D0435792

Oxford Spanish Desk Dictionary
Diccionario Oxford Desk

Diccionario Oxford Desk

Español-Inglés/Inglés-Español

Dirección editorial
Carol Styles Carvajal • Jane Horwood

Oxford New York
OXFORD UNIVERSITY PRESS
1997

Oxford Spanish Desk Dictionary

Spanish-English/English-Spanish

Chief editors
Carol Styles Carvajal • Jane Horwood

Oxford New York
OXFORD UNIVERSITY PRESS
1997

Oxford University Press
Oxford New York
Athens Auckland Bangkok Bogota Bombay Buenos Aires
Calcutta Cape Town Dar es Salaam Delhi Florence
Hong Kong Istanbul Karachi Kuala Lumpur Madras Madrid Melbourne Mexico City Nairobi Paris
Singapore Taipei Tokyo Toronto Warsaw

and associated companies in

Berlin Ibadan

Published by Oxford University Press, Inc.
198 Madison Avenue, New York, New York 10016

Published in paperback as The Pocket Oxford Spanish Dictionary:
Spanish-English/English-Spanish.

Published in paperback in Latin America as El Diccionario Oxford Compacto:
Español-Inglés/Inglés-Español.

Library of Congress Cataloging-in-Publication Data
The pocket Oxford Spanish dictionary: Spanish—English, English—Spanish /
chief editors, Carol Styles Carvajal, Jane Horwood.
p. cm.
Added title page title: Diccionario Oxford compact: español—inglés, inglés—español.
ISBN 0-19-521352-1
ISBN 0-19-521346-7 (Pbk.)
ISBN 0-19-511885-5 (Latin American edition)
1. Spanish language—Dictionaries—English. 2. English language—Dictionaries—Spanish. I. Carvajal, Carol Styles. II. Horwood, Jane.
III. Oxford Spanish dictionary. IV. Title: Diccionario Oxford compact :
PC4640.P63 1997 *97-3814*
463'.21—dc21 *CIP*

9 8 7 6 5 4 3 2 1
Printed in the United States of America
on acid-free paper

Preface
Prólogo

The *Oxford Spanish Desk Dictionary* has been designed to meet the needs of students, travelers, and all those who need quick and reliable answers to their translation problems.

Based on the *Oxford Spanish Dictionary*, the *Desk Dictionary* aims to reflect the breadth of Spanish and English used worldwide within a compact and easy-to-use format. Words and phrases restricted to particular areas of the Spanish-speaking world are precisely labeled for country or wider region. Likewise, American and British English variants are clearly distinguished. Universal translations applicable to all regions are given wherever possible; where such translations do not exist, clearly marked regional variants appear. The dictionary covers basic everyday vocabulary, together with a range of specialist terminology, from such diverse areas as computing, finance, music, communications, and sport.

A special feature of the dictionary is the use of detailed usage boxes to help with important areas of grammar and vocabulary. They highlight differences between Spanish and English which may create difficulty for the translator, explaining them in detail, and giving clear examples of how they are used. The boxes also cover such topics as numbers, forms of address, and measurements. In addition, grammatical points relating to particular entries are explained in notes within the entries.

Combining the authority of the *Oxford Spanish Dictionary* with the convenience of a smaller format, the *Oxford Spanish Desk Dictionary* is an invaluable tool for anyone needing up-to-date, clear, and practical guidance on English and Spanish.

The Editors

El *Diccionario Oxford Desk* ha sido diseñado para satisfacer las necesidades de los estudiantes, viajeros y todo aquél que necesite una respuesta rápida y fiable frente a problemas de traducción.

El texto de este diccionario se basa en el *Diccionario Oxford* y su objetivo es reflejar con amplitud el español y el inglés que se emplean por todo el mundo, dentro de un formato compacto y fácil de utilizar. Las palabras y frases que se restringen al uso dentro de un país o región más amplia del mundo hispanohablante, se señalan con indicadores precisos de ese país o esa región respectivamente. De la misma manera se distinguen claramente las variantes del inglés norteamericano y el inglés británico. Siempre que es posible se dan las traducciones universales que se aplican a todas las regiones.

El diccionario cubre el vocabulario básico de uso cotidiano junto con una variada terminología especializada de áreas tan diversas como la informática, las finanzas, las música, las comunicaciones y el deporte.

Una característica relevante de este diccionario es la inclusión de recuadros con información detallada acerca del uso de algunas palabras y que sirven de ayuda en importantes áreas de la gramática y del vocabulario. Estos recuadros destacan las diferencias que existen entre el español y el inglés, y que podrían crear dificultades para el traductor, señalándolas en detalle e ilustrándolas con ejemplos claros sobre su uso. Los recuadros cubren también temas tales como números, tratamientos y medidas. Además se incluyen notas, dentro de algunas entradas, las que explican puntos gramaticales relacionados con esa entrada en particular.

Al combinarse la autoridad del *Diccionario Oxford* con la comodidad del formato más pequeño, el *Diccionario Oxford Desk* resulta una herramienta inapreciable para todo el que necesite una guía actual, clara y práctica.

Los Editores

List of contributors
Lista de colaboradores

Project direction/Dirección
Michael Clark

Chief Editors/Dirección editorial
Carol Styles Carvajal • Jane Horwood

Senior Editor/Editor
Michael Britton

Editors/Redactores
Spanish-English/Español-Inglés
Ana Cristina Llompart
Malihe Forghani-Nowbari

English-Spanish/Inglés-Español
Julie Watkins

Data input/Entrada de datos
Susan Wilkin
Philip Gerrish

Contents

Índice

Proprietary names

This dictionary includes some words which have, or are asserted to have, proprietary status as trademarks or otherwise. Their inclusion does not imply that they have acquired for legal purposes a non-proprietary or general significance, nor is any other judgment implied concerning their legal status. In cases where the editorial staff have some evidence that a word has proprietary status this is indicated in the entry for that word by the symbol ®, but no judgment concerning the legal status of such words is made or implied thereby.

Marcas registradas

Este diccionario incluye palabras que constituyen, o se afirma que constituyen, marcas registradas o nombres comerciales. Su inclusión no significa que a efectos legales hayan dejado de tener ese carácter, ni supone un pronunciamiento respecto de su situación legal.
Cuando al editor le consta que una palabra es una marca registrada o un nombre comercial, esto se indica por medio del símbolo ®, lo que tampoco supone un pronunciamiento acerca de la situación legal de esa palabra.

Structure of a Spanish–English entry

Headword
Vocablo cabeza de artículo

acertijo *m* riddle, puzzle

All entries are listed in strict alphabetical order
Todos los artículos aparecen en riguroso orden alfabético

Variant form of headword
Variante del vocablo cabeza de artículo

achichincle, **achichinque** *mf* (Méx fam & pey) hanger-on (colloq & pej)

acomodar [A1] *vt* **1** (adaptar, amoldar) to adapt **2** ‹*huésped*› to put ... up **3 (a)** (AmL) (arreglar) to arrange; (poner) to put **(b)** (fam) ‹*persona*› (en puesto): **su tío lo acomodó en su sección** his uncle fixed him up with a job in his department

Sense divisions
Divisiones correspondientes a las distintas acepciones

A change of part of speech within an entry is marked by a box ■
Todo cambio de categoría gramatical dentro de una entrada se indica con el símbolo ■

acomplejado -da *adj*: **es muy ~** he's full of complexes; **está ~ por su gordura** he has a complex about being fat ■ *m, f*: **es un ~** he's a mass of complexes

acomplejar [A1] *vt* to give ... a complex
■ **acomplejarse** *v pron* to get a complex

acondicionar [A1] *vt* **(a)** ‹*vivienda*/*local*› to equip, fit out **(b)** (Col) ‹*carro*› to soup up

Part of speech
Función gramatical

aconsejable *adj* advisable

Irregular plural form
Plurales irregulares

acusetas *mf* (*pl* **~**), **acusete -ta** *m, f* (fam) tattletale (AmE colloq), telltale (BrE colloq)

adecuar [A1] *or* [A18] *vt* **~ algo a algo** to adapt sth TO sth

Every verb has a reference to the verb tables on p 939
Cada verbo se remite a la tabla de conjugaciones en la página 939

The use of ser or estar with adjectives is marked when necessary
El uso de ser o estar con adjetivos se indica donde es necesario

agarrado[1] **-da** *adj* **(a)** [SER] (fam) (tacaño) tightfisted (colloq) **(b)** [ESTAR] (CS fam) (enamorado) in love

águila *f*‡ **(a)** (ave) eagle; ***ser un* ~** to be very sharp **(b)** (Méx) (de moneda) ≈ heads (*pl*); **¿~ o sol?** heads or tails?

The part of speech *f*‡ indicates a feminine noun that takes the masculine article in the singular
La función gramatical *f*‡ indica un sustantivo femenino usado con el artículo masculino en el singular

Grammatical constructions in which the headword commonly occurs are indicated by small capitals
Las construcciones gramaticales en las que suele aparecer el vocablo cabeza de artículo se destacan mediante versalitas

■ **alimentarse** *v pron* «*persona/animal*» to feed oneself; **~se CON** *or* **DE algo** to live ON sth

antojarse [A1] *v pron* (+ *me/te/le etc*): **se me antojó una cerveza** I felt like (having) a beer; **de embarazada se me antojaban las uvas** when I was pregnant, I had a craving for grapes; **hace lo que se le antoja** he does as he pleases; **porque no se me antoja** because I don't feel like it

Spanish verbs (or senses of them) which are typically used with the indirect object pronouns me, te, le, nos, os and les
El indicador (+ me/te/le etc) señala las acepciones de los verbos españoles en las que éstos se emplean con los pronombres personales de objeto indirecto me, te, le, nos, os, y les

Pronominal verbs are labeled to indicate whether they are reflexive (refl), reciprocal (recípr), emphatic (enf) or causative (caus)
Los verbos pronominales llevan indicadores que denotan su uso reflexivo (refl), recíproco (recípr), enfático (enf) o causativo (caus)

anudar [A1] *vt* ‹*cordón/corbata*› to tie
■ **anudarse** *v pron* (*refl*) ‹*corbata/pañuelo*› to tie

■ **apostarse** *v pron* **(a)** (*recípr*): **se ~on una comida** they bet a meal on it **(b)** (*enf*) to bet

aprobación *f* (de proyecto de ley, moción) passing; (de préstamo, acuerdo, plan) approval, endorsement; (de actuación, conducta) approval

Sense indicators
Indicadores semánticos

Field labels
Indicadores de campo semántico

arco *m* **1** (Arquit) arch; (Anat) arch; (Mat) arc; **~ de triunfo** triumphal arch; **~ iris** rainbow **2** (AmL) (en fútbol) goal **3 (a)** (Arm, Dep) bow **(b)** (de violín) bow

arete *m* (Col, Méx) earring

Regional labels
Indicadores de uso regional

argolla *f* ring; **~ de compromiso/de matrimonio** (AmL) engagement/wedding ring; ***tener ~*** (AmC fam) to have contacts (colloq)

armario *m* **(a)** (para ropa — mueble) wardrobe; (— empotrado) closet (AmE), wardrobe (BrE) **(b)** (de cocina) cupboard; (de cuarto de baño) cabinet

Stylistic labels
Indicadores de estilo

armatoste *m* (fam) huge great thing (colloq)

arrechar [A1] *vt* **(a)** (AmL vulg) (excitar sexualmente) to turn ... on (colloq) **(b)** (AmL fam) (enojar) to bug (colloq)

ascendencia *f* **(a)** (linaje) descent, ancestry; **es de ~ francesa** he is of French descent **(b)** (origen) origins (*pl*); **su ~ humilde** her humble origins

Examples
Ejemplos

Idioms and proverbs appear in bold italics after examples
Los modismos y los proverbios aparecen en negritas redondas después de los ejemplos

ascua *f*‡ ember; ***estar en/tener a algn en ~s*** (fam) to be on/to keep sb on tenterhooks

aspereza *f* **1 (a)** (de superficie, piel) roughness **(b)** (de sabor) sharpness; (de voz, clima) harshness **2** (parte áspera): **usar papel de lija para quitar las ~s** use sandpaper to remove any roughness; ***limar ~s*** to smooth things over

aviso *m* **1 (a)** (notificación) notice; Ⓢ **aviso al público** notice to the public; **dio ~ a la policía** he notified *o* informed the police; **sin previo ~** without prior warning; **último ~ para los pasajeros** ... last call for passengers ... **(b)** (advertencia) warning; ***poner sobre ~ a algn*** to warn sb **(c)** (Cin, Teatr) bell **(d)** (Taur) warning **2** (AmL) (anuncio, cartel) advertisement, ad

Ⓢ indicates the use of the headword in signs, notices, warnings, etc
El símbolo Ⓢ indica el uso del vocablo cabeza de artículo en letreros, anuncios, advertencias, etc

Universally valid translation(s) followed by regional alternative(s)
Traducción universalmente válida seguida de alternativas regionales

balancín *m* (de niños) seesaw, teeter-totter (AmE)

balompié *m* soccer, football (BrE)

Words often used with the headword, shown to help select the correct translation for each context
Palabras que suelen acompañar al vocablo cabeza de artículo y que ayudan a elegir la traducción que corresponde a cada contexto

bancario -ria *adj* ‹*interés/préstamo*› bank (*before n*); ‹*sector*› banking (*before n*)

Nouns modified by an adjective
Sustantivos calificados por un adjetivo

bañar [A1] *vt* **1** ‹*niño/enfermo*› to bath, give ... a bath **2** ‹*pulsera/cubierto*› to plate

Objects of a verb
Complementos de un verbo

bifurcarse [A2] *v pron* «*camino*» to fork, diverge (frml); «*vía férrea*» to diverge

Subjects of a verb appear in double angled parentheses
Los posibles sujetos de un verbo aparecen entre paréntesis angulares dobles

A definition is provided where no equivalent exists in English
Se da una definición cuando no existe una palabra equivalente en inglés

boleador -dora *m,f* **1** (Méx) (lustrabotas) bootblack **2** (en las pampas) *person who uses bolas to catch cattle*

The sign ≈ is used to indicate approximate equivalence
El símbolo ≈ indica un equivalente aproximado en la lengua de destino

canciller *m* **(a)** (jefe de estado) chancellor **(b)** (AmS) (ministro) ≈ Secretary of State (*in US*), ≈ Foreign Secretary (*in UK*)

carnet /kar'ne/ *m* (*pl* **-nets**) ⇒ CARNÉ

ceder [E1] *vt* **1 (a)** ‹*derecho*› to transfer, assign; ‹*territorio*› to cede; ‹*puesto*/*título*› (voluntariamente) to hand over; (a la fuerza) to give up; **~ el poder** to hand over power; **me cedió el asiento** he let me have his seat; ⇒ PASO 1(b) **(b)** ‹*balón*/*pelota*› to pass **2** (prestar) ‹*jugador*› to loan

An arrow directs the user to another entry with the same meaning or to where a compound or idiomatic expression is to be found
Se utiliza una flecha para remitir al usuario a una variante sinónima o a otro artículo donde aparece un compuesto o un modismo

'ver tb' directs the user to a headword where additional information is to be found
'ver tb' remite al usuario a otro artículo donde se hallará información complementaria

chiva *f* **1** (AmL) (barba) goatee **2** (Col) (bus) rural *o* country bus **3** (Col period) (primicia) scoop, exclusive **4** (Chi fam) (mentira) cock-and-bull story (colloq); *ver tb* CHIVO **5 chivas** *fpl* (Méx fam) (cachivaches) junk (colloq)

Estructura del artículo Inglés–Español

Vocablo cabeza de artículo. Todos los artículos aparecen en riguroso orden alfabético, a excepción de los verbos con partícula
Headword. All entries appear in strict alphabetical order, except for phrasal verbs

alligator /ˈæləgeɪtər‖ˈælɪgeɪtə(r)/ *n* [C] aligátor *m*

all: **~-important** /ˈɔːlɪmˈpɔːrtn̩t‖ˌɔːlɪmˈpɔːtn̩t/ *adj* de suma importancia; **~-night** /ˈɔːlˈnaɪt/ *adj* ‹*party*/*show*› que dura toda la noche; ‹*cafe*/*store*› que está abierto toda la noche

Nombres compuestos
Compounds

La transcripción fonética aparece inmediatamente después del vocablo cabeza de artículo [ver página xxi]
Pronunciation is shown immediately after the headword [see p. xxi]

allocate /ˈæləkeɪt/ *vt* asignar; (distribute) repartir; **$3 million has been ~d for research** se han destinado tres millones de dólares a la investigación

allot /əˈlɑːt‖əˈlɒt/ *vt* **-tt-** (distribute) repartir; (assign) asignar

Cuando la pronunciación británica difiere de la norteamericana, la variante británica aparece precedida por barras verticales
Vertical lines indicate British English pronunciation, always shown if different from the American pronunciation

Variante del vocablo cabeza de artículo
Variant form of a headword

amoeba, (AmE also) **ameba** /əˈmiːbə/ *n* ameba *f*, amiba *f*

answer[1] /ˈænsər ‖ ˈɑːnsə(r)/ *n* **1 (a)** (reply) respuesta *f*, contestación *f*; **in ~ to your question** para contestar tu pregunta **(b)** (response): **her ~ to his rudeness was to ignore it** respondió a su grosería ignorándola; **Britain's ~ to Elvis Presley** el Elvis Presley británico **2 (a)** (in exam, test, quiz) respuesta *f* **(b)** (solution) solución *f*; **~** TO **sth** solución DE algo

Divisiones correspondientes a las distintas acepciones
Sense divisions

Los verbos con partícula aparecen al final del artículo correspondiente, precedidos por el símbolo ●
Phrasal verbs appear at the end of the root word entry and are marked by the symbol ●

answer² *vt* **1 (a)** (reply to) ‹*person*/*letter*› contestar **(b)** ‹*telephone*› contestar, atender* (AmL), coger* (Esp); **will you ~ the door?** ¿vas tú (a abrir)? **(c)** ‹*critic*/*criticism*› responder a **2** (fit): **to ~ (to) a description** responder a una descripción ■ **~** *vi* contestar, responder
● **answer back 1** [*v* + *adv*] (rudely) contestar **2** [*v* + *o* + *adv*] **to ~ sb back** contestarle mal *or* de mala manera a algn
● **answer for** [*v* + *prep* + *o*] (accept responsibility for) ‹*conduct*/*consequences*› responder de; **his parents have a lot to ~ for** sus padres tienen mucha culpa

appreciate /ə'pri:ʃieɪt/ *vt* **(a)** (value) ‹*food*/*novel*› apreciar **(b)** (be grateful for) agradecer* **(c)** (understand) ‹*danger*/*difficulties*› darse* cuenta de; **I ~ that, but** ... lo comprendo, pero ... ■ **~** *vi* «*shares*/*property*» (re)valorizarse*

Todo cambio de categoría gramatical de un verbo se indica con el símbolo ■
A change of part of speech of a verb is marked by a box ■

Función gramatical
Part of speech

approximate /ə'prɑ:ksəmət ‖ ə'prɒksɪmət/ *adj* aproximado
approximately /ə'prɑ:ksəmətli ‖ ə'prɒksɪmətli/ *adv* aproximadamente

artery /'ɑ:rtəri ‖ 'ɑ:təri/ *n* (*pl* **-ries**) arteria *f*

auditorium /'ɔ:də'tɔ:riəm ‖ ,ɔ:dɪ'tɔ:riəm / *n* (*pl* **-riums** *or* **-ria** /-riə/) auditorio *m*

Inflexiones irregulares
Irregular inflections

El comparativo y el superlativo del adjetivo
Comparative and superlative forms of an adjective

baggy /'bægi/ *adj* **-gier, -giest** ancho, guango (Méx)

balance¹ /'bæləns/ *n* **1** [C] (apparatus) balanza *f* **2** [U] (equilibrium) equilibrio *m*; **to lose one's ~** perder* el equilibrio **3** [C] **(a)** (in accounting) balance *m* **(b)** (*bank* **~**) saldo *m* **(c)** (difference, remainder) resto *m*; (of sum of money) saldo *m*

Acepciones numerables [C] y no numerables [U] de un sustantivo
Countable [C] or uncountable [U] senses of a noun

Las construcciones gramaticales en las que suele aparecer el vocablo cabeza de artículo se destacan mediante versalitas
Grammatical constructions in which the headword commonly occurs are indicated with the use of small capitals

bang² *vt* **(a)** (strike) golpear **(b)** (slam): **he ~ed the door** dio un portazo (fam) ■**~** *vi* **(a)** (strike) **to ~ ON sth** golpear algo; **to ~ INTO sth** darse* CONTRA algo **(b)** (slam) «*door*» cerrarse* de un golpe

Fórmulas que demuestran el comportamiento sintáctico de cada verbo con partícula. Señalan las posibles combinaciones de verbo [v], adverbio [adv], preposición [prep] y complemento [o]
Syntactical pattern of phrasal verbs, showing the possible combinations of verb [v], adverb [adv], preposition [prep] and object [o]

• **bear out** [*v* + *o* + *adv*, *v* + *adv* + *o*] ‹*theory*› confirmar
• **bear up** [*v* + *adv*]: **she bore up well under the strain** sobrellevó muy bien la situación

beg /beg/ **-gg-** *vt* **1** ‹*money/food*› pedir*, mendigar* **2** (frml) **(a)** (entreat) ‹*person*› suplicarle* a, rogarle* a **(b)** (ask for) ‹*forgiveness*› suplicar*, rogar* ■ ~ *vi* «*beggar*» pedir*, mendigar*; **to ~ for mercy** pedir* *or* suplicar* clemencia

Un asterisco señala los verbos de conjugación irregular en la traducción al español
An asterisk indicates an irregular verb in the translation

Indicadores semánticos
Sense indicators

belief /bəˈliːf ‖ bɪˈliːf/ *n* **(a)** [U C] (conviction, opinion) creencia *f* **(b)** [U] (confidence) ~ IN **sb/sth** confianza *f or* fe *f* EN algn/algo **(c)** [U C] (Relig) fe *f*

belt¹ /belt/ *n* **1** (Clothing) cinturón *m* **2** (Mech Eng) correa *f*

Indicadores de campo semántico
Field labels

Indicadores de uso regional
Regional labels

Biro ®, **biro** /ˈbaɪrəʊ ‖ ˈbaɪərəʊ/ *n* (*pl* **biros**) (BrE) bolígrafo *m*, birome *f* (RPl), esfero *m* (Col), lápiz *m* de pasta (Chi), boli *m* (Esp fam)

biscuit /ˈbɪskɪt/ *n* [C] (Culin) **(a)** (AmE) bollo *m*, panecillo *m*, bísquet *m* (Méx) **(b)** (cookie, cracker) (BrE) galleta *f*, galletita *f* (RPl)

bitch /bɪtʃ/ *n* **1** (female dog) perra *f* **2** (spiteful woman) (AmE vulg, BrE sl) bruja *f* (fam), arpía *f* (fam), cabrona *f* (Esp, Méx vulg)

Indicadores de estilo
Stylistic labels

Ejemplos
Examples

bounce² *n* **(a)** [C] (action) rebote *m*, pique *m* (AmL) **(b)** [U] (springiness, vitality): **this shampoo puts the ~ back into your hair** este champú les da nueva vida a sus cabellos; **she's full of ~** es una persona llena de vida

breath /breθ/ *n* [C U] (air exhaled or inhaled) aliento *m*; **to have bad ~** tener* mal aliento; **out of ~** sin aliento; ***to hold one's ~*** contener* la respiración; ***to take sb's ~ away*** dejar a algn sin habla

Los modismos y los proverbios aparecen en negritas cursivas después de los ejemplos
Idioms and proverbs appear in bold italics after examples

El símbolo Ⓢ indica el uso del vocablo cabeza de artículo en letreros, anuncios, advertencias, etc
Ⓢ indicates the use of the headword in signs, notices, warnings, etc

customer /'kʌstəmər || 'kʌstəmə(r)/ *n* cliente, -ta *m,f*; (*before n*) Ⓢ **customer services** información y reclamaciones

dump¹ /dʌmp/ *n* **1** (place for waste) vertedero *m* (de basura), basural *m* (AmL), tiradero *m* (Méx)

Traducción universalmente válida seguida de alternativas regionales
Universal Spanish translation followed by regional alternatives

Traducción de uso extendido excepto en las regiones que se especifican
Translation used in all areas except those specified

dust: **~bin** /'dʌstbɪn, 'dʌsbɪn/ *n* (BrE) cubo *m or* (CS, Per) tacho *m or* (Méx) tambo *m or* (Col) caneca *f or* (Ven) tobo *m* de la basura

Palabras que suelen acompañar al vocablo cabeza de artículo y que ayudan a elegir la traducción que corresponde a cada contexto
Words often used with the headword, shown to help select the correct translation for each context

ease² *vt* **1 (a)** (relieve) ‹*pain*› calmar, aliviar; ‹*tension*› hacer* disminuir, aliviar; ‹*burden*› aligerar; **to ~ sb's mind** tranquilizar* a algn **(b)** (make easier) ‹*situation*› paliar; ‹*transition*› facilitar; **to ~ the way for sth** preparar el terreno para algo

Complementos de un verbo
Objects of a verb

• ease off [*v + adv*] «*rain*» amainar; «*pain*» aliviarse, calmarse; «*pressure/traffic*» disminuir*

Los posibles sujetos de un verbo aparecen entre paréntesis angulares dobles
Subjects of a verb appear in double angled brackets

efficient /ɪ'fɪʃənt/ *adj* ‹*person/system*› eficiente; ‹*machine/engine*› de buen rendimiento

Sustantivos calificados por un adjetivo
Nouns modified by an adjective

Se da una definición cuando no existe una palabra equivalente en español
A definition is provided where no equivalent exists in Spanish

exhibit² *n* **(a)** (in gallery, museum) *objeto en exposición* **(b)** (Law) *documento u objeto que se exhibe en un juicio como prueba* **(c)** (exhibition) (AmE) exposición *f*

Inland Revenue /'ɪnlənd/ *n* (in UK) **the ~ ~** ≈Hacienda, ≈la Dirección General Impositiva (*en RPl*), ≈Impuestos Internos (*en Chi*)

El símbolo ≈ indica un equivalente aproximado en la lengua de destino
The sign ≈ is used to indicate approximate equivalence

Se utiliza una flecha para remitir al usuario a una variante sinónima o a otro artículo donde aparece un compuesto o un modismo
An arrow directs the user to another entry with the same meaning or to where a compound or idiomatic expression is to be found

inmost /ˈɪnməʊst/ *adj* ⇒ INNERMOST

jersey /ˈdʒɜrzi‖ˈdʒɜːzi/ *n* (*pl* **-seys**) **1 (a)** [C] (sports shirt) camiseta *f* **(b)** [U] (Tex) jersey *m* **(c)** [C] (BrE) ⇒ SWEATER **2 Jersey** (la isla de) Jersey

jetsam /ˈdʒetsəm/ *n* [U] echazón *f*; *see also* FLOTSAM

'see also' remite al usuario a otro artículo donde se hallará información complementaria
'see also' directs the user to a headword where the additional information is to be found

The pronunciation of Spanish

Symbols used in this dictionary

The pronunciation of Spanish words is directly represented by their written form and therefore phonetic transcriptions have only been supplied for loan words which retain their original spelling.

1 Consonants and semi-vowels

Symbol	Example	Approximation
/b/	**boca** /'boka/ **vaso** /'baso/	English *b* in *bin* but without the aspiration that follows it.
/β/	**cabo** /'kaβo/ **ave** /'aβe/	Very soft *b*, produced with the lips hardly meeting.
/d/	**dolor** /do'lor/	English *d* in *den*.
/ð/	**cada** /'kaða/	English *th* in *rather*.
/f/	**fino** /'fino/	English *f* in *feat*.
/g/	**gota** /'gota/	English *g* in *goat*.
/ɣ/	**pago** /'paɣo/ **largo** /'larɣo/	Very soft continuous sound, not punctuated like /g/.
/ɹ/	**mayo** /'maɹo/ **llave** /'ɹaβe/	English *y* in *yet*. For regional variants see points 7 and 14 of **General Rules of Spanish Pronunciation** on page xix.
/j/	**tiene** /'tjene/	English *y* in *yet*.
/k/	**cama** /'kama/ **cuna** /'kuna/ **quiso** /'kiso/ **kilo** /'kilo/	English *c* in *cap* but without the aspiration that follows it.
/l/	**lago** /'laɣo/	English *l* in *lid*.
/m/	**mono** /'mono/	English *m* in *most*.
/n/	**no** /no/	English *n* in *nib*.
/ŋ/	**banco** /'baŋko/	English *ng* in *song*.
/ɲ/	**año** /'aɲo/	Like *gn* in French *soigné*, similar to the *ni* in *onion*.
/p/	**peso** /'peso/	English *p* in *spin*.
/r/	**aro** /'aro/ **árbol** /'arβol/	A single flap with a curved tongue against the palate.
/rr/	**rato** /'rrato/ **parra** /'parra/	A rolled *'r'* as found in some Scottish accents.
/s/	**asa** /'asa/ **celo** /'selo/ **cinco** /'siŋko/ **azote** /a'sote/ } Latin-American Spanish	English *s* in *stop*.
/θ/	**celo** /'θelo/ **cinco** /'θiŋko/ **azote** /a'θote/ } European Spanish	English *th* in *thin*.
/t/	**todo** /'toðo/	English *t* in *step*.
/tʃ/	**chapa** /'tʃapa/	English *ch* in *church*.
/w/	**cuatro** /'kwatro/	English *w*.
/x/	**jota** /'xota/ **general** /xene'ral/ **gigante** /xi'ɣante/	*ch* in Scottish *loch*.
/z/	**desde** /'dezðe/	English *s* in *is*.

2 Vowels

None of the five Spanish vowels corresponds exactly to an English vowel.

Symbol	Example	Approximation
/a/	**casa** /'kasa/	Shorter than *a* in *father*.
/e/	**seco** /'seko/	English *e* in *pen*.
/i/	**fin** /fin/	Between English *ee* in *seen* and *i* in *sin*.
/o/	**oro** /'oro/	Shorter than English *o* in *rose*.
/u/	**uña** /'uɲa/	Between English *oo* in *boot* and *oo* in *foot*.

3 The stress mark

When phonetic transcriptions of Spanish headwords are given in the dictionary, the symbol ' precedes the syllable that carries the stress:

footing /'futin/

For information about where other words should be stressed, see section **2 Stress** on the next page.

General rules of Spanish pronunciation

1 Consonants

1 The letters *b* and *v* are pronounced in exactly the same way: /b/ when at the beginning of an utterance or after *m* or *n* (**barco** /'barko/, **vaca** /'baka/, **ambos** /'ambos/), and /β/ in all other contexts (**rabo** /'rraβo/, **ave** /'aβe/, **árbol** /'arβol/).

2 *C* is pronounced /k/ when followed by a consonant other than *h* or by *a, o* or *u* (**acto** /'akto/, **casa** /'kasa/, **coma** /'koma/). When it is followed by *e* or *i,* it is pronounced /s/ in Latin America and parts of southern Spain and /θ/ in the rest of Spain (**cero** /'sero/, /'θero/; **cinco** /'siŋko/, /'θiŋko/).

3 *D* is pronounced /d/ when it occurs at the beginning of an utterance or after *n* or *l* (**digo** /'diɣo/, **anda** /'anda/) and /ð/ in all other contexts (**hada** /'aða/, **arde** /'arðe/). It is often not pronounced at all at the end of a word (**libertad** /liβer'ta(ð)/, **Madrid** /ma'ðri(ð)/).

4 *G* is pronounced /x/ when followed by *e* or *i* (**gitano** /xi'tano/, **auge** /'awxe/). When followed by *a, o, u, ue* or *ui* it is pronounced /g/ if at the beginning of an utterance or after *n* (**gato** /'gato/, **gula** /'gula/, **tango** /'taŋgo/, **guiso** /'giso/) and /ɣ/ in all other contexts (**hago** /'aɣo/, **trague** /'traɣe/). Note that the *u* is not pronounced in the combinations *gue* and *gui,* unless it is written with a diaeresis (**paragüero** /para'ɣwero/, **agüita** /a'ɣwita/).

5 *H* is mute in Spanish, (**huevo** /'weβo/, **almohada** /almo'aða/) except in the combination *ch,* which is pronounced /tʃ/ (**chico** /'tʃiko/, **leche** /'letʃe/).

6 *J* is always pronounced /x/ (**jamón** /xa'mon/, **jefe** /'xefe/).

7 The pronunciation of *ll* varies greatly throughout the Spanish-speaking world. (*a*) It is pronounced rather like the *y* in English *yes* by the majority of speakers, who do not distinguish between the pronunciation of *ll* and that of *y* (e.g. between *haya* and *halla*). The sound is pronounced slightly more emphatically when at the beginning of an utterance. (*b*) In some areas, particularly Bolivia, parts of Chile, Peru and Castile in Spain, the distinction between *ll* and *y* has been preserved. In these areas *ll* is pronounced similarly to *lli* in *million.* (*c*) In the River Plate area *ll* is pronounced /ʒ/ (as in English *measure*), sometimes tending toward /ʃ/ (as in *shop*).

8 *Ñ* is always pronounced /ɲ/.

9 *Q* is pronounced /k/, and the *u* that always follows it is silent (**quema** /'kema/, **quiso** /'kiso/).

10 *R* is pronounced /r/ when it occurs

between vowels or in syllable-final position (**aro** /'aro/, **barco** /'barko/, **cantar** /kan'tar/). It is pronounced /rr/ when in initial position (**rama** /'rrama/). The double consonant *rr* is always pronounced /rr/.

11 *S* is pronounced /s/ but it is aspirated by speakers in many regions when it occurs in syllable-final position (**hasta** /'ahta/, **los cuatro** /loh'kwatro/). In other regions it is voiced when followed by a voiced consonant (**mismo** /'mɪzmo/, **los dos** /loz'ðos/).

12 *V* see 1 above.

13 *X* is pronounced /ks/, although there is a marked tendency to render it as /s/ before consonants (**extra** /'ekstra/, /'estra/).

In some words derived from Nahuatl and other Indian languages it is pronounced /x/ (**México** /'mexiko/) and in others it is pronounced /s/ (**Xochimilco** /sotʃi'milko/).

14 (*a*) When followed by a vowel within the same syllable *y* is pronounced rather like the *y* in English *yes* (slightly more emphatically when at the beginning of an utterance). In the River Plate area it is pronounced /ʒ/ (as in English *measure*), sometimes tending toward /ʃ/ (as in *shop*).

As the conjunction *y* and in syllable-final position, *y* is pronounced /i/.

15 *Z* is pronounced /s/ in Latin America and parts of southern Spain and /θ/ in the rest of Spain.

2 Stress

When no phonetic transcription is given for a Spanish headword, the following rules determine where it should be stressed:

1 If there is no written accent:
(*a*) a word is stressed on the penultimate syllable if it ends in a vowel, or in *n* or *s*:
arma /'arma/
mariposas /mari'posas/
ponen /'ponen/

(*b*) words which end in a consonant other than *n* or *s* are stressed on the last syllable:
cantar /kan'tar/
delantal /delan'tal/
maguey /ma'ɣei/

2 If a word is not stressed in accordance with the above rules, the written accent indicates the syllable where the emphasis is to be placed:
balcón /bal'kon/
salí /sa'li/
carácter /ka'rakter/

It should be noted that unstressed vowels have the same quality as stressed vowels and are not noticeably weakened as they are in English. For example, there is no perceptible difference between any of the e's in *entenderé* or between the a's in *Panamá*.

3 Combinations of vowels

A combination of a strong vowel (*a, e* or *o*) and a weak vowel (*i* or *u*) or of two weak vowels forms a diphthong and is therefore pronounced as one syllable. The stress falls on the strong vowel if there is one. In a combination of two weak vowels, it falls on the second element:

cuando /'kwando/ (stressed on the /a/)
aula /'awla/ (stressed on the /a/)
viudo /'bjuðo/ (stressed on the /u/)

A combination of two strong vowels does not form a diphthong and the vowels retain their separate values. They count as two separate syllables for the purposes of applying the above rules on stress:

faena /fa'ena/ (stressed on the /e/)
polea /po'lea/ (stressed on the /e/)

La pronunciación del inglés

La transcripción fonética que sigue a cada palabra cabeza de artículo corresponde a la pronunciación norteamericana de uso más extendido en los Estados Unidos. Se ha incluido la pronunciación británica (precedida por el símbolo ‖) únicamente en aquellos casos en que ésta difiere sustancialmente de la pronunciación norteamericana. Ejemplo:

address[1] /'ædres ‖ə'dres/
induce /ɪn'duːs ‖ɪn'djuːs/

Se reconoce la validez de muchas variantes regionales, tanto norteamericanas como británicas, pero éstas no se han incluido por razones de espacio.

Los símbolos empleados en las transcripciones son los del Alfabeto Fonético Internacional (AFI). Éstos se enumeran a continuación, seguidos de un ejemplo y una breve aproximación o descripción del sonido que representan. Estas descripciones no siguen criterios fonéticos estrictos.

1 Consonantes y semivocales

Símbolo	Ejemplo		Aproximación
/b/	**bat**	/bæt/	Sonido más explosivo que el de una *b* inicial española.
/d/	**dig**	/dɪg/	Sonido más explosivo que el de una *d* inicial española.
/dʒ/	**jam**	/dʒæm/	Similar a una *ch* pero más cercano al sonido inicial de *Giuseppe* en italiano.
/f/	**fit**	/fɪt/	Como la *f* española.
/g/	**good**	/gʊd/	Sonido más explosivo que el de una *g* inicial española.
/h/	**hat**	/hæt/	Sonido de aspiración más suave que la *j* española, articulado como si se estuviera intentando empañar un espejo con el aliento.
/hw/	**wheel**	/hwiːl/	Una /w/ con la aspiración de la /h/ (muchos hablantes no distinguen entre /hw/ y /w/ y pronuncian *whale* de la misma manera que *wail*).
/j/	**yes**	/jes/	Como la *y* española en *yema* y *yo* (excepto en el español rioplatense).
/k/	**cat**	/kæt/	Sonido más explosivo que el de una *c* española en *cama* o *acto*.
/l/	**lid**	/lɪd/	Como la *l* española.
/l̩/	**tidal**	/'taɪdl̩/	*l* alargada y resonante.
/m/	**mat**	/mæt/	Como la *m* española.

Símbolo	Ejemplo		Aproximación
/n/	**nib**	/nɪb/	Como la *n* española.
/n̩/	**threaten**	/ˈθretn̩/	*n* alargada y resonante.
/ŋ/	**sing**	/sɪŋ/	Como la *n* española en *banco* o *anca*.
/p/	**pet**	/pet/	Sonido más explosivo que el de una *p* española.
/r/	**rat**	/ræt/	Entre la *r* y la *rr* españolas, pronunciado con la punta de la lengua curvada hacia atrás y sin llegar a tocar el paladar.
/s/	**sip**	/sɪp/	Como la *s* española.
/ʃ/	**ship**	/ʃɪp/	Sonido similar al de la interjección *¡sh!*, utilizada para pedir silencio (ver también tʃ).
/t/	**tip**	/tɪp/	Sonido más explosivo que el de una *t* española.
/tʃ/	**chin**	/tʃɪn/	Como la *ch* española.
/θ/	**thin**	/θɪn/	Como la *c* o la *z* del español europeo en *cinco* o *zapato*.
/ð/	**the**	/ðə/	Sonido similar a una *d* intervocálica española como la de *cada* o *modo*.
/v/	**van**	/væn/	Sonido sonoro que se produce con los incisivos superiores sobre el labio inferior.
/w/	**win**	/wɪn/	Similar al sonido inicial de *huevo*.
/x/	**loch**	/lɑːx/	Como la *j* española.
/z/	**zip**	/zɪp/	*s* sonora (con zumbido).
/ʒ/	**vision**	/ˈvɪʒən/	Sonido similar al de la *y* o la *ll* del español rioplatense en *yo* o *llave,* o al de la *j* francesa en *je* (ver también /dʒ/).

2 Vocales y diptongos

(El símbolo **ː** indica que la vocal precedente es larga)

Símbolo	Ejemplo		Aproximación
/ɑː/	**father**	/ˈfɑːðər/	Sonido más largo que el de una *a* española.
/æ/	**fat**	/fæt/	Sonido que se obtiene al pronunciar una *a* española con los labios en la posición de pronunciar la *e*.
/ʌ/	**cup**	/kʌp/	Sonido más breve que la *a* española y que se pronuncia en la parte posterior de la boca.
/e/	**met**	/met/	Sonido parecido a la *e* española en *mesa*.

Símbolo	Ejemplo		Aproximación
/ə/	**ago**	/ə'gəʊ/	Sonido similar al de la *e* francesa en *je* (ver también /əʊ/).
/ɜː/	**fur**	/fɜːr/	Sonido que se obtiene al pronunciar una *e* española con los labios en la posición de pronunciar la *o*.
/ɪ/	**bit**	/bɪt/	Sonido más breve que el de la *i* española.
/iː/	**beat**	/biːt/	Sonido más largo que el de la *i* española.
/i/	**very**	/'veri/	Sonido similar al de la *i* española en *papi*.
/ɔː/	**paw**	/pɔː/	Sonido más largo que el de la *o* española.
/uː/	**boot**	/buːt/	Sonido más largo que el de una *u* española.
/ʊ/	**book**	/bʊk/	Sonido más breve que el de la *u* española.
/aɪ/	**fine**	/faɪn/	Como *ai* en las palabras españolas *aire, baile*.
/aʊ/	**now**	/naʊ/	Como *au* en las palabras españolas *pausa, flauta*.
/eɪ/	**fate**	/feɪt/	Como *ei* en las palabras españolas *peine, aceite*.
/əʊ/	**goat**	/gəʊt/	Como una *o* pronunciada sin redondear demasiado los labios.
/ɔɪ/	**boil**	/bɔɪl/	Como *oy* en *voy, coypu*.
/uə/	**sexual**	/'sekʃuəl/	Como una *u* pronunciada sin redondear demasiado los labios y seguida de una /ə/.

3 Símbolos adicionales utilizados en la transcripción de sonidos vocálicos británicos

Símbolo	Ejemplo		Aproximación
/ɒ/	**dog**	/dɒg/	Similar a una *o* española.
/eə/	**fair**	/feə(r)/	Como una *e* española seguida de /ə/.
/ɪə/	**near**	/nɪə(r)/	Como una *i* española seguida de /ə/.
/ʊə/	**tour**	/tʊə(r)/	Como una *u* española pronunciada sin redondear demasiado los labios y seguida de /ə/.

4 Acentuación

El símbolo ' precede a la sílaba sobre la cual recae el acento tónico primario:

ago /ə'gəʊ/
dinosaur /'daɪnəsɔːr/

El símbolo ˌ precede a la sílaba sobre la cual recae el acento tónico secundario:

blackmailer /'blækˌmeɪlər/

Abbreviations and labels / Abreviaturas e indicadores

Español/ Spanish	abreviatura/ abbreviation	Inglés/ English
adjetivo	**adj**	adjective
adjetivo invariable	**adj inv**	invariable adjective
Administración	**Adm**	Administration
adverbio	**adv**	adverb
Espacio	**Aerosp**	Aerospace
Agricultura	**Agr**	Agriculture
América Central	**AmC**	Central America
inglés norteamericano	**AmE**	American English
América Latina	**AmL**	Latin America
América del Sur	**AmS**	South America
Anatomía	**Anat**	Anatomy
Andes	**Andes**	Andes
anticuado	**ant**	dated
Antropología	**Anthrop**	Anthropology
arcaico	**arc, arch**	archaic
Arqueología	**Archeol**	Archeology
Arquitectura	**Archit**	Architecture
argot	**arg**	slang
Argentina	**Arg**	Argentina
Armas	**Arm**	Arms
Arqueología	**Arqueol**	Archeology
Arquitectura	**Arquit**	Architecture
artículo	**art**	article
Arte	**Arte, Art**	Art
Astrología	**Astrol**	Astrology
Astronomía	**Astron**	Astronomy
Audio	**Audio**	Audio
Automovilismo	**Auto**	Cars
Aviación	**Aviac, Aviat**	Aviation
Biblia	**Bib**	Bible
Biología	**Biol**	Biology
Bolivia	**Bol**	Bolivia
Botánica	**Bot**	Botany
inglés británico	**BrE**	British English
Comercio	**Busn**	Business
numerable	**C**	countable
causativo	**caus**	causative
Química	**Chem**	Chemistry
Chile	**Chi**	Chile
Cine	**Cin**	Cinema
Ingeniería civil	**Civil Eng**	Civil Engineering
Indumentaria	**Clothing**	Clothing
Cocina	**Coc**	Cookery
Colombia	**Col**	Colombia
familiar	**colloq**	colloquial
Comercio	**Com**	Business
Informática	**Comput**	Computing
conjunción	**conj**	conjunction
Construcción	**Const**	Building
Correspondencia	**Corresp**	Correspondence
numerable	**count**	countable
Costa Rica	**CR**	Costa Rica
uso criticado	**crit**	criticized usage
Cono Sur	**CS**	Southern Cone
Cuba	**Cu**	Cuba
Cocina	**Culin**	Cookery
anticuado	**dated**	dated
artículo definido	**def art**	definite article
Odontología	**Dent**	Dentistry
Deporte	**Dep**	Sport
Derecho	**Der**	Law
dialecto	**dial**	dialect
Ecuador	**Ec**	Ecuador
Comunidad Europea	**EC**	European Community
Ecología	**Ecol**	Ecology
Economía	**Econ**	Economics
Educación	**Educ**	Education
Electricidad	**Elec**	Electricity
Electrónica	**Electrón, Electron**	Electronics
enfático	**enf**	emphatic
Ingeniería	**Eng**	Engineering
Equitación	**Equ**	Equestrianism
especialmente	**esp**	especially
España	**Esp**	Spain
Espacio	**Espac**	Aerospace
Espectáculos	**Espec**	Entertainment
eufemismo	**euf, euph**	euphemism
excepto	**exc**	excluding
femenino	**f**	feminine
véase página ix	**f‡**	*see page ix*
familiar	**fam**	colloquial

Español/ Spanish	abreviatura/ abbreviation	Inglés/ English
Farmacología	**Farm**	Pharmacology
Ferrocarriles	**Ferr**	Railways
Filosofía	**Fil**	Philosophy
Finanzas	**Fin**	Finance
Física	**Fís**	Physics
Fisco	**Fisco**	Tax
Fisiología	**Fisiol**	Physiology
Fotografía	**Fot**	Photography
femenino plural	**fpl**	feminine plural
frase hecha	**fr hecha**	set phrase
formal	**frml**	formal
Juegos	**Games**	Games
generalmente	**gen**	generally
Geografía	**Geog**	Geography
Geología	**Geol**	Geology
gerundio	**ger**	gerund
Gobierno	**Gob, Govt**	Government
Historia	**Hist**	History
Horticultura	**Hort**	Horticulture
humorístico	**hum**	humorous
Imprenta e Industria editorial	**Impr**	Printing and Publishing
artículo indefinido	**indef art**	indefinite article
Indumentaria	**Indum**	Clothing
Informática	**Inf**	Computing
Ingeniería	**Ing**	Engineering
interjección	**interj**	exclamation
irónico	**iró, iro**	ironical
lenguaje periodístico	**journ**	journalese
Periodismo	**Journ**	Journalism
Juegos	**Jueg**	Games
Relaciones Laborales	**Lab Rel**	Labor Relations
Derecho	**Law**	Law
Ocio	**Leisure**	Leisure
lenguaje infantil	**leng infantil**	used to or by children
Lingüística	**Ling**	Linguistics
Literatura	**Lit**	Literature
literario	**liter**	literary
locución	**loc**	phrase
locución adjetiva	**loc adj**	adjectival phrase
locución adverbial	**loc adv**	adverbial phrase

Español/ Spanish	abreviatura/ abbreviation	Inglés/ English
locución preposicional	**loc prep**	prepositional phrase
masculino	**m**	masculine
Márketing	**Marketing**	Marketing
Matemáticas	**Mat, Math**	Mathematics
Mecánica	**Mec, Mech Eng**	Mechanical Engineering
Medicina	**Med**	Medicine
Metalurgia	**Metal, Metall**	Metallurgy
Meteorología	**Meteo**	Meteorology
México	**Méx**	Mexico
masculino y femenino	**mf**	masculine and feminine
masculino, femenino	**m, f**	masculine, feminine
Militar	**Mil**	Military
Minería	**Min**	Mining
Mitología	**Mit**	Mythology
masculino plural	**mpl**	masculine plural
Música	**Mús, Mus**	Music
Mitología	**Myth**	Mythology
nombre, sustantivo	**n**	noun
Náutica	**Náut, Naut**	Nautical
negativo	**neg**	negative
Ocultismo	**Occult**	Occult
Ocio	**Ocio**	Leisure
Odontología	**Odont**	Dentistry
Óptica	**Ópt, Opt**	Optics
Panamá	**Pan**	Panama
Paraguay	**Par**	Paraguay
participio pasado	**past p**	past participle
peyorativo	**pej**	pejorative
Perú	**Per**	Peru
lenguaje periodístico	**period**	journalese
Periodismo	**Period**	Journalism
peyorativo	**pey**	pejorative
Farmacología	**Pharm**	Pharmacology
Filosofía	**Phil**	Philosophy
Fotografía	**Phot**	Photography
Física	**Phys**	Physics
Fisiología	**Physiol**	Physiology
plural	**pl**	plural
sustantivo plural	**pl n**	plural noun
poético	**poet**	poetic
Política	**Pol**	Politics

Español/ Spanish	abreviatura/ abbreviation	Inglés/ English
Correo	**Post**	Post
participio pasado	**pp**	past participle
prefijo	**pref**	prefix
preposición	**prep**	preposition
participio presente	**pres p**	present participle
Imprenta	**Print**	Printing
pronombre	**pron**	pronoun
pronombre demostrativo	**pron dem**	demonstrative pronoun
pronombre personal	**pron pers**	personal pronoun
pronombre relativo	**pron rel**	relative pronoun
Psicología	**Psic, Psych**	Psychology
Industria editorial	**Publ**	Publishing
Química	**Quím**	Chemistry
marca registrada	**®**	registered trademark
Radio	**Rad**	Radio
Ferrocarriles	**Rail**	Railways
recíproco	**recípr**	reciprocal
reflexivo	**refl**	reflexive
Religión	**Relig**	Religion
Relaciones Laborales	**Rels Labs**	Labor Relations
Río de la Plata	**RPl**	River Plate area
inglés de Escocia	**Scot**	Scottish English
Servicios Sociales	**Servs Socs**	Social Administration
singular	**sing**	singular
argot	**sl**	slang
Servicios Sociales	**Soc Adm**	Social Administration
Sociología	**Sociol**	Sociology
Deporte	**Sport**	Sport
sufijo	**suf, suff**	suffix
Tauromaquia	**Taur**	Bullfighting
Fisco	**Tax**	Tax
también	**tb**	also
Teatro	**Teatr**	Theater
Tecnología	**Tec, Tech**	Technology
lenguaje técnico	**téc, tech**	technical language
Telecomunicaciones	**Telec**	Telecommunications
Textiles	**Tex**	Textiles
Teatro	**Theat**	Theater
Turismo	**Tourism**	Tourism
Transporte	**Transp**	Transport
Televisión	**TV**	Television
no numerable	**U**	uncountable
no numerable	**uncount**	uncountable
Uruguay	**Ur**	Uruguay
verbo	**v**	verb
verbo auxiliar	**v aux**	auxiliary verb
verbo	**vb**	verb
Venezuela	**Ven**	Venezuela
Veterinaria	**Vet, Vet Sci**	Veterinary Science
verbo intransitivo	**vi**	intransitive verb
Video	**Video, Vídeo**	Video
verbo impersonal	**v impers**	impersonal verb
Vinicultura	**Vin**	Wine
verbo modal	**v mod**	modal verb
verbo pronominal	**v pron**	pronominal verb
verbo transitivo	**vt**	transitive verb
vulgar	**vulg**	vulgar
Zoología	**Zool**	Zoology

Aa

A, **a** *f* (*pl* **aes**) (*read as* /a/) *the letter* A, a

a *prep*

■ **Nota** La preposición *a* suele emplearse precedida de ciertos verbos como *empezar*, *ir*, *oler*, *sonar* etc, en cuyo caso ver bajo el respectivo verbo.
— No se traduce cuando introduce el complemento directo de persona (ser humano, pronombres personales que lo representan, como *quien*, *alguien*, *algún* etc) o un nombre con un objeto o animal personalizado: *amo a mi patria* = I love my country, *paseo a mi perro* = I walk my dog.
— En los casos en que precede al artículo definido *el* para formar la contracción *al*, ver bajo la siguiente entrada, donde también se encontrarán otros ejemplos y usos de *a*.

1 (a) (indicando dirección) to; **voy a México/la tienda** I'm going to Mexico/to the shop; **voy a casa** I'm going home; **se cayó al río** she fell into the river **(b)** (indicando posición): **estaban sentados a la mesa** they were sitting at the table; **a orillas del Ebro** on the banks of the Ebro; **se sentó al sol** he sat in the sun; **se sentó a mi derecha** he sat down on my right **(c)** (indicando distancia): **a diez kilómetros de aquí** ten kilometers from here **2 (a)** (señalando hora, momento) at; **a las ocho** at eight o'clock; **a la hora de comer** at lunch time; **¿a qué hora vengo?** what time shall I come?; **a mediados de abril** in mid-April; **al día siguiente** the next *o* following day **(b)** (señalando fecha): **hoy estamos a lunes/a 20** today is Monday/it's the 20th today **(c) al** + INF: **se cayó al bajar del tren** she fell as she was getting off the train; **al enterarse de la noticia** when he learnt *o* on learning the news **(d)** (indicando distancia en el tiempo): **a escasos minutos de su llegada** (después) a few minutes after she arrived; (antes) a few minutes before she arrived; **de lunes a viernes** (from) Monday to Friday **3** (en relaciones de proporción, equivalencia): **tres veces al día** three times a day; **sale a 100 pesetas cada uno** it works out at 100 pesetas each; **a 100 kilómetros por hora** (at) 100 kilometers per hour; **nos ganaron cinco a tres** they beat us five three *o* (AmE) five to three **4** (indicando modo, medio, estilo): **a pie/a caballo** on foot/on horseback; **a crédito** on credit; **funciona a pilas** it runs on batteries; **a mano** by hand; **a rayas** striped; **vestirse a lo punk** to wear punk clothes **5 (a)** (introduciendo el complemento directo de persona): **¿viste a José?** did you see José?; **no he leído a Freud** I haven't read (any) Freud **(b)** (introduciendo el complemento indirecto) to; **le escribió una carta a su padre** he wrote a letter to his father, he wrote his father a letter; **dáselo a ella** give it to her; **les enseña inglés a mis hijos** she teaches my children English; **le echó (la) llave a la puerta** she locked the door **(c)** (indicando procedencia): **se lo compré a una gitana** I bought it from *o* (colloq) off a gipsy

abadía *f* (monasterio) abbey; (dignidad) abbacy

abajo *adv* **1 (a)** (lugar, parte): **aquí ~** down here; **en el estante de ~** (el siguiente) on the shelf below; (el último) on the bottom shelf; **más ~** further down; **por ~** underneath; **la parte de ~** the bottom (part) **(b)** (en un edificio) downstairs; **los vecinos de ~** the people downstairs **(c)** (en una escala, jerarquía): **del jefe para ~** from the boss down *o* downward(s); **de 20 años para ~** 20 or under **2** (expresando dirección, movimiento) down; **calle/escaleras ~** down the street/stairs; **tire hacia ~** pull down *o* downward(s); **desde ~** from below **3 abajo de** (AmL) under; **~ de la cama** under the bed **4** (en interjecciones) down with; **¡~ la dictadura!** down with the dictatorship!

abalanzarse [A4] *v pron*: **se abalanzaron hacia las salidas** they rushed toward(s) the exits; **~ SOBRE algn/algo** to leap ON sb/sth

abandonado -da *adj* **1** [ESTAR] (deshabitado) deserted **2** [ESTAR] ‹*niño/perro/coche*› abandoned **3** [ESTAR] (desatendido, descuidado) ‹*jardín/parque*› neglected

abandonar [A1] *vt* **1 (a)** (frml) ‹*lugar*› to leave **(b)** ‹*familia/bebé*› to leave, abandon; ‹*marido/amante*› to leave; ‹*coche/barco*› to abandon; **los abandonó a su suerte** he abandoned them to their fate **2** «*fuerzas*» to desert **3 (a)** ‹*actividad/propósito/esperanza*› to give up; **~ los estudios** to drop out of school/college **(b)** (Dep) ‹*carrera/partido*› to retire from, pull out of ■ **~** *vi* (Dep) **(a)** (en carrera, competición) to pull out **(b)** (en ajedrez) to resign; (en boxeo, lucha) to concede defeat

■ **abandonarse** *v pron* **1** (entregarse) **~se A algo** ‹*a vicios/placeres*› to abandon oneself TO sth **2** (en el aspecto personal) to let oneself go

abandono *m* **1 (a)** (de una persona) abandonment; **~ del hogar** desertion **2** (Dep) (antes de la carrera, competición) withdrawal; (iniciada la carrera, competición) retirement; (en ajedrez) resignation **3** (descuido, desatención) neglect

abanicar [A2] *vt/vi* to fan

■ **abanicarse** *v pron* to fan oneself

abanico *m* (utensilio) fan

abaratar [A1] *vt* ‹*precios/costos*› to reduce; ‹*producto*› to make … cheaper, reduce the price of

■ **abaratarse** *v pron* «*costos*» to drop, come down; «*producto*» to become cheaper, come down in price

abarcar [A2] *vt* **(a)** ‹*temas/materias*› to cover; ‹*superficie/territorio*› span, cover; ‹*siglos/generaciones*› to span; **la conversación abarcó varios temas** the conversation ranged over many topics **(b)** (dar abasto con) ‹*trabajos/actividades*› to cope with; ***quien mucho abarca poco aprieta*** you shouldn't bite off more than you can chew **(c)** (con los brazos, la mano) to encircle

abarrotado -da *adj* crammed, packed; **~ DE algo** ‹*de gente*› packed *o* crammed WITH sth

abarrotar [A1] *vt* ‹*sala/teatro*› to pack

abarrotería *f* (Méx) grocery store (AmE), grocer's (shop) (BrE)

abarrotero -ra *m,f* (Chi, Méx) (tendero) storekeeper (AmE), shopkeeper (BrE)

abarrotes *mpl* (AmL exc RPl) (comestibles) groceries (*pl*); (tienda) grocery store (AmE), grocer's (shop) (BrE)

abastecedor -dora *m,f* supplier

abastecer [E3] *vt* to supply; **~ a algn DE algo** to supply sb WITH sth

■ **abastecerse** *v pron* **~se DE algo** (obtener) to obtain sth; (almacenar) to stock up WITH sth

abastecimiento *m* supply

abasto *m* **(a)** (aprovisionamiento) supply; ***no dar ~***: **no dan ~ con el trabajo** they can't cope with all the work **(b)** (provisiones) *tb* **~s** *mpl* basic provisions (*pl*) (*esp foodstuffs*)

abatible *adj* ‹*respaldo*› reclining (*before n*) ; (hacia adelante) folding (*before n*)

abatido -da *adj* [ESTAR] (deprimido, triste) depressed; (desanimado) downhearted, dispirited

abdicación *f* abdication

abdicar [A2] *vi* «*soberano*» to abdicate; **~ EN algn** to abdicate IN FAVOR OF sb ■ **~** *vt* ‹*trono/corona*› to give up, abdicate

abdomen *m* abdomen

abdominal *adj* abdominal ■ *m* sit-up

abecedario *m* alphabet

abedul *m* birch

abeja *f* bee; **~ obrera/reina** worker/queen bee

abejorro *m* bumblebee

aberración *f* (disparate, extravío) outrage; **robarle a un ciego es una ~** stealing from sb who's blind is outrageous

abertura *f* (en general) opening; (agujero) hole; (rendija) gap; (corte, tajo) slit

abeto *m* fir (tree)

abierto[1] -ta *adj* **1 (a)** ‹*ventana/boca*› open; **está ~** it's open; **con los ojos muy ~s** with eyes wide open; **un sobre ~** an unsealed envelope; **los espacios ~s de la ciudad** the city's open spaces **(b)** [ESTAR] ‹*válvula*› open; **dejaste la llave ~** you left the faucet (AmE) *o* (BrE) tap running **(c)** (desabrochado) undone **(d)** ‹*herida*› open; ‹*madera/costura*› split **2** [ESTAR] ‹*comercio/museo*› open **3** (Ling) ‹*vocal*› open **4 (a)** [SER] (espontáneo) open **(b)** (receptivo) open-minded; **~ A algo** open TO sth **5** (manifiesto, directo) open

abierto[2] *m* (Dep) open (tournament)

abismante *adj* (Andes) ‹*valentía*› extraordinary; ‹*belleza*› breathtaking ‹*cifra/cantidad*› staggering

abismo *m* abyss; **hay un profundo ~ entre ellos** there's a deep rift between them

ablandar [A1] *vt* **(a)** ‹*cera/cuero*› to soften; ‹*carne*› to tenderize **(b)** ‹*persona*› to soften; ‹*corazón*› to melt

■ **ablandarse** *v pron* **(a)** «*cera/cuero*» to soften **(b)** «*persona*» to soften up; «*mirada*» to soften

abnegación *f* self-denial, abnegation (frml)

abnegado -da *adj* self-sacrificing, selfless

abofetear [A1] *vt* to slap

abogacía *f* law; **ejercer la ~** to practice law

abogado -da *m,f* (en general) lawyer, solicitor (*in UK*); (ante un tribunal superior) attorney (*in US*), barrister (*in UK*); **~ defensor** defense lawyer (AmE), defence counsel (BrE); **~ del diablo** devil's advocate

abolición *f* abolition

abolir [I32] *vt* to abolish

abolladura *f* dent

abollar [A1] *vt* ‹*coche/cacerola*› to dent

■ **abollarse** *v pron* to get dented

abombado -da *adj* **1** ‹*superficie*› convex; ‹*techo*› domed **2** (AmL fam) (atontado) dopey (colloq), dozy (colloq) **3** (AmS) (en mal estado) ‹*alimento*›: **esta carne está abombada** this meat has gone bad *o* (BrE) is off

abombarse [A1] *v pron* (AmS) to go bad, go off

abominable *adj* abominable

abominar [A1] *vt* to detest, abominate (frml)

abonado -da *m,f* (del teléfono, a revista) subscriber; (del gas) consumer, customer; (a espectáculo, transporte) season-ticket holder

abonar [A1] *vt* **1** ‹*tierra/campo*› to fertilize **2 (a)** (frml) (pagar) ‹*cantidad/honorarios*› to pay; **el cheque se lo ~án en caja** you can cash the check at the cash desk **(b)** (depositar) to credit; **hemos abonado la cantidad en su cuenta** we have credited your account with the amount **(c)** (Andes, Méx) (dar a cuenta) to give ... on account

■ **abonarse** *v pron* **~se A algo** ‹*a espectáculo*› to buy a season ticket FOR sth; ‹*a revista*› to subscribe TO sth

abono *m* **1** (Agr) fertilizer **2** (para espectáculos, transporte) season ticket **3** (frml) **(a)** (pago) payment **(b)** (en una cuenta) credit **(c)** (Andes, Méx) (cuota) installment*

abordar [A1] *vt* **1 (a)** (encarar) ‹*problema*› to tackle, deal with **(b)** (plantear) ‹*tema/asunto*› to raise **2** ‹*persona*› to approach; (agresivamente) to accost **3** (Méx) «*pasajero*» ‹*barco/avión*› to board; ‹*automóvil*› to get into ■ **~** *vi* (Méx) (subir a bordo) to board

aborigen *adj* aboriginal, indigenous ■ *mf* aborigine, aboriginal

aborrecer [E3] *vt* **(a)** ‹*persona/actividad*› to detest, loathe **(b)** ‹*crías*› to reject

aborrecible *adj* loathsome, detestable

abortar [A1] *vi* (Med) (de forma espontánea) to have a miscarriage, miscarry; (de forma provocada) to have an abortion, abort ■ **~** *vt* ‹*maniobra/aterrizaje*› to abort

aborto *m* (Med) (espontáneo) miscarriage; (provocado) abortion

abotagado -da *adj* ‹*cara*› swollen; ‹*cuerpo*› bloated

abotonar [A1] *vt* to button up, do up

■ **abotonarse** *v pron* ‹*chaqueta/camisa*› to button up, do up

abrasador -dora *adj* burning (*before n*)

abrasar [A1] *vt* **(a)** (quemar) to burn; **murieron abrasados** they were burned to death **(b)** «*bebida*» to scald, burn; «*comida*» to burn ■ ~ *vi* «*sol*» to burn, scorch

■ **abrasarse** *v pron* «*bosque*» to be burned (down); «*planta*» to get scorched; **nos abrasábamos bajo el sol** we were sweltering under the sun

abrasivo -va *adj/m* abrasive

abrazar [A4] *vt* ‹*persona*› to hug; (con más sentimiento) to embrace; **abrázame fuerte** hold me tight

■ **abrazarse** *v pron* (*recípr*) to hug each other; (con más sentimiento) to embrace each other; **~se A algn/algo** to hold on *o* cling TO sb/sth

abrazo *m* hug; (con más sentimiento) embrace; **me dio un ~** he gave me a hug, he hugged/embraced me; **dale un ~ de mi parte** give my love to her; **un ~, Miguel** (en cartas) best wishes, Miguel, regards, Miguel; (más íntimo) love, Miguel

abrebotellas *m* (*pl* ~) bottle opener

abrecartas *m* (*pl* ~) letter opener

abrelatas *m* (*pl* ~) can opener, tin opener (BrE)

abreviar [A1] *vt* ‹*permanencia/visita*› to cut short; ‹*plazo*› to shorten; ‹*texto/artículo*› to abridge; ‹*palabra*› to abbreviate ■ ~ *vi*: **abreviando** ... in short ...

abreviatura *f* abbreviation

abridor *m* (de botellas) bottle opener; (de latas) can opener, tin opener (BrE)

abrigado -da *adj* **(a)** [ESTAR] ‹*lugar*› sheltered **(b)** [ESTAR] ‹*persona*›: **¿estás bien ~ con esas mantas?** are you warm enough with those blankets?; **está demasiado ~** he has too many clothes on; **iba bien ~** he was wrapped up warm **(c)** [SER] (RPl, Ven) ‹*ropa*› warm

abrigador -dora *adj* [SER] (Andes, Méx) ‹*ropa*› warm

abrigar [A3] *vt* **1** (con ropa) to wrap ... up warm; **el pañuelo me abriga el cuello** the scarf keeps my neck warm **2** ‹*idea/esperanza*› to cherish; ‹*sospecha/duda*› to harbor*, entertain ■ ~ *vi* «*ropa*» to be warm

■ **abrigarse** *v pron* (*refl*) to wrap up warm

abrigo *m* **1 (a)** (prenda) coat **(b)** (calor que brinda la ropa): **necesita más ~** she needs to be wrapped up more warmly; **con una manta no tengo suficiente ~** I'm not warm enough with one blanket; **ropa de ~** warm clothes **2** (refugio, protección) shelter; **al ~ de la lluvia/los árboles** sheltered from the rain/under the trees; **al ~ de la lumbre** by the fireside

abril *m* ▶ 193 April; *para ejemplos ver* ENERO

abrillantar [A1] *vt* to polish

abrir [I33] *vt* **1** (en general) to open; ‹*paraguas*› to open, put up; ‹*mapa*› to open out, unfold; ‹*cortinas*› to open, draw back; ‹*persianas*› to raise, pull up; ‹*cremallera*› to undo **2** ‹*llave/gas*› to turn on; ‹*válvula*› to open; ‹*cerradura*› to unlock **3 (a)** ‹*zanja/túnel*› to dig; ‹*agujero*› to make **(b)** (fam) ‹*paciente*› to open ... up (colloq) **4 (a)** ‹*comercio/museo*› (para el quehacer diario) to open; (inaugurar) to open (up); **¿a qué hora abren la taquilla?** what time does the box office open? **(b)** ‹*carretera/aeropuerto*› to open; ‹*frontera*› to open (up) **5 (a)** (iniciar) ‹*cuenta bancaria*› to open; ‹*negocio*› to start, set up; ‹*suscripción*› to take out; ‹*investigación*› to begin, set up; **no han abierto la matrícula aún** registration hasn't begun yet; **~ fuego** to open fire **(b)** ‹*acto/debate/baile*› to open **(c)** ‹*desfile/cortejo*› to head, lead **(d)** ‹*paréntesis/comillas*› to open **6** ‹*apetito*› to whet

■ **abrirse** *v pron* **1 (a)** «*puerta/ventana*» to open; **~se A algo** ‹*a jardín/corredor*› to open ONTO sth **(b)** «*flor/almeja*» to open; «*paracaídas*» to open **2** (*refl*) ‹*chaqueta/cremallera*› to undo **3 (a)** «*porvenir*» to lie ahead; «*perspectivas*» to open up; **con este descubrimiento se abren nuevos horizontes** this discovery opens up new horizons **(b)** «*período/era*» to begin

abrochar [A1] *vt* ‹*chaqueta/botón*› to fasten, do up; ‹*collar/cinturón de seguridad*› to fasten

■ **abrocharse** *v pron* ‹*chaqueta/botón*› to fasten, do up; ‹*collar/cinturón de seguridad*› to fasten

abrumador -dora *adj* **(a)** ‹*victoria/mayoría*› overwhelming **(b)** ‹*trabajo/tarea*› exhausting

abrumar [A1] *vt* to overwhelm; **~ a algn CON algo** ‹*con problemas/quejas*› to wear sb out WITH sth; **la ~on con sus atenciones** she was overwhelmed by their kindness

abrupto -ta *adj* **(a)** ‹*camino/pendiente*› steep; ‹*terreno*› rough **(b)** ‹*tono*› abrupt **(c)** ‹*cambio/descenso*› abrupt, sudden

absolución *f* **(a)** (Relig) absolution **(b)** (Der) acquittal

absolutamente *adv* totally, absolutely; **no se ve ~ nada** you can't see a thing; **~ nadie** not a soul; **¿estás segura? — ~** are you sure? — absolutely *o* I'm positive

absoluto -ta *adj* **1** ‹*monarca/poder*› absolute **2 (a)** (total) total, absolute, complete; **tengo la absoluta certeza** I am absolutely convinced **(b) en absoluto** (*loc adv*): **¿te gustó? — en ~** did you like it? — no, not at all; **no lo consentiré en ~** there is absolutely no way I will agree to it

absolver [E11] *vt* **(a)** (Relig) to absolve **(b)** (Der) ‹*acusado*› to acquit, find ... not guilty

absorbente *adj* **1** ‹*esponja/papel*› absorbent **2** ‹*persona*› demanding; ‹*hobby/tarea*› time-consuming; ‹*profesión*› demanding

absorber [E1] *vt* **(a)** ‹*líquido/ruido/calor*› to absorb **(b)** ‹*tiempo*› to occupy, take up; ‹*recursos/energía*› to absorb

absorción *f* (de líquido, calor, ruido) absorption

absorto -ta *adj* engrossed, absorbed

abstemio -mia *adj* teetotal ■ *m,f* teetotaler*

abstención *f* abstention

abstenerse [E27] *v pron* **(a)** (en votación) to abstain **(b)** (frml) (no hacer): **~ DE hacer algo** to refrain FROM doing sth **(c)** (privarse de): **~ del alcohol** to avoid alcohol

abstinencia *f* abstinence

abstracto -ta *adj* abstract

abstraerse [E23] *v pron* **~se DE algo** ‹*de pensamiento/preocupación*› to block out FROM sth

abstraído -da *adj*: **estar ~ en algo** to be absorbed in sth; **lo noté como ~** he seemed rather preoccupied

absuelto -ta *pp*: *see* ABSOLVER

absurdo -da *adj* absurd, ridiculous

abuchear [A1] *vt* to boo

abucheo *m* booing

abuelito -ta *m,f* (*m*) grandpa (colloq), granddad (colloq); (*f*) grandma (colloq), granny (colloq)

abuelo -la *m,f* **1** (pariente) (*m*) grandfather; (*f*) grandmother; **mis ~s** my grandparents; ***¡cuéntaselo a tu abuela!*** (fam) pull the other one! (colloq) **2** (fam) (persona mayor) (*m*) old man, old guy (colloq); (*f*) old woman, old lady; **¡oiga ~!** hey, granddad! (colloq)

abultado -da *adj* **(a)** ‹*ojos/vientre*› bulging; ‹*labios*› thick; ‹*cartera*› bulging **(b)** (abundante) ‹*deuda/suma*› enormous, huge **(c)** (exagerado) ‹*cifra/cantidad*› inflated

abultar [A1] *vi* **(a)** (formar un bulto) to make a bulge **(b)** (ocupar lugar) to be bulky ■ **~** *vt* ‹*cifras/resultados*› to inflate

abundancia *f* **1** (gran cantidad) abundance; **la ~ de peces** the abundance of fish; **hay comida en ~** there's an abundance of food; **darse en ~** to be plentiful **2** (riqueza): **tiempos de ~** times of plenty; **viven en la ~** they're well-off; ***nadar en la ~*** to be rolling in money (colloq)

abundante *adj* ‹*reservas/cosecha*› plentiful, abundant; **la pesca es ~** the fishing is good; **aguas ~s en especies marinas** waters which abound in marine life

abundar [A1] *vi* **(a)** (existir en gran número o cantidad) «*especie/mineral*» to be abundant **(b)** (tener mucho) **~ EN algo** to abound *o* be rich IN sth

aburrido -da *adj* **1** [ESTAR] ‹*persona*› **(a)** (sin entretenimiento) bored; **estoy muy ~** I'm bored stiff **(b)** (harto) fed up; **~ DE algo** tired OF sth, fed up WITH sth; **~ DE + hacer algo** tired OF doing sth **2** [SER] ‹*película/persona*› boring; ‹*trabajo*› boring, tedious ■ *m,f* bore

aburridor -dora *adj* (AmL) ⇨ ABURRIDO 2

aburrimiento *m* **(a)** (estado) boredom **(b)** (cosa aburrida): **¡qué ~!** what a bore!

aburrir [I1] *vt* to bore

■ **aburrirse** *v pron* **(a)** (por falta de entretenimiento) to get bored **(b)** (hartarse) **~se DE algo/algn** to get tired OF *o* fed up WITH sth/sb; **~se DE hacer algo** to get tired OF doing sth

abusador -dora *adj* (aprovechado) ‹*comerciante*› opportunist; **¡qué ~ eres!** you really take advantage of the situation! ■ *m,f*: **estos comerciantes son unos ~es** these shopkeepers really take advantage; **es un ~ con sus padres** he takes advantage of his parents

abusar [A1] *vi* **1 (a)** (aprovecharse): **es muy hospitalaria pero no abuses** she's very hospitable but don't take advantage of her; **~ DE algo** ‹*de autoridad/posición/generosidad*› to abuse sth; **no quisiera ~ de su amabilidad** I don't want to impose (on you); **~ DE algn** ‹*de padres/amigo*› to take advantage OF sb **(b)** (sexualmente) **~ DE algn** to sexually abuse sb **2** (usar en exceso): **abusa de los tranquilizantes** he takes too many tranquilizers; **no se debe ~ del alcohol** alcohol should be drunk in moderation

abusivo -va *adj* ‹*precio/interés*› outrageous

abuso *m* **(a)** (uso excesivo) abuse; **~ de autoridad** abuse of authority; **el ~ en la bebida** excessive drinking **(b)** (de hospitalidad, generosidad): **espero no lo considere un ~** I hope you don't think it an imposition; **¡qué ~ de confianza!** (fam) what a nerve! (colloq) **(c)** (injusticia) outrage; **¡esto es un ~!** this is outrageous!; **prestarse a ~s** to lay itself open to abuse

abusón -sona *adj/m,f* (Esp, Méx fam) ⇨ ABUSADOR

acá *adv* **1** (en el espacio) here; **¡ven ~!** come here!; **ya viene para ~** he's on his way over; **nos pasamos el día de ~ para allá** we spent the whole day going to and fro; **un poquito más ~** a little closer *o* nearer (to me) **2** (en el tiempo): **del verano (para) ~** since the summer

acabado[1] -da *adj* [ESTAR] **(a)** ‹*trabajo*› finished; **son todos productos muy bien ~s** they are all well-finished products **(b)** ‹*persona*› finished

acabado[2] *m* finish

acabar [A1] *vi* **I (a)** «*reunión/película*» to finish, end; «*persona*» to finish; «*novios*» to split up; **ya casi acabo** I've nearly finished **(b)** (en un estado, situación) to end up; **acabó en la cárcel** he ended up in jail; (+ *compl*) **acabamos cansadísimos** by the end we were exhausted; **ese chico va a ~ mal** that boy will come to no good; **la película acabó bien** the movie had a happy ending; **~án aceptándolo** *o* **por aceptarlo** they'll end up accepting it; **~ DE algo** to end up AS sth; **acabó de camarero** he ended up (working) as a waiter **(c)** (rematar) **~ EN algo** to end IN sth

II acabar con (a) ~ CON algo (terminar) ‹*con libro/tarea*› to finish WITH sth; ‹*con bombones/bebidas*› to finish off sth; ‹*con salud/carrera*› to ruin sth; ‹*con sueldo/herencia*› to fritter AWAY sth; ‹*con abuso/problema*› to put an end TO sth **(b)** (fam) **~ CON algn** (pelearse) to finish WITH sb; (matar) to do away WITH sb (colloq); **este niño va a ~ conmigo** this child will be the death of me

III acabar de (a) (terminar) **~ DE hacer algo** to finish doing sth; **cuando acabes de leerlo** when you've finished reading it **(b)** (para referirse a acción reciente): **acaba de salir** she's just gone out; **acababa de meterme en la cama cuando** ... I had just got into bed when ... **(c)** (llegar a): **no acabo de entenderlo** I just don't understand; **no acababa de gustarle** she wasn't totally happy about it ■ **~** *vt* ‹*trabajo/libro*› to finish; ‹*curso/carrera*› to finish, complete

■ **acabarse** *v pron* **1** (terminarse) «*provisiones/comida*» to run out; «*problema*» to be over; «*reunión/fiesta/curso*» to end; «*proyecto*» to finish, come to an end; «*año*» to come to an end; **se nos acabó el café** we ran out of coffee; **se le ~on las**

fuerzas he ran out of energy; **un trabajo que no se acaba nunca** a never-ending *o* an endless task; **¡esto se acabó!** that's it! **2** (*enf*) (comer) to finish (up)

acabóse *m* (fam): **¡esto es el ~!** this is the end *o* limit! (colloq)

academia *f* **(a)** (sociedad) academy **(b)** (Educ) school; **~ de conductores** *or* (AmL) **choferes** driving school; **~ de idiomas** language school

académico -ca *adj* ‹*estudios/año*› academic (*before n*); ‹*estilo/lenguaje*› academic ■ *m,f* academician

acalorado -da *adj* **1** [SER] ‹*discusión/riña*› heated **2** [ESTAR] ‹*persona*› (enfadado) worked up; (con calor) hot

acalorarse [A1] *v pron* (enfadarse) to get worked up; (sofocarse) to get hot

acampada *f* camp; **ir de ~** to go camping

acampanado -da *adj* ‹*falda/pantalones*› bell-bottomed (AmE), flared (BrE)

acampante *mf* camper

acampar [A1] *vi* to camp

acantilado *m* cliff

acaparador -dora *adj* (egoísta) selfish, greedy; (posesivo) possessive ■ *m,f* **(a)** (de productos) hoarder **(b)** (persona egoísta) selfish person

acaparar [A1] *vt* **(a)** ‹*productos/existencias*› to hoard, stockpile **(b)** ‹*interés/atención*› to capture; **el trabajo acapara todo su tiempo** work takes up all his time

acaramelado -da *adj* **(a)** ‹*pareja*›: **estaban ~s** they were hugging and kissing **(b)** ‹*voz*› sugary **(c)** (Coc) toffee-coated; ‹*molde*› coated with caramel

acariciar [A1] *vt* ‹*persona*› to caress; ‹*mejilla/pelo*› to stroke, caress; ‹*perro/gato*› to stroke

acarrear [A1] *vt* **(a)** ‹*problema*› to give rise to, lead to; **esto le acarreó problemas** this caused her problems **(b)** ‹*materiales/paquetes*› to carry

acaso *adv* **1** (en preguntas): **¿~ no te lo dije?** I told you, didn't I?; **¿~ tengo yo la culpa?** is it *my* fault? **2** (*en locs*) **por si acaso** just in case; **si acaso** (quizás) maybe, perhaps; (en caso de que) if

acatar [A1] *vt* ‹*leyes/orden*› to obey, comply with

acatarrado -da *adj*: **estar ~** to have a cold

acatarrarse [A1] *v pron* (resfriarse) to catch a cold

acceder [E1] *vi* **1** (consentir) to agree; **~ A algo** to agree TO sth **2** (entrar) **~ A algo** to gain access TO sth

accesible *adj* **(a)** ‹*lugar*› accessible; ‹*persona*› approachable; ‹*precio*› affordable **(b)** ‹*novela/lenguaje*› accessible

acceso *m* **1 (a)** (a un lugar) access; **rutas de ~** approach roads **(b)** (a persona, información) access **(c)** (Inf) access **2** (a curso) entrance; **pruebas de ~** entrance examinations; **curso de ~** preparatory course

accesorio *m* accessory; **~s del vestir** accessories; **~s de baño** bathroom fittings

accidentado -da *adj* **1 (a)** ‹*viaje*› eventful; ‹*historia*› turbulent; ‹*carrera/pasado*› checkered* (*before n*); ‹*vida*› troubled **(b)** ‹*terreno*› rough, rugged; ‹*costa*› broken **2** ‹*persona*› hurt, injured ■ *m, f*: **llevaron a los ~s al hospital** those injured *o* hurt in the accident were taken to hospital

accidental *adj* ‹*encuentro*› chance (*before n*), accidental; ‹*circunstancias*› coincidental

accidente *m* **1** (percance) accident; **tener** *or* **sufrir un ~** to have an accident; **~ aéreo** plane crash; **~ de circulación/tráfico** traffic *o* road accident; **~ laboral** industrial accident **2** (hecho fortuito) coincidence; **por ~** by chance **3** (del terreno) unevenness; **~ geográfico** geographical feature

acción *f* **1** (acto, hecho) act; **acciones dignas de elogio** praiseworthy acts *o* actions; **hacer una buena ~** to do a good deed; **~ de gracias** thanksgiving **2 (a)** (actividad) action; **poner algo en ~** to put sth into action; **novela de ~** adventure story **(b)** (Mil) action **(c)** (Cin, Lit) (trama) action, plot **3 (a)**(Der) action, lawsuit **(b)** (Fin) share; **acciones** shares, stock **8** (Per) (de una rifa) ticket

accionar [A1] *vt* ‹*palanca*› to pull; ‹*mecanismo/dispositivo*› activate, trigger

accionista *mf* stockholder, shareholder

acebo *m* holly; (árbol) holly tree

acechar [A1] *vt* ‹*enemigo/presa*› to lie in wait for; **el peligro que nos acecha** the danger that lies ahead of us

acecho *m*: **al ~** lying in wait

aceite *m* oil; **~ lubricante** lubricating oil; **~ de oliva/girasol** olive/sunflower oil; **~ de ricino** cod liver oil

aceitera *f* (Tec) oilcan; (Coc) cruet

aceitoso -sa *adj* oily

aceituna *f* olive; **~s rellenas/sin hueso** stuffed/pitted olives

aceitunado -da *adj* ▶ **97** olive (*before n*)

aceleración *f* acceleration

acelerado -da *adj* ‹*curso*› intensive, crash (*before n*); **a paso ~** at a brisk pace

acelerador *m* (Auto) accelerator

acelerar [A1] *vt* **(a)** ‹*coche/motor*›: **aceleró el coche** (en marcha) he accelerated; (sin desplazarse) he revved the engine *o* car (up) **(b)** ‹*proceso/cambio*› to speed up; ‹*paso*› to quicken ■ **~** *vi* **(a)** (Auto) to accelerate **(b)** (fam) (darse prisa) to hurry (up)

acelgas *fpl* Swiss chard

acento *m* **(a)** (Ling) (tilde) accent; (de intensidad) stress, accent **(b)** (énfasis) emphasis **(c)** (dejo, pronunciación) accent; **tiene ~ francés** he has a French accent

acentuado -da *adj* **(a)** ‹*palabra/sílaba*› accented **(b)** ‹*diferencia/cambio*› marked, distinct

acentuar [A18] *vt* **(a)** (Ling) (al hablar) to stress, accent; (al escribir) to accent **(b)** (intensificar, hacer resaltar) to accentuate, emphasize

■ **acentuarse** *v pron* ‹*diferencias/problemas*› to become accentuated

acepción *f* sense, meaning

aceptable *adj* acceptable, passable

aceptación *f* **(a)** (éxito) success; **de gran ~ entre los jóvenes** very popular *o* successful with young people **(b)** (acción) acceptance

aceptar [A1] *vt* ‹*excusas/invitación/cargo*› to accept; ‹*términos/condiciones*› to agree to; **aceptan cheques** they take checks; **aceptó venir** she agreed to come; **no acepto que me digas eso** I won't have you saying that to me

acequia *f* irrigation ditch *o* channel

acera *f* sidewalk (AmE), pavement (BrE)

acerca de *loc prep* about

acercamiento *m* (entre posturas, países) rapprochement; (entre personas): **ese incidente produjo un ~ entre ellos** that incident brought them closer together

acercar [A2] *vt* **1 (a)** (aproximar) to bring … closer *o* nearer; **~on la mesa a la puerta** they moved the table closer *o* nearer to the door; **acercó las manos al fuego** he held his hands closer to the fire; **¿puedes ~me ese libro?** can you pass *o* give me that book? **(b)** (unir) ‹*posturas/países*› to bring … closer **2** (llevar): **me acercó a la parada** she gave me a ride (AmE) *o* (BrE) lift to the bus stop

■ **acercarse** *v pron* **(a)** (aproximarse) to approach, to get closer *o* nearer; **acércate más** (acercándose al hablante) come *o* get closer *o* nearer; (alejándose del hablante) go *o* get closer *o* nearer; **se le ~on dos policías** two policemen came up to *o* approached him **(b)** «*amigos/países*» to draw *o* come closer together **(c)** «*hora/momento*» to draw near, approach; **ahora que se acerca la Navidad** now that Christmas is coming

acero *m* (Metal) steel; **~ inoxidable** stainless steel

acérrimo -ma *adj* ‹*partidario/defensor*› staunch; ‹*enemigo*› bitter

acertado -da *adj* ‹*comentario*› pertinent; ‹*solución/elección*› good

acertante *adj* winning (*before n*) ■ *m, f* winner

acertar [A5] *vt* ‹*respuesta/resultado*› to get … right; **a ver si aciertas quién es** see if you can guess who it is ■ **~** *vi* **1 (a)** (dar, pegar): **~le A algo** to hit sth; **tiró pero no le acertó** he shot at it but (he) missed **(b)** (atinar) to be right; **acertaste con el regalo** your present was perfect **2** (lograr) **~ A hacer algo** to manage to do sth

acertijo *m* riddle, puzzle

acetona *f* (Quím) acetone; (quitaesmaltes) nail-polish remover

achacar [A2] *vt*: **~le la culpa a algn** to lay *o* put the blame on sb

achaques *mpl* ailments (*pl*); **mis acostumbrados ~** my usual aches and pains

achatar [A1] *vt* to flatten

achicar [A2] *vt* **1 (a)** ‹*chaqueta/vestido*› to take in **(b)** ‹*persona*› to intimidate, daunt **2** ‹*agua*› to bail out

■ **achicarse** *v pron* **(a)** (de tamaño) to shrink **(b)** (amilanarse) to be intimidated, be daunted

achicharrante *adj* (fam) ‹*sol*› scorching; **hizo un calor ~** it was scorching

achicharrar [A1] *vt* (fam) **(a)** ‹*carne/comida*› to burn … to a cinder (colloq) **(b)** «*sol*» ‹*planta*› to scorch; **hace un sol que te achicharra** the sun is scorching hot

■ **achicharrarse** *v pron* (fam) **(a)** «*persona*» to fry (colloq); «*planta*» to get scorched **(b)** «*carne/comida*» to be burned to a crisp (colloq)

achichincle, **achichinque** *mf* (Méx fam & pey) hanger-on (colloq & pej)

achicopalar [A1] *vt* (Col, Méx fam) to intimidate

■ **achicopalarse** *v pron* (Col, Méx fam) to feel intimidated

achicoria *f* chicory

achinado -da *adj* ‹*ojos*› slanting

achiote *m* (AmL) annatto

achispado -da *adj* (fam) tipsy (colloq)

achuras *fpl* (RPl) offal

acicalarse [A1] *v pron* to dress up, get dressed up

acicate *m* **(a)** (estímulo) incentive **(b)** (espuela) spur

acidez *f* (Quím) acidity; (Med) (en el estómago) acidity; (en el esófago) heartburn

ácido[1] -da *adj* **(a)** ‹*sabor*› acid; ‹*fruta*› acid, tart, sharp; ‹*vino*› sharp **(b)** ‹*carácter/tono*› acid, caustic

ácido[2] *m* **(a)** (Quím) acid **(b)** (arg) (droga) acid (sl).

acierta, **aciertas, etc** *see* ACERTAR

acierto *m* **(a)** (decisión correcta) good decision, good *o* wise move **(b)** (respuesta correcta) correct answer

acitronar [A1] *vt* (Méx) to fry … until golden brown

aclamación *f* acclaim

aclamar [A1] *vt* to acclaim, applaud

aclaración *f* explanation; **quisiera hacer una ~** I'd like to make one thing clear

aclarado *m* (Esp) rinse

aclarar [A1] *v impers* **(a)** (amanecer): **aclara temprano** it gets light early; **cuando nos levantamos estaba aclarando** dawn *o* day was breaking when we got up **(b)** (escampar) to clear up ■ **~** *vi* **(a)** «*día*» (empezar) to break, dawn **(b)** «*tiempo/día*» (escampar) to clear up ■ **~** *vt* **1** (quitar color a) to lighten **2** ‹*ideas*› to get … straight; ‹*duda*› to clear up, clarify; **quiero ~ que** … I want to make it clear that … **3** (Esp) ‹*ropa/vajilla*› to rinse

■ **aclararse** *v pron* **1 ~se la voz** to clear one's throat **2** (Esp fam) (entender) to understand; ***a ver si nos aclaramos*** let's see if we can sort things out *o* get things straight

aclimatarse [A1] *v pron* to acclimatize, get *o* become acclimatized

acné *m or f* acne

acobardar [A1] *vt* ‹*persona*› to unnerve, intimidate

■ **acobardarse** *v pron* to lose one's nerve; **~se ante el peligro** to lose one's nerve in the face of danger

acogedor -dora *adj* ‹*casa/habitación*› cozy*, welcoming; ‹*ambiente*› warm, friendly

acoger [E6] *vt* **(a)** ‹*huérfano/anciano*› to take in; ‹*refugiado*› to accept, admit **(b)** (+ *compl*) ‹*propuesta/persona*› to receive; **acogieron la noticia con satisfacción** the news was well received

■ **acogerse** *v pron* **~se A algo** ‹*a la ley*› to have recourse TO sth; ‹*a un régimen*› to opt FOR sth

acogida *f* **(a)** (de persona) welcome; (de noticia, propuesta) reception **(b)** (de huérfano) taking in; (de refugiado) acceptance

acolchar, **acolchonar** [A1] *vt* ‹*bata/tela*› to quilt; ‹*pared/puerta*› to pad

acomedido -da *adj* (Chi, Méx, Per) obliging, helpful

acomedirse [I14] *v pron* (Méx) to offer to help

acometer [E1] *vi* to attack; **~ CONTRA algo/algn** to attack sth/sb

acomodado -da *adj* **1** ‹*familia/gente*› well-off, well-to-do; **de posición acomodada** well-off, well-to-do **2** (CS, Méx fam) (que tiene palanca): **estar ~** to have contacts *o* connections

acomodador -dora *m,f* (*m*) usher; (*f*) usherette

acomodar [A1] *vt* **1** (adaptar, amoldar) to adapt **2** ‹*huésped*› to put ... up **3 (a)** (AmL) (arreglar) to arrange; (poner) to put **(b)** (fam) ‹*persona*› (en puesto): **su tío lo acomodó en su sección** his uncle fixed him up with a job in his department

■ **acomodarse** *v pron* **(a)** (ponerse cómodo) to make oneself comfortable **(b)** (adaptarse, amoldarse) **~se A algo** to adapt TO sth **(c)** (AmL) (arreglarse) ‹*ropa/anteojos*› to adjust

acompañado -da *adj* accompanied; **bien/mal ~** in good/bad company; **vino ~ de un amigo** he came with a friend

acompañamiento *m* **(a)** (Mús) accompaniment **(b)** (Coc) accompaniment; **¿con qué ~ lo quiere?** what would you like it served with?

acompañar [A1] *vt* **1 (a)** (a un lugar) to go with, accompany (frml); **acompáñalo hasta la puerta** see him to the door, see him out; **la acompañé a su casa** I walked her home; **¿me acompañas?** will you come with me? **(b)** (hacer compañía) to keep ... company **(c)** (Mús) to accompany **2** (frml) (adjuntar) to enclose; **acompañado de un certificado médico** accompanied by a medical certificate

acomplejado -da *adj*: **es muy ~** he's full of complexes; **está ~ por su gordura** he has a complex about being fat ■ *m,f*: **es un ~** he's a mass of complexes

acomplejar [A1] *vt* to give ... a complex

■ **acomplejarse** *v pron* to get a complex

acondicionador *m* **(a)** *tb* **~ de pelo** (hair) conditioner **(b) ~ de aire** air conditioner

acondicionar [A1] *vt* **(a)** ‹*vivienda/local*› to equip, fit out **(b)** (Col) ‹*carro*› to soup up

aconsejable *adj* advisable

aconsejar [A1] *vt* to advise; **~le a algn hacer algo/que haga algo** to advise sb to do sth; **has sido mal aconsejado** you've been given bad advice; **necesito que alguien me aconseje** I need some advice

acontecimiento *m* event; **adelantarse a los ~s** to jump the gun

acoplar [A1] *vt* **(a)** ‹*piezas*› to fit *o* put together **(b)** (Elec) to connect **(c)** (Ferr) to couple

acorazado *m* battleship

acordar [A10] *vt* ‹*términos*› to agree; ‹*precio/fecha*› to agree (on) ■ **~** *vi* (Andes) (recordar) **~le a algn DE hacer algo/que haga algo** to remind sb to do sth

■ **acordarse** *v pron* to remember; **si mal no me acuerdo** if I remember right; **~se DE algn/algo** to remember sb/sth; **no quiero ni ~me** I don't even want to think about it; **~se DE hacer algo** (de una acción que hay/había que realizar) to remember to do sth; (de una acción que ya se realizó) to remember *o* recall doing sth; **se acordó de haberlo visto allí** she remembered *o* recalled seeing him there; **~se (DE) QUE** ... to remember THAT ...

acorde *adj* (en armonía) ‹*sonidos*› harmonious; **colores ~s** colors that go *o* blend well together; **con un salario ~** with a salary to match; **~ CON** *or* **A algo** appropriate TO sth, in keeping WITH sth ■ *m* (Mús) chord

acordeón *m* **1** (Mús) accordion **2** (Méx fam) (para un examen) crib

acordeonista *mf* accordionist

acordonar [A1] *vt* **(a)** ‹*lugar*› to cordon off **(b)** ‹*zapatos*› to lace (up)

acorralar [A1] *vt* **(a)** ‹*animal/fugitivo*› to corner **(b)** ‹*ganado*› to round up

acortar [A1] *vt* ‹*falda/vestido*› to shorten; ‹*texto/artículo*› to cut, shorten; ‹*vacaciones/permanencia*› to cut short; ‹*película/carrera*› to reduce the length of; **~ camino** to take a short cut

■ **acortarse** *v pron* to get shorter

acosar [A1] *vt* **(a)** ‹*persona*› to hound; (sexualmente) to harass; **me ~on con preguntas** they plagued *o* bombarded me with questions **(b)** ‹*presa*› to hound, pursue relentlessly

acosijar [A1] *vt* (Méx) to badger, pester

acoso *m* **(a)** (de persona) hounding, harassment; **~ sexual** sexual harassment **(b)** (de presa) hounding, relentless pursuit

acostar [A10] *vt* ‹*persona*› to put ... to bed

■ **acostarse** *v pron* **(a)** (irse a dormir) to go to bed **(b)** (tenderse, tumbarse) to lie down; **~se boca abajo** to lie face down **(c)** (tener relaciones sexuales) to go to bed together, sleep together; **~se CON algn** to go to bed WITH sb, sleep WITH sb

acostumbrado -da *adj* **(a)** (habituado): **está mal ~** he's got into bad habits; **~ A algo/hacer algo** used TO sth/doing sth; **estamos ~s a cenar temprano** we're used to having dinner early; **está ~ a que le sirvan** he's used to being served **(b)** (habitual) customary, usual

acostumbrar [A1] *vt* **~ a algn A algo/hacer algo** to get sb used TO sth/doing sth ■ **~** *vi*: **~ A hacer algo** to be accustomed TO doing sth, be in the habit OF doing sth

■ **acostumbrarse** *v pron* **~se A algo/algn** to get used TO sth/sb; **~se A hacer algo** to get used TO doing sth

acotación *f* (en texto) marginal note, annotation

acotamiento *m* (Méx) shoulder (AmE), hard shoulder (BrE)

acrecentar [A5] *vt* to increase

■ **acrecentarse** *v pron* to increase, grow

acreditado -da *adj* **(a)** ‹*establecimiento/marca*› reputable, well-known **(b)** ‹*diplomático/periodista*› accredited; ‹*agente/representante*› authorized, official

acreditar [A1] *vt* **1** ‹*diplomático/periodista*› to accredit; ‹*representante*› to authorize **2** (frml) **(a)** (probar, avalar) ‹*pago*› to prove; **este libro lo acredita como un gran pensador** this book confirms him as a great thinker **(b)** (dar renombre): **con la calidad que lo acredita** with the quality for which it's renowned **3** (Fin) to credit

acreedor -dora *m,f* creditor

acribillar [A1] *vt* **(a)** (llenar de agujeros): **lo ~on a balazos** they riddled him with bullets **(b)** (asediar): **me ~on a preguntas** they fired a barrage of questions at me

acrílico *m* acrylic

acristalar [A1] *vt* to glaze

acrobacia *f* (arte) acrobatics: **hacer ~s** to perform acrobatics; **~ aérea** aerobatics

acróbata *mf* acrobat

acta *f*‡ (de reunión) minutes (*pl*); **levantar (el) ~** to take (the) minutes; **~ de defunción** (Col, Méx, Ven) entry in the register of deaths; **~ de matrimonio/nacimiento** (Méx) marriage/birth certificate; **~ notarial** notarial deed

actitud *f* (disposición) attitude; **adoptar una ~ firme (con algn)** to be firm (with sb)

activar [A1] *vt* **(a)** (agilizar) ‹*proceso/crecimiento*› to speed up; ‹*economía/producción*› to stimulate; ‹*circulación*› to stimulate; ‹*negociaciones*› to give fresh impetus to **(b)** (poner en funcionamiento) ‹*alarma*› to activate, trigger; ‹*dispositivo*› to activate; ‹*máquina*› to set ... in motion

■ **activarse** *v pron* «*alarma*» to go off; «*dispositivo*» to start working

actividad *f* activity; **un volcán en ~** an active volcano

activista *mf* activist

activo¹ -va *adj* active

activo² *m* assets (*pl*)

acto *m* **1 (a)** (acción) act; **morir en ~ de servicio** «*soldado*» to die on active service; «*policía/bombero*» to die in the course of one's duty; **~ sexual** sexual act (frml) **(b)** (*en locs*) **acto seguido** immediately after; **en el acto** ‹*morir*› instantly; ‹*acudir*› immediately; **lo despidieron en el ~** he was fired on the spot **2 (a)** (ceremonia) ceremony **(b)** (Teatr) act

actor *m* actor

actriz *f* actress

actuación *f* **(a)** (acción) action **(b)** (Cin, Dep, Teatr) performance; **la ~ es pésima** the acting is appalling **(c)** (conducta) conduct **(d)** (recital, sesión) performance, concert

actual *adj* ‹*ley/situación/dirección*› present, current; **en el Chile ~** in present-day Chile; **en el mundo ~** in the modern world, in today's world

actualidad *f* **(a)** (tiempo presente): **en la ~** currently, at present; **la ~ cubana** the current situation in Cuba **(b)** (de tema, noticia) topicality; **las noticias de ~** today's (*o* this week's *etc*) news; **un tema de ~** (period) a topical subject

actualizar [A4] *vt* ‹*salarios/pensiones/legislación*› to bring ... up to date; ‹*información/manual*› to update

actualmente *adv* (hoy en día) nowadays; (en este momento) at present; **se encuentra ~ en Suecia** she is currently in Sweden, she is in Sweden at present

actuar [A18] *vi* **(a)** «*persona*» (obrar) to act; **forma de ~** behavior* **(b)** «*medicamento*» to work, act **(c)** «*actor*» to act; «*torero*» to perform; **¿quién actúa en esa película?** who's in the movie?

acuarela *f* watercolor*

acuario *m* aquarium

Acuario *m* (signo) Aquarius; **es (de) ~** he's an Aquarius *o* Aquarian ■ *mf* (persona) *tb* **acuario** Aquarian, Aquarius

acuático -ca *adj* aquatic

acuatizaje *m*: *landing on water*

acuatizar [A4] *vi* to land on water

acuchillar [A1] *vt* ‹*persona*› to stab

acudir [I1] *vi* **1** (frml) (ir) to go; (venir) to come; **nadie acudió en su ayuda** nobody went/came to his aid; **~ A algo** ‹*a cita*› to arrive FOR sth; ‹*a reunión*› to attend sth; **la policía acudió al lugar de los hechos** the police arrived at the scene (of the incident) **2** (recurrir) **~ A algn** to turn TO sb; **no tenía a quien ~** he had nobody to turn to

acueducto *m* aqueduct

acuerdo *m* **(a)** (arreglo, pacto) agreement; **llegar a un ~** to reach an agreement; **~ de paz** peace agreement *o* (frml) accord **(b) estar de ~** to agree; **ponerse de ~** to come to *o* reach an agreement; **estar de ~ EN algo** to agree ON something; **estar de ~ CON algn/algo** to agree WITH sb/sth; **¿mañana a las ocho? — de ~** (*indep*) tomorrow at eight? — OK *o* all right **(c) de ~ con** *or* **a** in accordance with

acuesta, acuestas, etc *see* ACOSTAR

acumulación *f* accumulation

acumular [A1] *vt* ‹*riquezas/poder*› to accumulate; ‹*experiencia*› to gain

■ **acumularse** *v pron* «*trabajo*» to pile up, mount up; «*intereses*» to accumulate; «*deudas*» to mount up; «*polvo*» to accumulate

acunar [A1] *vt* to rock

acuñar [A1] *vt* ‹*moneda*› to mint; ‹*frase/palabra*› to coin

acuoso -sa *adj* watery

acupuntura *f* acupuncture

acupunturista *mf* acupuncturist

acurrucarse [A2] *v pron* to curl up

acusación *f* **(a)** (imputación) accusation **(b)** (Der) charge;

acusado -da *m,f*: **el/la ~** the accused, the defendant

acusador -dora *adj* accusing, accusatory (frml); **una mirada ~a** an accusing look ■ *m,f* prosecuting attorney (AmE), prosecuting counsel (BrE)

acusar [A1] *vt* **1 (a)** (culpar) to accuse; **~ a algn DE algo** to accuse sb OF sth; **me acusan de haber**

mentido they accuse me of lying **(b)** (Der) **~ a algn DE algo** to charge sb WITH sth **(c)** (fam) (delatar) to tell on (colloq) **2** (reconocer): **~ recibo de algo** (Corresp) to acknowledge receipt of sth

acusetas *mf (pl* **~***)*, **acusete -ta** *m,f* (fam) tattletale (AmE colloq), telltale (BrE colloq)

acústica *f* (ciencia) acoustics; (de local) acoustics *(pl)*

acústico -ca *adj* acoustic

adaptable *adj* adaptable

adaptación *f* **(a)** (proceso) adaptation, adjustment **(b)** (cosa adaptada) adaptation; **la ~ cinematográfica** the screen version

adaptador *m* adaptor

adaptar [A1] *vt ‹cortinas/vestido›* to alter; *‹habitación›* to convert; *‹pieza/motor›* to adapt; *‹obra/novela›* to adapt; (Inf) to convert

■ **adaptarse** *v pron* to adapt; **~se A algo/hacer algo** to adapt TO sth/doing sth; **un coche que se adapta a cualquier terreno** a car which is well suited to any terrain

a. de C. (= **antes de Cristo**) BC, before Christ

adecentar [A1] *vt ‹habitación›* to tidy up

adecuado -da *adj* **(a)** (apropiado) *‹vestido/regalo›* suitable; *‹momento›* right; *‹medios›* adequate; **la persona adecuada para el cargo** the right person for the job **(b)** (aceptable) adequate

adecuar [A1] *or* [A18] *vt* **~ algo A algo** to adapt sth TO sth

adefesio *m* (cosa) eyesore; (persona): **es un ~** he's so ugly; **ir hecho un ~** to look a sight *o* fright (colloq)

adelantado -da *adj* **1 (a)** (desarrollado) *‹país›* advanced **(b)** (aventajado): **va muy ~ en sus estudios** he is doing very well in his studies; **va ~ para su edad** he's advanced for his age **2** [ESTAR] *‹reloj›* fast **3** (Com, Fin): **pago ~** payment in advance; **por ~** in advance **4** (avanzado): **las obras están muy adelantadas** construction is already well underway; **vamos bastante ~s** we're quite far ahead with it **5** (Dep) *‹pase›* forward

adelantamiento *m* passing maneuver (AmE), overtaking manoeuvre (BrE)

adelantar [A1] *vt* **1 (a)** *‹fecha/viaje›* to bring forward **(b)** *‹pieza/ficha›* to move ... forward **2** (sobrepasar) to overtake, pass **3 (a)** *‹reloj›* to put ... forward **(b)** *‹balón›* to pass ... forward **(c)** *‹trabajo›* to get on with **4** (conseguir) to gain; **con llorar no adelantas nada** crying won't get you anywhere ■ **~** *vi* **1 (a)** (avanzar) to make progress **(b)** *«reloj»* to gain **2** (Auto) to pass, overtake (BrE)

■ **adelantarse** *v pron* **1 (a)** (avanzar) to move forward **(b)** (ir delante) to go ahead; **se adelantó para comprar las entradas** she went (on) ahead to buy the tickets **2 (a)** *«cosecha»* to be early; *«verano/frío»* to arrive early **(b)** *«reloj»* to gain **3** (anticiparse): **se adelantó a su época** he was ahead of his time; **~se a los acontecimientos** to jump the gun; **yo iba a pagar, pero él se me adelantó** I was going to pay, but he beat me to it

adelante *adv* **1** (en el espacio) **(a)** (expresando dirección, movimiento) forward; **para/hacia ~** forward; **seguir ~** to go on; **¡~!** *(como interj)* (autorizando la entrada) come in!; (ordenando marchar) forward! **(b)** (lugar, posición): **se sentó ~** (en coche) she sat in front; (en clase, cine) she sat at the front; **más ~ la calle se bifurca** further on, the road forks; **la parte de ~** the front **2** (en el tiempo): **más ~** later; **(de ahora) en ~** from now on; **de hoy en ~** as of *o* from today **3 adelante de** *(loc prep)* (AmL) in front of

adelanto *m* **1** (avance) step forward; **los ~s de la ciencia** the advances of science **2** (del sueldo) advance; (depósito) deposit **3** (en el tiempo): **llegó con un poco de ~** he/she/it arrived slightly early

adelgazamiento *m* slimming

adelgazante *adj* weight-reducing *(before n)*, slimming *(before n)* (BrE)

adelgazar [A4] *vt ‹caderas/cintura›* to reduce; *‹kilos›* to lose ■ **~** *vi* to lose weight

ademán *m* (expresión) expression; (movimiento, gesto) gesture; **hizo ~ de levantarse** he made as if to get up

además *adv* **1 (a)** (también) as well, too; **~ habla ruso** she speaks Russian as well *o* too **(b)** (lo que es más) what's more **(c)** (por otra parte) anyway, besides; **~ ¿a mí qué me importa?** anyway, what do I care? **2 además de** besides, apart from; **~ de hacerte mal, engorda** besides *o* apart from being bad for you, it's also fattening; **~ de hacerlos, los diseña** he designs them as well as making them

adentro *adv* **1 (a)** (expresando dirección, movimiento): **vamos para ~** let's go in *o* inside; **ven aquí ~** come in here **(b)** (lugar, parte) inside; [*European Spanish prefers* DENTRO *in many of these examples*] **¡qué calor hace aquí ~!** it's so hot in here!; **¿comemos ~?** shall we eat indoors *o* inside?; **la parte de ~** the inside **2 adentro de** (AmL) in, inside

adentros *mpl*: **dije para mis ~** I said to myself; **se rió para sus ~s** he chuckled to himself

adepto -ta *adj*: **ser ~ A algo** *‹a secta›* to be a follower OF sth; *‹a partido›* to be a supporter OF sth ■ *m,f* (de secta) follower; (de partido) supporter

aderezar [A4] *vt ‹guiso›* to season; *‹ensalada›* to dress

aderezo *m* (de guiso) seasoning; (de ensalada) dressing

adherencia *f* **(a)** (acción) adherence **(b)** (Auto) grip, roadholding **(c)** (Med) adhesion

adherente *adj* adhesive

adherir [I11] *vt* to stick

■ **adherirse** *v pron* **(a)** (pegarse) to stick **(b)** (unirse) **~se A algo** *‹a propuesta/causa›* to give one's support TO sth; *‹a movimiento/partido›* to join sth

adhesión *f* **(a)** (a una superficie) adhesion **(b)** (apoyo) support **(c)** (a una organización) joining

adhesivo[1] -va *adj* adhesive, sticky

adhesivo[2] *m* (sustancia) adhesive; (lámina, estampa) sticker

adicción *f* addiction; **~ a la heroína** heroin addiction

adición *f* **(a)** (Mat) addition **(b)** (RPl) (cuenta) check (AmE), bill (BrE)

adicional *adj* additional; **una cantidad ~** a supplement

adicto -ta *adj* (a la bebida, la droga) addicted; **~ A algo** addicted TO sth ■ *m,f* addict; **los ~s a la cocaína** cocaine addicts

adiestrar [A1] *vt* to train

adinerado -da *adj* wealthy, moneyed

adiós *m/interj* (al despedirse) goodbye, bye (colloq); (al pasar) hello; ⇒ DECIR *vt* 3(b)

aditivo *m* additive

adivinanza *f* riddle; **jugar a las ~s** to play at guessing riddles

adivinar [A1] *vt* **(a)** (por conjeturas, al azar) to guess **(b)** (por magia) to foretell, predict ■ ~ *vi* to guess

adivino -na *m,f* fortune-teller

adjetivo¹ -va *adj* adjectival

adjetivo² *m* adjective

adjudicación *f* **(a)** (de premio, contrato) awarding; (de viviendas) allocation **(b)** (en subasta) sale

adjudicar [A2] *vt* **(a)** ‹*premio/contrato*› to award; ‹*vivienda*› to allot, allocate **(b)** (en subasta): **le ~on la alfombra al anticuario** the carpet was sold to *o* went to the antique dealer; **¡adjudicado!** sold!

adjuntar [A1] *vt* to enclose

adjunto -ta *adj* **(a)** ‹*director*› deputy (*before n*); **profesor ~** associate professor (AmE), senior lecturer (BrE) **(b)** ‹*lista/copia*› enclosed, attached

administración *f* **1 (a)** (de empresa, bienes) management **(b)** (Pol) administration; **~ pública** civil service **2 (a)** (conjunto de personas) management **(b)** (oficina, departamento) administration

administrador -dora *m,f* (de empresa) manager, administrator; (de bienes) administrator

administrar [A1] *vt* **(a)** ‹*empresa/bienes*› to manage, administer (frml) **(b)** (frml) (dar) ‹*sacramentos/medicamento*› to give

■ **administrarse** *v pron*: **~se bien/mal** to manage one's money well/badly

administrativo -va *adj* administrative ■ *m,f* administrative assistant (*o* officer *etc*); (con funciones más rutinarias) clerk

admirable *adj* admirable

admiración *f* **(a)** (respeto) admiration **(b)** (sorpresa) amazement

admirador -dora *m,f* **(a)** (de persona) admirer, fan **(b)** (hum) (pretendiente) admirer (hum)

admirar [A1] *vt* **(a)** (respetar) ‹*persona/cualidad*› to admire **(b)** (contemplar) to admire **(c)** (sorprender) to amaze

■ **admirarse** *v pron* **~se DE algo** to be amazed AT *o* ABOUT sth

admisible *adj* ‹*comportamiento*› admissible, acceptable; ‹*excusa*› acceptable

admisión *f* admission; **examen** *or* **prueba de ~** entrance examination *o* test

admitir [I1] *vt* **1 (a)** (aceptar) to accept; Ⓢ **se admiten tarjetas de crédito** we take *o* accept credit cards **(b)** (permitir) to allow **(c)** (reconocer) to admit **2** (dar cabida a) «*local*» to hold

ADN *m* (= **ácido desoxirribonucleico**) DNA

adobar [A1] *vt* ‹*carne/pescado*› (condimentar) to marinade; (para conservar) to pickle; (para curar) to cure

adobe *m* adobe

adobo *m* (condimento) marinade; (para conservar) pickle

adoctrinar [A1] *vt* to indoctrinate

adolecer [E3] *vi* **~ DE algo** ‹*de enfermedad/defecto*› to suffer FROM sth

adolescencia *f* adolescence; **durante su ~** (when he was) in his teens, in adolescence (frml)

adolescente *adj* adolescent; **tiene dos hijos ~s** she has two teenage *o* adolescent children ■ *mf* (en contextos no técnicos) teenager; (Med, Psic) adolescent

adolorido -da *adj* (esp AmL) ⇒ DOLORIDO (a)

adonde *adv* where; **el lugar ~ se dirigían** the place where *o* to which they were going

adónde *adv* where

adondequiera *adv*: **~ que vayas** wherever you go

adopción *f* adoption

adoptar [A1] *vt* **(a)** ‹*actitud/costumbre*› to adopt; ‹*decisión/medida/posición*› to take **(b)** ‹*niño/nacionalidad*› to adopt

adoptivo -va *adj* **(a)** ‹*hijo*› adopted; ‹*padres*› adoptive **(b)** ‹*patria/país*› adopted

adoquín *m* **(a)** (de piedra) paving stone; (ovalado) cobblestone **(b)** (Per) (helado) popsicle® (AmE), ice lolly (BrE)

adorable *adj* adorable

adoración *f* **(a)** (de persona) adoration **(b)** (de deidad) adoration, worship

adorar [A1] *vt* **(a)** ‹*persona/cosa*› to adore **(b)** ‹*deidad*› to worship, adore

adormecer [E3] *vt* **(a)** ‹*persona*› to make ... sleepy *o* drowsy; ‹*sentidos*› to numb, dull **(b)** ‹*pierna/mano*› to numb

■ **adormecerse** *v pron* to fall asleep, doze off

adormecimiento *m* **(a)** (somnolencia) sleepiness, drowsiness **(b)** (de un miembro) numbness

adormilarse [A1] *v pron* to doze

adornar [A1] *vt* **(a)** ‹*habitación/sombrero/comida*› to decorate **(b)** ‹*relato/discurso*› to embellish **(c)** «*flores/banderas*» to adorn

■ **adornarse** *v pron* (*refl*) ‹*cabeza/pelo*› to adorn

adorno *m* **(a)** (objeto) ornament; **los ~s de Navidad** the Christmas decorations **(b)** (decoración) adornment; **de ~** for decoration

adosado -da *adj* **~ A algo** fixed TO sth; ⇒ CASA

adosar [A1] *vt* **(a)** ‹*armario/escritorio*› **~ algo A algo** to fix sth TO sth **(b)** (Méx) ‹*documento*› to enclose, attach

adquiera, adquirió, etc *see* ADQUIRIR

adquirir [I13] *vt* ‹*casa/coche*› to acquire, obtain; (comprar) to purchase, buy; ‹*conocimientos/colección/fortuna*› to acquire; ‹*fama*› to attain, achieve; ‹*experiencia*› to gain; **~ malas costumbres** to get into bad habits

adquisición *f* acquisition; (compra) purchase

adquisitivo -va *adj* purchasing

adrede *adv* on purpose, deliberately

adrenalina *f* adrenaline
aduana *f* customs; **libre de derechos de ~** duty free
aduanero -ra *adj* customs (*before n*) ■ *m,f* customs officer
adulación *f* flattery
adulador -dora *adj* flattering ■ *m,f* flatterer
adular [A1] *vt* to flatter
adulterar [A1] *vt* ‹*alimento/vino*› to adulterate; ‹*información*› to falsify
adulterio *m* adultery
adulto -ta *adj* **(a)** ‹*persona/animal*› adult (*before n*) **(b)** ‹*reacción/opinión*› adult ■ *m,f* adult
adusto -ta *adj* ‹*persona/expresión*› austere, severe; ‹*paisaje*› bleak, harsh
advenedizo -za *adj* upstart (*before n*) ■ *m,f* social climber
adverbio *m* adverb
adversario -ria *adj* opposing (*before n*) ■ *m,f* opponent, adversary
adversidad *f* adversity; **en la ~** in adversity
adverso -sa *adj* ‹*circunstancias/resultado*› adverse
advertencia *f* warning; **que les sirva de ~** let it be a warning to them
advertir [I11] *vt* **(a)** (avisar) to warn; **¡te lo advierto!** I'm warning you!; **~le A algn DE algo** to warn sb ABOUT sth; **le advertí que tuviera cuidado** I warned him to be careful; **te advierto que no me sorprendió nada** I must say I wasn't at all surprised **(b)** (notar) to notice
adviento *m* Advent
advierta, advirtió, etc *see* ADVERTIR
adyacente *adj* adjacent
aéreo -rea *adj* ‹*vista*› aerial; ‹*tráfico*› air (*before n*)
aerobic /e'roβik/ *m*, (Méx) **aerobics** *mpl* aerobics
aerodinámica *f* aerodynamics
aerodinámico -ca *adj* aerodynamic
aeródromo *m* aerodrome, airfield
aeroespacial *adj* aerospace (*before n*)
aerograma *m* aerogram, air (mail) letter
aerolínea *f* airline
aeromodelismo *m* model airplane making
aeromozo -za *m,f* (AmL) flight attendant
aeronáutica *f* **(a)** (ciencia) aeronautics **(b)** (RPl) (aviación militar) air force
aeronáutico -ca *adj* aeronautic, aeronautical
aeronave *f* **(a)** (globo dirigible) airship **(b)** (frml) (avión) airliner, aircraft
aeropuerto *m* airport
aerosol *m* aerosol, spray can
afable *adj* affable
afán *m* **1 (a)** (anhelo) eagerness; **su ~ de aventuras** his thirst for adventure; **~ DE hacer algo** eagerness TO do sth; **su ~ de agradar** their eagerness to please; **tiene ~ de aprender** she's eager to learn **(b)** (empeño) effort **2** (Col fam) (prisa) hurry
afanado -da *adj* **1** [ESTAR] ‹*persona*› busy **2** [ESTAR] (Col, Per fam) (con prisa) in a hurry
afanarse *v pron* (esforzarse) to work, toil; **~se EN** *or* **POR hacer algo** to strive TO do sth
afear [A1] *vt* **(a)** ‹*persona*› to make ... look ugly; ‹*paisaje*› to spoil **(b)** ‹*conducta*› to criticize
■ **afearse** *v pron* to lose one's looks
afectación *f* affectation
afectado -da *adj* **(a)** ‹*gestos/acento*› affected **(b)** ‹*área/órgano*› affected; **está afectado de una grave enfermedad** (frml) he is suffering from a serious disease
afectar [A1] *vt* **1 (a)** (tener efecto en) to affect; **esto nos afecta a todos** this affects us all **(b)** (afligir) to affect (frml); **la noticia lo afectó mucho** the news upset him terribly **2** (fingir) ‹*admiración/indiferencia*› to affect, feign
afectísimo -ma *adj* (Corresp) (frml): **suyo ~** yours truly
afectivo -va *adj* emotional
afecto *m* (cariño) affection; **tenerle ~ a algn** to be fond of sb; **tomarle ~ a algn** to grow fond of sb
afectuoso -sa *adj* ‹*persona*› affectionate; **reciba un ~ saludo** (Corresp) with warm *o* kind regards
afeitadora *f* shaver, electric razor
afeitar [A1] *vt* ‹*persona/cabeza*› to shave; ‹*barba*› to shave off
■ **afeitarse** *v pron* (*refl*) to shave; **se afeitó la barba** he shaved off his beard
afeminado -da *adj* effeminate
aferrarse [A1] *v pron*: **~se A algo/algn** to cling (ON) TO sth/sb
affmo. affma. (Corresp) (frml) = **afectísimo, -ma**
Afganistán *m* Afghanistan
afgano -na *adj/m,f* Afghan
afianzar [A4] *vt* ‹*posición/postura*› to consolidate
■ **afianzarse** *v pron* «*prestigio/sistema*» to become consolidated
afiche *m* (esp AmL) poster
afición *f* **(a)** (inclinación, gusto) love, liking; **~ a la lectura/música** love of reading/music **(b)** (pasatiempo) hobby **(c)** (Dep, Taur): **la ~** the fans (*pl*)
aficionado -da *adj* [SER] **(a)** (entusiasta) **~ A algo** fond OF *o* keen ON sth **(b)** (no profesional) amateur ■ *m,f* **(a)** (entusiasta) enthusiast; **para los ~s al bricolaje** for do-it-yourself enthusiasts; **un ~ a la música** a music lover; **los ~s al tenis/fútbol** tennis/football fans **(b)** (no profesional) amateur
aficionarse [A1] *v pron* **~se A algo** to become interested IN sth
afilado -da *adj* **1 (a)** ‹*borde/cuchillo*› sharp **(b)** ‹*nariz*› pointed; ‹*rasgos*› sharp; ‹*dedos*› long **2** (mordaz) ‹*lengua*› sharp; ‹*pluma*› biting
afilar [A1] *vt* ‹*navaja/cuchillo*› to sharpen, hone
afiliación *f* affiliation
afiliado -da *m,f* member
afiliarse [A1] *v pron* **~se A algo** ‹*a partido/sindicato*› to become a member OF sth, to join sth; ‹*a sistema*› to join sth

afín *adj* ‹*temas/lenguas*› related; ‹*culturas/ideologías*› similar; ‹*intereses*› common; **ideas afines a las nuestras** ideas which have a lot in common with our own

afinación *f* tuning

afinar [A1] *vt* **1 (a)** ‹*instrumento*› to tune **(b)** ‹*coche*› to tune up; ‹*motor*› to tune **2** ‹*punta*› to sharpen

afinidad *f* (entre personas, caracteres) affinity; **no tengo ninguna ~ con él** I have nothing in common with him

afirmación *f* (declaración) statement, assertion; (respuesta positiva) affirmation

afirmar [A1] *vt* **1** (aseverar) to state, declare, assert (frml); **no lo afirmó ni lo negó** she neither confirmed nor denied it **2** ‹*escalera*› to steady ■ **~** *vi:* **afirmó con la cabeza** he nodded
■ **afirmarse** *v pron* (físicamente) to steady oneself; **~se EN algo/algn** to hold ON to sth/sb

afirmativo -va *adj* ‹*respuesta/frase*› affirmative

afligido -da *adj* distressed

afligir [I7] *vt* **(a)** (afectar) to afflict **(b)** (apenar) to upset
■ **afligirse** *v pron* to get upset

aflojar [A1] *vt* **1** ‹*cinturón/tornillo*› to loosen; ‹*cuerda/riendas*› to slacken; ‹*presión/tensión*› to ease; ‹*marcha/paso*› to slow down **2** (fam) ‹*dinero*› to hand over **3** (AmL) ‹*motor*› to run in ■ **~** *vi* «*tormenta*» to ease off; «*fiebre/viento*» to drop; «*calor*» to let up; «*tensión/presión*» to ease off
■ **aflojarse** *v pron* **(a)** (*refl*) ‹*cinturón*› to loosen **(b)** «*tornillo/tuerca*» to come *o* work loose

afónico -ca *adj*: **estar/quedarse ~** to loose one's voice

afortunado *adj* ‹*persona*› lucky, fortunate; ‹*encuentro/coincidencia*› happy, fortunate; **una elección poco afortunada** a rather unfortunate choice

África *f*‡ *tb* **el ~** Africa

África del Sur *f*‡ South Africa

africano -na *adj/m,f* African

afrikaans *m* Afrikaans

afrikaner *adj/mf* (*pl* **-ners**) Afrikaner

afrodisíaco¹ -ca *adj* aphrodisiac

afrodisíaco² *m* aphrodisiac

afrontar [A1] *vt* ‹*problema/responsabilidad*› to face up to; ‹*desafío/peligro*› to face

afuera *adv* **1 (a)** (expresando dirección, movimiento) outside; **ven aquí ~** come out here; **¡~!** get out of here! **(b)** (lugar, parte) outside; [*European Spanish prefers* FUERA *in many of these examples*] **aquí ~ se está muy bien** it's really nice out here; **comimos ~** (en el jardín) we ate outside *o* outdoors; (en un restaurante) we ate out; **por ~ es rojo** it's red on the outside **2 afuera de** (AmL): **¿qué haces ~ de la cama?** what are you doing out of bed?; **~ del edificio** outside the building

afueras *fpl*: **las ~** the outskirts

agachar [A1] *vt* ‹*cabeza*› to lower
■ **agacharse** *v pron* **(a)** (ponerse en cuclillas) to crouch down; (inclinarse) to bend down **(b)** (AmL fam) (rebajarse) to eat humble pie *o* (AmE) crow (colloq)

agallas *fpl* (fam) (valor) guts (*pl*) (colloq); **con ~s** gutsy (colloq); **hay que tener ~s** it takes guts (colloq)

agarrado¹ -da *adj* **(a)** [SER] (fam) (tacaño) tightfisted (colloq) **(b)** [ESTAR] (CS fam) (enamorado) in love ■ *m,f* (fam) (tacaño) skinflint (colloq), tightwad (AmE colloq)

agarrado² *adv*: **bailar ~** to dance closely

agarrar [A1] *vt* **1** (sujetar) to grab, get hold of; **me agarró del brazo** (para apoyar) she took hold of my arm; (con violencia, rapidez) she grabbed me by the arm **2** (esp AmL) ‹*objeto*› (tomar) to take; (atajar) to catch; **agarra un papel y toma nota** get a piece of paper and take this down **3** (AmL) (pescar, atrapar) to catch; **si lo agarro, lo mato** if I get *o* lay my hands on him, I'll kill him **4** (esp AmL) (adquirir) ‹*resfriado/pulmonía*› to catch; ‹*costumbre/vicio*› to pick up; ‹*ritmo*› to get into; ‹*velocidad*› to gather, pick up; **~le cariño a algn** to grow fond of sb; **le agarró asco** he got sick of it; **le he agarrado odio** I've come to hate him **5** (AmL) (entender) ‹*indirecta/chiste*› to get ■ **~** *vi* **1** (asir, sujetar) to take hold of, hold; **toma, agarra** here, hold this **2** «*planta/injerto*» to take; «*tornillo*» to grip, catch; «*ruedas*» to grip; «*tinte*» to take
■ **agarrarse** *v pron* **1** (asirse) to hold on; **agárrate bien** *or* **fuerte** hold on tight; **~se A** *or* **DE algo** to hold on TO sth; **iban agarrados del brazo** they were walking along arm in arm **2** ‹*dedo/manga*› to catch; **me agarré el dedo en el cajón** I caught my finger in the drawer **3** (esp AmL) ‹*resfriado/pulmonía*› to catch; **~se una borrachera** to get drunk; **~se un disgusto/una rabieta** to get upset/into a temper **4** (AmL fam) (pelearse) to get into a fight; **se ~on a patadas** they started kicking each other; **~se CON algn** to have a set-to WITH sb (colloq)

agarre *m* (de neumático) grip; (de coche) roadholding

agarrotar [A1] *vt* ‹*piernas/músculos*› to make ... stiff
■ **agarrotarse** *v pron* **(a)** «*manos/músculos*» to stiffen up; **tengo las manos agarrotadas** my hands are stiff **(b)** «*motor/máquina*» to seize up

agazaparse [A1] *v pron* «*animal*» to crouch; «*persona*» to crouch (down)

agencia *f* (oficina) office; (sucursal) branch; **~ de colocaciones** employment agency *o* bureau (*generally for domestic staff*); **~ de prensa** *or* **de noticias** press *o* news agency; **~ de viajes** travel agent's, travel agency

agenda *f* (libreta) appointment book (AmE), diary (BrE); (programa) agenda; **~ de bolsillo** pocket diary; **~ de trabajo** engagement book

agente *mf* **1** (Com, Fin) agent; **~ de publicidad** advertising agent; **~ de seguros** insurance broker; **~ de viajes** travel agent **2** (frml) (funcionario) employee; **~ de policía** police officer; **~ de tráfico** *or* (Arg, Méx) **de tránsito** ≈ traffic policeman (*in US*), ≈ traffic warden (*in UK*); **~ secreto** secret agent

ágil *adj* ‹*persona/movimiento*› agile; ‹*estilo/programa*› lively

agilidad *f* (de persona) agility; (de estilo) liveliness

agilizar [A4] *vt* ‹*gestiones/proceso*› to speed up; ‹*pensamiento*› to sharpen; ‹*ritmo/presentación*› to make … livelier *o* more dynamic

agitación *f* **(a)** (nerviosismo) agitation **(b)** (de calle, ciudad) bustle

agitado -da *adj* **(a)** ‹*mar*› rough, choppy **(b)** ‹*día/vida*› hectic, busy **(c)** ‹*persona*› worked up, agitated

agitador -dora *m,f* (persona) agitator

agitar [A1] *vt* **(a)** ‹*líquido/botella*› to shake **(b)** ‹*brazo/pañuelo*› to wave; ‹*alas*› to flap
■ **agitarse** *v pron* **(a)** «*mar*» to get rough; «*barca*» to toss; «*toldo*» to flap **(b)** (inquietarse) to get worked up

aglomeración *f* **(a)** (de gente): **se prudujo una ~ a la entrada** people crowded at the entrance; **para evitar las aglomeraciones** to avoid crowding; **las aglomeraciones urbanas** the built-up urban areas **(b)** (de tráfico) buildup

aglomerarse [A1] *v pron* to crowd (together)

agnóstico -ca *adj/m,f* agnostic

agobiado -da *adj* [ESTAR] **~** DE **algo** ‹*de trabajo*› snowed under WITH sth; ‹*de deudas*› overwhelmed WITH sth; **estaba agobiada con tantos problemas** she was weighed down by all those problems

agobiante, **agobiador -dora** *adj* ‹*trabajo/día*› exhausting; ‹*calor*› stifling; **es una carga ~ para él** it's/he's/she's a terrible burden on him

agobiar [A1] *vt* «*problemas/responsabilidad*» to weigh *o* get … down; «*calor*» to oppress, get … down; **te agobia con tanta amabilidad** she smothers you with kindness; **este niño me agobia** this child is too much for me

agobio *m*: **una sensación de ~** a sense of oppression

agonía *f* **(a)** (de moribundo) death throes (*pl*) **(b)** (sufrimiento) suffering

agonizar [A4] *vi* «*persona*» to be dying, be in the throes of death; «*imperio/régimen*» be in its death throes

agosto *m* ▶ **193** August; *para ejemplos ver* ENERO; ***hacer su ~*** to make a fortune, to make a killing (colloq)

agotado -da *adj* **(a)** [ESTAR] ‹*recursos*› exhausted; ‹*edición*› sold out; ‹*pila*› dead, flat; Ⓢ **agotadas todas las localidades** sold out **(b)** [ESTAR] ‹*persona*› exhausted

agotador -dora *adj* exhausting

agotamiento *m* exhaustion

agotar [A1] *vt* **(a)** ‹*recursos*› to exhaust, use up; ‹*pila*› to wear out, run down; ‹*mina/tierra*› to exhaust **(b)** (cansar) ‹*persona*› to tire … out, wear … out
■ **agotarse** *v pron* **(a)** «*existencias/reservas*» to run out, be used up; «*pila*» to run down; «*mina/tierra*» to become exhausted; «*edición*» to sell out; **se me está agotando la paciencia** my patience is running out **(b)** «*persona*» to wear *o* tire oneself out

agraciado -da *adj* ‹*persona/figura*› attractive; **es muy poco ~** he's not very attractive

agradable *adj* ‹*persona*› pleasant, nice; ‹*carácter*› pleasant; ‹*día/velada*› enjoyable, nice; ‹*sensación/efecto*› pleasant, pleasing; ‹*sabor/olor*› pleasant, nice; **~ a la vista** pleasing to the eye

agradar [A1] *vi* (frml): **¿le agrada éste, señora?** is this one to your liking, madam? (frml); **la idea no me agrada** the idea doesn't appeal to me; **le agrada verlo contento** it gives her pleasure to see him happy; **me ~ía mucho verlos allí** I would be very pleased to see you there ■ **~** *vt* to please

agradecer [E3] *vt* **(a)** (sentir gratitud por) ‹*ayuda/amabilidad*› to appreciate, to be grateful for; **~le algo** A **algn** to be grateful TO sb for sth; **le ~ía (que) me llamara** (frml) I would appreciate it if you would call me (frml) **(b)** (dar las gracias por) to thank; **~le algo** A **algn** to thank sb for sth; **¡y así es como me lo agradece!** and this is all the thanks I get!

agradecido -da *adj* ‹*persona*› grateful; **estar ~** to be grateful; **¡qué poco ~ eres!** you're so ungrateful!

agradecimiento *m* gratitude; **demostrar ~** to show gratitude; **en ~ por todo lo que ha hecho** in appreciation of all you have done

agradezca, **agradezcas, etc** *see* AGRADECER

agrado *m* (frml): **espero que sea de su ~** I hope this is to your liking; **con sumo ~** gladly; **tuve el ~ de verla** I had the pleasure of seeing her

agrandar [A1] *vt* **(a)** ‹*casa*› to extend; ‹*agujero/pozo*› to make … larger *o* bigger; ‹*fotocopia*› to enlarge, blow up; ‹*vestido*› to let out **(b)** (exagerar) to exaggerate
■ **agrandarse** *v pron* «*agujero/bulto*» to grow larger, get bigger

agrario -ria *adj* ‹*sector/política*› agricultural (*before n*); ‹*sociedad*› agrarian

agravante *adj* aggravating ■ *f or m* (Der) aggravating factor *o* circumstance; **con la ~ de que estaba borracho** what makes it even worse is that he was drunk

agravar [A1] *vt* to make … worse, aggravate
■ **agravarse** *v pron* «*problema/situación*» to become worse, worsen; «*enfermo*» to deteriorate, get worse

agredir [I32] *vt* (frml) to attack, assault

agregar [A3] *vt* (añadir) to add; **~ algo** A **algo** to add sth TO sth

agresión *f* aggression; **una ~ brutal** a brutal attack

agresividad *f* aggressiveness

agresivo -va *adj* aggressive

agresor -sora *adj* ‹*ejército*› attacking (*before n*); ‹*país*› aggressor (*before n*) ■ *m,f* (país, ejército) aggressor; (persona) attacker, assailant (frml)

agreste *adj* ‹*terreno/camino*› rough; ‹*paisaje*› rugged; ‹*vegetación/animal*› wild

agriarse [A1 *or* A17] *v pron* «*leche/vino*» to turn *o* go sour; «*persona*» to become bitter *o* embittered

agrícola *adj* ‹*técnicas*› agricultural, farming (*before n*)

agricultor -tora *m,f* farmer

agricultura *f* agriculture

agridulce *adj* bittersweet; (Coc) sweet-and-sour

agrietarse [A1] *v pron* «*tierra/pared*» to crack; «*piel*» to chap, become chapped

agringado -da *adj* (AmL fam & pey) ‹*persona*› Americanized; ‹*acento/costumbres*› (norteamericanizado) Americanized; (extranjero) foreign

agrio, **agria** *adj* **(a)** ‹*manzana*› sour, tart; ‹*naranja/limón*› sour, sharp **(b)** ‹*tono/persona*› sour, sharp; ‹*disputa*› bitter

agriparse [A1] *v pron* (Andes) to get the flu (AmE), to get flu (BrE); **está agripado** he has (the) flu

agronomía *f* agronomy

agrónomo -ma *m,f* agronomist

agrupación *f* **1** (grupo) group; (asociación) association; **~ coral** choral group, choir **2** (acción) grouping (together)

agrupar [A1] *vt* **(a)** (formar grupos) to put ... into groups, to group **(b)** (reunir) ‹*organizaciones/partidos*› to bring together

■ **agruparse** *v pron* **(a)** (formar un grupo) «*niños/policías*» to gather; «*partidos*» to come together **(b)** (dividirse en grupos) to get into groups

agua *f*‡ **1** water; **~ de lluvia/mar** rainwater/seawater; **~ corriente/destilada** running/distilled water; **~ de colonia** eau de cologne; **~ dulce** fresh water; **~ mineral** mineral water; **~ ~ con gas/sin gas** sparkling/still mineral water; **~ oxigenada** peroxide, hydrogen peroxide (tech); **~ potable/salada** drinking/salt water; ***como ~ para chocolate*** (Méx fam) furious; ***estar con el ~ al cuello*** to be up to one's neck; ***estar más claro que el ~*** to be (patently) obvious; ***hacérsele ~ la boca a algn*** (AmL): **se me hizo ~ la boca** it made my mouth water; ***ser ~ pasada*** to be a thing of the past; **~ *que no has de beber déjala correr*** if you're not interested, don't spoil things for me/for other people; ***nunca digas de esta ~ no beberé*** you never know when the same thing might happen to you **2** (lluvia) rain **3** (AmC, Andes) (infusión) herb tea (AmE), herbal tea (BrE); **~ de menta** mint tea **4 aguas** *fpl* **(a)** (de mar, río) waters (*pl*) **(b)** (de balneario, manantial) waters (*pl*); **tomar las ~s** to take the waters; **~ termales** *fpl* thermal waters (*pl*)

aguacate *m* (árbol) avocado; (fruto) avocado (pear)

aguacero *m* downpour

aguado -da *adj* **1** ‹*leche/vino*› watered-down; ‹*sopa*› watery, thin; ‹*café*› weak; ‹*salsa*› thin **2** (AmC, Méx fam) (aburrido) [ESTAR] ‹*fiesta/película*› boring, dull; [SER] ‹*persona*› boring, dull

aguafiestas *mf* (*pl* **~**) (fam) wet blanket (colloq), party pooper (AmE colloq)

aguaitar [A1] *vt* (AmS fam) (espiar) to spy on; (vigilar) to keep an eye on ■ **~** *vi* (AmS fam) (espiar) to snoop (colloq); (mirar) to have a look

aguanieve *f* sleet

aguantador -dora *adj* (AmL) **1** (fam) (resistente) ‹*tela/ropa/zapatos*› hard-wearing; ‹*coche*› sturdy **2** (fam) **(a)** (paciente, tolerante): **es muy ~** he puts up with a lot (colloq) **(b)** (del dolor, sufrimiento) tough (colloq)

aguantar [A1] *vt* **1** ‹*dolor/sufrimiento*› to bear, endure; **aguanto bien el calor** I can take the heat; **no tengo por qué ~ esto** I don't have to put up with this; **este calor no hay quien lo aguante** this heat is unbearable; **no sabes ~ una broma** you can't take a joke; **no los aguanto** I can't stand them; **no puedo ~ este dolor de muelas** this toothache's unbearable **2 (a)** ‹*peso/carga*› to support, bear; ‹*presión*› to withstand **(b)** (durar): **estas botas ~án otro invierno** these boots will last (me/you/him) another winter **3** (sostener) to hold **4** (contener, reprimir) ‹*risa/lágrimas*› to hold back; **~ la respiración** to hold one's breath ■ **~** *vi:* **¡ya no aguanto más!** I can't take any more!; **no creo que este clavo aguante** I don't think this nail will hold

■ **aguantarse** *v pron* **1** (conformarse, resignarse): **me tendré que ~** I'll just have to put up with it; **si no le gusta, que se aguante** if he doesn't like it, he can lump it (colloq) **2** (euf) (reprimirse, contenerse): **no me pude ~ y me puse a llorar** I couldn't contain myself and burst into tears; **aguántate un poquito que ya llegamos** just hold *o* hang on a minute, we'll soon be there **3** (AmL fam) (esperarse) to hang on (colloq)

aguar [A16] *vt* **(a)** ‹*leche/vino*› to water down **(b)** (fam) (estropear) to put a damper on (colloq)

■ **aguarse** *v pron* (fam) to be spoiled

aguardar [A1] *vt* ‹*persona*› to wait for; ‹*acontecimiento*› to await ■ **~** *vi* «*noticia/destino*» to await; **les aguardaba una sorpresa** there was a surprise in store for them

aguardiente *m* eau-de-vie (*clear brandy distilled from fermented fruit juice*)

aguarrás *m* turpentine, turps (colloq)

aguayo *m* (Bol) *multicolored cloth*

agudeza *f* **1 (a)** (de voz, sonido) high pitch **(b)** (de dolor — duradero) intensity; (— momentáneo) sharpness **2** (perspicacia) sharpness; (de sentido, instinto) keenness, sharpness **3** (comentario ingenioso) witty comment

agudizar [A4] *vt* ‹*sensación*› to heighten; ‹*crisis/conflicto*› make worse; ‹*instinto*› to heighten; ‹*sentido*› to sharpen

■ **agudizarse** *v pron* «*sensación*» to heighten; «*dolor*» to get worse; «*crisis*» to worsen; «*instinto*» to become heightened; «*sentido*» to become sharper

agudo -da *adj* **1 (a)** ‹*filo/punta*› sharp **(b)** ‹*ángulo*› acute **2 (a)** ‹*voz/sonido*› high-pitched; ‹*nota*› high **(b)** ‹*dolor*› (duradero) intense, acute; (momentáneo) sharp **(c)** ‹*crisis*› severe **(d)** ‹*aumento/descenso*› sharp **3 (a)** (perspicaz) ‹*persona*› quick-witted, sharp; ‹*comentario*› shrewd **(b)** (gracioso) ‹*comentario/persona*› witty **(c)** ‹*sentido/instinto*› sharp

agüero *m*: **ser de mal/buen ~** (presagio) to be a bad/good omen; (causa) to bring bad/good luck

agüevado -da *adj* (AmC fam) [ESTAR] upset

aguijón *m* **(a)** (vara) goad **(b)** (Zool) sting

águila *f*‡ **(a)** (ave) eagle; ***ser un ~*** to be very sharp **(b)** (Méx) (de moneda) ≈ heads (*pl*); **¿~ o sol?** heads or tails?

aguileño -ña *adj* ‹*nariz*› aquiline

aguinaldo *m* **1 (a)** (propina) Christmas bonus (AmE), Christmas box (BrE) **(b)** (paga extra) *extra month's salary paid at Christmas*, Christmas bonus (AmE) **2** (Col, Ven) (canción) ≈ Christmas carol

aguja *f* **(a)** (de coser, tejer) needle; (para inyecciones) needle; (de tocadiscos) stylus, needle; (de instrumento) needle; (de balanza) pointer, needle; (de reloj) hand; ***buscar una ~ en un pajar*** to look for a needle in a haystack **(b)** (Inf) pin

agujereado -da *adj*: **está ~** it has holes in it

agujerear [A1] *vt* (hacer agujeros en) to make holes in; (atravesar) to pierce

agujero *m* hole; **hacerse ~s en las orejas** to have one's ears pierced

agujeta *f* **1** (Méx) (de zapato) (shoe) lace **2 agujetas** *fpl* (Esp) stiffness; **tengo ~s en las piernas** my legs are stiff

aguzar [A4] *vt* to sharpen; **aguzó el oído** he pricked up his ears

ah *interj* (expresando sorpresa, lástima, asentimiento) oh!

ahí *adv* **1 (a)** (en el espacio) there; **~ está/viene** there he is/here he comes; **~ arriba/abajo** up/down there; **~ mismo** *or* (AmL) **nomás** *o* (Méx) **mero** right *o* just there **(b) por ahí** somewhere; **debe estar por ~** it must be around somewhere; **fue a dar una vuelta por ~** she went off for a walk; **se fue por ~** she went that way; **yo he estado por ~** I've been around there; **tendrá unos 35 años o por ~** he must be 35 or thereabouts **2 (a)** (refiriéndose a un lugar figurado): **~ está el truco/problema** that's the secret/problem; **de ~ a la drogadicción sólo hay un paso** from there it's just a short step to becoming a drug addict; ***hasta ~ llego yo*** that's as far as I'm prepared to go **(b) de ahí** hence; **de ~ mi sorpresa** hence my surprise; **de ~ que hayan fracasado** that is why they failed; **de ~ a que venga es otra cosa** whether or not he actually comes is another matter **3** (en el tiempo) then; **de ~ en adelante** from then on; **~ mismo** there and then

ahijado -da *m,f* (por bautizo) (*m*) godson; (*f*) goddaughter; **mis ~s** my godchildren

ahogado -da *adj* **1** (en agua): **dos niños resultaron ~s** two children were drowned; **morir ~** (en agua) to drown; (asfixiarse) to suffocate; (atragantarse) to choke to death **2** ‹*llanto/grito*› stifled **3** (Méx fam) (borracho) blind *o* rolling drunk (colloq)

ahogador *m* (Chi, Méx) (Auto) choke

ahogar [A3] *vt* **1 (a)** ‹*persona/animal*› (en agua) to drown; (asfixiar) to suffocate **(b)** ‹*motor*› to flood **2 (a)** ‹*palabras/voz*› to drown (out); ‹*llanto/grito*› to stifle **(b)** ‹*penas*› to drown

■ **ahogarse** *v pron* **(a)** «*persona/animal*» (en agua) to drown; (asfixiarse) to suffocate; (atragantarse) to choke **(b)** «*motor*» to flood

ahogo *m* breathlessness; **tiene ~s** he gets out of breath

ahora *adv* **1 (a)** (en el momento presente) now; **~ que lo pienso** now I come to think of it; **la juventud de ~** young people today; **hasta ~** so far, up to now; **de ~ en adelante** from now on; **por ~** for the time being; **por ~ va todo bien** everything's going all right so far **(b)** (inmediatamente, pronto): **~ mismo** right now *o* away; **~ te lo muestro** I'll show it to you in a minute *o* second *o* moment; **¡~ voy!** I'm coming!; **¡hasta ~!** (esp Esp) see you soon! **(c)** (hace un momento) a moment ago **2 ahora bien** (*indep*) however

ahorcar [A2] *vt* to hang

■ **ahorcarse** *v pron* (*refl*) to hang oneself

ahorita *adv* (esp AmL fam) **(a)** (en este momento) just *o* right now **(b)** (inmediatamente, pronto): **~ te lo doy** I'll give it to you in a second *o* moment **(c)** (hace un momento) a moment ago

ahorrador -dora *adj* thrifty; **no soy muy ~a** I'm not very good at saving (money) ■ *m,f* saver, investor

ahorrante *mf* (Chi) saver, investor

ahorrar [A1] *vt* **1** ‹*dinero/energía/agua*› to save; ‹*tiempo*› to save **2** (evitar) ‹*molestia/viaje*› (+ *me/te/le etc*) to save, spare ■ ~ *vi* to save

■ **ahorrarse** *v pron* (*enf*) **(a)** ‹*dinero*› to save (oneself) **(b)** (evitarse) ‹*molestia/viaje*› to save oneself

ahorrista *mf* (RPl) saver, investor

ahorro *m* **(a)** (acción) saving **(b) ahorros** *mpl* (cantidad) savings (*pl*)

ahuecar [A2] *vt* **(a)** ‹*tronco/calabaza*› to hollow out; ‹*mano*› to cup **(b)** ‹*almohadón*› to plump up; ‹*pelo*› to give volume to

ahumado *adj* **(a)** (Coc) smoked **(b)** ‹*cristal*› smoked; ‹*gafas*› tinted

ahumar [A23] *vt* **(a)** ‹*jamón/pescado*› to smoke **(b)** ‹*paredes/techo*› to blacken

ahuyentar [A1] *vt* **(a)** (hacer huir) ‹*ladrón/animal*› to frighten off *or* away **(b)** (mantener a distancia) ‹*fiera/mosquitos*› to keep ... away

aimará *adj* Aymara ■ *mf* Aymara Indian

aire *m* **1** air; **sintió que le faltaba el ~** she felt as if she was going to suffocate; **salir a tomar el ~** to go outside for a breath of fresh air; **al ~ libre** outdoors, in the open air; **~ acondicionado** air-conditioning; **con ~ acondicionado** air-conditioned; ***a mi/tu/su ~***: **ellos salen en grupo, yo prefiero ir a mi ~** they go out in a group, I prefer doing my own thing (colloq); ***quedar en el ~***: **todo quedó en el ~** everything was left up in the air; ***saltar*** *or* ***volar por los ~s*** to explode, blow up; **2** (viento) wind; (corriente) draft (AmE), draught (BrE) **3** (Rad, TV): **estar en el ~** to be on the air **4 (a)** (aspecto) air; **tiene un ~ aristocrático** she has an aristocratic air; **la protesta tomó ~s de revuelta** the protest began to look like a revolt; ***darse ~s (de grandeza)*** to put on *o* give oneself airs **(b)** (parecido) resemblance; **tienen un ~** they look a bit alike; **~ de familia** family resemblance

airear [A1] *vt* **(a)** (ventilar) to air **(b)** (hacer público) ‹*asunto*› to air **(c)** ‹*masa/tierra*› to aerate

■ **airearse** *v pron* **(a)** «*persona*» to get some (fresh) air **(b)** «*manta/abrigo*» to air; **para que se airee el cuarto** to let some air into the room

aislado -da *adj* **(a)** (alejado) remote, isolated **(b)** (sin comunicación) cut off; **quedar ~** to be cut off; **vive ~ del mundo** he's cut himself off from the world **(c)** ‹*caso*› isolated **(d)** (Elec) insulated

aislamiento *m* **(a)** (en general) isolation **(b)** (Elec) insulation

aislante *adj* insulating, insulation (*before n*) ■ *m* insulator

aislar [A19] *vt* **(a)** (apartar, separar) ‹*enfermo*› to isolate, keep in isolation; ‹*preso*› to place ... in solitary confinement; ‹*virus*› to isolate **(b)** (dejar sin communicación) ‹*lugar*› to cut off **(c)** (Elec) to insulate

■ **aislarse** *v pron* (*refl*) to cut oneself off

ajado -da *adj* ‹*ropa*› worn; ‹*manos*› wrinkly; ‹*piel*› wrinkled

ajedrecista *mf* chess player

ajedrez *m* (juego) chess; (tablero y fichas) chess set

ajeno -na *adj* [SER] **(a)** (que no corresponde, pertenece): **mis ideales le son totalmente ~s** my ideals are completely alien to him; **aquel ambiente me era ~** that environment was alien *o* foreign to me; **por razones ajenas a nuestra voluntad** for reasons beyond our control **(b)** (que pertenece, corresponde a otro): **conduce un coche ~** he drives someone else's car; **por el bien ~** for the good of others; **las desgracias ajenas** other people's misfortunes

ajetreado -da *adj* hectic, busy

ajetreo *m* hustle and bustle; **un día de mucho ~** a hectic day

ají *m* **(a)** (chile) chili* **(b)** (Andes) (salsa) chili* sauce **(c)** (RPl) (pimiento) pepper

ajo *m* (Coc) garlic; **un diente de ~** a clove of garlic

ajonjolí *m* sesame

ajuar *m* (de novia) trousseau; (de bebé) layette

ajustado -da *adj* **(a)** (ceñido) tight; **me queda muy ~** it's too tight (for me) **(b)** ‹*presupuesto*› tight

ajustar [A1] *vt* **1 (a)** (apretar) to tighten (up) **(b)** ‹*volumen/temperatura*› to adjust; **~ la entrada de agua** to regulate the flow of water **(c)** ‹*retrovisor/asiento/cinturón de seguridad*› to adjust **(d)** (encajar) ‹*piezas*› to fit **2** (en costura) to take in **3 (a)** ‹*gastos/horarios*› **~ algo A algo** to adapt sth TO sth **(b)** ‹*sueldos/precios*› to adjust **4** (concertar) to fix, set **5** ‹*cuentas*› (sacar el resultado de) to balance; (saldar) to settle ■ **~** *vi* to fit

■ **ajustarse** *v pron* **1** (*refl*) ‹*cinturón de seguridad*› to adjust **2** «*piezas*» to fit

al ▶ **1** *contraction of* AL *and* EL

ala *f*‡ **1** (de ave, de avión) wing; **~ delta** (deporte) hang gliding; (aparato) hang glider; ***cortarle las ~s a algn*** to clip sb's wings; ***darle ~s a algn***: **si le das ~s, luego no podrás controlarlo** if you let him have his own way, you won't be able to control him later **2** (de sombrero) brim **3 (a)** (de edificio) wing **(b)** (facción) wing **(c)** (flanco) flank, wing **(d)** (Dep) (posición) wing ■ *mf*‡ (jugador) wing, winger

alabanza *f* praise; **digno de ~** praiseworthy

alabar [A1] *vt* to praise

alacena *f* larder

alacrán *m* scorpion

alambrada *f* (valla) wire fence; (material) wire fencing

alambrado *m* (AmL) **(a)** (acción) fencing in/off **(b)** (valla) wire fence

alambrar [A1] *vt* to fence in/off

alambre *m* (hilo metálico) wire; **~ de púas** barbed wire, barbwire (AmE)

alameda *f* (avenida) tree-lined avenue; (terreno con álamos) poplar grove

álamo *m* poplar

alarde *m* show, display; **hacer ~ de fuerza** to show off strength

alardear [A1] *vi* **~ DE algo** to boast ABOUT *o* OF sth; **alardea de tener dinero** she boasts about being well-off

alargado -da *adj* ‹*forma*› elongated; ‹*hoja*› elongate

alargador *m* extension cord (AmE), extension lead (BrE)

alargar [A3] *vt* **1 (a)** ‹*vestido/pantalón*› to let down, lengthen; ‹*manguera/cable*› to lengthen, extend; ‹*riendas/soga*› to let out; ‹*paso*› to lengthen **(b)** ‹*cuento/discurso*› to drag out; ‹*vacaciones/plazo*› to extend; **puede ~le la vida** it could prolong her life **2 (a)** (extender) ‹*mano/brazo*› to hold out **(b)** (alcanzar) **~le algo A algn** to hand *o* give *o* pass sth TO sb

■ **alargarse** *v pron* «*cara/sombra*» to get longer; «*días*» to grow longer; «*reunión/fiesta*» to go on

alarido *m* (de miedo) shriek; (de dolor) scream

alarma *f* **1** (ante peligro) alarm; **dar la voz de ~** to sound *o* raise the alarm **2** (dispositivo) alarm; **~ contra robos/incendios** burglar/fire alarm

alarmante *adj* alarming

alarmar [A1] *vt* to alarm

■ **alarmarse** *v pron* to be alarmed

alba *f*‡ (del día) dawn, daybreak; **al rayar el ~** (liter) at the break of day (liter); **al** *or* **con el ~** at the crack of dawn

albacora *f* (atún) albacore; (pez espada) (Chi) swordfish

albahaca *f* basil

albanés¹ -nesa *adj/m,f* Albanian

albanés² *m* (idioma) Albanian

Albania *f* Albania

albañil *m* (constructor) builder; (que coloca ladrillos) bricklayer

albaricoque *m* (Esp) apricot

albaricoquero *m* (Esp) apricot tree

albedrío *m* (free) will; **lo hizo a su ~** he did it of his own free will; **lo dejo a tu libre ~** I leave it entirely up to you

alberca *f* **(a)** (embalse) reservoir **(b)** (Méx) (piscina) swimming pool **(c)** (Col) (lavadero) sink (*for washing clothes*) **(d)** (Bol, Per) (comedero) trough

albergar [A3] *vt* ‹*personas*› to house, accommodate; ‹*biblioteca/exposición*› to house

■ **albergarse** *v pron* **(a)** (hospedarse) to lodge **(b)** (refugiarse) to shelter, take refuge

albergue *m* **(a)** (alojamiento) lodging, accommodations (*pl*) (AmE); **darle ~ a algn** to take sb in **(b)** (hostal) hostel; **~ juvenil** youth hostel **(c)** (en la montaña) refuge, shelter; (para vagabundos, mendigos) shelter

albino -na *adj/m,f* albino
albóndiga *f* meatball
albornoz *m* bathrobe
alborotado -da *adj* **1 (a)** (nervioso) agitated; (animado, excitado) excited **(b)** (ruidoso) noisy, rowdy; (amotinado) riotous **2**‹*mar*› rough; ‹*pelo*› untidy, disheveled*
alborotador -dora *adj* rowdy, noisy ■ *m,f* troublemaker
alborotar [A1] *vi* to make a racket ■ ~ *vt* **(a)** (agitar) to agitate, get ... agitated; (excitar) to get ... excited **(b)** ‹*muchedumbre*› to stir up
■ **alborotarse** *v pron* **(a)** (agitarse) to get agitated *o* upset; (excitarse) to get excited **(b)** (amotinarse) to riot
alboroto *m* **(a)** (agitación, nerviosismo) agitation; (excitación) excitement **(b)** (ruido) racket **(c)** (disturbio, jaleo) disturbance, commotion; (motín) riot
álbum *m* **(a)** (de fotos, sellos) album; (libro de historietas) comic book **(b)** (disco) album
alcachofa *f* **(a)** (Bot, Coc) artichoke **(b)** (de ducha) shower head; (de regadera) sprinkler (AmE), rose (BrE)
alcahuete -ta *m,f* **(a)** (ant) (mediador) procurer (arch) **(b)** (CS fam) (chismoso) gossip (colloq); (soplón) tattletale (AmE colloq), telltale (BrE colloq)
alcahuetear [A1] *vi* **(a)** (hacer de mediador) to act as a go-between, to procure **(b)** (Andes fam) (tapar): **les alcahuetea las travesuras** he lets them get away with all kinds of things; **le alcahuetea las mentiras** she covers up for him when he lies **(c)** (CS fam) (chismear) to gossip (colloq) ■ ~ *vt* (fam) (delatar) to tell *o* snitch on (colloq)
alcalde -desa *m,f* **1** (Gob) mayor **2 alcaldesa** *f* (mujer del alcalde) mayoress
alcance *m* **(a)** (de persona) reach; **fuera del ~ de los niños** out of reach of children; **está fuera de mi ~** it is beyond my means **(b)** (de arma, emisora) range; **misiles de largo ~** long-range missiles **(c)** (de ley, proyecto) scope; (de declaración, noticia) implications (*pl*) **(d)** (*en locs*) **al alcance de** within reach of; **precios al ~ de su bolsillo** prices to suit your pocket; **un lujo que no está a mi ~** a luxury I can't afford
alcancía *f* (AmL) (de niño) piggy bank; (para colectas) collection box
alcanfor *m* camphor
alcantarilla *f* (cloaca) sewer; (sumidero) drain
alcantarillado *m* sewer system, drains (*pl*)
alcanzar [A4] *vt* **1 (a)** ‹*persona*› (llegar a la altura de) to catch up with, to catch ... up (BrE); (pillar, agarrar) to catch; **lo alcancé en la curva** I caught up with him on the bend; **¡a que no me alcanzas!** I bet you can't catch me! (colloq) **(b)** (en tarea, estatura) to catch up with **2** (llegar a) ‹*lugar*› to reach, get to; ‹*temperatura/nivel/edad*› to reach; **casi no alcanzo el tren** I almost missed the train; **estos árboles alcanzan una gran altura** these trees can reach *o* grow to a great height; **~ la mayoría de edad** to come of age **3** (conseguir, obtener) ‹*objetivo/éxito*› to achieve; ‹*acuerdo*› to reach **4** (acercar, pasar) **~le algo a algn** to pass sb sth, to pass sth TO sb ■ ~ *vi* **1** (llegar con la mano) to reach; **hasta donde alcanzaba la vista** as far as the eye could see; **~ a hacer algo** to manage to + do sth **2** (ser suficiente) «*comida/provisones*» to be enough; **el sueldo no le alcanza** he can't manage on his salary
alcaparra *f* caper
alcaucil *m* (RPl) artichoke
alcázar *m* (fortaleza) fortress; (palacio) palace
alcista *adj* ‹*tendencia*› upward; ‹*mercado*› bull (*before n*)
alcoba *f* bedroom, bedchamber (liter)
alcohol *m* **1**(Quím) alcohol; (Farm) *tb* **~ de 90 (grados)** rubbing alcohol (AmE), surgical spirit (BrE) **2** (bebida) alcohol, drink
alcoholemia *f*: **hacerle la prueba de la ~ a algn** to breathalyze sb
alcohólico -ca *adj* alcoholic; **bebida no alcohólica** nonalcoholic drink ■ *m,f* alcoholic
alcoholímetro *m* Breathalyzer®, drunkometer (AmE)
alcoholismo *m* alcoholism
alcornoque *m* **(a)** (árbol) cork oak **(b)** (fam) (persona) idiot
aldaba *f* (llamador) doorknocker; (cerrojo) latch
aldea *f* small village, hamlet
aldeano -na *adj* village (*before n*) ■ *m,f* villager
alebrestarse [A1] *v pron* **(a)** (Col, Méx) (alterarse, agitarse) to get worked up, agitated **(b)** (Ven fam) (animarse) to get excited; (excesivamente) to get overexcited
alegación *f* declaration, statement
alegar [A3] *vt* ‹*motivos/causas*› to cite; ‹*razones*› to put forward; ‹*ignorancia/defensa propia*› to plead; ‹*inmunidad diplomática*› to claim; **alegó que no lo sabía** she claimed not to know ■ ~ *vi* (AmL) **(a)** (discutir) to argue; **~ DE algo** to argue ABOUT sth **(b)** (protestar) to complain; **~ POR algo** to complain ABOUT sth
alegata *f* (Méx) argument
alegato *m* **(a)** (exposición) statement, declaration **(b)** (Der) (escrito) submission **(c)** (Andes) (discusión) argument
alegrar [A1] *vt* **(a)** (hacer feliz) ‹*persona*› to make ... happy; **me alegra saberlo** I'm glad *o* pleased to hear it **(b)** (animar) ‹*persona*› to cheer up; ‹*fiesta*› to liven up; ‹*habitación*› to brighten up; **¡alegra esa cara!** cheer up!
■ **alegrarse** *v pron* **(a)** (ponerse feliz, contento): **me alegro mucho por ti** I'm really happy for you; **se alegró muchísimo cuando lo vio** she was really happy when she saw him; **¡cuánto me alegro!** I'm so happy *o* pleased!; **está mucho mejor — me alegro** she's much better — I'm glad (to hear that); **~se CON algo** to be glad *o* pleased ABOUT sth; **me alegro de verte** it's good *o* nice to see you; **me alegro de que todo haya salido bien** I'm glad *o* pleased that everything went well **(b)** (animarse) to cheer up **(c)** (por el alcohol) to get tipsy (colloq)
alegre *adj* **(a)** ‹*persona/carácter*› happy, cheerful; ‹*color*› bright; ‹*fiesta/música*› lively; **su habitación es muy ~** her room is nice and bright; **es**

muy ~ she's very cheerful, she's a very happy person **(b)** [ESTAR] (por el alcohol) tipsy (colloq)

alegría *f* (dicha, felicidad) happiness, joy; **¡qué ~ verte!** it's great to see you!; **saltar de ~** to jump for joy

alejado -da *adj* **(a)** ‹*lugar*› remote **(b)** (distanciado) ‹*persona*›: **hace tiempo que está ~ de la política** he's been away from *o* out of politics for some time; **está ~ de su familia** he's estranged from his family

alejar [A1] *vt* **(a)** (poner lejos, más lejos) to move ... (further) away; **~ algo/a algn** DE **algo/algn** to move sth/sb away FROM sth/sb **(b)** (distanciar) **~ a algn** DE **algn** to distance sb FROM sb **(c)** ‹*dudas/temores*› to dispel

■ **alejarse** *v pron* to move away; (caminando) to walk away; **no se alejen demasiado** don't go too far; **se alejó de su familia** he drifted apart from his family; **necesito ~me de todo** I need to get away from everything

aleluya *interj* halleluja!

alemán[1] -mana *adj/m,f* German

alemán[2] *m* (idioma) German

Alemania *f* Germany

alentador -dora *adj* encouraging

alentar [A5] *vt* **(a)** ‹*persona*› to encourage; ‹*jugador/equipo*› to cheer ... on **(b)** ‹*esperanza/ilusión*› to cherish

alergia *f* allergy; **le produce ~** she's allergic to it; **~** A **algo** allergy TO sth; **tiene ~ a la penicilina** he's allergic to penicillin

alérgico -ca *adj* **(a)** [SER] ‹*persona*› allergic; **~** A **algo** allergic TO sth **(b)** ‹*afección/reacción*› allergic

alerta *adj* alert; **estar ~** (tener cuidado) to be alert; (estar en guardia) to be on the alert; **mantener el oído ~** to keep one's ears open ■ *f*: **dar la (voz de) ~** to raise the alarm; **en estado de ~** on alert

alertar [A1] *vt* **~ a algn** DE **algo** to alert sb TO sth

aleta *f* **(a)** (de pez) fin; (de foca) flipper **(b)** (para natación) flipper **(c)** (de la nariz) wing

aletargado -da *adj* lethargic, drowsy

aletargar [A3] *vt* ‹*persona*› to make ... feel lethargic *o* drowsy

aletear [A1] *vi* «*pájaro/gallina*» to flap its wings; «*mariposa*» to flutter its wings

alfabético -ca *adj* alphabetical

alfabetización *f* teaching of basic literacy; **campaña de ~** literacy campaign

alfabetizar [A4] *vt* **(a)** (Educ) to teach ... to read and write **(b)** ‹*sistema/fichero*› to put ... in alphabetical order, to alphabetize (frml)

alfabeto *m* alphabet

alfajor *m*: *type of candy or cake varying from region to region*

alfalfa *f* alfalfa, lucerne (BrE)

alfarería *f* pottery

alfarero -ra *m,f* potter

alféizar *m* sill; **el ~ de la ventana** the windowsill

alférez *m* second lieutenant

alfil *m* bishop

alfiler *m* (en costura) pin; (broche) brooch, pin; **~ de corbata** tiepin; **~ de gancho** (CS, Ven) *or* (Col) **de nodriza** safety pin

alfombra *f* **(a)** (suelta) rug; (más grande) carpet **(b)** (AmL) (de pared a pared) carpet

alfombrado -da *adj* carpeted

alfombrar [A1] *vt* to carpet

alfombrilla *f* **1** (de coche) mat; (de baño) bath mat **2** (Med) *type of measles*

alforja *f* (para caballerías) saddlebag; (sobre el hombro) knapsack

alga *f*‡ (en el mar) seaweed; (en agua dulce) weed, waterweed; (nombre genérico) alga

algarroba *f* carob (bean)

algarrobo *m* carob (tree)

álgebra *f*‡ algebra

álgido -da *adj* ‹*punto/momento*› culminating (*before n*), decisive

algo[1] *pron* **▶ 19** **(a)** something; (en frases interrogativas, condicionales, etc) anything; (esperando respuesta afirmativa) something; **quiero decirte ~** I want to tell you something; **si llegara a pasarle ~** if anything happened to her; **¿quieres ~ de beber?** do you want something *o* anything to drink?; **por ~ será** there must be some *o* a reason; **le va a dar ~** he'll have a fit; **~ así** something like that; **eso ya es ~** at least that's something; **sé ~ de francés** I know some French; **¿queda ~ de pan?** is there any bread left? **(b)** (en aproximaciones): **serán las once y ~** it must be some time after eleven; **pesa tres kilos y ~** it weighs three kilos and a bit; **o ~ así** or something like that

algo[2] *adv* a little, slightly; **está ~ nublado** it's a bit cloudy; **es ~ para ti** it's a bit too big for you

algodón *m* **1** (Bot, Tex) cotton **2** (Farm) **(a)** (material) *tb* **~ hidrófilo** cotton (AmE), cotton wool (BrE) **(b)** (trozo) piece of cotton (AmE), piece of cotton wool (BrE); **~ de azúcar** cotton candy (AmE), candy floss (BrE)

algodonal, **algodonar** *m* cotton field

algodonero -ra *adj* cotton (*before n*) ■ *m,f* (agricultor) cotton planter *o* farmer; (vendedor) cotton dealer

alguacil -cila *m,f* **(a)** (agente de autoridad) sheriff **(b)** (de tribunal de justicia) bailiff (AmE), constable (BrE)

alguien *pron* somebody, someone; (en frases interrogativas, condicionales, etc) anybody, anyone; (esperando respuesta afirmativa) somebody, someone; **~ con experiencia** somebody *o* someone with experience; **¿ha llamado ~?** has anybody *o* anyone called?; **si ~ preguntara** if anybody *o* anyone should ask

algún *adj*: *apocopated form of* ALGUNO *used before masculine singular nouns*

alguno[1] -na *adj* **1** (*delante del n*) **(a)** (indicando uno indeterminado) some; **algún día** some *o* one day; **en algún lugar** somewhere **(b)** (en frases interrogativas, condicionales, etc) any; **¿tocas algún instrumento?** do you play any instruments?; **si tienes algún**

Algo

Algunas observaciones respecto del pronombre algo

En términos generales; para su correcta traducción se debe hacer la siguiente distinción:

En oraciones afirmativas algo *se traduce por* something:

he perdido algo	=	I've lost something
vi algo que quiero comprar	=	I've seen something I want to buy

En oraciones interrogativas su traducción es anything, *salvo cuando encierra una suposición por parte del hablante, en cuyo caso la traducción puede ser* something:

¿sabes algo de coches?	=	do you know anything about cars?
¿queda algo?	=	is there anything left?
estás un poco inquieto ¿ te pasa algo?	=	you're a bit restless, is something the matter?
¿quieres comer algo?	=	would you like something to eat?

En oraciones condicionales su traducción es anything, *salvo cuando la oración encierra una sugerencia, en cuyo caso su traducción puede ser* something:

si algo sale mal	=	if anything goes wrong
si crees que algo está mal, dímelo	=	if you think something's wrong, tell me

Para otros ejemplos y usos, ver bajo la respectiva entrada

problema if there's any problem, if you have any problems **(c)** (indicando cantidad indeterminada): **esto tiene alguna importancia** this is of some importance; **hace ~s años** some years ago, a few years ago; **me quedan tres tazas y algún plato** I have three cups and one or two plates; **escribió algún que otro artículo** he wrote one or two articles **2** (*detrás del n*) (con valor negativo): **esto no lo afectará en modo ~** this won't affect it in the slightest *o* at all

alguno² -na *pron* **(a)** (cosa, persona indeterminada) one; **~ de nosotros** one of us; **siempre hay ~ que no está conforme** there's always someone who doesn't agree **(b)** (en frases interrogativas, condicionales, etc): **buscaba una guía ¿tiene alguna?** I was looking for a guide, do you have one *o* any?; **si tuviera ~** if I had one **(c)** (una cantidad indeterminada — de personas) some (people); (— de cosas) some; **~s creen que fue así** some (people) believe that was the case; **he visto algunas** I've seen some; **he tenido ~ que otro** I've had one *or* two

alhaja *f* **(a)** (joya) piece of jewelry* **(b)** (persona) gem, treasure

alhajero *m*, **alhajera** *f* (AmL) jewel case

alharaca *f* fuss; **hacer ~s** to make a fuss

alhelí *m* wallflower

aliado -da *adj* allied ■ *m, f* (Hist, Pol) ally; **los A~s** the Allies

alianza *f* **(a)** (pacto, unión) alliance **(b)** (anillo) wedding ring

aliarse [A17] *v pron* to join forces; **~se CON algn** to form an alliance WITH sb, ally oneself WITH sb

alias *adv* alias ■ *m* (*pl* ~) alias

alicaído -da *adj* low, down in the dumps (colloq)

alicate *m*, **alicates** *mpl* (Tec) pliers (*pl*); (para uñas) nail clippers (*pl*); (para cutícula) cuticle clippers (*pl*)

aliciente *m* incentive

aliento *m* **1 (a)** (respiración, aire) breath; **sin ~** out of breath, breathless **(b)** (aire espirado) breath; **mal ~** bad breath **2** (ánimo, valor): **dar ~ a algn** to encourage sb

aligerar [A1] *vt* **(a)** ‹*carga*› to lighten; **~ a algn DE algo** to relieve sb OF sth **(b)** (acelerar): **~ el paso** to quicken one's pace

alijo *m* consignment

alimaña *f* pest; **~s** vermin

alimentación *f* **(a)** (nutrición, comida) diet; **la ~ integral va ganando adeptos** health food *o* (BrE) wholefood is growing in popularity **(b)** (de máquina, motor) fuel supply

alimentar [A1] *vt* **1** ‹*persona/animal*› to feed **2 (a)** ‹*ilusión/esperanza*› to nurture, cherish; ‹*ego*› to boost **(b)** ‹ *odio/pasión*› to fuel **3** ‹*máquina/motor*› to feed; ‹*caldera*› to stoke ■ **~** *vi* to be nourishing

■ **alimentarse** *v pron* «*persona/animal*» to feed oneself; **~se CON** *or* **DE algo** to live ON sth

alimenticio -cia, **alimentario -ria** *adj* **(a)** ‹*industria*› food (*before n*); **productos ~s** foodstuffs; **hábitos ~s** eating habits **(b)** ‹*valor*› nutritional; ‹*comida/plato*› nutritious, nourishing

alimento *m* **1** (frml) (comida) food; **la leche es un ~ completo** milk is a complete food **2** (valor nutritivo): **no tiene ~ ninguno** it has no nutritional value; **de mucho ~** very nutritious

alineación *f* **1 (a)** (Dep) (de equipo) lineup; (de jugador) selection **(b)** (puesta en fila) lining up **2** (Pol, Tec) alignment

alinear [A1] *vt* **1** ‹*equipo/jugador*› to select, pick **2 (a)** (poner en fila, línea) to line up **(b)** (Tec) to align, line up

■ **alinearse** *v pron* «*tropa*» to fall in; «*niños/presos*» to line up

aliñar [A1] *vt* ‹*ensalada*› to dress; ‹*carne/pescado*› to season

aliño *m* (para ensalada) dressing; (para otros alimentos) seasoning

alioli *m* (mayonesa) garlic mayonnaise; (salsa) garlic and olive oil vinaigrette

alisar [A1] *vt* ‹*colcha/papel*› to smooth out; ‹*pared/superficie*› to smooth down

■ **alisarse** *v pron* (*refl*) **(a)** ‹*vestido/falda*› to smooth out **(b)** ‹*pelo*› (con la mano) to smooth down; (quitar los rizos) to straighten

alistamiento *m* (acción) enlistment, recruitment; (soldados alistados) call-up, draft (AmE)

alistarse [A1] *v pron* **(a)** (Mil) to enlist, join up; **~ en el ejército** to join the army **(b)** (AmL) (prepararse) to get ready

alivianar *vt* [A1] (AmL) to lighten

aliviar [A1] *vt* ‹*dolor*› to relieve, soothe; ‹*síntomas*› to relieve; ‹*tristeza/pena*› to alleviate; ‹*persona*› to make ... feel better

■ **aliviarse** *v pron* **(a)** «*dolor*» to let up **(b)** «*persona*» to get better

alivio *m* relief; **¡qué ~!** what a relief!

aljibe *m* **(a)** (pozo) well; (depósito de agua) cistern, tank **(b)** (Per) (cárcel) dungeon

allá *adv* **1 (a)** (en el espacio): **ya vamos para ~** we're on our way (over); **~ en América** over in America; **lo pusiste muy ~** you've put it too far away; **¡~ voy!** here I come/go! **(b)** (*en locs*) **más allá** further away; **más allá de** (más lejos que) beyond; (aparte de) over and above; **~ *tú/él*** that's your/his lookout *o* problem (colloq) **2** (en el tiempo): **~ por los años 40** back in the forties; **~ para enero** sometime in January

allanamiento *m* **(a)** (AmL) (con autorización judicial) raid; **orden de ~** search warrant **(b)** (Esp, Méx) (sin autorización judicial) breaking and entering

allanar [A1] *vt* **1 (a)** (AmL) «*autoridad/policía*» to raid **(b)** (Esp, Méx) «*delincuente*» to break into **2** ‹*problemas*› to solve, resolve; ‹*obstáculo*› to remove, overcome; ‹*terreno*› to level out; ***~(le) el terreno a algn*** to smooth the way *o* path for sb

allegado -da *adj* close; **mis amigos y parientes más ~s** my close family and friends ■ *m, f* (amigo, pariente): **los ~s del difunto** those closest to the deceased; **un ~ de la familia** a close friend of the family

allí *adv* there; **~ arriba/dentro** up/in there; **~ donde estés/vayas** wherever you are/go

alma *f*‡ **1** (espíritu) soul; **tener ~ de niño** to be a child at heart; **~ mía** *or* **mi ~** (*como apelativo*) my love; ***con toda el*** *or* ***mi/tu/su ~*** with all my/your/his/ heart; ***del ~***: **su amigo del ~** his bosom friend; ***en el ~***: **lo siento en el ~** I'm really *o* terribly sorry; **te lo agradezco en el ~** I can't tell you how grateful I am; ***llegarle a algn al ~***: **aquellas palabras me llegaron al ~** (me conmovieron) I was deeply touched by those words; (me dolieron) I was deeply hurt by those words; ***me/le parte el ~*** it breaks my/his heart **2** (persona) soul; ***ni un ~ viviente*** not a living soul; ***ser ~s gemelas*** to be soul mates; ***ser un ~ bendita*** *or* ***de Dios*** to be a kind soul

almacén *m* **(a)** (depósito) warehouse **(b)** (CS) (de comestibles) grocery store (AmE), grocer's (shop) (BrE) **(c)** (AmC, Col, Ven) (de ropa, etc) store (AmE), shop (BrE) **(d)** (de mayorista) wholesaler's **(e) almacenes** *mpl* department store

almacenar [A1] *vt* ‹*mercancías/datos*› to store

almanaque *m* (calendario — de escritorio) almanac, desk calendar; (— de pared) calendar

almeja *f* clam

almendra *f* **(a)** (fruta) almond **(b)** (centro) kernel

almendro *m* almond tree

almíbar *m* syrup

almibarar [A1] *vt* ‹*fruta*› to preserve ... in syrup; ‹*pastel*› to soak ... in syrup

almidón *m* starch

almidonar [A1] *vt* to starch

almirante *m* admiral

almohada *f* pillow; ***consultarlo con la ~*** to sleep on it

almohadilla *f* **1** (para alfileres) pincushion; (para entintar) ink pad; (para sellos) damper **2** (para sentarse) cushion; (en béisbol) bag

almohadón *m* (cuadrado, redondo) cushion; (cilíndrico) bolster; (en la iglesia) kneeler

almorranas *fpl* (fam) piles (*pl*)

almorzar [A11] *vi* **(a)** (a mediodía) to have lunch **(b)** (en algunas regiones) (a media mañana) to have a mid-morning snack ■ **~** *vt* **(a)** (a mediodía) to have ... for lunch **(b)** (en algunas regiones) (a media mañana) to have ... mid-morning

almuerza, almuerzas, etc *see* ALMORZAR

almuerzo *m* **(a)** (a mediodía) lunch **(b)** (en algunas regiones) (a media mañana) mid-morning snack

aló *interj* **▶ 405** (AmS excl RPl) (al contestar el teléfono) hello?

alocado -da *adj* (irresponsable, imprudente) crazy, wild; (irreflexivo, impetuoso) rash, impetuous; (despistado) scatterbrained ■ *m, f* (imprudente) crazy *o* reckless fool; (irreflexivo) rash fool; (despistado) scatterbrain

alojado -da *m, f* (Chi) guest; **pieza de ~s** guest-room

alojamiento *m* accommodations (*pl*) (AmE), accommodation (BrE); **nos dio ~** he put us up

alojar [A1] *vt* **1 (a)** (en hotel): **los hemos alojado en el hotel Plaza** we've booked them into the Plaza Hotel; **el hotel en el que estaban alojados** the hotel where they were staying **(b)** (en casa particular) to put ... up **2** (albergar) ‹*evacuados/refugiados*› to house

■ **alojarse** *v pron* **(a)** (hospedarse) to stay **(b)** «*proyectil/bala*» to lodge

alondra *f* lark

alpaca *f* **1** (Zool, Tex) alpaca; **lana de ~** alpaca (wool) **2** (Metal) nickel silver, German silver

alpargata *f* espadrille

Alpes *mpl*: **los ~** the Alps

alpinismo *m* mountaineering, (mountain) climbing

alpinista *mf* mountaineer, (mountain) climber

alpino -na *adj* Alpine

alpiste *m* (semillas) birdseed

alquilar [A1] *vt* **1** (dar en alquiler) ‹*casa/local*› to rent (out), let (BrE); ‹*televisor*› to rent; ‹*coche/bicicleta*› to rent (out) (AmE), to hire out (BrE) **2** (tomar en alquiler) ‹*casa/local/televisor*› to rent; ‹*coche/bicicleta/disfraz*› to rent (AmE), to hire (BrE)

alquiler *m* **(a)** (renta — de apartamento) rent; (— de televisor, bicicleta) rental **(b)** (acción de alquilar — una casa) renting, letting (BrE); (— un televisor) rental; (— un coche, disfraz) rental (AmE), hire (BrE); **se dedica al ~ de coches** he's in the car-rental (AmE) *o* (BrE) car-hire business; **contrato de ~** tenancy agreement; **coches de ~** rental (AmE) *o* (BrE) hire cars

alquitrán *m* tar

alrededor *adv* **(a)** (en torno) around; **a mi ~** around me **(b) alrededor de** (*loc prep*) (en torno a) around; (aproximadamente) around, about

alrededores *mpl* **(a)** (barrios periféricos, extrarradio de ciudad) outskirts (*pl*); (otras localidades) surroundings (*pl*) **(b)** (de edificio, calle) surrounding area; **en los ~ de la iglesia** in the area around the church

alta *f*‡ **1** (Med) discharge; **dar el ~ a** *or* **dar de ~ a un enfermo** to discharge a patient **2** (Fisco, Servs Socs): **los dieron de ~ en la Seguridad Social** they registered them with Social Security

altanero -ra *adj* arrogant, haughty

altar *m* altar

altavoz *m* (Audio) loudspeaker; (megáfono) megaphone

alteración *f* **(a)** (de plan, texto) change, alteration **(b)** (de hechos, verdad) distortion **(c)** (del orden, de la paz) disturbance; (agitación) agitation ;**~ del orden público** breach of the peace

alterado -da *adj* [ESTAR] ‹*persona*› upset

alterar [A1] *vt* **1 (a)** ‹*plan/texto*› to change, alter **(b)** ‹*hechos/verdad*› to distort **(c)** ‹*alimento*› to make ... go off, turn ... bad **2** (perturbar) **(a)** ‹*paz*› to disturb; **~ el orden público** to cause a breach of the peace **(b)** ‹*persona*› to upset

■ **alterarse** *v pron* **1** «*alimentos*» to go off, go bad **2** «*pulso/respiración*» to become irregular; «*color*» to change **3** «*persona*» to get upset

altercado *m* argument

alternar [A1] *vt* **~ algo** CON **algo** to alternate sth WITH sth; **alternamos la gimnasia con el tenis** we alternate gymnastics with tennis ■ **~** *vi* «*persona*» to socialize; **~** CON **algn** to mix WITH sb

■ **alternarse** *v pron* to take turns

alternativa *f* (opción) alternative; **la ~ es clara** the choice is clear

alternativo -va *adj* ‹*medicina/prensa/música*› alternative

Alteza *mf* (tratamiento) Highness; **sí, (su) ~** yes, your Highness

altibajos *mpl* **(a)** (cambios bruscos) ups and downs (*pl*) **(b)** (del terreno) undulations (*pl*)

altillo *m* (desván) attic; (en habitación) (sleeping) loft

altiplanicie *f*, **altiplano** *m* high plateau, high plain; **el altiplano boliviano** the Bolivian altiplano

altiro *adv* (Chi fam) right away, immediately

altitud *f* altitude

altivo -va *adj* (arrogante) arrogant, haughty; (noble, orgulloso) proud

alto¹ -ta *adj* **1 (a)** [SER] ‹*persona/edificio/árbol*› tall; ‹*pared/montaña*› high; **una blusa de cuello ~** a high-necked blouse **(b)** [ESTAR]: **¡qué ~ estás!** haven't you grown!; **está tan alta como yo** she's as tall as me now **2** (indicando posición, nivel) **(a)** [SER] high; **los techos eran muy ~s** the rooms had very high ceilings **(b)** [ESTAR]: **el río está muy ~** the river is very high; **la marea está alta** it's high tide; **los pisos más ~s** the top floors; **salgan con los brazos en ~** come out with your hands in the air; **con la moral bastante alta** in pretty high spirits; **en lo ~ de la montaña** high up on the mountainside; **en lo ~ del árbol** high up in the tree; ***por todo lo ~*** in style **3** (en cantidad, calidad) high; **el alto nivel de contaminación** the high level of pollution; **productos de alta calidad** high-quality products; ***tirando por lo ~*** at the most **4 (a)** [ESTAR] (en intensidad) ‹*volumen/televisión*› loud; **pon la radio más alta** turn the radio up **(b) en alto** *or* **en voz alta** aloud, out loud **5** (*delante del n*) **(a)** (en importancia, trascendencia) ‹*ejecutivo/funcionario*› high-ranking, top; **conversaciones de ~ nivel** high-level talks **(b)** ‹*ideales/opinión*› high; **un ~ sentido del deber** a strong sense of duty **(c)** (en nombres compuestos) **alta burguesía** *f* upper-middle classes (*pl*); **alta costura** *f* haute couture; **alta fidelidad** *f* high fidelity, hi-fi; **alta mar** *f*: **en alta mar** on the high seas; **flota/pesca de alta mar** deep-sea fleet/fishing; **alta sociedad** *f* high society; **alta tensión** *f* high tension *o* voltage; **~ cargo** *m* (puesto) high-ranking position; (persona) high-ranking official; **~ mando** *m* high-ranking officer

alto² *adv* **1** ‹*volar/subir*› high **2** ‹*hablar*› loud, loudly; **habla más ~** speak up a little

alto³ *interj* halt!; **¡~ el fuego!** cease fire!

alto⁴ *m* **1 (a)** (altura) **de alto** high; **tiene tres metros de ~** it's three meters high **(b)** (en el terreno) high ground; **construido en un ~** built on high ground **2 (a)** (parada, interrupción): **hacer un ~** to stop; **~ el fuego** (Esp) (Mil) cease-fire **(b)** (Méx) (Auto): **pasarse el ~** (un semáforo) to run the red light (AmE), to jump the lights (BrE); (un stop) to go through the stop sign

altoparlante *m* (AmL) ⇨ ALTAVOZ

altruismo *m* altruism

altruista *adj* altruistic ■ *mf* altruist

altura *f* **1** (de persona, edificio, techo) height; **el muro tiene un metro de ~** the wall is one meter high **2** (indicando posición) height; **ponlos a la misma ~** put them at the same height; **a la ~ de los ojos** at eye level; ***estar/ponerse a la ~ de algo/algn***: **para ponernos a la ~ de la competencia** to put ourselves on a par with our competitors; **estar a la ~ de las circunstancias** to rise to the occasion; **no está a la ~ de su predecesor** he doesn't match up to his predecessor **3 (a)** (Aviac, Geog) (altitud) altitude; **a 2.240 metros de ~** at an altitude of 2,240 meters **(b) de altura** ‹*pesquero/flota*› deep-sea (*before n*); ‹*remolcador*› oceangoing (*before n*) **4** (en sentido horizontal): **¿a qué ~ de Serrano vive?** how far up Serrano do you live?; **cuando llegamos a la ~ de la plaza** when we reached the square **5** (en sentido temporal): **a estas ~s ya debe haber llegado** he should have arrived by now; **¡a estas ~s me vienes con eso!** you wait till now to bring this to me!; **a estas ~s del año** this late on in the year; **a esas ~s ya no me importaba** by that stage I didn't mind **6** (Mús) pitch

alturado -da *adj* (Per) calm

alubia *f* (haricot) bean

alucinación *f* hallucination

alucinado -da *adj* (fam): **los dejó a todos ~s** she left everybody stunned

alucinante *adj* **(a)** (Med) hallucinatory **(b)** (Esp, Méx fam) (increíble), amazing (colloq), mind-boggling (colloq)

alucinar [A1] *vi* to hallucinate

alud *m* (de nieve) avalanche; (de tierra) landslide, landslip

aludir [I1] *vi* **(a)** (sin nombrar) **~ A algn/algo** to refer TO sb/sth, allude TO sb/sth; **se sintió aludido** he thought we were referring to him; **no se dio por aludido** he didn't take the hint **(b)** (mencionar) **~ A algn/algo** to refer TO sb/sth, mention sb/sth

alumbrado *m* lighting

alumbramiento *m* (frml) birth

alumbrar [A1] *vt* (iluminar) to light, illuminate; **está muy mal alumbrado** it's very poorly lit; **alumbra este rincón** shine the light in this corner ■ **~** *vi* «*sol*» to be bright; «*lámpara/bombilla*» to give off light

aluminio *m* aluminum (AmE), aluminium (BrE)

alumnado *m* (de colegio) students (*pl*) (AmE), pupils (*pl*) (BrE); (de universidad) students (*pl*)

alumno -na *m,f* (de colegio) pupil; (de universidad) student; **~ interno** boarder

alunizar [A4] *vi* to land on the moon

alusión *f* **~ (A algo/algn)** allusion *o* reference (TO sth/sb); **hacer ~ a algo/a algn** to make reference *o* an allusion to sth/sb

alverjilla *f* (AmL) sweet pea

alza *f*‡ rise; **el ~ de los precios** the rise in prices; **en ~** ‹*intereses/precios*› rising (*before n*); **una escritora en ~** an up-and-coming writer; **estar en ~** to be on the rise

alzado -da *adj* **(a)** (Andes, Ven fam) (levantisco): **la servidumbre anda medio alzada** the servants have been rather uppity lately (colloq); **un chiquillo ~** a cocky little brat (colloq) **(b)** (Méx, Ven fam) (altivo) stuck-up (colloq)

alzamiento *m* uprising

alzar [A4] *vt* **1** (levantar) **(a)** ‹*brazo/cabeza/voz*› to raise; **alzó al niño para que viera el desfile** she lifted the little boy up so he could see the parade; **alzó la mirada** she looked up **(b)** (AmL) ‹*bebé*› to pick up **2** ‹*edificio/monumento*› to erect **3** (Méx) (poner en orden) ‹*juguetes*› to pick up; ‹*cuarto/casa*› to clean (up)

■ **alzarse** *v pron* (sublevarse) to rise up; **~se en armas** to take up arms

ama *f*‡ **(a)** (de bebé) *tb* **~ de leche** *or* **de cría** wet nurse **(b)** (de niño mayor) nanny **(c) ~ de casa/de llaves** housewife/housekeeper; *ver tb* AMO

amabilidad *f* **(a)** (cualidad) kindness **(b)** (gesto): **tuvo la ~ de invitarnos** she was kind enough to invite us; **¿tendría la ~ de cerrar la puerta?** would you be so kind as to close the door?; **tenga la ~ de esperar aquí** would you mind waiting here?

amable *adj* **(a)** ‹*persona/gesto*› kind; **es muy ~ de su parte** that's very kind of you; **¿sería tan ~ de ...?** would you be so kind as to ...? **(b)** (AmS) ‹*rato/velada*› pleasant

amado -da *adj* dear, beloved ■ *m,f* love, sweetheart

amadrinar [A1] *vt* ‹*niño*› to be godmother to; ‹*boda*› to act as MADRINA at; ‹*barco*› to launch, christen

amaestrar [A1] *vt* ‹*animales*› to train

amago *m*: **tuvo un ~ de infarto** he had a mild heart attack; **un ~ de revuelta** a threat of revolt; **hacer un ~** (Dep) to make a feint

amainar [A1] *vi* «*lluvia*» to ease up *o* off, abate; «*temporal/viento*» to die down, abate

amamantar [A1] *vt/vi* «*mujer*» to breastfeed; «*animal*» to suckle

amanecer[1] [E3] *v impers*: **¿a qué hora amanece?** what time does it get light?; **amanecía cuando partieron** dawn was breaking when they left ■ **~** *vi* (+ *compl*) **(a)** «*persona*»: **amaneció con fiebre** he woke up with a temperature; **amanecieron bailando** they were still dancing at dawn **(b)** (aparecer por la mañana): **amaneció nublado** it was cloudy first thing in the morning; **todo amaneció cubierto de nieve** in the morning everything was covered in snow

■ **amanecerse** *v pron* (Chi, Méx) to stay up all night

amanecer[2] *m* dawn, daybreak; **al ~** at dawn *o* at daybreak

amanerado -da *adj* (afectado) affected, mannered; (afeminado) (fam) mannered, camp (colloq)

amansar [A1] *vt* ‹*caballo*› to break in; ‹*fiera*› to tame

■ **amansarse** *v pron* «*fiera*» to become tame; «*caballo*» to quiet (AmE) *o* (BrE) quieten down

amante *mf* lover

amañar [A1] *vt* (fam) ‹*elecciones*› to rig; ‹*partido/pelea*› to fix; ‹*carnet/documento*› to tamper with; ‹*informe*› to alter, doctor (pej); ‹*excusa/historia*› to dream *o* cook up, concoct

■ **amañarse** *v pron* **1** *tb* **amañárselas** (ingeniarse) to manage **2** (Col, Ven) (acostumbrarse) to settle in

amapola *f* poppy

amar [A1] *vt* to love

■ **amarse** *v pron* (*recipr*) to love each other

amarga *f* (Col) beer

amargado -da *adj* bitter, embittered ■ *m,f* bitter *o* embittered person

amargar [A3] *vt* ‹*ocasión/día*› to spoil; ‹*persona*› to make ... bitter

■ **amargarse** *v pron* to become bitter; **no te amargues la existencia** (fam) don't get all uptight about it

amargo -ga *adj* **1 (a)** ‹*fruta/sabor*› bitter **(b)** (sin azúcar) unsweetened, without sugar **2** ‹*experiencia/recuerdo*› bitter, painful

amargor *m* bitterness

amargura *f* bitterness; **con ~** bitterly

amarillento -ta *adj* ▶ **97** yellowish

amarillista *adj* (Period) (pey): **prensa ~** sensationalist *o* yellow press

amarillo¹ -lla *adj* ▶ 97 **1** ‹*color/blusa*› yellow; **el semáforo estaba (en) ~** the light was yellow (AmE), the lights were (on) amber (BrE) **2 (a)** ‹*piel*› (de raza oriental) yellow **(b)** ‹*piel/cara*› (por enfermedad) yellow, jaundiced

amarillo² *m* ▶ 97 yellow

amarra *f* mooring rope; **~s** moorings (*pl*); **echar (las) ~s** to moor

amarradero *m* **(a)** (poste) bollard; (argolla) mooring ring **(b)** (lugar) berth, slip (AmE)

amarrado -da *adj* (Col, Méx, Ven fam) stingy (colloq), tightfisted (colloq)

amarrar [A1] *vt* **(a)** ‹*embarcación*› to moor; ‹*animal/persona*› to tie up; **le ~on las manos** they tied his hands together; **~ algo/a algn A algo** to tie sth/sb TO sth **(b)** (AmL exc RPl) ‹*zapatos/cordones*› to tie; ‹*paquete*› to tie ... up
■ **amarrarse** *v pron* (AmL exc RPl) ‹*zapatos/cordones*› to tie up, do up; ‹*pelo*› to tie up

amarrete -ta *adj* (AmS fam) stingy (colloq), tightfisted (colloq) ■ *m,f* (AmS fam) scrooge (colloq), skinflint (colloq)

amasar [A1] *vt* **1** ‹*pan*› to knead; ‹*yeso/argamasa*› to mix **2** ‹*fortuna/riquezas*› to amass

amateur /ama'ter/ *adj/mf* (*pl* **-teurs**) amateur

amazona *f* (Mit) Amazon; (Equ) horsewoman

Amazonas *m*: **el ~** the Amazon

amazónico -ca *adj* Amazonian, Amazon (*before n*)

ámbar *m* **(a)** (piedra) amber **(b)** ▶ 97 (color) amber

ambición *f* ambition

ambicionar [A1] *vt* to aspire to

ambicioso -sa *adj* ambitious; (codicioso) overambitious

ambidextro -tra *adj* ambidextrous ■ *m,f* ambidextrous person

ambientación *f* **(a)** (de obra, película) atmosphere **(b)** (de persona) adjustment

ambientador *m* air freshener

ambiental *adj* environmental

ambientar [A1] *vt* **(a)** ‹*obra/película*› to set **(b)** ‹*fiesta/local*› to give ... some atmosphere
■ **ambientarse** *v pron* to adjust, adapt

ambiente *m* **(a)** (entorno físico, social, cultural) environment; **crecí en un ~ rural** I grew up in a rural environment; **se encuentra realmente en su ~** he's really in his element; **había una cierta tensión en el ~** there was a feeling of tension in the air **(b)** (creado por la decoración, arquitectura, la gente) atmosphere; **un ~ de camaradería/de fiesta** a friendly/festive atmosphere **(c)** (animación) life

ambigüedad *f* ambiguity

ambiguo -gua *adj* ambiguous

ámbito *m* **(a)** (campo, círculo) sphere, field **(b)** (alcance) scope, range; **el ~ (de aplicación) de la ley** the scope of the law

ambo *m* (CS) (two-piece) suit

ambos -bas *adj pl* both; **a ~ lados** on both sides ■ *pron pl* both; **~ aceptaron la propuesta** they both accepted the proposal; **~ me gustan** I like both of them

ambulancia *f* ambulance

ambulanciero -ra *m,f* (*m*) ambulance man; (*f*) ambulance woman; **los ~s** the ambulance crew

ambulante *adj* traveling* (*before n*); **biblioteca ~** bookmobile (AmE), mobile library (BrE)

ambulatorio¹ -ria *adj* outpatient (*before n*)

ambulatorio² *m* (Esp) outpatients' department

ameba *f* amoeba

amén *m* amen; **~ de** ... as well as ...

amenaza *f* threat; **no me vengas con ~s** don't threaten me; **~ de bomba/muerte** bomb/death threat

amenazador -dora, **amenazante** *adj* threatening, menacing

amenazar [A4] *vt* **(a)** «*persona*» to threaten; **nos amenazó con llamar a la policía** he threatened to call the police **(b)** (dar indicios de): **esas nubes amenazan lluvia** those clouds look threatening ■ **~** *vi* **~ CON hacer algo** to threaten to do sth ■ **~** *v impers* (Meteo): **amenaza tormenta** there's a storm brewing; **amenaza lluvia** it's threatening to rain

amenizar [A4] *vt* ‹*conversación/discurso*› to make ... more enjoyable; **la fiesta fue amenizada por un payaso** a clown provided the entertainment for the party

ameno -na *adj* pleasant, enjoyable

América *f* (continente) America

americana *f* jacket

americanismo *m* Americanism

americano -na *adj/m,f* American

amerindio -dia *adj/m,f* American Indian, Amerindian

ameritado -da *adj* (AmL) meritorious (frml)

ameritar [A1] *vt* (AmL) to deserve

ametralladora *f* machine gun

ametrallar [A1] *vt* to machine-gun

amianto *m* asbestos

amiba *f* amoeba

amigable *adj* ‹*persona*› friendly; ‹*trato*› friendly, amicable; **un tono poco ~** a rather unfriendly manner

amígdalas *fpl* tonsils (*pl*)

amigdalitis *f* tonsillitis

amigo -ga *adj*: **son/se hicieron muy ~s** they are/they became good friends; **hacerse ~ de algn** to become friends with sb; **es muy ~ mío** he's a close friend of mine; **un país ~** a friendly country; **es muy ~ de contradecir** he's a great one for contradicting people (colloq); **no es amiga de las fiestas** she's not keen on parties ■ *m,f* friend; **un ~ mío** a friend of mine; **somos íntimos ~s** we're very close friends; **¡un momento, ~!** now, just a minute, pal *o* buddy (AmE) *o* (BrE) mate! (colloq)

amilanar [A1] *vt* to daunt
■ **amilanarse** *v pron* to be daunted

amistad *f* **(a)** (entre personas, países) friendship; **entabló** *or* **hizo ~ con ella** he struck up a friendship with her **(b) amistades** *fpl* (amigos) friends (*pl*)

amistoso -sa *adj* ‹*consejo/palmadita/charla*› friendly; ‹*partido*› friendly (*before n*)

amnesia *f* amnesia

amnistía *f* amnesty

amnistiado -da *m,f*: *person pardoned under an amnesty*

amnistiar [A17] *vt* ‹*persona*› to grant an amnesty to; ‹*delito*› to amnesty

amo, **ama** *m,f* (de animal, criado) (*m*) master; (*f*) mistress; **son los ~s del pueblo** they own the whole village; *ver tb* AMA

amoblar [A10] *vt* (CS) to furnish

amoldable *adj* adaptable

amoldar [A1] *vt* to adjust

■ **amoldarse** *v pron* to adapt; **~se A algo** ‹*a un trabajo/una situación*› to adjust TO sth; **estos zapatos todavía no se me han amoldado al pie** I haven't broken these shoes in yet

amonestación *f* (reprimenda) warning; (en fútbol) caution, booking

amonestar [A1] *vt* (reprender) to reprimand, admonish (frml); (en fútbol) to caution, book

amoníaco *m* ammonia

amontonar [A1] *vt* **(a)** (apilar) to pile ... up **(b)** (juntar) to accumulate

■ **amontonarse** *v pron* «*personas*» to gather *o* crowd together; «*objetos/trabajo*» to pile up

amor *m* **1 (a)** (sentimiento) love; **~ no correspondido** unrequited love; **~ a primera vista** love at first sight; **~ al prójimo/a la patria** love for one's neighbor/one's country; **~ propio** pride, self-esteem; **un gran ~ a la vida/a los animales** a great love of life/animals; ***por ~ al arte*** (fam) just for the fun of it; ***por (el) ~ de Dios*** (mendigando) for the love of God; (expresando irritación) for God's sake! **(b)** (el acto sexual): **hacer el ~ a/con algn** to make love to/with sb **(c)** (persona, cosa amada) love; **~ mío** *or* **mi ~** my darling, my love **(d)** (esmero, dedicación): **hacer algo con ~** to do sth lovingly **2** (fam) (persona encantadora) darling (colloq), dear (colloq)

amoral *adj* amoral

amoratado -da *adj* (de frío) blue; (por un golpe) ‹*piernas/brazos*› bruised; **ojo ~** black eye

amordazar [A4] *vt* ‹*persona*› to gag; ‹*perro*› to muzzle

amorío *m* love affair

amoroso -sa *adj* **(a)** (AmL) ‹*persona/casa*› lovely **(b)** ‹*vida*› love (*before n*); **sus relaciones amorosas** his relationships

amortajar [A1] *vt* to shroud

amortiguador *m* shock absorber

amortiguar [A16] *vt* ‹*golpe*› to cushion, absorb; ‹*sonido*› to muffle

amortizable *adj* redeemable

amortización *f* (de inversión) recovery; (de préstamo) repayment; (de bonos, hipoteca) redemption

amortizar [A4] *vt* **(a)** ‹*compra*› to recoup the cost of **(b)** (recuperar) ‹*inversión*› to recoup, recover **(c)** (pagar) ‹*deuda*› to repay, amortize (frml); ‹*valores/hipoteca*› to redeem

amotinado -da *adj* ‹*soldado/ejército*› rebel (*before n*), insurgent (*before n*); ‹*pueblo/ciudadanos*› rebellious, insurgent (*before n*) ■ *m,f* insurgent

amotinar [A1] *vt* ‹*tropa*› to incite ... to mutiny *o* rebellion; ‹*población/pueblo*› to incite ... to rebellion

■ **amotinarse** *v pron* «*soldados/oficiales*» to mutiny, rebel; «*población civil*» to rise up

amparar [A1] *vt* **(a)** (proteger) to protect; **¡que Dios nos ampare!** may the Lord help us! **(b)** (ofrecer refugio) to shelter, give shelter to

■ **ampararse** *v pron* **(a) ~se EN algo** ‹*en la ley*› to seek protection IN sth; **se amparó en su inmunidad diplomática** he used his diplomatic immunity to protect himself **(b)** (resguardarse) **~se DE** *or* **CONTRA algo** to shelter FROM sth

amparo *m* **(a)** (protección) protection **(b)** (refugio) refuge; **dar ~ A algn** to give sb refuge

amperio *m* amp, ampere (frml)

ampliación *f* **(a)** (de local, carretera) extension; (de negocio) expansion **(b)** (Com, Fin): **una ~ de capital/de personal** an increase in capital/in the number of staff **(c)** (de conocimientos, vocabulario) widening **(d)** (de plazo, período) extension **(e)** (Fot) enlargement

ampliar [A17] *vt* **(a)** ‹*local/carretera*› to extend; ‹*negocio*› to expand **(b)** ‹*capital/personal*› to increase **(c)** ‹*conocimientos/vocabulario*› to increase; ‹*explicación*› to expand (on); ‹*campo de acción*› to widen, broaden; **para ~ sus estudios** to further her studies **(d)** ‹*plazo/período*› to extend **(e)** ‹*fotografía*› to enlarge, blow up

amplificador *m* amplifier

amplificar [A2] *vt* to amplify

amplio -plia *adj* **(a)** ‹*calle/valle/margen*› wide; ‹*casa*› spacious; ‹*vestido/abrigo*› loose-fitting; ‹*sonrisa*› broad **(b)** ‹*criterio/sentido*› broad; **por amplia mayoría** by a large majority; **una amplia gama de colores** a wide range of colors **(c)** ‹*garantías/programa*› comprehensive

amplitud *f* **(a)** (de calle, margen) width; (de casa) spaciousness; (de vestido) looseness **(b)** (de miras, criterios) range; (de facultades, garantías) extent; **la ~ de sus conocimientos** the breadth *o* depth of his knowledge **(c)** (Fís) amplitude

ampolla *f* **1** (por quemadura, rozamiento) blister **2** (con medicamento) ampoule (frml), vial (AmE), phial (BrE)

ampolleta *f* (Chi) light bulb

amputar [A1] *vt* ‹*brazo/pierna*› to amputate

amueblar [A1] *vt* to furnish; **casa amueblada/sin ~** furnished/unfurnished house

amuleto *m* charm, amulet

anacardo *m* cashew (nut)

anaconda *f* anaconda

anacrónico -ca *adj* anachronistic

anacronismo *m* anachronism

ánade *mf* duck

anafe, **anafre** *m* (Chi, Méx) portable stove

anagrama *m* anagram

anal *adj* anal

anales *mpl* annals (*pl*)

analfabetismo *m* illiteracy

analfabeto -ta *adj* illiterate ■ *m,f* **(a)** (que no sabe leer) illiterate (person) **(b)** (fam & pey) (ignorante) ignoramus (colloq & pej)

analgésico *m* analgesic, painkiller

análisis *m* (*pl* ~) analysis; **hacerse un ~ de sangre** to have a blood test

analista *mf* analyst

analítico -ca *adj* analytic

analizar [A4] *vt* **(a)** (examinar) to analyze*, examine **(b)** (Med, Quím) to analyze* **(c)** (Ling) to parse ■ **analizarse** *v pron* to undergo *o* have analysis

analogía *f* analogy

ananá *m* (*pl* **-nás**) (RPl) pineapple

anaquel *m* shelf

anaranjado -da *adj* ▶97| orangish (AmE), orangey (BrE)

anarquía *f* anarchy

anárquico -ca *adj* anarchic

anarquismo *m* anarchism

anarquista *adj* anarchist (*before n*) ■ *mf* anarchist

anarquizar [A4] *vt* to cause chaos *o* anarchy in

anatomía *f* anatomy

anatómico -ca *adj* **(a)** (Anat) anatomical **(b)** ‹*asiento/respaldo*› anatomically designed

anca *f*‡ (de animal) haunch; **~s de rana** frogs' legs; **llevar a algn en ~s** (AmL) to take sb on the crupper

ancestral *adj* ‹*costumbre*› ancient; ‹*temor*› primitive, ancient

ancestro *m* ancestor

ancho¹ -cha *adj* **1 (a)** ‹*camino/río/mueble*› wide; **a todo lo ~ de la carretera** right across the road; **a lo ~** breadthways *o* (BrE) widthways **(b)** ‹*manos/cara/espalda*› broad; **es ~ de espaldas** he's broad-shouldered **(c)** ‹*ropa*› loose-fitting, loose; **me queda ~ de cintura** it's too big around the waist for me **2** (cómodo, tranquilo): **allí estaremos más ~s** (Esp) we'll have more room there; ***estar/sentirse/ponerse a sus anchas*** to be/feel/make oneself at home

ancho² *m* width; **¿cuánto mide de ~?** how wide is it?; **tiene 6 metros de ~** it's 6 meters wide

anchoa *f* anchovy

anchura *f* **(a)** (de camino, río, mueble) width **(b)** (medida): **~ de caderas** hip measurement

ancianato *m* (Col, Ven) old people's home

anciano -na *adj* elderly ■ *m,f* (*m*) elderly man; (*f*) elderly woman

ancla *f*‡ anchor; **echar el ~** to drop anchor; **levar ~s** to weigh anchor

anclar [A1] *vt/vi* to anchor

andadera *f* (Méx, Ven) ⇒ ANDADOR 1

andador *m* **1 (a)** (con ruedas) baby walker **(b)** **andadores** *mpl* (arnés) baby harness, reins (*pl*) **2** (para ancianos) Zimmer® frame

Andalucía *f* Andalusia

andaluz -luza *adj/m,f* Andalusian

andamio *m*: *tb* **~s** scaffolding

andanzas *fpl* adventures (*pl*)

andar¹ [A24] *vi* **1 (a)** (esp Esp) (caminar) to walk; **¿has venido andando?** did you come on foot?, did you walk? **(b)** (AmL): **~ a caballo/en bicicleta** to ride (a horse/a bicycle) **(c)** (AmS) (ir) to go; **anda a comprar el periódico** go and buy the newspaper **2** (marchar, funcionar) to work; **el coche anda de maravilla** the car's running *o* (BrE) going like a dream **3** (+ *compl*) **(a)** (estar) to be; **¿cómo andas?** how are you?, how's it going? (colloq); **¿quién anda por ahí?** who's there?; **anda en Londres** he's in London; **anda buscando pelea** he's out for *o* he's looking for a fight; **me anda molestando** (AmL) he keeps bothering me **(b) ~ CON algn** (juntarse) to mix WITH sb; (salir con) to go out WITH sb; ***dime con quién andas y te diré quién eres*** a man is known by the company he keeps **(c) ~ DETRÁS DE** *or* **TRAS algn/algo** (buscar, perseguir) to be AFTER sb/sth **4** (rondar): **~á por los 60 (años)** he must be around *o* about 60 **5 ~ CON algo** (esp AmL fam) ‹*con revólver/dinero*› to carry sth; ‹*con traje/sombrero*› to wear sth **6** (en exclamaciones) **(a)** (expresando sorpresa, incredulidad): **¡anda! ¡qué casualidad!** good heavens! what a coincidence!; **¡anda! ¡mira quién está aquí!** well, well! look who's here! **(b)** (expresando irritación, rechazo): **¡anda! ¡déjame en paz!** oh, leave me alone!; **¡anda! ¡se me ha vuelto a olvidar!** damn! I've forgotten it again! (colloq) **(c)** (instando a hacer algo): **préstamelo, anda** go on, lend it to me!; **¡ándale** (Méx) *or* (Col) **ándele que llegamos tarde!** come on, we'll be late! (colloq) ■ **~** *vt* **1** (caminar) to walk **2** (AmC) (llevar): **no ando dinero** I don't have any money on me; **siempre ando shorts** I always wear shorts ■ **andarse** *v pron* **1 ~se CON algo**: **ése no se anda con bromas** he's not one to joke; **ándate con cuidado** take care, be careful **2** (*en imperativo*) (AmL) (irse): **ándate de aquí** get out of here; **ándate luego** get going, get a move on (colloq)

andar² *m*, **andares** *mpl* gait, walk

andarivel *m* **(a)** (AmL) (cable) ferry cable **(b)** (AmS) (en una piscina — carril) lane; (— soga) lane divider

andas *fpl* portable platform (*used in religious processions*); ***llevar a algn en ~*** (CS) to carry sb on one's shoulders

ándele, **ándale** *interj*: *ver* ANDAR¹ 6 (b), (c)

andén *m* **(a)** (en estación) platform **(b)** (AmC, Col) (acera) sidewalk (AmE), pavement (BrE)

Andes *mpl*: **los ~** the Andes

andinismo *m* (AmL) mountaineering, mountain climbing, climbing

andinista *mf* (AmL) mountaineer, mountain climber, climber

andino -na *adj* Andean

andrajo *m* rag

andrajoso -sa *adj* ragged

anduve, **anduviste, etc** *see* ANDAR

anécdota *f* anecdote

anecdótico -ca *adj* **(a)** ‹*relato*› anecdotal **(b)** ‹*interés/valor*› incidental

anegar [A3] *vt* to flood ■ **anegarse** *v pron* «*campo/terreno*» to be flooded

anemia *f* anemia*
anémico -ca *adj* anemic* ■ *m,f* anemic person
anestesia *f* (proceso) anesthesia*; (droga) anesthetic*; **bajo los efectos de la ~** under (the) anesthetic; **lo operaron con ~** he was operated on under (an) anesthetic; **sin ~** without an anesthetic
anestesiar [A1] *vt ‹encía/dedo›* to anesthetize*; **me ~on** they gave me an anesthetic
anestesista *mf* anesthetist*
anexo¹ -xa *adj* **(a)** *‹edificio/local›* joined, annexed **(b)** *‹cláusula›* added, appended (frml); *‹documento›* (en informe) attached; (en carta) enclosed
anexo² *m* **(a)** (edificio) annex* **(b)** (documento — en informe) appendix; (— en carta) enclosure **(c)** (Chi) (del teléfono) extension
anfetamina *f* amphetamine
anfibio¹ -bia *adj* amphibious; **avión ~** seaplane
anfibio² *m* amphibian
anfiteatro *m* (Arquit) amphitheater*; (Geol) natural amphitheater*; (en la universidad) lecture hall
anfitrión -triona *m,f* (*m*) host; (*f*) hostess
ánfora *f*‡ (cántaro) amphora
angas (Andes, Méx fam): **por ~ o por mangas, nunca estás trabajando** for one reason or another, you're never working; **por ~ o por mangas tengo que salir** I have to go out whether I like it or not
ángel *m* **(a)** (Relig) angel; **~ guardián** *or* **de la guarda** guardian angel; **que sueñes con los angelitos** sweet dreams; **pobre angelito** poor little darling **(b)** (encanto) charm; **tener ~** to be charming
angelical *adj* angelic
angelito *m* (AmL) dead child; *ver tb* ÁNGEL
angina *f* **1** (Arg, Col, Ven) (de la garganta) *inflammation of the palate, tonsils and/or pharynx* **2** *tb* **~ de pecho** angina (pectoris)
anginas *fpl* **(a)** (Esp, Méx) (inflamación) throat infection **(b)** (Méx, Ven) (amígdalas) tonsils (*pl*)
anglicano -na *adj/m,f* Episcopalian (*in US and Scotland*), Anglican (*in UK*)
anglicismo *m* Anglicism
angloparlante *adj* English-speaking
Angola *f* Angola
angoleño -leña *adj/m,f* Angolan
angora *f* angora
angosto -ta *adj ‹calle/cama›* narrow; *‹falda›* tight
anguila *f* eel
angular *adj* angular
ángulo *m* (Mat) angle; (rincón, esquina) corner; (punto de vista) angle; **~ recto** right angle
anguloso -sa *adj* angular
angustia *f* **(a)** (congoja) anguish, distress; **gritos de ~** anguished cries **(b)** (desasosiego) anxiety; **vive con la ~ de que**… she's constantly worried that… **(c)** (Psic) anxiety
angustiado -da *adj* **(a)** (acongojado) distressed **(b)** (preocupado) worried, anxious; **vive angustiada** she lives in a constant state of anxiety
angustiar [A1] *vt* **(a)** (acongojar) to distress **(b)** (preocupar) to worry, make … anxious
■ **angustiarse** *v pron* (acongojarse) to get distressed, get upset; (preocuparse) to get worried, become anxious
angustioso -sa *adj ‹situación›* distressing; *‹mirada/grito›* anguished
anhelante *adj* (liter) *‹mirada›* longing (*before n*); **esperaba ~ su regreso** she longed *o* she yearned for his return; **con voz ~** in a voice full of longing
anhelar [A1] *vt* (liter) *‹fama/poder›* to yearn for, to long for; **~ hacer algo** to long to do sth, yearn to do sth; **anhelaba que su hijo fuera feliz** his greatest wish was for his son to be happy
anhelo *m* (liter) wish, desire; **mi mayor ~** my greatest wish
anhídrido *m* anhydride; **~ carbónico** carbon dioxide
anidar [A1] *vi «aves»* to nest
aniego *m* (Per) flood
anilla *f* **(a)** (de cortina, llavero) ring; (de puro) band; (de lata) ringpull; (de ave) ring **(b) anillas** *fpl* (Dep) rings (*pl*)
anillo *m* **1** (sortija) ring; **~ de boda/compromiso** wedding/engagement ring; ***como ~ al dedo*** (fam) *‹sentar/quedar›* to suit down to the ground; *‹venir›* to come in very handy (colloq) **2** (aro, arandela) ring; (de columna) annulet; (en árbol) ring
ánima *f*‡ (liter) (alma) soul
animación *f* **1** (bullicio, actividad) activity; **un bar con mucha ~** a very lively bar **2** (de una velada) entertainment **3** (Cin) animation
animado -da *adj* **1 (a)** *‹fiesta/ambiente›* lively; *‹conversación/discusión›* lively, animated **(b)** (optimista, con ánimo) cheerful, in good spirits **2** (impulsado) **~** DE *or* POR **algo** inspired *o* motivated BY sth
animador -dora *m,f* **(a)** (de programa) (*m*) presenter, host; (*f*) presenter, hostess **(b) animadora** *f* (de equipo) cheerleader
animal *adj* **1** *‹instinto›* animal (*before n*) **2** (fam) **(a)** (estúpido) stupid **(b)** (grosero) rude, uncouth ■ *m* **(a)** (Zool) animal; **~ doméstico** (de granja) domestic animal; (mascota) pet **(b)** (fam) (persona — violenta) brute, animal; (— grosera) lout
animar [A1] *vt* **1 (a)** (alentar) to encourage; (levantar el espíritu) to cheer … up; **tu visita lo animó mucho** your visit cheered him up a lot; **~ a algn** A **hacer algo** *or* A **que haga algo** to encourage sb to do sth **(b)** *‹fiesta/reunión›* to liven up; **el vino empezaba a ~los** the wine was beginning to liven them up **(c)** (con luces, colores) to brighten up **2** *‹programa›* to present, host **3** (impulsar) to inspire
■ **animarse** *v pron* **(a)** (alegrarse, cobrar vida) *«fiesta/reunión»* to liven up, warm up; *«persona»* to liven up **(b)** (cobrar ánimos) to cheer up; **si me animo a salir te llamo** if I feel like going out, I'll call you **(c)** (atreverse): **¿quién se anima a decírselo?** who's going to be brave enough to tell him?; **no me animo a saltar** I can't bring myself to jump; **al**

final me animé a confesárselo I finally plucked up the courage to tell her

anímicamente *adv* emotionally

anímico -ca *adj*: **su estado ~** her state of mind

ánimo *m* **1 (a)** (espíritu): **no estoy con el ~ para bromas** I'm not in the mood for jokes; **tu visita le levantó el ~** your visit cheered her up; **con el ~ por el suelo** in very low spirits, feeling very downhearted; **apaciguar los ~s** to calm everyone down; ***hacerse el ~ de hacer algo*** to bring oneself to do sth **(b)** (aliento, coraje) encouragement; **darle ~(s) a algn** (animar) to encourage sb; (con aplausos, gritos) to cheer sb on; **¡~, que ya falta poco para llegar!** come on! it's not far now!; **no tengo ~(s) de** *or* **para nada** I don't feel up to anything **2 (a)** (intención, propósito) intention; **lo dije sin ~ de ofender** I meant no offense, no offense intended (colloq) **(b)** (mente, pensamiento) mind

animosidad *f* animosity, hostility; **~ CONTRA algn** animosity *o* hostility TOWARD(s) sb

aniquilar [A1] *vt* ‹*enemigo/población*› to annihilate, wipe out; ‹*defensas/instalaciones*› to destroy

anís *m* **(a)** (Bot) (planta) anise; (semilla) aniseed **(b)** (licor) anisette

aniversario *m* anniversary

ano *m* anus

anoche *adv* last night

anochecer¹ [E3] *v impers* to get dark ■ **anochecerse** *v pron* (Chi, Méx) to stay up till really late

anochecer² *m* nightfall; **al ~** at nightfall

anomalía *f* anomaly

anonadado -da *adj* dumbfounded, speechless

anonimato *m* anonymity; **salir del ~** to rise from obscurity

anónimo -ma *adj* anonymous

anorak /ano'rak/ *m* parka (AmE), anorak (BrE)

anorexia *f* anorexia

anoréxico -ca *adj/m,f* anorexic

anormal *adj* abnormal ■ *mf* (fam) idiot

anormalidad *f* abnormality

anotación *f* **(a)** (nota) note **(b)** (AmL) (en fútbol) goal; (en fútbol americano) touchdown; (en básquetbol) point

anotador -dora *m,f* (AmL) (en fútbol) scorer, goalscorer; (en fútbol americano, básquetbol) scorer

anotar [A1] *vt* **1 (a)** (tomar nota de) ‹*dirección/nombre*› to make a note of **(b)** ‹*texto*› to annotate **(c)** (RPl) ⇨ APUNTAR *vt* 1(b) **2** (AmL) ‹*gol/tanto*› to score ■ **anotarse** *v pron* **1** (AmL) ‹*gol/tanto*› to score **2** (RPl) (inscribirse) ⇨ APUNTARSE 1(a)

anquilosado -da *adj* **(a)** ‹*articulación*› (atrofiado) ankylosed; (entumecido) stiff **(b)** ‹*ideas/economía*› stagnant

anquilosarse [A1] *v pron* **(a)** «*miembro/articulación*» (atrofiarse) to ankylose; (entumecerse) to get stiff **(b)** «*ideas/economía*» to stagnate

ansia *f*‡ **(a)** (avidez, deseo): **con ~** ‹*comer/beber*› eagerly; **~ DE algo** ‹*de paz/libertad*› longing FOR sth, yearning FOR sth; ‹*de poder*› thirst FOR sth, craving FOR sth; **sentir ~ de hacer algo** to long *o* yearn to do sth; **sus ~s de aprendar** her eagerness to learn **(b)** (Psic) anxiety **(c) ansias** *fpl* (Col, Ven fam) (náuseas) nausea

ansiar [A17] *vt* (liter) ‹*libertad/poder*› to long for, yearn for; **~ hacer algo** to long to do sth

ansiedad *f* **(a)** (preocupación) anxiety; **con ~** anxiously **(b)** (Med, Psic) anxiety

ansioso -sa *adj* **(a)** (deseoso) eager; **está ~ por saberlo** he's eager *o* (colloq) dying to know; **estoy ~ de verlos** I can't wait to see them **(b)** [SER] (fam) (voraz) greedy

antagónico -ca *adj* conflicting

antagonismo *m* antagonism

antagonista *adj* antagonistic ■ *mf* antagonist

antártico -ca *adj* Antarctic

Antártida *f*: **la ~** Antarctica, the Antarctic

ante *prep* **1 (a)** (frml) (delante de) before; **ante el juez** before the judge **(b)** (frente a): **~ la gravedad de la situación** in view of the seriousness of the situation; **iguales ~ la ley** equal in the eyes of the law; **nos hallamos ~ un problema** we are faced with a problem **2 ante todo** (primero) first and foremost; (sobre todo) above all ■ *m* (cuero) suede

anteanoche *adv* the night before last

anteayer *adv* the day before yesterday

antebrazo *m* ▶ 123 forearm

antecedente *m* **1 (a)** (precedente) precedent; **no hay ningún ~ de la enfermedad en mi familia** there's no history of the illness in my family **(b)** (causa) cause; ***estar/poner a algn en ~s*** to be/put sb in the picture **2** (Fil, Ling) antecedent **3 antecedentes** *mpl* (historial) background, record; **~s penales** (criminal) record

anteceder [E1] *vt* to precede, come before; **~ A algo** to come BEFORE sth, precede sth

antecesor -sora *m,f* (predecesor) predecessor; (antepasado) ancestor

antecomedor *m* (Méx) breakfast room

antelación *f*: **con ~** ‹*reservar/pagar*› in advance; ‹*avisar/salir*› in plenty of time; **saqué la entrada con un mes de ~** I got the ticket one month in advance; **llegó con dos días de ~** she arrived two days early; **con ~ a su boda** prior to her wedding

antemano: **de ~** (*loc adv*) in advance

antena *f* **1** (de radio, televisión, coche) antenna (AmE), aerial (BrE); **en ~** on the air; **~ colectiva** communal antenna *o* aerial; **~ de radar** radar dish; **~ repetidora** relay mast **2** (Zool) antenna

antenoche *adv* (AmL) the night before last

anteojo *m* **(a)** (telescopio) telescope **(b) anteojos** *mpl* (esp AmL) ⇨ GAFAS

antepasado -da *adj* ‹*año/semana*› before last ■ *m,f* ancestor

antepenúltimo -ma *adj* (*delante del n*) third from last, antepenultimate (frml) ■ *m,f*: **fue el ~ en la carrera** he came third from last on the race; **es el ~ en la lista** he's third from bottom on the list

anteponer [E22] *vt* **~ algo A algo** (poner delante) to put sth BEFORE *o* IN FRONT OF sth; (dar preferencia) to put sth BEFORE sth

anteproyecto *m* draft; **~ de ley** bill

anterior *adj* **(a)** (en el tiempo) previous; **el día ~** the previous day, the day before; **en épocas ~es** in earlier times; **~ A algo** prior TO sth **(b)** (en un orden) previous, preceding; **el capítulo ~ a éste** the previous chapter **(c)** (en el espacio) front (*before n*); **la parte ~** the front (part); **las patas ~es** the forelegs *o* front legs

anterioridad *f* (frml) anteriority (frml); **con ~** (antes) before, previously; (con antelación) beforehand, in advance; **con ~ a algo** before sth, prior to sth

antes *adv* **1 (a)** (con anterioridad) before; **lo compré el día ~** I bought it the day before; **lo ~ posible** as soon as possible **(b)** (más temprano) earlier; **no pude llegar ~** I couldn't arrive earlier **(c)** (*en locs*) **antes de** before; **~ de Jesucristo** before Christ, BC; **no van a llegar ~ de dos horas** they won't be here for two hours; **le daré la respuesta ~ de una semana** I will give you my reply within a week; **~ de lo esperado** earlier than expected; **~ DE hacer algo** before doing sth; **~ (de) que me olvide** before I forget; **no se lo des ~ (de) que yo lo vea** don't give it to him until I've seen it **(d)** (en el espacio) before **2** (en tiempos pasados) before, in the past; **ya no es el mismo de ~** he's not the same person any more **3 (a)** (indicando orden, prioridad) first; **~ que nada** first of all; **yo estaba ~** I was here first **(b)** (indicando preferencia): **¡~ me muero!** I'd rather *o* sooner die!; **cualquier cosa ~ que eso** anything but that

antiaéreo -rea *adj* antiaircraft (*before n*)

antialérgico -ca *adj* antiallergenic

antibalas *adj inv* bulletproof

antibiótico *m* antibiotic

anticiclón *m* anticyclone

anticipación *f* (antelación): **con (mucha) ~** (well) in advance; **con un mes de ~** a month in advance

anticipado -da *adj* ‹*pago*› advance (*before n*); ‹*elecciones*› early; **por ~** in advance

anticipar [A1] *vt* **(a)** ‹*viaje/elecciones*› to move up (AmE), to bring forward (BrE) **(b)** ‹*dinero/sueldo*› to advance; **¿nos podría ~ de qué se trata?** could you give us an idea of what it is about?

■ **anticiparse** *v pron* **(a)** «*verano/lluvias*» to be *o* come early **(b)** (adelantarse): **se anticipó a su tiempo** he was ahead of his time; **no nos anticipemos a los acontecimientos** let's not jump the gun

anticipo *m* **(a)** (del sueldo, dinero) advance **(b)** (pago inicial) down payment

anticonceptivo¹ -va *adj* contraceptive (*before n*); **métodos ~s** methods of contraception

anticonceptivo² *m* contraceptive

anticongelante *adj/m* antifreeze

anticuado -da *adj* old-fashioned ■ *m,f*: **eres un ~** you're so old-fashioned

anticuario -ria *m,f* **(a)** (persona) antique dealer **(b) anticuario** *m* (tienda) antique shop

anticucho *m* (Bol, Chi, Per) kebab

anticuerpo *m* antibody

antidemocrático -ca *adj* (poco democrático) undemocratic; (opuesto a la democracia) antidemocratic

antideportivo -va *adj* unsportsmanlike

antideslizante *adj* ‹*superficie/suela*› nonslip; ‹*neumático/freno*› antiskid (*before n*)

antidisturbios *adj inv* riot (*before n*)

antídoto *m* antidote

antiestético -ca *adj* unsightly

antifaz *m* mask

antigripal *adj* ‹*vacuna*› flu (*before n*) ■ *m* flu remedy

antiguamente *adv* in the past, in the old days

antigüedad *f* **(a)** (de monumento, objeto) age; **esas ruinas tienen varios siglos de ~** those ruins are several centuries old **(b)** (en el trabajo) seniority **(c)** (objeto) antique; **tienda de ~es** antique shop **(d)** (época): **en la ~** in ancient times

antiguo -gua *adj* **1 (a)** (viejo) ‹*ciudad/libro*› old; ‹*ruinas/civilización*› ancient; ‹*mueble/lámpara*› antique, old; ‹*coche*› vintage, old; ‹*costumbre/tradición*› old; **el Antiguo Testamento** the Old Testament **(b)** (veterano) old, long-standing **(c)** (*en locs*) **a la antigua** in an old-fashioned way; ***chapado a la antigua*** old-fashioned; **de** *or* **desde antiguo** from time immemorial **2** (*delante del n*) (de antes) old (*before n*), former (*before n*); **la antigua capital del Brasil** the former capital of Brazil **3** (anticuado) old-fashioned

antiguos *mpl*: **los ~** the ancients

antihigiénico -ca *adj* unhygienic

antiincendios *adj inv* firefighting (*before n*)

antiinflamatorio *m* anti-inflammatory

antillano -na *adj/m,f* West Indian

Antillas *fpl*: **las ~** the West Indies

antílope *m* antelope

antimanchas *adj inv* stain-resistant

antimisil *adj* antiballistic (*before n*) ■ *m* antiballistic missile

antimonárquico -ca *adj* antimonarchical, antimonarchist (*before n*) ■ *m,f* antimonarchist

antinatural *adj* unnatural

antioxidante *adj* (Quím) antioxidant (*before n*); ‹*pintura*› antirust (*before n*)

antipatía *f* dislike, antipathy; **tomarle ~ a algo/algn** to take a dislike to sth/sb

antipático -ca *adj* **(a)** ‹*persona*› unpleasant; **¡qué tipo más ~!** what a horrible man! **(b)** (fam) ‹*tarea*›: **esto de planchar es de lo más ~** ironing is such a drag (colloq) ■ *m,f*: **es un ~** he's really unpleasant

antipatriótico -ca *adj* unpatriotic

antipedagógico -ca *adj* pedagogically unsound

antiperspirante *m* antiperspirant

antípodas *fpl*: **las ~** the antipodes

antirreglamentario -ria *adj* (Dep): **una jugada antirreglamentaria** a foul; **estaba en posición antirreglamentaria** (period) he was offside

antirrobo *m* antitheft device

antisemita *adj* anti-Semitic ■ *mf* anti-Semite

antiséptico *m* antiseptic

antisocial *adj* antisocial ■ *mf* (Andes period) delinquent

antiterrorista *adj* antiterrorist (*before n*)

antítesis *f* (*pl* ~) antithesis

antojarse [A1] *v pron* (+ *me/te/le etc*): **se me antojó una cerveza** I felt like (having) a beer; **de embarazada se me antojaban las uvas** when I was pregnant, I had a craving for grapes; **hace lo que se le antoja** he does as he pleases; **porque no se me antoja** because I don't feel like it

antojitos *mpl* (Méx) *typical Mexican snacks, usually bought at street stands*

antojo *m* **(a)** (capricho) whim; **tiene que hacerlo todo a su ~** she has to do everything her own way; **maneja al marido a su ~** she has her husband twisted around her little finger **(b)** (de embarazada) craving **(c)** (en la piel) birthmark

antología *f* anthology; ***de ~*** (muy bueno) excellent, fantastic (colloq); (muy malo) terrible

antorcha *f* torch

antro *m* (local sórdido) dive (colloq); **~ de perdición** den of iniquity

antropología *f* anthropology

antropólogo -ga *m,f* anthropologist

anual *adj* **(a)** ‹*cuota/asamblea*› annual, yearly; ‹*interés/dividendo*› annual; **cinco mil pesetas ~es** five thousand pesetas a year **(b)** ‹*planta*› annual

anualidad *f* (inversión) annuity; (cuota anual) annual payment (*o* subscription *etc*)

anuario *m* yearbook

anudar [A1] *vt* ‹*cordón/corbata*› to tie

■ **anudarse** *v pron* (*refl*) ‹*corbata/pañuelo*› to tie

anulación *f* (de contrato, viaje) cancellation; (de matrimonio) annulment; (de sentencia) quashing, overturning; **protestó la ~ del gol** he protested when the goal was disallowed

anular *vt* **(a)** ‹*contrato/viaje*› to cancel; ‹*matrimonio*› to annul; ‹*fallo/sentencia*› to quash, overturn; ‹*resultado*› to declare ... null and void; ‹*tanto/gol*› to disallow **(b)** ‹*cheque*› (destruir) to cancel; (dar orden de no pagar) to stop ■ *m* ▶ **123** finger ring

anunciador -dora *m,f*, **anunciante** *mf* advertiser

anunciar [A1] *vt* **(a)** ‹*noticia/decisión*› to announce, make ... public; ‹*lluvias/tormentas*› to forecast **(b)** (frml) ‹*persona*› to announce **(c)** ‹*producto*› to advertise, promote

anuncio *m* **(a)** (de noticia) announcement; (presagio) sign, omen **(b)** (en periódico) advertisement, ad (colloq); (en televisión) commercial; **~s clasificados** *or* **por palabras** classified advertisements (*pl*)

anverso *m* obverse

anzuelo *m* hook; ***morder*** *or* ***tragarse el ~*** to swallow *o* take the bait

añadir [I1] *vt* to add

añejo -ja *adj* ‹*vino/queso*› mature; ‹*costumbre*› old, ancient

añicos *mpl*: **hacerse ~** to shatter; **tiró el florero y lo hizo ~** he knocked the vase over and smashed it to smithereens

año *m* **1** ▶ **193** (período) year; **los ~s 50** the 50s; **el ~ pasado** last year; **una vez al ~** once a year; **hace ~s que no lo veo** I haven't seen him for *o* in years; ***el ~ de la pera*** *or* ***de Maricastaña*** (fam): **ese peinado es del ~ de la pera** that hairstyle went out with the ark (colloq), that hairstyle is really old-fashioned; **un disco del ~ de la pera** a record that's really ancient; **~ bisiesto** leap year; **~ fiscal** fiscal year (AmE), tax year (BrE); **~ luz** light year; **Año Nuevo** New Year **2** ▶ **125**, **159** (indicando edad): **soltero, de 30 ~s de edad** single, 30 years old *o* (frml) 30 years of age; **¿cuántos ~s tienes?** how old are you?; **tengo 14 ~s** I'm 14 (years old); **hoy cumple 29 ~s** she's 29 today; **ya debe de tener sus añitos** he must be getting on (a bit); ***quitarse ~s***: **se quita ~s** she's older than she admits *o* says **3** (curso) year; **~ académico/escolar** academic/school year

añoranza *f* yearning; **siente ~ de** *or* **por su país** he yearns for his country

añorar [A1] *vt* ‹*patria/tranquilidad*› to yearn for; ‹*persona*› to miss

aorta *f* aorta

apabullante *adj* ‹*victoria/éxito*› resounding (*before n*), overwhelming; ‹*rapidez/habilidad*› incredible, extraordinary; ‹*personalidad*› overpowering

apabullar [A1] *vt* (vencer) to overwhelm, crush; (dejar confuso) to overwhelm

apache *adj* Apache (*before n*) ■ *mf* Apache

apachurrar [A1] *vt* (AmL fam) to squash

apacible *adj* ‹*carácter/persona*› calm, placid; ‹*vida*› quiet, peaceful; ‹*clima*› mild; ‹*mar*› calm; ‹*viento*› gentle

apaciguar [A16] *vt* ‹*ánimos*› to pacify; ‹*persona*› to calm ... down, to pacify

■ **apaciguarse** *v pron* «*persona*» to calm down; «*mar*» to become calm; «*temporal/viento*» to abate, die down

apadrinar [A1] *vt* ‹*niño*› to be godfather/godparent to; ‹*boda*› to act as PADRINO at; ‹*artista/novillero*› to sponsor, be patron to; ‹*político/idea/candidatura*› to support, back; ‹*barco*› to launch, christen

apagado -da *adj* **1** ‹*persona*› [SER] spiritless, lifeless; [ESTAR] subdued **2 (a)** ‹*sonido*› muffled **(b)** ‹*color*› muted, dull **3 (a)** (no encendido): **la televisión/luz está apagada** the TV/light is off; **el horno está ~** the oven is switched off; **con el motor ~** with the engine off **(b)** ‹*volcán*› extinct

apagar [A3] *vt* ‹*luz/televisión/motor*› to turn off, switch off; ‹*cigarrillo/fuego*› to put out; ‹*vela/cerilla*› to put out; (soplando) to blow out

■ **apagarse** *v pron* «*luz/fuego/vela*» to go out

apagón *m* power cut, blackout

apalabrar [A1] *vt*: **lo había apalabrado pero no llegué a firmar nada** it was all arranged *o* fixed but I never actually signed anything; **ya tengo apalabrado a un albañil** (fam) I've already fixed up with a builder

apalancar [A2] *vt* **(a)** (para levantar) to jack up (AmE), to lever up (BrE) **(b)** (para abrir) to force open

apalear [A1] *vt* **(a)** ‹*persona, alfombra*› to beat; ‹*árbol*› to beat the branches of **(b)** ‹*arena/carbón*› to shovel

apanar [A1] *vt* (Andes) ⇒ EMPANAR

apantallar [A1] *vt* **1** (Méx) (impresionar) to impress **2** (RPl) (abanicar) to fan

apañar [A1] *vt* **1** (fam) ‹*elecciones*› to fix (colloq), to rig **2** (AmS fam) (encubrir) to cover up for

■ **apañarse** *v pron* (Esp fam) ⇒ ARREGLARSE 4

apapachar [A1] *vt* (Cu, Méx fam) (abrazar) to cuddle; (acariciar) to stroke, caress

apapacho *m* (Cu, Méx fam) (abrazo) cuddle; (caricia) caress

aparador *m* **(a)** (mueble) sideboard **(b)** (AmL exc CS) (vitrina) store window (AmE), shop window (BrE)

aparato *m* **1 (a)** (máquina): **uno de esos ~s para hacer pasta** one of those pasta machines; **~s eléctricos** electrical appliances **(b)** (de televisión) set; (de radio) receiver **(c)** (dispositivo) device; **~ ortopédico** surgical appliance; **~ auditivo** hearing aid **(d)** (Odont) *tb* **~s** braces (*pl*) **(e)** (teléfono) telephone; **ponerse al ~** to come to the phone **2** (para gimnasia) piece of apparatus; **los ~s** the apparatus, the equipment **3** (frml) (avión) aircraft **4** (estructura, sistema) machine; **el ~ del partido** the party machine; **~ circulatorio/digestivo/respiratorio** circulatory/digestive/respiratory system

aparatoso -sa *adj* ‹*gesto*› flamboyant; ‹*sombrero*› showy, flamboyant; ‹*caída/accidente*› spectacular, dramatic

aparcamiento *m* (Esp) **(a)** (acción) parking **(b)** (lugar — en ciudad) parking lot (AmE), car park (BrE); (— en carretera) rest area *o* stop (AmE), lay-by (BrE)

aparcar [A2] *vt/vi* (Esp) to park; **~ en doble fila** to double-park

aparear [A1] *vt* ‹*animales*› to mate; ‹*objetos*› to match, pair up

■ **aparearse** *v pron* to mate

aparecer [E3] *vi* **1 (a)** «*síntoma/mancha*» to appear **(b)** «*objeto perdido*» to turn up; **hizo ~ un ramo de flores** he produced a bouquet of flowers **(c)** (en documento) to appear; **mi nombre aparece en la lista** my name appears on the list **(d)** «*revista/libro*» to come out **2** «*persona*» **(a)** (fam) (llegar) to appear, turn up **(b)** (fam) (dejarse ver) to appear, show up (colloq) **(c)** (en película, televisión) to appear

■ **aparecerse** *v pron* **(a)** «*fantasma/aparición*» **~se A algn** to appear TO sb **(b)** (AmL fam) «*persona*» to turn up; **¡no te vuelvas a ~ por aquí!** don't you dare show your face round here again!

aparejar [A1] *vt* ‹*caballos*› (para montar) to saddle; (a carro) to harness

aparejo *m* (de caballo) tack; (de pesca) tackle; (polea) block and tackle

aparentar [A1] *vt* **(a)** (fingir) ‹*indiferencia/interés*› to feign; **quiere ~ que no le importa** he's trying to make out he's not bothered about it **(b)** (parecer): **no aparentas la edad que tienes** you don't look your age ■ **~** *vi* **(a)** «*persona*» to show off; **sólo por ~** just for show **(b)** «*regalo/joya*» to look impressive

aparente *adj* **1** (que parece real) ‹*timidez/interés*› apparent (*before n*); **la ~ victoria se tornó en derrota** what had seemed like victory turned into defeat **2** (obvio, palpable) apparent, obvious

apariencia *f* appearance; **un hombre de ~ fuerte** a strong-looking man; **a juzgar por las ~s** judging by appearances; **guardar las ~s** to keep up appearances; **las ~s engañan** appearances can be deceptive

apartado[1] -da *adj* **(a)** ‹*zona/lugar*› isolated **(b)** ‹*persona*›: **se mantuvo ~ de la vida pública** he stayed out of public life; **vive ~ de la familia** he has little to do with his family

apartado[2] *m* **1** (Corresp) *tb* **~ de correos** *or* **~ postal** post office box, P.O. Box **2** (de artículo, capítulo) section

apartamento *m* apartment

apartar [A1] *vt* **1 (a)** (alejar) to move ... away; **sus amigos lo ~on del buen camino** his friends led him astray; **apartó los ojos** he averted his eyes **(b)** ‹*obstáculo*› to move, move ... out of the way **(c)** (frml) (de un cargo) to remove **(d)** (separar) to separate **2** (guardar, reservar) to set aside; **aparta un poco de comida para él** put a bit of food aside for him

■ **apartarse** *v pron* (*refl*) **(a)** (despejar el camino) to stand aside **(b)** (alejarse, separarse): **apártate de ahí** get/come away from there; **no se aparta de su lado** he never leaves her side; **¡apártate de mi vista!** get out of my sight!; **se apartó de su familia** she drifted away from her family; **nos estamos apartando del tema** we're going off the subject

aparte *adv* **1** (a un lado, por separado): **pon las verduras ~** put the vegetables to *o* on one side; **¿me lo podría envolver ~?** could you wrap it separately?; **lo llamó ~ y lo reprendió** she called him aside and reprimanded him; **bromas ~** joking aside; **~ de** (excepto) apart from; **~ de eso me encuentro bien** apart from that I'm all right; (además de) as well as; **~ de hacerlos, los diseña** she designs them as well as making them **2** (además) as well; (por otra parte) anyway, besides ■ *adj inv*: **esto merece un capítulo ~** this deserves a separate chapter; **es un caso ~** he's a special case

apasionado -da *adj* ‹*amor/persona*› passionate; ‹*discurso*› impassioned ■ *m,f* enthusiast

apasionante *adj* ‹*obra*› exciting, enthralling; ‹*tema*› fascinating

apasionar [A1] *vi*: **le apasiona la música** she has a passion for music; **no es un tema que me apasione** the subject doesn't exactly fascinate me

apatía *f* apathy

apático -ca *adj* apathetic

apátrida *mf* **(a)** (sin patria) stateless person **(b)** (RPl) (que no ama a su país) unpatriotic person

apearse [A1] *v pron* (frml) (bajarse) to get off, alight (frml); **~ DE algo** ‹*de un tren/caballo/una bicicleta*› to get OFF sth

apechugar [A3] *vi* (fam) to grin and bear it (colloq), to put up with it (colloq); **~ con las consecuencias** to put up with *o* suffer the consequences

apedrear [A1] *vt* **(a)** (tirar piedras a) to throw stones at **(b)** (matar a pedradas) to stone (to death)

Los apellidos

En los países de habla inglesa las personas utilizan un solo apellido, el del padre.

Tradicionalmente las mujeres adoptan el apellido del marido al casarse, pero es cada vez mayor el número de mujeres que prefieren conservar su apellido de soltera.

Hasta hace algunos años era usual referirse a una mujer casada utilizando el nombre y apellido del marido, por ejemplo 'Mrs John Ashdown', pero esta costumbre está cayendo en desuso.

No se suele usar el apellido para dirigirse a un compañero o colega, salvo en algunos colegios privados. Suele usarse, sin embargo, sobre todo entre hombres, para referirse a personas a las que se conoce a través del trabajo pero con quienes no se tiene mayor intimidad.

apego *m* ~ A **algo/algn** attachment TO sth/sb; **tenerle ~ a algn/algo** to be attached to sb/sth; **les tiene poco ~ a las cosas materiales** he attaches little importance to material things

apelación *f* appeal

apelar [A1] *vi* **(a)** (Der) to appeal; **~ ante el Tribunal Supremo** to appeal to the Supreme Court **(b)** (invocar, recurrir a) ~ A **algo/algn** to appeal TO sth/sb

apelativo *m* **(a)** (sobrenombre) name **(b)** (Ling) form of address; **un ~ cariñoso** a term of endearment

apellido *m* surname, last name (AmE); **~ de soltera/de casada** maiden/married name

apelmazarse [A4] *v pron* **(a)** «*arroz/pasta*» to stick together **(b)** «*colchón/cojín*» to go lumpy; «*lana*» to get *o* become matted

apenar [A1] *vt* to sadden

■ **apenarse** *v pron* **1** (entristecerse): **se sintió apenado por su muerte** he was saddened by her death; **se apenó mucho cuando lo supo** he was very upset *o* sad when he learned of it **2** (AmL exc CS) (sentir vergüenza) to be embarrassed

apenas *adv* **(a)** (a duras penas) hardly; **~ podíamos oírlo** we could hardly hear him; **hace ~ dos horas** only two hours ago **(b)** (no bien): **~ había llegado cuando** ... no sooner had he arrived than ... **(c)** (Méx, Ven fam) (recién): **~ el lunes la podré ir a ver** I won't be able to go and see her until Monday; **~ va por la página 10** he's only on page 10 ■ *conj* (esp AmL) (en cuanto) as soon as

apendejarse [A1] *v pron* (AmL exc CS fam) (volverse estúpido) to go soft in the head (colloq)

apéndice *m* **(a)** (del intestino) appendix; (de otro miembro) appendage; **lo operaron del ~** his appendix was removed **(b)** (de texto, documento) appendix

apendicitis *f* appendicitis

apergaminado -da *adj* ‹*papel*› parchment-like; ‹*piel*› leathery; ‹*cara*› wizened

aperitivo *m* **(a)** (bebida) aperitif; **nos invitaron a tomar el ~** they invited us for drinks before lunch (*o* dinner *etc*) **(b)** (comida) snack, appetizer

apersonarse [A1] *v pron* **(a)** (comparecer) to appear **(b)** (Col) ~ DE **algo** to take charge OF sth, take sth in hand **(c)** (RPl, Ven fam) (presentarse) to appear in person

apertura *f* **1 (a)** (de caja, sobre, cuenta) opening **(b)** (inauguración) opening; **la sesión de ~** the opening session **(c)** (de curso, año académico) beginning, start **(d)** (Fot) aperture **2** (actitud abierta) openness; (proceso) opening-up

apestado -da *adj* **(a)** (con la peste): **gente apestada** plague victims **(b)** ‹*lugar*›: **~ de turistas** crawling *o* infested with tourists

apestar [A1] *vi* (fam) to stink (colloq); ~ A **algo** to stink *o* reek OF sth (colloq) ■ ~ *vt* (fam) to stink out (colloq)

apetecer [E3] *vi* (esp Esp): **me apetece un helado/pasear** I feel like an ice-cream/going for a walk; **haz lo que te apetezca** do whatever you like

apetecible *adj* ‹*manjar*› appetizing, mouth-watering; ‹*puesto*› desirable

apetito *m* appetite; **no tengo ~** I don't feel hungry, I'm not hungry; **tiene buen ~** he has a good appetite; **esta caminata me ha abierto el ~** this walk has given me an appetite

apetitoso -sa *adj* ‹*plato/manjar*› appetizing, mouthwatering

apiadarse [A1] *v pron* ~ DE **algn** to take pity ON sb

apiario *m* (AmL) apiary

apicultura *f* beekeeping, apiculture (tech)

apilar [A1] *vt* to pile up, put ... into a pile

apiñarse [A1] *v pron* «*gente*» to crowd together

apio *m* celery

apiolarse [A1] *v pron* (RPl fam) to wise up (colloq)

apisonadora *f* road roller, steamroller

apisonar [A1] *vt* (con apisonadora) to roll, steamroll; (con pisón) to tamp

aplacar [A2] *vt* **(a)** ‹*ira*› to soothe; **supo ~ los ánimos** she was able to calm people down **(b)** ‹*sed*› to quench; ‹*hambre*› to satisfy; ‹*dolor*› to soothe

aplanadora *f* (AmL) road roller, steamroller

aplanar [A1] *vt* (con niveladora) to level; (con apisonadora) to roll

aplastante *adj* ‹*mayoría*› overwhelming; ‹*victoria/derrota*› overwhelming, crushing; ‹*lógica*› devastating

aplastar [A1] *vt* **1 (a)** (algo blando) to squash; (algo duro) to crush **(b)** (hacer puré) ‹*plátanos/papas*› to mash **2 (a)** ‹*rebelión*› to crush, quash **(b)** ‹*rival*› to crush, overwhelm; (moralmente) to devastate

aplaudir [I1] *vt* to applaud ■ ~ *vi* to applaud, clap

aplauso *m* **(a)** (ovación) applause; **un ~ para** ... a round of applause for ...; **fuertes ~s** loud applause **(b)** (elogio) praise; **ser digno de ~** to be commendable *o* praiseworthy

aplazamiento *m* **(a)** (de reunión — antes de iniciarse) postponement; (— una vez iniciada) adjournment **(b)** (de pago) deferment

aplazar [A4] *vt* **1 (a)** ‹*viaje*› to postpone, put off **(b)** ‹*juicio/reunión*› (antes de iniciarse) to postpone; (una vez iniciado) to adjourn **(c)** ‹*pago*› to defer **2** (RPl, Ven) ‹*estudiante*› to fail

aplazo *m* (RPl) fail

aplicable *adj* applicable

aplicación *f* **1 (a)** (frml) (de crema) application (frml); (de pintura, barniz) coat, application (frml) **(b)** (de sanción) imposition; (de técnica, método) application; (de plan, medida) implementation **2** (uso práctico) application, use **3** (Col, Ven) (solicitud) application

aplicado -da *adj* ‹*ciencias/tecnología*› applied (*before n*); ‹*estudiante*› diligent, hard-working

aplicar [A2] *vt* **1** (frml) ‹*pomada/maquillaje/barniz*› to apply (frml) **2** ‹*sanción*› to impose; ‹*descuento*› to allow; **el acuerdo se aplica sólo a los afiliados** the agreement only applies to members **3** ‹*método/sistema*› to put into practice ■ **~** *vi* (Col, Ven) to apply; **~ a un puesto/una beca** to apply for a job/a scholarship

■ **aplicarse** *v pron* to apply oneself

aplique, **apliqué** *m* **(a)** (lámpara) wall light **(b)** (adorno — en mueble) overlay; (— en prenda) appliqué

aplomo *m* composure

apocado -da *adj* **(a)** [SER] (de poco carácter) timid **(b)** [ESTAR] (deprimido) depressed, down (colloq)

apocalipsis *m* apocalypse

apocarse [A2] *v pron*: **se apocó** she lost all her self-confidence; **no se apoca ante** *or* **por nada** nothing intimidates *o* daunts him

apócope *f or m* apocope; (vocablo) apocopated form

apodar [A1] *vt* to nickname, call

apoderado -da *m,f* **(a)** (Der) proxy, representative; **nombrar a algn ~** to give sb power of attorney **(b)** (de deportista) agent, manager

apoderarse [A1] *v pron* **~ DE algo** ‹*de ciudad/fortaleza*› to seize sth, take sth; **se apoderó del control de la empresa** he took control of the company

apodo *m* nickname

apogeo *m* height

apolillado -da *adj* ‹*ropa*› moth-eaten; ‹*madera*› worm-eaten; ‹*ideas*› antiquated, fusty

apolillarse [A1] *v pron* «*ropa*» to get moth-eaten; «*madera*» to get infested with woodworm

apolítico -ca *adj* apolitical

apología *f* apologia (frml); **hizo ~ del terrorismo** he made a statement (*o* speech *etc*) justifying terrorism

apoltronarse [A1] *v pron* (en asiento) to settle oneself

aporrear [A1] *vt* ‹*puerta/mesa*› to bang *o* hammer on; ‹*persona*› (fam) to beat

aportación *f* **(a)** (contribución) contribution **(b)** (de socio) investment

aportar [A1] *vt* **(a)** (contribuir) ‹*dinero/tiempo/idea*› to contribute **(b)** «*socio*» to invest ■ **~** *vi* (RPl) (a la seguridad social) to pay contributions

aporte *m* **(a)** (esp AmL) ⇒ APORTACIÓN **(b)** (RPl) (a la seguridad social) social security contribution, ≈ National Insurance contribution (*in UK*)

aposento *m* (arc *o* hum) (habitación) chamber (dated)

apostar [A10] *vt* to bet; **te apuesto una cerveza** I bet you a beer; **~ algo POR algo/algn** to bet sth ON sth/sb ■ **~** *vi* to bet; **~ a las carreras** to bet on the horses; **te apuesto (a) que gana** I bet (you) he wins

■ **apostarse** *v pron* **(a)** (*recípr*): **se ~on una comida** they bet a meal on it **(b)** (*enf*) to bet

apóstol *m* (Relig) apostle

apostolado *m* (Relig) ministry, preaching

apostólico -ca *adj* apostolic

apóstrofo *m* apostrophe

apoteósico -ca *adj* tremendous

apoteosis *f* **(a)** (exaltación) apotheosis; **cuando salió en escena aquello fue la ~** (fam) the audience went wild when she came on stage (colloq) **(b)** (Teatr) finale

apoyabrazos *m* (*pl* **~**) armrest

apoyacabezas *m* (*pl* **~**) headrest

apoyar [A1] *vt* **1** (hacer descansar) **~ (algo EN algo)** to rest (sth ON sth); **apóyalo contra la pared** lean it against the wall **2 (a)** (respaldar) ‹*propuesta/persona*› to back, support **(b)** ‹*teoría*› to support, bear out

■ **apoyarse** *v pron* **1** (para sostenerse, descansar) **~se EN algo** to lean ON sth **2** (basarse, fundarse) **~se EN algo** to be based ON sth

apoyo *m* support; **~ A algo** support FOR sth

apreciable *adj* ‹*cambio/mejoría*› appreciable, substantial; ‹*suma/cantidad*› considerable, substantial

apreciación *f* **1 (a)** (percepción, enfoque) interpretation **(b)** (juicio) appraisal, assessment **2** (aprecio, valoración) appreciation; **~ musical** musical appreciation

apreciado -da *adj* ‹*amigo*› valued; **su piel es muy apreciada** its fur is highly prized

apreciar [A1] *vt* **1** ‹*persona*› to be fond of **2** ‹*interés/ayuda/arte*› to appreciate **3** (percibir, observar) to see; **para ~ la magnitud de los daños** in order to appreciate the extent of the damage

aprecio *m* (estima) esteem; **siente gran ~ por él** she holds him in great esteem; **goza del ~ de sus compañeros** she is highly regarded by her colleagues

apremiante *adj* ‹*necesidad*› pressing, urgent

apremiar [A1] *vt* (presionar): **me están apremiando para que lo termine** they are putting pressure on me to get it finished; **estamos apremiados de tiempo** we are pushed for *o* short of time ■ **~** *vi* to be urgent; **el tiempo apremia** time is getting on *o* is pressing

aprender [E1] *vi/vt* to learn; **~ A hacer algo** to learn to do sth

■ **aprenderse** *v pron* (*enf*) ‹*lección/parte*› to learn; **me la aprendí de memoria** I learnt it by heart

aprendiz -diza *m,f* apprentice, trainee; **es ~ de mecánico** he's an apprentice mechanic

aprendizaje *m* **(a)** (proceso) learning **(b)** (período como aprendiz) apprenticeship, training period

aprensión *f* **(a)** (preocupación, miedo) apprehension **(b)** (asco) squeamishness; **me da ~ ver sangre** I get squeamish at the sight of blood

aprensivo -va *adj*: **es muy ~** he's such a worrier

apresar [A1] *vt* **(a)** ‹*nave*› to seize, arrest; ‹*delincuente*› to capture, catch **(b)** «*animal*» ‹*presa*› to capture, catch

aprestarse [A1] *v pron* (*refl*) **~se** PARA **algo/**A **hacer algo** to prepare *o* get ready FOR sth/to do sth

apresurado -da *adj* **(a)** ‹*despedida*› quick, hurried; ‹*visita*› rushed, hurried **(b)** ‹*decisión*› rushed, hasty; ‹*respuesta/comentario*› hasty

apresurar [A1] *vt* **(a)** (meter prisa a) to hurry **(b)** (acelerar) ‹*proceso/cambio*› to speed up; ‹*paso*› to quicken

■ **apresurarse** *v pron:* **¡apresúrate!** hurry up!; **no nos apresuremos demasiado** let's not be hasty; **se apresuró a defenderla** he hastened *o* rushed to her defense

apretado -da *adj* **1 (a)** (ajustado) tight; **me queda muy ~** it is too tight for me **(b)** (sin dinero): **andamos** *or* **estamos algo ~s** we're a little short of money (colloq) **(c)** (apretujado) cramped **2** ‹*calendario/programa*› tight; ‹*victoria*› narrow **3** (fam) (tacaño) tight (colloq), tightfisted (colloq)

apretar [A5] *vt* **1** ‹*botón*› to press, push; ‹*acelerador*› to put one's foot on, press; ‹*gatillo*› to pull, squeeze **(b)** ‹*nudo/tapa/tornillo*› to tighten; ‹*puño/mandíbulas*› to clench; **apreté los dientes** I gritted my teeth **2 (a)** (apretujar): **apretó al niño contra su pecho** he clasped *o* clutched the child to his breast; **me apretó el brazo con fuerza** he squeezed *o* gripped my arm firmly **(b)** (presionar) to put pressure on ■ **~** *vi* **1** «*ropa/zapatos*» (+ *me/te/le etc*) to be too tight; **el vestido le aprieta** the dress is too tight for her **2** (hacer presión) to press down (*o* in *etc*)

■ **apretarse** *v pron* to squeeze *o* squash together

apretón *m* (abrazo) hug; **se dieron un ~ de manos** they shook hands

apretujado -da *adj* cramped; **tuvimos que comer todos ~s** we had to eat all squashed together round the table

apretujar [A1] *vt* (fam): **no me apretujes, que me haces daño** don't squeeze me so hard, you're hurting me; **me ~on mucho en el tren** I got squashed on the train

■ **apretujarse** *v pron* to squash *o* squeeze together

aprieta, aprietas, etc *see* APRETAR

aprieto *m* ⇒ APURO 2

aprisa *adv* ⇒ DEPRISA

aprisionar [A1] *vt* to trap

aprobación *f* (de proyecto de ley, moción) passing; (de préstamo, acuerdo, plan) approval, endorsement; (de actuación, conducta) approval

aprobado *m* (Educ) pass

aprobar [A10] *vt* **1** ‹*proyecto de ley/moción*› to pass; ‹*préstamo/acuerdo/plan*› to approve, sanction; ‹*actuación/conducta*› to approve of **2** (Educ) to pass ■ **~** *vi* «*estudiante*» to pass

aprontarse [A1] *v pron* (CS) (*refl*) to get ready

apropiado -da *adj* suitable; **el discurso fue muy ~ a la ocasión** the speech was very fitting for the occasion; **no era el momento ~** it wasn't the right moment

apropiarse [A1] *v pron* **~** (DE) **algo** to take *o* (frml) appropriate sth

aprovechable *adj* usable

aprovechado -da *adj* **1** (oportunista) opportunistic; **no seas ~** don't take advantage (of the situation) **2** ‹*estudiante*› hardworking ■ *m,f* opportunist

aprovechar [A1] *vt* **(a)** ‹*tiempo/espacio/talento*› to make the most of; **dinero/tiempo bien aprovechado** money/time well spent; **es espacio mal aprovechado** it's a waste of space **(b)** ‹*oportunidad*› to take advantage of; **aprovecho la ocasión para decirles que** ... I would like to take this opportunity to tell you that ... **(c)** (usar) to use; **no tira nada, todo lo aprovecha** she doesn't throw anything away, she makes use of everything ■ **~** *vi:* **aproveché para venir a verte** I thought I'd take the opportunity to come and see you; **¡que aproveche!** enjoy your meal, bon appétit; **aprovechen ahora, que son jóvenes** make the most of it now, while you're young

■ **aprovecharse** *v pron* **(a)** (abusar) **~se** DE **algo/algn** to take advantage OF sth/sb, to exploit sth/sb **(b)** (abusar sexualmente) **~se** DE **algn** ‹*de una mujer*› to take advantage OF sb; ‹*de un niño*› to abuse sb

aprovisionar [A1] *vt* ‹*buque/tropas*› to provision, to supply ... with provisions

■ **aprovisionarse** *v pron* **~se** DE **algo** to stock up WITH sth

aproximado -da *adj* ‹*cálculo/traducción/idea*› rough (*before n*); ‹*costo/velocidad*› estimated (*before n*)

aproximar [A1] *vt* **(a)** (acercar): **aproximó la mesa a la ventana** she moved (*o* brought *etc*) the table over to the window **(b)** ‹*países*› to bring ... closer together

■ **aproximarse** *v pron* **(a)** (acercarse) «*fecha/persona/vehículo*» to approach; **se aproximó a mí** she came up to me **(b)** **~se** A **algo** ‹*a la realidad/una cifra*› to come close TO sth

aprueba, apruebas, etc *see* APROBAR

aptitud *f* flair; **tener ~ para los idiomas** to have a flair for languages; **carece de ~es para el ballet** she shows no talent for ballet

apto -ta *adj* [SER] **~** PARA **algo** suitable FOR sth; **no es ~ para el cargo** he's not suitable *o* right for the job; **~ para el servicio militar** fit for military service; **no ~ para el consumo** not fit for consumption

apuesta *f* bet; **le hice una ~** I had a bet with him

apuesta, **apuestas**, **etc** *see* APOSTAR

apuesto -ta *adj* (liter) ‹*hombre/figura*› handsome

apunamiento *m* (AmS) altitude *o* mountain sickness

apunarse [A1] *v pron* (AmS) to get altitude *o* mountain sickness

apuntalar [A1] *vt* ‹*edificio/túnel*› to shore up, brace; ‹*cimientos*› to underpin

apuntar [A1] *vt* **1 (a)** (tomar nota de) to make a note of, note down **(b)** (para excursión, actividad) to put ... down **2** (señalar, indicar) to point at; **no la apuntes con el dedo** don't point (your finger) at her ■ ~ *vi* **(a)** (con arma) to aim; **preparen ... apunten ... ¡fuego!** ready ... take aim ... fire!; **le apuntó con una pistola** she pointed/aimed a gun at him **(b)** (indicar, señalar) to point

■ **apuntarse** *v pron* **(a)** (inscribirse) **~se** A *or* EN **algo** ‹*a curso*› to enroll* ON sth; ‹*a clase*› to sign up FOR sth; **me apunté para ir a la excursión** I put my name down for the outing **(b)** (obtener) ‹*tanto*› to score; ‹*victoria*› to chalk up, achieve

apunte *m* **1 (a)** (nota) note **(b) apuntes** *mpl* (Educ) notes (*pl*); (texto preparado) handout; **tomar** *or* (CS) **sacar ~s** to take notes **2 (a)** (Art) sketch; (Lit) outline **(b)** (AmL) (Teatr, TV) sketch **3** (Com) entry

apuñalar [A1] *vt* to stab

apurado -da *adj* **1** (avergonzado) embarrassed **2** (AmL) (con prisa) in a hurry; **andaba ~** he was in a hurry; ***a las apuradas*** (RPl fam) in a rush **3** (en apuros): **se vio muy ~ para contestar las preguntas** he was hard put to answer the questions; **si te encuentras ~, dímelo** if you run into any difficulties, let me know **4 (a)** (agobiado): **~ de trabajo** overwhelmed with work **(b)** (escaso) **~** DE **algo** ‹*de dinero/tiempo*› short OF sth

apurar [A1] *vt* **1** ‹*copa/botella*›: **apuró la cerveza y se fue** he finished (off) his beer and left **2** (meter prisa): **nos están apurando para que lo terminemos** they're pushing us to finish it; **no me apures** (AmL) don't hurry *o* rush me ■ **~** *vi* (Chi) (+ *me/te/le etc*) (urgir): **no me apura** I'm not in a hurry for it

■ **apurarse** *v pron* **1** (preocuparse) to worry **2** (AmL) (darse prisa) to hurry; **¡apúrate!** hurry up!

apuro *m* **1** (vergüenza): **¡qué ~!** how embarrassing!; **me daba ~ pedirle dinero** I was too embarrassed to ask him for money **2** (aprieto, dificultad) predicament; **estar/verse en ~s** to be/find oneself in a predicament *o* tight spot; **me sacó del ~** he got me out of trouble; **me puso en un ~** she put me in a real predicament; **pasaron muchos ~s** they had an uphill struggle *o* they went through a lot **3** (AmL) (prisa) rush; **esto tiene ~** this is urgent

aquel, **aquella** *adj dem* (*pl* **aquellos, aquellas**) that; (*pl*) those

aquél, **aquélla** *pron dem* (*pl* **aquéllos, aquéllas**) **(a)** (refiriéndose a cosa) that one; (*pl*) those; **ése no, ~** not that one, the *o* that other one **(b)** (refiriéndose a persona): **todo ~ que lo necesite** (frml) anyone *o* (frml) any person needing it; **el cuento de ~ que** ... the story about the man who ...

aquello *pron dem* (*neutro*): **¿qué es ~ que se ve allá?** what's that over there?; **~ que te dije el otro día** what I told you the other day

aquí *adv* **1** (en el espacio) here; **está ~ dentro** it's in here; **~ mismo** right here; **no soy de ~** I'm not from these parts *o* from around here; **pase por ~** come this way; **viven por ~** they live around here; **el agua me llegaba hasta ~** the water came up to here; **dando vueltas de ~ para allá** going to and fro *o* from one place to another **2** (en el tiempo): **de ~ a 2015** from now until 2015; **de ~ en adelante** from now on; **de ~ a un año** a year from now

ara *f*‡ (altar) altar; (piedra consagrada) altar stone

árabe *adj* **(a)** ‹*país/plato*› Arab; ‹*escritura/manuscritos*› Arabic **(b)** (Hist) (de Arabia) Arabian; (de los moros) Moorish ■ *mf* **(a)** (de país árabe) Arab **(b)** (Hist) (de Arabia) Arabian; (moro) Moor ■ *m* (idioma) Arabic

Arabia Saudí, **Arabia Saudita** *f* Saudi Arabia

arado *m* plow* (AmE), plough (BrE)

arancel *m* (tarifa) tariff; (impuesto) duty

arancelario -ria *adj* ‹*derecho/tarifa/barrera*› customs (*before n*)

arandela *f* washer

araña *f* (Zool) spider

arañar [A1] *vt/vi* to scratch

arañazo *m* scratch

arar [A1] *vt/vi* to plow (AmE), to plough (BrE)

araucano -na *adj/m,f* Araucanian

arbitraje *m* **(a)** (en fútbol, boxeo) refereeing; (en tenis, béisbol) umpiring **(b)** (Der, Rels Labs) (acción) arbitration; (resolución) decision, judgment

arbitrar [A1] *vt/vi* **(a)** (en fútbol, boxeo) to referee; (en tenis, béisbol) to umpire **(b)** (en conflicto, disputa) to arbitrate

arbitrario -ria *adj* arbitrary

árbitro -tra *m,f* **(a)** (en fútbol, boxeo) referee; (en tenis, béisbol) umpire; **los ~s de la moda** the arbiters of fashion **(b)** (en conflicto) arbitrator

árbol *m* (Bot) tree; **~ de Navidad** *or* (Andes) **de Pascua** Christmas tree; **~ genealógico** family tree; ***los ~es no dejan ver el bosque*** you can't see the forest (AmE) *o* (BrE) wood for the trees

arbolado -da *adj* ‹*terreno*› wooded; ‹*calle*› tree-lined (*before n*)

arboleda *f* grove

arbusto *m* shrub, bush

arca *f*‡ **1** (cofre) chest; **el Arca de Noé** Noah's Ark **2 arcas** *fpl* (de institución) coffers (*pl*)

arcada *f* **1** (Med): **tener ~s** to retch; **me provocó ~s** it made me retch **2** (Arquit) arcade; (de puente) arch

arcaico -ca *adj* archaic

arcángel *m* archangel

arce *m* maple

arcén *m* shoulder (AmE), hard shoulder (BrE)

archidiócesis *f* (*pl* **~**) archdiocese

archiduque -quesa *m,f* (*m*) archduke; (*f*) archduchess

archipiélago *m* archipelago

archivador *m* (mueble) filing cabinet; (carpeta) ring binder, file

archivar [A1] *vt* ‹*documentos*› to file; ‹*investigación/asunto*› (por un tiempo) to shelve; (para siempre) to close the file on

archivo *m* **(a)** (local) archive; (conjunto de documentos) *tb* **~s** archives (*pl*), archive; **los ~s de la policía** the police files *o* records **(b)** (Inf) file

arcilla *f* clay

arco *m* **1** (Arquit) arch; (Anat) arch; (Mat) arc; **~ de triunfo** triumphal arch; **~ iris** rainbow **2** (AmL) (en fútbol) goal **3 (a)** (Arm, Dep) bow **(b)** (de violín) bow

arcón *m* large chest

arder [E1] *vi* **1** (quemarse) to burn **2** (estar muy caliente) to be boiling (hot); ***estar que arde*** «*persona*» to be fuming; **la cosa está que arde** things have reached boiling point **3** (escocer) «*herida/ojos*» to sting, smart

ardid *m* trick, ruse

ardiente *adj* ‹*defensor*› ardent; ‹*deseo*› ardent, burning; ‹*amante*› passionate

ardilla *f* squirrel

ardor *m* (dolor) burning; (escozor) smarting; **~ de estómago** heartburn

arduo -dua *adj* arduous

área *f*‡ area; **~ chica** *or* **pequeña** goal area; **~ de castigo** penalty area; **~ de servicio** service area, services (*pl*)

arena *f* **1** (Const, Geol) sand; **~ movediza** quicksand **2** (palestra) arena; **en la ~ política** in the political arena

arenoso -sa *adj* ‹*playa/terreno*› sandy

arenque *m* herring; **~ ahumado** kipper

arepa *f*: *cornmeal roll*

arete *m* (Col, Méx) earring

argamasa *f* mortar

Argel *m* Algiers

Argelia *f* Algeria

argelino -na *adj/m,f* Algerian

Argentina *f*: *tb* **la ~** Argentina

argentino -na *adj* ‹*gobierno/presidente*› Argentine (*before n*); ‹*escritor/música*› Argentinian ■ *m, f* Argentinian

argolla *f* ring; **~ de compromiso/de matrimonio** (AmL) engagement/wedding ring; ***tener ~*** (AmC fam) to have contacts (colloq)

argot *m* (*pl* **-gots**) slang

argüendero -ra *m,f* (Méx fam) gossip

argumentación *f* line of argument (frml)

argumentar [A1] *vt* to argue

argumento *m* **(a)** (razón) argument **(b)** (Cin, Lit) plot, story line

aria *f*‡ aria

aridez *f* aridity, dryness

árido -da *adj* arid, dry

Aries *m* (signo, constelación) Aries; **es (de) ~** she's an Aries *o* an Arian ■ *mf* (*pl* **~**) (persona) *tb* **aries** Aries, person born under (the sign of) Aries

arisco -ca *adj* **(a)** [SER] (huraño) ‹*persona*› unfriendly, unsociable; ‹*animal*› unfriendly **(b)** [ESTAR] (Méx fam) (enojado) upset, angry

arista *f* (Mat) edge; (de viga) arris; (de bóveda) groin; (en montañismo) arête, ridge

aristocracia *f* aristocracy

aristócrata *mf* aristocrat

aristocrático -ca *adj* aristocratic

aritmética *f* arithmetic

aritmético -ca *adj* arithmetic

arma *f*‡ **(a)** (Arm, Mil) weapon; **~ nuclear** nuclear weapon; **~ blanca** *any sharp instrument used as a weapon*; **~ de fuego** firearm; **deponer las ~s** to lay down one's arms; **tomar (las) ~s** to take up arms; **no llevaba ~s** he wasn't carrying a weapon; ***de ~s tomar*** formidable; ***ser un ~ de doble filo*** to be a double-edged sword **(b)** (instrumento, medio) weapon

armada *f* navy

armadillo *m* armadillo

armado -da *adj* ‹*lucha/persona*› armed; **~ DE** *or* **CON algo** armed WITH sth

armador -dora *m,f* shipowner

armadura *f* **1** (Hist, Mil) armor* **2** (Const) framework

armamentista *adj* arms (*before n*)

armamento *m* armaments (*pl*)

armar [A1] *vt* **1 (a)** (Mil) ‹*ciudadanos/país*› to arm, supply ... with arms **(b)** (equipar) ‹*embarcación*› to fit out, equip **2 (a)** ‹*estantería/reloj*› to assemble; ‹*tienda/carpa*› to pitch, put up **(b)** (AmL) ‹*rompecabezas*› to do, piece together **(c)** (Col, RPl) ‹*cigarro*› to roll **3** (fam) ‹*alboroto/ruido/lío*› to make; **~ jaleo** to kick up *o* make a racket (colloq); **~ un escándalo** to kick up a fuss; ***~la*** (fam): **¡buena la has armado!** you've really done it now! (colloq); **la que me armó porque llegué tarde** you should have seen the way he went on because I was late

■ **armarse** *v pron* **1 (a)** (Mil) to arm oneself **(b)** **~se DE algo** ‹*de armas/herramientas*› to arm oneself WITH sth; **~se de paciencia** to be patient; **~se de valor** to pluck up courage **2 (a)** (fam) «*pelea/discusión*» to break out; **¡qué jaleo se armó!** there was a real commotion **(b)** (fam) «*persona*»: **me armé un lío/una confusión** I got into a mess (colloq)

armario *m* **(a)** (para ropa — mueble) wardrobe; (— empotrado) closet (AmE), wardrobe (BrE) **(b)** (de cocina) cupboard; (de cuarto de baño) cabinet

armatoste *m* (fam) huge great thing (colloq)

armazón *m or f* **1** (Const) skeleton; (de avión) airframe; (de barco, mueble) frame; (de gafas) frames (*pl*) **2** (de obra literaria) framework, outline

Armenia *f* Armenia

armenio[1] **-nia** *adj/m,f* Armenian

armenio[2] *m* (idioma) Armenian

armisticio *m* armistice

armonía *f* harmony

armónica *f* harmonica, mouth organ

armónico -ca *adj* **(a)** (Mús) harmonic **(b)** (armonioso) harmonious

armonioso -sa *adj* harmonious
armonizar [A4] *vt* **(a)** (Mús) to harmonize **(b)** ‹*tendencias/opiniones*› to reconcile, harmonize; ‹*diferencias*› to reconcile ■ ~ *vi* «*estilos/colores*» to blend in, harmonize; ~ CON **algo** «*color/estilo*» to blend (in) WITH sth
arnés *m* (para niño) baby reins (*pl*); (Dep) harness; (arreos) harness
aro *m* **(a)** (Jueg) hoop **(b)** (Arg, Chi) (para el lóbulo) earring; (en forma de aro) hooped earring **(c)** (de servilleta) napkin ring
aroma *m* (de flores) scent, perfume; (del café, de hierbas) aroma; (del vino) bouquet
aromaterapia *f* aromatherapy
aromático -ca *adj* aromatic
arpa *f*‡ harp
arpegio *m* arpeggio
arpillera *f* sacking, hessian, burlap (AmE)
arpista *mf* harpist
arpón *m* harpoon; ~ **submarino** speargun
arquear [A1] *vt* ‹*espalda*› to arch; ‹*cejas*› to raise, arch; ‹*estante*› to bow, bend
■ **arquearse** *v pron* «*estante*» to sag, bend; «*persona*» to arch one's back
arqueología *f* archaeology
arqueológico -ca *adj* archaeological
arqueólogo -ga *m,f* archaeologist
arquero *m* **1** (Hist, Mil) archer **2** (AmL) (en fútbol) goalkeeper
arquetipo *m* archetype
arquitecto -ta *m,f* architect
arquitectónico -ca *adj* architectural
arquitectura *f* architecture
arrabal *m* poor quarter *o* area
arraigado -da *adj* ‹*costumbre*› deeply rooted, deep-rooted; ‹*vicio*› deeply entrenched
arraigar [A3] *vi* «*costumbre*» to become rooted, take root; «*vicio*» to become entrenched; «*planta*» to take root
■ **arraigarse** *v pron* «*costumbres/ideas*» to take root; «*persona*» to settle
arrancar [A2] *vt* **1** ‹*hoja de papel*› to tear out; ‹*etiqueta*› to tear off; ‹*botón/venda*› to pull off; ‹*planta*› to pull up; ‹*flor*› to pick; ‹*diente/pelo*› to pull out; **le arrancó el bolso** he snatched her bag **2** ‹*confesión/declaración*› to extract **3** ‹*motor/coche*› to start ■ ~ *vi* «*motor/vehículo*» to start
■ **arrancarse** *v pron* **1** (*refl*) ‹*pelo/diente*› to pull out; ‹*piel/botón*› to pull off **2** (Chi fam) (huir) to run away
arranque *m* **(a)** (Auto, Mec) starting mechanism; **tengo problemas con el** ~ I have problems starting the car **(b)** (arrebato) ~ DE **algo** fit OF sth
arrasar [A1] *vi* ~ CON **algn** ‹*con contrincante*› to demolish; ‹*con enemigo*› to destroy; **nuestro equipo volvió a** ~ our team swept to victory again; ~ CON **algo**: **la inundación arrasó con las cosechas** the flood devastated the crops; ~**on con toda la comida** they polished off all the food (colloq) ■ ~ *vt* ‹*zona*› to devastate; ‹*edificio*› to destroy

arrastrar [A1] *vt* **1 (a)** (por el suelo) to drag **(b)** ‹*remolque/caravana*› to tow **(c)** (llevar consigo): **arrastró todo a su paso** it swept away everything in its path; **la corriente lo arrastraba mar adentro** the current was carrying him out to sea **2 (a)** ‹*problema/enfermedad*›: **arrastra esa tos desde el invierno** that cough of hers has been dragging on since the winter; **vienen arrastrando el problema desde hace años** they've been dragging out the problem for years **(b)** (atraer) to draw; **se dejan** ~ **por la moda** they are slaves to fashion ■ ~ *vi* «*mantel/cortina*» to trail along the ground
■ **arrastrarse** *v pron* **(a)** (por el suelo) «*persona*» to crawl; «*culebra*» to slither **(b)** (humillarse) to grovel, crawl
arrastre *m* **(a)** (acción) dragging; ***estar para el*** ~ (fam) to be done in (colloq) **(b)** (CS fam) (atractivo) appeal
arre *interj* (a un caballo) gee up!, giddy up!
arrear [A1] *vt* **(a)** ‹*ganado*› to drive, herd; ‹*caballerías*› to spur, urge on **(b)** (AmL fam) ‹*gente*› to chivy* (colloq), to hurry ... along **(c)** (AmL fam) (llevar) ~ CON **algo/algn** to cart sth/sb off (colloq)
arrebatador -dora *adj* ‹*belleza*› breathtaking; ‹*sonrisa*› dazzling; ‹*mirada*› captivating
arrebatar [A1] *vt* (quitar) to snatch
arrebato *m* (arranque) ~ DE **algo** fit OF sth; **le dio un** ~ he flew into a rage **(b)** (éxtasis) ecstasy, rapture
arrechar [A1] *vt* **(a)** (AmL vulg) (excitar sexualmente) to turn ... on (colloq) **(b)** (AmL fam) (enojar) to bug (colloq)
■ **arrecharse** *v pron* **(a)** (AmL vulg) (sexualmente) «*persona*» to get horny (sl); «*animal*» to come in (AmE) *o* (BrE) on heat **(b)** (AmL fam) (enfurecerse) to get furious
arrecho -cha *adj* **1 (a)** (AmL vulg) (sexualmente excitado) ‹*persona*› horny (sl), turned-on (colloq); ‹*animal*› in heat (AmE), on heat (BrE) **(b)** (Col, Ven fam) (valiente) gutsy (colloq) **2** (AmL fam) (enojado) furious, mad (AmE colloq) **3** (AmC, Ven fam) (difícil) tough
arrecife *m* reef
arreglado -da *adj* **1 (a)** (limpio, ordenado) tidy **(b)** (ataviado) smartly turned out, smart **2** (AmL fam) ‹*partido/elecciones*› fixed (colloq)
arreglar [A1] *vt* **1** ‹*aparato/reloj*› to mend, fix; ‹*zapatos*› to mend, repair; ‹*falda/vestido*› to alter; ‹*calle*› to repair; **el dentista me está arreglando la boca** (fam) the dentist is fixing my teeth (colloq); **esto te** ~**á el estómago** (fam) this'll sort your stomach out (colloq) **2 (a)** ‹*casa/habitación*› (ordenar) to straighten up, to tidy (up) (BrE); (hacer arreglos en) to do up (colloq) **(b)** (preparar, organizar): **ve arreglando a los niños ¿quieres?** can you start getting the children ready?; **tengo todo arreglado para el viaje** I've got everything ready for the trip; **un amigo me está arreglando los papeles** a friend is sorting out the papers for me; ~ **una entrevista** to arrange an interview **(c)** (disponer) ‹*flores/muebles*› to arrange **3** (solucionar) ‹*situación*› to sort out; ‹*asunto*› to settle, sort out; **lo quiso** ~

diciendo que … she tried to put things right by saying that …

■ **arreglarse** *v pron* **1** (*refl*) (ataviarse): **tarda horas en ~se** she takes hours to get ready; **no te arregles tanto** you don't need to get so dressed up; **sabe ~se** she knows how to make herself look good **2** ‹*pelo/manos*› **(a)** (*refl*) to do **(b)** (*caus*): **tengo que ir a ~me el pelo** I must go and have my hair done **3** (solucionarse) «*situación/asunto*» to get sorted out **4** (fam) (amañarse): **ya me ~é para volver a casa** I'll make my own way home; **la casa es pequeña pero nos arreglamos** it's a small house, but we manage; ***arreglárselas*** (fam) to manage; **no sé cómo se las arreglan** I don't know how they manage; **arréglatelas como puedas** sort *o* work it out as best you can; **ya me las ~é** I'll manage, I'll be OK **5** «*día/tiempo*» to get better, clear up

arreglo *m* **1 (a)** (reparación) repair; **hacerle ~s a algo** to carry out repairs on sth; **la casa necesita algunos ~s** the house needs some work done on it; ***no tiene ~*** «*reloj/máquina*» it's beyond repair; «*persona*» he/she is a hopeless case **(b)** (de ropa) alteration **(c)** (Mús) *tb* **~ musical** musical arrangement **2** (acuerdo) arrangement, agreement

arrellanarse [A1] *v pron*: **se arrellenó en el sofá** he settled himself into the sofa

arremangarse [A3] *v pron* ⇒ REMANGARSE

arremeter [E1] *vi* (embestir) to charge; (atacar) to attack; **~ CONTRA algo/algn** (acometer) to charge AT sth/sb; (atacar, criticar) to attack sth/sb

arremolinarse [A1] *v pron* «*agua/hojas*» to swirl; «*personas/animales*» to mill around

arrendador -dora *m,f* (*m*) landlord, lessor (frml); (*f*) landlady, lessor (frml)

arrendamiento *m* **(a)** (de casa) renting, letting (BrE); (de tierras, local) renting, leasing; **contrato de ~** tenancy agreement **(b)** (de otra cosa — por el propietario) renting (out); (— por el que la recibe) renting **(c)** (precio — de casa, local) rent; (— de otra cosa) rental

arrendar [A5] *vt* **1** (Der) **(a)** (dar en arriendo) ‹*casa*› to rent (out), let (BrE); ‹*local/tierras*› to rent (out), lease **(b)** (tomar en arriendo) ‹*casa*› to rent; ‹*local/tierras*› to rent, lease **(c)** (contratar) ‹*servicios*› to hire **2** (Andes) ‹*coche/bicicleta*› (dar en arriendo) to rent (out) (AmE), to hire out (BrE); (tomar en arriendo) to rent (AmE), to hire (BrE); Ⓢ **se arriendan coches** cars for rent (AmE), car hire (BrE)

arrendatario -ria *m,f* (de propiedad) lessee, tenant; (de contrata) contractor

arrepentido -da *adj* ‹*pecador*› repentant; **estaba ~ de lo que había hecho** he was sorry for *o* feeling remorse for what he had done; **estoy ~ de haberlo dicho** I regret having said it

arrepentimiento *m* remorse, repentance

arrepentirse [I11] *v pron* **(a)** (lamentar) to be sorry; **~ DE algo** to regret sth; **~ DE hacer algo** to regret doing sth **(b)** (cambiar de idea) to change one's mind

arrepienta, **arrepintió**, **etc** *see* ARREPENTIRSE

arrestar [A1] *vt* to arrest

arresto *m* (Der, Mil) **(a)** (detención) arrest; **bajo ~** under arrest **(b)** (prisión) detention

arriar [A17] *vt* ‹*bandera/vela*› to lower

arriba *adv* **1 (a)** (lugar, parte): **ahí/aquí ~** up there/here; **en el estante de ~** (el siguiente) on the shelf above; (el último) on the top shelf; **ponlo un poco más ~** put it a little higher up; **la parte de ~** the top (part); **~ del ropero** (AmL) on top of the wardrobe; **~ de la cocina está el baño** (AmL) the bathroom is above the kitchen; ***de ~ abajo***: **me miró de ~ abajo** he looked me up and down; **limpiar la casa de ~ abajo** to clean the house from top to bottom **(b)** (en edificio) upstairs; **los vecinos de ~** the people upstairs **(c)** (en escala, jerarquía) above; **órdenes de ~** orders from above; **las puntuaciones de 80 para ~** scores of 80 or over **2** (expresando dirección, movimiento): **corrió escaleras ~** he ran upstairs; **calle ~** up the street; **miró hacia ~** he looked up **3** (en interjecciones) **(a)** (expresando aprobación): **¡~ la democracia!** long live democracy! **(b)** (expresando estímulo) come on!; (llamando a levantarse) get up!

arribista *adj* socially ambitious ■ *mf* arriviste, social climber

arriendo *m* (esp Andes) ⇒ ARRENDAMIENTO

arriesgado -da *adj* ‹*acción/empresa*› risky, hazardous; ‹*persona*› brave, daring

arriesgar [A3] *vt* **(a)** ‹*vida/dinero*› to risk **(b)** ‹*opinión*› to venture

■ **arriesgarse** *v pron*: **¿nos arriesgamos?** shall we risk it *o* take a chance?; **~se A hacer algo** to risk doing sth

arrimar [A1] *vt* (acercar) to move/bring … closer; **arrimó la cama a** *or* **contra la pared** he pushed *o* moved the bed up against the wall

■ **arrimarse** *v pron* **1** (*refl*) (acercarse): **se arrimó mucho a la orilla** he went too close to the edge; **arrímate al fuego** come (up) closer to the fire; **se arrimó a** *or* **contra la pared** he moved up against the wall; **~se A algn** to move closer TO sb; (buscando calor, abrigo) to snuggle up TO sb **2** (Méx, Ven fam) (en casa de algn): **se ~on en mi casa** they came to live *o* stay with me, they dumped themselves on me (pey)

arrinconado -da *adj* **(a)** (bloqueado) blocked in, boxed in **(b)** (acorralado, acosado) cornered **(c)** (arrumbado) lying around

arrinconar [A1] *vt* **(a)** (poner en rincón) to put … in a corner **(b)** (acosar, acorralar) to corner **(c)** (marginar) to exclude **(d)** (arrumbar) to leave, dump (colloq)

arrocero -ra *adj* ‹*cultivo/producción*› rice (*before n*); ‹*región*› rice-growing (*before n*) ■ *m,f* rice grower

arrodillarse [A1] *v pron* to kneel (down)

arrogancia *f* arrogance; **con ~** arrogantly

arrogante *adj* arrogant, haughty

arrojar [A1] *vt* **1 (a)** (tirar) to throw **(b)** ‹*lava*› to spew (out); ‹*humo*› to belch out; ‹*luz*› to shed **2** (vomitar) to bring up, throw up

■ **arrojarse** *v pron* (*refl*) to throw oneself; **~se SOBRE algo/algn** «*persona*» to throw oneself ONTO sth/sb; «*perro/tigre*» to pounce ON sth/sb

arrollador -dora *adj* **(a)** ‹*éxito/mayoría/victoria*› overwhelming **(b)** ‹*fuerza/ataque*› devastating **(c)** ‹*personalidad/elocuencia*› overpowering

arrollar [A1] *vt* **(a)** «*vehículo*» to run over; «*muchedumbre/agua/viento*» to sweep *o* carry away **(b)** (derrotar, vencer) to crush, overwhelm

arropar [A1] *vt* ‹*niño/enfermo*› (abrigar) to wrap ... up; (en la cama) to tuck ... in

■ **arroparse** *v pron* (abrigarse) to wrap up warm; (en la cama) to pull the covers up

arroyo *m* **(a)** (riachuelo) stream **(b)** (cuneta) gutter **(c)** (AmC) (torrentera) gully **(d)** (Méx) (Auto) slow lane

arroz *m* rice; **~ a la cubana** *rice with fried egg, plantain and tomato sauce*; **~ con leche** rice pudding; **~ integral** brown rice

arrozal *m* ricefield, paddy

arruga *f* (en piel) wrinkle, line; (en tela, papel) crease

arrugado -da *adj* ‹*persona/manos/piel*› wrinkled; ‹*ropa*› wrinkled (AmE), creased (BrE); ‹*papel*› crumpled

arrugar [A3] *vt* ‹*piel*› to wrinkle; ‹*tela*› to wrinkle (AmE), to crease (BrE); «*papel*» to crumple; ‹*ceño*› to knit; ‹*nariz*› to wrinkle; ‹*cara*› to screw up; **arrugó el entrecejo** he frowned

■ **arrugarse** *v pron* **(a)** «*persona/piel*» to become wrinkled **(b)** (por acción del agua) «*piel/manos*» to shrivel up, go wrinkled **(c)** «*tela*» to wrinkle *o* get wrinkled (AmE), to crease *o* get creased (BrE); «*papel*» to crumple

arruinar [A1] *vt* to ruin

■ **arruinarse** *v pron* to be ruined

arrullo *m* (de palomas) cooing; (para adormecer) lullaby

arrumbar [A1] *vt* ⇒ ARRINCONAR (c), (d)

arsenal *m* **(a)** (Mil) arsenal; **un ~ de datos** a mine of information **(b)** (Esp) (Náut) navy yard (AmE), naval dockyard (BrE)

arsénico *m* arsenic

arte (*gen m en el singular y f en el plural*) **1** (Art) art; **el ~ por el ~** art for art's sake; **no trabajo por amor al ~** (hum) I'm not working for the good of my health (hum); ***(como) por ~ de magia*** as if by magic **2** (habilidad, destreza) art; **el ~ de la conversación** the art of conversation; **tiene ~ para arreglar flores** she has a flair *o* gift for flower arranging

artefacto *m* (instrumento) artifact; (dispositivo) device; **~s de baño** (CS) bathroom fixtures (*pl*), sanitary ware (frml); **un raro ~** a contraption

arteria *f* artery

arterial *adj* arterial

artesa *f* trough

artesanal *adj*: **de fabricación ~** ‹*muebles*› handcrafted; ‹*queso*› farmhouse; **productos ~es** handicrafts, craftwork

artesanía *f* **(a)** (actividad) handicraft; **una ~** a piece of craftwork; **objetos de ~** craftwork, handicrafts **(b) artesanías** *fpl* (AmL) (productos) crafts (*pl*), craftwork; **mercado de ~s** craft market

artesano -na *m,f* (*m*) craftsman, artisan; (*f*) craftswoman, artisan

ártico -ca *adj* Arctic

Ártico *m*: **el ~** (región) the Arctic; (océano) the Arctic Ocean

articulación *f* **1 (a)** (Anat, Mec) ▶ **123** joint **(b)** (organización) organization, coordination **2** (Ling) articulation

articulado -da *adj* articulated

articular [A1] *vt* (Tec, Ling) to articulate

articulista *mf* feature writer, columnist

artículo *m* **1** (Com): **~s del hogar/de consumo** household/consumer goods; **~ de primera necesidad** essential item, essential; **~s de escritorio** stationery; **~s de tocador** toiletries; **~s de punto** knitwear **2 (a)** (en periódico, revista) article **(b)** (de ley) article **3** ▶ **39** (Ling) article

artífice *mf* **(a)** (responsable, autor): **fue el ~ del secuestro** he planned the kidnapping; **el ~ de esta victoria** the architect of this victory **(b)** (artista) (*m*) craftsman, artisan; (*f*) craftswoman, artisan

artificial *adj* ‹*flor/satélite/sonrisa*› artificial; ‹*fibra*› man-made, artificial

artificio *m* **(a)** (artimaña) trick, artful device **(b)** (afectación) affectation **(c)** (artilugio) device

artillería *f* artillery

artilugio *m* **(a)** (aparato) device, contraption **(b) artilugios** *mpl* (de oficio) equipment

artimaña *f* trick

artista *mf* **(a)** (Arte) artist **(b)** (actor) actor; (actriz) actress; (cantante, músico) artist; **una ~ de cine** a movie star (AmE) *o* (BrE) film star

artístico -ca *adj* artistic

artritis *f* arthritis

arveja *f* (AmL) pea

arvejilla, **arverjilla** *f* (RPl) sweet pea

arzobispado *m* archbishopric

arzobispal *adj* ‹*sede/comisión*› archiepiscopal (frml)

arzobispo *m* archbishop

as *m* ace

asa *f*‡ (asidero) handle

asadera *f* (RPl) roasting pan *o* dish *o* tin

asadero *m* (Coc) griddle

asado¹ -da *adj* **1 (a)** ‹*carne/pollo*› (en horno) roast (*before n*); (con espetón) spit-roast (*before n*); (a la parrilla) barbecued, grilled **(b)** ‹*castaña/papa*› roast (*before n*); ‹*papa con piel*› baked **2** (fam) [ESTAR] (acalorado) roasting (colloq)

asado² *m* **(a)** (al horno) roast; **~ de cordero** roast lamb **(b)** (AmL) (a la parrilla) barbecued meat **(c)** (AmL) (reunión) barbecue

asador¹ *m* (espetón) spit; (aparato — de espetones) rotisserie; (— de parrilla) barbecue

asador² -dora *m,f* (RPl) cook (*person who cooks the meat at a barbecue*)

asalariado -da *adj* wage-earning (*before n*) ■ *m,f* wage *o* salary earner

asaltante *mf* **(a)** (ladrón) robber **(b)** (atacante) attacker; **los ~s de la embajada** those who stormed the embassy

asaltar [A1] *vt* **(a)** (atracar) ‹*banco/tienda*› to hold up; ‹*persona*› to rob, mug **(b)** (tomar por asalto) ‹*ciudad/embajada*› to storm **(c)** (atacar) to attack, assault **(d)** «*idea*» to strike; **me asaltó una duda** I was struck *o* seized by a sudden doubt

El Artículo Definido

En términos generales, el artículo definido masculino o femenino (el, la, los, las) *se traduce al inglés por* the *(invariable)*

No se traduce:

— Cuando se emplea con algunas instituciones

empiezo el colegio mañana	=	I start school tomorrow
este año termina la universidad	=	he finishes university this year
la universidad de Oxford	=	Oxford University

Nótese que si se refiere al edificio por lo general se traduce

demolieron el colegio	=	they demolished the school
lo vi en la universidad	=	I saw him at the university

— Cuando precede a un nombre abstracto

la paciencia es una virtud	=	patience is a virtue
el tiempo vuela	=	time flies

— Con nombres de materiales, nacionalidades o colores, especialmente si éstos tienen el carácter de sujetos de la oración

el oro es un metal precioso	=	gold is a precious metal
el lino/el azul está de moda	=	linen/blue is in fashion
los venezolanos son más extrovertidos	=	Venezuelans are more extrovert

— Cuando se emplea con los días de la semana y en expresiones de porcentaje

el lunes/los domingos	=	Monday/Sundays
el dos por ciento de la población	=	two per cent of the population

— Con apellidos y nombres propios, cuando el artículo precede a la palabra señor, señora *o* señorita *o a un adjetivo*

la señora/señorita López	=	Mrs/Miss López
los señores García viajan hoy	=	Mr and Mrs García travel today
el pobre Miguel	=	poor Miguel

— Con apellidos, cuando éstos van precedidos de la profesión

el Dr Ramos la atendrá	=	Dr Ramos will see you now
conozco al profesor Ramírez	=	I know Professor Ramírez

— Con algunos nombres geográficos

vive en La Habana	=	he lives in Havana
la India	=	India

— Con nombres geográficos que se califican

el Chile actual	=	present-day Chile
la Inglaterra imperial	=	imperial England

— Con algunos nombres de equipos deportivos

el Real Madrid	=	Real Madrid
el Boca Junior	=	Boca Junior

— Cuando precede a un infinitivo

el estudiar es aburrido	=	studying is boring
el viajar amplía los horizontes	=	travel broadens one's horizons

Cuando se emplea con partes del cuerpo ver página 123

Otros ejemplos típicos y usos se encontrarán bajo la entrada respectiva

asalto *m* **1 (a)** (atraco — a banco, tienda) holdup, robbery; (— a persona) mugging; **un ~ a mano armada** an armed robbery *o* raid **(b)** (ataque) attack, assault; **tomar algo por ~** to take sth by storm **2** (en boxeo) round; (en esgrima) bout

asamblea *f* **(a)** (reunión) meeting **(b)** (cuerpo) assembly

asar [A1] *vt* **(a)** ‹*carne/pollo*› (en horno) to roast; (a la parrilla) to grill; (con espetón) to spit-roast **(b)** ‹*castaña/papa*› to roast; ‹*papa con piel*› to bake ■ **asarse** *v pron* **(a)** (en horno) to roast **(b)** (fam) (de calor) to roast (colloq)

asbesto *m* asbestos

ascendencia *f* **(a)** (linaje) descent, ancestry; **es de ~ francesa** he is of French descent **(b)** (origen) origins (*pl*); **su ~ humilde** her humble origins

ascendente *adj* ‹*movimiento/tendencia*› upward; ‹*astro/marea*› rising

ascender [E8] *vi* **1** (frml) «*temperatura/precios*» to rise; «*globo*» to rise, ascend (frml); «*escalador/alpinista*» to climb, to ascend (fml) **2** (frml) «*gastos/pérdidas*» **~ A algo** to amount TO sth **3** «*empleado/oficial*» to be promoted; **ascendió rápidamente en su carrera** he advanced rapidly in his career; **~ al trono** to ascend the throne ■ **~** *vt* ‹*empleado/oficial*› to promote

ascendiente *mf* (antepasado) ancestor

Ascensión *f*: **la ~** the Ascension

ascenso *m* **(a)** (de temperatura, precios) rise **(b)** (a montaña) ascent; **una industria en ~** a growing industry **(c)** (de empleado, equipo, oficial) promotion

ascensor *m* elevator (AmE), lift (BrE)

ascensorista *mf* elevator operator (AmE), lift attendant (BrE)

asco *m* **(a)** (repugnancia): **¡qué ~!** how revolting!, how disgusting!; **me dio ~** it made me feel sick; **poner cara de ~** to make *o* (BrE) pull a face; **tanta corrupción da ~** all this corruption is sickening **(b)** (fam) (cosa repugnante, molesta): **tienen la casa que es un ~** their house is like a pigsty; **el parque está hecho un ~** the park is in a real state (colloq); **¡qué ~ de tiempo!** what foul *o* lousy weather!

ascua *f*‡ ember; ***estar en/tener a algn en ~s*** (fam) to be on/to keep sb on tenterhooks

aseado -da *adj* (limpio) clean; (arreglado) neat, tidy

asear [A1] *vt* (limpiar) to clean; (arreglar) to straighten (up), to tidy up (BrE)
■ **asearse** *v pron* (*refl*) (lavarse) to wash; (arreglarse) to straighten *o* (BrE) tidy oneself up

asediar [A1] *vt* **(a)** (Mil) ‹*ciudad*› to lay siege to, besiege; ‹*ejército*› to surround, besiege **(b)** (acosar) ‹*persona*› to besiege

asegurado -da *adj* insured; **tengo el coche ~ a todo riesgo** I have fully comprehensive insurance for the car ■ *m,f* (persona que contrata el seguro) policy-holder; (persona asegurada): **el ~/la asegurada** the insured

asegurador -dora *adj* ‹*compañía*› insurance (*before n*) ■ *mf* **(a)** (persona) insurer **(b) aseguradora** *f* (compañía) insurance company

asegurar [A1] *vt* **1 (a)** (prometer) to assure; **te lo aseguro** I assure you; **asegura no haberlo visto** she maintains that she did not see **(b)** (garantizar) ‹*funcionamiento/servicio*› to guarantee **2** (Com, Fin) ‹*persona/casa*› to insure; **aseguró el coche a todo riesgo** she took out fully comprehensive insurance for *o* on the car **3 (a)** (sujetar, fijar) ‹*puerta/estante*› to secure **(b)** ‹*edificio/entrada*› to secure, make ... secure
■ **asegurarse** *v pron* **1 (a)** (cerciorarse) to make sure **(b)** (garantizarse, procurarse): **con ese gol se ~on el triunfo** by scoring that goal they guaranteed themselves victory **2** (Com, Fin) to insure oneself

asemejar [A1] *vt* **(a)** (hacer parecido) to make ... (look) like **(b)** (comparar) to compare, liken
■ **asemejarse** *v pron* «*personas*» to be *o* look alike; «*objetos*» to be similar; **~se A algo/algn** to resemble sth/sb, look like sth/sb

asentado -da *adj* **(a)** [ESTAR] (situado) to be situated; **el pueblo está ~ a orillas de un río** the village lies *o* is situated on the banks of a river **(b)** [ESTAR] (establecido) ‹*creencia/tradición*› deep-rooted, deeply rooted; ‹*persona*› settled (in) **(c)** [SER] (esp AmL) (maduro, juicioso) mature

asentamiento *m* settlement

asentar [A5] *vt* **1** ‹*campamento*› to set up; ‹*damnificados/refugiados*› to place **2 (a)** ‹*objeto*› to place carefully (*o* firmly *etc*) **(b)** ‹*conocimientos/postura*› to consolidate **3** (Com, Fin) to enter
■ **asentarse** *v pron* **1** «*café/polvo/terreno*» to settle **2** (estar situado) «*ciudad/edificio*» to be situated, be built **3 (a)** (establecerse) to settle **(b)** (esp AmL) (adquirir madurez) to settle down

asentir [I11] *vi* to agree, consent; **asintió con la cabeza** she nodded

aseo *m* (limpieza) cleanliness; **~ personal** personal hygiene; Ⓢ **aseos** ▶**52**⌋ rest room (AmE), toilets (BrE)

asequible *adj* ‹*precio*› affordable, reasonable; ‹*meta*› attainable, achievable; ‹*proyecto*› feasible; ‹*persona*› approachable; ‹*obra/estilo*› accessible

aserradero *m* sawmill

aserrar [A5] *vt* to saw

aserrín *m* (esp AmL) sawdust

aserrío *m* (Col, Ec) sawmill

aserruchar [A1] *vt* (Chi) to saw

asesinar [A1] *vt* to murder; (por razones políticas) to assassinate

asesinato *m* murder; (por razones políticas) assassination

asesino -na *adj* ‹*instinto/odio*› murderous, homicidal; ‹*animal*› killer (*before n*) ■ *m,f* murderer; (por razones políticas) assassin; **~ a sueldo** hired killer; **~ en serie** serial killer

asesor -sora *adj* ‹*consejo*› advisory; ‹*arquitecto/ingeniero*› consultant (*before n*) ■ *m,f* advisor*, consultant

asesoramiento *m* advice

asesorar [A1] *vt* to advise
■ **asesorarse** *v pron* **~se CON algn** to consult sb

asesoría *f* consultancy; **~ fiscal/jurídica** tax/legal consultancy

asestar [A1] *vt*: **me asestó una puñalada/un puñetazo** he stabbed/punched me

asexuado -da *adj* asexual

asfaltado -da *adj* asphalt (*before n*), asphalted

asfaltar [A1] *vt* to asphalt

asfalto *m* asphalt

asfixia *f* **(a)** (Med) asphyxia, suffocation **(b)** (fam) (agobio) suffocation

asfixiante *adj* **(a)** ‹*gas/humo*› asphyxiating (*before n*) **(b)** (fam) ‹*calor*› suffocating, stifling; ‹*ambiente/relación*› oppressive, stifling

asfixiar [A1] *vt* **(a)** (ahogar) to asphyxiate, suffocate; **murió asfixiado** he died of asphyxiation *o* suffocation **(b)** (agobiar) to suffocate, stifle
■ **asfixiarse** *v pron* **(a)** (ahogarse) to be asphyxiated, to suffocate; (por obstrucción de la tráquea) to choke to death; **me asfixiaba de calor** (fam) I was suffocating in the heat **(b)** (fam) (agobiarse) to suffocate, feel stifled

así[1] *adj inv* like that; **no seas ~** don't be like that; **con gente ~ yo no me meto** I don't mix with people like that; **yo soy ~** that's the way I am; **~ es la vida** (fr hecha) that's life; **es un tanto ~ de hojas** it's about *that* many pages; **esperamos horas ¿no es ~?** we waited for hours, didn't we?; **tanto es ~ que** ... so much so that ...

así[2] *adv* **1** (de este modo) like this; (de ese modo) like that; **¿por qué me tratas ~?** why are you treating me like this?; **no le hables ~** don't talk to him like that; **¡~ cualquiera!** that's cheating! (colloq & hum); **~ es como pasó** this is how it happens; **no te pongas ~** don't get so worked up; **~ me podré comprar lo que quiera** that way I'll be able to buy whatever I want; **~ es** that's right; **¿está bien ~ o quieres más?** is that enough, or do you want some more?; **y ~ sucesivamente** and so on **2 ¡~ de fácil!** it's as easy as that; **~ de alto/grueso** *this* high/thick **3** (*en locs*) **así así** (fam) so-so; **así como así** just like that; **¡así me gusta!** (fr hecha) that's what I like to see!; **así nomás** (AmL) just like that; **así pues** so; **así que** (por lo tanto) so; **así y todo** even so; **por así decirlo** so to speak

Asia *f*‡ Asia

asiático -ca *adj/m,f* Asian, Asiatic

asidero *m* **(a)** (asa) handle **(b)** (punto de sujeción) hand (hold); **sin ~s en la realidad** with no grip on reality

asiduo -dua *adj* **(a)** (persistente) ‹*estudiante/lector*› assiduous; ‹*admirador*› devoted **(b)** (frecuente) ‹*cliente*› regular, frequent ■ *m,f* regular

asiento *m* **1 (a)** (para sentarse) seat; **~ anatómico** anatomically designed seat; **por favor, tome ~** (frml) please take a seat (frml) **(b)** (de bicicleta) saddle **(c)** (de silla) seat **(d)** (base, estabilidad) base **2** (en contabilidad) entry

asignación *f* **1 (a)** (de tarea, función) assignment **(b)** (de fondos, renta) allocation, assignment **2** (sueldo) wages (*pl*); (paga) allowance **3** (AmC) (Educ) homework

asignar [A1] *vt* **(a)** (dar, adjudicar) ‹*renta/función/tarea*› to assign; ‹*valor*› to ascribe; ‹*fondos/parcela*› to allocate; **me ~on la vacante** I was appointed to the post; **le ~on una beca** he was awarded a grant **(b)** (destinar) ‹*persona*› to assign; **~ a algn A algo** to assign sb TO sth

asignatura *f* subject; **~ pendiente** (Educ) subject which one has to retake; (asunto sin resolver) unresolved matter

asilado -da *m,f* inmate; **~ político** political refugee (*who has been granted asylum*)

asilar [A1] *vt* **(a)** (acoger) ‹*anciano/huérfano*› to take ... into care; ‹*refugiado*› to grant ... asylum **(b)** (internar) to put ... in a home

■ **asilarse** *v pron* «*anciano/huérfano*» to take refuge; «*refugiado*» to seek asylum

asilo *m* **1** (Servs Socs) home, institution; (para vagabundos, mujeres maltratadas) shelter; **~ de ancianos** *or* **de la tercera edad** old people's home **2** (Pol) asylum; **pedir ~ político** to seek political asylum

asimétrico -ca *adj* asymmetric

asimilación *f* assimilation

asimilar [A1] *vt* **1** ‹*alimentos/ideas/cultura*› to assimilate **2** (en boxeo) ‹*golpes*› to take, soak up (colloq)

asimismo *adv* **(a)** (también) also **(b)** (igualmente) likewise

asistencia *f* **1** (presencia) attendance; **~ A algo** attendance AT sth **2** (frml) (ayuda) assistance; **prestarle ~ a algn** to give sb assistance; **~ en carretera** breakdown service; **~ médica** (servicio) medical care; (atención médica) medical attention; **~ pública** (en CS) municipal health service (*esp for emergencies*); **~ técnica** after-sales service **3** (Dep) assist

asistencial *adj* welfare (*before n*)

asistenta *f* (Esp) cleaning lady *o* woman

asistente *mf* **1** (ayudante) assistant; **~ social** social worker **2** (frml) **los ~s** (a una reunión) those present; (a un espectáculo) the audience

asistir [I1] *vi* (estar presente) **~ A algo** ‹*a reunión/acto/clases*› to attend sth; **asistió a una sola clase** he only came/went to one class; **~ a misa** to go to *o* attend Mass ■ **~** *vt* (frml) (ayudar): **en el consulado lo ~án** you will receive assistance at the consulate (frml); **~ a los pobres** to care for the poor

asma *f*‡ asthma

asmático -ca *adj/m,f* asthmatic

asno *m* (Zool) donkey; (tonto) (fam) dimwit (colloq)

asociación *f* association; **~ de ideas** association of ideas

asociado -da *adj* associate (*before n*) ■ *m,f* (Com) associate; (de club, asociación) member

asociar [A1] *vt* ‹*ideas/palabras*› to associate; **~ algo/a algn CON algo/algn** to associate sth/sb WITH sth/sb; **no logro ~la con nada** I can't place her

■ **asociarse** *v pron* **(a)** «*empresas/comerciantes*» to collaborate; **~se CON algn** to go into partnership WITH sb **(b)** «*hechos/factores*» to combine **(c)** (a grupo, club) **~se A algo** to become a member OF sth

asolar [A1 *or* A10] *vt* «*guerra/huracán/sequía*» to devastate

asoleada *f* (Andes) (de una persona): **pegarse una ~** (fam) to sunbathe

asoleado -da *adj* sunny

asolear [A1] *vt* (exponer al sol) ‹*ropa*› to hang ... out in the sun; ‹*uvas*› to dry ... in the sun

■ **asolearse** *v pron* (AmL) to sunbathe

asomar [A1] *vi* to show; **empiezan a ~ los primeros brotes** the first shoots begin to show *o* appear ■ **~** *vt* ‹*cabeza*›: **asomó la cabeza por la ventanilla** she stuck her head out of the window; **abrió la puerta y asomó la cabeza** she opened the door and stuck her head out/in

■ **asomarse** *v pron:* **~se POR algo** to lean out OF sth; **se asomó a la ventana** she looked out of the window; **se ~on al balcón** they came out onto the balcony

asombrar [A1] *vt* to amaze, astonish; **me asombró su reacción** I was astonished *o* taken aback by his reaction

■ **asombrarse** *v pron* to be astonished *o* amazed; **se asombró con los resultados** she was amazed *o* astonished at the results; **yo ya no me asombro por nada** nothing surprises me any more

asombro *m* astonishment; **no salía de su ~** he couldn't get over his surprise

asombroso -sa *adj* amazing, astonishing

asonante *adj* assonant

asorocharse [A1] *v pron* **(a)** (Chi, Per) (por la altura) to get mountain *o* altitude sickness **(b)** (Chi) (por calor, vergüenza) to flush

aspa *f*‡ (de molino) sail; (de ventilador) blade; (cruz) cross

aspaviento *m*: **deja de hacer ~s** stop getting in such a flap

aspecto *m* **1 (a)** (de persona, lugar) look, appearance; **un hombre de ~ distinguido** a distinguished-looking man; **¿qué ~ tiene?** what does he look like?; **a juzgar por su ~** judging by the look of her; **tiene mal ~** «*persona*» she doesn't look well; «*cosa*» it doesn't look nice **(b)** (de problema, asunto): **no me gusta el ~ que van tomando las cosas** I don't like the way things are going *o* looking **2** (rasgo, faceta) aspect; **en ese ~ tienes razón** in that respect you're right

aspereza *f* **1 (a)** (de superficie, piel) roughness **(b)** (de sabor) sharpness; (de voz, clima) harshness **2** (parte áspera): **usar papel de lija para quitar las ~s** use sandpaper to remove any roughness; ***limar ~s*** to smooth things over

áspero -ra *adj* **1** ‹*superficie/piel*› rough; ‹*tela*› coarse **2 (a)** ‹*sabor*› sharp **(b)** ‹*voz/sonido/clima*› harsh **3 (a)** (en el trato) abrupt, surly **(b)** ‹*discusión*› acrimonious

aspersor *m* sprinkler

aspiración *f* **1** (deseo, ambición) aspiration **2** (Fisiol) inhalation; (Ling) aspiration; (Mús) breath

aspiradora *f*, **aspirador** *m* (electrodoméstico) vacuum cleaner; **pasé la ~ por la habitación** I vacuumed *o* (BrE) hoovered the bedroom

aspirante *mf*: **las ~s al título** the contenders for the title; **ocho ~s al puesto de redactor** eight candidates *o* applicants for the post of editor

aspirar [A1] *vi* **1** (desear, pretender) **~ A algo/hacer algo** to aspire TO sth/do sth **2 (a)** «*aparato*» to suck; «*aspiradora*» to pick up **(b)** (Fisiol) to breathe in **(c)** (AmL) (pasar la aspiradora) to vacuum, hoover (BrE) ■ **~** *vt* **(a)** «*aparato*» to suck up *o* in; «*aspiradora*» to pick up **(b)** (Fisiol) to inhale **(c)** (Ling) to aspirate

aspirina *f* aspirin

asqueante *adj* sickening, nauseating

asquear [A1] *vt* (dar asco a) to sicken; (aburrir, hartar): **está asqueado de todo** he's fed up with everything (colloq)

asqueroso -sa *adj* **1 (a)** ‹*libro/película*› digusting, filthy **(b)** ‹*olor/comida/costumbre*› disgusting, revolting **(c)** (sucio) filthy **2** (lascivo): **¡viejo ~!** you dirty old man!

asquiento -ta *adj* (AmL) ⇒ ASQUEROSO 1

asta *f*‡ **(a)** (de bandera) flagpole; **con la bandera a media ~** with the flag at half-mast **(b)** (cuerno) horn **(c)** (de lanza, flecha) shaft

astabandera *f* (Méx) flagpole

asterisco *m* asterisk

asteroide *m* asteroid

astigmatismo *m* astigmatism

astilla *f* **(a)** (fragmento) chip; (de madera, hueso) splinter; **se me metió una ~ en el dedo** I have a splinter in my finger **(b) astillas** *fpl* (para el fuego) kindling

astillarse [A1] *v pron* «*madera/hueso*» to splinter; «*piedra*» to chip

astillero *m* shipyard

astracán *m* astrakhan

astringente *adj* ‹*loción*› astringent; ‹*alimento/medicamento*› binding (*before n*) ■ *m* astringent

astro *m* (Astrol, Astron) heavenly body; (Espec) star

astrología *f* astrology

astrólogo -ga *m,f* astrologist

astronauta *mf* astronaut

astronomía *f* astronomy

astronómico -ca *adj* astronomical

astrónomo -ma *m,f* astronomer

astucia *f* **(a)** (cualidad — de sagaz) astuteness, shrewdness; (— de ladino) (pey) craftiness, cunning; **la ~ del zorro** the slyness of a fox **(b)** (ardid) trick, ploy

astuto -ta *adj* (sagaz) shrewd, astute; (ladino) (pey) crafty, sly, cunning

asueto *m* time off; **tomarse un día de ~** to take a day off

asumir [I1] *vt* **1 (a)** ‹*cargo/tarea/responsabilidad*› to take on, assume (frml); ‹*riesgo*› to take **(b)** (adoptar) ‹*actitud*› to assume (frml) **(c)** (aceptar) to come to terms with **2** (AmL) (suponer) to assume

asunceno -na, **asunceño -ña** *adj* of/from Asunción ■ *m,f* person from Asunción

Asunción *f* (Geog) Asunción

asunto *m* **(a)** (cuestión, problema) matter; **~s de negocios** business matters; **un ~ muy delicado** a very delicate matter *o* issue; **está implicado en un ~ de drogas** he's mixed up in something to do with drugs; **no es ~ mío/tuyo** it's none of my/your business **(b)** (pey) (relación amorosa) affair

asustado -da *adj* (atemorizado) frightened; (preocupado) worried

asustar [A1] *vt* to frighten; **me asustó cuando se puso tan serio** he gave me a fright when he went all serious

■ **asustarse** *v pron* to get frightened; **me asusté cuando vi que no estaba allí** I got a fright *o* I got worried when I saw he wasn't there; **no se asuste, no es nada grave** there's no need to worry, it's nothing serious

atacante *mf* attacker, assailant (frml)

atacar [A2] *vt* to attack

atado *m* **(a)** (de ropa) bundle **(b)** (CS) (de espinacas, zanahorias) bunch; ***ser un ~ de nervios*** (CS) to be a bundle of nerves **(c)** (RPl) (de cigarrillos) pack (AmE), packet (BrE)

ataduras *fpl* ties (*pl*)

atajada *f* (CS) save

atajador -dora *m,f* (Méx) (*m*) ballboy; (*f*) ballgirl

atajar [A1] *vt* **1 (a)** (AmL) (agarrar) ‹*pelota*› to catch **(b)** (Esp) (interceptar) ‹*pase/pelota*› to intercept **2 (a)** ‹*golpe/puñetazo*› to parry, block **(b)** ‹*persona*› (agarrar) to stop, catch; (interrumpir, detener) to stop **3** ‹*enfermedad/problema*› to keep ... in check; ‹*incendio*› to contain; ‹*rumor*› to quell

atajo *m* short cut

atañer [E7] *vi* (*en 3ª pers*) to concern; **por lo que a mí atañe** as far as I'm concerned

ataque *m* **1 (a)** (Dep, Mil) attack; **~ aéreo** air raid **(b)** (verbal) attack **2** (Med) attack; **~ de asma** asthma attack; **~ al corazón** heart attack; **~ epiléptico** epileptic fit; **me dio un ~ de nervios** I got into a panic; **un ~ de risa** a fit of hysterics

atar [A1] *vt* **1 (a)** ‹*caja/paquete*› to tie; **le até el pelo con una cinta** I tied her hair back with a ribbon **(b)** ‹*persona/caballo*› to tie ... up; ‹*cabra*› to tether; **lo ~on de pies y manos** they bound him hand and foot; **ató al perro a un poste** she tied the dog to a lamppost **2** «*trabajo/hijos*» to tie ... down

■ **atarse** *v pron* (*refl*) ‹*zapatos/cordones*› to tie up, do up; ‹*pelo*› to tie up

atarantado -da *adj* **(a)** (Col, Méx, Per fam) (por golpe) dazed, stunned **(b)** (Méx, Per fam) (confundido) in a spin, dazed **(c)** (Chi fam) (precipitado) harum-scarum (colloq)

atarantar [A1] *vt* (Col, Méx, Per fam): **con tantas preguntas me ~on** they made my head spin with all their questions; **el golpe lo atarantó** the blow left him dazed

■ **atarantarse** *v pron* **(a)** (Col, Méx, Per fam) (aturdirse, confundirse) to get flustered, get in a dither **(b)** (Chi fam) (precipitarse): **no te atarantes** don't rush into it (colloq)

atardecer¹ [E3] *v impers* to get dark

atardecer² *m* dusk; **al ~** at dusk

atareado -da *adj* busy

atascar [A2] *vt* **(a)** ‹*cañería*› to block **(b)** (Méx) ‹*motor*› to stall

■ **atascarse** *v pron* **1 (a)** «*cañería/fregadero*» to block, get blocked **(b)** «*tráfico*» to get snarled up **2 (a)** «*mecanismo*» to jam, seize up **(b)** (Méx) «*motor*» to stall

atasco *m* **(a)** (de tráfico) traffic jam; (en proceso) holdup, delay **(b)** (en tubería) blockage

ataúd *m* coffin

ateísmo *m* atheism

atemorizar [A4] *vt* (liter) ‹*persona*› to frighten, intimidate; ‹*barrio/población*› to terrorize

Atenas *f* Athens

atención¹ *f* **1 (a)** (concentración) attention; **pon/presta ~ a esto** pay attention to this; **con ~** attentively **(b) llamar la ~: se viste así para llamar la ~** he dresses like that to attract attention (to himself); **una chica que llama la ~** a very striking girl; **me llamó la ~ que estuviera sola** I was surprised she was alone; **llamarle la ~ a algn** (reprenderlo) to reprimand sb (frml), to give sb a talking to **2 (a)** (en hotel, tienda) service; Ⓢ **horario de atención al público** (en banco) hours of business; (en oficina pública) opening hours **(b)** (cortesía): **nos colmaron de atenciones** we were showered with attention *o* (BrE) attentions; **no tuvo ninguna ~ con ella a pesar de su hospitalidad** he didn't show the slightest appreciation despite her hospitality

atención² *interj* **(a)** (para que se atienda) attention; **¡~, por favor!** (your) attention, please! **(b)** (para avisar de peligro) look out!, watch out!

atender [E8] *vi* **(a)** (prestar atención) to pay attention; **~ A algo/algn** to pay attention TO sth/sb **(b)** (cumplir con) **~ A algo** ‹*a compromisos/gastos/obligaciones*› to meet sth **(c)** (prestar un servicio): **el doctor no atiende los martes** the doctor does not see anyone on Tuesdays; **en esa tienda atienden muy mal** the service is very bad in that store ■ **~** *vt* **1 (a)** ‹*paciente*›: **¿qué médico la atiende?** which doctor usually sees you?; **los atendieron enseguida en el hospital** they were seen immediately at the hospital; **no tiene quien lo atienda** he has no one to look after him **(b)** ‹*cliente*› to attend to, see to; (en tienda) to serve; **¿la están atendiendo?** are you being served? **(c)** ‹*asunto*› to deal with; ‹*llamada*› to answer; ‹*demanda*› to meet **2** ‹*consejo/advertencia*› to listen to

■ **atenderse** *v pron* (AmL): **¿con qué médico se atiende?** which doctor usually sees you?

atenerse [E27] *v pron* **(a)** (ajustarse, someterse) **~ A algo** ‹*a las reglas*› to abide BY *o* comply WITH sth; ‹*a los órdenes*› to obey sth; ‹*a las consecuencias*› to live WITH *o* abide BY sth; **no sé a que atenerme** I don't know where I stand **(b)** (limitarse): **si nos atenemos a lo que dijeron ellos** ... if we go by what they said ...; **aténgase a los hechos** confine yourself to the facts

atentado *m* **(a)** (ataque): **un ~ terrorista** a terrorist attack; **un ~ contra el presidente** an assassination attempt on the president **(b)** (afrenta) **~ CONTRA** *or* **A algo** ‹*a honor/dignidad*› affront TO sth; **un ~ contra la moral** an offense against decency

atentamente *adv* **(a)** ‹*escuchar/mirar*› attentively, carefully **(b)** (amablemente) thoughtfully, kindly; **lo saluda ~** (Corresp) sincerely (AmE), yours faithfully/sincerely (BrE)

atentar [A1] *vi*: **~on contra su vida** they made an attempt on her life; **~ contra la seguridad del Estado** to threaten national security

atento -ta *adj* **1 (a)** (que presta atención) ‹*alumno/público*› attentive; **estar ~ (A algo)** to pay attention (TO sth) **(b)** (alerta): **estáte ~ y avísame si viene alguien** stay alert and let me know if anyone comes; **estar ~ A algo** to be on the alert FOR sth **2 (a)** (amable) ‹*esposo/anfitrión/camarero*› attentive; **ser ~ CON algn** to be kind TO sb **(b)** (cortés) courteous

atenuar [A18] *vt* (disminuir, moderar) ‹*luz*› to dim; ‹*color*› to tone down; **deberías ~ el tono de tus críticas** you should tone down your criticism

ateo, **atea** *adj* atheistic ■ *m,f* atheist

aterrador -dora *adj* terrifying

aterrar [A1] *vt* ‹*persona*› to terrify; **le aterra la idea** she's terrified at the thought

aterrizaje *m* landing; **un ~ forzoso** an emergency landing

aterrizar [A4] *vi* to land, touch down

aterrorizado -da *adj* terrified

aterrorizar [A4] *vt* to terrorize

atesorar [A1] *vt* ‹*dinero*› to amass

atestado -da *adj* packed, crammed; **~ DE algo** packed *o* crammed full OF sth; **el salón estaba ~ (de gente)** the hall was packed *o* crammed (with people)

atestiguar [A16] *vt* **(a)** (Der) to testify **(b)** (probar) to bear witness to

atiborrar [A1] *vt* **~ algo/a algn DE algo** to stuff sth/sb WITH sth; **atiborrado de gente** packed *o* jam-packed with people

■ **atiborrarse** *v pron* **~se DE algo** to stuff oneself WITH sth

ático *m* **(a)** (apartamento) top-floor apartment *o* (BrE) flat; (de lujo) penthouse; (de techo bajo) garret (AmE), attic flat (BrE) **(b)** (desván) attic, loft (BrE)

atienda, **atiendas, etc** *see* ATENDER

atinado -da *adj* ‹*respuesta/comentario*› pertinent, spot-on (colloq); ‹*decisión/medida*› sensible, wise; ‹*solución*› sensible

atinar [A1] *vi*: **~ en el blanco** to hit the target; **¡atinaste!** you're dead right!; **no atiné a decir nada** I couldn't say a word; **~ CON algo** ‹*con solución/respuesta*› to hit ON *o* UPON sth, come up WITH sth; **atinaste con el regalo** the gift you got him/her was perfect; **no atinaba con la calle** I couldn't find the street

atizador *m* poker

atizar [A4] *vt* ‹*fuego*› to poke

Atlántico *m*: **el (océano) ~** the Atlantic (Ocean)

Atlántida *f*: **la ~** Atlantis

atlas *m* (*pl* **~**) atlas

atleta *mf* athlete

atlético -ca *adj* **(a)** ‹*club/competición*› athletics (*before n*) **(b)** ‹*figura*› athletic

atletismo *m* athletics

atmósfera *f* atmosphere

atole *m* (Méx) hot corn *o* maize drink

atolladero *m* **(a)** (lugar cenagoso) mire **(b)** (aprieto, apuro) predicament, awkward situation

atolondrado -da *adj* **(a)** [SER] (impetuoso) rash, impetuous; (despistado) scatterbrained **(b)** [ESTAR] (por golpe) dazed, stunned ■ *m,f* scatterbrain

atolondrar [A1] *vt* **(a)** (confundir) to fluster **(b)** «*golpe*» to daze, stun

■ **atolondrarse** *v pron* **(a)** (confundirse) to get flustered **(b)** (precipitarse): **no te atolondres, piénsalo bien** don't rush into it, think it over carefully

atómico -ca *adj* atomic

atomizador *m* spray, atomizer

átomo *m* atom

atónito -ta *adj* astonished, amazed; **se quedó mirándola ~** he stared at her in amazement

atontado -da *adj* (por golpe, asombro) stunned, dazed; (distraído): **contesta, que estás medio ~** answer me, you're in a daze; *ver tb* ATONTAR

atontar [A1] *vt* «*golpe*» to stun, daze; **estas pastillas me atontan** these pills make me groggy; **la televisión los atonta** television turns them into vegetables *o* zombies

atorar [A1] *vt* **1** (esp AmL) ‹*cañería*› to block (up) **2** (Méx) (sujetar): **atoramos la puerta con una silla** we jammed the door shut/open with a chair; **atóralo con este alambre** secure it with this bit of wire

■ **atorarse** *v pron* (esp AmL) **(a)** (atragantarse) to choke **(b)** «*cañería*» to get blocked; «*puerta/cajón*» to jam; (+ *me/te/le etc*) **se me atoró el cierre** my zipper got stuck; **se le atoró el chicle en la garganta** the chewing gum got stuck in her throat

atormentar [A1] *vt* «*persona*» (físicamente) to torture; (mentalmente) to torment

■ **atormentarse** *v pron* (*refl*) to torment oneself

atornillar [A1] *vt* to screw on (*o* down *etc*)

atorrante *adj* **(a)** (Andes, CS fam) (holgazán) lazy; (desaseado) scruffy **(b)** (Bol, RPl fam) (sinvergüenza) crooked **(c)** (Col, Per fam) (pesado, cargante): **no seas ~** don't be such a pain in the neck (colloq) ■ *mf* **(a)** (Andes, CS fam) (vagabundo) tramp; (holgazán) good-for-nothing, layabout; (desaseado) slob (colloq) **(b)** (Bol, RPl fam) (sinvergüenza): **es un ~** he's a bit of a crook (colloq) **(c)** (Col, Per fam) (pesado, cargante) pain in the neck (colloq)

atosigar [A3] *vt* (importunar) to pester, hassle (colloq); (presionar) to pressure (AmE), to pressurize (BrE)

atrabancado -da *adj* (Méx fam) (precipitado) rash, reckless

atracador -dora *m,f* (de banco) bank robber, raider (journ); (de persona) mugger

atracar [A2] *vi* «*barco*» to dock, berth ■ **~** *vt* (asaltar) ‹*banco*› to hold up; ‹*persona*› to mug

atracción *f* attraction; **la ~ más concurrida** the most popular attraction; **una ~ turística** a tourist attraction; **las atracciones están en la playa** the funfair is on the beach; **siente una gran ~ por ella** he feels strongly attracted to her

atraco *m* (a banco) robbery, raid (journ); (a persona) mugging; **~ a mano armada** armed robbery *o* (journ) raid

atracón *m* (fam): **se dio un ~ de paella** he stuffed himself with paella (colloq)

atractivo[1] -va *adj* attractive

atractivo[2] *m* **(a)** (encanto) charm, attractiveness; **tiene mucho ~** she's very charming; **el mayor ~ de la ciudad** the city's main attraction *o* appeal **(b)** (interés) appeal; **para mí viajar no tiene ningún ~** travel holds no appeal to me

atraer [E23] *vt* **(a)** (Fís) to attract **(b)** (traer, hacer venir) to attract; **un truco para ~ al público** a gimmick to attract the public **(c)** (cautivar, gustar): **se siente atraído por ella** he feels attracted to her; **no me atrae la idea** the idea doesn't attract me *o* appeal to me **(d)** ‹*atención/miradas*› to attract

■ **atraerse** *v pron* **(a)** (ganarse) ‹*amistad*› to gain; ‹*interés*› to attract **(b)** (*recípr*) to attract (each other)

atragantarse [A1] *v pron* (al tragar) to choke; **se le atragantó una espina** he choked on a fish bone

atraiga, atrajo, etc *see* ATRAER

atrancar [A2] *vt* ‹*cañería*› to block (up); ‹*puerta/ventana*› to bar

■ **atrancarse** *v pron* **(a)** «*cañería*» to get blocked **(b)** (fam) «*persona*» (en tarea) to get stuck

atrapar [A1] *vt* to catch

atrás *adv* **1** (en el espacio) **(a)** (expresando dirección) back; **muévelo para** *or* **hacia ~** move it back; **da un paso ~** take one step back **(b)** **¡~!** (*como interj*) get back! **(c)** (lugar, parte): **está allí ~** it's back there; **me senté ~** (en coche) I sat in the back; (en clase, cine) I sat at the back; **la parte de ~** the back; **me estaba quedando ~** I was getting left behind; **dejamos ~ la ciudad** we left the city behind us; ***estar hasta ~*** (Méx fam) to be as high as a kite (colloq) **2** (en el tiempo): **sucedió tres años ~** it happened three years ago; **había sucedido tres años ~** it had happened three years earlier *o* before **3 atrás de** (*loc prep*) (AmL) behind

atrasado -da *adj* **1 (a)** [ESTAR] ‹*reloj*› slow **(b)** (con respecto a lo esperado): **está muy ~ en los estudios** he's really behind in his studies; **el proyecto está ~** the project is behind schedule; **el tren**

llegó/salió ~ (AmL) the train arrived/left late; **apúrate que voy ~** (AmL) hurry up, I'm late **2** (acumulado, pasado): **tengo mucho sueño ~** I have a lot of sleep to catch up on; **tengo trabajo ~** I'm behind with my work; **todas las cuotas atrasadas** all outstanding payments; **un ejemplar ~** a back number *o* issue **3 (a)** (anticuado, desfasado) ‹*ideas/persona*› old-fashioned **(b)** ‹*país/pueblo*› backward

atrasar [A1] *vt* **(a)** ‹*reloj*› to put back **(b)** ‹*reunión/viaje*› to postpone, put back ■ **~** *vi* «*reloj*» to lose time

■ **atrasarse** *v pron* **1 (a)** «*reloj*» to lose time; **se me ha atrasado 15 minutos** it's 15 minutes slow **(b)** (esp AmL) (llegar tarde) «*avión/tren*» to be late, be delayed; «*persona*» to be late **2 (a)** (en estudios, trabajo, pagos) to fall behind, get behind **(b)** «*país/industria*» to fall behind

atraso *m* **(a)** (de país, ideas) backwardness **(b)** (esp AmL) (retraso) delay; **perdona el ~** I'm sorry about the delay; **salió con unos minutos de ~** it left a few minutes late; **viene con una hora de ~** it's (running) an hour late

atravesado -da *adj* (cruzado): **el piano estaba ~ en el pasillo** the piano was stuck (*o* placed *etc*) across the corridor; **un árbol/camión ~ en la carretera** a tree lying across/a truck blocking the road

atravesar [A5] *vt* **1 (a)** ‹*río/frontera*› to cross; **atravesó el río a nado** she swam across the river **(b)** «*bala/espada*» to go through; **le atravesó la pierna** it went through his leg **(c)** ‹*crisis/período*› to go through **2** (colocar) to put ... across

■ **atravesarse** *v pron:* **se nos atravesó un camión** a truck crossed right in front of us; **se me atravesó una espina en la garganta** I got a fish bone stuck in my throat

atraviesa, atraviesas, etc *see* ATRAVESAR

atrayente *adj* appealing

atreverse [E1] *v pron* to dare; **¡anda, atrévete!** go on then, I dare you (to); **no me atrevo a decírselo** I daren't tell him; **¿cómo te atreves a pegarle?** how dare you hit him?; **¿a que conmigo no te atreves?** I bet you wouldn't dare take me on

atrevido -da *adj* **(a)** (insolente) sassy (AmE colloq), cheeky (BrE colloq) **(b)** (osado) ‹*escote/persona*› daring; ‹*chiste*› risqué; ‹*diseño*› bold **(c)** (valiente) brave

atrevimiento *m* nerve

atribuir [I20] *vt* **(a) ~ algo A algn/algo** to attribute sth TO sb/sth; **le atribuyen algo que no dijo** they attribute words to him which he did not say; **le atribuyen propiedades curativas** it is held *o* believed to have healing powers **(b)** ‹*funciones/poder*› to confer

■ **atribuirse** *v pron* (*refl*) **(a)** ‹*éxito/autoría*› to claim **(b)** ‹*poderes/responsabilidad*› to assume

atributo *m* (cualidad) attribute, quality; (símbolo) insignia

atril *m* (para partituras) music stand; (para libros) lectern

atrincherar [A1] *vt* to entrench

■ **atrincherarse** *v pron* to entrench oneself

atrocidad *f* (cualidad) barbarity; (acto) atrocity; **¡qué ~!** how atrocious! *o* how awful!

atrofiarse [A1] *v pron* to atrophy

atropellado -da *adj*: **¡qué ~ eres!** you always do things in such a rush!

atropellar [A1] *vt* **(a)** «*coche/camión*» to knock ... down; (pasando por encima) to run ... over **(b)** ‹*libertades/derechos*› to violate, ride roughshod over

■ **atropellarse** *v pron* **(a)** (al hablar, actuar) to rush **(b)** (*recípr*) (empujarse): **salieron corriendo, atropellándose unos a otros** they came running out, pushing and shoving as they went

atropello *m* (abuso) outrage; **~ DE *or* A algo** violation OF sth

atroz *adj* atrocious

atte. (Corresp) (= **atentamente**): **lo saluda ~** sincerely yours (AmE), yours sincerely/faithfully (BrE)

atuendo *m* (frml) outfit

atún *m* tuna (fish)

aturdimiento *m* (perplejidad) bewilderment; (por golpe, noticia) daze

aturdir [I1] *vt* **(a)** «*música/ruido*»: **la música te aturdía** the music was deafening; **este ruido me aturde** I can't think straight with this noise **(b)** (dejar perplejo) to bewilder, confuse **(c)** «*golpe/noticia/suceso*» to stun, daze

■ **aturdirse** *v pron* (confundirse) to get confused *o* flustered; (por golpe, noticia) to be stunned *o* dazed

audacia *f* (valor) courage, daring; (osadía) boldness, audacity

audaz *adj* (valiente) brave, courageous; (osado) daring, bold

audición *f* **1** (facultad de oír) hearing **2** (prueba) audition **3** (RPl) (Rad) program*

audiencia *f* **1** (cita) audience; **pedir ~** to seek an audience **2** (Der) **(a)** (tribunal) court **(b)** (sesión) hearing **3** (espectadores, oyentes) audience; **un programa de mucha ~** a program with a large audience

audífono *m* **(a)** (para sordos) hearing aid, deaf-aid (BrE) **(b)** (de radio) earphone **(c) audífonos** *mpl* (AmL) headphones (*pl*)

audiovisual *adj* audiovisual ■ *m* audiovisual presentation

auditar [A1] *vt* to audit

auditivo -va *adj* **(a)** ‹*nervio/conducto*› auditory **(b)** ‹*problemas*› hearing (*before n*)

auditor -tora *m,f* **(a)** (persona) auditor **(b) auditora** *f* (empresa) auditors (*pl*), firm of auditors

auditoría *f* audit

auditorio *m* (público) audience; (sala) auditorium

auge *m* **(a)** (punto culminante) peak; **en el ~ de su carrera** at the peak *o* height of his career **(b)** (aumento): **la comida vegetariana está en ~** vegetarian food is on the increase; **un período de ~ económico** a period of economic growth

augurar [A1] *vt* «*futuro*» to predict, foretell

augurio *m* (presagio): **sus ~s no se cumplieron** his predictions did not come true; **es un ~ de mala suerte** it's (a sign of) bad luck *o* a bad omen

aula *f*‡ **(a)** (en escuela) classroom **(b)** (en universidad) lecture (*o* seminar *etc*) room; **~ magna** main lecture theater* *o* hall

aullar [A23] *vi* «*lobo/viento*» to howl

aullido *m* howl; **los ~s del perro** the howling of the dog

aumentar [A1] *vt* **(a)** (en general) to increase; ‹*precio/sueldo*› to increase, raise **(b)** (Opt) to magnify ■ **~** *vi* «*temperatura/presión*» to rise; «*velocidad*» to increase; «*precio/producción/valor*» to increase, rise; **~á el frío** it will become colder; **~** DE **algo** ‹*de volumen/tamaño*› to increase IN sth; **aumentó de peso** he put on *o* gained weight

aumento *m* **(a)** (incremento) rise, increase; **~ de peso** increase in weight; **~ de temperatura** rise in temperature; **~ de precio** price rise *o* increase; **~ de sueldo** salary increase, pay raise (AmE), pay rise (BrE) **(b)** (Ópt) magnification; **lentes de mucho ~** glasses with very strong lenses

aun *adv* even; **ni ~ trabajando 12 horas al día** (not) even if we worked 12 hours a day; **~ así, creo que** ... even so, I think ...; **ni ~ así me quedaría** even then I wouldn't stay

aún *adv* **1** (todavía) **(a)** (en frases afirmativas o interrogativas) still; **~ falta un mes** there's still a month to go; **¿~ estás aquí?** are you still here? **(b)** (en frases negativas) yet; **~ no ha llamado** she hasn't called yet **2** (en comparaciones) even

aunar [A23] *vt* ‹*ideas*› to combine
■ **aunarse** *v pron* to unite, come together

aunque *conj* **1** (a pesar de que) **(a)** (refiriéndose a hechos) although; **~ no estaba bien fue a trabajar** although he wasn't well he went to work **(b)** (respondiendo a una objeción) (+ *subjuntivo*): **es millonario, ~ no lo parezca** he's a millionaire though he may not look it; **~ no lo creas** ... believe it or not ... **2** (refiriéndose a posibilidades, hipótesis) (+ *subjuntivo*) even if; **iré ~ llueva** I'll go even if it rains

au pair /o'per/ *mf* (*pl* **-pairs**) au pair

aura *f*‡ (halo) aura

aureola *f* **(a)** (Relig) halo, aureole (liter) **(b)** (de gloria, fama) aura **(c)** (Astron) aureole, corona **(d)** (CS) (de mancha) ring

auricular *m* **(a)** (del teléfono) receiver **(b) auriculares** *mpl* (Audio) headphones (*pl*), earphones (*pl*)

aurora *f* dawn

auscultar [A1] *vt* to auscultate (tech); **el médico me auscultó** the doctor listened to my chest (with a stethoscope)

ausencia *f* **(a)** (de persona) absence; ***brillar por su ~*** to be conspicuous by one's absence; **el orden brilla por su ~** there's a distinct lack of order **(b)** (no existencia) lack, absence **(c)** (frml) (inasistencia) absence

ausentarse [A1] *v pron* (frml) to go away; **pidió permiso para ~ un momento** he asked to leave the room (*o* class *etc*)

ausente *adj* [ESTAR] **(a)** (no presente) absent; **todos los alumnos ~s** all those pupils who are absent **(b)** (distraído) ‹*persona*› distracted; ‹*mirada/expresión*› absent (*before n*)

ausentismo *m* absenteeism; **~ escolar** absenteeism, truancy

auspiciar [A1] *vt* **(a)** (patrocinar) ‹*exposición/función*› to back, sponsor **(b)** (propiciar, facilitar) to foster, promote

austeridad *f* austerity

austero -ra *adj* ‹*vida/costumbres/estilo*› austere; **es ~ en el comer** he is frugal in his eating habits

austral *adj* southern

Australia *f* Australia

australiano -na *adj/m,f* Australian

Austria *f*‡ Austria

austriaco -ca, **austríaco -ca** *adj/m,f* Austrian

autenticar [A2] *vt* **(a)** ‹*firma/documento*› to authenticate **(b)** (RPl) ‹*fotocopia*› to attest

autenticidad *f* authenticity

auténtico -ca *adj* **(a)** ‹*cuadro*› genuine, authentic; ‹*perla/piel*› real; ‹*documento*› authentic **(b)** ‹*interés/cariño/persona*› genuine **(c)** ‹*pesadilla/catástrofe*› (*delante del n*) real (*before n*)

autista *adj* autistic

auto *m* **1** (esp CS) (Auto) car, automobile (AmE); **~ de carrera** (CS) racing car; **autitos chocadores** (RPl) bumper cars **2** (Lit, Teatr) play

autoabastecerse [E3] *v pron* to be self-sufficient; **~** DE *or* EN **algo** to be self-sufficient IN sth

autoadhesivo -va *adj* self-adhesive

autobiografía *f* autobiography

autobomba *m* (RPl) water tender, fire engine

autobús *m* bus; **~ de dos pisos** double-decker bus; **~ de línea** (inter-city) bus

autocar *m* (Esp) bus, coach (BrE)

autocine *m* drive-in

autocross *m* autocross

autóctono -na *adj* ‹*flora/fauna*› indigenous, native; **el elefante es ~ de la India** the elephant is indigenous *o* native to India

autodefensa *f* self-defence

autodeterminación *f* self-determination

autodidacta *mf* self-taught person, autodidact (frml)

autodisciplina *f* self-discipline

auto-escuela, **autoescuela** *f* driving school

autoestop *m* ⇨ AUTOSTOP

autoestopista *mf* hitchhiker

autogol *m* own goal

autografiar [A17] *vt* to autograph

autógrafo *m* autograph

autómata *m* automaton

automático[1] -ca *adj* automatic; **es ~, se sienta a ver la tele y se queda dormido** (fam) it happens every time, he sits down in front of the TV and falls asleep

automático[2] *m* **(a)** (Fot) self-timer; (Elec) circuit breaker, trip switch **(b)** (cierre) snap fastener (AmE), press stud (BrE)

automatizado -da *adj* automated

automatizar [A4] *vt* to automate

automercado *m* (AmC) supermarket

automotor¹ -triz *or* **-tora** *adj* (frml) ‹*vehículo/industria*› motor (*before n*)

automotor² *m* (Ferr) railcar (*diesel or electric motor unit*)

automóvil *m* car, automobile (AmE)

automovilismo *m* motoring; **~ deportivo** motor racing

automovilista *mf* motorist

automovilístico -ca *adj* ‹*carrera*› motor (*before n*); ‹*accidente*› car (*before n*)

autonomía *f* **1 (a)** (independencia) autonomy; **obran con ~** they act autonomously **(b)** (en Esp, comunidad autónoma) autonomous region **2** (Aviac, Náut) range

autonómico -ca *adj* **(a)** (independiente) autonomous **(b)** ‹*presidente/elecciones*› (en Esp) regional

autónomo -ma *adj* **(a)** ‹*departamento/entidad*› autonomous **(b)** (Pol) (en Esp) ‹*región*› autonomous **(c)** ‹*trabajador*› self-employed; ‹*fotógrafo/periodista*› freelance ■ *m,f* (trabajador) self-employed worker *o* person; (fotógrafo, periodista) freelancer

autopista *f* expressway (AmE), motorway (BrE); **~ de peaje** *or* (Méx) **de cuota** turnpike (road) (AmE), toll motorway (BrE); **la ~ de la información** (Inf) the information superhighway

autopsia *f* autopsy, post mortem; **hacerle la ~ a algn** to perform an autopsy *o* a post mortem on sb

autor -tora *m,f* **(a)** (de libro, poema) author, writer; (de canción) writer; (de obra teatral) playwright **(b)** (de delito) perpetrator (frml); **el ~ del gol** the goalscorer

autoridad *f* **1 (a)** (poder, competencia) authority **(b)** (persona, institución): **la máxima ~ en el ministerio** the top official in the ministry; **se entregó a las ~es** she gave herself up to the authorities **2** (experto) authority; **una ~ en la materia** an authority on the subject

autoritario -ria *adj* authoritarian

autorización *f* authorization (frml); **los menores necesitan la ~ paterna** minors need their parents' consent; **no tiene ~ de sus padres** he doesn't have his parents' permission

autorizado -da *adj* ‹*fuente/portavoz*› official; ‹*distribuidor*› authorized, official; ‹*opinión*› expert (*before n*)

autorizar [A4] *vt* **(a)** ‹*manifestación/documento/firma*› to authorize; ‹*aumento/pago/obra*› to authorize, approve **(b)** ‹*persona*›: **¿quién te autorizó?** who gave you permission?; **lo autoricé para recibir el pago** I authorized him to receive the payment; **me autorizó para salir** he gave me permission to go out; **eso no te autoriza a** *or* **para hablarme así** that doesn't give you the right to talk to me like that

autorretrato *m* self-portrait

autoservicio *m* (tienda) supermarket; (restaurante) self-service restaurant, cafeteria

autostop, auto-stop /auto'(e)stop/ *m* hitchhiking; **hacer ~** to hitchhike

autosuficiente *adj* **(a)** (Econ) self-sufficient **(b)** (presumido) smug, self-satisfied

autovagón *m* (Per) railcar

autovía *f* divided highway (AmE), dual carriageway (BrE)

auxiliar¹ *adj* **(a)** ‹*profesor*› assistant (*before n*); ‹*personal/elementos*› auxiliary (*before n*) **(b)** ‹*servicios*› auxiliary **(c)** (Tec) auxiliary **(d)** (Inf) peripheral ■ *mf* **(a)** (persona) assistant; **~ de vuelo** flight attendant **(b) auxiliar** *f* (RPl) (Auto) spare tire

auxiliar² [A1] *vt* to help

auxilio *m* **(a)** (ayuda) help; **pedir ~** to ask for help; **~ en carretera** breakdown *o* recovery service; **acudieron en ~ de las víctimas** they went to the aid of the victims **(b)** (RPl) (grúa) recovery *o* breakdown truck

Av. *f* (= **Avenida**) Ave.

aval *m* (Com, Fin) guarantee; (respaldo) backing, support; (recomendación) reference

avalancha *f* avalanche

avalar [A1] *vt* (Com, Fin) ‹*documento*› to guarantee; ‹*persona/préstamo*› to guarantee, act as guarantor for

avaluar [A18] *vt* (AmL) to value

avalúo *m* (AmL) valuation

avance *m* **(a)** (adelanto) advance; **un ~ en este campo** an advance *o* a step forward in this field **(b)** (movimiento) advance; (Mil) advance; (Dep) move forward

avanzar [A4] *vi* **(a)** «*persona/tráfico*» to advance, move forward **(b)** «*ciencia/medicina*» to advance **(c)** «*cinta/rollo*» to wind on **(d)** «*persona*» (en los estudios, el trabajo) to make progress; «*negociaciones/proyecto*» to progress **(e)** «*tiempo*» to draw on ■ **~** *vt* **(a)** (adelantarse) to move forward, advance **(b)** (mover) to move ... forward, advance

avaricia *f* avarice; ***la ~ rompe el saco*** if you're too greedy you end up with nothing

avaricioso -sa, avariento -ta *adj* greedy, avaricious ■ *m,f* greedy *o* avaricious person

avaro -ra *adj* miserly ■ *m,f* miser

avasallador -dora, avasallante *adj* **(a)** ‹*persona/actitud*› domineering, overbearing **(b)** ‹*triunfo*› resounding (*before n*)

Avda. *f* (= **Avenida**) Ave.

ave *f*‡ bird; **~ de corral** fowl; **~ de mal agüero** bird of ill omen; **~ rapaz** *or* **de rapiña** (Zool) bird of prey; (persona) shark

avecinarse [A1] *v pron* to approach

avejentado -da *adj*: **está muy ~** he's aged a lot; **un rostro ~** an old face

avejentar [A1] *vt* to age, make ... look older

avellana *f* hazelnut

avellano *m* hazel

Avemaría *f*‡ (Relig) Hail Mary; (Mús) Ave Maria

avena *f* oats (*pl*)

avenida *f* **(a)** (calle) avenue, boulevard **(b)** (de río) freshet, flood

avenido -da *adj*: **bien ~** well-matched; **es una pareja mal avenida** they don't get on well as a couple

avenirse [I31] *v pron* **(a)** (ponerse de acuerdo) **~se** EN **algo** to agree ON sth **(b)** (llevarse bien) **~se** CON **algn** to get on WITH sb

aventajado -da *adj* outstanding, excellent

aventajar [A1] *vt* (estar por delante de) to be ahead of; (adelantarse) to overtake, get ahead of

aventar [A5] *vt* **(a)** (Col, Méx, Per) ‹*pelota/piedra*› to throw; **le aventé un sopapo** (fam) I smacked *o* (BrE) thumped him (colloq) **(b)** (Méx) (empujar) to push

■ **aventarse** *v pron* **(a)** (Méx fam) (atreverse) to dare; **~se** A **hacer algo** to dare to do sth **(b)** (*refl*) (Col, Méx) (arrojarse, tirarse) to throw oneself; **se aventó al agua** he dived into the water

aventón *m* (Méx) (fam) lift; **darle ~ a algn** to give sb a lift *o* ride; **pedir ~** to hitch *o* thumb a lift; **ir de ~** to go hitching

aventura *f* **(a)** (suceso extraordinario) adventure **(b)** (empresa arriesgada) venture **(c)** (relación amorosa — pasajera) fling; (— ilícita) affair

aventurado -da *adj* risky, hazardous

aventurar [A1] *vt* ‹*opinión*› to venture, put forward; ‹*conjetura*› to hazard

■ **aventurarse** *v pron* to venture; **me ~ía a decir que** ... I would go so far as to say that ...

aventurero -ra *adj* adventurous ■ *m,f* adventurer

avergonzado -da *adj* **(a)** (por algo reprensible) ashamed; **~** POR *or* DE **algo** ashamed OF sth **(b)** (en situación embarazosa) embarrassed

avergonzar [A13] *vt* **(a)** (por algo reprensible): **¿no te avergüenza salir así a la calle?** aren't you ashamed to go out looking like that? **(b)** (en situación embarazosa) to embarrass; **me avergüenza decírselo** I'm embarrassed to tell him

■ **avergonzarse** *v pron* to be ashamed (of oneself); **~se** DE **algo** to be ashamed OF sth; **se avergonzó de haberle mentido** she was ashamed of herself for having lied to him

avergüenza, **avergüenzas, etc** *see* AVERGONZAR

avería *f* (Auto, Mec) breakdown

averiado -da *adj* [ESTAR] ‹*coche/máquina*› broken down; ‹*ascensor/teléfono*› out of order

averiarse [A17] *v pron* to break down

averiguación *f* inquiry

averiguar [A16] *vt* to find out ■ **~** *vi* (Méx) to quarrel, argue; ***averiguárselas*** (Méx) to manage

aversión *f* aversion

avestruz *m* ostrich

aviación *f* (civil) aviation; (Mil) air force

aviador -dora *m,f* (Aviac, Mil) pilot

avícola *adj* poultry (*before n*)

avicultura *f* poultry farming

avidez *f* eagerness, avidity; **lee con ~** he reads avidly

ávido -da *adj* **~** DE **algo** ‹*de noticias/aventuras*› eager FOR sth; ‹*de poder*› hungry FOR sth

avinagrar [A1] *vt* ‹*vino*› to make ... taste vinegary; ‹*carácter*› to make ... sour *o* bitter

■ **avinagrarse** *v pron* «*vino*» to turn *o* go vinegary; «*persona*» to become bitter *o* sour

avión *m* (Aviac) plane, aircraft (frml), airplane (AmE), aeroplane (BrE); **viajar en ~** to fly; Ⓢ **por avión** (Corresp) air mail; **~ a chorro** *or* **a reacción** jet (plane); **~ de combate/de pasajeros** fighter/passenger plane

avionazo *m* (Méx) plane crash

avioneta *f* light aircraft

avisar [A1] *vt* **(a)** (notificar): **¿por qué no me avisaste que venías?** why didn't you let me know you were coming?; **nos han avisado que**... they've notified us that... **(b)** (Esp, Méx) (llamar) to call; **~ al médico** to call the doctor **(c)** (advertir) to warn; **quedas** *or* **estás avisado** you've been warned ■ **~** *vi:* **llegó sin ~** she showed up without any prior warning *o* unexpectedly; **avísame cuando acabes** let me know when you've finished; **~ a algn** DE **algo** to let sb know ABOUT sth

aviso *m* **1 (a)** (notificación) notice; Ⓢ **aviso al público** notice to the public; **dio ~ a la policía** he notified *o* informed the police; **sin previo ~** without prior warning; **último ~ para los pasajeros** ... last call for passengers ... **(b)** (advertencia) warning; ***poner sobre ~ a algn*** to warn sb **(c)** (Cin, Teatr) bell **(d)** (Taur) warning **2** (AmL) (anuncio, cartel) advertisement, ad

avispa *f* wasp

avispado -da *adj* (fam) sharp, bright

avispero *m* (nido) wasps' nest

avivar [A1] *vt* ‹*fuego*› to get ... going; ‹*color*› to make ... brighter; ‹*pasión/deseo*› to arouse; ‹*dolor*› to intensify

■ **avivarse** *v pron* **(a)** «*fuego*» to revive, flare up; «*debate*» to come alive, liven up **(b)** (AmL fam) (despabilarse) to wise up (colloq)

axila *f* ▶ **123** (Anat) armpit, axilla (tech)

axilar *adj* underarm (*before n*)

ay *interj* **(a)** (expresando — dolor) ow!, ouch!; (— susto, sobresalto) oh! **(b)** (expresando aflicción) oh dear! **(c)** (expresando amenaza): **¡~ del que se atreva!** woe betide anyone who tries it!

ayer *adv* (refiriéndose al día anterior) yesterday; **~ hizo un mes** a month ago yesterday; **~ por** *or* (esp AmL) **en la mañana** yesterday morning; **antes de ~** the day before yesterday; **el periódico de ~** yesterday's paper

ayuda *f* (asistencia) help; **nadie acudió en su ~** nobody went to his aid; **~s para la inversión** incentives for investment; **ha sido de gran ~** it has been a great help

ayudante *mf* assistant; **~ de cátedra** assistant professor (AmE), (junior) lecturer (BrE); **~ de cocina** kitchen assistant

ayudar [A1] *vt* to help; **~ al prójimo** to help one's neighbor; **¿te ayudo?** do you need any help?; **vino a ~me** she came to help me out; **ayúdame a poner la mesa** help me (to) set the table ■ **~** *vi* to help; **¿puedo ~ en algo?** can I do anything to help?

ayunar [A1] *vi* to fast

ayunas: **en ~** (*loc adv*): **estoy en ~** I haven't eaten anything; **debe tomarse en ~** it should be taken on an empty stomach

ayuno *m* fast, fasting

ayuntamiento *m* (corporación) town/city council; (edificio) town/city hall

azabache *m* jet; **negro como el ~** jet black

azada *f* hoe

azadón *m* mattock

azafata *f* **1 (a)** (en avión) flight attendant, air hostess; **~ de tierra** ground stewardess **(b)** (en programa, concurso) hostess; **~ de congresos** conference hostess **2** (Per) (bandeja) tray

azafate *m* (AmS) tray

azafrán *m* saffron

azahar *m* (del naranjo) orange blossom; (del limonero) lemon blossom

azar *m* **(a)** (casualidad) chance; **dejar algo al ~** to trust sth to chance; **al ~** at random **(b) azares** *mpl* (vicisitudes) ups and downs (*pl*), vicissitudes (*pl*)

azaroso -sa *adj* ‹*viaje*› hazardous; ‹*proyecto*› risky; ‹*vida*› eventful

Azerbaiyán, Azerbaiján *m* Azerbaijan, Azerbaidzhan

azerbaiyaní *adj/mf* Azerbaijani, Azeri ■ *m* (idioma) Azerbaijani

azorado -da *adj* **(a)** (turbado) embarrassed **(b)** (Col, Méx, RPl) (asombrado) amazed, astonished

azorar [A1] *vt* (turbar) to embarrass ■ **azorarse** *v pron* to get embarrassed

azotador *m* (Méx) caterpillar

azotaina *f* (fam) spanking

azotar [A1] *vt* **1** (con látigo) to whip, flog **2** (Méx) ‹*puerta*› to slam

azote *m* **1 (a)** (látigo) whip, lash; (latigazo) lash **(b)** (fam) (a un niño): **te voy a dar unos ~s** I'm going to spank you **2** (calamidad) scourge

azotea *f* terrace roof, flat roof

azteca *adj/mf* Aztec

azúcar *m or f* sugar; **el nivel de ~ en la sangre** the blood-sugar level; **chicle sin ~** sugar-free gum; **~ blanca** white sugar; **~ en terrones** *or* (RPl) **pancitos** sugar lumps *o* cubes (*pl*); **~ glasé** *or* (Méx) **glas** confectioners sugar (AmE), icing sugar (BrE); **~ lustre/morena** castor*/brown sugar

azucarar [A1] *vt* ‹*café/leche*› to add sugar to; ‹*fruta*› to sprinkle ... with sugar

azucarera *f* **(a)** (AmL) (recipiente) sugar bowl **(b)** (fábrica) sugar refinery

azucarero[1] -ra *adj* ‹*industria*› sugar (*before n*); ‹*zona*› sugar-producing (*before n*)

azucarero[2] *m* sugar bowl

azucena *f* Madonna lily, Annunciation lily

azufre *m* sulfur*

azul *adj/m* ▶ **97** blue; **de un ~ intenso** deep blue; **~ verdoso (a)** *m* greenish blue **(b)** *adj inv* greenish-blue (*before n*); **~ cielo** *or* **celeste (a)** *m* sky blue **(b)** *adj inv* sky-blue (*before n*); **~ marino (a)** *m* navy blue **(b)** *adj inv* navy blue, navy-blue (*before n*)

azulado -da *adj* ▶ **97** bluish

azulejo *m* (glazed ceramic) tile

azuzar [A4] *vt* **(a)** ‹*perros*› to sic; **~le los perros a algn** to set the dogs on sb **(b)** ‹*persona*› to egg ... on

Bb

B, b *f* (*read as* /be ('larɣa)/) *the letter* B, b

baba *f* **(a)** (de niño) dribble, drool (AmE) **(b)** (de adulto) saliva; ***caérsele a algn la ~ por*** *or* ***con algn*** to drool over sb **(c)** (de perro, caballo) slobber; (de caracol) slime

babear [A1] *vi* **(a)** «*persona*» to dribble, drool (AmE) **(b)** «*animal*» to slaver, slobber

babero *m* bib

babor *m* port; **a ~** to port

babosa *f* slug

babosada *f* (AmL fam) drivel; **decir ~s** to talk drivel

baboso -sa *adj* **1** (con babas) slimy **2** (AmL fam) (estúpido) ‹*persona*› dim (colloq); ‹*libro/espectáculo*› ridiculous ■ *m,f* (AmL fam) (tonto) dimwit (colloq)

babucha *f* (zapatilla) slipper

baca *f* roof-rack, luggage-rack

bacalao *m* cod, codfish (AmE); **~ seco** salt cod

bacenilla *f* (Col, Ven) chamber pot

bache *m* **(a)** (Auto) pothole **(b)** (Aviac) air pocket **(c)** (mal momento) bad time *o* (BrE) patch

bachillerato *m* **(a)** (educación secundaria) *secondary education and the qualification obtained*, ≈ high school diploma (*in US*) **(b)** (Per) (licenciatura) bachelor's degree

bacinica *f* (AmL exc RPl fam) chamber pot, potty (colloq)

bacteria *f* bacterium; **~s** bacteria (*pl*)

badén *m* **(a)** (vado) ford **(b)** (depresión) dip

bádminton /'baðminton/ *m* badminton

baffle /'bafle/, **bafle** *m* (altavoz) speaker, loudspeaker

bagaje *m*: **~ cultural** (de persona) cultural knowledge; (de un pueblo) cultural heritage

bagatela *f* (alhaja) trinket; (adorno) knickknack

bah *interj* (expresando — desprecio) huh!, bah!; (— conformidad) oh well!

bahía *f* bay

bailaor -laora *m,f* flamenco dancer

bailar [A1] *vi* **1** (Mús) to dance; **salir a ~** to go out dancing; **la sacó a ~** he asked her to dance **2** «*trompo/peonza*» to spin **3** (fam) (quedar grande) (+ *me/te/le etc*): **estos zapatos me bailan** these shoes are too big for me (colloq) ■ **~** *vt* to dance; **~ un tango** to (dance a) tango

bailarín -rina *m,f* dancer

baile *m* **(a)** (acción) dancing; **abrir el ~** to start the dancing **(b)** (arte, composición, fiesta) dance; **~ de disfraces/máscaras** fancy-dress/masked ball

baja *f* **1** (descenso) fall, drop; **una ~ en los precios** a fall *o* drop in prices; **la ~ de las tasas de interés** the cut in interest rates; **tendencia a la ~** downward trend **2 (a)** (Esp) (Rels Labs) (permiso) sick leave; (certificado) medical certificate; **está (dado) de ~** he's off sick *o* on sick leave; **~ por maternidad** (Esp) maternity leave **(b)** (Dep): **el equipo tiene varias ~s** the team is missing several regulars **(c)** (Mil) (muerte) loss, casualty **3** (en entidad): **darse de ~** (en club) to cancel one's membership, leave; (en partido) to resign, leave; (Mil) (cese) discharge; **dar de ~** to discharge

bajada *f* **1** (acción) descent; **durante la ~** on the way down; **tuvo una ~ de tensión** his blood pressure dropped; **~ de bandera** (en taxi) minimum fare **2 (a)** (pendiente) slope; **una ~ muy empinada** a very steep slope **(b)** (camino): **la ~ a la playa es muy empinada** the path (*o* road *etc*) down to the beach is very steep

bajamar *f* low tide

bajar [A1] *vi* **1 (a)** «*ascensor/persona*» (alejándose) to go down; (acercándose) to come down; **~ por las escaleras** to go/come down the stairs; **ya bajo** I'll be right down **(b)** (apearse) **~ DE algo** ‹*de tren/avión*› to get off sth; ‹*de coche*› to get out OF sth; ‹*de caballo/bicicleta*› to get off sth **(c)** (Dep) «*equipo*» to go down **2 (a)** «*marea*» to go out **(b)** «*fiebre/tensión*» to go down, drop; «*hinchazón*» to go down; «*temperatura*» to fall, drop **(c)** «*precio/valor*» to fall, drop; «*calidad*» to deteriorate; «*popularidad*» to diminish; **~ de precio** to go down in price ■ **~** *vt* **1** ‹*escalera/cuesta*› to go down **2** ‹*brazo/mano*› to put down, lower **3 (a) ~ algo (DE algo)** ‹*de armario/estante*› to get sth down (FROM sth); ‹*del piso de arriba*› (traer) to bring sth down (FROM sth); (llevar) to take sth down (TO sth) **(b) ~ a algn DE algo** ‹*de mesa/caballo*› to get sb off sth **4 (a)** ‹*persiana/telón*› to lower; ‹*ventanilla*› to open **(b)** ‹*cremallera*› to undo **5** ‹*precio*› to lower; ‹*fiebre*› to bring down; ‹*volumen*› to turn down; ‹*voz*› to lower

■ **bajarse** *v pron* **1** (apearse) **~se DE algo** ‹*de tren/autobús*› to get off sth; ‹*de coche*› to get out OF sth; ‹*de caballo/bicicleta*› to get off sth; ‹*de pared/árbol*› to get down off sth **2** ‹*pantalones*› to take down; ‹*falda*› to pull down

bajativo *m* (CS) liqueur, digestif

bajío *m* **(a)** (zona poco profunda) shallows (*pl*); (banco de arena) sandbank **(b)** (AmL) (terreno bajo) low-lying area

bajista *mf* bass player, bassist

bajo[1] -ja *adj* **1** [SER] ‹*persona*› short **2 (a)** [SER] ‹*techo*› low; ‹*tierras*› low-lying **(b)** [ESTAR] ‹*lámpara/cuadro/nivel*› low; **la marea está baja** the tide is out; **están ~s de moral** their morale is low; **está ~ de defensas** his defenses are low **3 (a)** ‹*calificación/precio/temperatura*› low; **~ en calorías** low-calorie; **de baja calidad** poor-quality **(b)** ‹*volumen/luz*› low; **en voz baja** quietly, in a low voice **4** (grave) ‹*tono/voz*› deep, low **5** (vil) ‹*acción/instinto*› low, base; **los ~s fondos** *mpl* the underworld

bajo[2] *adv* **(a)** ‹*volar/pasar*› low **(b)** ‹*hablar/cantar*› softly, quietly; **¡habla más ~!** keep your voice down! ■ *m* **1 (a)** (planta baja) first (AmE) *o* (BrE) ground floor **(b) los bajos** (CS) the first (AmE) *o* (BrE) ground floor **2** (contrabajo) (double) bass ■ *prep* under; **~ techo** under cover, indoors; **tres grados ~ cero** three degrees below zero; **~ juramento** under oath

bajón *m* (fam) **(a)** (descenso fuerte) sharp drop *o* fall **(b)** (de ánimo) depression

bajorrelieve *m* bas-relief

bala *f* **1** (Arm) (de pistola, rifle) bullet; (de cañón) cannon ball; **~ de fogueo** blank (round *o* cartridge); **~ de goma/plástico** rubber/plastic bullet; **a prueba de ~s** bulletproof; **una ~ perdida** a stray bullet; ***como (una) ~*** ‹*salir/entrar*› like a shot (colloq) **2** (AmL) (Dep) shot; **lanzamiento de ~** shot put

balaca *f* (Col) **(a)** (Indum) hair-band **(b)** (Dep) sweat-band, headband

balacera *f* (AmL) shooting

balada *f* ballad

balance *m* **1 (a)** (resumen, valoración) assessment, evaluation; **hacer ~ DE algo** to take stock OF sth, to evaluate sth **(b)** (resultado) result, outcome **2** (Com, Fin) (cálculo, cómputo) balance; (documento) balance sheet; (de cuenta) balance

balancear [A1] *vt* **1** ‹*paquetes/carga*› to balance **2** ‹*pierna/brazo*› to swing; ‹*barco*› to rock

■ **balancearse** *v pron* **(a)** «*árbol/ramas*» to sway; «*objeto colgante*» to swing **(b)** «*barco*» to rock

balanceo *m* (de hamaca) swinging; (de árboles) swaying; (de barco) rocking

balancín *m* (de niños) seesaw, teeter-totter (AmE)

balanza *f* scales (*pl*); (de dos platillos) scales (*pl*), balance; **~ comercial/de pagos** balance of trade/of payments; ***poner en la ~*** to weigh (AmE), to weigh up (BrE)

balar [A1] *vi* to bleat, baa

balazo *m* (Arm) (tiro) shot; (herida) bullet wound; **recibió un ~** he was shot

balboa *m* balboa (*Panamanian unit of currency*)

balbucear [A1] *vt* to stammer ■ **~** *vi* «*adulto*» to mutter, mumble; «*bebé*» to babble

balbuceo *m* (de adulto) mumbling, muttering; (de bebé) babble

balcón *m* balcony

balde *m* **1** (cubo) bucket, pail; ***caer como un ~ de agua fría*** to come as a complete shock **2** (*en locs*) **de balde** ‹*trabajar/viajar*› for nothing, for free; **en balde** in vain

baldío[1] -día *adj* **(a)** (sin cultivar): **terreno ~** waste land **(b)** ‹*esfuerzo*› vain, useless

baldío² *m* **(a)** (terreno sin cultivar) area of waste land **(b)** (Bol, Méx, RPl) (solar) piece *o* plot of land, vacant lot (AmE)

baldosa *f* floor tile; **suelo de ~s** tiled floor

baldosín *m* tile

balear [A1] *vt* (AmL) to shoot; **murió baleado** he was shot dead

baleo *m* (AmL) shooting

balero *m* (Méx, RPl) (juguete) *cup-and-ball toy*

balido *m* bleat, baa

balín *m* (perdigón) pellet; (bala pequeña) shot

balística *f* ballistics

baliza *f* **(a)** (boya) buoy; (señal fija) marker **(b)**(Aviac) beacon

ballena *f* (Zool) whale

ballenato *m* whale calf

ballenero -ra *m,f* **(a)** (persona) whaler **(b) ballenero** *m* (barco) whaleboat, whaler

ballet /ba'le/ *m* (*pl* **-llets**) ballet

balneario *m* **1** (de baños medicinales) spa **2** (AmL) (núcleo residencial) seaside resort, (holiday) resort

balompié *m* soccer, football (BrE)

balón *m* **(a)** (Dep) ball **(b)** (recipiente) cylinder; **~ de oxígeno** oxygen cylinder

baloncesto *m* basketball

balonmano *m* handball

balonvolea *m* volleyball

balsa *f* (embarcación) raft; **~ inflable/salvavidas** inflatable/life raft

bálsamo *m* **(a)** (Farm, Med) balsam, balm **(b)** (Chi) (para el pelo) conditioner

baluarte *m* bastion

bambalina *f* (Teatr) drop (curtain); ***entre ~s*** behind the scenes

bambolearse *v pron* «*persona/árbol/torre*» to sway; «*objeto colgante*» to swing; «*barco/tren*» to rock; «*avión/ascensor*» to lurch

bambú *m* (*pl* **-búes** *or* **-bús**) bamboo

banal *adj* banal

banana *f* (Per, RPl) banana

bananal, **bananar** *m* (AmL) banana plantation

bananero¹ -ra *adj* (AmL) banana (*before n*)

bananero² *m* (AmL) banana tree

banano *m* (árbol) banana tree; (fruta) (AmC, Col) banana

banca *f* **1 la ~** (sector) banking; (bancos) the banks **2** (AmL) **(a)** (asiento) bench; (pupitre) desk **(b)** (Dep) (asiento) bench; (jugadores) substitutes (*pl*)

bancario -ria *adj* ‹*interés/préstamo*› bank (*before n*); ‹*sector*› banking (*before n*)

bancarrota *f* bankruptcy; **en ~** bankrupt; **ir a la ~** to go bankrupt

banco *m* **1 (a)** (de parque) bench; (de iglesia) pew; (de barca) thwart; (pupitre) (Chi) desk **(b)** (de carpintero) workbench **2** (Com, Fin) bank; (de órganos, sangre) bank; (de información) bank; **~ de datos** data base *o* bank **3** (de peces) shoal; (bajío) bar, bank; **~ de arena** sandbank

banda *f* **1** (en la cintura, cruzando el pecho) sash; (franja, lista) band; (para pelo) (Méx) hair-band; (en brazo) armband; **~ sonora** (Cin) sound track; **~ transportadora** (Méx) conveyor belt **2** (de barco) side; (en billar) cushion; (en fútbol, rugby) touchline; **saque de ~** (en fútbol) throw-in; (en rugby) put-in **3 (a)** (de delincuentes) gang; **(b)** (Mús) band

bandada *f* (de pájaros) flock; (de peces) shoal

bandazo *m*: ***dar ~s*** «*equipaje*» to move about; «*coche*» to swerve about

bandeja *f* tray; ***servirle algo a algn en ~*** to hand sb sth on a platter (AmE) *o* (BrE) plate

bandera *f* **(a)** (de nación, club) flag; (de regimiento) colors* (*pl*); **izar la ~** to run up *o* raise the flag; **arriar la ~** to lower *o* strike the flag **(b)** (para señales) flag, pennant; **~ ajedrezada** *or* **a cuadros** checkered* flag **(c)** (de taxi): **bajar la ~** to start the meter **(d)** (Inf) flag

banderilla *f* (Taur) banderilla (*barbed dart stuck into the bull's neck*)

banderillero *m* banderillero (*person who sticks the banderillas into the bull's neck*)

banderín *m* (banderita triangular) pennant; (Dep) flag

banderola *f* (enseña) banderole

bandido -da *m,f* (delincuente) bandit; (granuja) crook; (pícaro) rascal

bando *m* **1** (edicto) edict **2** (facción) side, camp; **están en ~s contrarios** they're on opposing sides

bandolera *f* (cinturón) Sam Browne (belt); (para cartuchos) bandolier; **en ~** slung across one's shoulder

bandolero -ra *m,f* bandit

bandoneón *m*: *type of accordion*

banjo /'bandʒo/ *m* banjo

banquero -ra *m,f* banker

banqueta *f* **(a)** (taburete) stool; (para los pies) footstool **(b)** (Méx) (acera) sidewalk (AmE), pavement (BrE)

banquete *m* banquet; **~ de bodas/de gala** wedding/gala reception

banquillo *m* **(a)** (Der): **el ~ (de los acusados)** the dock **(b)** (Dep) bench

banquina *f* (RPl) (en autopista) shoulder (AmE), hard shoulder (BrE); (cuneta) ditch

bañado -da *adj* (Bol, RPl) **~ EN algo** (en sangre/sudor) covered WITH sth; ‹*en lágrimas*› bathed IN sth; **~ en oro/plata** gold-/silver-plated

bañador *m* (Esp) (de mujer) bathing suit (esp AmE), swimming costume (BrE); (de hombre) swimming trunks

bañar [A1] *vt* **1** ‹*niño/enfermo*› to bath, give ... a bath **2** ‹*pulsera/cubierto*› to plate
■ **bañarse** *v pron* (*refl*) **(a)** (en bañera) to have *o* take a bath, to bathe (AmE) **(b)** (en mar, río) to swim, bathe

bañera *f* bath, bathtub

bañero -ra *m,f* (RPl) lifeguard

bañista *mf* bather

baño *m*

■ **Nota** Con referencia al cuarto de baño de una casa particular, el inglés americano emplea normalmente *bathroom*. El inglés británico emplea *toilet*, *lavatory* o (coloquialmente) *loo*. Cuando se habla de los servicios de un edificio público, el inglés americano utiliza *washroom*, *restroom*, *men's room* o *ladies' room*. El inglés británico emplea *the Gents*, *the ladies*, o *the toilets*. En la calle y en los parques públicos se emplea *public toilets*, o en inglés británico más formal, *public conveniences*.

1 (en bañera) bath; (en mar, río) swim; **darse un ~** to have a bath/to go for a swim; **~ de sangre** bloodbath; **~s públicos** public baths (*pl*); **~ turco** Turkish bath **2 (a)** (bañera) bath **(b)** (esp AmL) (en casa privada) bathroom (AmE), toilet (BrE); (en edificio público) restroom (AmE), toilet (BrE) **~ público** (AmL) public toilet **3** (de metal) plating

baptista *adj* Baptist (*before n*) ■ *mf* Baptist

baqueta *f* **(a)** (Arm) ramrod **(b)** (Mús) drumstick

baquiano -na *m,f* (AmL) guide

bar *m* (local) bar; (mueble) liquor cabinet (AmE), drinks cabinet (BrE)

baraja *f* deck *o* (BrE) pack (of cards)

barajar [A1] *vt* **1** ‹*cartas*› to shuffle **2** ‹*nombres/posibilidades*› to consider, look at; ‹*cifras*› to talk about, mention

baranda, ((Esp)) **barandilla** *f* (de balcón) rail; (de escalera) handrail, banister

barata *f* **1** (Chi) (cucaracha) cockroach **2** (Méx) (liquidación) sale

baratija *f* (alhaja) trinket; (adorno) knickknack

barato¹ -ta *adj* **(a)** ‹*vestido/restaurante/viaje*› cheap, low-priced **(b)** (como adv) ‹*costar/comprar*› cheap

barato² *adv* ‹*comer/vivir*› cheaply; **se compra más ~ en el mercado** you can get things cheaper in the market

barba *f* ▶ 123 **(a)** (de quien se la afeita) stubble; **una ~ de dos días** two days' growth of stubble **(b)** (de quien se la deja) beard; **dejarse (la) ~** to grow a beard; **un hombre con ~** a man with a beard; ***hacerle la ~ a algn*** (Méx fam) to suck up to sb (colloq) **(c)** (mentón, barbilla) chin

barbacoa *f* **(a)** (parrilla) barbecue; (carne) barbecued meat **(b)** (Méx) *meat roasted in an oven dug in the earth*

barbaridad *f* **(a)** (acto atroz) atrocity **(b)** (disparate): **pagar tanto es una ~** it's madness to pay that much; **lo que hiciste/dijiste es una ~** what you did/said is outrageous; **es capaz de cualquier ~** he's quite capable of doing something really terrible *o* stupid; **¡qué ~!** good heavens!; ***una ~*** (fam) ‹*comer*› like a horse; ‹*fumar*› like a chimney; ‹*pagar/costar*› a fortune

barbarie *f* (de tribu, pueblo) barbarism, savagery; (brutalidad) barbarity

barbarismo *m* (extranjerismo) loan word, borrowing; (solecismo) barbarism

bárbaro¹ -ra *adj* **1** (Hist) barbarian **2** (bruto): **el muy ~ la hizo llorar** the brute made her cry; **no seas ~, no se lo digas** don't be crass *o* cruel, don't tell him **3** (fam) (como intensificador) ‹*casa/coche*› fantastic; **tengo un hambre bárbara** I'm starving

bárbaro² *adv* (fam): **lo pasamos ~** we had a fantastic time (colloq)

bárbaro³ -ra *m,f* **1** (Hist) Barbarian **2** (fam) (bruto) lout, thug

barbecho *m* (estado): **dejar la tierra en ~** to leave the land fallow; ***estar en ~*** (CS) to be in preparation

barbería *f* barber's (shop)

barbero¹ *m* barber

barbero² -ra *m,f* (Méx fam) toady

barbilampiño *adj*: **un hombre ~** a man with a light beard

barbilla *f* chin

barbitúrico *m* barbiturate

barbudo *m* bearded man, man with a beard

barca *f* boat; **~ de remos** rowboat (AmE), rowing boat (BrE)

barcaza *f* (en canales, ríos) barge; (entre barco y tierra) lighter

barco *m* (Náut) boat; (grande) ship, vessel (frml); **un viaje en ~** a journey by sea (*o* river *etc*); **ir/viajar en ~** to go/travel by boat/ship; **~ de guerra** warship; **~ de vapor** steamboat, steamer; **~ de vela** sailing boat, sailboat (AmE)

barda *f* (Méx) (de cemento) wall; (de madera) fence

barítono -na *adj/m* baritone

barman /ˈbarman/ *m* (*pl* **-mans**) barman, bartender (AmE)

barniz *m* **(a)** (para madera) varnish **(b)** (de cultura, educación) veneer; **~ de** *or* **para las uñas** nail polish (AmE), nail varnish (esp BrE

barnizar [A4] *vt* to varnish

barómetro *m* barometer

barón *m* (título nobiliario) baron; (de organización) influential member

baronesa *f* baroness

barquero -ra (*m*) boatman; (*f*) boatwoman

barquilla *f* (de globo) basket, carriage; (Náut) log

barquillo *m* (galleta) wafer; (cono) ice-cream cone *o* (BrE) cornet

barra *f* **1 (a)** (de armario) rail; (para cortinas) rod, pole; (de bicicleta) crossbar **(b)** (de oro, jabón, chocolate) bar; (de turrón, helado) block; (de desodorante) stick; (de pan) (Esp, Méx) stick, French loaf; **~ de labios** lipstick **2 (a)** (banda, franja) bar **(b)** (Mús) bar (line) **(c)** (signo de puntuación) oblique, slash **3** (para ballet, gimnasia) bar; **~ fija** horizontal bar; **~s asimétricas/paralelas** asymmetric/parallel bars (*pl*) **4** (de bar, cafetería) bar **5** (AmL fam) **(a)** (de hinchas, seguidores) supporters (*pl*) **(b)** (de amigos) gang (colloq)

barrabasada *f* (fam) prank; **hacer ~s** to play pranks

barraca *f* **(a)** (puesto) stall; (caseta) booth **(b)** (Mil) barrack hut **(c)** (casa) adobe house (*typical of Valencia and Murcia*) **(d)** (CS) (de materiales de construcción) builders merchant *o* yard

barranca *f*, **barranco** *m* (barranco) gully; (más profundo) ravine

barrena *f* (punzón) gimlet; (taladro, perforadora) drill

barrenar [A1] *vt* (perforar) to drill; (volar) ‹*roca*› to blast

barrendero -ra *m,f* road sweeper, street cleaner

barreno *m* (barrena) drill; (para explosivo) shot hole

barrer [E1] *vt* **1** ‹*suelo/cocina*› to sweep **2 (a)** (arrastrar) to sweep away **(b)** ‹*rival*› to thrash, trounce ■ ~ *vi* **1** (con escoba) to sweep **2** (arrasar) «*equipo/candidato*» to sweep to victory; ~ CON **algo** ‹*con premios/medallas*› to walk off WITH sth; **la inundación barrió con todo** the flood swept everything away; **barrió con todos los premios** she walked off with all the prizes
■ **barrerse** *v pron* (Méx) «*vehículo*» to skid; (en fútbol, béisbol) to slide

barrera *f* barrier; ~ **de peaje** toll barrier; ~ **generacional** generation gap; ~ **idiomática** language barrier

barriada *f* **(a)** (barrio) area, district (*often poor or working-class*) **(b)** (AmL) (barrio marginal) slum area, shantytown

barrial *m* (AmL) quagmire

barricada *f* barricade

barriga *f* ▶ **123** (fam) (vientre) belly (colloq), tummy (colloq); **dolor de** ~ bellyache (colloq), tummy ache (colloq); **echar** ~ to develop a paunch *o* (colloq) gut

barrigón -gona *adj* (fam): **se está volviendo barrigona** she's getting a bit of a belly *o* tummy (colloq); **un viejo** ~ an old man with a paunch

barril *m* barrel; (de pólvora, cerveza) keg; ***ser un ~ sin fondo*** (AmL fam) to be a bottomless pit (colloq)

barrio *m* **(a)** (zona) neighborhood*; **la gente del** ~ people in the neighborhood, local people; **el mercado del** ~ the local market; ~ **alto** (Chi) smart neighborhood; ~ **chino** (Esp) red-light district; ~ **espontáneo** (AmC) shantytown; ~**s bajos** poor neighborhoods (*pl*); ~ **de invasión** (Col) shantytown **(b)** (de las afueras) suburb

barriobajero -ra *adj* (pey) common (pej)

barrizal *m* quagmire, muddy area

barro *m* (lodo) mud; (Art) clay, earthenware (*before n*)

barroco -ca *adj* ‹*estilo*› baroque; (recargado) overelaborate

barrote *m* (de celda, ventana) bar; (en carpintería) crosspiece

bartola *f*: ***echarse a la ~*** (fam) (estar sin trabajar) to laze about

bártulos *mpl* (fam) gear (colloq), stuff (colloq)

barullo *m* (alboroto) racket (colloq), ruckus (AmE); (desorden) muddle, mess

basar [A1] *vt* ‹*teoría/idea*› ~ **algo** EN **algo** to base sth ON sth
■ **basarse** *v pron* **(a)** «*persona*» ~**se** EN **algo**: **¿en qué te basas para decir eso?** and what basis *o* grounds do you have for saying that?; **se basó en esos datos** he based his argument (*o* theory *etc*) on that information **(b)** «*teoría/creencia/idea/opinión*» ~**se** EN **algo** to be based ON sth

báscula *f* scales (*pl*); ~ **de baño** bathroom scales

base *f* **1 (a)** (parte inferior) base **(b)** *tb* ~ **de maquillaje** foundation **2 (a)** (fundamento) basis; **la** ~ **de una buena salud** the basis of good health; **tengo suficiente** ~ **para asegurar eso** I have sufficient grounds to claim that; **sentar las** ~**s de algo** to lay the foundations of sth; **tomar algo como** ~ to take sth as a starting point **(c)** (conocimientos básicos): **tiene una sólida** ~ **científica** he has a sound grounding in science; **llegó al curso sin ninguna** ~ he didn't have the basics when he began the course; ~ **de datos** database **3** (*en locs*) **a base de**: **un régimen a** ~ **de verdura** a vegetable-based diet; **vive a** ~ **de pastillas** he lives on pills **4** (centro de operaciones) base; ~ **aérea/naval/militar** air/naval/military base **5 bases** *fpl* (de concurso) rules (*pl*) **6 (a)** (en béisbol) base **(b)** **base** *mf* (en baloncesto) guard

básica *f* (Esp) primary *o* elementary education

básico -ca *adj* **(a)** (fundamental, esencial) basic; **alimento** ~ staple food **(b)** ‹*requisito*› essential, fundamental

basílica *f* basilica

basket, **básquet** *m* basketball

básquetbol, **basquetbol** *m* (AmL) basketball

basquetbolista *mf* (AmL) basketball player

bastante *adj* ▶ **54** **(a)** (suficiente) enough; ~**s vasos**/~ **vino** enough glasses/wine **(b)** (cantidad considerable) plenty of, quite a lot of; **había** ~ **gente**/~**s coches** there were plenty of people/cars ■ *pron* **1** (suficiente) enough; **ya tenemos** ~**s** we already have enough **2** (demasiado): **deja** ~ **que desear** it leaves rather a lot to be desired ■ *adv* **1** (suficientemente) enough; **no te has esforzado** ~ you haven't tried hard enough **2** (considerablemente) (*con verbos*) quite a lot; (*con adjetivos, adverbios*) quite; **le gusta bastante** she likes him quite a lot; **me pareció** ~ **agradable/aburrido** I thought he was quite pleasant/rather boring

bastar [A1] *vi* to be enough; **¿basta con esto?** will this be enough?; **basta con marcar el 101** just dial 101; **¡basta ya!** that's enough!; (+ *me/te/le etc*) **me basta con tu palabra** your word is good enough for me

bastardilla *f* italic type, italics (*pl*)

bastardo -da *adj* **(a)** (ilegítimo) illegitimate **(b)** (innoble) base ■ *m,f* bastard

bastidor *m* (Teatr) wing; ***entre ~es*** behind the scenes

basto -ta *adj* coarse

bastón *m* (para caminar) walking stick, cane; (en desfiles) baton; (de esquí) ski stick *o* pole

basura *f* **(a)** (recipiente) garbage *o* trash can (AmE), dustbin (BrE); **echar** *or* **tirar algo a la** ~ to throw sth in the garbage *o* trash (can) *o* dustbin **(b)** (desechos) garbage (AmE), trash (AmE), rubbish (BrE); (en sitios públicos) litter; **sacar la** ~ to take out the garbage *o* trash *o* rubbish **(c)** (fam) (porquería) trash (AmE colloq), rubbish (BrE colloq)

basural *m* (AmL) ⇒ BASURERO 2(a)

basurero -ra *m,f* **1** (persona) garbage collector (AmE), dustman (BrE) **2 (a) basurero** *m* (vertedero)

Bastante

Algunas observaciones generales respecto del adjetivo

Cuando bastante *tiene el sentido de* suficiente, *se traduce por* enough:

tenemos bastantes sillas/ bastante leche	=	we have enough chairs/milk

Respecto del adverbio

Cuando bastante tiene el sentido de suficientemente, lo suficiente, *se traduce por* enough:

no sales bastante	=	you don't go out enough
las cerezas no están bastante maduras	=	the cherries are not ripe enough
no estudiaste bastante	=	you didn't study enough

Cuando bastante *va seguido de* para *y tiene el sentido de* demasiado, *se traduce por* rather:

es bastante mayor para tener hijos	=	she's rather old to have children
¿no crees que eres bastante mayorcito para estas cosas?	=	don't you think you're rather old to be doing things like that?

Cuando se emplea para atenuar un juicio, suele traducirse por quite:

toca el violín bastante bien	=	she plays the violin quite well
suele hacer bastante frío	=	it's usually quite cold
es bastante alto para su edad	=	he's quite tall for his age

Nótese que otras posibles traducciones en este caso son fairly *y* pretty

Para el pronombre, otros usos y ejemplos, véase entrada

garbage dump (AmE), rubbish dump *o* tip (BrE); **(b)** (recipiente) (Chi, Méx) trash can (AmE), dustbin (BrE)

bata *f* (para estar en casa) dressing gown, robe; (de médico) white coat; (de colegio) work coat (AmE), overall (BrE)

batahola *f* (esp AmL fam) racket, din, ruckus (AmE)

batalla *f* battle; **librar ~** to do battle; **~ campal** pitched battle; **de ~** (fam) ‹*zapatos/abrigo*› everyday (*before n*)

batallar [A1] *vi* **(a)** (luchar) to battle; **~ CON algn/algo** (lidiar) to battle WITH sb/sth **(b)** (Mil) to fight

batallón *m* (Mil) battalion

batata *f* sweet potato, yam

bate *m* (en béisbol, cricket) bat

batea *f* **(a)** (bandeja) tray **(b)** (AmL) (recipiente) shallow pan *o* tray (*for washing*)

bateador -dora *m,f* (en béisbol, softbol) batter; (en cricket) batsman

batear [A1] *vi* to bat ■ **~** *vt* to hit

batería *f* **1** (Auto) battery; **se me descargó la ~** my battery went dead (AmE) *o* (BrE) flat **2 (a)** (Mús) drums (*pl*), drum kit **(b) batería** *mf* drummer

baterista *mf* (AmL) drummer

batido *m* (de leche) (milk) shake; (para panqueques) (AmL) batter

batidor *m* **(a)** (manual) whisk, beater; (eléctrico) mixer, blender **(b) batidora** *f* (máquina eléctrica) mixer, blender

batir [I1] *vt* **1** ‹*huevos*› to beat, whisk; ‹*crema/nata*› to whip; ‹*mantequilla*› to churn **2** ‹*marca/récord*› to break; ‹*enemigo/rival*› to beat **3 (a)** ‹*ala*› to beat, flap **(b) ~ palmas** to clap
■ **batirse** *v pron* **1** (enfrentarse): **~se a** *or* **en duelo** to fight a duel **2** (Méx) (ensuciarse) to get dirty; **llegó todo batido de lodo** he arrived all covered in mud

batracio *m* batrachian

batuta *f* baton; ***llevar la ~*** (fam) to be the boss (colloq)

baúl *m* (arca) chest; (de viaje) trunk; (del coche, carro) (Col, Ven, RPl) trunk (AmE), boot (BrE)

bautismo *m* (de bebé) baptism, christening; (de adulto) baptism

bautizar [A4] *vt* **(a)** (Relig) ‹*bebé*› to baptize, christen; ‹*adulto*› to baptize; **la ~ron con el nombre de Ana** she was christened Ana **(b)** ‹*barco*› to name

bautizo *m* **(a)** (de bebé) christening, baptism; (de adulto) baptism; (fiesta) christening party **(b)** (de barco) naming, launching

bayeta *f* **(a)** (para limpiar) cloth **(b)** (Bol, Col) (tela) baize

bayoneta *f* bayonet

bazar *m* **(a)** (mercado oriental) bazaar **(b)** (tienda) hardware store (*often selling a wide range of electrical goods and toys*)

bazo *m* ▶ 123 spleen

bazofia *f* (fam) (comida) crap (colloq); (libro, película) garbage (AmE colloq), rubbish (BrE colloq)

bazooka /ba'suka, ba'θuka/, **bazuca** *f* bazooka

be *f*: *name of the letter* b, *often called* BE LARGA *or* GRANDE *to distinguish it from* v

beato -ta *adj* (Relig) blessed; (piadoso) pious; (santurrón) (pey) excessively devout

bebe -ba *m,f* (RPl, Per) baby

bebé *m* baby; **~ probeta** test-tube baby

bebedero *m* (paraje) watering hole; (recipiente) trough; (para personas) (CS, Méx) drinking fountain

bebedor -dora *m,f* drinker; **un ~ empedernido** a hardened drinker

beber [E1] *vt/vi* to drink; **¿quieres ~ algo?** do you want something to drink?; **~ a sorbos** to sip; **~ a la salud de algn** to drink sb's *o* (BrE) to sb's health; **~ POR algn** to drink TO sb/sth
■ **beberse** *v pron* (*enf*) to drink up; **nos bebimos la botella entera** we drank the whole bottle

bebida *f* (líquido) drink, beverage (frml); (vicio) drink

bebido -da *adj* [ESTAR] (borracho) drunk

beca *f* (ayuda económica) grant; (que se otorga por méritos) scholarship

becado -da *m,f* (AmL) ⇒ BECARIO

becar [A2] *vt* (dar ayuda económica) to give *o* (frml) award a grant to; (dar beca por méritos) to give *o* (frml) award a scholarship to

becario -ria *m,f* recipient of a grant; (por méritos) scholarship holder, scholar

becerro -rra *m,f* calf, young bull; (piel) calfskin

bedel *mf* ≈ porter

beduino -na *adj/m,f* bedouin

beige, (Esp) **beis** /beʒ, beis/ *adj inv/m* ▶ 97 beige

béisbol, (Méx) **beisbol** *m* baseball

belén *m* nativity scene, crib, crèche (AmE)

Belén *m* Bethlehem

belga *adj/mf* Belgian

Bélgica *f* Belgium

bélico -ca *adj* ‹*conflicto/material*› military; **preparativos ~s** preparations for war

belicosidad *f* aggressiveness

belicoso -sa *adj* ‹*pueblo*› warlike; ‹*persona/carácter*› bellicose, belligerent

beligerante *adj* belligerent; **los países ~s** the belligerent *o* warring nations

bellaco -ca *m,f* (fam & hum) rogue (colloq & hum)

belleza *f* **(a)** (cualidad) beauty **(b)** (mujer bella) beauty **(c)** (cosa bella): **este paisaje es una ~** this is beautiful countryside

bello -lla *adj* **(a)** ‹*mujer/paisaje/poema*› (liter) beautiful; ***ser una bella persona*** to be a good person **(b)** (Art) **bellas artes** *fpl* fine art

bellota *f* acorn

bemba *f* (AmL fam) thick lips (*pl*)

bemol *adj* flat; **si ~** B flat

bencina *f* **(a)** (Quím) benzine, petroleum ether **(b)** (Andes) (gasolina) gasoline (AmE), petrol (BrE)

bencinera *f* (Andes) filling station, gas station (AmE), petrol station (BrE)

bencinero -ra *m,f* (Andes) filling station attendant

bendecir [I25] *vt* to bless; **¡que Dios te bendiga!** God bless you!; **~ la mesa** to say grace

bendice, etc *see* BENDECIR

bendición *f* **(a)** (Relig) blessing, benediction **(b)** (aprobación) blessing; (regalo divino) godsend

bendiga, bendijo, etc *see* BENDECIR

bendito -ta *adj* **(a)** (Relig) blessed; **¡~ sea Dios!** (expresando contrariedad) good God *o* grief!; (expresando alivio) thank God! **(b)** ‹*agua/pan*› holy ■ *m,f* simple soul

benedictino -na *adj/m,f* Benedictine

benefactor -tora *m,f* benefactor

beneficencia *f* (caridad) charity; **asociación/obra de ~** charitable organization/work

beneficiar [A1] *vt* (favorecer) to benefit, to be of benefit to; **esto beneficia a ambas partes** this benefits both sides; **salir beneficiados con algo** to be better off with sth
■ **beneficiarse** *v pron* to benefit; **~se CON/DE algo** to benefit FROM sth

beneficiario -ria *m,f* beneficiary; (de cheque) payee

beneficio *m* **(a)** (Com, Fin) profit; **producir** *or* **reportar ~s** to yield *o* bring returns *o* profits **(b)** (ventaja, bien) benefit; **a ~ de** in aid of; **en ~ de todos** in the interests of everyone

beneficioso -sa *adj* beneficial

benéfico -ca *adj* ‹*influencia*› benign, beneficial; ‹*espectáculo*› charity (*before n*), benefit (*before n*)

beneplácito *m* approval

benevolencia *f* (indulgencia) leniency, indulgence; (bondad) kindness, benevolence (frml)

benevolente, **benévolo -la** *adj* (indulgente) lenient, indulgent; (bondadoso) kind, benevolent (frml)

bengala *f* flare

benigno -na *adj* ‹*clima/invierno*› mild; ‹*tumor*› benign

benjamín -mina *m,f* (*m*) youngest son, (*f*) youngest daughter

beodo -da *adj* (frml *o* hum) inebriated (frml *or* hum) ■ *m,f* (frml *o* hum) drunkard, toper (liter *o* hum)

berberecho *m* cockle

berenjena *f* eggplant (AmE), aubergine (BrE)

Berlín *m* Berlin

berlinés -nesa *adj* of/from Berlin ■ *m,f* Berliner

berma *f* (Andes) (de asfalto) shoulder (AmE), hard shoulder (BrE); (de tierra) verge

bermudas *fpl or mpl* Bermuda shorts (*pl*)

Bermudas *fpl*: **las ~** Bermuda; **el triángulo de las ~** the Bermuda Triangle

berrear [A1] *vi* «*becerro/ciervo*» to bellow

berrido *m* (de becerro, ciervo) bellow

berrinche *m* (fam) tantrum; **le dio un** *or* (Méx) **hizo un ~** he threw *o* had a tantrum

berro *m* watercress

besar [A1] *vt* to kiss
■ **besarse** *v pron* (*recipr*) to kiss (each other)

beso *m* kiss; **darle un ~ a algn** to give sb a kiss

bestia *adj* (fam) **(a)** (grosero) rude **(b)** (violento, brusco): **¡qué hombre más ~! ha vuelto a pegarle** what a brute *o* an animal! he's hit her again ■ *f* beast; **~ salvaje** *or* **feroz** wild animal ■ *mf* (persona violenta) animal, brute

bestial *adj* (fam) (muy grande): **tengo un hambre ~** I'm starving; **hace un frío ~** it's incredibly cold

best-seller /bes'seler/ *m* (*pl* **-llers**) best-seller

besugo *m* (Coc, Zool) red bream

besuquear [A1] *vt* (fam) to smother ... with kisses

■ **besuquearse** *v pron* (*recípr*) (fam) to neck (colloq)

betabel *m* (Méx) beet, beetroot (BrE)

betún *m* (para calzado) shoe polish; **dales ~ a esos zapatos** give those shoes a polish

bianual *adj* biannual

biberón *m* (baby's *o* feeding) bottle; **hay que darle el ~** I have to give the baby his bottle *o* feed

biblia *f* bible

bíblico -ca *adj* biblical

bibliografía *f* (en libro, informe) bibliography; (para curso) booklist

biblioteca *f* **(a)** (institución, lugar) library; **~ pública/de consulta** public/reference library **(b)** (colección) book collection **(c)** (mueble) bookshelves (*pl*), bookcase

bibliotecario -ria *m,f* librarian

bicameral *adj* bicameral (frml)

bicampeón -peona *m,f* twice champion

bicarbonato *m* bicarbonate

bicentenario *m* bicentenary

bíceps *m* (*pl* ~) biceps

bicho *m* **1** (fam) **(a)** (insecto) bug (colloq), creepy-crawly (colloq) **(b)** (animal) animal, creature; **me picó** *or* (Esp) **ha picado un ~** I've been bitten by something **2** (fam) (persona) nasty piece of work (colloq); **~ raro** weirdo (colloq); **todo ~ viviente** everyone

bici *f* (fam) bike (colloq)

bicicleta *f* bicycle; **va en ~ al trabajo** she cycles to work; **¿sabes montar** *or* (AmL) **andar en ~?** can you ride a bicycle?; **~ de carreras/ejercicio** racing/exercise bike

bicimoto *m* (Méx) moped

bicolor *adj* two-colored*

bidé, **bidet** /bi'ðe/ *m* bidet

bidón *m* **(a)** (para gasolina, agua) can; (más grande) jerry can **(b)** (barril) barrel

bien[1] *adj inv* **1** [ESTAR] (de salud, en general) well; **sentirse** *or* **encontrarse ~** to feel well; **¿cómo estás? — muy ~, gracias** how are you? — (I'm) very well, thank you; **¡qué ~ estás!** you look really well!; **¡tú no estás ~ de la cabeza!** you are not right in the head **2** [ESTAR] **(a)** (cómodo, agradable): **¿vas ~ ahí atrás?** are you all right in the back?; **se está ~ a la sombra** it's nice in the shade; **la casa está muy ~** the house is very nice **(b)** [ESTAR] (correcto, adecuado) right; **la fecha/el reloj está ~** the date/the clock is right; **¿está ~ así?** is this all right?; **si te parece ~** if that's all right with you; **el cuadro no queda ~ ahí** the picture doesn't look right there **(c)** (suficiente): **estar** *or* **andar ~ de algo** to be all right for sth; **¿estamos ~ de aceite?** are we all right for oil?; **ya está ~** that's enough **3** [ESTAR] **(a)** (en calidad) good; **¿lo has leído? está muy ~** have you read it? it's very good **(b)** (fam) (sexualmente atractivo) good-looking, attractive **4** (fam) **(a)** (de buena posición social) ‹*familia*/*gente*› well-to-do **(b)** ‹*barrio*› well-to-do, (BrE) posh

bien[2] *adv* **1 (a)** (de manera satisfactoria) ‹*dormir*/*funcionar*/*cantar*› well; **no le fue ~ en Alemania** things didn't work out for her in Germany **(b)** (correctamente) well; **habla muy ~ inglés** she speaks English very well *o* very good English; **¡~ hecho/dicho!** well done/said!; **pórtate bien** behave yourself; **hiciste ~ en decírselo** you were right to tell him; **siéntate ~** sit properly **(c)** (de manera agradable) ‹*oler*/*saber*› good **2 (a)** (a fondo, completamente) well, properly; **~ cocido** well *o* properly cooked; **¿cerraste ~?** did you lock the door properly?; **~ sabes que** ... you know perfectly well that ... **(b)** (con cuidado, atención) ‹*escuchar*/*mirar*› carefully **3 (a)** (como intensificador) (muy) very; **canta ~ mal** he sings really badly; **~ entrada la noche** very late at night; **¿estás ~ seguro?** are you positive? **(b)** (en locs) **más bien** rather; **no bien** as soon as; **si bien** although ■ *interj*: **¡(muy) ~!** well done!, (very) good!; **¡qué ~!** great! ■ *conj*: **~ ... o ...** either ... or ...; **se puede subir ~ a pie o a caballo** you can go up either on foot or on horseback

bien[3] *m* **1** (Fil) good; **el ~ y el mal** good and evil; **hacer el ~** to do good deeds; **un hombre de ~** a good man **2 (a)** (beneficio, bienestar) good; **es por mi/tu ~** it's for my/your own good **(b) hacer bien** (+ *me*/*te*/*le etc*): **esto te hará ~** this will do you good **3** (en calificaciones escolares) *grade of between 6 and 6.9 on a scale of 1-10* **4 bienes (a)** (Com) goods; **~es de consumo** consumer goods **(b)** (Der) property; **le dejó todos sus ~es** she left him everything she owned; **~es inmuebles** *or* **raíces** real estate (AmE), property (BrE); **~es muebles** personal property, goods and chattels; **~es públicos** public property

bienal *adj* biennial

bienaventurado -da *adj* blessed

bienestar *m* well-being, welfare; **estado de ~** social welfare state; **~ social** social welfare

bienhablado -da *adj* well-spoken

bienintencionado -da *adj* well-meaning, well-intentioned

bienvenida *f* welcome; **darle la ~ a algn** to welcome sb; **un discurso de ~** a welcoming speech

bienvenido -da *adj* welcome; **ser ~** to be welcome

bies *m*: **al ~** on the cross

bife *m* (CS) (Coc) steak

bifocal *adj* bifocal

bifurcación *f* (en carretera) fork; (en la vía férrea) junction

bifurcarse [A2] *v pron* «*camino*» to fork, diverge (frml); «*vía férrea*» to diverge

bigamia *f* bigamy

bígamo -ma *adj* bigamous ■ *m,f* bigamist

bigote *m* **1** (de persona) *tb* **~s** mustache* **2** (de gato, ratón) whisker

bigotudo -da, (Méx) **bigotón -tona** *adj* (fam): **un hombre ~** a man with a big mustache*

bigudí *m* (*pl* **-díes -dís**) curler, roller

bikini *m* (RPl) *f* bikini

bilateral *adj* bilateral
bilingüe *adj* bilingual
bilis *f* (Fisiol) bile
billar *m* (con tres bolas) billiards; (con 16 bolas) pool; (con 22 bolas) snooker
billete *m* **1** (Fin) bill (esp AmE), note (BrE) **2** (de lotería, rifa, de transporte) ticket; **sacar/pagar un ~** to get/ pay for a ticket; **~ de ida y vuelta** (Esp) round-trip ticket (AmE), return (ticket) (BrE); **~ sencillo** *or* **de ida** (Esp) one-way ticket, single (ticket) (BrE)
billetera *f*, **billetero** *m* wallet, billfold (AmE); (con monedero) change purse (AmE), purse (BrE)
billetero -ra *m,f* (Méx, Ven) lottery ticket vendor
billón *m* trillion (AmE), billion (BrE)
billonario -ria *m,f* billionaire
bimensual *adj* (dos veces al mes) twice-monthly, fortnightly (BrE)
bimestral *adj* (cada dos meses) bimonthly; (que dura dos meses) two-month (*before n*)
bimestre *m* (period of) two months; (pago) bimonthly payment
bimotor *m* twin-engined aircraft
binario -ria *adj* binary
bingo *m* (juego) bingo; (sala) bingo hall
binoculares, (Col, Ven) **binóculos** *mpl* binoculars (*pl*)
biodegradable *adj* biodegradable
biografía *f* biography
biográfico -ca *adj* biographical
biógrafo -fa *m,f* biographer
biología *f* biology
biológico -ca *adj* (Biol) biological; ‹*verduras*› organic
biólogo -ga *m,f* biologist
biombo *m* folding screen
biopsia *f* biopsy
bioquímica *f* biochemistry
bioquímico -ca *adj* biochemical ■ *m,f* biochemist
bióxido *m* dioxide
bip *m* **(a)** (sonido) pip, beep **(b)** (Méx) (aparato) pager, beeper, bleeper (BrE)
bipartidismo *m* two-party system
bípedo *m* biped
biplaza *m* two-seater
biquini *m* bikini
birlar [A1] *vt* (fam) to swipe (colloq), to pinch (BrE colloq)
Birmania *f* Burma
birmano¹ -na *adj/m,f* Burmese; **los ~s** the Burmese
birmano² *m* (idioma) Burmese
birome *f* (RPl) ballpoint pen, Biro®
birrete *m* **(a)** cap (*worn by lawyers, professors, etc*) **(b)** (birreta) biretta
bis *m* encore
bisabuelo -la (*m*) great-grandfather; (*f*) great-grandmother; **mis ~s** my great-grandparents
bisagra *f* hinge
biselar [A1] *vt* to bevel
bisexual *adj/mf* bisexual
bisexualidad *f* bisexuality
bisiesto *adj*: **1992 fue (año) ~** 1992 was a leap year
bisne *m* (AmC fam) hustling (colloq), black marketeering
bisnieto -ta (*m*) great-grandson; (*f*) great-granddaughter; **mis ~s** my great-grandchildren
bisonte *m* bison
bisoñé *m* toupee, hairpiece
bisoño -ña *adj* inexperienced; **soldados ~s** raw recruits
bistec /bi'stek/ *m* (*pl* **-tecs**) steak, beefsteak
bisturí *m* scalpel
bisutería *f* costume *o* imitation jewelry*
bit *m* (Inf) bit
bividí /biβi'ði/ *m* (Per) undershirt (AmE), vest (BrE)
bizantino -na *adj* (Hist) Byzantine
bizco -ca *adj* cross-eyed ■ *m,f* cross-eyed person
bizcocho *m* (pastel) sponge (cake); (galleta) sponge finger
blanca *f* **1** (Mús) half note (AmE), minim (BrE) **2** (en dominó) blank; (en ajedrez) white piece
Blancanieves Snow White
blanco¹ -ca *adj* **1 (a)** ▶ **97** ‹*color/vestido/pelo*› white; **en ~** ‹*cheque/página*› blank; **rellenar los espacios en ~** fill in the blanks; **me quedé en ~** my mind went blank **(b)** (pálido) [SER] fair-skinned, pale-skinned; [ESTAR] white; **estoy muy ~** I'm very white *o* pale **2** ‹*persona/raza*› white **3** ‹*vino*› white ■ *m,f* white person
blanco² *m* **1** (color) ▶ **97** white; **en ~ y negro** black and white **2** (Dep, Jueg) (objeto) target; (centro) bullseye; **tirar al ~** to shoot at the target; **dar en el ~** to hit the target/bullseye **3** (vino) white (wine)
blancura *f* whiteness
blandir [I1] *vt* to brandish, wave
blando -da *adj* **1 (a)** ‹*carne*› tender; ‹*queso/mantequilla*› soft; **ponerse ~** to go soft **(b)** ‹*cama/madera/agua*› soft; **un cepillo de cerdas blandas** a soft brush **2** ‹*carácter*› (débil) weak; (poco severo) soft
blandura *f* **1** (en general) softness; (de la carne) tenderness **2** (falta de severidad) leniency; **trata a sus alumnos con demasiada ~** she's too lenient with *o* too soft on her pupils
blanqueador *m* (para visillos) whitener; (lejía) (Col, Méx) bleach
blanquear [A1] *vt* **(a)** ‹*ropa*› to bleach; ‹*pared*› to whitewash **(b)** ‹*dinero*› to launder
blanqueo *m* **(a)** (de paredes) whitewashing **(b)** (de dinero) laundering
blasfemia *f* blasphemy
blindado -da *adj* ‹*coche*› armor-plated*, armored*; ‹*puerta*› reinforced
blindar [A1] *vt* ‹*barco/coche*› to armor-plate*; ‹*puerta*› to reinforce
bloc *m* (*pl* **blocs**) (de papel) pad; **~ de notas** note *o* writing pad
blof *m* (Col, Méx) bluff

blofear [A1] *vi* (Col, Méx) **(a)** (en el juego) to bluff **(b)** (fam) (alardear) to show off

bloque *m* **1** (de piedra, hormigón) block **2** (edificio) block; **un ~ de departamentos** (AmL) *or* (Esp) **pisos** an apartment block, a block of flats (BrE) **3** (Inf) block **4** (fuerza política) bloc; **en ~** (*loc adv*) en bloc, en masse

bloquear [A1] *vt* **1 (a)** ‹*camino/entrada/salida*› to block; **estamos bloqueados por un camión** there's a truck blocking our way **(b)** (Mil) to blockade **2** ‹*cuenta/fondos*› to freeze, block

■ **bloquearse** *v pron* **1** «*mecanismo*» to jam; «*frenos*» to jam, lock on; «*ruedas*» to lock **2** «*negociaciones*» to reach deadlock

bloqueo *m* (de ciudad) blockade, siege; (de puerto) blockade; (Dep) block

bluff /bluf/ *m* (*pl* **bluffs**) **(a)** (Jueg) bluff **(b)** (fam) (fanfarronería): **es puro ~** he's all talk (colloq)

blusa *f* blouse

blusón *m* loose shirt *o* blouse

blvar. *m* (= **bulevar**) Blvd (*in US*)

Bº = **Banco**

boa *f* (Zool) boa

bobada *f* (cosa boba) silly thing; **deja de hacer ~s** stop being so stupid *o* silly; **deja de decir ~s** stop talking nonsense

bobina *f* **(a)** (de hilo) reel **(b)** (Auto, Elec) coil

bobo -ba *adj* (fam) silly ■ *m,f* (fam) fool

boca *f* **1 (a)** ▶**123** (Anat, Zool) mouth **(b)** (*en locs*) **boca abajo/arriba** ‹*dormir/echarse*› on one's stomach/back; **puso los naipes ~ arriba** she laid the cards face up; **en boca de**: **la pregunta que anda en ~ de todos los niños** the question which is on every child's lips; **el escándalo andaba en ~ de todos** the scandal was common knowledge; **por boca de** from; **lo supe por ~ de su hermana** I heard it from his sister; ***a pedir de ~*** just fine; ***hacerle el ~ a ~ a algn*** to give sb the kiss of life; ***hacérsele la ~ agua a algn*** (Esp): **se le hacía la ~ agua mirando los pasteles** looking at the cakes made her mouth water; ***quedarse con la ~ abierta*** to be dumbfounded *o* (colloq) flabbergasted **2** (de buzón) slot; (de túnel) mouth, entrance; (de puerto) entrance; (de vasija, botella) rim; **~ de incendios** fire hydrant, fireplug (AmE); **~ del estómago** (fam) pit of the stomach; **~ de metro** *or* (RPl) **subte** subway entrance (AmE), underground *o* tube station entrance (BrE)

bocacalle *f*: *entrance to a street*; **la primera ~ a la derecha** the first turning on the right

bocadillo *m* **1** (Esp) (emparedado) roll **2** (Col, Ven) (dulce) guava jelly

bocado *m* **(a)** (de comida) bite; **de un ~** in one bite; **no ha probado ~** she hasn't had a bite to eat **(b)** (comida ligera) snack

bocajarro: **a ~** (*loc adv*) **(a)** ‹*disparar*› at point-blank range **(b)** ‹*decir/preguntar*› point-blank

bocamanga *f* cuff

bocanada *f* (de humo, aliento) puff, mouthful; (ráfaga) gust, blast

bocatoma *f* (Andes) water inlet

boceto *m* (dibujo) sketch; (de proyecto) outline

bochar [A1] *vt* **(a)** (RPl fam) ‹*sugerencia/propuesta*› to squash (colloq) **(b)** (RPl arg) (en examen) ‹*estudiante*› to fail, to flunk (AmE colloq)

bochas *fpl* (RPl) (Jueg) bowls

bochinche *m* (esp AmL fam) **(a)** (riña, pelea) fight, brawl **(b)** (barullo, alboroto) racket (colloq), ruckus (AmE colloq), row (BrE colloq) **(c)** (confusión, lío) muddle, mess (colloq)

bochinchear [A1] *vi* (AmL fam) to fight

bochinchero -ra *adj* (AmL fam) rowdy

bochorno *m* **1** (calor) sultry *o* muggy weather **2** (vergüenza) embarrassment; **¡qué ~!** how embarrassing!

bochornoso -sa *adj* **1** ‹*tiempo*› sultry, muggy; ‹*calor*› sticky; **hacía un día ~** it was a close *o* muggy day **2** ‹*espectáculo/situación*› embarrassing

bocina *f* **1** (de coche) horn; (de fábrica) hooter, siren; (de faro) foghorn **2** (AmL) (auricular) receiver **3** (Méx) (Audio) loudspeaker

bocio *m* goiter*

boda *f* wedding; **~s de oro/plata** (de matrimonio) golden/silver wedding anniversary; (de organización) golden/silver jubilee

bodega *f* **1 (a)** (Vin) (fábrica) winery; (almacén) wine cellar; (tienda) wine merchant's, wine shop **(b)** (taberna) bar **(c)** (en casa) cellar **2 (a)** (AmC, Per, Ven) (tienda de comestibles) grocery store (AmE), grocer's (BrE) **(b)** (AmL exc RPl) (depósito) store, warehouse

bodeguero -ra *m,f* **1** (Vin) (productor) wine-producer **2 (a)** (AmC, Per, Ven) (tendero) shopkeeper **(b)** (AmL exc RPl) (depósito) warehouseman

bodrio *m* (fam): **es un ~** it is garbage (AmE) *o* (BrE) rubbish (colloq)

bofetada *f*, **bofetón** *m* slap; **le di** *or* **pegué una ~** I slapped him (in the face)

boga *f*: **estar en ~** to be in fashion *o* in vogue

Bogotá *m* Bogotá

bogotano -na *adj* of/from Bogotá

bohemio -mia *adj* **(a)** ‹*vida/artista*› bohemian **(b)** (de Bohemia) Bohemian ■ *m,f* bohemian

bohío *m* (AmC, Col, Ven) hut

boicot /boj'kot/ *m* (*pl* **-cots**) boycott

boicotear [A1] *vt* to boycott

boina *f* beret

boite /bwat/ *f* night club

bol *m* bowl

bola *f* **1** (cuerpo redondo) ball; (de helado) scoop; (Dep) ball; (de petanca) boule; (canica) (Col, Per) marble; **~ de cristal** crystal ball; **~ de nieve** snowball; **~ de partido/de set** match/set point **2 bolas** *fpl* (fam: en algunas regiones vulg) (testículos) balls (*pl*) (colloq *or* vulg); ***estar en ~s*** (fam *o* vulg) to be stark naked (colloq); ***hacerse ~s con algo*** (Méx) to get in a mess over sth **3** (fam) (mentira) lie, fib (colloq); **me metió una ~** he told me a fib; **contar/decir ~s** to fib (colloq), to tell fibs (colloq) **4** (Méx fam) (montón): **una ~ de** loads of (colloq)

bolchevique *adj/mf* Bolshevik

boleador -dora *m,f* **1** (Méx) (lustrabotas) bootblack **2** (en las pampas) *person who uses bolas to catch cattle*

boleadoras *fpl* bolas

bolear [A1] *vi* (Col) to knock up, knock a ball about ■ ~ *vt* (Méx) to polish, shine

bolera *f* bowling alley

bolero[1] *m* **1** (Mús) bolero **2** (Indum) bolero jacket/top

bolero[2] -ra *m,f* (Méx) bootblack

boleta *f* **(a)** (AmL) (en rifa) ticket **(b)** (CS) (de multa) ticket **(c)** (CS) (recibo) receipt **(d)** (Col) (entrada) ticket; **~ de calificaciones** (Méx) school report, report card (AmE); **~ de depósito** (RPl) deposit slip (AmE), paying-in slip (BrE); **~ electoral** (Méx, RPl) ballot paper

boletaje *m* (Méx, Per) tickets (*pl*)

boletería *f* (AmL) (de teatro, cine) box office; (de estación, estadio) ticket office

boletín *m* bulletin; **~ de calificaciones** *or* **notas** school report, report card (AmE)

boleto *m* (de lotería, rifa) ticket; (de quinielas) (Esp) coupon; (de tren, autobús) (AmL) ticket; **~ de ida** (AmL) one-way ticket, single (ticket) (BrE); **~ de ida y vuelta** (AmL) round trip (ticket) (AmE), return (ticket) (BrE); **~ de viaje redondo** (Méx) round trip (ticket) (AmE), return (ticket) (BrE)

boliche *m* **1 (a)** (en petanca) jack **(b)** (juguete) *cup-and-ball toy* **(c)** (Col) (bolo) tenpin **2** (Méx) (juego) bowling, ten pin bowling (BrE); (lugar) bowling alley **3 (a)** (CS) (tienda pequeña) (fam) small store (AmE), small shop (BrE) **(b)** (Bol, RPl) (taberna) bar

bolígrafo *m* ballpoint pen, Biro®

bolillo *m* (en pasamanería) bobbin; **encaje de ~s** bobbin lace

bolita *f* (AmS) (Jueg) marble; **jugar a las ~s** to play marbles

bolívar *m* bolivar (*Venezuelan unit of currency*)

Bolivia *f* Bolivia

boliviano -na *adj/m,f* Bolivian

bollo *m* (Coc) (bread) roll, bun; ***ser un ~*** (RPl fam) to be a piece of cake (colloq)

bolo *m* **(a)** (palo) skittle, tenpin; **(b) bolos** *mpl* (juego) bowling, ten pin bowling (BrE); **jugar a los ~s** to play skittles, to go bowling

bolsa *f* **1 (a)** (en general) bag; **~ de plástico/de la compra** plastic/shopping bag; **~ de (la) basura** garbage *o* trash bag (AmE), rubbish bag *o* bin liner (BrE); **una ~ de patatas fritas** (Esp) a bag of chips (AmE), a packet *o* bag of crisps (BrE); **~ de agua caliente** hot-water bottle **(b)** (Méx) (bolso) handbag, purse (AmE) **2 (a)** (de marsupial) pouch **(b)** (Méx) (bolsillo) pocket **3** (de aire, gas, agua) pocket **4** (Econ, Fin) *tb* **B~** *or* **~ de valores** stock exchange, stock market; **jugar a la ~** to play the market; **se cotizará en ~** it will be listed on the stock exchange; **~ de empleo** (Col) employment agency; **~ de trabajo** *job vacancies and place where they are advertised*

bolsear [A1] *vt* **(a)** (Méx fam) (robar): **me ~on en el camión** I had my pocket picked on the bus **(b)** (Chi fam) ‹*comida/cigarillos*› **~le algo** A **algn** to scrounge sth FROM *o* OFF sb

bolsillo *m* pocket; **de ~** ‹*calculadora/diccionario*› pocket (*before n*); ***meterse a algn en el ~*** to get sb eating out of one's hand

bolso *m* (de mujer) (Esp) handbag, purse (AmE); **~ de mano** (de viaje) (overnight) bag; (de mujer) (Esp) handbag, purse (AmE); **~ de viaje** (overnight) bag

boludo -da *adj* (Col, RPl, Ven vulg) (imbécil): **es tan ~** he's such a jerk (colloq) *o* (vulg) prick ■ *m,f* (Col, RPl, Ven vulg) asshole (vulg), dickhead (BrE vulg)

bomba *f* **1 (a)** (Arm, Mil) bomb; **lanzar/arrojar ~s** to drop bombs; **poner una ~** to plant a bomb; **~ atómica** atom *o* atomic bomb; **~ de tiempo** time bomb; **~ lacrimógena** tear gas canister; ***caer como una ~*** «*noticia*» to come as a bombshell **(b)** (notición) big news **(c)** (en fútbol americano) bomb **2** (Tec) pump; **~ de aire** pump; **~ de agua** water pump **3** (Andes, Ven) (gasolinera) gas station (AmE), petrol station (BrE) **4** (Chi) (vehículo) fire engine, fire truck (AmE); (estación) fire station

bombacha *f* **(a)** (CS) (de gaucho) baggy trousers (*pl*) **(b)** (RPl) (de mujer) panties (*pl*), knickers (*pl*) (BrE)

bombardear [A1] *vt* (desde avión) to bomb; (con artillería) to bombard, shell; **me ~on a preguntas** they bombarded me with questions

bombardeo *m* (desde aviones) bombing; (con artillería) bombardment, shelling

bombardero *m* bomber

bombazo *m* **1** (Méx) (explosión) bomb explosion **2** (fam) (noticia) bombshell

bombear [A1] *vt* to pump

bombero *mf*, **bombero -ra** *m,f* (de incendios) (*m*) firefighter, fireman; (*f*) firefighter; **llamar a los ~s** to call the fire department (AmE) *o* (BrE) brigade; **cuerpo de ~s** fire department (AmE) *o* (BrE) brigade

bombilla *f* **1** (Esp) (Elec) light bulb **2** (para el mate) *tube through which mate tea is drunk*

bombillo *m* (AmC, Col, Ven) light bulb

bombín *m* **1** (Indum) derby (AmE), bowler hat (BrE) **2** (para inflar) pump

bombita *f* (RPl) (Elec) light bulb

bombo *m* **1** (Mús) (instrumento) bass drum; (músico) bass drummer; **tengo la cabeza como un ~** my head's about to explode; ***con ~s y platillos*** *or* (Esp) ***a ~ y platillo*** with a great fanfare; ***darle ~ a algo*** to give sth a lot of hype (colloq) **2** (de sorteo) drum

bombón *m* **(a)** (confite) chocolate **(b)** (fam) (persona) stunner (colloq) **(c)** (Méx) (malvavisco) marshmallow

bombona *f* gas cylinder *o* canister

bombonería *f* candy store (AmE), sweet shop (BrE)

bonachón -chona *adj* (fam) (amable) good-natured, kind ■ *m,f* (fam) (persona amable) good-natured *o* kind person

bonaerense *adj*: *of/from the province of Buenos Aires*

bonche *m* **1** (AmC, Col fam) (riña) fight; (contienda) contest **2** (Ven fam) (fiesta) party, rave-up (BrE sl)

bondad *f* **(a)** (afabilidad, generosidad) goodness, kindness; **¿tendría la ~ de cerrar la puerta?** (fml) would you mind closing the door? **(b)** (del clima) mildness

bondadoso -sa *adj* kind, kindhearted, kindly

bongó, **bongo** *m* bongo

boniato *m* sweet potato

bonificación *f* **(a)** (aumento, beneficio) bonus **(b)** (descuento) discount

bonito[1] -ta *adj* pretty; ‹*canción/apartamento*› nice, lovely

bonito[2] *m* tuna, bonito

bono *m* (vale) voucher; (Econ, Fin) bond

boquera *f* cold sore

boquerón *m* anchovy

boquete *m* hole

boquiabierto -ta *adj*: **quedarse ~** to be speechless *o* dumbfounded

boquilla *f* (de instrumento musical) mouthpiece; (de pipa) stem; (para cigarrillos) cigarette holder

borbotón: **a borbotones** ‹*hervir*› fiercely; ‹*salir*› «*sangre/agua*» to gush out

borda *f* gunwale, rail; ***echar*** *or* ***tirar algo por la ~*** to throw sth overboard

bordado[1] -da *adj* ‹*mantel/sábana*› embroidered

bordado[2] *m* embroidery

bordar [A1] *vt* ‹*sábana/blusa*› to embroider; **lo bordó a mano** she embroidered it by hand

borde *m* (de mesa, cama, andén) edge; (de moneda, taza, vaso) rim; **llenó el vaso hasta el ~** she filled the glass to the brim; **al ~ de algo** ‹*de la guerra/locura*› on the brink of sth; ‹*de las lágrimas/del caos/de la ruina*› on the verge of sth; **al ~ de la muerte** on the point of death

bordear [A1] *vt* **(a)** (seguir el borde de) ‹*costa*› to go along, ‹*isla*› to go around **(b)** (estar a lo largo del borde): **un camino bordeado de álamos** a road lined with poplars

bordillo *m* curb (AmE), kerb (BrE)

bordo *m*: **a ~** on board; **subir a ~** to go aboard *o* on board

borgoña *m* (Vin) Burgundy, burgundy

borra *f* (sedimento — del café) dregs; (— del vino) lees (*pl*), sediment

borrachera *f*: **pegarse** *or* (Esp) **cogerse** *or* (esp AmL) **agarrarse una ~** to get drunk

borracho -cha *adj* **(a)** [ESTAR] drunk **(b)** [SER]: **es muy ~** he is a drunkard *o* a heavy drinker ■ *m, f* drunk; (habitual) drunkard, drunk

borrador *m* **1** (de redacción, carta) rough draft; (de contrato, proyecto) draft; (de dibujo) sketch; **lo hice en ~** I did a rough draft **2** (para la pizarra) eraser (AmE), board rubber (BrE)

borraja *f* borage

borrar [A1] *vt* **(a)** ‹*palabra/dibujo*› (con goma) to rub out, erase; (con líquido corrector) to white out, tippex out (BrE); ‹*pizarra*› to clean; ‹*huellas digitales*› to wipe off **(b)** ‹*cassette/disquete*› to erase, wipe; (Inf) delete **(c)** ‹*recuerdos/imagen*› to blot out

■ **borrarse** *v pron* «*inscripción/letrero*» to fade; **se borró con la lluvia** the rain washed it away *o* off

borrasca *f* **(a)** (área de bajas presiones) area of low pressure **(b)** (tormenta) squall

borrascoso -sa *adj* ‹*viento*› squally; ‹*tiempo*› stormy, squally

borrego -ga *m,f* (cordero) lamb; (oveja) sheep

borrón *m* (mancha) inkblot; (mancha borroneada) smudge; **~ *y cuenta nueva*** let's make a fresh start

borronear [A1] *vt* to smudge

borroso -sa *adj* ‹*foto/imagen*› blurred; ‹*inscripción*› worn; ‹*contorno*› indistinct, blurred

boscoso -sa *adj* wooded

bosque *m* wood; (más grande) forest, woods (*pl*); (terreno) woodland; **~ ecuatorial** *or* **pluvial** (equatorial) rainforest

bosquejar [A1] *vt* (Art) to sketch, make a sketch of; ‹*idea/proyecto*› to outline, sketch out

bosquejo *m* (Art) sketch; (de novela) outline

bostezar [A4] *vi* to yawn

bostezo *m* yawn

bota *f* **1** (calzado) boot; **~s de caña alta/de media caña** knee-high/calf-length boots; **~s de agua** rubber boots (*pl*), wellingtons (*pl*) (BrE); **~s de esquí/montar** ski/riding boots (*pl*) **2** (para vino) small wineskin

botadero *m* (Andes) *tb* **~ de basura** garbage dump (AmE), rubbish dump *o* tip (BrE)

botado -da *adj* [ESTAR] (AmS exc RPl fam) **(a)** (barato) dirt cheap (colloq) **(b)** (fácil) dead easy (colloq)

botadura *f* launching

botana *f* (Méx) snack, appetizer

botánico -ca *adj* botanical

botar [A1] *vt* **1** ‹*barco*› to launch **2** ‹*pelota*› to bounce **3** (AmL exc RPl) (tirar) to throw ... out; **no lo botes al suelo** don't throw it on the ground; **bótalo a la basura** chuck *o* throw it out (colloq); **~ el dinero** to throw your money away **4** (AmL exc RPl fam) **(a)** (echar — de lugar) to throw ... out (colloq); (— de trabajo) to fire (colloq), to sack (BrE colloq) **(b)** (abandonar) ‹*novio/novia*› to chuck (colloq), to ditch (colloq); ‹*marido/esposa*› to leave; **el tren nos dejó botados** we missed the train **5** (AmL exc RPl fam) (derribar) ‹*puerta/árbol*› to knock down; ‹*botella/taza*› to knock over; **no empujes que me botas** stop pushing, you're going to knock me over **6** (AmL exc RPl) (perder) ‹*aceite/gasolina*› to leak ■ **~** *vi* (Esp) «*pelota*» to bounce

■ **botarse** *v pron* (AmL exc CS fam) **(a)** (apresurarse) to rush **(b)** (arrojarse) to jump

botarate *mf* **(a)** (fam) (irresponsable) irresponsible fool **(b)** (AmL exc RPl) (derrochador) spendthrift

bote *m* **1** (Náut) boat; **~ de** *or* **a remos** rowboat (AmE), rowing boat (BrE); **~ salvavidas** lifeboat **2** (recipiente — de lata) tin; (— de vidrio, plástico) storage jar; (— de cerveza) (Esp) can; (— de mermelada) (Esp) jar; **el ~ de la basura** (Méx) the trash can (AmE), the rubbish bin (BrE); ***de ~ en ~*** packed **3** (de pelota) bounce; **dio dos ~s** it bounced twice

botella *f* bottle; **una ~ de vino** (recipiente) a wine bottle; (con contenido) a bottle of wine; **cerveza de** *or* **en ~** bottled beer

botijo *m*: *drinking jug with spout*

botillería *f* (Chi) liquor store (AmE), off licence (BrE)

botín *m* **1** (bota corta) ankle boot; (de bebé) bootee; (de futbolista) (CS) boot **2** (de guerra) plunder, booty; (de ladrones) haul, loot

botiquín *m* **(a)** (armario — para medicinas) medicine chest *o* cabinet; (para colonias, jabón, etc) bathroom cabinet **(b)** (maletín) *tb* **~ de primeros auxilios** first-aid kit

botón *m* **1** (Indum) button; **~ de presión** (AmL) snap fastener (AmE), press stud (BrE) **2** (de mecanismo) button; **el ~ del volumen** the volume control **3** (AmL) (insignia) badge, button (AmE) **4** (de flor) bud

botones *mf* (*pl* **~**) (de hotel) bellboy; (de oficina) (*m*) office boy; (*f*) office girl

bouquet /bu'ke/ *m* (*pl* **-quets**) **(a)** (del vino) bouquet **(b)** (ramillete) bouquet

boutique /bu'tik/ *f* boutique

bóveda *f* **1** (Arquit) vault; **~ de seguridad** (AmL) bank vault **2** (RPl) (sepulcro) tomb

bovino -na *adj* bovine

bowling /'boulin/ *m* **(a)** (deporte) tenpins (AmE), tenpin bowling (BrE) **(b)** (lugar) bowling alley

box /boks/ *m* (AmL) (boxeo) boxing

boxeador -dora *m,f* boxer

boxear [A1] *vi* to box

boxeo *m* boxing

boya *f* (Náut) buoy; (en pesca) float

boyante *adj* ‹*situación/economía*› buoyant

bozal *m* (de perro) muzzle; (de caballo) halter

bozo *m* down (*on upper lip*)

bracero -ra *m,f* temporary farm worker

bragas *fpl* (Esp) (de mujer) panties (*pl*), knickers (*pl*) (BrE)

braguero *m* truss

bragueta *f* fly, flies (*pl*)

braille /'brajle/ *adj* braille (*before n*) ■ *m* braille

bramante *m* twine, string

bramar [A1] *vi* «*toro/ciervo*» to bellow; «*elefante*» to trumpet

bramido *m* (de toro, ciervo) bellowing; (de elefante) trumpeting; **dio un ~** it bellowed/trumpeted

branquia *f* gill

brasa *f* ember; **carne/pescado a la(s) ~(s)** charcoal-grilled meat/fish

brasero *m* (de carbón — para interiores) small brazier; (— para la intemperie) brazier; (eléctrico) electric heater

brasier *m* (Col, Méx, Ven) bra

Brasil *m*: *tb* **el ~** Brazil

brasileño -ña, (AmL) **brasilero -ra** *adj/m,f* Brazilian

bravío -vía *adj* ‹*toro*› fierce, wild; ‹*potro*› wild, unmanageable

bravo[1] -va *adj* **(a)** [SER] ‹*toro/perro*› fierce; *ver tb* TORO **(b)** [ESTAR] ‹*mar*› rough **(c)** [ESTAR] (AmL fam) (enojado) angry

bravo[2] *interj* (expresando aprobación) well done!, good job! (AmE); (tras actuación) bravo!

bravucón -cona *adj* (fam) bragging (*before n*)

bravuconada *f* piece of bravado; **~s** bravado

braza *f* (Esp) (en natación) breaststroke; **nadar a ~** to swim (the) breaststroke

brazada *f* (al nadar) stroke

brazalete *m* **(a)** (pulsera — de una pieza) bangle, bracelet; (— de eslabones) bracelet **(b)** (de tela) armband

brazo *m* **1** (Anat) ▶ **123** arm; (parte superior) upper arm; **llevaba una cesta al ~** she had a basket on one arm; **caminar/ir del ~** to walk arm in arm; **llevaba al niño en ~s** he was carrying the child in his arms; ***cruzado de ~s***: **no te quedes ahí cruzado de ~s** don't just stand/sit there (doing nothing); ***dar el ~ a torcer*** to give in; **no dio el** *or* **su ~ a torcer** he didn't let them/her twist his arm **2** (de sillón) arm; (de tocadiscos) arm; (de grúa) jib; (de río) branch, channel; **~ de gitano** (Coc) jelly roll (AmE), swiss roll (BrE); **~ de mar** inlet, sound **3 brazos** *mpl* (trabajadores) hands (*pl*)

brea *f* pitch, tar

brebaje *m* potion; **un ~ mágico** a magic potion

brecha *f* (en muro) breach, opening; (en la frente, cabeza) gash; **~ generacional** generation gap

bretel *m* (CS) strap

bretón[1] -tona *adj/m,f* Breton

bretón[2] *m* (idioma) Breton

breva *f* (Bot) early fig, black fig

breve *adj* (frml) brief, short; ‹*viaje/distancia*› short; **dentro de ~s momentos** in a few moments; **sea usted ~, por favor** please be brief; **en ~** shortly, soon

brevete *m* (Per) driver's license (AmE), driving licence (BrE)

bribón -bona *m,f* (fam) rascal (colloq), scamp (colloq)

bricolaje, **bricolage** *m* do-it-yourself, DIY

brida *f* bridle

briega *f* (Col) hard work, struggle

brigada *f* (Mil) brigade; (de policía) squad; **~ antidroga/de explosivos** drug/bomb squad; **~ de salvamento** rescue team

brillante *adj* **(a)** ‹*luz/estrella/color*› bright; ‹*zapatos/metal/pelo*› shiny; ‹*pintura*› gloss (*before n*); ‹*papel*› glossy; ‹*tela*› with a sheen **(b)** ‹*escritor/porvenir*› brilliant; **su actuación fue ~** she performed brilliantly ■ *m* (diamante) diamond; **un anillo de ~s** a diamond ring

brillar [A1] *vi* **(a)** «*sol/luz*» to shine; «*estrella*» to shine, sparkle; «*zapatos/suelo/metal*» to shine, gleam; «*diamante/ojos*» to sparkle **(b)** (destacarse) «*persona*» to shine ■ **~** *vt* (Col) to polish

brillo *m* **(a)** (en general) shine; (de estrella) brightness, brilliance; (de diamante, ojos) sparkle; (de tela) sheen; **darle ~ al suelo** to polish the floor; **fotos con ~** gloss finish photos; **dale un poco de ~** (TV) turn the brightness up a bit **(b)** (esplendor, lucimiento) splendor*; **sin ~** ‹*discurso/interpretación*› dull **(c)** (para labios) lip gloss; (para uñas) clear nail polish

brilloso -sa *adj* (AmL) shiny

brincar [A2] *vi* «*niño*» to jump up and down; «*cordero*» to gambol, skip around; «*liebre*» to hop; **~ de alegría** to jump for joy ■ **~** *vt* (Méx) ‹*valla/obstáculo*› to jump

brinco *m* jump, leap, bound; **pegó** *or* **dio un ~ del susto** (fam) he jumped with fright

brindar [A1] *vi* to drink a toast; **~ POR algn/algo** to drink a toast TO sb/sth ■ **~** *vt* (frml) (proporcionar) to give; **le brindó su apoyo** she gave him her support

■ **brindarse** *v pron* (frml) **~se A hacer algo** to offer *o* volunteer to do sth; **se brindó a acompañarme** he offered *o* volunteered to accompany me

brindis *m* (*pl* **~**) toast; **hacer un ~ por algn** to drink a toast to sb

brío *m* **(a)** (ánimo, energía) spirit; **luchó con ~** he fought with great spirit *o* determination **(b)** (de caballo) spirit

brioso -sa *adj* ‹*caballo*› spirited

brisa *f* breeze

británico -ca *adj* British ■ *m,f* British person, Briton; **los ~s** the British, British people

brizna *f* (hebra) strand; (de hierba) blade

briznar [A1] *v impers* (Ven) to drizzle

broca *f* (drill) bit

brocado *m* brocade

brocha *f* (de pintor) paintbrush, brush; (de afeitar) shaving brush; (en cosmética) blusher brush

broche *m* **(a)** (joya) brooch **(b)** (de collar, monedero) clasp; **~ de presión** (AmL) snap fastener (AmE), press stud (BrE) **(c)** (Méx, Ur) (para el pelo) barrette (AmE), hair slide (BrE) **(d)** (Arg) (grapa) staple

brocheta *f* (aguja) brochette, skewer; (plato) kebab

brócoli *m* broccoli

broma *f* joke; **hacerle** *or* **gastarle una ~ a algn** to play a (practical) joke on sb; **déjate de ~s** stop kidding around (colloq); **no estoy para ~s** I'm not in the mood for jokes; **~s aparte** joking apart; **lo dije de** *or* **en ~** I was joking; ***ni en ~*** no way (colloq)

bromear [A1] *vi* to joke

bromista *adj*: **es muy ~** he's always joking; **¡qué ~ eres!** you're such a joker ■ *mf* joker

bromuro *m* bromide

bronca *f* **1 (a)** (fam) (disputa, lío) row; **armar** *or* **montar una ~** to kick up a fuss (colloq); **buscar ~** to look for trouble *o* a fight **(b)** (alboroto, bullicio) racket (colloq) **2** (esp Esp fam) (regañina) scolding, telling off (colloq); **echarle la ~ a algn** to tell sb off **3** (AmL fam) (rabia): **está con una ~** he's furious; **me da mucha ~** it really gets to *o* bugs me (colloq); **tenerle ~ a algn** to have it in for sb (colloq)

bronce *m* **(a)** (para estatuas, cañones) bronze; **una medalla de ~** a bronze medal **(b)** (para llamadores, placas) (AmL) brass

bronceado[1] **-da** *adj* tanned, suntanned

bronceado[2] *m* (de la piel) tan, suntan; (Metal) bronzing

bronceador *m* suntan lotion

broncear [A1] *vt* «*piel*» to tan

■ **broncearse** *v pron* to get a tan *o* a suntan

bronconeumonía *f* bronchopneumonia

bronquio *m* bronchial tube

bronquitis *f* bronchitis

brotar [A1] *vi* **(a)** «*planta*» to sprout, come up; «*hoja*» to appear, sprout; «*flor*» to come out **(b)** «*sarampión/grano*» to appear

■ **brotarse** *v pron* (AmL) to come out in spots

brote *m* **(a)** (Bot) shoot; **echar ~s** to sprout, put out shoots **(b)** (de violencia, enfermedad) outbreak **(c)** (Col) (sarpullido) rash

bruces: **de ~** (*loc adv*) face down; **se cayó de ~** he fell flat on his face

brujería *f* witchcraft

brujo -ja *adj* **(a)** ‹*ojos/amor*› bewitching **(b)** (AmC, Méx fam) (sin dinero) broke (colloq) ■ *m,f* (*m*) warlock; (*f*) witch

brújula *f* compass

bruma *f* (marina) (sea) mist; (del alba) mist

brumoso -sa *adj* misty

bruñir [I9] *vt* to polish

brusco -ca *adj* **(a)** ‹*movimiento/cambio*› abrupt, sudden; ‹*subida/descenso*› sharp, sudden **(b)** ‹*carácter/modales*› rough; ‹*tono/gesto*› brusque, abrupt; ‹*respuesta*› curt, brusque

Bruselas *f* Brussels

brusquedad *f* **(a)** (en el trato) roughness; **con ~** ‹*hablar/actuar*› abruptly **(b)** (de movimiento) abruptness, suddenness; **frenó con ~** he braked sharply

brutal *adj* ‹*crimen*› brutal; ‹*atentado*› savage

brutalidad *f* brutality, savageness

bruto -ta *adj* **1** ‹*persona*› **(a)** (ignorante) ignorant **(b)** (violento, brusco): **¡qué ~!** what a brute! **2** ‹*peso/sueldo*› gross; **en ~** ‹*diamante*› uncut; ‹*mineral*› crude ■ *m,f* **(a)** (ignorante) ignorant person **(b)** (persona violenta) brute, animal

bucal *adj* ‹*lesión*› mouth (*before n*); ‹*antiséptico/higiene*› oral (*before n*)

buceador -dora *m,f* diver

bucear [A1] *vi* to swim underwater, to dive

buceo *m* underwater swimming, diving

buchaca *f* (Col) pocket

buche *m* **1 (a)** (de aves) crop **(b)** (de otros animales) maw **2** (Med, Odont): **hacer ~s con algo** to rinse one's mouth out with sth

bucle *m* **(a)** (en el pelo) ringlet **(b)** (Inf) loop

bucólico -ca *adj* bucolic, pastoral

budín *m* **(a)** (dulce) pudding **(b)** (salado) pie

budismo *m* Buddhism

budista *adj/mf* Buddhist

buen *adj ver* BUENO

buenaventura *f* **(a)** (buena suerte) good fortune **(b)** (futuro): **me dijo/leyó la ~** she told my fortune

buen mozo, -na moza *adj* ‹*hombre*› good-looking, handsome; ‹*mujer*› attractive, good-looking

bueno[1] **-na** *adj* [BUEN *is used before masculine singular nouns*] **I 1** [SER] **(a)** ‹*hotel/producto/trabajo*› good; **ropa buena** good-quality clothes; **la buena mesa** good cooking **(b)** ‹*remedio/método*› good; **es ~ para la gripe/los dolores de cabeza** it's good for the flu/headaches **(c)** ‹*médico/alumno*› good; **es un buen padre/amigo** he's a good father/friend; **es muy buena en francés** she's very good at French; **es buena para los negocios** she's got a good head for business **(d)** (amable, bondadoso) good, kind; **fueron muy ~s conmigo** they were very good *o* kind to me **(e)** (conveniente, correcto) good; **no es buena hora** it's not a good time; **no es ~ comer tanto** it isn't good to eat so much; **es ~ para la salud** it's good for your health; **su inglés es ~** her English is good **2 (a)** (agradable) nice; **hace muy buen tiempo** the weather is nice **(b)** ‹*comida*› (en general) **ser ~** to be good, be nice; (en particular) **estar ~** to be good, be nice; **el guacamole es buenísimo** guacamole is really good; **esta sopa está muy buena** this soup is very good **(c)** (favorable) ‹*oferta/crítica*› good; **una buena noticia** a piece of good news **3** [ESTAR] **(a)** (en buen estado) ‹*leche/pescado*› fresh; **esta leche no está buena** this milk is off *o* sour **(b)** (fam) (sexualmente atractivo): **está buenísimo** he's really gorgeous **4** (saludable, sano) ‹*costumbre/alimentación*› good; **estar en buena forma** to be in good shape **5 (a)** ▶ 378 (en fórmulas, saludos) good; **¡~s días!** good morning; **¡buenas tardes!** (temprano) good afternoon; (más tarde) good evening; **¡buenas noches!** (al llegar) good evening; (al despedirse) good night; **¡buen viaje!** have a good trip!; **¡buen provecho!** enjoy your meal **(b)** (*delante del n*) (uso enfático) ‹*susto*› terrible; **una buena cantidad** a fair amount; **un ~ día** one day **(c) ¡qué ~!** (AmL) great **(d) de buenas a primeras** suddenly; **por las buenas** willingly ■ *m,f* **(a)** (hum *o* leng infantil) (en películas, cuentos) goody (colloq); **los ~s y los malos** the good guys and the bad guys (colloq) **(b)** (bonachón, buenazo): **el ~ de Juan/la buena de Pilar** good old Juan/Pilar

bueno² *interj* **1 (a)** (expresando — duda) well; (— conformidad) OK (colloq), all right; **¿un café? — bueno** coffee? — OK *o* all right **(b)** (expresando resignación): **~, otra vez será** never mind, maybe next time **(c)** (expresando irritación): **~, se acabó ¡a la cama!** right, that's it, bed!; **¡y ~! ¿qué querías que hiciera?** (RPl) well, what did you expect me to do? **2** (Méx) ▶ 405 (al contestar el teléfono) **¡~!** hello

Buenos Aires *m* Buenos Aires

buey *m* (Agr, Zool) ox ■ *adj* (Méx fam) dumb (colloq)

búfalo¹ -la *adj* (AmC fam) great (colloq), fantastic (colloq)

búfalo² *m* buffalo

bufanda *f* scarf

bufar [A1] *vi* to snort

bufet /bu'fe/, **bufé** *m* **1** (Coc) buffet **2** (Andes) (aparador) sideboard

bufete *m* (Der) (despacho) lawyer's office; (negocio) legal practice, law firm

bufido *m* snort

bufón *m* (Hist) jester; (gracioso) (fam) clown (colloq)

buhardilla *f* **(a)** (desván) attic **(b)** (apartamento) attic apartment (AmE) *o* (BrE) room **(c)** (ventana) dormer window

búho *m* owl

buitre *m* vulture

bujía *f* **(a)** (Auto) spark plug **(b)** (AmC) (Elec) light bulb

bula *f* (Relig) bull; **~ papal** papal bull

bulbo *m* bulb

bulevar *m* boulevard

Bulgaria *f* Bulgaria

búlgaro¹ -ra *adj/m,f* Bulgarian

búlgaro² *m* (idioma) Bulgarian

bulín *m* **1** (RPl fam) **(a)** (de soltero) bachelor pad **(b)** (vivienda): **se compraron un bulincito** they bought a little place of their own (colloq) **2** (Per) (burdel) brothel

bulla *f* (ruido) racket (colloq), ruckus (AmE colloq); (actividad) bustle; **armar** *or* **meter ~** to make a racket, to create a ruckus

bullanguero -ra *adj* (fam) ‹*persona*› fun-loving; ‹*música/ambiente*› lively

bullicio *m* **(a)** (ruido) racket, noise **(b)** (actividad): **el ~ de la gran ciudad** the hustle and bustle of the city

bullicioso -sa *adj* noisy

bullir [I9] *vi*: **la calle bullía de gente** the street was teeming *o* swarming with people; **el lugar bullía de actividad** the place was a hive of activity

bulto *m* **1 (a)** (cuerpo, forma) shape; **vi un ~ que se movía** I saw a shape moving; ***escurrir el ~*** (fam) (en el trabajo) to duck out; (en entrevista) to dodge the issue **(b)** (volumen): **hace mucho/poco ~** it is/isn't very bulky **2** (Med) lump **3 (a)** (maleta, bolsa) piece of luggage; **~ de mano** piece *o* item of hand baggage *o* luggage; **cargada de ~s** laden with packages (*o* bags *etc*) **(b)** (Col, Méx) (saco) sack

búnker /'buŋker/ *m* (*pl* **-kers**) bunker

buñuelo *m* fritter

buque *m* ship, vessel; **~ cisterna/de guerra** tanker/warship

burbuja *f* (de gas, aire) bubble; **una bebida con/sin ~s** a fizzy/still drink

burbujear [A1] *vi* **(a)** «*champán/agua mineral*» to fizz **(b)** (al hervir) to bubble

burdel *m* brothel

burdeos *adj inv* ▶ 97 (color) burgundy

burdo -da *adj* **(a)** ‹*persona/modales*› coarse **(b)** ‹*mentira*› blatant; ‹*imitación*› crude; ‹*excusa*› flimsy **(c)** ‹*paño/tela*› rough, coarse

burgués -guesa *adj* (Hist) bourgeois; (de clase media) middle-class; (pey) bourgeois (pej) ■ *m,f* **(a)** (Hist) bourgeois **(b)** (persona de clase media) member of the middle class; (pey) bourgeois

burguesía *f* (Hist) bourgeoisie; (clase media) middle class, middle classes (*pl*); (pey) bourgeoisie

burla *f* **(a)** (mofa): **hacerle ~ a algn** to make fun of sb, to mock sb **(b)** (atropello): **esto es una ~ del reglamento** this makes a mockery of the regulations

burladero *m*: *barrier behind which the bullfighter takes refuge*

burlar [A1] *vt* **(a)** ‹*medidas de seguridad*› to evade, get around; **~on la vigilancia de la policía** they slipped past the police **(b)** ‹*enemigo*› to outwit ■ **burlarse** *v pron* **~se DE algo/algn** to make fun OF sth/sb

burlesco -ca *adj* ‹*género*› burlesque; ‹*espectáculo*› comic

burlete *m* draft* excluder

burlón -lona *adj* **(a)** (de mofa) ‹*actitud/tono*› mocking; ‹*risa*› sardonic, derisive **(b)** (de broma) ‹*actitud*› joking, teasing

buró *m* **(a)** (escritorio) writing desk, bureau (BrE) **(b)** (Méx) (mesa de noche) bedside table

burocracia *f* bureaucracy

burócrata *mf* **(a)** (pey) bureaucrat (pej) **(b)** (Méx) (funcionario) civil servant, official

burocrático -ca *adj* **(a)** (pey) ‹*trámite/proceso*› bureaucratic **(b)** (Méx) ‹*empleado/jerarquía*› government (*before n*), state (*before n*)

burrada *f* (fam) (necedad, barbaridad): **decir ~s** to talk nonsense *o* drivel; **¿cómo pudiste hacer semejante ~?** how could you do such a stupid thing?

burro[1] -rra *adj* **(a)** (fam) (ignorante) stupid, dumb (AmE colloq), thick (BrE colloq) **(b)** (fam) (obstinado, cabezón) pigheaded (colloq) ■ *m,f* **1** (Zool) (asno) (*m*) donkey; (*f*) female donkey, jenny; ***trabajar como un ~*** to slog one's guts out **2** (fam) **(a)** (ignorante) idiot **(b)** (cabezón, obstinado) stubborn mule, obstinate pig (colloq)

burro[2] *m* **(a)** (en carpintería) sawhorse; (en herrería) workbench **(b)** (Méx) (para planchar) ironing board; (caballete) trestle; (escalera) stepladder

bursátil *adj* stock market *o* exchange (*before n*)

bus *m* (Auto, Transp) bus; (Inf) bus

busca *f* (búsqueda) search; **en ~ de algo** in search of sth; **salieron en su ~** they set out to look for him ■ *m* (Esp fam) pager, beeper (AmE), bleeper (BrE)

buscador -dora *m,f*: **~ de oro** gold prospector; **~ de tesoros** treasure hunter

buscapleitos *mf* (*pl* ~) (fam) troublemaker

buscar [A2] *vt* **1 (a)** (intentar encontrar) to look for; ‹*fama/fortuna*› to seek; **te buscan en la portería** someone is asking for you at reception **(b)** (en libro, lista) to look up; **busca el número en la guía** look up the number in the directory **2 (a)** (recoger) to collect, pick up; **fui a ~lo al aeropuerto** (para traerlo — en coche) I went to pick him up from the airport; (— en tren, a pie) I went to meet him at the airport; **vengo a ~ mis cosas** I've come to collect *o* pick up my things **(b)** (conseguir) to get; **yo le busqué trabajo** I found him a job; **fue a ~ un médico/un taxi** he went to get a doctor/a taxi; **¿qué buscas con eso?** what are you trying to achieve by that? ■ **~** *vi* to look; **busca en el cajón** look *o* have a look in the drawer

■ **buscarse** *v pron* **1** (intentar encontrar) to look for **2** ‹*problemas*› to ask for; **no quiero ~me complicaciones/problemas** I don't want any trouble; **tú te lo has buscado** you've brought it on yourself, it serves you right; ***buscársela(s)*** (fam): **te la estás buscando** you're asking for trouble, you're asking for it (colloq)

buseta *f* (Col, Ven) small bus

búsqueda *f* **~** (DE **algo/algn**) search (FOR sth/sb)

busto *m* bust

butaca *f* **(a)** (con respaldo) (esp Esp) armchair; (sin respaldo) (esp AmL) stool **(b)** (en teatro, cine) seat; **~ de patio** (Esp) orchestra (AmE) *o* (BrE) stall seat

buzo *m* **1** (Náut) diver **2** (Indum) **(a)** (Chi, Per) (para hacer ejercicio) track suit **(b)** (Col) (suéter de cuello alto) turtleneck sweater (AmE), polo-neck jumper (BrE) **(c)** (Arg, Col) (camiseta) sweatshirt **(d)** (Ur) (jersey) sweater, jumper (BrE)

buzón *m* (en la calle) postbox, mailbox (AmE), letterbox (BrE); (en una casa) mailbox (AmE), letter-box (BrE); **echar una carta al** *or* **en el ~** to mail (AmE) *o* (BrE) post a letter

Cc

C, c *f* (*read as* /se/ *or* (Esp) /θe/) *the letter* C, c

c/ (= **calle**) St, Rd

C *m* (= **centígrado** *or* **Celsius**) C, Centigrade, Celsius

cabales *mpl*: **no está en sus ~** he's not in his right mind

cabalgar [A3] *vi* (liter) «*jinete*» to ride

cabalgata *f* (desfile) parade; **la ~ de los Reyes Magos** the Epiphany parade *o* procession

caballa *f* mackerel

caballerango *m* (Méx) groom

caballería *f* (Mil) cavalry

caballeriza *f* (edificio) stable; (caballos) stable, stables (*pl*)

caballero *m* **(a)** (en general) gentleman; **es todo un ~** he's a perfect gentleman; **sección de ~s** men's department; **¿en qué puedo servirle, ~?** how can I help you, sir?; Ⓢ **caballeros** Men *o* Gentlemen *o* Gents **(b)** (Hist) knight

caballeroso -sa *adj* gentlemanly, gallant

caballete *m* (para mesa) trestle; (para lienzo, pizarra) easel; (de moto) kickstand; (del tejado) ridge

caballito *m* **(a)** (juguete — que se mece) rocking horse; (— con palo) hobbyhorse; **~ de mar** sea horse; *ver tb* CABALLO **(b) caballitos** *mpl* (carrusel) carousel, merry-go-round

caballo[1] -lla *adj* (AmC fam) (estúpido) stupid

caballo[2] *m* **1 (a)** (Equ, Zool) horse; **montar** *or* (AmL) **andar a ~** to ride (a horse); **dieron un paseo a ~** they went for a ride (on horseback); **~ de carga/de tiro** packhorse/carthorse; **~ de carreras** racehorse; ***a ~ entre*** … halfway between …; ***llevar a algn a ~*** to give sb a piggyback **(b)** (en ajedrez) knight; (en naipes) ≈ queen (*in a Spanish pack of cards*) **(c)** (Méx) (en gimnasia) horse

2 (Auto, Fís, Mec) *tb* **~ de vapor** (metric) horsepower

cabaña *f* (choza) cabin, shack

cabaré, **cabaret** /kaβa're/ *m* (*pl* **-rets**) cabaret

cabeceada *f* **(a)** (AmL) ⇒ CABEZADA **(b)** (CS) (Dep) header

cabecear [A1] *vi* **(a)** «*persona*» to nod off **(b)** «*caballo*» to toss its head; «*barco*» to pitch ■ ~ *vt* ‹*balón*› to head

cabecera *f* **(a)** (de la cama) headboard **(b)** (de una mesa) head, top **(c)** (de una manifestación) head, front

cabecero *m* headboard

cabecilla *mf* ringleader

cabellera *f* **(a)** (melena) hair **(b)** (de un cometa) tail

cabello *m* ▶ **123**, **97** hair; **~s de ángel** (fideos) vermicelli

caber [E15] *vi* **1 (a)** (en un lugar) to fit; **no cabe en la caja** it won't fit in the box; **no cabemos los cuatro** there isn't room for all four of us; **en esta botella caben diez litros** this bottle holds ten liters; ***no ~ en sí de alegría*** to be beside oneself with joy **(b)** (pasar) to fit, go; **~ POR algo** to go THROUGH sth **(c)** «*falda/zapatos*» to fit; **estos pantalones ya no me caben** these trousers don't fit me any more **2** (*en 3ª pers*) (frml) (ser posible): **cabe la posibilidad de que haya perdido el tren** he may have missed the train; **no cabe duda de que** ... there is no doubt that ...; **cabría decir que** ... it could be said that ...; **es, si cabe, aún mejor** it is even better, if such a thing is possible; ***dentro de lo que cabe*** all things considered **3** ▶ **294** (Mat): **17 entre 5 cabe a 3 y sobran 2** 5 into 17 goes 3 times and 2 over

cabestrillo *m* sling; **llevaba el brazo en ~** he had his arm in a sling

cabeza *f* **1 (a)** ▶ **123** (Anat) head; **de la ~ a los pies** from head to toe *o* foot; **me duele la ~** I've got a headache; **marcó de ~** he scored with a header; **pararse en la** *or* **de ~** (AmL) to do a headstand; **~ rapada** skinhead **(b)** (medida) head; **me saca una ~** he's a head taller than me **(c)** (pelo) hair; **me lavé la ~** I washed my hair **(d)** (inteligencia): **usa la ~** use your head; **¡qué poca ~!** have you/has he no sense? **(e)** (mente): **¡que ~ la mía!** what a memory!; **tú estás mal de la ~** you're out of your mind; **se me ha ido de la ~** it's gone right out of my head; **se le ha metido en la ~ que** ... she's got it into her head that ...; **no se me pasó por la ~** it didn't cross my mind; **~ de chorlito** *mf* (fam) scatterbrain (colloq); ***írsele a algn la ~*** to feel dizzy; ***levantar ~*** (fam) (superar problemas) to get back on one's feet; ***perder la ~***: **no perdamos la ~** let's not panic *o* lose our heads; **perdió la ~ por esa mujer** he lost his head over that woman; ***quitarle a algn algo de la ~*** to get sth out of sb's head; ***romperse la ~*** (fam) (preocuparse) to rack one's brains; (lastimarse) to break one's neck (colloq); ***subírsele a algn a la ~*** «*vino/éxito*» to go to one's head; ***tener la ~ llena de pájaros*** (fam) to have one's head in the clouds **2 (a)** (individuo): **por ~** each, a head **(b)** (de ganado) head; **50 ~s de ganado** 50 head of cattle **3** (primer lugar, delantera): **estamos a la ~ del sector** we are the leading company in this sector; **a la ~ de la manifestación** at the front *o* head of the demonstration; **el equipo va en ~ de la clasificación** the team is at the top of the division; **~ de familia** head of the family; **~ de serie** seed **4 (a)** (de alfiler, clavo, fósforo) head **(b)** (de misil) warhead **5** (Audio, Video) head **6** (de plátanos) hand, bunch; **~ de ajo** bulb of garlic

cabezada *f* (movimiento) nod; **iba dormido, dando ~s** his head kept nodding in his sleep; ***dar*** *or* ***echar una ~*** (fam) to have a nap (colloq)

cabezal *m* **1 (a)** (almohada) bolster **(b)** (de sillón) headrest **(c)** (AmL) (de cama) headboard/footboard **2** (AmL) (terminal) terminal **3** (Audio, Video) head

cabezazo *m* **(a)** (golpe): **se dio un ~ en el estante** he hit *o* banged his head on the shelf **(b)** (Dep) header

cabezón -zona *adj* **(a)** (fam) (terco) pigheaded (colloq) **(b)** (fam) (de cabeza grande): **¡qué ~ es!** what a big head he has! **(c)** ‹*vino*› heady ■ *m,f* (fam): **¡eres un ~!** you're so pigheaded! (colloq)

cabezota *adj/mf* ⇒ CABEZÓN (a),(b)

cabezudo[1] -da *adj* (de cabeza grande): **es ~** he has a very big head

cabezudo[2] *m*: *carnival figure with a large head*

cabida *f* (capacidad de recipiente, estadio, teatro) capacity; **sólo hay ~ para diez pasajeros** there's only room *o* space for ten passengers; **el estadio puede dar ~ a 100.000 personas** the stadium can hold 100,000 people

cabina *f* **1 (a)** (vestuario) cubicle, stall (AmE) **(b)** (de laboratorio de idiomas, estudio de radio) booth; **~ telefónica** telephone booth *o* (BrE) box **2 (a)** (de camión, grúa) cab **(b)** (Aviac) (para pilotos — en avión grande) flight deck; (— en avión pequeño) cockpit; (para pasajeros) cabin

cabizbajo -ja *adj* (alicaído) downcast; **caminaba ~** he walked along, head bowed

cable *m* (Elec, Telec) cable

cablevisión *f* (esp AmL) cable television

cabo *m* **1** (Geog) cape **2 (a)** (Mil) corporal **(b)** (en remo) stroke **3** (extremo) end; **al ~ de** after; ***de ~ a rabo*** (fam) from beginning to end; ***llevar a ~*** ‹*misión*› to carry out; **lleva a ~ una excelente labor** he does an excellent job

cabra *f* goat; ***estar como una ~*** (fam) to be completely nuts (colloq)

cabrá, **cabré, etc** *see* CABER

cabreado -da *adj* (fam) furious, mad (colloq)

cabrear [A1] *vt* (fam) (enfadar) to make ... mad (colloq), to piss ... off (sl)

■ **cabrearse** *v pron* (fam) (enojarse) to get mad (colloq)

cabreo *m* (fam) (enojo, irritación): **¡qué ~ tiene!** he's in a foul *o* a terrible mood! (colloq); **agarrarse un ~** to get mad (colloq), to hit the roof (colloq)

cabría, **etc** *see* CABER

cabriola *f*: **hacer ~s** «*niño*» to caper *o* jump around; «*caballo*» to buck, prance around

cabritas *fpl* (Chi) popcorn

cabrito *m* (Zool) kid

cabro -bra *adj* (Chi fam): **es muy ~ para eso** he's too young for that ■ *m,f* (Chi fam) (niño) kid (colloq)

cabrón¹ -brona *adj* (Esp, Méx vulg): **el muy ~/la muy cabrona** the bastard *o* (AmE) son of a bitch (vulg)/the bitch (vulg) ■ *m,f* (Esp, Méx vulg) (*m*) bastard (vulg), son of a bitch (AmE vulg); (*f*) bitch (vulg)

cabrón² *m* (vulg) (cornudo) cuckold; (proxeneta) (Andes fam *o* vulg) pimp, ponce (BrE)

cabús *m* (Méx) caboose (AmE), guard's van (BrE)

caca *f* (fam *o* leng infantil): **hacer ~** to go to the bathroom (AmE) *o* (BrE) toilet (euph), to do a poop (AmE) *o* (BrE) pooh (used to or by children); **hacerse ~** to mess oneself; **el niño se hizo ~** the baby dirtied his diaper (AmE) *o* (BrE) nappy (colloq); **~ de perro** dog mess; **¡no toques eso! ¡~!** don't touch that, it's dirty!

cacahuete, cacahuate *m* peanut, monkey nut; ***me/te/le importa un (reverendo) ~*** (Méx fam) I/you/he couldn't give a damn (colloq)

cacao *m* **1 (a)** (Coc) (polvo, bebida) cocoa **(b)** (Bot) (planta) cacao; (semillas) cocoa beans (*pl*) **(c)** (Esp) (para los labios) lipsalve **2** (fam) (jaleo) ruckus (AmE), to-do (BrE); **¡qué ~ se armó!** all hell broke loose (colloq)

cacarear [A1] *vi* **(a)** «*gallo*» to crow; «*gallina*» to cluck **(b)** (fam) (presumir) to brag

cacatúa *f* (Zool) cockatoo

cacería *f* (de zorro, jabalí) hunt; (de conejo, perdiz) shoot; **ir de ~** to go hunting/shooting

cacerola *f* saucepan, pan

cachalote *m* sperm whale

cachapa *f* (Ven) *corn-based pancake*

cachar [A1] *vt* **(a)** (AmL fam) ‹*pelota*› to catch; ‹*persona*›: **la caché del brazo** I caught *o* grabbed her by the arm **(b)** (AmL fam) (sorprender, pillar) to catch **(c)** (RPl fam) (gastar una broma) to kid (colloq) **(d)** (Andes fam) (enterarse) to get (colloq)

cacharrería *f* (Col) hardware store, ironmonger's (BrE)

cacharro *m* **(a)** (de cocina) pot **(b)** (fam) (cachivache) thing; (coche viejo) jalopy (AmE), old banger (BrE colloq); (aparato) gadget

cachaza *f* (bebida) *type of rum*

cachear [A1] *vt* **1** (fam) (registrar) to frisk, search **2** (AmL) (Taur) to gore

cachemir *m*, **cachemira** *f* cashmere

cachetada *f* (AmL) slap

cachete *m* **1** (mejilla) (esp AmL) cheek; (nalga) (CS fam) cheek **2** (esp Esp) (bofetada) slap

cachetear [A1] *vt* (AmL) to slap

cachetón -tona *adj* (Andes, Méx fam) (carrilludo) chubby-cheeked

cachimba *f* pipe; **fumar ~** to smoke a pipe

cachiporra *f* (palo) billy club (AmE), truncheon (BrE)

cachito *m* **1** (Méx) (de lotería) *one twentieth of a lottery ticket*; *ver tb* CACHO 1 **2** (Ven) (Coc) croissant

cachivache *m* (fam) (trasto inútil) piece of junk; **tiró todos los ~s que tenía** she threw out all her old junk (colloq)

cacho *m* **1** (fam) (pedazo) bit **2 (a)** (AmS) (cuerno) horn **(b)** (Andes) (juego) poker dice; (cubilete) shaker

cachondearse [A1] *v pron* (Esp fam) **~ DE algn/algo** to make fun OF sb/sth

cachondeo *m* (Esp fam): **estar de ~** to be joking; **se lo toma a ~** he treats it as a joke

cachondo -da *adj* (fam) **(a)** (Esp) (divertido) funny **(b)** (Esp, Méx) (sexualmente) hot (colloq), horny (sl)

cachorro -rra *m,f* (de perro) puppy, pup; (de león) cub

cachucha *f* (Col, Méx, Ven) (Indum) cap

cacillo *m* (cacerola) small saucepan; (cucharón) ladle

cacique *m* (Hist) chief, cacique; (Pol) local political boss; (hombre poderoso) tyrant

caco *m* (fam) burglar

cactus (*pl* ~), **cacto** *m* cactus

cada *adj inv* **1 (a)** (con énfasis en el individuo o cosa particular) each; (con énfasis en la totalidad del conjunto) every; **los ganadores de ~ grupo** the winners from each group; **hay un bar en ~ esquina** ther's a bar in every corner; **~ día** every day, each day; **¿~ cuánto viene?** how often does she come?; **hay cinco para ~ uno** there are five each; **cuestan $25 ~ uno** they cost $25 each; **~ uno** *or* **cual sabe qué es lo que más le conviene** everyone *o* each individual knows what's best for him or her; **~ vez que viene** every time *o* whenever he comes **(b)** (delante de numeral) every; **~ dos días** every two days, every other day; **siete de ~ diez** seven out of (every) ten **2** (indicando progresión): **~ vez más rápido** faster and faster; **lo hace ~ vez mejor** she's getting better all the time; **~ vez más gente** more and more people; **~ vez menos tiempo** less and less time

cadalso *m* (patíbulo) scaffold; (horca) gallows (*pl*)

cadáver *m* (de persona) corpse; (de animal) carcass

cadavérico -ca *adj* cadaverous, ghastly

caddie, caddy /'kaði/ *mf* (*pl* **-dies**) caddy

cadena *f* **1 (a)** (de eslabones) chain; (para la nieve) (snow) chain; **~ antirrobo** bicycle lock; **~ perpetua** life imprisonment **(b)** (del wáter) chain; **tirar de la ~** to flush the toilet **2 (a)** (de hechos, fenómenos) chain; **una larga ~ de atentados** a long series of attacks; **~ de fabricación** *or* **producción** production line; **~ de montañas** mountain range *o* chain; **en ~** ‹*transmisión*› simultaneous; **una choque en ~** a pileup **(b)** (de hoteles, supermercados) chain; **~ de radiodifusión** radio network **3** (TV) channel

cadencia *f* cadence

cadeneta *f* (labor) chain stitch; (de papel) paper chain

cadera *f* ▶ 123 hip

cadete *m* (Mil, Náut) cadet

caducar [A2] *vi* **(a)** «*carné/pasaporte*» to expire; **el plazo caduca el 17 de enero** the closing date (*for enrollment, etc*) is January 17; **estar caducado** to be out of date; «*yogurt*» to be past its sell-by date/use-by date **(b)** «*medicamento*» to expire (frml); Ⓢ **caduca a los tres meses** use within three months

caduco -ca *adj* **(a)** ‹*hoja*› deciduous **(b)** ‹*teoría/costumbres/valores*› outdated

caer [E16] *vi* **1** (de una altura) to fall; (de posición vertical) to fall over; **el coche cayó por un precipicio** the car went over a cliff; **cayó muerto allí mismo** he dropped down dead on the spot; **cayó en el mar** it came down in the sea; **~ *parado*** (AmL) to land on one's feet; ***dejar* ~ *algo*** ‹*objeto*› to drop; ‹*indirecta*› to drop; **dejó ~ la noticia que** ... she let drop the news that ... **2 (a)** «*chaparrón/nevada*»: **cayó un chaparrón** it poured down; **cayó una fuerte nevada** it snowed heavily; **el rayo cayó cerca** the lightning struck nearby **(b)** «*noche*» to fall; **al ~ la tarde/noche** at sunset *o* dusk/nightfall **3 (a)** (pender) «*cortinas/falda*» to hang **(b)** «*terreno*» to drop; **~ en pendiente** to slope down **4** (en error, trampa): **no caigas en ese error** don't make that mistake; **todos caímos (en la trampa)** we all fell for it; **cayó en la tentación de mirar** she succumbed to the temptation to look; **~ *muy bajo*** to stoop very low **5** (fam) (entender, darse cuenta): **¡ah, ya caigo!** (ya entiendo) oh, now I get it! (colloq); (ya recuerdo) oh, now I remember; **no caigo** I'm not sure what (*o* who *etc*) you mean; **no caí en que tú no tenías llave** I didn't realize *o* (fam) I didn't click that you didn't have keys **6** (en un estado): **~ en el olvido** to sink into oblivion; **~ enfermo** to fall ill **7** «*gobierno/ciudad*» to fall; «*soldado*» (morir) to fall, die **8** «*precios/temperatura*» to fall, drop **9 (a)** (sentar): **el pescado me cayó mal** the fish didn't agree with me; **le cayó muy mal que no la invitaran** she was very upset about not being invited **(b)** «*persona*»: **tu primo me cae muy bien** I really like your cousin; **me cae muy mal** (fam) I can't stand him (colloq); **¿qué tal te cayó?** what did you think of him? **10** «*cumpleaños/festividad*» to fall on; **¿el 27 en qué (día) cae?** what day's the 27th?

■ **caerse** *v pron* **(a)** (de una altura) to fall; (de posición vertical) to fall, to fall over; **me caí por las escaleras** I fell down the stairs; **~se del caballo/de la cama** to fall off one's horse/out of bed; **está que se cae de cansancio** (fam) she's dead on her feet (colloq) **(b) caérsele algo A algn**: **oiga, se le cayó un guante** excuse me, you dropped your glove; **no se te vaya a ~** don't drop it; **se me cayó de las manos** it slipped out of my hands; **se me están cayendo las medias** my stockings are falling down **(c)** (desprenderse) «*diente*» to fall out; «*hojas*» to fall off; «*botón*» to come off, fall off; **se le empieza a ~ el pelo** he's started to lose his hair

café *adj* (*gen inv*) ▶97 (AmC, Chi, Méx) (marrón) brown; **ojos ~(s)** brown eyes ■ *m* **1** (cultivo, bebida) coffee; **me sirvió un ~** he gave me a cup of coffee, he gave me a coffee (BrE); **~ cerrero** (Col) large strong black coffee; **~ con leche** (bebida) regular coffee (AmE), white coffee (BrE); **~ cortado** *coffee with a dash of milk*; **~ expreso** espresso; **~ instantáneo** *o* **soluble** instant coffee; **~ natural/torrefacto** light roast/high roast coffee; **~ negro** (AmL) *or* (Chi) **puro** *or* (Col) **tinto** *or* (Esp) **solo** black coffee **2** (cafetería) café; **~ bar** café **3** (AmC, Chi, Méx) (marrón) ▶97 brown

cafeína *f* caffeine

cafetal *m* coffee plantation

cafetera *f* **(a)** (para hacer café) coffee maker; (para servir café) coffeepot; ***estar como una* ~** (fam) to be off one's rocker *o* head (colloq) **(b)** (fam) (coche viejo) old heap (colloq)

cafetería *f* (café) café; (en museo, fábrica) cafeteria

cafetero -ra *adj* ‹*industria/finca*› coffee (*before n*); ‹*país*› coffee-producing (*before n*), coffee-growing (*before n*); **ser muy ~** to be a real coffee addict ■ *m,f* coffee planter *o* grower

cafeto *m* coffee tree

caficultor -tora *m,f* (Col) coffee grower

cagar [A3] *vi* (vulg) (defecar) to have a shit (vulg) ■ **cagarse** *v pron* (vulg) to shit oneself (vulg)

caída *f* **1** (en general) fall; **sufrir una ~** «*persona*» to have a fall; **~ libre** free fall; **la ~ del gobierno** the fall of the government; **la ~ del cabello** hair loss **2** (de tela, falda): **necesitas una tela con más ~** you need a heavier material; **tiene buena ~** it hangs well **3** (descenso) **~ DE algo** ‹*del dólar/de los precios/de la demanda*› fall IN sth; ‹*de temperatura/voltaje*› drop IN sth; **~ de agua** waterfall

caído[1] -da *adj* **1 (a)** (en el suelo) fallen **(b)** ‹*pechos*› drooping, sagging; **tener los hombros ~s** to be round-shouldered **(c)** (en la guerra): **soldados ~s en combate** soldiers who fell in combat **2** (Col) ‹*vivienda*› dilapidated, run-down

caído[2] *m*: **los ~s** the fallen

caiga, caigas, etc *see* CAER

caimán *m* (Zool) caiman, cayman, alligator

Cairo *m*: **el ~** Cairo

caja *f* **1 (a)** (recipiente) box; **una ~ de fósforos** (con fósforos) a box of matches; (vacía) a matchbox; **una ~ de vino** a crate of wine; **~ de cambios** gearbox; **~ de herramientas** toolbox; **~ de música** music box; **~ de resonancia** (Mús) soundbox; **~ de seguridad** safe-deposit box, safety deposit box; **~ fuerte** safe, strongbox **(b)** (de reloj) case, casing **(c)** (Mús) (de violín, guitarra) soundbox; (tambor) drum **(d)** (fam) (ataúd) coffin **2** (Com) **(a)** (lugar — en banco) window; (— en supermercado) checkout; (— en tienda, restaurante) cash desk, till **(b)** (máquina) *tb* **~ registradora** till, cash register **(c)** (dinero) cash; **hicimos una ~ de medio millón** we took half a million pesos (*o* pesetas *etc*); **~ de ahorros** savings bank; ***hacer* (*la*) ~** to cash up

cajero -ra *m,f* (en tienda) cashier; (en banco) teller, cashier; (en supermercado) check out operator; **~ automático** *or* **permanente** cash dispenser, automated teller machine (AmE), ATM (AmE)

cajeta *f* (Méx) caramel topping/filling

cajetilla *f* pack (AmE), packet (BrE)

cajón *m* **1 (a)** (en mueble) drawer **(b)** (caja grande) *tb* **~ de embalaje** crate; (para mudanzas) packing case **(c)** (AmL) (ataúd) coffin, casket (AmE) **2** (Méx) (en un estacionamiento) parking space

cajuela *f* (Méx) trunk (AmE), boot (BrE)

cal *f* lime

cala *f* **(a)** (ensenada) cove **(b)** (Náut) hold

calabacín *m*, (Méx) **calabacita** *f* zucchini (AmE), courgette (BrE)

calabaza *f* (fruto — redondo) pumpkin; (— alargado) squash (AmE), marrow (BrE)

calabozo *m* (en comisaría, cárcel) cell; (en cuartel) guardroom; (Hist) dungeon

calada *f* (Esp fam) (de cigarro) drag (sl), puff (colloq)

caladero *m* fishing ground

calado -da *adj* **1** (empapado) [ESTAR] soaked, drenched **2** ‹*jersey/tela*› openwork (*before n*)

calamar *m* squid; **~es a la romana** squid fried in batter

calambre *m* **(a)** (espasmo) cramp; **me ha dado un ~ en el pie** I have a cramp (AmE) *o* (BrE) I've got cramp in my foot **(b)** (sacudida eléctrica) electric shock; **me dio un ~** I got an electric shock

calamidad *f* **(a)** (desastre, desgracia) disaster, calamity; **¡las ~es que ha pasado!** the terrible things he's gone through! **(b)** (persona inútil) disaster (colloq)

calar [A1] *vt* **1** «*líquido*» (empapar) to soak; (atravesar) to soak through; **el agua me caló los calcetines** water soaked through my socks **2** (fam) ‹*persona/intenciones*› to rumble (colloq), to suss ... out (BrE colloq) **3** «*barco*» to draw **4** (Esp) ‹*coche/motor*› to stall ■ **~** *vi* **1** «*moda*» to catch on; «*costumbre/filosofía*» to take root **2** «*zapatos/tienda de campaña*» to leak, let water in

■ **calarse** *v pron* **1** (empaparse) to get soaked, get drenched **2** (Esp) «*coche/motor*» to stall

calavera[1] *f* **1** (Anat) skull **2** (Méx) (Auto) taillight

calavera[2] *m* (fam) rake

calcado -da *adj* **(a)** [SER] (fam): **ser ~ a algn** to be the spitting image of sb (colloq); **ser ~ a algo** to be exactly the same as sth **(b)** [ESTAR] (fam): **están ~s** one is a carbon copy of the other; **está ~ del de Serra** it's a straight copy of Serra's

calcar [A2] *vt* **(a)** ‹*dibujo/mapa*› to trace **(b)** (plagiar) to copy

calceta *f* (labor) knitting; **hacer ~** to knit

calcetín *m* sock

calcinar [A1] *vt* **(a)** (abrasar) «*fuego*» to burn; **cadáveres calcinados** charred bodies **(b)** (Quím) to calcine

calcio *m* calcium

calco *m* (copia) exact replica

calcomanía *f* transfer, decal (AmE)

calculador -dora *adj* calculating

calculadora *f* calculator

calcular [A1] *vt* **1 (a)** (Mat) to calculate, work out; **calculé mal la distancia** I miscalculated the distance **(b)** (evaluar) ‹*pérdidas/gastos*› to estimate **(c)** (conjeturar) to reckon, to guess (esp AmE); **yo le calculo unos sesenta años** I reckon *o* guess he's about sixty **(d)** (imaginar) to imagine **2** (planear) to work out; **lo tenía todo calculado** he had it all worked out

cálculo *m* **1** (Mat) **(a)** (operación) calculation; **según mis ~s** according to my calculations; **hizo un ~ aproximado** she made a rough estimate; **~ mental** mental arithmetic **(b)** (disciplina) calculus **2** (plan): **eso no entraba en mis ~s** I hadn't allowed for that in my plans *o* calculations; **le fallaron los ~s** things didn't work out as he had planned; **un error de ~** a miscalculation **3** (Med) stone, calculus (tech)

caldear [A1] *vt* ‹*habitación/local*› to heat, heat ... up

■ **caldearse** *v pron* **(a)** «*habitación/local*» to warm up, heat up **(b)** (enardecerse): **se estaban empezando a ~ los ánimos** feelings started to run high

caldera *f* **(a)** (industrial, de calefacción) boiler **(b)** (caldero) caldron*, copper (BrE)

calderilla *f* change, small *o* loose change

caldero *m* caldron*, copper (BrE)

caldo *m* (Coc) clear soup; (con arroz, etc) soup; (para cocinar) stock; (salsa de asado, etc) juices (*pl*); **~ de pollo** chicken stock

calé *adj* gypsy (*before n*) ■ *mf* gypsy

calefacción *f* heating; **~ a gas** gas heating; **~ central** central heating

caleidoscopio *m* kaleidoscope

calendario *m* **(a)** (en general) calendar; **~ de taco** tear-off calendar; **~ escolar** school calendar **(b)** (programa) schedule; **tiene un ~ muy apretado** she has a very tight schedule

calentador *m* **(a)** (para agua) (water) heater; (estufa) heater **(b) calentadores** *mpl* (Dep, Indum) legwarmers (*pl*)

calentamiento *m* **(a)** (Dep) warm-up **(b)** (Fís) warming; **~ global** *or* **del planeta** global warming

calentar [A5] *vt* **1 (a)** ‹*agua/comida*› to heat (up); ‹*habitación*› to heat **(b)** ‹*motor/coche*› to warm up **(c)** (Dep): **~ los músculos** to warm up **2** (AmL fam) (enojar) to make ... mad (colloq) ■ **~** *vi*: **¡cómo calienta hoy el sol!** the sun's really hot today!; **esta estufa casi no calienta** this heater is hardly giving off any heat

■ **calentarse** *v pron* **1 (a)** «*horno/plancha*» to heat up; «*habitación*» to warm up, get warm **(b)** «*motor/coche*» (al arrancar) to warm up; (en exceso) to overheat **2** (vulg) (excitarse sexualmente) to get turned on (colloq) **3** «*debate*» to become heated; **los ánimos se ~on** tempers flared **4** (AmL fam) (enojarse) to get mad (colloq)

calentura *f* **(a)** (fiebre) temperature **(b)** (en la boca) cold sore

calesita *f* (Per, RPl) merry-go-round, carousel

caleta *f* (ensenada) cove

calibrar [A1] *vt* **(a)** ‹*arma/tubo*› to calibrate **(b)** ‹*consecuencias/situación*› to weigh up

calibre *m* caliber*; **de ~ 22** 22 caliber; **de grueso ~** ‹*arma/proyectil*› large-bore; ‹*error*› (AmL) serious

calidad *f* **1** (de producto, servicio) quality; **un artículo de primera ~** a top-quality product; **productos de mala ~** poor-quality products; **~ de vida** quality of life **2** (condición): **asistió en ~ de observador** he attended as an observer; **en su ~ de presidente** in his capacity as president

cálido -da *adj* **(a)** ▶ 409 (Meteo) hot **(b)** ‹*acogida/bienvenida*› warm **(c)** ‹*color/tono*› warm

calidoscopio *m* kaleidoscope

calienta, **etc** *see* CALENTAR

caliente *adj* **1** ‹*agua/comida/horno*› hot; **aquí estaremos más calentitas** we'll be warmer here; **tomó la decisión en ~** she made the decision in the heat of the moment **2** (fam) (sexualmente) hot (colloq), horny (sl)

caliento *see* CALENTAR

califa *m* caliph

calificación *f* **(a)** (Educ) grade (AmE), mark (BrE) **(b)** (descripción) description **(c)** (de película) rating

calificado -da *adj* (esp AmL) ‹*mano de obra*› skilled; ‹*profesional*› qualified

calificar [A2] *vt* **1 ~ algo/a algn DE algo** (describir) to describe sth/sb AS sth; (categorizar) to label sth/sb AS sth **2** (Educ) **(a)** ‹*examen*› to grade (AmE), to mark (BrE); ‹*alumno*› to give a grade (AmE) *o* (BrE) mark to **(b)** (habilitar) «*título/diploma*» **~ a algn PARA hacer algo** to qualify sb TO do sth **3** (Ling) to qualify

California *f* California

californiano -na *adj/m,f* Californian

caligrafía *f* (arte) calligraphy; (de persona) writing, handwriting

calipso *m* **(a)** (Mús) calypso **(b)** ▶ **97** **(de) color ~** deep turquoise

cáliz *m* **(a)** (Relig) chalice **(b)** (Bot) calyx

caliza *f* limestone

calizo -za *adj* ‹*tierra*› limy; **piedra caliza** limestone

callado -da *adj* **(a)** [ESTAR] (silencioso) quiet; **estuvo ~ durante toda la reunión** he kept quiet throughout the whole meeting; **lo escucharon ~s** they listened to him quietly **(b)** [SER] (poco hablador) quiet

callampa *f* (Chi) **(a)** (hongo) mushroom **(b)** (vivienda) shanty (dwelling) **(c) callampas** *fpl* (poblaciones marginales) shantytown

callar [A1] *vi* to be quiet, shut up (colloq); **no pude hacerlo ~** I couldn't get him to be quiet; **hacer ~ a la oposición** to silence the opposition ■ **~** *vt* **(a)** ‹*secreto/información*› to keep ... quiet **(b)** (AmL) ‹*persona*› to get ... to be quiet, to shut ... up (colloq) ■ **callarse** *v pron* **(a)** (guardar silencio) to be quiet; **¡cállate!** be quiet!, shut up! (colloq); **cuando entró todos se ~on** when he walked in everyone went quiet *o* stopped talking; **la próxima vez no me ~é** next time I'll say something **(b)** (no decir) ‹*noticia*› to keep ... quiet, keep ... to oneself

calle *f* **1** (vía) street; **~ ciega** (Andes, Ven) dead end, cul-de-sac (BrE); **~ de dirección única** *or* (Col) **de una vía** one-way street; **~ peatonal** pedestrian street; **hoy no he salido a la ~** I haven't been out today; **el libro saldrá a la ~ mañana** the book comes out tomorrow; **el hombre de la ~** the man in the street; **el lenguaje de la ~** colloquial language; ***echar a algn a la ~*** to throw sb out (on the street); ***en la ~*** ‹*estar/quedar*› (en la ruina) penniless; (sin vivienda) homeless; (sin trabajo) out of work **2** (Esp) (en atletismo, natación) lane; (en golf) fairway

callejear [A1] *vi* to hang around the streets (colloq)

callejero[1] -ra *adj* ‹*riña/venta/músico*› street (*before n*); ‹*perro*› stray (*before n*)

callejero[2] *m* (Esp) street map *o* plan

callejón *m* alley, narrow street; **~ sin salida** (calle) dead end, blind alley; (situación) dead end

callejuela *f* narrow street

callista *mf* chiropodist

callo *m* **(a)** (en los dedos del pie) corn; (en la planta del pie, en las manos) callus; (en una fractura) callus **(b) callos** *mpl* (Esp) (Coc) tripe

callosidad *f* callus

calma *f* calm; **con ~** calmly; **mantener la ~** to keep calm; **tómatelo con ~** take it easy; **no hay que perder la ~** the thing is not to lose your cool; **el mar está en ~** the sea is calm; **¡~, por favor!** (en situación peligrosa) please, keep calm! *o* don't panic!; (en discusión acalorada) calm down, please!

calmante *m* (para dolores) painkiller; (para los nervios) tranquilizer

calmar [A1] *vt* **(a)** (tranquilizar) ‹*persona*› to calm ... down; ‹*nervios*› to calm; **esto calmó los ánimos** this eased the tension **(b)** (aliviar) ‹*dolor*› to relieve, ease; ‹*sed*› to quench; ‹*hambre*› to take the edge off ■ **calmarse** *v pron* **(a)** «*persona*» to calm down **(b)** «*mar*» to become calm

calmo -ma *adj* (esp AmL) calm

caló *m* gypsy slang

calor *m* [*Use of the feminine gender, although common in some areas, is generally considered to be archaic or non-standard*] **1 (a)** ▶ **409** (Fis, Meteo) heat; **hace ~** it's hot; **hacía un ~ agobiante** the heat was stifling *o* suffocating **(b)** (sensación): **tener ~** to be hot; **pasamos un ~ horrible** it was terribly hot; **entrar en ~** to get warm; **esta chaqueta me da mucho ~** I feel very hot in this jacket; **al ~ del fuego** by the fireside **2** (afecto) warmth **3 calores** *mpl* (de la menopausia) hot flashes (*pl*) (AmE), hot flushes (*pl*) (BrE)

caloría *f* calorie

calumnia *f* (oral) defamation, slander; (escrita) libel; **levantaron ~s contra la institución** they spread slanderous rumors about the institution

calumniar [A1] *vt* (por escrito) to libel; (oralmente) to slander

caluroso -sa *adj* **(a)** ▶ **409** ‹*día/clima*› hot **(b)** ‹*acogida/aplauso*› warm; **recibe un ~ saludo** (Corresp) best wishes

calva *f* (cabeza sin pelo) bald head; (parte sin pelo) bald patch

calvicie *f* baldness

calvo -va *adj* ‹*persona*› bald; **quedarse ~** to go bald ■ *m,f* bald person

calza *f* **(a)** (cuña) chock **(b)** (Col) (en una muela) filling

calzada *f* (camino) road; (de calle) road; (de autopista) side, carriageway

calzado *m* (frml) footwear (frml)

calzador *m* shoehorn

calzar [A4] *vt* **1 (a)** ‹*persona*› (proveerla de calzado) to provide ... with shoes; (ponerle los zapatos): **calzó a los niños** she put the children's shoes on **(b)** ▶ **401** (llevar): **calzo (un) 39** I take (a) size 39, I'm a 39; **calzaba zapatillas de deporte** he was wearing training shoes **2** ‹*rueda*› to chock, wedge a block under **3** (Col) ‹*muela*› to fill

■ **calzarse** *v pron* (*refl*) **(a)** (ponerse los zapatos) to put one's shoes on **(b)** ‹*zapato*› to put on

calzoncillos *mpl*, **calzoncillo** *m* underpants, shorts (*pl*) (AmE), pants (*pl*) (BrE); ~ **largos** long underwear, long johns (*pl*) (colloq)

calzones *mpl*, **calzón** *m* **1 (a)** (antiguos) long underwear, long johns (*pl*) (colloq) **(b)** (AmS) (modernos) panties (*pl*), knickers (*pl*) (BrE) **2 calzón** *m* (Esp) (para deporte) shorts (*pl*)

cama *f* (para dormir) bed; **hacer** *or* (AmL) **tender la** ~ to make the bed; **¡métete en la** ~**!** get into bed!; **guardar** ~ to stay in bed; **está en** ~ she's in bed; ~ **camarote** (AmL) bunk bed; ~ **doble** *or* **de matrimonio** *or* (AmL) **de dos plazas** double bed; ~ **individual** *or* (AmL) **de una plaza** single bed; ~ **solar** sunbed; ***caer en*** ~ to fall ill

camada *f* (Zool) litter; (de ladrones, sinvergüenzas) (pey) gang

camaleón *m* chameleon

cámara *f* **1 (a)** (arc) (aposento) chamber (frml) **(b)** (recinto): ~ **acorazada** *or* **blindada** strongroom, vault; ~ **de descompresión** decompression chamber; ~ **de gas** gas chamber; ~ **frigorífica** cold store **2** (Gob, Pol): **C**~ **de los Diputados** Chamber of Deputies; **C**~ **de los Comunes/de los Lores** House of Commons/of Lords; **C**~ **de Representantes** House of Representatives **3** (Com, Fin) association; ~ **de comercio** chamber of commerce **4** (aparato) camera; **en** *or* (Esp) **a** ~ **lenta** in slow motion; ~ **de cine** film camera; ~ **de video** *or* (Esp) **vídeo** video camera; ~ **fotográfica** camera

camarada *mf* **(a)** (de partido político) comrade **(b)** (de colegio) school friend; (de trabajo) colleague

camaradería *f* camaraderie, comradeship

camarero -ra *m,f* **1** (esp Esp) (en bar, restaurante) (*m*) waiter; (*f*) waitress; (detrás de mostrador) (*m*) barman, bartender (AmE); (*f*) barmaid, bartender (AmE) **2 (a)** (en hotel) (*m*) bellboy; (*f*) maid **(b)** (Transp) (*m*) steward; (*f*) stewardess

camarín *m* (CS) **(a)** (Teatr) dressing room **(b)** (en vestuarios) changing cubicle **(c) camarines** *mpl* (Chi) (Dep) changing rooms (*pl*), locker rooms (*pl*)

camarógrafo -fa *m,f* (*m*) cameraman; (*f*) camerawoman

camarón *m* (crustáceo — pequeño) shrimp; (— más grande) shrimp (AmE), prawn (BrE)

camarote *m* cabin

cambalache *m* **(a)** (fam) (trueque) swap (colloq); **hacer** ~**s** to swap (colloq) **(b)** (RPl fam & pey) (tienda) thrift store (AmE), junk shop (BrE)

cambiante *adj* ‹*tiempo*› changeable, unsettled; ‹*persona/carácter*› moody, temperamental

cambiar [A1] *vt* **1 (a)** (alterar, modificar) ‹*horario/imagen/persona*› to change **(b)** (de lugar, posición): ~ **los muebles de lugar** to move the furniture around; **cambié las flores de florero** I put the flowers in a different vase **(c)** (reemplazar) ‹*pieza/fecha/sábanas*› to change; **le cambió la pila al reloj** she changed the battery in the clock; ~**le el nombre a algo** to change the name of sth **(d)** ‹*niño/bebé*› to change **(e)** (Fin) to change; **cambié 100 libras a** *or* (Esp) **en dólares** I changed 100 pounds into dollars **2** (canjear) ‹*sellos/estampas*› to swap, to trade (esp AmE); ~ **algo** POR **algo** ‹*sellos/estampas*› to swap *o* (esp AmE) trade sth FOR sth; ‹*compra*› to exchange *o* change sth FOR sth; **¿quieres que te cambie el lugar?** do you want me to swap *o* change places with you? ■ ~ *vi* **(a)** «*ciudad/persona*» to change; ~ **para peor** to change for the worse; **le está cambiando la voz** his voice is breaking **(b)** (Auto) to change gear **(c)** (hacer transbordo) to change; ~ **de avión/tren** to change planes/train **(d)** ~ DE **algo** ‹*de tema/canal/color*› to change sth; ~ **de idea** to change one's mind; ~ **de sentido** to make (AmE) *o* (BrE) do a U-turn

■ **cambiarse** *v pron* **(a)** (*refl*) (de ropa) to change, get changed **(b)** (*refl*) ‹*camisa/nombre/peinado*› to change; ~**se** DE **algo** ‹*de pantalones/zapatos*› to change sth; **me cambié de sitio** I changed places; ~**se de casa** to move house; **cámbiate de camisa** change your shirt **(c)** ~**se** POR **algn** to change places WITH sb **(d)** (*recípr*) ‹*sellos/estampas*› to swap, to trade (esp AmE) **(e)** (CS) (mudarse de casa) to move

cambio *m* **1 (a)** (alteración) change; ~ DE **algo** ‹*de planes/domicilio*› change OF sth; **un** ~ **de aire(s)** *or* **ambiente** a change of scene **(b)** (Auto) gearshift (AmE), gear change (BrE); **un coche con cinco** ~**s** (AmL) a car with a five-speed gearbox; ~ **de sentido** U-turn **2 (a)** (canje) exchange; Ⓢ **no se admiten cambios** goods cannot be exchanged **(b)** (*en locs*) **a cambio (de)** in exchange (for), in return (for); **en cambio**: **el viaje en autobús es agotador, en** ~ **en tren es muy agradable** the bus journey is exhausting; by train however *o* on the other hand is very pleasant **3 (a)** (Fin) (de moneda extranjera) exchange; ~ **de divisas** foreign exchange; **¿a cómo está el** ~**?** what's the exchange rate?; Ⓢ **cambio** bureau de change, change **(b)** (diferencia) change; **me ha dado mal el** ~ he's given me the wrong change **(c)** (dinero suelto) change

cambista *mf* moneychanger

cambur *m* (Ven) (fruta) banana

camelia *f* camellia

camello *m* (Zool) camel

camellón *m* (Méx) (en la calle) traffic island

camelo *m* (fam) (timo) con (colloq); (mentira) lie

camerino *m* **(a)** (Teatr) dressing room **(b) camerinos** *mpl* (Col) (Dep) changing rooms (*pl*)

camilla *f* (de lona) stretcher; (con ruedas) trolley, gurney (AmE); (en un consultorio) couch

camillero -ra *m,f* stretcher-bearer

caminante *mf* hiker; (liter) traveler*

caminar [A1] *vi* **1** (andar) to walk; **salieron a** ~ they went out for a walk; **podemos ir caminando** we can walk, we can go on foot; ~ HACIA **algo** ‹*hacia meta/fin*› to move TOWARD(s) sth **2** (AmL) «*reloj/motor*» to work; «*asunto*» (fam): **el asunto va caminando** things are moving (colloq) ■ ~ *vt* ‹*distancia*› to walk

caminata *f* long walk; (en el campo) long walk, hike; **después de darme semejante** ~ after walking *o* (colloq) trekking all that way

camino *m* **1** (en general) road; (de tierra) track; (sendero) path; ~ **vecinal** minor road (*built and* *maintained by local council*) **2 (a)** (ruta, dirección) way; **saberse el ~** to know the way; **me salieron al ~** «*asaltantes*» they blocked my path *o* way; «*amigos*» they came out to meet me; **éste es el mejor ~ a seguir** this is the best course to follow; **el ~ a la fama** the road *o* path to fame; **se abrió ~ entre la espesura** she made her way through the dense thickets; **abrirse ~ en la vida** to get on in life; ***buen/mal* ~: este niño va por mal ~** this boy's heading for trouble; **ibas por buen ~ pero te equivocaste** you were on the right track but you made a mistake; **llevar a algn por mal ~** to lead sb astray **(b)** (trayecto, viaje): **el ~ de regreso** the return journey; **se pusieron en ~** they set off; **todavía nos quedan dos horas de ~** we still have two hours to go **(c)** (*en locs*) **camino de/a** ... on my/his/her way to ...; ***ir* ~ *de algo*: una tradición que va ~ de desaparecer** a tradition which looks set to disappear; **de camino** on the way; **pilla de ~** it's on the way; **me queda de ~** I pass it on my way; **de ~ a la estación** on the way to the station; **en camino** on the way; **deben estar ya en ~** they must be on their way already; **por el camino** on the way; ***a mitad de*** or ***a medio* ~** halfway through

camión *m* **(a)** (de carga) truck, lorry (BrE); (contenido) truckload; **~ cisterna** tanker; **~ de la basura** garbage truck (AmE), dustcart (BrE); **~ de mudanzas** moving van (AmE), removal van (BrE) **(b)** (AmC, Méx) (autobús) bus

camionero -ra *m,f* truck driver, lorry driver (BrE); (conductor de autobús) (AmC, Méx) bus driver

camioneta *f* **(a)** (furgoneta) van; (camión pequeño) light truck, pickup truck **(b)** (AmL) (coche familiar) station wagon (AmE), estate car (BrE)

camisa *f* **▶401** shirt; **en mangas de ~** in shirtsleeves; **~ de fuerza** straitjacket; ***cambiar de* ~** to change sides

camiseta *f* **(a)** (prenda interior) undershirt (AmE), vest (BrE) **(b)** (prenda exterior) T-shirt; (de fútbol) shirt, jersey (AmE); (sin mangas) jersey (AmE), vest (BrE)

camisón *m* nightdress

camomila *f* camomile, chamomile

camorra *f* (fam) (bronca, riña) fight; **armar ~** to start a fight; **buscar ~** to look for a fight (colloq)

camorrero -ra *adj/mf* (Col, CS) ⇒ CAMORRISTA

camorrista *adj* (fam) (pendenciero): **no seas ~** stop being a troublemaker ■ *mf* troublemaker (colloq)

camote *m* (Bot) (Andes, Méx) (batata) sweet potato; ***hacerse* ~** (Méx fam) to get in a muddle (colloq)

campamento *m* camp; **nos fuimos a Bariloche de ~** we went camping in Bariloche

campana *f* **(a)** (de iglesia, colegio) bell; **oía las ~s** I could hear the bells ringing; **tocar la ~** to ring the bell; **¿ya ha sonado la ~?** has the bell gone yet? **(b)** (de chimenea) hood; (de cocina) extractor hood

campanada *f* **(a)** (de campana) chime, stroke; (de reloj) stroke; **el reloj dio 12 ~s** the clock struck 12 **(b)** (fam) (sorpresa): **la noticia fue una ~** the news came like a bolt from the blue (colloq); ***dar la* ~** to cause a stir

campanario *m* bell tower, belfry

campanazo *m* (AmL) ⇒ CAMPANADA

campanilla *f* **(a)** (campana pequeña) small bell, hand bell **(b)** (Anat) uvula **(c)** (Bot) campanula, bellflower

campante *adj*: **se quedó tan ~** he didn't bat an eyelid; **nosotros muertos de miedo y él tan ~** we were scared stiff but he was as cool as a cucumber

campaña *f* campaign; **~ electoral** electoral *o* election campaign; **~ publicitaria** advertising campaign; **hacer una ~** to run *o* conduct a campaign

campechano -na *adj* (sin complicaciones) straightforward; (bondadoso) good-natured

campeón -peona *adj* champion (*before n*) ■ *m, f* champion; **el ~ del mundo** the world champion

campeonato *m* championship

cámper *f* (Chi, Méx) camper (van)

campera *f* **(a)** (RPl) (chaqueta) jacket **(b) camperas** *fpl* (Esp) (botas) cowboy boots

campero *m* (Col) (Auto) jeep

campesino -na *adj* ‹*vida/costumbre*› rural, country (*before n*); ‹*modales/aspecto*› peasant-like ■ *m,f* (persona del campo) country person; (con connotaciones de pobreza) peasant; **son ~s** they are country people *o* folk; **los obreros y los ~s** the manual workers and the agricultural workers

campestre *adj* ‹*escena/vida*› rural, country (*before n*); ‹*casa/club*› country (*before n*)

camping /'kampin/ *m* (*pl* **-pings**) **(a)** (actividad) camping; **irse de ~** to go camping **(b)** (lugar) campsite, campground (AmE)

campiña *f* countryside; **la ~ inglesa** the English countryside

campista *mf* camper

campo *m* **1** (zona no urbana) country; (paisaje) countryside; **la gente del ~** the country people; **el ~ se ve precioso** the countryside looks beautiful; **~ a través** or **a ~ traviesa** ‹*caminar/ir*› cross-country **2** (zona agraria) land; (terreno) field; **trabajar el ~** to work the land; **las faenas del ~** farm work; **los ~s de cebada** the field of barley; **~ de aterrizaje** landing field; **~ de batalla** battlefield; **~ de minas** minefield; **~ petrolífero** oilfield **3** (Dep) (de fútbol) field, pitch (BrE); (de golf) course; **jugar en ~ propio/contrario** to play at home/away; **~ a través** cross-country running; **~ de tiro** firing range **4** (ámbito, área de acción) field; **el ~ de la informática** the field of computing **5** (campamento) camp; **~ de concentración/de refugiados** concentration/refugee camp

camposanto *m* (liter) graveyard, cemetery

campus *m* (*pl* **~**) campus

camuflaje *m* camouflage

camuflar [A1] *vt* ‹*tanques/contrabando*› to camouflage; ‹*intenciones*› to disguise ■ **camuflarse** *v pron* «*persona*» to camouflage oneself; «*animal*» to camouflage itself

cana[1] *f* **1** (pelo) gray* hair, white hair; ***echar una* ~ *al aire*** to let one's hair down; (colloq) **2** (AmS arg) (cárcel) slammer (sl), nick (BrE colloq) **3** (RPl arg) (cuerpo de policía): **la ~** the cops (*pl*) (colloq)

cana² *mf* (RPl arg) (agente) cop (colloq)

Canadá *m*: *tb* **el ~** Canada

canadiense *adj/mf* Canadian

canal *m* **1** (Náut) (cauce artificial) canal; (Agr, Ing) channel; **~ de la Mancha** English Channel; **~ de Panamá** Panama Canal; **~ de San Lorenzo** St Lawrence Seaway **2 (a)** (Rad, Telec, TV) channel; **cambia de ~** change *o* switch channels **(b)** (medio) channel ■ *f or m* (canalón) gutter; (ranura) groove

canalizar [A4] *vt* to channel

canalla *mf* (fam) (bribón, granuja) swine (colloq)

canallada *f* (fam): **¡qué ~!** what a rotten *o* mean thing to do (colloq)

canalón *m* (Esp) gutter

canapé *m* **1** (Coc) canapé **2** (sofá) couch

Canarias *fpl*: *tb* **las (Islas) ~** the Canaries, the Canary Islands

canario¹ -ria *adj* of/from the Canary Islands ■ *m, f* (de las Canarias) person from the Canary Islands

canario² *m* (Zool) canary

canasta *f* **(a)** (para la compra) basket **(b)** (AmL) (en rifa) hamper **(c)** (en baloncesto) basket; **meter una ~** to make *o* score a basket **(d)** (Jueg) canasta

canastilla *f* layette

canasto *m* basket (*gen large and with a lid*)

cancel *m* (contrapuerta) inner door; (tabique) (Col, Méx) partition; (biombo) (Méx) folding screen

cancelar [A1] *vt* **(a)** ‹*reunión/viaje/pedido*› to cancel **(b)** ‹*deuda*› to settle, pay off; ‹*cuenta*› to pay

cáncer *m* (Med) cancer; **tiene (un) ~ de mama** she has breast cancer

Cáncer *m* (signo) Cancer; **es (de) ~** he's a Cancer *o* Cancerian ■ *mf* (persona) *tb* **cáncer** Cancerian, Cancer

cancha *f* **1 (a)** (Dep) (de baloncesto, frontón, squash, tenis) court; (de fútbol, rugby) (AmL) field, pitch; (de golf) (CS) course; (de polo) (AmL) field; (de esquí) (CS) slope **(b)** (Chi) (Aviac) *tb* **~ de aterrizaje** runway **2** (AmL fam) (desenvoltura): **un político con mucha ~** a politician with a great deal of experience, a seasoned politician

canchita *f* (Per) popcorn

canciller *m* **(a)** (jefe de estado) chancellor **(b)** (AmS) (ministro) ≈ Secretary of State (*in US*), ≈ Foreign Secretary (*in UK*)

cancillería *f* **(a)** (de embajada) chancery, chancellery **(b)** (AmS) (ministerio) ≈ State Department (*in US*), ≈ Foreign Office (*in UK*)

canción *f* song; **~ de cuna** lullaby; **~ nacional** (Chi) national anthem

candado *m* (cerradura) padlock; **está cerrada con ~** it is padlocked

candela *f* **(a)** (fuego) fire; **¿tienes ~?** (fam) have you got a light? **(b)** (vela) candle

candelabro *m* candelabra

candente *adj* **(a)** ‹*hierro*› red-hot **(b)** ‹*tema*› burning

candidato -ta *m,f* candidate; **~ a la presidencia** presidential candidate; **los ~s al puesto de** ... the applicants for the post of ...; **presentarse como ~ para algo** (Pol) to run (AmE) *o* (BrE) stand for sth

candidatura *f* **(a)** (propuesta) candidacy, candidature **(b)** (Esp) (lista) list of candidates

cándido -da *adj* naive

candil *m* oil lamp

candilejas *fpl* footlights (*pl*)

candor *m* innocence, naivety

caneca *f* (Col) (papelera) wastebasket, waste-paper basket (BrE); (cubo de la basura) garbage *o* trash can (AmE), dustbin (BrE)

canela *f* (Bot, Coc) cinnamon; **~ en polvo/en rama** ground/stick cinnamon

canelón *m* **(a)** (Const) gutter **(b) canelones** *mpl* canneloni

cangrejo *m* (de mar) crab; (de río) crayfish

canguro *m* **1** (Zool) kangaroo **2 (a)** (anorak) cagoule **(b)** (para llevar a un niño) sling **3** (Esp) **canguro** *mf* babysitter; **hacer de ~** to babysit

caníbal *mf* (antropófago) cannibal

canica *f* marble

caniche *mf* /ka'nitʃe, ka'niʃ/ poodle

canijo -ja *adj* **1** (fam) (pequeño) tiny, puny (hum *or* pej) **2** (Méx fam) (terco) stubborn, pig-headed (colloq)

canilla *f* **(a)** (RPl) (grifo) faucet (AmE), tap (BrE); **cerrar la ~** to turn off the faucet *o* tap **(b)** (bobina) bobbin

canillita *mf* (Bol, CS) newspaper vendor *o* seller

canino *m* (Odont) canine (tooth); (Zool) canine

canjear [A1] *vt* to exchange

cannabis *m* cannabis

cano -na *adj* white

canoa *f* canoe

canódromo *m* greyhound stadium, dog track (colloq)

canon *m* **1** (norma) rule, canon (frml) **2** (Mús) canon

canónico -ca *adj* canonical, canonic

canonizar [A4] *vt* to canonize

canoso -sa *adj* ▶**97** ‹*persona*› gray-haired*, white-haired; ‹*pelo/barba*› gray*, white

cansado -da *adj* **1** [ESTAR] **(a)** (fatigado) tired; **~s de tanto caminar** tired from so much walking; **tienes cara de ~** you look tired; **en un tono ~** in a weary tone of voice **(b)** (aburrido) **~ DE algo/hacer algo** tired OF sth/doing sth **2** [SER] ‹*viaje/trabajo*› tiring

cansador -dora *adj* (AmS) tiring

cansancio *m* tiredness; **me caigo de ~** I'm absolutely worn out *o* exhausted

cansar [A1] *vt* **(a)** (fatigar) to tire, tire ... out; **le cansa la vista** it makes her eyes tired, it strains her eyes **(b)** (aburrir): **¿no te cansa oír la misma música?** don't you get tired of listening to the same music? ■ **~** *vi* **(a)** (fatigar) to be tiring **(b)** (aburrir) to get tiresome

■ **cansarse** *v pron* **(a)** (fatigarse) to tire oneself out; **se le cansa la vista** her eyes get tired **(b)** (aburrirse) to get bored; **~se DE algo/algn** to get tired OF sth/sb, get bored WITH sth/sb, **~se DE hacer algo** to get tired OF doing sth

cantábrico -ca *adj* Cantabrian

Cantábrico *m*: **el (mar) ~** the Bay of Biscay

cantante *adj* singing (*before n*) ■ *mf* singer

cantar [A1] *vt* ‹*canción*› to sing ■ **~** *vi* **1 (a)** (Mús) to sing **(b)** «*pájaro*» to sing; «*gallo*» to crow; «*cigarra/grillo*» to chirp, chirrup **2** (fam) (confesar) to talk (colloq) ■ *m* poem (*gen set to music*)

cántara *f* churn

cantarín -rina, (CS) **cantarino -na** *adj* ‹*voz/tono/risa*› singsong; ‹*fuente/aguas*› (liter) babbling

cántaro *m* pitcher, jug; ***llover a ~s*** to pour with rain

cantautor -tora *m,f* singer-songwriter

cante *m* (Mús) Andalusian folk song; **~ flamenco** flamenco (singing)

cantera *f* (de piedra) quarry

cántico *m* canticle

cantidad *f* **(a)** (volumen) quantity, amount **(b)** (suma de dinero) sum, amount **(c)** (número) number; **la ~ de cartas recibidas** the number of letters received **(d)** (volumen impresionante): **había ~ de turistas** there were lots of tourists; **¡qué ~ de gente/de comida había!** there were so many people/there was so much food!; **tenemos ~** *or* **~es** (fam) we have lots *o* tons (colloq); ***cualquier ~ de*** (AmS) lots of, loads of (colloq)

cantimplora *f* water bottle, canteen

cantina *f* **1 (a)** (en estación) buffet, cafeteria; (en universidad) refectory; (en fábrica) canteen **(b)** (AmL exc RPl) (bar) bar **(c)** (RPl) (restaurante italiano) trattoria **2** (Col) (para la leche) churn

cantinela *f*: **siempre la misma ~** always the same old story (*o* thing *etc*)

cantinflear [A1] *vi* (fam) to babble

canto *m* **1** (Mús) (acción, arte) singing; (canción) chant **2** (de pájaro) song; (del gallo) crowing **3** (Lit) (canción) hymn **4** (borde, filo) edge; **colocó el ladrillo de ~** he lay the brick on its side **5** (Geol) *tb* **~ rodado** (roca) boulder; (guijarro) pebble

cantor -tora *adj* singing (*before n*) ■ *m,f* (cantante) singer

canturrear [A1] *vi* to sing softly to oneself ■ **~** *vt* to sing ... softly to oneself

canuto *m* (tubo) document tube

caña *f* **(a)** (planta) reed **(b)** (tallo del bambú, azúcar) cane; **muebles de ~** cane furniture; **~ de azúcar** sugar cane **(c)** (de pescar) rod **(d)** (de la bota) leg; **botas de media ~** calf-length boots

cañada *f* **(a)** (Geog) gully; (más profunda) ravine **(b)** (AmL) (arroyo) stream

cáñamo *m* (planta) cannabis plant, hemp; (tela) canvas

cañaveral *m* (de juncos) reedbed; (de cañas de azúcar) (Col) sugar-cane plantation

cañería *f* (tubo) pipe; (conjunto de tubos) piping, pipes (*pl*)

cañero -ra *adj* (AmL) (Agr) sugarcane (*before n*)

cañizal *m* reedbed

caño *m* (conducto) pipe; (de una fuente) spout; (grifo) (Per) faucet (AmE), tap (BrE)

cañón *m* **(a)** (Arm) (arma) cannon; (de una escopeta, pistola) barrel **(b)** (valle) canyon; **el Gran C~ del Colorado** the Grand Canyon **(c)** (de pluma) quill

cañonazo *m* (Arm, Mil) cannonshot; **una salva de 21 ~s** a 21-gun salute

caoba *f* **(a)** (árbol) mahogany tree; (madera) mahogany **(b)** ▶ **97** | **(de) color ~** mahogany

caos *m* chaos; **será un verdadero ~** there'll be absolute chaos

caótico -ca *adj* chaotic

capa *f* **1 (a)** (en general) layer; **una ~ de nieve** a layer *o* carpet of snow; **la ~ de ozono** the ozone layer; **lleva el pelo cortado en** *or* (Esp) **a ~s** she has layered hair **(b)** (de barniz, pintura) coat **(c)** (estrato) stratum; **las ~s de la sociedad** the social strata **2 (a)** (Indum) cloak, cape; **~ de agua** raincape **(b)** (Taur) cape

capacidad *f* **1 (a)** (competencia) ability **(b)** (potencial) capacity; **su gran ~ de trabajo** her great capacity for work; **~ DE** *or* **PARA hacer algo** ability *o* capacity to do sth **(c)** (Der) capacity **2** (cupo) capacity

capacitado -da *adj* **~ PARA algo/hacer algo** qualified FOR sth/to do sth

capacitar [A1] *vt* (formar) to prepare; (profesionalmente) **~ a algn PARA algo** to qualify sb FOR sth; **~ a algn PARA hacer algo** to qualify *o* entitle sb to do sth

■ **capacitarse** *v pron* (formarse) to train; (obtener un título) to qualify, become qualified

capar [A1] *vt* **1** (castrar) to castrate **2** (Col fam) (esp AmE colloq) **~ clase** to play hooky, to skive off (school) (BrE colloq)

caparazón *m or f* shell

capataz *mf* (*m*) foreman; (*f*) forewoman

capaz *adj* **(a)** (competente) capable, able **(b)** (de una hazaña) capable; **es ~ de grandes logros** he's capable of great things; **¿te sientes ~ de enfrentarte con ella?** do you feel able to face her?; **¿a qué no eres ~ de saltar esto?** I bet you can't jump over this; **es (muy) ~ de irse sin pagar** he's quite capable of leaving without paying

capazo *m* (cesta) basket; (para un niño) portacrib® (AmE), carrycot (BrE)

capea *f*: *amateur bullfight using young bulls*

capear [A1] *vt* **1** (Taur) to make passes at (*with the cape*) **2** (Chi fam) ‹*trabajo*› to skip, to skive off (BrE colloq); **~ clase** to play hooky (esp AmE colloq), to skive off (school) (BrE colloq)

capellán *m* chaplain

Caperucita Roja Little Red Riding Hood

caperuza *f* **(a)** (Indum) pointed hood **(b)** (de un bolígrafo) top, cap

capicúa *adj* ‹*número*› palindromic (frml); **era un número ~** the number read the same both ways

capilar *adj* **(a)** ‹*loción*› hair (*before n*) **(b)** ‹*vaso/tubo*› capillary (*before n*) ■ *m* capillary

capilla *f* chapel; **~ ardiente** funeral chapel

capital *adj* ‹*importancia*› cardinal, prime; ‹*influencia*› seminal (frml); ‹*obra*› key, seminal (frml)

■ *m* **(a)** (Com, Fin) capital **(b)** (recursos, riqueza) resources (*pl*) ■ *f* (de país) capital; (de provincia) provincial capital, ≈ county seat (*in US*), ≈ county town (*in UK*); **Valencia ~** the city of Valencia

capitalino -na *adj* (AmL) of/from the capital ■ *m, f* (AmL) inhabitant of the capital

capitalismo *m* capitalism

capitalista *adj* capitalist (*before n*) ■ *mf* capitalist

capitán -tana *m,f* **1** (Dep) captain **2** capitán *m* **(a)** (del ejército) captain; (de la Fuerza Aérea) captain (AmE), flight lieutenant (BrE) **(b)** (Náut) (de transatlántico, carguero) captain, master; (de buque de pesca) skipper **(c)** (Aviac) captain

capitel *m* capital

capítulo *m* (de libro) chapter; (de serie) episode

capó *m* hood (AmE), bonnet (BrE)

capón *adj* castrated ■ *m* (gallo) capon

caporal *m* (Méx) foreman, charge hand (BrE)

capot /ka'po/ *m* hood (AmE), bonnet (BrE)

capota *f* (de automóvil) convertible top; (de cochecito de bebé) canopy, hood

capote *m* **1** (capa) cloak; (de militar, torero) cape **2** (Méx) (Auto) hood (AmE), bonnet (BrE)

capricho *m* **1** (antojo) whim, caprice (liter); **le consienten todos los ~s** they indulge his every whim; **se lo compró por puro ~** he bought it on a whim; **entran y salen a ~** they come in and go out at will *o* as they please **2** (Mús) capriccio

caprichoso -sa *adj* **(a)** (inconstante) ‹*carácter/persona*› capricious; ‹*tiempo/moda*› changeable **(b)** (difícil, exigente) fussy ■ *m,f*: **es un ~** (es inconstante) he's always changing his mind; (es difícil, exigente) he's so fussy

Capricornio *m* (signo, constelación) Capricorn; **es (de) ~** she's a Capricorn ■ *mf* (persona) *tb* **capricornio** Capricornean, Capricorn

cápsula *f* **(a)** (Farm, Espac) capsule **(b)** (Audio) cartridge

captar [A1] *vt* **(a)** ‹*atención/interés*› to capture; ‹*clientes*› to win, gain; ‹*partidarios/empleados*› to attract, recruit **(b)** ‹*sentido/matiz*› to grasp; ‹*significado/indirecta*› to get **(c)** ‹*emisora/señal*› to pick up, receive

captura *f* (de delincuente, enemigo, animal) capture; (de un alijo) seizure; (en pesca) catch

capturar [A1] *vt* ‹*delincuente/enemigo/animal*› to capture; ‹*alijo*› to seize, confiscate; ‹*peces*› to catch

capucha *f* hood

capuchón *m* (de pluma, bolígrafo) top, cap; (Indum) hood

capullo *m* **(a)** (Bot) bud **(b)** (Zool) cocoon

caqui *adj inv/m* ▶ 97 khaki

cara *f* **1 (a)** ▶ 123 (Anat) face; **dímelo a la ~** say it to my face; **se le rió en la ~** she laughed in his face; **mírame a la ~** look at me **(b)** (*en locs*) **cara a cara** face to face; **de cara**: **el sol me da de ~** the sun is in my eyes; **se puso de ~ a la pared** she turned to face the wall, she turned her face to the wall; ***dar la ~***: **nunca da la ~** he never does his own dirty work; ***dar la ~ por algn*** to stand up for sb; ***echarle algo en ~ a algn*** to throw sth back in sb's face; ***romperle la ~ a algn*** (fam) to smash sb's face in (colloq **2 (a)** (expresión): **no pongas esa ~ que no es para tanto** don't look like that, it's not that bad; **alegra esa ~** cheer up; **le cambió la ~ cuando ...** her face changed when ...; **poner ~ de bueno** to play *o* act the innocent; **poner ~ de asco** to make *o* (BrE) pull a face; **andaba con/puso ~ larga** (fam) he had/he pulled a long face **(b)** (aspecto) look; **tiene ~ de cansado** he looks tired; **tienes mala ~** you don't look well; **¡qué buena ~ tiene la comida!** the food looks delicious! **3 (a)** (Mat) face **(b)** (de disco, papel) side; **~ o cruz** *or* (Arg) **ceca** *or* (Andes, Ven) **sello** heads or tails; **lo echaron a ~ o cruz** they tossed for it **4** (fam) (frescura, descaro) nerve (colloq), cheek (BrE colloq); **¡qué ~ (más dura) tienes!** you have some nerve! ■ *mf*: *tb* **~ dura** (fam) (persona) sassy devil (AmE colloq), cheeky swine (BrE colloq)

carabina *f* **(a)** (Arm) carbine **(b)** (Esp fam) (acompañante); **ir de ~** to play gooseberry (colloq)

carabinero -ra *m,f* **(a)** (policía) (*m*) police officer, policeman; (*f*) police officer, policewoman **(b)** (agente fronterizo) border guard **(c) carabineros** *mpl* (institución) police (force); (policía fronteriza) border police

Caracas *m* Caracas

caracol *m* **(a)** (Zool) (de mar) winkle; (de tierra) snail **(b)** (AmL) (concha) conch

caracola *f* conch

carácter *m* (*pl* **-racteres**) **(a)** (en general) character; **tenemos un ~ muy distinto** we have very different characters; **el restaurante tiene mucho ~** the restaurant has lots of character; **une persona de ~ fuerte** a person of strong character; **una persona de buen ~** a good-natured person; **un ~ abierto** an open nature; **tener mal ~** to have a (bad) temper **(b)** (índole, naturaleza) nature; **una visita de ~ oficial** a visit of an official nature; **heridas de ~ leve** (period) minor wounds **(c)** (Biol) characteristic **(d)** (Col, Méx) (personaje) character

característica *f* **(a)** (rasgo) feature, characteristic **(b)** (RPl) (Telec) exchange code

característico -ca *adj* characteristic

caracterizar [A4] *vt* **1** (distinguir) to characterize; **con la franqueza que lo caracteriza** with his characteristic frankness **2** (describir) to portray, depict **3** (Teatr) (encarnar) to play, portray

■ **caracterizarse** *v pron*: **~se** POR **algo** «*enfermedad/región/raza*» to be characterized BY sth; «*persona*» to be noted FOR sth

caradura *adj* (fam) sassy (AmE colloq), cheeky (BrE colloq) ■ *mf* (fam) sassy devil (AmE colloq), cheeky swine (BrE colloq) ■ *f* (fam) nerve (colloq), cheek (BrE colloq)

carajillo *m* (café) *coffee with brandy or similar*

carajito -ta *m,f* (Ven fam) (niño) kid (colloq)

caramba *interj* (expresando — sorpresa) good heavens!; (— disgusto) dammit! (colloq)

carámbano *m* icicle

carambola *f* **(a)** (en billar) carom (AmE), cannon (BrE) **(b)** (fam) (casualidad): **fue de ~** it was pure chance **(c)** (Méx) (choque múltiple) pileup

caramelo *m* **(a)** (golosina) candy (AmE), sweet (BrE); **un ~ de menta** a mint **(b)** (azúcar fundida) caramel

carantoña *f* (Esp fam) caress

caraota *f* (Ven) bean

caraqueño -ña *adj* of/from Caracas

carátula *f* **(a)** (de disco) jacket (AmE), sleeve (BrE); (de video) case **(b)** (Méx) (de reloj) face, dial **(c)** (máscara) mask

caravana *f* **1 (a)** (de tráfico — retención) backup (AmE) tailback (BrE); (— hilera) convoy; **ir en ~** to drive in (a) convoy **(b)** (remolque) trailer (AmE), caravan (BrE) **2** (Méx) (reverencia) bow

carbón *m* **(a)** (mineral) coal; ***negro como el ~*** as black as coal **(b)** (vegetal) charcoal

carboncillo *m* charcoal; **dibujo al ~** charcoal drawing

carbonilla *f* **(a)** (polvo de carbón) cinders (*pl*) **(b)** (RPl) (Art) charcoal

carbonizarse [A4] *v pron* **(a)** «*edificio/muebles*» to be reduced to ashes; **los cuerpos carbonizados de las víctimas** the victims' charred remains **(b)** (Quím) to carbonize

carbono *m* carbon

carburador *m* carburetor*

carburante *m* fuel

carburar [A1] *vi* **(a)** «*motor*» to carburet **(b)** (fam) (funcionar) «*electrodoméstico/coche*» to work ■ ~ *vt* (Andes) ‹*motor*› to tune

carca *adj* (fam) old-fashioned, fuddy-duddy (colloq) ■ *mf* old fogey (colloq)

carcacha *f* (Andes, Méx fam) (auto viejo) wreck (colloq), old heap (colloq); (otro aparato) contraption (colloq)

carcajada *f* guffaw; **soltar una ~** to give a guffaw, to burst out laughing; **reírse a ~s** to roar with laughter

carcasa *f* **(a)** (armazón, estructura) frame; (de aparato) casing; (de bara) hulk **(b)** (esqueleto de animal) skeleton

cárcel *f* (prisión) prison, jail; **la metieron en la ~** she was put in prison

carcelero -ra *m,f* jailer

carcoma *f* (Zool) woodworm

carcomer [E1] *vt* **(a)** «*carcoma*» to eat away (at); **el marco está carcomido** the frame is worm-eaten **(b)** ‹*salud*› to undermine; **la envidia lo carcomía** he was eaten up with envy

cardar [A1] *vt* **(a)** ‹*lana*› to card **(b)** ‹*pelo*› to backcomb, tease

■ **cardarse** *v pron* (*refl*) to backcomb

cardenal *m* **1** ▶420 (Relig) cardinal **2** (fam) (moretón) bruise

cardíaco, **cardiaco -ca** *adj* heart (*before n*), cardiac (tech); **enfermos ~s** heart patients

cárdigan *m* (*pl* **-gans**) cardigan

cardiólogo -ga *m,f* cardiologist

cardo *m* (Bot) thistle

carecer [E3] *vi* (frml) **~ DE algo** to lack sth; **carece de interés** it is lacking in interest, it lacks interest; **carece de valor** it has no value, it is worthless

carencia *f* **(a)** (escasez) lack, shortage; **~ de recursos financieros** lack of financial resources **(b)** (Med) deficiency; **~ de vitamina A** vitamin A deficiency

carente *adj* (frml): **lugares ~s de interés** places which are of no interest; **niños ~s de cariño** children lacking affection

carero -ra *adj* (fam) ‹*comerciante*› pricey (colloq)

carestía *f* (costo elevado) high cost; **la ~ de la vida** the high cost of living

careta *f* mask

carey *m* (Zool) hawksbill turtle; (material) tortoiseshell

carga *f* **1 (a)** (de barco, avión) cargo; (de camión) load; (de tren) freight; Ⓢ **zona de carga y descarga** loading and unloading only **(b)** (peso) load; **no lleves tanta ~** don't carry such a heavy load **2 (a)** (de escopeta, cañón) charge **(b)** (de bolígrafo, pluma) refill; (de lavadora) load **3** (Elec) (de cuerpo) charge; (de circuito) load **4** (responsabilidad) burden; **es una ~ para la familia** he is a burden to his family **5 (a)** (de tropas, policía) charge; **¡a la ~!** charge! **(b)** (Dep) *tb* **~ defensiva** blitz

cargada *f* (RPl fam) practical joke

cargaderas *fpl* (Col) suspenders (*pl*) (AmE), braces (*pl*) (BrE)

cargado -da *adj* **1 (a)** (con peso): **iba muy cargada** she had a lot to carry; **~ DE algo** ‹*de regalos*› laden WITH sth; ‹*de paquetes/maletas*› loaded down WITH sth; **~ de deudas** heavily in debt; **un árbol ~ de fruta** a tree laden with fruit; **~ de trabajo** overloaded with work **(b)** ‹*ambiente/atmósfera*› (bochornoso) heavy, close; (con humo, olores desagradables) stuffy; (tenso) strained, tense **(c)** ‹*café*› strong **2 ~ de hombros** *or* **de espaldas** with bowed shoulders

cargador *m* **(a)** (Arm) clip, magazine **(b)** (de pilas, baterías) battery charger

cargamento *m* (de camión) load; (de barco, avión) cargo; (de tren) freight

cargante *adj* **(a)** (CS fam) (antipático) unpleasant, horrible (colloq) **(b)** (Esp fam) annoying

cargar [A3] *vt* **1 (a)** ‹*barco/avión/camión*› to load; **cargaron la camioneta de cajas** they loaded the van with boxes; **no cargues tanto el coche** don't put so much in the car **(b)** ‹*pistola/escopeta*› to load; ‹*pluma/encendedor*› to fill; ‹*cámara*› to load, put a film in **(c)** (Elec) to charge **2 (a)** ‹*mercancías*› to load **(b)** ‹*combustible*› to fuel; **tengo que ~ nafta** (RPl) I have to fill up with gasoline (AmE) *o* (BrE) petrol **(c)** (Inf) to load **3** (de obligaciones) **~ a algn DE algo** to burden sb WITH sth; **me ~on la culpa** they put *o* laid the blame on me **4 (a)** ‹*paquetes/bolsas*› to carry; ‹*niño*› (AmL) to carry **(b)** (AmL exc RPl) ‹*armas*› to carry **(c)** (Ven fam) (llevar puesto) to wear; (tener consigo): **cargo las llaves** I have the keys **5** (a una cuenta) to charge **6** (Méx fam) (matar) to kill ■ **~** *vi* **1 ~ CON algo** ‹*con bulto*› to carry sth; **tiene que ~ con todo el peso de la**

casa she has to shoulder all the responsibility for the household **2** ~ CONTRA **algn** «*tropas/policía*» to charge ON *o* AT sb **3** «*batería*» to charge **4** (fam) (fastidiar): **me cargan los fanfarrones** I can't stand show-offs

■ **cargarse** *v pron* **1 (a)** «*pilas/flash*» to charge; «*partícula*» to become charged **(b)** **~se DE algo** ‹*de bolsas/equipaje*› to load oneself down WITH sth; ‹*de responsabilidades*› to take on a lot OF sth; ‹*de deudas*› to saddle oneself WITH sth **2 (a)** (fam) (matar) to kill **(b)** (Esp fam) ‹*motor*› to wreck; ‹*jarrón*› to smash

cargo *m* **1** (puesto) post, position (frml); (de presidente, ministro) office; **tener un ~ público** to hold public office; **un ~ de responsabilidad** a responsible job *o* post **2** (responsabilidad, cuidado): **los niños están a mi ~** the children are in my care; **estar al cargo de algo** to be in charge of sth; **los gastos corren a ~ de la empresa** expenses will be paid *o* met by the company; **hacerse ~ de algo** ‹*de puesto/tarea*› to take charge of sth; ‹*de gastos*› to take care of sth; **me da ~ de conciencia** I feel guilty **3 (a)** (Com, Fin) charge; **sin ~** free of charge **(b)** (Der) charge

cargoso -sa *adj* (CS, Per fam) annoying

cargue *m* (Col, Ven) loading; Ⓢ **zona de cargue y descargue** loading and unloading only

carguero *m* freighter, cargo ship

Caribe *m*: **el (mar) ~** the Caribbean (Sea)

caribeño -ña *adj* Caribbean ■ *m,f*: *person from the Caribbean region*

caribú *m* caribou

caricatura *f* (dibujo) caricature

caricaturizar [A4] *vt* to caricature

caricia *f* caress; **hacer ~s** to caress; **le hizo una ~ al perro** she stroked the dog

caridad *f* charity; **vivir de la ~** to live on charity; **por ~** for pity's sake

caries *f* (*pl* ~) **(a)** (proceso) tooth decay, caries (*pl*) (tech) **(b)** (cavidad) cavity

cariño *m* **(a)** (afecto) affection; **les tengo mucho ~** I am very fond of them; **te ha tomado mucho ~** he's become very fond of you; **~s por tu casa/a tu mujer** (AmL) (send my) love to your family/your wife; **~s, Beatriz** (en cartas) (AmL) love, Beatriz **(b)** (caricia): **le hice un cariñito al niño** I gave the little boy a cuddle (*o* kiss *etc*) **(c)** (como apelativo) dear, honey, love (BrE)

cariñoso -sa *adj* ‹*persona*› affectionate; ‹*bienvenida*› warm; **un ~ saludo de mi parte** regards

carioca *adj* of/from Rio de Janeiro

carisma *m* charisma

carismático -ca *adj* charismatic

caritativo -va *adj* charitable; **una organización con fines ~s** a charitable organization

cariz *m*: **el ~ que están tomando las cosas** the way things are going *o* developing; **la situación está tomando mal ~** the situation is beginning to look bad

carmín *adj inv* ▶97 carmine ■ *m* **(a)** (para labios) lipstick **(b)** ▶97 (color) carmine

carnada *f* bait

carnal *adj* ‹*amor/deseo*› carnal ■ *m* (Méx arg) pal (colloq), buddy (AmE colloq), mate (BrE colloq)

carnaval *m* (fiesta) carnival

carne *f* **1 (a)** (de mamífero, ave) meat; (de pescado) flesh; **~ de cerdo** *or* (Chi, Per) **chancho** *or* (Ven) **cochino** *or* (Méx) **puerco** pork; **~ de cordero** lamb; **~ de ternera** veal; **~ de vaca** *or* (AmC, Col, Méx, Ven) **res** beef; **~ molida** *or* (Esp, RPl) **picada** ground beef (AmE), mince (BrE) **(b)** (de fruta) flesh **2** (de una persona) flesh; **es ~ de mi ~** he's my flesh and blood; **tenía la herida en ~ viva** her wound was raw; **(de) color ~** flesh-colored*; ***en ~ y hueso*** in the flesh; ***me pone la ~ de gallina*** it gives me goose pimples (colloq)

carné *m* identity card; **sacar el ~** to have one's identity (*o* membership *etc*) card issued; **~ de conducir** driver's license (AmE), driving licence (BrE); **~ de estudiante** student card; **~ de identidad** identity card; **~ de socio** (de club, mutual) membership card; (de biblioteca) library card

carnear [A1] *vt* (CS) to slaughter ■ ~ *vi* (CS) to slaughter a cow (*o* lamb *etc*)

carnecería *f* butcher's shop (*o* stall *etc*)

cárneo -nea *adj* (CS) meat (*before n*)

carnero *m* ram

carnet /kar'ne/ *m* (*pl* **-nets**) ⇒ CARNÉ

carnicería *f* **(a)** (tienda) butcher's shop (*o* stall *etc*) **(b)** (fam) (matanza) slaughter

carnicero -ra *m,f* **(a)** (vendedor) butcher **(b)** (fam & pey) (cirujano) butcher (colloq & pej)

carnitas *fpl* (Méx) pieces of barbecued pork (*pl*)

carnívoro¹ -ra *adj* carnivorous, meat-eating

carnívoro² *m* carnivore

caro¹ -ra *adj* **(a)** ‹*coche/entrada/ciudad*› expensive; **la vida está muy cara** everything costs so much nowadays **(b)** (*como adv*): **me costó muy ~** I had to pay a lot of money for it; **pagarás ~ tu error** you'll pay dearly for your mistake

caro² *adv*: **vender ~** to charge a lot; *ver tb* CARO¹ (b)

carpa *f* **1 (a)** (de circo) big top; (para actuaciones) marquee **(b)** (AmL) (para acampar) tent **2** (Zool) carp

carpeta *f* (para documentos, dibujos) folder; **~ de anillos** *or* (Esp) **anillas** *or* (RPl) **ganchos** ring binder

carpintería *f* **(a)** (taller) carpenter's workshop; (actividad) carpentry **(b)** (de construcción, casa) woodwork; **~ metálica** metalwork

carpintero -ra *m,f* carpenter

carraca *f* **(a)** (matraca) rattle **(b)** (fam) (trasto) wreck (colloq))

carraspear [A1] *vi* to clear one's throat

carraspera *f*: **tener ~** to have a rough throat

carrasposo -sa *adj* **(a)** ‹*garganta*› rough **(b)** (Col) ‹*superficie*› rough

carrera *f* **1** (Dep) (competición) race; **~ de caballos** horse race; **la ~ de los 100 metros vallas** the 100 meters hurdles; **te echo una ~** I'll race you; **~ armamentista** arms race; **~ contra reloj** (Dep) time trial; **~ de fondo** long-distance race; **~ de postas** *o* **relevos** relay race **2** (fam) (corrida):

darse *or* **pegarse una ~** to run as fast as one can; **me fui de una ~ a su casa** I raced *o* rushed round to her house (colloq); ***a la(s) ~(s)*** in a rush **3 (a)** (Educ) degree course; **está haciendo la ~ de Derecho** he's doing a degree in law **(b)** (profesión, trayectoria) career; **un diplomático de ~** a career diplomat; **~ media/superior** *three-year/five-year university course* **4** (en la media) run, ladder (BrE); (en el pelo) (Col, Ven) part (AmE), parting (BrE)

carrerear [A1] *vt* (Méx fam) to push (colloq)

carrerilla *f*: **se lo saben de ~** they know it (off) by heart; **me lo dijo de ~** he reeled it off parrot-fashion; ***coger* ~** (Esp) to take a run-up

carreta *f* (con toldo) wagon; (sin toldo) cart

carrete *m* (de hilo, cinta) spool, reel (BrE); (de película) film; (de caña de pescar) reel

carretear [A1] *vi* (AmL) (Aviac) to taxi

carretela *f* (Chi) cart

carretera *f* road; **~ de circunvalación** bypass, beltway (AmE), ring road (BrE); **~ nacional** ≈ highway (*in US*), ≈ A-road (*in UK*)

carretilla *f* **1** (de mano) wheelbarrow **2** (CS) (quijada) jaw, jawbone

carricoche *m* covered wagon

carril *m* **(a)** (Auto) lane **(b)** (Ferr) rail **(c)** (AmL) (Dep) lane; **~ bus** bus lane; **~ de adelantamiento** overtaking lane, fast lane; **~ de bicicletas** cycleway, cycle path

carrillo *m* cheek

carriola *f* (Méx) baby carriage (AmE), baby buggy (BrE)

carrito *m* **(a)** (para el equipaje) trolley; (en supermercado) shopping cart (AmE), trolley (BrE); (de la compra) shopping trolley *o* (AmE) cart; **~ chocón** (Méx, Ven) bumper car **(b)** (mesita de servir) trolley

carro *m* **1 (a)** (carreta) cart; **un ~ de tierra** a cartload of earth; **~ de combate** tank **(b)** (AmL exc CS) (Auto) car, automobile (AmE); **~ bomba** (Col) car bomb; **~ loco** (Andes) bumper car (BrE); **~ sport** (AmL exc CS) sports car; **~ de bomberos** (Andes, Méx) fire engine **(c)** (Chi, Méx) (vagón) coach, carriage (BrE); **~ comedor/dormitorio** (Méx) dining/sleeping car **(d)** (Hist) (romano) chariot **2** (de máquina de escribir) carriage

carrocería *f* (de automóvil) bodywork

carroña *f* **(a)** (de animal muerto) carrion **(b)** (gente despreciable) riffraff (+ *sing or pl vb*)

carroza *f* **(a)** (coche de caballos) carriage **(b)** (de carnaval) float **(c)** (Chi, Ur) (coche fúnebre) hearse

carruaje *m* carriage

carrusel *m* **(a)** (para diapositivas) carousel, slide tray **(b)** (para niños) merry-go-round, carousel (AmE)

carta *f* **1** (Corresp) letter; **¿hay ~ para mí?** are there any letters for me?; **echar una ~ al correo** to mail (esp AmE) *o* (esp BrE) post a letter; **~ blanca** carte blanche; **~ certificada** registered letter; **~ de amor** love letter; **~ de recomendación** reference, letter of recommendation; **~ urgente** special-delivery letter **2** (naipe) card; **jugar a las ~s** to play cards; **dar las ~s** to deal the cards; ***echarle las ~s a algn*** to tell sb's fortune; ***poner las ~s sobre la mesa*** to put *o* lay one's cards on the table **3** (en restaurante) menu; **comer a la ~** to eat à la carte; **~ de vinos** wine list

cartearse [A1] *v pron*: **nos carteamos durante años** we wrote to each other *o* corresponded for years; **~ CON algn** to correspond WITH sb

cartel *m* (de publicidad, propaganda) poster; (letrero) sign; **~ luminoso** neon sign; **lleva dos meses en ~** ‹*obra/película*› it has been on for two months; **de ~** ‹*cantante/actor*› famous; ‹*torero*› star (*before n*)

cartelera *f* **(a)** (Cin, Teatr) publicity board; **la película sigue en ~** the movie is still on *o* still showing **(b)** (en el periódico) listings (*pl*); **~ de espectáculos** entertainment guide **(c)** (AmL) (tablón de anuncios) bulletin board (AmE), notice board (BrE)

cárter *m* (del cigüeñal) crankcase, sump; (del embrague) housing

cartera *f* **1 (a)** (billetera) wallet, billfold (AmE) **(b)** (para documentos) document case, briefcase; (de colegial) satchel; (de cobrador) money bag; (de cartero) sack, bag **(c)** (AmS) (bolso de mujer) purse (AmE), handbag (BrE) **2** (Com, Fin) portfolio

carterear [A1] *vt* (Chi): **me ~on en la micro** my handbag was picked on the bus

carterista *mf* pickpocket

cartero (*m*) mailman (AmE), postman (BrE); (*f*) mailwoman (AmE), postwoman (BrE)

cartílago *m* cartilage

cartilla *f* **(a)** (para aprender a leer) reader, primer **(b)** (libreta) book; **~ de ahorros** passbook, savings book; **~ de racionamiento** ration book

cartón *m* **(a)** (material) cardboard; **~ ondulado** corrugated cardboard; **~ piedra** papier-mâché **(b)** (de cigarrillos, leche) carton; (de huevos) tray

cartoné *m*: **en ~** hardback

cartuchera *f* **1 (a)** (estuche — para cartuchos) cartridge clip; (— para pistola) holster **(b)** (cinturón — para cartuchos) cartridge belt; (— para pistola) gun belt **2** (RPl) (de escolar) pencil case

cartucho *m* cartridge

cartuja *f* charterhouse, monastery

cartulina *f* card

casa *f* **1 (a)** (vivienda) house; **cambiarse de ~** to move house; **casita del perro** kennel; **~ adosada** *or* **pareada** semi-detached *o* terraced house; **C~ Blanca** White House; **~ de huéspedes** boardinghouse; **~ de socorro** first-aid post; **~ de vecinos** *or* (Méx) **de vecindad** tenement house; **C~ Real** Royal Household; **~ refugio** refuge *o* hostel for battered women; **~ rodante** (CS) trailer (AmE), caravan (BrE) **(b)** (hogar) home; **a los 18 años se fue de ~** *or* (AmL) **de la ~** she left home at 18; **no está nunca en ~** *or* (AmL) **en la ~** he's never (at) home; **está en casa de Ana** she's (over) at Ana's (house); **¿por qué no pasas por ~** *or* (AmL) **por la ~?** why don't you drop in?; ***de or para andar por ~*** ‹*vestido*› for wearing around the house; ‹*definición/terminología*› crude, rough; ***echar or tirar la ~ por la ventana*** to push the boat out **2 (a)** (empresa) company, firm (BrE); **una ~ de discos** a record company; **~ de cambios**

bureau de change **(b)** (bar, restaurante): **especialidad de la ~** house specialty (AmE), speciality of the house (BrE); **invita la ~** it's on the house **3** (Dep): **perdieron en ~** they lost at home

casabe *m* (Col, Ven) cassava bread

casaca *f* (chaqueta) jacket; (Equ) riding jacket

casado -da *adj* ▶ 378 married; **está ~ con una japonesa** he's married to a Japanese woman ■ *m, f(m)* married man; *(f)* married woman; **los recién ~s** the newlyweds

casamiento *m* (unión) marriage; (boda) wedding

casar [A1] *vt* «*cura/juez*» to marry ■ ~ *vi* **(a)** (encajar) «*dibujos*» to match up; «*piezas*» to fit together; «*cuentas*» to match, tally **(b)** (armonizar) «*colores/estilos*» to go together; ~ CON **algo** to go well WITH sth

■ **casarse** *v pron* to get married; **~se por la Iglesia** to get married in church; **se casó con un abogado** she married a lawyer; **~se en segundas nupcias** to marry again, to remarry

cascabel *m* **(a)** (campanita) bell **(b)** (Chi) (sonajero) rattle ■ *f* (Zool) rattlesnake

cascada *f* (Geog) waterfall, cascade

cascajo *m* (fam) **1** (trasto viejo) wreck (colloq) **2** (Col) (Const) piece of gravel

cascanueces *m* (*pl* ~) (a pair of) nutcrackers

cascar [A2] *vt* ‹*nuez/huevo*› to crack; ‹*taza*› to chip

■ **cascarse** *v pron* «*huevo*» to crack; «*taza*» to chip

cáscara *f* (de huevo, nuez) shell; (del queso) rind; (de naranja, limón) peel, rind; (de plátano, papa) skin; (de manzana) peel

cascarilla *f* (de cacao) roasted cacao husks (*pl*) (*used in infusions*); (de cereal) husk

cascarón *m* (de huevo, nuez) shell

cascarrabias *adj inv* (fam) cantankerous, grumpy ■ *mf* (*pl* ~) grouch (colloq)

casco *m* **1 (a)** (para la cabeza) helmet; **~ protector** (de obrero) safety helmet; (de motorista) crash helmet **(b) cascos** *mpl* (Audio) headphones (*pl*) **2** (Equ, Zool) hoof **3** (Náut) hull **4 (a)** (de ciudad): **~ antiguo** old quarter; **~ urbano** urban area, built-up area **(b)** (RPl) (de estancia) farmhouse and surrounding buildings **5** (Col) (gajo) segment **6** (Esp, Méx) (envase) bottle

cascote *m* piece of rubble; **~s** rubble

caserío *m* (poblado) hamlet; (finca) (Esp) farmhouse

casero -ra *adj* **(a)** ‹*vino/flan*› homemade; ‹*reparación*› amateur; ‹*trabajo*› domestic **(b)** ‹*persona*› home-loving ■ *m,f* **1 (a)** (propietario) *(m)* landlord; *(f)* landlady **(b)** (cuidador) caretaker **2** (Chi) (cliente) customer; (vendedor) storekeeper (AmE), stallholder

caseta *f* **(a)** (en la playa, de guardia etc) hut **(b)** (en exposición) stand **(c)** (para perro) kennel **(d)** (en fútbol) dugout

casete *m or f* (cinta) cassette ■ *m* (Esp) (grabador) cassette recorder/player

casi *adv* **1** (cerca de) almost, nearly; **~ me caigo** I nearly fell over **2** (en frases negativas): **~ no se le oía** you could hardly hear him; **~ nunca** hardly ever; **no nos queda ~ nada de pan** there's hardly any bread left; **¿pudiste dormir? — ~ nada** did you manage to sleep? — hardly at all; **~ no vengo** I almost didn't come **3** (expresando una opinión tentativa): **~ sería mejor venderlo** maybe it would be better to sell it

casilla *f* **1** (para cartas, llaves) pigeonhole; **~ postal** *or* **de correo** (CS, Per) post office box, P.O. Box **2** (en ajedrez, crucigrama) square; (en formulario) box **3 (a)** (de guardia, sereno) hut **(b)** (de perro) kennel **(c)** (Méx) (de votación) polling booth

casillero *m* **(a)** (mueble) set of pigeonholes; (compartimento) pigeonhole **(b)** (CS) (en formulario) box

casino *m* **1** (de juego) casino **2** (club social) club

casitas *fpl* (Chi fam & euf) (baño) bathroom (euph)

caso *m* **1** (situación, coyuntura) case; **en esos ~s** in cases like that; **yo en tu caso** ... if I were you ...; **en último ~** if it comes to it, if the worst comes to the worst; **en el mejor de los ~s** at (the very) best; **en el peor de los ~s te multarán** the worst they can do is fine you; **eso no venía al ~** that had nothing to do with what we were talking about; **pongamos por ~ que** ... let's assume that ...; **en ~ de incendio** in case of fire; **en ~ contrario** otherwise; **en cualquier ~** in any case; **en tal ~** in that case, in such a case (frml); **en todo ~ dijo que llamaría** in any case she said she'd ring; **llegado el ~** if it comes to it; **según el ~** as appropriate; ***no hay/hubo caso*** (AmL fam) it is no good *o* no use/it was no good *o* no use **2** (Der, Med) case; ***ser un ~ perdido*** (fam) to be a hopeless case (colloq) **3** (atención): **hacerle ~** A **algn** to pay attention TO sb, take notice OF sb; **hacer ~** DE **algo** to pay attention TO sth, to take notice OF sth; **hacer ~ omiso de algo** to ignore sth

caspa *f* dandruff

casquillo *m* **(a)** (de bala, cartucho) case **(b)** (portalámparas) lampholder, bulbholder; (de bombilla): **~ de rosca/bayoneta** screw-in/bayonet fitting

cassette *m or f* /ka'set/ ⇒ CASETE

casta *f* caste; **de ~** ‹*toro*› thoroughbred; ‹*torero*› top-class

castaña *f* (fruto) chestnut; **~ de Indias** horse chestnut; **~ de Pará** (RPl) Brazil nut; **~ pilonga** dried chestnut

castañetear [A1] *vi*: **me castañetean los dientes** my teeth are chattering

castaño[1] -ña *adj* ▶ 97 ‹*pelo*› chestnut; ‹*ojos*› brown

castaño[2] *m* **(a)** (Bot) chestnut tree; **~ de Indias** horse chestnut **(b)** ▶ 97 (color) chestnut

castañuela *f* castanet

castellano[1] -na *adj* (de Castilla) Castilian; (español) Spanish ■ *m,f* (persona) Castilian

castellano[2] *m* (idioma — de Castilla) Castilian; (— español) Spanish

castidad *f* chastity

castigar [A3] *vt* **(a)** (en general) to punish; **fueron castigados con la pena máxima** they received the maximum sentence **(b)** ‹*niño*› (a quedarse en el colegio) to keep ... in detention; (a quedarse en casa) to keep ... in as a punishment, to ground (esp AmE colloq); **lo ~on sin postre** as a punishment he was made to go without dessert

castigo *m* punishment; **~ corporal** corporal punishment; **les impusieron ~s severos** they were severely punished; **levantar un ~** to lift a punishment

Castilla *f* Castile

castillo *m* castle; **~ de arena** sandcastle; ***construir ~s en el aire*** to build castles in the air

castizo -za *adj* **(a)** (puro, tradicional) ‹*estilo/costumbre*› traditional **(b)** (típicamente castellano): **un lenguaje muy ~** very pure Castilian/Spanish

casto -ta *adj* chaste

castor *m* beaver

castrar [A1] *vt* ‹*caballo*› to geld; ‹*toro/hombre*› to castrate; ‹*gato*› to neuter

casual *adj* chance (*before n*)

casualidad *f* chance; **por (pura) ~** by (sheer) chance; **si por ~ la ves** if you happen to see her; **¿no tendrás su dirección por ~?** you wouldn't (happen to) have her address by any chance?; **¡qué ~!** what a coincidence!; **da la ~ de que** … as it happens …

cataclismo *m* natural disaster, cataclysm (frml)

catacumbas *fpl* catacombs (*pl*)

catador -dora *m,f* taster

catalán[1] -lana *adj/m,f* Catalan

catalán[2] *m* (idioma) Catalan

catalejo *m* (ant) telescope, spyglass

catalizador *m* (Auto) catalytic converter

catalogar [A3] *vt* **(a)** (en un catálogo) to catalog (AmE), to catalogue (BrE); (en una lista) to record, list **(b)** (considerar) to class

catálogo *m* (Art, Com) catalog (AmE), catalogue (BrE); **compra por ~** mail-order shopping

Cataluña *f* Catalonia

catamarán *m* catamaran

cataplasma *f* poultice, cataplasm (tech)

catapulta *f* catapult

catapultar [A1] *vt* to catapult

catar [A1] *vt* ‹*vino*› to taste

catarata *f* **(a)** (Geog) waterfall; **las ~s del Iguazú** Iguaçú Falls **(b)** (Med) cataract

catarro *m* **(a)** (resfriado) cold; **pescarse** *or* (esp Esp) **coger un ~** to catch a cold **(b)** (inflamación) catarrh

catastro *m* (censo) cadastre, land registry; (impuesto) property tax

catástrofe *f* catastrophe, disaster

catastrófico -ca *adj* catastrophic, disastrous

catear [A1] *vt* **1** (Esp arg) (suspender) to fail **2 (a)** (Chi) (Min) to prospect **(b)** (Méx) (registrar) ‹*persona*› to frisk; ‹*vivienda*› to search

catecismo *m* catechism

cátedra *f* (en universidad) professorship, chair; (en colegio) post of head of department

catedral *f* cathedral

catedrático -ca *m,f* (de universidad) professor; (en colegio) head of department

categoría *f* **(a)** (grupo) category; **~ gramatical** part of speech; **hotel de primera ~** first-class hotel **(b)** (calidad): **de ~** ‹*actor/espectáculo/revista*› first-rate; **un periódico de poca ~** a second-rate newspaper; **el hotel de más ~** the finest *o* best hotel **(c)** (estatus): **tiene ~ de embajador** he has ambassadorial status; **gente de cierta ~** people of some standing

categórico -ca *adj* ‹*respuesta*› categorical

cateo *m* (Chi, Méx) (cacheo) body search

catequesis *f*: *teaching of the catechism*

catire -ra *adj* (Ven) (de piel blanca) fair-skinned; (de pelo rubio) fair, fair-haired ■ *m,f* (Ven) (de piel blanca) fair-skinned person; (de pelo rubio) fair-haired person

catita *f* (CS) budgerigar

catolicismo *m* Catholicism

católico -ca *adj* **(a)** (Relig) Catholic; **es ~** he's a Catholic **(b)** (ortodoxo) orthodox ■ *m,f* Catholic

catorce *adj inv/m/pron* **▶ 293** fourteen; *para ejemplos ver* CINCO

catre *m* **(a)** (cama — plegable) folding bed; (— de campaña) camp bed **(b)** (CS) (armazón) bedstead

catsup *m* ketchup, catsup (AmE)

cauce *m* **(a)** (Geog) bed; **el río se salió de su ~** the river burst its banks; **desviaron el ~ del arroyo** they changed the course of the stream **(b)** (rumbo, vía): **desvió la conversación hacia otros ~s** he steered the conversation onto another tack; **seguir los ~s establecidos** to go through the normal channels

cauchera *f* (Col) (tirachinas) (fam) slingshot (AmE), catapult (BrE)

caucho *m* **(a)** (sustancia) rubber; (árbol) (Col) rubber tree **(b)** (neumatico) (Ven) tire*; (gomita) (Col) rubber band, elastic band (BrE)

caudal *m* **(a)** (de un fluido) volume of flow; **el río tiene muy poco ~** the water level is very low **(b)** (riqueza) fortune **(c)** (abundancia) wealth; **un ~ de conocimientos** a wealth of knowledge

caudaloso -sa *adj* ‹*río*› large

caudillo *m* (líder) leader

causa *f* **1** (motivo) cause; **la ~ de todas mis desgracias** the cause of *o* the reason for all my misfortunes; **se enfadó sin ~ alguna** she got annoyed for no reason at all *o* for no good reason; **a** *or* **por ~ de** because of **2** (ideal) cause; **una ~ perdida** a lost cause **3** (Der) (pleito) lawsuit; (proceso) trial

causante *adj*: **los factores ~s de la crisis** the factors which caused the crisis ■ *mf* (causa) cause; **la ~ de todas mis desgracias** the cause of all my misfortunes

causar [A1] *vt* ‹*daños/problema/sufrimiento*› to cause; ‹*indignación*› to cause, arouse; ‹*alarma*› to cause, provoke; ‹*placer*› to give; **le causó mucha pena** it made him very sad; **me causó muy buena impresión** I was very impressed with her

cautela *f* caution; **con ~** cautiously

cauteloso -sa *adj* [SER] ‹*persona*› cautious

cautivador -dora *adj* captivating

cautivar [A1] *vt* (atraer) to captivate

cautiverio *m* captivity

cautivo -va *adj/m,f* captive

cauto -ta *adj* careful, cautious

cava *f* cellar ■ *m* cava (*sparkling wine*)

cavar [A1] *vt* **(a)** ‹*fosa/zanja*› to dig; ‹*pozo*› to sink **(b)** ‹*tierra*› to hoe

caverna *f* cave, cavern

cavernícola *adj* (Hist) cave-dwelling; **un hombre ~** a caveman ■ *mf* (Hist) cave dweller

caviar *m* caviar

cavidad *f* cavity

cavilar [A1] *vi* to ponder, think deeply; **después de mucho ~** after much thought *o* deliberation

cayena *f* cayenne (pepper)

cayera, **cayese, etc** *see* CAER

caza *f* **(a)** (para subsistir) hunting; (como deporte — caza mayor) hunting; (— caza menor) shooting; **ir de ~** to go hunting/shooting; **~ del tesoro** treasure hunt; **~ furtiva** poaching; **salieron a la ~ del ladrón** they set off in pursuit of the thief; ***dar ~ a algn*** (perseguir) to pursue *o* chase sb; (alcanzar) to catch sb **(b)** (animales) game ■ *m* fighter

cazabombardero *m* fighter-bomber

cazador -dora *m,f* hunter; **~ furtivo** poacher

cazadora *f* (Esp) (Indum) jacket

cazamariposas *m* (*pl* **~**) butterfly net

cazar [A4] *vt* **(a)** (para subsistir) to hunt; (como deporte) (—caza mayor) to hunt; (— caza menor) to shoot **(b)** ‹*mariposas*› to catch **(c)** (fam) (conseguir, atrapar): **ha cazado un millonario/buen empleo** she's landed herself a millionaire/good job ■ **~** *vi* to hunt; (con fusil) to shoot; **salimos a ~** we went out hunting/shooting

cazo *m* (cacerola) small saucepan; (cucharón) ladle

cazuela *f* casserole

cazurro -rra *adj* (fam) (huraño) sullen, surly; (obstinado) stubborn, pig-headed (colloq) ■ *m,f* (fam) (huraño) sullen *o* surly person; (obstinado) stubborn *o* (colloq) pig-headed person

c.c. (= **centímetros cúbicos**) cc

CD *m* (= **compact disc**) CD

ce *f*: *name of the letter* c

cebada *f* barley

cebar [A1] *vt* **1** ‹*animal*› to fatten ... up **2** ‹*anzuelo/cepo*› to bait **3** (CS) ‹*mate*› to prepare (*and serve*)

cebo *m* **(a)** (en pesca, caza) bait **(b)** (Arm) primer

cebolla *f* onion

cebolleta *f*, **cebollino** *m* **(a)** (con tallo verde) scallion (AmE), spring onion (BrE) **(b)** (hierba) chive

cebra *f* zebra

cebú *m* (*pl* **-bús** *or* **-búes**) zebu

cedazo *m* sieve

ceder [E1] *vt* **1 (a)** ‹*derecho*› to transfer, assign; ‹*territorio*› to cede; ‹*puesto/título*› (voluntariamente) to hand over; (a la fuerza) to give up; **~ el poder** to hand over power; **me cedió el asiento** he let me have his seat; ⇨ PASO 1(b) **(b)** ‹*balón/pelota*› to pass **2** (prestar) ‹*jugador*› to loan ■ **~** *vi* **1** (cejar) to give way; **no cedió ni un ápice** she didn't give *o* yield an inch; **cedió en su empeño** she gave up the undertaking; **~ A algo** to give in TO sth **2** «*fiebre/lluvia/viento*» to ease off; «*dolor*» to ease **3** «*muro/puente/cuerda*» to give way; «*zapatos/muelle*» to give

cedro *m* cedar

cédula *f* (Fin) bond, warrant; **~ de identidad** identity card

cegador -dora *adj* blinding

cegar [A7] *vt* **1 (a)** (deslumbrar) to blind **(b)** (ofuscar) to blind; **cegado por los celos** blinded by jealousy **2** ‹*conducto/cañería*› to block

ceguera *f* blindness

ceja *f* **(a)** ▶ 123 (Anat) eyebrow; **arquear las ~s** to raise one's eyebrows **(b)** (Mús) capo

cejilla *f* capo

celador -dora *m,f* **(a)** (en museo, biblioteca) security guard **(b)** (en la cárcel) (AmL) prison guard (AmE), prison warder (BrE) **(c)** (en hospital) orderly, porter

celda *f* cell

celebración *f* celebration

celebrar [A1] *vt* **1 (a)** ‹*éxito/cumpleaños/festividad*› to celebrate **(b)** (liter) ‹*belleza/valor/hazaña*› to celebrate (liter) **(c)** ‹*chiste/ocurrencia*› to laugh at **2** (frml) (alegrarse) to be delighted at, be very pleased at; **celebro su éxito** I'm delighted to hear about your success **3 (a)** (frml) ‹*reunión/elecciones/juicio*› to hold; ‹*partido*› to play **(b)** ‹*misa*› to say, celebrate; ‹*boda*› to perform ■ **~** *vi* «*sacerdote*» to say *o* celebrate mass

célebre *adj* **(a)** (famoso) famous, celebrated **(b)** (Col) ‹*mujer*› elegant

celebridad *f* (fama) fame; (persona) celebrity

celeste ▶ 97 *adj* **1** (del cielo) heavenly, celestial **2** ‹*ojos*› blue; ‹*pintura/vestido*› (claro) light *o* pale blue; (intenso) sky-blue (*before n*) ■ *m* (claro) light *o* pale blue; (intenso) sky blue

celestial *adj* **(a)** (Relig) celestial **(b)** ‹*placer*› heavenly

célibe *adj/mf* celibate

celo *m* **1** (esmero, fervor) zeal **2** (Zool) **(a)** (de los machos) rut **(b)** (de las hembras) heat; **estar en ~** to be in season, to be in heat (AmE) *o* (BrE) on heat **3 celos** *mpl* jealousy; **tener ~s DE algn** to be jealous OF sb; **darle ~s a algn** to make sb jealous **4** (Esp) (cinta adhesiva) Scotch® tape (AmE), Sellotape® (BrE)

celofán *m* cellophane

celoso -sa *adj* **(a)** ‹*marido/novia*› jealous; **estar ~ DE algn** to be jealous OF sb **(b)** (diligente, esmerado) conscientious, zealous

celta *adj* Celtic ■ *mf* (persona) Celt ■ *m* (Ling) Celtic

célula *f* cell

celular *adj* cellular ■ *m* **(a)** (AmL) (teléfono) mobile phone **(b)** (Esp) (furgoneta para presos) patrol wagon (AmE), police van (BrE)

celulitis *f* (gordura) cellulite; (inflamación) cellulitis

cementerio *m* cemetery; (junto a una iglesia) graveyard; **~ de coches** salvage *o* wrecker's yard (AmE), scrapyard (BrE)

cemento *m* **(a)** (Const, Odont) cement; **~ armado** reinforced concrete **(b)** (AmL) (pegamento) glue, adhesive

cena *f* dinner, supper; (en algunas regiones del Reino Unido) tea; (formal, fuera de casa) dinner; **¿qué hay**

de ~? what's for dinner *o* supper?; **~ de gala** banquet

cenagal *m* (barrizal) bog, mire

cenar [A1] *vi* to have dinner *o* supper; (en algunas regiones del Reino Unido) to have tea; **nos invitaron a ~** they invited us for *o* to dinner; **salimos a ~** we went out for dinner ■ **~** *vt* ‹*tortilla/pescado*› to have ... for dinner *o* supper

cencerro *m* cowbell

cenefa *f* (en ropa, sábanas) border; (en techos, muros) frieze

cenicero *m* ashtray

cenicienta *f* drudge; **la C~** Cinderella

cenit *m* zenith

ceniza *f* ash

censo *m* **1 (a)** (de población) census **(b)** (Esp) *tb* **~ electoral** electoral roll *o* register **2** (Der, Fin) charge; (sobre una finca) ground rent

censor -sora *m,f* **(a)** (Cin, Period) censor **(b)** (crítico) critic **(c)** (Der, Fin) *tb* **~ de cuentas** auditor

censura *f* **(a)** (reprobación) censure (frml), condemnation **(b)** (de libros, películas) censorship

censurar [A1] *vt* **(a)** (reprobar) to censure (frml), to condemn **(b)**‹*libro/película*› to censor, ‹*escena/párrafo*› to cut, censor

centavo *m* **(a)** (en AmL) *hundredth part of many currencies*; ***estar sin un*** **~** to be penniless **(b)** (del dólar) cent

centella *f* (rayo) flash of lightning; (chispa) spark; ***como una*** **~** like greased lightning

centelleante *adj* ‹*estrella*› twinkling; ‹*luz/joya*› sparkling; ‹*ojos*› blazing

centellear [A1] *vi* «*luz/joya*» to sparkle, «*estrella*» to twinkle

centena *f* ▶ **293**: **una ~** a hundred; **unidades, decenas y ~s** units, tens and hundreds

centenar *m*: **un ~ de personas** a hundred or so people; **~es de cartas** hundreds of letters

centenario *m* centenary, centennial (AmE)

centeno *m* rye

centésima *f* ▶ **294** hundredth; **en una ~ de segundo** in a fraction of a second

centésimo *m* ▶ **294** (Fis, Mat) hundredth

centígrado -da *adj* ▶ **406** centigrade, Celsius

centigramo *m* ▶ **322** centigram

centímetro *m* ▶ **679** centimeter*

céntimo *m*: *hundredth part of the Spanish peseta, the Venezuelan bolivar and the Paraguayan guarani*; ***no tener un*** **~** to be penniless *o* (colloq) broke; ***no vale ni un*** **~** it's totally worthless

centinela *mf* (Mil) guard, sentry; (no militar) lookout; **estar de ~** (Mil) to be on sentry duty

centolla *f*, **centollo** *m* spider crab

centrado -da *adj* (equilibrado) stable, well-balanced; (en un trabajo, lugar) settled

central *adj* central; **~ teléfonica** telephone exchange; **~ hidroeléctrica/nuclear** hydroelectric/nuclear power station ■ *f* head office

centralista *adj/mf* centralist

centralita *f* switchboard

centralizar [A4] *vt* to centralize

centrar [A1] *vt* **(a)** ‹*imagen*› to center* **(b)** (Dep) to center* **(c)** ‹*atención/investigación/esfuerzos*› **~ algo EN algo** to focus sth ON sth ■ **~** *vi* (Dep) to center*, cross

■ **centrarse** *v pron* **~se EN algo** «*investigación/atención/esfuerzos*» to focus *o* center* ON sth

céntrico -ca *adj* ‹*área/calle*› central; **un bar ~** a downtown bar (AmE), a bar in the centre of town (BrE)

centrifugado *m* spin

centrifugar [A3] *vt* **(a)** ‹*ropa*› to spin **(b)** (Tec) to centrifuge

centrista *adj/mf* centrist

centro *m* **(a)** (en general) center*; **~ ciudad/urbano** downtown (AmE), city/town centre (BrE); **ser el ~ de atención** to be the center of attention; **se convirtió en el ~ de interés** it became the focus of attention; **~ turístico** tourist resort *o* center; **~ comercial** shopping mall (AmE), shopping centre (BrE); **~ de planificación familiar** family planning clinic **(b)** (en fútbol) cross, center* ■ *mf* (jugador) center*; **~ delantero** center* forward

Centroamérica *f* Central America

centroamericano -na *adj/m,f* Central American

centrocampista *mf* midfield player

ceñido -da *adj* tight; **me queda muy ~** it's very tight on me

ceñir [I15] *vt*: **esa falda te ciñe demasiado** that skirt is too tight for you; **el vestido le ceñía el talle** the dress clung to her waist

■ **ceñirse** *v pron* **~se A algo** ‹*a las reglas*› to adhere TO *o* (colloq) stick TO sth; **~se al tema** to keep to the subject

ceño *m*: **arrugó el ~** he frowned; **me miró con el ~ fruncido** she frowned at me

cepa *f* (Bot) stump; (Vin) stock (*of a vine*)

cepillar [A1] *vt* **(a)** ‹*ropa/dientes/pelo*› to brush **(b)** ‹*madera*› to plane

■ **cepillarse** *v pron* (*refl*) ‹*ropa*› to brush; ‹*dientes*› to brush, clean

cepillo *m* **1** (para ropa, zapatos, pelo) brush; (para suelo) scrubbing brush; **lleva el pelo cortado al ~** he has a crew cut; **~ de dientes/uñas** toothbrush/nailbrush **2** (de carpintería) plane **3** (en la iglesia) collection box (*o* plate *etc*)

cepo *m* (trampa) trap; (Auto) wheel clamp; (Hist) stocks (*pl*)

cera *f* (para velas) wax; (para pisos, muebles) wax polish; (de abejas) beeswax; (de los oídos) wax; **le di ~ al suelo** I polished the floor

cerámica *f* (arte) ceramics, pottery; (pieza) piece of pottery

cerca *adv* **(a)** (en el espacio) near, close; **~ DE algo/algn** near sth/sb; **¿hay algún banco ~?** is there a bank nearby *o* close by?; **está por aquí ~** it's near here (somewhere); **mirar algo/a algn de ~** to look at sth/sb close up *o* close to; ***seguir algo de*** **~** to follow sth closely **(b)** (en el tiempo) close; **los exámenes estaban ~** the exams were close; **estás tan ~ de lograrlo** you're so close to achieving it; **serán ~ de las dos** it must be nearly

2 o'clock **(c)** (indicando aproximación): **~ de** almost, nearly ■ *f* (de alambre, madera) fence; (de piedra) wall

cercado *m* **(a)** (de alambre, madera) fence; (de piedra) wall **(b)** (terreno) enclosure **(c)** (Per) (distrito) district

cercanía *f* **1** (en el espacio) closeness, proximity; (en el tiempo) proximity, imminence **2 cercanías** *fpl*: **Madrid y sus ~s** Madrid and its environs; **en las ~s del aeropuerto** in the vicinity of the airport

cercano -na *adj* **1 (a)** (en el espacio) nearby, neighboring*; **~ A algo** near sth, close TO sth; **el C~ Oriente** the Near East **(b)** (en el tiempo) close, near; **en fecha cercana** soon; **~ A algo** close TO sth **2** ‹*pariente/amigo*› close

cercar [A2] *vt* **(a)** ‹*campo/terreno*› to enclose, surround; (con valla) to fence in **(b)** ‹*persona*› to surround **(c)** (Mil) ‹*ciudad*› to besiege; ‹*enemigo*› to surround

cerciorarse *v pron* **~ se DE algo** to make certain OF sth

cerco *m* **(a)** (asedio) siege **(b)** (de una mancha) ring **(c)** (AmL) (valla) fence; (seto) hedge

cerda *f* **(a)** (animal) sow **(b)** (fam) (mujer — sucia) slob (colloq); (— despreciable) bitch (sl) **(c)** (pelo) bristle

cerdo *m* **(a)** (animal) pig, hog (AmE) **(b)** (carne) pork **(c)** (fam) (hombre — sucio) slob (colloq); (— despreciable) bastard (sl), swine (colloq)

cereal *m* cereal

cereales *mpl* (Esp) (para desayunar) cereal

cerebral *adj* ‹*actividad/tumor/derrame*› brain (*before n*); ‹*persona*› cerebral

cerebro *m* **(a)** ▶ **123** (Anat) brain; ***lavarle el ~ a algn*** to brainwash sb **(b)** (persona) brains; **el ~ de la operación** the brains behind the operation

ceremonia *f* ceremony; **no andemos con ~s** let's not stand on ceremony

cereza *f* (fruta) cherry

cerezo *m* cherry tree

cerilla *f* **1** (esp Esp) (fósforo) match **2** (de los oídos) wax

cerillo *m* (esp AmC, Méx) match

cernícalo *m* (Zool) kestrel

cero *m* ▶ **293**, **406** **(a)** (Fís, Mat) zero; (en números de teléfono) zero (AmE), oh (BrE); **~ coma cinco** zero point five; **empezar** *or* **partir de ~** to start from scratch; ***ser un ~ a la izquierda*** to be useless **(b)** (en fútbol, rugby) zero (AmE), nil (BrE); (en tenis) love; **ganan por tres a ~** they're winning three-zero (AmE) *o* (BrE) three-nil **(c)** (Educ) zero, nought (BrE)

cerquillo *m* (AmL) (flequillo) bangs (*pl*) (AmE), fringe (BrE)

cerrado -da *adj* **1 (a)** ‹*puerta/ventana/ojos/boca*› closed, shut; ‹*mejillones/almejas*› closed; ‹*sobre/carta*› sealed; ‹*puño*› clenched; ‹*cortinas*› drawn, closed; **estaba ~ con llave** it was locked **(b)** ‹*válvula*› closed, shut off; ‹*grifo/llave*› turned off **2** ‹*tienda/restaurante/museo*› closed, shut **3** ‹*espacio/recinto*› enclosed; ‹*curva*› sharp **4** ‹*acento/dialecto*› broad **5** ‹*persona*› (poco comunicativo) uncommunicative; **está ~ a todo cambio** his mind is closed to change; **~ a influencias externas** shut off from outside influence

cerradura *f* lock; ⇨ OJO

cerrajería *f* locksmith's shop

cerrajero -ra *m,f* locksmith

cerrar [A5] *vt* **1 (a)** ‹*puerta/ventana*› to close, shut; ‹*ojos/boca*› to shut, close; **cierra la puerta con llave** lock the door **(b)** ‹*botella*› to put the top on/cork in; ‹*frasco*› to put the lid on; ‹*sobre*› to seal **(c)** ‹*paraguas/abanico/mano*› to close; ‹*libro*› to close, shut; ‹*puño*› to clench **(d)** ‹*cortinas*› to close, draw; ‹*persianas*› to lower, pull down; ‹*abrigo*› to fasten, button up; ‹*cremallera*› to do ... up **(e)** ‹*grifo/agua/gas*› to turn off; ‹*válvula*› to close, shut off **2 (a)** ‹*fábrica/comercio/oficina*› (en el quehacer diario) to close; (definitivamente) to close (down) **(b)** ‹*aeropuerto/carretera/frontera*› to close **3 (a)** ‹*cuenta bancaria*› to close **(b)** ‹*caso/juicio*› to close **(c)** ‹*acuerdo/negociación*› to finalize **(d)** ‹*acto/debate*› to bring ... to an end ■ **~** *vi* **1** (hablando de puerta, ventana): **cierra, que hace frío** close *o* shut the door (*o* window *etc*), it's cold; **¿cerraste con llave?** did you lock up? **2** «*puerta/ventana/cajón*» to close, shut **3** «*comercio/oficina*» (en el quehacer diario) to close, shut; (definitivamente) to close (down)

■ **cerrarse** *v pron* **1 (a)** «*puerta/ventana*» to shut, close; **la puerta se cerró de golpe** the door slammed shut **(b)** «*ojos*» to close; **se le cerraban los ojos** his eyes were closing **(c)** «*flor/almeja*» to close up **(d)** «*herida*» to heal (up) **2** (*refl*) ‹*abrigo*› to fasten, button up; ‹*cremallera*› to do ... up **3** «*acto/debate/jornada*» to end

cerrazón *m* (terquedad) stubbornness; (mentalidad poco flexible) blinkered attitude

cerro *m* (Geog) hill

cerrojo *m* bolt; **echar el ~** to bolt the door

certamen *m* competition, contest

certero -ra *adj* **(a)** ‹*tiro*› accurate; ‹*golpe*› well-aimed **(b)** ‹*juicio*› sound; ‹*respuesta*› good

certeza, **certidumbre** *f* certainty; **no lo sé con ~** I'm not sure, I don't know for sure

certificado[1] **-da** *adj* ‹*paquete/carta*› registered; **mandé la carta certificada** I sent the letter by registered mail

certificado[2] *m* certificate

certificar [A2] *vt* to certify

cervatillo *m* fawn

cerveza *f* beer; **~ tirada** *o* **de barril** draft beer (AmE), draught beer (BrE); **~ rubia** lager; **~ negra** dark beer

cesante *adj* [ESTAR] (Chi) (sin empleo) unemployed; **quedó ~** he lost his job ■ *mf* (Chi) (sin empleo) unemployed person

cesantía *f* (desempleo) (Chi) unemployment; (despido) (RPl frml) dismissal; (pago) (Col) severance pay

cesar [A1] *vi* **1** (parar) to stop; **~ DE hacer algo** to stop doing sth; **sin ~** incessantly **2** (frml *o* period) (dimitir): **cesó en su cargo** she left her post, she resigned

cesárea *f* cesarean* (section); **le tuvieron que hacer una ~** she had to have a cesarean

cese *m* (frml *o* period) **(a)** (interrupción) cessation (frml); **el ~ de hostilidades** the cessation of hostilities; **~ del fuego** (AmL) ceasefire **(b)** (renuncia) resignation

césped *m* **(a)** (planta) grass; (extensión) lawn, grass; Ⓢ **prohibido pisar el césped** keep off the grass **(b)** (Dep) field, pitch (BrE); (en tenis) (AmL) grass

cesta *f* **(a)** (recipiente) basket; **~ de Navidad** Christmas hamper; **~ punta** (deporte) pelota; (canasta) basket (*for playing pelota*) **(b)** (esp AmL) (en baloncesto) basket

cesto *m* **(a)** (esp Esp) (recipiente) basket; **el ~ de la ropa sucia** the laundry basket **(b)** (esp AmL) (en baloncesto) basket

cetro *m* scepter*

cg. (= **centigramo**) cg

Ch, **ch** *f* (*read as* /tʃe/ *or* /se 'atʃe/ *or* (Esp) /θe 'atʃe/) *combination traditionally considered as a separate letter in the Spanish alphabet*

chabacano¹ -na *adj* ‹*ropa/decoración*› gaudy, tasteless; ‹*espectáculo/persona*› vulgar; ‹*chiste/cuento*› coarse, tasteless

chabacano² *m* (Méx) (árbol) apricot tree; (fruta) apricot

chabola *f* (Esp) **(a)** (en los suburbios) shack, shanty dwelling **(b) chabolas** *fpl* shantytown

chacal *m* jackal

chacarero -ra *m,f* (CS, Per) farmer (*who works a* CHACRA)

cháchara *f* **1** (fam) (conversación) chatter; **se pasa la mañana de ~** she spends the whole morning chattering **2** (Méx) (objeto de poca importancia) piece of junk; **un cajón lleno de ~s** a drawer's full of junk

chacharear [A1] *vi* (fam) to chatter

Chaco *m*: *tb* **el Gran ~** *region of scrub and swamp plains covering parts of Paraguay, Bolivia and Argentina*

chacra *f* (CS, Per) (granja) small farm; (casa) farmhouse

chafar [A1] *vt* (fam) **(a)** ‹*peinado*› to flatten; ‹*plátano/pulpa*› to mash; ‹*huevos*› to break; ‹*ajo*› to crush **(b)** ‹*vestido/falda*› to wrinkle (AmE), to crumple (BrE)
■ **chafarse** *v pron* to get squashed

chal *m* shawl, wrap

chala *f* **(a)** (RPl) (Bot) corn husk **(b)** (Chi) (Indum) sandal

chalado -da *adj* (fam) [ESTAR] crazy (colloq), nuts (colloq) ■ *m,f* nutter (colloq)

chale *interj* (Méx fam) you're kidding! (colloq)

chalé *m* ⇒ CHALET

chaleca *f* (Chi) cardigan

chaleco *m* (de traje) vest (AmE), waistcoat (BrE); (jersey sin mangas) sleeveless sweater; (acolchado) body warmer; (chaqueta de punto) (CS) cardigan; **~ antibalas** bulletproof vest; **~ de fuerza** straitjacket; **~ salvavidas** lifejacket; ***a* ~** (Méx) no matter what

chalet /tʃa'le/ *m* (*pl* **-lets**) (en urbanización) house; (en el campo) cottage; (en la montaña) chalet; (en la playa) villa

chalote *m*, **chalota** *f* shallot, scallion (AmE)

chalupa *f* **1** (barca) skiff; (canoa) (AmL) small canoe **2** (Méx) (Coc) stuffed tortilla

chamaco -ca *m,f* (Méx fam) (muchacho) kid (colloq), youngster (colloq)

chamagoso -sa *adj* (Méx fam) dirty, filthy

chamarra *f* (chaqueta) jacket

chamba *f* **1** (Méx, Per, Ven fam) (trabajo) work; (empleo) job; (lugar) work **2** (Col) **(a)** (zanja) ditch **(b)** (herida) wound, gash

chambear [A1] *vi* (Méx, Per fam) to work

chambón -bona *adj* (AmL fam) clumsy, klutzy (AmE colloq)

chambonada *f* (AmL fam) botch (colloq)

chamizo *m* **1 (a)** (leña quemada) charred log **(b)** (Col) (ramas secas) *tb* **~s** brushwood **2** (choza) thatched hut

chamo -ma *m,f* (Ven fam) (niño, muchacho) kid (colloq)

champán *m*, **champaña** *m or f* champagne

champiñón *m* mushroom

champú *m* (*pl* **-pús** *or* **-púes**) shampoo

champurrear [A1] *vt* (CS) ⇒ CHAPURREAR

chamuscar [A2] *vt* to scorch, singe; **madera chamuscada** charred wood
■ **chamuscarse** *v pron*: **~se el pelo** to singe one's hair

chamuyar [A1] *vi* (RPl fam) to chatter ■ **~** *vt* (RPl fam) to mutter

chan *m* (AmC) mountain guide

chancaca *f* **(a)** (Andes) (melaza) brown sugarloaf **(b)** (Per) (dulce de maíz) maize cake

chancar [A2] *vt* **1** (Andes) (triturar) to crush, grind **2** (Per arg) (estudiar) to cram

chance *f or m* (AmL) (oportunidad) chance; **dar ~ a algn** to give sb the chance; **tiene pocas ~s de ganar** he doesn't have *o* stand much chance of winning

chancear [A1] *vi* (Col fam) to joke, kid around (colloq)
■ **chancearse** *v pron* **~se** DE **algn** to make fun OF sb

chanchada *f* (AmL fam) **(a)** (porquería, suciedad) mess **(b)** (acción indigna) dirty trick (colloq); **hacerle una ~ a algn** to play a dirty trick on sb

chanchería *f* (AmL) pork butcher's shop

chanchito *m* (fam) **1** (Andes, CS) (Zool) woodlouse **2** (CS) (alcancía) piggy bank

chancho¹ -cha *adj* (AmL fam) (sucio) filthy, gross (colloq); (miserable, ruin) mean ■ *m,f* (AmL) **(a)** (Zool) pig **(b)** (fam) (persona sucia) dirty *o* filthy pig (colloq)

chancho² *m* (Chi, Per) (Coc) *tb* **carne de ~** pork

chanchullero -ra *adj* (fam) shady (colloq), crooked (colloq) ■ *m,f* (fam) racket (colloq)

chanchullo *m* (fam) racket (colloq), fiddle (BrE colloq)

chancla *f* (sandalia) thong (AmE), flip-flop (BrE); (pantufla) (Col) slipper

chancleta *f* (sandalia) thong (AmE), flip-flop (BrE)

chándal *m* (*pl* **-dals**) (Esp) tracksuit

changador *m* (RPl) porter

changarro *m* (Méx) small store

chango -ga *m,f* (Méx) monkey

changuito® *m* (Arg) (para las compras) shopping cart (AmE), shopping trolley (BrE); (para el bebé) stroller (AmE), pushchair (BrE)

chanquetes *mpl* whitebait (*pl*)

chanta *adj* (RPl arg) (informal) unreliable; (mentiroso) deceitful ■ *mf* (RPl arg) (informal) unreliable person; (mentiroso) liar

chantaje *m* blackmail; **le hacen ~** he is being blackmailed

chantajear [A1] *vt* to blackmail

chantajista *mf* blackmailer

chantillí, **chantilly** /ʃanti'ʝi, tʃanti'ʝi/ *m*: *tb* **crema ~** *f* whipped cream, chantilly

chao *interj* (fam) bye (colloq), bye-bye (colloq)

chapa *f* **1 (a)** (plancha — de metal) sheet; (— de madera) panel **(b)** (lámina de madera) veneer **(c)** (carrocería) bodywork **2 (a)** (distintivo) badge; (de policía) shield (AmE), badge (BrE); (con el nombre) nameplate; (de perro) identification disc *o* tag **(b)** (RPl) (de matrícula) license plate (AmE), numberplate (BrE) **3** (de botella) cap, top **4** (AmL) (cerradura) lock **5 chapas** *fpl* (AmL fam) (en las mejillas): **le salieron ~s** (por vergüenza) her cheeks flushed (red); (por el aire fresco) her cheeks were red **6** (AmC fam) (joya) earring; (dentadura postiza) false teeth (*pl*)

chapado -da *adj* ‹*metal*› plated; **un reloj ~ en oro** a gold-plated watch

chaparrastroso -sa *adj* (Méx fam) scruffy

chaparro -rra *adj* (AmL fam) short, squat; **quedarse ~** to stop growing ■ *m,f* (AmL fam) shorty (colloq), titch (colloq)

chaparrón *m* (Meteo) downpour, cloudburst

chape *m* (Chi) (trenza) braid (AmE), plait (BrE); (pelo atado) bunch

chapetes *mpl* (Méx) ⇒ CHAPA 5

chapista *mf* panel beater

chapopote *m* (Méx) (alquitrán) tar; (asfalto) asphalt

chapotear [A1] *vi* (en agua) splash (around); (en barro) squelch (around)

chapucero -ra *adj* ‹*persona*› sloppy, slapdash; ‹*trabajo/reparación*› botched ■ *m,f*: **es un ~** his work is very slapdash

chapulín *m* (AmC, Méx) (Zool) locust

chapurrear [A1] *vt* (fam): **~ el inglés** to speak broken *o* poor English

chapuza *f* (fam) (trabajo mal hecho) botched job (colloq), botch (colloq)

chapuzón *m* dip; **darse un ~** to have a dip

chaquet (*pl* **-quets**), **chaqué** *m* morning coat

chaqueta *f* **1** (Indum) jacket; **~ de punto** cardigan **2** (Col) (Odont) crown

chaquetón *m* three-quarter length coat

charanga *f* brass band; (militar) military band

charango *m* small five-stringed guitar

charca *f* pond, pool

charco *m* **(a)** puddle, pool **(b) el ~** (fam) (océano Atlántico) the Atlantic, the Pond (colloq & hum)

charcutería *f* delicatessen, charcuterie (AmE)

charla *f* **(a)** (conversación) chat; **estábamos de ~** we were having a chat **(b)** (conferencia) talk

charlar [A1] *vi* to chat, talk

charlatán -tana *adj* (fam) talkative ■ *m,f* (fam) **(a)** (parlanchín) chatterbox (colloq) **(b)** (vendedor) dishonest hawker; (curandero) charlatan

charlestón *m* charleston

charme /ʃarm/ *m* charm

charol *m* **1** (barniz) lacquer; (cuero) patent leather; **zapatos de ~** patent leather shoes **2** (Col, Per) (bandeja) tray

charola *f* (Bol, Méx, Per) tray

charqui *m* (AmS) charqui, jerked beef

charrasquear [A1] *vt* **1** (AmL) ‹*guitarra*› to strum **2** (Méx) ‹*persona*› to stab

charrería *f* (Méx) *the culture of horsemanship and rodeo riding*

charretera *f* epaulette

charro -rra *adj* **1** (fam) (de mal gusto) gaudy, garish **2** (en Méx) ‹*tradiciones/música*› of/relating to the CHARRO ■ *m,f* (en Méx) (jinete) (*m*) horseman, cowboy; (*f*) horsewoman, cowgirl

chárter *adj inv* charter (*before n*) ■ *m* charter (flight)

chasco *m* (decepción) disappointment, let-down (colloq); **me llevé un ~** I felt let down *o* disappointed

chasis, **chasís** *m* (*pl* **~**) (Auto) chassis; (Fot) plateholder

chasquear [A1] *vt* **(a)** ‹*lengua*› to click; ‹*dedos*› to click, snap **(b)** ‹*látigo*› to crack

chasquido *m* **(a)** (de la lengua) click; (de los dedos) click, snap **(b)** (de látigo) crack; (de rama seca) crack, snap

chasquilla *f* (Chi) bangs (*pl*) (AmE), fringe (BrE)

chatarra *adj inv* (Méx): **comida ~** junk food; **productos ~** cheap goods ■ *f* (Metal) scrap (metal); **el coche es pura ~** the car is just a heap of scrap

chatarrero -ra *m,f* scrap merchant

chatel -tela *m,f* (AmC fam) (*m*) little boy; (*f*) little girl

chato -ta *adj* **(a)** ‹*nariz*› snub (*before n*) **(b)** (Per fam) (bajo) short **(c)** (AmS) ‹*nivel*› low; ‹*obra*› pedestrian

chaucha *f* (RPl) (Bot, Coc) French bean

chauvinismo /tʃoβi'nismo/ *m* chauvinism

chauvinista /tʃoβi'nista/ *adj* chauvinistic ■ *mf* chauvinist

chaval -vala *m,f* (esp Esp fam) (niño) kid (colloq), youngster

chavalo -la *m,f* (AmC, Méx) ⇒ CHAVAL

chavo -va *adj* (Méx fam) young ■ *m,f* (Méx) **(a)** (fam) (muchacho) guy (colloq); (muchacha) girl **(b)** (como apelativo) kid (colloq)

chayote *m* (planta, fruto) chayote, mirliton

che *interj* (RPl fam): **no te hagas el bobo, ~** come on, don't act the innocent; **~, Marta, ¿qué tal?** hey Marta, how are you?; **¡pero ~! ¡cómo le dijiste eso!** for Heaven's sake! whatever made you tell him that?

checar [A2] *vt* (Méx) **(a)** (revisar, mirar) to check; **me chequé la presión** (Med) I had my blood pressure checked; **¿por qué no vas a que te chequen?** why don't you go for a checkup? **(b)** (verificar) to check **(c)** (vigilar) to check up on

checo[1] -ca *adj/m,f* Czech

checo[2] *m* (idioma) Czech

checoslovaco -ca *adj/m,f* (Hist) Czechoslovakian, Czechoslovak

Checoslovaquia *f* (Hist) Czechoslovakia

chef /ʃef, tʃef/ *m* chef

chele -la *adj* (AmC) (de piel) light-skinned; (de pelo) blond-haired

chelín *m* shilling

chelista *mf* cellist

chelo *m* cello

cheque *m* check (AmE), cheque (BrE); **pagar con ~** to pay by check; **un ~ a nombre de** ... a check made out to *o* made payable to ...; **~ bancario** *o* (AmL) **de gerencia** banker's draft; **~ cruzado/en blanco** crossed/blank check*; **~ de viaje** *or* **de viajero** traveler's check (AmE), traveller's cheque (BrE); **~ sin fondos** bad *o* (frml) dishonored* check*

chequear [A1] *vt* **1** (revisar, verificar) to check; **~ algo** CON **algo** to check sth AGAINST sth **2** (AmL) ‹*equipaje*› to check in

■ **chequearse** *v pron* **(a)** (Col, Ven) (Aviac) to check in **(b)** (Ven) (Med) to have a checkup

chequeo *m* **(a)** (Med) checkup; (para entrar en el ejército, a trabajar) medical; **someterse a un ~ médico** to have a medical/a checkup **(b)** (control, inspección) check; **mostradores de ~ de tiquetes** (Col) check-in desks

chequera *f* checkbook (AmE), chequebook (BrE)

chévere *adj* (AmL exc CS fam) great (colloq), fantastic (colloq); **¡qué ~!** that's great!

chic /ʃik, tʃik/ *adj inv* chic, fashionable ■ *m* chic; **tiene ~** she's very chic

chica *f* (fam) maid; *ver tb* CHICO

chicanero -ra *adj* (Andes, Méx) tricky, crafty

chicano -na *adj/m,f* Chicano

chicha *f* **1 (a)** (bebida alcohólica) *alcoholic drink made from fermented maize, also called* CHICHA BRUJA; **~ andina** *alcoholic drink made with corn flour and pineapple juice*; **~ de manzana/uva** *alcoholic drink made from apple/grape juice* **(b)** (bebida sin alcohol) *cold drink made with maize or fruit* **2** (AmC vulg) (teta) tit (sl)

chícharo *m* (esp Méx) pea

chicharra *f* **(a)** (Zool) cicada **(b)** (timbre) buzzer

chicharrón *m* piece of crackling; **chicharrones** cracklings (*pl*) (AmE), pork scratchings (*pl*) (BrE)

chiche *adj* (AmC fam) dead easy (colloq) ■ *m* **1** (juguete) (CS fam) toy; (adorno) (Chi) trinket **2** (AmC fam) (pecho) tit (sl)

chichi *f* (Méx fam) (de mujer) tit (sl); (de animal) teat

chicho -cha *adj* (Méx fam) **(a)** (bonito) nice, neat (AmE colloq) **(b)** ‹*persona*›: **es muy chicha para los deportes** she's brilliant at sport (colloq)

chichón *m* swelling *o* bump on the head

chicle, **chiclé** *m* chewing gum

chiclero -ra *m,f* **1** (Méx) (vendedor) street vendor (*selling chewing gum, candy, etc*) **2** (AmC) (Agr) rubber tapper

chico -ca *adj* (esp AmL) **(a)** (joven) young; **cuando éramos ~s** when we were little (colloq) **(b)** (bajo) small **(c)** (pequeño) small ■ *m,f* **1 (a)** (niño) (*m*) boy; (*f*) girl **(b)** (hijo) (*m*) son, boy; (*f*) daughter, girl **(c)** (joven) (*m*) guy (colloq), boy (colloq), bloke (BrE colloq); (*f*) girl; **unos ~s** (varones) some boys; (varones y hembras) some boys and girls **(d)** (empleado joven) (*m*) boy; (*f*) girl **(e)** (como apelativo): **¡~! ¿tú por aquí?** well, well! what brings *you* here? **2 chico** *m* (AmL) (en billar) frame; (en bolos) game

chicoria *f* chicory

chicotazo *m* (AmL) whipping

chicote *m* (fam) (AmL) (látigo) whip

chicotear [A1] *vt* (AmL) to whip

chifa *m* (Per fam) Chinese (restaurant)

chifla *f* whistling, catcalls (*pl*)

chiflado -da *adj* (fam) crazy (colloq), mad (BrE); **estar ~** POR **algo/algn** to be crazy *o* mad ABOUT sth/sb (colloq) ■ *m,f* (fam) nutter (colloq)

chiflar [A1] *vt* ‹*actor/cantante*› to whistle at (*as sign of disapproval*), ≈ to boo ■ **~** *vi* **1** (silbar) to whistle **2** (fam) (gustar mucho): **le chiflan los coches** he's crazy about cars (colloq)

■ **chiflarse** *v pron* (fam) **~se** POR **algo/algn** to be crazy ABOUT sth/sb (colloq)

chihuahua *mf* chihuahua

chilaba *f* djellaba

chilango -ga *adj* (Méx) of/from Mexico City

chilaquiles *mpl* (Méx) *corn tortilla in tomato and chili sauce*

chile *m* **1** (AmC, Méx) (Bot, Coc) chili, hot pepper; **~ con carne** chili con carne **2** (AmC fam) (chiste) joke

Chile *m* Chile

chilear [A1] *vi* (AmC fam) to tell jokes

chileno -na *adj/m,f* Chilean

chilicote *m* (AmS) cricket

chillar [A1] *vi* **(a)** «*pájaro*» to screech; «*cerdo*» to squeal; «*ratón*» to squeak **(b)** «*persona*» to shout, yell (colloq); (de dolor, miedo) to scream; **~le** A **algn** to yell *o* shout AT sb **(c)** «*bebé/niño*» (llorar) to scream

chillido *m* **(a)** (de ave) screech; (de cerdo) squeal; (de ratón) squeak **(b)** (grito) shout, yell; (de dolor, miedo) scream, shriek; **dar ~s** *o* **un ~** (fam) to shout, to yell

chillón -llona *adj* (fam) ‹*voz*› shrill, piercing; ‹*color*› loud

chilote *m* (AmC) baby sweetcorn

chiltoma *f* (AmC) sweet pepper

chimbo -ba *adj* **(a)** (Col fam) (falsificado) ‹*perfume*› fake (*before n*); ‹*whisky/grabación*› bootleg (*before n*); **un cheque ~** a dud check (colloq) **(b)** (Ven arg) (malo) lousy (colloq)

chimbomba *f* (AmC) balloon

chimenea *f* **1 (a)** (de casa) chimney; (de locomotora, fábrica) smokestack (AmE), chimney (BrE) **(b)** (de volcán) vent **2** (hogar) fireplace, hearth

chimpancé *mf* chimpanzee

chimpún *m* (Per) football boot

china *f* **(a)** (piedra) pebble, small stone **(b)** (Esp) (porcelana) porcelain

China *f*: *tb* **la ~** China

chinamo *m* (AmC fam) (en feria) stall; (bar) small bar

chinchar [A1] *vt* (fam) to pester (colloq)

chinche *adj* (fam) (pesado) irritating; (quisquilloso): **es muy ~** he's a real nit-picker ■ *f or m* **1** (insecto) bedbug **2** (RPl fam) (mal humor) bad mood ■ *mf* **(a)** (fam) (pesado) nuisance, pain in the neck (colloq) **(b)** (fam) (quisquilloso) nit-picker (colloq) ■ *f (en algunas regiones m)* (clavito) thumbtack (AmE), drawing pin (BrE)

chincheta *f* (Esp) thumbtack (AmE), drawing pin (BrE)

chinchilla *f* chinchilla

chin-chin *interj* (fam) cheers!

chinchorro *m* (Col, Ven) (hamaca) hammock

chinchulines *mpl* (Bol, RPl) chitterlings (*pl*)

chincol *m* (Chi) (pájaro) crown sparrow

chinela *f* (pantufla) slipper; (chancla) (AmC) thong (AmE), flip-flop (BrE)

chingada *f* (Méx vulg): **está pa' la ~** he's/she's had it (colloq); **¡vete a la ~!** screw you! (vulg); **la casa estaba en la ~** the house was in the middle of nowhere (colloq); **¡hijo de la ~!** you son-of-a-bitch! (sl)

chingadera *f* (Méx vulg) trash (colloq), crap (sl)

chingar [A3] *vi* **(a)** (esp Méx vulg) (copular) to screw (vulg), to fuck (vulg) **(b)** (Méx vulg) (molestar): **te lo dijo para ~ nada más** he only said it to annoy you; **¡deja de ~!** stop being such a pain in the ass! (vulg); **¡no chingues!** (no digas) you're kidding! (colloq) ■ **~** *vt* **(a)** (AmL vulg) (en sentido sexual) to fuck (vulg), to screw (vulg) **(b)** (Méx vulg) (jorobar) to screw (vulg); **~*la***: **¡no la chingues!** (Méx vulg) shit! (vulg) ■ **chingarse** *v pron* **1 (a)** (*enf*) (AmL vulg) (en sentido sexual) to fuck (vulg), to screw (vulg) **(b)** (esp Méx vulg) (jorobarse): **creyó que ganaría pero se chingó** he thought he'd win but he got a shock; **se chingó el motor** the engine's had it (colloq); **estamos chingados** we're in deep shit (vulg) **2** (Méx vulg) **(a)** (aguantarse): **si no te gusta, te chingas** if you don't like it, tough (colloq) **(b)** (robar) to rip ... off (colloq)

chingaste *m* (AmC) coffee grounds (*pl*)

chingo¹ -ga *adj* (AmC fam) (desnudo) stark naked (colloq) ■ *m,f* (Ven fam) snub-nosed person

chingo² *m* (Méx fam *o* vulg): **un ~ de** loads of (colloq); **me costó un ~** it cost me a bundle *o* (BrE) packet (colloq)

chingón -gona *adj* (Méx vulg) ‹*partido/película*› fantastic (colloq); ‹*persona*› cool (sl)

chingue *m* (Chi) **(a)** (Zool) skunk **(b)** (fam) (persona hedionda) smelly person

chinguear [A1] *vi/vt* (AmC) ⇒ CHINGAR

chinita *f* (Chi) ladybug (AmE), ladybird (BrE)

chino¹ -na *adj* **1** (de la China) Chinese **2** (Méx) ‹*pelo*› curly ■ *m,f* **1** (de la China) (*m*) Chinese man; (*f*) Chinese woman; **los ~s** the Chinese **2 (a)** (Arg, Per) (mestizo) mestizo, person of mixed Amerindian and European parentage **(b)** (Col fam) (joven) kid (colloq)

chino² *m* **1** (idioma) Chinese; ***me suena a ~*** it's all Greek to me **2** (Méx) (pelo rizado) curly hair; (para rizar el pelo) curler, roller **3** (Per fam) (tienda) convenience store, corner shop (BrE)

chip *m* (*pl* **chips**) **(a)** (Inf) chip **(b)** (papa frita) potato chip (AmE), crisp (BrE) **(c)** (Arg) (pancito) bridge roll

chipirón *m* small cuttlefish

chipote *m* (Méx fam) bump, lump

Chipre *f* Cyprus

chipriota *adj/mf* Cypriot

chiqueado *adj* (Méx fam) spoilt

chiquear [A1] *vt* (Méx fam) to spoil

chiquero *m* (AmL) (pocilga) pigpen (AmE), pigsty (BrE)

chiquilín -lina *adj* (AmL fam) (infantil) childish; **ser ~** to be childish, to act like a kid (colloq) ■ *m,f* (fam) (persona infantil) (AmL) big kid (colloq); (niño) (Ur) kid (colloq)

chiquillada *f*: **se pelearon por una ~** they fought over something really silly

chiquillo -lla *adj*: **no seas ~** don't be childish ■ *m,f* kid (colloq)

chiquito¹ -ta, **chiquitito -ta** *adj* (esp AmL fam) small

chiquito² -ta *m,f* (esp AmL fam) (niño) (*m*) little boy; (*f*) little girl

chiribita *f* **(a)** (chispa) spark **(b) chiribitas** *fpl* (en la vista) spots in front of the eyes; **los ojos le hacían ~s** his eyes glowed

chirigota *f* (fam) (broma) joke; **estar de ~** to be kidding around (colloq)

chirimiri *m* fine drizzle

chirimoya *f* custard apple

chiripa *f* **1** (fam) (casualidad) fluke; **de** *or* **por ~** (fam) by sheer luck, by a fluke **2** (Ven) **(a)** (insecto) cockroach **(b)** (palmera) palm

chirla *f* (Coc, Zool) baby clam

chirona *f* (Esp fam) can (AmE sl), nick (BrE sl)

chiros *mpl* (Col) rags (*pl*)

chirriar [A17] *vi* «*puerta/gozne*» to squeak, creak; «*frenos/neumáticos*» to screech

chirrido *m* (de puerta) squeaking, creaking; (de frenos, neumáticos) screech, screeching

chis, **chist** *interj* shush!, ssh!

chisme *m* **(a)** (chismorreo) piece of gossip; **~s** gossip, tittle-tattle (colloq); **contar ~s** to gossip **(b)** (Esp, Méx fam) (trasto, cacharro) thing, thingamajig (colloq); **un cuarto lleno de ~s** a room full of junk *o* stuff (colloq)

chismear, **chismorrear** [A1] *vi* (fam) to gossip

chismorreo *m* (fam) gossip, tittle-tattle (colloq)

chismoso -sa *adj* gossipy (colloq) ■ *m,f* gossip, scandalmonger (colloq)

chispa *f* **1 (a)** (del fuego) spark **(b)** (Auto, Elec) spark **2** (fam) (pizca) little bit **3** (gracia, ingenio) wit; **tener ~** to be witty ■ *adj inv* (Esp fam) tipsy (colloq)

chisparse [A1] *v pron* (Méx) to come loose

chispazo *m* (Elec, Tec) spark

chispeante *adj* **(a)** ‹*leña/fuego*› crackling **(b)** ‹*lenguaje/personalidad*› witty; ‹*ingenio*› lively, sparkling **(c)** ‹*ojos*› (de alegría) sparkling; (de ira) flashing

chispear [A1] *vi* **(a)** «*leña*» to spark **(b)** (Elec) to spark, give off sparks ■ ~ *v impers* (fam) (lloviznar) to spit, spot

chispero *m* (AmC) (encendedor) (fam) lighter; (Auto) spark plug

chisporrotear [A1] *vi* «*leña/fuego*» to spark, crackle; «*aceite*» to spit, splutter; «*carne/pescado*» to sizzle

chistar [A1] *vi*: **¡y sin ~!** and not another word!; **no chistó** he didn't say a word

chiste *m* **(a)** (cuento gracioso) joke; **contar** *or* (Col) **echar un ~** to tell a joke; **~ picante** *or* **verde** *or* (Bol, Méx) **colorado** dirty joke **(b)** (Bol, CS, Méx) (broma) joke; **hacerle un ~ a algn** to play a joke *o* trick on sb; **me lo dijo en ~** he was joking **(c)** (Col, Méx fam) (gracia): **el ~ está en hacerlo rápido** the idea *o* point is to do it quickly; ***tener su ~*** (Méx) to be tricky **(d) chistes** *mpl* (RPl) (historietas) comic strips (*pl*), funnies (*pl*) (AmE colloq)

chistera *f* top hat

chistoso -sa *adj* funny, amusing ■ *m,f* comic, joker

chiva *f* **1** (AmL) (barba) goatee **2** (Col) (bus) rural *o* country bus **3** (Col period) (primicia) scoop, exclusive **4** (Chi fam) (mentira) cock-and-bull story (colloq); *ver tb* CHIVO **5 chivas** *fpl* (Méx fam) (cachivaches) junk (colloq)

chivarse [A1] *v pron* (Esp fam) to tell; (a la policía) to squeal (sl)

chivatazo *m* (Esp fam) tip-off (colloq); **les dieron el ~** they were tipped off

chivato[1] -ta *m,f* (Esp, Ven fam) **(a)** (informador) informer, stool pigeon (colloq) **(b)** (acusetas) tattletale (AmE colloq), telltale (BrE colloq)

chivato[2] *m* (Esp fam) (dispositivo sonoro) bleeper (colloq); (luz piloto) pilot light

chivearse [A1] *v pron* (Méx) (fam) (turbarse) to get embarrassed

chivo -va *m,f* **1 (a)** (cría de la cabra) kid **(b)** (Ven) (cabra) goat; *ver tb* CHIVA **2 chivo** *m* **(a)** (AmL) (macho cabrío) billy goat **(b) ~ expiatorio** scapegoat

chocado -da *adj* (AmL fam) smashed up (colloq); (superficialmente) dented

chocante *adj* **(a)** (que causa impresión): **su reacción me pareció ~** I was shocked *o* taken aback by his reaction, his reaction shocked me **(b)** (en cuestiones morales) shocking **(c)** (Col, Méx, Ven) (desagradable) unpleasant

chocar [A2] *vi* **1 (a)** (colisionar) to crash; (entre sí) to collide; **~ de frente** to collide *o* crash head-on; **~** CON *or* CONTRA **algo** «*vehículo*» to crash *o* run INTO sth; (con otro en marcha) to collide WITH sth; **el balón chocó contra el poste** the ball hit the goalpost; **~** CON **algn** «*persona*» to run INTO sb; (con otra en movimiento) to collide WITH sb **(b)** (entrar en conflicto) **~** CON **algn** to clash WITH sb **(c) ~** CON **algo** ‹*con problema/obstáculo*› to come up AGAINST sth **2 (a)** (extrañar): **me chocó que no me lo dijera** I was surprised that he hadn't told me **(b)** (escandalizar) to shock; **me chocó su lenguaje** I was shocked by her language **3** (Col, Méx, Ven fam) (irritar, molestar) to annoy, bug (colloq) ■ **~** *vt* **(a)** ‹*copas*› to clink; **¡chócala!** (fam) put it there! (colloq), give me five! (colloq) **(b)** (AmL) ‹*vehículo*› (que se conduce) to crash; (de otra persona) to run into ■ **chocarse** *v pron* (Col) **1** (en vehículo) to have a crash *o* an accident **2** (fam) (molestarse) to get annoyed

chochada *f* (AmC fam) silly little thing (colloq)

chochear [A1] *vi* (fam) **(a)** «*anciano*» to be gaga (colloq) **(b)** (sentir adoración) **~** POR **algn** to dote ON sb

chocho -cha *adj* (fam) ‹*viejo*› gaga (colloq) **(b)** (fam) (encantado): **está ~ con su hijita** he dotes on his daughter; **se quedó ~ con el regalo** he was delighted with his present

choclo *m* **1** (CS, Per) (mazorca) corn cob; (granos) sweet corn; (cultivo) corn (AmE), maize (BrE) **2** (Méx fam) (Indum) brogue

chocolate *m* **1 (a)** (para comer) chocolate; **~ blanco/con leche** white/milk chocolate; **~ negro** plain chocolate, dark chocolate; **sirvieron unos ~s con el café** (AmL) they gave us chocolates with our coffee **(b)** (bebida) hot chocolate **2** (Esp arg) (hachís) dope (sl), pot (colloq)

chocolatería *f* (cafetería) *café serving hot chocolate as a speciality*

chocolatina *f*, (RPl) **chocolatín** *m* chocolate bar

chocoyo *m* (AmC) parakeet

chofer, (Esp) **chófer** *mf* **(a)** (asalariado — de coche particular) chauffeur; (— de transporte colectivo) driver **(b)** (persona que maneja) driver

cholga *f* (Chi) mussel

chollo *m* (Esp fam) (trabajo fácil) cushy job *o* number (colloq); (ganga) steal (colloq), bargain

chomba *f* (sin botones) (Chi) sweater; (con botones) (Arg) polo shirt

chompa *f* (chaqueta) (Col, Ec) jacket; (suéter) (Bol, Per) sweater

chompipe *m* (AmC, Méx) turkey

choncho -cha *adj* (Méx fam) **(a)** ‹*problema/situación*› serious **(b)** ‹*persona*› hefty (colloq), big

chongo *m* (Méx) (moño) bun

chopo *m* (Bot) black poplar

choque *m* **(a)** (de vehículos) crash, collision; **~ múltiple** pile-up; **~ frontal** (Auto) head-on collision; (enfrentamiento) head-on confrontation **(b)** (conflicto) clash **(c)** (sorpresa, golpe) shock

chorear [A1] *vt* (fam) **1** (CS, Per) (robar) to swipe (colloq) **2** (Chi) **(a)** (aburrir): **esto me choreó** I'm fed up with this (colloq) **(b)** (molestar, enojar) to annoy ■ **chorearse** *v pron* (fam) **1** (CS) (robarse) to swipe (colloq) **2** (Chi) **(a)** (fam) (aburrirse) to get bored, get fed up **(b)** (molestarse, enojarse) to get annoyed

choreto -ta *adj* (Ven fam) crooked

chorito *m* (Chi) baby mussel

chorizar [A4] *vt* (Esp fam) to swipe

chorizo *m* (embutido curado) chorizo (*highly-seasoned pork sausage*); (salchicha) (RPl) sausage

chorlito *m* plover

choro *m* (Chi, Per) **1** (Coc, Zool) mussel **2** (fam) (delincuente) crook (colloq)

chorrada *f* (Esp fam) **(a)** (estupidez): **decir ~s** to talk drivel *o* twaddle (colloq) **(b)** (cosa insignificante) little thing

chorrear [A1] *vi* to drip; **estaba chorreando** (muy mojado) it was dripping wet; **chorreando de sudor** dripping with sweat; **la sangre le chorreaba de la nariz** blood was pouring from his nose ■ **~** *vt* **1** (AmL fam) (manchar): **chorreado de café** covered in coffee stains **2** (Col, RPl arg) (robar) to swipe (colloq)

■ **chorrearse** *v pron* (*refl*) (CS, Per fam) (mancharse): **cuidado con ~te** mind you don't get it all over yourself

chorrillo *m* (Méx fam) diarrhea*, the runs (colloq)

chorro *m* **1** (de agua) stream, jet; (de vapor, gas) jet; **un chorrito de agua** a trickle of water; **a ~** ‹*motor/avión*› jet (*before n*); **el agua salía a ~s** water gushed out **2** (AmC, Ven) (llave) faucet (AmE), tap (BrE) **3** (Méx fam) (cantidad): **¡qué ~ de gente!** what a lot of people!; **~s de dinero** loads of money (colloq); **me gusta un ~ salir** I really love going out

chotis *m* schottische

chovinismo *m* chauvinism

chovinista *adj/mf* chauvinist

choza *f* hut, shack

christmas /'krismas/ *m* (*pl* **~**) (Esp) Christmas card

chubasco *m* heavy shower

chubasquero *m* slicker (AmE), cagoule (BrE)

chuchería *f* **(a)** (alhaja) trinket; (adorno) knickknack **(b)** (dulce) tidbit (AmE), titbit (BrE)

chucho -cha *m,f* **1** (Esp fam) (perro) mongrel **2** **chucho** *m* (RPl fam) (escalofrío) shiver; **tengo ~s de frío** I have the shivers (colloq)

chueca *f* (Chi) (juego) *game similar to hockey, and the stick with which it's played*

chueco[1] -ca *adj* **1** (AmL) (torcido) crooked, askew **2** (Chi, Méx fam) (deshonesto) ‹*persona*› crooked (colloq); ‹*documento*› false; ‹*elecciones*› rigged ■ *m,f* (Chi, Méx fam) (deshonesto): **es un ~** he's crooked (colloq)

chueco[2] *adv* (AmL fam) **(a)** (torcido): **camina/escribe ~** he can't walk/write straight **(b)** ‹*jugar/pelear*› dirty (colloq)

chufa *f* tiger nut, earth almond

chuico *m* (Chi) demijohn

chulear [A1] *vt* **1** (Arg fam) (provocar) to needle (colloq) **2** (Méx fam) (piropear) to compliment; ‹*vestido/peinado*› to make nice comments about **3** (Col) (con un signo) to check (AmE), to tick (BrE)

chuleta *f* **1** (Coc) chop; **~ de cordero** lamb chop **2** (Esp arg) (para copiar) crib (colloq) **3** (Chi fam) (patilla) sideburn

chulla *mf* (Ec) (quiteño) *person from Quito*

chulo[1] -la *adj* **1** (fam) (bonito) **(a)** (Esp, Méx) ‹*vestido/casa*› neat (AmE colloq), lovely (BrE) **(b)** (Méx) ‹*hombre*› good-looking, cute (esp AmE); ‹*mujer*› pretty, cute (esp AmE) **2** (Esp fam) (bravucón) nervy (AmE colloq), cocky (BrE colloq) **3** (Chi fam) (de mal gusto) tacky (colloq) ■ *m,f* (Esp fam) (bravucón) flashy type

chulo[2] *m* (Esp fam) **1** (proxeneta) pimp **2** (Col) (Zool) black vulture **3** (Col) (signo) check mark (AmE), tick (BrE)

chumero -ra *m,f* (AmC) apprentice

chunche *m* (AmC) (fam) (cosa) thing, thingamajig (colloq)

chuño *m* (CS) (fécula de papa) potato flour

chupachups® *m* (*pl* **~**) (Esp) lollipop

chupada *f* (fam) (de helado) lick; (de cigarrillo) puff; **le dio unas ~s a la pipa** he puffed on his pipe a few times

chupado -da *adj* **1** [ESTAR] (fam) (flaco) skinny **2** [ESTAR] (Esp fam) (fácil) dead easy (colloq) **3** [ESTAR] (AmL fam) (borracho) plastered (colloq) **4 (a)** [ESTAR] (Chi, Per) (inhibido) withdrawn **(b)** [SER] (Chi, Per fam) (tímido) shy

chupalla *f* (Chi) straw hat

chupamedias *mf* (*pl* **~**) (CS, Ven fam) bootlicker (colloq)

chupar [A1] *vt* **(a)** (extraer) ‹*sangre/savia*› to suck **(b)** ‹*biberón/chupete*› to suck (on); ‹*naranja/caramelo*› to suck; ‹*pipa/cigarrillo*› to puff on **(c)** (AmL fam) (beber) to drink ■ **~** *vi* **(a)** «*bebé/cría*» to suckle **(b)** (AmL fam) (beber) to booze (colloq)

■ **chuparse** *v pron* ‹*dedo*› to suck

chupeta *f* (Col) lollipop

chupete *m* **1 (a)** (de bebé) pacifier (AmE), dummy (BrE) **(b)** (CS) (del biberón) nipple (AmE), teat (BrE) **2** (Chi, Per) (golosina) lollipop **3** (Chi) (Auto) choke

chupetín *m* (RPl) lollipop

chupón *m* **(a)** (AmL) ⇒ CHUPETE 1(a) **(b)** (Méx) (del biberón) nipple (AmE), teat (BrE) **(c)** (Col) (chupada) lick

churrasquería *f* (AmS) steak house

churrusco *m* (Col) (Zool) caterpillar; (cepillo) bottle brush

chusco -ca *adj* **1** (gracioso) ‹*persona/humor*› earthy **2** (Chi, Per fam & pey) **(a)** (ordinario) ‹*persona*› common (pej); ‹*perro*› mongrel; ‹*barrio/lugar*› plebeian (pej) **(b)** ‹*mujer*› loose (colloq)

chusma *f* rabble (*pl*), plebs (*pl*) (colloq)

chuspa *f* (Col) (para lápices) pencil case; (para gafas) glasses case

chutar [A1] *vi* (Dep) to shoot

chute *m* (Dep) shot

chutear [A1] *vt/vi* (CS) to shoot

chuza *f* (Méx) (Dep) (jugada) strike; (marca) mark

chuzo *adj* (CS fam) ‹*pelo*› dead straight (colloq); ‹*persona*› hopeless (colloq) ■ *m*: ***llover a ~s*** (fam) to pour (down with rain)

Cía. *f* (= **Compañía**) Co

cianuro *m* cyanide

ciática *f* sciatica

ciberespacio *m* (Inf) cyberspace

cibernética *f* cybernetics

cicatero -ra *adj* (fam) tightfisted (colloq) ■ *m,f* (fam) skinflint (colloq)

cicatriz *f* scar; **la herida le dejó ~** the wound left her with a scar

cicatrizar [A4] *vi*, **cicatrizarse** [A4] *v pron* to heal (up), cicatrize (tech)

cicerone *mf* (liter) guide, cicerone (liter)

ciclismo *m* cycling, biking (colloq)

ciclista *adj* cycle (*before n*) ■ *mf* cyclist

ciclo *m* **(a)** (de fenómenos, sucesos) cycle **(b)** (de películas) season; (de conferencias) series **(c)** (Educ): **el primer ~** primary school

ciclocross *m* cyclo-cross; **bicicleta de ~** mountain bike

ciclomotor *m* moped

ciclón *m* cyclone

ciclovía *f* (Col) cycle path

cicuta *f* hemlock

ciego -ga *adj* **1 (a)** (invidente) blind; **es ~ de nacimiento** he was born blind; **se quedó ~** he went blind; **anduvimos a ciegas por el pasillo** we groped our way along the corridor **(b)** (ante una realidad) **estar ~ A algo** to be blind TO sth **(c)** (ofuscado) blind; **~ de ira** blind with fury **2** ‹*fe/obediencia*› blind **3** ‹*conducto/cañería*› blocked; ■ *m,f* (invidente) (*m*) blind man; (*f*) blind woman; **los ~s** the blind

cielo *m* **1** (firmamento) sky; **~ cubierto** overcast sky; **a ~ abierto** (Min) opencast (*before n*); **este dinero me viene como caído del ~** this money is a godsend **2** (Relig) **(a) el ~** (Paraíso) heaven; **ir al ~** to go to heaven; ***ganarse el ~*** to earn oneself a place in heaven **(b)** (*como interj*): **¡~s!** (good) heavens! **3** (techo) ceiling **~ raso** ceiling **4 (a)** (aplicado a personas) angel **(b)** (como apelativo) sweetheart, darling; **¡mi ~!** my darling

ciempiés *m* (*pl* **~**) centipede

cien ▶ 293 *adj inv/pron* a/one hundred; **~ mil** a/one hundred thousand; **es ~ por ~ algodón** (esp Esp) it's a hundred percent cotton ■ *m*: **el ~** (number) one hundred

ciénaga *f* swamp

ciencia *f* **(a)** (rama del saber) science; (saber, conocimiento) knowledge, learning; **~ ficción** science fiction; ***a ~ cierta*** for sure, for certain **(b) ciencias** *fpl* (Educ) science; **C~s Empresariales/de la Información** Business/Media Studies; **C~s Políticas/de la Educación** Politics/Education

cieno *m* silt, mud

científico -ca *adj* scientific ■ *m,f* scientist

ciento ▶ 293 *adj/pron* (*delante de otro número*) a/one hundred; **~ dos** a/one hundred and two; *para ejemplos ver* QUINIENTOS ■ *m* **(a)** (número) ▶ 293: **~s de libros** hundreds of books; **vinieron a ~s** they came in the (AmE) *o* (BrE) in their hundreds **(b)** ▶ 130 **por ciento** percent; **cien por ~** a hundred percent

cierra, cierras, etc *see* CERRAR

cierre *m* **1** (acción) **(a)** (de fábrica, empresa, hospital) closure **(b)** (de establecimiento) closing **(c)** (de frontera) closing **(d)** (de emisión) end, close **(e)** (Fin) close **2 (a)** (de bolso, pulsera) clasp, fastener; (de puerta, ventana) lock **(b)** (cremallera) zipper (AmE), zip (BrE); **~ metálico** (en tienda) metal shutter *o* grille; **~ relámpago** (CS, Per) zipper (AmE), zip (BrE)

cierro *see* CERRAR

cierto -ta *adj* **1** (verdadero) true; **no hay nada de ~ en ello** there is no truth in it; **una cosa es cierta** one thing's certain; **¡ah!, es ~** oh yes, of course; **parece más joven, ¿no es ~?** he looks younger, doesn't he *o* don't you think?; **estabas en lo ~** you were right; **lo ~ es que** ... the fact is that ...; **si bien es ~ que** ... while *o* although it's true to say that ...; **por ~** (a propósito) by the way, incidentally **2** (*delante del n*) (que no se especifica, define) certain; **cierta clase de gente** a certain kind of people; **de cierta edad** of a certain age; **en cierta ocasión** on one occasion; **en ~ modo** in some ways; **hasta ~ punto** up to a point; **durante un ~ tiempo** for a while

ciervo -va *m,f* (especie) deer; (macho) stag; (hembra) hind

cifra *f* **1 (a)** (dígito) figure; **un número de cinco ~s** a five-figure number **(b)** (número, cantidad) number; **la ~ de muertos** the number of dead, the death toll (period) **(c)** (de dinero) figure, sum **2** (clave) code, cipher; **en ~** in code

cifrar [A1] *vt* **1** ‹*mensaje/carta*› to write ... in code, encode (frml) **2** ‹*esperanza*› to place, pin

cigala *f* crawfish, crayfish

cigarra *f* cicada

cigarrería *f* (Andes) tobacco shop (AmE), tobacconist's (BrE)

cigarrillo *m* cigarette; **~ con filtro** filter tipped cigarette

cigarro *m* (puro) cigar; (cigarrillo) cigarette

cigüeña *f* stork

cigüeñal *m* crankshaft

cilantro *m* coriander

cilindrada *f*, **cilindraje** *m* cubic capacity

cilíndrico -ca *adj* cylindrical

cilindro *m* cylinder; **un motor de cuatro ~s** a four-cylinder engine

cima *f* (de montaña) top, summit; (de árbol) top; (de profesión) top; (de carrera) peak, height; **está en la ~ de su carrera** she is at the peak of her career

cimarra *f* (Chi): **hacer la ~** to play hooky (esp AmE colloq); to skive off (school) (BrE colloq)

cimentar [A1] *or* [A5] *vt* **(a)** ‹*edificio*› to lay the foundations of **(b)** (consolidar) to consolidate, strengthen **(c)** (basar) **~ algo EN algo** to base sth ON sth

cimientos *mpl* foundations (*pl*); **poner los ~ de algo** to lay the foundations of sth

cinc *m* ⇒ ZINC

cincel *m* (de escultor, albañil) chisel; (de orfebre) graver

cincelar [A1] *vt* ‹*piedra*› to chisel, carve; ‹*metal*› to engrave

cinco ▶ 293, 221, 193, 159 *adj inv/pron* five; [*nótese que algunas frases requieren el uso del número ordinal 'fifth' en inglés*] **noventa y ~** ninety-five; **quinientos ~** five hundred and five; **la fila ~** row five, the fifth row; **vinimos los ~** the five of us came; **somos ~** there are five of us; **entraron de ~ en ~** they went in five at a time; **tiene ~ años** she's five (years old); **son las ~ de la mañana** it's five (o'clock) in the morning; **las ocho y ~** five after (AmE) *o* (BrE) past eight; **~ para las dos** (AmL exc RPl) five to two; *ver tb* MENOS *prep* 2(b); **hoy estamos a ~** today is the fifth ■ *m*

1 ▶ 293 (número) (number) five; **el ~ de corazones** the five of hearts **2** (Per) (momento) moment

cincuenta ▶ 293, 159 *adj inv/m/pron* fifty; **los (años) ~** *or* **la década de los ~** the fifties; **tiene unos ~ años** she's about 50 years old; **~ y tantos/pico** fifty-odd, fifty something; **la página ~** page fifty; **el ~ aniversario** the fiftieth anniversary

cincuentón -tona ▶ 159 *adj* (fam): **es ~** he's in his fifties ■ *m,f* (fam): **una cincuentona** a woman in her fifties

cine *m* **(a)** (arte, actividad) cinema; **el ~ francés** French cinema; **actor de ~** movie *o* film actor; **hacer ~** to make movies *o* films **(b)** (local) movie house *o* theater (AmE), cinema (BrE); **¿vamos al ~?** shall we go to the movies (AmE) *o* (BrE) cinema?; **~ de barrio** local movie theater (AmE), local cinema (BrE); **~ de estreno** *movie theater where new releases are shown*

cineclub, cine-club *m* film club

cinematografía *f* cinematography

cinematográfico -ca *adj* movie (*before n*), film (BrE) (*before n*)

cínico -ca *adj* cynical ■ *m,f* cynic

cinismo *m* cynicism

cinta *f* **(a)** (para adornar, envolver) ribbon; **~ adhesiva** (en papelería) adhesive tape; (Med) sticking plaster; **~ durex®** (AmL excl CS) *or* (AmL) **scotch®** *or* (Col) **pegante** Scotch tape® (AmE), Sellotape® (BrE); **~ métrica** tape measure; **~ negra** (Méx) *mf* (Dep) black belt; **~ transportadora** conveyor belt **(b)** (en gimnasia rítmica) ribbon; (en carreras) tape **(c)** (Audio, Video) tape; **~ virgen** blank tape

cintura *f* ▶ 123 (de persona, prenda) waist; **me tomó de la ~** he grabbed me round the waist; **me queda grande de ~** it's too big for me round the waist

cinturilla *f* waistband

cinturón *m* **(a)** (Indum) belt; **~ de castidad** chastity belt; **~ de seguridad** seat belt, safety belt; **~ negro/verde** (Dep) black/green belt **(b)** (de ciudad) belt; **el ~ industrial** the industrial belt

ciprés *m* cypress

circo *m* (Espec, Hist) circus

circuito *m* **(a)** (pista) track, circuit; (de circo, exposición) circuit **(b)** (Elec, Electrón) circuit

circulación *f* **(a)** (en general) circulation; **tener mala ~** to have poor circulation **(b)** (movimiento) movement; (Auto) traffic

circular[1] *adj* circular; **de forma ~** circular ■ *f* circular

circular[2] [A1] ■ *vi* **(a)** «*sangre/savia*» to circulate, flow; «*agua/corriente*» to flow **(b)** «*transeúnte/peatón*» to walk; (referido al tráfico): **circulan por la izquierda** they drive on the left **(c)** «*autobús/tren*» (estar de servicio) to run, operate **(d)** «*dinero/billete/sello*» to be in circulation **(e)** «*noticia/rumor/memo*» to circulate, go around ■ ~ *vt* to circulate

circulatorio -ria *adj* circulation (*before n*)

círculo *m* **(a)** (en general) circle; **coloca las mesas en ~** arrange the tables in a circle; **en (los) ~s teatrales** in theatrical circles; **C~ Polar Antártico/Ártico** Antarctic/Arctic Circle; **~ vicioso** vicious circle **(b)** (asociación) society; **~ de Bellas Artes** Fine Arts Association *o* Society

circuncisión *f* circumcision

circundante *adj* surrounding (*before n*)

circunferencia *f* **(a)** (Mat) circle; **dibujar una ~** to draw a circle **(b)** (perímetro) circumference; **tiene 1 km de ~** it has a circumference of 1 km

circunscripción *f* (distrito) district

circunstancia *f* **1** (particularidad): **si por alguna ~ no puede ir** if for any reason you cannot go; **se da la ~ de que** ... as it happens ...; **bajo ninguna ~** under no circumstances **2 circunstancias** *fpl* (situación) circumstances (*pl*); **dadas las ~s** given the circumstances; **debido a sus ~s familiares** due to her family situation

cirio *m* candle

cirrosis *f* cirrhosis

ciruela *f* (Bot, Coc) plum; **~ pasa** *or* (CS) **seca** prune

ciruelo *m* plum tree

cirugía *f* surgery; **hacerse la ~ estética/plástica** to have cosmetic/plastic surgery

cirujano -na *m,f* surgeon; **~ dentista** dental surgeon

Cisjordania *f* the West Bank

cisma *m* (Rel) schism; (en partido) split

cisne *m* (Zool) swan

cisterna *f* (depósito) tank; (subterránea) cistern; (del retrete) cistern

cistitis *f* cystitis

cita *f* **1 (a)** (con profesional) appointment; **pedir ~** to make an appointment; **concertar una ~** to arrange an appointment **(b)** (con novio, amigo): **tengo una ~ con mi novio/con un amigo** I have a date with my boyfriend/I'm going out with a friend; **faltó a la ~** he didn't show up (colloq) **2** (en texto, discurso) quote; **una ~ de Cervantes** a quotation *o* quote from Cervantes

citadino -na *adj* (AmL) urban, city (*before n*) ■ *m,f* **(a)** (AmL) (ciudadano) city dweller **(b)** (Méx) (defeño) inhabitant of México City

citar [A1] *vt* **1 (a)** (dar una cita) «*doctor/jefe de personal*» to give ... an appointment; **estar citado con algn** to have an appointment with sb **(b)** (convocar): **nos citó a todos a una reunión** she called us all to a meeting **(c)** (Der) to summon; **~ a algn como testigo** to call sb as a witness **2 (a)** (mencionar) to mention **(b)** ‹*escritor/pasaje*› to quote

■ **citarse** *v pron* **~se** CON **algn** to arrange to meet sb; **se ~on en la plaza** (*recípr*) they arranged to meet in the square

citófono *m* (Andes) internal phone system

citología *f* (análisis) smear test

cítrico[1] **-ca** *adj* citrus (*before n*)

cítrico[2] *m* citrus

ciudad *f* town; (de mayor tamaño) city; Ⓢ **centro ciudad** town *o* city center; **~ balneario** (AmL) coastal resort; **C~ del Vaticano/de México** Vatican/Mexico City; **~ perdida** (Méx) shantytown; **~ satélite** satellite town; **~ universitaria** university campus

ciudadano -na *adj* ‹*vida*› city (*before n*); **la inseguridad ciudadana** the lack of safety in towns *o* cities; **es un deber ~** it's the duty of every citizen ■ *m,f* (habitante) citizen

cívico -ca *adj* **(a)** ‹*deberes/derechos*› civic **(b)** ‹*acto*› public-spirited, civic-minded

civil *adj* **(a)** ‹*derechos/responsabilidades*› civil **(b)** (no religioso) civil; **casarse por lo ~** *or* (Per, RPl, Ven) **sólo por ~** *or* (Chi, Méx) **por el ~** to be married in a civil ceremony (AmE), to have a registry office wedding (BrE) **(c)** (no militar) civilian (*before n*); **iba (vestido) de ~** he was in civilian clothes ■ *mf* **(a)** (persona no militar) civilian **(b)** (Esp) (guardia civil) Civil Guard

civilización *f* civilization

civilizado -da *adj* civilized

civilizar [A4] *vt* ‹*país/pueblo*› to civilize; ‹*persona*› to teach ... to behave properly
■ **civilizarse** *v pron* «*pueblo*» to become civilized; «*persona*» to learn to behave properly

civismo *m* public-spiritedness

cizaña *f* darnel

clamar [A1] *vi* **~ CONTRA algo** to protest AGAINST sth; **~ POR algo** to clamor* FOR sth, cry out FOR sth ■ **~** *vt:* **~ venganza** to cry out for vengeance

clamor *m* clamor*

clamoroso -sa *adj* ‹*acogida*› rousing (*before n*); ‹*ovación*› rapturous, thunderous; ‹*éxito*› resounding (*before n*)

clan *m* clan

clandestinidad *f* secrecy, secret nature; **trabajar en la ~** to work underground; **pasar a la ~** to go underground

clandestino -na *adj* ‹*reunión/relación*› clandestine, secret; ‹*periódico*› underground ■ *m,f* (fam) illegal immigrant

claqué *m* tap (dancing)

claqueta *f* clapperboard

clara *f* **(a)** *tb* **~ de huevo** (egg) white **(b)** (Esp) (bebida) shandy

claraboya *f* skylight

clarear [A1] *v impers* **(a)** (amanecer): **estaba clareando** it was getting light *o* day was breaking **(b)** (Meteo): **comenzó a ~** the sky/the clouds began to clear ■ **~** *vi* «*pelo*» to go gray*/white

clarete *m* (rosado) rosé; (tinto) claret

claridad *f* **(a)** (luz) light **(b)** (luminosidad) brightness **(c)** (de explicación, imagen, sonido) clarity; **con ~** clearly

clarificar [A2] *vt* to clarify

clarín *m* bugle

clarinete *m* clarinet

clarinetista *mf* clarinetist

clarividente *adj* (que adivina el futuro) clairvoyant; (perspicaz) discerning, clear-sighted ■ *mf* clairvoyant

claro¹ -ra *adj* **(a)** (luminoso) ‹*cielo/habitación*› bright **(b)** ▶97 (pálido) ‹*color/verde/azul*› light, pale; ‹*piel*› fair; **tiene los ojos ~s** she has blue/green/gray eyes **(c)** ‹*salsa/sopa*› thin **(d)** ‹*agua/sonido*› clear; ‹*ideas/explicación/instrucciones*› clear; ‹*situación/postura*› clear; **tener algo ~** to be clear about sth; **¿está ~?** is that clear?; **quiero dejar (en) ~ que** ... I want to make it clear that ...; ***sacar algo en ~ de algo*** to make sense of sth **(e)** (evidente) clear, obvious; **está ~ que** ... it is clear *o* obvious that ...; **a no ser, ~ está, que esté mintiendo** unless, of course, he's lying

claro² *adv* **1** ‹*ver*› clearly; **voy a hablarte ~** I'm not going to beat around *o* about the bush; **me lo dijo muy ~** he made it very quite clear (to me) **2** (*indep*) (en exclamaciones de asentimiento) of course ■ *m* **(a)** (en bosque) clearing; (en pelo, barba) bald patch **(b)** (Meteo) sunny spell *o* period

clase *f* **1** (tipo) kind, sort, type; **distintas ~s de arroz** different kinds of rice **2** (Transp, Sociol) class; **viajar en segunda ~** to travel (in) second class; **~ económica** *or* **turista** economy *o* tourist class; **~ ejecutiva** *or* **preferente** business class; **~ alta/baja/media** upper/lower/middle class; **~ dirigente** *or* **dominante** ruling class; **~ obrera** working class **3 (a)** (distinción, elegancia) class; **tiene ~** she has class **(b)** (categoría): **productos de primera ~** top-quality products **4** (Educ) **(a)** (lección) class; **~s de conducir** *or* **manejar** driving lessons; **dictar ~ (DE algo)** (AmL frml) to lecture (IN sth); **dar ~** *or* (Chi) **hacer ~s (DE algo)** «*profesor*» to teach (sth); **da ~s de piano** (Esp) she has piano lessons; **~ particular** private class *o* lesson **(b)** (grupo de alumnos) class **(c)** (aula — en escuela) classroom; (— en universidad) lecture hall *o* room

clásico¹ -ca *adj* **(a)** ‹*lengua/mundo*› classical; ‹*decoración/estilo/ropa*› classical **(b)** ‹*método*› standard, traditional; ‹*error/malentendido/caso*› classic

clásico² *m* **(a)** (obra) classic **(b)** (AmL) (Dep) traditional big game

clasificación *f* **1** (de documentos, animales, plantas) classification; (de cartas) sorting **2** (de película) certificate **3 (a)** (Dep) (para una etapa posterior) qualification; **partido de ~** qualifying match **(b)** (tabla) placings (*pl*); (puesto) position, place; **quinto en la ~ final del rally** fifth in the final placings for the rally

clasificar [A2] *vt* **(a)** ‹*documentos/datos*› to sort, put in order; ‹*cartas*› to sort **(b)** ‹*planta/animal/elemento*› to classify **(c)** ‹*hotel*› to class, rank; ‹*fruta*› to class; ‹*persona*› to class, rank
■ **clasificarse** *v pron* (Dep) **(a)** (para etapa posterior) to qualify; **~ para la final** to qualify for the final **(b)** (en tabla, carrera): **se clasificó en sexto lugar** he finished in sixth place

clasista *adj* ‹*actitud/sociedad*› classist; ‹*persona*› class-conscious

claustro *m* **(a)** (Arquit, Relig) cloister **(b)** (Educ) (de universidad) senate; (de colegio) staff; (reunión) senate/staff meeting

claustrofobia *f* claustrophobia; **siento ~ allí dentro** I get claustrophobia in there

cláusula *f* (clause

clausura *f* **(a)** (de congreso, festival) closing ceremony; **de ~** ‹*ceremonia/discurso*› closing (*before n*) **(b)** (de local) closure

clausurar [A1] *vt* **(a)** ‹*congreso/sesión*› «*acto/discurso*» to bring ... to a close; «*persona*» to close **(b)** ‹*local/estadio*› to close ... down

clavada *f* (Méx) (en natación) dive

clavadista *mf* (Méx) diver

clavado[1] **-da** *adj* **1 (a)** ~ EN **algo** ‹*puñal/tachuela/espina*› stuck IN sth; ‹*estaca*› driven INTO sth **(b)** (fijo): **con la vista clavada en un punto** staring at a point, with his gaze fixed on a point; **se quedó ~ en el lugar** he was rooted to the spot **2** (fam) **(a)** (idéntico) **ser ~ A algn** «*persona*» to be the spitting image of sb (colloq); **ser ~ A algo** «*objeto*» to be identical TO sth **(b)** (en punto): **llegó a las cinco clavadas** he arrived on the dot of five (colloq)

clavado[2] *m* (AmL) dive

clavar [A1] *vt* **1 (a) ~ algo EN algo** ‹*clavo*› to hammer sth INTO sth; ‹*puñal/cuchillo*› to stick sth IN sth; ‹*estaca*› to drive sth INTO sth; **me clavó los dientes/las uñas** he sank his teeth/dug his nails into me **(b)** ‹*cartel/estante*› to put up (*with nails, etc*) **(c)** ‹*ojos/vista*› to fix ... on **2** (fam) **(a)** (cobrar caro) to rip ... off (colloq); **nos ~on $10,000** they stung us for $10,000 **(b)** (CS) (engañar) to cheat **(c)** (Méx) (robar) to swipe (colloq), to filch (colloq)
■ **clavarse** *v pron* **1 (a)** ‹*aguja*› to stick ... into one's finger (*o* thumb *etc*); **me clavé una espina en el dedo** I got a thorn in my finger **(b)** (*refl*) ‹*cuchillo/puñal*›: **se clavó el puñal en el pecho** he plunged the dagger into his chest **2** (CS fam) **~se CON algo** (por no poder venderlo) to get stuck WITH sth (colloq); (por ser mala compra): **se clavó con el auto que compró** the car turned out to be a bad buy **3** (Méx) (Dep) to dive

clave *adj* (*pl* ~ *or* **-ves**) key (*before n*); **un factor ~** a key factor ■ *f* **(a)** (código) code; **en ~** in code **(b)** (de problema, misterio) key **(c)** (Mús) clef; **~ de fa/sol** bass/treble clef ■ *m* harpsichord

clavel *m* carnation

clavicordio *m* clavichord

clavícula *f* ▶ 123 collarbone, clavicle (tech)

clavija *f* **(a)** (Mec) pin **(b)** (Elec) (enchufe) plug; (de enchufe) pin **(c)** (de guitarra) tuning peg

clavo *m* **(a)** (Tec) nail; ***dar en el ~*** to hit the nail on the head **(b)** (Med) pin **(c)** (en montañismo) piton **(d)** (Bot, Coc) *tb* **~ de olor** clove

claxon /ˈklakson/ *m* (*pl* **-xons**) horn; **tocar el ~** to sound *o* blow one's horn, to honk

clemencia *f* mercy, clemency (frml)

clementina *f* clementine

cleptómano -na *m,f* kleptomaniac

clérigo -ga *m,f* **1** (en el clero protestante) (*m*) clergyman, cleric; (*f*) clergywoman, cleric **2 clérigo** *m* (en el clero católico) clergyman, priest

clero *m* clergy

cliché *m* **(a)** (expresión, idea) cliché **(b)** (de multicopista) stencil; (Impr) plate; (Fot) negative

cliente -ta *m,f* (de tienda, restaurante) customer; (de empresa, abogado) client; (de hotel) guest; (en taxi) fare, customer; **~ habitual** regular customer (*o* client *etc*)

clientela *f* (de tienda, restaurante) clientele, customers (*pl*); (de hotel) guests (*pl*); (de abogado) clients (*pl*)

clima *m* **(a)** (Meteo) climate **(b)** (ambiente) atmosphere; **un ~ festivo** a festive atmosphere; **el ~ económico** the economic climate

climatizado -da *adj* ‹*local/casa*› air-conditioned; ‹*piscina*› heated

clímax *m* (*pl* ~) climax

clínica *f* private hospital *o* clinic; **~ dental** dental office (AmE), dental surgery (BrE); **~ de reposo** convalescent *o* rest home

clínico -ca *adj* ‹*ensayo*› clinical (*before n*); ⇒ HOSPITAL ■ *m,f* (RPl) general practitioner

clip *m* (*pl* **clips**) **1 (a)** (sujetapapeles) paperclip **(b)** (para el pelo) bobby pin (AmE), hairgrip (BrE) **(c)** (cierre) clip; **aretes** *or* **pendientes de ~** clip-on earrings **2** (Video) (pop) video

cloaca *f* **1** (alcantarilla) sewer **2** (de ave, reptil) cloaca

clon *m* clone

cloro *m* (Quím) chlorine; (lejía) (AmC, Chi) bleach

clorofila *f* chlorophyll

cloroformo *m* chloroform

clóset *m* (*pl* **-sets**) (AmL exc RPl) (en dormitorio) built-in closet (AmE), fitted *o* built-in wardrobe (BrE)

clotch /ˈklotʃ/ ⇒ CLUTCH

clown /ˈklaun/ *m* (*pl* **clowns**) clown

club *m* (*pl* **clubs** *or* **-es**) club; **~ nocturno** nightclub

clueca *adj* broody

clutch /ˈklʊtʃ/ *m* (AmC, Col, Méx, Ven) clutch

cm. (= **centímetro**) cm.

coacción *f* coercion; **bajo ~** under duress

coaccionar [A1] *vt* to coerce

coagular [A1] *vt* to clot, coagulate
■ **coagularse** *v pron* to clot, coagulate

coágulo *m* clot

coalición *f* coalition; **gobierno de ~** coalition government

coartada *f* alibi

coartar [A1] *vt* ‹*persona*› to inhibit; ‹*libertad/voluntad*› to restrict

coba *f* (Ven arg) (mentira, engaño) lie; ***darle ~ a algn*** (adular) (Esp, Méx, Ven fam) to suck up to sb (colloq)

cobarde *adj* cowardly ■ *mf* coward

cobardía *f* cowardice; **fue una ~** it was an act of cowardice

cobaya *f*, **cobayo** *m* guinea pig

cobertizo *m* shed

cobertura *f* **(a)** (de seguro) cover **(b)** (Period, Rad, TV) coverage; **~ informativa** news coverage

cobija *f* (AmL) **(a)** (manta) blanket **(b) cobijas** *fpl* (ropa de cama) bedclothes (*pl*)

cobijar [A1] *vt* ‹*persona*› (proteger) to shelter; (hospedar) to give ... shelter, take ... in
■ **cobijarse** *v pron* to shelter, take shelter

cobijo *m* shelter; **darle ~ a algn** to shelter sb

cobra *f* cobra

cobrador -dora *m,f* (a domicilio) collector; (de autobús) bus conductor

cobrar [A1] *vt* **1 (a)** ‹*precio/suma/intereses*› to charge; **nos cobran 30.000 pesos de alquiler** they charge us 30,000 pesos in rent; **~ algo POR algo/hacer algo** to charge sth FOR sth/doing sth; **vino a ~ el alquiler** she came for the rent *o* to collect the rent; **¿me cobra estas cervezas?** can

I pay for these beers, please?; **me cobró el vino dos veces** he charged me twice for the wine **(b)** ‹*sueldo*› to earn; ‹*pensión*› to draw; **cobra 200.000 pesetas al mes** he earns/draws 200,000 pesetas a month; **todavía no hemos cobrado junio** we still haven't been paid for June **(c)** ‹*deuda*› to recover; **nunca llegó a ~ esas facturas** he never received payment for those bills **(d)** ‹*cheque*› to cash **2 (a)** (Chi) (pedir): **le cobré los libros que le presté** I asked him to give back the books I'd lent him **(b)** (Chi) ‹*gol/falta*› to give **3** (adquirir) ‹*fuerzas*› to gather; **~ fama/importancia** to become famous/important **4** (period) ‹*vidas/víctimas*› to claim ■ *~ vi* **(a) ~** POR **algo/hacer algo** to charge FOR sth/doing sth; **¿me cobra, por favor?** can you take for this, please?, can I pay, please?; **llámame por ~** (Chi, Méx) call collect (AmE), reverse the charges (BrE) **(b)** (recibir el sueldo) to be paid

■ **cobrarse** *v pron* **(a)** (recibir dinero): **tenga, cóbrese** here you are; **cóbrese las cervezas** can you take for the beers, please? **(b)** (period) ‹*vidas/víctimas*› to claim

cobre *m* (Metal, Quím) copper

cobrizo -za *adj* ▶ 97 coppery, copper-colored*

cobro *m* **(a)** (de cheque) cashing; (de sueldo, pensión): **para el ~ de la pensión** in order to collect your pension **(b)** (Telec): **llamó a ~ revertido** she called collect (AmE), she reversed the charges (BrE)

coca *f* (Bot) coca; (cocaína) (arg) coke (sl)

cocaína *f* cocaine

cocainómano -na *m,f* cocaine addict

cocaví *m* (Chi) things (*pl*) to eat

cocer [E10] *vt* **(a)** (Coc) (cocinar) to cook; (hervir) to boil; **~ algo a fuego lento** to simmer sth, cook sth over a low heat **(b)** ‹*ladrillos/cerámica*› to fire

■ **cocerse** *v pron* **1** «*verduras/arroz*» (hacerse) to cook; (hervir) to boil; **tardan unos 15 minutos en ~se** they take 15 minutes to cook **2** (Chi) «*bebé*» to have a diaper (AmE) *o* (BrE) nappy rash

coche *m* **(a)** (Auto) car, auto (AmE), automobile (AmE); **nos llevó en ~ a la estación** he drove us to the station; **~ bomba** car bomb; **~ de bomberos** fire engine, fire truck (AmE); **~ de carreras** racing car; **~ de choque** bumper car; **~ fúnebre** hearse **(b)** (Ferr) car (AmE), carriage (BrE); **~ cama** *or* (CS) **dormitorio** sleeper, sleeping car **(c)** (de bebé) baby carriage (AmE), pram (BrE); (en forma de sillita) stroller (AmE), pushchair (BrE) **(d)** (carruaje) coach, carriage; **~ de caballos** carriage

cochera *f* **(a)** (para autobuses) depot, garage; **las ~s** the depot **(b)** (garaje) (Esp, Méx) garage

cochinada *f* (fam) **(a)** (suciedad) filth **(b)** (palabra, acción): **¡no digas esas ~s!** don't use such filthy language!; **eso es una ~** that's a disgusting thing to do **(c)** (mala pasada) dirty trick

cochino -na *adj* **(a)** (fam) (sucio) ‹*persona/manos*› filthy **(b)** (fam) (indecoroso) ‹*persona*› disgusting; ‹*revista/película*› dirty (colloq) **(c)** (Chi) (Dep, Jueg) (violento) dirty (colloq); (tramposo): **es muy ~** he's a terrible cheat ■ *m,f* **(a)** (Zool) pig, hog (AmE) **(b)** (fam) (persona sucia) filthy pig (colloq), slob (colloq)

cocido¹ -da *adj* **(a)** (hervido) ‹*huevos/verduras*› boiled **(b)** (CS) (no crudo) cooked; **muy/poco ~** well done/rare **(c)** ‹*arcilla*› fired

cocido² *m* **(a)** (Esp) stew (*made with meat and chickpeas*) **(b)** (Col, Ven) stew (*made with meat, plantains and cassava*)

cociente *m* quotient

cocina *f* **(a)** (habitación) kitchen **(b)** (aparato) stove, cooker (BrE); **~ de** *or* **a gas** gas stove *o* (BrE) cooker; **~ eléctrica** electric stove *o* (BrE) cooker **(c)** (arte) cookery; (gastronomía) cuisine; **libro de ~** cookbook, cookery book (BrE); **la ~ casera** home cooking

cocinar [A1] *vt/vi* to cook; **¿quién cocina en tu casa?** who does the cooking in your house?

cocinero -ra *m,f* cook

cocineta *f* (Méx) (cocina) kitchenette

cocinilla *f* camp stove (AmE), camping stove (BrE)

cocktail /'koktel/ *m* (*pl* **-tails**) ⇒ CÓCTEL

coco *m* **(a)** (Bot, Coc) coconut **(b)** (fam) (cabeza) head; **está mal del ~** he's off his head (colloq) **(c)** (fam) (fantasma, espantajo) boogeyman (AmE), bogeyman (BrE)

cocoa *f* (AmL) cocoa

cocodrilo *m* crocodile

cocol *m* (Méx) (bizcocho) cookie (*covered in sesame seeds*)

cocotero *m* coconut palm

cóctel *m* (*pl* **-teles** *or* **-tels**) **(a)** (bebida) cocktail; **~ de frutas** (AmC, Col) fruit salad, fruit cocktail; **~ de gambas** (Esp) shrimp (AmE) *o* (BrE) prawn cocktail; **~ Molotov** Molotov cocktail **(b)** (fiesta) cocktail party

cocuyo *m* **(a)** (AmL) (insecto) firefly **(b)** (Col, Ven) (Auto) parking light (AmE), sidelight (BrE)

codazo *m*: **darle un ~ a algn** (leve) to nudge sb; (fuerte) to elbow sb; **se abrió camino a ~s** he elbowed his way through

codearse [A1] *v pron* **~** CON **algn** to rub shoulders WITH sb

codera *f* (Indum) elbow patch

codicia *f* (avaricia) greed, avarice

codiciar [A1] *vt* to covet

codicioso -sa *adj* ‹*persona/mirada*› covetous, greedy ■ *m,f* covetous *o* greedy person

codificar [A2] *vt* **(a)** ‹*leyes/normas*› to codify **(b)** (Inf) ‹*información*› to code **(c)** (Ling) ‹*mensaje*› to encode

código *m* **(a)** (de signos) code; **~ barrado** *or* **de barras** bar code; **~ postal** zipcode (AmE), postcode (BrE) **(b)** (de leyes, normas) code; **~ de la circulación** Highway Code

codillo *m* **(a)** (Zool) elbow **(b)** (Coc) knuckle

codo¹ -da *adj* (Méx fam) tight fisted (colloq)

codo² *m* ▶ 123 elbow; **~ *con*** *or* ***a* ~** side by side; ***empinar el* ~** (fam) to prop up the bar; ***hablar (hasta) por los ~s*** (fam) to talk nineteen to the dozen (colloq)

codorniz *f* quail

coeficiente *m* (Mat) coefficient; **~ intelectual** *or* **de inteligencia** IQ, intelligence quotient

coexistir [I1] *vi* to coexist

cofia *f* cap

cofradía *f* (Relig) brotherhood

cofre *m* **(a)** (joyero) jewel case, jewelry* box **(b)** (arcón) chest **(c)** (Méx) (capó) hood (AmE), bonnet (BrE)

coger [E6] *vt* **1** (esp Esp) **(a)** (tomar) to take; **lo cogió del brazo** she took him by the arm; **coge un folleto** pick up *o* take a leaflet **(b)** (quitar) to take; **siempre me está cogiendo los lápices** she's always taking my pencils **(c)** ‹*flores/fruta*› to pick **(d)** (levantar) to pick up; **coge esa revista del suelo** pick that magazine up off the floor; **no cogen el teléfono** (Esp) they're not answering the phone **2** (atrapar) (esp Esp) **(a)** ‹*ladrón/pelota*› to catch **(b)** ‹*pescado/liebre*› to catch **(c)** (descubrir) to catch; **lo cogieron robando** he was caught stealing **(d)** «*toro*» to gore **3** **(a)** ‹*tren/autobús/taxi*› to catch, take **(b)** ‹*calle/camino*› to take **4** (Esp fam) **(a)** (obtener) ‹*billete/entrada*› to get; **~ hora para el médico** to make an appointment to see the doctor; **~ sitio** to save a place **(b)** (aceptar) ‹*dinero/trabajo/casa*› to take **(c)** (admitir) ‹*alumnos/solicitudes*› to take **5** (esp Esp) (adquirir) **(a)** ‹*enfermedad*› to catch; ‹*insolación*› to get; **vas a ~ frío** you'll catch cold **(b)** ‹*acento*› to pick up; ‹*costumbre/vicio*› to pick up; **le cogí cariño** I got quite fond of him **6** (esp Esp) (captar) **(a)** ‹*sentido/significado*› to get **(b)** ‹*emisora*› to pick up, get **7** (Méx, RPl, Ven vulg) to screw (vulg), to fuck (vulg) ■ **~** *vi* **1** (esp Esp) «*planta*» to take; «*tinte/permanente*» to take **2** (Méx, RPl, Ven vulg) to screw (vulg), to fuck (vulg)

■ **cogerse** *v pron* (esp Esp) **(a)** (agarrarse, sujetarse) to hold on; **cógete de la barandilla** hold on to the railing **(b)** (*recípr*): **se cogieron de la mano** they held hands

cogida *f* (Taur) goring; **sufrió una ~** he was gored

cognac *m* brandy

cogollo *m* (de lechuga, col) heart; (de hinojo) bulb

cogote *m* (fam) (nuca) scruff of the neck; (cuello) (AmL) neck

coherencia *f* **(a)** (congruencia) coherence, logic; **con ~** coherently *o* logically **(b)** (consecuencia) consistency; **actuar con ~** to be consistent **(c)** (Fís) coherence

coherente *adj* **(a)** (congruente) ‹*discurso/razonamiento*› coherent, logical **(b)** (consecuente) ‹*actitud*› consistent; **una mujer ~** a woman who acts according to her beliefs

cohesión *f* **(a)** (de ideas, pensamientos) coherence **(b)** (en grupo) cohesion, unity

cohete *m* **1** (Espac, Mil) rocket **2** **cohetes** *mpl* fireworks (*pl*)

cohibido -da *adj* (tímido) shy; (inhibido) inhibited; (incómodo) awkward

cohibir [I22] *vt* **(a)** (inhibir) to inhibit; **su presencia me cohíbe** I feel inhibited in front of him **(b)** (hacer sentir incómodo): **hablar en público lo cohíbe** he feels awkward about speaking in public

■ **cohibirse** *v pron* **(a)** (inhibirse) to feel inhibited **(b)** (sentirse incómodo) to feel awkward

coincidencia *f* **(a)** (casualidad) coincidence; **se dio la ~ de que él también estaba allá** by coincidence *o* chance he was there too; **¡que ~!** what a coincidence! **(b)** (de opiniones) agreement

coincidir [I1] *vi* **(a)** «*fechas/sucesos/líneas*» to coincide; «*dibujos*» to match up; «*versiones/resultados*» to coincide, match up, tally; **~ CON algo** to coincide (*o* match up *etc*) WITH sth **(b)** (en opiniones, gustos): **coinciden en sus gustos** they share the same tastes; **todos coincidieron en que ...** everyone agreed that ...; **~ CON algn** to agree WITH sb **(c)** (en un lugar): **a veces coincidimos en el supermercado** we sometimes see each other in the supermarket

coito *m* intercourse, coitus (frml)

cojear [A1] *vi* **(a)** (por herida, dolor) to limp; (permanentemente) to be lame; **entró cojeando** he limped *o* hobbled in **(b)** «*silla/mesa*» to wobble **(c)** (fam) «*explicación/definición*» to fall short

cojera *f* limp

cojín *m* cushion

cojo -ja *adj* **(a)** ‹*persona/animal*› lame; **está ~ del pie derecho** he's lame in his right leg; ***andar a la pata coja*** *or* (Méx) ***brincar de cojito*** (fam) to hop **(b)** ‹*mesa/silla*› wobbly **(c)** (fam) ‹*razonamiento*› shaky, weak ■ *m,f* lame person

cojones *mpl* (vulg) (testículos) balls (*pl*) (sl *o* vulg); ***estar hasta los ~*** (vulg) to be pissed off (sl); ***tener ~*** (vulg) to have guts (colloq), to have balls (sl)

col *f* (Esp, Méx) cabbage; **~ de Bruselas** Brussels sprout

cola *f* **1** **(a)** (Zool) tail; **~ de caballo** (en el pelo) ponytail **(b)** (de vestido) train; (de frac) tails (*pl*) **(c)** (de avión, cometa) tail **(d)** (RPl fam) (nalgas) bottom (colloq) **2** (fila) line (AmE), queue (BrE); **hacer ~** to line up (AmE), to queue (up) (BrE); **pónganse a la ~ por favor** please join the (end of the) line *o* queue; **brincarse la ~** (Méx) to jump the line *o* queue; **a la ~ del pelotón** at the tail end of the group **3** **(a)** (pegamento) glue **(b)** (bebida) Coke®, cola **4** (Ven) (Auto): **pedir ~** to hitchhike; **darle la ~ a algn** to give sb a lift *o* a ride

colaboración *f* collaboration; **en ~ con algn/algo** in collaboration with sb/sth

colaborador -dora *m,f* (en revista) contributor; (en tarea) collaborator

colaborar [A1] *vi* to collaborate; **~ CON algn** to collaborate WITH sb; **~ con dinero** to contribute some money; **~ EN algo** ‹*en proyecto/tarea*› to collaborate ON sth; ‹*en revista*› to contribute TO sth

colada *f* (Esp) (lavado) laundry, washing

coladera *f* **(a)** (Méx) (sumidero) drain **(b)** (Col) ⇒ COLADOR

colador *m* (para té) tea strainer; (para pastas, verduras) colander

colapso *m* **(a)** (Med) collapse; **sufrió un ~** he collapsed **(b)** (paralización) standstill

colar [A10] *vt* **(a)** ‹*verdura/pasta*› to strain, drain; ‹*caldo/té*› to strain **(b)** ‹*billete falso*› to pass ■ **~** *vi* (fam) «*cuento/historia*»: **no va a ~** it won't wash (colloq)

■ **colarse** *v pron* (fam) **(a)** (en cola) to jump the line (AmE) *o* (BrE) queue **(b)** (entrar a hurtadillas) to sneak in; (en cine, autobús) to sneak in without paying (colloq); (en fiesta) to gatecrash

colcha *f* bedspread

colchón *m* (de cama) mattress; **~ de muelles** sprung mattress

colchoneta *f* (de playa) air bed, Lilo® (BrE); (de gimnasia) mat; (de cama) (Méx) comforter (AmE), duvet (BrE)

colección *f* collection

coleccionar [A1] *vt* to collect

coleccionista *mf* collector

colecta *f* (de donativos) collection; **hacer una ~** (para comprar un regalo) to have a collection; (con fines caritativos) to collect

colectar [A1] *vt* to collect

colectivero -ra *m,f* (de autobús) (Arg) bus driver

colectividad *f* group, community; **en ~** collectively

colectivo[1] -va *adj* collective

colectivo[2] *m* **(a)** (period) (agrupación) group **(b)** (Andes) (taxi) collective taxi (*with a fixed route and fare*) **(c)** (Arg) (autobús) bus **(d)** (Per, Ur) (para regalo) collection

colega *mf* **(a)** (de profesión) colleague **(b)** (homólogo) counterpart **(c)** (fam) (amigo) buddy (AmE), mate (BrE colloq)

colegiado -da *m,f* (profesional) member (*of a professional association*)

colegial -giala *m,f* (de colegio) (*m*) schoolboy; (*f*) schoolgirl; **los ~es** (the) schoolchildren

colegiatura *f* (Méx) school fees (*pl*)

colegio *m* **(a)** (Educ) school; **los niños están en el ~** the children are at school; **un ~ de monjas** convent school; **un ~ de curas** a Catholic boys' school; **~ privado** *or* **de pago** fee-paying *o* private school; **~ electoral** electoral college; **~ estatal** *or* **público** public school (AmE), state school (BrE) **(b)** (de profesionales): **C~ de Abogados** ≈ Bar Association; **C~ Oficial de Médicos** ≈ Medical Association

cólera[1] *m* cholera

cólera[2] *f* rage, anger

colérico -ca *adj* **(a)** [ESTAR] (furioso) furious **(b)** [SER] (malhumorado) quick-tempered

colesterol *m* cholesterol

coleta *f* ponytail; (de torero) braid (AmE), ponytail (BrE)

coletazo *m* **(a)** (con la cola) thrash of the tail; **dar ~s** to thrash about **(b)** (Auto): **el coche dio un ~** the rear of the car skidded

coletilla *f* tag

colgado -da *adj*: **dejar a algn ~** (dejarlo en la estacada) to leave sb in the lurch; *ver tb* COLGAR

colgante *adj* hanging; ⇒ PUENTE 1 ■ *m* pendant

colgar [A8] *vt* **(a)** ‹*cuadro*› to hang, put up; ‹*lámpara*› to put up; ‹*ropa lavada*› to hang (out); **~ algo DE algo** to hang sth ON sth; **el abrigo estaba colgado de un gancho** the coat was hanging on a hook **(b)** (ahorcar) to hang **(c)** ‹*teléfono/auricular*› to put down; **tienen el teléfono mal colgado** their phone is off the hook ■ **~** *vi* **(a)** (pender) to hang; **colgaba del techo** it was hanging from the ceiling; **el vestido me cuelga de un lado** my dress is hanging down on one side **(b)** ▶ **405** (Telec) to hang up; **no cuelgue, por favor** hold the line please, please hold; **me colgó** he hung up on me

■ **colgarse** *v pron* (*refl*) **1 (a)** (ahorcarse) to hang oneself **(b)** (agarrarse, suspenderse): **no te cuelgues de ahí** don't hang off there; **no te cuelgues de mí** don't cling on to me; **se pasa colgada del teléfono** (fam) she spends her time on the phone **2** (Chi, Méx) (Elec): **~se del suministro eléctrico** to tap into the electricity supply

colibrí *m* hummingbird

cólico *m* colic

coliflor *f*, (RPl) *m* cauliflower

colilla *f* (de cigarrillo) cigarette end *o* butt

colina *f* hill

colirio *m* eye drops (*pl*)

colisión *f* **(a)** (de trenes, aviones) collision, crash; **~ en cadena** pileup **(b)** (conflicto) conflict, clash

colitis *f* colitis

collado *m* (colina) hill; (entre montañas) pass

collage /ko'laʒ/ *m* (*pl* **-llages**) collage

collar *m* **(a)** (alhaja) necklace; **~ de perlas** string of pearls **(b)** (para animales) collar **(c)** (plumaje) collar, ruff

colleras *fpl* (Chi) (gemelos) cuff links (*pl*)

colmado -da *adj* ‹*cucharada*› heaped; *ver tb* COLMAR

colmar [A1] *vt* **(a)** ‹*vaso/cesta*› to fill … to the brim **(b)** ‹*deseos/aspiraciones*› to fulfill* **(c)** ‹*paciencia*› to stretch … to the limit; **~ a algn DE algo** ‹*de atenciones*› to lavish sth on sb; ‹*de regalos*› to shower sb WITH sth

colmena *f* beehive

colmillo *m* (de persona) eyetooth, canine (tech); (de elefante, jabalí, morsa) tusk; (de perro, lobo) fang, canine

colmo *m*: **el ~ de la vagancia** the height of laziness; **para ~ de desgracias** to top *o* cap it all; **sería el ~ que** … it would be too much if …; **¡esto es el ~!** this is the limit *o* the last straw!

colocación *f* **(a)** (empleo) job; **buscar ~** to look for a job **(b)** (acción) positioning, placing; (de losas, alfombra) laying

colocar [A2] *vt* **1 (a)** (en lugar) to place, put; ‹*losas/alfombra*› to lay; ‹*cuadro*› to hang; ‹*bomba*› to plant **(b)** (Com, Fin) ‹*acciones*› to place; ‹*dinero*› to place, invest **2** ‹*persona*› **(a)** (en lugar) to put **(b)** (en trabajo) to get … a job

■ **colocarse** *v pron* **(a)** (situarse, ponerse): **se colocó a mi lado** she stood/sat beside me **(b)** (en trabajo) to get a job

colocho -cha *m,f* (AmC) **(a)** (persona) curly-haired person **(b) colocho** *m* (rizo) curl

Colombia *f* Colombia

colombiano -na *adj/m,f* Colombian

colón *m* colon (*Costa Rican and Salvadoran unit of currency*)

Colón (Hist) Columbus; **Cristóbal ~** Christopher Columbus

colonia *f* **1 (a)** (Hist, Pol, Zool, Biol) colony **(b)** (de viviendas) residential development; **~ militar** housing estate (*for service families*); **~ penal** (Per) penal colony **(c)** (Méx) (barrio) quarter, district **(d)** (campamento) camp; **~ de vacaciones** holiday camp **2** (perfume) (eau de) cologne

colonial *adj* colonial

colonialismo *m* colonialism

colonización *f* colonization

colonizador -dora *m,f* colonizer

colonizar [A4] *vt* to colonize

colono *m* **(a)** (inmigrante) colonist **(b)** (Agr) (en tierras baldías) settler; (en tierras arrendadas) tenant farmer

coloquial *adj* colloquial

coloquio *m* **(a)** (debate) discussion, talk; (simposio) (AmL) colloquium, symposium; **conferencia ~** talk (*followed by discussion*) **(b)** (Lit) dialogue

color *m* **(a)** ▶ 97 color*; **¿de qué ~ es?** what color is it?; **cambiar de ~** to change color; **un sombrero de un ~ oscuro/claro** a dark/light hat; **las de ~ amarillo** the yellow ones; **ilustraciones a todo ~** full color illustrations; **cintas de ~es** colored ribbons; **fotos en ~es** *or* (Esp) **en ~** color photos; **sin distinción de credo ni ~** regardless of creed or color; **una chica de ~** (euf) a colored girl (dated); **tomar ~** «*pollo*» to brown; «*cebolla frita/pastel*» to turn golden-brown; «*fruta*» to ripen; «*piel*» to become tanned; ***ponerse ~ de hormiga*** (AmL) to start looking pretty grim; ***subido de ~*** (chiste) risqué **(b) colores** *mpl* (lápices) colored* pencils (*pl*), crayons (*pl*)

colorado[1] -da *adj* **(a)** ▶ 97 red; ***ponerse ~*** to blush, turn red, go red (BrE) **(b)** (Méx fam) ‹*chiste*› risqué

colorado[2] *m* ▶ 97 red

colorante *m* coloring*; Ⓢ **no contiene colorantes** no artificial colors

colorear [A1] *vt* (Art) to color*; **~ algo DE algo** to color* sth IN sth

colorete *m* blusher, rouge

colorido *m* colors* (*pl*); **un desfile de gran ~** a very colorful parade

colosal *adj* ‹*estatua/obra/fortuna*› colossal; ‹*ambiente/idea*› (fam) great (colloq)

coloso *m* (estatua) colossus; (gigante) giant

columna *f* **(a)** (Arquit) column, pillar **(b)** (Anat) ▶ 123 *tb* **~ vertebral** spine, backbone **(c)** (Impr, Period, Mil) column

columnista *mf* columnist

columpiar [A1] *vt* to push (*on a swing*) ■ **columpiarse** *v pron* (*refl*) to swing

columpio *m* **(a)** (Jueg, Ocio) swing **(b)** (sofá de jardín) couch hammock

colza *f* rape, colza; **aceite de ~** rapeseed oil

coma *m* **(a)** (Med) coma; **entrar en (estado de) ~** to go into a coma **(b)** (Ling) comma; ⇒ PUNTO 1(a) **(c)** (Mat) ▶ 130 point

comadre *f*: *godmother of one's child or mother of one's godchild*

comadreja *f* (mustélido) weasel

comadrona *f* midwife

comal *m* (Méx) *ceramic dish or metal hotplate for cooking* TORTILLAS 2

comandante *mf* **(a)** (en el ejército) major; (en las fuerzas aéreas) major (AmE), squadron leader (BrE); **~ en jefe** commander in chief **(b)** (oficial al mando) commanding officer **(c)** (Aviac) captain

comando *m* **1 (a)** (grupo de combate) commando group; **~ terrorista** terrorist cell *o* squad **(b)** (AmL) (mando militar) command **2** (Inf) command

comarca *f* region

comarcal *adj* regional

comba *f* **(a)** (de viga, cable) sag; (de pared) bulge **(b)** (Esp) (Jueg) jump rope (AmE), skipping rope (BrE); **saltar la ~** to jump rope (AmE), to skip (BrE)

combarse [A1] *v pron* «*viga/cable*» to sag; «*pared*» to bulge; «*disco*» to warp

combate *m* **(a)** (Mil) combat; **zona de ~** combat zone; **avión de ~** fighter plane **(b)** (en boxeo) fight

combatiente *mf* combatant (frml); **antiguo** *or* **ex ~** veteran

combatir [I1] *vi* «*soldado/ejército*» to fight ■ **~** *vt* ‹*enemigo/enfermedad/fuego*› to fight, to combat (frml); ‹*proyecto/propuesta*› to fight; ‹*frío*› to fight off

combativo -va *adj* **(a)** (luchador) spirited, combative; **espíritu ~** fighting spirit **(b)** (agresivo) combative

combi® *f* (Méx, Per, RPl) VW® van, combi (van) (BrE)

combinación *f* **(a)** (de colores, sabores) combination **(b)** (de caja fuerte) combination **(c)** (Mat) permutation **(d)** (Indum) slip **(e)** (Transp) connection

combinado *m* **(a)** (bebida) cocktail **(b)** (Andes period) (Dep) team, line-up (journ)

combinar [A1] *vt* **(a)** (en general) to combine **(b)** ‹*colores*› to put together; ‹*ropa*› to coordinate; **~ el rojo con el violeta** to put red and purple together ■ **~** *vi* «*colores/ropa*» to go together; **~ CON algo** to go WITH sth

combustible *adj* combustible ■ *m* (Fís, Quím) combustible; (Transp) (carburante) fuel

combustión *f* combustion

comedero *m* (Agr) (para el ganado) feeding trough

comedia *f* **(a)** (Teatr) (obra) play; (cómica) comedy; **~ musical** musical **(b)** (serie cómica) comedy series **(c)** (AmL) (telenovela) soap (opera); (radionovela) radio serial

comediante -ta *m,f* **(a)** (Teatr) (*m*) actor; (*f*) actress **(b)** (farsante) fraud

comedido -da *adj* **(a)** (moderado) moderate, restrained **(b)** (AmL) (atento) obliging, well-meaning

comedor *m* **(a)** (en casa, hotel) dining room; (sala — en colegio, universidad) dining hall, refectory; (— en fábrica, empresa) canteen, cafeteria **(b)** (muebles) dining-room furniture

comedura de coco *f* (Esp fam) **(a)** (lavado de cerebro): **la tele es una ~ de ~** TV just tries to brainwash you **(b)** (preocupación): **tener una ~ de ~** to worry nonstop

comentar [A1] *vt* **(a)** ‹*suceso/película*› to talk about, discuss; ‹*obra/poema*› to comment on **(b)** (mencionar) to mention; (hacer una observación) to remark on; **comentó que** ... he remarked that ... **(c)** (CS) (Rad, TV) ‹*partido*› to commentate on

Los colores

En las explicaciones siguientes se empleará el color azul en los ejemplos; los otros adjetivos y nombres de colores se utilizan de igual manera

Los adjetivos

¿de qué color es/son?	=	what color is it/are they?
es azul	=	it's blue
son azules	=	they're blue
un vestido azul	=	a blue dress

Cuando en español se emplea la palabra color *antepuesta al vocablo que lo señala, ésa no se traduce al inglés*:

el color azul	=	blue
un coche (de) color azul	=	a blue car
son de color azul	=	they're blue

Los nombres

En inglés, por lo general, los nombres de los colores no se usan con el artículo definido:

prefiero el azul	=	I prefer blue
el azul no combina con marrón	=	blue doesn't go with brown
está de moda el azul	=	blue is in fashion
me encanta el azul	=	I love blue

La expresión de azul, *cuando se utiliza como locución adverbial o adjetiva, se traduce al inglés por* in blue:

vestirse de azul	=	to dress in blue
vestido de azul	=	(dressed) in blue
pintado de azul	=	painted in blue
el hombre de azul	=	the man in blue
los niños de azul	=	the boys in blue

Otros usos:

¿la tienen en azul?	=	do you have it in blue?
las hay en azul y verde	=	they do them in blue and green
la tienen en todos los azules	=	they have them in all shades of blue

Los matices

Los matices en español se suelen expresar con un adjetivo invariable:

azul intenso/oscuro	=	deep/dark blue
un sombrero azul claro	=	a light blue hat
zapatos azul oscuro	=	dark blue shoes
un azul más oscuro	=	a darker blue
el vestido era (de un) azul más claro	=	the dress was a lighter blue

Tanto en inglés como en español se pueden expresar matices utilizando el nombre de una cosa cuyo color es típico. Nótese que el adjetivo en inglés lleva un guión, no así el sustantivo:

el azul cielo	=	sky blue
una tela azul cielo	=	a sky-blue material
el azul marino	=	navy blue
zapatos azul marino	=	navy-blue shoes

Asimismo tenemos verde manzana (apple green), verde botella (bottle green) *etc. En caso de duda consultar el diccionario, bajo la correspondiente entrada*

En estos casos cuando en español se utiliza la palabra color, *el inglés utiliza un adjetivo compuesto, formado por el sufijo* -colored *(AmE)* o *(BrE)* -coloured, *y el nombre respectivo*:

medias color carne	=	flesh-colored stockings
un vestido color fresa	=	a strawberry-colored dress
una camisa (de) color crema	=	a cream-colored shirt

Otras maneras de expresar colores:

azulado *or* azuloso	=	bluish
verdoso	=	greenish
rojizo	=	reddish
negruzco	=	blackish
azul verdoso	=	greenish blue
verde azuloso	=	bluish green

Para otras expresiones, consultar el diccionario

El color del pelo

pelo negro/marrón	=	black/brown hair
pelo castaño/rojizo	=	chestnut/reddish hair
pelo rubio	=	blond *o* fair hair
pelo blanco	=	white hair

El color de los ojos

ojos azules	=	blue eyes
ojos azul claro	=	light blue eyes
ojos azul verdoso	=	greenish blue eyes
ojos marrones/color avellana	=	brown/hazel eyes

Nótense las siguientes traducciones:

ojos negros	=	dark eyes
ojos claros	=	blue/green/gray eyes

Para otros colores, ver bajo respectiva entrada

comentario *m* **1 (a)** (observación) comment; **hacer un ~** to make a comment; **fue un ~ de mal gusto** it was a tasteless remark; **sin ~(s)** no comment **(b)** (mención): **no hagas ningún ~ sobre esto** don't mention this **(c)** (análisis) commentary; **~ de texto** textual analysis **2** (Rad, TV) commentary

comentarista *mf* commentator

comenzar [A6] *vt* to begin, commence (frml) ■ ~ *vi* to begin; **al ~ el día** at the beginning of the day; **~ haciendo algo/POR hacer algo** to begin BY doing sth; **~ A hacer algo** to start doing *o* to do sth; **~on a disparar** they started firing *o* to fire; **~ POR algo** to begin WITH sth

comer [E1] *vi* **(a)** (en general) to eat; **no tengo ganas de ~** I'm not hungry; **este niño no me come nada** (fam) this child won't eat anything (colloq); **dar(le) de ~ a algn (en la boca)** to spoonfeed sb; **darle de ~ al gato/al niño** to feed the cat/the kid; **salir a ~ (fuera)** to go out for a meal, to eat out; **¿qué hay de ~?** (a mediodía) what's for lunch?; (por la noche) what's for dinner *o* supper? **(b)** (esp Esp, Méx) (almorzar) to have lunch; **nos invitaron a ~** they asked us to lunch **(c)** (esp AmL) (cenar) to have dinner ■ ~ *vt* **(a)** ‹*fruta/verdura/carne*› to eat; **¿puedo ~ otro?** can I have another one?; **no tienen qué ~** they don't have anything to eat **(b)** (fam) (hacer desaparecer) ⇒ COMERSE 3 **(c)** (en ajedrez, damas) to take

■ **comerse** *v pron* **1 (a)** (al escribir) ‹*acento/palabra*› to leave off; ‹*línea/párrafo*› to miss out **(b)** (al hablar) ‹*letra*› to leave off; ‹*palabra*› to swallow **2** (*enf*) ‹*comida*› to eat; **cómetelo todo** eat it all up; **~se las uñas** to bite one's nails **3** (fam) (hacer desaparecer) **(a)** «*acido/óxido*» to eat away (at); «*polilla/ratón*» to eat away (at) **(b)** «*inflación/alquiler*» ‹*sueldo/ahorros*› to eat away at

comercial *adj* **(a)** ‹*zona/operación/carta*› business (*before n*); **una firma ~** a company; **el déficit ~** the trade deficit; ⇒ GALERÍA, CENTRO **(b)** ‹*película/arte*› commercial ■ *m* **(a)** (anuncio) commercial, advert (BrE) **(b)** (CS) (Educ) business school

comercializar [A4] *vt* ‹*producto*› to market; ‹*lugar/deporte*› to commercialize

■ **comercializarse** *v pron* to become commercialized

comerciante *mf* **(a)** (dueño de tienda) storekeeper (AmE), shopkeeper (BrE); (negociante) dealer, trader **(b)** (mercenario) money-grubber (colloq)

comerciar [A1] *vi* to trade, do business; **~ EN algo** to trade *o* deal IN sth

comercio *m* **(a)** (actividad) trade; **el ~ de armas** the arms trade; **el mundo del ~** the world of commerce **(b)** (tiendas): **hoy cierra el ~** the stores (AmE) *o* (BrE) shops are closed today **(c)** (tienda) store (AmE), shop (BrE)

comestible *adj* edible

comestibles *mpl* food; **tienda de ~** grocery store (AmE), grocer's (shop) (BrE)

cometa *m* comet ■ *f* kite; **hacer volar una ~** *or* (RPl) **remontar una ~** to fly a kite

cometer [E1] *vt* ‹*crimen/delito/pecado*› to commit; ‹*error/falta*› to make

cometido *m* **(a)** (tarea, deber) task, mission **(b)** (Chi) (actuación) performance

comezón *f* (Med) itching, itch; **tenía ~ en la espalda** his back was itching

comic /'komik/, **cómic** *m* (*pl* **-mics**) (esp Esp) (tira ilustrada) comic strip; (revista) comic

comicios *mpl* elections (*pl*)

cómico -ca *adj* ‹*actor/género/obra*› comedy (*before n*); ‹*situación/mueca*› comical, funny ■ *m,f* (actor) comedy actor, comic actor; (humorista) comedian, comic

comida *f* **(a)** (en general) food; **~ para perros** dog food; **~ basura/rápida** junk/fast food **(b)** (ocasión en que se come) meal; **la ~ fuerte del día** the main meal of the day; **¿quién hace la ~ en tu casa?** who does the cooking in your house?; **todavía no he hecho la ~** I still haven't cooked the meal **(c)** (esp Esp, Méx) (almuerzo) lunch **(d)** (esp AmL) (cena) dinner, supper; (en algunas regiones del Reino Unido) tea

comidilla *f*: **ser la ~ del pueblo** to be the talk of the town

comience, **comienza, etc** *see* COMENZAR

comienzo *m* beginning; **al ~** at first, in the beginning; **dar ~** to begin; **dar ~ a algo** «*persona*» to begin sth; «*ceremonia/acto*» to mark the beginning of sth; **el proyecto está en sus ~s** the project is still in its early stages

comillas *fpl* quotation marks (*pl*), inverted commas (BrE) (*pl*); **poner algo entre ~** to put sth in quotation marks *o* in inverted commas

comilona *f* (fam) feast (colloq); **nos dimos una ~** we had a blowout

comino *m* (Bot, Coc) cumin

comisaría *f* (edificio) *tb* **~ de policía** (police) station

comisario *m* **(a)** (de policía) captain (AmE), superintendent (BrE) **(b)** (delegado) commissioner

comisión *f* **(a)** (delegación, organismo) committee; **C~ Europea** European Commission **(b)** (Com) commission; **trabajar a ~** to work on a commission basis

comisionista *mf* commission agent

comiso *m* (Col) packed lunch

comisura *f* (de los labios) corner

comité *m* (junta) committee; **~ de redacción** editorial board *o* committee

comitiva *f* **(a)** (séquito) procession; **~ fúnebre** funeral procession, cortège **(b)** (grupo) delegation

como *prep* **(a)** (en calidad de) as; **quiero hablarte ~ amigo** I want to speak to you as a friend **(b)** (con el nombre de) as; **se la conoce ~ 'flor de luz'** it's known as 'flor de luz' **(c)** (en comparaciones, contrastes) like; **uno ~ el tuyo** one like yours; **¡no hay nada ~ un buen coñac!** there's nothing like a good brandy!; **es ~ para echarse a llorar** it's enough to make you want to cry **(d)** (*en locs*) **así como** (frml) as well as; **como mucho/poco** at (the) most/at least; **como ser** (CS) such as, for example; **como si** (+ *subj*) as if, as though ■ *conj* **(a)** (de la manera que) as; **tal ~ había prometido** just as he had promised; **~ era de esperar** as was to be expected; **no me gustó ~ lo dijo** I didn't

Cómo

Algunas observaciones generales sobre el adverbio

Cuando significa de qué manera, *el adverbio se traduce generalmente por* how:

no sé cómo pasó = I don't know how it happened
¿cómo se escribe? = how is it spelled?

Nótese que en este tipo de oraciones, cuando se emplea el verbo llamar, cómo *se traduce al inglés por* what:

¿cómo te llamas? = what's your name?
no sé cómo se llama = I don't know what her name is

En oraciones en que cómo *aparece seguido del verbo* ser *o* estar *más la preposición* de *más un adjetivo, por lo general el inglés emplea* how *inmediatamente seguido del adjetivo correspondiente*:

¿cómo es de grande? = how big is it?
¡(si) hubieras visto cómo estaba de sucio! = you should have seen how dirty he was

Nótese la falta de equivalencia en inglés de la preposición de

Cuando cómo *seguido del verbo* ser *o* estar *sugiere una descripción, la traducción al inglés suele ser* what . . . like?:

¿cómo es su novio? = what's her boyfriend like? (como persona)
= what does her boyfriend look like? (físicamente)
¿cómo está el tiempo allí? = what's the weather like there?

En oraciones exclamativas que expresan cierta sorpresa, cómo *puede traducirse por* what:

¡cómo! ¿no lo sabías? = what! you mean you didn't know?

Se encontrarán otros usos y ejemplos suplementarios en la siguiente entrada

like the way she said it; **(tal y) ~ están las cosas** as things stand; **hazlo ~ quieras/~ mejor puedas** do it any way you like/as best as you can; **no voy — ~ quieras** I'm not going — please yourself **(b)** (puesto que) as, since; **~ era temprano, fui a dar una vuelta** as it was early, I went for a walk **(c)** (si) (+ *subj*) if; **~ te pille** ... if I catch you ... ■ *adv* (expresando aproximación) about; **está ~ a cincuenta kilómetros** it's about fifty kilometers away; **un sabor ~ a almendras** a kind of almondy taste

cómo *adv* **(a)** (de qué manera) how; **¿~ estás?** how are you?; **¿~ es tu novia?** what's your girlfriend like?; **¿~ es de grande?** how big is it?; **¿~ te llamas?** what's your name? **(b)** (por qué) why, how come (colloq); **¿~ no me lo dijiste antes?** why didn't you tell me before? **(c)** (al solicitar que se repita algo) sorry?, pardon?; **¿~ dijo?** sorry, what did you say? **(d)** (en exclamaciones): **¡~ llueve!** it's really raining!; **¡~ comes!** the amount you eat!; **¡~! ¿no te lo han dicho?** what! haven't they told you? **(e)** (*en locs*) **¿a cómo ...?**: **¿a ~ están los tomates?** (fam) how much are the tomatoes?; **¿a ~ estamos hoy?** (AmL) what's the date today?; **¡cómo no!** of course!; **¿cómo que ...?**: **¿~ que no fuiste tú?** what do you mean it wasn't you?; **aquí no está — ¿~ que no?** it isn't here — what do you mean it isn't there?

cómoda *f* chest of drawers

comodidad *f* **1 (a)** (confort) comfort; **la ~ del hogar** the comfort of home **(b)** (conveniencia) convenience; **por ~** for the sake of convenience **(c)** (holgazanería): **no lo hace por ~** he doesn't do it because he's lazy **2 comodidades** *fpl* (aparatos, servicios) comforts (*pl*)

comodín *m* **(a)** (Jueg) (mono) joker; (otra carta) wild card **(b)** (Inf) wild card

cómodo -da *adj* **(a)** (confortable) comfortable, comfy (colloq); **ponte ~** make yourself comfortable **(b)** (conveniente, fácil) ‹*horario/sistema*› convenient; **ésa es una actitud muy cómoda** that's a very easy attitude to take **(c)** (holgazán) lazy, idle

compact disc /kompac'ðis(k)/ *m* (*pl* **-discs**) (disco) compact disc, CD; (aparato) compact disc player, CD player

compacto -ta *adj* **(a)** ‹*tejido*› close; ‹*estructura/coche*› compact **(b)** ‹*muchedumbre*› dense

compadecer [E3] *vt* to feel sorry for

■ **compadecerse** *v pron* (apiadarse) **~se DE algn** to take pity ON sb; **~se de sí mismo** to feel sorry for oneself

compadre *m* **(a)** (padrino) *godfather of one's child or father of one's godchild* **(b)** (esp AmL fam) (amigo) buddy (AmE colloq), mate (BrE colloq)

compaginar [A1] *vt* ‹*actividades/soluciones*› to combine; **compagina el trabajo con los estudios** she combines work with studying ■ **~** *vi* **(a)** (combinar) to go together **(b)** (llevarse bien) to get on; **~ CON algn** to get on well WITH sb

compañerismo *m* comradeship

compañero -ra *m,f* **(a)** (en actividad): **un ~ de equipo** a fellow team member; **fuimos ~s de universidad** we were at college together; **~ de clase/de trabajo** classmate/workmate **(b)** (pareja sentimental, en juegos) partner; (de guante, calcetín) (fam) pair **(c)** (Pol) comrade

compañía *f* **1** (acompañamiento) company; **llegó en ~ de sus abogados** he arrived accompanied by his lawyers; **hacerle ~ a algn** to keep sb company; **andar en malas ~s** to keep bad company **2**

(empresa) company, firm; ~ **de seguros** insurance company; ~ **de teatro** theater* company; Ⓢ **Muñoz y Compañía** Muñoz and Co. **3** (Mil) company

comparable *adj* comparable; ~ A *or* CON comparable TO *o* WITH

comparación *f* comparison; **hacer una** ~ to make a comparison; **en** ~ **a** *or* **con el año pasado** compared to *o* with last year; **no tienen ni punto de** ~ you cannot even begin to compare them

comparar [A1] *vt* to compare; ~ **algo/a algn** A *or* CON **algo/algn** to compare sth/sb TO *o* WITH sth/sb; **no puede ni ~se al otro** it doesn't even compare at all to *o* with the other one ■ ~ *vi* to make a comparison, to compare

comparecer [E3] *vi* to appear (in court)

compartimento, **compartimiento** *m* compartment

compartir [I1] *vt* to share; ~ **algo** CON **algn** to share sth WITH sb

compás *m* **1** (Mús) **(a)** (ritmo) time, meter (esp AmE); **marcar/llevar el** ~ to beat/keep time; **perder el** ~ to get out of time; **se movía al** ~ **de la música** she moved in time to the music **(b)** (división) measure (AmE), bar (BrE); ~ **de dos por cuatro** two-four time; ~ **mayor/menor** four-four/two-four time **2** (Mat, Náut) (instrumento) compass

compasión *f* pity, compassion; **lo hace por** ~ he does it out of compassion

compasivo -va *adj* compassionate

compatible *adj* compatible

compatriota *m,f* (*m*) fellow countryman, compatriot; (*f*) fellow countrywoman, compatriot

compendio *m* (libro) textbook, coursebook; (resumen) summary, compendium (BrE)

compenetrarse [A1] *v pron* ~ CON **algo** ‹*con ideas/objetivos*› to identify WITH sth; ~ CON **algn** to have a good relationship WITH sb; (en trabajo) to work well WITH sb; **se han compenetrado a la perfección** they understand each other perfectly

compensación *f* (contapartida) compensation; **en** ~ by way of compensation; **en** ~ **por algo** in compensation for sth

compensar [A1] *vi*: **no compensa hacer un viaje tan largo** it's not worth making such a long journey; **no me compensa** it's not worth my while ■ ~ *vt* **1 (a)** (contrarrestar) ‹*pérdida/deficiencia*› to compensate for, make up for; ‹*efecto*› to offset; **su entusiasmo compensa su falta de experiencia** his enthusiasm makes up for his lack of experience **(b)** ‹*persona*› ~ **a algn** POR **algo** ‹*por pérdidas/retraso*› to compensate sb FOR sth; **lo ~on con $2.000 por los daños** he was awarded $2,000 compensation in damages **2** ‹*cheque*› to clear

■ **compensarse** *v pron* «*fuerzas*» (*recípr*) to compensate each other, cancel each other out

competencia *f* **1 (a)** (pugna) competition, rivalry; **hacerse la** ~ to be rivals *o* in competition; **hacerle la** ~ **a algn** to compete with sb **(b)** (persona, entidad) competition; **la** ~ **se nos adelantó** the competition got in first **(c)** (AmL) (certamen) competition **2 (a)** (de juez, tribunal) competence; **este asunto no es de mi** ~ I have no authority *o* say in this matter **(b)** (habilidad, aptitud) competence, ability; **falta de** ~ incompetence

competente *adj* competent

competición *f* (Esp) **(a)** (rivalidad): **espíritu de** ~ competitive spirit **(b)** (certamen) competition

competidor -dora *m,f* competitor, rival

competir [I14] *vi* **(a)** (pugnar, luchar) to compete; ~ CON *or* CONTRA **algn** (POR **algo**) to compete WITH *o* AGAINST sb (FOR sth) **(b)** (estar al mismo nivel): **los dos modelos compiten en calidad** the two models rival each other in quality

competitividad *f* competitiveness

competitivo -va *adj* competitive

compilar [A1] *vt* to compile

compinche *mf* (compañero) (fam) buddy (AmE colloq), mate (BrE colloq); (cómplice en crimen) partner in crime

complacer [E3] *vt* to please

■ **complacerse** *v pron* **~se** EN **algo** to take pleasure IN sth

complaciente *adj* indulgent

complejidad *f* complexity

complejo[1] -ja *adj* complex

complejo[2] *m* **(a)** (de edificios) complex; ~ **deportivo/industrial** sports/industrial complex **(b)** (Psic) complex; **tiene** ~ **porque es bajito** he's got a complex about being short; ~ **de culpa** *or* **culpabilidad** guilt complex; ~ **de inferioridad/superioridad** inferiority/superiority complex

complementar [A1] *vt* to complement

■ **complementarse** *v pron* (*recípr*) to complement each other

complementario -ria *adj* **(a)** ‹*personalidades/ángulos/colores*› complementary **(b)** (adicional) additional

complemento *m* **(a)** (Ling, Mat) complement; ~ **directo/indirecto** direct/indirect object **(b)** (acompañamiento) accompaniment **(c) complementos** *mpl* (Auto, Indum) accessories (*pl*)

completar [A1] *vt* **(a)** (terminar) to finish, complete **(b)** (AmL) ‹*cuestionario/impreso*› to complete, fill out *o* in

completo -ta *adj* **1 (a)** (entero) complete; **las obras completas de Neruda** the complete works of Neruda **(b)** (total, absoluto) complete, total; **lo olvidé por** ~ I completely forgot about it **(c)** (exhaustivo) ‹*explicación*› detailed; ‹*obra/diccionario*› comprehensive; ‹*tesis/ensayo*› thorough **(d)** ‹*deportista/actor*› complete, very versatile **2** (lleno) ‹*vagón/hotel*› full; Ⓢ **completo** (en hostal) no vacancies; (en taquilla) sold out

complexión *f* constitution

complicación *f* **(a)** (contratiempo, dificultad) complication **(b)** (cualidad) complexity **(c)** (esp AmL) (implicación) involvement

complicado -da *adj* **(a)** ‹*problema/sistema/situación*› complicated, complex **(b)** ‹*carácter*› complex; ‹*persona*› complicated **(c)** ‹*diseño/adorno*› elaborate

complicar [A2] *vt* **(a)** ‹*situación/problema/asunto*› to complicate, make ... complicated **(b)** (implicar) ‹*persona*› to involve, get ... involved ■ **complicarse** *v pron* **(a)** «*situación/problema/asunto*» to get complicated; «*enfermedad*»: **se le complicó con un problema respiratorio** he developed respiratory complications; ⇒ VIDA 2 **(b)** (implicarse) **~se** EN **algo** to get involved IN sth

cómplice *mf* accomplice; **~** EN **algo** accomplice TO sth

complicidad *f* complicity

compló, **complot** *m* (*pl* **-plots**) plot, conspiracy

compondré, **compondría, etc** *see* COMPONER

componente *m* **(a)** (de sustancia) constituent (part), component (part); (de equipo, comisión) member **(b)** (Tec) component

componer [E22] *vt* **(a)** (constituir) ‹*jurado/equipo/plantilla*› to make up; **el tren estaba compuesto por ocho vagones** the train was made up of eight cars **(b)** ‹*sinfonía/canción/verso*› to compose **(c)** (esp AmL) (arreglar) ‹*reloj/radio/zapatos*› to repair **(d)** (AmL) ‹*hueso*› to set ■ **~** *vi* to compose ■ **componerse** *v pron* **1** (estar formado) **~se** DE **algo** to be made up OF sth, to consist OF sth; **un conjunto compuesto de falda y chaqueta** an outfit consisting of a skirt and a jacket **2** (esp AmL fam) «*persona*» to get better

comportamiento *m* **(a)** (conducta) behavior*; **mal ~** bad behavior **(b)** (Mec) performance

comportarse [A1] *v pron* to behave; **~ mal** to behave badly, misbehave

composición *f* composition

compositor -tora *m,f* composer

compostura *f* **(a)** (circunspección) composure; **guardar la ~** to maintain *o* keep one's composure **(b)** (RPl) (arreglo) repair

compota *f* compote

compra *f* **(a)** (acción): **ir de ~s** to go shopping; **hacer las ~s** *or* (Esp) **la ~** to do the shopping **(b)** (cosa comprada) buy, purchase (frml); **fue una buena ~** it was a good buy

comprador -dora *m,f* buyer, purchaser (frml)

comprar [A1] *vt* **(a)** ‹*casa/regalo/comida*› to buy, purchase (frml); **~le algo** A **algn** (a quien lo vende) to buy sth FROM sb; (a quien lo recibe) to buy sth FOR sb **(b)** (fam) (sobornar) to buy (colloq)

comprender [E1] *vt* **1 (a)** (entender) to understand, comprehend (frml); **nadie me comprende** nobody understands me **(b)** (darse cuenta) to realize, understand; **comprendió que lo habían engañado** he realized that he had been tricked **2** (abarcar, contener) «*libro*» to cover; «*factura/precio*» to include ■ **~** *vi* (entender) to understand; **hacerse ~** to make oneself understood

comprensible *adj* understandable

comprensión *f* understanding; **capacidad de ~** comprehension; **~ auditiva** listening comprehension

comprensivo -va *adj* understanding

compresa *f* **(a)** (Med) compress **(b)** (Esp) *tb* **~ higiénica** sanitary napkin (AmE) *o* (BrE) towel

comprimido *m* (Farm) pill, tablet

comprimir [I1] *vt* to compress

comprobación *f* **(a)** (acción) verification, checking **(b)** (Col) (examen) test

comprobante *m* proof; **~ de pago** proof of payment

comprobar [A10] *vt* **(a)** (verificar) ‹*operación/resultado/funcionamiento*› to check **(b)** (demostrar) to prove **(c)** (darse cuenta) to realize **(d)** «*hecho*» (confirmar) to confirm

comprometedor -dora *adj* compromising

comprometer [E1] *vt* **(a)** (poner en un apuro) to compromise **(b)** ‹*vida/libertad*› to jeopardize, threaten **(c)** (obligar) **~ a algn** A **algo** to commit sb TO sth; **esto no me compromete a nada** this does not commit me to anything ■ **comprometerse** *v pron* **(a)** (dar su palabra) **~se** A **hacer algo** to promise to do sth; **me he comprometido para salir esta noche** I've arranged to go out tonight **(b)** «*autor/artista*» to commit oneself politically **(c)** «*novios*» to get engaged; **~se** CON **algn** to get engaged TO sb

comprometido -da *adj* **(a)** [SER] ‹*asunto/situación*› awkward, delicate **(b)** [SER] ‹*cine/escritor*› politically committed **(c)** [ESTAR] (para casarse) engaged; **~** CON **algn** engaged TO sb

compromiso *m* **(a)** (moral, financiero) commitment; **adquirir un ~ con algn** to make a commitment to sb; **sin ~ alguno** without obligation; **los invitó por ~** she felt obliged to invite them; **yo con ellos no tengo ningún ~** I'm under no obligation to them **(b)** (cita) engagement; **~s sociales** social engagements *o* commitments **(c)** (de matrimonio) engagement **(d)** (acuerdo) agreement; (con concesiones recíprocas) compromise; **llegaron a un ~** they came to *o* reached an agreement/a compromise **(e)** (apuro) awkward situation; **me puso en un ~** he put me in an awkward position

compuesto -ta *adj* ‹*oración/número/flor*› compound (*before n*); *ver tb* COMPONER

compungido -da *adj* (arrepentido) remorseful, contrite; (triste) sad

compuse, **compuso, etc** *see* COMPONER

computadora *f*, **computador** *m* (esp AmL) computer; **~ personal/de mesa** personal/desktop computer

computerizar [A4] *vt* to computerize

comulgar [A3] *vi* (Relig) to receive *o* take communion

común *adj* **(a)** ‹*intereses/características*› common (*before n*); ‹*amigo*› mutual **(b)** (*en locs*) **de común acuerdo** by common consent; **de ~ acuerdo con algn** in agreement with sb; **en común** ‹*esfuerzo/regalo*› joint (*before n*); **no tenemos nada en ~** we have nothing in common **(c)** (corriente, frecuente) common; **es un nombre muy ~** it's a very common name; **un modelo fuera de lo ~** a very unusual model; **~ *y corriente*** (normal, nada especial) ordinary

comuna *f* **(a)** (de convivencia) commune **(b)** (CS, Per) (municipio) town, municipality (frml)

comunal *adj* **(a)** (de todos) communal **(b)** (CS, Per) (del municipio) town (*before n*), municipal

comunicación *f* **(a)** (enlace) link; **~ vía satélite** satellite link **(b)** (contacto) contact; **ponerse en ~ con algn** to get in contact *o* in touch with sb **(c)** (por teléfono): **se ha cortado la ~** I've/we've been cut off **(d)** (entendimiento, relación) comunicación **(e) comunicaciones** *fpl* (por carretera, teléfono, etc) communications (*pl*)

comunicado *m* communiqué; **~ de prensa** press release

comunicar [A2] *vt* **1** (frml) **(a)** (informar) to inform; **~le algo A algn** to inform sb OF sth **(b)** (AmL) (por teléfono) ‹*persona*› to put ... through **2** (transmitir) **(a)** ‹*entusiasmo/miedo*› to convey, communicate **(b)** ‹*conocimientos*› to impart, pass on; ‹*información*› to convey, communicate; ‹*idea*› to put across **(c)** ‹*fuerza/calor*› to transmit **3** ‹*habitaciones/ciudades*› to connect, link; **un barrio bien comunicado** an area easily accessible by road/well served by public transport; **~ algo CON algo** to connect sth WITH sth ■ **~** *vi* **1** «*habitaciones*» to be connected **2** (Esp) «*teléfono*» to be busy (AmE) *o* (BrE) engaged

■ **comunicarse** *v pron* **1 (a)** (*recípr*) (relacionarse) to communicate; **~ por señas** to communicate using sign language; **~se CON algn** to communicate WITH sb **(b)** (ponerse en contacto) **~se CON algn** to get in touch *o* in contact WITH sb **2** «*habitaciones/ciudades/lagos*» (*recípr*) to be connected; **~se CON algo** to be connected TO sth

comunicativo -va *adj* communicative

comunidad *f* community; **C~ (Económica) Europea** European (Economic) Community

comunión *f* (Relig) communion; **hacer la primera ~** to make one's first Holy Communion

comunismo *m* communism

comunista *adj/mf* communist

comunitario -ria *adj* **(a)** ‹*bienes*› communal; ‹*espíritu/trabajo*› community (*before n*) **(b)** (de la CE) EC (*before n*), Community (*before n*)

con *prep* **(a)** (en general) with; **vive ~ su novio** she lives with her boyfriend; **¡~ mucho gusto!** with pleasure!; **córtalo ~ la tijera** cut it with the scissor; **amaneció ~ fiebre** he woke up with a temperature; **hablar ~ algn** to talk to sb; **está casada ~ mi primo** she's married to my cousin; **portarse mal ~ algn** to behave badly toward(s) sb; **tener paciencia ~ algn** to be patient with sb; **pan ~ mantequilla** bread and butter; **¿vas a ir ~ ese vestido?** are you going in that dress? **(b)** (indicando una relación de causa): **¿cómo vamos a ir ~ esta lluvia?** how can we go in this rain?; **ella se lo ofreció, ~ lo que** *or* **lo cual me puso a mí en un aprieto** she offered it to him, which put me in an awkward position; **~ lo tarde que es, ya se debe haber ido** it's really late, he should have gone by now **(c) ~** + INF: **~ llorar no se arregla nada** crying won't solve anything; **~ llamarlo por teléfono ya cumples** as long as you call him, that should do; **me contento ~ que apruebes** as long as you pass I'll be happy; ⇒ TAL *adv* 2 **(d)** (AmL) (indicando el agente, destinatario): **me peino ~ Gerardo** Gerardo does my hair; **se estuvo quejando ~migo** she was complaining to me

cóncavo -va *adj* concave

concebir [I14] *vt* **1** (Biol) to conceive **2** ‹*plan/idea*› to conceive **3** (entender, imaginar): **no concibe la vida sin él** she can't conceive of life without him; **yo concibo la amistad de modo distinto** I have a different conception of friendship ■ **~** *vi* to conceive

conceder [E1] *vt* **1 (a)** ‹*premio/beca*› to give, award; ‹*descuento/préstamo*› to give; ‹*privilegio/favor/permiso*› to grant; **nos concedió una entrevista** she agreed to give us an interview; **¿me podría ~ unos minutos?** could you spare me a few minutes? **(b)** ‹*importancia/valor*› to give **2** (admitir, reconocer) to admit, acknowledge

concejal -jala *m,f* town/city councilor*

concejero -ra *m,f* (AmL) town/city councilor*

concejo *m* council

concentración *f* **(a)** (Psic, Quim) concentration; **falta de ~** lack of concentration **(b)** (acumulación) concentration **(c)** (Pol) rally, mass meeting

concentrado[1] -da *adj* concentrated (*before n*)

concentrado[2] *m* (de verdura, tomate) concentrate; **~ de carne** meat extract

concentrar [A1] *vt* **(a)** ‹*solución/caldo*› to make ... more concentrated **(b)** ‹*esfuerzos*› to concentrate; ‹*atención*› to focus **(c)** (congregar) ‹*multitud/tropas*› to assemble, bring ... together

■ **concentrarse** *v pron* **(a)** (Psic) to concentrate; **~se EN algo** to concentrate ON sth **(b)** (reunirse) to assemble, gather together

concéntrico -ca *adj* concentric

concepción *f* (Biol) conception

concepto *m* **(a)** (idea): **el ~ de la libertad** the concept of freedom; **tener un ~ equivocado de algo/algn** to have a mistaken idea of sth/sb; **tengo (un) mal ~ de su trabajo** I have a very low opinion of her work; ***bajo*** *or* ***por ningún ~*** on no account **(b)** (Com, Fin): **en** *or* **por ~ de** in respect of

conceptuoso -sa *adj* (CS) (amable, elogioso): **una conceptuosa felicitación** warm congratulations

concerniente *adj* **~ A algo** concerning sth; **en lo ~ a este problema** as far as this problem is concerned

concernir [I12] *vi* (*en 3ª pers*) to concern; **~ A algn** to concern sb; **por lo que a mí concierne** as far as I'm concerned; **en lo que concierne a su pedido** with regard to your order

concertar [A5] *vt* ‹*cita/entrevista*› to arrange, set up; ‹*plan*› to arrange; ‹*precio*› to agree (on)

concertista *mf* soloist; **~ de piano** concert pianist

concesión *f* **(a)** (de premios) awarding; (de préstamo) granting **(b)** (en una postura) concession; **hacer concesiones** to make concessions **(c)** (Com) dealership, concession, franchise

concesionario *m* dealer, concessionaire

concha *f* **(a)** (de moluscos) shell; **~ nácar** (Méx) *or* (Chi) **de perla** mother-of-pearl **(b)** (carey) tortoise shell **(c)** (Teatr) prompt box **(d)** (Ven) (cáscara — de verduras, fruta) skin; (— del queso) rind; (— del pan) crust; (— de nueces) shell

cónchale *interj* (Ven fam) good heavens!

concho *m* (Chi) **(a)** (del vino) lees (*pl*); (del café) dregs (*pl*) **(b)** (fam) (parte final) end, last bit **(c) conchos** *mpl* (restos) leftovers (*pl*)

conciencia *f* **(a)** (en moral) conscience; **tener la ~ tranquila** to have a clear *o* clean conscience; **tener la ~ sucia** to have a bad *o* guilty conscience; **me remuerde la ~** my conscience is pricking me; **no siente ningún cargo de ~** she feels no remorse; ***hacer algo a ~*** to do something conscientiously **(b)** (conocimiento) awareness; **tener/tomar ~ de algo** to be/become aware of sth

concienciar [A1] *vt* (Esp) ⇒ CONCIENTIZAR

concientizar [A4] *vt* (esp AmL) ‹*población/sociedad*› to make ... aware; **~ a algn DE algo** to raise sb's consciousness ABOUT *o* awareness OF sth
■ **concientizarse** *v pron* (esp AmL) **~se DE algo** to become aware OF sth

concienzudo -da *adj* ‹*trabajador/estudiante*› conscientious; ‹*estudio/repaso/análisis*› thorough, painstaking

concierto *m* (Mús) **(a)** (obra) concerto **(b)** (función) concert, recital

conciliación *f* conciliation

conciliar [A1] *vt* **1 (a)** ‹*personas*› to conciliate **(b)** ‹*ideas*› to reconcile; ‹*actividades*› to combine **2** ‹*sueño*›: **~ el sueño** to get to sleep

concilio *m* council

conciso -sa *adj* concise

conciudadano -na *m,f* fellow citizen

concluir [I20] *vt* **(a)** (frml) (terminar) ‹*obras*› to complete, finish; ‹*trámite*› to complete; ‹*acuerdo/tratado*› to conclude **(b)** (frml) (deducir) to conclude, come to the conclusion; **~ algo DE algo** to conclude sth FROM sth ■ **~** *vi* (frml) **(a)** «*congreso/negociaciones*» to end, conclude; **el plazo concluyó el día 17** the time limit expired on the 17th **(b)** «*persona*» **~ DE hacer algo** to finish doing sth

conclusión *f* **(a)** (terminación) completion **(b)** (deducción) conclusion; **saqué la ~ de que** ... I came to the conclusion that ...; **tú saca tus propias conclusiones** you can draw your own conclusions; **en ~** (en suma) in short; (en consecuencia) so

concluyente *adj* ‹*razón/respuesta/prueba*› conclusive; **fue ~ al responder** he answered categorically

concordante *adj* concordant (frml), concurrent

concordar [A10] *vi* **(a)** (Ling) to agree; **~ CON algo** to agree WITH sth **(b)** «*cifras*» to tally; «*versiones*» to agree, coincide; **~ CON algo** ‹*con documento/versión*› to coincide WITH sth; **su comportamiento no concuerda con sus principios** his behavior is not in keeping with his principles

concretamente *adv* (específicamente) specifically; **vive en Wisconsin, ~ en Madison** he lives in Wisconsin, in Madison to be precise

concretar [A1] *vt* **(a)** (concertar) ‹*fecha/precio*› to fix, set **(b)** (precisar, definir) to be specific about; **no concretamos nada** we didn't settle on anything definite ■ **~** *vi:* **a ver si concretas** try and be more specific; **llámame para ~** give me a call to arrange the details
■ **concretarse** *v pron* to become a reality

concreto¹ -ta *adj* **(a)** (específico) ‹*política/solución/acusación*› concrete, specific; ‹*motivo/ejemplo/pregunta*› specific; ‹*fecha/hora*› definite; ‹*caso*› particular; ‹*lugar*› specific, particular; **en tu caso ~** in your particular case; **en ~** specifically; **en una zona en ~** in a particular *o* specific area; **no sé nada en ~** I don't know anything definite **(b)** (no abstracto) concrete

concreto² *m* (AmL) concrete; **~ armado** reinforced concrete

concubina *f* concubine

concuñado -da *m,f*: **mi ~** my wife's brother-in-law; **mi concuñada** my husband's sister-in-law

concurrido -da *adj* **(a)** [ESTAR] (con mucha gente) ‹*discoteca/local*› busy, crowded; ‹*concierto/exposición*› well-attended **(b)** [SER] (frecuentado) popular

concursante *mf* (en concurso) competitor, contestant; (para empleo) candidate

concursar [A1] *vi* (en concurso) to take part; (para puesto) to compete (*through interviews and competitive examinations*)

concurso *m* **(a)** (certamen) competition; **presentarse a un ~** to take part in a competition; **~ de belleza** beauty contest *o* (esp AmE) pageant; **~ hípico** show jumping competition **(b)** (para puestos, vacantes) *selection process involving interviews and competitive examinations* **(c)** (TV) (de preguntas y respuestas) quiz show; (de juegos y pruebas) game show **(d)** (licitación) tender; **sacar algo a ~** to put sth out to tender

condado *m* (división territorial) county

conde -desa *m,f* (en Gran Bretaña) (*m*) earl; (*f*) countess; (en otros países) (*m*) count; (*f*) countess

condecoración *f* decoration

condecorar [A1] *vt* to decorate

condena *f* **(a)** (Der) sentence; **está cumpliendo su ~** he is serving his sentence **(b)** (reprobación) **~ DE** *or* **A algo** condemnation OF sth

condenado -da *adj* **(a)** (destinado) **~ A algo** doomed TO sth **(b)** (obligado) **~ A hacer algo** condemned *o* forced to do sth **(c)** (fam) (expresando irritación) wretched (colloq), damn (colloq) ■ *m,f* **(a)** (Der) convicted person; **el ~ a muerte** the condemned man **(b)** (Relig): **los ~s** the damned; ***como (un) ~*** (fam) ‹*correr*› like hell (colloq); ‹*work*› like mad

condenar [A1] *vt* **(a)** (Der) to sentence, condemn; **~ a algn A algo** to sentence sb TO sth; **~ a algn a muerte** to sentence sb to death; **lo ~on por robo** he was found guilty of robbery **(b)** (reprobar, censurar) to condemn

condensación *f* condensation

condensar [A1] *vt* to condense
■ **condensarse** *v pron* to condense

condesa *f* countess

condescendiente *adj* **(a)** ‹*actitud/respuesta*› (con aires de superioridad) condescending **(b)** (comprensivo) understanding

condición *f* **1** (requisito) condition; **sin condiciones** unconditionally; **a ~** *or* **con la ~ de que** on condition (that); **acepto con una ~** I accept on one condition; **me puso una ~** she made one condition **2 (a)** (calidad, situación): **en su ~ de sacerdote** as a priest; **en su ~ de jefe de la delegación** in his capacity as head of the delegation **(b)** (naturaleza) condition; **la ~ humana** the human condition **3 condiciones** *fpl* **(a)** (estado, circunstancias) conditions (*pl*); **condiciones de trabajo/de vida** working/living conditions; **estar en perfectas condiciones** «*coche/mueble*» to be in perfect condition; «*persona*» to be in good shape; **estar en condiciones de hacer algo** (de ayudar, exigir) to be in a position to do sth; (de correr, viajar, jugar) to be fit to do sth **(b)** (aptitudes) talent; **tener condiciones para algo** (para la música, el arte) to have a talent for sth; (para un trabajo) to be suited for sth

condicional *adj* conditional

condicionar [A1] *vt* **(a)** (determinar) to condition, determine **(b)** (supeditar) **~ algo A algo** to make sth conditional ON sth

condimentar [A1] *vt* to season

condimento *m*: **el comino es un ~** cumin is a condiment; **le falta ~** it needs some seasoning; **los ~s usados en la cocina india** the herbs and spices used in Indian cooking

condominio *m* **(a)** (propiedad) joint ownership, joint control **(b)** (Pol) (territorio) condominium **(c)** (AmL) (edificio) condominium (esp AmE), block of flats (BrE)

condón *m* condom

cóndor *m* condor

conducción *f* **(a)** (Elec, Fís) conduction **(b)** (esp Esp) (Auto) driving **(c)** (AmL) (de programa) presentation; **está a cargo de la ~ del programa** he's in charge of presenting the program **(d)** (Arg) (cúpula) leadership

conducir [I6] *vi* **(a)** (llevar) **~ A algo** «*camino/sendero*» to lead TO sth; **esa actitud no conduce a nada** that attitude won't achieve anything *o* (colloq) won't get us anywhere **(b)** (esp Esp) (Auto) to drive; **~ por la izquierda** to drive on the left ■ **~** *vt* **(a)** (guiar, dirigir) to lead; **~ a algn A algo** to lead sb TO sth; **~ a algn ANTE algn** to take sb BEFORE sb **(b)** (AmL) ‹*programa*› to host, present; ‹*debate*› to chair **(c)** (esp Esp) ‹*vehículo*› to drive **(d)** ‹*electricidad/calor*› to conduct

conducta *f* behavior*, conduct; **mala ~** bad behavior, misconduct (frml)

conducto *m* **(a)** (Anat) duct, tube **(b)** (Tec) (canal, tubo) pipe, tube

conductor[1] **-tora** *adj* conductive; **materiales ~es de la electricidad** materials which conduct electricity ■ *m,f* **(a)** (de vehículo) driver **(b)** (AmL) (de programa) host

conductor[2] *m* (Elec, Fís) conductor

conduje, **condujiste, etc** *see* CONDUCIR

conduzca, **conduzcas, etc** *see* CONDUCIR

conectar [A1] *vt* **(a)** ‹*cables/aparatos*› to connect (up); ‹*luz/gas/teléfono*› to connect **(b)** (relacionar) ‹*hechos/sucesos*› to connect, link **(c)** (AmL) (poner en contacto) **~ a algn CON algn** to put sb in touch *o* in contact WITH sb ■ **~** *vi* **(a)** (Rad, TV) **~ CON algn/algo** to go over TO sb/sth **(b)** (empalmar) to connect, link up **(c)** (llevarse bien, entenderse) to get along *o* on well **(d)** (AmL) **~ CON algo** «*vuelo/tren*» to connect WITH sth; **conectamos con el vuelo a Lima** we took a connecting flight to Lima

conecte *mf* **(a)** (Méx arg) (traficante) (drug) dealer **(b)** (AmC fam) (contacto) friend on the inside (colloq)

conector *m* connector

conejera *f* (madriguera) burrow; (para crianza) (rabbit) hutch

conejillo de Indias *m* guinea pig

conejo -ja *m,f* (Zool) rabbit

conexión *f* **(a)** (Elec) connection; **~ a tierra** ground (AmE), earth (BrE); **~ a la red** connection to the mains **(b)** (relación entre hecho, etc) connection **(c)** (Transp) connection; **perdí la ~ con Roma** I missed my connection to Rome **(d) conexiones** *fpl* (AmL) (amistades) connections (*pl*), contacts (*pl*)

confabularse [A1] *v pron* **~ (CONTRA algn)** to plot *o* conspire (AGAINST sb)

confección *f* **(a)** (de trajes) tailoring; (de vestidos) dressmaking; **industria de la ~** clothing industry; **de ~** ready-to-wear, off-the-peg **(b)** (de lista) drawing-up

confeccionar [A1] *vt* ‹*falda/vestido*› to make (up); ‹*artefactos*› to make; ‹*lista*› to draw up

confederación *f* confederation

conferencia *f* **(a)** (charla — formal) lecture; (— más informal) talk; **dar una ~ SOBRE algo** to give a lecture/talk ON sth **(b)** (reunión) conference; **~ de prensa** press conference **(c)** (Esp) (Telec) long distance call; **poner una ~** to make *o* (AmE) place a long-distance call; **~ a cobro revertido** collect call (AmE), reverse charge call (BrE)

conferenciante, (AmL) **conferencista** *mf* lecturer

conferencista *mf* (AmL) lecturer

confesar [A5] *vt* **(a)** (Relig) ‹*pecado*› to confess; **el cura que la confiesa** the priest who hears her confession **(b)** ‹*sentimiento/ignorancia/delito*› to confess; ‹*error*› to admit ■ **~** *vi* **(a)** (Relig) to hear confession **(b)** (admitir culpabilidad) to confess, make a confession

■ **confesarse** *v pron* **(a)** (Relig) to go to confession; **~se DE algo** to confess sth; **~se CON algn** (Relig) to go to sb for confession; (hacer confidencias) to open up one's heart to sb **(b)** (declararse) (+ *compl*) to confess to being, admit to being

confesión *f* confession

confesionario *m* confessional

confesor *m* confessor

confeti *m* confetti

confiable *adj* (esp AmL) **(a)** ‹*estadísticas*› reliable **(b)** ‹*persona*› (cumplidor) reliable, dependable; (honesto) trustworthy

confiado -da *adj* **(a)** [SER] (crédulo) trusting **(b)** [ESTAR] (seguro): **está muy ~ en que lo van a llevar** he's convinced they're going to take him; **no estés tan ~** don't get over-confident

confianza *f* **(a)** (fe) confidence; **ella me inspira ~** I feel I can trust her; **lo considero digno de toda ~** he has my complete trust; **~ EN algn/algo** confidence IN sb/sth; **tiene ~ en sí misma** she is self-confident; **había puesto toda mi ~ en él** I had put all my trust *o* faith in him; **de ~** ‹*persona*› trustworthy, reliable; ‹*producto*› reliable; ‹*puesto/posición*› of trust; **nombró a alguien de su ~** he appointed someone he trusted **(b)** (intimidad): **tenemos mucha ~** we are close friends; **no les des tanta(s) ~(s)** don't let them be so familiar with you; **estamos en ~** we're among friends; **te lo digo en ~** I'm telling you in confidence; **tratar a algn con ~** to be friendly with sb

confianzudo -da *adj* (esp AmL fam) forward

confiar [A17] *vi* **(a)** (tener fe) **~ EN algn/algo** to trust sb/sth; **no confío en ella** I don't trust her; **confiamos en su discreción** we rely *o* depend on your discretion **(b)** (estar seguro) **~ EN algo** to be confident OF sth; **~ en la victoria** to be confident of victory; **confiamos en poder llevarlo a cabo** we are confident that we can do it; **confiemos en que venga** let's hope she comes ■ **~** *vt* **~le algo A algn** ‹*secreto*› to confide sth TO sb; ‹*trabajo/responsabilidad*› to entrust sb with sth

■ **confiarse** *v pron* **(a)** (hacerse ilusiones) to be overconfident; **no te confíes demasiado** don't get overconfident *o* too confident **(b)** (desahogarse, abrirse) **~se A algn** to confide IN sb

confidencia *f* secret, confidence (frml); **hacer una ~ a algn** to tell sb a secret

confidencial *adj* confidential

confidente *mf* **(a)** (amigo) (*m*) confidant; (*f*) confidante **(b)** (de la policía) informer

confinar [A1] *vt* **~ a algn A algo** ‹*a hospital/a calabozo*› to put sb INTO sth; ‹*a casa*› to confine sb TO sth; ‹*a isla*› to banish sb TO sth; **la parálisis lo confinó a una silla de ruedas** he was confined to a wheelchair because of paralysis

confirmación *f* **1** (de noticia, de boleto) confirmation **2** (Relig) confirmation; **hacer la ~** to be confirmed

confirmar [A1] *vt* to confirm; **la excepción que confirma la regla** the exception that proves the rule

confiscar [A2] *vt* **(a)** ‹*contrabando/armas*› to confiscate, seize **(b)** (para uso del estado) to requisition

confitería *f* **(a)** (tienda) patisserie, cake shop (*also selling sweets*) **(b)** (Bol, RPl) (salón de té) tearoom

confitura *f* preserve, jam

conflictivo -va *adj* **(a)** (problemático) ‹*situación*› difficult; ‹*época*› troubled; **una zona conflictiva** a trouble spot **(b)** (polémico) ‹*tema/persona*› controversial

conflicto *m* **(a)** (enfrentamiento) conflict; **estar en ~** to be in conflict; **entrar en ~ con algn/algo** to come into conflict with sb/sth **(b)** (Psic) conflict **(c)** (apuro) difficult situation

confluir [I20] *vi* **(a)** «*calles/ríos*» to converge, meet; «*corrientes/ideologías*» to come together, merge **(b)** «*grupos/personas*» to congregate, come together

conformar [A1] *vt* **(a)** (contentar) ‹*persona*› to satisfy **(b)** ‹*cheque*› to authorize payment of

■ **conformarse** *v pron* **(a)** (contentarse) **~se CON algo** to be satisfied WITH sth; **no se conforma con nada** he's never satisfied; **tuvo que ~se con lo que tenía** he had to make do with what he had **(b)** (esp AmL) (resignarse): **no tienes más remedio que ~te** you'll just have to accept it *o* to resign yourself to it; **no se puede ~** she can't get over it

conforme *adj* [ESTAR] **(a)** (satisfecho) satisfied, happy; **~ CON algo/algn** satisfied *o* happy WITH sth/sb **(b)** (de acuerdo); **¡~!** agreed!, fine!; **estoy ~ en que se haga así** I agree that it should be done like that; **~ A algo** in accordance WITH sth (frml) **(c)** (en regla) in order ■ *conj* as; **~ se entra, está a mano izquierda** it's on the left as you go in

conformidad *f* **(a)** (aprobación) consent, approval **(b)** (esp AmL) (resignación) resignation

conformista *adj/mf* conformist

confort /kom'for/ *m* comfort; **apartamento todo ~** well-appointed *o* fully equipped apartment

confortable *adj* comfortable

confortar [A1] *vt* to reassure, comfort

confrontación *f* **(a)** (enfrentamiento) confrontation **(b)** (de textos) comparison

confrontar [A1] *vt* **(a)** ‹*textos/versiones*› to compare **(b)** ‹*testigos/equipos*› to bring ... face to face; ‹*ejércitos*› to bring ... into conflict **(c)** ‹*dificultad/peligro*› to confront, face

■ **confrontarse** *v pron* **~se CON algo** to face up to sth

confundir [I1] *vt* **(a)** (por error) ‹*fechas/datos*› to confuse, get ... mixed *o* muddled up; ‹*personas*› to confuse, mix up; **~ algo/algn CON algo/a algn** to mistake sth/sb FOR sth/sb; **me confundió con mi hermana** he mistook me for my sister **(b)** (desconcertar) to confuse **(c)** (turbar) to embarrass

■ **confundirse** *v pron* **(a)** (equivocarse) to make mistakes/a mistake; **me confundí de calle** I got the wrong street **(b)** (desconcertarse) to get confused

confusión *f* **(a)** (en general) confusion; **para que no haya confusiones** to avoid any confusion **(b)** (turbación) embarrassment, confusion

confuso -sa *adj* **(a)** ‹*idea/texto/explicación*› confused; ‹*recuerdo*› confused, hazy; ‹*imagen*› blurred, hazy; ‹*información*› confused **(b)** (turbado) embarrassed, confused

congelado -da *adj* **(a)** ‹*alimentos*› frozen **(b)** (Med) frostbitten; *ver tb* CONGELAR

congelador *m* (en el refrigerador) freezer compartment; (independiente) freezer, deepfreeze

congelar [A1] *vt* to freeze

■ **congelarse** *v pron* **(a)** «*agua/lago*» to freeze **(b)** (Med): **se le congeló el pie** he got frostbite in his foot **(c)** (tener mucho frío) to be freezing; **me estoy congelando** I'm freezing!

congeniar [A1] *vi* to get along (esp AmE), to get on (esp BrE); **~ CON algn** to get along *o* on WITH sb

congénito -ta *adj* congenital

congestión *f* congestion

congestionado -da *adj* **(a)** (Med) congested **(b)** ‹*cara*› flushed **(c)** ‹*calle/área*› congested

congestionarse [A1] *v pron* **(a)** «*cara*» to become flushed **(b)** (Med) to become congested *o* blocked **(c)** «*calle/área*» to become congested

conglomerado *m* conglomeration

conglomerarse [A1] *v pron* to conglomerate

congratular [A1] *vt* (frml) to congratulate; **~ a algn** POR **algo** to congratulate sb ON sth
■ **congratularse** *v pron* **~se** DE *or* POR **algo** (alegrarse) to be pleased ABOUT sth, congratulate oneself ON sth (frml)

congregar [A3] *vt* to bring together
■ **congregarse** *v pron* to assemble, gather

congreso *m* **1** (reunión) conference, congress **2 Congreso** (Gob, Pol) **(a)** (asamblea) Parliament; (in US) Congress; **C~ de los Diputados** (Esp) Chamber of Deputies (*lower chamber of Spanish Parliament*) **(b)** (edificio) Parliament (*o* Congress *etc*) building

congrio *m* (Coc, Zool) conger eel

congruente *adj* (coherente) coherent; **ser ~ con algo** to be consistent with sth

cónico -ca *adj* ‹*pieza/forma*› conical, conic (tech); ‹*sección*› conic

conífera *f* conifer

conjetura *f* conjecture, speculation; **hacer ~s** to surmise, conjecture (frml); **son simples ~s** that's pure conjecture *o* speculation

conjugar [A3] *vt* (Ling) to conjugate

conjunción *f* **(a)** (Ling, Astron) conjunction **(b)** (unión) combination; **en ~ con** in conjunction with

conjuntivitis *f* conjunctivitis

conjunto[1] -ta *adj* ‹*esfuerzo/accion*› joint (*before n*)

conjunto[2] *m* **(a)** (de objetos, obras) collection; (de personas) group; **en su ~** (referido a — obra, exposición) as a whole; (— comité, partido) as a group; **~ residencial** residential complex **(b)** (Mús) *tb* **~ musical** (de música clásica) ensemble; (de música popular) pop group **(c)** (Indum) (de pulóver y chaqueta) twinset; (de prendas en general) outfit; **un ~ de chaqueta y pantalón** matching jacket and trousers; **hacer ~ con algo** to go well with sth **(d)** (Mat) set

conjura, **conjuración** *f* conspiracy, plot

conjurar [A1] *vi* to conspire, plot

conjuro *m* (fórmula mágica) spell

conllevar [A1] *vt* **(a)** (*en 3ª pers*) (comportar, implicar) to entail; **conlleva mucha responsabilidad** it entails a great deal of responsibility **(b)** ‹*desgracia/enfermedad*› to bear ■ **~** *vi* (Ven) **~** A **algo** to lead TO sth

conmemoración *f* commemoration; **en ~ de** in commemoration of

conmemorar [A1] *vt* to commemorate

conmigo *pron pers* with me; **vino ~** she came with me; **estoy furiosa ~ misma** I'm furious with myself; **ha sido muy bueno ~** he's been very good to me

conmoción *f* **(a)** (Med) *tb* **~ cerebral** concussion **(b)** (trastorno, agitación): **la noticia produjo una ~ familiar** the news shocked the whole family **(c)** (Geol) shock

conmocionar [A1] *vt* to shake

conmovedor -dora *adj* moving, touching

conmover [E9] *vt* **(a)** (emocionar) to move **(b)** (inducir a piedad) to move ... to pity
■ **conmoverse** *v pron* (enternecerse, emocionarse) to be moved

conmutar [A1] *vt* (Der) ‹*pena*› to commute

connotación *f* connotation

cono *m* cone; **el C~ Sur** the Southern Cone (*Argentina, Chile, Paraguay and Uruguay*)

conocedor -dora *m,f* connoisseur, expert

conocer [E3] *vt* **1** ‹*persona*› to know; (por primera vez) to meet; ‹*ciudad/país*› to know; **¿conoces a Juan?** do you know *o* have you met Juan?; **te conocía de oídas** he'd heard of you; **lo conozco de nombre** I know the name; **~ a algn de vista** to know sb by sight; **es de todos conocido** he's well known; **quiero que conozcas a mi novio** I want you to meet my boyfriend; **nunca llegué a ~lo bien** I never really got to know him; **¿conoces Irlanda** do you know *o*? have you been to Ireland?; **quiere ~ mundo** she wants to see the world; **me encantaría ~ tu país** I'd love to visit your country **2** (estar familiarizado con, dominar) ‹*tema/autor/obra*› to know, be familiar with; ‹*lengua*› to speak, know **3 (a)** (saber de la existencia de) to know, know of; **conocían sus actividades** they knew of *o* about his activities **(b) dar a ~** (frml) ‹*noticia/resultado*› to announce; ‹*identidad/intenciones*› to reveal; **darse a ~** «*persona*» to make oneself known; **intentó no darse a ~** he tried to keep his identity a secret **4** (reconocer) to recognize*; **te conocí por la voz** I knew it was you by your voice **5** (*impers*) (notar): **se conoce que no están en casa** they don't seem to be in; **se conoce que ya llevaba algún tiempo enfermo** apparently he'd been ill for some time ■ **~** *vi* (saber) **~** DE **algo** ‹*de tema/materia*› to know ABOUT sth
■ **conocerse** *v pron* **1** (*recipr*) (tener cierta relación con) to know each other; (por primera vez) to meet; (aprender cómo se es) to get to know each other **2** (*refl*) **(a)** (aprender cómo se es) to get to know oneself **(b)** (saber cómo se es) to know oneself

conocido -da *adj* **(a)** (famoso) ‹*actor/cantante*› famous, well-known **(b)** ‹*cara/voz*› familiar **(c)** ‹*hecho/nombre*› well-known; **más ~ como** ... better known as ... ■ *m,f* acquaintance

conocimiento *m* **(a)** (saber) knowledge; **tiene algunos ~s de inglés** he has some knowledge of English; **poner algo en ~ de algn** to inform sb of sth; **tener ~ de algo** to be aware of sth **(b)** (sentido) consciousness; **perder/recobrar el ~** to lose/regain consciousness; **estar sin ~** to be unconscious

conozca, **conozco, etc** *see* CONOCER

conque *conj* so; **~ ya lo sabes** so now you know

conquista *f* **(a)** (de territorio, pueblo) conquest; **la C~** (Hist) the Spanish conquest (*of America*) **(b)** (logro) achievement **(c)** (fam) (amorosa) conquest

conquistador -dora *adj* ‹*ejército*› conquering
■ *m,f* **(a)** (Hist) conqueror; (en la conquista de América) conquistador **(b)** (fam) (en el amor) (*m*) lady-killer; (*f*) femme fatale

conquistar [A1] *vt* **(a)** ‹*territorio/pueblo/montaña*› to conquer; ‹*mercado*› to capture **(b)** ‹*victoria/título*› to win; ‹*éxito/fama*› to achieve **(c)** ‹*simpatía/respeto*› to win; ‹*persona/público*› to captivate; ‹*corazón*› to capture; **acabó conquistándola** he won her heart in the end

consagrado -da *adj* **(a)** (Relig) consecrated **(b)** ‹*artista*› acclaimed **(c)** ‹*costumbre/procedimiento*› established

consagrar [A1] *vt* **(a)** (Relig) to consecrate **(b)** **~ algo** A **algo/algn** ‹*monumento/edificio*› to dedicate sth TO sth/sb; ‹*vida/tiempo/esfuerzo*› to dedicate *o* devote sth TO sth/sb; ‹*programa/publicación*› to devote sth TO sth/sb **(c)** (establecer) ‹*artista/profesional*› to establish; **la película que la consagró como actriz** the movie that established her as an actress

■ **consagrarse** *v pron* (*refl*) (dedicarse) **~se** A **algo/algn** to devote oneself TO sth/sb

consciencia *f* ⇨ CONCIENCIA (b)

consciente *adj* **(a)** [ESTAR] (Med) conscious **(b)** (de problema, hecho) **ser** *or* (Chi, Méx) **estar ~** DE **algo** to be aware *o* conscious OF sth **(c)** [SER] (sensato) sensible; (responsable) responsible

conscripto *m* (AmL) conscript

consecuencia *f* consequence; **atenerse a las ~s** to accept the consequences; **esto trajo como ~ su renuncia** this resulted in his resignation; **a ~ de** as a result of; **en ~** (frml) (por consiguiente) consequently, as a result; ‹*actuar/obrar*› accordingly

consecuente *adj* consistent; **hay que ser ~** you have to be consistent; **es ~ con sus ideas** she acts according to her beliefs (*o* principles *etc*)

consecutivo -va *adj* consecutive

conseguir [I30] *vt* ‹*objetivo/fin/resultado*› to achieve, obtain; ‹*entrada/permiso/empleo*› to get; ‹*medalla/título*› to win; **si lo intentas, al final lo ~ás** if you try, you'll succeed in the end; **la película consiguió un gran éxito** the film was a great success; **~ hacer algo** to manage to do sth; **no consigo entenderlo** I can't work it out; **conseguí que me lo prestara** I got him to lend it to me

consejero -ra *m,f* **(a)** (asesor) adviser **(b)** (Adm, Com) director **(c)** (en embajada) counselor*

consejo *m* **(a)** (recomendación) piece of advice; **te voy a dar un ~** let me give you some advice *o* a piece of advice; **me pidió ~** he asked me for advice *o* asked (for) my advice; **sus ~s son siempre acertados** she always gives good advice **(b)** (organismo) council, board; **~ de administración** board of directors; **~ de guerra** court-martial; **~ de ministros** (grupo) cabinet; (reunión) cabinet meeting

consenso *m* consensus; **por ~** by general consent *o* assent

consentido -da *adj* spoiled ■ *m,f*: **es un ~** he's spoiled

consentimiento *m* (autorización) consent

consentir [I11] *vt* **(a)** (permitir, tolerar) to allow; **¡no te consiento que me hables así!** I won't have you speak to me like that; **se lo consienten todo** he's allowed to do whatever he likes **(b)** (mimar) ‹*niño*› to spoil ■ **~** *vi*: **~** EN **algo** to consent *o* agree TO sth

conserje *mf* **(a)** (de establecimiento público) superintendent (AmE), caretaker (BrE) **(b)** (de colegio) custodian (AmE), caretaker (BrE) **(c)** (de hotel) receptionist

conserjería *f* reception

conserva *f*: **latas de ~** cans *o* (BrE) tins of food; **piña en ~** canned *o* (BrE) tinned pineapple

conservación *f* **(a)** (de alimentos) preserving **(b)** (Ecol) conservation **(c)** (de monumentos, obras de arte) preservation

conservador -dora *adj* conservative ■ *m,f* **(a)** (Pol) conservative **(b)** (de museo) curator

conservante *m* preservative

conservar [A1] *vt* **(a)** (mantener, preservar) ‹*alimentos*› to preserve; ‹*sabor/calor*› to retain; ‹*tradiciones/costumbres*› to preserve; ‹*amigo/cargo*› to keep; ‹*naturaleza*› to conserve; **conservo buenos recuerdos suyos** I have good memories of him; **~ la calma** to keep calm; **~ la línea** to keep one's figure **(b)** (guardar) ‹*cartas/fotografías*› to keep

■ **conservarse** *v pron* **(a)** «*alimentos*» to keep **(b)** (perdurar) «*restos/tradiciones*» to survive **(c)** «*persona*» (+ *compl*) to keep; **se conserva joven** she keeps herself young; **está muy bien conservada** she's very well preserved

conservatorio *m* conservatory, conservatoire

considerable *adj* considerable

consideración *f* consideration; **tomar algo en ~** to take sth into consideration *o* account; **por ~ a su familia** out of consideration for his family; **en ~ a sus méritos** in recognition of her merits; **la trataron sin ninguna ~** they treated her most inconsiderately; **¡qué falta de ~!** how thoughtless!; **de ~** serious

considerado -da *adj* [SER] considerate; **ser ~** CON **algn** to be considerate TOWARD(S) sb

considerar [A1] *vt* ‹*asunto/posibilidad/oferta*› to consider; ‹*ventajas/consecuencias*› to weigh up, consider; **considerando que ha estado enfermo** considering (that) he's been ill; **tenemos que ~ que** ... we must take into account that ...; **eso se considera de mala educación** that's considered bad manners; **está muy bien considerado** he is very highly regarded

■ **considerarse** *v pron* «*persona*» (juzgarse) to consider oneself; **se considera afortunado** he considers himself (to be) lucky

consiga, consigas, etc *see* CONSEGUIR

consigna *f* **(a)** (eslogan) slogan **(b)** (para equipaje) baggage room (AmE), left-luggage (office) (BrE); **~ automática** (coin-operated *o* automatic) luggage locker (AmE) *o* (BrE) left-luggage locker

consigo *pron pers* (con él) with him; (con ella) with her; (con uno) with you *o* one; (con usted, ustedes) with you; **no está satisfecho ~ mismo** he's not happy with himself; **traigan ~ todo lo necesario** bring everything you'll need with you; **hablaba ~ misma** she was talking to herself

consigo, consigues, etc *see* CONSEGUIR

consiguiente *adj* resulting (*before n*), consequent (*before n*) (frml); **por ~** consequently

consistencia *f* **(a)** (de mezcla, masa) consistency; **tomar ~** to thicken **(b)** (de teoría, argumento) soundness; **un argumento sin ~** a flimsy argument

consistente *adj* **(a)** ‹*salsa/líquido*› thick; ‹*masa*› solid **(b)** ‹*argumentación/tesis*› sound **(c)** (Andes, Méx) ‹*conducta*› consistent; ‹*persona*› ⇒ CONSECUENTE

consistir [I1] *vi* **(a)** (expresando composición) **~ EN algo** to consist OF sth; **el mobiliario consistía en una cama y una sella** the furniture consisted of a bed and a chair **(b)** (expresando naturaleza): **¿en qué consiste el juego?** what does the game involve?; **~ EN hacer algo** to involve *o* entail doing sth **(c)** (radicar) **~ EN algo** to lie IN sth; **en eso consiste su gracia** that is where its charm lies

consola *f* **(a)** (mueble) console table **(b)** (panel de controles) console

consolar [A10] *vt* to console, comfort; **si en algo te consuela** if it's any consolation to you
■ **consolarse** *v pron* (*refl*): **me consuelo pensando que** ... I take comfort *o* I find some consolation in the thought that ...

consolidar [A1] *vt* **(a)** ‹*situación/posición/acuerdo*› to consolidate; ‹*amistad*› to strengthen **(b)** ‹*deuda/préstamo*› to consolidate
■ **consolidarse** *v pron* «*situación/acuerdo*» to be consolidated; «*amistad/relación*» to grow stronger

consomé *m* consommé

consonante *f* consonant

conspiración *f* conspiracy, plot

conspirador -dora *m,f* conspirator

conspirar [A1] *vi* to conspire, plot

constancia *f* **1** (perseverancia) perseverance **2** (prueba) proof; **dejar ~ DE algo** (en registro, acta) to record sth (in writing); (verbalmente) to state sth; (atestiguar) to prove sth

constante *adj* **(a)** (continuo) constant **(b)** (perseverante) ‹*persona*› persevering ■ *f* **(a)** (Mat) constant **(b)** (característica) constant feature **(c) constantes** *fpl* (Med) *tb* **~s vitales** vital signs (*pl*)

constar [A1] *vi* **(a)** (figurar) **~ EN algo** ‹*en acta/documento*› to be stated *o* recorded IN sth; ‹*en archivo/catálogo*› to be listed IN sth; ‹*en libro/texto*› to appear IN sth **(b)** (quedar claro): **(que) conste que yo no fui** it certainly wasn't me; **yo nunca dije eso, que conste** just to set the record straight, I never actually said that; **eso me consta** I am sure of that **(c) hacer ~ algo** (manifestar) to state sth; (por escrito) to register sth, to put sth on record **(d)** (estar compuesto de) **~ DE algo** to consist OF sth

constelación *f* constellation

consternación *f* consternation, dismay

consternar [A1] *vt* to fill ... with dismay

constipación *f* (esp AmL) constipation

constipado[1] -da *adj* **(a)** (resfriado) **está muy ~** he has a bad cold **(b)** (AmL) (estreñido) constipated

constipado[2] *m* cold

constiparse [A1] *v pron* to catch a cold

constitución *f* **(a)** (establecimiento) setting-up **(b)** (Pol) (de país) constitution **(c)** (complexión) constitution; **un hombre de ~ fuerte** a man with a strong constitution

constitucional *adj* constitutional

constituir [I20] *vt* (frml) **(a)** (componer, formar) to make up, constitute (frml) **(b)** (ser, representar) to represent, constitute (frml); **esta acción no constituye delito** this action does not constitute a crime **(c)** (crear) ‹*comisión/compañía*› to set up, establish

construcción *f* **(a)** (acción) construction, building; **en ~** under construction; **obrero de la ~** building *o* construction worker **(b)** (edificio, estructura) construction **(c)** (Ling) construction

constructivo -va *adj* constructive

constructor -tora *m,f* **(a)** (Const) builder, building contractor **(b) constructora** *f* construction company, building firm

construir [I20] *vt* **(a)** ‹*edificio/barco/sociedad*› to build **(b)** ‹*figura/frases/oraciones*› to construct

construya, etc *see* CONSTRUIR

consuegro -gra *m,f* (*m*) *father-in-law of one's son or daughter*; (*f*) *mother-in-law of one's son or daughter*

consuelo *m* consolation, comfort

cónsul *mf* consul

consulado *m* (oficina) consulate; (cargo) consulship

consulta *f* **(a)** (pregunta, averiguación): **¿te puedo hacer una ~?** can I ask you something?; **de ~** ‹*biblioteca/libro*› reference (*before n*) **(b)** (Med) (entrevista) consultation; (consultorio) office (AmE), practice (AmE), surgery (BrE); **¿a qué horas tiene ~s el Dr. Sosa?** what are Dr Sosa's office hours (AmE) *o* (BrE) surgery times?; **~ a domicilio** home *o* house visit

consultar [A1] *vt* ‹*persona/obra*› to consult; ‹*dato/duda*› to look up; **~ algo CON algn** to consult sb ABOUT sth ■ **~** *vi:* **~ CON algn** to consult sb

consultor -tora *m,f* consultant

consultorio *m* **(a)** (de médico, dentista) office (AmE), practice (AmE), surgery (BrE); (de abogado) office **(b)** (consultoría) consultancy; **~ sentimental** (en revista) problem page; (en la radio) phone-in (*about personal problems*)

consumición *f* (esp Esp) (bebida) drink; **~ mínima** minimum charge

consumido -da *adj* [ESTAR] (por enfermedad, hambre) emaciated; *ver tb* CONSUMIR

consumidor -dora *m,f* consumer

consumir [I1] *vt* **(a)** (frml) ‹*comida/bebida*› to eat/drink, consume (frml) **(b)** ‹*gasolina/energía/producto*› to consume, use; ‹*tiempo*› to take up **(c)** ‹*salud*› to ruin **(d)** (destruir) «*fuego/llamas*» to consume; «*envidia/celos*»: **la envidia la consumían** she was consumed by *o* with envy
■ **consumirse** *v pron* **(a)** «*enfermo/anciano*» to waste away; **se consumía de pena** she was being consumed by grief **(b)** «*vela/cigarrillo*» to burn down **(c)** «*líquido*» to reduce

consumismo *m* consumerism

consumo *m* consumption; **~ mínimo** (AmL) minimum charge

contabilidad *f* **(a)** (ciencia) accounting **(b)** (profesión) accountancy **(c)** (cuentas) accounts (*pl*), books (*pl*); **lleva la ~** she does the accounts *o* the books

contabilizar [A4] *vt* (en contabilidad) to enter; (contar) to count

contable *mf* (Esp) accountant

contactar [A1] *vi* **~ CON algn** to contact sb, get in touch WITH sb ■ **~** *vt* to contact

contacto *m* **(a)** (entre dos cuerpos) contact; **entrar en ~** to come into contact; **hacer ~** to make contact **(b)** (comunicación) contact; **estar/ponerse en ~ con algn** to be/get in touch *o* contact with sb **(c)** (entrevista, reunión) encounter **(d)** (persona, conocido) contact **(e)** (Auto) ignition **(f)** (Méx) (Elec) socket, power point

contado[1] -da *adj* few; **en contadas ocasiones** on (a) very few occasions; **salimos con los minutos ~s** we left with only a few minutes to spare

contado[2] *m* **(a) al ~** *or* (Col) **de ~** ‹*pago/precio*› cash (*before n*); ‹*pagar*› (in) cash; **lo compré al ~** I paid cash for it, I paid for it in cash **(b)** (Col) (cuota, plazo) installment*

contador[1] *m* **(a)** (de luz, de gas) meter; (taxímetro) meter, taximeter **(b)** (AmL) (ábaco) abacus

contador[2] -dora *m,f* (AmL) accountant; **~ público** (AmL) certified public (AmE) *o* (BrE) chartered accountant

contagiar [A1] *vt* ‹*enfermedad*› to pass on, transmit (tech); **me contagió la gripe** she passed her flu on to me; **no te acerques que te voy a ~** don't come near or I'll give it to you

■ **contagiarse** *v pron* **(a)** «*persona/animal*» to become infected; **se ha contagiado de mí** she has caught it from me **(b)** «*enfermedad*» to be transmitted; «*manía/miedo*» to spread; **se contagia con facilidad** it is very contagious

contagioso -sa *adj* **(a)** (por contacto — directo) contagious; (— indirecto) infectious **(b)** ‹*risa/alegría*› infectious

contaminación *f* (del mar, aire) pollution; (de agua potable, comida) contamination; (por radiactividad) contamination; **~ acústica** noise pollution

contaminar [A1] *vt* ‹*mar/atmósfera*› to pollute; ‹*agua potable/comida*› to contaminate; (por radiactividad) to contaminate

contar [A10] *vt* **1** ‹*dinero/votos/días*› to count; **eran 6 sin ~ al conductor** there were 6 of them not counting the driver; **y eso sin ~ las horas extras** and that's without including overtime; **lo cuento entre mis amigos** I consider him (to be) one of my friends **2** ‹*cuento/chiste/secreto*› to tell; **no se lo cuentes a nadie** don't tell anyone; **es muy largo de ~** it's a long story; **¿qué cuentas (de nuevo)?** (fam) how're things? (colloq) ■ **~** *vi* **1** (en general) to count; **~ con los dedos** to count on one's fingers; **¿este trabajo cuenta para la nota final?** does this piece of work count toward(s) the final grade?; **ella no cuenta para nada** what she says (*o* thinks *etc*) doesn't count for anything **2** **contar con (a)** ‹*persona/ayuda/discreción*› to count on, rely on; **cuento contigo para la fiesta** I'm counting *o* relying on you being at the party; **sin ~ con que** ... without taking into account that ... **(b)** (prever) to expect; **no contaba con que hiciera tan mal tiempo** I wasn't expecting the weather to be so bad **(c)** (frml) (tener) to have; **cuenta con 10 años de experiencia** she has 10 years of experience

■ **contarse** *v pron* **(a)** (frml) (estar incluido): **me cuento entre sus partidarios** I count myself as one of their supporters; **su novela se cuenta entre las mejores** his novel is among the best **(b)** **¿qué te cuentas?** how's it going? (colloq)

contemplación *f* **1** (observación) contemplation **2 contemplaciones** *fpl* (miramientos): **tienes demasiadas contemplaciones con él** you're too soft on him; **lo echaron sin contemplaciones** they threw him out without ceremony

contemplar [A1] *vt* **(a)** ‹*paisaje/cuadro*› to gaze at, contemplate **(b)** ‹*posibilidad/idea*› to consider, contemplate

contemporáneo -nea *adj* contemporary; **ser ~ DE algn** to be a contemporary OF sb, be contemporary WITH sb ■ *m,f* contemporary

contenedor *m* container; (para basuras) bin, container; (para escombros) Dumpster® (AmE), skip (BrE); **~ de recogida de vidrio** bottle bank

contener [E27] *vt* **(a)** «*recipiente/producto/libro*» to contain **(b)** (parar, controlar) ‹*infección/epidemia*› to contain; ‹*tendencia*› to curb; ‹*respiración*› to hold; ‹*risa/lágrimas*› to contain (frml), to hold back; ‹*invasión/revuelta*› to contain

■ **contenerse** *v pron* (*refl*) to contain oneself; **no se pudo ~ más** he could contain himself no longer

contenido *m* (de recipiente, producto, mezcla) contents; (de libro, carta) content

contentar [A1] *vt* to please; **¡qué difícil de ~ eres!** you're so hard to please!

■ **contentarse** *v pron* **~se CON algo** to be satisfied WITH sth; **se contenta con muy poco** he's easy to please

contento -ta *adj* [ESTAR] **(a)** (feliz, alegre) happy; **se puso muy ~ al oír que venías** he was very happy to hear you were coming; **~ CON algo/algn** happy WITH sth/sb **(b)** (satisfecho) pleased; **estamos ~s con la nueva secretaria** we're pleased with the new secretary; **no ~ con que le prestara el coche** ... not content *o* satisfied with me lending him the car ...

conteo *m* (Andes, Ven) count

contestación *f* (respuesta) answer, reply

contestador -dora *adj* (CS fam) ⇒ CONTESTÓN

contestador automático *m* answering machine

contestar [A1] *vt* ‹*pregunta/teléfono*› to answer; ‹*carta*› to answer, reply to; **me contestó que no** he said no ■ **~** *vi* **(a)** (a pregunta, al teléfono) to answer; (a carta, a invitación) to answer, reply; **no contesta nadie** (Telec) there's no answer **(b)** (insolentarse) to answer back

contestón -tona *adj* (fam): **es muy ~** he's always answering back

contexto *m* context

contigo *pron pers* with you; **¿puedo ir ~?** can I go with you?; **en paz ~ misma** at peace with yourself; **ha sido muy amable ~** she's been very kind to you

contiguo -gua *adj* adjoining

continental *adj* continental

continente *m* (Geog) continent

continuación *f* **(a)** (acción) continuation **(b)** (de calle) continuation **(c)** (de novela) sequel; (de serie) next part *o* episode **(d) a continuación** next, then; **a ~ de** after, following

continuamente *adv* (con frecuencia, repetidamente) continually, constantly; (sin interrupción) continuously

continuar [A18] *vt* to continue ■ ~ *vi* «*guerra/espectáculo/vida*» to continue; **si las cosas continúan así** if things go on *o* continue like this; Ⓢ **continuará** to be continued; **la película continúa en cartelera** the movie is still showing; ~ CON **algo** to continue WITH sth; **continuó diciendo que** ... she went on to say that ...

continuidad *f* continuity

continuo -nua *adj* **(a)** (sin interrupción) ‹*dolor*› constant; ‹*movimiento/sonido*› continuous, constant; ‹*lucha*› continual **(b)** (frecuente) ‹*llamadas/viajes*› continual, constant

contonearse [A1] *v pron* to swing one's hips

contorno *m* **(a)** (forma) outline **(b)** (de árbol, columna) girth; **medir el ~ de cintura** to take the waist measurement **(c)** (de ciudad) surrounding area

contorsión *f* contortion; **hacer contorsiones** to contort one's body

contorsionista *mf* contortionist

contra *prep* against; **lo puso ~ la pared** he put it against the wall; **nos estrellamos ~ un árbol** we crashed into a tree; **dos ~ uno** two against one; **yo estoy en ~** I'm against it; **40 votos en ~** 40 votes against; **en ~ de** (opuesto a) against; (contrariamente a) contrary to ■ *f* **(a)** (esp AmL fam) (dificultad) snag; ***llevarle la ~ a algn*** to contradict sb **(b)** (Col) (antídoto) antidote **(c)** (Pol, Hist) (grupo): **la ~** the Contras (*pl*) ■ *mf* (individuo) Contra rebel ■ *m* ⇒ PRO

contraatacar [A2] *vi* to counterattack

contraataque *m* counterattack

contrabajo *m* (instrumento) double bass; (cantante) basso profundo ■ *mf* double-bass player

contrabandista *mf* smuggler

contrabando *m* **(a)** (actividad) smuggling; **~ de armas** gunrunning; **pasaba relojes de ~** he smuggled watches **(b)** (mercancías) smuggled goods (*pl*), contraband

contracción *f* contraction

contracorriente *f* crosscurrent; ***ir a ~*** «*barco*» to go against the current; «*nadador*» to swim against the current; «*diseñador/escritor*» to go *o* swim against the tide

contradecir [I24] *vt* ‹*persona/argumento*› to contradict

■ **contradecirse** *v pron* **(a)** «*persona*» to contradict oneself **(b)** (*recipr*) «*afirmaciones/órdenes*» to contradict each other, be contradictory; **~se** CON **algo** to conflict WITH sth, contradict sth

contradicción *f* contradiction; **eso está en ~ con lo que predica** that is a contradiction of what he advocates

contradictorio -ria *adj* contradictory

contraer [E23] *vt* **1** (frml) **(a)** ‹*enfermedad*› to contract (frml), to catch **(b)** ‹*obligación/deudas*› to contract (frml); ‹*compromiso*› to make; **~ matrimonio con algn** to marry sb **2 (a)** ‹*músculo*› to contract, tighten; ‹*facciones/cara*› to contort **(b)** ‹*metal/material*› to cause ... to contract

■ **contraerse** *v pron* to contract

contrafuerte *m* (Arquit) buttress

contraincendios *adj inv* fire-prevention (*before n*)

contraindicado -da *adj* ‹*remedio/preparado*› contraindicated (tech)

contralto *m,f* (*f*) (en coro) alto; (solista) contralto; (*m*) countertenor

contraluz *m or f* back light; **a ~** against the light

contramano: **el coche venía a ~** (en calle de dirección única) the car was coming the wrong way down the street; (por el lado contrario) the car was on the wrong side of the road

contraofensiva *f* counteroffensive

contraparte *f* (Andes) opposing party

contrapartida *f* **(a)** (compensación) compensation; (contraste) contrast; **como ~** in contrast **(b)** (Com) balancing entry

contrapelo: **cepillar a ~** ‹*tela*› to brush ... against the nap; ‹*pelo*› to brush ... the wrong way

contrapeso *m* (del ascensor) counterweight; (de equilibrista) balancing pole; **siéntate al otro lado para hacer ~** sit on the other side to balance it

contraportada *f* (de libro, revista) back cover; (de periódico) back page

contraposición *f* comparison; **en ~ a** *or* **con algo** in comparison to *o* with sth

contraproducente *adj* counterproductive

contrapunto *m* counterpoint

contrariado -da *adj* (disgustado) upset; (enojado) annoyed

contrariar [A17] *vt* (disgustar) to upset; (enojar) to annoy

contrariedad *f* **(a)** (dificultad, problema) setback, hitch; **nos surgió una ~** something came up; **¡qué ~!** how annoying! **(b)** (disgusto) annoyance, vexation (frml)

contrario -ria *adj* **1** (opuesto) ‹*opiniones/intereses*› conflicting; ‹*dirección/lado*› opposite; ‹*equipo*› opposing; ‹*bando*› opposite; **yo pienso lo ~** I think the opposite; **mientras no se demuestre lo ~** until proven otherwise; **sería ~ a mis intereses** it would be against *o* (frml) contrary to my interests; ⇒ SENTIDO *m* 4 **2** (*en locs*) **al contrario** on the contrary; **al ~ de su hermano** ... unlike his brother, ...; **de lo contrario** or else, otherwise; **por el contrario** on the contrary; **en el sur, por el ~, el clima es seco** the south, on the other hand, has a dry climate; **todo lo contrario** quite the opposite; ***llevarle la contraria a algn*** to contradict sb ■ *m,f* opponent

contrarreloj *adj* ‹*carrera/etapa*› timed; **a ~** against the clock

contrarrestar [A1] *vt* to counteract

contrasentido *m* contradiction in terms

contraseña *f* (Mil) watchword, password; (Teatr, Cin) stub

contrastar [A1] *vi* **~** CON **algo** to contrast WITH sth ■ **~** *vt* **~ algo** CON **algo** to contrast sth WITH sth

contraste *m* contrast; **hacer ~ con algo** to contrast with sth; **en ~ con algo** in contrast to sth

contrata *f* contract

contratar [A1] *vt* **(a)** ‹*empleado/obrero*› to hire, take on; ‹*artista/deportista*› to sign up; ‹*servicios*› to contract **(b)** (Const) ‹*ejecución de una obra*› to put ... out to contract

contratiempo *m* (problema) setback, hitch; (accidente) mishap; **sufrir** *or* **tener un ~** to have a setback/a mishap

contratista *mf* contractor

contrato *m* contract; **~ de alquiler** rental agreement; **~ de compraventa/de trabajo** contract of sale and purchase/of employment

contravenir [I31] *vt* to contravene

contraventana *f* shutter

contravía (Col): **ir en ~** to drive the wrong way down the road; **un carro que venía en ~** an oncoming car

contribución *f* (colaboración, donación) contribution; (Fisco) tax

contribuir [I20] *vi* **(a)** (en general) to contribute; **contribuyó con 100 pesetas** he contributed 100 pesetas; **~** A **algo** to contribute TO sth **(b)** (Fisco) to pay taxes

contribuyente *mf* taxpayer

contrincante *mf* opponent

control *m* **1** (en general) control; **bajo ~** under control; **sin ~** out of control; **perdí el ~** I lost control (of myself); **hacerse con el ~ de algo** to gain control of sth; **lleva el ~ de los gastos** she keeps a check on the money that is spent; **~ de (la) natalidad** birth control; **~ de calidad** quality control *o* check; **~ de pasaportes** passport control; **~ remoto** remote control **2** (en carretera, rally) checkpoint **3 (a)** (Educ) test **(b)** (Med) check-up; **~ antidoping** dope test, drug test

controlador -dora *m,f* controller; **~ aéreo** *or* **de vuelo** air traffic controller

controlar [A1] *vt* **1** ‹*nervios/impulsos/persona*› to control; ‹*incendio*› to bring ... under control; **controlamos la situación** we are in control of the situation; **pasaron a ~ la empresa** they took control of the company **2** ‹*inflación/proceso*› to monitor; ‹*persona*› to keep a check on; **~ el peso/la línea** to watch one's weight/one's waistline; **controlé el tiempo que me llevó** I timed how long it took me **3** (regular) ‹*presión/inflación*› to control

■ **controlarse** *v pron* (dominarse) to control oneself; (vigilar) ‹*peso/colesterol*› to check, monitor

controversia *f* controversy

controversial *adj* (Ven) ⇒ CONTROVERTIDO

controvertido -da *adj* [SER] ‹*persona/tema*› controversial

contundente *adj* **(a)** ‹*objeto/instrumento*› blunt; ‹*golpe*› severe, heavy **(b)** ‹*argumento/respuesta*› forceful; ‹*prueba*› convincing; ‹*fracaso/victoria*› resounding (*before n*); **fue ~ en sus declaraciones** he was categorical in his statements

conurbano *m* (Arg): **el ~** the suburbs (*pl*)

convalecencia *f* convalescence

convaleciente *adj* convalescent

convalidar [A1] *vt* ‹*estudios/título*› to validate, recognize

convencer [E2] *vt* **(a)** (de hecho, idea) to convince; **no se dejó ~** she wouldn't be convinced; **la convencí de que estaba equivocada** I convinced her that she was wrong **(b)** (para hacer algo) to persuade; **no pude ~lo de que** *or* **para que me prestara dinero** I couldn't persuade him to lend me any money **(c)** (*en frases negativas*) (satisfacer): **no me convence del todo la idea** I'm not absolutely sure about the idea; **su explicación no convenció a nadie** his explanation wasn't at all convincing

■ **convencerse** *v pron* to be convinced; **¿te convenciste?** are you convinced?; **~se** DE **algo** to accept sth; **¿te convences de que tenía razón?** do you believe *o* accept I was right?

convención *f* convention

convencional *adj* conventional

convenenciero -ra *m,f* (Méx fam) user (colloq)

convenible *adj* ‹*solución*› suitable; ‹*precio*› reasonable

conveniencia *f* **(a)** (interés, provecho): **sólo piensa en su propia ~** he only thinks of his own interests; **lo hizo por ~** she only did it because it was in her own interest; **se casó por ~** it was a marriage of convenience **(b)** (de proyecto, acción) advisability

conveniente *adj* **(a)** (cómodo) convenient **(b)** (aconsejable, provechoso) advisable; **sería ~ que guardaras cama** it would be advisable for you to stay in bed

convenio *m* agreement

convenir [I31] *vi* **1 (a)** (ser aconsejable): **no conviene que nos vean juntos** we'd better not be seen together; **convendría que descansaras** it would be a good idea if you rest; **no te conviene venderlo** it's not worth your while selling it; **no le conviene que eso se sepa** it's not in his interest for anybody to know that **(b)** (venir bien): **el jueves no me conviene** Thursday's no good for me; **te convendría tomarte unas vacaciones** it would do you good to take a vacation **2** (acordar) **~** EN **algo** ‹*en fecha/precio*› to agree (ON) sth ■ **~** *vt* ‹*precio/fecha*› to agree (on); **a la hora convenida** at the agreed *o* (frml) appointed time

conventillo *m* (CS) tenement; **esta oficina es un ~** (fam) this office is a hotbed of gossip

convento *m* convent

convergente *adj* convergent

conversación *f* **(a)** (charla) conversation; **trabar ~ con algn** to strike up a conversation with sb; **no tiene ~** she has no conversation **(b) conversaciones** *fpl* (negociaciones) talks (*pl*)

conversador -dora *adj* chatty ■ *m,f* conversationalist

conversar [A1] *vi* **(a)** (hablar) to talk **(b)** (esp AmL) (charlar) to chat, gab (AmE colloq); **conversé largo rato con ella** I had a long talk *o* chat with her

conversión *f* conversion

convertible *m* (AmL) convertible

convertir [I11] *vt* **1 (a)** (transformar) **~ algo/a algn EN algo** to turn sth/sb INTO sth **(b)** (a una religión) to convert; **~ a algn A algo** to convert sb TO sth **(c)** ‹*medida/peso*› **~ algo A algo** *or* (Esp) **EN algo** to convert sth INTO sth **2** (period) (Dep) to score ■ **convertirse** *v pron* **(a)** (transformarse) **~se EN algo** to turn INTO sth **(b)** (a una religión) to convert, be converted; **~se A algo** to convert TO sth

convicción *f* **(a)** (convencimiento) conviction; **tengo la ~ de que lo sabe** I'm certain *o* convinced he knows it **(b)** (persuasión) persuasion; **poder de ~** powers of persuasion **(c) convicciones** *fpl* (ideas, creencias) convictions (*pl*)

convicto -ta *m,f* prisoner, convict

convidado -da *m,f* guest

convidar [A1] *vt* **(a)** (invitar) to invite; **~ a algn A algo** ‹*a una boda/fiesta*› to invite sb TO sth; **nos ~on a unas copas** they invited us for a few drinks; **~ a algn a cenar** to invite sb to *o* for dinner **(b)** (AmL) (ofrecer) to offer; **~ a algn CON algo** *or* (Chi, Méx) **~ algo A algn** to offer sth TO sb, offer sb sth

convincente *adj* convincing

convivencia *f* (de etnias, sectas) coexistence; (de individuos): **la ~ pone el amor a prueba** living together puts love to the test

convivir [I1] *vi* «*personas*» to live together; «*ideologías/etnias*» to coexist; **~ CON algn** to live WITH sb

convocar [A2] *vt* ‹*huelga/elecciones*› to call; ‹*manifestación*› to organize; ‹*concurso/certamen*› to announce; ‹*reunión/asamblea*› to call, convene (frml); **~ a algn A algo** to summon sb TO sth

convocatoria *f* **(a)** (llamamiento a huelga, elecciones) call; **la ~ de huelga** the strike call **(b)** (anuncio — para una reunión) notification; (— de exámenes, concursos) official announcement **(c)** (Esp) (Educ) (período de exámenes): **la ~ de junio** the June exams

convoy *m* (de barcos, camiones) convoy; (Ferr) (period) train

convulsión *f* (Med) convulsion

convulsionar [A1] *vt* to throw ... into confusion

conyugal *adj* (frml) marital, conjugal (frml); **problemas ~es** marital problems

cónyuge *mf* (frml) spouse (frml); **los ~s** the married couple

coñac, coñá *m* brandy, cognac

coñazo *m* **(a)** (Esp fam *o* vulg) (persona o cosa pesada) pain (in the neck) (colloq); ***dar el ~*** (fam) to be a pain (colloq) **(b)** (Col, Ven fam) (golpe) blow

coño *m* (vulg) (de la mujer) cunt (vulg), beaver (AmE sl), fanny (BrE sl)

cooperación *f* cooperation

cooperador -dora *adj* cooperative, helpful

cooperar [A1] *vi* to cooperate; **~ CON algn** to cooperate WITH sb; **~ en la lucha contra el cáncer** to work together in the fight against cancer

cooperativa *f* (asociación) cooperative; (tienda) company store

coordinación *f* coordination

coordinado -da *adj* coordinate

coordinador -dora *m,f* **(a)** (organizador) coordinator **(b) coordinadora** *f* coordinating committee

coordinar [A1] *vt* ‹*movimientos/actividades/ropa*› to coordinate; **no lograba ~ las ideas** he couldn't speak/think coherently ■ **~** *vi* «*colores*» to match, go together

copa *f* **1 (a)** (para vino) glass (*with a stem*); (para postres) parfait dish; (para helado) sundae dish; **~ de champán/coñac** champagne/brandy glass; **~ de vino** wineglass **(b)** (contenido) drink; **vamos a tomar una(s) ~(s)** let's go for a drink **2** (Dep) cup **3 (a)** (de árbol) top, crown **(b)** (de un sostén) cup **(c)** (de sombrero) crown **4 copas** *fpl* (en naipes) *one of the suits in a Spanish pack of cards*

Copenhague *m* Copenhagen

copera *f* (AmS) hostess

coperacha *f* (Méx fam) (recaudación) kitty (colloq), collection; (contribución) contribution; **hacer una ~** to get up a collection (AmE colloq), to have a whip round (BrE colloq)

copetín *m* (RPl) aperitif

copia *f* copy; **saqué dos ~s** I made two copies

copiadora *f* photocopier, copier

copiar [A1] *vt* to copy; **copió el artículo a máquina** he typed out a copy of the article; **le copia todo al hermano** he copies his brother in everything; **le copié la respuesta a Ana** I copied the answer from Ana ■ **~** *vi* to copy

copihue *m* Chile-bells (*national flower of Chile*)

copiloto *mf* (Aviac) copilot; (Auto) co-driver

copión -piona *m,f* (fam) copycat (colloq)

copioso -sa *adj* ‹*cosecha/comida*› abundant, plentiful; ‹*nevada/lluvia*› heavy; ‹*información/ejemplos*› copious; ‹*llamadas*› numerous

copla *f* **(a)** (Lit) stanza **(b)** (Mús) popular folk song

copo *m* (de nieve) flake, snowflake; (de algodón) ball; **~s de avena** *mpl* rolled oats (*pl*); **~s de maíz** *mpl* cornflakes (*pl*)

coproducción *f* coproduction, joint production

copucha *f* (Chi fam) (rumor, chisme) rumor*; (curiosidad) nosiness (colloq)

copuchar [A1] *vi* (Chi fam) (conversar) to chat (colloq); (curiosear) to nose around (colloq)

cópula *f* **(a)** (Biol, Zool) copulation **(b)** (Ling) copula

copular [A1] *vi* to copulate

copulativo -va *adj* copulative

copyright /kopi'rraj(t)/ *m* (*pl* **-rights**) copyright

coqueta *f* **(a)** (chica que flirtea) flirt, coquette (liter); (presumida) vain girl/woman; **eres una ~** you are so vain **(b)** (mueble) dressing table

coquetear [A1] *vi* to flirt; **~ CON algn** to flirt WITH sb

coqueto -ta *adj* **(a)** (en el arreglo personal): **es muy coqueta** she's very concerned about her appearance **(b)**‹*casa/dormitorio*› cute, sweet **(c)** ‹*sonrisa/mirada/mujer*› flirtatious, coquettish (liter)

coraje *m* **(a)** (valor) courage **(b)** (fam) (desfachatez) nerve; **¡qué ~!** what a lot of nerve! (AmE), what a nerve! (BrE)

coral *adj* **▶ 97** choral ■ *m* (Zool) coral; **color ~** coral (*before n*), coral-colored* ■ *f* (Mús) (coro) choir

Corán *m*: **el ~** the Koran

coraza *f* **(a)** (armadura) cuirasse **(b)** (de tortuga) shell

corazón *m* **1 (a) ▶ 123** (en general) heart; **sufre del ~** she has heart trouble; **es un hombre de buen/gran~** he's very kind-hearted/big-hearted; **no tener ~** to be heartless (colloq); **con todo mi ~** with all my heart; **de (todo) ~** sincerely; **le partió el ~** it broke her heart; ***tener un ~ de oro/de piedra*** to have a heart of gold/of stone **(b)** (apelativo cariñoso) (fam) sweetheart (colloq) **2 (a)** (de manzana, pera) core; (de alcachofa) heart **(b)** (de ciudad, área) heart **3** (en naipes) **(a)** (carta) heart **(b) corazones** *mpl* (palo) hearts (*pl*)

corazonada *f* hunch; **tuve la ~ de que ibas a venir** I had a hunch *o* feeling you'd come

corbata *f* (Indum) tie, necktie (AmE); **hay que ir de ~** you have to wear a tie; **~ de lazo** *or* (AmL) **de moño** *or* (Chi) **de humita** bow tie

corbatín *m* bow tie

corchete *m* **(a)** (Impr) square bracket **(b)** (en costura) hook and eye **(c)** (Chi) (para sujetar papeles) staple

corchetear [A1] *vt* (Chi) to staple

corchetera *f* (Chi) stapler

corcho *m* cork; (para pescar, nadar) float

corcholata *f* (Méx) bottle top

corcovear [A1] *vi* to buck

cordel *m* **(a)** (fino) cord, string **(b)** (Chi) (cuerda) rope; **saltar al ~** to jump rope (AmE), to skip (BrE)

cordero *m* **(a)** (cría) lamb **(b)** (carne — de cordero) lamb; (— de oveja) mutton **(c)** (piel) lambskin **(d)** (fam) (persona dócil): **ser un corderito** to be as good as gold

corderoy *m* (AmS) corduroy

cordial *adj* (frml) (amistoso) cordial, friendly; ‹*ambiente*› congenial; **recibe un ~ saludo** (Corresp) (kindest) regards

cordialidad *f* (frml) cordiality

cordillera *f* (mountain) range; **la ~ de los Andes** the Andes

cordillerano -na *adj* (AmL) Andean, mountain (*before n*)

córdoba *m* cordoba (*Nicaraguan unit of currency*)

cordón *m* **1 (a)** (cuerda) cord; **~ umbilical** umbilical cord **(b)** (de zapatos) shoelace, lace **(c)** (Elec) cord **(d)** (de personas) cordon; **~ policial** police cordon **2 (a)** (CS) (de cerros) chain **(b)** (RPl) (de la vereda) curb (AmE), kerb (BrE)

cordura *f* (Psic) sanity; (sensatez) good sense; **obrar con ~** to act sensibly

Corea *f* Korea

coreano -na *adj/m,f* Korean

corear [A1] *vt* ‹*consignas/insultos*› to chant, chorus; ‹*marcha/estrofa*› to sing ... in unison

coreografía *f* choreography

coreógrafo -fa *m,f* choreographer

corista *f* (en revista musical) chorus girl

cornada *f* (golpe) thrust (*with the horns*); (herida) wound (*caused by a bull's horn*); **darle una ~ a algn** to gore sb

córnea *f* cornea

córner *m* (*pl* **-ners**) corner (kick); **lanzar un ~** to take a corner

corneta *f* **(a)** (Mús) (sin llaves) bugle; (con llaves) cornet **(b)** (Ven) (Auto) horn

cornetista *mf* (de corneta sin llaves) bugler; (de corneta con llaves) cornet player

cornisa *f* (Arquit) cornice

corno *m* (Mús) horn; **~ inglés** English horn (AmE), cor anglais (BrE)

cornudo -da *m,f* (fam) (*m*) deceived husband; (*f*) deceived wife

coro *m* **(a)** (conjunto vocal) choir; (en revista musical) chorus line; **a ~** ‹*repetir*› together, in unison; ‹*cantar*› in chorus, together **(b)** (composición) chorus **(c)** (Arquit) choir

corola *f* corolla

corona *f* **1 (a)** (de soberano) crown **(b)** (institución): **la ~** the Crown **(c)** (de flores) crown, wreath; (para funerales) wreath **2** (moneda) crown **3** (Odont) crown

coronación *f* **(a)** (de soberano) coronation **(b)** (culminación) culmination

coronar [A1] *vt* **(a)** ‹*soberano*› to crown; **lo ~on rey** he was crowned king **(b)** ‹*montaña/cima*› to reach the top of **(c)** (en damas) to crown

coronel -nela *m,f* (en el ejército) colonel; (en las fuerzas aéreas) ≈ Colonel (*in US*), ≈ Group Captain (*in UK*)

coronilla *f* crown (of the head); ***estar hasta la ~ (de algo/algn)*** (fam) to be fed up to the back teeth (with sth/sb) (colloq)

coronta *f* (Chi, Per) *tb* **~ de choclo** *stripped corn cob*

coroto *m* **(a)** (Col, Ven fam) (trasto) piece of junk (colloq); **recoge tus ~s** get your things *o* stuff together **(b)** (Ven) (poder político) (political) power

corpiño *m* (chaleco) bodice; (del vestido) bodice; (prenda interior) (RPl) brassière

corporación *f* (Com, Fin) corporation

corporal *adj* ‹*trabajo*› physical; ‹*necesidades*› bodily (*before n*); ‹*castigo*› corporal (*before n*)

corpulento -ta *adj* ‹*persona/animal*› hefty, burly; ‹*árbol*› solid, sturdy

corpus *m* (*pl* **~**) corpus

Corpus, Corpus Christi Corpus Christi

corral *m* **(a)** (en granja) yard, farmyard **(b)** (para ganado) corral **(c)** *tb* **corralito** (para niños) playpen

corralón *m* **(a)** (Méx) (de la policía) car pound **(b)** (Per) (terreno baldío) piece of waste land (*sometimes with shanty dwellings*) **(c)** (Arg) (Const) lumberyard

correa *f* **(a)** (tira) strap; (cinturón) belt; (de perro) leash; **~ de reloj** watchband (AmE), watchstrap (BrE) **(b)** (Mec) belt; **~ del ventilador** fan belt

corrección *f* **1 (a)** (buenos modales): **es un hombre de una gran ~** he is very well-mannered *o* correct; **vestir con ~** to dress correctly *o* properly **(b)** (honestidad) correctness **(c)** (propiedad): **habla el francés con ~** he speaks French well *o* correctly **2** (de exámenes, errores) correction; **~ de pruebas** proofreading

correccional *f or* (Esp) *m*: *tb* **~ de menores** reformatory (AmE), detention centre (BrE)

correctamente *adv* **(a)** (sin errores) correctly **(b)** (con cortesía) politely **(c)** (honestamente) honorably

correcto -ta *adj* **(a)** (educado) correct, polite; (honesto) honest **(b)** ‹*respuesta/solución*› correct, right **(c)** ‹*funcionamiento/procedimiento*› correct

corrector -tora *m,f* (de exámenes) marker; **~ de pruebas** proofreader

corredor[1] -dora *m,f* **1** (Dep) runner; (ciclista) cyclist; **~ de coches** racing driver; **~ de fondo** long-distance runner **2 (a)** (agente) agent; **~ de Bolsa** stockbroker; **~ de bienes raíces** *or* (Esp) **de fincas** real estate broker (AmE), estate agent (BrE) **(b)** (RPl) (viajante) sales representative

corredor[2] *m* (Arquit, Geog, Pol) corridor

corregir [I8] *vt* (en general) to correct; ‹*modales*› to improve, mend; ‹*examen/prueba*› to correct; (puntuar) to grade (AmE), to mark (BrE)

■ **corregirse** *v pron* **(a)** (en el comportamiento) to change *o* mend one's ways **(b)** (*refl*) (al hablar) to correct oneself; **un defecto físico que se corrige solo** a defect which corrects itself

correlación *f* correlation

correntoso -sa *adj* (CS) fast-flowing

correo *m* **(a)** mail, post (BrE); **envíamelo por ~** mail (AmE) *o* (BrE) post it to me; **echar una carta al ~** to mail (AmE) *o* (BrE) post a letter; **~ aéreo** air mail; **~ certificado** *o* (Col, Ur) **recomendado** registered mail; **~ urgente** special delivery; **de ~s** ‹*servicio/huelga*› postal (*before n*) **(b)** (tren) mail train **(c)** (oficina) *tb* **C~s** (Esp) post office **(d)** (mensajero) messenger

correoso -sa *adj* tough, leathery

correr [E1] *vi* **1 (a)** (en general) to run; **bajó/subió las escaleras corriendo** she ran down/up the stairs; **salieron corriendo del banco** they ran out of the bank; **echó a ~** he started to run **(b)** (Auto, Dep) «*piloto/conductor*» to race **2 (a)** (apresurarse): **¡corre, ponte los zapatos!** hurry *o* quick, put your shoes on!; **no corras tanto que te equivocarás** don't do it so quickly, you'll only make mistakes ; **corrí a llamarte** I rushed to call you; **me tengo que ir corriendo** I have to rush off **(b)** (fam) «*vehículo*» to go fast; «*conductor*» to drive fast **3 (a)** «*carretera/río*» to run; «*agua*» to run; «*sangre*» to flow; **corría una brisa suave** there was a gentle breeze **(b)** «*rumor*»: **corre el rumor/la voz de que** ... there is a rumor going around that ... **4** (pasar, transcurrir): **corría el año 1973 cuando** ... it was 1973 when ...; **con el ~ de los años** as time went/goes by; **¡cómo corre el tiempo!** how time flies! **5** (hacerse cargo) **~ CON algo** ‹*con gastos*› to pay sth; ‹*con organización*› to be responsible FOR sth ■ **~** *vt* **1 (a)** (Dep) ‹*maratón*› to run **(b)** (Auto, Dep) ‹*prueba/gran premio*› to race in **2** (exponerse a): **corres el riesgo de perderlo** you run the risk of losing it; **aquí no corres peligro** you're safe here **3 (a)** ‹*botón/ficha/silla*› to move; ‹*cortina*› (cerrar) to draw, close; (abrir) to open, pull back; **corre el cerrojo** bolt the door **(b)** (Inf) ‹*texto*› to scroll

■ **correrse** *v pron* **1 (a)** «*silla/cama*» to move; «*pieza/carga*» to shift **(b)** (fam) «*persona*» to move up *o* over **2 (a)** «*tinta*» to run; «*rímel/maquillaje*» to run, smudge; **se me corrió el rímel** my mascara ran **(b)** (AmL) «*media*» to ladder

correspondencia *f* **(a)** (relación por correo) correspondence; (cartas) mail, post (BrE); **mantener ~ con algn** to correspond with sb **(b)** (equivalencia) correspondence

corresponder [E1] *vi* **1 (a)** (en un reparto): **le corresponde la mitad de la herencia** he's entitled to half the inheritance; **la parte que te corresponde** your part *o* share **(b)** (incumbir): **te corresponde a ti preparar el informe** it's your job to prepare the report; **el lugar que le corresponde** his rightful place **(c)** (*en 3ª pers*) (ser adecuado): **debe disculparse, como corresponde** he must apologize, as is right and proper (frml); **según corresponda** as appropriate **2** (encajar, cuadrar): **su aspecto corresponde a la descripción** his appearance fits *o* matches the description; **el texto no corresponde a la foto** the text doesn't belong with *o* match the photograph **3 ~ A algo** ‹*a un favor*› to return sth; ‹*a amabilidad/generosidad*› to repay sth ■ **~** *vt* ‹*favor/atención*› to return; **un amor no correspondido** an unrequited love

correspondiente *adj* **(a)** (en general) corresponding (*before n*); **la etiqueta ~** the corresponding label; **los números ~s a cada página** the numbers corresponding to each page **(b)** (propio) own; **viene con su ~ caja** it comes with its own box **(c)** (pertinente) relevant; **rellene el impreso ~** complete the relevant form

corresponsal *mf* (Period, Rad, TV) correspondent; **~ extranjero/de guerra** foreign/war correspondent

corretear [A1] *vi* (correr) to run around ■ **~** *vt* **1** (esp AmL) (perseguir) to chase, pursue **2** (RPl) (Com) to wholesale

corrida *f* **1** (Taur) bullfight **2** (Chi) (serie) series; (fila) row; (de bebidas) round

corrido *m*: *Mexican folk song*

corriente *adj* **1** (que se da con frecuencia) common; (normal, no extraño) usual, normal; **es un error muy ~** it's a very common mistake; **lo ~ es pagar al contado** the normal thing is to pay cash; **un tipo normal y ~** an ordinary guy **2 (a)** (en curso) ‹*mes/año*› current **(b) al corriente**: **estoy al ~ en los pagos** I'm up to date with the payments; **empezó con retraso pero se ha puesto al ~** she started late but she has caught up; **mantener a algn al ~ de algo** to keep sb informed about sth ■ *f* **(a)** (de agua) current; **~s marinas** ocean currents; ***dejarse llevar por la ~*** to go along with the crowd; ***seguirle la ~ a algn*** to humor* sb **(b)** (de aire) draft (AmE), draught (BrE) **(c)** (Elec) current; **me dio (la) ~** I got a shock *o* an electric shock; **se cortó la ~** there was a power cut

corro *m* **(a)** (círculo) circle, ring; **hacer un ~** to stand/sit in a circle; **se formó un ~ a su alrededor** a circle of people formed around her **(b)** (Jueg): **jugar al ~** *to play a singing game standing in a ring*

corroborar [A1] *vt* to corroborate

corroer [E13] *vt* ‹*metal*› to corrode; ‹*mármol*› to erode

corromper [E1] *vt* **(a)** ‹*persona/lengua/sociedad*› to corrupt **(b)** ‹*materia orgánica*› to rot

■ **corromperse** *v pron* **(a)** «*costumbres/persona/lengua*» to become corrupted **(b)** «*materia orgánica*» to rot

corrompido -da *adj* **(a)** ‹*persona/sociedad*› corrupt **(b)** ‹*materia orgánica*› rotten

corrosión *f* corrosion

corrosivo -va *adj* ‹*sustancia/acción*› corrosive

corrupción *f* **(a)** (de moral, persona, lengua) corruption; **~ de menores** corruption of minors **(b)** (de materia) decay

corrupto -ta *adj* corrupt

corsé, **corset** /kor'se/ *m* (*pl* **-sets**) corset

cortacésped *m* lawnmower

cortada *f* **(a)** (Col, Méx) (herida) cut; **hacerse una ~** to cut oneself **(b)** (RPl) (calle sin salida) no through road

cortado[1] -da *adj* **1** ‹*persona*› **(a)** [ESTAR] (Chi, Esp) (turbado, avergonzado) embarrassed **(b)** [ESTAR] (Esp, CS) (aturdido) stunned; **me quedé ~ con su respuesta** I was stunned by her reply **(c)** [SER] (Esp) (tímido) shy **2** [ESTAR] **(a)** ‹*calle/carretera*› closed, closed off **(b)** ‹*película*› cut **3 (a)** [ESTAR] ‹*mayonesa/salsa*› separated; **la leche está cortada** the milk is curdled *o* off **(b)** ‹*café*› with a dash of milk

cortado[2] *m* expresso with a dash of milk

cortante *adj* **(a)** ‹*instrumento/objeto*› sharp **(b)** ‹*viento*› biting **(c)** ‹*respuesta/tono*› sharp

cortaplumas *m or f* (*pl* ~) penknife

cortar [A1] *vt* **1** (dividir) ‹*cuerda/pastel*› to cut, chop; ‹*asado*› to carve; ‹*leña/madera*› to chop; ‹*baraja*› to cut; **~ algo por la mitad** to cut sth in half *o* in two; **~ algo en rodajas/en cuadritos** to slice/dice sth; **~ algo en trozos** to cut sth into pieces **2** (quitar, separar) ‹*rama/punta/pierna*› to cut off; ‹*árbol*› to cut down, chop down; ‹*flores*› (CS) to pick; **me cortó un trozo de melón** she cut me a piece of melon **3** (hacer más corto) ‹*pelo/uñas*› to cut; ‹*césped/pasto*› to mow; ‹*seto*› to cut; ‹*rosal*› to cut back; ‹*texto*› to cut down **4** (en costura) ‹*falda/vestido*› to cut out **5** (interrumpir) **(a)** ‹*agua/gas/luz/teléfono*› to cut off; ‹*película/programa*› to interrupt **(b)** ‹*calle*› «*policía/obreros*» to close, block off; «*manifestantes*» to block; **me cortó el paso** he stood in my way **6** (censurar, editar) ‹*película*› to cut; ‹*escena/diálogo*› to cut (out) **7** «*frío*»: **el frío me cortó los labios** my lips were chapped *o* cracked from the cold weather ■ **~** *vi* **1** «*cuchillo/tijeras*» to cut **2 (a)** (Cin): **¡corten!** cut! **(b)** (CS) (por teléfono) to hang up; **no me cortes** don't hang up on me **(c)** (en naipes) to cut

■ **cortarse** *v pron* **1** (interrumpirse) «*proyección/película*» to stop; «*llamada/gas*» to get cut off; **se cortó la luz** there was a power cut; **se me cortó la respiración** I could hardly breathe **2 (a)** (*refl*) (hacerse un corte) to cut oneself; ‹*brazo/cara*› to cut; **me corté un dedo** I cut my finger **(b)** (*refl*) ‹*uñas/pelo*› to cut; **se corta el pelo ella misma** she cuts her own hair **(c)** (*caus*) ‹*pelo*› to have ... cut; **tengo que ~me el pelo** I have to have my hair cut **(d)** «*piel/labios*» to crack, become chapped **3** (cruzarse) «*líneas/calles*» to cross **4** «*leche*» to curdle; «*mayonesa/salsa*» to separate **5** (Chi, Esp) «*persona*» (turbarse, aturdirse) to get embarrassed

cortaúñas *m* (*pl* ~) nail clippers (*pl*)

corte *m* **1** (en general) cut; **se hizo un ~ en la cabeza** he cut his head; **~ de pelo** haircut; **~ a (la) navaja** razor cut; **un ~ de luz** a power cut; **tuvimos varios ~s de agua** the water was cut off several times; **~ de digestión** stomach cramp; **~ publicitario** (RPl) commercial break **2 (a)** (de tela) length, length of material **(b)** (en costura) cut; **un traje de buen ~** a well-made *o* well-cut suit; **~ y confección** dressmaking **3** (Esp fam) (vergüenza) embarrassment; **me da ~ ir sola** I'm embarrassed to go by myself; **¡qué ~!** how embarrassing! **4** (RPl fam) (atención): **darle ~ a algn** to take notice of sb ■ *f* **(a)** (del rey) court **(b)** (esp AmL) (Der) Court of Appeal; **C~ Suprema (de Justicia)** (AmL) Supreme Court **(c)** **las Cortes** *fpl* (Pol) (en Esp) Parliament, the legislative assembly

cortejo *m* (de rey) retinue, entourage; (de ministro) entourage; **~ fúnebre** funeral procession *o* (frml) cortege

cortés *adj* polite, courteous

cortesía *f* **(a)** (urbanidad, amabilidad) courtesy, politeness; **la trató con ~** he was polite to her; **tuvo la ~ de invitarnos** she was kind enough to invite us **(b) de cortesía** ‹*entrada*› complimentary; ‹*visita*› courtesy (*before n*)

corteza *f* (de árbol) bark; (del pan) crust; (del queso) rind; (de naranja, limón) peel, rind; **la ~ terrestre** the earth's crust

cortijo *m* (en Esp) (finca) country estate; (casa) country house

cortina *f* curtain, drape (AmE); **~ de ducha** shower curtain; **~ de humo** smokescreen

cortisona *f* cortisone

corto[1] -ta *adj* **1 (a)** (en longitud) ‹*calle/río*› short; **de manga corta** short-sleeved; **el vestido le quedó ~** the dress is too short for her now; **iba vestida de ~** she was wearing a short dress/skirt **(b)** (en duración) ‹*película/curso/viaje*› short; ‹*visita/conversación*› short, brief; ***a la corta o a la larga*** sooner or later **2** (escaso, insuficiente): **un niño de corta edad** a very young child; **~ de vista** nearsighted, shortsighted (BrE); **andar ~ de tiempo** to be pressed for time **3** (fam) (poco inteligente) stupid;

~ **de entendederas** *or* **alcances** dim, dense (colloq)

corto² *m* (Cin) **(a)** (cortometraje) short (movie *o* film) **(b) cortos** *mpl* (Col, Méx, Ven) (de película) trailer

cortocircuito *m* short circuit; **hacer ~** to short-circuit

cortometraje *m* short (movie *o* film)

cosa *f* **1** (en general) thing; **cualquier ~** anything; **¿alguna otra ~?** anything else?; **pon cada ~ en su lugar** put everything in its place; **entre una(s) ~(s) y otra(s)** ... what with one thing and another ...; **¡qué ~s dices!** really, what a thing to say!; **dime una ~** ... tell me something ...; **tengo que contarte una ~** there's something I have to tell you; **fue ~ fácil** it was easy; **se enfada por cualquier ~** he gets angry over the slightest thing; **si por cualquier ~ no puedes venir** if you can't come for any reason; **por una ~ o por otra** for one reason or another; **esto no es ~ de risa/broma** this is no laughing matter/no joke **2 cosas** *fpl* (pertenencias) things (*pl*); **mis ~s de deporte** my sports things **3** (situación, suceso): **así están las ~s** that's how things are *o* stand; **la ~ se pone fea** things are starting to get unpleasant; **¿cómo (te) van las ~s?** how are things?; **son ~s de la vida** that's life!; **¡qué ~ más extraña!** how strange *o* funny! **4 (a)** (fam) (ocurrencia): **¡tienes cada ~!** the things you come up (AmE) *o* (BrE) out with!; **esto es ~ de tu padre** this is your father's doing *o* idea **(b)** (comportamiento típico): **son ~s de niños** children are like that; **son ~s de Ana** that's one of Ana's little ways **5** (asunto): **no es ~ tuya** it's none of your business; **no te preocupes, eso es ~ mía** don't worry, I'll handle it **6** (*en locs*) **cosa de** (AmS fam) so as to; **~ de terminarlo** so as to finish it; **cosa que** (AmS fam) so that; **~ que no me olvide** so that I don't forget; **no sea cosa que: llévate el paraguas, no sea ~ que llueva** take your umbrella just in case; **átalo, no sea ~ que se escape** tie it up so that it doesn't get away; ***ser ~ de*** ... (fam): **es ~ de unos minutos** it'll (only) take a couple of minutes; **es ~ de intentarlo** you just have to give it a go

cosecha *f* **(a)** (acción, época) harvest; **un vino de la ~ del 70** a 1970 vintage wine **(b)** (producto) crop

cosechador -dora *m,f* **(a)** (persona) harvester **(b) cosechadora** *f* (máquina) combine (harvester)

cosechar [A1] *vt* **(a)** (recoger) ‹*cereales*› to harvest; ‹*legumbres*› to pick **(b)** (Esp) (cultivar) ‹*cereales/patatas*› to grow **(c)** ‹*aplausos/premios/honores*› to win; ‹*éxitos*› to achieve ■ ~ *vi* to harvest

coser [E1] *vt* **(a)** ‹*dobladillo*› to sew; ‹*botón*› to sew on; ‹*agujero*› to sew (up); **cóselo a máquina** sew it on the machine **(b)** ‹*herida*› to stitch ■ ~ *vi* to sew

cosmético¹ -ca *adj* cosmetic (*before n*)

cosmético² *m* cosmetic

cósmico -ca *adj* cosmic

cosmopolita *adj/mf* cosmopolitan

cosmos *m* cosmos

cosquillas *fpl*: **hacerle ~ a algn** to tickle sb; **tener ~** to be ticklish

costa *f* **1** (Geog) (del mar — área) coast; (— perfil) coastline; **una ~ muy accidentada** a very rugged coastline; **la ~ atlántica** the Atlantic coast **2** (*en locs*) **a costa de**: **lo terminó a ~ de muchos sacrificios** he had to make a lot of sacrifices to finish it; **a ~ mía/de los demás** at my/other people's expense; **a toda costa** at all costs **3 costas** *fpl* (Der) costs (*pl*)

costado *m* side; **pasar de ~** to go through sideways; **duerme de ~** she sleeps on her side

costal *m* sack, bag

costanera *f* (CS) (de río) riverside path (*o* road *etc*); (del mar) promenade; (de lago) lakeside path (*o* road *etc*)

costar [A10] *vt* **(a)** (en dinero) to cost; **¿cuánto me ~á arreglarlo?** how much will it cost to fix it? **(b)** (en perjuicios): **el atentado que le costó la vida** the attack in which he lost his life; **le costó el puesto** it cost him his job **(c)** (en esfuerzo): **me costó mucho trabajo** it took me a lot of hard work; **cuesta abrirlo** it's hard to open; **me cuesta trabajo creerlo** I find it hard *o* difficult to believe ■ ~ *vi* **(a)** (en dinero) to cost; **el reloj me costó caro** the watch cost a lot **(b)** (resultar perjudicial): **esto te va a ~ caro** you're going to pay dearly for this **(c)** (resultar difícil): **cuesta un poco acostumbrarse** it's not easy to get used to; **no te cuesta nada intentarlo** it won't do you any harm to give it a try; **la física le cuesta** he finds physics difficult; **me costó dormirme** I had trouble getting to sleep

Costa Rica *f* Costa Rica

costarricense *adj/mf* Costa Rican

costarriqueño -ña *adj/m,f* Costa Rican

coste *m* (Esp) ⇒ COSTO

costear [A1] *vt* (financiar) to finance ■ **costearse** *v pron* (*refl*) (financiarse): **yo me costeé el viaje** I paid for the trip myself

costeño -ña *adj* coastal ■ *m,f*: **los ~s** people from coastal regions

costero -ra *adj* ‹*camino/pueblo*› coastal

costilla *f* **(a)** (Anat) rib **(b)** (AmS) (chuleta — de vaca) T-bone steak; (— de cerdo, cordero) chop

costipado -da *adj/m* ⇒ CONSTIPADO

costo *m* (Com, Econ, Fin) cost; **de bajo ~** low-cost, budget; **precio de ~** cost price; **al ~** at cost price; **~ de (la) vida** cost of living

costoso -sa *adj* **(a)** ‹*casa/coche/joya*› expensive **(b)** ‹*error*› costly **(c)** ‹*trabajo/tarea*› difficult

costra *f* **(a)** (de herida) scab **(b)** (de suciedad) layer, coating

costumbre *f* **(a)** (de individuo) habit; **tenía (la) ~ de madrugar** he was in the habit of getting up early; **agarró la ~ de** ... she got into the habit of ...; **hacer algo por ~** to do sth out of habit; **a la hora de ~** at the usual time; **como de ~** as usual; **se quejó menos que de ~** he complained less than he usually does **(b)** (de país, pueblo) custom

costura *f* **(a)** (acción) sewing **(b)** (puntadas) seam

costurera *f* seamstress

costurero *m* (caja, estuche) workbox; (canasta) sewing basket; **~ de viaje** sewing kit

cotejar [A1] *vt* ‹*documentos*› to compare; ‹*información/respuesta*› to collate; **~ algo CON algo** to check sth AGAINST sth
cotelé *m* (Chi) corduroy
cotidiano -na *adj* daily; ‹*vida*› everyday, daily
cotilla *mf* (Esp fam) gossip (colloq)
cotillear [A1] *vi* (Esp fam) to gossip
cotización *f* **(a)** (de moneda) value; (de acciones, valores, producto) price; **su ~ llegó a 500 pesos** it reached 500 pesos **(b)** (Andes) (evaluación) valuation; (presupuesto) estimate
cotizado -da *adj* sought-after
cotizar [A4] *vt* **(a)** (Fin) ‹*acciones*› to quote; **las acciones se cotizan a 525 pesos** the shares are quoted at 525 pesos; **la libra se cotizó a 198 pesetas** the pound stood at 198 pesetas **(b)** (Andes) ‹*cuadro/joyas*› to value; ‹*obra/reparación*› to give an estimate for
coto *m* (Dep, Ecol) reserve; **~ de caza/pesca** game/fishing preserve
cotorra *f* **(a)** (Zool) (loro) parrot **(b)** (fam) (persona) chatterbox (colloq)
cototo *m* (Chi fam) bump (*on the head*)
cottolengo /koto'leŋgo/ *m* (RPl) (para ancianos) old people's home; (para niños) children's home; (para drogadictos, desamparados, etc) shelter, refuge
cotufas *fpl* (Ven) (maíz tostado) popcorn
COU /kou/ *m* (en Esp) = **Curso de Orientación Universitaria**
courier /ku'rje(r)/ *mf* courier
coya *mf*: *indian from the Andean region of Bolivia, Peru and the NW of Argentina*
coyote *m* (Zool) coyote
coyuntura *f* (Anat) joint
coz *f* kick; **dar coces** to kick
crac *m* (*pl* **cracs**) **(a)** (sonido) crack, snap **(b)** (Fin) crash
crack *m* (*pl* **cracks**) (droga) crack
cráneo *m* ▶ **123** skull, cranium (tech)
cráter *m* crater
crawl /krol/ *m*: *tb* **estilo ~** crawl, front crawl
crayón *m* (Méx, RPl) wax crayon
creación *f* **(a)** (en general) creation **(b)** (Relig) **la C~** the Creation
creador -dora *adj* creative ■ *m,f* **(a)** (en general) creator; **~es de moda** fashion designers **(b)** (Relig) **el C~** the Creator
crear [A1] *vt* to create; ‹*producto*› to develop; ‹*institución/comisión/fondo*› to set up; ‹*fama/prestigio*› to bring; ‹*reputación*› to earn; **crea muchos problemas** it causes *o* creates a lot of problems; **no quiero ~ falsas expectativas** I don't want to raise false hopes
■ **crearse** *v pron* ‹*problema*› to create ... for oneself; ‹*enemigos*› to make
creatividad *f* creativity
creativo -va *adj* creative
crecer [E3] *vi* **1 (a)** «*ser vivo/pelo/uñas*» to grow; **dejarse ~ la barba** to grow a beard **(b)** (criarse) to grow up; **crecieron en un pueblo** they grew up in a village **2 (a)** «*río*» to rise; «*ciudad*» to grow; «*luna*» to wax **(b)** «*sentimiento/interés*» to grow; «*rumor*» to spread **(c)** «*economía*» to grow; **el número de desempleados ha crecido** the number of unemployed has risen **(d)** (en importancia, sabiduría) **~ EN algo** to grow IN sth
creces: **pagar con ~ un error** to pay dearly for a mistake; **superar algo con ~** ‹*nivel/previsiones*› to far exceed sth
crecida *f* **(a)** (subida de nivel): **el río experimentó una fuerte ~** the river level rose sharply **(b)** (desbordamiento): **las ~s del Paraná** the flooding of the Paraná
creciente *adj* **(a)** ‹*interés/necesidad*› increasing **(b)** (Astron): **luna ~** waxing moon
crecimiento *m* growth; **una industria en ~** a growth industry; **durante el ~** while they are growing
credibilidad *f* credibility
crédito *m* **1 (a)** (en negocio) credit; **tengo ~ aquí** they let me have credit here; **a ~** on credit **(b)** (cuenta) account **(c)** (préstamo) loan; **~ hipotecario** mortgage loan **2** (credibilidad): **fuentes dignas de ~** reliable sources; **no di ~ a sus palabras** I doubted his words (frml) **3** (Cin, TV, Educ) credit
credo *m* creed
crédulo -la *adj* credulous, gullible
creencia *f* belief
creer [E13] *vi* **(a)** (tener fe, aceptar como verdad) to believe; **~ EN algo/algn** to believe IN sth/sb; **¿me crees?** do you believe me? **(b)** (pensar, juzgar) to think; **¿tú crees?** do you think so?; **no creo** I don't think so; **no creas, es bastante difícil** believe me, it's quite hard ■ **~** *vt* **(a)** (dar por cierto) to believe; **hay que verlo para ~lo** it has to be seen to be believed; **aunque no lo creas** believe it or not; **¡no lo puedo ~!** I don't believe it!; **¡ya lo creo!** of course! **(b)** (pensar, juzgar) to think; **creo que sí/creo que no** I think so/I don't think so; **creo que va a llover** I think it's going to rain; **no la creo capaz** I do not think she is capable; **se cree que el incendio fue provocado** the fire is thought to have been started deliberately; **no lo creí necesario** I didn't think it necessary; **no creo que pueda ir** I doubt if *o* I don't think I'll be able to go; **creí oír un ruido** I thought I heard a noise; **creo recordar que** ... I seem to remember that ...
■ **creerse** *v pron* **(a)** (*enf*) (con ingenuidad) to believe; **eso nadie se lo cree** no one believes that **(b)** (con arrogancia) to think; **se cree muy listo** he thinks he's really clever; **¿quién se ~á que es?** who does he think he is? **(c)** (CS fam) (estimarse superior) to think one is special (*o* great *etc*) **(d)** (Méx) (fiarse) **~se DE algn** to trust sb
creído -da *adj* [SER] (engreído) conceited
crema *f* **(a)** (plato dulce) *type of custard* **(b)** (esp AmL) (de la leche) cream; **~ batida** whipped cream; **~ agria** *or* **ácida** (AmL) sour *o* soured cream; **~ chantilly** *or* **chantillí** (AmL) whipped cream (*with sugar, vanilla and egg white*); **~ doble/líquida** (AmL) double/single cream; **~ pastelera** crème pâtissière, confectioner's custard **(c)** (sopa) cream **(d)** (en cosmética) cream; **~ bronceadora** suntan lotion *o* cream; **~ de afeitar** shaving cream; **~ de**

calzado (Esp) shoe cream; **~ hidratante** moisturizer, moisturizing cream ■ *adj inv* ▶97 cream; **(de) color ~** cream, cream-colored

cremallera *f* **(a)** (Indum) zipper (AmE), zip (BrE) **(b)** (Mec, Tec) rack

cremar [A1] *vt* to cremate

crematorio *m* crematorium

cremoso -sa *adj* ‹*salsa*› creamy; ‹*queso*› soft, creamy

crep *m* (*pl* **creps**), (Méx) **crepa** *f* crepe

crepe /krep/ *m or f* (Coc) crepe

crepé *m* (Tex) crepe

crepería *f* creperie

crepúsculo *m* (del anochecer) twilight; (del amanecer) dawn light

crespo[1] -pa *adj* (rizado) (AmL) curly; (muy rizado) frizzy

crespo[2] *m* (AmL) curl

cresta *f* **(a)** (Zool) crest; (de gallo) comb **(b)** (de ola, monte) crest

cretino -na *adj* cretinous ■ *m,f* cretin

creyente *adj*: **es muy ~** she has a strong faith ■ *mf* believer; **los no ~s** the nonbelievers

creyera, **creyese, etc** *ver* CREER

cría *f* **(a)** (crianza) rearing, raising; (para la reproducción) breeding **(b)** (Zool) (camada) litter; (nidada) brood **(c)** (animal): **una ~ de ciervo** a baby deer

criadero *m* farm; **~ de pollos/de truchas** poultry/trout farm; **~ de perros** kennel (AmE), kennels (BrE); **~ de ostras** oyster bed

criado -da *m,f* (*m*) servant; (*f*) servant, maid

criador -dora *m,f* breeder

crianza *f* **1** (Agr) raising, rearing; (para la reproducción) breeding **2** (de niños) upbringing

criar [A17] *vt* **1** ‹*niño*› **(a)** (cuidar, educar) to bring up, raise **(b)** (amamantar) to breast-feed; **criado con biberón** bottle-fed **2 (a)** ‹*ganado*› to raise, rear; (para la reproducción) to breed **(b)** ‹*pollos/pavos*› to breed

■ **criarse** *v pron* to grow up; **me crié en el campo** I grew up in the country; **me crié con mi abuela** I was brought up by my grandmother

criatura *f* **(a)** (niño — pequeño) child; (— recién nacido) baby **(b)** (cosa creada) creature

criba *f* **(a)** (instrumento) sieve **(b)** (proceso de selección): **la primera ~** the first stage of the selection process; **hicimos una ~ de las solicitudes** we went through the applications

cribar [A1] *vt* to sieve, sift

cricket /'krike(t)/ *m* cricket

crimen *m* (delito grave) serious crime; (asesinato) murder; **~ de guerra** war crime; **~ pasional** crime of passion; **es un ~ tirar esta comida** it's a crime to throw away this food; **¡qué ~!** it's wicked *o* criminal

criminal *adj/mf* criminal

criminalidad *f* **(a)** (cualidad) criminality **(b)** (número de crímenes) crime

criminalista *adj* criminal (*before n*) ■ *mf* criminal lawyer

crin *f* **(a)** (del caballo) *tb* **~es** mane **(b)** (pelo de caballo) horsehair **(c)** (esparto) esparto grass

crío, **cría** (esp Esp fam) *m,f* kid (colloq)

criollo -lla *adj* **(a)** (Hist) Creole **(b)** (AmL) (por oposición a extranjero) Venezuelan (*o* Peruvian *etc*); ‹*plato/artesanía/cocina*› national ■ *m,f* **(a)** (Hist) Creole (*of European descent born in a Spanish American colony*) **(b)** (AmL) (nativo) Venezuelan (*o* Peruvian *etc*)

cripta *f* crypt

criquet *m* (Dep) cricket

crisantemo *m* chrysanthemum

crisis *f* (*pl* **~**) **(a)** (en general) crisis; **~ nerviosa** nervous breakdown **(b)** (period) (remodelación ministerial) *tb* **~ de Gobierno** cabinet reshuffle

crismas *m* (*pl* **~**) (Esp) Christmas card

crispar [A1] *vt* **(a)** (contraer): **con la expresión crispada por el dolor** his face tensed/contorted with pain **(b)** (exasperar) to infuriate; **me crispa los nervios** it really irritates me *o* gets on my nerves

■ **crisparse** *v pron* «*rostro/expresión*» to tense up; «*persona*» to get irritated

cristal *m* **1 (a)** (vidrio fino) crystal; **~ de roca** rock crystal; **~ tallado** *or* (AmL) **cortado** cut glass **(b)** (lente) lens **2** (Esp) (vidrio) glass; (trozo) piece of glass; (de ventana) pane; **puerta de ~** glass door; **~es rotos** pieces of glass; **limpiar los ~s** to clean the windows; **~ delantero** (Esp) windshield (AmE), windscreen (BrE); **~ trasero** (Esp) rear windshield (AmE), rear windscreen (BrE)

cristalera *f* (Esp) **(a)** (mueble) display cabinet, dresser **(b)** (escaparate) shop window **(c)** (puertas) French windows (*pl*), French doors (*pl*) (AmE); (ventanas) windows (*pl*)

cristalería *f* (objetos) glassware; (juego) set of glasses

cristalero -ra *m,f* (Esp) (persona que instala) glazier

cristalino -na *adj* crystalline

cristalizar [A4] *vi/vt* to crystallize

cristiandad *f* Christendom

cristianismo *m* Christianity

cristiano -na *adj/m,f* Christian; **¿eres ~?** are you a Christian?

Cristo Christ; **antes/después de ~** before Christ *o* BC/AD

criterio *m* **(a)** (norma, principio) criterion; **tenemos que unificar ~s** we have to agree on our criteria **(b)** (capacidad para juzgar, discernir) discernment (frml), judgment*; **lo dejo a tu ~** I leave that to your discretion *o* judgment; **no tiene ~** he has no common sense **(c)** (opinión, juicio) opinion

crítica *f* **(a)** (ataque, censura) criticism; **fue objeto de numerosas ~s** she was the object of a lot of criticism **(b)** (reseña) review; (ensayo) critique; **la película recibió muy buenas ~s** the movie had very good reviews; **la ~** (los críticos) the critics (*pl*); **~ literaria** literary criticism

criticar [A2] *vt* **(a)** (censurar) to criticize **(b)** (Art, Espec, Lit) ‹*libro/película*› to review ■ **~** *vi* to gossip, backbite

crítico -ca *adj* critical ■ *m,f* critic

criticón -cona *adj* (fam & pey) critical, hypercritical ▪ *m,f* (fam & pey) faultfinder

Croacia *f* Croatia

croar [A1] *vi* to croak

croata *adj* Croatian, Croat ▪ *mf* Croat; **los ~s** the Croats, Croatian people

crochet /kro'tʃe/ *m* crochet; **hacer ~** to crochet

croissant /krwa'san/ *m* (*pl* **-ssants**) croissant

crol *m* (Dep) crawl

cromo *m* **(a)** (metal) chromium, chrome **(b)** (Esp) (estampa) picture card, sticker

cromosoma *m* chromosome

crónica *f* **(a)** (Period) report, article; (Rad, TV) report; **~ deportiva/de sociedad** sport(s)/society page (*o* section *etc*) **(b)** (Hist) chronicle

crónico -ca *adj* chronic

cronista *mf* **(a)** (esp AmL) (periodista) journalist, reporter; **~ de radio** radio broadcaster **(b)** (Hist) chronicler

cronología *f* chronology

cronológico -ca *adj* chronological

cronometrar [A1] *vt* to time

cronómetro *m* (Tec) chronometer; (Dep) stopwatch

croqueta *f* croquette

croquis *m* (*pl* **~**) sketch

cross /kros/ *m* **(a)** (deporte — en atletismo) cross-country running; (— en motociclismo) motocross **(b)** (carrera — a pie) cross country, cross-country race; (— en moto) motocross race

cruce *m* **1 (a)** (acción) crossing **(b)** (de calles) crossroads; Ⓢ **cruce peligroso** dangerous junction; **~ peatonal** *or* **de peatones** pedestrian crossing **(c)** (Telec): **hay un ~ en las líneas** there's a crossed line **2** (Agr, Biol) cross

cruceiro *m* (unidad monetaria) cruzeiro (*former Brazilian unit of currency*)

crucero *m* **(a)** (viaje) cruise; **hizo un ~ por el Caribe** he went on a Caribbean cruise **(b)** (barco de guerra) cruiser **(c)** (Méx) (de carreteras) crossroads; (Ferr) grade crossing (AmE), level crossing (BrE)

crucial *adj* crucial

crucificar [A2] *vt* to crucify

crucifijo *m* crucifix

crucigrama *m* crossword, crossword puzzle

cruda *f* (AmC, Méx fam) hangover

crudeza *f* harshness; (del clima) severity, harshness

crudo -da *adj* **1** [ESTAR] ‹*carne/verduras/pescado*› (sin cocinar) raw; (poco hecho) underdone **2** [SER] **(a)** ‹*invierno/clima*› severe, harsh **(b)** ‹*lenguaje/imágenes/realidad*› harsh

cruel *adj* cruel; **ser ~ con algn** to be cruel to sb

crueldad *f* cruelty; **eso es una ~** that's cruel; **~ mental** mental cruelty

crujido *m* **(a)** (de tablas, muelles, ramas) creaking **(b)** (de papel, hojas secas) rustling; (de seda) rustle **(c)** (de los nudillos, las rodillas) cracking **(d)** (de la grava, nieve) crunching **(e)** (de los dientes) grinding

crujiente *adj* ‹*galletas/tostadas*› crunchy; ‹*pan*› crusty

crujir [I1] *vi* **(a)** «*tabla/muelles/ramas*» to creak; «*hojas secas*» to rustle **(b)** «*nudillos/rodillas*» to crack **(c)** «*grava/nieve*» to crunch **(d)** «*galletas/tostadas*» to be crunchy **(e)** «*dientes*»: **le crujen los dientes** he grinds his teeth

crustáceo *m* crustacean

cruz *f* **1 (a)** (figura) cross; **ponte con los brazos en ~** stand with your arms stretched out to the sides; **la C~** (Relig) the Cross; **~ gamada** swastika; **C~ Roja** Red Cross **(b)** (ornamento, condecoración) cross **2** (de moneda) reverse; **cara o ~** heads or tails

cruzada *f* crusade

cruzado -da *adj* **1 (a)** (atravesado): **había un árbol ~ en la carretera** there was a tree lying across the road **(b)** ‹*abrigo/chaqueta*› double-breasted **2** ‹*cheque*› crossed; *ver tb* CRUZAR

cruzar [A4] *vt* **1** (atravesar) ‹*calle/mar/puente*› to cross **2** ‹*piernas*› to cross; ‹*brazas*› to cross, fold **3 (a)** ‹*cheque*› to cross **(b)** (tachar) to cross out **(c)** ‹*palabras/saludos*› to exchange **4** (llevar al otro lado) to take (*o* carry *etc*) ... across **5** ‹*animales/plantas*› to cross ▪ **~** *vi* (atravesar) to cross; **~on por el puente** they went across the bridge

▪ **cruzarse** *v pron* **1** (*recípr*) **(a)** «*caminos/líneas*» to intersect, meet **(b)** (en viaje, camino): **nos cruzamos en el camino** we met *o* passed each other on the way; **nuestras cartas se han debido de ~** our letters must have crossed in the post; **~se** CON **algn** to see *o* pass sb **2** (interponerse): **se me cruzó una moto** a motorcycle pulled out in front of him; **se me cruzó otro corredor** another runner cut in front of me

cta. (= **cuenta**) a/c

cuaderno *m* (de ejercicios) exercise book; (de notas) notebook; **~ (de) borrador** rough notebook; **~ de espiral** *o* (Chi) **de anillos** spiral-bound notebook

cuadra *f* **(a)** (Equ) stable, stables (*pl*) **(b)** (AmL) (distancia entre dos esquinas) block

cuadrado[1] -da *adj* **1 (a)** (de forma) square **(b)** (Mat) ‹*metro/centímetro*› square (*before n*); **2 m² ~s** (*read as: dos metros cuadrados*) m² (*léase: two square meters*) **2** [ESTAR] (fam) (fornido) well-built, big, hefty (colloq) **3** [SER] (AmL) (cerrado de mente) (fam) inflexible

cuadrado[2] *m* square; **25 elevado al ~** 25 squared

cuadrar [A1] *vi* **(a)** «*cuentas*» to tally, balance **(b)** «*declaraciones/testimonias*» to tally; **~** CON **algo** to fit in WITH sth, tally WITH sth **(c)** (Ven) (para una cita) **~** CON **algn** to arrange to meet sb; **~** PARA **hacer algo** to arrange to do sth

▪ **cuadrarse** *v pron* **(a)** «*soldado*» to stand to attention **(b)** «*caballo/toro*» to stand stock-still **(c)** (Col, Ven fam) (estacionarse) to park

cuadriculado -da *adj* ‹*papel*› squared; **mapa ~** grid map

cuadrilátero *m* **(a)** (Mat) quadrilateral **(b)** (period) (de boxeo) ring

cuadrilla *f* **(a)** (Taur) cuadrilla (*team of matador's assistants*) **(b)** (de obreros) team, gang; (de soldados) squad; (de maleantes) gang

cuadro *m* **1 (a)** (Art) (pintura) painting; (grabado, reproducción) picture **(b)** (Teatr) scene **(c)** (gráfico) table, chart **2 (a)** (cuadrado) square, check; **tela a ~s** checked material; **zanahorias cortadas en cuadritos** diced carrots **(b)** (tablero) board, panel; **~ de mandos** *or* **instrumentos** (Auto) dashboard; (Aviac) instrument panel **(c)** (de bicicleta) frame **3** (en organización): **los ~s directivos del partido** the top party officials; **los ~s superiores de la empresa** the company's senior management; **~s de mando** (Mil) commanders (*pl*)

cuadrúpedo -da *adj/m* quadruped (*before n*)

cuádruple, **cuádruplo** *m*: **esta cifra es el ~ de la que esperábamos** this figure is four times what we expected

cuajada *f* junket, curd

cuajar [A1] *vi* **1 (a)** «*leche*» to curdle; «*flan/yogur*» to set **(b)** «*nieve*» to settle **2 (a)** «*ideología*» to be accepted; «*plan/proyecto*» to come off; «*moda*» to catch on, take off **(b)** «*persona*» to fit in ■ **~** *vt* ‹*leche*› to curdle

cuajo *m* **1** (sustancia) rennet **2** (raíz): **arrancar algo de ~** ‹*planta*› to pull sth out by the roots; ‹*vicio/corrupción*› to root out (completely)

cual *pron* **1 (a) el/la ~/los/las ~es** (hablando de personas) (*sujeto*) who; (*complemento*) who, whom (frml); (hablando de cosas) which; **mis vecinos, a los ~es no conocía** my neighbors who I didn't know *o* (frml) whom I did not know; **el motivo por el ~ lo hizo** the reason why he did it; **según lo ~** ... by which ...; **dos de los ~es** two of whom/which **(b) lo ~** which; **por lo ~** as a result, therefore; **con lo ~** so **2** (*en locs*) **cada cual** everyone, everybody; **sea cual sea** *or* **fuera** *or* **fuere** whatever

cuál *pron* (uno en particular) which; (uno en general) what; **¿~ quieres?** which (one) do you want?; **¿y ~ es el problema?** so, what's the problem? ■ *adj* (esp AmL): **¿a ~ colegio vas?** what *o* which school do you go to?

cualidad *f* quality

cualificado -da *adj* (Esp) ⇒ CALIFICADO

cualificar [A2] *vt* (Esp) ⇒ CALIFICAR 2(b)

cualquier *adj*: *apocopated form of* CUALQUIERA *used before nouns*

cualquiera *adj* (*pl* **cualesquiera** *or* (crit) **cualquiera**) [*see also note under* CUALQUIER] any; **en cualquier momento** (at) any time; **cualquier cosa/persona** anything/anyone; **en cualquier lado** anywhere; **de cualquier forma que se haga** whichever way you do it; **lo voy a hacer de ~ forma** I'm going to do it anyway; **es un mercenario ~** he's nothing but a mercenary ■ *pron* (refiriéndose — a dos personas o cosas) either (of them); (— a más de dos personas) anybody, anyone; (— a más de dos cosas) any one; **¿cuál de los dos? — cualquiera** which one? — either (of them); **pregúntaselo a ~** ask anybody *o* anyone (you like); **~ que elijas estará bien** whichever (one) you choose *o* any one you choose will be fine ■ *m*: **un ~** a nobody

cualquiera *mf*: **un ~** a nobody; **una ~** a floozy *o* (BrE) a tart (colloq & pej)

cuando *conj* ▶ **121** **(a)** (con valor temporal) when; **ven ~ quieras** come when *o* whenever you like; **~ se mejore** when she gets better; **ahora es ~ me viene mejor** now is the best time for me **(b)** (si) if; **será verdad ~ él lo dice** it must be true if he says so **(c)** (*en locs*) **cada cuando** (esp AmL) every so often; **de vez en cuando** from time to time, every so often

cuándo *adv* ▶ **193** when; **¿de ~ es esa foto?** when was that photo taken?; **¿desde ~ lo sabes?** how long have you known?; **¿desde ~?** since when?; **¡~ no!** (AmL) as usual!

cuantificar [A2] *vt* ‹*valor/daños/pérdidas*› to quantify, assess

cuantioso -sa *adj* substantial

cuanto[1] *adv* **(a)** (tanto como) as much as; **grita ~ quieras** shout as much as you like **(b)** (*como conj*): **~s más/menos seamos, mejor** the more/the fewer of us there are the better; **~ antes empecemos, más pronto terminaremos** the sooner we begin, the sooner we'll finish **(c)** (*en locs*) **cuanto antes** as soon as possible; **en cuanto** (tan pronto como) as soon as; **en cuanto a** (en lo que concierne) as for, as regards

cuanto[2] **-ta** *adj*: **llévate ~s discos quieras** take as many records as you want *o* like; **unos ~s amigos** a few friends; **tiene ~ libro hay sobre el tema** she has every book there is on the subject ■ *pron*: **le di todo ~ tenía** I gave her everything I had; **fuimos sólo unos ~s** only a few of us went

cuánto[1] *adv* **(a)** (en preguntas) how much **(b)** (uso indirecto): **si supieras ~ la quiero/lo siento** if you knew how much I love her/how sorry I am

cuánto[2] **-ta** *adj* **(a)** (en preguntas) (*sing*) how much; (*pl*) how many; **¿~ café queda?** how much coffee is there left?; **¿~s alumnos tienes?** how many students do you have?; **¿~s años tienes?** how old are you?; **¿~ tiempo tardarás?** how long will you take? **(b)** (uso indirecto) (*sing*) how much; (*pl*) how many; **no sé ~ dinero/~s libros tengo** I don't know how much money/how many books I have **(c)** (en exclamaciones): **¡~ vino!** what a lot of wine!; **¡~ tiempo sin verte!** I haven't seen you for ages! (colloq) ■ *pron* **1** (en preguntas) **(a)** (*sing*) how much; (*pl*) how many; **¿~ pesas?** how much do you weigh?; **¿~ mides?** how tall are you?; **¿~s quieres?** how many do you want?; **¿a ~ estamos hoy?** what's the date today? **(b)** (refirido a tiempo) how long; **¿~ falta para llegar?** how long before we get there? **(c)** (refirido a precios, dinero) how much; **¿~ cuesta?** how much is it?; **¿~ es?** how much is that (altogether)? **2** (uso indirecto): **pregúntale ~ va a demorar** ask her how long she'll be; **no sé ~ puede costar/~s tiene** I don't know how much it might cost/how many she has **3** (en exclamaciones): **¡~ has tardado!** it's taken you a long time!

cuarenta ▶ **293** *adj inv/pron/m* forty; *para ejemplos ver* CINCUENTA

cuarentena *f* (aislamiento) quarantine

cuarentón -tona ▶ **159** *m,f* (fam) person in his/her forties

Cuaresma *f* Lent

Cuando

Algunas observaciones sobre la conjunción

En los casos en que cuando *precede al subjuntivo, se traduce al inglés por* when *seguido de indicativo*:

llámame cuando vayas a salir	=	call me when you're about to leave
cuando sea viejo	=	when I'm old
cuando todos hayan llegado	=	when everybody has arrived

Cuando la conjunción significa siempre que *o* cada vez que *se puede traducir también por* whenever:

cuando oigas esa canción te acordarás de mí	=	whenever you hear that song, you'll remember me
cuando necesites ayuda, llámame	=	whenever you need help, just call me

Para otros usos y más ejemplos ver entrada

cuarta *f* (Auto) fourth (gear); **mete la ~** put it in fourth

cuartel *m* **(a)** (Mil) barracks (*sing o pl*); **~ de bomberos** (RPl) fire station, fire house (AmE); **~ general** headquarters (*sing o pl*) **(b)** (tregua): **no dieron ~ a los rebeldes** they showed no mercy to the rebels; **una lucha sin ~** a merciless fight

cuarteto *m* (Mús) quartet

cuarto[1] **-ta** *adj/pron* fourth; **la cuarta parte** a quarter; *para ejemplos ver* QUINTO

cuarto[2] *m* **1** (habitación) room; (dormitorio) room, bedroom; **~ de baño** bathroom; **~ de estar** living room, parlor (AmE), sitting room (BrE); **~ de (los) huéspedes** guest room, spare room; **~ trastero** lumber room, junk room **2 (a)** ▶ **294** (cuarta parte) quarter; **un ~ de kilo** a quarter (of a) kilo; **un ~ de pollo** a quarter chicken; **~ creciente/menguante** first/last quarter; **~s de final** quarterfinals (*pl*) **(b)** ▶ **221** (en expresiones de tiempo) quarter; **un ~ de hora** a quarter of an hour; **la una y ~** (a) quarter after (AmE) *o* (BrE) past one, one fifteen; **es un ~ para las dos** *or* (Esp, RPl) **son las dos menos ~** it is a quarter to two

cuarzo *m* quartz

cuate *mf* (Méx) **(a)** (mellizo) twin **(b)** (fam) (amigo) pal (colloq) **(c)** (fam) (tipo, tipa) (*m*) guy (colloq); (*f*) woman

cuatrapearse [A1] *v pron* (Méx) «*aparato*» to break; «*planes*» to fall through

cuatrero -ra *m,f* rustler

cuatrillizo -za *m,f* quadruplet, quad

cuatro ▶ **293** *adj inv/pron* four; **¿llueve? — no, sólo son ~ gotas** is it raining? no, it's just a drop or two; **le escribí ~ líneas** I wrote him a couple of lines; *para más ejemplos ver tb* CINCO ■ *m* **(a)** (número) ▶ **293** (number) four; *para ejemplos ver* CINCO **(b)** (Ven) (guitarra) four-stringed guitar

cuatrocientos -tas ▶ **293** *adj/pron* four hundred; *para ejemplos ver* QUINIENTOS

cuba *f* **(a)** (barril) barrel, cask **(b)** (tina) tub, vat

Cuba *f* Cuba

cubalibre *m* (de ron) rum and coke; (de ginebra) gin and coke

cubano -na *adj/m,f* Cuban

cubertería *f* cutlery; **una ~ de plata** a set of silver cutlery

cubeta *f* **(a)** (Fot, Quím) tray; (de paredes más altas) tank **(b)** (para hielo) ice tray **(c)** (barril) keg, small cask **(d)** (Méx) (balde) bucket

cúbico -ca *adj* cubic; **$2m^3$** (*read as: dos metros cúbicos*) $2m^3$ (*léase: two cubic meters*)

cubierta *f* **1 (a)** (funda) cover; (de libro) cover, sleeve **(b)** (Auto) tire* **2** (Náut) (en barco) deck; **salir a ~** to go up on deck

cubierto[1] **-ta** *adj* ‹*cielo*› overcast, cloudy; *ver tb* CUBRIR

cubierto[2] *m* **1 (a)** (pieza) piece of cutlery; **los ~s de plata** the silver cutlery **(b)** (servicio de mesa) place setting; **pon otro ~** can you set another place? **2** (*en locs*) **a cubierto**: **ponerse a ~ de la lluvia** to take cover *o* to shelter from the rain

cubilete *m* **(a)** (vaso) beaker; (para dados) shaker, cup **(b)** (Col) (sombrero) top hat

cubitera *f* (bandeja) ice tray; (cubo) ice bucket

cubo *m* **1** (Esp) bucket; **~ de (la) basura** (de la cocina) garbage can (AmE), (kitchen) bin (BrE); (de edificio) garbage can (AmE), rubbish bin (BrE) **2 (a)** (cuerpo geométrico) cube; **cubito de hielo** ice cube; **cubito de caldo** stock cube **(b)** (Mat) cube; **elevar un número al ~** to cube a number

cubrecama *m* bedspread

cubrir [I33] *vt* **(a)** (en general) to cover; **~ algo** DE **algo** to cover sth WITH sth; **cubrí al niño con una manta** I covered the child with a blanket **(b)** ‹*demanda/necesidad*› to meet **(c)** ‹*plaza/vacante*› to fill

■ **cubrirse** *v pron* **1 (a)** (*refl*) (taparse) to cover oneself; ‹*cara*› to cover **(b)** (ponerse el sombrero) to put one's hat on **(c)** (protegerse) to take cover **(d)** (contra riesgo) to cover oneself **2** (llenarse): **las calles se habían cubierto de nieve** the streets were covered with snow

cucaracha *f* (Zool) cockroach

cuchara *f* spoon; **~ de postre** dessertspoon; **~ sopera** *or* **de sopa** soup spoon

cucharada *f* spoonful; **~ sopera** ≈ tablespoonful

cucharadita *f* teaspoon, teaspoonful

cucharilla, **cucharita** *f* (Coc) teaspoon

cucharón *m* ladle

cucheta *f* (RPl) trundle bed, truckle bed

cuchichear [A1] *vi* (fam) to whisper

cuchilla *f* **(a)** (de segadora, batidora, cuchillo) blade; (de arado) coulter, share **(b)** *tb* **~ de afeitar** (hoja) razor blade; (maquinilla) razor

cuchillada *f*, **cuchillazo** *m* **(a)** (golpe) stab; **le dio una ~** she stabbed him **(b)** (herida) stab wound

cuchillo *m* knife; **~ de cocina** kitchen knife

cuchitril *m* hole (colloq), hovel

cucho -cha *m,f* **1** (Col fam) **(a)** (padre) dad (colloq); (madre) mom (AmE colloq), mum (BrE colloq) **(b)** (profesor) teacher **(c)** (viejecito) (*m*) old guy (colloq); (*f*) old girl (colloq) **2** (Chi fam) (gato) puss (colloq)

cuclillas *fpl*: **en ~** squatting, crouching; **ponerse en ~** to squat

cuco *m* **1** (Zool) cuckoo **2** (Esp) (de bebé) Moses basket **3** (CS, Per leng infantil) bogeyman

cucú *m* cuckoo

cucurucho *m* **(a)** (de papel, cartón) cone; (de barquillo) cone **(b)** (helado) cone, cornet (BrE) **(c)** (capirote) hood, pointed hat

cuece, **cuecen, etc** *see* COCER

cuello *m* **(a)** (Anat) ▶ **123** neck; **le cortaron el ~** they slit *o* cut his throat **(b)** (de botella) neck; **~ de botella** (Auto) bottleneck **(c)** (se prenda de vestir) collar; **sin ~** collarless **(d)** (escote) neck; **~ alto** *or* **vuelto** *or* (AmL) **tortuga** turtleneck (AmE), polo neck (BrE); **~ de pico** V neck; **~ redondo** round neck

cuenca *f* **(a)** (Geog, Geol) basin **(b)** (del ojo) socket

cuenco *m* (recipiente) bowl

cuenta *f*

■ **Nota** Cuando la frase *darse cuenta* va seguida de una oración subordinada introducida por *de que*, en el español latinoamericano existe cierta tendencia a omitir la preposición *de* en el lenguaje coloquial: *se dio cuenta que no iba a convencerla* = he realized (that) he wasn't going to convince her

1 (a) (operación, cálculo) calculation, sum; **hacer una ~** to do a calculation *o* sum; **saca la ~** add it up, work it out; **hacer** *or* **sacar ~s** to do some calculations; ***a fin de ~s*** after all **(b) cuentas** *fpl* (contabilidad) accounts: **yo llevo las ~s del negocio** I do the accounts for the business, I handle the money side of the business (colloq); **ella se ocupa de las ~s de la casa** she pays all the bills and looks after the money **(b)** (cómputo) count; **llevar/perder la ~** to keep/lose count; **~ atrás** countdown; ***más de la ~*** too much **2 (a)** (factura) bill; **¿nos trae la ~, por favor?** could we have the check (AmE) *o* (BrE) bill, please?; **la ~ del gas** the gas bill; **a cuenta** on account; **entregó $2.000 a ~** she gave me/him/them $2,000 on account; **este dinero es a ~ de lo que te debo** this money is to go toward(s) what I owe you **(b)** (Com, Fin) (en banco, comercio) account; **abrir/cerrar/liquidar una ~** to open/close/to settle an account; **~ corriente/de ahorro(s)** current/savings account **3 cuentas** *fpl* (explicaciones): **no tengo por qué darte ~s** I don't have to explain *o* justify myself to you; **dar** *or* **rendir ~s de algo** to account for sth; ***en resumidas ~s*** in short **4** (cargo, responsabilidad): **los gastos corren por ~ de la empresa** the expenses are covered *o* paid by the company; **se instaló por su ~** she set up (in business) on her own; **trabaja por ~ propia** she's self-employed **5 darse ~ (de algo)** (comprender) to realize (sth); (notar) to notice (sth); **se da ~ de todo** she's aware of everything that's going on (around her); **date ~ de que es imposible** you must realize (that) it's impossible; **tener algo en ~** to bear sth in mind; **ten en ~ que es joven** bear in mind that he's young; **sin tener en ~ los gastos** without taking the expenses into account; **tomar algo en ~** to take sth into consideration **6** (de collar, rosario) bead

cuenta, **cuentas**, **etc** *see* CONTAR

cuentagotas *m* (*pl* **~**) dropper

cuentakilómetros *m* (*pl* **~**) (de distancia recorrida) odometer (AmE), mileometer (BrE); (de velocidad) speedometer

cuentero -ra *adj* (Méx, RPl fam) **(a)** (mentiroso): **ser ~** to be a fibber (colloq) **(b)** (chismoso) gossipy

cuentista *adj* **(a)** (fam) (exagerado): **no seas ~, que no duele tanto** don't exaggerate, it doesn't hurt that much **(b)** (fantasioso): **ser ~** to be a fibber (colloq) ■ *mf* **(a)** (Lit) short-story writer **(b)** (fam) (exagerado): **no te fíes de ese ~, es puro teatro** don't fall for his playacting, he's just putting it on **(c)** (fantasioso) fibber (colloq)

cuento *m* **(a)** (narración corta) short story; (para niños) story, tale; **cuéntame un ~** tell me a story; **~ de hadas** fairy story, fairy tale; ***venir a ~***: **eso no viene a ~** that doesn't come into it; **sin venir a ~** for no reason at all **(b)** (chiste) joke, story **(c)** (fam) (mentira, excusa) story (colloq); **no me vengas con ~s** I'm not interested in your excuses *o* stories **(d)** (fam) (exageración): **todo ese llanto es puro ~** all that crying is just put on; **eso es un ~ chino** what a load of baloney; **el ~ del tío** a con trick

cuento *see* CONTAR

cuerda *f* **1 (a)** (gruesa) rope; (delgada) string; **~ floja** (Espec) tightrope **(b)** (Jueg) jump rope (AmE), skipping rope (BrE); **saltar a la ~** to jump rope (AmE), to skip (BrE) **(c)** (para tender ropa) washing line, clothes line **(d)** (de arco) bowstring **2** (Mús) **(a)** (de guitarra, violín) string **(b) cuerdas** *fpl* (instrumentos) strings (*pl*); **~s vocales** *fpl* vocal chords (*pl*) **3** (de reloj, juguete): **un juguete de ~** a clockwork toy; **le dio ~ al despertador** she wound up the alarm clock

cuerdo -da *adj* [ESTAR] sane; **no está ~** he is insane

cuerno *m* **(a)** (de toro) horn; (de caracol) feeler; (de ciervo) antler; ***irse al ~*** (fam) «*plan*» to fall through; «*fiesta*» to be ruined *o* spoiled; ***ponerle los ~s a algn*** (fam) to be unfaithful to sb **(b)** (Mús) horn

cuero *adj* (Méx fam) gorgeous (colloq) ■ *m* (piel) leather; (sin curtir) skin, hide; **chaqueta de ~** leather jacket; **~ de chancho** (AmL) pigskin; **~ de vaca** cowhide; ***en ~s (vivos)*** (fam) (desnudo) stark naked (colloq); ***ser un ~*** (Chi, Méx fam) «*mujer*» she's a real stunner (colloq); «*hombre*» he's a real hunk (colloq)

cuerpo *m* **1 (a)** (Anat) ▶ **123** body; **el ~ humano** the human body; **retrato/espejo de ~ entero** full-length portrait/mirror; **~ a ~** hand-to-hand **(b)** (cadáver) body, corpse **(c)** (Fís) (objeto) body, object **2** (conjunto de personas, de ideas, normas)

El cuerpo humano

En los casos en que el español utiliza el artículo definido para referirse a alguna parte del cuerpo, el inglés usa el adjetivo posesivo:

abrió la boca = he opened his mouth
se llevó la mano a la boca = she put her hand over her mouth
le cortó el pelo = she cut his hair
le brillaban los ojos = his eyes sparkled
se le cansaron los brazos = his arms got tired
inclinó la cabeza = he tilted his head

Para describir a las personas

Cuando el español emplea el verbo tener (tiene el pelo largo) *el inglés utiliza el verbo* to be (her hair is long) *o bien el verbo* to have (she has long hair):

tiene los pies grandes = she has big feet
tiene los ojos verdes = she has green eyes

Cuando la parte del cuerpo mencionada es un nombre singular, el inglés antepone al artículo indefinido a *cuando se emplea el verbo* to have:

tiene la cara redonda = she has a round face
= her face is round
tiene el cuello largo = he has a long neck

Nótense los siguientes ejemplos

el muchacho de los ojos azules = the boy with blue eyes
un hombre con el pelo rizado = a man with curly hair

Dolores y dolencias

¿Qué/dónde le duele? = where does it hurt?

Cuando el español emplea la construcción gramatical dolerle algo a alguien, *la traducción al inglés debe obtenerse en contexto*:

me duele el brazo = my arm hurts
= my arm aches
le duelen las piernas = her legs hurt
= her legs ache
me dolía la cabeza = I had a headache
= my head hurt (a causa de un golpe, herida etc.)

Nótese el uso del artículo indefinido a *en la primera traducción del ejemplo anterior*

le duelen los oídos = he has (an) earache
me dolía el estómago = I had stomach ache

Nótense las siguientes traducciones:

me duele todo el cuerpo = I'm aching all over
= my whole body aches

Otros usos:

tengo un fuerte dolor de espalda = I have a bad backache
fuertes dolores de estómago/pecho = sharp *o* severe stomach/chest pains
tengo un dolor en la pierna = I have a pain in my leg
tengo dolor de garganta = I have a sore throat
tengo el brazo muy dolorido = I have a very sore arm
tiene los músculos doloridos = his muscles are sore

Para dolencias nótense las siguientes traducciones:

tiene problemas de corazón/espalda = he has heart/back trouble *o* problems
sufre *or* (frml) padece del hígado/de los riñones = she has *o* suffers from a liver/kidney complaint
tuvo *or* le dió un ataque al corazón = he had a heart attack

Accidentes

Cuando el español emplea los verbos pronominales con el artículo definido (se quemó la mano), *el inglés utiliza un verbo transitivo, seguido del correspondiente adjetivo posesivo* (he burnt his hand):

se rompió la nariz = she broke her nose
me hice daño en *or* (AmL) me lastimé la pierna = I hurt my leg
se lesionó la rodilla = he injured his knee
me di un golpe en el brazo = I hit my arm
me mordí la lengua = I bit my tongue

En otros casos cuando el español emplea los pronombres complemento indirecto (me/te/le *etc*), *el inglés utiliza el correspondiente sujeto* (I/you/he *etc*) *y el respectivo adjetivo posesivo*:

le rompió la nariz = he/she broke his/her nose
le mordió la mano = he/she bit his/her hand
les cayó en la cabeza = it fell on their heads

Nótese el plural en la última traducción

body; **~ de bomberos** fire department (AmE), fire brigade (BrE); **~ de policía** police force; **~ diplomático** diplomatic corps **5** (consistencia, densidad) body; **de mucho ~** ‹*tela*› heavy; ‹*vino*› full-bodied

cuervo *m* raven; (como nombre genérico) crow

cuesco *m* (Bot) stone

cuesta *f* **(a)** (pendiente) slope; **una ~ muy pronunciada** a very steep slope; **ir ~ arriba** to go uphill; **iba corriendo ~ abajo** I was running downhill **(b) a cuestas: llevar algo a ~s** to carry sth on one's shoulders/back; **echarse algo a ~s** ‹*carga/bulto*› to put sth on one's back; ‹*problema*› to burden oneself with sth

cuesta, cuestan, etc *see* COSTAR

cuestión *f* **(a)** (tema, problema) question, matter; **cuestiones de derecho internacional** matters *o* questions of international law; **llegar al fondo de la ~** to get to the heart of the matter **(b)** (*en locs*) **en cuestión** in question; **en cuestión de** in a matter of; **la cuestión es** ... the thing is ...; **la ~ es divertirnos** the main thing is to enjoy ourselves; **ser cuestión de** to be a matter of; **todo es ~ de** ... it's just a question of ...

cuestionar [A1] *vt* to question

cuestionario *m* (encuesta) questionnaire; (Educ) question paper, questions (*pl*)

cuete *m* **1** (Méx, RPl fam) (borrachera): **agarrar un ~** to get plastered (colloq) **2** (AmL fam) (petardo) firecracker **3** (Per fam) (pistola) shooter (colloq), rod (sl) **4** (Méx) (Coc) braising steak

cueva *f* cave

cueza, cuezan, etc *see* COCER

cuidado[1] -da *adj* ‹*presentación*› meticulous, careful; ‹*aspecto*› impeccable; ‹*dicción*› precise

cuidado[2] *m* **(a)** (precaución): **tener ~** to be careful; **lo envolvió con mucho ~** she wrapped it very carefully; **¡~ con el escalón!** mind the step!; **~ con lo que haces** watch *o* be careful what you do; ***de ~*** (fam) ‹*problema/herida*› serious **(b)** (atención) care; **pone mucho ~ en su trabajo** he takes a great deal of care over his work **(c)** (de niños, enfermos): **no tiene experiencia en el ~ de los niños** he has no experience of looking after children; **estar al ~ de algn/algo** (cuidar) to look after sb/sth; (ser cuidado por) to be in sb's care **(d) cuidados** *mpl* (Med) attention, care, treatment; **necesita los ~s de una enfermera** she needs to be looked after by a nurse; **~s intensivos** intensive care **(e)** (preocupación): **pierde ~** (AmL) don't worry; **me tiene sin ~** it doesn't matter to me in the slightest ■ *interj* be careful!, watch out!

cuidador -dora *m,f* (de niños) baby sitter (AmE), childminder (BrE); (de animales) zookeeper

cuidadoso -sa *adj* **(a)** ‹*persona*› careful; **~** CON **algo** careful WITH sth **(b)** ‹*búsqueda/investigación*› careful, thorough

cuidar [A1] *vt* **(a)** ‹*juguetes/plantas/casa*› to look after; ‹*niño*› to look after, take care of; ‹*enfermo*› to care for, look after **(b)** ‹*estilo/apariencia*› to take care over; **debes ~ la ortografía** you must take care over your spelling ■ **~** *vi* **~** DE **algo/algn** to take care OF sth/sb; **~ré de que no les falte nada** I'll make sure they have everything they need

■ **cuidarse** *v pron* (*refl*) to take care of oneself, look after oneself; **¡cuídate!** take care!; **se cuidó bien de no volver por ahí** he made very sure he didn't go back there; **cuídate de decir algo que te comprometa** take care not to say something which might compromise you

cuije *mf* (Méx) office junior

culantro *m* coriander

culata *f* **(a)** (de escopeta, revólver) butt; (de cañón) breech **(b)** (de motor) cylinder head

culebra *f* (Zool) snake

culebrón *m* soap opera, soap (colloq)

culinario -ria *adj* culinary (frml)

culminación *f* **(a)** (de carrera, negociaciones) culmination; (de fiesta) climax **(b)** (realización) fulfillment*

culminante *adj*: **punto ~** (de carrera) peak, high point; (de historia, película) climax; (de negociaciones) crucial stage

culminar [A1] *vi* (llegar al clímax): **la novela culmina cuando** ... the novel reaches its climax when ...; **~** EN *or* CON **algo** to culminate IN sth

culo *m* (fam: en algunas regiones vulg) **(a)** (nalgas) backside (colloq), butt (AmE colloq), bum (BrE colloq), ass (AmE vulg), arse (BrE vulg); **te voy a pegar en el ~** I'm going to spank *o* smack you **(b)** (de vaso, botella) bottom

culpa *f* **(a)** (responsabilidad) fault; **yo no tengo la ~** it's not my fault; **echarle la ~ a algn (de algo)** to blame sb *o* put the blame on sb (for sth); **llegó tarde por ~ del tráfico** he arrived late because of the traffic **(b)** (falta, pecado) sin

culpabilidad *f* (Der,Psic) guilt

culpable *adj* [SER] ‹*persona*› guilty; **sentirse ~ de algo** to feel guilty about sth; **ser ~ de algo** to be to blame for sth; (Der) to be guilty of sth ■ *mf* **(a)** (de delito) culprit **(b)** (de problema, situación): **tú eres el ~ de todo esto** this is all your fault, you're to blame for all this

culpar [A1] *vt* to blame; **~ a algn** DE **algo** to blame sb FOR sth, blame sth ON sb

cultivado -da *adj* cultivated

cultivar [A1] *vt* **(a)** ‹*campo/tierras*› to cultivate, farm; ‹*plantas*› to grow, cultivate **(b)** ‹*bacterias/perlas*› to culture **(c)** ‹*amistad*› to cultivate; ‹*inteligencia/memoria*› to develop; ‹*artes/interés*› to encourage

cultivo *m* **(a)** (de tierra) farming, cultivation; (de plantas, frutas) growing, cultivation; **~ intensivo** intensive farming **(b)** (cosa cultivada) crop; **~s de secano** dry-farmed crops **(c)** (Biol, Med) (acción) culturing; (producto) culture **(d)** (de las artes) promotion, encouragement

culto[1] -ta *adj* **(a)** ‹*persona/pueblo*› educated, cultured **(b)** (Ling) ‹*palabra*› learned; ‹*literatura/música*› highbrow

culto[2] *m* **(a)** (adoración, creencia) worship; **rendir ~ a algo/algn** to worship sth/sb; **libertad de ~(s)** freedom of worship **(b)** (interés obsesivo) cult; **el ~ del dinero** the cult of money

cultura *f* **(a)** (civilización) culture **(b)** (conocimientos, ilustración): **una persona de gran ~** a very well-educated *o* cultured person; **~ general/musical**

Cumplir

El verbo cumplir seguido de años (edad), debe traducirse en contexto

cuando cumpla 21 años	=	when I'm twenty one
voy a cumplir 21 años el mes que viene	=	it's my twenty first birthday next month
acaba de cumplir 16 años *o or* tiene 16 años recién cumplidos	=	he's just sixteen *o* he's just turned sixteen
al cumplir los 18 años	=	shortly after her eighteenth birthday
cumplió 5 años en diciembre	=	he was 5 last December

Para ejemplos suplementarios, ver bajo entrada

general/musical knowledge; **la ~ popular** popular culture

cultural *adj* cultural; **un acto ~** a cultural event; **bajo nivel ~** low standard of general education

culturismo *m* bodybuilding

cumbre *f* **(a)** (de montaña) top **(b)** (apogeo) height; **en la ~ del éxito** at the height of his success **(c)** (Pol) summit (meeting)

cumpleaños *m* (*pl* ~) **(a)** (aniversario) birthday; **¡feliz ~!** happy birthday!; **¿qué vas a hacer el día de tu ~?** what are you going to do on your birthday? **(b)** (fiesta) birthday party

cumplido[1] -da *adj* [SER] **(a)** (atento, cortés) polite **(b)** (considerado) thoughtful **(c)** (Col) (puntual) punctual; *ver tb* CUMPLIR

cumplido[2] *m*: **hacerle un ~ a algn** to pay sb a compliment; **una visita de ~** a duty *o* courtesy call; **la invitó por ~** he invited her because he felt he ought to

cumplidor -dora *adj* reliable

cumplir [I1] *vt* **1 (a)** (ejecutar) ‹*orden*› to carry out; ‹*ley*› to obey; **la satisfacción del deber cumplido** the satisfaction of having done one's duty **(b)** ‹*promesa/palabra*› to keep; ‹*compromiso*› to honor*, fulfill*; ‹*obligación/contrato*› to fulfill* **(c)** (alcanzar) ‹*objetivo/ambición*› to achieve; ‹*requisitos*› fulfill; **¡misión cumplida!** mission accomplished **(d)** (desempeñar) ‹*papel*› to perform, fulfill* **2** ‹*condena/sentencia*› to serve; ‹*servicio militar*› to do **3** ‹*años/meses*›: **mañana cumple 20 años** she'll be 20 tomorrow; **¡que cumplas muchos más!** many happy returns!; **mañana cumplimos 20 años de casados** (AmL) tomorrow we'll have been married 20 years ■ ~ *vi* **(a)** ~ CON **algo** ‹*con obligación*› to fulfill* sth, satisfy sth; ‹*con tarea*› to carry out sth; ‹*con trámite*› to comply WITH sth; ‹*con requisito/condición*› to fulfill* sth; **cumple con su deber** he does his duty **(b)** (con una obligación social): **nos invitó sólo por ~** she only invited us because she felt she ought to; **con los Lara ya hemos cumplido** we've done our bit as far as the Laras are concerned (colloq)

■ **cumplirse** *v pron* **(a)** «*deseo/predicción*» to come true; «*ambición*» to be realized, be fulfilled **(b)** «*plazo*»: **mañana se cumple el plazo para pagar el impuesto** tomorrow is the last day for paying the tax; **hoy se cumple el primer aniversario de** ... today marks the first anniversary of ...

cuna *f* **(a)** (tradicional) cradle; (cama con barandas) crib (AmE), cot (BrE); (portabebé) portacrib (AmE), carrycot (BrE) **(b)** (liter) (lugar de nacimiento) birthplace

cuncho *m* (Col) (poso — del café) grounds (*pl*); (— del vino) lees (*pl*)

cuncuna *f* (Chi) (Zool) caterpillar

cundir [I1] *vi* **(a)** «*rumor*» to spread; «*miedo*» to grow; **¡que no cunda el pánico!** don't panic!; **cundió la alarma** there was widespread alarm **(b)** (rendir) «*detergente/lana*» to go a long way; **hoy no me ha cundido el trabajo** I haven't got much work done today

cuneta *f* **(a)** (en carretera) ditch **(b)** (Chi) (de calle) curb (AmE), kerb (BrE)

cuña *f* **1 (a)** (pieza triangular) wedge; **en ~** in a V-formation *o* wedge formation **(b)** (Col) (muesca) groove **2** (CS fam) ⇒ PALANCA 2

cuñado -da *m,f* **(a)** (pariente político) (*m*) brother-in-law; (*f*) sister-in-law; **mis ~s** (sólo varones) my brothers-in-law; (varones y mujeres) my brothers and sisters-in-law **(b)** (Per fam) (compañero) buddy (AmE colloq), mate (BrE colloq)

cuño *m* (troquel) die; (sello) stamp; ***de nuevo ~*** ‹*palabra*› newly-coined (*before n*)

cuota *f* **(a)** (de club, asociación) membership fees (*pl*); (de sindicato) dues (*pl*); **~ inicial** deposit, down payment **(b)** (AmL) (plazo) installment*, payment; (parte proporcional) quota; **~s de producción** production quotas **(c)** (Méx) (Auto) toll

cupe *see* CABER

Cupido *m* Cupid

cupiera, **cupiese, etc** *see* CABER

cupimos, **cupisteis, etc** *see* CABER

cupo *m* **(a)** (cantidad establecida) quota **(b)** (AmL) (capacidad) room; **una sala con ~ para 300 personas** a hall with room for 300 people **(c)** (AmL) (plaza) place

cupo, **cupiste, etc** *see* CABER

cupón *m* **(a)** (vale) coupon, voucher **(b)** (Esp) (de lotería) ticket

cúpula *f* (Arquit) dome, cupola

cura *m* (sacerdote) priest; **se metió de** *or* **a ~** he became a priest ■ *f* **(a)** (curación, tratamiento) cure; **tener/no tener ~** to be curable/incurable; **~ de urgencias** first aid **(b)** (vendaje) dressing; (curita) (Col) Band-Aid® (AmE), (sticking) plaster (BrE)

curable *adj* curable

curación *f* **(a)** (tratamiento) treatment **(b)** (recuperación—de enfermo) recovery; (— de herida) healing

curado -da *adj* **1** ‹*jamón/carne*› cured; ‹*cuero/piel*› tanned **2** (fam) (borracho) plastered (colloq)

curandero -ra *m,f* (en medicina popular) folk healer; (hechicero) witch doctor; (charlatán) (pey) quack doctor (pej)

curar [A1] *vt* **1 (a)** (poner bien) ‹*enfermo/enfermedad*› to cure; ‹*herida*› to heal **(b)** (tratar) ‹*enfermo/enfermedad*› to treat; ‹*herida*› (desinfectar) to clean; (vendar) to dress **2** ‹*jamón/pescado*› to cure; ‹*cuero/piel*› to tan

■ **curarse** *v pron* «*enfermo*» to recover, get better; «*herida*» to heal up; **~se DE algo** to get over sth

curda *mf* (RPl fam) (borracho) soak (colloq)

curiosear [A1] *vi* **(a)** (fisgonear) to pry; **~ en la vida ajena** to pry into other people's affairs; **estaba curioseando en mis cajones** he was going *o* looking through my drawers **(b)** (por las tiendas, en una biblioteca) to browse

curiosidad *f* (cualidad) curiosity; **por ~** out of curiosity; **siente mucha ~** he is very curious; **tengo ~ por saberlo** I'm curious to know; **están muertos de ~** they are dying to see him (*o* to know *etc*)

curioso -sa *adj* **1** (interesante, extraño) curious, strange, odd **2 (a)** [SER] (inquisitivo) inquisitive; (entrometido) (pey) nosy* (colloq) **(b)** [ESTAR] (interesado) curious ■ *m,f* **(a)** (espectador) onlooker **(b)** (fam) (fisgón) busybody (colloq)

curita *f* (AmL) Band-Aid® (AmE), (sticking) plaster (BrE)

currículo *m* (Educ) curriculum

curriculum, **currículum** *m* (*pl* **-lums**) **(a)** (antecedentes) *tb* **~ vitae** curriculum vitae, CV **(b)** (Educ) curriculum

curry /'kurri/ *m* (*pl* **-rries**) (polvo) curry powder; (plato) curry; **pollo al ~** curried chicken

cursar [A1] *vt* (estudiar): **cursa segundo (año)** she is in her second year; **cursó estudios de Derecho** she did *o* studied *o* (BrE) read Law

cursi *adj* (fam) ‹*objeto*› corny, twee (BrE); ‹*idea*› sentimental, twee (BrE); ‹*decoración*› chichi; ‹*persona*› affected; ■ *mf* (fam): **es un ~** he's so affected *o* (BrE) twee

cursillo *m* **(a)** (curso corto) short course; **~ de natación** swimming lessons **(b)** (ciclo de conferencias) series of lectures

cursiva *f* italics (*pl*)

curso *m* **1** (Educ) **(a)** (año académico) year; **está en (el) tercer ~** he's in the third year; **el ~ escolar/universitario** the academic year **(b)** (de inglés, mecanografía) course; **~ intensivo** crash *o* intensive course; **C~ de Orientación Universitaria** (en Esp) pre-university course; **~ por correspondencia** correspondence course **2 (a)** (transcurso, desarrollo) course; **dejar que algo siga su ~** to let sth take its course **(b)** (de río) course **3** (circulación): **monedas de ~ legal** legal tender, legal currency

cursor *m* cursor

curtido -da *adj* ‹*rostro/piel*› weather-beaten; ‹*manos*› hardened

curul *f* (Col, Méx) (Pol) seat

curva *f* **(a)** (línea) curve **(b)** (en camino, carretera) curve; (más pronunciada) bend; **una ~ cerrada** a sharp bend **(c)** (Dep) curveball **(c) curvas** *fpl* (de una mujer) curves (*pl*); **con ~s** curvaceous

curvo -va *adj* curved

cúspide *f* **(a)** (de montaña) top, summit; (de pirámide) top, apex **(b)** (de fama, poder) height, pinnacle **(c)** (de organización) leadership

cusuco *m* (AmC) armadillo

cutáneo -nea *adj* skin (*before n*), cutaneous (tech)

cutícula *f* cuticle

cutis *m* (*pl* **~**) skin

cuy *m* (AmS) guinea pig

cuye *m* (Chi) guinea pig

cuyo -ya *adj* whose; **un amigo ~s hijos van a ese colegio** a friend whose children go to that school; **vocablos ~ uso es extendido** words which are in widespread use, **en ~ caso** in which case

C.V. *m* (= **curriculum vitae**) CV

Dd

D, d *f* (*read as* /de/) *the letter* D, d

D. = **Don**

dactilar *adj* finger (*before n*); ⇒ HUELLA (a)

dactilografía *f* typing, typewriting

dactilógrafo -fa *m,f* typist

dado¹ -da *adj* **1** (determinado) given; **en un momento ~** at a given moment **2** (*como conj*) given; **dadas las circunstancias** given *o* in view of the circumstances; **~ que** given that **3** [SER] (proclive) **~ A algo/hacer algo** given TO sth/doing sth

dado² *m* **1** (Jueg) dice, die (frml); **jugar a los ~s** to play dice **2** (Arquit) dado

daga *f* dagger

dalia *f* dahlia

daltónico -ca *adj* color-blind* ■ *m,f*: **los ~s** people suffering from color-blindness*

daltonismo *m* color-blindness*

dama *f* **1** (frml) (señora) lady; **~s y caballeros** ladies and gentlemen; **~ de honor** (de novia) bridesmaid; (de reina) lady-in-waiting **2** (figura — en damas) king; (— en ajedrez, en naipes) queen **3 damas** *fpl* (juego) checkers (AmE), draughts (BrE); **jugar a las ~s** to play checkers *o* draughts

damasco *m* **1** (Tex) damask **2** (AmS) (fruta) apricot; (árbol) apricot tree

Damasco *m* Damascus

damnificado -da *m,f* (frml) victim

danés -nesa *adj* Danish ■ *m,f* **(a)** (persona) (*m*) Dane, Danish man; (*f*) Dane, Danish woman **(b) danés** *m* (idioma) Danish

danza *f* dance; **~ moderna** modern dance

danzar [A4] *vi* (frml) (bailar) to dance

dañar [A1] *vt* (en general) to damage; ‹*salud/organismo*› to be bad for

■ **dañarse** *v pron* **1** (en general) to be/get damaged; ‹*salud*› to damage **2** (Col, Ven) **(a)** «*carne/comida*» to rot, go bad **(b)** «*carro*» to break down; «*aparato*» to break

dañino -na *adj* [SER] ‹*planta/sustancia*› harmful; **~** PARA **algo** harmful TO sth

daño *m* **(a)** (dolor físico): **hacerse ~** to hurt oneself; **me he hecho ~ en la espalda** I've hurt my back; **hacerle ~ a algn** «*persona*» to hurt sb; **el picante me hace ~** hot, spicy food doesn't agree with me **(b)** (destrozo) damage; **sufrir ~s** to be damaged, to suffer damage **(c) ~s y perjuicios** damages (*pl*)

dar [A25] *vt* **I 1 (a)** (entregar) to give; **dale las llaves a Pedro** give the keys to Pedro; **déme un kilo de peras** can I have a kilo of pears?; ⇒ CONOCER *vt* 3 (b), ENTENDER *vt* **(b)** ‹*cartas/mano*› to give **2 (a)** (donar, regalar) ‹*sangre/limosna*› to give; **me dio su reloj** she gave me her watch **(b)** (proporcionar) ‹*fuerzas/valor/esperanza*› to give; ‹*información/idea*› to give **3 (a)** (conferir, aportar) ‹*sabor/color/forma*› to give **(b)** (aplicar) ‹*mano de pintura/barniz*› to give **(c)** ‹*sedante/masaje*› to give **4** (conceder) ‹*prórroga/permiso*› to give; **el dentista me dio hora para el miércoles** I have an appointment with the dentist on Wednesday; **nos dieron un premio** we won *o* got a prize **5 (a)** (expresar, decir) ‹*parecer/opinón*› to give; **¿le diste las gracias?** did you thank him?, did you say thank you?; **dales saludos** give/send them my regards; **tuve que ~le la noticia** I was the one who had to break the news to him **(b)** (señalar, indicar): **me da ocupado** *or* (Esp) **comunicando** the line's busy *o* (BrE) engaged; **el reloj dio las cinco** the clock struck five

II 1 (a) (producir) ‹*fruto/flor*› to bear; ‹*dividendos*› to pay; **un negocio que da mucho dinero** a business which makes a lot of money **(b)** (AmL) (alcanzar hasta): **da 150 kilómetros por hora** it can do *o* go 150 kilometres an hour; **venía a todo lo que daba** it was travelling at full speed; **ponen la radio a todo lo que da** they turn the radio on full blast **2** (causar, provocar) ‹*placer/susto*› to give; ‹*problemas*› to cause; **~ trabajo** to be hard work; **el calor le dio sueño/sed** the heat made him sleepy/thirsty

III 1 (presentar) ‹*concierto*› to give; **¿qué dan esta noche en la tele?** what's on TV tonight? (colloq); **¿dónde están dando esa película?** where's that film showing? **2 (a)** ‹*fiesta/conferencia*› to give; ‹*baile/banquete*› to hold; ‹*discurso*› (AmL) to make **(b)** (CS) ‹*examen*› to take *o* (BrE) sit; *ver tb* CLASE 4

IV (realizar la acción que se indica) ‹*grito*› to give; **~ un paso atrás** to take a step back; **dame un beso** give me a kiss; *ver tb* GOLPE, PASEO, VUELTA, ETC

V (considerar) **~ algo/a algn** POR **algo**: **lo dieron por muerto** they gave him up for dead; **ese tema lo doy por sabido** I'm assuming you've already covered that topic; **¡dalo por hecho!** consider it done! ■ **~** *vi* **I 1 dar a** «*puerta*» to give onto, open onto; «*ventana/balcón*» to look onto, give onto; «*fachada/frente*» to face **2** (ser suficiente, alcanzar) **~** PARA **algo/algn** to be enough FOR sth/sb; **no me dio (el) tiempo** I didn't have time; **~ *de sí*** ‹*zapatos/jersey*› to stretch **3** (arrojar un resultado): **el análisis le dio positivo** her test was positive; **¿cuánto da la cuenta?** what does it come to?; **a mí me dio 247** I made it (to be) 247 **4** (importar): **da lo mismo** it doesn't matter; **¡qué más da!** what does it matter!; **¿qué más da?** what difference does it make?; **me da igual** I don't mind **5** (en naipes) to deal

II 1 (a) (pegar, golpear): **~le** A **algn** to hit sb; (como castigo) to smack sb; **dale al balón** kick the ball; **el balón dio en el poste** the ball hit the post **(b)** (acertar) to hit; **~ en el blanco** to hit the target **2** (accionar, mover) **~le** A **algo** ‹*a botón/tecla*› to press sth; ‹*a interruptor*› to flick sth; ‹*a manivela/volante*› to turn sth **3 dar con** (encontrar) ‹*persona*› to find; ‹*solución*› to hit upon, find; ‹*palabra*› to come up with **4** (hablando de manías, ocurrencias) **~le a algn** POR **hacer algo** ‹*por pintar/cocinar*› to take to doing sth; **le ha dado por decir que** ... he's started saying that ... **5** «*sol/luz*»: **aquí da el sol toda la mañana** you get the sun all morning here; **la luz le daba de lleno en los ojos** the light was shining right in his eyes

■ **darse** *v pron* **I 1** (producirse) «*fruta/trigo*» to grow **2** (presentarse) «*oportunidad/ocasión*» to arise **3** (resultar) (+ *me/te/le etc*): **se le dan los idiomas** she's good at languages

II (a) (*refl*) (realizar lo que se indica) ‹*ducha/banquete*› to have; ***dárselas de algo***: **se las da de valiente/de que sabe mucho** he likes to make out he's brave/he knows a lot; **dárselas de listo** to act smart **(b)** (golpearse, pegarse): **se dio con el martillo en el dedo** he hit his finger with the hammer; **se dieron contra un árbol** they crashed into a tree; **se dio ~ un golpe en la rodilla** he hit his knee

IV (considerarse) **~se** POR **algo**: **con eso me ~ía por satisfecha** I'd be quite happy with that; *ver tb* ALUDIR (a), ENTERADO 1

dardo *m* **(a)** (Jueg) dart; **jugar a los ~s** to play darts **(b)** (arma) small spear

datar [A1] *vi* to date; **data del siglo XII** it dates from the 12th century; **data de hace muchos años** it goes back many years

de

Algunas observaciones generales

Cuando la preposición de *introduce el complemento de verbos intransitivos como* hablar de, dudar de, presumir de, *se debe consultar la respectiva entrada, asimismo cuando introduce el complemento de ciertos sustantivos como* deseo de, falta de *etc., o de adjetivos como* lleno de, temeroso de, harto de *etc.*

Expresiones de origen

En las oraciones que denotan origen o pertenencia a cierto lugar, de *suele traducirse por* in:

todos los maestros de Lima	=	all the teachers in Lima
el mejor vino de Chile/ del mundo	=	the best wine in Chile/ in the world
visitamos varias iglesias de la ciudad	=	we visited several churches in the city

Relaciones de pertenencia/posesión

La mayoría de las frases que expresan relaciones de pertenencia o posesión se traducen al inglés mediante el genitivo sajón, cuyas reglas son las siguientes:

Cuando el poseedor en español es un nombre singular o propio, el inglés añade -'s *(apóstrofo s) a la traducción del mismo*:

la casa de mi amiga	=	my friend's house
el coche de John	=	John's car

Cuando el poseedor en español es un nombre plural, el inglés añade -' *(apóstrofo) a la traducción de éstos*:

la habitación de las niñas	=	the girls' room
el coche de mis padres	=	my parents' car

En todo caso se deben tener en cuenta los nombres irregulares en inglés que no acaban en s*, el genitivo sajón se construye añadiendo* -'s *(apóstrofo s)*:

los libros de los niños	=	the children's books

Son de notar también los siguientes usos del genitivo:

fuimos a casa de Pedro	=	we went to Pedro's (place)
la tienda de comestibles	=	the grocer's (BrE)

así como el uso del genitivo en inglés coloquial:

es una amiga de mi madre	=	she's a friend of my mother's
fue una receta de María	=	it was a recipe of María's

Para otros usos y ejemplos suplementarios de *la preposición* de *ver entrada*

dátil *m* (Bot) date

datívo *m* (Ling) dative

dato *m* **(a)** (elemento de información) piece of information; **no dispongo de todos los ~s** I don't have all the information; **~s personales** personal details (*pl*) **(b) datos** *mpl* (Inf) data (*pl*), information

d. de C. (= **después de Jesucristo**) AD

de *prep* **1 (a)** (pertenencia, posesión): **la casa ~ ~ mis padres** my parents' house; **el rey ~ Francia** the king of France; **no es ~ él** it isn't his; **es un amigo ~ mi hijo** he's a friend of my son's; **un estudiante ~ quinto año** a fifth-year student; **la tapa ~ la cacerola** the saucepan lid; **un avión ~ Mexair** a Mexair plane **(b)** (con un nombre en aposición) of; **la ciudad ~ Lima** the city of Lima; **el aeropuerto ~ Barajas** Barajas airport; **el mes ~ enero** the month of January **2 (a)** (procedencia, origen, tiempo) from; **es ~ Bogotá** she's/she comes from Bogotá; **una carta ~ Julia** a letter from Julia; **un amigo ~ la infancia** a childhood friend; **la literatura ~ ese período** the literature of *o* from that period; **~ aquí a tu casa** from here to your house **(b)** (material, contenido, composición): **son ~ plástico** they're (made of) plastic; **una mesa ~ caoba** a mahogany table; **un vaso ~ agua** a glass of water; **un millón ~ dólares** a million dollars **(c)** (causa, modo): **murió ~ viejo** he died of old age; **~ tanto gritar** from shouting so much; **verde ~ envidia** green with envy; **temblando ~ miedo** trembling with fear; **~ memoria** by heart; **lo tumbó ~ un golpe** he knocked him down with one blow **(d)** (en oraciones pasivas) by; **un poema ~ Neruda** a poem by Neruda; **rodeada ~ árboles** surrounded by trees **3 (a)** (cualidades, características): **de gran inteligencia** of great intelligence; **objetos ~ mucho valor** objects of great value; **¿~ qué color lo quiere?** what color do you want it?; **tiene cara ~ aburrido** he looks bored; **una botella ~ un litro** a liter bottle; **la chica ~ azul** the girl in blue **(b)** (al definir, especificar): **el botón ~ abajo** the bottom button; **tiene dos metros ~ ancho** it's two meters wide; **es fácil de pronunciar** it's easy to pronounce; **uno ~ los míos** one of mine; **el mayor ~ los Soto** the eldest of the Soto children **4 (a)** (con cifras): **pagan un interés ~l 15%** they pay 15% interest *o* interest at 15% **(b)** (en comparaciones de cantidad) than; **más ~ £100** more than *o* over £100; **pesa menos ~ un kilo** it weighs less than *o* under a kilo; **un número mayor/menor ~ 29** a number over/under 29 **(c)** (con un superlativo): **es el más caro ~ todos** it's the most expensive one; **la ciudad más grande ~l mundo** the biggest city in the world **(d)** (refiriéndose a una parte del día): **~ día/noche** during the day/at night; **~ madrugada** early in the morning **5 (a)** (en calidad de) as; **trabaja ~ secretaria** she works as a secretary; **hace ~ rey en la**

obra he plays (the part of) a king in the play **(b)** (en expresiones de estado, actividad): **~ mal humor** in a bad mood; **estamos ~ fiesta** we're having a party **(c)** (indicando uso, destino, finalidad): **el cepillo ~ la ropa** the clothes brush; **copas ~ vino** wine glasses; **ropa ~ cama** bed clothes; **dales algo ~ comer** give them something to eat; **¿qué hay ~ postre?** what's for dessert? **6** (con sentido condicional): **~ haberlo sabido** if I had known, had I known; **~ no ser así** otherwise

de *f: name of the letter* d

dé *see* DAR

deambular [A1] *vi* to wander around *o* about

debajo *adv* **1** [*Latin American Spanish also uses* ABAJO *in many of these examples*] underneath; **no hay nada ~** there's nothing underneath; **el que está ~** the one below, the next one down **2 debajo de** (*loc prep*) under, underneath; **~ del coche** under *o* underneath the car; **~ del agua** underwater; **por ~ de la puerta** under the door; **temperaturas por ~ de lo normal** temperatures below average

debate *m* debate; (más informal) discussion

debatir [I1] *vt* to debate; (más informal) to discuss

debe *m* debit

deber¹ [E1] *vt* ‹*dinero/favor/explicación*› to owe; **te debo las entradas de ayer** I owe you for the tickets from yesterday ■ **~** *v aux* **1** (expresando obligación): **debemos trabajar más** we must work harder; **no debes usarlo** you must not use it; **~ías** *or* **debías habérselo dicho** you ought to have *o* you should have told her; **no se debe mentir** you mustn't tell lies; **no ~ías haberlo dejado solo** you shouldn't have left him alone **2** (expresando suposición, probabilidad): **deben (de) ser más de las cinco** it must be after five o'clock; **deben (de) haber salido** they must have gone out; **debe (de) estar enamorado** she/he must be in love; **no deben (de) saber la dirección** they probably don't know the address; **no les debe (de) interesar** they can't be interested

■ **deberse** *v pron* **1** (tener su causa en) **~se A algo** to be due TO sth; **se debe a que no estudia** it's due to the fact that she doesn't study; **¿a qué se debe este escándalo?** what's all this racket about? **2** «*persona*» (tener obligaciones hacia) **~se A algn** to have a duty TO sb

deber² *m* **1** (obligación) duty; **cumplió con su ~** he carried out *o* did his duty **2 deberes** *mpl* (tarea escolar) homework, assignment (AmE)

debido -da *adj* **(a)** (apropiado): **a su ~ tiempo** in due course; **tratar a algn con el ~ respeto** to show due respect to sb; **tomó las debidas precauciones** she took the necessary precautions; **como es ~** ‹*sentarse/comer*› properly; ‹*comida/regalo*› proper; **más de lo ~** too much **(b)** (*en locs*) **debido a** owing to, on account of; **debido a que** owing to the fact that

débil *adj* **(a)** ‹*persona/economía/gobierno*› weak **(b)** ‹*sonido/voz*› faint; ‹*moneda/argumento*› weak; ‹*excusa*› feeble, lame; ‹*luz*› dim, faint; ‹*sílaba/vocal*› unstressed, weak

debilidad *f* weakness; **siento una gran ~** I feel terribly debilitated *o* weak; **se aprovechan de su ~** they take advantage of his weak character; **tener ~ por algn/algo** to have a soft spot for sb/a weakness for sth

debilitar [A1] *vt* to weaken

■ **debilitarse** *v pron* **(a)** «*persona*» to become weak; «*salud*» to deteriorate; «*voluntad*» to weaken **(b)** «*sonido*» to get *o* become faint/fainter **(c)** «*economía*» to grow *o* become weak/weaker

débito *m* debit; **~ bancario** (AmL) direct debit, direct billing (AmE)

debutante *mf* (Dep, Espec) *player or artist making his/her public debut*

debutar [A1] *vi* to make one's debut

década *f* ▶ **193** decade; **la ~ de los ochenta** the eighties

decadencia *f* **(a)** (proceso) decline **(b)** (estado) decadence

decadente *adj* **(a)** ‹*moral/costumbres*› decadent **(b)** ‹*salud*› declining

decaer [E16] *vi* **(a)** «*ánimo/fuerzas*» to flag; «*enfermo*» to deteriorate; «*interés/popularidad*» to wane **(b)** «*barrio/restaurante*» to go downhill; «*calidad/prestigio*» to decline **(c)** «*imperio/civilización*» to decay, decline

decaído -da *adj* [ESTAR] low, down (colloq)

decálogo *m* decalogue

decano -na *m,f* (de una facultad) dean; (de una profesión, un grupo) senior member

decapitar [A1] *vt* to behead, decapitate

decatlón *m* decathlon

decena *f*: ▶ **293** **unidades, ~s y centenas** (Mat) units, tens and hundreds; **una ~ de personas** about ten people; **~s de personas lo presenciaron** dozens *o* scores of people witnessed it

decencia *f* decency

decenio *m* decade

decente *adj* **(a)** (honrado, decoroso) decent, respectable **(b)** (aceptable) ‹*sueldo/vivienda*› decent, reasonable **(c)** [ESTAR] (de apariencia aceptable) respectable

decepción *f* disappointment, letdown (colloq); **me llevé una gran ~** I was very disappointed

decepcionado -da *adj* disappointed; **estar ~ con algo/de algn** to be disappointed with sth/sb

decepcionante *adj* disappointing

decepcionar [A1] *vt* to disappoint; **la película me decepcionó** I was disappointed with the movie

decidido -da *adj* **(a)** [SER] ‹*persona/tono*› (resuelto, enérgico) decisive, determined **(b)** [ESTAR] **~ A hacer algo** determined *o* resolved to do sth

decidir [I1] *vt* **1 (a)** (tomar una determinación) to decide; **decidí comprarlo** I decided to buy it **(b)** ‹*persona*› to make … decide; **lo que me decidió** what made me decide **2** ‹*asunto*› to settle; ‹*resultado*› to decide ■ **~** *vi* to decide; **tiene que ~ entre los dos** she has to choose *o* decide between the two; **~ SOBRE algo** to decide ON sth

Decimales, Fracciones y Porcentajes

Decimales y fracciones

En inglés se utiliza el punto para separar los números enteros de los decimales:

10.5 ten point five
12.76 twelve point seven six

Las fracciones se expresan de la siguiente manera:

½ one half *o* a half
⅓ one third *o* a third
⅔ two thirds
¼ one quarter *o* a quarter
¾ three quarters
⅕ one fifth

En todos los demás casos, el denominador se expresa por medio del número ordinal correspondiente:

⅜ three eighths

Fracciones fuera del contexto estrictamente matemático:

media naranja	half an orange
quiero la mitad del dinero	I want half (of) the money
las dos terceras partes de los estudiantes	two thirds of the students
las tres cuartas partes de la población	three quarters of the population

Porcentajes

En inglés no se utiliza el artículo delante del numeral:

el 10% de la población	10% (ten per cent) of the population
los precios han subido un 15%	prices have gone up by 15% (fifteen per cent)
si el 40% de los socios vota en contra	if 40% (forty per cent) of the members vote against

▪ **decidirse** *v pron* to decide, to make up one's mind; **~se a hacer algo** to decide to do sth; **~se por algo** to decide on sth

décima *f* ▶ 294, 406 (de segundo, grado) tenth; **tiene 39 y tres ~s** his temperature is 39.3 (degrees)

decimal *m* (número) decimal (number)

décimo[1] -ma *adj/pron* tenth; *para ejemplos ver* QUINTO; **la décima parte** a tenth

décimo[2] *m* **(a)** ▶ 294 (partitivo) tenth **(b)** (de lotería) *tenth share in a lottery ticket*

decir[1] *m*: **¿cientos de personas? — bueno, es un ~** hundreds of people? — well, figuratively speaking

decir[2] [I24] *vt* **1 (a)** ‹*palabra/frase/poema*› to say; ‹*mentira/verdad*› to tell; [*para ejemplos con complemento indirecto ver división 2*] **no digas estupideces** don't talk nonsense!; **¿eso lo dices por mí?** are you referring to me?; **¡no lo dirás en serio!** you can't be serious!; **dijo que sí con la cabeza** he nodded; **no se dice 'andé', se dice 'anduve'** it isn't 'andé', it's 'anduve'; **¡eso no se dice!** you mustn't say that!; **¿cómo se dice 'amor' en ruso?** how do you say 'love' in Russian?; **¿lo encontró? — dice que sí/no** did he find it? — he says he did/he didn't **(b) decir misa** to say mass **2 ~le algo a algn** to tell sb sth; **voy a ~le a papá que** ... I'm going to tell Dad ...; **¡ya te lo decía yo!** I told you so! **3 (a)** (expresando órdenes, deseos, advertencias): **¡porque lo digo yo!** because I say so!; **harás lo que yo diga** you'll do as I say; **dice que llames cuando llegues** she says (you are) to phone when you get there; **dijo que tuviéramos cuidado** she said to be careful; **diles que empiecen** tell them to start; **le dije que no lo hiciera** I told him not to do it **(b) ~(le) adiós (a algn)** to say goodbye (to sb) **4 (a)** (opinar, pensar) to think; **¿y los padres qué dicen?** what do her parents think of it?, how do her parents feel about it?; **¡quién lo hubiera dicho!** who would have thought *o* believed it?; **es muy fácil — si tú lo dices** ... it's very easy — if you say so ... **(b)** (sugerir, comunicar): **el tiempo lo dirá** time will tell; **¿te dice algo ese nombre?** does that name mean anything to you? **5 querer decir** «*palabra/persona*» to mean; **¿qué quieres ~ con eso?** what do you mean by that? **6** (*en locs*) **a decir verdad** to tell you the truth, to be honest; **como quien dice** so to speak; **es decir** that is; **¡he dicho!** that's that *o* final!; **ni que decir tiene que** ... it goes without saying that ...; **¡no me digas!** no!, you're kidding *o* joking! (colloq); **por así decirlo** so to speak; ***el qué dirán*** (fam) what other people (might) think; *ver tb* DICHO[1] ▪ **~** *vi* **(a)** (invitando a hablar): **papá — dime, hijo** dad — yes, son?; **quería pedirle un favor — usted dirá** I wanted to ask you a favor — certainly, go ahead **(b)** ▶ 405 (Esp) (al contestar el teléfono): **¿diga?** *or* **¿dígame?** hello?

▪ **decirse** *v pron* **(a)** (*refl*) to say ... to oneself **(b)** (*recípr*) to say .... to each other; **se decían secretos al oído** they were whispering secrets to each other

decisión *f* **(a)** (acción) decision; **tomar una ~** to make a decision; **su ~ de marcharse** her decision to leave **(b)** (cualidad) decisiveness, decision; **una mujer con ~** a woman of decision **(c)** (AmL) (en boxeo): **ganó por ~** he won on points *o* by a decision

decisivo -va *adj* ‹*fecha/voto/resultado*› crucial, decisive; ‹*prueba*› conclusive; ‹*papel*› decisive

declaración *f* **1 (a)** (afirmación) declaration; **una ~ de amor** a declaration of love **(b)** (a la prensa, en público) statement; **hacer una ~** to issue a statement **(c)** (proclamación) declaration; **~ de guerra** declaration of war **2** (Der) statement, testimony; **el policía me tomó ~** the policeman took my statement; **prestar ~ como testigo** to give evidence, to testify; **~ del impuesto sobre la renta** income tax return

declarado -da *adj* declared, professed

declarar [A1] *vt* **1 (a)** (manifestar) ‹*apoyo/oposición/intención*› to declare, state; **le declaró su amor** he declared his love to her **(b)** (proclamar) ‹*guerra/independencia*› to declare; **el jurado lo declaró inocente** the jury found him not guilty **2 (a)** (en la aduana) to declare **(b)** (Fisco) ‹*bienes/ingresos*› to declare ■ **~** *vi* to give evidence, testify; **~ como testigo** to give evidence, to testify

■ **declararse** *v pron* **1 (a)** (manifestarse) to declare oneself; **~se en quiebra** to declare oneself bankrupt; **~se culpable/inocente** to plead guilty/not guilty; **~se en huelga** to go on strike **(b)** (confesar amor): **se le declaró** he declared himself *o* his love to her **2** «*incendio/epidemia*» to break out

declinación *f* (Ling) declension

declinar [A1] *vt* **(a)** ‹*invitación/oferta/honor*› to turn down, decline (frml) **(b)** (Ling) to decline

declive *m* **(a)** (de una superficie) slope, incline (frml); **terreno en ~** sloping ground **(b)** (decadencia) decline

decolaje *m* (AmL) take-off

decolar [A1] *vi* (AmL) to take off

decoración *f* **(a)** (de pasteles, platos) decoration; (de habitación) decor; (de árbol de Navidad) (AmL) decoration **(b)** (interiorismo) *tb* **~ de interiores** interior decoration

decorado *m* set

decorador -dora *m,f*: *tb* **~ de interiores** interior decorator

decorar [A1] *vt* to decorate

decorativo -va *adj* decorative

decoro *m* (pudor, respeto) decorum

decoroso -sa *adj* decent, respectable

decrecer [E3] *vi* **(a)** «*afición/interés*» to wane, decrease; «*importancia*» to decline **(b)** «*número/cantidad*» to decline, fall **(c)** «*aguas*» to drop, fall

decreciente *adj* decreasing (*before n*)

decrépito -ta *adj* decrepit

decretar [A1] *vt* to order, decree (frml)

decreto *m* decree

dedal *m* thimble

dedicación *f* dedication

dedicar [A2] *vt* **(a)** (consagrar) **~ algo A algo/hacer algo** ‹*tiempo/esfuerzos*› to devote sth TO sth/doing sth; **dedicó su vida a la ciencia/ayudar a los pobres** she devoted her life to science/to helping the poor **(b)** (ofrendar, ofrecer) ‹*obra/canción*› to dedicate

■ **dedicarse** *v pron* **(a)** (consagrarse) **~se A algo/hacer algo** to devote oneself TO sth/doing sth **(b)** (tener cierta ocupación, profesión): **¿a qué se dedica tu padre?** what does your father do?; **se dedica a la investigación** she does research; **se dedica a pintar en sus ratos libres** she spends her free time painting

dedicatoria *f* dedication

dedillo *m*: **conocer algo al ~** to know sth like the back of one's hand; **sabía la lección al ~** I knew the lesson (off) by heart

dedo *m* ▶ 123 (de mano, guante) finger; (del pie) toe; **señalar con el ~** to point; **~ anular/(del) corazón** ring/middle finger; **~ gordo** (fam) (del pie) big toe; (de la mano) thumb; **~ índice** forefinger, index finger; **~ meñique** little finger; **~ pulgar** thumb; ***a* ~** (fam): **ir a ~** to hitchhike, hitch (colloq); **recorrió Europa a ~** she hitchhiked around Europe; ***hacer* ~** (fam) to hitchhike, hitch (colloq); ***poner el ~ en la llaga*** to hit *o* touch a raw nerve; ***señalar a algn con el ~*** (literal) to point at sb; (culpar) to point the finger at sb

deducción *f* deduction

deducible *adj* **1** (que se puede inferir) deducible **2** (Com, Fin) deductible

deducir [I6] *vt* **1** (inferir) to deduce; **~ algo DE algo** to deduce sth FROM sth **2** (descontar) to deduct

deduje, deduzca, etc *see* DEDUCIR

defecto *m* **(a)** (en un sistema) fault, flaw, defect; **~ de fábrica** manufacturing fault *o* defect **(b)** (de una persona) fault, shortcoming; **~ físico** physical handicap

defectuoso -sa *adj* faulty, defective

defender [E8] *vt* to defend; ‹*intereses*› to protect; **~ a algo/algn DE algo/algn** to defend sth/sb AGAINST sth/sb

■ **defenderse** *v pron* **(a)** (*refl*) (contra una agresión) to defend *o* protect oneself; (Der) to defend oneself; **~se DE algo/algn** to defend oneself AGAINST sth/sb **(b)** (fam) (arreglárselas) to get by (colloq); **me defiendo bastante bien en francés** I can get by quite well in French

defensa *f* **1 (a)** (protección) defense*; **salir en ~ de algn** to come to sb's defense; **actuó en ~ propia** he acted in self-defense; **~ DE algo/algn** defense* OF sth/sb; **~ personal** self-defense* **(b)** (Dep) defense* **2 (a) Defensa** *f* the Defense Department (AmE), the Ministry of Defence (BrE) **(b) defensas** *fpl* (Biol, Med) defenses* (*pl*) **(c) defensa** *mf* (jugador) defender

defensivo -va *adj* ‹*arma/actitud/táctica*› defensive; **estar/ponerse a la defensiva** to be/get on the defensive

defensor -sora *adj* **(a)** ‹*ejército*› defending (*before n*) **(b)** (Der) ‹*abogado*› defense* (*before n*) ■ *m,f* **(a)** (Mil) defender **(b)** (de una causa) champion **(c)** (Der) defense counsel (AmE), defence lawyer (BrE)

defeño -ña *m,f* (Méx) person from the DISTRITO FEDERAL

deferencia *f* (frml) deference; **por ~ a algn/algo** out of *o* in deference to sb/sth

deficiencia *f* **(a)** (defecto) fault **(b)** (insuficiencia alimentaria, inmunológica) deficiency

deficiente *adj* poor, inadequate; ‹*salud*› poor; **~ EN algo** deficient IN sth ■ *mf* (persona) *tb* **~ mental** mentally subnormal

déficit *m* (*pl* **~** *or* **-cits**) **(a)** (Com, Fin) deficit **(b)** (en la producción) shortfall; (de lluvias) shortage

defienda, **defiendas, etc** *see* DEFENDER

definición *f* (de palabra, postura) definition

definido -da *adj* clearly-defined

definir [I1] *vt* to define

definitivamente *adv* ‹*resolver/rechazar*› once and for all; ‹*quedarse/instalarse*› permanently, for good

definitivo -va *adj* ‹*texto/solución/respuesta*› definitive; ‹*cierre*› permanent, definitive; **ya es ~ que no viene** he's definitely not coming

deforestar [A1] *vt* to deforest

deformación *f* **(a)** (en general) distortion **(b)** (Anat, Med) deformity

deformar [A1] *vt* **(a)** (en general) to distort **(b)** (Anat, Med) to deform

■ **deformarse** *v pron* **(a)** (en general) to become distorted **(b)** (Anat, Med) to become deformed

deforme *adj* deformed

defraudar [A1] *vt* **(a)** (decepcionar) to disappoint **(b)** (estafar) to defraud; **defraudó al fisco** he evaded his taxes

defunción *f* (frml) death; Ⓢ **cerrado por defunción** closed owing to bereavement

degenerado -da *adj/m,f* degenerate

degenerar [A1] *vi* to degenerate; **~ EN algo** to degenerate INTO sth

degollar [A12] *vt* ‹*persona/animal*›: **lo ~on** they slit his/its throat

degradante *adj* degrading

degradar [A1] *vt* **(a)** (Mil) to demote **(b)** (envilecer) to degrade **(c)** (empeorar) ‹*calidad/valor*› to diminish

■ **degradarse** *v pron* «*persona*» to demean oneself, degrade oneself

dehesa *f* **(a)** (terreno) meadow, pasture **(b)** (hacienda) farm

dejación *f* (AmC, Chi) ⇒ DEJADEZ

dejadez *f* **(a)** (en el aseo personal) slovenliness **(b)** (en tarea, trabajo) laziness, slackness

dejado -da *adj* **(a)** (en aseo personal, aspecto) slovenly **(b)** (en tarea, trabajo) slack, lazy

dejar [A1] *vt* **I 1 (a)** (en lugar determinado) to leave; **lo dejé en recepción** I left it in reception; **dejó a los niños en el colegio** she dropped the children (off) at school; **~ un recado** to leave a message; **~ propina** to leave a tip; **deja ese cuchillo** put that knife down; **déjala, ella no tuvo la culpa** leave her alone, it wasn't her fault; **~ *mucho que desear*** to leave a great deal to be desired **(b)** (olvidar) ‹*dinero/objeto*› to leave; **¡déjalo!** forget it! **(c)** (como herencia) to leave **2 (a)** ‹*mancha/huella/sabor*› to leave **(b)** ‹*ganancia*› to produce; **el negocio dejó pérdidas** the business made a loss **3** (abandonar) ‹*novia/marido*› to leave; ‹*familia*› to leave, abandon; ‹*trabajo*› to give up, leave; ‹*lugar*› to leave; **quiere ~ el ballet** he wants to give up ballet dancing **4** (+ *compl*) (en cierto estado) to leave; **dejé la ventana abierta** I left the window open; **me dejó esperando afuera** she left me waiting outside; **¡déjame en paz!** leave me alone!; **me lo dejó en 1.000 pesos** he let me have it for 1,000 pesos; ⇒ LADO 3 **5 (a)** (posponer) leave; **no lo dejes para después, hazlo ahora** don't put it off *o* leave it until later, do it now **(b)** (reservar, guardar) ‹*espacio/margen/comida*› to leave

II 1 (permitir) **~a algo/algn hacer algo** to let sth/sb do sth; **déjalo entrar** let it/him in; **deja correr el agua** let the water run; **¿me dejas ir?** will you let me go?; **~ que algo/algn haga algo** to let sb/sth do sth; **déjame que te ayude** let me help you; ⇒ CAER 1, PASO 1 (b) ■ **~** *vi* **~ DE hacer algo** to stop doing sth; **~ de fumar** to give up *o* to stop smoking; **no dejes de escribirme** make sure you write to me

■ **dejarse** *v pron* **1 (a)** (abandonarse) to let oneself go **(b) ~se + INF: se deja dominar por la envidia** he lets his feelings of envy get the better of him; **se deja influir fácilmente** he's easily influenced; **~se llevar por la música** to let oneself be carried along by the music; ***~se estar*** (AmL); (descuidarse) to be careless; (abandonarse) to let oneself go **2** ‹*barba/bigote*› to grow **3 ~se DE hacer algo** to stop doing sth; **déjate de lamentarte** stop complaining **4** (esp Esp fam) (olvidar) to leave

deje *m* ⇒ DEJO (a)

dejo *m* **(a)** (acento) (slight) accent, lilt **(b)** (de una bebida, comida) aftertaste; **~ A algo** slight taste OF sth **(c)** (de arrogancia, ironía) touch, hint **(d)** (impresión, sensación): **me quedó un ~ triste** I was left with a feeling of sadness

del: ▶ **128**, **39** *contraction of* DE *and* EL

delantal *m* (para cocinar) apron; (de escolar) pinafore

delante *adv* **1** (lugar, parte) [*Latin American Spanish also uses* ADELANTE *in many of these examples*]: **yo voy ~** I'll go ahead *o* in front; **no te pongas ~** don't stand in front of me; **lo tengo aquí ~** I have it right here; **el asiento de ~** the front seat; **la parte de ~** the front; **el pasajero de ~** the passenger in the front **2 delante de** (*loc prep*) in front of

delantera *f* **(a)** (en general) lead; **llevar/tomar la ~** to be in/to take the lead **(b)** (Dep) (de equipo) forwards (*pl*), forward line

delantero -ra *adj* **(a)** ‹*asiento/rueda*› front (*before n*) **(b)** (Dep) ‹*línea/posición*› forward (*before n*), offensive (*before n*) (AmE) ■ *m,f* (Dep) forward; **~ forward** center* forward

delatar [A1] *vt* «*persona*» (acusar) to denounce, inform on

■ **delatarse** *v pron* (*refl*) to give oneself away

delator -tora *adj* **(a)** ‹*prueba/arma*› incriminating **(b)** ‹*mirada/sonrisa*› revealing ■ *m,f* informer

delegación *f* **1** (grupo) delegation **2** (de poderes) delegation **3 (a)** (Méx) (comisaría) police station **(b)** (Esp) (oficina local) regional *o* local office

delegado *m,f* (representante) delegate; **~ de curso** student representative

delegar [A3] *vt* to delegate; **~ algo EN algn** to delegate sth TO sb ■ **~** *vi* to delegate

deleitar [A1] *vt* to delight
■ **deleitarse** *v pron* **~se haciendo algo** to delight IN doing sth, enjoy doing sth

deleite *m* delight

deletrear [A1] *vt* to spell

delfín *m* (Zool) dolphin

delgado -da *adj* **(a)** ‹*persona/piernas*› (esbelto) slim; (flaco) thin **(b)** ‹*tela/lámina/pared*› thin; ‹*hilo*› fine, thin

deliberado -da *adj* deliberate

delicadeza *f* **1** (cuidado, suavidad) gentleness; **con mucha ~** very gently **2 (a)** (tacto, discreción) tact; **fue una falta de ~** it was tactless of him (*o* you *etc*) **(b)** (gesto amable): **fue una ~ de su parte traerme** it was very kind of him to bring me; **ni siquiera tuvo la ~ de informarme** he didn't even have the courtesy to inform me

delicado -da *adj* **1** (fino) ‹*rasgos/manos*› delicate; ‹*sabor*› delicate, subtle; ‹*lenguaje/modales*› refined **2 (a)** (que requiere cuidados) ‹*cerámica/cristal*› fragile; ‹*tela*› delicate; ‹*piel*› sensitive **(b)** ‹*salud/estómago*› delicate; ‹*corazón*› weak **3** ‹*asunto/cuestión/tema*› delicate, sensitive; ‹*situación*› delicate, tricky **4 (a)** (melindroso) delicate, fussy **(b)** (susceptible) touchy

delicia *f* delight; **ser una ~** to be delicious

delicioso -sa *adj* ‹*comida/bebida/sabor*› delicious; ‹*tiempo*› delightful

delimitar [A1] *vt* **(a)** ‹*terreno/espacio*› to demarcate (frml), to delimit (frml) **(b)** ‹*poderes/responsabilidades*› to define, specify

delincuencia *f* crime, delinquency (frml); **~ juvenil** juvenile delinquency

delincuente *mf* criminal; **~ común** common criminal; **~ juvenil** juvenile delinquent

delinear [A1] *vt* **(a)** ‹*dibujo/plano*› to outline, draft; ‹*contorno*› to delineate **(b)** ‹*programa/proyecto*› to formulate, draw up

delinquir [I3] *vi* to commit a criminal offense*

delirar [A1] *vi* (Med) to be delirious; **la fiebre lo hacía ~** the fever made him delirious

delirio *m* (Med) delirium; **~s de grandeza** *mpl* delusions of grandeur (*pl*)

delito *m* crime, offense*

delta *m* (Geog) delta ■ *f* (letra griega) delta

demacrado -da *adj* haggard, drawn

demagogia *f* demagogy, demagoguery

demagogo -ga *m,f* demagogue, demagog (AmE)

demanda *f* **1** (Com) demand; **tiene mucha ~** it's in great demand **2 (a)** (Der) lawsuit; **presentar una ~ contra algn** to bring a lawsuit against sb **(b)** (petición) request; **accedí a su ~** I agreed to his request

demandado -da *m,f* defendant

demandante *mf* plaintiff

demandar [A1] *vt* **1** (Der) to sue **2** (AmL) (requerir) to require

demarcar [A2] to demarcate

demás *adj inv* (*delante del n*): **los ~ estudiantes** the rest of the *o* the remaining students ■ *pron* **1 (a) lo ~** the rest; **todo lo ~** everything else **(b)** (*en locs*) **por lo demás** apart from that, otherwise; **por demás** extremely **2 los/las ~** (referido a cosas) the rest, the others; (referido a personas) the rest, everybody else; **me dio uno y se quedó con los ~** he gave me one and kept the rest *o* the others; **los ~ han terminado** the rest (of them) have finished, everybody else has finished

demasía: **en ~** ‹*beber/comer*› to excess; **todo alimento, tomado en ~, es perjudicial** any food, when eaten in excess, can be harmful

demasiado[1] -da *adj* (*delante del n*): **~ dinero** too much money; **había ~s coches** there were too many cars; **hace ~ calor** it's too hot ■ *pron*: **es ~** it's too much; **somos ~s** there are too many of us; **hizo ~s** she made too many

demasiado[2] *adv* **1** ‹*pequeño/caliente/caro*› too; **fue un esfuerzo ~ grande para él** it was too much of an effort for him **2** ‹*comer/hablar/preocuparse*› too much; ‹*trabajar*› too hard

demencia *f* dementia

demente *adj* insane ■ *mf* insane person

democracia *f* democracy

demócrata *mf* democrat

democratacristiano -na *adj/m,f* Christian Democrat

democrático -ca *adj* democratic

demografía *f* demography

demoledor -dora *adj* **(a)** ‹*máquina*› demolition (*before n*) **(b)** ‹*ataque/crítica*› devastating

demoler [E9] *vt* **(a)** ‹*edificio*› to demolish, pull down **(b)** ‹*mito/teoría*› (fam) to debunk, demolish

demonio *m* **1** (diablo) devil **2** (fam) (uso expletivo): **¡cómo ~s lo hizo!** how on earth did he do it?; **¿qué ~s ... ?** what the hell ... ? (colloq); **¡~(s)!** (expresando enfado) damn! (colloq); (expresando sorpresa) goodness!, heavens!

demora *f* **1** (esp AmL) (retraso) delay; **perdón por la ~** I'm sorry I'm late; **~ EN hacer algo** delay IN doing sth; **sin ~** without delay **2** (Náut) bearing

demorar [A1] *vt* **(a)** (AmL) (tardar): **demoró tres horas en llegar** he took *o* it took him three hours to arrive **(b)** (AmL) (retrasar) ‹*viaje/decisión*› to delay ■ **~** *vi* (AmL): **¡no demores!** don't be long!
■ **demorarse** *v pron* (AmL) **(a)** (tardar cierto tiempo): **¡qué poco te demoraste!** that didn't take you very long; **me demoro 3 horas** it takes me 3 hours **(b)** (tardar demasiado) to be *o* take too long; **~se EN hacer algo** to take a long time TO do sth

demoroso -sa *adj* (Bol, Chi) ‹*persona/vehículo*› slow; ‹*trabajo*› time-consuming

demostración *f* demonstration; (de teorema) proof

demostrar [A10] *vt* **1** ‹*verdad/teorema*› to prove, demonstrate; ‹*ignorancia*› to show, prove; **ha demostrado ser muy capaz** he's shown himself to be very able; **~ que algo es/no es cierto** to prove sth right/wrong **2 (a)** ‹*interés/sentimiento*› to show **(b)** ‹*funcionamiento/método*› to demonstrate

demostrativo -va *adj* **(a)** ‹*ejemplo*› illustrative **(b)** ‹*adjetivo/pronombre*› demonstrative **(c)** (AmL) ‹*persona/carácter*› demonstrative

denantes *adv* (Chi fam) a moment ago, just now

denegar [A7] *vt* (frml) ‹*permiso/autorización*› to refuse; ‹*petición*› to turn down; ‹*recurso*› (Der) to refuse

dengue *m* (Med) dengue fever

denigrante *adj* degrading, humiliating

denigrar [A1] *vt* **(a)** (hablar mal de) to denigrate **(b)** (degradar) to degrade

denominar [A1] *vt* (frml) **(a)** (dar nombre a) to call; **el denominado efecto invernadero** the so-called greenhouse effect **(b)** (con carácter oficial) to designate

densidad *f* density; (de vegetación, niebla) thickness, denseness

denso -sa *adj* dense

dentado -da *adj* ‹*filo*› serrated; **una rueda dentada** a gearwheel, a cogwheel

dentadura *f* teeth (*pl*); **~ postiza** false teeth (*pl*), dentures (*pl*)

dental *adj* dental

dentera *f* (sensación): **darle ~ a algn** to set sb's teeth on edge

dentífrico *m* toothpaste

dentista *mf* dentist

dentística *f* (Chi) dentistry, dental surgery

dentro *adv* **1** (lugar, parte) [*Latin American Spanish also uses* ADENTRO *in this sense*] inside; **aquí/ahí ~** in here/there; **el perro duerme ~** the dog sleeps indoors; **por ~** on the inside; **la parte de ~** the inside **2 dentro de (a)** (en el espacio) in, inside; **~ del edificio** in *o* inside the building **(b)** (en el tiempo) in; **~ de dos semanas** in two weeks' time **(c)** (de límites, posibilidades) within; **~ de nuestras posibilidades** within our means

denuncia *f* **1** (de robo, asesinato) report; **hizo la ~ del robo del coche** he reported the theft of his car; **presentar una ~** to make a formal complaint **2** (crítica pública) denunciation

denunciar [A1] *vt* **1** ‹*robo/asesinato/persona*› to report **2** (condenar públicamente) to denounce, condemn

Dep., **Dept.** (= **Departamento**) Dept

departamento *m* **1 (a)** (de empresa, institución) department **(b)** (provincia, distrito) department **2** (AmL) (apartamento) apartment (esp AmE), flat (BrE)

dependencia *f* **1** (condición) dependence; **~** DE **algo** dependence ON sth **2 dependencias** *fpl* (edificios) buildings (*pl*); (salas) rooms (*pl*)

depender [E1] *vi* **(a)** «*resultado/solución*» to depend; **~** DE **algo/algn** to depend ON sth/sb **(b)** «*persona*» **~** DE **algn/algo** to be dependent ON sb/sth

dependiente -ta *m,f* salesclerk (AmE), shop assistant (BrE)

depilación *f* (con cera) waxing; (con crema) hair-removal, depilation (frml); (de cejas) plucking

depilar [A1] *vt* ‹*piernas/axilas*› to wax (*o* shave *etc*); ‹*cejas*› to pluck

■ **depilarse** *v pron*: **~se las piernas** to shave (*o* wax *etc*) one's legs; (*caus*) to have one's legs waxed

deplorable *adj* deplorable

deportar [A1] *vt* to deport

deporte *m* sport; **no practican ningún ~** they don't play *o* do any sport(s); **hace ~ para estar en forma** she does sports (AmE) *o* (BrE) some sport to keep fit; **~ acuático/de invierno** water/winter sport

deportista *adj* sporty; **fue muy ~ en su juventud** he was a keen sportsman in his youth; ■ *mf* (*m*) sportsman (*f*) sportswoman

deportividad *f* sportsmanship

deportivo[1] **-va** *adj* **(a)** ‹*club/centro*› sports (*before n*) **(b)** ‹*ropa*› (para deporte) sports (*before n*); (informal) sporty, casual

deportivo[2] *m* sports car

depositar [A1] *vt* **1** (frml) **(a)** (colocar) to place, deposit (frml) **(b)** (dejar) to leave, deposit (frml) **2** (Fin) ‹*dinero*› to deposit; (en cuenta corriente) (AmL) to deposit, pay in (BrE)

depósito *m* **1 (a)** (almacén) warehouse; **~ de armas** arms depot; **~ de cadáveres** morgue, mortuary (BrE) **(b)** (tanque) tank; **~ de gasolina** gas tank (AmE), petrol tank (BrE) **2** (sedimento) deposit, sediment; (yacimiento) deposit **3** (Fin) **(a)** (AmL) (en una cuenta) deposit **(b)** (garantía) deposit

depravado -da *m,f* degenerate

depreciarse [A1] *v pron* to depreciate, fall in value

depredador[1] **-dora** *adj* (Zool) ‹*animal/ave*› predatory

depredador[2] *m* predator

depresión *f* depression

deprimente *adj* depressing

deprimido -da *adj* depressed

deprimir [I1] *vt* to depress

■ **deprimirse** *v pron* to get/become depressed

deprisa *adv* fast; **trabajar más ~** to work faster; **¡~! escóndelo** quick! hide it

depurado -da *adj* ‹*lenguaje/estilo*› polished, refined; ‹*gusto*› refined

depuradora *f* **(a)** (de aguas residuales) sewage treatment plant **(b)** (en piscina) filter system

depurar [A1] *vt* **1 (a)** ‹*agua*› to purify, treat; ‹*aguas residuales*› to treat **(b)** ‹*sangre*› to cleanse **2 (a)** ‹*organización/partido*› to purge **(b)** ‹*lenguaje/estilo*› to polish, refine

derecha *f* **1 (a)** (lado derecho) right; **la primera calle a la ~** the first street on the right; **dobla a la ~** turn right; **por la ~** ‹*conducir/caminar*› on the right; **mantenga su ~** keep to the right **(b)** (mano derecha) right hand **2** (Pol): **la ~** the Right; **un político de ~** *or* (Esp) **~s** a right-wing politician

derecho[1] **-cha** *adj* **1** ‹*mano/ojo/zapato*› right; ‹*lado*› right, right-hand; **el ángulo superior ~** the top right-hand corner; **queda a mano derecha** it's on the right-hand side *o* on the right **2 (a)** (recto) straight; **ese cuadro no está ~** that picture isn't straight; **siéntate ~** sit up straight **(b)** (fam) (justo, honesto) honest, straight

derecho² *adv* straight; **siga todo ~** go *o* keep straight on

derecho³ *m* **1 (a)** (facultad, privilegio) right; **~s humanos** human rights (*pl*); **estás en tu ~** you're within your rights; **~ A algo** right TO sth; **el ~ al voto** the right to vote; **tengo ~ a saber** I have a *o* the right to know; **esto da ~ a participar** this entitles you to participate; **¡no hay ~!** (fam) it's not fair! **(b)** (Com, Fin) tax; **~s de aduana** customs duties (*pl*); **~ de matrícula** registration fee **2** (Der) law **3** (de prenda) right side, outside; (de tela) right side, face; **póntelo al ~** put it on properly *o* right side out

deriva *f*: **a la ~** adrift

derivar [A1] *vi* **(a)** (proceder) **~ DE algo** «*palabra*» to derive FROM sth, come FROM sth; «*problema/situación*» to arise FROM sth **(b)** (traer como consecuencia) **~ EN algo** to result IN sth, lead TO sth ■ **~** *vt* (Med) (AmL) **~ a algn a un especialista** to refer sb to a specialist

■ **derivarse** *v pron* (proceder) **~se DE algo** «*palabra*» to be derived FROM sth, come FROM sth; «*problema/situación*» to arise FROM sth

dermatólogo -ga *m,f* dermatologist

derogar [A3] *vt* to abolish, repeal

derramar [A1] *vt* **(a)** ‹*agua/leche/azúcar*› to spill; ‹*cuentas/sangre*› to shed **(b)** ‹*lentejas/botones*› to spill, scatter

■ **derramarse** *v pron* **(a)** «*tinta/leche*» to spill; «*corriente*» to pour out **(b)** «*cuentas/botones*» to scatter, spread

derrame *m* **(a)** (Med): **tengo un ~ en el ojo** I have a burst blood vessel in my eye; **~ cerebral** brain hemorrhage* **(b)** (de líquido) spillage

derrapar [A1] *vi* «*vehículo*» to skid; «*embrague*» to slip; «*llantas*» to spin

derredor: **al/en ~** (*loc adv*) around

derretir [I14] *vt* ‹*mantequilla/helado*› to melt; ‹*hielo/nieve*› to melt, thaw

■ **derretirse** *v pron* «*mantequilla/helado*» to melt; «*nieve/hielo*» to thaw, melt

derribar [A1] *vt* **(a)** ‹*edificio/muro*› to demolish, knock down; ‹*puerta*› to break down **(b)** ‹*avión*› to shoot down, bring down **(c)** ‹*persona*› to floor, knock ... down; ‹*novillo*› to knock ... over **(d)** «*viento*» to bring down **(e)** ‹*gobierno*› to overthrow, topple

derrocar [A2] *vt* to overthrow, topple

derrochador -dora *adj*: **es muy ~** he's a real spendthrift ■ *m,f* squanderer, spendthrift

derrochar [A1] *vt* (malgastar) ‹*dinero*› to squander, waste; ‹*electricidad/agua*› to waste ■ **~** *vi* to throw money away, to squander money

derroche *m* (de dinero, bienes) waste

derrota *f* (Dep, Mil) defeat

derrotado -da *adj* **(a)** ‹*ejército*› defeated; ‹*equipo/contrincante*› defeated, beaten **(b)** (desesperanzado) despondent

derrotar [A1] *vt* ‹*ejército/partido*› to defeat; ‹*equipo/contrincante*› to defeat, beat

derrotista *adj/mf* defeatist

derruido -da *adj* ‹*casa*› ruined; **medio ~** virtually in ruins

derrumbamiento *m* collapse

derrumbar [A1] *vt* ‹*casa/edificio*› to demolish, pull down

■ **derrumbarse** *v pron* **(a)** «*edificio*» to collapse **(b)** «*persona*» to go to pieces; «*esperanzas/ilusiones*» to be shattered, collapse

desabastecimiento, (Méx) **desabasto** *m* shortage of supplies (*o* food *etc*)

desabotonarse [A1] *v pron* **(a)** «*prenda*» to come undone **(b)** (*refl*) «*persona*» ‹*camisa/abrigo*› to unbutton, undo

desabrido -da *adj* (comida) tasteless, bland

desabrigado -da *adj* ‹*lugar*› exposed; **estás muy ~** you're not wearing warm enough clothes

desabrochar [A1] *vt* ‹*prenda/zapatos/pulsera*› to undo; **¿me desabrochas?** can you undo me? (colloq)

■ **desabrocharse** *v pron* **(a)** «*prenda*» to come undone **(b)** (*refl*) «*persona*» ‹*camisa/abrigo*› to undo

desaconsejar [A1] *vt* to advise against

desacostumbrarse [A1] *v pron* to get out of the habit; **~ A hacer algo** to get out of the habit OF doing sth; **se desacostumbró al tráfico de la ciudad** she forgot what city traffic was like

desacreditar [A1] *vt* to discredit

■ **desacreditarse** *v pron* (*refl*) to discredit oneself, damage one's reputation

desactivar [A1] *vt* ‹*bomba/explosivo*› to defuse, deactivate

desacuerdo *m* disagreement; **~ CON algo/algn** disagreement WITH sth/sb

desadaptado -da *adj*: **un niño ~** a child who has problems settling in *o* adjusting; **sentirse ~** to feel unsettled

desafiante *adj* ‹*gesto/palabras*› defiant

desafiar [A17] *vt* **(a)** ‹*persona*› to challenge; **~ a algn A algo/hacer algo** to challenge sb TO sth/do sth **(b)** ‹*peligro/muerte*› to defy

desafilado -da *adj* blunt

desafinado -da *adj* out of tune

desafinar [A1] *vi* «*instrumento*» to be out of tune; «*músico/cantante*» to be off key *o* out of tune

desafío *m* (a una persona) challenge; (al peligro, a la muerte) defiance

desaforado -da *m,f*: **como un ~** ‹*correr*› hell for leather; ‹*gritar*› at the top of one's voice

desafortunado -da *adj* **(a)** (desdichado) ‹*persona*› unlucky; ‹*suceso*› unfortunate **(b)** (desacertado) ‹*medidas/actuación*› unfortunate

desagradable *adj* unpleasant; ‹*respuesta/comentario*› unkind

desagradar [A1] *vt*: **me desagrada el calor/tener que decírselo** I don't like the heat/having to tell her

desagradecido -da *adj* ‹*persona*› ungrateful; ‹*trabajo/tarea*› thankless

desagrado *m* displeasure; **lo hizo con ~** she did it reluctantly *o* unwillingly

desagüe *m* **(a)** (de lavabo, lavadora) wastepipe; (de patio, azotea) drain **(b)** (acción) drainage

desahogado -da *adj* ‹*posición económica/vida*› comfortable; ‹*casa/habitación*› uncluttered, spacious

desahogar [A3] *vt* ‹*penas/ira*› to give vent to ■ **desahogarse** *v pron* to let off steam ; **se desahogó dándole patadas a la rueda** he vented his anger (*o* frustration *etc*) by kicking the wheel; **~se CON algn** to pour one's heart out to sb

desahogo *m* **(a)** (alivio) relief; **llorar le servirá de ~** crying will make him feel better **(b) con ~** comfortably; **vivir con ~** to be comfortably off

desahuciar [A1] *vt* **1** ‹*enfermo*› to declare ... terminally ill **2 (a)** ‹*inquilino*› to evict **(b)** (Chi) ‹*empleado*› (despedir) to dismiss; (notificar el despido) to give ... notice

desaire *m* snub, slight; **hacerle un ~ a algn** to snub *o* slight sb

desalentador -dora *adj* disheartening, discouraging

desalentar [A5] *vt* to discourage, dishearten

desaliento *m* dejection, despondency

desaliñado -da *adj* slovenly

desalojar [A1] *vt* **(a)** ‹*edificio/recinto*› «*ocupantes*» to vacate; «*policía/juez*» to clear **(b)** ‹*residentes*› to evacuate; ‹*inquilino*› (esp AmL) to evict

desamarrar [A1] *vt* (AmL exc RPl) ‹*embarcación*› to cast off; ‹*zapatos/paquete*› to undo, untie; ‹*animal/persona*› to untie
■ **desamarrarse** *v pron* (AmL exc RPl) **1** «*paquete/zapatos*» to come undone; «*bultos/barco*» to come untied **2** (*refl*) «*persona*» to get free; «*animal*» to get loose *o* free

desamparado -da *adj* ‹*niño/anciano*› defenseless*; ‹*lugar*› bleak, unprotected

desamparo *m* neglect

desangrarse *v pron* to bleed to death

desanimado -da *adj* discouraged, dispirited

desanimar [A1] *vt* to discourage
■ **desanimarse** *v pron* to become disheartened *o* discouraged

desánimo *m* dejection, despondency

desaparecer [E3] *vi* «*persona/objeto*» to disappear; «*dolor/síntoma/cicatriz*» to disappear, go; «*costumbre*» to disappear, die out; «*mancha*» to come out
■ **desaparecerse** *v pron* (Andes) to disappear

desaparecido -da *adj* **(a)** (que no se encuentra) missing **(b)** (period) (muerto) late (*before n*), deceased (frml) ■ *m,f* **(a)** (en un accidente) missing person **(b)** (Pol): **los ~s** the disappeared *o* those who have disappeared

desaparición *f* disappearance; **una especie en vías de ~** an endangered species

desapercibido -da *adj*: **pasar ~** to go unnoticed

desaprovechar [A1] *vt* ‹*oportunidad*› to waste; ‹*tiempo/comida*› to waste

desarmable *adj* ‹*mueble/mecanismo*› which can be dismantled *o* taken apart

desarmado -da *adj* ‹*policía/criminal*› unarmed

desarmador *m* (Méx) **(a)** (herramienta) screwdriver **(b)** (bebida) screwdriver

desarmar [A1] *vt* **1** ‹*mueble/mecanismo*› to dismantle; ‹*carpa*› (AmL) to take down; ‹*rifle/motor*› to strip (down); ‹*rompecabezas*› to take ... to pieces, break up; ‹*juguete/maqueta*› to take ... apart **2 (a)** (quitar armas) to disarm **(b)** (dejar sin argumentos) to disarm

desarme *m* disarmament

desarrollado -da *adj* developed; **un niño muy/poco ~** a well-developed/an underdeveloped child

desarrollar [A1] *vt* **1** (en general) to develop **2 (a)** (exponer) ‹*teoría/tema*› to explain **(b)** (llevar a cabo) ‹*actividad/labor*› to carry out
■ **desarrollarse** *v pron* **1** (en general) to develop **2** «*acto/entrevista/escena*» to take place

desarrollo *m* development; **países en vías de ~** developing countries; **según el ~ de los acontecimientos** according to how things develop

desastrado -da *adj* ‹*persona*› scruffy, untidy; ‹*habitación/trabajo*› untidy

desastre *m* disaster; **como cantante es un ~** he's a hopeless singer; **tienes la habitación hecha un ~** your room is a shambles; **vas hecha un ~** you look a real mess (colloq)

desastroso -sa *adj* disastrous

desatado -da *adj*: **estar ~** ‹*perro*› to be loose; ‹*cordón/nudo*› to be undone

desatar [A1] *vt* **(a)** ‹*nudo/lazo*› to untie, undo **(b)** ‹*persona*› to untie; ‹*perro*› to let ... loose
■ **desatarse** *v pron* **(a)** «*nudo/cordones*» to come undone *o* untied; «*perro/caballo*» to get loose **(b)** (*refl*) «*persona*» to untie oneself; ‹*cordones/zapatos*› to untie, undo

desatascador *m* (instrumento) plunger; (producto) nitric acid (*o* caustic soda *etc*) (*used to clear blocked drains*)

desatascar [A2] *vt* ‹*cañería/fregadero*› to unblock, clear
■ **desatascarse** *v pron* «*cañería/fregadero*» to unblock; «*carretera*» to clear

desatender [E8] *vt* **(a)** ‹*trabajo/familia*› to neglect **(b)** ‹*tienda/mostrador*› to leave ... unattended

desatento -ta *adj* **(a)** [SER] (desconsiderado) thoughtless, inconsiderate **(b)** [ESTAR] (distraído) inattentive

desatornillador *m* (AmC, Chi) screwdriver

desatornillar [A1] *vt* to unscrew

desautorizar [A4] *vt* **(a)** (restar autoridad a) ‹*persona*› to undermine the authority of; ‹*declaraciones*› to disavow (frml) **(b)** (retirar la autorización para) ‹*marcha/huelga*› to ban

desayunar [A1] *vt* to have ... for breakfast; **¿qué desayunaste?** what did you have for breakfast? ■ **~** *vi* to have breakfast

■ **desayunarse** *v pron* (AmL) (tomar el desayuno) to have breakfast; **~se** CON **algo** to have sth FOR breakfast

desayuno *m* breakfast; **tomar el ~** to have breakfast

desbarajuste *m* (fam) mess; **un ~ económico** an economic mess *o* chaos

desbaratar [A1] *vt* **(a)** ‹*planes*› to spoil, ruin; ‹*sistema*› to disrupt **(b)** (Méx) ‹*papeles*› to jumble (up), muddle (up); ‹*mecanismo*› to ruin, destroy
■ **desbaratarse** *v pron* **(a)** «*plan*» to be ruined, be spoiled; «*sistema*» to be disrupted, break down **(b)** (Méx) «*papeles*» to get jumbled up, get muddled (up); «*mecanismo*» to break, get broken

desbarrancarse [A2] *v pron* to go over a sheer drop

desbloquear [A1] *vt* **(a)** ‹*carretera/entrada*› to clear; ‹*mecanismo*› to release, free **(b)** ‹*negociaciones/diálogo*› to break the deadlock in **(c)** (Com, Fin) ‹*cuenta*› to unfreeze

desbocado -da *adj* **(a)** ‹*caballo*› runaway (*before n*) **(b)** ‹*cuello/escote*› loose, wide

desbocarse [A2] *v pron* «*caballo*» to bolt

desbordante *adj* ‹*entusiasmo/júbilo*› boundless; **está ~ de entusiasmo** he's bursting with enthusiasm

desbordarse [A1] *v pron* **(a)** «*río/canal*» to burst its banks **(b)** «*vaso/cubo*» to overflow **(c)** «*multitud*» to get out of hand, get out of control

descabellado -da *adj* crazy, ridiculous

descafeinado -da *adj* decaffeinated

descalabro *m* **(a)** (desastre) disaster **(b)** (Mil) defeat

descalificación *f* (Dep) disqualification

descalificar [A2] *vt* ‹*deportista/equipo*› to disqualify

descalzarse [A4] *v pron* to take off one's shoes

descalzo -za *adj* ‹*pie*› bear; ‹*persona*› barefoot

descaminado -da *adj*: **andar ~** to be on the wrong track

descampado *m* **(a)** (terreno) area *o* piece of open ground *o* land **(b) al descampado** (AmS) ‹*dormir*› in the open (air)

descansado -da *adj* **(a)** [ESTAR] ‹*persona*› rested, refreshed **(b)** [SER] ‹*actividad/trabajo*› easy, undemanding; ‹*vida*› quiet, peaceful

descansar [A1] *vi* **(a)** (de actividad, trabajo) to rest, have a rest; **sin ~** without a break; **~** DE **algo** to have a rest *o* break FROM sth **(b)** (yacer) to lie; **que en paz descanse** God rest his soul ■ **~** *vt* **~ la vista** to rest one's eyes, to give one's eyes a rest; **~ la mente** to give one's mind a break *o* rest

descansillo *m* (Esp) landing

descanso *m* **1 (a)** (reposo) rest **(b)** (en trabajo, colegio) break; **sin ~** without a break **(c)** (Mil): **estar en posición de ~** to be standing at ease **2** (intervalo) (Dep) half time; (Teatr) interval **3** (alivio, tranquilidad) relief **4** (AmL) (rellano) landing

descapotable *adj/m* convertible

descarado -da *adj* ‹*persona/actitud*› brazen, shameless; **es un ~** he has a lot of nerve

descarga *f* **1** (de mercancías) unloading **2** (Elec) discharge; **una ~ eléctrica** an electric shock **3** (de arma) shot, discharge (frml); (de conjunto de armas) volley

descargar [A3] *vt* **1** ‹*vehículo/mercancías*› to unload **2 (a)** ‹*pistola*› (extraer las balas) to unload; (disparar) to fire, discharge (frml); **la pistola está descargada** the pistol is not loaded **(b)** ‹*tiro*› to fire; ‹*golpe*› to deal, land **3** ‹*ira/agresividad*› to vent; ‹*preocupaciones/tensiones*› to relieve ■ **~** *v impers* «*aguacero*» to pour down; «*temporal*» to break
■ **descargarse** *v pron* **1** (Elec) «*pila*» to run down; «*batería*» to go dead *o* flat **2** «*tormenta*» to break; «*lluvias*» to come down, fall

descaro *m* audacity, nerve (colloq); **¡qué ~!** what a nerve!

descarriado -da *adj*: **hoy día la juventud anda descarriada** the youth of today has lost its way; ⇒ OVEJA

descarrilamiento *m* derailment

descarrilar [A1] *vi* to derail, be derailed
■ **descarrilarse** *v pron* (AmL) to derail, be derailed

descartar [A1] *vt* to rule out

descascararse [A1] *v pron* «*pared/pintura*» to peel; «*taza/plato*» to chip

descendencia *f* descendants (*pl*)

descender [E8] *vi* **1 (a)** «*temperatura/nivel*» to fall, drop **(b)** (frml) (desde una altura) «*avión*» to descend; «*persona*» to descend (frml), to come/go down **2** (en clasificación) to go down **3** (proceder) **~** DE **algn** to be descended FROM sb

descendiente *mf* descendant

descenso *m* **1 (a)** (de temperatura, nivel) fall, drop; (de precios) fall **(b)** (desde una altura) descent **2** (Dep) relegation

descentrado -da *adj* **(a)** ‹*eje/rueda*› off-center* **(b)** ‹*persona*› disoriented, disorientated (BrE)

descentralizar [A4] *vt* to decentralize

descifrar [A1] *vt* **(a)** ‹*mensaje*› to decode, decipher; ‹*escritura/jeroglífico/código*› to decipher **(b)** ‹*misterio/enigma*› to work out, figure out

descodificador *m* decoder

descolgar [A8] *vt* **(a)** ‹*cuadro/cortina*› to take down **(b)** ‹*teléfono*› to pick up; **dejar el teléfono descolgado** to leave the phone off the hook
■ **descolgarse** *v pron* **1** (por una cuerda) to lower oneself **2** (en carrera) to pull away, break away

descollar [A10] *vi* to be outstanding

descolorido -da *adj* ‹*tela/papel*› faded

descomponer [E22] *vt* **1** ‹*alimento/cadáver*› to rot, cause … to decompose *o* rot **2** (esp AmL) ‹*máquina/aparato*› to break; ‹*peinado*› to mess up **3** ‹*persona*› **(a)** (producir malestar) «*olor*» to make … queasy **(b)** (producir diarrea) to give … diarrhea*
■ **descomponerse** *v pron* **1** «*luz*» to split; «*sustancia*» to break down, separate **2** «*cadáver/alimento*» to rot, decompose (frml) **3** (esp AmL) «*máquina/aparato*» to break down **4** «*persona*» (sentir malestar) to feel sick; (del estómago) to have an attack

of diarrhea* **6** (CS) «*tiempo*» to become unsettled; «*día*» to cloud over

descompuesto -ta *adj* **1** ‹*alimento*› rotten, decomposed (frml); ‹*cadáver*› decomposed **2** ‹*expresión*› changed, altered **3** (esp AmL) [ESTAR] ‹*máquina/aparato*› broken; ‹*teléfono*› out of order **4** **estar ~** (indispuesto) to feel sick; (del estómago) to have diarrhea*/an upset stomach

descompuse, **descompuso, etc** *see* DESCOMPONER

desconcertado -da *adj* disconcerted; **quedarse ~** to be taken aback

desconcertante *adj* disconcerting

desconcertar [A5] *vt* to disconcert; **su respuesta me desconcertó** I was disconcerted by her reply

desconchado *m* (en taza, plato) chip; (en pared) *place where plaster or paint has come off*

desconcharse [A1] *v pron* «*taza/plato*» to chip, get chipped; «*pared/piel*» to peel

desconcierto *m*: **su llamada los llenó de ~** they were disconcerted by his call; **el ~ reinante** the prevailing atmosphere of uncertainty

desconectar [A1] *vt* ‹*alarma/teléfono*› to disconnect; ‹*calefacción*› to switch off, turn off; **~ algo** DE **algo** to disconnect sth FROM sth
■ **desconectarse** *v pron* «*aparato*» to switch *o* turn off

desconfiado -da *adj* (receloso) distrustful; (suspicaz) suspicious

desconfianza *f* distrust, suspicion

desconfiar [A17] *vi* **~** DE **algn** to mistrust sb, to distrust sb; **~** DE **algo** ‹*de motivos*› to mistrust sth; ‹*de honestidad*› to doubt sth

descongelante *m* deicer

descongelar [A1] *vt* ‹*refrigerador*› to defrost; ‹*alimentos*› to defrost, thaw
■ **descongelarse** *v pron* «*refrigerador*» to defrost; «*alimentos*» to defrost, thaw

descongestionar [A1] *vt* to clear

desconocer [E3] *vt* **(a)** (no conocer): **por razones que desconocemos** for reasons unknown to us; **desconocía este hecho** I was unaware of this fact **(b)** (no reconocer): **te desconocí** I didn't recognize you

desconocido -da *adj* (en general) unknown; **un cantante ~** an unknown singer; **una persona desconocida** a stranger ■ *m,f* (no conocido) stranger

desconocimiento *m* ignorance

desconsiderado -da *adj* thoughtless, inconsiderate

desconsolado -da *adj* **estar ~** POR **algo** to be heartbroken OVER sth; **lloraba ~** he cried inconsolably

desconsuelo *m* grief, despair

descontado *adj*: **eso dalo por ~** you can be sure of that; **doy por ~ que vendrás a cenar** I'm assuming that you're coming to dinner

descontaminar [A1] *vt* ‹*alimentos/cultivos*› to decontaminate; ‹*atmósfera*› to clean up

descontar [A10] *vt* **1 (a)** (rebajar): **me descontó el 15%** he gave me a 15% discount **(b)** (restar) ‹*gastos/impuestos*› to deduct, take off; ‹*horas*› to deduct **2** (exceptuar): **si descontamos a Pedro/los domingos** ... if we don't count Pedro/Sundays ... **3** ‹*letra/pagaré*› to discount

descontento[1] -ta *adj* [ESTAR] dissatisfied; **~** CON **algo/algn** unhappy *o* dissatisfied WITH sth/sb

descontento[2] *m* discontent

descontrolado -da *adj* out of control

descontrolarse [A1] *v pron* to get out of control

descorazonar [A1] *vt* to dishearten, discourage

descorchar [A1] *vt* to uncork, open

descorrer [E1] *vt* ‹*cortinas*› to draw (back); ‹*cerrojo*› to draw back

descortés *adj* ‹*persona*› impolite, ill-mannered; ‹*comportamiento*› rude, impolite

descortesía *f* **(a)** (acto descortés) discourtesy **(b)** (cualidad) rudeness, impoliteness

descoserse [E1] *v pron* «*prenda/costura*» to come unstitched

descosido -da *adj* ‹*dobladillo/costura*› unstitched

descremado -da *adj* skimmed

describir [I34] *vt* to describe

descripción *f* description

descriptivo -va *adj* descriptive

descrito -ta *pp*: *see* DESCRIBIR

descuartizar [A4] *vt* **(a)** ‹*res*› to quarter **(b)** «*asesino*» to chop ... (up) into pieces

descubierto -ta *adj* **1** ‹*piscina/terraza*› open-air, outdoor (*before n*); ‹*carroza*› open-top **2** ‹*cielos*› clear **3 al descubierto**: **quedar al ~** «*planes/escándalo*» to come to light; **han puesto al ~ sus chanchullos** his shady dealings have been exposed; **girar al** *or* **en ~** (Com, Fin) to overdraw

descubridor -dora *m,f* discoverer

descubrimiento *m* discovery

descubrir [I33] *vt* **1** ‹*tierras/oro/artista*› to discover **2 (a)** (enterarse de, averiguar) ‹*razón/solución*› to discover, find out; ‹*complot/engaño*› to uncover; ‹*fraude*› to detect **(b)** ‹*persona escondida*› to find, track down **(c)** ‹*culpable*› find ... out **(d)** (delatar) to give ... away **3 (a)** ‹*estatua/placa*› to unveil **(b)** (revelar) ‹*planes/intenciones*› to reveal

descuento *m* **1 (a)** (rebaja) discount; **hacen un ~ del 15%** they give a 15% discount **(b)** (del sueldo) deduction **2** (Dep) injury time **3** (de letra, pagaré) discount

descuidado -da *adj* **(a)** [SER] (negligente) careless; (en el vestir) sloppy **(b)** [ESTAR] (desatendido) neglected

descuidar [A1] *vt* ‹*negocio/jardín*› to neglect ■ **~** *vi*: **descuide, yo me ocuparé de eso** don't worry, I'll see to that
■ **descuidarse** *v pron* **(a)** (no prestar atención, distraerse): **se descuidó un momento y el perro se le escapó** his attention strayed for a moment and the dog ran off; **si te descuidas, te roban** if you don't watch out, they'll rob you; **como te descuides, te van a quitar el puesto** if you

don't look out, they'll take your job from you **(b)** (en el aspecto físico) to neglect one's appearance

descuido *m* **(a)** (distracción): **en un ~ el niño se le escapó** she took her eyes off the child for a moment and he ran off; **basta el más pequeño ~** the smallest lapse of concentration is enough **(b)** (error) slip; (omisión) oversight

desde *prep* **1** (en el tiempo) since; **~ entonces/~ que se casó** since then/since he got married; **¿~ cuándo trabajas aquí?** how long have you been working here?; **~ el primer momento** right from the start; **no los veo ~ hace meses** I haven't seen them for months; **~ el 15 hasta el 30** from the 15th to *o* until the 30th **2** (en el espacio) from; **~ aquí/allá** from here/there; **¿~ dónde tengo que leer?** where do I have to read from?; **~ la página 12 hasta la 20** from page 12 (up) to page 20 **3** (en escalas, jerarquías) from; **blusas ~ 2.000 ptas.** blouses from 2,000 ptas.

desdén *m* disdain, scorn

desdeñable *adj* insignificant

desdeñar [A1] *vt* **(a)** (menospreciar) to scorn **(b)** ‹*pretendiente*› to spurn

desdeñoso -sa *adj* disdainful

desdicha *f* (desgracia) misfortune; (infelicidad) unhappiness

desdichado -da *adj* **(a)** (infeliz) unhappy **(b)** [SER] ‹*día*› ill-fated; **ser ~ en amores** to be unlucky in love ■ *m,f*: **es un pobre ~** he's a poor unfortunate wretch

desdoblar [A1] *vt* ‹*servilleta/pañuelo*› to unfold
■ **desdoblarse** *v pron* to divide into two, split into two

deseable *adj* desirable

desear [A1] *vt* **1** ‹*suerte/éxito/felicidad*› to wish; **te deseo un feliz viaje** I hope you have a good trip **2** (querer): **un embarazo no deseado** an unwanted pregnancy; **las tan deseadas vacaciones** the long-awaited holidays; **lo que más deseo es** ... my greatest wish is ...; **si tú lo deseas** if you want to; **~ía una respuesta ahora** I would like a reply now; **está deseando verte** he's really looking forward to seeing you; **¿desea que se lo envuelva?** (frml) would you like me to wrap it for you? **3** ‹*persona*› to desire, want

desechable *adj* disposable

desechar [A1] *vt* **(a)** ‹*ayuda/propuesta*› to reject; ‹*idea/plan*› (rechazar) to reject; (renunciar a) to drop, give up **(b)** ‹*restos/residuos*› to throw away *o* out; ‹*ropa*› to throw out

desecho *m* waste

desembarcar [A2] *vi* (de barco, avión) «*pasajeros*» to disembark; «*tropas*» to land, disembark ■ ~ *vt* ‹*mercancías*› to unload; ‹*pasajeros*› to disembark; (en emergencia) to evacuate

desembocadura *f* mouth, estuary

desembocar [A2] *vi* **~ EN algo** ‹*en mar/río*› to flow INTO sth; ‹*en calle*› to come out ONTO sth; ‹*en plaza*› to come out INTO sth

desembolsar [A1] *vt* to spend, pay out

desembolso *m* expenditure; (gasto inicial) outlay

desempacar [A2] *vt/vi* (esp AmL) to unpack

desempaquetar [A1] *vt* to unwrap

desempatar [A1] *vi* **(a)** (Dep) to break the tie (AmE), to break the deadlock (BrE) **(b)** (en una votación) to break the deadlock

desempate *m* **(a)** (Dep): **el ~ se produjo en el minuto 36** the breakthrough came in the 36th minute; **un partido de ~** a decider; **~ a penaltys** penalty shoot-out **(b)** (en concurso) tiebreak, tiebreaker; (en una votación) run-off

desempeñar [A1] *vt* **(a)** (Teatr) ‹*papel*› to play **(b)** ‹*funciones*› to carry out, perform; ‹*cargo*› to hold
■ **desempeñarse** *v pron* (AmL): **se desempeña bien en su trabajo** she does her job well; **se desempeñó muy bien** she did *o* managed very well

desempleado -da *m,f*: **un ~** someone who is out of work *o* unemployed; **los ~s** the unemployed

desempleo *m* **(a)** (situación) unemployment **(b)** (subsidio) unemployment benefit

desencadenar [A1] *vt* **(a)** ‹*crisis/protesta/reacción*› to trigger **(b)** ‹*perro*› to unleash; ‹*preso*› to unchain
■ **desencadenarse** *v pron* «*explosión/reacción*» to be triggered off; «*guerra*» to break out; «*tempestad*» to break

desencajado -da *adj* **(a)** ‹*pieza*› out of position **(b)** ‹*mandíbula/rótula*› dislocated **(c)** (alterado) shaken

desencajar [A1] *vt* **(a)** (Mec) to knock out of position **(b)** ‹*mandíbula/rótula*› to dislocate
■ **desencajarse** *v pron* **(a)** (Mec) to be knocked/come out of position **(b)** «*mandíbula/rótula*» to become/get dislocated

desencaminado -da *adj* (AmL) ⇒ DESCAMINADO

desencanto *m* disillusionment, disenchantment

desenchufar [A1] *vt* to unplug, disconnect

desenfadado -da *adj* **(a)** (seguro de sí mismo) self-assured, confident; (sin inhibiciones) uninhibited **(b)** ‹*estilo/moda/actitud*› free-and-easy, carefree

desenfocado -da *adj* out of focus

desenganchar [A1] *vt* ‹*caballos/remolque*› to unhitch; ‹*vagones*› to uncouple

desengañar [A1] *vt* (decepcionar) to disillusion; (sacar del engaño, error) to get ... to face the facts
■ **desengañarse** *v pron* **(a)** (decepcionarse) **~se DE algo** to become disillusioned WITH *o* ABOUT sth **(b)** (salir del engaño, error) to stop fooling oneself

desengaño *m* disappointment; **llevarse un ~** to be disappointed; **un ~ amoroso** an unhappy love affair

desenlace *m* (de película, libro) ending; (de aventura) outcome

desenredar [A1] *vt* ‹*pelo/lana*› to untangle, disentangle; ‹*lío*› to straighten out, sort out
■ **desenredarse** *v pron* (*refl*) ‹*pelo*› to get the knots out of

desenrollar [A1] *vt* ‹*alfombra/póster*› to unroll; ‹*persiana*› to let down; ‹*ovillo/cuerda*› to unwind

desenroscar [A2] *vt* to unscrew

desentenderse [E8] *v pron* ~ DE **algo** ‹*de un asunto*› to wash one's hands OF sth; **se desentiende de los hijos** he doesn't take an interest in the children

desenterrar [A5] *vt* ‹*cadáver*› to exhume, dig up; ‹*ruinas/tesoro*› to unearth, dig up

desentonar [A1] *vi* **(a)** (Mús) to go out of tune *o* off key **(b)** «*color*» to clash **(c)** «*atuendo/comentario*» to be out of place

desentrenado -da *adj* out of condition *o* training

desenvoltura *f* self-assurance

desenvolver [E11] *vt* to unwrap, open
■ **desenvolverse** *v pron* **(a)** (manejarse) to get by, manage; **se desenvuelve muy bien en inglés** she gets by very well in English; **se desenvolvió bien en la entrevista** she managed the interview all right **(b)** (en situaciones difíciles) to cope **(c)** «*hechos/sucesos*» to develop

desenvuelto -ta *adj* ‹*persona*› self-assured, confident

deseo *m* **(a)** (anhelo) wish; **formular un** ~ to make a wish **(b)** (apetito sexual) desire

desequilibrado -da *adj* ‹*rueda/mecanismo*› out of balance; ‹*persona*› unbalanced

desequilibrar [A1] *vt* **(a)** ‹*embarcación/vehículo*› to unbalance, make ... unbalanced; ‹*persona*› (físicamente) to throw ... off balance; (mentalmente) to unbalance **(b)** ‹*fuerzas/poder*› to upset the balance of
■ **desequilibrarse** *v pron* «*ruedas/mecanismo*» to get out of balance

desequilibrio *m* **(a)** (desigualdad) imbalances**(b)** (Psic) unbalanced state of mind

desertar [A1] *vi* (Mil) to desert; (de partido) to defect

desértico -ca *adj* ‹*zona/clima*› desert (*before n*)

desertor -tora *m,f* (Mil) deserter; (de un partido) defector

desesperación *f* **(a)** (angustia) desperation; **con** ~ ‹*luchar/gritar*› desperately; ‹*mirar/suplicar*› despairingly; ‹*llorar*› bitterly; **de** ~ out of desperation **(b)** (desesperanza) despair

desesperado -da *adj* desperate

desesperante *adj* **(a)** (exasperante) exasperating **(b)** (angustioso) distressing

desesperar [A1] *vt* to drive ... to distraction *o* despair ■ ~ *vi* to despair, give up hope
■ **desesperarse** *v pron* to become exasperated

desestabilizar [A4] *vt* to destabilize

desfachatez *f* audacity, nerve (colloq)

desfalco *m* embezzlement

desfallecer [E3] *vi* **(a)** (flaquear) «*persona*» to become weak; «*fuerzas*» to fade, fail; «*ánimos*» to flag; **lucharon sin** ~ they fought tirelessly **(b)** (desmayarse) to faint, pass out

desfasado -da *adj* ‹*ideas/persona*› old-fashioned

desfavorable *adj* unfavorable*; **el tiempo nos ha sido** ~ we had unfavorable weather conditions

desfigurado -da *adj* disfigured

desfigurar [A1] *vt* **1** «*quemaduras/cicatriz*» ‹*persona*› to disfigure **2** ‹*hechos*› to distort, twist; ‹*realidad*› to distort

desfiladero *m* (barranco) ravine, narrow gorge; (puerto) narrow pass

desfilar [A1] *vi* **(a)** «*soldados*» to parade **(b)** «*manifestantes*» to march; **la manifestación desfiló por la Gran Vía** the demonstration passed along the Gran Via **(c)** «*modelo*» to parade up and down the catwalk

desfile *m* (de carrozas) parade, procession; (Mil) parade, march past; ~ **de modelos** fashion show

desgajar [A1] *vt* ~ **algo** DE **algo** ‹*rama*› to break *o* snap sth OFF sth; ‹*páginas*› to tear *o* rip sth OUT OF sth
■ **desgajarse** *v pron* «*rama*» to break off, snap off

desgana *f* **(a)** (inapetencia) lack of appetite **(b)** (falta de entusiasmo): **con** *or* **a** ~ ‹*trabajar*› half-heartedly; ‹*obedecer*› reluctantly

desganado -da *adj* **(a)** (inapetente): **me siento** ~ I'm not hungry **(b)** (apático) lethargic

desgano *m* (AmL) ⇨ DESGANA

desgarbado -da *adj* ‹*persona/aspecto*› gangling, gawky; ‹*movimientos/andar*› ungainly

desgarrador -dora *adj* heartbreaking, heartrending

desgarrar [A1] *vt* **(a)** ‹*vestido/papel*› to tear, rip **(b)** ‹*corazón*› to break
■ **desgarrarse** *v pron* **(a)** «*vestido/camisa*» to tear, rip **(b)** (Med) to tear

desgarro *m* (de ligamento, músculo): **sufrió un** ~ she tore a muscle

desgastar [A1] *vt* **(a)** (gastar) ‹*suelas/ropa*› to wear out; ‹*roca*› to wear away, erode **(b)** (debilitar) to wear ... down
■ **desgastarse** *v pron* **(a)** (gastarse) «*ropa*» to wear out; «*roca*» to wear away; «*tacón*» to wear down **(b)** «*persona*» to wear oneself out; «*relación*» to grow stale

desgaste *m* **(a)** (de ropa, suelas) wear; (de rocas) erosion, wearing away **(b)** (debilitamiento físico) debilitation

desgracia *f* **(a)** (desdicha, infortunio) misfortune; **tiene la** ~ **de ser ciego** he has the misfortune to be blind; ***caer en*** ~ to fall from favor **(b) por desgracia** (*indep*) unfortunately

desgraciado -da *adj* **(a)** [SER] (infeliz) unhappy **(b)** [SER] (desafortunado) ‹*viaje*› ill-fated **(c)** (desacertado) ‹*elección/coincidencia*› unfortunate, unwise ■ *m,f* **1** (desdichado) wretch **2** (persona vil) swine (colloq)

desgravación *f* tax exemption (AmE), tax relief (BrE)

desgravar [A1] *vt* **(a)** ‹*gastos/suma*› to claim tax exemption on (AmE), to claim tax relief on (BrE) **(b)** ‹*producto/importación*› to eliminate the tax *o* duty on ■ ~ *vi* to be tax-deductible

desguazar [A4] *vt* to scrap

deshabitado -da *adj* ‹*región*› uninhabited; ‹*edificio*› empty, unoccupied

deshacer [E18] *vt* **1 (a)** ‹*costura/bordado*› to unpick **(b)** ‹*nudo/lazo/trenza*› to undo; ‹*ovillo*› to unwind **2 (a)** (desarmar, desmontar) ‹*maqueta/mecanismo*› to take ... apart; ‹*paquete*› to undo, unwrap **(b)** ‹*cama*› (para cambiarla) to strip; (desordenar) to mess up; ‹*maleta*› to unpack **3 (a)** (derretir) ‹*nieve/helado*› to melt **(b)** (desmenuzar) to break up **(c)** (en líquido) to dissolve **4** ‹*acuerdo/trato*› to break; ‹*noviazgo*› to break off; ‹*planes/compromiso*› to cancel

■ **deshacerse** *v pron* **1** «*dobladillo/costura*» to come undone *o* unstitched; «*nudo/trenza/moño*» to come undone; «*peinado*» to get messed up, be ruined **2 (a)** (desintegrarse) to disintegrate **(b)** «*nieve/helado*» to melt **(c)** (en líquido) to dissolve **3 ~se** EN **algo**: **~se en llanto** to dissolve into tears; **me deshice en cumplidos** I went out of my way to be complimentary **4 deshacerse de (a)** (librarse de) to get rid of **(b)** (desprenderse de) to part with

deshaga, deshagas, etc *see* DESHACER

deshecho -cha *adj* [ESTAR] **(a)** (cansado, agotado) exhausted **(b)** (destrozado moralmente) shattered, devastated **(c)** (estropeado) ruined

deshelar [A5] *vt* ‹*cañería*› to thaw out, unfreeze; ‹*nevera/congelador*› to defrost; ‹*parabrisas*› to deice

■ **deshelarse** *v pron* «*nieves*» to thaw, melt; «*río/lago*» to thaw; «*relaciones*» to thaw

desheredar [A1] *vt* to disinherit

deshice, deshiciera, etc *see* DESHACER

deshidratarse [A1] *v pron* to become dehydrated

deshielo *m* **(a)** (de ríos, nieves) thaw; **agua de ~** meltwater **(b)** (de relaciones) thaw, thawing-out

deshizo *see* DESHACER

deshojar [A1] *vt* ‹*flor*› to pull the petals off; ‹*cuaderno*› to tear *o* rip the pages out of

deshonesto -ta *adj* **(a)** (tramposo, mentiroso) dishonest **(b)** (indecente) ‹*proposiciones*› improper, indecent

deshonor *m* ⇒ DESHONRA (a)

deshonra *f* **(a)** (vergüenza) disgrace; **ese chico es una ~ para su familia** that boy is a disgrace to his family **(b)** (pérdida de la honra) dishonor*

deshonrar [A1] *vt* ‹*familia/patria*› to dishonor*, disgrace; ‹*mujer*› to dishonor*

deshonroso -sa *adj* dishonorable*, disgraceful

deshora: **a ~(s)** off hours (AmE), out of hours (BrE)

deshuesar [A1] *vt* **1 (a)** ‹*aceitunas*› to pit **(b)** ‹*pollo*› to bone **2** (Méx) ‹*coche/barco*› to scrap

desidia *f* **(a)** (apatía) slackness, indolence (frml) **(b)** (desaseo) slovenliness

desierto[1] -ta *adj* ‹*lugar*› deserted

desierto[2] *m* desert

designar [A1] *vt* **1** (frml) (elegir) **(a)** ‹*persona*› to appoint, designate (frml) **(b)** ‹*lugar/fecha*› to fix, set; (con carácter oficial) to designate **2** (frml) (denominar) to designate (frml)

designio *m* plan

desigual *adj* **1 (a)** (diferente) uneven; **las mangas quedaron ~es** one sleeve turned out longer (*o* wider *etc*) than the other **(b)** (desequilibrado) ‹*lucha*› unequal; ‹*fuerzas*› unevenly-matched **2** (irregular) ‹*terreno/superficie*› uneven; ‹*letra*› uneven, irregular; ‹*calidad*› variable, varying (*before n*); ‹*rendimiento*› inconsistent, erratic

desigualdad *f* **1 (a)** (diferencia) inequality **(b)** (desequilibrio) inequality, disparity **2** (de superficie) unevenness

desilusión *f* (decepción) disappointment; **se llevó una ~** she was disappointed

desilusionado -da *adj* (decepcionado) disappointed

desilusionar [A1] *vt* to disappoint

■ **desilusionarse** *v pron* (decepcionarse) to be disappointed; (perder las ilusiones) to become disillusioned

desinfectante *m* disinfectant

desinfectar [A1] *vt* to disinfect

desinflar [A1] *vt* ‹*globo/balón/neumático*› to let the air out of, to deflate, let down (esp BrE)

■ **desinflarse** *v pron* «*globo/balón/neumático*» to deflate, go down

desinhibido -da *adj* uninhibited

desintegrarse [A1] *v pron* to disintegrate, break up; «*familia*» to break up

desinterés *m* (falta de interés) lack of interest; (altruismo) unselfishness

desinteresado -da *adj* ‹*consejo/ayuda*› disinterested; ‹*persona*› selfless

desintoxicación *f* detoxification

desintoxicarse [A2] *v pron* to undergo detoxification

desistir [I1] *vi* to give up; **~** DE **algo** ‹*de propósito*› to give up sth, desist FROM sth (frml); ‹*de demanda/derecho*› to relinquish sth; **~** DE **hacer algo** to give up doing sth, desist FROM doing sth (frml)

desleal *adj* [SER] disloyal; **~** CON *or* A **algn/algo** disloyal TO sb/sth

desligarse [A3] *v pron* **(a)** (librarse) **~se** DE **algo** ‹*de obligaciones*› to free oneself OF sth; ‹*de compromiso*› to get out OF sth **(b)** (apartarse) **~se** DE **algo/algn** to cut oneself off FROM sth/sb

desliz *m* (error, falta) slip; (al hablar) gaffe, faux pas

deslizador *m* (Méx) (ala delta) hang glider

deslizar [A4] *vt* (hacer resbalar) to slip, slide

■ **deslizarse** *v pron* **(a)** «*patinador/bailarines*» to glide; «*esquiador*» to ski, slide; «*serpiente*» to slither, glide; **~se** POR **algo** to slide down sth; **se deslizó por la cuerda** he slid down the rope **(b)** «*barco/cisne*» to glide; **~se** SOBRE **algo** to glide OVER sth **(c)** «*cajón/argollas de cortina*» to slide **(d)** «*agua/arroyo*» to flow gently **(e)** (escurrirse, escaparse) to slip away

deslucido -da *adj* ‹*actuación/desfile*› dull, lackluster*; ‹*colores/paredes*› faded, drab; ‹*plata*› tarnished

deslumbrante, deslumbrador -dora *adj* ‹*luz*› blinding; ‹*belleza*› dazzling, stunning

deslumbrar [A1] *vt* to dazzle

desmadrarse [A1] *v pron* (fam) «*persona*» to go wild (colloq)

desmán *m* (exceso, abuso) outrage, excess

desmanchar [A1] *vt* (AmL) to get the stains out of

desmandarse [A1] *v pron* «*niños/tropas*» to get out of control *o* hand

desmano: **a ~** (*loc adv*) ‹*estar/quedar*› out of the way; **me pilla a ~** it's out of my way

desmantelar [A1] *vt* to dismantle; ‹*coche*› to strip

desmarcarse [A2] *v pron* (Dep) to slip the coverage (AmE), to slip one's marker (BrE)

desmayado -da *adj* ‹*persona*› unconscious (*from having fainted*)

desmayarse [A1] *v pron* to faint

desmayo *m* **(a)** (Med) faint; **sufrir un ~** to faint **(b) sin ~** ‹*luchar/trabajar*› resolutely, tirelessly

desmedido -da *adj* excessive; **le han dado una importancia desmedida** they have attributed too much importance to it

desmejorado -da *adj* **(a)** (de salud): **lo encontré muy ~** he didn't look at all well to me **(b)** (de atractivo): **está desmejorada** she's lost her looks

desmemoriado -da *adj* forgetful, absent-minded

desmentir [I11] *vt* ‹*noticia/rumor*› to deny; ‹*acusación*› to deny, refute

desmenuzar [A4] *vt* ‹*pescado*› to flake; ‹*pollo*› to shred; ‹*pan*› to crumble

desmigajarse [A1] *v pron* to crumble

desmilitarizar [A4] *vt* to demilitarize

desmontable *adj* **(a)** (desarmable) ‹*mecanismo/mueble*› which can be dismantled *o* taken apart **(b)** (separable) ‹*forro/pieza*› detachable, removable

desmontar [A1] *vt* **(a)** (desarmar) ‹*mueble/mecanismo*› to dismantle, take apart; ‹*tienda de campaña*› to take down **(b)** (separar) ‹*forro/pieza*› to detach, remove ■ **~** *vi* «*jinete*» to dismount

desmoralizar [A4] *vt* to demoralize, dishearten ■ **desmoralizarse** *v pron* to get demoralized *o* disheartened, to lose heart

desmoronarse [A1] *v pron* **(a)** «*muro/edificio*» to collapse; «*imperio/sociedad*» to crumble, collapse **(b)** «*fe/moral*» to crumble; «*persona*» to go to pieces

desnatado -da *adj* (Esp) skimmed

desnaturalizado -da *adj* **(a)** ‹*aceite/vino*› denatured **(b)** ‹*madre*› unnatural

desnivel *m* **1** (en superficie) **(a)** (irregularidad) unevenness, irregularity; **es un terreno lleno de ~es** it is a very uneven piece of land; **un ~ entre la cocina y el comedor** a difference in floor level between the kitchen and the dining room **(b)** (inclinación, pendiente) slope, incline (frml) **(c)** (depresión) drop (*in the level of the ground*) **2** (diferencia) difference, disparity

desnivelado -da *adj* **(a)** (irregular) ‹*terreno*› uneven **(b)** (fuera de nivel): **la mesa está desnivelada** the table isn't level

desnucarse [A2] *v pron* to break one's neck

desnuclearizar [A4] *vt* to denuclearize; **zona desnuclearizada** nuclear-free zone

desnudar [A1] *vt* (desvestir) to undress ■ **desnudarse** *v pron* (*refl*) (desvestirse) to undress, take one's clothes off; **~se de (la) cintura para arriba** to strip to the waist

desnudez *f* (de persona) nakedness, nudity

desnudo[1] -da *adj* **(a)** (sin ropa) ‹*persona*› naked; **nadar ~** to swim in the nude; **totalmente ~** stark naked; **~ de la cintura para arriba** naked to the waist **(b)** (descubierto) ‹*hombros/brazos/torso*› bare

desnudo[2] *m* (Art) nude

desnutrido -da *adj* malnourished, undernourished

desobedecer [E3] *vt/vi* to disobey

desobediente *adj* disobedient

desocupado -da *adj* **1** (vacío, libre) ‹*casa/habitación*› unoccupied, vacant; ‹*asiento/baño*› free **2** (desempleado) unemployed

desodorante *m* deodorant; **~ en barra** stick deodorant; **~ ambiental** (CS) air freshener

desolado -da *adj* **1** ‹*paisaje/campos*› desolate; ‹*ciudad*› devastated **2** (afligido) desolated, devastated

desolador -dora *adj* **1** (devastador) ‹*tormenta/epidemia*› devastating **2** (triste, penoso) ‹*noticia*› devastating; ‹*espectáculo*› distressing

desollar [A10] *vt* ‹*animal*› to skin, flay

desorbitado -da *adj* **(a)** ‹*precios*› exorbitant, astronomical **(b) con los ojos ~s** with her/his eyes popping out of her/his head (colloq)

desorden *m* **1 (a)** (de persona, cuarto, cajón) untidiness, mess (colloq); **perdona el ~** sorry about the mess; **en ~** ‹*salir/entrar*› in a disorderly fashion; **todo estaba en ~** everything was in disorder *o* in a mess **(b)** (confusión) disorder **2 desórdenes** *mpl* (disturbios) disturbances (*pl*), disorder

desordenado -da *adj* **1 (a)** ‹*persona/habitación*› untidy, messy (colloq); **tengo la casa toda desordenada** my house is in a mess *o* is very untidy **(b)** [ESTAR] ‹*naipes/hojas*› out of order **2** ‹*vida*› disorganized

desordenar [A1] *vt* ‹*mesa/habitación*› to make ... untidy, mess up (colloq); ‹*naipes/hojas*› to get ... out of order

desorganización *f* lack of organization

desorganizado -da *adj* disorganized

desorientado -da *adj* disoriented, disorientated (BrE)

desorientar [A1] *vt* to confuse ■ **desorientarse** *v pron* to lose one's bearings, become disoriented

despabilado -da *adj* ⇒ ESPABILADO

despabilar [A1] *vt* ⇒ ESPABILAR

despachar [A1] *vt* **1 (a)** ‹*asunto/tarea/*› to take care of, deal with; ‹*correspondencia*› to deal with, attend to **(b)** ‹*carta/paquete*› to send; ‹*mercancías*› (por barco) to ship; (por avión, tren) to send, dispatch **2** (Com) (en tienda) to serve, deal with ■ **~** *vi* (Com) «*dependiente*» to serve

despacho *m* **1 (a)** (oficina) office; (estudio) study **(b)** (mobiliario) office furniture **2** (envío) dispatch, despatch **3** (comunicado) communiqué; (Mil) dispatch; (Period) report

despacio *adv* **1** (lentamente) slowly **2** (CS) (en voz baja) quietly, softly; (sin hacer ruido) quietly

despampanante *adj* (fam) stunning (colloq)

desparpajo *m* (desenvoltura) self-confidence; (desfachatez) audacity, nerve (colloq)

desparramado -da *adj* (esparcido) scattered; (derramado) spilt

desparramar [A1] *vt* ‹*líquido/azúcar*› to spill; ‹*botones/monedas*› to spill, scatter; ‹*papeles/juguetes*› to scatter

■ **desparramarse** *v pron* «*líquido/azúcar*» to spill; «*botones/monedas*» to scatter, spill

despavorido -da *adj* terrified, petrified

despecho *m* spite; **por ~** out of spite

despectivo -va *adj* ‹*trato/gesto/actitud*› contemptuous; ‹*tono*› disparaging; ‹*término*› pejorative, derogatory

despedazar [A4] *vt* **(a)** (cortar en trozos) to cut ... into pieces **(b)** ‹*presa*› to tear ... to pieces *o* shreds

despedida *f* **(a)** (acción) goodbye, farewell (liter) **(b)** (celebración) farewell party; **regalo de ~** a farewell gift; **~ de soltera/soltero** hen/stag night *o* party

despedir [I14] *vt* **1** (decir adiós): **vinieron a ~me al aeropuerto** they came to see me off at the airport **2** (del trabajo) to dismiss, fire (colloq); (por reducción de personal) to lay off **3** ‹*olor*› to give off; ‹*humo/vapor*› to emit, give off; **salir despedido** «*corcho/pelota*» to shoot out; **el conductor salió despedido del asiento** the driver was thrown out of his seat

■ **despedirse** *v pron* (decir adiós) to say goodbye; **~se DE algn** to say goodbye TO sb

despegar [A3] *vt* ‹*etiqueta/esparadrapo*› to remove, peel off; ‹*piezas/ensambladura*› to get ... unstuck *o* apart; **no despegó los labios** she didn't say a word ■ **~** *vi* «*avión*» to take off; «*cohete*» to lift off, be launched

■ **despegarse** *v pron* «*sello/etiqueta*» to come unstuck, peel off; «*esparadrapo/empapelado*» to come off

despegue *m* (de avión) takeoff; (de cohete) launch, lift-off

despeinado -da *adj* ‹*pelo/melena*› unkempt, disheveled*; **estar ~** to have one's hair in a mess

despeinar [A1] *vt*: **~ a algn** to mess up sb's hair

■ **despeinarse** *v pron* to mess one's hair up

despejado -da *adj* **1** ▶ **409** (Meteo) ‹*día/cielo*› clear **2** (libre, vacío) ‹*carretera/camino*› clear **3 (a)** ‹*persona*› clearheaded; ‹*mente*› clear **(b)** [ESTAR] (sobrio) sober

despejar [A1] *vt* **1 (a)** (desocupar, desalojar) to clear **(b)** ‹*nariz*› to unblock, clear; **el paseo me despejó** the walk cleared my head **2** ‹*balón*› (en fútbol) to clear; (en fútbol americano) to punt ■ **~** *vi* (en fútbol) to clear; (en fútbol americano) to punt ■ **~** *v impers* (Meteo) to clear up

■ **despejarse** *v pron* (espabilarse) to wake (oneself) up; (desembotarse) to clear one's head; «*borracho*» to sober up

despellejar [A1] *vt* ‹*animal*› to skin

■ **despellejarse** *v pron* to peel; **se me despellejó la nariz** my nose peeled

despelote *m* (AmL fam) (caos, lío) shambles (colloq)

despenalizar [A4] *vt* to legalize, decriminalize

despensa *f* larder, pantry

despeñadero *m* cliff, precipice

despeñarse [A1] *v pron* to go over a cliff (*o* precipice *etc*)

desperdiciar [A1] *vt* ‹*comida/papel/tela*› to waste; ‹*oportunidad*› to miss, waste

desperdicio *m* **(a)** (de comida, papel) waste **(b) desperdicios** *mpl* (residuos) scraps (*pl*)

desperdigado -da *adj* scattered

desperezarse [A4] *v pron* to stretch

desperfecto *m* **(a)** (daño) damage **(b)** (defecto) flaw

despertador *m* alarm clock; **poner el ~** to set the alarm

despertar [A5] *vt* **(a)** ‹*persona*› to wake, wake ... up **(b)** ‹*sentimientos/pasiones*› to arouse; ‹*apetito*› to whet; ‹*recuerdos*› to evoke; ‹*interés*› to awaken, stir up ■ **~** *vi* (del sueño) to wake (up); (de la anestesia) to come round

■ **despertarse** *v pron* (del sueño) to wake (up)

despiadado -da *adj* ‹*persona*› ruthless, heartless; ‹*ataque/crítica*› savage, merciless

despida, **despidas, etc** *see* DESPEDIR

despido *m* dismissal; (por falta de trabajo) redundancy, layoff (AmE)

despierta, **despiertas, etc** *see* DESPERTAR

despierto -ta *adj* **(a)** [ESTAR] (del sueño) awake **(b)** [SER] ‹*persona/mente*› bright, alert

despilfarrar [A1] *vi* to waste *o* squander money ■ **~** *vt* to squander, waste

despilfarro *m* waste

despistado -da *adj* **(a)** [SER] vague, absent-minded; **soy muy ~ para los nombres** I never remember names **(b) estar ~** to be miles away (colloq) *o* daydreaming; (desorientado, confuso) to be bewildered *o* lost ■ *m, f* scatterbrain (colloq)

despistar [A1] *vt* **(a)** (desorientar, confundir) to confuse **(b)** ‹*perseguidor*› to shake off; ‹*sabueso*› to throw ... off the scent

■ **despistarse** *v pron* (confundirse) to get confused *o* muddled; (distraerse) to lose concentration

despiste *m* **(a)** (distracción) absentmindedness; **fue un ~** it was a lapse of concentration **(b)** (equivocación) slip, mistake

desplazamiento *m* **1** (movimiento) movement, displacement (frml) **2** (frml) (traslado, viaje) trip; **gastos de ~** traveling expenses

desplazar [A4] *vt* **1** (frml) (mover, correr) to move **2** (suplantar, relegar) ‹*persona*› to displace; **~ A algo** to take the place OF sth

■ **desplazarse** *v pron* (frml) (trasladarse, moverse) «*animal*» to move around; «*avión/barco*» to travel, go; «*persona*» to get around

desplegar [A7] *vt* **1 (a)** ‹*alas*› to spread; ‹*mapa*› to open out, spread out; ‹*velas*› to unfurl **(b)** (demostrar) ‹*talento/ingenio*› to display; (emplear) ‹*en-*

cantos/poder› to use **(c)** (llevar a cabo) ‹*campaña*› to mount; ‹*esfuerzo*› to make **2** (Mil) ‹*tropas/misiles*› to deploy

■ **desplegarse** *v pron* (Mil) to deploy

despliegue *m* **1** (de tropas, recursos) deployment **2** (de riqueza, sabiduría) display

desplomarse [A1] *v pron* «*persona/edificio*» to collapse

desplumar [A1] *vt* **(a)** ‹*ave*› to pluck **(b)** (fam) ‹*persona*› to fleece (colloq)

despoblación *f* depopulation

despoblado -da *adj* (sin habitantes) deserted, uninhabited; (subpoblado) underpopulated, sparsely populated **2** ‹*cejas*› thin, sparse

despojar [A1] *vt* (frml) **~ A algn DE algo** ‹*de privilegios/poderes*› to divest sb OF sth (frml); ‹*de título/posesiones*› to dispossess (frml) *o* strip sb OF sth

■ **despojarse** *v pron* (frml *o* liter) **~se DE algo** ‹*de ropa*› to remove sth; ‹*de bienes*› to relinquish sth

despojos *mpl* **(a)** (restos) remains (*pl*) **(b)** (presa, botín) spoils (*pl*), loot **(c)** (de aves) *head, wings, feet and giblets*; (de reses) *head, feet and offal*

desportillado -da *adj* chipped

desposeído -da *m,f*: **los ~s** the destitute, the dispossessed

déspota *mf* tyrant, despot

despótico -ca *adj* despotic, tyrannical

despotricar [A2] *vi* (fam) **~ (CONTRA algo/algn)** to rant and rave (ABOUT sth/sb)

despreciable *adj* **(a)** ‹*persona/conducta*› despicable, contemptible **(b) no/nada ~** ‹*suma/número*› not inconsiderable, significant

despreciar [A1] *vt* **(a)** (menospreciar) ‹*persona*› to look down on; (profundamente) to despise **(b)** (rechazar) ‹*oferta/ayuda*› to reject

despreciativo -va *adj* disdainful

desprecio *m* **(a)** (menosprecio) disdain; (más intenso) contempt; **me miró con ~** she gave me a disdainful *o* scornful look **(b)** (indiferencia por el peligro, la vida) disregard **(c)** (desaire) snub, slight; **hacerle un ~ a algn** to snub *o* slight sb

desprender [E1] *vt* (soltar, separar) ‹*teja*› to dislodge; ‹*etiqueta*› to detach

■ **desprenderse** *v pron* **1** «*teja*» to come loose; «*botón*» to come off; «*retina*» to become detached; **~se DE algo** to come away FROM sth **2** (renunciar, entregar) **~se DE algo** ‹*de posesiones*› to part WITH sth

desprendido -da *adj* [SER] generous, openhanded; *ver tb* DESPRENDER

desprendimiento *m* detachment; **~ de retina** detachment of the retina; **~ de tierras** landslide

despreocupado -da *adj* **(a)** (sin preocupaciones) ‹*vida*› carefree **(b)** (descuidado) negligent **(c)** (indiferente) unworried

despreocuparse [A1] *v pron* **(a)** ⇒ DESENTENDERSE **(b)** (dejar de preocuparse): **despreocúpate de todo** don't worry about anything

desprestigiar [A1] *vt* to discredit

■ **desprestigiarse** *v pron* «*persona/producto/empresa*» to lose prestige

desprestigio *m* **(a)** (pérdida de prestigio) loss of prestige; **ir en ~ de algo/algn** to bring discredit on *o* upon sth/sb **(b)** (falta de prestigio) bad reputation

desprevenido -da *adj*: **estar ~** to be unprepared *o* unready; **pillar a algn ~** «*pregunta*» to catch sb unawares *o* off guard; «*lluvia*» to catch sb by surprise

desprolijo -ja *adj* (CS) **(a)** [ESTAR] ‹*trabajo*› untidy, messy **(b)** [SER] ‹*persona*› careless

desproporción *f* disparity, disproportion

desproporcionado -da *adj* out of proportion

desprovisto -ta *adj* **~ DE algo** lacking IN sth

después *adv* **1 (a)** (más tarde) later; **para ~** for later **(b)** (en una serie de sucesos) then, afterward(s); **~ no lo he vuelto a ver** I haven't seen him since then **(c)** (*en locs*) **después de** after; **~ de Cristo** AD; **~ DE hacer algo** after doing sth; **después de todo** after all; **después (de) que** after; (refiriéndose al futuro) once, when; **~ (de) que todos se hayan ido** once *o* when everybody has left; **después que** after **2** (en el espacio): **bájate dos paradas ~** get off two stops further on; **hay una casa y ~ está el colegio** there is a house and then you come to the school; **está justo ~ del puente** it's just past the bridge

despuntado -da *adj* blunt

despuntar [A1] *vt* to blunt ■ **~** *vi* **(a)** «*día*» to break, dawn; **al ~ el día** at daybreak **(b)** «*flor*» to bud; «*plantas*» to sprout **(c)** «*persona*» **~ EN algo** to excel AT *o* IN sth

desquiciado -da *adj* ‹*mundo/persona*› crazy; **tengo los nervios ~s** my nerves are in tatters

desquiciante *adj* maddening, infuriating

desquicio *m* (RPl fam) chaos

desquitarse [A1] *v pron* to get even; **lo hizo para ~ de él** she did it to get even with him; **~ CON algn/algo** to take it out ON sb/sth

destacado -da *adj* **1** ‹*profesional/artista*› prominent, distinguished; ‹*actuación*› outstanding **2** [ESTAR] ‹*tropas*› stationed

destacar [A2] *vt* **1** (recalcar, subrayar) to emphasize, stress **2** (realzar) ‹*belleza/figura*› to enhance; ‹*color/plano*› to bring out **3 (a)** (Mil) ‹*tropas*› to post **(b)** ‹*periodista/fotógrafo*› to send ■ **~** *vi* to stand out; **~ EN algo** to excel AT *o* IN sth

destajo *m* (Com, Rels Labs) piecework; **trabajar a ~** to do piecework

destapado -da *adj* **(a)** (sin tapa) ‹*olla*› uncovered; **dejó la botella destapada** he left the top off the bottle **(b)** (en la cama): **siempre duerme ~** he always sleeps with the covers thrown back

destapador *m* (AmL) bottle opener

destapar [A1] *vt* **1 (a)** ‹*botella/caja*› to open, take the top/lid off; ‹*olla*› to uncover, take the lid off **(b)** (descubrir) ‹*mueble*› to uncover; ‹*escándalo*› to uncover **(c)** (en la cama) to pull the covers off **2** (AmL) ‹*cañería/inodoro*› to unblock

■ **destaparse** *v pron* (*refl*) **1** (en la cama) to throw the covers *o* bedclothes off **2** «*nariz/oídos*» to unblock

destaponar [A1] *vt* ‹*cañería*› to unblock

destartalado -da *adj* (fam) ‹*coche*› beat-up (AmE colloq), clapped-out (BrE colloq); ‹*mueble*› shabby; ‹*casa*› ramshackle, rundown

destellar [A1] *vi* «*brillante/joya*» to sparkle, glitter; «*estrella*» to twinkle, sparkle

destello *m* (de estrella) twinkle, sparkle; (de brillante, joya) sparkle, glitter

destemplado -da *adj* **1** ‹*persona*›: **estoy ~** (con fiebre) I have a slight fever; (indispuesto) I'm feeling off-color* **2 (a)** ‹*instrumento/voz/tono*› discordant **(b)** ‹*nervios*› frayed

destemplar [A1] *vt* **1** ‹*guitarra/violín*› to make ... go out of tune **2** ‹*ánimos/nervios*› to fray **3** (AmL) ‹*dientes*› to set ... on edge

desteñir [I15] *vi* «*prenda/color*» to run; (decolorarse) to fade

■ **desteñirse** *v pron* to run; (decolorarse) to fade

desternillarse [A1] *v pron* (fam): **~ de risa** to split one's sides (laughing) (colloq)

desterrado -da *m,f* exile

desterrar [A5] *vt* ‹*persona*› to exile, banish (liter)

destiempo: **a ~** ‹*marchar*› out of step; ‹*tocar*› out of time; **habló a ~** she picked the wrong moment to say it

destierro *m* exile, banishment

destilar [A1] *vt* **(a)** ‹*alcohol/petróleo*› to distill*; ‹*hulla/madera*› to char **(b)** (rezumar) to ooze

destilería *f* distillery

destinado -da *adj* **1 (a)** (predestinado): **~ a triunfar/al fracaso** destined to succeed/to fail **(b)** (dirigido, asignado): **~ A algn** ‹*carta/paquete*› addressed TO sb; ‹*víveres*› intended FOR sb; ‹*libro/novela*› aimed AT sb; **las cajas destinadas a Montevideo** the boxes destined for Montevideo; **los aviones ~s a este fin** the planes used for this purpose **2 (a)** ‹*militar*›: **~ en Ceuta** stationed in Ceuta **(b)** ‹*funcionario/diplomático*›: **ahora está ~ en Lima** now he's been posted to Lima

destinar [A1] *vt* **1** ‹*funcionario/militar*› to post, send, assign **2** (asignar un fin): **destinó todos sus ahorros a pagar las deudas** she used all her savings to pay her debts; **~on el dinero a la investigación** the money was used for research; **~on parte de los fondos a este fin** they earmarked part of the funds for this purpose

destinatario -ria *m,f* (de carta, paquete) addressee; (de giro, transferencia) payee

destino *m* **1** (sino) fate **2 (a)** (de avión, autobús) destination; **con ~ a Roma** ‹*vuelo/tren*› to Rome; ‹*pasajero*› travelling to Rome; ‹*carga*› destined for Rome; **salieron con ~ a Lima** they set off for Lima **(b)** (puesto) posting, assignment **3** (uso, fin) use

destituir [I20] *vt* (frml) (despedir) to dismiss

destornillador *m* screwdriver

destornillar [A1] *vt* to unscrew

destreza *f* skill; **con gran ~** very skillfully

destronar [A1] *vt* ‹*rey*› to dethrone, depose; ‹*líder/campeón*› to depose, topple

destrozar [A4] *vt* **(a)** (romper, deteriorar) ‹*zapatos*› to ruin; ‹*cristal/jarrón*› to smash; ‹*juguete*› to pull ... apart; ‹*coche*› to wreck; ‹*libro*› to pull apart **(b)** ‹*felicidad/matrimonio/vida*› to wreck, destroy; ‹*corazón*› to break; **tiene los nervios destrozados** he's a nervous wreck

■ **destrozarse** *v pron* **(a)** (romperse) «*zapatos*» to be ruined; «*jarrón/cristal*» to smash **(b)** ‹*estómago/hígado*› to ruin

destrozo *m*: *tb* **~s** damage

destrucción *f* destruction

destructivo -va *adj* destructive

destructor *m* destroyer

destruir [I20] *vt* **(a)** ‹*documentos/pruebas*› to destroy; ‹*ciudad*› to destroy; ‹*medio ambiente*› to damage **(b)** (echar por tierra) ‹*reputación*› to ruin; ‹*plan*› to wreck; ‹*esperanzas*› to dash, shatter

desubicado -da *adj* (AmS) **(a)** [ESTAR] (desplazado) out of position **(b)** [ESTAR] (desorientado) confused, disoriented **(c)** [SER] (en cuestiones sociales): **es tan ~** he just doesn't have a clue (colloq)

desuso *m* disuse; ***caer en* ~** to fall into disuse

desvaído -da *adj* ‹*color*› faded, washed-out; ‹*persona*› colorless*, insipid

desvalido -da *m,f* helpless person

desvalijar [A1] *vt* **(a)** ‹*casa/tienda*› to strip ... bare **(b)** ‹*persona*› (robar) to rob; (en juego) (fam) to clean ... out (colloq)

desván *m* attic, loft

desvanecerse [E3] *v pron* **(a)** «*humo/nubes/niebla*» to clear, disperse; «*dudas/temores/sospechas*» to vanish, be dispelled; «*fantasma/visión*» to disappear, vanish **(b)** «*color*» to fade

desvariar [A17] *vi* (Med) to be delirious; (decir tonterías) to talk nonsense, rave

desvelado -da *adj*: **estoy ~** I can't sleep

desvelar [A1] *vt* **1** ‹*persona*› to keep ... awake, stop ... from sleeping **2** (Esp) ⇒ DEVELAR

■ **desvelarse** *v pron* (perder el sueño): **me desvelé anoche** I couldn't sleep last night

desvelo *m* **1** (insomnio) sleeplessness **2 desvelos** *mpl* (esfuerzos) efforts (*pl*), pains (*pl*)

desvencijado -da *adj* ‹*silla/cama*› rickety; ‹*coche*› dilapidated, beat-up (AmE colloq), clapped-out (BrE colloq)

desventaja *f* disadvantage; **en ~** at a disadvantage

desvergonzado -da *m,f*: **ser un ~** (impúdico) to have no shame; (descarado) to be very impertinent

desvestir [I14] *vt* to undress

■ **desvestirse** *v pron* to undress, get undressed; **~se de la cintura para arriba** to strip to the waist

desviación *f* **(a)** (en general) diversion **(b)** (Med) curvature **(c)** (alejamiento) **~ DE algo** deviation FROM sth

desviar [A17] *vt* ‹*tráfico/vuelo/fondos*› to divert; ‹*río*› to alter the course of; ‹*golpe/pelota*› to deflect, parry; **~ la conversación** to change the subject; **desvió la mirada** he looked away

■ **desviarse** *v pron* **1** «*carretera*» to branch off; «*vehículo*» to turn off; **la conversación se desvió hacia otros temas** the conversation turned to other things **2** «*persona*» **~se DE algo** ‹*de ruta*› to deviate FROM sth; ‹*de tema*› to get off sth

desvincularse [A1] *v pron* **~se DE algn/algo** to dissociate oneself FROM sth/sb; **está desvinculado de la política** he is no longer involved in politics

desvío *m* **(a)** (por obras) diversion, detour (AmE); **tomar un ~** to make a detour **(b)** (Esp) (salida, carretera) exit

desvivirse [I1] *v pron* **~ POR algn** to be completely devoted TO sb; **~ POR hacer algo** to go out of one's way to do sth

detallado -da *adj* ‹*factura/cuenta*› itemized

detallar [A1] *vt* to detail

detalle *m* **1 (a)** (pormenor) detail; **entrar en ~s** to go into details; **describir algo con todo ~** to describe sth in great detail **(b)** (elemento decorativo) detail **2 (a)** (pequeño regalo) little gift **(b)** (Esp, Méx) (atención, gesto) nice (*o* thoughtful *etc*) gesture; **tener un ~ CON algn** to do sth nice FOR sb **3** (Com) **al detalle** retail

detallista *adj* (minucioso) precise, meticulous

detectar [A1] *vt* to detect

detective *mf* detective

detector *m* detector; **~ de mentiras/metales** lie/metal detector

detención *f* **1** (arresto) arrest; (encarcelamiento) detention **2** ⇒ DETENIMIENTO

detener [E27] *vt* **1** (parar) ‹*vehículo/máquina*› to stop; ‹*trámite/proceso*› to halt; ‹*hemorragia*› to stop, staunch **2** (arrestar) to arrest; (encarcelar) to detain; **¡queda usted detenido!** you're under arrest!

■ **detenerse** *v pron* **(a)** (pararse) «*vehículo/persona*» to stop; **~se A hacer algo** to stop to do sth **(b)** (tomar mucho tiempo) **~se EN algo**: **no nos detengamos demasiado en los detalles** let's not spend too much time discussing the details

detenido -da *adj* **(a)** ‹*vehículo/tráfico*› held up **(b)** ‹*investigación/estudio*› detailed, thorough **(c)** [ESTAR] ‹*persona*› under arrest; (por período más largo) in custody ■ *m,f* person under arrest; (durante un período más largo) detainee, person held in custody

detenimiento *m*: **con ~** carefully *o* in detail

detergente *m* **(a)** (para ropa) laundry detergent (AmE), washing powder (BrE) **(b)** (Bol, CS) (para vajilla) dishwashing liquid (AmE), washing-up liquid (BrE)

deteriorado -da *adj* ‹*mercancías*› damaged; ‹*edificio*› dilapidated, run down; ‹*mueble/cuadro*› in bad condition

deteriorar [A1] *vt* ‹*relaciones/salud/situación*› to cause ... to deteriorate

■ **deteriorarse** *v pron* «*relaciones/salud/situación*» to deteriorate, worsen; «*mercancías*» to get damaged

deterioro *m* **(a)** (de edificio, muebles) deterioration, wear **(b)** (empeoramiento) deterioration, worsening

determinación *f* (cualidad) determination, resolve; (decisión) decision; **tomar una ~** to make a decision

determinado -da *adj* ‹*fecha/lugar*› certain; **en determinadas circunstancias** in certain circumstances; **una determinada dosis** a particular dosage

determinante *adj* ‹*causa*› main (*before n*); ‹*factor*› deciding (*before n*)

determinar [A1] *vt* **1** (establecer, precisar) **(a)** «*ley/contrato*» to state; «*persona*» to determine **(b)** (por deducción) to establish, determine **2** (motivar) to cause, bring about

detestar [A1] *vt* to hate, detest

detiene, detienes, etc *see* DETENER

detonación *f* **(a)** (ruido) explosion; (acción) detonation **(b)** (Auto) (de motor) backfire

detonador *m* detonator

detonar [A1] *vi* to detonate, explode

detrás *adv* **1** (lugar, parte) [*Latin American Spanish also uses* ATRÁS *in this sense*]: **iba corriendo ~** he ran along behind; **las cajas de ~** the boxes at the back; **por ~** ‹*abrocharse*› at the back; ‹*atacar*› from behind **2 detrás de** (*loc prep*) behind; **~ de la puerta** behind the door; **~ de mí/ti** behind me/you; **un cigarrillo ~ de otro** one cigarette after another

detuve, detuvo, etc *see* DETENER

deuda *f* **(a)** (Com, Fin) debt; **pagar una ~** to pay (off) a debt; **contraer una ~** to run up *o* (frml) contract a debt **(b)** (compromiso moral): **estoy en ~ con usted** I am indebted to you

deudor -dora *adj* debtor (*before n*) ■ *m,f* debtor

devaluación *f* devaluation

devaluar [A18] *vt* to devalue

■ **devaluarse** *v pron* «*moneda*» to fall; «*terrenos/propiedad*» to depreciate, fall in value

devanar [A1] *vt* ‹*hilo/lana/alambre*› to wind

devaneo *m* **(a)** (amorío) affair; (pasajero) fling **(b)** (pasatiempo frívolo) idle pursuit

devastador -dora *adj* devastating

develar [A1] *vt* (AmL) ‹*secreto*› to reveal, disclose; ‹*misterio*› to uncover; ‹*monumento/placa*› to unveil

devoción *f* devotion; **siente ~ por sus hijos** she's devoted to her children

devolución *f* (de artículo) return; (de dinero) refund

devolver [E11] *vt* **1 (a)** (restituir) ‹*objeto prestado*› to return, give back; ‹*dinero*› to give back, pay back; ‹*envase*› to return; ‹*objeto comprado*› to bring/take ... back; **devuélvelo a su lugar** put it back in its place; **~le algo A algn** to return sth TO sb; ‹*dinero*› to give *o* pay sth back TO sb; **me devolvieron los documentos** I got my papers back; **el teléfono me devolvía las monedas** the telephone kept rejecting my coins; **la operación le devolvió la vista** the operation restored his sight **(b)** ‹*refugiado*› to return, send back **(c)** (Fin) ‹*letra*› to return **2** (corresponder) ‹*visita/favor*› to return **3** (vomitar) to bring up, throw up (colloq) ■ **~** *vi* to bring up; **tengo ganas de ~** I feel sick

■ **devolverse** *v pron* (AmL exc RPl) (regresar) to go/come/turn back

devorar [A1] *vt* «*animal*» to devour; «*persona*» to devour, wolf down (colloq); **~ a algn con los ojos** *or* **la mirada** to devour sb with one's eyes (colloq); **fue devorado por las llamas** it was consumed by the flames

devoto -ta *adj* ‹*persona*› devout; ‹*lugar/obra*› devotional ■ *m,f* **(a)** (Relig) **~ DE algn** devotee OF sb **(b)** (aficionado) **~ DE algo/algn** devotee OF sth/admirer of sb

devuelva, **devuelvas, etc** *see* DEVOLVER

DF *m* (en Méx) = **Distrito Federal**

di *see* DAR, DECIR

día *m* **1 (a)** (en general) day; **todos los ~s** every day; **~ a ~** day by day; **de** *or* **durante el ~** during the day; **el ~ anterior** the day before, the previous day; **el ~ siguiente** the next *o* the following day; **un ~ sí y otro no** *or* (AmL) **~ (de) por medio** every other day, on alternate days; **dentro de quince ~s** in two weeks *o* (BrE) a fortnight; **cada ~** every day; **buenos ~s** *or* (RPl) **buen ~** good morning; ***al* ~**: **una vez al ~** once a day; **estoy al ~ en los pagos** I'm up to date with the payments; **poner algo al ~** to bring sth up to date; **ponerse al ~ con algo** (con noticias) to get up to date with sth; (con trabajo) to catch up on sth; **mantenerse al ~** to keep up to date; ***de un ~ para otro*** overnight; ***hoy en ~*** nowadays, these days **(b)** ▶ **193** (fecha): **¿qué ~ es hoy?** what day is it today?; **empieza el ~ dos** it starts on the second; **el ~ de Año Nuevo** New Year's Day; **~ de los enamorados** (St) Valentine's Day; **~ festivo** *or* (AmL) **feriado** public holiday; **~ laborable** working day; **~ libre** (sin trabajo) day off; (sin compromisos) free day **2 (a)** (tiempo indeterminado) day; **algún ~** one day; **lo haremos otro ~** we'll do it some other time; **un ~ de estos** one of these days; **¡hasta otro ~!** so long!, see you!; ***el ~ menos pensado*** when you least expect it **(b) días** *mpl* (vida, tiempo) days (*pl*); **tiene los ~s contados** his days are numbered; **hasta nuestros ~s** (up) to the present day

diabetes *f* diabetes

diabético -ca *adj/m,f* diabetic

diablo *m* **1** (demonio) devil; ***como* (*el* or *un*) ~** like crazy *o* mad (colloq); ***del ~*** *or* ***de mil ~s*** (fam) devilish (colloq); **está de un humor de mil ~s** she's in a devil of a mood (colloq); ***donde el ~ perdió el poncho*** (AmS fam) (en un lugar — aislado) in the back of beyond; (— lejano) miles away (colloq); ***mandar algo/a algn al ~*** (fam) to pack sth in/to tell sb to go to hell (colloq) **2** (fam) (uso expletivo): **¿cómo/dónde/qué/quién ~s ... ?** how/where/what/who the hell ... ? (colloq)

diablura *f* (fam) prank

diabólico -ca *adj* (del diablo) diabolic, satanic; ‹*persona*› evil; ‹*plan/intenciones*› devilish, fiendish

diadema *f* (para el pelo) hair-band; (corona) crown, diadem; (media corona) tiara

diafragma *m* (Anat, Fot, Med) diaphragm

diagnosticar [A2] *vt* to diagnose

diagnóstico *m* diagnosis

diagonal *f* **(a)** (Mat) diagonal **(b)** (en fútbol americano) endzone

diagrama *m* diagram

dial *m* (Rad, Tec) dial; (del teléfono) dial

dialecto *m* dialect

dialogar [A3] *vi* to talk; **~ CON algn** to talk TO sb

diálogo *m* **(a)** (conversación) conversation; (Lit) dialogue, dialog (AmE) **(b)** (Pol, Rels Labs) talks (*pl*), negotiations (*pl*)

diamante *m* **(a)** (piedra) diamond; **un anillo de ~s** a diamond ring **(b)** (Dep) diamond **(c) diamantes** *mpl* (en naipes) diamonds (*pl*)

diámetro *m* diameter

diana *f* **1** (Mil) reveille **2** (Dep, Jueg) (objeto) target; (para dardos) dartboard; (centro) bull's-eye

diapasón *m* (para afinar) tuning fork; (de instrumento de cuerda) fingerboard

diapositiva *f* slide, transparency

diariero -ra *m,f* (CS) newspaper vendor

diario -ria *adj* **(a)** (de todos los días) ‹*tarea/clases*› daily; ‹*gastos*› everyday, day-to-day **(b)** (por día): **trabaja cuatro horas diarias** she works four hours a day **(c)** (*en locs*) **a diario** every day; **de diario** ‹*roba/vajilla*› everyday (*before n*); **para diario** for everyday (use) ■ *m* **1** (periódico) newspaper; **~ mural** (Chi) bulletin board (AmE), notice board (BrE) **2** (libro personal) diary, journal (AmE) **3** (Méx, Col, Ven) (gastos cotidianos): **el ~** day-to-day expenses

diarrea *f* diarrhea*

dibujante *mf* (*m*) draftsman*; (*f*) draftswoman*; (de cómics) comic book artist, strip cartoonist

dibujar [A1] *vt/vi* to draw; **~ a mano alzada** to draw freehand

dibujo *m* **(a)** (arte) drawing; **clase de ~** drawing class; **~ lineal** line drawing **(b)** (representación) drawing; **un ~ al carboncillo** a charcoal drawing; **~s animados** cartoons (*pl*) **(c)** (estampado) pattern

diccionario *m* dictionary; **~ bilingüe** bilingual dictionary; **~ de sinónimos** dictionary of synonyms, ≈ thesaurus

dice, **dices, etc** *see* DECIR

dicharachero -ra *adj* (que habla mucho) chatty (colloq), talkative; (gracioso) witty

dicho[1] -cha *pp* [*ver tb* DECIR[2]]: **~ esto, se fue** having said this, he left; **con eso queda todo ~** that says it all; **~ de otro modo** to put it another way, in other words; **~ sea de paso** incidentally, by the way; **y ¡~ y hecho! en diez minutos estaba listo** and, sure enough, ten minutes later there it was ■ *adj dem* (frml): **en dichas cuidades ...** in these cities ...; **dicha información** that information; **~s documentos** (en escrito, documento) the above *o* (frml) said documents

dicho[2] *m* saying

dichoso -sa *adj* **1** (feliz) happy; (afortunado) fortunate, lucky **2** (*delante del n*) (fam) (maldito) blessed (colloq), damn (sl)

diciembre *m* ▶ **193** December; *para ejemplos ver* ENERO

diciendo *see* DECIR

dictado *m* dictation; **nos hizo un ~** she gave us a dictation; **escribir al ~** to take dictation

dictador -dora *m,f* dictator

dictadura *f* dictatorship

dictar [A1] *vt* **(a)** ‹*carta/texto*› to dictate **(b)** ‹*leyes/medidas*› to announce; ‹*sentencia*› to pronounce, pass **(c)** ‹*acción/tendencia/moda*› to dictate **(d)** (AmL) ‹*clase/curso/conferencia*› to give ■ ~ *vi* to dictate

didáctico -ca *adj* ‹*juguete/programa*› educational; ‹*poema/exposición*› didactic

diecinueve *adj inv/m/pron* ▶ 293 nineteen; *para ejemplos ver* CINCO

dieciocho *adj inv/m/pron* ▶ 293 eighteen; *para ejemplos ver* CINCO

dieciséis *adj inv/m/pron* ▶ 293 sixteen; *para ejemplos ver* CINCO

diecisiete *adj inv/m/pron* ▶ 293 seventeen; *para ejemplos ver* CINCO

diente *m* **(a)** ▶ 123 (Anat, Zool) tooth; **lavarse** *or* **cepillarse los ~s** to clean *o* brush one's teeth; **~ de leche** milk tooth; ***daba ~ con ~*** my/his teeth were chattering; ***hablar*** *or* ***murmurar entre ~s*** to mutter (under one's breath) **(b)** (de engranaje, sierra) tooth; (de tenedor) prong, tine; **~ de ajo** clove of garlic

diera, dieras, etc *see* DAR

diéresis *f* (*pl* ~) diaeresis

diese, dieses, etc *see* DAR

diestra *f* (liter *o* period) right hand; ***a ~ y siniestra*** left and right (AmE), left, right and centre (BrE)

diestro[1] -tra *adj* **(a)** (frml) ‹*mano*› right; ‹*persona*› right-handed **(b)** (hábil) ‹*persona/jugada*› skillful*

diestro[2] *m* matador, bullfighter; ***a ~ y siniestro*** (Esp) left and right (AmE), left, right and centre (BrE)

dieta *f* **1** (alimentación, régimen) diet; **ponerse a ~** to go on a diet **2 (a)** (para viajes) allowance **(b)** (de parlamentario) salary

diez *adj inv/m/pron* ▶ 293 ten; *para ejemplos ver* CINCO

difamar [A1] *vt* (por escrito) to libel, defame (frml); (oralmente) to slander, defame (frml)

diferencia *f* **(a)** (disparidad) difference; **la ~ de precio** the difference in price; **a ~ del marido, ella es encantadora** unlike her husband, she's really charming **(b)** (distinción) distinction; **hacer una ~** to make a distinction **(c)** (desacuerdo) difference; **resolver sus** (*or* **mis** *etc*) **~s** to resolve one's differences **(d)** (resto) difference; **yo pagué la ~** I paid the difference

diferenciar [A1] *vt* ‹*colores/sonidos*› to tell the difference between, differentiate between

■ **diferenciarse** *v pron*: **¿en qué se diferencia esta especie?** what makes this species different?; **no se diferencian en nada** there's no difference between them; **~se** DE **algo/algn** to differ FROM sth/sb; **sólo se diferencia del otro en** *or* **por el precio** the only difference between this one and the other one is the price

diferente *adj* **(a)** (distinto) different; **ser ~** A *or* DE **algn/algo** to be different FROM sb/sth **(b)** (*en pl, delante del n*) ‹*motivos/soluciones/maneras*› various; **nos vimos en ~s ocasiones** we've met on several occasions

diferido: **una transmisión en ~** a prerecorded broadcast

difícil *adj* **1 (a)** ‹*problema/situación*› difficult; ‹*examen*› hard, difficult; **me fue muy ~ decírselo** it was very hard *o* difficult for me to tell him; **es ~ de hacer/entender** it's difficult *o* hard to do/understand **(b)** ‹*persona/carácter*› difficult **2** (poco probable) unlikely; **va a ser ~ que acepte** it's unlikely that he'll accept; **veo ~ que gane** I doubt if she'll win

dificultad *f* difficulty; **respira con ~** he has difficulty breathing; **tiene ~es en hacerse entender** she has difficulty in making herself understood; **me pusieron muchas ~es para entrar** they made it very hard for me to get in; **meterse en ~es** to get into difficulties

dificultar [A1] *vt* to make … difficult

difteria *f* diphtheria

difundir [I1] *vt* ‹*noticia/rumor*› to spread; ‹*ideas/doctrina*› to spread, disseminate; ‹*cultura*› to disseminate; ‹*comunicado*› to issue; (por radio) to disseminate; **muy difundidas** very widespread

difunto -ta *adj* (frml) late (*before n*), deceased (frml); **su ~ marido** her late husband ■ *m,f* (frml) deceased (frml)

difusión *f* (de noticia, rumor) spreading; (de ideas, doctrina, cultura) spreading, diffusion (frml); **los medios de ~** the media

difuso -sa *adj* ‹*luz*› dim, diffused; ‹*idea/conocimientos*› vague

diga, digas, etc *see* DECIR

digerir [I11] *vt* to digest

digestión *f* digestion; **hacer la ~** to let one's food go down

digestivo -va *adj* ‹*aparato*› digestive

digital *adj* **(a)** (dactilar) finger (*before n*), digital (frml) **(b)** ‹*aparato/sonido*› digital

dignarse [A1] *v pron* **~** (A) **hacer algo** to condescend *o* deign TO sth

dignatario -ria *m,f* dignitary

dignidad *f* **(a)** (cualidad) dignity **(b)** (título) rank; (cargo) position

digno -na *adj* **1 (a)** ‹*persona/actitud*› honorable* **(b)** ‹*sueldo*› decent, living (*before n*); ‹*vivienda*› decent **2** (merecedor) **~** DE **algo/algn** worthy OF sth/sb; **una persona digna de admiración** a person worthy of admiration; **una medida digna de elogio** a praiseworthy measure; **un espectáculo ~ de verse** a show worth seeing

dije *adj* (Chi fam) **(a)** (agradable) nice, lovely **(b)** (bondadoso) kind ■ *m* charm

dije, dijera, etc *see* DECIR

dilapidar [A1] *vt* to squander

dilatado -da *adj* ‹*pupila/conducto*› dilated

dilatarse [A1] *v pron* **1** «*cuerpo/metal*» to expand; «*corazón*» to expand, dilate; «*pupila*» to dilate; «*embarazada*» to dilate **2 (a)** (prolongarse) to be prolonged **(b)** (diferirse) to be postponed, be put off **3** (Méx, Ven) ⇒ DEMORARSE (b)

dilema *m* (disyuntiva) dilemma

diligencia *f* **(a)** (aplicación) diligence, conscientiousness; **con ~** diligently **(b)** (gestión):

tengo que hacer unas ~s I have some business to attend to

diligente *adj* (trabajador) diligent, conscientious

diluir [I20] *vt* ‹*líquido*› to dilute; ‹*pintura*› to thin (down); ‹*sólido*› to dissolve

diluviar [A1] *vi* to pour (with rain)

diluvio *m* (lluvia) heavy rain, deluge; (inundación) flood; **el D~ Universal** the Flood

diluyente *m* thinner

dimensión *f* **1 (a)** (Fís, Mat) dimension; **una figura en tres dimensiones** a three-dimensional figure **(b) dimensiones** *fpl* (tamaño) dimensions (*pl*); **de enormes dimensiones** huge, enormous **2** (alcance, magnitud — de problema) magnitude, scale; (— de tragedia) scale

diminutivo *m* diminutive

diminuto -ta *adj* tiny, minute

dimisión *f* resignation

dimitir [I1] *vi* to resign; **~ DE algo** to resign FROM sth

dimos *see* DAR

Dinamarca *f* Denmark

dinámico -ca *adj* dynamic

dinamita *f* dynamite

dinamitar [A1] *vt* to dynamite

dínamo, dinamo *m or* (Esp) *f* dynamo

dinastía *f* dynasty

dineral *m* fortune, huge amount of money

dinero *m* money; **estar escaso de ~** to be short of money; **gente de ~** well-off *o* wealthy people; ***hacer ~*** to make money; **~ de bolsillo** pocket money; **~ (en) efectivo** cash; **~ suelto** change; ***~ contante y sonante*** (fam) hard cash

dinosaurio *m* dinosaur

dio *see* DAR

diócesis *f* diocese

dioptría *f* diopter*; **¿cuántas ~s tiene?** what's your correction *o* gradation?

dios, diosa *m,f* **1** (Mit) (*m*) god; (*f*) goddess **2 Dios** *m* (Relig) God; **el D~ de los musulmanes** the Muslim God; **gracias a D~** thank God *o* heaven; **si D~ quiere** God willing; **te lo juro por D~** I swear to God; **¡por (el) amor de D~!** for God's sake *o* for heaven's sake!; **que D~ te bendiga** God bless you; **¡D~ me libre!** God *o* heaven forbid!; **¡sabe D~!** God knows!; **¡vaya por D~!** oh dear!; **¡por D~!** for God's *o* heaven's sake!; **¡D~ mío!** *or* **¡D~ santo!** (expresando angustia) my God!, oh God!; (expresando sorpresa) (good) God!; ***como D~ manda***: **un coche como D~ manda** a real *o* a proper car; **pórtate como D~ manda** behave properly; ***hacer algo a la buena de D~*** to do sth any which way (AmE) *o* (BrE) any old how

diploma *m* diploma, certificate

diplomacia *f* **1** (Pol) (carrera) diplomacy; (cuerpo) diplomatic corps **2** (tacto) diplomacy, tact

diplomado -da *adj* qualified; **~ en peluquería** qualified hairdresser

diplomarse [A1] *v pron* **(a)** (AmL) (obtener un título universitario) to graduate; **~ DE/EN algo** to graduate AS/IN sth **(b)** (obtener otro título) to obtain a diploma (*o* certificate *etc*)

diplomático -ca *adj* **1** (Pol) ‹*carrera/pasaporte*› diplomatic **2** (en el trato) diplomatic, tactful ■ *m,f* diplomat

diptongo *m* diphthong

diputación *f* **(a)** (delegación) deputation, delegation **(b)** (Gob) (en Esp) council

diputado -da *m,f* deputy, ≈representative (*in US*), ≈member of parliament (*in UK*)

dique *m* dike*

diré, dirá, etc *see* DECIR

dirección *f* **1** (señas) address **2** (sentido, rumbo) direction; **ellos venían en ~ contraria** they were coming the other way *o* from the opposite direction; **¿en qué ~ iba?** which way was he heading *o* going?; **señal de ~ prohibida** no-entry sign; **~ obligatoria** one way only **3** (Auto) (mecanismo) steering **4** (Adm) **(a)** (cargo — en escuela) principalship (AmE), headship (BrE); (— en empresa) post *o* position of manager **(b)** (cuerpo directivo — de empresa) management; (— de periódico) editorial board; (— de prisión) authorities (*pl*); (— de partido) leadership **(c)** (oficina — en escuela) principal's office (AmE), headmaster's/headmistress's office (BrE); (— en empresa) manager's/director's office; (— en periódico) editorial office

direccional *f* (Col, Méx) turn signal (AmE), indicator (BrE)

directiva *f* **1** (de empresa) board (of directors); (de partido) executive committee, leadership **2** (directriz) guideline

directo -ta *adj* **1** ‹*vuelo*› direct, nonstop; ‹*ruta/acceso*› direct; ‹*tren*› direct, through (*before n*) **2** (Rad, TV): **en ~** live **3** ‹*lenguaje/pregunta*› direct; ‹*respuesta*› straight; ‹*persona*› direct, straightforward

director -tora *m,f* **(a)** (de escuela) (*m*) head teacher, principal (AmE), headmaster (BrE); (*f*) head teacher, principal (AmE), headmistress (BrE); (de periódico, revista) editor (in chief); (de hospital) administrator; (de prisión) warden (AmE), governor (BrE) **(b)** (Com) (gerente) manager; (miembro de junta directiva) director, executive **(c)** (Cin, Teatr) director; **~ de orquesta** conductor

directorio *m* (AmL exc CS) (guía telefónica) telephone directory, directory

directriz *f* (Mat) directrix; (guía) guideline, principle; (instrucción) directive

dirigente *mf* (de partido, país) leader

dirigible *m* airship, dirigible

dirigir [I7] *vt* **1 (a)** ‹*empresa*› to manage, run; ‹*periódico/revista*› to run, edit; ‹*investigación/tesis*› to supervise; ‹*debate*› to lead, chair; ‹*tráfico*› to direct **(b)** ‹*obra/película*› to direct; ‹*orquesta*› to conduct **2 (a) ~ algo A algn** ‹*mensaje/carta*› to address sth TO sb; ‹*críticas*› to direct sth TO sb; **la pregunta iba dirigida a usted** the question was meant for you; **no me dirigió la palabra** he didn't say a word to me **(b) ~ algo HACIA** *or* **A algo/algn** ‹*telescopio*› to point sth TOWARD(S) sth/sb; ‹*pistola*› to point sth TOWARD(S) sth/sb; **~ la**

mirada hacia *or* **a algo/algn** to look at sth/sb; **dirigió sus pasos hacia la esquina** he walked toward(s) the corner **3** (encaminar) **~ algo** A **hacer algo** ‹*esfuerzos*› to channel sth INTO doing sth; ‹*energía/atención*› to direct sth TOWARD(S) doing sth
■ **dirigirse** *v pron* **1** (encaminarse): **~se** HACIA **algo** to head FOR sth **2 ~se** A **algn** (oralmente) to speak *o* talk TO sb; (por escrito) to write TO sb

discado *m* (AmL) dialing*; **~ automático** *or* **directo** (AmL) direct dialing*

discapacitado -da *m,f* disabled person, handicapped person

discar [A2] *vt/vi* (AmL) to dial

disciplina *f* discipline; **mantener la ~** to keep *o* maintain discipline

discípulo -la *m,f* disciple

disco *m* **1 (a)** (Audio) record; **grabar un ~** to make a record; **poner un ~** to put on a record; **~ compacto** CD, compact disc; **~ de larga duración** album, LP; **~ volador** (CS) flying saucer **(b)** (Inf) disk; **~ duro** hard disk; **~ flexible** *or* **floppy** floppy disk **2 (a)** (Dep) discus **(b)** (Anat) disk*; (Auto, Mec) disk **(c)** (del teléfono) dial **3** (señal de tráfico) (road) sign

disconforme *adj* **(a)** (no satisfecho) dissatisfied; **~** CON **algo/algn** dissatisfied WITH sth/sb **(b)** (en desacuerdo) **~** CON **algo** in disagreement WITH sth

discontinuo -nua *adj* ‹*línea*› broken; ‹*sonido*› intermittent

discordante *adj* (Mús) discordant; ‹*opiniones/versiones*› conflicting

discordia *f* discord

discoteca *f* **(a)** (local) discotheque **(b)** (colección de discos) record collection **(c)** (AmC) (tienda) record store *o* shop

discreción *f* **1 (a)** (tacto, mesura) tact, discretion **(b)** (reserva) discretion **2 a discreción** ‹*comer/beber*› as much as you (*o* we *etc*) like; **esto queda a ~ del juez** this is left to the discretion of the judge

discreto -ta *adj* **(a)** ‹*persona/carácter/comportamiento*› discreet **(b)** ‹*color/vestido*› discreet **(c)** ‹*cantidad/sueldo/actuación*› modest

discriminación *f* discrimination

discriminar [A1] *vt* **(a)** ‹*persona/colectividad*› to discriminate against **(b)** (distinguir) to differentiate, distinguish

disculpa *f* apology; **me debe una ~** she owes me an apology; **un error que no tiene ~** an inexcusable error; **pedir(le) ~s (a algn) por algo** to apologize (to sb) for sth

disculpar [A1] *vt* **(a)** ‹*error/falta/comportamiento*› to forgive, excuse; **le disculpó la indiscreción** he forgave her her indiscretion; **disculpa mi tardanza** I am sorry I'm late **(b)** ‹*persona*› to make excuses for; **su madre siempre lo está disculpando** his mother's always making excuses for him ■ **~** *vi:* **disculpe, no lo volveré a hacer** I'm sorry *o* (frml) I apologize, I won't do it again
■ **disculparse** *v pron* to apologize; **~se** CON **algn** to apologize TO sb

discurso *m* speech; **pronunciar un ~** to give *o* make a speech

discusión *f* **(a)** (de asunto, tema) discussion **(b)** (altercado, disputa) argument

discutible *adj* debatable

discutido -da *adj* controversial

discutir [I1] *vt* **(a)** (debatir) ‹*problema/asunto*› to discuss; ‹*proyecto de ley*› to debate, discuss **(b)** (cuestionar) ‹*derecho/afirmación*› to question, challenge ■ **~** *vi* to argue, quarrel; **discutió de política con su padre** he argued with his father about politics; **~** POR **algo** to argue ABOUT sth; **~le** A **algn** to argue WITH sb

disecar [A2] *vt* **(a)** ‹*animal muerto*› (para estudiarlo) to dissect; (para conservarlo) to stuff **(b)** ‹*planta*› to preserve

disección *f* dissection

diseccionar [A1] *vt* to dissect

diseminado -da *adj* scattered; **los pueblos ~s por la región** the villages scattered throughout the region; **los hoteles están muy ~s** the hotels are very spread out

diseminarse [A1] *v pron* «*personas*» to scatter, disperse; «*ideas/cultura*» to spread

diseñador -dora *m,f* designer; **~ de moda(s)** fashion designer

diseñar [A1] *vt* ‹*moda/mueble/máquina*› to design; ‹*parque/edificio*› to design, plan

diseño *m* design; **~ de moda** fashion design; **blusas de ~ francés** French-designed blouses; **ropa de ~** designer clothes

disforzarse [A11] *v pron* (Per fam) to clown around

disfraz *m* **(a)** (Indum) (para jugar, fiestas) costume, fancy dress outfit (BrE); (para engañar) disguise; **un fiesta de disfraces** a costume *o* (BrE) fancy dress party **(b)** (simulación) front

disfrazar [A4] *vt* **(a) ~ a algn** DE **algo** (para fiesta) to dress sb up AS sth; (para engañar) to disguise sb AS sth **(b)** (disimular, ocultar) ‹*sentimiento/verdad*› to conceal, hide; ‹*voz/escritura/intención*› to disguise
■ **disfrazarse** *v pron* **(a)** (por diversión) to dress up; **~se** DE **algo/algn** to dress up AS sth/sb **(b)** (para engañar) to disguise oneself; **~se** DE **algo/algn** to disguise oneself AS sth/sb, dress up AS sth/sb

disfrutar [A1] *vi* **(a)** (divertirse) to enjoy oneself, have fun; **~** CON/DE **algo** to enjoy sth; **~ haciendo algo** to enjoy doing sth **(b)** (tener) **~** DE **algo** ‹*de privilegio/derecho/buena salud*› to enjoy, have ■ **~** *vt* ‹*viaje/espectáculo*› to enjoy; ‹*beneficio/derecho*› to have, enjoy

disgregarse [A3] *v pron* **(a)** «*grupo/familia*» to break up, split up; «*multitud/manifestantes*» to break up, disperse **(b)** (Tec) to disintegrate

disgustado -da *adj* [ESTAR] upset

disgustar [A1] *vt:* **me disgustó mucho que me mintiera** I was very upset that he lied to me; **me disgusta tener que decírselo** I don't like having to tell her
■ **disgustarse** *v pron* to get upset

disgusto *m* **1** (sufrimiento, pesar): **tiene un ~ tremendo** he's very upset; **me ha dado muchos ~s** he's given me lots of upset *o* heartache; **lo hizo a ~** she did it reluctantly **2** (discusión) argument, quarrel

disidente *mf* (que discrepa) dissident; (escindido) member of a splinter *o* breakaway group

disimulado -da *adj* **(a)** (disfrazado, oculto) disguised; **un mal ~ descontento** ill-concealed displeasure **(b)** (discreto) discreet; **sé más ~** be more discreet ■ *m,f*: **me vio pero se hizo el ~** he saw me but he pretended he hadn't

disimular [A1] *vt* **(a)** ‹*alegría/rabia/dolor*› to hide, conceal **(b)** ‹*defecto/imperfección*› to hide, disguise

disimulo *m*: **con ~** without anyone noticing; **sin ~** openly

disiparse [A1] *v pron* «*nubes/niebla*» to clear; «*temores/sospechas*» to be dispelled; «*ilusiones*» to vanish, disappear

dislexia *f* dyslexia

disléxico -ca *adj/m,f* dyslexic

dislocado -da *adj* ‹*articulation*› dislocated

dislocarse [A2] *v pron* ‹*articulation*› to dislocate

disminución *f* decrease, fall; (de temperatura) drop; (de tarifa) reduction

disminuido -da *m,f*: **~ psíquico/físico** mentally/physically handicapped person

disminuir [I20] *vi* (menguar) «*número/cantidad*» to decrease, fall; «*precios/temperaturas*» to drop, fall; «*dolor*» to diminish, lessen ■ **~** *vt* (reducir) ‹*gastos/producción*› to cut back on; ‹*impuestos*› to cut; ‹*velocidad/número/cantidad*› to reduce

disolución *f* **(a)** (de contrato, matrimonio) annulment; (de organización, del parlamento) dissolution **(b)** (de manifestación) breaking up **(c)** (Quím) (acción) dissolving

disolvente *m* solvent; (de pintura) thinner

disolver [E11] *vt* **(a)** ‹*matrimonio/contrato*› to annul; ‹*parlamento/organización*› to dissolve **(b)** ‹*manifestación/reunión*› to break up **(c)** (en líquido) to dissolve **(d)** (Med) to dissolve, break up
■ **disolverse** *v pron* «*manifestación/reunión*» to break up; «*azúcar/aspirina*» to dissolve

disonante *adj* (Mús) dissonant; ‹*voz*› discordant; ‹*colores*› clashing

dispar *adj* **(a)** (irregular) uneven **(b)** (diferente) different, disparate (frml)

disparado -da *adj* (fam): ***salir disparado*** (irse de prisa) to shoot off (colloq); **con el choque salió ~ del asiento** the impact catapulted him from his seat; *ver tb* DISPARAR

disparador *m* (de arma) trigger; (Fot) shutter release; (de reloj) escapement

disparar [A1] *vi* **(a)** (con arma) to shoot, fire; **~ al aire** to fire *o* shoot into the air; **~ a matar** to shoot to kill; **le disparó por la espalda** he shot him in the back; **~ a quemarropa** *or* **a bocajarro** to fire at point-blank range; **~ CONTRA algn** to shoot *o* fire AT sb **(b)**(Dep) to shoot ■ **~** *vt* **1 (a)** ‹*arma/flecha*› to shoot, fire; ‹*tiro/proyectil*› to fire; **le ~on un tiro en la nuca** they shot him in the back of the head **(b)** (Dep): **disparó el balón a portería** he shot at goal **2** (Méx fam) (pagar) to buy
■ **dispararse** *v pron* **1 (a)** «*arma*» to go off **(b)** (*refl*): **se disparó un tiro en la sien** he shot himself in the head **2** (fam) «*precio*» to shoot up, rocket

disparatado -da *adj* ‹*acto/proyecto/idea*› crazy, ludicrous; ‹*gasto/precio*› outrageous, ridiculous

disparate *m* **(a)** (acción insensata, cosa absurda): **hacer ~s** to do stupid things; **decir ~s** to make foolish remarks; **es un ~ casarse tan joven** it's crazy to get married so young; **temo que haga algún ~** I'm afraid he might do something crazy **(b)** (fam) (cantidad exagerada) ridiculous (*o* crazy *etc*) amount

disparo *m* shot

dispersar [A1] *vt* **(a)** ‹*manifestantes/multitud/enemigo*› to disperse **(b)** ‹*rayos*› to scatter, diffuse; ‹*niebla/humo*› to clear, disperse
■ **dispersarse** *v pron* **(a)** «*manifestantes/manifestación/multitud*» to disperse **(b)** «*rayos*» to diffuse, scatter; «*niebla/humo*» to disperse, clear

disperso -sa *adj* (diseminado) scattered, dispersed (frml)

displicente *adj* (indiferente) indifferent, blasé; (frío) disdainful

disponer [E22] *vt* **1** (frml) (establecer, ordenar) «*ley*» to provide (frml), to stipulate (frml); «*rey*» to decree; «*general/juez*» to order **2** (frml) (colocar, arreglar) to arrange, set out, lay out ■ **~** *vi*: **~ DE algo** ‹*de tiempo/ayuda*› to have sth; **con los recursos de que dispongo** with the means available to me *o* at my disposal
■ **disponerse** *v pron* (frml) **mientras se disponían a tomar el tren** as they were about to catch the train; **la tropa se dispuso a atacar** the troops prepared to attack

disponible *adj* available; ‹*tiempo*› free (*before n*), available; **cuando estés ~** when you're free

disposición *f* **1** (norma) regulation **2 (a)** (actitud) disposition **(b)** (talento) aptitude **(c)** (inclinación, voluntad) willingness **3 (a)** (de un bien) disposal **(b) a ~ de algn** «*coche/chofer*» at sb's disposal; **estoy a tu ~ para lo que sea** I'm here to help if you need anything; **será puesto a ~ del juez** he will appear before the judge; **puso su casa a mi ~** he offered me his house

dispositivo *m* **1** (mecanismo) mechanism; (aparato) device **2** (frml) (destacamento): **un fuerte ~ policial/militar** a large police/military presence

dispuesto -ta *adj* **(a)** (preparado) ready **(b)** (con voluntad) willing; **~ A hacer algo** prepared to do sth

dispuse, **dispuso, etc** *see* DISPONER

disputa *f* **(a)** (discusión, pelea) quarrel, argument **(b)** (combate) fight **(c)** (controversia) dispute

disputar [A1] *vt* **(a)** **~le algo A algn** ‹*título*› to challenge sb for sth; **le disputaban su derecho a la herencia** they contested his right to the inheritance **(b)** ‹*partido*› to play; ‹*combate*› to fight
■ **disputarse** *v pron*: **se disputan el primer puesto** they are competing for first place

disquete, **disquette** /dis'kete/ *m* diskette, floppy disk

distancia *f* **(a)** distance; **la ~ que separa dos puntos** the distance between two points; **¿a qué ~ está Londres?** how far is it to London?, **se situó a una ~ de un metro** she stood a meter away; ⇒ LLAMADA **(b)** (*en locs*) **a distancia**: **se situó a ~ para verlo en conjunto** she stood back to see it as a whole; **se veía a ~** one could see it from a distance; **mantenerse a ~** to keep at a distance; **en la distancia** in the distance

distanciado -da *adj* (afectivamente): **estamos algo distanciadas** we're not as close as we were

distanciar [A1] *vt* **(a)** (espaciar) to space ... out **(b)** (en lo afectivo) «*amigos/familiares*» to make ... drift apart; **~ a algn** DE **algn** to distance sb FROM sb

▪ **distanciarse** *v pron* **(a)** (en el espacio) **~se** DE **algo** to get far FROM sth **(b)** (en lo afectivo) (*recípr*) to grow *o* drift apart; (*refl*) **~se** DE **algn** to distance oneself FROM sb

distante *adj* distant

distar [A1] *vi* (*en 3ª pers*) (estar a): **el colegio dista unos dos kilómetros de su casa** the school is about two kilometers from her house

diste, **etc** *see* DAR

distinción *f* **(a)** (diferencia) distinction; **hacer una ~** to make a distinction; **sin ~ de raza o credo** regardless of race or creed; **no hago distinciones con nadie** I don't give anyone preferential treatment **(b)** (elegancia) distinction, elegance **(c)** (honor, condecoración) award

distinguido -da *adj* ‹*escritor/actor/aire*› distinguished; ‹*alumno*› outstanding

distinguir [I2] *vt* **1 (a)** (diferenciar) to distinguish **(b)** (caracterizar) to characterize **2** (percibir) ‹*figura/sonido*› to make out **3** (con medalla, honor) to honor*

▪ **distinguirse** *v pron* (destacarse): **~se** POR **algo** «*persona*» to distinguish oneself BY sth; «*producto*» to be distinguished BY sth

distintivo¹ -va *adj* ‹*rasgo/característica*› distinctive

distintivo² *m* (insignia) emblem; (símbolo) sign

distinto -ta *adj* **1** (diferente) different; **ser ~** A *or* DE **algo/algn** to be different FROM *o* TO *o* (AmE) THAN sth/sb; **estás/te encuentro ~** you look different **2** (*en pl, delante del n*) (varios) several, various

distorsionar [A1] *vt* to distort

distracción *f* **(a)** (entretenimiento) entertainment **(b)** (descuido): **en un momento de ~se la robaron** she took her eye off it for a moment and someone stole it; **la más mínima ~ puede ser fatal** the slightest lapse of concentration could be fatal **(c)** (de fondos) embezzlement

distraer [E23] *vt* **(a)** ‹*persona/atención*› to distract; **~ a algn** DE **algo** ‹*de trabajo/estudios*› to distract sb FROM sth ‹*de preocupaciones*› to take sb's mind OFF sth **(b)** (entretener) ‹*persona*› to keep ... entertained

▪ **distraerse** *v pron* **(a)** (despistarse, descuidarse) to get distracted **(b)** (entretenerse): **se distraen viendo la televisión** they pass the time watching television; **se distrae con cualquier cosa** she doesn't need much to keep amused

distraído -da *adj* **(a)** [SER] ‹*persona*› absent-minded, vague **(b) estaba/iba ~** he was miles away (colloq)

distribución *f* **(a)** (reparto — de dinero, víveres) distribution; (— de tareas) allocation **(b)** (de producto, película) distribution **(c)** (disposición, división) layout, arrangement **(d)** (Auto) valve-operating gear

distribuidor¹ -dora *m,f* (Com) distributor

distribuidor² *m* (Auto, Mec) distributor

distribuidora *f* (empresa) distributor, distribution company

distribuir [I20] *vt* **(a)** ‹*dinero/víveres/panfletos*› to hand out, distribute; ‹*ganancias*› to distribute; ‹*tareas*› to allocate, assign; ‹*carga/peso*› to distribute, spread **(b)** ‹*producto/película*› to distribute **(c)** «*canal/conducto*» ‹*agua*› to distribute **(d)** (disponer) to lay out **(e)** (dividir) to divide ... up; **los distribuyeron en tres grupos** they divided them (up) into three groups

▪ **distribuirse** *v pron* (*refl*) to divide up

distrito *m* district

Distrito Federal *m* Federal District (*including Mexico City*)

disturbio *m* **(a)** (perturbación del orden) disturbance **(b) disturbios** *mpl* (motín) riot, disturbances (journ)

disuadir [I1] *vt* to deter, discourage; **~** A **algn** DE **algo**/DE **que haga algo** to dissuade sb FROM sth/doing sth

disuasión *f* (Mil, Pol) deterrence

disuasivo -va, **disuasorio -ria** *adj* ‹*tono/palabras*› dissuasive, discouraging; ‹*efecto*› deterrent; ‹*medida*› designed to act as a deterrent

disuelto -ta *pp*: *see* DISOLVER

diurético *m* diuretic

diurno -na *adj* day (*before n*); **clases diurnas** daytime classes

diva *f* diva, prima donna; *ver tb* DIVO

divagación *f* digression

divagar [A3] *vi* **(a)** (desviarse del tema) to digress **(b)** (hablar sin sentido) to ramble

diván *m* couch

diversidad *f* diversity

diversión *f* **(a)** (esparcimiento) fun **(b)** (espectáculo, juego): **aquí hay pocas diversiones** there isn't much to do here

diverso -sa *adj* **1** (variado, diferente): **su obra es muy diversa** his work is very diverse; **seres de diversa naturaleza** various types of creatures; **ha desempeñado las más diversas actividades** she has engaged in a very wide range of activities **2** (*pl*) (varios) various, several

divertido -da *adj* **(a)** (que interesa, divierte) ‹*espectáculo/fiesta*› fun, enjoyable; ‹*momento/situación*› entertaining; **es un tipo muy ~** he's a really fun guy, he's really fun to be with **(b)** (gracioso) funny

divertir [I11] *vt* to amuse

▪ **divertirse** *v pron* (entretenerse) to amuse oneself; (pasarlo bien) to have fun, enjoy oneself; **¡que**

te diviertas! have fun!, enjoy yourself!; **nos divertimos mucho en la fiesta** we had a really good time at the party

dividendo *m* dividend

dividir [I1] *vt* **(a)** (partir) to divide; **lo dividió en partes iguales** he divided it (up) into equal portions **(b)** (repartir) to divide, share (out) **(c)** (enemistar) ‹*partido/familia*› to divide ■ ~ *vi* (Mat) to divide

■ **dividirse** *v pron* **(a)** «*célula*» to split; «*grupo/partido*» to split up; «*camino/río*» to divide **(b)** ~ EN **algo** «*obra/período*» to be divided INTO sth **(c)** (repartirse) to divide up, share out

divierta, divirtió, etc *see* DIVERTIR

divinidad *f* **(a)** (deidad) deity, god **(b)** (cualidad) divinity **(c)** (fam) (preciosidad) delight

divinizar [A4] *vt* to deify

divino -na *adj* divine

divisa *f* **1** (Com, Fin) currency; **la fuga de ~s** the flight of capital; **una fuente de ~s** a source of foreign currency **2** (emblema) emblem, insignia

divisar [A1] *vt* ‹*tierra/barco*› to sight, make out; **a lo lejos se divisaba un poblado** they (*or* he *etc*) could make out a village in the distance

divisible *adj* ~ POR **algo** divisible BY sth

división *f* (en general) division; **hacer una ~** (Mat) to do a division

divisor *m* divisor

divisorio -ria *adj* dividing (*before n*)

divo -va *m,f* (estrella) celebrity, star; (con actitud soberbia) prima donna; *ver tb* DIVA

divorciado -da *adj* divorced ■ *m,f* (*m*) divorcé (esp AmE), divorcee (esp BrE); (*f*) divorcée (esp AmE), divorcee (esp BrE)

divorciarse [A1] *v pron* to get divorced; **~se** DE **algn** to divorce sb, get divorced FROM sb

divorcio *m* (Der) divorce

divulgar [A3] *vt* ‹*noticia/información*› to spread, circulate; ‹*secreto/plan*› to divulge; ‹*cultura*› to spread, disseminate

■ **divulgarse** *v pron* to spread

dizque, diz que *adv* (AmL) **(a)** (según parece) apparently **(b)** (expresando escepticismo): **esta ~ democracia** this so-called democracy; **estaban allí, ~ trabajando** they were there, supposedly working

Dn. = **Don**

DNA *m* DNA

Dña. = **Doña**

do *m* (nota) C; (en solfeo) do, doh (BrE); **~ de pecho** high C, top C

dobladillo *m* hem

doblar [A1] *vt* **1** ‹*camisa/papel*› to fold; ‹*brazo/vara*› to bend **2** ‹*esquina*› to turn, go around; ‹*cabo*› to round **3** (aumentar al doble) ‹*oferta/apuesta/capital*› to double; (tener el doble que): **la dobla en edad** he's twice her age **4** ‹*actor*› (en banda sonora) to dub; (en escena) to double for; ‹*película*› to dub; **doblada al castellano** dubbed into Spanish ■ ~ *vi* **1** (torcer, girar) «*persona*» to turn; «*camino*» to bend, turn; **dobla a la izquierda** turn left **2** «*campanas*» to toll

■ **doblarse** *v pron* **1** «*rama/alambre*» to bend **2** «*precios/población*» to double

doble[1] *adj* **1** ‹*whisky/flor/puerta*› double; ‹*café*› large; ‹*costura/hilo/consonante*› double; **lo veo todo ~** I'm seeing double; **cerrar con ~ llave** to double-lock; **tiene ~ sentido** it has a double meaning; **calle de ~ sentido** two-way street; **~ crema** *f* (Méx) double cream; **~ fondo** *m* false bottom; **~ ve** *or* **~ u** *f*: *name of the letter* W; **~ ventana** *f* double glazing **2** (Andes, Ven fam) ‹*persona*› two-faced

doble[2] *m* **1** (Mat): **los precios aumentaron el ~** prices doubled; **tardó el ~** she took twice as long; **el ~ de tres es seis** two threes are six; **el ~** QUE **algn/algo** twice as much AS sb/sth; **el ~ de largo/rápido** twice as long/quick **2 (a)** (en béisbol) double **(b) dobles** *mpl* (en tenis) doubles **3 doble** *mf* (actor, actriz) stand-in, double; (en escenas peligrosas) (*m*) stuntman; (*f*) stuntwoman; (persona parecida) (fam) double

doblez *m* **1** (en tela, papel) fold **2 doblez** *m or f* (falsedad) deceitfulness

doce *adj inv/m/pron* ▶ 293, 221 twelve; **son las ~ de la noche** it's twelve o'clock, it's midnight; *para más ejemplos ver tb* CINCO

docena *f* ▶ 293 dozen; **una ~ de huevos** a dozen eggs; **media ~** half a dozen

dócil *adj* ‹*niño/comportamiento*› meek, docile; ‹*perro/caballo*› docile, well-trained; ‹*pelo*› manageable

doctor -tora *m,f* doctor; **~ en derecho** Doctor of Law

doctorado *m* doctorate, PhD

doctorarse [A1] *v pron* to earn *o* get one's doctorate, do one's PhD

doctrina *f* (ideología) doctrine; (enseñanza) teaching

documentación *f* **1** (de persona) papers (*pl*); (de vehículo, envío) documents (*pl*), documentation (frml) **2** (información) information, data (*pl*)

documental *adj* **(a)** (Cin, TV) ‹*programa/serie*› documentary (*before n*) **(b)** (Der) ‹*prueba*› documentary ■ *m* documentary

documentar [A1] *vt* **1** ‹*trabajo/hipótesis/solicitud*› to document **2** (Méx) ‹*equipaje*› to check in

■ **documentarse** *v pron* **1** (informarse) to do research **2** (Méx) «*pasajero*» to check in

documento *m* (Adm, Der) document

dogma *m* dogma

dogmático -ca *adj* dogmatic

dólar *m* dollar

dolencia *f* ▶ 123 ailment, complaint

doler [E9] *vi* ▶ 123 **(a)** «*inyección/herida/brazo*» to hurt; **no duele nada** it doesn't hurt at all; (+ *me/te/le etc*) **le dolió mucho** it hurt a lot; **le duele una muela/la cabeza** she has (a) toothache/a headache; **me dolía el estómago** I had (a) stomachache; **me duele la garganta** I have a sore throat; **me duelen los pies** my feet ache; **me duele todo (el cuerpo)** I ache all over **(b)** (apenar) (+ *me/te/le etc*): **me duele tener que decirte esto** I'm sorry to have to tell you this;

me dolió muchísimo lo que me dijo I was deeply hurt by what he said

dolido -da *adj* hurt; **estar ~ POR algo** to be hurt AT sth

dolor *m* ▶ 123 **(a)** (físico) pain; **sentía mucho ~** he was in a lot of pain; **tener ~ de muelas/cabeza/garganta** to have a toothache/a headache/a sore throat **(b)** (pena, tristeza) pain, grief

dolorido -da *adj* ▶ 123 **(a)** (físicamente): **estoy toda dolorida** I'm aching all over; **tengo el brazo muy ~** I've got a very sore arm **(b)** (afligido) hurt

doloroso -sa *adj* **(a)** ‹*tratamiento/enfermedad*› painful **(b)** ‹*decisión/momento/recuerdo*› painful; ‹*separación/espectáculo*› distressing, upsetting

domador -dora *m,f* (de fieras) tamer; (de caballos) horsebreaker, broncobuster (AmE)

domar [A1] *vt* **(a)** ‹*fieras*› to tame; ‹*caballo*› to break in **(b)** (fam) ‹*niño*› to bring *o* get ... under control **(c)** (fam) ‹*zapatos*› to break in

domesticado -da *adj* tame, domesticated

domesticar [A2] *vt* to domesticate

doméstico -ca *adj* **1** ‹*vida/problemas/servicio*› domestic; ‹*gastos*› household; **tareas domésticas** housework **2** ‹*vuelo*› domestic

domiciliar [A1] *vt* (Esp) ‹*pago/letras*› to pay ... by direct debit *o* (AmE) direct billing; ‹*sueldo*› to have ... paid direct into one's bank account
■ **domiciliarse** *v pron* (frml) (residir) to reside (frml), to be domiciled (frml)

domicilio *m* (frml) address; **en su ~ particular** at his home address; **sin ~ fijo** of no fixed abode (frml); **Pat Lee, con ~ en Londres** Pat Lee currently living in London

dominante *adj* **1 (a)** ‹*color/tendencia*› predominant, dominant; ‹*opinión*› prevailing (*before n*); ‹*cultura*› dominant **(b)** (Biol, Mús, Astrol) dominant **2** ‹*persona*› domineering

dominar [A1] *vt* **(a)** (controlar) ‹*nación/territorio/persona*› to dominate; ‹*pasión/cólera*› to control; ‹*vehículo/caballo*› to control; **dominado por la ambición/los celos** ruled by ambition/consumed by jealousy **(b)** ‹*idioma*› to have a good command of; ‹*tema/asignatura*› to know ... very well **(c)** (abarcar con la vista): **desde allí se domina toda la bahía** there's a view over the whole bay from there ■ ~ *vi* «*color/tendencia*» to predominate; «*opinión*» to prevail; «*equipo*» to dominate
■ **dominarse** *v pron* «*persona*» to restrain *o* control oneself

domingo *m* ▶ 193 (día) Sunday; (Relig) Sabbath; **traje de ~** Sunday best; **~ de Pascua** *or* **de Resurrección** Easter Sunday; **~ de Ramos** Palm Sunday; *para más ejemplos ver* LUNES

dominicano -na *adj/m,f* (Geog) Dominican

dominio *m* **1 (a)** (control) control; **perdió el ~ de sí mismo** he lost his self-control **(b)** (de idioma, tema) command; ***ser del ~ público*** to be public knowledge **2 (a)** (Hist, Pol) dominion **(b) dominios** *mpl* (colonias) dominions (*pl*)

dominó *m* (*pl* **-nós**) **(a)** (juego) dominoes; **jugar** *or* (Esp, RPl) **al ~** to play dominoes **(b)** (ficha) domino

don *m* **1 (a)** (liter) (dádiva) gift **(b)** (talento) talent, gift; **el ~ de la palabra** the gift of speech; **~ de gentes** ability to get on well with people; **~ de mando** leadership qualities (*pl*) **2** (tratamiento de cortesía) ≈ Mr; **buenos días ~ Miguel** good morning Mr López; ***ser un ~ nadie*** to be a nobody

dona *f* (Méx) (Coc) doughnut, donut (AmE)

donación *f* donation

donador -dora *m,f*, **donante** *mf* donor

donar [A1] *vt* ‹*bienes/dinero*› to donate, give; ‹*sangre*› to give, donate; ‹*órganos*› to donate

donativo *m* donation

doncella *f* **(a)** (arc) (virgen) maiden (liter) **(b)** (ant) (criada) maid

donde ▶ 155 *conj* where; **la ciudad ~ se conocieron** the city where they met; **siéntate ~ quieras** sit wherever *o* where you like; **déjalo ~ sea** leave it anywhere; **de ~ se deduce que** ... from which it can be deduced that ...; **la ventana por ~ había entrado** the window through which he had got in ■ *prep* (esp AmL, en algunas regiones crit): **ve ~ tu hermana y dile que** ... (a su casa) go over to your sister's and tell her ...; (al lugar donde está ella) go and tell your sister ...

dónde *adv* **1** where; **¿~ está?** where is it?; **¿de ~ es?** where is he from?; **¿por ~ quieres ir?** which way do you want to go? **2** (Chi, Méx, Per) (cómo) how; **¡~ íbamos a imaginar que ...!** how were we to imagine that ...!

dondequiera *adv*: **~ QUE** wherever

donjuán *m* (tenorio) womanizer, Don Juan

doña *f* (tratamiento de cortesía) ≈ Mrs/Ms; **~ Cristina Fuentes** Mrs/Ms Cristina Fuentes

dopado -da *adj* [ESTAR] drugged

dopar [A1] *vt* ‹*enfermo*› to drug, dope (colloq); ‹*caballo*› to dope
■ **doparse** *v pron* (*refl*) to take drugs

doping *m* (Equ) doping; (Dep) drug-taking

dorada *f* gilthead (bream)

dorado¹ -da *adj* **(a)** ‹*botón/galones*› gold; ‹*pintura*› gold, gold-colored*; ‹*cabello*› (liter) golden **(b)** ‹*época*› golden

dorado² *m* (acción) gilding; (capa) gilt

dorar [A1] *vt* ‹*marco/porcelana*› to gild; (Coc) ‹*cebolla/papas*› to brown
■ **dorarse** *v pron* (Coc) to brown

dormida *f* (AmL) sleep

dormido -da *adj* **(a)** (durmiendo) asleep; **estar/quedarse ~** to be/to fall asleep **(b)** (sin sensibilidad): **tengo la pierna dormida** my leg's gone to sleep (colloq)

dormilón -lona *adj* (fam): **es muy ~** he's a real sleepyhead (colloq) ■ *m,f* (fam) (persona) sleepyhead (colloq)

dormir [I16] *vi* to sleep; **no dormí nada** I didn't sleep a wink; **dormimos en un hotel** we spent the night in a hotel; **durmió de un tirón** she slept right through (the night); **se fue a ~ temprano** he went off to bed early, he had an early night; **~ *a pierna suelta*** (fam) to sleep the sleep of the dead; **~ *como un lirón*** *or* ***tronco*** to sleep

Donde

Algunas observaciones sobre la conjunción

En términos generales su traducción es where:

quédate donde estás = stay where you are

Sin embargo, en oraciones subordinadas en las que donde *va precedido de una preposición, la traducción suele ser distinta*:

la ventana desde donde la observaba = the window from which he watched her
= the window which he watched her from

la bolsa en donde lo metí = the bag (which) I put it in

Obsérvese que algunos casos admiten varias traducciones distintas:

los pueblos por donde pasamos = the villages (that) we passed through
= the villages which we passed through
= the villages through which we passed

Cuando donde *precede al subjuntivo y tiene el sentido de* en cualquier parte que, *la traducción es* wherever:

ponlo donde quieras = put it wherever you want

lo encontraré esté donde esté = I'll find him wherever he is

Nótese que en su uso preposicional, donde *puede significar* en casa de *o* a casa de *especialmente en algunas regiones de Latinoamérica*:

los vi donde Alfonso = I saw them at Alfonso's (place)

fuimos donde Lucía = we went to Lucía's (place)

Para otros usos y ejemplos suplementarios, ver entrada

like a log (colloq) ■ ~ *vt* **(a)** (hacer dormir) ‹*niño/bebé*› to get … off to sleep; **sus clases me duermen** his classes send *o* put me to sleep **(b)** (anestesiar) ‹*persona*› to put to sleep, put out (colloq); **todavía tengo este lado dormido** this side is still numb **(c)** ~ **la siesta** to have a siesta *o* nap
■ **dormirse** *v pron* **(a)** (conciliar el sueño) to fall asleep; (lograr conciliar el sueño) to get to sleep; **casi me duermo en la clase** I almost fell asleep *o* (colloq) dropped off in class **(b)** (no despertarse) to oversleep, sleep in (AmE) **(c)** «*pierna/brazo*» (+ *me/te/le etc*) to go to sleep (colloq); **se me durmió el pie** my foot went to sleep **(d)** (fam) (distraerse, descuidarse): **no te duermas** don't waste any time

dormitar [A1] *vi* to doze, snooze (colloq)

dormitorio *m* (en casa) bedroom; (en colegio, cuartel) dormitory

dorso *m* **(a)** (de un papel) back; **al ~** ‹*ver*› overleaf; ‹*escribir*› on the back **(b)** (de la mano, animal) back

dos *adj inv/m/pron* ▶ **293** two; **lo hicimos entre los ~** we did it between the two of us; **sujétalo con las ~ manos** hold it with both hands; **llamó ~ veces** he called twice; **caminaban de ~ en ~** they walked in pairs; **entraron de ~ en ~** they came in two at a time *o* two by two; **~ puntos** *mpl* colon; ***en un ~ por tres*** in a flash; *para más ejemplos ver* CINCO

doscientos[1] -tas *adj/pron* two hundred; *para ejemplos ver* QUINIENTOS

doscientos[2] *m* ▶ **293** (number) two hundred

dosel *m* (de cama) canopy; (de trono, púlpito) baldachin

dosificar [A2] *vt* ‹*medicamento*› to dose

dosis *f* (*pl* ~) dose

dotado -da *adj* ‹*persona*› gifted; **estar ~ DE algo** «*persona*» to be blessed WITH sth; «*cocina/oficina*» to be equipped WITH sth

dotar [A1] *vt* **(a)** (fml) ‹*institución/organismo*› ~ (A) **algo DE** *or* **CON algo** ‹*de fondos*› to provide sth WITH sth; ‹*de técnica/maquinaria*› to equip sth WITH sth; ‹*de poderes*› to invest sth WITH sth **(b)** «*naturaleza/Dios*» ~ **a algn DE** *or* **CON algo** to endow *o* bless sb WITH sth

dote *f* **1** (de novia) dowry **2 dotes** *fpl*: **~s para el canto** a talent for singing; **~s de mando** leadership qualities

doy *see* DAR

Dr. *m* (= **Doctor**) Dr

Dra. *f* (= **Doctora**) Dr

dracma *m* drachma

dragar [A3] *vt* ‹*río*› to dredge; ‹*minas*› to sweep for

dragón *m* (Mit) dragon

drama *m* drama; ***hacer un ~ de algo*** (fam) to make a big deal out of sth

dramático -ca *adj* dramatic; **un autor ~** a playwright *o* dramatist

dramatismo *m* dramatic quality *o* character

dramatización *f* dramatization

dramaturgo -ga *m,f* dramatist, playwright

drástico -ca *adj* drastic

driblar, **driblear** [A1] *vt* to dribble past *o* around

drible *m* dribble

droga *f* drug; **~s duras/blandas** hard/soft drugs

drogadicción *f* (drug) addiction

drogadicto -ta *adj* addicted to drugs ■ *m,f* drug addict

drogar [A3] *vt* to drug
■ **drogarse** *v pron* (*refl*) to take drugs

drogodependiente[1] *adj* (fml) drug-dependent

drogodependiente[2] *mf* (fml) drug addict

droguería *f* **(a)** (Esp) (tienda) *store selling cleaning materials and other household goods* **(b)** (Col) (farmacia) drugstore (AmE), chemist's (BrE) **(c)** (RPl) (de productos químicos) pharmaceutical wholesaler's

dromedario *m* dromedary

dual *adj/m* dual
Dublín *m* Dublin
dublinés -nesa *m,f* Dubliner
ducado *m* (título) dukedom; (territorio) duchy, dukedom
ducha *f* shower; **darse una ~** to take *o* (BrE) have a shower
ducharse [A1] *v pron* (*refl*) to take *o* (BrE) have a shower
ducto *m* **(a)** (Méx) (de gas, petróleo) pipeline **(b)** (Ur) (para la basura) garbage chute (AmE), rubbish chute (BrE) **(c)** (Col, Ven) (de ventilación) duct, shaft
duda *f* **1** (interrogante, sospecha) doubt; **expuso sus ~s sobre** ... he expressed his reservations about ...; **tengo unas ~s para consultar** I have a few points I'd like to check; **me ha surgido una ~** there's something I'm not sure about; **¿tienen alguna ~?** are there any queries *o* questions?; **nunca tuve la menor ~ de que tenía razón** I never doubted that he was right; **fuera de (toda) ~** beyond (all) doubt; **de eso no cabe la menor ~** there's absolutely no doubt about that; **lo pongo en ~** I doubt it; **sin ~** *or* **sin lugar a ~s** undoubtedly; **sin ~ ya te lo habrás preguntado** no doubt you'll have already asked yourself that question; **para salir de ~s** just to be doubly sure **2** (estado de incertidumbre, indecisión): **ahora me has hecho entrar en (la) ~** now you've made me wonder; **a ver si puedes sacarme de la ~** do you think you can clear something up for me?; **si estás en (la) ~ no lo compres** if you're not sure don't buy it
dudar [A1] *vt* to doubt; **dudo que lo haya terminado** I doubt if *o* whether he's finished it ■ **~** *vi:* **duda entre comprar y alquilar** she can't make up her mind whether to buy or rent; **~ EN hacer algo** to hesitate to do sth; **~ DE algo/algn** to doubt sth/sb
dudoso -sa *adj* **(a)** (incierto) doubtful; **lo veo ~** I doubt it **(b)** (cuestionable) dubious **(c)** (indeciso) hesitant, undecided
duela *f* (Méx) (del suelo) floorboard
duele, **duelen, etc** *see* DOLER
duelo *m* **1** (dolor) sorrow, grief; (luto) mourning; **estar de ~** to be in mourning **2** (desafío) duel; **retar a ~** to challenge ... to a duel; **batirse en ~** to fight a duel; **~ a muerte** duel to the death
duende *m* **(a)** (en cuentos) goblin, imp **(b)** (espíritu) spirit (*which inhabits a house or room*)
dueño -ña *adj* **1** [SER] (libre) **~ DE hacer algo** free to do sth, at liberty to do sth (frml) **2** [SER] (indicando control): **ser ~ DE algo** to be in control OF sth; **hacerse ~ DE algo** to gain control OF sth ■ *m,f* **(a)** (de casa, pensión) (*m*) owner, landlord; (*f*) owner, landlady; (de negocio) (*m*) owner, proprietor; (*f*) owner, proprietress; **~ de casa** (AmL) (propietario) householder; (en fiesta) (*m*) host; (*f*) hostess **(b)** (de perro) owner
duerma, **duermas, etc** *see* DORMIR
dulce *adj* **(a)** ‹*fruta/vino*› sweet; **prefiero lo ~** I prefer sweet things **(b)** ‹*agua*› fresh; **pez de agua ~** freshwater fish **(c)** ‹*persona*› gentle, kind; ‹*sonrisa/voz*› sweet; ‹*música*› soft, sweet ■ *m* **(a)** (AmL exc RPl) (golosina) candy (AmE), sweet (BrE) **(b)** (RPl) (mermelada) jam; **~ de leche** caramel spread (*made by boiling down milk and sugar*) **(c)** (AmC) (azúcar) *type of sugarloaf* **(d) dulces** *mpl* (cosas dulces) sweet things (*pl*)
dulcificar [A2] *vt* ‹*persona*› to mellow; ‹*vejez*› to make ... more pleasant
■ **dulcificarse** *v pron* «*carácter/persona*» to mellow, soften
dulzor *m* sweetness, sweet taste
dulzura *f* sweetness; **habló con ~** she spoke kindly *o* gently; **los trata con mucha ~** she's very sweet *o* gentle with them
duna *f* dune
dúo *m* **(a)** (composición) duet, duo **(b)** (de músicos, instrumentos) duo; **a ~** ‹*contestar*› in unison; **lo cantaron a ~** they sang it as a duet
duodécimo -ma *adj/pron* ▶ **294** twelfth
dúplex *m* (*pl* **~**) **(a)** (apartamento) duplex apartment, maisonette (BrE) **(b)** (Méx) (casa) semi-detached house
duplicado¹ -da *adj* duplicated; **por ~** in duplicate
duplicado² *m* copy, duplicate
duplicar [A2] *vt* ‹*documento/llave*› to copy, duplicate
■ **duplicarse** *v pron* «*número*» to double
duplo *m*: **el ~ de dos es cuatro** two times two is four
duque *m* duke
duquesa *f* duchess
duración *f* **(a)** (de película, acto, curso) length, duration **(b)** (de pila, bombilla) life; **pila de larga ~** long-life battery; ⇒ DISCO 1 (a)
duradero -ra *adj* ‹*amistad/recuerdo*› lasting (*before n*); ‹*ropa/zapatos*› hardwearing, longwearing (AmE)
durante *prep* ▶ **157** (en el transcurso de) during; (cuando se especifica la duración) for; **~ 1980** during *o* in 1980; **gobernó el país ~ casi dos décadas** she governed the country for almost two decades; **los precios aumentaron un 0,3% ~ el mes de diciembre** prices rose by 0.3% in December; **~ todo el invierno** throughout the winter
durar [A1] *vi* **(a)** «*reunión/guerra/relación*» to last; **¿cuánto dura la película?** how long is the film? **(b)** «*coche/zapatos*» to last **(c)** (Col, Ven) ⇒ DEMORAR (a)
■ **durarse** *v pron* (Ven) ⇒ DEMORARSE
durazno *m* (esp AmL) (fruto) peach; (árbol) peach tree
durex® *m* (AmL) Scotch tape® (AmE), Sellotape® (BrE)
dureza *f* **1** (en general) hardness; (de la carne) toughness **2 (a)** (severidad, inflexibilidad) harshness; **nos trataban con ~** they treated us harshly; **fue castigado con ~** he was severely punished **(b)** (en el deporte) roughness
durmiera, **durmió, etc** *see* DORMIR
duro¹ -ra *adj* **1** (en general) hard; ‹*carne*› tough; ‹*pan*› stale; **las peras están duras** the pears

Durante

Algunas observaciones generales

Cuando la preposición se emplea para referirse al tiempo o al momento en que se desarolla una acción y contesta a la pregunta ¿cuándo? (when?), *se traduce al inglés por* during:

empecé a sentirme mal durante el viaje	=	I started feeling ill during the journey
no solemos salir durante la semana	=	we don't normally go out during the week

Cuando se emplea para referirse a la duración de la acción y contesta a la pregunta ¿por cuánto tiempo? (how long?), *su traducción es* for:

lloró durante media hora	=	he cried for half an hour
estuve sin trabajo durante tres meses	=	I was unemployed for three months

Cuando durante *va seguido de* todo, *y se quiere poner especial énfasis en la longitud de la duración de una acción, se puede traducir por* throughout:

vivió allí durante toda su vida	=	he lived there throughout his life
llovió durante toda la noche	=	it rained throughout the night

aren't ripe **2** ‹*luz/voz*› harsh; ‹*facciones*› hard, harsh **3 (a)** (severo, riguroso) harsh; ‹*juego*› rough, hard; **fuiste demasiado ~ con él** you were too hard on him; **una postura más dura** a tougher line **(b)** (difícil, penoso) ‹*trabajo/vida*› hard, tough; **fue un golpe muy ~** it was a very hard blow

duro² *adv* (esp AmL) ‹*trabajar/estudiar/llover*› hard; ‹*hablar*› (Col, Ven) loudly

duro³ *m* (en España) five-peseta coin

E, e *f* (*pl* **es**) (*read as* /e/) *the letter* E, e

e *conj* [*used instead of* Y *before* I- *or* HI-] and

E. (= **Este**) ▶ 346 E, East

EAU *mpl* (= **Emiratos Árabes Unidos**) UAE

ebanista *mf* cabinetmaker

ébano *m* ebony

ebrio, ebria *adj* (frml) inebriated (frml), drunk

ebullición *f* **(a)** (Coc, Fís): **entrar en ~** to come to the boil; **punto de ~** boiling point **(b)** (agitación) turmoil

eccema *m* eczema

echado -da *adj* (acostado): **está ~ en el sofá** he's lying down on the sofa

echador -dora *adj* (Méx fam) boastful ■ *m,f* (Méx fam) boaster (colloq)

echar [A1] *vt* **I 1 (a)** (lanzar, tirar) to throw; **lo eché a la basura** I threw it out *o* away; **echó la moneda al aire** he tossed the coin; **~on el ancla/la red** they cast anchor/their net; **echó la cabeza hacia atrás** she threw her head back; **~ *algo a perder*** to ruin sth; **~ *de menos algo/a algn*** to miss sth/sb **(b) echar abajo** ‹*edificio*› to pull down; ‹*gobierno*› to bring down; ‹*proyecto*› to destroy; ‹*esperanzas*› to dash; ‹*moral*› to undermine; ‹*puerta/valla*› to break ... down **2** (expulsar) ‹*persona*› (de trabajo) to fire (colloq), to sack (BrE colloq); (de bar, casa) to throw ... out; (de colegio) to expel **3** ‹*carta*› to mail (AmE), to post (BrE) **4 (a)** (pasar, correr) ‹*cortinas*› to pull, draw; **échale (la) llave** lock it; **¿echaste el cerrojo?** did you bolt the door? **(b)** (mover): **lo echó para atrás/a un lado** she pushed (*o* moved *etc*) it backward(s)/to one side **5 (a)** (expeler, despedir) ‹*olor, humo, chispas*› to give off **(b)** (producir) ‹*hojas*› to sprout; **ya está echando flores** it's flowering already

II 1 (a) (poner) ‹*leña/carbón*› to put; ‹*gasolina*› to put in; **¿le echas azúcar al café?** do you take sugar in your coffee? **(b)** (servir, dar) to give; **échame un poco de vino** can you give me a little wine? **(c)** ‹*trago*› to have **2 (a)** ‹*sermón/discurso*› (fam) (+ *me/te/le etc*) to give; **le echó una maldición** she put a curse on him **(b)** (fam) ‹*condena/multa*› (+ *me/te/le etc*) to give; **~le la culpa a algn** to put *o* lay the blame on sb **3** (fam) (calcular) (+ *me/te/le etc*): **¿cuántos años me echas?** how old do you think I am?; **de aquí a tu casa échale una hora** it's *o* it takes about an hour from here to your house **4** (Esp fam) (dar, exhibir) ‹*programa/película*› to show

■ **echarse** *v pron* **1 (a)** (tirarse, arrojarse) to throw oneself; **me eché al suelo** I threw myself to the ground; **~se de cabeza al agua** to dive into the water; **~*se a perder*** «*comida*» to go bad, go off (BrE); «*cosecha/proyecto/plan*» to be ruined **(b)** (tumbarse, acostarse) to lie down **(c)** (apartarse, moverse) (+ *compl*): **se echó a un lado** she moved to one side; **échate un poco para allá** move over that way a bit; **~*se atrás*** to back out **2 (a)** (ponerse) ‹*crema/bronceador*› to put on **(b)** ‹*cigarillo*› to have **(c)** (Esp fam) ‹*novio/novia*›: **se ha echado novia** he's found *o* got himself a girlfriend **(d)** (Méx fam) (beberse) to drink **3** (Méx fam) (romper) to break **4** (Col fam) (tardar) ‹*horas/días*› to take **5** (empezar) **~se** A to start *o* begin to, start *o* begin; **se echó a correr** he started to run *o* started running; **las palomas se ~on a volar** the doves flew off

echarpe *m* shawl, stole

ecléctico -ca *adj/m,f* eclectic

eclesiástico -ca *adj* ecclesiastical, church (*before n*)

eclipse *m* eclipse

eco *m* (Fís) echo; **la cueva tiene ~** there's an echo in the cave; **hacer ~** to echo

ecografía *f* ultrasound scan

ecología *f* ecology

ecológico -ca *adj* ‹*problema/estudio*› ecological

ecologista *adj* ecology (*before n*), environmentalist (*before n*) ■ *mf* ecologist, environmentalist

economato *m* **(a)** (de empresa) company store **(b)** (Mil) PX (AmE), NAAFI shop (BrE)

economía *f* **(a)** (ciencia) economics **(b)** (de país) economy; **~ de (libre) mercado** (free) market economy **(c)** (ahorro): **hacer ~s** to economize **(d)** (de persona, familia) finances (*pl*)

económico -ca *adj* **1** ‹*crisis/situación*› economic (*before n*); ‹*problema/independencia*› financial **2 (a)** ‹*piso/comida*› cheap; ‹*restaurante/hotel*› cheap, inexpensive **(b)** (que gasta poco) ‹*motor*› economical; ‹*persona*› thrifty

economista *mf* economist

economizar [A4] *vt* ‹*tiempo*› to save; ‹*combustible/recursos*› to economize on, save ■ ~ *vi* to economize, save money

ECU, ecu /'eku/ *m* ECU, ecu

ecuación *f* equation

ecuador *m* **1** (línea) equator **2 Ecuador** (país) Ecuador

ecuatorial *adj* equatorial

ecuatoriano -na *adj/m,f* Ecuadorean

eczema *m* eczema

edad *f* **1** ▶ **159** (de persona, árbol) age; **tienen la misma ~** they are the same age; **un joven de unos quince años de ~** a boy of about fifteen; **¿qué ~ tiene?** how old is he?; **aún no tiene la ~ suficiente** he's still not old enough ...; **de ~ madura** *or* **de mediana ~** middle-aged; **niños en ~ escolar** children of school age; ***estar en la ~ del pavo*** to be at that awkward age **2** (Hist) (época) age, period; **la E~ de bronce/de hierro/de piedra** the Bronze/Iron/Stone Age; **la E~ media** the Middle Ages (*pl*)

edema *m* edema*

Edén *m*: **el ~** (the Garden of) Eden

edición *f* **1** (Impr, Period) (tirada) edition; (acción) publication; **~ de bolsillo** pocket edition; **Ediciones Rivera** Rivera Publications **2** (Rad, TV) program*, edition

edificado -da *adj* built-up

edificar [A2] *vt/vi* to build

edificio *m* building

Edimburgo *m* Edinburgh

editar [A1] *vt* **1** (publicar) ‹*libro/revista*› to publish **2** (modificar) ‹*película/grabación/texto*› to edit; (Inf) to edit

editor -tora *adj* publishing (*before n*) ■ *m,f* (que publica) publisher; (que revisa, modifica) editor

editorial *adj* ‹*casa/actividad*› publishing (*before n*); ‹*puesto/decisión*› editorial ■ *f* (empresa) publishing company *o* house ■ *m* (en periódico) editorial, leading article

edredón *m* eiderdown, comforter (AmE); (que se usa sin mantas) duvet, continental quilt (BrE)

educación *f* **1** (enseñanza) education; (para la convivencia) upbringing; **~ a distancia** correspondence courses (*pl*), distance learning; **~ física** physical education; **~ primaria/secundaria/superior** primary/secondary/higher education; **~ universitaria** university education, college education (AmE); **~ vocacional** (AmS) careers guidance **2** (modales) manners (*pl*); **es una falta de ~** it's rude, it's bad manners

educado -da *adj* polite, well-mannered

educar [A2] *vt* **1 (a)** (Educ) to educate, teach **(b)** (para la convivencia) ‹*hijos*› to bring up; ‹*ciudadanos*› to educate **2** ‹*oído/voz*› to train

■ **educarse** *v pron* (hacer los estudios) to be educated

educativo -va *adj* ‹*programa/juego*› educational; ‹*establecimiento*› educational, teaching (*before n*); ‹*sistema*› education (*before n*)

EEUU *or* **EE.UU.** (= **Estados Unidos**) USA

efe *f*: *name of the letter* f

efectista *adj* theatrical, dramatic

efectividad *f* (eficacia) effectiveness

efectivo¹ -va *adj* ‹*remedio/medio/castigo*› effective; **hacer ~** ‹*cheque*› to cash; ‹*pago*› to make

efectivo² *m* (Fin) cash; **pagar en ~** to pay cash

efecto *m* **1** (resultado, consecuencia) effect; **hacer ~** to take effect; **un calmante de ~ inmediato** a fast-acting painkiller; **mecanismo de ~ retardado** delayed-action mechanism; **~ invernadero** greenhouse effect; **~ óptico** optical illusion **2** (impresión): **su conducta causó mal ~** his behavior made a bad impression *o* (colloq) didn't go down well; **no sé qué ~ le causaron mis palabras** I don't know what effect my words had on him **3** (Dep) (desvío) swerve; (movimiento rotatorio) spin; **le dio a la bola con ~** she put some spin on the ball **4 ~s personales** personal effects (*pl*)

efectuar [A18] *vt* (frml) ‹*maniobra/redada*› to carry out, execute (frml); ‹*pago*› to make; ‹*viaje/cambio*› to make; ‹*disparo*› to fire; **el tren ~á su salida a las 10.50** the train will depart at 10:50

efervescente *adj* ‹*pastilla*› effervescent; ‹*bebida*› sparkling, fizzy (colloq)

eficacia *f* **(a)** (de acción, remedio) effectiveness, efficacy (frml) **(b)** (eficiencia) efficiency

eficaz *adj* **(a)** ‹*fórmula/remedio*› effective, efficacious (frml) **(b)** (eficiente) efficient

eficiencia *f* efficiency

eficiente *adj* efficient

efigie *f* (cuadro) image, picture; (estatua) statue, effigy

La edad

En inglés no se emplea el verbo to have = tener *para referirse a la edad, sino el verbo* to be = ser

¿qué edad tienes? *or* ¿cuántos años tienes? = how old are you? *o* what's your age?

Nótese que cuando en español se dice tener . . . año(s), *su equivalente en inglés es* to be . . . year(s) old. *Las palabras* 'year(s) old' *se pueden omitir, salvo que se esté hablando de cosas*:

tengo 18 años = I'm eighteen *o* (más formal) I'm eighteen years old

el castillo tiene 200 años = the castle is 200 years old

En comparaciones

Cuando se emplea más *o* menos *que*:

Pedro tiene 2 años más que María = Pedro is 2 years older than María

tengo 5 años menos que él = I'm 5 years younger than him

Cuando se emplea mayor *y* menor, *el verbo* ser *se traduce por* to be:

es 3 años mayor/menor que yo = he's 3 years older/younger than me

es algunos años mayor/menor = he's a few years older/younger

Para ejemplos suplementarios con mayor/menor, *ver bajo la respectiva entrada*

Cuando el español utiliza la expresión llevarle años a alguien, *su traducción en contexto es la siguiente*:

me lleva 2 años = he's 2 years older than me

se llevan 10 años = one is 10 years older than the other

Otros ejemplos:

son de la misma edad = they're the same age

le dobla la edad *or* la dobla en edad = he's twice her age

La edad con preposiciones

una mujer de 50 años = a woman of fifty
= a fifty-year-old woman

Nótese en la segunda traducción del ejemplo anterior, el empleo de guiones y la falta del plural del vocablo year, *el que en este caso se trata como parte del adjetivo*

un bebé de 10 meses = a ten-month-old baby

mi hija de 6 años = my six-year-old daughter

una carrera para niños de 12 años = a race for twelve-year-olds

a los 5 años (de edad) = at five (years of age)
= at the age of five

a esa edad ya se había casado = by that age she was already married

La edad aproximada

tendrá alrededor de *or* unos 30 años = she must be around *o* about thirty

tiene entre 30 y 40 años = she must be in her thirties

tiene más/menos de 40 años = he's over/under forty

tiene un poco más de 20 años = she's just over twenty
= she's in her early twenties

va para los 50 = she's going on fifty
= she's pushing fifty

Otras maneras de referirse a la edad

En lenguaje coloquial (*por lo general denota desaprobación*):

una cuarentona = a woman in her forties

es cincuentón = he's in his fifties

una mujer setentona = a woman in her seventies

ver tambien página 125

efímero -ra *adj* ephemeral

efusivo -va *adj* ‹*temperamento/recibimiento*› effusive; ‹*persona*› demonstrative; ‹*recibimiento*› warm

egipcio -cia *adj/m,f* Egyptian

Egipto *m* Egypt

ego *m* ego

egocéntrico -ca *adj* egocentric, self-centered*

egoísmo *m* selfishness, egotism

egoísta *adj* selfish, egotistic ■ *mf* (Psic) egotist; **es una ~** she is very selfish

egresado -da *adj* (AmL): **los alumnos ~s** (de universidad) the graduates; (de colegio) the high school graduates (AmE), the school leavers (BrE) ■ *m,f* (AmL) (de universidad) graduate; (de colegio) high school graduate (AmE), school leaver (BrE)

egresar [A1] *vi* (AmL) (de universidad) to graduate; (de colegio) to graduate from high school (AmE), to leave school (*o* college *etc*) (BrE) ■ **~** *vt* (Andes) (Fin) to withdraw, take out

egreso *m* (AmL) (de universidad) graduation; (de colegio) graduation (AmE)

eh *interj* **(a)** (para llamar la atención) hey! **(b)** (expresando amenaza, advertencia) eh?, huh?, OK? **(c)** (contestando una pregunta) eh?, what?

Ej., ej. (*read as* **por ejemplo**) eg

eje *m* **1 (a)** (Astron, Fís, Mat) axis **(b)** (Auto, Mec) (barra) axle **2** (de asunto, política) core, central theme

ejecución *f* **1** (de persona) execution **2 (a)** (de plan) implementation; (de orden) carrying out **(b)** (Mús) performance

ejecutar [A1] *vt* **1** ‹*condenado/reo*› to execute **2** ‹*plan*› to implement, carry out; ‹*orden/trabajo*› to carry out; ‹*sentencia*› to execute, enforce; ‹*ejercicio/salto*› to perform; ‹*sinfonía/himno nacional*› to play, perform

ejecutivo[1] **-va** *adj* ‹*función/comisión*› executive ■ *m,f* (Bot, Com) executive

ejecutivo[2] *m* (Gob) executive

ejemplar *adj* ‹*conducta/vida/castigo*› exemplary; ‹*trabajador/padre*› model (*before n*) ■ *m* **(a)** (de libro, documento) copy **(b)** (Bot, Zool) specimen

ejemplarizador -dora *adj* (Chi, Per) exemplary

ejemplo *m* example; **dar (el) ~** to set an example; **pongamos por ~ el caso de Elena** let's take Elena's case as an example; **por ejemplo** for example

ejercer [E2] *vt* **1 (a)** ‹*profesión*› to practice*; **~ la abogacía** to practice law **(b)** ‹*derecho*› to exercise **2** ‹*influencia/poder/presión*› to exert ■ **~** *vi* «*abogado/médico*» to practice*; **es maestra pero no ejerce** she's a teacher but she doesn't practice her profession

ejercicio *m* **1** (actividad física) exercise; **hacer ~** to exercise **2** (Educ) **(a)** (trabajo de práctica) exercise **(b)** (prueba, examen) test, exam **3** (de profesión) practice **4** (Mil) exercise, maneuver*

ejercitar [A1] *vt* **1** ‹*músculo/dedos/memoria*› to exercise **2** ‹*caballos*› to train; ‹*tropa*› to drill, train; ‹*alumnos*› to train

ejército *m* army; **~ del aire** air force; **~ de tierra** army

ejidal *adj* (en Méx) cooperative (*before n*)

ejidatario -ria *m,f* (en Méx) member of a cooperative

ejido *m* (en Méx) (sistema) *system of communal or cooperative farming*; (sociedad) cooperative; (terreno) *land belonging to a cooperative*

ejote *m* (Méx) green bean

el (*pl* **los**), **la** (*pl* **las**) *art* ▶**39** [*the masculine article* EL *is also used before feminine nouns which begin with accented* A *or* HA, *e.g.* EL AGUA PURA, EL HADA MADRINA] **1 (a)** (en general) the; **la Tierra** the Earth **(b)** (con sustantivos en sentido genérico): **odio el pescado** I hate fish; **así es la vida** that's life; **(nosotros) los mexicanos** we Mexicans; **¿ya vas a la escuela?** do you go to school yet? **(c)** (refiriéndose a algo que se conoce o se está definiendo): **en la calle Solis** in Solis street; **las tuyas** yours; **el último** the last one; **el estúpido del marido** that stupid husband of hers **2 (a) el** + DE: **la del sombrero** the one with the hat; **el de las nueve** the nine o'clock one; **el de mi hijo** my son's **(b) el** + QUE: **las que yo ví** the ones I saw; **los que estén cansados**; those who are tired, anyone who's tired; **la que te guste** whichever you like **3** (en expresiones de tiempo): **ocurrió el domingo** it happened last Sunday; **mi cumpleaños es el 28 de mayo** my birthday's on May 28; **el mes pasado** last month; **toda la mañana** all morning; **a las ocho** at eight o'clock **4** (cada): **$80 el metro/kilo** $80 a meter/a kilo, $80 per kilo/meter **5** ▶**130** (con fracciones, porcentajes, números): **la mitad/la cuarta parte del dinero** half the money/a quarter of the money; **el 20% de** ... 20% of ... **6** ▶**123** (con partes del cuerpo, prendas de vestir, artículos personales, etc): **tenía las manos en los bolsillos** she had her hands in her pockets; **¡te cortaste el pelo!** you've had your hair cut!; **tiene los ojos azules** he has blue eyes **7 (a)** ▶**420** (con apellidos acompañados de título, adjetivos, etc): **el señor Ortiz/la doctora Vidal** Mr Ortiz/Doctor Vidal; **los Ortega** the Ortegas **(b)** (con algunos nombres geográficos): **en la India** in India; *ver* ÁFRICA, ARGENTINA, ETC

él *pron pers* **(a)** (como sujeto) he; **¿quién se lo va a decir? — él** who's going to tell her? — he is; **lo hizo ~ mismo** he did it himself; **fue ~** it was him **(b)** (en comparaciones, con preposiciones) him; (refiriéndose a cosas) it; **llegué antes que ~** I arrived before him *o* before he did; **con/para ~** with/for him; **son de ~** they're his

elaboración *f* (de producto, vino) production, making; (de pan) baking, making

elaborado -da *adj* elaborate

elaborar [A1] *vt* **1** ‹*producto/vino*› to produce, make; ‹*pan*› to bake, make **2** ‹*plan/teoría*› to devise, draw up; ‹*informe/estudio*› to prepare, write

elasticidad *f* (de material) elasticity; (de horario) flexibility

elástico[1] **-ca** *adj* ‹*membrana/cinta*› elastic; ‹*medias/venda*› elastic, stretch (*before n*); ‹*horario*› flexible

elástico[2] *m* **(a)** (material) elastic; (cordón) piece of elastic; (en géneros de punto) rib, ribbing **(b)** (Chi) (goma) rubber band

ele *f*: *name of the letter l*

elección *f* **(a)** (acción de escoger) choice; **llévate tres, a tu ~** take *o* choose any three **(b)** (Pol) (de candidato) election **(c) elecciones** *fpl* (Pol) election; **convocar elecciones** to call an election

elector -tora *m,f* (Pol) voter, elector

electorado *m* electorate

electoral *adj* ‹*campaña/discurso*› election (*before n*)

electricidad *f* electricity

electricista *mf* electrician

eléctrico -ca *adj* ‹*tren/motor/luz*› electric; ‹*instalación/aparato*› electrical; ‹*carga*› electrical, electric

electrocardiograma *m* electrocardiogram

electrocutar [A1] *vt* to electrocute ■ **electrocutarse** *v pron* to be electrocuted

electrodoméstico *m* electrical appliance

electrón *m* electron

electrónica *f* electronics

electrónico -ca *adj* electronic

elefante -ta *m,f* elephant

elegancia *f* **(a)** (en el vestir) smartness, elegance; (garbo, gracilidad) elegance; (de barrio, restaurante) smartness **(b)** (de estilo) elegance

elegante *adj* **1 (a)** ‹*moda/vestido*› elegant, smart; **iba muy ~** he was very well *o* very smartly dressed **(b)** ‹*barrio/restaurante/fiesta*› smart **2** ‹*estilo/frase*› elegant, polished

elegir [I8] *vt* **(a)** (escoger) to choose; **me dieron a ~** I was given a *o* the choice **(b)** (por votación) to elect

elemental *adj* **(a)** (esencial) ‹*norma/principio*› fundamental **(b)** (básico) ‹*curso/nivel/texto*› elementary; ‹*conocimientos/nociones*› rudimentary, basic

elemento *m* **(a)** (en general) element; **se siente en su ~** he's in his element; **los ~s** (fuerzas naturales) the elements **(b)** (persona): **un ~ pernicioso** a bad influence; **~s subversivos** subversive elements; **es un ~ de cuidado** (Esp fam & pey) he's a nasty piece of work **(c)** (RPl) (tipo de gente) crowd

elepé *m* album, LP

elevado -da *adj* **1** ‹*terreno/montaña*› high; ‹*edificio*› tall, high **2 (a)** ‹*cantidad*› large; ‹*precio/impuestos*› high; ‹*pérdidas*› heavy, substantial **(b)** ‹*categoría/calidad/posición*› high **(c)** ‹*ideas/pensamientos*› noble, elevated; ‹*estilo*› lofty, elevated

elevador *m* (montacargas) hoist; (ascensor) (Méx) elevator (AmE), lift (BrE)

elevar [A1] *vt* **1** (frml) **(a)** (levantar) ‹*objeto*› to raise, lift **(b)** ‹*espíritu/mente*› to uplift **(c)** ‹*muro/nivel*› to raise, make … higher **2** (frml) **(a)** (aumentar) ‹*precios/impuestos*› to raise, increase; ‹*nivel de vida*› to raise **(b)** ‹*voz/tono*› to raise

■ **elevarse** *v pron* **1** (tomar altura) «*avión/cometa*» to climb, gain height; «*globo*» to rise, gain height **2** (frml) (aumentar) «*temperatura*» to rise; «*precios/impuestos*» to rise, increase; «*tono/voz*» to rise **3** (frml) (ascender): **la cifra se elevaba ya al 13%** the figure had already reached 13%

elige, elija, etc *see* ELEGIR

eliminación *f* elimination; (de residuos) disposal

eliminar [A1] *vt* **(a)** ‹*obstáculo*› to remove; ‹*párrafo*› to delete, remove **(b)** ‹*candidato*› to eliminate; (Dep) to eliminate, knock out **(c)** (euf) (matar) to eliminate (euph), to get rid of (euph) **(d)** ‹*residuos*› to dispose of **(e)** ‹*toxinas/grasas*› to eliminate

eliminatoria *f* (en torneo) qualifying round; (para carrera) heat; (certamen) qualifying competition

eliminatorio -ria *adj* ‹*examen/fase*› qualifying (*before n*), preliminary (*before n*)

elite /e'lit/, **élite** /'elite e'lit/ *f* elite, élite

elitista *adj* ‹*sociedad/actitud*› elitist; ‹*colegio/club*› exclusive

elixir *m* **(a)** (Mit) elixir **(b)** (Esp) (Farm) mouthwash

ella *pron pers* **(a)** (como sujeto) she; **¿quién lo va a hacer? — ella** who's going to do it? — she is; **lo hizo ~ misma** she did it herself; **fue ~** it was her **(b)** (en comparaciones, con preposiciones) her; (referido a cosas) it; **salí después que ~** I left after her *o* after she did; **con/para ~** with/for her; **son de ~** they're hers

elle *f*: *name of the letter* ll

ello *pron pers* it; **ya que estamos en ~** while we're at it; **todo ~ exquisitamente presentado** all beautifully presented; **para ello hay que obtener un permiso** (frml) you need a permit for this

ellos, ellas *pron pers pl* **(a)** (como sujeto) they; **lo hicieron ~ mismos** they did it themselves; **fueron ellas** it was them **(b)** (en comparaciones, con preposiciones) them; **llegué antes que ~** I arrived before them *o* before they did; **con/para ~/ellas** with/for them; **son de ~** they're theirs, they belong to them

elocuencia *f* eloquence; **con ~** eloquently

elocuente *adj* eloquent

elogiar [A1] *vt* to praise

elogio *m* praise; **digno de ~** praiseworthy

elote *m* (mazorca) (AmC, Méx) corncob, ear of corn (AmE); (granos) (Méx) corn (AmE), sweetcorn (BrE)

El Salvador *m* El Salvador

eludir [I1] *vt* **(a)**‹*problema/compromiso/pago*› to evade, avoid **(b)**‹*persona*› to avoid

emancipación *f* emancipation

emancipado -da *adj* emancipated

embadurnar [A1] *vt* **~ algo DE algo** to smear sth WITH sth

■ **embadurnarse** *v pron* (*refl*) **~se DE algo** to plaster *o* smear oneself WITH sth

embajada *f* (sede, delegación) embassy; (cargo) ambassadorship

embajador -dora *m,f* (Adm, Pol) ambassador

embalaje *m* **1** (acción) packing; (envoltura) packaging, wrapping **2** (Col) (Dep) sprint

embalar [A1] *vt* to pack

embaldosar [A1] *vt* to tile

embalsamar [A1] *vt* to embalm

embalse *m* (depósito) reservoir

embarazada *adj* pregnant; **(se) quedó ~** she got *o* became pregnant; **está ~ de dos meses** she's two months pregnant; **la dejó ~** he got her pregnant ■ *f* pregnant woman

embarazo *m* (Med) pregnancy

embarazoso -sa *adj* embarrassing, awkward

embarcación *f* (frml) vessel (frml), craft (frml)

embarcadero *m* (atracadero) jetty; (para mercancías) wharf

embarcar [A2] *vi* (Aviac) to board; (Náut) to embark, board ■ **~** *vt* **1** ‹*mercancías/equipaje*› to load **2** (Ven) to let … down

■ **embarcarse** *v pron* **(a)** «*pasajero*» (en barco) to board, embark; (en tren, avión) to board, get on; **se ~on para América** they set sail for America **(b)** (en asunto, negocio) **~se EN algo** to embark ON sth

embargar [A3] *vt* ‹*bienes*› to seize, to sequestrate (frml); ‹*vehículo*› to impound

embargo *m* **1 (a)** (Der) (incautación, decomiso) seizure, sequestration (frml) **(b)** (Mil, Pol) embargo **2 sin embargo**: **sin ~, tiene algunas desventajas** however *o* nevertheless, it has some disadvantages; **sin ~, ayer no decías eso** you weren't saying that yesterday, though; **tiene de todo y sin embargo y todavía se queja** he has everything and yet he still complains

embarrada *f* (AmS fam) (metedura de pata) blunder, boo-boo (colloq)

embarrar [A1] *vt* to cover … in mud; **~*la*** (AmS fam) to mess up (AmE colloq), to mess things up (BrE colloq)

■ **embarrarse** *v pron* «*persona*» to get covered in mud; ‹*prenda/ropa*› to get…muddy

embaucador -dora *adj* deceitful ■ *m,f* trickster

embaucar [A2] *vt* to trick, con (colloq)

embelesado -da *adj* spellbound

embelesar [A1] *vt* to captivate

embellecer [E3] *vt* ‹*persona*› to make … beautiful; ‹*campiña/ciudad*› to beautify, improve the appearance of

embestida *f* charge

embestir [I14] *vi* to charge; ~ CONTRA **algo/algn** to charge AT sth/sb ■ ~ *vt* «*toro*» to charge (at)

embetunar [A1] *vt* **1** ‹*zapatos*› to polish, put polish on **2** (CS) (ensuciar) to get … dirty

emblema *m* emblem

embobado -da *adj* spellbound; **la miraban ~s** they were watching her open-mouthed; **está ~ con ella** he's besotted with her

embolador -dora *m,f* (Col) bootblack

embolar [A1] *vt* **1** (RPl arg) (fastidiar) to bug (colloq), to piss … off (sl) **2** (Col) ‹*zapatos*› to shine, polish

■ **embolarse** *v pron* (AmC fam) to get plastered (colloq)

embolia *f* embolism

embolsarse [A1] *v pron* ‹*dinero ajeno*› to pocket; ‹*premio*› to collect, receive; ‹*ganancia*› to make

embonar [A1] *vi* (Méx) ‹*tubos/ventana/piezas*› to fit; ~ CON **algo** to fit in WITH sth

emborrachar [A1] *vt* «*bebida*» to make … drunk; «*persona*» to get … drunk

■ **emborracharse** *v pron* to get drunk

emborronar [A1] *vt* (manchar) to smudge; (con tinta) to make blots on, to blot

■ **emborronarse** *v pron* to smudge, get smudged

emboscada *f* ambush

emboscar [A2] *vt* to ambush

embotado -da *adj* ‹*punta/filo*› dull, blunt; **estoy totalmente ~** my brain's seized up, I can't take in any more

embotar [A1] *vt* ‹*mente/sentidos*› to dull

embotellado -da *adj* **(a)** ‹*agua/vino*› bottled **(b)** ‹*calle/tráfico*› jammed solid

embotellamiento *m* (del tráfico) traffic jam

embotellar [A1] *vt* to bottle

embragar [A3] *vi* to engage the clutch

embrague *m* clutch

embriagado -da *adj* (frml) (borracho) inebriated (frml)

embriagador -dora *adj* ‹*vino*› heady; ‹*sensación*› (liter) intoxicating (liter)

embriagarse [A3] *v pron* (frml) (con alcohol) to become intoxicated (frml)

embrión *m* (Biol) embryo

embrollar [A1] *vt* **(a)** ‹*hilo/madeja*› to tangle (up) **(b)** (confundir) ‹*situación*› to complicate; ‹*persona*› to muddle, confuse **(c)** (implicar) ~ **a algn** EN **algo** to embroil sb IN sth, get sb involved IN sth

■ **embrollarse** *v pron* «*hilo/madeja*» to get tangled; «*situación*» to get confused *o* muddled; «*persona*» to get muddled, to get mixed up (colloq)

embrollo *m* (de hilos, cables) tangle; (de callejuelas, pasillos) maze; (situación confusa) muddle, mess; **el argumento es un ~** the plot is extremely involved *o* complicated

embromado -da *adj* **1** [ESTAR] (AmS fam) (enfermo, delicado) in a bad way; **tiene un pie ~** she has a bad foot **2** (AmS fam) ‹*situación*› tricky; ‹*problema*› thorny

embromar [A1] *vt* (AmS fam) **(a)** (molestar) to pester **(b)** (estropear) ‹*aparato*› to ruin (colloq); ‹*plan*› to ruin, spoil **(c)** (perjudicar): **la guerra nos embromó a todos** we all suffered because of the war; **¡me embromaste!** now you've really landed me in it! (colloq)

■ **embromarse** *v pron* (AmS fam) **(a)** (jorobarse): **que se embrome por estúpido** it serves him right for being so stupid; **si no te gusta, te embromas** if you don't like it, tough! **(b)** (hacerse daño) to hurt oneself; ‹*rodilla/hígado*› to screw up (AmE colloq), to do … in (BrE colloq) **(c)** (enfermarse) to get ill (colloq) **(d)** «*aparato/frenos*» to go wrong

embrujado -da *adj* [ESTAR] ‹*persona*› bewitched; ‹*casa/lugar*› haunted

embrujar [A1] *vt* **(a)** (hechizar) to bewitch, put … under a spell **(b)** (fascinar, enamorar) to bewitch

embrujo *m* **(a)** (hechizo) spell; (maleficio) curse **(b)** (encanto, atractivo) magic, enchantment

embrutecer [E3] *vt* «*trabajo*» to stultify; «*televisión*» to make … mindless

embudo *m* funnel

embuste *m* tall story, story (colloq)

embustero -ra *adj*: **¡qué niño más ~!** what a little fibber (colloq) ■ *m,f* fibber (colloq), liar

embutido *m* (salchicha) sausage; (fiambre) cold meat

eme *f*: *name of the letter* m

emergencia *f* emergency

emerger [E6] *vi* **(a)** «*submarino*» to surface **(b)** «*persona*» to emerge **(c)** (sobresalir) to emerge

emigración *f* (de personas) emigration; (de animales) migration

emigrante *adj/mf* emigrant

emigrar [A1] *vi* «*persona*» to emigrate; «*animal*» to migrate

eminencia *f* **(a)** (personalidad) expert **(b)** (frml) (Relig) Eminence (frml)

eminente *adj* eminent

Emiratos Árabes Unidos *mpl* United Arab Emirates

emisario -ria *m,f* emissary

emisión *f* **(a)** (Tec) emission **(b)** (Fin) issue **(c)** (Rad, TV) (acción) broadcasting; (programa) (frml) program*, broadcast

emisor *m* (aparato) transmitter

emisora *f* (Rad) radio station

emitir [I1] *vt* ‹*sonido/luz/señal*› to emit, give out; ‹*acciones/sellos/comunicado*› to issue; ‹*programa*› to broadcast; ‹*película*› to show; ‹*veredicto*› to deliver, announce; ‹*voto*› to cast

emoción *f* (sentimiento) emotion; (expectación, excitación) excitement; **¡qué ~!** how exciting!

emocionado -da *adj* (conmovido) moved; (entusiasmado) excited

emocional *adj* emotional

emocionante *adj* (conmovedor) moving; (excitante, apasionante) exciting

emocionar [A1] *vt* to move, affect

■ **emocionarse** *v pron* (conmoverse) to be moved; (entusiasmarse) to get excited

emotivo -va *adj* ‹*desarrollo/mundo/persona*› emotional; ‹*acto/discurso*› moving, emotional

empacar [A2] *vt* **(a)** (empaquetar) to pack **(b)** ‹*algodón/heno*› to bale **(c)** (AmL) ‹*maleta*› to pack ■ ~ *vi* to pack

empachar [A1] *vt* (fam) (indigestar) to give ... an upset stomach

■ **empacharse** *v pron* (fam) (indigestarse) **~se** DE **algo** to get an upset stomach FROM sth

empacho *m* (fam) (indigestión): **agarrarse un ~** to get *o* have an upset stomach

empadronarse [A1] *v pron* to register

empalagar [A3] *vt*: **los bombones me empalagan** chocolates are too sweet *o* sickly for my taste ■ ~ *vi* «*licor/dulce*» to be too sweet *o* sickly; «*estilo/sentimentalismo*» to be cloying

empalagoso -sa *adj* ‹*tarta/licor*› sickly; ‹*persona/sonrisa*› sickly sweet, cloying

empalizada *f* palisade

empalmar [A1] *vt* ‹*cuerdas/películas/cintas*› to splice; ‹*cables*› to connect ■ ~ *vi* «*líneas/carreteras*» to converge, meet

empalme *m* (de cables) connection; (de cuerdas) splice; (de carreteras, líneas) junction

empanada *f* **(a)** (AmL) (individual) pasty, pie **(b)** (Esp) (grande) pie

empanadilla *f* (Esp) tuna/meat pasty

empanar [A1], (Méx) **empanizar** [A4] *vt* to coat ... in breadcrumbs

empantanado -da *adj* ‹*camino/campo*› swampy

empantanarse [A1] *v pron* «*camino/campo*» to become swamped; «*coche*» to get bogged down

empañar [A1] *vt* ‹*vidrio/espejo*› to steam *o* mist up

■ **empañarse** *v pron* «*vidrio/espejo*» to steam *o* mist up

empapar [A1] *vt* **(a)** (embeber) ‹*esponja/toalla/galleta*› to soak **(b)** (mojar mucho) ‹*persona*› to soak, drench

■ **empaparse** *v pron* (mojarse mucho) «*persona/zapatos/ropa*» to get soaking wet

empapelar [A1] *vt* ‹*habitación/pared*› to wallpaper, paper

empaque *m* **1** (Col, Méx, Ven) (Tec) seal; (de llave de agua) washer **2** (Col) (acción de empaquetar) packing; (de regalo) wrapping

empaquetar [A1] *vt* (embalar) to pack

emparedado *m* sandwich

emparejar [A1] *vt* **1** ‹*personas*› to pair ... off; ‹*calcetines/zapatos*› to pair up **2** (nivelar) ‹*pelo*› to make ... even; ‹*dobladillo*› to even up; ‹*pared/suelo*› to level, make ... level; ‹*montones/pilas*› to make ... the same height

■ **emparejarse** *v pron* **(a)** (formar parejas) to pair off **(b)** (nivelarse) to level off, even up

emparentado -da *adj* [ESTAR] related; **~** CON **algn** related TO sb

empastar [A1] *vt* ‹*diente/muela*› to fill

empaste *m* (Odont) filling; (Chi) (pasta) filler

empatar [A1] *vi* **1 (a)** (durante un partido) to draw level, equalize; (como resultado) to tie, draw (BrE); **~on a dos** they tied two-two (AmE), it was a two-all draw (BrE); **van empatados** they're equal *o* level at the moment **(b)** (en una votación) to tie **2** (Col, Ven) «*listones/piezas*» to fit together ■ ~ *vt* **(a)** (Ven) (amarrar) to tie *o* join ... together **(b)** (Col, Per, Ven) ‹*cables/tubos*› to connect

■ **empatarse** *v pron* (Ven) **(a)** (unirse) «*calles/líneas*» to join, meet (up); «*huesos*» to knit together **(b)** (fam) «*pareja*» to get together (colloq), to start going out together

empate *m* **1 (a)** (en partido, certamen) tie (AmE), draw (BrE); **terminó con ~ a cero** it finished in a scoreless tie (AmE) *o* (BrE) goalless draw; **el gol del ~** the equalizer *o* (AmE) the tying goal **(b)** (en una votación) tie **2** (Col, Per, Ven) (unión — en carpintería) joint; (— de tubos, cables) connection **3** (Ven fam) (novio) boyfriend; (novia) girlfriend

empecinado -da *adj* (esp AmL) (terco) stubborn; (determinado) determined

empecinarse [A1] *v pron* (obstinarse) to get an idea into one's head; (empeñarse) to persist

empedernido -da *adj* ‹*bebedor/fumador*› hardened, inveterate; ‹*jugador*› compulsive; ‹*solterón*› confirmed

empedrado *m* (de adoquines) paving; (de piedras irregulares) cobbled paving

empedrar [A5] *vt* to pave

empeine *m* instep

empellón *m* shove; **se abrió paso a empellones** she shoved her way through

empeñado -da *adj* **1 (a)** (resuelto) determined; **está ~ en hacerlo** he's determined to do it **(b)** (obstinado): **está ~ en que nos quedemos** he's insistent that we should stay **2** (endeudado) in debt

empeñar [A1] *vt* **(a)** ‹*joyas/pertenencias*› to pawn, hock (colloq) **(b)** ‹*palabra*› to give

■ **empeñarse** *v pron* **1** (endeudarse) to get *o* go into debt **2 ~se** EN **hacer algo** (esforzarse) to strive to do sth (frml), to make an effort to do sth; (proponerse) to be determined to do sth; (obstinarse) to insist ON doing sth

empeño *m* **(a)** (afán) determination; (esfuerzo) effort; **estudiar con ~** to study hard; **pondré todo mi ~** I will do my best **(b)** (obstinación) **~** EN **algo** insistence ON sth **(c)** (intento, empresa) undertaking, endeavor*

empeñoso -sa *adj* (AmL) hard-working

empeoramiento *m* (de la salud) deterioration, worsening; (del tiempo, de una situación) worsening

empeorar [A1] *vi* «*salud*» to deteriorate, get worse; «*tiempo/situación*» to get worse, worsen ■ ~ *vt* to make ... worse

emperador *m* (soberano) emperor

emperatriz *f* empress

empezar [A6] *vi* **1** «*película/conferencia/invierno*» to begin, start; **empezó a nevar** it started to snow *o* snowing **2** «*persona*» to start; **volver a ~** to start again; **todo es (cuestión de) ~** it'll be fine once we/you get started; **no sé por dónde ~**

I don't know where to begin; **vamos a ~ por ti** let's start with you; **~ A hacer algo** to start doing sth, start to do sth; **empezó diciendo que ...** she started *o* began by saying that ...; **empezó trabajando de mecánico** he started out as a mechanic; **empecemos por estudiar el contexto histórico** let's begin *o* start by looking at the historical context **3 para empezar** first of all, to start with ■ **~** *vt* **(a)** ‹*tarea/actividad*› to start **(b)** ‹*frasco/mermelada*› to start, open

empiece, empieza *etc see* EMPEZAR

empinado -da *adj* ‹*calle/pendiente*› steep

empinar [A1] *vt* ‹*bota/botella/vaso*› to raise ■ **empinarse** *v pron* (de puntillas) to stand on tiptoe

emplasto *m* **(a)** (Farm, Med) dressing **(b)** (fam) (cosa blanda, pegajosa) sticky mess (colloq)

empleada *f* maid; **~ de planta** (Méx) live-in maid; **~ doméstica** *or* **de servicio** (frml) maid, domestic servant (frml); *ver tb* EMPLEADO

empleado -da *m,f* **(a)** (trabajador) employee; **una nómina de 300 ~s** a staff of 300; **~ público** civil servant **(b)** (en oficina) office *o* clerical worker; (en banco) bank clerk, teller; (en tienda) (AmL) clerk (AmE), shop assistant (BrE)

empleador -dora *m,f* employer

emplear [A1] *vt* **1 (a)** «*empresa/organización*» to employ **(b)** (colocar) ‹*hijo/sobrino*› to fix ... up with a job **2** (usar) ‹*energía/imaginación/material*› to use ■ **emplearse** *v pron* (esp AmL) to get a job

empleo *m* **1 (a)** (trabajo) employment; **la creación de ~** job creation **(b)** (puesto) job; **está sin ~** she's out of work **2** (uso) use; Ⓢ **modo de empleo** instructions for use

emplomadura *f* (RPl) filling

emplomar [A1] *vt* (RPl) to fill

empobrecer [E3] *vt* ‹*población/tierra/lenguaje*› to impoverish ■ **empobrecerse** *v pron* «*país/lenguaje/vocabulario*» to become impoverished

empobrecimiento *m* impoverishment

empollar [A1] *vi* **1** «*gallina*» to brood **2** (Esp fam) «*estudiante*» to cram (colloq), to swot (BrE colloq) ■ **~** *vt* **1** ‹*huevos*› to hatch, sit on **2** (Esp fam) ‹*lección*› to cram (colloq), to swot up (on) (BrE colloq)

empollón -llona *m,f* (Esp fam & pey) grind (AmE colloq), swot (BrE colloq & pej)

empolvarse [A1] *v pron* (*refl*) ‹*nariz/cara*› to powder

empotrado -da *adj* built-in, fitted (*before n*)

empotrarse [A1] *v pron*: **el coche se empotró en el muro** the car crashed into the wall

emprendedor -dora *adj* enterprising

emprender [E1] *vt* ‹*viaje*› to embark on; ‹*proyecto/aventura*› to undertake; ‹*ataque/ofensiva*› to launch; **~ la marcha** to set out; **~ el regreso** to begin one's return journey

empresa *f* **1** (compañía) company, firm (BrE); **~ pública** public sector company **2** (tarea, labor) venture, undertaking

empresario -ria *m,f* **(a)** (Com, Fin) (*m*) businessman; (*f*) businesswoman; **~ de pompas fúnebres** undertaker **(b)** (Teatr) impresario **(c)** (en boxeo) promoter

empujar [A1] *vt* **(a)** ‹*coche/columpio*› to push; **¡empújame!** give me a push! **(b)** (incitar, presionar) to spur ... on; (obligar) to force **(c)** (Tec) to drive ■ **~** *vi* **(a)** (hacer presión) to push **(b)** (dar empellones) to push, shove

empuje *m* (dinamismo) drive

empujón *m* **(a)** (empellón) shove, push; **abrió la puerta de un ~** he pushed the door open; **abrirse paso a (los) empujones** to shove one's way through **(b)** (fam) (para animar, incitar) prod (colloq); **voy a darle un ~ al asunto** I'm going to push things along a bit (colloq)

empuñadura *f* (de espada) hilt; (de daga, navaja) handle; (de bastón, paraguas) handle

empuñar [A1] *vt* ‹*arma/espada*› to take up; ‹*bastón/palo*› to brandish

en *prep* **1** (en expresiones de lugar) **(a)** (refiriéndose a ciudad, edificio): **viven ~ París/~ el número diez/~ un hotel** they live in Paris/at number ten/in a hotel; **~ el último piso** on the top floor; **está ~ la calle Goya** it's on *o* (BrE) in Goya Street; **~ casa** at home **(b)** (dentro de) in; **~ una caja** in a box **(c)** (sobre) on; **~ una silla** on a chair; **se le nota ~ la cara** you can see it in his face **2** (expresando circunstancias, ambiente) in; **~ peligro** in danger **3 (a)** (indicando tema, especialidad): **un experto ~ la materia** an expert on the subject; **doctor ~ derecho** Doctor of Law **(b)** (indicando proporción, precio): **~ un diez por ciento** by ten per cent; **~ dólares** in dollars **4 (a)** (indicando estado, manera) in; **~ malas condiciones** in bad condition; **~ llamas** in flames, on fire **(b)** (en forma de): **termina ~ punta** it's pointed; **colóquense ~ círculo** get into *o* in a circle **(c)** (con medios de transporte) by; **ir ~ taxi** to go by taxi; **fueron ~ bicicleta** they cycled, they went on their bikes; **dimos una vuelta ~ coche** we went for a ride in the car **5 (a)** (indicando el material): **~ seda natural** in natural silk; **una escultura ~ bronce** a bronze (sculpture) **(b)** (indicando el modo de presentación o expresión) in; **~ azul/ruso** in blue/Russian **6** (con expresiones de tiempo): **~ verano** in (the) summer; **~ varias ocasiones** on several occasions; **~ la mañana/noche** (esp AmL) in the morning/at night **7 (a)** (seguido de construcción verbal): **no hay nada de malo ~ lo que hacen** there's nothing wrong in what they're doing; **fuí el último ~ salir** I was the last to leave **(b)** (con complementos de persona) in; **no sé qué ve ~ ella** I don't know what he sees in her

enagua *f*, **enaguas** *fpl* **(a)** (prenda interior) petticoat, underskirt **(b)** (AmC) (falda) skirt

enamorado -da *adj* [ESTAR] in love; **~ DE algn** in love WITH sb; **están muy ~s** they are very much in love ■ *m,f* lover; **una pareja de ~s** two lovers; **vino con su ~** (Bol, Per) she came with her boyfriend; **es un ~ de su profesión** he loves his work

enamoramiento *m* infatuation

enamorarse [A1] *v pron* to fall in love; **~ DE algo/algn** to fall in love WITH sth/sb

enano -na *m,f* (de proporciones normales) midget; (de cabeza más grande) dwarf; (en los cuentos) dwarf ■ *adj* ‹*especie/planta*› dwarf (*before n*); ‹*ración*› (fam) minute, tiny

encabezado *m* (Chi, Méx) headline

encabezamiento *m* **(a)** (en carta — saludo) opening; (— dirección, fecha) heading **(b)** (en ficha, documento) heading

encabezar [A4] *vt* **1** ‹*artículo/escrito*› to head **2 (a)** ‹*liga/clasificación/lista*› to head, be at the top of; ‹*carrera/movimento/revolución*› to lead **(b)** ‹*delegación/comité*› to head, lead

encabritarse [A1] *v pron* «*caballo*» to rear up

encachado -da *adj* (Chi fam) **(a)** (bonito) ‹*ropa/lugar*› lovely, nice; ‹*persona*› attractive **(b)** (arreglado) well-dressed **(c)** (entretenido) ‹*historia*› entertaining

encadenar [A1] *vt* ‹*prisionero/bicicleta*› to chain (up)

encajar [A1] *vt* **1** (meter, colocar) to fit **2** (esp AmL fam) (endilgar): **me ~on a mí el trabajito** I got saddled *o* landed with the job (colloq); **le encaja los hijos a la suegra** she dumps the kids on her mother-in-law (colloq); **les ~on tres goles** they put three goals past them ■ **~** *vi* **(a)** «*pieza/cajón*» to fit; **no encaja bien** it doesn't fit properly; **las piezas ~on** the pieces fitted together **(b)** (corresponder, cuadrar) «*hechos/descripción*» to fit; **no encaja con la decoración** it doesn't fit in with the decor

encaje *m* (Indum) lace; **pañuelo de ~** lace handkerchief

encajonar [A1] *vt* (en lugar estrecho) **~ algo/a algn EN algo** to cram *o* pack sth/sb INTO sth; **me ~on el coche** my car *o* I got boxed in

encalar [A1] *vt* to whitewash

encalillarse [A1] *v pron* (Chi fam) to get into debt

encallar [A1] *vi* to run aground

encallecido -da *adj* ‹*manos*› callused

encamar [A1] *vt* (Méx) to confine … to bed

encaminado -da *adj*: **el proyecto va bien ~** the project is shaping up well *o* is going well; **iba bien ~** he was on the right track; **medidas encaminadas a reducir** … measures designed to reduce *o* aimed at reducing …

encaminar [A1] *vt* **(a)** ‹*intereses/esfuerzos*› to direct, channel **(b)** ‹*estudiante/niño*› to point … in the right direction

encandilar [A1] *vt* **(a)** «*luz*» to dazzle **(b)** (asombrar, pasmar) to dazzle

encanecer [E3] *vi* to (go) gray*

encantado -da *adj* **1 (a)** (muy contento) delighted; **estoy ~ de haber venido** I am delighted *o* very glad that I came **(b)** (en fórmulas de cortesía): **~ de conocerla** pleased to meet you; **~ de poder ayudarte** I'm glad to be/to have been of help **2** ‹*bosque/castillo*› enchanted

encantador -dora *adj* ‹*persona/lugar*› charming, delightful ■ *m,f* magician; **~ de serpientes** snake charmer

encantar [A1] *vi* (+ *me/te/le etc*): **me encantó la obra** I loved *o* I really enjoyed the play; **me ~ía que me acompañaras** I'd love you to come with me ■ **~** *vt* to cast *o* put a spell on, bewitch

encanto *m* **1 (a)** (atractivo) charm; **sabe utilizar sus ~s** she knows how to use her charms; **su sencillez es su mayor ~** its most appealing feature is its simplicity **(b)** (fam) (maravilla): **¡qué ~ de hombre!** what a lovely *o* charming man!; **tienen un jardín que es un ~** they have a lovely garden **2 (a)** (hechizo) spell; **como por ~** as if by magic **(b)** (Ven fam) (fantasma) ghost

encapotado -da *adj* ▶ **409** overcast, cloudy

encapricharse [A1] *v pron*: **se ha encaprichado con esa moto** he's really taken a liking *o* (BrE) a fancy to that motorbike; **~ CON** *or* (Esp) **DE algn** to fall for sb (colloq)

encarado -da *adj* (Esp, Méx): **mal ~** (enojado) bad-tempered; (de mal aspecto) nasty-looking

encaramarse [A1] *v pron* **~ A** *or* **EN algo** ‹*a árbol/valla*› to climb up; ‹*a taburete*› to climb on to

encarar [A1] *vt* **1** (enfocar) ‹*tarea*› to approach; (afrontar) ‹*desgracia/problema*› to face up to; ‹*futuro*› to face **2** (AmL) ‹*persona*› to stand up to
■ **encararse** *v pron* **~se CON algn** to face up to *o* stand up to sb

encarcelar [A1] *vt* to imprison, jail

encarecer [E3] *vt* (hacer más caro): **el envase encarece el producto** the container makes the product more expensive; **~á los alquileres** it will push rents up
■ **encarecerse** *v pron* «*precios*» to increase, rise; «*productos/vida*» to become more expensive

encargado -da *adj* **~ DE algo/hacer algo** responsible FOR sth/doing sth, in charge OF sth/doing sth ■ *m,f* **(a)** (de negocio) manager **(b)** (de tarea): **tú serás el ~ de avisarles** it will be your responsibility to tell them

encargar [A3] *vt* **1 (a) ~le algo A algn** ‹*tarea*› to entrust sb WITH sth; **me encargó una botella de whisky escocés** she asked me to buy *o* get her a bottle of Scotch **(b) ~ a algn QUE haga algo** to ask sb to do sth **2** ‹*mueble/paella/libro*› to order; ‹*informe/cuadro*› to commission
■ **encargarse** *v pron* **~se DE algo/algn** to take care OF sth/sb; **me tuve que ~ del asunto** I had to take charge of the matter

encargo *m* **(a)** (recado, pedido): **¿te puedo hacer unos ~s?** could you buy *o* get a few things for me?; **mi hijo está haciendo un ~** my son is out on *o* is running an errand **(b)** (Com) order; **los hacemos por ~** we make them to order **(c)** (cargo, misión) job, assignment

encariñarse [A1] *v pron* **~ CON algo/algn** to grow fond OF sth/sb

encarnación *f* incarnation

encarnado -da *adj* **1** ‹*color/vestido*› red **2** ‹*uña*› ingrowing

encarnarse [A1] *v pron* **(a)** (Relig) to become incarnate **(b)** «*uña*» to become ingrown

encarrilar [A1] *vt* ‹*trabajo/asunto*› to direct; ‹*persona*› to guide, give guidance to

encasillar [A1] *vt* to class, categorize, pigeonhole

encauzar [A4] *vt* to channel; **~ algo** HACIA **algo** to channel sth INTO sth

encefalograma *m* encephalogram

enceguecedor -dora *adj* (AmL) blinding

enceguecer [E3] *vt* (AmL) to blind

■ **enceguecerse** *v pron* (AmL) (por la luz) to be blinded; (de ira) to become furious

encendedor *m* lighter

encender [E8] *vt* **(a)** ‹*cigarrillo/hoguera/vela*› to light; ‹*fósforo*› to strike, light **(b)** ‹*luz/calefacción*› to switch on, turn on; ‹*motor*› to start; **no dejes el televisor encendido** don't leave the television on ■ **~** *vi* «*fósforo*» to light; «*leña*» to catch light; «*luz/radio*» to come on

■ **encenderse** *v pron* «*aparato/luz*» to come on; «*fósforo/piloto*» to light; «*leña*» to catch light

encendido *m* ignition

enceradora *f* polisher

encerar [A1] *vt* to polish, wax

encerrado -da *adj*: **está ~ en su habitación** he's shut away *o* shut up in his room; **se quedó ~ en el cuarto de baño** he got locked in the bathroom; **siguen ~s en la universidad** they are still occupying the university; **oler a ~** (AmL) to be stuffy

encerrar [A5] *vt* **1** ‹*ganado*› to shut up, pen; ‹*perro*› to shut ... in; ‹*persona*› (en cárcel, calabozo) to lock up; **me encerró en mi habitación** he shut me *o* locked me in my room; **me dejaron encerrada en la oficina** I got locked in the office **2** (conllevar) ‹*peligro/riesgo*› to involve, entail

■ **encerrarse** *v pron* (*refl*) (en habitación) to shut oneself in; (en fábrica, universidad) «*obreros/estudiantes*» to lock oneself in

encerrona *f* (trampa) trap

encestar [A1] *vi* to score (a basket)

enchapar [A1] *vt* (de metal) to plate; (de madera) to veneer

encharcarse [A2] *v pron* «*terreno/zona*» to become waterlogged *o* flooded; «*agua*» to form a pool/pools

enchastrar [A1] *vt* (RPl fam) ‹*ropa/cocina*› to make a mess of

■ **enchastrarse** *v pron* (RPl fam) to get dirty

enchastre *m* (RPl fam) mess

enchilada *f* enchilada (*tortilla with a meat or cheese filling, served with a tomato and chili sauce*)

enchilado[1] -da *adj* (Méx) (Coc) seasoned with chili

enchilado[2] *m* stew (*with chili*)

enchilar [A1] *vt* (Méx) (Coc) to add chili to

■ **enchilarse** *v pron* (Méx) (comiendo): **ya me enchilé** my mouth's burning; **con este plato me enchilo** this dish is too hot for me

enchinar [A1] *vt* (Méx) to perm

■ **enchinarse** *v pron* (Méx): **se me enchina la piel** I come out in goose bumps *o* goose pimples

enchuecar [A2] *vt* (AmL fam) ‹*metal*› to bend; ‹*madera/lámina*› to warp; ‹*cara/boca*› to twist; ‹*cuadro*› to tilt

■ **enchuecarse** *v pron* (Chi fam) «*metal*» to bend, get bent; «*madera/lámina*» to warp; «*cara/boca*» to become twisted

enchufado -da *adj* (fam): **está ~** he knows all the right people; **estar ~ con** ... to be well in with ... (colloq)

enchufar [A1] *vt* **1** (fam) ‹*radio/televisión*› to plug in **2** (fam) ‹*persona*›: **me enchufó en la empresa** he set me up with a job in the company (colloq)

enchufe *m* **1 (a)** (Elec) (macho) plug; (hembra) socket, power point (BrE) **(b)** (del teléfono) socket, point (BrE) **2** (Esp fam) (influencia): **necesitas algún ~** you need to have connections; **por ~** by pulling some strings

encía *f* ▶ **123** gum

enciclopedia *f* encyclopedia*

encienda, **enciendas, etc** *see* ENCENDER

encierra, **encierras, etc** *see* ENCERRAR

encierro *m* **(a)** (en fábrica, universidad) sit-in **(b)** (reclusión): **salió de su ~ después de ocho meses** she emerged after being holed up for eight months **(c)** (Taur) (conducción) *running of bulls through the streets*; (toros) *bulls to be used in a bullfight*

encima *adv* **1** (en el espacio): **le puso una piedra ~** he put a stone on it; **no llevo dinero ~** I don't have any money on me; **se tiró el café ~** she spilled the coffee over herself; **se me vino el armario ~** the cupboard came down on top of me **2** (además): **¡y ~ se queja!** and then she goes and complains!; **y ~ no me lo devolvió** and on top of that, he didn't give it back! **3** (*en locs*) **encima de**: **~ de la mesa** on the table; **~ del armario** on top of the cupboard; **llevaba un chal ~ de la chaqueta** she wore a shawl over her jacket; **viven ~ de la tienda** they live over *o* above the shop; **~ de caro es feo** not only is it expensive, it's also ugly; **por encima** over; **saltó por ~** he jumped over; **le eché un vistazo por ~** I just looked over it quickly; **una limpieza por ~** a quick clean; **por encima de** above; **por ~ de la media** above average; **por ~ de todo** above everything; **volaban por ~ de las nubes/del pueblo** they flew above the clouds/over the town; **está por ~ del jefe de sección** she's above the head of department; ***quitarse algo de ~*** ‹*problema/tarea*› to get sth out of the way; ***quitarse a algn de ~*** to get rid of sb

encimar [A1] *vt* **(a)** (Col) (regalar): **me encimó dos más** she gave me two extra **(b)** (Méx, RPl) ‹*cajas/libros*› to stack up

encina *f* holm oak, ilex

encinta *adj* ⇒ EMBARAZADA

enclenque *adj* **(a)** ‹*persona*› (enfermizo) sickly; (delgado) weak, weedy (colloq) **(b)** ‹*estructura*› rickety

encoger [E6] *vi* to shrink ■ **~** *vt* **(a)** ‹*ropa*› to shrink **(b)** ‹*piernas*› to tuck ... in; **encogió el cuerpo de miedo** he shrank back in fear

■ **encogerse** *v pron* **1** «*ropa/tela*» to shrink **2** «*persona*» **(a)** (físicamente): **~se de hombros** to shrug one's shoulders; **caminar encogido** to walk with one's shoulders hunched **(b)** (por la edad)

to shrink, get shorter **(c)** (acobardarse) to be intimidated

encomendería *f* (Per) grocery store (AmE), grocer's shop (BrE)

encomendero *m* (Per) (tendero) grocer

encomienda *f* (AmL) (Corresp) package (AmE), parcel (BrE)

encontrar [A10] *vt* **1 (a)** (buscando) ‹*casa/trabajo/persona*› to find; **no encontré entradas para el teatro** I couldn't get tickets for the theater; **no le encuentro lógica** I can't see the logic in it **(b)** (casualmente) ‹*cartera/billete*› to find, come across **(c)** (descubrir) ‹*falta/error*› to find, spot; ‹*cáncer/quiste*› to find, discover **(d)** ‹*obstáculo/dificultad*› to meet (with), encounter **2** (+ *compl*): **te encuentro muy cambiado** you look very different; **lo encuentro ridículo** I find it ridiculous; **¿cómo encontraste el país?** how did the country seem to you?

■ **encontrarse** *v pron* **1** (por casualidad) **~se** CON **algn** to meet sb, bump INTO sb (colloq) **2** (*recípr*) **(a)** (reunirse) to meet; (por casualidad) to meet, bump into each other (colloq) **(b)** «*carreteras/líneas*» to meet **3** (*enf*) (inesperadamente) ‹*billete/cartera*› to find, come across; **me encontré con que todos se habían ido** I found they had all gone **4** (frml) (estar) to be; **me encuentro mejor** I am feeling better; **el hotel se encuentra cerca de la estación** the hotel is (located) near the station

encorvado -da *adj*: **anda ~** he walks with a stoop

encorvarse [A1] *v pron* to develop a stoop

encrespar [A1] *vt* ‹*pelo*› to make ... go curly; ‹*mar*› to make ... rough *o* choppy

■ **encresparse** *v pron* «*pelo*» to curl, go curly; «*mar*» to get rough *o* choppy

encrucijada *f* crossroads

encuadernación *f* **(a)** (cubierta) binding **(b)** (acción) book binding

encuadernador -dora *m,f* bookbinder

encuadernar [A1] *vt* to bind

encuadrar [A1] *vt* **(a)** (clasificar) to class, classify **(b)** (Cin, Fot, TV) to frame, center*

encubrir [I33] *vt* **(a)** ‹*delincuente*› to harbor* **(b)** ‹*delito*› to cover up; **siempre lo está encubriendo** she's always covering up for him **(c)** ‹*temor/verdad/problema*› to mask

encuclillarse [A1] *v pron* to squat (down)

encuentra, encuentras, etc *see* ENCONTRAR

encuentro *m* **(a)** (acción) meeting, encounter; **una secretaria le salió al ~** he was met by a secretary **(b)** (Dep) (period) game

encuerarse [A1] *v pron* (*refl*) (AmL fam) (desnudarse) to strip off (colloq), get undressed; (en el escenario) to strip

encuesta *f* **(a)** (sondeo) survey; **~ de opinión** opinion poll **(b)** (investigación) inquiry

encuestado -da *m,f*: **el 50% de los ~s** 50% of those polled

encumbrar [A1] *vt* (Chi) ‹*volantín*› to fly

endeble *adj* weak; ‹*salud*› delicate, poor

endemoniado -da *adj* **(a)** (inaguantable) ‹*niño/asunto*› wretched (*before n*); ‹*genio/humor*› foul, wicked **(b)** (poseído del demonio) possessed (by the devil)

enderezar [A4] *vt* **(a)** (destorcer) ‹*clavo*› to straighten **(b)** (poner vertical) ‹*poste/espalda*› to straighten; ‹*planta*› to stake; ‹*barco*› to right **(c)** ‹*persona*› to straighten ... out

■ **enderezarse** *v pron* (ponerse derecho) «*persona*» to stand up straight, straighten up; «*árbol*» to straighten up

endeudado -da *adj* in debt; **~** CON **algn** indebted TO sb

endeudarse [A1] *v pron* to get (oneself) into debt; **~** CON **algn** to get into debt WITH sb

endiablado -da *adj* **(a)** (malo) ‹*carácter/genio*› terrible; **¡este ~ niño!** this wretched child! **(b)** (peligroso) ‹*velocidad*› reckless, dangerous

endibia *f* endive, chicory (BrE)

endilgar [A3] *vt* (fam): **nos endilgó un sermón** he lectured us; **me ~on el trabajito** I got saddled *o* landed with the job (colloq); **me endilgó a los niños** she dumped the kids on me (colloq)

endivia *f* endive, chicory (BrE)

endrogarse [A3] *v pron* (Méx) to get into debt

endulzar [A4] *vt* **(a)** ‹*café*› to sweeten **(b)** ‹*tono/respuesta*› to soften; ‹*vida/vejez*› to brighten up; ‹*carácter*› to mellow

endurecer [E3] *vt* **1** (en general) to harden **2** ‹*persona/carácter*› (volver insensible) to harden; (fortalecer) to toughen ... up; **ese corte te endurece las facciones** that haircut makes you look harsher

■ **endurecerse** *v pron* **(a)** (en general) to harden; «*pan*» to go stale **(b)** «*persona/carácter*» (volverse insensible) to harden; (fortalecerse) to toughen up **(c)** «*facciones*» to become harder *o* harsher

ene *f*: *name of the letter* n

eneldo *m* dill

enemigo -ga *adj* **(a)** ‹*tropas/soldados/país*› enemy (*before n*) **(b) ser ~** DE **algo** to be against sth; **era enemiga de pegarles a los niños** she was against hitting children ■ *m,f* enemy

enemistad *f* enmity

enemistado -da *adj*: **están ~s** they're been at odds (with each other); **quedó ~ con ellos** she fell out with them

enemistar [A1] *vt* ‹*dos facciones/países*› to make enemies of; **~ un país con otro** to turn one country against the other; **ella los enemistó** she turned them against each other

■ **enemistarse** *v pron* to fall out; **~se** CON **algn** (POR **algo**) to fall out WITH sb (OVER sth)

energético -ca *adj* ‹*crisis/política/recursos*› energy (*before n*); ‹*alimento*› energy-giving, fuel (*before n*) (AmE)

energía *f* **1** (Fís) energy; **~ nuclear/solar** nuclear/solar power **2 (a)** (vigor, empuje) energy; **protestar con ~** to protest vigorously **(b)** (firmeza) firmness

enérgico -ca *adj* **(a)** (físicamente) energetic **(b)** (firme, resuelto) ‹*carácter*› forceful; ‹*protesta/ataque*› vigorous; ‹*medidas*› firm, strong; ‹*negativa/rechazo*› flat, firm

enero *m* ▶ **193** January; **a principios de ~** at the beginning of January; **a mediados de ~** in the middle of January, in mid-January; **el tres de ~** the third of January, January the third, January third (AmE); **en (el mes de) ~** in (the month of) January; **Lima, 8 de ~ de 1987** (Corresp) Lima, January 8 *o* January 8th, 1987

enfadado -da *adj* (esp Esp) angry; (en menor grado) annoyed; **están ~s** they've fallen out; **está ~ contigo** he's angry/annoyed with you

enfadar [A1] *vt* (esp Esp) (enojar) to anger, make ... angry; (en menor grado) to annoy
■ **enfadarse** *v pron* (esp Esp) **(a)** (enojarse) to get angry, get mad (esp AmE colloq); (en menor grado) to get annoyed, get cross (BrE colloq); **~se CON algn** to get angry/annoyed WITH sb **(b)** «*novios*» to fall out

enfado *m* (esp Esp) anger; (menos serio) annoyance

énfasis *m* emphasis; **poner ~ en algo** to stress *o* emphasize sth

enfático -ca *adj* emphatic

enfatizar [A4] *vt* to emphasize, stress

enfermar [A1] *vi* to fall ill, get sick (AmE)
■ **enfermarse** *v pron* **(a)** (esp AmL) (caer enfermo) to fall ill, get sick (AmE); **~se del estómago** to develop stomach trouble **(b)** (CS euf) (menstruar) to get one's period

enfermedad *f* illness; **contraer una ~** to contract an illness/a disease (frml); **después de una larga ~** after a long illness; **está con permiso por ~** he's off sick; **~es de la piel** skin diseases; **~ mental** mental illness; **~ nerviosa** nervous disorder

enfermería *f* **1** (sala) infirmary, sickbay **2** (carrera) nursing

enfermero -ra *m,f* nurse; **~ jefe** ≈ head nurse (AmE), ≈ charge nurse (BrE)

enfermizo -za *adj* unhealthy, sickly; **de aspecto ~** unhealthy-looking

enfermo -ma *adj* **(a)** (Med) ill, sick; **gravemente ~** seriously ill; **está ~ del corazón** he has heart trouble; **está enferma de los nervios** she suffers with her nerves; **se puso ~** he fell *o* got ill, he got sick (AmE); ***poner ~ a algn*** (fam) to get on sb's nerves (colloq), to get sb (colloq) **(b)** (CS euf) (con la menstruación): **estoy enferma** I've got my period, it's the time of the month (euph) ■ *m,f* (en hospital) patient; **quiere cuidar ~s** she wants to care for sick people *o* the sick; **~s del corazón** people with heart trouble; **~s de cáncer** cancer sufferers

enfocar [A2] *vt* **1** ‹*objeto/persona*› (con cámara, prismáticos) to focus on; **los ~on con la linterna** they shone the torch on them **2 (a)** (Fot, Ópt) ‹*telescopio/cámara*› to focus **(b)** ‹*tema/asunto*› to approach, look at

enfoque *m* **(a)** (Fot, Ópt) (acción) focusing*; (efecto) focus **(b)** (de asunto) approach; **todo depende del ~ que se le dé** everything depends on the way you look at it; **~ DE algo** approach TO sth

enfrentamiento *m* clash; **~ bélico** military confrontation

enfrentar [A1] *vt* **1** ‹*problema/peligro/realidad*› to confront, face up to; ‹*futuro*› to face **2 (a)** ‹*contrincantes/opositores*› to bring ... face to face **(b)** (enemistar) to bring ... into conflict
■ **enfrentarse** *v pron* **(a)** (hacer frente a) **~se CON algn** ‹*con rival/enemigo*› to confront sb; **~se A algo** ‹*a dificultades/peligros*› to face sth; ‹*a realidad/responsabilidad*› to face up to sth **(b)** (*recípr*) «*equipos/atletas*» to meet; «*tropas/oponentes*» to clash

enfrente *adv* **1** (al otro lado de una calle, etc) opposite; **~ de mí/del parque** opposite me/the park **2** (delante) in front; **~ DE algo** in front of sth

enfriamiento *m* **(a)** (catarro) chill **(b)** (de amor, entusiasmo, relaciones) cooling (off)

enfriar [A17] *vt* **(a)** ‹*alimento*› to cool; (en el refrigerador) to chill, cool **(b)** ‹*entusiasmo/relación*› to cool, cause ... to cool ■ **~** *vi:* **no dejes ~ el café** don't let your coffee go *o* get cold; **deja ~ el motor** let the engine cool down; **ponlo a ~** put it in the refrigerator to chill
■ **enfriarse** *v pron* **1 (a)** «*comida/bebida*» (ponerse — demasiado frío) to get cold, go cold; (— lo suficientemente frío) to cool down **(b)** «*manos*» to get cold **(c)** «*entusiasmo/relaciones*» to cool (off) **2** (tomar frío) to catch *o* get cold; (resfriarse) to catch a cold, catch a chill

enfurecer [E3] *vt* to infuriate, make ... furious
■ **enfurecerse** *v pron* to fly into a rage, get furious

enfurecido -da *adj* [ESTAR] ‹*persona*› furious

enfurruñarse [A1] *v pron* (fam) to go into a sulk (colloq), to get into a huff (colloq)

enganchar [A1] *vt* **(a)** ‹*cable/cadena*› to hook **(b)** ‹*remolque*› to hitch up, attach; ‹*caballos*› to harness; ‹*vagón*› to couple, attach **(c)** ‹*pez*› to hook
■ **engancharse** *v pron* **(a)** (quedar prendido) to get caught; **se me enganchó la media en el clavo** my tights got caught on the nail **(b)** (fam) (hacerse adicto) **~se (A algo)** to get hooked (ON sth)

enganche *m* **1** (pieza, mecanismo) (Auto) towing hook; (Ferr) coupling **2** (Esp) (de la luz, del teléfono) connection **3** (Méx) (Fin) down payment

engañar [A1] *vt* **(a)** (hacer errar en el juicio) to deceive, mislead; **me engañó la vista** my eyes deceived me; **tú a mí no me engañas** you can't fool me; **lo engañó haciéndole creer que ...** she deceived him into thinking that ...; **~ a algn PARA QUE haga algo** to trick sb INTO doing sth **(b)** (estafar, timar) to cheat, con (colloq) **(c)** (ser infiel a) to be unfaithful to, cheat on
■ **engañarse** *v pron* (*refl*) (mentirse) to deceive oneself, kid oneself (colloq)

engaño *m* **(a)** (mentira) deception **(b)** (timo, estafa) swindle, con (colloq) **(c)** (ardid) ploy, trick

engañoso -sa *adj* ‹*palabras*› deceitful; ‹*apariencias*› deceptive

engarce *m* setting

engarzar [A4] *vt* **1** ‹*piedra/brillante*› to set **2** (Col, Ven) (enganchar) to hook
■ **engarzarse** *v pron* (Col) (engancharse) to get caught

engatusar [A1] *vt* to sweet-talk; **~ a algn PARA QUE haga algo** to sweet-talk sb INTO doing sth

engendrar [A1] *vt* ‹*hijos*› to father; ‹*odio/sospecha*› to breed, engender (frml)

engendro *m* **(a)** (feto) fetus* **(b)** (criatura malformada) malformed creature **(c)** (creación monstruosa) freak, monster

engentado -da *adj* (Méx) dazed, confused

engomado -da *adj* ‹*etiqueta*› gummed, self-adhesive; ‹*sobre*› gummed, self-sealing

engordar [A1] *vt* **(a)** (aumentar) to put on, gain **(b)** (cebar) to fatten (up) **(c)** ‹*cifras/estadísticas*› to swell ■ **~** *vi* **(a)** «*persona*» to put on *o* gain weight; «*animales*» to fatten **(b)** «*alimentos*» to be fattening

engorroso -sa *adj* ‹*problema*› complicated, thorny; ‹*situación*› awkward, difficult; ‹*asunto*› trying, tiresome

engranaje *m* **1** (Mec) gear assembly (*o* mechanism *etc*), gears (*pl*); **el ~ del reloj** the cogs of the watch **2** (de partido, sociedad) machinery

engrandecer [E3] *vt* (ennoblecer) to ennoble (frml)

engrapadora *f* (AmL) stapler

engrapar [A1] *vt* (AmL) to staple

engrasado *m* lubrication, greasing

engrasar [A1] *vt* **(a)** (Auto, Mec) (con grasa) to grease, lubricate; (con aceite) to oil, lubricate **(b)** (Coc) ‹*molde*› to grease

engreído -da *adj* **(a)** (vanidoso) conceited, bigheaded (colloq) **(b)** (Per) (mimado) spoiled* ■ *m,f* **(a)** (vanidoso) bighead (colloq) **(b)** (Per) (mimado) spoiled brat

engrupir [I1] *vt* (CS fam) to fool (colloq)

engullir [I9] *vt* to bolt (down)

enhebrar [A1] *vt* ‹*aguja*› to thread; ‹*perlas*› to string

enhorabuena *f* congratulations (*pl*); **darle a algn la ~** to congratulate sb ■ *interj* congratulations!

enigma *m* enigma, mystery

enigmático -ca *adj* enigmatic, mysterious

enjabonar [A1] *vt* to soap

■ **enjabonarse** *v pron* (*refl*) to soap oneself; **~se las manos** to soap one's hands

enjambre *m* (Zool) swarm

enjaular [A1] *vt* ‹*pájaro/fiera*› to cage, put ... in a cage

enjuagar [A3] *vt* ‹*boca/ropa/vajilla*› to rinse; ‹*palangana/cubo*› to swill out

■ **enjuagarse** *v pron* (*refl*) to wash off the soap; **~se el pelo** to rinse one's hair

enjuague *m* **(a)** (acción de enjuagar) rinse **(b)** (AmL) (para el pelo) conditioner **(c) ~ bucal** mouthwash

enjugar [A3] *vt* (liter) ‹*lágrimas/sudor*› to wipe away

■ **enjugarse** *v pron* (*refl*) (liter) ‹*lágrimas*› to wipe away; ‹*frente*› to mop, wipe

enlace *m* **(a)** (conexión, unión) link **(b)** (de vías, carreteras) intersection, junction **(c)** *tb* **~ matrimonial** marriage **(d)** (persona) liaison; **~ sindical** (Esp) shop steward, union rep

enlatado[1] -da *adj* **(a)** ‹*alimentos*› canned, tinned (BrE) **(b)** ‹*música/programa*› canned **(c)** (Inf) ‹*programa*› stored

enlatado[2] *m* **1** (proceso) canning **2** (AmL pey) (TV) poor-quality program

enlazar [A4] *vt* **1 (a)** ‹*ciudades*› to link (up); ‹*ideas/temas*› to link, connect **(b)** ‹*cintas*› to tie ... together **2** (Col, RPl) ‹*res/caballo*› to lasso, rope (AmE) **3** (Méx frml) (casar) to marry ■ **~** *vi* **~ CON algo** «*tren/vuelo*» to connect WITH sth; «*carretera*» to link up WITH sth

enlistarse [A1] *v pron* (AmC, Col, Ven) to enlist, join up

enloquecedor -dora *adj* ‹*dolor*› excruciating; **el ruido era ~** the noise was enough to drive you crazy

enloquecer [E3] *vt* to drive ... crazy *o* mad ■ **~** *vi* (perder el juicio) to go crazy *o* mad; **enloqueció de celos** he was driven crazy *o* insane with jealousy

enlozado -da *adj* (AmL) ‹*cacerola*› enameled*; ‹*fuente*› glazed

enmarañado -da *adj* **(a)** ‹*pelo/lana*› tangled **(b)** (complicado, confuso) complicated, involved

enmarcar [A2] *vt* ‹*lámina/foto*› to frame

enmascarado -da *adj* masked ■ *m,f* (*m*) masked man; (*f*) masked woman

enmendar [A5] *vt* ‹*conducta*› to improve, amend (frml); ‹*actitud*› to change; ‹*error*› to amend, rectify

■ **enmendarse** *v pron* (*refl*) to mend one's ways

enmienda *f* amendment

enmohecer [E3] *vt* ‹*ropa*› to make ... moldy*; ‹*metal*› to rust

■ **enmohecerse** *v pron* «*ropa/pan/queso*» to become moldy*; «*metal*» to rust, become rusty

enmoquetar [A1] *vt* (Esp) to carpet

enmudecer [E3] *vi* to fall silent

ennegrecer [E3] *vt* (poner negro) to blacken; (oscurecer) to darken

■ **ennegrecerse** *v pron* **(a)** (ponerse negro) to go black **(b)** (ponerse oscuro) «*cielo/nubes*» to darken, go dark; «*plata*» to tarnish

enojadizo -za *adj* (esp AmL) irritable, touchy

enojado -da *adj* (esp AmL) angry, mad (esp AmE colloq); (en menor grado) annoyed, cross (BrE colloq); **esta ~ contigo** he's angry/annoyed with you; **están ~s** they've fallen out

enojar [A1] *vt* (esp AmL) to make ... angry; (en menor grado) to annoy

■ **enojarse** *v pron* (esp AmL) to get angry, get mad (esp AmE colloq); (en menor grado) to get annoyed, get cross (BrE colloq); **~se CON algn** to get angry/annoyed WITH sb

enojo *m* (esp AmL) anger; (menos serio) annoyance; **¿ya se te pasó el ~?** are you still angry/annoyed?

enojón -jona *adj* (Chi, Méx fam) irritable, touchy

enojoso -sa *adj* (esp AmL) (violento) awkward; (aburrido) tedious, tiresome

enorgullecer [E3] *vt*: **mi hijo me enorgullece** I am proud of my son

■ **enorgullecerse** *v pron* to be proud; **no es para ~se** it's nothing to be proud of; **~se DE algo** to take pride IN sth

enorme *adj* ‹*edificio/animal/suma*› huge, enormous; ‹*zona*› vast, huge; **sentí una pena ~** I felt tremendously sad

enraizado -da *adj* ‹*prejuicio*› deep-seated, deep-rooted; ‹*tradición*› deeply rooted

enrarecido -da *adj* **(a)** ‹*atmósfera/aire*› rarefied **(b)** ‹*ambiente/relaciones*› strained, tense

enredadera *f* creeper, climbing plant

enredado -da *adj* **1** ‹*lana/cuerda*› tangled; ‹*pelo*› tangled, knotted; ‹*asunto/idea*› complicated **2 (a)** (involucrado) **~ EN algo** mixed up IN sth **(b)** (fam) (en lío amoroso) **~ CON algn** involved WITH sb

enredar [A1] *vt* **(a)** ‹*cuerdas/cables*› to get ... tangled up, tangle up **(b)** (embarullar) ‹*persona*› to muddle ... up, confuse; ‹*asunto/situación*› to complicate **(c)** (fam) (involucrar) **~ a algn EN algo** to get sb mixed up *o* caught up IN sth ■ **~** *vi* (fam) **(a)** (intrigar) to make trouble, stir up trouble **(b)** (Esp) (molestar) to fidget; **~ CON algo** to fiddle (around) WITH sth

■ **enredarse** *v pron* **1** «*lana/cuerda*» to get tangled, become entangled; «*pelo*» to get tangled *o* knotted; «*planta*» to twist itself around **2** (fam) **(a)** (en lío amoroso) **~se CON algn** to get involved WITH sb **(b)** (involucrarse) **~se EN algo** to get mixed up *o* involved IN sth **(c)** (fam) (embarullarse) to get mixed up, get muddled up

enredo *m* **(a)** (de hilos) tangle; (en el pelo) tangle, knot **(b)** (embrollo) mess; **tengo un ~ en las cuentas** ... my accounts are in a terrible mess **(c)** (fam) (lío amoroso) affair

enrejado *m* (de verja, balcón) railing, railings (*pl*); (rejilla) grating, grille; (para plantas) trellis

enrevesado -da *adj* complicated

enrielar [A1] *vt* ⇒ ENCARRILAR

enriquecer [E3] *vt* **1** ‹*país/población*› to make ... rich **2** ‹*espíritu/lengua/alimento*› to enrich

■ **enriquecerse** *v pron* **1** (hacerse rico) to get rich **2** «*cultura/relación/lengua*» to be enriched

enrojecer [E3] *vt* ‹*rostro/mejillas*› to redden, make ... go red; ‹*pelo*› to turn ... red, make ... go red ■ **~** *vi* (liter) (ruborizarse) to redden, blush; (de ira, rabia) to go red in the face

■ **enrojecerse** *v pron* «*rostro/mejillas*» to redden, blush; «*pelo*» to go *o* turn red; «*cielo*» to turn red

enrolarse [A1] *v pron* to enlist, join up; **~ en la marina** to enlist in *o* join the navy; **~ en un partido** to join a party

enrollado -da *adj* **1 (a)** ‹*papel*› rolled up **(b)** ‹*cable*› coiled (up) **2** (Esp) **(a)** (fam) **estar ~ CON algn** to have a thing (going) WITH sb (colloq); **están ~s** they've got sth going between them (colloq) **(b) estar ~ CON algo** ‹*con exámenes/preparativos*› wrapped up IN sth **(c)** (arg) (en la onda) ‹*persona/música/coche*› cool (sl) **3** (Ven fam) (preocupado) uptight (colloq), freaked out (sl)

enrollar [A1] *vt* **1** ‹*papel/persiana*› to roll up; ‹*cable/manguera*› to coil; **~ el hilo en el carrete** wind the thread onto the spool **2** (Esp arg) ‹*persona*› (confundir) to confuse, get ... confused; (en asunto) to involve, get ... involved

■ **enrollarse** *v pron* **1** «*papel*» to roll up; «*cuerda/cable*» to coil up; **la cadena se enrolló en la rueda** the chain wound itself around the wheel **2** (Esp fam) **(a)** (hablar mucho): **no te enrolles** stop jabbering on (colloq); **se ~on hablando** they got deep into conversation **(b)** (tener relaciones amorosas): **se ~on en la discoteca** they made out (AmE colloq) *o* (BrE colloq) they got off together in a disco; **~se CON algn** to make out WITH sb (AmE colloq), to get off WITH sb (BrE colloq)

enroque *m* (en ajedrez) castling

enroscar [A2] *vt* ‹*tornillo*› to screw in; ‹*cable/cuerda*› to coil; **~ algo EN algo** to wind sth AROUND *o* ONTO sth

■ **enroscarse** *v pron* **(a)** «*víbora*» to coil up **(b)** «*gato/persona*» to curl up

enrular [A1] *vt* (Col, CS) to curl

ensalada *f* (Coc) salad; **~ de fruta** fruit salad

ensaladera *f* salad bowl

ensalzar [A4] *vt* ‹*virtudes*› to extol; ‹*persona*› to praise, sing the praises of

ensamblar [A1] *vt* to assemble

ensanchar [A1] *vt* **(a)** ‹*calle*› to widen; ‹*vestido*› to let out **(b)** ‹*horizontes/posibilidades*› to expand

■ **ensancharse** *v pron* **(a)** «*calle/acera*» to widen, get wider; «*jersey*» to stretch **(b)** «*horizontes*» to expand

ensangrentado -da *adj* bloodstained

ensangrentar [A5] *vt* to stain ... with blood

ensañarse [A1] *v pron*: **se ensañaron con los prisioneros** they showed the prisoners no mercy *o* pity; **no te ensañes con él** don't take it out on him (colloq)

ensartar [A1] *vt* **(a)** ‹*perlas/cuentas*› to string **(b)** (con pincho) to skewer **(c)** (enhebrar) to thread **(d)** (clavar) **~ algo EN algo** to stick sth IN(TO) sth

ensayar [A1] *vt* **(a)** ‹*obra/baile*› to rehearse **(b)** ‹*método*› to test, try out ■ **~** *vi* to rehearse

ensayo *m* **1 (a)** (Espec) rehearsal; **~ general** (de obra teatral) dress rehearsal; (de concierto) final rehearsal **(b)** (prueba) trial, test; (intento) attempt **2** (Lit) essay **3** (en rugby) try

enseguida *adv* at once, immediately, right away; **¡~ voy!** I'll be right with you; **~ de almorzar** (esp AmL) right *o* straight after lunch

enseñado -da *adj*: **bien/mal ~** ‹*niño*› well/badly brought up; ‹*animal*› well/badly trained

enseñanza *f* **(a)** (docencia) teaching **(b)** (educación) education; **~ a distancia** distance learning; **~ media** *or* **secundaria** high school (AmE) *o* (BrE) secondary education; **~ primaria** elementary (AmE) *o* (BrE) primary education; **~ universitaria** college (AmE) *o* (BrE) university education

enseñar [A1] *vt* **1 (a)** ‹*asignatura/niño*› to teach; ‹*animal*› to train; **~le a algn A hacer algo** to teach sb to do sth **(b)** (dar escarmiento) to teach **2** (mostrar) ‹*camino/procedimiento*› to show

■ **enseñarse** *v pron* (Méx fam) **~se A hacer algo** (aprender) to learn to do sth; (acostumbrarse) to get used TO doing sth

ensillar [A1] *vt* to saddle (up)

ensimismado -da *adj* [ESTAR] lost in thought; **~ EN algo** engrossed IN sth, absorbed IN sth

ensordecedor -dora *adj* deafening

ensuciar [A1] *vt* **(a)** ‹*ropa/mantel*› to get ... dirty, dirty; **lo vas a ~ todo de barro** you'll get mud everywhere **(b)** (liter) ‹*honor/nombre*› to sully, tarnish

■ **ensuciarse** *v pron* **(a)** (*refl*) «*persona*» to get dirty; **no te ensucies los dedos** don't get your fingers dirty **(b)** «*falda/suelo*» to get dirty; **que no se te ensucie** don't get it dirty; **se me ensució el vestido de grasa** I got grease on my dress

entablar [A1] *vt* **(a)** (iniciar) ‹*conversación/amistad*› to strike up; ‹*negociaciones*› to enter into **(b)** ‹*partida*› to set up

entablillar [A1] *vt* to splint, put ... in a splint

entallado -da *adj* ‹*chaqueta/vestido*› waisted; ‹*camisa*› tailored, fitted

ente *m* **(a)** (ser) being, entity **(b)** (organismo, institución) body

entender [E8] *vt* to understand; ‹*chiste*› to understand, get (colloq); **no te entiendo la letra** I can't read your writing; **no entendí su nombre** I didn't get his name; **lo entendió todo al revés** he got it all completely wrong; **tú ya me entiendes** you know what I mean; **me has entendido mal** you've misunderstood me; **se hace ~** *or* (AmL) **se da a ~** he makes himself understood; **me dio a ~ que** ... she gave me to understand that ...; **dar algo a ~** to imply sth ■ **~** *vi* **(a)** (comprender) to understand **(b)** (saber) **~ DE algo** to know ABOUT sth

■ **entenderse** *v pron* **1 (a)** (comunicarse) to communicate; **se entienden por señas** they communicate using sign language; **~se CON algn** to communicate WITH sb; **a ver si nos entendemos ¿quién te pegó?** let's get this straight, who hit you? **(b)** (llevarse bien); **lo que pasa es que no nos entendemos** the thing is we just don't get on very well; **~se CON algn** to get along *o* on WITH sb **2** (*refl*): **déjame, yo me entiendo** leave me alone, I know what I'm doing

entendido -da *adj* **1** [ESTAR] (comprendido) understood; **según tengo ~** as I understand it; **tenía ~ que** ... I was under the impression that ...; **eso se da por ~** that goes without saying **2** [SER] (experto): **no soy muy ~ en estos temas** I'm not very well up on these subjects; **es muy ~ en política** he knows a lot about politics ■ *m,f* expert

entendimiento *m* **(a)** (acuerdo) understanding **(b)** (capacidad para entender) mind; **todavía no tiene suficiente ~** he's not old enough to understand

enterado -da *adj* **1** (de hecho, suceso): **¿estás ~ de lo ocurrido?** have you heard what's happened?; **no estoy enterada de nada** I have no idea what's going on; ***darse por ~*** to get the message, take the hint **2** (Esp) (que sabe mucho) knowledgeable, well-informed

enterarse [A1] *v pron* **1** (de suceso, noticia): **ahora me entero** this is the first I've heard of it; **me enteré por tus padres** I found out from your parents; **le robaron el reloj y ni se enteró** they stole her watch and she didn't even notice *o* realize; **me enteré de la noticia por la radio** I heard the news on the radio; **si papá se entera de esto** ... if Dad finds out about this ... **2** (averiguar) to find out; **~ DE algo** to find out ABOUT sth **3** (esp Esp fam) (entender): **te voy a castigar ¿te enteras?** I'll punish you, have I made myself clear?; **¡para que te enteres!** (fam) so there! (colloq)

entereza *f* (serenidad, fortaleza) fortitude; (rectitud) integrity; (firmeza) determination, strength of mind

enternecedor -dora *adj* moving, touching

enternecer [E3] *vt* to move, touch

■ **enternecerse** *v pron* to be moved *o* touched

entero¹ -ra *adj* **(a)** (en su totalidad) whole; **una caja entera de bombones** a whole *o* an entire box of chocolates; **en el mundo ~** all over the world; **por ~** completely, entirely **(b)** (intacto) intact **(c)** ‹*número*› whole

entero² *m* **(a)** (Fin) point **(b)** (Mat) whole number, integer **(c)** (de lotería) (whole) lottery ticket

enterrador -dora *m,f* gravedigger

enterrar [A5] *vt* to bury; **lo entierran mañana** the funeral is tomorrow

entibiar [A1] *vt* ‹*líquido*› (enfriar) to cool; (calentar) to warm (up)

entidad *f* (frml) (organización, institución) entity, body; **~ deportiva** sporting body

entienda, **entiendas, etc** *see* ENTENDER

entierro *m* (acto) burial; (ceremonia) funeral; (procesión) funeral procession; **ir a un ~** to attend a funeral

entoldado *m* (marquesina) awning; (carpa) marquee

entonación *f* intonation

entonado -da *adj* **1** (Mús) in tune **2** [ESTAR] (fam) (por el alcohol) tipsy (colloq), merry (BrE colloq)

entonar [A1] *vt* **1** ‹*canción*› to intone, sing; ‹*voz*› to modulate; ‹*nota*› to sing, give **2** (animar) «*café/sopa*» ‹*persona*› to perk ... up ■ **~** *vi* (Mús) to sing in tune

entonces *adv* **1** (en aquel momento) then; **por** *or* **en aquel ~** in those days **2 (a)** (introduciendo conclusiones) so; **¿~ vienes o te quedas?** so are you coming with us or staying here? **(b)** (uso expletivo) well, anyway; **~, como te iba diciendo** ... well *o* anyway, as I was saying ...

entornado -da *adj* ‹*puerta*› ajar, half-open; ‹*ventana*› slightly open; ‹*ojos*› half-closed

entorno *m* **(a)** (situación) environment **(b)** (Lit) setting **(c)** (Inf) environment

entorpecer [E3] *vt* **(a)** (dificultar) ‹*tráfico*› to hold up, slow down; ‹*planes/movimiento*› to hinder; **estas cajas entorpecen el paso** these boxes are (getting) in the way **(b)** ‹*entendimiento/reacciones*› to dull

■ **entorpecerse** *v pron* «*entendimiento/reacciones*» to become dulled

entrada *f* **1** (acción) entrance; **la ~ es gratuita** admission *o* entrance is free; **vigilaban sus ~s y salidas** they watched his comings and goings; Ⓢ **prohibida la entrada** no entry; Ⓢ **entrada libre** admission free; **la ~ de divisas** the inflow of foreign currency; **~ EN** *or* (esp AmL) **A algo** entry

INTO sth; **forzaron su ~ en el** *or* **al edificio** they forced an entry into the building; ***de*** **~** right from the start **2 (a)** (en etapa, estado): **la ~ en vigor del nuevo impuesto** the coming into effect of the new tax **(b)** (ingreso, incorporación) entry; **la ~ de Prusia en la alianza** Prussia's entry into the alliance; **esto le facilitó la ~ a la universidad** that made it easier for him to get into university **(c)** (lugar de acceso) entrance; **espérame en** *or* **a la ~** wait for me at the entrance; **repartían folletos a la ~** they were handing out leaflets at the door **(d)** (vestíbulo) hall **3** (Espec) ticket; **los niños pagan media ~** it's half-price for children **4** (Com, Fin) **(a)** (Esp) (depósito) deposit **(b)** (ingreso) income; **~s y salidas** income and expenditure, receipts and outgoings **5** (de comida) starter **6** (Dep) **(a)** (en fútbol) tackle; **hacerle una ~ a algn** to tackle sb **(b)** (en béisbol) inning **7** (en el pelo): **tiene ~s** he has a receding hairline

entrado -da *adj*: **era entrada la noche** it was dark *o* night-time; **duró hasta bien entrada la tarde** it went on well into the evening

entrador -dora *adj* (AmL fam) (lanzado) daring, forward

entrante *adj* **(a)** (próximo): **el año ~** next year, the coming year **(b)** (nuevo) ‹*gobierno/presidente*› new, incoming (*before n*)

entrañable *adj* **(a)** ‹*amistad*› close, intimate; ‹*amigo*› very close, bosom (*before n*); ‹*recuerdo*› fond (*before n*) **(b)** ‹*persona*› pleasant, likable*

entrañar [A1] *vt* to entail, involve

entrañas *fpl* (vísceras) entrails (*pl*)

entrar [A1] *vi* **1** (acercándose) to come in; (alejándose) to go in; **déjame ~** let me in; **hazla ~** tell her to come in, show her in; **entró corriendo** he ran in, he came running in; **¿se puede ~ con el coche?** can you drive in?; **había gente entrando y saliendo** there were people coming and going; **¿cómo entró?** how did he get in?; **~ EN** *or* (esp AmL) **A algo** ‹*a edificio/habitación*› to go INTO sth; **entró en el** *or* **al banco** she went into the bank **2** (en etapa, estado) **~ EN algo** ‹*en periodo/guerra/negociaciones*› to enter sth; **~ en calor** to get warm; **entró en coma** he went into a coma **3 (a)** (introducirse, meterse): **cierra la puerta, que entra frío** close the door, you're letting the cold in; **me entró arena en los zapatos** I've got sand in my shoes **(b)** (poderse meter): **¿entrará por la puerta?** will it get through the door?; (+ *me/te/le etc*): **estos vaqueros no me entran** I can't get into these jeans; **el zapato no le entra** he can't get his shoe on; **no me entra la segunda** (Auto) I can't get it into second (gear) **4** «*hambre*» (+ *me/te/le etc*): **le entró hambre** she felt *o* got hungry; **me ha entrado la duda** I'm beginning to have my doubts; **me entró sueño** I got *o* began to feel sleepy **5** (empezar) to start, begin; **entró de aprendiz** he started *o* began as an apprentice **6** (incorporarse) **~ EN** *or* (esp AmL) **A algo** ‹*en empresa/ejército/club*› to join sth; ‹*en convento*› to enter sth; **el año que entré en** *or* **a la universidad** the year I started college I've just joined the association **7** (estar incluido): **el postre no entra en el precio** dessert is not included in the price; **¿cuántas entran en un kilo?** how many do you get in a kilo? ■ **~** *vt* (traer) to bring in; (llevar) to take in; **¿cómo van a ~ el sofá?** how are they going to get the sofa in?

entre *prep* **1 (a)** (dos personas, cosas) between; **lo decidieron ~ ellos dos** they decided it between the two of them; **está ~ las dos casas** it's between the two houses; **~ paréntesis** in brackets; **cuando hablan ~ los dos** when they talk to each other **(b)** (más de dos personas, cosas) among; **los alumnos hablaban ~ ellos** the pupils were talking among themselves; **~ otras cosas** among other things; **se perdió ~ la muchedumbre** he disappeared into the crowd; **~ estas cuatro paredes** within these walls **(c)** (indicando cooperación, distribución): **~ los tres logramos levantarlo** we managed to lift it between the three of us; **le hicimos con regalo ~ todos** we all got together and brought him a present; **repártelos ~ los niños/~ todos** share them out among the children/between everybody **2** (en expresiones de tiempo): **abierto ~ semana** open during the week; **llegaré ~ las tres y las cuatro** I'll be arriving between three and four; **cualquier semana ~ julio y agosto** any week in July or August **3 entre tanto** meanwhile, in the meantime ■ *adv* (esp AmL): **~ más come más/menos engorda** the more he eats the less he puts on weight

entreabierto -ta *adj* ‹*puerta*› ajar, half-open; ‹*ventana/ojos/boca*› half-open

entreabrir [I33] *vt* to half-open

entrecejo *m* space between the eyebrows; **fruncir el ~** to frown

entrecortado -da *adj* ‹*respiración*› difficult, labored*; **con la voz entrecortada por la emoción** in a voice choked with emotion

entrecruzar [A4] *vt* to intertwine, interweave

entredicho *m* **1** (duda): **estar en ~** to be in doubt *o* question; **poner algo en ~** «*persona*» to question sth **2** (CS, Per) (entre dos personas) argument; (entre dos países) dispute

entrega *f* **1** (de pedido, paquete, carta) delivery; (de premio) presentation; **~ de premios**, prize-giving; **la ~ de los documentos** the handing over of the documents; **el plazo para la ~ de solicitudes** the deadline for handing in *o* (frml) submitting applications; **servicio de ~ a domicilio** delivery service **2 (a)** (partida) delivery, shipment **(b)** (plazo, cuota) installment* **(c)** (de enciclopedia) installment*, fascicle; (de revista) issue **3** (dedicación) dedication, devotion; (abandono) surrender

entregar [A3] *vt* **1** (llevar) ‹*pedido/paquete/carta*› to deliver **2 (a)** (dar) to give; **me entregó un cuestionario** she gave me *o* handed me a questionnaire; **no quiso entregármelo** he refused to hand it over to me **(b)** ‹*premio/trofeo*› to present; **~le algo A algn** to present sb WITH sth **(c)** ‹*trabajo/deberes/informe*› to hand in, give in; ‹*solicitud/impreso*› to hand in, submit (frml) **3 (a)** ‹*ciudad/armas*› to surrender; ‹*poder/control*› to hand over **(b)** ‹*delincuente/prófugo*› to turn in, hand over; ‹*rehén*› to hand over **(c)** ‹*novia*› to give away **(d)** (dedicar) to devote

■ **entregarse** *v pron* **1** (dedicarse) **~se A algo/algn** to devote oneself TO sth/sb **2 (a)** (rendirse) to surrender, give oneself up; **~se A algo/algn** ‹*al enemigo/a la policía*› to give oneself up *o* surrender TO sth/sb **(b)** (abandonarse): **se entregó a la bebida** he gave himself over to drink

entrelazar [A4] *vt* ‹*cintas/hilos*› to interweave, intertwine; **con las manos entrelazadas** hand in hand

■ **entrelazarse** *v pron* to intertwine, interweave

entremedias, **entremedio** *adv* **(a)** (entre dos cosas) in between; **son muy caros o muy baratos, no hay nada ~** they're very expensive or very cheap, there's nothing in between; **lo metí ~** I put it in between **(b)** (mezclado con) **~ DE algo** among; **~ de mis papeles/de la gente** among my papers/the people **(c)** (en el tiempo) in between

entremés *m* (Coc) hors d'oeuvre, starter

entremezclar [A1] *vt* to intermingle

■ **entremezclarse** *v pron* «*recuerdos*» to intermingle, become intermingled; «*culturas*» to mix, intermingle

entrenador -dora *m,f* (manager) coach (AmE), manager (BrE); (preparador físico) trainer

entrenamiento *m* **(a)** (por el entrenador) coaching, training **(b)** (ejercicios) training **(c)** (sesión) training session

entrenar [A1] *vt/vi* to train

■ **entrenarse** *v pron* to train

entrepierna *f* (Anat) crotch; (medida) inside leg measurement

entrepiso *m* (AmL) mezzanine

entreplanta *f* mezzanine

entretanto *adv* meanwhile, in the meantime

entretejer [E1] *vt* ‹*hilos*› (en tela) to weave; (entrelazar) to interweave

entretelones *mpl* (CS, Per) (de un caso) ins and outs (*pl*)

entretención *f* (AmL) ⇒ ENTRETENIMIENTO

entretener [E27] *vt* **1** «*crucigrama/libro*» to keep ... amused; «*obra/payaso*» to entertain; **pintar me entretiene** I enjoy painting **2 (a)** (distraer, apartar de una tarea) to distract **(b)** (retener) to keep, detain; **no te entretengo más** I won't keep *o* detain you any longer

■ **entretenerse** *v pron* **1 (a)** (divertirse) to amuse oneself; **se entretiene con cualquier cosa** «*adulto*» she's easily amused; «*niño*» she's happy playing with anything **(b)** (pasar el tiempo) to keep (oneself) busy *o* occupied **2** (demorarse) to hang around, dally about

entretenido -da *adj* **1** [SER] ‹*película/conversación*› entertaining, enjoyable; ‹*persona*› entertaining **2** [ESTAR] ‹*persona*› (ocupado) busy

entretenimiento *m* entertainment; **lo hace por ~** he does it for pleasure *o* for fun

entretiempo *m* **(a)** (período entre estaciones): **de ~** ‹*abrigo*› lightweight; ‹*ropa*› spring/autumn (*before n*) **(b)** (Chi) (Dep) halftime

entrever [E29] *vt* **(a)** (ver confusamente) to make out **(b)** ‹*solución/acuerdo*› to begin to see; **ha dejado ~ que** ... she has hinted *o* suggested that ...

entreverado -da *adj* **(a)** (intercalado) interspersed **(b)** (fam) (desordenado, mezclado) muddled up, mixed up

entrevista *f* **(a)** (para trabajo, en periódico) interview **(b)** (period) (reunión) meeting

entrevistador -dora *m,f* interviewer

entrevistar [A1] *vt* to interview

entristecer [E3] *vt* to sadden

■ **entristecerse** *v pron* to grow sad

entrometerse [E1] *v pron* to meddle

entrometido -da *adj* meddling (*before n*), interfering (*before n*) ■ *m,f* meddler, busybody (colloq)

entronque *m* (AmL) (Ferr) junction

entumecerse [E3] *v pron* (perder la sensibilidad) to go numb; (perder la flexibilidad) to get stiff; **estar entumecido de frío** to be numb with cold

entusiasmado -da *adj* excited, enthusiastic; **está ~ con la idea** he's excited *o* enthusiastic about the idea

entusiasmar [A1] *vt* (apasionar): **lo entusiasma el fútbol** he's crazy about football; **no me entusiasma mucho la idea** I'm not very enthusiastic about the idea

■ **entusiasmarse** *v pron* **~se CON algo** to get excited *o* enthusiastic ABOUT sth

entusiasmo *m* enthusiasm

entusiasta *adj* enthusiastic ■ *mf* enthusiast

enumerar [A1] *vt* to list, enumerate (frml)

envainar [A1] *vt* ‹*espada*› to sheathe

envalentonar [A1] *vt* to make ... bolder, encourage

■ **envalentonarse** *v pron* (ponerse valiente) to become bolder *o* more daring; (insolentarse) to become defiant

envasar [A1] *vt* (en botellas) to bottle; (en latas) to can; (en paquetes, cajas) to pack

envase *m* (en general) container; (botella) bottle; (lata) can, tin (BrE)

envejecer [E3] *vi* **(a)** «*persona*» (hacerse más viejo) to age, grow old; (parecer más viejo) to age **(b)** «*vino/queso*» to mature, age ■ **~** *vt* **(a)** ‹*persona*› «*tragedia/experiencia*» to age; «*ropa/peinado*» to make ... look older **(b)** ‹*madera*› to make ... look old; ‹*vaqueros*› to give ... a worn look

envejecido -da *adj* **(a)** ‹*persona*›: **está tan ~** he's aged so much, he looks so old **(b)** ‹*cuero/madera*› distressed

envenenamiento *m* poisoning

envenenar [A1] *vt* to poison

■ **envenenarse** *v pron* (involuntariamente) to be poisoned; (voluntariamente) to poison oneself

envergadura *f* (importancia) magnitude (frml), importance; **de cierta ~** of some importance

enviado -da *m,f* (Pol) envoy; (Period) reporter, correspondent

enviar [A17] *vt* **(a)** ‹*carta/paquete*› to send; ‹*pedido/mercancías*› to send, dispatch **(b)** ‹*persona*› to send; **me envió por pan** she sent me out for bread

enviciarse [A1] *v pron* to become addicted, get hooked (colloq); **~ CON algo** to become addicted TO sth *o* (colloq) hooked ON sth

envidia *f* envy, jealousy; **le da ~ que yo vaya** he's envious *o* jealous because I'm going; **le tienes ~** you are jealous of him; **me muero de ~** I'm green with envy; **¡qué ~!** I'm so jealous!

envidiable *adj* enviable

envidiar [A1] *vt* to envy; **~le algo A algn** to envy sb sth

envidioso -sa *adj* envious

envío *m* **1** (acción): **el ~ de los fondos** the remittance *o* sending of the money; **fecha de ~** date of dispatch, date sent; **~ contra reembolso** COD, cash on delivery **2** (partida — de mercancías) consignment, shipment; (— de dinero) remittance

enviudar [A1] *vi* to be widowed

envoltorio *m* **(a)** (de paquete, regalo) wrapping; (de caramelo) wrapper **(b)** (bulto) bundle

envolver [E11] *vt* **1** ‹*paquete/regalo*› to wrap (up); **¿me lo puede ~ para regalo?** could you gift wrap it?; **~ algo/a algn EN algo** to wrap sth/sb (up) IN sth **2** (rodear) «*membrana/capa*» to surround; «*humo/tristeza*» to envelop **3** (involucrar) to involve

■ **envolverse** *v pron* **(a)** (*refl*) (en manta) to wrap oneself (up) **(b)** (en delito, asunto) to become involved

envuelto -ta *adj* **1** ‹*paquete/regalo*› wrapped; **~ para regalo** gift-wrapped **2** (rodeado) **~ EN algo** ‹*en humo/niebla*› enveloped IN sth; ‹*en misterio*› cloaked *o* shrouded IN sth; ‹*en una manta*› wrapped (up) IN sth **3** (involucrado) **~ EN algo** involved IN sth

enyesar [A1] *vt* **(a)** (Const) to plaster **(b)** ‹*brazo/pierna*› to put ... in a plaster cast, put ... in plaster (BrE)

enzarzarse [A4] *v pron* **~ EN algo** to get involved IN sth

eñe *f*: *name of the letter* ñ

epicentro *m* epicenter*

épico -ca *adj* epic

epidemia *f* epidemic

epilepsia *f* epilepsy

epiléptico -ca *adj/m,f* epileptic

epílogo *m* (Lit) epilogue; (de suceso) conclusion

episodio *m* (Cin, Rad, TV) episode; (suceso) episode, incident

epístola *f* (frml *o* hum) epistle (frml *or* hum)

epitafio *m* epitaph

época *f* **(a)** (período de tiempo) time, period; **en la ~ de Franco** in Franco's time; **la ~ de los Tudor** the Tudor period; **muebles de ~** period furniture; **en aquella ~** in those days *o* at that time; **esa ~ de mi vida** that period of my life; **es música de mi ~** it's music from my time **(b)** (parte del año) time of year; **la ~ de lluvias** the rainy season

epopeya *f* **(a)** (Lit) (poema) epic, epic poem **(b)** (empresa difícil): **el viaje fue toda una ~** the journey turned out to be a real ordeal

equilátero -ra *adj* equilateral

equilibrado -da *adj* ‹*persona/dieta*› well-balanced, balanced; ‹*lucha/partido*› close

equilibrar [A1] *vt* ‹*peso/carga/ruedas*› to balance; **~ las diferencias económicas** to redress economic imbalances

■ **equilibrarse** *v pron* «*fuerzas*» to even up; «*balanza de pagos*» to be restored; «*platillos de la balanza*» to balance out

equilibrio *m* (de fuerzas, estabilidad) balance; **perdió el ~** he lost his balance; **en estado de ~** in equilibrium

equilibrista *mf* (Espec) tightrope walker

equinoccio *m* equinox; **~ de primavera/de otoño** vernal/autumnal equinox

equipaje *m* baggage (esp AmE), luggage (BrE); **facturar el ~** to check in one's baggage *o* luggage; **~ de mano** hand baggage *o* luggage; **viaja con poco ~** he travels light

equipar [A1] *vt* **(a)** ‹*persona*› to equip, fit ... out; **~ a algn CON *or* DE algo** to equip sb WITH sth **(b)** ‹*casa*› to furnish; ‹*local/barco*› to fit out; (de víveres) to provision; **una cocina bien equipada** a well-equipped kitchen

equiparable *adj* comparable

equiparar [A1] *vt* **(a)** (poner al mismo nivel) **~ algo/a algn A *or* CON algo/algn** to put sth/sb on a level WITH sth/sb **(b)** (comparar) **~ algo CON algo** to compare sth TO *o* WITH sth

equipo *m* **1** (de trabajadores, jugadores) team; **el ~ local/visitante** the home/visiting team; **trabajo de ~** team work; **trabajar en ~** to work as a team **2** (de materiales, utensilios) equipment; **~ de pesca** fishing tackle; **~ de gimnasia** gym kit; **~ de alta fidelidad** hi-fi system

equis *f*: *name of the letter* x

equitación *f* riding, horseback riding (AmE), horse riding (BrE); **practica (la) ~** he rides

equitativo -va *adj* ‹*persona*› fair; ‹*reparto*› equitable

equivalente *adj* equivalent; **~ A algo** equivalent TO sth ■ *m* equivalent; **~ A *or* DE algo** equivalent OF sth

equivaler [E28] *vi* **~ A algo** to be equivalent TO sth; **¿a cuánto equivalen mil pesetas en libras?** how much is a thousand pesetas equivalent to *o* worth in pounds?

equivocación *f* mistake; **por ~** by mistake, in error (frml)

equivocado -da *adj* **(a)** ‹*dato/número/respuesta*› wrong **(b)** [ESTAR] ‹*persona*› mistaken, wrong

equivocar [A2] *vt* ‹*persona*› to make ... make a mistake, to make ... go wrong

■ **equivocarse** *v pron* (cometer un error) to make a mistake; (estar en un error) to be wrong *o* mistaken; **me equivoqué con él** I was wrong about him; **me equivoqué de autobús** I took the wrong bus; **no te equivoques de fecha** don't get the date wrong; **se equivocó de camino** he went the wrong way

era *f* (período, época) era, age

era, éramos, etc *see* SER

eras *see* SER

erección *f* erection

erecto -ta *adj* erect

eres *see* SER

erguido -da *adj* upright

erguir [I26] *vt* (liter) ‹*cabeza*› to raise, lift; ‹*cuello*› to straighten
■ **erguirse** *v pron* (liter) «*persona*» to stand up; «*edificio/torre*» to rise

erizado -da *adj* (de punta): **tenía el pelo ~** her hair was standing on end

erizar [A4] *vt* ‹*pelo/vello*› to make ... stand on end
■ **erizarse** *v pron* «*pelo*» to stand on end

erizo *m* hedgehog; **~ de mar** sea urchin

ermita *f* chapel

ermitaño -ña *m,f* (asceta) hermit

erosión *f* erosion

erosionar [A1] *vt* to erode
■ **erosionarse** *v pron* to be/become eroded

erótico -ca *adj* erotic

erotismo *m* eroticism

erradicar [A2] *vt* (frml) to eradicate

errado -da *adj* **1** (desacertado): **cinco tiros ~s** five misses **2** (esp AmL) **(a)** [ESTAR] ‹*persona*› mistaken, wrong; **están muy ~s en estos cálculos** they're way off the mark with these calculations **(b)** [SER] ‹*decisión*› wrong; ‹*política*› misguided

errante *adj* **(a)** ‹*persona*› wandering (*before n*), roaming (*before n*); ‹*pueblo*› wandering (*before n*) **(b)**‹*mirada*› faraway, distant; **una vida ~** a nomadic existence

errar [A26] *vt* ‹*tiro/golpe*› to miss; **erró su vocación** she chose the wrong vocation/career ■ **~** *vi* «*tirador*» to miss; **erró en su decisión** he made the wrong decision

errata *f* (error de imprenta) misprint, printer's error; (error de mecanografía) typing error

erre *f*: *name of the letter* r

erróneo -nea *adj* (frml) ‹*decisión/afirmación*› wrong, erroneous (frml)

error *m* mistake; **cometer un ~** to make a mistake *o* an error; **~ de ortografía** spelling mistake; **~ de cálculo** miscalculation; **~ de imprenta** misprint, printer's error; **por ~** by mistake, in error (frml)

eructar [A1] *vi* to belch, burp (colloq)

eructo *m* belch, burp (colloq)

erudición *f* erudition (frml), learning

erudito -ta *adj* ‹*lenguaje/obra*› erudite; ‹*persona*› learned, knowledgeable; **~ EN algo** learned IN sth, knowledgeable ABOUT sth ■ *m,f* scholar

erupción *f* **(a)** (de volcán) eruption; **el volcán entró en ~** the volcano erupted **(b)** (en la piel) rash, eruption (frml)

es *see* SER

esbelto -ta *adj* slender

esbozar [A4] *vt* **(a)** ‹*figura*› to sketch **(b)** ‹*idea/tema*› to outline

esbozo *m* **(a)** (Art) sketch **(b)** (de proyecto) outline, rough draft

escabeche *m* pickling brine (*made with oil, vinegar, peppercorns and bay leaves*)

escabroso -sa *adj* **(a)** ‹*terreno*› rugged, rough **(b)** ‹*asunto/problema/tema*› thorny, tricky; ‹*escena/relato*› shocking

escabullirse [I9] *v pron* (escaparse) to slip away; **logró ~ entre la multitud** he managed to slip away into the crowd; **no puedes escabullirte de tus responsabilidades** you can't get away from your responsibilities

escafandra *f* diving suit

escala *f* **1** (en general) scale; **~ centígrada/Fahrenheit** centigrade *o* Celsius/Fahrenheit scale ▶ **406**; **~ de valores** set of values; **~ musical** (musical) scale; **la ~ social** the social scale; **hecho a ~** done to scale; **a gran ~** on a large scale **2** (Aviac, Náut) stopover; **hicimos ~ en Roma** we stopped over in Rome

escalada *f* **1** (Dep) (de montaña) climb, ascent **2** (aumento, subida): **una ~ de la violencia** an escalation of violence; **la ~ de los precios** the increase *o* escalation in prices

escalador -dora *m,f* (de montañas) mountaineer, climber; (de rocas) rock-climber; (en ciclismo) climber, mountain rider

escalafón *m* scale; **subir un puesto en el ~** to go up one step on the promotion ladder

escalar [A1] *vt* ‹*montaña/pared*› to climb, scale; (en jerarquía, clasificación) to climb (up) ■ **~** *vi* (Dep) to climb, go climbing

escaldar [A1] *vt* **(a)** ‹*acelgas/tomates*› to blanch, scald **(b)** ‹*manos/persona*› to scald
■ **escaldarse** *v pron* **(a)** (con agua, vapor) to scald oneself **(b)** «*bebé*» to get diaper (AmE) *o* (BrE) nappy rash

escalera *f* **1** (de edificio) stairs (*pl*), staircase; **bajó las ~s** he came downstairs *o* down the stairs; **el hueco de la ~** the stairwell; **~ (de) caracol** spiral staircase; **~ mecánica** escalator **2** (portátil) *tb* **~ de mano** ladder; (de tijera) stepladder **3** (en naipes) run; (juego de tablero) snakes and ladders

escalfar [A1] *vt* to poach

escalinata *f* staircase, steps (*pl*)

escalofriante *adj* ‹*crimen/escena*› horrifying; ‹*cifra*› staggering, incredible

escalofrío *m* shiver; **me da ~s** it makes me shiver *o* shudder; **tiene ~s** she's shivering

escalón *m* (peldaño) step; (travesaño) rung

escalonar [A1] *vt* ‹*pagos/vacaciones*› to stagger; ‹*terreno*› to terrace

escalope *m* escalope

escama *f* **(a)** (Zool) scale **(b)** (en la piel) flake

escamotear [A1] *vt* **(a)** (ocultar) ‹*naipe*› to palm; ‹*informe*› to keep ... secret; **nos escamoteaban la información** they were keeping the information (secret) from us **(b)** (robar) to swipe

escampar [A1] *v impers* to stop raining, to clear up ■ **~** *vi* (Col) to shelter

escanciar [A1] *vt* (frml) ‹*vino*› to serve; ‹*sidra*› to pour (*from a height*)

escandalizar [A4] *vt/vi* to shock
■ **escandalizarse** *v pron* to be shocked

escándalo *m* **1** (hecho, asunto chocante) scandal; **¡qué ~! ¡qué manera de vestir!** what a shocking *o* an outrageous way to dress! **2** (alboroto, jaleo) fuss; **tanto ~ para náda** all this fuss over nothing; **cuando lo sepa va a armar un ~** when she finds out she'll kick up a fuss; **no armen tanto ~**

don't make such a racket *o* row (colloq); **nada de ~s dentro del local** we don't want any trouble in here

escandaloso -sa *adj* **(a)** ‹*conducta*› shocking, scandalous; ‹*ropa*› outrageous; ‹*película*› shocking; ‹*vida*› scandalous **(b)** (ruidoso) ‹*persona/griterío*› noisy; ‹*risa*› loud, uproarious

Escandinavia *f* Scandinavia

escandinavo -va *adj/m,f* Scandinavian

escaño *m* (Esp) (Pol) (cargo, asiento) seat; (banco) bench

escapada *f* **(a)** (huida) breakout, escape **(b)** (de un peligro) escape **(c)** (en ciclismo) breakaway

escapar [A1] *vi* **1** to escape; **~ DE algo** ‹*de cárcel/rutina/peligro*› to escape FROM sth; ‹*de castigo/muerte*› to escape sth **2 dejar escapar** ‹*carcajada/suspiro*› to let out, give; ‹*oportunidad*› to pass up; ‹*persona/animal*› to let ... get away

■ **escaparse** *v pron* **1** «*prisionero*» to escape; «*animal/niño*» to run away; **~se DE algo** ‹*de cárcel/jaula*› to escape FROM sth; ‹*de situación/castigo*› to escape sth; **~se DE algn** ‹*de policía/perseguidor*› to escape (FROM) sth; **~se de casa** to run away from home; **se me escapó el peno** the dog got away from me **2** (+ *me/te/le etc*) **(a)** (involuntariamente): **se le escapó un grito** he cried out, he let out a cry **(b)** (pasar inadvertido): **no se le escapa nada** he doesn't miss anything; **se me escapó ese detalle** that detail escaped my notice **3** «*gas/aire/agua*» to leak

escaparate *m* **(a)** (esp Esp) (de tienda) shop window **(b)** (Col) (vitrina) display cabinet; (aparador) sideboard **(c)** (Ven) (armario) wardrobe

escapatoria *f* (salida, solución) way out

escape *m* **(a)** (fuga) escape **(b)** (de gas, fluido) leak **(c)** (Auto) exhaust

escapismo *m* escapism

escarabajo *m* beetle

escaramuza *f* (Mil) skirmish; (Dep) scrimmage

escarbadientes *m* (*pl* ~) toothpick

escarbar [A1] *vi* **(a)** (en la tierra — haciendo un hoyo) to dig; (— superficialmente) to scrabble *o* scratch around **(b)** (buscando algo) **~ EN algo** ‹*en cajón/armario*› to rummage (about *o* around) IN sth; **perros escarbando en la basura** dogs rummaging through the garbage ■ **~** *vt*: **~ la tierra** (hacer un hoyo) to dig a hole; (superficialmente) to scratch around in the soil

■ **escarbarse** *v pron* (*refl*) ‹*nariz/dientes*› to pick

escarcha *f* frost

escarchar [A1] *vt* to crystallize

escarlata *adj inv/m* scarlet

escarlatina *f* scarlet fever, scarlatina

escarmentar [A5] *vi* to learn one's lesson; **¡para que escarmientes!** that'll teach you!; **no escarmienta** she never learns ■ **~** *vt* to teach ... a lesson

escarmiento *m* lesson; **habrá que darle un buen ~** he needs to be taught a good lesson

escarola *f* escarole, endive (BrE)

escarpado -da *adj* ‹*montaña/terreno*› precipitous; ‹*pared/acantilado*› sheer, steep

escarpín *m* (AmL) (calcetín — de bebé) bootee; (— de adulto) bed sock

escasear [A1] *vi*: **empiezan a ~ los alimentos** food is running short; **va a ~ el café** there's going to be a coffee shortage

escasez *f* shortage; **hubo ~ de agua** there was a water shortage; **por ~ de medios** owing to a lack of resources

escaso -sa *adj* **(a)** ‹*recursos económicos*› limited, scant; ‹*posibilidades*› slim, slender; ‹*visibilidad*› poor; ‹*conocimientos/experiencia*› limited **(b)** [ESTAR] (falto) **~ DE algo** ‹*de dinero/tiempo*› short OF sth

escatimar [A1] *vt* ‹*comida/tela*› to skimp on, be sparing with; **no ~on esfuerzos** they spared no effort

escayola *f* (Esp) (material) plaster; (Med) plaster cast

escayolar [A1] *vt* (Esp) to put ... in a (plaster) cast, to put ... in plaster (BrE)

escena *f* **1 (a)** (de obra) scene; **la ~ del duelo** the duel scene **(b)** (*sin art*) (escenario): **poner en ~** to stage; **entrar en ~** to come/go on stage **2 la ~ del accidente** (period) the scene of the accident; **no me hagas una ~** there's no need to make a scene

escenario *m* (Teatr) stage

escenografía *f* (decorado) scenery; (arte) scenography, set design

escenógrafo -fa *m,f* scenographer, set designer

escepticismo *m* skepticism*

escéptico -ca *adj* skeptical* ■ *m,f* skeptic*

esclarecer [E3] *vt* ‹*situación/hechos*› to clarify, elucidate (frml); ‹*crimen/misterio*› to clear up

esclavitud *f* slavery

esclavizar [A4] *vt* to enslave; **está esclavizado por el trabajo** he's a slave to his work

esclavo -va *m,f* slave; **es un ~ del trabajo** he is a slave to his work

esclerosis *f* sclerosis; **~ múltiple** multiple sclerosis

esclusa *f* (de canal) lock; (de presa) floodgate

escoba *f* (para barrer) broom; (de bruja) broomstick

escobilla *f* **(a)** (de motor) brush **(b)** (del limpiaparabrisas) wiper-blade, blade **(c)** (del inodoro) toilet brush

escocedura *f* irritation; (de bebé) diaper rash (AmE), nappy rash (BrE)

escocer [E10] *vi* «*herida/ojos*» to sting, smart

escocés -cesa *adj* **(a)** ‹*ciudad/persona*› Scottish; ‹*dialecto*› Scots **(b)** ‹*whisky*› Scotch; ‹*tela/manta*› tartan ■ *m,f* (*m*) Scotsman, Scot; (*f*) Scotswoman, Scot

Escocia *f* Scotland

escocido -da *adj* ‹*cuello/axila*› sore, chafed; **tiene las nalgas escocidas** he has diaper rash (AmE) *o* (BrE) nappy rash

escoger [E6] *vt* to choose; **escoge que quieras** pick *o* choose whichever (one) you want; **no hay mucho (de) donde ~** there isn't a great deal of choice, there isn't much to choose from

escogido -da *adj* **(a)** (selecto) ‹*mercancía*› choice; ‹*clientela*› select **(b)** (Méx fam) (manoseado) picked over

escolar *adj* school (*before n*) ■ *m,f* (*m*) schoolboy, schoolchild; (*f*) schoolgirl, schoolchild

escolarizar [A4] *vt* to educate, provide schooling for; **niños sin ~** children without any (formal) education *o* schooling

escoleta *f* (Méx) **(a)** (banda) band (*of amateur musicians*) **(b)** (ensayo) rehearsal

escollo *m* (Náut) reef; (dificultad) obstacle, hurdle

escolta *mf* (persona) escort; (en baloncesto) guard ■ *f* (grupo) escort

escoltar [A1] *vt* to escort

escombros *mpl* rubble

esconder [E1] *vt* to hide, conceal (frml) ■ **esconderse** *v pron* **1** (*refl*) «*persona*» to hide; **~se DE algn** to hide FROM sb **2** (estar oculto) to hide, lie hidden

escondidas *fpl* **1** (AmL) (Jueg): **jugar a las ~** to play hide-and-seek **2 a escondidas** in secret, secretly; **hacer algo a ~ de algn** to do sth behind sb's back

escondido -da *adj* **(a)** (oculto) hidden **(b)** (lejano) remote

escondite *m* **(a)** (para personas) hideout; (para cosas) hiding place **(b)** (Jueg): **jugar al ~** to play hide-and-seek

escondrijo *m* hidden place, recess (liter)

escopeta *f* shotgun

escoria *f* (de fundición) slag; **la ~ de la sociedad** the dregs of society

Escorpio *m* (signo) Scorpio; **es (de) ~** he's a Scorpio ■ *mf* (*pl* **~** *or* **-pios**) (persona) *tb* **escorpio** Scorpio

escorpión *m* scorpion

escotado -da *adj* **(a)** ‹*blusa/vestido*› low-cut; **~ por detrás** cut low at the back **(b)** (RPl) ‹*zapato*› strapless

escote *m* (Indum) neck, neckline; (profundo) low-cut neck *o* neckline; **~ redondo** round neck; (en suéters) crew neck; **~ en pico** V neck; ***pagar a ~*** (Esp fam) to go Dutch

escotilla *f* hatch, hatchway

escozor *m* **(a)** (Med) stinging, burning sensation **(b)** (resentimiento, amargura) bitterness

escribanía *f* (RPl) (Der) (oficina) notary's office; (profesión): **ejerce la ~** he is a practicing notary (public)

escribano -na *m,f* **(a)** (Hist) (amanuense) scribe **(b)** (RPl) (notario) notary (public)

escribir [I34] *vt* **1 (a)** (anotar) to write; **escríbelo aquí** write it down here **(b)** (ser autor de) ‹*libro/canción/carta*› to write **2** (ortográficamente) to write; **la escribió sin acento** she wrote it without an accent; **no sé cómo se escribe** I don't know how you spell it; **se escribe sin acento** it's written without an accent ■ **~** *vi* to write; **nunca le escribe** she never writes him (AmE) *o* (BrE) writes to him; **~ a máquina** to type

■ **escribirse** *v pron* (*recípr*): **me escribo con ella** we write to each other; **se escribe con un peruano** she has a Peruvian penfriend *o* penpal

escrito¹ -ta *adj* ‹*examen*› written; **por ~** in writing

escrito² *m* (documento) document

escritor -tora *m,f* writer, author

escritorio *m* **(a)** (mueble) desk **(b)** (AmL) (oficina, despacho) office; (en casa particular) study; **~ público** (en Méx) *office or stall offering letter writing, form-filling or typing services*

escritura *f* **1** (sistema de signos) writing; (letra) writing, handwriting **2** (Der) (documento) deed; **la ~ de la casa** the deeds to *o* of the house

escrúpulo *m* scruple

escrupuloso -sa *adj* **(a)** (honrado) honest, scrupulous **(b)** (meticuloso) meticulous **(c)** (Esp) (aprensivo) fastidious

escrutinio *m* **(a)** (Pol) count; **los resultados del ~** the results of the ballot **(b)** (inspección) scrutiny

escuadra *f* **1** (instrumento — triangular) set square; (— de carpintero) square **2** (en el ejército) squad; (en la marina) squadron

escuadrón *m* **(a)** (Aviac) squadron **(b)** (de caballería) squadron; (más pequeño) troop

escuálido -da *adj* ‹*persona/animal*› skinny, scrawny

escuchar [A1] *vt* **(a)** (prestar atención) ‹*música/persona*› to listen to **(b)** (esp AmL) (oír) to hear ■ **~** *vi* to listen

escudarse [A1] *v pron*: **quiso ~ en su inmunidad diplomática** he tried to hide behind his diplomatic immunity

escudilla *f* bowl

escudo *m* **(a)** (Hist, Mil) shield **(b)** (emblema) *tb* **~ de armas** coat of arms **(c)** (en la solapa, etc) badge

escudriñar [A1] *vt* **(a)** (liter) (mirar intensamente) ‹*horizonte*› to scan **(b)** (examinar) ‹*persona*› to scrutinize, examine; ‹*casa/habitación*› to search ... thoroughly

escuela *f* school; **~ de conductores** *or* **choferes** (AmL) driving school; **~ primaria** primary school; **~ militar/naval** military/naval academy; **~ pública** public (AmE) *o* (BrE) state school; **E~ de Medicina** Medical Faculty *o* School

escueto -ta *adj* ‹*explicación*› succinct; ‹*lenguaje/estilo*› concise, plain; **fue muy ~** he was very succinct

escuincle -cla *m,f* (Méx fam) kid (colloq)

esculcar [A2] *vt* (AmC, Col, Méx, Ven) ‹*cajones/papeles*› to go through; ‹*persona/casa*› to search

esculpir [I1] *vt* ‹*estatua/busto*› to sculpt, sculpture; ‹*inscripción*› to engrave, carve ■ **~** *vi* to sculpt, sculpture

escultor -tora *m,f* sculptor

escultura *f* sculpture; **~ en madera** wood carving

escupida *f* (RPl) gob (of spit) (colloq)

escupir [I1] *vi* to spit; **~le A algn** to spit AT sb; **le escupió en la cara** he spat in her face ■ **~** *vt* **(a)**

‹*comida*› to spit out; ‹*sangre*› to spit, cough up **(b)** ‹*llamas/lava*› to belch out

escupitajo *m* gob (of spit) (colloq)

escupo *m* (Chi, Ven) gob (of spit) (colloq)

escurreplatos *m* (*pl* ~) (mueble) *cupboard with built-in plate rack*; (rejilla) plate rack

escurridizo -za *adj* ‹*piel/jabón*› slippery; ‹*persona/respuesta*› evasive; ‹*idea/concepto*› elusive

escurrir [I1] *vt* ‹*ropa*› to wring out, wring; ‹*verduras/pasta*› to strain, drain; ‹*líquido*› to drain (off) ■ ~ *vi* to drain; **dejar ~** ‹*platos*› to leave ... to drain; ‹*camisa*› to leave ... to drip-dry
■ **escurrirse** *v pron* **1 (a)** «*líquido*»: **cuelga la camisa para que se escurra el agua** hang the shirt out to drip-dry **(b)** «*verduras/vajilla*» to drain **2 (a)** (fam) (escaparse, escabullirse) to slip away; **~se DE algo** to wriggle *o* get out OF sth **(b)** (resbalarse, deslizarse) to slip

escúter *m* scooter

esdrújula *f* word with the stress on the antepenultimate syllable

ese[1] *f*: *name of the letter* s

ese[2], **esa** *adj dem* (*pl* **esos, esas**) that; (*pl*) those; **en ~ país/esos países** in that country/those countries

ése, **ésa** *pron dem* (*pl* **ésos, ésas**) **(a)** that one; (*pl*) those; **~ es el tuyo** that (one) is yours; **prefiero ésos** I prefer those (ones); [*usually indicates disapproval when used to refer to a person*] **ésa no sabe lo que dice** (fam) she doesn't know what she's talking about **(b) ésas** (fam) (esas cosas, esos asuntos): **¡conque ésas tenemos!** so *that's* it!; **¡no me vengas con ésas!** don't give me that! (colloq)

esencia *f* essence

esencial *adj* (fundamental) essential; **coincidimos en lo ~** we agree on the essentials *o* on the main points; **lo ~ es** ... the main *o* the most important thing is ...

esfera *f* **(a)** (Astron, Mat) sphere **(b)** (de reloj) face **(c)** (ámbito) sphere; **en las altas ~s de la política** in the highest political circles

esférico -ca *adj* spherical

esfero *m* (Col fam) ballpoint pen, biro® (BrE)

esfinge *f* sphinx

esforzar [A11] *vt* ‹*voz/vista*› to strain
■ **esforzarse** *v pron*: **se esforzó mucho** he tried very hard, he put in a lot of effort; **tienes que ~te más** you'll have to work harder; **~se POR** *o* **EN hacer algo** to strive to do sth

esfuerzo *m* effort; **hizo el ~ de ser amable** he made an effort *o* tried to be friendly

esfumarse [A1] *v pron* **(a)** «*ilusiones/sueños*» to evaporate; «*temores*» to melt away, be dispelled **(b)** (fam) «*persona/dinero*» to vanish, disappear

esgrima *f* fencing

esgrimista *mf* fencer

esguince *m* sprain; **sufrió un ~ en el tobillo** he sprained his ankle

eslabón *m* link

eslálom (*pl* **-loms**), **eslalon** *m* slalom

eslavo -va *adj* Slavic, Slavonic ■ *m,f* Slav

eslogan *m* (*pl* **-lóganes**) slogan

eslovaco[1] **-ca** *adj* Slovakian ■ *m,f* Slovak

eslovaco[2] *m* (idioma) Slovak

Eslovaquia *f* Slovakia

esmaltar [A1] *vt* ‹*metal*› to enamel; ‹*cerámica*› to glaze

esmalte *m* **(a)** (capa — sobre metales) enamel; (— sobre cerámica) glaze; **~ de** *or* **para uñas** nail polish *o* (BrE) varnish **(b)** (Odont) enamel **(c)** (Art) enamel

esmerado -da *adj* ‹*persona*› conscientious, painstaking; ‹*presentación*› careful, painstaking; ‹*trabajo*› carefully done

esmeralda *f* emerald

esmerarse [A1] *v pron* to go to a lot of trouble; **se esmera en hacerlo bien** she goes to great pains to do it properly

esmero *m* care

esmirriado -da *adj* (fam) ‹*persona*› skinny (colloq), scrawny (colloq); ‹*animal*› scrawny

esmog *m* smog

esmoquin *m* (*pl* **-móquines**) tuxedo (AmE), dinner jacket (BrE)

esnifar [A1] *vt* ‹*cocaína*› (arg) to snort (sl); ‹*pegamento*› to sniff (colloq)

esnob *adj* (*pl* **-nobs**) snobbish ■ *mf* (*pl* **-nobs**) snob

esnobismo *m* snobbery, snobbishness

eso *pron dem* **(a)** (*neutro*) that; **no digas ~** don't say that; **~ que te contaron** what they told you **(b)** (*en locs*) **a eso de** (at) around *o* about; **en eso**: **en ~ llegó su madre** (just) at that moment her mother arrived; **¡eso es!** that's it!; **y eso que** ... even though ... **(c) ¡eso!** (*interj*) exactly!

esófago *m* ▶ 123 esophagus*

esos, **esas** *adj dem*: *ver* ESE[2]

ésos, **ésas** *pron dem*: *ver* ÉSE

espabilado -da *adj* **(a)** (despierto) awake **(b)** (vivo, listo) bright, smart; **tienes que ser más ~** you have to keep more on the ball ■ *m,f*: **los ~s de la clase** the smart ones of the class

espabilar [A1] *vt* **(a)** (quitar el sueño) to wake ... up **(b)** (avivar) to wise ... up (colloq) ■ ~ *vi* **(a)** (sacudirse el sueño) to wake up **(b)** (darse prisa) to get a move on (colloq) **(c)** (avivarse) to wise up (colloq)
■ **espabilarse** *v pron* **(a)** (sacudirse el sueño) to wake (oneself) up **(b)** (darse prisa) to get a move on (colloq) **(c)** (avivarse) to wise up (colloq)

espaciado -da *adj* **(a)** (en el espacio): **los árboles están muy ~s** the trees are too far apart **(b)** (en el tiempo): **sus visitas se hicieron más espaciadas** her visits became more infrequent

espacial *adj* **(a)** ‹*cohete/vuelo*› space (*before n*) **(b)** (Fís, Mat) spatial

espacio *m* **1 (a)** (amplitud) space, room; **ocupan demasiado ~** they take up too much space *o* room **(b)** (entre líneas, palabras) space; (entre objetos) space, gap; **rellenar los ~s en blanco** fill in the blank spaces *o* the blanks **(c)** (recinto, área) area **2** (Espac): **el ~** space; **~ aéreo** airspace **3** (de tiempo): **un**

corto ~ de tiempo a short space of time; **por ~ de 24 horas** for 24 hours *o* for a period of 24 hours **4 (a)** (Rad, TV) (programa) program*; **~ publicitario** advertising slot **(b)** (en periódico, revista) space

espacioso -sa *adj* spacious

espada *f* **1** (arma) sword **2 (a)** (carta) *any card of the* ESPADAS *suit* **(b) espadas** *fpl* (palo) *one of the suits in a Spanish pack of cards*

espagetis, **espaguettis** *mpl* spaghetti

espalda *f* ▶ 123 back; **ancho de ~s** broad-shouldered; **perdona, te estoy dando la ~** sorry, I've got my back to you; **de ~s a nosotros** with his/her back to us; **vuélvete de ~s** turn around *o* (BrE) round; **los 100 metros ~** the 100 meters backstroke; **tenderse de ~s** to lie on one's back; **lo atacaron por la ~** he was attacked from behind; ***hacer algo a ~s de algn*** to do sth behind sb's back

espantado -da *adj* **(a)** (asustado) frightened, scared; **salieron ~s** they ran off in fright **(b)** (horrorizado) horrified, appalled

espantapájaros *m* (*pl* ~) scarecrow

espantar [A1] *vt* **1 (a)** (ahuyentar) ‹*peces/pájaros*› to frighten away **(b)** (asustar) ‹*caballo*› to frighten, scare **2** (fam) (horrorizar) to horrify, appall* ■ ~ *vi* **(a)** (fam) (asustar): **es tan feo que espanta** he's absolutely hideous (colloq) **(b)** (Bol, Col, Ven fam) «*fantasma*»: **en esa casa espantan** that house is haunted

■ **espantarse** *v pron* «*pájaro/peces*» to get frightened away; «*caballo*» to take fright, be startled

espanto *m* **1 (a)** (miedo) fright, horror **(b)** (uso hiperbólico): **la noticia nos llenó de ~** we were horrified *o* appalled at the news; **hace un frío de ~** (fam) it's freezing *o* terribly cold (colloq); **ya está curada de ~** (fam) she's seen/heard it all before **2** (Bol, Col, Ven fam) (espíritu) ghost, spook (colloq)

espantoso -sa *adj* **(a)** ‹*escena/crimen*› horrific, appalling **(b)** (fam) (uso hiperbólico) ‹*comida/letra/tiempo*› atrocious; ‹*vestido/color*› hideous; ‹*ruido/voz*› terrible, awful; **pasé un frío ~** I was absolutely freezing (colloq)

España *f* Spain

español[1] -ñola *adj* Spanish ■ *m,f* (persona) (*m*) Spaniard, Spanish man; (*f*) Spaniard, Spanish woman; **los ~es** the Spanish, Spaniards, Spanish people

español[2] *m* (idioma) Spanish

esparadrapo *m* surgical tape

esparcir [I4] *vt* **(a)** ‹*libros/juguetes*› to scatter **(b)** ‹*rumor*› to spread **(c)** (Chi) ‹*mantequilla*› to spread

■ **esparcirse** *v pron* **(a)** «*líquido*» to spread; «*papeles/semillas*» to be scattered **(b)** «*noticia/rumor*» to spread

espárrago *m* asparagus; ***mandar a algn a freír ~s*** (fam) to tell sb to get lost (colloq)

espasmo *m* spasm

espátula *f* **(a)** (paleta) spatula; (Art) palette knife **(b)** (para quitar pintura, papel) scraper

especia *f* (condimento) spice

especial *adj* **(a)** (en general) special; **en ~** especially, particularly; **nadie en ~** nobody in particular; **un día muy ~ para mí** a very special day for me **(b)** (difícil) ‹*persona/carácter*› fussy

especialidad *f* **(a)** (actividad, estudio) specialty (AmE), speciality (BrE); **hizo dos años de ~** she did two years' specialization **(b)** (de restaurante) specialty (AmE), speciality (BrE)

especialista *adj* specialist (*before n*) ■ *mf* **(a)** (experto) specialist, expert **(b)** (Med) specialist; **un ~ de(l) corazón** a heart specialist **(c)** (Cin, TV) (*m*) stuntman; (*f*) stuntwoman

especialización *f* specialization

especializado -da *adj* **(a)** ‹*librería/restaurante*› specialty (*before n*) (AmE), specialist (*before n*) (BrE); **~** EN **algo** specializing IN sth **(b)** ‹*lenguaje*› technical, specialized **(c)** ‹*obrero*› skilled, specialized (*before n*)

especializarse [A4] *v pron* to specialize

especie *f* **(a)** (Biol, Bot, Zool) species **(b)** (clase) kind, sort

especificar [A2] *vt* to specify

específico -ca *adj* specific

espécimen *m* (*pl* **-pecímenes**) (ejemplar) specimen; (muestra) sample, specimen

espectacular *adj* spectacular

espectáculo *m* **1** (representación) show; ⓢ **espectáculos** (en periódicos) entertainment guide; **el mundo del ~** showbusiness **2** (visión, panorama) sight; **un triste ~** a sad sight *o* spectacle

espectador -dora *m,f* (Dep) spectator; (Espec) member of the audience; **asistieron al estreno dos mil ~es** two thousand people attended the premiere

espectro *m* **1** (gama) spectrum **2** (fantasma) specter*, ghost; (amenaza) specter*

especulación *f* speculation

especulador -dora *m,f* speculator

especular [A1] *vi* to speculate

espejismo *m* (fenómeno óptico) mirage; (ilusión) illusion

espejo *m* mirror; **~ de cuerpo entero** full-length mirror; **~ lateral/retrovisor** wing/rear-view mirror; **mirarse al ~** to look (at oneself) in the mirror; **la obra es ~ de esa sociedad** the play mirrors that society

espeleología *f* spelunking, potholing (BrE)

espeluznante *adj* ‹*tragedia/estado/experiencia*› horrific, horrifying; ‹*grito*› terrifying, bloodcurdling

espera *f* **1** (acción, período) wait; **una larga ~** a long wait; **estoy a la ~ de una oferta concreta** I am waiting for a concrete offer; **en ~ de su respuesta saluda a Vd. atte.** (frml) I look forward to hearing from you, yours faithfully **2** (Der) respite

esperado -da *adj* **(a)** (aguardado) ‹*acontecimiento/carta*› eagerly awaited **(b)** (que es de esperar): **no obtuvo los resultados ~s** he didn't get the results he expected

esperanza *f* hope; **mi única ~** my only hope; **puso todas sus ~s en su hijo** he pinned all his hopes on his son; **hay ~s de éxito** there are hopes that he/it/they will succeed; **perdimos toda ~ de encontrarlos vivos** we gave up *o* lost hope of finding them alive; **fue con la ~ de que** ... he went in the hope that ...; **me dio ~s de que el niño mejoraría** he gave me hope that the child would recover

esperanzado -da *adj* hopeful

esperanzador -dora *adj* encouraging

esperar [A1] *vt* **1 (a)** ‹*autobús/persona/acontecimiento*› to wait for; **¿qué estás esperando para decírselo?** tell him! what are you waiting for? **(b)** (recibir) to meet; **la fuimos a ~ al aeropuerto** we went to meet her at the airport **(c)** «*sorpresa*» to await; **le espera un futuro difícil** he has a difficult future ahead of him **2 (a)** (contar con, prever) to expect; **tal como esperábamos** just as we expected; **cuando uno menos lo espera** when you least expect it; **te espero alrededor de las nueve** I'll expect you around nine; **¿esperabas que te felicitara?** did you expect me to congratulate you?; **era de ~ que el proyecto fracasara** the project was bound to fail **(b)** ‹*niño/bebé*› to be expecting **3** (con esperanza) to hope; **eso espero** *or* **espero que sí** I hope so; **espero que no** I hope not; **~ hacer algo** to hope to do sth; **espero que no llueva** I hope it doesn't rain; **esperemos que no sea nada grave** let's hope it's nothing serious ■ **~** *vi* **(a)** (aguardar) to wait; **no podemos ~ más** we can't wait any longer; **espera a estar seguro** wait until you're sure; **~on (a) que él se fuera para entrar** they waited for him to go before they went in **(b)** «*embarazada*»: **estar esperando** to be expecting

■ **esperarse** *v pron* **1** (fam) (aguardar) to hang on (colloq), to hold on (colloq) **2** (fam) (prever) to expect; **¡quién se lo iba a ~!** who would have thought it!

esperma *m or f* (Biol) sperm ■ *f* **(a)** (sustancia) spermaceti **(b)** (Col) (vela) candle

espesar [A1] *vt/vi* to thicken

■ **espesarse** *v pron* «*salsa*» to thicken; «*vegetación*» to become thick, become dense

espeso -sa *adj* **(a)** ‹*salsa*› thick; ‹*vegetación/niebla*› dense, thick; ‹*nieve*› thick, deep; ‹*cabello/barba*› bushy, thick **(b)** (Per fam) (cargoso) annoying

espesor *m* thickness

espesura *f* vegetation; **se abrieron paso por entre la ~** they hacked a path through the vegetation

espía *adj inv* ‹*avión/satélite*› spy (*before n*); ‹*cámara*› hidden (*before n*), secret (*before n*) ■ *mf* (persona) spy

espiar [A17] *vt* ‹*enemigo/movimientos*› to spy on, keep watch on ■ **~** *vi* to spy

espiga *f* (Agr, Bot) (de trigo) ear, spike; (de flores) spike

espigón *m* **(a)** (rompeolas) breakwater **(b)** (Per, RPl) (en aeropuerto) terminal (building)

espina *f* **(a)** (de rosal, zarza) thorn; (de cactus) prickle **(b)** (de pez) bone **(c)** (Anat) spine; **~ dorsal** spine, backbone; ***darle a algn mala ~*** to make sb feel uneasy; **esto me da mala ~** I don't like the look of this

espinaca *f* spinach

espinazo *m* spine, backbone

espinilla *f* **1** (Anat) shin **2** (en la piel) **(a)** (de cabeza negra) blackhead **(b)** (AmL) (barrito) pimple, spot

espino *m* hawthorn

espinoso -sa *adj* **1 (a)** ‹*rosal/zarza*› thorny; ‹*cactus*› prickly **(b)** ‹*pescado*› bony **2** ‹*problema/asunto*› thorny, knotty

espionaje *m* spying, espionage; **novela de ~** spy novel

espiral *f* **(a)** (forma, movimiento) spiral; **un cuaderno de ~(es)** a spiral-bound notebook; **escalera de ~** spiral staircase **(b)** (muelle) hairspring **(c)** (dispositivo intrauterino) coil

espirar [A1] *vi* to breathe out, exhale

espiritismo *m* spiritualism; **sesión de ~** séance

espiritista *adj/mf* spiritualist

espíritu *m* **(a)** (en general) spirit; **un ~ maligno** an evil spirit; **E~ Santo** Holy Ghost *o* Spirit; **con ~ de sacrificio** in a spirit of self-sacrifice; **el ~ de la ley** the spirit of the law **(b)** (naturaleza, carácter) nature; **tiene un ~ rebelde** she has a rebellious nature

espiritual *adj* spiritual ■ *m*: *tb* **~ negro** (Negro) spiritual

espita *f* spigot (AmE), tap (BrE)

espléndido -da *adj* **(a)** ‹*fiesta/comida*› splendid, magnificent; ‹*día/tiempo*› splendid, marvelous*; ‹*regalo/joya/abrigo*› magnificent **(b)** (generoso) ‹*persona*› generous; ‹*regalo*› lavish, generous

esplendor *m* **(a)** (magnificencia) splendor*, magnificence **(b)** (apogeo) splendor*

espolear [A1] *vt* ‹*caballo*› to spur (on)

espoleta *f* (Arm) fuse

espolvorear [A1] *vt* to sprinkle

esponja *f* sponge

esponjoso -sa *adj* ‹*masa/bizcocho*› spongy, fluffy; ‹*tejido*› soft; ‹*lana*› fluffy

espontaneidad *f* spontaneity

espontáneo -nea *adj* ‹*persona/gesto/ayuda*› spontaneous; ‹*actuación*› impromptu ■ *m,f*: *spectator who jumps into the ring to join in the bullfight*

esporádico -ca *adj* ‹*sucesos/visitas*› sporadic, intermittent

esposado -da *adj* handcuffed, in handcuffs

esposas *fpl* handcuffs (*pl*)

esposo -sa *m,f* (*m*) husband; (*f*) wife

espray *m* (*pl* **-prays**) **(a)** (atomizador) spray **(b)** (pintura) spray paint

esprint *m* (*pl* **-prints**) sprint

espuela *f* spur

espuelear [A1] *vt* (AmL) to spur (on)

espuma *f* **1 (a)** (del mar) foam; (al romper las olas) surf; (en agua revuelta) foam, froth **(b)** (del jabón) lather; **este jabón no hace ~** this soap doesn't lather; **un baño de ~** a foam *o* bubble bath; **~ de afeitar** shaving foam; **~ seca** carpet shampoo **(c)** (de la cerveza) head, froth **(d)** (Coc) (capa) scum **2 (a)** (caucho celular) foam rubber **(b)** (tejido elástico) stretch nylon

espumadera *f* skimmer, slotted spoon

espumante *m* sparkling wine
espumillón *m* tinsel
espumoso[1] -sa *adj* ‹*ola*› foaming; ‹*cerveza*› frothy; ‹*vino*› sparkling
espumoso[2] *m* sparkling wine
esqueje *m* (para plantar) cutting; (para injertar) scion
esquela *f* **(a)** (AmL) (carta) note **(b)** (Andes) (papel) stationery set **(c)** (Esp) (aviso fúnebre) *tb* **~ mortuoria** death notice
esqueleto *m* **(a)** (Anat) skeleton **(b)** (de edificio, novela) framework
esquema *m* **1** (croquis) sketch, diagram; (sinopsis) outline **2** (de ideas): **el ~ liberal** liberal philosophy *o* thinking; **no se sale de sus ~s** she doesn't change her way of thinking
esquemático -ca *adj* schematic; **el libro es algo ~** the book is a little oversimplified
esquematizar [A4] *vt/vi* to schematize
esquí *m* (*pl* **-quís** *or* **-quíes**) (tabla) ski; (deporte) skiing; **pista de ~** ski run, piste; **~ acuático** *or* **náutico** waterskiing; **hacer ~ acuático** to water-ski
esquiador -dora *m,f* skier
esquiar [A17] *vi* to ski
esquilar [A1] *vt* to shear, clip
esquimal *adj/mf* Eskimo
esquina *f* **(a)** (en calle) corner; **en la calle Vidal, ~ (a) Cádiz** on the corner of Vidal (Street) and Cadiz (Street); **doblar la ~** to go round *o* turn the corner; **hace ~ con la plaza** it's on the corner of the square **(b)** (Dep): **sacar de ~** to take a corner (kick)
esquinazo *m* **1** (Esp): **darle (el) ~ a algn** (dejar plantado) to stand sb up; (esquivar) to give sb the slip **2** (Chi) (serenata) *serenade of traditional singing and dancing*
esquirol *mf* (pey) strikebreaker, scab (pej)
esquivar [A1] *vt* ‹*persona/problema/dificultad*› to avoid; ‹*golpe/pregunta*› to dodge, evade; ‹*responsabilidad*› to avoid, evade
esquivo -va *adj* **(a)** ‹*persona*› (difícil de encontrar) elusive; (huraño) aloof, unsociable; (tímido) shy **(b)** ‹*respuesta*› elusive, evasive
esquizofrenia *f* schizophrenia
esquizofrénico -ca *adj/m,f* schizophrenic
estabilidad *f* stability
estabilizar [A4] *vt* to stabilize
■ **estabilizarse** *v pron* to stabilize
estable *adj* stable; ‹*trabajo*› steady
establecer [E3] *vt* **1 (a)** ‹*colonia/dictadura*› to establish; ‹*campamento*› to set up; **estableció su residencia en Mónaco** he took up residence in Monaco **(b)** ‹*relaciones/contacto*› to establish **2** (dejar sentado) **(a)** ‹*criterios/bases*› to establish, lay down; ‹*precio*› to fix, set; ‹*precedente*› to establish, set **(b)** (frml) «*ley/reglamento*» (disponer) to state, establish **(c)** ‹*récord/marca/moda*› to set; ‹*uso*› to establish **3** (determinar) to establish
■ **establecerse** *v pron* «*colono/emigrante*» to settle; «*comerciante/empresa*» to set up
establecimiento *m* establishment
establo *m* stable
estaca *f* **(a)** (poste) stake, post **(b)** (para carpa) tent peg **(c)** (garrote) club, stick **(d)** (clavo de madera) peg
estación *f* **1** (de tren, metro, autobús) station; **~ de bomberos** (Col, Méx, Ven) fire station; **~ de policía** (Col, Ven) police station; **~ de esquí** ski resort; **~ de servicio** service station, gas (AmE) *o* (BrE) petrol station; **~ terminal** *or* **término** terminal, terminus (BrE) **2** (del año) season **3** (AmL) (emisora) radio station
estacionamiento *m* **(a)** (acción de estacionar) parking **(b)** (espacio para estacionar) parking space; (en recinto cerrado) (AmL) parking lot (AmE), car park (BrE)
estacionar [A1] *vt* to park ■ **~** *vi* to park; Ⓢ **prohibido estacionar** no parking; **~ en doble fila** to double-park
■ **estacionarse** *v pron* **(a)** «*crecimiento*» to stop; «*peso*» to stabilize; «*proceso/enfermedad*» to halt **(b)** (Chi, Méx) «*conductor*» to park
estadía *f* (AmL) (en un lugar) stay
estadio *m* stadium
estadista *mf* (*m*) statesman; (*f*) stateswoman
estadística *f* **(a)** (estudio) statistical study **(b)** (cifra) statistic, figure **(c)** (disciplina) statistics
estadístico -ca *adj* statistical
estado *m* **1 (a)** (en general) state; **~ de ánimo** state of mind; **~ de cuenta** bank statement; **~ de emergencia** *or* **excepción** state of emergency; **la casa está en buen ~** the house is in good condition **(b)** (Med) condition; ***estar en ~*** (euf) to be expecting (colloq); ***quedarse en ~*** (euf) to get pregnant **(c) estado civil** marital status **2** (nación, gobierno) state; **la seguridad del E~** national *o* state security
Estados Unidos *m*: *tb* **los ~ ~** *mpl* the United States (+ *sing or pl vb*)
Estados Unidos Mexicanos *mpl* (frml) United States of Mexico (frml)
estadounidense *adj* American, US (*before n*) ■ *mf* American
estafa *f* **(a)** (Der) fraud, criminal deception **(b)** (fam) (timo) rip-off (colloq), con (colloq)
estafador -dora *m,f* **(a)** (Der) fraudster **(b)** (fam) (timador) swindler (colloq)
estafar [A1] *vt* **(a)** (Der) to swindle, defraud; **~le algo A algn** to defraud sb OF sth, swindle sb OUT OF sth **(b)** (fam) (timar) to rip ... off (colloq), to con (colloq)
estafeta *f*: *tb* **~ de correos** mail office (AmE), sub-post office (BrE)
estallar [A1] *vi* **(a)** «*bomba*» to explode; «*neumático*» to blow out, burst; «*globo*» to burst; «*vidrio*» to shatter; **hizo ~ el dispositivo** he detonated the device **(b)** «*guerra/revuelta*» to break out; «*tormenta/escándalo/crisis*» to break **(c)** «*persona*» (ponerse furioso) to blow one's top (colloq); **~ EN algo** ‹*en llanto/carcajadas*› to burst INTO sth
estallido *m* **(a)** (de bomba) explosion; (de neumático) bursting; (de cristal) shattering **(b)** (de guerra) outbreak
estamento *m* (de sociedad) stratum, class

estampado¹ -da *adj* patterned, printed
estampado² *m* pattern; **los ~s están de moda** patterned *o* printed fabrics are in fashion
estampar [A1] *vt* (imprimir) ‹*tela/diseño*› to print; ‹*metal*› to stamp; (formando relieve) to emboss
estampida *f* stampede; **salir en** *or* **de ~** to stampede out
estampido *m* (de pistola) bang, report; (de bomba) bang
estampilla *f* **(a)** (AmL) (sello — postal) postage (stamp); (— fiscal) tax stamp **(b)** (sello de goma) rubber stamp
estampillar [A1] *vt* (AmL) (con sello fiscal o de correos) to stamp
estancado -da *adj* **(a)** ‹*agua*› stagnant **(b)** (detenido): **las negociaciones están estancadas** negotiations are at a standstill **(c)** (con un problema) stuck, bogged down
estancamiento *m* stagnation
estancarse [A2] *v pron* **(a)** «*agua*» to become stagnant, to stagnate **(b)** «*negociación/proceso*» to come to a halt *o* standstill **(c)** (con un problema) to get bogged down *o* stuck
estancia *f* **1** (frml) (habitación) large room **2** (Esp, Méx) (permanencia) stay **3** (en el CS) (Agr) farm; (de ganado) ranch
estanciero -ra *m,f* (en el CS) (Agr) farmer; (de ganado) rancher
estanco *m* (tienda) tobacconist's
estándar *adj/m* standard
estandarte *m* standard, banner
estanque *m* pond
estanquillo *m* (Méx) general store (AmE), grocer's shop (BrE)
estante *m* shelf
estantería *f* shelves (*pl*); (para libros) bookcase, bookshelves (*pl*)
estaño *m* (elemento) tin; (para soldar) solder; (peltre) pewter
estar¹ [A27] *cópula* **1 (a)** (seguido de adjetivos) [ESTAR *denotes a changed condition or state as opposed to identity or nature, which is normally expressed by* SER. ESTAR *is also used when the emphasis is on the speaker's perception of things, of their appearance, taste, etc. The examples given below should be contrasted with those to be found in* SER¹ *cópula* 1] to be; **estás más gordo** you've put on weight; **estoy cansada** I'm tired; **está muy simpático conmigo** he's being *o* he's been so nice to me (recently); **¡todo está tan caro!** things are *o* have become so expensive! **(b)** (*con* BIEN, MAL, MEJOR, PEOR): **están todos bien, gracias** they're all fine, thanks; **¡qué bien estás en esta foto!** you look great in this photo!; **está mal que no se lo perdones** it's wrong of you not to forgive him; *ver tb* BIEN, MAL, MEJOR, PEOR **2** ▶ **378** (hablando de estado civil) to be; **está casada con un primo mío** she's married to a cousin of mine **3** (seguido de participios) **~ sentado** to be sitting; **estaban abrazados** they had their arms around each other; *ver tb v aux* 2 **4** (seguido de preposición) to be; (*para más ejemplos ver tb la preposición o el nombre correspondiente*); **estoy a régimen** I'm on a diet; **¿a cómo está la uva?** how much are the grapes?; **está con el sarampión** she has (the) measles; **estoy de cocinera** I'm doing the cooking; **estamos sin electricidad** the electricity is off at the moment; **está sin pintar** it hasn't been painted yet ■ **~** *vi* **1** (en un lugar) to be; **¿dónde está Chiapas?** where's Chiapas?; **está a 20 kilómetros de aquí** it's 20 kilometers from here; **¿sabes dónde está Pedro?** do you know where Pedro is?; **¿está Rodrigo?** is Rodrigo in?; **sólo ~é unos días** I'll only be staying a few days; **¿cuánto tiempo ~ás en Londres?** how long are you going to be in London (for)? **2** ▶ **193** (en el tiempo): **¿a qué (día) estamos?** what day is it today?; **¿a cuánto estamos hoy?** what's the date today?; **estamos a 28 de mayo** it's May 28th (AmE) *o* (BrE) the 28th of May; **estamos en primavera** it's spring ▶ **99** **3 (a)** (tener como función, cometido): **para eso están los amigos** that's what friends are for; **estamos para ayudarlos** we're here to help them **(b)** (radicar) to lie; **en eso está el problema** that's where the problem lies **4** (estar listo, terminado): **la carne todavía no está** the meat's not ready yet; **lo atas con un nudo y ya está** you tie a knot in it and that's it *o* there you are; **enseguida estoy** I'll be right with you **5** (Esp) (quedar) (+ *me/te/le etc*) (+ *compl*): **te está pequeña** it's too small for you; **la 46 te está mejor** the 46 fits you better ■ **~** *v aux* **1** (con gerundio): **está lloviendo** it's raining; **estoy viendo que va a ser imposible** I'm beginning to see that it's going to be impossible **2** (con participio): **ese asiento está ocupado** that seat is taken; **ya está hecho un hombrecito** he's a proper young man now; *ver tb* ESTAR *cópula* 3
■ **estarse** *v pron* (*enf*) (permanecer) to stay; **¿no te puedes ~ quieto?** can't you stay *o* keep still?; **estése tranquilo** don't worry
estar² *m* (esp AmL) living room
estárter *m* choke
estatal *adj* state (*before n*)
estático -ca *adj* static
estatua *f* statue
estatura *f* height; **mide dos metros de ~** he's two meters (tall); **¿qué ~ tenía?** how tall was she?
estatus *m* status
estatuto *m* **(a)** (Der, Pol) statute; (regla) rule **(b) estatutos** *mpl* (de empresa) articles of association (*pl*)
este¹ *adj inv* ▶ **346** ‹*región*› eastern; **iban en dirección ~** they were heading east *o* eastward(s); **el ala/la costa ~** the east wing/coast ■ *m* **(a)** (parte, sector): **el ~** the east; **al ~ de Lima** to the east of Lima **(b)** (punto cardinal) east, East; **vientos del E~** easterly winds; **las ventanas dan al ~** the windows face east **(c) el Este** (Hist, Pol) the East; **los países del E~** the Eastern Bloc countries
este², **esta** *adj dem* (*pl* **estos, estas**) **(a)** this; (*pl*) these; **este chico** this boy; **estos dólares** these dollars; [*usually indicates a pejorative or emphatic tone when placed after the noun*] **la estúpida esta no me avisó** (fam) this idiot here didn't tell me **(b)** (como muletilla) well, er

éste, **ésta** *pron dem* (*pl* **éstos, éstas**) this one; (*pl*) these; **~ es el mío** this (one) is mine; **un día de éstos** one of these days; **~ es el que yo quería** this is the one I wanted; **prefiero éstos** I prefer these (ones); [*sometimes indicates irritation, emphasis or disapproval*] **¡qué niña ésta!** (fam) honestly, this child!; **residente en ésta** resident in Seville (*o* Lima *etc*)

estela *f* (de barco) wake; (de avión, cohete) trail

estelarizar [A4] *vt* (Méx) to star in

estepa *f* steppe

estera *f* mat

estercolero *m* dunghill, dung heap

estéreo *adj inv/m* stereo

estereofónico -ca *adj* stereophonic

estereotipado -da *adj* ‹*frase*› clichéd; ‹*idea/personaje*› stereotyped

estereotipo *m* stereotype

estéril *adj* **(a)** ‹*animal/persona*› sterile; ‹*terreno*› infertile, barren **(b)** ‹*esfuerzo/discusión*› futile **(c)** ‹*gasa/jeringa*› sterile

esterilizar [A4] *vt* to sterilize

esterilla *f* **(a)** (alfombrilla) mat **(b)** (AmS) (mimbre) wicker

esternón *m* sternum, breastbone

estero *m* **(a)** (AmS) (laguna, pantano) marsh **(b)** (Chi) (arroyo) stream

esteroide *m* steroid

estética *f* **(a)** (Art) aesthetics **(b)** (Med) cosmetic surgery

esteticien, **esteticista** *mf* aesthetician, beautician

estético -ca *adj* aesthetic

estetoscopio *m* stethoscope

estiércol *m* (excremento) dung; (abono) manure

estigma *m* stigma

estilar [A1] *vi* (Chi) (gotear) to drip; (escurrir) to drain ■ **estilarse** *v pron* «*moda/peinado*» to be fashionable

estilista *mf* **(a)** (Lit) stylist **(b)** (diseñador de modas) designer **(c)** (AmL) (peluquero) hairstylist

estilístico -ca *adj* stylistic

estilizado -da *adj* **(a)** (Art) stylized **(b)** ‹*cuerpo/figura*› slender, slim

estilo *m* **(a)** (en general) style; **~ barroco** baroque style; **~ de vida** way of life, lifestyle; **ropa ~ deportivo** casual wear; **vestir con ~** to dress stylishly; **al ~ de mi tierra** the way they do it back home; ***por el ~***: **son todos por el ~** they are all the same; **algo por el ~** something like that **(b)** (en natación) stroke, style; **~ libre** freestyle; **~ mariposa** butterfly; **~ pecho** *or* (Esp) **braza** breaststroke

estima *f* esteem; **ganarse la ~ de algn** to raise oneself in sb's esteem; **tener(le) ~ a algn** to think highly of sb; **tiene en gran ~ tu amistad** he values your friendship very highly

estimación *f* **1** (cálculo) estimate **2** (aprecio) esteem

estimado -da *adj* dear

estimar [A1] *vt* **1 (a)** ‹*persona*› (respetar) to respect, hold ... in high esteem (frml); (tener cariño) to be fond of **(b)** ‹*objeto*› to value; **su piel es muy estimada** its skin is highly prized **2** (frml) (considerar) (+ *compl*) to consider, deem (frml)

estimulante *adj* stimulating

estimular [A1] *vt* **(a)** (en general) to stimulate **(b)** (alentar) ‹*persona*› to encourage

estímulo *m* **(a)** (incentivo) incentive **(b)** (Biol, Fisiol) stimulus

estirado -da *adj* (fam) stuck-up (colloq), snooty (colloq)

estirar [A1] *vt* **1 (a)** ‹*goma/elástico/suéter*› to stretch; ‹*cable/soga*› to pull out, stretch **(b)** ‹*sábanas/mantel*› (con las manos) to smooth out; (con la plancha) to run the iron over **2** ‹*brazos/piernas/músculo*› to stretch; **estiró el cuello para poder ver** she craned her neck to be able to see **3** ‹*dinero/comida/recursos*› to make ... go further ■ **estirarse** *v pron* to stretch

estirón *m*: **dar** *or* **pegar un ~** (fam) to shoot up (colloq)

estirpe *f* stock, lineage

estítico -ca *adj* (Chi) constipated

estitiquez *f* (Chi) constipation

esto *pron dem* (*neutro*) this; **¿qué es ~?** what's this?; **~ es lo que quiero** this is what I want

estofado[1] -da *adj* stewed; (con menos líquido) braised

estofado[2] *m* stew

estoico -ca *adj* stoic, stoical

estomacal *adj* stomach (*before n*)

estómago *m* ▶ 123 (Anat) stomach; **tengo dolor de ~** I have a stomachache, my stomach hurts; **beber con el ~ vacío** to drink on an empty stomach; ***revolverle el ~ a algn*** to turn sb's stomach

estoperol *m* **1** (Andes) (en carretera) cat's eye **2** (Chi) (Dep) stud

estoque *m* sword (*used for killing bull*)

estorbar [A1] *vi* to be/get in the way ■ **~** *vt* to obstruct; **el piano estorbaba el paso** the piano was in the way

estorbo *m* (obstáculo) hindrance; (molestia) nuisance

estornudar [A1] *vi* to sneeze

estornudo *m* sneeze

estos -tas *adj dem*: *ver* ESTE[2]

éstos -tas *pron dem*: *ver* ÉSTE

estoy *see* ESTAR

estrabismo *m* squint, strabismus (tech)

estrado *m* (tarima) platform, dais

estrafalario -ria *adj* ‹*persona/ideas/conducta*› eccentric; ‹*vestimenta*› outlandish, bizarre ■ *m,f* eccentric

estragón *m* tarragon

estragos *mpl*: **los ~ de la guerra** the ravages of war; **causar/hacer ~s** «*terremoto/inundación*» to wreak havoc; **la epidemia causó ~ entre la población** the epidemic devastated the population

estrambótico -ca *adj* ‹*persona/idea/conducta*› eccentric; ‹*vestimenta*› outlandish, bizarre

estrangulador -dora *m,f* strangler

estrangular [A1] *vt* **(a)** ‹*persona/animal*› to strangle, throttle **(b)** ‹*vena/conducto*› to strangulate

estraperlo *m* black market

estratagema *f* stratagem

estrategia *f* strategy

estratégico -ca *adj* strategic

estratosfera *f* stratosphere

estrechar [A1] *vt* **1 (a)** ‹*falda/pantalones*› to take ... in; ‹*carretera*› to make ... narrower **(b)** ‹*relaciones/lazos*› to strengthen **2** (abrazar, apretar): **la estrechó entre sus brazos** he held her tightly in his arms; **me estrechó la mano** he shook my hand

■ **estrecharse** *v pron* **1 (a)** «*carretera/acera*» to narrow, get narrower **(b)** «*relaciones/lazos*» to strengthen **2** (*recípr*) (apretarse): **se ~on en un abrazo** they embraced; **se ~on la mano** they shook hands

estrecho[1] **-cha** *adj* **1** ‹*calle/pasillo*› narrow; ‹*falda*› tight; **íbamos muy ~s** it was very cramped **2** ‹*amistad/colaboración/vigilancia*› close **3** (limitado) ‹*criterio*› narrow; **es muy ~ de miras** he's very narrow-minded

estrecho[2] *m* (Geog) strait, straits (*pl*)

estrella *f* **(a)** (en general) star; **~ de mar** starfish; **~ fugaz** shooting star; **~ polar** Pole Star; **un hotel de tres ~s** a three-star hotel; **una ~ de cine** a movie star **(b)** (asterisco) asterisk

estrellado -da *adj* (lleno de estrellas) starry; (en forma de estrella) star-shaped

estrellar [A1] *vt*: **estrelló un plato contra la pared** he smashed a plate against the wall; **estrelló el coche contra un árbol** he smashed his car into a tree

■ **estrellarse** *v pron* (chocar) to crash; **se estrelló con la moto** he had a motorcycle accident; **~se CONTRA algo** «*coche*» to crash INTO sth; «*olas*» to crash AGAINST sth; **se estrelló contra el vidrio** he walked smack into the glass door

estremecedor -dora *adj* ‹*escena/noticia*› horrifying; ‹*grito/relato*› spine-chilling, hair-raising

estremecer [E3] *vt* to make ... shudder ■ **~** *vi* to shudder; **hacer ~ a algn** to make sb shudder

■ **estremecerse** *v pron* **(a)** «*persona*» **~se DE algo** ‹*de miedo/horror*› to shudder WITH sth; ‹*de frío*› to shiver *o* tremble WITH sth; **se estremeció sólo de pensarlo** he shuddered at the mere thought of it **(b)** «*edificio/ventana*» to shake

estremecimiento *m* (de miedo) shudder; **tenía ~s de frío** he was shivering with cold

estrenar [A1] *vt* **1** (Cin, Teatr): **la película se estrenó en marzo** the movie opened *o* (journ) had its premiere in March; **acaban de ~ la obra en Madrid** the play's just started showing *o* just opened in Madrid **2** (usar por primera vez): **voy a ~ corbata** I'm going to wear a new tie; **todavía no he estrenado la blusa** I still haven't worn the blouse; **todavía no estrenamos el gimnasio** we still haven't tried out the gymnasium

estreno *m* **1** (de película, nueva obra) premiere; (de nueva puesta en escena) opening night **2** (primer uso): **ir de ~** to be wearing new clothes; **el ~ del local** the opening of the new premises

estreñido -da *adj* constipated

estreñimiento *m* constipation

estreñir [I15] *vi* to cause constipation ■ **~** *vt* to make ... constipated, bind (colloq)

estrés *m* stress

estresado -da *adj* under stress

estresante *adj* stressful

estría *f* **(a)** (de la piel) stretch mark **(b)** (de columna) groove, stria (tech)

estriado -da *adj* **(a)** ‹*piel*› stretch-marked **(b)** ‹*columna*› fluted

estribillo *m* (Lit) refrain; (Mús) chorus

estribo *m* **(a)** (Equ) stirrup; ***perder los ~s*** to fly off the handle, lose one's cool; ***tomarse la del ~*** to have one for the road (colloq) **(b)** (de vehículo) running board; (de moto) footrest

estribor *m* starboard

estricto -ta *adj* strict

estridente *adj* **(a)** ‹*pitido/chirrido*› shrill **(b)** ‹*voz*› (agudo) shrill; (fuerte) strident **(c)** ‹*color*› garish, loud

estrofa *f* stanza, verse

estropajo *m* scourer

estropeado -da *adj*: **estar ~** «*zapato/sillón*» to be falling apart; «*motor/coche*» to be broken down; *ver tb* ESTROPEAR

estropear [A1] *vt* **1 (a)** ‹*aparato/mecanismo*› to damage, break; ‹*coche*› to damage **(b)** (malograr) ‹*plan/vacaciones*› to spoil, ruin **2** (deteriorar, dañar) ‹*piel*› to damage, ruin; ‹*juguete*› to break; ‹*ropa*› to ruin; **el calor estropeó la fruta** the heat made the fruit go bad

■ **estropearse** *v pron* **1 (a)** (averiarse) «*motor/coche*» to break down; **la lavadora está estropeada** the washing machine is broken **(b)** «*plan/vacaciones*» to go wrong **2** (deteriorarse) «*fruta*» to go bad; «*leche/pescado*» to go off; «*zapatos/chaqueta*» to get ruined

estructura *f* structure

estructurar [A1] *vt* to structure, to organize

estruendo *m* (de las olas) roar; (de cascada, tráfico) thunder, roar; (de maquinaria) din

estrujar [A1] *vt* **1 (a)** (apretar arrugando) ‹*papel*› to crumple up, scrunch up; ‹*tela*› to crumple (up) **(b)** (para escurrir) to wring (out) **(c)** ‹*uvas*› to press **2** ‹*persona*› to squeeze, hold ... tightly

estuche *m* (de gafas, lápices, violín) case; (de cubiertos) canteen; (de collar, reloj) box, case

estudiante *mf* (de universidad) student; (de secundaria) (high-school) student (AmE), (secondary school) pupil (BrE)

estudiantil *adj* student (*before n*)

estudiar [A1] *vt* **1 (a)** ‹*asignatura*› to study; (en la universidad) to study, read (fml); **¿qué carrera**

estudió? what subject did he do at college/university? **(b)** ‹*instrumento*› to learn **(c)** ‹*lección/tablas*› to learn **2** (observar) ‹*rostro/comportamiento*› to study **3** (considerar, analizar) ‹*mercado/situación/proyecto*› to study; ‹*propuesta*› to study, consider; ‹*causas*› to look into, investigate ■ ~ *vi* to study; **estudia en un colegio privado** he goes to a private school; **debes ~ más** you must work harder; **dejó de ~ a los 15 años** she left school at 15; ~ PARA **algo** to study to be sth

■ **estudiarse** *v pron* (*enf*) ‹*lección*› to study; ‹*papel*› to learn

estudio *m* **1 (a)** (Educ) (actividad): **primero está el ~** studying *o* your studies *o* work must come first **(b)** (investigación, análisis) study; **~ de mercado** market research **(c)** (de asunto, caso) consideration; **está en ~** it is being considered **2** (lugar) **(a)** (de artista) studio; (de arquitecto) office, studio **(b)** (Cin, Rad, TV) studio **(c)** (en casa) study; (apartamento) studio apartment **3 estudios** *mpl* (Educ) education; **~s superiores** higher education; **quiso darle ~s a su hijo** she wanted to give her son an education; **tener ~s superiores** to have a degree; **dejar los ~s** to give up one's studies

estudioso -sa *adj* studious ■ *m,f* scholar

estufa *f* **(a)** (de calefacción) stove; **~ eléctrica** electric heater **(b)** (Col, Méx) (cocina) stove; **~ de gas** gas stove *o* (BrE) cooker

estupefaciente *m* narcotic (drug); **tráfico de ~s** drug trafficking

estupefacto -ta *adj* astonished, amazed

estupendo[1] -da *adj* **(a)** (excelente) marvelous*, fantastic (colloq), great (colloq); **¡~!** great! **(b)** (guapo) gorgeous

estupendo[2] *adv* ‹*cantar*› marvelously*; **lo pasé ~** I had a great *o* wonderful time

estupidez *f* **(a)** (cuálidad) stupidity, foolishness **(b)** (dicho): **no digas estupideces** don't talk nonsense **(c)** (acto): **eso sería una ~** that would be stupid *o* foolish

estúpido -da *adj* ‹*persona*› stupid; ‹*argumento*› stupid, silly; **¡ay, qué estúpida soy!** oh, how stupid of me! ■ *m,f* idiot, fool

estupor *m* astonishment

estuve, **estuviste, etc** *see* ESTAR

esvástica *f* swastika

etapa *f* stage; **por ~s** in stages; **la ~ más feliz de mi vida** the best *o* happiest time of my life

etcétera etcetera, and so on (and so forth)

etéreo -rea *adj* ethereal

eternidad *f* eternity

eterno -na *adj* eternal; ‹*amor*› everlasting

ética *f* ethics

ético -ca *adj* ethical

etimología *f* etymology

etíope, **etiope** *adj/mf* Ethiopian

Etiopía *f* Ethiopia

etiqueta *f* **1 (a)** (adherida) label **(b)** (atada) tag; (en prenda) label **2** (protocolo) etiquette; **baile/traje de ~** formal ball/dress

etiquetar [A1] *vt* ‹*producto*› to label; ‹*persona*› **~ a algn** DE **algo** to label sb (AS) sth

étnico -ca *adj* ethnic

eucalipto *m* eucalyptus

Eucaristía *f* Eucharist

eufemismo *m* euphemism

euforia *f* elation, euphoria

eufórico -ca *adj* ecstatic, euphoric

eurodiputado -da *m,f* Euro MP, MEP, Member of the European Parliament

Europa *f* Europe

europeísta *adj* pro-European

europeo -pea *adj/m,f* European

Eurotunnel®, **eurotúnel** *m* Channel Tunnel

Euskadi *f* the Basque Country

euskera, **eusquera** *adj/m* Basque

eutanasia *f* euthanasia

evacuación *f* (desalojo) evacuation

evacuar [A1] *vt* ‹*local/zona/población*› to evacuate

evadir [I1] *vt* **(a)** ‹*pregunta/peligro/responsabilidad*› to avoid; ‹*tema*› to dodge, evade **(b)** ‹*impuestos*› to evade

■ **evadirse** *v pron* **(a)** «*preso*» to escape **(b)** **~se** DE **algo** ‹*de responsabilidad/problema*› to run away FROM sth; ‹*de la realidad*› to escape FROM sth

evaluación *f* **(a)** (de daños, situación) assessment; (de datos, informes) evaluation, assessment **(b)** (Educ) (acción) assessment; (prueba, examen) test

evaluar [A18] *vt* ‹*pérdidas/situación*› to assess; ‹*datos*› to evaluate; ‹*alumno*› to assess

evangélico -ca *adj* **(a)** (del evangelio) evangelical **(b)** (protestante) protestant (*before n*) ■ *m,f* Protestant

evangelio *m* gospel

evaporación *f* evaporation

evaporarse [A1] *v pron* «*líquido*» to evaporate; «*ayuda/dinero*» to evaporate; «*persona*» (fam) to vanish *o* disappear into thin air

evasión *f* escape, breakout; **~ de impuestos** tax evasion

evasiva *f*: **me contestó con ~s** she avoided *o* dodged the issue

evasivo -va *adj* evasive, noncommital

evento *m* **(a)** (period) (suceso) event **(b)** (caso) case; **en este ~** in such a case

eventual *adj* **1** (posible) ‹*problema/conflicto*› possible; ‹*gastos*› incidental; ‹*riesgos/pasivos*› contingent **2** ‹*trabajo/trabajador*› casual, temporary; ‹*cargo*› temporary

evidencia *f* **(a)** (pruebas) evidence, proof; **negar la ~** to deny the obvious *o* the facts **(b)** (cualidad) obviousness; ***dejar*** *or* ***poner a algn en ~*** to show sb up

evidente *adj* obvious, clear

evitar [A1] *vt* **(a)** (eludir, huir de) to avoid; **~ hacer algo** to avoid doing sth **(b)** (impedir) to avoid, prevent; **para ~ que sufran** to avoid *o* prevent them suffering **(c)** (remediar): **me puse a llorar, no lo puede ~** I started to cry, I couldn't help it **(d)** (ahorrar) **~le algo** A **algn** ‹*molestia/preocupación*› to save *o* spare sb sth

■ **evitarse** *v pron* ‹*problemas*› to save oneself; **evítese la molestia de ir a la tienda** avoid the inconvenience of going to the store

evolución *f* **(a)** (Biol) evolution **(b)** (de ideas, sociedad, enfermedad) development; (de enfermo) progress

evolucionado -da *adj* ‹*especie*› highly developed *o* evolved; ‹*sociedad/ideas*› advanced, highly developed

evolucionar [A1] *vi* **(a)** (Biol) to evolve **(b)** «*ideas/sociedad/ciencia*» to develop, evolve **(c)** «*enfermo*» to progress

exactitud *f* **(a)** (precisión) accuracy, precision; **las órdenes se cumplieron con ~** the orders were carried out to the letter **(b)** (veracidad, rigor) accuracy

exacto -ta *adj* **(a)** ‹*medida/cantidad*› exact; **40 kilos ~s** exactly 40 kilos; **hay que ser muy ~ en los cálculos** you have to be very accurate *o* precise in your calculations **(b)** ‹*informe/mapa/descripción*› accurate **(c)** ‹*copia*› exact; ‹*reproducción*› accurate

exageración *f* exaggeration

exagerado -da *adj* **(a)** ‹*persona*›: **¡qué ~ eres!** you do exaggerate! **(b)** ‹*historia/relato*› exaggerated **(c)** (excesivo) ‹*precio*› exorbitant; ‹*cariño/castigo*› excessive; ‹*moda*› extravagant, way-out (colloq)

exagerar [A1] *vt* ‹*suceso/noticia*› to exaggerate ■ ~ *vi* (al hablar) to exaggerate; (al hacer algo) to overdo it, go over the top (colloq)

exaltado -da *adj* **(a)** (vehemente) ‹*discurso*› impassioned **(b)** (excitado): **los ánimos estaban ~s** feelings were running high; **estaba muy ~** he was really worked up **(c)** [SER] ‹*persona*› hotheaded ■ *m,f* hothead

exaltar [A1] *vt* **1 (a)** (excitar) ‹*personas*› to excite; ‹*pasiones*› to arouse **(b)** (hacer enojar) to anger **2** (frml) (alabar) to extol (frml)

■ **exaltarse** *v pron* to get worked up

exalumno -na *m,f* (de colegio) ex-pupil; (de universidad) ex-student

examen *m* **(a)** (Educ) exam, examination (frml); **~ de admisión** entrance examination *o* test; **~ parcial** modular exam *o* test; **hacer** *or* (CS) **dar un ~** to take an exam; **presentarse a un ~** to take *o* (BrE) sit an exam **(b)** (estudio, investigación) examination; **someter algo a ~** to examine sth; **~ médico** medical examination, medical

examinador -dora *adj* examining (*before n*) ■ *m,f* examiner

examinar [A1] *vt* to examine; ‹*situación/caso*› to study, consider

■ **examinarse** *v pron* (Esp) to take an exam

exasperante *adj* exasperating

exasperar [A1] *vt* to exasperate

■ **exasperarse** *v pron* to get worked up *o* exasperated

excavación *f* excavation

excavadora *f* excavator

excavar [A1] *vt* **(a)** ‹*túnel/fosa*› to dig **(b)** (Arqueol) to excavate ■ ~ *vi* to dig, excavate

excedencia *f* (Esp) extended leave of absence

excedente *adj* **(a)** ‹*producción*› excess (*before n*), surplus (*before n*) **(b)** (con permiso) (Esp) on extended leave of absence ■ *m* surplus

exceder [E1] *vt* **(a)** ‹*límite/peso*› to exceed **(b)** (superar, aventajar) **~ A algo** to be superior TO sth

■ **excederse** *v pron* (al beber, trabajar) to overdo it; **se excedió en sus críticas** she went too far in her criticism

excelencia *f* **1** (cualidad) excellence **2** (frml) (tratamiento): **Su E~** (*m*) His Excellency; (*f*) Her Excellency

excelente *adj* excellent

excéntrico -ca *adj/m,f* eccentric

excepción *f* exception; **esta norma tiene una ~** there is an exception to this rule; **hacer una ~ (con algn)** to make an exception (for sb); **a excepción de** with the exception of, except for

excepcional *adj* ‹*caso/circunstancia/talento*› exceptional; ‹*contribución/labor*› outstanding

excepto *prep* except, apart from; **todos ~ yo** everyone but me

exceptuar [A18] *vt* to except (frml); **exceptuando un pequeño incidente** except for *o* with the exception of a minor incident

excesivo *adj* excessive

exceso *m* **(a)** (excedente) excess; **~ de equipaje** excess baggage **(b)** (demasía): **un ~ de ejercicio** too much exercise; **me multaron por ~ de velocidad** I was fined for speeding; **en ~** ‹*beber/fumar/trabajar*› too much **(c) excesos** *mpl* (abusos) excesses (*pl*)

excitación *f* **(a)** (entusiasmo) excitement **(b)** (sexual) arousal, excitement

excitante *adj* ‹*espectáculo/libro*› exciting

excitar [A1] *vt* **(a)** (hacer enojar): **la discusión lo excitó mucho** he got very excited *o* worked up during the argument **(b)** (sobreexcitar) to get ... overexcited; **el café me excita** coffee makes me jumpy **(c)** (en sentido sexual) to arouse, excite **(d)** ‹*deseo/odio/curiosidad*› to arouse

■ **excitarse** *v pron* **(a)** (enojarse) to get agitated, get worked up **(b)** (sobreexcitarse) to get overexcited **(c)** (sexualmente) to get aroused, get excited

exclamación *f* exclamation

exclamar [A1] *vt* to exclaim

excluir [I20] *vt* to exclude; ‹*posibilidad*› to rule out

exclusión *f* exclusion

exclusiva *f* **(a)** (Period) (derechos) exclusive rights (*pl*); (reportaje) exclusive **(b)** (Esp) (Com) exclusive rights (*pl*); **tendrán la ~ de nuestros productos** they will be sole distributors of our products

exclusive *adj inv* (*detrás del n*): **del tres al quince, ambos ~** from the third to the fifteenth not inclusive

exclusividad *f* **(a)** (de club, colegio, diseño) exclusiveness, exclusivity **(b)** (AmL) (Com) exclusive rights (*pl*), sole rights (*pl*)

exclusivo -va *adj* ‹*club/diseño*› exclusive; ‹*distribuidor*› sole; ‹*derechos*› exclusive, sole

excombatiente *mf* (*m*) veteran (AmE), ex-serviceman (esp BrE); (*f*) veteran (AmE), ex-servicewoman (esp BrE)

excomulgar [A3] *vt* to excommunicate

excomunión *f* excommunication

excremento *m* excrement

excursión *f* (viaje organizado) excursion, day trip; (paseo, salida) trip, excursion; **ir de ~ al campo** to go on a trip to the countryside

excursionista *mf* (que hace una excursión) tripper; (que hace excursionismo) hiker

excusa *f* **(a)** (pretexto) excuse **(b) excusas** *fpl* (disculpas) apologies (*pl*)

excusar [A1] *vt* **(a)** (disculpar) ‹*comportamiento*› to excuse **(b)** (eximir) **~ a algn** DE **algo/hacer algo** to excuse sb (FROM) sth/doing sth

■ **excusarse** *v pron* (frml) **(a)** (pedir perdón) to apologize **(b)** (ofrecer excusas) to excuse oneself

exento -ta *adj* (frml) [ESTAR] exempt; **~** DE **algo** exempt FROM sth; **~ de impuestos** tax-exempt, tax-free (BrE)

exfoliador *m* (Col) notepad

exhaustivo -va *adj* exhaustive

exhausto -ta *adj* exhausted

exhibición *f* **(a)** (demostración) display **(b)** (de cuadros, artefactos) exhibition, display; **estar en ~** to be on show *o* display

exhibicionista *mf* **(a)** (pervertido) exhibitionist, flasher (colloq) **(b)** (ostentoso) exhibitionist, show-off (colloq)

exhibir [I1] *vt* **(a)** ‹*colección/modelos*› to show, display **(b)** ‹*película*› to show, screen; ‹*cuadro/obras de arte*› to exhibit **(c)** (con orgullo) ‹*regalos/trofeos*› to show off ■ **~** *vi* (period) (Art) to exhibit

■ **exhibirse** *v pron* (mostrarse en público) to show oneself; (hacerse notar) to draw attention to oneself

exhumar [A1] *vt* to exhume, disinter

exigencia *f* **(a)** (pretensión) demand; **¡no me vengas con ~s!** don't start making demands **(b)** (requisito) requirement

exigente *adj* ‹*persona/prueba*› demanding; ‹*clientela/paladar*› discerning

exigir [I7] *vt* **(a)** ‹*pago/respuesta/disciplina*› to demand; **exigió que se retiraran** he demanded that they leave **(b)** (requerir) ‹*concentración/paciencia*› to call for, demand **(c)** (esperar de algn) (+ *me/te/le etc*): **le exigen demasiado en ese colegio** they ask too much of him at that school

exiliado -da *adj* exiled, in exile ■ *m,f* exile

exiliarse [A1 *or* A1] *v pron* to go into exile

exilio *m* exile

eximir [I1] *vt* (frml) to exempt; **~ a algn** DE **algo/hacer algo** to exempt sb FROM sth/doing sth; **esto me exime de toda culpa** this relieves *o* absolves me of all responsibility

existencia *f* **1 (a)** (hecho de existir) existence **(b)** (vida) life; **amargarle la ~ a algn** to make sb's life a misery **2** (Com) stock

existir [I1] *vi* **(a)** (*en 3ª pers*) (haber): **siempre ha existido rivalidad entre ellos** there has always been rivalry between them; **no existen pruebas** there is no evidence **(b)** (ser) to exist; **ya no existe** it doesn't exist anymore

éxito *m* success; **con ~** successfully; **tener ~** to be successful; **~ de ventas** best-seller

exitoso -sa *adj* (AmL) ‹*campaña/gira*› successful

éxodo *m* exodus

exorbitante *adj* exorbitant

exorcismo *m* exorcism

exorcizar [A4] *vt* to exorcize

exótico -ca *adj* exotic

expandirse [I1] *v pron* to expand

expansión *f* expansion; **en ~** expanding

expatriado -da *m,f* expatriate

expatriarse [A1] *or* [A17] *v pron* (emigrar) to leave one's country; (exiliarse) to go into exile

expectación *f* sense of expectancy *o* anticipation

expectante *adj* expectant; **esperaba ~** she waited expectantly

expectativa *f* **(a)** (espera): **estar a la ~ (de algo)** (espera) to be waiting (for sth) **(b)** (esperanza) expectation; **defraudó las ~s de su padre** he failed to live up to his father's expectations **(c) expectativas** *fpl* (perspectivas) prospects (*pl*); **tienen pocas ~s de ganar** they have little hope of winning; **~s de vida** life expectancy

expedición *f* expedition; **~ de salvamento** (misión) rescue mission; (equipo) rescue party

expediente *m* **(a)** (documentos) file, dossier; **~ académico** student record **(b)** (investigación) investigation, inquiry **(c)** (medidas disciplinarias) disciplinary action; **le abrieron ~** disciplinary action was taken against him

expedir [I14] *vt* ‹*pasaporte/visa*› to issue

expendio *m* (AmL) (tienda) store (AmE), shop (BrE); (venta) sale; **un ~ de licores** a package store (AmE), an off-licence (BrE)

expensas: **a expensas de algo** ‹*de ideales/salud*› at the expense of; **vive a ~ de su familia** he lives off his family

experiencia *f* **(a)** (conocimiento, suceso) experience; **saber algo por ~** to know sth by *o* from experience; **~ piloto** pilot scheme **(b)** (experimento) experiment

experimentado -da *adj* experienced

experimental *adj* experimental

experimentar [A1] *vi* **~** CON **algo** to experiment ON *o* WITH sth ■ **~** *vt* **(a)** ‹*sensación*› to experience, feel; ‹*tristeza/alegría*› to feel **(b)** (sufrir) ‹*cambio*› to undergo; **ha experimentado una leve mejoría** there's been a slight improvement in his condition

experimento *m* experiment

experto -ta *adj*: **es ~ en casos de divorcio** he's an expert on divorce cases; **~** EN **hacer algo** very good AT doing sth ■ *m,f* expert

expiar [A17] *vt* to expiate, atone for

explanada *f* (plataforma) raised area, terrace; (delante de un edificio) leveled* area; (al lado del mar) esplanade

explayarse [A1] *v pron* **(a)** (sobre un tema) to speak at length **(b)** (desahogarse) to unburden oneself **(c)** (esparcirse) to relax

explicación *f* explanation

explicar [A2] *vt* to explain; **no sé ~lo** I don't know how to explain it
■ **explicarse** *v pron* **(a)** (comprender, concebir) to understand; **no me lo explico** I can't understand it *o* (colloq) I just don't get it **(b)** (hacerse comprender) to express oneself; **explícate** explain what you mean; **¿me explico?** do you understand what I mean?

explícito -ta *adj* explicit

exploración *f* **(a)** (de territorio) exploration; (de yacimientos) prospecting **(b)** (Mil) reconnaisance **(c)** (Med) examination, exploration

explorador -dora *m,f* **1** (expedicionario) explorer; (Mil) scout **2 exploradora** *f* (Col) (Auto) fog lamp

explorar [A1] *vt* **(a)** ‹*región*› to explore; ‹*yacimientos*› to prospect for **(b)** ‹*posibilidades*› to explore, investigate; ‹*situación*› to investigate, examine **(c)** (Mil) to reconnoiter*, scout

explosión *f* **(a)** (de bomba) explosion; **la bomba hizo ~** (period) the bomb exploded *o* went off **(b)** (de cólera, júbilo) outburst **(c)** (crecimiento brusco) explosion

explosivo¹ -va *adj* explosive; **materiales ~s** explosives

explosivo² *m* explosive

explotación *f* **(a)** (de tierra, mina) exploitation, working; (de negocio) running, operation **(b)** (de trabajador) exploitation

explotador -dora *adj* exploitative ■ *m,f* exploiter

explotar [A1] *vt* **(a)** ‹*tierra*› to exploit, work; ‹*mina*› to operate, work; ‹*negocio*› to run, operate **(b)** ‹*idea/debilidad*› to exploit **(c)** ‹*trabajador*› to exploit ■ ~ *vi* **(a)** «*bomba*» to explode, go off; «*caldera/máquina*» to explode, blow up **(b)** (fam) «*persona*» to explode, to blow a fuse (colloq)

exponer [E22] *vt* **1 (a)** (en museo) ‹*cuadro/escultura*› to exhibit, show **(b)** (en vitrina) to display **2** ‹*razones/hechos*› to set out, state; ‹*ideas/teoría*› to put forward; ‹*tema*› to present **3 (a)** (poner en peligro) to put ... at risk **(b)** (al aire, sol) **~ algo A algo** to expose sth TO sth ■ ~ *vi* to exhibit, exhibit *o* show one's work
■ **exponerse** *v pron* **~se (A algo)** to expose oneself (TO sth); **te expones a que te multen** you're risking a fine

exportación *f* **(a)** (acción) exportation, export **(b) exportaciones** *fpl* (mercancías) exports (*pl*)

exportador -dora *adj*: **países ~es de petróleo** oil-exporting countries; **una región ~a de cítricos** a region that exports citrus fruit ■ *m,f* exporter

exportar [A1] *vt* to export

exposición *f* **1 (a)** (acción) exhibition, showing **(b)** (muestra — de cuadros, esculturas) exhibition; (— de productos, maquinaria) show **2** (de hechos, razones) statement; (de tema, teoría) presentation **3** (al aire, sol) exposure; (Fot) exposure

expositor -tora *m,f* **1** (de cuadros, maquinaria) exhibitor **2** (Col, Ven) (conferenciante) speaker

exprés *adj inv* (Esp) ‹*servicio/envío*› express (*before n*) ■ *m* (Esp) ⇒ EXPRESO¹

expresar [A1] *vt* to express
■ **expresarse** *v pron* to express oneself

expresión *f* expression

expresividad *f* expressiveness

expresivo -va *adj* ‹*persona/rostro/lenguaje*› expressive

expreso¹ -sa *adj* **1** (explícito) express (*before n*) **2** ‹*tren*› express (*before n*), fast (*before n*); ‹*carta/envío*› express (*before n*); **por correo ~** express **3** ‹*café*› espresso

expreso² *m* **1** (Ferr) express train, fast train **2** (café) espresso

exprimidor *m* (manual) reamer (AmE), lemon squeezer (BrE); (eléctrico) juicer

exprimir [I1] *vt* **(a)** ‹*naranja/limón*› to squeeze; ‹*ropa*› to wring **(b)** (explotar) ‹*trabajadores*› to exploit

expropiación *f* (sin indemnización) expropriation; (con indemnización) compulsory purchase

expropiar [A1] *vt* (sin indemnización) to expropriate; (con indemnización) to acquire ... by compulsory purchase

expulsar [A1] *vt* **1 (a)** (de institución) to expel; (de local) to throw ... out, eject (frml) **(b)** (de territorio) to expel, drive out **(c)** (Dep) to send off **2** ‹*aire/cálculo*› to expel

expulsión *f* expulsion; (Dep) sending-off

expurgar [A3] *vt* to expurgate

exquisito -ta *adj* ‹*comida*› delicious; ‹*tela/poema/música*› exquisite; ‹*persona*› refined

éxtasis *m* ecstasy

extático -ca *adj* ecstatic

extender [E8] *vt* **1** ‹*periódico/mapa*› to open ... up *o* out; ‹*mantel/toalla*› to spread ... out **2** ‹*brazos*› to stretch out; ‹*alas*› to spread; **le extendió la mano** he held out his hand to her **3** ‹*pintura/mantequilla*› to spread **4** (ampliar) ‹*poderes/plazo/permiso*› to extend **5** (frml) ‹*factura/cheque/escritura*› to issue; ‹*receta*› to make out, write
■ **extenderse** *v pron* **1** (en el espacio) **(a)** «*fuego/epidemia/noticia*» to spread **(b)** «*territorio/propiedad*» to stretch; **se extiende hasta el río** it stretches down to the river **(c)** «*influencia/autoridad*» to extend; **~se A algo** to extend TO sth **2** (en el tiempo) **(a)** «*época/debate*» to last **(b)** «*persona*»: **se extendió demasiado en ese tema** he spent too much time on that subject; **¿quisiera ~se sobre ese punto?** would you like to expand on that point?

extendido -da *adj* **(a)** ‹*costumbre/error*› widespread **(b)** ‹*brazos/alas*› outstretched

extensión *f* **1 (a)** (superficie): **una gran ~ de terreno** a large expanse *o* stretch of land; **una ~ de 20 hectáreas** an area of 20 hectares **(b)** (longitud) length; **la ~ de la novela** the length of the novel; **por ~** by extension **2** (grado, importancia) extent; **en toda la ~ de la palabra** in every sense of the word **3 (a)** (prolongación) extension; **pidió una ~ del plazo** she asked for an extension on the deadline **(b)** (de cable) extension lead; (línea telefónica) extension

extenso -sa *adj* extensive

exterior *adj* **1 (a)** ‹*aspecto*› external (*before n*), outward (*before n*); ‹*bolsillo/temperatura/mundo*› outside (*before n*); ‹*revestimiento/capa*› outer (*before n*) **(b)** ‹*habitación/apartamento*› outward-facing **2** ‹*comercio/política*› foreign (*before n*) ■ *m* **1** (fachada) outside, exterior; (espacio circundante) outside; **desde el ~ de la iglesia** from outside the church **2 el exterior** (países extranjeros): **la influencia del ~** foreign influence; **las relaciones con el ~** relations with other countries

exteriorizar [A4] *vt* to externalize, exteriorize

exterminar [A1] *vt* to exterminate

exterminio *m* extermination

externar [A1] *vt* (Méx) to display, show

externo -na *adj* **(a)** ‹*apariencia/signos*› outward (*before n*), external; ‹*influencia*› outside, external; ‹*superficie*› external; ‹*ángulo*› exterior **(b)** ‹*alumno*› day (*before n*) ■ *m,f* day pupil

extinción *f* (de especie, volcán) extinction

extinguidor *m* (AmL) fire extinguisher

extinguir [I2] *vt* **(a)** ‹*especie*› to wipe out; ‹*violencia/injusticia*› to put an end to **(b)** ‹*fuego*› to extinguish, put out

■ **extinguirse** *v pron* **(a)** «*especie*» to become extinct, die out **(b)** «*fuego*» to go out; «*volcán*» to become extinct; «*sonido*» to die away **(c)** «*entusiasmo/amor*» to die

extintor *m* (Esp): *tb* **~ de incendios** fire extinguisher

extirpar [A1] *vt* (Med) to remove

extorsión *f* extortion

extorsionar [A1] *vt* to extort money from

extra *adj* **(a)** (Com) top quality, fancy grade (AmE) **(b)** (adicional) ‹*gastos/ración*› additional, extra; ‹*edición*› special ■ *adv* extra ■ *mf* (Cin) extra ■ *m* (gasto) extra expense; (paga) bonus

extracción *f* **(a)** (en general) extraction **(b)** *tb* **~ social** background, origins (*pl*); **de ~ humilde** of humble origins

extraconyugal *adj* extramarital

extracto *m* **(a)** (resumen) summary, abstract; **~ de cuenta** (bank) statement **(b)** (esencia) extract

extractor *m* extractor; **~ de aire** extractor fan

extradición *f* extradition

extraer [E23] *vt* (en general) to extract; ‹*bala*› to remove; ‹*conclusión*› to draw

extraescolar *adj* extramural, out-of-school (*before n*)

extralimitarse [A1] *v pron* to exceed one's authority

extramatrimonial *adj* extramarital

extranjero -ra *adj* foreign ■ *m,f* **(a)** (persona) foreigner **(b) extranjero** *m*: **al/en el ~** abroad; **noticias del ~** foreign news

extrañar [A1] *vt* (esp AmL) ‹*amigo/país*› to miss ■ **~** *vi* **1** (sorprender) (+ *me/te/le etc*) to surprise; **me extraña que no lo sepas** I'm surprised you didn't know that; **ya me extrañaba a mí que** ... I thought it was strange that ... **2** (RPl) (tener nostalgia) to be homesick

■ **extrañarse** *v pron* **~se** DE **algo** to be surprised AT sth

extrañeza *f* surprise; **me miró con ~** she looked at me in surprise

extraño -ña *adj* (raro) strange, odd; **eso no tiene nada de ~** there's nothing unusual about that ■ *m,f* (desconocido) stranger

extraoficial *adj* unofficial

extraordinario -ria *adj* (en general) extraordinary; ‹*edición*› special; ‹*contribución*› extra, additional; **la película no fue nada ~** the movie was nothing special *o* nothing out of the ordinary

extraplano -na *adj* ‹*reloj/calculadora*› slimline; ‹*compresa*› extra-slim

extrarradio *m* outlying districts (*pl*), outskirts (*pl*)

extrasensorial *adj* extrasensory

extraterrestre *adj/mf* alien, extraterrestrial

extravagancia *f* (acto) outrageous thing (to do); (cualidad) extravagance

extravagante *adj* ‹*comportamiento/ideas*› outrageous, extravagant; ‹*persona/ropa*› flamboyant, outrageous

extraviado -da *adj* ‹*objeto/niño*› lost, missing; ‹*perro/gato*› stray

extraviar [A17] *vt* (frml) to mislay (frml), to lose

■ **extraviarse** *v pron* (frml) «*persona/animal*» to get lost; «*documento*» to go missing

extremado -da *adj* extreme

extremar [A1] *vt* (frml) to maximize (frml)

extremaunción *f* extreme unction

extremidad *f* **(a)** (extremo) end **(b) extremidades** *fpl* (Anat) extremities

extremista *adj* (extremo) extreme; (Pol) extremist ■ *mf* (Pol) extremist

extremo[1] -ma *adj* extreme; **un caso de extrema gravedad** an extremely serious case; **en caso ~** as a last resort; **~ derecha/izquierda** (Pol) extreme right/left; **~ derecho/izquierdo** (Dep) right/left wing; **E~ Oriente** Far East

extremo[2] *m* **(a)** (de palo, cable) end **(b)** (postura extrema) extreme; **va de un ~ a otro** she goes from one extreme to the other; **son ~s opuestos** they are complete opposites **(c)** (límite): **si se llega a ese ~** ... if it gets that bad *o* to that point ...; **en último ~** as a last resort

extrovertido -da *adj/m,f* extrovert

exuberante *adj* exuberant; ‹*mujer*› voluptuous

eyaculación *f* ejaculation

eyacular [A1] *vi* to ejaculate

Ff

F, f *f* (*read as* /'efe/) *the letter* F, f

fa *m* (nota) F; (en solfeo) fa, fah (BrE)

fábrica *f* factory; **una ~ de zapatos** a shoe factory; **~ de textiles/papel** textile/paper mill; **~ de cerveza** brewery; **~ de conservas** cannery

fabricación *f* manufacture; **la ~ de coches** car manufacture; **de ~ japonesa** made in Japan; **de ~ casera** home-made; **~ en serie** mass production

fabricante *mf* manufacturer

fabricar [A2] *vt* to manufacture; **~ en cadena/serie** to mass-produce; Ⓢ **fabricado en Perú** made in Peru

fábula *f* (Lit) fable; (mentira) fabrication

fabuloso -sa *adj* (maravilloso) (fam) fabulous (colloq)

facción *f* **(a)** (Pol) faction **(b) facciones** *fpl* (rasgos) features (*pl*)

faceta *f* facet

facha *f* (fam) (aspecto) look; **no me gustó su ~** I didn't like the look of him; **¿vas a salir con esa ~?** are you going out looking like that?; ***estar hecho una ~*** to be *o* look a sight (colloq)

fachada *f* **(a)** (de edificio) facade (tech), front **(b)** (apariencia) facade

fácil *adj* **1 (a)** ‹*problema/lección/vida*› easy; **~ de entender** easy to understand **(b)** (pey) (en lo sexual) easy (pej), loose (pej) **2** (probable): **es ~ que se le olvide** he'll probably forget; **no es ~ que me lo den** they are unlikely to let me have it

facilidad *f* **1 (a)** (cualidad de fácil) ease; **con ~** easily **(b)** (de una tarea) simplicity **2** (aptitud): **tener ~ para los idiomas/los números** to have a gift for languages/to be good at figures; **tiene ~ de palabra** he has a way with words **3 facilidades** *fpl* **(a)** (posibilidades, oportunidades): **se le dieron todas las ~es** they gave her every chance **(b)** (Fin) *tb* **~es de pago** credit facilities (*pl*)

facilitar [A1] *vt* **(a)** (hacer más fácil) ‹*tarea*› to make ... easier, facilitate (frml) **(b)** (frml) (proporcionar) ‹*datos/información*› to provide

factible *adj* possible, feasible

factor *m* factor; **el ~ tiempo** the time factor

factoría *f* (fábrica) factory; (astillero) shipyard; (fundición) foundry

factura *f* **1** (Com) invoice (frml), bill; **pasarle ~ a algn** (Fin) to invoice sb **2** (RPl) (Coc) *rolls, croissants, etc*

facturación *f* **1** (Com) **(a)** (acción) invoicing **(b)** (volumen) turnover **2** (Ferr) registration; (Aviac) check-in

facturar [A1] *vt* **1** (Com) **(a)** ‹*mercancías/arreglo*› to invoice for, bill for **(b)** (refiriéndose al volumen de ventas) to turn over, have a turnover of **2** (Ferr) to register; (Aviac) to check in ■ **~** *vi* (Ferr) to register; (Aviac) to check in

facultad *f* **1** (capacidad) faculty; **está perdiendo ~es** he's losing his faculties; **~es mentales** (mental) faculties (*pl*) **2** (Educ) faculty; **F~ de Filosofía y Letras** Faculty of Arts

facultar [A1] *vt* (frml) **~ a algn PARA hacer algo** «*jefe/presidente*» to authorize sb to do sth; «*carnet/documento*» to entitle sb to do sth; «*ley*» to allow sb to do sth

faena *f* **1** (tarea) task, job; **es una ~ dura** it's hard work; **~s domésticas** housework; **~s agrícolas** farm work **2** (fam) **(a)** (mala pasada) dirty trick; **hacerle una ~ a algn** to play a dirty trick on sb (colloq) **(b)** (contratiempo) drag (colloq), pain (colloq)

fagot /fa'ɣo(t)/ *m* (instrumento) bassoon ■ *mf* (músico) bassoonist

faisán *m* pheasant

faja *f* **(a)** (prenda interior) girdle **(b)** (cinturón — de traje regional) wide belt; (— de sotana) sash; (— de smoking) cummerbund **(c)** (franja, zona) strip

fajo *m* (de billetes) wad, roll (AmE); (de papeles) bundle, sheaf

falda *f* **(a)** (Indum) skirt; **~ escocesa** (de mujer) tartan skirt, kilt; (de hombre) kilt; **~ pantalón** split skirt, culottes (*pl*); **se enemistaron por un asunto de ~s** they fell out over a woman **(b)** (de montaña) side

faldón *m*, **faldones** *mpl* **(a)** (de camisa) shirttails; (de frac, chaqué) coattails **(b)** (de bebé) christening robe

falla *f* **1 (a)** (de tela, cristal) flaw; **la pieza tenía una ~** the part was defective **(b)** (Geol) fault **2 (a)** (de motor, máquina, sistema — en la composición) defect, fault; (— en el funcionamiento) failure; **~s en el sistema de seguridad** security failures **(b)** (de persona) mistake; **~ humana** (AmL) human error; **¡qué ~!** what a stupid mistake! **(c)** (Dep) miss **3** (AmL exc CS fam) (lástima) pity, shame

fallado -da *adj* (CS) flawed, defective

fallar [A1] *vi* **1** «*juez/jurado*» **~ a** *or* **en favor/en contra de algn** to rule in favor* of/against sb **2 (a)** «*frenos/memoria*» to fail; «*planes*» to go wrong; **le falló el corazón** his heart failed; **le falló la puntería** he missed; **a ti te falla** (AmL) (fam) you've a screw loose (colloq) **(b)** «*persona*» (+ *me/te/le etc*) to let ... down ■ **~** *vt* (errar) to miss; **fallé el tiro** I missed (the shot)

fallecer [E3] *vi* (frml *o* euf) to pass away (frml *or* euph), to die

fallecimiento *m* (frml) death, passing (frml *or* euph)

fallo *m* **(a)** (en concurso, certamen) decision; (Der) ruling, judgment **(b)** (Esp) ⇒ FALLA (2)

falluca *f* (Méx fam) (comercio ilegal) black market (*gen in smuggled goods*); (mercancía) smuggled goods (*pl*)

falsear [A1] *vt* ‹*hechos/datos*› to falsify; ‹*verdad/realidad*› to distort

falsedad *f* **(a)** (de afirmación) falseness; (de persona) insincerity, falseness **(b)** (mentira) lie

falsificador -dora *m,f* forger

falsificar [A2] *vt* **(a)** ‹*firma/billete/cheque*› to forge **(b)** ‹*documento*› (copiar) to forge, counterfeit; (alterar) to falsify

falso -sa *adj* **(a)** ‹*billete*› counterfeit, forged; ‹*cuadro*› forged; ‹*documento*› false, forged; ‹*diamante/joya*› fake; ‹*cajón/techo*› false **(b)** (insincero) ‹*persona*› insincere, false; ‹*sonrisa/promesa*› false **(c)** (no cierto) ‹*dato/nombre/declaración*› false; **eso es ~** that is not true *o* is untrue; **falsa alarma** false alarm; **~ testimonio** *m* (Der) false testimony, perjury

falta *f* **1** (carencia, ausencia) **~** DE **algo** ‹*de interés/dinero*› lack OF sth; **~ de personal** staff shortage; **es la ~ de costumbre** it's because I'm/you're not used to it; **fue una ~ de respeto** it was very rude of you/him/her/them; **eso es una ~ de educación** that's bad manners; **a ~ de más información** in the absence of more information **2** (inasistencia) *tb* **~ de asistencia** absence; **le pusieron ~** they marked her down as absent **3 (a)** **hacer falta**: **no hace ~ que se queden** there's no need for you to stay; **si hace ~** ... if necessary ...; **hacen ~ dos vasos más** we need two more glasses; **le hace ~ descansar** he/she needs to rest **(b)** **sin falta** without fail **4** (defecto) fault; **a pesar de todas sus ~s** in spite of all his faults; **sacarle** *or* **encontrarle ~s a algo** to find fault with sth; **~ de ortografía** spelling mistake **5** (Dep) **(a)** (infracción — en fútbol, baloncesto) foul; (— en tenis) fault **(b)** (tiro libre — en fútbol) free kick; (— en balonmano) free throw

faltar [A1] *vi* **1 (a)** (no estar) to be missing; **¿quién falta?** who's missing?; (en colegio, reunión) who's absent?; **te falta un botón** you have a button missing; **a esta taza le falta el asa** there's no handle on this cup **(b)** (no haber suficiente): **va a ~ vino** there won't be enough wine; **nos faltó tiempo** we didn't have enough time **(c)** (hacer falta): **le falta alguien que la aconseje** she needs someone to advise her; **les falta cariño** they need affection **2** (quedar): **yo estoy lista ¿a ti te falta mucho?** I'm ready, will you be long?; **nos falta poco para terminar** we're almost finished; **me faltan tres páginas para terminar el libro** I have three pages to go to finish the book; **sólo me falta pasarlo a máquina** all I have to do is type it out; **falta poco para Navidad** it's not long until Christmas; **faltan cinco minutos para que empiece** there are five minutes to go before it starts; ***¡no faltaba más!*** (respuesta — a un agradecimiento) don't mention it!; (— a una petición) of course, certainly; (— a un ofrecimiento) I wouldn't hear of it! **3 (a)** (no asistir): **te esperamos, no faltes** we're expecting you, make sure you come; **~** A **algo** ‹*al colegio/a clase*› to be absent FROM sth; ‹*a una cita*› to miss sth; **ha faltado dos veces al trabajo** she's been off work twice **(b)** (no cumplir): **faltó a su promesa** he didn't keep his promise; **¡no me faltes al respeto!** don't be rude to me

fama *f* **(a)** (renombre, celebridad) fame; **una marca de ~ mundial** a world-famous brand; **dar ~ a algo/algn** to make sth/sb famous **(b)** (reputación) reputation; **tener mala ~** to have a bad reputation; **tiene ~ de ser severo** he has a reputation for being strict; **tiene ~ de bromista** he's well known as a joker

familia *f* **(a)** (parientes) family; **una ~ numerosa** a large family; **mi ~ política** my wife's/husband's family, my in-laws (colloq); **es de buena ~** *or* **de ~ bien** he's from a good family; **somos como de la ~** we're just like family; **le viene de ~** it runs in the family **(b)** (hijos) children; **no tienen ~** they don't have any children

familiar *adj* **(a)** ‹*vida/vínculo*› family (*before n*); ‹*envase/coche*› family (*before n*) **(b)** ‹*trato/tono*› familiar, informal; ‹*lenguaje/expresión*› colloquial **(c)** (conocido) ‹*cara/lugar*› familiar; **su voz me resulta ~** her voice is familiar ■ *mf* relative, relation

familiaridad *f* familiarity

familiarizarse [A4] *v pron* **~** CON **algo** to familiarize oneself WITH sth, become familiar WITH sth

famoso -sa *adj* famous; **~** POR **algo** famous FOR sth ■ *m,f* celebrity, famous person

fan *mf* (*pl* **fans**) fan

fanático -ca *adj* fanatical ■ *m,f* (en general) fanatic; **es un ~ de la gimnasia** he's a gym fanatic; (de fútbol) (AmS period) fan

fanatismo *m* fanaticism

fanfarrón -rrona *adj* (fam) (al hablar) loudmouthed (colloq); (al actuar): **no seas ~** stop showing off ■ *m,f* (fam) (al hablar) loudmouth (colloq); (al actuar) show-off (colloq)

fanfarronear [A1] *vi* (fam) **(a)** (al hablar) to boast, brag **(b)** (al actuar) to show off (colloq)

fango *m* mud

fantasear [A1] *vi* to fantasize

fantasía *f* **1 (a)** (imaginación) imagination **(b)** (ficción) fantasy; **vive en un mundo de ~** he's living in a fantasy world **2** (bisutería): **joyas de ~** costume jewelry*; **una pulsera de ~** an imitation diamond (*o* ruby *etc*) bracelet

fantasma *m* **(a)** (aparición) ghost **(b)** (amenaza) specter*

fantástico -ca *adj* fantastic

fantochear [A1] *vi* (AmL fam) ⇒ FANFARRONEAR

faquir *m* fakir

faraón *m* Pharaoh

fardar [A1] *vi* (Esp fam) «*persona*» ⇒ FANFARRONEAR

fardo *m* (de algodón, paja) bale; (de ropa) bundle

faringe *f* pharynx

faringitis *f* pharyngitis

farmacéutico -ca *adj* pharmaceutical ■ *m,f* druggist (AmE), chemist (BrE)

farmacia *f* **(a)** (tienda) drugstore (AmE), chemist's (BrE); **~ de guardia** *or* **de turno** duty chemist **(b)** (disciplina) pharmacy

faro *m* **(a)** (Náut) lighthouse **(b)** (Auto) headlight, headlamp; **~ antiniebla** fog light *o* (BrE) lamp

farol *m* (de alumbrado público) streetlight, streetlamp; (en jardín, portal) lantern, lamp; **~ de papel** paper lantern

farola *f* (luz) streetlight, streetlamp; (poste) lamppost

farolillo *m* (de papel) Chinese lantern

farra *f* (fam) ⇒ JUERGA

farrear [A1] *vi* (AmL fam) to go out partying (colloq), go out on the town (colloq)
■ **farrearse** *v pron* (AmL fam) ‹*fortuna/dinero*› to blow (colloq); ‹*oportunidad*› to throw away

farrero -ra *adj/m,f* (AmL fam) ⇒ FARRISTA

farrista *adj* (AmL fam): **estudiantes ~s** students who are always out living it up ■ *mf* (AmL fam): **es un ~** he's always out living it up

farsa *f* (Teatr) farce; (engaño) sham, farce

farsante *mf* fraud, fake

fascículo *m* part (*of a serialized publication*), fascicle (tech)

fascinación *f* fascination

fascinante *adj* fascinating

fascinar [A1] *vi* (fam): **me fascinó ese programa** I found that program fascinating; **me fascina viajar** I love travelling ■ **~** *vt* to fascinate, captivate

fascismo *m* fascism

fascista *adj/mf* fascist

fase *f* **(a)** (etapa) stage, phase; **la ~ de clasificación** the preliminary round; **está todavía en ~ de negociación** it is still being negotiated **(b)** (Astron, Elec, Fis, Quím) phase

fastidiado -da *adj* (esp Esp fam): **estoy un poco ~** I'm not too good *o* too well; **anda ~ de los riñones** he's having trouble with his kidneys

fastidiar [A1] *vt* **(a)** (molestar, irritar) ‹*persona*› to bother, pester **(b)** (esp Esp fam) (estropear) ‹*mecanismo/plan*› to mess up; ‹*fiesta/excursión*› to spoil; ‹*estómago*› to upset ■ **~** *vi:* **me fastidia tener que repetir las cosas** it annoys me to have to repeat things; **¡no fastidies! ¿de veras?** go on! you're kidding! (colloq)
■ **fastidiarse** *v pron* **(a)** (AmL fam) (molestarse) to get annoyed **(b)** (fam) (jorobarse): **tendré que ~me** I'll have to put up with it (colloq); **¡te fastidias!** (Esp) tough! (colloq) **(c)** (Esp fam) (estropearse) «*velada/plan*» to be ruined

fastidio *m* (molestia) annoyance; **¡qué ~!** what a nuisance!

fastidioso -sa *adj* **(a)** (molesto) ‹*persona*› tiresome, annoying; ‹*trabajo*› tiresome, irksome **(b)** (Méx, Per fam) (quisquilloso) fussy (colloq)

fastuoso -sa *adj* ‹*salón*› magnificent; ‹*banquete*› lavish

fatal *adj* **1** ‹*accidente/enfermedad/consecuencias*› fatal **2** (fam) (muy malo) terrible, awful; **fue un fin de semana ~** it was a terrible weekend; **me encuentro ~** I feel awful; **su padre está ~** his father's in a really bad way (colloq) ■ *adv* (esp Esp fam): **viste ~** he dresses really badly; **me caen ~** I can't stand them (colloq)

fatiga *f* **(a)** (cansancio) tiredness, fatigue (frml) **(b)** (ahogo) breathlessness

fatigado -da *adj* tired, weary

fatigar [A3] *vt* (físicamente) to tire ... out; (mentalmente) to tire
■ **fatigarse** *v pron* **(a)** (cansarse) to get tired, wear oneself out (colloq) **(b)** (ahogarse) to get breathless

fatigoso -sa *adj* ‹*trabajo*› tiring, exhausting

faul *m* (*pl* **fauls**) (AmL) foul

faulear [A1] *vt* (AmL) to foul

fauna *f* fauna

favor *m* **(a)** (ayuda, servicio) favor*; **¿me puedes hacer un ~?** can you do me a favor?; **vengo a pedirte un ~** I've come to ask you (for) a favor; **¿me harías el ~ de copiarme esto?** would you copy this for me, please?; **hagan el ~ de esperar** would you mind waiting, please? **(b)** (*en locs*) **a favor** in favor*; **dos votos a ~** two votes in favor; **en ~ de** in favour of; **estar a ~ de algo/algn/hacer algo** to be in favor* of sth/sb/doing sth; **por favor** please

favorable *adj* favorable*

favorecedor -dora *adj* becoming

favorecer [E3] *vt* **(a)** (ayudar, beneficiar) to favor* **(b)** «*peinado/color*» (sentar bien) to suit

favoritismo *m* favoritism*

favorito -ta *adj/m,f* favorite*

fax *m* fax; **mándaselo por ~** fax it to him

faxear [A1] *vt* to fax, send ... by fax

Fdo (= **firmado**) (en correspondencia) signed

fe *f* **(a)** (Relig) faith; (creencia, confianza) faith; **tener ~ en algo/algn** to have faith in sth/sb; **puse toda mi ~ en ti** I put all my trust in you **(b)** (intención): **no dudo de su buena ~** I don't doubt his good intentions; **actuar de buena/mala ~** to act in good/bad faith

febrero *m* ▶ **193** February; *para ejemplos ver* ENERO

fecha *f* date; **¿qué ~ es hoy?** what's the date today?, what date is it today?; **con ~ 7 de marzo** (Corresp) dated March 7 *o* (BrE) 7th March; **hasta la ~** to date; **el año pasado por estas ~s** this time last year; **en ~ próxima** soon; **~ de caducidad** *or* (AmL) **vencimiento** (de medicamento) expiration date (AmE), expiry date (BrE); (de alimento) use-by date; **~ límite** *or* **tope** (para solicitud, suscripción) closing date; (para proyecto, trabajo) deadline

fechar [A1] *vt* to date

fechoría *f* misdeed

fecundación *f* fertilization; **~ in vitro** in vitro fertilization

fecundar [A1] *vt* ‹*óvulo*› to fertilize; ‹*animal*› to inseminate

fecundo -da *adj* **(a)** (Biol) ‹*mujer*› fertile **(b)** ‹*región/tierra*› fertile; ‹*labor*› fruitful

federación *f* federation

federal *adj* federal

La fecha

Los días y los meses

Los nombres de los días de la semana y los meses del año se escriben con mayúscula en inglés:

lunes	Monday
martes	Tuesday
miércoles	Wednesday
jueves	Thursday
viernes	Friday
sábado	Saturday
domingo	Sunday
enero	January
febrero	February
marzo	March
abril	April
mayo	May
junio	June
julio	July
agosto	August
septiembre *or* setiembre	September
octubre	October
noviembre	November
diciembre	December

En inglés se emplean los números ordinales para referirse a los días del mes:

today's the ninth	hoy es nueve
he arrived on the third	llegó el tres
we'll meet again on the twentieth	nos volveremos a reunir el día veinte

En el inglés norteamericano la fecha normalmente se escribe de la siguiente manera:

March 3rd (*léase* March third)

En el inglés británico puede escribirse de dos maneras distintas:

3rd March (*léase* the third of March)
March 3rd (*léase* March the third)

Para preguntar la fecha

¿a cuánto estamos?	what's the date?
¿qué fecha es hoy?	what date is it today?
hoy es siete	it's the seventh
(el) siete de enero	January seventh (AmE) January the seventh (BrE) the seventh of January (BrE)
¿qué día es hoy?	what day is it today?
es miércoles	it's Wednesday

Años y décadas

En inglés los años se expresan de la siguiente manera:

55 aC/dC	fifty-five BC/AD
763	seven sixty-three
900	nine hundred

Los años a partir del año 1000 se expresan en centenas y no en miles:

1066	ten sixty-six
1200	twelve hundred
1996	nineteen ninety-six

Cuando se añade el año a la fecha, sólo hace falta agregar una coma:

nació el 27 de mayo de 1913	she was born on May 27th, 1913

Esta coma suele omitirse en correspondencia formal, donde la fecha puede escribirse:

September 8th 1994
8th September 1994
September 8 1994
8 September 1994

Cuando la fecha se escribe en cifras, el inglés norteamericano indica primero el mes y luego el día, mientras que en Gran Bretaña se expresa primero el día y luego el mes:

10.28.93 (AmE) 28.10.93 (BrE)	28 de octubre de 1993

Las cifras pueden ir separadas por puntos, guiones o barras:

5.10.94 5-10-94 5/10/94

Para referirse a una década se utiliza el plural:

the twenties	los años veinte
the eighteen fifties	la década 1850–1860

Siglos

Se utilizan los números ordinales para referirse a los siglos:

el siglo quinto	the fifth century
el siglo dieciocho	the eighteenth century

Cuando se escriben en cifras, se utilizan números arábigos:

el siglo XIV	the 14th century
s.XIX	19c C19

¿Cuándo?

¿Cuándo sucedió/sucede/sucederá?
When did it/does it/will it happen?

el jueves	on Thursday
el jueves 6	on Thursday 6th
el jueves por la tarde	on Thursday afternoon
el 26 de febrero	on February 26th
el 10 de junio de 1979	on June 10th, 1979
en enero	in January
en primavera	in (the) spring
en la primavera de 1994	in the spring of 1994
en 1970	in 1970
en la década de los 80	in the eighties
en el siglo XXI	in the 21st century
a principios de agosto	in early August
a mediados de enero	in mid-January
a fines de diciembre	in late December
a principios de la primavera	in the early spring
a principios de este año	at the beginning of this year
a mediados de la década de los 60	in the mid-1960s
a fines del s.XVIII	in the late 18c

felicidad *f* **(a)** (alegría) happiness **(b) ¡felicidades!** *interj* (por cumpleaños) Happy Birthday!; (en Navidad) Merry Christmas!; (por un logro) congratulations!

felicitación *f* **(a)** (escrito — por un logro) letter of congratulation; (— en Navidad) Christmas card (*or letter wishing sb Merry Christmas*) **(b) felicitaciones** *fpl* (deseo — por un logro) congratulations (*pl*); (— en Navidad) greetings (*pl*) **(c) ¡felicitaciones!** *interj* (AmL) congratulations!

felicitar [A1] *vt* **(a)** (por un logro) to congratulate; **¡te felicito!** congratulations!; **me felicitó por el premio** he congratulated me on winning the prize **(b)** (por Navidad) to wish ... (a) Merry Christmas; (por cumpleaños) to wish ... (a) Happy Birthday

feligrés -gresa *m,f* parishioner

feliz *adj* happy; **les deseo que sean muy felices** I wish you every happiness; **¡~ cumpleaños!** happy birthday!; **¡~ Navidad!** Merry Christmas!; **¡~ Año Nuevo!** Happy New Year!; **¡~ viaje!** have a good trip!

felpa *f* (Tex) (para toallas) toweling*; (en tapicería) plush

felpudo *m* doormat

femenil *adj* (Méx) ‹*equipo/moda*› ladies' (*before n*), women's (*before n*)

femenino -na *adj* **(a)** ‹*equipo/moda*› ladies' (*before n*), women's (*before n*); ‹*hormona/sexo*› female **(b)** ‹*vestido/modales/chica*› feminine **(c)** (Ling) feminine

feminismo *m* feminism

feminista *adj/mf* feminist

fenomenal *adj* (fam) great (colloq) ■ *adv* (fam): **lo pasamos ~** we had a great time (colloq); **me vino ~** it was exactly *o* just what I needed; **¡~!** great! (colloq)

fenómeno[1] -na *adj/adv* (AmL) ⇒ FENOMENAL

fenómeno[2] *m* (suceso) phenomenon

feo[1], fea *adj* **(a)** ‹*persona/edificio*› ugly; ‹*peinado*› unflattering; **es fea de cara** she has a very plain face; **es un barrio ~** it's not a very nice neighborhood **(b)** ‹*asunto/situación*› unpleasant; ‹*olor/sabor*› (esp AmL) unpleasant; **¡qué ~ está el día!** what an awful day!; **la cosa se está poniendo fea** things are getting nasty *o* ugly; **es** *or* (Esp) **está muy ~ hablar así** it's not nice to talk like that

feo[2] *adv* (AmL) ‹*oler/saber*› bad; **me miró ~** she gave me a dirty look

féretro *m* coffin

feria *f* **1 (a)** (exposición comercial) fair; **~ de muestras** trade fair **(b)** (CS, Per) (mercado) (street) market **2 (a)** (fiesta popular) festival **(b)** (parque de atracciones) fair **3** (Méx fam) (cambio, suelto) small change; (dinero) cash (colloq)

feriado *m* (AmL) (public) holiday

fermentar [A1] *vi/vt* to ferment

fermento *m* ferment

feroz *adj* **(a)** ‹*animal*› ferocious, fierce; ‹*ataque/mirada/odio*› fierce, vicious; ‹*viento/tempestad*› fierce, violent **(b)** (Col, Méx, Ven fam) (feo) horrendous (colloq)

ferretería *f* (tienda) hardware store, ironmonger's (BrE); (mercancías) hardware, ironmongery (BrE)

ferrocarril *m* railroad (AmE), railway (BrE)

ferrocarrilero -ra *adj* (Chi, Méx) rail (*before n*)

ferroviario -ria *adj* rail (*before n*)

ferry /'ferri/ *m* (*pl* **-rrys**) ferry

fértil *adj* fertile

fertilización *f* fertilization; **~ in vitro** in vitro fertilization

fertilizante *m* fertilizer

fertilizar [A4] *vt* to fertilize, put fertilizer on

ferviente *adj* ‹*admiración/creyente*› fervent; ‹*deseo*› burning; ‹*fe/defensor*› passionate

fervor *m* fervor*; **con ~** fervently

festejado -da *m,f* (CS) *person celebrating his/her birthday* (*o saint's day etc*)

festejar [A1] *vt* (AmL) (celebrar) to celebrate

festejo *m* celebration, festivity

festín *m* feast, banquet

festival *m* festival; **~ de cine** film festival

festividad *f* **(a)** (fiesta religiosa) feast, festivity **(b) festividades** *fpl* (festejos) festivities (*pl*)

festivo -va *adj* festive; ⇒ DIA 1(b)

fetidez *f* (cualidad) smelliness; (olor) stench

fétido -da *adj* fetid, foul-smelling

feto *m* fetus*

feúcho -cha *adj* (fam) ‹*mujer*› plain, homely (AmE colloq); **es ~** he's not much to look at

feudalismo *m* feudalism

fiable *adj* reliable

fiaca *adj inv* (RPl fam) bone idle (colloq), lazy ■ *f* (Andes, CS fam) (pereza): **me da ~** I can't be bothered

fiador -dora *m,f* (Com, Der, Fin) guarantor

fiambre *m* (Coc): *tb* **~s** cold cuts (*pl*) (AmE), cold meats (*pl*) (BrE)

fiambrería *f* (AmL) delicatessen

fianza *f* **(a)** (Der) bail; **salió bajo ~** she was released on bail **(b)** (Com) deposit

fiar [A17] *vt* ‹*mercancías*› to sell ... on credit ■ **~** *vi* **(a)** (dar crédito) to give credit **(b) ser de ~** «*persona*» (digno de confianza) to be trustworthy; (responsable) to be reliable; «*mecanismo/motor*» to be reliable

■ **fiarse** *v pron:* **no me fío de lo que dice** I don't believe what he says; **~se** DE **algn** to trust sb

fiasco *m* fiasco

fibra *f* fiber*; **~s artificiales** man-made fibers; **~ de vidrio** fiberglass*; **~ óptica** optical fiber*

ficción *f* fiction

ficha *f* **1** (para datos) card; (de fichero) index card; **~ médica** medical records (*pl*); **~ policial** police record **2 (a)** (de teléfono, estacionamiento) token **(b)** (Jueg) (de dominó) domino; (de damas) checker(AmE), draught (BrE); (de otros juegos de mesa) counter; (de ruleta, póker) chip

fichaje *m* (Dep) (acción) signing (up); (jugador) signing, trade (AmE)

fichar [A1] *vt* **(a)** «*policía*» to open a file on **(b)** «*equipo/club*» to sign (up) ■ **~** *vi* (en fábrica, oficina

— a la entrada) to clock in, punch in (AmE); (— a la salida) to clock out *o* (BrE) off, to punch out (AmE)

fichero *m* **(a)** (mueble para carpetas) filing cabinet **(b)** (cajón — de carpetas) filing draw; (— para tarjetas) card index draw **(c)** (caja) index card file (AmE), card index box (BrE) **(d)** (conjunto de fichas) file; (Inf) file

ficticio -cia *adj* ‹*personaje/suceso*› fictitious

fidelidad *f* **(a)** (de persona, animal) fidelity, faithfulness **(b)** (de reproducción) faithfulness, fidelity; (de instrumento) accuracy, precision

fideo *m* **(a)** (pasta fina) noodle; (muy finos) vermicelli **(b) fideos** *mpl* (RPl) (pasta en general) pasta

fiebre *f* **(a)** (Med) fever; **tener ~** to be feverish, to have a fever (esp AmE), to have a temperature (esp BrE); **le bajó la ~** his fever *o* temperature came down; **~ del heno** hay fever; **~ palúdica** malaria **(b)** (furor) obsession; **le dio la ~ de la limpieza** he went crazy and started cleaning the whole house (colloq); **~ del oro** gold fever

fiel *adj* **(a)** ‹*persona/animal*› faithful; **serle ~ a algn** to be faithful to sb; **~ al rey** loyal to the king **(b)** ‹*traducción/copia*› faithful, accurate ■ *mf* (Relig) **los ~es** the faithful

fieltro *m* felt

fiera *f* (animal) wild animal, beast (liter); ***ponerse como*** or ***hecho una ~*** to go wild (colloq)

fiero -ra *adj* ‹*animal*› fierce, ferocious

fierro *m* **(a)** (AmL) (hierro) iron; (fam) (trozo de metal) piece of metal **(b) fierros** *mpl* (Méx fam) (en los dientes) braces (*pl*) (AmE), brace (esp BrE)

fiesta *f* **(a)** (celebración) party; **~ de cumpleaños** birthday party; **dieron una gran ~** they threw *o* had a big party; **estar de ~** to be having a party; ***aguar la ~*** to spoil the fun **(b)** (día festivo) (public) holiday; **el lunes es ~** Monday is a holiday; **~ nacional** (día festivo) public holiday; (Taur) bullfighting; **~ patria** (AmL) independence day **(c) fiestas** *fpl* (festejos) fiesta, festival; (de fin de año, etc) festive season; **¡felices ~s!** Merry Christmas!; **¿dónde vas a pasar estas ~s?** where are you going to spend the vacation (AmE) *o* (BrE) holidays?

FIFA /'fifa/ *f*: **la ~** FIFA

figura *f* figure; **tiene buena ~** she has a good figure; **una ~ de las letras** an important literary figure; **~ paterna** father figure

figuración *f* (imaginación) imagining; **son figuraciones tuyas** it's all in your imagination

figurado -da *adj* figurative; **en sentido ~** in a figurative sense

figurar [A1] *vi* (en lista, documento) to appear ■ **figurarse** *v pron* to imagine; **me figuro que sí** I imagine so, I figure she (*o* he *etc*) will (AmE); **me figuro que tardaremos una hora** I reckon *o* (AmE) figure that it'll take us one hour; **¡figúrate, tardamos dos horas!** just imagine! it took us two hours; **ya me lo figuraba yo** I thought as much, so I thought

figurita *f* (de adorno) figurine; (lámina) (RPl) picture card

fijación *f* (Psic) fixation, obsession; **¡que ~ tienes con ese tema!** you're obsessed with that subject!

fijar [A1] *vt* **1 (a)** (poner, clavar) ‹*poste/estantería*› to fix; ⊖ **prohibido fijar carteles** stick no bills; **fijó la mirada en el horizonte** she fixed her gaze on the horizon **(b)** ‹*atención/mente*› to focus **2 (a)** ‹*residencia*› to take up, establish (frml) **(b)** ‹*fecha/cifra/precio*› to set **(c)** «*reglamento/ley*» to state ■ **fijarse** *v pron* **(a)** (prestar atención): **fíjate bien en cómo lo hace** watch carefully how she does it; **fíjate en lo que haces** watch *o* pay attention to what you're doing **(b)** (darse cuenta) to notice; **¿te has fijado en que no discuten nunca?** have you noticed that they never quarrel?; **¡fíjate lo que ha crecido!** just look how she's grown!

fijo¹ -ja *adj* **(a)** (no movible) fixed; **una lámpara fija a la pared** a lamp fixed to the wall; **con los ojos ~s en ella** with his eyes fixed on her; **asegúrate de que la escalera está bien fija** make sure the ladder is steady **(b)** ‹*sueldo/precios*› fixed; ‹*trabajo/empleado*› permanent; ‹*cliente*› regular **(c)** (definitivo) ‹*fecha*› definite, firm

fijo² *adv* (fam): **¿crees que vendrá? — fijo** do you think she'll come? — definitely *o* (colloq) sure; **~ que el domingo llueve** it's bound to rain on Sunday

fila *f* **(a)** (hilera) line; **formen ~ aquí** line up *o* form a line here; **en ~ india** in single file; **estacionado en doble ~** double-parked **(b)** (en teatro, aula) row **(c) filas** *fpl* (Mil) ranks (*pl*); **incorporarse a ~s** to join up; **lo llamaron a ~s** he was drafted

filamento *m* (Elec) filament; (hilo, fibra) thread

filatelia *f* stamp collecting, philately

filete *m* (de pescado), fillet; (de carne — bistec) steak; (— corte entre las costillas y el lomo) (Chi, Méx) fillet

filiación *f* (afiliación) affiliation; **~ política** political affiliation

filial *adj* **(a)** ‹*amor*› filial **(b)** ‹*compañía/asociación*› affiliate (*before n*), subsidiary ■ *f* subsidiary (company)

Filipinas *fpl*: *tb* **las ~** the Philippines

filipino -na *adj* Philippine, Filipino ■ *m,f* Filipino

film *m* (*pl* **films**) **(a)** (Cin, TV) movie, film (BrE) **(b)** (Coc) *tb* **~ transparente** Saran wrap® (AmE), clingfilm (BrE)

filmadora *f* (AmL) movie camera (AmE), cinecamera (BrE)

filmar [A1] *vt* ‹*película*› to shoot; ‹*persona/suceso*› to film

filmina *f* slide

filmoteca *f* film library

filo *m* **(a)** (de cuchillo, espada) cutting edge, blade; **no tiene mucho ~** it isn't very sharp; **le voy a dar ~** I'm going to sharpen it **(b)** (borde) edge; **el ~ de la mesa** the edge of the table; **al ~ de las siete** at seven o'clock sharp

filología *f* philology; **una licenciatura en ~ francesa** a degree in French

filólogo -ga *m,f* philologist; **soy ~** I have a degree in languages

filón *m* **(a)** (Min) seam, vein **(b)** (fam) (negocio) gold mine (colloq)

filoso -sa *adj* (AmL) ‹*cuchillo/hoja*› sharp

filosofía *f* philosophy

filosófico -ca *adj* philosophical

filósofo -fa *m,f* philosopher

filtración *f* (en general) leak ; (de información) leak; **la ~ de un informe** the leaking of a report

filtrar [A1] *vt* **(a)** ‹*líquido/rayos*› to filter **(b)** ‹*informaciones/noticias*› to leak

■ **filtrarse** *v pron* **(a)** «*agua*» to leak; «*humedad*» to seep; **la luz se filtraba por entre las persianas** light filtered through the shutters **(b)** «*noticia*» to leak

filtro *m* filter; **~ solar** sunscreen

fin *m* **1 (a)** (final) end; **a ~es de junio** at the end of June; **a ~ de mes** at the end of the month; **~ de año** New Year's Eve; **~ de semana** (sábado y domingo) weekend; **puso ~ a la discusión** she put an end to the discussion **(b)** (*en locs*) **por** *or* **al fin** at last; **en fin** (expresando resignación) ah well; **en ~ ¡sigamos!** anyway, let's carry on!; ***a ~ de cuentas*** in the end, at the end of the day; ***al ~ y al cabo*** after all **2 (a)** (objetivo, finalidad) purpose; **el ~ de esta visita** the aim *o* purpose of this visit **(b)** (*en locs*) **a fin de que** (frml) in order to; **con este fin** (frml) with this aim (frml), to this end (frml); **con el fin** *or* **a fin de** (frml) with the aim *o* purpose of

final *adj* ‹*decisión*› final; ‹*objetivo*› ultimate ■ *m* end; **a ~es de junio** at the end of June; **un ~ feliz** a happy ending; **al ~ de la lista** at the bottom of the list; **al ~ tendrá que decidirse** he'll have to make his mind up in the end *o* eventually ■ *f* (Dep) **(a)** (en fútbol, tenis etc) final; **la ~ de copa** the cup final; **pasar a la ~** to go through to *o* make it to the final **(b) finales** *fpl* (en béisbol, baloncesto, fútbol americano) playoffs (*pl*)

finalidad *f* (propósito, utilidad) purpose, aim

finalista *adj*: **los dos equipos ~s** the two teams that reach (*o* reached *etc*) the final ■ *mf* finalist

finalizar [A4] *vt* to finish ■ **~** *vi* to end; **una vez finalizada la reunión** once the meeting is/was over

financiación *f*, **financiamiento** *m* financing

financiar [A1] *vt* **(a)** ‹*empresa/proyecto*› to finance, fund **(b)** (AmL) (vender a plazos) to give credit facilities for

financiero -ra *adj* financial ■ *m,f* financier

financista *mf* (AmL) financier

finanzas *fpl* finances (*pl*)

finca *f* **(a)** (explotación agrícola) farm **(b)** (casa de campo) country estate **(c)** (Esp) (propiedad urbana) building

fincar [A2] *vt* (Méx) to build

fingido -da *adj* hypocritical, false

fingir [I7] *vt* **(a)** ‹*alegría/desinterés*› to feign, fake; **fingió no verme** she pretended not to see me **(b)** ‹*voz*› to imitate ■ **~** *vi* to pretend

■ **fingirse** *v pron:* **se fingió apenado** he pretended to be sorry

finlandés¹ -desa *adj* Finnish ■ *m,f* (persona) Finn

finlandés² *m* (idioma) Finnish

Finlandia *f* Finland

fino¹ -na *adj* **1** (en grosor) ‹*papel/capa/hilo*› fine, thin; ‹*loncha*› thin; ‹*arena/pelo/lluvia*› fine; ‹*labios*› thin; ‹*cintura/dedos*› slender; ‹*punta/lápiz*› fine **2** (en calidad) ‹*pastelería/bollería*› high quality; ‹*porcelana*› fine; ‹*lencería*› sheer **3** (en modales) refined **4 (a)** ‹*oído/olfato*› acute **(b)** ‹*ironía/humor*› subtle

fino² *m* fino, dry sherry

firma *f* **1** (nombre) signature; (acción) signing **2** (empresa) company, firm (BrE)

firmar [A1] *vt/vi* to sign

firme *adj* **1** ‹*escalera/silla/mesa*› steady; **terreno ~** solid ground; **con paso/pulso ~** with a firm step/steady hand; **una oferta en ~** a firm offer; ***de ~*** ‹*estudiar/trabajar*› hard **2** (Mil): **¡~s!** attention! **3 (a)** ‹*persona*› firm; **mostrarse ~ con algn** to be firm with sb; **me mantuve ~ en mi idea** I stuck *o* kept to my idea **(b)** (*delante del n*) ‹*creencia/convicción*› firm

firmeza *f* **(a)** (de convicciones, carácter) strength; **con ~** firmly **(b)** (del terreno) firmness

fiscal *adj* fiscal, tax (*before n*) ■ *mf* ≈ district attorney (*in US*), ≈ public prosecutor (*in UK*)

fiscalizar [A4] *vt* to supervise, control

fisco *m* ≈ Treasury (*in US*), ≈ Exchequer (*in UK*)

fisgar [A3] *vi* (fam) to snoop (colloq); **andaba fisgando por las oficinas** he was snooping around the offices

fisgón -gona *adj* (fam) nosy (colloq) ■ *m,f* (fam) busybody (colloq)

fisgonear [A1] *vi* (fam) to nose around (colloq)

física *f* physics; **~ nuclear** nuclear physics

físico¹ -ca *adj* physical ■ *m,f* physicist

físico² *m* (cuerpo — de hombre, atleta) physique; (— de mujer) figure; (apariencia) appearance

fisionomía, **fisonomía** *f* **(a)** (de persona) features (*pl*) **(b)** (de objeto, lugar) appearance

fisioterapia *f* physiotherapy, physical therapy (AmE)

flaccidez *f* flaccidity

fláccido -da *adj* flaccid, flabby

flaco -ca *adj* thin, skinny (colloq)

flama *f* (Méx) flame

flamable *adj* (Méx) inflammable, flammable

flamante *adj* (*gen delante del n*) (nuevo) brand-new; (vistoso) smart (colloq)

flamenco¹ -ca *adj* **1** ‹*cante/baile*› flamenco (*before n*) **2** (de Flandes) Flemish ■ *m,f* Fleming; **los ~s** the Flemish

flamenco² *m* **1** (Mús) flamenco **2** (idioma) Flemish **3** (Zool) flamingo

flan *m* **(a)** (dulce) crème caramel **(b)** (de arroz) mold*; (de pescado, verduras) terrine

flanco *m* **(a)** (Mil) flank **(b)** (de animal) flank, side; (de persona) side

Flandes *m* Flanders

flaquear [A1] *vi* «*persona/fuerzas*» to flag; **su voluntad empezó a ~** she began to lose heart

flaqueza *f* weakness

flash /'flas/ *m* (*pl* **flashes**) (Fot) flash

flato *m* **(a)** (Esp) (dolor en el costado): **tengo ~** I have a stitch **(b)**(Chi fam) (eructo) burp (colloq)

flauta *f* (Mús) flute; **~ dulce** recorder ■ *mf* flute player, flutist (AmE), flautist (BrE)

flautín *m* piccolo ■ *mf* piccolo (player)

flautista *mf* flute player, flutist (AmE), flautist (BrE)

flecha *f* arrow

flechazo *m* **(a)** (fam) (enamoramiento): **fue un ~** it was love at first sight **(b)** (herida) arrow wound

fleco *m* (Méx) (en el pelo) bangs (*pl*) (AmE), fringe (BrE)

flecos *mpl* **(a)** (adorno) fringe; **un chal con ~** a fringed shawl **(b)** (borde deshilachado) frayed edge

flema *f* phlegm

flemático -ca *adj* phlegmatic

flemón *m* boil, abscess; (en la encía) gumboil

flequillo *m* bangs (*pl*) (AmE), fringe (BrE)

fletar [A1] *vt* (Com, Transp) ‹*barco/avión*› to charter; ‹*autobús/camión*› to hire, rent (AmE)

flete *m* **(a)** (contratación — de barco, avión) charter; (— de autobús, camión) hire **(b)** (precio de contratación — de barco, avión) charter fee; (— de autobús, camión) hire charge, rental charge (AmE)

flexibilidad *f* flexibility

flexible *adj* flexible

flexión *f* (Dep) (de brazos) push-up, press-up (BrE); (de piernas) squat; **hacer flexiones** (de brazos) to do push-ups *o* press-ups; (de cintura) to touch one's toes

flexionar [A1] *vt* (Dep) ‹*pierna/rodillas*› to bend

flirt /ˈflirt/ *m* (*pl* **flirts**) **(a)** (relación) fling **(b)** (persona) (*m*) boyfriend; (*f*) girlfriend

flirtear [A1] *vi* to flirt

flojear [A1] *vi* **(a)** (debilitarse) to grow *o* get weak; **me flojean las piernas** my legs are getting weak **(b)** (fam) (holgazanear) to laze around

flojera *f* **(a)** (fam) (debilidad) lethargy **(b)** (fam) (pereza) laziness; **me da ~** I can't be bothered; **tengo ~** I feel lazy

flojo -ja *adj* **1 (a)** ‹*nudo/tornillo/vendaje*› loose; ‹*cuerda/goma*› slack **(b)** (débil) weak **(c)** ‹*vientos*› light **(d)** ‹*café/té*› weak **2** (mediocre) ‹*trabajo/examen*› poor; ‹*película/vino*› second-rate; ‹*estudiante*› poor; **está ~ en física** he's weak in (AmE) *o* (BrE) at physics **3** ‹*persona*› (fam) (perezoso) lazy ■ *m,f* (fam) (perezoso) lazybones (colloq)

floppy /ˈflopi/ *m* (*pl* **floppys**) floppy disk, diskette

flor *f* (de planta) flower; (de árbol frutal) blossom; **~es secas** dried flowers; **un vestido de ~es** a flowery dress; **en ~** in flower *o* bloom/in blossom; **~ de azahar** orange/lemon blossom; ***la ~ y nata*** the cream, the crème de la crème

flora *f* flora

florear [A1] *vi* **(a)** (Chi, Méx) (Bot) to flower, blossom **(b)** (Méx) (halagar): **le ~on mucho su vestido** her dress got a lot of compliments

florecer [E3] *vi* **(a)** «*tulipán/rosa*» to flower, bloom; «*árbol*» to flower, blossom **(b)** (prosperar) to flourish, thrive

floreciente *adj* flourishing, thriving

Florencia *f* Florence

florentino -na *adj/m,f* Florentine

florería *f* (AmL) florist's, flower shop

florero *m* vase

florido -da *adj* **(a)** ‹*campo*› full of flowers **(b)** ‹*estilo/lenguaje*› flowery

florín *m* (moneda holandesa) guilder

floristería *f* florist's, flower shop

flota *f* **1** (de barcos, camiones, aviones) fleet **2** (Col) (autobús) bus (AmE), coach (BrE)

flotador *m* (en general) float; (para la cintura) rubber ring; (para los brazos) armband

flotante *adj* floating

flotar [A1] *vi* to float

flote: **a ~** afloat; **mantenerse a ~** to stay afloat; **logró mantener el negocio a ~** he managed to keep the business afloat; **salir a ~** «*cuerpo sumergido*» to float to the surface; «*país/persona en apuros*» to get back on its/one's feet

flotilla *f* (Náut) flotilla; (Aviac) fleet

fluctuar [A18] *vi* to fluctuate

fluidez *f* **(a)** (de expresión) fluency; **habla griego con ~** she speaks Greek fluently **(b)** (de tráfico) smooth flow **(c)** (Fís, Quím) fluidity

fluido *adj* ‹*estilo/lenguaje*› fluent; ‹*circulación*› free-flowing; ‹*movimientos*› fluid, fluent ■ *m* fluid

fluir [I20] *vi* to flow

flujo *m* **1** (circulación, corriente) flow; **~ sanguíneo** blood flow **2** (Med) (secreción) discharge; **~ menstrual** menstrual flow **3** (Náut) tide; **~ y reflujo** ebb and flow

fluminense *adj* of/from Rio de Janeiro

flúor, **fluor** *m* (gas) fluorine; (fluoruro) fluoride

fluorescente *adj* fluorescent

fluvial *adj* river (*before n*)

fobia *f* phobia; **tiene ~ a los aviones** he has a phobia about flying

foca *f* (animal) seal; (piel) sealskin

focal *adj* focal

foco *m* **1 (a)** (Fís, Fot, Mat) focus **(b)** (centro, núcleo) focus; **fue el ~ de todas las miradas** everybody's eyes were focused on him **(c)** (de incendio) seat **2 (a)** (reflector) (Cin, Teatr) spotlight; (en estadio, monumento) floodlight **(b)** (AmL) (Auto) light **(c)** (Ec, Méx, Per) (de lámpara) light bulb **(d)** (AmC) (linterna) flashlight (AmE), torch (BrE)

fogata *f* bonfire

fogón *m* (quemador) burner; (fogata) (AmL) bonfire, campfire; (de caldera) firebox

fogonazo *m* flash, explosion

fogueado -da *adj* (AmS fam) experienced

fogueo *m* (Mil): **un cartucho de ~** a blank (cartridge)

folio *m* **(a)** (hoja) sheet (of paper); **papel tamaño ~** A4 paper **(b)** (de un trabajo, una tesis) page

folk /ˈfo(l)k/ *adj* folk (*before n*) ■ *m* folk (music)

folklore *m* folklore

folklórico -ca *adj* **(a)** ‹*danza/música/leyenda*› folk (*before n*) **(b)** (fam) (pintoresco) quaint

follaje *m* foliage

folletín *m* (en periódicos, revistas) newspaper serial; (revista mala) rag (colloq); (película, novela mala) melodrama

folleto *m* (hoja) leaflet, flier (AmE); (librito) brochure, pamphlet

follón *m* (Esp fam) **(a)** (trifulca) commotion, ruckus; (ruido) racket (colloq), din (AmE colloq); **armó un buen ~** (montó una trifulca) he kicked up a hell of a fuss (colloq); (hizo ruido) he made such a racket *o* din (colloq) **(b)** (situación confusa, desorden) mess **(c)** (problema) trouble; **no te metas en follones** don't get into trouble

fomentar [A1] *vt* ‹*industria/turismo*› to promote; ‹*ahorro/inversión*› to encourage, boost; ‹*disturbio/odio*› to incite, foment (frml); ‹*interés/afición*› to encourage

fonda *f* **(a)** (esp AmL) (restaurant) cheap restaurant **(b)** (esp Esp) (pensión) boarding house **(c)** (Chi) (puesto) refreshment stand

fondista *mf* (Dep) long-distance runner

fondo *m* **1 (a)** (parte más baja) bottom; **el ~ del mar** the bottom of the sea; **llegaré al ~ de esta cuestión** I'll get to the bottom of this matter **(b)** (parte de atrás — de pasillo, calle) end; (— de habitación) back; **al ~ de la sala** at the back of the room **(c)** (profundidad): **tiene poco ~** it is not very deep **(d)** (de edificio) depth **(e)** (en cuadro, fotografía) background **2** (Lit) (contenido) content **3** (Fin) **(a)** (de dinero) fund; **hacer un ~ común** to start a joint fund *o* (colloq) a kitty **(b) fondos** *mpl* (dinero) money, funds (*pl*); **recaudar ~s** to raise money; **un cheque sin ~s** a dud *o* (AmE) rubber check (colloq) **4** (Dep) (en atletismo): **de ~** ‹*corredor/carrera/prueba*› long-distance (*before n*) **5** (Méx) (Indum) slip, underskirt **6** (*en locs*) **a fondo** (*loc adj*) ‹*estudio/investigación*› in-depth (*before n*); ‹*limpieza*› thorough; (*loc adv*) ‹*prepararse/entrenar*› thoroughly; **conoce el tema a ~** she knows the subject really well; **de fondo** ‹*ruido/música*› background (*before n*); ***en el ~*: en el ~ nos llevamos bien** we get on all right, really; **en el ~ no es malo** deep down he's not a bad person

fonética *f* phonetics

fonógrafo *m* phonograph

fontanería *f* (esp Esp) plumbing

fontanero -ra *m,f* (esp Esp) plumber

footing /'futin/ *m* jogging; **hacer ~** to jog

forajido -da *m,f* fugitive, outlaw

foráneo -nea *adj* foreign, strange

forastero -ra *m,f* stranger, outsider

forcejear [A1] *vi* to struggle

forcejeo *m* struggle

fórceps *m* (*pl* ~) forceps (*pl*)

forense *adj* forensic ■ *mf* forensic scientist

forestal *adj* forest (*before n*)

forjar [A1] *vt* **(a)** ‹*utensilio/pieza*› to forge; ‹*metal*› to work **(b)** ‹*porvenir*› to shape, forge; ‹*plan*› to make; ‹*ilusiones/esperanzas*› to build up **(c)** ‹*nación/bases*› to create; ‹*amistad/alianza*› to forge
■ **forjarse** *v pron* ‹*porvenir*› to shape, forge; ‹*ilusiones*› to build up

forma *f* **1 (a)** (contorno, apariencia) shape; **en ~ de cruz** in the shape of a cross; **tiene la ~ de un platillo** it's the shape of a saucer; **dar ~ a algo** (al barro) to shape sth; (a proyecto) to give shape to sth **(b)** (tipo, modalidad) form; **distintas ~s de vida animal** different forms of animal life; **~ de pago** form *o* method of payment **2** (Dep, Med): **estar en ~** to be fit; **está en baja ~** he's not on form; **en plena ~** on top form; ***en ~*: nos divertimos en ~** we had a really good time **3** (manera, modo) way; **es su ~ de ser** it's just the way he is; **¡vaya ~ de conducir!** what a way to drive!; **de ~ distinta** differently; ***de cualquier ~*** *or* ***de todas ~s*** anyway, in any case **4 formas** *fpl* **(a)** (de mujer) figure **(b)** (apariencias) appearances (*pl*); **guardar las ~s** to keep up appearances **5** (Méx) (formulario) form

formación *f* **1** (en general) formation; **la ~ de un gobierno** the formation of a government **2** (educación recibida) education; (para trabajo) training; **~ profesional** *or* (CS) **vocacional** professional *o* vocational training

formal *adj* **1** (en general) formal; ‹*promesa/oferta*› firm **2** ‹*persona*› (cumplidora) reliable, dependable; (responsable) responsible

formalidad *f* **1** (de persona) reliability; **no tiene ~** he's so unreliable **2** (requisito) formality

formalizar [A4] *vt* ‹*noviazgo/relación*› to make ... official; ‹*transacción/contrato*› to formalize

formar [A1] *vt* **1 (a)** (crear) ‹*círculo/figura*› to make, form; ‹*asociación/gobierno*› to form, set up; ‹*barricada*› to set up; **¡formen parejas!** (en clase) get into pairs *o* twos!; (en baile) take your partners! **(b)** (Ling) to form **(c)** (Mil) ‹*tropas*› to have ... fall in **2** (componer) to make up; **un equipo formado por cinco personas** a team made up of five people; **~ parte de algo** to be part of sth, to belong to sth **3** ‹*carácter/espíritu*› to form, shape **4** (educar) to bring up; (para trabajo) to train ■ **~** *vi* (Mil) to fall in
■ **formarse** *v pron* **1 (a)** (hacerse, crearse) «*grupo/organismo*» to form; **se formó una cola** a line (AmE) *o* (BrE) queue formed **(b)** (desarrollarse) «*niño/huesos*» to develop **(c)** ‹*idea/opinión*› to form **2** (educarse) to be educated; (para trabajo) to be trained

formato *m* **1** (tamaño, forma) format **2** (Méx) (formulario, solicitud) form

formidable *adj/interj* (fam) fantastic (colloq)

fórmula *f* **1 (a)** (Mat, Quím) formula **(b)** (manera, sistema) way **(c)** (frase, expresión) standard expression, formula; **~s de cortesía** polite expressions **(d)** (Col) (receta médica) prescription **2** (Auto) formula; **un coche de F~ 1** a Formula 1 car

formular [A1] *vt* **1** ‹*queja*› to make, lodge; ‹*teoría/plan*› to formulate **2** (Col) «*médico*» to prescribe

formulario *m* form

forrado -da *adj* **1** ‹*prenda*› lined; ‹*sillón/libro*› covered; **un abrigo ~ de seda** a coat lined with silk **2** [ESTAR] (fam) (de dinero) loaded (colloq)

forrar [A1] *vt* ‹*prenda*› to line; ‹*libro/sillón*› to cover
■ **forrarse** *v pron* (fam) *tb* **~se de dinero** to make a killing *o* mint

forro *m* (de abrigo) lining; (de sillón) cover; (de libro) cover, jacket

fortalecer [E3] *vt* ‹*organismo/músculos/amistad*› to strengthen

■ **fortalecerse** *v pron* «*organismo/músculo*» to get stronger

fortaleza *f* **1** (física) strength; (moral) fortitude, strength of spirit **2** (Mil) fortress

fortificar [A2] *vt* **(a)** (Mil) ‹*lugar/plaza*› to fortify **(b)** (dar fuerza) to strengthen, make ... stronger

fortín *m* (fuerte pequeño) (small) fort; (emplazamiento) pillbox, bunker

fortuito -ta *adj* ‹*encuentro/suceso*› chance (*before n*), fortuitous

fortuna *f* **(a)** (riqueza) fortune **(b)** (azar, suerte) fortune; **por ~** fortunately; ***probar* ~** to try one's luck

forzado -da *adj* forced, unnatural

forzar [A11] *vt* **1** (obligar) to force **2 (a)** ‹*vista*› to strain; **estaba forzando la vista** I was straining my eyes **(b)** ‹*sonrisa*› to force **3** ‹*puerta/cerradura*› to force

forzoso -sa *adj* ‹*aterrizaje/anexión/paro*› forced; ‹*jubilación/liquidación*› compulsory

fosa *f* (zanja) ditch; (hoyo) pit; (tumba) grave; **~ común** common *o* communal grave

fosforescente *adj* **(a)** (Fís) phosphorescent **(b)** ‹*color/pintura*› fluorescent

fósforo *m* **(a)** (Quím) phosphorus **(b)** (cerilla) match

fósil *adj* fossilized, fossil (*before n*) ■ *m* fossil

foso *m* **(a)** (zanja) ditch; (en fortificaciones) moat; (Equ) water jump **(b)** (Teatr) pit; **~ de la orquesta** orchestra pit **(c)** (Auto) (inspection) pit

foto *f* picture, photo (esp BrE); **me sacó** *or* **tomó una ~** he took a picture *o* photo of me; **~ de carné/pasaporte** passport photo

fotocopia *f* photocopy, Xerox®; **hizo** *or* **sacó una ~ de la carta** he made *o* took a photocopy of the letter

fotocopiadora *f* photocopier, Xerox® machine

fotocopiar [A1] *vt* to photocopy, xerox

fotogénico -ca *adj* photogenic

fotografía *f* (técnica, arte) photography; (retrato, imagen) photograph

fotografiar [A17] *vt* to photograph, take a photograph of

fotográfico -ca *adj* photographic

fotógrafo -fa *m,f* photographer

fotomatón *m* photo booth

fotómetro *m* (Fot) exposure *o* light meter; (Fís) photometer

foul /'faul/ *m* (*pl* **fouls**) (AmL) foul

frac *m* (*pl* **fracs** *or* **fraques**) (chaqueta) tail coat, tails (*pl*); (traje) morning suit

fracasado -da *adj* failed, unsuccessful ■ *m,f* failure

fracasar [A1] *vi* to fail

fracaso *m* failure

fracción *f* ▶ **130** fraction

fractura *f* **(a)** (Med) fracture **(b)** (Geol) fault

fracturar [A1] *vt* to fracture

■ **fracturarse** *v pron* to fracture

fragancia *f* fragrance, perfume

fragata *f* frigate

frágil *adj* **(a)** ‹*cristal/fuente*› fragile **(b)** ‹*salud/constitución*› delicate; ‹*persona*› frail; ‹*economía*› fragile

fragmento *m* **(a)** (de jarrón) shard; (de hueso) fragment **(b)** (de conversación) snippet, snatch **(c)** (extracto de novela, carta) extract, passage

fragua *f* forge

fraguar [A16] *vt* **(a)** (Metal) to forge **(b)** ‹*complot*› to hatch; ‹*plan*› to conceive ■ **~** *vi* «*cemento*» to set

fraile *m* friar, monk

frailecillo *m* puffin

frambuesa *f* raspberry

francés[1] -cesa *adj* French ■ *m,f* (*m*) Frenchman; (*f*) Frenchwoman; **los franceses** the French, French people

francés[2] *m* (idioma) French

Francia *f* France

franco[1] -ca *adj* **1** (sincero) ‹*persona*› frank; ‹*sonrisa*› natural; **para serte ~ ...** to be frank *o* honest ...; **una mirada franca** an honest *o* open expression **2** (*delante del n*) (patente) ‹*mejoría/decadencia*› marked; **un clima de franca cordialidad** an atmosphere of genuine warmth **3** (Com) free; **~ de porte** carriage free; **paso ~** free passage; **~ de derechos** duty-free **4** [ESTAR] **(a)** (Mil) off duty **(b)** (RPl) (libre de trabajo): **el lunes estoy ~** I have Monday off

franco[2] *m* (unidad monetaria) franc

francotirador -dora *m,f* sniper

franela *f* **(a)** (Tex) flannel **(b)** (Ven) (camiseta) T-shirt **(c)** (Col) (camiseta de interior) undershirt (AmE), vest (BrE)

franja *f* (banda) stripe, band; (cinta, adorno) border, fringe

franquear [A1] *vt* **1** ‹*paso/entrada*› to clear; ‹*puerta*› to go through; ‹*umbral/río*› to cross **2** ‹*carta*› (pagar) to pay the postage on

■ **franquearse** *v pron* **~se** CON **algn** to confide IN sb

franqueo *m* postage

franqueza *f* frankness, openness; **hablar con (toda) ~** to be (perfectly) frank *o* honest

franquicia *f* **1** (exención) exemption; (en seguros) excess; **~ aduanera** (condición) duty-free status; (cantidad) duty-free allowance **2** (concesión) franchise

frasco *m* bottle; (de mermelada) jar

frase *f* (oración) sentence; (sintagma) phrase; **~ hecha** set phrase

fraternal *adj* brotherly, fraternal

fraude *m* fraud; **~ fiscal** tax evasion

fraudulento -ta *adj* ‹*negocio*› fraudulent; ‹*elecciones*› rigged

fray *m* (*delante de n propio*) Brother

frazada *f* (AmL) blanket; **~ eléctrica** electric blanket

frecuencia *f* frequency; **con ~** frequently; **~ modulada** frequency modulation, FM

frecuentar [A1] *vt* to frequent

frecuente *adj* ‹*llamada/visita*› frequent

freelance /'frilans/ *mf* freelancer; **trabaja de ~** he works freelance

freezer /'friser/ *m* **(a)** (AmL) (electrodoméstico) freezer, deep freeze **(b)** (Chi, Ven) (en el refrigerador) freezer (compartment)

fregadero *m* (de la cocina) kitchen sink; (para lavar ropa) (Méx) sink

fregado -da *adj* (AmL exc RPl fam) **(a)** (molesto) annoying; **¡no seas ~, hombre!** stop being such a pain (colloq) **(b)** (difícil) ‹*examen/tema*› tricky (colloq), tough (colloq); ‹*persona/carácter*› difficult **(c)** [ESTAR] (enfermo, delicado) in a bad way (colloq); (sin dinero) broke (colloq) ■ *m,f* (AmL exc RPl fam) (persona difícil) difficult person

fregar [A7] *vt* **1** (lavar, limpiar) to wash; **fregué el suelo** I washed the floor; (con cepillo) I scrubbed the floor; **~ los platos** to wash the dishes, to do the dishes (colloq) **2** (AmL exc RPl fam) **(a)** (molestar) to bug (colloq) **(b)** ‹*planes/vacaciones*› to ruin ■ **~** *vi* **1** (lavar los platos) to wash the dishes, to do the dishes (colloq); (limpiar) to clean; (restregar) to scrub **2** (AmL exc RPl fam) (molestar): **¡déjate de ~!** stop being such a pest!; **¡no friegues!** (no digas) you're kidding! (colloq)

■ **fregarse** *v pron* **1** (AmL fam) (embromarse): **¡te friegas!** tough! (colloq); **¡me fregué!** I've really done it now! (colloq) **2** (AmL exc RPl fam) (malograrse): **se ~on nuestros planes** that's ruined *o* messed up our plans (colloq)

fregona *f* (Esp) (utensilio) mop

freidora *f* deep fryer

freír [I35] *vt* to fry

■ **freírse** *v pron* to fry

frenada *f* (esp AmL) ⇒ FRENAZO

frenar [A1] *vt* **1** (Transp) to brake **2** ‹*proceso/deterioro*› to slow ... down; ‹*alza/inflación*› to curb, check; ‹*progreso/desarrollo*› to hold ... back ■ **~** *vi* to brake, apply the brake(s) (frml)

frenazo *m* (fam): **oí el ~** I heard the screeching of brakes; **dio un ~** she slammed *o* jammed on her brakes

frenético -ca *adj* frenzied, frenetic; **ponerse ~** (fam) to go crazy *o* wild

frenillos *mpl* (AmL) (para los dientes) braces (*pl*) (AmE), brace (esp BrE)

freno *m* **(a)** (Mec, Transp) brake; **~ de mano** emergency brake (AmE), handbrake (BrE) **(b)** (Equ) bit **(c)** (contención): **poner ~ a algo** (a gastos, importaciones) to curb sth; (a abusos) to put a stop to sth **(d) frenos** *mpl* (Méx) ⇒ FRENILLOS

frente *f* ▶ 123 forehead, brow (liter); **arrugar la ~** to frown ■ *m* **1 (a)** (de edificio) front, facade (frml); ***hacer(le) ~ a algo*** (a la realidad, una responsabilidad) to face up to sth; (a gastos, obligaciones) to meet sth; ***hacerle ~ a algn*** (a enemigo, atacante) to face sb **(b)** (*en locs*) **al frente**: **dar un paso al ~** to take a step forward; **vive al ~** (Chi) she lives opposite; **estar al ~ de algo** (de una clasificación) to be at the top of sth; (de una empresa) to be in charge of sth; **de frente** ‹*chocar*› head on; **una foto de ~** a full-face photo; **de frente a** (AmL) facing; **frente a** opposite; **estamos ~ a un grave problema** we are faced with a serious problem **2** (Meteo, Mil, Pol) front

fresa *f* ▶ 97 (planta) strawberry plant; (fruta) strawberry

fresco¹ -ca *adj* **1 (a)** ‹*viento*› cool, fresh; ‹*agua*› cold; ‹*bebida*› cool, cold; **el tiempo está ~** the weather is a bit chilly **(b)** ‹*ropa/tela*› cool **2 (a)** ‹*pescado/fruta*› fresh; **trae noticias frescas** she has the latest news; Ⓢ **pintura fresca** wet paint **(b)** ‹*cutis/belleza*› fresh, young **(c)** (no viciado) ‹*aire*› fresh **3** ‹*persona*› **(a)** [SER] (fam) (descarado): **¡qué tipo más ~!** that guy sure has some nerve! (colloq) **(b)** [ESTAR] (descansado) refreshed; (no cansado) fresh **(c)** (tranquilo): **él estaba tan ~** he was as cool as a cucumber ■ *m,f* (fam) (descarado): **¡eres un ~!** you have a lot of nerve! (colloq)

fresco² *m* **1 (a)** (aire) fresh air; **tomar el ~** to get some fresh air **(b)** (frío moderado): **hace un fresquito que da gusto** it's lovely and cool; **hace ~** it's chilly **2** (Art) fresco; **pintura al ~** fresco painting **3** (AmL) (gaseosa) soda (AmE), fizzy drink (BrE); (refresco de frutas) fruit drink

frescura *f* (descaro) nerve (colloq)

fresón *m* (long stem) strawberry

frialdad *f* (en general) coldness; **la ~ de su mirada** the coldness in his eyes; **me trató con ~** he treated me coldly *o* frostily; **la ~ del público** the audience's lack of enthusiasm

friega *f* (fricción) rub; **date una(s) ~(s) en el pecho con esto** rub this on your chest

friega, friegas, etc *see* FREGAR

frígido -da *adj* frigid

frigorífico *m* **(a)** (Esp) (nevera) refrigerator, fridge **(b)** (en tiendas) cold store **(c)** (AmS) (de carne) meat processing plant

frijol *m* (AmL exc CS) (Bot, Coc) bean; **~ colorado/negro** kidney/black bean; ***ganarse los ~es*** to earn a living

frío¹, fría *adj* **1** ▶ 409 ‹*comida/agua/motor/viento*› cold; **tengo los pies ~s** my feet are cold; ***dejar ~ a algn***: **la noticia lo dejó ~** (indiferente) he was quite unmoved by the news; (atónito) he was staggered by the news; **el jazz me deja fría** jazz does nothing for me **2 (a)** ‹*persona*› cold; ‹*público*› unresponsive; ‹*recibimineto*› cool; **estuvo ~ conmigo** he was cold towards me **(b)** ‹*decoración/color*› cold

frío² *m* ▶ 409 cold; **no salgas con este ~** don't go out in this cold; **¡qué ~ hace!** it's so cold!; **tener/pasar ~** to be cold; **tengo ~ en los pies** my feet are cold; ***tomar*** *or* (Esp) ***coger ~*** to catch cold

friolento -ta *adj* (AmL): **es muy ~** he really feels the cold

friolero -ra *adj* (Esp) ⇒ FRIOLENTO

friso *m* frieze

fritanga *f* **(a)** (AmC, Andes, Méx) (alimento frito) fried snack **(b)** (pey) (comida frita) greasy fried food

frito -ta *adj* **1** (Coc) fried **2 (a)** (fam) (harto) fed up (colloq); **me tienes ~** I'm fed up with you **(b)** (CS, Méx fam) (en apuros) done for (colloq)

frivolidad *f* (cualidad) frivolousness, frivolity; (cosa vana) triviality, frivolous thing

frívolo -la *adj* frivolous

frondoso -sa *adj* ‹*árbol*› leafy; ‹*vegetación*› lush; ‹*bosque*› thick

frontal *adj* ‹*colisión*› head-on; ‹*ataque*› direct, frontal (frml); ‹*oposición*› direct

frontenis *m* pelota (*played with tennis rackets*)

frontera *f* border, frontier (frml)

frontón *m* (juego) pelota; (cancha) pelota court; (pared) fronton

frotar [A1] *vt/vi* to rub
■ **frotarse** *v pron* (*refl*) ‹*ojos/rodillas*› to rub; ‹*manos*› to rub ... together

fructífero -ra *adj* fruitful, productive

fruncir [I4] *vt* **(a)** ‹*tela*› to gather **(b)** **~ el ceño** *or* **entrecejo** to frown

frustración *f* frustration

frustrado -da *adj* **(a)** ‹*persona*› frustrated; ‹*actor/bailarina*› frustrated (*before n*) **(b)** ‹*atentado/intento*› failed (*before n*)

frustrar [A1] *vt* ‹*persona*› to frustrate; ‹*planes*› to thwart; ‹*esperanzas*› to dash; **me frustra que no entiendan** I find it frustrating that they don't understand
■ **frustrarse** *v pron* «*planes*» to be thwarted, fail; «*esperanzas*» to come to nothing

fruta *f* fruit; **una ~** a piece of fruit; **~ confitada** *or* **escarchada** crystallized fruit, candied fruit; **~ del tiempo** *or* **de (la) estación** seasonal fruit

frutal *adj* fruit (*before n*) ■ *m* fruit tree

frutería *f* fruit store *o* shop, greengrocer's (BrE)

frutero[1] -ra *m,f* (vendedor) fruit seller, greengrocer (BrE)

frutero[2] *m* (recipiente) fruit bowl

frutilla *f* (Bol, CS) strawberry

fruto *m* **1** (Bot) fruit; **~s secos** nuts and dried fruit (*pl*) **2** (resultado, producto) fruit; **dar** *or* **rendir ~s** to bear fruit; **~ DE algo** ‹*de inversión*› return ON sth; ‹*de trabajo/investigación*› fruits OF sth; **todo fue ~ de su imaginación** it was all a figment of his imagination

fucsia *f* fuchsia ■ *m/adj inv* ▶ **97** fuchsia

fue *see* IR, SER

fuego *m* **(a)** (en general) fire; **¡~!** fire!; **le prendieron ~ a la casa** they set the house on fire; **abrieron ~ sobre los manifestantes** they opened fire on the demonstrators; **~s artificiales** fireworks (*pl*) **(b)** (para cigarrillo): **¿me da ~, por favor?** have you got a light, please? **(c)** (Coc): **cocinar a ~ lento** to cook over a low heat; (apenas hirviendo) to simmer; **poner la sartén al ~** put the frying pan on to heat

fuel, **fuel-oil** *m* fuel oil

fuelle *m* bellows (*pl*)

fuente *f* **1 (a)** (manantial) spring; **~ termal** thermal spring **(b)** (origen) source; **la ~ del río** the source of the river; **~ de ingresos** source of income; **información de buena ~** information from reliable sources **2** (construcción) fountain; **~ de soda** (Chi, Méx) soda fountain (AmE), (*place where drinks and ice creams are bought and consumed*) **3** (plato) dish; **~ de horno** ovenproof dish

fuera *adv* **1 (a)** (lugar, parte) [*Latin American Spanish also uses* AFUERA *in this sense*] outside; **comeremos ~** (en el jardín) we'll eat outside; **por ~ es rojo** it's red on the outside; **aquí ~ se está muy bien** it's very nice out here; **se pasa el día ~** she's out all day; (en un restaurante) we'll eat out; **¡~ (de aquí)!** get out (of here)! **(b)** (en el extranjero) abroad, out of the country; (del lugar de trabajo, de la ciudad, etc) away **2 fuera de** (*loc prep*) **(a)** (en el exterior de, más allá de) out of; **está ~ del país** he's out of the country; **ocurrió ~ del edificio** it happened outside the building; **~ de peligro/lugar** out of danger/place **(b)** (excepto) apart from; **~ de eso, me encuentro bien** apart *o* (AmE) aside from that, I feel fine **3** (*en otras locs*): **fuera de combate**: **lo dejó ~ de combate** (Dep) he knocked him out; **fuera de serie** ‹*jugador/cantante*› exceptional, outstanding; **fuera de sí**: **estaba ~ de sí** he was beside himself; **fuera de temporada** out of season

fuera, **fuéramos, etc** *see* IR, SER

fueraborda *m* outboard

fuereño -ña *m,f* (Méx fam): **un ~** some guy from out of town (colloq)

fuero *m* **(a)** (jurisdicción) jurisdiction **(b)** (privilegio, derecho) privilege; ***en mi/su ~ interno*** in my/his heart of hearts, deep down inside

fuerte *adj* **1** (en general) strong; **un equipo/una cuerda ~** a strong team/rope **2 (a)** ‹*viento*› strong; ‹*terremoto*› severe; ‹*lluvia/nevada*› heavy **(b)** ‹*dolor*› intense, bad; ‹*golpe*› heavy; ‹*resfriado*› bad; ‹*abrazo/beso*› big **(c)** ‹*ruido/música*› loud **(d)** ‹*olor/sabor/medicina*› strong; ‹*comida/dosis*› heavy **(e)** ‹*acento*› strong, thick **3** (violento) ‹*discusión*› violent, heated; ‹*película/escena*› shocking ■ *adv* **1** ‹*golpear/empujar*› hard; ‹*agarrar/apretar*› tightly; ‹*llover*› heavily **2** ‹*hablar*› loudly; **pon la radio más ~** turn the radio up; **habla más ~** speak up ■ *m* **(a)** (Mil) fort **(b)** (especialidad) strong point, forte

fuerza *f* **1 (a)** (vigor, energía) strength; **tener ~** to be strong; **no me siento con ~s** I don't have the strength; **tiene mucha ~ en los brazos** she has very strong arms; **agárralo con ~** hold on to it tightly; **empuja con ~** push hard; **le fallaron las ~s** his strength failed him; **recuperar ~s** to get one's strength back; **gritó con todas sus ~s** she shouted with all her might; **~ de voluntad** willpower **(b)** (del viento, de olas) strength, force **(c)** (de estructura, material) strength **2** (violencia) force; **recurrir a la ~** to resort to force; **~ bruta** brute force **3** (Mil, Pol, Fís) force; **~s políticas** political forces; **las ~s armadas** the armed forces; **las ~s de orden público** (period) the police; **~ de gravedad** (force of) gravity **4** (*en locs*) **a la fuerza**: **a la ~ tuvo que verme** he must have seen me; **lo llevaron a la ~** they dragged him there; **comí a la ~** I forced myself to eat; **entraron a la ~** they forced their way in; **a fuerza de** by; **aprobó a ~ de estudiar** he managed to pass by studying hard; **por fuerza**: **por ~ tiene que saberlo** he *must* know about it; **por la fuerza** by force

fuerza, **fuerzas, etc** *see* FORZAR

fuese, **fuésemos, etc** *see* IR, SER

fuete *m* (AmL exc CS) riding crop; (más largo) whip

fuga *f* **1** (huida) escape; **un intento de ~** an attempted escape; **se dieron a la ~** they fled; **~**

de capitales *or* **divisas** flight of capital; **~ de cerebros** brain drain **2** (de líquido, gas) leak, escape (frml) **3** (Mús) fugue

fugarse [A3] *v pron* **(a)** (huir) to flee, run away; «*preso*» to escape; **~ DE algo** to escape FROM sth **(b)** «*enamorados*» to run away together

fugaz *adj* ‹*sonrisa/visión/amor*› fleeting; ‹*visita/tregua*› brief

fugitivo -va *adj* fugitive; **anda ~** he is on the run

fui, fuimos, etc *see* IR, SER

fuiste, etc *see* IR, SER

fulano -na *m,f* (fam) (persona cualquiera) so-and-so; **don ~ de tal** Mr so-and-so ■ *m* (fam) (tipo) guy (colloq)

fulminante *adj* ‹*enfermedad*› sudden and devastating; ‹*mirada*› withering; **tuvo un efecto ~** it had an immediate and devastating effect

fulminantes *mpl* (AmL) (Jueg) caps (*pl*); **pistola de ~** cap gun

fumador -dora *m,f* smoker; **sección de ~es/no ~es** smoking/no-smoking section

fumar [A1] *vt* **1** ‹*cigarrillo/puro*› to smoke **2** (Méx fam) (hacer caso) to take notice of ■ **~** *vi* to smoke; **~ en pipa** to smoke a pipe

fumigar [A3] *vt* ‹*campo/cultivo*› to spray, dust; ‹*local*› to fumigate

función *f* **1 (a)** (cometido, propósito) function; **tiene la ~ de** ... it performs the function of ...; **salario en ~ de la experiencia** salary according to experience **(b) funciones** *mpl* duties (*pl*); **en el ejercicio de sus funciones** in the performance of her duties; **el secretario en funciones** the acting secretary; **entrar en funciones** (AmL) «*empleado*» to take up one's post; «*presidente*» to assume office **2** (Fisiol, Mat, Ling) function **3** (de teatro, circo) performance; (de cine) showing, performance; **~ de noche** late night performance

funcionamiento *m*: **me explicó su ~** he explained (to me) how it works (*o* worked *etc*); **para el buen ~ de la escuela** for the smooth running of the school; **ponerse en ~** «*hospital/estación/fábrica*» to become operational; «*central nuclear*» to come into operation; «*mecanismo/máquina*» to start up; «*servicio/sistema*» to start; **estar en ~** to be running; **poner en ~** ‹*central/fábrica*› to bring into operation; ‹*mecanismo/máquina*› to start ... up

funcionar [A1] *vi* «*aparato/máquina*» to work; «*servicio*» to operate; Ⓢ **no funciona** out of order; **~ con pilas/gasolina** to run off batteries/on gasoline

funcionario -ria *m,f* **(a)** (empleado público) *tb* **~ público** *or* **del Estado** government employee; **un alto ~** a senior *o* high-ranking official **(b)** (de organización internacional) member of staff, staff member **(c)** (RPl) (de empresa, banco) employee

funda *f* **(a)** (de libro) dustjacket; (de disco) sleeve **(b)** (de raqueta, cojín, sillón) cover **(c)** *tb* **~ de almohada** pillowcase, pillowslip **(d)** (Odont) cap

fundación *f* **1** (institución) foundation; **una ~ benéfica** a charity **2** (de ciudad, escuela) founding; (de empresa, partido) establishment

fundado -da *adj* ‹*temor/sospecha*› justified, well founded

fundador -dora *m,f* founder

fundamental *adj* fundamental

fundamento *m* **(a)** (base, sustentación) foundation; **los rumores carecen de ~** the rumors are totally without foundation **(b) fundamentos** *mpl* (nociones básicas) fundamentals (*pl*), basics (*pl*)

fundar [A1] *vt* **(a)** ‹*ciudad/hospital/escuela*› to found; ‹*partido/empresa*› to establish **(b)** (basar) ‹*sospecha/argumento*› **~ algo EN algo** to base sth ON sth

■ **fundarse** *v pron* **~se EN algo** «*afirmación/sospecha*» to be based ON sth; **¿en qué te fundas para decirlo?** what grounds do you have for saying that?

fundir [I1] *vt* **1 (a)** ‹*metal/hierro*› to melt; ‹*mineral*› to smelt **(b)** ‹*estatua/campana*› to cast **2** (Elec) to blow **3** (fusionar) to merge

■ **fundirse** *v pron* **1** «*metal*» to melt; «*nieve/hielo*» to melt, thaw **2** (Elec): **se ha fundido la bombilla** the bulb has gone (colloq); **se fundieron los fusibles** the fuses blew **3** (fusionarse) «*empresas/partidos*» to merge; **~se EN algo** to merge sth INTO sth

fundo *m* (Chi) country estate, large farm

fúnebre *adj* ‹*música/ambiente*› funereal; ⇒ COCHE (a), CORTEJO, ETC

funeral *m*, **funerales** *mpl* (exequias) funeral; (oficio religioso) funeral service

funeraria *f* undertaker's, funeral parlor*

funesto -ta *adj* disastrous, terrible

fungir [I7] *vi* (Méx, Per) **~ COMO** *or* **DE algo** to act AS sth

funicular *m* (tren) funicular (railway); (teleférico) cable car

furgón *m* (Auto) truck, van; (Ferr) boxcar (AmE), goods van (BrE)

furgoneta *f* (para carga) van; (para pasajeros) van, minibus

furia *f* fury; ***estar/ponerse hecho una ~*** (fam) to be/to get furious

furioso -sa *adj* furious; **se puso ~** he was furious, he flew into a rage

furor *m* **(a)** (rabia) fury, rage **(b)** (de las olas, del viento, de una tempestad) fury **(c)** (entusiasmo) enormous enthusiasm; ***causar*** *or* ***hacer ~*** to be all the rage (colloq)

furtivo -va *adj* **(a)** (ilegal): **la caza/pesca furtiva** poaching; **un cazador ~** a poacher **(b)** ‹*mirada/caricia*› furtive

furúnculo *m* boil

fusible *m* (Elec) fuse; **saltaron los ~s** the fuses blew

fusil *m* **1** (Arm) rifle **2** (Méx fam) (plagio) plagiarism

fusilar [A1] *vt* **1** (Mil) to shoot; **fue fusilado** he was executed by firing squad **2** (fam) (plagiar) to plagiarize, lift (colloq)

fusión *f* **1** (de empresas, partidos) merger **2 (a)** (de un metal) melting; (de metales, piezas) fusion, fusing together **(b)** (Fís) fusion

fusionar [A1] *vt* **(a)** ‹*piezas/metales*› to fuse, fuse

together **(b)** ‹*empresas/partidos*› to merge **(c)** (Inf) to merge
■ **fusionarse** *v pron* **(a)** «*piezas/metales*» fuse (together) **(b)** «*empresas/partidos*» to merge; «*ideas*» to fuse

fusta *f* riding crop; (más larga) whip

fustigar [A3] *vt* ‹*caballo*› to whip

futbito *m* (Esp) five-a-side soccer *o* football, ≈ indoor soccer (AmE)

fútbol, (AmC, Méx) **futbol** *m* soccer, football (esp BrE); **~ americano** American football; **~ sala** five-a-side soccer *o* football, ≈ indoor soccer (AmE)

futbolín *m* **(a)** (juego) table football **(b)** **futbolines** *mpl* (local) amusement arcade

futbolista *mf* soccer *o* football player

futuro[1] -ra *adj* future (*before n*); **las futuras generaciones** future generations; **la futura mamá** the mother-to-be

futuro[2] *m* **1** (porvenir) future; **¿qué nos deparará el ~?** what will the future bring?; **en un ~ cercano** *or* **próximo** in the near future; **en el** *or* **en lo ~** in future; **un empleo con/sin ~** a job with good prospects/with no prospects; **su relación no tiene ~** their relationship has no future **2** (Ling) future (tense)

Gg

G, g *f* (*read as* /xe/) *the letter* G, g

gabacho -cha *m,f* **(a)** (Chi, Esp fam & pey) (francés) frog (colloq & pej) **(b)** (Méx fam & pey) (extranjero) foreigner (*of North American or European origin*)

gabán *m* (abrigo — largo) overcoat; (— corto) jacket

gabardina *f* (prenda) raincoat; (tela) gabardine

gabinete *m* **1** (despacho) office; (en una casa) study **2** (conjunto de profesionales) department; (Pol) cabinet **3** (armario —de la cocina) (Méx) kitchen cabinet *o* cupboard; (— del baño) (Col, Ven) bathroom cabinet

gacela *f* gazelle

gacho -cha *adj* **(a)** ‹*orejas*› drooping (*before n*); **con la cabeza gacha** with his head bowed **(b)** **a gachas** (agachado) crouching; (a gatas) on all fours

gachupín *m* (Méx pey) Spaniard

gaélico[1] -ca *adj* Gaelic

gaélico[2] *m* (idioma) Gaelic

gafar [A1] *vt* (Esp fam) to jinx

gafas *fpl* **(a)** (anteojos) glasses (*pl*), spectacles (*pl*) (frml); **unas ~s nuevas** a new pair of glasses; **~ de sol** sunglasses; **~ oscuras** dark glasses **(b)** (de protección) goggles (*pl*)

gafe *adj* (Esp fam): **es ~** she has a jinx on her; **no seas ~** don't say that, you'll bring us bad luck

gafo -fa *adj* (Ven fam) (estúpido) dumb (colloq)

gagá *adj inv* **1** (fam) (senil) gaga (colloq) **2** (Per fam) (elegante) smart (colloq)

gaita *f tb* **~ gallega/escocesa** (Galician/Scottish) bagpipes (*pl*)

gaitero -ra *m,f* (Mús) (bag)piper

gajes *mpl*: **son (los) ~ del oficio** it's all part of the job

gajo *m* **1** (de naranja, limón) segment **2** (Col) (de pelo) lock

gala *f* **(a)** (cena) gala; **cena de ~** gala (dinner); (en el teatro) *tb* **función de ~** gala (evening *o* performance); **vestido de ~** formal *o* full dress; ***hacer ~ de algo*** to display sth **(b)** **galas** *fpl* (ropa) clothes (*pl*); **mis/tus mejores ~s** my/your best clothes *o* Sunday best

galán *m* **(a)** (actor) hero **(b)** (hum) (novio) young man (hum)

galante *adj* ‹*hombre*› gallant, attentive

galantería *f* **(a)** (caballerosidad) gallantry **(b)** (piropo) compliment; (gesto cortés) polite gesture, attention

galápago *m* (Zool) (tortuga — gigante) giant turtle; (— europea) terrapin

galaxia *f* galaxy

galera *f* **1** (Hist, Náut) galley **2** (RPl) (sombrero) top hat

galería *f* **(a)** (interior) corridor; (exterior) gallery **(b)** (Teatr) gallery **(c)** **~ comercial** shopping mall (AmE), shopping arcade (BrE); **~ de arte** art gallery

Gales *m*: *tb* **el país de ~** Wales

galés[1] -lesa *adj* Welsh ■ *m,f* (persona) (*m*) Welshman; (*f*) Welshwoman; **los galeses** the Welsh, Welsh people

galés[2] *m* (idioma) Welsh

galgo *mf* greyhound

galgódromo *m* (Méx) dog track

galicismo *m* gallicism

galimatías *m* (*pl* **~**) (lenguaje incomprensible) gibberish; (de cosas, ideas) jumble

gallada *f* (Andes fam): **la ~** the crowd

gallego[1] -ga *adj* **(a)** (de Galicia) Galician **(b)** (AmL fam) (español) Spanish ■ *m,f* **(a)** (de Galicia) Galician **(b)** (AmL fam) (español) Spaniard

gallego[2] *m* (idioma) Galician

galleta *f* (Coc) (dulce) cookie (AmE), biscuit (BrE); (salada) cracker

gallina *f* **1** (Zool) hen; (Coc) chicken; **~ clueca** (empollando) broody hen; (cuidando la pollada) mother hen; **gallinita ciega** blind man's buff **2** **gallina** *mf* (fam) (cobarde) chicken (colloq)

gallinazo *m* (Zool) (de cabeza roja) turkey buzzard *o* vulture; (de cabeza negra) black vulture

gallinero *m* **(a)** (Zool) (corral) henhouse, coop **(b)** (fam) (sitio ruidoso) madhouse (colloq) **(c)** (fam) (en el cine, teatro): **el ~** the gods (colloq)

gallito *m* **1** (fam) (persona) tough guy (colloq) **2** (Col, Méx) (Dep) shuttlecock, birdie (AmE)

gallo[1] *m* **1** (Zool) (ave) cockerel; **~ de pelea** *or* (AmS) **de riña** fighting *o* game cock; (más grande) rooster; ***en menos (de lo) que canta un ~*** in no time at all; ***otro ~ cantaría*** *or* ***otro ~ me/te/nos cantara*** (fam) things would be very different **2** (Méx fam) (bravucón) macho, tough guy (colloq) **3** (fam) **(a)** (de un cantante) false note **(b)** (de adolescente): **soltó un ~** his voice went squeaky **4** (Méx) (serenata) serenade

gallo[2] **-lla** *adj* (AmL fam) tough (colloq) ■ *m,f* (Chi fam) (*m*) guy (colloq); (*f*) woman; **hola ~** hi, buddy (AmE) *o* (BrE) mate (colloq)

galón *m* **1** (Mil) stripe **2** ▶ **322** (medida) gallon

galopante *adj* ‹*inflación/tuberculosis*› galloping (*before n*)

galopar [A1] *vi* (Equ) to gallop

galope *m* gallop; **a** *or* **al ~** at a gallop

galpón *m* (AmL) (cobertizo) shed; (almacén) storehouse

gama *f* **(a)** (de colores, productos) range **(b)** (de notas musicales) scale

gamba *f* (esp Esp) (Coc, Zool) shrimp (AmE), prawn (BrE)

gamberrada *f* (Esp) (grosería) loutish act; (acto violento) act of hooliganism

gamberrismo *m* (Esp) (comportamiento — escandaloso) loutishness; (— violento) hooliganism

gamberro -rra *m,f* (Esp) (grosero) lout; (vándalo) hooligan

gamín -mina *m,f* (Col) street urchin

gamo -ma *m,f* fallow deer

gamulán® *m* (CS) (prenda) sheepskin coat/jacket

gamuza *f* **(a)** (Zool) chamois **(b)** (piel) chamois (leather); (de otros animales) suede

gana *f* (deseo): **¡con qué ~s me comería un helado!** I'd love an ice cream!; **lo hizo sin ~s** he did it very half-heartedly; **siempre hace lo que le da la ~** she always does just as she pleases; **quería ir pero me quedé con las ~s** (fam) I wanted to go, but it wasn't to be; **tener ~s de hacer algo** to feel like doing sth; **(no) tengo ~s de ir** I (don't) feel like going; **tengo ~s de volver a verte** I'm looking forward to seeing you again; **le dieron ~s de reírse** she felt like bursting out laughing; **se me quitaron las ~s de ir** I don't feel like going any more; **tengo ~s de que llegue el verano** I'm looking forward to the summer; ***con ~s***: **llover con ~s** to pour down; **es feo/tonto con ~s** he is so ugly/stupid!; ***de buena/mala ~*** willingly/reluctantly

ganadería *f* (actividad) ranching, stockbreeding; (ganado) cattle (*pl*), livestock (+ *sing or pl vb*)

ganadero -ra *adj* ranching (*before n*), stockbreeding (*before n*) ■ *m,f* rancher, stockbreeder

ganado *m* cattle (*pl*), livestock (+ *sing or pl vb*); **~ bovino** *or* **vacuno** cattle (*pl*); **~ caballar** *or* **equino** horses (*pl*); **~ en pie** (AmL) cattle on the hoof (*pl*); **~ ovino/porcino** sheep (*pl*)/pigs (*pl*)

ganador -dora *adj* ‹*equipo/caballo*› winning (*before n*); **la película ~a del Oscar** the Oscar-winning film ■ *m,f* winner

ganancia *f* (Com, Fin) profit; **~ neta/bruta** net/gross profit

ganar [A1] *vt* **1 (a)** ‹*sueldo*› to earn; **lo único que quiere es ~ dinero** all he's interested in is making money **(b)** ‹*tiempo*› to gain; **¿qué ganas con eso?** what do you gain by (doing) that? **(c)** (adquirir) ‹*experiencia*› to gain **2** ‹*partido/guerra/premio*› to win; **le gané la apuesta** I won my bet with him ■ **~** *vi* **(a)** (vencer) to win; **van ganando 2 a 1** they're winning 2-1; **~le A algn** to beat sb; **nos ~on por cuatro puntos** they beat us by four points **(b)** (aventajar): **le ganas en estatura** you're taller than him; **me gana en todo** he beats me on every count; ***salir ganando***: **salió ganando con el trato** he did well out of the deal; **al final salí ganando** in the end I came out of it better off

■ **ganarse** *v pron* **1** (*enf*) (mediante el trabajo) to earn; **~se la vida** to earn a/one's living **2** (*enf*) ‹*premio/apuesta*› to win **3** ‹*afecto/confianza*› to win; **se ganó el respeto de todos** she won *o* earned everyone's respect **4** ‹*descanso*› to earn oneself; **te lo has ganado** you've earned it, you deserve it

ganchillo *m* (aguja) crochet hook; (labor) crochet; **hacer ~** to crochet

gancho *m* **(a)** (garfio) hook **(b)** (AmL) (para la ropa) hanger **(c)** (Andes, Ven) (imperdible) safety pin **2 (a)** (en boxeo) hook **(b)** (en baloncesto) hook shot

gandalla *mf* (Méx fam) (persona deshonesta) crook (colloq); (sinvergüenza) swine (colloq)

gandul -dula *m,f* (fam) lazybones (colloq)

ganga *f* (compra ventajosa) bargain; **a precio de ~** at a bargain *o* giveaway price

ganglio *m* (en los vasos linfáticos) gland; (de células nerviosas) ganglion

gangrena *f* gangrene

ganso -sa *m,f* **1** (Zool) (*m*) goose, gander; (*f*) goose **2** (fam) **(a)** (persona torpe) clumsy oaf (colloq) **(b)** (tonto) idiot, clown (colloq)

ganzúa *f* picklock

garabatear [A1] *vi/vt* (escribir) to scribble, scrawl; (dibujar) to doodle

garabato *m* **1 (a)** (dibujo) doodle **(b) garabatos** *mpl* (escritura) scrawl, scribble **2** (Chi) (palabrota) swearword

garaje /ga'raxe/ *m*, (esp AmL) **garage** /ga'raʒ/ *m* garage

garantía *f* **1** (Com) guarantee, warranty; **estar bajo** *or* **en ~** to be under guarantee *o* warranty **2 (a)** (Der) (fianza) surety, guarantee **(b)** (seguridad) guarantee **(c) ~s constitucionales** constitutional rights (*pl*)

garantizar [A4] *vt* **1** (Com) ‹*producto*› to guarantee, warrant (AmE) **2** (asegurar) to guarantee

garapiña *f* (Méx) pineapple squash

garbanzo *m* chickpea

garbo *m* (elegancia) poise, grace; (gracia, desenvoltura) jauntiness
garfio *m* hook
gargajo *m* (fam) gob (sl)
garganta *f* **1** ▶ **123** **(a)** (Anat) throat; **me dolía la ~** I had a sore throat **(b)** (cuello) neck **2** (desfiladero) gorge, ravine; (entre montañas) narrow pass ■ *mf* (Per fam) scrounger (colloq)
gargantilla *f* choker, necklace
gárgara *f* gargle; **hacer ~s** to gargle
garita *f* (de centinela) sentry box; (de portero) lodge
garito *m* gambling den
garra *f* **1** (de animal) claw; (de águila) talon **2** (arrojo, valor) fighting spirit; (personalidad) personality **3 garras** *fpl* (poder, dominio) clutches (*pl*)
garrafa *f* **(a)** (para vino) demijohn **(b)** (RPl) (para gas) cylinder
garrafal *adj* terrible; ‹*error*› monumental
garrapata *f* tick
garrapiñada *f* (esp AmL) caramel-coated peanuts/almonds (*pl*)
garrobo *m* (AmC) iguana
garrocha *f* **1** (Taur) lance, goad **2** (AmL) (Dep) pole
garrochista *mf* (AmL) pole-vaulter
garrotazo *m* (golpe) blow (*with a club*)
garrote *m* (palo) club, stick; (método de ejecución) garrotte
garúa *f* (AmL) drizzle
garuar [A18] *v impers* ▶ **409** (AmL) to drizzle
garza *f* (Zool) heron
garzón -zona *m,f* (Chi) (*m*) waiter; (*f*) waitress
gas *m* **1** (Fís, Quím) gas; **~es tóxicos** toxic fumes; **~ ciudad** town gas; **~ lacrimógeno/licuado** tear/liquified gas **2 gases** *mpl* (Fisiol) wind, gas (AmE)
gasa *f* (Med, Tex) gauze
gaseosa *f* **(a)** (bebida efervescente) soda (AmE), fizzy drink (BrE) **(b)** (CS) (cualquier refresco) soft drink
gaseoso -sa *adj* **(a)** ‹*cuerpo/estado*› gaseous **(b)** ‹*bebida*› carbonated, fizzy (BrE)
gásfiter *mf* (*pl* **-ters**) (Chi) plumber
gasfitería *f* (Chi, Per) plumbing
gasfitero -ra *m,f* (Per) plumber
gasoducto *m* gas pipeline
gas-oil, gasóleo *m* (para calefacción) (gas) oil; (para motores) diesel (fuel *o* oil)
gasolina *f* gasoline (AmE), gas (AmE), petrol (BrE); **~ normal** regular gasoline (AmE), two-star petrol (BrE); **~ sin plomo** unleaded gasoline (AmE) *o* (BrE) petrol; **~ super** premium gasoline (AmE), four-star petrol (BrE)
gasolinera *f* gas station (AmE), petrol station (BrE)
gastado -da *adj* ‹*ropa/zapatos*› worn-out; ‹*político/cantante*› washed-up (colloq)
gastador -dora *adj/m,f* spendthrift
gastar [A1] *vt* **1** (consumir) **(a)** ‹*dinero*› to spend; **~ algo EN algo** to spend sth ON sth **(b)** ‹*gasolina/electricidad*› to use **2** (desperdiciar, malgastar) ‹*dinero/tiempo/energía*› to waste **3** (desgastar) ‹*ropa/zapatos*› to wear out; ‹*tacones*› to wear down **4** (fam) (llevar, usar) ‹*ropa/gafas*› to wear; **gasto el 37** I'm a size 37 **5** ‹*broma*› to play; **le ~on una broma** they played a joke *o* trick on him
■ **gastarse** *v pron* **1** (*enf*) ‹*dinero*› to spend **2** «*pilas/batería*» to run down; **se me gastó la tinta** I ran out of ink **3** «*ropa/zapatos*» (desgastarse) to wear out **4** (*enf*) (fam) (tener) to have; **se gasta un genio** ... he has a terrible temper!
gasto *m* expense; **un ~ innecesario** an unnecessary expense; **este mes he tenido muchos ~s** this has been an expensive month for me; **el ~ público** public expenditure; **~s de correo** postage; **~s de envío** postage and handling (AmE) *o* (BrE) packing
gastritis *f* gastritis
gastronomía *f* gastronomy
gata *f* **1** (Chi, Per) (Auto) jack; *ver tb* GATO[1] **2 a gatas** (*loc adv*) (a cuatro patas): **ir** *or* **andar a ~s** to crawl; **tuve que entrar a ~s** I had to go in on all fours
gatear [A1] *vi* (andar a gatas) to crawl
gatera *f* cathole (AmE), cat flap (BrE)
gatillero *m* (Méx) gunman
gatillo *m* trigger; **apretar el ~** to pull the trigger
gatito -ta *m,f* kitten
gato[1] -ta *m,f* (Zool) cat; **~ montés** wild cat; ***aquí hay ~ encerrado*** there's something fishy going on here; ***le dieron ~ por liebre*** he was conned *o* had! (colloq); ***llevarse el ~ al agua*** (fam) to pull it off (colloq)
gato[2] *m* **1** (Auto) jack **2** (Chi, Méx) (Jueg) ticktacktoe (AmE), noughts and crosses (BrE) **3** (Méx) (signo) hash sign
gauchada *f* (Bol, CS fam) favor*, good turn
gaucho *m* gaucho
gaveta *f* drawer
gavilán *m* sparrowhawk
gavilla *f* (de cereales) sheaf
gaviota *f* seagull, gull
gay /gai, gei/ *adj* (*pl* **~** *or* **gays**) gay ■ *mf* (*m*) gay man, gay; (*f*) gay woman, lesbian
gazmoño -ña *adj* (pudoroso) prudish; (mojigato) sanctimonious
gaznate *m* (garganta) (fam) throat, gullet; **refrescar el ~** (fam) to have a drink
gazpacho *m*: *tb* **~ andaluz** gazpacho (*cold soup made from tomatoes, peppers, etc*)
ge *f*: *name of the letter* G
gel *m* gel
gelatina *f* **(a)** (sustancia) gelatin* **(b)** (postre) Jell-O® (AmE), jelly (BrE)
gelatinoso -sa *adj* gelatinous
gema *f* gem
gemelo[1] -la *adj* twin (*before n*) ■ *m,f* twin
gemelo[2] *m* **(a)** (de camisa) cuff link **(b) gemelos** *mpl* (Ópt) binoculars (*pl*)
gemido *m* **(a)** (de dolor, pena) groan, moan **(b)** (de animal) whine
Géminis *m* (signo, constelación) Gemini; **es (de) ~** she's (a) Gemini, she's a Geminian ■ *mf* (*pl* **~**) (persona) *tb* **géminis** Geminian, Gemini

gemir [I14] *vi* **(a)** «*persona*» to moan, groan **(b)** «*animal*» to whine

gen *m* gene

gendarme *mf* gendarme

gendarmería *f* gendarmerie

genealógico -ca *adj* genealogical

generación *f* generation

generacional *adj* generation (*before n*), generational

generador *m* generator

general *adj* **(a)** (no específico, global) general; **de interés ~** of general interest; **hablando en líneas ~es** broadly speaking; **un panorama ~ de la situación** an overall view of the situation **(b)** (*en locs*) **en general** on the whole, in general; **el público en ~** the general public; **por lo general** as a (general) rule ■ *mf* (Mil) general

generalidad *f* (vaguedad) general comment, generality; (mayoría) majority

generalizado -da *adj* widespread

generalizar [A4] *vi* to generalize, make generalizations

■ **generalizarse** *v pron* to spread

generar [A1] *vt* to generate

género *m* **1 (a)** (clase, tipo) kind, type; **el ~ humano** the human race, mankind **(b)** (Biol) genus **(c)** (Lit, Teatr) genre; **el ~ dramático** drama **(d)** (Ling) gender **2** (tela) cloth, material

generosidad *f* generosity

generoso -sa *adj* generous

genética *f* genetics

genético -ca *adj* genetic

genial *adj* **(a)** ‹*idea/escritor/pintor*› brilliant **(b)** (fam) (estupendo) great (colloq), fantastic (colloq); (fam) (ocurrente, gracioso) witty, funny

genialidad *f* (cualidad) genius; (ocurrencia) brilliant idea, stroke of genius

geniecillo *m* elf

genio *m* **(a)** (carácter) temper; **tener buen/mal ~** to be even-tempered/bad-tempered **(b)** (lumbrera) genius **(d)** (ser fantástico) genie

genitales *mpl* genitals (*pl*), genital organs (*pl*)

genocidio *m* genocide

Génova *f* Genoa

gente *f*

■ **Nota** Nótese que en español, cuando el nombre *gente* significa *personas*, se traduce al inglés por *people* con verbo en plural — *allí la gente es muy amable* = people are very nice there

Cuando tiene el sentido de *familia* se traduce al inglés por *family* con el verbo en singular o plural — *mi gente está de vacaciones* = my family is *o* are on holiday

---

(a) (personas) people (*pl*); **la gente está asustada** people are frightened; **había muy poca/tanta ~** there were very few/so many people; **~ bien** (de respeto) respectable people; (adinerada) well-to-do people; **la ~ de a pie** the man in the street; ***ser buena* ~** to be nice (*o* kind *etc*); ***ser* ~** (AmS) to behave (properly) **(b)** (Méx) (persona) person ■ *adj* (AmL) (de buenas maneras) respectable; (amable) kind, good ■ *adv* (Chi, Méx): **se portó muy ~ conmigo** she was very good *o* kind to me

gentil *adj* (amable) kind

gentileza *f* (cualidad) kindness; (atención, gesto): **tuvo la ~ de cederme el asiento** she was kind enough to let me have her seat; **ni siquiera tuvo la ~ de avisarnos** he didn't even have the courtesy to inform us

gentilicio *m*: *name given to the people from a particular region or country*

gentío *m* crowd

gentuza *f* (pey) riffraff (pej), rabble (pej)

genuflexión *f* genuflection

genuino -na *adj* genuine

geografía *f* geography

geográfico -ca *adj* geographical

geología *f* geology

geólogo -ga *m,f* geologist

geometría *f* geometry

geométrico -ca *adj* geometric

geranio *m* geranium

gerencia *f* **(a)** (cargo) post *o* position of manager **(b)** (personas) management **(c)** (oficina) manager's office

gerenciar [A1] *vt* (AmL) to manage

gerente *mf* manager; **~ comercial** business manager

geriatría *f* geriatrics

germen *m* **1** (microbio) germ **2 (a)** (embrión) germ **(b)** (origen) seeds (*pl*)

germicida *m* germicide

germinar [A1] *vi* to germinate

gerundio *m* gerund

gestación *f* gestation

gesticular [A1] *vi* to gesticulate

gestión *f* **(a)** (trámite) step; **la única ~ que había hecho** the only step he had taken; **hizo gestiones para adoptar un niño** he went through the procedure for adopting a child; **su apoyo a las gestiones de paz** their support for the peace process **(b) gestiones** *fpl* (negociaciones) negotiations (*pl*)

gestionar [A1] *vt* ‹*compra/préstamo*› to negotiate; **le están gestionando el permiso de trabajo** they are getting his work permit sorted out *o* arranged

gesto *m* **1** (en general) gesture; **un ~ grosero** a rude gesture; **le hizo un ~ para que se callara** she gestured to him to be quiet **2** (expresión) expression; **hacer ~s** to make faces

gestoría *f* agency (*which obtains official documents on clients' behalf*)

ghetto /'geto/ *m* ghetto

Gibraltar *m* Gibraltar

gibraltareño -ña *adj/m,f* Gibraltarian

gigante¹ *adj* giant (*before n*)

gigante² -ta *m,f* (en cuentos) (*m*) giant; (*f*) giantess; (persona alta) giant

gigantesco -ca *adj* huge, gigantic

gil *mf* (RPl fam *o* vulg) jerk (sl)

gilipollas *adj inv* (Esp fam *o* vulg): **¡qué ~ es ese tío!** that guy's such a jerk! (sl & pej) ■ *mf* (*pl* ~) (Esp fam *o* vulg) jerk (sl & pej)

gilipollez *f* (Esp fam *o* vulg): **decir gilipolleces** to talk garbage (AmE) *o* (BrE) rubbish; **no discutáis por esa ~** don't argue over a stupid *o* silly thing like that; **pagar tanto es una ~** it's stupid paying that much

gimnasia *f* gymnastics; (como asignatura) gym, PE (BrE); **hago ~ todos los días** I do exercises every day; **~ de mantenimiento** keep-fit

gimnasio *m* gymnasium, gym

gimnasta *mf* gymnast

gimotear [A1] *vi* to whine, whimper

ginebra *f* gin

Ginebra *f* Geneva

ginecólogo -ga *m,f* gynecologist*

gira *f* tour; **de ~** on tour

girar [A1] *vi* **1 (a)** «*rueda*» to turn, go around; «*disco*» to revolve, go around; «*trompo*» to spin; **~ ALREDEDOR DE algo/algn** to revolve AROUND sth/sb **(b)** (darse la vuelta) to turn **2** (torcer, desviarse) to turn; **~on a la derecha** they turned right ■ **~** *vt* **1** ‹*manivela/volante*› to turn **2** (Com, Fin) ‹*cheque/letra de cambio*› to draw

girasol *m* sunflower

giratorio -ria *adj* revolving (*before n*)

giro *m* **1** (en general) turn; **hizo un ~ a la derecha** she made a right turn; **un ~ de 180 grados** a volte-face, an about-turn; **el ~ que estaba tomando la conversación** the direction the conversation was taking **2** (Fin): **enviar un ~** (a través de un banco) to transfer money; (por correo) to send a money order; **~ bancario** (cheque) bank *o* banker's draft; (transferencia) credit transfer; **~ postal** money order

gis *m* (Méx) chalk

gitano -na *adj* gypsy (*before n*) ■ *m,f* gypsy

glacial *adj* **(a)** ‹*zona/período*› glacial **(b)** ‹*viento/temperatura*› icy

glaciar *m* glacier

gladiador *m* gladiator

gladiolo *m* gladiolus

glamoroso -sa *adj* glamorous

glándula *f* gland

glandular *adj* glandular

glicerina *f* glycerin

global *adj* global; ‹*informe*› full, comprehensive; ‹*resultado*› overall; ‹*precio/cantidad*› total

globo *m* **1 (a)** (Aviac, Jueg, Meteo) balloon; **~ aerostático/sonda** hot-air/observation balloon **(b)** (de chicle) bubble **(c)** (de lámpara) globe **(d) ~ ocular** eyeball **2** (mundo) world; *tb* **~terráqueo** globe

glóbulo *m* (cuerpo esférico) globule; (corpúsculo) corpuscle; **~ blanco/rojo** white/red corpuscle

gloria *f* **1 (a)** (Relig) glory; ***estar/sentirse en la ~*** to be in seventh heaven **(b)** (fama, honor) glory; **cubrirse de ~** to win glory **2** (personalidad) figure; **es una de las ~s del deporte** he is one of the great sporting figures *o* heroes

glorieta *f* **(a)** (plaza) square; (Auto) traffic circle (AmE), roundabout (BrE) **(b)** (en el jardín) arbor*

glorioso -sa *adj* ‹*hecho*› glorious; ‹*personaje*› great

glotón -tona *adj* gluttonous, greedy ■ *m,f* glutton

glotonería *f* gluttony

glúteo *m* gluteus

gnomo *m* gnome

gobelino *m* Gobelin

gobernador -dora *m,f* governor

gobernante *adj* ‹*partido/organismo*› ruling (*before n*), governing (*before n*) ■ *mf* leader, ruler

gobernar [A5] *vt* ‹*país*› to govern, rule; ‹*barco*› to steer ■ **~** *vi* (Gob, Pol) to govern; (Náut) to steer

gobierna, **gobiernas** *see* GOBERNAR

gobierno *m* government

goce *m* **(a)** (de derecho, título) enjoyment; **en pleno ~ de sus facultades** in full possession of her faculties **(b)** (placer) pleasure

gol *m* goal; **marcar** *or* **meter un ~** to score a goal

goleada *f* heavy defeat

goleador -dora *adj* high-scoring ■ *m,f* scorer, goal-scorer

golear [A1] *vt*: **el Madrid goleó al Osasuna** Madrid thrashed Osasuna

golero -ra *m,f* (CS) goalkeeper

golf *m* golf

golfa *f* (fam) (prostituta) whore (colloq)

golfillo -lla *m,f* street urchin

golfista *mf* golfer

golfito *m* (AmL) mini-golf, miniature golf

golfo[1] -fa *m,f* **(a)** (holgazán) good-for-nothing, layabout **(b)** (fam) (niño travieso) rascal (colloq), little devil (colloq)

golfo[2] *m* (Geog, Náut) gulf; **G~ de México** Gulf of Mexico; **G~ de Vizcaya** Bay of Biscay

golilla *f* **1** (Indum) **(a)** (cuello fruncido) ruff **(b)** (RPl) (pañuelo) neckerchief **2** (arandela) washer

gollete *m* neck (*of a bottle*); ***estar hasta el ~*** (fam) to be fed up to the back teeth (colloq); ***no tiene ~*** (RPl fam) it's the limit

golondrina *f* (Zool) swallow

golosa *f* (Col) hopscotch

golosina *f* (dulce) candy (AmE), sweet (BrE)

goloso -sa *adj* (amante de lo dulce): **es muy ~** he has a really sweet tooth

golpe *m* **1** (choque, impacto) knock; **me di un ~ en la cabeza** I got a knock on the head, I hit *o* banged my head; **darse un ~ contra algo** to bang *o* knock into sth; **dio unos ~s en la mesa** he tapped on the table; (más fuerte) he knocked on the table; (aún más fuerte) he banged on the table; ***a ~ de*** (Ven) around; ***de ~ (y porrazo)*** suddenly; **se abrió/cerró de ~** it flew open/slammed shut; ***de un ~*** (de una vez) all at once; (de un trago) in one go *o* gulp **2 (a)** (al pegarle a algn) blow; **lo derribó de un ~** he knocked him down with one blow; **casi lo matan a ~s** they almost beat him to death; **siempre andan a ~s** they're always fighting **(b)**

(marca) bruise, mark **3** (Dep) stroke **4 (a)** (desgracia) blow **(b) ~ de suerte** stroke of luck **5** (fam) (atraco, timo) job (colloq); **dar el ~** to do the job **6** (Pol) *tb* **~ de estado** coup (d'état)

golpear [A1] *vt* **1** ‹*objeto/superficie*› to bang; (repetidamente) to beat; **no golpees la puerta al salir**; don't slam *o* bang the door as you go out; **la lluvia golpeaba los cristales** the rain beat against the window panes; **golpeó la mesa con el puño** he banged his fist on the table **2** (pegar) to hit; **algo me golpeó en la cara** something hit me in the face; **su marido la golpea** her husband hits her ■ **~** *vi* **(a)** (dar, pegar) **~** CONTRA **algo** to beat AGAINST sth **(b)** (AmS) (llamar a la puerta) to knock **(c)** (en fútbol americano) to scrimmage
■ **golpearse** *v pron* **(a)** (*refl*) ‹*cabeza/codo*› to bang, hit **(b)** (AmL) «*puerta*» to bang

golpista *adj* ‹*minoría/tendencia*› in favor of a coup; **los militares ~s** the soldiers who took part in the coup

golpiza *f* (AmL) beating

goma *f* **1 (a)** (caucho) rubber; **suelas de ~** rubber soles **(b)** (pegamento) glue, gum; **~ de mascar** chewing gum **2 (a)** (para sujetar) rubber band, elastic band (BrE) **(b)** (de borrar) eraser **(c)** (RPl) (neumático) tire* **3** (AmC fam) (resaca) hangover; **ando de ~** I've got a hangover

gomina *f* hair gel

gomita *f* **1** (RPl) (para sujetar) rubber band, elastic band (BrE) **2** (Chi, Méx, Ven) (dulce) gumdrop, gum (BrE)

góndola *f* gondola

gondolero *m* gondolier

gordo[1] -da *adj* **1** ‹*persona/piernas*› fat; **siempre ha sido ~** he's always been overweight *o* fat; **estás ~** you've put on weight; **es más bien gordita** she's quite plump **2** (grueso) ‹*libro/lana/suéter*› thick **3** ‹*carne/tocino*› fatty ■ *m,f* **(a)** (persona) (*m*) fat man; (*f*) fat woman **(b)** (fam) (como apelativo ofensivo) fatso (colloq), fatty (colloq)

gordo[2] *m* (Jueg) (premio mayor) jackpot (*in the state lottery*)

gordura *f* (grasa) fat; (exceso de peso) fatness; **me preocupa su ~** I'm worried about how fat he is

gorgorito *m* trill

gorgotear [A1] *vi* (en cañería) to gurgle; (al hervir) to bubble

gorila *m* **1** (Zool) gorilla **2** (fam) **(a)** (matón) thug **(b)** (guardaespaldas) heavy (colloq) **(c)** (reaccionario) fascist **(d)** (Esp) (en un club) bouncer

gorjear [A1] *vi* «*pájaro*» to trill, warble; «*niño*» to gurgle

gorra *f* cap; (con visera) peaked cap; (de bebé) bonnet

gorrear [A1] *vt* **1** (fam) (pedir) to scrounge (colloq); **me gorreó $20** he scrounged $20 off me **2** (Chi fam) ‹*conyuge*› to cheat on (colloq)

gorrero -ra *m,f* (AmL fam) (aprovechado) scrounger (colloq)

gorrión *m* sparrow

gorro *m* cap; **~ de baño** (para nadar) bathing cap; (para la ducha) shower cap; ***estar hasta el ~*** (fam) to be fed up to the back teeth (colloq)

gorrón -rrona *m,f* (Esp, Méx fam) scrounger (colloq)

gorronear [A1] *vt/vi* (Esp, Méx fam) to scrounge (colloq)

gota *f* **1** (de líquido) drop; **~s de sudor** beads of sweat; ***la ~ que colma*** *or* ***rebasa el vaso*** the last straw; ***parecerse/ser como dos ~s de agua*** to be as like as two peas in a pod **2** (enfermedad) gout

gotear [A1] *vi* «*líquido/grifo/vela*» to drip; «*cañería*» to leak ■ **~** *v impers* ▶ **409** (lloviznar) to spit, drizzle

goteo *m* dripping

gotera *f* **(a)** (filtración) leak **(b)** (mancha) damp stain

gótico -ca *adj* Gothic

gourde *m* gourde (*Haitian unit of currency*)

gozador -dora *adj* (AmL) fun-loving

gozar [A4] *vi*: **~** DE **algo** to enjoy sth; **~ de la vida** to enjoy life; **goza viéndolos jugar** she enjoys watching them play; **~** CON **algo** to enjoy sth; **goza de perfecta salud** he enjoys perfect health; **goza de una buena posición** he has a good position

gozne *m* hinge

gozque *mf* (Col) mongrel

grabación *f* recording; **~ en video** video recording

grabado *m* engraving

grabador -dora *m,f* **1** (Art) engraver **2 grabadora** *f* **(a)** (casa discográfica) record company **(b)** (magnetófono) tape recorder

grabar [A1] *vt/vi* **(a)** (Audio, TV) to record, tape **(b)** (Art) to engrave
■ **grabarse** *v pron:* **sus palabras se me ~on en la memoria** her words are etched on my memory; **su cara se me quedó grabada** I'll never forget her face

gracia *f* **I 1** (comicidad): **yo no le veo la ~** I don't think it's funny; **tener ~** «*chiste/broma*» to be funny; **me hace ~ que digas eso** it's funny you should say that; **no me hace ninguna ~ tener que ir** I don't relish the idea of having to go **2 (a)** (chiste) joke; (broma) joke, trick **(b)** (de niño) party piece **3** (encanto, elegancia) grace; **con ~** ‹*moverse/bailar*› gracefully; **un vestido sin ~** a very plain dress; **tiene mucha ~ para arreglar flores** she has a real flair for flower arranging
II gracias *fpl* **(a)** (expresión de agradecimiento): **darle las ~s a algn** to thank sb; **no dieron ni las ~s** they didn't even say thank you **(b)** (*como interj*) thank you, thanks (colloq); **muchas ~s** thank you very much, thanks a lot (colloq); **un millón de ~s por ayudarme/tu ayuda** thank you very much for helping me/your help **(c) gracias a** thanks to; **~s a Dios** thank God

gracioso -sa *adj* **1** (divertido) ‹*chiste/persona*› funny; **¡qué ~!** how funny!; ***hacerse el ~*** to play the fool **2** (atractivo) ‹*cara/figura*› attractive; **las pecas le dan un aspecto muy ~** those freckles make her look really cute *o* sweet

grada *f* **(a)** (peldaño) step **(b) gradas** *fpl* (Dep) stand, grandstand

gradería *f*, (Esp) **graderío** *m* stands (*pl*)

gradiente *f* (AmL) (pendiente) slope, gradient

grado *m* **1** ▶ 406 (en general) degree; **estamos a tres ~s bajo cero** it's three degrees below zero; **~ centígrado** *or* **Celsius/Fahrenheit** degree centigrade *o* Celsius/Fahrenheit; **el ~ de confusión reinante** the degree of confusion that prevails; ***en ~ sumo*** extremely **2** (de escalafón) grade; (Mil) rank **3** (disposición): **de buen/mal ~** willingly/unwillingly **4 (a)** (esp AmL) (Educ) (curso, año) year **(b)** (título): **tiene el ~ de licenciado** he has a college (AmE) *o* (BrE) university degree

graduable *adj* adjustable

graduación *f* **(a)** (acción de regular) adjustment **(b)** (de bebida alcohólica) alcohol content **(c)** (Mil) rank **(d)** (Educ) graduation

graduado -da *adj* **(a)** ‹*gafas/lentes*› prescription (*before n*) **(b)** ‹*termómetro*› graduated ■ *m,f* (Educ) graduate

gradual *adj* gradual

graduar [A18] *vt* **(a)** (regular) to adjust **(b)** (marcar) ‹*instrumento/termómetro*› to calibrate

■ **graduarse** *v pron* **(a)** (Educ) to graduate **(b)** (Mil) to take a commission

graffiti /gra'fiti/ *mpl* graffiti

gráfico[1] -ca *adj* graphic; ‹*gesto*› expressive

gráfico[2] *m* **(a)** (Mat) graph **(b)** (Inf) graphic

grafología *f* graphology

gragea *f* **(a)** (Farm) tablet **(b)** (Coc) small candy (AmE) *o* (BrE) sweet

Gral. *m* (= **General**) Gen.

grama *f* (AmC, Ven) (césped) lawn

gramática *f* (disciplina) grammar; (libro) grammar (book)

gramatical *adj* grammatical

gramo *m* ▶ 322 gram

gran *adj*: *ver* GRANDE

granada *f* **1** (Bot) pomegranate **2** (Arm, Mil) grenade; **~ de mano** hand grenade

Granada *f* (en España) Granada; (en el Caribe) Grenada

granadilla *f* (fruta — redonda, oscura) passion fruit; (— más grande, amarilla) granadilla

granate *adj inv* ▶ 97 maroon (*before n*) ■ *m* (color) maroon

Gran Bretaña *f* Great Britain

grande *adj* [GRAN *is used before singular nouns*] **1 (a)** (en dimensiones) ‹*casa/área/nariz*› big, large; **un tipo ~** a big guy; **unos ~s almacenes** a department store **(b)** (en demasía) too big; **me queda ~** it's too big for me **(c)** (en número) ‹*familia*› large, big; ‹*clase*›big; **la gran parte** *or* **mayoría** the great majority **2 (a)** (alto) tall; **¡qué ~ está Andrés!** isn't Andrés tall! **(b)** (en edad): **cuando sea ~** when I grow up; **ya son ~s** they are all grown up now **3** (Geog): **el Gran Santiago** Greater Santiago **4** (*delante del n*) **(a)** (notable, excelente) great; **un gran hombre** a great man **(b)** (poderoso) big; **los ~s bancos** the big banks; ***a lo ~*** in style **5 (a)** (en intensidad, grado) ‹*pena/honor/ventaja*› great; ‹*explosión*› powerful; **¡me llevé un susto más ~ ... !** I got such a fright!; **una temporada de gran éxito** a very *o* a highly successful season; **son ~s amigos** they're great friends; **eso es una gran verdad** that is absolutely true; **¡qué mentira más ~!** that's a complete lie! **(b)** (elevado): **a gran velocidad** at high *o* great speed; **volar a gran altura** to fly at a great height; **un gran número de personas** a large number of people; **objetos de gran valor** objects of great value; ***en ~***: **lo pasamos en ~** we had a great time (colloq) ■ *m,f* **(a)** (mayor): **la grande ya está casada** their eldest (daughter) is already married **(b)** (adulto): **los ~s** the grown-ups

grandilocuencia *f* grandiloquence

grandiosidad *f* grandeur

grandioso -sa *adj* **(a)** ‹*espectáculo/obra*› impressive, magnificent **(b)** (rimbombante) ‹*gesto/palabras*› grandiose

granel: **a ~ (a)** (*loc adj*) (en abundancia) ‹*comida/bebida*› stacks of **(b)** (*loc adv*) **comprar/vender a ~** ‹*vino/aceite*› to buy/sell ... by the liter (*o* pint *etc*); ‹*galletas/nueces*› to buy/sell ... loose; (en grandes cantidades) to buy/sell ... in bulk

granero *m* granary, barn

granito *m* (roca) granite

granizado *m* (bebida) *drink served on crushed ice*

granizar [A4] *v impers* ▶ 409 to hail

granizo *m* (grano, bola) hailstone; (conjunto) hail

granja *f* (Agr) farm; **~ avícola** poultry farm

granjearse [A1] *v pron* to earn, win

granjero -ra *m,f* farmer

grano *m* **1** (de arena, azúcar, trigo, arroz) grain; (de café) bean; (de mostaza) seed; **~s de pimienta** peppercorns; ***ir al ~*** (fam) to get (straight) to the point **2** (Med) spot, pimple (esp AmE) **3 (a)** (de la piedra, la madera) grain **(b)** (Fot) grain

granuja *mf* rascal

grapa *f* **1 (a)** (para papeles) staple; (para cables) cable clip **(b)** (Arquit) cramp iron **2** (CS) (aguardiente) grappa

grapadora *f* stapler

grapar [A1] *vt* to staple

grasa *f* **1 (a)** (Biol, Coc) fat; **la comida tenía mucha ~** the food was very greasy **(b)** (suciedad) grease; **está lleno de ~** it's all greasy **(c)** (Mec) grease **2** (Méx) (betún) shoe polish

grasiento -ta *adj* greasy

grasitud *f* (AmL) greasiness

graso -sa *adj* **(a)** ‹*pelo/cutis*› greasy **(b)** (Coc) greasy, oily, fatty; **queso ~** full fat cheese

grasoso -sa *adj* (AmL) greasy

gratificación *f* **(a)** (bonificación) bonus; (recompensa) reward **(b)** (satisfacción) gratification

gratificador -dora *adj* (AmL) rewarding, gratifying (frml)

gratificante *adj* rewarding, gratifying (frml)

gratificar [A2] *vt* **(a)** ‹*persona*› to give ... a bonus **(b)** (recompensar) to give ... a reward; Ⓢ **se gratificará** reward offered

gratinado -da *adj* au gratin

gratinador *m* grill

gratis *adj/adv* free; **es ~** it is free (of charge); **entramos ~** we got in free *o* for nothing

gratitud *f* gratitude

grato -ta *adj* pleasant
gratuito -ta *adj* **(a)** (gratis) free **(b)** (infundado) ‹*afirmaciones*› unwarranted; ‹*insulto*› gratuitous
grava *f* gravel
gravamen *m* (impuesto) tax; (carga) burden; (sobre finca, casa) encumbrance
gravar [A1] *vt* (con impuesto) ‹*ingresos/productos*› to tax
grave *adj* **1 (a)** [ESTAR] ‹*enfermo*› seriously ill **(b)** [SER] ‹*herida/enfermedad*› serious **2** ‹*situación/asunto/error*› serious **3 (a)** ‹*tono/expresión/gesto*› grave, solemn **(b)** ‹*voz*› deep **(c)** ‹*sonido/nota*› low **4** (Ling) ‹*acento*› grave; ‹*palabra*› paroxytone
gravedad *f* **1** (en general) seriousness; **está herido de ~** he is seriously injured; **es un asunto de mucha ~** it is a very serious matter **2** (Fís) gravity
gravilla *f* gravel
graznar [A1] *vi* «*cuervo*» to caw; «*ganso*» to honk; «*pato*» to quack
graznido *m* (del cuervo) caw; (del ganso) honk; (del pato) quack
Grecia *f* Greece
greda *f* (para cerámica) clay
grei *m* (Col) grapefruit
greifrú *mf* (*pl* **-frús**) (AmC, Ven fam) grapefruit
gremial *adj* **(a)** (profesional) ‹*asociación*› professional **(b)** (AmL) (sindical) union (*before n*)
gremialista *mf* (AmL) trade unionist
gremio *m* **(a)** (de oficio, profesión) trade **(b)** (CS, Per) (sindicato) union
greña *f* **(a)** (enredo) tangle **(b) en greña** (Méx) ‹*trigo*› unthreshed; ‹*plata/azúcar*› unrefined; ‹*tabaco*› leaf (*before n*) **(c) greñas** *fpl* untidy hair
gresca *f* (fam) (jaleo) rumpus (colloq); (riña) fight
griego[1] -ga *adj/m,f* Greek
griego[2] *m* (idioma) Greek
grieta *f* (en una pared) crack; (en la tierra) crack, crevice; (en la piel) crack
grifo[1] *m* **1** (Esp) (de lavabo, bañera) faucet (AmE), tap (BrE); **abrir/cerrar el ~** to turn the faucet *o* tap on/off **2** (Per) (gasolinera) filling station **3** (Chi) (de incendios) fire hydrant, fireplug (AmE)
grifo[2] -fa *m,f* (Méx fam) pothead (sl), dopehead (sl)
grillo *m* **1** (Zool) cricket **2 grillos** *mpl* (de los presos) fetters (*pl*), shackles (*pl*)
grima *f* (Esp fam): **darle ~ a algn** (repulsión) to make sb's flesh crawl; (dentera) to set sb's teeth on edge
gringo -ga *adj* **(a)** (AmL fam & pey) gringo, foreign (*of or relating to a person from a non-Spanish speaking country*) **(b)** (Andes fam) (rubio) fair-haired ■ *m,f* **(a)** (AmL fam & pey) (extranjero) gringo, foreigner (*from a non-Spanish speaking country*); (norteamericano) Yank (colloq & pej), Yankee (colloq & pej) **(b)** (Andes fam) (rubio) (*m*) fair-haired boy/man; (*f*) fair-haired girl/woman
Gringolandia *f* (Andes fam & pey) Yankeeland (colloq & pej)
gripa *f* (Col, Méx) ⇒ GRIPE
gripe *f* flu; **estar con/tener ~** to have (the) flu
gris ▶ 97 *adj/m* gray*
gritar [A1] *vi* to shout; **no hace falta que grites** there's no need to shout *o* yell; **~ de dolor** to scream with pain; **~ de alegría** to shout for joy; **~ pidiendo ayuda** to shout for help; **~le A algn** to shout AT sb; (para llamarlo) to shout (out) TO sb ■ **~** *vt* to shout
griterío *m* shouting, clamor*
grito *m* **(a)** (de dolor, alegría) shout, cry; (de terror) scream; **un ~ de socorro** a cry for help; **~s de protesta** shouts *o* cries of protest; **hablar a ~s** to talk at the top of one's voice; ***ser el último ~*** to be the last word in fashion **(b)** (de pájaro, animal) call, cry
groenlandés -desa *adj* of/from Greenland
Groenlandia *f* Greenland
grosella *f* redcurrant
grosería *f* **(a)** (acción): **fue una ~ de su parte** it was very rude of him **(b)** (comentario) rude comment; **¡qué ~!** how rude!; **decir ~s** to swear
grosero -ra *adj* **(a)** (descortés) ‹*persona/lenguaje*› rude **(b)** (vulgar) crude, vulgar ■ *m,f*: **es un ~** (vulgar) he's so vulgar *o* crude!; (descortés) he's so rude!
grosor *m* thickness
grotesco -ca *adj* ‹*personaje/mueca*› grotesque; ‹*espectáculo*› hideous, grotesque
grúa *f* **(a)** (Const) crane **(b)** (Auto) (de taller) wrecker (AmE), breakdown van (BrE); (de la policía) tow truck; **se lo llevó la ~** it was towed (away)
grueso -sa *adj* thick
grulla *f* crane
grumete *m* cabin boy
grumo *m* lump
grumoso -sa *adj* lumpy
gruñido *m* grunt; (del perro) growl
gruñir [I9] *vi* **(a)** «*cerdo*» to grunt; «*perro*» to growl **(b)** (fam) «*persona*» to grumble
gruñón -ñona *adj* (fam) grumpy (colloq)
grupa *f* rump, hindquarters (*pl*)
grupo *m* **(a)** (de personas, empresas, países) group; (de árboles) clump; **~ sanguíneo** blood group; **~s sociales** social groups; **de ~** ‹*terapia/trabajo*› group (*before n*); **en ~** ‹*salir/trabajar*› in a group/in groups **(b)** (Mús) *tb* **~ musical** group, band
gruta *f* (natural) cave; (artificial) grotto
guaca *f* (Andes) *pre-Columbian tomb*
guacal *m* **(a)** (Col, Méx, Ven) (caja) wooden crate **(b)** (Ven) (medida) crate, crateload **(c)** (AmC) (calabaza) large gourd (*used for storing tortillas*)
guacamaya *f* (Méx) **1** (ave) macaw **2** (fam) (persona) loudmouth (colloq)
guacamayo *m* macaw
guacamole *m* guacamole
guachimán *m* (AmS fam) watchman
guachinango *m* (Méx) red snapper
guacho[1] -cha *adj* **1** (Andes, RPl) **(a)** (fam) ‹*niño*› orphaned; ‹*perro*› stray **(b)** (fam & pey) ‹*hijo*› bastard (*before n*) (pej) **2** (Chi, Per fam) ‹*calcetín/guante*› odd

■ *m,f* **1** (Andes, RPl) **(a)** (fam) (niño abandonado) orphan, waif; (perro) stray **(b)** (fam & pey) (hijo ilegítimo) bastard (vulg) **(c)** (insulto — a un hombre) bastard (pej); (— a una mujer) bitch (sl & pej)

guacho² *m* (Per) (de la lotería) *tenth share in a lottery ticket*

guaco *m* (Andes) pot (*found in pre-Columbian tomb*)

guadaña *f* scythe

guagua *f* (fam) **1** (Andes) (bebé) baby **2** (Cu) (autobús) bus

guaje -ja *m,f* **1** (Méx fam) sucker (colloq); ***hacerle ~ a algn*** (serle infiel) to cheat on sb (colloq); (engañarlo) to rip sb off (colloq); ***hacerse ~*** to act dumb (colloq) **2 guaje** *m* (Méx) **(a)** (planta, fruto) bottle gourd **(b)** (vasija) gourd **(c)** (instrumento) maraca (*made from a bottle gourd*)

guajiro -ra *m,f* **(a)** (en Cuba) peasant **(b)** (en Col, Ven) *native of the Guajira peninsula*

guajolote -ta *m,f* (Méx) turkey

guanábana *f* (fruto) soursop; (árbol) soursop tree

guanaco *m* **1** (Zool) guanaco **2** (Chi fam) (de la policía) water cannon

guanera *f* guano deposit

guanero -ra *adj* guano (*before n*)

guano *m* guano

guante *m* glove; **~s de lana/boxeo** woollen/ boxing gloves; ***echarle el ~ a algn*** (fam) to nab sb (colloq)

guantera *f* glove compartment

guapetón -tona *adj* (fam) ‹*chico*› handsome; ‹*chica*› pretty

guapo -pa *adj* **1** ‹*hombre*› handsome, good-looking; ‹*mujer*› attractive, good-looking; ‹*bebé*› beautiful; **estás muy ~ con ese traje** you look very nice in that suit **2 (a)** (fam) (bravucón): **ponerse ~** to get cocky (colloq) **(b)** (AmS fam) (valiente) gutsy (colloq)

guarangada *f* (RPl, Ven fam) ⇒ GROSERÍA (b)

guarango -ga *adj* (CS, Ven fam) (grosero) rude, loutish ■ *m,f* (CS, Ven fam) (grosero) lout (colloq)

guaraní *adj/m,f* Guarani ■ *m* (idioma) Guarani

guarapear [A1] *vi* (Per fam) to get plastered (colloq)

guarda *mf* (de museo, parque) keeper; (de edificio público) *tb* **~ jurado** security guard

guardabarros *m* (*pl* ~) **(a)** (Auto) fender (AmE), mudguard (BrE) **(b)** (de bicicleta) mudguard

guardabosque *mf* (en parque nacional) forest ranger

guardacostas *mf* (*pl* ~) **(a)** (persona) coastguard **(b) guardacostas** *m* (buque) coastguard vessel

guardaespaldas *mf* (*pl* ~) bodyguard

guardalíneas *mf* (*pl* ~) (Chi) (*m*) linesman; (*f*) lineswoman

guardameta *mf* goalkeeper

guardapelo *m* locket

guardapolvo *m* (bata — de niño) overall; (— de profesor, tendero) workcoat (AmE), overall (BrE)

guardar [A1] *vt* **1** (reservar) to save, keep; **guarda algo para después** save *o* keep sth for later **2 (a)** (poner en un lugar) ‹*juguetes/libros*› to put ... away; **ya guardé toda la ropa de invierno** I've already put away all my winter clothes **(b)** (conservar, mantener) to keep; **lo guardó durante años** she kept it for years; **~ las apariencias** to keep up appearances **(c)** ‹*secreto*› to keep; ‹*rencor*› to bear, harbor*; **guardo muy buenos recuerdos de él** I have very good memories of him

■ **guardarse** *v pron* **1 (a)** (quedarse con) to keep **(b)** (reservar) to save, keep **2** (poner en un lugar): **se guardó el cheque en el bolsillo** he put the check (away) in his pocket

guardarropa *m* **(a)** (en restaurantes, teatros) cloakroom **(b)** (ropa) wardrobe **(c)** (armario) dressing room

guardavallas *mf* (*pl* ~) (AmL) goalkeeper

guardería *f*: *tb* **~ infantil** nursery

guardia *f* **1 (a)** (vigilancia): **estar de ~** «*soldado*» to be on guard duty; «*médico*» to be on duty *o* call; «*empleado*» to be on duty; «*marino*» to be on watch; **montar ~** to stand guard; ***poner en ~ a algn*** to warn sb **(b)** (en esgrima): **en ~** on guard **2** (cuerpo militar) guard; **cambio de ~** changing of the guard **3 guardia** *mf* (*m*) policeman; (*f*) policewoman

guardiamarina *mf* midshipman

guarecer [E3] *vt* to shelter, protect

■ **guarecerse** *v pron* (*refl*) to shelter, take shelter

guarén *m* water rat

guargüero *m* (AmL fam) (garganta) throat

guarida *f* (de animales) den, lair; (de personas) hideout

guarnecer [E3] *vt* (Coc) to garnish

guarrada *f* (Esp fam) **(a)** (porquería, suciedad) mess (colloq) **(b)** (mala pasada) dirty trick (colloq) **(c)** (indecencia, vulgaridad): **no digas ~s** don't be filthy; **esa película es una ~** that's a filthy movie

guarro -rra *m,f* (Esp fam) **(a)** (persona sucia) filthy pig (colloq) **(b)** (indecente, vulgar): **es un ~** he's really disgusting

guarura *m* (Méx) bodyguard

guasa *f* (fam) (broma, burla) joke; **de ~** as a joke; **no te lo tomes a ~** it's no joke, it's no laughing matter

guasca *f* (Chi, Per) (ramal de cuero) strap

guasón -sona *m,f* (fam) (bromista) joker

guata *f* **1** (Esp) (algodón) wadding **2** (Andes fam) (barriga) paunch; **echar ~** to get a paunch; **me duele la ~** I've got a tummy ache (colloq)

Guatemala *f* Guatemala

guatemalteco -ca *adj/m,f* Guatemalan

guateque *m* (Esp, Méx fam) (fiesta) bash (colloq), party

guatitas *fpl* (Chi) tripe

guatón -tona *adj* (Chi, Per fam): **está muy ~** he has a real paunch (colloq) ■ *m,f* (Chi, Per fam) fatty (colloq)

guau *interj* (del perro) woof!, bow-wow!

guayaba *f* (fruta) guava

guayabera *f*: *loose lightweight shirt*

guayabo *m* **1** (Bot) guava tree **2** (Col fam) (resaca) hangover

Guayana *f*: *tb* **la ~ Francesa** French Guiana

gubernatura *f* (Méx) government

güero -ra *adj* (Méx fam) (rubio) blond, fair-haired; (amarillo) yellow ■ *m,f* (Méx fam) (*m*) blond *o* fair-haired man; (*f*) blonde *o* fair-haired woman

guerra *f* **1** (Mil, Pol) war; **nos declararon la ~** they declared war on us; **estar en ~** to be at war; **hacerle la ~ a algn** to wage war on *o* against sb; **~ bacteriológica** *or* **biológica** germ *o* biological warfare **2** (fam) (problemas) trouble, hassle (colloq); **estos niños me dan mucha ~** these kids give me a lot of hassle

guerrera *f* army jacket

guerrero -ra *adj* ‹*pueblo/espíritu*› warlike; **canto ~** war cry ■ *m,f* warrior

guerrilla *f* **(a)** (grupo) guerrillas (*pl*) **(b)** (lucha) guerrilla warfare

guerrillero -ra *m,f* guerrilla

guía *f* **1** (libro, folleto) guide (book); (de calles) map; **~ turística/de hoteles** tourist/hotel guide; **~ telefónica** *or* **de teléfonos** telephone directory, phone book **2 guía** *mf* (persona) guide; **~ de turismo** tourist guide

guiar [A17] *vt* to guide
■ **guiarse** *v pron* **~se POR algo** ‹*por mapa/consejo*› to follow sth; **~se por las apariencias** to be led by appearances; **~se por el instinto** to follow one's instincts

guijarro *m* pebble

guillotina *f* guillotine

guillotinar [A1] *vt* to guillotine

guinda *f* morello cherry; (confitada) glacé cherry

guindar [A1] *vt* **1** (Esp arg) (robar) ‹*novia/trabajo*› to steal **2 (a)** (Col, Méx, Ven fam) ‹*ropa*› to hang up **(b)** (Col fam) ‹*hamaca*› to hang
■ **guindarse** *v pron* (Col, Méx, Ven) (colgarse) to hang

guindilla *f* chili

guindo *m* morello cherry tree

guiñar [A1] *vt* to wink; **~le el ojo** *or* **un ojo a algn** to wink at sb

guiño *m* wink; **hacerle un ~ a algn** to give sb a wink

guión *m* **1 (a)** (Cin, TV) script; **~ cinematográfico** screenplay **(b)** (esquema) outline, plan **2** (Impr) (en diálogo) dash; (en palabras compuestas) hyphen; **lleva ~** it's hyphenated

guionista *mf* scriptwriter, screenwriter

güirila *f* (AmC) maize pancake

guirnalda *f* garland

guisante *m* (Esp) pea

guisar [A1] *vi* (Esp) to cook; **guisa muy bien** he's a very good cook ■ **~** *vt* (con bastante líquido) to stew; (con poco líquido) to braise

guiso *m* stew, casserole

guita *f* (arg) cash (colloq), dough (sl)

guitarra *f* guitar; **~ eléctrica/española/clásica** electric/Spanish/classical guitar

guitarrear [A1] *vi* (Mús) to play the guitar

guitarrista *mf* guitarist

gula *f* greed, gluttony

gusano *m* **1 (a)** (como nombre genérico) worm; (lombriz de tierra) earthworm, worm **(b)** (larva — de mariposa) caterpillar; (— de mosca) maggot; **~ de luz** glowworm; **~ de seda** silkworm **2** (pey) (persona despreciable) worm (pej)

gustar [A1] *vi* **1** (+ *me/te/le etc*): **¿te gustó el libro?** did you like *o* enjoy the book?; **me gusta su compañía** I enjoy her company; **los helados no me/te/nos gustan** I/you/we don't like ice cream; **le gusta mucho la música** he likes music very much; **a Juan le gusta María** Juan likes María; **le gusta tocar la guitarra** she likes to play the guitar (AmE), she likes playing the guitar (BrE); **le gusta mucho viajar** she's very fond of traveling (colloq); **nos gusta dar un paseo después de comer** we like to have a walk after lunch; **¿te ~ía visitar el castillo?** would you like to visit the castle?; **me ~ía que vinieras temprano** I'd like you to come early **2** (en frases de cortesía) to wish (frml); **como guste** as you wish; **cuando usted guste** whenever it is convenient for you ■ **~** *vt* (AmL) (querer) to like; **¿gustan tomar algo?** would you like something to drink?

gusto *m* **1 (a)** (sentido, sabor) taste; **resulta amargo al ~** it has a bitter taste; **tiene un ~ medio raro** it has a funny taste to it; **tiene ~ a fresa** it tastes of strawberry; **deja un ~ a menta** it has a minty aftertaste **(b)** (sentido estético) taste; **tiene muy buen ~ para vestirse** she has very good taste in clothes; **una broma de mal ~** a tasteless joke; **para todos los ~s** to suit all tastes **2 (a)** (placer, agrado) pleasure; **tendré mucho ~ en acompañarlos** (frml) it will be a pleasure for me to accompany you (frml); **da ~ estar aquí** it's so nice (being) here; **me dio mucho ~ volverlo a ver** it was lovely to see him again; **por ~** for fun, for pleasure; **un lugar donde se está a ~** a place where you feel comfortable *o* at ease **(b)** (en fórmulas de cortesía): **mucho ~ (en conocerla)** pleased *o* nice to meet you

gustoso -sa *adj* willingly

gutural *adj* guttural

H, **h** *f* (*read as* /'atʃe/) *the letter* H, h (*ver tb* HACHE)
h. (= **hora**) hr
ha *interj* ah!, ha!
Ha. (= **hectárea**) ha., hectare
haba *f*‡ (Bot) (broad) bean
Habana *f*: **La ~** Havana
habanero -ra *adj/m,f* Havanan
habano *m* (cigarro) Havana cigar
haber[1] [E17] *v aux* (en tiempos compuestos) to have; **no habían llegado** they hadn't arrived; **de ~lo sabido** had I known, if I'd known; **¡deberías ~lo dicho!** you should have said so! ■ **~** *v impers* **I** (existir, estar, darse): **hay una carta/varias cartas para ti** there's a letter/there are several letters for you; **¿hay un banco por aquí?** is there a bank near here?; **hubo dos accidentes** there were two accidents; **¿hay helado?** do you have any ice cream?; **no hay como un buen descanso** there's nothing like a good rest; **hubo varios heridos** several people were injured; **las hay rojas y verdes** there are red ones and green ones; **gracias — no hay de qué** thank you — don't mention it *o* not at all *o* you're welcome; **no hay de qué preocuparse** there's nothing to worry about; **¿qué hay de nuevo?** (fam) what's new?; **¿qué hubo?** (Andes, Méx, Ven fam) how are things?
II (ser necesario) **~** QUE + INF: **hay que estudiar** you/we/they must study; **hubo que romperlo** we/they had to break it; **no hay que lavarlo** (no es necesario) you don't need *o* have to wash it; (no se debe) you mustn't wash it
haber[2] *m* **(a)** (bienes) assets (*pl*) **(b)** (en contabilidad) credit side **(c) haberes** *mpl* (frml) (ingresos) income, earnings (*pl*)
habichuela *f* **(a)** (semilla) bean **(b)** (Col) (con vaina) green bean, French bean (BrE)
hábil *adj* **1 (a)** (diestro) ‹*carpintero*› skilled, adept; ‹*conductor*› good, skillful*; ‹*juego/táctica*› skillful* **(b)** (astuto, inteligente) clever, able **2** ‹*horas/días*› working (*before n*) **3** (Der) competent
habilidad *f* **1 (a)** (para actividad manual, física) skill; **tiene ~ para la carpintería** he is good at carpentry **(b)** (astucia, inteligencia) skill, cleverness; **con ~** cleverly, skillfully **2** (Der) competence
habilidoso -sa *adj* [SER] good with one's hands, handy
habilitación *f* **1** (de lugar) fitting out **2** (autorización) authorization **3** (Col) (Educ): **exámenes de ~** retakes
habilitar [A1] *vt* **1** ‹*lugar*› to fit out **2** ‹*persona/institución*› to authorize; «*título*» to qualify, authorize; «*documento*» to authorize, empower **3** (Col) (Educ) to retake, to make up (AmE)
habiloso -sa *adj* (Chi fam) (inteligente) bright, smart (colloq)
habitable *adj* habitable
habitación *f* (cuarto) room; (dormitorio) bedroom; **~ individual** single room
habitacional *adj* (CS) housing (*before n*)
habitante *mf* (Geog, Sociol) inhabitant; (de barrio) resident
habitar [A1] *vt* ‹*vivienda*› to live in; ‹*isla/planeta*› to inhabit ■ **~** *vi* (frml) to dwell (frml)
hábitat /'aβita(t)/ *m* (*pl* **-tats**) (Ecol, Zool) habitat; (Geog, Sociol) environment
hábito *m* **1** (costumbre) habit; **adquirir/tener el ~** DE **hacer algo** to get into/have the habit OF doing sth **2** (de religioso) habit
habitual *adj* ‹*sitio/hora*› usual; ‹*cliente/lector*› regular
habituar [A18] *vt* **~ a algn** A **algo** to get sb used TO sth
■ **habituarse** *v pron* **~se** A **algo** to get used TO sth, get *o* become accustomed TO sth
habla *f*‡ **1** (facultad) speech; **perder el ~** to lose one's powers of speech; **al verla me quedé sin ~** when I saw her I was speechless **2 (a)** (idioma): **países de ~ hispana** Spanish-speaking countries **(b)** (manera de hablar): **el ~ de esta región** the local way of speaking **3 al habla** (en el teléfono) speaking; **estamos al ~ con nuestro corresponsal** we have our correspondent on the line
hablado -da *adj* **(a)** ‹*lenguaje*› spoken **(b) bien/mal ~** ‹*persona*› well-spoken/foul-mouthed
hablador -dora *adj* **(a)** (charlatán) talkative, chatty (colloq) **(b)** (chismoso) gossipy **(c)** (Méx fam) (mentiroso): **es tan ~** he's such a fibber (colloq); ■ *m,f* **(a)** (charlatán) chatterbox (colloq) **(b)** (chismoso) gossip (colloq) **(c)** (Méx fam) (mentiroso) storyteller, fibber (colloq)
habladurías *fpl* idle gossip *o* talk
hablar [A1] *vi* **1 (a)** (articular palabras) to speak; **habla más alto** speak up; **habla más bajo** keep your voice down **(b)** (expresarse) to speak; **~ claro** (claramente) to speak clearly; (francamente) to speak frankly; **~ por señas** to use sign language; **un político que habla muy bien** a politician who is a very good speaker; **~ *por* ~** to talk for the sake of it **2 (a)** (conversar) to talk; **habla mucho** he talks a lot; **tenemos que ~** we must (have a) talk; **~** CON **algn** to speak *o* talk TO sb; **tengo que ~te** *or* **que ~ contigo** I need to speak to you *o* have a word with you; **está hablando por teléfono** he's on the phone; **¡ni ~!** no way! (colloq), no chance! (colloq) **(b)** (bajo coacción) to talk **(c)** (murmurar) to talk, gossip; ***dar que* ~** to start people talking **(d)**

(rumorear): **se habla ya de miles de víctimas** there is already talk of thousands of casualties; **se habla de que va a renunciar** it is said *o* rumored that she's going to resign **(e)** (al teléfono): **¿con quién hablo?** who am I speaking with (AmE) *o* (BrE) speaking to? **4 (a)** (tratar, referirse a) **~ DE algo/algn** to talk ABOUT sth/sb; **~ de negocios** to talk (about) *o* discuss business; **siempre habla mal de ella** he never has a good word to say about her; **hablan muy bien de él** people speak very highly of him; **me ha hablado mucho de ti** she's told me a lot about you; **en tren sale caro, y no hablemos ya del avión** going by train is expensive, and as for flying ...; **háblame de tus planes** tell me about your plans; **~ SOBRE** *or* **ACERCA DE algo** to talk ABOUT sth **(b)** (dirigirse a) to speak; **no me hables así** don't speak to me like that; **háblale de tú** use the 'tú' form with him **(c)** (anunciar propósito) **~ DE hacer algo** to talk OF doing sth; **habla de jubilarse** he's talking of retiring **5** (Méx) (por teléfono) to call, phone ■ **~** *vt* **1** ‹*idioma*› to speak **2** (tratar): **tenemos que ~ las cosas** we must talk things over; **ya lo ~emos más adelante** we'll talk about *o* discuss that later

■ **hablarse** *v pron:* **llevan meses sin ~se** they haven't spoken to each other for months; **no se habla con ella** he's not speaking *o* talking to her, he's not on speaking terms with her

habrá, habría, etc *see* HABER

hacendado -da *adj* landowning (*before n*) ■ *m, f* landowner, owner of a ranch (*o* farm *etc*)

hacendoso -sa *adj* hardworking (*esp referring to housework*)

hacer [E18] *vt* **I 1 (a)** (crear) ‹*mueble/vestido*› to make; ‹*casa/carretera*› to build; ‹*nido*› to build, make; ‹*túnel*› to make, dig; ‹*dibujo/plano*› to do, draw; ‹*lista*› to make, draw up; ‹*resumen*› to do, make; ‹*película*› to make; ‹*nudo/lazo*› to tie; ‹*pan/pastel*› to make, bake; ‹*vino/café/tortilla*› to make; ‹*cerveza*› to make, brew; **me hizo un lugar en la mesa** he made room for me at the table; **hacen buena pareja** they make a lovely couple **(b)** (producir, causar) ‹*ruido*› to make; **los chistes no me hacen gracia** I don't find jokes funny; **estos zapatos me hacen daño** these shoes hurt my feet **2 (a)** (efectuar, llevar a cabo) ‹*sacrificio*› to make; ‹*milagro*› to work, perform; ‹*deberes/ejercicios/limpieza*› to do; ‹*mandado*› to run; ‹*transacción/investigación*› to carry out; ‹*experimento*› to do, perform; ‹*entrevista*› to conduct; ‹*gira/viaje*› to do; ‹*regalo*› to give; ‹*favor*› to do; ‹*trato*› to make; **me hicieron una visita** they paid me a visit; **aún queda mucho por ~** there is still a lot (left) to do; **dar que ~** to make a lot of work **(b)** ‹*cheque/factura*› to make out, write out **3** (formular, expresar) ‹*declaración/promesa/oferta*› to make; ‹*proyecto/plan*› to make, draw up; ‹*crítica/comentario*› to make, voice; ‹*pregunta*› to ask; **nadie hizo ninguna objeción** nobody raised any objections **4 (a)** (refiriéndose a necesidades fisiológicas): **~ caca** (fam) to do a poop (AmE) *o* (BrE) a pooh (colloq); **~ pis** *or* **pipí** (fam) to have a pee (colloq); **~ sus necesidades** (euf) to go to the bathroom *o* toilet (euph) **(b)** (refiriéndose a sonidos onomatopéyicos) to go; **las vacas hacen 'mu'** cows go 'moo' **5** (adquirir) ‹*dinero/fortuna*› to make; ‹*amigo*› to make **6** (preparar, arreglar) ‹*cama*› to make; ‹*maleta*› to pack; **hice el pescado al horno** I did *o* cooked the fish in the oven; **tengo que ~ la comida** I must make lunch; *ver tb* COMIDA 2(b) **7** (recorrer) ‹*trayecto/distancia*› to do, cover **8** (en cálculos, enumeraciones): **son 180 ... y 320 hacen 500** that's 180 ... and 320 is *o* makes 500

II 1 (a) (ocuparse en actividad) to do; **~ la(s) compra(s)** to do the shopping; **¿hacemos algo esta noche?** shall we do something tonight?; **~ ejercicio** to do (some) exercise; **¿hace algún deporte?** do you play *o* do any sports?; ⇒ AMOR 1b **(b)** (como profesión, ocupación) to do; **¿qué hace tu padre?** what does your father do? **(c)** (estudiar) to do **2** (realizar cierta acción, actuar de cierta manera) to do; **¡eso no se hace!** you shouldn't do that!; **¡qué le vamos a ~!** what can you *o* (frml) one do?; **toca bien el piano — antes lo hacía mejor** she plays the piano well — she used to play better; **~*la buena*** (fam): **¡ahora sí que la hice!** now I've really done it!; ⇒ TONTO *m, f*

III 1 (transformar en, volver) to make; **ella lo hizo posible** she made it possible; **hizo pedazos la carta** she tore the letter into tiny pieces; **ese vestido te hace más delgada** that dress makes you look thinner; **~ algo DE algo** to turn sth INTO sth; **quiero ~ de ti un gran actor** I want to make a great actor of you **2 (a)** (obligar a, ser causa de que) **~ a algn hacer algo** to make sb do sth; **me hizo abrirla** he made me open it; **me hizo llorar** it made me cry; **hágalo pasar** tell him to come in; **me hizo esperar tres horas** she kept me waiting for three hours; **~ que algo/algn haga algo** to make sth/sb do sth **(b) hacer hacer algo** to have *o* get sth done/made; **hice acortar las cortinas** I had *o* got the curtains shortened ■ **~** *vi* **I 1** (obrar, actuar): **déjame ~ a mí** just let me handle this *o* take care of this; **¿cómo se hace para que te den la beca?** what do you have to do to get the scholarship?; **hiciste bien en decírmelo** you did *o* were right to tell me; **haces mal en mentir** it's wrong of you to lie **2** (fingir, simular): **hice como que no oía** I pretended not to hear; **haz como si no lo conocieras** act as if *o* pretend you don't know him **3** (servir): **esta sábana hará de toldo** this sheet will do for *o* as an awning; **la escuela hizo de hospital** the school served as *o* was used as a hospital **4** (interpretar personaje) **~ DE algo/algn** to play (the part of) sth/sb

II (+ *compl*) (sentar): **tanto sol hace mal** (AmL) too much sun is not good for you; (+ *me/te/le etc*) **el descanso le hizo bien** the rest did him good; **la trucha me hizo mal** (AmL) the trout didn't agree with me ■ **~** *v impers* **1** ▶ **409** (refiriéndose al tiempo atmosférico): **hace frío/sol** it's cold/sunny; **hace tres grados** it's three degrees; **(nos) hizo un tiempo espantoso** the weather was terrible **2** (expresando tiempo transcurrido): **hace dos años que murió** he's been dead for two years; **hace mucho que lo conozco** I've known him for a long time; **hacía años que no lo veía** I hadn't seen him for *o* in years; **¿cuánto hace que se fue?** how long ago did she leave?; **hace poco/un año** a short time/a year ago; **hasta hace poco** until recently

■ **hacerse** *v pron* **I 1** (producirse) (+ *me/te/le etc*): **se me hizo un nudo en el hilo** I got a knot in the thread; **se le hizo una ampolla** she got a blister; ***hacérsele algo a algn*** (Méx): **por fin se le hizo ganar el premio** she finally got to win the award **2 (a)** (*refl*) (hacer para sí) ‹*café/falda*› to make oneself; **se hicieron una casita** they built themselves a little house **(b)** (*caus*) (hacer que otro haga): **se hicieron una casita** they had a little house built; **se hizo la cirugía estética** she had plastic surgery **3** (causarse): **¿qué te hiciste en el brazo?** what did you do to your arm?; **¿te hiciste daño?** did you hurt yourself? **4** (refiriéndose a necesidades fisiológicas): **todavía se hace pis/caca** (fam) she still wets/messes herself **5** (*refl*) (adquirir) to make; **~se un nombre** to make a name for oneself **II 1 (a)** (volverse, convertirse en) to become; **se hicieron amigos** they became friends; **se están haciendo viejos** they are getting *o* growing old **(b)** (resultar): **se hace muy pesado** it gets very boring; (+ *me/te/le etc*) **se me hizo interminable** it seemed interminable; **se me hace difícil creerlo** I find it very hard to believe **(c)** (*impers*): **se hace de noche muy pronto** it gets dark very early; **se está haciendo tarde** it's getting late **(d)** (cocinarse) «*pescado/guiso*» to cook **(e)** (AmL) (pasarle a): **¿qué se habrá hecho María?** what can have happened to María? **2** (acostumbrarse) **~se A algo** to get used TO sth **3** (fingirse): **no te hagas el inocente** don't act the innocent; **¿es bobo o se (lo) hace?** (fam) is he stupid or just a good actor? (colloq); **~se pasar por algn** (por periodista, doctor) to pass oneself off as sb **4** (moverse) (+ *compl*) to move; **~se a un lado** to move to one side **5 hacerse de** (AmL) (de fortuna, dinero) to get; (de amigos) to make

hacha *f*‡ (herramienta) ax (AmE), axe (BrE)

hache *f*: *the name of the letter* h

hachís *m* hashish, hash (colloq)

hacia *prep* **(a)** (dirección) toward (esp AmE) , towards (esp BrE): **~ el sur** southward(s), toward(s) the south; **~ adentro/arriba** inward(s)/upward(s); **el centro queda ~ allá** the center is (over) that way; **¿~ dónde tenemos que ir?** which way do we have to go? **(b)** (aproximación) toward(s); **llegaremos ~ las dos** we'll arrive toward(s) *o* at around two **(c)** (con respecto a) toward(s); **su actitud ~ mí** his attitude toward(s) *o* to me

hacienda *f* **1 (a)** (esp AmL) (finca) estate; (dedicada a ganadería) ranch **(b)** (bienes) possessions (*pl*), property **2 Hacienda (a)** (ministerio) ≈ the Treasury Department (*in US*), ≈ the Treasury (*in UK*) **(b)** (oficina) tax office; **el dinero que debo a H~** the money I owe the IRS (AmE) *o* (BrE) the Inland Revenue

hada *f*‡ fairy; **el ~ madrina** the fairy godmother

haga, etc *see* HACER

hago *see* HACER

Haití *m* Haiti

haitiano -na *adj/m,f* Haitian

hala *interj* (Esp) **(a)** (para animar) come on! **(b)** (expresando sorpresa) wow!

halagador -dora *adj* flattering

halagar [A3] *vt* to flatter; **me halaga que me lo ofrezcas a mí** I am flattered that you're offering it to me; **le ~on el vestido** they complimented her on her dress

halago *m* praise; **~s** praise, flattery

halagüeño -ña *adj* ‹*palabras/frases*› flattering, complimentary; ‹*situación*› promising, encouraging; ‹*noticia*› encouraging; ‹*futuro*› promising

halcón *m* (Zool) falcon

hall /'xol/ *m* (*pl* **halls**) (de casa) hall, hallway; (de teatro, cine) foyer

hallaca *f* (Ven) *cornmeal, meat and vegetables wrapped in banana leaves*

hallar [A1] *vt* **1** (frml) (encontrar) to find; **halló la puerta abierta** she found the door open **2** (esp AmL) **(a)** (*en frases negativas*) (saber): **no halla cómo sentarse** she can't find a comfortable position to sit in; **no hallo cómo decírselo** I don't know how to tell her **(b)** (opinar, creer) to find

■ **hallarse** *v pron* **(a)** (frml) (estar, encontrarse) (+ *compl*) to be **(b)** (sentirse) (+ *compl*) to feel

hallazgo *m* find

hallulla *f* **1** (Chi) (pan) *slightly leavened white bread* **2** (Chi) (sombrero) straw boater

halo *m* **(a)** (aureola) halo **(b)** (de inocencia, santidad) aura

halógeno -na *adj* halogen (*before n*)

halterofilia *f* weightlifting

hamaca *f* **(a)** (para colgar) hammock **(b)** (RPl) (mecedora) rocking chair; (columpio) swing **(c)** (Esp) (asiento plegable) deckchair

hamacar [A2] *vt* (columpiar) (RPl) to swing; (mecer) (CS) to rock

■ **hamacarse** *v pron* (columpiarse) to swing; (mecerse) to rock (oneself)

hambre *f*‡ **(a)** (sensación) hunger; **tengo ~** I'm hungry; **pasar ~** to go hungry; **morirse de ~** to starve to death; **me muero de ~** (fam) I'm starving (colloq) **(b)** (como problema) **el ~** hunger

hambreado -da *adj* (Andes, Méx, RPl) hungry, starving

hambriento -ta *adj* [ESTAR] hungry, starving (colloq); **~ DE algo** hungry FOR sth ■ *m,f*: **los ~s** hungry people

hamburguesa *f* (bistec) hamburger, beefburger (BrE); (sandwich) hamburger, burger

hampa *f*‡: **el ~** criminals (*pl*), the underworld

hámster /'xamster/ *m* (*pl* **-ters**) hamster

handicap /'xandikap/ *m* (*pl* **-caps**) handicap

hangar *m* hangar

haragán -gana *adj* lazy, idle ■ *m,f* shirker, layabout

harapiento -ta *adj* ragged

harapo *m* rag

haré, etc *see* HACER

harén *m* harem

haría, etc *see* HACER

harina *f* flour; **~ de avena/maíz** oatmeal/cornmeal

harinoso -sa *adj* floury

hartar [A1] *vt* **1** (cansar, fastidiar): **me hartó con sus quejas** I got tired of his complaints **2** (fam) (llenar): **nos hartaban a** *or* **de sopa** they fed us on nothing but soup; **lo ~on a palos** they gave him a real beating
■ **hartarse** *v pron* **1** (cansarse, aburrirse) to get fed up; **~se DE algo/algn** to get tired *o* sick OF sth/sb, get fed up WITH sth/sb; **~se DE hacer algo** to get tired *o* sick of doing sth, get fed up WITH doing sth **2** (llenarse): **~se (DE algo)** to gorge oneself (ON sth), to stuff oneself (WITH sth) (colloq)

harto¹ -ta *adj* **1 (a)** (cansado, aburrido) fed up; **~ DE algo/algn** fed up WITH sth/sb, tired OF sth/sb; **~ DE hacer algo** tired OF doing sth, fed up WITH doing sth; **estaba harta de que le dijeran eso** she was tired of *o* fed up with them telling her that **(b)** (de comida) full **2** (*delante del n*) (mucho) (AmL exc RPl): **te llamé hartas veces** I phoned you lots of times; **tiene hartas ganas de verte** he really wants to see you ■ *pron* (AmL exc RPl): **tenía ~ que hacer** I had an awful lot to do; **¿tienes amigos allí? — ¡sí, ~s!** do you have friends there? — yes, lots

harto² *adv* **(a)** (AmL exc RPl) (modificando un adjetivo) very; **es ~ mejor que el hermano** he's much *o* a lot better than his brother **(b)** (modificando un verbo): **me gustó ~** I really liked it; **bailamos ~** we danced a lot

hasta *prep* **1** (en el tiempo) **(a)** until; **no descansó ~ terminar** she didn't rest until she'd finished; **~ el momento** so far, up to now **(b) hasta que** until, till; **espera ~ que pare de llover** wait until *o* till it stops raining **(c) hasta tanto** until such time as **(d)** (AmC, Col, Méx) (con valor negativo): **cierran ~ las nueve** they don't close until *o* till nine **(e)** (en saludos): **~ mañana** see you tomorrow; **~ luego/pronto** see you (colloq), see you soon **2** (en el espacio) to; **el agua me llegaba ~ los hombros** the water came up to my shoulders; **el pelo le llega hasta la cintura** her hair goes down to her waist; **¿~ dónde llega?** how far does it go? **3** (en cantidades) up to; **~ cierto punto** up to a point ■ *adv* even

hastiante *adj* boring, sickening

hastiarse [A17] *v pron* **~se DE algo** to grow tired *o* weary OF sth; **hastiado de la vida** tired *o* weary of life

Hawai *m* Hawaii

hawaiano -na *adj/m,f* Hawaiian

hay *see* HABER

haya *f*‡ (árbol, madera) beech

haya, hayas, etc *see* HABER

hayaca *f* (Ven) ⇒ HALLACA

haz *m* (de leña, paja) bundle; (de trigo) sheaf; (de luz) beam

haz *see* HACER

hazaña *f* (acción — heróica) great *o* heroic deed, exploit; (— de mucho esfuerzo) feat, achievement

hazmerreír *m* (fam) laughing stock

he *see* HABER

hebilla *f* (de zapato) buckle; (de cinturón) clasp, buckle

hebra *f* **(a)** (Tex) thread, strand **(b)** (fibra vegetal, animal) fiber* **(c)** (del gusano de seda) thread **(d)** (de la madera) grain

hebreo¹ -brea *adj/m,f* Hebrew

hebreo² *m* (idioma) Hebrew

heces *fpl*: *ver* HEZ

hechicero -ra *adj* ‹*persona*› enchanting, captivating; ‹*ojos/sonrisa*› captivating ■ *m,f* **(a)** (brujo) (*m*) sorcerer, wizard; (*f*) sorceress, witch **(b)** (de tribu) witch doctor

hechizar [A4] *vt* **(a)** «*brujo*» to cast a spell on, bewitch **(b)** (cautivar) to captivate

hechizo¹ -za *adj* (Chi, Méx) home-made

hechizo² *m* **(a)** (maleficio) spell **(b)** (atractivo, encanto) charm

hecho¹ -cha *pp* [*ver tb* HACER] **1** (manufacturado) made; **~ a mano** handmade; **un traje ~ a (la) medida** a made-to-measure suit; **bien/mal ~** well/badly made **2** (refiriéndose a acción): **¡bien ~!** well done!; **no le avisé — pues mal ~** I didn't let him know — well you should have (done); ***lo ~, ~ está*** what's done is done **3** (convertido en): **estaba ~ una fiera** he was furious; **tú estás ~ un vago** you've become *o* turned into a lazy devil ■ *adj* **(a)** ‹*ropa*› ready-to-wear **(b)** (terminado) ‹*trabajo*› done **(c)** (esp Esp) ‹*carne*› done; **un filete muy/poco ~** a well-done/rare steak

hecho² *m* **1 (a)** (acto, acción): **yo quiero ~s** I want action, I want something done; **demuéstramelo con ~s** prove it to me by doing something about it **(b)** (suceso, acontecimiento) event; **el lugar de los ~s** the scene of the crime **2** (realidad, verdad) fact; **de hecho** in fact

hechura *f* **(a)** (de traje, vestido): **no cobran por la ~** they don't charge for making it up **(b)** (modelo, estilo) style; **la falda tiene una ~ muy simple** the skirt is cut very simply **(c)** (forma) shape, form

hectárea *f* ▶ 679 hectare

hediondez *f* stench, stink

hediondo -da *adj* (fétido) foul-smelling, stinking

hegemonía *f* hegemony, dominance

helada *f* frost

heladera *f* (para hacer helados) ice-cream maker; (nevera) (RPl) refrigerator, fridge; (para picnic) (Arg, Col) cool *o* cold box

heladería *f* ice-cream parlor*

heladero -ra *m,f* (esp AmL) ice-cream vendor *o* seller

helado¹ -da *adj* **1 (a)** ‹*persona/manos*› freezing (colloq), frozen (colloq); ‹*casa/habitación*› freezing (colloq); ***quedarse ~*** (de asombro) to be stunned **(b)** ‹*comida*› stone-cold; ‹*líquido/bebida*› (muy frío) freezing; (que se ha enfriado) stone-cold; **servir el vino bien ~** (AmL) serve the wine well chilled **2** ‹*agua/estanque*› frozen

helado² *m* ice cream; **~ de agua** (Andes) water ice, sherbet (AmE); (con palo) Popsicle® (AmE), ice lolly (BrE)

helar [A5] *vt/vi* to freeze ■ **~** *v impers* ▶ 409: **anoche heló** it went below freezing last night (AmE), there was a frost last night (BrE)

■ **helarse** *v pron* **1** «*río/charco*» to freeze (over); «*agua/plantas/cosecha*» to freeze **2** (fam) **(a)** «*persona*» to freeze **(b)** «*comida/café*» to get *o* go cold

helecho *m* (como nombre genérico) fern; (más específico) bracken

hélice *f* (de barco) propeller, screw; (de avión) propeller

helicóptero *m* helicopter

hematoma *m* (tumor) hematoma*; (moretón) bruise

hembra *adj inv* female ■ *f* **(a)** (Zool) female; **la ~ del faisán** the hen pheasant **(b)** (mujer) female, woman**(c)** (de enchufe, corchete) female (part)

hemisferio *m* **(a)** (Geog, Mat) hemisphere; **el ~ norte** the northern hemisphere **(b)** (Anat) cerebral hemisphere

hemofilia *f* hemophilia*

hemofílico -ca *adj/m,f* hemophiliac*

hemorragia *f* hemorrhage*

hemorroides *fpl* piles, hemorrhoids (tech)

hendidura *f* (en madera) crack; (en roca) fissure, crack

heno *m* hay

hepatitis *f* hepatitis

heráldica *f* heraldry

herbáceo -cea *adj* herbaceous

herbicida *m* herbicide, weedkiller

herbívoro -ra *adj* herbivorous ■ *m,f* herbivore

herboristería *f* herbalist's

heredar [A1] *vt* ‹*bienes/título/tradiciones*› to inherit; ‹*trono*› to succeed to; **heredó los ojos de su madre** he has his mother's eyes

heredero -ra *m,f* (*m*) heir; (*f*) heir, heiress; **príncipe ~** crown prince; **~ DE algo** heir TO sth

hereditario -ria *adj* hereditary

herejía *f* heresy

herencia *f* **(a)** (Der) inheritance; **le dejó en ~ la finca** he bequeathed *o* left her the farm **(b)** (patrimonio cultural, nacional) heritage **(c)** (Biol) heredity

herida *f* **(a)** (en el cuerpo): **sufrir ~s de carácter grave** to suffer serious injuries; **se hizo una ~ en la rodilla** he cut his knee; **curar una ~** to clean/dress a wound **(b)** (pena, sufrimiento) wound

herido -da *adj* **(a)** (físicamente) injured; **está gravemente ~** (por accidente) he is seriously injured; (por agresión) he has been seriously wounded; **~ de muerte** fatally wounded **(b)** (en sentimiento) ‹*persona*› hurt ■ *m,f*: **los ~s** the injured/wounded

herir [I11] *vt* **(a)** (físicamente) to wound **(b)** ‹*orgullo*› to hurt **(c)** ‹*vista*› to hurt

hermanar [A1] *vt* **(a)** (en sentimiento, propósito) to unite **(b)** ‹*ciudades*› to twin **(c)** ‹*calcetines*› to match up, put ... in pairs; ‹*fichas/naipes*› to match up

hermanastro -tra *m,f* **(a)** (con vínculo sanguíneo) (*m*) half brother; (*f*) half sister **(b)** (sin vínculo sanguíneo) (*m*) stepbrother; (*f*) stepsister

hermandad *f* **(a)** (de hombres) brotherhood, fraternity; (de mujeres) sisterhood **(b)** (asociación) association

hermano -na ■ *m,f* **1** (pariente) (*m*) brother; (*f*) sister; **mis ~s** (sólo varones) my brothers; (varones y mujeres) my brothers and sisters; **~ gemelo/hermana gemela** twin brother/twin sister; **~ político/hermana política** brother-in-law/sister-in-law **2** (como apelativo) (Col, Per, Ven fam) buddy (AmE colloq), mate (BrE colloq) **3 (a)** (religioso) (*m*) brother; (*f*) sister **(b)** (prójimo) (*m*) brother; (*f*) sister **4** (de guante, calcetín) pair ■ *adj* ‹*buque*› sister (*before n*); ‹*ciudades*› twin (*before n*)

hermético -ca *adj* **(a)** ‹*envase/cierre*› airtight, hermetic (tech) **(b)** ‹*persona/rostro*› inscrutable, secretive

hermoso -sa *adj* **(a)** (bello) beautiful, lovely **(b)** (magnífico) splendid **(c)** (lozano, corpulento) big and healthy, bonny (BrE) **(d)** (noble) noble

hermosura *f* **(a)** (cualidad) beauty, loveliness **(b)** (persona, cosa hermosa): **¡qué ~ de niño/paisaje!** what a beautiful child/landscape!

hernia *f* hernia, rupture; **~ discal** slipped disk*

herniarse [A1] *v pron* to get a hernia, rupture oneself

héroe *m* hero

heroico -ca *adj* heroic

heroína *f* **1** (persona) heroine **2** (droga) heroin

heroinómano -na *m,f* heroin addict

heroísmo *m* heroism

herpes *m* (*pl* ~) (en boca, genitales) herpes; (en cintura) shingles

herradura *f* horseshoe

herramienta *f* tool

herrería *f* blacksmith's, smithy

herrero -ra *m,f* blacksmith

herrumbre *f* rust

hervidero *m* (de moscas) swarm; (de chismes, delincuencia) hotbed; **un ~ de gente** a seething mass of people; **la casa era un ~** the house was buzzing

hervidor *m* (de agua) kettle; (de leche) milk pan

hervir [I11] *vi/vt* to boil; **el café está hirviendo** the coffee is boiling

heterosexual *adj/mf* heterosexual

hez *f* **(a)** (escoria) dregs (*pl*) **(b)** (Vin) *tb* **heces** sediment, lees (*pl*) **(c) heces** *fpl* (excrementos) feces* (*pl*)

hibernar [A1] *vi* to hibernate

híbrido[1] -da *adj* hybrid (*before n*)

híbrido[2] *m* hybrid

hice, hiciera, etc *see* HACER

hidalgo *m* gentleman, nobleman (*from the lower ranks of the nobility*)

hidratante *adj* moisturizing (*before n*)

hidratar [A1] *vt* ‹*verduras*› to hydrate; ‹*piel*› to moisturize

hidrato *m* hydrate; **~s de carbono** carbohydrates

hidráulico -ca *adj* hydraulic

hidroavión *m* seaplane

hidroeléctrico -ca *adj* hydroelectric

hidrofobia *f* hydrophobia (tech), rabies

hidrógeno *m* hydrogen

hiedra *f* ivy

hiel *f* bile

hiela, **hielas, etc** *see* HELAR

hielo *m* ice; ***romper el ~*** to break the ice

hiena *f* hyena

hierba *f* **1** (césped) grass; ***~ mala nunca muere*** the Devil looks after his own **2 (a)** (Bot, Coc, Med) herb; **malas ~s** weeds **(b)** (arg) (marihuana) grass (colloq)

hierbabuena *f* mint

hierbajo *m* (esp Esp) weed

hierro *m* **(a)** (Metal) iron; **~ forjado** wrought iron; **~ fundido** cast iron; ***de ~*** iron (*before n*) **(b)** (de lanza, flecha) head, tip **(c)** (en golf) iron; **un ~ cuatro** a four iron

hígado *m* ▸ **123** liver

higiene *f* hygiene

higiénico -ca *adj* hygienic

higo *m* (de la higuera) fig; **~ chumbo** (Esp) prickly pear

higuera *f* fig tree

hijastro -tra *m,f* (*m*) stepson; (*f*) stepdaughter; **mis ~s** (varones y mujeres) my stepchildren

hijo -ja *m,f* **1** (pariente) (*m*) son; (*f*) daughter; **mis ~s** (sólo varones) my sons; (varones y mujeres) my children; **espera un ~** she's expecting a baby; **no tienen ~s** they don't have any children; **~ adoptivo/hija adoptiva** adopted son/daughter; **~/hija de papá** rich kid (colloq); **~/hija natural** illegitimate son/daughter; **~ político/hija política** son-in-law/daughter-in-law; **~ único/hija única** only child; **M. Pérez, ~** M. Pérez Junior; ***~ de tigre sale pintado*** (AmL fam) he's just like his father/mother **2** (apelativo): **¡~, por Dios!** (hablándole a un niño) for heaven's sake, child!; (hablándole a un adulto) for heaven's sake, Pedro (*o* Luis *etc*)!

híjole *interj* (Méx) jeez! (AmE colloq), gosh (colloq)

hilacha *f* loose thread

hilar [A1] *vi* to spin; ***~ fino*** to split hairs ■ **~** *vt* **(a)** ‹*algodón/lana*› to spin; «*araña*» to spin **(b)** ‹*ideas/hechos*› to string together

hilera *f* **(a)** (fila) row, line **(b)** (Mil) file (frml *or* liter) **(c)** (de ladrillos) course **(d)** (de semillas) row, drill

hilo *m* **1 (a)** (en costura) thread; **~ dental** dental floss **(b)** (lino) linen **(c)** (de araña) thread **(d)** (fam) (de las judías) string **2** (Elec) wire; **~ musical** (Esp) piped music **3** (de relato, conversación) thread **4** (de sangre, agua) trickle

hilvanar [A1] *vt* **1** (coser) to baste (AmE), to tack (BrE) **2** ‹*frases/ideas*› to put together

himen *m* hymen

himno *m* **(a)** (religioso) hymn; (de colegio) school song *o* anthem; **~ nacional** national anthem **(b)** (Lit) ode

hincada *f* (Col, Per) sharp pain

hincapié *m*: **hacer ~ en algo** to stress *o* emphasize sth

hincar [A2] *vt* (clavar) **~ algo EN algo** ‹*estaca*› to drive *o* thrust sth INTO sth; **me hincó los dientes en la mano** it buried its teeth in *o* sunk its teeth into my hand

■ **hincarse** *v pron tb* **~se de rodillas** to kneel

hincha *mf* (fam) (Dep) fan (colloq), supporter

hinchado -da *adj* ‹*vientre/pierna*› swollen; ‹*estilo/lenguaje*› overblown

hinchar [A1] *vt* (Esp) ‹*globo*› to inflate (frml), to blow up; ‹*rueda*› to inflate, pump up; ‹*suceso/noticia*› (fam) to blow ... up (colloq) ■ **~** *vi* (CS fam) (fastidiar) «*persona*» to be a pain in the ass (AmE vulg) *o* (BrE vulg) arse; (+ *me/te/le etc*) **me hincha su actitud** his attitude really pisses me off (sl)

■ **hincharse** *v pron* **(a)** «*vientre/pierna*» (+ *me/te/le etc*) to swell up **(b)** (fam) (enorgullecerse) to swell with pride **(c)** (Esp fam) (hartarse) **~se DE algo** ‹*de pasteles/ostras*› to stuff oneself WITH sth

hinchazón *f* swelling

hindú *adj/mf* **(a)** (Relig) Hindu **(b)** (crit) (de la India) Indian

hinojo *m* (Bot, Coc) fennel

hiperactivo -va *adj* hyperactive

hipermercado *m* large supermarket, hypermarket (BrE)

hípica *f* equestrian sports (*pl*); (carreras) horse racing

hípico -ca *adj* ‹*deportes/centro*› equestrian (*before n*)

hipnosis *f* hypnosis

hipnotismo *m* hypnotism

hipnotizador -dora *adj* ‹*mirada*› hypnotic ■ *m,f* hypnotist

hipnotizar [A4] *vt* (Psic) to hypnotize; (fascinar) to mesmerize

hipo *m* hiccups (*pl*), hiccoughs (*pl*)

hipocondríaco -ca *m,f* hypochondriac

hipocresía *f* hypocrisy

hipócrita *adj* hypocritical ■ *mf* hypocrite

hipodérmico -ca *adj* hypodermic

hipódromo *m* (Equ, Ocio) racecourse, racetrack (AmE); (Hist) hippodrome

hipopótamo *m* hippopotamus

hipoteca *f* mortgage

hipotecar [A2] *vt* to mortgage

hipotecario -ria *adj* mortgage (*before n*)

hipótesis *f* hypothesis

hipotético -ca *adj* hypothetical

hippy, **hippie** /'xipi/ *adj* (*pl* **hippies**) hippy (*before n*), hippie (*before n*) ■ *mf* hippy, hippie

hiriente *adj* hurtful, wounding (*before n*)

hirviendo *see* HERVIR

hisopo *m* **(a)** (bastoncillo) cotton swab (AmE), cotton bud (BrE) **(b)** (Chi) (de afeitar) shaving brush

hispánico -ca *adj* **(a)** (de los países de habla hispana) Hispanic **(b)** (relativo a España) Spanish

hispanismo *m* (giro propio del español de España) word/expression peculiar to Spain; (palabra derivada del español) hispanicism; (estudio) Hispanic studies

hispano -na *adj* **(a)** (español) Spanish, Hispanic (frml); **países de habla hispana** Spanish-speaking countries **(b)** (hispanoamericano) Spanish American, Latin American; (en EE UU) Hispanic ■ *m,f* **(a)** (liter) (español) Spaniard **(b)** (hispanoamericano) Spanish American, Latin American; (en EE UU) Hispanic

Hispanoamérica *f* Spanish America

hispanoamericano -na *adj/m,f* Spanish American

hispanohablante, **hispanoparlante** *mf* Spanish speaker

histeria *f* hysteria; **~ colectiva** mass hysteria

histérico -ca *adj* (Med, Psic) hysterical; (exaltado): **ponerse ~** to have hysterics *o* a fit; **me pones ~** you drive me mad ■ *m,f* (Med, Psic) hysteric; (exaltado): **es un ~** he gets quite hysterical about things

historia *f* **1** (Hist) history; **~ antigua** ancient history; **~ clínica** medical history; ***pasar a la ~*** (por ser importante) to go down in history; (perder actualidad) (fam): **aquello ya pasó a la ~** that's ancient history now (colloq) **2** (relato) story; **la ~ de su vida** the story of his life **3** (fam) (cuento, asunto): **me vino con la ~ de que** ... he came up with this story *o* tale about ...; **déjate de ~s** stop making excuses; **se quejó de no sé qué ~s** he complained about something or other (colloq)

historiador -dora *m,f* historian

historial *m* record; **~ clínico** *or* **médico** medical history; **~ personal** resumé (AmE), curriculum vitae (BrE)

histórico -ca *adj* (real) historical; (importante) historic

historieta *f* comic strip, cartoon story

hit /'xit/ *m* (*pl* **hits**) hit

hito *m* (hecho trascendental) landmark, milestone

hizo *see* HACER

Hnos. (= **hermanos**) Bros.

hobby /'xoβi/ *m* (*pl* **-bbies**) hobby

hocico *m* (de cerdo) snout; (de perro, lobo) snout, muzzle

hocicón -cona *m,f* (CS, Méx fam & pey) bigmouth (colloq & pej), blabbermouth (colloq & pej)

hockey /'(x)oki/ *m* hockey; **~ sobre hielo** ice hockey

hogar *m* home; **formar un ~** to set up home; **artículos para el ~** household goods; **las labores del ~** housework; **quedarse sin ~** to be left homeless; **~ de ancianos** residential home for the elderly, old people's home (colloq)

hogareño -ña *adj* ‹*persona*› home-loving; ‹*vida/escena*› domestic (*before n*)

hoguera *f* bonfire; **murió en la ~** he was burned at the stake

hoja *f* **1** (Bot) leaf **2 (a)** (folio) sheet; **~ de vida** (Col, Ven) resumé (AmE), curriculum vitae (BrE) **(b)** (de libro) page, leaf; **pasar las ~s** to turn the pages **(c)** (formulario) form, sheet **3 (a)** (de puerta, mesa) leaf **(b)** (de madera, metal) sheet **(c)** (de cuchillo) blade; **~ de afeitar** razor blade

hojalata *f* tinplate

hojalatería *f* (Méx) body work (AmE), panel-beating (BrE)

hojalatero -ra *m,f* (Auto) (Méx) body shop worker (AmE), panel beater (BrE)

hojaldre *m* puff pastry, puff paste (AmE)

hojear [A1] *vt* to leaf *o* glance through

hojilla *f* (Ven) razor blade

hojuela *f* (AmL exc CS) flake

hola *interj* ▶ **378** (saludo) hello, hi! (colloq)

holá *interj* ▶ **405** (RPl) (por teléfono) hello?

holán *m* (Méx) flounce, frill

Holanda *f* Holland

holandés[1] -desa *adj* Dutch ■ *m,f* (*m*) Dutchman; (*f*) Dutchwoman; **los holandeses** the Dutch, Dutch people

holandés[2] *m* (idioma) Dutch

holgado -da *adj* **(a)** ‹*prenda*› loose-fitting, baggy **(b)** ‹*posición*› comfortable; **viven ~s** they're comfortably off **(c)** ‹*victoria/mayoría*› comfortable **(d)** (de espacio): **así iremos más ~s** we'll be more comfortable like that

holgar [A8] *vi* (*en 3ª pers*) (frml) (estar de más): **huelga decir que** ... it goes without saying that ...; **huelgan los comentarios** what can one say?

holgazán -zana *adj* lazy ■ *m,f* idler, lazybones (colloq)

holgazanear [A1] *vi* to idle, laze *o* loaf around

holgura *f* **(a)** (bienestar económico, comodidad): **vivir con ~** to live comfortably **(b)** (de prenda) fullness, looseness

hollejo *m* skin

hollín *m* soot

hombre *m* **(a)** (varón) man; **~s, mujeres y niños** men, women and children; **no es lo bastante ~ para** ... he's not man enough to ...; **¡~ al agua!** man overboard!; **este ~ no sabe lo que dice** this guy doesn't know what he's talking about; **~ de confianza** right-hand man; **~ del tiempo** weatherman; **~ de negocios** businessman; **~ lobo** werewolf; **~ medio** man in the street; **~ rana** frogman, diver; ***~ precavido vale por dos*** forewarned is forearmed **(b)** (especie humana): **el ~** man ■ *interj*: **¡~! ¡qué sorpresa!** well! what a nice surprise!; **¿te gustaría venir? — ¡~!** would you like to come? — you bet! what do you think?; **~, no es lo mismo** come off it, it's not the same thing at all (colloq)

hombrera *f* (almohadilla) shoulder pad; (Mil) (de uniformes) epaulet

hombría *f* manliness

hombrillo *m* (Ven) shoulder (AmE), hard shoulder (BrE)

hombro *m* ▶ **123** shoulder; **encogerse de ~s** to shrug (one's shoulders); **lo llevaron a ~s** they carried him on their shoulders *o* shoulder high; ***arrimar el ~*** to pull one's weight, put one's shoulder to the wheel; ***mirar a algn por encima del ~*** to look down on sb

hombruno -na *adj* (pey) ‹*mujer*› mannish, butch (colloq & pej); ‹*gestos/modales*› masculine, mannish

homenaje *m* **(a)** (tributo) tribute; **rendir(le) ~ a algn** to pay tribute *o* homage to sb; **en ~ a** in honor of **(b)** (acto): **le ofrecieron un ~** they held a party (*o* reception, *etc*) in his honor

homeópata *mf* homeopath
homeopatía *f* homeopathy
homeopático -ca *adj* (Med) homeopathic
homicida *adj* (frml) ‹*instinto*› homicidal; ‹*arma*› murder (*before n*) ■ *mf* (frml) murderer, homicide (frml)
homicidio *m* (frml) homicide
homogéneo -nea *adj* ‹*grupo*› homogeneous; ‹*masa/mezcla*› smooth
homologar [A3] *vt* **(a)** ‹*producto*› (recomendar) to approve, endorse; (autorizar) to authorize, approve **(b)** (Dep) ‹*récord*› to ratify, recognize **(c)** ‹*convenio*› to recognize
homólogo -ga *adj* equivalent ■ *m,f* (period) counterpart
homosexual *adj/mf* homosexual
honda *f* (de cuero) sling; (con elástico) slingshot (AmE), catapult (BrE)
hondo[1] -da *adj* **(a)** ‹*piscina/río*› deep; **en lo más ~ de mi corazón** in my heart of hearts, deep down; **en lo ~ del valle** at the bottom of the valley **(b)** (*gen delante del n*) (frml) ‹*pena/pesar*› profound (frml), deep
hondo[2] *adv*: **respirar ~** to breathe deeply
hondonada *f* hollow
Honduras *f* Honduras
hondureño -ña *adj/m,f* Honduran
honestidad *f* integrity, honesty
honesto -ta *adj* (íntegro) honest, honorable*
hongo *m* **(a)** (Bot, Med) fungus **(b)** (AmL) (Coc) mushroom **(c)** *tb* **sombrero de ~** derby (AmE), bowler hat (BrE) **(d) ~ atómico** mushroom cloud
honor *m* **(a)** honor*; **tengo el ~ de ...** it is my honor *o* I have the honor to ...; **me hizo el ~ de recibirme** he did me the honor of receiving me; ***en ~ a la verdad*** to be truthful; ***hacer ~ a su nombre*** to live up to one's reputation **(b) honores** *mpl* (homenaje) honors* (*pl*); **le rindieron los ~es correspondientes a su rango** he was accorded the honors befitting his rank (frml)
honorable *adj* honorable*
honorario -ria *adj* honorary
honorarios *mpl* fees (*pl*)
honorífico -ca *adj* honorary
honra *f* **(a)** (en general) honor*; ***¡y a mucha ~!*** and proud of it! **(b) ~s fúnebres** *fpl* funeral rites (*pl*)
honradez *f* (honestidad) honesty; (decencia) decency
honrado -da *adj* **(a)** (honesto) honest, honorable* **(b)** ‹*mujer*› respectable
honrar [A1] *vt* **1** «*comportamiento/actitud*» to do ... credit *o* honor*; **nos honra hoy con su presencia** she is honoring us with her presence here today **2** (respetar) to honor*
hora *f* **1** (período de tiempo) hour; **media ~** half an hour, a half hour (AmE); **las ~s de mayor afluencia** the busiest time; **cobrar por ~s** to be paid by the hour; **8.000 pesetas por ~** 8,000 pesetas an hour; **~ libre** free period; **~ pico** (AmL) *or* (Esp) **punta** rush hour; **~s extra(s)** overtime **2 (a)** (momento puntual) time; **¿tiene ~, por favor?** have you got the time, please?; **¿qué ~ es?** what's the time?, what time is it?; **pon el reloj en ~** put the clock right; **todavía no es la ~** it's not time yet; **nunca llegan a la ~** they never arrive on time; **el avión llegó antes de (su) ~** the plane arrived early **(b)** (momento sin especificar) time; **es ~ de irse a la cama** it's bedtime *o* time for bed; **a la ~ de almorzar** at lunchtime; **ya es ~ de irnos** it's time for us to go; **¡ya era ~ de que llamases!** it's about time you called; **a primera ~ de la mañana** first thing in the morning; **a última ~** at the last moment; ***a la ~ de***: **a la ~ traducirlo** when it comes to translating it; **a la ~ de la verdad** when it comes down to it; ***entre ~s*** between meals; ***hacer ~*** (Chi) to kill time **3** (cita) appointment; **pedir ~** to make an appointment
horadar [A1] *vt* ‹*roca*› to bore through; ‹*pared*› to drill a hole in
horario *m* **1** (de trenes, aviones) schedule (AmE), timetable (BrE); (de clases) timetable; **tiene un ~ muy flexible** his hours are very flexible; **~ continuo** *or* (AmL) **corrido** *or* (Esp) **intensivo** *continuous working day* (*usually from eight to three*) *with no break for lunch*; **~ de visitas** visiting hours (*pl*); **~ partido** *working day with a long break for lunch* **2** (de reloj) hour hand
horca *f* **1** (patíbulo) gallows (*pl*); (juego): **la ~** hangman **2** (Agr) pitchfork, hayfork
horcajadas : **a ~** (*loc adv*) astride
horchata *f* (de chufas) horchata (*cold drink made from tiger nuts*); (en Méx) *drink made from ground melon seeds*
horda *f* horde
horizontal *adj/f* horizontal
horizonte *m* **(a)** (línea) horizon **(b) horizontes** *mpl* (perspectivas) horizons (*pl*)
horma *f* (para hacer zapatos) last; (para conservar su forma) shoetree
hormiga *f* ant
hormigón *m* concrete
hormigueo *m* pins and needles (*pl*), tingling
hormiguero *m* **(a)** (Zool) (nido) ant's nest; (montículo) anthill **(b)** (de personas): **era un ~ de gente** it was swarming with people
hormona *f* hormone
hornada *f* (de pan, pasteles) batch
hornalla *f* (RPl) ⇒ HORNILLO 1
hornilla *f* **(a)** (AmL exc CS) ⇒ HORNILLO 1 **(b)** (Chi) ⇒ HORNILLO 2
hornillo *m* **1** (Esp) **(a)** (de gas) burner **(b)** (de una cocina eléctrica — espiral) ring; (— placa) hotplate **2** (cocinilla portátil) portable electric stove
horno *m* **(a)** (de cocina) oven; **resistente al ~** ovenproof; **pollo al ~** roast chicken; **pescado al ~** baked fish **(b)** (Metal, Tec) furnace **(c)** (para cerámica) kiln
horóscopo *m* horoscope
horqueta *f* (Chi) (de jardinero) fork; (de campesino) pitchfork
horquilla *f* **(a)** (para pelo) hairpin **(b)** (Agr) pitchfork **(c)** (en bicicleta) fork
horrendo -da *adj* ⇒ HORROROSO

La Hora

Unidades de tiempo

a second	un segundo
a minute	un minuto
an hour	una hora
a quarter of an hour	un cuarto de hora
half an hour	media hora
three quarters of an hour	tres cuartos de hora

Para preguntar la hora

what time is it? what's the time?	¿qué hora es?
can you tell me the time?	¿me dice(s) or me da(s) la hora?
do you have the time? have you got the time (on you)?	¿tiene(s) hora?
what time do you have (AmE) what time do you make it? (BrE)	¿qué hora tiene(s)?

Respuestas

it's twelve o'clock	son las doce
it's exactly ten o'clock	son las diez en punto

Para expresar los minutos después de la hora se utiliza after *en el inglés norteamericano y* past *en el inglés británico*:

it's five after seven (AmE) it's five past seven (BrE)	7:05
it's a quarter after three (AmE) it's a quarter past three (BrE)	3:15

El caso de la hora y media es ligeramente diferente:

it's four thirty it's half past four (BrE)	4:30

Para expresar los minutos que faltan para la hora se emplea to. *En el inglés norteamericano también se utiliza* of:

it's twenty to twelve it's twenty of twelve (AmE)	11:40

Respuestas menos precisas:

it's just after five o'clock it's just gone five (colloq)	son las cinco pasadas
it's coming up to three o'clock it's nearly three o'clock	son casi las tres
it must be about seven it must be around seven	serán las siete

De la mañana/de la tarde/de la noche

Para especificar si se trata de antes o después del mediodía se utilizan las siguientes expresiones:

7 in the morning	las 7 de la mañana
3 in the afternoon	las 3 de la tarde
8 in the evening	las 8 de la tarde/noche
11.30 at night	las 11.30 de la noche

In the evening *se emplea normalmente para referirse al período comprendido entre las seis y las nueve. A veces se usa* at night *si el hablante quiere dar a entender que es muy tarde*:

seven o'clock in the morning
three o'clock in the afternoon
the concert starts at nine in the evening
she didn't leave the office until nine o'clock at night

También se pueden utilizar las abreviaturas a.m. y p.m.:

three fifteen a.m.	las tres y cuarto de la madrugada
four thirty p.m.	las cuatro y media de la tarde

(*la forma escrita es 3:15 a.m. en el inglés norteamericano y 3.15 a.m. en el inglés británico*)

Existen varias alternativas para hablar de las doce del mediodía y las doce de la noche:

12:00	24:00
it's twelve o'clock it's midday it's twelve a.m. it's twelve midday it's noon	it's twelve o'clock it's midnight it's twelve p.m. it's twelve midnight

¿A qué hora?

What time did you arrive?

at five (o'clock)	a las cinco
at six (o'clock) on the dot	a las seis en punto
at exactly 4:45 a.m.	a las cuatro cuarenta y cinco
around o about 3 p.m.	alrededor de las tres de la tarde
soon after midnight	poco después de (la) medianoche
just after ten	a las diez pasadas
sometime between eight and nine in the morning	entre las ocho y las nueve de la mañana

El sistema de 24 horas

Este sistema se emplea fundamentalmente cuando se trata de horarios. Es poco usado en el inglés norteamericano:

twenty thirty	20:30
fourteen ten	14:10
eighteen forty-four	18:44

Para la hora en punto se suele agregar hundred hours:

it arrives at sixteen hundred hours	llega a las 16:00
the sixteen hundred (hours) departure	el tren/avión de las 16:00

horrible *adj* **(a)** ‹*accidente/muerte*› horrible, horrific **(b)** (feo) ‹*persona*› hideous, ugly; ‹*camisa/adorno*› horrible, hideous **(c)** ‹*tiempo*› terrible, awful **(d)** (inaguantable) unbearable

horripilante *adj* terrifying, horrifying

horror *m* **1 (a)** (miedo, angustia) horror; **me causa ~ verlo** it horrifies me to see it; **les tengo ~ a los hospitales** I'm terrified of hospitals **(b)** (fam) (uso hiperbólico): **¡qué ~!** how awful *o* terrible! **2 horrores** *mpl* (cosas terribles) horrors (*pl*); **los ~s de la guerra** the horrors of the war

horrorizar [A4] *vt* to horrify, appall ■ **horrorizarse** *v pron* to be horrified, be appalled; **~se DE algo** to be horrified BY *o* AT sth

horroroso -sa *adj* ‹*crimen*› horrific, horrifying; ‹*película/novela*› terrible, awful; ‹*persona/vestido*› awful, horrific (colloq); **tengo un hambre horrorosa** I'm absolutely starving (colloq)

hortaliza *f* vegetable

hortelano -na *m,f* truck farmer (AmE), market gardener (BrE)

hortensia *f* hydrangea

hortera *adj* (Esp fam) ‹*vestido/canción*› tacky (colloq); **es muy ~** he has very tacky taste

horticultor -ra *m,f* horticulturalist, gardener

horticultura *f* horticulture, gardening

hosco -ca *adj* ‹*persona/semblante*› surly, sullen

hospedaje *m* accommodations (AmE), accommodation (BrE)

hospedar [A1] *vt* to provide … with accommodations (AmE) *o* (BrE) accommodation ■ **hospedarse** *v pron* to stay, put up (AmE colloq)

hospicio *m* (para niños huérfanos) orphanage

hospital *m* hospital; **~ clínico** teaching hospital

hospitalario -ria *adj* **(a)** ‹*pueblo/persona*› hospitable, welcoming **(b)** (Med) hospital (*before n*)

hospitalidad *f* hospitality

hospitalizar [A4] *vt* to hospitalize ■ **hospitalizarse** *v pron* (AmL) to go into the hospital (AmE) *o* (BrE) into hospital

hostal *m* cheap hotel; **~ residencia** guesthouse, boarding house

hostelería *f* (Esp) ⇒ HOTELERÍA

hostia *f* **1** (Relig) host **2** (Esp vulg *o* fam) (golpe) slap, smack in the face (*o* mouth *etc*); **se pegó una ~ con el coche** he smashed his car up badly (colloq) **3** (uso expletivo) (Esp vulg *o* fam) **¡~(s)!** jeez! (AmE colloq), bloody hell! (BrE sl); **hace un frío de la ~** it's goddamn (AmE) *o* (BrE) bloody freezing! (sl); **¡qué ~s …!** what the hell …! (sl)

hostigar [A3] *vt* **1 (a)** (acosar) to bother, pester **(b)** (Mil) to harass **(c)** ‹*caballo*› to whip **2** (Andes fam) «*comida/bebida*» to pall on

hostigoso -sa *adj* (Andes) ‹*comida/bebida*› sickly, sickly-sweet; ‹*persona*› annoying, irritating

hostil *adj* [SER] ‹*medio/clima*› hostile; ‹*gente/actitud*› hostile, unfriendly

hostilidad *f* **(a)** (del clima) hostility; (de actitud) hostility, unfriendliness **(b) hostilidades** *fpl* hostilities (*pl*)

hotel *m* hotel; **~ residencia** guesthouse, boarding house

hotelería *f* (AmL) (negocio, industria) hotel and catering trade *o* business; (profesión) hotel management

hotelero -ra *adj* hotel (*before n*) ■ *m,f* hotel manager, hotelier

hoy *adv* **1** (este día) today; **~ hace un año** a year ago today; **¿a cuánto estamos ~?** what's the date today? **2 (a)** (actualmente) today, nowadays **(b)** (*en locs*) **hoy (en) día** nowadays, these days; **hoy por hoy** at this precise moment, at this moment in time

hoyo *m* (agujero) hole; (depresión) hollow; (fosa) pit; (en golf) hole; (sepultura) (fam) grave

hoyuelo *m* dimple

hoz *f* sickle

huacal *m* (Col, Méx, Ven) (caja) wooden crate

huachafo -fa *adj* (Per fam) **(a)** ‹*persona*› pretentious, affected **(b)** ‹*vestido/adorno*› tacky (colloq)

huachinango *m* (Méx) red snapper

huacho -cha *adj/m,f* ⇒ GUACHO[1,2]

huarache *m* (Méx) (Indum) sandal

huasca *f* (Chi, Per) ⇒ GUASCA

huaso -sa *m,f* (Chi) **(a)** (campesino) peasant **(b)** (fam) (persona — rústica) hick (AmE colloq), country bumpkin (colloq); (—sin modales) uncouth yob (colloq)

hube, hubo, etc *see* HABER

hucha *f* (Esp) moneybox, piggybank

hueco[1] -ca *adj* **(a)** [ESTAR] ‹*árbol/bola*› hollow; ‹*nuez*› empty, hollow; **tienes la cabeza hueca** (fam & hum) you've got a head full of sawdust (colloq & hum) **(b)** [SER] (vacío) ‹*palabras*› empty; ‹*estilo*› superficial; ‹*persona*› shallow, superficial **(c)** (esponjoso) ‹*lana*› soft; ‹*colchón*› soft, spongy **(d)** ‹*sonido/tos*› hollow; ‹*voz*› resonant

hueco[2] *m* **(a)** (cavidad en árbol, roca) hollow; (de ascensor) shaft; **suena a ~** it sounds hollow; **el ~ de la escalera** the stairwell **(b)** (espacio) space; (entre dos dientes) gap; **un ~ para aparcar** a parking space; **hazme un ~** make room for me; **llenar un ~ en el mercado** to fill a gap in the market **(c)** (concavidad) hollow

huela, huele, etc *see* OLER

huelga *f* strike; **hacer ~** to (go on) strike; **estar en ~** to be on strike

huelga, huelgan, etc *see* HOLGAR

huelguista *mf* striker

huella *f* **(a)** (pisada — de persona) footprint, footstep; (— de rueda) track; **las ~s del animal** the animal's tracks *o* pawprints (*o* hoofmarks *etc*); **~s dactilares** fingerprints **(b)** (vestigio) mark; **sin dejar ~** without (a) trace

huelo *see* OLER

huemul *m* deer (*native to the Southern Andes*)

huérfano -na *adj*: **un niño ~** an orphan; **quedó ~** he was orphaned; **es ~ de padre** he doesn't have a father ■ *m,f* orphan

huerta *f* **(a)** (huerto grande) (vegetable) garden; (con frutales) orchard **(b)** (explotación agrícola) truck farm (AmE), market garden (BrE)

huerto *m* (para verduras) vegetable garden; (con frutales) orchard

hueso *m* ▶ 123 | **1 (a)** (Anat) bone; ***en los* ~*s*** (fam) nothing but skin and bone(s) (colloq) **(b) (de) color ~** off-white, bone-colored **2** (de fruta) pit (AmE), stone (BrE)

huésped *mf* (en casa, hotel) guest

huesudo -da *adj* bony

hueva *f* **1** *tb* **~s** (Coc) roe; (Zool) spawn **2** (Andes vulg) (testículo): **~s** balls (vulg), bollocks (BrE vulg)

huevada *f* (Andes vulg) (estupidez): **¿dónde compraste esa ~?** where did you buy that crap (sl) *o* (vulg) that shit?; **¡no digas ~s!** don't talk crap! (sl); **déjate de ~s y ponte a trabajar** stop screwing around (AmE) *o* (BrE) pissing about and get on with some work (vulg)

huevear [A1] *vi* (Chi, Per vulg) (perder el tiempo) to goof off (AmE colloq), to piss around (BrE sl) ■ **~** *vt* (Chi vulg) ‹*persona*› (molestar) to bug (colloq), to hassle (colloq); (tomar el pelo a) to kid

hueveo *m* (Chi vulg) (tomadura de pelo) pisstake (vulg); **agarrar a algn para el ~** to make fun of sb, to take the piss out of sb (BrE sl)

huevera *f* **1** (para guardar huevos) egg box; (para servir huevos) eggcup **2** (Per) (huevas) roe

huevo *m* **1** (Biol, Coc, Zool) egg; **~ a la copa** (Chi) boiled egg; **~ de Pascua** Easter egg; **~ duro** *or* (Ven) **sancochado** hard-boiled egg; **~ escalfado** *or* (Méx, RPl) **poché** poached egg; **~ estrellado** (frito) fried egg; **~ pasado por agua** *or* (Col, Méx) **tibio** soft boiled egg; **~s revueltos** *or* (Col) **pericos** scrambled eggs (*pl*); ***a* ~: tuve que leer el libro a ~** (Méx vulg) I had no damn *o* (BrE) bloody choice but to read the book (sl); **comprar/vender a ~** (Andes fam) to buy/sell for peanuts (colloq); **mirar a ~** (Chi fam) to look down on **2** (vulg) (testículo) ball (vulg); *para modismos ver* COJONES 1

huevón -vona *adj* **(a)** (Andes, Ven fam *o* vulg) (tonto, estúpido) (fam) dumb (colloq); **es tan ~** he's so fucking stupid (vulg) **(b)** (Méx vulg) (holgazán) lazy (colloq) ■ *m, f* **(a)** (Andes, Ven vulg) (imbécil) dickhead (vulg), asshole (AmE vulg) **(b)** (Méx vulg) (holgazán) lazy bum (colloq)

huida *f* (fuga) flight; **emprender la ~** to take flight (frml)

huidizo -za *adj* ‹*mirada*› evasive, shy; ‹*carácter/persona*› elusive; ‹*animal*› timid

huila *f* (Chi) rag

huincha *f* **(a)** (Andes) (cinta) ribbon; (en carrera) tape **(b)** (Andes) (para pelo) hair-band **(c)** (Bol, Chi, Per) (para medir) tape measure

huipil *m* (en AmC, Méx) huipil (*traditional embroidered dress worn by Indian women*)

huir [I20] *vi* **(a)** (escapar) to flee (liter *or* journ), escape; **huyó de la cárcel** he escaped from prison; **~ del país** to flee the country **(b)** (tratar de evitar) **~ DE algo** to avoid sth; **~le A algn** to avoid sb

huira *f* (Per) rope

huiro *m* (Chi, Per) seaweed

hule *m* **1** (para mantel) oilcloth; (para ropa impermeable) oilskin **2** (Méx) (goma) rubber

hule-espuma *m* (Méx) foam rubber

hulera *f* (AmC) slingshot (AmE), catapult (BrE)

hulla *f* coal

humanidad *f* **(a)** (los humanos): **la ~** the human race, humanity, mankind **(b)** (piedad, benevolencia) humanity **(c) humanidades** *fpl* (estudios de letras) humanities (*pl*); (enseñanza secundaria) (Chi) secondary education

humanista *mf* humanist

humanitario -ria *adj* humanitarian

humano¹ -na *adj* **(a)** ‹*naturaleza*› human (*before n*) **(b)** (benevolente) humane

humano² *m* human being; **los ~s** humans

humareda *f* cloud of smoke

humeante *adj* ‹*leño/lava*› smoking; ‹*sopa/café*› steaming (hot), piping hot

humear [A1] *vi* «*chimenea/hoguera*» to smoke; «*sopa/café*» to steam

humectante *m* moisturizer

humedad *f* **(a)** (Meteo) dampness; (con calor) humidity **(b)** (en paredes, suelo) damp

humedecer [E3] *vt* to moisten, dampen ■ **humedecerse** *v pron* «*paredes/ropa*» to get damp

húmedo -da *adj* **(a)** (Meteo) damp; (con calor) humid **(b)** ‹*suelo/casa/ropa*› damp **(c)** ‹*labios*› moist

humildad *f* **(a)** (sumisión) humility; **con ~** humbly **(b)** (pobreza) humbleness, lowliness

humilde *adj* ‹*carácter/tono*› meek; ‹*vivienda/ropa*› humble, lowly

humillación *f* humiliation

humillante *adj* humiliating

humillar [A1] *vt* to humiliate ■ **humillarse** *v pron:* **no se humilla ante nadie** she doesn't kowtow to anyone; **no me voy a ~ a pedirle que vuelva** I'm not going to demean myself by begging him to come back

humita *f* **1** (CS) (Coc) *flavored corn paste wrapped in corn leaves* **2** (Chi) (Indum) bow tie

humo *m* **1** (de tabaco, incendio) smoke; (gases) fumes (*pl*); **echaba ~** smoke was pouring out of it; ***hacerse* ~** (AmL fam) to make oneself scarce (colloq) **2 humos** *mpl* (aires) airs (*pl*); **¡qué ~s se da!** she really gives herself airs (colloq); ***bajarle los* ~*s a algn*** to take sb down a peg or two

humor *m* **(a)** (estado de ánimo) mood; **estar de buen ~** to be in a good mood; **no estoy de ~ para salir** I'm not in the mood to go out **(b)** (gracia) humor*

humorada *f* **(a)** (extravagancia): **hacer una ~** to do something crazy **(b)** (broma) little joke, witticism

humorista *mf* (autor) humorist, comic writer; (dibujante) cartoonist; (cómico) comic, comedian

humorístico -ca *adj* humorous

hundido -da *adj* **(a)** ‹*barco*› sunken **(b)** ‹*ojos*› deep-set; (por enfermedad) sunken

hundimiento *m* **(a)** (de barco) sinking **(b)** (de negocio) collapse **(c)** (de edificio — bajada de nivel) subsidence; (— derrumbe) collapse

hundir [I1] *vt* ‹*barco*› to sink; ‹*persona*› to destroy; ‹*negocio/empresa*› to drive ... under ■ **hundirse** *v pron* **(a)** «*barco*» to sink **(b)** (en barro, nieve) to sink **(c)** «*empresa/negocio*» to fold **(d)** «*edificio*» (bajar de nivel) to sink, subside; (derrumbarse) to collapse

húngaro¹ -ra *adj/m,f* Hungarian
húngaro² *m* (idioma) Hungarian
Hungría *f* Hungary
huracán *m* hurricane
huraño -ña *adj* ‹*persona*› unsociable; ‹*animal*› timid
hurgar [A3] *vi* ~ EN **algo** ‹*en basura*› to rummage *o* rake THROUGH sth; ~ **en el pasado** to delve into the past
■ **hurgarse** *v pron* (*refl*): ~**se la nariz** to pick one's nose
hurguetear [A1] *vi* (CS) ~ EN **algo** ‹*en papeles*› to nose THROUGH sth; ‹*en cartera*› to rummage *o* ferret around IN sth ■ ~ *vt* ‹*cajón/cartera*› to rummage around in, rummage through
■ **hurguetearse** *v pron* (*refl*) (esp AmL) ⇨ HURGARSE
hurra, **hurrah** *interj* hurrah!, hooray!
hurtadillas *fpl*: **entrar/salir a** ~ to sneak in/out
hurtar [A1] *vt* (frml) to purloin (frml), to steal
hurto *m* (frml) (robo) robbery, theft
husmear [A1] *vt* to sniff ■ ~ *vi* **(a)** «*perro*» to sniff around **(b)** (fam) (fisgonear) to snoop, sniff (around) (colloq)
huso *m* spindle
huy *interj* (fam) (para expresar— dolor) ouch!, ow!; (— asombro) wow!; (— alivio) phew!
huya, **huyas, etc** *see* HUIR

Ii

I, **i** *f* (*pl* **íes**) (*read as* /i/) *tb* **i latina** *the letter* I, i; **i griega** *the letter* Y
iba, **íbamos, etc** *see* IR
Iberia *f* Iberia
ibérico -ca *adj* Iberian
Iberoamérica *f* Latin America
iberoamericano -na *adj/m,f* Latin American
icaco *m* (Col, Méx, Ven) coco plum
iceberg /'aɪsβer, 'iθe'βer/ *m* (*pl* **-bergs**) iceberg
icono, **ícono** *m* icon
ictericia *f* jaundice
ida *f* **(a)** (viaje) outward journey; **a la** ~ on the way out; **¿cuánto cuesta la** ~**?** how much does it cost one way?; **¿saco de** ~ **y vuelta?** shall I buy a round-trip ticket (AmE) *o* (BrE) return ticket? **(b)** (partida) departure
idea *f* idea; **la** ~ **de libertad** the idea *o* concept of freedom; **es de** ~**s fijas** he has very set ideas about things; **no tiene** ~ **de cómo funciona** he has no idea how it works; **no tengo** ~ I don't have a clue; **hacerse una** ~ **de la situación** to get an idea of the situation; **se me ocurre una** ~ I've got an idea; **cambió de** ~ she changed her mind; ***hacerse (a) la*** ~ ***de algo*** to get used to the idea of sth
ideal *adj* ideal ■ *m* **(a)** (prototipo) ideal **(b)** (aspiración) dream **(c) ideales** *mpl* (valores, principios) ideals (*pl*)
idealismo *m* idealism
idealista *adj* idealistic ■ *mf* idealist
idealizar [A4] *vt* to idealize
ídem *adv* ditto, idem (frml)
idéntico -ca *adj* identical; **es** ~ **al padre** (físicamente) he looks just like his father, he's the spitting image of his father (colloq); (en el carácter) he's exactly like his father; ~ A **algo** identical TO sth
identidad *f* identity
identificar [A2] *vt* to identify
■ **identificarse** *v pron* **(a)** (compenetrarse, solidarizarse) ~**se** CON **algo/algn** to identify WITH sth/sb **(b)** (demostrar la identidad) to identify oneself
ideología *f* ideology
ideológico -ca *adj* ideological
idílico -ca *adj* idyllic
idilio *m* **(a)** (Lit) idyll **(b)** (romance) romance
idioma *m* language
idiota *adj* (fam) (tonto) stupid, idiotic; **¡no seas** ~**!** don't be such an idiot! ■ *mf* (tonto) (fam) idiot, stupid fool (colloq)
idiotez *f* (fam) (cosa estúpida): **decir idioteces** to talk nonsense; **fue una** ~ **hacer eso** that was a stupid thing to do
ido, **ida** *adj* (distraído) ‹*mirada*› faraway (*before n*); **estás como** ~ you seem miles away
ídolo *m* idol
idóneo -nea *adj* ideal, perfect; **es la persona idónea para el cargo** he's perfect for the job, he's the ideal person for the job
iglesia *f* church; **no van a la** ~ they don't go to church; **casarse por la** ~ *or* (Bol, Per, RPl) **por** ~ to have a church wedding
iglú *m* igloo
ignorancia *f* ignorance; **por** ~ out of *o* through ignorance
ignorante *adj* **(a)** (sin instrucción) ignorant **(b)** (sin información): **estar** ~ **de algo** to be unaware of sth ■ *mf* ignoramus, ignorant fool (colloq)
ignorar [A1] *vt* **(a)** (desconocer): **lo ignoro** I've no idea; **ignoran las causas del accidente** they do not know what caused the accident; **ignora los peligros que le acechan** he's unaware of the dangers which await him **(b)** (no hacer caso de) to ignore

igual *adj* **1 (a)** (idéntico): **de ~ peso** of equal *o* the same weight; **son ~es** they are the same *o* alike; **de forma son ~es** they're the same shape; **~ A** *or* QUE **algo/algn** the same AS sth/sb; **es ~ita a** *or* **que su madre** (físicamente) she looks just like her mother; (en personalidad) she's exactly the same as *o* just like her mother; **es ~ a x** (Mat) it equals x; **me/nos es** *or* **da ~** I/we don't mind, it makes no difference to me/to us **(b)** (en una jerarquía) equal; **~es ante la ley** equal in the eyes of the law **2** (en tenis): **quince ~es** fifteen all; **van ~es** they're even ■ *adv* **1 (a)** (de la misma manera): **los trato a todos ~** I treat them all the same **(b)** (*en locs*) **igual que**: **tiene pecas, ~ que su hermano** she has freckles, (just) like her brother; **se llama ~ que su padre** he's named after his father; **me aburrí — ~ que yo** I got bored — so did I *o* me too; **opino ~ que tú** I agree with you; **por igual** equally **2** (de todos modos) anyway **3** (expresando posibilidad): **~ llueve y no podemos salir** it might rain and then we won't be able to go out; **~ llamaron y no estábamos** they may have called and we weren't in ■ *mf* (par) equal; **le habló de ~ a ~** he spoke to him on equal terms; **me trató de ~ a ~** she treated me as an equal; **sin ~** ‹*belleza/talento*› unequaled*, matchless (frml); **es un compositor sin ~** he's unrivaled as a composer ■ *m* (signo) equals sign

igualado -da *adj* **1 (a)** (Dep): **van muy ~s** they're very close, they're neck and neck; **quedaron ~s** they drew; **iban ~s a tres** they were level at three-three **(b)** ‹*superficie*› even, level **2** (Méx fam) (irrespetuoso) sassy (AmE colloq), cheeky (BrE colloq)

igualar [A1] *vt* **1 (a)** ‹*superficie/terreno*› to level, level off; ‹*flequillo/dobladillo*› to even up, make ... straight **(b)** ‹*salarios*› to make ... equal *o* the same; **~ algo** CON *or* A **algo** to make sth the same AS sth **2** ‹*éxito/récord*› to equal, match
■ igualarse *v pron:* **nada se le iguala** it has no equal, there's nothing like it; **~se** A *or* CON **algo** to match *o* equal sth

igualdad *f* equality; **~ de oportunidades** equal opportunities; **en ~ de condiciones** on equal terms

igualmente *adv* **(a)** (en fórmulas de cortesía): **que lo pases muy bien — igualmente** have a great time — you too *o* and you **(b)** ‹*bueno/malo*› equally **(c)** (frml) (también) likewise

iguana *f* (Zool) iguana

ilegal *adj* illegal; **de manera ~** illegally

ilegible *adj* illegible, unreadable

ilegítimo -ma *adj* ‹*hijo*› illegitimate

ileso -sa *adj* unhurt, unharmed

ilícito -ta *adj* illicit

ilimitado -da *adj* unlimited

ilógico -ca *adj* illogical

iluminación *f* (de habitación) lighting; (de monumento) illumination; (Teatr) lighting

iluminar [A1] *vt* **(a)** ‹*calles*› to light, illuminate; ‹*monumento*› to illuminate; ‹*escenario*› to light **(b)** (con focos muy potentes) ‹*estadio*› to floodlight **(c)** ‹*rostro/ojos*› (liter) to light up

ilusión *f* **1 (a)** (esperanza) hope; **no te hagas ilusiones** don't build your hopes up; **no me hago muchas ilusiones** I'm not very hopeful; **su mayor ~ es** ... her dearest *o* fondest wish is ... **(b)** (esp Esp) (alegría, satisfacción): **me hizo mucha ~** I was thrilled; **le hace ~ el viaje** he's looking forward to the trip; **¡qué ~!** isn't it wonderful! **2** (noción falsa) illusion

ilusionar [A1] *vt*: **me ilusiona mucho** I'm very excited about it; **no la ilusiones** don't raise her hopes
■ ilusionarse *v pron* **(a)** (hacerse ilusiones) to build one's hopes up **(b)** (entusiasmarse) **~se** CON **algo** to get excited ABOUT sth

iluso -sa *adj* naive ■ *m,f* dreamer

ilustración *f* illustration

ilustrado -da *adj* **(a)** ‹*revista/libro*› illustrated **(b)** (frml) ‹*persona*› erudite, learned

ilustrar [A1] *vt* to illustrate

ilustre *adj* illustrious, distinguished

imagen *f* **1 (a)** (Fís, Ópt) image; (TV) picture, image **(b)** (foto) picture **(c)** (en espejo) reflection; ***ser la viva ~ de algn*** to be the image of sb **(d)** (en la mente) picture **2** (de político, cantante, país) image

imaginación *f* imagination; **¡ni (se) me pasó por la ~!** it never even crossed my mind!; **son imaginaciones tuyas** you're imagining things

imaginar [A1] *vt* **(a)** (suponer, figurarse) ⇒ IMAGINARSE **(b)** (idear) ‹*plan/método*› to think up, come up with
■ imaginarse *v pron* to imagine; **me imagino que no querrá ir** I don't imagine *o* suppose he feels like going; **no te puedes ~ lo mal que nos trató** you've no idea how badly she treated us; **¿quedó contento? — ¡imagínate!** was he pleased? — what do you think!; **me imagino que sí** I suppose so; **me lo imaginaba más alto** I imagined he'd be taller

imaginario -ria *adj* imaginary

imaginativo -va *adj* imaginative

imán *m* magnet

imbécil *adj* **(a)** (fam) (tonto) stupid **(b)** (Med) imbecilic ■ *mf* **(a)** (fam) (tonto) stupid idiot, moron (colloq & pej) **(b)** (Med) imbecile

imberbe *adj*: **un joven ~** (sin barba) a beardless youth; (sin experiencia) a callow youth, a fresh-faced youth

imborrable *adj* lasting (*before n*), indelible

imitación *f* **(a)** (acción) imitation **(b)** (parodia) impression **(c)** (copia) imitation; **bolso ~ cuero** imitation-leather bag

imitador -dora *m,f* (Teatr) impressionist, impersonator; (plagiario) imitator

imitar [A1] *vt* **(a)** ‹*persona*› (copiar) to copy, imitate; (para hacer reír) to do an impression of, mimic; **se sentó y todos lo ~on** he sat down and everyone followed suit **(b)** ‹*voz/gesto/estilo*› to imitate; (para reírse) to imitate, mimic **(c)** (tener el aspecto de) to simulate

impaciencia *f* impatience

impacientarse [A1] *v pron* (por retraso) to get impatient; (exasperarse) to lose (one's) patience, get exasperated

impaciente *adj* **(a)** [SER] impatient **(b)** [ESTAR]: **estaba ~** he was (getting) impatient; **~ POR hacer algo** impatient to do sth

impactante *adj* ‹*noticia*› shocking; ‹*libro/imagen*› powerful; ‹*espectáculo/efecto*› stunning, impressive

impactar [A1] *vt* **(a)** (golpear) to hit **(b)** (impresionar) to have a profound impact on ■ **~** *vi* **(a)** (impresionar) to shock **(b)** (chocar) to hit, strike

impacto *m* **(a)** (choque) impact; **recibió un ~ de bala** she was shot **(b)** (huella, señal) hole, mark; **el cadáver tiene varios ~s de bala** there are several bullet wounds in the body **(c)** (en el ánimo, público) impact

impago -ga *adj* (AmL) ‹*persona*› unpaid; ‹*deuda/impuesto*› unpaid, outstanding

impalpable *adj* impalpable

impar *adj* ‹*número*› odd ■ *m* odd number

imparcial *adj* impartial, unbiased

imparcialidad *f* impartiality

impasible *adj* impassive

impecable *adj* impeccable; **va siempre ~** she is always impeccably dressed

impedido -da *adj* disabled ■ *m, f* disabled person

impedimento *m* obstacle, impediment; **si no surge ningún ~** if there are no hitches; **~ físico** physical handicap

impedir [I14] *vt* **(a)** (imposibilitar) to prevent; **nadie te lo impide** nobody's stopping you; **~le a algn hacer algo** to prevent sb FROM doing sth; **quiso ~ que nos viéramos** she tried to stop us seeing each other **(b)** ‹*paso/entrada*› to block **(c)** (dificultar) to hamper, hinder

impenetrable *adj* **(a)** ‹*bosque*› impenetrable; ‹*fortaleza*› impregnable **(b)** ‹*persona/expresión*› inscrutable; ‹*misterio/secreto*› unfathomable

impensable *adj* unthinkable, inconceivable

imperante *adj* ‹*moda/tendencia/condiciones*› prevailing (*before n*); ‹*dinastía/régimen*› ruling (*before n*)

imperativo[1] -va *adj* **(a)** (Ling) imperative **(b)** ‹*voz/tono*› commanding, authoritative

imperativo[2] *m* imperative

imperdible *m* safety pin

imperdonable *adj* ‹*error/comportamiento*› unforgivable, inexcusable

imperfección *f* **(a)** (en tela) flaw; (en mecanismo) defect **(b)** (cualidad) imperfection

imperfecto[1] -ta *adj* **1** ‹*trabajo/tela/facciones*› flawed **2** (Ling) imperfect

imperfecto[2] *m* imperfect (tense)

imperial *adj* ‹*dinastía/corona*› imperial

imperialismo *m* imperialism

imperialista *adj/mf* imperialist

imperio *m* empire

impermeable *adj* ‹*material/tela*› waterproof, impermeable (tech) ■ *m* (Indum) raincoat

impersonal *adj* impersonal

impersonar [A1] *vt* (Méx) to impersonate

impertinencia *f* **(a)** (cualidad) impertinence **(b)** (hecho, dicho): **me dijo que me callara — ¡qué ~!** he told me to shut up — how impertinent!; **me contestó con una ~** she gave me a very cheeky reply

impertinente *adj* ‹*persona/pregunta/tono*› impertinent; ‹*comentario*› uncalled-for ■ *mf* (persona): **eres una ~** you're extremely impertinent

imperturbable *adj* **(a)** [SER] (sereno) imperturbable **(b)** [ESTAR] (ante un peligro) unperturbed **(c)** ‹*rostro/sonrisa*› impassive

ímpetu *m* **(a)** (Fís, Mec) impetus, momentum **(b)** (energía, ardor) vigor*, energy **(c)** (violencia) force

impetuoso -sa *adj* impetuous, impulsive

impida, **impidas, etc** *see* IMPEDIR

implacable *adj* **(a)** ‹*odio/furia*› implacable; ‹*avance/lucha*› relentless; ‹*sol*› relentless **(b)** ‹*juez/crítico*› implacable **(c)** ‹*enemigo/contrincante*› ruthless

implantar [A1] *vt* **1** ‹*método/norma/moda*› to introduce; ‹*régimen político*› to establish; ‹*estado de excepción*› to impose **2** ‹*embrión/cabello*› to implant

implante *m* implant

implementar [A1] *vt* **1** ‹*medidas/plan*› to implement **2** (Ven) (instalar) to install*, set up

implicación *f* **1** (participación) involvement **2 implicaciones** *fpl* (consecuencias) implications (*pl*)

implicancia *f* (AmL) (consecuencia) implication

implicar [A2] *vt* **1** (significar, conllevar) to entail, involve **2** (envolver, enredar) to involve; **estuvo implicado en un delito** (participó) he was involved in a crime; (estuvo bajo sospecha) he was implicated in a crime

■ **implicarse** *v pron* to get involved

implícito -ta *adj* implicit

implorar [A1] *vt* ‹*perdón/ayuda*› to beg for; **~le algo A algn** to beg sth OF sb; **~le a algn QUE haga algo** to implore *o* beg sb TO do sth

imponente *adj* ‹*belleza*› impressive; ‹*edificio/paisaje*› imposing, impressive

imponer [E22] *vt* (frml) **(a)** to impose (frml); **le impusieron una pena de un año de cárcel** he was sentenced to one year in prison **(b)** ‹*respeto*› to command; ‹*temor*› to inspire, instill* **(c)** ‹*moda*› to set

■ **imponerse** *v pron* **1 (a)** (*refl*) ‹*horario/meta*› to set oneself **(b)** «*idea*» to become established **(c)** «*color/estilo*» to come into fashion **2** (hacerse respetar) to assert oneself *o* one's authority **3** (frml) (vencer) to win; **se impondrá el sentido común** common sense will prevail

importación *f* **(a)** (acción) importation; **de ~** ‹*artículos/mercancías*› imported; ‹*permiso*› import (*before n*) **(b) importaciones** *fpl* (mercancías) imports (*pl*)

importado -da *adj* imported

importador -dora *adj*: **países ~es de petróleo** oil-importing countries ■ *m, f* importer

importancia *f* importance; **darle ~ a algo** to attach importance to sth; **quitarle ~ a algo** to play down the importance of sth; **detalles sin ~** minor *o* insignificant details; **no tiene ~** it doesn't matter; ***darse ~*** to give oneself airs

importante *adj* **(a)** ‹*noticia/persona*› important; ‹*acontecimiento/cambio*› important, significant; ***dárselas de*** *or* ***hacerse el ~*** to give oneself airs **(b)** ‹*pérdidas*› serious, considerable; ‹*daños*› severe, considerable; ‹*cantidad*› considerable, significant

importar [A1] *vi* **(a)** (tener importancia, interés) to matter; **no importa quién lo haga** it doesn't matter *o* it makes no difference who does it; **lo que importa es que te recuperes** the important thing is for you to get better; **no me importa lo que piense** I don't care what he thinks; **¿a mí qué me importa?** what do I care?; **¿a ti qué te importa?** what business is it of yours?; **yo no le importo** I don't mean a thing to him; ***me importa un bledo*** *or* ***un comino*** *or* ***un pepino*** *or* ***un rábano*** (fam) I couldn't care less, I don't give a damn (colloq); ***meterse en lo que no le importa*** (fam) to poke one's nose into other people's business (colloq); **no te metas en lo que no te importa** mind your own business! **(b)** (molestar): **no me ~ía venir el sábado** I wouldn't mind coming on Saturday; **no me importa que me llame a casa** I don't mind him calling me at home ■ **~** *vt* (Com, Fin) ‹*productos*› to import

importe *m* **(a)** (de factura, letra) amount; **el ~ total** the full *o* total amount; **el ~ de la compra** the purchase price **(b)** (costo) cost

importunar [A1] *vt* (frml) to inconvenience, disturb ■ **~** *vi*: **espero no ~** I hope it's not inconvenient, I hope I'm not disturbing you

importuno -na *adj* inopportune

imposibilitado -da *adj* [ESTAR] (Med) disabled

imposibilitar [A1] *vt* **(a)** (hacer imposible) to make ... impossible **(b)** (impedir) to prevent

imposible *adj* **1** [SER] ‹*sueño/amor*› impossible; **me es ~ acompañarte** I won't be able to go with you; **es ~ que lo sepan** they can't possibly know; **hicieron lo ~** they did everything they could **2** (inaguantable) ‹*persona*› impossible; **está ~ hoy** he's (being) impossible today

impositivo -va *adj* ‹*sistema/reforma*› tax (*before n*)

impostor -tora *m,f* impostor

impotencia *f* (falta de poder) powerlessness, helplessness; (Med) impotence

impotente *adj* (incapaz, sin poder) powerless, helpless; (Med) impotent

impreciso -sa *adj* vague, imprecise; **un número ~ de personas** an indeterminate number of people

impredecible *adj* unpredictable

imprenta *f* (taller) printer's; (aparato) (printing) press

imprescindible *adj* ‹*requisito/herramienta/factor*› essential, indispensable; **lleva lo ~** take the bare essentials; **es ~ hacerlo** it is essential to do it; **es ~ que nos acompañe** it is essential that you come with us

impresión *f* **(a)** (idea, sensación) impression; **nos causó** *or* **nos hizo muy buena ~** he made a very good impression on us; **da la ~ de ser demasiado ancho** it looks too wide; **me da/tengo la ~ de que me está mintiendo** I have a feeling he's lying to me; **cambiar impresiones** to exchange ideas **(b)** (sensación desagradable): **el accidente me produjo mucha ~** the accident really shocked me

impresionable *adj* squeamish, easily affected

impresionante *adj* ‹*éxito/cantidad/paisaje*› amazing, incredible; ‹*accidente*› horrific

impresionar [A1] *vt* **1 (a)** (causar buena impresión): **París me impresionó** I was really taken with Paris **(b)** (afectar) to affect; **verlo llorar me impresionó mucho** seeing him cry really affected *o* moved me **(c)** (alarmar) to shock; **me impresionó verla tan delgada** it shocked me to see her looking so thin **(d)** (sorprender) to strike **2** (Fot) ‹*película*› to expose ■ **~** *vi* to impress

impresionismo *m* impressionism

impresionista *adj* ‹*movimiento/pintor*› Impressionist; ‹*estilo/descripción*› impressionistic

impreso[1] -sa *pp*: *see* IMPRIMIR

impreso[2] *m* (formulario) form; **~ de solicitud** application form

impresora *f* (Inf) printer

imprevisible *adj* ‹*hecho/factor*› unforeseeable; ‹*persona*› unpredictable

imprevisión *f* lack of foresight

imprevisto[1] -ta *adj* unforeseen, unexpected; **de modo ~** unexpectedly

imprevisto[2] *m* unforeseen event (*o* factor *etc*); **si no surge ningún ~** if nothing unexpected happens

imprimir [I36] *vt* (Impr) to print; **impreso en Perú** printed in Peru

improbable *adj* unlikely, improbable

impropio -pia *adj* **(a)** ‹*actitud/respuesta*› inappropriate; **un comportamiento ~ de una persona educada** behavior unbecoming to an educated person (frml) **(b)** (incorrecto) incorrect

improvisación *f* (acción) improvisation; (actuación) impromptu performance

improvisar [A1] *vt* to improvise; **~ una comida** to rustle up a meal ■ **~** *vi* «*actor/músico*» to improvise

improviso: **de ~** (*loc adv*) ‹*llegar/aparecer*› unexpectedly, out of the blue

imprudencia *f* imprudence; **no cometas esa ~** don't be so rash *o* reckless; **su ~ al conducir** his reckless driving

imprudente *adj* (que actúa sin cuidado) imprudent, careless; (temerario) reckless; **fuiste muy ~ al decírselo** it was very rash *o* imprudent of you to tell him

impúdico -ca *adj* (frml *o* hum) **(a)** (obsceno) indecent **(b)** (desvergonzado) shameless

impuesto *m* tax; **libre de ~s** tax-free, duty-free; **~ a** *or* **sobre la renta** income tax; **~ de circulación** road tax

impugnar [A1] *vt* ‹*decisión/fallo*› to contest, challenge

impulsar [A1] *vt* **(a)** ‹*motor/vehículo*› to propel, drive **(b)** ‹*persona*› to drive **(c)** ‹*comercio, producción*› to boost, give a boost to; ‹*cultura/relaciones*› to promote

impulsivo -va *adj* impulsive

impulso *m* **(a)** (empuje): **un fuerte ~ para el comercio** a major boost for trade; **dar ~ a algo** (a comercio) to give a boost to sth; (a iniciativa) to give impetus to sth; **tomar** *or* **darse ~** to gather momentum, to get up speed **(b)** (reacción, deseo) impulse; **mi primer ~ fue** ... my first instinct was ... **(c)** (Fís) impulse

impuntualidad *f* unpunctuality

impureza *f* impurity

impuro -ra *adj* impure

impuse, **impuso, etc** *see* IMPONER

in *adj inv* ‹*discoteca*› trendy (colloq); **lo que está muy ~** the in thing (colloq), the trendy thing (colloq)

inaccesible *adj* **(a)** ‹*montaña/persona/concepto*› inaccessible **(b)** (crit) ‹*precios*› prohibitive; ‹*objetivo*› unattainable

inaceptable *adj* unacceptable

inactividad *f* inactivity

inactivo -va *adj* inactive

inadecuado -da *adj* ‹*color/traje*› inappropriate, unsuitable; ‹*norma/sistema*› inadequate

inadmisible *adj* **(a)** ‹*comportamiento/pretensiones*› unacceptable, inadmissible **(b)** (Der) inadmissible

inadvertido -da *adj* (no notado): **pasar ~** to go unnoticed

inagotable *adj* ‹*fuente/reservas*› inexhaustible, endless

inaguantable *adj* unbearable

inalámbrico -ca *adj* ‹*teléfono*› cordless; ‹*comunicaciones*› wireless

inalcanzable *adj* unattainable, unachievable

inanimado -da *adj* inanimate

inapetente *adj* lacking in appetite

inapreciable *adj* **1** (muy valioso) ‹*ayuda/amistad*› invaluable; **un cuadro de un valor ~** a priceless painting **2** (insignificante) negligible

inapropiado -da *adj* inappropriate

inaudible *adj* inaudible

inaudito -ta *adj* ‹*decisión/suceso*› unprecedented

inauguración *f* opening, inauguration (frml)

inaugurar [A1] *vt* ‹*teatro/hospital*› to open, inaugurate (frml); ‹*monumento*› to unveil; ‹*exposición/sesión*› to open

inca *mf* Inca

incaico -ca *adj* Inca, Incaic

incalculable *adj* inestimable, incalculable

incandescente *adj* incandescent

incansable *adj* tireless

incapacidad *f* **1** (física) disability, physical handicap; (mental) mental handicap **2** (ineptitud) incompetence; (falta de capacidad) inability **3** (Col) (baja) sick leave

incapacitado -da *adj* (físicamente) disabled, physically handicapped; (mentalmente) mentally handicapped

incapacitar [A1] *vt* «*enfermedad*» to incapacitate; **la lesión lo incapacita para su trabajo** the injury has made him unfit for work

incapaz *adj* [SER] (de un logro, una hazaña): **no lo conseguirá nunca, es ~** he'll never do it, he simply isn't capable; **es ~ de una cosa así** he's incapable of doing something like that; **es ~ de llamarme** he can't even be bothered to phone me ■ *mf* (inútil, inepto) incompetent (fool)

incendiar [A1] *vt* **(a)** (prender fuego a) to set fire to **(b)** (quemar) ‹*edificio*› to burn down; ‹*coche*› to burn; ‹*pueblo/bosque*› to burn ... to the ground

■ **incendiarse** *v pron* **(a)** (empezar a arder) to catch fire **(b)** (destruirse) «*edificio*» to be burned down; **los bosques que se ~on** the forests that were destroyed by fire

incendiario -ria *m,f* arsonist

incendio *m* fire; **~ provocado** arson attack

incentivo *m* incentive

incertidumbre *f* uncertainty

incesto *m* incest

incestuoso -sa *adj* incestuous

incidente *m* incident

incienso *m* incense; (Bib) frankincense

incierto -ta *adj* (dudoso, inseguro) uncertain

incinerador *m* incinerator

incinerar [A1] *vt* ‹*basura*› to incinerate, burn; ‹*cadáver*› to cremate

incitar [A1] *vt* **~ a algn** A **algo** to incite sb TO sth; **~ a algn** CONTRA **algn** to incite sb AGAINST sb

incivilizado -da *adj* uncivilized

inclinación *f* **1 (a)** (pendiente) slope **(b)** (ángulo) inclination **2** (movimiento del cuerpo) bow; **asintió con una ~ de la cabeza** he nodded (his head) in agreement **3** (interés, tendencia): **tener ~ por** *or* **hacia la música** to have a musical bent *o* musical inclinations; **inclinaciones políticas/sexuales** political/sexual leanings

inclinado -da *adj* **1** ‹*tejado/terreno*› sloping; ‹*torre*› leaning (*before n*); ‹*cuadro*› crooked; **una pendiente muy inclinada** a very steep slope *o* incline **2** (predispuesto): **sentirse ~ a hacer algo** to feel inclined to do sth

inclinar [A1] *vt* **1** ‹*botella/sombrilla/plato*› to tilt; **inclinó la cabeza a un lado** she tilted her head to one side; **inclinó la cabeza en señal de asentimiento** he nodded (his head) in agreement; **~ el cuerpo** to bend over; (en señal de respeto) to bow; **el viento inclinaba los árboles** the wind bent the trees **2** (inducir, predisponer) ‹*persona*›: **ello me inclina a pensar que** ... this inclines me to think that ... (frml)

■ **inclinarse** *v pron* **1** (tender) **~se** A **hacer algo** to be inclined to do sth; **me inclino por su candidato** I'm inclined to go for your candidate; **me ~ía por esta opción** I would tend to favor this option **2** (doblarse) to bend; (en señal de respeto) to bow; **~se ante algn** to bow to sb; **se inclinó sobre**

la cuna she leaned over the cradle; **~se hacia adelante/atrás** to lean forward/back

incluir [I20] *vt* **1** (comprender) **(a)** ‹*impuestos/gastos*› to include; **$500 todo incluido** $500 all inclusive *o* all in **(b)** ‹*tema/sección*› to include, contain **2** (poner, agregar) **(a)** (en un grupo) to include **(b)** (en una carta) to enclose

inclusive *adj inv* inclusive; **del 10 al 18, ambos ~** from 10 to 18 inclusive; **domingos ~** including Sundays

incluso *adv* even

incógnita *f* **(a)** (Mat) unknown (factor *o* quantity) **(b)** (misterio) mystery

incógnito: **de ~** (loc adv) incognito

incoherente *adj* incoherent, illogical

incoloro -ra *adj* colorless*

incomible *adj* inedible, uneatable

incómodo -da *adj* **(a)** (en general) uncomfortable; **¿no estás ~ en esa silla?** aren't you uncomfortable in that chair?; **se siente muy ~ en las fiestas** he feels ill at ease *o* uncomfortable at parties **(b)** (inconveniente) inconvenient; **es muy ~ vivir tan lejos** it's very inconvenient living so far away

incompatible *adj* ‹*personas/caracteres*› incompatible; **el horario de clases es ~ con el de mi trabajo** the times of the classes clash with my work hours

incompetente *adj/mf* incompetent

incompleto -ta *adj* incomplete

incomprensible *adj* incomprehensible

incomprensión *f* lack of understanding

incomunicado -da *adj* ‹*prisonero*› in solitary confinement; **hay varios pueblos ~s** several villages have been cut off

inconcebible *adj* inconceivable

incondicional *adj* **(a)** ‹*apoyo*› unconditional, wholehearted; ‹*obediencia*› absolute; ‹*aliado/admirador*› staunch; ‹*amigo*› true, loyal **(b)** ‹*rendición*› unconditional

inconexo -xa *adj* unconnected

inconfesable *adj* unmentionable

inconformista *adj/mf* nonconformist

inconfundible *adj* unmistakable

incongruente *adj* ‹*imágenes*› unconnected; **decía palabras ~s** his words didn't make sense

inconsciencia *f* **(a)** (Med) unconsciousness **(b)** (insensatez) irresponsibility

inconsciente *adj* **1** [ESTAR] (Med) unconscious **2** [SER] (insensato) irresponsible **3** [SER] (no voluntario) ‹*movimiento/gesto*› unwitting, unconscious; **de una manera ~** unconsciously ■ *mf* irresponsible person; **son unos ~s** they are very irresponsible

inconsecuente *adj*: **ser ~ con uno mismo** to be inconsistent with one's principles

inconsistente *adj* **(a)** ‹*material*› flimsy, weak **(b)** ‹*argumento*› (falto de solidez) weak, flimsy; (falto de coherencia) inconsistent, flawed

inconsolable *adj* inconsolable

inconstante *adj* **(a)** (falto de perseverancia) lacking in perseverance **(b)** (voluble) fickle

inconstitucional *adj* unconstitutional

incontable *adj* countless, innumerable

incontrolado -da *adj* **(a)** ‹*furia/pasión/ira*› uncontrolled, unbridled (liter) **(b)** ‹*llanto/risa*› uncontrollable

inconveniencia *f* **(a)** (cualidad) inconvenience **(b)** (comentario inoportuno) tactless remark

inconveniente *adj* (incómodo) ‹*hora/fecha*› inconvenient ■ *m* **(a)** (problema) problem; **si no surge ningún ~** if everything goes according to plan; if there are no problems; **¿habría algún ~ en que nos quedemos?** would it be alright if we stayed? **(b)** (desventaja) drawback; **tiene sus ~s** it has its disadvantages *o* drawbacks **(c)** (objeción) objection; **no tengo ~** I have no objection; **no tengo ~ en decírselo** I don't mind telling him; **no veo ningún ~ en que venga** I see no reason why he shouldn't come

incordiar [A1] *vt* (Esp fam) to annoy, to pester (colloq) ■ **~** *vi* (Esp): **¡no incordies!** don't be such a nuisance!

incordio *m* (Esp fam) nuisance, pain in the neck (colloq)

incorporación *f* incorporation

incorporado -da *adj* integral, built-in

incorporar [A1] *vt* (frml) **1 (a)** (agregar) to add; **~ algo A algo** to add sth TO sth **(b)** (integrar) to incorporate **2** ‹*enfermo/niño*› to sit ... up

■ **incorporarse** *v pron* (frml) **1** (a equipo, puesto) to join; **~se A algo** to join sth **2** (levantarse) to sit up

incorrecto -ta *adj* **(a)** ‹*respuesta/interpretación*› incorrect, wrong **(b)** ‹*comportamiento*› impolite, discourteous (frml)

incorregible *adj* ‹*mentiroso/idealista*› incorrigible; ‹*defecto*› irremediable, irreparable

incredulidad *f* skepticism*

incrédulo -la *adj* skeptical* ■ *m,f* skeptic*

increíble *adj* incredible, unbelievable

incrementar [A1] *vt* (frml) to increase

incremento *m* (frml) increase

incrustación *f* **(a)** (de madera, metal) inlay **(b)** (Col) (Odont) filling

incrustar [A1] *vt* ‹*piedra preciosa*› **~ algo EN algo** to set sth IN sth

■ **incrustarse** *v pron* **~se EN algo** «*bala*» to embed itself IN sth; «*suciedad*» to get embedded IN sth

incubadora *f* incubator

incubar [A1] *vt* to incubate

inculcar [A2] *vt* to instill*, inculcate (frml); **las ideas que les inculcan** the ideas they fill their heads with

inculto -ta *adj* (sin cultura) uncultured, uneducated; (ignorante) ignorant ■ *m,f* **(a)** (persona sin cultura): **es un ~** he's uneducated **(b)** (persona ignorante) ignorant person

incumplido -da *adj* (AmL exc CS) unreliable

incumplidor -dora *adj* (CS) unreliable

incumplir [I1] *vt* ‹*ley/promesa*› to break; ‹*contrato*› to breach ■ **~** *vi* (AmL exc CS): **no me vayas a**

~ don't let me down; **incumplió a la cita** she didn't show *o* turn up

incurable *adj* incurable

indagación *f* (frml) investigation; **hacer indagaciones** to make inquiries, to investigate

indagar [A3] (frml) *vi* to investigate; ~ SOBRE **algo** to investigate sth

indecencia *f* **(a)** (cualidad) indecency **(b)** (cosa, hecho): **presentarse así en público es una ~** it's indecent to appear in public like that

indecente *adj* ‹*persona/vestido*› indecent; ‹*película/lenguaje*› obscene ■ *mf* rude *o* shameless person

indecisión *f* indecision

indeciso -sa *adj* ‹*persona*› **(a)** [SER] indecisive **(b)** [ESTAR] undecided ■ *m,f* **(a)** (en general) indecisive person **(b)** (sobre un tema): **hay un gran número de ~s** there are a lot of people who are as yet undecided

indecoroso -sa *adj* unseemly, indecorous (frml)

indefenso -sa *adj* ‹*niño/animal*› defenseless*; ‹*fortaleza*› undefended

indefinido -da *adj* **(a)** ‹*forma*› undefined, vague; **un color ~** a difficult color to describe **(b)** (ilimitado) indefinite, unlimited; **por tiempo ~** for an indefinite *o* unlimited period

indemnización *f* **(a)** (por pérdidas sufridas) compensation, indemnity (frml); (por posibles pérdidas) indemnity (frml); **~ por daños y perjuicios** damages (*pl*) **(b)** (por despido) severance pay

indemnizar [A4] *vt* **(a)** (por pérdidas sufridas) to compensate, indemnify (frml); (por posibles pérdidas) to indemnify (frml); **fue indemnizado con dos millones de pesetas** he was given two million pesetas (in) compensation **(b)** (por despido) to pay severance pay to

independencia *f* independence

independentista *adj* ‹*político/ideas*› pro-independence (*before n*) ■ *mf* supporter of the independence movement

independiente *adj/mf* independent

independizarse [A4] *v pron* to become independent, gain independence; ~ DE **algn** to become independent OF sb

indescriptible *adj* indescribable

indestructible *adj* indestructible

indeterminado -da *adj* **(a)** (indefinido) indefinite; **por tiempo ~** indefinitely **(b)** (no establecido) undetermined **(c)** (vago, impreciso) ‹*contorno/forma*› indeterminate **(d)** (Ling) indefinite

India *f*: **la ~** India

indicación *f* **(a)** (instrucción) instruction; **me dio indicaciones de cómo llegar** ▶ 235 he gave me directions as to how to get there **(b)** (muestra) indication; **no dio ninguna ~ de sus intenciones** she gave no indication of her intentions

indicado -da *adj* **(a)** (adecuado) suitable; **es el menos ~ para hacerlo** he's the last person who should do it; **lo más ~ sería** ... the best thing to do would be ... **(b)** (señalado) ‹*hora/fecha*› specified

indicador *m* (Auto) **(a)** *tb* **~ de dirección** indicator **(b)** (señal de tráfico) sign **(c)** (del aceite, la gasolina) gauge; **~ de velocidad** speedometer

indicar [A2] *vt* to indicate, show; **hay una flecha que indica el camino** there's an arrow indicating the way; **¿me podría ~ cómo llegar allí?** could you tell me how to get there?; **me indicó el lugar en el mapa** he showed me *o* pointed out the place on the map; **todo parece ~ que** ... there is every indication that ...; **el asterisco indica que** ... the asterisk indicates *o* shows that ...

indicativo *m* (Ling) indicative; **presente de ~** present indicative

índice *m* **1** (de una publicación) index; (catálogo) catalog* **2** (Anat) index finger, forefinger **3** (tasa, coeficiente) rate; **~ de natalidad** birth rate

indicio *m* **(a)** (señal, huella) sign, indication **(b)** (vestigio) trace, sign; **~s de potasio** traces of potassium

Índico *adj*: **el (Océano) ~** the Indian Ocean

indiferencia *f* indifference

indiferente *adj* **(a)** (poco importante, de poco interés): **es ~ que venga hoy o mañana** it doesn't matter *o* it makes no difference whether he comes today or tomorrow; **me es ~ su amistad** I'm not concerned *o* (colloq) bothered about his friendship **(b)** (poco interesado) indifferent; **~** A **algo** indifferent TO sth

indígena *adj* indigenous, native (*before n*) ■ *mf* native

indigestión *f* indigestion

indignación *f* indignation, anger; (más fuerte) outrage; **sentí una gran ~** I was outraged

indignado -da *adj* indignant, angry; (más fuerte) outraged, incensed

indignante *adj* outrageous

indignar [A1] *vt* to make ... angry *o* indignant; (más fuerte) to outrage

■ **indignarse** *v pron* to get angry, become indignant; (más fuerte) to be outraged *o* incensed

indigno -na *adj* **(a)** (impropio) unworthy; **~** DE **algn** unworthy OF sb **(b)** (no merecedor) unworthy **(c)** (humillante) degrading, humiliating **(d)** (vergonzoso) shameful, disgraceful

indio -dia *adj* **(a)** (de América) (American) Indian, Amerindian **(b)** (de la India) Indian, of/from India ■ *m,f* **(a)** (de América) (American) Indian, Amerindian **(b)** (de la India) Indian

indirecta *f* hint; **lanzar** *or* **soltar una ~** to drop a hint

indirecto -ta *adj* indirect

indisciplinado -da *adj* ‹*alumno*› undisciplined, unruly; ‹*soldado*› insubordinate

indiscreción *f* **(a)** (dicho, declaración — que molesta) indiscreet *o* tactless remark; (— que revela un secreto) indiscreet *o* unguarded remark; **¿su edad, si no es ~?** how old are you, if you don't mind my asking?; **cometió la ~ de preguntárselo** he was indiscreet *o* tactless enough to ask her **(b)** (cualidad) lack of discretion

indiscreto -ta *adj* **(a)** (falto de tacto) indiscreet, tactless **(b)** (que revela un secreto) indiscreet

indiscutible *adj* **(a)** ‹*pruebas/hecho/verdad*› indisputable **(b)** ‹*líder/campeón*› undisputed

indispensable *adj* ‹*persona*› indispensable; ‹*objeto*› indispensable, essential; **lleva lo ~** take the bare essentials

indispuesto -ta *adj* **(a)** (enfermo) unwell, indisposed (frml) **(b)** (CS euf) ‹*mujer*›: **está indispuesta** it's the time of the month (euph)

individual *adj* **(a)** ‹*características/libertades*› individual **(b)** ‹*cama/habitación*› single (*before n*); **mantel ~** place mat **(c)** ‹*caso*› one-off (*before n*), isolated **(d)** (Dep) ‹*prueba/final*› singles (*before n*) ■ *m* (Dep) singles (*pl*); **~ femenino** women's singles

individualismo *m* individualism

individualista *adj* individualistic ■ *mf* individualist

individuo *m* **(a)** (persona indeterminada): **un ~ alto** a tall man **(b)** (pey) (tipo) character (colloq), individual (colloq); **ese ~ que iba contigo** (fam) that guy you were with (colloq)

indivisible *adj* indivisible

Indochina *f* Indo-China

índole *f* **(a)** (tipo, clase) kind, nature; **un problema de ~ afectiva** a problem of an emotional nature **(b)** (manera de ser) nature; **ser de buena/mala ~** to be good-natured/ill-natured

indolente *adj* lazy, slack, indolent

indoloro -ra *adj* painless

indomable *adj* **(a)** ‹*animal salvaje*› untamable*; ‹*caballo*› unbreakable **(b)** ‹*pueblo/tribu*› indomitable, unconquerable; ‹*persona*› indomitable **(c)** (fam) ‹*pelo/remolino*› unruly, unmanageable

Indonesia *f* Indonesia

indonesio -sia *adj/m,f* Indonesian

indudable *adj* unquestionable; **es ~ que ...** there is no doubt that ...

indulgente *adj* (tolerante) indulgent; (para perdonar castigos) lenient; **~ con algn** indulgent WITH/lenient TOWARD(S) sb

indultar [A1] *vt* (Der) to pardon; (la pena de muerte) to reprieve

indulto *m* (Der) pardon; (de la pena de muerte) reprieve

indumentaria *f* clothing, clothes (*pl*), attire (frml)

industria *f* (Com, Econ) industry; **~ pesquera** fishing industry

industrial *adj* industrial ■ *mf* industrialist

industrialización *f* industrialization

industrializarse [A4] *v pron* to become industrialized

inédito -ta *adj* **(a)** ‹*obra/autor*› unpublished **(b)** (nuevo, sin precedente) unprecedented; **una técnica inédita en nuestro país** a technique unknown in our country

ineficacia *f* (de medida) ineffectiveness; (de método, persona) inefficiency

ineficaz *adj* **(a)** ‹*remedio/medida*› ineffectual, ineffective **(b)** ‹*método/sistema/persona*› inefficient

ineficiencia *f* inefficiency

ineficiente *adj* inefficient

inepto -ta *adj* inept, incompetent ■ *m,f* incompetent

inercia *f* **(a)** (Fís) inertia **(b) por ~** (por rutina) out of habit; (por apatía) out of inertia *o* apathy

inescrutable *adj* inscrutable

inesperado -da *adj* unexpected; **de manera inesperada** unexpectedly

inestabilidad *f* instability

inestable *adj* **(a)** (en general) unstable **(b)** ‹*tiempo*› changeable, unsettled

inestimable *adj* ‹*ayuda*› invaluable

inevitable *adj* (ineludible) inevitable; ‹*cambio/conflicto/controversia*› unavoidable; **era ~ que empeorase la situación** the situation was bound to get worse

inexcusable *adj* ‹*comportamiento/error*› inexcusable, unforgivable; ‹*deber*› inescapable, unavoidable

inexistente *adj* nonexistent

inexperiencia *f* inexperience

inexperto -ta *adj* (falto de experiencia) inexperienced; (falto de habilidad) inexpert, unskilled

inexplicable *adj* inexplicable

inexpresivo -va *adj* expressionless, inexpressive

infalible *adj* ‹*persona/método*› infallible; ‹*puntería*› unerring

infancia *f* (período) childhood

infante -ta *m,f* (hijo del Rey) (*m*) prince, infante; (*f*) princess, infanta

infantería *f* infantry; **~ de marina** marines (*pl*), Marine Corps

infantil *adj* **(a)** ‹*enfermedad*› children's (*before n*), childhood (*before n*); ‹*literatura/programa/moda*› children's (*before n*); ‹*rasgos/sonrisa*› childlike; ‹*población*› child (*before n*) **(b)** (pey) ‹*persona/actitud/reacción*› childish (pej), infantile (pej)

infarto *m* heart attack

infección *f* infection

infeccioso -sa *adj* infectious

infectar [A1] *vt* to infect
■ **infectarse** *v pron* to become infected

infelicidad *f* unhappiness

infeliz *adj* **(a)** ‹*persona/vida*› unhappy **(b)** ‹*intervención/tentativa*› unfortunate ■ *mf* poor wretch, poor devil

inferior *adj* **1** (en el espacio) ‹*piso/planta*› lower **2** (en jerarquía) ‹*especie/rango*› inferior **3** (en comparaciones) lower; **temperaturas ~es a los 10°** temperatures lower than *o* below 10°; **un número ~ al 20** a number below twenty

inferioridad *f* inferiority

infernal *adj* ‹*ruido*› infernal, hideous; ‹*música*› diabolical; **hacía un calor ~** it was baking hot (colloq)

infértil *adj* infertile

infertilidad *f* infertility

infestado -da *adj* **~ DE algo** ‹*de insectos, parásitos*› infested WITH sth; **~ de turistas** crawling with tourists

infestar [A1] *vt* to infest

infidelidad *f* infidelity, unfaithfulness

infiel *adj* **(a)** (desleal) unfaithful; **ser ~ A algn/algo** to be unfaithful TO sb/sth **(b)** (Relig) unbelieving (*before n*), infidel (*before n*) (dated)

infiernillo *m* (Esp) kerosene stove, primus® stove (BrE)

infierno *m* **(a)** (en general) hell; **¡vete al ~!** (fam) go to hell! (sl); **su vida es un ~** her life is hell **(b)** (fam) (lugar — ruidoso) madhouse (colloq), bedlam (colloq); (— horrendo) hellhole (colloq)

infílder *mf* (Col, Ven) infielder

infiltración *f* infiltration

infiltrado -da *m,f* infiltrator

infiltrar [A1] *vt* to infiltrate; **~ a algn EN algo** to infiltrate sb INTO sth
■ **infiltrarse** *v pron* to infiltrate; **~se EN algo** ‹*en partido/organización*› to infiltrate sth

infinidad *f* (gran cantidad): **en ~ de ocasiones** on countless occasions; **~ de veces** innumerable *o* countless times

infinitivo *m* infinitive

infinito[1] -ta *adj* **(a)** (Fil, Mat) infinite **(b)** ‹*bondad/sabiduría*› infinite; ‹*amor*› boundless **(c)** (*delante del n, en pl*) (innumerables) innumerable, countless

infinito[2] *m* **(a) el ~** (Fil) the infinite; **mirar al ~** to look into the distance **(b)** (Mat) infinity

inflación *f* inflation

inflador *m* (Bol, Per, RPl) bicycle pump

inflamable *adj* flammable, inflammable

inflamación *f* (Med) inflammation; (Quím) ignition

inflamar [A1] *vt* **(a)** (Med) to inflame **(b)** (Quím) to ignite, set ... on fire
■ **inflamarse** *v pron* **(a)** (Med) to become inflamed **(b)** (Quím) to ignite

inflar [A1] *vt* **(a)** ‹*balón/rueda*› to inflate; ‹*globo*› to blow up **(b)** ‹*noticia/acontecimiento*› to exaggerate
■ **inflarse** *v pron* «*velas*» to swell, fill

inflexible *adj* inflexible; **se mostró ~** he refused to give in

inflexión *f* inflection

influencia *f* **1** (influjo) influence; **bajo la ~ del alcohol** under the influence of alcohol; **~ EN** *or* **SOBRE algo** influence ON *o* UPON sth; **~ SOBRE algn** influence ON sb **2 influencias** *fpl* (contactos) contacts (*pl*)

influenciable *adj* easily influenced

influenciar [A1] *vt* to influence

influir [I20] *vi* **~ EN algo/algn** to influence sth/sb, have an influence ON sth/sb ■ **~** *vt* to influence

influyente *adj* influential

información *f* **1 (a)** (datos, detalles) information; **el mostrador de ~** the information desk **(b)** (Telec) information (AmE), directory enquiries (BrE) **2** (Period, Rad, TV) news; **la ~ internacional** the foreign news **3** (Inf) data (*pl*)

informado -da *adj* (sobre tema, noticia) informed; **está usted muy mal informada** you have been misinformed *o* wrongly informed; **fuentes bien informadas** reliable sources

informal *adj* **1 (a)** ‹*persona*› unreliable **(b)** ‹*ropa/estilo*› informal, casual; ‹*cena/ambiente*› informal **(c)** (no oficial) ‹*reunión*› informal **2** (AmL) ‹*economía/sector*› black (*before n*), informal (*before n*)

informar [A1] *vt* ‹*persona/prensa*› to inform; **te han informado mal** you've been misinformed; **¿podría ~me sobre los cursos de idiomas?** could you give me some information about language courses? ■ **~** *vi* (dar noticias, información) to report; **~ SOBRE algo** to report ON sth, give a report ON sth; **~ DE algo** to announce sth
■ **informarse** *v pron* to get information; **~se SOBRE algo** to find out *o* inquire ABOUT sth

informática *f* computer science, computing

informático -ca *adj* computer (*before n*)

informativo -va *adj* **(a)** ‹*servicios/campaña*› information (*before n*); **programa ~** news program* **(b)** (instructivo) informative

informatizar [A4] *vt* to computerize

informe *m* **1** (exposición, dictamen) report; **~ médico** medical report **2 informes** *mpl* **(a)** (datos) information, particulars (*pl*) **(b)** (de empleado) reference, references (*pl*); **pedir ~s** to ask for a reference/for references

infracción *f* offense*, infraction (frml); **~ de tráfico** traffic violation (AmE), driving offence (BrE)

infraestructura *f* infrastructure

in fraganti *loc adv* red-handed

infrarrojo -ja *adj* infrared

infringir [I7] *vt* to infringe, break

ínfulas *fpl*: **darse** *or* **tener muchas ~** to put on *o* give oneself airs

infundado -da *adj* unfounded, groundless

infundir [I1] *vt* ‹*confianza/respeto*› to inspire; ‹*sospechas*› to arouse; **les infundía miedo** it filled them with fear; **para ~les ánimo** to give them encouragement

infusión *f* infusion; **~ de manzanilla** chamomile tea

ingeniar [A1] *vt* ‹*método/sistema*› to devise, think up; ***ingeniárselas*** (fam): **se las ingenió para arreglarlo** he managed to fix it

ingeniería *f* engineering; **~ civil** civil engineering

ingeniero -ra *m,f* engineer; **~ agrónomo** agriculturist; **~ civil/industrial** civil/industrial engineer; **~ técnico** engineer (*qualified after a three-year university course*)

ingenio *m* **1 (a)** (talento) ingenuity, inventiveness; ***aguzar el ~*** to rack one's brains **(b)** (chispa, agudeza) wit **2** (aparato) device **3** (AmL) (refinería) *tb* **~ azucarero** sugar refinery

ingenioso -sa *adj* **(a)** (lúcido) ‹*persona/idea*› clever, ingenious **(b)** (con chispa, agudeza) ‹*persona/dicho/chiste*› witty **(c)** ‹*aparato/invención*› ingenious

ingenuidad *f* naivety, ingenuousness

ingenuo -nua *adj* naive, ingenuous ■ *m,f*: **es un ~** he's so naive

Inglaterra *f* England

ingle *f* groin

inglés[1] -glesa *adj* **(a)** (de Inglaterra) English **(b)** (crit) (británico) British, English (crit) ■ *m,f* **(a)** (de Inglaterra) (*m*) Englishman; (*f*) Englishwoman; **los ingleses** the English, English people **(b)** (crit) ⇒ BRITÁNICO

inglés[2] *m* (idioma) English

ingratitud *f* ingratitude

ingrato -ta *adj* **(a)** (desagradecido) ‹*persona*› ungrateful; **~ con ella** ungrateful to her **(b)** (desagradable, difícil) ‹*vida*› hard; ‹*trabajo/tarea*› unrewarding ■ *m,f* ungrateful wretch (*o* swine *etc*) (coloq), ingrate (liter)

ingrediente *m* ingredient

ingresar [A1] *vi* **1** «*persona*» (en organización, club) to join; (en colegio) to enter; (en el ejército) to join; **después de ~ en el hospital** after being admitted to (the) hospital; **ingresó cadáver** (Esp) he was dead on arrival **2** «*dinero*» to come in ■ **~** *vt* **1** ‹*persona*› (en hospital): **el médico decidió ~lo** the doctor decided to send him to hospital; **hubo que ~lo de urgencia** he had to be admitted as a matter of urgency; **fueron ingresados en esta prisión** they were taken to this prison **2** (Esp) (Fin) ‹*dinero/cheque*› to pay in; **~ una cantidad en una cuenta** «*persona*» to pay a sum into an account; «*banco*» to credit an account with a sum

ingreso *m* **1 (a)** (en organización): **el año de mi ~ a** *or* **en la universidad/el ejército/la compañía** the year I started *o* entered university/joined the army/joined the company; **examen de ~** entrance examination **(b)** (en hospital) admission **2** (Fin) **(a)** (Esp) (depósito) deposit **(b) ingresos** *mpl* (ganancias) income; **~s brutos/netos** gross/net income

íngrimo -ma *adj* (Col, Méx, Ven fam) **(a)** (sin compañía) all alone, all by oneself **(b)** ‹*lugar*› lonely, deserted

inhábil *adj* **(a)** (torpe) unskillful*, clumsy **(b)** (no apto) **~** PARA **algo** unsuited TO sth

inhabitado -da *adj* uninhabited

inhalación *f* inhalation; **hacer inhalaciones** to inhale; **~ de pegamento** *or* (Méx) **cemento** glue sniffing

inhalador *m* inhaler

inhalar [A1] *vt* to inhale; ‹*pegamento*› to sniff

inhibición *f* inhibition

inhibir [I1] *vt* to inhibit

■ **inhibirse** *v pron* to become inhibited

inhóspito -ta *adj* inhospitable

inhumano -na *adj* **(a)** (falto de compasión) inhumane **(b)** (cruel) inhuman

iniciación *f* **(a)** (frml) (comienzo) beginning, start **(b)** (introducción) introduction; **curso de ~** introductory course **(c)** (a secta) initiation

inicial *adj* initial ■ *f* **(a)** (letra) initial **(b)** (en béisbol) first base

iniciar [A1] *vt* **(a)** (frml) ‹*curso/viaje*› to begin, commence (frml); ‹*negociaciones/diligencias*› to initiate, commence (frml) **(b) ~ a algn** EN **algo** ‹*en secta*› to initiate sb INTO sth; ‹*en un arte*› to introduce sb TO sth

■ **iniciarse** *v pron* **1** «*ceremonia/negociaciones*» to begin, commence (frml) **2** «*persona*» **~se** EN **algo** ‹*en secta*› to be initiated INTO sth; ‹*en un arte*› to take one's first steps IN sth

iniciativa *f* initiative; **tomó la ~** he took the initiative

inicio *m* beginning, start

inigualable *adj* ‹*belleza*› matchless, incomparable; ‹*precios/oferta*› unbeatable

ininteligible *adj* unintelligible, incomprehensible

ininterrumpido -da *adj* ‹*lluvias/trabajo*› continuous, uninterrupted; ‹*sueño*› uninterrupted; ‹*línea*› continuous

injertar [A1] *vt* to graft

injerto *m* **(a)** (Agr) (acción) grafting; (tallo) graft, scion **(b)** (Med) graft

injusticia *f* **(a)** (acto injusto) injustice, act of injustice; **es una ~ que te hayan dicho eso** it's unfair of them to have said that to you **(b)** (cualidad) unfairness, injustice

injustificable *adj* unjustifiable

injustificado -da *adj* unwarranted, unjustified; **despido ~** unfair dismissal

injusto -ta *adj* unfair; **ser ~** CON **algn** to be unfair TO *o* ON sb

inmaculado -da *adj* **(a)** ‹*presentación/vestido/superficie*› immaculate **(b)** ‹*fama*› impeccable

inmadurez *f* immaturity, lack of maturity

inmaduro -ra *adj* ‹*persona/animal*› immature; ‹*fruta*› unripe

inmediaciones *fpl* vicinity, surrounding area; **el hotel está en las ~ del aeropuerto** the hotel is in the vicinity of the airport; **en las ~ de la capital** in the area around the capital

inmediato -ta *adj* **(a)** ‹*efecto/respuesta*› immediate; **de ~** immediately, right away, straightaway (BrE) **(b)** ‹*zona*› immediate; ‹*lugar/pueblo*› **~** A **algo** close TO sth

inmejorable *adj* ‹*resultados/posición*› excellent, unbeatable; **está en una situación ~** it is superbly located

inmenso -sa *adj* ‹*fortuna/cantidad*› immense, vast, huge; ‹*casa/camión*› huge, enormous; ‹*alegría/pena*› great, immense; **¡es ~!** it's absolutely huge!

inmerecido -da *adj* undeserved, unmerited

inmerso -sa *adj* ‹*submarino/buzo*› submerged; ‹*objeto*› immersed

inmigración *f* immigration

inmigrante *mf* immigrant

inmigrar [A1] *vi* to immigrate

inmiscuirse [I20] *v pron* **~** EN **algo** to interfere IN sth, meddle IN sth

inmobiliaria *f* **(a)** (agencia) real estate agency (AmE), estate agent's (BrE) **(b)** (empresa propietaria) real estate company (AmE), property company (BrE) **(c)** (empresa constructora) property developer

inmoral *adj* immoral ■ *mf*: **eres un ~** you have no morals

inmoralidad *f* immorality

inmortal *adj/mf* immortal

inmortalidad *f* immortality

inmovible *adj* immovable
inmóvil *adj* still
inmovilismo *m* resistance to change, immobilism (frml)
inmovilizar [A4] *vt* **1** ‹*persona/país/vehículo*› to immobilize **2** (Com, Fin) ‹*capital*› to tie up
inmundo -da *adj* **(a)** ‹*lugar*› filthy **(b)** ‹*sabor/comida*› foul, disgusting **(c)** (repulsivo) ‹*escena/película*› filthy, disgusting
inmune *adj* immune; **~ A algo** immune TO sth
inmunidad *f* immunity
inmunizar [A4] *vt* to immunize; **~ a algn CONTRA algo** to immunize sb AGAINST sth
inmunodeficiencia *f* immunodeficiency
inmunológico -ca *adj* ‹*tolerancia*› immunological; ‹*sistema/reacción*› immune (*before n*)
inmutarse [A1] *v pron* «*persona*»: **cuando se lo dije ni se inmutó** she didn't bat an eyelid when I told her (colloq); **lo escuchó sin ~se** she listened to him unperturbed
innato -ta *adj* innate, inborn
innavegable *adj* ‹*río*› unnavigable; ‹*embarcación*› unseaworthy
innecesario -ria *adj* unnecessary
innegable *adj* undeniable
innovación *f* innovation
innovador -dora *adj* innovative ■ *m,f* innovator
innovar [A1] *vi* to innovate
innumerable *adj* innumerable
inocencia *f* innocence
inocentada *f* ≈ April Fools' joke (*played on 28 December*); **gastarle** *or* **hacerle ~s a algn** to play practical jokes on sb
inocente *adj* **(a)** (sin culpa) innocent; (Der) innocent, not guilty; **lo declararon ~** he was found not guilty **(b)** ‹*broma*› harmless **(c)** (ingenuo) naive, gullible ■ *mf* innocent; **no te hagas el ~** don't play the innocent
inodoro *m* **(a)** ▶**52** (wáter) toilet, lavatory **(b)** (taza) bowl, pan
inofensivo -va *adj* harmless, inoffensive
inolvidable *adj* unforgettable
inoportuno -na *adj* **(a)** ‹*visita/llamada*› untimely, inopportune; **llamó en un momento ~** he phoned at a bad moment **(b)** ‹*comentario/crítica*› ill-timed, inopportune
inquebrantable *adj* ‹*fe*› unshakable, unyielding; ‹*lealtad*› unswerving; ‹*voluntad/salud*› iron (*before n*)
inquietante *adj* ‹*noticia/cifras*› disturbing, worrying; ‹*síntoma*› worrying
inquietarse [A1] *v pron* to worry; **~ POR algo/algn** to worry ABOUT sth/sb
inquieto -ta *adj* **(a)** [ESTAR] (preocupado) worried **(b)** [SER] (emprendedor) enterprising; (vivo) lively, inquiring (*before n*) **(c)** (que se mueve mucho) restless
inquietud *f* **(a)** (preocupación) worry; **~ POR algo** concern ABOUT sth **(b)** (interés): **es una persona sin ~es** she has no interest in anything; **su ~ filosófica** his philosophical preoccupations
inquilino -na *m,f* (arrendatario) tenant
Inquisición *f* (Hist): **la Inquisición** the Inquisition
inquisidor *m* inquisitor
insaciable *adj* insatiable; ‹*sed*› unquenchable
insalubre *adj* unhealthy
insalvable *adj* insurmountable, insuperable
insatisfacción *f* dissatisfaction
insatisfactorio -ria *adj* unsatisfactory
insatisfecho -cha *adj* **(a)** (descontento) dissatisfied; **~ CON algo/algn** dissatisfied WITH sth/sb **(b)** ‹*hambre/deseo*› unsatisfied
inscribir [I34] *vt* (en registro) to register; (en curso, escuela) to register, enroll*
■ **inscribirse** *v pron* «*persona*» (en curso, colegio) to enroll*, register; (en concurso) to enter; (en congreso) to register
inscripción *f* **(a)** (para curso) enrollment*, registration; (para concurso) entry; (en congreso) registration; **la ~ se cierra el** ... the last day for enrollment is ... **(b)** (de un nacimiento) registration **(c)** (leyenda, lema) inscription
inscrito -ta, (RPl) **inscripto -ta** *pp*: *see* INSCRIBIR
insecticida *m* insecticide
insecto *m* insect
inseguridad *f* **(a)** (falta de confianza) insecurity **(b)** (falta de firmeza, estabilidad) unsteadiness **(c)** (falta de garantías) insecurity, lack of security **(d)** (en ciudad, barrio): **la ~ ciudadana** the lack of safety on our streets
inseguro -ra *adj* **(a)** (falto de confianza) insecure **(b)** (falto de firmeza, estabilidad) unsteady **(c)** ‹*situación/futuro*› insecure **(d)** ‹*ciudad/barrio*› unsafe, dangerous
inseminación *f* insemination; **~ artificial** artificial insemination
insensatez *f* **(a)** (cualidad) foolishness, senselessness **(b)** (dicho, hecho): **lo que has dicho/hecho es una ~** that was a stupid thing to say/do
insensato -ta *adj* foolish ■ *m,f* fool
insensible *adj* insensitive; **~ al frío** insensitive to the cold
inseparable *adj* inseparable
insertar [A1] *vt* to insert
inservible *adj* (inútil) useless; (inutilizable) unusable
insignia *f* **(a)** (distintivo, emblema) insignia, emblem; (prendedor) badge, button (AmE) **(b)** (bandera) flag; (estandarte) standard, banner
insignificante *adj* ‹*asunto/detalle/suma*› insignificant, trivial; ‹*objeto/regalo*› small; ‹*persona*› insignificant
insinuación *f* hint; (que ofende) insinuation; **hacerle insinuaciones (amorosas) a algn** ⇒ INSINUARSE
insinuante *adj* ‹*mirada/voz*› suggestive; ‹*escote*› provocative
insinuar [A18] *vt* to imply, hint at; (algo ofensivo) to insinuate
■ **insinuarse** *v pron*: **insinuársele a algn** to make advances to sb, to make a pass at sb
insípido -da *adj* insipid, bland

insistencia *f* insistence; **con ~** insistently

insistente *adj* ‹*persona*› insistent; ‹*recomendaciones/pedidos*› repeated (*before n*), persistent; ‹*timbrazos*› insistent, repeated (*before n*)

insistir [I1] *vi* to insist; **ya que insistes** if you insist; **es inútil que insistas** there's no point going on about it; **~ EN hacer algo** to insist ON doing sth; **insiste en que lo hagamos** he insists (that) we do it; **insiste en que es suyo** she is adamant that it's hers; **~ SOBRE** *or* **EN algo** to stress sth

insociable *adj* unsociable

insolación *f* (Med) sunstroke; **agarrar una ~** to get sunstroke

insolencia *f* **(a)** (cualidad) insolence **(b)** (dicho): **no pienso tolerar sus ~s** I don't intend putting up with his insolence *o* his insolent behavior; **contestarle así fue una ~** it was very rude of you to answer him like that

insolente *adj* rude, insolent ■ *mf*: **es una ~** she's so rude *o* insolent

insólito -ta *adj* unusual

insomnio *m* insomnia

insonorizado -da *adj* soundproof

insoportable *adj* unbearable, intolerable

insostenible *adj* **(a)** ‹*situación/gasto*› unsustainable **(b)** ‹*posición/tesis*› untenable

inspección *f* inspection

inspeccionar [A1] *vt* to inspect

inspector -tora *m,f* inspector; **~ de Hacienda** revenue agent (AmE), tax inspector (BrE); **~ de policía** (police) inspector

inspiración *f* (Art, Lit, Mús) inspiration

inspirado -da *adj* inspired

inspirar [A1] *vt* **1** ‹*confianza*› to inspire; ‹*compasión*› to arouse, inspire; **sabe ~les confianza** she knows how to inspire confidence in them **2** «*obra/canción/persona*» to inspire

■ **inspirarse** *v pron* **~se EN algo** «*persona/obra/ley*» to be inspired BY sth

instalación *f* **(a)** (colocación) installation **(b)** (equipo, dispositivo) system; **la ~ sanitaria** the plumbing **(c) instalaciones** *fpl* (dependencias) installations (*pl*); **instalaciones deportivas** sports facilities

instalar [A1] *vt* **(a)** (colocar y conectar) ‹*teléfono/lavaplatos*› to install; ‹*antena*› to erect, put up **(b)** (colocar) ‹*archivador/piano*› to put **(c)** ‹*oficina/consultorio*› to open, set up

■ **instalarse** *v pron* to settle, install oneself

instantánea *f* snapshot

instantáneo -nea *adj* **(a)** ‹*resultado/crédito*› instant (*before n*); ‹*reacción*› instantaneous, immediate **(b)** ‹*café*› instant (*before n*)

instante *m* moment; **un ~, por favor** just a second *o* moment, please; **me llama a cada ~** he calls me all the time; **al ~** right away, straightaway (BrE)

instigar [A3] *vt* **~ a algn A algo/hacer algo** to incite sb TO sth/do sth

instintivo -va *adj* instinctive

> ## Instrucciones para encontrar el camino
>
> **¿cómo se llega?**
>
> When you come out of the station, turn left and go down the road till you get to the traffic lights. Turn left there into Main Street and carry on along past the pub and the theatre. At the second set of traffic lights turn right and then take the first right. That will bring you to a small square. Cross (over) the square and you'll come to a narrow passage in the corner. Go down there and you'll come out into Washington Avenue. Cross over the street toward(s) the fountain and the office is on the right, between a gym and an office block.
>
> *Nótese que también se puede usar el indicativo en lugar del imperativo*:
>
> *ej.* you turn left, you take the first turning on the right, etc.

instinto *m* instinct; **por ~** instinctively; **~ de conservación** survival instinct

institución *f* institution

instituto *m* institute; **~ nacional de bachillerato** (Esp) high school (AmE), secondary school (BrE)

institutriz *f* governess

instrucción *f* **1** (educación) education; (práctica) training; **~ militar** military training **2 instrucciones** *fpl* **(a)** (de aparato, juego) instructions (*pl*); (para llegar a un lugar) directions (*pl*) **(b)** (órdenes) instructions

instructor -tora *m,f* instructor

instruir [I20] *vt* (adiestrar, educar) **~ a algn EN algo** to instruct *o* train sb IN sth

■ **instruirse** *v pron* (*refl*) to broaden one's mind, improve oneself

instrumental *m* (Med) equipment, set of instruments

instrumento *m* **1** (en general) instrument; **~ de cuerda** string instrument; **~s de precisión** precision instruments **2** (medio) means

insubordinación *f* insubordination

insubordinarse [A1] *v pron* **~** (**CONTRA algn**) (desobedecer) to be insubordinate (TO sb); (sublevarse) to rebel (AGAINST sb)

insuficiencia *f* (escasez): **~ de medios** lack of resources; **~ de personal** staff shortage

insuficiente *adj* **(a)** ‹*medios/cantidad*› inadequate, insufficient **(b)** (Educ) ‹*trabajo*› poor, unsatisfactory ■ *m* fail

insular *adj* insular

insulina *f* insulin

insulso -sa *adj* **(a)** ‹*comida*› insipid, tasteless **(b)** ‹*persona*› insipid, dull; ‹*conversación/libro*› dull

insultante *adj* insulting

insultar [A1] *vt* **(a)** (proferir insultos) to insult **(b)** (ofender) to insult, offend

insulto *m* insult

insumos *mpl* (esp AmL) consumables (*pl*)

insuperable *adj* **(a)** (insalvable) ‹*problema/dificultad*› insurmountable, insuperable **(b)** (inmejorable) ‹*calidad/precio*› unbeatable

insurgente *mf* (frml) rebel, insurgent (frml)

insurrección *f* (frml) uprising, insurrection (frml)

intachable *adj* impeccable, irreproachable

intacto -ta *adj* (íntegro, no dañado) intact

integración *f* integration

integrado -da *adj* integrated

integral *adj* **(a)** (completo, total) comprehensive **(b)** (incorporado) built-in

integrante *mf* member

integrar [A1] *vt* **1** (formar) ‹*grupo/organización*› to make up **2** (incorporar) ‹*idea/plan*› to incorporate **3** (Mat, Sociol) to integrate **4** (CS) ‹*suma/cantidad*› to pay

■ **integrarse** *v pron* **(a)** (asimilarse) to integrate, fit in; **~se** A *or* EN **algo** to integrate INTO sth, fit INTO sth **(b)** (unirse) **~se** A *or* EN **algo** to join sth

integridad *f* integrity

íntegro -gra *adj* **1** ‹*texto*› unabridged; **se proyectó en versión íntegra** they screened the full-length version **2** ‹*persona*› upright

intelecto *m* intellect

intelectual *adj/mf* intellectual

inteligencia *f* **1 (a)** (facultad, ser inteligente) intelligence **(b)** (comprensión) understanding **2** (Mil, Pol) intelligence

inteligente *adj* intelligent; ‹*persona*› intelligent, clever

inteligible *adj* intelligible

intemperie *f*: **pasar la noche a la ~** to spend the night out in the open

intención *f* intention; **no fue mi ~ ofenderte** I didn't mean to offend you; **tiene buenas/malas intenciones** she's well-intentioned/up to no good; **lo dijo con segunda** *or* **doble ~** she had an ulterior motive for saying it; **con la mejor ~** with the best of intentions; **lo que cuenta es la ~** it's the thought that counts; **vine con (la) ~ de ayudarte** I came to help you; **tiene (la) ~ de abrir un bar** she plans *o* intends to open a bar; **no tengo la menor ~ de venderlo** I have no intention whatsoever of selling it

intencionado -da *adj* (hecho a propósito) deliberate, intentional; **mal ~** malicious, hostile; **bien ~** well-intentioned

intendencia *f* **(a)** (Andes) (división territorial) administrative division **(b)** (RPl) (gobierno municipal) town/city council; (edificio) town/city hall

intendente *mf* **(a)** (Andes) governor **(b)** (RPl) mayor

intensidad *f* **(a)** (de terremoto) intensity, strength; (del viento) strength; (de dolor, sentimiento) intensity **(b)** (Elec, Fís) intensity

intensivo -va *adj* intensive

intenso -sa *adj* **(a)** ‹*frío/luz/color*› intense **(b)** ‹*emoción/mirada*› intense; ‹*dolor/sentimiento*› intense, acute **(c)** ‹*esfuerzo*› strenuous; ‹*negociaciones*› intensive

intentar [A1] *vt* to try; **¡inténtalo otra vez!** try again!; **~ un aterrizaje de emergencia** to attempt an emergency landing; **~ hacer algo** to try to do sth; **¿has intentado que te lo arreglen?** have you tried getting *o* to get it fixed?

intento *m* **(a)** (tentativa) attempt **(b)** (Méx) (propósito) intention, aim

intercalar [A1] *vt* **~ algo** EN **algo** ‹*en texto*› to insert sth INTO sth; **intercaló algunas citas en su discurso** she interspersed her speech with some quotations; **intercala uno rojo cada dos azules** put a red one between every two blue ones

intercambiable *adj* interchangeable

intercambiar [A1] *vt* ‹*impresiones/ideas*› to exchange; ‹*sellos/revistas*› to swap

intercambio *m* **(a)** (de ideas, información, bienes) exchange **(b)** (de sellos, revistas) swap; (de estudiantes, prisioneros) exchange

interceder [E1] *vi* (frml) to intercede; **intercedió por ellos ante el rey** he interceded for them with the king

interceptar [A1] *vt* **(a)** ‹*correspondencia/mensaje*› to intercept **(b)** ‹*teléfono*› to tap **(c)** (Dep) ‹*balón/pase*› to intercept; ‹*golpe*› to block **(d)** ‹*calzada/carretera*› to block; **~ el paso** to block the way

intercomunicar [A2] *vt* to link (up)

interés *m* **1** (en general) interest; **de ~ turístico** of interest to tourists; **pon más ~ en tus estudios** take more interest in your schoolwork; **tengo especial ~ en que** ... I am particularly concerned *o* keen that ...; **tienen gran ~ en verlo** they are very interested in seeing it; **por tu propio ~** in your own interest, for your own good; **actúa sólo por ~** he acts purely in his own interest *o* out of self-interest; **conflicto de intereses** conflict of interests **2** (Fin) interest; **a** *or* **con un ~ del 12%** at 12% interest *o* at an interest rate of 12%; **ganar intereses** to earn interest; **tipo de ~** rate of interest

interesado -da *adj* **(a)** [ESTAR] (que muestra interés) interested; **~** EN **algo** interested IN sth **(b)** [SER] (egoísta) selfish; **actuó de manera interesada** he acted selfishly **(c)** (parcial) biased, biassed ■ *m,f* **(a)** (que tiene interés) interested party (frml); **los ~s deberán** ... all those interested *o* (frml) all interested parties should ... **(b)** (que busca su provecho): **es un ~** he always acts in his own interest *o* out of self-interest

interesante *adj* interesting; ***hacerse el ~*** (fam) to try to draw attention to oneself

interesar [A1] *vi* **(a)** (suscitar interés): (+ *me/te/le etc*) **no me interesa la política** I'm not interested in politics; **esto a ti no te interesa** this doesn't concern you, this is no concern of yours **(b)** (convenir): **~ía comprobar los datos** it would be useful/advisable to check the data; **me interesa este tipo de préstamo** this sort of loan would suit me ■ **~** *vt* **~ a algn** EN **algo** to interest sb IN sth, get sb interested IN sth

■ **interesarse** *v pron* **(a)** (tener interés) to take interest; **~se** EN *or* POR **algo** to take an interest IN sth **(b)** (preguntar) **~se** POR **algo/algn** to ask *o* inquire ABOUT sth/sb

interferencia *f* interference

interferir [I11] *vt* **(a)** (obstaculizar) to interfere in **(b)** ‹*emisión*› to jam ■ ~ *vi* to interfere, meddle; ~ EN **algo** ‹*en asunto*› to interfere *o* meddle IN sth ■ **interferirse** *v pron* **~se** EN **algo** to interfere *o* meddle IN sth

interfono *m* **(a)** (portero automático) intercom (AmE), entryphone (BrE); (intercomunicador) intercom **(b)** (para bebés) baby alarm

interinato *m* (esp AmL) (cargo) temporary post *o* position

interino -na *adj* ‹*secretario/director*› acting (*before n*); ‹*profesor*› substitute (AmE) (*before n*), supply (BrE) (*before n*); ‹*gobierno*› interim (*before n*); **médico ~** locum ■ *m,f* (funcionario) temporary clerk (*o* accountant *etc*); (profesor) substitute teacher (AmE), supply teacher (BrE); (médico) locum

interior *adj* **(a)** ‹*patio/escalera*› interior, internal, inside (*before n*); ‹*habitación/piso*› *with windows facing onto a central staircase or patio* **(b)** ‹*bolsillo/revestimiento*› inside (*before n*); **en la parte ~** inside *o* on the inside **(c)** ‹*vida/mundo*› inner **(d)** ‹*política/comercio*› domestic, internal ■ *m* **1 (a)** (de cajon, maleta, coche) inside; (de edificio) interior, inside; (de un país) interior; **en el ~ de la habitación** inside the room **(b)** (Méx, RPl, Ven) (provincias) provinces (*pl*) **(c)** (de una persona): **en su ~ estaba muy intranquilo** inside he was very worried; **allá en su ~ la amaba** deep down he really loved her **2 Interior** *m* (period) (Ministerio del Interior) Ministry of the Interior, ≈ Department of the Interior (*in US*), ≈ Home Office (*in UK*) **3 interiores** *mpl* (Col, Ven) (Indum) underwear

interjección *f* interjection

intermediario -ria *adj* intermediary ■ *m,f* **(a)** (Com) middleman, intermediary **(b)** (mediador) intermediary, mediator, go-between

intermedio[1] -dia *adj* **(a)** ‹*punto/etapa*› intermediate; **alumnos de nivel ~** students at intermediate level **(b)** ‹*calidad/tamaño*› medium (*before n*); **un color ~ entre el gris y el verde** a color halfway between gray and green

intermedio[2] *m* (Espec) intermission, interval

interminable *adj* ‹*serie/discusión/espera*› interminable, never-ending; ‹*cola/fila*› endless, never-ending

intermitente *adj* **(a)** ‹*lluvia*› intermittent, sporadic **(b)** ‹*luz*› flashing; ‹*señal*› intermittent **(c)** ‹*fiebre*› intermittent ■ *m* turn signal (AmE), indicator (BrE)

internacional *adj* international; ‹*noticia*› foreign (*before n*), international (*before n*); ‹*política*› foreign (*before n*); **de fama ~** internationally famous; Ⓢ **salidas internacionales** international departures

internado[1] -da *adj* (AmL): **está ~** he's been admitted to (the) hospital, he's been hospitalized

internado[2] *m* **(a)** (Educ) boarding school **(b)** (Med) *position or term as an intern or a houseman at a hospital*, internship (AmE)

internar [A1] *vt*: **la ~on en un manicomio** she was put in an asylum; **lo ~on en el hospital** he was admitted to (the) hospital; **tuvimos que ~lo** we had to take him to (the) hospital ■ **internarse** *v pron* **(a)** (adentrarse) **~se** EN **algo** ‹*en bosque/espesura*› to penetrate INTO sth, to go deep INTO sth **(b)** (AmL) (en hospital) to go into the hospital

Internet /inter'ne/ *m*: **el ~** the Internet

interno[1] -na *adj* **1** (en general) internal **2 (a)** (Educ): **está ~ en un colegio inglés** he is a boarder at an English school **(b)** (Med): **médico ~** ≈ intern (*in US*), ≈ houseman (*in UK*) ■ *m,f* **(a)** (Educ) boarder **(b)** (en cárcel) inmate **(c)** (médico) ≈ intern (*in US*), ≈ houseman (*in UK*)

interno[2] *m* (RPl) (Telec) (extensión) extension

interponerse [E22] *v pron*: **se interpuso y paró la pelea** he stepped in and stopped the fight; **nada se interpone en su camino** nothing stands in her way

interpretación *f* **(a)** (de un texto) interpretation **(b)** (Cin, Mús, Teat) interpretation **(c)** (traducción oral) interpreting; **~ simultánea** simultaneous interpreting

interpretar [A1] *vt* **1** ‹*texto/comentario/sueño*› to interpret; **interpretó mal tus palabras** she misinterpreted what you said **2 (a)** ‹*papel/personaje*› to play **(b)** ‹*pieza/sinfonía*› to play, perform; ‹*canción*› to sing

intérprete *mf* **1** (traductor oral) interpreter; **~ jurado** sworn interpreter **2** (Mús) performer; (cantante) singer

interpuesto -ta *pp*: *see* INTERPONERSE

interrogación *f* **(a)** (de un sospechoso) interrogation **(b)** (Chi) (Educ) test

interrogar [A3] *vt* ‹*testigo/acusado*› to question, examine; ‹*detenido/sospechoso*› to interrogate, question; ‹*examinando*› to examine

interrogatorio *m* (de acusado, testigo) questioning, examination; (de detenido) interrogation, questioning

interrumpir [I1] *vt* **1** (temporalmente) **(a)** ‹*persona/reunión*› to interrupt **(b)** ‹*suministro*› to cut off; ‹*servicio*› to suspend; ‹*tráfico*› to hold up; **las obras no ~án el paso** the work will not block the road **2 (a)** (acortar) ‹*viaje/vacaciones/reunión*› to cut short **(b)** ‹*embarazo*› to terminate ■ ~ *vi* to interrupt

interrupción *f* interruption

interruptor *m* switch

intersección *f* **(a)** (en geometría) intersection **(b)** (frml) (Transp) intersection, junction

intertanto *m*: **en el ~** (AmL) in the meantime

interurbano -na *adj* ‹*transporte/autobús/llamada*› long-distance; ‹*tren*› intercity

intervalo *m* **(a)** (de tiempo) interval; (entre clases) recess (AmE), break (BrE) **(b)** (Mús) interval **(c)** (Teatr) (intermedio) intermission (AmE), interval (BrE) **(d)** (en el espacio) gap

intervención *f* **(a)** (en general) intervention; **se probó su ~ en el atraco** his involvement in the robbery was proved; **una política de no ~** a policy of nonintervention; **~ quirúrgica** operation **(b)** (de droga, armas) seizure, confiscation

intervenir [I31] *vi* **(a)** (en debate, operación) to take part; (en espectáculo) to appear, perform **(b)** (mediar) to intervene, intercede (frml); **en mi decisión intervinieron muchos factores** there were many factors involved in my decision; **~ en una pelea** to intervene *o* step in to stop a fight; (involucrarse) to get involved in a fight ■ **~** *vt* **1 (a)** ‹*teléfono*› to tap **(b)** (tomar control de) ‹*empresa*› to place ... in administration **(c)** (inspeccionar) ‹*cuentas*› to audit, inspect **(d)** ‹*armas/droga*› to seize, confiscate **2** (operar) to operate on; **fue intervenido en una clínica privada** he underwent surgery in a private clinic

interviú *f* interview

intestinal *adj* intestinal

intestino *m* intestine, gut

inti *m* inti (*former Peruvian unit of currency*)

intimar [A1] *vi* **~ CON algn** to get close TO sb

intimidación *f* intimidation

intimidad *f* **1 (a)** (ambiente privado) privacy; **en la ~ del hogar** in the privacy of one's home **(b)** (relación estrecha) intimacy **2 intimidades** *fpl* **(a)** (cosas íntimas) private life, personal *o* private affairs (*pl*) **(b)** (euf) (partes pudendas) private parts (*pl*) (euph), privates (*pl*) (colloq)

intimidante *adj* intimidating

intimidar [A1] *vt* **(a)** (atemorizar) to intimidate **(b)** (amenazar) to threaten

íntimo -ma *adj* **(a)** ‹*vida/diario/ceremonia*› private; ‹*secreto*› intimate; ‹*ambiente*› intimate; **una cena íntima** a small dinner (with a few friends/ members of the family); (en pareja) a candlelit *o* romantic dinner **(b)** ‹*amistad*› close; ‹*amigo*› close, intimate (*before n*)

intocable *adj* **(a)** (sagrado) sacred, sacrosanct **(b)** ‹*tema*› taboo **(c)** ‹*casta*› untouchable

intolerable *adj* intolerable

intolerancia *f* intolerance

intolerante *adj* intolerant

intoxicación *f* (Med) intoxication, poisoning

intoxicar [A2] *vt* to poison
■ **intoxicarse** *v pron* to get food poisoning

intranquilizar [A4] *vt* to worry

intranquilo -la *adj* **(a)** [ESTAR] (preocupado) worried, anxious **(b)** (agitado) restless

intranscendente *adj* ⇒ INTRASCENDENTE

intransferible *adj* not transferable, untransferable

intransigente *adj* intransigent

intransitivo -va *adj* intransitive

intrascendente *adj* ‹*episodio/detalle*› insignificant, unimportant; ‹*comentario*› trivial

intriga *f* intrigue; **novela/película de ~** thriller

intrigante *mf* schemer, intriguer (AmE)

intrigar [A3] *vt* to intrigue ■ **~** *vi* to scheme

intrincado -da *adj* **(a)** ‹*problema/asunto*› intricate, complex; ‹*laberinto/sistema*› complicated **(b)** ‹*nudo*› tangled

introducción *f* introduction; **~ A algo** introduction TO sth

introducir [I6] *vt* **1** (en general) to put ... in; ‹*moneda*› to insert; **~ algo EN algo** to put sth INTO sth; ‹*moneda*› to insert sth IN sth **2 (a)** ‹*cambios/medidas/ley*› to introduce, bring in; ‹*producto*› to introduce **(b)** ‹*contrabando/drogas*› to bring in, smuggle in **3** (presentar) ‹*acto/cantante*› to introduce
■ **introducirse** *v pron* **(a)** (meterse) «*ladrón*» to gain access; **la moneda se introdujo por una grieta** the coin fell down a crack **(b)** (entrar en uso) «*moda*» to come in; «*costumbre*» to be introduced **(c)** (hacerse conocido) «*escritor/actor*» to become known

introductorio -ria *adj* introductory

introvertido -da *adj* introverted ■ *m,f* introvert

intruso -sa *m,f* intruder

intuición *f* intuition; **hacer algo por ~** to do sth intuitively; **tuve la ~ de que** ... I had a feeling that ...

intuir [I20] *vt* to sense; **intuía que me iba a llamar** I had a feeling he was going to ring me

intuitivo -va *adj* intuitive

inundación *f* (en área limitada, casa) flood; (en zona más amplia) floods (*pl*), flooding

inundar [A1] *vt* **(a)** «*riada/aguas*» to flood, inundate (frml); «*turistas/manifestantes*» to inundate, crowd **(b)** «*persona*» (con agua) to flood; (con productos) to flood, swamp; **~ algo DE** *or* **CON algo** to flood sth WITH sth
■ **inundarse** *v pron* (de agua) to be flooded

inusitado -da *adj* unusual, rare

inútil *adj* useless; **es ~ que insistas** there's no point (in) insisting ■ *mf*: **es un ~** he's useless

invadir [I1] *vt* **(a)** «*ejército/fuerzas*» to invade **(b)** ‹*espacio aéreo/aguas*› to enter, encroach upon **(c)** «*tristeza/alegría*» to overcome, overwhelm

invalidez *f* (Med) disability, disablement

inválido -da *adj* (Med) ‹*persona*› disabled, handicapped ■ *m,f* invalid, disabled person

invariable *adj* **(a)** ‹*precio/estado*› constant, stable **(b)** (Ling) invariable

invasión *f* **1** (de zona, país) invasion **2** (Col) (chabolas) shantytown

invasor -sora *m,f* invader

invencible *adj* **(a)** ‹*luchador/equipo*› unbeatable, invincible **(b)** ‹*miedo/timidez*› insuperable, insurmountable

invención *f* **(a)** (en general) invention **(b)** (mentira) fabrication

inventar [A1] *vt* **(a)** ‹*aparato/sistema*› to invent **(b)** ‹*juego/palabra*› to make up, invent; ‹*cuento/ excusa/mentira*› to make up

inventario *m* (de negocio) inventory, stock list; (de casa) inventory

inventiva *f* inventiveness; **tiene mucha ~** she's very inventive

invento *m* invention

inventor -tora *m,f* inventor

invernadero *m* greenhouse

invernal *adj* ‹*lluvias*› winter (*before n*); ‹*frío*› wintry

inverosímil *adj* implausible

inversión *f* **1** (de dinero, tiempo, esfuerzos) investment **2** (de posiciones, términos) reversal; (de una imagen) inversion; **~ térmica** thermal inversion

inversionista *mf* investor

inverso -sa *adj* ‹*sentido/orden*› reverse; **puedes ordenarlo así o a la inversa** you can arrange it like this or the other way around

inversor -sora *m,f* investor

invertido -da *adj* ‹*posición/orden*› reversed; ‹*imagen/figura*› inverted, reversed

invertir [I11] *vt* **1** ‹*dinero/capital*› to invest; ‹*tiempo*› to invest, devote **2** ‹*orden/papeles/términos*› to reverse; ‹*imagen/figura*› to invert, reverse ■ **~** *vi* to invest; **~ EN algo** to invest IN sth

■ **invertirse** *v pron* «*papeles/funciones*» to be reversed

investigación *f* **(a)** (de caso, delito) investigation; (por comisión especial) inquiry **(b)** (Educ, Med, Tec) research; **~ científica** scientific research; **~ de mercados** market research

investigador -dora *m,f* **(a)** (que indaga) investigator **(b)** (Educ, Med, Tec) researcher

investigar [A3] *vt* **(a)** ‹*delito/caso*› to investigate **(b)** (Educ, Med, Tec) «*persona*» to research, do research into ■ **~** *vi* **(a)** «*policía*» to investigate **(b)** (Educ, Med, Tec) **~ SOBRE algo** to research *o* do research INTO sth

invierno *m* winter; (en la zona tropical) rainy season; **en ~** in winter, in wintertime; **ropa de ~** winter clothes

invierta, inviertas, etc *see* INVERTIR

invirtiera, invirtió, etc *see* INVERTIR

invisible *adj* invisible

invitación *f* invitation

invitado -da *m,f* guest; **tenemos ~s a cenar** we have people coming to dinner; **los ~s a la boda** the wedding guests

invitar [A1] *vt* to invite; **~ a algn A algo** to invite sb TO sth; **te invito a una copa** I'll buy *o* get you a drink; **~ a algn A + INF** *or* **A QUE + SUBJ** to invite sb to + INF; **me invitó a cenar** (en casa) she invited me (round) to dinner; (en restaurante) she invited me out to dinner ■ **~** *vi* «*persona*»: **invito yo** it's on me, I'm buying; **invita la casa** it's on the house

invocar [A2] *f* **(a)** ‹*divinidad/santos*› to invoke (frml), to call on **(b)** ‹*auxilio/protección*› to appeal for

involucrar [A1] *vt* **(a)** (implicar) to involve; **~ a algn EN algo** ‹*en asunto/crimen*› to involve sb IN sth **(b)** (AmL) (conllevar) to involve

■ **involucrarse** *v pron* «*persona*» to get involved

involuntario -ria *adj* ‹*error/movimiento/gesto*› involuntary; ‹*testigo/cómplice*› unwitting

inyección *f* (Med) injection; (dosis) injection, shot (colloq); **le puso una ~** she gave him an injection

inyectado -da *adj*: **ojos ~s en sangre** bloodshot eyes

inyectar [A1] *vt* to inject; **le ~on morfina** they gave him morphine injections/a shot of morphine

■ **inyectarse** *v pron* (*refl*) «*persona*» to give oneself an injection, inject oneself; **se inyectó heroína** he injected himself with heroin

ion *m* ion

ir [I27] *vi* **I 1 (a)** (trasladarse, desplazarse) to go; **~ en taxi** to go by taxi; **iban a caballo/a pie** they were on horseback/on foot; **~ por mar** to go by sea; **¡Fernando! — ¡voy!** Fernando! — (just) coming! *o* I'll be right there!; **el ~ y venir de los invitados** the coming and going of the guests; **vamos a casa** let's go home; **¿adónde va este tren?** where's this train going (to)?; **~ de compras/de caza** to go shopping/hunting; **ya vamos para allá** we're on our way; **¿por dónde se va a ...?** how do you get to ...?; ***~ por*** *or* (Esp) ***a por algo/algn*** to go to get sth/sb; **voy (a) por pan** I'm going to get some bread **(b)** (asistir) to go to; **voy a clases nocturnas** I go to evening classes; **ya va al colegio** she's already at school **2** (expresando propósito) **~ A + INF**: **¿has ido a verla?** have you been to see her?; **ve a ayudarla** go and help her; *ver tb* V AUX 1 **3** (al arrojar algo, arrojarse): **tírame la llave — ¡allá va!** throw me the key — here you are *o* there you go!; **tírate del trampolín — ¡allá voy!** jump off the board! — here I go/come! **4** «*comentario*»: **no iba con mala intención** it wasn't meant unkindly; **eso va por ti también** that goes for you too, and the same goes for you

II 1 (*+ compl*) (sin énfasis en el movimiento): **iban cantando por el camino** they sang as they went along; **¿van cómodos?** are you comfortable?; **íbamos sentados** we were sitting down; **vas muy cargada** you have a lot to carry; **yo iba a la cabeza** I was in the lead **2** (refiriéndose al atuendo): **iban de largo** they wore long dresses; **voy a ~ de Drácula** I'm going to go as Dracula; **iba de verde** she was dressed in green **3** (en calidad de) **~ DE algo** to go (along) AS sth; **yo fui de intérprete** I went along as interpreter

III 1 «*camino/sendero*» (llevar) **~ A algo** to lead TO sth, to go TO sth **2** (extenderse, abarcar): **la autopista va desde Madrid hasta Valencia** the highway goes from Madrid to Valencia; **el período que va desde ... hasta ...** the period from ... to ...

IV 1 (marchar, desarrollarse): **¿cómo va el nuevo trabajo?** how's the new job going?; **va de mal en peor** it's going from bad to worse; **¿cómo te va?** how's it going?, how are things? (colloq), what's up? (AmE colloq); **¿cómo les fue en Italia?** how was Italy?, how did you get on in Italy?; **me fue mal/bien en el examen** I did badly/well in the exam; **¡que te vaya bien!** all the best!, take care!; **¡que te vaya bien (en) el examen!** good luck in the exam **2** (en competiciones): **¿cómo van? — 3-1** what's the score? — 3-1; **voy ganando yo** I'm ahead, I'm winning **3** (en el desarrollo de algo): **¿por dónde van en historia?** where have you got (up) to in history?; **¿todavía vas por la página 20?** are you still on page 20? **4** (estar en camino): **¡vamos para viejos!** we're getting on *o* old!; **va para los cincuenta** she's going on fifty; **ya va para dos años que ...** it's getting on for two years since ... **5** (sumar, hacer): **ya van tres veces que te lo digo** this is the third time I've told you; **con éste van**

seis six, counting this one **6** (haber transcurrido): **en lo que va del** *or* (Esp) **de año/mes** so far this year/month

V 1 (deber colocarse) to go; **¿dónde van las toallas?** where do the towels go?; ***¡qué va!*** (fam): **¿has terminado? — ¡qué va!** have you finished? — you must be joking!; **¿se disgustó? — ¡qué va!** did she get upset? — not at all!; **vamos a perder el avión — ¡qué va!** we're going to miss the plane — no way! **2 (a)** (combinar) **~** CON **algo** to go WITH sth **(b)** (sentar bien, convenir) (+ *me/te/le etc*): **el negro no te va bien** black doesn't suit you; **te ~á bien un descanso** a rest will do you good **3** (Méx) (tomar partido por, apoyar) **~le** A **algo/algn** to support sth/sb; **le va al equipo peruano** he supports the Peruvian team

VI 1 vamos (a) (expresando incredulidad, fastidio): **¡vamos! ¿eso quién se lo va a creer?** come off it *o* come on! who do you think's going to believe that? **(b)** (intentando tranquilizar, animar, dar prisa): **vamos, mujer, dile algo** go on, say something to him; **¡vamos, date prisa!** come on, hurry up! **(c)** (al aclarar, resumir): **eso sería un disparate, vamos, digo yo** that would be a stupid thing to do, well, that's what I think anyway; **vamos, que no es una persona de fiar** basically, he's not very trustworthy; **es mejor que el otro, vamos** it's better than the other one, anyway **2 vaya (a)** (expresando sorpresa, contrariedad): **¡vaya! ¡tú por aquí!** what a surprise! what are you doing here?; **¡vaya! ¡se ha vuelto a caer!** oh no *o* (colloq) damn! it's fallen over again! **(b)** (Esp) (para enfatizar): **¡vaya cochazo!** what a car! ■ **~** *v aux* **~** A + INF: **1 (a)** (para expresar tiempo futuro, propósito) to be going to + INF; **voy a estudiar medicina** I'm going to study medicine; **va a hacer dos años que** ... it's getting on for two years since ... **(b)** (en propuestas, sugerencias): **vamos a ver ¿cómo dices que te llamas?** now then, what did you say your name was?; **bueno, vamos a trabajar** all right, let's get to work **2** (al prevenir, hacer recomendaciones): **que no se te vaya a caer** make sure you don't drop it; **cuidado, no te vayas a caer** mind you don't fall (colloq); **lleva el paraguas, no vaya a ser que llueva** take the umbrella, in case it rains **3** (expresando un proceso paulatino): **poco a poco irá aprendiendo** she'll learn little by little; **ya puedes ~ haciéndote a la idea** you'd better get used to the idea; **la situación ha ido empeorando** the situation has been getting worse and worse

■ **irse** *v pron* **1** (marcharse) to leave; **¿por qué te vas tan temprano?** why are you leaving *o* going so soon?; **vámonos** let's go; **bueno, me voy** right then, I'm taking off (AmE) *o* (BrE) I'm off; **no te vayas** don't go; **vete a la cama** go to bed; **se fue de casa/de la empresa** she left home/the company; **vete de aquí** get out of here; **se han ido de viaje** they're away, they've gone away **2** (consumirse, gastarse): **¡cómo se va el dinero!** I don't know where the money goes!; **se me va medio sueldo en el alquiler** half my salary goes on the rent **3** (desaparecer) «*mancha/dolor*» to go; **se ha ido la luz** the electricity's gone off; (+ *me/te/le etc*) **¿se te ha ido el dolor de cabeza?** has your headache gone? **4** (salirse, escaparse) «*líquido/gas*» to escape; **se le está yendo el aire al globo** the balloon's losing air *o* going down **5** (caerse, perder el equilibrio) (+ *compl*): **~se de boca/espaldas** to fall flat on one's face/back; **me iba para atrás** I was falling backwards; **frenó y nos fuimos todos para adelante** he braked and we all went flying forwards

ira *f* rage, anger

Irak, **Iraq** *m* Iraq

Irán *m* Iran

iraní *adj/mf* Iranian

iraquí *adj/mf* Iraqi

irguieron, **irguió, etc** *see* ERGUIR

iris *m* (*pl* **~**) iris

Irlanda *f* Ireland; **~ del Norte** Northern Ireland

irlandés[1] -desa *adj* Irish ■ *m,f* (persona) (*m*) Irishman; (*f*) Irishwoman; **los irlandeses** the Irish, Irish people

irlandés[2] *m* (idioma) Irish (Gaelic)

ironía *f* irony

irónico -ca *adj* **(a)** ‹*situación*› ironic **(b)** ‹*persona/comentario/tono*› sarcastic; **en tono ~** sarcastically

irracional *adj* irrational

irradiar [A1] *vt* **(a)** ‹*calor/luz*› to radiate **(b)** ‹*simpatía/felicidad*› to radiate, irradiate

irrazonable *adj* unreasonable

irreal *adj* unreal

irrealizable *adj* ‹*proyecto*› unfeasible; ‹*deseo*› unattainable, unrealizable

irreconocible *adj* unrecognizable

irrecuperable *adj* unrecoverable, irretrievable

irreemplazable *adj* irreplaceable

irregular *adj* (en general) irregular; ‹*letra/superficie*› irregular, uneven

irregularidad *f* irregularity

irrelevante *adj* irrelevant

irremediable *adj* irreparable

irrepetible *adj* unrepeatable

irreprochable *adj* irreproachable

irresistible *adj* **(a)** ‹*sonrisa/mujer/hombre*› irresistible; ‹*deseo/tentación*› irresistible **(b)** ‹*dolor*› unbearable

irrespetar [A1] *vt* (Col, Ven) ‹*persona*› to be disrespectful *o* rude to; ‹*lugar sagrado*› to desecrate

irrespetuoso -sa *adj* disrespectful

irrespirable *adj* unbreathable

irresponsabilidad *f* irresponsibility

irresponsable *adj* irresponsible ■ *mf*: **es un ~** he's irresponsible, he's an irresponsible person

irreversible *adj* irreversible

irritable *adj* irritable

irritación *f* **(a)** (Med) irritation, inflammation **(b)** (enfado) irritation, annoyance

irritante *adj* ‹*situación/actitud*› irritating, annoying

irritar [A1] *vt* **(a)** ‹*piel/garganta*› to irritate; **tiene la garganta irritada** his throat is sore *o* inflamed **(b)** ‹*persona*› to annoy, irritate

■ **irritarse** *v pron* **(a)** «*piel/ojos*» to become irritated **(b)** «*persona*» to get annoyed, get irritated

irrompible *adj* unbreakable

isla *f* **(a)** (Geog) island, isle (liter) **(b)** (Ven) (en autopistas) median strip (AmE), central reservation (BrE); **~ peatonal** safety island (AmE), traffic island (BrE)

Isla de Pascua *f*: **la ~ de ~** Easter Island

Islam *m*: **el ~** Islam

islámico -ca *adj* Islamic

islandés¹ -desa *adj* Icelandic ■ *m,f* (persona) Icelander

islandés² *m* (idioma) Icelandic

Islandia *f* Iceland

Islas Británicas *fpl* British Isles (*pl*)

Islas Canarias *fpl* Canary Islands (*pl*), Canaries (*pl*)

Islas Malvinas *fpl* Falkland Islands (*pl*)

isleño -ña *adj* ‹*población/productos*› island (*before n*) ■ *m,f* (habitante de una isla) islander

islote *m* small island, islet

Israel *m* Israel

israelí *adj/mf* Israeli

itacate *m* (Méx) pack, bundle

Italia *f* Italy

italiano¹ -na *adj/m,f* Italian

italiano² *m* (idioma) Italian

ítem *m* (*pl* **ítems**) item

itinerario *m* itinerary, route

IVA /'iβa/ *m* (= **Impuesto al Valor Agregado** *or* **sobre el Valor Añadido**) VAT

izar [A4] *vt* ‹*vela/bandera*› to hoist, raise, run up

izquierda *f* **1 (a)** (mano izquierda): **la ~** the left hand **(b)** (lado) left; **la puerta de la ~** the door on the left, the left-hand door; **torció a la ~** he turned left; **ahí enfrente a la ~** over there on the left; **conducen por la ~** they drive on the left **2** (Pol) left; **de ~** *or* (Esp) **de ~s** left-wing

izquierdo -da *adj* left (*before n*)

Jj

J, j *f* (*read as* /'xota/) *the letter* J, j

ja *interj* ha!

jabalí *m* (*pl* **-líes**) wild boar

jabalina *f* **(a)** (Arm, Dep) javelin **(b)** (Zool) wild sow

jabón *m* (producto) soap; **una barra** *or* **pastilla de ~** a bar *o* cake of soap; **~ de afeitar** shaving soap

jabonada *f* (con jabón): **dale una buena ~** wash it well in soapy water

jabonar [A1] *vt* ⇒ ENJABONAR

jabonera *f* soap dish

jabonoso -sa *adj* soapy

jacal *m* (Méx) hut, small house (*made of adobe or reeds*)

jacarandá *m or f* jacaranda

jacinto *m* (Bot) hyacinth

jactarse [A1] *v pron* to boast, brag; **~ DE algo** to boast *o* brag ABOUT sth

Jacuzzi® /dʒə'kuzi/ *m* Jacuzzi®

jade *m* ▶97 jade

jadeante *adj*: **venía ~ por la cuesta** he came up the hill (puffing and) panting; **con voz ~** in a breathless voice

jadear [A1] *vi* to pant

jadeo *m* panting

jaguar *m* jaguar

jagüey, jagüel *m* (AmL) pool

jai *f* (AmS fam) (alta sociedad) high society

jai alai *m* jai alai, pelota

jaiba *f* (AmL) crab; (de río) freshwater crab

jaibol *m* (Méx) highball (AmE), whisky and soda (BrE)

jalada *f* (Méx fam) **1** (tirón) pull, tug **2** (tontería, exageración): **esas son puras ~s** that's a load of garbage (AmE) *o* (BrE) rubbish (colloq)

jalado¹ -da *adj* **1** (AmC, Col, Méx fam) (borracho) tight (colloq) **2** (Méx fam) (descabellado) crazy (colloq) **3** (Per fam) ‹*ojos*› slanting *m,f* (Per fam) oriental-looking person

jalado² *m* (Per arg) (Educ) fail

jalador -dora *adj* **1** (Méx fam) **(a)** (trabajador) hardworking **(b)** (animoso) willing **(c)** (que atrae) ‹*oferta*› attractive; ‹*cantante/actor*› popular **2** (Per arg) ‹*profesor*› tough (colloq)

jalapeño *m* (Méx) jalapeño pepper

jalar [A1] *vt* **1 (a)** (AmL exc CS) (tirar de) to pull; **me jaló la manga** he pulled *o* tugged at my sleeve **(b)** (Méx) (agarrar y acercar) ‹*periódico/libro*› to pick up, take; ‹*silla*› to draw up **2** (Per arg) ‹*alumno*› to fail, flunk (esp AmE colloq) **3** (Per fam) (en automóvil, moto) to give ... a lift *o* ride ■ **~** *vi* **1** (AmL exc CS) (tirar) to pull; **~ DE algo** to pull sth; **~ *con algn*** (Méx fam) (llevarse bien) to get on *o* along well with sb **2 (a)** (Méx fam) (apresurarse) to hurry up, get a move on (colloq); **¡jálale!** hurry up! **(b)** (Col, Méx fam) (ir) to go; **jálale por el pan** go and get the bread **3** (Méx fam) «*motor/aparato*» to work; **mi coche no jalaba en la mañana** my car wouldn't start this morning; **¿cómo van los negocios? — jalando, jalando** how's business? — oh, not so bad (colloq) **5** (AmC fam) «*pareja*» to date, go out; «*persona*» **~ CON algn** to date sb, go out WITH sb

■ **jalarse** *v pron* **1** (Méx) (*enf*) ⇒ JALAR *vt* 1(b) **2** (Méx) (*enf*) **(a)** (irse) to go **(b)** (venir) to come **3** (Col, Méx fam) (emborracharse) to get tight (colloq)

jalea *f* jelly; **~ real** royal jelly

jaleo *m* (fam) **(a)** (alboroto, ruido) racket (colloq), row (colloq) **(b)** (confusión) muddle, mess; (desorden) mess; (problemas) hassle (colloq) **(c)** (actividad intensa): **hemos tenido mucho ~ en casa** everything's been very hectic at home; **con todo el ~ de la mudanza** with all the upheaval of the move **(d)** (riña) brawl

jallán *m* (AmC, Col) lout

jalón *m* **(a)** (AmL exc CS fam) (tirón) pull, yank; ***de un*** **~** in one go **(b)** (Méx) (tramo) stretch

jalonazo *m* (AmL exc CS fam) tug, yank; **el carro iba a ~s** the car jerked *o* lurched along

jalonear [A1] *vt* (Méx, Per fam) to tug (at) ■ **~** *vi* **(a)** (AmL exc CS fam) (dar tirones) to pull, tug **(b)** (AmC fam) (regatear) to haggle

jamaica *f* (Bot) hibiscus

Jamaica *f* Jamaica

jamaicano -na *adj/m,f* Jamaican

jamás *adv* ▶ 289 never; **~ volverá a suceder** it will never happen again; **nunca ~** never ever; **por** *or* **para siempre ~** for ever and ever

jamón *m* (Coc) ham; **~ serrano** ≈ Parma ham

jaña *f* (AmC fam) (compañera) girlfriend; (chica) girl

Japón *m*: *tb* **el ~** Japan

japonés[1] -nesa *adj/m,f* Japanese

japonés[2] *m* (idioma) Japanese

jaque *m* check; **~ mate** checkmate

jaqueca *f* migraine, severe headache

jarabe *m* **1** (Coc, Farm, Med) syrup; **~ para la tos** cough mixture *o* syrup **2** (Mús) *Mexican folk dance and music*

jarana *f* **1** (fam) **(a)** (bromas): **basta de ~** that's enough fun and games *o* fooling around (colloq) **(b)** (juerga): **salir de ~** to go out on the town *o* out partying (colloq) **2 (a)** (baile) *folk dance from southeast Mexico* **(b)** (Per) (fiesta) party (*with folk music*)

jaranero -ra *adj* (fam): **es muy ~** he's always out on the town *o* out partying (colloq)

jardín *m* **1** (con plantas) garden; **~ botánico** botanical garden; **~ zoológico** zoological garden, zoo; **~ de infancia** *or* **de niños** nursery school, kindergarten; **2 los jardines** *mpl* (en béisbol) the outfield; **~ central** center* field

jardinear [A1] *vi* **1** (en béisbol) to field **2** (Chi) (en el jardín) to do the gardening

jardinera *f* (para la ventana) window box; (con pedestal) jardinière

jardinería *f* gardening

jardinero -ra *m,f* **1** (persona) gardener **2** (Dep) outfielder

jareta *f* **(a)** (para pasar una cinta) casing; (de adorno) tuck **(b)** (AmC) (bragueta) fly

jaripeo *m*: *Mexican rodeo*

jarra *f* **1 (a)** (para servir) pitcher (AmE), jug (BrE) **(b)** (para beber) stein (AmE), tankard (BrE); ***en*** **~*s***: **con los brazos en ~s** (with) arms akimbo, hands on hips **2** (Méx fam) bender (colloq); **irse de ~** to go on a bender

jarro *m* **(a)** (para servir) pitcher (AmE), jug (BrE) **(b)** (AmS) (tazón) mug; (para cerveza) beer mug

jarrón *m* vase

jaspe *m* (piedra) jasper; (mármol) veined marble

jaspeado -da *adj* ‹*mármol*› veined; ‹*tela/lana*› flecked; ‹*plumaje/huevos*› speckled

jauja *f* (fam): **piensan que la universidad es ~** they think that university is a bed of roses; **¡esto es ~!** this is the life!

jaula *f* cage

jauría *f* (de perros) pack (of hounds)

jayán -yana *adj* (AmC fam) foul (colloq); **no seas ~** don't be a jerk *o* creep (colloq)

jazmín *m* jasmine

jazz /(d)ʒas/ *m* jazz

jebo -ba *m,f* (Ven arg) **(a)** (novio) (*m*) boyfriend; (*f*) girlfriend **(b) jeba** *f* (muchacha) chick (AmE colloq), bird (BrE colloq)

Jeep® /(d)ʒip/ *m* (*pl* **Jeeps**) Jeep®

jefatura *f* **1** (sede) headquarters (*sing o pl*) **2** (de partido) leadership

jefe -fa *m,f*, **jefe** *mf* **(a)** (superior) boss; **~ de estudios** director of studies; **~ de personal/ventas** personnel/sales manager; **~ de redacción** editor-in-chief **(b)** (de empresa) manager; (de sección) head; (de tribu) chief **(c)** (Pol) leader; **~ de Estado/gobierno** head of state/government

jején *m*: *small mosquito*

jengibre *m* ginger

jeque *m* sheik, sheikh

jerarca *mf* leader

jerarquía *f* **(a)** (organización) hierarchy **(b)** (categoría, rango) rank

jerez *m* sherry

jerga *f* **1 (a)** (de gremio, profesión) jargon; (de los adolescentes) slang **(b)** (galimatías) mumbo jumbo (colloq) **2** (Méx) (trapo) floorcloth

jergón *m* straw mattress

jeringa *f* (Med) syringe

jeringuilla *f* syringe

jeroglífico *m* (escritura) hieroglyphic, hieroglyph; (acertijo) rebus

jersey *m* (*pl* **-seys**) **(a)** /'ʒersi/ (AmL) (tela) jersey **(b)** /xer'sei/ (Esp) (prenda) sweater

Jerusalén *m* Jerusalem

Jesucristo Jesus Christ

jesuita *adj/m* Jesuit

Jesús **(a)** (Relig) Jesus **(b)** (*como interj*) **¡~!** (expresando — dolor, fatiga) heavens!; (— susto, sorpresa) good heavens!, good grief!; (cuando alguien estornuda) (Esp) bless you!

jet /'(d)ʒet/ *m* (*pl* **jets**) (Aviac) jet

jeta *f* (fam) **(a)** (cara) face, mug (colloq) **(b)** (AmL fam) (boca) trap (sl)

jet lag /'(d)ʒetlaɣ/ *m* jet lag

jet set /'(d)ʒetset/ *m or* (Esp) *f* jet set

jíbaro -ra *adj/m,f* Jivaro

jibia *f* cuttlefish

jícama *f* yam bean

jícara *f* **1** (Méx) (Bot) calabash **2 (a)** (Méx) (taza) (drinking) bowl **(b)** (Col, Méx) (vasija — de calabaza) gourd, calabash; (— de otro material) pot

jicote *m* (Méx) wasp

jicotera *f* **(a)** (Méx) (nido) wasp's nest **(b)** (ruido) row (colloq)

jilguero *m* goldfinch

jinete *mf* (Equ) (*m*) horseman, rider; (*f*) horsewoman, rider

jinetear [A1] *vt* **1** (Equ) (Chi) (montar) to ride **2** (Méx fam) ‹*dinero*› to speculate with

jirafa *f* (Zool) giraffe

jirón *m* **1** (de tela) shred; **hecho jirones** in tatters *o* shreds **2** (Per) (avenida) avenue, street

jitomate *m* (Méx) tomato

jo *interj* (Esp fam) (expresando — sorpresa) wow! (colloq); (— enfado, disgusto) damn it! (colloq)

jockey /'(d)ʒoki/ *mf* (*pl* **-ckeys**) jockey

jocoso -sa *adj* humorous, jocular

joda *f* (AmL fam) **(a)** (molestia) pain (colloq), drag (colloq) **(b)** (broma): **en ~** as a joke

joder[1] [E1] *vi* **1** (vulg) (copular) to screw (vulg), fuck (vulg) **2** (fam: en algunas regiones vulg) (molestar) to annoy (sl); **lo hace sólo por ~** he only does it to annoy ■ **~** *vt* **1** (vulg) (copular con) to screw (vulg), fuck (vulg) **2** (fam: en algunas regiones vulg) **(a)** (molestar) to bug (colloq) **(b)** (engañar) to rip ... off (colloq) **3** (fam: en algunas regiones vulg) ‹*televisor/reloj*› to bust (colloq), to fuck up (vulg); ‹*planes*› to mess up (colloq), to screw up (vulg); **~ *la*** (fam) to screw up (vulg)

■ **joderse** *v pron* (fam: en algunas regiones vulg) **(a)** (jorobarse): **y si no te gusta, te jodes** and if you don't like it, that's tough! (colloq) **(b)** ‹*espalda*› to do ... in (colloq); ‹*hígado/estómago*› to mess up (colloq) **(c)** «*planes*» to get screwed up (vulg), fucked up (vulg); **se ha jodido el motor** the engine's had it (colloq)

joder[2] *interj* (esp Esp fam: en algunas regiones vulg) (expresando — fastidio) for heaven's sake! (colloq), for fuck's sake! (vulg); (— asombro) good grief!, holy shit! (vulg)

jodido -da *adj* **1** (fam: en algunas regiones vulg) **(a)** [SER] (difícil) ‹*trabajo*› tricky, tough (colloq); ‹*persona*› difficult, pain in the neck (colloq) **(b)** (*delante del n*) (maldito) damn (colloq), fucking (vulg) **(c)** [SER] (AmL) (exigente) demanding, tough (colloq) **2** [ESTAR] (fam: en algunas regiones vulg) **(a)** (estropeado) ‹*ascensor/radio*› bust (colloq), fucked (vulg) **(b)** (enfermo) in a bad way (colloq) **(c)** (deprimido) down (colloq) **3** [SER] (Col fam) (astuto) sharp

jogging /(d)ʒoɣin/ *m* **(a)** (Dep, Ocio) jogging; **hacer ~** to jog, go jogging **(b)** (RPl) (Indum) jogging suit

jojoto *m* (Ven) corn (AmE), maize (BrE)

jolgorio *m* revelry, merrymaking; **irse de ~** (fam) to go out on the town *o* out partying (colloq)

jonrón *m* (AmL) home run

Jordania *f* Jordan

jordano -na *adj/m,f* Jordanian

jornada *f* **1 (a)** (period) (día) day **(b)** (Rels Labs) *tb* **~ laboral** working day; **trabajar ~ completa/media ~** to work full-time/part-time; **~ continuada** *or* **intensiva** *working day with no break for lunch so as to finish earlier*; **~ partida** split shift (*working day with long break for lunch*); **~ única** (Chi) ⇒ JORNADA CONTINUADA **2** (esp Col) (viaje) journey

jornal *m* day's wages (*pl*), day's pay; **trabajar a ~** to be paid on a daily basis

jornalero -ra *m,f* day laborer*

joroba *f* **(a)** (de persona, camello) hump **(b)** (fam) (molestia) drag (colloq), pain in the neck (colloq)

jorobado -da *adj* **1** (giboso) hunchbacked **2** (fam) **(a)** (enfermo, delicado): **todavía anda algo jorobada** she's still a bit low (colloq); **está ~ del estómago** his stomach's been playing (him) up (colloq) **(b)** (sin dinero) broke (colloq) **(c)** ‹*asunto*› tricky ■ *m,f* hunchback

jorobar [A1] *vt* (fam) **(a)** (molestar) to bug (colloq) **(b)** (malograr) to ruin, spoil ■ **~** *vi* (fam) (molestar) to annoy; **lo que más me joroba es** ... what really bugs *o* gets me is ... (colloq)

■ **jorobarse** *v pron* (fam) **(a)** (aguantarse): **y si no te gusta, te jorobas** and if you don't like it, that's tough (colloq) **(b)** (dañarse) ‹*hígado/estómago*› to mess up (colloq); ‹*espalda*› to do ... in (colloq) **(c)** «*plan*» to be scuppered (colloq); «*fiesta*» to be ruined

jorongo *m* (Méx) poncho

joropo *m*: *Colombian/Venezuelan folk dance*

jota *f* **(a)** (letra) *name of the letter* j; ***ni* ~** (fam): **no entiendo/no veo ni ~** I don't understand/I can't see a thing; **no sabe ni ~** he doesn't have a clue (colloq) **(b)** (Mús) jota (*Aragonese folk song/dance*) **(c)** (en naipes) jack

joven *adj* young ■ *mf* (*m*) young person, young man; (*f*) young person, young woman; **de aspecto ~** youthful looking; **los jóvenes de hoy** ... young people today ...

jovial *adj* jovial, cheerful

joya *f* **1** (alhaja) piece of jewelry*; **~s** jewelry *o* jewels; **~ de fantasía** piece *o* item of costume jewelry **2** (persona) gem, treasure; (cosa): **este coche es una ~** this is a real gem of a car

joyería *f* (tienda) jeweler's*

joyero -ra *m,f* **(a)** (persona) jeweler* **(b) joyero** *m* (estuche) jewelry* box, jewel case

joystick /'(d)ʒojstik/ *m* joystick

jr (en Perú) (= **jirón**) street

Jr. (= **Júnior**) Jr

juanete *m* (Med) bunion

jubilación *f* (retiro) retirement; (pensión) pension; **~ anticipada/forzosa** early/compulsory retirement

jubilado -da *adj* retired ■ *m,f* pensioner, retired person (*o* worker *etc*)

jubilar [A1] *vi* (Andes) to retire

■ **jubilarse** *v pron* (del trabajo) to retire

júbilo *m* jubilation

judaísmo *m* Judaism

judía *f* (Esp) bean; **~ verde** green bean

judicial *adj* judicial ■ *m* (Méx) policeman

judío -día *adj* **1** (Relig, Sociol) Jewish **2** (fam & pey) (tacaño) miserly, tightfisted (colloq) ■ *m,f* Jewish person, Jew

judo /'(d)ʒuðo/ *m* judo

juega, juegas, etc *see* JUGAR

juego *m* **1 (a)** (en general) play; ***entrar en*** ~ «*jugador*» to come on; «*factores/elementos*» to come into play; ***estar en*** ~ to be at stake; ~ ***limpio/sucio*** fair/foul play; ***seguirle el*** ~ ***a algn*** to go *o* play along with sb **(b)** (por dinero): **el** ~ gambling **(c)** (fam) (maniobras, estratagemas) game (colloq) **(d)** (en naipes) hand, cards (*pl*) **2 (a)** (de mesa, de niños, etc) game; ~ **de azar** game of chance; ~ **de manos** conjuring trick; ~ **de palabras** pun, play on words; ~**s malabares** juggling; **J**~**s Olímpicos** Olympic Games (*pl*), Olympics (*pl*) **(b)** (AmL) (en la feria) fairground attraction, ride **(c)** (en tenis) game **(d) juegos** *mpl* (columpios, etc) swings, slide, etc (*in a children's playground*); **3** (conjunto) set; **un** ~ **de cuchillos/llaves** a set of knives/keys; **un** ~ **de platos** a dinner service; ~ **de café/té** coffee/tea set; ~ **de escritorio** desk set; ***hacer*** ~ «*colores/cortinas*» to go together; **te hace** ~ **con los zapatos** it goes with your shoes

juerga *f* (fam): **ir de** ~ to go out on the town *o* out partying (colloq); **organizar una** ~ to have *o* throw a party

juerguista *mf* (fam) reveller

jueves *m* ▶ **193** (*pl* ~) Thursday; *para ejemplos ver* LUNES; **J**~ **Santo** Maundy Thursday

juez *mf*, **juez -za** *m,f* **(a)** (Der) judge **(b)** (Dep) referee; ~ **de banda** *or* **línea** (en fútbol, tenis) (*m*) linesman; (*f*) lineswoman; (en fútbol americano, rugby) line judge

jugada *f* **(a)** (con pelota — individual) move; (— entre varios) play **(b)** (en ajedrez, damas, etc) move; ***hacerle una (mala)*** ~ ***a algn*** to play a (dirty) trick on sb

jugado -da *adj* (Col, Méx) experienced

jugador -dora *m,f* (Dep) player; (en naipes, juegos de mesa) player; (que juega habitualmente por dinero) gambler

jugar [A15] *vi* **1 (a)** (en general) to play; ~ A **algo** to play sth; ~ **a la pelota** to play ball; ~ **al fútbol** (Esp, RPl) to play football; ~ **a las muñecas** to play with dolls; ~ ***limpio/sucio*** to play fair/dirty **(b)** (en ajedrez, damas) to move; (en naipes) to play; (en otros juegos) to play; **me tocaba** ~ **a mí** it was my turn/move/go **(c)** (apostar fuerte) to gamble **2 jugar con (a)** ‹*persona/sentimientos*› to play with, toy with **(b)** (manejar) ‹*colores/luz/palabras*› to play with ■ ~ *vt* **1 (a)** ‹*partido/carta*› to play **(b)** (AmL exc RPl) ‹*tenis/fútbol/ajedrez*› to play **2** (apostar) ~ **algo** A **algo** to bet sth ON sth **3** ‹*rol/papel*› to play

■ **jugarse** *v pron* **(a)** (gastarse en el juego) ‹*sueldo*› to gamble (away) **(b)** (arriesgar) ‹*reputación/vida*› to risk, put … at risk; ~**se el pellejo** (fam) to risk one's neck (colloq) **(c)** (apostarse) (*recipr*): **nos jugamos una comida** we bet a meal on it

jugarreta *f* (fam) dirty trick (colloq); **hacerle una** ~ **a algn** to play a dirty trick on sb

juglar *m* minstrel, jongleur

jugo *m* (líquido) juice; ~ **de tomate** tomato juice

jugoso -sa *adj* **(a)** ‹*fruta/carne*› juicy **(b)** ‹*historia/anécdota*› colorful*; ‹*chisme*› juicy **(c)** ‹*artículo/guión*› meaty **(d)** ‹*negocio*› lucrative, profitable

juguera *f* (CS) (para hacer jugos) juicer

juguete *m* toy; **un tren de** ~ a toy train

juguetear [A1] *vi* to play

juguetería *f* (tienda) toy store; (ramo) toy trade *o* business

juguetón -tona *adj* playful

juicio *m* **1** (facultad) judgment; **no está en su sano** ~ he's not in his right mind; ***perder el*** ~ to go out of one's mind **2** (prudencia, sensatez) sense **3** (opinión) opinion; **a mi** ~ in my opinion, to my mind; **lo dejo a tu** ~ I'll leave it up to you; ~ **de valor** value judgment **4** (Der) trial; **llevar a** ~ **a algn** to take sb to court; **ir a** ~ to go to court; ~ **civil/criminal** civil/criminal proceedings (*pl*); **el J**~ **Final** (Relig) the Final Judgment

juicioso -sa *adj* sensible

jul. (= **julio**) Jul

julepe *m* **1** (Jueg) *card game similar to whist* **2** (AmS fam) (susto) fright; **le da** ~ **la oscuridad** she's terrified of the dark

julia *f* (Méx fam) Black Maria (colloq)

julio *m* ▶ **193** (mes) July; *para ejemplos ver* ENERO

jumbo /'(d)ʒumbo/ *m* jumbo jet

jun. (= **junio**) Jun

junco *m* **1** (planta) rush, reed **2** (Náut) *tb* ~ **chino** junk

jungla *f* jungle

junio *m* ▶ **193** June; *para ejemplos ver* ENERO

júnior /'(d)ʒunjo(r)/ *adj inv* ‹*equipo/categoría*› junior (*before n*), youth (*before n*) (BrE) ■ *mf* (*pl* ~**s**) **(a)** (Dep): **los** ~**s** the juniors **(b)** (el más joven, el hijo) Junior ■ *m* **(a)** (Chi) (en oficina) office junior **(b)** (Méx) (hijo de papá) rich kid (colloq)

junta *f* **1 (a)** (comité, comisión) board, committee; (de empresa) board; (reunión) meeting; ~ **directiva** board of directors **(b)** (de militares) junta **(c)** (gobierno regional) *autonomous government in some regions of Spain* **2** (Mec) (acoplamiento) joint; (para cerrar herméticamente) gasket

juntar [A1] *vt* **(a)** (unir) ‹*pies/manos/camas*› to put … together **(b)** (reunir) ‹*fichas/piezas*› to collect up, gather together; ‹*dinero*› to save (up); ~ **sellos** (esp AmL) to collect stamps **(c)** (cerrar) ‹*puerta*› to push … to

■ **juntarse** *v pron* **1** «*personas*» **(a)** (acercarse) to move *o* get closer together **(b)** (reunirse) to get together; ~**se con algn** to join sb, meet up with sb **(c)** (como pareja) to live together; **se volvieron a** ~ they got back together again **2 (a)** «*desgracias/sucesos*» to come together **(b)** «*carreteras/conductos*» to meet, join

junto -ta *adj* **1 (a)** (unido, reunido) together; **nunca había visto tanto dinero** ~**/tanta gente junta** I'd never seen so much money/so many people in one place **(b)** (*pl*) (cercanos, contiguos) together; **están demasiado** ~**s** they're too close together; **bailaban muy** ~**s** they were dancing very close **2** (*como adv*) **(a)** ‹*estudiar/trabajar/vivir*› together **(b)** ‹*llegar/saltar*› at the same time; **¡ahora todos** ~**s!** all together now! **3** (*en locs*) **junto a** next to; **junto con** (together) with

juntura *f* join, joint

Júpiter *m* Jupiter

jurado *m* (cuerpo) (Der) jury; (de concurso) panel of judges, jury ■ *mf* (persona) (Der) juror, member of a jury; (de concurso) judge, member of the jury

juramento *m* oath; **prestar ~** to take an oath; **tomarle ~ a algn** (Der) to swear sb in; **bajo ~** under *o* on oath

jurar [A1] *vt* to swear; **juró su cargo el 22 de julio** he was sworn in on July 22; **~on (la) bandera** *or* (AmL) **a la bandera** they swore allegiance to the flag; **juró vengarse** he swore to get his revenge; **no lo entiendo, te lo juro** I honestly don't understand ■ **~** *vi* **(a)** (maldecir) to curse, swear **(b)** (prometer): **~ en falso** *or* **vano** to commit perjury

jurídico -ca *adj* legal (*before n*)

jurisdicción *f* jurisdiction

justicia *f* **(a)** (equidad) justice; **pedir ~** to call for justice; **en ~** in all fairness, to be fair; **la ~ de su decisión** the fairness of her decision; **nunca se le ha hecho ~ como escritor** he has never received due recognition as a writer **(b)** (sistema, leyes): **la ~** the law; **huir de la ~** to flee from justice *o* the law; **tomarse la ~ por su mano** to take the law into one's own hands

justificable *adj* justifiable

justificación *f* (disculpa, razón) justification; (Der) (prueba) proof

justificante *m* receipt; **~ de pago** receipt, proof of payment; **~ de asistencia** certificate of attendance; **~ de ausencia** note explaining reasons for one's absence

justificar [A2] *vt* **(a)** (en general) to justify; **eso no justifica su actitud** that does not justify her attitude; **sus sospechas no estaban justificadas** his suspicions were not justified; **trabajar por tan poco no se justifica** it isn't worth working for so little **(b)** (disculpar) ‹*persona*› to find *o* make excuses for ■ **justificarse** *v pron* to justify oneself, excuse oneself

justo[1] -ta *adj* **1** ‹*persona/castigo/sociedad*› just, fair; ‹*causa*› just **2 (a)** (exacto) ‹*medida/peso/cantidad*› exact; **me dio el dinero ~** he gave me the right money; **son 5.000 pesetas justas** that's 5,000 pesetas exactly; **buscaba la palabra justa** he was searching for exactly *o* just the right word **(b)** (apenas suficiente): **tener lo ~ para vivir** to have just enough to live on; **andan muy ~s de dinero** they're very short of money; **teníamos las sillas justas** we had just enough chairs for everybody **(c)** (ajustado): **estos zapatos me quedan demasiado ~s** these shoes are too tight (for me)

justo[2] *adv* **(a)** (exactamente) just; **~ a tiempo** just in time; **es ~ lo que quería** it's just *o* exactly what I wanted; **vive ~ al lado** he lives just *o* right next door; **y ~ hoy que pensaba salir** and today of all days, when I was planning to go out **(b)** (ajustado): **con el sueldo que gana vive muy ~** he only just manages to scrape by on what he earns; **me cupo todo, pero muy ~** I managed to get everything in, but only just

juvenil *adj* ‹*moda*› young; ‹*aspecto*› youthful; ‹*categoría/competición*› junior (*before n*), youth (*before n*) (BrE) ■ *mf* junior; **los ~es** the juniors

juventud *f* (edad) youth; (gente joven) youth; **¡esta ~ de hoy!** young people today!

juzgado *m* court

juzgar [A3] *vt* **(a)** (Der) ‹*acusado*› to try; ‹*caso*› to try, judge **(b)** ‹*conducta/persona*› to judge; **~ mal a algn** to misjudge sb **(c)** (considerar) to consider; **a ~ por las apariencias** judging by appearances

K, k *f* (*read as* /ka/) *the letter* K, k

ka *f*: *name of the letter* k

kaleidoscopio *m* kaleidoscope

karate, kárate *m* karate

kárdex *m* (archivo) file; (mueble) filing cabinet

kart *m* (*pl* **karts**) kart

Kenia, Kenya *f* Kenya

kermesse /ker'mes/ *f* (CS, Méx) charity fair, kermess (AmE), fête (BrE)

ketchup /'katʃup 'katsup/ *m* ketchup, catsup (AmE)

Kg. (= **kilogramo**) kg

kilo *m* ▶ 322 kilogram, kilo

kilogramo *m* ▶ 322 kilogram

kilometraje *m* ≈ mileage

kilométrico -ca *adj* (fam) ‹*pasillo*› endless; **una cola kilométrica** a line (AmE) *o* (BrE) queue a mile long

kilómetro *m* ▶ 681 kilometer*

kilovatio *m* kilowatt

kimono *m* kimono

kindergarten *m* (*pl* **~** *or* **-tens**) kindergarten

kiosco, kiosko *m* **(a)** (de periódicos) newsstand, newspaper kiosk; (de refrescos) drinks stand; (de helados) ice-cream stand; (de caramelos, tabaco) kiosk **(b)** (para orquesta) bandstand

kiwi /'kiwi/ *m* **(a)** (Bot) kiwifruit, Chinese gooseberry **(b)** (Zool) kiwi

Kleenex®, kleenex /'klineks/ *m* (*pl* **~**) tissue

Km. (= **kilómetro**) km

K.O. KO; **lo dejó ~** he knocked him out

koala *m* koala (bear)

kuchen /'kuxen/ *m* (Chi) (Coc) tart

Kurdistán *m* Kurdistan

kurdo -da *adj* Kurdish ■ *m,f* Kurd

Kuwait *m* Kuwait

Kuwaití *adj/mf* Kuwaiti

L, l *f* (*read as* /'ele/) *the letter* L, l

l. (= **litro**) l, liter*

la *art* ▶ 39 ■ *pron pers* **(a)** (referido — a ella) her; (— a usted) you; (— a cosa) it; **no ~ conozco** I don't know her; **¿~ atienden?** can I help you?; **yo se ~ llevo** I'll take it to him **(b)** (*impers*) you, one (frml) ■ *m* (nota) A; (en solfeo) la

laberinto *m* (de caminos, pasillos) maze, labyrinth; (en jardín, parque) maze

labia *f* (fam) gift of the gab (colloq)

labio *m* ▶ 123 lip; **leer los ~s** to lip-read; **sin dispegar los ~s** without uttering a single word

labor *f* **(a)** (trabajo) work; **una ~ de equipo** teamwork; **~es domésticas** housework; **~es agrícolas** *or* **del campo** farm work **(b)** (de coser, bordar) needlework; (de punto) knitting

laborable *adj* **(a)** ‹*día*› working (*before n*) **(b)** ‹*tierra*› arable

laboral *adj* ‹*problemas/conflictos*› labor* (*before n*), work (*before n*); ⇒ ACCIDENTE

laboratorio *m* laboratory

laborioso -sa *adj* ‹*persona*› hardworking, industrious; ‹*abejas*› industrious; ‹*tarea*› laborious

laborista *adj* Labour (*before n*) ■ *mf* member of the Labour Party

labrador -dora *m,f* (Agr) (propietario) farmer; (trabajador) farmworker

labrar [A1] *vt* **1** (Agr) ‹*tierra*› to work **2** ‹*madera*› to carve; ‹*piedra*› to cut; ‹*cuero*› to tool, work; ‹*metales*› to work

■ **labrarse** *v pron* (forjarse): **~se un porvenir** to carve out a future for oneself

labriego -ga *m,f* farmworker

laburar [A1] *vi* (CS fam) to work

laca *f* (resina) lac, shellac; (barniz) lacquer; (para el pelo) hairspray

lacear [A1] *vt* (CS) ‹*ganado*› to lasso

lacio -cia *adj* ‹*pelo*› straight; ‹*cuerpo*› limp, weak

lacónico -ca *adj* laconic

lacrar [A1] *vt* (con cera) to seal

lacre *adj* ▶ 97 (AmL) bright-red; (Chi) red ■ *m* sealing wax

lactancia *f* (secreción de leche) lactation; **durante el período de ~** while breastfeeding

lácteo -tea *adj* dairy (*before n*), milk (*before n*)

ladeado -da *adj*: **el cuadro está ~** the picture is on a slant *o* is askew; **llevaba el sombrero ~** he wore his hat at an angle; **con la cabeza ladeada** with his head tilted to one side

ladear [A1] *vt* ‹*cabeza*› to tilt ... to one side; ‹*objeto*› to tilt

■ **ladearse** *v pron* (inclinarse) to lean to one side

ladera *f* hillside, mountainside; **la ~ norte** the northern slope *o* side

ladino -na *adj* **1** (taimado) sly, cunning **2** (AmC, Méx) **(a)** (mestizo) mestizo, of mixed race **(b)** (hispanohablante) Spanish-speaking (*often used to refer to Indians who adopt Spanish ways*) **3** (Méx fam) (agudo) high-pitched, piercing ■ *m,f* (AmC, Méx) **(a)** (mestizo) mestizo, person of mixed race **(b)** (hispanohablante) Spanish-speaking Indian

lado *m* **1 (a)** (en general) side; **está en el ~ derecho** it is on the right-hand side; **hacerse a un ~** to move to one side; **echarse a un ~** «*coche*» to swerve; «*persona*» to move over; **ponlas a un ~** set them aside; **¿de qué ~ estás?** whose side are you on?; **cambiar de ~** (Dep) to change sides (AmE) *o* (BrE) ends; **ver el ~ positivo de las cosas** to look on the bright side of things; **por el ~ de mi padre** on my father's side (of the family) **(b)** (de papel, moneda, tela) side **2** (sitio, lugar): **a/en/por todos ~s** everywhere; **en algún ~** somewhere; **en cualquier ~** anywhere; **ir de un ~ para otro** to run around **3** (*en locs*) **al lado**: **viven en la casa de al ~** they live next door; **los vecinos de al ~** the next-door neighbors; **al lado de algn/algo** (contiguo a) next to sb/sth, beside sb/sth; (en comparación con) compared to sb/sth; **de lado** ‹*meter/colocar*› sideways; ‹*tumbarse/dormir*› on one's side; **de ~ a lado** ‹*extenderse/cruzar*› from one side to the other; **por otro lado** (en cambio) on the other hand; (además) apart from anything else; **por un ~ ..., pero por otro ~** ... on the one hand ..., but on the other hand ...; ***dejar algo de ~*** to leave sth aside *o* to one side; ***ir cada uno por su ~***: **cada uno se fue por su ~** they went their separate ways

ladrar [A1] *vi* **(a)** «*perro*» to bark **(b)** (fam) «*persona*» to yell (colloq), to bark (colloq)

ladrido *m* bark; **~s** barking

ladrillo *m* brick; **(de) color ~** brick-red

ladrón -drona *m,f* **1** (de bolsos, coches) thief; (de bancos) bank robber; (de casas) burglar **2 ladrón** *m* (Elec) adaptor

ladronzuelo -la *m,f* petty thief

lagartija *f* wall lizard

lagarto *m* **1** (Zool) lizard **2** (Col fam) (persona) crawler (colloq)

lago *m* lake

lágrima *f* (Fisiol) tear; **le caían las ~s** tears were running down her face; **se le saltaron las ~s** it brought tears to his eyes; **~s de cocodrilo** crocodile tears (*pl*); ***llorar a ~ viva*** to cry one's eyes *o* heart out

lagrimal *m* **(a)** (extremo del ojo) corner of the eye **(b)** *tb* **conducto ~** tear duct

laguna *f* **1** (de agua dulce) lake, pool; (de agua salada) lagoon **2 (a)** (en estudio, artículo) gap **(b)** (en la memoria) memory lapse

laico -ca *adj* secular, lay (*before n*) ■ *m,f* (*m*) layman, layperson; (*f*) laywoman, layperson

laísmo *m*: *use of* LA/LAS *instead of* LE/LES (*as in* LA/LAS DIJE QUE NO), *common in certain regions of Spain but not acceptable to most speakers*

laja *f* (AmS) slab

lama *m* lama ■ *f* (AmL) (musgo) moss; (verdín) green slime; (moho) mold*

lambetear [A1] *vt* (Col, Méx, Ven) to lick

lambiscón -cona *m,f* (Méx fam) bootlicker (colloq)

lambisquear [A1] *vt* **(a)** (Col) (lamer) to lick **(b)** (Méx fam) (lisonjear) to suck up to (colloq)

lamentable *adj* **(a)** ‹*conducta/error/suceso*› deplorable, terrible **(b)** ‹*pérdida*› sad; ‹*estado/aspecto*› pitiful; ‹*error*› regrettable

lamentar [A1] *vt* to regret; **lamento molestarlo** I'm sorry to disturb you; **lamentamos tener que comunicarle que** ... (frml) we regret to have to inform you that ...; **lo lamento mucho** I am very sorry

■ **lamentarse** *v pron* to complain, to grumble (colloq)

lamento *m* **(a)** (quejido — por un dolor físico) groan; (— por tristeza) wail **(b)** (elegía) lament

lamer [E1] *vt* «*persona/animal*» to lick

lámina *f* **1** (hoja, plancha) sheet **2** (Impr) **(a)** (plancha, ilustración) plate; (estampa) picture card **(b)** (Educ) wall chart

laminar [A1] *vt* to laminate, roll

lámpara *f* lamp; **~ de pie/mesa** standard/table lamp

lamparín *m* (Per) kerosene lamp

lamparita *f* (RPl) (light) bulb

lampiño -ña *adj* (sin barba) smooth-faced; (con poco vello) with little body hair

lana *f* **1** (material) wool; (vellón, pelambre) fleece; **~ virgen** new wool; **una bufanda de ~** a wool *o* woolen scarf **2** (AmL fam) (dinero) dough (sl); **tienen mucha ~** they're loaded (colloq)

lanceta *f* **(a)** (Med) lancet **(b)** (Andes, Méx) (aguijón) sting

lancha *f* (barca grande) launch, cutter; (bote) motorboat; **~ fuera borda** (outboard) launch; **~ neumática** inflatable (dinghy); **~ salvavidas** lifeboat

langosta *f* (crustáceo) lobster; (insecto) locust

langostino *m* (grande) king prawn; (pequeño) prawn; **~ de río** crayfish, crawfish (esp AmE)

langüetear [A1] *vt* (Chi) to lick

languidecer [E3] *vi* «*persona*» to languish (liter); «*entusiasmo/conversación*» to flag

lánguido -da *adj* **(a)** (débil) listless, weak **(b)** ‹*mirada/aspecto*› languid

lanolina *f* lanolin

lanudo -da *adj* long-haired, shaggy

lanza *f* (arma — en las lides) lance; (— arrojadiza) spear ■ *m* (Chi) (delincuente) pickpocket, thief

lanzacohetes *m* (*pl* ~) rocket launcher

lanzado -da *adj* **1** [SER] (fam) (precipitado) impulsive, impetuous; (decidido, atrevido) forward **2** (fam) (rápido): **ir ~** to shoot along (colloq); **pasar ~** to shoot past

lanzador -dora *m,f* (Dep) (de disco, jabalina) thrower; (en béisbol) pitcher; **~ de bala** *or* (Esp) **de peso** shot-putter

lanzamiento *m* **1 (a)** (de objetos, pelota) throwing; (de misil, torpedo) launch; (de bomba) dropping **(b)** (de cohete, satélite) launch **(c)** (Dep) (de disco, jabalina) throw; (de bala) put; (en béisbol) pitch; **~ de bala** *or* (Esp) **de peso** shot put; **~ de disco/jabalina** discus/javelin throwing **2** (de producto, libro) launch, launching **3** (CS) (Der) *tb* **orden de ~** eviction order

lanzamisiles *adj inv* missile-launching (*before n*) ■ *m* (*pl* ~) missile launcher

lanzar [A4] *vt* **1 (a)** ‹*pelota/objetos/jabalina*› to throw; (en béisbol) to pitch **(b)** ‹*misil/satélite*› to launch; ‹*bomba*› to drop **2** ‹*producto/libro*› to launch **3 (a)** ‹*ofensiva/ataque/crítica*› to launch **(b)** ‹*mirada*› to shoot, give; ‹*indirecta*› to drop; ‹*grito*› to give; **lanzó un grito de dolor** he cried out in pain ■ ~ *vi* (en béisbol) to pitch

■ **lanzarse** *v pron* **(a)** (*refl*) (arrojarse) to throw oneself; **~se al agua/al vacío** to leap into the water/the void; **~se en paracaídas** to parachute; (en una emergencia) to bale out **(b)** (abalanzarse, precipitarse): **~se sobre algo/algn** to pounce on sth/sb; **~se al ataque** to attack

lapa *f* **(a)** (molusco) limpet **(b)** (Ven) (mamífero) paca **(c)** (AmC) (ave) macaw

lapicera *f* (CS) pen; **~ fuente** *or* **estilográfica** (CS) fountain pen

lapicero *m* **(a)** (portaminas) automatic pencil (AmE), propelling pencil (BrE) **(b)** (Esp) (lápiz) pencil **(c)** (AmC, Per) (bolígrafo) ballpoint pen

lápida *f* (en tumba) tombstone, gravestone; (losa conmemorativa) stone plaque

lapislázuli *m* lapis lazuli

lápiz *m* (de madera) pencil; (portaminas) automatic pencil (AmE), propelling pencil (BrE); **con** *or* **a ~** in pencil; **lápices de colores** crayons (*pl*); **~ de labios** lipstick; **~ de ojos** eye pencil; **~ de pasta** (Chi) ballpoint pen

lapso *m* **(a)** (de tiempo) space **(b)** (error, olvido) ⇨ LAPSUS

lapsus *m* (*pl* ~) (error) slip, blunder; (olvido): **tuve un pequeño ~** it slipped my mind

laptop *m* laptop (computer)

larga *f* **(a)** (largo plazo): **a la ~** in the long run; ***darle ~s a algn/algo*** to put sb/sth off **(b)** (Auto) high beam (AmE), full *o* main beam (BrE)

largar [A3] *vt* **1 (a)** (Náut) ‹*amarras/cabo*› to let out, pay out **(b)** (RPl) (soltar, dejar caer) to let ... go **2** ‹*discurso/sermón*› to give; ‹*palabrota/insulto*› to let fly **3** (fam) (despedir) to fire, to give ... the boot (colloq); ‹*novio*› to ditch **5** (CS, Méx) (Dep) ‹*pelota*› to throw; ‹*carrera*› to start

■ **largarse** *v pron* **(a)** (fam) (irse) to beat it (colloq); **¡yo me largo!** I'm taking off! (AmE), I'm off! (BrE) (colloq) **(b)** (CS fam) (empezar) to start, get going (colloq); **~se A hacer algo** to start to do sth, to start doing sth

largavistas *m* (*pl* ~) (CS) binoculars (*pl*)

largo¹ -ga *adj* **(a)** (en general) long; **me queda largo** it's too long (for me); **es muy ~ de contar** it's a long story; **un tren de ~ recorrido** a long-distance train **(b)** (*en locs*) **a lo largo** ‹*cortar/partir*› lengthways; **a lo largo de** (de camino, río) along; (de jornada, novela) throughout; (de una semana, vida) in the course of; **de largo** ‹*vestirse*› to wear a long skirt/dress; *ver tb* PASAR I 1(a); ***va para ~*** (fam) it's going to be a while

largo² *m* **(a)** (longitud) length; **¿cuánto mide de ~?** how long is it? **(b)** (en natación) lap (AmE), length (BrE) ■ *interj* (fam) *tb* **¡~ de aquí!** get out of here!

largometraje *m* feature film, full-length film

larguero *m* **(a)** (Arquit, Const) (viga) crossbeam; (de puerta) jamb **(b)** (de cama) side **(c)** (Dep) crossbar

larguirucho -cha *adj* (fam) gangling (*before n*)

laringe *f* larynx

laringitis *f* laryngitis

larva *f* larva, grub

lasaña *f* lasagna, lasagne

lascivo -va *adj* lascivious, lustful

láser *m* laser

lástima *f* **(a)** (pena) shame, pity; **¡qué ~!** what a shame *o* pity!; **me da ~ tirarlo** it seems a pity *o* shame to throw it out **(b)** (compasión): **sentir ~ por algn** to feel sorry for sb; **digno de ~** worthy of compassion

lastimadura *f* (AmL) graze

lastimar [A1] *vt* to hurt

■ **lastimarse** *v pron* (*refl*) (esp AmL) to hurt oneself; ‹*dedo/rodillas*› to hurt

lastimero -ra *adj* pitiful

lastre *m* **(a)** (de buque, globo) ballast **(b)** (carga, estorbo) burden

lata *f* **1 (a)** (hojalata) tin **(b)** (envase) can, tin (BrE); **sardinas en ~** canned *o* tinned sardines **(c)** (para galletas, etc) tin **2** (fam) (pesadez) nuisance, pain (colloq); **¡qué ~!** what a nuisance!; ***dar (la) ~*** (fam) to be a nuisance; **¡deja ya de darme ~!** stop bugging *o* pestering me! (colloq)

latente *adj* latent

lateral *adj* ‹*puerta/salida/calle*› side (*before n*); ‹*línea/sucesión*› indirect, lateral ■ *m* (Dep) (poste) goalpost ■ *m or f* (Auto) (calle perpendicular) side street; (calle paralela) service road, frontage road (AmE) ■ *mf* (Dep) (alero) wing, winger; (defensa) left/right back

latido *m* (del corazón) heartbeat; (en la sien, una herida) throbbing

latifundio *m* large estate

latigazo *m* **(a)** (golpe) lash **(b)** (chasquido) crack of the whip

látigo *m* whip

latín *m* Latin

latino -na *adj* **(a)** ‹*literatura/gramática/pueblo*› Latin **(b)** (fam) (latinoamericano) Latin American ■ *m,f* **(a)** (español, italiano, etc) Latin **(b)** (fam) (latinoamericano) Latin American

Latinoamérica *f* Latin America

latinoamericano -na *adj/m,f* Latin American

latir [I1] *vi* **1** «*corazón*» to beat; «*vena*» to pulsate; «*herida/sien*» to throb **2 (a)** (Chi, Méx fam) (parecer) (+ *me/te/le etc*): **me late que no vendrá** I have a feeling *o* something tells me he isn't going to come **(b)** (Méx fam) (parecer bien, gustar) (+ *me/te/le etc*): **¿te late ir al cine?** do you feel like going to the movies?

latitud *f* (Astron, Geog) latitude; **la flora de otras ~es** the flora of other parts of the world

latón *m* **(a)** (Metal) brass **(b)** (RPl) (palangana) metal bowl

latonería *f* (Col) body shop

latoso -sa *adj* **(a)** (fam) (molesto) annoying, tiresome; **no seas ~** don't be such a pain (colloq) **(b)** (Andes fam) (aburrido) dull, boring ■ *m,f* **(a)** (fam) (pesado) pain (in the neck) (colloq) **(b)** (Andes fam) (aburrido) bore

laucha *f* (CS) mouse

laúd *m* lute

laurel *m* (árbol) laurel; (Coc) bay leaf

lava *f* lava

lavable *adj* washable

lavabo *m* **(a)** (pila) sink (AmE), washbasin (BrE) **(b)** ▶ **052** (retrete) toilet, bathroom; Ⓢ **lavabos** rest rooms (*in US*), toilets (*in UK*)

lavadero *m* **(a)** (habitación) utility room, laundry room; (pila) sink; (al aire libre) washing place **(b)** (RPl) (lavandería) laundry **(c)** (Col) (tina de lavar) washtub

lavado¹ -da *adj* **(a)** ‹*ropa/manos*› washed **(b)** (RPl fam) ‹*color*› (descolorido) washed-out; (muy claro) light; ‹*persona*› pale

lavado² *m* **1 (a)** (de ropa) wash, washing; (de coche) wash; **~ en seco** dry cleaning; **hacerle un ~ de cerebro a algn** to brainwash sb; **le hicieron un ~ de estómago** they pumped his stomach out **(b)** (ropa, tanda) wash **2** (AmL) (de dinero) laundering

lavadora *f* washing machine

lavamanos *m* sink (AmE), washbasin (BrE)

lavanda *f* lavender ■ *m* ▶ **97** lavander

lavandería *f* laundry; **~ automática** Laundromat® (AmE), launderette (BrE)

lavaplatos *mf* (*pl* ~) (persona) dishwasher ■ *m* (*pl*) **(a)** (máquina) dishwasher **(b)** (Andes) (fregadero) sink

lavar [A1] *vt* **1** ‹*ropa/coche*› to wash; ‹*suelo*› to mop; ‹*fruta/verdura*› to wash; **hay que ~lo en seco/a mano** it has to be dry-cleaned/hand-washed **2** (AmL) ‹*dinero*› to launder ■ **~** *vi* **(a)** (lavar ropa) to do

the laundry *o* (BrE) washing **(b)** (en peluquería): **~ y marcar** to shampoo and set
■ **lavarse** *v pron* **(a)** (*refl*) to have a wash; ‹*cara/manos*› to wash; ‹*dientes*› to clean, brush; **~se el pelo** *or* **la cabeza** to wash one's hair **(b)** (Col fam) (empaparse) to get soaked

lavarropas *m* (*pl* ~) (RPl) washing machine

lavatorio *m* **(a)** (CS) (lavamanos) sink (AmE), washbasin (BrE) **(b)** (Chi, Per) (palangana) washbowl (AmE), washbasin (BrE)

lavavajillas *m* (*pl* ~) (detergente) dishwashing liquid (AmE), washing-up liquid (BrE); (máquina) dishwasher

laxante *adj* laxative (*before n*) ■ *m* laxative

lazar [A4] *vt* (Méx) to rope, lasso

lazo *m* **1 (a)** (cinta) ribbon; (nudo decorativo) bow; **¿te hago un ~?** shall I tie it in a bow? **(b)** (Méx) (del matrimonio) *cord with which the couple are symbolically united during the wedding ceremony* **2 (a)** (Agr) lasso **(b)** (cuerda) (Col, Méx) rope; (para saltar) (Col) ⇒ CUERDA 1(b) **(c)** (para cazar) snare, trap **3** (vínculo) bond, tie

le *pron pers* **1** (como objeto indirecto): **~ dije la verdad** (a él) I told him the truth; (a ella) I told her the truth; (a usted) I told you the truth; **~ di otra mano de barniz** I gave it another coat of varnish; **~ robaron el dinero** they stole the money from him; **a este libro ~ faltan páginas** there are some pages missing from this book **2** (como objeto directo) (esp Esp) (referido — a él) him; (— a usted) you; **¿le conoces?** do you know him?; **hoy no ~ puedo recibir** I can't see him/you today

leal *adj* loyal, trusty; ‹*tropas*› loyal

lealtad *f* loyalty

leasing /'lisin/ *m* (contrato) lease; (sistema) leasing

lección *f* lesson; **no me supe la ~** I hadn't learned the lesson; **eso te servirá de ~** let that be a lesson to you

lechal *adj* suckling

leche *f* **1** (de madre, de vaca) milk; **~ descremada** *or* (Esp) **desnatada** skim milk (AmE), skimmed milk (BrE); **~ en polvo** powdered milk; **~ entera** whole milk, full-cream milk **2** (en cosmética) milk, lotion **3** (Esp vulg) (mal humor): **tiene una ~** ... he's got a foul temper; ***hacer algo con mala ~*** to do sth deliberately *o* to be nasty; ***tener mala ~*** to be bad-tempered **4** (Andes fam) (suerte) luck; **estar con** *or* **de ~** to be lucky

lechera *f* (para transportar) churn; (para servir) milk jug

lechería *f* dairy, creamery

lechero -ra *adj* **1 (a)** ‹*industria/vaca*› dairy (*before n*) **(b)** ‹*producción*› milk (*before n*) **2** (Col, Per fam) (afortunado) lucky ■ *m,f* (vendedor) (*m*) milkman; (*f*) milkwoman

lecho *m* **1** (liter) (cama) bed; **en su ~ de muerte** on her deathbed **2** (de río) bed; (capa, estrato) layer

lechón *m* (Coc) (cochinillo) suckling *o* sucking pig

lechosa *f* (AmC, Col, Ven) papaya

lechoso -sa *adj* ‹*líquido*› milky; ‹*piel*› pale

lechuga *f* lettuce

lechuza *f* owl

lectivo -va *adj* ‹*día*› school (*before n*); ‹*año*› academic (*before n*)

lector -tora *m,f* **(a)** (de libros, revistas) reader **(b)** (Esp) (Educ) foreign language assistant

lectura *f* **(a)** (acción) reading; **la ~ es su pasatiempo preferido** reading is her favorite pastime **(b)** (texto) reading matter; **~s para niños** reading material for children

leer [E13] *vt* **(a)** ‹*libro/texto*› to read; **~ los labios** to lip-read; **~le el pensamiento a algn** to read sb's mind **(b)** (Educ) ‹*tesis doctoral*› to defend **(c)** (Inf) to scan ■ ~ *vi* to read

legado *m* (Der) bequest, legacy

legal *adj* **1** (Der) **(a)** ‹*trámite/documentos*› legal **(b)** (lícito, permitido) lawful; **lo haré si es ~** I'll do it as long as it's within the law **2** (Col, Per arg) (estupendo) great (colloq)

legalización *f* (Der) (de droga, aborto) legalization; (de documento) authentication

legalizar [A4] *vt* (Der) ‹*droga/aborto*› to legalize; ‹*documento*› to authenticate

legaña *f* sleep; **tienes ~s en los ojos** you have (some) sleep in your eyes

legar [A3] *vt* (en testamento) to bequeath, leave

legendario -ria *adj* legendary

legible *adj* legible

legión *f* (Hist, Mil) legion; (multitud) crowd

legionario¹ -ria *adj* legionary

legionario² *m* (romano) legionary; (de otras asociaciones) legionnaire

legislación *f* legislation

legislar [A1] *vi* to legislate

legislatura *f* **(a)** (mandato) term (of office); (año parlamentario) session **(b)** (AmL) (cuerpo) legislature, legislative body

legítimo -ma *adj* **1** ‹*hijo*› legitimate; ‹*esposa*› lawful (*before n*); ‹*heredero*› rightful (*before n*); ‹*derechos/reclamación/representante*› legitimate; **en legítima defensa** in self-defense **2** ‹*cuero*› genuine, real; ‹*oro*› real

lego -ga *adj* **1** (seglar) lay (*before n*) **2** (ignorante): **soy ~ en la materia** I know nothing at all about the subject ■ *m,f* **(a)** (fiel laico) layperson **(b)** (religioso) (*m*) lay brother; (*f*) lay sister **(c)** (Col) (curandero) quack

legua *f* league

legumbre *f* (garbanzo, lenteja, etc) pulse, legume; (hortaliza) vegetable

leído -da *adj*: **ser muy ~** to be well-read

leísmo *m*: *use of* LE/LES *instead of* LO/LOS/LA/LAS (*as in* ESTE LIBRO NO TE LE PRESTO), *common in certain regions of Spain but not acceptable to most speakers*

lejanía *f* remoteness; **en la ~** in the distance

lejano -na *adj* **(a)** ‹*época/futuro*› distant; ‹*lugar*› remote, far-off; **el L~ Oriente** the Far East **(b)** ‹*pariente*› distant

lejía *f* bleach

lejísimos *adv* ‹*quedar/estar*› very far (away); **vive ~** she lives miles away

lejos *adv* **1 (a)** (en el espacio) far; **no está muy ~** it isn't very far; **queda ~ del centro** it's a long way from the center; **estaba ~ de imaginarme la verdad** I was far from guessing the truth **(b)**

(*en locs*) **a lo lejos** in the distance; **de lejos** from a distance; ***ir demasiado*** **~** to go too far; ***sin ir más*** **~** for example, for instance **(c)** (fam) (con mucho): **es ~** (CS) *o* (Col, Méx) **de ~** by far **2** (en el futuro) a long way off; **las vacaciones aún están ~s** the holidays are still a long way off

lelo -la *adj* (fam) (tonto) slow on the uptake; (pasmado) speechless

lema *m* (de insignia, de persona) motto; (de partido, anuncio publicitario) slogan

lempira *m* lempira (*Honduran unit of currency*)

lencería *f* lingerie

lengua *f* **1 (a)** ▶ **123** (Anat) tongue; **se me traba la ~** I get tongue-tied (colloq); ***irse de la ~*** *or* ***írsele la ~ a algn*** (fam): **no debía haberlo dicho pero se me fue la ~** I shouldn't have said it but it just slipped out; **no te vayas a ir de la ~** make sure you don't tell anybody; ⇒ MALO 2 **(b)** (Coc) tongue **(c)** (de tierra) spit, tongue; (de fuego) tongue **2** (Ling) language; **~ materna** mother tongue

lenguado *m* sole

lenguaje *m* language

lengüeta *f* (de zapato) tongue; (Mús) reed

lente *m* [*en algunas regiones f*] lens; **~ de contacto** contact lens; *ver tb* LENTES

lenteja *f* lentil

lentejuela *f* sequin

lentes *mpl* (esp AmL) ⇒ GAFAS (a)

lentilla *f* (Esp) contact lens

lentitud *f* slowness; **con ~** slowly

lento[1] **-ta** *adj* slow

lento[2] *adv* slowly

leña *f* wood, firewood

leñador -dora *m,f* woodcutter

leño *m* log

Leo *m* (signo) Leo; **es (de) ~** he's (a) Leo ■ *mf* (*pl* ~) (persona) *tb* **leo** Leo

león -ona *m,f* (de África) (*m*) lion; (*f*) lioness

leonera *f* **(a)** (de león) lion's den **(b)** (Esp fam) (lugar desordenado) tip (colloq)

leopardo *m* leopard; **~ hembra** leopardess

leotardo *m tb* **~s** (woolen) tights (*pl*)

lépero -ra *adj* (Méx) coarse

lepra *f* leprosy

leproso -sa *adj* leprous ■ *m,f* leper

lerdo -da *adj* (fam) (torpe) clumsy; (tonto) slow

les *pron pers* **1** (como objeto indirecto): **~ quiero mostrar algo** (a ellos, ellas) I want to show them something; (a ustedes) I want to show you something; **~ puse fundas a los muebles** I put covers on the furniture **2** (como objeto directo) (esp Esp) (referido — a ellos) them; (— a ustedes) you; **no ~ reconocí** I didn't recognize them/you; **¿~ atienden?** can I help you?

lesbiana *f* lesbian

lesear [A1] *vi* (Chi fam) (tontear) to clown *o* fool around (colloq); (bromear) to joke (colloq); (flirtear) to flirt; (perder el tiempo) to laze around

lesera (Chi fam) nonsense, tripe (colloq)

lesión *f* injury; **sufrió una ~ cerebral** he suffered brain damage

lesionado -da *adj* injured

lesionar [A1] *vt* ‹*persona*› to injure; **le ~on la pierna en el partido** his leg was hurt *o* injured in the game

■ **lesionarse** *v pron* «*persona*» to injure oneself; ‹*pierna/rodilla*› to injure

leso -sa *adj* (Chi fam) dumb (colloq); ***hacer ~ a algn*** (fam) to make a monkey out of sb (colloq)

letárgico -ca *adj* lethargic

letargo *m* lethargy

letra *f* **1 (a)** (Impr, Ling) letter; **~ bastardilla** *or* **cursiva** italic script, italics (*pl*); **~ de imprenta** print; **~ negrita** boldface, bold type; **~ pequeña** *or* (AmS) **chica** small print **(b)** (caligrafía) writing, handwriting; **no entiendo tu ~** I can't read your writing **(c) letras** *fpl* (carta breve): **sólo unas ~s para decirte que** ... just a few lines to let you know that ... **2** (Mús) (de canción) words (*pl*), lyrics (*pl*) **3** (Fin) *tb* **~ de cambio** bill of exchange, draft; **me quedan tres ~s por pagar** I still have three payments to make **4 letras** *fpl* (Educ) arts (*pl*), liberal arts (*pl*) (AmE)

letrado -da *adj* learned ■ *m,f* (frml) lawyer

letrero *m* sign, notice; **~ luminoso** neon sign

letrina *f* latrine

leucemia *f* leukemia

levadura *f* yeast; **pan sin ~** unleavened bread; **~ de cerveza** brewer's yeast; **~ en polvo** (Esp) baking powder

levantado -da *adj*: **estar ~** to be up

levantador -dora *m,f* (Dep) *tb* **~ de pesas** weightlifter

levantamiento *m* **(a)** (sublevación) uprising **(b)** (de embargo, sanción) lifting; **~ de pesas** weightlifting

levantar [A1] *vt* **1 (a)** (del suelo) ‹*bulto/peso*› to lift, pick up **(b)** ‹*tapadera/mantel*› to lift (up); ‹*cabeza/mano/copa*› to raise; ‹*alfombra*› to lift up **(c)** ‹*persiana*› to pull up, raise **(d)** (elevar) ‹*voz*› to raise: **sin ~ la vista del libro** without looking up from her book **(e)** ‹*polvo*› to raise **(f)** (Jueg) ‹*carta*› to pick up **2 (a)** ‹*ánimo*› to boost; ‹*moral*› to raise, boost **(b)** ‹*industria/economía*› to help ... to pick up **3** ‹*estatua/muro/edificio*› to erect, put up **4** ‹*embargo/sanción*› to lift; **le levantó el castigo** he let him off; **se levanta la sesión** the meeting is adjourned **5** ‹*rumor/protestas*› to spark (off); ‹*polémica*› to cause; **~ sospechas** to arouse suspicion **6** ‹*campamento*› to strike; **~ la mesa** (AmL) to clear the table **7** (en brazos) ‹*persona*› to pick up; (de la cama) to get ... out of bed; (poner de pie) to get ... up **8** (AmS) ‹*mujer*› to pick up (colloq)

■ **levantarse** *v pron* **1 (a)** (de la cama) to get up; ⇒ PIE[1] **(b)** (ponerse en pie) to stand up, to rise (frml); **¿me puedo ~ de la mesa?** may I leave the table? **2** «*polvareda*» to rise; «*temporal*» to brew; «*viento*» to begin to blow, rise **3** (sublevarse) to rise (up) **4** (*refl*) ‹*solapas/cuello*› to turn up **5** (AmS fam) ‹*mujer*› to pick up (colloq)

levante *m* **1 (a)** (Geog) (este) east **(b)** (viento) east wind **2** (AmS fam) (conquista) pick up

levar [A1] *vt*: **~ anclas** to weigh anchor

leve *adj* **(a)** ‹*perfume/gasa*› delicate **(b)** ‹*sospecha/duda*› slight; ‹*sonrisa*› slight; ‹*brisa*› gentle, slight; ‹*golpe*› gentle, light; ‹*enfermedad*› mild; ‹*herida/lesión*› slight; ‹*pecado*› venial; ‹*castigo/sanción*› light; ‹*infracción*› minor

levita *f* (Indum) frock coat

léxico¹ -ca *adj* lexical

léxico² *m* (vocabulario) vocabulary, lexis (tech); (diccionario) lexicon; (glosario) glossary, lexicon

ley *f* **1** (en general) law; **violar la ~** to break the law; **iguales ante la ~** equal in the eyes of the law; **~ de la oferta y la demanda** law of supply and demand; ***la ~ del más fuerte*** the survival of the fittest; ***~ pareja no es dura*** (CS) a rule isn't unfair if it applies to everyone **2** (de oro, plata) assay value

leyenda *f* **(a)** (Lit) (narración) legend **(b)** (de moneda, escudo) legend; (de ilustración) caption, legend

leyeron, **leyó, etc** *see* LEER

liado -da *adj* (fam) **(a)** (ocupado) tied up **(b)** (relacionado) **~ CON algn** involved WITH sb

liana *f* liana

liar [A17] *vt* **1 (a)** ‹*cigarrillo*› to roll **(b)** (atar) to tie (up); (envolver) to wrap (up); (en un fardo, manojo) to bundle (up) **2** (fam) **(a)** ‹*situación/asunto*› to complicate **(b)** (confundir) ‹*persona*› to confuse, get ... in a muddle **(c)** (en un asunto) ‹*persona*› to involve
■ **liarse** *v pron* **1** (fam) **(a)** «*asunto*» to get complicated **(b)** «*persona*» to get confused **2** (Esp fam) **(a)** (entretenerse): **nos liamos a hablar y** ... we got talking and ... **(b)** (emprenderla): **se ~on a golpes** they started throwing punches at each other

libanés -nesa *adj/m,f* Lebanese

Líbano *m*: *tb* **el ~** Lebanon

libélula *f* dragonfly

liberación *f* (de preso, rehén) release, freeing; (de pueblo, país) liberation; **la ~ de la mujer** Women's Liberation, Women's Lib

liberado -da *adj* ‹*mujer*› liberated

liberal *adj* liberal ■ *mf* Liberal

liberalismo *m* liberalism

liberalizar [A4] *vt* ‹*comercio/importaciones*› to relax the restrictions on

liberar [A1] *vt* **(a)** ‹*prisionero/rehén*› to release, free; ‹*pueblo/país*› to liberate **(b)** (de una obligación) **~ a algn DE algo** to free sb FROM sth
■ **liberarse** *v pron* **~se DE algo** ‹*de ataduras/deudas*› to free oneself FROM sth

libertad *f* **1** (para actuar) freedom; **queda usted en ~** you are free to go; **poner a algn en ~** to release sb; **~ bajo fianza** bail; **~ condicional** parole; **~ de expresión/de prensa** freedom of speech/of the press **2** (confianza): **pídelo con toda ~** feel free to ask; **habla con toda ~** speak freely; **tomarse la ~ de hacer algo** to take the liberty of doing sth

libertador -dora *m,f* liberator

libertinaje *m* licentiousness

libertino -na *adj* dissolute, licentious ■ *m,f* libertine

Libia *f* Libya

libidinoso -sa *adj* lustful

libido, **líbido** *f* libido

libio -bia *adj/m,f* Libyan

libra *f* pound; **~ esterlina** pound sterling

Libra *m* (signo) Libra; **es (de) ~** she's (a) Libra, she's a Libran ■ *mf* (*pl* **~** *or* **-bras**) (persona) *tb* **libra** Libran, Libra

libramiento *m* (Méx) (Transp) beltway (AmE), relief road (BrE)

librar [A1] *vt* **1** (liberar) **~ a algn DE algo** ‹*de peligro*› to save sb FROM sth; ‹*de obligación/responsabilidad*› to free sb FROM sth; **¡Dios nos libre!** God forbid! **2** ‹*batalla/combate*› to fight
■ **librarse** *v pron:* **se libró por poco** he had a lucky escape; **~se DE algo** ‹*de tarea/obligación*› to get out of sth; **~se de un castigo** to escape punishment; **se libró de tener que ayudarlo** she got out of having to help him; **se ~on de morir asfixiados** they escaped being suffocated; **~se DE algn** to get rid OF sb

libre *adj* **1** ‹*país/pueblo*› free; **lo dejaron ~** they set him free; **eres ~ de ir donde quieras** you're free to go wherever you want; **~ albedrío** free will; **~ mercado** free market **2** ‹*traducción/adaptación*› free; **los 200 metros ~s** the 200 meters freestyle **3** (no ocupado) ‹*persona/tiempo/asiento*› free; **¿tienes un rato ~?** do you have a (spare) moment?; **en sus ratos ~s** in her spare *o* free time; **tengo el día ~** I have the day off **4** (exento): **artículos ~s de impuestos** duty-free goods

librecambista *adj* free-trade (*before n*)

librería *f* **1** (tienda) bookstore (AmE), bookshop (BrE); **~ de ocasión** second-hand bookstore **2** (Esp) (mueble) bookcase

librero -ra *m,f* **(a)** (Com) bookseller **(b) librero** *m* (Chi, Méx) (mueble) bookcase

libreta *f* notebook; **~ de ahorro** passbook, bankbook; **~ de calificaciones** (AmL) school report

libretearse [A1] *v pron* (AmC fam) to play hooky (esp AmE colloq), to skive off (school) (BrE colloq)

libreto *m* **1 (a)** (de ópera) libretto **(b)** (AmL) (guión) script **2** (Chi) *tb* **~ de cheques** checkbook*

libro *m* (Impr) book; **un ~ de cocina** a cookbook; **llevar los ~s** (Fin) to do the bookkeeping; **~ de bolsillo** paperback; **~ de consulta** reference book; **~ de escolaridad** school record; **~ de familia** *booklet recording details of one's marriage, children's birthdates, etc*; **~ de texto** textbook

liceal *mf* (Ur) high school student (AmE), secondary school pupil (BrE)

liceano -na *m,f* (Chi) ⇒ LICEAL

liceísta *mf* (Ven) ⇒ LICEAL

licencia *f* **1** (documento) license*; **~ de caza** hunting permit; **~ de conducir** *or* (AmC, Méx, Ven) **de manejar** driver's license (AmE), driving licence (BrE) **2 (a)** (Mil) leave; **con ~** on leave **(b)** (AmL) (de un trabajo) leave; **estar de ~** to be on leave

licenciado -da *m,f* **(a)** (Educ) graduate; **~ en Filosofía y Letras** ≈ arts *o* (AmE) liberal arts graduate **(b)** (AmC, Méx) (abogado) lawyer

licenciar [A1] *vt* ‹*soldado*› to discharge

■ **licenciarse** *v pron* «*estudiante*» to graduate
licenciatura *f* degree
licencioso -sa *adj* dissolute
liceo *m* (CS, Ven) high school (AmE), secondary school (BrE)
licitación *f* (esp AmL) tender; **se llamará a ~ para la construcción del puente** the construction of the bridge will be put out to tender
licitar [A1] *vt* (esp AmL) (llamar a concurso para) to invite tenders for; (presentar una propuesta para) to put in a tender for
lícito -ta *adj* **(a)** (dentro de la ley) ‹*acto/conducta*› legal, lawful; ‹*jugada*› legal **(b)** (admisible) justifiable, reasonable
licor *m* (bebida dulce) liqueur; (alcohol) liquor, spirits (*pl*)
licuado *m* (AmL) (con leche) (milk) shake; (de frutas) fruit drink
licuadora *f* blender, liquidizer (BrE)
licuar [A18] *vt* **(a)** (Coc) ‹*frutas/verduras*› to blend, liquidize **(b)** (Fís, Quím) to liquefy
líder[1] *mf* **(a)** (Com, Dep, Pol) leader **(b)** (*como adj*) ‹*equipo/marca/empresa*› leading (*before n*)
líder[2] lideresa *m,f* (Méx) (Dep, Pol) leader
liderazgo, **liderato** *m* leadership
lidiar [A1] *vt* ‹*toro*› to fight ■ **~** *vi:* **~ CON algn/algo** to battle WITH sb/sth
liebre *f* **1** (Zool) hare **2** (Chi) (Transp) small bus
liendre *f* nit
lienzo *m* **1 (a)** (Art) canvas **(b)** (Tex) cloth **2** (Arquit) (pared) wall
lifting /'liftin/ *m* facelift
liga *f* **1** (asociación) league; (Dep) league, conference (esp AmE) **2 (a)** (Indum) garter **(b)** (AmL) (gomita) rubber *o* (BrE) elastic band
ligado *adj* [ESTAR] (conectado) connected, linked; (apegado) **~ A algn** attached TO sb; **se siente muy ~ a su país** he feels a strong bond with his country
ligadura *f* **(a)** (Med) ligature **(b) ligaduras** *fpl* (ataduras) bonds (*pl*), ties (*pl*)
ligamento *m* ligament
ligar [A3] *vt* **(a)** (unir) to bind; **los ligaba una gran amistad** they were bound together by a strong friendship **(b)** (atar): **le ~on las manos** they tied his hands together; **un fajo de billetes ligados con una goma elástica** a bundle of bills held together with a rubber band **(c)** ‹*metales*› to alloy; ‹*salsa*› to bind ■ **~** *vi* (fam) (con el sexo opuesto): **salieron a ~** they went out on the make *o* (BrE) pull (colloq); **~ CON algn** to make out WITH sb (AmE), to get off WITH sb (BrE)
■ **ligarse** *v pron* (fam) (conquistar) to make out with (AmE colloq), to get off with (colloq BrE)
ligazón *f* connection, link
ligereza *f* **1** (de objeto) lightness **2 (a)** (de carácter) flippancy; **con ~** ‹*actuar/hablar*› flippantly **(b)** (acto, dicho irreflexivo): **cometió la ~ de mencionarlo** he thoughtlessly mentioned it **3** (agilidad) agility, nimbleness; (rapidez) speed
ligero[1] -ra *adj* **1** (liviano) **(a)** ‹*paquete/gas/metal*› light; ‹*tela*› light, thin; **~ de ropa** lightly dressed; **viajar ~ de equipaje** to travel light **(b)** ‹*comida/masa*› light **2** (leve) **(a)** ‹*dolor/sabor/olor*› slight; ‹*inconveniente*› slight, minor; ‹*golpe*› gentle, slight; **tener el sueño ~** to be a light sleeper **(b)** ‹*sensación/sospecha*› slight **3** (no serio) ‹*conversación*› lighthearted; ‹*película/lectura*› lightweight; ***a la ligera*** ‹*actuar*› without thinking, hastily; **todo se lo toma a la ligera** he doesn't take anything seriously **4** (ágil) ‹*movimiento*› agile, nimble; (rápido) ‹*persona/animal/vehículo*› fast
ligero[2] *adv* quickly, fast
light /lajt/ *adj inv* ‹*cigarrillos*› low-tar; ‹*alimentos*› low-calorie; ‹*refresco*› diet (*before n*)
ligue *m* (Esp, Méx fam) **(a)** (persona): **el nuevo ~ de Ana** Ana's new man (colloq) **(b)** (acción): **ir de ~** to go out on the make *o* (BrE) pull
liguero *m* garter belt (AmE), suspender belt (BrE)
lija *f* **(a)** (para madera, metales) *tb* **papel de ~** sandpaper **(b)** (Ven) ⇒ LIMA 1b
lijar [A1] *vt* to sand (down)
lila *f* (Bot) lilac ■ *adj* (*gen inv*) ▶ 97 ‹*color*› lilac ■ *m* (color) lilac
lima *f* **1 (a)** (herramienta) file **(b)** (para uñas — de metal) nail file; (—de papel) emery board **2** (Bot) (fruto) lime; (árbol) lime (tree)
Lima *f* Lima
limar [A1] *vt* ‹*uñas/metal*› to file
■ **limarse** *v pron* ‹*uñas*› to file
limeño -ña *adj* of/from Lima ■ *m,f* person from Lima
limitación *f* **(a)** (restricción) restriction, limitation **(b)** (carencia) limitation; (defecto) shortcoming
limitado -da *adj* ‹*poder/número/edición*› limited; **estar ~ A/POR algo** to be restricted TO/BY sth
limitar [A1] *vt* ‹*funciones/derechos*› to limit, restrict ■ **~** *vi* **~ CON algo** «*país/finca*» to border ON sth
■ **limitarse** *v pron:* **el problema no se limita a las ciudades** the problem is not confined *o* limited to cities; **me limité a repetir lo dicho** I just repeated what was said
límite *m* **1** (Geog, Pol) boundary **2** (tope) limit; **el ~ de velocidad** the speed limit; **su ambición no tiene ~s** his ambition knows no limits; **sin ~s** unlimited; **¡todo tiene un ~!** enough is enough! **3** (*como adj inv*): **tiempo ~** time limit; **situación ~** extreme situation; **fecha ~** deadline
limítrofe *adj* ‹*país/provincia*› neighboring* (*before n*); ‹*conflicto*› border (*before n*)
limo *m* **1** (barro) mud, slime **2** (Col) (Bot) lime (tree)
limón *m* **(a)** (fruto amarillo) lemon **(b)** (AmL) (árbol) lemon tree **(c)** (Méx, Ven) (fruto verde) lime
limonada *f* lemonade
limonero *m* lemon tree
limosna *f* alms (*pl*) (arch); **pedir ~** to beg; **dar ~** to give money to beggars
limosnear [A1] *vi* (AmL) to beg
limosnero -ra *m,f* (AmL) beggar
limpiabotas *mf* (*pl* **~**) bootblack; (niño) shoeshine boy

limpiacristales *m* (*pl* ~) (Esp) (líquido) window cleaner ■ *mf* (persona) window cleaner

limpiador[1] **-dora** *m,f* (persona) cleaner

limpiador[2] *m* (Méx) (Auto) ⇒ LIMPIAPARABRISAS

limpiamuebles *m* (*pl* ~) furniture polish

limpiaparabrisas *m* (*pl* ~) windshield wipers (*pl*) (AmE), windscreen wipers (*pl*) (BrE)

limpiar [A1] *vt* **1 (a)** ‹*casa/mueble/zapatos*› to clean; ‹*arroz/lentejas*› to wash; ‹*pescado*› to clean; ‹*aire/atmósfera*› to clear; **lo limpió con un trapo** he wiped it with a cloth; **~ algo en seco** to dry-clean sth **(b)** ‹*nombre*› to clear; ‹*honor*› to restore **2** (dejar libre) **~ algo** DE **algo** to clear sth OF sth **3** (fam) **(a)** (en el juego) ‹*persona*› to clean … out (colloq) **(b)** «*ladrones*» ‹*casa*› to clean … out (colloq) ■ **~** *vi* to clean

■ **limpiarse** *v pron* (*refl*) ‹*boca/nariz*› to wipe; **se ~on los zapatos al entrar** they wiped their shoes as they came in

limpiavidrios *mf* (*pl* ~) (esp AmL) (persona) window cleaner ■ *m* (líquido) window cleaner

limpieza *f* **1** (estado, cualidad) cleanliness **2** (acción) cleaning; **la señora de la ~** the cleaning lady; **~ de cutis** skin cleansing; **~ en seco** drycleaning; **~ general** spring-cleaning (AmE), spring-clean (BrE); **~ étnica** ethnic cleansing **3** (por la policía) clean-up operation; (Pol) purge

limpio[1] **-pia** *adj* **1 (a)** [ESTAR] ‹*casa/vestido/vaso*› clean **(b)** ‹*aire*› clean; ‹*cielo*› clear **(c) pasar algo en** *or* (Esp) **a ~** to make a clean (AmE) *o* (BrE) fair copy of sth **2** [SER] **(a)** ‹*persona*› clean **(b)** ‹*dinero/campaña*› clean; ‹*elecciones/juego*› fair, clean; **un asunto poco ~** an underhand business **(c)** (libre) **~** DE **algo** ‹*de impurezas/polvo*› free OF sth **3** (neto): **saca unos $70 ~s por mes** she makes $70 a month after deductions; ***sacar en ~***: **no sacó nada en ~ de todo lo que dijo** he didn't make sense of anything he said; **lo único que saqué en ~ es que** … the only thing that I got clear was that …

limpio[2] *adv* ‹*jugar/pelear*› fairly, clean

linaje *m* descent, lineage (frml)

linaza *f* linseed

lince *m* (Zool) lynx; (persona): **es un ~ para los negocios** he's a very shrewd businessman

linchar [A1] *vt* to lynch

lindar [A1] *vi* **~** CON **algo** (limitar) to adjoin sth; (aproximarse a) to border ON sth, verge ON sth

lindo[1] **-da** *adj* **1** (bonito) ‹*bebé*› cute, sweet; ‹*casa/canción*› lovely; ‹*cara*› pretty **2** (esp AmL) (agradable) ‹*gesto/detalle*› nice; ‹*fiesta/viaje*› wonderful; ‹*ceremonia*› beautiful; **¡es una persona tan linda!** she's such a lovely person; ***de lo ~*** (fam): **nos divertimos de lo ~** we had a great time

lindo[2] *adv* (AmL) ‹*cantar/bailar*› beautifully; **se siente ~** (Méx) it feels wonderful

lindura *f* (AmL) delight; **me pareció una ~** I thought it was lovely

línea *f* **1** (en general) line; **la ~ de puntos** the dotted line; **escribirle unas ~s a algn** to drop sb a line; **seguir la ~ del partido** to follow the party line; **en ~s generales** broadly speaking; **por ~ materna** on his (*o* her *etc*) mother's side; **~ de montaje** assembly line; **~ de gol** goal line; **~ de llegada** finishing line, wire (AmE); **~ de salida** starting line; ***de primera ~*** ‹*tecnología*› state-of-the-art; ‹*producto*› top-quality, high-class; ‹*actor/jugador*› first-rate; ***leer entre ~s*** to read between the lines **2** (Transp, Tele) line; **~ aérea** airline; **final de la ~** end of the line; **no hay ~ directa a Córdoba** there is no direct service to Cordoba; **intenté llamarte pero no había ~** I tried to ring you but the phone *o* the line was dead; **la ~ está ocupada** the line is busy **3 (a)** (gama, colección) line, range; **nuestra nueva ~ de cosméticos** our new line *o* range of cosmetics **(b)** (estilo): **una ~ más clásica** a more classic look **4** (figura): **cuidar la ~** to watch one's figure

lineal *adj* linear

lingo *m* (Per) leapfrog

lingote *m* ingot

lingüística *f* linguistics

lingüístico -ca *adj* ‹*fenómeno/aptitud*› linguistic; ‹*barrera*› language (*before n*)

lino *m* (planta) flax; (tela) linen

linóleo *m* lino, linoleum

linterna *f* (fanal) lantern; (de pilas) flashlight (AmE), torch (BrE)

lío *m* **1 (a)** (fam) (embrollo, confusión) mess; **armarse/hacerse un ~ (con algo)** to get into a mess (with sth) (colloq) **(b)** (fam) (problema, complicación) trouble; **meterse en un ~** to get oneself into trouble; **tiene ~s con la policía** he's in trouble with the police (colloq); **¡qué ~ se va a armar!** there's going to be hell to pay! (colloq) **(c)** (fam) (amorío) affair **2** (fardo) bundle

lioso -sa *adj* (fam) confusing, muddling

liquidación *f* **1** (en tienda) sale; **~ total** clearance sale **2** (de negocio, activo) liquidation **3 (a)** (de cuenta, deuda) settlement **(b)** (Méx) (compensación por despido) severance pay

liquidar [A1] *vt* **1** ‹*existencias*› to sell off **2** ‹*negocio*› to wind up; ‹*activo*› to liquidate **3 (a)** ‹*deuda/cuenta*› to settle; ‹*sueldo/pago*› to pay **(b)** (Méx) ‹*trabajador*› to pay … off **4** (fam) ‹*persona*› (matar) to do away with (colloq); (destruir) (AmL) to destroy (colloq)

liquidez *f* liquidity

líquido[1] **-da** *adj* **1** ‹*sustancia*› liquid **2** ‹*sueldo/renta*› net

líquido[2] *m* **1** (sustancia) liquid; **~ de frenos** brake fluid **2** (dinero) cash

lira *f* **(a)** (Mús) lyre **(b)** (Fin) lira

lírico -ca *adj* **(a)** (Lit, Mús) lyric **(b)** (Per, RPl fam) ‹*persona*› dreamy, starry-eyed (colloq)

lirio *m* iris

lirón *m* dormouse; ⇒ DORMIR *vi*

lis *f* lily

lisiado -da *adj* crippled ■ *m,f* cripple; **un ~ de guerra** a disabled veteran

lisiarse [A1] *v pron* (*refl*): **se lisió la columna vertebral** he damaged his spine

liso -sa *adj* **1** ‹*piel/superficie*› smooth; ‹*pelo*› straight; ‹*terreno*› flat **2** (sin dibujos) plain **3** (Per fam) (insolente) fresh (AmE colloq), cheeky (BrE colloq)

lisonjero -ra *adj* ‹*palabras*› flattering; **es un hombre muy ~** he's a terrible flatterer

lista *f* **(a)** (de nombres, números) list; **pasar ~** (Educ) to take roll call, to take the register (BrE); **~ de boda** wedding list; **~ de espera** waiting list; **~ de éxitos** (Mús) charts (*pl*); (Lit) best-seller list **(b)** (raya) stripe; **a ~s** striped

listado *m* (Inf) printout; (lista) list; **~ electoral** (RPl) electoral roll *o* register

listar [A1] *vt* to list

listín *m* (Esp) *tb* **~ de teléfonos** telephone directory

listo -ta *adj* **1** [SER] ‹*persona*› clever, bright, smart (colloq); **se pasó de ~** he tried to be too clever; ***estar* ~** (fam): **ahora sí que estamos ~s** we're in real trouble now (colloq); **está lista si cree eso** if that's what she thinks, she's got another think coming (colloq) **2 (a)** [ESTAR] (preparado) ready; **~ PARA algo/hacer algo** ready FOR sth/to do sth **(b)** [ESTAR] (terminado) finished; **lo doblas así y ~** you fold it like this and that's it (finished) **(c)** (Andes fam) (manifestando acuerdo) okay (colloq) ■ *m,f* (esp Esp) **(a)** (inteligente) clever one; **el ~ de la clase** (pey) the class know-it-all (colloq & pej) **(b)** (vivo, astuto) tricky customer (colloq)

listón *m* **(a)** (de madera) strip; (en salto de altura) bar **(b)** (Méx) (cinta) ribbon

lisura *f* (Per) **(a)** (fam) (grosería) four-letter word (colloq) **(b)** (gracia) gracefulness

litera *f* (en dormitorio) bunk; (en barco) bunk, berth; (en tren) berth, couchette (BrE)

literal *adj* literal

literalmente *adv* ‹*traducir*› literally; ‹*repetir*› word for word

literario -ria *adj* literary

literato -ta *m,f* (*m*) man of letters; (*f*) woman of letters

literatura *f* literature; **~ infantil** juvenile books (AmE), children's books (BrE)

litigar [A3] *vi* to be at law *o* in litigation (frml), to be in dispute

litigio *m* **(a)** (Der) lawsuit **(b)** (disputa) dispute

litografía *f* (sistema) lithography; (grabado) lithograph

litoral *adj* coastal ■ *m* coast; **un largo ~** a long coastline

litro *m* liter*

Lituania *f* Lithuania

lituano¹ -na *adj/m,f* Lithuanian

lituano² *m* (idioma) Lithuanian

liturgia *f* liturgy

liviano -na *adj* (esp AmL) **(a)** ‹*paquete/tela*› light **(b)** ‹*comida*› light; **tiene un sueño muy ~** she's a very light sleeper **(c)** ‹*obra/película*› lightweight

lívido -da *adj* (pálido) pallid; (morado) livid

living /'lißin/ *m* (*pl* **-vings**) (esp AmS) living room

Ll, ll *f* (*read as* /'eʎe/) Ll, ll

llaga *f* (Med) sore, ulcer; (Bib) wound

llama *f* **1** (de fuego) flame; **la casa ardía en ~s** the house was in flames; **~ piloto** pilot light **2** (Zool) llama

llamada *f* ▶ 405 call; **hacer una ~** to make a phone call; **~ a cobro revertido** collect call (AmE), reverse-charge call (BrE); **~ de larga distancia** long-distance call; **~ local** *or* **urbana** local call; **~ al orden** call to order

llamado¹ -da *adj* **1** (por un nombre) called; **un lugar ~ La Dehesa** a place called La Dehesa; **el 747, también ~ 'jumbo'** the 747, also known as the jumbo jet; **el ~ 'boom' de los sesenta** the so-called 'boom' of the sixties **2** (a la fama, éxito) ⇒ DESTINADO 1(a)

llamado² *m* **(a)** (AmL) (al público) ⇒ LLAMAMIENTO **(b)** (Arg) (Telec) ⇒ LLAMADA

llamamiento *m* call; **hacer un ~ a la calma** to appealfor calm

llamar [A1] *vt* **1** ‹*bomberos/policía*› to call; ‹*médico*› to call (out); ‹*camarero/criada/ascensor*› to call; ‹*súbditos/servidores*› to summon; ‹*taxi*› (por teléfono) to call; (en la calle) to hail; **lo llamó por señas** she beckoned to him; **el sindicato los llamó a la huelga** the union called them out on strike **2** ▶ 405 (por teléfono) to phone, to call; **te llamó Eva** Eva phoned (for you) **3 (a)** (dar el nombre de) to call, name; (dar el título, apodo de) to call **(b)** (considerar) to call; **eso es lo que yo llamo un amigo** that's what I call a friend ■ **~** *vi* **1** (con los nudillos) to knock; (tocar el timbre) to ring (the doorbell); **llaman a la puerta** there's someone at the door **2** ▶ 405 (Telec) «*persona*» to telephone, phone, call; «*teléfono*» to ring; **¿quién llama?** who's calling?; *ver tb* COBRO (b)
■ **llamarse** *v pron* to be called; **su padre se llama Pedro** his father is called Pedro, his father's name is Pedro; **¿cómo te llamas?** what's your name?

llamarada *f* (de fuego) sudden blaze, flare-up

llamativo -va *adj* ‹*color*› bright; ‹*mujer/vestido*› striking

llanamente *adv*: ***lisa*** *or* ***simple y ~*** ‹*explicar/hablar*› in straightforward terms; **lisa y ~, hay que despedirlos** they should be fired, it's as simple as that

llanero -ra *m,f* **(a)** (habitante del llano) (*m*) plainsman; (*f*) plainswoman **(b)** (vaquero) cattle herder, cowboy (*of the Colombian/Venezuelan* LLANOS)

llaneza *f* simplicity

llano¹ -na *adj* **(a)** ‹*terreno/superficie*› (horizontal) flat; (sin desniveles) even; **los 100 metros ~s** (RPl) the 100 meters dash *o* sprint **(b)** ‹*persona*› straightforward; ‹*trato*› natural; ‹*lenguaje*› plain

llano² *m* **(a)** (Geog) (llanura) plain **(b)** (extensión de terreno) area of flat ground

llanta *f* **(a)** (de metal) rim **(b)** (AmL) (neumático) tire*; **~ de repuesto** *or* (Méx) **de refacción** spare tire*

llanto *m* (de niño) crying; (de adulto) crying, weeping (liter)

llanura *f* (Geog) plain, prairie

llapa *f* ⇒ YAPA

llave *f* **1** (en general) key; **cierra la puerta con ~** lock the door; **bajo ~** under lock and key; **la ~ del éxito** the key to success; **~ de contacto** ignition key; **~ maestra** master key, passkey **2** (Mec) (herramienta) wrench (AmE), spanner (BrE); **~ inglesa** monkey wrench **3 (a)** (interruptor) switch; (en tubería) valve; **la ~ del gas** the gas jet (AmE) *o* (BrE) tap; **cerrar la ~ de paso** to turn the water/gas off at the main valve (AmE) *o* (BrE) at the mains **(b)** (AmL) (de lavabo, bañera) faucet (AmE), tap (BrE) **4** (en un texto) brace **5** (en lucha, judo) hold; **lo inmovilizó con una ~ (de brazo)** she got him in an armlock

llavero *m* key ring

llegada *f* **(a)** (de un viaje) arrival; **(b)** (Dep) (meta) finishing line, wire (AmE); (Equ) winning post

llegar [A3] *vi* **1** «*persona/tren/carta*» to arrive; **tienen que estar por** *or* **al ~** they'll be arriving any minute now; **~on cansadísimos** they were exhausted when they arrived; **¿falta mucho para ~?** is it much further (to go)?; **siempre llega tarde** he's always late; **no me llegó el telegrama** I didn't get the telegram; **~ A algo** ‹*a país/ciudad*› to arrive IN sth; ‹*a edificio*› to arrive AT sth; **~ a casa** to arrive *o* get home; **el rumor llegó a oídos del alcalde** the rumor reached the mayor **2** «*camino/ruta/tren*» (ir) **~ A** *or* **HASTA** to go all the way to, go as far as; **sólo llega al tercer piso** it only goes (up) to the third floor **3** «*día/invierno*» to come, arrive; **ha llegado el momento de** ... the time has come to ... **4 (a)** (alcanzar) to reach; **~ A algo** ‹*a acuerdo/conclusión*› to reach sth, come to sth; ‹*a estante/techo*› to reach; **llegué a la conclusión de que**... I reached *o* came to the conclusion that ...; **los pies no le llegan al suelo** her feet don't touch the floor; **la falda le llegaba a los tobillos** her skirt came down to her ankles; **el agua le llegaba al cuello** the water came up to her neck; **las cosas ~on a tal punto que** ... things reached such a point that ... **(b)** (expresando logro): **~á lejos** she'll go far *o* a long way; **así no vas a ~ a ningún lado** you'll never get anywhere like that; **llegó a (ser) director** he became director; **~ a viejo** to live to old age; **llegué a conocerlo mejor** I got to know him better **5 ~ A + INF (a)** (al extremo de): **llegó a amenazarme** she even threatened me; **no llegó a pegarme** he didn't actually hit me **(b)** (en oraciones condicionales): **si lo llego a saber, no vengo** if I'd known, I wouldn't have come; **si llego a enterarme de algo, te aviso** if I happen to hear anything, I'll let you know

llenador -dora *adj* (CS) ‹*comida*› filling

llenar [A1] *vt* **1 (a)** ‹*vaso/plato/cajón*› to fill; ‹*tanque*› to fill (up); ‹*maleta*› to fill, pack; **no me llenes el vaso** don't fill my glass right up; **~ algo DE/CON algo** to fill sth WITH sth **(b)** ‹*formulario*› to fill out, to fill in (esp BrE) **2 (a)** (cubrir) **~ algo DE algo** to cover sth WITH sth **(b)** ‹*vacante*› to fill **3** (colmar) ‹*persona*›: **la noticia nos llenó de alegría** we were overjoyed by the news; **nos llenó de atenciones** he made a real fuss of us **4** (hacer sentirse realizado) ‹*persona*›: **su carrera no la llena** she doesn't find her career fulfilling ■ **~** *vi* «*comida*» to be filling

■ **llenarse** *v pron* **1 (a)** «*recipiente/estadio*» to fill (up); **el teatro sólo se llenó a la mitad** the theater only filled to half capacity *o* was only half full; **~se DE algo** to fill WITH sth **(b)** (cubrirse) **~se DE algo** ‹*de polvo/pelos*› to be covered IN sth **2** ‹*bolsillo/boca*› to fill; **~se algo DE algo** to fill sth WITH sth **3** (colmarse): **su corazón se llenó de alegría** she filled with joy; **se ~on de deudas** they got heavily into debt **4** «*persona*» (de comida): **con un plato de ensalada ya se llena** one plate of salad and she's full; **me llené** (colloq) I'm full (up) (colloq)

lleno -na *adj* **1 (a)** ‹*estadio/autobús/copa*› full; **~ DE algo** full OF sth **(b)** (cubierto) **~ DE algo** ‹*de granos/manchas/polvo*› covered IN sth **(c)** (después de comer) full (up) (colloq) **2 de lleno** ‹*consagrarse/dedicarse*› fully; **el sol nos daba de ~** the sun was shining down on us

llevadero -ra *adj* bearable

llevar [A1] *vt* **I 1 (a)** (de un lugar a otro) to take; **le llevé unas flores** I took her some flowers; **te lo ~é cuando vaya** I'll bring it when I come; **¿qué llevas en la bolsa?** what have you got in your bag?; **comida para ~** take out (AmE) *o* (BrE) take-away meals **(b)** (transportar) ‹*carga*› to carry; **la ayudé a ~ las bolsas** I helped her carry her bags **(c)** ‹*persona*› to take; **nos llevó a cenar** he took us out to dinner; **me llevó (en su coche) hasta la estación** she gave me a lift to the station; **lo llevaba en brazos/de la mano** she was carrying him in her arms/holding her hand **(d)** (tener consigo) ‹*llaves/dinero/documentación*› to have **2 (a)** (guiar, conducir) to take; **la llevaba de la mano** I/he was holding her hand; **esto no nos ~á a ninguna parte** this won't get us anywhere **(b)** (impulsar, inducir) to lead; **esto me lleva a pensar que** ... this leads me to believe that ... **3 (a)** ‹*ropa/perfume/reloj*› to wear **(b)** (tener) ‹*barba/bigote*› to have; **llevaba el pelo corto** she had short hair

II 1 (tener a su cargo) ‹*negocio/tienda*› to run; ‹*caso*› to handle; ‹*contabilidad*› to do **2** (esp Esp) (conducir) ‹*vehículo*› to drive; ‹*moto*› to ride **3** ‹*vida*› to lead; **~ una vida tranquila** to lead a quiet; **¿cómo llevas el informe?** how are you getting on with the report? **4** (seguir, mantener): **~ el ritmo** *or* **el compás** to keep time; **¿llevas la cuenta de lo que te debo?** are you keeping track of what I owe you?; **¿qué dirección llevaban?** which direction were they going in?

III 1 (a) (requerir) ‹*tiempo*› to take; **le llevó horas aprendérselo** it took her hours to learn it **(b)** (aventajar) (+ *me/te/le etc*): **me lleva un año** he's a year older than me; **nos llevan un día de ventaja** they have a one-day lead over us **2** (Esp) (cobrar) to charge ■ **~** *v aux:* **llevo una hora esperando** I've been waiting for an hour; **lleva tres días sin comer** he hasn't eaten for three days; **el tren lleva una hora de retraso** the train's an hour late; **llevo revisada la mitad** I've already checked half of it ■ **~** *vi* «*camino/carretera*» to go, lead

■ **llevarse** *v pron* **1 (a)** (a otro lugar) to take; **la policía se llevó al sospechoso** the police took the suspect away; **¿quién se llevó mi paraguas?** who took my umbrella?; **el agua se llevó las casas** the water swept away the houses **(b)** ‹*premio/dinero*› to win **(c)** (quedarse con, comprar) to take; **me llevo éste** I'll take this one **(d)** (Mat) to carry; **9 y 9 son 18, me llevo una** 9 plus 9 is 18, carry one **(e)** (Arg) ‹*asignatura*› to carry over **2** ‹*susto/*

regañina› to get; **me llevé una decepción** I was disappointed; **se llevó un buen recuerdo** he left here with pleasant memories **3 ~se bien con algn** to get along with sb **4** (hablando de modas) to be in fashion; **vuelven a ~se las faldas cortas** short skirts are back in fashion

llorar [A1] *vi* (derramar lágrimas) **(a)** «*persona*» to cry; **estaba a punto de ~** she was on the verge of tears; **~ DE algo** ‹*de risa/rabia*› to cry WITH sb; ‹*de emoción*› to weep WITH sth; **~ POR algo/algn** to cry over sth/sb **(b)** «*ojos*» (+ *me/te/le etc*) to water

lloriquear [A1] *vi* (fam) to whine (colloq)

llorón -rona *adj* (fam): **es muy ~** he cries a lot; **no seas tan ~** don't be such a crybaby (colloq) ■ *m,f* **(a)** (fam) (que llora mucho) crybaby (colloq) **(b)** (Col, RPl, Ven fam) (quejón) whiner (colloq)

llover [E9] *v impers* ▶ **409** to rain; **aquí llueve mucho** it rains a lot here; ***llueve a cántaros*** *or* ***mares*** it's pouring (with rain)

llovizna *f* ▶ **409** drizzle

lloviznar [A1] *v impers* ▶ **409** to drizzle

llueva, llueve *see* LLOVER

lluvia *f* ▶ **409** **(a)** (Meteo) rain; **un día de ~** a rainy day; **zonas de mucha ~** areas of heavy rainfall; **~ radiactiva** nuclear fallout **(b)** (de balas) hail; (de críticas) hail, barrage

lluvioso -sa *adj* ‹*tiempo/día/época*› rainy; ‹*región*› wet

lo *art* **1** : **prefiero ~ dulce** I prefer sweet things; **~ interesante del caso es** ... the interesting thing about the case is ...; **¿estoy en ~ cierto?** am I right?; **en ~ alto de la sierra** high up in the mountains; **ser ~ más objetivo posible** to be as objective as possible; **me dijo ~ de siempre** he came out with the same old story; **se ha enterado de ~ nuestro/de ~ de Pablo** she's found out about us/about Pablo; **voy a ~ de Eva** (RPl) I'm going to Eva's (place) **2 (a) lo cual** which; **~ cual fue desmentido por el gobierno** which was denied by the Government; **(b) lo que** what; **no entiendo ~ que dices** I don't understand what you're saying; **pide ~ que quieras** ask for whatever you want; **límpialo con un trapo o ~ que sea** clean it with a cloth or whatever; **¡~ que debe haber sufrido!** how she must have suffered!; **¡no te imaginas ~ que fue aquello!** you can't imagine what it was like!; **¡~ que es saber idiomas!** it sure is something (AmE) *o* (BrE) what it is to be able speak languages ■ *pron pers* **1 (a)** (referido — a él) him; (— a usted) you; (— a cosa, etc) it; **¿~ conozco?** do I know you?; **~ compré hoy** I bought it today; **ya ~ sé** I know **(b)** (*impers*): **duele que a uno ~ traten así** it hurts when people treat you like that **2** (*con* **estar, ser**): **¿que si estoy harta? pues sí, ~ estoy** am I fed up? well, yes, I am; **si ella es capaz, yo también ~ soy** if she can, so can I

loable *adj* commendable, praiseworthy

lobezno -na *m,f* wolf cub

lobo -ba *m,f* (Zool) wolf; **~ marino** seal

lóbrego -ga *adj* gloomy

lóbulo *m* ▶ **123** lobe

locación *f* (Méx) (lugar): **visite el museo Rivera, ~: Calle Altavista** visit the Rivera Museum on Altavista Street; **¿en qué ~?** whereabouts?

local *adj* local; **el equipo ~** the home team ■ *m* premises (*pl*)

localidad *f* **1** (población) town, locality (frml) **2** (Espec) seat, ticket

localizar [A4] *vt* **(a)** ‹*persona/lugar/tumor*› to locate; **estoy intentando ~la** I am trying to get hold of her **(b)** ‹*incendio/epidemia*› to localize

loción *f* lotion

loco[1] -ca *adj* **(a)** (Med, Psic) mad, insane **(b)** (chiflado) crazy (colloq), nuts (colloq); **este tipo está medio ~** (fam) the guy's not all there (colloq); **eso no lo hago (pero) ni ~** there's no way I'd do that; **hacer algo a lo ~** to do sth any which way (AmE) *o* (BrE) any old how (colloq); ***estar ~ de remate*** (fam) to be completely nuts (colloq); ***tener*** *or* (Esp) ***traer ~ a algn*** to be driving sb crazy (colloq); ***volver ~ a algn*** to drive sb crazy (colloq); ***volverse ~*** to go mad **(c)** (entusiasmado): **está loca por él** she's crazy about him (colloq); **está ~ por volver** he's dying to come back (colloq) **(d)** (fam) (ajetreado): **anda (como) ~ con los preparativos** the preparations are driving him mad (colloq) **(e)** (indicando gran cantidad): **tengo unas ganas locas de verla** I'm dying to see her (colloq); **tuvo una suerte loca** she was incredibly lucky **(f) estar ~ DE algo** ‹*de entusiasmo/furia/celos*› to be wild WITH sth; ‹*de dolor/remordimiento*› to be racked WITH sth; **estaba loca de alegría** she was blissfully happy ■ *m,f* (enfermo mental) (*m*) madman; (*f*) madwoman; **se puso como un ~** he went crazy *o* mad; **corrimos como ~s** (fam) we ran like crazy *o* mad (colloq); ***hacerse el ~*** to act dumb (colloq)

loco[2] *m* (Chi) (Zool) abalone

locomoción *f* **(a)** (acción) locomotion **(b)** (Chi) (Transp) *tb* **~ colectiva** public transport

locomotora *f* (Ferr) locomotive, engine

locuaz *adj* talkative, loquacious (frml)

locución *f* phrase

locura *f* **(a)** (demencia) madness, insanity; **lo que hizo/dijo fue una ~** what he did/said was sheer madness **(b)** (inclinación exagerada): **siente ~ por la pequeña** she's absolutely besotted with the little one; **la quiero con ~** I'm crazy about her (colloq)

locutor -tora *m,f* (en general) broadcaster; (informativo) newscaster (AmE), newsreader (BrE); (deportivo) sports commentator; (de continuidad) commentator, announcer (BrE)

lodo *m* mud; *para modismos ver* BARRO

logia *f* **(a)** (de los masones) lodge **(b)** (Arquit) loggia

lógica *f* logic

lógico[1] -ca *adj* **(a)** (normal, natural) natural, logical; **como es ~** naturally, obviously; **es ~ que así sea** it's (only) natural that it should be so; **lo ~ sería** ... the logical thing would be ... **(b)** ‹*conclusión/consecuencia*› logical

lógico[2] *adv* (*indep*) (fam) of course

logotipo *m* logo, logotype

logrado -da *adj* (satisfactorio) successful; (verosímil) ‹*retrato/personaje*› lifelike

lograr [A1] *vt* ‹*objetivo*› to attain, achieve; ‹*éxito*› to achieve; **logró el quinto puesto** she managed fifth place; ~ **hacer algo** to manage to do sth

logro *m* (de un objetivo) achievement; (éxito) success

loísmo *m*: *use of* LO/LOS *instead of* LE/LES (*as in* LO/ LOS DIJE QUE NO), *common in certain regions of Spain but not acceptable to most speakers*

lolo -la *m,f* (Chi fam) teenager

loma *f* hill; (más pequeño) hillock

lombriz *f* (de tierra) worm, earthworm; (en el intestino) (fam) worm (colloq)

lomo *m* **(a)** (de animal) back; ~ **de burro** (RPl) *or* (Chi) **de toro** (Auto) speed bump **(b)** (Coc) (de cerdo) loin; (de vaca) (AmL) fillet steak **(c)** (de libro) spine; (de cuchillo) back

lona *f* canvas

loncha *f* slice

lonche *m* (Per) (merienda) tea

lonchera *f* (AmL) lunch box

londinense *adj* ‹*público/teatro/periódico*› London (*before n*); **es** ~ she's from London, she's a Londoner ■ *mf* Londoner

Londres *m* London

longaniza *f*: *spicy pork sausage*

longitud *f* **(a)** ▶ **679** (largo) length; **de 30 metros de** ~ 30 meters long **(b)** (Astron, Geog) longitude

lonja *f* **1 (a)** (loncha) slice **(b)** (RPl) (de cuero) strip **2 (a)** (Esp) (mercado de pescado) fish market **(b)** (institución mercantil) guild; ~ **de propiedad raíz** (Col) association of realtors (AmE) *o* (BrE) estate agents

loro[1] -ra *m,f* (Zool) parrot

loro[2] *m* (fam) (charlatán) chatterbox (colloq), gasbag (colloq)

los, **las** *art* ▶ **39** ■ *pron pers* **1** (referido — a ellos, ellas, cosas, etc) them; (— a ustedes) you; **¿las atienden?** can I help you? **2** (*con el verbo* **haber**): **las hay de muchos tamaños** they come in many different sizes; **también** ~ **hay de chocolate** we have chocolate ones too

losa *f* (de sepulcro) tombstone; (de suelo) flagstone

lote *m* **(a)** (de un producto) batch; (en subastas) lot **(b)** (terreno) plot (of land)

lotería *f* lottery; **me tocó** *or* **me gané la** ~ I won the lottery

loto *m* lotus

loza *f* **(a)** (material) china **(b)** (vajilla) crockery; (de mejor calidad) china

lozano -na *adj* ‹*persona*› healthy-looking; ‹*cutis*› fresh; ‹*verduras*› fresh

Ltda (= **Limitada**) Ltd, Limited

lubina *f* sea bass

lubricante *adj* lubricating ■ *m* lubricant

lubricar [A2] *vt* to lubricate

lucero *m* bright star; ~ **del alba** morning star

luces *fpl* ⇒ LUZ

lucha *f* **(a)** (combate, pelea) fight; (para conseguir algo) struggle; ~ **de clases** class struggle; **la** ~ **contra el cáncer** the fight against cancer **(b)** (Dep) wrestling; ~ **libre** all-in wrestling

luchador -dora *m,f* **(a)** (persona esforzada) fighter **(b)** (Dep) wrestler

luchar [A1] *vi* **(a)** (combatir, pelear) to fight **(b)** (para conseguir algo) to struggle, fight; ~ **para salir adelante** struggle hard to get on in life; ~ **por la paz** to fight for peace **(c)** (batallar) ~ CON **algo** ‹*con problema*› to wrestle WITH sth **(d)** (Dep) to wrestle

luche *m* (Chi) (Jueg) hopscotch

lucidez *f* lucidity

lucido -da *adj* ‹*fiesta*› magnificent, splendid; **su actuación no fue muy lucida** her performance wasn't particularly brilliant

lúcido -da *adj* **(a)** [SER] ‹*mente/análisis*› lucid, clear; ‹*persona*› clear-thinking **(b)** [ESTAR] ‹*enfermo*› lucid

luciérnaga *f* glowworm; (insecto volador) firefly

lucir [I5] *vi* (aparentar) to look good, look special; **gasta mucho en ropa pero no le luce** she spends a fortune on clothes but it doesn't do much for her ■ ~ *vt* **(a)** (period) ‹*vestido/modelo*› to wear, sport (journ); ‹*peinado/collar*› to sport (journ) **(b)** ‹*figura/piernas*› to show off, flaunt

■ **lucirse** *v pron* **(a)** (destacarse) to excel oneself **(b)** (presumir) to show off

lucrativo -va *adj* lucrative, profitable; **una entidad sin fines** ~**s** a nonprofit (AmE) *o* (BrE) non-profit-making organization

lucro *m* profit, gain; **sin ánimo de** ~ with no profit motive in mind

lúcuma *f* eggfruit

lúdico -ca *adj* ‹*fantasías/diversiones*› playful, ludic (*before n*) (liter)

luego *adv* **1 (a)** (más tarde) later (on); (después de otro suceso — en el futuro) afterwards; (— en el pasado) then, next; **¡hasta** ~**!** goodbye!, see you!; ~ DE **hacer algo** after doing sth **(b)** (Chi, Méx) (pronto) soon, quickly; ~ ~ (Méx) immediately **2 (a)** (en el espacio): **hay una tienda y** ~ **está el banco** you come to a shop and the bank is next **(b)** (Méx) (cerca) nearby; **aquí** ~ just here **(c)** (indicando orden, prioridad) then; **primero está él y** ~ **nosotros** he's first and then we're next **3 desde luego** of course; **desde** ~ **que no** of course not ■ *conj* (frml) therefore

lugar *m* **1** (en general) place; **éste es el** ~ this is the place; **en cualquier otro** ~ anywhere else; **en algún** ~ somewhere; **cambiar los muebles de** ~ to move the furniture around; **el** ~ **del suceso** the scene of the incident; **yo en tu** ~ ... if I were you ...; **ponte en mi** ~ put yourself in my place; **se clasificó en primer** ~ she finished in first place **2** (localidad, región): **los habitantes del** ~ the local people; ~ **y fecha de nacimiento** place and date of birth **3 (a)** (espacio libre) room; **hacer** ~ **para algn/algo** to make room *o* space for sb/sth; **me hizo un** ~ he made me some room **(b)** (asiento) seat **4 dar lugar a** (a disputa, comentarios) to provoke, give rise to **5** (*en locs*) **en lugar de** instead of; **ella firmó en mi** ~ she signed on my behalf; **en primer lugar** (antes que nada) first of all, firstly; **en último lugar** (finalmente) finally, lastly; ***sin*** ~ ***a dudas*** without doubt, undoubtedly; ***tener*** ~ to take place

lugareño -ña *adj/mf* local

lugarteniente *mf* deputy

lúgubre *adj* gloomy

lujo *m* luxury; **no puedo permitirme el ~ de llegar tarde** I can't afford to be late; **nos dimos el ~ de viajar en primera** we treated ourselves and traveled first class; **a todo ~** in style; **de ~** luxury (*before n*); **con ~ de detalles** with a wealth of detail

lujoso -sa *adj* luxurious

lujuria *f* (liter) lust, lechery

lumbago *m* lumbago

lumbre *f* (de hoguera, chimenea) fire; (de la cocina): **puso el cazo en la ~** she put the saucepan on the stove

lumbrera *f* (fam) (persona brillante) genius, whiz* (colloq)

luminoso -sa *adj* **(a)** ‹*habitación*› bright, light; ‹*fuente*› luminous; ‹*letrero*› illuminated **(b)** ‹*idea*› bright, brilliant

luna *f* **1** (Astron) moon; **a la luz de la ~** in the moonlight; **hay ~** the moon's out; **~ creciente/menguante/llena/nueva** waxing/waning/full/new moon; **~ de miel** honeymoon; ***estar en la ~*** (fam) to have one's head in the clouds **2** (espejo) mirror; (de puerta, ventana) glass; (escaparate) window; (parabrisas) windshield (AmE), windscreen (BrE) **3** (de la uña) half-moon, lunule (tech)

lunar *adj* lunar ■ *m* **(a)** (en la piel) mole; (pintado) beauty spot **(b)** (en el pelo) gray* patch **(c)** (en un diseño) polka-dot

lunático -ca *adj* lunatic (*before n*) ■ *m,f* lunatic

lunes *m* ▶ 193 (*pl* ~) Monday; **el ~ por la mañana/noche** on Monday morning/night; **todos los ~** every Monday; **el próximo ~** next Monday; **el ~ pasado** last Monday; **el ~ es fiesta** Monday is a holiday; **nos vemos el ~** I'll see you on Monday; **los ~ voy a nadar** on Mondays I go swimming

luneta *f* **1** (Auto) window **2** (Col, Méx) (Teatr) orchestra seats (*pl*) (AmE), front stalls (*pl*) (BrE)

lunfardo *m* Buenos Aires slang

lupa *f* magnifying glass

lustrabotas *mf* (*pl* ~) ⇨ LUSTRADOR

lustrada *f* (AmS) polish, shine

lustrador -dora *m,f* (AmS) bootblack; (niño) shoeshine boy

lustrar [A1] *vt* (esp AmL) ‹*zapatos/muebles*› to polish

■ **lustrarse** *v pron* **1** (esp AmL) ‹*zapatos*› to polish **2** (AmC) (en una actividad) to excel

lustre *m* **(a)** (brillo) shine, luster*; **darle** *or* **sacarle ~ a algo** to polish sth **(b)** (distinción) glory, distinction

lustrín *m* (AmS) (cajón) bootblack's box; (puesto) shoeshine stand

lustro *m* period of five years

luterano -na *adj/m,f* Lutheran

luto *m* mourning; **estar de ~** to be in mourning; **~ riguroso** deep mourning; **ir de ~** to wear mourning (clothes); **ponerse de ~** to go into mourning

Luxemburgo *m* Luxembourg

luxemburgués -guesa *adj* of/from Luxembourg

luz *f* **1** (en general) light; **la ~ del sol** the sunlight; **me da la ~ en los ojos** the light's in my eyes; **a plena ~ del día** in broad daylight; **este reflector da mucha ~** this spotlight is very bright; **leer con poca ~** to read in poor light; **a la ~ de los últimos acontecimientos** in the light of recent events; ***a todas luces***: whichever way you look at it; ***dar a ~*** to give birth; ***sacar algo a la ~*** ‹*secreto/escándalo*› to bring sth to light; ‹*publicación*› to bring out; ***salir a la ~*** «*secreto/escándalo*» to come to light; «*publicación*» to come out **2 (a)** (fam) (electricidad) electricity; **les cortaron la ~** their electricity was cut off; **se fue la ~** (en una casa) the electricity went off; (en una zona) there was a power cut **(b)** (dispositivo) light; **encender** *or* (AmL) **prender** *or* (Esp) **dar la ~** to turn on *o* switch on the light; **apagar la ~** to turn off *o* switch off the light; **cruzar con la luz roja** to cross when the lights are red; **luces de estacionamiento** *or* (Esp) **de situación** parking lights (*pl*) (AmE), sidelights (*pl*) (BrE); **luces de cruce** *or* **cortas** *or* (AmL) **bajas** dipped headlights (*pl*); **poner las luces largas** *or* **altas** to put the headlights on high (AmE) *o* (BrE) full beam; **~ de frenado** stoplight, brake light (BrE); **~ de giro** (Arg) indicator

luzca, luzcan, etc *see* LUCIR

Mm

M, **m** *f* (*read as* /'eme/) *the letter* M, m
m (= **metro**) m, meter*
macabro -bra *adj* macabre
macaco -ca *m,f* (Zool) macaque
macana *f* **1** (AmL) (de policía) billy club (AmE), truncheon (BrE) **2** **(a)** (CS fam) (tontería, disparate): **decir ~s** to talk nonsense; **no hagas la ~ de renunciar** don't be so stupid as to resign (colloq) **(b)** (CS fam) (problema) trouble, snag; **¡qué ~ que no puedas venir!** what a shame *o* (colloq) drag you can't come! **(c)** (RPl fam) (mentira) lie
macanear [A1] *vt* (Méx) (golpear) to beat ■ ~ *vi* (RPl fam) (mentir) to lie; (decir tonterías) to talk garbage (AmE) *o* (BrE) rubbish (colloq)
macanudo -da *adj* (CS, Per fam) great (colloq)
macarrón *m* **(a)** (pasta) piece of macaroni; **macarrones** macaroni **(b)** (galleta) macaroon
macedonia *f* (de frutas) fruit salad, macedoine; (de verduras) mixed vegetables (*pl*), macedoine
macerar [A1] *vt* ‹*fruta*› to soak, macerate; ‹*carne*› to marinate, marinade
maceta *f* flowerpot
macetero *m* **(a)** (para tiestos) flowerpot holder **(b)** (AmS) (tiesto) large flowerpot; (jardinera) window box
machacar [A2] *vt* **(a)** ‹*ajo*› to crush; ‹*almendras*› to grind, crush; ‹*piedra*› to crush, pound **(b)** (fam) ‹*contrincante*› to thrash (colloq) ■ ~ *vi* **(a)** (fam) (insistir): **~ con** *or* **sobre algo** to go on *o* harp on about sth (colloq) **(b)** (fam) (para un examen) to cram (colloq)
machacón -cona *adj* (insistente) insistent; (pesado) tiresome
machamartillo: **a ~** (*loc adj*) ‹*monárquico/feminista*› ardent, staunch; (*loc adv*) firmly
machete *m* (cuchillo) machete ■ *adj inv* (Ven fam) great (colloq)
machetero -ra *m,f* (cañero) cane cutter ■ *adj* (Méx fam) persevering
machismo *m* (actitud, ideología) sexism, male chauvinism
machista *adj* sexist, chauvinist ■ *mf* sexist, male chauvinist
macho *m* **1** (Biol, Zool) male; **~ cabrío** billy goat **2** (fam) (hombre fuerte) tough guy (colloq); (pey) macho man (colloq & pej) **3** (Mec, Tec) pin; (Elec) male (plug); (de un corchete) hook; (en carpintería) peg, pin ■ *adj* **1** ‹*animal/planta*› male; **ballena/elefante ~** bull whale/elephant; **gato ~** tomcat **2** (fam) (valiente, fuerte) tough, brave; (pey) macho (pej) **3** ‹*pieza*› male
machote -ta *m,f* **(a)** (fam) (hombre) tough guy (colloq); (pey) macho man (colloq & pej) **(b)** (fam & pey) (mujer) butch woman (colloq & pej)
machucar [A2] *vt* **(a)** ‹*fruta*› to bruise **(b)** (fam) ‹*dedo*› to crush **(c)** (Méx) ‹*ajo*› to crush
machucón *m* (AmL fam) (moretón) bruise
macilento -ta *adj* **(a)** ‹*persona/cara*› gaunt, haggard **(b)** ‹*luz*› wan (liter)
macillo *m* hammer
macizo[1] -za *adj* **(a)** [SER] (sólido) solid **(b)** [ESTAR] (fam) ‹*persona*› (robusto) strapping (colloq)
macizo[2] *m* (de montañas) massif; (de flores, arbustos) clump
maco *m* (Col) monkey
macramé *m* macramé
macrobiótico -ca *adj* macrobiotic
macroeconomía *f* macroeconomics
macuco -ca *adj* (Chi, Per fam) cute (AmE colloq), sharp (BrE colloq)
macuto *m* back pack, rucksack (BrE)
madalena *f* ≈ cupcake (AmE), ≈ fairycake (BrE)
madeja *f* (de lana, hilo) hank, skein
madera *f* (material) wood; (para construcción, carpintería) lumber (esp AmE), timber (BrE); **~ blanda/dura** softwood/hardwood; **es de ~** it's made of wood, it's wooden; **mesa de ~** wooden table; **~ de pino** pine (wood); ***tener ~ de algo*** to have the makings of sth; ***tocar ~*** to knock (on) wood (AmE), touch wood (BrE)
maderero -ra *adj* timber (*before n*); lumber (*before n*) (esp AmE) ■ *m,f* timber merchant
madero *m* (piece of) timber
madrastra *f* stepmother
madrazo *m* (Méx fam) blow; **darle un ~ a algn** to give sb a beating; **películas de ~** violent movies
madre *f* mother; **ser ~** to be a mother; **~ de familia** mother; **~ política** mother-in-law; **~ soltera** single *o* unmarried mother; **~ superiora** Mother Superior; **¡~ mía!** *or* **¡mi ~!** (my) goodness!, (good) heavens!; ***me vale ~s*** (Méx vulg) I don't give a damn (colloq) *o* (vulg) shit; ***salirse de ~*** «*río*» to burst its banks; «*situación*» to get out of hand
madreperla *f* mother-of-pearl
madreselva *f* honeysuckle
Madrid *m* Madrid
madriguera *f* **(a)** (de conejos) warren, burrow; (de zorros) earth; (de tejones) set **(b)** (de maleantes) den, lair
madrileño -ña *adj* of/from Madrid ■ *m,f* person from Madrid
madrina *f*

■ **Nota** En inglés *godmother* no se usa como apelativo

---

1 (a) (en bautizo) godmother; (en boda) ≈matron of honor* **(b)** (de barco) *woman who launches a ship* **2** (Méx fam) paddy wagon (AmE sl), police van (BrE)

madroño *m* (Bot) tree strawberry

madrugada *f* **(a)** (amanecer, alba) dawn, daybreak; **se levantó de ~** (muy temprano) she got up very early (in the morning); (al amanecer) she got up at dawn *o* daybreak **(b)** (después de medianoche) (early) morning; **las tres de la ~** three o'clock in the morning; **llegó de ~** he arrived in the early hours of the morning *o* in the small hours

madrugador -dora *adj*: **ser ~** to be an early riser

madrugar [A3] *vi* to get up early

maduración *f* **(a)** (de fruta) ripening (process) **(b)** (de persona) maturing (process) **(c)** (de idea) development, maturing

madurar [A1] *vi* **(a)** «*fruta*» to ripen **(b)** «*persona*» to mature **(c)** «*ideas*» to mature, come to fruition ■ **~** *vt* **(a)** ‹*fruta*› to ripen **(b)** ‹*plan*› to develop, bring to fruition

madurez *f* **(a)** (de fruta) ripeness **(b)** (de persona) maturity

maduro -ra *adj* **1** [ESTAR] ‹*fruta*› ripe **2 (a)** [SER] (entrado en años) mature, of mature years **(b)** [SER] (sensato) mature; **es joven pero muy ~** he's young but very mature for his age

maestría *f* **1** (liter) (habilidad) skill, mastery **2** (esp AmL) (Educ) (postgrado) master's degree, master's

maestro -tra *m,f* **1 (a)** (Educ) teacher, schoolteacher; **maestra jardinera** (Arg, Col) kindergarten teacher, nursery school teacher (BrE) **(b)** (en un arte): **es un ~ de la danza española** he is a master of Spanish dance; **un ~ de las letras españolas** a leading authority *o* an expert on Spanish literature **(c)** (en un oficio) master (*before n*); **~ carpintero** master carpenter **(d)** (Chi) (obrero) builder **2** (Mús) maestro **3** (en ajedrez) master

mafia *f* mafia

mafioso -sa *adj* mafia (*before n*) ■ *m,f* (criminal) gangster, racketeer; (de la Mafia siciliana) mafioso

magdalena *f* (Esp) ≈cupcake (AmE), ≈fairy-cake (BrE)

magia *f* magic; **hacer ~** to do magic (tricks)

mágico -ca *adj* **(a)** ‹*poderes/número*› magic (*before n*) **(b)** ‹*belleza/ambiente*› magical

magisterio *m* (enseñanza) teaching; (carrera) teacher training; **estudia ~** he's training to be a teacher

magistrado -da *m,f* judge

magistral *adj* ‹*actuación/libro*› masterly; ‹*tono/actitud*› magisterial (frml)

magnánimo -ma *adj* magnanimous

magnate *mf* magnate, tycoon; **los ~s de la prensa** the press barons

magnesia *f* magnesia

magnesio *m* magnesium

magnético -ca *adj* magnetic

magnetismo *m* magnetism

magnetófono, **magnetofón** *m* (reel-to-reel) tape recorder

magnífico -ca *adj* **(a)** (estupendo) ‹*edificio/panorama*› magnificent, superb; ‹*espectáculo/escritor/oportunidad*› marvelous*, wonderful; **¡~!** excellent! **(b)** (suntuoso) magnificent, splendid

magnitud *f* magnitude; **la ~ de la tragedia** the extent *o* magnitude of the tragedy

magnolia *f* magnolia

mago -ga *m,f* **(a)** (prestidigitador) conjurer, magician **(b)** (en cuentos) wizard, magician **(c)** (persona habilidosa) wizard

magro -gra *adj* lean

magulladura *f* bruise

magullar [A1] *vt* to bruise
■ **magullarse** *v pron* to bruise

mahometano -na *adj* Islamic ■ *m,f* follower of Islam

mahonesa *f* mayonnaise

maicena® *f* cornstarch (AmE), cornflour (BrE)

maillot /ma'ʝo(t)/ *m* **(a)** (traje de baño) swimsuit **(b)** (de ciclista) jersey

maíz *m* (planta) maize, corn (AmE); (Coc) corn (AmE), sweet corn (esp BrE); **~ tostado** *or* **pira** *or* **tote** (Col) popcorn

maizal *m* cornfield (AmE), maize field (BrE)

maizena® *f* cornstarch (AmE), cornflour (BrE)

majadería *f* (fam) **(a)** (cualidad) stupidity **(b)** (dicho, acto): **no dice más que ~s** he talks a lot of rubbish *o* nonsense (colloq); **fue una ~** it was a stupid thing to do

majadero -ra *adj* (fam) (insensato) stupid ■ *m,f* clown (colloq)

majar [A1] *vt* to crush

maje *mf* **1** (AmC arg) (individuo) (*m*) guy (colloq), bloke (BrE colloq); (*f*) girl **2** (Méx fam) (persona crédula) sucker (colloq)

majestad *f* **1** (aspecto grandioso) majesty **2 su Majestad** (al referirse — al rey) His Majesty; (— a la reina) Her Majesty; (al dirigirse al rey, a la reina) Your Majesty; **sus M~es los Reyes** Their Majesties the King and Queen

majestuosidad *f* majesty

majestuoso -sa *adj* majestic

majo -ja *adj* (Esp fam) **(a)** (simpático) nice **(b)** (guapo) ‹*hombre*› handsome, good-looking; ‹*mujer*› good-looking, pretty **(c)** ‹*casa/vestido*› lovely, nice

mal *adj*: *ver* MALO ■ *adj inv* **1** [ESTAR] (enfermo) ill; (anímicamente) in a bad way (colloq); (incómodo) uncomfortable; **andar ~ del estómago** to have trouble with one's stomach; **¡éste está ~ de la cabeza!** he's not right in the head; **esas cosas me ponen ~** things like that really upset me **2** (fam) (*en frases negativas*) (refiriéndose al aspecto): **no está nada ~** she's/he's/it's not at all bad (colloq) **3** (insatisfactorio): **estoy** *or* **salí muy ~ en esta foto** I look awful in this photograph; **le queda ~ ese color** that color doesn't suit her **4** [ESTAR] (incorrecto) wrong **5** (indicando escasez) **estar** *or* **ir ~ DE algo** ‹*de dinero/tiempo*› to be short OF sth ■ *adv* **1** (de manera no satisfactoria) ‹*vestir/cantar/jugar*› badly; **le fue ~ en los exámenes** his exams went badly; **te oigo muy ~** I can hardly hear you; **el negocio marcha ~** the business isn't doing well;

de ~ en peor from bad to worse **2** (desfavorablemente) badly, ill; **hablar ~ de algn** to speak badly *o* ill of sb **3 (a)** (de manera errónea) wrong, wrongly; **te han informado ~** you've been badly *o* wrongly informed; **te entendí ~** I misunderstood you **(b)** (de manera reprensible) ‹*obrar/partarse*› badly; **haces ~ en no ir a verla** it's wrong of you not to go and see her; **me contestó muy ~** she answered me very rudely **4** (desagradable) ‹*oler/saber*› bad; **aquí huele ~** there's a horrible smell *o* it smells in here **5** (*en locs*) **hacer mal** (AmL) (a la salud): **esto hace ~ al hígado** this is bad for the liver; **el pescado me hizo ~** the fish didn't agree with me; **menos mal**: **¡menos ~!** thank goodness!; **¡menos ~ que le avisaron a tiempo!** it's just as well they told him in time!; ***tomarse algo a ~*** to take sth to heart ■ *m* **1** (Fil) evil; **el bien y el ~** good and evil, right and wrong **2** (daño, perjuicio): **el divorcio de sus padres le hizo mucho ~** her parents' divorce did her a lot of harm **3** (cosa dañina) ill, evil; **los ~es sociales** the social ills; ***no hay ~ que por bien no venga*** every cloud has a silver lining **4** (Med) (liter) (enfermedad) illness; **tiene ~ de amores** (fam) he's lovesick; **~ de (las) altura(s)** altitude sickness, mountain sickness **5** (pena) trouble

malabarismo *m* juggling; ***hacer ~s*** «*malabarista*» to juggle; (en situación difícil) to do a juggling *o* balancing act

malabarista *mf* juggler

malacostumbrado -da *adj* spoiled*, pampered

malacostumbrar [A1] *vt* to spoil ■ **malacostumbrarse** *v pron* to become spoilt

malacrianza *f* (AmL) rudeness

malaria *f* malaria

Malasia *f* Malaysia

malasio -sia *adj/m,f* Malaysian

malayo[1] -ya *adj/m,f* Malay

malayo[2] *m* (idioma) Malay

malcriado -da *adj* (mimado) spoiled*; (travieso) bad-mannered, badly brought up

malcriar [A17] *vt* to spoil, bring … up badly

maldad *f* **(a)** (cualidad) evilness, wickedness **(b)** (acto) evil deed, wicked thing

maldecir [I25] *vt* to curse ■ **~** *vi* **(a)** (renegar) to curse; **~** DE **algo/algn** to speak ill OF sth/sb **(b)** (blasfemar) to swear, curse (AmE)

maldición *f* **(a)** (imprecación) curse; **nos echó una ~** she put a curse on us **(b)** (palabrota) swearword; **soltó una ~** he swore

maldiga, **maldijo, etc** *see* MALDECIR

maldito -ta *adj* (fam) (expresando irritación) damn (*before n*) (colloq), wretched (*before n*) (colloq); **¡este ~ ruido!** this damn *o* wretched noise!; **¡maldita/~ sea!** damn (it)! (colloq)

maldoso -sa *adj* (Méx) mischievous

malecón *m* **(a)** (rompeolas) breakwater; (embarcadero) jetty **(b)** (AmL) (paseo marítimo) seafront

maleducado -da *adj* rude, bad-mannered

maléfico -ca *adj* ‹*poderes/espíritus*› evil; ‹*influencia*› harmful

malenseñado -da *adj* (CS) (maleducado) rude, bad-mannered; (mimado) spoiled

malenseñar [A1] *vt* (CS) to spoil

malentender [E8] *vt* to misunderstand

malentendido *m* misunderstanding

malestar *m* **(a)** (Med) discomfort **(b)** (desazón, inquietud) unease

maleta *f* **1** (valija) suitcase, case; **hacer la ~** to pack (one's case) **2** (Chi, Per) ⇒ MALETERA

maletera *f* (Chi, Per) trunk (AmE), boot (BrE)

maletero *m* **(a)** (Auto) trunk (AmE), boot (BrE) **(b)** (mozo de estación) porter

maletín *m* (para documentos) briefcase; (maleta pequeña) overnight bag, small case; (de médico) bag

malévolo -la *adj* malevolent, malicious

maleza *f* **1** (espesura) undergrowth; (malas hierbas) weeds (*pl*) **2** (AmL) (mala hierba) weed

malformación *f* malformation

malgastador -dora *adj* wasteful, spendthrift ■ *m,f* squanderer, spendthrift

malgastar [A1] *vt* ‹*tiempo/esfuerzo*› to waste; ‹*dinero/herencia*› to squander

malhablado -da *adj* foul-mouthed

malhechor -chora *m,f* criminal, delinquent

malhumorado -da *adj* **(a)** [SER] ‹*persona/gesto*› bad-tempered **(b)** [ESTAR] ‹*persona*› in a bad mood

malicia *f* **(a)** (intención malévola) malice, malevolence **(b)** (picardía) mischief

malicioso -sa *adj* **(a)** (malintencionado) malicious, spiteful **(b)** (pícaro) mischievous

maligno -na *adj* **(a)** ‹*tumor*› malignant **(b)** ‹*persona/intención*› evil; ‹*influencia*› harmful, evil

malinchista *adj* (Méx) *preferring foreign things*

malinformar [A1] *vt* (CS frml) to misinform (frml)

malintencionado -da *adj* ‹*persona/palabras*› malicious, spiteful; ‹*golpe*› malicious

malinterpretar [A1] *vt* to misinterpret

malla *f* **1** (red) mesh; **una ~ para los insectos** a screen *o* mesh to stop insects **2 (a)** (para gimnasia) leotard; **~ de baño** (RPl) bathing suit, swimsuit **(b) mallas** *fpl* (medias) tights (*pl*); (sin pie) leggings (*pl*)

Mallorca *f* Majorca

mallorquín[1] -quina *adj/m,f* Majorcan

mallorquín[2] *m* (idioma) Majorcan

mallugar [A3] *vt* (Méx, Ven) to bruise

malnutrición *f* malnutrition

malnutrido -da *adj* malnourished

malo -la *adj* [*The form* MAL *is used before masculine singular nouns*] **1 (a)** [SER] (en general) bad; **una novela mala** a bad novel; **un mal amigo** a bad friend; **una mala caída** a bad fall; **soy muy ~ para los números** I'm very bad with figures; **¡qué mala suerte** *or* (fam) **pata!** what bad luck!, how unlucky!; **lo ~ es que** … the thing *o* trouble is that …; **las malas compañías** bad company; **mala hierba** weed; **~s tratos** ill-treatment; **es ~ tomar tanto sol** it's not good to sunbathe so much; **tienes mala cara** *or* **mal aspecto** you don't look well **(b)** ‹*calidad/visibilidad*› poor; **tiene mala ortografía** her spelling is poor; ***estar de malas*** (de mal humor) (fam) to be in a bad mood; (con mala suerte) (esp AmL) to be unlucky; ***más vale ~ conocido que bueno por conocer*** better the devil you know (than the devil you don't) **2** [SER] ‹*persona*› (en sentido ético) nasty; (travieso) naughty; **¡qué ~ eres con tu hermano!** you're really horrible *o* nasty to your brother; **no seas mala, préstamelo** don't be mean *o* rotten, lend it to me (colloq); **una mala mujer** a loose woman; **una mujer mala** a wicked *o* an evil woman; **lo hizo a** *or* **con mala idea** he did it deliberately *o* to be nasty; **mala palabra** (esp AmL) rude *o* dirty word; **dicen las malas lenguas que** ... (fam) there's a rumor going around that ..., people are saying that ...; *ver tb* LECHE 3 **3** [ESTAR] **(a)** (en mal estado) ‹*alimento*›: **el pescado/queso está ~** the fish/cheese has gone bad, that fish/cheese is off (BrE) **(b)** (Esp, Méx fam) (enfermo) sick (AmE), ill (BrE); **el pobre está malito** the poor thing's not very well (colloq); ***hacerse mala sangre*** to get upset ■ *m,f* (leng infantil *o* hum) baddy (colloq)

malograr [A1] *vt* ‹*oportunidad*› to waste; ‹*trabajo*› to ruin, spoil

■ **malograrse** *v pron* **1** «*proyecto/cosecha*» to fail **2 (a)** «*persona*» (morir joven) to die young *o* before one's time **(b)** (Per) «*reloj*» to stop working; «*lavadora*» to break down

maloliente *adj* stinking, smelly

malparado -da *adj*: **salir ~** to come off badly

malpensado -da *adj*: **no seas ~** why do you always think the worst of people?

malsano -na *adj* ‹*clima/lugar*› unhealthy; ‹*influencia*› bad, unhealthy

malsonante *adj* rude

malta *f* **(a)** (cereal) malt **(b)** (Chi) (cerveza) stout

malteada *f* (AmL) milk shake

maltratar [A1] *vt* **(a)** ‹*persona/animal*› to maltreat, ill-treat, mistreat; (pegar) ‹*niño/mujer*› to batter **(b)** ‹*juguete/coche*› to mistreat, treat ... very roughly

maltrecho -cha *adj*: **lo dejaron muy ~** they left him in a bad way

malucho -cha *adj* (fam) (algo enfermo): **estar ~** to be *o* feel under the weather (colloq)

malva *adj inv/m* ▶ 97 mauve ■ *f* mallow; **~ real** hollyhock, rose mallow (AmE)

malvado -da *adj* wicked, evil

malvavisco *m* marshmallow

malvender [E1] *vt* to sell ... off cheap, sell ... at a loss

malversación *f tb* **~ de fondos** embezzlement (of funds)

malversar [A1] *vt* to embezzle, misappropriate

Malvinas *fpl*: **las ~** the Falkland Islands, the Falklands

malvón *m* (RPl, Méx) geranium

mama *f* (Anat) ▶ 123 breast; (Zool) mammary gland

mamá *f* (*pl* **-más**) (fam) mom (AmE colloq), mum (BrE colloq); (usado por niños) mommy (AmE colloq), mummy (BrE colloq)

mamadera *f* (CS, Per) (biberón) (feeding) bottle, baby bottle

mamado -da *adj* **(a)** (fam) (borracho) tight(colloq), sloshed (colloq) **(b)** (Col, Ven fam) (cansado) dead beat (colloq), shattered (colloq); (aburrido) bored

mamar [A1] *vi* **1 (a)** «*bebé*» to feed; **dar de ~** to breastfeed **(b)** «*gato/cordero*» to suckle **2** (fam) (beber alcohol) to booze (colloq)

mameluco *m* (AmL) **(a)** (de niño, bebé) rompers (*pl*), romper suit (BrE) **(b)** (pantalón con peto) overalls (*pl*) (AmE), dungarees (*pl*) (BrE); (de trabajo) coveralls (*pl*) (AmE), overalls (*pl*) (BrE)

mamífero *adj* mammalian ■ *m* mammal

mamila *f* (Méx) (biberón) (feeding) bottle; (tetilla) nipple (AmE), teat (BrE)

mampara *f* **(a)** (biombo, tabique) screen, partition **(b)** (Chi, Per) (puerta) inner door

mampostería *f* masonry

manada *f* **(a)** (Zool) (de elefantes) herd; (de leones) pride; (de lobos) pack **(b)** (fam) (de gente) herd

Managua *f* Managua

managüense *adj* of/from Managua

manantial *m* (de agua) spring

manar [A1] *vi* to pour

manatí *m* manatee

mancha *f* **1 (a)** (de suciedad) spot, mark; (difícil de quitar) stain; **una ~ de grasa** a grease stain; **~s de humedad** damp patches; **~ de petróleo** oil slick **(b)** (borrón) blot **2 (a)** (en la piel) mark **(b)** (en el pelaje, las plumas) patch; (del leopardo) spot **3** (liter) (imperfección, mácula) stain; **sin ~** ‹*alma*› pure; ‹*reputación*› spotless **4** (Per fam) (pandilla) gang

manchado -da *adj* ‹*mantel/vestido*› stained; **está ~ de vino** it has wine stains on it; **~ de sangre** blood-stained

manchar [A1] *vt* **1** (ensuciar) to mark, get ... dirty; (de algo difícil de quitar) to stain **2** ‹*reputación/honra/memoria*› to tarnish ■ **~** *vi* to stain

■ **mancharse** *v pron* **(a)** «*ropa/mantel*» to get dirty; (de algo difícil de quitar) to get stained; **~se** DE *or* CON **algo** to get stained WITH sth **(b)** (*refl*) «*persona*» to get dirty; **me manché la blusa de aceite** I got oil stains on my blouse

manchego -ga *adj* of/from La Mancha

manco -ca *adj*: **es ~ de un brazo/una mano** he only has one arm/hand

mancomunidad *f* community, association; **M~ Británica de Naciones** British Commonwealth

mancorna *f* (Col) cufflink

mancuernilla *f* (Méx) cufflink

manda *f* (Chi, Méx) offering, promise

mandadero -ra *m,f* (esp AmL) (*m*) office boy; (*f*) office girl

mandado[1] -da *adj* (Méx fam): **es muy ~** he's a real opportunist; **no seas mandada, sólo te ofrecí uno** don't be so greedy, I only offered you one (colloq) ■ *m,f* (esp Esp) (subordinado) minion (hum *or* pej); **no soy más que un ~** I'm just following orders

mandado² *m* **(a)** (esp AmL) (compra): **hacer los ~s** *or* (Méx) **ir al ~** to do the shopping **(b)** (Méx) (cosa comprada): **¿me trajiste el ~?** did you get the shopping *o* the things I asked you for? **(c)** (diligencia) errand

mandamiento *m* **1** (Relig) commandment **2** (orden) order; (Der) warrant, order

mandar [A1] *vt* **1 (a)** (ordenar): **a mí nadie me manda** nobody tells me what to do, nobody orders me about; **haz lo que te mandan** do as you're told; **la mandó callar** he told *o* ordered her to be quiet; **mandó que sirvieran la comida** she ordered lunch to be served **(b)** (recetar) to prescribe; **el médico le mandó descansar** the doctor advised him to rest **2** (enviar) to send; **la mandé por el pan** I sent her out to buy the bread **3** (AmL) (tratándose de encargos): **mis padres me ~on llamar** my parents sent for me; **mandó decir que** ... she sent a message to say that ...; **~ algo a arreglar** to get *o* have sth mended **4** (AmL fam) (arrojar, lanzar): **mandó la pelota fuera de la cancha** he kicked/sent/hit the ball out of play ■ **~** *vi* (ser el jefe) to be in charge, be the boss (colloq); **¿mande?** (Méx) (I'm) sorry?, pardon?; **¡María! — ¿mande?** (Méx) María! — yes?

mandarina *f* (Bot, Coc) mandarin (orange), tangerine

mandatario -ria *m,f* (Pol) *tb* **primer ~/primera mandataria** head of state

mandato *m* **1 (a)** (período) term of office **(b)** (orden) mandate **2** (Der) mandate

mandíbula *f* jaw

mandil *m* (delantal) leather apron

mandioca *f* (planta) cassava; (fécula) tapioca

mando *m* **1** (en general) command; **entregarle el ~ a algn** to hand over command to sb; **dotes de ~** leadership qualities; **estar al ~ (de algo)** to be in charge (of sth) **2** (Auto, Elec) control; **~ a distancia** remote control

mandolina *f* mandolin

mandón -dona *adj* bossy

mandonear [A1] *vt* (fam) to boss ... around (colloq)

mandril *m* (Zool) mandrill

manearse [A1] *v pron* (Chi fam) to get in a tangle (colloq), to be all fingers and thumbs (colloq)

manecilla *f* hand; **la ~ grande/pequeña** the minute/hour hand

manejable *adj* **1** ‹*coche*› maneuverable*; ‹*máquina*› easy-to-use; ‹*pelo*› manageable **2** ‹*persona*› easily led, easily manipulated

manejar [A1] *vt* **1** (usar) ‹*herramienta/arma/diccionario*› to use; ‹*máquina*› to use, operate **2** (dirigir, llevar) ‹*negocio/empresa*› to manage; ‹*asuntos*› to manage, handle **3** (manipular) to manipulate **4** (AmL) ‹*auto*› to drive ■ **~** *vi* (AmL) to drive

■ **manejarse** *v pron* **1** (desenvolverse) to get by, manage **2** (Col) (comportarse) to behave

manejo *m* **1** (uso): **el ~ de la máquina es muy sencillo** the machine is easy to use *o* operate; **su ~ de la lengua** his use of the language **2** (de asunto, negocio) management **3** (AmL) (Auto) driving

manera *f* **1** (modo, forma) way; **yo lo hago a mi ~** I do it my way; **a ~ de** by way of; **de todas ~s** anyway; **su ~ de ser** the way she is; **se puede ir vestido de cualquier ~** you can dress however you want; **no lo pongas así, de cualquier ~** don't just put it in any which way (AmE) *o* (BrE) any old how; **de ninguna ~ lo voy a permitir** there's no way I'm going to allow it; **de alguna ~ tendré que conseguirlo** I'll have to get it somehow (or other); **no hay/hubo ~** it is/it was impossible; **de ~ que** so; **de mala ~** ‹*contestar*› rudely; ‹*tratar*› badly **2 maneras** *fpl* (modales) manners (*pl*)

manga *f* **1 (a)** (de abrigo, blusa) sleeve; **sin ~s** sleeveless; **de ~ corta/larga** short-sleeved/long-sleeved; **en ~s de camisa** in shirtsleeves; ***tener (la) ~ ancha*** to be tolerant *o* lenient **(b)** (capa de jerga) (AmC) poncho **2** (Coc) (filtro) strainer; (para repostería) *tb* **~ pastelera** pastry bag **3** (Dep) round **4** (manguera) hose; **~ de incendio** fire hose; **~ de riego** hosepipe **5** (AmL) (de langostas) swarm

manglar *m* mangrove swamp

mangle *m* mangrove

mango *m* **1** (de cuchillo, paraguas) handle **2** (Bot) (árbol) mango (tree); (fruta) mango **3** (Méx fam & hum) (persona atractiva): **es un ~** «*mujer*» she's a real stunner (colloq); «*hombre*» he's a real hunk (colloq)

mangonear [A1] *vi* (fam) **(a)** (mandonear) to order *o* (colloq) boss people around **(b)** (entrometerse) to meddle ■ **~** *vt* (fam) to boss ... around (colloq)

mangosta *f* mongoose

manguera *f* (para regar) hose, hosepipe; (de bombero) hose

maní *m* (*pl* **-níes** *or* (crit) **-nises**) (AmC, AmS) peanut

manía *f* **1** (obsesión, capricho): **tiene sus ~s** he has his funny little ways; **tiene la ~ de la limpieza** she has a mania for cleanliness *o* (colloq) a thing about cleaning; **le ha dado la ~ de vestirse de negro** she has this fad *o* craze of dressing in black; **~ persecutoria** *or* **de persecución** persecution complex *o* mania **2** (antipatía): **tenerle ~ a algn** to have it in for sb (colloq)

maniaco -ca, maníaco -ca *m,f* **(a)** (Psic) manic **(b)** (fam) (loco) maniac; **~ sexual** sex maniac

maniatar [A1] *vt* **(a)** ‹*persona*›: **los ladrones lo ~on** the burglars tied his hands **(b)** ‹*animal*› to hobble

maniático -ca *adj* **(a)** (delicado, difícil) finicky, fussy **(b)** (obsesionado) obsessive

manicero -ra *m,f* (AmC, AmS) peanut seller

manicomio *m* mental hospital, lunatic asylum

manicura *f* manicure; **hacerse la ~** (*refl*) to do one's nails; (*caus*) to have a manicure

manido -da *adj* ‹*frase*› hackneyed; ‹*tema*› stale

manifestación *f* **1** (Pol) demonstration **2** (expresión, indicio) sign; **las manifestaciones artísticas/culturales de la época** the artistic/cultural expression of the era

manifestante *mf* demonstrator

manifestar [A5] *vt* **(a)** (expresar) ‹*desaprobación/agradecimiento*› to express; **~on su apoyo a esta propuesta** they expressed their support for the proposal **(b)** (demostrar) ‹*emociones*› to show
■ **manifestarse** *v pron* **1** (hacerse evidente) to become apparent *o* evident; (ser evidente) to be apparent *o* evident **2** (Pol) to demonstrate, take part in a demonstration **3** (dar opinión): **~se en contra/a favor de algo** to express one's opposition to/support for sth

manifiesta, **manifiestas, etc** *see* MANIFESTAR

manifiesto¹ -ta *adj* (frml) manifest (frml), evident (frml); **poner algo de ~** to highlight sth; **quedar de ~** to become plain *o* obvious *o* evident

manifiesto² *m* (Pol) manifesto

manija *f* (esp AmL) handle

manilla *f* **(a)** (de reloj) hand **(b)** (de cajón) handle **(c)** (Col) (guante) baseball glove

manillar *m* (esp Esp) handlebars (*pl*)

maniobra *f* maneuver*; **estar de ~s** (Mil) to be on maneuvers

maniobrar [A1] *vi/vt* to maneuver*

manipulador -dora *adj* manipulative ■ *m,f* (aprovechado) manipulator

manipular [A1] *vt* **1 (a)** ‹*mercancías*› to handle **(b)** ‹*aparato/máquina*› to operate, use **2** ‹*persona/información/datos*› to manipulate; **~ los resultados** to fix *o* rig the results

maniquí *mf* **(a)** (persona) model **(b) maniquí** *m* (de sastre, escaparate) mannequin, dummy

manirroto -ta *adj* **(a)** (fam) extravagant **(b)** (generoso) generous, open-handed ■ *m,f* (fam) spendthrift

manitas *mf* (Esp, Méx fam) handyman (colloq)

manito -ta *m,f*: *ver* MANO²

manivela *f* crank, handle

manjar *m* delicacy; **~ blanco** (Andes) ⇨ DULCE DE LECHE

mano¹ *f* **1 (a)** (Anat) ▶ **123** hand; **tengo las ~s sucias** my hands are dirty; **levantar la ~** to raise one's hands, put one's hand up; **¡~s arriba!** *or* **¡arriba las ~s!** hands up!; **con la ~ en el corazón** hand on heart; **le hizo adiós con la ~** he waved goodbye to her; **su carta pasó de ~ en ~** her letter was passed around; **darle la ~ a algn** (para saludar) to shake hands with sb, to shake sb's hand; (para ayudar, ser ayudado) to give sb one's hand; **dame la ~** hold my hand; **me tendió la ~** he held out his hand to me; **me tomó de la ~** she took me by the hand; **ir (tomados) de la ~** to walk hand in hand; **~ de obra** labor **(b)** (Zool) (de oso, perro) paw; (de mono) hand; (Equ) forefoot, front foot **2** (control, posesión) *gen* **~s** hands (*pl*); **ha cambiado de ~s** it has changed hands; **cayó en ~s del enemigo** it fell into the hands of the enemy; **haré todo lo que esté en mis ~s** I will do everything in my power; **la oportunidad se nos fue de las ~s** we let the opportunity slip through our fingers; **se tomó la justicia por su propia ~** he took the law into his own hands **3** (en fútbol) handball **4** (del mortero) pestle **5** (de pintura, barniz) coat **6** (Jueg) (vuelta, juego) hand; (conjunto de cartas) hand; (jugador): **soy/eres ~** it's my/your lead **7** (*en locs*) **a mano** (no a máquina) by hand; **hecho a ~** handmade; **escrito a ~** handwritten; **tejido a ~** handwoven; **las tiendas me quedan muy a ~** the shops are very close by *o* near; **siempre tengo un diccionario a ~** I always keep a dictionary by me; **a la mano** (AmL) close at hand; **de mano** hand (*before n*); **en mano** ‹*lápiz/copa*› in hand; ***agarrar*** *or* (esp Esp) ***coger a algn con las ~s en la masa*** to catch sb red-handed; ***agarrarle*** *or* ***tomarle la ~ a algo*** (CS fam) to get the hang of sth (colloq); ***bajo ~*** on the quiet, on the sly (colloq); ***con las ~s vacías*** empty-handed; ***darse la ~*** (para saludar) to shake hands; (para cruzar, jugar, etc) to hold hands; ***de segunda ~*** secondhand; ***echar*** *or* ***dar una ~*** to give *o* lend a hand; ***echar ~ a algo*** (fam) to grab sth; ***estar/quedar a ~*** (AmL fam) to be even *o* quits (colloq); ***lavarse las ~s*** to wash one's hands; ***levantarle la ~ a algn*** to raise one's hand to sb; ***llegar*** *or* ***pasar a las ~s*** to come to blows; ***pedir la ~ de algn*** to ask for sb's hand in marriage; ***ser la ~ derecha de algn*** to be sb's right-hand man/woman; ***tenderle una ~ a algn*** to offer sb a (helping) hand; ***tener ~ dura*** to have a firm hand; ***tener ~ para algo*** to be good at sth; ***traerse algo entre ~s*** to be up to sth (colloq) **8 (a)** (lado) side; **queda de esta ~** it's on this side of the street; **a ~ derecha** on the right **(b)** (Auto) side of the road

mano² -na *m,f* (AmL fam) (apelativo) buddy (AmE colloq), mate (BrE colloq)

manojo *m* bunch; ***ser un ~ de nervios*** to be a bundle of nerves

manoseado -da *adj* **(a)** ‹*libro*› well-thumbed; **fruta manoseada** fruit that has been handled by lots of people **(b)** ‹*tema*› hackneyed, well-worn

manosear [A1] *vt* **(a)** ‹*objeto*› to handle **(b)** (fam) ‹*persona*› to grope (colloq)

manotada *f* (Col) handful

manotazo *m* swipe

mansalva: **a ~** (*loc adv*) ‹*disparar*› at close range

mansión *f* mansion; **~ señorial** stately home

manso -sa *adj* **(a)** ‹*caballo*› tame; ‹*toro*› docile; ‹*perro*› friendly **(b)** (liter) ‹*río*› gently-flowing (liter)

manta *f* **1** (de cama) blanket **2** (Chi) (poncho) poncho **3** (Méx) (tela) *a coarse muslin-like cloth*, calico (BrE)

manteca *f* **(a)** (grasa) fat; (de cerdo) lard **(b)** (mantequilla) (RPl) butter; **~ de cacao** cocoa butter; **~ de maní** (RPl) peanut butter

mantecoso -sa *adj* greasy

mantel *m* (de mesa) tablecloth; (del altar) altar cloth; **~ individual** place mat

mantelería *f* table linen

mantención *f* (CS) maintenance

mantener [E27] *vt* **1** (económicamente) ‹*familia/persona*› to support, maintain; ‹*amante*› to keep **2** (conservar, preservar) to keep; **~ la calma** to keep calm; **~ el equilibrio** to keep one's balance; **~ algo en equilibrio** to balance sth; **para ~ su peso actual** to maintain his present weight **3 (a)** ‹*conversaciones*› to have; ‹*contactos*› to maintain,

keep up; ‹*correspondencia*› to keep up; ‹*relaciones*› to maintain **(b)** (cumplir) ‹*promesa/palabra*› to keep **4** (afirmar, sostener) to maintain
■ **mantenerse** *v pron* **1** (sustentarse económicamente) to support oneself **2** (en cierto estado, cierta situación) to keep; **~se en forma** to keep fit; **la torre aún se mantiene en pie** the tower is still standing; **~se en contacto (con algn)** to keep in touch (with sb) **3** (alimentarse): **~se a base de latas** to live off tinned food

mantenimiento *m* maintenance; **ejercicios de ~** keep-fit exercises

mantequilla *f* butter; **~ de cacao** (Chi, Per) cocoa butter

mantequillera *f* butter dish

mantiene, mantienes, etc *see* MANTENER

mantilla *f* **(a)** (de mujer) mantilla **(b)** (de bebé) terry diaper (AmE), terry nappy (BrE)

manto *m* (Indum) cloak

mantón *m* shawl

mantuve, mantuvo, etc *see* MANTENER

manual *adj* ‹*trabajo/destreza*› manual; **tener habilidad ~** to be good with one's hands ■ *m* manual, handbook

manualidades *fpl* handicrafts (*pl*)

manubrio *m* **(a)** (manivela) crank, handle **(b)** (AmL) (de bicicleta) handlebars (*pl*) **(c)** (Chi, Par) (de auto) steering wheel

manufacturar [A1] *vt* to manufacture

manuscrito[1] -ta *adj* hand-written, manuscript (frml)

manuscrito[2] *m* manuscript

manutención *f* maintenance

manzana *f* **1** (Bot) apple **2** (de edificios) block; **dar una vuelta a la ~** to go round the block **3** (AmL) (Anat) *tb* **~ de Adán** Adam's apple

manzanar *m* apple orchard

manzanilla *f* (planta) camomile; (infusión) camomile tea ■ *m* manzanilla (*dry sherry*)

manzano *m* apple tree

maña *f* **1** (habilidad) skill, knack (colloq); **tener** *or* **darse ~ para algo** to be good at sth; ***más vale ~ que fuerza*** brain is better than brawn **2 mañas** *fpl* (artimañas) wiles (*pl*), guile **3** (capricho) bad habit; (manía) (AmL fam): **tiene ~s de viejo** he's like an old man with all his funny little ways (colloq); **tiene la ~ de morderse las uñas** he has the annoying habit of biting his nails

mañana *adv* **▶ 193** tomorrow; **pasado ~** the day after tomorrow; **~ por la ~** tomorrow morning; **adiós, hasta ~** goodbye, see you tomorrow; **el día de ~** tomorrow ■ *m* future ■ *f* **▶ 221** morning; **a la ~ siguiente** (the) next *o* the following morning; **a media ~ nos reunimos** we met midmorning; **a las nueve de la ~** at nine (o'clock) in the morning; **en** *or* (esp Esp) **por** *or* (RPl) **a la(s) ~(s)** in the morning; **muy de ~** very early in the morning; **el tren de la ~** the morning train

mañanero -ra *adj* (fam): **soy muy ~** I'm a very early riser

mañanitas *fpl* (en Méx) *song often sung on birthdays*

mañosear [A1] *vi* (Chi fam) to play *o* act up (colloq)

mañoso -sa *adj* **1** (habilidoso) good with one's hands **2** (AmL) (caprichoso) difficult

mapa *m* map; **~ de carreteras** road map; **cambios en el ~ político** changes in the political scene *o* landscape; ***desaparecer del ~*** to disappear off the face of the earth

mapache *m* racoon

mapamundi *m* map of the world, world map

mapurite *m* (AmC, Ven) skunk

maqueta *f* (de edificio) model, mock-up

maquiladora *f* (Méx) (cross-border) assembly plant

maquillador -dora *m,f* makeup artist

maquillaje *m* makeup; **~ de fondo** foundation

maquillar [A1] *vt* to make up
■ **maquillarse** *v pron* to put one's makeup on, to make up

máquina *f* **1 (a)** (aparato) machine; **¿se puede lavar a ~?** can it be machine-washed?; **escribir a ~** to type; **~ de afeitar** safety razor; (eléctrica) electric razor, shaver; **~ de coser/lavar** sewing/washing machine; **~ de escribir** typewriter; **~ expendedora** vending machine; **~ tragamonedas** *or* (Esp) **tragaperras** slot machine, fruit machine **(b)** (Jueg) fruit machine; (Fot) camera **2 (a)** (Ferr, Náut) engine **(b)** (Ven fam) (auto) car

maquinación *f* plot, scheme

maquinar [A1] *vt* to plot, scheme

maquinaria *f* **(a)** (conjunto) machinery **(b)** (mecanismo) mechanism; **la ~ del estado** the state machinery

maquinilla *f* **1** *tb* **~ de afeitar** safety razor; (eléctrica) electric razor, shaver **2** (AmC) (máquina de escribir) typewriter

maquinista *mf* **1** (operador de una máquina) machine operator **2** (Ferr) engine driver, engineer (AmE); (Náut) engineer

mar *m* (*sometimes f in literary language and in set idiomatic expressions*) **1** (Geog) sea; **a orillas del ~** by the sea; **el fondo del ~** the seabed, the bottom of the sea; **~ abierto** open sea; **la corriente llevó la barca ~ adentro** the boat was swept out to sea by the current; **hacerse a la ~** (liter) to set sail; **por ~** by sea; **~ Cantábrico** Bay of Biscay; **~ de las Antillas** Caribbean Sea; **~ Mediterráneo** Mediterranean Sea; **~ gruesa** rough *o* heavy sea; **2** (costa): **prefiero el ~ a la montaña** I prefer the seaside to the mountains

maraca *f* maraca

maracuyá *m* passion fruit

maraña *f* tangle; **la ~ burocrática** the tangle of bureaucracy

maratón *m or f* marathon

maravilla *f* **1** (portento, prodigio) wonder; **las ~s de la tecnología moderna** the wonders of modern technology; **mi secretaria es una verdadera ~** my secretary is absolutely wonderful; ***a las mil ~s*** marvelously; ***de ~*** wonderfully; ***hacer ~s*** to work wonders **2** (Bot) marigold

maravillar [A1] *vt* to amaze, astonish

■ **maravillarse** *v pron* to be amazed *o* astonished; **~se** DE **algo/algn** to marvel AT sth/sb

maravilloso -sa *adj* marvelous*, wonderful

marca *f* **1 (a)** (señal, huella) mark **(b)** (en el ganado) brand **2** (Com) (de coches, cámaras) make; (de productos alimenticios, cosméticos, etc) brand; **comprar artículos de ~** to buy brand products *o* brand names; **ropa de ~** designer clothes; **~ patentada** *or* **registrada** registered trademark **3** (Dep) record; **superar** *or* **batir una ~** to break a record

marcado[1] -da *adj* marked; **un ~ acento escocés** a marked *o* pronounced Scottish accent

marcado[2] *m* **(a)** (del pelo) set **(b)** (de reses) branding

marcador *m* **1** (Dep) scoreboard; **¿cómo va el ~?** what's the score? **2 (a)** (para libros) bookmark **(b)** (AmL) (rotulador) felt-tip pen, fiber-tip* pen

marcaje *m* (Dep) coverage, cover

marcapasos *m* (*pl* **~**) pacemaker

marcar [A2] *vt* **1 (a)** (con señal) ‹*ropa/página/baraja*› to mark; ‹*ganado*› to brand **(b)** «*experiencia/suceso*» (dejar huella) to mark **2 (a)** (indicar, señalar) to mark; **el precio va marcado en la tapa** the price is marked on the lid; **el reloj marca las doce en punto** the time is exactly twelve o'clock **(b)** (hacer resaltar) ‹*cintura/busto*› to accentuate **(c)** (Mús): **~ el compás/el ritmo** to beat time/the rhythm **3** ‹*pelo*› to set **4** (Telec) to dial **5** (Dep) **(a)** ‹*gol/tanto*› to score **(b)** ‹*jugador*› to mark ■ **~** *vi* **1** (Dep) to score **2** (Telec) to dial

■ **marcarse** *v pron:* **~se el pelo** (*refl*) to set one's hair; (*caus*) to have one's hair set

marcha *f* **1 (a)** (Mil) march; (manifestación) march; (caminata) hike, walk; **ir de ~** to go walking *o* hiking; **recojan todo y ¡en ~!** pick up your things and off you/we go!; ***ponerse en ~*** to set off **(b)** (en atletismo) *tb* **~ atlética** walk **2** (paso, velocidad) speed; **el vehículo disminuyó la ~** the car reduced speed *o* slowed down; **acelerar la ~** to speed up; ***a toda ~*** at full *o* top speed, flat out **3** (Auto) gear; **cambiar de ~** to change gear; **meter la ~ atrás** to put the car into reverse; ***dar*** *or* ***hacer ~ atrás*** (Auto) to go into reverse; (arrepentirse, retroceder) to pull out, back out **4** (funcionamiento) running; ***estar en ~*** «*motor*» to be running; «*proyecto*» to be up and running, to be under way; «*gestiones*» to be under way; ***poner en ~*** ‹*coche/motor*› to start; ‹*plan/sistema*› to set ... in motion; ***ponerse en ~*** «*tren*» to move off; «*persona*» to set off **5** (curso, desarrollo) course; **la ~ de los acontecimientos** the course of events; ***sobre la ~*: hago correcciones sobre la ~** I make corrections as I go along; **lo decidiremos sobre la ~** we'll play it by ear **6** (partida) departure **7** (Mús) march; **~ nupcial** wedding march **8** (Esp fam) (animación, ambiente): **una ciudad con mucha ~** a very lively city; **¡qué ~ tiene!** he's so full of energy

marchante -ta *m,f* **1** (de obras de arte) art dealer **2** (Méx) (en mercado — vendedor) stallholder; (— comprador) customer

marchar [A1] *vi* **1** «*coche*» to go, run; «*reloj/máquina*» to work; «*negocio/relación/empresa*» to work; **su matrimonio no marcha muy bien** his marriage isn't going *o* working very well **2 (a)** (Mil) to march **(b)** (caminar) to walk

■ **marcharse** *v pron* (esp Esp) to leave; **se marcha a Roma** he's leaving for *o* going off to Rome

marchitarse [A1] *v pron* **(a)** «*flores*» to wither **(b)** (liter) «*belleza/juventud*» to fade

marchito -ta *adj* **(a)** ‹*flores*› withered **(b)** (liter) ‹*belleza/juventud*› faded

marchoso -sa *adj* (Esp fam) ‹*ambiente/ciudad*› lively; **es un tío ~** he's really into the night life (colloq), he's really into having a good time (colloq)

marcial *adj* martial

marciano -na *adj/m,f* Martian

marco *m* **1 (a)** (de cuadro) frame; (de puerta) doorframe **(b)** (Dep) goalposts (*pl*), goal **(c)** (Andes) (de bicicleta) frame **2** (contexto) framework; **dentro del ~ de la ley** within the framework of the law **3** (Fin) mark

marea *f* tide; **cuando baja/sube la ~** when the tide goes out/comes in; **~ creciente** rising tide, flood tide; **~ menguante** falling tide, ebb tide; **~ negra** oil slick

mareado -da *adj* **(a)** (Med): **está ~** (con náuseas) he's feeling sick *o* queasy; (con pérdida del equilibrio, etc) he's feeling dizzy *o* giddy; (a punto de desmayarse) he's feeling faint **(b)** (confundido): **me tienes ~ con tanta cháchara** all your chatter is making my head spin

marear [A1] *vt* **(a)** (Med) (con náuseas) to make ... feel sick *o* queasy; (con pérdida de equilibrio) to make ... dizzy **(b)** (confundir) to confuse, get ... confused *o* muddled; **me mareas con tantas preguntas** you're confusing me with all these questions

■ **marearse** *v pron* **(a)** (al viajar — en coche) to get carsick; (— en barco) to get seasick; (— en avión) to get airsick; (perder el equilibrio) to feel dizzy; (con alcohol) to get tipsy **(b)** (confundirse) to get muddled *o* confused

marejada *f* heavy sea, swell

maremoto *m* **(a)** (sismo) seaquake **(b)** (ola) tidal wave

mareo *m* **(a)** (del estómago) sickness, nausea; (producido por movimiento) motion sickness; (en coche) carsickness; (en avión) airsickness; (en barco) seasickness; (pérdida de equilibrio, etc) dizziness, giddiness; **me dio un ~** I felt dizzy **(b)** (confusión) muddle, mess

marfil *m* ivory

margarina *f* margarine

margarita *f* (Bot) (pequeña) daisy; (grande) marguerite

margen *f* (*a veces m*) (de río) bank; (de carretera) side ■ *m* **1** (en general) margin; **~ de beneficio** *or* **ganancias** profit margin; **~ de error** margin of error; **ver nota al ~** see margin note; **al ~ de la ley** on the fringes of the law; **mantenerse al ~ de algo** to keep out of sth; **dejar a algn al ~** to leave sb out; **~ de acción/tiempo** leeway **2** **márgenes** *mpl* (límites, parámetros) limits (*pl*); **dentro de ciertos márgenes** within certain limits

marginación *f* (Sociol) marginalization

marginado -da *adj* **(a)** (Sociol) marginalized **(b)** (excluido) excluded ■ *m,f* social outcast

marginal *adj* **1** (Sociol): **en los barrios ~es** in the poor, outlying areas of the city **2** (secundario) ‹*posición*› peripheral; ‹*asunto*› marginal, peripheral **3** (Impr): **una nota ~** a note in the margin, a marginal note

marginar [A1] *vt* (en la sociedad) to marginalize; (en un grupo) to ostracize

mariachi *m* mariachi musician

marialuisa *f* (Méx) mount, passe-partout

maricón¹ -cona *adj* (fam & pey) **(a)** (homosexual) queer (colloq & pej), bent (sl & pej) **(b)** (como insulto): **el muy ~** the bastard *o* (AmE) son of a bitch (vulg); **la muy maricona** the bitch (vulg) **(c)** (AmL) (cobarde) wimpy (colloq), wimpish (colloq)

maricón² *m* (fam & pey) fag (AmE colloq & pej), poof (BrE colloq & pej)

mariconera *f* (fam & hum) (men's) handbag

marido *m* husband

marihuana *f* marijuana

marihuanero -ra *m,f* (fam) dope fiend (colloq)

marimacho *m or f* (fam & pey) **(a)** (niña) tomboy (colloq) **(b)** (mujer hombruna) butch woman (colloq)

marimba *f* marimba (*type of xylophone*)

marina *f* **1** (organización) navy; (barcos) fleet; **~ de guerra** navy **2** (Art) seascape

marinar [A1] *vt* to marinate, marinade

marinera *f* **1** (blusa) sailor top; (chaqueta) (Col) sailor jacket **2** (baile) *Andean folk dance*

marinero *m* sailor

marino¹ -na *adj* ‹*brisa/corriente*› sea (*before n*); ‹*fauna/biología*› marine (*before n*)

marino² *m* (marinero) sailor; (oficial) naval officer; **~ mercante** merchant seaman

marioneta *f* puppet, marionette

mariposa *f* butterfly; **~ nocturna** moth; **estilo ~** butterfly; **nadar ~** *or* (Esp) **a** *or* (Méx) **de ~** to swim butterfly

mariquita *f* (Zool) ladybug (AmE), ladybird (BrE) ■ *m* (fam & pey) fag (AmE colloq & pej), poof (BrE colloq & pej)

mariscal *m* (Hist, Mil) marshal; **~ de campo** (Mil) field marshal; (en fútbol americano) quarterback

marisco *m* shellfish (*pl*), seafood

marisma *f* marsh

marisquería *f* seafood *o* shellfish restaurant/bar/shop

marital *adj* ‹*relaciones*› marital (*before n*); ‹*vida*› married (*before n*)

marítimo -ma *adj* ‹*comercio*› maritime; ‹*ruta/agente*› shipping (*before n*); ‹*transporte*› sea (*before n*); ‹*ciudad*› coastal, maritime; **un puerto ~** a seaport

marketing /'marketin/ *m* marketing

mármol *m* marble

marmota *f* **(a)** (Zool) marmot **(b)** (fam) (persona dormilona) sleepyhead (colloq)

maroma *f* **1** rope **2 (a)** (Andes) (acrobacia, malabarismo) trick, stunt; **las ~s del payaso** the clown's antics **(b)** (Méx) (voltereta) somersault, tumble; **dar una ~** to do a somersault

marqués -quesa *m,f* **1** (persona) (*m*) marquis, marquess (BrE); (*f*) marquise, marchioness (BrE) **2 marquesa** *f* (Chi) (catre) bed

marquesina *f* (en parada, andén) shelter; (de teatro, hotel) marquee (AmE), canopy (BrE); (en estadio) roof

marquetería *f* marquetry

marranada *f* (fam) (faena) dirty trick

marrano -na *adj* filthy ■ *m,f* (fam) **(a)** (animal) (*m*) pig, hog; (*f*) pig, sow **(b)** (Col) (carne) pork **(c)** (persona grosera) dirty swine (colloq)

marraqueta *f* (Chi) bread roll

marrón ▶ 97 *adj/m* brown; **zapatos ~ oscuro** dark brown shoes

marroquí *adj/mf* Moroccan

marroquinería *f* **(a)** (artículos de cuero) leather goods (*pl*) **(b)** (tienda) leather goods shop

marrueco *m* (Chi) fly, flies (*pl*)

Marruecos *m* Morocco

marsupial *adj/m* marsupial

marta *f* (pine) marten; **~ cibelina** sable

Marte *m* Mars

martes *m* ▶ 193 (*pl* ~) Tuesday; **~ (y) trece** ≈ Friday the thirteenth; **~ de carnaval** Shrove Tuesday, Mardi Gras; *para ejemplos ver* LUNES

martillar, martillear [A1] *vt/vi* to hammer

martilleo *m* hammering; **un ~ terrible en las sienes** a terrible pounding in the temples

martillero -ra *m,f* (CS, Per) auctioneer

martillo *m* hammer; **~ neumático** jackhammer, pneumatic drill

martín pescador *m* kingfisher

mártir *mf* martyr

martirio *m* **(a)** (muerte) martyrdom **(b)** (sufrimiento) torment, ordeal

martirizar [A4] *vt* **(a)** (matar) to martyr **(b)** (atormentar) to torment

marxismo *m* Marxism

marxista *adj/mf* Marxist

marzo *m* ▶ 193 March; *para ejemplos ver* ENERO

mas *conj* (liter) but

más *adv* **1 (a)** (comparativo): **¿tiene algo ~ barato/moderno?** do you have anything cheaper/more modern; **duran ~** they last longer; **me gusta ~ sin azúcar** I prefer it without sugar; **ahora la vemos ~** we see more of her now; **tendrás que estudiar ~** you'll have to study harder; **~ lejos/atrás** further away/back; **el ~ allá** the other world; **~ que nunca** more than ever; **me gusta ~ el vino seco que el dulce** I prefer dry wine to sweet, I like dry wine better than sweet; **pesa ~ de lo que parece** it's heavier than it looks; **es ~ complicado de lo que tú crees** it's more complicated than you think; **eran ~ de las cinco** it was after five o'clock; **~ de 30** more than 30, over 30 **(b)** (especialmente) particularly, especially **2** (superlativo): **la ~ bonita/la ~ inteligente** the prettiest/the most intelligent; **el que ~ sabe** the one who knows most; **el que ~ me gusta** the one I like best; **estuvo de lo ~ divertido** it was great fun **3** (*en frases negativas*): **no tiene ~ que tres**

meses she's only three months old; **nadie ~ que ella** nobody but her; **no tengo ~ que esto** this is all I have; **no tuve ~ remedio** I had no alternative; **no juego ~** I'm not playing any more; **nunca ~** never again **4** (con valor ponderativo): **¡cantó ~ bien...!** she sang so well!; **¡qué cosa ~ rara!** how strange! ■ *adj inv* **1** (comparativo) more; **~ dinero** more money; **una vez ~** once more; **ni un minuto ~** not a minute longer; **hoy hace ~ calor** it's warmer today; **son ~ que nosotros** there are more of them than us **2** (superlativo) most; **el equipo que ganó ~ partidos** the team that won most games; **las ~ de las veces** more often than not **3** (con valor ponderativo): **¡me da ~ rabia ...!** it makes me so mad!; **¡tiene ~ amigos ...!** he has so many friends! **4 ¿qué ~?** what else?; **nada/nadie ~** nothing/nobody else; **algo/alguien ~** something/somebody else; **¿quién ~ vino?** who else came?; **¿algo ~? — nada ~ gracias** anything else? — no, that's all, thank you ■ *pron* **1** more; **¿te sirvo ~?** would you like some more? **2** (*en locs*) **a lo más** at the most; **a más no poder**: **corrimos a ~ no poder** we ran as fast *o* hard as we could; **a más tardar** at the latest; **cuanto más** at the most; **de más**: **¿tienes un lápiz de ~?** do you have a spare pencil?; **me dio cinco dólares de ~** he gave me five dollars too much; **no está de ~ repetirlo** there's no harm in repeating it; **es más** in fact; **más bien** (un poco) rather; **más o menos** (aproximadamente) more or less; (no muy bien) so-so; **ni más ni menos** no less; **no más** ⇒ NOMÁS; **por más**: **por ~ que llores** however much you cry; **por ~ que trataba** however hard he tried; **¿qué más da?** what does it matter?; **sin más (ni más)** just like that ■ *prep* **(a)** ▶ 294 (Mat) (en sumas) plus; **8 + 7 = 15** (*read as: ocho más siete (es) igual (a) quince*) eight plus seven equals fifteen **(b)** (además de) plus; **mil pesos, ~ los gastos** a thousand pesos, plus expenses ■ *m* plus sign

masa *f* **1** (Coc) **(a)** (para pan, pasta) dough; (para empanadas, tartas) pastry; (para bizcocho) mixture; (para crepes) batter; **~ de hojaldre** puff pastry **(b)** (RPl) (pastelito) pastry, cake **2** (Pol, Sociol, Fís) mass; **educar a las ~s** to educate the masses **3 en masa (a)** (*loc adj*) ‹*fabricación/despidos*› mass (*before n*) **(b)** (*loc adv*) ‹*acudir*› en masse

masacrar [A1] *vt* to massacre

masacre *f* massacre

masaje *m* massage; **darle ~s** *or* **un ~ a algn** to give sb a massage

masajear [A1] *vt* to massage

masajista *mf* **1** (que da masajes) (*m*) masseur; (*f*) masseuse **2** (en fútbol) coach, trainer

mascada *f* **(a)** (Chi) (mordisco) bite **(b)** (Méx) (pañuelo grande) scarf

mascar [A2] *vt* to chew

máscara *f* mask; **~ de oxígeno** oxygen mask; **~ facial** face pack

mascarilla *f* mask; (en cosmética) face pack

mascota *f* (talismán) mascot; (animal doméstico) pet

masculino[1] -na *adj* **(a)** ‹*actitud/hormona*› male; ‹*mujer/aspecto*› masculine, manly **(b)** (Ling) masculine

masculino[2] *m* masculine

mascullar [A1] *vt* to mumble, mutter

masía *f* (granja) farm; (casa) country house

masificado -da *adj* ‹*universidad*› overcrowded

masilla *f* (para cristales) putty; (para rellenar grietas) mastic, filler

masivo -va *adj* **(a)** ‹*ejecución/migración*› mass (*before n*); ‹*protesta*› large-scale (*before n*), mass (*before n*); ‹*concurrencia*› massive **(b)** ‹*dosis*› massive, huge

masón *adj* Masonic ■ *m* Freemason, Mason

masonería *f* Freemasonry

masoquismo *m* masochism

masoquista *adj* masochistic ■ *mf* masochist

máster /'master/ *m* (*pl* **-ters**) **1** (Audio, Vídeo) master **2** (Educ) master's degree

masticar [A2] *vt/vi* to chew

mástil *m* **(a)** (Náut) mast; (para una bandera) flagpole, flagstaff **(b)** (de guitarra, violín) neck **(c)** (de carpa) centerpole*

mastín *m* mastiff

mastodonte *m* **(a)** (animal prehistórico) mastodon **(b)** (fam) (persona grande) giant

mastuerzo *m* (planta) (garden) cress

masturbación *f* masturbation

masturbarse [A1] *v pron* to masturbate

mata *f* **1** (arbusto) bush, shrub; (planta) (AmL) plant **2** (ramita) sprig; (de hierba) tuft **3** (fam) (de pelo) mane (colloq), mop (colloq)

matadero *m* slaughterhouse, abattoir

matado -da *m,f* (Méx fam & pey) grind (AmE colloq), swot (BrE colloq)

matador *m* matador

matamoscas *m* (*pl* ~) **(a)** (paleta) flyswatter **(b)** (spray) fly spray, fly killer

matanza *f* (acción de matar) killing, slaughter; (de res, cerdo) slaughter

matapolillas *m* (*pl* ~) moth killer

matar [A1] *vt* **1 (a)** ‹*persona*› to kill **(b)** (sacrificar) ‹*perro/caballo*› to put down, destroy; ‹*reses*› to slaughter; **lo mató un coche** he was run over and killed by a car **(c)** (en sentido hiperbólico): **la vas a ~ a disgustos** you'll be the death of her; **es para ~los** I could murder *o* kill them (colloq); **nos mataban de hambre** they used to starve us; **estos zapatos me están matando** these shoes are killing me! **2** (fam) ‹*sed*› to quench; ‹*tiempo*› to kill; **compraron fruta para ~ el hambre** they bought some fruit to keep them going ■ **~** *vi* to kill ■ **matarse** *v pron* **1 (a)** (morir violentamente) to be killed; **casi me mato** I almost got killed **(b)** (*refl*) (suicidarse) to kill oneself; **se mató de un tiro** she shot herself **2** (fam) **(a)** (esforzarse): **me maté estudiando** *or* (Esp) **a estudiar** I studied like crazy *o* mad (colloq) **(b)** (Méx fam) (para un examen) to cram (colloq), to swot (BrE colloq)

matarife *m* (en matadero) slaughterman

matarratas *m* (*pl* ~) (veneno) rat poison

matasellos *m* (*pl* ~) **(a)** (marca) postmark **(b)** (instrumento) datestamp, stamp

matazón *f* (Col, Méx, Ven fam) massacre, slaughter

mate *adj or adj inv* ‹*pintura/maquillaje*› matt; **fotos ~** photos with a matt finish ■ *m* **1** (en ajedrez) *tb* **jaque ~** checkmate, mate **2 (a)** (infusión) maté; **cebar ~** to brew maté **(b)** (AmL) (calabaza) gourd

matear [A1] *vi* (CS fam) to drink maté ■ **matearse** *v pron* (*Chi fam*) to cram (colloq), to swot (BrE colloq)

matemáticas *fpl* mathematics, math (AmE), maths (BrE)

matemático -ca *adj* mathematical ■ *m,f* mathematician

mateo -tea *m,f* (Chi fam) grind (AmE colloq), swot (BrE colloq)

materia *f* **1** (sustancia) matter; **~ gris** gray* matter; **~ prima** (Econ, Tec) raw material; (Fin) commodity **2 (a)** (tema, asunto) subject; **en ~ de** as regards, with regard to **(b)** (asignatura) subject

material *adj* **(a)** ‹*necesidades/ayuda/valor*› material; **daños ~es** damage to property, material damage **(b)** ‹*autor/causante*› actual ■ *m* **1** (en general) material; **~es para la construcción** building materials **2** (útiles) materials (*pl*); **~ de oficina** office stationery; **~ didáctico/escolar** teaching/school materials (*pl*)

materialismo *m* materialism

materialista *adj* materialistic ■ *mf* **1** (persona) materialist **2** (Méx) (constructor) building contractor; (camionero) truck driver, lorry driver (BrE)

maternal *adj* ‹*instinto*› maternal; ‹*amor*› motherly, maternal

maternidad *f* **(a)** (estado) motherhood, maternity **(b)** (hospital) maternity hospital; (sala) maternity ward

materno -na *adj* ‹*amor*› motherly; ‹*pariente*› maternal; ‹*lengua*› mother

matinal *adj* morning (*before n*)

matinée, **matiné** *f* **(a)** (AmS) (de tarde) matinée **(b)** (Méx) (de mañana) morning performance

matiz *m* **(a)** (de color) shade, hue **(b)** (de palabra, frase) nuance, shade of meaning; **tiene cierto ~ peyorativo** it has a slightly pejorative nuance **(c)** (de ironía) touch, hint

matizar [A4] *vt* **1** ‹*colores*› to blend **2** (concretar, puntualizar) to qualify, clarify

matón *m* (del barrio) thug; (en la escuela) bully; (criminal) thug, heavy (colloq)

matorral *m* **(a)** (conjunto de matas) thicket, bushes (*pl*) **(b)** (terreno) scrubland

matraca *f* **1** (juguete) rattle **2** (Méx fam) (coche) rattletrap (colloq)

matrero -ra *adj* **1** (Col fam) (basto) shoddy **2** (RPl) (fugitivo): **un gaucho ~** a gaucho on the run from the law **3** (Col) (traicionero) sly, crafty

matriarcado *m* matriarchy

matriarcal *adj* matriarchal

matrícula *f* **1** (Educ) (inscripción) registration, enrollment*; **derechos** *or* **tasas de ~** registration fees; **~ de honor** (Esp) ≈ distinction, ≈ magna cum laude **2** (Transp) (número) registration number; (placa) license* plate, number plate (BrE)

matricular [A1] *vt* **(a)** ‹*persona*› to register, enroll* **(b)** ‹*coche/barco*› to register ■ **matricularse** *v pron* (*refl*) to register, enroll*; **~se EN algo** to enroll ON sth

matrimonial *adj* marital

matrimonio *m* **(a)** (institución) marriage, matrimony (frml); **contraer ~** (frml) to marry **(b)** (pareja) (married) couple; **el ~ Garrido** Mr and Mrs Garrido, the Garridos **(c)** (AmS exc RPl) (boda) wedding; **~ civil/religioso** civil/church wedding

matriz *f* **(a)** (útero) womb, uterus **(b)** (molde) mold* **(c)** (de talonario) stub

matrona *f* (comadrona) midwife

matutino[1] -na *adj* morning (*before n*)

matutino[2] *m* morning paper

maullar [A23] *vi* to miaow

maullido *m* miaow

mausoleo *m* mausoleum

maxilar *m* jawbone, maxilla (tech)

máxima *f* maxim

máxime *adv* especially

máximo[1] -ma *adj* ‹*temperatura/velocidad*› top (*before n*), maximum (*before n*); ‹*carga/altura*› maximum (*before n*); ‹*punto*› highest; ‹*esfuerzo/ambición*› greatest(*before n*); **el ~ dirigente francés** the French leader

máximo[2] *m* maximum; **como ~** at the most; **aprovechar algo al ~** to make the most of sth; **se esforzó al ~** she did her utmost; **rendir al ~** «*persona*» to give a hundred percent; «*máquina*» to work to its full capacity

maya *adj* Mayan ■ *mf* Maya, Mayan; **los ~s** the Maya *o* Mayas

mayo *m* ▶ **193** May; **el primero de ~** May Day; *para ejemplos ver* ENERO

mayonesa *f* mayonnaise, mayo (AmE) (colloq)

mayor *adj* **1 (a)** (comparativo de GRANDE) ‹*número/porcentaje*› greater, higher; ‹*beneficio*› greater; **vuelan a ~ altura** they fly at a greater height; **a ~ escala** on a larger scale; **un número ~ que 40** a number greater than 40 **(b)** (superlativo de GRANDE): **el ~ número de accidentes** the greatest *o* highest number of accidents; **su ~ preocupación** her greatest *o* biggest worry; **a la ~ brevedad posible** as soon as possible; **la ~ parte de los estudiantes** most students, the majority of students **2** ▶ **159** (en edad) **(a)** (comparativo) older; **~ QUE algn** older THAN sb **(b)** (superlativo): **es la ~ de las dos** she is the older *o* elder of the two; **mi hijo ~** my eldest *o* oldest son **(c)** (anciano) elderly **(d)** (adulto): **las personas ~es** adults, grown-ups (colloq); **cuando sea ~** when I grow up; **ser ~ de edad** (Der) to be of age; **soy ~ de edad y haré lo que quiera** I'm over 18 (*o* 21 *etc*) and I'll do as I please **3** (en nombres) (principal) main; **Calle M~** Main Street (*in US*), High Street (*in UK*) **4** (Mús) major **5** (Com): **(al) por ~** wholesale ■ *mf* (adulto) adult, grown-up (colloq); **sólo para ~es** adults only; **mis/tus ~es** my/your elders; **~ de edad** person who is legally of age

mayoral *m* (capataz) foreman; (de finca) farm manager, steward

mayordomo *m* (criado principal) butler, majordomo; (capataz) (CS) foreman; (portero) (Chi) superintendent (AmE), caretaker (BrE)

mayoría *f* majority; **la gran ~ de** ... the great majority of ...; **ser ~** *or* **estar en ~** to be in the majority; **gobierno de la ~** majority rule; **~ absoluta/relativa** absolute/simple majority; **llegar a la ~ de edad** to come of age

mayorista *adj* wholesale ■ *mf* wholesaler

mayoritario -ria *adj* **(a)** ‹*apoyo/decisión/partido*› majority (*before n*) **(b)** (Fin) ‹*socio/accionista*› principal

mayúscula *f* capital (letter), uppercase letter (tech); **se escribe con ~** it is written with a capital letter; **rellenar en** *or* **con ~s** write in block capitals *o* in capital letters

mayúsculo -la *adj* **(a)** ‹*letra*› capital (*before n*), upper-case (tech) **(b)** ‹*susto/error*› terrible

maza *f* **(a)** (Const) drop hammer **(b)** (de bombo) drumstick **(c)** (arma) mace

mazacote *m* **(a)** (fam) (Coc): **un ~** a lumpy mess **(b)** (fam) (obra tosca) eyesore

mazamorra *f* **(a)** (AmS) *milky pudding made with maize* **(b)** (Per) *pudding made with corn starch, sugar and honey* **(c)** (Col) *maize soup*

mazapán *m* marzipan

mazmorra *f* dungeon

mazo *m* **1 (a)** (herramienta) mallet; (del mortero) pestle; (para la carne) meat tenderizer; (porra) club **(b)** (en croquet, polo) mallet **2** (esp AmL) (manojo) bunch; (de naipes) deck (of cards) (AmE), pack (of cards) (BrE)

mazorca *f* (Bot, Coc) cob; **~ de maíz** corncob

mazurca *f* mazurka

me *pron pers* me; **¿~ lo prestas?** will you lend it to me *o* lend me it?; **~ arregló el televisor** he fixed the television for me; **~ lo quitó** he took it off me *o* away from me; **~ robaron el reloj** my watch was stolen; **~ miré en el espejo** (*refl*) I looked at myself in the mirror; **~ corté el pelo** (*refl*) I cut my hair; (*caus*) I had my hair cut; **~ equivoqué** I made a mistake; **~ alegro mucho** I'm very pleased; **se ~ murió el gato** my cat died

mear [A1] *vi* (vulg) to (have a) piss (vulg)
■ **mearse** *v pron* (fam) to wet oneself; **me estoy meando** I'm dying for a pee (colloq)

mecánica *f* mechanics

mecánico -ca *adj* mechanical ■ *m,f* (de vehículos) mechanic; (de maquinaria industrial) fitter; (de fotocopiadoras, lavadoras) engineer

mecanismo *m* mechanism; **~ de defensa** defense* mechanism

mecanizado -da *adj* mechanized

mecanizar [A4] *vt* to mechanize

mecanografía *f* typing

mecanografiar [A17] *vt* to type

mecanógrafo -fa *m,f* typist

mecate *m* (AmC, Méx, Ven) string, cord; (más grueso) rope

mecedora *f* rocking chair

mecenas *mf* (*pl* ~) patron, sponsor

mecer [E2] *vt* ‹*bebé/cuna*› to rock; ‹*niño*› (en columpio) to push
■ **mecerse** *v pron* **(a)** (en mecedora) to rock; (en columpio) to swing **(b)** (bambolearse) to sway

mecha *f* **1** (de vela) wick; (de armas, explosivos) fuse **2 mechas** *fpl* (en peluquería) highlights (*pl*)

mechero *m* **(a)** (Esp) (encendedor) lighter **(b)** (Col) (candil) oil lamp

mechón¹ *m* **(a)** (de pelo) lock **(b)** (de lana) tuft **(c) mechones** *mpl* (Col) (en peluquería) highlights (*pl*)

mechón² -chona *m,f* (Chi) (estudiante) freshman, fresher (BrE)

medalla *f* (Dep, Mil) medal; (Relig) medallion (*with religious engraving on it*)

medallón *m* medallion

media *f* **1** (Indum) **(a)** (hasta el muslo) stocking; **~s con/sin costura** seamed/seamless stockings **(b) medias** *fpl* (hasta la cintura) panty hose (*pl*) (AmE), tights (*pl*) (BrE); **~s bombacha(s)** (RPl) *or* (Col, Ven) **pantalón** panty hose (*pl*) (AmE), tights (BrE) (*pl*) **(c)** (AmL) (calcetín) sock **2** (Mat) average; **la ~ de velocidad** the average speed **3 a medias** (*loc adv*) **(a)** (incompleto): **dejó el trabajo a ~s** he left the work half-finished; **me dijo la verdad a ~s** she didn't tell me the whole truth *o* story **(b)** (entre dos): **pagar a ~s** to pay half each, go halves; **lo hicimos a ~s** we did half (of it) each

mediación *f* mediation; **por ~ de** through

mediador -dora *m,f* mediator

mediados: ▶ 193 **a ~ de mes** halfway through the month, in the middle of the month; **a ~ de los años 30** in the mid thirties

mediagua *f* (Andes) hut, shack

medialuna *f* **(a)** (esp RPl) (Coc) croissant (*often with ham and cheese*) **(b)** (Chi) (corral) ring

mediana *f* (Auto) median strip (AmE), central reservation (BrE)

medianero -ra *adj* dividing (*before n*)

mediano -na *adj* **(a)** ‹*tamaño/porción*› medium; ‹*coche*› medium-sized; **de mediana estatura/inteligencia** of average height/intelligence; **de mediana edad** middle-aged **(b)** (mediocre) average, mediocre

medianoche *f* midnight; **a ~** at midnight

mediante *prep* through, by means of

mediar [A1] *vi* **(a)** (intervenir) to mediate; **~ EN algo** ‹*en conflicto/negociaciones*› to mediate IN sth, to act as mediator IN sth **(b)** (interceder) **~ POR algn** to intercede FOR sb; **~ ANTE algn** to intercede *o* intervene WITH sb

mediasnueves *fpl* (Col) mid-morning snack, elevenses (BrE colloq)

medicamento *m* (frml) medicine, medicament (frml)

medicatura *f* (Ven) first aid post, clinic

medicina *f* medicine

medicinal *adj* ‹*aguas/planta*› medicinal; ‹*champú/jabón*› medicated

medición *f* **(a)** (acción) measuring **(b)** (frml) (medida) measurement

médico[1] **-ca** *adj* medical; **un reconocimiento ~** a medical (examination)

médico[2] *mf* doctor; **~ de cabecera** family doctor *o* (AmE) physician, general practitioner, GP; **~ de medicina general** general practitioner, GP

medida *f* **1** (Mat) (dimensión) measurement; **tomarle las ~s a algn** to take sb's measurements; **tomar las ~s de algo** to measure something **2** (*en locs*) **a (la) medida** ‹*traje/zapato*› custom-made (AmE), made-to-measure (BrE); **a medida que** as; **a ~ que fue creciendo** as he grew up **3** (utensilio) measure; (contenido) measure **4** (grado, proporción): **en gran/cierta ~** to a large/certain extent; **en la ~ de lo posible** as far as possible **5** (disposición) measure; **tomar ~s** to take steps *o* measures

medido -da *adj* (CS) ‹*persona/comportamiento*› restrained; **es muy ~ con la bebida** he's a very moderate drinker

medidor *m* (AmL) meter

medieval *adj* medieval

medio[1] **-dia** *adj* **1 ▶ 130** (*delante del n*) (la mitad de): **~ kilo** half a kilo; **media manzana** half an apple; **pagar ~ pasaje** to pay half fare *o* half price; **media hora** half an hour, a half hour (AmE); **dos horas y media** two and a half hours; **a las cinco y media** at half past five; **a media mañana/tarde** in the middle of the morning/afternoon; **a ~ camino** halfway; **media pensión** (en hoteles) half board; **(se) dio ~ vuelta y se fue** she turned on her heel and left; **un jugador de ~ campo** a midfield player; **~ tiempo** (AmL) half-time; ***mi media naranja*** (fam & hum) my better half (colloq & hum) **2** (mediano, promedio) average; **el ciudadano ~** the average citizen; **a ~ y largo plazo** in the medium and long term

medio[2] *adv* half; **está ~ loca** she's half crazy; **todo lo deja a ~ terminar** he leaves everything half finished ■ *m* **1 ▶ 130** (Mat) (mitad) half **2** (centro) middle; **en (el) ~ de la habitación** in the middle *o* center of the room; **quitarse de en** *or* **del ~** to get out of the way **3 (a)** (recurso, manera) means (*pl*); **como ~ de coacción** as a means of coercion; **los ~s de comunicación** the media; **~ de transporte** means of transport **(b) medios** *mpl* (recursos económicos) *tb* **~s económicos** means (*pl*), resources (*pl*) **4** (*en locs*) **en medio de**: **en ~ de tanta gente** (in) among so many people; **en ~ de la confusión** in *o* amid all the confusion; **por medio** (CS, Per): **día/semana por ~** every other day/week; **dos casas por ~** every two houses; **por medio de** (de proceso, técnica) by means of; **por ~ de tu primo** from *o* through your cousin **5 (a)** (círculo, ámbito): **en ~s literarios/políticos** in literary/political circles; **no está en su ~** he's out of his element **(b)** (Biol) environment; **la adaptación al ~** adaptation to one's environment; **~ ambiente** environment

mediocampista *mf* midfield player

mediocre *adj* mediocre

mediocridad *f* mediocrity

mediodía *m* **(a) ▶ 221** (las doce de la mañana) midday, noon; **a ~** *or* **al ~** at midday **(b)** (hora de comer) lunch time

Medio Oriente *m* Middle East, Mid-East (AmE)

medir [I14] *vt* **1** ‹*habitación/distancia/velocidad*› to measure **2** (tener ciertas dimensiones) to be, measure; **mido 60 cm de cintura** I measure *o* I'm 60 cm round the waist; **¿cuánto mide de alto/largo?** how tall/long is it?; **mide casi 1,90 m** he's almost 1.90 m (tall) **3** (calcular, considerar) to consider, weigh up; **~ los pros y los contras de algo** to weigh up the pros and cons of sth

■ **medirse** *v pron* **1** (*refl*) to measure oneself; ‹*caderas/pecho*› to measure **2** (Col, Méx, Ven) (probarse) to try on

meditación *f* meditation

meditar [A1] *vi* to meditate; **~ sobre algo** to reflect *o* meditate on sth ■ **~** *vt* (considerar) to think about; (durante más tiempo) to ponder, meditate on; **una decisión muy meditada** a very carefully thought-out decision

mediterráneo -nea *adj* Mediterranean

Mediterráneo *m*: *tb* **el (mar) ~** the Mediterranean (sea)

médula *f* (Anat) marrow, medulla (tech); **~ ósea** bone marrow; **británico hasta la ~** British through and through

medusa *f* jellyfish, medusa

megafonía *f* PA system

megáfono *m* megaphone

mejicano -na *adj/m,f* Mexican

Méjico *m* ⇒ MEXICO

mejilla *f* **▶ 123** cheek; ***poner la otra ~*** to turn the other cheek

mejillón *m* mussel

mejor *adj* **1 (a)** (comparativo de BUENO) ‹*producto/profesor*› better; ‹*calidad*› better, higher, superior; **tanto ~** so much the better; **cuanto más grande ~** the bigger the better **(b)** (comparativo de BIEN) better; **está ~ así** it's better like this **2 (a)** (superlativo de BUENO) (entre dos) better; (entre varios) best; **mi ~ amiga** my best friend; **productos de la ~ calidad** products of the highest quality; **lo ~ es que se lo digas** the best thing (to do) is to tell her; **le deseo lo ~** I wish you the very best *o* all the best **(b)** (superlativo de BIEN): **la que está ~ de dinero** the one who has the most money ■ *adv* **1** (comparativo) better; **luego lo pensé ~** then I thought better of it; **pintas cada vez ~** your painting is getting better and better; **me lleva dos años, ~ dicho, dos y medio** she's two years older than me, or rather, two and a half **2** (superlativo) best; **éste es el lugar desde donde se ve ~** this is where you can see best (from); **la versión ~ ambientada de la obra** the best-staged production of the play; **lo hice lo ~ que pude** I did it as best I could *o* (frml) to the best of my ability; **a lo ~** maybe, perhaps; **a lo ~ vamos a Italia** we may *o* might go to Italy **3** (esp AmL) (en sugerencias): **~ lo dejamos para otro día** why don't we leave it for another day?; **~ me callo** I think I'd better shut up ■ *mf*: **el/la ~** (de dos) the better; (de varios) the best; **es la ~ de la clase** she's the best in the class

mejora *f* improvement

mejorana *f* marjoram

mejorar [A1] *vt* ‹*condiciones/situación/oferta*› to improve; ‹*marca*› to improve on, beat; **el tratamiento la mejoró** the treatment made her a lot better ■ ~ *vi* «*tiempo/calidad/situación*» to improve, get better; «*persona*» (Med) to get better; **ha mejorado de aspecto** he looks a lot better ■ **mejorarse** *v pron* «*enfermo*» to get better; **que te mejores** get well soon, I hope you get better soon

mejoría *f* improvement; **le deseamos una pronta ~** we wish you a speedy recovery

melancolía *f* melancholy, sadness

melancólico -ca *adj* melancholy ■ *m,f* melancholic

melaza *f* molasses

melé *f* (Dep) (libre) ruck, maul; (organizada) scrum

melena *f* **(a)** (pelo suelto) long hair **(b)** (estilo de corte) bob **(c)** (del león) mane

melenudo -da *adj* (fam) long-haired

melindroso -sa *adj* **(a)** (remilgado) affected **(b)** (Méx) (delicado) choosy, finicky **(c)** (mojigato) prudish

mellado -da *adj* ‹*diente/taza*› chipped; ‹*cuchillo/borde*› jagged

mellar [A1] *vt* **(a)** ‹*cuchillo/hoja*› to notch, nick; ‹*diente/porcelana*› to chip **(b)** (esp AmL) ‹*honor/fama*› to damage

mellizo -za *adj* twin (*before n*) ■ *m,f* (*m*) twin (brother); (*f*) twin (sister); **tuvo ~s** she had twins

melocotón *m* **(a)** (esp Esp) (fruta redonda) peach **(b)** (AmC) (fruta en forma de estrella) star fruit

melodía *f* melody, tune

melodioso -sa *adj* melodious, tuneful

melodrama *m* melodrama

melodramático -ca *adj* melodramatic

melón *m* (Bot) melon

meloso -sa *adj* ‹*persona/voz*› sickly-sweet; ‹*música/canción*› schmaltzy, slushy

membrana *f* membrane

membresía *f* (AmL frml) membership

membrete *m* letterhead; **papel con ~** headed paper

membrillo *m* (árbol) quince (tree); (fruta) quince; **dulce de ~** quince jelly

memorable *adj* memorable

memorándum *m* (*pl* **-dums**), **memorando** *m* (nota) memorandum, memo

memoria *f* **1** (en general) memory; **tener buena/mala ~** to have a good/poor memory; **si la ~ no me falla** *or* **engaña** if my memory serves me right; **desde que tengo ~** for as long as I can remember; **aprender/saber algo de ~** to learn/know sth by heart; **respetar la ~ de algn** to respect the memory of sb; **a la** *or* **en ~ de algn** in memory of sb **2 memorias** *fpl* (Lit) memoirs (*pl*) **3 (a)** (Adm, Com) report; **~ anual** annual report **(b)** (Educ) written paper

memorial *m* memorial

memorizar [A4] *vt* to memorize

menaje *m*: **artículos de ~** household items; **sección de ~ del hogar** household department

mención *f* mention; **hacer ~ de algo** to mention sth

mencionar [A1] *vt* to mention; **no quiero oír ~ ese nombre** I don't want to hear that name mentioned

mendicidad *f* begging

mendigar [A3] *vi* to beg ■ ~ *vt* «*mendigo*» to beg for

mendigo -ga *m,f* beggar

mendrugo *m*: *tb* **~ de pan** piece of stale bread

menear [A1] *vt* ‹*rabo*› to wag; ‹*cabeza*› to shake; ‹*caderas*› to wiggle ■ **menearse** *v pron* **(a)** (con inquietud) to fidget **(b)** (provocativamente) to wiggle one's hips

menestra *f* vegetable stew

menguar [A16] *vi* **1** (frml) «*temperatura/nivel*» to fall, drop; «*cantidad/número/reservas*» to diminish **2** (al tejer) to decrease ■ ~ *vt* **1** (frml) ‹*responsabilidad/influencia*› to diminish; ‹*reputación*› to damage **2** ‹*puntos*› (en tejido) to decrease

meningitis *f* meningitis

menisco *m* cartilage, meniscus (tech)

menopausia *f* menopause

menopáusico -ca *adj* menopausal

menor *adj* **1 (a)** (comparativo de PEQUEÑO) ‹*número/porcentaje*› lower, smaller; **en ~ medida/grado** to a lesser extent *o* degree; **~ QUE algo** lower THAN sth; **un ingreso ~ que el mío** an income lower than mine **(b)** (superlativo de PEQUEÑO): **el país con el ~ número de parados** the country with the lowest unemployment figures; **haciendo el ~ ruido posible** making as little noise as possible; **el de ~ tamaño** the smallest one **2** ▶ 159 (en edad) **(a)** (comparativo) younger; **~ QUE algn** younger THAN sb **(b)** (superlativo): **¿cuál es el ~ de los hermanos?** who's the youngest of the brothers?; **el ~ de los dos niños** the younger of the two boys **3** (secundario) ‹*escritor/obra*› minor; **lesiones de ~ importancia** minor injuries **4** (Mús) minor **5** (Com): **(al) por ~** retail ■ *mf*: *tb* **~ de edad** minor; Ⓢ **película no apta para menores** film not suitable for under-18s

menorista *mf* (Col, Méx, Ven) retailer

menos *adv* **1** (comparativo) less; **cada vez estudia ~** she's studying less and less; **ya me duele ~** it hurts less now; **ahora lo vemos ~** we don't see him so often now, we don't see so much of him now; **pesa ~ de 50 kilos** it weighs less than *o* under 50 kilos; **éramos ~ de diez** there were fewer than ten of us; **los niños de ~ de 7 años** children under seven **2** (superlativo) least; **es la ~ complicada** it is the least complicated one; **el que ~ me gusta** the one I like (the) least; **se esfuerza lo ~ posible** he makes as little effort as possible; **cuando ~ lo esperaba** when I was least expecting it ■ *adj inv* **1** (comparativo) (en cantidad) less; (en número) fewer; **alimentos con ~ fibra/calorías** food with less fiber/fewer calories; **hay ~ errores** there are fewer mistakes; **mide medio metro ~** it's half a meter shorter; **~ estudiantes que el año pasado** fewer students than last year; **tengo ~ tiempo que tú** I haven't as *o* so much time as you **2** (superlativo) (en cantidad) least; (en número) fewest; **donde hay ~ luz** where there's least light; **el que obtuvo ~ votos** the one who got (the) fewest votes ■ *pron* **1** (en cantidad) less; (en número) fewer; **sírveme ~** give me less; **ya falta ~** it won't be long now **2** (*en locs*) **al menos** at least; **a menos que** unless; **cuando menos** at least; **de menos**: **me dió 100 pesos de ~** he gave me 100 pesos too little; **me cobró de ~** he undercharged me; **lo menos** the least; **menos mal** just as well, thank goodness; **por lo menos** at least; ***eso es lo de ~*** that's the least of my (*o* our *etc*) problems ■ *prep* **1** (excepto): **todos ~ Alonso** everybody except *o* but Alonso; **~ estos dos,** ... apart from *o* with the exception of these two, ...; **tres latas de pintura, ~ la que usé para la puerta** three cans of paint, less what I used on the door **2 (a)** ▶ **294** (Mat) (en restas, números negativos) minus **(b)** ▶ **221** (Esp, RPl) (en la hora): **son las cinco ~ diez/cuarto** it's ten to five/(a) quarter to five; **son ~ veinte** it's twenty to

menoscabar [A1] *vt* ‹*autoridad/fortuna*› to diminish, reduce; ‹*derechos*› to impinge upon, infringe; ‹*honor/fama/salud*› to damage, harm

menospreciar [A1] *vt* **(a)** (despreciar) ‹*persona/obra*› to despise, look down on **(b)** (subestimar) to underestimate

menosprecio *m* contempt, scorn

mensaje *m* (en general) message; (nota) note

mensajero -ra *adj* messenger (*before n*) ■ *m, f* (en general) messenger; (Com) messenger, courier (BrE)

menso -sa *adj* (AmL fam) stupid ■ *m,f* (AmL fam) fool

menstruación *f* menstruation; **estar con la ~** to have one's period

menstruar [A3] *vi* to menstruate

mensual *adj* ‹*publicación/sueldo*› monthly; **9.000 pesos ~es** 9,000 pesos a month

mensualidad (a) *f* (sueldo) monthly salary **(b)** (cuota) monthly payment *o* installment*

menta *f* mint; **licor de ~** crème de menthe; **caramelos de ~** mints, peppermints

mentada *f* (Col, Méx, Ven euf) *tb* **~ de madre** insult (*usually about a person's mother*)

mental *adj* mental

mentalidad *f* mentality; **tener una ~ muy cerrada** a very closed mind

mentalizar [A4] *vt* **~ a algn DE algo** to make sb aware OF sth

■ **mentalizarse** *v pron* **(a)** (prepararse mentalmente) to prepare oneself (mentally), get into the right frame of mind **(b)** (tomar conciencia): **tuve que ~me de que mi carrera se había acabado** I had to come to terms with the fact that my career was over

mentar [A5] *vt* to mention

mente *f* mind; **tenía la ~ en blanco** my mind was a blank; **de repente me vino a la ~** it suddenly came to me; ***tener algo en ~*** to have sth in mind

mentecato -ta *m,f* fool

mentir [I11] *vi* to lie; **me mintió** he lied to me

mentira *f* lie; **eso es ~** that's a lie; **¡~! yo no le pegué** that's a lie, I didn't hit him!; **¡parece ~! ¡cómo pasa el tiempo!** isn't it incredible! doesn't time fly!; **~ piadosa** white lie; **una araña de ~** *or* (Méx) **de ~s** (leng infantil) a toy spider; ***una ~ como una casa*** *or* ***un templo*** (fam) a whopping great lie (colloq), a whopper (colloq)

mentiroso -sa *adj*: **es muy ~** he's an awful *o* terrible liar; (dicho sin ánimo de ofender) he's a real fibber (colloq) ■ *m,f* liar; (dicho sin ánimo de ofender) fibber (colloq)

mentolado -da *adj* menthol (*before n*)

mentón *m* ▶ **123** chin

menú *m* (*pl* **-nús**) menu; **~ del día** set menu

menudencia *f* **1** (cosa insignificante): **eso es una ~** that's not important **2 menudencias** *fpl* (AmL) (Coc) giblets (*pl*)

menudeo *m* (Col, Méx) retail trade; **ventas al ~** retail sales

menudillos *mpl* giblets (*pl*)

menudo[1] -da *adj* **1 (a)** ‹*persona*› slight **(b)** ‹*letra/pie*› small **2** (Esp) (en exclamaciones) (*delante del n*): **¡~ lío!** what a mess!; **¡~ cochazo!** that's some car! **3 a menudo** often

menudo[2] *m* (Col, Ven) (dinero suelto) loose change

meñique *m* ▶ **123** little finger

meollo *m* **(a)** (Anat) marrow **(b)** (de un tema) heart

mercadería *f* (esp AmS) merchandise

mercadillo *m* street market

mercado *m* market; **ir al ~** *or* (Col, Méx) **hacer el ~** to go to market; **~ de abastos** market (*selling fresh food*); **~ de (las) pulgas** flea market; **~ persa** (CS) bazaar, street market; **el ~ del petróleo** the oil market; **salir al ~** to come onto the market; **el M~ Común** the Common Market; **~ de divisas** foreign exchange market; **~ negro** black market

mercancía *f*, **mercancías** *fpl* (Com) goods (*pl*), merchandise

mercante *adj* merchant (*before n*)

mercantil *adj* ‹*ley/operación*› commercial, mercantile

merced *f* (arc) (favor) favor*; **conceder una ~** to grant a favor; **a (la) ~ de** at the mercy of

mercenario -ria *adj/m,f* (Mil) mercenary

mercería *f* (tienda de hilos, botones) notions store (AmE), haberdashery (BrE); (ferretería) (Chi) hardware store

Mercosur *m*: *economic community comprising Argentina, Brazil, Paraguay and Uruguay*

mercurio *m* mercury

Mercurio *m* Mercury

merecedor -dora *adj* **~ DE algo** worthy OF sth, deserving OF sth (frml)

merecer [E3] *vt* ‹*premio/castigo*› to deserve; **merece que le den el puesto** she deserves to get the job

■ **merecerse** *v pron* (*enf*) ‹*premio/castigo*› to deserve; **te lo tienes bien merecido** it serves you right; **se merece que la asciendan** she deserves to be promoted

merecido *m*: **recibió** *or* **se llevó su ~** he got what he deserved

merendar [A5] *vi* to have a snack in the afternoon, have tea; **merendamos en el campo** we had a picnic (tea) in the country ■ ~ *vt* to have ... as an afternoon snack

merendero *m* (bar) outdoor bar; (instalaciones para picnics) picnic area

merengada *f* (Ven) milkshake

merengue *m* **1** (pastel) meringue **2** (baile) merengue

meridiano *m* meridian; **~ cero** *or* **de Greenwich** /ˈgrinɪtʃ/ Greenwich Meridian

meridional *adj* southern ■ *mf* southerner

merienda *f* afternoon snack, tea; (para la escuela) (RPl) snack; **ir de ~ al campo** to go for a picnic (tea) in the country

mérito *m* merit, worth; **no le veo ningún ~ a eso** I can't see any merit in that; **una persona de ~** a worthy person; **tener ~** to be praiseworthy; **quitarle ~s a algn** to take the credit away from sb; **atribuirse el ~ de algo** to take the credit for sth

meritorio -ria *adj* [SER] (frml) commendable, praiseworthy (frml); **~ DE algo** worthy OF sth ■ *m, f* unpaid trainee

merluza *f* (Coc, Zool) hake

mermar [A1] *vi* (frml) «*viento/frío*» to abate (frml); «*luz*» to fade ■ ~ *vt* (frml) to reduce

mermelada *f* (de cítricos) marmalade; (de otras frutas) jam

mero[1] **-ra** *adj* (*delante del n*) **1** (solo, simple) mere; **el ~ hecho de** ... the mere *o* simple fact of ...; **es un ~ juego** it's only *o* just a game **2** (AmC, Méx fam) (uso enfático): **¿cuántas quedaron? — una mera** how many were left? — just one; **el ~ día de su boda** the very day of her wedding; **el ~ patrón** the boss himself; **en la mera esquina** right on the corner

mero[2] *m* grouper; ***el ~ ~*** (Méx fam) the boss ■ *adv* (Méx fam) **(a)** (casi) nearly, almost **(b)** (uso enfático): **así ~ me gustan los tacos** this is just how I like tacos; **ya ~** right now; **aquí merito** right here

merodear [A1] *vi* to prowl

mersa *adj* (RPl fam & pey) ‹*ropa/lugar*› tacky (colloq); ‹*persona*› common (pej) ■ *mf* (RPl fam & pey) **(a)** (persona): **es un ~** he's so common (pej) **(b) la mersa** *f* the plebs (*pl*) (colloq & pej), the riffraff (hum *or* pej)

mes *m* ▶ 193 month; **el ~ pasado/que viene** last/next month; **una vez al ~** once a month; **tiene siete ~es** he's seven months old; **nos deben dos ~es** they owe us two months' rent (*o* pay *etc*)

mesa *f* **1** (mueble) table; **poner/recoger la ~** to lay/clear the table; **bendecir la ~** to say grace; **sentarse a la ~** to sit at the table; **se levantó de la ~** he got up from *o* left the table; **reservar ~** to reserve a table; **~ de centro** coffee table; **~ de noche** *or* (RPl) **de luz** bedside table **2** (conjunto de personas) committee; **~ redonda/de negociaciones** round/negotiating table

mesada *f* (AmL) (dinero) monthly allowance; (para niños) pocket money

mesero -ra *m,f* (AmL) (*m*) waiter; (*f*) waitress

meseta *f* (Geog) plateau

Mesías *m* Messiah

Mesoamérica *f* Middle America (*most of Mexico and Central America*)

mesón *m* **1** (bar) *old-style bar/restaurant* **2** (Chi) (en tienda) counter; (de bar) bar, counter; **~ de información** information desk

mesonero -ra *m,f* **(a)** (de bar) (*m*) landlord; (*f*) landlady **(b)** (Ven) (camarero) (*m*) waiter; (*f*) waitress

mestizo -za *adj* **(a)** ‹*persona*› of mixed race (*particularly of Indian and white parentage*); **de sangre mestiza** of mixed blood **(b)** ‹*animal*› crossbred ■ *m,f* mestizo, person of mixed race

meta *f* **1 (a)** (en atletismo) finishing line; (en ciclismo, automovilismo) finish; (en carreras de caballos) winning post **(b)** (en fútbol) goal **2 (a)** (propósito) aim; **su única ~ es ganar dinero** his only aim *o* ambition is to earn money **(b)** (objetivo) goal; **trazarse ~s** to set oneself targets *o* goals

metabolismo *m* metabolism

metafísico -ca *adj* metaphysical

metáfora *f* metaphor

metal *m* **(a)** (material, elemento) metal; **~ noble** *or* **precioso** precious metal **(b)** *tb* **metales** (Mús) brass (section)

metálico[1] **-ca** *adj* **(a)** (de metal) metallic, metal (*before n*) **(b)** ‹*sonido/brillo/color*› metallic

metálico[2] *m*: **pagar en ~** to pay (in) cash; **un premio en ~** a cash prize

metalurgia *f* metallurgy

metalúrgico -ca *adj* metallurgical ■ *m,f* metalworker

metamorfosis, metamórfosis *f* (*pl* ~) metamorphosis

metate *m* (AmC, Méx) *flat stone used for grinding corn*

metedura de pata *f* (esp Esp fam) blunder, gaffe

metegol *m* (Arg) table football

meteorito *m* meteorite

meteoro *m* meteor

meteorología *f* meteorology

meteorológico -ca *adj* meteorological, weather (*before n*)

meteorólogo -ga *m,f* meteorologist

meter [E1] *vt* **1 (a)** (introducir, poner) to put; **~ algo EN algo** to put sth IN(TO) sth; **~ la llave en la cerradura** to put the key into the lock; **logró ~ todo en la maleta** he managed to fit everything into the suitcase **(b)** (hacer entrar): **~ a algn en la cárcel** to put sb in prison; **consiguió ~lo en la empresa** she managed to get him a job in the company **(c)** (involucrar) **~ a algn EN algo** to involve sb IN sth, get sb involved IN sth **2 (a)** (invertir) ‹*ahorros/dinero*› to put **(b)** ‹*tanto/gol*› to score **(c)** (en costura) ‹*dobladillo*› to turn up **(d)** (Auto): **mete (la) tercera** put it into third (gear); **~ la marcha**

atrás to get into reverse **3** (provocar, crear): **~le prisa a algn** to rush sb; **~le miedo a algn** to frighten *o* scare sb; **no metas ruido** keep the noise down

■ **meterse** *v pron* **1 (a)** (entrar): **me metí en el agua** (en la playa) I went into the water; (en la piscina) I got into the water; **nos metimos en un museo** we went into a museum; **~se en la cama/la ducha** to get into bed/the shower; **¿dónde se habrá metido el perro?** where can the dog have got to?; **se me metió algo en el ojo** I got something in my eye **(b)** (introducirse): **me metí el dedo en el ojo** I stuck my finger in my eye; **se metió el dinero en el bolsillo** he put the money in(to) his pocket **2 (a)** (en trabajo): **se metió de secretaria** she got a job as a secretary; **~se de** *or* **a cura/monja** to become a priest/nun **(b)** (involucrarse) **~se EN algo** to get involved IN sth; **te has metido en un buen lío** you've got yourself into a fine mess; **no te metas en lo que no te importa** mind your own business; ***~se con algn*** (fam) to pick on sb; ***~se por medio*** to interfere

metiche *adj* (AmL fam) nosy (colloq) ■ *mf* busybody (colloq)

meticuloso -sa *adj* ‹*trabajo/investigación*› meticulous, thorough; ‹*persona*› meticulous

metida de pata *f* (AmL fam) blunder, gaffe

metódico -ca *adj* methodical

metodista *adj/mf* Methodist

método *m* method; **con ~** methodically

metodología *f* methodology

metomentodo *mf* (*pl* ~) (fam) busybody (colloq)

metralla *f* (trozos) shrapnel; (munición) grapeshot

metralleta *f* submachine gun

métrico -ca ▶ 322 *adj* metric, metrical

metro *m* **1 (a)** ▶ 679 (medida) meter*; **~ cuadrado/cúbico** square/cubic meter; **vender algo por ~(s)** to sell sth by the meter; **los 100 ~s valla** the 100-meter hurdles **(b)** (cinta métrica) tape measure **2** (Transp) subway (AmE), tube (BrE) **3** (en poesía) meter*

metrónomo *m* metronome

metrópolis (*pl* ~), **metrópoli** *f* metropolis

metropolitano[1] -na *adj* metropolitan

metropolitano[2] *m* subway (AmE), underground (BrE)

mexicanismo *m* Mexicanism

mexicano -na *adj/m,f* Mexican

México *m* Mexico; (capital) Mexico City

mexiquense *adj* (Méx) of/from Mexico City

mezcal *m* mescal

mezcla *f* **1** (proceso) **(a)** (en general) mixing **(b)** (de vinos, tabacos, cafés) blending **2** (combinación) **(a)** (de cosas diversas) mixture; (de vinos, tabacos, cafés) blend; (de tejidos) mix; **una ~ de harina y azúcar** a mixture of flour and sugar **(b)** (de razas, culturas) mix **(c)** (Audio) mix

mezclador -dora *m,f* (persona) *tb* **~ de sonido** *or* **audio** sound mixer

mezcladora *f* (Const) mixer

mezclar [A1] *vt* **1 (a)** (combinar) to mix; **~ algo CON algo** to mix sth WITH sth **(b)** ‹*café/vino/tabaco*› to blend **2** ‹*documentos/ropa*› to mix up, get ... mixed up; **~ algo CON algo** to get sth mixed up WITH sth **3** (involucrar) **~ a algn EN algo** to get sb mixed up *o* involved IN sth

■ **mezclarse** *v pron* **1 (a)** (involucrarse) **~se EN algo** to get mixed up *o* involved IN sth **(b)** (tener trato con) **~se CON algn** to mix WITH sb **2** «*razas/culturas*» to mix

mezclilla *f* **(a)** (tela de mezcla) cloth of mixed fibers **(b)** (Chi, Méx) (tela de jeans) denim

mezcolanza *f* (pey) hodgepodge (esp AmE), hotchpotch (BrE)

mezquindad *f* **(a)** (cualidad — de tacaño) meanness, stinginess (colloq); (— de vil): smallmindedness, pettiness **(b)** (acción egoísta) mean thing to do

mezquino[1] -na *adj* **(a)** (tacaño) mean, stingy (colloq); (vil) mean, small-minded **(b)** (escaso) ‹*sueldo/ración*› paltry, miserable

mezquino[2] *m* (Col, Méx) wart

mezquita *f* mosque

mezzo-soprano *f* mezzo soprano

mg. (= **miligramo**) mg

mi *adj* (*delante del n*) my; **~s libros** my books; **sí, ~ vida** yes, darling; **sí, ~ capitán** yes, sir ■ *m* (nota) E; (en solfeo) mi

mí *pron pers* me; **¿es para ~?** is it for me?; **por ~ no hay problema** as far as I'm concerned that's fine, that's fine by me; **¿y a ~ qué?** so what?, what do I care?; **a ~ no me importa** I couldn't care less; **~ mismo/misma** (*refl*) myself

miau *m* miaow; **hacer ~** to miaow

mica *f* **1 (a)** (Min) mica **(b)** (AmL) (de un reloj) crystal **2** (Col) (de niño) potty (colloq)

mico -ca *m,f* (Zool) long-tailed monkey; (como término genérico) monkey

micrero -ra *m,f* (Chi) bus driver

micro *m* **1** (fam) (microbús) small bus; (autobús) (Arg) bus, coach (BrE) **2** (fam) (micrófono) mike (colloq) ■ *f* (Chi) bus

microbio *m* microbe

microbiología *f* microbiology

microbús *m* small bus

microchip /mikro'tʃip/ *m* (*pl* **-chips**) microchip

microcosmos (*pl* ~), **microcosmo** *m* microcosm

microfilm (*pl* **-films**), **microfilme** *m* microfilm

micrófono *m* microphone; **hablar por el ~** to speak over the microphone

microondas *m* (*pl* ~) microwave (oven)

microorganismo *m* microorganism

microscópico -ca *adj* microscopic

microscopio *m* microscope; **mirar algo al** *or* **por el ~** to look at sth under the microscope

mida, midas, etc *see* MEDIR

miedo *m* fear; **¡qué ~ pasamos!** we were so frightened *o* scared!; **temblaba de ~** he was trembling with fear; **me da ~ salir de noche** I'm afraid to go *o* of going out at night; **~ A algo/algn** fear OF sth/sb; **el ~ a lo desconocido** fear of the unknown; **le tiene ~ a su padre** he's scared *o* afraid of his father; **agarrarle** *or* (esp Esp) **cogerle**

~ **a algo/algn** to become frightened *o* scared of sth/sb; **por ~ a** for fear of; **tener ~** to be afraid *o* frightened *o* scared; **tiene ~ de caerse** he's afraid he might fall; **tengo ~ de que se ofenda** I'm afraid he will take offense

miedoso -sa *adj*: **¡no seas ~! no te va a hacer daño** don't be frightened *o* scared! it won't hurt you; **¡qué ~ es!** he's such a coward! ■ *m, f* coward, scaredy cat (colloq)

miel *f* honey; **~ de palma** palm syrup

miembro *m* **1 (a)** (de organización, asociación) member **(b)** (*como adj*) ‹*estado/países*› member (*before n*) **2** (Anat) limb; **~s anteriores/posteriores** fore/back limbs

mienta, mientas, etc *see* MENTIR

mientras *adv* **1** (al mismo tiempo) *tb* **~ tanto** in the meantime, meanwhile **2** (esp AmL) (cuanto): **~ más se le da, más pide** the more you give him, the more he wants; **~ menos coma, mejor** the less I eat the better ■ *conj* **1** (indicando simultaneidad) while; **~ dormíamos** while we were asleep **2** (con idea de futuro, condición, etc) as long as; **~ viva/él no se entere** as long as I live/he doesn't find out **3 mientras que** (con valor adversativo) whereas, while

miércoles *m* ▶ **193** (*pl* ~) Wednesday; **~ de ceniza** Ash Wednesday; *para ejemplos ver* LUNES

mierda *f* **1** (vulg) (excremento) shit (vulg) **2** (vulg) **(a)** (cosa despreciable): **una ~ de empleo** a crappy *o* lousy job (colloq); **la película es una ~** the movie is (a load of) crap (sl) **(b)** (mugre) filth, crap (sl); ***¡a la ~ con ... !*** (vulg) to hell with ... ! (colloq); ***irse a la ~*** (vulg) «*proyecto/empresa*» to go to the dogs, go to pot (colloq); ***mandar a algn a la ~*** (vulg) to tell sb to go to hell (colloq) *o* (vulg) to screw himself/herself; ***¡vete a la ~!*** (vulg) go to hell! (colloq), fuck off! (vulg)

mies *f* ripe grain; **~es** cornfields

miga *f* **1** (de pan) crumb **2 migas** *fpl* (Coc) *breadcrumbs fried with garlic, etc* **3** (contenido, sustancia) substance; (dificultad) difficulties (*pl*); **el asunto tiene su ~** it has its difficulties *o* it's quite tricky

migajas *fpl* (de pan) breadcrumbs (*pl*); (sobras) leftovers (*pl*), scraps (*pl*)

migración *f* migration

migraña *f* migraine

mijo[1] *m* millet

mijo[2] **-ja** *pron* (apelativo) (AmL fam) dear; **¿qué le pasa, mijita?** what's the matter, darling? (colloq)

mil *adj inv/pron* ▶ **293** thousand; **~ quinientos pesos** fifteen hundred pesos, one thousand five hundred pesos; **20 ~ millones** 20 billion (AmE), 20 thousand million (BrE); **tengo ~ cosas que hacer** I have a thousand and one things to do ■ *m* ▶ **293** (number) one thousand

milagro *m* miracle; **alcancé el tren de ~** by a miracle I caught the train; **escaparon de ~** they had a miraculous escape; ***hacer ~s*** to work wonders

milagroso -sa *adj* miraculous

milanesa *f*: *thin breaded cutlet of meat/chicken*

milano *m* kite

milenio *m* millennium

milésima *f* ▶ **294** thousandth

milésimo -ma *adj/pron* ▶ **294** thousandth; **la milésima parte** a thousandth

milhojas *f* (*pl* ~) (Coc) millefeuille

mili *f* (Esp fam) military service; **hacer la ~** to do one's military service

milicia *f* militia

miliciano -na *m, f* militiaman

milico *m* (AmL fam & pey) soldier; **los ~s** the military

miligramo *m* ▶ **322** milligram

mililitro *m* milliliter*

milímetro *m* ▶ **679** millimeter*

militancia *f* (filiación) political affiliation; (militantes) members (*pl*)

militante *adj* politically active ■ *mf* activist

militar[1] *adj* military ■ *mf* soldier, military man; **los ~es** the military

militar[2] [A1] *vi* to be politically active; **~ en un partido político** to be an active member of a political party

milla *f* ▶ **679** mile

millar *m* ▶ **293** thousand; **un ~ de seguidores** about a thousand supporters

millón *m* ▶ **293** million; **15 mil millones** 15 billion (AmE), 15 thousand million (BrE); **un ~ de gracias** thank you very much

millonario -ria *adj*: **es ~** he's a millionaire ■ *m, f* millionaire

milonga *f* **1** (Mús) *a type of dance and music from the River Plate region* **2** (RPl arg) **(a)** (fiesta) party, bash (colloq) **(b)** (mujer fácil) slut (colloq & pej)

milonguero -ra *m, f* (RPl arg) reveler, raver (BrE colloq)

milpa *f* (AmC, Méx) (campo) field (*used mainly for the cultivation of maize*); (cultivo) crop

mimado -da *adj* spoiled, pampered ■ *m, f* spoiled child; **este niño es un ~** this child is spoiled *o* (pej) is a spoiled brat

mimar [A1] *vt* to spoil, pamper

mimbre *m* (material) wicker; **silla de ~** wicker *o* basket chair

mimbrera *f* (arbusto) osier; (sauce) willow

mímica *f* (Teatr) mime; (gestos, señas) sign language, mime

mimo *m* **(a)** (caricia) cuddle; **hacerle ~s a algn** to cuddle sb **(b)** (trato indulgente) pampering; **lo criaron con mucho ~** he had a very pampered upbringing ■ *mf* mime

mimosa *f* mimosa

min (= **minuto**) min

mina *f* **1** (yacimiento, excavación) mine; **~ de carbón** coalmine; **~ a cielo abierto** *or* (Andes) **a tajo abierto** strip mine (AmE), opencast mine (BrE); **es una ~ de información** he's a mine of information **2** (Mil, Náut) mine; **un campo de ~s** a minefield **3** (de lápiz) lead **4** (CS arg) (mujer) broad (AmE sl), bird (BrE sl)

minar [A1] *vt* **(a)** ‹*campo/mar*› to mine **(b)** (debilitar) ‹*salud*› to damage; ‹*autoridad/moral*› to undermine

minarete *m* minaret

mineral *adj* mineral ■ *m* **(a)** (sustancia) mineral **(b)** (de un metal) ore

minería *f* mining industry

minero -ra *adj* mining (*before n*) ■ *m,f* miner

mini *f* (fam) miniskirt, mini (colloq)

miniatura *f* (Art) miniature; **¡qué ~ de pie!** (fam) what a tiny little foot!

minicomputadora *f* (esp AmL) minicomputer

minifalda *f* miniskirt

minifundio *m* (propiedad) smallholding

mini-golf *m* miniature golf

mínima *f* minimum temperature

minimizar [A4] *vt* (reducir al mínimo) to minimize; (quitar importancia) to make light of, play down

mínimo¹ -ma *adj* **(a)** ‹*temperatura/peso*› minimum (*before n*); **no le importa lo más ~** he couldn't care less; **el trabajo no le interesa en lo más ~** he is not in the slightest (bit) interested in his work; **no tengo la más mínima idea** I haven't the faintest idea **(b)** (insignificante) ‹*detalle*› minor; ‹*diferencia/beneficios*› minimal

mínimo² *m* minimum; **reducir los gastos al ~** to keep costs to a minimum; **como ~** at least

miniordenador *m* (Esp) minicomputer

ministerial *adj* ‹*reunión*› cabinet (*before n*); ‹*orden*› ministerial

ministerio *m* **1** (Pol) ministry, department (AmE); **M~ de Hacienda** ≈Treasury Department (*in US*), ≈Treasury (*in UK*); **M~ del Interior** ≈Department of the Interior (*in US*), ≈Home Office (*in UK*); **M~ de Relaciones** *or* **Asuntos Exteriores** ≈State Department (*in US*), ≈Foreign Office (*in UK*) **2** (Relig) ministry

ministro -tra *m,f* minister, government minister; **M~ de Hacienda** ≈Secretary of the Treasury (*in US*), ≈Chancellor of the Exchequer (*in UK*); **M~ del Interior** ≈Secretary of the Interior (*in US*), ≈Home Secretary (*in UK*); **M~ de Relaciones** *or* **Asuntos Exteriores** ≈Secretary of State (*in US*), ≈Foreign Secretary (*in UK*)

minoría *f* minority; **estar en ~** to be in a/the minority; **~ de edad** minority

minorista *adj* retail (*before n*) ■ *mf* retailer

minoritario -ria *adj* minority (*before n*)

mintiera, mintió, etc *see* MENTIR

minucia *f* **(a)** (detalle pequeño) minor detail **(b)** (cualidad) detail; **explicar algo con ~** to explain sth in detail *o* thoroughly

minuciosidad *f* attention to detail

minucioso -sa *adj* ‹*búsqueda/investigación/persona*› meticulous, thorough; ‹*informe*› detailed

minúscula *f* lower case letter, minuscule (tech)

minúsculo -la *adj* **(a)** (diminuto) minute, tiny **(b)** ‹*letra*› lower case

minusvalía *f* **1** (física) physical handicap *o* disability; (psíquica) mental handicap **2** (Econ) drop *o* fall in value

minusválido -da *adj* (físico) physically handicapped, disabled; (psíquico) mentally handicapped ■ *m,f* (físico) disabled person, physically handicapped person; (psíquico) mentally handicapped person; **coches para ~s** cars for the disabled

minuta *f* **1** (de abogado, notario) bill **2** (plato rápido) (RPl) quick meal

minutero *m* minute hand

minuto *m* ▶ 221 minute; **a tres ~s de su casa** three minutes (away) from his house

mío, mía *adj* (*detrás del n*) mine; **un primo ~** a cousin of mine; **eso es asunto ~** that's my business; **Muy señor ~** (Corresp) (frml) Dear Sir ■ *pron*: **el ~/la mía, etc** mine; **sus hijos y los ~s** their children and mine; **los idiomas no son lo ~** languages are not my thing; **los ~s** my family and friends

miope *adj* **(a)** (Med, Ópt) myopic (tech), nearsighted (AmE), short-sighted (BrE) **(b)** (falto de perspicacia) short-sighted ■ *mf* myopic person (tech), nearsighted person (AmE), short-sighted person (BrE)

miopía *f* **(a)** (Med, Ópt) myopia (tech), nearsightedness (AmE), short-sightedness (BrE) **(b)** (falta de perspicacia) shortsightedness

mira *f* **(a)** (Arm, Ópt) sight; **(b)** (intención, objetivo): **con ~s a reducir los gastos** with a view to reducing costs; **con la ~ puesta en el porvenir** with one's sight set on the future; **es muy estrecho de ~s** he's very narrow-minded

mirada *f* **(a)** (modo de mirar) look; **una ~ reprobatoria** a disapproving look; **su ~ era triste** he had a sad look in his eyes; **lo fulminó con la ~** she looked daggers at him **(b)** (vistazo, ojeada) glance; **echarle una ~ por encima a algo** to take a quick glance at sth; **échales una ~ a los niños** have a look at the children **(c)** (vista): **tenía la ~ fija en el suelo** she had her eyes fixed on the ground; **recorrió la habitación con la ~** she cast her eyes over the room; **bajar/levantar la ~** to look down/up

miradero *m* (Col) viewpoint

mirado -da *adj* (considerado): **eso no está bien ~** that's not approved of, that's looked down on; **está muy mal ~ en el barrio** he is not at all well thought of *o* well regarded in the neighborhood; *ver tb* MIRAR *vt* 3

mirador *m* viewpoint

miramiento *m*: **tratar a algn sin ningún ~** to treat sb with a total lack of consideration

mirar [A1] *vt* **1 (a)** (observar, contemplar) to look at; **~ un cuadro** to look at a picture; **no me mires así** don't look at me like that; **~ a algn a los ojos** to look sb in the eye; **se me quedó mirando** he just stared at me; **miraba distraída por la ventana** he was gazing absent-mindedly out of the window; **miraba cómo lo hacía** he was watching how she did it; **ir a ~ escaparates** *or* (AmL) **vidrieras** to go window shopping **(b)** ‹*programa/partido/televisión*› to watch **2** (fijarse) to look; **¡mira lo que has hecho!** look what you've done!; **mira bien que esté apagado** make sure *o* check it's off; **miré a ver si estaba listo** I had a look to see if he was ready **3** (considerar): **míralo desde otro punto de vista** look at it from another point of view; **lo**

mires por donde lo mires whatever *o* whichever way you look at it; **mirándolo bien** (pensándolo detenidamente) all things considered; (pensándolo mejor) on second thoughts; **~ *a algn en menos*** to look down on sb; **~ *mal a algn*** to disapprove of sb **4** (expresando incredulidad, irritación, etc): **¡mira que poner un plato de plástico en el horno** ...! honestly *o* really! imagine putting a plastic dish in the oven ...! (colloq); **¡mira que eres tacaño!** boy, you're mean! (colloq); **¡mira las veces que te lo habré dicho** ...! the times I've told you! ■ **~** *vi* **1** (en general) to look; **he mirado por todas partes** I've looked everywhere; **~ por la ventana** to look out of the window; **¿miraste bien?** did you have a good look?, did you look properly?; **~ *atrás*** to look back **2** (estar orientado) **~** A/HACIA **algo** «*fachada*» to face sth; «*terraza/habitación*» to look out over sth, overlook sth; **ponte mirando hacia la ventana** stand (*o* sit *etc*) facing the window **3 mirar por (a)** (preocuparse por) to think of **(b)** (Col) (cuidar) to look after

■ **mirarse** *v pron* **(a)** (*refl*) to look at oneself; **~se en el espejo** to look at oneself in the mirror **(b)** (*recípr*) to look at each other

mirilla *f* peephole, spyhole

mirlo *m* blackbird

mirto *m* myrtle

misa *f* mass; **están en ~** they're at mass; **ir a ~** to go to mass; **decir ~** «*sacerdote*» to say *o* celebrate mass; **~ de cuerpo presente** funeral mass; **~ de difuntos** Requiem (mass); **~ de** *or* **del gallo** midnight mass (*on Christmas Eve*)

miscelánea *f* **(a)** (variedad) miscellany **(b)** (Méx) (tienda) small general store, corner shop (BrE)

misceláneo -nea *adj* miscellaneous

miserable *adj* **(a)** (pobre) ‹*vivienda*› miserable, wretched; ‹*sueldo*› paltry, miserable **(b)** (avaro) mean, stingy (colloq) **(c)** (malvado) malicious, nasty ■ *mf* wretch, scoundrel

miseria *f* **1** (pobreza) poverty, destitution **2** (cantidad insignificante) miserable amount, paltry amount; **gana una ~** she earns a pittance **3** (desgracia) misfortune; **las ~s de la guerra** the miseries of war

misericordia *f* mercy, compassion

misericordioso -sa *adj* merciful

mísero -ra *adj* miserable

misil *m* missile; **~ antiaéreo/balístico** antiaircraft/ballistic missile

misión *f* **1** (tarea) mission **2** (delegación): **una ~ científica** a team of scientists; **una ~ diplomática** a diplomatic delegation

misionero -ra *adj* missionary (*before n*) ■ *m,f* missionary

Misisipí *m* (río): **el (río) ~** the Mississippi (River); (estado) Mississippi

mismo¹ -ma *adj* **1 (a)** (*delante del n*) (expresando identidad) same; **hacer dos cosas al ~ tiempo** to do two things at once *o* at the same time **(b)** (*como pron*) same; **Roma ya no es la misma** Rome isn't the same any more; **el ~ que vimos ayer** the same one we saw yesterday **2** (uso enfático) **(a)** (refiriéndose a lugares, momentos, cosas): **en el ~ centro de Lima** right in the center of Lima; **en este ~ instante** this very minute; **eso ~ pienso yo** that's exactly what I think **(b)** (refiriéndose a personas): **el mismísimo presidente** the president himself; **te perjudicas a ti ~** you're only hurting yourself; **ella misma lo trajo** she brought it herself **3 lo mismo**: **siempre dice lo ~** he always says the same thing; **lo ~ para mí** the same for me, please; **nuestra empresa, lo ~ que tantas otras** our company, like so many others; **los niños pueden ir lo ~ que los adultos** children can go as well as adults; **o lo que es lo ~** in other words; ***da lo ~*** it doesn't matter; ***me/le da lo ~*** I don't care/he/she doesn't care

mismo² *adv* (uso enfático): **aquí/ahora ~** right here/now; **hoy ~ te mando el cheque** I'll send you the check today; **ayer ~ hablé con él** I spoke to him only yesterday

miss /mis/ *f* beauty queen; **M~ Universo** Miss Universe

misterio *m* mystery

misterioso -sa *adj* mysterious

misticismo *m* mysticism

místico -ca *adj* ‹*experiencia*› mystic, mystical; ‹*escritor*› mystic (*before n*) ■ *m,f* mystic

mitad *f* **1** (parte) half; **la ~ de la población** half (of) the population; **sólo quiero la ~** I only want half; **a ~ de precio** half price; **lo hizo en la ~ del tiempo** she did it in half the time; **~ *y* ~** half and half **2** (medio, centro): **cortar algo por la ~** to cut sth in half; **dividir algo por la ~** to halve sth; **a** *or* **en (la) ~ de la reunión** in the middle of the meeting; **a ~ de camino** halfway; **en la ~ de la película/del libro** halfway through the movie/the book

mítico -ca *adj* mythical

mitigar [A3] *vt* ‹*dolor*› to relieve, ease; ‹*pena/sufrimiento*› to alleviate, mitigate (frml); ‹*sed*› to quench

mitin, **mitín** *m* (Pol) political meeting, rally

mito *m* **(a)** (leyenda) legend **(b)** (invención, mentira) myth

mitología *f* mythology

mitológico -ca *adj* mythological

mixto¹ -ta *adj* mixed; **educación mixta** coeducation

mixto² *m* toasted sandwich (*with two different fillings*)

ml. (= **mililitro**) ml

mm. (= **milímetro**) mm

moaré *m* moiré

mobiliario *m* furniture, furnishings (*pl*); **renovar el ~ del comedor** to refurnish the dining room; **~ de baño** bathroom furnishings (*pl*); **~ de cocina** kitchen fittings *o* units (*pl*)

moca *m*: *tb* **café ~** mocha; **tarta de ~** coffee cake

mocasín *m* moccasin

mochila *f* (de excursionista, soldado) backpack; (de escolar) satchel

mochilear [A1] *vi* (CS) to backpack

mochilero -ra *m,f* (CS) backpacker

moción *f* motion; **presentar una ~** to propose *o* (BrE) table a motion; **~ de censura** vote of censure *o* no confidence

moco *m* **(a)** (líquido) snot (colloq); **límpiate los ~s** wipe *o* blow your nose; **le colgaban los ~s** he had a runny nose (colloq) *o* (sl) snotty nose **(b)** (seco) booger (AmE colloq), bogey (BrE colloq)

mocoso -sa *m,f* (fam) squirt (colloq), pipsqueak (colloq)

moda *f* fashion; **la ~ joven** *or* **juvenil** young fashion; **la ~ de los 30** 30's fashion; **ir a la ~** to be trendy; **estar de ~** to be in fashion, be in (colloq); **ponerse/pasar de ~** to come into/go out of fashion; **seguir la ~** to follow fashion

modales *mpl* manners (*pl*); **tener buenos/malos ~** to be well-mannered/bad-mannered

modalidad *f*: **varias ~es de pago** several methods *o* modes of payment; **la medalla de oro en la ~ de esquí alpino** the gold medal for downhill skiing

modelaje *m* (Andes, Ven) modeling*; **hacer ~** to model

modelar [A1] *vt* (Art) ‹*arcilla*› to model; ‹*estatua/figura*› to model, sculpt; ‹*carácter*› to mold* ■ **~** *vi* **1** (Art) to model **2** (Andes) (para fotos, desfiles) to model

modelo *adj inv* **(a)** ‹*niño/estudiante*› model (*before n*); ‹*comportamiento/carácter*› exemplary **(b)** (de muestra): **visité la casa ~** I visited the model home (AmE) *o* (BrE) the showhouse ■ *m* **1** (en general) model; **tomar/utilizar algo como ~** to take/use sth as a model; **tomó a su padre como ~** he followed his father's example; **~ en** *or* **a escala** scale model **2** (Indum) design; **un ~ de Franelli** a Franelli (design); **llegó con un nuevo modelito** (fam) she arrived wearing a new little number ■ *mf* model; **desfile de ~s** fashion show

módem *m* (*pl* **-dems**) modem

moderación *f* moderation; **beber con ~** to drink in moderation

moderado -da *adj* **(a)** ‹*persona/comportamiento*› restrained **(b)** ‹*temperatura*› moderate; ‹*precio*› reasonable; ‹*ideología/facción*› moderate ■ *m,f* moderate

moderador -dora *m,f* (en debate) moderator, chair; (Rad, TV) presenter

moderar [A1] *vt* **1 (a)** ‹*impulsos/aspiraciones*› to curb, moderate; **por favor modera tu vocabulario** please mind your language **(b)** ‹*gasto/consumo*› to curb; ‹*velocidad*› to reduce **2** ‹*debate/coloquio*› to moderate, chair

■ **moderarse** *v pron*: **modérate, estás comiendo mucho** restrain yourself *o* (colloq) go easy, you're eating too much; **~se en los gastos** to cut down on spending

modernismo *m* (Arquit, Art, Lit) modernism; (cualidad) modernness, modernity

modernista *adj/mf* modernist

modernizar [A4] *vt* ‹*fábrica/técnica/sociedad*› to modernize; ‹*costumbres*› to update; ‹*vestido/abrigo*› to do up

■ **modernizarse** *v pron*: **debes ~te** you have to keep up with the times

moderno -na *adj* **(a)** (actual) modern; **el hombre ~** modern man; **una edición más ~** a more up-to-date edition **(b)** (a la moda) ‹*vestido/peinado*› fashionable, trendy **(c)** ‹*edad/historia*› modern

modestia *f* modesty

modesto -ta *adj* **(a)** (falto de pretensión) modest **(b)** (humilde) ‹*familia*› humble; ‹*posición social*› modest, humble **(c)** ‹*sueldo/ingresos*› modest

módico -ca *adj* reasonable

modificar [A2] *vt* **(a)** ‹*aparato*› to modify; ‹*plan*› to change; ‹*horario/ley*› to change, alter **(b)** (Ling) to modify; **modifica al verbo** it modifies the verb

■ **modificarse** *v pron* to change, alter

modismo *m* idiom

modista *mf* (que diseña) couturier, designer; (que confecciona) dressmaker

modistería *f* (Col) (actividad) dressmaking; (establecimiento) dressmaker's shop/workshop

modisto *m* couturier, designer

modo *m* **1 (a)** (manera, forma) way, manner (frml); **el ~ de hacerlo** the way of doing it; **del siguiente ~** in the following manner; **a mi ~ de ver** to my way of thinking, in my opinion; **no lo digas de ese ~** don't say it like that; **de un ~ u otro** one way or another; Ⓢ **modo de empleo** instructions for use, directions; **me lo pidió de muy mal ~** (AmL) she asked me (for it) very rudely **(b)** (*en locs*) **a mi/tu/su modo** (in) my/your/his (own) way; **de cualquier modo** (de todas formas) (*indep*) in any case, anyway; (sin cuidado) anyhow; **del mismo** *or* **de igual modo que** just as, in the same way (that); **de modo que** (así que) so; (para que) so that; **de ningún modo** no way; **de ningún ~ puedo aceptar** there's no way I can accept; **de todos modos** anyway, anyhow; **en cierto modo** in a way; **ni modo** (AmL exc CS fam) no way; **traté de persuadirlo pero ni ~** I tried to persuade him but it was no good; **ni ~ que te quedes aquí** there's no way you're staying here (colloq) **2 modos** *mpl* (modales) manners (*pl*); **con buenos/malos ~s** politely/rudely *o* impolitely

modulación *f* modulation; **~ de amplitud/frecuencia** amplitude/frequency modulation

modular [A1] *vt/vi* to modulate

módulo *m* **(a)** (de mueble) unit, module **(b)** (de prisión) unit **(c)** (Espac, Educ) module

mofarse [A1] *v pron* **~ DE algo/algn** to make fun of sth/sb

mofle *m* (AmC, Méx) muffler (AmE), silencer (BrE)

moflete *m* (fam) chubby cheek

mofletudo -da *adj* (fam) chubby-cheeked

mogolla *f* (Col) bread roll

mohair /mo'er/ *m* mohair

mohín *m* face; **hacer un ~** to make *o* (BrE) pull an angry face

moho *m* **(a)** (en fruta, pan) mold*, mildew; **criar ~** «*fruta/queso*» to go moldy* **(b)** (en cobre) patina, verdigris; (en hierro) rust

moisés *m* (cuna) cradle, Moses basket; (portátil) portacrib (AmE), carrycot (BrE)

mojado -da *adj* wet ■ *m,f* (Méx fam) wetback (colloq & pej)

mojar [A1] *vt* **(a)** ‹*suelo/papel/pelo*› (accidentalmente) to get *o* make ... wet; (a propósito) to wet; **pasó un coche y me mojó** a car went by and splashed me; **~ la cama** (euf) to wet the bed **(b)** (sumergiendo) ‹*galleta/bizcocho*› to dip, dunk (colloq)
■ **mojarse** *v pron* **(a)** «*persona/ropa/suelo*» to get wet; **se me ~on los zapatos** my shoes got wet; **me mojé toda** I got soaked **(b)** ‹*pelo/pies*› (a propósito) to wet; (accidentalmente) to get ... wet

mojigatería *f* prudishness

mojigato -ta *adj* prudish ■ *m,f* prude

mojón *m* (señal) marker, boundary stone; (hito) landmark; (Auto) *tb* **~ kilométrico** ≈ milestone

molar *m* molar, back tooth

molcajete *m* (Méx) mortar

molde *m* **(a)** (para hornear) baking pan (AmE), baking tin (BrE); (para flanes, gelatina) mold*; **~ de pan** loaf pan (AmE) *o* (BrE) tin **(b)** (Tec) cast; **un ~ de yeso** (Art) a plaster cast **(c)** (AmL) (para coser) pattern

moldeable *adj* **(a)** ‹*barro*› moldable*, malleable **(b)** ‹*persona/carácter*› malleable

moldear [A1] *vt* **(a)** (en bronce) to cast; (en barro) to mold*, model **(b)** ‹*persona/carácter*› to mold*, shape; ‹*pelo*› to style

moldura *f* molding*

mole *f* mass; **una ~ de hormigón** a huge mass of concrete ■ *m* (Méx) (salsa) chili sauce (*with chocolate and peanuts*); (plato) *turkey, chicken or pork with* MOLE *sauce*

molécula *f* molecule

moler [E9] *vt* ‹*especias/café*› to grind; ‹*trigo*› to grind, mill; ‹*aceitunas*› to crush; ‹*carne*› to grind (AmE), to mince (BrE); ‹*plátano*› (Chi, Méx) to mash; **café molido** ground coffee

molestar [A1] *vt* **1 (a)** (importunar) to bother; **perdone que lo moleste** sorry to trouble *o* bother you **(b)** (interrumpir) to disturb **2** (ofender, disgustar) to upset ■ **~** *vi* **1** (importunar): **¿le molesta si fumo?** do you mind if I smoke?; **me molesta su arrogancia** her arrogance irritates *o* annoys me; **no me duele, pero me molesta** it doesn't hurt but it's uncomfortable **2** (fastidiar) to be a nuisance; **no quiero ~** I don't want to be a nuisance *o* to cause any trouble
■ **molestarse** *v pron* **1** (disgustarse) to get upset; **~se POR algo** to get upset ABOUT sth; **~se CON algn** to get annoyed WITH sb **2** (tomarse el trabajo) to bother, trouble oneself (frml); **ni se molestó en llamarme** he didn't even bother to call me; **se molestó en venir hasta aquí a avisarnos** she took the trouble to come all this way to tell us

molestia *f* **1 (a)** (incomodidad, trastorno): **ser una ~** to be a nuisance; **siento causarte tantas ~s** I'm sorry to cause you so much trouble; **perdona la ~, pero** ... sorry to bother you, but ... **(b)** (trabajo) trouble; **se tomó la ~ de escribirnos** she took the trouble to write to us; **¿para qué te tomaste la ~?** why did you bother to do that?; **no es ninguna ~** it's no trouble *o* bother **2** (malestar): **~s estomacales** stomach problems *o* upsets; **no es un dolor, sólo una ~** it's not a pain, just a feeling of discomfort

molesto -ta *adj* **1** [SER] **(a)** (fastidioso) ‹*ruido/tos*› annoying, irritating; ‹*sensación/síntoma*› unpleasant **(b)** (violento, embarazoso) awkward, embarrassing **2** [ESTAR] (ofendido) upset; (irritado) annoyed; **está muy ~ por lo que hiciste** he's very upset/annoyed about what you did

molestoso -sa *adj* (AmL fam) annoying

molido -da *adj* **(a)** (fam) (agotado) bushed (AmE colloq), shattered (BrE colloq) **(b)** (Andes fam) (dolorido) stiff

molinero -ra *m,f* miller

molinillo *m* **(a)** (de café, especias) grinder, mill; **~ de carne** grinder (AmE), mincer (BrE) **(b)** (juguete) pinwheel (AmE), windmill (BrE) **(c)** (Col, Méx) (para batir) whisk

molino *m* **(a)** (máquina — para el trigo) mill; (— para la carne) grinder (AmE), mincer (BrE) **(b)** (fábrica) mill; **~ de agua** waterwheel; **~ de viento** windmill; **~ de papel** paper mill

molleja *f* (de res) sweetbread; (de ave) gizzard

mollera *f* (fam) head; **está mal de la ~** he's off his head *o* rocker (colloq); ***cerrado** or **duro de ~*** pigheaded (colloq)

molo *m* (Chi) *tb* **~ de abrigo** breakwater, mole

molusco *m* mollusk*

momentáneo -nea *adj* **(a)** (breve) momentary **(b)** (pasajero) temporary

momento *m* **1 (a)** (instante puntual) moment; **justo en ese ~** just at that moment; **a partir de ese ~** from that moment on; **en todo ~** at all times **(b)** (lapso breve) minute, moment; **dentro de un ~** in a minute *o* moment; **¡un momentito!** (por teléfono) just a moment, just a minute; **eso te lo arreglo en un ~** I'll fix that for you in no time at all **(c)** (época, período) time, period; **atravesamos ~s difíciles** we're going through a difficult time *o* period; **está en su mejor ~** he is at his peak **(d)** (ocasión) time; **llegas en buen/mal ~** you've arrived at the right time/at a bad time; **en ningún ~** at no time **2** (*en locs*) **al momento** at once; **de momento** (ahora mismo) right now; (mientras tanto) for the time being; (por ahora) for the moment; **de un momento al otro** (dentro de muy poco) any minute now; **en cualquier momento** at any time; **en el momento** immediately; **en el momento menos pensado** when they (*o* you *etc*) least expect it; **por el momento** for the time being **3** (Fís, Mec) momentum

momia *f* mummy

mona *f* **1** (fam) (borrachera): **agarrar una ~** to get plastered (colloq); **dormir la ~** to sleep it off **2 (a)** (en naipes) old maid **(b)** (Col) (para un álbum) picture card; ***como la ~*** (CS fam) terrible

monada *f* (fam) **(a)** (cosa bonita): **¡qué ~ de vestido!** what a lovely dress! **(b)** (persona bonita): **su novia es una ~** his girlfriend's really pretty; **¡qué ~ de niño!** what a lovely *o* (colloq) cute kid **(c)** (RPl) (persona encantadora) angel (colloq)

monaguillo *m* altar boy, acolyte, server

monarca *mf* monarch

monarquía *f* monarchy

monárquico -ca *adj* ‹*régimen*› monarchical; ‹*persona/ideas*› monarchist (*before n*) ■ *m,f* monarchist, royalist

monasterio *m* monastery

monástico -ca *adj* monastic

mondadientes *m* (*pl* ~) toothpick

mondar [A1] *vt* (Esp) ‹*fruta/patatas*› to peel ■ **mondarse** *v pron* (*refl*): **se mondaba los dientes** she was picking her teeth; ***~se de risa*** (Esp fam) to die laughing

moneda *f* **1 (a)** (pieza) coin; **una ~ de cinco pesos** a five-peso coin *o* piece **(b)** (de país) currency; **acuñar ~** to mint money **2 la Moneda** (en Chi) Presidential Palace

monedero *m* change purse (AmE), purse (BrE)

monerías *fpl* (fam): **hacer ~** (tontear) to mess around (colloq); (hacer payasadas) to monkey *o* clown around (colloq)

mongólico -ca *adj* **(a)** (ant *o* crit) (Med) ‹*rasgos*› mongoloid (dated *or* crit); **niños ~s** Down's syndrome children **(b)** (fam & pey) (tonto) moronic (colloq & pej)

mongolismo *m* (ant *o* crit) Down's syndrome

monigote *m* (muñeco) rag doll; (de papel) paper doll; (dibujo) doodle

monitor -tora *m,f* **1 (a)** (CS) (Dep): **~ de esquí/natación** ski/swimming instructor; **~ de tenis** tennis coach **(b)** (Educ) (en la escuela) (RPl) monitor; (en la universidad) (Col) *student who acts as an assistant teacher* **2 monitor** *m* (Inf, Med, Tec) monitor

monja *f* nun; **meterse a** *or* **de ~** to become a nun

monje *m* monk

mono[1] -na *adj* **1** (fam) ‹*mujer*› pretty, lovely-looking (colloq); ‹*niño*› lovely, cute (colloq); ‹*vestido/piso*› gorgeous, lovely **2** (Col) (rubio) ‹*hombre/niño*› blond; ‹*mujer/niña*› blonde **3** (Audio) mono ■ *m,f* **1** (Zool) monkey; ***ser el último ~*** (fam) to be the lowest of the low

mono[2] **1** *m* (monigote) doodle; **una revista de monitos** (Andes, Méx) a comic; **~ animado** (Chi) cartoon; **~ de nieve** (Chi) snowman **2 (a)** (de mecánico) coveralls (*pl*) (AmE), overalls (*pl*) (BrE) **(b)** (de moda — de cuerpo entero) jumpsuit; (— con peto) overalls (*pl*) (AmE), dungarees (*pl*) (BrE) **(c)** (Méx) (malla de bailarina) leotard

monocarril *m* monorail

monocolor *adj* one-color* (*before n*)

monóculo *m* monocle

monogamia *f* monogamy

monógamo -ma *adj* monogamous ■ *m,f* monogamist

monografía *f* monograph

monográfico -ca *adj* monographic

monolingüe *adj* monolingual

monolítico -ca *adj* monolithic

monolito *m* monolith

monólogo *m* monologue

monopatín *m* (con manillar) (CS) scooter; (sin manillar) (Esp) skateboard

monopolio *m* monopoly

monopolizar [A4] *vt* to monopolize

monorriel *m* (AmL) monorail

monosílabo *m* monosyllable

monoteísmo *m* monotheism

monotonía *f* (de tarea) monotony; (de sonido) monotone

monótono -na *adj* monotonous

monóxido *m* monoxide; **~ de carbono** carbon monoxide

monseñor *m* Monsignor

monstruo *m* **(a)** (en general) monster **(b)** (fenómeno) phenomenon; **un ~ de la música pop** a pop phenomenon

monstruosidad *f* **(a)** (cosa fea, grande) monstrosity **(b)** (atrocidad) atrocity **(c)** (cualidad) monstrous nature, monstrousness

monstruoso -sa *adj* **(a)** ‹*crimen/comportamiento*› monstrous, atrocious **(b)** ‹*ser/facciones*› hideous, grotesque

monta *f* (monto) total (value); ***de poca ~*** ‹*asunto*› of little importance *o* note; ‹*escritor*› third-rate; ‹*daños*› slight, minor

montacargas *m* (*pl* ~) freight *o* service elevator (AmE), service *o* goods lift (BrE)

montado -da *adj* ‹*policía*› mounted; **iba ~ a caballo** he was riding a horse; **estaba montada en su bicicleta** she was sitting on her bicycle; *ver tb* MONTAR

montador -dora *m,f* (Mec, Tec) fitter; (Cin, TV) film editor

montaje *m* **(a)** (de máquina, mueble) assembly **(b)** (de obra) staging; (de película) editing; **seguro que todo es un ~** I bet it's all a big con *o* a set-up (colloq)

montallantas *m* (*pl* ~) (Col) (taller) *workshop where tires* are retreaded*; (mecánico) *person who retreads tires**

montaña *f* **1** (Geog) mountain; **tienen un chalet en la ~** they have a chalet in the mountains; **~ rusa** roller coaster **2** (montón) pile

montañero -ra *m,f* mountaineer, mountain climber

montañés -ñesa *adj* mountain (*before n*), highland (*before n*) ■ *m,f* highlander

montañismo *m* mountaineering, mountain climbing

montañoso -sa *adj* ‹*cadena*› mountain (*before n*); ‹*terreno/país*› mountainous

montar [A1] *vt* **1 (a)** ‹*caballo*› (subirse a) to mount, get on; (ir sobre) to ride **(b)** (subir, colocar): **montó al niño en el poni** he lifted the boy up onto the pony **2** ‹*vaca/yegua*› to mount **3 (a)** (poner, establecer) ‹*feria/exposición*› to set up; ‹*negocio*› to start up, set up **(b)** ‹*máquina/mueble*› to assemble; ‹*estantería*› to put up; ‹*tienda de campaña*› to put up, pitch **(c)** ‹*piedra preciosa*› to set; ‹*diapositiva*› to mount **(d)** (organizar) ‹*obra/producción*› to stage **4** (Esp) ‹*nata*› to whip; ‹*claras*› to whisk ■ **~** *vi* **1 (a)** (ir): **~ a caballo/en bicicleta** to ride a horse/bicycle **(b)** (Equ) to mount **2** (cubrir parcialmente) **~** SOBRE **algo** to overlap sth ■ **montarse** *v pron* (en coche) to get in; (en tren, autobús, bicicleta) to get on; (en caballo) to mount, get on; **¿me dejas ~me en tu bicicleta?** can I have a ride on your bicycle?

monte *m* (Geog) **(a)** (montaña) mountain **(b)** (terreno — cubierto de maleza) scrubland, scrub; (— cubierto de árboles) woodland

montera *f* (gorra) cap; (de torero) bullfighter's hat

montés *adj* ‹*animal/planta*› wild

montevideano -na *adj* of/from Montevideo

Montevideo *m* Montevideo

montgomery *m* (CS) duffle coat

montículo *m* mound

montón *m* **(a)** (pila) pile; ***del*** **~** (fam) ordinary, average **(b)** (fam) (gran cantidad): **un ~ de gente** loads of people (colloq); **me gusta un ~** I like her/him/it a lot

montonero -ra *m,f* (guerrillero) guerrilla

montura *f* **1** (Equ) (silla) saddle; (animal) mount **2** **(a)** (de anteojos) frame **(b)** (engarce) setting, mount

monumental *adj* (fam) **(a)** ‹*cocina/jardín*› huge, massive **(b)** ‹*error/esfuerzo*› monumental

monumento *m* **1** (obra conmemorativa) monument; **~ histórico/nacional** historical/national monument; **~ a los caídos** war memorial; **~ funerario** commemorative stone **2** (obra excepcional) masterpiece, classic **3** (fam) (mujer atractiva) stunner (colloq)

monzón *m* monsoon

moña *f* (Taur) ribbon; (lazo) (RPl) bow

moño *m* **(a)** (peinado) bun; **se hizo un ~** she put her hair up in a bun; ***estar hasta el*** **~** to be fed up (to the back teeth) (colloq) **(b)** (AmL) (lazo) bow

moñona *f* (Col fam) strike; **hacer ~** to get a strike

moqueta *f* (Esp) wall-to-wall carpet, fitted carpet (BrE)

moquillento -ta *adj* (Andes fam) **(a)** (resfriado) coldy (colloq) **(b)** (con mocos) ‹*nariz*› runny, snotty (colloq); ‹*niño*› runny-nosed, snotty-nosed (colloq)

moquillo *m* distemper

mora *f* (de zarzamora) blackberry; (de moral) mulberry; (de morera) white mulberry

morada *f* (frml *o* liter) dwelling (frml), abode (frml *or* liter)

morado[1] -da *adj* ▶ **97** ‹*color*› purple; **~ del frío** blue with cold; **ponerle a algn un ojo ~** to give sb a black eye

morado[2] *m* (Esp, Ven) bruise

moral *adj* moral ■ *f* **1** (Fil, Relig) **(a)** (doctrina) moral doctrine **(b)** (moralidad) morality, morals (*pl*) **2** (estado de ánimo) morale; **levantarle la ~ a algn** to raise sb's morale, lift sb's spirits; **estar bajo de ~** to be feeling low; **tener la ~ alta** to be in good spirits ■ *m* mulberry (tree)

moraleja *f* moral

moralidad *f* morality, ethics (*pl*)

morar [A1] *vi* (liter) to dwell (liter)

moratón *m* bruise

morboso -sa *adj* ‹*escena/película*› gruesome; ‹*persona/mente*› ghoulish; (truculento, retorcido) morbid ■ *m,f* (fam) ghoul

morcilla *f* blood sausage (AmE), black pudding (BrE)

mordaz *adj* ‹*estilo/lenguaje*› scathing, caustic; ‹*crítica*› sharp, scathing

mordaza *f* **(a)** (en la boca) gag **(b)** (Tec) clamp

mordedura *f* bite

morder [E9] *vt* **1** (con los dientes) to bite; **el perro le mordió la mano** the dog bit her hand **2** (Méx fam) «*policía/funcionario*» to extract a bribe from ■ **~** *vi* to bite

■ **morderse** *v pron* (*refl*) to bite oneself; **~se las uñas** to bite one's nails

mordida *f* **1** (CS) (en general) bite; (huella) toothmarks (*pl*) **2** (Méx fam) (soborno) bribe, backhander (BrE colloq)

mordisco *m* bite; **le dio un ~ en el brazo** it bit her (on the) arm

mordisquear [A1] *vt* to nibble

moreno -na *adj* **(a)** [SER] ‹*persona*› (de pelo oscuro) dark, dark-haired; (de tez oscura) dark; (de raza negra) (euf) dark-skinned (euph) **(b)** [ESTAR] (bronceado) brown, tanned **(c)** ‹*piel*› brown, dark ■ *m,f* **(a)** (de pelo oscuro) (*m*) dark-haired man (*o* boy *etc*); (*f*) dark-haired woman (*o* girl *etc*), brunet* **(b)** (de tez oscura) dark person (*o* man *etc*); (de raza negra) (euf) dark-skinned person (*o* man *etc*) (euph), coloured man (*o* woman *etc*) (BrE euph)

morera *f* white mulberry tree

moretón *m* bruise

morfar [A1] *vi* (RPl arg) to eat

morfina *f* morphine

morgue *f* (AmL) morgue, mortuary

moribundo -da *adj* dying, moribund (frml) ■ *m, f* dying man (*o* woman *etc*)

morir [I37] *vi* **(a)** «*persona/animal*» to die; **~ ahogado** to drown; **murió asesinada** she was murdered; **~ DE algo** ‹*de vejez/cáncer*› to die OF sth; **murió de hambre** she starved to death; **¡y allí muere!** (AmC fam) and that's all there is to it! **(b)** (liter) «*civilización/costumbre*» to die out

■ **morirse** *v pron* «*persona/animal/planta*» to die; **se les murió la madre** their mother died; **se me murió la perra** my dog died; **no te vas a ~ por ayudarlo** (fam) it won't kill you to help him (colloq); **como se entere me muero** (fam) I'll die if she finds out (colloq); **~se DE algo** ‹*de un infarto/de cáncer*› to die OF sth; **se moría de miedo/aburrimiento** he was scared stiff/bored stiff; **me muero de frío** I'm freezing; **me estoy muriendo de hambre** I'm starving (colloq); **me muero por una cerveza** I'm dying for a beer (colloq); **se muere por verla** he's dying to see her (colloq)

morisco -ca *adj* Moorish, Morisco

morisqueta *f* (CS): **hacer ~s** to make *o* (BrE) pull faces

mormado -da *adj* (Méx) ‹*nariz*› blocked; **estoy ~** I'm all stuffed up (colloq)

mormón -mona *adj/m,f* Mormon

moro -ra *adj* **1** (Hist) Moorish **2** (Esp) (de África del Norte) (fam & pey) North African; (referido a un hombre machista) (fam) chauvinistic, sexist ■ *m,f* **1** **(a)** (Hist) Moor **(b)** (mahometano) Muslim **2** (Esp) (de África del Norte) (fam & pey) North African ■ *m* (hombre machista) (fam) sexist, male chauvinist pig

morocho -cha *adj* (AmS fam) (de pelo oscuro) dark, dark-haired; (de piel oscura) dark ■ *m, f* (de pelo oscuro) dark-haired person (*o* man *etc*); (de piel oscura) dark person (*o* man *etc*)

morral *m* **(a)** (al hombro) rucksack, haversack; (a la espalda) backpack, rucksack **(b)** (para el pienso) nosebag

morralla *f* **1** (cosas sin valor) junk **2** (chusma) riffraff, rabble **3** (Méx) (dinero suelto) loose change

morriña *f* (fam) homesickness; **tener ~** to feel *o* be homesick

morro *m* **1 (a)** (hocico) snout **(b)** (Esp fam) (boca) *tb* **~s** mouth, chops (*pl*) (BrE colloq); ***estar de ~s (con algn)*** (Esp fam) to be in a bad mood (with sb) **(c)** (Esp fam) (descaro) nerve (colloq) **(d)** (Esp fam) (de coche, avión) nose **2** (cerro) hill

morrón *m* (CS) (pimiento) red pepper

morsa *f* walrus

mortadela *f* mortadella

mortaja *f* **1** (sábana) shroud **2** (Tec) mortise

mortal *adj* **1 (a)** ‹*ser*› mortal **(b)** ‹*herida*› fatal, mortal; ‹*dosis*› fatal, lethal; ‹*enfermedad/veneno*› deadly; **un golpe ~** a death blow **2** ‹*odio/enemigo*› mortal ■ *mf* mortal

mortalidad *f* mortality

mortecino -na *adj* ‹*luz*› weak; ‹*color*› pale

mortero *m* mortar

mortífero -ra *adj* deadly, lethal

mortificar [A2] *vt* **(a)** (atormentar) to torment; **los celos lo mortifican** he's tortured *o* tormented by jealousy **(b)** (Relig) to mortify

■ **mortificarse** *v pron* (*refl*) (atormentarse) to fret, distress oneself; (Relig) to mortify the flesh

mortuorio -ria *adj* funeral (*before n*)

mosaico *m* **(a)** (Art) mosaic **(b)** (Méx, RPl) (baldosa) floor tile; **piso de ~** tiled floor **(c)** (Col) (foto) school/college photograph

mosca *f* fly; **no se oía ni una ~** you could have heard a pin drop (colloq); ***por si las ~s*** (fam) just in case (colloq)

moscardón *m* botfly

moscatel *adj* muscat (*before n*) ■ *m* muscatel

moscovita *adj/mf* Muscovite

Moscú *m* Moscow

mosqueado -da *adj* (esp Esp fam) **(a)** (molesto, disgustado) annoyed, sore (AmE colloq), cross (BrE colloq) **(b)** (desconfiado, suspicaz) suspicious, wary

mosquearse [A1] *v pron* (esp Esp fam) **(a)** (sospechar, desconfiar) to get suspicious, smell a rat (colloq) **(b)** (disgustarse) to get annoyed, get sore (AmE colloq), to get cross (BrE colloq)

mosquetero *m* musketeer

mosquitero *m*, **mosquitera** *f* (de ventana) mosquito netting; (de tela) mosquito net

mosquito *m* mosquito

mostaza *f* mustard; (color) ▶ **97**: **(de) color ~** mustard, mustard-colored*

mosto *m* grape juice, must

mostrador *m* (en tienda) counter; (en bar) bar; (en aeropuerto) check-in desk

mostrar [A10] *vt* to show; **muéstrame cómo funciona** show me how it works

■ **mostrarse** *v pron* (+ *compl*): **se mostró muy atento con nosotros** he was very obliging (to us); **se ~on partidarios de la propuesta** they expressed support for the proposal

mota *f* **1** (partícula) tiny bit, dot; **una ~ de polvo** a speck of dust **2** (Tex): **una tela a ~s** a spotted fabric; **una lana azul con ~s de colores** blue wool with flecks of colors **3** (AmC, Méx arg) (marihuana) grass (colloq), weed (sl) **4** (Méx) **(a)** (para empolvarse) powder puff **(b)** (borla) pom-pom

mote *m* **1** (apodo) nickname; **le pusieron como ~ 'el Oso'** they nicknamed him 'the Bear' **2** (Andes) (trigo) boiled wheat; (maíz) boiled corn (AmE) *o* (BrE) maize

moteado -da *adj* ‹*tela*› (jaspeado) flecked; (a lunares) dotted, spotted; ‹*piel*› mottled

motel *m* motel

motín *m* (de tropas, tripulación) mutiny; (de prisioneros) riot, rebellion

motivación *f* (incentivo) motivation; (motivo) motive

motivar [A1] *vt* **1** (en general) to motivate; **motivado por la venganza** motivated by revenge; **¿qué te motivó a hacerlo?** what made you do it? **2** (causar) to bring about, cause

motivo *m* **1 (a)** (razón, causa) reason, cause; **el ~ de su viaje** the reason for her trip; **por este ~ nos hallamos aquí** that's (the reason) why we're here; **con ~ de algo** on the occasion of sth; **no des ~s para que te critiquen** don't give them cause to criticize you; **hay ~s para preocuparse** there is cause for concern; **el adulterio es ~ suficiente de divorcio** adultery is sufficient grounds for divorce; **sin ningún ~** for no reason at all; ***¡que sea un ~!*** (Col fam) let's drink to that! (colloq) **(b)** (propósito, finalidad) purpose; **el ~ de esta carta es** ... the purpose of this letter is ... **2** (Art, Lit, Mús) motif; **~s decorativos** decorative motifs

moto *f* (motocicleta) motorcycle, motorbike (BrE); (motoneta, escúter) (motor) scooter; **fue en ~** he went on his motorcycle

motocicleta *f* motorcycle

motociclismo *m* motorcycling

motociclista *mf* motorcyclist

motocross, **moto-cross** *m* motocross

motoneta *f* (AmL) (motor) scooter

motor[1] **-triz**, **motor -tora** *adj* motor (*before n*)

motor[2] *m* **1** (Tec) engine; **~ fuera (de) borda** outboard motor **2** (impulsor) driving force

motora *f* small motorboat, powerboat

motorismo *m* motorcycling

motorista *mf* **(a)** (que va en moto) motorcyclist **(b)** (Col) (automovilista) motorist (frml), driver

motorizado -da *adj* ‹*ejército*› motorized ■ *m, f* (Ven) motorcycle messenger *o* (BrE) courier

motudo -da *adj* (CS fam) frizzy

mousse /mus/ *f or m* mousse

mouton /mu'ton/ *m* sheepskin

mover [E9] *vt* **1 (a)** (trasladar, desplazar) to move **(b)** (Jueg) ‹*ficha/pieza*› to move **(c)** (agitar): **no muevas**

la cámara keep the camera still; **el viento movía los árboles** the wind shook the trees; **movió la cabeza** (asintiendo) he nodded (his head); (negando) she shook her head; **mueve la cola** it wags its tail **(d)** (accionar) to drive **2** (inducir): **~ a algn a hacer algo** to move sb to do sth ■ **~** *vi* (Jueg) to move
■ **moverse** *v pron* **(a)** (en general) to move; **no te muevas de ahí** don't move; **la lámpara se movía con el viento** the lamp was moving *o* swaying in the wind **(b)** (apresurarse) to hurry up, get a move on (colloq)

movida *f* **1** (Jueg) move **2** (Esp) (fam) **(a)** (asunto, rollo): **no me interesa la ~ ecológica** I'm not into this ecology thing (colloq); **anda en ~s chuecas** (Méx) he's into some shady deals (colloq) **(b)** (actividad cultural): **la ~ madrileña** the Madrid scene; **donde está la ~** where it's all going on

movido -da *adj* **(a)** (Fot) blurred **(b)** (agitado) ‹*mar*› rough, choppy; ‹*día/año*› hectic, busy; ‹*fiesta*› lively

móvil *adj* mobile ■ *m* **1** (frml) (impulso) motive **2** (adorno) mobile

movilidad *f* mobility

movilización *f* **1 (a)** (Mil) mobilization **(b)** (Rels Labs) (manifestación) demonstration; **un calendario de movilizaciones** a program of industrial action **2** (Chi) (Transp) public transportation (AmE), public transport (BrE)

movilizar [A4] *vt* ‹*tropas/población*› to mobilize
■ **movilizarse** *v pron* **1** (Mil, Rels Labs) to mobilize **2** (CS) (desplazarse) to move *o* get around

movimiento *m* **1 (a)** (en general) movement; **el menor ~ de la mano** the slightest movement of the hand; **el ~ surrealista** the surrealist movement; **~ pictórico** school of painting; **~ sísmico** earth tremor **(b)** (Fís, Tec) motion, movement; **poner algo en ~** to set sth in motion; **se puso en ~** it started moving **(c)** (agitación, actividad) activity; **una calle de mucho ~** a very busy street **2** (Mús) (parte de obra) movement; (compás) tempo **3** (Jueg) move

mozárabe *adj* Mozarabic ■ *mf* Mozarab

mozo -za *adj*: **en mis años ~s** in my youth; **sus hijos ya son ~s** her children are quite grown-up now ■ *m,f* **(a)** (ant) (joven) (*m*) young boy; (*f*) young girl; **los ~s del pueblo** the young people in the village **(b)** (AmS) (camarero) (*m*) waiter; (*f*) waitress **(c)** (Ferr) *tb* **~ de equipajes** *or* **de estación** porter

muaré *m* moiré

mucamo -ma (AmL) (*m*) servant; (*f*) maid, servant; **mucama de hotel** chambermaid

muchacha *f*: *tb* **~ de servicio** maid; *ver tb* MUCHACHO

muchacho -cha *m,f* (*m*) kid (colloq), boy, guy (colloq); (*f*) girl

muchedumbre *f* crowd

mucho[1] *adv* **(a)** ‹*salir/ayudar*› a lot; ‹*trabajar*› hard; **no salen ~** they don't go out much *o* a lot; **me gusta muchísimo** I like it very much *o* a lot; **~ mejor** a lot better; **por ~ que insistas** no matter how much you insist; **después de ~ discutir** after much discussion **(b)** (en respuestas): **¿estás preocupado? — mucho** are you worried? — (yes, I am,) very; **¿te gusta? — sí, ~** do you like it? — yes, very much

mucho[2] **-cha** *adj* **(a)** (*sing*) a lot of; (en oraciones negativas, interrogativas) much, a lot of; **~ vino** a lot of wine; **no gano ~ dinero** I don't earn much *o* a lot of money; **¿ves mucha televisión?** do you watch much *o* a lot of television; **tiene mucha hambre** he's very hungry **(b)** (*pl*) many, a lot of; **había ~s extranjeros/muchas personas allí** there were many *o* a lot of foreigners/people there; **hace ~s años** many years ago ■ *pron* **1** (referido a cantidad) **(a)** (*sing*) a lot; (en oraciones negativas) much; **~ de lo dicho** a lot of what was said; **tengo ~ que hacer** I have a lot to do; **eso no es ~** that's not much; **no queda mucha** there isn't much left **(b)** (*pl*) many; **~s creen que** ... many (people) believe that ...; **~s de nosotros** many of us **2 mucho (a)** (referido a tiempo): **hace ~ que no la veo** I haven't seen her for a long time; **¿te falta ~ para terminar?** will it take you long to finish?; **~ antes** long before; **¿tuviste que esperar ~?** did you have to wait long? **(b)** (*en locs*) **como mucho** at (the) most; **con mucho** by far, easily; **ni mucho menos** far from it; **por mucho que** ... however much ...

mucosidad *f* mucus, mucosity

muda *f* (de ropa) change of clothes; (de la piel) shedding, sloughing off

mudanza *f* move, removal (BrE); **camión de ~s** moving (AmE) *o* (BrE) removal van; **estoy de ~** I'm in the process of moving (house)

mudar [A1] *vi* **1** (cambiar): **las serpientes mudan de piel** snakes slough off *o* shed their skin; **cuando mudó de voz** when his voice broke **2** (Méx) (cambiar los dientes) to lose one's milk teeth ■ **~** *vt* **1** ‹*bebé/sábanas*› to change **2** (Zool) ‹*piel/plumas*› to molt, shed
■ **mudarse** *v pron* **(a)** (de casa) to move (house); **se ~on a una casa más grande** they moved to a bigger house **(b)** (de ropa) to get changed, change (one's) clothes

mudéjar *adj/mf* Mudejar

mudo -da *adj* **(a)** (Med) dumb, mute; **es ~ de nacimiento** he was born mute; **se quedó ~ de asombro** he was dumbfounded **(b)** ‹*letra*› silent, mute ■ *m,f* mute

mueble *m* piece of furniture; **los ~s del dormitorio** the bedroom furniture; **~ bar** drinks cabinet, cocktail cabinet; **~ cama** foldaway bed

mueca *f*: **hacerle ~s a algn** to make *o* (BrE) pull faces at sb; **sus graciosísimas ~s** her funny faces; **una ~ burlona** a sneer

muela *f* **1** ▶ **123** (Odont) molar, back tooth; (como término genérico) tooth; **me sacaron una ~** I had a tooth taken out; **tengo dolor de ~s** I have (a) toothache; **~ del juicio** wisdom tooth **2** (de molino) millstone; (para afilar) whetstone **3** (Col) (en calle) parking bay; (en carretera) rest stop (AmE), lay-by (BrE)

muelle *m* **1** (Náut) (saliente) pier, mole; (rústico, más pequeño) jetty; (sobre la costa) quay, wharf **2** (resorte) spring

muera, **mueras, etc** *see* MORIR

muérdago *m* mistletoe

muerte *f* death; **condenado a ~** sentenced to death; **a la ~ de su padre** on her father's death; **~ de cuna** crib death (AmE), cot death (BrE); **me dio un susto de ~** (fam) she scared me to death (colloq); **dar ~ a algn** (frml) to kill sb; ***de mala ~*** (fam) ‹*pueblo/hotel*› grotty (colloq); ***ser la ~*** (fam) (ser atroz) to be hell *o* murder (colloq); (ser estupendo) to be fantastic (colloq)

muerto -ta *adj* **1** [ESTAR] **(a)** ‹*persona/animal/planta*› dead; **lo dieron por ~** he was given up for dead; **resultaron ~s 30 mineros** 30 miners died *o* were killed; **caer ~** to drop dead **(b)** (fam) (cansado) dead beat (colloq) **(c)** (fam) (pasando, padeciendo): **estar ~ de hambre/frío/sueño** to be starving/freezing/dead-tired (colloq); **estaba ~ de miedo** he was scared stiff (colloq); ***~ de (la) risa*** (fam): **estaba ~ de risa** he was laughing his head off **2 (a)** ‹*pueblo/zona*› dead, lifeless **(b)** (inerte) limp ■ *m,f* **1** (persona muerta): **hubo dos ~s** two people died *o* were killed; **hacerse el ~** to pretend to be dead; ***cargar con el ~*** (fam) (con un trabajo pesado) to do the dirty work; ***cargarle el ~ a algn*** (fam) (responsabilizar) to pin the blame on sb; (endilgarle la tarea) to give sb the dirty work (colloq); ***hacer el ~*** to float on one's back **2 muerto** *m* (en naipes) dummy

muesca *f* **(a)** (hendidura) nick, notch **(b)** (para encajar) slot, groove

muesli /'musli/ *m* muesli

muestra *f* **1 (a)** (de mercancía) sample **(b)** (de sangre, orina) specimen, sample **(c)** (en estadísticas) sample **2** (prueba, señal) sign; **una ~ de cansancio/falta de madurez** a sign of tiredness/immaturity; **como** *or* **en ~ de mi gratitud** as a token of my gratitude **3** (exposición) exhibition, exhibit (AmE); (de teatro, cine) festival

mueva, muevas, etc *see* MOVER

mufa *f* (RPl fam) **(a)** (mal humor) bad mood **(b)** (moho) mold*

mugido *m* moo; **los ~s de las vacas** the mooing of the cows

mugir [I7] *vi* «*vaca*» to moo; «*toro*» to bellow

mugre *f* (suciedad) dirt, filth; (grasa) grime, grease

mugriento -ta *adj* filthy

mugroso -sa *adj* (Chi, Méx fam) filthy

mujer *f* **(a)** woman; **ser ~** to be a woman; **~ de la limpieza** cleaning lady, cleaner; **~ de mala vida** *or* **de mal vivir** prostitute; ***hacerse ~*** (euf) to reach puberty, become a woman (euph) **(b)** (esposa) wife

mujeriego *m* womanizer

mújol *m* gray* mullet

mula *f* mule; **~ de carga** pack mule; ***terco/tozudo como una ~*** as stubborn as a mule (colloq) ■ *adj* (Méx fam) stubborn

mulato -ta *adj* of mixed race (*black and white*), mulatto (dated *or* pej) ■ *m,f* person of mixed race (*of a black and a white parent*), mulatto (dated *or* pej)

muleta *f* **1** (bastón) crutch; (apoyo) crutch, prop **2** (Taur) red cape (*attached to a stick*)

muletilla *f* tag, filler (tech)

mulita *f* (Per) (de pisco) glass, shot

mullido -da *adj* ‹*colchón/sofá*› soft; ‹*hierba*› springy

mulo *m* (male) mule

multa *f* fine; **le pusieron una ~** she was fined

multar [A1] *vt* to fine

multicine *m* multiscreen movie complex (AmE), multiscreen cinema (BrE)

multicolor *adj* multicolored*

multicultural *adj* multicultural

multimillonario -ria *adj*: **es ~** he is a multimillionaire; **un contrato ~** a multi-million dollar (*o* pound *etc*) contract ■ *m,f* multimillionaire

multinacional *adj/f* multinational

múltiple *adj* **1** ‹*aplicaciones/causas*› many, numerous **2** ‹*flor/imagen/fractura*› multiple

multiplicación *f* **1** (Biol, Mat) multiplication **2** (incremento) increase

multiplicar [A2] *vt* ▶ **294** to multiply; **~ algo** POR **algo** to multiply sth BY sth ■ **~** *vi* to multiply ■ **multiplicarse** *v pron* **1** «*especie*» to multiply, reproduce **2** (aumentar) to increase several times over

múltiplo *m* multiple

multitud *f* **1** (muchedumbre) crowd **2 ~** DE **algo** (muchos): **tengo (una) ~ de cosas que hacer** I have dozens of things to do (colloq); **una ~ de usos** an enormous variety of uses

multitudinario -ria *adj* ‹*manifestación/movilizaciones*› mass (*before n*); ‹*concierto*› with mass audiences

mundano -na *adj* **(a)** ‹*problemas/placeres*› worldly **(b)** ‹*fiesta*› society (*before n*)

mundial *adj* ‹*historia/mercado*› world (*before n*); **la marca ~** the world record; **de fama ~** world-famous; **es un problema ~** it's a global *o* worldwide problem ■ *m*: *tb* **~es** *mpl* World Championship(s); **el ~ de fútbol** the World Cup

mundo *m* **1** (en general) world; **artistas venidos de todo el ~** artists from all over the world; **el mejor del ~** the best in the world; **me parece lo más normal del ~** it seems perfectly normal to me; **es conocido en todo el ~** he is known worldwide; **el ~ árabe** the Arab world; **el ~ de la droga** the drugs world; **el ~ del espectáculo** showbusiness; **todo el ~ lo sabe** everybody knows it; ***el ~ es un pañuelo*** it's a small world; ***por nada del*** *or* ***en el ~***: **yo no me lo pierdo por nada del ~** I wouldn't miss it for the world; **no lo vendería por nada en el ~** I wouldn't sell it for anything in the world *o* (colloq) for all the tea in China; ***traer a algn/venir al ~*** to bring sb/come into the world; ***ver ~*** to see the world **2** (planeta, universo) planet, world; **él vive en otro ~** he's on another planet *o* in another world

munición *f* (carga) *tb* **municiones** ammunition, munitions (*pl*)

municipal *adj* ‹*impuesto*› local; ‹*elecciones/piscina/mercado*› municipal

municipalidad *f* ⇒ MUNICIPIO

municipio *m* (territorio) municipality; (entidad) town council; (edificio) town hall

muñeca *f* **1 (a)** (Jueg) doll; ~ **de trapo** rag doll; **jugar a las ~s** to play with dolls; ***ser*** *or* ***parecer una*** ~ to be a little doll **(b)** (fam) (como apelativo) darling, honey (colloq) **2** ▶ **123** (Anat) wrist

muñeco *m* **1 (a)** (con forma humana) doll; (con forma de animal) toy animal; ~ **de peluche** stuffed animal (AmE), soft toy (BrE); ~ **de nieve** snowman **(b)** (de ventrílocuo, sastre, etc) dummy **(c)** (dibujo) figure **2 muñecos** *mpl* (Per fam): **estar con los ~s** to be very nervous

muñequera *f* (Dep) wristband; (Med) wrist bandage

muñón *m* (de un miembro) stump

mural *adj* wall (*before n*), mural (*before n*) ■ *m* mural

muralista *adj/mf* muralist

muralla *f* **(a)** (de ciudad) walls (*pl*), city wall; (de convento) wall; **la M~ China** the Great Wall of China **(b)** (Chi) (pared) wall

murciélago *m* bat

muriera, murió, etc *see* MORIR

murmullo *m* (de voces) murmur

murmuraciones *fpl* gossip

murmurador -dora *adj* gossipy ■ *m,f* gossip

murmurar [A1] *vt* **(a)** (hablar bajo) to murmur; **le murmuró algo al oído** he whispered something in her ear **(b)** (con enojo) to mutter; **— no pienso hacerlo — murmuró** I won't do it, she muttered **(c)** (en son de crítica): **cosas que se murmuran en la oficina** rumors that go around the office ■ ~ *vi* (criticar) to gossip (*maliciously*); ~ DE **algn** to gossip ABOUT sb

muro *m* wall; **M~ de las Lamentaciones** *or* **los Lamentos** Wailing Wall

mus *m*: *a Spanish card game*

musa *f* (Mit) Muse; (inspiración) muse

muscular *adj* muscular

musculatura *f* muscles (*pl*), musculature (tech)

músculo *m* muscle; **sacar** ~ to flex one's muscles

musculoso -sa *adj* muscular

muselina *f* muslin

museo *m* museum; ~ **de cera** wax museum, waxworks (*pl*); ~ **de ciencias naturales** natural science museum

musgo *m* moss

música *f* music; **pon algo de** ~ put some music on; ~ **ambiental** background music; (en tienda, fábrica) piped *o* canned music

musical *adj/m* musical

músico -ca *m,f* (compositor) composer; (instrumentista) musician; ~ **callejero** street musician, busker (BrE)

musitar [A1] *vt* to whisper, murmur

muslera *f* thighband

muslo *m* (Anat) ▶ **123** thigh (Coc): **~s de pollo** chicken legs

mustio -tia *adj* **1** ‹*flor/planta*› withered **2** (Méx fam) (hipócrita) two-faced (colloq)

musulmán -mana *adj/m,f* Muslim, Moslem

mutable *adj* changeable, mutable (frml)

mutación *f* mutation

mutilado -da *m,f* disabled person; **un ~ de guerra** a disabled serviceman

mutilar [A1] *vt* **(a)** ‹*persona/pierna*› to mutilate; **quedó mutilado en el accidente** he was maimed as a result of the accident **(b)** ‹*árbol/estatua*› to vandalize

mutua *f* benefit society (AmE), friendly society (BrE)

mutual *f* (CS) (de asistencia económica) benefit society (AmE), friendly society (BrE)

mutuo -tua *adj* mutual; **de ~ acuerdo** by mutual *o* joint agreement; **redundará en beneficio ~** it will be to our mutual benefit

muy *adv* **(a)** very; ~ **poca gente** very few people; **son ~ amigos** they're great friends; ~ **admirado** much admired; ~ **respetado** highly respected; ~ **bien, sigamos adelante** OK *o* fine, let's go on; **por ~ cansado que estés** however *o* no matter how tired you are **(b)** (demasiado) too; **quedó ~ dulce** it's rather *o* too sweet

Nn

N, n *f* (*read as* /'ene/) *the letter* N, n

N. (= **norte**) ▶ **346** North, N

nabo *m* turnip

nácar *m* mother-of-pearl, nacre

nacer [E3] *vi* **1 (a)** «*niño/animal*» to be born; **¿dónde naciste?** where were you born?; **al ~** at birth; **nació para (ser) músico** he was born to be a musician **(b)** «*pollito/insecto*» to hatch **(c)** «*hoja/rama*» to sprout **(d)** «*río*» to have its source; «*carretera*» to start **(e)** «*pelo/plumas*» to grow **2** (surgir) «*amistad/relación*» to spring up; ~ DE **algo** «*problema/situación*» to arise *o* spring FROM sth; **nació de ella invitarlo** it was her idea to invite him

nacido -da *adj* born; **un niño recién ~** a newborn baby

naciente *adj* ‹*sol*› rising (*before n*); **el ~ interés por la ecología** the new interest in ecology

nacimiento *m* **1** (de niño, animal) birth; **es argentino de ~** he's Argentinian by birth; **es sorda de ~** she was born deaf **2** (de idea, movimiento) birth; **el ~ de una amistad duradera** the start *o* beginning of a lasting friendship **3** (belén) crib

nación *f* nation; **las Naciones Unidas** the United Nations (*pl*)

nacional *adj* **(a)** (de la nación) ‹*deuda/reservas/industria*› national; **en todo el territorio ~** throughout the country; **un programa de difusión ~** a program broadcast nationwide **(b)** ‹*vuelo*› domestic ■ *mf* (frml) (ciudadano) national

nacionalidad *f* (ciudadanía) nationality

nacionalismo *m* nationalism

nacionalista *adj* nationalist (*before n*) ■ *mf* nationalist

nacionalización *f* (de industria) nationalization; (naturalización) naturalization

nacionalizar [A4] *vt* ‹*industria*› to nationalize; ‹*persona*› to naturalize

■ **nacionalizarse** *v pron* «*persona*» to become naturalized

naco -ca *adj* (Méx fam & pey) plebby (colloq & pej) ■ *m,f* pleb (colloq & pej)

nada *pron* **1 (a)** nothing; **es mejor que ~** it's better than nothing; **de ~ sirve que le compres libros** there's no point in buying him books; **antes que** *or* **de ~** first of all; **no quiere ~** he doesn't want anything; **¡no sirves para ~!** you're useless; **sin decir ~** without a word **(b)** (*en locs*) **de nada** you're welcome; **nada de nada** (fam) not a thing; **nada más: no hay ~ más** there's nothing else; **¿algo más? — ~ más** anything else? — no, that's it *o* that's all; **~ más fui yo** (Méx) I was the only one who went; **salí ~ más comer** I went out right *o* straight after lunch; **sacó (~ más ni) ~ menos que el primer puesto** she came first no less; **para nada: no me gustó para ~** I didn't like it at all; **por nada: la compraron por ~** they bought it for next to nothing; **discuten por ~** they argue over nothing; **llora por ~** she cries at the slightest little thing **2** (Esp) (en tenis) love; **quince-~** fifteen-love ■ *adv* **▶ 289** : **no está ~ preocupado** he isn't at all *o* the least bit worried; **esto no me gusta ~** I don't like this at all *o* (colloq) one bit

nadador -dora *m,f* swimmer

nadar [A1] *vi* **(a)** «*persona/pez*» to swim; **¿sabes ~?** can you swim?; **~ (estilo) mariposa/pecho** to do (the) butterfly/breaststroke; **~ de espalda** *or* (Méx) **de dorso** to do (the) back stroke **(b)** «*ramas/hojas*» (flotar) to float **(b) nadar en** (tener mucho): **~ en dinero** to be rolling in money (colloq); **el pollo nadaba en grasa** the chicken was swimming in grease ■ **~** *vt* to swim

nadie *pron* **▶ 289** nobody, no one; **no me ayudó ~** nobody helped me; **no vi a ~** I didn't see anybody; **sin que ~ se diera cuenta** without anyone noticing

nado *m* **(a) a nado: cruzó el río a ~** he swam across the river **(b)** (Méx, Ven) (natación) swimming

nafta *f* **(a)** (Quím) naphtha **(b)** (RPl) (gasolina) gas (AmE), petrol (BrE)

naftalina *f* (Quím) naphthalene; (para ropa) mothballs (*pl*)

naguas *fpl* (Méx fam) petticoat

náhuatl[1] *adj/mf* (*pl* **nahuas**) Nahuatl

náhuatl[2] *m* (idioma) Nahuatl

nailon *m* nylon

naipe *m* (playing) card; **juegos de ~s** card games

nalga *f* (Anat) buttock; **una inyección en la ~** an injection in the buttock *o* bottom

nalgada *f* (Méx) smack on the bottom

nana *f* **(a)** (canción de cuna) lullaby **(b)** (fam) (abuela) grandma (colloq), granny (colloq) **(c)** (Andes, Ven) (niñera) nanny

naranja *f* (fruta) orange; **~ amarga** Seville orange ■ *m* **▶ 97** (color) orange ■ *adj* (*gen inv*) orange

naranjada *f* orangeade

naranjal *m* orange grove

naranjo *m* orange tree

narciso *m* **(a)** (Bot) daffodil; (género) narcissus **(b)** (persona) narcissist

narcótico *m* narcotic

narcotráfico *m* drug trafficking

nardo *m* spikenard, nard

nariz *f* **(a) ▶ 123** (Anat) nose; **sonarse la ~** to blow one's nose; **no te metas los dedos en la ~** don't pick your nose; ***en mis/sus propias narices*** (fam) right under my/his nose; ***estar hasta las narices de algo/algn*** (fam) to be fed up (to the back teeth) with sth/sb (colloq); ***meter las narices*** *or* ***la ~ en algo*** (fam) to poke one's nose into sth (colloq) **(b)** (de avión) nose

narizota *f* (fam) schnozzle (AmE colloq), conk (BrE colloq)

narración *f* (relato) story; (acción de contar) account

narrador -dora *m,f* narrator

narrar [A1] *vt* (frml) **(a)** «*película/libro*» ‹*hazañas/experiencias*› to tell of (frml), to relate; ‹*historia*› to tell, relate **(b)** «*persona*» ‹*historia*› to tell, narrate (frml)

narrativa *f* (género) fiction; (narración) narrative

narrativo -va *adj* narrative

nasal *adj* nasal

nata *f* **(a)** (sobre leche hervida) skin **(b)** (Esp) ⇒ CREMA (b)

natación *f* swimming

natal *adj* **(a)** ‹*país*› native (*before n*); ‹*ciudad*› home (*before n*) **(b)** (Méx) (originario): **es ~ de Chiapas** she was born in Chiapas

natalidad *f* birthrate

natillas *fpl* custard

natividad *f* **(a) la ~** (nacimiento de Cristo) the Nativity **(b) la N~** (navidad) Christmas

nativo -va *adj* **(a)** ‹*tierra/país/lengua*› native **(b)** ‹*flora/fauna*› native; **~ DE algo** native TO sth ■ *m, f* (aborigen) native; (hablante) native speaker

nato -ta *adj* ‹*artista/deportista*› born (*before n*)

natural *adj* **1 (a)** ‹*fenómeno/ingrediente*› natural; ‹*fruta*› fresh; ***al ~*** ‹*mejillones*› in brine **(b)** (a temperatura ambiente) ‹*cerveza/gaseosa*› unchilled **(c)** (Mús) natural **2 (a)** (espontáneo) ‹*gesto/persona*› natural **(b)** (inherente) natural, innate **(c)** (normal) natural; **me parece lo más ~ del mundo** it seems perfectly natural to me **3** (frml) (nativo) **ser ~ DE** to be a native OF, to come FROM ■ *m* **(a)** (carácter) nature **(b)** (nativo) native; **los ~es del lugar** people from the area

naturaleza *f* **(a)** (Ecol): **la ~** nature; **~ muerta** still life **(b)** (índole) nature

naturalidad *f*: **su ~** her natural manner; **con la mayor ~ del mundo** as if it were the most natural thing in the world

naturalización *f* naturalization

naturalizarse [A4] *v pron* to become naturalized

naturismo *m* (estilo de vida) natural lifestyle

naturista *adj* ‹*médico/tratamiento*› natural

naufragar [A3] *vi* **(a)** «*barco*» to be wrecked; «*persona*» to be shipwrecked **(b)** «*plan/negocio*» to go under

naufragio *m* **(a)** (Náut) shipwreck **(b)** (fracaso) failure

náufrago -ga *adj* shipwrecked ■ *m,f* (Naút) shipwrecked person

náuseas *fpl* nausea, sickness; **sentir** *or* **tener ~** to feel sick *o* nauseous; **me da ~** it makes me sick

náutico -ca *adj* nautical

navaja *f* (de bolsillo) penknife; (para afeitar) razor

navajazo *m* (herida) knife wound

naval *adj* naval

nave *f* **1** (Náut) (arc *o* liter) ship; **~ espacial** spacecraft, spaceship **2** (de iglesia) nave

navegabilidad *f* (de río) navigability; (de embarcación) seaworthiness

navegable *adj* ‹*río*› navigable; ‹*barco*› seaworthy

navegación *f* (acción de navegar) navigation; (tráfico) shipping; **~ aérea** aerial navigation; **~ fluvial** river navigation

navegar [A3] *vi* **(a)** «*nave*» to sail **(b)** «*persona*» (a vela) to sail **(c)** (determinar el rumbo) to navigate ■ **~** *vt* (liter) to sail

Navidad *f* Christmas; **el día de ~** Christmas Day; **¡feliz ~!** happy Christmas!; **en ~** at Christmas (time)

navideño -ña *adj* Christmas (*before n*)

navío *m* ship

nazi *adj/mf* Nazi

nazismo *m* Nazism

NE ▶ 346 (= **nordeste**) NE

neblina *f* ▶ 409 mist

nebuloso -sa *adj* **(a)** ▶ 409 (Meteo) misty **(b)** ‹*idea/imagen*› hazy, nebulous

necedad *f* **(a)** (cualidad) crassness **(b)** (dicho, acto): **decir ~es** to talk nonsense; **es una ~** it's sheer stupidity

necesario -ria *adj* (imprescindible) necessary; **haré lo que sea ~** I'll do whatever's necessary; **si es ~** if necessary, if need be; **no es ~** there's no need, it isn't necessary; **me sentía ~** I felt needed

neceser *m* (estuche) toilet kit (AmE), toilet bag (BrE); (maleta pequeña) overnight bag

necesidad *f* **1 (a)** (urgencia, falta) need; **no hay ~ de que se entere** there's no need for her to know; **en caso de ~** if necessary, if need be **(b)** (cosa necesaria) necessity, essential **(c)** (pobreza) poverty, need **2 necesidades** *fpl* **(a)** (requerimientos) needs (*pl*), requirements (*pl*) **(b)** (privaciones) hardship; **pasar ~es** to suffer hardship **(c) hacer sus ~es** (euf) to relieve oneself (euph)

necesitado -da *adj* **(a)** (falto) **~ DE algo** ‹*de dinero*› short OF sth; ‹*de afecto*› in need OF sth **(b)** (pobre) in need, needy ■ *m,f* needy person; **los ~s** the needy

necesitar [A1] *vt* to need; Ⓢ **se necesita vendedora** saleswoman required; **necesito verte hoy** I need to see you today ■ **~** *vi* (frml) **~ DE algo** to need sth

necio -cia *adj* **(a)** (tonto) stupid **(b)** (AmC, Col, Ven fam) (travieso) naughty

néctar *m* nectar

nectarina *f* nectarine

nefasto -ta *adj* ‹*consecuencias*› disastrous; ‹*influencia*› harmful; ‹*tiempo/fiesta*› (fam) awful (colloq)

negación *f* (acción) denial, negation; (antítesis) antithesis; (Ling) negative

negado -da *adj*: **ser ~ para algo** to be useless *o* hopeless at sth

negar [A7] *vt* **(a)** ‹*acusación/rumor*› to deny; **no puedo ~lo** I can't deny it; **niega habértelo dicho** she denies having told you **(b)** (no conceder) ‹*permiso/favor*› to refuse; **les ~on la entrada** they were refused entry ■ **~** *vi*: **~ con la cabeza** to shake one's head

■ **negarse** *v pron* (rehusar) to refuse; **~se A hacer algo** to refuse to do sth; **se negó a que llamáramos a un médico** he refused to let us call a doctor

negativa *f* (ante acusación) denial; (a propuesta) refusal

negativo[1] -va *adj* negative

negativo[2] *m* (Fot) negative

negligé /neɣli'ʒe/ *m* negligee

negligencia *f* negligence

negociable *adj* negotiable

negociación *f* **1** (Pol, Rels Labs) negotiation **2** (Méx) (empresa) business

negociado *m* **1** (departamento) department **2** (AmS fam) (negocio sucio) shady deal (colloq)

negociador -dora *adj* negotiating (*before n*) ■ *m,f* negotiator

negociante *mf* **(a)** (Com, Fin) (*m*) businessman; (*f*) businesswoman **(b)** (pey) (mercenario) money-grubber (colloq & pej)

negociar [A1] *vt/vi* to negotiate

negocio *m* **(a)** (Com) business; **montar** *or* **poner un ~** to set up a business; **dedicarse a los ~s** to be in business; **hablar de ~s** to talk business; **en el mundo de los ~s** in the business world **(b)** (transacción) deal; **un buen ~** a good deal **(c)** (CS) (tienda) store (AmE), shop (BrE) **(d)** (fam) (asunto) business (colloq)

negra *f* **(a)** (Mús) crotchet **(b)** (en ajedrez): **las ~s** the black pieces

negrita *f* boldface, bold type; **en ~(s)** in boldface, in bold (type)

Negativos

Algunas observaciones generales

Oraciones negativas

Para traducir el adverbio de negación 'no' cuando modifica a un verbo, se debe tener en cuenta que la negación de la mayoría de los verbos ingleses requiere el uso del auxiliar do *o de un verbo modal seguido de la negación* not *(por lo general en la forma contraída)*:

no entiende francés = he doesn't understand French

no pudo venir = he couldn't come

Se debe hacer especial mención del verbo to be *cuya negación sólo requiere el adverbio* not

no es caro = it's not expensive

no eran ricos = they weren't rich

Cuando en español se emplea el imperativo precedido del adverbio 'no', *el inglés siempre utiliza el auxiliar* do *seguido de la negación* not:

no sean/seas egoísta = don't be selfish

Sin embargo, si se trata de la primera persona plural, se emplea let's not:

no seamos egoístas = let's not be selfish

no discutamos = let's not argue

Respuestas negativas

El adverbio 'no' *como respuesta se traduce por* no, *pero el inglés suele agregar el verbo auxiliar o el modal empleado en la pregunta pero en la forma negativa*:

¿vives aquí? = do you live here?
– no – no, I don't

¿puedes venir? = can you come?
– no – no, I can't

¿lo vas a ver hoy? = will you be seeing him today?
– no – no, I won't

¿vienes? = are you coming?
– no – no, I'm not

Nótese que en las respuestas cortas en las que 'no' *modifica a un adverbio, el negativo* not *en inglés se coloca delante del adverbio*:

todavía no = not yet

aquí/ahora no = not here/now

Preguntas negativas

Para traducir las preguntas en español que empiezan con el negativo 'no' *el inglés* not, *utiliza un verbo auxiliar o modal seguido del adverbio* not *(por lo general en la forma contraída)*:

¿no dejó recado? = didn't he leave a message?

¿no estarán allí tus padres? = won't your parents be there?

De la misma manera, la pregunta ¿no? (coletilla interrogativa) al final de una oración se traduce al inglés mediante el uso de un verbo auxiliar o modal seguido del adverbio not:

usted habla español ¿no? = you speak Spanish, don't you?

sabes nadar ¿no? = you can swim, can't you?

tiene una hermana ¿no? = she has a sister, hasn't she?

fuiste tú ¿no? = it was you, wasn't it?

Negativos dobles

En español son corrientes las oraciones construidas con dos negativos. En inglés, por el contrario, estas construcciones no son posible. Así pues, oraciones que en español se inician con el adverbio 'no' *y contienen vocablos como* nada, nadie, ningún, ninguno, nunca, jamás, tampoco *etc, admiten en inglés dos traducciones distintas las que incluyen un solo negativo respectivamente*:

no vi nada/a nadie = I didn't see anything/anybody
= I saw nothing/nobody

no quedaba ningún asiento = there weren't any seats left
= there were no seats left

no hablé con ninguno (de los dos) = I didn't speak to either (of them)
= I spoke to neither (of them)

no se había sentido nunca *or* jamás tan humillada = she had never felt so humiliated before
= never before had she felt so humiliated (más formal)

Nótese la inversión de verbo sujeto en la traducción anterior

El inglés también evita el doble negativo al traducir las oraciones en español construidas con la conjunción ni *y otro negativo*:

no vino ni llamó = he neither came nor called
= he didn't come or call

nunca nos visitó ni nos escribió = he never visited us or wrote (to us)

Las construcciones españolas con ni . . . ni *se traducen de la misma manera*:

ni vino ni llamó = he neither came nor called

Para más información, usos y ejemplos suplementarios de nunca, ninguno, tampoco *etc., ver bajo respectiva entrada*

negro[1] **-gra** *adj* **(a)** ▶97 ‹*pelo/hombre/raza*› black; ‹*ojos*› dark **(b)** (fam) (por el sol) tanned **(c)** (sombrío) black, gloomy; **lo ve todo tan ~** she's always so pessimistic; ***pasarlas negras*** (fam) to have a rough time of it (colloq) ■ *m, f* (persona de raza negra) black person

negro[2] *m* ▶97 (color) black

negrura *f* blackness

nene -na *m, f* (Esp, RPl fam) **(a)** (niño pequeño) (*m*) little boy; (*f*) little girl; **los ~s** the kids (colloq) **(b)** (apelativo cariñoso) darling, honey **(c) nena** *f* (arg) (mujer) chick (AmE colloq), bird (BrE colloq)

nené *mf* (Ven fam) (*m*) little boy; (*f*) little girl

neocelandés -desa *adj* of/from New Zealand ■ *m,f* New Zealander

neologismo *m* neologism

neonazi *adj/mf* neonazi

neoyorquino -na *adj* of/from New York ■ *m,f* New Yorker

nepotismo *m* nepotism

Neptuno *m* Neptune

nervio *m* **1 (a)** (Anat) nerve **(b)** (en la carne) sinew; **carne con ~s** gristly meat **2 nervios** *mpl* nerves (*pl*); **tiene los ~s destrozados** his nerves are in shreds; **está enfermo de los ~s** he suffers with his nerves; **tengo unos ~s** ... I'm *o* I feel so nervous; **me muero de ~s** I'm a nervous wreck (colloq); ***ponerle a algn los ~s de punta*** to get on sb's nerves

nerviosismo *m* nervousness; **el ~ que producen los exámenes** the feeling of nervousness *o* nerves that exams produce

nervioso -sa *adj* **1** ‹*persona/animal*› **(a)** [SER] (excitable) nervous **(b)** [ESTAR] (preocupado, tenso) nervous; **estoy muy ~ por lo de los exámenes** I'm very nervous about the exams **(c)** [ESTAR] (agitado) agitated; **últimamente se le nota ~** he's been on edge *o* (colloq) uptight lately; **ese ruido me pone muy nerviosa** that noise is getting on my nerves; **me pongo ~ cada vez que la veo** I get flustered every time I see her **2** ‹*trastorno*› nervous; ‹*célula*› nerve (*before n*)

nervudo -da *adj* sinewy

neto -ta *adj* **(a)** ‹*sueldo/precio*› net **(b)** (claro) ‹*silueta/perfil*› distinct, clear

neumático *m* tire (AmE), tyre (BrE)

neumonía *f* pneumonia

neura *adj* (fam): **eso me pone ~** that drives me crazy *o* (BrE) mad (colloq); **es tan ~** he's so neurotic ■ *mf* (fam) **1** (persona): **es un ~** he's a complete neurotic (colloq) **2 neura** *f*: **está con la ~** she's in a real state (colloq)

neurasténico -ca *adj/m,f* **(a)** (Med) neurasthenic **(b)** (fam) ⇨ NEURA

neurólogo -ga *m,f* neurologist

neurosis *f* neurosis

neurótico -ca *adj/m,f* neurotic

neutral *adj* neutral

neutralizar [A4] *vt* to neutralize

neutro[1] **-tra** *adj* **(a)** (Elec, Fís) neutral **(b)** (Biol, Ling) neuter

neutro[2] *m* **(a)** (Ling) neuter **(b)** (AmL) (Auto) neutral

nevada *f* ▶ 409 snowfall

nevado -da *adj* ‹*cumbres/picos*› snowcapped, snow-covered; ‹*campos/techos*› covered with snow

nevar [A5] *v impers* ▶ 409 to snow

nevasca *f*, (CS) **nevazón** *f* ▶ 409 blizzard, snowstorm

nevera *f* **(a)** (refrigerador) refrigerator, fridge, icebox (AmE); **~ congelador** fridge-freezer **(b)** (para picnic) cooler (AmE), cool bag/box (BrE)

nexo *m* (enlace, vínculo) link

ni *conj* **(a)** ▶ 289 (con otro negativo): **no vino él ~ su mujer** neither he nor his wife came; **yo no pienso ir — ~ yo (tampoco)** I don't intend going — neither do I; **~ fumo ~ bebo** I don't smoke or drink, I neither smoke nor drink; **no nos avisó ~ a él ~ a mí** he didn't tell him or me (either); **~ siquiera** not even; **¿ ~ siquiera piensas llamarlo?** aren't you even going to call him?; **no vendieron ~ un libro** they didn't sell a single book **(b)** (expresando rechazo, enfado): **¡~ hablar!** out of the question!; **~ aunque me lo ruegue** not even if he gets down on his knees

Nicaragua *f* Nicaragua

nicaragüense *adj/mf* Nicaraguan

nicho *m* (Arquit) niche; (en cementerio) *deep recess in a wall used as a tomb*

nicotina *f* nicotine

nidada *f* (de huevos) clutch; (de crías) clutch, brood

nido *m* nest; **un ~ de ladrones** a den of thieves; **un ~ de amor** a love nest

niebla *f* ▶ 409 fog; **había ~** it was foggy

niega, niegas, etc *see* NEGAR

nieto -ta *m,f* (*m*) grandson, grandchild; (*f*) granddaughter, grandchild; **mis ~s** my grandchildren

nieva *see* NEVAR

nieve *f* **(a)** ▶ 409 (Meteo) snow **(b)** (Coc): **batir las claras a (punto de) ~** whisk the egg whites until stiff **(c)** (Méx) (helado) sorbet, water ice

nimiedad *f* triviality

nimio -mia *adj* trivial, petty

ningún *adj*: *apocopated form of* NINGUNO *used before masculine singular nouns*

ningunear [A1] *vt* (Méx fam) to treat ... like dirt (colloq)

ninguno -na *adj* ▶ 289 (*see note under* NINGÚN) (*delante del n*): **no prestó ninguna atención** he didn't pay any attention; **en ningún momento** never; **no lo encuentro por ningún lado** I can't find it anywhere; **no hay problema ~** there's absolutely no problem ■ *pron* ▶ 289 **(a)** (refiriéndose — a dos personas o cosas) neither; (— a más de dos) none; **~ de los dos vino** neither of them came; **no trajo ~ de los dos** she didn't bring either of them; **~ de nosotros la conoce** none of us know her **(b)** (nadie) nobody, no-one

niña *f* pupil; *ver tb* NIÑO *m,f*

niñera *f* nanny, nursemaid (AmE)

niñería *f* (pey): **déjate de ~s** stop being so childish

niñez *f* childhood

niño -ña *adj* (joven) young; (infantil, inmaduro) immature, childish ■ *m,f* **(a)** (*m*) boy, child; (*f*) girl, child; (bebé) baby; **¿te gustan los ~s?** do you like children?; **de ~** as a child; **~ bien** rich kid (colloq); **~ de pecho** small *o* young baby; **el ~ mimado de la maestra** the teacher's favorite* *o* pet; **~ prodigio** child prodigy **(b)** (con respecto a los padres) (*m*) son, child; (*f*) daughter, child; **tengo que llevar al ~ al dentista** I have to take my son to the dentist

nipón -pona *adj/m,f* Japanese

níquel *m* nickel

níspero *m* loquat

nitidez *f* (de imagen, del día) clarity; (de recuerdo) vividness

nítido -da *adj* ‹*foto/imagen*› clear

nitrógeno *m* nitrogen

nivel *m* **(a)** (altura) level **(b)** (en escala, jerarquía) level; **conversaciones de alto ~** high-level talks; **~ de vida** standard of living; **no está al ~ de los demás** he's not up to the same standard as the others; **el ~ de las universidades mexicanas** the standard of Mexican universities

nivelar [A1] *vt* **(a)** (Const) ‹*suelo/terreno*› to level; ‹*estante*› to get ... level **(b)** ‹*presupuesto*› to balance

no *adv* **▶ 289** **(a)** (como respuesta) no; (modificando adverbios, oraciones, verbos) not [*la negación de la mayoría de los verbos ingleses requiere el uso del auxiliar 'do'*] **¿te gustó? — no** did you like it? — no, I didn't; **¿vienes o ~?** are you coming or not?; **~ te preocupes** don't worry; **¿por qué ~ quieres ir? — porque ~** why don't you want to go? — I just don't **(b)** (con otro negativo): **~ veo nada** I can't see a thing *o* anything; **~ viene nunca** she never comes **(c)** (en coletillas interrogativas): **está mejor ¿~?** she's better, isn't she?; **ha dimitido ¿~?** he has resigned, hasn't he? **(d)** (expresando incredulidad): **se ganó la lotería — ¡no!** he won the lottery — he didn't! *o* no! **(e)** (sustituyendo a una cláusula): **creo que ~** I don't think so; **¿te gustó? a mí ~** did you like it? *I* didn't **(f)** (*delante de n, adj, pp*): **los ~ fumadores** nonsmokers; **la ~ violencia** nonviolence; **un hijo ~ deseado** an unwanted child ■ *m* (*pl* **noes**) no

NO (= **noroeste**) **▶ 346** NW

Nobel *m* **(a)** *tb* **Premio ~** Nobel Prize **(b)** (ganador) Nobel prizewinner

noble *adj* **(a)** (en general) noble; **un caballero de ~ linaje** (liter) a knight of noble lineage (liter) **(b)** ‹*madera*› fine ■ *mf* (*m*) nobleman; (*f*) noblewoman; **los ~** the nobles, the nobility

nobleza *f* nobility

nocaut *adj* (AmL): **lo dejó ~** he/it knocked him out; **está ~** he's out for the count ■ *m* (*pl* **-cauts**) (AmL) knockout

noche *f* **▶ 221** **(a)** night; **la ~ anterior** the night before, the previous evening; **esta ~** tonight, this evening; **¡buenas ~s!** (al saludar) good evening!; (al despedirse) goodnight **(b)** (*en locs*) **de noche** ‹*trabajar/conducir*› at night; ‹*vestido/función*› evening (*before n*) **hacerse de ~** to get dark; **en la** *or* (esp Esp) **por la** *or* (RPl) **a la noche**: **en la ~ fuimos al teatro** in the evening we went to the theater; **el lunes en la ~** on Monday evening/night; ***de la ~ a la mañana*** overnight

Nochebuena *f* Christmas Eve

Nochevieja *f* New Year's Eve (*in the evening*)

noción *f* **(a)** (idea, concepto) notion, idea; **no tiene la menor ~ del tema** he doesn't know the first thing about the subject **(b) nociones** *fpl* (conocimientos): **tengo nociones de ruso** I have a smattering of Russian; **las nociones de electrónica** the basics *o* rudiments of electronics

nocivo -va *adj* ‹*sustancia*› harmful; ‹*influencia*› damaging

> **Los Nombres Compuestos**
>
> Los nombres compuestos en español pueden estar o no unidos por la preposición *de*, ej. *caja de cambio = gear box*; *perro policía = police dog.*
>
> El plural de los nombres compuestos en español generalmente recae en el primer elemento de los mismos, en inglés, sin embargo, el plural recae en el segundo, ej. *tarjetas de embarque = boarding cards*; *países satelite = satelite nations.* Se deben tener presente los casos de plurales irregulares en inglés, como en los ejemplos: *niños prodigio = prodigy children*; *hombres rana = frogmen.*

noctámbulo -la *adj*: **siempre ha sido ~** he's always been a night bird *o* (AmE) nighthawk (colloq)

nocturno -na *adj* **(a)** ‹*vuelo/tren/vida*› night (*before n*); ‹*clases*› evening (*before n*) **(b)** ‹*animal/planta*› nocturnal

nodriza *f* (ama de cría) wet nurse; (niñera) (ant) nursemaid

nogal *m* (árbol) walnut tree; (madera) walnut

nómada *adj* nomadic ■ *mf* nomad

nomás *adv* **(a)** (AmL): **pase ~** come on in; **no lo vas a convencer así ~** you're not going to convince him as easily as that; **déjelo aquí ~** just leave it here; **lo dijo por molestar ~** she only said it to be difficult **(b) nomás (que)** (Col, Méx fam) as soon as; **~ (que) tenga dinero** as soon as I have some money

nombramiento *m* (designación) appointment; (documento) letter of appointment

nombrar [A1] *vt* **(a)** (citar, mencionar) to mention; **no lo volvió a ~** she never mentioned his name *o* him again **(b)** (designar) to appoint

nombre *m* **(a)** (de cosa, persona, animal) name; **~ y apellidos** full name, name in full; **~ artístico** stage name; **~ de pila** first name, christian name; **~ de soltera** maiden name; **¿qué ~ le pusieron?** what did they call him?; **lo conozco de ~** I know him by name; **en ~ de** (en representación de) on behalf of; (apelando a) in the name of; **a ~ de** ‹*paquete/carta*› made payable to, made out to; **lo que ha hecho no tiene ~** what she has done is unspeakable **(b)** (Ling) noun; **~ compuesto** compound noun **(c)** (fama): **un científico de ~** a renowned scientist; **hacerse un ~ en la vida** to make a name for oneself

nómina *f* (lista de empleados) payroll; (hoja de pago) payslip; (suma de dinero) salary, wages (*pl*)

nominación *f* nomination

nominar [A1] *vt* to nominate

nominativo *adj* (Fin): **un cheque ~ a favor de** ... a check made out to *o* payable to ...

nomo *m* gnome

non *adj* odd ■ *m* odd number; **pares y ~es** odds and evens

noqueada *f* knockout

noquear [A1] *vt* to knock out

noratlántico -ca *adj* north-Atlantic (*before n*)

nordeste, **noreste** ▶346 *adj inv* ‹región› northeastern; **iban en dirección ~** they were heading northeast ■ *m* (punto cardinal) northeast, Northeast; **vientos del ~** northeasterly winds

nórdico -ca *adj* ‹país/pueblo› Nordic (*esp Scandinavian*)

noria *f* **(a)** (para sacar agua) waterwheel **(b)** (Ocio) Ferris wheel (AmE), big wheel (BrE)

norma *f* **(a)** (regla) rule, regulation; **~s de conducta** rules of conduct; **~s de seguridad** safety regulations; **tengo por ~ ...** I make it a rule ... **(b)** (manera común de hacer algo): **la ~ es que acudan los directivos** it is standard practice for the directors to attend

normal *adj* normal; **es ~ que reaccionen así** it's normal for them to react like that; **hoy en día es muy ~** it's very common nowadays; **no es ~ que haga tanto frío** it's unusual *o* it isn't normal for it to be so cold; **superior a lo ~** above-average; ***~ y corriente*** ordinary ■ *f* **(a)** (escuela): **la N ~** teacher training college **(b)** (gasolina) regular gas (AmE), two-star petrol (BrE)

normalidad *f* **(a)** (cualidad): **con ~** normally **(b)** (situación) normality, normalcy (AmE); **el país volvió a la ~** the country returned to normal

normalización *f* **(a)** (de situación) normalization **(b)** (estandarización) standardization

normalizar [A4] *vt* **(a)** ‹situación/relaciones› to normalize **(b)** (estandarizar) to standardize
■ **normalizarse** *v pron* **(a)** «situación/relaciones» to return to normal **(b)** (estandarizarse) to become standardized

noroeste ▶346 *adj inv* ‹región› northwestern; **iban en dirección ~** they were heading northwest ■ *m* (punto cardinal) northwest, Northwest; **vientos del ~** northwesterly winds

norte ▶346 *adj inv* ‹región› northern; ‹costa/ala› north (*before n*); **iban en dirección ~** they were heading north *o* northward(s) ■ *m* north, North; **al ~ de Matagalpa** to the north of Matagalpa; **vientos del N~** northerly winds; **caminaron hacia el N~** they walked north *o* northward(s); **la casa da al ~** the house faces north

Norteamérica *f* (América del Norte) North America; (EEUU) America, the States (colloq)

norteamericano -na *adj/m,f* (de América del Norte) North American; (estadounidense) American

norteño -ña, (Chi, Per) **nortino -na** *adj* ▶346 northern ■ *m,f* northerner

Noruega *f* Norway

noruego[1] **-ga** *adj/m,f* Norwegian

noruego[2] *m* (idioma) Norwegian

nos *pron pers* **(a)** (como complemento directo, indirecto) us; **~ ayudaron mucho** they helped us a lot; **escúchanos** listen to us; **~ han robado el coche** our car's been stolen **(b)** (*refl*) ourselves; **~ hicimos daño** we hurt ourselves; **sentémonos** let's sit down **(c)** (*recípr*): **~ conocemos desde hace años** we have known each other for years

nosotros -tras *pron pers pl* **(a)** we; **¿quién lo trajo? — nosotros** who brought it? — we did; **ábrenos, somos nosotras** open the door, it's us; **~ mismos lo arreglamos** we fixed it ourselves **(b)** (en comparaciones, con preposiciones) us; **antes/después que ~** before/after us; **ven con ~** come with us

nostalgia *f* nostalgia; **siente ~ por su país** he feels homesick

nostálgico -ca *adj* nostalgic

nota *f* **1** (apunte, mensaje) note; **tomar ~ de algo** (apuntar) to make a note of sth; (fijarse) to take note of sth; **tomar ~s** to take notes; **~ a pie de página** footnote **2 (a)** (Educ) (calificación) grade (AmE), mark (BrE); **sacar buenas ~s** to get good grades *o* marks **(b)** (Mús) note **3** (detalle) touch; **una ~ de humor** a touch of humor

notable *adj* ‹diferencia/mejoría› notable; **una actuación ~** an outstanding performance; **posee una ~ inteligencia** she is remarkably *o* extremely intelligent ■ *m* **(a)** (Educ) *grade between 7 and 8.5 on a scale from 1 to 10* **(b)** (persona importante) dignitary

notar [A1] *vt* **(a)** (advertir) to notice; **no noté nada extraño** I didn't notice anything strange; **hacer(le) ~ algo (a algn)** to point sth out (to sb); **te noto muy triste** you look very sad; **se le notaba indeciso** he seemed hesitant **(b)** (*impers*): **se nota que es novato** you can tell *o* see he's a beginner; **se te nota en la cara** it's written all over your face
■ **notarse** ■ *v pron* (+ *compl*) to feel; **me noto rara con este vestido** I feel funny in this dress

notaría *f* **(a)** (profesión) *profession of notary*; (oficina) notary's office **(b)** (Col) (registro civil) registry office

notarial *adj* notarial

notario -ria *m,f* notary, notary public

noticia *f* **1** (información): **una ~** a piece *o* an item of news; **buenas/malas ~s** good/bad news; **la última ~ del programa** the final item on the news **2 noticias** *fpl* **(a)** (referencias) news; **no hemos tenido ~s suyas** (provenientes de él) we haven't heard from him; (provenientes de otra persona) we haven't had (any) news of him **(b)** (Rad, TV) news

noticiario *m*, (AmL) **noticiero** *m* (Rad, TV) news; (Cin) newsreel

notificación *f* (frml) notification (frml)

notificar [A2] *vt* (frml) to notify

notorio -ria *adj* **(a)** (evidente) evident, obvious **(b)** (conocido) well-known **(c)** (notable) ‹descenso/mejora› marked

nov. (= **noviembre**) Nov

novato -ta *adj* inexperienced, new ■ *m,f* novice, beginner

novecientos -tas ▶293 *adj/pron* nine hundred; *para ejemplos ver* QUINIENTOS

novedad *f* **1 (a)** (innovación) innovation; **la última ~ en el campo de la informática** the latest innovation in the field of computing **(b)** (cualidad, cosa nueva) novelty; **eran una ~ en aquel entonces** they were a novelty then **2** (noticia): **¿alguna ~?** any news?; **eso no es ninguna ~** everybody knows that; **sin ~** ‹llegar› safely; **¿cómo sigue? — sin ~** how is he? — much the same

Números 1

Números cardinales

1	one
2	two
3	three
4	four
5	five
6	six
7	seven
8	eight
9	nine
10	ten
11	eleven
12	twelve
13	thirteen
14	fourteen
15	fifteen
16	sixteen
17	seventeen
18	eighteen
19	nineteen
20	twenty
21	twenty-one
22	twenty-two
23	twenty-three
30	thirty
31	thirty-one
32	thirty-two
33	thirty-three
40	forty
50	fifty
60	sixty
70	seventy
80	eighty
90	ninety
100	a hundred
101	a hundred and one
102	a hundred and two
103	a hundred and three
200	two hundred
300	three hundred
400	four hundred
500	five hundred
600	six hundred
700	seven hundred
800	eight hundred
900	nine hundred

En inglés se usa una coma para separar los millares de las centenas y los millones de los cientos de millares:

1,000	one thousand
1,001	one thousand and one
10,000	ten thousand
90,000	ninety thousand
100,000	one hundred thousand
1,000,000	one million
12,000,000	twelve million
1,000,000,000	one billion *or* one thousand million

El numeral 'billion' *equivale a mil millones, aunque en el inglés británico puede significar también un millón de millones.*

Nótese el uso de 'and' *entre las centenas y las decenas*:

220 two hundred and twenty

pero no entre las decenas y las unidades:

76 seventy-six
333 three hundred and thirty-three

Las palabras 'million' *y* 'dozen' *funcionan igual que* 'hundred' *y* 'thousand' *en cuanto al uso de la preposición* 'of':

un millón de personas	a million people
una docena de huevos	a dozen eggs
un millón de ellos	a million of them
una docena de sus amigos	a dozen of his friends

El cero en inglés

En el inglés norteamericano se prefiere el uso de la palabra 'zero', *mientras que en el inglés británico se emplea más la palabra* 'nought':

0.25 point two five
zero point two five
nought point two five

Al leer un número cifra por cifra, el cero suele leerse 'zero' *en el inglés norteamericano y como la letra 'o' en el inglés británico*:

250674 two – five – zero – six – seven – four (esp AmE)
two – five – oh – six – seven – four (esp BrE)

Nótese el uso inglés cuando se trata de dar el resultado de un encuentro deportivo. El cero puede expresarse de las siguientes maneras:

ganaron seis a cero — they won six – nothing *o* six to nothing
they won six – zero (AmE)
they won six – zip (AmE)
they won six – nil (BrE)

En tenis se usa la palabra 'love':

iba ganando treinta a cero — he was winning thirty-love

Números 2

Números ordinales

1º	1st	first
2º	2nd	second
3º	3rd	third
4º	4th	fourth
5º	5th	fifth
6º	6th	sixth
7º	7th	seventh
8º	8th	eighth
9º	9th	ninth
10º	10th	tenth
11º	11th	eleventh
12º	12th	twelfth
13º	13th	thirteenth
14º	14th	fourteenth
15º	15th	fifteenth
16º	16th	sixteenth
17º	17th	seventeeth
18º	18th	eighteenth
19º	19th	nineteenth
20º	20th	twentieth
21º	21st	twenty-first
22º	22nd	twenty-second
23º	23rd	twenty-third
24º	24th	twenty-fourth
30º	30th	thirtieth
40º	40th	fortieth
50º	50th	fiftieth
60º	60th	sixtieth
70º	70th	seventieth
80º	80th	eightieth
90º	90th	ninetieth
100º	100th	hundredth
1,000º	1,000th	thousandth
1,000,000º	1,000,000th	millionth

Los números ordinales se emplean:

— *en títulos*:

Queen Elizabeth II (Queen Elizabeth the Second)
Pope John XXIII (Pope John the Twenty-third)

— *para referirse a siglos*:

the 19th century

— *para indicar la fecha*:

April 3rd

(*Ver también página 193*)

Operaciones matemáticas

13 + 3 = 16	thirteen plus three is sixteen thirteen plus three equals sixteen thirteen and three are sixteen
4 – 1 = 3	four minus one is three
3 x 2 = 6	three times two is six three twos are six
20 ÷ 4 = 5	twenty divided by four is five
a > b	a is greater than b
b < c	b is less than c

novedoso -sa *adj* ‹*idea/enfoque*› novel, original

novela *f* (Lit) novel; (TV) soap opera; **~ policíaca** detective novel *o* story; **~ rosa** (pey) novelette (pej), romantic novel

novelesco -ca *adj* ‹*vida/historia*› like something out of a novel; ‹*viajes/andanzas*› fabulous

novelista *mf* novelist

noveno¹ -na ▶ 294 *adj/pron* ninth; **la novena parte** a ninth; *para ejemplos ver* QUINTO

noveno² *m* ▶ 294 ninth

noventa ▶ 293 *adj inv/pron/m* ninety; *para ejemplos ver* CINCUENTA

noviar [A1] *vi* (AmL fam) to go out together, to date (AmE); **~** CON **algn** to go out WITH sb, to date sb (AmE)

noviazgo *m*: **el ~ duró un año** they went out (together) for one year; **~s a larga distancia** long-distance relationships

novicio -cia *m,f* novice

noviembre ▶ 193 *m* November; *para ejemplos ver* ENERO

novillo -lla *m,f* (*m*) young bull; (*f*) heifer; ***hacer ~s*** (fam) to play hooky (esp AmE colloq), to skive off (school) (BrE colloq)

novio -via *m,f* **(a)** (no formal) (*m*) boyfriend; (*f*) girlfriend; (después del compromiso) (*m*) fiancé; (*f*) fiancée **(b)** (el día de la boda) (*m*) groom; (*f*) bride; **los ~s** the bride and groom

nubarrón *m* storm cloud

nube *f* (Meteo) cloud; (de polvo, humo) cloud; (de insectos) cloud, swarm; **un cielo cubierto de ~s** an overcast *o* a cloudy sky; **~ atómica** mushroom cloud; ***estar*** or ***andar en las ~s*** (fam) to have one's head in the clouds

nublado -da *adj* ▶ 409 ‹*cielo/día*› cloudy, overcast

nublar [A1] *vt* **(a)** ‹*vista*› to cloud **(b)** (liter) ‹*felicidad*› to cloud (liter)

■ **nublarse** ■ *v pron* **(a)** ▶ 409 «*cielo*» to cloud over **(b)** «*vista*» to cloud over

nubosidad *f*: **la ~ irá en aumento** it will become increasingly cloudy; **un día con mucha ~** a day with a lot of cloud about

nuboso -sa *adj* ▶ 409 cloudy

nuca *f* back *o* nape of the neck

nuclear *adj* nuclear

núcleo *m* **(a)** (Biol, Fís) nucleus **(b)** (Elec) core

nudillo *m* ▶ 123 knuckle

nudismo *m* nudism

nudista *adj/mf* nudist

nudo *m* **(a)** (en general) knot; **se hizo un ~ en el hilo** the thread got into a knot; **¿me haces el ~ de la corbata?** can you do my tie for me?; **tenía un ~ en la garganta** I had a lump in my throat **(b)** (de carreteras, vías férreas) junction

nuera *f* daughter-in-law

nuestro -tra *adj* our; **~ coche** our car; **un amigo ~** a friend of ours ■ *pron*: **el ~, la nuestra**

etc ours; **es de los ∼s** he's one of us; **nosotros a lo ∼** let's just get on with our own business; **sabe lo ∼** he knows about us

Nueva York *f* New York

Nueva Zelandia, **Nueva Zelanda** *f* New Zealand

nueve ▶ 293 *adj inv/pron/m* nine; *para ejemplos ver* CINCO

nuevo -va *adj* **(a)** [SER] ‹*estilo/coche/novio*› new; **soy ∼ en la oficina** I'm new in the office; **de ∼** again; **¿qué hay de ∼** what's new? (colloq); **∼ rico** nouveau riche **(b)** (*delante del n*) ‹*intento/cambio*› further; **ha surgido un ∼ problema** another *o* a further problem has arisen; **N∼ Testamento** New Testament **(c)** [ESTAR] (no desgastado) as good as new

Nuevo México *m* New Mexico

nuez *f* **1 (a)** (del nogal) walnut **(b)** (Méx) (pacana) pecan (nut) **(c) ∼ moscada** nutmeg **2** (Anat) Adam's apple

nulidad *f* **1** (Der) nullity **2** (fam) (calamidad) dead loss (colloq); **soy una ∼ para los idiomas** I'm useless at languages

nulo -la *adj* **(a)** (Der) ‹*testamento/votación*› null and void; ‹*voto*› void **(b)** ‹*persona*› useless (colloq), hopeless (colloq) **(c)** (inexistente): **mis conocimientos del tema son ∼s** my knowledge of the subject is virtually nil

Núm., **núm.** (= **número**) no.

numerable *adj* countable

numeración *f* (acción) numbering; (números) numbers (*pl*); (sistema) numerals (*pl*)

numeral *adj/m* numeral

numerar [A1] *vt* to number

número *m* **1 (a)** ▶ 293, 294 (Mat) number; **∼ de identificación personal** PIN number, Personal Identification Number; **∼ de matrícula** license number (AmE), registration number (BrE); **∼ de teléfono/fax** phone/fax number; **una suma de seis ∼s** a six figure sum; **problemas sin ∼** innumerable *o* countless problems **(b)** ▶ 401 (de zapatos) size; **¿qué ∼ calzas?** what size shoe do you take? **(c)** (billete de lotería) lottery ticket **2 (a)** (Espec) act **(b)** (de publicación) issue

numeroso -sa *adj* ‹*clase/grupo*› large; ‹*ocasiones/ejemplos*› numerous, many

nunca *adv* ▶ 289 never; **como ∼** like never before; **casi ∼** hardly ever; **más que ∼** more than ever (before); **∼ más** never again

nuncio *m* (Relig) *tb* **∼ apostólico** papal nuncio

nupcial *adj* ‹*festejos*› (liter) nuptial (liter); ‹*ceremonia*› wedding (*before n*)

nutria *f* otter

nutrición *f* nutrition

nutrido -da *adj*: **mal ∼** undernourished, malnourished; **bien ∼** well-nourished

nutrir [I1] *vt* ‹*organismo*› to nourish; ‹*niño/planta*› to nourish, feed

nutritivo -va *adj* ‹*alimento*› nutritious; ‹*valor*› nutritional

nylon /'najlon, ni'lon/ *m* nylon

Ññ

Ñ, **ñ** *f* (*read as* /'eɲe/) *the letter* Ñ, ñ

ñandú *m* rhea

ñandutí *m* nanduti (*fine Paraguayan lace*)

ñango -ga *adj* (Méx fam) wimpish (colloq)

ñapa *f* (AmL fam) *small amount of extra goods given free*, lagniappe (AmE); **dar algo de ∼** to throw sth in (for free) (colloq); **me dio dos de ∼** she threw in a couple extra

ñato -ta *adj* (AmS fam) ‹*persona*› snub-nosed; ‹*animal*› pug-nosed

ñauca (Chi), (RPl) **ñaupa** *f* (fam): **es del año de ∼** it's really ancient (colloq); **ropa del año de ∼** clothes that went out with the ark (colloq)

ñoquis *mpl* (Coc) gnocchi (*pl*)

ñorbo *m* (Ec, Per) passionflower

ñu *m* gnu, wildebeest

Oo

O, o *f* (*read as* /o/) *the letter* O, o

o *conj* or; **¿vienes o no?** are you coming or not?; **o ... o ...** either ... or ...; **o mañana o el jueves** either tomorrow or Thursday; [*between two digits* o *is written with an accent*: **unas 100 ó 120** about 100 or 120]; **o sea** *ver* SER *vi* II

O. (= **oeste**) ▶ 346 W, West

oasis *m* (*pl* ~) oasis

obcecarse [A2] *v pron* to become obsessed; **está obcecado con la idea** he's obsessed with the idea

obedecer [E3] *vt* **(a)** ‹*orden/norma*› to obey, comply with **(b)** ‹*persona*› to obey; **obedece a tu madre** do as your mother tells you ■ ~ *vi* **(a)** «*persona*» to obey; **para que aprendas a ~** to teach you to do as you're told **(b)** «*mecanismo*» to respond **(c)** (frml) (a motivo, causa) ~ A **algo** to be due TO sth

obediente *adj* obedient

obelisco *m* obelisk

obertura *f* overture

obesidad *f* obesity

obeso -sa *adj* obese

obispo *m* bishop

objeción *f* objection; **nadie puso objeciones** nobody objected *o* made any objection; **~ de conciencia** conscientious objection

objetar [A1] *vt* to object; **¿tienes algo que ~?** do you have any objection? ■ ~ *vi* (Esp fam) to declare oneself a conscientious objector

objetividad *f* objectivity; **con ~** objectively

objetivo¹ -va *adj* objective

objetivo² *m* **1** (finalidad) objective, aim; (Mil) objective **2** (Fot, Ópt) lens

objeto *m* **1** (cosa) object; **~s de valor** valuables; **~s de uso personal** items *o* articles for personal use; **~s perdidos** lost and found (AmE), lost property (BrE); **~ volador no identificado** unidentified flying object, UFO **2 (a)** (finalidad) aim, object; **con el ~ de hacer algo** in order to do sth, with the aim of doing sth; **con el ~ de que se conozcan** so that they can get to know each other; **ser ~ de algo** (de admiración/críticas) to be the object of sth; (de investigación/estudio) to be the subject of sth; **ser ~ de malos tratos** to be ill-treated **(b)** (Ling) object

objetor -tora *m,f* objector; **~ de conciencia** conscientious objector

oblicuo -cua *adj* ‹*línea*› oblique

obligación *f* (deber) obligation; **cumplió con sus obligaciones** he fulfilled his obligations; **tiene (la) ~ de ...** it is his duty to ..., he has an obligation to ...; **es mi ~ decírtelo** it is my duty to tell you; **lo hace por ~** she does it out of obligation; **si sus obligaciones se lo permiten** if her commitments permit

obligado -da *adj* [ESTAR] ‹*persona*› obliged; **~ A hacer algo** obliged to do sth; **se vio ~ a acompañarla** he was obliged to accompany her

obligar [A3] *vt* **(a) ~ a algn A hacer algo** to force sb to do sth, to make sb do sth; **no lo obligues a comer** don't force him to eat; **nos obligan a llevar uniforme** we are required to wear uniform; **~ a algn A QUE haga algo** to make sb do sth **(b)** «*ley/disposición*» to bind

obligatorio -ria *adj* compulsory, obligatory; **no es ~ firmarlo** it doesn't have to be signed

oboe *m* (instrumento) oboe ■ *mf* (músico) oboist

obra *f* **1** (creación artística) work; **sus primeras ~s** her earliest works; **una ~ de artesanía** a piece of craftsmanship; **sus ~s de teatro** her plays; **~ de arte** work of art; **~ maestra** masterpiece **2** (acción): **mi buena ~ del día** my good deed for the day; **~ benéfica** (acto) act of charity; (organización) charity, charitable organization **3** (Arquit, Const) **(a)** (construcción) building work; **estamos de ~s** we're having some building work done **(b)** (sitio) building *o* construction site

obrar [A1] *vi* (actuar) to act; **~ de buena fe** to act in good faith ■ ~ *vt* ‹*milagros*› to work

obrera *f* (hormiga) worker (ant); (abeja) worker (bee); *ver tb* OBRERO²

obrero -ra *adj* ‹*barrio*› working-class; **el movimiento ~** the workers' movement; **la clase obrera** the working class ■ *m,f* (de fábrica, industria) worker; **los ~s dejaron la arena en el jardín** the workmen left the sand in the garden

obsceno -na *adj* obscene

obscuro, etc ⇒ OSCURO, ETC

obsequio *m* (frml) gift

observación *f* **1** (examen, vigilancia) observation; **tener a algn en ~** (Med) to keep sb under observation; **tener mucha capacidad de ~** to be very observant **2** (comentario) observation, remark; (en texto) note

observador -dora *m,f* observer

observar [A1] *vt* **(a)** (en general) to observe; **alguien la observaba** someone was watching *o* (frml) observing her **(b)** (notar) to observe (frml); **¿has observado algún cambio?** have you noticed *o* observed any changes?

observatorio *m* observatory

obsesión *f* obsession

obsesionar [A1] *vt* to obsess; **estaba obsesionado con la idea** he was obsessed with the idea

■ **obsesionarse** *v pron* to become obsessed
obsesivo -va *adj* obsessive
obsidiana *f* obsidian
obsoleto -ta *adj* obsolete
obstaculizar [A4] *vt* ‹*progreso/trabajo*› to hinder, hamper; ‹*tráfico*› to hold up; **no obstaculice el paso** don't stand in the way
obstáculo *m* obstacle
obstante: **no obstante** (sin embargo) nevertheless, nonetheless; (a pesar de) despite, in spite of
obstinado -da *adj* **(a)** (tozudo) obstinate, stubborn **(b)** (tenaz) tenacious, dogged
obstinarse [A1] *v pron* **~ EN hacer algo** to (obstinately) insist ON doing sth; **se obstinó en no ir** he obstinately refused to go; **se ha obstinado en que hay que terminarlo hoy** he is bent on finishing it today
obstrucción *f* obstruction
obstruir [I20] *vt* **1** (bloquear) ‹*conducto*› to block; ‹*salida*› to block, obstruct **2** (entorpecer) ‹*plan/proceso*› to obstruct; ‹*tráfico*› to obstruct, hold up; ‹*progreso*› to impede **3** (Dep) to obstruct
■ **obstruirse** *v pron* to get blocked (up)
obtener [E27] *vt* ‹*premio*› to win, receive; ‹*resultado/autorización*› to obtain; ‹*calificación*› to obtain, set
obturador *m* (Fot) shutter
obtuve, obtuvo, etc *see* OBTENER
obvio -via *adj* obvious
oca *f* (Zool) goose
ocasión *f* **1 (a)** (vez, circunstancia) occasion; **con ~ de** on the occasion of; **en alguna ~** occasionally **(b)** (momento oportuno) opportunity; **no tuve ~ de hablarle** I didn't have an opportunity *o* a chance to talk to him **2** (ganga) bargain; **de ~** ‹*precios*› bargain (*before n*); ‹*muebles*› (usados) secondhand; (baratos) cut-rate *o* (BrE) cut-price; ‹*coches*› secondhand
ocasional *adj* ‹*encuentro*› chance (*before n*); ‹*trabajo*› temporary
ocasionar [A1] *vt* to cause
occidental *adj* ‹*zona*› ▶ 346 western; ‹*cultura/países*› Western; **África O~** West Africa ■ *mf* westerner
occidentalizarse [A4] *v pron* to become westernized
occidente *m* ▶ 346 west
Oceanía *f* Oceania
océano *m* ocean
ochenta ▶ 293 *adj inv/pron/m* eighty; *para ejemplos ver* CINCUENTA
ocho ▶ 293 *adj inv/pron/m* eight; *para ejemplos ver* CINCO
ochocientos -tas ▶ 293 *adj/pron* eight hundred; *para ejemplos ver* QUINIENTOS
ocio *m* **(a)** (tiempo libre) spare time, leisure time **(b)** (inactividad, holgazanería) inactivity, idleness
ociosidad *f* inactivity, idleness
ocioso -sa *adj* (inactivo) idle
ocre *m* ▶ 097: **(de) color ~** ocher-colored*
oct. (= **octubre**) Oct
octavilla *f* pamphlet
octavo¹ -va ▶ 294 *adj/pron* eighth; **la octava parte** an eighth; *para ejemplos ver* QUINTO
octavo² *m* ▶ 294 eighth; **~s de final** *round before the quarter-finals*
octubre *m* ▶ 193 October; *para ejemplos ver* ENERO
oculista *mf* ophthalmologist
ocultar [A1] *vt* (en general) to conceal, hide; ‹*persona*› to hide; **~le algo A algn** to conceal *o* hide sth FROM sb
■ **ocultarse** *v pron* **(a)** «*persona*» to hide **(b)** (estar oculto) to hide, lie hidden **(c)** «*sol*» to disappear
ocultismo *m* occult, occultism
oculto -ta *adj* **(a)** [ESTAR] (escondido) hidden **(b)** [SER] (misterioso) ‹*razón/designio*› mysterious, secret
ocupación *f* (empleo) occupation; (actividad) activity
ocupado -da *adj* **(a)** (atareado) busy **(b)** ‹*línea telefónica*› busy, engaged (BrE); **¿este asiento está ~?** is this seat taken? **(c)** ‹*territorio*› occupied
ocupante *mf* occupant
ocupar [A1] *vt* **1** ‹*espacio/tiempo*› to take up; **me ocupó toda la mañana** it took up my whole morning; **¿en qué ocupas tu tiempo libre?** how do you spend your spare time? **2** «*persona*» **(a)** (situarse en) ‹*asiento*› to take; **volvió a ~ su asiento** she returned to her seat, she took her seat again; **ocupaban (todo) un lado de la sala** they took up one (whole) side of the room **(b)** (estar en) ‹*vivienda*› to live in, occupy; ‹*habitación*› to be in; ‹*asiento*› to be (sitting) in **(c)** (en clasificación): **¿qué lugar ocupan en la liga?** what position are they in the division? **(d)** ‹*cargo*› to hold, occupy (frml); ‹*vacante*› to fill **3** ‹*fábrica/territorio*› to occupy **4** (AmC, Chi, Méx) (usar) to use
■ **ocuparse** *v pron* **~se DE algo/algn** ‹*de tarea/trabajo*› to take care OF sth; ‹*de problema/asunto*› to deal WITH sth; **yo me ~é de eso** I'll see to that; **~se DE algn** ‹*de niño/enfermo*› to take care OF sb, to look after sb
ocurrencia *f* (comentario gracioso) witty *o* funny remark, witticism; (idea disparatada) crazy idea
ocurrente *adj* (gracioso) witty; (ingenioso) clever
ocurrir [I1] *vi* (*en 3ª pers*) to happen; **ocurra lo que ocurra** whatever happens; **lo que ocurre es que** ... the trouble is (that) ...; **lamento lo ocurrido** I'm sorry about what happened
■ **ocurrirse** *v pron* (*en 3ª pers*): **se me ha ocurrido una idea** I've had an idea; **no se les ocurría nada** they couldn't think of anything; **di lo primero que se te ocurra** say the first thing that comes into your head; **¿cómo se te ocurrió comprarlo?** whatever made you buy it?
odiar [A1] *vt* to hate; **odio planchar** I hate ironing
odio *m* hate, hatred; **tenerle ~ a algn** to hate sb
odioso -sa *adj* ‹*trabajo/tema*› horrible, hateful; ‹*persona*› horrible, odious
oeste *adj inv* ▶ 346 ‹*región*› western; **conducían en dirección ~** they were driving west *o*

westward(s); **la costa ~** the west coast ■ *m* ▶ 346 **1 (a)** (parte, sector): **el ~** the west; **en el ~ de la provincia** in the west of the province; **al ~ de Oaxaca** to the west of Oaxaca **(b)** (punto cardinal) west, West; **vientos del O~** westerly winds; **caminaron hacia el O~** they walked west *o* westward(s) **2 el Oeste** (de los Estados Unidos) the West; **una película del O~** a Western

ofender [E1] *vt* to offend
■ **ofenderse** *v pron* to take offense*

ofensa *f* (agravio) insult

ofensiva *f* offensive

ofensivo -va *adj* offensive

oferta *f* **1 (a)** (proposición) offer **(b)** (Econ, Fin) supply **2** (Com) offer; **están de** *or* **en ~** they are on special offer

oficial *adj* official ■ *mf* (de policía) police officer (*above the rank of sergeant*); (Mil) officer

oficialismo *m* (AmL): **representantes del ~** representatives of the ruling *o* governing party

oficialista *adj* (AmL) ‹*periódico*› pro-government; ‹*candidato*› fielded by the party in power

oficina *f* (despacho) office; **en horas de ~** during office hours; **~ de empleo/turismo** unemployment/tourist office

oficinista *mf* office worker

oficio *m* **1** (trabajo) trade; **carpintero de ~** carpenter by trade **2** (Der) **de ~** court-appointed (*before n*) **3** (Relig) service, office

ofrecer [E3] *vt* **1 (a)** ‹*ayuda/cigarrillo/empleo*› to offer **(b)** ‹*dinero*› to offer; (en una subasta) to bid **(c)** ‹*fiesta*› to give; ‹*recepción*› to lay on **(d)** ‹*sacrificio/víctima*› to offer (up) **2 (a)** ‹*oportunidad/posibilidad*› to give, provide; ‹*dificultad*› to present **(b)** «*persona*» ‹*resistencia*› to put up, offer
■ **ofrecerse** *v pron* **1** «*persona*» to offer, volunteer; **~se A** *or* **PARA hacer algo** to offer *o* volunteer TO do sth **2** (frml) (querer, necesitar) (*gen neg o interrog*): **¿qué se le ofrece, señora?** what would you like, madam? (frml); **si no se le ofrece nada más** if there's nothing else I can do for you

ofrecimiento *m* offer

ofrenda *f* offering

ofuscarse [A2] *v pron* to get worked up

ogro *m* ogre

oídas: **de ~** (*loc adv*) **lo conozco de ~** I've heard of him, I know of him

oído *m* **(a)** ▶ 123 (Anat) ear; **me lo susurró al ~** she whispered it in my ear **(b)** (sentido) hearing; (para la música, los idiomas) ear; **es duro de ~** he's hard of hearing; **aguzar el ~** to prick up one's ears; **no tiene ~** she's tone-deaf, she has no ear for music; ***tocar de ~*** (Mús) to play by ear

oiga, **oigas, etc** *see* OÍR

oír [I28] *vt* **1** (percibir sonidos) to hear; **no oigo nada** I can't hear anything *o* a thing; **se oyeron pasos** I (*or* you *etc*) heard footsteps; **he oído hablar de él** I've heard of him **2** (escuchar) ‹*música/radio*› to listen to **3 oír misa** to go to mass **4 oiga/oye** (para llamar la atención) excuse me; **¡oiga! se le cayó la cartera** excuse me, you've dropped your wallet; **oye, si ves a Gustavo dile que me llame** listen, if you see Gustavo tell him to call me ■ **~** *vi* to hear

ojal *m* buttonhole

ojalá *interj*: **seguro que apruebas — ¡~!** I'm sure you'll pass — I hope so!; **¡~ que todo salga bien!** let's hope everything turns out all right!; **~ fuera rico!** if only I were rich!, I wish I was rich!

ojeada *f* glance; **echar una ~ a algo** to have a quick glance *o* look at sth

ojear [A1] *vt* to (have a) look at

ojeras *fpl* rings under the eyes (*pl*)

ojeriza *f* grudge; **tenerle ~ a algn** to have a grudge against sb

ojeroso -sa *adj*: **estar ~** to have rings under one's eyes

ojo *m* **1 (a)** ▶ 123 (en general) eye; **un niño de ~s negros** a boy with dark eyes; **mirar fijamente a los ~s** to stare straight into sb's eyes; **no me quita los ~s de encima** he won't take his eyes off me; **a los ~s de la sociedad** in the eyes of society; **~ de la cerradura** keyhole; **~ de buey** porthole; **~ de vidrio** *or* (Esp) **cristal** glass eye; **~ mágico** (AmL) spyhole, peephole; **~ morado** *or* (Méx) **moro** *or* (CS fam) **en tinta** black eye; ***costar un ~ de la cara*** (fam) to cost an arm and a leg (colloq); ***cuatro ~s ven más que dos*** two heads are better than one; ***en un abrir y cerrar de ~s*** in the twinkling of an eye; **~ *por* ~** an eye for an eye **(b)** (vista): **bajó los ~s avergonzada** she lowered her eyes in shame; **sin levantar los ~s del libro** without looking up from her book; ***a ~*** (***de buen cubero***) *or* (AmS) ***al ~*** at a guess; ***echar un ~ a algo/algn*** (fam) to have *o* take a (quick) look at sth/sb; ***tener ~ de lince*** *or* ***de águila*** to have eyes like a hawk **2** (perspicacia): **¡vaya ~ que tiene!** he's pretty sharp *o* on the ball!; **tener ~ para los negocios** to have a good eye for business **3** (fam) (cuidado, atención): **hay que andar** *or* **ir con mucho ~** you have to keep your eyes open; **¡~! que viene un coche** watch out! *o* be careful! there's a car coming

ojota *f* (CS) (para playa, piscina) thong (AmE), flip-flop (BrE); (calzado rústico) sandal

okey *interj* (esp AmL) OK!, okay!

ola *f* wave; **~ de calor** heat wave; **~ de frío** cold spell

olán *m* (Méx) flounce, frill

olé, **ole** *interj* olé!, bravo!

oleada *f* wave

oleaje *m* swell

óleo *m* (sustancia) oil; (cuadro) oil painting; **pintura al ~** oil painting

oleoducto *m* (oil) pipeline

oler [E12] *vi* **1** (percibir olores) **~ A algo** to smell sth; **¿no hueles a humo?** can't you smell smoke? **2** (despedir olores) «*comida/perfume*» to smell; **¡qué bien/mal huele!** it smells good/awful!; **le huelen los pies** his feet smell; **~ A algo** ‹*a rosas/ajo*› to smell OF sth **3** (fam) (expresando sospecha) (+ *me/te/le etc*): **esto me huele mal** it sounds fishy to me; **me huele que fue ella** I have a feeling it was her ■ **~** *vt* «*persona*» to smell; «*animal*» to sniff, smell
■ **olerse** *v pron* (fam) to suspect; **ya me lo olía** I thought so

olfatear [A1] *vt* **(a)** (oler con insistencia) to sniff **(b)** ‹*rastro/presa*› to scent, follow

olfato *m* (sentido) smell; (perspicacia, intuición) nose

oligarquía *f* oligarchy

olimpiada, olimpíada *f*: *tb* **~s** Olympic Games (*pl*), Olympics (*pl*)

olímpico -ca *adj* **(a)** ‹*campeón/récord*› Olympic (*before n*) **(b)** (AmL fam) ‹*pase/gol*› fantastic (colloq), sensational (colloq)

olisquear [A1] *vt* to sniff

oliva *f* olive

olivar *m* olive grove

olivo *m* olive (tree)

olla *f* pot; **~ a presión** pressure cooker

olmo *m* elm (tree)

olor *m* smell; **tiene un ~ raro** it has a funny smell; **tomarle el ~ a algo** (AmL) to smell sth; **~ A algo** smell OF sth

oloroso -sa *adj* **(a)** ‹*jabón/flor*› scented, fragrant **(b)** ‹*queso/pies*› smelly

olote *m* (AmC, Méx) cob, corncob

olvidadizo -za *adj* forgetful

olvidar [A1] *vt* **1** ‹*pasado/nombre*› to forget; **había olvidado que** ... I had forgotten that ...; **~ hacer algo** to forget to do sth **2** (dejar en un lugar) to forget, leave ... behind; **olvidó el pasaporte en casa** she left her passport at home

■ **olvidarse** *v pron* **1** (en general) to forget; **~se DE algo** to forget sth; **~se DE hacer algo** to forget to do sth; (+ *me/te/le etc*) **¡ah! se me olvidaba** ah! I almost forgot; **se me olvidó decírtelo** I forgot to tell you **2** (dejar en un lugar) to forget, leave ... behind

olvido *m* **(a)** (abandono, indiferencia) obscurity; **caer en el ~** to fall *o* sink into obscurity *o* oblivion **(b)** (descuido) oversight; **fue un ~** it was an oversight, I forgot

ombligo *m* **▶ 123** navel, belly button (colloq)

omisión *f* omission

omitir [I1] *vt* ‹*frase/nombre*› to omit, leave out; **omitió mencionar que** ... he omitted *o* failed to mention that ...

ómnibus *m* (*pl* **~** *or* **-buses**) (autobús — urbano) (Per, Ur) bus; (— de larga distancia) (Arg) bus, coach (BrE)

omnipotente *adj* omnipotent

omoplato, omóplato *m* shoulder blade, scapula (tech)

once **▶ 293** *adj inv/pron/m* eleven; *para ejemplos ver* CINCO

onces *fpl* (Andes) tea

onda *f* (en general) wave; **~ corta/larga** short/long wave; **~ expansiva** blast, shock wave; **longitud de ~** wavelength; ***agarrarle la ~ a algo*** (AmL fam) to get the hang of sth (colloq); ***estar en la ~*** (fam) (a la moda) to be trendy (colloq); (al tanto) to be bang up to date (colloq); ***¡qué buena/mala ~!*** (AmL fam) that's great/terrible! (colloq); ***¿qué ~?*** (AmL fam) what's up? (colloq)

ondear [A1] *vi* «*bandera*» to fly

ondulado *adj* ‹*pelo*› wavy; ‹*terreno*› undulating, rolling

ondulante *adj* ‹*movimiento*› undulatory; ‹*terreno*› undulating, rolling

ondularse [A1] *v pron* to go wavy

onix *m* onyx

onomatopeya *f* onomatopoeia

onomatopéyico -ca *adj* onomatopoeic

ONU /'onu/ *f* (= **Organización de las Naciones Unidas**): **la ~** the UN, the United Nations

onza *f* **1** **▶ 322** (peso) ounce **2** (de chocolate) square

opaco -ca *adj* (no transparente) opaque; (sin brillo) dull

ópalo *m* opal

opción *f* option; **no tenía ~** I had no option *o* choice; **con ~ a compra** with option to buy

opcional *adj* optional

open *m* open championship *o* tournament

ópera *f* (obra musical) opera; (edificio) opera house

operación *f* **(a)** (Mat) **▶ 294** operation **(b)** (Med) operation; **una ~ a corazón abierto** open-heart surgery **(c)** (Fin) transaction **(d)** (misión) operation; **~ de rescate** rescue operation

operador -dora *m,f* **(a)** (Inf, Tec, Telec) operator **(b)** (Cin, TV) (de cámara) (*m*) cameraman; (*f*) camerawoman; (de proyección) projectionist **(c)** (Chi, Méx) (obrero) ⇒ OPERARIO **(d)** **~ turístico** tour operator

operar [A1] *vt* **1** (Med) to operate on; **me van a ~ de la vesícula** I'm having a gallbladder operation; **lo ~on de apendicitis** he had his appendix taken out **2** (frml) ‹*cambio/transformación*› to produce, bring about **3** (Chi, Méx) ‹*máquina*› to operate ■ **~** *vi* **(a)** (Med) to operate **(b)** (frml) «*servicio/vuelo*» to operate

■ **operarse** *v pron* **1** (Med) (*caus*) to have an operation; **~se del corazón** to have a heart operation **2** (frml) «*cambio/transformación*» to take place

operario -ria *m,f* (frml) operator; **el ~ de la máquina** the machine operator

opinar [A1] *vi* to express an opinion; **prefiero no ~** I would prefer not to comment ■ **~** *vt* **(a)** (pensar) to think; **¿qué opinas del aborto?** what do you think about abortion?; **¿qué opinas de ella?** what do you think of her?; **no opino lo mismo** I do not share that view *o* opinion; **opino que debería renunciar** in my opinion he should resign **(b)** (expresar un juicio): **opinó que deberían aplazarlo** he expressed the view that it should be postponed

opinión *f* opinion; **en mi ~** in my opinion; **cambió de ~** he changed his mind; **la ~ pública** public opinion

opio *m* (Bot, Farm) opium

oponente *mf* opponent

oponer [E22] *vt* ‹*resistencia*› to offer, put up; ‹*objeción*› to raise

■ **oponerse** *v pron* (ser contrario) to object; **~se A algo** to oppose sth; **nuestros caracteres se oponen** (*recipr*) we are opposites

oporto *m* (vino) port

oportunidad *f* **1** (momento oportuno, posibilidad) chance, opportunity; **a la primera ~** at the earliest opportunity; **tuve la ~ de conocerla** I got to meet her; **igualdad de ~es** equal opportunities

2 (AmL) (vez, circunstancia) occasion; **en aquella ~** that time *o* on that occasion

oportunismo *m* opportunism

oportunista *mf* opportunist

oportuno -na *adj* **(a)** ‹*visita/lluvia*› timely, opportune; **llegó en el momento ~** he arrived at just the right moment **(b)** ‹*medida/respuesta*› appropriate; **sería ~ avisarle** we ought to inform her; **estuvo muy ~** what he said was very much to the point

oposición *f* **1** (en general) opposition **2** (Esp, Ven) (concurso) (public) competitive examination; **hacer oposiciones** to take *o* (BrE) sit a competitive examination

opresión *f* (de un pueblo) oppression; (en el pecho) tightness

opresivo -va *adj* oppressive

oprimido -da *adj* ‹*pueblo*› oppressed

oprimir [I1] *vt* **(a)** (frml) (apretar, presionar) to press **(b)** (tiranizar) to oppress

optar [A1] *vi* **1** (decidirse) **~ POR algo** to choose sth, opt FOR sth; **~ POR hacer algo** to choose *o* opt to do sth **2 ~ A algo** ‹*a plaza/puesto*› to apply FOR sth

optativo -va *adj* optional

óptica *f* (Fís, Ópt) optics; (tienda) optician's

óptico -ca *adj* optical ■ *m,f* optician

optimismo *m* optimism

optimista *adj* optimistic ■ *mf* optimist

óptimo -ma *adj* ‹*posición*› ideal, optimum; **en condiciones óptimas** ‹*persona*› in peak condition; ‹*coche*› in perfect condition; ‹*alimento*› fresh

opuesto -ta *adj* ‹*versiones/opiniones*› conflicting; ‹*extremo/polo/lado*› opposite; **tienen caracteres ~s** they have very different personalities; **venía en dirección opuesta** he was coming from the opposite direction

opulento -ta *adj* opulent, affluent

oración *f* **(a)** (Relig) prayer **(b)** (Ling) sentence

orador -dora *m,f* speaker

oral *adj* oral

órale *interj* (Méx fam) (expresando acuerdo) right!, OK!; (para animar) come on!

orangután *m* orangutan

orar [A1] *vi* (frml) (Relig) to pray

oratorio *m* (Relig) oratory, chapel; (Mús) oratorio

órbita *f* **1** (Astron) orbit; **poner en ~** to put into orbit **2** (Anat) (eye) socket, orbit (tech)

orca *f* killer whale

orden[1] *f* **1** (mandato) order; **deja de darme órdenes** stop ordering me about; **hasta nueva ~** until further notice; **estamos a la ~ para lo que necesite** (AmL) just let us know if there's anything we can do for you; **¡a la ~!** (Mil) yes, sir!; (fórmula de cortesía) (Andes, Méx, Ven) you're welcome, not at all; **~ de arresto** *or* **de busca y captura** arrest warrant; **~ de registro** *or* (Chi, Méx) **de cateo** search warrant; **~ judicial** court order **2** (Fin) order; **~ bancaria** banker's order **3** (Hist, Mil, Relig) order **4** (AmL) (pedido) order

orden[2] *m* **1** (en general) order; **en** *or* **por ~ alfabético** in alphabetical order; **por ~ de estatura** according to height; **vayamos por ~** let's begin at the beginning; **poner algo en ~** ‹*habitación/armario/juguetes*› to straight sth (up) (esp AmE), to tidy sth up (esp BrE); ‹*asuntos/papeles*› to sort sth up; ‹*fichas*› to put sth in order; **mantener el ~ en la clase** to keep order in the classroom; **~ del día** agenda; **~ público** public order; **alterar el ~ público** to cause a breach of the peace **2 (a)** (frml) (carácter, índole) nature; **problemas de ~ económico** problems of an economic nature **(b)** (cantidad): **del ~ de** (frml) on the order of (AmE), in *o* of the order of (BrE)

ordenado -da *adj* **(a)** [ESTAR] (en orden) tidy **(b)** [SER] ‹*persona*› (metódico) organized, orderly; (para la limpieza) tidy

ordenador *m* (Esp) ⇒ COMPUTADORA

ordenanza *m* (en oficinas) porter; (Mil) orderly, batman (BrE)

ordenar [A1] *vt* **1** ‹*habitación/armario/juguetes*› to straighten (up) (esp AmE), to tidy (up) (BrE); ‹*fichas*› to put in order; **ordené los libros por materias** I arranged the books according to subject **2 (a)** (dar una orden) to order; **le ordenó salir de la oficina** she ordered him to leave the office **(b)** (AmL) (pedir) ‹*taxi/bebida/postre*› to order **3** ‹*sacerdote*› to ordain

■ **ordenarse** *v pron* to be ordained

ordeñar [A1] *vt* to milk

ordinal *m* ordinal (number)

ordinariez *f* **(a)** (falta de refinamiento) vulgarity; (grosería) rudeness, bad manners (*pl*); (en la manera de hablar) vulgarity, coarseness **(b)** (comentario — poco refinado) vulgar comment; (— grosero) rude comment

ordinario -ria *adj* **1** (poco refinado) vulgar, common (pej); (grosero) rude, bad-mannered; (en el hablar) vulgar, coarse **2** (de mala calidad) poor *o* bad quality **3** (no especial) ordinary; **correo ~** regular (AmE) *o* (BrE) normal delivery **4 de ordinario** usually, normally; **hay menos gente que de ~** there are fewer people than usual *o* normal ■ *m,f* (persona — poco refinada) vulgar *o* (pej) common person; (— grosera) rude *o* bad-mannered person

orégano *m* oregano

oreja *f* ▶ **123** (Anat) ear; **el perro puso las ~s tiesas** the dog pricked up its ears; **tirarle a algn de las ~s** *or* (AmL) **tirarle las ~s a algn** to pull sb's ears ■ *mf* (Méx fam) (soplón — de la policía) stool pigeon (colloq), grass (BrE colloq); (que escucha a escondidas) eavesdropper

orfanato, (Méx) **orfanatorio** *m* orphanage

orfelinato *m* orphanage

orgánico -ca *adj* organic

organismo *m* (Biol) organism; (Adm, Pol) organization

organización *f* organization

organizado -da *adj* organized

organizador -dora *m,f* organizer

organizar [A4] *vt* to organize, arrange

■ **organizarse** *v pron* to organize oneself

órgano *m* organ

orgasmo *m* orgasm

orgía *f* orgy

orgullo *m* pride; **con ~** proudly

orgulloso -sa *adj* **(a)** [ESTAR] (satisfecho) proud; **~ DE algn/algo** proud OF sb/sth **(b)** [SER] (soberbio) proud

orientación *f* **(a)** (de habitación, edificio) aspect (frml); **¿cuál es la ~ de la casa?** which way does the house face?; **la ~ de la antena** the way the antenna (AmE) *o* (BrE) aerial is pointing **(b)** (enfoque, dirección) orientation **(c)** (guía) guidance, direction; (acción de guiar) orientation; **~ profesional** (para estudiantes) vocational guidance, careers advice; (para desempleados) career guidance *o* advice **(d)** (en un lugar) bearings (*pl*)

oriental *adj* (del este) **▶376** eastern; (del Lejano Oriente) oriental; (uruguayo) (AmL) Uruguayan ■ *mf* (del Lejano Oriente) oriental; (uruguayo) (AmL) Uruguayan

orientar [A1] *vt* **1 (a)** ‹*reflector/antena*› to position; **la casa está orientada al sur** the house faces south (frml) **(b)** (Náut) ‹*velas*› to trim **2** (encaminar) ‹*esfuerzos/política*› to direct **3** ‹*persona*› **(a)** «*faro/estrellas*» to guide **(b)** (aconsejar) to advise; (mostrar el camino): **una mujer nos orientó** a woman told us the way

■ **orientarse** *v pron* (ubicarse) to get one's bearings, orient oneself; **~se por las estrellas** (Náut) to steer by the stars

oriente *m* (punto cardinal) **▶346** east; (viento) east wind; **O~ Medio/Próximo** Middle/Near East

orificio *m* (frml) (de bala) hole; **los ~s de la nariz** the nostrils

origen *m* origin; **en su ~** originally, in the beginning; **dar ~ a algo** to give rise to sth; **país de ~** country of origin; **de ~ humilde** of humble origin(s)

original *adj/m* original

originalidad *f* (cualidad) originality; (comentario) clever remark

originar [A1] *vt* to start, give rise to

■ **originarse** *v pron* «*idea/costumbre*» to originate; «*movimiento*» to start, come into being, originate; «*incendio/disputa*» to start

originario -ria *adj* (de un lugar) native; **ser ~ de algo** «*persona*» to come from sth; «*especie*» to be native to sth

orilla *f* **(a)** (del mar, de lago) shore; (de río) bank; **viven a la ~ del mar** they live by the sea; **un paseo a la ~ del mar** a walk along the seashore **(b)** (de mesa, plato) edge **(c)** (dobladillo) hem

orillar [A1] *vt* **1 (a)** ‹*muro/costa/zona*› to skirt (around) **(b)** (Col, Méx, Ven) (hacer a un lado): **orilló el coche** he pulled over **2** (Méx) (obligar) **~ a algn A algo** to drive sb TO sth

■ **orillarse** *v pron* (Col, Méx, Ven) to move over

orina *f* urine

orinal *m* (de dormitorio) chamber pot; (para niños) pot, potty (colloq); (para enfermos) bedpan

orinar [A1] *vi* to urinate ■ **~** *vt*: **~ sangre** to pass blood

■ **orinarse** *v pron* to wet oneself; **se orina en la cama** he wets the bed

Orinoco *m*: **el (río) ~** the Orinoco (River)

oriundo -da *adj* ⇒ ORIGINARIO

ornamentación *f* ornamentation

oro *adj inv* gold ■ *m* **1** (metal) gold; **~ (de) 18 quilates** 18-carat gold; **bañado en ~** gold-plated; **~ negro** black gold; ***ni por todo el ~ del mundo*** not for all the tea in China (colloq) **2** (en naipes) **(a)** (carta) *any card of the* OROS *suit* **(b) oros** *mpl* (palo) *one of the suits in a Spanish pack of cards*

orquesta *f* orchestra; **~ de jazz** jazz band

orquídea *f* orchid

ortiga *f* (stinging) nettle

ortodoxo -xa *adj* orthodox

ortografía *f* spelling, orthography (frml)

ortopédico -ca *adj* orthopedic*; ‹*pierna*› artificial

oruga *f* (Zool) caterpillar; (Auto) caterpillar *o* crawler track

orzuela *f* (Méx): **tengo ~** I've got split ends

orzuelo *m* sty*

os *pron pers* (Esp) **(a)** (complemento directo, indirecto) you; **~ veo mañana** I'll see you tomorrow; **~ lo prometió** she promised it to you **(b)** (*refl*) yourselves; **no ~ engañéis** don't kid yourselves **(c)** (*recípr*): **creía que ~ conocíais** I thought you knew each other

oscar /'oskar/ *m* (*pl* **~** *or* **-cars**) Oscar

oscilación *f* (movimiento) oscillation; (fluctuación) fluctuation

oscilar [A1] *vi* **1** «*péndulo*» to swing, oscillate (tech); «*aguja*» to oscillate; «*torre/columna*» to sway **2** (fluctuar) «*cotización/valores*» to fluctuate; **sus edades oscilaban entre** ... their ages ranged between ...

oscuras: **a ~** (*loc adv*) in darkness

oscurecer [E3] *v impers* to get dark ■ **~** *vt* ‹*habitación/color*› to darken, make ... darker

■ **oscurecerse** *v pron* to get darker

oscuridad *f* (de la noche, de lugar) darkness, dark; **¡qué ~!** it's so dark in here!

oscuro -ra *adj* **1 (a)** ‹*calle/habitación*› dark; **a las seis ya está ~** at six it's already dark **(b) ▶097** ‹*color/ojos/pelo*› dark; **vestía de ~** she was wearing dark clothes **2 (a)** ‹*intenciones*› dark; ‹*asunto*› dubious **(b)** (poco claro) ‹*significado/asunto*› obscure **(c)** (poco conocido) ‹*escritor/orígenes*› obscure

oso, **osa** *m,f* bear; **~ de felpa** *or* **peluche** teddy bear; **~ hormiguero** anteater, ant bear (AmE); **~ panda** panda; **~ polar** polar bear

ostensible *adj* obvious, evident

ostentación *f* ostentation

ostentar [A1] *vt* **1** (frml) (tener) ‹*cargo/título*› to hold **2** (exhibir) ‹*alhajas/dinero*› to flaunt ■ **~** *vi* to show off

ostentoso -sa *adj* ostentatious

ostión *m* **(a)** (CS) scallop **(b)** (Méx) oyster

ostra *f* oyster; ***aburrirse como una ~*** (fam) to get bored stiff *o* to death (colloq)

otitis *f* inflammation of the ear, otitis (tech)

otoñal *adj* ‹*colores/paisaje*› autumnal, fall (*before n*) (AmE), autumn (*before n*) (BrE)

Otro, Otra

Algunas observaciones sobre el adjetivo

Cuando en español otro *se utiliza con nombres en singular, se traduce al inglés por* another:

eso es otra cosa	=	that is another matter
¿quieres otro café?	=	do you want another coffee?

Cuando se emplea con nombres en plural, se traduce por other *(invariable)*:

otras veces íbamos a la playa	=	other times we would go to the beach
¿lo tienen en otras tallas?	=	do you have it in other sizes?

El adjetivo plural otros, otras *se traduce por* another *cuando tiene el sentido de* más *y va seguido de numeral*:

nos hacen falta otras tres sillas	=	we need another three chairs
todavía tengo otras cinco libras	=	I still have another five pounds
agrégale otros dos huevos	=	add another two eggs

Cuando va precedido de artículo definido o adjetivo posesivo, se traduce por other *(invariable)*:

el otro día	=	the other day
mi otro hermano	=	my other brother
ponte esos otros zapatos	=	put those other shoes on

Cuando va precedido de un adjetivo indefinido como algún, alguno, *etc., la traducción suele ser* other:

algunas otras cosas	=	some other things
cualquier otro libro	=	any other book
¿algún otro problema?	=	any other problems?

Nótese la traducción plural del nombre singular en el ejemplo anterior

En todo caso se debe prestar especial atención a los siguientes ejemplos:

¿alguna otra cosa?	=	anything else?
cualquier otra persona/cosa	=	anyone else/ anything else

otoño *m* fall (AmE), autumn (BrE); **en ~** in the fall, in (the) autumn

otorgar [A3] *vt* (frml) ‹*premio*› to award; ‹*favor/préstamo*› to grant; ‹*poderes*› to bestow (frml), to give

otro, otra *adj* **1** (con carácter adicional) (*sing*) another; (*pl*) other; (con numerales) another; **¿puedo comer ~ trozo?** can I have another piece?; **prueba otra vez** try again; **una y otra vez** time and time again; *ver* TANTO[2] 2 **2** (diferente) (*sing*) another; (*pl*) other; **otra manera de hacerlo** another way of doing it; **¿no sabes ninguna otra canción?** don't you know any other songs?; **en ~ sitio** somewhere else; **en ~ momento** some other time **3** (estableciendo un contraste) other; **queda del ~ lado de la calle** it's on the other side of the street **4** (siguiente, contiguo) next; *ver tb* DÍA ■ *pron* **1** (con carácter adicional) (*sing*) another (one); **¿quieres ~?** would you like another (one)? **2** (diferente): **parece otra** she looks like a different person; **no voy a aceptar ningún ~** I won't accept any other; **lo cambié por ~** I changed it for another one; **¿no tiene ~s?** have you any other ones?; **~s piensan que no es así** others feel that this is not so **3** (estableciendo un contraste): **los ~s no están listos** (hablando — de personas) the others aren't ready; (— de cosas) the others *o* the other ones aren't ready **4** (siguiente, contiguo): **la semana que viene no, la otra** not next week, the week after; **uno detrás del ~** one after the other

ovación *f* (frml) ovation

ovalado, -da *adj* oval

óvalo *m* oval

ovario *m* ovary

oveja *f* (nombre genérico) sheep; (hembra) ewe; **un rebaño de ~s** a flock of sheep; **la ~ negra** the black sheep; **la ~ descarriada** (Bib) the lost sheep

overol *m* (AmL) (pantalón con peto) overalls (*pl*) (AmE), dungarees (*pl*) (BrE); (con mangas) coveralls (*pl*) (AmE), overalls (*pl*) (BrE)

ovillo *m* ball (*of yarn*); ***hacerse un ~*** to curl up (in a ball)

ovni, OVNI /'oβni/ *m* (= **objeto volador no identificado**) UFO

ovular [A1] *vi* to ovulate

óvulo *m* (Biol) ovule; (Farm) pessary

oxidado -da *adj* rusty

oxidarse [A1] *v pron* «*hierro*» to rust, go rusty, oxidize (tech); «*cobre*» to oxidize, form a patina

óxido *m* (herrumbre) rust; (Quím) oxide

oxígeno *m* oxygen

oye, etc *see* OÍR

oyente *mf* **(a)** (Educ) occasional student, auditor (AmE) **(b)** (Rad) listener

oyera, oyese, etc *see* OÍR

ozono *m* ozone; **la capa de ~** the ozone layer

Pp

P, p *f* (*read as* /pe/) *the letter* P, P

pabellón *m* **1 (a)** (en hospital, cuartel) block, building; (en feria, exposición) pavilion; (de palacio) pavilion; (en jardín) summerhouse **(b)** (de instrumento de viento) bell **2** (frml) (bandera) flag

paceño -ña *adj* of/from La Paz ■ *m,f* person from La Paz

pacer [E3] *vi* to graze

pacha *f* (AmC) baby's bottle

pachanga *f* (esp AmL fam) ⇒ PARRANDA

pachanguero -ra *adj* (esp AmL fam) ⇒ PARRANDERO

pachón -chona *adj* (Méx) ‹*suéter*› chunky; ‹*perro*› wooly*

pachucho -cha *adj* [ESTAR] (Esp fam) ‹*persona*› poorly (colloq); ‹*fruta*› overripe

pachuco -ca *m,f* (Méx) *young Mexican influenced by US culture*

paciencia *f* patience; **perder la ~** to lose patience; **ten ~** be patient, have a little patience

paciente *adj* (tolerante) patient ■ *mf* patient

pacificador -dora *adj* peace (*before n*) ■ *m,f* peacemaker

pacificar [A2] *vt* (Mil) to pacify (frml); (calmar) to pacify, appease; **~ los ánimos** to calm people down

pacífico -ca *adj* **(a)** ‹*manifestación/medios*› peaceful, pacific (frml) **(b)** ‹*carácter/persona*› peace-loving, peaceable; ‹*animal*› peaceful

Pacífico *m*: **el (océano) ~** the Pacific (Ocean)

pacifista *adj/mf* pacifist

paco -ca *m,f* (Andes fam) cop (colloq)

pacotilla *f* trash; **de ~** ‹*escritor/novela*› second-rate; ‹*reloj*› cheap, shoddy

pactar [A1] *vt* ‹*paz/tregua*› to negotiate, agree terms for; ‹*plazo/indemnización*› to agree on ■ **~** *vi* to make a pact, negotiate an agreement

pacto *m* pact, agreement; **cumplir/romper un ~** to abide by the terms of/to break an agreement

padecer [E3] *vt* ‹*enfermedad/hambre*› to suffer from; ‹*desgracias/injusticias/privaciones*› to suffer, undergo ■ **~** *vi* to suffer; **~ DE algo** to suffer FROM sth; **padece del corazón** he has heart trouble

padrastro *m* **1** (pariente) stepfather **2** (Anat) hangnail

padre *m* **1** (pariente) father; **mis ~s** my parents; **~ de familia** father, family man **2** (Relig) (sacerdote) father ■ *adj* **(a)** (fam) (grande) terrible (colloq) **(b)** [ESTAR] (Méx fam) ‹*coche/persona*› great (colloq), fantastic

padrenuestro *m* Lord's Prayer

padrino *m*

■ **Nota** En inglés *godfather* no se usa como apelativo. Nótese también que cuando el plural *padrinos* se refiere al padrino y a la madrina se traduce por *godparents*.

(a) (en bautizo) godfather; (de boda) *man who gives away the bride, usually her father* **(b)** (en duelo) second **(c)** (protector) sponsor, patron

padrón *m* **(a)** (Gob, Pol) register **~ electoral** (AmL) electoral roll *o* register **(b)** (Chi) (Auto) registration documents (*pl*)

paella *f* paella

pág. *f* (= **página**) p.; **760 págs.** 760 pp.

paga *f* **(a)** (acción de pagar) payment **(b)** (sueldo) pay; **~ de Navidad** *extra month's salary paid at Christmas*; **~ extra** *or* **extraordinaria** *extra month's salary gen paid twice a year*

paganismo *m* paganism

pagano -na *adj/m,f* pagan; (pey) heathen

pagar [A3] *vt* **(a)** (abonar) ‹*cuenta/alquiler*› to pay; ‹*deuda*› to pay (off), repay; ‹*comida/entradas/mercancías*› to pay for; **¿cuánto pagas de alquiler?** how much rent do you pay?; **le pagan los estudios** they are paying for his education; **no puedo ~ tanto** I can't afford (to pay) that much; **~ algo POR algo** to pay sth FOR sth **(b)** ‹*favor/desvelos*› to repay **(c)** (expiar) ‹*delito/atrevimiento*› to pay for; **~ algo CON algo** to pay FOR sth WITH sth; ***¡me las vas a ~!*** you'll pay for this! ■ **~** *vi* (Com, Fin) to pay; **~le a algn** to pay sb

pagaré *m* promissory note, IOU

página *f* page; **~s amarillas** yellow pages

pago *m* **(a)** (Com, Fin) payment; **~ adelantado** *or* **anticipado** payment in advance; **~ inicial** down payment; **~ al contado/a plazos/en especie** payment in cash/by installments/in kind **(b)** (recompensa) reward; **en ~ a algo** as a reward for sth

pagoda *f* pagoda

pai *m* (AmC, Méx) pie

país *m* **(a)** (unidad política) country; **~ de origen** (de persona) home country, native land; (de producto) country of origin; **los P~es Bajos** the Netherlands; **el P~ de Gales** Wales; **el P~ Vasco** the Basque Country **(b)** (ciudadanos) nation **(c)** (en ficción) land

paisaje *m* **(a)** (panorama) landscape, scenery **(b)** (Art) landscape

paisano -na *m,f* **1 (a)** (compatriota) (*m*) fellow countryman, compatriot; (*f*) fellow countrywoman, compatriot **(b)** (de la misma zona, ciudad): **es un ~ mío** he's from the same area/place as I am **2**

(Indum): **vestir de ~** «*soldado*» to wear civilian clothes *o* (colloq) civvies; «*policía*» to be in/to wear plain clothes; «*sacerdote*» to be in/to wear secular dress **3 (a)** (Per) *mountain-dweller of Indian origin* **(b)** (RPl) peasant

paja *f* **1 (a)** (Agr, Bot) straw; **sombrero de ~** straw hat; **techo de ~** thatched roof **(b)** (para beber) (drinking) straw **2 (a)** (fam) (en texto, discurso) padding, waffle (BrE colloq) **(b)** (Col fam): **hablar** *or* **echar ~** (decir mentiras) to tell lies; (charlar) to chat, gab (colloq) **3** (AmC) (grifo) faucet (AmE), tap (BrE)

pajar *m* (granero) barn; (desván) hayloft

pajarita *f* **(a)** *tb* **~ de papel** origami bird **(b)** (Esp) (Indum) bow tie

pajarito *m* (cría) baby bird; (pájaro) (fam) little bird, birdie (colloq)

pájaro *m* **1** (Zool) bird; **~ carpintero** woodpecker; ***más vale ~ en mano que cien*** *or* ***ciento volando*** a bird in the hand is worth two in the bush **2** (fam) (granuja) nasty piece of work (colloq)

pajarraco *m* (fam) **(a)** (Zool) big, ugly bird **(b)** (granuja) rogue

paje *m* **(a)** (Hist) page **(b)** (en boda) page (boy)

pajita, **pajilla** *f* (drinking) straw

pajizo -za *adj* straw-colored*

pajuerano -na *m,f* (RPl fam) country bumpkin, hick (AmE colloq)

Pakistán *m* Pakistan

pakistaní *adj/mf* Pakistani

pala *f* **1** (para cavar, de niño) spade; (para mover arena, carbón) shovel; (para recoger la basura) dustpan **2** (Coc) (para servir — pescado) slotted spatula (AmE), fish slice (BrE); (— tarta) cake slice **3** (de remo, hélice) blade; (de frontenis) racket; (de ping-pong) paddle, bat (BrE); (en piragüismo) paddle

palabra *f* **1** (vocablo) word; **una ~ de seis letras** a six-letter word; **no son más que ~s** it's all talk; **en pocas ~s, es un cobarde** in a word, he's a coward; **~ por ~** word for word; **yo no sabía ni una ~ del asunto** I didn't know a thing *o* anything about it; **no entendí (ni) una ~** I didn't understand a (single) word; **sin decir (una) ~** without a word; **~ compuesta** compound word; ***tener la última ~*** to have the final say **2** (promesa) word; **~ de honor** word of honor*; **una mujer de ~** a woman of her word; **cumplió con su ~** she kept her word; **nunca falta a su ~** he never breaks *o* goes back on his word **3 (a)** (habla) speech; **el don de la ~** the gift of speech; **un acuerdo de ~** a verbal agreement; **no me dirigió la ~** she didn't speak to me; ***dejar a algn con la ~ en la boca*** to cut sb off in mid-sentence **(b)** (frml) (en ceremonia, asamblea): **pedir la ~** to ask for permission to speak; **tener/tomar la ~** to have/to take the floor (frml)

palabrería *f*, **palabrerío** *m* talk; **no dice más que ~s** he's full of hot air (colloq)

palabrota *f* (fam) swearword; **decir ~s** to swear

palacio *m* **(a)** (residencia) palace; **el personal de ~** the Royal Household; **P~ Episcopal** Bishop's Palace; **P~ Real** Royal Palace **(b)** (edificio público) *large public building*; **P~ de Justicia** lawcourts (*pl*)

paladar *m* ▶ **123** palate

paladear [A1] *vt* to savor*

palanca *f* **1** (en general) lever; (para forzar, abrir algo) crowbar; **lo levanté haciendo ~** I lifted it using a lever; **~ de cambios** gearshift (AmE), gear lever *o* stick (BrE); **~ de mando** joystick **2** (fam) (influencia) influence; (persona influyente) contact

palangana *f* **(a)** (para fregar) bowl **(b)** (jofaina) washbowl (AmE), washbasin (BrE)

palanquear [A1] *vt* **1** (AmL) ⇒ APALANCAR **2** (AmL fam) (usando influencias): **le ~on un puesto** they pulled some strings to get him a job (colloq) ■ **~** *vi* (AmL fam) to pull strings (colloq)

palapa *f* (Méx) palm shelter

palco *m* box

palenque *m* **1** (RPl) (poste) tethering post **2** (Méx) **(a)** (fiesta popular) festival (*with cockfights, music, etc*) **(b)** (para gallos) cockpit

Palestina *f* Palestine

palestino -na *adj/m,f* Palestinian

paleta *f* **1 (a)** (de pintor) palette; (de cocina) spatula; (de ventilador) blade; (de albañil) trowel **(b)** (Dep) (de ping-pong) paddle, bat (BrE); (Jueg) (AmL) beach tennis **2** (fam) (diente) front tooth **3** (Coc) shoulder; (Anat, Zool) (Andes) shoulder blade **4 (a)** (Andes, Méx) (helado) Popsicle® (AmE), ice lolly (BrE) **(b)** (Méx) (dulce) lollipop

paletilla *f* **(a)** (Anat, Zool) shoulder blade **(b)** (Coc) shoulder

paleto -ta *m,f* (Esp fam & pey) country bumpkin, hick (AmE colloq & pej)

paliacate *m* (Méx) brightly colored* scarf

palidecer [E3] *vi* «*persona*» to turn *o* go pale

palidez *f* paleness

pálido -da *adj* ‹*persona/luz/color*› pale; **estás ~** you're very pale; **se puso ~** he went pale

paliducho -cha *adj* (fam) pale, peaky (colloq)

palillo *m* **(a)** (mondadientes) *tb* **~ de dientes** toothpick **(b)** (para comida oriental) chopstick; (de tambor) drumstick; (para tejer) (Chi) knitting needle **(c)** (fam) (persona flaca): **es un ~** he's as thin as a rake

palio *m* **(a)** (dosel) canopy **(b)** (prenda) pallium

paliza *f* **1 (a)** (zurra) hiding, beating; **su padre le dio una buena ~** his father gave him a good hiding; **los matones le pegaron una ~** the thugs beat him up **(b)** (fam) (derrota) thrashing (colloq) **2** (fam) **(a)** (esfuerzo): **fue una ~ de viaje** the journey was a real killer; ***darse la ~*** (fam) (trabajando, estudiando) to work one's butt off (AmE colloq), to slog one's guts out (BrE colloq) **(b)** (aburrimiento) drag (colloq)

palizada *f* (valla) palisade; (terreno) fenced enclosure

pallar *m* (Per) (Bot, Coc) butter bean

palma *f* **1** ▶ **123** (de la mano) palm; ***conocer algo como la ~ de la mano*** to know sth like the back of one's hand **2 (a)** (Bot) (planta) palm; (hoja) palm leaf; **~ de coco** (Col) coconut palm **(b)** (gloria, triunfo) distinction **3 palmas** *fpl*: **dar** *or* **batir ~s** (aplaudir) to clap (one's hands), applaud; **tocar las ~s** (marcando el ritmo) to clap in time

palmada *f* **(a)** (golpecito amistoso) pat; **le dio una ~ en la espalda** he gave him a pat on the back; **me dio unas palmaditas en la mejilla** he patted me on the cheek **(b)** (para llamar la atención) clap; **dio unas ~s para pedir silencio** he clapped his hands for silence **(c)** (AmL) (golpe, azote) smack, slap

palmado *adj* **(a)** (AmC fam) (sin dinero) broke (colloq) **(b)** (Arg fam) (cansado) worn out (colloq)

palmatoria *f* candlestick

palmera *f* **(a)** (Bot) palm tree **(b)** (Coc) palmier

palmito *m* (planta) European fan palm; (tallo) palm heart

palmo *m* span, handspan; **casi un ~** several inches; ***conocer algo ~ a ~*** to know sth like the back of one's hand

palo *m* **1 (a)** (trozo de madera) stick; (de valla, portería) post; (de herramienta) handle; (de tienda, carpa) tent pole; **~ de escoba** broomstick, broomhandle; ***de tal ~, tal astilla*** a chip off the old block, like father like son (*o* like mother like daughter *etc*) **(b)** (AmC, Col fam) (árbol) tree **(c)** (Dep) (de golf) (golf) club; (de hockey) hockey stick **(d)** (Náut) mast; **~ mayor** mainmast **2** (madera) wood; **cuchara de ~** wooden spoon **3** (fam) (golpe) blow (with a stick); **lo molieron a ~s** they beat him till he was black and blue **4** (en naipes) suit

paloma *f* (Zool) pigeon; (blanca) dove; (como símbolo) dove; **~ de la paz** dove of peace; **~ mensajera** carrier pigeon; **~ torcaz** *or* **torcaza** ringdove, wood pigeon (BrE)

palomar *m* dovecot, pigeon loft

palomilla *f* **1** (mariposa nocturna) moth; (crisálida) chrysalis **2** (tuerca) wing nut, butterfly nut; (soporte) wall bracket **3** (Méx fam) (pandilla, grupo) gang ■ *mf* (Andes fam) (muchacho — callejero) street kid (colloq); (— travieso) little monkey (colloq), little devil (colloq)

palomita *f* **1** (Méx fam) (marca) check (AmE), tick (BrE) **2 palomitas** *fpl*: *tb* **~s de maíz** popcorn

palomo *m* (ave) cock pigeon

palote *m* **1** (en caligrafía) line, stroke **2** (RPl) (de amasar) rolling pin

palpable *adj* (claro, evidente) palpable (frml), obvious; (al tacto) palpable, tangible

palpar [A1] *vt* (Med) to palpate; (tantear) to touch, feel
■ **palparse** *v pron* ‹*bolsillo*› to feel

palpitación *f* palpitation

palpitar [A1] *vi* **(a)** «*corazón*» to beat **(b)** «*vena/sien*» to throb

pálpito *m* (AmS fam) feeling (colloq); **me dio el** *or* **tuve un ~** I had a feeling *o* a hunch

palta *f* (Bol, CS, Per) (Bot, Coc) avocado (pear)

palto *m* (Bol, CS, Per) avocado tree

paludismo *m* malaria

palurdo -da *m,f* (fam) yokel (pej & hum), hick (AmE colloq & pej)

pamela *f* picture hat

pampa *f* pampa, pampas (*pl*); **la ~ argentina** the Argentinian Pampas; **la ~ salitrera** *region of nitrate deposits in northern Chile*

pampeano -na *adj* pampas (*before n*)

pamplinas *fpl* (fam) **(a)** (zalamerías) sweet talk (colloq); **no me vengas con ~** don't try to sweet-talk me (colloq) **(b)** (tonterías) nonsense

pan *m* (Coc) bread; (pieza) loaf; (panecillo) roll; **¿quieres ~?** would you like some bread?; **una rebanada de ~** a slice of bread; **~ blanco/de centeno/integral** white/rye/whole wheat bread; **~ de molde** *bread/loaf baked gen in a rectangular tin*, tin *o* pan loaf (BrE); **~ de Pascua** (Chi) panettone; **~ dulce** (con pasas) (RPl) panettone; (bollo) (AmC, Méx) bun, pastry; **~ rallado** breadcrumbs (*pl*); **~ tostado** toast; **un ~ tostado** (Chi, Méx) a piece of toast; ***ganarse el ~*** to earn one's daily bread; ***ser ~ comido*** (fam) to be a piece of cake (colloq)

pana[1] *f* **1** (tela) corduroy; **panatalones de ~** corduroy trousers **2** (Chi) (avería) breakdown

pana[2] *mf* (Ven fam) pal (colloq), buddy (AmE colloq), mate (BrE colloq)

panacea *f* panacea

panadería *f* (tienda) bakery, baker's (shop); (fábrica) bakery

panadero -ra *m,f* baker

panal *m* honeycomb

panamá *m* panama hat

Panamá *m* **(a)** (país) Panama; **el Canal de ~** the Panama Canal **(b)** (capital) *tb* **ciudad de ~** Panama (City)

panameño -ña *adj/m,f* Panamanian

Panamericana *f*: **la ~** the Pan-American Highway

pancarta *f* banner, placard

panceta *f* **(a)** (Esp) (sin curar) belly pork **(b)** (RPl) (curada) streaky bacon

pancho[1] **-cha** *adj* (tranquilo) calm; ***quedarse tan ~*** (fam): **se lo dije y se quedó tan ~** he didn't bat an eyelash *o* (BrE) eyelid when I told him

pancho[2] *m* (RPl) hot dog

pancito *m* (AmL) (bread) roll

páncreas *m* (*pl* **~**) pancreas

panda *mf* panda ■ *f* (Esp fam) gang

pandemónium *m* pandemonium

pandereta *f* (Mús) tambourine

pandero *m* **1** (Mús) tambourine **2** (Per) (Fin) *co-operative savings scheme*

pandilla *f* (fam) gang

panecillo *m* (Esp) bread roll

panecito *m* (AmL) bread roll

panel *m* **1 (a)** (de puerta, pared) panel **(b)** (tablero — de anuncios) noticeboard; (— en exposición) exhibition panel; (— en estación) arrivals/departures board **(c)** (Chi) (de auto) dashboard **(d) ~ de instrumentos** instrument panel *o* console **2** (de personas) panel

panela *f* (Col, Ven) *brown sugarloaf*

panera *f* (para servir pan) bread basket; (para guardar pan) bread box (AmE), bread bin (BrE)

pánfilo -la *adj* (fam) dimwitted (colloq) ■ *m,f* (fam) dimwit (colloq)

panfleto *m* pamphlet

pánico *m* panic; **tenerle ~ a algo** to be terrified of sth; ***sembrar el ~*** to spread panic

panocha *f* **1** (de maíz, trigo) ear **2** (Méx) (melaza) *candy made from molasses*

panorama *m* **(a)** (vista, paisaje) view, panorama **(b)** (perspectiva) outlook, prospect

panorámica *f* (Cin, TV) pan; (perspectiva) outlook

panorámico -ca *adj* panoramic

panque *m* (Méx) sponge cake

panqueque *m* (AmL) pancake, crepe

pantaletas *fpl* (AmC, Ven) panties (*pl*), knickers (*pl*) (BrE)

pantalla *f* **1** (Cin, Inf, TV) screen; **~ de radar** radar screen; **la ~ chica** (AmL) the small screen **2 (a)** (de lámpara) shade **(b)** (de chimenea) fireguard **(c)** (cobertura) front

pantalones *mpl*, **pantalón** *m* pants (*pl*) (AmE), trousers (*pl*) (BrE); **unos ~** a pair of pants *o* trousers; **~ cortos** shorts (*pl*); **~ de peto** overalls (*pl*) (AmE), dungarees (*pl*) (BrE); **~ tejanos** *or* **vaqueros** jeans (*pl*)

pantano *m* **1** (natural) marsh, swamp; (artificial) reservoir **2** (dificultad) mess, predicament

pantanoso -sa *adj* **1** ‹*terreno*› marshy, swampy **2** ‹*asunto/negocio*› difficult, tricky (colloq)

panteón *m* **(a)** (monumento) pantheon, mausoleum; **~ de familia** family vault **(b)** (AmL) (cementerio) cemetery

pantera *f* panther

panti *m* (*pl* **-tis**), (Méx) **pantimedia** *f* ⇒ PANTY

pantomima *f* pantomime

pantorrilla *f* ▶ 123 calf

pants *mpl* (Méx) tracksuit, sweat suit (AmE)

pantufla *f* slipper

panty *m* (*pl* **-tys**) panty hose (*pl*) (AmE), tights (*pl*) (BrE)

panza *f* **(a)** (fam) (barriga) belly, paunch (colloq); **tener ~** to have a belly *o* paunch **(b)** (de cántaro) belly **(c)** (de rumiante) rumen

panzada *f* (fam) **1** (en el agua) belly flop (colloq); **se dio una ~** he did a belly flop **2** (comilona): **darse una ~ de algo** to pig out on sth (colloq)

panzón -zona *adj* (fam) potbellied (colloq)

pañal *m* diaper (AmE), nappy (BrE)

pañito *m* doily

paño *m* **(a)** (Tex) woollen cloth; **abrigo de ~** wool coat **(b)** (para limpiar) cloth; **~ de cocina** (para limpiar) dishcloth; (para secar) teatowel; **~ higiénico** sanitary napkin (AmE), sanitary towel (BrE) **(c)** (de adorno) antimacassar

pañolenci *m* (CS) baize, felt

pañoleta *f* (de mujer) shawl; (de torero) neckerchief

pañuelo *m* (para la nariz) handkerchief; (para la cabeza) headscarf, scarf; (para el cuello) scarf, neckerchief

papa¹ *m* pope; **el P~** the Pope

papa² *f* (esp AmL) (Bot) potato; **~ caliente** hot potato; **~ dulce** (AmL) sweet potato; **~s fritas** (esp AmL); (de paquete) potato chips (AmE) *o* (BrE) crisps (*pl*); (de cocina) French fries (*pl*) (AmE), chips (*pl*) (BrE) ***ni ~*** (fam) not a thing; **no sé ni ~ de coches** I haven't a clue about cars (colloq)

papá *m* (*pl* **-pás**) (fam) daddy (colloq), pop (AmE colloq); **mis ~s** (AmL) my parents, my mom and dad (AmE), my mum and dad (BrE colloq); **P~ Noel** Santa Claus, Father Christmas

papada *f* (de persona) double chin, jowl

papagayo *m* **1** (ave) parrot; ***recitar algo como un ~*** to recite sth parrot-fashion **2** (Ven) (juguete) kite

papalote *m* (AmC, Méx) (juguete) kite; (ala delta) hang glider

Papanicolau *m* (AmL) smear test

papaya *f* papaya, pawpaw

papel *m* **1** (material) paper; **un ~** a piece of paper; **toalla de ~** paper towel; **~ carbón** carbon paper; **~ cuadriculado/rayado** squared/lined paper; **~ de aluminio** tinfoil, aluminum* foil; **~ de embalar/de envolver/de regalo** wrapping paper; **~ higiénico** *or* **de water** toilet paper; **~ picado** (RPl) confetti **2** (documento) document, paper; **no tenía los ~es en regla** her papers were not in order **3 (a)** (Cin, Teatr) role, part; **hace el ~ de monja** she plays the part of a nun **(b)** (actuación) performance; **hizo un lamentable ~ en el congreso** his performance at the conference was abysmal **(c)** (función) role; **juega un ~ importante en** ... it plays an important role in ...

papeleo *m* (fam) red tape, paperwork

papelera *f* **(a)** (de oficina) wastepaper basket; (en la calle) litter basket (AmE), litter bin (BrE) **(b)** (fábrica) paper mill

papelería *f* (tienda) stationery store (AmE), stationer's (BrE); **artículos de ~** stationery

papelero -ra *adj* paper (*before n*) ■ *m,f* **1** (fabricante) paper manufacturer; (vendedor) stationer **2 papelero** *m* (CS) ⇒ PAPELERA (a)

papeleta *f* **(a)** (de votación) ballot (paper); **~ en blanco** blank ballot (paper) **(b)** (de rifa) raffle ticket **(c)** (de calificación) grade slip **(d)** (de empeño) pawn ticket

papelillo *m* cigarette paper

papelitos *mpl* (Ur) confetti

papelón *m* (fam) (cosa vergonzosa): **hacer un ~** to make a fool of oneself; **¡qué ~!** how embarrassing!

paperas *fpl* mumps

papi *m* (fam) ⇒ PAPÁ

papilla *f* (para bebés) baby food, formula (AmE); (para enfermos) puree, pap; *estar hecho ~* ‹*persona*› to be absolutely shattered (colloq)

papiro *m* papyrus

paprika *f* paprika

paquete¹ -ta *adj* (RPl fam) smart, chic

paquete² *m* **1 (a)** (bulto envuelto) package, parcel; **hacer un ~** to wrap up a parcel; **~ bomba** parcel bomb; **~ postal** parcel (*sent by mail*) **(b)** (de galletas, cigarrillos) pack (AmE), packet (BrE); **un ~ de papas fritas** (AmL) a bag of chips (AmE), a packet of crisps (BrE) **2** (conjunto) package; (Inf) package **3** (Méx fam) (problema) headache (colloq)

Paquistán *m* Pakistan

paquistaní *adj/mf* Pakistani

par *adj* ‹*número*› even; **jugarse algo a ~es o nones** *to decide sth by guessing whether the number* *of objects held is odd or even* ■ *m* **1 (a)** (de guantes, zapatos) pair; **un ~ de preguntas/de veces** a couple of questions/of times; ***a ~es*** two at a time **(b)** (comparación) equal; **sin ~** (liter) incomparable, matchless (liter) **2** (Arquit) rafter; **(*abierto*) *de ~ en ~*** wide open **3** (en golf) par; **sobre/bajo ~** over/under par ■ *f* par; **a la ~** (Fin) at par (value); **sabroso a la ~ que sano** both tasty and healthy; **baila a la ~ que canta** he dances and sings at the same time

para *prep* **I 1** (destino, finalidad, intención) for; **una carta para él** a letter for him; **¿~ qué sirve esto?** what's this (used) for?; **champú ~ bebés** baby shampoo; **~ eso no voy** I might as well not go; **~** + INF: **ahorra ~ comprarse un coche** he's saving up to buy a car; **tomé un taxi ~ no llegar tarde** I took a taxi so I wouldn't be late; **está listo ~ pintar** it's ready to be painted *o* for painting; **~ aprobar** (in order) to pass; **entró en puntillas para no despertarla** he went in on tiptoe so as not to wake her; **lo dice ~ que yo me preocupe** he (only) says it to worry me; **cierra ~ que no nos oigan** close the door so (that) they don't hear us **2 (a)** (suficiencia) for; **no hay ~ todos** there isn't enough for everybody; **no es ~ tanto** it's not that bad; **soy lo bastante viejo (como) ~ recordarlo** I'm old enough to remember it **(b)** (en comparaciones, contrastes): **hace demasiado frío ~ salir** it's too cold to go out; **son altos ~ su edad** they're tall for their age; **~ lo que come, no está gordo** considering how much he eats, he's not fat; **¿quién es él ~ hablarte así?** who does he think he is, speaking to you like that ?; **es mucho ~ que lo haga sola** it's too much for you to do it on your own

II 1 (dirección): **salieron ~ el aeropuerto** they left for the airport; **empuja ~ arriba** push up *o* upward(s); **¿vas ~ el centro?** are you going to *o* toward(s) the center? **2** (tiempo) **(a)** (señalando una fecha, un plazo): **estará listo ~ el día 15** it'll be ready by *o* for the 15th; **deberes ~ el lunes** homework for Monday; **faltan cinco minutos ~ que termine** there are five minutes to go before the end; **me lo prometió ~ después de Pascua** he promised me it for after Easter; **¿cuánto te falta ~ terminar?** how much have you got left to do?; **~ entonces estaré en Madrid** I'll be in Madrid (by) then; **tengo hora ~ mañana** I have an appointment (for) tomorrow **(b)** (AmL exc RPl) (al decir la hora) to; **son cinco ~ las diez** it's five to ten **(c)** (duración): **~ siempre** forever; **tengo ~ rato** (fam) I'm going to be a while (yet)

parábola *f* **(a)** (Relig) parable **(b)** (Mat) parabola

parabrisas *m* (*pl* ~) windshield (AmE), windscreen (BrE)

paracaídas *m* (*pl* ~) (Aviac) parachute; **tirarse** *or* **lanzarse en ~** to parachute

paracaidismo *m* parachuting

paracaidista *adj* parachute (*before n*) ■ *mf* **(a)** (Mil) paratrooper; (Dep) parachutist **(b)** (AmL fam) (en fiesta) gatecrasher; **llegar de ~** to come/go uninvited (*to a party*)

parachoques *m* (*pl* ~) (Auto) bumper

parada *f* **1** (Transp) **(a)** (acción) stop **(b)** (lugar) *tb* **~ de autobús** (*or* **de ómnibus** *etc*) bus stop; **me bajo en la próxima ~** I'm getting off at the next stop; **~ de taxi** taxi stand, taxi rank (BrE) **2** (Dep) (en fútbol) save, stop **3** (desfile) parade **4** (Per) (mercado) street market

paradero *m* **(a)** (frml) (de persona) whereabouts (*pl*) **(b)** (AmL exc RPl) ⇒ PARADA 1(b)

parado -da *adj* **1** (detenido): **un coche ~ en medio de la calle** a car sitting *o* stopped in the middle of the street; **no te quedes ahí ~, ven a ayudarme** don't just stand there, come and help me **2** (AmL) **(a)** (de pie): **estar ~** to stand, be standing **(b)** (erguido): **tengo el pelo todo ~** my hair's standing on end; *ver tb* ⇒ PARAR *vt* 2(b) **3** (Esp) (desempleado) unemployed **4 salir (de algo) bien/mal parado** (de pelea, discusión) to come off well/badly (in sth); **es el que mejor ~ ha salido** he's the one who's come off best ■ *m,f* (Esp) unemployed person; **los ~s** the unemployed

paradoja *f* paradox

paradójico -ca *adj* paradoxical

parador *m* **(a)** (mesón) roadside bar/hotel **(b)** (en Esp) parador, state-owned hotel

parafina *f* **(a)** (sólida) paraffin (wax); **~ líquida** mineral oil (AmE), liquid paraffin (BrE) **(b)** (AmL) (combustible) kerosene

paragolpes *m* (*pl* ~) (RPl) bumper

paraguas *m* (*pl* ~) umbrella

Paraguay *m*: *tb* **el ~** Paraguay

paraguayo -ya *adj/m,f* Paraguayan

paragüero *m* umbrella stand

paraíso *m* (Relig) **el ~** paradise, heaven; **~ fiscal** tax haven

paraje *m* spot, place

paralela *f* **1** (línea) parallel (line) **2 paralelas** *fpl* (Dep) parallel bars (*pl*)

paralelismo *m* parallelism, parallel

paralelo[1] -la *adj* **(a)** ‹*líneas/planos*› parallel; **~ A algo** parallel TO sth **(b)** (*como adv*) ‹*marchar/crecer*› parallel

paralelo[2] *m* parallel

paralelogramo *m* parallelogram

parálisis *f* paralysis; **~ cerebral** cerebral palsy; **~ infantil** poliomyelitis, infantile paralysis

paralítico -ca *adj* paralytic (*before n*); **se quedó ~** he was paralyzed ■ *m,f* paralytic

paralizar [A4] *vt* **(a)** (Med) to paralyze; **se quedó paralizada de un lado** she was paralyzed down one side **(b)** ‹*industria/economía*› to paralyze; ‹*circulación/producción*› to bring ... to a halt *o* standstill

paramilitar *adj* paramilitary

páramo *m* high plateau, bleak upland *o* moor

paramuno -na *m,f* (Col) *person from the high plateau*

paraninfo *m* main hall *o* auditorium

paranoia *f* paranoia

paranoico -ca *adj/m,f* paranoid

paranormal *adj* paranormal

parapetarse [A1] *v pron* to take cover

parapeto *m* (Arquit) parapet; (barricada) barricade

paraplejía, **paraplejia** *f* paraplegia

parapléjico -ca *adj/m,f* paraplegic

parapsicología *f* parapsychology

parar [A1] *vi* **1** (detenerse) to stop; **paró en seco** she stopped dead; ***ir/venir a*** **~** to end up; **fue a ~ a la cárcel** he ended up in prison; **¿a dónde habrá ido a ~ aquella foto?** what can have happened to that photo?; **¡a dónde iremos a ~!** I don't know what the world's coming to **2** (cesar) to stop; **para un momento** hang on a minute; **ha estado lloviendo sin ~** it hasn't stopped raining; **no para quieto ni un momento** he can't keep still for a minute; **no para en casa** she's never at home; **~** DE + INF to stop -ING; **paró de llover** it stopped raining **3** (AmL) «*obreros/empleados*» to go on strike ■ **~** *vt* **1 (a)** ‹*coche/tráfico/persona*› to stop; ‹*motor/máquina*› to stop, switch off **(b)** ‹*hemorragia*› to stanch (AmE), to staunch (BrE) **(c)** ‹*balón/tiro*› to save, stop; ‹*golpe*› to block, ward off **2** (AmL) **(a)** (poner de pie) to stand **(b)** (poner vertical) ‹*vaso/libro*› to stand ... up; **el perro paró las orejas** the dog pricked up its ears

■ **pararse** *v pron* **1** (detenerse) **(a)** «*persona*» to stop **(b)** «*reloj/máquina*» to stop; «*coche/motor*» to stall; **se me paró el reloj** my watch stopped **2 (a)** (AmL) (ponerse de pie) to stand up; **párate derecho** stand up straight; **se paró en una silla** she stood on a chair; **¿te puedes ~ de cabeza/de manos?** can you do headstands/handstands? **(b)** (AmL) «*pelo*» (hacia arriba) to stick up; (en los lados) to stick out **(c)** (Méx, Ven) (levantarse de la cama) to get up

pararrayos *m* (*pl* **~**) (en edificio) lightning rod (AmE), lightning conductor (BrE)

parásito *m* parasite

parasol *m* (sombrilla) parasol, sunshade

parcela *f* plot (of land), lot (AmE)

parchar [A1] *vt* (AmL) (arreglar) to repair; (con parche) to patch (up)

parche *m* patch

parchís *m* (Esp, Méx) Parcheesi® (AmE), ludo (BrE)

parcial *adj* **1** ‹*solución/victoria*› partial **2** (no equitativo) biased, partial ■ *m* (examen) assessment examination (*taken during the year and counting towards the final grade*)

parcialidad *f* **(a)** (cualidad) partiality, bias **(b)** (seguidores) supporters (*pl*)

parco -ca *adj* **(a)** (lacónico) laconic **(b)** (sobrio, moderado) frugal; **ser ~ en palabras** to be sparing with words

pardo -da *adj* ‹*color*› dun, brownish-gray*

parecer¹ [E3] *vi* **1** (aparentar ser): **parece fácil** it looks easy; **no pareces tú en esta foto** this picture doesn't look like you (at all); **parecía de cuero** it looked like leather; **parece ser muy inteligente** she seems to be very clever **2** (expresando opinión) (+ *me/te/le etc*): **todo le parece mal** he's never happy with anything; **¿qué te parecieron?** what did you think of them?; **vamos a la playa ¿te parece?** what do you think, shall we go to the beach?; **si te parece bien** if that's alright with you; **me parece que sí** I think so; **¿a ti qué te parece?** what do you think?; **me parece importante** I think it's important; **me pareció que no era necesario** I didn't think it necessary; **hazlo como mejor te parezca** do it however *o* as you think best; **me parece mal que vaya sola** I don't think it's right that she should go on her own **3** (dar la impresión) (*en 3ª pers*): **así parece** *or* **parece que sí** it looks like it; **aunque no lo parezca, está limpio** it might not look like it, but it's clean; **parece que va a llover** it looks like (it's going to) rain; **parece que fue ayer** it seems like only yesterday; **parece mentira que tenga 20 años** it's hard to believe *o* I can't believe that he's 20; **parece que fuera más joven** you'd think she was much younger

■ **parecerse** *v pron* **(a)** (asemejarse) **~se** A **algn/algo** (en lo físico) to look *o* to be like sb/sth; (en el carácter) to be like sb/sth **(b)** (*recípr*) to be alike; **no se parecen en nada** they're not/they don't look in the least bit alike; **se parecen mucho** they are very similar

parecer² *m* (opinión) opinion; **a mi ~** in my opinion; **son del mismo ~** they're of the same opinion

parecido¹ -da *adj* [SER] ‹*personas*› alike; ‹*cosas*› similar; **son muy parecidas de cara** they have very similar features; **una especie de capa o algo ~** a cape or something like that; **~** A **algo** similar TO sth; **eres muy ~ a tu padre** you're a lot like your father

parecido² *m* resemblance, similarity; **tiene cierto ~ con su hermano** he bears some *o* a certain resemblance to his brother; **hay un ~ en sus estilos** there is a resemblance *o* similarity in their styles

pared *f* **1 (a)** (Arquit, Const) wall; **viven ~ por medio** they live next door; ***las ~es oyen*** walls have ears **(b)** (de recipiente) side **(c)** (de montaña) face **2** (en fútbol) one-two

paredón *m* **(a)** (de roca) rock face, wall of rock **(b)** (pared gruesa) thick wall **(c)** (de fusilamiento) wall

pareja *f* **1 (a)** (equipo, conjunto) pair; **salieron por ~s** they came out in pairs; **formar ~s** to get into pairs **(b)** (en una relación) couple; **hacen buena ~** they make a good couple **(c)** (en naipes) pair **2 (a)** (compañero) partner **(b)** (de guante, zapato) pair; **no encuentro la ~ de este guante** I can't find the pair for this glove; **un calcentin sin ~** an odd sock

parejo -ja *adj* **1 (a)** (esp AmL) (sin desniveles) even; **los dos ciclistas van muy ~s** the two cyclists are neck and neck; **el nivel en la clase es muy ~** the class are all at the same level **(b)** (afín, semejante) similar **(c)** (CS, Méx) (equitativo) ‹*trato*› equal; ‹*ley*› fair, impartial **2** (Méx fam) **al ~** (a la par): **trabajan al ~** they all do the same amount of work; **al ~ de los mejores del mundo** on a par with the world's best

parentela *f* (fam) clan (colloq), tribe (colloq)

parentesco *m* relationship; **tener ~ con algn** to be related to sb

paréntesis *m* (*pl* **~**) **(a)** (signo) parenthesis, bracket (BrE); **cerrar el ~** close parentheses *o* brackets; ***entre*** **~** (literal) in parentheses, in brackets; (a propósito) by the way **(b)** (digresión) digression, parenthesis

parezca, parezcas, etc *see* PARECER[1]

paria *mf* pariah

pariente *mf*, **pariente -ta** *m,f* (familiar) relative, relation; **~ lejano** distant relative *o* relation; **~ político** in-law

parir [I1] *vi* «*mujer*» to give birth; «*vaca*» to calve; «*yegua/burra*» to foal; «*oveja*» to lamb ■ **~** *vt* **(a)** «*mujer*» to give birth to, have **(b)** «*mamíferos*» to have, bear (frml)

París *m* Paris

parisiense *adj/mf* Parisian

parisino -na *adj/m,f* Parisian

parking /'parkin/ *m* (esp Esp) parking lot (AmE), car park (BrE)

parlamentar [A1] *vi* **~ (CON algn)** to talk (TO sb)

parlamentario -ria *m,f* member of parliament, parliamentarian

parlamento *m* (asamblea) parliament; (Lit, Teatr) speech

parlanchín -china *adj* (fam) chatty (colloq) ■ *m, f* (fam) chatterbox (colloq)

parlante *m* (AmL) (en lugar público) loudspeaker; (de equipo de música) speaker

paro *m* **1** (esp AmL) (huelga) strike; **hacer un ~ de 24 horas** to go on a 24-hour strike; **están en** *or* **de ~** (AmL) they're on strike; **~ cívico** (Col) community protest; **~ general** (esp AmL) general strike **2** (Esp) **(a)** (desempleo) unemployment; **está en ~** he's unemployed **(b)** (subsidio) unemployment benefit; **cobrar el ~** to claim unemployment benefit **3 ~ cardíaco** *or* **cardiaco** cardiac arrest

parodia *f* parody, send-up (colloq)

parpadear [A1] *vi* **(a)** «*persona/ojo*» to blink **(b)** «*luz*» to flicker; «*estrellas*» to twinkle

párpado *m* ▶ **123** eyelid

parque *m* **1** (terreno) park; **~ de atracciones** *or* (Col, RPl) **de diversiones** *or* (Chi) **de entretenciones** amusement park, funfair; **~ de bomberos** (Esp) fire station; **~ natural** nature reserve; **~ zoológico** zoo **2** (para niños) playpen

parqué *m* (suelo) parquet (flooring)

parqueadero *m* (Col) parking lot (AmE), car park (BrE)

parquear [A1] *vt* (Col) to park
■ **parquearse** *v pron* (Col) to park

parquet *m* (*pl* **-quets**) ⇒ PARQUÉ

parquímetro *m* parking meter

parra *f* vine

párrafo *m* paragraph; **~ aparte** new paragraph

parral *m* (en un jardín) vine arbor*; (viñedo) vineyard

parranda *f* (fam): **estar/irse de ~** to be/go out on the town *o* out partying (colloq)

parrilla *f* **1 (a)** (Coc) grill, broiler (AmE); **pescado a la ~** grilled *o* (AmE) broiled fish **(b)** (restaurante) grillroom, grill bar **(c)** (de la chimenea) grate **2** (AmL) (para el equipaje) luggage rack, roof rack

parrillada *f* **(a)** (comida) grill, barbecue **(b)** (RPl) (restaurante) grillroom, grill bar

párroco *m* parish priest

parroquia *f* (iglesia) parish church; (área) parish; (feligreses) parishioners (*pl*)

parroquiano -na *m,f* **(a)** (Relig) parishioner **(b)** (cliente) regular customer *o* (frml) patron

parsimonia *f* **(a)** (calma) calm **(b)** (frugalidad) parsimony

parsimonioso -sa *adj* **(a)** (tranquilo) phlegmatic, unhurried **(b)** (frugal) parsimonious

parte *m* **1** (informe, comunicación) report; **dar ~ de un incidente** «*particular*» to report an incident; «*autoridad*» to file a report about an incident; **dar ~ de enfermo** to call in sick; **~ meteorológico** weather report **2** (Andes) (multa) ticket (colloq), fine ■ *f* **1 (a)** (porción, fracción) part; **tres ~s iguales** three equal parts; **pasa gran ~ del tiempo al teléfono** she spends most of her *o* the time on the phone; **la mayor ~ de los participantes** the majority of *o* most of the participants **(b)** (en una distribución) share; **su ~ de la herencia** his share of the inheritance **(c)** (de lugar) part; **¿de qué ~ de México eres?** what part of Mexico are you from?; **en la ~ de atrás** at the back **2** (*en locs*) **en parte** partly; **en gran ~** to a large extent, largely; **en su mayor ~** for the most part; **de un tiempo a esta ~** for some time now; **de parte de algn** on behalf of sb; **llamo de ~ de María** I'm ringing on behalf of María; **dale recuerdos de mi ~** give him my regards; **vengo de ~ del señor Díaz** Mr Díaz sent me; **¿de ~ de quién?** (por teléfono) who's calling?, who shall I say is calling? (frml); **formar parte de algo** «*pieza/sección*» to be part of sth; «*persona/país*» to belong to sth; **entrar a formar ~ de algo** to join sth; **por mi/tu/su parte** as far as I'm/you're/he's concerned; **por partes**: **revisémoslo por ~s** let's go over it section by section; **vayamos por ~s** let's take it step by step; **por otra parte** (además) anyway, in any case; (por otro lado) however, on the other hand; **por una parte ..., por la otra** ... on the one hand ..., on the other ... **3** (participación) part; **tomar ~** to take part **4** (lugar): **vámonos a otra ~** let's go somewhere else *o* (AmE) someplace else; **esto no nos lleva a ninguna ~** this isn't getting *o* leading us anywhere; **¿adónde vas? — a ninguna ~** where are you going? — nowhere; **en cualquier ~** anywhere; **a/en/por todas ~s** everywhere; **en alguna ~** somewhere **5** (en negociación, contrato, juicio) party **6** (Teatr) part, role **7** (Méx) (repuesto) part, spare (part)

participación *f* **1** (intervención) participation; **la ~ del público** audience participation; **~ EN algo** ‹*en debate/clase/huelga*›) participation IN sth; ‹*en robo/fraude*› involvement IN sth; ‹*en obra/película*› role IN sth **2 (a)** (en ganancias) share **(b)** (en empresa) stockholding, interest **(c)** (de lotería) share (*in a lottery ticket*)

participante *adj* participating (*before n*) ■ *mf* (en debate) participant; (en concurso) contestant; (en carrera) competitor

participar [A1] *vi* **(a)** (tomar parte) ~ (EN **algo**) to take part (IN sth), participate (IN sth) (frml) **(b)** ~ EN **algo** ‹*en ganancias*› to have a share IN sth; ‹*en empresas*› to have a stockholding IN sth

participio *m* participle; ~ **pasado** *or* **pasivo** past participle

partícula *f* particle

particular *adj* **(a)** (privado) ‹*clases/profesor*› private; ‹*teléfono*› home (*before n*) **(b)** (específico) ‹*caso/aspecto*› particular; **en ~** in particular, particularly **(c)** (especial) ‹*estilo/gusto*› individual, personal; **es un tipo muy ~** (fam) he's a very peculiar guy; **no tiene nada de ~ que vaya** there's nothing unusual *o* strange in her going; **la casa no tiene nada de ~** there's nothing special about the house

partida *f* **1** (Jueg) game; **una ~ de ajedrez/cartas** a game of chess/cards; **echar una ~** to have a game **2** (en registro, contabilidad) entry; (en presupuesto) item **3** (certificado) certificate; **~ de defunción/nacimiento** death/birth certificate **4** (frml) (salida) departure, leaving

partidario -ria *adj* (a favor) ~ DE **algo/hacer algo** in favor* OF sth/doing sth ■ *m,f* supporter; **los ~s de Gaztelu** Gaztelu's supporters; **los ~s de la violencia** those who favor *o* advocate the use of violence

partido[1] -da *adj* **1** ‹*labios*› chapped; ‹*barbilla*› cleft **2** (Mat): **siete ~ por diez** seven over ten; **nueve ~ por tres da** ... nine divided by three gives ...

partido[2] *m* **1 (a)** (de fútbol) game, match (BrE); (de tenis) match; **echar un ~** to have a game; **un ~ de béisbol** a baseball game; **~ amistoso** friendly game *o* match; **~ de desempate** deciding game, decider **(b)** (AmL) (partida) game; **un ~ de ajedrez** a game of chess **2** (Pol) party; **~ de la oposición** opposition party; ***tomar ~*** to take sides **3** (provecho): **sacar ~ de algo** to benefit from sth; **sacarle ~ a algo** to make the most of sth **4** (para casarse): **un buen ~** a good catch

partir [I1] *vt* **(a)** (con cuchillo) ‹*tarta/melón*› to cut; **lo partió por la mitad** he cut it in half **(b)** (romper) ‹*piedra/coco*› to break, smash; ‹*nuez/avellana*› to crack; ‹*rama/palo*› to break **(c)** (con golpe) ‹*labio*› to split (open); ‹*cabeza*› to split open **(d)** «*frío*» ‹*labios*› to chap ■ ~ *vi* **1 (a)** (frml) (marcharse) to leave, depart (frml) **(b)** «*auto*» (Chi) to start **2 (a)** ~ DE **algo** ‹*de una premisa/un supuesto*› to start FROM sth **(b) a partir de** from; **a ~ de ahora/ese momento** from now on/that moment on; **a ~ de hoy** (as *o* starting) from today

■ **partirse** *v pron* **(a)** «*mármol/roca*» to split, smash **(b)** (*refl*) ‹*labio*› to split; ‹*diente*› to break, chip

partitura *f* (de obra orquestada) score

parto *m* (Med) labor*; **estar de ~** to be in labor; **fue un ~ difícil** it was a difficult birth; **provocar el ~** to induce labor; **~ sin dolor** pain-free labor*

parvulario *m* kindergarten, nursery school (BrE)

pasa *f* raisin

pasable *adj* (tolerable) passable

pasabordo *m* (Col) boarding pass

pasada *f* **(a)** (con un trapo) wipe; (de barniz, cera) coat **(b)** (paso): **trató el tema de ~** he dealt with the subject in passing; ***hacerle*** *or* ***jugarle una mala ~ a algn*** to play a dirty trick on sb

pasadizo *m* passageway, passage

pasado[1] -da *adj* **1** (en expresiones de tiempo): **el año/sábado ~** last year/Saturday; **~s dos días** after two days; **son las cinco pasadas** it's after *o* past five o'clock; **~ mañana** the day after tomorrow **2** (anticuado) *tb* **~ de moda** old-fashioned **3** ‹*fruta*› overripe; ‹*arroz/pastas*› overcooked; ‹*leche*› sour; **el pescado está ~** the fish is bad; **el filete muy ~, por favor** I'd like my steak well done

pasado[2] *m* **(a)** (época pasada) past **(b)** (Ling) past (tense)

pasador *m* **(a)** (de pelo — decorativo) barrette (AmE), hair slide (BrE); (— en forma de horquilla) (Méx) bobby pin (AmE), hair clip (BrE) **(b)** (de corbata) tiepin **(c)** (Per) (cordón) shoelace

pasaje *m* **1** (esp AmL) (Transp) ticket; **un ~ de ida/de ida y vuelta** a one-way/round-trip ticket (AmE), a single/return ticket (BrE) **2** (callejón) passage, narrow street; (galería comercial) arcade, mall **3** (Lit, Mús) passage

pasajero -ra *adj* ‹*capricho/moda*› passing (*before n*); ‹*amor*› fleeting (*before n*); ‹*molestia/dolor*› temporary ■ *m,f* passenger

pasamanos *m* (*pl* ~) banister

pasamontañas *m* (*pl* ~) balaclava

pasapalo *m* (Ven fam) nibble (colloq)

pasaporte *m* passport; **sacar el ~** to get a passport

pasapurés *m* (*pl* ~) (con manivela) food mill; (para aplastar) potato masher

pasar [A1] *vi* **I 1 (a)** (ir por un lugar) to come/go past; **no ha pasado ni un taxi** not one taxi has come/gone past; **los otros coches no podían ~** the other cars weren't able to get past; **no dejan ~ a nadie** they're not letting anyone through; **~ de largo** to go right *o* straight past; **~ por la aduana** to go through customs; **es un vuelo directo, no pasa por Miami** it's a direct flight, it doesn't go via Miami; **¿este autobús pasa por el museo?** does this bus go past the museum?; **pasamos por delante de su casa** we went past her house; **pasaba por aquí y** ... I was just passing by *o* I was in the area and ... **(b)** (deteniéndose en un lugar): **¿podríamos ~ por el banco?** can we stop off at the bank?; **pasa un día por casa** why don't you drop *o* come by the house sometime?; **puede ~ a recogerlo mañana** you can come and pick it up tomorrow **(c)** (atravesar) to cross; **~ de un lado a otro** «*persona/barco*» to go *o* cross from one side to the other; «*humedad*» to go through from one side to the other **(d)** (caber): **no ~á por la puerta** it won't go through the door **2** (entrar — acercándose al hablante) to come in; (— alejándose del hablante) to go in; **pase, por favor** please, do come in; **¡que pase el siguiente!** next, please!; **haga ~ al Sr Díaz** show Mr Díaz in please **3 (a)** (transmitirse, transferirse) «*corona/título*» to pass; **pasó de mano en mano** it was passed around (to everyone) **(b)** (comunicar): **te paso con Javier** (en el mismo teléfono) I'll hand *o* pass you over to Javier; (en otro teléfono) I'll put you through to Javier **4 (a)** (Educ) to pass; **~ de curso** to get through *o* pass one's end-of-year exams **(b)** (ser aceptable): **no está perfecto, pero puede ~** it's not perfect, but it'll do; **por esta vez (que) pase** I'll let it pass *o* go this time **5 pasar por (a)** (ser tenido por): **podrían ~ por hermanas** they could pass for sisters; *ver tb* HACERSE 3 **(b)** (experimentar) to go through; **~ por una crisis** to go through a crisis

II (suceder) to happen; **cuéntame lo que pasó** tell me what happened; **lo que pasa es que**... the thing *o* the problem is ...; **pase lo que pase** whatever happens, come what may; **siempre pasa igual** *or* **lo mismo** it's always the same; **¿qué pasa?** what's the matter?, what's up? (colloq); **¿qué te pasa?** what's the matter with you?; **¿qué te pasó en el ojo?** what happened to your eye?; **¿qué le pasa a la tele?** what's wrong with the TV?; **eso le pasa a cualquiera** that can happen to anybody; **no le pasó nada** nothing happened to him

III 1 (transcurrir) «*tiempo/años*» to pass, go by; **~on muchos años** many years went by *o* passed; **ya han pasado dos horas** it's been two hours now; **un año pasa muy rápido** a year goes very quickly; **¡cómo pasa el tiempo!** doesn't time fly! **2** (cesar) «*crisis/mal momento*» to be over; «*efecto*» to wear off; «*dolor*» to go away **3** (arreglárselas) **~ SIN algo** to manage WITHOUT sth ■ **~** *vt* **I 1 (a)** (cruzar, atravesar) ‹*frontera*› to cross; ‹*pueblo/ciudad*› to go through **(b)** (dejar atrás) ‹*edificio/calle*› to go past **(c)** (adelantar, sobrepasar) to overtake **2 (a)** (hacer atravesar) **~ algo POR algo** to put sth THROUGH sth; **~ la salsa por un tamiz** to put the sauce through a sieve **(b)** (por la aduana —legalmente) to take through; (— ilegalmente) to smuggle **3** (exhibir, mostrar) ‹*película/anuncio*› to show **4** ‹*examen/prueba*› to pass **5** ‹*página/hoja*› to turn; ***~ por alto*** ‹*falta/error*› to overlook; ‹*tema/punto*› to leave out, omit

II (entregar, hacer llegar): **pásaselo a Miguel** pass it on to Miguel; **¿me pasas el martillo?** can you pass me the hammer?

III 1 (a) ‹*tiempo*› to spend; **pasamos las Navidades en casa** we spent Christmas at home; **fuimos a Toledo a ~ el día** we went to Toledo for the day **(b)** (con idea de continuidad): **pasé toda la noche en vela** I was awake all night; **pasa toda el día al teléfono** she spends all day on the phone **(c) pasarlo** *or* **pasarla bien** to have a good time; **¿qué tal lo pasaste en la fiesta?** did you have a good time at the party?, did you enjoy the party?; **lo pasé mal** I didn't enjoy myself **2** (sufrir, padecer) ‹*penalidades/desgracias*› to go through, to suffer; **pasé mucho miedo/frío** I was very frightened/cold

■ **pasarse** *v pron* **I 1** (cambiarse): **~se al enemigo** to go over to the enemy **2 (a)** (ir demasiado lejos) to go too far; **nos pasamos de estación** we went past our station; **esta vez te has pasado** (fam) you've gone too far this time **(b)** (*enf*) (fam) (ir): **pásate por casa** come round; **¿podrías ~te por el mercado?** could you go down to the market? **3 (a)** «*peras/tomates*» to go bad, get overripe; «*carne/pescado*» to go off, go bad; «*leche*» to go off, go sour **(b)** (recocerse) «*arroz/pasta*» to get overcooked

II 1 (a) (desaparecer) «*efecto*» to wear off; «*dolor*» to go away; (+ *me/te/le etc*) **ya se me pasó el dolor** the pain's gone *o* eased now; **espera a que se le pase el enojo** wait until he's calmed *o* cooled down **(b)** (transcurrir): **el año se ha pasado muy rápido** this year has gone very quickly; *ver tb* PASAR *vt* III 1(b), (c) **2** (+ *me/te/le etc*) **(a)** (olvidarse): **se me pasó su cumpleaños** I forgot his birthday **(b)** (dejar escapar): **se me pasó la oportunidad** I missed the opportunity

pasarela *f* **(a)** (en desfiles de modelos) runway (AmE), catwalk (BrE) **(b)** (Náut) gangway

pasatiempo *m* **(a)** (entretenimiento) hobby, pastime **(b) pasatiempos** *mpl* (en periódico) puzzles (*pl*)

Pascua *f* **(a)** (fiesta de Resurrección) Easter **(b)** (Navidad) Christmas **(c)** (fiesta judía) Passover

pase *m* **1 (a)** (permiso) pass; **~ de abordar** (Méx) boarding pass; **~ de periodista** press pass **(b)** (para espectáculo) *tb* **~ de favor** complimentary ticket **(c)** (Col) (licencia de conducción) license* **2 (a)** (Dep) (en fútbol, baloncesto, rugby) pass; (en esgrima) feint **(b)** (Taur) pass **(c)** (en magia) sleight of hand

pasear [A1] *vi* **(a)** (a pie) to go for a walk *o* stroll; **salir a ~** to go out for a walk *o* stroll **(b)** (en bicicleta) to go for a (bike) ride; (en coche) to go for a drive ■ **~** *vt* ‹*perro*› to walk

paseo *m* **1 (a)** (caminata) walk; **dar un ~** to go for a walk *o* (colloq) stroll; ***mandar a algn a ~*** (fam) to tell sb to get lost (colloq) **(b)** (en bicicleta) ride; (en coche) drive; **fuimos a dar un ~ en coche** we went for a drive **(c)** (AmL) (excursión) trip, outing; **no vivo aquí, estoy de ~** I don't live here, I'm just visiting **2** (en nombres de calles) walk, avenue; **~ marítimo** esplanade, seafront

pasillo *m* (corredor) corridor; (en avión) aisle

pasión *f* passion; **tiene ~ por el fútbol** he has a passion for football

pasional *adj*: **un crimen ~** a crime of passion

pasito *adv* (Col, Ven) ‹*hablar*› quietly, softly; **poner ~ la música** to turn the music down

pasivo[1] **-va** *adj* passive

pasivo[2] *m* (en negocio) liabilities (*pl*); (en cuenta) debit side

pasmado -da *adj* (fam) ‹*persona*›: **la noticia me dejó pasmada** I was stunned by the news (colloq)

pasmar [A1] *vt* (fam) to amaze, stun

paso *m* **1 (a)** (acción): **el ~ del tren** the passing of the train; **el ~ del tiempo** the passage of time; **el ~ de la dictadura a la democracia** the transition from dictatorship to democracy; ***de ~***: **están de ~** they're just visiting *o* just passing through; **me pilla de ~** it's on my way; **y dicho sea de ~** ... and incidentally ... **(b)** (camino, posibilidad de pasar) way; **abrir/dejar ~ (a algn/algo)** to make way (for sth/sb); **me cerró el ~** she blocked my way; **dejen el ~ libre** leave the way clear; Ⓢ **ceda el paso** yield (*in US*), give way (*in UK*); Ⓢ **prohibido el paso** no entry; **~ de cebra** zebra crossing; **~ de peatones** crosswalk (AmE), pedestrian crossing (BrE); **~ nivel** grade (AmE) *o* (BrE) level crossing;

~ **elevado** *or* (Méx) **a desnivel** overpass (AmE), flyover (BrE); ~ **subterráneo** (para peatones) underpass, subway (BrE); (para vehículos) underpass; ***abrirse*** ~ to make one's way; (a codazos) to elbow one's way; ***salir al ~ de algn*** (abordar) to waylay sb; (detener) to stop sb **2** (Geog) (en montaña) pass; ***salir del*** ~ to get out of a (tight) spot *o* (AmE) crack (colloq) **3 (a)** (al andar, bailar) step; **dio un ~ para atrás** he took a step backward(s); **oyó ~s** she heard footsteps; **entró con ~ firme** he came in purposefully; **~ a ~** step by step; **seguirle los ~s a algn** to tail sb; ***seguir los ~s de algn*** to follow in sb's footsteps **(b)** (distancia corta): **vive a dos ~s de mi casa** he lives a stone's throw (away) from my house; **está a un ~ de aquí** it's just around the corner/down the road from here **(c)** (avance) step forward; **eso ya es un ~ (adelante)** that's a step forward in itself **(d)** (de gestión) step **4** (ritmo, velocidad): **apretó/aminoró el ~** he quickened his pace/he slowed down; **a este ~** ... at this rate ...; ***a ~ de hormiga*** *or* ***tortuga*** at a snail's pace; ***marcar el*** ~ to mark time **5** (en contador) unit

pasodoble *m* paso doble

pasota *mf* (Esp fam): **ese tío es un ~** that guy couldn't give a damn about anything (colloq)

pasparse [A1] *v pron* (RPl) «*cara/labios*» to get chapped

pasta *f* **1** (Coc) **(a)** (fideos, macarrones, etc) pasta **(b)** (Esp) (masa de harina) pastry; (galleta) *tb* **~ de té** cookie **(c)** (de tomates, anchoas, etc) paste **2 (a)** (materia moldeable) paste; **~ dentífrica** *or* **de dientes** toothpaste; **un libro en ~** a book in boards; **libros de ~ blanda** (Méx) paperback books **(b)** (Chi) (betún) polish **3** (Esp fam) (dinero) money, dough (sl)

pastar [A1] *vi* to graze

pastel *m* **1 (a)** (dulce) cake; **~ de boda/cumpleaños** wedding/birthday cake **(b)** (cubierto de masa) pie; **~ de papas** shepherd's pie, cottage pie **2** (Art) pastel; **al ~** pastel (*before n*) ■ *adj inv* pastel

pastelería *f* (tienda) cake shop, patisserie (BrE); (actividad) (cake) baking

pastelero -ra *m,f* (fabricante) patissier, pastry cook; (vendedor) cake seller

pasteurizado -da, **pasterizado -da** *adj* pasteurized

pastilla *f* **1 (a)** (Farm, Med) (para tragar) pill, tablet; (para chupar) pastille, lozenge; **~s para dormir** sleeping tablets *o* pills; **~s para los nervios** tranquilizers **(b)** (caramelo) candy (AmE), sweet (BrE); **~ de menta** mint **2** (de jabón) bar; (de chocolate) bar; (de caldo) cube **3** (Electrón) chip, microchip

pasto *m* **(a)** (Agr) pasture **(b)** (AmL) (hierba) grass; (extensión) lawn, grass

pastor -tora *m,f* **1** (Agr) (*m*) shepherd; (*f*) shepherdess; **~ alemán** German shepherd, Alsatian **2** (Relig) minister

pastoso -sa *adj* **(a)** ‹*sustancia/masa*› doughy **(b)** ‹*boca/lengua*› furry **(c)** ‹*voz/tono*› rich, mellow

pata *f* **1** (Zool) **(a)** (pierna — de animal, ave) leg; **las ~s delanteras/traseras** the front/hind legs **(b)** (pie — de perro, gato) paw; (— de ave) foot **2** (de persona) (fam & hum) (pierna) leg; (pie) (AmL) foot; **~ de palo** wooden leg; ***a*** ~ (fam & hum) on foot; ***meter la*** ~ (fam) to put one's foot in it (colloq); ***~s (para) arriba*** (fam) upside down; ***saltar a (la) ~ coja*** to hop; ***tener*** ~ (AmL fam) to have contacts; ⇒ MALO[1] **3** (de mueble) leg ■ *m* (Per fam) **(a)** (tipo) guy (colloq), bloke (BrE colloq) **(b)** (amigo) buddy (AmE colloq), mate (BrE colloq)

patada *f* **1** (puntapié) kick; **le dio una ~ al balón** he kicked the ball, he gave the ball a kick; **tiró la puerta abajo de una ~** he kicked the door down; **dio una ~ en el suelo** he stamped his foot; **los echaron a ~s** they were kicked out **2** (AmL) **(a)** (de arma) kick **(b)** (fam) (producida por la electricidad) shock (colloq); **me dio tremenda ~** I got a real shock

Patagonia *f*: **la ~** Patagonia

patagónico -ca *adj* Patagonian

patalear [A1] *vi* **(a)** (con enfado) to stamp (one's feet) **(b)** (en el aire, agua) to kick (one's legs in the air/water) **(c)** (fam) (protestar) to kick up a fuss (colloq)

pataleta *f* (fam) (de niño pequeño) tantrum; **le dio una ~** «*niño*» he threw a tantrum; «*adulto*» he had a fit (colloq)

patán *adj* (fam) loutish, uncouth; **no seas ~** don't be such a lout *o* so uncouth ■ *m* **1** (fam) (grosero) lout, yob (BrE colloq) **2** (Chi) (holgazán) good-for-nothing

patata *f* (Esp) potato; **~ frita** (Esp) (de sartén) French fry, chip (BrE); (de bolsita) (potato) chip (AmE), (potato) crisp (BrE)

patatús *m* (fam) fit (colloq)

paté, **pâté** *m* pâté; **~ de hígado** liver pâté

patear [A1] *vt* **(a)** «*persona*» to kick, boot (colloq) **(b)** (AmL) «*animal*» to kick ■ ~ *vi* **(a)** (dar patadas en el suelo) to stamp (one's feet) **(b)** (AmL) «*animal*» to kick

patentado -da *adj* ‹*invento*› patented; ⇒ MARCA 2

patentar [A1] *vt* **1** ‹*marca*› to register; ‹*invento*› to patent **2** (CS) ‹*coche*› to register

patente *adj* clear, evident; **dejó ~ cuál era su objetivo** he made his aim quite clear ■ *f* **1** (de invento) patent **2** (Auto) **(a)** (CS) (impuesto) road tax; (placa) license* plate, numberplate (BrE); **el número de la ~** the registration number, (AmE) the license number **(b)** (Col) (carnet de conducir) driving license*

paternal *adj* paternal

paternalismo *m* paternalism

paternalista *adj* paternalistic

paternidad *f* **1** (del padre) **(a)** (Der) paternity (frml) **(b)** (circunstancia) fatherhood; **la ~ lo ha cambiado** fatherhood *o* being a father has changed him **2** (de los padres) parenthood

paterno -na *adj* **(a)** ‹*abuelo*› paternal (*before n*) **(b)** ‹*autoridad/herencia*› paternal; ‹*cariño*› paternal, fatherly; **su domicilio ~** her parents' home

patético -ca *adj* pathetic, moving

patetismo *m* pathos (liter); **imágenes de (un) gran ~** very moving images

patíbulo *m* **(a)** (tablado) scaffold **(b)** (horca) gallows

patilla *f* **1 (a)** (barba) sideburn, sideboard (BrE) **(b)** (de las gafas) sidepiece, arm **2** (fruta) (Col, Ven) watermelon; (esqueje) (Chi) cutting

patín *m* **(a)** (con ruedas) (roller) skate; (para el hielo) (ice) skate; **le regalé unos patines** I gave him a pair of skates **(b)** (tabla) skateboard **(c)** (Esp) (bote) pedalo, pedal boat

pátina *f* patina

patinador -dora *m,f* (Dep) (sobre ruedas) (roller) skater; (sobre hielo) (ice) skater

patinaje *m* (sobre ruedas) roller skating; (sobre hielo) ice skating; **~ artístico/de velocidad** figure/speed skating

patinar [A1] *vi* **1 (a)** (Dep) (con ruedas) to skate, roller-skate; (sobre hielo) to skate, ice-skate **(b)** (resbalar) «*persona*» to slip, slide; «*vehículo*» to skid; «*embrague*» to slip **2** (fam) (equivocarse) to slip up

patinazo *m* **1** (de vehículo) skid; **el coche pegó un ~** the car skidded **2** (fam) (equivocación) blunder, slip-up (colloq)

patineta *f* **(a)** (con manillar) scooter **(b)** (CS, Méx, Ven) (sin manillar) skateboard

patinete *m* scooter

patio *m* **1** (en una casa) courtyard, patio; (de escuela) playground, schoolyard **2** (Esp) (Cin, Teatr) *tb* **~ de butacas** (Esp) orchestra (AmE), stalls (*pl*) (BrE) orchestra (AmE), stalls (*pl*) (BrE)

patizambo -ba *adj* (con las piernas arqueadas — hacia adentro) knock-kneed; (— hacia afuera) bowlegged

pato[1] -ta *m,f* (Zool) duck

pato[2] *m* **1** (Esp fam) (persona) clodhopper (colloq) **2** (Andes, Méx) (Med) bedpan

patochada *f* (fam) piece of nonsense; **decir ~s** talk nonsense

patología *f* pathology

patológico -ca *adj* pathological

patón -tona *adj* (AmL fam) ⇒ PATUDO 1

patoso -sa[1] *adj* (Esp fam) clumsy ■ *m,f* (Esp fam) clumsy idiot (colloq)

patoso[2] -sa *m,f* (Esp fam) clumsy idiot (colloq)

patota *f* (AmL fam) mob, gang

patraña *f* tall story

patria *f* homeland, motherland, fatherland; **luchar por la ~** to fight for one's country

patriarca *m* patriarch

patrimonio *m* patrimony; **~ personal** personal assets (*pl*); **el ~ nacional** national wealth; **~ histórico** heritage; **~ artístico/cultural** artistic/cultural heritage

patriota *adj* patriotic ■ *mf* patriot

patriotero -ra *adj* jingoistic, chauvinistic ■ *m,f* jingoist, chauvinist

patriótico -ca *adj* patriotic

patriotismo *m* patriotism

patrocinador -dora *m,f* (de acto, proyecto) sponsor; (Art) patron

patrocinar [A1] *vt* **1** ‹*acto/proyecto*› to sponsor **2** (Chi, Méx) «*abogado*» to represent

patrón -trona *m,f* **1 (a)** (Rels Labs) employer (frml), boss **(b)** (Esp) (de casa de huéspedes) (*m*) landlord; (*f*) landlady **2** (Relig) patron saint **3** (CS fam) (como apelativo) (*m*) sir; (*f*) madam **4 patrón** *m* **(a)** (en costura) pattern **(b)** (para mediciones) standard

patrono -na *m,f* **(a)** (esp AmL) (Relig) patron saint **(b)** (Rels Labs) employer

patrulla *f* patrol; **están de ~** they are on patrol; **la ~ costera** the coastguard (patrol) ■ *m or f* (coche) patrol *o* squad car

patrullar [A1] *vi/vt* to patrol

patrullera *f* (lancha) patrol boat

patrullero *m* (barco) patrol boat; (avión) patrol plane; (coche — militar) patrol car; (— policial) (CS, Per) patrol *o* squad car

patudo -da *adj* **1** (AmL fam) (de pies grandes) with big feet; **¡qué niño tan ~!** what big feet he/she has! **2** (Chi fam) (descarado) nervy (AmE colloq), cheeky (BrE colloq)

paulatino -na *adj* gradual

paulista *adj* of/from São Paulo

pausa *f* **(a)** (interrupción) pause; (Rad, TV) break; **hacer una ~** to pause/have a break **(b)** (Mús) rest

pauta *f* **1** (guía) guideline; **~s de comportamiento** rules *o* norms of behavior **2** (de un papel) lines (*pl*)

pava *f* **1** (para calentar agua) kettle **2** (Col fam) (de cigarrillo) butt; *ver tb* PAVO

pavada *f* (RPl fam) **(a)** (dicho, acción) silly thing to say/do **(b)** (cosa insignificante) little thing

pavimentar [A1] *vt* (con asfalto) to surface, asphalt; (con cemento, adoquines) to pave

pavimento *m* (de asfalto) road surface; (de cemento, adoquines) paving

pavo -va *m,f* (Coc, Zool) turkey; **~ real** peacock; ***de* ~** (Chi, Per fam) ‹*viajar/entrar*› without paying ■ *adj* **(a)** (fam) (tonto, bobo) silly, dumb (AmE colloq) **(b)** (Chi fam) (ingenuo) naive (colloq)

pavonearse [A1] *v pron* (fam) to show off; **~** DE **algo** to brag *o* crow ABOUT sth (colloq)

pavor *m* terror; **me da ~** it terrifies me; **les tiene ~ a los perros** (fam) she's terrified of dogs

pavoroso -sa *adj* terrifying, horrific

paya (Chi), **payada** (RPl) *f*: *improvised musical dialogue*

payador *m* (CS) singer (*who performs* PAYADAS)

payasada *f* **1** (bufonada): **deja de hacer ~s** stop clowning around *o* acting the clown (colloq) **2** (Chi fam) **(a)** (tontería) stupid thing to say/do; **son puras ~s** that's utter nonsense **(b)** (cosa) thingamajig (colloq)

payasear [A1] *vi* (AmL fam) to clown around (colloq)

payaso -sa *m,f* **(a)** (Espec) clown; ***hacer(se) el* ~** to clown around (colloq) **(b)** (persona — cómica) clown, comedian; (— poco seria) joker (colloq & pej)

payo -ya *m,f* (Esp) *word used by gypsies to refer to a non-gypsy*

paz *f* **(a)** (Mil, Pol) peace; **firmar la ~** to sign a peace agreement *o* treaty; **en época de ~** in peacetime; ***hacer las paces*** to make (it) up **(b)** (calma) peace; **no me dejan vivir en ~** they don't give me a moment's peace; **dejar algo/a algn en ~** to leave sth/sb alone; **descanse en ~** (frml) rest in peace (frml)

PC *m or f* personal computer, PC

P.D. (= **post data**) PS

pe *f: name of the letter* P
peaje *m* (dinero) toll; (lugar) toll barrier; **carretera de ~** toll road
pearse [A1] *v pron* (AmL fam) to fart (sl)
peatón *m* pedestrian
peatonal *adj* pedestrian (*before n*)
pebete -ta *m,f* (RPl fam) kid (colloq)
pebre *m: sauce made with onion, chili, coriander, parsley and tomato*
peca *f* freckle
pecado *m* **(a)** (Relig) sin; **~ capital** deadly sin; **~ mortal** mortal sin **(b)** (lástima) crime, sin
pecador -dora *m,f* sinner
pecaminoso -sa *adj* sinful
pecar [A2] *vi* (Relig) to sin
pecera *f* (redonda) goldfish bowl; (rectangular) fish tank
pechera *f* (de camisa, vestido) front
pecho *m* **▶ 123** (tórax) chest; (mama) breast; **dar (el) ~ a un niño** to breast-feed *o* suckle a child; ***tomarse algo a ~*** ‹*crítica*› to take sth to heart; ‹*responsabilidad*› to take sth seriously
pechuga *f* (de pollo) breast
pechugona *f* (fam & hum) big-breasted woman
pecoso -sa *adj* freckly
pectoral *adj* **1 ▶ 123** ‹*músculos*› pectoral (*before n*) **2** (Med): **jarabe ~** cough mixture *o* syrup
peculiar *adj* **1** (característico) particular; **un rasgo ~** a particular trait; **con su ~ buen humor** with his characteristic good humor **2** (poco común, raro) ‹*sensación*› peculiar, unusual
peculiaridad *f* peculiarity
pedagogía *f* pedagogy, teaching
pedagógico -ca *adj* pedagogical, teaching (*before n*)
pedagogo -ga *m,f* (estudioso) educationalist; (educador) educator, teacher, pedagogue (frml)
pedal *m* pedal; **~ de embrague/de freno** clutch/brake pedal; **~ de arranque** kickstart
pedalear [A1] *vi* to pedal
pedante *adj* pedantic ■ *mf* pedant
pedantería *f* pedantry
pedazo *m* **1** (trozo) piece; **un ~ de pan** a piece of bread; **se hizo ~s** it smashed (to pieces); **el coche saltó** *or* **voló en ~s** the car was blown to pieces; **lo hice ~s** I smashed it; ***caerse a ~s*** to fall to pieces **2** (fam) (en insultos): **¡~ de idiota!** you idiot! (colloq)
pederasta *m* (homosexual) homosexual; (pedófilo) pederast
pedernal *m* flint
pedestal *m* pedestal
pedestre *adj* prosaic
pediatra *mf* pediatrician*
pediatría *f* pediatrics*
pediátrico -ca *adj* pediatric*
pedicuro -ra *m,f* chiropodist
pedido *m* **1** (Com) order; **hacer un ~** to place an order **2** (AmL) (solicitud) request; **a ~ de** at the request of
pedigree /peðiˈɣri/, **pedigrí** *m* pedigree; **un perro de** *or* **con ~** a pedigree dog
pedinche *mf* (Méx fam) scrounger (colloq)
pedir [I14] *vt* **1 (a)** ‹*dinero/ayuda*› to ask for; **pidieron un préstamo al banco** they asked the bank for a loan; **pidió permiso para salir** she asked permission to leave; **pide limosna** he begs (for money); **~le algo a algn** to ask sb for sth; **le pidió ayuda** he asked her for help; **me pidió disculpas** *or* **perdón** he apologized (to me); **~ hora** to make an appointment; **~ la palabra** to ask for permission to speak; **me pidió que le enseñara** he asked me to teach him; *ver* PRESTADO **(b)** (en bar, restaurante) ‹*plato/bebida*› to order; ‹*cuenta*› to ask for **2** (Com) **(a)** (como precio) **~ algo POR algo** to ask sth FOR sth; **¿cuánto pide por la casa?** how much is she asking for the house? **(b)** ‹*mercancías*› to order ■ **~** *vi* **(a)** (en bar, restaurante) to order **(b)** (mendigar) to beg
pedo *m* **1** (fam) (ventosidad) fart (sl); **tirarse un ~** to fart (sl), to let off (BrE colloq); ***al ~*** (RPl fam) for nothing **2** (arg) (borrachera): **agarró un buen ~** he got really plastered (colloq); **tenía un ~ que no veía** he was blind drunk (colloq) **3** (Méx fam) (problema, lío) hassle (colloq); ***hacérsela de ~ a algn*** (Méx vulg) to give sb hell (colloq)
pedofilia *f* pedophilia*
pedófilo *m* pedophile*
pedorreta *f* (fam) raspberry (colloq)
pedrada *f* **1** (golpe): **me dio una ~ en la cabeza** she hit me on the head with a stone **2** (Méx fam) (indirecta) hint
pedrisco *m* hail
pega *f* **1** (Col fam) (broma) trick; **de ~** (Esp fam) ‹*araña/culebra*› joke (*before n*), trick (*before n*); ‹*revólver*› dummy (*before n*) **2** (Esp fam) (dificultad, inconveniente) problem, snag (colloq); **te ponen muchas ~s** they make it really difficult for you **3** (Andes fam) **(a)** (trabajo) work; (empleo) work; **está sin ~** he's out of work **(b)** (lugar) work
pegadizo -za *adj* catchy
pegado -da *adj* [ESTAR] **(a)** (junto) **~ A algo**: **su casa está pegada a la mía** her house is right next to mine; **iba muy ~ al coche de delante** he was too close to the car in front; **pon la cama pegada a la pared** put the bed right up against the wall **(b)** (adherido) stuck; (con cola, goma) glued; **está ~ al suelo** it's stuck to the floor; **las piezas están pegadas** the pieces are glued together
pegajoso -sa *adj* **(a)** ‹*superficie/sustancia*› sticky **(b)** ‹*calor*› sticky **(c)** (fam) ‹*persona*› clinging (colloq) **(d)** (AmL fam) ‹*canción/música*› catchy
pegamento *m* glue, adhesive
pegar [A3] *vt* **1 (a)** ‹*bofetada/patada*› to give; **le pegó una paliza terrible** he gave him a terrible beating; **le ~on un tiro** they shot her **(b)** ‹*grito/chillido*› to let out; **~ un salto de alegría** to jump for joy; **~le un susto a algn** to give sb a fright **2 (a)** (adherir) to stick; (con cola) to glue, stick **(b)** (coser) ‹*mangas/botones*› to sew on **(c)** (arrimar) to move ... closer **3** (fam) (contagiar) ‹*enfermedad*› to give; **me pegó la gripe** he gave me the flu ■ **~** *vi* **1 (a)** (golpear): **~le A algn** to hit sb; (a un niño, como

castigo) to smack sb; **le pega a su mujer** he beats his wife; **la pelota pegó en el poste** the ball hit the goalpost **(b)** (fam) (hacerse popular) «*producto/moda*» to take off; «*artista*» to be very popular **2 (a)** (adherir) to stick **(b)** (armonizar) to go together; **~ con algo** to go WITH sth; **no pega con el vestido** it doesn't go (very well) with the dress
■ **pegarse** *v pron* **1 (a)** (golpearse): **me pegué con la mesa** I knocked *o* hit myself on the table; **me pegué en la cabeza** I banged *o* knocked my head **(b)** (*recípr*) (darse golpes) to hit each other **2** ‹*susto*› to get; **~se un tiro** to shoot oneself **3** (contagiarse) «*enfermedad*» to be infectious; **eso se pega** you can easily catch it; **se te va a ~ mi catarro** you'll catch my cold; **se le ha pegado el acento mexicano** he's picked up a Mexican accent

pegatina *f* (Esp) sticker

pegoste *mf* (Méx fam) hanger-on (colloq)

peinado¹ -da *adj*: **no estaba peinada** she hadn't combed her hair; **siempre va muy bien peinada** her hair always looks very nice

peinado² *m* (arreglo del pelo) hairstyle; **lavado y ~** shampoo and set

peinador -dora *m,f* (Méx, RPl) (persona) hairdresser, stylist

peinar [A1] *vt* **1 (a)** ‹*melena/flequillo*› (con peine) to comb; (con cepillo) to brush **(b)** «*peluquero*»: **¿quién te peina?** who does your hair? **2** ‹*lana*› to card **3** (period) ‹*área/zona*› to comb
■ **peinarse** *v pron* **(a)** (*refl*) (con peine) to comb one's hair; (con cepillo) to brush one's hair **(b)** (*caus*) to have one's hair done; **me peino en esta peluquería** I have my hair done at this salon

peine *m* comb

peineta *f* **(a)** (para sujetar, adornar) ornamental comb **(b)** (Chi) (peine) comb

p. ej. (= **por ejemplo**) eg, for example

Pekín *m* Peking, Beijing

pekinés -nesa *m,f* Pekinese

pela *f* (Esp fam) (peseta) peseta

peladez *f* (Méx) rude word

pelado -da *adj* **1 (a)** (con el pelo corto): **lo dejaron ~** *or* **con la cabeza pelada (al rape)** they cropped his hair very short **(b)** (CS) (calvo) bald **2 (a)** ‹*manzana*› peeled; ‹*hueso*› clean; ‹*almendras*› blanched **(b)** ‹*nariz/espalda*›: **tengo la nariz/espalda pelada** my nose/back is peeling **3** (Chi fam) ‹*pies/trasero*› bare; **ir a pie ~** to go barefoot **4** (Méx fam) (grosero) foulmouthed ■ *m,f* (CS fam) (calvo) baldy (colloq)

peladura *f* **(a)** (de fruta) peel; **~s de papa** potato peelings **(b)** (Andes) (en la piel) graze

pelaje *m* (de animal) coat, fur

pelar [A1] *vt* **1 (a)** ‹*fruta/zanahoria*› to peel; ‹*habas/marisco*› to shell; ‹*caramelo*› to unwrap **(b)** ‹*ave*› to pluck **2** (rapar): **lo ~on al cero** *or* **al rape** they cropped his hair very short **3** (fam) (en el juego) to clean ... out (colloq) **4** (Chi fam) ‹*persona*› to badmouth (AmE colloq), to slag off (BrE colloq)
■ **pelarse** *v pron* (a causa del sol) «*persona*» to peel; «*cara/hombros*» (+ *me/te/le etc*) to peel; **se te está pelando la nariz** your nose is peeling

peldaño *m* (escalón) step, stair; (travesaño) rung

pelea *f* **(a)** (discusión) quarrel, fight (colloq), argument; **buscar ~** to try to pick a quarrel *o* fight; **tuvimos una ~** we quarreled *o* had an argument **(b)** (en sentido físico) fight; **~ de gallos** cockfight

peleado -da *adj* **(a)** (enfadado): **están ~s** they've fallen out; **estar ~ con algn** to have fallen out with sb **(b)** ‹*partido/carrera/elecciones*› keenly-contested

peleador -dora *adj* (fam) (que discute) argumentative; (que pelea): **es muy ~** he's always fighting

pelear [A1] *vi* **(a)** (discutir) to quarrel; **~on por una tontería** they quarreled *o* (colloq) had a fight over a silly little thing **(b)** «*novios*» (discutir) to quarrel, argue; (terminar) to break up, split up **(c)** (en sentido físico) to fight; **~ POR algo** to fight OVER sth
■ **pelearse** *v pron* **(a)** (discutir) to quarrel; (pegarse) to fight; **~se POR algo** to quarrel/fight OVER sth **(b)** «*novios*» (discutir) to quarrel; (terminar) to break up, split up

pelele *m* **(a)** (de trapo) rag doll; (de paja) straw doll **(b)** (persona — manipulada) puppet; (— débil) (fam) wimp (colloq)

peletería *f* (oficio) fur trade; (tienda) furrier's, fur shop; (género) furs (*pl*)

peliagudo -da *adj* ‹*problema*› difficult, tricky; ‹*asunto*› thorny

pelícano *m* pelican

película *f* **1 (a)** (Cin, TV) movie, film (BrE); **hoy dan** *or* (Esp) **echan** *or* **ponen una ~** there's a movie *o* film on today, they're showing a movie *o* film today; **~ de dibujos animados** cartoon; **~ del Oeste** *or* **de vaqueros** Western; **~ de miedo** *or* **de terror** horror movie *o* film; **~ de suspenso** *or* (Esp) **suspense** thriller; **~ muda** silent movie *o* film **(b)** (Fot) film **2** (capa fina — de aceite) film; (— de polvo) thin layer

peligrar [A1] *vi* to be at risk; **hacer ~ algo** to put sth at risk

peligro *m* danger; **estar en** *or* **correr ~** «*persona*» to be in danger; «*vida*» to be in danger *o* at risk; **un ~ para la salud** a health risk; **poner algo/a algn en ~** to put sth/sb at risk; **corren el ~ de perder la final** they're in danger of losing the final; **corres el ~ de que te despidan** you run the risk of being fired; **estar fuera de ~** to be out of danger; Ⓢ **peligro de incendio** fire hazard

peligrosidad *f* dangerousness

peligroso -sa *adj* dangerous

pelillo *m* small hair

pelirrojo -ja *adj* ▶ 97 red-haired, ginger-haired ■ *m,f* redhead

pellejerías *fpl* (Andes fam) hard times (*pl*)

pellejo *m* **(a)** (piel — de animal) skin, hide; (— de persona) (fam) skin (colloq); ***ponerse en el ~ de algn*** (fam) to put oneself in sb's shoes **(b)** (fam) (vida) neck (colloq); **jugarse** *or* **arriesgar el ~** to risk one's neck (colloq) **(c)** (odre) wineskin

pellizcar [A2] *vt* ‹*persona/brazo*› to pinch

pellizco *m* **(a)** (en la piel) pinch; **me dio un ~ en la pierna** she pinched my leg **(b)** (fam) (cantidad pequeña) little bit; **un ~ de sal** a pinch of salt

pelmazo *adj* (fam) boring ■ *m* (fam) bore

pelo *m* **1** (de personas) ▶ **123**, **97** hair; ~ **rizado/liso** *or* **lacio** curly/straight hair; **tiene mucho/poco** ~ he has really thick/thin hair; **llevar el** ~ **suelto** to wear one's hair down *o* loose; **se le está cayendo el** ~ he's losing his hair; ***con*** **~*s y señales*** (fam) down to the last detail; ***no tiene*** **~*s en la lengua*** (fam) he doesn't mince his words; ***se me/le ponen los*** **~*s de punta*** (fam) it sends shivers down my/his spine, it makes my/his hair stand on end; ***tomarle el*** **~ *a algn*** (fam) (bromeando) to pull sb's leg (colloq); (burlándose) to mess around with sb (AmE), to mess sb around (BrE) **2** (Zool) (filamento) hair; (pelaje — de perro, gato) hair, fur; (— de conejo, oso) fur; ~ **de camello** camelhair **3** (de alfombra) pile

pelón -lona *adj* (fam) (sin pelo) bald ■ *m,f* **1** (fam) (sin pelo) baldy (colloq) **2 pelón** *m* (RPl) (duranzo) nectarine

pelota *f* **1** (Dep, Jueg) ball; **una** ~ **de fútbol** (esp AmL) a football; **jugar a la pelota** to play ball; ~ **vasca** jai alai, pelota; ***darle*** **~ *a algn*** (CS fam) to take notice of sb; ***hacerle la*** **~ *a algn*** (Esp fam) to suck up to sb (colloq) **2 pelotas** *fpl* (vulg) (testículos) balls (*pl*) (colloq *or* vulg); ***en*** **~*s*** (vulg) (sin ropa) stark naked; (sin dinero) flat broke (colloq) ■ *mf* **1** (AmS vulg) (imbécil) jerk (sl) **2** (Esp fam) (adulador) creep (colloq)

pelotari *mf* jai alai *o* pelota player

pelotazo *m* (golpe): **me dio un** ~ he hit me with the ball

pelotera *f* (fam) **(a)** (lío, jaleo) ruckus (AmE colloq), rumpus (BrE colloq) **(b)** (riña) argument, row (colloq)

pelotero -ra *m,f* **(a)** (AmL) (jugador — de béisbol) baseball player; (— de fútbol) soccer *o* football player, footballer **(b)** (Chi) (recogepelotas) (*m*) ballboy; (*f*) ballgirl

pelotón *m* **(a)** (Mil) squad; ~ **de ejecución** *or* **fusilamiento** firing squad **(b)** (en ciclismo) bunch, pack; (en atletismo) pack **(c)** (fam) (de gente) gang (colloq)

pelotudo -da *adj* (AmS vulg): **¡qué ~!** what a jerk! (sl) ■ *m,f* (AmS vulg) jerk (sl)

peluca *f* wig

peluche *m* felt, plush; **un juguete de** ~ a cuddly toy; ⇒ oso

pelucón -cona *adj* (Chi, Per fam) (con mucho pelo) hairy; (de pelo largo) long-haired

peludo -da *adj* ‹*hombre/brazo*› hairy; ‹*barba*› bushy; ‹*animal*› hairy, furry; ‹*cola*› bushy; ‹*lana/jersey*› hairy

peluquería *f* **(a)** (establecimiento) hairdresser's, hairdressing salon **(b)** (oficio) hairdressing, hairstyling

peluquero -ra *m,f* hairdresser, hairstylist

peluquín *m* toupee, hairpiece

pelusa¹, **pelusilla** *f* **1** (en la cara) down, fuzz; (de fruta) down; (en jersey) ball of fluff *o* fuzz; (de suciedad) ball of fluff **2** (Esp fam) (celos) jealousy; **tener** ~ to be jealous

pelusa² *mf* (Chi fam) (niño — callejero) street kid (colloq); (— travieso) little rascal (colloq)

pelvis *f* (*pl* ~) pelvis

pena *f* **1 (a)** (tristeza): **tenía/sentía mucha** ~ he was *o* felt very sad; **me da** ~ **verlo** it upsets me *o* it makes me sad to see it; **a mí la que me da** ~ **es su mujer** it's his wife I feel sorry for; **está que da** ~ she's in a terrible state **(b)** (lástima) pity, shame; **¡qué ~!** what a pity *o* shame!; **es una** ~ **que** … it's a pity (that) …; ***vale*** *or* ***merece la*** **~** it's worth it; **vale la** ~ **leerlo/visitarlo** it's worth reading/a visit **2 penas** *fpl* **(a)** (problemas) sorrows (*pl*); **ahogar las ~s** to drown one's sorrows; **me contó sus ~s** he told me his troubles; ***a duras*** **~*s*** (apenas) hardly; (con dificultad) with difficulty **(b)** (penalidades) hardship **3** (Der) sentence; **la** ~ **máxima** the maximum sentence; ~ **capital** *or* **de muerte** death penalty **4** (AmL exc CS) (vergüenza) embarrassment; **¡qué ~!** how embarrasing!; **me da mucha** ~ **pedírselo** I'm too embarrassed to ask him

penal *adj* criminal (*before n*) ■ *m* **1** (cárcel) prison, penitentiary (AmE) **2** (AmL period) (Dep) penalty

pénal *m* (Andes) penalty

penalidades *fpl* hardship, suffering

penalizar [A4] *vt* (Der) to penalize

penalty /'penalti, pe'nalti/ *m* (*pl* **-tys**) penalty; **pitar** *or* **señalar** ~ to award *o* give a penalty

penca *f* **(a)** (de hoja) main rib **(b)** (del nopal) stalk **(c)** (Méx) (de bananas) bunch

pendejada *f* **(a)** (AmL exc CS fam) (estupidez) stupid thing to say/do **(b)** (Per vulg) (mala jugada) dirty trick

pendejear [A1] *vi* (Méx fam) to clown around (colloq)

pendejez *f* (Méx vulg) stupidity

pendejo -ja *adj* **(a)** (AmL exc CS fam) (estúpido) dumb (AmE colloq), thick (BrE colloq) **(b)** (Per fam) (listo) sly, sharp (colloq) ■ *m,f* **(a)** (AmL exc CS fam) (estúpido) dummy (colloq), nerd (colloq); ***hacerse el*** **~** (fam) (hacerse el tonto) to act dumb (colloq); (no hacer nada) to loaf around (colloq) **(b)** (Per fam) (persona lista) sly devil

pendenciero -ra *adj* quarrelsome ■ *m,f* troublemaker

pendiente *adj* **1** ‹*asunto/problema*› unresolved; ‹*cuenta*› outstanding **2** (atento): **está** ~ **del niño a todas horas** she devotes every minute of the day to the child; **estoy** ~ **de que me llamen** I'm waiting for them to call me ■ *m* (Esp) earring ■ *f* (de terreno) slope, incline; (de tejado) slope; **una** ~ **muy pronunciada** a very steep slope *o* incline; **tiene mucha** ~ it slopes steeply

péndulo *m* pendulum

pene *m* penis

penetración *f* penetration

penetrante *adj* **1 (a)** ‹*mirada/voz*› penetrating, piercing; ‹*olor*› pungent, penetrating; ‹*sonido*› piercing **(b)** ‹*viento/frío*› bitter, biting **2** ‹*inteligencia/mente/ironía*› sharp

penetrar [A1] *vi* (entrar) ~ POR **algo** «*agua/humedad*» to seep THROUGH sth; «*luz*» to shine THROUGH sth; «*ladrón*» to enter THROUGH sth; ~ EN **algo** to penetrate sth ■ ~ *vt* to penetrate; **la bala le penetró el pulmón** the bullet penetrated *o* entered his lung

penicilina *f* penicillin

península *f* peninsula

peninsular *adj* peninsular ■ *mf*: **los ~es** people from mainland Spain

penique *m* penny

penitencia *f* **1** (Relig) penance; **en ~** as (a) penance **2 (a)** (Andes) (en juegos) forfeit; (castigo) **(b)** (RPl) (fam) punishment; **el maestro me puso en ~** the teacher punished me

penitenciaría *f* penitentiary

penitente *mf* penitent

penoso -sa *adj* **1** (lamentable) terrible, awful **2 (a)** (triste) sad **(b)** ‹*viaje*› grueling*; ‹*trabajo*› laborious, difficult **3** (AmL exc CS fam) **(a)** ‹*persona*› shy **(b)** (embarazoso) embarrassing

pensamiento *m* **1 (a)** (facultad) thought **(b)** (cosa pensada) thought **(c)** (doctrina) thinking **(d)** (máxima) thought **2** (Bot) pansy

pensar [A5] *vi* to think; **después de mucho ~** ... after much thought ...; **actuó sin ~** he did it without thinking; **pensé para mí** *or* **para mis adentros** I thought to myself; **~ EN algo/algn** to think ABOUT sth/sb; **cuando menos se piensa** ... just when you least expect it ...; **~ mal/bien de algn** to think ill *o* badly/well of sb; ***dar que*** *or* ***hacer ~ a algn*** to make sb think ■ **~** *vt* **1 (a)** (creer, opinar) to think; **pienso que no** I don't think so; **¿qué piensas del divorcio/del jefe?** what do you think about divorce/the boss? **(b)** (considerar) to think about; **lo ~é** I'll think about it; **piénsalo bien antes de decidir** think it over before you decide; **pensándolo bien,** ... on second thought(s) *o* thinking about it, ...; **¡y ~ que ...!** (and) to think that ...!; **¡ni ~lo!** no way! (colloq), not on your life! (colloq) **(c)** (Col) ‹*persona*› to think about **2** (tener la intención de): **~ hacer algo** to think of doing sth; **pensamos ir al teatro** we're thinking of going to the theater; **no pienso ir** I'm not going ■ **pensarse** *v pron* (*enf*) (fam) ‹*decisión/respuesta*› to think about; *ver tb* PENSAR *vt* 1(b)

pensativo -va *adj* pensive, thoughtful

pensión *f* **1** (Servs Socs) pension; **cobrar la ~** to draw one's pension; **~ alimenticia** maintenance; **~ de invalidez** disability (allowance) (AmE), invalidity benefit (BrE) **2 (a)** (casa — de huéspedes) guesthouse, rooming house (AmE), boarding house (BrE); (— para estudiantes) student hostel; **~ completa** full board **(b)** (alojamiento) accommodations (*pl*) (AmE), lodging, accommodation (BrE); ⇒ MEDIO[1] **3** (Col) (mensualidad) tuition (AmE), school fees (*pl*) (BrE)

pensionado -da *m,f* **1** (Servs Socs) pensioner **2 pensionado** *m* **(a)** (Esp) (internado) boarding school **(b)** (CS) (pensión para estudiantes) student hostel

pensionarse [A1] *v pron* (Col) to retire

pensionista *mf* **1** (Servs Socs) pensioner **2** (en casa de huéspedes) resident, lodger

pentágono *m* **(a)** (Mat) pentagon **(b) el Pentágono** the Pentagon

pentagrama *m* (Mús) stave, staff

pentatlón *m* pentathlon

penúltimo -ma *adj* penultimate ■ *m,f*: **ser el ~** to be second to last

penumbra *f* (media luz) half-light, semidarkness

penuria *f* **(a)** (escasez) shortage, dearth; **pasar ~s** to suffer hardship **(b)** (pobreza) poverty

peña *f* **1** (roca) crag, rock **2 (a)** (grupo) circle, group; **~ taurina** bullfighting club **(b)** (AmL) *tb* **~ folklórica** folk club

peñasco *m* crag, rocky outcrop

peón *m* **1** (Const) laborer*; (Agr) (esp AmL) agricultural laborer*, farm worker; **~ albañil** (building) laborer*; **~ caminero** road worker **2** (en ajedrez) pawn; (en damas) piece, checker (AmE), draughtsman (BrE)

peonza *f* spinning top

peor *adj/adv* **1** (uso comparativo) worse; **va a ser ~ para él como no estudie** if he doesn't study so much the worse for him; **y si vienen los dos, tanto ~** and it'll be even worse if the two of them come; **cada vez ~** worse and worse; **su situación es ~ que la mía** his situation is worse than mine; **está ~ que nunca** it's worse than ever **2** (uso superlativo) worst; **el ~ alumno de la clase** the worst pupil in the class; **lo ~ que puede pasar** the worst (thing) that can happen; **en el ~ de los casos** if the worst comes to the worst; **el lugar donde ~ se come** the worst place to eat in ■ *mf*: **el/la ~** (de dos) the worse; (de varios) the worst

pepa *f* (AmS) (semilla — de uva, naranja) pip; (— de durazno, aguacate) stone, pit

Pepe: *diminutive of José*

pepenador -dora *m,f* (Méx) scavenger (*on garbage dumps*)

pepenar [A1] *vt* (Méx fam) (en la basura) to scavenge

pepinillo *m* gherkin

pepino *m* cucumber

pepita *f* **(a)** (de uva) pip; (de tomate) seed; (de calabaza) (Méx) dried pumpkin seed **(b)** (de oro) nugget

pepona *f* large doll

pequeño -ña *adj* **(a)** (de tamaño) small; **me queda ~** it's too small for me; **en ~** in miniature **(b)** (de edad) young, small; **mi hermano ~** my younger *o* little brother; **cuando era ~** when I was small *o* little **(c)** (de poca importancia) ‹*distancia*› short; ‹*retraso*› short, slight; ‹*cantidad*› small; ‹*esfuerzo*› slight; ‹*problema/diferencia*› slight, small ■ *m,f*: **el ~/la pequeña** the little one (colloq); (edad — de dos) the younger; (— de muchos) the youngest

pera *f* **1** (Bot) pear; **~ de agua** dessert pear **2** (de goma) bulb **3** (en boxeo) punching ball (AmE), punchball (BrE) **4** (CS fam) (mentón) chin; (barba) goatee

peral *m* pear tree

percal *m* percale

percance *m* (contratiempo) mishap; (accidente) minor accidente

percatarse [A1] *v pron* to notice; **~ DE algo** to notice sth

percebe *m* (molusco) goose barnacle

percepción *f* (por los sentidos) perception; **~ extrasensorial** extrasensory perception, ESP

perceptible *adj* (por los sentidos) perceptible, noticeable

percha *f* **(a)** (para el armario) (coat) hanger **(b)** (gancho) coat hook; (perchero) coat stand

perchero *m* (de pared) coat rack; (de pie) coat stand

percibir [I1] *vt* **1** ‹*sonido/olor*› to perceive; ‹*peligro*› to sense **2** (frml) ‹*sueldo/cantidad*› to receive

percusión *f* percussion

perdedor -dora *adj* losing (*before n*) ■ *m,f* loser; **es un mal ~** he's a bad loser

perder [E8] *vt* **1** (en general) to lose; **perdí el pasaporte** I lost my passport; **quiere ~ peso** he wants to lose weight; **con preguntar no se pierde nada** we've/you've nothing to lose by asking; **~ la vida** to lose one's life, to perish; ⇒ CABEZA, VISTA[2] 3; **yo no pierdo las esperanzas** I'm not giving up hope; **~ la práctica** to get out of practice; **~ el equilibrio** to lose one's balance; **~ el conocimiento** to lose consciousness, to pass out; **~ el ritmo** (Mús) to lose the beat; (en trabajo) to get out of the rhythm **2 (a)** ‹*autobús/tren/avión*› to miss **(b)** ‹*ocasión/oportunidad*› to miss; **sin ~ detalle** without missing any detail **(c)** ‹*tiempo*› to waste; **¡no me hagas ~ (el) tiempo!** don't waste my time!; **no hay tiempo que ~** there's no time to lose **3 (a)** ‹*guerra/pleito/partido*› to lose **(b)** ‹*curso/año*› to fail; ‹*examen*› (Ur) to fail **4** ‹*agua/aceite/aire*› to lose ■ **~** *vi* **1** (ser derrotado) to lose; **perdieron 3 a 1** they lost 3-1; **no sabes ~** you're a bad loser; **llevar las de ~** to be onto a loser; **la que sale perdiendo soy yo** I'm the one who loses out *o* comes off worst **2** «*cafetera/tanque*» to leak **3 echar(se) a perder** *ver* ECHAR I 1(a), ECHARSE I 1(a)

■ **perderse** *v pron* **1** «*persona/objeto*» to get lost; **siempre me pierdo en esta ciudad** I always get lost in this town; **se le perdió el dinero** he's lost the money; **cuando se ponen a hablar rápido me pierdo** when they start talking quickly I get lost **2** ‹*fiesta/película/espectáculo*› to miss

perdición *f* ruin

pérdida *f* **(a)** (en general) loss; **~ de calor/energía** heat/energy loss; **tuvo una ~ de conocimiento** he lost consciousness, he passed out; ***no tiene ~*** (Esp) you can't miss it **(b)** (Fin) loss; **la compañía sufrió grandes ~s** the company made a huge loss; **~s materiales** damage; **~s y ganancias** profit and loss **(c)** (desperdicio) waste; **fue una ~ de tiempo** it was a waste of time **(d)** (escape de gas, agua) leak

perdido -da *adj* **1** [ESTAR] **(a)** ‹*objeto/persona*› lost; ***dar algo por ~*** to give sth up for lost; ***de ~*** (Méx fam) at least **(b)** (confundido, desorientado) lost, confused **(c)** ‹*bala/perro*› stray (*before n*) **2** [ESTAR] (en un apuro): **si se enteran, estás ~** if they find out, you've had it *o* you're done for (colloq) **3** (aislado) ‹*lugar*› remote, isolated; ‹*momento*› idle, spare **4** ‹*idiota*› complete and utter (*before n*), total (*before n*); ‹*loco*› raving (*before n*); ‹*borracho*› out and out (*before n*) ■ *m,f* degenerate

perdidoso *m,f* (Méx) loser

perdigón *m* (Arm) pellet

perdiz *f* partridge

perdón *m* (Der) pardon; (Relig) forgiveness; **me pidió ~ por su comportamiento** he apologized to me for his behavior, he said he was sorry about his behavior; ***con ~*** if you'll pardon the expression ■ *interj* (expresando disculpas) I beg your pardon (frml), excuse me (AmE), sorry; (para atraer la atención) excuse me, pardon me (AmE); (al pedir que se repita algo) sorry?, pardon me? (AmE)

perdonar [A1] *vt* **(a)** ‹*persona/falta/pecado*› to forgive; **te perdono** I forgive you; **perdona mi curiosidad, pero** ... forgive my asking but ...; **perdone que lo moleste, pero** ... sorry to bother you *o* (AmE) pardon me for bothering you, but ... **(b)** (Der) to pardon **(c)** ‹*deuda*› to write off; **le perdonó el castigo** she let him off the punishment ■ **~** *vi*: **perdone ¿me puede decir la hora?** excuse me *o* (AmE) pardon me, can you tell me the time?; **perdone ¿cómo ha dicho?** sorry? what did you say?, excuse *o* pardon me? what did you say? (AmE); **perdona, pero yo no dije eso** I'm sorry but that's not what I said

perdurar [A1] *vi* «*duda/sentimiento/recuerdo*» to remain, last; «*crisis/situación/relación*» to last

perecear [A1] *vi* (Col) to laze around

perecedero -ra *adj* ‹*producto*› perishable

perecer [E3] *vi* (frml) to die, perish (journ *or* liter)

peregrinación *f*, **peregrinaje** *m* pilgrimage

peregrino -na *adj* **1** ‹*idea/respuesta*› outlandish, peculiar **2 (a)** ‹*ave*› migratory **(b)** ‹*monje*› wandering (*before n*) ■ *m,f* pilgrim

perejil *m* (Bot, Coc) parsley

perenne *adj* perennial; **árbol de hoja ~** evergreen tree

pereza *f* laziness; **me da ~ ir** I can't be bothered to go; **tengo una ~ horrible** I feel terribly lazy; **¡qué ~ tener que ir!** what a bind *o* drag having to go! (colloq)

perezosa *f* (Col, Per) deck chair

perezoso -sa *adj* lazy, idle ■ *m,f* **1** (holgazán) lazybones (colloq) **2 perezoso** *m* (Zool) sloth

perfección *f* perfection; **habla francés a la ~** she speaks perfect French

perfeccionar [A1] *vt* (mejorar) to improve; (hacer perfecto) to perfect

perfeccionista *mf* perfectionist

perfecto[1] -ta *adj* **(a)** (ideal, excelente) perfect **(b)** (*delante del n*) (absoluto): **un ~ caballero** a perfect gentleman; **es un ~ desconocido** he is completely unknown

perfecto[2] *interj* fine!

perfil *m* **(a)** (del cuerpo, la cara) profile; **una foto de ~** a profile photograph; **visto de ~** seen from the side **(b)** (contorno, silueta) profile, silhouette

perfilar [A1] *vt* ‹*plan/estrategia*› to shape

■ **perfilarse** *v pron* **(a)** «*silueta/contorno*» to be outlined **(b)** (tomar forma) «*posición/actitud*» to become clear

perforación *f* **(a)** (en general) drilling, boring; (pozo) borehole **(b)** (Med) perforation **(c)** (en papeles, sellos) perforation

perforadora *f* **1** (Min, Tec) drill **2** (de papeles) hole puncher; (de sellos) perforator

perforar [A1] *vt* **1 (a)** ‹*pozo*› to sink, drill, bore **(b)** ‹*madera*› to drill *o* bore holes/a hole in **(c)**

«*ácido*» to perforate; «*bala*» to pierce **2** ‹*papel/tarjeta*› to perforate
■ **perforarse** *v pron* «*úlcera/intestino*» to become perforated

perfumar [A1] *vt* to perfume
■ **perfumarse** *v pron* (*refl*) to put perfume *o* scent on

perfume *m* perfume, scent

perfumería *f* perfumery

pergamino *m* (material) parchment; (documento) scroll

pérgola *f* pergola

pericia *f* (destreza) skill

periferia *f* **(a)** (de círculo) periphery, circumference **(b)** (de ciudad) outskirts (*pl*) **(c)** (Inf) peripherals (*pl*)

periférico[1] **-ca** *adj* ‹*barrio/zona*› outlying (*before n*)

periférico[2] *m* **1** (Inf) peripheral **2** (AmC, Méx) (carretera) beltway (AmE), ring road (BrE)

perilla *f* (barba) goatee; ***venir de ~s*** (fam) to come in very handy (colloq)

perímetro *m* perimeter

periódico[1] **-ca** *adj* periodic

periódico[2] *m* newspaper, paper

periodiquero -ra *m,f* (Méx) news *o* newspaper vendor

periodismo *m* journalism

periodista *mf* journalist, reporter; **~ gráfico** press photographer

período, **periodo** *m* period

peripecia *f* **(a)** (incidente): **un viaje lleno de ~s** an eventful journey; **sus ~s en el extranjero** her adventures abroad **(b)** (problema) vicissitude

periquito *m* (americano) parakeet; (australiano) budgerigar, budgie (colloq)

periscopio *m* periscope

peritaje *m* **(a)** (informe) expert's report; (de casa) survey (report) **(b)** (Educ) technical studies (*pl*)

perito -ta *m,f* (experto) expert; **~ agrónomo** agricultural technician; **~ industrial** engineer; **~ mercantil** qualified accountant

peritonitis *f* (*pl* **~**) peritonitis

perjudicado -da *adj*: **el que resultó ~** the one who lost out *o* who was worst hit; **los más ~s** the worst hit, the worst affected ■ *m,f*: **el ~ fui yo** I was the one who lost out

perjudicar [A2] *vt* (dañar) to be detrimental to (frml), damage; **el tabaco perjudica tu salud** smoking is detrimental to *o* damages your health; **estas medidas perjudican a los jóvenes** these measures are detrimental to *o* harm young people

perjudicial *adj* [SER] damaging, harmful, detrimental (frml); **~ PARA algo/algn** damaging *o* harmful *o* detrimental TO sth/sb

perjuicio *m* (daño) damage; **no sufrió ningún ~** it did him no harm *o* damage; **le causó un gran ~** it was very damaging to him; **redunda** *o* **va en ~ de todos** it works against *o* (frml) is detrimental to everyone; **sin ~ para su salud** without detriment to his health (frml); **sin ~ de que cambiemos de opinión** even though we may change our minds later

perjurio *m* perjury

perla *f* (joya) pearl; **~ cultivada** *or* **de cultivo** cultured pearl

permanecer [E3] *vi* (frml) **(a)** (en lugar) to stay, remain (frml) **(b)** (en actitud, estado) to remain; **permaneció en silencio** he was *o* remained silent

permanencia *f* (en lugar) stay; (en organización, cargo) continuance (frml)

permanente *adj* permanent ■ *f* **1** (en el pelo) perm; **hacerse la ~** to have one's hair permed, to have a perm **2** (Col) (juzgado) emergency court (*for cases of violent crime*)

permisible *adj* permissible

permisionario -ria *m,f* (Méx) concessionaire, official agent

permisivo -va *adj* permissive

permiso *m* **1** (autorización) permission; (documento) permit, license*; **me dio ~** she gave me permission; **(con) permiso** (al abrirse paso) excuse me; (al entrar) may I come in?; **~ de conducir** driver's license (AmE), driving licence (BrE); **~ de residencia** residence permit/green card (AmE); **~ de trabajo** work permit **2** (días libres) leave; **de ~** on leave

permitir [I1] *vt* **(a)** (autorizar) to allow, permit (frml); **no le permitieron verla** he was not allowed to see her; **no van a ~les la entrada** they're not going to let them in; **¿me permite?** (frml) may I? **(b)** (tolerar, consentir): **no te permito que me hables así** I won't have you speak *o* I won't tolerate you speaking to me like that; **si se me permite la expresión** if you'll pardon the expression **(c)** (hacer posible) to enable, to make ... possible; **esto ~á mejores comunicaciones** this will enable better communications; **si el tiempo lo permite** weather permitting
■ **permitirse** *v pron* (*refl*) to allow oneself; (económicamente): **puedo/no puedo ~me ese lujo** I can/can't afford that luxury

permutación *f* permutation

pernera *f* (del pantalón) leg

pero *conj* but; **ella fue, ~ yo no** she went, but I didn't; **¡~ si queda lejísimos!** but it's miles (away)!; **¿~ tú estás loca?** are you crazy? ■ *m* **(a)** (defecto) defect, bad point; (dificultad, problema) drawback; ***ponerle ~s a algo/algn*** to find fault with sth/sb **(b)** (excusa) objection; ***¡no hay ~ que valga!*** I don't want any excuses (*o* arguments *etc*)

perogrullada *f* (fam) platitude, truism

Perogrullo *m*: **ser de ~** to be patently obvious

perol *m* (pequeño) saucepan; (grande) pot

peroné *m* fibula

perorata *f* (fam) lecture (colloq)

perpendicular *adj/mf* perpendicular

perpetrar [A1] *vt* to perpetrate (frml), to carry out

perpetuar [A18] *vt* to perpetuate

perpetuo -tua *adj* perpetual

perplejidad *f* perplexity, puzzlement

perplejo -ja *adj* perplexed, puzzled; **estar ~ con algo** to be puzzled *o* perplexed by sth

perra *f* **1** (Zool) dog, bitch [BITCH *sólo se emplea cuando se quiere hacer referencia al sexo del animal*] *ver tb* PERRO **2** (Esp fam) **(a)** (rabieta) tantrum; **coger una ~** to have *o* throw a tantrum **(b)** (manía) obsession; **le ha dado la ~ de tener uno** he's obsessed with having one

perrada *f* (AmL fam) dirty trick

perrera *f* **(a)** (lugar) dog pound, dog's home **(b)** (vehículo) dog catcher's van

perrería *f* (fam) terrible thing (colloq)

perrero -ra *m,f* dog catcher, dog warden (BrE)

perrito *m* **1** (Zool) little dog; *ver tb* PERRO **2** (AmL) (Bot) snapdragon

perro -rra *m,f* (Zool) dog; **~ callejero** stray (dog); **~ de compañía** pet dog; **~ guardián** guard dog; **~ guía** *or* **lazarillo** guide dog; **~ pastor** sheepdog; **perrito caliente** (Coc) hot dog; **perrito faldero** lapdog; **~ policía** German shepherd, Alsatian (BrE); **~ salchicha** dachshund, sausage dog (colloq); ***de ~s*** (fam) foul; **hace un tiempo de ~s** the weather's foul *o* horrible; **está de un humor de ~s** he's in a foul mood; ***llevarse como (el) ~ y (el) gato*** to fight like cats and dogs (AmE) *o* (BrE) cat and dog ■ *adj* (fam) **(a)** ‹*vida/suerte*› rotten (colloq), lousy (colloq) **(b)** ‹*persona*› nasty

persa *adj/mf* Persian ■ *m* (idioma) Persian

persecución *f* **(a)** (en sentido físico) pursuit; **salir en ~ de algn** to set off in pursuit of sb **(b)** (por la ideología) persecution; **sufrir persecuciones** to be subjected to persecution, to be persecuted

perseguir [I30] *vt* **1 (a)** ‹*fugitivo/delincuente/presa*› to pursue, chase **(b)** (por la ideología) to persecute **2** ‹*objetivo/fin*› to pursue; **~ la fama** to be in pursuit of fame; **me persigue la mala suerte** I'm dogged by bad luck

perseverante *adj* persevering, persistent

perseverar [A1] *vi* to persevere

Persia *f* Persia

persiana *f* **(a)** (que se enrolla o levanta) blind; **~ veneciana** *or* **de lamas** Venetian blind **(b)** (AmL) (contraventana, postigo) shutter

persignarse [A1] *v pron* to cross oneself

persistencia *f* persistence

persistente *adj* persistent

persistir [I1] *vi*: **persiste el temporal** there is still a storm blowing; **~ EN algo** to persist IN sth

persona *f* **(a)** (ser humano) person; **una ~ muy educada** a very polite person; **dos o más ~s** two or more people; **las ~s interesadas** ... all those interested ... **(b)** (*en locs*) **en persona** ‹*ir/presentarse*› in person; **no lo conozco en ~** I don't know him personally; **por persona** per person; **sólo se venden dos entradas por ~** you can only get two tickets per person; **la comida costó 20 dólares por ~** the meal cost 20 dollars per *o* a head **(c)** (Ling) person

personaje *m* **(a)** (Cin, Lit) character **(b)** (persona importante) important figure, personage (frml); **un ~ de la política** an important political figure; **es todo un ~ en el pueblo** he's something of a local celebrity

personal *adj* personal; **objetos de uso ~** personal effects ■ *m* (de fábrica, empresa) personnel (*pl*), staff (*sing or pl*); **estamos escasos de ~** we're short-staffed

personalidad *f* **(a)** (Psic) personality **(b)** (persona importante) ⇒ PERSONAJE (b)

personalizar [A4] *vi*: **no quiero ~** I don't want to name names *o* mention any names ■ **~** *vt* to personalize

personería *f* (Col, RPl) legal capacity

personero -ra *m,f* (AmL) (representante) representative; (portavoz) (*m*) spokesman, spokesperson; (*f*) spokeswoman, spokesperson

personificar [A2] *vt* to personify; **es la bondad personificada** she is kindness itself

perspectiva *f* **(a)** (Arquit, Art) perspective; **en ~** in perspective **(b)** (vista, paisaje) view, perspective (frml) **(c)** (punto de vista) perspective **(d)** (posibilidad) prospect; **las ~s son buenas** the prospects are good; **no tengo ningún plan en ~** I've no plans for the immediate future

perspicacia *f* shrewdness, insight

perspicaz *adj* shrewd, perceptive

persuadir [I1] *vt* to persuade; **~ a algn DE QUE** *or* **PARA QUE haga algo** to persuade sb to do sth

persuasión *f* persuasion

persuasivo -va *adj* persuasive

pertenecer [E3] *vi* **(a)** (ser propiedad) **~ A algn/algo** to belong TO sb/sth **(b)** (formar parte) **~ A algo** to belong TO sth, be a member OF sth

perteneciente *adj*: **los países ~s al grupo** the countries belonging to *o* which are members of the group

pertenencia *f* **(a)** (a grupo, organización) membership **(b)** (frml) (propiedad): **los objetos de su ~** his belongings **(c) pertenencias** *fpl* belongings (*pl*), possessions (*pl*)

pértiga *f* **(a)** (vara) pole **(b)** (Esp) (Dep) pole; **salto con ~** pole vault

pertinente *adj* **(a)** (oportuno, adecuado) ‹*medida*› appropriate **(b)** (relevante) ‹*observación/comentario*› relevant, pertinent

perturbación *f* (alteración) disruption; (Psic) disturbance

perturbado -da *adj* disturbed ■ *m,f*: *tb* **~ mental** mentally disturbed person

perturbar [A1] *vt* to disturb

Perú *m*: *tb* **el ~** Peru

peruanismo *m* Peruvianism, Peruvian word/expression

peruano -na *adj/m,f* Peruvian

perversión *f* **(a)** (maldad) evil, wickedness **(b)** (corrupción) perversion

perverso -sa *adj* evil ■ *m,f* evil *o* wicked person

pervertido -da *m,f* pervert

pervertir [I11] *vt* to corrupt, pervert ■ **pervertirse** *v pron* to become corrupted

pesa *f* **(a)** (de balanza, reloj) weight **(b)** (Dep) (grande) weight; (pequeña) dumbbell; **levantamiento de**

~s weightlifting; ***hacer ~s*** to do weight training **(c)** (balanza) scales (*pl*)

pesadez *f* **1** (sensación de cansancio) heaviness **2** (fam) **(a)** (aburrimiento, molestia) drag (colloq); **¡qué ~ de conversación!** what a boring conversation! **(b)** (Andes) (broma) tiresome joke; (comentario) nasty remark

pesadilla *f* **(a)** (sueño) nightmare, bad dream **(b)** (situación) nightmare; **de ~** ‹*viaje/visión*› nightmare (*before n*)

pesado -da *adj* **1** (en general) heavy; ‹*estómago*› bloated; ‹*sueño*› deep **2 (a)** (fam) (fastidioso, aburrido) ‹*libro/película*› tedious; ‹*persona*›: **¡qué ~ es!** he's such a pain in the neck! (colloq); **no te pongas ~** don't be so annoying *o* (colloq) such a pest! **(b)** (AmL) (difícil, duro) ‹*trabajo/tarea*› heavy, hard **3** (Andes fam) (antipático) unpleasant; **¡qué tipo tan ~!** what a jerk! (colloq) ■ *m,f* **(a)** (fam) (latoso) pain (colloq), pest (colloq) **(b)** (Andes fam) (antipático) jerk (colloq)

pesadumbre *f* grief, sorrow

pésame *m* condolences (*pl*); **darle el ~ a algn** to offer sb one's condolences; **mi más sentido ~** (fr hecha) my deepest sympathies

pesar[1] *m* **1 (a)** (pena, tristeza) sorrow; **a ~ mío** *or* **muy a mi ~** much to my regret **(b)** (remordimiento) regret, remorse **2 a pesar de** despite, in spite of; **a ~ de todo** in spite of *o* despite everything; **a pesar de que** even though

pesar[2] [A1] *vi* **1** «*paquete/maleta*» to be heavy; **estas gafas no pesan** these glasses don't weigh much; **no me pesa** it's not heavy **2** (causar arrepentimiento) (+ *me/te/le etc*): **ahora me pesa mucho** now I deeply regret it; **me pesa haberlo ofendido** I'm very sorry I offended him **3 pese a** despite, in spite of; **pese a que** even though; **mal que me/le pese** whether I like/he likes it or not ■ ~ *vt* **(a)** ‹*niño/maleta*› to weigh; ‹*manzanas*› to weigh (out) **(b)** (tener cierto peso) to weigh; **pesa 80 kilos** he weighs 80 kilos

■ **pesarse** *v pron* (*refl*) to weigh oneself

pesca *f* **(a)** (en general) fishing; **ir** *or* **salir de ~** to go fishing; **~ con caña** angling; **~ con red** net fishing; **~ submarina** underwater fishing **(b)** (peces) fish (*pl*); **aquí hay mucha ~** there are a lot of fish here **(c)** (lo pescado) catch

pescada *f* hake

pescadería *f* fish shop, fishmonger's (BrE)

pescadero -ra *m,f* fish dealer (AmE), fishmonger (BrE)

pescadilla *f* whiting, young hake

pescado *m* (Coc) fish; (pez) (AmL) fish; **~ azul/blanco** blue/white fish

pescador -dora (*m*) fisherman; (*f*) fisherwoman

pescar [A2] *vt* **1** ‹*trucha/corvina*› to catch; **fuimos a ~ trucha(s)** we went trout-fishing, we went fishing for trout **2** (fam) **(a)** ‹*catarro/gripe*› to catch **(b)** ‹*novio/marido*› to get, hook (colloq & hum) **(c)** ‹*chiste/broma*› to get (colloq) **(d)** (pillar) to catch; **lo ~on robando** they caught him red-handed (as he was stealing something) ■ ~ *vi* to fish; **~ a mosca** to fly-fish

pescuezo *m* (fam) neck

pese a *loc prep ver* PESAR[2] 3

pesebre *m* (en establo) manger, trough; (de Navidad) crib

pesebrera *f* (Col) stable

pesero *m* (Méx) minibus

peseta *f* peseta (*Spanish unit of currency*)

pesimismo *m* pessimism

pesimista *adj* pessimistic ■ *mf* pessimist

pésimo -ma *adj* dreadful, terrible, abysmal

peso *m* **1 (a)** ▶ **322** (Fís, Tec) weight; **ganar/perder ~** to gain *o* put on/lose weight; **~ bruto/neto** gross/net weight; ⇒ CAERSE **(b) al peso** by weight **2 (a)** (carga, responsabilidad) weight, burden; ***quitarle un ~ de encima a algn*** to take a load *o* a weight off sb's mind **(b)** (influencia) weight; **todo el ~ de la ley** the full weight of the law **(c) de peso** ‹*argumento*› strong, weighty; ‹*razón*› forceful **3** (Dep) **(a)** (Esp) (en atletismo) shot; **lanzamiento de ~** shot-put, shot-putting **(b)** (Esp) (en halterofilia) weight; **levantamiento de ~s** weightlifting **(c)** (en boxeo) weight; **~ ligero/mosca/pesado/pluma** lightweight/flyweight/heavyweight/featherweight **4** (báscula) scales (*pl*) **5** (Fin) peso (*unit of currency in many Latin American countries*); **no tiene un ~** he doesn't have a cent *o* penny

pespunte *m* backstitch

pesquero -ra *adj* fishing (*before n*)

pesquisa *f* investigation, inquiry

pestaña *f* (Anat) ▶ **123** eyelash

pestañear [A1] *vi* to blink; ***sin ~*** (literal) without blinking; (sin inmutarse) without batting an eyelash (AmE) *o* (BrE) eyelid

peste *f* **(a)** (Med, Vet) plague, epidemic; **~ cristal** (Chi) chickenpox; **~ negra** Black Death **(b)** (AmL fam) (enfermedad contagiosa) bug (colloq); (resfriado) cold **(c)** (fam) (mal olor) stink

pesticida *m* pesticide

pestilente *adj* ‹*olor*› foul

pestillo *m* (cerrojo) bolt; (de cerradura) latch, catch; **echó** *or* **corrió el ~** she put the bolt across

petaca *f* **(a)** (cigarrera) cigarette case; (para tabaco — de cuero) tobacco pouch; (— de metal) tobacco tin **(b)** (para bebidas alcohólicas) hipflask

pétalo *m* petal

petanca *f* petanque

petardo *m* firecracker, banger (BrE)

petate *m* **1** (Mil) (para dormir) bedroll; (bolsa) knapsack **2** (Col, Méx) (estera) matting **3 petates** *mpl* (CS fam) (pertenencias) gear (colloq)

petición *f* **(a)** (acción) request; **a ~ del público** by popular request *o* demand; **a ~ fiscal** at the prosecutor's request **(b)** (escrito) petition; **~ de divorcio** petition for divorce; **~ de extradición** application for extradition

petirrojo *m* robin

petiso -sa *m,f* **1** (AmS fam) (de baja estatura) shorty (colloq) **2 petiso** *m* (CS) (Equ) small horse, pony

peto *m* **(a)** (de pantalón, delantal) bib; **pantalones de ~** (Esp) overalls (*pl*) (AmE), dungarees (*pl*) (BrE) **(b)**

Peso/Weight

Sistema métrico *Metric system*				Sistema estadounidense y británico *US/UK system*
10 miligramos	=	1 centigramo		
10 milligrams	=	1 centigram		
10 centigramos	=	1 decigramo		
10 centigrams	=	1 decigram		
100 centigramos	=	1 gramo	=	0.0352 ounces
100 centigrams	=	1 gram		
10 gramos	=	1 decagramo	=	0.352 ounces
10 grams	=	1 dekagram		
1.000 gramos	=	1 kilo(gramo)	=	2.205 pounds
1,000 grams	=	1 kilo(gram)		
1.000 kilogramos	=	1 tonelada	=	0.9842 tons
1,000 kilograms	=	1 metric ton		
	=	1 tonne		

US/UK system *Sistema estadounidense y británico*				Metric system *Sistema métrico*
	=	1 ounce	=	28,35 gramos
	=	1 onza		
16 ounces	=	1 pound	=	0,454 kilogramos
	=	1 libra		
14 pounds	=	1 stone*	=	6,35 kilogramos
112 pounds	=	1 hundredweight	=	50,8 kilogramos
20 hundredweight	=	1 ton	=	1.016 kilogramos
2000 pounds	=	1 short ton	=	0,907 toneladas
2,240 pounds	=	1 long ton	=	1,016 toneladas

** En EEUU el peso de una persona se suele expresar en libras y no en 'stone':*

She weighs 129 pounds (US)
She weighs 9 stone 3 pounds (UK)

(de armadura) breastplate **(c)** (Taur) protective covering (*for picador's horse*) **(d)** (en béisbol) chest protector

petrificado -da *adj* ‹*madera*› petrified; ‹*animal*› fossilized; **al oírlo se quedó ~** he was thunderstruck when he heard

petrificar [A2] *vt* to petrify ■ **petrificarse** *v pron* to become petrified, turn to stone

petrodólar *m* petrodollar

petróleo *m* **(a)** (Min) oil, petroleum; **~ crudo** crude oil **(b)** (combustible) kerosene, paraffin (BrE)

petrolero¹ -ra *adj* oil (*before n*)

petrolero² *m* oil tanker

petrolífero -ra *adj* oil (*before n*); ⇒ YACIMIENTO

petulante *adj* smug, self-satisfied ■ *mf* smug *o* self-satisified fool

petunia *f* petunia

peyorativo -va *adj* pejorative

pez *m* fish; **~ de río** freshwater fish; **~ de colores** goldfish; **~ espada** swordfish; **~ gordo** (fam) (persona importante) bigwig (colloq); (en delito) big shot (colloq); **~ volador** flying fish; ***estar** or **sentirse como ~ en el agua*** to be in one's element ■ *f* (sustancia) pitch, tar

pezón *m* (Anat) nipple; (Zool) teat

pezuña *f* (Zool) hoof

piadoso -sa *adj* ‹*personas*› devout, pious; ‹*obra*› kind

pianista *mf* pianist

piano *m* piano; **~ de cola/de media cola** grand piano/baby grand; **~ vertical** upright piano

pianola *f* Pianola®, player piano

piar [A17] *vi* to chirp, tweet

PIB *m* (Esp) (= **Producto Interior Bruto**) GDP

pibe -ba *m,f* (RPl fam) kid (colloq)

pica *f* **1** (Arm) pike; (Taur) lance, goad; (para cavar) pick, pickax* **2** (Jueg) **(a)** (carta) spade **(b) picas** *fpl* (palo) spades

picada *f* **1** (AmL) (descenso pronunciado): **caer en ~** «*avión*» to nose-dive; «*pájaro*» to plunge, to dive; «*acciones/valores*» to plummet **2** (AmL) (aperitivo) nibbles (*pl*)

picadero *m* (para caballos) exercise ring; (escuela) riding school

picado[1] -da *adj* **(a)** ‹*diente/muela*› decayed, bad; ‹*manguera/llanta*› perished **(b)** ‹*ajo/perejil*› chopped; ‹*carne*› (Esp, RPl) ground (AmE), minced (BrE) **(c)**‹*manzana*› rotten; ‹*vino*› sour **(d)** (fam) (enfadado, ofendido) put out (colloq), miffed (colloq) **(e)** ‹*mar*› choppy

picado[2] *m* (Esp) ⇒ PICADA 1

picador *m* **(a)** (Taur) picador **(b)** (en mina) face worker

picadura *f* **1** (de mosquito, serpiente) bite; (de abeja) sting; (de polilla) hole **2** (en diente, muela) cavity

picaflor *m* (AmL) (Zool) hummingbird; (donjuán) (fam) womanizer

picana *f* (AmL) **(a)** (para bueyes) prod, goad **(b)** *tb* **~ eléctrica** cattle prod

picante *adj* **(a)** (Coc) ‹*comida*› hot **(b)** ‹*chiste/libro*› risqué; ‹*comedia*› racy

picaporte *m* (manivela) door handle; (mecanismo) latch

picar [A2] *vt* **1 (a)** «*mosquito/víbora*» to bite; «*abeja/avispa*» to sting; **me ~on los mosquitos** I got bitten by mosquitoes; **una manta picada por las polillas** a moth-eaten blanket **(b)** «*ave*» ‹*comida*› to peck at; ‹*enemigo*› to peck **(c)** ‹*anzuelo*› to bite **(d)** (fam) (comer) to eat; **sólo quiero ~ algo** I just want a snack *o* a bite to eat **(e)** ‹*billete/boleto*› to punch **(f)** (Taur) to jab **2 (a)** (Coc) ‹*carne*› (Esp, RPl) to grind (AmE), to mince (BrE); ‹*cebolla/perejil*› to chop (up) **(b)** ‹*hielo*› to crush; ‹*pared*› to chip; ‹*piedra*› to break up, smash **3** ‹*dientes/muelas*› to rot, decay ■ **~** *vi* **1 (a)** (morder el anzuelo) to bite, take the bait **(b)** (comer) to nibble **2 (a)** (ser picante) to be hot **(b)** (producir comezón) «*lana/suéter*» to itch, be itchy; **me pica la espalda** my back itches *o* is itchy; **me pican los ojos** my eyes sting **3** (AmL) «*pelota*» to bounce **4** (RPl arg) (irse, largarse) to split (sl); **~le** (Méx fam) to get a move on (colloq)
■ **picarse** *v pron* **1 (a)** «*muelas*» to decay, rot; «*manguera/llanta*» to perish; «*cacerola/pava*» to rust; «*ropa*» to get moth-eaten **(b)** «*manzana*» to go rotten; «*vino*» to go sour **2** «*mar*» to get choppy **3** (fam) (enfadarse) to get annoyed; (ofenderse) to take offense

picardía *f* **(a)** (astucia) craftiness, cunning **(b)** (malicia) mischief **(c)** (travesura) prank

pícaro -ra *adj* **(a)** (ladino) crafty, cunning **(b)** (malicioso) ‹*persona*› naughty, wicked (colloq); ‹*chiste/comentario*› naughty, racy; ‹*mirada/sonrisa*› mischievous, cheeky (BrE) ■ *m,f* **(a)** (Lit) rogue, villain **(b)** (astuto) cunning *o* crafty devil (colloq)

picatoste *m* (para sopa) crouton

picazón *f* irritation, itch

pichanga *f* (Chi) (partido — improvisado) kickabout, friendly game; (— malo) bad game

pichi *m* (Esp) jumper (AmE), pinafore (BrE)

pichí *m* (CS fam) wee-wee (used to or by children)

pichicatearse [A1] *v pron* (CS, Per fam) to take drugs

pichincha *f* (RPl fam) (ganga) bargain, steal (colloq)

pichirre *mf* (Ven fam) skinflint (colloq)

pichón -chona *m,f* (de paloma) young pigeon; (de otros pájaros) chick

picnic *m* (*pl* **-nics**) picnic

pico *m* **1 (a)** (de pájaro) beak **(b)** (fam) (boca) mouth; **¡cierra el ~!** shut up (colloq), keep your trap shut! (colloq) **2 (a)** (cima, montaña) peak **(b)** (en gráfico) peak **(c)** (en diseños, costura) point; **cuello de ~** V neck **(d)** (de jarra, tetera) spout **3** (fam) (algo): **tiene 50 y ~ de años** she's fifty odd *o* fifty something (colloq); **son las dos y ~** it's past *o* gone two; **tres metros y ~** (just) over three meters **4 picos** *mpl* (Méx) (zapatillas) spikes (*pl*)

picor *m* irritation, itch

picoso *adj* (Méx) hot, spicy

picotazo *m* peck

picotear [A1] *vt* to peck ■ **~** *vi* (fam) (entre comidas) to nibble, snack

picudo -da *adj* **(a)** ‹*nariz*› pointed, sharp **(b)** ‹*ave*› long-beaked

pida, **pidas**, **etc** *see* PEDIR

pie[1] *m* **1 (a)** (Anat) ▶ **123** foot; **un dedo del ~** a toe; **tiene (los) ~s planos** she has flat feet; **~ de atleta** athlete's foot **(b)** (*en locs*) **a pie** on foot; **ir a ~** to go on foot, walk; **hoy ando a ~** (AmL) I'm without wheels today; **de pie** standing; **ponte de ~** stand up; **en pie**: **estoy en ~ desde las siete** I've been up since seven o'clock; **no puedo tenerme en ~** I can hardly walk/stand; **sólo la iglesia quedó en ~** only the church remained standing; **mi oferta sigue en ~** my offer still stands; ***a ~ pelado*** (Chi) barefoot, in one's bare feet; ***de a ~*** common, ordinary; ***de la cabeza a los ~s*** *or* ***de ~s a cabeza*** from head to foot *o* toe, from top to toe (colloq); ***en ~ de guerra*** on a war footing; ***en (un) ~ de igualdad*** on an equal footing; ***hacer ~*** to be able to touch the bottom; ***levantarse con el ~ derecho*** to get off to a good start; ***no tener ni ~s ni cabeza*** to make no sense whatsoever; ***por mi/tu/su (propio) ~*** unaided, without any help **2 (a)** (de calcetín, media) foot **(b)** (de lámpara, columna) base; (de copa — base) base; (— parte vertical) stem; (de montaña) foot **(c)** (de página, escrito) foot, bottom; **una nota a** *or* **al ~ de página** a footnote; **~ de fotografía** caption; ***al ~ de la letra*** ‹*copiar/repetir*› word by word, exactly **(d)** (de cama) *tb* **~s** foot **3 (a)** ▶ **681** (medida) foot **(b)** (Lit) foot

pie[2] /paɪ/ *m* (AmL) pie

piedad *f* **(a)** (compasión) mercy; **ten ~ de nosotros** have mercy on us; **es un hombre sin ~** he's merciless; **¡por ~!** for pity's sake! **(b)** (devoción) devotion

piedra *f* **1** (material) stone; (trozo) stone, rock (esp AmE); **casas de ~** stone houses; **me tiró una ~** he threw a stone *o* rock at me; **~ caliza** *or* **de cal** limestone; **~ de molino** millstone; **~ pómez** pumice stone; **~ preciosa** precious stone; ***dejar a algn de ~*** (fam) to stun sb; ***(duro) como una ~*** ‹*pan/asado*› rock hard; **tiene el corazón duro como una ~** he has a heart of stone **2 (a)** (de mechero) flint **(b)** (cálculo) stone; **tiene ~s en el riñón/la vesícula** she has kidney stones/gallstones

piel *f* **1** ▶ 123 (Anat, Zool) skin; ~ **grasa/seca** oily *o* greasy/dry skin; ~ **roja** *mf* (fam & pey) redskin (colloq & pej), Red Indian; ***se me/te pone la ~ de gallina*** I/you get gooseflesh *o* goose pimples **2** (Indum) **(a)** (Esp, Méx) (cuero) leather; **guantes de ~** leather gloves; ~ **de cocodrilo** crocodile skin; ~ **de serpiente** snakeskin; ~ **sintética** (cuero sintético) (Esp, Méx) synthetic leather; (imitación nutria, visón, etc) synthetic fur **(b)** (de visón, zorro, astracán) fur; **abrigo de ~(es)** fur coat **(c)** (sin tratar) pelt **3** (Bot) (de cítricos, papa) peel; (de manzana) peel, skin; (de otras frutas) skin

pienso *m* (comida) fodder, feed

pierda, pierdas, etc *see* PERDER

pierna *f* **(a)** (Anat) ▶ 123 leg; **con las ~s cruzadas** cross-legged; ***abrirse de ~s*** (en gimnasia) to do the splits **(b)** (Coc) leg; ~ **de cordero** leg of lamb

pieza *f* **1** **(a)** (elemento, parte) piece; *ver tb* DOS[1] **(b)** (de motor, reloj) part; ~ **de recambio** *or* **de repuesto** spare part; ***quedarse de una ~*** to be dumbfounded; ***ser de una sola ~*** (AmL) to be as straight as a die **(c)** (en ajedrez) piece; (unidad, objeto) piece; ***una ~ de museo*** a museum piece **(d)** (en caza) piece, specimen **2** (Mús, Teatr) piece **3** (esp AmL) (dormitorio) bedroom; (en hotel) room

pifia *f* **1** **(a)** (fam) (error) boob (colloq) **(b)** (en billar) miscue **(c)** (Chi) (defecto) fault **2** (Chi, Per) (del público) booing and hissing

pifiar [A1] *vt* **1** (fam) (fallar) to fluff (colloq); **~*la*** (fam) to blow it (colloq) **2** (Chi, Per) « *público* » to boo

pigmentación *f* pigmentation

pigmento *m* pigment

pigmeo -mea *adj/m,f* pygmy

pijama *m* pajamas (*pl*) (AmE), pyjamas (*pl*) (BrE)

pije *adj/mf* (Chi) ⇒ PIJO

pijo -ja *adj* (Esp fam & pey) ‹*persona/moda/lugar*› posh (colloq & pej) ■ *m,f* (Esp fam & pey) rich kid (colloq & pej)

pila *f* **1** (Elec, Fís) battery; **funciona a ~(s)** *or* **con ~s** it runs on batteries, it's battery-operated **2** (fregadero) sink; (de una fuente) basin, bowl; ~ **bautismal** baptismal font **3** (fam) (de libros, platos) pile, stack

pilar *f* (Arquit) pillar, column; (de puente) pier ■ *mf* (en rugby) prop (forward)

pilchas *fpl* (CS fam) clothes (*pl*), gear (colloq)

píldora *f* **(a)** (pastilla) pill, tablet **(b)** *tb* ~ **anticonceptiva** (contraceptive) pill; **tomar la ~** to be on the pill; ~ **del día siguiente** morning-after pill

pileta *f* **(a)** (RPl) (fregadero) kitchen sink; (del baño) washbowl (AmE), washbasin (BrE) **(b)** (RPl) (piscina) swimming pool **(c)** (Chi) (estanque) pond; (bebedero) drinking fountain

pillaje *m* pillage

pillar [A1] *vt* **1** (fam) **(a)** (atrapar) to catch; **le pilló un dedo** it caught *o* trapped her finger; **¡te pillé!** caught *o* got you! **(b)** ‹*catarro/resfriado*› to catch **2** (Esp fam) « *coche* » to hit

■ **pillarse** *v pron* (fam) ‹*dedos/manga*› to catch

pillo -lla *adj* (fam) (travieso) naughty, wicked (colloq); (astuto) crafty, cunning ■ *m,f* (fam) (travieso) rascal (colloq); (astuto) crafty *o* cunning devil (colloq)

pilón *m* **1** **(a)** (de fuente) basin **(b)** (Arquit) pillar; (de puente) pylon **2** (Méx fam) (en la compra) *small amount of extra goods given free*; **me dio tres manzanas de ~** he threw in three extra apples (for free)

pilotar [A1] *vt* **(a)** ‹*avión*› to pilot, fly; ‹*barco*› to pilot, steer; ‹*coche*› to drive; ‹*moto*› to ride **(b)** ‹*empresa/país*› to guide, steer

pilotear [A1] *vt* (AmL) ⇒ PILOTAR

piloto *mf* **1** (Aviac, Náut) pilot; (de coche) driver; (de moto) rider; ~ **de carreras** racing driver; ~ **de pruebas** (de avión) test pilot; (de coche) test driver; (de moto) test rider **2** **piloto** *m* **(a)** (de aparato eléctrico, a gas) pilot light **(b)** (CS) (impermeable) raincoat **3** (*como adj inv*) ‹*programa/producto*› pilot (*before n*)

piltrafa *f* **(a)** (de comida) scrap **(b)** (cosa inservible) useless thing

pimentón *m* **(a)** (dulce) paprika; (picante) cayenne pepper **(b)** (AmS exc RPl) (fruto) pepper, capsicum

pimienta *f* pepper

pimiento *m* pepper, capsicum; ~ **rojo/verde** red/green pepper

pimpón *m* Ping-Pong®, table tennis

pin *m* (broche) pin

pináculo *m* (Arquit) pinnacle; (apogeo) pinnacle, peak

pinar *m* pine forest

pincel *m* (Art) paintbrush; (para maquillarse) brush

pincelada *f* brushstroke

pinchar [A1] *vt* **1** **(a)** ‹*globo/balón*› to burst; ‹*rueda*› to puncture **(b)** (con alfiler, espina) to prick **(c)** (para recoger) to spear **2** (fam) (poner una inyección) to give ... a shot (colloq) **3** ‹*teléfono*› to tap, bug **4** (Esp fam) ‹*discos*› to play ■ ~ *vi* **1** « *planta* » to be prickly **2** (Auto) to get a flat (tire*), get a puncture **3** (Chi fam) (con el sexo opuesto) ⇒ LIGAR *vi*

■ **pincharse** *v pron* **1** **(a)** (*refl*) « *persona* » (accidentalmente) to prick oneself; (inyectarse) (fam) to shoot up (sl), to jack up (sl) **2** « *rueda* » to puncture; « *globo/balón* » to burst; **se me pinchó un neumático** I got a flat (tire*) *o* a puncture

pinchazo *m* **(a)** (herida) prick; (inyección) shot (colloq) **(b)** (en una rueda) flat, puncture **(c)** (dolor agudo) sharp pain **(d)** (fam) (de droga) fix (colloq)

pinche *adj* **(a)** (AmL exc CS fam) (*delante del n*) (maldito): **¡~ vida!** what a (lousy *o* rotten) life!; **por unos ~s pesos** for a few measly pesos (colloq); **vámonos de este ~ lugar** let's get out of this damn place! **(b)** (Méx fam) (de poca calidad) lousy (colloq); (despreciable) horrible **(c)** (AmC fam) (tacaño) tightfisted (colloq) ■ *mf* (Coc) kitchen assistant

pincho *m* **1** (de rosa, zarza) thorn, prickle (colloq); (de cactus) spine, prickle (colloq) **2** (Esp) (de aperitivo) bar snack

pingo -ga *m,f* (Méx fam) little scamp *o* rascal (colloq)

Ping-Pong® *m* Ping-Pong®, table tennis

pingüino *m* penguin

pino *m* **1** (Bot) (árbol) pine (tree); (madera) pine **2** (Esp) (en gimnasia): **hacer el ~** to do a handstand **3** (Méx) (en bolos) pin

pinolillo *m* (AmC) (maíz) cornstarch (AmE), maize flour (BrE); (bebida) *drink made with cornstarch and water*

pinta *f* **1** (fam) (aspecto) look; **eso le da ~ de intelectual** it gives him an intellectual look; **tiene ~ de extranjero** he looks foreign; **¿dónde vas con esa(s) ~(s)?** where are you going looking like that?; ***echar*** *or* ***tirar*** (Andes) *or* (RPl) ***hacer*** **~** (fam) to impress **2** (en tela, animal) spot **3** (medida) pint **4** (Méx fam) (de la escuela): **irse de ~** to play hooky* (esp AmE colloq), to skive off (school) (BrE colloq)

pintada *f* piece of graffiti; (Pol) slogan

pintado -da *adj* ‹*vaca*› spotted; ‹*caballo*› dappled, pied

pintalabios *m* (*pl* **~**) (fam) lipstick

pintar [A1] *vt* **(a)** (en general) to paint; **pintó la puerta de rojo** she painted the door red **(b)** (fam) (dibujar) to draw ■ **~** *vi* **1 (a)** (con pintura) to paint **(b)** (fam) (dibujar) to draw **2** (en naipes) to be trumps

■ **pintarse** *v pron* (*refl*) (maquillarse) to put on one's makeup; **~se los labios** to put on some lipstick; **~se los ojos** to put on eye makeup; **~se las uñas** to paint one's nails

pintarrajear [A1] *vt* to daub

pintor -tora *m,f* (de cuadros) painter, artist; (de paredes) (house) painter; **~ de brocha gorda** (de casas, barcos) painter

pintoresco -ca *adj* picturesque

pintura *f* **(a)** (arte, cuadro) painting; **~ a la acuarela/al óleo** watercolor*/oil painting **(b)** (material) paint; (en cosmética) makeup

pinza *f* **1 (a)** (para la ropa) clothespin (AmE), clothes peg (BrE) **(b)** (para el pelo) bobby pin (AmE), hairgrip (BrE) **(c)** (de un cangrejo) pincer **(d)** (en costura) dart; **un pantalón con ~s** pleated pants (AmE) *o* (BrE) trousers **2** *tb* **~s (a)** (para depilar) tweezers (*pl*); (de cirujano) forceps (*pl*); (de cocina, chimenea) tongs (*pl*) **(b)** (alicates) pliers (*pl*)

piña *f* (Bot) (fruta) pineapple; (del pino) pine cone

piñata *f*: *container hung up during festivities and hit with a stick to release candy inside*

piñón *m* **1** (Bot) pine kernel *o* nut **2** (Mec) pinion; (de bicicleta) sprocket wheel

pío¹, **pía** *adj* devout, pious

pío² *m* peep, tweet; ***no decir ni*** **~** (fam) not to say a word

piojo *m* louse; **~s** lice

piojoso -sa *adj* **(a)** (con piojos) lousy, lice-ridden **(b)** (fam) (sucio) filthy

piola *adj inv* (RPl fam) **(a)** (divertido) fun (*before n*) (colloq) **(b)** (astuto) crafty (colloq) **(c)** ‹*ropa*› trendy (colloq) ■ *f* (AmL) cord

piolet /pjo'le(t)/ *m* (*pl* **-lets**) ice ax*

pionero -ra *adj* pioneering (*before n*) ■ *m,f* pioneer

pipa *f* **1** (para fumar) pipe; **fumar (en) ~** to smoke a pipe **2** (tonel) cask, barrel **3** (Esp) (de sandía, mandarina) pip; (de girasol, calabaza) seed; ***pasarlo*** **~** (fam) to have a great time **4** (Méx) (camión) tanker

pipí *m* (fam) pee (colloq), wee (BrE colloq); **hacer ~** to have a pee *o* (BrE) wee

pique *m* **1 a pique**: **una caída a** *or* (Méx) **en ~ hasta el mar** a vertical *o* sheer drop to the sea below; **a pique de** on the point of, about to; ***irse a*** **~** «*barco*» to sink; «*negocio*» to go under **2** (fam) **(a)** (enfado, resentimiento): **tener un ~ con algn** to be at odds with sb **(b)** (rivalidad) rivalry, needle **3 (a)** (carta) spade **(b) piques** *fpl* (palo) spades (*pl*)

piqueta *f* pick, pickax*

piquete *m* **1**(de huelguistas) picket; (de soldados) squad, picket (arch) **2** (Méx fam) **(a)** (herida) prick; (inyección) shot (colloq), jab (colloq) **(b)** (de insecto) sting, bite

pira *f* pyre

piragua *f* (Dep) canoe

piragüismo *m* canoeing

pirámide *f* pyramid

piraña *f* (Zool) piranha

pirarse [A1] *v pron* (Esp fam) to make oneself scarce (colloq)

pirata *adj* **(a)** ‹*barco*› pirate (*before n*) **(b)** (clandestino) ‹*casete/copia*› pirate (*before n*), bootleg (*before n*) (colloq) ■ *mf* **(a)** (Náut) pirate; **~ aéreo** hijacker **(b)** (de casetes, videos) pirate

piratear [A1] *vt* ‹*videos/casetes*› to pirate; ‹*sistema*› to hack into

piratería *f* piracy; **~ informática** hacking (colloq)

Pirineos *mpl*, **Pirineo** *m*: **los ~** *or* **el Pirineo** the Pyrenees (*pl*)

pirinola *mf* (Andes, Méx) (peonza) spinning top

pirómano -na *m,f* pyromaniac

piropear [A1] *vt* to make flirtatious/flattering comments to

piropo *m* flirtatious/flattering comment

pirueta *f* (en danza) pirouette; (de un caballo) pesade

pis *m* ⇒ PIPÍ

pisada *f* (acción) footstep; (huella) footprint

pisapapeles *m* (*pl* **~**) paperweight

pisar [A1] *vt* **1 (a)** (con el pie) ‹*mina/clavo*› to step on; ‹*charco*› to step in, tread in (esp BrE); **la pisó sin querer** he accidentally stepped *o* (esp BrE) trod on her foot; 🅢 **prohibido pisar el césped** keep off the grass **(b)** (humillar) to trample on, walk all over **2** (RPl, Ven) **(a)** (Coc) to mash **(b)** (fam) (atropellar) to run over ■ **~** *vi* to tread; **pisó mal y se cayó** she lost her footing and fell

pisca *f* (Méx) harvest

piscina *f* swimming pool; **~ cubierta/climatizada** covered/heated swimming pool

Piscis *m* (signo, constelación) Pisces; **es (de) ~** he's (a) Pisces, he's a Piscean ■ *mf* (*pl* **~**) (persona) *tb* **piscis** Piscean, Pisces

pisco *m* (aguardiente) ≈ grappa

piso *m* **1 (a)** (de edificio) floor, story*; (de autobús) deck; **una casa de seis ~s** a six-story building; **un autobús de dos ~s** a double-decker bus **(b)** (de pastel) layer **2** (AmL) **(a)** (suelo) floor **(b)** (de carretera) road surface **3** (Esp) (apartamento) apartment (esp AmE), flat (BrE); **~ piloto** (Esp) show apartment *o* (BrE) flat **4** (Chi) (taburete) stool; (alfombrita) rug; (felpudo) doormat

pisotear [A1] *vt* **(a)** (con los pies) to trample, stamp on **(b)** ‹*persona/derecho*› to ride roughshod over

pisotón *m* stamp; **darle un ~ a algn** (intencional) to stamp on sb's foot *o* toes; (sin querer) to tread *o* step on sb's foot *o* toes

pista *f* **1 (a)** (rastro) trail, track; **seguirle la ~ a algn** to be/get on sb's trail **(b)** (indicio) clue **2 (a)** (carretera) road, track **(b)** (Chi) (carril) lane **(c)** (Audio) track **3 (a)** (en el circo) ring; (en el picadero) ring; (en el hipódromo) track (AmE), course (BrE); **~ de aterrizaje** runway, landing strip; **~ de baile** dance floor; **~ de esquí** ski slope, piste; **~ de hielo/de patinaje** ice/skating rink **(b)** (Esp) (de tenis) court

pistacho *m* pistachio (nut)

pistola *f* **(a)** (Arm) pistol; **a punta de ~** at gunpoint **(b)** (para pintar) spray gun

pistolero *m* gunman

pistón *m* **(a)** (émbolo) piston **(b)** (de arma) percussion cap **(c)** (de instrumento) key

pitada *f* **1 (a)** (pitido) beep **(b)** (en espectáculo) ≈ booing and hissing, whistling (*as sign of disapproval*) **2** (AmL) (de cigarrillo) puff, drag (colloq)

pitar [A1] *vi* **(a)** «*guardia/árbitro*» to blow one's whistle **(b)** «*vehículo*» to blow the horn, to hoot **(c)** «*público*» (como protesta) to boo and hiss ■ **~** *vt* ‹*falta*› to blow for, award, call (AmE)

pítcher *mf* pitcher

pitido *m* (sonido agudo) whistle, whistling; (de claxon) beep, hoot, honk

pitillera *f* cigarette case

pitillo *m* **1** (fam) (cigarrillo) smoke (colloq), fag (BrE colloq) **2** (Col) (para beber) straw

pito *m* **1 (a)** (silbato) whistle; **tocar el ~** to blow the whistle; **tener voz de ~** (fam) to have a squeaky voice **(b)** (fam) (de coche) horn, hooter; (de tren) whistle; **tocar el ~** to hoot, honk **2** (Chi fam) (de marihuana) joint (colloq), spliff (sl) **3** (fam) (pene) weenie (AmE colloq), willy (BrE colloq)

pitón *f or m* python

pitonisa *f* fortuneteller

pitorrearse [A1] *v pron* (Esp fam) **~** DE **algn** to make fun OF sb

pituco -ca *adj* (CS, Per fam) **(a)** (elegante) posh (colloq) **(b)** (engreído) **es un ~** he's stuck-up (colloq) ■ *m, f* (CS, Per fam) **es un ~** he's stuck-up (colloq)

pituto *m* (Chi fam) (para conseguir algo) contact

pívot *mf* (*pl* **-vots**) (Dep) center*, pivot

piyama *m or f* (AmL) pajamas (*pl*) (AmE), pyjamas (*pl*) (BrE)

pizarra *f* **(a)** (Min) slate **(b)** (en el aula) blackboard, chalkboard; (del alumno) slate **(c)** (Cin) clapperboard **(d)** (en béisbol) scoreboard

pizarrón *m* (AmL) blackboard, chalkboard

pizca *f* **1** (cantidad pequeña): **una ~ de algo** (de sal, azúcar) a pinch of sth; (de vino, agua) a drop of sth; **no tiene ni ~ de gracia** it's not the slightest bit funny **2** (Méx) (cosecha) harvest

pizcar [A2] *vt* (Méx) ‹*maíz*› to harvest; ‹*algodón*› to pick ■ **~** *vi* (Méx) to take in the harvest

pizza /'pitsa, 'pisa/ *f* pizza

pizzería /pitse'ria, pise'ria/ *f* pizzeria

Pl. (= **Plaza**) Sq, Square

placa *f* **1** (lámina, plancha) sheet **2 (a)** (con inscripción) plaque; **una ~ con el nombre** a nameplate; **~ de matrícula** license (AmE) *o* (BrE) number plate **(b)** (de policía) badge **3** (Chi) (dentadura) dentures (*pl*), dental plate

placaje *m* (en fútbol americano) block; (en rugby) tackle

placar [A2] *vt* (en fútbol americano) to block; (en rugby) to tackle

placard /pla'kar/ *m* (RPl) built-in closet (AmE), fitted wardrobe (BrE)

placenta *f* placenta, afterbirth

placentero -ra *adj* pleasant, agreeable

placer [E4] *vi* (*en 3ª pers*) (+ *me/te/le etc*): **haz lo que te plazca** do as you please; **me place informarle que** ... (frml) it is my pleasure to inform you that ... (frml) ■ *m* (gusto, satisfacción) pleasure; **ha sido un ~ conocerla** (frml) it has been a pleasure to meet you; **un viaje de ~** a pleasure trip

placero *m* (Per) street vendor

placidez *f* placidity, placidness, calmness

plácido -da *adj* placid, calm

plaga *f* **(a)** (de insectos, ratas) plague; **las ardillas son consideradas una ~** squirrels are considered to be a pest **(b)** (calamidad, azote) plague

plagado -da *adj*: [ESTAR] **~** DE **algo** ‹*de faltas/errores*› riddled WITH sth; ‹*de turistas/insectos*› swarming WITH sth

plagiar [A1] *vt* ‹*idea/libro*› to plagiarize

plagio *m* (copia) plagiarism

plan *m* **1** (proyecto, programa) plan; **hacer ~es** to make plans; **~ de estudios** syllabus **2** (fam) (cita, compromiso): **si no tienes otros ~es** if you're not doing anything else; **¿tienes algún ~ para esta noche?** do you have any plans for tonight? **3** (fam) (actitud): **vienen en ~ de diversión** they're here to have fun; **lo dijo en ~ de broma** he was only kidding (colloq); **en ~ económico** cheaply, on the cheap (colloq)

plana *f* **1** (de periódico) page; **en primera ~** on the front page **2** (Educ) (ejercicio) handwriting exercise **3 la ~ mayor** (Mil) the staff officers (*pl*); (jefes) (fam) the top brass (colloq)

plancha *f* **1 (a)** (electrodoméstico) iron **(b)** (acto) ironing; (ropa para planchar) ironing **2 (a)** (Const, Tec) sheet **(b)** (Impr) plate **3** (utensilio de cocina) griddle; **filete a la ~** grilled steak **4 (a)** (fam) (metedura de pata) boo-boo (colloq), boob (colloq) **(b)** (Chi fam) (vergüenza) embarrassment

planchar [A1] *vt* ‹*sábana/mantel*› to iron; ‹*pantalones*› to press, iron; ‹*traje*› to press ■ **~** *vi* (con la plancha) to do the ironing

plancton *m* plankton

planeación *f* (Méx) planning

planeador *m* glider

planear [A1] *vt* to plan ■ **~** *vi* (Aviac) to glide; «*águila*» to soar; (Náut) to plane

planeta *m* planet

planetario *m* planetarium

planificación *f* planning; ~ **familiar** family planning

planificar [A2] *vt* to plan, draw up a plan for

planilla *f* **1 (a)** (tabla) table, chart; (lista) list **(b)** (AmL) (nómina) payroll; **estar en** ~ to be on the payroll **(c)** (AmL) (personal) staff **2 (a)** (Méx) (en elección) list of candidates **(b)** (Col) (censo electoral) electoral register

plano[1] -na *adj* **1** ‹*superficie/terreno/zapato*› flat; **los 100 metros** ~**s** (AmL) the hundred meters dash *o* sprint **2** ‹*figura/ángulo*› plane

plano[2] *m* **1** (de edificio) plan; (de ciudad) street plan, map **2** (Mat) plane **3 (a)** (nivel) level; **en el** ~ **afectivo** on an emotional level **(b)** (Cin, Fot) shot **4** **de plano** ‹*rechazar/rehusar*› flatly

planta *f* **1** (Bot) plant; ~ **de interior** houseplant, indoor plant **2** (Arquit) **(a)** (plano) plan **(b)** (piso) floor; **una casa de dos** ~**s** a two-story house; ~ **baja** first floor (AmE), ground floor (BrE) **3** (Tec) (instalación) plant **4** (del pie) sole

plantación *f* **(a)** (terreno plantado) field; (de árboles) plantation **(b)** (explotación agrícola) plantation **(c)** (acción) planting

plantado -da *adj* ~ DE **algo** planted WITH sth; ***dejar*** ~ ***a algn*** ⇒ PLANTAR 2(b)

plantar [A1] *vt* **1 (a)** ‹*árboles/cebollas*› to plant **(b)** ‹*postes*› to put in; ‹*tienda*› to pitch, put up **2** (fam) **(a)** (abandonar) ‹*novio*› to ditch (colloq), to dump (colloq); ‹*estudios*› to give up, to quit (AmE) **(b)** (dejar plantado) ‹*persona*› (en cita) to stand … up; (el día de la boda) to jilt

■ **plantarse** *v pron* **1** (fam) (quedarse, pararse) to plant oneself (colloq) **2** (Jueg) (en cartas, apuesta) to stick

planteamiento *m* **(a)** (enfoque) approach **(b)** (exposición): **no les sabe dar el** ~ **adecuado a sus ideas** he doesn't know how to set his ideas out; **ése no es el** ~ **que me hicieron** that's not the way they explained the situation to me

plantear [A1] *vt* **1 (a)** ‹*teoría/razones*› to set out **(b)** (exponer) ‹*tema/pregunta*› to raise; **me lo planteó de la siguiente manera** he explained it to me in the following way; ~**le algo a algn** to raise sth with sb; **le** ~**é la cuestión a mi jefe** I'll raise the matter with my boss; **nos** ~**on dos opciones** they presented us with *o* gave us two options; **le planteé la posibilidad de ir a Grecia** I suggested going to Greece **2** ‹*problemas/dificultades*› to pose

■ **plantearse** *v pron* **1** (considerar) ‹*problema/posibilidad*› to think about, consider **2** (presentarse) «*problema/posibilidad*» to arise

plantel *m* **1** (cuerpo) staff **2** (Agr) nursery **3** (AmL frml) (escuela) educational establishment (frml)

plantilla *f* **1** (de zapato) insole **2** (Esp) (personal) staff; (nómina) payroll; **estar en** ~ to be on the staff *o* payroll **3** (para marcar, cortar) template; (para corregir exámenes) mask

plantón *m* **(a)** (fam) (espera) long wait; ***darle el*** ~ ***a algn*** ⇒ PLANTAR 2(b) **(b)** (Méx) (para protestar) sit-in

plasma *m* (Biol, Fís) plasma

plasta *f* (fam) (masa — blanda) soft lump; (— aplastada) flat *o* shapeless lump

plasticina® *f* (CS) Plasticine®

plástico[1] -ca *adj* plastic

plástico[2] *m* **(a)** (material) plastic **(b)** (explosivo) plastic explosive, plastique **(c)** (fam) (tarjetas de crédito) credit cards (*pl*), plastic (colloq)

plastificar [A2] *vt* ‹*tela*› to plasticize; ‹*carné/documento*› to laminate

plata *f* **1 (a)** (metal) silver; ~ **de ley** hallmarked silver **(b)** (vajilla) silver, silverware **2** (AmS fam) (dinero) money; **tiene mucha** ~ she has a lot of money

plataforma *f* platform; ~ **de lanzamiento** launchpad

platal *m* (AmS fam) fortune (colloq)

platanal, platanar *m* banana plantation

platanera *f* (empresa) banana company

platanero *m* (árbol) banana tree

plátano *m* **1** (árbol) *tb* ~ **oriental** plane tree **2 (a)** (fruto que se come crudo) banana; (árbol) banana tree **(b)** (fruto para cocinar) plantain; (árbol) plantain

platea *f* **(a)** (patio de butacas) orchestra (AmE), stalls (*pl*) (BrE) **(b)** (localidad) seat (*in the orchestra/stalls*)

plateado -da *adj* **(a)** ▶ **97** (del color de la plata) silver **(b)** (con baño de plata) silver-plated

platería *f* **(a)** (arte) silverwork **(b)** (objetos) silver(ware) **(c)** (tienda) silversmith's

plática *f* **(a)** (conferencia) talk **(b)** (esp AmL) (conversación) [*this noun is widely used in Mexico and Central America but is literary in other areas*] talk; **estar de** ~ to talk, to chat (colloq)

platicar [A2] *vi* (esp AmL) [*this verb is widely used in Mexico and Central America but is literary in other areas*] to talk, chat (colloq) ■ ~ *vt* (Méx) (contar) to tell

platillo *m* **1 (a)** (plato pequeño) saucer; (de balanza) pan; (para limosnas) collection plate *o* bowl; ~ **volador** *or* (Esp) **volante** flying saucer **(b)** (Mús) cymbal **(c)** (Dep) clay pigeon **2** (Méx) (en una comida) course

platino *m* **1** (metal) platinum **2** **platinos** *mpl* (Auto, Mec) (contact breaker) points (*pl*)

plato *m* **1 (a)** (utensilio) plate; **lavar** *or* **fregar los** ~**s** to wash *o* do the dishes; ~ **de postre** dessert plate; ~ **hondo** *or* **sopero** soup dish; ~ **llano** *or* (RPl) **playo** *or* (Chi) **bajo** *or* (Méx) **extendido** (dinner) plate **(b)** (para taza) *tb* **platito** saucer **2** (contenido) plate, plateful **3 (a)** (receta) dish; ~ **típico** typical dish **(b)** (en una comida) course; ~ **central** (Ven) main course; ~ **combinado** (Esp) *meal served on one plate, eg burger, eggs and fries*; ~ **del día** dish of the day; ~ **fuerte** (Coc) main course **4 (a)** (de balanza) (scale) pan **(b)** (de tocadiscos) turntable **(c)** (Dep) clay pigeon **(d)** (en béisbol) home plate

plató *m* set

platónico -ca *adj* platonic

platudo -da *adj* (AmS fam) well-heeled (colloq)

playa *f* **(a)** (extensión de arena) beach; (lugar de veraneo) seaside **(b)** ~ **de estacionamiento** (CS, Per) parking lot (AmE), car park (BrE)

playera *f* (zapatilla) canvas shoe, beach shoe; (camiseta) (Méx) T-shirt

plaza *f* **1** (espacio abierto) square; **~ de armas** (Mil) parade ground; (lugar público) (Andes) main square; **~ de toros** bullring; **~ mayor** main square **2 (a)** (esp AmL) (bolsa) market **(b)** (Esp) (mercado) market (place) **3 (a)** (puesto de trabajo) post, position; (en una clase, universidad) place; **hay varias ~s vacantes** there are several vacancies **(b)** (asiento) seat

plazo *m* **1** (de tiempo) period; **dentro de un ~ de dos meses** within a two-month period; **el ~ vence el próximo lunes** (para proyecto, trabajo) the deadline is next Monday; (para entrega de solicitudes) next Monday is the closing date; **tenemos un mes de ~ para pagar** we have one month to pay; **un objetivo a corto/largo ~** a short-term/long-term objective **2** (mensualidad, cuota) installment*; **pagar a ~s** to pay in installments; **comprar a ~s** to buy on installments

plebe *f* **(a)** (Hist) **la ~** the masses (*pl*), the populace **(b)** (pey) (chusma) rabble (pej), plebs (*pl*) (colloq & pej)

plebeyo -ya *adj/m,f* plebeian

plebiscito *m* plebiscite

plegable *adj* folding (*before n*)

plegar [A7] *vt* ‹*papel*› to fold; ‹*silla*› to fold up ■ **plegarse** *v pron* **1** (ceder) to yield, submit; **~se A algo** to yield TO sth, submit TO sth **2** (AmS) (unirse) to join in; **~se A algo** to join sth

plegaria *f* prayer

pleitear [A1] *vi* (AmL fam) (discutir) to argue

pleito *m* **1** (Der) action, lawsuit **2** (AmL) **(a)** (disputa, discusión) argument, fight (colloq) **(b)** (de boxeo) fight, boxing match

plenario -ria *adj* plenary, full

plenitud *f*: **en la ~ de algo** (de la vida) in the prime of sth; (de la carrera) at the height *o* peak of sth; **vivir la vida con ~** to live life to the full

pleno¹ -na *adj* **(a)** (completo, total) full; **en ~ uso de sus facultades** in full possession of his faculties **(b)** (uso enfático): **en ~ verano** in the middle of summer; **le dio una bofetada en plena cara** he slapped her right across the face; **a plena luz del día** in broad daylight; **a ~ sol** in the full sun

pleno² *m* **1** (reunión) plenary *o* full meeting/session **2** (Jueg) (en bolos) strike; (en lotería, bingo) full house; (en las quinielas) correct forecast *o* prediction

pliego *m* **(a)** (hoja de papel) sheet of paper **(b)** (Impr) section, signature **(c)** (documento) document

pliegue *m* **(a)** (en papel) fold, crease; (en la piel) fold; (en tela) pleat **(b)** (Geol) fold

plinto *m* (en gimnasia) box

plomería *f* (AmL) plumbing

plomero -ra *m,f* (AmL) plumber

plomizo -za *adj* ‹*cielo*› gray*, leaden (liter)

plomo *m* **1 (a)** (metal) lead; **soldado de ~** tin soldier **(b)** (arg) (balas) lead (sl) **2** (fam) (persona aburrida): **este profesor es un ~** this teacher is deadly boring (colloq) **3** (Esp) (fusible) fuse

pluma *f* **1** (de aves) feather; (antigua para escribir) quill; (como adorno) plume, feather; **mudar la ~** to molt* **2** (para escribir) pen; **~ atómica** (Méx) ballpoint pen; **~ estilográfica** *or* (AmL) **fuente** fountain pen

plumaje *m* (de ave) plumage; (en un casco) plume, crest

plumero *m* **(a)** (para limpiar) feather duster **(b)** (estuche) pencil case; (recipiente) pen holder

plumilla *f* **1** (para escribir) nib **2 (a)** (del limpiaparabrisas) blade **(b)** (Mús) brush **(c)** (Dep) shuttlecock

plumón *m* **1 (a)** (pluma suave) down **(b)** (edredón) down-filled quilt *o* (BrE) duvet **2** (Chi) (rotulador) felt-tip pen

plural *adj/m* plural; **tercera persona del ~** third person plural; **en ~** in the plural

pluralizar [A4] *vi* to generalize

pluscuamperfecto *m* pluperfect, past perfect

Plutón *m* Pluto

plutonio *m* plutonium

población *f* **1** (habitantes) population; (Zool) population, colony; **~ activa/pasiva** working/non-working population **2** (ciudad) town, city; (aldea) town, village; **~ callampa** (Chi) shantytown **3** (acción) settlement

poblado¹ -da *adj* **1** (habitado) populated; **poco ~** sparsely populated **2** ‹*barba/cejas*› bushy, thick; ‹*pestañas*› thick

poblado² *m* village

poblador -dora *m,f* **(a)** settler **(b)** (Chi) *inhabitant of a shantytown*

poblar [A10] *vt* **1** ‹*territorio/región*› **(a)** «*colonos/inmigrantes*» (ir a ocupar) to settle, populate **(b)** (habitar) to inhabit **2 ~ algo DE algo** ‹*bosque*› to plant sth WITH sth; ‹*río/colmena*› to stock sth WITH sth
■ **poblarse** *v pron* «*tierra/colonia*» to be settled

pobre *adj* **1 (a)** ‹*persona/barrio/nación*› poor; ‹*vestimenta*› poor, shabby **(b)** (escaso) ‹*vocabulario*› poor, limited; **aguas ~s en minerales** water with a low mineral content **(c)** (mediocre) ‹*examen/trabajo/actuación*› poor; ‹*salud*› poor, bad; ‹*argumento*› weak **(d)** ‹*tierra*› poor **2** (*delante del n*) (digno de compasión) poor; **~ animal** poor animal; **~, tiene hambre** poor thing, he's hungry; **¡~ de mí!** poor (old) me! ■ *mf* (necesitado) poor person, pauper (arch); **los ~s** the poor

pobreza *f* **(a)** (económica) poverty; **extrema ~** abject poverty **(b)** (mediocridad) poverty, poorness **(c)** (de la tierra) poorness, poor quality

poceta *f* (Ven) toilet bowl *o* pan

pocho -cha *adj* **(a)** (Esp fam) [ESTAR] ‹*persona*› off-color, peaked (AmE colloq) **(b)** ‹*fruta*› overripe; ‹*flor*› withered

pocilga *f* pigsty

pócima *f* (Farm) potion; (bebida) (fam) concoction (colloq)

poción *f* potion

poco¹ *adv* ▶ 329: **habla ~** he doesn't say much *o* a lot; **es muy ~ agradecido** he is very ungrateful; **un autor muy ~ conocido** a very little-known author; **viene muy ~ por aquí** he hardly ever comes around; *para locs ver* POCO² 4

poco² -ca *adj* ▶ 329 (con sustantivos no numerables) little; (en plural) few; **muy ~ vino** very little wine; **muy ~s niños** very few children; **había poquísimos coches** there were hardly any cars ■ *pron* **1** ▶ 329 (poca cantidad, poca cosa): **había ~ que hacer** there was little to do; **por ~ que gane** ...

Poco

Algunas observaciones sobre el adverbio

Cuando el español emplea poco *para modificar a un verbo, el inglés prefiere utilizar la oración negativa* do not . . . much *o* a lot *generalmente en la forma contraída*:

sale poco = he doesn't go out much *o* a lot
dijeron poco = they didn't say much *o* a lot

En todo caso cuando poco *va precedido por un adverbio como* muy, realmente *etc., el inglés prefiere utilizar oraciones positivas con el respectivo adverbio según el contexto*:

sale muy poco = he goes out very little
salen realmente poco = they hardly go out (at all) = they seldom go out

Nótese que cuando el español emplea poco *para modificar a un adjetivo, muchas veces el inglés prefiere utilizar el prefijo* un-:

poco realista = unrealistic
poco práctico = unpractical
poco amistoso/sociable = unfriendly/unsociable
poco sentimental = unsentimental
poco comprensivo = unsympathetic

pero

poco cuidadoso = careless

En caso de duda consultar el diccionario
Para ejemplos suplementarios, ver entrada

Respecto del adjetivo

En términos generales, cuando éste califica a un nombre no numerable, siempre lo precede y su traducción al inglés es little, *aunque se debe tener presente que el inglés en ciertos casos prefiere utilizar la oración negativa* not much:

poca diferencia = little difference
poca paciencia = little patience
poca leche = not much milk
poco dinero = not much money

Cuando el nombre al que califica es plural (numerable), su traducción es few:

tengo pocos amigos = I have few friends
a los pocos días = a few days later
con pocas excepciones = with few exceptions

Para más ejemplos ver entrada

Acerca del pronombre

En términos generales cuando en español el pronombre se presenta en singular, el inglés prefiere utilizar la oración negativa do not . . . much *(generalmente en la forma contraída) o* not much, *según el contexto:*

había mucha cerveza, pero bebió poca = there was plenty of beer, but he didn't drink much
¿vas a menudo al teatro? — no, poco = do you go to the theater often? — no, not much

En todo caso cuando el pronombre va precedido de un adverbio como muy, realmente *etc., el inglés prefiere utilizar una oración positiva precedida por el adverbio correspondiente*:

compra más, porque queda muy poca = buy some more, because there's very little left

Cuando el pronombre es plural, su traducción es few *o* not many *según el caso*:

son pocos los escogidos = few are chosen *o* not many are chosen
hay pocos como él = there are few like him *o* there aren't many like him
los pocos/las pocas que vinieron = the few who came
las pocas/los pocos que compré = the few (that) I bought

Para otros usos y ejemplos suplementarios, ver entrada. Ver también página 289

no matter how little *o* however little she earns ...; **se conforma con ~** he's easily satisfied; **todo le parece ~** she is never satisfied; **~s quisieron ayudar** few were willing to help; **~s pueden permitirse ese lujo** not many people can afford to do that **2 poco** (refiriéndose a tiempo): **lo vi hace ~** I saw him recently *o* not long ago; **hace muy ~ que lo conoce** she hasn't known him for very long; **tardó ~ en hacerlo** it didn't take him long to do it; **falta ~ para las navidades** it's not long till Christmas; **a ~ de venir él** soon *o* shortly after he came; **dentro de ~** soon; **~ antes de que** ... a short while *o* shortly before ... **3 un poco (a)** (refiriéndose a cantidades) a little; (refiriéndose a tiempo) a while; **dame un ~** I'll have some *o* a little; **espera un ~** wait a while **(b) un poco de** a little, a bit of **(c) un poco** + ADJ/ADV: **un ~ caro/tarde** a bit *o* a little expensive/late **4** (*en locs*) **a poco** (Méx): **¡a ~ no está fabuloso Acapulco!** isn't Acapulco just fantastic!; **¡a ~ ganaron!** don't tell me they won!; **de a poco** (AmL) gradually, little by little; **poco a poco** gradually; **poco más o menos** approximately, roughly; **por poco** nearly

poda *f* (acción) pruning; (temporada) pruning season

podar [A1] *vt* ‹*árbol*› to prune

poder¹ [E21] *v aux* **I 1** (tener la capacidad o posibilidad de): **puedo ir ahora o mañana** I can go now or tomorrow; **no puedo pagar tanto** I can't pay that much; **no podía dormir** I couldn't sleep; **no va a ~ venir** he won't be able to come; **no pudo asistir** he was unable to *o* he couldn't attend; **¿pudiste**

hacerlo sola? were you able to do it on your own? **2 (a)** (expresando idea de permiso): **¿puedo servirme otro?** can *o* may I have another one?; **¿podría irme más temprano hoy?** could I leave earlier today?; **puedes hacer lo que quieras** you can do whatever you like; **no puede comer sal** he isn't allowed to eat salt; **¿se puede? — ¡adelante!** may I? — come in; **aquí no se puede fumar** smoking is not allowed here **(b)** (solicitando un favor): **¿puedes bajar un momento?** can you come down for a moment?; **¿podrías hacerme un favor?** could you do me a favor? **3** (expresando derecho moral): **no podemos hacerle eso** we can't do that to her **4** (en quejas, reproches): **podías** *or* **podrías haberme avisado** you could *o* might have warned me!
II (con idea de esfuerzo) **1 ~ con algo/algn**: **¿puedes con todo eso?** can you manage all that?; **no puedo con este niño** I can't cope with this child; **estoy que no puedo más** (cansado) I'm exhausted; (lleno) I can't eat anything else; **ya no puedo más** I can't go on like this **2** (con idea de eventualidad, posibilidad): **te podrías** *or* **podías haber matado** you could have killed yourself!; **no podía haber estado más amable** she couldn't have been kinder; **podría volver a ocurrir** it could happen again; **no pudo ser** it wasn't possible; **puede (ser) que tengas razón** you may *o* could be right; **puede que sí, puede que no** maybe, maybe not **3** (Méx) (doler): **nos pudo mucho la muerte de Julio** we were terribly upset by Julio's death

poder² *m* **1 (a)** (control, influencia) power; **tiene mucho ~** he has a great deal of power; **estamos en su ~** we are in her power **(b)** (Pol) **el ~** power; **estar en el ~** to be in power; **tomar el ~** to take *o* seize power **2** (posesión): **la carta está en ~ de** ... the letter is in the hands of ... **3 (a)** (derecho, atribución) power; **tener amplios ~es para hacer algo** to have wide-ranging powers to do sth **(b)** (Der) (documento) letter of authorization; (hecho ante notario) power of attorney; **casarse por ~** (AmL) *or* (Esp) **por ~es** to get married by proxy **4 (a)** (capacidad, facultad) power; **su ~ de convicción** her power of persuasion; **~ adquisitivo** purchasing power **(b)** (de motor, aparato) power

poderío *m* power

poderoso -sa *adj* powerful

poderosos *mpl*: **los ~s** (los ricos) the wealthy; (los que tienen poder) the powerful

podio *m*, **pódium** *m* (*pl* **-diums**) (Dep) podium; (Mús) podium, rostrum

podólogo -ga *m,f* chiropodist, podiatrist (AmE)

podré, **etc** *see* PODER¹

podría, **etc** *see* PODER¹

podrido -da *adj* **1 (a)** (descompuesto) rotten; **huele a** *or* (AmL) **hay olor a ~** there's a smell of something rotting *o* rotten **(b)** (corrompido) rotten, corrupt; ***estar ~ de dinero*** *or* (AmS) ***estar ~ en plata/oro*** (fam) to be stinking *o* filthy rich (colloq) **2** (RPl fam) (harto, aburrido) fed up (colloq)

podrir [I38] *vt* ⇒ PUDRIR

poema *m* poem

poesía *f* (género) poetry; (poema) poem

poeta -tisa *m,f*, **poeta** *mf* poet

poético -ca *adj* poetic

póker *m* ⇒ PÓQUER

polaco -ca *adj* Polish ■ *m,f* **1** (persona) Pole **2** **polaco** *m* (idioma) Polish

polar *adj* polar

polarizar [A4] *vt* **(a)** (Fot, Ópt) to polarize **(b)** ‹*atención*› to focus **(c)** ‹*nación/opiniones*› to polarize

polea *f* (Tec) pulley; (Náut) tackle

polémica *f* controversy, polemic (frml)

polémico -ca *adj* controversial, polemic (frml)

polemizar [A4] *vi* to argue

polen *m* pollen

poleo *m* pennyroyal

polera *f* (suéter) (RPl) polo neck (camiseta); (Chi) T-shirt

polichinela *m* (títere) string puppet

policía *f* **1** (cuerpo) police; **la ~ está investigando el caso** the police are investigating the case; **~ antidisturbios** riot police; **~ de tráfico** *or* (AmL) **de tránsito** traffic police, highway patrol (AmE); **~ municipal** local *o* city police; **~ nacional** (state) police **2 policía** (agente) (*m*) policeman, police officer; (*f*) policewoman, police officer

policíaco -ca, **policiaco -ca** *adj* ‹*novela/serie*› crime (*before n*), detective (*before n*)

policial *adj* police (*before n*)

polideportivo *m* sports center*

poliéster *m* polyester

polifacético -ca *adj* versatile, multifaceted

poligamia *f* polygamy

polígamo -ma *m,f* polygamist

políglota *mf* polyglot

polígono *m* **1** (Mat) polygon **2** (Esp) (zona) area, zone; (urbanización) development, housing estate; **~ industrial** (Esp) industrial area *o* zone

polilla *f* (Zool) moth; **~ de la madera** woodworm

Polinesia *f* Polynesia

polinesio¹ -sia *adj/m,f* Polynesian

polinesio² *m* (idioma) Polynesian

polinización *f* pollination

polio *f* polio

poliomielitis *f* poliomyelitis

politécnico -ca *adj* ‹*universidad*› *specializing in technical or practical subjects*; **escuela politécnica** technical college

politeísmo *m* polytheism

política *f* **1** (Pol) politics **2** (postura) policy; **~ interior/exterior** domestic/foreign policy

político -ca *adj* **1** (Pol) political **2** (diplomático) diplomatic, tactful **3** (en relaciones de parentesco): **la familia política** the in-laws ■ *m,f* politician

politizarse [A4] *v pron* to become politicized

póliza *f* **1** (de seguros) policy **2** (esp Esp) (sello) fiscal stamp

polizón *mf* stowaway; **viajar de ~** to stow away

polla *f* **1** (Esp vulg) (pene) cock (vulg), prick (vulg) **2 (a)** (AmL) (apuesta) bet **(b)** (Per) (quiniela) ≈ sports lottery (*in US*), ≈ pools (*in UK*) **(c)** (Chi) (lotería) lottery; *ver tb* POLLO

pollera *f* (CS) (Indum) skirt
pollería *f* poultry store, poulterer's store
pollito -ta *m,f* chick
pollo -lla *m,f* (Zool) **(a)** (cría) chick **(b)** (adulto) chicken **(c)** (Coc) chicken; **~ asado** roast chicken
polluelo *m* chick
polo *m* **1 (a)** (Geog) pole; **P~ Norte/Sur** North/South Pole **(b)** (Elec, Fís) pole; **~ negativo** negative pole; ***ser ~s opuestos*** (fam) to be poles apart **2** (centro) center*, focus **3 (a)** (Dep) polo **(b)** (Indum) polo shirt **4** (Esp) (helado) Popsicle® (AmE), ice lolly (BrE)
pololear [A1] *vi* (Chi) to have a boyfriend/girlfriend; **~ CON algn** to go out WITH sb
pololo -la *m,f* (Chi fam) (*m*) boyfriend; (*f*) girlfriend
Polonia *f* Poland
poltrona *f* armchair, easy chair
polución *f* pollution
polvareda *f* dust cloud
polvera *f* powder compact
polvo *m* **(a)** (suciedad) dust; **limpiar** *or* **quitar el ~** to do the dusting, to dust; ***estar hecho ~*** (agotado) to be all in (fam); (deprimido) to be devastated; (destruido) to be a wreck **(b)** (Coc, Quím) powder **(c) polvos** *mpl* (en cosmética) face powder; **~s de talco** talcum powder, talc (colloq)
pólvora *f* **(a)** (explosivo) gunpowder **(b)** (fuegos artificiales) fireworks (*pl*)
polvoriento -ta *adj* dusty
polvorín *m* **(a)** (almacén de explosivos) magazine **(b)** (lugar, país peligroso) powder keg
pomada *f* (Farm) ointment, cream; **~ de zapatos** (RPl) shoe polish
pomelo *m* (fruto) grapefruit; (árbol) grapefruit tree
pomo *m* (de puerta, mueble) handle, knob; (de espada) pommel
pompa *f* **1** *tb* **~ de jabón** bubble **2** (esplendor) pomp, splendor*; **~s fúnebres** *fpl* (ceremonia) funeral ceremony; (funeraria) funeral parlor*, funeral director's
pomposo -sa *adj* **(a)** ‹*boda/fiesta*› magnificent, splendid; ‹*lenguaje/estilo*› pompous, high-sounding **(b)** (ostentoso) pompous, ostentatious
pómulo *m* ▶ **123** (hueso) cheekbone; (mejilla) cheek
pon *see* PONER
ponchadura *f* (Méx) flat, puncture
ponchar [A1] *vt* (Méx) ‹*llanta/balón*› to puncture ■ **poncharse** *v pron* **1** (Méx) «*balón*» to puncture; **se nos ponchó una llanta** we had a flat *o* a puncture **2** (Col, Ven) (en béisbol) to fan (colloq), to strike out
ponche *m* (bebida) punch
poncho *m* poncho
ponderar [A1] *vt* **(a)** ‹*cálculo/índice*› to weight, adjust **(b)** (considerar) to weigh up, consider, ponder **(c)** (alabar) to praise, speak highly of
pondré, pondría, etc *see* PONER
ponedora *f* layer, laying hen
poner [E22] *vt* **I 1 (a)** (colocar) to put; **ponlo en el suelo** put it on the floor; **ponle el collar al perro** put the dog's collar on **(b)** ‹*anuncio/aviso*› to place, put **(c)** ‹*ropa*› (+ *me/te/le etc*): **le puse el sombrero** I put his hat on (for him) **2** (agregar) to put **3** ‹*inyección/supositorio*› to give **4 poner la mesa** to lay *o* set the table **5** (instalar, montar) **(a)** ‹*oficina/restaurante*› to open **(b)** ‹*cocina/teléfono/calefacción*› to install **(c)** ‹*cerradura/armario*› to fit **6** «*ave*» ‹*huevo*› to lay **7** (Esp) (servir, dar): **póngame un café, por favor** I'll have a coffee, please; **¿cuántos le pongo?** how many would you like?
II 1 ‹*dinero*› (contribuir) to put in; **pusimos 500 pesos cada uno** we put in 500 pesos each **2** ‹*atención*› to pay; ‹*cuidado/interés*› to take; **pon más cuidado en la presentación** take more care over the presentation **3 (a)** (imponer) ‹*deberes*› to give, set; ‹*examen/problema*› to set; **le pusieron una multa** he was fined **(b)** (oponer) ‹*inconvenientes*› to raise; **me pusieron problemas para entrar** they made it difficult for me to get in **(c)** (adjudicar) ‹*nota*› to give **4** (dar) ‹*nombre/apodo*› to give; ‹*ejemplo*› to give; **le pusieron Eva** they called her Eva **5** (enviar) ‹*telegrama*› to send **6** (escribir) ‹*dedicatoria/líneas*› to write **7** (Esp) (exhibir, dar) ‹*película*› to show; **¿ponen algo interesante en la tele?** is there anything interesting on TV?; **¿qué ponen en el Royal?** what's on *o* what's showing at the Royal?
III 1 (a) (conectar, encender) ‹*televisión/calefacción*› to turn on, switch on, put on; ‹*programa/canal*› to put on; ‹*cinta/disco/música*› to put on; **puso el motor en marcha** she switched on *o* started the engine **(b)** (ajustar, graduar) ‹*despertador*› to set; **pon la música más alta** turn the music up; **puso el reloj en hora** she put the clock right **2** (Esp) (al teléfono): **~ a algn CON algo/algn** to put sb THROUGH TO sth/sb
IV (en estado, situación) (+ *compl*): **~ a algn nervioso** to make sb nervous; **~ a algn en un aprieto** to put sb in an awkward position ■ *vi* «*ave*» to lay
■ **ponerse** *v pron* **I 1** (*refl*) (colocarse): **pongámonos ahí** let's stand (*o* sit *etc*) there; **~se de pie** to stand (up); **~se de rodillas** to kneel (down), get down on one's knees **2** «*sol*» to set **3** (*refl*) ‹*calzado/maquillaje/alhaja*› to put on; **no tengo nada que ~me** I don't have a thing to wear
II 1 (en estado, situación) (+ *compl*): **~se enfermo** to get sick; **se puso triste** she became sad; **cuando lo vio se puso muy contenta** she was so happy when she saw it; **se puso como loco** he went mad; **~se cómodo** to make oneself comfortable **2** (empezar) **~se A + INF** to start -ING, to start + INF; **se puso a llover** it started raining, it started to rain
III (Esp): **~se al teléfono** to come to the phone
ponga, pongas, etc *see* PONER
poni *m* ⇒ PONY
poniente *m* (occidente) west; (viento) west wind
pontífice *m* pontiff, pope
pony /'poni/ *m* (*pl* **-nies** *or* **-nys**) pony
pop *m* **1** (Mús) pop (music) **2** (Ur) (Coc) popcorn
popa *f* stern
popis, popoff *adj inv* (Méx fam) posh
popote *m* (Méx) straw

popular *adj* **1 (a)** ‹*cultura/tradiciones*› popular (*before n*); ‹*canción/baile/costumbres*› traditional **(b)** (Pol) ‹*movimiento/rebelión*› popular (*before n*) **2** (que gusta) ‹*actor/programa/deporte*› popular

popularidad *f* popularity

popularizar [A4] *vt* to popularize, make … popular

■ **popularizarse** *v pron* to become popular

popurrí *m* (de cosas, colores) potpourri

póquer *m* (juego — de naipes) poker; (— de dados) poker dice; **un ~ de ases** four aces

poquísimo *adj*: *ver* POCO

por *prep* **I 1** (causa) because of; **~ falta de dinero** because of *o* owing to lack of money; **~ naturaleza** by nature; **~ necesidad** out of necessity; **fue ~ eso que vine** that was why I came; **si no fuera ~ mi hijo …** if it wasn't for my son …; **me pidió perdón ~ haberme mentido** he apologized for lying *o* for having lied to me **2** (*en locs*) **por qué** why; **no dijo por qué** he didn't say why; **¿por qué no vienes conmigo?** why don't you come with me?; **por si** in case; **por si no entiende** in case he doesn't understand; ⇒ ACASO, MOSCA[2] **3** (en expresiones concesivas): **~ más que me esfuerzo** however hard *o* no matter how hard I try; **~ (muy) fácil que sea** however easy *o* no matter how easy it is **4 (a)** (modo): **colócalos ~ orden de tamaño** put them in order of size; **~ adelantado** in advance; **~ escrito** in writing **(b)** (medio): **se lo comunicaron ~ teléfono** they told him over the phone; **lo dijeron ~ la radio** they said it on the radio; **~ avión** by air; **la conocí ~ la voz** I recognized her by her voice; **me enteré ~ un amigo** I heard from *o* through a friend **5 (a)** (proporción): **cobra $30 ~ clase** he charges $30 a *o* per class; **120 kilómetros ~ hora** 120 kilometers an *o* per hour; **~ metro/docena** by the meter/dozen; **tú comes ~ tres** you eat enough for three people; **tiene tres metros de largo ~ uno de ancho** it's three meters long by one meter wide; **uno ~ uno** one by one; ⇒ CIENTO[2] **(b)** ▶ **294** (en multiplicaciones): **tres ~ cuatro (son) doce** three times four is twelve, three fours are twelve **6 (a)** (sustitución) for; **su secretaria firmó ~ él** his secretary signed for him *o* on his behalf; **pasa ~ inglesa** she passes for an Englishwoman **(b)** (como): **~ ejemplo** for example **7** (introduciendo el agente) by; **compuesto ~ Mozart** composed by Mozart

II 1 (finalidad, objetivo): **pelearse ~ algo** to fight over sth; **lo hace ~ el dinero** he does it for the money; **no entré ~ no molestar** I didn't go in because I didn't want to disturb him; **~** QUE + SUBJ (*here* POR QUE *can also be written* PORQUE): **estaba ansioso ~ que lo escucharan** he was eager for them to listen to him **2** (indicando inclinación, elección): **su amor ~ la música** her love of music; **no siento nada ~ él** I don't feel anything for him; **votó ~ ella** he voted for her **3** (en busca de): **salió/fue ~** *or* (Esp) **a ~ pan** he went (out) for some bread, he went (out) to get some bread **4** (en lo que respecta a): **~ mí que haga lo que quiera** as far as I'm concerned, he can do what he likes **5** (esp AmL) **estar ~** + INF (estar a punto de) to be about to + INF; **está ~ terminar** he's about to finish; **deben (de) estar ~ llegar** they should be arriving any minute

III 1 (a) (lugar): **entró ~ la ventana** he came in through the window; **sal ~ aquí** go out this way; **se cayó ~ la escalera** he fell down the stairs; **¿el 121 va ~ (la) Avenida Rosas?** does the 121 go along Rosas Avenue?; **¿~ dónde has venido?** which way did you come?; **está ~ ahí** he's over there somewhere; **¿~ dónde está el hotel?** whereabouts is the hotel?; **viven ~ mi barrio** they live around my area; **voy ~ la página 15** I'm up to *o* I'm on page 15; **empieza ~ el principio** start at the beginning; **agárralo ~ el mango** hold it by the handle **(b)** (indicando extensión): **~ todos lados** *or* **~ todas partes** everywhere; **viajamos ~ el norte de Francia** we traveled around *o* in the North of France; *ver tb* DENTRO, FUERA, ENCIMA, ETC **2** (tiempo) for; **~ un mes** for a month; **~ el momento** *or* **~ ahora** for the time being, for now; *ver tb* MAÑANA, TARDE[2], NOCHE **3** (Esp) (ocasión) for; **me lo regaló ~ mi cumpleaños** she gave it to me for my birthday

porcelana *f* **(a)** (material) china; (de mejor calidad) porcelain **(b)** (objeto) piece of china/porcelain

porcentaje *m* ▶ **130** percentage

porche *m* (de casa) porch; (soportal) arcade

porción *f* (de un todo) portion; (en reparto) share; (de comida) portion, helping, serving

pordiosero -ra *m,f* beggar

porfiado -da *adj* stubborn, pig-headed (colloq) ■ *m,f* (persona) stubborn creature (colloq)

porfiar [A17] *vi* (insistir) to insist; **no me porfíes, ya te dije que no** don't keep on *o* go on about it, I said no

pormenor *m* detail; **los ~es del incidente** the details of the incident; **entrar en ~es** to go into detail

pornografía *f* pornography

pornográfico -ca *adj* pornographic

poro *m* **1** (Anat, Biol) pore **2** (Méx) (puerro) leek

pororó *m* (RPl) popcorn

poroso -sa *adj* porous

poroto *m* (CS) bean; **~ verde** (Chi) green bean

porque *conj* **(a)** (indicando causa) because; **¿por qué no vas a ir? — ~ no** why don't you go? — because I don't want to **(b)** (indicando finalidad) *ver* POR II 1

porqué *m* reason; **quiero saber el ~** I want to know the reason

porquería *f* **1 (a)** (suciedad) dirt **(b)** (cochinada): **no hagas ~s** don't do disgusting *o* filthy things like that; **la casa está hecha una ~** (fam) the house is in such a state (colloq) **2** (cosa de mala calidad): **el libro es una ~** the book's a piece of junk; **la comida es una ~** the food is dreadful *o* terrible

porra *f* **1** (de guardia, policía) nightstick (AmE), truncheon (BrE) **2** (fam) (expresando disgusto, enojo): ***mandar a algn a la ~*** (colloq) to tell sb to get lost (colloq); **¡vete** *or* **ándate a la ~!** go to hell! (colloq), get lost! (colloq); ***mandar algo a la ~*** (colloq) ‹*trabajo*› to chuck sth in (colloq) **3** (Jueg) draw, lottery **4** (Col, Méx fam) **(a)** (seguidores, hinchas) fans (*pl*) **(b)** (canto, grito): **¡una ~ para Villalva!** three cheers

for Villalva!; **la ~ de la universidad** the college chant; ***echarle ~s a algn*** (Méx fam) ‹*a equipo/corredor*› to cheer sb (on)
porrista *mf* **(a)** (Col, Méx) (seguidor) fan **(b) porrista** *f* (Col, Méx) (animadora) cheerleader
porro *m* (Esp arg) (de hachís) joint (colloq), spliff (sl)
porrón *m* **1 (a)** (de vino) wine bottle (*with a long spout for drinking from*) **(b)** (Arg) (de cerveza) bottle of beer **2** (CS) (pimiento) green pepper; (puerro) leek
portabebés *m* (*pl* ~) portacrib® (AmE), carrycot (BrE)
portada *f* **1** (de libro) title page; (de periódico) front page; (de revista) cover **2** (de iglesia) front, facade
portadocumentos *m* (*pl* ~) (AmL) (grande) briefcase, attaché case; (pequeño) document wallet
portador -dora *m,f* **1** (Med) (de virus, germen) carrier **2** (Com, Fin) bearer; **páguese al ~** pay the bearer
portaequipajes *m* (*pl* ~) **(a)** (Auto) (para el techo) roofrack; (maletero) trunk (AmE), boot (BrE) **(b)** (en tren, autobús) luggage rack
portafolios *m* (*pl* ~) (maletín) briefcase
portal *m* **(a)** (de casa — entrada) doorway; (— vestíbulo) hall **(b)** (de iglesia, palacio) portal **(c)** (en muralla) gate
portarse [A1] *v pron* (comportarse): **~se bien** to behave (oneself); **~se mal** to behave badly; **~se bien/mal CON algn** to treat sb well/badly
portátil *adj* portable
portaviones *m* (*pl* ~) aircraft carrier
portavoz *mf* (*m*) spokesperson, spokesman; (*f*) spokesperson, spokeswoman
portazo *m* slam, bang; **dar un ~** to slam the door
porte *m* **1** (tamaño) size; **es de este ~** (AmL) it's about *this* big **2** (acción de portar) carrying; (costo) carriage; **~s pagados** freight/postage paid
porteño -ña *adj* of/from the city of Buenos Aires
portería *f* **1 (a)** (de edificio) *desk/area from where the super/caretaker supervises the building* **(b)** (vivienda) super's *o* superintendent's apartment (AmE), caretaker's flat (*o* house *etc*) (BrE) **2** (Dep) goal
portero -ra *m,f* **1** (que abre la puerta) doorman, porter; (que cuida el edificio) super (AmE), superintendent (AmE), caretaker (BrE); **~ eléctrico** *or* (Esp) **automático** *m* entryphone **2** (Dep) goalkeeper
portezuela *f* door
pórtico *m* (entrada) portico, porch; (galería) arcade
portón *m* (puerta grande) large door; (puerta principal) front door; (en cerca) gate
portorriqueño -ña *adj/m,f* Puerto Rican
Portugal *m* Portugal
portugués[1] -guesa *adj/m,f* Portuguese
portugués[2] *m* (idioma) Portuguese
porvenir *m* future; **un joven sin ~** a young man with no future *o* no prospects
posaderas *fpl* (fam) backside (colloq), butt (AmE colloq), bum (BrE colloq)
posar [A1] *vi* to pose
■ **posarse** *v pron* «*pájaro/insecto*» to alight, land; «*avión/helicóptero*» to land
posavasos *m* (*pl* ~) coaster; (de cartón) beermat
pose *f* **(a)** (para foto) pose **(b)** (pey) (afectación) pose
poseedor -dora *m,f* (frml) (de título, récord, billete) holder
poseer [E13] *vt* **(a)** ‹*tierras/fortuna*› to own **(b)** ‹*conocimientos*› to have **(c)** ‹*récord/título*› to hold
posesión *f* possession; **tomar ~ de algo** (de casa) to take possession of sth; (de cargo) to take up sth; **está en ~ de todas sus facultades** he is in full possession of his faculties
posesivo -va *adj* possessive
posguerra *f* postwar period
posibilidad *f* **1** (circunstancia) possibility; **tener la ~ de hacer algo** to have the chance of doing sth; **tiene muchas ~es de salir elegido** he has a good chance of being elected; **existe la ~ de que estés equivocado** you might just be wrong **2 posibilidades** *fpl* **(a)** (medios económicos) means (*pl*); **vivo de acuerdo a mis ~es** I live within my means; **la casa está por encima de mis ~es** I can't afford the house **(b)** (potencial) potential; **un cantante con muchas ~es** a singer of great potential
posibilitar [A1] *vt* to make … possible
posible *adj* possible; **es ~** it's possible; **a ser ~** *or* **si es ~** if possible; **hicieron todo lo ~** they did everything possible *o* everything they could; **prometió ayudarlo dentro de lo ~** *or* **en lo ~** she promised to do what she could to help (him); **¡no es ~!** that can't be true! (colloq); **en cuanto te sea ~** as soon as you can; **no creo que me sea ~** I don't think I'll be able to; **es ~ hacerlo más rápido** it's possible to do it more quickly; **no me fue ~ terminarlo** I wasn't able to finish it; **es ~ que sea cierto** it might *o* may *o* could be true
■ *adv*: **lo más pronto ~** as soon as possible; **lo mejor ~** the best you can
posición *f* **(a)** (en general) position; **en ~ vertical** in an upright position **(b)** (en la sociedad) social standing; **gente de buena ~** people of high social standing **(c)** (actitud) position, stance; **adoptar una ~ intransigente** to take a tough stand *o* stance
positivo -va *adj* positive
poso *m* (del vino) sediment, lees (*pl*), dregs (*pl*); (del café) dregs (*pl*), grounds (*pl*)
posponer [E22] *vt* (aplazar) to postpone, put off
posta *f* **1** (AmL) (Dep) relay (race) **2** (AmC) (Mil) sentry post **3** (Esp) **a posta** on purpose, deliberately **4** (Chi) (centro médico) accident and emergency center*
postal *adj* ‹*distrito/servicio*› postal ■ *f* postcard
postdata *f* postscript
poste *m* **(a)** (de alambrado) (fence) post; (de teléfono, telégrafo) pole **(b)** (Dep) post, upright
postemilla *f* (AmL) gumboil, abscess
póster *m* (*pl* **-ters**) poster
postergar [A3] *vt* **1** (esp AmL) (aplazar) ‹*juicio/reunión*› to postpone, put back **2** (relegar) ‹*empleado*› to pass over
posteridad *f* posterity
posterior *adj* **1 (a)** (en el tiempo) later, subsequent; **en años nes** in later *o* subsequent years; **ese incidente fue ~ a su llegada** that incident happened after his arrival **(b)** (en orden) subsequent **2** (trasero)

‹patas› back (*before n*), rear (*before n*); **la parte ~** the back *o* rear

posterioridad *f*: **con ~** subsequently, later

postgrado *m* postgraduate course

postgraduado -da *adj/m,f* postgraduate

postguerra *f* postwar period

postigo *m* shutter

postizo[1] -za *adj* **(a)** ‹*pestañas*› false; **dentadura postiza** dentures, false teeth **(b)** ‹*manga/cuello*› detachable

postizo[2] *m* hairpiece

postor *m* bidder

postrarse [A1] *v pron* (frml) (arrodillarse) to kneel

postre *m* dessert, pudding (BrE) ■ *f*: **a la ~** (*loc adv*) (frml) in the end

postulante -ta *m,f* **(a)** (AmL) (Pol) (candidato) candidate **(b)** (CS) (para puesto) applicant

postular [A1] *vt* (AmL) (Pol) ‹*candidato*› to nominate, propose ■ *vi* **~** PARA **algo** (CS) ‹*para puesto*› to apply FOR sth

■ **postularse** *v pron* (AmL) to stand, run

póstumo -ma *adj* posthumous

postura *f* **1** (del cuerpo) position **2 (a)** (actitud) stance, stand; **adoptar una ~ firme con respecto a algo** to take a tough stance *o* stand on sth **(b)** (opinión) opinion; ***tomar* ~** to take a stand **3** (AmL) (de ropa, zapatos): **se le rompieron a la primera ~** they broke the first time she wore them; **~ de argollas** (Chi) (acción) exchange of rings (*to seal one's engagement*); (fiesta) engagement party

potable *adj* ‹*agua*› drinkable, potable (frml); **Ⓢ agua no potable** not drinking water

potaje *m* (Coc) vegetable stew/soup (*gen with pulses*)

potasio *m* potassium

pote *m* (olla) pot; (de crema, maquillaje) (CS) pot, jar

potencia *f* power; **~ militar/nuclear** military/nuclear power; **este niño es un artista en ~** this child has the makings of an artist

potencial *adj* (posible) potential; (Ling) conditional ■ *m* (capacidad, posibilidades) potential

potenciar [A1] *vt* (period) **(a)** ‹*desarrollo/investigación/exportaciones*› to boost; ‹*relaciones/unidad/talento*› to foster; ‹*cultura*› to promote **(b)** (mejorar) ‹*seguridad*› to improve

potentado -da *m,f* tycoon

potente *adj* **(a)** (en general) powerful **(b)** ‹*hombre*› virile

potestad *f* legal authority

potingue *m* (fam) cream, lotion

poto *m* (Andes fam) (de persona) butt (AmE colloq), bum (BrE colloq); (de botella) bottom

potpourrí /popu'rri/ *m* medley

potrero *m* (AmL) (terreno cercado) field; (para pastar) pasture

potrillo -lla *m,f* (Zool) foal

potro -tra *m,f* **1** (caballo joven) (*m*) colt; (*f*) filly **2 potro** *m* (instrumento de tortura) rack; (cepo) stocks (*pl*); (en gimnasia) vaulting horse, buck

pozo *m* **(a)** (de agua) well; **~ ciego** *or* **negro** *or* **séptico** septic tank, cesspool, cesspit; **~ de petróleo** oil well **(b)** (en mina) shaft **(c)** (en río) deep pool

práctica *f* **1 (a)** (en actividad) practice; (en trabajo) experience; **perder la ~** to be out of practice **(b)** (de profesión) practicing* **2** (aplicación) practice; **en la ~** in practice; **poner algo en ~** *or* **llevar algo a la ~** to put sth into practice **3 prácticas** *fpl* (de Anatomía, Química) practicals (*pl*); (de maestro) teaching practice; **~s de tiro** target practice **4** (costumbre) practice

practicante *adj* (Rel) practicing* (*before n*) ■ *mf* (Med) nurse (*specializing in giving injections, dressing wounds, etc*)

practicar [A2] *vt* **1 (a)** ‹*idioma/pieza musical*› to practice*; ‹*tenis*› to play; **~ la natación** to swim; **no practica ningún deporte** he doesn't play *o* do any sport(s) **(b)** ‹*profesión*› to practice* **2** (frml) (llevar a cabo, realizar) ‹*corte/incisión*› to make; ‹*autopsia/operación*› to perform, do; ‹*redada/actividad*› to carry out; ‹*detenciones*› to make ■ **~** *vi* (repetir) to practice*; (ejercer) to practice*

práctico -ca *adj* **1** ‹*envase/cuchillo*› useful, handy; ‹*falda/diseño*› practical; **es muy ~ tener el coche para hacer la compra** it's very handy *o* convenient having the car to do the shopping **2** (no teórico) practical **3** ‹*persona*› [SER] (desenvuelto) practical

pradera *f* meadow; **las ~s de los Estados Unidos** the prairies of the United States

prado *m* **(a)** (Agr) meadow, field **(b)** (lugar de paseo) park (*with lawns*) **(c)** (Col) (jardín) garden, yard (AmE)

Praga *f* Prague

pragmático -ca *adj* pragmatic ■ *m,f* pragmatist

pragmatismo *m* pragmatism

preámbulo *m* **(a)** (de obra) introduction; (de constitución) preamble **(b)** (rodeo): **sin más ~s** without further ado; **dímelo sin tanto ~** stop beating about the bush and tell me **(c)** (de curso, negociaciones) preliminary

preaviso *m* notice

precalentamiento *m* **(a)** (Dep) warm-up **(b)** (del horno) preheating **(c)** (de motor) warming up

precalentar [A5] *vt* ‹*horno*› to preheat; ‹*motor*› to warm up

precario -ria *adj* ‹*vivienda*› poor; ‹*medios*› scarce, meager*; ‹*salud/situación*› precarious, unstable; ‹*gobierno/puesto*› unstable

precaución *f* **1** (medida) precaution **2** (prudencia): **medida de ~** precautionary measure; **actuar con ~** to act with caution

precaverse [E1] *v pron* to take precautions

precavido -da *adj* cautious, prudent

precedencia *f* precedence, priority

precedente *adj* previous ■ *m* precedent; **sentar (un) ~** to set a precedent

preceder [E1] *vt* to precede

precepto *m* rule, precept (frml)

preciado -da *adj* ‹*bien/objeto*› prized, valued; ‹*don*› valuable

preciarse [A1] *v pron* **(a)** (estimarse): **un abogado que se precie no haría eso** no self-respecting lawyer would do that **(b)** (jactarse) ~ DE **algo** to pride oneself ON sth

precintar [A1] *vt* **(a)** ‹*paquete/botella*› to seal **(b)** ‹*local*› (tras crimen) to seal; (clausurar) to close down (*often on health or safety grounds*)

precinto *m* seal

precio *m* **1** (de producto) price; ~ **al contado/a plazos** cash/credit price; **¿qué ~ tiene este vestido?** how much is this dress?; ~ **de costo** *or* (Esp) **coste** cost price; ~ **de venta al público** (de alimento, medicamento) recommended retail price; (de libro) published price; ***no tener*** ~ to be priceless **2** (sacrificio, costo) price, cost; **a cualquier** ~ at any price, whatever the cost

preciosidad *f*: **ser una** ~ to be absolutely beautiful

precioso -sa *adj* (hermoso) beautiful, gorgeous, lovely; (de gran valor) precious, valuable

preciosura *f* (AmL) ⇒ PRECIOSIDAD

precipicio *m* (despeñadero) precipice

precipitación *f* **1** (prisa) rush, hurry; **lo hizo con mucha** ~ she did it in a rush *o* hurry **2** (Meteo) rainfall; **la** ~ **mensual** the monthly rainfall; **habrá precipitaciones débiles** there will be some light rain

precipitado -da *adj* ‹*decisión/actuación*› hasty; ‹*juicio*› snap (*before n*)

precipitarse [A1] *v pron* **1** (en decisión, juicio) to be hasty; **te precipitaste juzgándolo así** you were rash to judge him like that **2** (apresurarse) to rush; ~**se** A **hacer algo** to rush to do sth **3 (a)** (caer) to plunge **(b)** (*refl*) (arrojarse) to throw oneself

precisado -da *adj* (AmL frml): **verse** ~ **a hacer algo** to be forced *o* obliged to do sth

precisar [A1] *vt* **1** (determinar con exactitud) to specify **2** (necesitar) to need

precisión *f* **(a)** (exactitud) precision; **no puedo decírtelo con** ~ I can't tell you exactly; **de** ~ ‹*instrumento/máquina*› precision (*before n*) **(b)** (claridad, concisión) precision

preciso -sa *adj* **1 (a)** (exacto, claro) precise **(b)** (*delante del n*) (como intensificador) very; **en este** ~ **momento** this very minute, right now; **en el** ~ **momento en que salía** just as he was going out; **en este** ~ **lugar** in this very spot **2** (necesario) necessary; **si es** ~ if necessary, if need be; **ser** ~ **hacer algo** to be necessary to do sth; **es** ~ **que la veas** you must see her; **no es** ~ **que vayamos todos** there's no need for all of us to go

preconcebido -da *adj* preconceived

precoz *adj* ‹*niño/desarrollo*› precocious; ‹*diagnóstico/fruto/helada*› early

predecesor -sora *m,f* predecessor

predecir [I25] *vt* to predict, foretell (frml)

predestinación *f* predestination

predestinar [A1] *vt* to predestine; **estar** ~ **a algo/hacer algo** to be predestined to sth/do sth

predeterminar [A1] *vt* to predetermine

predicado *m* predicate

predicador -dora *m,f* preacher

predicamento *m* (AmL) (situación difícil) predicament

predicar [A2] *vi* to preach

predicativo -va *adj* predicative

predicción *f* prediction, forecast

predicible *adj* (Andes) predictable

predilección *f* predilection; **tiene/siente** ~ **por su hijo** she's especially fond of her son

predilecto -ta *adj/m,f* favorite*

predisponer [E22] *vt* **1** (Med) to predispose **2** (influir en) to prejudice; **lo predispusieron en contra mía** they prejudiced him against me

predisposición *f* **1** (Med) predisposition **2** (inclinación): **tener** ~ **contra algn** to be prejudiced against sb

predispuesto -ta *adj* **(a)** [SER] (propenso) ~ A **algo** prone TO sth **(b)** [ESTAR] (prejuiciado) ~ A FAVOR/EN CONTRA DE **algo/algn** biased TOWARDS/AGAINST sth/sb

predominante *adj* predominant

predominar [A1] *vi* «*actitud/opinión*» to prevail; ~ EN **algo** to dominate sth; **el tema predominó en el congreso** the subject dominated the conference; ~ SOBRE **algo** to be predominant OVER sth

predominio *m* predominance

preescolar *adj* ‹*edad/educación*› preschool (*before n*); **centro de educación** ~ kindergarten, nursery school (BrE)

preestreno *m* preview

prefabricado -da *adj* prefabricated

prefacio *m* preface

preferencia *f* **(a)** (prioridad) priority, precedence; (Auto) right of way, priority (BrE) **(b)** (predilección) preference; **tiene** ~ **por el más pequeño** the youngest one is her favorite **(c)** (Espec) (localidad) grandstand

preferente *adj* (especial) special

preferible *adj* preferable, better; **es** ~ **quedarse callado** it's better to stay quiet; **es** ~ **a uno de plástico** it's better than *o* preferable to a plastic one; **es** ~ **que no vayas** you'd better not go

preferido -da *adj/m,f* favorite*

preferir [I11] *vt* to prefer; **prefiero esperar aquí** I'd rather wait here, I'd prefer to wait here; ~ **algo** A **algo** to prefer sth TO sth; **prefiero que te quedes** I'd rather you stayed, I prefer you to stay

prefiera, **prefieras, etc** *see* PREFERIR

prefijo *m* (Ling) prefix; (de teléfono) (dialing*) code

prefiriera, **prefirió, etc** *see* PREFERIR

pregonar [A1] *vt* **(a)** ‹*noticia/secreto*› to make ... public **(b)** ‹*virtudes/méritos*› to extol **(c)** ‹*mercancía*› to hawk, cry

pregunta *f* question; **hacer/contestar una** ~ to ask/answer a question

preguntar [A1] *vt* to ask; **eso no se pregunta** you shouldn't ask things like that; **la maestra me preguntó la lección** the teacher tested me on the lesson ■ ~ *vi* to ask; **le preguntó sobre** *or* **acerca de lo ocurrido** he asked her (about) what had

happened; ~ POR **algo/algn** to ask ABOUT sth/sb; **preguntaban por un tal Mario** they were looking for *o* asking for someone called Mario
■ **preguntarse** *v pron* (*refl*) to wonder

prehistoria *f* prehistory

prehistórico -ca *adj* prehistoric

prejuiciado -da *adj* (AmL) prejudiced

prejuicio *m* prejudice

prejuzgar [A3] *vt/vi* to prejudge

prelavado *m* prewash

preliminar *adj* preliminary

preludio *m* prelude

premamá *adj inv* (Esp fam) maternity (*before n*)

prematrimonial *adj* ‹*relaciones*› premarital

prematuro -ra *adj* premature

premeditación *f* premeditation

premeditado -da *adj* premeditated

premeditar [A1] *vt* to premeditate

premenstrual *adj* premenstrual

premiación *f* (AmL) (acción) awarding of prizes; (ceremonia) awards ceremony, prize-giving (BrE)

premiado -da *adj* ‹*número/boleto*› winning; ‹*novela/película/escritor*› prizewinning (*before n*); *ver tb* PREMIAR

premiar [A1] *vt* **(a)** ‹*actor/escritor*› to award a/the prize to, award ... a/the prize **(b)** ‹*generosidad/sacrificio*› to reward

premio *m* **(a)** (en general) prize; **conceder** *or* **dar un ~** to award *o* give a prize; **ganar** *or* **llevarse un ~** to win a prize; **el ~ a la mejor película** the award *o* prize for the best movie; **~ de consolación** *or* (CS) **(de) consuelo** consolation prize; **~ gordo** jackpot; **P~ Nobel** (galardón) Nobel Prize; (galardonado) Nobel Prize winner **(b)** (a esfuerzos, sacrificios) reward; **como ~ a su dedicación** as a reward for your dedication

premisa *f* premise

premonición *f* premonition

prenatal *adj* prenatal (AmE), antenatal (BrE)

prenda *f* **1** (de vestir) garment; **~ íntima** undergarment, item of underwear **2** (señal, garantía) security, surety **3** (Jueg) forfeit

prendarse [A1] *v pron* (liter) ~ DE **algn** to fall in love WITH sb

prender [E1] *vt* **1** ‹*persona*› to catch, seize **2** (sujetar) to pin; ‹*bajo/dobladillo*› to pin up **3 (a)** ‹*cigarrillo/cerilla*› to light; **~(le) fuego a algo** to set fire to sth **(b)** (AmL) ‹*gas*› to light; ‹*estufa/horno*› to turn on; ‹*radio/luz/televisión*› to turn on, switch on
■ ~ *vi* **1** «*rama/planta*» to take **2 (a)** «*fósforo/piloto*» to light; «*leña*» to catch (light) **(b)** (AmL) «*luz/radio/televisión*» to come on; **la televisión no prende** the TV won't come on **3** «*idea/moda*» to catch on
■ **prenderse** *v pron* **(a)** (con fuego) to catch fire **(b)** (AmL) «*luz/radio/televisión*» to come on

prensa *f* **(a)** (Impr, Period, Tec) press; **la ~ oral** radio and television; **estar en ~** to be in *o* at the press **(b)** (periodistas) **la ~** the press; **~ amarilla** gutter press, yellow press; **~ del corazón** gossip magazines (*pl*); **~ roja** (CS) sensationalist press (*specializing in crime stories*)

preñado -da *adj* ‹*animal*› pregnant

preocupación *f* **(a)** (problema) worry; **les causa muchas preocupaciones** she causes them a lot of worry *o* problems **(b)** (inquietud) concern

preocupado -da *adj* worried; **~ POR algo** worried ABOUT sth

preocupante *adj* worrying

preocupar [A1] *vt* to worry; **no quiero ~lo** I don't want to worry him; **le preocupa el futuro** she's worried *o* concerned about her future; **me preocupa que no haya llamado** it worries me that she hasn't phoned; **no me preocupa** it doesn't bother *o* worry me
■ **preocuparse** *v pron* **1** (inquietarse) to worry; **~se** POR **algo/algn** to worry ABOUT sth/sb **2** (ocuparse) **~se** DE **algo**: **me preocupé de que no faltara nada** I made sure *o* I saw to it that we had everything; **no se preocupó más del asunto** he gave the matter no further thought

preparación *f* **1** (de examen, discurso) preparation **2 (a)** (conocimientos, educación) education; (para trabajo) training **(b)** (de deportista) training; **su ~ física es muy buena** he's in peak condition **3** (Farm, Med) preparation

preparado -da *adj* **1** [ESTAR] (listo, dispuesto) ready; **~ PARA algo** ready FOR sth; **¡~s, listos, ya!** get ready, get set, go! (AmE), on your marks, get set, go! (BrE) **2** [SER] (instruido, culto) educated; **un profesional muy bien ~** a highly-trained professional

preparar [A1] *vt* **1** ‹*plato*› to make, prepare; ‹*comida*› to prepare, get ... ready; ‹*medicamento*› to prepare, make up; ‹*habitación*› to prepare, get ... ready; ‹*cuenta*› to draw up (AmE), make up (BrE) **2** ‹*examen/prueba*› to prepare **3** ‹*persona*› (para examen) to tutor, coach (BrE); (para partido) to train, coach, prepare; (para tarea, reto) to prepare
■ **prepararse** *v pron* **1** (*refl*) (disponerse): **~se** PARA **algo** to get ready FOR sth **2** (*refl*) (formarse) to prepare; **~se PARA algo** ‹*para examen/competición*› to prepare FOR sth

preparativos *mpl* preparations (*pl*)

preparatoria *f* (Méx) *three-year pre-university course and college where this is taught*

preparatorio -ria *adj* ‹*curso*› preparatory; ‹*ejercicios*› warm-up (*before n*)

preponderante *adj* predominant, preponderant (frml)

preposición *f* preposition

prepotencia *f* arrogance

prepotente *adj* ‹*persona*› arrogant, overbearing; ‹*actitud*› high-handed

prepucio *m* foreskin, prepuce (tech)

presa *f* **1** (en caza) prey; ***ser ~ de algo*** (de terror, pánico) to be seized with sth **2** (dique) dam; (embalse) reservoir, lake **3** (AmS) (de pollo) piece

presagio *m* **(a)** (señal) omen **(b)** (premonición) premonition

prescindir [I1] *vi* **1** (arreglárselas sin) **~ DE algo/algn** to do WITHOUT sth/sb **2** (omitir) **~ DE algo** ‹*de detalles/formalidades*› to dispense WITH sth

prescribir [I34] *vt* to prescribe

prescripción *f* prescription; **por ~ facultativa** *or* **médica** on doctor's orders

prescrito -ta, **prescripto -ta** *pp*: *see* PRESCRIBIR

preselección *f*: **hacer una ~ de los candidatos** to draw up a shortlist of candidates; **una vez terminada la ~** once the initial selection process is/was complete

preseleccionar [A1] *vt* ‹*candidatos/solicitantes*› to shortlist

presencia *f* **(a)** (en lugar, acto) presence; **su ~ me cohíbe** I feel awkward in his presence; **en ~ de algn** in the presence of sb **(b)** (euf) (aspecto físico) appearance; **se requiere buena ~** good *o* (BrE) smart appearance required **(c) ~ de ánimo** (serenidad) presence of mind; (valor) courage, strength

presenciar [A1] *vt* ‹*suceso/asesinato*› to witness; ‹*acto/espectáculo*› to be present at, to attend

presentable *adj* presentable

presentación *f* (en general) presentation; (de personas) **▶378** introduction

presentador -dora *m,f* presenter

presentar [A1] *vt* **1 (a)** (mostrar) to present **(b)** (exponer por primera vez) ‹*libro/disco*› to launch; ‹*obra de arte*› to present; ‹*colección de moda*› to present, exhibit **(c)** (entregar) ‹*informe/solicitud*› to submit; ‹*trabajo*› to hand in; ‹*renuncia*› to hand in, submit **(d)** (enseñar) ‹*carnet/pasaporte*› to show **(e)** ‹*disculpas/excusas*› to make; ‹*queja*› to file, make; ‹*cargos*› to bring; **~on una denuncia** they reported the matter (to the police), they made an official complaint; **~ pruebas** to present evidence **(f)** (Mil): **~ armas** to present arms **2** (TV) ‹*programa*› to present, introduce **3** **▶378** ‹*persona*› to introduce; **te presento a mi hermana** I'd like you to meet my sister, this is my sister **4** ‹*novedad/ventaja*› to offer; ‹*síntoma*› to show

■ **presentarse** *v pron* **1 (a)** (en lugar) to turn up, appear; **~se (como) voluntario** to volunteer **(b) ~se** A **algo** ‹*a examen*› to take sth; ‹*a concurso*› to enter sth; ‹*a elecciones*› to take part IN sth; **se presenta como candidato independiente** he's running (AmE) *o* (BrE) he's standing as an independent; **~se para un cargo** to apply for a post **2** «*dificultad/problema*» to arise, come up; «*oportunidad*» to arise **3** (darse a conocer) to introduce oneself

presente *adj* **1** (en un lugar) [ESTAR] present; Ⓢ **Presente** (CS) (Corresp) ≈ by hand; ***tener algo ~*** to bear sth in mind **2** (actual) present; **hasta el momento ~** up to the present time; **el día 15 del ~ mes** the 15th of this month; **en su atenta carta del 3 ~** (Méx frml) (Corresp) in your letter of the 3rd of this month *o* (frml) of the 3rd inst. ■ *m* **1 (a)** (en el tiempo) **el ~** the present **(b)** (Ling) present (tense) **2 los presentes** *mpl* (asistentes) those present

presentimiento *m* premonition; **tengo el ~ de que** ... I have a feeling that ...

presentir [I11] *vt* ‹*desgracia*› to have a premonition of; **presiento que** ... I have a feeling that ...

preservar [A1] *vt* **(a)** (proteger) to preserve **(b)** (AmL) (conservar, mantener) to maintain

preservativo *m* **1** (condón) condom **2** (Andes) (conservante) preservative

presidencia *f* **(a)** (Gob, Pol) (cargo) presidency; **~ municipal** (Méx) town hall **(b)** (de compañía, banco) presidency (esp AmE), chairmanship (BrE); (de reunión, comité) chairmanship, chair

presidente -ta *m,f* **(a)** (Gob, Pol) president; **el ~ del gobierno** the premier, the prime minister **(b)** (de compañía, banco) president (AmE), chairman (BrE) **(c)** (de reunión, comité, acto) chairperson, chair **(d)** (Der) (de tribunal) presiding judge/magistrate **(e)** (de jurado) chairman/chairwoman

presidiario -ria *m,f* convict, inmate, prisoner

presidio *m* (lugar) prison; (pena) prison sentence; **condenado a cinco años de ~** sentenced to five years imprisonment

presidir [I1] *vt* ‹*país*› to be president of; ‹*reunión*› to chair, preside at *o* over; ‹*comité*› to chair; ‹*tribunal/cortes/jurado*› to preside over; ‹*compañía*› to be president of (AmE), to be chairman of (BrE)

presilla *f* (para abrochar) eye; (lazo) loop

presión *f* **(a)** (Fís, Med, Meteo) pressure; **~ arterial** *or* **sanguínea** blood pressure **(b)** (coacción) pressure; **bajo ~** under pressure

presionar [A1] *vt* **(a)** (coaccionar) to put pressure on, to pressure (esp AmE), to pressurize (esp BrE) **(b)** ‹*botón/timbre*› to press ■ **~** *vi* (Dep) to put on the pressure

preso -sa *adj*: **estuvo ~ diez años** he was in prison for ten years; **llevarse a algn ~** to take sb prisoner ■ *m,f* prisoner

prestaciónes *fpl* (Servs Socs) benefits (*pl*), assistance

prestado -da *adj*: **el libro está ~** the book is on loan *o* (colloq) is already out; **esta chaqueta es prestada** this jacket is borrowed; **pedir algo ~** to borrow sth; **me pidió el coche ~** she asked if she could borrow my car; **pídeselo ~** ask (him) if you can borrow it

prestamista *mf* moneylender

préstamo *m* (Econ, Fin) (acción — de prestar) lending; (— de tomar prestado) borrowing; (cosa prestada) loan

prestar [A1] *vt* **1** ‹*dinero/libro*› to lend; **¿me prestas el coche?** will you lend me your car?, can I borrow your car? **2 (a)** ‹*ayuda*› to give; ‹*servicio*› to render; ‹*servicio militar*› to do **(b)** ‹*atención*› to pay **3** ‹*juramento*› to swear

■ **prestarse** *v pron* **1** (dar ocasión) **~se** A **algo** ‹*a críticas/malentendidos/abusos*› to be open TO sth **2** (ser apto, idóneo) **~se** PARA **algo** to be suitable FOR sth **3** (*refl*) **(a)** (ofrecerse) **~se a hacer algo** to offer to do dth **(b)** (en frases negativas): **no me presto a negocios sucios** I won't take part in anything underhand

prestidigitador -dora *m,f* conjurer

prestigio *m* prestige; **de ~** prestigious

prestigioso -sa *adj* famous, prestigious

presumido -da *adj* **(a)** (engreído) conceited, full of oneself; (arrogante) arrogant **(b)** (coqueto) vain

presumir [I1] *vi* to show off; **~** DE **algo** ‹*de dinero*› (hablando) to boast *o* brag ABOUT sth; (enseñándolo) to flash sth around; **presume de guapo** he thinks he's good-looking ■ ~ *vt:* **se presume una reacción violenta** there is likely to be a violent reaction

presunto -ta *adj* (*delante del n*) (frml) ‹*asesino/terrorista*› alleged (*before n*)

presuntuoso -sa *adj* conceited, vain

presuponer [E22] *vt* to presuppose (frml), assume

presupuesto *m* **1 (a)** (Fin) budget **(b)** (precio estimado) estimate; **hacer un ~** to give an estimate **2** (supuesto) assumption, supposition

pretencioso -sa *adj* ‹*casa/película*› pretentious

pretender [E1] *vt:* **¿qué pretendes con esa actitud?** what do you hope to gain with that attitude?; **pretendía entrar sin pagar** he was trying to get in without paying; **no pretendo saberlo todo** I don't claim to know everything; **lo único que pretendía era ayudar** I was only trying to help; **¿pretendes que te crea?** do you expect me to believe you?

pretendido -da *adj* (*delante del n*) ‹*interés/amabilidad*› feigned; **el ~ duque** the so-called duke; **con ~ interés** with false interest

pretendiente *mf* **1** (al trono) pretender; (a un puesto) applicant **2 pretendiente** *m* (de una mujer) suitor

pretensión *f* **1** (a trono, herencia) claim **2 pretensiones** *fpl* (ínfulas): **tener pretensiones** to be pretentious; **una película sin pretensiones** an unpretentious film

pretensioso -sa *adj* (AmL) vain

pretérito *m* preterit*; **~ indefinido** simple past, preterit*; **~ perfecto/pluscuamperfecto** present/past perfect

pretexto *m* pretext; **volvió con el ~ de recoger el paraguas** he went back on the pretext of getting his umbrella; **siempre sale con algún ~** she always comes out with some excuse; **bajo ningún ~** under no circumstances

prevalecer [E3] *vi* to prevail

prevención *f* **(a)** (de un mal, problema) prevention **(b)** (medida) precaution; **tomar prevenciones** to take precautionary measures

prevenido -da *adj* **(a)** [SER] (precavido) well-prepared, well-organized; **es muy prevenida** she likes to be prepared *o* ready for all eventualities **(b)** [ESTAR] (advertido) forewarned; **ahora ya estás ~** you've been warned

prevenir [I31] *vt* **(a)** ‹*enfermedad/accidente*› to prevent **(b)** (advertir, alertar) to warn

■ **prevenirse** *v pron* **~se** CONTRA **algo** to take preventive *o* preventative measures AGAINST sth, take precautions AGAINST sth

preventiva *f* (Méx) yellow (AmE) *o* (BrE) amber light

preventivo -va *adj* preventive, preventative

prever [E29] *vt* **(a)** (anticipar) ‹*acontecimiento/consecuencias*› to foresee, anticipate; ‹*tiempo*› to forecast; **se prevé un aumento de precios** a rise in prices has been predicted **(b)** (proyectar, planear): **medidas previstas por el gobierno** measures planned by the government; **tiene prevista su llegada a las 11 horas** it is due *o* scheduled to arrive at 11 o'clock; **todo salió tal como estaba previsto** everything turned out just as planned **(c)** «*ley*» to envisage ■ **~** *vi:* **como era de ~** as was to be expected

previo -via *adj* **(a)** (anterior) ‹*experiencia/conocimientos*› previous; **sin ~ aviso** without (prior) warning **(b)** ‹*reunión/asunto*› preliminary

previsible *adj* foreseeable

previsión *f* **(a)** (precaución) precaution; **en ~ de ...** as a precaution against ...; **por falta de ~** owing to a lack of foresight **(b)** (predicción) forecast

previsor -sora *adj* (con visión de futuro) farsighted; (precavido) well-prepared

prieta *f* (Chi) blood sausage, black pudding (BrE)

prieto -ta *adj* (Méx fam) (oscuro) dark; (de piel oscura) dark-skinned

prima *f* **(a)** (de seguro) premium **(b)** (pago extra) bonus; **~ de** *or* **por peligrosidad** danger money

primar [A1] *vi:* **debería ~ el interés público** the public interest should be (a) top priority; **~** SOBRE **algo** to take precedence *o* priority OVER sth

primaria *f* **1** (Educ) elementary *o* (BrE) primary education **2** (Pol) (en EEUU) primary

primario -ria *adj* **(a)** (básico) ‹*necesidades/objetivo*› primary, basic **(b)** (primitivo) ‹*instintos*› primitive

primavera *f* **1** (estación) spring; **en ~** in spring, in springtime **2** (Bot) primrose

primaveral *adj* ‹*tiempo/moda*› spring (*before n*); ‹*ambiente*› spring-like

primer *ver* PRIMERO

primera *f* **(a)** (Auto) first (gear) **(b)** (Transp) (clase) first class; **viajar en ~** to travel first class; *ver tb* PRIMERO

primerizo -za *m,f* **(a)** novice, beginner **(b) primeriza** *f* first-time mother

primero -ra *adj/pron* [PRIMER *is used before masculine singular nouns*] **1** ▶ **294** (en el espacio, el tiempo) first; **el primer piso** the second (AmE) *o* (BrE) first floor; **en primer lugar** ... first (of all), ..., firstly, ...; **1º de julio** (*read as: primero de julio*) 1st July, July 1st (*léase: July the first*); **Olaf I** (*read as: Olaf primero*) Olaf I (*léase: Olaf the First*); **a primeras horas de la madrugada** in the early hours of the morning; **primera plana** front page; **~s auxilios** *mpl* first aid; **primer plano** (Fot) close-up (shot) **2** (en calidad, jerarquía): **un artículo de primera calidad** a top-quality product; **de primera (categoría)** first-class, first-rate; **es el ~ de la clase** he is top of the class; **primer ministro** Prime Minister **3** (básico, fundamental): **nuestro primer objetivo** our primary objective; **artículos de primera necesidad** basic necessities; **lo ~ es** ... the most important thing is ... ■ *adv* **1** (en el tiempo) first **2** (en importancia): **estar ~** to come first

primicia *f* (Period): **conseguimos la ~ del reportaje** we were the first to carry the report; **una ~ informativa** a scoop

primitivo -va *adj* primitive

primo -ma *adj* ‹*número*› prime; ‹*materia*› raw; ■ *m,f* (pariente) cousin; **~ hermano** first cousin

primogénito -ta *m,f* first *o* firstborn child

primordial *adj* ‹*objetivo*› fundamental, prime (*before n*); ‹*interés/importancia*› paramount
prímula *f* primula; (amarilla) primrose
princesa *f* princess
principal *adj* main; **lo ~ es que**… the main thing is that…
príncipe *m* prince; **~ heredero** crown prince
principiante *mf* beginner; **un error de ~** a basic mistake
principio *m* **1** (comienzo) beginning; **a ~s de temporada** at the beginning of the season; **empieza por el ~** start at the beginning; **eso es un buen ~** that's a good start; **en un** *or* **al ~** at first, in the beginning **2 (a)** (postulado, norma moral) principle; **es una mujer de ~s** she's a woman of principle; **por ~** on principle
pringar [A3] *vt* (fam) (ensuciar) to get … dirty (with grease, oil etc)
■ **pringarse** *v pron* (fam) (ensuciarse) **~se** DE **algo** ‹*de grasa/mermelada*› to get covered IN sth
pringoso -sa *adj* greasy
prioridad *f* priority
prisa *f* **1** (rapidez, urgencia) rush, hurry; **¿a qué viene tanta ~?** what's the rush *o* hurry?; **con las ~s olvidé decírselo** in the rush I forgot to tell her; **tenía ~ por llegar a casa** he was in a rush to get home; **no me metas ~** don't rush *o* hurry me; **tengo ~** (Esp, Méx) I'm in a rush *o* a hurry; **darse ~** to hurry (up) **2** (*en locs*) **a** *or* **de prisa** ⇒ DEPRISA; **a toda prisa** as fast as possible; **correr prisa: éstos no (me) corren ~** there's no rush for these
prisco *m* (CS) *type of peach*
prisión *f* **1** (edificio) prison, jail, penitentiary (AmE) **2** (pena) prison sentence; **seis años de ~** six years' imprisonment
prisionero -ra *m,f* prisoner; **lo hicieron ~** he was taken prisoner *o* captured
prisma *m* (Fís, Ópt) prism; (perspectiva) perspective
prismáticos *mpl* binoculars (*pl*), field-glasses (*pl*); **unos ~** a pair of binoculars
privacidad *f* privacy
privación *f* **(a)** (acción) deprivation; **la ~ de libertad** deprivation of liberty **(b)** (falta, carencia) privation, deprivation; **pasar privaciones** to suffer privations *o* deprivations
privada *f* (Méx) private road (*with security control*)
privado -da *adj* **(a)** ‹*reunión/vida*› private; **en ~** in private **(b)** (Col, Méx) (desmayado) unconscious **(c)** (Méx) ‹*teléfono/número*› unlisted (AmE), ex-directory (BrE)
privar [A1] *vt* **1 ~ a algn** DE **algo** ‹*de derecho/libertad*› to deprive sb OF sth **2** (Col, Méx) (dejar inconsciente) to knock … unconscious
■ **privarse** *v pron* **1 ~se** DE **algo** ‹*de lujos/placeres*› to deprive oneself OF sth **2** (Col, Méx) (desmayarse) to lose consciousness, pass out
privatización *f* privatization
privatizar [A4] *vt* to privatize
privilegiado -da *adj* **(a)** ‹*persona/clase*› privileged **(b)** (excelente) ‹*posición*› privileged; ‹*clima/inteligencia/memoria*› exceptional ■ *m,f*: **unos pocos ~s** a privileged few
privilegio *m* privilege
pro *m* (ventaja) advantage; **sopesar los ~s y los contras de algo** to weigh up the pros and cons of sth ■ *prep*: **los sectores ~ amnistía** the sectors in favor of an amnesty
proa *f* bow, prow
probabilidad *f* (Mat) probability; **con toda ~** in all probability *o* likelihood; **¿qué ~es tiene de ganar?** what are her chances of winning?
probable *adj* (posible) probable; **es ~** probably; **es ~ que llegue hoy** he will probably arrive today
probado -da *adj* (*delante del n*) proven
probador *m* fitting room, changing room (BrE)
probar [A10] *vt* **1** (demostrar) ‹*teoría/inocencia*› to prove **2 (a)** ‹*vino/sopa*› to taste; (por primera vez) to try **(b)** ‹*método*› to try; ‹*coche/mecanismo*› to try out **(c)** ‹*ropa*› to try on; **~le algo** A **algn** to try sth ON sb **(d)** (poner a prueba) ‹*empleado/honradez*› to test; ‹*arma/vehículo*› to test (out) ■ **~** *vi* (intentar) to try; **~** A **hacer algo** to try doing sth
■ **probarse** *v pron* ‹*ropa/zapatos*› to try on
probeta *f* test tube ■ *adj inv* ‹*gemelos/hijos*› test-tube (*before n*)
problema *m* problem; **resolver/solucionar un ~** to solve a problem; **los coches viejos dan muchos ~s** old cars give a lot of trouble; **no te hagas ~** (AmL) don't worry about it
problemático -ca *adj* problematic, difficult
procaz *adj* ‹*comentario/chiste*› indecent, lewd; ‹*lenguaje*› obscene
procedencia *f* **(a)** (origen) origin **(b)** (de barco) port of origin
procedente *adj*: **el vuelo/tren ~ de París** the flight/train from Paris
proceder [E1] *vi* **1** (provenir) **~** DE **algo** to come FROM sth **2** (actuar) to act, to proceed (frml); **procedió con mucha corrección** he behaved very correctly **3** (frml) (iniciar) **~** A **algo** to proceed TO sth **4** (ser conveniente): **procede actuar rápidamente** it would be wise to act swiftly; **rellenar lo que proceda** complete as appropriate
procedimiento *m* **1** (método) procedure; (Tec) process **2** (Der) proceedings (*pl*)
prócer *m* national hero (*esp of a struggle for independence*)
procesado -da *m,f* (Der) accused, defendant
procesador *m* processor; **~ de textos** word processor
procesamiento *m* **1** (Der) prosecution, trial **2** (Tec, Inf) processing; **~ de textos** word processing
procesar [A1] *vt* **1** (Der) to try, prosecute **2** ‹*materia prima/datos/solicitud*› to process
procesión *f* procession
proceso *m* **1** (serie de acciones, sucesos) process **2** (Der) trial **3** (Inf) processing; **~ de datos/textos** data/word processing **4** (transcurso) course
proclamación *f* proclamation, declaration
proclamar [A1] *vt* to proclaim

■ **proclamarse** *v pron* to proclaim oneself

procrear [A1] *vi* to procreate, breed

procurador -dora *m,f* (Der) (abogado) attorney, lawyer; (asistente) ≈ paralegal (*in US*), ≈ clerk (*in UK*)

procurar [A1] *vt* (intentar) **~ hacer algo** to try to do sth; **procura que no te vea** try not to let him see you

prodigio *m* **(a)** (maravilla) wonder **(b)** (milagro) miracle

prodigioso -sa *adj* prodigious, phenomenal; ‹*éxito/jugador/músico*› phenomenal

producción *f* **1** (Com, Econ) (proceso, acción) production; (cantidad) output, production; **~ en cadena** *or* **serie** mass production **2** (Cin, Teatr, TV) production

producir [I6] *vt* **1 (a)** (en general) to produce **(b)** ‹*sonido*› to cause, generate **2** (causar) ‹*conmoción/reacción/explosión*› to cause; **le produjo una gran alegría** it made her very happy

■ **producirse** *v pron* **1** (frml) (tener lugar) «*accidente/explosión*» to occur (frml), to take place; «*cambio*» to occur (frml), to happen; **se produjeron 85 muertes** there were 85 deaths, 85 people died *o* were killed **2** (*refl*) (frml) ‹*heridas*› to inflict ... on oneself (frml)

productividad *f* (cualidad) productivity; (rendimiento) productivity, output

productivo -va *adj* productive; ‹*empresa/negocio*› lucrative

producto *m* **(a)** (artículo producido) product; **~s agrícolas/de granja** agricultural/farm produce; **~ alimenticio** foodstuff; **~ lácteo** dairy product **(b)** (resultado) result, product

productor -tora *adj* producing (*before n*) ■ *m,f* **(a)** (en general) producer **(b) productora** *f* (empresa) production company

produje, produzca, etc *see* PRODUCIR

proeza *f* (logro) feat, exploit; (Mil) heroic deed *o* exploit

profanar [A1] *vt* ‹*templo/sepultura*› to desecrate, defile

profano -na *adj* **1 (a)** (no sagrado) ‹*escritor/música*› secular, profane (frml); ‹*fiesta*› secular **(b)** (antirreligioso) profane (frml), irreverent **2** (no especializado): **soy ~ en la materia** I'm not an expert on the subject ■ *m,f* **1** (Relig) (*m*) layman; (*f*) laywoman **2** (no especialista) non-specialist

profecía *f* prophecy

proferir [I11] *vt* ‹*palabras/amenazas*› to utter; ‹*insultos*› to hurl

profesar [A1] *vt* **(a)** (declarar) ‹*religión/doctrina*› to profess **(b)** (sentir) ‹*cariño*› to feel; ‹*respeto*› to have

profesión *f* (ocupación) profession; (en formularios) occupation; **~ liberal** profession

profesional *adj* ‹*fotógrafo/deportista*› professional (*before n*) ■ *mf* professional

profesionalidad *f* professionalism

profesionista *mf* (Méx) professional

profesor -sora *m,f* (de escuela secundaria) teacher, schoolteacher; (de universidad) professor (AmE), lecturer (BrE); **tiene un ~ particular** he has a private tutor

profeta *m* prophet

profetizar [A4] *vt* to prophesy

prófugo -ga *m,f* (Der) fugitive; (Mil) deserter

profundidad *f* **(a)** (de pozo, río, mar) depth; **tiene 20 metros de ~** it's 20 meters deep **(b)** (de conocimientos, ideas) depth; **en ~** ‹*analizar*› in depth; ‹*reformar*› radically

profundizar [A4] *vi* **~ EN algo** ‹*en tema*› to go into sth in depth

profundo -da *adj* **(a)** ‹*herida/pozo/raíz*› deep; **un río poco ~** a shallow river **(b)** ‹*pensamiento*› profound, deep; ‹*respeto/desprecio*› profound; ‹*lazos*› strong; ‹*desengaño*› grave, terrible **(c)** ‹*misterio*› profound; ‹*silencio*› deep, profound **(d)** ‹*voz/suspiro*› deep **(e)** ‹*sueño*› deep, sound

progenitor -tora *m,f* **(a)** (antepasado) ancestor **(b)** (frml) (*m*) (padre) father; (*f*) (madre) mother

programa *m* **1 (a)** (Rad, TV) program*; **~ concurso** quiz show **(b)** (folleto) program* **2** (programación, plan) program* **3 (a)** (político) program*; **su ~ electoral** their election manifesto **(b)** (Educ) (de asignatura) syllabus; (de curso) curriculum, syllabus **4** (Inf, Elec) program*

programación *f* **1 (a)** (Rad, TV) programs* (*pl*) **(b)** (de festejos, visitas — lista) program*; (— organización) organization, planning **2** (Inf) programming

programador -dora *m,f* programmer

programar [A1] *vt* **1 (a)** (Rad, TV) to schedule **(b)** ‹*actividades/eventos*› to plan, draw up a program* for; ‹*horario/fecha*› to schedule, program*; ‹*viaje*› to organize **(c)** (Transp) ‹*llegadas/salidas*› to schedule, timetable (BrE) **2** (Inf) to program

progresar [A1] *vi* «*persona*» to make progress, to progress; «*negociaciones/proyecto*» to progress

progresión *f* (Mat, Mús) progression

progresista *adj/mf* progressive

progresivo -va *adj* progressive

progreso *m* **(a)** (adelanto): **supuso un gran ~** it was a great step forward; **hacer ~s** to make progress **(b)** (evolución, desarrollo) progress

prohibición *f* (acción) prohibition, banning; (orden) ban

prohibir [I22] *vt* **(a)** ‹*acto/venta*› to ban, prohibit (frml); **iba en dirección prohibida** I was going the wrong way up a one-way street; **Ⓢ prohibido el paso** *or* **prohibida la entrada** no entry; **Ⓢ prohibido fumar** no smoking; **Ⓢ se prohíbe la entrada a menores de 16 años** over 16s only, no admission to persons under 16 years of age **(b) ~le algo A algn** to ban sb FROM sth; **~le A algn hacer algo** to forbid sb to do sth, prohibit sb FROM doing sth (frml); **~ A algn QUE haga algo** to forbid sb to do sth

prohibitivo -va *adj* prohibitive

prójimo *m* (semejante) fellow man; **amar al ~** to love one's neighbor

prole *f* kids (*pl*) (colloq), offspring (hum)

proletario -ria *adj/m* proletarian

proliferar [A1] *vi* to proliferate, spread
prolífico -ca *adj* prolific
prolijo -ja *adj* **1** (extenso) protracted, long-winded; (minucioso) detailed **2** (RPl) (ordenado, aseado) ‹*persona/casa*› tidy; ‹*cuaderno*› neat
prólogo *m* (de libro) preface, foreword; (de acto) prelude
prolongación *f* extension
prolongado -da *adj* prolonged, lengthy
prolongar [A3] *vt* **(a)** ‹*contrato/plazo*› to extend; ‹*vacaciones/visita*› to prolong, extend **(b)** ‹*línea/calle*› to extend
■ **prolongarse** *v pron* **(a)** (en el tiempo) «*debate/fiesta*» to go on, carry on **(b)** (en el espacio) «*carretera/línea*» to extend
promedio *m* **(a)** (Mat) average; **el ~ de mis ingresos** my average earnings; **como ~** on average **(b)** (nota media) average grade *o* (BrE) mark **(c)** (punto medio) mid-point
promesa *f* **(a)** (palabra) promise; **cumplí (con) mi ~** I kept my promise *o* word; **romper una ~** to break a promise **(b)** (persona) hope
prometedor -dora *adj* promising
prometer [E1] *vt* **(a)** (dar su palabra) to promise; **te lo prometo** I promise **(b)** (augurar) to promise ■ **~** *vi* «*persona/negocio*» to show *o* have promise
■ **prometerse** *v pron* **(a)** (en matrimonio) to get engaged **(b)** (*refl*) ‹*viaje/descanso*› to promise oneself
prometido -da *adj* **(a)** (para casarse) engaged **(b)** ‹*aumento/regalo*› promised; **cumplir con lo ~** to keep one's promise *o* word ■ *m,f* (*m*) fiancé; (*f*) fiancée
prominente *adj* prominent
promiscuo -cua *adj* promiscuous
promoción *f* **1 (a)** (de actividad, producto) promotion; **hacer la ~ de un producto** to promote a product **(b)** (ascenso) promotion **2** (Educ): **somos de la misma ~** we graduated at the same time
promocionar [A1] *vt* to promote
promontorio *m* (en tierra) hill, rise; (en el mar) promontory, headland
promotor -tora *m,f* (persona) **(a)** (Const) developer **(b)** (Espec) promoter **(c)** (de rebelión, huelga) instigator
promover [E9] *vt* ‹*ahorro/turismo*› to promote; ‹*conflicto/enfrentamientos*› to provoke; ‹*querella/pleito*› to bring
promulgar [A3] *vt* to enact, to promulgate (frml)
pronombre *m* pronoun
pronosticar [A2] *vt* ‹*tiempo/resultado*› to forecast; ‹*victoria/muerte*› to predict
pronóstico *m* **(a)** (predicción) forecast, prediction; **el ~ del tiempo** the weather forecast **(b)** (Med) prognosis **(c)** (en carreras de caballos) tip
prontitud *f* promptness
pronto[1] -ta *adj* **(a)** (rápido) ‹*entrega/respuesta*› prompt **(b)** (RPl) (preparado) ready
pronto[2] *adv* **1 (a)** (en poco tiempo) soon; **¡hasta ~!** see you soon!; **lo más ~ posible** as soon as possible **(b)** (Esp) (temprano) early **2** (*en locs*) **de pronto** (repentinamente) suddenly; **por lo pronto** *or* **por de pronto** for the moment, for now; **tan pronto como** as soon as
pronunciación *f* pronunciation
pronunciado -da *adj* **(a)** ‹*curva*› sharp, pronounced; ‹*pendiente*› steep, pronounced **(b)** ‹*facciones/rasgos*› pronounced, marked **(c)** ‹*tendencia*› marked, noticeable
pronunciamiento *m* rebellion, military uprising
pronunciar [A1] *vt* **1 (a)** (Ling) to pronounce **(b)** ‹*discurso*› to deliver, give **2** (resaltar) to accentuate
■ **pronunciarse** *v pron* **1** (dar una opinión) **~se A FAVOR/EN CONTRA DE algo** to declare oneself to be IN FAVOR OF/AGAINST sth **2** (acentuarse) to become more marked, become more pronounced
propaganda *f* **(a)** (Pol) propaganda **(b)** (Com, Marketing) advertising; **hacer ~ de un producto** to advertise a product **(c)** (material publicitario) advertisements (*pl*); **no trae más que ~** it has nothing but advertisements in it; **repartir ~** to hand out advertising leaflets
propagar [A3] *vt* **(a)** ‹*doctrina/rumores/enfermedad*› to spread, propagate **(b)** ‹*especie*› to propagate
■ **propagarse** *v pron* to spread; «*especie/sonido/luz*» to propagate
propasarse [A1] *v pron* **(a)** (excederse) to go too far, overstep the mark **(b)** (en sentido sexual) **~ CON algn** to make a pass AT sb
propenso -sa *adj* **~ A algo** prone TO sth
propiamente *adv* exactly; **no vive en Londres ~ dicho** he doesn't live in London proper
propiciar [A1] *vt* (favorecer) to favor*; (causar) to bring about
propicio -cia *adj* ‹*momento*› opportune, propitious (frml); ‹*condiciones*› favorable*, propitious (frml)
propiedad *f* **1 (a)** (pertenencia) property; **son ~ del museo** they are the property of the museum; **la casa es ~ de mi hijo** the house belongs to my son **(b)** (lo poseído) property; **~ intelectual** copyright; **~ privada/pública** private/public property **2** (cualidad) property; (corrección): **con ~** ‹*hablar*› correctly; ‹*comportarse*› with decorum
propietario -ria *m,f* **(a)** (de comercio) owner, proprietor **(b)** (de casa) owner **(c)** (de tierras) landowner
propina *f* **(a)** (a camarero, empleado) tip, gratuity (frml); **dejó 25 pesos de ~** she left a 25 peso tip; **dar ~ a algn** to tip sb **(b)** (Per) (de niño) pocket money
propio -pia *adj* **1 (a)** (indicando posesión) own; **¿es ~ o alquilado?** is it your own or is it rented?; **tienen piscina propia** they have their own swimming pool **(b)** (de uno mismo) own; **por tu ~ bien** for your own good; **todo lo hace en beneficio ~** everything he does is for his own gain; **lo vi con mis ~s ojos** I saw it with my own two eyes *o* with my (very) own eyes **2** (característico, típico): **esa actitud es muy propia de él** that kind of attitude is very typical of him; **una enfermedad propia de la vejez** an illness common among old people; **no es un comportamiento ~ de una señorita** it's not ladylike behaviour **3** (*delante del n*) (mismo): **fue el ~ presidente** it was the president himself;

debe ser el ~ interesado quien lo pida it must be the person concerned who makes the request

proponer [E22] *vt* **(a)** ‹*idea*› to propose, suggest; ‹*brindis*› to propose; **nos propuso ir al campo** she suggested we go to the countryside; **te voy a ~ un trato** I'm going to make you a proposition **(b)** ‹*persona*› (para cargo) to put forward, nominate; (para premio) to nominate **(c)** ‹*moción*› to propose **(d)** ‹*teoría*› to propound

■ **proponerse** *v pron:* **~se hacer algo** to set out to do sth; **me lo propuse como meta** I set myself that goal; **me propuse decírselo** I made up my mind *o* I decided to tell her

proporción *f* **1** (relación) proportion; **en ~ a los ingresos** in proportion to income **2 proporciones** *fpl* (dimensiones) proportions (*pl*)

proporcionado -da *adj*: **~ a la figura humana** in proportion to the human body; **mal ~** ‹*dibujo*› poorly proportioned; **es bajo pero bien ~** he's short but he's well-proportioned

proporcional *adj* proportional, proportionate

proporcionar [A1] *vt* ‹*materiales/información/comida*› to provide; **~ algo A algn** to provide sb WITH sth

proposición *f* proposal, proposition; **~ de matrimonio** proposal of marriage

propósito *m* **(a)** (intención) intention, purpose; **con el ~ de verla** with the intention *o* purpose of seeing her; **tiene el firme ~ de dejar de fumar** she's determined to give up smoking; **buenos ~s** good intentions **(b) a propósito** (adrede) deliberately, on purpose; (por cierto) (*indep*) by the way

propuesta *f* **(a)** (sugerencia) proposal **(b)** (oferta) offer

propulsar [A1] *vt* ‹*desarrollo/actividad*› to promote, stimulate; ‹*avión/cohete*› to propel; ‹*vehículo*› to drive, propel

propulsión *f* propulsion; **~ a chorro** jet propulsion

propulsor -sora *adj* ‹*mecanismo*› driving (*before n*), propulsion (*before n*); ‹*cohete*› propulsion (*before n*) ■ *m,f* **(a)** (de actividad, idea) promoter **(b) propulsor** *m* (Tec) propellant

propuse, **propuso, etc** *see* PROPONER

prórroga *f* **(a)** (extensión) extension; (Dep) overtime (AmE), extra time (BrE) **(b)** (aplazamiento) deferral, deferment

prorrogar [A3] *vt* **(a)** (alargar) to extend **(b)** (aplazar) ‹*fecha*› to postpone, put back

prosa *f* prose

prosaico -ca *adj* ‹*existencia/vida*› mundane, prosaic

proseguir [I30] *vi/vt* (frml) to continue

prospecto *m* **(a)** (de fármaco) directions for use (*pl*), patient information leaflet **(b)** (de propaganda) pamphlet, leaflet

prosperar [A1] *vi* **(a)** «*negocio/país*» to prosper, thrive; «*persona*» to do well, make good **(b)** «*iniciativa/proyecto*» (aceptarse) to be accepted, prosper

prosperidad *f* prosperity

próspero -ra *adj* prosperous

próstata *f* prostate (gland)

prostíbulo *m* brothel

prostitución *f* prostitution

prostituir [I20] *vt* to prostitute

■ **prostituirse** *v pron* to prostitute oneself

prostituto -ta *m,f* (*m*) male prostitute; (*f*) prostitute

protagonista *mf* **(a)** (personaje principal) main character **(b)** (actor) **el ~ de la nueva serie** the actor who is playing the leading role in the new series; **los principales ~s de nuestra historia** the major figures of our history

protagonizar [A4] *vt* **(a)** (Cin, Teatr) to star in, play the lead *o* leading role in **(b)** ‹*tiroteo*› to be involved in; ‹*debate*› to take part in; ‹*disturbios*› to be responsible for

protección *f* protection

proteccionista *adj/mf* protectionist

protector -tora *adj* protective; **sociedad ~a de animales** society for the prevention of cruelty to animals ■ *m,f* (defensor) protector; (benefactor) patron

protectorado *m* protectorate

proteger [E6] *vt* **(a)** (en general) to protect; **~ algo/a algn** DE *or* CONTRA **algo/algn** to protect sth/sb FROM *o* AGAINST sth/sb **(b)** ‹*artes*› to champion, patronize; ‹*pintor/poeta*› to act as patron to

■ **protegerse** *v pron* (*refl*) **~se** DE *or* CONTRA **algo** to protect oneself FROM *o* AGAINST sth; **~se de la lluvia** to shelter from the rain

protegido -da *adj* **(a)** ‹*especie*› protected **(b)** ‹*vivienda*› subsidized **(c)** (Inf) write-protected ■ *m,f* (*m*) protegé; (*f*) protegée

proteína *f* protein

prótesis *f* prosthesis

protesta *f* **1 (a)** (queja) protest; **en señal de ~** in protest **(b)** (manifestación) demonstration, protest march (*o* rally *etc*) **2** (Méx) **(a)** (promesa) promise; **cumplieron con su ~** they kept their promise *o* word **(b)** ⇒ JURAMENTO

protestante *adj/mf* Protestant

protestantismo *m* Protestantism

protestar [A1] *vi* **(a)** (mostrar desacuerdo) to protest; **~** CONTRA **algo** to protest AGAINST *o* ABOUT sth **(b)** (quejarse) to complain; **~** POR *or* DE **algo** to complain ABOUT sth

protocolo *m* protocol

prototipo *m* **(a)** (de especie) archetype, prototype **(b)** (Tec) prototype

protuberancia *f* bulge, protuberance (frml)

provecho *m* **(a)** (beneficio, utilidad) benefit; **no sacó mucho ~ de la experiencia** she didn't benefit much from the experience; **le sacó mucho ~ a su estancia** she got a lot out of her stay; **sólo piensa en su propio ~** he's only out for himself (colloq); **de ~** ‹*estudiante*› hardworking; ‹*experiencia/visita*› worthwhile **(b)** (en la mesa): **¡buen ~!** (dicho por uno mismo) bon appetit!; (dicho por camarero) enjoy your meal!

provechoso -sa *adj* profitable, fruitful

proveedor -dora *m,f* supplier, purveyor (frml)

proveer [E14] *vt* (suministrar) to provide; **~ a algn** DE **algo** to provide sb WITH sth; **iban provistos**

de botes salvavidas they were equipped with *o* they carried lifeboats
■ **proveerse** *v pron (refl)*: **~se** DE **algo** ‹*de herramientas/armas*› to equip oneself WITH sth; ‹*de comida*› to get sth

provenir [I31] *vi* **~** DE **algo/algn** to come FROM sth/sb

proverbio *m* proverb

providencia *f* (Relig): **la (divina) P~** (divine) Providence

providencial *adj* **(a)** (oportuno) fortunate, lucky, providential (frml); **fue ~ que** ... it was fortunate that ... **(b)** (Relig) providential

provincia *f* **1** (Gob, Relig) province **2 provincias** *fpl* (por oposición a la capital) provinces (*pl*); **la vida de ~s** provincial life

provinciano -na *adj* **(a)** (de provincias) provincial **(b)** (pey) (estrecho de miras) provincial, parochial ■ *m, f* **(a)** (de provincias): **los ~s** people from the provinces **(b)** (pey) (de mentalidad estrecha) provincial **(c)** (paleto) country bumpkin, hick (AmE colloq)

provisional *adj* provisional

provisiones *fpl* (víveres) provisions (*pl*)

provisto -ta *pp*: *ver* PROVEER

provocación *f* provocation

provocador -dora *adj* provocative ■ *m, f* agitator

provocar [A2] *vt* **1 (a)** ‹*explosión*› to cause; ‹*incendio*› to start; ‹*polémica*› to spark off, prompt; ‹*reacción*› to cause **(b)** (Med) ‹*parto*› to induce **2** ‹*persona*› (al enfado) to provoke; (sexualmente) to lead ... on ■ **~** *vi* (Andes) (apetecer): **¿le provoca un traguito?** do you want a drink?, do you fancy a drink? (BrE colloq)

provocativo -va *adj* **1** (insinuante) provocative **2** (Col, Ven) (apetecible) tempting, mouthwatering

proximidad *f* **(a)** (en el tiempo, espacio) closeness, proximity (frml) **(b) proximidades** *fpl* (cercanías) vicinity

próximo -ma *adj* **1 (a)** (siguiente) next; **el ~ jueves** next Thursday **(b)** (*como pron*): **esto lo dejamos para la próxima** we'll leave this for next time; **tome la próxima a la derecha** take the next (on the) right **2** [ESTAR] (cercano) **(a)** (en el tiempo) close; **la fecha ya está próxima** the day is close; **en fecha próxima** in the near future **(b)** (en el espacio) near, close; **~** A **algo** close *o* near TO sth

proyección *f* **(a)** (Cin) showing **(b)** (de sombra) casting; (de luz) throwing

proyectar [A1] *vt* **1** (planear) to plan; **~ hacer algo** to plan to do sth **2 (a)** ‹*película*› to show, screen; ‹*diapositivas*› to project, show **(b)** ‹*sombra*› to cast; ‹*luz*› to throw, project

proyectil *m* projectile, missile

proyecto *m* **(a)** (plan) plan; **¿qué ~s tienes para el próximo año?** what are your plans for next year?; **tiene un viaje en ~** she's planning a trip; **~ de ley** bill **(b)** (trabajo) project **(c)**(Arquit, Ing) plans and costing

proyector *m* **1** (Cin, Fot) projector **2** (Teatr) spotlight; (para monumentos) floodlight; (Mil) searchlight

prudencia *f* (cuidado) caution; (sabiduría) wisdom, prudence; **conduce con ~** drive carefully

prudente *adj* (sensato. responsable) prudent, sensible; (cauto, precavido) cautious, prudent

prueba *f* **1 (a)** (demostración, testimonio) proof; **no hay ~s de que eso sea verdad** there's no proof that that's true; **eso es ~ de que le caes bien** that proves he likes you; **en** *or* **como ~ de mi agradecimiento** as a token of my gratitude **(b)** (Der) piece of evidence **2** (Educ) test; (Cin) screen test, audition; (Teatr) audition **3 (a)** (ensayo, experimento) test; **vamos a hacer la ~** let's try; **~ de la alcoholemia** Breathalyzer® test, sobriety test (AmE), drunkometer test (AmE); **~ del embarazo** pregnancy test **(b)** (*en locs*) **a prueba**: **tomar a algn a ~** to take sb on for a trial period; **tener algo a ~** to have sth on trial; **poner algo a ~** to put sth to the test; **a ~ de golpes/de balas** shockproof/bulletproof **(c)** (en costura) fitting **4** (Fot, Impr) proof; **corregir ~s** to proofread **5** (Dep): **en las ~s de clasificación** in the qualifying heats; **la ~ de los 1.500 metros** the 1,500 meters (event *o* race)

prueba, **pruebas**, **etc** *see* PROBAR

psicoanálisis *m* psychoanalysis

psicoanalista *mf* psychoanalyst

psicodélico -ca *adj* psychedelic

psicología *f* psychology

psicológico -ca *adj* psychological

psicólogo -ga *m, f* (Psic) psychologist

psicópata *mf* psychopath

psicosis *f* (*pl* **~**) psychosis

psicosomático -ca *adj* psychosomatic

psicoterapia *f* psychotherapy

psiquiatra *mf* psychiatrist

psiquiatría *f* psychiatry

psiquiátrico[1] **-ca** *adj* psychiatric (*before n*)

psiquiátrico[2] *m* psychiatric hospital, mental hospital

psíquico -ca *adj* psychic

ptas, **pts** = **pesetas**

púa *f* **1 (a)** (de erizo) spine, quill; (de alambre) barb; (de peine) tooth **(b)** (Chi, Ven) (en zapatos de atletismo) spike **2** (para guitarra) plectrum, pick; (de tocadiscos) (RPl) needle

pub /puβ, pʌβ/ *m* (*pl* **pubs** *or* **pubes**) bar (*gen with music, open late at night*)

pubertad *f* puberty

pubis *m* (*pl* **~**) pubis

publicación *f* publication

publicar [A2] *vt* **(a)** ‹*artículo/noticia*› to publish **(b)** (divulgar) to divulge, disclose

publicidad *f* **(a)** (de tema, suceso) publicity **(b)** (Com, Marketing) advertising; **hacer ~ de algo** to advertise sth

publicista *mf* **(a)** (AmL) (Com) advertising executive *o* agent, publicist **(b)** (Period) publicist

publicitario -ria *adj* ‹*campaña/espacio*› advertising (*before n*); ‹*truco/montaje*› publicity (*before n*)

público¹ -ca *adj* public; **hacer ~ algo** to announce sth; **es un peligro ~** he's a danger to the public

público² *m* (en teatro) audience, public; (Dep) spectators (*pl*); Ⓢ **horario de atención al público** (en oficinas públicas) opening hours; (en bancos) hours of business; **película apta para todo(s) (los) ~(s)** 'G' movie (AmE), 'U' film (BrE); **el ~ en general** the general public; **en ~** ‹*hablar*› in public; ‹*cantar/bailar*› in front of an audience; ***salir al*** **~** (Andes) «*periódico/revista*» to come out, appear; «*noticia/información*» to be published

puchero *m* **1** (Coc) (recipiente) pot, stewpot; (cocido) stew **2** (mueca) pout; **hacer ~s** to pout

pucho *m* (AmS fam) **(a)** (cigarrillo — de tabaco) smoke (colloq), fag (BrE colloq); (— de marihuana) joint (colloq) **(b)** (resto — de cigarrillo) butt, fag end (BrE colloq); (— de comida) scrap; (— de bebida) drop

pude *see* PODER

púdico -ca *adj* ‹*ropa*› modest; ‹*comportamiento/beso*› chaste

pudiera, **pudiese**, **etc** *see* PODER

pudín *m* ⇒ BUDÍN

pudiste, **etc** *see* PODER

pudor *m* **(a)** (recato sexual) modesty; **no se desnudó por ~** she was too embarrassed *o* shy to take her clothes off; **es una falta de ~** it shows a lack of (a sense of) decency **(b)** (reserva) reserve; **nos habló sin ~** he talked to us very openly

pudoroso -sa *adj* ⇒ PÚDICO

pudrir [I38] *vt* (descomponer) ‹*carne/fruta/madera*› to rot, decay

■ **pudrirse** *v pron* **1** (descomponerse) «*fruta/carne*» to rot, decay; «*madera/tela*» to rot; «*cadáver*» to decompose, rot **2** (fam) (por el abandono): **~se en la cárcel** to rot in jail

pueblerino -na *adj* ‹*aire*› provincial; **¡qué ~ eres!** you're such a country bumpkin *o* (AmE colloq) hick!

pueblo *m* **1** (poblado) village; (más grande) small town; **~ joven** (Per) shantytown **2 (a)** (comunidad) people; **un ~ nómada** a nomadic people **(b)** (ciudadanos, nación) people; **el ~ vasco** the Basque people

pueda, **puedas**, **etc** *see* PODER

puente *m* **1** (Ing) bridge; **~ colgante/giratorio** suspension/swing bridge; **~ levadizo** (en castillo) drawbridge; (en carretera) lifting bridge; **~ aéreo** (servicio frecuente) shuttle (service); (Mil) airlift **2** (Mús, Odont) bridge; (de anteojos) bridge **3** (Elec) bridge (circuit) **4** (vacación) ≈long weekend (*linked to a public holiday by an extra day's holiday in between*) **5** (Náut) *tb* **~ de mando** bridge

puerco -ca *adj* (fam & pey) (sucio) dirty; (despreciable) low-down (colloq) ■ *m,f* **1 (a)** (animal) (*m*) pig, hog, boar; (*f*) pig, hog, sow; **~ espín** porcupine **(b)** (Méx) (carne) pork **2** (fam) (persona — sucia) pig (colloq); (— despreciable) swine (colloq)

puericultor -tora *m,f*: *nurse or doctor who specializes in babycare/childcare*

puericultura *f* babycare, childcare

pueril *adj* **(a)** (infantil) childish, puerile (fml) **(b)** (ingenuo) naive

puerro *m* leek

puerta *f* (de casa, coche, horno) door; (en jardín, valla) gate; **llamar a la ~** to ring the doorbell/knock on the door; **te espero en la ~ del teatro** I'll meet you at the entrance of the theater; **te acompaño a la ~** I'll see *o* show you out; **servicio ~ a ~** door-to-door service; **un coche de dos ~s** a two-door car; **~ de embarque** gate; **~ principal** *or* **de la calle** (de casa) front door; (de edificio público) main door *or* entrance; **~ trasera** back door

puerto *m* **1** (Náut) port, harbor*; **entrar a ~** to enter port *o* harbor; **~ deportivo** marina; **~ franco** *or* **libre** free port; **~ pesquero** fishing port **2** (Geog) *tb* **~ de montaña** (mountain) pass

Puerto Príncipe *m* Port-au-Prince

Puerto Rico *m* Puerto Rico

pues *conj* **(a)** (en general) well **(b)** (indicando consecuencia) then; **~ si te gusta tanto, cómpralo** if you like it that much, then buy it

puesta *f* **1** (acción de poner): **hasta la ~ en servicio de los autobuses** until the buses come into service; **la ~ en libertad de los prisoneros** the freeing *o* release of the prisoners; **~ a punto** (de vehículo) tune-up; (de máquina) adjustment; **~ de sol** sunset; **~ en escena** production; **~ en marcha** (de vehículo, motor) starting (up); **~ al día** updating **2** (de huevos) lay

puestero -ra *m,f* (AmL) **(a)** (vendedor) stallholder, market vendor **(b)** (en una estancia) farmer (*responsible for the running of part of a large ranch*)

puesto¹ -ta *adj*: **¿qué haces con el abrigo ~?** what are you doing with your coat on?; **tenía las botas puestas** she was wearing her boots; **la mesa estaba puesta** the table was laid; *ver tb* PONER

puesto² *m* **1 (a)** (lugar, sitio) place; **se sentó en mi ~** he sat in my place **(b)** (en una clasificación) place, position; **sacó el primer ~ de su clase** she came top *o* (AmE) came out top of the class **2** (empleo) position, job; **~ de trabajo** (empleo) job; (Inf) workstation **3 (a)** (Com) (en mercado) stall; (quiosco) kiosk; (tienda) stand, stall **(b)** (de la policía, del ejército) post; **~ de socorro** first-aid post/station **4 puesto que** (*conj*) (fml) since

puf *m* (*pl* **pufs**) hassock (AmE), pouffe (BrE) ■ *interj* (expresando — repugnancia) ugh! (colloq), pee-yoo! (AmE); (— cansancio, sofoco) whew!, oof!

púgil *m* (period) boxer, pugilist (fml)

pugna *f* **(a)** (lucha) struggle **(b)** (conflicto): **tendencias/intereses en ~** conflicting trends/interests; **entrar en ~ con algo/algn** to clash *o* come into conflict with sth/sb

pujante *adj* booming (*before n*)

pujanza *f* vigor*, strength

pujar [A1] *vi* **1** (luchar) **~ POR algo/hacer algo** to struggle FOR sth/to do sth **2** (Esp) (en subasta) to bid **3** (Méx fam) (gemir) to moan, whimper

pulcro -cra *adj* ‹*persona/aspecto*› immaculate, neat and tidy; ‹*informe/trabajo*› meticulous

pulga *f* (Zool) flea; ***tener malas ~s*** (fam) to be bad-tempered

pulgada *f* ▶ 681 inch

pulgar *m* ▶ 123 (de la mano) thumb; (del pie) big toe

pulgón *m* aphid, plant louse

pulido -da *adj* ‹*estilo/trabajo/lenguaje*› polished; ‹*modales*› refined

pulir [I1] *vt* **1 (a)** ‹*metal/piedra/vidrio*› to polish **(b)** ‹*madera*› to sand **(c)** (lustrar) to polish **2** (refinar) ‹*estilo/trabajo*› to polish up; ‹*persona*› to make ... more refined; ‹*idioma*› to brush up

pulla *f* gibe

pulmón *m* ▶ 123 lung; **~ de acero** iron lung

pulmonía *f* pneumonia; **~ doble** double pneumonia

pulóver *m* (*pl* **-vers**) (suéter) pullover, sweater, jumper (BrE)

pulpa *f* (de fruta, vegetal) pulp; (de madera) (wood) pulp

pulpería *f* (AmL) local store

pulpero -ra *m* (AmL) local storekeeper

púlpito *m* pulpit

pulpo *m* (Zool) octopus

pulque *m* pulque (*drink made from fermented cactus sap*)

pulquería *f* (Méx) bar, restaurant (*serving pulque*)

pulquero -ra *m,f* (Méx) *owner of a* PULQUERÍA

pulsación *f* **1** (latido) beat **2** (en mecanografía) keystroke; **¿cuántas pulsaciones piden por minuto?** ≈ how many words a minute do they want?

pulsar [A1] *vt* **1 (a)** (Mús) ‹*cuerda*› to pluck; ‹*tecla*› to press **(b)** ‹*botón*› to push, press; ‹*timbre*› press, ring **2** ‹*opinión/situación*› to gauge, assess

pulsera *f* bracelet; **~ de tobillo** ankle bracelet, anklet

pulso *m* **(a)** (Med) pulse; **tomarle el ~ a algn** to take sb's pulse; ***tomarle el ~ a algo*** to gauge sth **(b)** (firmeza en la mano): **tengo muy mal ~** I have a very unsteady hand; **me temblaba el ~** my hand was shaking; **a ~** ‹*levantar*› with one's bare hands; ‹*dibujar*› freehand

pulular [A1] *vi* **(a)** (bullir) «*muchedumbre*» to mill around **(b)** (abundar): **aquí pululan los mosquitos** there are swarms of mosquitos here

pulverizador *m* (de perfume) atomizer, spray; (de pintura) spray gun; (del carburador) jet

pulverizar [A4] *vt* ‹*líquido*› to atomize, spray; ‹*sólido*› to pulverize, crush

puma *m* (animal) cougar, mountain lion, puma

puna *f* **(a)** (páramo) *high Andean plateau* **(b)** (Andes) (soroche) mountain *o* altitude sickness

punki /'puŋki, 'pʌŋki/ *adj/mf* (fam) punk

punta *f* **1 (a)** (de lengua, dedos) tip; (de nariz) end, tip; (de pan) end; (de pincel) tip; **vivo en la otra ~ de la ciudad** I live on the other side *o* at the other end of town; **con la ~ del pie** with the point of one's foot; ***la ~ del iceberg*** the tip of the iceberg; ***tener algo en la ~ de la lengua*** to have sth on the tip of one's tongue **(b) puntas** *fpl* (del pelo) ends (*pl*) **2 (a)** (de aguja, clavo, cuchillo, lápiz) point; (de flecha, lanza) tip; **~ de lanza** spearhead; **sácale ~ al lápiz** sharpen the pencil; **de ~** point first; **en ~** pointed; **por un extremo acaba en ~** it's pointed at one end **(b) a punta de** (AmL fam): **a ~ de repetírselo mil veces** by telling him it a thousand times; **a ~ de palos lo hicieron obedecer** they beat him until he did as he was told **3** (de pañuelo) corner ■ *adj inv*: **la hora ~** the rush hour

puntabola *f* (Bol) ballpoint pen, Biro® (BrE)

puntada *f* **1** (en costura) stitch **2** (CS) (de dolor) stab of pain, sharp pain **3** (Méx fam) (comentario ingenioso) quip, witticism

puntaje *m* (AmL) (en competencia, prueba) score; (Educ) grades (*pl*) (AmE), marks (BrE)

puntal *m* **(a)** (Const) prop **(b)** (sostén, apoyo) mainstay

puntapié *m* kick; **darle** *or* **pegarle un ~ a algo/algn** to kick sth/sb, to give sth/sb a kick; *para modismos ver* PATADA

puntear [A1] *vt* **1** (Mús) to pluck **2** (AmL) (Dep) to lead

punteo *m* plucking

puntería *f* aim **tener buena/mala ~** to have a good/poor aim; **afinar la ~** to take careful aim; **¡qué ~!** what a shot!

puntero *m* **1** (para señalar) pointer; (de reloj) (Andes) hand **2** (Dep) **(a)** (equipo) leader, leaders (*pl*) **(b)** (Andes, RPl) (en fútbol) winger

puntiagudo -da *adj* (acabado en punta) pointed; (afilado) sharp

puntilla *f* **1** (Taur) dagger (*used to administer the coup de grâce in a bullfight*); ***dar la ~*** (Taur) to administer the coup de grâce **2** (punta del pie): **de ~s** *or* (AmL) **en ~s** on tiptoe; **entró de ~s** she tiptoed into the room **3** (encaje) lace edging

puntilloso -sa *adj* particular, punctilious

punto *m* **1 (a)** (señal, marca) dot **(b)** (Ling) (sobre la 'i', la 'j') dot; (signo de puntuación) period (AmE), full stop (BrE); **~ decimal** decimal point ▶ 130; **~ final** period (AmE), full stop (BrE); **~s suspensivos** ellipsis (tech), suspension points (*pl*) (AmE), dot, dot, dot; **~ y aparte** period (AmE) *o* (BrE) full stop, new paragraph; **~ y coma** semicolon; ***a ~ fijo*** exactly, for certain; ... ***y punto*** ... and that's that, ... period (AmE); ⇒ DOS **2 (a)** (momento, lugar) point; **en ese ~ de la conversación** at that point in the conversation; **el ~ donde ocurrió el accidente** the spot *o* place where the accident happened; **~ cardinal** cardinal point ▶ 346; **~ ciego** blind spot; **~ de apoyo** (de palanca) fulcrum; **no hay ningún ~ de apoyo para la escalera** there is nowhere to lean the ladder; **~ de vista** (perspectiva) viewpoint, point of view; (opinión) views; **~ flaco/fuerte** weak/strong point; **~ muerto** (Auto) neutral; (en negociaciones) deadlock **(b)** (en geometría) point **3** (grado) point, extent; **hasta cierto ~ tiene razón** she's right, up to a point; **hasta tal ~ que** ... so much so that ... **4** (asunto, aspecto) point; **analizar algo ~ por ~** to analyze sth point by point; **los ~s a tratar en la reunión** the matters *o* items on the agenda for the meeting **5** (*en locs*) **a punto** (a tiempo) just in time; **estábamos a ~ de cenar** we were about to have dinner; **estuvo a ~ de caerse** he

Puntos cardinales

En español como en inglés la lista de los cuatro puntos cardinales se da, tradicionalmente, en el mismo orden:

norte	N	north	N
sur	S	south	S
este	E	east	E
oeste	O	west	W

En las explicaciones siguientes tanto en lo que se refiere al punto cardinal como a la parte o sección, se empleará norte *como ejemplo. Los otros puntos cardinales se utilizan de la misma manera*:

noreste	NE	northeast	NE
nordeste *or* nornoreste	NNE	north-northeast	NNE
nornoroeste	NNO	north-northwest	NNW

¿dónde?

viven en el norte = they live in the north *o* (menos formal) they live up north
queda al norte = it's to the north
al norte de Londres = to the north of London
está justo *or* exactamente al norte del río = it's due north of the river

Cuando se utilizan con el carácter de adjetivo (invariable), el inglés suele utilizar también la terminación -ern:

la costa norte = the north *o* northen coast
la cara norte de la montaña = the north *o* northern face of the mountain
las regiones norte del país = the northern regions of the country

También en los siguientes casos:

un pueblo/acento del norte = a northern town/accent
la ciudad más al norte del país = the northernmost *o* the most northerly town of the country

En inglés también se emplea la terminación -ern *para designar las regiones del interior de un país o de un continente*:

Europa del norte = northern Europe
el norte de Inglaterra = northern England
el hemisferio norte = the northern hemisphere

Para los países que incluyen en su nombre el punto cardinal (Corea del Norte), consultar el diccionario

¿En qué dirección?

En inglés también se utilizan los adjetivos terminados en -ward, -erly *y los adverbios terminados en* -ward *(AmE) o* -wards *(BrE) para indicar una dirección vaga*:

en dirección norte = in a northward direction
hacia el norte = in a northerly direction
iban/navegaban hacia el norte = they were going/sailing northward(s)
viajar al norte = to travel north *o* northward(s)
doble hacia el norte = turn north *o* northward(s)
venir del norte = to come from the north
va de Norte a Sur = it runs North to South

Para describir el desplazamiento de un objeto, el inglés suele utilizar un compuesto con terminación -bound:

el tráfico *or* los vehículos que van en dirección norte = northbound traffic
el tren que va hacia el norte = the northbound train

Otros ejemplos:

el tráfico *or* los vehículos que vienen del norte = traffic from the north
un balcón que da al norte = a north-facing balcony
el jardín está orientado al norte = the garden faces north

Nótense las traducciones siguientes cuando se habla de personas y del viento:

es del norte *or* es norteño = he's from the north *o* he's a northerner
los norteños = northerners *o* people from the north
el viento norte = the north wind
viento del norte = northerly wind *o* wind from the north
= northerly (Náut)
vientos preponderantes del norte = prevailing northerly winds

almost fell over; **batir las claras a ~ de nieve** beat the egg whites until they form stiff peaks; **en su punto** just right; **en punto**: **a las 12 en ~** at 12 o'clock sharp; **son las tres en ~** it's exactly three o'clock; **llegaron en ~** they arrived exactly on time **6 (a)** (en costura, labores) stitch; **artículos de ~** knitwear; **hacer ~** (Esp) to knit; **~ (de) cruz** cross-stitch **(b)** (en cirugía) *tb* **~ de sutura** stitch **7 (a)** (Dep, Jueg) point **(b) ~ para partido/set** (Méx) match/set point; (Educ) point, mark; (Fin) point

puntuación *f* **1** (Impr, Ling) punctuation **2 (a)** (acción) (Educ) grading (AmE), marking (BrE); (Dep) scoring **(b)** (esp Esp) (Educ) grade (AmE), mark (BrE); (Dep) score

puntual *adj* **1 (a)** ‹*persona*› punctual **(b)** (*como adv*) ‹*llegar*› punctually, on time **2** (detallado) detailed; (exacto) precise

puntualidad *f* punctuality

puntualizar [A4] *vt* **(a)** (especificar) to state **(b)** (señalar) to point out

puntuar [A18] *vt* **1** ‹*examen/prueba*› to grade (AmE), to mark (BrE) **2** ‹*texto*› to punctuate ■ ~ *vi* **(a)** «*partido/prueba*» ~ PARA **algo** to count TOWARD(s) sth **(b)** «*deportista*» score (points)

puntudo -da *adj* (Andes, RPl) ⇒ PUNTIAGUDO

punzada *f* sharp pain, stab of pain; **me dio una ~ en el costado** I felt a sharp pain *o* a stab of pain in my side

punzante *adj* ‹*objeto*› sharp; ‹*dolor*› sharp, stabbing (*before n*); ‹*palabras/comentario*› biting, incisive; ‹*estilo*› caustic

punzón *m* (para hacer agujeros) bradawl, awl; (para hacer ojetes) hole punch; (de grabador, escultor) burin

puñado *m* handful

puñal *m* dagger

puñalada *f* **(a)** (navajazo) stab; **lo mató a ~s** she stabbed him to death **(b)** (herida) stab wound

puñeta *f* (Esp fam): ***hacerle la ~ a algn*** to mess things up for sb; ***mandar a algn a hacer ~s*** to tell sb to go to hell; **¡vete a hacer ~s!** go to hell! (colloq)

puñetazo *m* punch; **darle** *or* **pegarle un ~ a algn** to punch sb; **pegó un ~ en la mesa** he thumped the table with his fist; **le rompió la cara de un ~** he smashed his face in (colloq)

puñetero -ra *adj* (Esp fam) **(a)** (*delante del n*) (uso enfático) damn, blasted **(b)** [SER] ‹*persona*›: **no seas ~** don't be a swine (colloq), don't be a jerk (colloq)

puño *m* **1** (Anat) **▶123** fist; **apretar los ~s** to clench one's fists **2** (de camisa) cuff **3** (de espada) hilt; (de bastón) handle, haft; (de moto) grip

pupa *f* **(a)** (fam) (en los labios) cold sore **(b)** (Esp leng infantil) (dolor, daño): **mamá, (tengo) ~** mummy, it hurts; **¿te has hecho ~?** have you hurt yourself?

pupila *f* **▶123** pupil

pupilo -la *m,f* **(a)** (de maestro) pupil; (de tutor) ward, charge **(b)** (RPl) (alumno interno) boarder

pupitre *m* desk

purasangre *mf* thoroughbred

puré *m*: **~ de verduras** puréed vegetables; **~ de tomates** tomato purée *o* paste; **~ de papas** *or* (Esp) **patatas** mashed *o* creamed potatoes

pureza *f* purity

purgante *adj/m* purgative, laxative

purgatorio *m* purgatory

purificador *m* purifier; **~ de ambientes** (Col) air freshener

purificadora *f tb* **~ de agua** water treatment plant, waterworks (*sing or pl*)

purificar [A2] *vt* to purify

puritanismo *m* puritanism

puritano -na *adj* (Relig) Puritanical, Puritan (*before n*); (mojigato) puritanical ■ *m,f* (Relig) Puritan; (mojigato) puritan

puro[1] **-ra** *adj* **1 (a)** (sin mezcla) pure; (limpio) ‹*aire*› frsh, clean **(b)** (casto, inocente) ‹*mujer*› chaste, pure; ‹*niño*› innocent; ‹*mirada/amor*› innocent, pure **2** (*delante del n*) **(a)** (mero, simple) ‹*verdad*› plain, honest (colloq); ‹*casualidad/coincidencia*› pure, sheer; **lo hizo por ~ capricho** she did it purely on a whim; **de ~ cansancio** from sheer exhaustion **(b)** (AmL fam) (sólo): **a ese bar van ~s viejos** only old men go to that bar; **son puras mentiras** it's just a pack of lies (colloq)

puro[2] *adv* (AmL fam) (muy, tan): **se murió de ~ vieja** she just died of old age; **lo hizo de ~ egoísta** he did it out of sheer selfishness ■ *m* cigar

púrpura *f*: **▶97** **(de) color ~** purple

purpurina *f* (en pinturas) metallic powder; (para adornar) glitter

pus *m* pus

puse, **pusiera, etc** *see* PONER

pusilánime *adj* fainthearted, pusillanimous (frml)

pusiste, **etc** *see* PONER

puso *see* PONER

puta *f* (vulg & pey) (prostituta) whore (colloq & pej), hooker (colloq); **hijo (de) ~** son of a bitch (vulg), bastard (vulg)

putada *f* (vulg): **hacerle una ~ a algn** to play a dirty trick on sb (colloq)

putrefacción *f* putrefaction

putrefacto -ta, **pútrido -da** *adj* putrid

puya *f* **(a)** (Taur) point (*of the picador's lance*) **(b)** (comentario irónico) gibe; **lanzar** *or* **echar una ~** to make a gibe

puzzle /'pusle/ *m* (rompecabezas) (jigsaw) puzzle

Pza. *f* (= **Plaza**) Sq

Qq

Q, **q** *f* (*read as* /ku/) *the letter* Q, q

que *conj* **1** (oraciones subordinadas) **(a)** that; **creemos ~ ésta es la solución** we believe that this is the solution; **estoy seguro de ~ vendrá** I'm sure (that) she'll come; **¿cuántos años crees ~ tiene?** how old do you think she is?; **eso de ~ estaba enfermo es mentira** (fam) this business about him being ill is a lie; **quiero ~ vengas** I want you to come; **dice ~ no vayas** she says you're not to go; **es importante ~ quede claro** it's important that it should be clear; **sería una lástima ~ no vinieras** it would be a shame if you didn't come **(b) es que: es ~ hoy no voy a poder** I'm afraid (that) I won't be able to today; **es ~ no tengo dinero** the trouble is I don't have any money **2 (a)** (en expresiones de deseo): **¡~ te mejores!** I hope you feel better soon; **¡~ se diviertan!** have a good time!; *ver tb* IR *v aux* 2 **(b)** (en expresiones de mandato): **¡~ te calles!** shut up! (colloq); **¡~ no!** I said no! **(c)** (en expresiones de sorpresa): **¿~ se casa?** she's getting married?; **¿cómo ~ no vas a ir?** what do you mean, you're not going? **(d)** (indicando persistencia): **se pasa dale ~ dale con lo mismo** he goes on and on about the same old thing; **y aquí llueve ~ llueve** and over here it just rains and rains **3** (introduciendo una consecuencia) that; **se parecen tanto ~ apenas los distingo** they're so alike (that) I can hardly tell them apart **4** (en comparaciones): **su casa es más grande ~ la mía** his house is bigger than mine; **tengo la misma edad ~ tú** I'm the same age as you **5** (fam) (en oraciones condicionales) if; **yo ~ tú** if I were you ■ *pron* **1** (refiriéndose a personas) **(a)** (*sujeto*) who; **los ~ estén cansados** those who are tired; **es la ~ manda aquí** she's the one who gives the orders here **(b)** (*complemento*): **la mujer ~ amo** the woman (that) I love; **las chicas ~ entrevistamos** the girls (that *o* who) we interviewed; **el único al ~ no le han pagado** the only one who hasn't been paid; **la persona de la ~ te hablé** the person (that *o* who) I spoke to you about **2** (refiriéndose a cosas, asuntos, etc) **(a)** (*sujeto*) that, which; **la pieza ~ se rompió** the part that *o* which broke; **eso es lo ~ me preocupa** that's what worries me **(b)** (*complemento*): **el disco ~ le regalé** the record (which *o* that) I gave her; **la casa en ~ vivo** the house (that) I live in; **¿sabes lo difícil ~ fue?** do you know how hard it was?; *ver tb* LO *art* 2 (b)

qué¹ *pron* **1** (interrogativo) **(a)** what; **¿~ es eso?** what's that?; **¿y ~?** so what?; **¿de ~ habló?** what did she talk about?; **¿sabes ~?** you know what *o* something?; **no sé ~ hacer** I don't know what to do **(b)** (al pedir que se nos repita algo) what; **¿qué?** what? **(c)** (en saludos): **¿~ tal?** how are you?; **¿~ es de tu vida?** how's life? **2** (en exclamaciones): **¡~ va a ser abogado ése!** him, a lawyer?; *ver tb* IR V ■ *adj* **1** (interrogativo) what, which; **¿~ color quieres?** what *o* which color do you want? **2** (en exclamaciones) what; **¡~ noche!** what a night! ■ *adv*: **¡~ lindo!** how lovely!; **¡~ inteligente eres!** aren't you clever!; **¡~ bien (que) se está aquí!** it's so nice here!; **¡~ bien!** great!, good!

quebrada *f* **(a)** (despeñadero) gully; (más profunda) ravine **(b)** (AmS) (arroyo) stream

quebradero de cabeza *m* problem, headache (colloq)

quebradizo -za *adj* **(a)** (frágil) fragile; ‹*uña/hueso*› brittle **(b)** (que se desmenuza con facilidad) crumbly

quebrado¹ -da *adj* **1 (a)** ‹*hueso*› broken; ‹*vaso/huevo*› (roto) broken; (rajado) cracked **(b)** ‹*voz*› faltering **2** ‹*empresa/comerciante*› bankrupt **3 (a)** ‹*línea*› crooked, zigzag (*before n*) **(b)** (Mat) **número ~** fraction

quebrado² *m* fraction

quebradura *f* (esp AmL) crack

quebrar [A5] *vt* **1** (esp AmL) ‹*lápiz/rama*› to snap; ‹*vaso/plato*› (romper) to break; (rajar) to crack **2** (Méx fam) (matar) to kill ■ **~** *vi* **1** (Com) «*empresa/persona*» to go bankrupt **2** (AmC) (romper una relación) to break up

■ **quebrarse** *v pron* **1** (esp AmL) **(a)** «*lápiz/rama*» to snap; «*vaso/plato*» (romperse) to break; (rajarse) to crack **(b)** ‹*pierna/brazo*› to break; ‹*diente*› to chip **2** (Col) (arruinarse) to go bankrupt

quechua *adj* Quechua ■ *mf* (persona) Quechuan ■ *m* (idioma) Quechua

quedar [A1] *vi* **I 1** (en un estado, una situación): **~ viudo/huérfano** to be widowed/orphaned; **quedó paralítico** he was left paralyzed; **el coche quedó como nuevo** the car is as good as new (now); **y que esto quede bien claro** and I want to make this quite clear; **¿quién quedó en primer lugar?** who was *o* came first? **2** (en la opinión de los demás): **si no voy ~é mal con ellos** it won't go down very well *o* it'll look bad if I don't turn up; **lo hice para ~ bien con el jefe** I did it to get in the boss's good books; **quedé muy bien con el regalo** I made a very good impression with my present; **me hiciste ~ muy mal diciendo eso** you really showed me up saying that; **nos hizo ~ mal a todos** he embarrassed us all; **quedó en ridículo** (por culpa propia) he made a fool of himself; (por culpa ajena) he was made to look a fool **3** (permanecer): **¿queda alguien adentro?** is there anyone left inside?; **le quedó la cicatriz** she was left with a scar; **esto no puede ~ así** we can't leave things like this; **nuestros planes ~on en nada** our plans came to nothing; **~ *atrás*** «*persona*» to fall behind; «*rencillas/problemas*» to be in the past **4** (+ *me/te/le etc*) **(a)** «*tamaño/talla*»: **me queda largo** it's too long for me; **la talla 12 le queda bien** the size 12 fits (you/him) fine **(b)** (sentar): **el azul le queda bien/mal** blue suits her/doesn't suit her

II (a) (acordar, convenir): **¿en qué ~on?** what did you decide?; **¿entonces en qué quedamos?** so, what's happening, then?; **~on en** *or* (AmL) **de no decirle nada** they agreed *o* decided not to tell him anything; **quedó en** *or* (AmL) **de venir a las nueve** she said she would come at nine **(b)** (citarse): **¿a qué hora quedamos?** what time shall we meet?; **quedé con unos amigos para cenar** I arranged to meet some friends for dinner

III (estar situado) to be; **queda justo enfrente de la estación** it's right opposite the station; **me queda muy lejos** it's very far from where I live (*o* work *etc*)

IV (*en 3ª pers*) **1 (a)** (haber todavía) to be left; **¿te queda algo de dinero?** do you have any money left?; **¿queda café?** is there any coffee left?; **sólo quedan las ruinas** only the ruins remain; **no nos queda más remedio que ir** we have no choice but to go **(b)** (sobrar) «*comida/vino*» to be left (over) **2** (faltar): **queda poco para que acabe la clase** it's not long till the end of the class; **¿cuántos kilómetros quedan?** how many kilometers are there to go?; **todavía le quedan dos años** he still has two years to go *o* do; **queda mucho por ver** there is still a lot to see; **aún me queda todo esto**

por hacer I still have all this to do; ***no me/le queda otra*** (AmL fam) I have/he has no choice

■ **quedarse** *v pron* **I 1 (a)** (en un lugar, país) to stay; **~se en la cama** to stay in bed **(b)** (en un estado, una situación) (+ *compl*): **te estás quedando calvo** you're going bald; **~se dormido** to fall asleep; **~se sin trabajo** to lose one's job **2** (+ *me/te/le etc*) **(a)** (permanecer): **~se soltera** to stay single; **no me gusta ~me sola en casa** I don't like being alone in the house; **no te quedes ahí parado** don't just stand there!; **nos quedamos charlando hasta tarde** we went on chatting until late in the evening; **se me quedó mirando** he sat/stood there staring at me; **de repente el motor se quedó** (AmL) the engine suddenly died on me **(b)** (Andes) (olvidarse): **se me quedó el paraguas** I left my umbrella behind **(c)** (Esp) (llegar a ser): **la casa se les está quedando pequeña** the house is getting (to be) too small for them
II ‹*cambio/lápiz*› to keep; **se quedó con mi libro** she kept my book; **me quedo con éste** I'll take this one

quehacer *m* (actividad, tarea) work; **~es domésticos** housework, household chores; **el ~ diario** the daily routine

queja *f* (protesta) complaint; **presentar una ~** to make a complaint

quejarse [A1] *v pron* **(a)** (protestar) to complain; (refunfuñar) to grumble; **~ DE algo/algn** to complain ABOUT sth/sb **(b)** (de una afección, un dolor) **~ DE algo** to complain OF sth **(c)** (gemir) to moan, groan

quejica *adj/m,f* (Esp fam) ⇒ QUEJÓN

quejido *m* groan, moan; (más agudo) whine; **un ~ de dolor** a cry of pain

quejón -jona *adj* (fam) whining (*before n*) (colloq) ■ *m,f* (fam) crybaby (colloq)

quemada *f* **(a)** (Andes, Ven fam) (del sol): **pegarse una ~** to get sunburned **(b)** (Méx) ⇒ QUEMADURA

quemado -da *adj* **1** [ESTAR] **(a)** ‹*comida/tostada*› burnt; **esto sabe a ~** this tastes burnt; **huele a ~** I can smell burning **(b)** (rojo) ‹*cara/espalda*› burnt **(c)** (AmL) (bronceado) tanned, brown **2** [ESTAR] (desgastado, agotado) burned-out

quemador *m* burner

quemadura *f* **(a)** (herida causada — por fuego, ácido) burn; (— por líquido caliente) scald **(b)** (en prenda — de cigarrillo) cigarette burn; (— al planchar) scorch mark; (en mueble) burn mark

quemar [A1] *vt* **1 (a)** ‹*basura/documentos/leña*› to burn **(b)** ‹*herejes/brujas*› to burn ... at the stake **2** ‹*calorías*› to burn up; ‹*grasa*› to burn off **3 (a)** ‹*comida/mesa/mantel*› to burn; (con la plancha) to scorch **(b)** «*líquido/vapor*» to scald **(c)** «*ácido*» ‹*ropa/piel*› to burn **(d)** ‹*motor*› to burn ... out; ‹*fusible*› to blow **(e)** «*sol*» ‹*plantas*› to scorch; ‹*piel*› to burn; (broncear) (AmL) to tan ■ **~** *vi* **(a)** «*plato/sartén*» to be very hot; «*café/sopa*» to be boiling (hot) (colloq) **(b)** «*sol*» to burn

■ **quemarse** *v pron* **1 (a)** (*refl*) (con fuego, calor) to burn oneself; (con líquido, vapor) to scald oneself; ‹*mano/lengua*› to burn; ‹*pelo/cejas*› to singe **(b)** (al sol — ponerse rojo) to get burned; (— broncearse) (AmL) to tan **2 (a)** (destruirse) «*papeles*» to get burned; «*edificio*» to burn down **(b)** (sufrir daños) «*alfombra/vestido*» to get burned; «*comida*» to burn; **se me ~on las tostadas** I burned the toast **3** «*persona*» (desgastarse) to burn oneself out

quemarropa: **a ~** (*loc adv*) ‹*disparar*› at point-blank range; ‹*preguntar*› point-blank

quemazón *f* (sensación de ardor) burning

quena *f* reed flute (*used in Andean music*)

quepa, **etc** *see* CABER

quepo *see* CABER

querella *f* **(a)** (Der) private prosecution; **presentar ~ contra algn** to bring a private prosecution against sb **(b)** (disputa) dispute

querendón -dona *adj* (AmL fam) (cariñoso) affectionate; (enamoradizo) flighty

querer [E24] *vt* **I** (amar) to love; **te queré siempre** I'll always love you; **sus alumnos lo quieren mucho** his pupils are very fond of him; **¡por lo que más quieras!** for pity's sake!, for God's sake!
II 1 (a) (expresando deseo, intención, voluntad): **no sabe lo que quiere** she doesn't know what she wants; **quisiera una habitación doble** I'd like a double room; **¿qué más quieres?** what more do you want?; **hazlo cuando/como quieras** do it whenever/however you like; **iba a hacerlo pero él no quiso** I was going to do it but he didn't want me to; **tráemelo mañana ¿quieres?** bring it tomorrow, will you?; **no quiero** I don't want to; **quiero ir** I want to go; **quisiera reservar una mesa** I'd like to book a table; **quisiera poder ayudarte** I wish I could help you; **no quiso comer nada** she wouldn't eat anything; **quiero que estudies más** I want you to study harder; **¡qué quieres que te diga ...!** quite honestly *o* frankly ...; **el destino así lo quiso** it was destined to be; **~ *es poder*** where there's a will there's a way **(b)** (al ofrecer algo): **¿quieres un café?** would you like a coffee?; (menos formal) do you want a coffee? **(c)** (introduciendo un pedido): **¿querrías hacerme un favor?** could you do me a favor?; **¿te quieres callar?** be quiet, will you? **2** (*en locs*) **cuando quiera que** whenever; **donde quiera que** wherever; **queriendo** (adrede) on purpose, deliberately; **sin querer** accidentally; **fue sin ~** it was an accident; **querer decir** to mean; **¿qué quieres decir con eso?** what do you mean by that? **3** (como precio): **¿cuánto quieres por el coche?** how much do you want *o* are you asking for the car?

■ **quererse** *v pron* (*recípr*): **se quieren mucho** they love each other very much

querido -da *adj* **(a)** (amado) ‹*patria*› beloved; **mis recuerdos más ~s** my fondest memories; **seres ~s** loved ones; **un profesor muy ~ por todos** a well-liked teacher **(b)** (Corresp) Dear **(c)** (Col fam) (simpático) nice ■ *m,f* **(a)** (como apelativo) darling, dear, sweetheart **(b)** (amante) (*m*) fancy man; (*f*) fancy woman

querré, **querría, etc** *see* QUERER

querubín *m* cherub

quesadilla *f* **(a)** (Méx) (tortilla): *tortilla filled with a savory mixture and topped with melted cheese* **(b)** (Ven) (panecillo) small roll (*flavored with cheese*)

quesera *f* cheese dish

queso *m* (Coc) cheese; ~ **crema** (AmL) cream cheese; ~ **fundido** processed cheese; ~ **para untar** cheese spread

quetzal *m* (Fin) quetzal (*Guatemalan unit of currency*)

quicio *m* doorjamb; ***sacar de ~ a algn*** to drive sb crazy (colloq)

quid *m*: **el ~ de la cuestión** the crux of the matter

quiebra[1] *f* (Com, Fin) (de empresa, individuo) bankruptcy; **declarse en ~** to go into liquidation

quiebra[2], quiebras, etc *see* QUEBRAR

quien *pron* **1 (a)** (*sujeto*) who, that; (*complemento*) who, that, whom (frml); **tienes que ser tú misma ~ lo decida** *you* are the one who *o* that has to decide; **es a él a ~ debemos agradecérselo** he's the one (who) we must thank; **la chica con ~ salía** the girl (who) I was going out with **(b)** (frml *o* liter) (en frases explicativas) who, whom (frml); **su hermano, a ~ no había visto, ...** her brother, who *o* whom she had not seen, ... **2** (la persona que): **~es hayan terminado** those who have finished; **~ lo haya encontrado** the person who found it; **~ se lo haya dicho** whoever told him

quién *pron* who; **¿~es eran?** who were they?; **¿~ de ustedes se atrevería?** which of you would dare?; **¿con ~es fuiste?** who did you go with?; **¿de ~ es esto?** whose is this?; **llegó una postal — ¿de ~?** there's a postcard — who's it from?

quienquiera *pron* (*pl* **quienesquiera**) whoever

quiera, quieras, etc *see* QUERER

quieto -ta *adj* still; **¡estáte ~!** keep still!

quietud *f* (ausencia de movimiento) stillness; (tranquilidad, sosiego) calm, peace

quihubo *interj* (Chi, Méx fam) hi! (colloq), how's it going? (colloq)

quihúbole *interj* (Méx fam) ⇒ QUIHUBO

quijada *f* jaw (bone)

Quijote *m*: **Don ~** Don Quixote

quilate *m* karat (AmE), carat (BrE); **oro de 18 ~s** 18-karat gold

quilla *f* keel

quilombo *m* (Bol, RPl arg) (lío, jaleo) mess

quiltro -tra *m,f* (Chi fam) mongrel

quimera *f* (ilusión) illusion, chimera (liter)

química *f* chemistry

químico -ca *adj* chemical ■ *m,f* chemist

quimioterapia *f* chemotherapy

quince ▶ **293** *adj inv/pron/m* fifteen; **dentro de ~ días** in two weeks' time, in a fortnight's time (BrE); *para ejemplos ver tb* CINCO

quinceañero -ra *m,f* ▶ **159** (de quince años) fifteen-year-old; (menos específico) teenager

quincena *f* (dos semanas) two weeks (*pl*), fortnight (BrE); **la primera ~ de marzo** the first two weeks in March

quincenal *adj* bimonthly (AmE), fortnightly (BrE)

quiniela *f* (Esp) (boleto) sports lottery ticket (AmE), pools coupon (BrE); (juego): **las ~s** the sports lottery (AmE), the football pools (BrE)

quinientos -tas *adj/pron* ▶ **293** five hundred; **~ cinco** five hundred and five; **~ y pico** five hundred odd; **el ~ aniversario** the five hundredth anniversary

quinqué *m* oil lamp

quinquenal *adj* ‹revisión/censo› five-yearly, quinquennial (frml); **un plan ~** a five-year plan

quinta *f* **1 (a)** (casa) *house in its own grounds, usually in the country* **(b)** (Agr) estate, farm **2** (Esp) (Mil) draft, call up

quintaesencia *f* quintessence (frml)

quinteto *m* quintet

quintillizo -za *m,f* quintuplet

quinto[1] -ta ▶ **294** *adj/pron* fifth; **llegó en ~ lugar** he came fifth; **Carlos V** (*read as: Carlos quinto*) Charles V (*read as: Charles the fifth*); **vive en el ~ (piso)** she lives on the sixth (AmE) *o* (BrE) fifth floor; **la quinta parte** a fifth

quinto[2] *m* **1 (a)** ▶ **294** (partitivo) fifth; **tres ~s** three-fifths **(b)** (en Méx) (moneda) five centavo coin; ***estar sin un ~*** (Méx fam) to be broke (colloq) **2** (Esp) (Mil) conscript

quíntuple *m* quintuple ■ *mf* (Chi, Ven) quintuplet

quíntuplo[1] -pla *adj* quintuple, fivefold

quíntuplo[2] *m* quintuple

quiosco *m* ⇒ KIOSCO

quirófano *m* operating room (AmE), operating theatre (BrE)

quiromancia *f* palmistry, chiromancy (frml)

quirúrgico -ca *adj* surgical; **fue sometido a una intervención quirúrgica** (frml) he underwent surgery (frml)

quise, quisiera, etc *see* QUERER

quisquilloso -sa *adj* (meticuloso, exigente) fussy, picky (colloq); (susceptible) touchy

quiste *m* cyst

quitaesmalte *m* nail polish remover

quitamanchas *m* (*pl* ~) stain remover

quitar [A1] *vt* **1** (apartar, retirar): **¡quítalo de aquí!** get it out of here!; **quité la silla de en medio** I got the chair out of the way; **quita tus cosas de mi escritorio** take your things off my desk; **~ la mesa** (Esp) to clear the table; **¡quítame las manos de encima!** take your hands off me!; **no le puedo ~ la tapa** I can't get the top off; **le quitó los zapatos** she took his shoes off **2** (+ *me/te/le etc*) **(a)** (de las manos): **le quitó la pistola al ladrón** he got *o* took the gun off the thief; **le quité el cuchillo** I took the knife (away) from her **(b)** (privar de) ‹*pasaporte/carnet de conducir*› to take away **(c)** ‹*cartera/dinero*› to take, steal; ‹*asiento/lugar*› to take **3** (restar) (+ *me/te/le etc*): **me quita mucho tiempo** it takes up a lot of my time; **~le años a algn** to take years off sb; **~le importancia a algo** to play sth down; **le quita valor** it detracts from its value **4** (hacer desaparecer) ‹*mancha*› to remove, get ... out; ‹*dolor*› to relieve, get rid of; ‹*sed*› to quench; ‹*apetito*› to take away; (+ *me/te/le etc*) **eso te ~á el hambre** that will stop you feeling hungry; **hay que ~le esa idea de la cabeza** we must get that idea out of his head **5 quitando** (*ger*) (fam) except for ■ ~ *vi* **1** (Esp fam): **¡quita (de ahí)!** get out of the way! **2** (*en locs*) **de quita y pon**

‹*funda/etiqueta*› removable; ***eso no quita que*** ... that doesn't mean that ...

■ **quitarse** *v pron* **1** (desaparecer) «*mancha*» to come out; «*dolor*» to go (away); **ya se me ~on las ganas** I don't feel like it any more **2** (apartarse, retirarse) to get out of the way; **¡quítate de mi vista!** get out of my sight! **3** (*refl*) **(a)** ‹*prenda/alhaja/maquillaje*› to take off **(b)** ‹*dolor/resfriado*› to get rid of; ‹*miedo*› to overcome, get over; **se quita la edad** she lies about her age; **~se algo/a algn de encima** to get rid of sth/sb

quitasol *m* sunshade

quiteño -ña *adj* of/from Quito

Quito *m* Quito

quiubo *interj* (Chi, Méx fam) ⇒ QUIHUBO

quizá, quizás *adv* maybe, perhaps

quórum /'kworum/ *m* (*pl* **-rums**) quorum

R, r *f* (*read as* /'ere/) *the letter* R, r

rábano *m* radish; ⇒ IMPORTAR

rabia *f* **1** (enfermedad) rabies **2 (a)** (expresando fastidio): **no sabes la ~ que me da** you've no idea how much it annoys *o* irritates me; **¡qué ~!** how annoying! **(b)** (furor, ira) anger, fury; **tener ~** to be angry; **con ~** angrily, in a rage **(c)** (antipatía, manía): **tenerle ~ a algn** to have it in for sb (colloq)

rabiar [A1] *vi* (de furor, envidia): **el jefe está que rabia contigo** the boss is furious with you; **no lo hagas ~** don't tease him

rabieta *f* tantrum; **le dio una ~** he threw a tantrum

rabino -na *m,f* rabbi

rabioso -sa *adj* **1** (Med, Vet) rabid **2** (furioso) furious

rabo *m* **(a)** (Zool) tail **(b)** (de letra) tail **(c)** (Bot) stem, stalk

racha *f* **(a)** (secuencia) **una ~ DE algo** ‹*de buena/mala suerte*› a run *o* spell OF sth; ‹*de enfermedades/éxitos*› a string OF sth; **pasar una mala ~** to go through bad times *o* (BrE) a bad patch; **tengo una buena ~, voy a seguir jugando** I'm on a winning streak so I'm going to carry on playing; **va/viene por ~s** it goes/comes in phases **(b)** (Meteo) gust of wind

racial *adj* racial; ‹*disturbio*› race (*before n*)

racimo *m* bunch

raciocinio *m* (facultad) reason; (argumento) reasoning

ración *f* **(a)** (parte) share **(b)** (porción de comida) portion, helping; **una ~ de calamares** a portion *o* plate of squid **(c)** (Mil) ration

racional *adj* rational

racionalizar [A4] *vt* to rationalize

racionamiento *m* rationing

racionar [A1] *vt* to ration

racismo *m* racism

racista *adj/mf* racist

radar *m* radar

radiación *f* radiation

radiactividad *f* radioactivity

radiactivo -va *adj* radioactive

radiador *m* radiator

radiante *adj* **(a)** (brillante) brilliant; **hace un sol ~** it's brilliantly *o* beautifully sunny; **un día ~** a bright, sunny day **(b)** [ESTAR] ‹*persona*› radiant; **~ de alegría** radiant with happiness

radical *adj/mf* radical

radicar [A2] *vi* «*problema/dificultad*» to lie

■ **radicarse** *v pron* to settle

radio *m* **(a)** (Mat) radius **(b)** (distancia) range, radius; **en un ~ de diez kilómetros** within a ten kilometer radius **(c)** (de rueda) spoke; **~ de acción** (de avión, barco) operational range; (de organización) area of operations ■ *f or* (AmL exc CS) *m* **(a)** (medio de comunicación) radio; **por (la) ~** on the radio; **escuchar la ~** to listen to the radio **(b)** (aparato) radio **(c)** (emisora) radio station

radioactividad *f* radioactivity

radioactivo -va *adj* radioactive

radioaficionado -da *m,f* radio ham

radiocassette /rraðioka'set/, **radiocasete** *m* radio cassette player

radiodifusora *f* (AmL frml) radio station

radiofónico -ca *adj* radio (*before n*)

radiografía *f* X-ray; **hacerse una ~** to have an X-ray taken

radiólogo -ga *m,f* radiologist

radionovela *f* radio serial

radiooperador -dora *m,f* (AmL) radio operator

radiopatrulla *m* radio patrol car

radioterapia *f* radiotherapy

radioyente *mf* listener

raer [E16] *vt* ‹*superficie*› to scrape; ‹*barniz/pintura*› to scrape off

ráfaga *f* (de viento) gust; (de ametralladora) burst

raid *m* (AmC) (en carro) ride; **pedir ~** to hitch a ride *o* lift

raído -da *adj* worn-out, threadbare

raíz *f* (en general) root; **arrancar de ~** ‹*planta*› to uproot; ‹*vello*› to remove ... at the roots; **~ cuadrada** (Mat) square root; **a ~ de** as a result of; ***echar raíces*** «*planta/costumbre/ideología*» to take root; «*persona*» to put down roots

raja *f* **(a)** (en pared, cerámica) crack **(b)** (rotura — en costura) split; (— en tela) tear, rip **(c)** (abertura — en falda) slit; (— en chaqueta) vent **(d)** (de melón, salami) slice

rajar [A1] *vt* **1 (a)** (agrietar) to crack, cause ... to crack **(b)** (con cuchillo, navaja) ‹*neumático/lienzo*› to slash **2 (a)** (CS fam) (criticar) to run ... down **(b)** (Andes) (en examen) (fam) to fail, flunk (AmE colloq)
■ **rajarse** *v pron* **1** «*pared/cerámica*» to crack; «*tela*» to split, tear, rip **2** (fam) (acobardarse) to back off

rajatabla: **a ~** (*loc adv*) to the letter

rallador *m* grater

ralladura *f*: **~ de limón** grated lemon rind

rallar [A1] *vt* to grate

ralo -la *adj* ‹*bosque*› sparse; ‹*monte*› bare; ‹*pelo/barba*› thin, sparse

rama *f* branch; **una ramita de perejil** a sprig of parsley; ***andarse/irse por las ~s*** to beat about the bush

ramada *f* **(a)** (AmS) (cobertizo) shelter (*made from branches*) **(b)** (Chi) (pérgola) arbor, arbour (BrE)

ramal *m* (Ferr) branch line; (Geog) branch; (cuerda) strap

rambla *f* **(a)** (RPl) (paseo marítimo) esplanade, promenade **(b)** (avenida) boulevard

ramera *f* prostitute

ramificación *f* ramification

ramificarse [A2] *v pron* **(a)** «*árbol/plantas/nervios*» to branch **(b)** «*carretera/ciencia*» to branch **(c)** «*problema*» to ramify (frml), to become complex

ramillete *m* **(a)** (de flores) posy **(b)** (iró) (grupo selecto) bunch (colloq)

ramo *m* **1** (de flores) bunch; (para novia, dignatario) bouquet **2 (a)** (en industria) industry **(b)** (Chi) (Educ) subject

rampa *f* (pendiente) ramp; **~ de lanzamiento** launch pad

rana *f* (Zool) frog

ranchera *f* (Mús) *Mexican folk song*

ranchería *f* **(a)** (Col) ⇒ RANCHERÍO **(b)** (Méx) dairy

rancherío *m* (CS) (poblado) settlement; (en suburbios) shantytown

ranchero -ra *adj* (Méx) fam) shy ■ *m,f* (Méx) rancher

rancho *m* **1** (comida) food (*for a group of soldiers, workers, etc*) **2 (a)** (AmL) (choza) hut; (casucha) hovel; (chabola) shack, shanty **(b)** (Méx) (hacienda) ranch

rancio -cia *adj* **1** ‹*mantequilla/tocino*› rancid **2 (a)** ‹*vino*› mellow **(b)** (*delante del n*) ‹*abolengo/tradición*› ancient, long-established

rango *m* **1 (a)** (Mil) rank **(b)** (categoría, nivel) level **2** (Chi) (lujo, pompa) luxury; (de persona) high social status

rangoso -sa *adj* (Chi) ‹*fiesta/casa*› lavish; ‹*persona*› of high social status

ranura *f* **(a)** (para monedas, tarjetas, cartas) slot; **por la ~ de la puerta** through the chink *o* gap in the door **(b)** (en ensambladura, tornillo) groove

rapapolvo *m* (Esp) telling-off (colloq), talking-to (colloq)

rapar [A1] *vt* ‹*cabeza*› to shave; ‹*pelo*› to crop

rapaz *adj* (Zool) predatory; **ave ~** bird of prey

rape *m* **(a)** (Coc, Zool) monkfish, goosefish (AmE) **(b)** **al ~**: **tiene el pelo cortado al ~** he has closely-cropped hair

rapidez *f* speed; **con ~** quickly; **¡qué ~!** that was quick!

rápido[1] *adv* ‹*hablar/trabajar*› quickly, fast; ‹*conducir/ir*› fast; **tráemelo ¡~!** bring it to me, quick!

rápido[2] -da *adj* ‹*aumento*› rapid; ‹*cambio*› quick, rapid, swift; ‹*desarrollo*› rapid, swift; **a paso ~** quickly, swiftly; **comida rápida** fast food ■ *m* (Ferr) express train, fast train ■ *m* **1** (Ferr) fast train **2 rápidos** *mpl* (Geog) rapids (*pl*)

rapiña *f* robbery, pillage

raptar [A1] *vt* (secuestrar) to kidnap, abduct (frml)

rapto *m* (secuestro) kidnapping, abduction (frml)

raptor -tora *m,f* kidnapper

raqueta *f* (de tenis, squash) racket; (para nieve) snowshoe

raquítico -ca *adj* ‹*niño/animal*› rickety, rachitic (tech); ‹*árbol*› stunted

rareza *f* **(a)** (de persona) peculiarity, quirk **(b)** (cosa poco común) rarity **(c)** (cualidad) rareness

raro -ra *adj* **(a)** (extraño) strange, odd, funny (colloq); **es ~ que** ... it's strange *o* odd *o* funny that ...; **¡qué ~!** how odd *o* strange!; **te noto muy ~ hoy** you're acting very strangely today **(b)** (poco frecuente) rare; **salvo raras excepciones** with a few rare exceptions; **aquí es ~ que nieve** it's very unusual *o* rare for it to snow here

ras: **a ras de** (*loc prep*): **llega a ~ del suelo** it reaches down to the floor; **volar a ~ de tierra** to fly very low

rasca *adj* (CS fam) **(a)** ‹*persona*› vulgar, common (pej); ‹*lugar/canción*› tacky (colloq) **(b)** (de mala calidad) trashy (colloq)

rascacielos *m* (*pl* **~**) skyscraper

rascar [A2] *vt* **(a)** (con las uñas) to scratch **(b)** (con cuchillo) ‹*superficie*› to scrape; ‹*pintura*› to scrape off
■ **rascarse** *v pron* (*refl*) to scratch (oneself)

rasgado -da *adj* ‹*ojos*› almond (*before n*), almond-shaped

rasgar [A3] *vt* to tear, rip
■ **rasgarse** *v pron* to tear, rip

rasgo *m* **1 (a)** (característica) characteristic, feature **(b)** (gesto) gesture **(c)** (de la pluma) stroke; (en pintura) brushstroke; ***a grandes ~s*** in outline, broadly speaking **2 rasgos** *mpl* (facciones) features (*pl*)

rasguear [A1] *vt* to strum

rasguñar [A1] *vt* to scratch
■ **rasguñarse** *v pron* (*refl*) (con uña, púa) to scratch oneself; (con algo áspero) to graze oneself; **me rasguñé la rodilla** I grazed my knee

rasguño *m* scratch

rasmillarse [A1] *v pron* (Chi fam) to graze oneself

raso[1] -sa *adj* ‹*taza/cucharada*› level (*before n*)

raso[2] *m* satin

raspado *m* (Col, Méx) ⇒ GRANIZADO

raspadura *f* (arañazo) scratch; (ralladura de metal, chocolate) shavings

raspar [A1] *vt* **(a)** (con espátula) ‹*superficie*› to scrape; ‹*pintura*› to scrape off **(b)** (limar) to file, rasp **(c)** ‹*piel*› to scrape, graze ■ ~ *vi* **(a)** «*toalla/manos*» to be rough; «*barba*» to scratch, be scratchy **(b)** «*garganta*» (+ *me/te/le etc*) to feel rough ■ **rasparse** *v pron* ‹*rodillas/codos*› (con algo puntiagudo) to scratch; (con algo áspero) to scrape, graze

raspón *m* (AmL) (por algo puntiagudo) scratch; (por algo áspero) graze, scrape; **hay un ~ en la puerta** the door is scratched

rastra: **a rastras** (*loc adv*): **llevar algo/a algn a ~s** to drag sth/sb; **fue a ~s hasta la puerta** she dragged herself to the door

rastreador -dora *m,f* tracker

rastrear [A1] *vt* **(a)** ‹*zona*› to comb **(b)** ‹*persona/satélite*› to track **(c)** ‹*río/lago*› «*pescadores*» to trawl; «*policías*» to drag, dredge

rastrero -ra *adj* **(a)** (despreciable) despicable, contemptible **(b)** ‹*tallo*› creeping (*before n*); ‹*animal*› crawling (*before n*)

rastrillo *m* **1** (Agr) rake **2** (Méx) (para afeitarse) safety razor

rastro *m* **1** (pista, huella) trail; (señal, vestigio) trace, sign; **sin dejar ~** without (a) trace **2** (mercado) flea market

rasurador *m*, **rasuradora** *f* (AmC, Méx) electric razor *o* shaver

rasurar [A1] *vt* (AmL) to shave ■ **rasurarse** *v pron* (AmL) to shave

rata *f* **1** (Zool) rat; ***hacerse la ~*** (RPl fam) to play hooky (esp AmE colloq), to skive off (school) (BrE colloq) **2** (Col) (Econ, Mat) (tasa) rate; (razón) ratio; (porcentaje) percentage ■ *mf* (fam) (tacaño) miser, stingy devil (colloq), tightwad (AmE colloq)

ratán *m* rattan

ratero -ra *m,f* (fam) (carterista) pickpocket; (ladrón) petty thief

ratificar [A2] *vt* ‹*tratado/contrato*› to ratify; ‹*persona*› (en un puesto) to confirm; ‹*noticia*› to confirm

rato *m* **(a)** (tiempo breve) while; **hace un ~** a while ago; **espera un ratito** wait a minute (colloq); **en mis ~s libres** in my spare time; **pasé un mal ~** it was terrible; **iré dentro de un ~** I'll go shortly **(b)** (*en locs*) **a cada rato** (AmL): **me interrumpe a cada ~** he keeps interrupting me; **al (poco) rato** shortly afterwards; **al poco ~ de irte tú** shortly *o* just after you left; **a ratos** from time to time; ***para ~*** (fam): **tengo para ~** I'll be a while, I'll be some time; **todavía hay para ~** there's still a long way to go; ***pasar el ~*** to while away the time

ratón[1] -tona *m,f* (Zool) mouse; **~ de biblioteca** (fam) bookworm

ratón[2] *m* **1** (Inf) mouse **2** (AmC) **(a)** (Coc) *sinewy cut of meat* **(b)** (fam) (bíceps) biceps **3** (Ven fam) (resaca) hangover

ratonera *f* (trampa) mousetrap; (madriguera) mousehole

raudal *m* (de agua) torrent; **el agua entraba a ~es** the water poured out in torrents

ravioles, **raviolis** *mpl* ravioli

raya *f* **1 (a)** (línea) line; (lista) stripe; **a** *or* **de ~s** ‹*tela/vestido*› striped; ***pasarse de la ~*** to overstep the mark, to go too far; ***tener a algn a ~*** to keep a tight rein on sb **(b)** (del pantalón) crease **(c)** (del pelo) part (AmE), parting (BrE); **hacerse la ~** to part one's hair **(d)** (Impr) dash **2** (Zool) ray, skate

rayado -da *adj* **1** ‹*papel*› lined, ruled (frml); ‹*tela/vestido*› striped, stripy (colloq) **2** [ESTAR] (AmS fam) (loco) screwy (colloq), nutty (colloq)

rayar [A1] *vt* **(a)** ‹*pintura/mesa*› to scratch **(b)** (garabatear) to scrawl ■ ~ *vi* **1** (dejar marca) to scratch **2** (aproximarse) ~ EN **algo** to border ON sth, verge ON sth **3** (Méx) «*obreros*» to get one's wages, get paid ■ **rayarse** *v pron* **1** «*superficie*» to get scratched **2** (AmS fam) (volverse loco) to crack up (colloq)

rayo *m* **1** (en general) ray; **un ~ de luz** a ray *o* beam (of light); **un ~ de luna** a moonbeam; **~ láser** laser beam; **~s ultravioleta** ultraviolet rays (*pl*); **~s X** X-rays (*pl*) **2** (Meteo) bolt (of lightning); ***como un ~*** (fam) ‹*salir/pasar*› like greased lightning (colloq) **3** (AmL) (de rueda) spoke

rayuela *f* **(a)** (juego de adultos) *game similar to pitch-and-toss* **(b)** (RPl) (juego de niños) hopscotch

raza *f* (etnia) race; (Agr, Zool) breed; **un perro de ~** a pedigree dog

razón *f* **1** (motivo, causa) reason; **la ~ por la que te lo digo** the reason (that) I'm telling you; **se enojó y con ~** she got angry and rightly so; **con ~ o sin ella** rightly or wrongly; **se quejan sin ~/con ~** they're complaining for no good reason/they have good reason to complain; **¡con ~ no contestaban!** no wonder they didn't answer!; **~ de más para** ... all the more reason to ... **2** (verdad, acierto): **tener** *or* **llevar ~** to be right; **tuve que darle la ~** I had to admit she was right; **tienes toda la ~** (fam) you're absolutely right **3** (habilidad para razonar) reason; **actuó guiado por la ~** he was guided by reason; **desde que tengo uso de ~** for as long as I can remember; **entrar en ~** to see reason *o* sense; **perder la ~** to go out of one's mind; (en sentido hiperbólico) to take leave of one's senses

razonable *adj* reasonable

razonamiento *m* reasoning

razonar [A1] *vi* to reason

re *m* (nota) D; (en solfeo) re, ray

reacción *f* **1** (en general) reaction **2** (Pol) (AmL) right wing

reaccionar [A1] *vi* to react; ~ A *or* FRENTE A *or* ANTE **algo** to react TO sth

reaccionario -ria *adj/m,f* reactionary

reacio -cia *adj* reluctant

reactor *m* **(a)** (Fís) reactor; **~ nuclear** nuclear reactor **(b)** (Aviac) (motor) jet engine; (avión) jet (plane)

readmitir [I1] *vt* ‹*trabajador*› to reemploy; ‹*alumno*› to readmit

reafirmar [A1] *vt* to reaffirm, reassert

reajuste *m* adjustment; **~ ministerial** cabinet reshuffle; **~ salarial** wage settlement

real *adj* **(a)** (verdadero, no ficticio): **un hecho ~** a true story; **en la vida ~** in real life; **historias de la vida ~** real-life *o* true-life stories **(b)** (de la realeza) royal; **porque me da la ~ gana** (fam) because I damn well want to (colloq) ■ *m* **(a)** (Hist) real (*old Spanish coin*); ***no valer un ~*** (fam) to be worth nothing **(b)** (Fin) real (*Brazilian unit of currency*) **(c) reales** *mpl* (AmC fam) (dinero) cash (colloq)

realce *m*: **dar ~ A algo** ‹*a belleza/figura*› to enhance sth; ‹*a ocasión*› to add luster TO sth

realeza *f* royalty; **la ~** (personas) the royal family

realidad *f* reality; **la ~ paraguaya** the reality of life *o* of the situation in Paraguay; **ésa es la dura ~** those are the harsh facts; **en ~** in reality, actually

realismo *m* realism

realista *adj* (pragmático) realistic; (Art, Lit, Fil) realist ■ *mf* realist

realizable *adj* feasible, practicable

realización *f* **1** (de tarea) carrying out, execution (frml); (de sueños, deseos) fulfillment*, realization **2** (Cin, TV) production

realizado -da *adj* fulfilled*

realizador -dora *m,f* producer

realizar [A4] *vt* **(a)** ‹*tarea*› to carry out, execute (frml); ‹*viaje/visita*› to make; ‹*entrevista/pruebas*› to conduct; ‹*encuesta/investigación*› to carry out; ‹*experimento*› to perform, do; ‹*compra/inversión*› to make; **realizó una magnífica labor** she did a magnificent job **(b)** ‹*ambiciones/ilusiones*› to fulfill*, realize
■ **realizarse** *v pron* «*sueños/ilusiones*» to come true, be realized; «*persona*» to fulfill* oneself

realmente *adv* really, in fact

realzar [A4] *vt* ‹*belleza/figura*› to enhance, set off; ‹*color*› to highlight, bring out

reanimar [A1] *vt* to revive
■ **reanimarse** *v pron* (recobrar fuerzas) to revive; (recobrar el conocimiento) to come to *o* around

reanudar [A1] *vt* (frml) ‹*conversaciones/negociaciones/viaje*› to resume; ‹*hostilidades*› to renew, resume; ‹*amistad/relación*› to renew, revive
■ **reanudarse** *v pron* to resume

reaparición *f* (de publicación, persona) reappearance; (de artista) comeback

reapertura *f* reopening

rearme *m* rearmament

reata *f* **(a)** (Méx) (cuerda) rope; (Agr) lasso **(b)** (Col) (correa) cartridge belt

reavivar [A1] *vt* to revive
■ **reavivarse** *v pron* to be revived

rebaja *f* **(a)** (descuento) discount, reduction; **nos hicieron una ~ del 10%** they gave us a 10% discount *o* reduction; **de ~** reduced **(b) rebajas** *fpl* (saldos) sale, sales (*pl*); **están de ~s** there's a sale on, they're having a sale

rebajar [A1] *vt* **1** ‹*precio*› to lower, bring ... down; ‹*artículo*› to reduce; **me rebajó $200** he took $200 off **2** ‹*peso/kilos*› to lose ■ ~ *vi* (humillar) to degrade, be degrading
■ **rebajarse** *v pron* **~se A hacer algo** to lower oneself TO doing sth; **~se ANTE algn** to humble oneself BEFORE sb

rebalsarse [A1] *v pron* (CS) «*agua/cauce/vaso*» to overflow; **se rebalsó el río** the river burst its banks

rebanada *f* slice

rebanar [A1] *vt* to slice, cut

rebaño *m* (de ovejas) flock; (de cabras) herd

rebasar [A1] *vt* **(a)** (sobrepasar) ‹*límite de velocidad*› to exceed, go over; ‹*cifras previstas*› to exceed; ‹*punto*› to go beyond; **el agua ha rebasado el límite** the water has risen above the limit **(b)** (Méx) (Auto) to pass, overtake ■ ~ *vi* (Méx) to pass, overtake (BrE)

rebatir [I1] *vt* to refute

rebeca *f* (Esp) cardigan

rebelarse [A1] *v pron* to rebel

rebelde *adj* **(a)** ‹*tropas/ejército*› rebel (*before n*) **(b)** ‹*niño/carácter*› unruly, rebellious **(c)** ‹*tos*› persistent; ‹*mancha*› stubborn ■ *mf* (Mil, Pol) rebel

rebeldía *f* (cualidad) rebelliousness

rebelión *f* rebellion, uprising

reblandecer [E3] *vt* to soften
■ **reblandecerse** *v pron* to become *o* go soft

rebobinar [A1] *vt* to rewind

rebosante *adj* **~ DE algo** ‹*de alegría/optimismo*› brimming WITH sth; ‹*de vino/agua*› filled to the brim WITH sth

rebosar [A1] *vi* **(a) ~ DE algo** ‹*de felicidad/entusiasmo*› to be brimming *o* bubbling over WITH sth; ‹*de salud*› to be bursting *o* brimming WITH sth **(b)** «*agua/embalse*» to overflow ■ ~ *vt* ‹*alegría/felicidad*›: **rebosaba felicidad** she was radiant with happiness

rebotar [A1] *vi* «*pelota/piedra*» to bounce; «*bala*» to ricochet

rebote *m* **(a)** (al golpear algo): **la pelota dio un ~ en el poste** the ball bounced off the post; **de ~** «*pelota*» ‹*pegar/entrar*› on the rebound; **la bala dio de ~** the bullet ricocheted **(b)** (en baloncesto) rebound

rebozar [A4] *vt* to coat ... in batter (*o* in egg and breadcrumbs *etc*)

rebozo *m* (AmL) (Indum) shawl, wrap

rebuscado -da *adj* ‹*explicación*› over-elaborate, overcomplicated; ‹*ejemplo/argumento*› far-fetched; ‹*estilo*› affected

rebuscar [A2] *vi*: **rebuscó entre los papeles** he searched through the papers; **rebuscaba en la basura** he was rummaging about in the garbage

rebuznar [A1] *vi* to bray

recadero *m* messenger, runner

recado *m* **(a)** (mensaje) message; **le mandó ~ de que volviera** she sent word that he should return **(b)** (Esp) (encargo, diligencia) errand; **hacer un ~** to run an errand

recaer [E16] *vi* **1** «*enfermo*» to have *o* suffer a relapse **2 (a)** «*sospechas/responsabilidad*» **~ SOBRE algn** to fall ON sb **(b)** «*premio/nombramiento*» **~ EN algn** to go TO sb

recaída *f* relapse

recalcar [A2] *vt* to stress, emphasize

recalentar [A5] *vt* **(a)** ‹*motor*› to cause ... to overheat **(b)** ‹*comida*› to heat up, warm up; **me dio un guiso recalentado** he gave me some reheated stew

▪ **recalentarse** *v pron* to overheat, become overheated

recámara *f* (Méx) (dormitorio) bedroom; (muebles) bedroom furniture

recamarera *f* (Méx) chambermaid

recambio *m* **(a)** (Auto, Mec) spare (part); **rueda de ~** spare wheel **(b)** (de bolígrafo) refill

recapacitar [A1] *vi* to reconsider, think again; **~ SOBRE algo** to reconsider sth

recargable *adj* ‹*batería/pila*› rechargeable; ‹*encendedor/pluma*› refillable

recargado -da *adj* ‹*decoración*› overelaborate; ‹*texto*› overwritten

recargar [A3] *vt* ‹*batería*› to recharge; ‹*encendedor/estilográfica*› to refill; ‹*arma/programa*› to reload

▪ **recargarse** *v pron* (Col, Méx, Ven) (apoyarse) **~se CONTRA algo** to lean AGAINST sth

recargo *m* surcharge; **sin ~** at no extra charge

recatado -da *adj* (pudoroso) demure, modest

recato *m* (pudor) modesty

recauchar, (Esp) **recauchutar** [A1] *vt* to retread, remold*

recaudación *f* **(a)** (acción) collection **(b)** (ganancia — en tienda) takings (*pl*); (— en cine) box office receipts (*pl*); (— en estadio) gate

recaudador -dora *m,f*: *tb* **~ de impuestos** tax collector

recaudar [A1] *vt* to collect

recelo *m* suspicion, distrust; **con ~** distrustfully

recepción *f* (en general) reception; (de mercancías) receipt (frml)

recepcionista *mf* receptionist

receptivo -va *adj* receptive

receptor -tora *m,f* **1** (Med, Ling) recipient **2** (Dep) (en fútbol americano) receiver; (en béisbol) catcher **3** **receptor** *m* (Rad) radio, receiver; (TV) television (receiver *o* set)

recesión *f* recession

receso *m* (AmL) recess

receta *f* (Coc) recipe; (Med) prescription

recetar [A1] *vt* to prescribe

rechazar [A4] *vt* **(a)** ‹*invitación/propuesta/individuo*› to reject; ‹*moción/enmienda*› to defeat; ‹*oferta/trabajo*› to turn down **(b)** ‹*ataque/enemigo*› to repel, repulse **(c)** (Med) ‹*órgano*› to reject

rechazo *m* (de invitación, individuo, órgano) rejection; (de moción, enmienda) defeat

rechifla *f* whistling (*as a sign of disapproval*), ≈ booing

rechinar [A1] *vi* «*polea/bisagra*» to creak, squeak; **le rechinan los dientes** he grinds his teeth

rechinón *m* (Méx) screech

rechistar [A1] *vi* ⇒ CHISTAR

rechoncho -cha *adj* (fam) dumpy (colloq), short and fat

rechupete (fam): **de rechupete** (*loc adj*) ‹*comida*› delicious, scrumptious (colloq)

recibidor *m* entrance hall

recibimiento *m* reception

recibir [I1] *vt* (en general) to receive; **recibió muchos regalos** she got lots of gifts; **reciba un atento saludo de ...** (Corresp) sincerely yours (AmE), yours faithfully/sincerely (BrE); **~ a algn con los brazos abiertos** to welcome sb with open arms; **van a ir a ~lo** they are going to meet him; **el encargado la ~á enseguida** the manager will see you right away

▪ **recibirse** *v pron* (AmL) (Educ) to graduate; **~se DE algo** to qualify AS sth

recibo *m* (en general) receipt; (de luz, teléfono) bill

reciclado, **reciclaje** *m* **(a)** (de papel, vidrio) recycling **(b)** (de persona) retraining

reciclar [A1] *vt* ‹*papel/vidrio*› to recycle

recién *adv* **1** (con participio): **pan ~ hecho** freshly baked bread; **está ~ pintado** it's just been painted; **tiene un año ~ cumplido** he's just one; **los ~ casados** the newlyweds; **un ~ nacido** a newborn baby **2** (AmL) **(a)** (hace poco tiempo) just; **~ llegaron** they have just arrived **(b)** (sólo ahora) only just; **~ me entero** I've only just found out **(c)** (sólo) only; **~ voy por la página 20** I'm only on page 20; **~ el lunes iré** the first day I'll be able to go is Monday

reciente *adj* ‹*acontecimiento/foto*› recent; ‹*huella*› fresh; **en fecha ~** recently

recinto *m* enclosure; **el público abandonó el ~** the public left the premises/building; **~ ferial** (de muestras) showground, exhibition site; (de atracciones) fairground

recio -cia *adj* ‹*hombre/aspecto*› robust, sturdy

recipiente *m* (utensilio) container, receptacle (frml)

recíproco -ca *adj* reciprocal

recital *m* recital

recitar [A1] *vt* to recite

reclamación *f* **(a)** (petición, demanda) claim **(b)** (queja) complaint

reclamar [A1] *vt* **(a)** «*persona*» ‹*derecho/indemnización*› to claim; (con insistencia) to demand **(b)** «*situación/problema*» to require, demand ▪ **~** *vi* to complain; **reclamó ante los tribunales** she took the matter to court

réclame *m or f* (AmL) commercial, advertisement; **~ publicitario** advertising

reclamo *m* **(a)** (de pájaro) call **(b)** (esp AmL) (para atraer la atención, provocar interés) lure **(c)** (AmL) (queja) complaint

reclinable *adj* reclining (*before n*)

reclinar [A1] *vt* to rest, lean

▪ **reclinarse** *v pron* to lean back; **reclinado contra la pared** leaning against the wall

recluir [I20] *vt* (en prisión) to imprison; (en hospital psiquiátrico), to intern (frml)

recluso -sa *m,f* prisoner, inmate

recluta *mf* (Mil) recruit; (en servicio militar) conscript, recruit

reclutar [A1] *vt* to recruit

recobrar [A1] *vt* **(a)** ‹*confianza/conocimiento*› to regain; ‹*salud/vista*› to recover; **~ las fuerzas** to recover one's strength **(b)** ‹*dinero/botín/joyas*› to recover, retrieve **(c)** ‹*ciudad/plaza fuerte*› to recapture

■ **recobrarse** *v pron* **~se DE algo** ‹*de enfermedad/susto*› to recover FROM sth, get over sth; ‹*de pérdidas económicas*› to recoup sth

recogedor *m* dustpan

recogepelotas *mf* (*pl* ~) (*m*) ball boy; (*f*) ball girl

recoger [E6] *vt* **1 (a)** (levantar) ‹*objeto/papeles*› to pick up; **recogí el agua con un trapo** I mopped the water up **(b)** ‹*casa/habitación*› to straighten (up) (AmE), to tidy (up) (BrE); ‹*platos*› to clear away; **~ la mesa** to clear the table **2 (a)** ‹*dinero/firmas*› to collect **(b)** ‹*deberes/cuadernos*› to collect, take in **(c)** ‹*trigo/maíz*› to harvest, gather in; ‹*fruta*› to pick; ‹*flores/hongos*› to pick, gather **(d)** ‹*tienda de campaña/vela*› to take down **(e)** ‹*pelo*› to tie ... back; **le recogió el pelo en una cola** he tied her hair back in a ponytail **3** (ir a buscar) ‹*persona*› to pick up, fetch, collect; ‹*paquete*› to collect, pick up; ‹*basura*› to collect ■ ~ *vi* (guardar) to clear up, to straighten up (AmE), to tidy up (BrE)

■ **recogerse** *v pron* ‹*pelo*› to tie up; ‹*falda*› to gather up

recogida *f* **(a)** (de basura, correo) collection **(b)** (Agr) harvest

recolección *f* **(a)** (Agr) harvest **(b)** (de fondos, dinero) collection

recolectar [A1] *vt* **(a)** ‹*trigo*› to harvest, gather in; ‹*fruta*› to pick, harvest **(b)** ‹*dinero*› to collect

recomendación *f* **(a)** (consejo) advice **(b)** (para empleo) reference, recommendation

recomendado -da *adj* **1 (a)** ‹*método/producto*› recommended **(b)** (apropiado) suitable; **no recomendada para menores de 15 años** not suitable for under-15s **2** (Col, Ur) ‹*carta*› registered

recomendar [A5] *vt* **(a)** ‹*libro/restaurante/persona*› to recommend **(b)** (aconsejar) to advise; **no te lo recomiendo** I wouldn't advise it

recomienda, recomiendas, etc *see* RECOMENDAR

recompensa *f* reward

recompensar [A1] *vt* to reward

reconciliación *f* reconciliation

reconciliar [A1] *vt* to reconcile

■ **reconciliarse** *v pron* **(a) ~se (CON algn)** to make (it) up (WITH sb) **(b) ~se CON algo** ‹*con idea/postura*› to reconcile oneself TO sth

reconfortante *adj* ‹*palabras/pensamientos*› comforting; ‹*baño*› relaxing

reconfortar [A1] *vt* to comfort

reconocer [E3] *vt* **1 (a)** ‹*hecho/error*› to admit; ‹*verdad/autoridad*› to acknowledge **(b)** ‹*hijo/gobierno/derecho*› to recognize **2** (identificar) ‹*persona/letra/voz*› to recognize **3** ‹*terreno*› to reconnoiter*

reconocimiento *m* **(a)** (en general) recognition **(b)** (Med) *tb* **~ médico** medical (examination) **(c)** (de territorio) reconnaissance

reconquista *f* reconquest; **la R~** the Reconquest

reconquistar [A1] *vt* ‹*territorio*› to reconquer, regain; ‹*cariño/afecto*› to win back

reconstituyente *m* tonic, restorative

reconstruir [I20] *vt* to reconstruct

recopilación *f* compilation, collection

recopilar [A1] *vt* to compile, gather together

récord, record *adj inv* record (*before n*) ■ *m* (*pl* **-cords**) record; **batir un ~** to break a record

recordar [A10] *vt* **1 (a)** ‹*nombre/fecha*› to remember, recall; **recuerdo que lo puse ahí** I remember *o* recall putting it there **(b)** (rememorar) ‹*niñez/pasado*› to remember **2 (a)** (traer a la memoria) **~le A algn algo/que haga algo** to remind sb ABOUT sth/to do sth; **les recuerdo que ...** I would like to remind you that ... **(b)** (por asociación, parecido) to remind; **me recuerdas a tu hermano** you remind me of your brother ■ ~ *vi* (acordarse) to remember; **si mal no recuerdo** if I remember right

recorrer [E1] *vt* **(a)** (viajar por): **recorrí toda España** I traveled *o* went all over Spain; (como turista) I toured all over Spain; **~ mundo** to travel all around the world; **recorrimos toda la costa** we traveled the whole length of the coast **(b)** ‹*distancia/trayecto*› to cover, do **(c)** (con la mirada): **recorrió la sala con la mirada** he looked around the hall

recorrido *m* **(a)** (viaje): **un ~ por Perú** a trip around Peru; (turístico) a tour around Peru **(b)** (trayecto) route; **cubrir el ~** to cover the route **(c)** (de proyectil) trajectory; (de balón) path **(d)** (en golf) round; (en esquí) run

recortable *adj* cutout (*before n*)

recortar [A1] *vt* **1 (a)** ‹*figura/artículo/anuncio*› to cut out **(b)** ‹*pelo/puntas*› to trim **2** ‹*gastos/plantilla*› to reduce

recorte *m* **1** (de periódico, revista) cutting, clipping **2** (Fin) (acción) cutting; (efecto) cut, reduction

recostar [A10] *vt* (apoyar) to lean

■ **recostarse** *v pron* **(a)** (acostarse) to lie down; **recuéstate en el almohadón** lie back on the pillow **(b)** (apoyarse) to lean; **recostados en el escritorio** leaning on the desk; **estaba recostado en un sillón** he was sitting back in an armchair

recoveco *m*: **un camino lleno de ~s** a road full of twists and turns; **en todos los ~s de la casa** in every nook and cranny of the house

recreativo -va *adj* recreational

recreo *m* **(a)** (diversión): **nos servía de ~** it served as entertainment; **viaje de ~** pleasure trip **(b)** (en el colegio) recess (AmE), break (BrE)

recriminar [A1] *vt* to reproach

recta *f* (Mat) straight line; (Dep) straight; **~ final** (Dep) home stretch

rectángulo *m* rectangle

rectificar [A2] *vt* to correct ■ ~ *vi* (corregirse) to correct oneself

rectitud *f* rectitude (frml), honesty

recto[1] -ta *adj* **(a)** ‹*línea/nariz/falda*› straight **(b)** (honrado) honest, upright

recto² *m* (Anat) rectum ■ *adv* straight; **todo ~** straight on

rector -tora *m,f* (de universidad) rector (AmE), vice-chancellor (BrE)

recuadro *m* box

recubrir [I33] *vt* ~ **algo** DE *or* CON **algo** to cover sth WITH sth

recuento *m* (de votos) recount

recuerdo *m* **1 (a)** (reminiscencia) memory **(b)** (souvenir) souvenir; (regalo) memento, keepsake; **un ~ de familia** a family heirloom **2 recuerdos** *mpl* regards (*pl*), best wishes (*pl*); **dale ~s** give him my regards

recuperación *f* **(a)** (en general) recovery **(b)** (Esp) (Educ) *tb* **examen de ~** retake, makeup (exam) (AmE)

recuperar [A1] *vt* **(a)** ‹*dinero/joyas/botín*› to recover, get back; ‹*pérdidas*› to recoup **(b)** ‹*vista/salud*› to recover; ‹*confianza*› to regain; **~ fuerzas** to get one's strength back **(c)** (compensar) ‹*tiempo perdido*› to make up for; **tienes que ~ esas tres horas** you have to make up those three hours **(d)** ‹*examen/asignatura*› to retake, make up (AmE)
■ **recuperarse** *v pron* **~se** DE **algo** ‹*de enfermedad*› to recover FROM sth, recuperate FROM sth (frml); ‹*de sorpresa/desgracia*› to get over sth, recover FROM sth

recurrir [I1] *vi* (frente a problema) **~** A **algn** to turn TO sb; **~** A **algo** to resort TO sth

recursivo *adj* (Col) resourceful

recurso *m* **1** (medio): **agoté todos los ~s** I exhausted all the options; **como último ~** as a last resort; **un hombre de ~s** a resourceful man **2 recursos** *mpl* (medios económicos — de país) resources (*pl*); (— de persona) means (*pl*); **~s humanos** human resources (*pl*)

red *f* **1 (a)** (para pescar) net **(b)** (Dep) net **(c)** (para pelo) hairnet **(d)** (en tren) (luggage) rack **2** (de comunicaciones, emisoras, transportes) network; (de comercios, empresas) chain, network; (de espionaje, contrabando) ring **3** (de electricidad) power supply, mains; (de gas) mains **4 la Red** (Inf) the Net

redacción *f* **1 (a)** (de carta) writing; (de borrador) drafting; (de tratado) drawing-up, drafting **(b)** (lenguaje, estilo) wording, phrasing **2** (Educ) composition, essay **3** (Period) **(a)** (acción) writing **(b)** (equipo) editorial staff *o* team **(c)** (oficina) editorial department *o* office

redactar [A1] *vt* ‹*informe/artículo/composición*› to write; ‹*acuerdo/tratado*› to draw up ■ **~** *vi*: **redacta muy bien** she writes very well

redactor -tora *m,f* editor; **~ jefe** editor in chief

redada *f* raid

redentor -tora *adj* redeeming ■ *m,f* redeemer

redimir [I1] *vt* to redeem

redoblar [A1] *vt* (aumentar) ‹*esfuerzos/críticas*› to redouble; ‹*vigilancia*› to step up, tighten ■ **~** *vi* «*tambor*» to roll

redoble *m* drumroll

redoma *f* (Ven) (Auto) traffic circle (AmE), roundabout (BrE)

redomado -da *adj* utter, out-and-out

redonda *f* **1** (Mús) semibreve **2 a la redonda**: **en diez metros a la ~** within a ten meter radius; **se oyó a varios kilómetros a la ~** it could be heard for miles around

redondear [A1] *vt* **(a)** (dar forma curva) to round (off) **(b)** ‹*cifra/número*› to round off; (por lo alto) to round up; (por lo bajo) to round down ■ **~** *vi*: **digamos 200, para ~** let's make it a round 200

redondel *m* (figura circular) ring

redondela *f* (Andes) ⇒ REDONDEL

redondo -da *adj* **1** ‹*cara/espejo*› round; ***caer(se)* ~** (desplomarse) to collapse; ***en* ~** ‹*girar*› (right) around **2** ‹*cifra/número*› round **3** (perfecto): **un negocio ~** a great *o* excellent deal; **nos salió todo ~** everything turned out perfectly for us **4** (Méx) ‹*boleto/pasaje*› return (*before n*), round-trip (*before n*) (AmE)

reducción *f* reduction; **~ de impuestos** tax cuts, reduction in taxes

reducido -da *adj* **(a)** (pequeño) ‹*espacio/presupuesto*› limited; ‹*tamaño*› small **(b)** (rebajado, achicado) ‹*precio/fotografía*› reduced; **un número ~ de personas** a small number of people; **trabaja jornada reducida** she is on short-time (working)

reducidor -dora *m,f* (AmS) (de objetos robados) receiver, fence (colloq)

reducir [I6] *vt* **1 (a)** ‹*gastos/costos*› to cut, reduce; ‹*velocidad/producción/consumo*› to reduce; **debería ~ el consumo de sal** you should cut down on salt; **~ algo** A **algo** to reduce sth TO sth; **~ algo** EN **algo** to reduce sth BY sth **(b)** ‹*fotocopia/fotografía*› to reduce **2 (a)** (transformar): **~ los gramos a milígramos** to convert the grams to milligrams; **quedaron reducidos a cenizas** they were reduced to ashes **(b)** (AmS) ‹*objeto robado*› to receive, fence (colloq) **3** (dominar) ‹*enemigo/rebeldes*› to subdue; ‹*ladrón*› to overpower
■ **reducirse** *v pron*: **todo se reduce a tener tacto** it all comes down to being tactful

redundancia *f* (Ling) tautology, redundancy; **valga la ~** if you'll forgive the repetition

redundante *adj* redundant

reedición *f* reissue, reprint

reeditar [A1] *vt* to reprint, reissue

reelegir [I8] *vt* to reelect

reembolsar [A1] *vt* ‹*gastos*› to refund, reimburse (frml); ‹*depósito*› to refund; ‹*préstamo*› to repay

reembolso *m* (de gastos) refund, reimbursement (frml); (de depósito) refund; (de préstamo) repayment; **contra ~** cash on delivery, COD

reemplazar [A4] *vt* ‹*persona*› (durante período limitado) to substitute for, stand in for; (durante más tiempo) to replace; ‹*aparato/pieza*› to replace; **~ algo/a algn** POR *or* CON **algo/algn** to replace sth/sb WITH *o* BY sth/sb

reemplazo *m* (durante período limitado) substitution; (durante más tiempo) replacement; **entró en ~ del jugador lesionado** he came on as a substitute for the injured player

reencarnación *f* reincarnation

reencarnarse [A1] *v pron* to be reincarnated; ~ EN **algn/algo** to be reincarnated AS sb/sth

reencuentro *m* reunion

reestreno *m* (de película) rerelease; (de obra teatral) revival

reestructurar [A1] *vt* to restructure

refacción *f* **1** (AmS) (para ampliar, mejorar) refurbishment **2** (Méx) (pieza de repuesto) spare part; **llanta de ~** spare tire

refaccionar [A1] *vt* (AmS) to refurbish

refaccionaria *f* (Méx) (tienda) auto spares store; (taller) garage

referencia *f* reference; **hacer ~ a algo** to refer to *o* mention sth; **con ~ a** ... with reference to ...; **número de ~** reference number; **tener buenas ~s** to have good references

referéndum *m* (*pl* **-dums**) referendum; **someter algo a ~** to hold a referendum on sth

referente *adj*: **las noticias ~s al accidente** the news about the accident; **en lo ~ a** ... regarding ...

réferi, **referí** *mf* (AmL) referee

referirse [I11] *v pron* **(a)** (aludir) **~se** A **algo/algn** to refer TO sth/sb **(b)** (estar relacionado con): **por lo que se refiere a este asunto** ... with regard to this matter ..., as far as this matter is concerned ...

refilón: **de refilón** (*loc adv*): **lo miré de ~** I gave him a sidelong glance; **la vi sólo de ~** I just caught a glimpse of her

refinado -da *adj* ‹*persona/modales*› refined; ‹*ironía*› subtle

refinar [A1] *vt* to refine; ‹*estilo*› to polish

refinería *f* refinery

reflector *m* **(a)** (pantalla reflectante) reflector **(b)** (foco) (Teatr) spotlight; (Dep) floodlight; (Mil) searchlight; (en monumento) floodlight

reflejar [A1] *vt* to reflect
■ reflejarse *v pron* **(a)** «*imagen*» to be reflected **(b)** «*emoción/cansancio/duda*» to show

reflejo[1] -ja *adj* reflex (*before n*)

reflejo[2] *m* **1 (a)** (en general) reflection; (luz reflejada) reflected light **(b) reflejos** *mpl* (en peluquería) highlights (*pl*) **2** (Fisiol) reflex

reflexionar [A1] *vi* to reflect (frml); **¿has reflexionado bien?** have you thought it over *o* through carefully?; **~** SOBRE **algo** to think ABOUT sth, reflect ON sth (frml)

reflexivo -va *adj* **(a)** (Ling, Mat) reflexive **(b)** ‹*persona*› thoughtful, reflective

reflujo *m* (de marea) ebb (tide)

reforestación *f* reforestation

reforestar [A1] *vt* to reforest

reforma *f* **(a)** (en general) reform; **la R~** (Relig) the Reformation **(b)** (en edificio, traje) alteration

reformar [A1] *vt* **(a)** (en general) to reform **(b)** ‹*casa/edificio*› to make alterations to
■ reformarse *v pron* to mend one's ways

reformatorio *m* reformatory

reforzar [A11] *vt* ‹*puerta/costura*› to reinforce; ‹*guardia*› to increase, strengthen; ‹*relaciones*› to reinforce; ‹*medidas de seguridad*› to step up, tighten

refrán *m* saying, proverb; **como dice el ~** as the saying goes

refregar [A7] *vt* ‹*puños/cuello*› to scrub

refrendar [A1] *vt* (Col, Méx) ‹*pasaporte*› to renew

refrescante *adj* refreshing

refrescar [A2] *vt* **(a)** ‹*bebida*› to cool; ‹*ambiente*› to make ... fresher *o* cooler **(b)** ‹*conocimientos*› to brush up (on) **■ ~** *v impers* to turn cooler

refresco *m* soft drink, soda (AmE)

refrigerador *m* **(a)** (nevera) refrigerator, fridge **(b)** (del aire acondicionado) cooling unit

refrigeradora *f* (Col, Per) refrigerator, fridge

refrigerar [A1] *vt* **(a)** ‹*alimentos/bebidas*› to refrigerate **(b)** ‹*motor*› to cool; ‹*cine/bar*› to air-condition; Ⓢ **local refrigerado** air-conditioned premises

refrito *m* (Coc): **un ~ de tomate y cebolla** fried onions and tomato

refuerzo *m* **(a)** (para puerta, pared, costura) reinforcement **(b)** (de vacuna) booster **(c) refuerzos** *mpl* (Mil) reinforcements (*pl*)

refugiado -da *adj* refugee (*before n*) **■** *m,f* refugee

refugiar [A1] *vt* to give ... refuge
■ refugiarse *v pron* to take refuge; **~se** DE **algo** ‹*de bombardeo/ataque*› to take refuge FROM sth; ‹*de lluvia/tormenta*› to take shelter FROM sth

refugio *m* **(a)** (contra la lluvia, bombardeo) shelter; (en montaña) refuge, shelter **(b)** (contra perseguidores) refuge **(c)** (en calzada) traffic island

refunfuñar [A1] *vi* (fam) to grumble, grouch (colloq)

refunfuñón -ñona *adj* (fam) grouchy (colloq), grumpy (colloq)

regadera *f* **(a)** (para jardín) watering can **(b)** (Col, Méx, Ven) (de ducha) rose, shower head (AmE); (ducha) shower

regadío *m* (sistema) irrigation; **tierras de ~** irrigated land

regalado -da *adj* **(a)** (fam) (muy barato): **precios ~s** giveaway prices (colloq); **esos zapatos están ~s** those shoes are dirt cheap *o* are a steal (colloq) **(b)** (Chi, Méx, Ven fam) (muy fácil) easy

regalar [A1] *vt* **(a)** (obsequiar): **¿qué te ~on para tu cumpleaños?** what did you get for your birthday?; **le ~on un reloj de oro** he was given a gold watch **(b)** (vender muy barato) to sell ... at bargain prices

regaliz *m* licorice (AmE), liquorice (BrE)

regalo *m* **(a)** (obsequio) gift, present **(b)** (cosa barata) steal (colloq) **(c)** (deleite, festín) treat

regalón -lona *adj* (CS fam) spoiled **■** *m,f* (CS fam) spoilt brat (colloq)

regalonear [A1] *vt* (CS fam) to spoil **■ ~** *vi* (CS fam): **le encanta ~ con su abuela** she loves being made a fuss of by her grandmother

regañadientes: **a regañadientes** (*loc adv*) reluctantly, unwillingly

regañar [A1] *vt* (esp AmL) to scold, to tell ... off (colloq) ■ ~ *vi* (Esp) (pelearse) to quarrel

regañina, (Méx) **regañiza** *f* (fam) scolding, talking-to (colloq), telling-off (colloq)

regaño *m* (AmL fam) scolding, telling-off (colloq)

regar [A7] *vt* **(a)** ‹*planta/jardín*› to water; ‹*tierra/campo*› to irrigate; ‹*calle*› to hose down **(b)** «*río*» to water **(c)** (AmC, Ven) ‹*noticia/versión*› to spread

regata *f* (carrera) yacht race; (serie de carreras) regatta

regate *m* (Esp) (en fútbol) feint

regatear [A1] *vi* (Com) to bargain, haggle ■ ~ *vt* **1** (escatimar): **no han regateado esfuerzos para** ... no efforts have been spared to ...; **sin ~ medios** whatever it takes **2** (Esp) (Dep) to get past, swerve past

regencia *f* (en lugar del soberano) regency

regenerar [A1] *vt* to regenerate
■ **regenerarse** *v pron* **(a)** (Biol, Tec) to be regenerated **(b)** «*persona*» to be reformed

regente *mf* regent

régimen *m* **1** (dieta) diet; **hacer ~** to be on a diet; **ponerse a ~** to go on a diet **2** (Pol) regime

regimiento *m* (Mil) regiment

regio -gia *adj* **(a)** (majestuoso) regal **(b)** (Col, CS fam) (estupendo) great (colloq); **te queda ~** it looks fantastic on you (colloq); **me viene ~** it suits me fine

región *f* region

regional *adj* regional

regir [I8] *vt* to govern ■ ~ *vi* «*ley/disposición*» to be in force, be valid; **ese horario ya no rige** that timetable is no longer valid
■ **regirse** *v pron* **~se** POR **algo** «*sociedad*» to be governed BY sth; «*economía/mercado*» to be controlled BY sth *o* subject TO sth

registrar [A1] *vt* **1 (a)** ‹*nacimiento/defunción/patente*› to register **(b)** ‹*sonido/temperatura*› to record; ‹*temblor*› to register **2** ‹*equipaje/lugar/persona*› to search; **estaba registrando mis cajones** (fam) he was going through my drawers **3** (Méx) ‹*carta*› to register
■ **registrarse** *v pron* (inscribirse) to register; (en hotel) to register, check in

registro *m* **1** (libro) register; (acción de anotar) registration; (cosa anotada) record, entry; **~ civil** (oficina) registry, registry office (BrE) **2** (por la policía) search; **orden de ~** search warrant

regla *f* **(a)** (utensilio) ruler **(b)** (norma) rule; **todo está en ~** everything is in order; **por ~ general** as a (general) rule **(c)** (menstruación) period; **tengo la ~** I have my period

reglamentario -ria *adj* ‹*horario*› set (*before n*); ‹*uniforme/arma*› regulation (*before n*)

reglamento *m* rules (*pl*), regulations (*pl*)

regocijarse [A1] *v pron* to rejoice; **~** DE *or* POR **algo** (por buena noticia) to rejoice AT sth; (por mal ajeno) to take delight IN sth, delight IN sth

regocijo *m* **(a)** (júbilo, alborozo) rejoicing; (alegría) joy, delight; **sintió gran ~ al verla** he was delighted to see her **(b)** (ante el mal ajeno) pleasure

regodearse [A1] *v pron* **(a)** (complacerse) to delight in, take great delight in; **se regodea haciéndeme sufrir** he delights in making me suffer; **~** EN *or* CON **algo** to delight IN sth, gloat OVER sth **(b)** (Chi) (al elegir) to hesitate

regordete -ta *adj* (fam) chubby

regresar [A1] *vi* to return, come/go back; **no sé cuándo va a ~** I don't know when he'll be back ■ ~ *vt* (AmL exc CS) **(a)** ‹*libro/llaves*› to return, give back **(b)** ‹*persona*› to send ... back
■ **regresarse** *v pron* (AmL exc RPl) to return, go/come back; **ya se regresó** she's back now

regreso *m* **(a)** (vuelta) return; **emprendió el ~** she set off on the return journey *o* trip; **de ~ paramos en León** on the way back we stopped in León **(b)** (AmL) (devolución) return

reguero *m* (rastro) trail

regulable *adj* adjustable

regulador *m* regulator

regular¹ *adj* **1** (en general) regular **2 (a)** (no muy bien): **¿qué tal te va? — regular** how's it going? — so-so; **¿qué tal la película? — regular** how was the movie? — nothing special **(b)** (de tamaño) medium-sized, middling ■ *m* (calificación) fair

regular² [A1] *vt* **1 (a)** ‹*espejo/asiento*› to adjust **(b)** ‹*caudal/temperatura/velocidad*› to regulate, control **2** «*ley/norma*» to regulate

regularidad *f* regularity; **con ~** regularly

regusto *m* aftertaste

rehabilitación *f* **(a)** (de enfermo, delincuente) rehabilitation **(b)** (en cargo) reinstatement **(c)** (de vivienda) renovation, restoration

rehabilitar [A1] *vt* **(a)** ‹*paciente/delincuente*› to rehabilitate **(b)** (en cargo) to reinstate **(c)** ‹*vivienda/local*› to renovate, restore

rehacer [E18] *vt* (volver a hacer) to redo; **trató de ~ su vida** she tried to rebuild her life
■ **rehacerse** *v pron* **~se** DE **algo** to get over sth

rehén *m* hostage

rehogar [A3] *vt* to fry ... lightly

rehuir [I21] *vt* to shy away from

rehusar [A23] *vt/vi* to refuse
■ **rehusarse** *v pron* (esp AmL) to refuse

reilón -lona *adj* (Per, Ven fam) smiley (colloq)

reina *f* queen; **~ de belleza** beauty queen

reinado *m* reign

reinante *adj* **(a)** ‹*casa/dinastía*› reigning **(b)** ‹*frío/lluvias*› prevailing; **el malestar ~ en el partido** the unease prevailing in the party

reinar [A1] *vi* **(a)** «*monarca/dinastía*» to reign **(b)** «*silencio/paz*» to reign; «*terror/buen tiempo*» to prevail

reincidir [I1] *vi* (Der) to reoffend

reincorporarse [A1] *v pron* to return; **~ a filas** to rejoin the army

reino *m* kingdom; **~ animal** animal kingdom; **el ~ de la fantasía** the realm of fantasy; ⇒ CIEGO

Reino Unido *m* United Kingdom

reinserción *f*: *tb* **~ social** social rehabilitation, reintegration into society

reintegrar [A1] *vt* **1** ‹*persona*› (a cargo) to reinstate; (a la comunidad) to reintegrate; **~ a algn** A *or* EN **algo** ‹*a cargo*› to reinstate sb IN sth; ‹*a la comunidad*› to reintegrate sb INTO sth **2** (frml) ‹*depósito*› to refund, return; ‹*gastos*› to reimburse; ‹*préstamo*› to repay
■ **reintegrarse** *v pron* to return; **~se** A **algo** ‹*a trabajo/equipo*› to return TO sth; **~se en la comunidad** to reintegrate into the community

reintegro *m* **(a)** (en banco) withdrawal; (de depósito) refund; (de gastos) reimbursement; (de préstamo) repayment **(b)** (en lotería) refund (*of the ticket price*)

reír [I18] *vi* to laugh; **se echaron a ~** they burst out laughing ■ **~** *vt* ‹*gracia/chiste*› to laugh at
■ **reírse** *v pron* to laugh; **~se a carcajadas** to guffaw; **~se** DE **algo/algn** to laugh AT sth/sb

reivindicación *f* **(a)** (demanda) demand, claim **(b)** (reconocimiento) recognition **(c)** (rehabilitación): **luchó por la ~ de su buen nombre** she fought to vindicate her good name **(d)** (de atentado): **la ~ del atentado** the claiming of responsibility for the attack

reivindicar [A2] *vt* **(a)** ‹*derecho*› to demand; ‹*tierras*› to claim **(b)** (rehabilitar) ‹*imagen/reputación*› to restore **(c)** ‹*atentado*› to claim responsibility for

reja *f* **(a)** (de ventana) grille **(b)** (para cercar) railing

rejego *adj* (Méx fam) ‹*persona*› mouthy (AmE), cheeky (BrE)

rejilla *f* **(a)** (de ventilación) grille; (Auto) grille; (del confesionario) screen; (del desagüe) grating **(b)** (para equipajes) luggage rack; (de horno) rack; (base de chimenea) grate

rejuntar [A1] *vt* (Méx fam) ‹*reses*› to round up; ‹*borregos*› to gather

rejuvenecer [E3] *vt* to rejuvenate
■ **rejuvenecerse** *v pron* to be rejuvenated

relación *f* **1 (a)** (conexión) connection; **con ~ a** *or* **en ~ con** (con respecto a) in connection with; (en comparación con) relative to; **en ~ con su carta** ... with regard to *o* regarding your letter ... **(b)** (correspondencia): **en una ~ de diez a uno** (Mat) in a ratio of ten to one; **una ~ causa-efecto** a relationship of cause and effect **2 (a)** (entre personas) relationship; **las relaciones entre padres e hijos** the relationship between parents and their children; **estoy en buenas relaciones con él** I'm on good terms with him **(b) relaciones** *fpl* (influencias) contacts (*pl*), connections (*pl*); (trato comercial, diplomático) relations (*pl*); (trato carnal) sex; **relaciones prematrimoniales** premarital sex; **relaciones sexuales** sexual relations; **relaciones públicas** (actividad) public relations (*pl*); (persona) public relations officer; (de cantante, artista) PR **3 (a)** (exposición) account **(b)** (lista) list

relacionado -da *adj* **(a)** [ESTAR] ‹*temas/ideas/hechos*› related, connected **(b)** ‹*persona*›: **está muy bien ~** he is very well connected; **estar ~** CON **algn/algo** to be connected WITH sb/sth

relacionar [A1] *vt* (conectar) to relate, connect; **~ algo** A *o* CON **algo** to relate *o* connect sth TO sth
■ **relacionarse** *v pron* **(a) ~se** CON **algo** ‹*con tema/asunto*› to be related TO sth **(b)** «*persona*» **~se** CON **algn** to mix WITH sb

relajación *f* (de músculos, mente) relaxation

relajado -da *adj* **(a)** (tranquilo) relaxed **(b)** ‹*costumbres*› dissolute, lax

relajante *adj* **1** ‹*música/baño*› relaxing **2** (CS fam) (empalagoso) sickly-sweet (pej)

relajar [A1] *vt* ‹*músculo/persona/mente*› to relax ■ **~** *vi* «*ejercicio/música*» to be relaxing
■ **relajarse** *v pron* **1 (a)** (físicamente, mentalmente) to relax; (tras período de tensión, mucho trabajo) to relax, unwind **(b)** «*tensión*» to ease; «*ambiente*» to become more relaxed **2** (degenerar) «*costumbres/moral*» to decline

relajo *m* **1** (de la moral) decline **2** (esp Esp fam) (relax): **¡qué ~!** how relaxing! **3 (a)** (Méx fam) (persona divertida) laugh (colloq) **(b)** (persona problemática) troublemaker

relamerse [E1] *v pron* (por algo sabroso) to lick one's lips; (de satisfacción) to smack one's lips

relámpago *m* (Meteo) bolt *o* flash of lightning; ***como un ~*** ‹*salir/pasar*› like greased lightning

relatar [A1] *vt* ‹*historia/aventura*› to recount, relate

relativo -va *adj* **1** (no absoluto) relative; **eso es muy ~** that depends; **una enfermedad de relativa gravedad** a relatively serious illness **2** (concerniente) **~** A **algo** relating TO sth; **todo lo ~ a la política** anything to do with *o* related to politics; **en lo ~ a este problema** with regard to this problem

relato *m* **(a)** (historia, cuento) story, tale **(b)** (relación) account

relax *m* relaxation

relegar [A3] *vt*: **se siente relegado** he feels left out; **el problema quedó relegado a un segundo plano** the matter was pushed into the background; **relegado al olvido** consigned to oblivion

relevante *adj* notable, outstanding

relevar [A1] *vt* **(a)** (sustituir) ‹*guarda/enfermera*› to relieve; ‹*jugador*› to replace, take over from; **~ la guardia** (Mil) to change the guard **(b)** (destituir) to remove
■ **relevarse** *v pron* to take turns, take it in turn(s)

relevo *m* **(a) de ~** ‹*conductor/equipo*› relief (*before n*) **(b)** (Dep) *tb* **~s** relay (race)

relieve *m* **1 (a)** (Art, Geog) relief; **la costa tiene un ~ muy accidentado** the coast is very rugged; **letras en ~** embossed letters **(b)** (parte que sobresale): **el marco tiene un centímetro de ~** the frame protrudes by a centimeter **2** (importancia) prominence; **personas de ~** prominent people; **dar ~ a algo** to lend (special) importance to sth; ***poner de ~*** to highlight

religión *f* religion

religioso -sa *adj* religious ■ *m,f* member of a religious order

relinchar [A1] *vi* to neigh, whinny

reliquia *f* relic; **una ~ de familia** a family heirloom

rellano *m* (de escalera) landing; (de ladera, montaña) shelf

rellenar [A1] *vt* **1 (a)** ‹*pavo/pimientos/cojín*› to stuff; ‹*pastel*› to fill; **~ algo** DE *or* CON **algo** to stuff/fill sth WITH sth **(b)** ‹*agujero/grieta*› to fill **2** (volver a llenar) to refill **3** ‹*impreso/formulario*› to fill out *o* in; ‹*examen/discurso*› to pad out

relleno[1] -na *adj* ‹*pavo/pimientos*› stuffed; **caramelos ~s de chocolate** candies with a chocolate filling

relleno[2] *m* (para pasteles, tortas) filling; (para pavo, pimientos, cojín) stuffing; (de ropa interior) padding; (para agujeros, grietas) filler

reloj *m* (de pared, mesa) clock; (de pulsera, bolsillo) watch; **funciona como un ~** it's going like clockwork; **contra ~** against the clock; **~ de arena** hourglass; **~ de pie** grandfather clock; **~ de sol** sundial; **~ despertador** alarm clock

relojería *f* (tienda, taller) clockmaker's, watchmaker's; (actividad) watchmaking

relojero -ra *m,f* (de relojes — de pulsera) watchmaker; (— de pared, mesa) clockmaker

reluciente *adj* ‹*dientes/coche*› gleaming; ‹*metal/suelo*› shiny, shining; **una mañana ~** a bright, sunny morning

relucir [I5] *vi* «*sol*» to shine; «*estrellas*» to twinkle, glitter; «*plata/zapatos*» to shine, gleam; ***salir/sacar a ~*** to come to the surface/to bring up

relumbrante *adj* brilliant, dazzling

relumbrar [A1] *vi* to shine brightly

remachar [A1] *vt* **(a)** ‹*clavo*› to clinch; ‹*perno/chapas*› to rivet **(b)** (recalcar) to repeat, reiterate; (finalizar) to round off, finish off ■ **~** *vi* (en tenis) to smash; (en voleibol) to spike

remache *m* **1** (perno) rivet **2** (en tenis) smash; (en vóleibol) spike

remangarse [A3] *v pron* (*refl*) ‹*pantalones/manga*› to roll up; **se remangó para lavar los platos** he rolled up his sleeves to wash the dishes

remanso *m* pool; **un ~ de paz** a haven of peace (liter)

remar [A1] *vi* (en bote) to row; (en canoa) to paddle

remarcar [A2] *vt* (hacer notar) to stress, emphasize

rematado -da *adj* complete, absolute; **es un loco ~** he's a raving lunatic

rematar [A1] *vt* **1 (a)** ‹*actuación/intervención*› to round off, finish off; ‹*negocio*› to conclude, close; ‹*torre/bastón*› to top, crown; ***y para ~la*** (fam) and to crown *o* cap it all (colloq) **(b)** ‹*costura*› to finish off **(c)** ‹*animal/persona*› to finish off **2** (en tenis) to smash; (en vóleibol) to spike; (en fútbol): **rematé el centro a la portería** he hit the cross straight into the goal **3** (AmL) **(a)** (en subasta — vender) to auction; (— comprar) to buy … at an auction **(b)** (liquidar) to sell … off cheaply ■ **~** *vi* **1** (terminar) **~** EN **algo** to end IN sth **2** (en tenis) to smash; (en vóleibol) to spike; (en fútbol) to shoot; **~ de cabeza** to head the ball

remate *m* **1 (a)** (de activades, esfuerzos) culmination; ***y como ~*** (fam) and to crown *o* cap it all (colloq) **(b)** (en costura) double stitch (*to finish off*) **2** (en tenis) smash; (en vóleibol) spike; (en fútbol) shot; **~ de cabeza** header **3** (AmL) (subasta) auction

remedar [A1] *vt* to mimic, ape

remediar [A1] *vt* **1** ‹*situación/problema*› to remedy; ‹*daño*› to repair; **¿qué piensas hacer para ~lo?** what are you going to do to put things right?; **con llorar no remedias nada** crying won't solve anything **2** (evitar): **no lo puedo/pude ~** I can't/couldn't help it

remedio *m* **1 (a)** (Med) (cura) remedy, cure **(b)** (esp AmL) (Farm) medicine **2** (solución) solution; **ya no tiene ~** there's nothing we (*or* you *etc*) can do now; **su matrimonio no tiene ~** her marriage is beyond hope; **un caso sin ~** a hopeless case **3** (alternativa, recurso) option; **no queda más ~ que** … we have no alternative *o* choice but …; **iré si no hay otro ~** I'll go if I really have to *o* if I must

remendar [A5] *vt* to mend

remera *f* (RPl) (camiseta) T-shirt

remero -ra *m,f* (*m*) rower, oarsman; (*f*) rower, oarswoman

remesa *f* (de mercancías) consignment, shipment; (de dinero) remittance

remezón *m* (Andes) (temblor) earth tremor; (sacudida brusca) shake; (suceso inesperado) shake-up

remiendo *m* (pedazo de tela, cuero) patch; **le hizo un ~** she mended *o* patched it

remilgado -da *adj* fussy

remilgón -gona, **remilgoso -sa** *adj* (delicado) (Andes, Méx) fussy; (difícil) (Méx) difficult

remisión *m* **1** (en texto) reference; **~** A **algo** reference TO sth **2** (de enfermedad) remission **3** (Relig, Der) remission

remite *m* (persona) sender; (dirección) return address

remitente *mf* sender

remitir [I1] *vt* **(a)** (frml) (mandar) to send **(b)** ‹*lector/estudiante*› **~** A **algn** A **algo** to refer sb TO sth ■ **~** *vi* «*fiebre*» to drop, go down; «*tormenta*» to abate, subside

■ **remitirse** *v pron* **~se** A **algo** ‹*a obra*› to refer TO sth

remo *m* (con soporte) oar; (sin soporte) paddle

remodelación *f* (Arquit) remodeling*, redesigning; (de organización) reorganization, restructuring; (del gabinete) (Pol) reshuffle

remodelar [A1] *vt* ‹*plaza/barrio*› to remodel, redesign; ‹*organización*› to reorganize; ‹*gabinete*› to reshuffle

remojar [A1] *vt* ‹*ropa/lentejas*› to soak

remojo *m* (en agua): **poner algo a** *or* **en ~** to put sth to soak; **dejar algo en ~** to leave sth to soak

remojón *m* **1** (fam) (en agua) soaking, drenching; **¿quién quiere darse un ~?** who's for a dip? (colloq) **2** (Méx fam) (de algo nuevo): **nos dio el ~** (en el coche) he took us for a spin in his new car; (en la casa) he had us over for a housewarming party

remolacha *f* beet (AmE), beetroot (BrE); **~ azucarera** sugar beet

remolcador *m* (Náut) tug; (Auto) tow truck (AmE), breakdown van (BrE)

remolcar [A2] *vt* ‹*barco*› to tug; ‹*coche*› to tow

remolino *m* **(a)** (de viento) eddy, whirl **(b)** (de agua) eddy; (más violento) whirlpool **(c)** (en el pelo) cowlick

remolón -lona *adj* (fam) idle, lazy ■ *m,f* (fam) slacker (colloq)
remolque *m* **(a)** (vehículo) trailer **(b)** (acción) towing; **ir a ~** (Auto) to be in tow **(c)** (AmS) (grúa) tow truck (AmE), breakdown van (BrE)
remontar [A1] *vt* **1** ‹*dificultad/problema*› to overcome, surmount (frml) **2 (a) ~ el vuelo** «*avión*» to gain height; «*pájaro*» to fly *o* soar up **(b) ~ el río** to go upriver **(c)** (RPl) ‹*barrilete*› to fly
■ **remontarse** *v pron* **1** «*avión*» to gain height; «*pájaro*» to soar up **2** (en el tiempo) to go back
remorder [E9] *vi* (+ *me/te/le etc*): **me remuerde haberlo dicho** I feel guilty for having said it; **¿no te remuerde la conciencia?** don't you feel guilty?
remordimiento *m* remorse; **sentir** *or* **tener ~s de conciencia** to suffer pangs of conscience
remoto -ta *adj* **(a)** ‹*tiempo/época*› distant, far-off (*before n*) **(b)** ‹*lugar/mares/tierras*› remote, far-off **(c)** ‹*posibilidad*› remote, slim; ‹*esperanza*› faint; **no tengo (ni) la más remota idea** I haven't the remotest *o* faintest idea
remover [E9] *vt* **1 (a)** ‹*líquido/salsa*› to stir; ‹*ensalada*› to toss; ‹*tierra/piedras*› to turn over; ‹*escombros*› to dig about in; ‹*brasas*› to poke, stir **(b)** ‹*asunto*› to bring ... up again; ‹*pasado*› to revive, stir up **2** (frml) **(a)** ‹*impedimento/obstáculo*› to remove **(b)** (esp AmL) (destituir) **~ A algn DE algo** to remove sb FROM sth
remunerar [A1] *vt* to pay, remunerate (frml)
renacentista *adj* Renaissance (*before n*)
renacer [E3] *vi* to be reborn; **sentí ~ la esperanza** I felt renewed hope
renacimiento *m* **(a)** (acción) revival, rebirth **(b)** (Art, Hist) **el R~** the Renaissance
renacuajo *m* (Zool) tadpole; (niño, persona baja) (fam) shrimp (colloq)
rencilla *f* quarrel, row
rencor *m* resentment; **con el corazón lleno de ~** with his heart full of resentment; **no te guardo ~** I don't bear you any grudge; **siento ~ por lo que me hizo** I feel bitter about what he did to me
rencoroso -sa *adj* [SER] resentful
rendición *f* surrender
rendido -da *adj* [ESTAR] (exhausto) exhausted; **cayó ~ (de cansancio)** he collapsed from exhaustion; *ver tb* RENDIR
rendidor -dora *adj* (AmL) ‹*tierra*› productive; **un detergente ~** a detergent that goes a long way
rendija *f* (grieta) crack, crevice; (hueco) gap
rendimiento *m* **(a)** (de persona, coche) performance **(b)** (de máquina, factoría) output; **funciona a pleno ~** it is working at full capacity **(c)** (de terreno) yield **(d)** (Fin) yield, return
rendir [I14] *vt* **1** ‹*homenaje/tributo*› to pay; **~le culto a algn** to worship sb **2** (Fin) to yield; (producir) to produce **3** ‹*persona*›: **me rindió el sueño** I was overcome by sleep; **tanto trabajo rinde a cualquiera** working that hard is enough to exhaust anyone **4** (CS) (Educ) ‹*examen*› to take, sit (BrE) ■ **~** *vi* **(a)** (cundir) (+ *me/te/le etc*): **me rindió mucho la mañana** I had a lot done this morning; **trabaja mucho pero no le rinde** he works hard but he doesn't make much headway **(b)** «*alumno/obrero/empleado*» to perform well **(c)** «*tela/arroz/jabón*» to go a long way
■ **rendirse** *v pron* (en pelea, guerra) to surrender; (en tarea, adivinanza) to give up
renegado -da *m,f* renegade
renegar [A7] *vi* **(a)** (Relig) to apostatize; **~ DE algo** ‹*de creencias/principios*› to renounce sth **(b)** (maldecir) to swear, curse; (blasfemar) to blaspheme **(c)** (refunfuñar) to grumble; **~ DE algo** to grumble ABOUT sth **(d)** (AmL) (enojarse) to get annoyed
renglón *m* (línea) line
rengo -ga *adj* (AmL) lame ■ *m,f* (AmL) lame person, cripple (pej)
renguear [A1] *vi* (AmL) to limp
renguera *f* (AmL) limp
reno *m* reindeer
renombrado -da *adj* well-known, renowned
renombre *m* renown; **de ~** renowned
renovación *f* **(a)** (de pasaporte, contrato) renewal **(b)** (del mobiliario) complete change; (de edificio, barrio) renovation **(c)** (de organización, sistema) updating **(d)** (reanudación) renewal
renovar [A10] *vt* **(a)** ‹*pasaporte/contrato*› to renew **(b)** ‹*mobiliario*› to change; ‹*edificio/barrio*› to renovate **(c)** ‹*organización/sistema*› to update, bring up to date **(d)** ‹*ataque/esperanza/promesa*› to renew
■ **renovarse** *v pron* **(a)** «*sospechas/dolor/interés*» to be renewed **(b)** «*persona*» to be revitalized
renta *f* **(a)** (beneficio) income; **inversiones de ~ fija** fixed interest investments; **vivir de las ~s** (de dinero) to live off the interest; (de propiedades) to live off **(b)** (esp Méx) (alquiler) rent
rentable *adj* ‹*inversión/negocio*› profitable
rentar [A1] *vt* (Méx) **(a)** ‹*departamento*› «*propietario*» to rent out, let (BrE); «*usuario*» to rent **(b)** ‹*coche*› to rent, hire (BrE)
renuncia *f* **1** (dimisión) resignation; **presentar la ~** to resign, tender one's resignation (frml) **2** (abandono) **~ A algo** renunciation OF sth **3** (abnegación) self-sacrifice
renunciar [A1] *vi* (dimitir) to resign; **~ A algo** ‹*a puesto*› to resign sth; ‹*a derecho*› to relinquish sth, renounce sth (frml); ‹*a título*› to give up sth, relinquish sth; ‹*a trono*› to renounce sth
reñido -da *adj* **1** ‹*partido/batalla*› hard-fought, tough **2** [ESTAR] **(a)** (peleado): **está ~ con su novia** he has fallen out with his girlfriend (colloq) **(b)** (en contradicción) **~ CON algo** ‹*con principios*› against sth
reñir [I15] *vi* (esp Esp) **(a)** (discutir) to argue, quarrel **(b) ~ CON algn** (pelearse) to quarrel *o* have a row WITH sb; (enemistarse) to fall out WITH sb ■ **~** *vt* (Esp) (regañar) to scold, tell ... off (colloq)
reo *mf* (en lo penal — acusado) accused, defendant; (— condenado) convicted offender; (en lo civil) (Méx) defendant
reojo: **de reojo** (*loc adv*): **mirar a algn de ~** to look at sb out of the corner of one's eye
reorganizar [A4] *vt* to reorganize

reparación *f* **(a)** (arreglo) repair; **taller de reparaciones** repair shop **(b)** (de daño, ofensa) redress, reparation

reparador -dora *adj* ‹*sueño/descanso*› refreshing

reparar [A1] *vt* **(a)** ‹*coche*› to repair, fix; ‹*gotera/avería*› to mend, fix **(b)** ‹*error*› to correct, put right; ‹*ofensa/agravio*› to make amends for, make up for; ‹*daño/perjuicio*› to make good, compensate for ■ ~ *vi* **1** ~ EN **algo** (darse cuenta) to notice sth; (considerar): **no repara en gastos** she spares no expense **2** (Méx) «*caballo/toro*» to rear, shy

reparo *m* **(a)** (inconveniente, objeción): **pone ~s a todo** she finds fault with everything; **no tengo ningún ~ en decírselo** I have no qualms about telling him **(b)** (duda) reservation

repartición *f* **(a)** (división) distribution, share-out **(b)** (CS) (departamento, sección) department; (del ejército) division

repartidor -dora *m,f* (*m*) delivery man; (*f*) delivery woman; (de periódicos) newspaper man (*o* boy *etc*)

repartir [I1] *vt* **(a)** ‹*ganancias/trabajo*› to distribute, share out **(b)** ‹*panfletos/propaganda*› to hand out, give out; ‹*periódicos/correo*› to deliver; ‹*naipes/fichas*› to deal **(c)** (esparcir) to spread, distribute ■ ~ *vi* (Jueg) to deal

reparto *m* **1 (a)** (distribución) distribution; (entre socios, herederos) share-out; **~ de premios** prizegiving **(b)** (servicio de entrega) delivery; **~ a domicilio** delivery service **2** (Cin, Teatr) cast

repasador *m* (RPl) dish towel (AmE), tea towel (BrE)

repasar [A1] *vt* ‹*lección/tema*› to review (AmE), to revise (BrE); ‹*lista/cuenta/carta*› to go over, check ■ ~ *vi* to review (AmE), to revise (BrE)

repaso *m* (revisión — para aprender algo) review (AmE), revision (BrE); (— para detectar errores) check; **dio un ~ a sus apuntes** she went *o* looked over her notes

repatriado -da *m,f* repatriate

repatriar [A1 *or* A17] *vt* to repatriate

repelar [A1] *vi* (Méx fam) to grumble, to moan (BrE colloq)

repelente *adj* ‹*persona*› repulsive, repellent; ‹*niño*› obnoxious ■ *m* insect repellent

repeler [E1] *vt* ‹*ataque/agresión*› to repel, repulse (frml) ■ ~ *vi* (+ *me/te/le etc*): **las serpientes me repelen** I find snakes repellent *o* repulsive

repente: **de repente** (*loc adv*) **(a)** (de pronto) suddenly **(b)** (RPl, Per) (quizás) maybe, perhaps

repentino -na *adj* sudden

repercusión *f* (consecuencia) repercussion

repercutir [I1] *vi* **(a)** «*sonido*» to reverberate **(b)** (afectar) ~ EN **algo** to have an effect *o* an impact ON sth

repertorio *m* repertoire

repetición *f* **(a)** (de experimento, palabra) repetition; (de un sueño, fenómeno) recurrence **(b)** (de programa) repeat, rerun

repetido *adj* **(a)** ‹*sello/disco*›: **éste lo tengo ~** I have two of these **(b)** (*delante del n*) ‹*casos/avisos/intentos*› repeated (*before n*)

repetir [I14] *vt* **(a)** ‹*pregunta/explicación*› to repeat; **¿me lo puedes ~?** could you repeat it, please?; **¡que no te lo tenga que volver a ~!** don't let me have to tell you again! **(b)** ‹*tarea*› to do ... again; ‹*programa*› to repeat, rerun; ‹*experimento/curso/asignatura*› to repeat **(c)** ‹*plato*› to have a second helping of, to have seconds of (colloq) ■ ~ *vi* **1** (volver a comer) to have a second helping, to have seconds (colloq) **2** «*pimientos/pepinos*» to repeat; **el ajo me repite** garlic repeats on me **3** (Educ) to repeat a year/course

■ **repetirse** *v pron* **(a)** «*fenómeno/incidente/sueño*» to recur, happen again; «*persona*» to repeat oneself **(b)** (Chi) (volver a comer) to have a second helping, have seconds (colloq)

repetitivo -va *adj* repetitive

repicar [A2] *vi* to ring out, peal

repiquetear [A1] *vi* **(a)** «*campanas*» to peal, ring out **(b)** (golpear) «*lluvia*» to patter; **~ con los dedos en la mesa** to drum *o* tap one's fingers on the table

repiqueteo *m* **(a)** (de campanas) ringing, pealing **(b)** (de lluvia) pattering, pitter-patter (colloq); (con los dedos) drumming, tapping

repisa *f* (estante) shelf; (de chimenea) mantelpiece

repita, **repitas, etc** *see* REPETIR

repleto -ta *adj* **(a)** ‹*calle/vehículo/sala*› ~ DE **algo** full OF sth, packed WITH sth; **el tren iba ~** the train was packed *o* (colloq) jam-packed **(b)** ‹*persona*› replete (frml *or* hum), full

réplica *f* **(a)** (copia) replica **(b)** (Chi, Méx) (de terremoto) aftershock

repoblar [A10] *vt* **(a)** ‹*río/lago*› to restock **(b)** (de árboles) to reforest **(c)** (de personas) to repopulate, resettle

repollo *m* cabbage

reponer [E22] *vt* **(a)** (reemplazar) ‹*existencias*› to replace; ‹*dinero*› to put back, repay; **~ fuerzas** to get one's strength back **(b)** ‹*funcionario/trabajador*› to reinstate **(c)** ‹*obra*› to put ... on again, revive; ‹*serie*› to repeat, rerun; ‹*película*› to show ... again

■ **reponerse** *v pron* to recover

reportaje *m* (en periódico, revista) article, feature; (en televisión) report, item; (entrevista) (AmL) interview

reportar [A1] *vt* **1** ‹*beneficios/pérdidas*› to produce, yield; **sólo me reportó disgustos** it brought *o* caused me nothing but trouble **2** (AmL) (denunciar, dar cuenta de) to report **3** (Méx) ⇒ REPORTEAR

■ **reportarse** *v pron* (AmL) (presentarse) to report

reporte *m* (Méx) (informe) report; (queja) complaint

reportear [A1] *vt* (Andes) to cover, report on ■ ~ *vi* (Andes) to report

reportero -ra *m,f* reporter; **~ gráfico** press photographer

reposacabezas *m* (*pl* ~) headrest

reposado -da *adj* [SER] ‹*persona/temperamento*› calm; ‹*ademanes/habla*› unhurried

reposar [A1] *vi* **(a)** (descansar) «*persona*» to rest; «*restos mortales*» to lie **(b)** «*líquido/solución*» to settle; **dejar ~ la masa** let the dough stand

reposición *f* **(a)** (reemplazo) replacement **(b)** (de serie) repeat, rerun; (de obra) revival; (de película) reshowing

reposo *m* **(a)** (descanso) rest **(b)** (Coc): **dejar en ~** leave to stand

repostar [A1] *vt* ‹*gasolina*› to fill up with; ‹*provisiones*› to stock up with ■ **~** *vi* (Auto) to fill up, to get some gas (AmE) *o* (BrE) petrol; (Aviac, Náut) to refuel

repostería *f* confectionery, baking (*of pastries, desserts*)

repostero -ra *m,f* (persona) confectioner, pastry-cook

reprender [E1] *vt* to scold, tell ... off (colloq)

represa *f* **(a)** (en río — dique) dam; (— embalse) reservoir **(b)** (de molino) millpond

represalia *f* reprisal; **como ~ por** ... in retaliation for ...

representación *f* **1** (acción) representation; **~ legal** legal representation; **asistió en ~ del Rey** she attended as the King's representative; **en ~ de mis compañeros** on behalf of my companions **2** (delegación) delegation **3** (Teatr) performance, production **4** (símbolo) representation

representante *mf* representative; (de artista, cantante) agent; **es ~ de una editorial** she represents a publishing house

representar [A1] *vt* **1** ‹*persona/organización/país*› to represent **2** ‹*obra*› to perform, put on; ‹*papel*› to play **3** (aparentar) to look; **no representa su edad** he doesn't look his age **4** (simbolizar) to represent, symbolize **5** (reproducir) «*dibujo/fotografía/escena*» to show, depict; «*obra/novela*» to portray, depict **6** (equivaler a, significar) to represent; **esto representa un aumento del 5%** this represents a 5% increase; **eso ~ía tres días de trabajo** that would mean *o* involve three days' work

representativo -va *adj* representative

represión *f* repression

reprimenda *f* reprimand

reprimido -da *adj* repressed ■ *m,f*: **es un ~** he's repressed

reprimir [I1] *vt* **(a)** ‹*rebelión*› to suppress, crush **(b)** ‹*risa/llanto/bostezo*› to suppress, stifle **(c)** (Psic) to repress

■ **reprimirse** *v pron* (*refl*) to control oneself

reprobar [A10] *vt* **(a)** ‹*actitud/conducta*› to condemn **(b)** (AmL) ‹*estudiante/materia/curso*› to fail; **me ~on en física** I failed physics

reprochar [A1] *vt* to reproach; **~le algo a algn** to reproach sb for sth

reproche *m* reproach; **hacerle ~s a algn** to reproach sb

reproducción *f* reproduction

reproducir [I6] *vt* to reproduce

■ **reproducirse** *v pron* **(a)** (Biol, Bot) to reproduce, breed **(b)** «*fenómeno*» to recur, happen again

reproductor -tora *adj* ‹*animal*› breeding (*before n*); ‹*órgano*› reproductive

reptar [A1] *vi* «*serpiente*» to slither; «*cocodrilo*» to crawl, slide

reptil *m* reptile

república *f* republic

República Dominicana *f* Dominican Republic

republicano -na *adj/m,f* republican

República Oriental del Uruguay *f* (frml) *official name of Uruguay*

repuesto *m* (pieza) (spare) part; **de ~** spare (*before n*)

repugnancia *f*: **me causa ~** I find him repulsive *o* repugnant; **siento ~ hacia las culebras** I find snakes repulsive

repugnante *adj* ‹*olor*› disgusting, revolting; ‹*crimen*› abhorrent, repugnant; ‹*persona*› (físicamente) repulsive, revolting; (moralmente) repugnant

repugnar [A1] *vi*: **me repugna beber de un vaso sucio** I find having to drink out of a dirty glass disgusting; **me repugna su comportamiento** I find his behavior disgusting *o* repulsive

repulsa *f* (condena) condemnation; (rechazo) rejection

repulsivo -va *adj* ‹*persona*› (físicamente) repulsive, revolting; (moralmente) repugnant; ‹*olor*› disgusting, revolting

reputación *f* reputation; **~ de algo** reputation as sth

requerir [I11] *vt* **(a)** (necesitar) to require **(b)** ‹*documento*› to require; ‹*persona*› to summon

requesón *m* curd (cheese)

requisar [A1] *vt* **(a)** (expropiar) ‹*vehículo/suministros*› to requisition; (confiscar) ‹*drogas/objetos robados*› to seize **(b)** (Col, Ven) (registrar) to search

requisito *m* requirement; **reunir los ~s** to fulfill *o* meet the requirements; **~ previo** prerequisite

res *f* **(a)** (animal) animal **(b)** (Col, Méx, Ven) (Coc) *tb* **carne de ~** beef

resaca *f* **1** (de las olas) undertow **2** (después de beber) hangover

resaltador *m* (Col) highlighter

resaltante *adj* (AmL) outstanding

resaltar [A1] *vi* (sobresalir, destacarse) to stand out; **hacer ~** ‹*color*› to bring out; ‹*importancia/necesidad*› to highlight, stress ■ **~** *vt* ‹*cualidad/importancia/necesidad*› to highlight

resarcir [I4] *vt* **~ a algn** DE **algo** ‹*de daños/inconvenientes*› to compensate sb FOR sth; ‹*de gastos*› to reimburse sb FOR sth

■ **resarcirse** *v pron* **~se** DE **algo** (desquitarse) to get one's own back FOR sth; (compensar) to make up FOR sth

resbalada *f* (AmL) slip

resbaladilla *f* (Méx) slide, chute

resbaladizo -za *adj* **(a)** ‹*superficie/carretera*› slippery **(b)** ‹*asunto/tema*› delicate, tricky (colloq)

resbalar [A1] *vi* **1** (caerse) to slip; **las lágrimas le resbalaban por las mejillas** the tears ran *o* trickled down his cheeks **2** (fam) (ser indiferente): **todo lo que le digas le resbala** anything you say to him is just like water off a duck's back (colloq); **todo**

le **resbala** he couldn't care less about anything (colloq)
■ **resbalarse** *v pron* (caerse) to slip

resbalín *m* (Chi) slide, chute

resbalón *m* slip

resbaloso -sa *adj* (AmL) ‹*superficie*› slippery

rescatar [A1] *vt* **(a)** (salvar) to rescue **(b)** ‹*dinero/pulsera*› to recover, get back

rescate *m* **(a)** (salvamento) rescue; **equipo de ~** rescue team **(b)** (precio) ransom **(c)** (de dinero, joya) recovery

rescoldo *m* embers (*pl*)

resecar [A2] *vt* ‹*piel/ambiente*› to make ... very dry
■ **resecarse** *v pron* to dry up, get very dry

reseco -ca *adj* ‹*planta*› dried-up; ‹*pan*› dry; ‹*tierra/garganta*› parched

resentido -da *adj* **(a)** (dolorido) painful **(b)** (disgustado) upset, hurt; (con rencor) resentful ■ *m,f*: **es un ~** he has a chip on his shoulder

resentimiento *m* resentment, bitterness

resentirse [I11] *v pron* **(a)** (sentir dolor): **aún se resiente de la lesión** he is still suffering the effects of the injury; **aún se resienten de la derrota** they're still smarting from the defeat **(b)** (sufrir las consecuencias) «*salud/trabajo*» to suffer **(c)** (ofenderse, molestarse) to get upset

reseña *f* **(a)** (de congreso, reunión) summary, report; (de libro) review; **una ~ biográfica** a biographical outline **(b)** (descripción) description; (sobre escritor, deportista) profile

reserva *f* **1** (de habitación, pasaje) reservation; (de mesa) booking, reservation; **¿tiene ~?** do you have a reservation?, have you booked? **2** (cantidad guardada) reserve; **tengo otro par de ~** I have a spare pair **3 (a)** (Dep) (equipo) reserves (*pl*), reserve team; (conjunto de suplentes) substitutes (*pl*) **(b)** (de indígenas) reservation; (de animales) reserve; **~ natural** nature reserve **4** (secreto, discreción): **en la más absoluta ~** in the strictest confidence **5 reservas** *fpl* **(a)** (dudas) reservations (*pl*) **(b)** (reparos): **habló sin ~s** he talked openly *o* freely **6** (Méx): **a ~ de que (no) llueva** as long as *o* provided (that) it doesn't rain ■ *mf* (Dep) reserve

reservación *f* (AmL) ⇒ RESERVA 1

reservado -da *adj* ‹*persona/actitud*› reserved; ‹*asunto/tema*› confidential; *ver tb* RESERVAR

reservar [A1] *vt* **1** ‹*asiento/habitación/mesa*› to reserve, book; ‹*pasaje/billete*› to book **2** (guardar) ‹*porción de comida/dinero*› to set aside; **nos reservaba una sorpresa** he had a surprise in store for us; **reservó lo mejor para el final** she kept the best till last
■ **reservarse** *v pron* **(a)** (para sí mismo) ‹*porción/porcentaje*› to keep ... for oneself; **~se la opinión** to reserve judgment **(b)** (*refl*) (para otra tarea) to save oneself

resfriado[1] **-da** *adj*: **estoy (algo) ~** I have a (slight) cold

resfriado[2] *m* cold

resfriarse [A17] *v pron* to catch a cold

resfrío *m* (esp AmS) cold

resguardar [A1] *vt* **~ algo/a algn DE algo** ‹*de peligro/frío*› to protect sth/sb FROM sth
■ **resguardarse** *v pron* (de peligro) to protect oneself; (de la lluvia, el frío) to shelter, take shelter

resguardo *m* **1** (Esp) (de depósito) deposit slip; (en tintorería, zapatería) slip, ticket **2** (Col) (reserva) reservation, reserve **3** (Méx) (control, vigilancia) control

residencia *f* **1 (a)** (en país, ciudad) residence; **fijar ~** to take up residence **(b)** (documento) *tb* **permiso de ~** residence permit **2 (a)** (casa) residence **(b)** (de estudiantes) dormitory (AmE), hall of residence (BrE); (de enfermeras) hostel, home; **~ de ancianos** old people's home **(c)** (hostal, fonda) boarding house, guest house (*not providing meals*) **3** (AmL) (Med) residency (AmE), time spent as a houseman (BrE)

residencial *adj* residential ■ *f* (CS) guest house, boarding house

residente *adj* resident ■ *m,f* **(a)** (en país) resident **(b)** (médico) resident (AmE), houseman (BrE)

residir [I1] *vi* **(a)** «*persona*» to live, reside (frml) **(b)** «*encanto/interés*» (radicar) **~ EN algo** to lie IN sth

residuo *m* **(a)** (Mat) remainder; (Quím) residue **(b) residuos** *mpl* (desperdicios) waste, waste materials *o* products (*pl*); **~s radiactivos** radioactive waste

resignación *f* resignation

resignado -da *adj* resigned; **~ A algo** resigned TO sth

resignarse [A1] *v pron* to resign oneself; **~ a hacer algo** to resign oneself to doing sth

resina *f* resin

resistencia *f* **1 (a)** (en general) resistance **(b)** (aguante físico) stamina; **prueba de ~** endurance test **2** (componente de circuito) resistor; (de secador, calentador) element

resistente *adj* ‹*material/metal*› resistant, tough; ‹*tela*› tough, hard-wearing; ‹*persona/animal/planta*› tough, hardy; **~ al calor** heat-resistant

resistir [I1] *vt* **(a)** (aguantar) ‹*dolor/calor/presión*› to withstand, take; **no la resisto** (Col, Per fam) I can't stand her **(b)** ‹*tentación/impulso*› to resist **(c)** ‹*ataque/enemigo*› to resist ■ **~** *vi* **(a)** (aguantar) «*cuerda/puerta*» to hold; **ya no resisto más** I can't take (it) any more **(b)** «*ejército*» to hold out, resist
■ **resistirse** *v pron* **(a)** (oponer resistencia) to resist **(b)** (tener reticencia): **se resiste a aceptarlo** she's unwilling *o* reluctant to agree to it; **me resisto a creerlo** I find it hard to believe

resolver [E11] *vt* **(a)** ‹*crimen/problema/misterio*› to solve, clear up; ‹*asunto/conflicto*› to resolve, settle; ‹*duda*› to clear up; **tiene resuelto su futuro** his future is sorted out **(b)** (decidir) to decide

resonancia *f* (Mús, Fís) resonance; (eco) echo; (de noticia, suceso) impact

resonante *adj* ‹*sonido*› resonant; ‹*éxito*› resounding, tremendous

resonar [A10] *vi* **(a)** (hacer eco) to echo, resound **(b)** «*gritos/risas*» to ring (out)

resoplar [A1] *vi* (por cansancio) to puff; (por enfado) to snort

resoplido *m* **(a)** (de enfado) snort **(b)** (de cansancio): **dando ~s** puffing and panting **(c)** (de caballo) snort

resorte *m* **(a)** (muelle) spring **(b)** (AmC, Col, Méx) (elástico) elastic

resortera *f* (Méx) slingshot (AmE), catapult (BrE)

respaldar [A1] *vt* ‹*persona*› (apoyar) to support, back; (en discusión) to back up; ‹*propuesta/plan*› to support, back; ‹*versión/teoría*› to support, back up

respaldo *m* **(a)** (de asiento) back **(b)** (apoyo) support, backing; **en ~ de** in support of **(c)** (Fin) backing

respectar [A1] *vi* (*en 3ª pers*): **en** *or* **por lo que a mí respecta** as far as I'm concerned

respectivo -va *adj* (correspondiente) respective

respecto *m*: **a este ~** on this respect, in this regard (frml); **(con) ~ a algo** regarding sth, with regard to sth

respetable *adj* (digno de respeto) respectable; (considerable) considerable

respetar [A1] *vt* **(a)** ‹*persona*› to respect; **se hizo ~ por todos** he won *o* gained everyone's respect **(b)** ‹*opinión/tradiciones*› to respect; ‹*señal/luz roja*› to obey; ‹*ley/norma*› to observe

respeto *m* **(a)** (consideración, deferencia) respect; **con ~** respectfully, with respect; **por ~ a algn/algo** out of consideration *o* respect for sb/sth; **faltarle al** *or* (CS) **el ~ a algn** to be rude *o* disrespectful to sb; **presentaron sus ~s a ...** they paid their repects to ... (frml) **(b)** (temor): **su presencia impone ~** her presence commands (a feeling of) respect; **les tengo mucho ~ a los perros** I have a healthy respect for dogs

respetuoso -sa *adj* ‹*persona/silencio*› respectful

respingado -da *adj* (AmL) ‹*nariz*› turned-up

respingo *m* start; **dio un ~** he gave a start

respingón -gona *adj* **(a)** ‹*nariz*› turned-up **(b)** (Méx fam) ‹*persona*› touchy

respiración *f* (Fisiol) breathing, respiration (frml); **me quedé sin ~** I was out of breath; **contener la ~** to hold one's breath; **~ boca a boca** mouth-to-mouth resuscitation, kiss of life

respirar [A1] *vi* to breathe; **respire hondo** take a deep breath ■ **~** *vt* **(a)** ‹*aire*› to breathe; ‹*humo/gases*› to breathe in **(b)** ‹*tranquilidad*›: **la paz que se respira aquí** the feeling of peace that you get here

respiratorio -ria *adj* respiratory

respiro *m* (descanso) break; **tomarse un ~** to take a break *o* (colloq) have a breather

resplandecer [E3] *vi* «*sol*» to shine; «*luna/metal/cristal*» to gleam; «*hoguera*» to blaze

resplandeciente *adj* **(a)** ‹*luna/metal/cristal*› gleaming; ‹*sol*› dazzling **(b)** (limpio) ‹*cocina/coche*› sparkling clean

resplandor *m* (del sol) glare, brightness; (de luna, metal, cristal) gleam; (de relámpago, explosión) flash

responder [E1] *vi* **1 (a)** (contestar) to reply, answer, respond (frml); **respondió con una evasiva** he gave an evasive reply **(b)** (replicar) to answer back **2** (reaccionar) to respond; **~ A algo** ‹*a amenaza/estímulo*› to respond TO sth **3** (corresponder): **no responden a la descripción** they do not answer the description; **las cifras no responden a la realidad** the figures do not reflect the true situation **4** (responsabilizarse): **si ocurre algo yo no respondo** if anything happens I will not be held responsible; **~ ante la justicia** to answer for one's acts in a court of law; **yo respondo de su integridad** I will vouch for his integrity; **no respondo de lo que hizo** I am not responsible for what he did; **~ POR algn** to vouch FOR sb ■ **~** *vt* **(a)** (contestar) to reply, answer **(b)** ‹*pregunta*› to answer **(c)** ‹*llamada/carta*› to answer, reply to

respondón -dona *adj* (fam) ‹*niño*› mouthy (AmE colloq), cheeky (BrE colloq) ■ *m,f* (fam): **es un ~** he's always answering back

responsabilidad *f* responsibility; **un puesto de mucha ~** a post which involves a great deal of responsibility; **tener sentido de la ~** to have a sense of responsibility; **cargó con toda la ~** she took full responsibility

responsabilizar [A4] *vt* **~ a algn DE algo** to hold sb responsible *o* accountable FOR sth

■ **responsabilizarse** *v pron* to take responsibility; **~se DE algo** ‹*de tarea/error/accidente*› to take responsibility FOR sth; ‹*de atentado*› to claim responsibility FOR sth; ‹*de delito*› to admit responsibility FOR sth

responsable *adj* [SER] (concienzudo) responsible; **~ DE algo** ‹*de tarea/error*› responsible FOR sth; (culpable) responsible FOR sth; ‹*de accidente/delito*› liable FOR sth; **nadie se ha hecho ~ del atentado** no one has claimed responsibility for the attack ■ *mf*: **el ~ de ventas** the person responsible for sales; **los ~s serán castigados** those responsible will be punished

respuesta *f* **(a)** (a carta, mensaje) reply, answer, response (frml) **(b)** (reacción) response **(c)** (solución) answer, solution

resquebrajar [A1] *vt* ‹*loza/roca*› to crack; ‹*madera*› to split

■ **resquebrajarse** *v pron* «*loza/roca*» to crack; «*madera*» to split

resquicio *m* **1** (grieta) crack; (abertura) gap **2** (huella, resto) trace

resta *f* subtraction

restablecer [E3] *vt* ‹*relaciones/comunicaciones*› to re-establish; ‹*orden/democracia/normalidad*› to restore

■ **restablecerse** *v pron* to recover

restablecimiento *m* (de relaciones, comunicaciones) re-establishment; (de orden, paz) restoration; (de enfermo) recovery

restante *adj* remaining

restantes *mpl/fpl*: **los ~s** the rest, the remainder

restar [A1] *vt* **(a)** ▶ **294** (Mat) ‹*número*› to subtract, take away; **~ algo DE algo** to take (away) *o* subtract sth FROM sth **(b)** ‹*gastos/cantidad*› to deduct, take away **(c)** (quitar): **~le importancia a algo** to minimize *o* play down the importance of sth ■ **~** *vi* **1** ▶ **294** (Mat) to subtract, take away **2** (Esp) (Dep) to return (service)

restauración *f* restoration

restaurante *m* restaurant

restaurar [A1] *vt* to restore

resto *m* **1 (a)** (lo demás, lo que queda) **el ~** the rest **(b)** (Mat) remainder **2 restos** *mpl* (humanos, arqueológicos) remains (*pl*); (de avión, barco siniestrado) wreckage; (de comida) leftovers (*pl*) **3** (Esp) (Dep) return (of service)

restregar [A7] *vt* ‹*suelo*› to scrub; ‹*ropa*› to rub, scrub

■ **restregarse** *v pron* (*refl*) ‹*ojos/mejilla*› to rub

restricción *f* restriction

restringido -da *adj* ‹*libertad*› restricted, limited; ‹*posibilidades/cantidad*› limited

restringir [I7] *vt* to restrict

resucitar [A1] *vt* **(a)** (Relig) to raise ... from the dead, to bring ... back to life **(b)** (Med) to resuscitate, revive **(c)** ‹*costumbres/rencores*› to revive, resurrect ■ **~** *vi* «*persona*» to rise (from the dead); «*costumbre/grupo*» to take on a new lease of life

resuelto -ta *adj* **(a)** [SER] ‹*persona*› decisive; **en tono ~** decisively **(b)** [ESTAR] (decidido) determined, resolved (frml); *ver tb* RESOLVER

resultado *m* result; **como ~ de** as a result of; **mi idea dio ~** my idea worked; **intentó convencerlo, pero sin ~** she tried to persuade him, but without success *o* to no avail; **~ final** (Dep) final score

resultar [A1] *vi* **1** (dar resultado) to work; **su idea no resultó** his idea didn't work (out) **2** (+ *compl*): **resulta más barato así** it works out cheaper this way; **me resulta simpático** I think he's very nice; **resultó ser un malentendido** it turned out to be *o* proved to be a misunderstanding; **resultó tal como lo planeamos** it turned out *o* worked out just as we planned **3** (*en 3ª pers*): **ahora resulta que era periodista** now it turns out that he was a journalist **4** (derivar) **~** EN **algo** to result IN sth, lead TO sth

resumen *m* summary; **hacer un ~ de un texto** to summarize a text; **en ~** in short

resumidero *m* (AmL) drain

resumir [I1] *vt* **(a)** (condensar) ‹*texto/libro*› to summarize **(b)** (recapitular) ‹*discurso/argumento*› to sum up ■ **~** *vi*: **resumiendo** ... in short ..., to sum up ...

resurgir [I7] *vi* to reemerge

resurrección *f* resurrection

retachar [A1] *vt* (Méx fam) **(a)** ‹*carta/trabajo*› to reject, refuse to accept **(b)** (no dejar entrar): **nos ~on** they turned us away ■ **~** *vi* (Méx) «*bala*» to ricochet

retador -dora *m,f* (AmL) challenger

retaguardia *f* (Mil) rearguard

retahíla *f* string

retaliación *f* (AmL) retaliation

retar [A1] *vt* **(a)** (desafiar) to challenge **(b)** (CS) (regañar) to tell ... off (colloq), to scold

retardado -da *adj* **1** (Tec) delayed; **de apertura retardada** with time-delay lock **2** ‹*persona*› mentally handicapped *o* retarded

retardar [A1] *vt* (frenar) to delay, hold up, retard (tech); (posponer) to postpone

retén *m* **(a)** (patrulla) patrol; (pelotón) squad; (puesto de policía) police post **(b)** (Ven) (correccional) reformatory (AmE), remand home (BrE)

retener [E27] *vt* **1 (a)** ‹*datos/información*› to keep back, withhold **(b)** ‹*pasaporte/tarjeta*› to retain **(c)** (Fin, Fisco) ‹*dinero/cuota*› to deduct, withhold **2 (a)** «*policía*» ‹*persona*› to detain, hold **(b)** (hacer permanecer): **no te retendré mucho** I won't keep you long **3** ‹*calor/carga/líquidos*› to retain **4** ‹*atención/interés*› to keep, retain **5** (recordar) to retain, keep ... in one's head

reticencia *f* **(a)** (renuencia) reluctance; **con ~** reluctantly **(b)** (reserva) reticence

reticente *adj* **(a)** (reacio) reluctant **(b)** (reservado) reticent

retina *f* retina

retintín *m* (fam) (tonillo sarcástico) sarcastic tone of voice; **con ~** sarcastically

retirada *f* **(a)** (en general) withdrawal **(b)** (Mil) retreat; **batirse en ~** to retreat **(c)** (de actividad profesional) retirement **(d)** (de competición — antes de iniciarse) withdrawal; (— una vez iniciada) retirement

retirado -da *adj* **1 (a)** ‹*lugar/casa*› remote, out-of-the-way; **una casa retirada de la calle** a house set back from the road; **un barrio ~ del centro** an outlying district **(b)** ‹*vida*› secluded, quiet **2** (jubilado) retired

retirar [A1] *vt* **1 (a)** (quitar) to remove, take away; (apartar) to move away; **retiró la cacerola del fuego** he removed the saucepan from the heat; **~ de la circulación** to withdraw from circulation **(b)** ‹*cabeza/mano*› to pull ... back **(c)** ‹*embajador/tropas*› to withdraw, pull out **(d)** (+ *me/te/le etc*) ‹*apoyo*› to withdraw; ‹*pasaporte/carnet*› to withdraw, take away **2** ‹*afirmaciones/propuesta*› to withdraw; **retiro lo dicho** I take back what I said **3** (de cuenta) ‹*dinero*› to withdraw

■ **retirarse** *v pron* **1 (a)** (apartarse) to move back *o* away; (irse) to leave, withdraw **(b)** «*ejército/tropas*» to withdraw, pull out **(c)** (irse a dormir) to go to bed, retire (frml) **2** (jubilarse) to retire; (de competición — antes de iniciarse) to withdraw, pull out; (— una vez iniciada) to pull out

retiro *m* **(a)** (jubilación) retirement; (pensión) (retirement) pension **(b)** (AmL) (de fuerzas, empleados) withdrawal; (de apoyo, fondos) withdrawal

reto *m* **(a)** (desafío) challenge **(b)** (CS) (regañina) telling-off (colloq), scolding

retobar [A1] *vi* (Méx fam) to answer back

retocar [A2] *vt* ‹*fotografía/maquillaje*› to touch up, retouch

retoño *m* (Bot) shoot

retoque *m*: **dar los últimos ~s a algo** to put the final *o* the finishing touches to sth

retorcer [E10] *vt* to twist

■ **retorcerse** *v pron* **1 (a)** (enrollarse) to become tangled (up) **(b)** «*serpiente*» to writhe **(c)** «*persona*»: **~se de dolor** to writhe in agony; ⇒ RISA **2** (*refl*) ‹*manos*› to wring

retorcido -da *adj* ‹*persona/mente*› twisted, devious; ‹*estilo/argumento*› convoluted, involved

retorcijón *m* (AmL) sharp pain (*in the stomach or gut*); **retorcijones de tripas** stomach cramps

retórico -ca *adj* rhetorical

retornable *adj* returnable; **no ~** non-returnable

retornar [A1] *vi/vt* (frml *o* liter) to return

retorno *m* (frml *o* liter) (regreso, devolución) return; (viaje de regreso) return journey

retortijón *m* (Esp, Méx) ⇒ RETORCIJÓN

retraído -da *adj* withdrawn, retiring (*before n*)

retransmisión *f* **(a)** (transmisión) transmission; **~ en directo** live broadcast *o* transmission **(b)** (repetición) repeat

retransmitir [I1] *vt* **(a)** (repetir) to repeat, rebroadcast (frml) **(b)** (Esp period) (Rad, TV) to broadcast

retrasado -da *adj* **(a)** [SER] (Med, Psic) mentally handicapped **(b)** [ESTAR] (en tarea, actividad): **está muy ~ con respecto a los demás** he lags a long way behind the others; **están ~s en los pagos** they are behind in their payments; **tengo trabajo ~** I have work to catch up on **(c)** ‹*país/sociedad*› backward **(d)** ‹*reloj*› slow ■ *m,f*: *tb* **~ mental** mentally handicapped person, (mentally) retarded person

retrasar [A1] *vt* **(a)** ‹*persona*› to make ... late; **el tráfico nos retrasó** we got held up in the traffic **(b)** ‹*producción/proceso*› to delay, hold up; **la niebla retrasó la salida del avión** the departure (of the plane) was delayed by fog **(c)** ‹*partida/fecha*› to postpone **(d)** ‹*reloj*› to put back

■ **retrasarse** *v pron* **(a)** (llegar tarde) to be late **(b)** «*producción/trámite*» to be delayed, be held up **(c)** (en trabajo, estudios, pagos) to fall behind; **se retrasó en presentarlo** she was late (in) submitting it **(d)** «*reloj*» to run slow

retraso *m* **(a)** (demora) delay; **viene con media hora de ~** it's (running) half an hour late; **llevamos un ~ de dos meses sobre lo previsto** we're two months behind schedule **(b)** (de país) backwardness

retratar [A1] *vt* **(a)** (pintar) to paint a portrait of; (fotografiar) to photograph **(b)** ‹*realidad/costumbres*› to portray, depict

retrato *m* **(a)** (Art, Fot) portrait; ***ser el vivo ~ de algn*** to be the (spitting) image of sb (colloq) **(b)** (descripción) depiction, portrayal

retreta *f* **1** (Mil) (toque) retreat **2** (AmL) (concierto) open-air concert

retribuir [I20] *vt* **(a)** ‹*esfuerzos/trabajo*› to pay **(b)** (recompensar) to reward **(c)** (AmL) ‹*favor*› to return

retroactivo -va *adj* retrospective, retroactive; **un aumento con efecto ~ desde enero** an increase backdated to January

retroceder [E1] *vi* **(a)** «*persona/coche*» to go back, move back; «*ejército*» to withdraw, retreat **(b)** (volverse atrás) to back down

retroceso *m* **(a)** (movimiento hacia atrás) backward movement; (en plan, desarrollo) backward step **(b)** (de ejército) withdrawal, retreat **(c)** (Arm) recoil **(d)** (Ven) (Auto) reverse

retrógrado -da *adj* ‹*persona/actitud*› reactionary; ‹*planteamiento/idea*› retrograde ■ *m,f* reactionary

retrovisor *m* (interior) (rear-view) mirror; (lateral) (wing) mirror

retumbar [A1] *vi* «*voz/explosión*» to boom; «*eco*» to resound; «*paso*» to echo; «*trueno*» to roll, boom; «*habitación*» to resound

reubicar [A2] *vt* (AmL) **(a)** ‹*trabajadores*› to relocate, redeploy; ‹*empresas*› to relocate; ‹*pobladores/damnificados*› to resettle **(b)** (cambiar de lugar) to put ... in a different place, change the position of

reuma, **reúma** *m or f* rheumatism

reumático -ca *adj* rheumatic

reunido -da *adj*: **estuvieron ~s tres horas** the meeting lasted three hours; **está reunida** (Esp) she's in a meeting; *ver tb* REUNIR

reunificar [A2] *vt* ‹*nación*› to reunify; ‹*familia*› to reunite, bring together

reunión *f* **(a)** (para discutir algo) meeting; (de carácter social) gathering; (reencuentro) reunion **(b)** (de datos, información) gathering, collecting

reunir [I23] *vt* **1** ‹*cualidades/características*› to have; ‹*requisitos*› to satisfy, meet; ‹*condiciones*› to fulfill, satisfy **2** ‹*datos*› to gather; ‹*dinero/fondos*› to raise; ‹*información*› to gather together, collect **3** ‹*amigos/familia*› to get ... together; **reunió a los jefes de sección** he called a meeting of the heads of department

■ **reunirse** *v pron* «*consejo/junta*» to meet; «*amigos/parientes*» to get together; **~se CON algn** (encontrarse) to meet up WITH sb; (tener una reunión) to have a meeting WITH sb, meet WITH sb (AmE)

reválida *f* (RPl) validation

revalidación *f* **(a)** (Chi, Méx) (convalidación) validation **(b)** (Col, Ven) (del pasaporte) renewal

revalidar [A1] *vt* **1** ‹*campeonato/título*› to defend, win ... again; ‹*victoria*› to repeat **2 (a)** (Chi, Méx) (convalidar) to validate **(b)** (Col, Ven) ‹*pasaporte*› to renew

revalorizar [A4] *vt* **(a)** ‹*moneda*› to revalue, revaluate (AmE); ‹*pensiones*› to increase, adjust **(b)** ‹*sistema/situación*› to reassess, reevaluate

■ **revalorizarse** *v pron* «*acciones/propiedad*» to appreciate; «*moneda*» to gain in value

revancha *f* **(a)** (Dep, Jueg) return game **(b)** (desquite): **¡me tomaré la ~!** I'll get my own back! (colloq)

revelación *f* **1** (de secreto, noticia) revelation, disclosure **2** (éxito, figura) revelation

revelado *m* developing

revelador -dora *adj* revealing

revelar [A1] *vt* **(a)** ‹*secreto/verdad*› to reveal **(b)** (Cin, Fot) to develop

revendedor -dora *m,f* (de entradas) scalper (AmE), ticket tout (BrE)

revender [E1] *vt* ‹*alimentos/artículos*› to resell; ‹*entradas*› to scalp (AmE), to tout (BrE); ‹*acciones*› to sell off

reventa *f* (de alimentos, artículos) resale; (de entradas) scalping (AmE), touting (BrE)

reventar [A5] *vi* **1** «*globo*» to burst, pop; «*neumático*» to blow out, burst; «*ampolla/tubería*» to burst; «*ola*» to break **2 (a)** «*persona*» (uso hiperbólico): **si sigue comiendo así va a ~** if he carries on eating like that, he'll burst! **(b)** (fam) (irritar) to rile (colloq), to make ... mad (colloq); **me revienta cocinar** I hate cooking ■ **~** *vt* ‹*globo/neumático*› to burst
■ **reventarse** *v pron* **(a)** «*globo/tubería*» ⇒ REVENTAR *vi* 1 **(b)** (*refl*) ‹*grano*› to squeeze; ‹*ampolla*› to burst

reventón *m* **1** (de neumático) blowout; (de tubería) burst **2** (Méx fam) (fiesta) party

reverencia *f* (de hombre, niño) bow; (de mujer, niña) curtsy; **hacer una ~** «*hombre*» to bow; «*mujer*» to curtsy

reverendo -da *adj* **(a)** (Relig) reverend (*before n*) **(b)** (esp AmL fam) (como intensificador) (*delante del n*); ⇒ SOBERANO 2

reversa *f* (Col, Méx) reverse; **meter ~** to put the car into reverse

reversible *adj* reversible

reverso *m* **(a)** (de papel, cuadro) back **(b)** (de moneda, medalla) reverse

revés *m* **1 (a) el ~** (de prenda) the inside; (de tela) the back, the wrong side; (de papel, documento) the back **(b) al revés** (*loc adv*) (con lo de adelante atrás) back to front; (con lo de arriba abajo) upside down; (con lo de dentro fuera) inside out; **así no, va al ~** not that way, it goes the other way around *o* (BrE) round; **se puso los zapatos al ~** he put his shoes on the wrong feet; **todo lo entiende al ~** she's always getting the wrong end of the stick; **todo me sale al ~** nothing goes right for me; ***saberse algo al ~ y al derecho*** to know sth (off) by heart **2** (Dep) backhand **3** (contratiempo) setback

revestir [I14] *vt* (cubrir) ‹*pared/suelo*› to cover; ‹*cable*› to sheathe, cover; ‹*tubería*› (con material aislante) to lag; **paredes revestidas de madera** wood-paneled walls

revienta, **revientas**, **etc** *see* REVENTAR

revisación *f* (RPl) (Med, Odont) examination; (periódica) checkup

revisar [A1] *vt* **(a)** ‹*documento*› to go through, look through; ‹*traducción/cuenta*› to check, go through **(b)** ‹*criterio/doctrina/edición*› to revise **(c)** ‹*máquina/instalación/frenos*› to check; ‹*coche*› (hacer revisión periódica) (Esp) to service **(d)** (AmL) ‹*equipaje/bolsillos*› to search, go through **(e)** (AmL) ‹*paciente*› to examine; ‹*dentadura*› to check; **se hizo ~ la dentadura** he had a dental checkup

revisión *f* **(a)** (de trabajo, documento) checking, check **(b)** (de criterio, doctrina) revision **(c)** (de instalación) inspection; (de frenos) check; (de coche) (Esp) service **(d)** (AmL) (de equipaje) inspection **(e)** (Med, Odont) checkup; **~ médica** (Esp) (periódica) checkup; (para trabajo) medical examination

revisor -sora *m,f* (Esp) ticket inspector

revista *f* **(a)** (publicación ilustrada) magazine; (de profesión) journal; **~ del corazón** real-life *o* true-romance magazine **(b)** (Espec, Teatr) revue; **teatro de ~** variety theater **(c)** (inspección) review; **pasar ~ a las tropas** to inspect *o* review the troops

revistero *m* magazine rack

revitalizar [A4] *vt* to revitalize

revivir [I1] *vi* to revive ■ **~** *vt* to relive

revolcar [A9] *vt*: **lo ~on por el suelo** they knocked him to the ground and pushed him around
■ **revolcarse** *v pron* to roll around; (en lodo) to wallow, roll around

revolcón *m* (caída) tumble; (vuelta) roll

revolotear [A1] *vi* «*mariposa*» to flutter; «*polilla*» to flit; «*pájaro*» to flutter around; «*papeles/hojas*» to fly *o* swirl around

revoltijo, **revoltillo** *m* (fam) **(a)** (desorden) mess, jumble **(b)** (comida, bebida) mixture, concoction

revoltoso -sa *adj* ‹*niño*› naughty; ‹*soldados/estudiantes*› rebellious

revolución *f* revolution

revolucionar [A1] *vt* **(a)** ‹*costumbres/industria*› to revolutionize **(b)** ‹*niños*› to get ... excited; ‹*estudiantes/obreros*› to stir up

revolucionario -ria *adj/m,f* revolutionary

revolver [E11] *vt* **(a)** ‹*salsa/guiso*› to stir; **me revuelve el estómago** it turns my stomach **(b)** (AmL) ‹*dados*› to shake **(c)** ‹*cajones/papeles*› to rummage through, go through; «*ladrones*» ‹*casa*› to turn ... upside down ■ **~** *vi*: **revolvió en mis cosas** he rummaged through my things

revólver *m* revolver

revuelo *m* (conmoción) stir

revuelta *f* **(a)** (de civiles) uprising; (de tropas) uprising, revolt; (de estudiantes, presos) riot **(b)** (jaleo) commotion, row (colloq)

revuelto[1] -ta *adj* **(a)** (desordenado) in a mess; ‹*pelo*› disheveled*; **tener el estómago ~** to feel sick *o* nauseous **(b)** ‹*mar*› rough; ‹*tiempo*› unsettled

revuelto[2] *m* vegetables sautéed with egg

rey *m* **1 (a)** (monarca) king; **los R~es de Suecia** the King and Queen of Sweden; **los R~es y sus hijos** the royal couple and their children **(b)** (en ajedrez, naipes) king **(c)** (como apelativo) pet (colloq), precious (colloq) **2 Reyes** Epiphany, January 6th; **Los R~es Magos** the Three Wise Men, The Three Kings

rezagado -da *adj*: **quedar(se) ~** to fall *o* drop behind; **iban ~s** they were lagging behind; **los alumnos más ~s** the slower students

rezar [A4] *vi* (Relig) to pray; **~ POR algn/algo** to pray FOR sb/sth; **reza por que todo salga bien** pray that everything turns out all right ■ **~** *vt* ‹*oración/rosario*› to say

rezo *m* prayer

rezongar [A3] *vi* to grumble ■ **~** *vt* (AmC, Ur fam) (regañar) to tell ... off (colloq)

rezumar [A1] *vt/vi* to ooze

RFA *f* (= **República Federal de Alemania**) FRG

ría *f* ria (*long, narrow, tidal inlet*)

ría, **rías**, **etc** *see* REÍR

riachuelo *m* stream, brook

riada *f* flood; (en área más extensa) flooding

ribera *f* **(a)** (orilla — de río) bank; (— de lago, mar) shore **(b)** (vega) strand, riverside

ribete *m* (adorno) trimming, edging

rico -ca *adj* **1 (a)** ‹*persona/país*› rich, wealthy **(b)** ‹*tierra*› rich; ‹*vegetación*› lush; ‹*lenguaje/historia*› rich; **~ EN algo** rich IN sth **2 (a)** ‹*comida*› good, nice; **¡esto está riquísimo!** this is delicious! **(b)** (esp CS) ‹*perfume*› nice, lovely; **¡qué ~ olor tiene!** what a lovely smell! **(c)** (fam) (mono) ‹*niño/chica*› lovely, cute **(d)** (AmL exc RPl) (agradable) lovely, wonderful ■ *m,f* **(a)** (*m*) rich *o* wealthy man; (*f*) rich *o* wealthy woman; **los ~s** rich people, the rich **(b)** (como apelativo) (fam & iró) sweetie (colloq & iro), honey (colloq & iro)

ricura *f* (fam): **tiene un bebé que es una ~** she has the cutest little baby (colloq); **ven, ~** come here, darling (colloq)

ridiculez *f* **(a)** (tontería, insignificancia): **lo que dijo fue una ~** what he said was ridiculous; **¡qué ~!** that's ridiculous!; **pagué una ~ por esto** I paid next to nothing for this **(b)** (cualidad) ridiculousness

ridiculizar [A4] *vt* to ridicule

ridículo[1] -la *adj* **(a)** ‹*persona/comentario/vestimenta*› ridiculous; **lo ~ de la situación era que** ... the ridiculous thing about the situation was that ...; **eso es ~** it's absurd *o* ridiculous **(b)** ‹*cantidad/precios*› ridiculous, ludicrous; ‹*sueldo*› ridiculous, laughable

ridículo[2] *m*: **sentido del ~** sense of the ridiculous *o* absurd; **dejar** *or* **poner a algn en ~** to make a fool of sb; **hacer el ~** to make a fool of oneself

ríe, etc *see* REÍR

riega, riegas, etc *see* REGAR

riego *m* **(a)** (Agr) irrigation **(b) falta de ~ sanguíneo** insufficient blood supply

riel *m* rail

rienda *f* rein; ***aflojar las ~s*** to slacken the reins; ***llevar las ~s*** to be in charge *o* control; ***tomar las ~s*** to take charge

riesgo *m* risk; **un ~ para la salud** a health hazard; **a ~ de perder su amistad** at the risk of losing his friendship; **~s que hay que correr** risks you have to take; **corres el ~ de perderlo** you run the risk of losing it; **un seguro a** *or* **contra todo ~** an all-risks *o* a comprehensive insurance policy

riesgoso -sa *adj* (AmL) risky

rifa *f* (sorteo) raffle, draw

rifar [A1] *vt* to raffle

rifle *m* rifle

rigidez *f* **(a)** (de material) stiffness, rigidity; (de un miembro) stiffness **(b)** (de ley, doctrina, horario) inflexibility; (de educación, dieta) strictness

rígido -da *adj* **(a)** ‹*material*› rigid, stiff **(b)** ‹*educación/dieta*› strict; ‹*regla/horario/carácter*› inflexible; ‹*actitud*› rigid, inflexible; ‹*moral/principios*› strict

rigor *m* (en general) rigor*; (de medidas, castigo) harshness, severity; **con todo el ~ de la ley** with the full rigor of the law; **el ~ del invierno** the rigors of winter; **con ~** rigorously, strictly; **los saludos de ~** the usual greetings

riguroso -sa *adj* **(a)** ‹*método*› rigorous; ‹*dieta/control/orden*› strict; ‹*examen*› thorough; **rigurosas medidas de seguridad** tight security **(b)** ‹*juez*› harsh; ‹*maestro*› strict; ‹*castigo*› severe, harsh **(c)** ‹*invierno*› hard; ‹*clima*› harsh

rima *f* (de sonidos) rhyme

rimar [A1] *vi* to rhyme

rimbombante *adj* ‹*estilo*› grandiose, overblown; ‹*palabras*› high-flown; ‹*boda/fiesta*› ostentatious, showy

rímel *m* mascara

rin *m* **1** (Col, Méx) (rueda) wheel; (llanta) rim **2** (Per) (teléfono) public telephone; (ficha) (telephone) token

rincón *m* **1** (de habitación, armario) corner **2** (lugar) spot, place; **bellos rincones de Perú** beautiful places *o* spots in Peru; **registraron hasta el último ~ de la casa** they searched every nook and cranny of the house

ring /rrin/ *m* (*pl* **rings**) (Dep) ring

rinoceronte *m* rhinoceros

riña *f* **(a)** (pelea) fight; **~ de gallos** (AmS) cockfight **(b)** (discusión) quarrel, argument, row (colloq)

riñón *m* **(a)** ▶ **123** (Anat) kidney **(b)** (Coc) kidney **(c) riñones** *mpl* (fam) (espalda baja) lower part of the back, kidneys (*pl*)

río *m* river; **~ abajo/arriba** downstream/upstream; **el R~ de la Plata** the River Plate

río, rió, etc *see* REÍR

Río de Janeiro *m* Rio de Janeiro

rioplatense *adj* of/from the River Plate

riqueza *f* **(a)** (bienes) wealth; **las ~s del museo** the treasures of the museum **(b)** (recursos): **las ~s del suelo** the earth's riches; **las ~s naturales de un país** a country's natural resources **(c)** (variedad, abundancia) richness

risa *f* laugh; **una risita nerviosa** a nervous giggle *o* laugh; **¡qué ~!** what a laugh!, how funny!; **entre las ~s del público** amid laughter from the audience; **me entró la ~** I got the giggles; **da ~ oírla hablar** it's very funny hearing her talk; ***morirse de (la) ~*** (fam) to die laughing (colloq); **estábamos muertos de (la) ~** we were killing ourselves laughing (colloq); ***retorcerse de la ~*** to double up with laughter; ***tomarse algo a ~*** (fam) to treat sth as a joke

risotada *f* guffaw

risueño -ña *adj* ‹*cara/expresión*› smiling; ‹*persona*› cheerful; ‹*porvenir/perspectivas*› bright

rítmico -ca *adj* rhythmic, rhythmical

ritmo *m* **(a)** (compás) rhythm; **al ~ de la música** to the rhythm of the music, in time to the music; **llevaba el ~ con los pies** he kept time with his feet; **seguir el ~** to keep in time, follow the beat **(b)** (velocidad) pace, speed; **llevan un buen ~ de trabajo** they work at a steady pace *o* speed; **a este ~ no terminaremos nunca** at this rate we'll never finish; **el ~ de crecimiento** the rate of growth

rito *m* (Relig) rite; (costumbre) ritual

ritual *adj/m* ritual

rival *adj* rival (*before n*) ■ *mf* rival; **sin ~** unrivaled

rivalidad *f* rivalry

rizado -da *adj* ‹*pelo*› curly; ‹*mar*› slightly choppy

rizar [A4] *vt* ‹*pelo/melena*› to curl, perm

■ **rizarse** *v pron* **(a)** «*pelo*» (con la humedad) to frizz, go frizzy **(b)** (*refl*) ‹*pelo*› to curl

rizo *m* **(a)** (de pelo) curl **(b)** (Tex) bouclé **(c)** (Aviac) loop

róbalo *m* sea bass

robar [A1] *vt* **1 (a)** ‹*dinero/bolso*› to steal; ‹*banco*› to rob; **~le algo A algn** to steal sth FROM sb; **le robó dinero a su jefe** he stole some money from his boss; **le robaron el bolso** she had her bag stolen **(b)** (raptar) ‹*niño*› to abduct, kidnap **2** (estafar) to cheat, rip off (colloq) **3** (Jueg) (en naipes, dominó) to draw, pick up (colloq) ■ **~** *vi* to steal; **~on en la casa de al lado** the house next door was broken into; **¡me han robado!** I've been robbed!

roble *m* (árbol) oak (tree); (madera) oak

robo *m* **(a)** (en banco, museo) robbery; (hurto de dinero, objeto) theft; **~ a mano armada** armed robbery **(b)** (en vivienda) burglary; (forzando la entrada) break-in **(c)** (fam) (estafa) rip-off (colloq)

robot *m* (*pl* **-bots**) robot

robustecer [E3] *vt* to strengthen

■ **robustecerse** *v pron* to become *o* grow stronger

robusto -ta *adj* ‹*árbol*› robust, strong; ‹*persona*› robust, sturdy; ‹*construcción*› sturdy

roca *f* rock

roce *m* **(a)** (contacto) rubbing; (fricción) friction; **no soporta el ~ de la sábana** he can't bear the sheet rubbing against his skin; **el ~ de su mejilla** the brush of her cheek; **tiene los puños gastados por el ~** his cuffs are worn **(b)** (trato frecuente) regular contact **(c)** (desacuerdo): **~s dentro del partido** friction within the party; **tener un ~ con algn** to have a brush with sb

rociar [A17] *vt* (con pulverizador) to spray; **lo ~on de keroseno** they doused it with kerosene; **rocíelo con limón** sprinkle with lemon

rocío *m* dew; **una gota de ~** a dewdrop

rock *adj inv* rock (*before n*) ■ *m* rock music; **~ duro** *or* (AmL) **pesado** hard rock

rockero -ra *adj* ‹*grupo/ambiente*› rock (*before n*) ■ *m,f* rock artist *o* musician, rocker (colloq)

rocola *f* (AmL) jukebox

rocoso -sa *adj* rocky

rocote, **rocoto** *m* (AmS) hot pepper

rodaballo *m* turbot

rodachina *f* (Col) caster, roller

rodaja *f* slice; **en ~s** sliced

rodaje *m* **(a)** (Cin) filming, shooting **(b)** (Auto) breaking-in (AmE), running-in (BrE); **estar en ~** to be breaking in (AmE) *o* (BrE) running in

rodapié *m* baseboard (AmE), skirting board (BrE)

rodar [A10] *vi* **1** «*moneda/pelota*» to roll; «*rueda*» to go round, turn; **la moneda rodó por la mesa** the coin rolled across the table; **rodó escaleras abajo** she went tumbling down the stairs **2** (Cin) to film, shoot; **¡se rueda!** action! ■ **~** *vt* (Cin) to shoot, film

rodeado -da *adj* **~ DE algo** surrounded BY sth

rodear [A1] *vt* **(a)** ‹*edificio/persona*› to surround; **~ algo DE algo** to surround sth WITH sth; **las circunstancias que ~on su muerte** the circumstances surrounding his death; **le rodeó la cintura con los brazos** he put his arms around her waist **(b)** (AmL) ‹*ganado*› to round up **2** (estar alrededor de) to surround; **todos los que lo rodean** everyone who works with him/knows him

■ **rodearse** *v pron* **~se DE algo/algn** to surround oneself WITH sth/sb

rodeo *m* **(a)** (desvío) detour; **dar un ~** to make a detour; ***andarse con rodeos*** to beat about the bush **(b)** (Espec) rodeo

rodilla *f* ▶ 123 knee; **ponerse de ~s** to kneel down, to get down on one's knees

rodillera *f* **(a)** (Dep) kneepad; (Med) knee bandage **(b)** (parche) knee patch

rodillo *m* (de cocina) rolling pin; (para pintar) paint roller; (de máquina de escribir) roller, platen

roedor -dora *m,f* rodent

roer [E13] *vt* ‹*hueso/cable*› to gnaw (at)

rogar [A8] *vt*: **te lo ruego** I beg you; **se ruega no fumar** you are kindly requested not to smoke; **te ruego que me perdones** please forgive me; **le rogó que tuviera misericordia** she begged him to have mercy ■ **~** *vi* (Relig) to pray; **roguemos al Señor** let us pray; ***hacerse (de)*** *or* (Méx) ***del ~*** to play hard to get; **aceptó sin hacerse (de) ~** he accepted immediately, without any persuading

rojizo -za *adj* ▶ 97 reddish

rojo[1] **-ja** *adj* **1 (a)** ▶ 97 ‹*color/vestido*› red; **ponerse ~** «*persona*» to blush, turn red; «*semáforo*» to turn red, go red (BrE); **ponerse ~ de ira** to turn *o* (BrE) go red with anger **(b)** ‹*piel*› (por el sol) sunburnt, red **2** (pey *o* hum) (Pol) **(a)** (de izquierda) red (pej *or* hum), commie (pej *or* hum) **(b)** (en la Guerra Civil española) Republican ■ *m,f* (pey *o* hum) **(a)** (izquierdista) red (pej *or* hum), commie (pej *or* hum) **(b)** (en la Guerra Civil española) Republican

rojo[2] *m* ▶ 97 red; ***al ~ vivo*** ‹*metal*› red-hot

rol *m* **(a)** (lista) roll, list **(b)** (papel) role

rolar [A1] *vi* (Méx fam) (dar vueltas) to wander around ■ **~** *vt* (Méx fam) ‹*persona*› to move

■ **rolarse** *v pron* (*recipr*) (Méx fam) (turnarse) to take turns; **tenemos que ~nos el libro** we have to take turns with the book *o* pass the book around

rollizo -za *adj* chubby

rollo *m* **1 (a)** (de papel, tela, película) roll **(b)** (de cable, cuerda) reel **(c)** (fam) (de gordura) roll of fat **2 (a)** (Esp fam) (cosa aburrida) bore; **¡qué ~ de conferencia!** what a boring lecture! **(b)** (Esp, Méx fam) (lata) nuisance, pain (colloq); **¡qué ~!** what a nuisance *o* pain! **3** (fam) **(a)** (perorata) speech (colloq), lecture (colloq); **siempre nos suelta el mismo ~** he always gives us the same speech; **bueno, corta el ~ ya** OK, can it, will you? (AmE colloq), OK, put a sock in it, will you? (BrE colloq) **(b)** (mentira) story **4** (Esp, Méx fam) (asunto) business ■ *adj inv* (Esp fam) boring; **¡qué tío más ~!** that guy's such a pain *o* bore! (colloq)

Roma *f* Rome

romance *m* romance

románico -ca *adj* ‹*arquitectura/columna*› Romanesque; ‹*lengua*› Romance (*before n*)

romano -na *adj* (Hist) Roman; (de la ciudad) of/from Rome, Roman ■ *m,f* (Hist) Roman; (de la ciudad) person from Rome

romanticismo *m* (Art, Lit, Mús) Romanticism; (sentimentalismo) romanticism

romántico -ca *adj/m,f* (Art, Lit, Mús) Romantic; (sentimental) romantic

rombo *m* **(a)** (Mat) rhombus **(b)** (carta) diamond **(c)** **rombos** *mpl* (palo) diamonds (*pl*)

romería *f* **(a)** (Relig) procession (*to a local shrine, gen followed by festivities*) **(b)** (AmL fam) (multitud) mass, crowd

romero *m* (Bot, Coc) rosemary

rompecabezas *m* (*pl* ~) puzzle

rompehielos *m* (*pl* ~) icebreaker

rompeolas *m* (*pl* ~) breakwater

romper [E30] *vt* **1 (a)** ‹*loza/mueble*› to break; ‹*ventana*› to break, smash; ‹*lápiz/cuerda*› to break, snap **(b)** ‹*hoja/póster*› (rasgar) to tear; (en varios pedazos) to tear up **(c)** ‹*camisa*› to tear, split **2 (a)** ‹*silencio/monotonía*› to break; ‹*tranquilidad*› to disturb **(b)** ‹*promesa/pacto*› to break; ‹*relaciones/compromiso*› to break off ■ ~ *vi* **1 (a)** «*olas*» to break **(b)** (liter) «*alba*» to break; **al ~ el día** at daybreak, at the crack of dawn **(c)** (empezar): **rompió a llorar/reír** she burst into tears/burst out laughing **2** «*novios*» to break up, split up; **~ CON algn** ‹*con novio*› to split *o* break up WITH sb; **~ CON algo** ‹*con el pasado*› to break WITH sth; ‹*con tradición*› to break away FROM sth

■ **romperse** *v pron* **(a)** «*vaso/plato*» to break, smash, get broken *o* smashed; «*papel*» to tear, rip, get torn *o* ripped; «*televisor/ascensor*» (RPl) to break down **(b)** «*pantalones/zapatos*» to wear out **(c)** (*refl*) ‹*brazo/pierna*› to break

rompevientos *m* (*pl* ~) (Méx, RPl) (pulóver) sweater; (anorak) windbreaker (AmE), windcheater (BrE)

ron *m* **(a)** (bebida) rum **(b)** (Per) (combustible) methanol

roncar [A2] *vi* (al dormir) to snore; (dormir) (fam) to sleep

roncha *f* (Med) (por picadura de insecto) bump; **se llenó de ~s** she came out in a rash

ronco -ca *adj* **(a)** ‹*persona*› hoarse; **se quedó ~ de tanto gritar** he shouted himself hoarse **(b)** ‹*voz*› husky

ronda *f* **1** (de soldado, guarda) patrol; (de enfermera) round; (de policía) patrol, beat; **hacer la ~** «*policía*» to patrol one's beat; «*soldado/guarda*» to be on patrol; «*repartidor*» to do one's round **2** (vuelta, etapa) round; (de bebidas) round **3** (CS, Per) (de niños): **formaron una ~ tomándose de la mano** they held hands in a circle; **danzaban en ~** they were dancing around in a circle **4** (Esp, Méx) (serenata) serenade

rondar [A1] *vt* **(a)** «*vigilante/patrulla*» to patrol **(b)** «*pensamiento*»: **hace días que me ronda esa idea** that idea has been going round and round in my head for days **(c)** ‹*lugar*› to hang around **(d)** (acercarse a): **debe estar rondando los 60** she must be getting on for 60 ■ ~ *vi* (merodear) to hang around

ronquido *m* snore

ronronear [A1] *vi* to purr

roña *f* **1 (a)** (mugre) dirt, grime; **lleno de ~** covered in dirt *o* grime **(b)** (en metal) rust **(c)** (Vet) mange **2** (Méx) (juego) tag; **jugar a la ~** to play tag

roñoso -sa *adj* **1** [ESTAR] **(a)** (mugriento) grubby **(b)** (oxidado) rusty **(c)** (Vet) mangy **2** [SER] (fam) (tacaño) tight-fisted (colloq), stingy (colloq) ■ *m,f* (fam) scrooge (colloq), skinflint (colloq)

ropa *f* clothes (*pl*); **cambiarse de ~** to get changed, to change (one's clothes); **la ~ sucia** the dirty laundry; **tengo un montón de ~ para planchar** I've got a stack of ironing to do; **~ interior** underwear, underclothes (*pl*)

ropero *m* (armario) wardrobe

roquero -ra *adj/m,f* ⇒ ROCKERO

rosa *f* **(a)** (flor) rose **(b)** (rosal) rosebush **(c)** (Chi) (nudo) bow ■ *adj* (*gen inv*) ▶ **97** pink; **un vestido (de color) ~** a pink dress; **verlo todo de color ~** to see things through rose-colored glasses *o* (BrE) rose-tinted spectacles ■ *m* ▶ **97** pink

rosado -da *adj* **(a)** ▶ **97** ‹*color/vestido*› pink **(b)** ‹*mejillas*› rosy; ‹*vino*› rosé ■ *m* **(a)** ▶ **97** (color) pink **(b)** (vino) rosé

rosal *m* (árbol) rosetree; (arbusto) rosebush

rosario *m* **(a)** (Relig) (rezo) rosary; (cuentas) rosary (beads) **(b)** (serie, sarta) string

rosca *f* **(a)** (de tornillo, tuerca) thread; **tapón de ~** screw top; ***pasarse de ~***: **el tornillo se pasó de ~** the screw isn't biting; **te has pasado de ~** (fam) you've gone too far **(b)** (Bol, Col) (círculo, grupo) clique, set

rosedal *m* (CS, Méx) rose garden

roseta *f* (Arquit) rose, rosette; (de ducha) showerhead; (de regadera) spinkler (AmE), rose (BrE)

rosetón *m* (ventana) rose window, rosette; (en el techo) ceiling rose

rosquilla *f*: *type of doughnut*

rosticería *f* (Méx) ⇒ ROTISERÍA

rostizar [A4] *vt* (Méx) to roast; **pollo rostizado** roast chicken

rostro *m* **(a)** (cara) face **(b)** (Esp fam) (desfachatez) nerve (colloq), cheek (BrE colloq)

rotación *f* rotation

rotar [A1] *vt/vi* to rotate

■ **rotarse** *v pron* (en trabajo) to work on a rota system; **~se para hacer algo** to take it in turns to do sth

rotativo *m* **(a)** (period) (diario) newspaper **(b)** (Chi) (Cin) movie theater (AmE), cinema (BrE) (*showing a continuous performance*)

rotería *f* (Chi) (fam) (hecho): **fue una ~ no invitarlo** it was incredibly rude not to invite him; **me hizo una ~** he was rude to me

rotisería *f* (CS) *delicatessen selling spit-roast chickens*

roto[1] **-ta** *adj* **1 (a)** ‹*camisa*› torn, ripped; ‹*zapato*› worn-out **(b)** ‹*vaso/plato/brazo*› broken **(c)** ‹*papel*› torn; **me devolvió el libro ~** the book was falling apart when he gave it back to me **(d)** (RPl) ‹*televisor/heladera*› broken; ‹*coche*› broken down **2** (Chi fam & pey) **(a)** ‹*barrio/gente*› lower-class (pej), plebby (colloq & pej) **(b)** (mal educado) rude ■ *m,f* **1** (Chi) **(a)** (fam & pey) (de clase baja) pleb (colloq & pej) **(b)** (fam & pey) (mal educado): **es una rota, nunca saluda** she's so rude, she doesn't even say hello **2** (Per fam) (chileno) Chilean

roto[2] *m* (Esp) (agujero) hole

rotonda *f* (glorieta) traffic circle (AmE), roundabout (BrE)

rotoso -sa *adj* **(a)** (CS, Per fam) ‹*persona/ropa*› scruffy **(b)** (Chi fam & pey) ‹*barrio/gente*› lower-class (pej)

rótula *f* (Anat) kneecap

rotulador *m* (Esp) felt-tip pen

rótulo *m* **(a)** (Impr) (título) title; (encabezamiento) heading **(b)** (etiqueta) label **(c)** (letrero) sign

rotundo -da *adj* **(a)** ‹*respuesta*› categorical, emphatic; ‹*negativa*› categorical, outright (*before n*); **me contestó con un 'no' ~** his answer was an emphatic 'no' **(b)** ‹*éxito/fracaso*› resounding

rotura *f*: **hay una ~ en la cañería** there's a burst in the pipe; **sufrió ~ de cadera** she fractured her hip; **tiene ~ de ligamentos** she has torn ligaments; **tiene una ~ en la manga** (CS) it has a rip in the sleeve

round /rraun/ *m* (Dep) round

rozado -da *adj* (gastado) worn; (sucio) grubby

rozadura *f* scratch; **le hizo una ~ al coche** he scratched the car; **los zapatos nuevos le hicieron una ~** her new shoes rubbed

rozagante *adj* (AmL) healthy

rozamiento *m* friction

rozar [A4] *vt* (tocar ligeramente): **el gato me rozó la pierna** the cat brushed against my leg; **sus labios ~on mi frente** her lips brushed my forehead; **las sillas rozan la pared** the chairs rub *o* scrape against the wall; **la bala le rozó el brazo** the bullet grazed his arm; **me roza el zapato** my shoe's rubbing

■ **rozarse** *v pron* **(a)** (*recipr*) «*cables/piezas*» to chafe; «*manos/labios*» to touch **(b)** (*refl*) ‹*brazo/rodillas*› to graze **(c)** «*cuello/puños*» to wear **(d)** (Méx) «*bebé*» to get diaper rash (AmE), get nappy rash (BrE); **el bebé está rozado** the baby has diaper (AmE) *o* (BrE) nappy rash

Rte. (= **remite** *or* **remitente**) sender

ruana *f* ruana (*Colombian, Venezuelan poncho*)

rubeola *f* German measles

rubí *m* **(a)** (Min) ruby **(b)** (de reloj) jewel **(c)** (color) **▶97**: **de color ~ rubí** ruby red

rubio -bia *adj* **▶97** ‹*pelo*› fair, blonde; ‹*hombre*› fair-haired, blond; ‹*mujer*› fair-haired, blonde ■ *m, f* (*m*) blond *o* fair-haired man; (*f*) blonde *o* fair-haired woman, blonde (colloq)

rublo *m* ruble*

rubor *m* **(a)** (liter) (sonrojo) flush; **el ~ de sus mejillas la delató** her flushed cheeks betrayed her **(b)** (Méx, RPl) (cosmética) rouge, blusher

ruborizarse [A4] *v pron* to blush, to turn red (in the face), to flush

rúbrica *f* (de firma) flourish; (firma) signing

rubro *m* (esp AmL) **(a)** (área) area; **nuestro ~ de peletería** our line in furs; **trabaja en el ~ de la computación** he works in computers **(b)** (en contabilidad — apartado) heading; (— renglón) item

rucio -cia *adj* **(a)** ‹*caballo*› gray* **(b)** (Chi fam) ‹*pelo*› fair, blonde; ‹*hombre*› fair-haired, blond; ‹*mujer*› fair-haired, blonde

ruco -ca *adj* (Méx fam) old

rudimentario -ria *adj* rudimentary

rudimento *m* rudiment

rudo -da *adj* (tosco) rough, rude (arch)

rueca *f* distaff

rueda *f* **(a)** (de vehículo, mecanismo) wheel; **~ de molino** millstone; **~ dentada** gear wheel, cogwheel; **~ de recambio** *or* **repuesto** *or* (RPL) **de auxilio** spare wheel; **patinar sobre ~s** to rollerskate; ***ir sobre ~s*** to go *o* run smoothly **(b)** (neumático) tire*; **se me pinchó una ~** I got a flat tire *o* a puncture **(c)** (de mueble) caster, roller **(d)** (corro) ring, circle; **~ de prensa** press conference **(e)** (en gimnasia) cartwheel

ruedo *m* **(a)** (Taur) bullring **(b)** (esp AmL) (de falda, pantalón) hem

ruego *m* **(a)** (súplica) plea; **de nada te servirán tus ~s** your pleading will get you nowhere **(b)** (petición) request; **en respuesta a un ~ de sus oyentes** in response to a request from his listeners

rufián *m* (granuja) rogue, scoundrel (dated); (chulo) pimp

rugby /'rruɣbi/ *m* rugby

rugido *m* roar

rugir [I7] *vi* «*león/mar/viento*» to roar

rugoso -sa *adj* rough, bumpy

ruibarbo *m* rhubarb

ruido *m* noise; **sin hacer ~** quietly; **no hagas tanto ~** don't make so much noise

ruidoso -sa *adj* ‹*calle/máquina/persona*› noisy

ruin *adj* (mezquino, vil) despicable, contemptible; (avaro) miserly, mean (BrE)

ruina *f* **(a)** (bancarrota) ruin; **dejar a algn en la ~** to ruin sb; **estar en la ~** «*empresario*» to be ruined; «*país*» to be in financial ruin; **la compañía está en la ~** the company has collapsed **(b)** (perdición) downfall; **el juego fue su ~** gambling was his downfall **(c)** (hundimiento) collapse; **la casa amenaza ~** the house is on the point of collapse **(d) ruinas** *fpl* (de edificio, ciudad) ruins (*pl*); **en ~s** in ruins

ruiseñor *m* nightingale

rulero *m* (Per, RPl) curler

ruleta *f* roulette

ruletero -ra *m,f* (Méx fam) cab *o* taxi driver, cabbie (colloq)

rulo *m* (para el pelo) curler, roller; (rizo) (CS, Per) curl

rulot *f* (Esp) trailer (AmE), caravan (BrE)

ruma *f* (Chi) pile, heap

Rumania, **Rumanía** *f* Romania

rumano[1] **-na** *adj/m,f* Romanian, Rumanian

rumano[2] *m* (idioma) Romanian, Rumanian

rumba *f* rumba

rumbo *m* (dirección) direction, course; (Náut) course; **caminar sin ~ fijo** to wander aimlessly; **partió (con) ~ a Toluca** he set off for Toluca; **navegar con ~ norte** to sail a northerly course; **los acontecimientos tomaron un ~ trágico** events took a tragic turn

rumiante *m* ruminant

rumiar [A1] *vi* «*vaca*» to chew the cud, ruminate

rumor *m* **(a)** (murmuración) rumor*; **circulan ~es de que** ... rumors are circulating that ..., rumor has it that ... **(b)** (sonido) murmur

rumorear [A1] *vt*: **se rumorea que** ... rumor has it that ...

rupestre *adj* ‹*pintura/dibujo*› cave (*before n*); ‹*planta*› rock (*before n*)

rupia *f* rupee

ruptura *f* **(a)** (de relaciones, negaciones) breaking-off; (de contrato) breach, breaking; (de matrimonio) break-up; (con pasado, tradición) break; **ésa fue la causa de la ~ de las negociaciones** that was what caused the negotiations to be broken off **(b)** (Dep) (en tenis) service break

rural *adj* rural

Rusia *f* Russia

ruso[1] **-sa** *adj/m,f* Russian

ruso[2] *m* (idioma) Russian

rústica (esp Esp): **en rústica** (*loc adj*) ‹*edición*› paperback (*before n*); **un libro en ~** a paperback

rústico -ca *adj* (del campo) rustic; (basto) coarse

ruta *f* **(a)** (itinerario) route **(b)** (RPl) (carretera) road

rutina *f* routine; **inspección de ~** routine inspection; **por pura ~** out of habit

rutinario -ria *adj* **(a)** ‹*trabajo/vida*› monotonous **(b)** ‹*inspección/procedimiento*› routine (*before n*)

Ss

S, **s** *f* (*read as* /'ese/) *the letter* S, s

s. *m* (= **siglo**) C; **s.XX** C20

S (= **sur**) ▶ 346 S, South

S. (= **santo**) St

S.A. (= **Sociedad Anónima**) ≈Inc (*in US*), ≈Ltd (*in UK*), ≈PLC (*in UK*)

sábado *m* ▶ 193 Saturday; (Relig) Sabbath; **~ de Gloria** *or* **Santo** Easter Saturday; **~ inglés** (CS) *non-working Saturday*

sabana *f* (Geog) savanna*, grassland

sábana *f* sheet; **~ ajustable** *or* (Méx) **de cajón** fitted sheet; **~ bajera/encimera** bottom/top sheet

sabandija *f* **1** (insecto) creepy-crawly (colloq), bug; (reptil) creepy-crawly (colloq) **2 sabandija** *mf* (AmL fam) (pícaro) rascal (colloq)

sabañón *m* chilblain; ⇒ COMER[1]

sabático -ca *adj* sabbatical

sabelotodo *mf* (fam) know-it-all (AmE colloq), know-all (BrE colloq)

saber[1] *m* knowledge; **una persona de gran ~** a person of great learning

saber[2] [E25] *vt* **1 (a)** ‹*nombre/dirección/canción*› to know; **ya lo sé** I know; **no lo sé** I don't know; **no sé cómo se llama** I don't know his name; **¡yo qué sé!** how (on earth) should I know! (colloq); **que yo sepa** as far as I know; **~ algo** DE **algo** to know sth ABOUT sth; **sé muy poco de ese tema** I know very little about the subject; **no sabe lo que dice** he doesn't know what he's talking about **(b)** (enterarse) to find out; **lo supe por mi hermana** I found out about it through my sister; **sin que lo supiéramos** without our knowing; **¡si yo lo hubiera sabido antes!** if I had only known before!; **¡cómo iba yo a ~ que ...!** how was I to know that ...! **2** (ser capaz de): **~ hacer algo** to know how to do sth; **¿sabes nadar?** can you swim?, do you know how to swim?; **sabe escuchar** she's a good listener; **sabe hablar varios idiomas** she can speak several languages ■ **~** *vi* **I (a)** (tener conocimiento) to know; **¿quién sabe?** who knows?; **~** DE **algo/algn** to know OF sth/sb; **yo sé de un lugar donde te lo pueden arreglar** I know of a place where you can get it fixed **(b)** (tener noticias, enterarse): **no sé nada de ella desde hace más de un mes** I haven't heard from her for over a month; **yo supe del accidente por la radio** I heard about the accident on the radio

II (a) (tener sabor) (+ *compl*) to taste; **sabe dulce/bien** it tastes sweet/nice; **~** A **algo** to taste OF sth; **no sabe a nada** it doesn't taste of anything; **sabe a podrido** it tastes rotten **(b)** (causar cierta impresión): **me sabe mal** *or* **no me sabe bien tener que decírselo** I don't like having to tell him

■ **saberse** *v pron* (*enf*) ‹*lección/poema*› to know

sabido -da *adj* [SER] well-known; **como es ~** as everybody knows

sabiduría *f* wisdom

sabiendas: **a ~** (*loc adv*): **lo hizo a ~ de que me molestaba** he did it knowing full well *o* perfectly well that I found it annoying

sabihondo -da *m,f* (fam) know-it-all (AmE colloq), know-all (BrE colloq)

sabio -bia *adj* (con grandes concocimientos) learned, wise; (sensato) ‹*persona/medida*› wise; ‹*consejo*› sound, wise ■ *m,f(m)* wise man, sage (liter); *(f)* wise woman

sable *m* **1** (Arm) saber*; (Náut) batten **2** (en heráldica) sable

sabor *m* **(a)** (de comida, bebida, etc) taste, flavor*; **con ~ a menta** mint-flavoured; **viene en tres ~es** it comes in three flavors; **no tiene ~** it has no taste to it **(b)** (carácter) flavor*

saborear [A1] *vt* to savor*; ‹*éxito/triunfo*› to relish

sabotaje *m* sabotage

saboteador -dora *m,f* saboteur

sabotear [A1] *vt* to sabotage

sabré, **sabría, etc** *see* SABER

sabroso -sa *adj* **1** ‹*comida*› tasty, delicious; ‹*chisme/historia*› spicy (colloq), juicy (colloq) **2** (AmL fam) (agradable) ‹*música/ritmo*› pleasant, nice; ‹*clima/agua*› beautiful

sabrosón -sona *adj* **(a)** (AmL fam) ‹*guiso*› tasty, delicious; ‹*fruta*› delicious **(b)** (AmL fam) ‹*clima*› mild **(c)** (Col, Méx, Ven fam) ‹*música*› pleasant

sabueso *m* (Zool) bloodhound

sacacorchos *m* (*pl* ~) corkscrew

sacapuntas *m* (*pl* ~) pencil sharpener

sacar [A2] *vt* **I 1** (extraer) **(a)** ‹*billetera/lápiz*› to take out, get out; ‹*pistola/espada*› to draw; **~ algo DE algo** to take *o* get sth OUT OF sth; **lo saqué del cajón** I took *o* got it out of the drawer **(b)** ‹*muela*› to pull out, take out; ‹*riñón/cálculo*› to remove; **me ~on sangre** they took some blood **(c)** ‹*diamantes/cobre/petróleo*› to extract **(d)** ‹*carta/ficha*› to draw **2** (poner, llevar fuera) **(a)** ‹*maceta/mesa/basura*› to take out; **sácalo aquí al sol** bring it out here into the sun; **tuvimos que ~lo por la ventana** we had to get it out through the window; **~ el perro a pasear** to take the dog out for a walk; **~ el coche del garaje** to get the car out of the garage **(b)** (invitar): **el marido no la saca nunca** her husband never takes her out; **~ a algn a bailar** to ask sb to dance **(c)** ‹*parte del cuerpo*› to put out; **me sacó la lengua** he stuck *o* put his tongue out at me **3** (retirar) to take out; **~ dinero del banco** to take out *o* withdraw money from the bank **4** (de una situación difícil) **~ a algn DE algo** ‹*de apuro/atolladero*› to get sb OUT OF sth **5** (Esp) ‹*dobladillo*› to let down; ‹*pantalón/falda*› (alargar) to let down; (ensanchar) to let out

II (obtener) **1** ‹*pasaporte/permiso*› to get; ‹*entrada/billete*› to get, buy **2 (a)** ‹*votos/puntos/calificación*› to get **(b)** ‹*premio*› to get, win **(c)** ‹*conclusión*› to draw **(d)** ‹*suma/cuenta*› to do, work out **3** ‹*beneficio*› to get; ‹*ganancia*› to make; **¿qué sacas con eso?** what do you gain by doing that?; **no sacó ningún provecho del curso** she didn't get anything out of the course **4 ~ algo DE algo** ‹*idea/información*› to get sth FROM sth; ‹*porciones/unidades*› to get sth OUT OF sth; **~le algo A algn** ‹*dinero/información*› to get sth OUT OF sb **5** ‹*brillo*› to bring out; **~le brillo a algo** to polish sth to a shine

III 1 (a) ‹*libro*› to publish, bring out; ‹*disco*› to bring out, release; ‹*modelo/producto*› to bring out **(b)** ‹*tema*› to bring up **(c)** ‹*foto*› to take; ‹*copia*› to make, take; ‹*apuntes*› to make, take; **~le una foto a algn** to take a photo of sb **(d)** (Esp) ‹*defecto/falta*› (+ *me/te/le etc*) to find; **a todo le tiene que ~ faltas** he always has to find fault with everything **2 sacar adelante** ‹*proyecto*› (poner en marcha) to get sth off the ground; (salvar de la crisis) to keep sth going; **luché tanto para ~ adelante a mis hijos** I fought so hard to give my children a good start in life **3** (Dep) ‹*tiro libre/falta*› to take

IV (quitar) **1** (esp AmL) **(a) ~le algo A algn** ‹*botas/gorro*› to take sth OFF sb **(b) ~le algo A algo** ‹*tapa/cubierta*› to take sth OFF sth **(c)** (retirar): **saca esto de aquí** take this away; **saquen los libros de la mesa** take the books off the table **(d)** (hacer desaparecer) ‹*mancha*› to remove, get ... out ■ **~** *vi* (Dep) (en tenis, vóleibol) to serve; (en fútbol) to kick off

■ **sacarse** *v pron* (*refl*) **1** (extraer) ‹*astilla/púa*› to take ... out; ‹*ojo*› to poke ... out; **me tengo que ~ una muela** (*caus*) I have to have a tooth out; **~se algo DE algo** to take sth OUT OF sth; **sácate las manos de los bolsillos** take your hands out of your pockets **2** (AmL) (quitarse) ‹*ropa/zapatos*› to take off; ‹*maquillaje*› to remove, take off **3 (a)** (*caus*) ‹*foto*›: **tengo que ~me una foto** I have to have my photo taken **(b)** (AmL) ‹*calificación/nota*› to get

sacarina *f* saccharin

sacerdote *m* priest

sacerdotisa *f* priestess

saciar [A1] *vt* ‹*hambre*› to satisfy; ‹*sed*› to quench; ‹*deseo*› (liter) to satiate (liter); ‹*ambición*› to fulfill*, realize

■ **saciarse** *v pron:* **comer/beber hasta ~se** to eat/drink one's fill

saco *m* **1** (continente) sack; (contenido) sack, sackful; **~ de dormir** sleeping bag **2** (AmL) (de tela) jacket; **~ sport** (AmL) sports coat (AmE), sports jacket (BrE)

sacramento *m* sacrament; **los últimos ~s** the last rites

sacrificado -da *adj* ‹*persona*› selfless, self-sacrificing

sacrificar [A2] *vt* **(a)** (Relig) ‹*cordero/víctimas*› to sacrifice **(b)** ‹*res/ganado*› to slaughter; ‹*perro/gato*› (euf) to put ... to sleep (euph) **(c)** ‹*carrera/juventud*› to sacrifice

■ **sacrificarse** *v pron* to make sacrifices

sacrificio *m* **(a)** (privación, renuncia) sacrifice **(b)** (inmolación) sacrifice **(c)** (de res) slaughter

sacrilegio *m* sacrilege

sacrílego -ga *adj* sacrilegious

sacristán *m* sacristan, verger

sacristía *f* vestry, sacristy

sacudida *f* **(a)** (agitando) shake, shaking; (golpeando) beating **(b)** (de terremoto) tremor; (de explosión) blast; (de tren, coche) jerk, jolt **(c)** (fam) (descarga) electric shock

sacudir [I1] *vt* **1 (a)** (agitar) ‹*toalla/alfombra*› to shake; (golpear) ‹*alfombra/colchón*› to beat; **sacudió la arena de la toalla** he shook the sand out of the towel **(b)** (fam) ‹*niño*› to clobber (colloq); **~ la cabeza** (para negar) to shake one's head; (para afirmar) to nod (one's head) **(c)** (hacer temblar) to shake **(d)** (CS, Méx) (limpiar) to dust, do the dusting **2** (conmover, afectar) to shake ■ **~** *vi* (CS, Méx) to dust

■ **sacudirse** *v pron* (*refl*) (quitarse) ‹*arena/polvo*› to shake off

sádico -ca *adj* sadistic ■ *m,f* sadist

sadismo *m* sadism

sadomasoquismo *m* sadomasochism

sadomasoquista *mf* sadomasochist

safari *m* **(a)** (gira, viaje) safari; **ir de ~** to go on safari **(b)** (zoológico) safari park

sagaz *adj* shrewd, astute

Sagitario *m* (signo, constelación) Sagittarius; **es (de) ~** she's (a) Sagittarian ■ *mf* (*pl* **~** *or* **-rios**) (persona) *tb* **sagitario** Sagittarian, Sagittarius

sagrado -da *adj* **1** (Relig) ‹*altar*› holy; ‹*lugar*› holy, sacred **2** (fundamental, intocable) sacred

Sahara /sa'ara/ *m*: **el (desierto del) ~** the Sahara (Desert)

sajón -jona *adj/m,f* Saxon

sal *f* **1** (Coc) salt; **mantequilla sin ~** unsalted butter; ***echarle la ~ a algn*** (Méx fam) to put a jinx on sb **2** (Quím) salt; **~ de fruta** liver salts (*pl*); **~es de baño** bath salts (*pl*)

sal *see* SALIR

sala *f* **(a)** (de casa) *tb* **~ de estar** living room, lounge (BrE) **(b)** (de hotel) lounge; (en hospital) ward; (para reuniones, conferencias) hall; (Teatr) theater*; (Cin) movie theater (AmE), cinema (BrE); **~ cuna** (Chi) day nursery, creche; **~ de clases** (CS frml) classroom; **~ de embarque** departure lounge; **~ de espera** waiting room; **~ de exposiciones** gallery, exhibition hall; **~ de fiestas** night club (*usually featuring dancing and cabaret*); **~ de profesores** staff room **(c)** (sede de tribunal) courtroom, court

salado -da *adj* **1** (Coc) **(a)** (con sal) ‹*almendras/bacalao*› salted; ‹*gusto*› salty; **está demasiado ~** it's too salty **(b)** [SER] (no dulce) ‹*plato/comida*› savory* **2 (a)** (fam) ‹*persona*› (gracioso) funny, witty **(b)** (fam) ‹*chiste*› risqué; ‹*anécdota*› spicy **3** (Méx fam) (que trae mala suerte) jinxed (colloq)

salamandra *f* (Zool) salamander; (estufa) salamander stove

salame *m* **(a)** (CS) (Coc) salami **(b)** (RPl fam) (tonto) idiot

salar[1] [A1] *vt* **(a)** (para conservar) ‹*carne/pescado*› to salt (down); ‹*pieles*› to salt **(b)** (para condimentar) to salt, add salt to

■ **salarse** *v pron* (Méx fam) (echarse a perder) «*planes*» to fall through; «*negocio*» to go bust

salar[2] *m* (Chi) salt pan, salt flat

salario *m* (frml) wage, salary

salchicha *f* sausage

salchichón *m*: *spiced sausage similar to salami*

salchichonería *f* (Méx) delicatessen

saldar [A1] *vt* **(a)** ‹*cuenta*› to settle; ‹*deuda*› to settle, pay (off) **(b)** ‹*mercancías/productos*› to sell off

saldo *m* **1** (de cuenta) balance; **~ a su/nuestro favor** credit/debit balance **2 (a)** (artículo): **los ~s no se cambian** sale goods cannot be exchanged; **precios de ~** sale prices; Ⓢ **venta de saldos** clearance sale **(b)** **saldos** *mpl* (rebajas) sales (*pl*)

saldré, **saldría**, **etc** *see* SALIR

salero *m* **1** (recipiente) salt shaker (AmE), saltcellar (BrE) **2** (fam) (gracia): **tener ~** (contando chistes) to be funny; (bailando) to be stylish

salga, **salgas, etc** *see* SALIR

salida *f* **I** (hacia el exterior) **1 (a)** (lugar, puerta) exit; **~ de emergencia/incendios** emergency/fire exit; **todas las ~s de Bilbao** all the roads out of Bilbao; **es una calle sin ~** it's a dead end **(b)** (de tubería) outlet, outflow; (de circuito) outlet **2 (a)** (acción): **me lo encontré a la ~** I met him on my way out; **nos encontramos a la ~ del concierto** we met at the door after the concert; **una ~ al campo** an outing *o* a trip to the country **(b)** (de líquido, gas, electricidad) output **(c)** **la ~ del sol** sunrise

II (partida) **1** (de tren, avión) departure; **el tren efectuará su ~ por la vía cinco** the train will leave from track five; Ⓢ **salidas nacionales/internacionales** domestic/international departures **2** (Dep) (en una carrera) start

III 1 (solución): **no le veo ninguna ~ a esta situación** I can see no way out of this situation; **no nos queda otra ~** we have no other option **2** (Com, Fin) (gasto) payment

salido -da *adj* ‹*ojos/dientes*› protruding; ‹*frente/mentón*› prominent

saliente *adj* ‹*pómulo/hueso*› prominent; ‹*cornisa/balcón*› projecting ■ *f or* (Esp) *m* (de edificio, muro) projection; (de precipicio) ledge

salir [I29] *vi* **I 1** (partir) to leave; **¿a qué hora sale el tren?** what time does the train leave?; **el jefe había salido de viaje** the boss was away; **salió corriendo** (fam) she was off like a shot (colloq); **~** DE **algo** to leave FROM sth; **¿de qué andén sale el tren?** what platform does the train leave from?; **salgo de casa a las siete** I leave home at seven; **~** PARA **algo** to leave FOR sth **2** (al exterior — acercándose al hablante) to come out; (— alejándose del hablante) to go out; **no salgas sin abrigo** don't go out without a coat; **no puedo ~, me he quedado encerrado** I can't get out, I'm trapped in here; **~** DE **algo** to come out/get out OF sth; **¡sal de ahí/de aquí!** come out of there/get out of here!; **¿de dónde salió este dinero?** where did this money come from?; **nunca ha salido de España** he's never been out of Spain; **~ por la ventana/por la puerta** to get out through the window/leave by the door; **salieron al balcón/al jardín** they went out onto the balcony/into the garden; **¿por aquí se sale a la carretera?** can I get on to the road this way?; **salió a hacer las compras** she's gone out (to do the) shopping **3** (habiendo terminado algo) to leave; **¿a qué hora sales de clase?** what time do you get out of class *o* finish your class?; **¿cuándo sale del hospital?** when is he coming out of (the) hospital? **4 (a)** (como entretenimiento) to go out; **salir a cenar** to go out for dinner **(b)** (tener una relación) to go out; **~** CON **algn** to go out WITH sb **5** «*clavo/tapón/mancha*» to come out; «*anillo*» to come off

II 1 (aparecer, manifestarse) **(a)** «*cana/sarpullido*» to appear; (+ *me/te/le etc*) **me empiezan a ~ canas** I'm starting to go gray; **le están saliendo los dientes** she's teething; **me salió una ampolla** I've got a blister; **le salió un sarpullido** he came out in a rash; **me salieron granos** I broke out *o* (BrE) came out in spots; **me sale sangre de la nariz** my nose is bleeding; **a la planta le están saliendo hojas nuevas** the plant's putting out new leaves **(b)** «*sol*» (por la mañana) to rise, come up; (de detrás de una nube) to come out **(c)** (surgir) «*tema/idea*» to come up **(d)** «*carta*» (en naipes) to come up **2 (a)** «*revista/novela*» to come out; «*disco*» to come out, be released; **~ al mercado** to come on to the market **(b)** (en televisión, el periódico) to appear **(c)** (en una foto) to appear; (+ *compl*) **saliste muy bien en la foto** you came out very well in the photo

III 1 (expresando logro) (+ *me/te/le etc*): **no me sale esta ecuación** I can't do this equation; **ahora mismo no me sale su nombre** (fam) I can't think of her name right now; **no le salían las palabras** he couldn't get his words out **2 (a)** (costar) to work out; **sale más barato/caro** it works out less/more expensive **(b)** (resultar): **todo salió bien** everything turned out *o* worked out well; **salió tal como lo planeamos** it turned out just as we planned; **no salió ninguna de las fotos** none of the photographs came out; **¿qué número salió premiado?** what was the winning number?; **~ bien/mal en un examen** (Chi fam) to pass/fail an exam; (+ *me/te/le etc*) **el postre no me salió bien** the dessert didn't come out right **3** (de situación, estado) **~ DE algo** ‹*de apuro*› to get out of sth; ‹*de depresión*› to get over sth; **salieron ilesos del accidente** they were not hurt in the accident; **~ *adelante*** «*negocio*» to stay afloat, survive; «*propuesta*» to prosper; **lograron ~ adelante** they managed to get through it **4** (con preposición) **(a) salir a** (parecerse a) to take after **(b) salir con** (Col) (combinar con) to go with

■ salirse *v pron* **1 (a)** (de borde, límite) «*agua*» to overflow; «*leche*» to boil over; **~se DE algo** ‹*de carretera*› to come/go off sth; ‹*de tema*› to get off sth; **el río se salió de su cauce** the river overflowed its banks; **procura no ~te del presupuesto** try to keep within the budget **(b)** (por orificio, grieta) «*agua/tinta*» to leak (out), come out; «*gas*» to escape, come out **2** (soltarse) «*pedazo/pieza*» to come off; (+ *me/te/le etc*) **estos zapatos se me salen** these shoes are too big for me **3** (irse) to leave; **~se DE algo** ‹*de asociación*› to leave sth; ***~se con la suya*** to get one's (own) way

saliva *f* saliva, spit (colloq)

salivar [A1] *vi* to salivate

salmo *m* psalm

salmón *m* salmon **■** *adj inv* ▶97 salmon-pink, salmon, salmon-colored*

salmonete *m* red mullet, surmullet (AmE)

salmuera *f* brine

salón *m* **(a)** (en casa particular) living room, sitting room (BrE), lounge (BrE) **(b)** (en hotel) reception room, function room **(c)** (en palacio) hall **(d)** (de clases) classroom; **~ de actos** auditorium (AmE), assembly hall (BrE); **~ de baile** ballroom; **~ de belleza** beauty salon, beauty parlor; **~ de fiestas** (AmL) function room, reception room; **~ náutico/del automóvil** boat/motor show

salpicadera *f* (Méx) (de coche, bicicleta) fender (AmE), mudguard (BrE)

salpicadero *m* (Esp) dashboard

salpicadura *f* splash

salpicar [A2] *vt* (de agua) to splash; (de barro, aceite) to splash, spatter

salpicón *m* (de pescado, ave) *chopped seafood or meat with onion, tomato and peppers*

salsa *f* **1** (Coc) sauce; (de jugo de carne) gravy; **~ bechamel** *or* **blanca** bechamel (sauce); **~ de tomate** (sofrito) tomato sauce; (catsup) (Col) ketchup, catsup (AmE) **2** (Mús) salsa

saltamontes *m* (*pl* **~**) grasshopper

saltar [A1] *vi* **1 (a)** (brincar) to jump; (más alto, más lejos) to leap; **~ a la cuerda** *or* (Esp) **comba** to jump rope (AmE), to skip (BrE); **~ de alegría** to jump for joy; **~ con** *or* **en una pierna** to hop; **~ de la cama/silla** to jump out of bed/one's chair **(b)** (en atletismo) to jump **(c)** «*pelota*» to bounce **(d)** (lanzarse) to jump; **~ al agua** to jump into the water; **~ en paracaídas** to parachute; **¿sabes ~ del trampolín?** can you dive off the springboard?; **saltó al vacío** he leapt into space; **~ SOBRE algo/algn** to jump ON sth/sb **2** (pasar) **~ DE algo A algo** to jump FROM sth TO sth; **saltaba de una idea a otra** she kept jumping from one idea to the next **3** «*botón*» to come off, pop off; «*chispas*» to fly; «*aceite*» to spit; «*corcho*» to pop out; «*fusibles*» to blow; **la bomba hizo ~ el coche por los aires** the bomb blew the car into the air **■ ~** *vt* ‹*obstáculo/valla/zanja*› to jump (over); (apoyándose) to vault (over)

■ saltarse *v pron* **1 (a)** (omitir) ‹*línea/página/nombre*› to skip, miss out; ‹*comida*› to miss, skip **(b)** ‹*semáforo/stop*› to jump **2** «*botón*» to come off, pop off; «*pintura*» to chip; **se le ~on las lágrimas** her eyes filled with tears **3** (Chi) «*diente/loza*» to chip

salteado -da *adj*: **¿se pueden contestar las preguntas salteadas?** can we answer the questions in any order?; **leí unos capítulos ~s** I read a few odd chapters

saltear [A1] *vt* (Coc) to sauté

saltimbanqui *m* (Espec, Hist) tumbler, acrobat

salto *m* **1 (a)** (brinco) jump; **se levantó de un ~** (de la cama) he leapt *o* sprang out of bed; (del suelo) he leapt *o* jumped up from the floor; **se puso en pie de un ~** she leapt *o* sprang to her feet; **los pájaros se acercaban dando saltitos** the birds were hopping closer to me/us; **dar** *or* **pegar un ~** (dar un brinco) to jump; (de susto) to start, jump; **daban ~s de alegría** they were jumping for joy **(b)** (Dep) (en atletismo, esquí, paracaidismo) jump; (en natación) dive; **~ con pértiga** *or* (AmL) **garrocha** pole vault; **~ de altura/longitud** high/long jump; **~ (en) alto/(en) largo** (AmL) high/long jump; **~ mortal** somersault **2** (Geog) *tb* **~ de agua** waterfall

saltón -tona *adj* ‹*ojos*› bulging

salud *f* **1** (Med) health; **estar bien de ~** to be in good health; **gozar de buena ~** to enjoy good health **2 ¡~!** (al brindar) cheers!; (cuando alguien estornuda) (AmL) bless you!

Saludos y presentaciones

Cuando el trato es familiar

hola ¿qué tal (estás)?	= hi, how are you?
muy bien gracias, ¿y tú?	= fine, thanks, how about you?
muy bien gracias	= fine, thanks
hola ¿qué hay? *or* ¿qué cuentas (de nuevo)?	= hi, how are things? *o* (AmE) what's up?
aquí ando, tirando	= not too bad

Otras posibles respuestas:

así así	= so-so
igual que siempre	= as ever
nada nuevo	= same as ever
hola, te presento a María/a mi hermana	= hi, this is María/my sister
	= hi, I'd like you to meet María, my sister
hola ¿qué tal?	= hello *o* hi, nice to meet you

Cuando el trato es formal

hola, buenos días ¿cómo está usted?	= hello, how are you?
muy bien gracias ¿y usted?	= very well, thank you, and yourself?
muy bien también, gracias	= I'm very well, thank you
buenos días, le presento al Sr. León	= good morning, this is Mr. León
Juan, le presento al	= Juan, meet Mr. León
Sr. León	= Juan, I'd like you to meet Mr. León
permítame presentarle *or* que le presente al Sr. León	= allow me to introduce Mr. León
¿cómo está? encantado (de conocerlo) *or* mucho gusto	= how do you do? *o* pleased to meet you

Conocer a la gente y hablar de uno mismo

¿cómo te llamas? ¿cómo se llama usted?	= what's your name?
José *or* me llamo José pero me dicen Pepe	= José *o* my name is José but people call me Pepe
yo soy María y ella es Ana	= I'm María and this is Ana
¿de dónde eres/ es usted?	= where are you from? *o* where do you come from?
soy de Madrid	= I'm *o* I come from Madrid
soy español	= I'm Spanish
¿dónde vives/vive?	= where do you live?
(vivo) en Londres	= (I live) in London
¿qué haces/hace usted? ¿en qué trabajas/ trabaja?	= what do you do?
soy profesora/ estudiante/escritora	= I'm a teacher/a student/ a writer

Nótese el uso del artículo indefinido a en inglés en la traducción anterior

soy *or* (esp Esp) estoy soltera/casada	= I'm single/married
soy *or* (esp Esp) estoy viuda	= I'm a widow

Nótese el uso del artículo indefinido a en esta última traducción

¿tiene usted/tienes hijos?	= do you have (any) children?
no *or* no, no tengo	= no, I don't
tengo tres hijos, dos niños y una niña	= I have three children, two boys and a girl

saludable *adj* ‹*clima/alimentación*› healthy; ‹*experiencia*› salutary

saludar [A1] *vt* **(a)** ‹*persona*› to greet, say hello to; **saluda a tu hermano de mi parte** give my regards to your brother; **lo saluda atentamente** (Corresp) Sincerely (yours) (AmE), Yours sincerely (BrE); **los saludó con la mano** she waved at them **(b)** (Mil) to salute ■ ~ *vi* **(a)** (de palabra) to say hello (*o* good morning *etc*) **(b)** (con la mano) to wave **(c)** (Mil) to salute

■ **saludarse** *v pron* (*recipr*) to say hello to *o* greet each other

saludo *m* **(a)** greeting; **te mandan ~s** they send (you) their regards *o* best wishes; **~s** (Corresp) best wishes; **le hice un ~ con la mano** I gave him a wave, I waved to him **(b)** (Mil) salute

salva *f*: **una ~ de 21 cañonazos** a 21-gun salute *o* salvo; **una ~ de aplausos** a burst *o* round of applause

salvación *f* salvation

salvado *m* bran

salvador -dora *m,f* savior*

Salvador *ver* EL SALVADOR

salvadoreño -ña *adj/m,f* Salvadoran, Salvadorean

salvaguardar [A1] *vt* to safeguard

salvaguardia *f* safeguard, defense*

salvaje *adj* **1 (a)** ‹*animal*› wild **(b)** (primitivo) ‹*tribu*› savage **(c)** ‹*vegetación/terreno*› wild **2** (cruel) ‹*persona/tortura*› brutal; ‹*ataque/matanza*› savage ■ *mf* (primitivo) savage; (bruto) (pey) animal, savage

salvamanteles *m* (*pl* ~) (para platos, fuentes) tablemat; (para vasos) coaster

salvamento *m* rescue; **equipo de ~** rescue team

salvar [A1] *vt* **1** (en general) to save; **~ algo/a algn** DE **algo** to save sth/sb FROM sth **2 (a)** ‹*dificultad/obstáculo*› to overcome **(b)** ‹*distancia*› to cover **(c)** (Per, Ur) ‹*examen*› to pass

■ **salvarse** *v pron* to survive; **¡sálvese quien pueda!** every man for himself!; **~se DE algo** ‹*de accidente/incendio*› to survive sth; **se ~on de una muerte segura** they escaped certain death

salvavidas *mf* (*pl* ~) **(a)** (persona) lifeguard **(b) salvavidas** *m* (flotador) life jacket, life preserver (frml)

salvia *f* sage

salvo: **a ~** (*loc adv*) **poner algo a ~** to put sth in a safe place; **los niños están a ~** the children are safe *o* unharmed; **ponerse a ~** to reach safety; **a ~ de** safe from ■ *prep* (excepto) except, apart from; **~ que** unless

salvoconducto *m* safe-conduct

samba *m or f* samba

San *adj* (*apócope de* SANTO *usado delante de nombres de varón excepto Domingo, Tomás y Tomé*) St, Saint

sanar [A1] *vi* «*enfermo*» to get well, recover; «*herida*» to heal; **~ DE algo** to recover FROM sth

sanatorio *m* **(a)** (para convalecientes) nursing home, sanitarium (AmE), sanatorium (BrE) **(b)** (hospital) clinic, hospital (*usually private*) **(c)** (Col, Ven) (hospital psiquiátrico) psychiatric hospital

sanción *f* **1** (castigo a empleado, obrero) disciplinary measure; (Der) sanction, penalty; **una ~ de tres partidos** a three-game ban *o* suspension; **~ económica** (multa) fine; **sanciones económicas** (a país) economic sanctions **2** (de ley) sanction; (de costumbre) sanction (frml), authorization

sancionar [A1] *vt* **1** (multar) to fine; (castigar) ‹*empleado/obrero*› to discipline; ‹*jugador*› to penalize **2** ‹*ley/disposición/acuerdo/huelga*› to sanction; ‹*costumbre*› to approve, sanction

sancochar [A1] *vt* (AmL) (cocer a medias) to parboil

sandalia *f* sandal

sándalo *m* sandalwood

sandez *f* (fam) silly *o* stupid thing to say; **¡no digas sandeces!** don't talk nonsense!

sandía *f* watermelon

sándwich /ˈsaŋgwitʃ/ *m*, **sándwiche** /ˈsaŋgwitʃe/ *m* (esp AmL) (de pan de molde) sandwich; (de pancito) (filled) roll

sanfermines *mpl*: *festival in Pamplona in which bulls are run through the streets*

sangrar [A1] *vi* «*persona/herida/nariz*» to bleed

sangre *f* **1** (Biol) blood; **una transfusión de ~** a blood transfusion; **no me salió ~** it didn't bleed; **te sale ~ de** *or* **por la nariz** your nose is bleeding; **los ojos inyectados en ~** bloodshot eyes; **animales de ~ fría/caliente** cold-blooded/warm-blooded animals; **~ *fría*** calmness and courage; **a ~ fría** ‹*matar*› in cold blood; ⇒ MALO[1], PURO[1] **2** (linaje) blood; **era de ~ noble** he was of noble blood *o* birth; **es de ~ mestiza** he is of mixed race; **no son de la misma ~** they are not from the same family; **~ azul** blue blood

sangría *f* **1** (bebida) sangria (*type of red wine punch*) **2 (a)** (Med) bleeding **(b)** (de capital, recursos) outflow, drain **3** (Impr) indentation

sangriento -ta *adj* bloody

sangrón -grona *adj* (Méx fam) annoying ■ *m,f* (Méx fam) nuisance

sanguijuela *f* **(a)** (Zool) leech **(b)** (fam) (persona) leech, bloodsucker

sanguinario -ria *adj* ‹*persona*› cruel, bloodthirsty; ‹*animal*› vicious, ferocious

sanidad *f* **1** (calidad de sano) health, healthiness **2 (a)** (salud pública) public health **(b) Sanidad** (*sin art*) (departamento) Department of Health

sanitario[1] -ria *adj* ‹*medidas*› public health (*before n*); ‹*condiciones*› sanitary (*before n*); **servicios ~s** sanitation; **asistencia sanitaria** health-care

sanitario[2] *m* **(a)** (Col, Méx, Ven) (retrete) toilet, lavatory **(b) sanitarios** *mpl* (para cuarto de baño) bathroom fittings (*pl*)

sano -na *adj* **1** ‹*persona/planta/cabello*› healthy; ‹*clima/vida*› healthy; ‹*alimentación*› healthy, wholesome; **~ *y salvo*** safe and sound **2** (en sentido moral) ‹*lecturas/ideas*› wholesome; ‹*ambiente*› healthy; ‹*persona*› good

San Salvador *m* San Salvador

sánscrito *m* Sanskrit

Santa Sede *f*: **la ~ ~** the Vatican, the Holy See (frml)

Santiago (de Chile) *m* Santiago

Santiago (de Compostela) *m* Santiago (de Compostela)

santiaguino -na *adj* of/from Santiago (*Chile*)

santiamén *m*: **en un ~** (fam) in no time at all

santiguarse [A16] *v pron* (*refl*) to cross oneself, make the sign of the cross

santo -ta *adj* **1** (Relig) **(a)** ‹*lugar/mujer/vida*› holy **(b)** (con nombre propio) St, Saint; **Santa Teresa** Saint Theresa; *ver tb* SAN **2** (fam) (uso enfático) blessed; **llovió todo el ~ día** it rained the whole blessed day (colloq) ■ *m,f* **1** (persona) saint; **una paciencia de ~** the patience of a saint; **no te hagas el ~** don't come over all virtuous; **~ y seña** password **2 santo** *m* (festividad) name day, saint's day; (cumpleaños) (esp AmL) birthday

Santo Domingo *m* (Geog) Santo Domingo; (Relig) Saint Dominic

santuario *m* (Relig) sanctuary, shrine; (refugio) sanctuary

saña *f* viciousness, brutality; **con ~** brutally, viciously

São Paulo *m* São Paulo

sapo *m* (Zool) toad

saque *m* **(a)** (en tenis, vóleibol) serve, service **(b)** (en fútbol) kickoff; **~ de banda** (en fútbol) throw-in; (en rugby) line-out; **~ de esquina** corner (kick); **~ de puerta** *or* (CS) **valla** goal kick; **~ inicial** kickoff

saquear [A1] *vt* ‹*ciudad/población*› to sack, plunder; ‹*tienda/establecimiento*› to loot

sarampión *m* measles

sarape *m* (Méx) ⇒ ZARAPE

sarcasmo *m* **(a)** (cualidad) sarcasm; **con ~** sarcastically **(b)** (comentario) sarcastic remark

sarcástico -ca *adj* sarcastic

sarcófago *m* sarcophagus

sardina *f* sardine

sardinel *m* (Col) **(a)** (de la acera) curb (AmE), kerb (BrE) **(b)** (de ventana) windowsill

sargento *mf* (Mil) (en el ejército) sergeant; (en las fuerzas aéreas) ≈ staff sergeant (*in US*), ≈ sergeant (*in UK*)

sari *m* sari

sarita *f* (Per) straw hat

sarna *f* (Med) scabies; (Vet) mange

sarpullido *m* rash, hives (*pl*)

sarro *m* (en los dientes) plaque, tartar; (en la lengua) fur; (en tetera eléctrica, cañería) scale

sarta *f* string

sartén *f*, (AmL) *m or f* frying pan, fry pan (AmE), skillet

sastre *mf* (persona) tailor

sastrería *f* tailor's shop

Satanás, **Satán** *m* Satan

satánico -ca *adj* (del diablo) satanic; (malvado) evil, satanic

satélite *m* satellite; **~ artificial** artificial satellite

satén, (AmL) **satín** *m* satin

sátira *f* satire

satírico -ca *adj* satirical

satirizar [A4] *vt* to satirize

satisfacción *f* satisfaction; **la ~ del deber cumplido** the satisfaction of a job well done; **es una ~ para mí estar aquí** it is a pleasure to be here

satisfacer [E20] *vt* to satisfy; **su respuesta no me satisface** I am not satisfied *o* happy with your reply
■ **satisfacerse** *v pron* **(a)** (contentarse) to be satisfied **(b)** (de agravio) to obtain satisfaction

satisfactorio -ria *adj* satisfactory

satisfaga, **satisfará, etc** *see* SATISFACER

satisfecho -cha *adj* [ESTAR] (complacido, contento) satisfied, pleased

saturado -da *adj* (en general) saturated; ‹*líneas telefónicas*› busy, engaged (BrE)

saturar [A1] *vt* to saturate

Saturno *m* Saturn

sauce *m* willow; **~ llorón** weeping willow

saudí, **saudita** *adj/mf* (Saudi) Arabian

sauna *f or* (AmL) *m* sauna

savia *f* (Bot) sap

sávila *f* (Méx) aloe vera

saxo *m* (fam) **(a)** (instrumento) sax (colloq) **(b) saxo** *mf* (persona) sax player (colloq)

saxofón, **saxófono** *m* saxophone

saxofonista *mf* saxophonist

sazonar [A1] *vt* to season

schop /ʃop/ *m* (Chi) (vaso) beer mug; (cerveza) keg beer

Scotch® /(e)s'kotʃ/ *m* (Andes) Scotch® tape (AmE), Sellotape® (BrE)

scout /(e)s'kau(t)/ *mf* scout

se *pron pers* **1** [*seguido de otro pronombre: sustituyendo a* LE, LES]: **ya ~ lo he dicho** (a él) I've already told him; (a ella) I've already told her; (a usted, ustedes) I've already told you; (a ellos) I've already told them; **el vestido tenía cuello pero ~ lo quité** the dress had a collar but I took it off **2** (*en verbos pronominales*): **¿no ~ arrepienten?** «*ellos/ellas*» aren't they sorry?; «*ustedes*» aren't you sorry?; **el barco ~ hundió** the ship sank; **~ secó/secaron** (*refl*) he dried himself/they dried themselves; **~ secó el pelo** (*refl*) she dried her hair; **~ hizo un vestido** (*refl*) she made herself a dress; (*caus*) she had a dress made; **no ~ hablan** (*recípr*) they're not on speaking terms, they're not speaking to each other; **~ lo comió todo** (*enf*) he ate it all **3 (a)** (*voz pasiva*): **~ oyeron unos gritos** there were shouts, I (*o* we *etc*) heard some shouts; **~ publicó el año pasado** it was published last year **(b)** (*impersonal*): **aquí ~ está muy bien** it's very nice here; **~ castigará a los culpables** those responsible will be punished **(c)** (en normas, instrucciones): **¿cómo ~ escribe tu nombre?** how is your name spelled?, how do you spell your name?; **~ pica la cebolla bien menuda** chop the onion finely

sé *see* SABER, SER

sea, **seas, etc** *see* SER

sebo *m* (grasa) grease, fat; (para jabón, velas) tallow; (Coc) suet

secador *m* **1** *tb* **~ de pelo** hairdryer **2** (Per) (paño) dishtowel (AmE), tea towel (BrE); (toalla) towel

secadora *f* (de ropa, tabaco) dryer; (para el pelo) (Méx) hairdryer

secano *m*: **de ~** ‹*campo/tierra*› dry, unirrigated

secar [A2] *vt* **(a)** ‹*ropa/pelo/platos*› to dry; ‹*pintura/arcilla*› to dry **(b)** ‹*tierra/plantas/hierba*› to dry up; ‹*piel*› to make ... dry ■ **~** *vi* to dry
■ **secarse** *v pron* **1 (a)** «*ropa/pintura/pelo*» to dry; «*piel*» to get dry; **se me seca mucho la piel** my skin gets very dry **(b)** «*herida*» to heal (up) **(c)** «*tierra/planta/hierba*» to dry up **(d)** «*río/pozo/fuente*» to dry up **(e)** «*arroz/guiso*» to go dry **2** (*refl*) «*persona*» to dry oneself; ‹*manos/pelo*› to dry; ‹*lágrimas*› to dry, wipe away

sección *f* **1** (corte) section **2 (a)** (división, área — en general) section; (— de empresa, en grandes almacenes) department **(b)** (de periódico, orquesta) section **3** (Mil) platoon

seccionar [A1] *vt* (cortar) to cut off; (dividir en secciones) to section

seco -ca *adj* **1 (a)** [ESTAR] ‹*ropa/platos/pintura*› dry; ‹*boca/garganta*› dry **(b)** [ESTAR] ‹*planta/río/comida*› dry **(c)** [SER] ‹*clima/región*› dry **2** ‹*higos/flores*› dried; **bacalao ~** stockfish, dried salt cod **3** [SER] (no graso) ‹*piel/pelo*› dry **4** [SER] (no dulce) ‹*vino/licor/vermut*› dry **5** ‹*golpe/sonido*› sharp; ‹*tos*› dry **6** ‹*respuesta/carácter*› dry; **estuvo muy ~ conmigo** he was very short with me **7** (*en locs*) **en seco** ‹*frenar/parar*› sharply, suddenly; **limpieza en ~** dry cleaning

secreción *f* (de glándula) secretion; (de herida) discharge

secretaría *f* **1 (a)** (cargo) office of secretary **(b)** (oficina) secretary's office **(c)** (departamento administrativo) secretariat **2** (Méx) (ministerio) department, ministry (BrE)

secretariado *m* secretarial work; **estudia ~** she's doing a secretarial course

secretario -ria *m,f* **1 (a)** (trabajador administrativo) secretary **(b)** (de asociación, sociedad) secretary; **~ general** secretary general **2** (Méx) (Gob, Pol) secretary of state, minister; **S~ de Gobernación** (en Méx) Minister of the Interior, ≈ Home Secretary (*in UK*)

secretear [A1] *vi* (AmL fam) to whisper ■ **secretearse** *v pron* (AmL fam) to whisper

secreter *m* writing desk

secreto¹ -ta *adj* secret

secreto² *m* **(a)** (información confidencial) secret; **los preparamos en ~** we prepared them secretly *o* in secret; **~ a voces** open secret **(b)** (truco) secret; **el ~ está en** ... the secret is in ...

secta *f* sect

sectario -ria *adj* sectarian

sector *m* **(a)** (grupo) sector, group **(b)** (Mat) sector **(c)** (de ciudad) area **(d)** (Com, Econ) sector

secuela *f* consequence

secuencia *f* sequence, series

secuestrador -dora *m,f* (de persona) kidnapper; (de avión) hijacker

secuestrar [A1] *vt* ‹*persona*› to kidnap; ‹*avión*› to hijack

secuestro *m* (de persona) kidnapping; (de avión) hijack(ing)

secundaria *f* **(a)** (AmL) (enseñanza media) secondary education, high school (AmE) **(b)** (Méx) (instituto) middle school

secundario -ria *adj* ‹*factor/problema*› secondary; ‹*actor/actriz*› supporting (*before n*)

sed *f* thirst; **el agua le quitó la ~** the water quenched his thirst; **tengo ~** I'm thirsty; **me da ~** it makes me (feel) thirsty

seda *f* (Tex) silk; (Odont) **~ dental** dental floss

sedal *m* fishing line

sedante *adj/m* (Med) sedative

sede *f* **(a)** (del gobierno) seat **(b)** (Relig) see **(c)** (de organización internacional) headquarters (*sing or pl*); (de compañía) headquarters (*sing or pl*), head office **(d)** (de congreso, feria) venue; **la ~ de los Juegos Olímpicos** the venue for the Olympic Games

sedentario -ria *adj* sedentary

sediento -ta *adj* thirsty

sedimento *m* sediment, deposit

sedoso -sa *adj* silky

seducción *f* seduction

seducir [I6] *vt* **(a)** (en sentido sexual) to seduce **(b)** (fascinar, cautivar) to captivate **(c)** «*idea/proposición*» (atraer) to attract, tempt; **no me seduce la idea** the idea doesn't appeal to me at all

seductor -tora *adj* **(a)** (en sentido sexual) seductive **(b)** (que cautiva, fascina) enchanting, charming **(c)** ‹*idea/proposición*› attractive, tempting ■ *m,f* (*m*) seducer; (*f*) seducer, seductress

seg. *m* (= **segundo/segundos**) sec.

segar [A7] *vt* ‹*mies*› to reap (liter), to cut

seglar *adj* lay (*before n*) ■ *mf* (*m*) layman; (*f*) laywoman

segmento *m* (Mat) segment; (Zool) segment; (Com) sector

segregación *f* segregation; **~ racial** racial segregation

segregar [A3] *vt* ‹*personas/grupos*› to segregate

seguida: **en ~** (*loc adv*) immediately, right *o* (BrE) straight away; **vinieron en ~** they came at once *o* right away; **en ~ voy/vuelvo** I'll be right there/back

seguido¹ -da *adj* consecutive, in a row; **faltó tres días ~s** she was absent three days running *o* in a row; **pasaron tres autobuses ~s** three buses went by one after the other; **~ DE algo/algn** followed BY sth/sb

seguido² *adv* **1** (recto, sin desviarse) straight on; **vaya todo ~** go straight on **2** (AmL) (a menudo) often

seguidor -dora *m,f* (de teoría, filósofo) follower; (Dep) supporter, fan

seguir [I30] *vt* **1** ‹*persona/vehículo/presa*› to follow; **camina muy rápido, no la puedo ~** she walks very fast, I can't keep up with her **2** ‹*camino/ruta*› to follow, go along; **siga esta carretera hasta llegar al puente** go along *o* follow this road as far as the bridge; **la saludé y seguí mi camino** I said hello to her and went on (my way); **la enfermedad sigue su curso normal** the illness is running its normal course **3 (a)** ‹*instrucciones/consejo/flecha*› to follow **(b)** ‹*autor/método/tradición/moda*› to follow; **~ los pasos de algn** to follow in sb's footsteps **4 (a)** ‹*trámite/procedimiento*› to follow; ‹*tratamiento*› to undergo **(b)** (Educ) ‹*curso*› to do, take **5** ‹*explicaciones/profesor*› to follow; **dicta demasiado rápido, no la puedo ~** she dictates too quickly, I can't keep up ■ **~** *vi* **1 (a)** (por un camino) to go on; **siga derecho** *or* **todo recto** keep *o* go straight on; **sigue por esta calle** go on down this street; **~ de largo** (AmL) to go straight past **(b) seguir adelante** to carry on; **resolvieron ~ adelante con los planes** they decided to go ahead with their plans **(c)** (Col, Ven) (entrar): **siga por favor** come in, please **2** (en lugar, estado): **¿tus padres siguen en Ginebra?** are your parents still in Geneva?; **espero que sigan todos bien** I hope you're all keeping well; **sigue soltera** she's still single; **si las cosas siguen así** ... if things carry on like this ... **3** «*tareas/buen tiempo/lluvia*» to continue; «*rumores*» to persist; **sigo pensando que deberíamos haber ido** I still think we ought to have gone; **~é haciéndolo a mi manera** I'll go on *o* carry on doing it my way **4 (a)** (venir después): **lee lo que sigue** read what comes next; **el capítulo que sigue** the next chapter **(b)** «*historia/poema*» to continue, go on

según *prep* **1** (de acuerdo con) according to; **~ Elena** according to Elena; **~ parece** apparently **2** (dependiendo de): **~ cómo lo hagas** depending (on) how you do it; **¿me llevas a casa? — ~ dónde vivas** will you take me home? — (it) depends where you live ■ *adv* it depends; **puede resultar o no, ~** it may or may not work, it depends ■ *conj* (a medida que) as; **~ van entrando** as they come in

segunda *f* **1 (a)** (Auto) (marcha) second (gear); **mete (la) ~** put it in second (gear) **(b)** (Transp) (clase) second class; **viajar en ~** to travel second class **2 segundas** *fpl*: **todo lo dice con ~s** there's a hidden meaning to everything he says

segundero *m* second hand

segundo¹ -da *adj/pron* **(a)** ▶ **294** (ordinal) second; **relegar a algn a un ~ plano** to push sb into the background; *para ejemplos ver tb* QUINTO **(b)** ‹*categoría/clase*› second ■ *m,f* deputy, second-in-command

segundo² *m* ▶ **221** second; **un ~, ahora te atiendo** just a second, I'll be right with you

seguridad *f* **1** (ausencia de peligro) safety; (protección contra robos, atentados) security; **medidas de ~** (contra accidentes, incendios) safety measures; (contra robos, atentados) security measures; **una prisión de alta ~** a high security prison; **~ ciudadana** public safety **2** (estabilidad, garantía) security; **~ social** social security **3 (a)** (certeza) certainty; **podemos decir con ~ que** ... we can say for sure *o* with certainty that ... **(b)** (confianza, aplomo) confidence, self-confidence

seguro¹ -ra *adj* **1 (a)** [SER] (exento de riesgo) safe; **en un lugar ~** in a safe place **(b)** (estable) secure; **un trabajo ~** a secure job; **esa escalera no está segura** that ladder isn't safe *o* steady **(c)** [SER] (fiable) ‹*test/método*› reliable; ‹*anticonceptivo*› safe; **el cierre de la pulsera es muy ~** the fastener on the bracelet is very secure **(d)** [ESTAR] (a salvo) safe **2 (a)** [ESTAR] (convencido) sure; **no estoy ~** I'm not sure; **~ DE algo** sure *o* certain OF sth **(b)** [SER] (que no admite duda) ‹*muerte/victoria*› certain; ‹*fecha*› definite; **todavía no es ~** it's not definite yet; **no te preocupes, ~ que no es nada** don't worry, I'm sure it's nothing; **~ que se le olvida** he's sure *o* bound to forget **(c)** (con confianza en sí mismo) self-assured, self-confident

seguro² *m* **1 (a)** (mecanismo — de armas) safety catch; (— de pulsera, collar) clasp, fastener; **echó el ~ antes de acostarse** he locked the door before going to bed **(b)** (Méx) (imperdible) safety pin **2 (a)** (contrato) insurance; **~ contra** *or* **a todo riesgo** comprehensive insurance, all-risks insurance; **~ contra** *or* **de incendios** fire insurance; **~ de desempleo** unemployment benefit; **~ de vida** life assurance, life insurance **(b)** (Seguridad Social): **el ~** *or* **el S~** the state health care system, ≈ Medicaid (*in US*), ≈ the National Health Service (*in UK*) ■ *adv*: **dijo que llegaría mañana ~** she said she'd definitely be arriving tomorrow; **no lo sabe ~** she doesn't know for sure *o* certain; **~ que sospecha lo nuestro** I'm sure he suspects we're up to something

seis *adj inv/pron/m* ▶ **293** six; *para ejemplos ver* CINCO

seiscientos -tas *adj/pron* ▶ **293** six hundred

seísmo *m* (Esp) (temblor) tremor; (terremoto) earthquake

selección *f* selection; **hizo una ~ de los mejores** she selected the best ones; **la ~ mexicana** (Dep) the Mexican national team

seleccionador -dora *m,f* (Dep) **(a)** (entrenador) coach (AmE), manager (BrE) **(b)** (miembro de una junta) selector

seleccionar [A1] *vt* to select, choose

selectivo -va *adj* selective

selecto -ta *adj* ‹*fruta/vino*› select, choice; ‹*ambiente/club*› select, exclusive

sellar [A1] *vt* **1 (a)** ‹*pasaporte*› to stamp **(b)** ‹*plata/oro*› to hallmark **2** (cerrar) to seal

sello *m* **1** (de correos) (postage) stamp; (útil de oficina) rubber stamp; (marca) stamp **2 (a)** (en el oro, la plata) hallmark **(b)** (AmL) (de una moneda) reverse; **¿cara o ~?** (Andes, Ven) heads or tails? **(c)** (anillo) signet ring, seal ring **(d)** (distintivo) hallmark **(e)** (Mús) *tb* **~ discográfico** record label **3** (precinto) seal

selva *f* (bosque) forest; (de vegetación tropical) jungle; **S~ Negra** Black Forest; **~ tropical** tropical rainforest, selva

semáforo *m* **(a)** (Auto) traffic lights (*pl*); **se pasó un ~ en rojo** she went through *o* (AmE) ran a red light **(b)** (Ferr) stop signal **(c)** (Náut) semaphore

semana *f* **1** (periodo) week; **S~ Santa** Easter **2** (Col) (dinero) allowance, pocket money

semanal *adj* weekly

semántico -ca *adj* semantic

sembrado¹ *m* sown field

sembrado² -da *m,f* (Méx) (Dep) seed

sembrar [A5] *vt* ‹*terreno/campo*› to sow; ‹*trigo/hortalizas*› to sow, plant; **~ algo DE algo** to plant sth WITH sth

semejante *adj* **(a)** (similar) similar; **~ A algo** similar TO sth **(b)** (*delante del n*) (para énfasis): **¡cómo puedes decir ~ cosa!** how can you say such a thing!; **nunca había oído ~ estupidez** I'd never heard such nonsense *o* anything so stupid ■ *m*: **nuestros ~s** our fellow men

semejanza *f* similarity; **a ~ de sus antepasados** like his ancestors

semen *m* semen

semental *m* (caballo) stud horse; (toro) stud bull

semestral *adj* **(a)** (en frecuencia) ‹*exámenes/reuniones*› half-yearly, six-monthly **(b)** (en duración) ‹*curso*› six-month (*before n*)

semestre *m* **(a)** (seis meses): **cada curso dura un ~** each course lasts six months **(b)** (Educ) (en algunos países latinoamericanos) *tb* **~ lectivo** semester (AmE), term (BrE)

semicírculo *m* semicircle

semicorchea *f* sixteenth note (AmE), semiquaver (BrE)

semidesnatado -da *adj* (Esp) semi-skimmed, half-cream (*before n*)

semifinal *f* semifinal

semifinalista *mf* semifinalist

semilla *f* seed

semillero *m* **(a)** (Agr, Bot) seedbed **(b)** (de discordias) source; (de delincuencia) hotbed, breeding ground

seminario *m* **(a)** (Relig) seminary **(b)** (Educ) seminar

seminarista *m* seminarian

semita *adj* Semitic ■ *mf* Semite

sémola *f* semolina; **~ de arroz** ground rice

Sena *m*: **el ~** the Seine

senado *m* senate

senador -dora *m,f* senator

sencillez *f* simplicity; **con ~** ‹*vestir*› simply; ‹*comportarse*› with modesty; **habla con ~** she uses plain language

sencillo[1] **-lla** *adj* **1 (a)** ‹*ejercicio/problema*› simple, straightforward; **no fue ~ hacerlos entrar** it wasn't easy getting them in **(b)** ‹*persona*› modest, unassuming; ‹*vestido/estilo*› simple, plain; ‹*casa/comida*› simple, modest **2** (Esp, Méx) (Transp) one-way (AmE), single (BrE)

sencillo[2] *m* **1** (disco) single **2** (AmL) (dinero suelto) change **3** (Esp, Méx) (Transp) one-way ticket (AmE), single (ticket) (BrE)

senda *f* **(a)** (camino) path **(b)** (Ur) (de carretera) lane

sendero *m* path, track

sendos -das *adj pl* (cada uno): **llevaban sendas pistolas** each of them was carrying *o* they were each carrying a gun; **con sendas fiestas en Madrid y Barcelona** with parties in both Madrid and Barcelona

Senegal *m* Senegal

senilidad *f* senility

seno *m* **(a)** ▶ 123 (mama) breast; (pecho) bosom; **los ~s** the breasts; **dar el ~** (Ven) to breastfeed **(b)** (de organización, empresa) heart

sensación *f* **1** (percepción, impresión) feeling; **una ~ de tristeza/impotencia** a feeling of sadness/ impotence; **una vaga ~ de placer** a vague sensation of pleasure; **una ~ de pérdida/espacio** a sense of loss/space; **tengo** *or* **me da la ~ de que no vamos a ganar** I have a feeling we're not going to win **2** (furor, éxito) sensation; **ser una ~** to be a sensation

sensacional *adj* sensational

sensacionalismo *m* sensationalism

sensacionalista *adj* ‹*prensa*› sensationalist (*before n*); ‹*artículo/foto*› sensationalistic

sensatez *f* sense; **tuvo la ~ de ...** she had the (good) sense to ...; **obró con ~** she acted sensibly

sensato -ta *adj* sensible

sensibilidad *f* **(a)** (en general) sensitivity **(b)** (en brazo, pierna) feeling

sensibilizar [A4] *vt* to raise ... awareness

sensible *adj* **1** (en general) sensitive; **~ A algo** sensitive TO sth **2** (*gen delante del n*) (frml) (ostensible) ‹*cambio/diferencia*› appreciable; ‹*mejoría*› noticeable; ‹*aumento/pérdida*› considerable

sensiblero -ra *adj* (pey) mawkish

sensitivo -va *adj* sensory

sensorial *adj* sensory

sensual *adj* ‹*boca/cuerpo*› sensual, sensuous; ‹*placeres/gesto*› sensual; ‹*descripción*› sensuous

sensualidad *f* (de boca, gesto) sensuality; (de descripción) sensuousness

sentada *f* **(a)** (protesta) sit-in, sit-down protest **(b) de** *or* **en una sentada** in one go

sentado -da *adj* sitting, seated (frml); **estaban ~s a la mesa** they were (sitting) at the table; ***dar algo por ~*** to assume sth

sentador -dora *adj* (AmL) flattering, fetching

sentar [A5] *vi* (+ *me/te/le etc*) **(a)** «*ropa/color*» (+ *compl*): **ese vestido le sienta de maravilla** that dress really suits her **(b)** «*comida/bebida/ clima*» (+ *compl*): **el café no le sienta bien** coffee doesn't agree with her; **me sentó bien el descanso** the rest did me a lot of good **(c)** «*actitud/ comentario*» (+ *compl*): **me sentó mal que no me invitaran** I was rather put out that they didn't ask me (colloq) ■ **~** *vt* **1** ‹*niño/muñeca*› to sit; ‹*invitado*› to seat, sit **2** (establecer) to establish

■ **sentarse** *v pron* to sit; **~se a la mesa** to sit at (the) table; **siéntese, por favor** please (do) sit down

sentencia *f* (Der) judgment, ruling

sentenciar [A1] *vt* to sentence; **la ~on a muerte** (Der) she was sentenced to death

sentido[1] **-da** *adj* **1** ‹*palabras/carta*› heartfelt; ‹*anhelo/dolor*› deep; **mi más ~ pésame** my deepest sympathy **2** [ESTAR] (AmL) (ofendido) hurt, offended

sentido[2] *m* **1 (a)** (Fisiol) sense **(b)** (noción, idea) **~ DE algo** sense OF sth; **su ~ del deber** her sense of duty; **~ común** common sense; **~ del humor** sense of humor* **2** (conocimiento) consciousness; **perder el ~** to lose consciousness; **el golpe lo dejó sin ~** he was knocked unconscious by the blow **3** (significado) sense; **en el buen ~ de la palabra** in the nicest sense of the word; **en ~ literal** in a literal sense; **lo dijo con doble ~** he was intentionally ambiguous; **el ~ de la vida** the meaning of life; **en cierto ~** ... in a sense ...; **no le encuentro ~ a lo que haces** I can't see any sense *o* point in what you're doing; **esa política ya no tiene ~** that policy doesn't make sense anymore *o* is meaningless now; **palabras sin ~** meaningless words **4** (dirección) direction; **gírese en ~ contrario al de las agujas del reloj** turn (round) in a counterclockwise (AmE) *o* (BrE) an anticlockwise direction; **venían en ~ contrario al nuestro** they were coming in the opposite direction to us; **calle de ~ único** *or* (Méx) **de un solo ~** one-way street

sentimental *adj* **(a)** (relativo a los sentimientos) sentimental **(b)** ‹*persona/canción/novela*› sentimental; **ponerse ~** to get sentimental **(c)** ‹*aventura/vida*› love (*before n*)

sentimentalismo *m* sentimentalism

sentimiento *m* **1 (a)** (emoción) feeling; **ser de buenos ~s** to be a caring person; **no se deja llevar por los ~s** she doesn't let herself get carried away by her emotions **(b)** (pesar): **les acompaño en el ~** my commiserations **2 sentimientos** *mpl* feelings (*pl*); **herir los ~s de algn** to hurt sb's feelings

sentir [I11] *vt* **1 (a)** ‹*dolor/pinchazo*› to feel; **~ hambre/frío/sed** to feel hungry/cold/thirsty **(b)** ‹*emoción*› to feel; **sentimos una gran alegría** we were overjoyed; **~ celos** to feel jealous **2 (a)** (oír) ‹*ruido/disparo*› to hear **(b)** (esp AmL) (percibir): **siento olor a gas** I can smell gas; **le siento gusto a vainilla** I can taste vanilla **3** (lamentar): **lo siento mucho** I'm really sorry; **sentí mucho no poder ayudarla** I was very sorry not to be able to help her; **ha sentido mucho la pérdida de su madre** she has been very affected by her mother's death

■ **sentirse** *v pron* **1** (+ *compl*) to feel; **me siento mal** I don't feel well, I'm not feeling well; **no me siento con ánimos** I don't feel up to it **2** (Chi, Méx) (ofenderse) to be offended *o* hurt; **~se** CON **algn** to be offended *o* upset WITH sb

seña *f* **1** (gesto) sign; **hacer una ~** to make a sign, to signal; **les hice ~s de que se callaran** I gestured *o* motioned to them to keep quiet **2 señas** *fpl* (dirección) address **3 señas** *fpl* (indicios): **dar ~s** DE **algo** to show signs OF sth **4** (RPl) ⇒ SEÑAL 5

señal *f* **1 (a)** (aviso, letrero) sign; **~es de tráfico** traffic signs; **S~ de la Cruz** sign of the cross **(b)** (signo) signal; **nos hacía ~es para que nos acercáramos** she was signaling *o* gesturing for us to come nearer; **~ de auxilio** *or* **socorro** distress signal **(c)** (Ferr) signal **2** (marca, huella): **pon una ~ en la página** mark the page; **~es de violencia** signs of violence **3 (a)** (Rad, TV) signal **(b)** (Telec): **la ~ para marcar** the dial (AmE) *o* (BrE) dialling tone; **la ~ de ocupado** *or* (Esp) **comunicando** the busy signal (AmE), the engaged tone (BrE) **4** (indicio) sign; **eso es mala ~** that's a bad sign; **no daba ~es de vida** he showed no signs of life; **en ~ de respeto/amor** as a token of respect/love **5** (Esp) (Com) (depósito) deposit, down payment

señalar [A1] *vt* **1** (indicar) ‹*ruta/camino*› to show; **el reloj señalaba las doce** the clock showed twelve; **me señaló con el dedo** he pointed at me (with his finger); **~le algo** A **algn** to show sb sth, point sth out TO sb; **me señaló con el dedo qué pasteles quería** he pointed out (to me) which cakes he wanted **2** (marcar con lápiz, rotulador) to mark **3** (afirmar) to point out; **señaló que** ... she pointed out that ... **4** (fijar) ‹*fecha*› to fix, set; **en el lugar señalado** in the appointed *o* agreed place **5** (anunciar) to mark ■ **~** *vi* to point

señalización *f* **(a)** (en carretera, calle) signposting; (en edificio, centro comercial) signs (*pl*) **(b)** (Ferr) signaling*

señalizar [A4] *vt* **(a)** ‹*carretera/calle/ciudad*› to signpost; ‹*edificio/centro comercial*› to put up directions on/in **(b)** (Ferr) ‹*tramo/vía*› to install signals on

señor -ñora *m,f* **1 (a)** (persona adulta) (*m*) man, gentleman; (*f*) lady; **peluquería de ~as** ladies' hairdresser's **(b)** (persona distinguida) (*m*) gentleman; (*f*) lady; **es todo un ~** he's a real gentleman **2** (dueño, amo): **el ~/la ~a de la casa** the gentleman/the lady of the house (frml) **3** (Relig) **(a) Señor** *m* Lord **(b) Señora** *f*: **Nuestra S~a de Montserrat** Our Lady of Montserrat **4 señora** *f* (esposa) wife **5** (tratamiento de cortesía) **(a)** (con apellidos) ▶ 420 (*m*) Mr; (*f*) Mrs; **los ~es de Paz** Mr and Mrs Paz **(b)** (frml) (con otros sustantivos): **la ~a directora está ocupada** the director is busy; **S~ Director** (Corresp) Dear Sir, Sir (frml) **(c)** (frml) (sin mencionar el nombre): ▶ 420 **perdón, ~ ¿tiene hora?** excuse me, could you tell me the time?; **muy ~ mío/~es míos** (Corresp) Dear Sir/Sirs; **Teresa Chaves — ¿~a o ~ita?** Teresa Chaves — Miss, Mrs or Ms?; **los ~es han salido** Mr and Mrs Paz (*o* López *etc*) are not at home

señorial *adj* ‹*casa*› stately; ‹*ciudad*› noble

señorita *f* **1 (a)** (mujer joven) young lady **(b)** (joven distinguida) young lady **(c)** (maestra) teacher **2** (tratamiento de cortesía) **(a)** (con apellidos) Miss ▶ 420 **(b)** (con nombres de pila): **~ Teresa ¿puede atender a la señora?** Teresa/Miss Chaves (*o* López *etc*), could you serve this lady please? **(c)** (maestra) Miss **(d)** (sin mencionar el nombre) (frml) Miss

señorito *m* (pey) rich young man, rich kid (colloq)

señuelo *m* (persona) bait; (para aves) decoy

sepa, **sepas**, **etc** *see* SABER

separación *f* **1 (a)** (división) separation; **la ~ de la Iglesia y del Estado** the separation of the Church and the State **(b)** (espacio) gap, separation **2** (del matrimonio) separation

separado -da *adj* **1** ‹*persona*› separated **2 (a)** ‹*camas*› separate **(b) por separado** separately ■ *m,f*: **es hijo de ~s** his parents are separated

separador *m* **1** (de carpeta) divider **2** (Col) (Auto) median strip (AmE), central reservation (BrE)

separar [A1] *vt* **1 (a)** (apartar, alejar) to separate; **~ los machos de las hembras** to separate the males from the females; **separa la cama de la pared** move the bed away from the wall **(b)** (dividir un todo) to divide **(c)** (guardar, reservar) to put *o* set aside **2 (a)** (actuar de división) «*valla/línea*» to separate; **los Andes separan a Chile de Argentina** the Andes separate Chile from Argentina **(b)** (despegar): **no puedo ~ estas dos fotos** I can't get these two photographs apart

■ **separarse** *v pron* **(a)** «*matrimonio*» to separate; **~se** DE **algn** to separate FROM sb **(b)** (seguir direcciones distintas) to split up; **a mitad de camino nos separamos** we split up half way **(c)** (apartarse, alejarse): **no se separen, que los pequeños se pueden perder** please stay together in case the children get lost; **no me he separado nunca de mis hijos** I've never been away *o* apart from my children

separatismo *m* separatism

separatista *mf* separatist

separo *m* (Méx) cell

sepia *f* **(a)** (Coc, Zool) cuttlefish, sepia (tech) **(b)** (en pintura) sepia ■ *m* (color) ▶ 97 sepia

septentrional *adj* northern

septiembre *m* ▶ 193 September; *para ejemplos ver* ENERO

séptimo[1] -ma *adj/pron* seventh; **la séptima parte** a seventh; **el ~ arte** the movies (*pl*) (AmE), the cinema (BrE); *para ejemplos ver* QUINTO

séptimo[2] *m* ▶ 294 seventh

sepulcral *adj* (liter) ‹*silencio*› deathly

sepulcro *m* tomb, sepulcher* (liter)

sepultar [A1] *vt* **(a)** (frml) ‹*muerto*› to inter (frml), to bury **(b)** (period) (cubrir): **fue sepultado por un alud de nieve** he was buried by an avalanche

sepultura *f* **(a)** (acción) burial **(b)** (tumba) tomb, grave

sepulturero -ra *m,f* gravedigger

sequedad *f* **(a)** (de terreno, región, piel) dryness **(b)** (de respuesta, tono) curtness

sequía *f* drought

séquito *m* (de rey) retinue, entourage

ser [E26] *cópula* **1** (seguido de adjetivos) to be [SER *expresses identity or nature as opposed to condition or state, which is normally conveyed by* ESTAR *The examples given below should be contrasted with those to be found in* ESTAR[1] *cópula* 1] ▶ 99 **es bajo/muy callado** he's short/very quiet; **es sorda de nacimiento** she was born deaf; **es inglés/católico** he's English/(a) Catholic; **era cierto** it was true; **sé bueno, estáte quieto** be a good boy and keep still; **que seas muy feliz** I hope you'll be very happy; (+ *me/te/le etc*) **siempre le he sido fiel** I've always been faithful to her; *ver tb* IMPOSIBLE, DIFÍCIL *etc* **2** (hablando de estado civil) ▶ 378 to be; **el mayor es casado** the oldest is married; **es viuda** she's a widow; *ver tb* ESTAR[1] *cópula* 2 **3** (seguido de nombre, pronombre) to be; **soy abogada** I'm a lawyer; **ábreme, soy yo** open the door, it's me **4** (con predicado introducido por 'de'): **esos zapatos son de plástico** those shoes are (made of) plastic; **soy de Córdoba** I'm from Cordoba; **es de los vecinos** it belongs to the neighbors, it's the neighbors'; **no soy de aquí** I'm not from around here **5** (hipótesis, futuro): **será un error** it must be a mistake; **¿será cierto?** can it be true? ■ ~ *vi* **I 1 (a)** (existir) to be **(b)** (liter) (en cuentos): **érase una vez** ... once upon a time there was ... **2 (a)** (tener lugar, ocurrir): **la fiesta va a ~ en su casa** the party is going to be (held) at her house; **¿dónde fue el accidente?** where did the accident happen? **(b)** (en preguntas): **¿qué habrá sido de él?** I wonder what happened to *o* what became of him; **¿qué es de Marisa?** (fam) what's Marisa up to (these days)? (colloq); **¿qué va a ser de nosotros?** what will become of us? **3** (sumar): **¿cuánto es (todo)?** how much is that (altogether)?; **son 3.000 pesos** that'll be *o* that's 3,000 pesos; **somos diez en total** there are ten of us altogether **4** (indicando finalidad, adecuación) ~ PARA **algo** to be FOR sth; **este agua es para beber** this water is for drinking

II (*en locs*) **a no ser que** (+ *subj*) unless; **¿cómo es eso?** why is that?, how come? (colloq); **como/cuando/donde sea**: **tengo que conseguir ese trabajo como sea** I have to get that job no matter what; **hazlo como sea, pero hazlo** do it any way *o* however you want but get it done; **el lunes o cuando sea** next Monday or whenever; **puedo dormir en el sillón o donde sea** I can sleep in the armchair or wherever you like *o* anywhere you like; **de ser así** (frml) should this be so *o* the case (frml); **¡eso es!** that's it!, that's right!; **es que** ...: **¿es que no lo saben?** do you mean to say they don't know?; **es que no sé nadar** the thing is I can't swim; **lo que sea**: **cómete una manzana, o lo que sea** have an apple or something; **estoy dispuesta a hacer lo que sea** I'm prepared to do whatever it takes; **o sea**: **en febrero, o sea hace un mes** in February, that is to say a month ago; **o sea que no te interesa** in other words, you're not interested; **o sea que nunca lo descubriste** so you never found out; **(ya) sea ..., (ya) sea ...** either ..., or ...; **sea como sea** at all costs; **sea cuando sea** whenever it is; **sea donde sea** no matter where; **sea quien sea** whoever it is; **si no fuera/hubiera sido por** ... if it wasn't *o* weren't/hadn't been for ...

III (en el tiempo) ▶ 193, 221 to be; **¿qué fecha es hoy?** what's the date today?, what's today's date; **serían las cuatro cuando llegó** it must have been (about) four (o'clock) when she arrived; *ver tb v impers* ■ ~ *v impers* to be; **era primavera** it was spring(time) ■ ~ *v aux* (en la voz pasiva) to be; **fue construido en 1900** it was built in 1900 ■ *m* **1 (a)** (ente) being; **~ humano/vivo** human/living being **(b)** (individuo, persona): **un ~ querido** a loved one **2** (naturaleza): **desde lo más profundo de mi ~** from the bottom of my heart

Serbia *f* Serbia

serbio[1] -bia *adj/m,f* Serbian

serbio[2] *m* (idioma) Serbian

serbocroata *adj/mf* Serbo-Croat, Serbo-Croatian ■ *m* (idioma) Serbo-Croat

seré, **seremos, etc** *see* SER

serenarse [A1] *v pron* (calmarse) to calm down

serenata *f* serenade; **dar una** *or* (Méx) **llevar ~** to serenade

serenidad *f* calmness, serenity; **no pierdas la ~** keep calm

sereno[1] -na *adj* **(a)** ‹*rostro/expresión/belleza*› serene; ‹*persona*› serene, calm **(b)** ‹*cielo*› cloudless, clear; ‹*tarde*› still; ‹*mar*› calm, tranquil (liter)

sereno[2] *m* (vigilante nocturno) night watchman

sería, **etc** *see* SER

serial *m*, (CS) **serial** *f* ⇒ SERIE 2

serie *f* **1 (a)** (sucesión) series; **una ~ de pueblos** a series of villages **(b)** (clase) series; **coches de ~** production cars; **fabricación en ~** mass production; **producir/fabricar en ~** to mass produce; ***fuera de ~*** (fam) out of this world (colloq) **(c)** (Dep) heat **2** (Rad, TV) series; (historia continua) serial

seriedad *f* **(a)** (en general) seriousness **(b)** (sensatez, responsabilidad): **se comportó con mucha ~** she behaved very sensibly *o* responsibly; **¡un poco de ~!** come on, let's be serious now!

serio -ria *adj* **1** (poco sonriente) serious **2** ‹*empleado*› responsible, reliable; ‹*empresa*› reputable **3 (a)** ‹*cine/tema*› serious **(b)** (grave) ‹*enfermedad/problema*› serious; **tengo serias dudas acerca de él** I have serious doubts about him **(c) en serio** ‹*hablar*› seriously, in earnest; **¿lo dices en ~?** are you (being) serious?, do you really mean it?; **tomarse algo en ~** to take sth seriously

sermón *m* sermon; **me echó un ~** (fam) he gave me a lecture

seropositivo -va *adj* (en general) seropositive; (con el VIH) HIV positive

serpentear [A1] *vi* «*río*» to meander, wind; «*camino*» to wind, twist

serpentina *f* streamer

serpiente *f* snake, serpent; **~ (de) cascabel** rattlesnake; **~ pitón** python

serrar [A5] *vt* to saw (up)

serrín *m* sawdust

serruchar [A1] *vt* (AmL) to saw

serrucho *m* handsaw

servicentro *m* (Andes) service station

servicial *adj* helpful, obliging

servicio *m* **1 (a)** (acción de servir) service; **estamos a su ~** we are at your service; **estar de ~** «*policía/bombero*» to be on duty; **~ público** public service; **~s informativos** broadcasting services (*pl*) **(b)** (favor) favor*, service **(c) servicios** *mpl* (asistencia) services (*pl*); **me ofreció sus ~s** he offered me his services **2** (funcionamiento) service, use; **está fuera de ~** it's out of service; **han puesto en ~ el nuevo andén** the new platform is now in use *o* is now open **3** (en hospital) department; **~ de urgencias** casualty department **4** (en restaurante, hotel) **(a)** (atención al cliente) service **(b)** (propina) service (charge) **5** (servidumbre): **entrada de ~** tradesman's entrance; **cuarto de ~** servant's quarters (frml), maid's room; **~ doméstico** (actividad) domestic service; (personas) servants (*pl*), domestic staff **6** (Mil) service; **~ militar** military service **7** (retrete) restroom (AmE), bathroom (esp AmE), toilet (esp BrE) **8** (en tenis) service, serve **9** (Relig) service **10** (AmL) (Auto) service

servidor -dora *m,f* **1 (a)** (sirviente) servant **(b)** (frml) (Corresp): **su (atento y) seguro ~** your humble servant (frml) **2 servidor** *m* (Inf) server

servidumbre *f* **1** (esclavitud) servitude **2** (conjunto de criados) domestic staff, servants (*pl*)

servil *adj* **(a)** ‹*persona/actitud*› servile, obsequious (frml) **(b)** ‹*trabajo*› menial

servilleta *f* napkin, serviette (esp BrE)

servilletero *m* napkin ring, serviette ring (BrE)

servir [I14] *vi* **1** (ser útil): **esta caja no sirve** this box won't do *o* is no good; **ya no me sirve** it's (of) no use to me anymore; **¿para qué sirve este aparato?** what's this device for?; **no lo tires, puede ~ para algo** don't throw it away, it might come in useful for something; **este cuchillo no sirve para cortar pan** this knife is no good for cutting bread; **no sirves para nada** you're useless; **no creo que sirva para este trabajo** I don't think he's right *o* suitable for this job; **~** DE **algo**: **de nada sirve llorar** it's no use *o* good crying; **¿de qué sirve?** what's the point *o* the use?; **esto te puede ~ de mesa** you can use this as a table **2 (a)** (en la mesa) to serve **(b)** (trabajar de criado) to be in (domestic) service **(c)** (Mil) to serve (frml) **3** (Dep) (en tenis) to serve ■ **~** *vt* **1** ‹*comida*› to serve; ‹*bebida*› to serve, pour **2** (estar al servicio de) ‹*persona/a la patria*› to serve; **¿en qué puedo ~la?** (frml) how can I help you?

■ **servirse** *v pron* (*refl*) ‹*comida*› to help oneself to; ‹*bebida*› to pour oneself, help oneself to

sésamo *m* sesame

sesear [A1] *vi*: *to pronounce the Spanish [Θ] as [s], eg* /ser'βesa/ instead of /θer'βeθa/ for CERVEZA

sesenta *adj inv/m/pron* ▶ **293** sixty; *para ejemplos ver* CINCUENTA

seseo *m*: *pronunciation of the Spanish* /θ/ as /s/, *eg* /ser'βesa/ *instead of* /θer'βeθa/ *for* CERVEZA

sesión *f* **(a)** (reunión) session; **~ de clausura** closing session **(b)** (de tratamiento, actividad) session; (de fotografía, pintura) sitting **(c)** (de cine) showing, performance; (de teatro) show, performance; **~ de noche** late evening performance

sesionar [A1] *vi* (AmL) to be in session

seso *m* **(a)** ▶ **123** (Anat, Zool) brain **(b) sesos** *mpl* (Coc) brains (*pl*)

set *m* (*pl* **sets**) set

seta *f* (comestible) mushroom; (venenosa) toadstool

setecientos -tas *adj/pron* ▶ **293** seven hundred; *para ejemplos ver* QUINIENTOS

setenta *adj inv/m/pron* ▶ **293** seventy; *para ejemplos ver* CINCUENTA

setiembre *m* ▶ **193** september

seto *m* hedge

seudónimo *m* pseudonym; (de escritor) pen name, pseudonym

severidad *f* (de castigo, pena) severity, harshness; (de padre, educador) strictness; (de clima) harshness

severo -ra *adj* ‹*padre/profesor*› strict; ‹*castigo*› severe, harsh; ‹*invierno*› hard, severe; ‹*dieta/régimen*› strict

Sevilla *f* Seville

sexismo *m* sexism

sexista *adj/mf* sexist

sexo *m* sex; **el ~ débil** the weaker sex; **~ seguro** safe sex

sexto[1] -ta *adj/pron* sixth; *para ejemplos ver* QUINTO; **la sexta parte** a sixth; **~ sentido** sixth sense

sexto[2] *m* ▶ **294** sixth

sexual *adj* ‹*relaciones/órganos/comportamiento*› sexual; ‹*educación/vida*› sex (*before n*)

sexualidad *f* sexuality

sexy /'seksi, 'sesi/ *adj* (fam) sexy

sh, **shh** *interj* shush!, ssh!, hush!

sha, **shah** *m* shah

sheriff /'ʃerif/ *mf* sheriff

shock /ʃok/ *m* **(a)** (Med) shock; **en estado de ~** in (a state of) shock **(b)** (sorpresa desagradable) shock

show /ʃou, tʃou/ *m* (*pl* **shows**) show

si *conj* **1 (a)** (en general) if; **~ pudiera** if I could; **~ lo hubiera** *or* **hubiese sabido** ... if I'd known ..., had I known ...; **empezó a decir que ~ esto, que ~ lo otro** he said this, that and the other **(b)** (en frases que expresan deseo) if only; **¡~ yo lo supiera!** if only I knew! **(c)** (en frases que expresan protesta, indignación, sorpresa): **¡pero ~ te avisé** ...! but I warned you ...! **(d)** (planteando eventualidades, sugerencias): **y ~ no quiere hacerlo ¿qué?** and if she doesn't want to do it, what then?; **¿y ~ lo probáramos?** why don't we give it a try? **(e)** (*en locs*) **si no** otherwise **2** (en interrogativas indirectas) whether; **no sé ~ marcharme o quedarme** I don't know whether to go or to stay ■ *m* (nota) B; (en solfeo) ti, te (BrE); **~ bemol/sostenido** B flat/sharp

sí *adv* **1** (respuesta afirmativa) yes; **¿has terminado? — sí** have you finished? — yes (I have); **decir que ~ con la cabeza** to nod **2** (uso enfático): **ahora ~ que lo has hecho bien** now you've really done it! (colloq); **tú ~ que sabes vivir** you certainly know how to live!; **eso ~ que es caro** that *is* expensive; **no puedo — ¡~ que puedes!** I can't — yes, you can! *o* of course, you can!; **que ~ cabe** it does fit; **es de muy buena calidad — eso ~** it's very good quality — (yes,) that's true **3** (sustituyendo a una cláusula): **creo que ~** I think so; **me temo que ~** I'm afraid so; **¿lloverá? — puede que ~** do you think it will rain? — it might; **un día ~ y otro no** every other day; **no puedo ir pero ella ~** I can't go but she can ■ *m* yes ■ *pron pers* **1 (a)** (*refl*) (él) himself; (ella) herself; (ellos, ellas) themselves; **sólo piensa en ~ (mismo)** he only thinks of himself; **parece muy segura de ~ (misma)** she seems very sure of herself; **fueron para convencerse a ~ mismos/mismas** they went to convince themselves **(b)** (*refl*) (usted) yourself; (ustedes) yourselves; **descríbase a ~ mismo** describe yourself; **léanlo para ~ (mismos)** read it (to) yourselves **(c)** (*impers*): **hay cosas que uno tiene que ver por ~ mismo** there are some things you have to see for yourself **2** (*en locs*) **entre sí** (entre dos) between themselves; (entre varios) among themselves; **lo discutieron entre ~** they discussed it between/among themselves; **no se respetan entre ~** they don't respect each other; **de por sí**: **es de por ~ nervioso** he is nervous by nature; **el sistema es de por ~ complicado** the system is in itself complicated; **en sí (mismo)**: **el hecho en ~ (mismo) no tenía demasiada importancia** this in itself was not so important

siamés -mesa *adj* Siamese ■ *m,f* (gemelo) Siamese twins

sibarita *mf* (amante de los lujos) lover of luxury, sybarite (frml); (en cuestiones de comida) gourmet, epicure (frml)

Siberia *f* Siberia

Sicilia *f* Sicily

siciliano -na *adj/m,f* Sicilian

sida *m* (= **Síndrome de Inmunodeficiencia Adquirida**) AIDS

sidecar /siðe'kar, 'saikar/ *m* (*pl* **-cares** *or* **-cars**) sidecar

sideral *adj* (Astron) sidereal

siderurgia *f* iron and steel industry

sidra *f* hard cider (AmE), cider (BrE)

siempre *adv* **1** always; **~ se sale con la suya** he always gets his own way; **como ~** as usual; **lo de ~** the usual thing; **a la hora de ~** at the usual time; **los conozco desde ~** I've known them for as long as I can remember; **para ~** (definitivamente) ‹*regresar/quedarse*› for good; (eternamente) ‹*durar/vivir*› for ever **2** (en todo caso) always; **~ podemos modificarlo después** we can always modify it later **3** (AmL) (todavía) still; **¿~ viven en Malvín?** do they still live in Malvín? **4** (*en locs*) **siempre que** (cada vez que) whenever; (a condición de que) (+ *subj*) provided (that), providing (that) **5** (Méx) (en definitiva) after all; **~ no se va** he's not leaving after all

sien *f* ▶ 123 temple

sienta, sientas, etc *see* SENTAR, SENTIR

sierra *f* **1** (Tec) saw; **~ de mano** handsaw; **~ mecánica** power saw **2** (Geog) (cordillera) mountain range; (zona montañosa): **fuimos a la ~** we went to the mountains

Sierra Leona *f* Sierra Leone

sierraleonés -nesa *adj* of/from Sierra Leone

siervo -va *m,f* serf, slave

siesta *f* siesta, nap; **dormir la ~** *or* **echar una ~** to have a siesta *o* nap

siete *adj inv/pron* seven; *para ejemplos ver* CINCO ■ *m* **(a)** (cardinal) ▶ 293 (number) seven; *para ejemplos ver* CINCO **(b)** (rotura) tear (*L-shaped*)

sietemesino -na *m,f* premature baby (*esp when born two months early*)

sífilis *f* syphilis

sifilítico -ca *m,f* person with *o* suffering from syphilis, syphilitic

sifón *m* **1 (a)** (botella) siphon* **(b)** (Esp fam) (soda) soda (water) **(c)** (Col) (cerveza) draft* beer **2** (para trasvasar líquidos) siphon; (en fontanería) U-bend, trap

siga, sigas, etc *see* SEGUIR

sigilo *m* stealth; **con ~** stealthily

sigiloso -sa *adj* stealthy

sigla *f* abbreviation; (pronunciado como una palabra) acronym

siglo *m* (período) ▶ 294, 193 century; **hace ~s** *or* **un ~ que no le escribo** (fam) I haven't written to her for ages (colloq)

significación *f* (importancia) significance, importance

significado *m* **1** (de palabra) meaning; (de símbolo) meaning, significance **2** (importancia) ⇒ SIGNIFICACIÓN

significar [A2] *vt* **(a)** (querer decir) to mean **(b)** (suponer, representar) ‹*mejora/ruina*› to represent; ‹*esfuerzo/riesgo*› to involve **(c)** (valer, importar) to mean

significativo -va *adj* **1** ‹*cambio/detalle*› significant **2** ‹*gesto/sonrisa*› meaningful

signo *m* **1** (en general) sign; **~ de admiración** exclamation point (AmE), exclamation mark (BrE); **~ de interrogación** question mark; **~ de la victoria** V-sign; **~ de puntuación** punctuation mark **2** (Astrol) *tb* **~ del zodiaco** sign; **¿de qué ~ eres?** what sign are you?

sigo, sigue, etc *see* SEGUIR

siguiente *adj* **1 (a)** (en el tiempo) following (*before n*); **al día ~** the next *o* the following day **(b)** (en secuencia) next; **en el capítulo ~** in the next *o* following chapter **(c)** (*como n*): **serán los ~s en entrar** they'll be the next to go; **¡(que pase) el ~!** next please! **2** (que se va a nombrar) following (*before n*); **la carta decía lo ~** ... the letter said the following ...

sílaba *f* syllable

silbar [A1] *vt* **(a)** ‹*melodía*› to whistle **(b)** ‹*cantante/obra*› (en señal de desaprobación) to whistle at, catcall ■ **~** *vi* **(a)** (Mús) to whistle **(b)** «*viento*» to whistle **(c)** «*oídos*»: **me silban los oídos** I've got a ringing *o* whistling in my ears

silbato *m* **(a)** (pito) whistle; **tocar el ~** to blow the whistle **(b)** (Col period) (árbitro) referee

silbido *m* **(a)** (con la boca, un silbato) whistle; **dio un ~** he whistled **(b)** (del viento, balas) whistling; (de respiración) wheezing **(c)** (en los oídos) ringing, whistling **(d)** **~s** (en señal de desaprobacion) catcalls

silenciador *m* **(a)** (Auto) muffler (AmE), silencer (BrE) **(b)** (de arma) silencer

silencio *m* **1** (en general) silence; **deben guardar ~** you must remain silent; **en el ~ más absoluto** in dead *o* total silence **2** (Mús) rest

silencioso -sa *adj* **1** ‹*máquina/motor*› quiet, silent, noiseless; ‹*persona*› silent, quiet **2** ‹*calle/barrio*› quiet

silicona *f* silicone

silicosis *f* silicosis

silla *f* **(a)** (mueble) chair; **~ de ruedas** wheelchair; **~ eléctrica** electric chair; **~ plegable** *or* **de tijera** folding chair **(b)** (Equ) *tb* **~ de montar** saddle

sillín *m* (de bicicleta) saddle

sillón *m* armchair, easy chair

silogismo *m* syllogism

silueta *f* **(a)** (cuerpo) figure **(b)** (contorno) silhouette

silvestre *adj* wild

simbólico -ca *adj* symbolic

simbolizar [A4] *vt* to symbolize, represent

símbolo *m* symbol

simetría *f* symmetry

simétrico -ca *adj* symmetric, symmetrical

símil *m* **(a)** (comparación) comparison **(b)** (Lit) simile

similar *adj* similar; **~ A algo** similar TO sth

similitud *f* similarity, resemblance

simio *m* ape, simian (tech)

simpatía *f* **(a)** (de una persona) friendliness **(b)** (sentimiento): **se ganó la(s) ~(s) de todos** everyone came to like him; **no le tengo mucha ~** I don't really like him

simpático -ca *adj* **(a)** ‹*persona*› nice; **me cae** *or* **me resulta muy ~** I really like him **(b)** ‹*gesto/detalle*› nice, lovely **(c)** ‹*ambiente*› pleasant, congenial; ‹*paseo*› pleasant, nice

simpatizante *mf* (de partido) sympathizer, supporter

simpatizar [A4] *vi* **(a)** (caerse bien) **~** (CON **algn**) to get on well (WITH sb); **~on desde el primer momento** they took to each other right from the start **(b)** (Pol) **~** CON **algo** to be sympathetic TO sth, to sympathize WITH sth

simple *adj* **1** (sencillo, fácil) simple; ⇒ LLANAMENTE **2** (*delante del n*) (mero) simple; **el ~ hecho de** ... the simple fact of ...; **es un ~ resfriado** it's just a common cold; **un ~ soldado** an ordinary soldier **3** (tonto) simple, simple-minded ■ *mf* simpleton

simpleza *f* **(a)** (falta de inteligencia) simpleness; (ingenuidad) gullibility **(b)** (tontería): **deja de hacer/decir ~s** stop being silly; **discutieron por una ~** they argued over a trifling matter

simplicidad *f* simplicity

simplificar [A2] *vt* to simplify

simplista *adj* simplistic

simposio, **simposium** *m* symposium

simulacro *m* **(a)** (cosa fingida): **no era de verdad, sólo fue un ~** it wasn't for real, they (*o* he *etc*) were (*o* was *etc*) just pretending **(b)** (farsa) sham; **~ de ataque** mock attack; **~ de incendio** fire drill, fire practice

simular [A1] *vt* ‹*sentimiento*› to feign; ‹*accidente*› to fake; ‹*efecto/sonido*› to simulate

simultánea *f* (en ajedrez) simultaneous match

simultáneo -nea *adj* simultaneous

sin *prep* **1** ▶**389** without; **~ azúcar** without sugar; **seguimos ~ noticias** we still haven't had any news; **agua mineral ~ gas** still mineral water; **cerveza ~ alcohol** non-alcoholic beer, alcohol-free beer; **me quedé ~ pan** I ran out of bread **2 (a)** (con significado activo) without; **se fue sin pagar** he left without paying; **estuvo una semana ~ hablarme** she didn't speak to me for a week; **sigo ~ entender** I still don't understand; **la pisé ~ querer** I accidentally trod on her foot **(b)** (con significado pasivo): **preguntas ~ contestar** unanswered questions; **esto está aún ~ terminar** it still isn't finished **3 ~** QUE + SUBJ: **no voy a ir ~ que me inviten** I'm not going if I haven't been invited; **quítaselo ~ que se dé cuenta** get it off him without his *o* without him noticing

sinagoga *f* synagogue

sinceridad *f* sincerity; **te voy a contestar con toda ~** I'm going to be quite honest *o* frank with you

sincero -ra *adj* sincere

sincronía *f* synchrony

sincronizar [A4] *vt* **(a)** ‹*frecuencias/relojes*› to synchronize; **~ algo** CON **algo** to synchronize sth WITH sth **(b)** (Col) ‹*carro*› to tune

sindical *adj* union (*before n*), labor union (*before n*) (AmE), trade union (*before n*) (BrE)

sindicalismo *m* **(a)** (movimiento) labor union movement (AmE), trade union movement (BrE) **(b)** (sistema, ideología) unionism, trade unionism (BrE)

sindicalista *mf* **(a)** (Rels Labs) member of the unions, trade unionist (BrE) **(b)** (Pol) syndicalist

sindicalizarse [A4] *v pron* (formar un sindicato) to unionize, form a union; (afiliarse a un sindicato) to join a union

sindicato *m* (Rels Labs) union, labor union (AmE), trade union (BrE)

síndrome *m* syndrome; **~ de abstinencia** withdrawal symptoms (*pl*); **~ de inmunodeficiencia adquirida** Acquired Immune Deficiency Syndrome, AIDS; **el ~ premenstrual** premenstrual syndrome *o* (BrE) tension, PMS, PMT (BrE)

sinfín *m*: **un ~ de** a great many

sinfonía *f* symphony

sinfónico -ca *adj* ‹*música*› symphonic; ‹*orquesta*› symphony (*before n*)

Singapur *m* Singapore

single /'siŋgel/ *m* **1** (Mús) single **2** (en tenis) **(a)** (CS) (partido) singles (match) **(b) singles** *mpl* (AmL) (partido) singles (match)

singular *adj* singular ■ *m* singular; **en ~** (Ling) in the singular

Sin

Algunas observaciones generales

Cuando la preposición 'sin' *va seguida de un sustantivo singular, la traducción inglesa* without, *puede requerir artículo indefinido*:

lo corté sin cuchillo = I cut it without a knife
un perro sin cola = a dog without a tail

Nótese que en muchas ocasiones cuando el español utiliza la preposición 'sin' *seguida de un sustantivo o de un infinitivo, el inglés prefiere utilizar un adjetivo encabezado por el prefijo* un- *o* in-:

sin educación/empleo = uneducated/unemployed
sin titulación = unqualified
sin terminar/abrir = unfinished/unopened
sin experiencia = inexperienced

o bien por un sustantivo terminado con el sufijo -less:

sin dolor = painless
sin hogar = homeless

En otras ocasiones cuando la preposición 'sin' *va seguida de infinitivo, el inglés prefiere el uso de un adverbio*:

sin querer = inadvertently
sin cesar = incessantly

En caso de duda consultar el diccionario
Para otros ejemplos y usos de la preposición, ver bajo entrada

siniestro[1] **-tra** *adj* ‹*mirada/aspecto*› sinister; ‹*intenciones*› sinister, evil

siniestro[2] *m* (frml) (accidente) accident; (causado por una fuerza natural) disaster, catastrophe

sino *conj* but; **se comió no uno, ~ tres** he ate not one, but three; **no hace ~ criticar a los demás** he does nothing but criticize everybody else; **no vino, ~ que llamó** he didn't come, he telephoned; **no sólo** ... **~ que** ... not only ... but ... ■ *m* (liter) fate

sínodo *m* synod

sinónimo[1] **-ma** *adj* synonymous; **~ DE algo** synonymous WITH sth

sinónimo[2] *m* synonym; **~ DE algo** synonym FOR sth

sinsabores *mpl* (problemas) troubles (*pl*); (experiencias tristes) heartaches (*pl*)

sintáctico -ca *adj* syntactic

sintagma *m* syntagm, syntagma

sintaxis *f* syntax

síntesis *f* (*pl* ~) **(a)** (resumen) summary **(b)** (deducción) synthesis; (combinación) synthesis, combination

sintético -ca *adj* ‹*fibra*› synthetic, man-made; ‹*suelas*› man-made

sintetizador *m* synthesizer

sintetizar [A4] *vt* **(a)** (resumir) to summarize **(b)** (combinar) to synthesize, combine

sintiera, **sintió, etc** *see* SENTIR

síntoma *m* (Med) symptom; (señal) sign, indication

sintonía *f* **(a)** (Rad, TV): **están ustedes en la ~ de Radio Victoria** you are listening to Radio Victoria; **para una mejor ~** for better reception **(b)** (armonía): **en ~ con el pueblo** in tune with the people

sintonizador *m* tuner

sintonizar [A4] *vt* ‹*emisora*› to tune (in) to ■ ~ *vi* (Rad, TV) to tune in

sinvergüenza *adj* **(a)** (canalla): **¡qué tipo más ~!** what a swine! (colloq) **(b)** (hum) (pícaro) naughty ■ *mf* **(a)** (canalla) swine (colloq); (estafador, ladrón) crook (colloq) **(b)** (hum) (pícaro) rascal (hum)

síper *m* (Méx) zipper (AmE), zip (BrE)

siquiera *adv* **1** (por lo menos) at least; **dile ~ adiós** at least say goodbye to her; **¡si (tan) ~ me hubiera avisado** ...! if only you'd warned me ...! **2** (en frases negativas) even; **ni ~ nos saludó** he didn't even say hello to us

sirena *f* **1** (Mit) mermaid; (en mitología clásica) siren **2** (de fábrica, ambulancia, alarma) siren **3** (Col) (en pirotecnia) rocket

Siria *f* Syria

sirope *m* syrup

sirviente -ta *m,f* (*m*) servant; (*f*) maid, servant

sísmico -ca *adj* seismic

sismo *m* (terremoto) earthquake; (temblor) earth tremor

sismógrafo *m* seismograph

sistema *m* **1** (método) system; **trabajar con ~** to work systematically *o* methodically **2** (conjunto organizado) system; **~ nervioso** nervous system; **~ solar** solar system

sistemático -ca *adj* ‹*persona*› systematic, methodical; ‹*método*› systematic

sistematizar [A4] *vt* to systematize

sitiar [A1] *vt* **(a)** (Mil) to besiege; **estamos sitiados** we are under siege **(b)** (acorralar) to corner

sitio *m* **1 (a)** (lugar) place; **pon ese libro en su ~** put that book back in its place; **cambié la tele de ~** I moved the TV; **déjalo en cualquier ~** leave it anywhere; **tiene que estar en algún ~** it must be around somewhere **(b)** (espacio) room, space;

¿hay ~ para todos? is there (enough) room for everyone?; ***hacer* ~** to make room **(c)** (plaza, asiento): **guárdame el ~** keep my seat *o* place; **le cambié el ~** I changed places with him **(d)** (Méx) (parada de taxis) taxi stand *o* rank **(e)** (Chi) (terreno urbano) vacant lot **2** (Mil) siege

situación *f* **1 (a)** (coyuntura) situation **(b)** (en la sociedad) position, standing **2** (emplazamiento) position, situation (frml), location (frml)

situado -da *adj* **(a)** (ubicado) situated **(b)** ‹*persona*›: **estar bien ~** to have a good position in society

situar [A18] *vt* **(a)** (colocar, ubicar) ‹*fábrica/aeropuerto*› to site, to locate (frml) **(b)** (Lit) ‹*obra/acción*› to set **(c)** ‹*soldados*› to post, station
■ **situarse** *v pron* **(a)** (colocarse, ubicarse): **con esta victoria se sitúan en primer lugar** this victory puts them in first place; **se situó entre los cinco mejores** she got a place among the top five **(b)** (socialmente): **se ha situado muy bien** he has done very well for himself

siútico -ca *adj/m,f* (Chi) ⇒ CURSI

skai®, **skay**® /(e)s'kai/ *m* imitation leather

S.L. *f* = **Sociedad Limitada**

slalom /(e)s'lalom/ *m* (*pl* **-loms**) slalom

slip /(e)s'lip/ (*pl* **slips**) *m* **1** (prenda interior) **(a)** (de hombre) underpants (*pl*), pants (*pl*) (BrE) **(b)** (de mujer) panties (*pl*), knickers (*pl*) (BrE) **2** (bañador) swimming trunks (*pl*)

smog /(e)s'moɣ/ *m* (AmL) smog

sobaco *m* armpit

sobado -da *adj* ‹*tapizado/cortinas/prenda*› worn, shabby; ‹*libro*› dog-eared, well-thumbed

sobajear [A1] *vt* (AmL fam) ⇒ SOBAR 1(a), (b)

sobar [A1] *vt* **1 (a)** (manosear) ‹*tela/ropa/tapizado*› to handle, finger **(b)** (fam) ‹*chica*› to feel up (colloq), to grope (esp BrE colloq) **(c)** (Méx, Per fam) (adular) to suck up to (colloq) **2** (Col, Ven) (dar masajes) to massage

soberanía *f* sovereignty

soberano -na *adj* **1** ‹*estado/pueblo/poder*› sovereign **2** (fam) (enorme) tremendous; **eso es una soberana estupidez** that's an absolutely ridiculous thing to say/do ■ *m,f* (Gob, Pol) sovereign

soberbia *f* (orgullo) pride; (altivez) arrogance, haughtiness

soberbio -bia *adj* **1** ‹*persona/carácter*› (orgulloso) proud; (altivo) arrogant, haughty **2** (magnífico) superb, magnificent

sobornar [A1] *vt* to bribe, suborn (frml)

soborno *m* (acción) bribery; (dinero, regalo) bribe

sobra *f* **1 de sobra (a)** (mucho): **hay comida de ~** there's plenty of food **(b)** (de más): **tengo una entrada de ~** I have a spare *o* an extra ticket; **tú aquí estás de ~** you're not wanted/needed here **(c)** (muy bien): **saber de ~ que** ... to know full well *o* perfectly well that ... **2 sobras** *fpl* (de comida) leftovers (*pl*)

sobrado -da *adj* **1 (a)** ‹*experiencia*› ample, more than enough; **tengo ~s motivos para sospechar** I have every reason to be suspicious **(b)** ‹*persona*›: **estar ~ de algo** to have plenty of sth; **no ando muy ~ de tiempo** I'm a bit short of time **2** (Andes fam) (engreído) full of oneself (colloq)

sobrar [A1] *vi* **(a)** (quedar, restar): **sobró mucha comida** there was a lot of food left over; **¿te ha sobrado dinero?** do you have any money left? **(b)** (estar de más): **ya veo que sobro aquí** I can see I'm not wanted/needed here; **a mí no me sobra el dinero** I don't have money to throw around (colloq); **sobra un cubierto** there's an extra place

sobre *m* **1** (Corresp) envelope **2** (AmL) (cartera) clutch bag ■ *prep* **1** (indicando posición) **(a)** (encima de) on; **lo dejé ~ la mesa** I left it on the table; **los puso uno ~ otro** she placed them one on top of the other; **estamos ~ su pista** we're on their trail **(b)** (por encima de) over; **volamos ~ Lima** we flew over Lima; **en el techo justo ~ la mesa** on the ceiling right above *o* over the table; **4.000 metros ~ el nivel del mar** 4,000 meters above sea level **(c)** (alrededor de) on; **gira ~ su eje** it spins on its axis **2** (en relaciones de jerarquía): **amar a Dios ~ todas las cosas** to love God above all else **3** (acerca de) on; **hay muchos libros ~ el tema** there are many books on *o* about the subject **4** (Esp) (con cantidades, fechas, horas) around, about (BrE); **~ unos 70 kilos** around *o* about 70 kilos **5 sobre todo** above all

sobrecama *f or m* (AmL exc CS) bedspread, counterpane

sobrecarga *f* **(a)** (en vehículo) excess load *o* weight **(b)** (de circuito, motor) overload; (de batería) overcharging

sobrecargar [A3] *vt* **(a)** ‹*vehículo/animal*› to overload **(b)** ‹*circuito/motor*› to overload; ‹*batería*› to overcharge **(c)** ‹*persona*› **~ a algn DE algo** ‹*de trabajo/responsabilidad*› to overburden sb WITH sth

sobrecargo *mf* **(a)** (Aviac) (supervisor) purser, chief flight attendant; (auxiliar de vuelo) flight attendant **(b)** (Náut) purser

sobrecogedor -dora *adj* shocking, horrific

sobrecoger [E6] *vt* **(a)** (conmover) to move **(b)** (asustar) to strike fear into

sobredosis *f* (*pl* ~) overdose

sobregirado -da *adj* (esp AmL) overdrawn

sobregirar [A1] *vt* (esp AmL) to overdraw (on)
■ **sobregirarse** *v pron* to overdraw

sobregiro *m* (esp AmL) overdraft

sobrehumano -na *adj* superhuman

sobrellevar [A1] *vt* ‹*dolor/enfermedad*› to endure, bear; ‹*tragedia*› to bear; ‹*soledad*› to endure

sobremesa *f* (conversación) after-lunch/after-dinner conversation; **estuvimos de ~** we sat around the table chatting

sobrenatural *adj* supernatural

sobrenombre *m* nickname

sobrepasar [A1] *vt* **(a)** ‹*nivel/cantidad*› to exceed, go above; **~ el límite de velocidad** to exceed *o* go over the speed limit **(b)** ‹*persona*› (en capacidad) to outstrip; (en altura) to overtake

sobrepeso *m* (AmL) (exceso — de equipaje) excess (baggage); (— de carga) excess load *o* weight

sobreponerse [E22] *v pron* (recuperarse) to pull oneself together; **~se A algo** to get over sth, recover FROM sth

sobrepuesto *pp*: *see* SOBREPONER

sobresaliente *adj* ‹*actuación*› outstanding; ‹*noticia/hecho*› most significant *o* important ■ *m* (Educ) *grade between 8.5 and 10 on a scale of 10*

sobresalir [I29] *vi* **(a)** «*alero/viga*» to project, overhang; «*borde*» to protrude **(b)** (destacarse, resaltar) to stand out; **sobresale entre los demás** it/she stands out from the rest; **~ EN algo** ‹*en deportes/idiomas*› to excel *o* shine AT sth

sobresaltar [A1] *vt* to startle, make ... jump ■ **sobresaltarse** *v pron* to jump, be startled

sobresalto *m* fright

sobretiempo *m* (Chi, Per) **(a)** (horas extra, pago) overtime **(b)** (Dep) overtime (AmE), extra time (BrE)

sobretodo *m* overcoat

sobrevenir [I31] *vi* «*desgracia/accidente*» to strike

sobrevivencia *f* survival

sobreviviente *adj/mf* ⇒ SUPERVIVIENTE

sobrevivir [I1] *vi* to survive; **~ A algo** to survive sth

sobrevolar [A10] *vt* to fly over

sobrino -na *m,f* (*m*) nephew; (*f*) niece; **mis ~s** (sólo varones) my nephews; (varones y mujeres) my nephews and nieces

sobrio -bria *adj* **1** [SER] **(a)** ‹*persona*› sober, restrained; ‹*hábitos*› frugal **(b)** ‹*decoración/estilo/color*› sober **2** [ESTAR] (no borracho) sober

sobros *mpl* (AmC) leftovers (*pl*)

socarrón -rrona *adj* (sarcástico) sarcastic, snide; (taimado) sly, crafty

socavón *m* (hoyo) hole; (excavación) shaft, tunnel; (cueva) cave

sociable *adj* sociable

social *adj* social

socialdemocracia *f* social democracy

socialdemócrata *adj* social democratic ■ *mf* social democrat

socialismo *m* socialism

socialista *adj/mf* socialist

socializar [A4] *vt* to socialize

sociedad *f* **1** (Sociol) society; **~ de consumo** consumer society **2** (asociación, club) society **3** (Der, Fin) company; **~ anónima** ≈public corporation (*in US*), ≈public limited company (*in UK*); **~ inmobilaria** (Esp) (que construye) construction company; (que administra) real estate (AmE) *o* (BrE) property management company; **~ mercantil** trading company **4** (clase alta) (high) society

socio -cia *m,f* **1** (miembro) member; **hacerse ~ de un club** to join a club **2** (Der, Fin) partner; **~ accionista** shareholder **3** (fam) (camarada) buddy (AmE colloq), mate (BrE colloq)

sociología *f* sociology

sociológico -ca *adj* sociological

sociólogo -ga *m,f* sociologist

socorrer [E1] *vt* to help, come to the aid of

socorrido -da *adj* ‹*excusa/recurso*› handy, useful

socorrismo *m* (en el agua) lifesaving; (en la montaña) mountain rescue; (primeros auxilios) first aid

socorrista *mf* (en el agua) lifeguard, lifesaver; (en la montaña) mountain rescue worker; (de primeros auxilios) first-aider

socorro *m* help; **pedir ~** to ask for help; **¡~!** help!; **un grito de ~** a cry for help

soda *f* **(a)** (bebida) soda water, soda (AmE) **(b)** (AmC) (cafetería) coffee bar

sodio *m* sodium

sofá *m* sofa, settee, couch

sofá-cama *m* sofa bed

sofisticado -da *adj* sophisticated

sofocante *adj* stifling

sofocar [A2] *vt* ‹*fuego*› to smother, put out; ‹*motín/revolución*› to stifle, put down ■ **sofocarse** *v pron* (acalorarse) to get upset *o* (colloq) worked up

sofoco *m* **(a)** (fam) (disgusto): **estaba con un ~ terrible** I was so upset **(b)** (por el calor) suffocation; (en la menopausia) hot flash (AmE), hot flush (BrE)

sofreír [I35] *vt* to sauté, fry lightly

sofrito *m*: *lightly fried tomatoes, onion, garlic, etc*

software /'sofwer/ *m* software

soga *f* (cuerda) rope

sois *see* SER

soja *f* (Esp) soy (AmE), soya (BrE)

sol *m* **1** (Astron, Meteo) sun; **brillaba el ~** the sun was shining; **al salir/ponerse el ~** at sunrise/sunset; **ayer hizo** *or* **hubo ~** it was sunny yesterday; **un día de ~** a sunny day; **en esa habitación no da el ~** that room doesn't get any sunlight *o* sun; **ayer hubo siete horas de ~** we had seven hours of sunshine yesterday; ***tomar el ~*** *or* (CS) ***tomar ~*** to sunbathe **2** (fam) (persona encantadora): **es un ~** she's an angel (colloq) **3** (Mús) (nota) G; (en solfeo) so*, sol; **~ bemol/sostenido** G flat/sharp **4** (moneda) sol (*Peruvian unit of currency*)

solamente *adv* ⇒ SÓLO

solapa *f* (de chaqueta) lapel; (de bolsillo, libro, sobre) flap

solapado -da *adj* ‹*persona*› sly, underhand (BrE); ‹*maniobra*› surreptitious, sly

solar *adj* ‹*energía/año/placa*› solar; **los rayos ~es** the sun's rays ■ *m* **1** (terreno) piece of land, site **2 (a)** (casa solariega) ancestral home **(b)** (linaje) lineage **3** (Per) (casa de vecindad) tenement building

solario, **solárium** *m* solarium

soldado *mf* soldier; **~ de caballería** cavalryman; **~ de infantería** infantryman; ; **~ raso** private; **~** *or* **soldadito de plomo** tin soldier

soldar [A10] *vt* (con estaño) to solder; (sin estaño) to weld

soleado -da *adj* sunny

soledad *f*: **en la ~ de su cuarto** in the solitude of his room; **bebe para olvidar su ~** she drinks to forget her loneliness; **no soporta la ~** he can't stand being alone; **pasó sus últimos años en ~** she spent her last years alone

solemne *adj* **1** (en general) solemn **2** (*delante del n*) (fam) ‹*mentira*› complete, downright

solemnidad *f* solemnity

soler [E9] *vi*: **suele venir una vez a la semana** she usually comes once a week; **no suele retrasarse** he's not usually late; **solía correr todos los días** he used to go for a run every day

solera *f* **1** (tradición, calidad): **una familia con ~** a family with a long pedigree, a long-established family **2** (CS) (Indum) sundress

solfeo *m* (asignatura) music theory, sol-fa

solicitado -da *adj* ‹*persona*› in demand; ‹*canción*› popular

solicitante *mf* applicant

solicitar [A1] *vt* ‹*empleo/plaza*› to apply for; ‹*permiso/entrevista/información*› to request, ask for; ‹*servicios/apoyo/cooperación*› to request, ask for

solícito -ta *adj* (dispuesto a ayudar) attentive; (amable) thoughtful, kind

solicitud *f* **(a)** (para trabajo) application; (para licencia) application, request; (para información, ayuda) request **(b)** (formulario) application form

solidaridad *f* solidarity; **en** *or* **por ~ con algn** in solidarity with *o* in sympathy with sb

solidario -ria *adj* (fraterno) supportive; **un gesto ~** a gesture of solidarity

solidarizar [A4] *vi* **~ CON algn** to support sb
■ **solidarizarse** *v pron* **~se CON algn** to support sb; **~se CON algo** to support sth, to back sth

solidez *f* (de muro, edificio) solidity; (de argumento, empresa) soundness; (de relación) strength

sólido[1] -da *adj* **1** (en sentido físico) solid **2 (a)** ‹*argumento/razonamiento*› solid, sound; ‹*preparación/principios*› sound **(b)** ‹*empresa*› sound; ‹*relación*› steady, strong

sólido[2] *m* **(a)** (Fís, Mat) solid **(b) sólidos** *mpl* (Med) solids (*pl*)

solista *mf* soloist

solitaria *f* tapeworm

solitario -ria *adj* **(a)** ‹*persona/animal*› solitary; ‹*vejez/niñez*› lonely; **lleva una vida muy solitaria** he leads a very solitary existence **(b)** ‹*calles*› empty, deserted; ‹*paraje/lugar*› lonely, solitary
■ *m,f* **1** (persona) loner **2 solitario** *m* **(a)** (Jueg) solitaire (AmE), patience (BrE) **(b)** (diamante) solitaire

sollozar [A4] *vi* to sob

sollozo *m* sob

solo[1] -la *adj* **(a)** (sin compañía): **estar/sentirse ~** to be/feel lonely; **lo dejaron ~** (sin compañía) they left him on his own *o* by himself; (para no molestar) they left him alone; **el niño ya camina ~** the baby's walking on his own now; **hacen los deberes ~s** they do their homework by themselves; **hablar ~** to talk to oneself; **a solas** alone, by oneself **(b)** ‹*café/té*› black; ‹*whisky*› straight, neat; ‹*pan*› dry **(c)** (*delante del n*) (único): **lo haré con una sola condición** I'll do it on one condition; **hay un ~ problema** there's just one problem

solo[2] *m* (Mús) solo

sólo *adv* only; **~ quería ayudarte** I only wanted to help, I was only *o* just trying to help; **~ de pensarlo me dan escalofríos** just *o* merely thinking about it makes me shudder

solomillo *m* fillet/tenderloin/sirloin steak

solsticio *m* solstice

soltar [A10] *vt* **1** (dejar ir) ‹*persona*› to release, to let ... go; **soltó al perro** he let the dog off the leash **2** (dejar de tener agarrado) to let go of; **no lo sueltes** don't let go of it; **soltó el dinero y huyó** he dropped/let go of the money and ran; **¡suelta la pistola!** drop the gun! **3 (a)** (desatar) ‹*cuerda/cable*› to undo, untie; **~ amarras** to cast off **(b)** (aflojar): **suelta la cuerda poco a poco** let *o* pay out the rope gradually **(c)** ‹*freno*› to release; ‹*embrague*› to let out **(d)** (desatascar) ‹*cable/cuerda*› to free; ‹*tuerca*› to ondo, get ... undone **4** (desprender) ‹*calor/vapor*› to give off; ‹*pelo*› to shed **5** ‹*carcajada*› to let out; ‹*palabrotas/disparates*› to come out with; ‹*grito*› to let out
■ **soltarse** *v pron* **1** (*refl*) «*perro*» to get loose; **no te sueltes (de la mano)** don't let go of my hand **2** (desatarse) «*nudo*» to come undone, come loose; (aflojarse) «*nudo*» to loosen, come loose; «*tornillo*» to come loose

soltería *f*: *the fact or state of being unmarried*; (en hombre) bachelorhood (frml); (en mujer) spinsterhood (frml)

soltero -ra *adj* ▶ 378 single; **soy** *or* (esp Esp) **estoy soltera** I'm single, I'm not married ■ *m,f* (*m*) single man, bachelor; (*f*) single woman, spinster (dated *or* pej)

solterón -rona *m,f* (pey) (*m*) old *o* confirmed bachelor; (*f*) old maid (pej)

soltura *f*: **habla dos idiomas con ~** he speaks two languages fluently; **se desenvuelve con ~ en cualquier situación** she is at ease in any situation

soluble *adj* **1** (Quím) soluble; **~ en agua** water-soluble **2** ‹*problema*› soluble, solvable

solución *f* solution; **encontrar una ~ a algo** to find a solution to sth

solucionar [A1] *vt* ‹*problema*› to solve; ‹*asunto/conflicto*› to settle, resolve
■ **solucionarse** *v pron* «*problema*» to be resolved; **al final todo se solucionó** everything worked out in the end

somalí *adj/mf* Somali

Somalia *f* Somalia

sombra *f* (lugar sin sol) shade; (proyección) shadow; **las ~s de los árboles** the shadows of the trees; **sentarse a** *or* **en la ~** to sit in the shade; **este árbol casi no da ~** this tree gives hardly any shade; **~ de** *or* **para ojos** eyeshadow

sombrero *m* hat; **~ de copa** top hat; **~ de jipijapa** Panama (hat); **~ hongo** derby (AmE), bowler (hat) (BrE); **~ jarano** Mexican sombrero

sombrilla *f* **(a)** (de mano) parasol; (de playa) sunshade **(b)** (Col, Ven) (paraguas) lady's umbrella

sombrío -bría *adj* (liter) ‹*lugar*› (umbrío) dark **(b)** (lúgubre) cheerless, dismal; ‹*persona*› gloomy

someter [E1] *vt* **1** (dominar) ‹*país*› to subjugate; **fue necesario usar la fuerza para ~lo** they had to use force to subdue him **2** (a torturas, presiones,

prueba) to subject; **lo sometieron a un interrogatorio** they subjected him to an interrogation; **~ algo a votación** to put sth to the vote
■ **someterse** *v pron* **(a)** (a autoridad) to submit to, yield to; (a capricho) to give in to; (a ley) to comply with **(b)** (a prueba, exámen, operación) to undergo

somier /so'mje(r)/ *m* (*pl* **-miers** *or* **-mieres**) sprung bed base

somnífero *m* sleeping pill, soporific (frml)

somnolencia *f* drowsiness, sleepiness

somnoliento -ta *adj* sleepy, drowsy

somos *see* SER

son *m* **1 (a)** (sonido) sound; **al ~ del violín** to the strains *o* to the sound of the violin **(b) en son de**: **lo dijo en ~ de burla** she said it mockingly; **venimos en ~ de paz** we come in peace **2** (canción latinoamericana) *song with a lively, danceable beat*

son *see* SER

sonado -da *adj* **1** ‹*boda/suceso/noticia*› much-talked-about **2 (a)** ‹*boxeador*› punch-drunk **(b)** (fam) (torpe) stupid (colloq) **3** (AmL fam) (en dificultades) [ESTAR] in a mess (colloq), in trouble (colloq)

sonaja *f* (Méx) rattle

sonajero *m* rattle

sonámbulo -la *adj* somnambulistic (frml); **es ~** he sleepwalks, he walks in his sleep ■ *m,f* sleepwalker, somnambulist (frml)

sonar [A10] *vi* **1** «*teléfono/timbre*» to ring; «*disparo*» to ring out; **el despertador sonó a las cinco** the alarm went off at five o'clock; **~on las doce en el reloj** the clock struck twelve; **me suenan las tripas** (fam) my tummy's rumbling (colloq) **2** (+ *compl*) **(a)** «*motor/instrumento*» to sound; «*persona*» to sound; **suena raro** it sounds funny; **sonaba preocupada** she sounded worried; **suena a hueco** it sounds hollow **(b)** «*palabra/expresión*» to sound **3 (a)** (resultar conocido) (+ *me/te/le etc*): **me suena tu cara** your face is *o* looks familiar; **¿te suena este refrán?** does this proverb ring a bell (with you) *o* sound familiar to you? **(b)** (parecer) **~ A algo** to sound like sth **4** (AmL fam) (fracasar): **soné en el examen** I blew it in the exam (colloq); **sonamos** we've blown it now (colloq) ■ **~** *vt* **1 (a)** (+ *me/te/le etc*) ‹*nariz*› to wipe **(b)** ‹*trompeta*› to play **2** (Méx fam) **(a)** (pegar) ‹*persona*› to thump (colloq), to clobber (colloq) **(b)** (en competición) to beat, thrash (colloq)
■ **sonarse** *v pron*: *tb* **~se la nariz** to blow one's nose

sonata *f* sonata

sonda *f* **(a)** (Med) catheter **(b)** (para perforar) drill **(c)** (Náut) sounding line, lead line **(d)** (Espac, Meteo) probe

sondeo *m* **1** (encuesta) poll, survey **2** (perforación) test drilling; (Náut) sounding; (Espac, Meteo) exploration

soneto *m* sonnet

sonido *m* sound

sonoro -ra *adj* ‹*golpe*› resounding (*before n*); loud; ‹*voz/lenguaje*› sonorous, resonant; (Ling) voiced

sonreír [I18] *vi* **(a)** «*persona*» to smile; **~(le) A algn** to smile AT sb **(b)** «*vida/fortuna*» (+ *me/te/le etc*) to smile on

sonriente *adj* ‹*ojos/expresión*› smiling (*before n*); ‹*persona*› cheerful

sonrisa *f* smile

sonrojarse [A1] *v pron* to blush

sonsacar [A2] *vt*: **me costó trabajo ~le la verdad** I had a hard time getting the truth out of her

soñado -da *adj* (AmL fam) divine (colloq), heavenly (colloq); *ver tb* SOÑAR

soñador -dora *adj* ‹*mirada*› dreamy, faraway; **soy muy ~** I'm a real dreamer ■ *m,f* dreamer

soñar [A10] *vt* **(a)** (durmiendo) to dream **(b)** (fantasear) to dream; **la casa soñada** her/his/their dream house ■ **~** *vi* **(a)** (durmiendo) to dream; **~ CON algo/algn** to dream ABOUT sth/sb; **que sueñes con los angelitos** (fr hecha) sweet dreams **(b)** (fantasear) to dream; **~ despierto** to daydream; **~ CON algo** to dream OF sth

sopa *f* (caldo) soup; **~ de sobre** packaged soup (AmE), packet soup (BrE)

sopapo *m* (fam) (bofetón) slap, smack (colloq)

sope *m* (Méx) *fried tortilla topped with refried beans, onion and hot sauce*

sopera *f* soup tureen

sopesar [A1] *vt* ‹*situación/ventajas*› to weigh up; ‹*palabras*› to weigh

soplar [A1] *vi* **1 (a)** (con la boca) to blow **(b)** «*viento*» to blow **2** (fam) (en examen) to whisper (*answers in an exam*) ■ **~** *vt* **1 (a)** ‹*vela*› to blow out; ‹*fuego/brasas*› to blow on **(b)** ‹*vidrio*› to blow **2** (fam) ‹*respuesta*› (en examen) to whisper **3** (fam) (robar) to swipe (colloq), to pinch (BrE colloq); (cobrar) to sting (colloq)
■ **soplarse** *v pron* (Méx, Per fam) (aguantar) ‹*persona*› to put up with; ‹*discurso/película*› to sit through, suffer

soplete *m* (para soldar) gas welding torch; (para quitar pintura) blowtorch

soplido *m* puff

soplo *m* **1 (a)** (soplido) puff; **de un ~** with one puff, in one go **(b)** (de aire) puff; (más fuerte) blast **(c)** (de viento) puff; (más fuerte) gust **2** (fam) (chivatazo): **alguien dio el ~ a la policía** someone tipped off the police (colloq) **3** (Med) heart murmur

soplón -plona *m,f* **(a)** (fam) (en colegio) tittle-tattle (AmE colloq), telltale (BrE colloq) **(b)** (fam) (a la policía) informer, stoolie (AmE colloq), grass (BrE colloq)

soponcio *m* (fam) **(a)** (desmayo): **le dio un ~** she fainted **(b)** (ataque de nervios) fit (colloq)

sopor *m* **(a)** (somnolencia) drowsiness, sleepiness **(b)** (letargo) torpor

soporífero -ra *adj* ‹*efecto/discurso/clase*› soporific

soportable *adj* bearable

soportal *m* **(a)** (de casa) porch **(b) soportales** *mpl* (de calle) arcade, colonnade

soportar [A1] *vt* **1 (a)** ‹*situación/frío/dolor*› to put up with, bear, endure (frml); ‹*persona*› to put up with; **no soporto este calor/la gente así** I can't stand this heat/people like that **2** ‹*peso/carga*› to support, withstand; ‹*presión*› to withstand

soporte *m* **(a)** (de estante) bracket; (de viga) support; (de maceta, portarretratos) stand **(b)** (Inf) medium

soprano *mf* soprano

soquete *m* **1** (CS) (Indum) ankle sock **2** (Chi) (Elec) lampholder, socket **3** (Col, Méx, RPl fam) (tonto) fool, idiot

sor *f* (Relig) sister

sorber [E1] *vt* **(a)** (beber) to suck in *o* up; (tomar poco a poco) to sip **(b)** «*esponja*» to absorb, soak up

sorbete *m* sherbet (AmE), sorbet (esp BrE)

sorbo *m* **(a)** (cantidad pequeña) sip; **bébetelo a sorbitos** sip it **(b)** (trago grande) gulp; **de un ~** in one gulp

sordera *f* deafness

sórdido -da *adj* ‹*lugar/ambiente*› squalid; ‹*asunto/libro*› sordid

sordina *f* (de trompeta, violín) mute; (de piano) damper

sordo -da *adj* **1** (Med) deaf; **se quedó ~** he went deaf; **es ~ de nacimiento** he was born deaf **2** ‹*ruido/golpe*› dull, muffled; ‹*dolor*› dull; (Ling) voiceless ■ *m,f* deaf person; ***hacerse el ~*** to pretend not to hear

sordomudo -da *adj* deaf-mute (*before n*), deaf and dumb (BrE) ■ *m,f* deaf-mute

soroche *m* (Andes) (en la montaña) mountain sickness, altitude sickness

sorprendente *adj* surprising

sorprender [E1] *vi* to surprise; **me sorprende que no lo sepas** I'm surprised you don't know ■ **~** *vt* (coger desprevenido) to surprise, catch … unawares; **nos sorprendió la lluvia** we got caught in the rain

■ **sorprenderse** *v pron* to be surprised

sorprendido -da *adj* surprised; **me miró ~** he looked at me in surprise; *ver tb* SORPRENDER

sorpresa *f* **(a)** (emoción) surprise; **se va a llevar una ~** she's going to be surprised, she's in for a surprise (colloq); ***tomar*** *or* (esp Esp) ***coger a algn de ~*** to take sb by surprise **(b)** (regalo) surprise ■ *adj inv* ‹*fiesta/ataque*› surprise (*before n*)

sorpresivo -va *adj* (AmL) surprise (*before n*), unexpected

sortear [A1] *vt* **1** ‹*premio/puesto*› to draw lots for; **se ~á un coche** there will be a prize draw for a car **2 (a)** ‹*bache/obstáculo*› to avoid, negotiate **(b)** ‹*problema/dificultad*› to get around

sorteo *m* draw; **por ~** by drawing lots

sortija *f* **(a)** (anillo) ring **(b)** (en el pelo) ringlet

sortilegio *m* (embrujo) spell, charm; (brujería) sorcery; (adivinación) fortune-telling

sos: *equivalent of 'eres' in Central America and the River Plate area*

SOS *m* SOS, distress call

sosa *f* soda

soslayo: **de ~** ‹*mirada*› sidelong (*before n*), sideways; ‹*mirar*› sideways

soso -sa *adj* **(a)** ‹*comida*› (sin sabor) bland, tasteless; **está ~** (sin sabor) it's bland *o* tasteless; (sin sal) it needs more salt **(b)** ‹*persona/película*› boring, dull; ‹*estilo*› flat, drab

sospecha *f* suspicion; **tengo la ~ de que** … I suspect *o* I have a feeling that …

sospechar [A1] *vt* to suspect ■ **~** *vi* **~** DE **algn** to suspect sb, have one's suspicions ABOUT sb

sospechoso -sa *adj* ‹*movimiento/comportamiento*› suspicious; ‹*paquete*› suspicious, suspect; **tres hombres de aspecto ~** three suspicious-looking men ■ *m,f* suspect

sostén *m* **(a)** (físico) support; (económico) means of support **(b)** (Indum) bra, brassiere

sostener [E27] *vt* **1** (apoyar) **(a)** ‹*estructura/techo*› to hold up, support; ‹*carga/peso*› to bear **(b)** (sustentar) ‹*familia*› to support, maintain **2** (sujetar, tener cogido) ‹*paquete*› to hold; **no tengas miedo, yo te sostengo** don't be afraid, I've got you *o* I'm holding you **3** ‹*conversación/relación/reunión*› to have **4 (a)** (opinar) to hold **(b)** ‹*argumento/afirmación*› to support, back up **5 (a)** ‹*lucha/ritmo/resistencia*› to keep up, sustain; **ella sostuvo mi mirada** she held my gaze **(b)** (Mús) ‹*nota*› to hold, sustain

■ **sostenerse** *v pron* **(a)** (no caerse): **la estructura se sostiene sola** the structure stays up without support; **apenas se sostenía en pie** he could hardly stand **(b)** (en un estado) to remain; **se sostuvo en el poder** she managed to remain in power

sostenido -da *adj* sharp; **re ~** D sharp

sostuve, sostuvo, etc *see* SOSTENER

sota *f* jack (*in Spanish pack of cards*)

sotana *f* cassock, soutane

sótano *m* (habitable) basement; (para almacenamiento) cellar, basement

souvenir /suβe'nir/ *m* (*pl* **-nirs**) souvenir

soviético -ca *adj/m,f* (Hist) Soviet

soy *see* SER

soya *f* (AmL) soy (AmE), soya (BrE)

sport /(e)s'por/ *m*: **ropa (de) ~** leisure wear, casual clothes (*pl*); **vestido de ~** casually dressed

spot /(e)s'pot/ *m* (*pl* **spots**) *tb* **~ publicitario** (espacio) slot; (anuncio) commercial, advertisement (BrE)

spray /(e)s'prai/ *m* (*pl* **sprays**) spray

Sr. *m* **▶ 420** (= **señor**) Mr

Sra. *f* **▶ 420** (= **señora**) Mrs

Sres. *mpl* = **señores**

Srta. *f* **▶ 420** (= **señorita**) Miss

SS.MM. = **Sus Majestades**

Sta. (= **Santa**) St

status /(e)s'tatus/ *m* (*pl* **~**) status

Sto. (= **Santo**) St

stop /(e)s'top/ *m* (disco) stop sign

su *adj* (*delante del n*) (de él) his; (de ella) her; (de usted, ustedes) your; (de ellos, ellas) their; (de animal, cosa) its

suave *adj* **1** ‹*piel/cutis*› smooth, soft; ‹*pelo*› soft; ‹*superficie/pasta*› smooth **2 (a)** ‹*tono*› gentle; ‹*acento/música*› soft **(b)** ‹*color*› soft, pale **(c)** ‹*sabor*› (no fuerte) delicate, mild; (sin acidez) smooth **3 (a)** ‹*movimiento/gesto*› gentle, slight **(b)** ‹*temperaturas/clima*› mild; ‹*brisa*› gentle **(c)** ‹*modales/carácter/reprimenda*› mild, gentle **(d)** ‹*cuesta/*

curva› gentle, gradual **(e)** ‹*jabón/champú*› gentle, mild **(f)** ‹*laxante/sedante*› mild **4** (Méx fam) (fantástico): **¡qué ~!** great! (colloq), fantastic! (colloq)

suavidad *f* (de la piel) smoothness, softness; (de jabón, champú) gentleness, mildness; (de tono, acento) gentleness, softness; (de color) softness, paleness; (de movimiento) gentleness; (de carácter) mildness, gentleness

suavizante *m* (para el pelo) (Esp) conditioner; (para la ropa) (fabric) softener *o* conditioner

suavizar [A4] *vt* ‹*piel*› to leave ... smooth/soft; ‹*color*› to soften, tone down; ‹*sabor*› to tone down; ‹*carácter*› to mellow, make ... gentler; ‹*dureza/severidad*› to soften, temper; ‹*situación*› to calm, ease ■ **suavizarse** *v pron* «*piel*» to become smoother/softer; «*carácter*» to mellow, become gentler; «*situación*» to calm down, ease

subalterno -na *m,f* **(a)** (en jerarquía) subordinate **(b)** (Taur) *member of a matador's support team*

subarrendar [A5] *vt* to sublease, sublet

subasta *f* **(a)** (venta) auction; **sacar algo a ~** to put sth up for auction **(b)** (de obras) invitation to tender

subastar [A1] *vt* ‹*cuadro*› to auction, sell ... at auction; ‹*contrato/obra pública*› to put ... out to tender

subcampeón -peona *m,f* (en liga) runner-up; (en torneo eliminatorio) losing finalist

subcomisión *f* subcommittee

subcomité *m* subcommittee

subconsciente *adj/m* subconscious

subcontratar [A1] *vt* to subcontract

subdesarrollado -da *adj* underdeveloped

subdesarrollo *m* underdevelopment

subdirector -ra *m,f* (de organización) deputy director; (de comercio) assistant manager, deputy manager

súbdito -ta *m,f* subject

subdividir [I1] *vt* to subdivide

subestimar [A1] *vt* to underestimate

subida *f* **(a)** (pendiente) rise, slope **(b)** (a montaña) ascent, climb; (al poder) rise **(c)** (de temperatura, precios, salarios) rise, increase

subido -da *adj* ‹*color*› intense, deep

subir [I1] *vi* **1 (a)** «*ascensor/persona/coche*» (ir arriba) to go up; (venir arriba) to come up; **hay que ~ a pie** you have to walk up; **ahora subo** I'll be right up; **el camino sube hasta la cima** the path goes up to *o* leads to the top of the hill **(b) ~ A algo** ‹*a autobús/tren/avión*› to get ON *o* ONTO sth; ‹*a coche*› to get IN *o* INTO sth; ‹*a caballo/bicicleta*› to get ON *o* ONTO sth, to mount sth (frml); **~ a bordo** to go *o* get on board **(c)** (de categoría) to go up; (en el escalafón) to be promoted **2 (a)** «*marea*» to come in; «*aguas/río*» to rise **(b)** «*fiebre/tensión*» to go up, rise; «*temperatura*» to rise **3** «*precio/valor/cotización/salario*» to rise, go up ■ **~** *vt* **1** ‹*montaña*› to climb; ‹*escaleras/cuesta*› to go up, climb **2 (a)** ‹*objeto/niño*› (traer arriba) to bring up; (llevar arriba) to take up; **tengo que ~ unas cajas al desván** I have to put some boxes up in the attic **(b)** (poner más alto) ‹*objeto*› to put up ... (higher); ‹*cuello de prenda*› to turn up; **sube al niño al caballo** lift the child onto the horse **(c)** ‹*persiana/telón/ventanilla*› to raise; ‹*pantalones*› to pull up; **¿me subes la cremallera?** will you zip me up?, will you fasten my zipper (AmE) *o* (BrE) zip? **(d)** ‹*dobladillo*› to take up; ‹*falda*› to take *o* turn up **3 (a)** ‹*precios/salarios*› to raise, put up **(b)** ‹*volumen/radio/calefacción*› to turn up ■ **subirse** *v pron* **1 (a)** (a coche, autobús, etc) ⇒ *vi* 1(b) **(b)** (trepar) to climb; **se subió al árbol/al muro** she climbed up the tree/(up) onto the wall; **estaba subido a un árbol** he was up a tree **(c)** (a la cabeza) (+ *me/te/le etc*): **el éxito se le subió a la cabeza** the success went to his head **2** (*refl*) ‹*calcetines/pantalones*› to pull up; ‹*cuello*› to turn up

subjetivo -va *adj* subjective

subjuntivo *m* subjunctive

sublevarse [A1] *v pron* to revolt, rise up, rebel

sublime *adj* ‹*acción/sacrificio*› noble; ‹*cuadro/música*› sublime

submarinismo *m* scuba diving

submarinista *mf* (buzo) scuba diver; (tripulante de submarino) submariner

submarino[1] -na *adj* underwater (*before n*), submarine (*before n*)

submarino[2] *m* submarine

subnormal *adj* **(a)** (Psic) mentally handicapped, subnormal **(b)** (fam & pey) (como insulto) moronic (colloq & pej) ■ *mf* **(a)** (Psic) mentally handicapped person **(b)** (fam & pey) (cretino) moron (colloq & pej), cretin (colloq & pej)

subordinado -da *adj/mf* subordinate

subordinar [A1] *vt* to subordinate; **~ algo A algo** to subordinate sth TO sth

subrayar [A1] *vt* **(a)** ‹*texto*› to underline, underscore **(b)** (poner énfasis en) to underline, emphasize, stress

subsanar [A1] *vt* ‹*error*› to rectify, correct; ‹*carencia*› to make up for; ‹*obstáculo/dificultad*› to overcome

subsidio *m* subsidy; **~ de enfermedad** sickness benefit; **~ de desempleo** unemployment compensation (AmE), unemployment benefit (BrE)

subsistencia *f* subsistence, survival

subsistir [I1] *vi* «*persona/planta*» to survive, subsist (frml); «*creencia/tradición*» to persist, survive

subte *m* (RPl fam) subway (AmE), tube (BrE colloq)

subterráneo[1] -nea *adj* underground, subterranean

subterráneo[2] *m* **(a)** (pasaje) subway, tunnel **(b)** (RPl) (Transp) subway (AmE), underground (BrE)

subtitular [A1] *vt* to subtitle; **versión original subtitulada** original version with subtitles

subtítulo *m* subtitle

suburbano -na *adj* suburban

suburbio *m* (extrarradio) suburb; (barrio pobre) depressed area (*on the outskirts of town*)

subvención *f* subsidy, subvention (frml)

subvencionar [A1] *vt* to subsidize

subversivo -va *adj* subversive

subyacer [E5] *vi* ~ (EN **algo**) to underlie (sth)

succionar [A1] *vt* to suck (up)

sucedáneo *m* substitute

suceder [E1] *vi* **1** (ocurrir) to happen; **¿le ha sucedido algo?** has something happened to him?; **le expliqué lo sucedido** I explained to him what had happened; **por lo que pueda ~** just in case **2** (en el tiempo) «*hecho/época*» ~ A **algo** to follow sth ■ ~ *vt* (en trono, cargo) to succeed

sucesión *f* **1 (a)** (al trono, en un cargo) succession **(b)** (herederos) heirs (*pl*), issue (frml) **(c)** (Der) (herencia) estate, inheritance **2** (serie) succession, series

sucesivo -va *adj* consecutive; **~s gobiernos lo han intentado** successive governments have tried it; **en lo ~** from now on, in future

suceso *m* **(a)** (acontecimiento) event **(b)** (accidente, crimen): **el lugar del ~** the scene of the incident/crime/accident

sucesor -sora *m,f* (al trono, en un puesto) successor; (heredero) heir, successor (frml)

suciedad *f* **(a)** (mugre) dirt **(b)** (estado) dirtiness

sucio -cia *adj* **1 (a)** [ESTAR] ‹*ropa/casa/vaso*› dirty; **hacer algo en ~** to do a rough draft of sth (AmE), do sth in rough (BrE) **(b)** ‹*lengua*› furred, coated **2** [SER] **(a)** ‹*trabajo*› dirty; ‹*dinero/negocio/juego*› dirty **(b)** ‹*lenguaje*› filthy; ‹*mente*› dirty; **una jugada sucia** a dirty trick

sucre *m* sucre (*Ecuadorean unit of currency*)

sucursal *f* (de banco, comercio) branch; (de empresa) office

sudadera *f* (Dep, Indum) (suéter) sweatshirt; (conjunto) (Col, Ven) tracksuit

Sudáfrica *f* South Africa

sudafricano -na *adj/m,f* South African

Sudamérica *f* South America

sudamericano -na *adj/m,f* South American

Sudán *m*: *tb* **el ~** (the) Sudan

sudanés -nesa *adj/m,f* Sudanese

sudar [A1] *vi* to sweat, perspire (frml)

sudario *m* shroud

sudeste ▶ 346 *adj inv* ‹*región*› southeastern; **iban en dirección ~** they were heading southeast ■ *m* **(a)** (parte, sector): **el ~** the southeast, the Southeast **(b)** (punto cardinal) southeast, Southeast

sudoeste ▶ 346 *adj inv* ‹*región*› southwestern; **iban en dirección ~** they were heading southwest ■ *m* **(a)** (parte, sector): **el ~** the southwest, the Southwest **(b)** (punto cardinal) southwest, Southwest

sudor *m* sweat, perspiration (frml)

sudoroso -sa *adj* sweaty

Suecia *f* Sweden

sueco[1] -ca *adj* Swedish ■ *m,f* (persona) Swede

sueco[2] *m* (idioma) Swedish

suegro -gra *m,f* (*m*) father-in-law; (*f*) mother-in-law; **mis ~s** my in-laws, my mother-and father-in-law

suela *f* sole

sueldo *m* (de funcionario, oficinista) salary; (de obrero) wage; **~ base** base salary (AmE), basic salary (BrE)

suelo *m* **(a)** (tierra) ground; **se cayó al ~** she fell over **(b)** (en casa) floor **(c)** (en calle, carretera) road (surface) **(d)** (Agr) land **(e)** (territorio) soil; **el ~ patrio** one's native soil *o* land

suelta, **sueltas, etc** *see* SOLTAR

suelto[1] -ta *adj* **1 (a)**. ‹*tornillo/tabla/hoja*› loose; ‹*cordones*› loose, untied **(b)** (libre): **el perro está ~ en el jardín** the dog's loose in the garden; **el asesino anda ~** the murderer is on the loose **(c)** ‹*vestido/abrigo*› loose; **déjate el pelo ~** leave your hair loose *o* down **(d)** (separado): **ejemplares ~s** individual *o* single issues; **no los vendemos ~s** ‹*yogures/sobres*› we don't sell them individually *o* separately; ‹*caramelos/tornillos*› we don't sell them loose **2 (a)** (fraccionado): **dinero ~** loose change; **mil pesetas sueltas** a thousand pesetas in change **(b)** ‹*lenguaje/estilo*› fluent; ‹*movimientos*› fluid **(c)** (euf) ‹*vientre*› loose

suelto[2] *m* (Esp, Méx) (monedas) (small) change

suena, **suenan, etc** *see* SONAR

sueño *m* **1 (a)** (estado) sleep; **oyó un ruido entre ~s** she heard a noise in her sleep; **tener el ~ ligero/pesado** to be a light/heavy sleeper; ***perder el ~ (por algo)*** to lose sleep (over sth) **(b)** (ganas de dormir): **¿tienes ~?** are you tired/sleepy?; **el vino me dio ~** the wine made me sleepy; **me empezó a entrar ~** I started feeling sleepy; **se me quitó el ~** I don't feel sleepy any more **2 (a)** (cosa soñada) dream; **un mal ~** a bad dream **(b)** (ilusión) dream; **la mujer de sus ~s** the woman of his dreams; **su ~ dorado es llegar a ser actriz** her (greatest) dream is to become an actress

suero *m* **(a)** (Med) (para alimentar) saline solution; (para inmunizar) serum **(b)** (de la sangre) blood serum **(c)** (de la leche) whey

suerte *f* **(a)** (fortuna) luck; **buena/mala ~** good/bad luck; **ha sido una ~ que vinieras** it was lucky you came; **¡qué mala ~!** how unlucky!; **¡qué ~ tienes!** you're so lucky!; **no tengo ~** I'm not a lucky person; **hombre de ~** lucky man; **por ~ no estaba sola** luckily *o* fortunately I wasn't alone; **¡(que tengas) buena ~!** good luck!; ***probar ~*** to try one's luck; ***traer** or **dar mala ~*** to bring bad luck **(b)** (azar) chance; ***echar algo a ~s*** (con monedas) to toss for sth; (con pajitas) to draw straws for sth **(c)** (destino) fate

suertero -tera *m,f* (Per) lottery ticket seller

suéter *m* sweater, pullover, jersey (BrE), jumper (BrE)

suficiencia *f* **(a)** (aptitud) aptitude **(b)** (presunción) self-satisfaction, smugness; **aire de ~** air of self-satisfaction

suficiente *adj* **(a)** (bastante) enough; **con esto hay más que ~** there's more than enough here **(b)** ‹*persona*› self-satisfied, smug ■ *m* pass (*equivalent to a grade of 5 on a scale from 0-10*)

sufijo *m* suffix

suflé *m* soufflé

sufragio *m* (sistema) suffrage; (voto) (frml) vote

sufrido -da *adj* ‹*persona*› long-suffering, uncomplaining; ‹*ropa/tejido*› hard-wearing; **un color ~** a color that doesn't show the dirt

sufrimiento *m* suffering; **pasar ~s** to suffer

sufrir [I1] *vt* **(a)** ‹*dolores/molestias*› to suffer; **sufre lesiones de gravedad** he has serious injuries **(b)** ‹*derrota/persecución/consecuencias*› to suffer; ‹*cambio*› to undergo; ‹*accidente*› to have; **sufrió un atentado** there was an attempt on his life; **el coche sufrió una avería** the car broke down ■ ~ *vi* to suffer; **~ DE algo** to suffer FROM sth

sugerencia *f* suggestion

sugerente *adj* ‹*mirada/pose*› suggestive; ‹*vestido/blusa*› sexy

sugerir [I11] *vt* to suggest; **me sugirió que lo probara** he suggested that I (should) try it; **¿qué te sugiere este cuadro?** what does this picture make you think of?

sugestión *f* (convencimiento): **es pura ~** it's all in your (*o* his *etc*) mind; **tiene gran poder de ~** he is very persuasive

sugestionarse [A1] *v pron* to get ideas into one's head

sugestivo -va *adj* ‹*mirada*› suggestive; ‹*escote*› sexy; ‹*libro/idea*› stimulating

suicida *adj* suicidal ■ *mf* suicide victim

suicidarse [A1] *v pron* to commit suicide

suicidio *m* suicide

suite /swit/ *f* (Mús) suite

Suiza *f* Switzerland

suizo -za *adj/m,f* Swiss

sujetador *m* (Esp) bra, brassiere

sujetar [A1] *vt* **1 (a)** (mantener sujeto) to hold; **sujétalo bien, que no se escape** hold it tight, don't let it go; **tuvimos que ~los para que no se pegaran** we had to hold them back to stop them hitting each other **(b)** (sostener) to hold; **sujétame los paquetes** hold on to the packages for me **(c)** (fijar, trabar — con clip) to fasten ... together; (— con alfileres) to pin ... together **2** (dominar) to subdue, conquer

■ **sujetarse** *v pron* **1 (a)** (agarrarse) **~se A algo** to hold on TO sth **(b)** (trabar, sostener): **se sujetaba los pantalones con la mano** he held his trousers up with his hand; **se sujetó la falda con un imperdible** she fastened her skirt with a safety pin **2** (someterse) **~se A algo** ‹*a ley/reglas*› to abide BY sth

sujeto[1] -ta *adj* **1** (sometido) **~ A algo** ‹*a cambios/revisión*› subject TO sth **2** (fijo) secure

sujeto[2] *m* **1** (individuo) character, individual **2** (Fil, Ling) subject

sultán *m* sultan

suma *f* **1** (cantidad) sum **2** (Mat) addition; **hacer ~s** to do addition, to do sums (BrE)

sumar [A1] *vt* **(a)** ‹*cantidades*› to add (up) **(b)** (totalizar) to add up to; **8 y 5 suman 13** 8 and 5 add up to *o* make 13 ■ ~ *vi* to add up

■ **sumarse** *v pron* **(a)** (agregarse) **~se A algo**: **esto se suma a los problemas ya existentes** this comes on top of *o* is in addition to any already existing problems **(b)** (adherirse) **~se A algo** ‹*a protesta/celebración*› to join sth

sumario *m* **1** (Der) **(a)** (en lo penal) indictment **(b)** (juicio administrativo) disciplinary action **2** (índice) (table of) contents

sumergible *adj* ‹*reloj*› waterproof; ‹*nave*› submersible

sumergido -da *adj* ‹*submarino*› submerged; ‹*ciudad*› submerged, sunken

sumergir [I7] *vt* (en líquido) to immerse, submerge ■ **sumergirse** *v pron* **(a)** «*submarino/buzo*» to dive, submerge **(b)** (en ambiente) to immerse oneself

sumidero *m* drain

suministrar [A1] *vt* (frml) to supply; **~ algo A algn** to supply sb WITH sth

suministro *m* supply; **el ~ de gas** the gas supply

sumir [I1] *vt* **1** (sumergir) **~ algo/a algn EN algo** ‹*en tristeza/desesperación*› to plunge sth/sb INTO sth **2** (Col, Méx) (abollar) to dent, make a dent in

■ **sumirse** *v pron* **1** (hundirse) **~se EN algo** ‹*en tristeza*› to plunge INTO sth; ‹*en pensamientos*› to become lost IN sth **2** (Col, Méx) (abollarse) to get dented

sumisión *f* (acción) submission; (actitud dócil) submissiveness

sumiso -sa *adj* submissive

sumo -ma *adj* utmost (*before n*); **de suma importancia** of the utmost importance; **con ~ cuidado** with great *o* the utmost care; **a lo ~** at the most

suntuoso -sa *adj* sumptuous; ‹*palacio*› magnificent

supe *see* SABER

súper *adv* (fam): **lo pasamos ~ bien** we had a great *o* fantastic time (colloq); **es ~ bueno** it's great *o* fantastic (colloq); **lo hizo ~ rápido** he did it incredibly quickly ■ *f* ≈ premium grade gasoline (*in US*), ≈ four-star petrol (*in UK*)

superación *f* (de problema) surmounting, overcoming; (de récord) breaking, beating; (de teoría) superseding

superar [A1] *vt* **1 (a)** (ser superior a) to exceed; **superó todas las expectativas** she exceeded all expectations; **nadie lo supera en experiencia** no one has more experience than him; **supera en estatura a su hermano** he's taller than his brother **(b)** (mejorar) ‹*marca*› to beat **2 (a)** (vencer, sobreponerse a) ‹*timidez/dificultad/etapa*› to overcome; ‹*trauma*› to get over **(b)** (frml) ‹*examen/prueba*› to pass

■ **superarse** *v pron* to better oneself

superbloque *m* (Ven) large apartment building

superdotado -da *adj* highly gifted ■ *m,f* highly-gifted person

superficial *adj* **1** (frívolo) ‹*persona*› superficial, shallow; ‹*charla/comentario*› superficial **2** ‹*herida*› superficial; ‹*marca/grieta*› surface (*before n*)

superficie *f* **1** (parte expuesta, aparente) surface; **salir a la ~** to surface, come to the surface **2** (Mat) (área) area

superfluo -flua *adj* superfluous, unnecessary; ‹*gastos*› unnecessary

superior[1] *adj* **1** (en posición) ‹*parte/piso*› top (*before n*), upper (*before n*); ‹*nivel*› higher; ‹*labio/mandíbula*› upper (*before n*) **2 (a)** (en calidad) superior; **~ A algo/algn** superior TO sth/sb; **se siente ~ a los demás** he thinks he's better than everyone else; **una inteligencia ~ a la media** above-average intelligence **(b)** (en jerarquía) ‹*oficial*› superior; ‹*clase social*› higher **(c)** (en cantidad, número): **los atacantes eran ~es en número** the attackers were greater *o* more in number; **~ A algo** above sth; **un número ~ a 9** a number greater than *o* higher than *o* above 9

superior[2] **-riora** *m,f* **(a)** (Relig) (*m*) Superior; (*f*) Mother Superior **(b) superior** *m* (en rango) superior

superioridad *f* superiority

superlativo *m* superlative

supermercado *m* supermarket

superpoblado -da *adj* ‹*mundo/país*› overpopulated; ‹*barrio/ciudad*› overcrowded

superpotencia *f* superpower

superstición *f* superstition

supersticioso -sa *adj* superstitious

supervisar [A1] *vt* to supervise

supervisor -sora *m,f* supervisor

supervivencia *f* survival

superviviente *adj* surviving (*before n*) ■ *mf* survivor

supiera, **supiste, etc** *see* SABER

suplantar [A1] *vt* ‹*persona*› to impersonate, pass oneself off as

suplementario -ria *adj* ‹*información/ingresos*› additional, supplementary; ‹*trabajo*› extra

suplemento *m* supplement

suplencia *f* **(a)** (sustitución): **hacer una ~** «*profesor*» to do substitute (AmE) *o* (BrE) supply teaching **(b)** (trabajo) temporary job

suplente *mf* **(a)** (de médico) covering doctor (AmE), locum (BrE) **(b)** (de actor) understudy **(c)** (Dep) substitute **(d)** (de profesor) substitute (teacher) (AmE), supply teacher (BrE)

supletorio -ria *adj* ‹*cama*› extra, additional; **teléfono ~** extension

súplica *f* (ruego) entreaty, plea; (Der) petition

suplicante *adj* imploring (*before n*)

suplicar [A2] *vt* (rogar) to beg; **~le a algn que haga algo** to beg *o* implore *o* (liter) beseech sb to do sth

suplicio *m* **(a)** (tortura) torture **(b)** (castigo) punishment

suplir [I1] *vt* **1** (compensar) ‹*falta/deficiencia*› to make up for **2** (reemplazar) ‹*profesor/médico*› to stand in for, substitute for; ‹*jugador*› to replace, substitute **3** (Col, Ven) (suministrar) to provide, supply

suponer [E22] *vt* **1 (a)** (tomar como hipótesis) to suppose, assume; **supongamos que lo que dice es cierto** let's suppose *o* assume what he says is true; **suponiendo que todo salga bien** assuming everything goes OK **(b)** (imaginar): **supongo que tienes razón** I suppose you're right; **¿va a venir hoy? — supongo que sí** is she coming today? — I should think so *o* I suppose so; **es de ~ que se lo habrán dicho** presumably *o* I should think he's been told; **se supone que empieza a las nueve** it's supposed to start at nine **2** (significar, implicar) to mean; **eso supondría tener que repetirlo** that would mean having to do it again

suposición *f* supposition

supositorio *m* suppository

supremo -ma *adj* supreme

suprimir [I1] *vt* **(a)** ‹*impuesto/ley/costumbre*› to abolish; ‹*restricción*› to lift; ‹*servicio*› to withdraw; ‹*gasto/ruido/alcohol*› to cut out **(b)** (Impr) ‹*párrafo/capítulo*› to delete **(c)** ‹*noticia/detalles*› to suppress

supuesto[1] **-ta** *adj* **(a)** (falso) false; **un nombre ~** a false name; **el ~ mendigo** the supposed beggar **(b)** (que se rumorea) ‹*milagro*› alleged (*before n*) **(c) por supuesto** of course; ***dar algo por ~*** to take sth for granted

supuesto[2] *m* supposition

supurar [A1] *vi* to weep, ooze, suppurate (tech)

supuse, **supuso, etc** *see* SUPONER

sur ▶ **346** *adj inv* ‹*región*› southern; **conducían en dirección ~** they were driving south *o* southward(s); **la costa ~** the south coast ■ *m* **(a)** (parte, sector): **el ~** the south; **al ~ de Cartagena** to the south of Cartagena **(b)** (punto cardinal) south, South; **vientos del ~** southerly winds; **viajábamos hacia el ~** we were travelling south *o* southward(s)

Suráfrica *f* South Africa

surafricano -na *adj/m,f* South African

Suramérica *f* South America

suramericano -na *adj/m,f* South American

surco *m* **1 (a)** (en la tierra) furrow **(b)** (en el agua) wake, track **(c)** (en disco) groove; (en superficie) groove, line; (marca de rueda) ruts, track **2** (Col) (de flores) flowerbed

sureño -ña *adj* ▶ **346** southern ■ *m,f* southerner

sureste *adj inv/m* ⇒ SUDESTE

surf /'surf/, **surfing** /'surfin/ *m* surfing

surfista *mf* surfer

surgir [I7] *vi* «*manantial*» to rise; «*problema/dificultad*» to arise, come up, emerge; «*interés/sentimiento*» to develop, emerge; «*idea*» to emerge, come up; «*tema*» to come up, crop up; «*movimiento/partido*» to come into being, arise

suroeste *adj inv/m* ⇒ SUDOESTE

surrealismo *m* surrealism

surrealista *adj* ‹*artista/exposición*› surrealist (*before n*); ‹*estilo/efecto*› surrealistic

surtido[1] **-da** *adj* **(a)** ‹*bombones/galletas*› assorted **(b)** (provisto) stocked; **una tienda bien/mal surtida** a well-stocked/poorly-stocked shop

surtido[2] *m* (de bombones, galletas) assortment; (de herramientas, ropa) range, selection, assortment

surtidor *m* (aparato) gas pump (AmE), petrol pump (BrE); (estación de servicio) gas station (AmE), petrol station (BrE)

surtir [I1] *vt* **(a)** (proveer) **~ a algn DE algo** to supply sb WITH sth **(b) surtir efecto** to take effect

■ **surtirse** *v pron* **~se DE algo** ‹*de provisiones*› to stock up WITH sth

susceptibilidad *f* sensitivity, touchiness

susceptible *adj* ‹*persona*› sensitive, touchy; **~ A algo** sensitive TO sth

suscribirse [I34] *v pron* (*refl*) **~ A algo** to take out a subscription TO sth

suscripción *f* (a publicación) subscription

suscriptor -tora *m,f* subscriber

suspender [E1] *vt* **1 (a)** ‹*pagos*› to suspend; ‹*garantía/derecho*› to suspend, withdraw; ‹*sesión*› to adjourn; ‹*vuelo*› (cancelar) to cancel; (aplazar) to postpone; ‹*viaje/reunión*› (cancelar) to call off; (aplazar) to put off; ‹*tratamiento*› to stop, suspend; ‹*servicio*› to suspend, discontinue; ‹*programa*› to cancel **(b)** ‹*empleado/jugador*› to suspend; ‹*alumno*› (AmL) to suspend **2** (colgar) **~ algo DE algo** to hang sth FROM sth **3** (Esp) ‹*asignatura/examen/alumno*› to fail ■ **~** *vi* (Esp) to fail

suspense *m* (Esp) ⇒ SUSPENSO 1

suspensión *f* suspension

suspenso *m* **1** (AmL) (Cin, Lit) suspense; **película/novela de ~** thriller **2** (Esp) (Educ) fail, failure; **no he tenido ningún ~** I haven't failed anything

suspensores *mpl* (Chi) (tirantes) suspenders (*pl*) (AmE), braces (*pl*) (BrE)

suspicacia *f* suspicion

suspicaz *adj* suspicious

suspirar [A1] *vi* **(a)** (de pena, alivio) to sigh **(b)** (anhelar) **~ POR algo** to yearn *o* long FOR sth

suspiro *m* sigh; **un ~ de alivio** a sigh of relief

sustancia *f* substance

sustantivo *m* noun, substantive (frml)

sustentar [A1] *vt* **(a)** ‹*peso*› to support **(b)** ‹*persona/familia*› to support, maintain

sustento *m* **(a)** (apoyo) means of support **(b)** (alimento) sustenance

sustitución *f* **(a)** (permanente) replacement **(b)** (transitoria) substitution

sustituir [I20] *vt* **(a)** (permanentemente) to replace; **~ A algo** to replace sth; **~ algo/a algn POR algo/algn** to replace sth/sb WITH sth/sb **(b)** (transitoriamente) ‹*trabajador/profesor*› to stand in for; ‹*deportista*› to come on as a substitute for

sustituto -ta *m,f* **(a)** (permanente) replacement **(b)** (transitorio) substitute; (de médico) covering doctor (AmE), locum (BrE); (de actor) understudy; **el ~ de la profesora de alemán** the substitute (AmE) *o* (BrE) stand-in for the German teacher

susto *m* (impresión momentánea) fright; **darle un ~ a algn** to give sb a fright; **darse** *or* **llevarse un ~** to get a fright (colloq)

susurrar [A1] *vi* **(a)** «*persona*» to whisper **(b)** (liter) «*agua*» to murmur; «*viento*» to sigh; «*hojas*» to rustle ■ **~** *vt* to whisper; **le susurró algo al oído** she whispered something in his ear

susurro *m* **(a)** (murmullo) whisper **(b)** (liter) (del agua) murmuring; (del viento) sighing; (de las hojas) rustling

sutil *adj* **(a)** ‹*diferencia*› subtle, fine; ‹*ironía*› subtle; ‹*mente/inteligencia*› keen, sharp **(b)** ‹*gasa/velo*› fine; ‹*fragancia*› subtle, delicate

sutileza *f* subtlety

suyo -ya *adj* (de él) his; (de ella) hers; (de usted, ustedes) yours; (de ellos, ellas) theirs; **Marta y un amigo ~** Marta and a friend of hers ■ *pron* **el ~, la suya, etc** (de él) his; (de ella) hers; (de usted, ustedes) yours; (de ellos, ellas) theirs; **él me prestó el ~** he lent me his

svástica *f* swastika

switch /(e)'switʃ/ *m* **(a)** (Col, Ven, Méx) (interruptor) light switch **(b)** (Méx) (Auto) ignition switch

Tt

T, t *f* (*read as* /te/) *the letter* T, t

tabaco *m* **(a)** (planta, producto) tobacco; **~ de hebra/de pipa** loose/pipe tobacco; **~ negro/rubio** dark/Virginia tobacco **(b)** (Esp) (cigarrillos) cigarettes (*pl*) **(c)** (Col) (puro) cigar

tábano *m* horsefly

tabasco *m* Tabasco® (sauce)

taberna *f* bar, tavern (arch), pub (BrE)

tabernáculo *m* tabernacle

tabernero -ra *m,f* (propietario) (*m*) bar owner, landlord (BrE); (*f*) bar owner, landlady (BrE); (camarero) (*m*) bartender; (*f*) barmaid

tabique *m* **(a)** (pared) partition **(b)** (Méx) (ladrillo) brick

tabla *f* **1** (de madera) plank; **las ~s del suelo** the floorboards; **~ de picar/planchar** chopping/ironing board; ***tener ~s*** «*actor/cantante*» (fam) to be an old hand *o* an expert **2** (de surfing) surfboard; (de windsurf) sailboard, windsurfer; (para natación) float **3** (gráfico, listado) table; (Mat) *tb* **~ de multiplicar** multiplication table **4** (de falda) pleat; **una falda de ~s** a pleated skirt **5 tablas** *fpl* (en ajedrez): **acabar** *or* **quedar en ~s** to end in a draw; ***estar ~s*** (Méx fam) to be even *o* quits (colloq)

tablado *m* (para discursos) platform; (para espectáculos) stage

tablao *m*: *tb* **~ flamenco** *bar or club where flamenco is performed*

tablero *m* **(a)** (en estación, aeropuerto) board; (para anuncios) bulletin board (AmE), noticeboard (BrE); **~ de dibujo** drawing board; **~ de instrumentos** *or* **de mandos** instrument panel **(b)** (Jueg) board; **un ~ de ajedrez** a chessboard; **un ~ de damas**

a checkerboard (AmE), a draughtboard (BrE) **(c)** (pizarra) blackboard **(d)** (de mesa) top

tableta *f* **(a)** (Farm) tablet, pill **(b)** (de chocolate) bar

tablilla *f* (Méx) (de chocolate) bar

tablón *m* **(a)** (de madera) plank **(b)** *tb* **~ de anuncios** (Esp) bulletin board (AmE), noticeboard (BrE)

tabú *adj inv* taboo ■ *m* (*pl* **-búes** *or* **-bús**) taboo

tabulador *m* tabulator, tab

taburete *m* stool

tacañería *f* stinginess, meanness (colloq)

tacaño -ña *adj* stingy, mean ■ *m,f* miser, tightwad (AmE colloq)

tacha *f* stain, blemish; **sin ~** ‹*reputación*› unblemished, spotless; ‹*conducta*› irreproachable

tachadura *f* crossing out, correction

tachar [A1] *vt* **1** (en escrito) to cross out **2** (tildar) **~ a algn DE algo** to brand *o* label sb AS sth

tacho *m* **(a)** (CS) (recipiente) (metal) container **(b)** (CS, Per) (papelero) wastebasket (AmE), wastepaper basket (BrE); **~ de la basura** (en la cocina) garbage can (AmE), rubbish bin (BrE); (en la calle) garbage *o* trash can (AmE), dustbin (BrE)

tachón *m* (en escrito) crossing out

tachuela *f* (clavo) tack; (en cinturón) stud

tácito -ta *adj* ‹*acuerdo*› tacit, unspoken

taciturno -na *adj* **(a)** [SER] (callado, silencioso) taciturn, uncommunicative **(b)** [ESTAR] (triste) glum, gloomy

taco *m* **1 (a)** (de madera) plug; (para tornillo) Rawl® (AmE), Rawplug® (BrE) **(b)** (de billetes) book; (de folletos) wad; (de queso, jamón) (Esp) cube **2 (a)** (en billar) cue **(b)** (Col) (de golf) tee **3 (a)** (de botas de deporte) cleat (AmE), stud (BrE) **(b)** (CS, Per) (tacón) heel; **zapatos de ~ alto/bajo** high-heeled/low-heeled *o* flat shoes **4 (a)** (Coc) taco **(b)** (Méx) (comida ligera) snack, bite to eat (colloq) **5** (Esp fam) (palabrota) swearword; **soltar ~s** to swear **6** (Chi) (embotellamiento) traffic jam

tacón *m* heel; **zapatos de ~ alto/bajo** high-heeled/low-heeled *o* flat shoes; **~ de aguja** spike heel

táctica *f* tactic, strategy

táctico -ca *adj* tactical

táctil *adj* tactile

tacto *m* **1 (a)** (sentido) sense of touch **(b)** (acción) touch; **áspero al ~** rough to the touch **(c)** (cualidad) feel **2** (delicadeza) tact; **¡qué falta de ~!** how tactless!; **tiene mucho ~** he's very tactful

Tahití *m* Tahiti

tailandés[1] -desa *adj/m,f* Thai

tailandés[2] *m* (idioma) Thai

Tailandia *f* Thailand

taimado -da *adj* **1** (astuto) crafty, cunning **2** (Chi) (malhumorado) sulky, huffy

taimarse [A1] *v pron* (Chi fam) **(a)** «*persona*» to get into a huff (colloq) **(b)** «*mula*» to balk

tajada *f* **(a)** (de melón, queso) slice **(b)** (Ven) (de plátano frito) slice of fried plantain

tajante *adj* ‹*respuesta*› categorical, unequivocal; ‹*tono*› sharp; **un 'no' ~** an emphatic *o* categorical 'no'

tajear [A1] *vt* (AmL) to slash

tajo *m* **1** (corte) cut **2 (a)** (Geol) gorge, ravine **(b)** (Min) face

tal *adj* **1** (dicho) such; **en ~es casos** in such cases; **nunca dije ~ cosa** I never said anything of the kind *o* such a thing **2** (seguido de consecuencia): **se llevó ~ disgusto que** ... she was so upset (that) ...; **había ~ cantidad de gente que** ... there were so many people that ... **3** (con valor indeterminado) such-and-such; **~ día, en ~ lugar** such-and-such a day, at such-and-such a place; **llamó un ~ Méndez** a Mr Méndez phoned ■ *pron*: **eres un adulto, compórtate como ~** you're an adult, behave like one; **que si ~ y que si cual** and so on and so forth; ***son ~ para cual*** they're as bad as each other ■ *adv* **1** (fam) (en preguntas): **hola ¿qué ~?** hello, how are you?; **¿qué ~ es Marisa?** what's Marisa like?; **¿qué ~ lo pasaron?** how did it go? **2** (*en locs*) **con tal de**: **hace cualquier cosa con ~ de llamar la atención** he'll do anything to get attention; **con ~ de no tener que volver** as long as I don't have to come back; **tal (y) como**: **~ (y) como están las cosas** the way things are; **hazlo ~ (y) como te indicó** do it exactly as she told you; **tal cual**: **lo dejé todo ~ cual** I left everything exactly as it was; **tal vez** maybe

talacha *f* **(a)** (Méx) (reparación de llantas) flat *o* puncture repair **(b)** (Méx fam) (trabajo manual) work

taladradora *f* pneumatic drill

taladrar [A1] *vt* ‹*pared/madera*› to drill (through)

taladro *m* **(a)** (mecánico) hand drill; (eléctrico) electric *o* power drill **(b)** (agujero) drill hole

talante *m* (humor) mood; **estar de buen ~** to be in a good mood

talar [A1] *vt* ‹*árbol*› to fell, cut down

talco *m* talc; **polvos de ~** talcum powder

talento *m* **(a)** (aptitud) talent; **tiene ~ para la música** he has a talent *o* gift for music; **un joven de ~** a talented young man **(b)** (persona) talented person

talismán *m* talisman, lucky charm

talla *f* **(a)** **▶ 401** (Indum) size; **¿cuál es su ~?** what size are you?; **de** *o* **en todas las ~s** in all sizes **(b)** (estatura) size, height; **de ~ mediana** of medium height

tallado *m* (de madera) carving; (de piedras preciosas) cutting

tallar [A1] *vt* **1** ‹*madera*› to carve; ‹*escultura/mármol*› to sculpt; ‹*piedras preciosas*› to cut **2** (Méx) **(a)** (para limpiar) to scrub **(b)** (para aliviar) to rub ■ **~** *vi* (Col) «*zapatos*» to be too tight

■ **tallarse** *v pron* (Méx) **(a)** (para limpiarse) to scrub oneself **(b)** (para aliviar) to rub oneself; ‹*ojos*› to rub

tallarín *m* noodle

talle *m* **(a)** (cintura) waist **(b)** (figura) figure **(c)** (en costura) trunk measurement; **es corta de ~** she's short-waisted

taller *m* **1 (a)** (Auto) *tb* **~ mecánico** garage, repair shop (AmE) **(b)** (de carpintero, técnico) workshop **2** (Educ) workshop

tallo *m* stem, stalk

Tallas/Sizes

(Equivalentes aproximados/Approximate equivalents)

América Latina y España *Latin America & Spain*	**EEUU** *US*	**Reino Unido** *UK*
Calzado de señora Ladies' shoes		
35	4½	3
36	5	3½
37	5½	4
37	6	4½
38	6½	5
39	7	5½
39	7½	6
40	8	6½
41	8½	7
Calzado de caballero Men's shoes		
39	7	6
41	8	7
42	9	8
43	10	9
44	11	10
Tallas de ropa de señora Women's clothing sizes		
36	6	8
38	8	10
40	10	12
42	12	14
44	14	16
46	16	18
48	18	20
50	20	22

América Latina y España *Latin America & Spain*	**EEUU** *US*	**Reino Unido** *UK*
Tallas de ropa de caballero Men's clothing sizes		
40	30	30
42	32	32
44	34	34
46	36	36
48	38	38
50	40	40
52	42	42
54	44	44
Camisa de caballero Men's collar sizes		
36	14	14
37	14½	14½
38	15	15
39	15½	15½
41	16	16
42	16½	16½
43	17	17
44	17½	17½
46	18	18

talón *m* **1 (a)** ▶ 123 (del pie) heel; **~ de Aquiles** Achilles' heel **(b)** (de zapato, calcetín) heel **2 (a)** (AmL) (matriz) stub, counterfoil **(b)** (Esp) (cheque) check (AmE), cheque (BrE); (vale) chit; **~ de compra** receipt

talonario *m* (de cheques) checkbook (AmE), chequebook (BrE); (de recibos) receipt book; (de volantes) book of vouchers

talonear [A1] *vt* (AmL) ‹*caballo*› to spur (on)

tamal *m* tamale

tamaño *m* ▶ 401 size; **pañuelos de todos los ~s** handkerchiefs in all sizes; **de ~ bolsillo** pocket-size; **un busto ~ natural** a life-size bust

tamarindo *m* **(a)** (Bot) tamarind **(b)** (Méx fam) (agente) traffic cop (colloq)

tambache *m* (Méx fam) (bulto) bundle; (montón) pile

tambalearse [A1] *v pron vi* «*silla/botella*» to wobble; «*persona*» to stagger; **caminaba tambaleándose** he was staggering; **todo empezó a ~** everything began to shake

también *adv* too, as well **~ habla ruso** she speaks Russian too *o* as well; **que te diviertas — tú ~** have fun! — you too *o* and you; **Pilar fuma — yo ~** Pilar smokes — so do I *o* (colloq) me too

tambo *m* **1** (Méx) **(a)** (recipiente) can (AmE), bin (BrE) **(b)** (fam) (cárcel) slammer (sl), can (AmE sl) **2** (Per) (tienda) wayside stall

tambor *m* **1 (a)** (instrumento) drum; **un redoble de ~es** a drum roll **(b)** (persona) drummer **2 (a)** (del freno) drum **(b)** (AmL) (barril) drum

tamborilear [A1] *vi* to drum, tap

Támesis *m*: **el ~** the (River) Thames

tamiz *m* sieve; **pasar algo por el ~** ‹*harina*› to sift sth; ‹*salsa*› to sieve sth

tamizar [A4] *vt* ‹*harina*› to sift; ‹*salsa*› to sieve

tampoco *adv* ▶ 289 not ... either; **yo ~ entendí** I didn't understand either; **él no va, ni yo ~** he isn't going and neither am I; **no he estado en Roma ni ~ en París** I've never been to Rome or Paris

tampón *m* **(a)** (para entintar) ink pad **(b)** (Farm, Med) tampon

tan *adv*: *apocopated form of* TANTO *used before adjectives (except some comparatives), adverbs, and adjectival or adverbial phrases*

tanda *f* **1** (grupo) batch, lot; **cada dos minutos hay una ~ de avisos** (AmL) every couple of minutes there's another lot of commercials; **los horneamos en dos ~s** we baked them in two batches **2** (AmC, Méx fam) (función — de teatro) performance; (— de cine) showing, performance **3** (Col, Méx) (ronda) round (of drinks)

tándem *m* (bicicleta) tandem

tanga *f* tanga

tangente *f* tangent; ***irse*** *or* ***salirse por la ~*** to go off at a tangent

tangerina *f* tangerine

tango *m* tango; **bailar el ~** to tango

tano -na *adj/m,f* (RPl fam & pey) Italian

tanque *m* **1** (Arm) (carro) tank **2** (de agua, gasolina) tank; (de gas, oxígeno) cylinder, bottle

tantear [A1] *vt* **(a)** (con el tacto) to feel **(b)** ‹*situación*› to weigh up, size up; ‹*persona*› to sound out **(c)** (calcular aproximadamente) to estimate ■ ~ *vi* to feel one's way

tanteo *m* (Dep) score

tantito *adv* (Méx fam) a bit; **espérame ~, ya voy** just wait a bit, I'm coming

tanto[1] *adv* **1** [*see note under* TAN] (aplicado a adjetivo o adverbio) so; (aplicado a verbo) so much; **es tan bonito** it's so beautiful; **¡es una chica tan amable!** she's such a nice girl!; **~ mejor** so much the better; **tan sólo** only; **~ es así que** ... so much so that ...; **ya no salimos ~** we don't go out so often *o* so much now; **llegó tan tarde que** ... he arrived so late (that) ...; **no es tan tímida como parece** she's not as shy as she looks; **sale ~ como tú** he goes out as much as you do; **tan pronto como puedas** as soon as you can; **~ Suárez como Vargas votaron en contra** both Suárez and Vargas voted against **2** (AmL exc RPl) **qué tanto/qué tan**: **¿qué ~ te duele?** how much does it hurt?; **¿qué tan alto es?** how tall is he? ■ *m* **1** (cantidad): **un ~ por ciento** a percentage; **hay que dejar un ~ de depósito** you have to put down a certain amount as a deposit **2** (punto — en fútbol) goal; (— en fútbol americano, tenis, juegos) point **3** (*en locs*) **al tanto**: **me puso al ~** she put me in the picture; **mantenerse al ~ de algo** to keep up to date with sth; **estar al ~** (pendiente, alerta) to be on the ball (colloq); **está al ~ de lo ocurrido** he knows what's happened; **un tanto** somewhat, rather; **un ~ triste** somewhat sad

tanto[2] -ta *adj* **(a)** (*sing*) so much; (*pl*) so many; **había ~ espacio/~s niños** there was so much space/there were so many children; **¡~ tiempo sin verte!** it's been so long!; **~ dinero/~s turistas como** ... as much money/as many tourists as ... **(b)** (fam) (expresando cantidades indeterminadas): **tenía setenta y ~s años** he was seventy something, he was seventy-odd (colloq) ■ *pron* **1 (a)** (*sing*) so much; (*pl*) so many; **¡tengo ~ que hacer!** I've so much to do!; **vinieron ~s que** ... so many people came (that) ...; **¿de verdad gana ~?** does he really earn that much?; ***no ser para ~*** (fam): **duele, pero no es para ~** it hurts, but it's not *that* bad **(b)** (fam) (expresando cantidades indeterminadas): **hasta las tantas de la madrugada** until the early hours of the morning; **treinta y ~s** thirty or so **(c)** (refiriéndose a tiempo): **hace ~ que no me llama** it's been so long since she called me; **aún faltan dos horas — ¿tanto?** there's still two hours to go — what? that long? **2** (*en locs*) **en tanto** while; **entre tanto** meanwhile, in the meantime; **otro tanto** as much again; **me queda otro ~ por hacer** I have as much again still to do; **por (lo) tanto** therefore

tapa *f* **1 (a)** (de caja, cacerola) lid; (de botella, frasco) top; **~ de rosca** screw top **(b)** (de lente, bolígrafo) cap; **la ~ del tanque de gasolina** the gas (AmE) *o* (BrE) petrol cap **2 (a)** (de libro, revista) cover; (de disco) sleeve **(b)** (de tacón) heelpiece **(c)** (de bolsillo) flap **(d)** (Auto) head **3** (Esp) (para acompañar la bebida) tapa, bar snack

tapabarros *m* (*pl* ~) (Chi, Per) (de coche) fender (AmE), wing (BrE); (de bicicleta) splashguard (AmE), mudguard (BrE)

tapadera *f* **(a)** (de cazo) lid **(b)** (de fraude, engaño) cover, front **(c)** (Méx) (de botella) cap, top

tapado *m* **1** (RPl, Ven) (abrigo) (winter) coat **2** (Méx) (Pol) potential candidate (*with official support*)

tapadura *f* (Andes, Méx) filling

tapar [A1] *vt* **1** (cubrir) ‹*caja*› to put the lid on; ‹*botella/frasco*› to put the top on; ‹*olla*› to cover, put the lid on; ‹*bebé/enfermo/cara*› to cover **2 (a)** ‹*agujero/hueco*› to fill in; ‹*puerta/ventana*› to block up **(b)** (Andes, Méx) ‹*muela*› to fill; **me ~on dos muelas** I had two fillings **(c)** ‹*defecto/error*› to cover up **3 (a)** ‹*vista/luz*› to block **(b)** ‹*salida/entrada*› to block; ‹*excusado/cañería*› (AmL) to block ■ **taparse** *v pron* **1** (*refl*) (cubrirse) to cover oneself up; ‹*cara*› to cover **2 (a)** «*oídos/nariz*» to get *o* become blocked; **tengo la nariz tapada** my nose is blocked **(b)** (AmL) «*cañería/excusado*» to get blocked

taparrabos *m* (*pl* ~) loincloth

tapatío -tía *adj* of/from Guadalajara (*in Mexico*)

tapete *m* **1** (para mesa) decorative table cloth; (para sofá) antimacassar **2** (Col, Méx, Ven) (alfombra) rug

tapia *f* (muro) wall; (cerca) fence; ***ser/estar más sordo que una ~*** (fam) to be as deaf as a post (colloq)

tapiar [A1] *vt* **(a)** ‹*espacio*› to wall in **(b)** ‹*puerta/ventana*› to brick up

tapicería *f* **(a)** (de coches, muebles) upholstery **(b)** (arte) tapestry making; (tapiz) tapestry

tapicero -ra *m,f* (de muebles) upholsterer

tapilla *f* (Chi) heelpiece

tapir *m* tapir

tapiz *m* (para pared) tapestry; (para suelo) carpet

tapizado *m* upholstery

tapizar [A4] *vt* ‹*sillón*› to upholster; ‹*pared*› to line

tapón *m* **1 (a)** (de vidrio, goma) stopper; (de corcho) cork; (del lavabo) plug; (de botella) (Esp) top **(b)** (para los oídos) earplug; (de cerumen) plug **2 (a)** (fam) (atasco) traffic jam, tailback (BrE) **(b)** (en baloncesto) block **3** (CS) (Elec) fuse

taponar [A1] *vt* ‹*agujero*› to block ■ **taponarse** *v pron* **(a)** «*oídos/nariz*» to get blocked **(b)** «*cañería*» to get blocked **(c)** (Col, RPl) «*ciudad/zona*» to block

taquigrafía *f* shorthand, stenography (AmE)

taquilla *f* **(a)** (de cine) box office; (en estación, estadio) ticket office **(b)** (cantidad recaudada) takings (*pl*) **(c)** (casillero) rack, pigeonholes (*pl*)

taquillero -ra *m,f* box-office clerk

tara *f* **1** (peso) tare **2** (defecto) defect

tarántula *f* tarantula

tararear [A1] *vt* to la-la-la

tardado -da *adj* (Méx) ‹*proceso/tarea*› time-consuming; ‹*persona*› slow

tardar [A1] *vt* (emplear cierto tiempo): **está tardando mucho** she's taking a long time; **tarda una hora en hacerse** it takes about an hour to cook; **tardó un mes en contestar** it took him a month to reply; **no tardo ni un minuto** I won't be a minute; **¿cuánto se tarda en coche?** how long does it take by car? ■ **~** *vi* (retrasarse) to be late; (emplear demasiado tiempo) to take a long time; **empieza a las seis, no tardes** it starts at six, don't be late; **parece que tarda** he seems to be taking a long time; **¡no tardo!** I won't be long!; **aún ~á en llegar** it'll be a while yet before he gets here; **no ~on en detenerlo** it didn't take them long to arrest him ■ **tardarse** *v pron* (Méx, Ven) ⇒ TARDAR *vt, vi*

tarde *adv* late; **llegar ~** to be late; **se está haciendo ~** it's getting late; **~ *o temprano*** sooner or later ■ *f* ▶ **221** (temprano) afternoon; (hacia el anochecer) evening; **a las seis de la ~** at six in the evening; **¡buenas ~s!** (temprano) good afternoon!; (hacia el anochecer) good evening!; **en la** *or* (esp Esp) **por la** *or* (RPl) **a la ~** in the afternoon/evening

tardón -dona *adj* (fam) slow ■ *m,f* (fam) slowpoke (AmE colloq), slowcoach (BrE colloq)

tarea *f* **(a)** (trabajo) task, job; **las ~s de la casa** the housework **(b)** (deberes escolares) homework

tarifa *f* **(a)** (baremo, escala) rate; **~s postales** postal rates **(b)** (Transp) fare **(c)** (lista de precios) price list **(d)** (arancel) tariff

tarima *f* (plataforma) dais

tarjar [A1] *vt* (Andes) to cross out, delete (frml)

tarjeta *f* card; **marcar** (AmL) *or* (Méx) **checar ~** to clock in/out, punch in/out (AmE); **~ amarilla/roja** yellow/red card; **~ de crédito** credit card; **~ de embarque** boarding pass *o* card; **~ de Navidad** Christmas card; **~ de visita** *or* (Méx) **de presentación** (personal) visiting card; (de negocios) business card; **~ postal/telefónica** postcard/phonecard

tarro *m* **1** (recipiente— de vidrio) jar; (— de cerámica) pot; (— de metal) (Chi) can, tin (BrE) **2** (Méx, Ven) (taza) mug

tarta *f* (Esp) cake; (de hojaldre — descubierta) tart; (— cubierta) pie

tartamudear [A1] *vi* to stutter, stammer

tartamudo -da *adj* stuttering (*before n*), stammering (*before n*); **es ~** he has a stutter *o* stammer ■ *m,f*: **hay un ~ en mi clase** one of the boys in my class has a stutter *o* stammer

tartera *f* (para cocinar) cake tin

tarumba *adj* crazy (colloq); **me vuelve ~** he drives me crazy (colloq)

tasa *f* **(a)** (valoración) valuation **(b)** (impuesto) tax **(c)** (índice) rate; **~ de desempleo** rate of unemployment; **~ de mortalidad/natalidad** mortality rate/birthrate

tasación *f* valuation

tasajear [A1] *vt* (Méx, Per) to slash

tasar [A1] *vt* ‹*objeto/coche*› to value

tasca *f* (taberna) bar, tavern

tata *m* (AmL fam) **(a)** (padre) dad (colloq), pop (AmE colloq) **(b)** (abuelo) grandpa (colloq)

tatarabuelo -la *m,f* (*m*) great-great-grandfather; (*f*) great-great-grandmother; **mis ~s** my great-great-grandparents

tataranieto -ta *m,f* (*m*) great-great-grandson; (*f*) great-great-granddaughter; **sus ~s** his great-great-grandchildren

ta-te-ti *m* (RPl) tic-tac-toe (AmE), noughts and crosses (BrE)

tatuaje *m* (acción) tattooing; (dibujo) tattoo

tatuar [A18] *vt* to tattoo

taurino -na *adj* ‹*temporada/afición*› bullfighting (*before n*), taurine (frml)

Tauro *m* (signo, constelación) Taurus; **es (de) ~** he's (a) Taurus, he's a Taurean ■ *mf* (*pl* **-ros**) (persona) *tb* **tauro** Taurean, Taurus

taxi *m* taxi, cab; **~ colectivo** (Col) minibus

taxímetro *m* taximeter

taxista *mf* taxi driver, cabdriver

taza *f* **(a)** (recipiente) cup; **~ de café/té** coffee cup/teacup **(b)** (contenido) cupful; **una ~ de azúcar** a cupful of sugar; **tomar una ~ de té** to have a cup of tea **(c)** (del retrete) (toilet) bowl **(d)** (de fuente) basin

tazón *m* bowl

te *pron pers* **(a)** you; **no ~ lo quiero prestar** I don't want to lend it to you; **¿~ lo paso a máquina?** shall I type it for you?; **voy a serte sincera** I'll be frank with you; **cuídate** (*refl*) look after yourself; **¿~ has cortado el pelo?** (*caus*) have you had your hair cut?; **¿~ sientes bien?** are you feeling all right?; **no ~ muevas** don't move **(b)** (*impers*): **cuando ~ pasa eso** ... when that happens ... ■ *f*: *name of the letter* t

té *m* **(a)** (infusión, planta) tea; **¿quieres un ~?** do you want a cup of tea? **(b)** (AmL) (reunión) tea party

tea *f* torch

teatral *adj* **(a)** (Teatr) ‹*grupo/temporada*› theater* (*before n*); **una obra ~** a play; **un autor ~** a playwright **(b)** ‹*persona/gesto/tono*› theatrical

teatro *m* **1** (Teatr) **(a)** (arte, actividad) theater*; **una obra de ~** a play; **actor de ~** stage actor; **~ de guiñol** puppet theater*; **~ de variedades** vaudeville (AmE), music hall (BrE) **(b)** (local) theater* **(c)** (cine) movie theater (AmE), cinema (BrE) **2** (fam) (exageración): **es puro ~** it's all an act

tebeo *m* (Esp) comic (*for children*)

techo *m* **(a)** (cielo raso) ceiling **(b)** (AmL) (tejado, cubierta) roof; ~ **corredizo** sunroof **(c)** (hogar, casa) house; **sin** ~ homeless; **bajo el mismo** ~ under the same roof

techumbre *f* roof

tecla *f* key

teclado *m* keyboard; ~ **numérico** numeric keypad

teclear [A1] *vt* ‹*palabra/texto*› to key in, type in ■ ~ *vi* (en máquina de escribir) to type; (en ordenador) to key

técnica *f* **1 (a)** (método) technique **(b)** (destreza) skill **2** (tecnología) technology **3** (en baloncesto) technical foul

tecnicismo *m* (cualidad) technical nature; (palabra) technical term

técnico -ca *adj* technical ■ *m,f* **(a)** (en fábrica) technician **(b)** (de lavadoras, etc) repairman (AmE), engineer (BrE) **(c)** (Dep) trainer, coach (AmE), manager (BrE)

tecnicolor *m* Technicolor®

tecnología *f* technology; ~ **punta** state-of-the-art technology

tecnológico -ca *adj* technological

tecolote *m* (Méx) (Zool) owl

tedio *m* boredom, tedium

teja *f* tile; ~**s de pizarra** slates

tejado *m* (esp Esp) roof

tejano -na *adj/m,f* Texan

Tejas *m* Texas

tejaván *m* (Méx) shed

tejedor -dora *m,f* **(a)** (con telar) weaver **(b)** (con agujas, máquina) knitter

tejer [E1] *vt* **(a)** (en telar) to weave; **tejido a mano** hand-woven **(b)** (con agujas, a máquina) to knit; (con ganchillo) to crochet; **máquina de** ~ knitting machine **(c)** «*araña*» to spin ■ ~ *vi* (en telar) to weave; (con agujas, a máquina) to knit; (con ganchillo) to crochet

tejido *m* **1 (a)** (tela) fabric; ~**s sintéticos** synthetic fabrics **(b)** (AmL) (con agujas, máquina) knitting; (con ganchillo) crochet **2** (Anat) tissue

tejo *m* **(a)** (disco) disc **(b)** (juego — de niños) hopscotch; (— de adultos) *game similar to pitch-and-toss*

tejolote *m* (Méx) pestle

tejón *m* badger

tela *f* **1** (Tex) (material) material, fabric; ~ **de lana** wool (fabric); ~ **de araña** ⇒ TELARAÑA; ~ **metálica** wire mesh **2** (Art) (cuadro) canvas, painting **3** (membrana) skin, film

telar *m* **(a)** (máquina) loom **(b) telares** *mpl* (fábrica) textile mill

telaraña *f* spiderweb (AmE), spider's web (BrE); (polvorienta) cobweb

tele *f* (fam) TV (colloq), telly (BrE colloq)

telebanco *m* cash dispenser

telecomunicación *f* telecommunication

teleculebra *f* (Ven fam) soap opera (colloq)

telediario *m* (Esp) (television) news

teledirigido -da *adj* ‹*coche*› radio-controlled, remote-controlled; **misiles** ~**s** guided missiles

teleférico *m* cable railway

telefonazo *m* (fam) buzz (colloq); **darle** *or* (Méx) **echarle un** ~ **a algn** to give sb a buzz (colloq)

telefonear [A1] *vt* to telephone, phone, call; **¿puedo** ~ **a Londres?** can I make a (telephone) call to London? ■ ~ *vi* to telephone, phone

telefónico -ca *adj* telephone (*before n*)

telefonista *mf* telephone operator

teléfono *m* **1** (Telec) telephone, phone; **número de** ~ phone number; **contestar el** ~ to answer *o* (colloq) get the phone; **me colgó el** ~ she hung up on me; **hablé por** ~ **con ella** I spoke to her on the phone; **está hablando por** ~ he's on the phone; **llamar a algn por** ~ to call sb (up), phone sb; ~ **celular** *or* (Esp) **móvil** mobile telephone; ~ **rojo** hotline **2** (de la ducha) shower head

telégrafo *m* telegraph

telegrama *m* telegram

telenovela *f* soap opera

telepatía *f* telepathy

telescopio *m* telescope

telespectador -dora *m,f* viewer

telesquí *m* ski lift

teletexto, **teletex** *m* teletext, videotex

televidente *mf* viewer

televisar [A1] *vt* to televise

televisión *f* **(a)** (sistema) television; **¿qué hay en (la)** ~**?** what's on television?; **lo transmitieron por** ~ it was broadcast on television; ~ **a** *or* **en color(es)** color* television; ~ **por cable/por satélite** cable/satellite television **(b)** (programación) television; **ver (la)** ~ to watch television **(c)** (televisor) television (set)

televisor *m* television (set)

télex *m* (*pl* ~) telex

telón *m* curtain; ~ **de fondo** (Teatr) backdrop

tema *m* **(a)** (asunto, cuestión) matter; (de conferencia, composición) topic; (de examen) subject; (Art, Cin, Lit) subject; **es un** ~ **delicado** it's a delicate matter; ~ **de conversación** topic of conversation; **cambiar de** ~ to change the subject **(b)** (Mús) (motivo) theme

temario *m* **(a)** (para examen) syllabus, list of topics **(b)** (en congreso) agenda

temblar [A5] *vi* **(a)** «*persona*» (de frío) to shiver; (por nervios, miedo) to shake, tremble; (+ *me/te/le etc*) «*párpado*» to twitch; «*mano*» to shake; «*voz*» to tremble; **la voz le temblaba de emoción** her voice was trembling with emotion **(b)** «*edificio/tierra*» to shake ■ ~ *v impers:* **¡está temblando!** (AmL) it's an earthquake!; **tembló ayer** there was an earthquake yesterday

temblor *m* **(a)** (de frío, fiebre) shivering; (de miedo, nervios) trembling, shaking; **con un ligero** ~ **en la voz** in a tremulous voice **(b)** *tb* ~ **de tierra** earth (tremor)

tembloroso -sa *adj* **(a)** ‹*manos*› trembling, shaking; ‹*voz*› trembling, tremulous; ~ **de frío** shivering with cold **(b)** ‹*llama/luz*› flickering, quivering

Telefonear

Números de teléfono

El cero se traduce normalmente por 'zero' *en el inglés norteamericano y por* 'oh' *en el inglés británico. En ambos idiomas se suele decir cada cifra por separado salvo que haya dos números iguales seguidos, en cuyo caso el inglés británico prefiere anteponer el vocablo* 'double'

013 821 99

zero – one – three – eight – two – one – nine – nine

oh – one – three – eight – two – one – double nine

Una llamada telefónica

En español la palabra que se emplea al contestar el teléfono, varía según la región: aló (*AmS*), diga *o* dígame (*Esp*), bueno (*Méx*), holá (*RPl*), *el inglés utiliza la palabra* hello

En los ejemplos se utilizará la variante aló *por corresponder a la región más amplia*:

¿alo? ¿está Juan?	=	hello? is Juan there, please?
¿es usted el Sr. León?	=	hello, is that Mr. León?
hola ¿Juan? *or* (esp Esp) ¿eres Juan?	=	hello, is that Juan?
podría hablar con Juan, por favor?	=	could I speak with (AmE) *o* (BrE) to Juan please?

Posibles respuestas:

con él (habla) *or* (esp Esp) soy yo	=	speaking
¿quién habla? *or* ¿con quién hablo?	=	who's speaking? *o* who am I speaking with (AmE) *o* (BrE) to?
un momento *or* momentito, por favor (no cuelgue)	=	just a moment *o* a minute, please
lo siento, no está *or* en este momento no está	=	I'm sorry, he isn't in *or* he's not in right now
¿de parte de quién?	=	who's calling *o* speaking please?
¿quiere dejar un recado?	=	would you like to leave a message? *o* can I take a message?
no gracias, volveré a llamar más tarde	=	it's OK, I'll call again later
¿podría decirle que llamó Ana?	=	could you tell her (that) Ana called?
¿podría decirle que me llame? ella sabe mi número de teléfono	=	could you ask her to call me back? she knows my phone number

Otros ejemplos:

¿me comunica *or* (esp Esp) me pone con el gerente por favor?	=	could you put me through to *o* could I speak with (AmE) *o* (BrE) to the manager, please?
¿me comunica *or* (esp Esp) me pone con la extensión 249?	=	extension 249 (two-four-nine) please
	=	could you put me through to *o* can I have extension 249 please?
por favor deje su mensaje después de la señal	=	please leave your message after the tone
éste es un mensaje para Juan (León): que se comunique con Ana por favor	=	this is a message for Juan (León): could he get in touch with Ana, please?

temer [E1] *vt* ‹*castigo/reacción*› to fear, dread; ‹*persona*› to be afraid of; **sus hijos le temen** her children are afraid of her; **temo ofenderlo** I'm afraid of offending him ■ **~** *vi* to be afraid; **no temas** don't be afraid

■ **temerse** *v pron* **(a)** (sospechar) to fear; **ya me lo temía** I knew this would happen; **me temo que tenía rázon** I fear that he was right **(b)** (en fórmulas de cortesía) to be afraid; **me temo que no ha llegado** I'm afraid he hasn't arrived

temeridad *f* **(a)** (acción): **eso fue una ~** that was a very rash *o* bold thing to do **(b)** (cualidad) temerity; **conduce con ~** she drives recklessly

temible *adj* fearsome, fearful

temor *m* fear; **no dije nada por ~ a ofenderlo** I didn't say anything for fear of offending him

témpano *m* ice floe

témpera *m* tempera

temperamental *adj* (irascible, cambiable) temperamental; (de mucho carácter) spirited

temperamento *m* **(a)** (manera de ser) temperament; **son de ~s muy diferentes** they have very different temperaments **(b)** (vigor de carácter): **un chico con mucho ~** a boy with a lot of spirit

temperatura *f* ▶ **406** temperature; **tomarle la ~ a algn** to take sb's temperature; **tiene ~** (CS) she has a fever (AmE) *o* (BrE) a temperature; **~ ambiente** room temperature

tempestad *f* storm, tempest (liter); **~ de arena** sandstorm

tempestuoso -sa *adj* stormy, tempestuous

templado -da *adj* **(a)** ‹*clima*› mild, temperate; ‹*zona*› temperate; ‹*día*› warm **(b)** ‹*agua/comida*› lukewarm

templo *m* temple

Temperaturas/Temperatures

Conversión/Conversion

De °F a °C	***From °F to °C***
Restar 32, multiplicar por 5 y dividir por 9	Subtract 32, multiply by 5 and divide by 9
De °C a °F	***From °C to °F***
Multiplicar por 9, dividir por 5 y añadir 32	Multiply by 9, divide by 5 and add 32

Escala centígrada *Centigrade scale*	**Escala Fahrenheit** *Fahrenheit scale*	
°C	**°F**	
100	212	Boiling point of water/Punto de ebullición del agua
90	194	
80	176	
70	158	
60	140	
50	122	
40	104	
37	98.4	Body temperature/Temperatura del cuerpo humano
30	86	
20	68	
10	50	
0	32	Freezing point/Punto de congelación del agua
–10	14	
–17,8	0	
–273,15	–459.67	Absolute Zero/Cero absoluto

temporada *f* **(a)** (época establecida) season; **verduras de ~** seasonal vegetables; **fuera de/en ~** out of/in season; **~ alta/baja** high/low season **(b)** (período de tiempo) spell; **una ~ de mucho trabajo** a very busy spell *o* period

temporal *adj* **1** (transitorio) temporary **2** (relativo al tiempo) temporal ■ *m* (Meteo) storm; **~ de nieve** snowstorm, blizzard

temporalero -ra *m,f* (Méx) seasonal worker

temporario -ria *adj* (AmL) temporary

temprano *adv* early; **levantarse ~** to get up early; **por la mañana ~** in the morning

ten *see* TENER

tenacidad *f* (perseverancia) tenacity

tenacillas *fpl* hair crimper

tenaz *adj* **(a)** ‹*persona*› tenacious **(b)** ‹*dolor*› persistent; ‹*mancha*› stubborn

tenaza *f*, **tenazas** *fpl* **(a)** (Mec, Tec) pliers (*pl*) **(b)** (de chimenea, cocina) tongs (*pl*) **(c)** (del cangrejo) pincer **(d)** (Méx) (de pelo) curling iron (AmE), hair crimper (BrE)

tendajón *m* (Méx) shack (*serving as a store or stall*)

tendal *m* (AmL) (para el café) drying area

tendedero *m* (cuerda) clothes-line; (caballete) clotheshorse

tendencia *f* tendency; **~s homosexuales** homosexual tendencies *o* leanings; **~ A algo** trend TOWARD(S) sth; **tiene ~ a exagerar** she has a tendency to exaggerate; **existe una ~ a la centralización** there is a trend toward centralization

tender [E8] *vt* **1** ‹*ropa*› (afuera) to hang out; (dentro de la casa) to hang (up); **tengo ropa tendida** I have some washing on the line **2 (a)** (extender) ‹*manta*› to spread out, lay out; ‹*mantel*› to spread; **le tendió la mano** he held out his hand to him **(b)** (AmL) ‹*cama*› to make; ‹*mesa*› to lay, set **(c)** ‹*persona*› to lay **3 (a)** ‹*cable*› (sobre superficie) to lay; (suspendido) to hang **(b)** ‹*vía férrea*› to lay **4** ‹*emboscada*› to lay, set; ‹*trampa*› to set ■ **~** *vi* (inclinarse) **~ A hacer algo** to tend to do sth; **tiende a encoger** it tends to shrink

■ **tenderse** *v pron* (tumbarse) to lie down

tendero -ra *m,f* storekeeper (esp AmE), shopkeeper (esp BrE)

tendido *m* **1** (Elec) (cables) cables (*pl*), wires (*pl*) **2** (Col, Ven) (ropa de cama) bedclothes (*pl*)

tendón *m* ▶ 123 tendon

tendré, tendría, etc *see* TENER

tenebroso -sa *adj* ‹*lugar*› dark, gloomy; ‹*asunto/maquinaciones*› sinister; ‹*porvenir*› dismal, gloomy

tenedor *m* (cubierto) fork

tenencia *f* (Méx) (Auto) road tax

tener [E27] *vt* [*El uso de 'got' en frases como 'I've got a new dress' está mucho más extendido en el inglés británico que en el americano. Éste prefiere la forma 'I have a new dress'*] **1 (a)** (poseer, disponer de) ‹*dinero/trabajo/tiempo*› to have; **¿tienen hijos?** do they have any children?, have they got any children?; **no tenemos pan** we don't have any bread, we haven't got any bread; **tiene el pelo largo** she has *o* she's got long hair **(b)** (llevar encima) ‹*lápiz/*

cambio› to have; **¿tiene hora?** have you got the time? **(c)** (hablando de actividades, obligaciones) to have; **tengo invitados a cenar** I have *o* I've got some people coming to dinner; **tengo cosas que hacer** I have *o* I've got things to do **(d)** (dar a luz) ‹*bebé/gemelos*› to have **2 (a)** (señalando características, tamaño) to be; **la casa tiene mucha luz** the house is very light; **tiene un metro de largo** it is one meter long; **(b)** (señalando edad) ▶ 159 to be; **¿cuántos años tienes?** how old are you?; **tengo veinte años** I'm twenty (years old); **le lleva 15 años — ¿y eso qué tiene?** (AmL fam) she's 15 years older than he is — so what does that matter? **3 (a)** (sujetar, sostener) to hold; **tenlo derecho** hold it upright **(b)** (tomar): **ten la llave** take *o* here's the key **4 (a)** (sentir): **tengo hambre/frío** I'm hungry/cold; **le tengo mucho cariño** I'm very fond of him; **tengo el placer de** ... it gives me great pleasure to ... **(b)** (refiriéndose a enfermedades) ▶ 000 ‹*gripe/cáncer*› to have; **tengo dolor de cabeza** I have *o* I've got a headache **(c)** (refiriéndose a experiencias) ‹*discusión/accidente*› to have; **que tengas buen viaje** have a good trip **5** (refiriéndose a actitudes): **ten más respeto** have a little more respect; **ten paciencia/cuidado** be patient/careful; **tiene mucho tacto** he's very tactful **6** (indicando estado, situación): **la mesa tiene una pata rota** one of the table legs is broken; **tengo las manos sucias** my hands are dirty; **tienes el cinturón desabrochado** your belt's undone; **me tiene muy preocupada** I'm very worried about it ■ ~ *v aux* **1 (a)** ~ QUE **hacer algo** (expresando obligación, necesidad) to have (got) to do sth; **tengo que estudiar hoy** I have to *o* I must study today; **tienes que comer más** you ought to eat more **(b)** (expresando propósito, recomendación): **tenemos que ir a ver esa película** we must go and see that movie; **tendrías que llamarlo** you should ring him **(c)** (expresando certeza): **tiene que estar en este cajón** it must be in this drawer; **¡tú tenías que ser!** it had to be you! **2** (con participio pasado): **tengo entendido que sí viene** I understand he *is* coming; **te tengo dicho que** ... I've told you before (that) ...; **teníamos pensado irnos hoy** we intended leaving today **3** (AmL) (en expresiones de tiempo): **tienen tres años de casados** they've been married for three years; **tenía un año sin verlo** she hadn't seen him for a year

■ **tenerse** *v pron* (sostenerse): **no podía ~se en pie** he couldn't stand; **no ~se de sueño** to be dead on one's feet

tenga, tengas, etc *see* TENER

tenia *f* (Med) tapeworm, taenia (tech)

tenida *f* (Chi) outfit

teniente *mf* **(a)** (en ejército) lieutenant **(b)** (en fuerzas aéreas) ≈ first lieutenant (*in US*), ≈ flying officer (*in UK*)

tenis *m* (*pl* ~) tennis; **~ de mesa** table tennis

tenista *mf* tennis player

tenor *m* (Mús) tenor

tensar [A1] *vt* ‹*músculo*› to tense; ‹*cuerda/cable*› to tighten; ‹*arco*› to draw; ‹*relaciones/lazos*› to strain

tensión *f* **1 (a)** (de cuerda, músculo) tension **(b)** *tb* **~ arterial** blood pressure; **tomarle la ~ a algn** to take sb's blood pressure; **~ nerviosa** nervous tension **2** (estrés) strain, stress; (en relaciones, situación) tension **3** (Elec) voltage

tenso -sa *adj* **1** ‹*cuerda/cable*› taut, tight; ‹*músculo*› tense **2** ‹*persona/situación*› tense; ‹*relación*› strained, tense

tentación *f* **(a)** (impulso) temptation; **no resistió la ~ de comérselo** he couldn't resist the temptation to eat it **(b)** (cosa, persona): **los bombones son mi ~** I can't resist chocolates (colloq)

tentáculo *m* tentacle

tentador -dora *adj* tempting

tentar [A5] *vt* **1** (atraer, seducir) «*plan/idea*» to tempt; «*persona*» to tempt; **me tienta tu propuesta** I am very tempted by your proposal; **estuve tentado de decírselo** I was tempted to tell him; **~ a algn** A **hacer algo** to tempt sb to do sth **2** (probar) **(a)** ‹*cuerda/tabla*› to test **(b)** (palpar) to feel

tentativa *f* attempt

tentempié *m* (bocado) snack

tenue *adj* **(a)** ‹*luz*› faint, weak; ‹*voz/sonido/sonrisa*› faint; ‹*neblina/llovizna*› light; ‹*línea*› faint, fine **(b)** ‹*color*› subdued, pale

teñir [I15] *vt* **(a)** ‹*ropa/zapatos/pelo*› to dye **(b)** (manchar) to stain; **la tinta le tiñó los dedos de rojo** the ink stained his fingers red

■ **teñirse** *v pron* (*refl*) ‹*pelo/zapatos*› to dye

teología *f* theology

teoría *f* theory; **en ~** in theory

teórico -ca *adj* ‹*existencia/valor/curso*› theoretical; **examen ~** theory (exam)

tequila *m* tequila

terapeuta *mf* therapist

terapéutico -ca *adj* therapeutic

terapia *f* therapy; **~ de pareja** marriage counseling*; **~ intensiva** (Méx, RPl) intensive care

tercer *ver* TERCERO[1]

tercera *f* (Auto) third (gear); **mete (la) ~** put it into third (gear)

tercermundista *adj* third-world (*before n*)

tercero[1] -ra ▶ 294, 130 *adj/pron* [TERCER *is used before masculine singular nouns*] third; **en el tercer piso** on the third floor; **el Tercer Mundo** the Third World; **personas de la tercera edad** senior citizens; **la tercera parte** a third; *para ejemplos ver* QUINTO

tercero[2] *m* third party; **seguro contra ~s** third party insurance

tercio *m* **(a)** ▶ 130 (tercera parte) third **(b)** (Taur) *each of the three main stages of a bullfight*

terciopelo *m* velvet

terco -ca *adj* stubborn, obstinate

tergiversar [A1] *vt* to distort, twist

termas *fpl* (baños) hot *o* thermal baths (*pl*); (manantial) hot *o* thermal springs (*pl*)

térmico -ca *adj* thermal

terminación *f* **(a)** (finalización) termination (frml) **(b)** (acabado) finish **(c)** (Ling) ending

terminal *adj* ‹*enfermedad/caso*› terminal; **los enfermos ~es** the terminally ill ■ *m* (Elec, Inf) terminal ■ *f* (de autobuses) terminus, bus station; (Aviac, Inf) terminal

terminante *adj* ‹*respuesta*› categorical; ‹*orden*› strict

terminar [A1] *vt* ‹*trabajo/estudio*› to finish; ‹*casa/obras*› to finish, complete; ‹*discusión/conflicto*› to put an end to; **termina esa sopa** finish up that soup; **~ la comida con un café** to end the meal with a cup of coffee ■ **~** *vi* **1** «*persona*» **(a)** (de hacer algo) to finish; **~ DE hacer algo** to finish doing sth; **déjame ~ de hablar** let me finish (speaking) **(b)** (en estado, situación) to end up; **terminé muy cansada** I ended up feeling very tired; **va a ~ mal** he's going to come to a bad end; **terminó marchándose** *or* **por marcharse** he ended up leaving **2 (a)** «*reunión/situación*» to end, come to an end; **al ~ la clase** when the class ended; **esto va a ~ mal** this is going to turn out *o* end badly **(b)** (rematar) **~ EN algo** to end IN sth; **termina en consonante** it ends in a consonant **(c)** (llegar a): **no termina de convencerme** I'm not totally convinced; **no terminaba de gustarle** she wasn't totally happy about it **3 terminar con (a)** (acabar) **~ CON algo** ‹*con libro/tarea*› to finish WITH sth; ‹*con problema/abuso*› to put an end to sth **(b) ~ CON algn** (pelearse) to finish WITH sb; (matar) to kill sb

■ **terminarse** *v pron* **1** «*azúcar/pan*» to run out; **se me terminó la lana** I've run out of wool **2** «*curso/reunión*» to come to an end, be over **3** (*enf*) ‹*libro/comida*› to finish, polish off

término *m* **1** (posición, instancia): **en primer ~** first, first of all; **~ medio** happy medium; ***por ~ medio*** on average **2** (Ling) term; **en ~s reales** in real terms **3 términos** *mpl* (condiciones, especificaciones) terms (*pl*) **4** (Col, Méx, Ven) (Coc): **¿qué ~ quiere la carne?** how would you like your meat (done)?

termita *f* termite

termo® *m* (recipiente) Thermos®, vacuum flask

termómetro *m* thermometer

termostato *m* thermostat

ternera *f* veal

ternero -ra *m,f* calf

terno *m* (AmS) suit (*in some countries specifically a three-piece suit*)

ternura *f* tenderness; **con ~** tenderly

terquedad *f* obstinacy, stubbornness

terracería *f* (Méx) (camino) rough dirt track

terracota *f* terra-cotta

terrateniente *mf* landowner

terraza *f* **(a)** (balcón) balcony **(b)** (azotea) terrace **(c)** (de bar) *area outside a bar or café where tables are placed*; **sentémonos en la ~** let's sit outside **(d)** (Agr) terrace

terregal *m* (Méx) loose topsoil

terremoto *m* earthquake

terrenal *adj* worldly, earthly

terreno¹ -na *adj* (Relig) earthly

terreno² *m* **1 (a)** (lote, parcela) plot of land, lot (AmE); **heredó unos ~s en Sonora** she inherited some land in Sonora; **un ~ plantado de viñas** a field planted with vines; **~ de juego** field, pitch **(b)** (extensión de tierra) land; **una casa con mucho ~** a house with a lot of land **2** (Geog) (refiriéndose al relieve) terrain; (refiriéndose a la composición) land, soil; **un ~ fértil** fertile land **3** (esfera, campo de acción) sphere, field; **en el ~ político** within the field of politics

terrestre *adj* **(a)** ‹*transportes/comunicaciones*› land (*before n*), terrestrial (frml); **por vía ~** overland, by land; **fuerzas ~s** ground *o* land forces; **la superficie ~** the earth's surface **(b)** (Relig) ‹*vida*› earthly

terrible *adj* **(a)** ‹*tortura/experiencia*› terrible, horrific **(b)** (uso hiperbólico) terrible; **tengo un sueño ~** I'm terribly tired

territorial *adj* territorial

territorio *m* territory

terrón *m* (de azúcar) lump; (de tierra) clod, lump

terror *m* **(a)** (miedo) terror; **le tengo ~** it terrifies me, I find it terrifying; **de ~** ‹*novela/relato*› horror (*before n*) **(b)** (persona) terror

terrorífico -ca *adj* horrific

terrorismo *m* terrorism

terrorista *adj/mf* terrorist

terso -sa *adj* smooth

tertulia *f* (reunión) gathering (*to discuss philosophy, politics, art, etc*)

tesina *f* dissertation (*submitted as part of a first degree*)

tesis *f* (*pl* **~**) **(a)** (Educ, Fil) thesis; **~ doctoral** doctoral thesis **(b)** (opinión): **los dos sostienen la misma ~** they are both of the same opinion; **esto confirma la ~ inicial** this confirms the initial theory

tesón *m* tenacity, determination

tesorería *f* (oficina) treasury; (cargo) post of treasurer

tesorero -ra *m,f* treasurer

tesoro *m* **(a)** (cosa valiosa) treasure **(b)** (persona) treasure, gem (colloq); **¿qué te pasa, ~?** what's the matter, darling?

test *m* (*pl* **tests**) test; **un examen tipo ~** a multiple-choice exam

testamento *m* will, testament (frml); **hacer ~** to make one's will

testarudo -da *adj* stubborn, pigheaded

testículo *m* testicle

testigo *mf* witness; **ser ~ de algo** to witness sth, be a witness to sth

testimonio *m* **(a)** (Der) (declaración) testimony, statement **(b)** (prueba) proof, testimony (frml); **dar ~ de algo** to bear witness to sth

tétanos, **tétano** *m* tetanus

tetera *f* **(a)** (para servir té) teapot **(b)** (Andes, Méx) (para hervir agua) kettle **(c)** (Méx) (biberón) baby's bottle

tetero *m* (Col, Ven) baby's bottle

tetilla *f* **(a)** (Anat) nipple; (Zool) teat **(b)** (del biberón) teat

tetina *f* teat

tétrico -ca *adj* dismal, gloomy

textil *adj* textile (*before n*)

texto *m* text

El tiempo atmosférico

¿qué tiempo hace? *or* ¿cómo está el tiempo?	=	what's the weather like?

Cuando en español, al hablar del tiempo, se emplea el verbo hacer, haber (*en sus formas impersonales*), *el inglés utiliza el verbo* to be:

hace buen tiempo	=	it's fine
hace un día precioso	=	it's a beautiful day
hace tan malo (Esp)	=	it's such horrible weather

Nótese que cuando en español se utiliza el verbo hacer *o* haber *seguido de un nombre, el inglés emplea el verbo* to be *seguido de un adjetivo*:

hace sol/frío	=	it's sunny/cold
hacía mucho calor	=	it was very hot
¡qué calor hace!	=	it's so hot!
hace or hay viento	=	it's windy
hay niebla/neblina	=	it's foggy/misty

En todo caso el uso de hacer *o* haber *no excluye la posibilidad de utilizar el nombre* tiempo (weather), día (day)*etc., como sujeto del verbo* ser *o* estar (to be) *con un complemento adjetivo*:

el tiempo estaba/ha estado excelente	=	the weather was/has been very good
en Madrid, en verano, el tiempo es bueno y caluroso	=	in Madrid, during the summer, the weather is fine and hot
¿cómo es el clima en Ciudad de México?	=	what's the weather like in Mexico City?
el día está nublado/ lluvioso/caluroso	=	it's a cloudy/rainy/ hot day
era una mañana fría y gris (liter)	=	it was a cold, gray morning

Cuando el español utiliza verbos impersonales como llover, nevar *etc., el inglés utiliza el respectivo verbo impersonal* to rain, snow *etc*:

llovió toda la noche	=	it rained all night
está lloviendo	=	it's raining

Para otros usos de verbos impersonales referidos al tiempo atmosférico, consultar el diccionario

Otros usos:

amaneció nublado/ lloviendo	=	it was cloudy/raining first thing in the morning
	=	it dawned cloudy/raining (liter)

Nótese en los siguientes ejemplos (*menos formales*)*, la falta de equivalencia en inglés de los pronombres* me/te/le *etc*:

nos hizo un tiempo estupendo	=	we had very good weather
les llovió toda la semana	=	they had rain all week

textual *adj* ‹*traducción*› literal; ‹*palabras*› exact; ‹*cita*› direct

textura *f* texture

tez *f* complexion

ti *pron pers* **(a)** you; **para ~** for you; **delante de ~** in front of you; **a mí me gusta ¿y a ~?** I like it, do you? **(b)** (*refl*): **~ mismo/misma** yourself; **piensa un poco en ~ mismo** just think of yourself a little **(c)** (*impers*) you; **si a ~ te cuentan que** ... if someone tells you that ...

tianguis *m* (Méx) street market

tibio -bia *adj* **(a)** ‹*agua/baño*› lukewarm, tepid **(b)** ‹*atmósfera/ambiente*› warm **(c)** ‹*relación*› lukewarm; ‹*acogida*› unenthusiastic, cool

tiburón *m* **(a)** (Zool) shark **(b)** (fam) (persona) shark **(c)** (Fin) raider

tic *m* **1** (movimiento) *tb* **~ nervioso** nervous tic **2** (marca en escrito) tick

tico -ca *adj/m,f* (AmL fam) Costa Rican

tiempo *m* **1 (a)** (en general) time; **¡cómo pasa el ~!** how time flies!; **te acostumbrarás con el ~** you'll get used to it in time; **perder el ~** to waste time; **¡no hay ~ que perder!** there's no time to lose!; **para ganar ~** (in order) to gain time; **¿cuánto ~ hace que no lo ves?** how long is it since you last saw him?; **hace ~ que no sé de él** I haven't heard from him for a long time; **ya hace ~ que se marchó** she left quite some time ago; **¡cuánto ~ sin verte!** I haven't seen you for ages; **la mayor parte del ~** most of the time; **me llevó mucho ~** it took me a long time; **no pude quedarme más ~** I couldn't stay any longer; **poco ~ después** a short time after; **de un ~ a esta parte** for some time (now); **a ~ completo/parcial** full time/part time; **no vamos a llegar a ~** we won't get there in time; **al mismo ~** at the same time; **avísame con ~** let me know in good time; **¡qué ~s aquellos!** those were the days!; **en aquellos ~s** at that time, in those days **(b)** (temporada) season; **fruta del ~** fruits in season **(c)** (momento propio, oportuno): **a su (debido) ~** in due course; **cada cosa a su ~** everything in (its own) good time **(d)** (edad de bebé): **¿cuánto ~ tiene?** how old is he? **2** (Dep) (en partido) half; **primer ~** first half **3** (Mús) (compás) tempo, time; (de sinfonía) movement **4** (Ling) tense **5** (Meteo) **▶ 409** weather; **hace buen/mal ~** the weather's good/bad; **del** *or* (Méx) **al ~** ‹*bebida*› at room temperature

tienda *f* **1** (Com) (en general) store (esp AmE), shop (esp BrE); **ir de ~s** to go shopping; **~ de comestibles** *or* (AmC, Andes, Méx) **abarrotes** grocery store (AmE), grocer's (shop) (BrE) **2** (Dep, Mil, Ocio) *tb* **~ de campaña** tent; **poner** *or* **montar una ~** to put up *o* pitch a tent; **desmontar una ~** to take down a tent

tiene, tienes, etc *see* TENER

tienta *f*: **a tientas** (*loc adv*): **andar** *or* **ir a ~s** to feel one's way; **buscó el timbre a ~s** he fumbled *o* felt around for the bell

tierno -na *adj* **1** ‹*carne*› tender; ‹*pan*› fresh;

‹*brote/planta*› young, tender **2** ‹*persona*› affectionate, loving; ‹*mirada/corazón*› tender

tierra *f* **1** (campo, terreno) land; **~s fértiles** fertile land; **~ de cultivo** arable land **2** (suelo, superficie) ground; (materia, arena) earth; **cavar la ~** to dig the ground; **un camión de ~** a truckload of soil *o* earth; **no juegues con ~** don't play in the dirt; **un camino de ~** a dirt road *o* track; ***echar algo por ~*** ‹*planes*› to wreck, ruin; ‹*argumentos*› to demolish, destroy; ‹*esperanzas*› to dash **3** (AmL) (polvo) dust **4** (Elec) ground (AmE), earth (BrE); **estar conectado a ~** *or* (AmL) **hacer ~** to be grounded *o* earthed **5** (por oposición al mar, al aire) land; **viajar por ~** to travel overland *o* by land; **~ firme** solid ground; ***tomar ~*** to land, touch down **6** (país, lugar): **su ~ (natal)** his homeland, his native land; **costumbres de aquellas ~s** customs in those places *o* countries; **la T~ Santa** the Holy Land **7** (planeta) **la T~** (the) Earth

tieso -sa *adj* **1 (a)** (rígido) stiff; **con las orejas tiesas** with ears pricked up **(b)** (Col, Ven) (duro) ‹*pan*› hard; ‹*carne*› tough **2** ‹*persona*› (erguido) upright, erect; (orgulloso) stiff; ***quedarse ~*** (fam) (helarse) to get frozen stiff (colloq)

tiesto *m* **(a)** (para plantas) flowerpot **(b)** (Chi) (palangana) basin

tifón *m* typhoon

tifus *m* **(a)** (transmitido por parásitos) typhus (fever) **(b)** (fiebre tifoidea) typhoid

tigre -gresa *m,f* (animal asiático) (*m*) tiger; (*f*) tigress

tijeras *fpl*, **tijera** *f* (para cortar papel, tela) scissors (*pl*); (para uñas) nail scissors (*pl*); (para césped) shears (*pl*); **unas ~s** a pair of scissors; **~ de podar** pruning shears (*pl*); ***de ~*** ‹*silla/cama*› folding (*before n*); **escalera de ~** stepladder

tila *f* (infusión) lime (blossom) tea

tilde *f* (acento) accent; (sobre la ñ) tilde, swung dash

tiliches *mpl* (Méx fam) stuff (colloq)

tilo *m* **(a)** (árbol) lime (tree) **(b)** (Chi) ⇒ TILA

timador -dora *m,f* swindler, cheat

timar [A1] *vt* to swindle, cheat

timbal *m* (Mús) kettledrum; **los ~es** the timpani, the timps (colloq)

timbrar [A1] *vt* ‹*documento*› to stamp; ‹*carta*› to frank ■ **~** *vi* (Col, Méx) to ring the bell

timbre *m* **1** (para llamar) (door)bell; **tocar el ~** to ring the bell; **~ de alarma** alarm bell **2** (de sonido, voz) tone, timbre **3 (a)** (sello) fiscal stamp **(b)** (Méx) (sello postal) (postage) stamp

timidez *f* (retraimiento) shyness; (falta de decisión, coraje) timidity

tímido -da *adj* (retraído) shy; (falto de decisión, coraje) timid

timo *m* (fam) con (colloq), scam (colloq)

timón *m* **(a)** (Aviac, Náut) rudder **(b)** (Col, Per) (volante) steering wheel; **ir al ~** to be at the wheel

timonel *mf* (*m*) helmsman; (*f*) helmswoman

tímpano *m* (Anat) eardrum

tinaco *m* (Méx) water tank

tinaja *f* large earthenware jar

tinca *f* (Andes) (fam) (empeño) effort

tincada *f* (Andes fam) feeling, hunch (colloq)

tincar [A2] *vi* (Andes fam) **(a)** (parecer): **me tinca que ya no viene** I get the feeling she's not coming **(b)** (parecer bien, gustar): **ese pescado me tinca** I like the look of that fish; **¿te tinca ir al cine?** do you feel like going to the movies?

tinieblas *fpl* darkness

tino *m* **(a)** (sentido común) sound judgment, good sense **(b)** (tacto) tact, sensitivity

tinta *f* ink; **escribir con ~** to write in ink; **~ China** India ink (AmE), Indian ink (BrE); ***saber algo de buena ~*** to have sth on good authority

tinte *m* **1** (acción) dyeing; (sustancia) dye **2** (Esp) (establecimiento) dry cleaner's

tintero *m* inkwell

tintín *m* (de campanilla) tinkling, jingling; (de copa) clinking

tinto¹ -ta *adj* ‹*vino/uva*› red

tinto² *m* **1** (Vin) red wine **2** (Col) (café) black coffee

tintorería *f* dry cleaner's

tiña *f* (Med) ringworm

tiñoso -sa *adj* (Med) scabby, mangy

tío, tía *m,f* **1** (pariente) (*m*) uncle; (*f*) aunt; **mis ~s** (varones) my uncles; (varones y mujeres) my aunts and uncles **2** (Esp) (individuo) (fam) ⇒ TIPO¹

tiovivo *m* (Esp) merry-go-round, carousel (AmE)

tipear [A1] *vt* (AmS) to type

típico -ca *adj* typical; ‹*plato/traje*› typical, traditional; **¡eso es ~ de él!** that's typical of him!

tipo¹ -pa *m,f* (fam) (*m*) guy (colloq), bloke (BrE colloq); (*f*) woman

tipo² *m* **1** (clase) kind, type, sort; **todo ~ de plantas** all kinds of plants; **no es mi ~** he's not my type **2** (figura — de mujer) figure; (— de hombre) physique **3** (*como adv*) (CS fam) around, about; **vénganse ~ cuatro** come around about four o'clock

tique, tiquet *m* **(a)** (de tren, bus) ticket **(b)** (recibo) receipt, sales slip (AmE)

tiquete *m* (Col) ⇒ TIQUE

tira *f* (de papel, tela) strip; (de zapato) strap; **~ cómica** comic strip, strip cartoon ■ *mf* **(a)** (Chi, Méx fam) (agente) cop (colloq) **(b)** (Per, RPl arg) (detective infiltrado) police plant (colloq), undercover cop (colloq) **(c) la tira** *f* (Méx fam) (cuerpo) the cops (colloq)

tirabuzón *m* **1** (sacacorchos) corkscrew **2** (rizo, bucle) ringlet **3** (en béisbol) screwball

tirada *f* **1** (Jueg) (en juegos de mesa) throw **2** (Impr) print run; **un periódico con una ~ de 300.000 ejemplares diarios** a newspaper with a daily circulation of 300,000 copies

tiradero *m* (Méx) (basurero) garbage (AmE) *o* (BrE) rubbish dump; (casa, habitación) mess, pigsty

tirado -da *adj* **1** (en desorden): **lo dejan todo ~** they leave everything lying around **2** (fam) [ESTAR] **(a)** (muy fácil) dead easy (colloq) **(b)** (muy barato) dirt cheap (colloq)

tirador¹ *m* **(a)** (de cajón, puerta) knob, handle **(b)** (tirachinas) slingshot (AmE), catapult (BrE) **(c) tiradores** *mpl* (Arg, Bol) (de pantalón) suspenders (*pl*) (AmE), braces (*pl*) (BrE)

tirador² -dora *m,f* (*m*) marksman; (*f*) markswoman; **es un buen ~** he's a good shot

tiraje *m* **(a)** (AmL) (Impr) ⇒ TIRADA 2 **(b)** (CS) (de la chimenea) damper

tiranía *f* tyranny

tirano -na *adj* tyrannical ■ *m,f* tyrant

tirantas *fpl* (Col) suspenders (*pl*) (AmE), braces (*pl*) (BrE)

tirante *adj* **(a)** ‹*piel/costura/cuerda*› taut **(b)** ‹*situación*› tense; ‹*relaciones*› tense, strained ■ *m* **1** (Const) strut, brace **2** (Indum) **(a)** (de prenda) strap, shoulder strap; **pantalones de ~s** overalls (*pl*) (AmE), dungarees (*pl*) (BrE) **(b) tirantes** *mpl* (Esp, Méx, Ven) (de pantalón) suspenders (*pl*) (AmE), braces (*pl*) (BrE)

tirar [A1] *vt* **1 (a)** (lanzar) to throw; **tiró la pelota al aire** he threw the ball up in the air; **~le algo A algn** (para que lo agarre) to throw sb sth; (con agresividad) to throw sth AT sb **(b)** (desechar) to throw out *o* away **(c)** (desperdiciar) to waste; **¡qué manera de ~ el dinero!** what a waste of money! **2 (a)** (hacer caer) ‹*jarrón/silla*› to knock over; **el perro me tiró al suelo** the dog knocked me over **(b)** (derribar) ‹*pared/puerta*› to knock down **3 (a)** ‹*bomba*› to drop; ‹*cohete*› to fire, launch; ‹*flecha*› to shoot **(b)** ‹*foto*› to take **4** (AmL) (atrayendo hacia sí) to pull; **tiró la cadena** he pulled the chain ■ **~** *vi* **1** (atrayendo hacia sí) to pull; **~ DE algo** to pull sth; **no le tires del pelo** don't pull her hair **2 (a)** (disparar) to shoot; **~ a matar** to shoot to kill **(b)** (Dep) to shoot; **~ al arco** (AmL) *or* (Esp) **a puerta** to shoot at goal **(c)** (Jueg) (descartarse) to throw away; (en juegos de dados) to throw; (en dardos) to throw; (en bolos) to bowl **3 (a)** «*chimenea/cigarro*» to draw **(b)** «*coche/motor*» to pull **4 tirando** *ger* (fam): **gano poco pero vamos tirando** I don't earn much but we're managing; **¿qué tal andas? — tirando** how are things? — not too bad **5 tirar a** (tender a): **tira más bien a azul** it's more of a bluish color; **ella tira más a la madre** she takes after her mother more

■ **tirarse** *v pron* **1 (a)** (lanzarse, arrojarse) to throw oneself; **se tiró por la ventana** he threw himself out of the window; **~se en paracaídas** to parachute; (en emergencia) to bale out; **~se al agua** to jump into the water; **~se de cabeza** to dive in, to jump in headfirst **(b)** (AmL) (tumbarse) to lie down **2** (fam) ‹*horas/días*› to spend; **se tiró dos años escribiéndolo** he spent two years writing it **3** (fam) (expulsar): **~se un pedo** to fart (sl)

tirita *f* (Esp) Band-Aid® (AmE), sticking plaster (BrE)

tiritar [A1] *vi* to shiver, tremble; **~ de frío** to shiver with cold

tiro *m* **1** (disparo) shot; **le dispararon un ~** they shot him; **lo mató de un ~** she shot him dead; ***al ~*** (Chi fam) right away, straightaway (BrE); ***errar el ~*** (literal) to miss; (equivocarse) to get it wrong **2** (en fútbol, baloncesto) shot; (deporte) shooting; **~ al arco** (deporte) archery; (en fútbol) (AmL) shot at goal; **~ al blanco** (deporte) target shooting; (lugar) shooting gallery; **~ al plato** skeet shooting (AmE), clay-pigeon shooting (BrE); **~ de esquina** (AmL) corner (kick); **~ libre** (en fútbol) free kick; (en baloncesto) free shot *o* throw **3** (de chimenea) flue; **tiene muy buen ~** it draws well **4 animal/caballo de ~** draught animal/horse

tirón *m* **(a)** (movimiento) tug, pull; **me dio un ~ de pelo** he pulled my hair; **dale un ~ de orejas** tweak his ears for him (colloq); **el autobús avanzaba a tirones** the bus jerked along; ***de un ~***: **me arrancó la cadena de un ~** he ripped the chain from my neck; **lo leyó/bebió de un ~** (fam) she read/downed it in one go **(b)** (de músculo): **sufrió un ~ en la pierna** he pulled a muscle in his leg **(c)** (forma de robo): **le dieron un** *or* **el ~** they snatched her bag

tironear [A1] *vi* (AmL fam) to tug, pull ■ **~** *vt* (AmL fam) to tug (at)

tiroteo *m* (tiros) shooting; (intercambio de tiros) shoot-out

tirria *f* (fam) grudge; **tenerle ~ a algn** to have a grudge against sb

tisú *m* (*pl* **-sús** *or* **-súes**) (pañuelo) tissue; (tela) lamé

titánico -ca *adj* huge, colossal (*before n*)

títere *m* **(a)** (marioneta, persona) puppet **(b) títeres** *mpl* (función) puppet show

titiritar [A1] *vi* to shiver, tremble

titiritero -ra *m,f* (de marionetas) puppeteer; (acróbata) acrobat

titubeante *adj* ‹*voz/respuesta*› faltering, halting; ‹*actitud*› hesitant

titubear [A1] *vi* **(a)** (dudar, vacilar) to hesitate; **sin ~** without hesitation **(b)** (balbucear) to stutter

titubeo *m* (duda, vacilación) hesitancy, hesitation

titulación *f* qualifications (*pl*); **personas con ~ universitaria** university graduates, college graduates (AmE)

titulado -da *adj* qualified ■ *m,f* graduate; **~ medio** *graduate with a qualification obtained after a three-year degree course as opposed to a five-year course*; **~ superior** *or* **universitario** university graduate, college graduate (AmE)

titular¹ *adj* ‹*médico/profesor*› permanent ■ *mf* (de pasaporte, cuenta, cargo) holder ■ *m* **(a)** (en periódico) headline **(b)** (Rad, TV) main story; **los ~es** the main stories, the news headlines

titular² [A1] *vt* ‹*obra*›: **su novela titulada 'Julia'** his novel called *o* (frml) entitled 'Julia'

■ **titularse** *v pron* **1** «*obra/película*» to be called, be entitled (frml) **2** (Educ) to graduate, get one's degree; **~se EN/DE algo** to graduate IN/AS sth

título *m* **1** (en general) title; **un poema que lleva por ~ ...** a poem called *o* (frml) entitled ...; **el ~ de campeón juvenil** the junior title; **~ nobiliario** title; ***a ~ de***: **a ~ de introducción** by way of introduction; **asiste a ~ de observador** he's attending as an observer **2** (Educ) degree; (diploma) certificate; **~ académico** academic qualification; **~ universitario** university degree, college degree (AmE)

tiza *f* (material) chalk; (barra) (piece of) chalk; (en billar) chalk

tizón *m* (leño) charred stick/log

toalla *f* **(a)** (tejido) toweling* **(b)** (para secarse) towel; **~ higiénica** sanitary napkin (AmE), sanitary towel (BrE); ***tirar*** *or* ***arrojar la ~*** to throw in the towel

toallero *m* (barra) towel rail; (aro) towel ring

tobillera *f* **(a)** (Med) ankle support **(b)** (de ciclista) cycle clip

tobillo *m* ▶ 123 ankle

tobogán *m* **(a)** (en parque) slide; (en piscina) water chute **(b)** (Aviac) escape chute **(c)** (trineo) toboggan

toca *f* (de religiosa) wimple; (de tocado) circlet

tocadiscos *m* (*pl* ~) record player

tocador *m* (mueble) dressing table

tocar [A2] *vt* **1 (a)** (en general) to touch; (palpar) to feel; (manosear) to handle; **¡no vayas a ~ ese cable!** don't touch that cable!; **mis ahorros no los quiero ~** I don't want to touch my savings; **la planta ya toca el techo** the plant is already touching the ceiling **(b)** (hacer sonar) ‹*timbre/campana*› to ring; ‹*claxon*› to blow, sound **(c)** (Mús) ‹*instrumento/pieza*› to play **2** ‹*tema*› (tratar) to touch on, refer to; (sacar) to bring up **3** (atañer, concernir) to affect; **un problema que nos toca de cerca** a problem which affects us directly ■ ~ *vi* **1 (a)** (AmL) (llamar) «*persona*» to knock at the door; **alguien está tocando (a la puerta)** there's somebody at the door **(b)** «*campana/timbre*» to ring; **las campanas tocaban a misa** the bells were ringing for mass **(c)** (Mús) to play **2 (a)** (corresponder en reparto, concurso, sorteo): **a ella le toca la mitad de la herencia** she gets half of the inheritance; **le tocó el primer premio** she won the first prize; **me tocó la maestra más antipática del colegio** I got the most horrible teacher in the school **(b)** (ser el turno): **te toca a ti** it's your turn; **¿a quién le toca cocinar?** whose turn is it to do the cooking?

■ **tocarse** *v pron* **(a)** (*refl*) ‹*herida/grano*› to touch; ‹*barba*› to play with **(b)** (*recípr*) «*personas*» to touch each other; «*cables*» to touch

tocayo -ya *m,f* namesake

tocino *m* (para guisar) pork fat; (con vetas de carne) fatty salt pork; (para freír) bacon

tocología *f* obstetrics

tocólogo -ga *m,f* obstetrician

todavía *adv* ▶ 413 **1 (a)** (aún) still; **¿~ estás aquí?** are you still here? **(b)** (en frases negativas) yet; **~ no está lista** she isn't ready yet **2** (en comparaciones) even, still; **sus primos son ~ más ricos** her cousins are even richer *o* richer still **3** (fam) (encima) still; **¡y ~ se queja!** and he still complains!

todo[1] -da *adj* ▶ 414 **1** (la totalidad de) all; **nos comimos ~ el pan** we ate all the bread; **toda la mañana** all morning, the whole morning; **invitó a toda la clase** she invited the whole class; **por ~s lados** all over the place; **~s ustedes lo sabían** you all knew **2** (cualquier, cada): **~ artículo importado** all imported items, any imported item; **~ aquél que quiera** anyone who wishes to; **~s los días** every day **3** (uso enfático): **a toda velocidad** at top speed; **con toda inocencia** in all innocence; **le dieron ~ tipo de facilidades** they gave him all kind of facilities; ***a ~ esto*** (mientras tanto) meanwhile, in the meantime; (a propósito) incidentally, by the way ■ *pron* **1 (a)** (sin excluir nada) everything; **lo perdieron ~** they lost everything; **~ le parece poco** he's never satisfied; **come ~ lo que quieras** eat as much as you like; **~ o nada** all or nothing **(b) ~s/todas** (referido a — cosas) all; (— a personas) all, everybody; **los compró ~s** she bought all of them; **vinieron ~s** they all came, everybody came; **buena suerte a ~s** good luck to everybody; **es el más alto de ~s** he's the tallest of the lot *o* of them all; **¿están ~s?** is everyone *o* everybody here?; **~s y cada uno** each and every one **2** (*en locs*) **con todo (y eso)** (fam) (aun así) all the same, even so; **de todo**: **come de ~** she'll eat anything; **venden de ~** they sell everything *o* all sorts of things; **hace de ~ un poco** he does a bit of everything; **del todo** totally **3** (*como adv*) **(a)** (completamente) all; **está ~ mojado** it's all wet **(b)** (en frases ponderativas) quite; **fue ~ un espectáculo** it was quite a show!

todo[2] *m*: **el/un ~** the/a whole; ***jugarse el ~ por el ~*** to risk *o* gamble everything on one throw

todopoderoso -sa *adj* all-powerful

Todopoderoso *m*: **el ~** the Almighty

todoterreno *m* (Auto) four-wheel-drive vehicle, 4 x 4 (*léase: four by four*)

Tokio *m* Tokyo

toldo *m* **(a)** (de terraza) canopy; (de tienda) awning; (en la playa) awning; (en camión) tarpaulin **(b)** (para fiestas) tent (AmE), marquee (BrE) **(c)** (de los indios) hut

tolerable *adj* tolerable

tolerancia *f* tolerance

tolerante *adj* tolerant

tolerar [A1] *vt* to tolerate; **¡eso no se puede ~!** that's intolerable!; Ⓢ **tolerada (para menores de 14 años)** (Esp) ≈ PG; **le toleras demasiado** you're too lenient with him

toma *f* **1 (a)** (Mil) capture, taking **(b)** (de universidad, fábrica) occupation; (de tierras) seizure **2** (Cin, Fot — imagen) shot; (— acción de filmar) take **3** (de medicamento) dose **4** (de datos) gathering; (de muestras) taking; **la ~ de decisiones** the decision-making **5** (AmL) (acequia) irrigation channel **6 (a) ~ de tierra** (Elec) ground (wire) (AmE), earth (wire) (BrE) **(b)** (Aviac) landing, touchdown

tomado -da *adj* **1** ‹*voz*›: **tengo la voz tomada** I'm hoarse **2** (AmL fam) ‹*persona*› drunk

tomadura de pelo *f* **(a)** (broma, chiste) joke **(b)** (burla): **esto es una ~ de ~** they're just messing around with us (AmE) *o* (BrE) messing us around

tomar [A1] *vt* **1** (en general) to take; **tomé un libro de la estantería** I took a book from the shelf; **la tomé de la mano** I took her by the hand; **toma lo que te debo** here's what I owe you; **¿lo puedo ~ prestado?** can I borrow it?; **tomó el asunto en sus manos** she took charge of the matter; **~ precauciones/el tren/una foto** to take precautions/the train/a picture; **~le la temperatura a algn** to take sb's temperature; **~ algo por escrito** to write sth down; **~ algo/a algn** POR **algo/algn** to take sth/sb FOR sth/sb; **¿por quién me has tomado?** who *o* what do you take me for?; **lo tomó a mal/a broma** he took it the wrong way/as a joke; **eso toma demasiado tiempo** that takes up too much time **2 (a)** (beber) to drink; **el niño**

Todavía

En términos generales todavía *se traduce por* still *cuando se trata de oraciones afirmativas o interrogativas*:

todavía estaba trabajando = I was still working
¿todavía tienes el mismo coche? = do you still have the same car?
¿su padre todavía vive? = is her father still alive?
podemos ganar todavía = we can still win
todavía queda una hora = there's still an hour to go

En frases negativas su traducción es por lo general yet:

todavía no ha llegado = she hasn't arrived yet *or* (AmL) no llega

Sin embargo, en estos casos el inglés puede emplear el adverbio still *cuando se quiere poner especial énfasis en el hecho de que aún no ocurre o no ha ocurrido la acción*:

todavía no ha llegado = she still hasn't arrived *or* (AmL) no llega

En comparaciones su traducción por lo general, es even:

allí hacía todavía más frio = it was even colder there

Para otros usos y ejemplos, ver entrada

toma (el) pecho the baby's being breast-fed **(b)** (servirse, consumir) to have; **¿qué vas a ~?** what are you going to have? **3** (esp AmL) **(a)** (contratar) to take on **(b)** «*profesor*» ‹*alumnos/clases*› to take on **(c)** «*colegio*» ‹*niño*› to take **4** (apoderarse de) ‹*fortaleza/tierras*› to seize; ‹*universidad/fábrica*› to occupy **5** (adquirir) ‹*forma*› to take; ‹*aspecto*› to take on; ‹*velocidad/altura*› to gain; ‹*costumbre*› to get into **6** (cobrar): **le he tomado cariño a esta casa/a la niña** I've become quite attached to this house/quite fond of the girl **7** (exponerse a): **~ el aire** to get some (fresh) air; **~ (el) sol** to sunbathe; **vas a ~ frío** (CS) you'll get *o* catch cold ■ **~** *vi* **1** (asir): **toma, aquí tienes tus tijeras** here are your scissors; **tome, yo no lo necesito** take it, I don't need it **2** (esp AmL) (beber alcohol) to drink **3** (AmL) (ir) to go; **~on para el norte** they went north; **~ a la derecha** to turn *o* go right **4** «*injerto*» to take
■ **tomarse** *v pron* **1** ‹*vacaciones/tiempo*› to take; **se tomó el día libre** he took the day off **2** ‹*molestia/libertad*› to take; **~se la molestia/libertad de hacer algo** to take the trouble to do sth/the liberty of doing sth **3** (*enf*) **(a)** ‹*café/vino*› to drink **(b)** ‹*medicamento/vitaminas*› to take **(c)** ‹*desayuno/merienda/sopa*› to eat, have; ‹*helado/yogur*› to have **4** ‹*autobús/tren/taxi*› to take **5** (Med) **(a)** (*refl*) to take; **se tomó la temperatura** she took her temperature **(b)** (*caus*): **~se la tensión** to have one's blood pressure taken **6** (*caus*) (esp AmL) ‹*foto*› to have ... taken **7** (*enf*) (reaccionar frente a) ‹*comentario/noticia*› to take; **no te lo tomes a mal** don't take it the wrong way **8** (Chi) ‹*universidad/fábrica*› to occupy

tomate *m* tomato; ***estar/ponerse* (*colorado*) *como un* ~** (de vergüenza) to be/turn as red as a beet (AmE), to be/go as red as a beetroot (BrE); (por el sol) to be/turn as red as a lobster

tomavistas *m* (*pl* **~**) movie camera

toma y daca *m* give-and-take

tómbola *f* tombola

tomillo *m* thyme

tomo *m* volume

ton *m*: **hacer algo sin ~ ni son** to do sth for no reason

tonada *f* **(a)** (melodía) tune; (canción) ballad, song **(b)** (AmL) (acento) accent

tonel *m* barrel

tonelada *f* ▶ 322 ton

tongo *m* (fam) (en partido, pelea) fix (colloq); **hubo ~** it was fixed (colloq)

tónica *f* **1** (bebida) tonic (water) **2** (tendencia, tono) trend, tendency

tónico[1] **-ca** *adj* **1** (Med) tonic (*before n*) **2 (a)** ‹*sílaba/vocal*› tonic (*before n*), stressed **(b)** (Mús) tonic

tónico[2] *m* (Med) tonic; (en cosmética) toner

tono *m* **1 (a)** (en general) tone; **en ~ cariñoso** in an affectionate tone of voice; **en ~ de reproche** reproachfully; **el ~ en que lo dijo** the way he said it; **el ~ general de la conversación** the general tone of the conversation **(b)** (Rad, Telec, TV) tone; **este teléfono no da** *or* **tiene ~** I can't get a dial tone (AmE) *o* (BrE) dialling tone on this phone; **~ de marcar** *or* (AmL) **de discado** *or* (AmS) **de discar** dial tone (AmE), dialling tone (BrE); **~ de ocupado** busy signal (AmE), engaged tone (BrE); ***no venir a* ~** to be out of place **2** (de color) shade; ***subido de* ~** risqué **3** (Mús) key

tontear [A1] *vi* **(a)** (hacer el tonto) to play the fool; (decir tonterías) to talk nonsense **(b)** (flirtear) to fool around (colloq)

tontería *f* **(a)** (cosa tonta) silly *o* stupid thing; (dicho tonto) silly remark; **¡déjate de ~s!** stop fooling around; **¡~s!** nonsense! **(b)** (cosa insignificante) silly thing, small thing; **se enoja por cualquier ~** she

Todo, Toda

Observaciones generales acerca del adjetivo

Cuando significa la totalidad de *y precede al artículo, a un posesivo o a un demonstrativo, su traducción es por lo general* all:

todo el vino = all the wine
todos los españoles = all (the) Spaniards
toda su inteligencia = all his intelligence
todo ese ruido = all that noise

Si 'todo' *se puede sustituir por* entero, *se puede también traducir por* whole. *Ambas traducciones no son siempre intercambiables por lo que se debe prestar atención al contexto*:

toda la mañana = all morning *o* the whole morning
todo el tiempo = all the time *o* the whole time
toda su familia = his whole family
toda la verdad = the whole truth

Nótese la siguiente traducción:

conoce todo México = he knows all of Mexico

Cuando 'todo' *se emplea en plural con el artículo definido seguido de un período de tiempo, su traducción es* every:

todos los días/meses = every day/month
todos los domingos/años = every Sunday/year

Nótese la traducción singular del nombre plural en español

Para ejemplos y usos suplementarios consultar entrada

Observaciones generales acerca del pronombre

En singular se traduce por everything *or* all, *aunque ambas traducciones no son siempre intercambiables*:

se lo comieron todo = they ate everything
= they ate it all (up)
eso es todo = that's all
el dinero no lo es todo = money isn't everything

En el plural si se refiere a cosas su traducción es all:

los vendió todos = they sold them all
= they sold all of them
están todos rotos = they're all broken

En el plural referido a personas, se traduce por all *o* everybody, *según si se hace referencia a la totalidad de las mismas o se pone énfasis en cada uno de los individuos respectivamente*:

todos lo sabían = they all knew
= everybody knew
estaban todos muy tristes = everybody was sad
= they were all sad

Para su uso adverbial y otros ejemplos, ver entrada

gets angry over the slightest little thing **(c)** (cualidad) stupidity

tonto -ta *adj* **1 (a)** [SER] (falto de inteligencia) stupid, dumb (colloq); (ingenuo) silly **(b)** [ESTAR] (intratable) difficult, silly; (disgustado) upset **2** ‹*excusa/error/historia*› silly ■ *m,f* (falto de inteligencia) idiot, dummy (colloq); (ingenuo) idiot, fool; ***hacer el ~*** (hacer payasadas) to play *o* act the fool; (actuar con necedad) to make a fool of oneself; ***hacerse el ~*** to act dumb

topacio *m* topaz

toparse [A1] *v pron* **~se CON algn** (tropezarse) to bump INTO sb; (encontrarse) to bump *o* run INTO sb; **~se CON algo** (tropezarse) to bump INTO sth; (encontrarse) to come across sth

tope *m* **1 (a)** (límite) limit; **han establecido un ~ máximo** an upper limit has been set **(b)** (*como adj inv*) ‹*edad/precio*› maximum (*before n*); **fecha ~** deadline **2 (a)** (para las puertas) doorstop; (Ferr) buffer **(b)** (Méx) (Auto) speed bump **3** (Andes) (cima) top **4 (a)** (Andes) (golpe, choque) bump **(b)** (Méx fam) (cabezazo): **me di un ~** I bumped my head

tópico[1] -ca *adj* **1** ‹*comentario/afirmación*› trite **2** (Farm): Ⓢ **uso tópico** for external use only

tópico[2] *m* **(a)** (tema, asunto) topic, subject **(b)** (tema trillado) hackneyed subject; (expresión) cliché

top-less, topless /'toples/ *m*: **el ~ es habitual aquí** it is quite normal for people to go topless here

topo *m* **(a)** (Zool) mole **(b)** (Col) (pendiente) earring

topografía *f* topography, surveying

toque *m* **1 (a)** (de timbre) ring; (de campana) stroke, chime; **al ~ de las doce** on the stroke of twelve; **~ de queda** curfew **(b)** (Esp fam) (llamada) call, ring (BrE colloq) **2** (en béisbol) bunt **3** (detalle) touch; **falta darle los últimos ~s** we have to put the finishing touches to it **4** (Méx fam) (descarga) electric shock

toquetear [A1] *vt* (fam) to touch; (sexualmente) to touch up

toquilla *f* shawl

tórax *m* ▶ 123 thorax

torbellino *m* **(a)** (de viento) whirlwind; (de polvo) dust storm **(b)** (de actividad) whirl **(c)** (persona inquieta) bundle of energy

torcedura *f* sprain

torcer [E10] *vt* **1** ‹*cuerpo*› to twist; ‹*cabeza*› to turn; **me torció el brazo** she twisted my arm **2** ‹*esquina*› to turn **3** ‹*curso/rumbo*› to change ■ ~ *vi* (girar) «*persona/vehículo*» to turn; «*camino*» to bend, curve

■ **torcerse** *v pron* **1** ‹*tobillo/muñeca*› to sprain **2** «*madera/viga*» to warp

torcido -da *adj* **1** [ESTAR] **(a)** (con respecto a otra cosa) crooked; **tiene la nariz torcida** he has a crooked nose; **llevas la falda torcida** your skirt's twisted **(b)** (curvo) bent; **una rama torcida** a bent branch; **tiene las piernas torcidas** (para adentro) he is knock-kneed; (para afuera) he is bowlegged **2** ‹*intenciones*› devious, crooked

torcijón *m* stomach cramp

tordo -da *m,f* **(a)** (caballo) dapple, dapple-gray* **(b)** (pájaro) thrush

torear [A1] *vi* to fight; **quiere** ~ he wants to be a bullfighter ■ ~ *vt* **1** ‹*toro/novillo*› to fight **2** (fam) **(a)** ‹*perseguidor/pregunta*› to dodge **(b)** (AmL) (provocar) to torment, needle

toreo *m* bullfighting

torero -ra *m,f* bullfighter, matador

tormenta *f* **1** (Meteo) storm; ~ **de nieve** snowstorm; (con viento) blizzard; ***hacer frente a la ~*** to weather the storm **2** (de pasiones) storm; (de celos) frenzy

tormentoso -sa *adj* stormy

tornado *m* tornado

tornamesa *f or m* (Col, Méx) (plato giratorio) turntable

torneo *m* tournament

tornero -ra *m,f* lathe operator

tornillo *m* (Tec) screw; ***te/le falta un ~*** you have/he has a screw loose (colloq)

torniquete *m* (Med) tourniquet

torno *m* **1 (a)** (de carpintero) lathe; ~ **de alfarero** potter's wheel **(b)** (Odont) drill **(c)** (para alzar pesos) winch **2 en torno a** around

toro *m* (animal) bull; ~ **bravo** *or* **de lidia** fighting bull; **los ~s** (el espectáculo) bullfighting; **ir a los ~s** to go to a bullfight

toronja *f* (AmL) grapefruit

torpe *adj* **(a)** (en las acciones) clumsy **(b)** (de entendimiento) slow (colloq) **(c)** (sin tacto) ‹*persona/comentario*› clumsy; **de manera** ~ clumsily

torpedo *m* **1** (Arm) torpedo **2** (Chi fam) (de estudiante) crib (note) (colloq)

torpeza *f* **1** (cualidad) **(a)** (en las acciones) clumsiness **(b)** (falta de inteligencia) stupidity; **perdona mi ~, pero no entiendo** I'm sorry to be so stupid *o* dim, but I don't understand **(c)** (falta de tacto) clumsiness **2** (dicho desacertado) gaffe; (acción desacertada) blunder

torrar [A1] *vt* to roast

torre *f* **(a)** (de castillo, iglesia) tower; (en punta) steeple, spire **(b)** (de cables de alta tensión) pylon; (de pozo de petróleo) derrick **(c)** (en ajedrez) rook, castle **(d)** (edificio alto) apartment block (AmE), tower block (BrE)

torreja *f* **1** (AmL) (pan frito) ⇒ TORRIJA **2** (Chi) (rodaja) slice

torrencial *adj* torrential

torrente *m* (Geog) torrent

torrentoso -sa *adj* (AmL) fast-flowing

torreón *m* tower

torrija *f* piece *o* slice of French toast; **~s** French toast

torsión *f* torsion

torso *m* (Anat) ▶ **123** torso, trunk; (Art) bust

torta *f* **1** (CS, Ven) (de cumpleaños, etc) cake; (decorada, con crema, etc) gateau **2** (Méx) (bocadillo) sandwich **3** (fam) (golpe): **darle una ~ a algn** to hit *o* wallop sb (colloq); **pegarse una ~** to bang one's head (*o* arm *etc*); **liarse a ~s** to come to blows

tortazo *m* (fam) ⇒ TORTA 3

tortícolis *f* stiff neck, torticollis (tech)

tortilla *f* **1** (de huevos) omelet*; ~ **de papas** *or* (Esp) **de patatas** Spanish omelet* (*made with potatoes and sometimes onion*) **2** (de maíz) tortilla

tortillero -ra *m,f* tortilla seller

tórtola *f* turtledove

tortuga *f* (Zool) (de tierra) tortoise, turtle (AmE); (de mar) turtle

tortuoso -sa *adj* **(a)** ‹*sendero*› tortuous, winding **(b)** ‹*maquinaciones/conducta*› devious; ‹*mente*› devious, twisted

tortura *f* torture

torturar [A1] *vt* (con violencia física) to torture; (angustiar) to torment, torture

tos *f* cough; **tener ~** to have a cough; ~ **convulsa** *or* **convulsiva** whooping cough

tosco -ca *adj* **(a)** ‹*utensilio/mueble/construcción*› crude, basic; ‹*tela*› coarse, rough **(b)** ‹*persona/manos*› rough; ‹*lenguaje*› unrefined; ‹*modales*› coarse; ‹*facciones*› coarse

toser [E1] *vi* to cough

tostada *f* **(a)** (de pan) piece *o* slice of toast; **desayuno café con ~s** I have coffee and toast for breakfast **(b)** (Méx) (de tortilla) tostada (*fried maize tortilla*)

tostado -da *adj* ‹*pan/almendras*› toasted; ‹*café*› roasted; ‹*piel*› tanned

tostadora *f*, **tostador** *m* (para pan) toaster; (para café) roaster

tostar [A10] *vt* **(a)** ‹*pan/almendras*› to toast; ‹*café*› to roast **(b)** ‹*piel/persona*› to tan

■ **tostarse** *v pron* (broncearse) to tan

tostón *m* **1 (a)** (Esp) (pan frito) crouton **(b)** (Ven) (plátano frito) fried plantain **2** (Esp fam) (cosa fastidiosa) drag (colloq); ***darle el ~ a algn*** (Esp fam) to pester somebody **3** (Méx fam) (moneda) fifty-cent coin

total *adj* **(a)** (absoluto) ‹*desastre/destrucción*› total; ‹*éxito*› resounding (*before n*), total; ‹*cambio*› complete **(b)** (global) ‹*costo/importe*› total ■ *m* total; **en ~** altogether ■ *adv* (*indep*) (fam) (al resumir una narración) so, in the end; **~, que me di por vencida** so in the end I gave up

totalidad *f*: **la ~ de la población** the whole *o* entire population; **fue destruido en su ~** it was totally destroyed; **se pagó en su ~** it was paid in full

totalitario -ria *adj* totalitarian

totalitarismo *m* totalitarianism

totogol *m* (Col) sports lottery (AmE), football pools (*pl*) (BrE)

totopo *m* (Méx) tortilla chip

totora *f* reed mace, bulrush

tóxico¹ -ca *adj* toxic

tóxico² *m* poison, toxin

toxicómano -na *m,f* drug addict

tozudo -da *adj* obstinate, stubborn ■ *m,f*: **es un ~** he's extremely stubborn *o* obstinate

traba *f* **1** (en ventana) catch; (de cinturón) belt loop **2** (dificultad, impedimento) obstacle; **me puso muchas ~s** he made things really difficult for me

trabajado -da *adj* ‹*diseño/bordado/plan*› elaborate

trabajador -dora *adj* (que trabaja mucho) hardworking ■ *m,f* worker; **un ~ no calificado** (AmL) *or* (Esp) **cualificado** an unskilled worker *o* laborer; **~ autónomo** self-employed worker *o* person; **~ de medio tiempo** (AmL) *or* (Esp) **a tiempo parcial** part-time worker; **~dora social** (Méx) social worker

trabajar [A1] *vi* **1** (en general) to work; **~ por cuenta propia** to be self-employed; **~ jornada completa** *or* **a tiempo completo** to work full-time; **~ media jornada** to work part-time; **~ mucho** to work hard; **¿en qué trabajas?** what do you do (for a living)?; **estoy trabajando en una novela** I'm working on a novel **~ DE** *or* **COMO algo** to work **2** (actuar) to act, perform; **¿quién trabaja en la película** who's in the movie? ■ **~** *vt* **1 (a)** ‹*campo/tierra/madera*› to work **(b)** ‹*masa*› (con las manos) to knead, work; AS sth **2** (perfeccionar, pulir) to work on

trabajo *m* **1 (a)** (empleo) job; **buscar ~** to look for work *o* for a job; **quedarse sin ~** to lose one's job; **un ~ fijo** a steady job; **un ~ de media jornada** a part-time job; **un ~ de jornada completa** *or* **a tiempo completo** a full-time job **(b)** (lugar) work; **está en el ~** she's at work; **ir al ~** to go to work **2** (actividad, labor) work; **~ en equipo** teamwork; **el ~ de la casa** housework; **los niños dan mucho ~** children are hard work; **¡buen ~!** well done!; **~ de campo** fieldwork; **~s forzados** hard labor*; **~s manuales** handicrafts (*pl*) **3 (a)** (tarea) job; **limpiar el horno es un ~ que odio** cleaning the oven is a job I hate **(b)** (obra escrita) piece of work; (en universidad, escuela) essay **4** (esfuerzo): **con mucho ~ consiguió levantarse** with great effort she managed to get up; **me cuesta ~ creerlo** I find it hard to believe

trabajoso -sa *adj* ‹*subida*› arduous; ‹*tarea*› laborious

trabalenguas *m* (*pl* **~**) tongue twister

trabar [A1] *vt* **1 (a)** ‹*puerta/ventana*› (para que no se abra) to hold ... shut; (para que no se cierre) to hold ... back *o* open **(b)** ‹*caballo*› to hobble **2 (a)** ‹*conversación/amistad/relación*› to strike up **(b)** ‹*historia*› to weave together **3** ‹*proceso/negociaciones*› to hamper the progress of

■ **trabarse** *v pron* «*cajón/cierre*» to get jammed *o* stuck; **se le traba la lengua** he gets tongue-tied

trabilla *f* (de pantalón) stirrup; (para cinturón) belt loop

trácala *m* (Méx, Ven fam) cheat ■ *f* (Méx, Ven fam) trick, swindle; **se la pasa haciendo ~** he's always cheating people

tracalada *f* (Andes fam) bunch (colloq)

tracalear [A1] *vt* (Méx, Ven fam) to cheat, swindle

tracalero -ra *adj* (Méx, Ven fam) dishonest

tracción *f* (Auto, Mec) traction, drive; **un vehículo con** *or* **de ~ a cuatro ruedas** a four-wheel-drive vehicle

tractor *m* tractor

tradición *f* (costumbre) tradition

tradicional *adj* traditional

tradicionalista *adj/mf* traditionalist

traducción *f* translation; **~ del inglés al español** translation from English into Spanish

traducir [I6] *vt* ‹*texto/escritor*› to translate; **~ DE algo A algo** to translate FROM sth INTO sth

traductor -tora *m,f* translator

traer [E23] *vt* **1** (de un lugar a otro) to bring; **me trajo en la moto** he brought me on his motorbike; **¿qué te trae por aquí?** what brings you here? **2** (ocasionar, causar) ‹*problemas/dificultades*› to cause; **~ buena suerte** to bring good luck **3** «*libro/artículo*» ‹*artículo/capítulo*› to have; **este diccionario no lo trae** it's not in this dictionary **4 (a)** ‹*ropa/sombrero*› to wear **(b)** (tener consigo) to bring; **traje poco dinero** I didn't bring much money (with me)

■ **traerse** *v pron* **1** (*enf*) (a un sitio) to bring (along); **lo invité a él y se trajo a toda la familia** I invited him and he brought the whole family along **2** (fam) (tramar) to be up to (colloq); **¿qué se ~án esas dos?** what are those two up to?

traficante *mf* dealer, trafficker; **~ de drogas** drug dealer *o* trafficker; **~ de esclavos** slave trader

traficar [A2] *vi* **~ EN** *or* **CON algo** to deal IN sth

tráfico *m* **1** (de vehículos) traffic; **accidente de ~** road accident **2** (de mercancías) trade; **~ de armas** arms trade; **~ de drogas** drug dealing *o* trafficking

tragaluz *m* (en el techo) skylight; (en una puerta, ventana) fanlight

traganíqueles *m* (*pl* **~**) (AmC) slot machine

tragaperras *m or f* (*pl* **~**) (Esp fam) slot machine

tragar [A3] *vt* **1** ‹*comida/agua/medicina*› to swallow **2** (fam) (aguantar): **no lo trago** I can't stand him ■ **~** *vi* **1** (Fisiol) to swallow **2** (RPl fam) (estudiar) to cram

■ **tragarse** *v pron* **1** (*enf*) **(a)** ‹*comida*› to swallow; **~se el humo** to inhale **(b)** ‹*lágrimas*› to choke back; ‹*orgullo*› to swallow **(c)** «*máquina*» ‹*dinero/tarjeta*› to swallow up **2** (fam) **(a)** (soportar) ‹*obra/recital*› to sit through **(b)** (creerse) ‹*excusa/cuento*› to swallow, fall for (colloq)

tragedia *f* tragedy

trágico -ca *adj* **(a)** ‹*actriz/obra*› tragic (*before n*) **(b)** ‹*vida/final/consecuencia*› tragic; **no te pongas ~** don't be so melodramatic

tragicomedia *f* tragicomedy

trago *m* **1 (a)** (de líquido) drink, swig; **un ~ de agua** a drink of water; **de un ~** in one gulp **(b)**

(esp AmL fam) (bebida alcohólica) drink; **¿vamos a tomar un ~?** shall we go for a drink? **2** (experiencia): **pasar un ~ amargo** to have a rough time

traición *f* **(a)** (delito) treason **(b)** (acto desleal) treachery, betrayal; **lo mataron a ~** they killed him by treachery

traicionar [A1] *vt* **(a)** ‹*patria/amigo*› to betray **(b)** (delatar) «*mirada/nerviosismo*» to give ... away

traicionero -ra *adj* **(a)** ‹*persona/acción*› treacherous **(b)** ‹*mar/carretera*› treacherous, dangerous

traidor -dora *adj* traitorous, treacherous ■ *m,f* traitor; **~ A algo** traitor TO sth

traiga, traigas, etc *see* TRAER

trailer /'trajler/ *m* **1 (a)** (AmL) (casa rodante) trailer (AmE), caravan (BrE) **(b)** (para caballos) horsebox **2** (Méx) (camión) semitrailer (AmE), articulated lorry (BrE)

tráiler *m* **1** (Esp) (Cin) trailer **2** ⇒ TRAILER 1

trailero -ra *m,f* (Méx) truck driver

traje *m* (de dos, tres piezas) suit; (vestido de mujer) dress; (Teatr) costume; (de país, región) dress; **~ de baño** (de hombre) swimming trunks (*pl*); (de mujer) bathing suit, swimsuit; **~ de etiqueta/gala** formal/evening dress; **~ largo** evening dress

traje, etc *see* TRAER

trajera, trajese, etc *see* TRAER

trajimos, trajiste, etc *see* TRAER

trajín *m*: **un día de mucho ~** a very hectic day; **con todo este ~** ... with all this coming and going...; **el ~ de las grandes ciudades** the hustle and bustle of big cities

trajinar [A1] *vi* (fam) to rush about (colloq)

trajiste, etc *see* TRAER

trama *f* **1** (de tejido) weave, weft **2** (de película, novela) plot

tramar [A1] *vt* ‹*engaño*› to devise; ‹*venganza*› to plot; ‹*complot*› to hatch, lay; **¿qué andan tramando?** what are you up to? (colloq)

tramitación *f* processing; **la ~ del divorcio tardó años** the divorce proceedings took years

tramitar [A1] *vt* ‹*préstamo*› «*funcionario*» to deal with; «*interesado*» to arrange; **están tramitando el divorcio** «*cónyuges*» they have started divorce proceedings; **~ un permiso de trabajo** «*organismo*» to deal with a work permit application; «*interesado*» to apply for one's work permit

trámite *m* (proceso) procedure; (etapa) step, stage; **simplificar los ~s aduaneros** to simplify customs procedures; **el préstamo está en ~** the loan application is being processed; **tengo que hacer unos ~s en el centro** I have some business to attend to in the centre

tramo *m* (de carretera, vía) stretch; (de escalera) flight

trampa *f* **(a)** (para animales) trap; (de lazo) snare **(b)** (ardid) trap; **le tendieron una ~** they laid *o* set a trap for him **(c)** (en el juego): **hacer ~(s)** to cheat; **eso es ~** that's cheating

trampilla *f* trapdoor

trampolín *m* (en natación — flexible) springboard; (— rígido) diving board; (en gimnasia) trampoline; (en esquí) ski jump

tramposo -sa *adj*: **ser ~** to be a cheat ■ *m,f* cheat

tranca *f* **1 (a)** (de puerta, ventana) bar **(b)** (palo) cudgel, club **2** (esp AmL fam) (borrachera) bender (colloq); **agarrarse una ~** to get plastered *o* smashed (colloq) **3** (Ven fam) (Auto) holdup, tailback

trancar [A1] *vt* ‹*puerta/ventana*› to bar

trance *m* (Psic, Relig) trance; **estar en ~** to be in a trance

tranque *m* (CS) reservoir

tranquilidad *f* **(a)** (calma) peace; **ni un minuto de ~** not a moment's peace; **con ~** (sin prisas) at my (*o* your *etc*) leisure; (sin nerviosismo) calmly **(b)** (falta de preocupación): **llámame a la hora que sea, con toda ~** feel free to call me at any time; **lo hice para mi propia ~** I did it for my own peace of mind

tranquilizante *adj* **(a)** ‹*noticia*› reassuring; ‹*música*› soothing **(b)** (Med) tranquilizing* ■ *m* tranquilizer*

tranquilizar [A4] *vt* **(a)** (apaciguar) to calm ... down; **intenté ~lo** I tried to calm him down; **sus palabras la ~on** his words reassured her **(b)** (atenuar la preocupación): **eso me tranquiliza mucho** that makes me feel a lot better

■ **tranquilizarse** *v pron* (calmarse) to calm down; (dejar de preocuparse): **al oir su voz me tranquilicé** when I heard his voice I felt reassured

tranquilo[1] -la *adj* **1 (a)** [SER] ‹*persona*› (pacífico) calm **(b)** ‹*mar/ambiente*› calm; ‹*lugar*› quiet, peaceful, tranquil **2** [ESTAR] **(a)** (libre de preocupacion) ‹*conciencia*› clear; ‹*persona*›: **ahora que trabaja estoy más ~** I feel better now that he's found a job; **¡tranquilo!** relax!; **tú, ~, de eso me encargo yo** there's no need for you to worry, I'll take care of that; **lo hice para quedarme ~** I did it for my own peace of mind; **déjalo ~** leave him alone **(b)** (sin inmutarse): **su hermano en el hospital y él tan ~** his brother's in hospital and he doesn't seem at all bothered; **...y se quedó tan tranquila** ...and she didn't bat an eyelash (AmE) *o* (BrE) eyelid

tranquilo[2] *adv* (Méx fam): **te cuesta ~ unas 2,000 libras** it costs 2,000 pounds easily (colloq)

tranquiza *f* (Méx fam) hiding (colloq)

transa *adj/mf* (Méx fam) ⇒ TRANZA

transacción *f* (Com, Fin) transaction, deal

transandino[1] -na *adj* trans-Andean

transandino[2] *m* trans-Andean railroad *o* railway

transar [A1] *vi* (AmL) **(a)** (hacer concesiones) ⇒ TRANSIGIR (a) **(b)** (llegar a un acuerdo) to reach an agreement *o* a compromise; **~ EN algo** to settle FOR sth

transatlántico[1] -ca *adj* transatlantic

transatlántico[2] *m* ocean liner

transbordador *m* ferry

transbordar [A1] *vt* ‹*mercancías/equipajes*› to transfer ■ **~** *vi* «*pasajeros*» to change

transbordo *m* **(a)** (de viajeros) change; **hacer ~** to change **(b)** (de equipaje, mercancías) transfer

transcribir [I34] *vt* to transcribe

transcurrir [I1] *vi* **(a)** «*tiempo/años*» to pass, go by **(b)** «*acontecimiento/acto*» to take place

transcurso *m* course; **en el ~ del año** during the course of the year; **con el ~ del tiempo** as time goes/went by

transeúnte *mf* (peatón) passer-by; (no residente) non-resident

transexual *adj/mf* transsexual

transferencia *f* transfer; **~ bancaria** credit *o* bank transfer

transferir [I11] *vt* to transfer

transformación *f* **(a)** (cambio) transformation, change **(b)** (en rugby) conversion **(c)** (Ling) transformation

transformador *m* transformer

transformar [A1] *vt* **(a)** (convertir) to convert; **~ algo EN algo** to convert sth INTO sth **(b)** (cambiar radicalmente) ‹*persona/situación/país*› to transform, change *o* alter ... radically **(c)** (en rugby) to convert ■ **transformarse** *v pron* **(a)** (convertirse) **~se EN algo** to turn into sth **(b)** (cambiar radicalmente) «*persona/país*» to change completely, be transformed

transfusión *f* transfusion; **le hicieron una ~ de sangre** they gave him a blood transfusion

transición *f* transition; **~ DE algo A algo** transition FROM sth TO sth

transigente *adj* accommodating

transigir [I7] *vi* **(a)** (hacer concesiones) to compromise, give way; **~ EN algo** to compromise ON sth **(b)** (tolerar) **~ CON algo** to tolerate sth, put up WITH sth

transistor *m* transistor

transitar [A1] *vi* «*vehículo*» to travel; «*peatón*» to walk

transitivo -va *adj* transitive

tránsito *m* **1** (tráfico) traffic; **~ rodado** vehicular traffic; **una calle de mucho ~** a very busy road; **un accidente de ~** (AmL) a road accident; **infracción de ~** (AmL) traffic violation (AmE), motoring offense (BrE) **2** (paso) movement; **el ~ de turistas en los meses de verano** the movement of tourists during the summer months; **pasajeros en ~** passengers in transit

transitorio -ria *adj* **(a)** ‹*medida*› provisional; ‹*situación*› temporary; ‹*período*› transitional **(b)** (efímero) transitory, fleeting

transmisión *f* **(a)** (acción) transmission **(b)** (Rad, TV) (señal) transmission; (programa) broadcast; **una ~ en directo/en diferido** a live/prerecorded broadcast; **~ de pensamiento** thought transference

transmisor *m* transmitter

transmitir [I1] *vt* **1** (Rad, TV) ‹*señal*› to transmit; ‹*programa*› to broadcast **2 (a)** ‹*sonido/movimiento*› to transmit **(b)** ‹*enfermedad/lengua/costumbres*› to transmit, pass on; ‹*conocimientos*› to pass on **(c)** ‹*saludos/felicidades*› to pass on ■ **~** *vi* (Rad, TV) to transmit

transparentarse [A1] *v pron* **(a)** «*blusa/falda*»: **una blusa que se transparenta** a see-through blouse; **con ese vestido se le transparenta el viso** her petticoat shows through that dress **(b)** «*intenciones*» to be evident, be apparent

transparente *adj* **(a)** ‹*cristal/agua*› transparent, clear; ‹*aire*› clear **(b)** ‹*tela/papel*› transparent; ‹*blusa*› see-through **(c)** ‹*persona/carácter*› transparent; ‹*intenciones*› clear, plain

transpirar [A1] *vi* (Fisiol) to perspire, sweat; (Bot) to transpire

transportador *m* (Mec) conveyor

transportar [A1] *vt* **(a)** ‹*personas/mercancías*› to transport; **~ algo por aire** to ship sth by air **(b)** ‹*energía/sonido*› to transmit

transporte *m* **1** (de pasajeros, mercancías) transportation (esp AmE), transport (esp BrE); **~ aéreo** airfreight; **~ público** public transportation (AmE), public transport (BrE) **2** (medio, vehículo) means of transport **3** (gastos de viaje) traveling expenses

transportista *mf* haulage contractor

transversal *adj* ‹*eje/línea*› transverse; **una calle ~ al Paseo de Recoletos** a street which crosses the Paseo de Recoletos; **un corte ~** a cross section ■ *f* (Mat) transversal

tranvía *m* **(a)** (vehículo urbano) streetcar (AmE), tram (BrE) **(b)** (Esp) (Ferr) local train

tranza *adj* (Méx fam) crooked ■ *mf* (Méx fam) (persona) con artist (colloq), shark (colloq) ■ *f* (Méx fam) (engaño, fraude) scam (colloq)

tranzar [A4] *vt* (Méx fam) ‹*persona*› to con (colloq)

trapear [A1] *vt* (AmL) to mop

trapecio *m* **(a)** (Mat) trapezoid (AmE), trapezium (BrE) **(b)** (Espec) trapeze

trapecista *mf* trapeze artist

trapero -ra *m,f* **1** (ropavejero) junkman (AmE), rag and bone man (BrE) **2 trapero** *m* (AmL) (para el suelo) floorcloth

trapo *m* (para limpiar) cloth; **pásale un ~ a la mesa** wipe the table; **~ de cocina** dishtowel (AmE), tea towel (BrE); **~ de sacudir** dust cloth (AmE), duster (BrE)

tráquea *f* windpipe, trachea

traquetear [A1] *vi* «*tren/carreta*» (hacer ruido) to clatter; (moverse) to jolt

traqueteo *m* (de tren, carreta — movimiento) jolting; (— ruido) clatter, clattering

tras *prep* **1 (a)** (frml) (después de) after; **~ interrogarlo lo pusieron en libertad** after questioning him they released him **(b)** (indicando repetición) after; **día ~ día** day after day **2 (a)** (detrás de) behind; **la puerta se cerró ~ él** the door closed behind him; **la policía anda ~ él** the police are after him **(b)** (más allá de) beyond

trascendental *adj* **(a)** (importante) ‹*noticia/ocasión*› momentous; (de gran alcance) ‹*decisión/cambio/efecto*› far-reaching **(b)** (Fil) transcendental

trascendente *adj* **(a)** (importante) ‹*hecho/suceso*› significant, important **(b)** (Fil) transcendent

trascender [E8] *vi* (ir más allá) ~ DE **algo** to transcend sth (frml), to go beyond sth ■ ~ *vt* to go beyond, transcend (frml)

trasero[1] -ra *adj* ‹*puerta/habitación/asiento*› back (*before n*); ‹*rueda/pata/asiento*› rear (*before n*), back (*before n*); ‹*motor*› rear-mounted

trasero[2] *m* (fam) (de persona) bottom, backside (colloq); (de animal) hindquarters (*pl*)

trasladar [A1] *vt* **1** (cambiar de sitio) ‹*objeto/oficina/tienda*› to move; ‹*preso/enfermo*› to move, transfer; ‹*información*› to transfer; **los heridos fueron trasladados al hospital** the injured were taken to hospital **2** (cambiar de destino) ‹*empleado/funcionario*› to transfer

■ **trasladarse** *v pron* (mudarse) to move

traslado *m* (de prisioneros transferal; (de oficina) removal; (de empleados) transfer; (de objeto): **el ~ del cuadro se llevó a cabo ayer** the picture was moved yesterday; **gastos de ~** relocation expenses

traslúcido -da *adj* translucent

trasluz *m*: **al ~** against the light

trasmano: **a trasmano** (*loc adv*) out of the way; **vive muy a ~** she lives in a very out-of-the-way place

trasnochar [A1] *vi* (no acostarse) to be up all night; (acostarse de madrugada) to stay up late

■ **trasnocharse** *v pron* (Col, Per, Ven) ⇒ TRASNOCHAR

traspasar [A1] *vt* **1 (a)** «*bala/espada*» to pierce, go through; «*líquido*» to go through, soak through **(b)** (sobrepasar) to go beyond **2** ‹*bar/farmacia*› (vender) to sell; (arrendar) to let, lease **3** ‹*poderes/fondos/negocio*› to transfer **4** (Dep) ‹*jugador*› to transfer, trade (AmE)

traspaso *m* **1 (a)** (de bar, farmacia — venta) sale; (— arrendamiento) leasing, letting **(b)** (suma) premium **2** (de poderes, fondos, negocio) transfer **3** (Dep) **(a)** (de jugador) transfer, trade (AmE) **(b)** (suma) transfer fee

traspié *m* (tropezón) stumble; **dar un ~** to stumble

trasplantar [A1] *vt* (Bot, Med) to transplant

trasplante *m* (Bot, Med) transplant

trasquilar [A1] *vt* **(a)** ‹*ovejas*› to shear, clip **(b)** (fam) ‹*pelo*› to hack … about (colloq); ‹*persona*› to scalp (colloq)

trastada *f* **(a)** (fam) (mala pasada) dirty trick; **hacerle una ~ a algn** to play a dirty trick on sb **(b)** (travesura) prank

traste *m* **1** (Mús) fret **2** (fam) (trasero) backside (colloq) **3** (AmC, Méx) (utensilio) utensil; **lavar los ~s** to do the dishes *o* (BrE) the washing-up

trastero *m* junk room, lumber room (AmE)

trastienda *f* back room (*of a shop*)

trasto *m* (fam) (cosa inservible) piece of junk (colloq); **el cuarto de los ~s** the junk room

trastornado -da *adj* ‹*persona/mente*› disturbed; **su muerte lo dejó ~** she was deeply disturbed *o* traumatized by his death

trastornar [A1] *vt* **1** (Psic) to disturb; **la muerte de su hijo la trastornó** her son's death left her deeply disturbed; **esa chica lo ha trastornado** (fam) he's lost his head over that girl (colloq) **2** (alterar la normalidad) to upset, disrupt

■ **trastornarse** *v pron* (Psic) to become disturbed

trastorno *m* **1** (Med, Psic) disorder **2** (alteración de la normalidad) disruption; **los ~s provocados por la huelga** the disruption caused by the strike; **me ocasionó muchos ~s** it caused me a great deal of inconvenience

trastrocar [A9] *vt* to alter, change; **~ algo** EN **algo** to transform *o* change sth INTO sth

trasvasar [A1] *vt* **(a)** ‹*vino/aceite*› to decant **(b)** (Inf) to download

tratado *m* **1** (Der, Pol) treaty; **~ de paz** peace treaty **2** (libro) treatise

tratamiento *m* **1 (a)** (en general) treatment; **estoy en ~ médico** I am undergoing medical treatment; **no me quejo del ~ que recibí** I can't complain about the treatment I received **(b)** (Inf) (de información, datos) processing; **~ de textos** word processing **2** (título de cortesía) form of address

tratar [A1] *vi* **1** (intentar) to try; **traten de llegar temprano** try to arrive early; **~é de que no vuelva a suceder** I'll try to make sure it doesn't happen again **2** «*obra/libro/película*» ~ DE **algo** to be ABOUT sth; ~ SOBRE **algo** to deal WITH sth; **la conferencia ~á sobre medicina alternativa** the lecture will deal with alternative medicine **3** (tener contacto, relaciones) ~ CON **algn** to deal WITH sb; **en mi trabajo trato con gente de todo tipo** in my job I deal with all kinds of people ■ ~ *vt* **1** ‹*persona/animal/instrumento*› to treat; **me tratan muy bien** they treat me very well **2** (frecuentar): **lo trataba cuando era joven** I saw quite a lot of him when I was young **3** ‹*tema/asunto*› to discuss, to deal with **4 (a)** (Med) to treat **(b)** ‹*sustancia/metal*› to treat

■ **tratarse** *v pron* **1 ~se** CON **algn** (ser amigo de) to be friendly WITH sb; (alternar) to socialize *o* mix WITH sb; **no nos tratamos mucho** (*recip*) we don't have much to do with each other **2** (+ *compl*) (*recipr*): **se tratan sin ningún respeto** they show no respect for each other **3** (Med) to have *o* undergo treatment **4 tratarse de** (*en 3ª pers*) **(a)** (ser acerca de) to be about; **¿de qué se trata?** what's it about? **(b)** (ser cuestión de) to be a question of; **se trata de participar, no de ganar** it's a question of taking part, not of winning; **sólo porque se trata de ti** just because it's you

trato *m* **1 (a)** (acuerdo) deal; **cerrar un ~** to finalize a deal; **¡~ hecho!** it's a deal! **(b) tratos** *mpl* (negociaciones): **estamos en ~s con otra compañía** we are talking to *o* negotiating with another company **2 (a)** (relación): **no tiene ~ con los vecinos** he doesn't have much to do with his neighbors; **tengo poco ~ con ella** I don't really have much contact with her *o* much to do with her **(b)** (manera de tratar) treatment; **le dan un ~ preferencial** they give him preferential treatment

trauma *m* trauma

traumatizado -da *adj* traumatized

traumatizar [A4] *vt* to traumatize

■ **traumatizarse** *v pron* (fam) to be traumatized

Tratamientos

Mr, Mrs, Miss, Ms

Estas formas se utilizan para dirigirse o referirse a un hombre (Mr), *una mujer casada* (Mrs), *una mujer soltera* (Miss) *y una mujer sin distinción de estado civil* (Ms).

Se emplean siempre con el apellido:

Mr Boyce

Ms King

Nótese que aunque estas formas son abreviaturas, ya no se suelen escribir con punto

Al referirse a una persona, se puede incluir también el nombre de pila:

the prizes were presented by Mr Michael Stein = el señor Michael Stein hizo entrega de los premios

Sir, Madam, Miss, Ms

Estas formas se utilizan sin mencionar el apellido, pero su uso es más limitado que el de 'señor', 'señora' *y* 'señorita' *en español. Se suelen emplear para dirigirse a un cliente en una tienda, restaurante, etc. y son más frecuentes en los Estados Unidos que en Gran Bretaña*:

Can I help you, sir?

Esq

'Esq.' *es la abreviatura de* 'esquire'. *Se usa en Gran Bretaña en correspondencia comercial u oficial dirigida a un hombre. Sustituye a* 'Mr' *y se coloca detrás del apellido*:

Roy Russell Esq.

En los Estados Unidos 'Esq.' *sólo se utiliza en cartas dirigidas a abogados*

través (a) a través de (*loc prep*) (de lado a lado) across; (por medio de) through; **pusieron barricadas a ~ de la calle** they erected barricades across the street; **se enteró a ~ de un amigo** she heard about it through a friend **(b) al** *or* (Méx) **de través** (*loc adv*) diagonally

travesaño *m* **(a)** (Const) crossbeam **(b)** (Dep) crossbar

travesía *f* **1** (viaje) crossing **2** (Esp) (callejuela) alleyway, side street

travesti, **travestí** *m* transvestite

travesura *f* prank; **hacer ~s** to play pranks

travieso -sa *adj* naughty, mischievous

trayecto *m* **(a)** (viaje) journey; **charlamos todo el ~** we chatted the whole journey **(b)** (ruta) route; **¿qué ~ hace este autobús?** which route does this bus take? **(c)** (trayectoria) trajectory, path

trayectoria *f* **(a)** (de proyectil, pelota) trajectory, path **(b)** (de persona, institución): **una brillante ~ profesional** a brilliant career; **una larga ~ democrática** a long democratic tradition

trayendo *see* TRAER

trazar [A4] *vt* **1 (a)** ‹*línea*› to trace, draw; ‹*plano*› to draw; **~on la ruta a seguir** they traced out the route to be followed; **~ el contorno de algo** to outline sth **(b)** (Arquit) ‹*puente/edificio*› to design **2** ‹*plan/proyecto/estrategia*› to draw up, devise

trazo *m* stroke

trébol *m* **1** (Bot) clover **2** (Jueg) **(a)** (carta) club **(b) tréboles** *mpl* (palo) clubs (*pl*)

trece ▶ **293** *adj inv/m/pron* thirteen; *para ejemplos ver* CINCO; ***mantenerse*** *or* ***seguir en sus ~*** to stand one's ground

trecho *m* **(a)** (tramo) stretch **(b)** (distancia) distance; **aún nos queda un buen ~** we still have a good distance *o* a fair way to go

tregua *f* **(a)** (Mil) truce; **acordar una ~** to agree to a truce **(b)** (interrupción): **sin ~** relentlessly

treinta ▶ **293** *adj inv/m/pron* thirty; *para ejemplos ver* CINCO, CINCUENTA

tremendo -da *adj* **1 (a)** (muy grande, extraordinario) ‹*diferencia/cambio*› tremendous, enormous; ‹*velocidad/éxito*› tremendous; ‹*chichón*› huge; **hace un frío ~** it's incredibly cold! (colloq); **me dio (una) tremenda patada** he kicked me really hard **(b)** (terrible) ‹*ruido/dolor/situación*› terrible; **la película tiene unas escenas tremendas** (AmL) the film has some horrific scenes **2** (fam) ‹*persona*› terrible

tren *m* **1** (Ferr) train; **tomar** *or* (esp Esp) **coger el ~** to take *o* catch the train; **ir en ~** to go by train; **cambiar de ~** to change trains; **~ correo** *or* **postal** mail train; **~ de cercanías** local *o* suburban train; **~ directo** through train; **~ expreso** *or* **rápido** express train **2** (fam) (ritmo) rate; **a este ~** at this rate (colloq); **~ de vida** lifestyle

trenazo *m* (Méx) train crash

trenca *f* (Esp) duffle *o* duffel coat

trenza *f* (de cintas, fibras) plait; (de pelo) braid (AmE), plait (BrE)

trepador -dora *m,f* **1** (Col, CS, Ven) social climber **2 trepadora** *f* (Bot) climber

trepar [A1] *vi* to climb; **~ a un árbol** to climb (up) a tree

tres ▶ **293** *adj inv/m/pron* three; **~ en raya** tic-tac-toe (AmE), noughts and crosses (BrE); *para ejemplos ver* CINCO

trescientos -tas ▶ **293** *adj/pron* three hundred; *para ejemplos ver* QUINIENTOS

tresillo *m* (Esp) (sofá) three-seater sofa; (juego de muebles) suite

treta *f* **(a)** (ardid) trick, ruse **(b)** (en esgrima) feint

trial /'trial/ *m* motocross

triangular *adj* triangular

triángulo *m* **1** (Mat) triangle; **~ rectángulo** right-angled triangle **2 (a)** (en relaciones amorosas) (love) triangle **(b)** (Mús) triangle **(c)** (Auto) *tb* **~ reflectante** advance-warning triangle

tribu *f* tribe

tribuna *f* **(a)** (para orador) platform, rostrum **(b)** (para autoridades) platform; (para espectadores) grandstand, stand; **la ~ de la prensa** the press box **(c)** (de iglesia) gallery

tribunal *m* **1** (Der) **(a)** (lugar) court; (jueces) judges (*pl*) **(b) tribunales** *mpl* (justicia): **acudir a los ~es** to go to court; **~ militar** court martial, military court; **~ supremo** ≈ supreme court (*in US*), ≈ high court (*in UK*); **~ (tutelar) de menores** juvenile court **2** (en examen) examining board; (en concurso) panel of judges

tributar [A1] *vt* **(a)** (Fisco) to pay **(b)** (rendir, ofrecer): **~ un homenaje a algn** to pay tribute to sb

tributo *m* **(a)** (Fisco) tax **(b)** (ofrenda, homenaje) tribute; **rendirle ~ a algn/algo** to pay tribute to sb/sth

triciclo *m* tricycle

tricotar [A1] *vt* (Esp) to knit

tridimensional *adj* three-dimensional

trifulca *f* (fam) rumpus, commotion

trigal *m* wheat field

trigo *m* wheat

trigueño -ña *adj* ‹*pelo*› light brown; ‹*persona*› dark; **una niña de tez trigueña** an olive-skinned girl

trillar [A1] *vt* to thresh

trillizo -za *m,f* triplet

trilogía *f* trilogy

trimestral *adj* ‹*publicación/pago*› quarterly; **examen ~** end-of-semester examination (AmE), end-of-term examination (BrE)

trimestre *m* **(a)** quarter, three-month period; **pago por ~s** I pay quarterly **(b)** (Educ) term, ≈ semester (*in US*)

trinar [A1] *vi* «*pájaro*» to sing

trinchar [A1] *vt* to carve

trinchera *f* **(a)** (Mil) trench **(b)** (Indum) trench coat

trineo *m* **(a)** (Dep, Jueg) sled (AmE), sledge (BrE) **(b)** (tirado por perros, caballos) sleigh

trinidad *f* trinity; **La T~** (Relig) the Trinity

trino *m* trill

trío *m* trio

tripa *f* **1 (a)** *tb* **tripas** *fpl* (intestino) intestine, gut; (vísceras) (fam) innards (*pl*) (colloq); **se me revuelven las ~s de sólo verlo** just looking at it turns my stomach **(b)** (material) gut **2** (Esp fam) (barriga) belly (colloq)

triple *adj* triple ■ *m* **1** (Mat): **el precio aumentó al ~** the price tripled *o* trebled; **tardó el ~** it took him three times as long; **el ~ de tres es nueve** three times three equals nine **2** (Elec) three-way adapter *o* adaptor

triplicado: **por triplicado** (*loc adv*) in triplicate

triplicar [A2] *vt* ‹*capacidad/precio/ventas*› to treble; ‹*longitud/cifra*› to triple

■ **triplicarse** *v pron* to treble, triple

trípode *m* tripod

tripulación *f* crew

tripulante *mf* crew member; **los ~s** the crew

tripular [A1] *vt* to crew, man

triquiñuela *f* (fam) trick, dodge (colloq)

trisílabo -ba *adj* trisyllabic

triste *adj* **1 (a)** [ESTAR] ‹*persona*› sad; **esa música me pone ~** that music makes me sad **(b)** ‹*expresión/mirada*› sad, sorrowful **(c)** [SER] (que causa tristeza) ‹*historia/película/noticia*› sad; ‹*paisaje/color*› dismal, gloomy; ‹*lugar/ambiente*› gloomy **2** (*delante del n*) (miserable, insignificante) miserable; **por cuatro ~s pesetas** for a few miserable pesetas; **es la ~ realidad** it's the sad truth

tristeza *f* (de mirada, persona) sadness, sorrow; (de lugar, ambiente) gloominess

triturador *m*: **~ de basura** garbage disposal unit (AmE), waste disposal unit (BrE); **~ de ajos** garlic press

trituradora *f* crushing machine, crusher

triturar [A1] *vt* ‹*almendras/ajo*› to crush; ‹*minerales*› to grind, crush

triunfador -dora *adj* ‹*ejército*› triumphant; ‹*equipo*› winning (*before n*), triumphant ■ *m,f* winner

triunfal *adj* ‹*marcha/arco*› triumphal; ‹*gesto/sonrisa/entrada*› triumphant

triunfalismo *m* triumphalism

triunfar [A1] *vi* **(a)** (ganar) **~ SOBRE algo/algn** to triumph OVER sth/sb; **triunfó en el concurso** she won the competition **(b)** (tener éxito) to succeed, be successful **(c)** «*justicia/verdad/razón*» (prevalecer) to prevail, win out (AmE) *o* (BrE) through

triunfo *m* **1 (a)** (victoria) victory; **el ~ del equipo irlandés** the Irish team's victory **(b)** (logro) triumph; **uno de dos ~s de la ciencia** one of the triumphs of science **(c)** (éxito) success **2** (en naipes) trump; **palo del ~** trumps (*pl*)

trivial *adj* trivial

trivialidad *f* **(a)** (cualidad) triviality **(b)** (dicho) trivial *o* trite remark; (cosa) triviality

trivializar [A4] *vt* ‹*asunto*› to trivialize; ‹*éxito*› to play down

trizarse [A4] *v pron* (Chi) (rajarse) «*anteojos/vaso*» to crack; «*diente*» to chip

trizas *fpl*: **hacer ~ algo** ‹*tela/carta*› to tear sth to shreds; **el jarrón se cayó y se hizo ~** the vase fell and smashed (to bits *o* smithereens); **tengo los nervios hechos ~** my nerves are in shreds *o* tatters

trofeo *m* (premio) trophy

troglodita *mf* **(a)** (cavernícola) troglodyte **(b)** (fam) (bruto) lout

trolebús *m* trolleybus

tromba *f* (terrestre) whirlwind, tornado; (marina) waterspout; **~ de agua** downpour

trombón *m* **1** (instrumento) trombone **2 trombón** *mf* (músico) trombonist

trombonista *mf* trombonist

trombosis *f* thrombosis

trompa *f* **1** (de elefante) trunk; (de insecto) proboscis **2** (boca) (AmL fam) lips (*pl*), mouth **3** (instrumento) horn **4 trompa** *mf* (músico) horn-player

trompada *f* (AmS fam) (puñetazo) punch; **darle** *or* **pegarle una ~ a algn** to punch sb

trompazo *m* (fam): **me di un ~ con la puerta** I walked (*o* ran *etc*) smack into the door (colloq)

trompear [A1] *vt* (AmL fam) to thump (colloq), to punch

trompeta *f* **1** (instrumento) trumpet **2 trompeta** *mf* (persona) trumpet player; (Mil) trumpeter

trompetista *mf* trumpet player

trompicón *m*: **iba dando trompicones** he was staggering; **a trompicones** in fits and starts

trompo *m* **(a)** (Jueg) (spinning) top **(b)** (Auto) spin

trona *f* (Esp) high chair

tronar [A10] *v impers* ▶ **409** to thunder ■ ~ *vi* **1** «*cañones/voz*» to thunder **2** (Méx fam) **(a)** (en relación) to split up (colloq) **(b)** (fracasar) to flop (colloq); (en examen) to fail ■ ~ *vt* **1** (AmC, Méx fam) (fusilar) to shoot **2** (Méx fam) ‹*examen/alumno*› to fail, flunk (AmE colloq)

tronchar [A1] *vt* ‹*tallo/rama*› to snap
■ **troncharse** *v pron* «*tallo/rama*» to break *o* snap off; ***~se de (la) risa*** (Esp fam) to die laughing (colloq)

tronco *m* **1** (Bot) trunk; (leño) log **2** (en genealogía) stock **3** (Anat) ▶ **123** trunk, torso

tronera *f* (en billar) pocket

trono *m* throne; **subir al ~** to come to the throne

tropa *f* **(a)** (soldados rasos): **la ~** the troops (*pl*) **(b) tropas** *fpl* (ejército, soldados) troops

tropel *m* (de personas) mob; **entraron al estadio en ~** they poured into the stadium

tropezar [A6] *vi* **(a)** (al caminar, correr) to stumble, trip; **~ CON algo** ‹*con piedra/escalón*› to trip OVER sth; ‹*con árbol/muro*› to walk (*o* run *etc*) INTO sth **(b)** (encontrarse) **~ CON algo** ‹*con dificultad/problema*› to come up AGAINST sth; **~ CON algn** to run *o* bump INTO sb (colloq)
■ **tropezarse** *v pron* (encontrarse) **~se CON algn** to run *o* bump INTO sb (colloq)

tropezón *m* **(a)** (acción de tropezar) stumble; **dio un ~ y cayó** he stumbled and fell; **a tropezones** (fam) in fits and starts **(b)** (equivocación) mistake, slip

tropical *adj* tropical

trópico *m* tropic

tropiece, tropieces, etc *see* TROPEZAR

tropieza, tropiezas, etc *see* TROPEZAR

tropiezo *m* (contratiempo) setback, hitch; (equivocación) mistake, slip

trotar [A1] *vi* **(a)** «*caballo/jinete*» to trot **(b)** (fam) (ir de un lado a otro) to rush around **(c)** (CS, Méx) (como ejercicio) to jog

trote *m* **1** (Equ) trot; **al ~** at a trot **2** (fam) (ajetreo): **¡que ~ he tenido hoy!** it's been so hectic today (colloq); **ya no estoy para esos ~s** I'm not up to that sort of thing any more

trovador *m* troubadour, minstrel

trozar [A4] *vt* (AmL) to cut … into pieces, cut up

trozo *m* **(a)** (de pan, pastel) piece, bit, slice; (de madera, papel, tela) piece, bit; (de vidrio, cerámica) piece, fragment; **cortar la zanahoria en trocitos** dice the carrot **(b)** (Lit, Mús) passage

trucar [A2] *vt* **(a)** ‹*dados/juego/elecciones*› to fix, rig **(b)** ‹*fotografía*› to touch up

trucha *f* (Coc, Zool) trout

truco *m* trick; **el ~ está en**… the trick *o* secret is…; **pillarle el ~ a algo** to get the hang of sth

trueno *m* **(a)** (Meteo) thunderclap, clap of thunder; **~s** thunder **(b)** (de cañones) thunder

trueque *m* (cambio) barter

trufa *f* truffle

truncar [A2] *vt* **(a)** ‹*frase/discurso/texto*› to cut short **(b)** ‹*vida*› to cut short; ‹*planes*› to frustrate, thwart; ‹*ilusiones*› to shatter

tu *adj* (*delante del n*) your; **~s amigos** your friends

tú *pron pers* [*familiar form of address*] **1** (como sujeto, en comparaciones, con preposición) you; **¿quién lo va a hacer? — tú** who's going to do it? — you are; **llegó después que ~** he arrived after you (did); **entre ~ y yo** between you and me; **tratar de ~ a algn** *to address sb using the familiar* TÚ *form* **2** (uno) you; **te dan varias opciones y tú eliges una** you're given several options and you choose one

tuba *f* tuba

tubérculo *m* (Bot) tuber

tuberculosis *f* tuberculosis

tuberculoso -sa *m,f* tuberculosis sufferer (*o* patient *etc*)

tubería *f* (cañería) pipe; (conjunto de tubos) piping, pipes (*pl*)

tubo *m* **1** **(a)** (cilindro hueco) tube; **~ de escape** exhaust (pipe) **(b)** (del órgano) pipe **(c)** (Chi, Méx) (para el pelo) roller, curler **2** (RPl) (del teléfono) receiver

tuco *m* (Per, RPl) (Coc) tomato sauce

tuerca *f* nut

tuerce, tuerces, etc *see* TORCER

tuerto -ta *adj* one-eyed; **es ~** (sin un ojo) he only has one eye; (ciego de un ojo) he's blind in one eye ■ *m,f*. *person blind in one eye or with only one eye*

tuerza, tuerzas, etc *see* TORCER

tuétano *m* marrow

tufo *m* (fam) (olor — a sucio, podrido) stink (colloq); (— a cerrado): **aquí dentro hay un ~ horrible** it smells really stuffy in here

tugurio *m* (vivienda) hovel; (bar) dive

tul *m* tulle

tulipa *f* lampshade

tulipán *m* tulip

tullido -da *adj* crippled ■ *m,f* cripple

tumba *f* (excavada) grave; (construida) tomb

tumbar [A1] *vt* **(a)** (hacer caer) to knock down; **lo tumbó en el primer asalto** he knocked him down in the first round; **un olor que te tumbaba** a smell that knocked you backward(s) **(b)** (AmL) ‹*árbol*› to fell, cut down; ‹*muro/casa*› to demolish, knock down
■ **tumbarse** *v pron* to lie down

tumbo *m* **1** (vaivén): **salió del bar dando ~s** he staggered out of the bar; **la carreta iba dando**

~s **por el camino** the cart jolted along the path **2** (Bol) (fruta) passion fruit

tumbona *f* (Esp) sun lounger, deck chair

tumor *m* tumor*

tumulto *m* (multitud) crowd; (alboroto) commotion, tumult

tumultuoso -sa *adj* tumultuous

tuna *f* **1** (Bot, Coc) (planta, fruto) prickly pear **2** (Mús) tuna (*musical group made up of university students*)

tundra *f* tundra

túnel *m* tunnel; **~ de lavado** car wash

túnica *f* (Hist) tunic; (Relig) robe

tuntún *m* (fam): **al ~** ‹*elegir*› at random; **contestó al ~** he just said the first thing that came into his head

tupé *m* **1** (fam) (descaro) nerve **2** (Esp) (peluquín) toupee; (mechón de pelo) forelock

tupido[1] -da *adj* ‹*follaje/vegetación*› dense; ‹*tela*› closely-woven; ‹*cejas*› bushy; ‹*niebla*› thick

tupido[2] *adv* (Méx) intensely

turbante *m* turban

turbina *f* turbine

turbio -bia *adj* **(a)** ‹*agua*› cloudy; ‹*río*› muddy **(b)** ‹*visión/ojos*› blurred, misty **(c)** ‹*asunto/negocio*› shady, murky

turbo *adj inv* turbocharged ■ *m* (turbocompresor) turbocharger; (automovíl) turbo

turbulencia *f* turbulence

turbulento -ta *adj* turbulent

turco[1] -ca *adj* (Geog) Turkish ■ *m,f* **(a)** (Geog) (persona) Turk **(b)** (AmL) (árabe) *term used (often pejoratively) to refer to someone of Middle Eastern origin*

turco[2] *m* (idioma) Turkish

turismo *m* (Com, Ocio) tourism; **los ingresos del ~** income from tourism *o* from the tourist industry; **dependen del ~ alemán** they rely on German tourists; **oficina de ~** tourist office; **hacer ~** to travel (around)

turista *adj* tourist (*before n*); **clase ~** tourist *o* economy class ■ *mf* tourist

turistear [A1] *vi* (Andes, Méx) (en país) to tour around; (en ciudad) to do some sightseeing

turístico -ca *adj* ‹*información/folleto*› tourist (*before n*); ‹*viaje*› sightseeing (*before n*); ‹*empresa*› travel (*before n*); ‹*atracción/actividad/lugar*› tourist (*before n*)

turnarse [A1] *v pron* to take turns

turnio -nia *adj* (Chi fam) ‹*persona*› cross-eyed; ‹*ojos*› squint

turno *m* **(a)** (horario de trabajo): **hacer el ~ de noche** to work the night shift; **estar de ~** to be on duty **(b)** (personas) shift **(c)** (en un orden): **cuando te toque el ~** when your turn comes; **cuidémoslo por ~s** let's take turns looking after him; **pedir ~** (Esp) *to ask who is last in the line* (AmE) *o* (BrE) queue

turquesa *f* (Min) turquoise ■ *m/adj inv* ▶ 97 turquoise

turrón *m*: *type of candy traditionally eaten at Christmas*

tute *m*: *card game in which the object is to win all the kings or queens*

tutear [A1] *vt*: *to address sb using the familiar* TÚ *form*

tutela *f* **(a)** (Der) guardianship, tutelage **(b)** (protección) protection

tuteo *m*: *use of the familiar* TÚ *form*

tutor -tora *m,f* **1** (Educ) (encargado de curso) course tutor, class teacher; (en la universidad) tutor **2** (Der) guardian

tutoría *f* **1** (Educ) tutorship **2** (Der) guardianship, tutelage

tutú *m* (Indum) tutu

tuve, tuviera, etc *see* TENER

tuyo -ya *adj* yours; **esto es ~** this is yours; **¿es amigo ~?** is he a friend of yours?; **fue idea tuya** it was your idea ■ *pron*: **el ~, la tuya etc** yours; **la música no es lo ~** music isn't your strong point *o* your forte; **los ~s** (tu familia) your family and friends

twist /twis(t)/ *m* twist

Uu

U, u *f* (*pl* **úes**) (*read as* /u/) *the letter* U, u

u *conj* [*used instead of* o *before* o- *or* HO-] or; **siete u ocho** seven or eight

ubicación *f* **(a)** (esp AmL) (situación, posición) location **(b)** (AmL) (localización): **se hizo difícil la ~ del avión** locating the airplane was very difficult

ubicar [A2] *vt* (AmL) **(a)** (colocar, situar): **me ~on a su lado** they placed me next to him; **~on las sillas para la reunión** they arranged the chairs for the meeting **(b)** (localizar) ‹*persona/lugar*› to find, locate **(c)** (identificar): **la ubico sólo de nombre** I only know her by name; **lo ubiqué por el color** I recognized it by the color; **me suena el nombre, pero no lo ubico** the name rings a bell, but I can't quite place him

■ **ubicarse** *v pron* **1** (AmL) **(a)** (colocarse, situarse): **se ubicó en la primera fila** he sat in the front row **(b)** (en empleo) to get oneself a good job **(c)** (orientarse) to find one's way around; **¿te ubicas?** have you got your bearings? **2** (esp AmL) (estar situado) to be, be situated *o* located

ud. = **usted**

uds. = **ustedes**

uf *interj* (expresando — cansancio, sofocación) whew! (colloq); (— repugnancia) yuck (colloq)

ufano -na *adj* **(a)** (satisfecho, orgulloso) proud **(b)** (engreído) self-satisfied, smug

ujier *m* uniformed doorman; (en tribunales) usher

úlcera *f* ulcer

ulpo *m* (Chi) *cold drink made with roasted flour and sugar*

ultimar [A1] *vt* **1** ‹*preparativos*› to complete; ‹*detalles*› to finalize **2** (AmL frml) (matar) to kill, murder

ultimátum *m* (*pl* ~ *or* **-tums**) ultimatum

último -ma *adj* (*delante del n*) **1** (en el tiempo) last; **a última hora** at the last minute *o* moment; **su ~ libro** his latest book; **en los ~s tiempos** recently; **¿cuándo fue la última vez que lo usaste?** when did you last use it? **2 (a)** (en una serie) last; **estar en ~ lugar** to be last; **por última vez** for the last time; **como ~ recurso** as a last resort; **última voluntad** last wishes (*pl*) **(b)** (*como adv*) (CS) ‹*salir/terminar*› last **3** (en el espacio): **el ~ piso** the top floor; **la última fila** the back row **4** (definitivo): **es mi última oferta** it's my final offer; ■ *m,f* last one; **era el ~ que me quedaba** it was my last one; **es el ~ de la clase** he's bottom of the class; **a ~s de** (Esp) toward(s) the end of; **por ~** finally, lastly

ultra *mf* (Esp) right-wing extremist

ultraderecha *f*: **la ~** the far *o* extreme right

ultrafino -na *adj* ultrafine, superfine

ultrajar [A1] *vt* (frml) ‹*persona*› to outrage, offend ... deeply; ‹*bandera*› to insult; ‹*honor*› to offend against

ultraje *m* outrage, insult

ultramarinos *mpl* (comestibles) groceries; **tienda de ~** grocery store (AmE), grocer's shop (BrE)

ultrasónico -ca *adj* ultrasonic

ultravioleta *adj* (*pl* ~ *or* **-tas**) ultraviolet

umbilical *adj* umbilical

umbral *m* **(a)** (de puerta) threshold **(b)** (borde, frontera) *tb* **~es** threshold; **en los ~es de la muerte** at death's door; **en los ~es de la civilización** at the dawn of civilization

un (*pl* **unos**), **una** (*pl* **unas**) *art* [*the masculine article* UN *is also used before feminine nouns which begin with stressed* A *or* HA *e.g.* UN ARMA PODEROSA, UN HAMBRE FEROZ] **1** (*sing*) a; (*delante de sonido vocálico*) an; (*pl*) some; **una nueva droga** a new drug; **un asunto importante** an important matter; **hay unas cartas para ti** there are some letters for you; **tiene unos ojos preciosos** he has lovely eyes **2** (con valor ponderativo): **tú haces unas preguntas** ... you do ask some questions! **3** (con nombres propios) a; **es un Miró** it's a Miró **4** (*pl*) (expresando aproximación) about; **tiene unos 30 años** she's about 30

una *pron* (*ver tb* UN, UNO): **a la ~, a las dos, ¡a las tres!** ready, steady, go!

unánime *adj* unanimous

unanimidad *f* unanimity; **por ~** unanimously

undécimo -ma *adj/pron* ▶**294**⌋ eleventh; *para ejemplos ver* QUINTO

ungüento *m* ointment

únicamente *adv* only

único -ca *adj* **1** (solo) only; **soy hijo ~** I'm an only child; **¡es lo ~ que faltaba!** that's all we needed!; **tarifa única** flat rate; **talla única** one size **2** (extraordinario) extraordinary ■ *m,f*. **el ~/las únicas que tengo** the only one/ones I have

unicornio *m* unicorn

unidad *f* **1** (Com, Mat) unit; **costo por ~** unit cost; **~ de peso** unit of weight; **~ de cuidados intensivos** *or* (Esp) **de vigilancia** *or* (Arg, Méx) **terapia intensiva** *or* (Chi) **de tratamiento intensivo** intensive care unit **2** (unión, armonía) unity

unido -da *adj* **(a)** ‹*familia/amigos*› close **(b)** (sobre un tema) united

unificación *f* unification

unificar [A2] *vt* ‹*país*› to unify; ‹*precios*› to standardize

uniforme *adj* ‹*velocidad/temperaturas*› constant, uniform; ‹*superficie*› even, uniform; ‹*terreno*› even, level; ‹*paisaje/estilo*› uniform; ‹*criterios/precios*› standard, uniform ■ *m* uniform

unilateral *adj* ‹*desarme/decisión*› unilateral; ‹*criterio/opinión*› one-sided

unión *f* **1 (a)** (acción): **la ~ de las dos empresas** the merger of the two companies; **la ~ de estos factores** the combination of these factors **(b)** (agrupación) association **(c) la U~ Americana** (Méx) (Period) the United States **2** (relación) union, relationship; (matrimonio) union, marriage **3** (juntura) joint

Unión Europea *f*: **la ~ ~** the European Union

Unión Soviética *f* (Hist): **la ~ ~** the Soviet Union

unir [I1] *vt* **1 (a)** ‹*cables*› to join; (con cola, pegamento) to stick ... together; ‹*esfuerzos*› to combine **(b)** «*sentimientos/intereses*» to unite **(c)** ‹*características/cualidades/estilos*› to combine; **~ algo** A **algo** to combine sth WITH sth **2** (comunicar) ‹*lugares*› to link **3** (fusionar) ‹*empresas/organizaciones*› to merge ■ **unirse** *v pron* **1** (aliarse) «*personas/colectividades*» to join together; **se unió a nuestra causa** he joined our cause **2** (juntarse) «*caminos*» to converge, meet **3** (fusionarse) «*empresas/organizaciones*» to merge

universal *adj* universal

universidad *f* university; **~ a distancia** *or* (Méx) **abierta** open university; **~ laboral** ≈ technical college (*school with emphasis on vocational training*)

universitario -ria *adj* university (*before n*) ■ *m, f* (estudiante) undergraduate, (university) student; (licenciado) (university) graduate

universo *m* universe

uno[1], **una** *adj* ▶**293**⌋ [UNO *becomes* **un** *before a masculine noun or noun phrase*] one; **no había ni un asiento libre** there wasn't one empty seat *o* a single empty seat; **treinta y un pasajeros** thirty-one passengers; **el capítulo uno** chapter one ■ *pron* **1** (numeral) ▶**293**⌋ one; **uno a** *or* **por uno** one by one; **es la una** it's one o'clock; ***más de uno/una*** (fam) quite a few **2** (personal) (*sing*) one; (*pl*) some; **uno es mío, el otro no** one's mine, the other isn't; **¿te gustaron? — unos sí, otros no**

did you like them? — some I did, others I didn't; **se ayudan los unos a los otros** they help one another **3** (fam) (alguien) (*m*) some guy (colloq); (*f*) some woman (colloq); **les pregunté a unos que estaban allí** I asked some people who were there **4** (uso impersonal) you; **uno no sabe qué decir** you don't *o* (frml) one doesn't know what to say; **nunca le dicen nada a uno** they don't tell you anything

uno[2] *m* ▶ 293 (number) one; *para ejemplos ver* CINCO

untar [A1] *vt* **(a)** (cubrir): **~ las galletas con miel** spread honey on the cookies; **se unta el molde con mantequilla** grease the cake tin (with butter) **(b)** (empapar) **~ algo EN algo** to dip sth IN sth
■ **untarse** *v pron* **(a)** (ensuciarse): **se untó las manos de pintura** he got paint all over his hands **(b)** (ponerse): **se untó los hombros con bronceador** she rubbed suntan lotion on her shoulders

uña *f* **(a)** ▶ 123 (Anat) (de la mano) nail, fingernail; (del pie) nail, toenail; ***arreglarse*** or ***hacerse las ~s*** (*refl*) to do one's nails; (*caus*) to have one's nails done **(b)** (de oso, gato) claw; (de caballo, oveja) hoof

uralita® *f* asbestos

uranio *m* uranium

Urano *m* Uranus

urbanidad *f* courtesy, urbanity (frml)

urbanismo *m* city (AmE) *o* (BrE) town planning

urbanización *f* (acción) urbanization, development; (núcleo residencial) (Esp) (housing) development

urbanizado -da *adj* built-up; **esta zona está muy urbanizada** this area is heavily developed

urbanizar [A4] *vt* ‹*zona/terreno*› to develop, urbanize; **una zona sin ~** an undeveloped area

urbano -na *adj* ‹*núcleo/transporte*› urban, city (*before n*); ‹*población*› urban

urdir [I1] *vt* **(a)** (en telar) to warp; ‹*puntos*› to cast on **(b)** ‹*plan*› to devise, hatch

urgencia *f* **(a)** (cualidad) urgency; **con ~** urgently **(b)** (Med) emergency; Ⓢ **urgencias** accident and emergency; **lo operaron de ~** he had an emergency operation

urgente *adj* ‹*asunto*› pressing, urgent; ‹*mensaje*› urgent; ‹*caso/enfermo*› emergency (*before n*); ‹*carta*› express (*before n*)

urgido -da *adj* (AmL): **estaban ~s de dinero** they were in urgent need of money; **estamos ~s de tiempo** we are pressed for time

urgir [I7] *vi* (*en 3ª pers*): **urge la finalización del proyecto** the project must be finished as soon as possible; **me urge estar allí el martes** I absolutely must be there on/by Tuesday; **le urge el préstamo** he needs the loan urgently

urinario *m* urinal

urna *f* **1** (vasija) urn; (de exposición) display case; (para votar) ballot box; **~ cineraria** funerary urn **2** (Chi, Ven) (ataúd) coffin, wooden box (euph)

urólogo -ga *m,f* urologist

urraca *f* magpie

URSS /urs/ *f* (Hist) (= **Unión de Repúblicas Socialistas Soviéticas**) USSR

urubú *m* black vulture

Uruguay *m* **(a)** (país) *tb* **el ~** Uruguay **(b)** (río): **el (río) ~** the Uruguay River

uruguayismo *m* Uruguayan word (*o* phrase *etc*)

uruguayo -ya *adj/m,f* Uruguayan

USA /'usa/ (fam) USA

usado -da *adj* **(a)** [SER] (de segunda mano) second-hand **(b)** [ESTAR] (gastado, viejo) worn

usar [A1] *vt* **(a)** (utilizar) to use; **¿qué champú usas?** what shampoo do you use?; **~ algo/a algn DE** or **COMO algo** to use sth/sb AS sth **(b)** (llevar) ‹*alhajas/ropa/perfume*› to wear; **estos zapatos están sin ~** these shoes are unworn, these shoes have never been worn
■ **usarse** *v pron* (*en 3ª pers*) (esp AmL) (estar de moda) «*color/ropa*» to be in fashion, to be popular; **ya no se usa hacer fiestas de compromiso** people don't tend to have engagement parties any more

usina *f* (AmS) (fábrica) large factory; (industria) industry

uso *m* **(a)** (de producto, medicamento, máquina) use; **instrucciones para su ~** instructions for use; **hacer ~ de algo** to use sth **(b)** (de facultad, derecho): **en pleno ~ de sus facultades mentales** in full possession of his mental faculties; **hacer ~ de un derecho** to exercise a right; **desde que tengo ~ de razón** ever since I can remember; **hacer ~ de la palabra** (frml) to speak **(c)** (de prenda): **ropa de ~ diario** everyday clothes; **los zapatos ceden con el ~** shoes give with wear

usted *pron pers* [*Polite form of address but also used in some areas, eg Colombia and Chile, instead of the familiar* TÚ *form*] **1** (como sujeto, en comparaciones, con preposición) you; **¿quién lo va a hacer? — usted** who's going to do it? — you (are); **tratar a algn de ~** to address sb using the USTED form; **muchas gracias — a ~** thank you very much — thank *you*; **son de ~** they're yours **2** (uso impersonal) you, one (frml); **le dicen eso y ~ no sabe qué contestar** when they say that you just don't know what to say in reply

ustedes *pron pers pl* [*Polite plural form of address also used in Latin American countries as the familiar plural form*] you; **¿quién lo va a hacer? — ustedes** who's going to do it? — you (are); **~ mismos lo dijeron** you said so yourselves; **son de ~** they're yours

usual *adj* usual, normal

usuario -ria *m,f* user

usurero -ra *m,f* usurer

usurpador -dora *m,f* usurper

usurpar [A1] *vt* (frml) ‹*propiedad/título*› to misappropriate; ‹*territorio*› to seize; ‹*poder*› to usurp

utensilio *m* (instrumento) utensil; (herramienta) tool; **~s de cocina** kitchen *o* cooking utensils; **~s de laboratorio** laboratory apparatus; **~s de pesca** fishing tackle

útero *m* womb, uterus (tech)

útil *adj* useful

utilería *f* (esp AmL) (Cin, Teatr) props (*pl*)

utilero -ra *m,f* (esp AmL) (Cin, Teatr) props manager

útiles *mpl* **(a)** (herramientas, instrumentos) tools (*pl*), implements (*pl*); **~ de pesca** fishing tackle; **~ de jardinería** gardening tools **(b)** (AmL) (artículos

escolares) *tb* ~ **escolares** *pencils, pens, rulers, etc for school*
utilidad *f* **(a)** (de aparato) usefulness; **un coche me sería de mucha** ~ a car would be of great use to me **(b) utilidades** *fpl* (AmL) (ganancia, beneficio) profits (*pl*)
utilitario *m* small (economical) car
utilización *f* use, utilization (frml)
utilizar [A4] *vt* to use, utilize (frml)
utopía *f* Utopia
utópico -ca *adj* Utopian
uva *f* grape; ~ **blanca/negra** white/black grape
uve *f* (Esp) *name of the letter* v; ~ **doble** (Esp) *name of the letter* w
uy *interj* (expresando — asombro) ooh! (colloq); (— malestar, disgusto) oh!; (— emoción súbita) ah!, oh!; (— dolor) ow!, ouch!

Vv

V, v *f* (*read as* /be/, /be 'korta/, /be 'tʃika/, /be pe'keɲa/ *or* (Esp) /'uβe/) *the letter* V, v
va, vas, etc *see* IR
vaca *f* **(a)** (Zool) cow; ***estar como una*** ~ (fam) to be very fat; ***hacer una*** ~ (AmL fam) to make a collection **(b)** (Coc): **(carne de)** ~ beef; **filete de** ~ fillet steak
vacacionar [A1] *vi* (Méx) to spend one's vacation(s) *o* holidays
vacaciones *fpl* vacation(s) (esp AmE), holiday(s) (esp BrE); ~ **de verano** summer vacation *o* holidays; **irse de** ~ to go away on vacation *o* on holiday; **estamos de** ~ we're on vacation *o* holiday; **tomarse unas** ~ to take a vacation *o* holiday
vacacionista *mf* (Méx) vacationer (AmE), holidaymaker (BrE)
vacante *adj* ‹*puesto/plaza*› vacant; ‹*piso/asiento*› empty, unoccupied ■ *f* vacancy; **cubrir una** ~ to fill a vacancy
vaciar [A17] *vt* **1 (a)** ‹*vaso/botella*› to empty; ‹*radiador*› to drain; ‹*bolsillo/cajón*› to empty; ‹*armario/habitación*› to clean out **(b)** ‹*contenido*› to empty (out) **2** (ahuecar) to hollow out
■ **vaciarse** *v pron* to empty
vacilación *f* hesitation, vacillation (frml); **tras un momento de** ~ after a moment's hesitation
vacilante *adj* **(a)** (oscilante) unsteady, shaky; **con paso** ~ unsteadily **(b)** (dubitativo) ‹*expresión*› doubtful; ‹*voz*› hesitant **(c)** ‹*luz*› flickering
vacilar [A1] *vi* **1 (a)** (dudar) to hesitate; **sin** ~ without hesitating; **no vaciló en aceptar** he did not hesitate to accept, he accepted without hesitation **(b)** «*fe/determinación*» to waver **(c)** «*luz*» to flicker **2** (oscilar) «*persona*» to stagger, totter **3** (AmL exc CS fam) (divertirse) to have fun
vacile *m* (fam) (tomadura de pelo) joke; **basta de** ~ that's enough kidding (colloq)
vacilón *m* (AmL fam) **(a)** (diversión): **le encanta el** ~ he loves having a good time; **la fiesta fue un** ~ the party was great fun **(b)** (tomadura de pelo) joke; **es puro** ~ it's just a joke
vacío¹ -cía *adj* **(a)** ‹*botella/caja*› empty; ‹*calle/ciudad*› empty, deserted; ‹*casa*› empty, unoccupied; ‹*palabras/retórica*› empty; **con el estómago** ~ on an empty stomach **(b)** (frívolo) ‹*persona*› shallow; ‹*vida/frase*› empty, meaningless
vacío² *m* **(a)** (Fís) vacuum; **envasado al** ~ vacuum-packed **(b)** (espacio vacío) space; **mirar al** ~ to gaze into space **(c)** (falta, hueco) gap; **dejó un** ~ **en su vida** she left a gap *o* a void in his life; **una sensación de** ~ a feeling of emptiness
vacuna *f* vaccine; **me tengo que poner la** ~ I have to have my vaccination
vacunar [A1] *vt* to vaccinate; ~ **a algn** CONTRA **algo** to vaccinate sb AGAINST sth
vacuno -na *adj* bovine; **ganado** ~ cattle (*pl*)
vado *m* (de río) ford; Ⓢ **vado permanente** no parking
vagabundear [A1] *vi* to drift (around)
vagabundo -da *adj* ‹*perro*› stray; **niños** ~**s** street urchins ■ *m,f* tramp, vagrant
vagar [A3] *vi* to wander, roam
vagina *f* vagina
vago -ga *adj* **1** (fam) ‹*persona*› lazy, idle **2** ‹*recuerdo/idea*› vague, hazy; ‹*contorno/forma*› vague, indistinct; ‹*explicación/parecido*› vague ■ *m,f* (fam) layabout, slacker (colloq); **deja ya de hacer el** ~ stop lazing around (colloq)
vagón *m* (de pasajeros) coach, car (AmE), carriage (BrE); ~ **restaurante** dining *o* (BrE) restaurant car
vagoneta *f* (Méx) (para pasajeros) van, minibus
vaho *m* **(a)** (aliento) breath **(b)** (vapor) steam, vapor* **(c)** (inhalación): **hacer** ~**s** to inhale
vaina *f* **1** (de espada) scabbard; (de navaja) sheath **2** (Bot) (de habas, etc) pod **3** (Col, Per, Ven fam) **(a)** (problema, contrariedad): **¡qué** ~**!** what a drag *o* pain (colloq); **la** ~ **es que no sé cómo** the thing *o* problem is that I don't know how; **estoy metida en una** ~ I'm in a spot of trouble (colloq) **(b)** (cosa, asunto) thing, thingamajig (colloq) **(c)** (comportamiento sospechoso): **tenían una** ~ they were up to something funny; **¿qué** ~ **te traes tú?** what are you up to?
vainilla *f* (Bot, Coc) vanilla
vais *see* IR
vaivén *m* (de columpio, péndulo) swinging; (de tren) rocking; (de barco) rolling; (de mecedora) rocking; (de gente) toing and froing

vajilla *f* (en general) dishes (*pl*); (juego) dinner service *o* set

valdré, valdría, etc *see* VALER

vale *m* **(a)** (para adquirir algo) voucher; (por devolución) credit note *o* slip; **un ~ de descuento** a money-off coupon **(b)** (pagaré) IOU ■ *interj*: *ver* VALER 4

valenciana *f* (Méx) cuff (AmE), turn-up (BrE)

valenciano[1] -na *adj/m,f* Valencian

valenciano[2] *m* (Ling) Valencian

valentía *f* bravery, courage; **con ~** courageously

valer [E28] *vt* **1** (tener un valor de) to be worth; (costar) to cost; **¿cuánto valen?** how much are they?, what do they cost? **2** (+ *me/te/le etc*) (ganar): **esta obra le valió un premio** this play earned *o* won her a prize ■ **~** *vi* **1** (+ *compl*) (tener cierto valor) to be worth; (costar) to cost; **vale más, pero es mejor** it costs more but it's better; **cada cupón vale por un regalo** each voucher is worth a gift **2** (tener valor no material): **ha demostrado que vale** he has shown his worth; **como profesor no vale (nada)** as a teacher he's useless; **vales tanto como él** you're as good as he is; ***hacerse ~*** to assert oneself; ***hacer ~ algo*** ‹*derecho*› to assert *o* enforce sth **3** (servir): **ésta no vale, es muy ancha** this one's no good, it's too wide; **no le valió de nada protestar** protesting got him nowhere; **no ~ PARA algo** to be useless *o* no good AT sth **4 vale** (Esp fam) **(a)** (expresando acuerdo) OK; **¿a las ocho? — ¡vale!** at eight o'clock? — sure *o* fine *o* OK!; **¿vale?** OK?, all right? **(b)** (basta): **¿~ así?** is that OK *o* enough? **5 más vale**: **más vale así** it's better that way; **más te vale ir** you'd better go **6 (a)** (ser válido) «*entrada/pasaporte*» to be valid; «*jugada/partido*» to count **(b)** (estar permitido): **eso no vale, estás haciendo trampa** that's not fair, you're cheating; **no vale mirar** you're not allowed to look **7** (Méx fam) **(a)** (no importar): **a mí eso me vale** I don't give a damn about that (colloq) **(b)** (no tener valor) to be useless *o* no good (colloq) **(c)** (estropearse): **mi coche ya valió** my car's had it (colloq)

■ **valerse** *v pron* **1** (servirse) **~se DE algo/algn** to use sth/sb **2** «*anciano/enfermo*»: **~se por sí mismo** to look after oneself **3** (estar permitido, ser correcto): **no se vale golpear abajo del cinturón** hitting below the belt is not allowed; **¡no se vale!** that's not fair!

valeroso -sa *adj* brave, courageous, valiant (liter)

valga, valgas, etc *see* VALER

validar [A1] *vt* to validate

validez *f* validity

válido -da *adj* valid

valiente *adj* ‹*persona*› brave, courageous

valija *f* (RPl) suitcase; **~ diplomática** diplomatic bag

valioso -sa *adj* ‹*joya/consejo/experiencia*› valuable; **un hombre ~** a man of great worth

valla *f* **(a)** (cerca) fence **(b)** (Dep) (en atletismo) hurdle; (en fútbol) goal; **~ publicitaria** billboard (AmE), hoarding (BrE)

valle *m* valley

valor *m* **1 (a)** (Com, Fin) value; **libros por ~ de $150** books to the value of $150; **objetos de ~** valuables; **~ adquisitivo** purchasing power; **~es** securities, stocks, shares **(b)** (importancia, mérito) value; **~ sentimental** sentimental value **(c)** (validez) validity; **sin la firma no tiene ningún ~** it's not valid without the signature **2 (a)** (coraje, valentía) courage; **me faltó ~** I didn't have the courage; **armarse de ~** to pluck up courage **(b)** (fam) (descaro, desvergüenza) nerve (colloq); **¡encima tiene el ~ de protestar!** and then she has the nerve to complain!

valoración *f* **(a)** (de bienes, joyas) valuation; (de pérdidas, daños) assessment **(b)** (frml) (de suceso, trabajo) assessment, appraisal (frml)

valorar [A1] *vt* **(a)** ‹*joya/cuadro*› to value; ‹*pérdida/daño*› to assess; **~ algo EN algo** to value/assess sth AT sth; **eso no se puede ~ en dinero** you cannot put a value on it **(b)** (frml) ‹*trabajo/actuación*› to assess **(c)** ‹*amistad/lealtad*› to value

valorización *f* **(a)** (tasación) ⇒ VALORACIÓN (a) **(b)** (AmL) (aumento de valor) appreciation

vals *m* waltz; **bailar un ~** to waltz

valuar *vt* [A18] (AmL) to value

válvula *f* valve

vamos *see* IR

vampiresa *f* femme fatale, vamp (dated)

vampiro *m* **(a)** (en historias de horror) vampire; (explotador) vampire, bloodsucker **(b)** (Zool) vampire (bat)

van *see* IR

vanagloriarse [A1] *v pron* **~ DE algo** to boast *o* brag ABOUT sth

vandalismo *m* vandalism, hooliganism

vándalo -la *m,f* (gamberro) vandal, hooligan

vanguardia *f* (Mil) vanguard; (Art, Lit) avant-garde; **teatro de ~** avant-garde theater; **ir** *or* **estar a la ~ (de algo)** to be in the vanguard (of sth)

vanguardista *adj* avant-garde

vanidad *f* vanity

vanidoso -sa *adj* (presumido) vain, conceited; (en cuanto al aspecto físico) vain ■ *m,f*: **es un ~** he's so vain *o* conceited

vano -na *adj* **(a)** (ineficaz) ‹*discusión/intento*› vain, futile; ‹*esfuerzo*› futile; **en ~** in vain **(b)** (falto de realidad) vain; **ilusiones vanas** wishful thinking **(c)** ‹*palabra/promesa*› empty

vapor *m* **(a)** (Fís, Quím) vapor*, steam **(b)** (Coc): **al ~** steamed **(c)** (Náut) steamer, steamship

vaquero[1] -ra *adj* **(a)** ‹*falda/cazadora*› denim; **un pantalón ~** a pair of jeans *o* denims **(b)** ‹*estilo*› cowboy (*before n*) ■ *m,f* (Agr) (*m*) cowboy, cowhand; (*f*) cowgirl, cowhand

vaquero[2] *m* (Indum) *tb* **~s**: **unos ~s** a pair of jeans *o* denims

vaquilla *f* heifer

vara *f* **1** (palo) stick, pole **2** (Per fam) (influencia) connections (*pl*) (colloq)

varado -da *adj* **1 (a)** (Náut) ‹*barco*› aground **(b)** (AmL) (detenido): **miles de turistas se quedaron ~s** thousands of tourists were left stranded; **me quedé ~ con el trabajo** I got stuck with my work **2 (a)** (Col, Méx fam) (sin dinero) broke (colloq) **(b)** (Andes) (sin empleo) out of work

variable *adj* ‹*carácter/humor*› changeable; **tiempo ~** unsettled *o* changeable weather

variación *f* variation

variado -da *adj* **(a)** ‹*programa/vida/trabajo*› varied **(b)** (diverso): **ropa de colores ~s** clothes in a variety of colors

variante *f* **1** (de palabra) variant **2** (carretera) turnoff

variar [A17] *vi* «*precio/temperatura*» to vary; **las temperaturas varían entre 20°C y 25°C** temperatures range *o* vary between 20°C and 25°C; **para ~** (iró) (just) for a change (iro) ■ **~** *vt* **1** (hacer variado) ‹*menú*› to vary; ‹*producción*› to vary, diversify **2** (cambiar) ‹*decoración/rumbo*› to change, alter

varicela *f* chicken pox

várices, (Esp) **varices** *fpl* ⇒ VARIZ

varicoso -sa *adj* varicose

variedad *f* **(a)** (en general) variety **(b) variedades** *fpl* (Espec) vaudeville (AmE), variety (BrE)

varilla *f* (en general) rod; (de abanico, paraguas) rib; (de jaula) bar; (de rueda de bicicleta) spoke; (para medir el aceite) dipstick

vario -ria *adj* **1 ~s/varias** (más de dos) several; **hace ~s años** several years ago **2** (variado, diverso) various; **asuntos ~s** various matters

varios -rias *pron* several; **lo compraron entre ~s** several of them got together to buy it

varita *f* wand; **~ mágica** magic wand

variz (*pl* **várices** *or* (Esp) **varices**) *f* varicose vein

varón *adj* ‹*heredero/descendiente*› male; **un hijo ~** a son ■ *m* (niño) boy; (hombre) man, male

varonil *adj* **(a)** (viril) manly, masculine; **voz ~** masculine voice **(b)** ‹*mujer*› (hombruna) mannish, masculine

vas *see* IR

vasallo *m* vassal

vasco[1] -ca *adj/m,f* Basque

vasco[2] *m* (idioma) Basque

vasectomía *f* vasectomy

vaselina *f* Vaseline®, petroleum jelly

vasija *f* (Arqueol) vessel (frml)

vaso *m* **1** (recipiente, contenido) glass; **un ~ de vino** (con vino) a glass of wine; (para vino) a wine glass; **~ de papel** paper cup **2** (Anat) vessel; **~ sanguíneo** blood vessel

vasto -ta *adj* (*gen delante del n*) ‹*mar/llanura*› vast, immense; ‹*conocimientos/experiencia*› vast, enormous

váter *m* (Esp fam) (inodoro) toilet, lavatory; ▶52 (cuarto) bathroom (esp AmE), toilet (BrE), loo (BrE colloq)

Vaticano *m*: **el ~** the Vatican

vatio *m* watt

vaya, **vayas, etc** *see* IR

Vd. = **usted**

ve *f* (AmL) *tb* **~ corta** *or* **chica** *or* **pequeña** *name of the letter* V

ve *see* IR, VER

vea, **veas, etc** *see* VER

vecindad *f* **1** (lugar, barrio) neighborhood*, area; (vecinos) residents (*pl*) **2** (Méx) (edificio) tenement house

vecindario ⇒ VECINDAD 1

vecino -na *adj* **(a)** (contiguo) neighboring*; **los países ~s** the neighboring countries; **~ A algo** bordering ON sth, adjoining sth **(b)** (cercano) neighboring*, nearby ■ *m,f* **(a)** (persona que vive cerca) neighbor*; **mi ~ de al lado** my next-door neighbor **(b)** (habitante — de población, municipio) inhabitant; (— de barrio, edificio) resident

veda *f* (en caza y pesca) closed (AmE) *o* (BrE) close season; **la perdiz está en ~** it is the closed *o* close season for partridge

vedar [A1] *vt* **(a)** ‹*caza/pesca*› to prohibit, ban (*during the closed season*) **(b)** (prohibir) to ban

vedette /be'ðet/ *f* cabaret star

vegetación *f* **(a)** (Bot) vegetation **(b)** (Med) **vegetaciones** *fpl* adenoids (*pl*)

vegetal *adj* ‹*vida*› plant (*before n*); ‹*aceite/reino*› vegetable (*before n*) ■ *m* plant, vegetable

vegetar [A1] *vi* **(a)** (Bot) to grow **(b)** (fam) «*persona*» to vegetate (colloq & pej)

vegetariano -na *adj/m,f* vegetarian

vehemente *adj* vehement

vehículo *m* vehicle

veía, **veíamos, etc** *see* VER

veinte ▶293 *adj inv/m/pron* twenty; *para ejemplos ver* CINCO, CINCUENTA

veintitantos -tas ▶293 *adj/pron* twenty-odd

veintiuno -na[1] ▶293 *adj/pron* [VEINTIÚN *is used before masculine nouns and before feminine nouns which begin with accented* A *or* HA] twenty-one; **veintiún años** twenty-one years; *para ejemplos ver tb* CINCO

veintiuno[2] *m* ▶293 (number) twenty-one

vejestorio *m* **(a)** (fam) (persona): **la profesora es un ~** the teacher is ancient (colloq) **(b)** (AmL fam) (cosa) old relic (colloq), piece of old junk (colloq)

vejez *f* old age

vejiga *f* ▶123 (Anat) bladder

vela *f* **1** (para alumbrar) candle **2** (vigilia): **pasé la noche en ~** (por preocupación, dolor) I couldn't get to sleep all night; (cuidando a un enfermo) I was up all night **3 (a)** (de barco) sail **(b)** (deporte) sailing; **hacer ~** to go sailing

velado -da *adj* ‹*película*› fogged; ‹*amenaza/referencia*› veiled; ‹*sonido*› muffled

velador[1] *m* **(a)** (mesa) pedestal table **(b)** (AmS) (mesilla de noche) bedside table, night stand (AmE)

velador[2] -dora *m,f* **1** (Méx) (de fábrica) watchman, guard **2 veladora** *f* (Méx) (vela) candle

velar [A1] *vt* **1 (a)** ‹*difunto*› to hold a wake over **(b)** ‹*enfermo*› to watch over **2** ‹*película*› to fog, expose ■ **~** *vi* **1** (permanecer despierto) to stay up *o* awake **2** (cuidar) **~ POR algo/algn** to watch OVER sth/sb ■ **velarse** *v pron* «*película*» to get fogged *o* exposed

velatorio *m* **(a)** (reunión) wake, vigil (frml) **(b)** (establecimiento) funeral parlor*; (sala) chapel of rest

velero *m* **(a)** (Náut) (grande) sailing ship; (pequeño) sailboat (AmE), sailing boat (BrE) **(b)** (Aviac) glider

veleta *f* **1** (para el viento) weather vane, weathercock **2 veleta** *mf* (fam) (persona inconstante) fickle person

vello *m* **1** (pelusa) down; (en las piernas, etc) hair **2** (Bot) bloom

velo *m* veil

velocidad *f* **1** (en general) speed; **cobrar ~** to pick up *o* gather speed; **¿a qué ~ iba?** how fast was he going?; **disminuir la ~** to slow down; **a toda ~** at top speed; **la ~ con que lo hizo** the speed with which he did it **2** (Auto, Mec) gear; **un modelo de cinco ~es** a five-gear model

velocímetro *m* speedometer

velódromo *m* cycle track, velodrome

veloz *adj* ‹*corredor*› fast; ‹*movimiento*› swift, quick

ven *see* VENIR, VER

vena *f* **1** (Anat) vein; **cortarse las ~s** to slash *o* cut one's wrists **2** (Geol, Min) vein, seam **3** (de madera) grain; (de piedra) vein, stripe

venado *m* **(a)** (Zool) deer; ***pintar ~*** (Méx fam) to play hooky (esp Ame colloq), skive off (school) (BrE colloq) **(b)** (Coc) venison

vencedor -dora *adj* ‹*ejército/país*› victorious; ‹*equipo/jugador*› winning (*before n*) ■ *m,f* (en guerra) victor; (en competición) winner

vencer [E2] *vt* **(a)** ‹*enemigo*› to defeat, vanquish (liter); ‹*rival/competidor*› to defeat, beat; **no te dejes ~** don't give in **(b)** ‹*miedo/pesimismo/obstáculo*› to overcome **(c)** (dominar): **me venció el sueño** I was overcome by sleep ■ **~** *vi* **1** «*ejército/equipo*» to win, be victorious; **¡~emos!** we shall overcome! **2 (a)** «*pasaporte/garantía*» to expire; **el lunes vence el plazo** Monday is the deadline **(b)** «*letra*» to be due for payment

■ **vencerse** *v pron* (AmL) «*pasaporte/garantía*» to expire; **se me venció el carnet** my card expired *o* ran out

vencido -da *adj* **1** ‹*ejército/país*› defeated, vanquished (liter); ‹*equipo/jugador*› losing (*before n*), beaten; ***darse por ~*** to give up *o* in **2 (a)** ‹*visa/pasaporte*› expired, out-of-date (*before n*); **estos antibióticos están ~s** (AmL) these antibiotics are past their expiration (AmE) *o* (BrE) expiry date **(b)** ‹*boleto/cheque*› out-of-date (*before n*) **(c)** ‹*letra/intereses*› due for payment ■ *m,f*: **los ~s** the defeated, the vanquished (liter)

vencimiento *m* (de letra, pago) due date; (de carnet, licencia) expiration (AmE) *o* (BrE) expiry date

venda *f* bandage; **~ elástica** elastic bandage

vendaje *m* dressing; **poner un ~** to put on a dressing

vendar [A1] *vt* to bandage

vendaval *m* gale, strong wind

vendedor -dora *m,f* **(a)** (en mercado) stallholder, stallkeeper (AmE); (en tienda) salesclerk (AmE), shop assistant (BrE); (viajante, representante) sales representative; **~ a domicilio** door-to-door sales agent; **~ ambulante** peddler, hawker; **~ de periódicos** newspaper vendor *o* seller **(b)** (Der) (propietario que vende) vendor

vender [E1] *vt* ‹*mercancías/casa*› to sell; **le vendí el reloj** I sold him the watch; **vendió la casa muy bien** she got a very good price for her house; Ⓢ **se vende** for sale; **lo venden a $500 el kilo** they sell it at $500 a kilo; **vendí el cuadro en** *or* **por $20.000** I sold the painting for $20,000; **se vende por kilo(s)/unidades** it's sold by the kilo/unit ■ **~** *vi* «*producto*» to sell

■ **venderse** *v pron* (dejarse sobornar) to sell out

vendimia *f* grape harvest, wine harvest

vendimiar [A1] *vt* to pick, harvest

vendré, vendría, etc *see* VENIR

venduta *f* (Col) public sale (*of household goods*)

Venecia *f* Venice

veneno *m* **(a)** (sustancia tóxica) poison; (de culebra) venom **(b)** (malevolencia) venom

venenoso -sa *adj* ‹*sustancia/planta*› poisonous; ‹*araña/serpiente*› poisonous, venomous; ‹*palabras/mirada*› venomous

venerable *adj/m,f* venerable

venerar [A1] *vt* (adorar) to revere, worship; (Relig) to venerate

venéreo -rea *adj* venereal

venezolanismo *m* Venezuelan word (*o* phrase *etc*), Venezuelanism

venezolano -na *adj/m,f* Venezuelan

Venezuela *f* Venezuela

venga *interj* (Esp fam) **(a)** (para animar) come on **(b)** (expresando insistencia): **y ~ a protestar** and they just kept *o* went on (and on) complaining

vengáis, vengamos, etc *see* VENIR

venganza *f* revenge, vengeance (liter)

vengar [A3] *vt* ‹*insulto/derrota*› to take revenge for, to avenge; ‹*persona*› to avenge

■ **vengarse** *v pron* to take revenge; **~se** DE *or* POR **algo** to take revenge FOR sth; **~se** DE/EN **algn** to take (one's) revenge ON sb

vengativo -va *adj* vindictive, vengeful (liter)

vengo *see* VENIR

venia *f* (AmS) (inclinación de cabeza) bow

venial *adj* venial

venida *f* **(a)** (llegada) arrival **(b)** (AmL) (vuelta): **a la** *or* **de ~** on the way back

venir [I31] *vi* **1 (a)** (a un lugar) to come; **vine en tren** I came by train; **¿a qué vino?** what did he come by *o* around for?; **vine dormida todo el tiempo** I slept (for) the whole journey; **~** POR *or* (Esp) A POR **algn/algo** to come FOR sb/sth, come to pick sb/sth up; **la vino a buscar su madre** her mother came to pick her up; **ven a ver esto** come and see this **(b)** (volver) to come back; **ahora vengo** I'll be back in a moment; **no vengas tarde** don't be late home *o* back **(c)** (salir): **me vino con un cuento** he came up with some excuse; **no me vengas con exigencias** don't start making demands **2 (a)** (tener lugar): **ahora viene esa escena que te conté** that scene I told you about is coming up now; **¿qué viene después de las noticias?** what's on after the news?; **ya vendrán**

tiempos mejores things will get better **(b)** (indicando procedencia) ~ DE **algo** to come FROM sth; **viene de la India** it comes from India; **le viene de familia** it runs in his family; **¿a qué viene eso?** why do you say that? **(c)** (indicando presentación) to come; **viene en tres tamaños** it comes in three sizes **(d)** (estar incluido): **viene en primera página** it's on the front page; **no viene nada sobre la huelga** there's nothing about the strike **3** (convenir): **estas cajas me vendrían muy bien** these boxes would come in handy; **el jueves no me viene bien** Thursday's no good for me; **me vendría bien un descanso** I could do with a rest **4** (*como aux*): **esto viene a confirmar mis sospechas** this confirms my suspicions; **hace mucho que lo venía diciendo** I'd been saying so all along ■ **venirse** *v pron* (*enf*) **(a)** (a un lugar) to come; **se vinieron a pie** they came on foot; ***~se abajo*** «*persona*» to go to pieces; «*techo*» to fall in, collapse; «*estante*» to collapse; «*ilusiones*» to go up in smoke; «*proyectos*» to fall through **(b)** (volver) to come back

venta *f* (Com) sale; **~ al contado** cash sale; **~ al por mayor/menor** wholesale/retail; **~ a plazos** installment plan (AmE), hire purchase (BrE); **~ por catálogo** *or* **correo** mail order; **pronto saldrá a la ~** it will be on sale soon; **estar en** *or* **a la ~** «*coche/bicicleta*» to be for sale; «*casa*» to be (up) for sale

ventaja *f* **(a)** (beneficio) advantage; **tiene la ~ de que está cerca** it has the advantage of being near; **tienes ~ por tu experiencia** you have an advantage because of your experience **(b)** (en carrera): **lleva una ~ de diez segundos** she has a ten-second lead; **jugar con ~** to be at an advantage

ventajero -ra *m,f* (RPl) opportunist

ventajoso -sa *adj* **(a)** ‹*negocio*› profitable; ‹*acuerdo/situación*› favorable*, advantageous **(b)** (Col) ‹*persona*› opportunistic

ventana *f* **1** (Arquit, Const, Inf) window **2** (de la nariz) nostril

ventanilla *f* **(a)** (de coche, tren) window **(b)** (en oficinas) window; (en cines, teatros) box office; **horario de ~** opening hours **(c)** (Inf) window

ventilación *f* **(a)** (posibilidad de ventilarse) ventilation **(b)** (acción de ventilar) airing

ventilador *m* (aparato) fan; (abertura) ventilator, air vent

ventilar [A1] *vt* ‹*habitación*› to air, ventilate; ‹*ropa/colchón*› to air ■ **ventilarse** *v pron* **1** «*habitación/ropa*» to air **2** (fam) (tomar el aire) to get a breath of fresh air, get some air

ventisca *f* snowstorm; (con más viento) blizzard

ventolera *f* gust of wind

ventosa *f* **(a)** (de goma, plástico) suction pad **(b)** (Zool) sucker

ventosidad *f* wind, flatulence

ventoso -sa *adj* windy

ventrículo *m* ventricle

ventrílocuo -cua *m,f* ventriloquist

ventura *f* **1** (liter) (suerte) fortune; **tiene la ~ de** ... he has the good fortune to ...; ***echarle la buena ~ a algn*** to tell sb's fortune **2** (*en locs*) **a la ventura**: **viven a la ~** they take each day as it comes; **salieron a la ~** they set out with no fixed plan

Venus *m* (Astron) Venus ■ *f* (Art, Mit) Venus

veo *see* VER [2]

ver[1] *m* **1** (aspecto): **ser de buen ~** to be good-looking *o* attractive **2** (opinión): **a mi/su ~** in my/his view

ver[2] [E29] *vt* **1 (a)** (percibir con la vista) to see; **¿ves algo?** can you see anything?; **no se ve nada aquí** you can't see a thing in here; **lo vi hablando con ella** I saw him talking to her **(b)** (mirar) ‹*programa/partido*› to watch; **~ (la) televisión** to watch television; **esa película ya la he visto** I've seen that movie before; ***no poder (ni) ~ a algn***: **no la puede ~** he can't stand her **2** (entender, notar) to see; **¿no ves lo que está pasando?** don't *o* can't you see what's happening?; **se la ve preocupada** she looks worried; ***hacerse ~*** (RPl) to show off **3 (a)** (constatar, comprobar) to see; **ve a ~ quién es** go and see who it is; **¡ya ~ás lo que pasa!** you'll see what happens; **¡ya se ~á!** we'll see **(b)** (ser testigo de) to see; **¡nunca he visto cosa igual!** I've never seen anything like it!; **¡si vieras lo mal que lo pasé!** you can't imagine how awful it was!; **¡hubieras visto cómo se asustaron!** (AmL) you should have seen the fright they got! **4 a ver**: **(vamos) a ~ ¿de qué se trata?** OK *o* all right, now, what's the problem?; **aquí está en el periódico — ¿a ~?** it's here in the newspaper — let's see; **apriétalo a ~ qué pasa** press it and see what happens; **a ~ si escribes pronto** make sure you write soon **5 (a)** (estudiar): **esto mejor que lo veas tú** you'd better have a look at this; **tengo que ~ cómo lo arreglo** I have to work out how I can fix it; **ya ~é qué hago** I'll decide what to do later **(b)** «*médico*» (examinar) to see; **¿la ha visto un médico?** has she been seen by a doctor yet? **6 (a)** (juzgar, considerar): **yo eso no lo veo bien** I don't think that's right; **a mi modo** *or* **manera de ~** the way I see it **(b)** (encontrar) to see; **no le veo salida a esto** I can't see any way out of this; **no le veo la gracia** I don't think it's funny **7** (visitar, entrevistarse con) ‹*amigo/pariente*› to see, visit; ‹*médico/jefe*› to see; **¡cuánto tiempo sin ~te!** I haven't seen you for ages! **8 tener ... que ver**: **¿y eso qué tiene que ~?** and what does that have to do with it?; **no tengo nada que ~ con él** I have nothing to do with him; **¿qué tiene que ~ que sea sábado?** what difference does it make that it's Saturday? ■ **~** *vi* **1** (percibir con la vista) to see; **así no veo** I can't see like this; **no veo bien de lejos/de cerca** I'm shortsighted/longsighted **2** (constatar): **¿hay cerveza? — no sé, voy a ~** is there any beer? — I don't know, I'll have a look; **pues ~ás, todo empezó cuando** ... well you see, the whole thing began when ... **3** (pensar) to see; **ya ~é** I'll see; ***estar/seguir en ~emos*** (AmL fam): **todavía está en ~emos** it isn't certain yet; **seguimos en ~emos** we still don't know anything

■ **verse** *v pron* **1** (*refl*) (percibirse, imaginarse) to see oneself **2** (hallarse) (+ *compl*) to find oneself; **me vi en un aprieto** I found myself in a tight spot; **me vi obligado a despedirlo** I had no choice but to dismiss him **3** (esp AmL) (parecer): **se ve bien con esa falda** she looks good in that skirt; **no se ve bien con ese peinado** that hairdo doesn't suit her **4** (*recípr*) **(a)** (encontrarse) to meet; **nos vemos a las siete** I'll meet *o* see you at seven; **¡nos vemos!** (esp AmL) see you! **(b)** (visitarse, encontrarse) to see each other; **nos vemos a menudo** we see each other often; **~se CON algn** to see sb

veraneante *mf* vacationer (AmE), holidaymaker (BrE)

veranear [A1] *vi*: **solía ~ en un pueblo** she used to spend her summer vacation (AmE) *o* (BrE) holidays in a small town

veraneo *m*: **fuimos de ~ al campo** we spent our summer vacation (AmE) *o* (BrE) holidays in the country; **lugar de ~** summer resort

veraniego -ga *adj* summer (*before n*)

verano *m* summer; (en la zona tropical) dry season; **ropa de ~** summer clothes

veras: **de veras** (*loc adv*) really; **lo siento de ~** I really am sorry; **¡no lo dirás de ~!** you can't be serious!

verbal *adj* verbal

verbena *f* **1** (Bot) verbena **2** (fiesta popular) festival; (baile) open-air dance

verbo *m* (Ling) verb

verdad *f* **(a)** (en general) truth; **dime me la ~** tell me the truth; **es la pura ~** it's the gospel truth; **a decir ~** ... to tell you the truth ...; **la ~, no lo sé** I don't honestly know; **¡no es ~!** that's not true!; **eso es una gran ~** that is *so* true! **(b) de verdad** (*loc adv*) really; (*loc adj*) real; **¡de ~ que me gusta!** I really do like it!; **una pistola de ~** a real gun **(c)** (buscando corroboración): **es guapa ¿~?** she's beautiful, isn't she?; **¿~ que tú me entiendes?** you understand me, don't you?

verdadero -ra *adj* **1 (a)** ‹*premisa/historia*› true; ‹*caso/nombre*› real **(b)** ‹*pieles/joyas*› real **2** (*delante del n*) (uso enfático) real; **se portó como un ~ imbécil** he behaved like a real *o* (colloq) proper idiot

verde *adj* **1** ▶ **97** ‹*color/ojos/vestido*› green; **zapatos ~ oliva** olive-green shoes; **ojos ~ azulado** bluish *o* (BrE) bluey green eyes **2** ‹*fruta*› green, unripe; ‹*leña*› green; ***estar* ~** (fam) (no tener experiencia) to be green (colloq); (en una asignatura): **está ~ en historia** he doesn't know much about history (colloq) **3** (Pol) Green **4** (fam) ‹*chiste*› dirty, blue (colloq) ■ *m* (color) ▶ **97** green; (Bot) greenery ■ *mf* (Pol) Green; **los ~s** the Greens

verdín *m* **(a)** (musgo) moss **(b)** (moho) mold*; (en el agua) slime; (en metal) verdigris

verdor *m* greenness

verdoso -sa *adj* ▶ **97** greenish

verdugo *m* **1 (a)** (en ejecuciones) executioner; (en la horca) hangman **(b)** (persona cruel) tyrant **2** (Indum) balaclava; (para el esquí) ski mask

verdulería *f* fruit and vegetable store, greengrocer's (BrE)

verdulero -ra *m,f* (persona) greengrocer

verdura *f* (Bot, Coc) vegetable; **sopa de ~** vegetable soup

vereda *f* **(a)** (senda) path **(b)** (CS, Per) (acera) sidewalk (AmE), pavement (BrE) **(c)** (Col) (distrito) district

veredicto *m* (Der) verdict; (dictamen) opinion, verdict

vergonzoso -sa *adj* **1** (tímido) shy, bashful **2** ‹*asunto/comportamiento*› disgraceful, shameful

vergüenza *f* **1** (turbación) embarrassment; **no lo hagas pasar ~** don't embarrass him; **me da ~ pedírselo otra vez** I'm embarrassed to ask him again; **sentí ~ ajena** I felt embarrassed for him (*o* her *etc*) **2** (sentido del decoro) (sense of) shame; **no tiene ~** he has no (sense of) shame **3** (escándalo, motivo de oprobio) disgrace; **ser una ~ para algo/algn** to be a disgrace to sth/sb; **estos precios son una ~** these prices are outrageous

verídico -ca *adj* true

verificar [A2] *vt* ‹*hechos*› to establish, verify; ‹*resultado*› to check; ‹*pagos/cuentas*› to check, audit; ‹*máquina/instrumento*› to check, test

verja *f* (cerca) railings (*pl*); (puerta) wrought-iron gate; (de ventana) (wrought-iron) grille

vermut /ber'mu(t)/ *m* (*pl* **-muts**) vermouth ■ *f* (CS) early evening performance

verosímil *adj* ‹*excusa/versión*› plausible; ‹*argumento/historia*› realistic

verruga *f* **(a)** (Med) (en la mano, cara) wart; (en los pies) verruca **(b)** (Bot) wart

versículo *m* verse

versión *f* **(a)** (de obra, suceso) version; **~ original** *movie in its original language* **(b)** (traducción) translation **(c)** (modelo) model

verso *m* (Lit) (línea) line, verse; (poema) poem; (género) verse; **en ~** in verse

vértebra *f* vertebra

vertebrado¹ -da *adj* vertebrate

vertebrado² *m* vertebrate; **los ~s** the vertebrates

vertedero *m* **1** (para basura) dump; **un ~ de residuos nucleares** a dumping site for nuclear waste **2** (desagüe) outlet

verter [E31] *or* [E8] *vt* **(a)** (en un recipiente) ‹*agua/vino/trigo*› to pour **(b)** (derramar) ‹*líquido*› to spill; ‹*lágrimas/sangre*› (liter) to shed (liter) **(c)** ‹*residuos radiactivos*› to dump

vertical *adj* **1 (a)** ‹*línea/madero*› vertical; **en posición ~** in a vertical position **(b)** (en crucigramas): **el tres ~** three down **2** (Pol, Rels Labs) vertical ■ *f* **(a)** (Mat, Tec) vertical line, vertical (tech) **(b)** (Dep) handstand

vértice *m* (de ángulo, figura) vertex, apex; (coronilla) crown

vertiente *f* **(a)** (de montaña, tejado) slope **(b)** (faceta, aspecto) aspect **(c)** (CS) (manantial) spring

vertiginoso -sa *adj* ‹*velocidad*› dizzy, giddy, vertiginous (frml)

vértigo *m* vertigo; **tener ~** to have vertigo; **me produce ~** it makes me dizzy *o* giddy

ves *see* VER

vesícula *f* ▶ 123 vesicle; **~ biliar** gallbladder

vespa® *f* Vespa®, scooter

vespertino -na *adj* evening (*before n*); **diario ~** evening newspaper

vespino® *m* moped

vestíbulo *m* (de casa particular) hall; (de edificio público) lobby; (de teatro, cine) foyer

vestido¹ -da *adj* dressed; **bien ~** well/badly dressed; **¿cómo iba ~?** what was he wearing?; **iba vestida de azul** she was wearing blue; **~ de uniforme** in uniform; **¿de qué vas a ir ~?** what are you going to go as?

vestido² *m* **(a)** (de mujer) dress; **~ de baño** (Col) swimsuit; **~ de noche** evening dress; **~ de novia** wedding dress *o* gown **(b)** (Col) (de hombre) suit

vestidor *m* (en casa) dressing room; (en club, gimnasio) (Chi, Méx) locker room (AmE), changing room (BrE)

vestier *m* (Col) (en tienda) fitting room; (en club, gimnasio) locker room (AmE), changing room (BrE)

vestir [I14] *vt* **1 (a)** ‹*niño/muñeca*› to dress **(b)** (proporcionar ropa a) to clothe (frml) **(c)** (confeccionar ropa a) «*modisto*» to dress **2** (liter *o* period) (llevar puesto) to wear ■ **~** *vi* **1** «*persona*» to dress; **~ bien** to dress well; **~ DE algo** ‹*de uniforme/azul*›) to wear sth; **~ de etiqueta** to wear formal dress **2** (ser elegante): **no sabe ~** he has no dress sense; **de ~** ‹*traje/zapatos*› smart

■ **vestirse** *v pron* (*refl*) **(a)** (ponerse ropa) to dress, get dressed; **date prisa, vístete** hurry up, get dressed **(b)** (de cierta manera): **se viste mal** he dresses badly; **se viste a la última moda** she wears the latest styles; **siempre se viste de verde** she always wears green **(c)** (disfrazarse) **~se DE algo** to dress up AS sth

vestón *m* (CS) jacket

vestuario *m* **1** (conjunto de ropa) wardrobe; (Cin, Teatr) wardrobe **2** (en club, gimnasio) locker room (AmE), changing room (BrE)

veta *f* **1 (a)** (en madera) streak **(b)** (en la carne) streak **(c)** (en roca, mármol) vein **2** (inclinación) bent, leanings (*pl*)

vetar [A1] *vt* to veto

veteranía *f* (experiencia) experience; (antigüedad) seniority

veterano -na *adj/m,f* veteran

veterinaria *f* (ciencia) veterinary science *o* medicine; (clínica) veterinary surgery

veterinario -ria *adj* ‹*clínica*› veterinary (*before n*); **médico ~** vet, veterinarian (AmE), veterinary surgeon (BrE) ■ *m,f* vet, veterinarian (AmE), veterinary surgeon (BrE)

veto *m* veto; **poner el ~ a algo** to veto sth

vez *f* **1** (ocasión) time; **una ~/dos veces** once/twice; **una ~ por semana** once a week; **me acuerdo de una/aquella ~ cuando** ... I remember once/that time when ...; **la última ~ que lo vi** the last time I saw him; **mil veces** *or* **miles de veces** a thousand times, thousands of times; **algunas veces** sometimes; **¿te has arrepentido alguna ~?** have you ever regretted it?; **érase una ~** (liter) once upon a time (liter); **por primera ~** for the first time; **otra ~** again; **déjalo para otra ~** leave it for another time *o* day; **otra ~ será** maybe next time; **una ~ más** once again **2** (*en locs*) **a la vez** at the same time; **a veces** sometimes; **cada vez** every *o* each time; **cada ~ más** more and more; **lo encuentro cada ~ más viejo** he looks older every time I see him; **cada ~ menos** less and less; **de una vez** (expresando impaciencia) once and for all; (simultáneamente) in one go; **de vez en cuando** from time to time, every now and then; **en vez de** instead of; **rara vez** seldom, hardly ever; **una vez** once; **una ~ que hayas terminado** once *o* when you have finished **3** (Esp) (turno en una cola): **¿quién tiene** *or* **me da la ~?** who's last?; **pedir la ~** to ask who's last

vi *see* VER

vía *f* **1 (a)** (ruta, camino): **la ~ rápida** the fast route; **una ~ al diálogo** a channel *o* an avenue for dialogue; **¡dejen ~ libre!** clear the way!; **~ de comunicación** road (*o* rail *etc*) link; **V~ Láctea** Milky Way; **~ marítima** sea route, seaway **(b)** (medio de transporte): **por ~ aérea/marítima/terrestre** by air/by sea/by land; Ⓢ **vía aérea** airmail **(c)** (medio, procedimiento) channels (*pl*); **por la ~ diplomática/política** through diplomatic/political channels **2 en vías de**: **está en ~s de solucionarse** it's in the process of being resolved; **países en ~s de desarrollo** developing countries; **una especie en ~s de extinción** an endangered species **3** (Ferr) track; **saldrá por la ~ dos** it will depart from track (AmE) *o* (BrE) platform two **4** (Anat, Med): **por ~ oral/venosa** orally/intravenously; **~s respiratorias/urinarias** respiratory/urinary tract ■ *prep* via; **~ Miami** via Miami

viable *adj* ‹*proyecto/plan*› viable, feasible; ‹*bebé*› viable

viaducto *m* viaduct

viajante *mf* traveling* salesman/saleswoman

viajar [A1] *vi* to travel; **~ en avión** to travel by plane; **~ en primera clase** to travel *o* go first class

viaje *m* trip, journey; **hacer un ~** to go on a trip *o* journey; **un ~ en tren** a train journey; **hizo el ~ en coche** he drove; **estar de ~** to be away; **salir de ~** to go on a trip; **en el ~ de vuelta** on the way back; **¡buen ~!** have a good trip!; **hicimos un ~ por todo Chile** we traveled all around Chile; **~ de negocios** business trip; **~ de novios** honeymoon; **~ organizado** package tour; **hice varios ~s para llevarlas todas** I made several trips to take them all

viajero -ra *m,f* traveler*; (pasajero) passenger

vial *adj* road (*before n*)

viáticos *mpl* (esp AmL) travel allowance

víbora *f* **(a)** (Zool) viper; **~ de cascabel** (Méx) rattlesnake **(b)** (fam & pey) (persona): **es una ~** he has a vicious tongue

vibración *f* vibration

vibrante *adj* ‹*voz*› vibrant, resonant; ‹*discurso*› vibrant

vibrar [A1] *vi* «*cuerdas/cristales*» to vibrate

vicaría *f* vicariate

vicario -ria *m,f* (párroco) vicar

vicecampeón -peona *m,f* runner-up

vicepresidencia *f* (Gob, Pol) vice presidency; (de empresa) vice presidency (AmE), deputy chairmanship (BrE)

vicepresidente -ta *m,f*, **vicepresidente** *mf* (Gob, Pol) vice president; (de empresa) vice president (AmE), deputy chairman/chairwoman (BrE)

vice versa *adv* vice versa

vichar [A1] *vi* (RPl fam) to peep (colloq) ■ ~ *vt* to peep at

viciado -da *adj* **1** ‹*atmósfera*› stuffy; **aquí dentro el aire está ~** it's very stuffy in here **2** ‹*estilo/dicción*› marred

viciar [A1] *vt* ‹*persona*› to get ... into a bad habit; ‹*estilo/lenguaje*› to mar

■ **viciarse** *v pron* **(a)** «*persona*»: **~ CON algo** to become addicted TO sth **(b)** «*estilo/lenguaje*» to deteriorate

vicio *m* **1** (corrupción) vice; **darse al ~** to give oneself over to vice **2** (hábito): **el único ~ que tengo** my only vice *o* bad habit; **el juego se convirtió en ~ para él** his gambling became an addiction; **se queja de ~** (fam) she complains for the sake of it

vicioso -sa *adj* ‹*persona*› depraved, debauched ■ *m,f* dissolute person

víctima *f* victim; **~ DE algo** victim OF sth; **fue ~ de una emboscada** he was the victim of an ambush; **~s del cáncer** cancer victims

victoria *f* victory; (Dep) win; **no cantes ~ antes de tiempo** don't count your chickens before they're hatched

victorioso -sa *adj* victorious

vicuña *f* vicuna

vid *f* vine

vida *f* **1 (a)** (Biol) life; **la ~ marina** marine life; **una cuestión de ~ o muerte** a matter of life and death; **quitarse la ~** to take one's (own) life (frml); **salir con ~** to escape alive **(b)** (viveza, vitalidad) life; **lleno de ~** full of life; **le falta ~** it's/she's/he's not very lively **2** (extensión de tiempo, existencia) life; **a lo largo de su ~** throughout his life; **toda una ~** a lifetime; **la ~ de un coche** the life-span of a car; **un amigo de toda la ~** a lifelong friend; ***amargarle la ~ a algn*** to make sb's life a misery; ***complicarse la ~*** to make life difficult for oneself; ***de por ~*** for life; ***hacerle la ~ imposible a algn*** to make sb's life impossible **3** (manera de vivir, actividades) life; **lleva una ~ muy ajetreada** she leads a very busy life; **¿qué es de tu ~?** what have you been up to?; **hace** *or* **vive su ~** he lives his own life; **¡esto sí que es ~!** this is the life!; **¡(así) es la ~!** that's life, such is life; **~ privada** private life; **su ~ sentimental** his love life; **una mujer de ~ alegre** a woman of easy virtue; **¡que ~ de perros!** it's a dog's life; **hacer ~ social** to socialize; ***estar encantado de la ~*** to be thrilled, to be over the moon (colloq) **4** (necesidades materiales): **la ~ está carísima** the cost of living is very high; **ganarse la ~** to earn one's *o* a living; **tiene la ~ resuelta** he's set up for life **5** (como apelativo) darling; **¡mi ~!** (my) darling!

vidente *mf* (que ve) sighted person; (que adivina) clairvoyant

video, (Esp) **vídeo** *m* **(a)** (medio, sistema) video; **en ~** on video **(b)** (cinta) videocassette, videotape, video (colloq); (grabación) video **(c)** (aparato) video (cassette recorder), VCR

videocámara *f* video camera, camcorder

videoclip *m* video

videoclub *m* (*pl* **-clubs** *or* **-clubes**) videoclub

videojuego *m* video game

videoteca *f* video library

videotex *m* videotex(t), teletext

vidriado -da *adj* glazed

vidriera *f* **(a)** (puerta) glazed door; (ventana) window; (en iglesia) *tb* **~ de colores** stained glass window **(b)** (AmL) (escaparate) shop window; **mirar ~s** to window-shop

vidrierista *mf* (AmL) window dresser

vidriero *m* glazier

vidrio *m* **(a)** (material) glass; **una botella de ~** a glass bottle; **fábrica de ~** glassworks **(b)** (esp AmL) (objeto): **limpiar los ~s** to clean the windows; **cambié uno de los ~s** I replaced one of the panes *o* windowpanes; **me corté con un ~** I cut myself on a piece of glass; **hay ~s rotos en la calle** there is broken glass in the street; ***pagar los ~s rotos*** to take the responsibility *o* blame **(c)** (de reloj) crystal, glass

vieira *f* (molusco) scallop; (concha) scallop shell

vieja *f* (Col, Méx, Ven fam) (mujer) broad (AmE sl), bird (BrE sl); *ver tb* VIEJO *m,f*

viejo -ja *adj* **1** [SER] ‹*persona/animal*› old; ‹*coche/ropa/casa*› old; **hacerse ~** to get old **2 (a)** [ESTAR] ‹*persona/animal*› (envejecido) old; **ya está ~** he's got(ten) old; **¡qué vieja estoy!** I look so old! **(b)** [ESTAR] ‹*zapatos/pantalones*› (desgastado) old **3** (*delante del n*) (antiguo) ‹*costumbre/amigo*› old; **los ~s tiempos** the old days; **~ Testamento** Old Testament ■ *m,f* **1** (*m*) old man; (*f*) old woman; **los ~s** old people, the elderly; **llegar a ~** to reach old age; **se casó de ~** he was an old man when he got married; **se murió de ~** he died of old age; **V~ Pascuero** (Chi) ⇒ PAPÁ NOEL; **~ verde** *or* (Méx) **rabo verde** (fam) dirty old man **2** (fam) (refiriéndose a los padres): **mi ~/mi vieja** my old man/lady (colloq); **tus ~s** your folks, your Mom and Dad **3** (AmL) (hablándole a un niño, al cónyuge etc) darling (colloq), love (colloq); (a un amigo) buddy (AmE), mate (BrE) **4** (Méx fam) (esposo) (*m*) old man (colloq); (*f*) old woman *o* lady (colloq)

Viena *f* Vienna

viendo *see* VER

viene, **vienes, etc** *see* VENIR

vienés -nesa *adj/m,f* Viennese

viento *m* **1** (en general) ▶ 346 wind; **correr** *or* **hacer ~** to be windy; **un ~ helado** an icy wind; **~ en contra/a favor** *or* **de cola** head/tail wind; **instrumento de ~** wind instrument **2** (de tienda de campaña) guy (rope)

vientre *m* **(a)** (cavidad) abdomen; **el bajo ~** the lower abdomen; **hacer de ~** to have a bowel movement **(b)** (región exterior) stomach, belly (colloq) **(c)** (de mujer embarazada) womb, belly (colloq)

viera, **vieras, etc** *see* VER

viernes *m* (*pl* ~) ▶ 193 Friday; **V~ Santo** Good Friday; *para ejemplos ver* LUNES

viese, **vieses, etc** *see* VER

viga *f* (de madera) joist, beam; (de metal) beam, girder

vigencia *f* validity; **entrar en ~** «*ley*» to come into force *o* effect

vigente *adj* ‹*pasaporte/contrato*› valid; ‹*legislación/precio*› current (*before n*); **estar ~** «*ley*» to be in force

vigésimo -ma ▶ 294 *adj/pron* twentieth; **~ primero** twenty-first; **el ~ aniversario** the twentieth anniversary; **la vigésima parte** a twentieth

vigía *mf* (persona) lookout

vigilancia *f* (atención, cuidado) vigilance; (por guardias, la policía) surveillance; **estar bajo ~** to be under surveillance; **servicio de ~** security patrol

vigilante *adj* vigilant, on the alert; **en actitud ~** on the alert ■ *mf* (en tienda) store detective; (en banco, edificio público) security guard; **~ jurado/nocturno** security guard/night watchman

vigilar [A1] *vt* **(a)** (cuidar, atender) to watch, keep an eye on **(b)** ‹*preso/local*› to guard, keep watch on; ‹*frontera/zona*› to guard, patrol; ‹*examen*› to proctor (AmE), to invigilate at (BrE) **(c)** (fam) (espiar) to watch ■ **~** *vi* to keep watch

vigilia *f* **1** (vela) wakefulness; **de ~** awake **2** (Relig) (víspera) vigil; (abstinencia) abstinence; (tiempo de abstinencia) day/period of abstinence

vigor *m* **(a)** (fuerza, energía) vigor*, energy; **con ~** vigorously **(b) en vigor** ‹*estar*› in force; **entrar en ~** to come into effect *o* force

vigoroso -sa *adj* ‹*persona/movimiento*› vigorous, energetic; ‹*esfuerzo*› strenuous

VIH *m* (= **virus de inmunodeficiencia humana**) HIV

vil *adj* (liter) ‹*acto/persona*› vile, despicable

villa *f* **1** (Hist) (población) town; **~ miseria** (Arg) shantytown **2** (casa) villa

villancico *m* (Christmas) carol

villano -na *m,f* (persona ruin) rogue, scoundrel

vilo: **en vilo** (*loc adv*): **la levantó en ~** he lifted her up; **permanecen en ~ esperando el resultado** they're on tenterhooks awaiting the result

vinagre *m* vinegar

vinagrera *f* **(a)** (para vinagre) vinegar bottle **(b) vinagreras** *fpl* (para aceite y vinagre) cruet set *o* stand

vinagreta *f* vinaigrette

vinatero -ra *adj* wine (*before n*) ■ *m,f* vintner (AmE), wine merchant (BrE)

vincha *f* (AmS) (elástica, rígida) hair-band; (hebilla del pelo) barrette (AmE), hair slide (BrE)

vinculación *f* (relación) links (*pl*), connections (*pl*); **~** CON *or* A **algo/algn** links *o* connections WITH sth/sb

vincular [A1] *vt* **(a)** (conectar, relacionar) **~ algo/algn** A *or* CON **algo/algn** to link sth/sb TO *o* WITH sth/sb; **están vinculados por lazos de amistad** they are linked by bonds *o* ties of friendship; **grupos estrechamente vinculados** closely linked groups **(b)** (comprometer) to bind, be binding on

vínculo *m* (unión, relación) tie, bond; **~s familiares** family ties

vine *see* VENIR

vinería *f* (AmL) wineshop, liquor store (*specializing in wines*)

vinero -ra *adj* (Chi, Per) wine (*before n*)

vinícola *adj* ‹*industria/producción*› wine (*before n*); ‹*región*› wine-producing, wine-growing

vinicultor -tora *m,f* wine producer, winegrower

viniera, **viniese, etc** *see* VENIR

viniste, **etc** *see* VENIR

vino *m* (bebida) wine; **~ dulce/seco** sweet/dry wine; **~ blanco/rosado/tinto** white/rosé/red wine; **~ de la casa** house wine

vino *see* VENIR

viña *f* vineyard

viñatero -ra *adj* (AmL) wine (*before n*), wine-growing (*before n*) ■ *m,f* (AmL) **(a)** (propietario) winegrower **(b)** (trabajador) vineyard worker

viñedo *m* vineyard

viola *f* **(a)** (instrumento) viola **(b) viola** *mf* (persona) viola player, violist (AmE)

violáceo -cea *adj* ▶ 97 purplish

violación *f* **(a)** (de persona) rape **(b)** (de ley, acuerdo, derecho) violation; (de templo) violation

violador -dora *m,f* **(a)** (de persona) rapist **(b)** (de ley, acuerdo) violator

violar [A1] *vt* **(a)** ‹*persona*› to rape **(b)** ‹*ley*› to violate, break; ‹*tratado/derecho*› to violate; ‹*templo*› to violate

violencia *f* violence; **recurrir a la ~** to resort to violence

violentar [A1] *vt* **(a)** (forzar) ‹*cerradura/puerta*› to force; ‹*persona*› to rape **(b)** (poner en situación embarazosa) to make … feel awkward
■ **violentarse** *v pron* to get embarrassed

violento -ta *adj* **1** (en general) violent; **utilizar medios ~s** to use violent means **2** (incómodo) ‹*situación*› embarrassing, awkward; **le resulta ~ hablar del tema** she finds it embarrassing to talk about it; **estaba muy ~** I felt very awkward

violeta *f* violet *m/adj inv* ▶ 97 violet

violín **(a)** *m* (instrumento) violin **(b) violín** *mf* (persona) violinist

violinista *mf* violinist

violón **(a)** *m* (instrumento) double bass **(b) violón** *mf* (persona) double bass player

violonchelista *mf* cellist

violonchelo *m* cello, violoncello

viral *adj* viral

virar [A1] *vi* **(a)** (Náut) to tack, go about **(b)** «*vehículo/conductor*» to turn; **viró bruscamente** she swerved **(c)** «*política/partido*» to veer

virgen *adj* **(a)** ‹*persona*›: **una mujer/un hombre ~** a virgin; **ser ~** to be a virgin **(b)** ‹*cinta*› blank; ‹*película*› unexposed **(c)** ‹*selva*› virgin ■ *f* virgin; **la V~** (Relig) the Virgin

virginidad *f* virginity

Virgo *m* (signo) Virgo; **es (de) ~** she's (a) Virgo, she's a Virgoan ■ *mf* (*pl* ~ *or* **-gos**) (persona) *tb* **virgo** Virgo, Virgoan

viril *adj* ‹*cualidades*› virile, manly

virilidad *f* virility

virreinato *m* viceroyalty

virtual *adj* **(a)** (potencial) virtual **(b)** (tácito) implicit

virtud *f* **(a)** (cualidad) virtue **(b)** (capacidad) power; **con ~es curativas** with healing powers

virtuoso -sa *adj* virtuous ■ *m,f* virtuoso

viruela *f* (enfermedad) smallpox; (marca) pockmark

virus *m* (*pl* ~) virus

viruta *f* shaving

visa *f*, (Esp) **visado** *m* visa

visar [A1] *vt* ‹*documento*› to endorse; ‹*pasaporte*› to visa

visceral *adj* **(a)** (Anat) visceral **(b)** ‹*odio/impresión*› visceral, deep; **un sentimiento ~** a gut feeling

vísceras *fpl* entrails (*pl*), viscera (*pl*)

visconde -desa *m,f* (*m*) viscount; (*f*) viscountess

viscosa *f* viscose

viscoso -sa *adj* viscous

visera *f* (de casco) visor; (de gorra) peak; (de jugador) eyeshade

visibilidad *f* visibility

visible *adj* **(a)** [SER] visible **(b)** (fam) [ESTAR] (presentable) presentable, decent

visillo *m* net curtain, lace curtain

visión *f* **1 (a)** (vista) vision, sight; **perdió la ~ de un ojo** she lost the sight of one eye **(b)** (aparición) vision; ***ver visiones*** to be seeing things **2** (enfoque, punto de vista) view; **una ~ romántica de la vida** a romantic view of life; **tener ~ de futuro** to be forward-looking

visionario -ria *adj/m,f* visionary

visir *m* vizier

visita *f* **(a)** (acción) visit; **hacer(le) una ~ (a algn)** to pay (sb) a visit; **ir de ~** to go visiting; **horario de ~** visiting hours *o* times; **~ a domicilio** house call; **~ de cortesía** courtesy call, duty visit; **~ guiada** (AmL) guided tour **(b)** (visitante) visitor; (invitado) guest; **espera una ~ importante** he's expecting an important visitor; **tener ~** to have visitors/guests

visitador social, **-dora social** *m,f* (AmL) social worker

visitante *adj* visiting (*before n*) ■ *mf* visitor

visitar [A1] *vt* **(a)** ‹*persona*› to visit, visit with (AmE) **(b)** ‹*lugar*› to visit

■ **visitarse** *v pron* (*recípr*) to visit each other

vislumbrar [A1] *vt* (en la distancia) to make out, discern (frml); (entre los árboles, las nubes) to glimpse; **a lo lejos se vislumbraba una iglesia** a church could just be made out in the distance

viso *m* (Indum) petticoat, underskirt

visón *m* mink

visor *m* **(a)** (en cámara) viewfinder; (para diapositivas) slide viewer **(b)** (Arm) sight

víspera *f* **(a)** (día anterior): **la ~** the day before **(b)** (tiempo anterior): **~s de fiesta** days prior to public holidays; **en ~s de un viaje** just before a journey

vista *f* **1 (a)** (sentido) sight, eyesight; **tener buena ~** to have good eyesight; **ser corto de ~** to be near-sighted; **perdió la ~** he lost his sight; **~ cansada** eyestrain **(b)** (ojos) eyes; **le hace daño a la ~** it hurts his eyes; **lo operaron de la ~** he had an eye operation **2** (mirada): **alzar/bajar la ~** to look up/down **3** (*en locs*) **a la vista**: **ponlo bien a la ~** put it where it can be seen easily; **estar/no estar a la ~** to be within/out of sight; **a la ~ de todos** in full view of everyone; **¿tienes algún proyecto a la ~?** do you have any projects in view?; **a primera** *or* **a simple vista** at first sight *o* glance; **con vistas a** with a view to; **en vista de** in view of; **en ~ de que** ... in view of the fact that ...; **¡hasta la vista!** see you!, so long! (colloq); ***perder algo/a algn de ~*** to lose sight of sth/sb; ***perderse de ~*** to disappear from view **4** (panorama) view; **con ~ al mar** with a sea view; **~ aérea** aerial view **5** (Der) hearing

vistazo *m* look; **darle** *or* **echarle un ~ a algo** to have a look at sth

viste, **visteis** *see* VER

viste, **vistieron, etc** *see* VESTIR

visto[1] -ta *adj* **1 (a)** (claro, evidente) obvious, clear; **está/estaba ~ que** ... it is/was clear *o* obvious that ... **(b) por lo visto** (*loc adv*) apparently **2** [ESTAR] (común, trillado): **un truco que está muy ~** an old trick; **eso ya está muy ~** that's not very original **3** (considerado): **en ciertos círculos eso no está bien ~** in some circles that is not considered correct; **estaba mal ~ que las mujeres fumaran** it was not the done thing *o* it was frowned upon for women to smoke

visto[2] *m* **(a)** (Esp) check (AmE), tick (BrE) **(b) visto bueno** approval; **tiene que dar el ~ bueno** she has to give her approval

visto *see* VESTIR, VER

vistoso -sa *adj* bright and colorful*

visual *adj* visual; **campo ~** field of vision

vital *adj* **1** (fundamental) vital; **de ~ importancia** of vital importance **2 (a)** (Biol, Med) ‹*órgano*› vital (*before n*) **(b)** ‹*persona*› dynamic, full of life

vitalicio -cia *adj* ‹*miembro/presidente*› life (*before n*); **cargo ~** post held for life

vitalidad *f* vitality

vitamina *f* vitamin

viticultor -tora *m,f* vine-grower

viticultura *f* vine-growing

vitorear [A1] *vt* to cheer

vitral *m* stained-glass window

vitrina *f* **(a)** (mueble — en tienda) showcase; (— en casa) glass cabinet, display cabinet **(b)** (AmL) (escaparate) shop window

vitrinear [A1] *vi* (Andes fam) to window-shop

viudez *f* (de mujer) widowhood; (de hombre) widowerhood

viudo -da ▶ 378 *adj*: **su madre es** *or* (Esp) **está viuda** her mother is a widow; **(se) quedó ~ a los 40 años** he lost his wife *o* he was widowed when he was 40 ■ *m,f* (*m*) widower; (*f*) widow

viva *m*: **dar ~s** to cheer; **fuera se oían ~s** cheering could be heard outside

vivacidad *f* (de persona) liveliness, vivacity; (de ojos) brightness

vivaracho -cha *adj* **(a)** ‹*ojos*› sparkling; ‹*niño*› lively **(b)** (AmL) (espabilado) crafty

vivaz *adj* ‹*persona*› lively, vivacious; ‹*ojos*› bright; ‹*imaginación*› vivid, lively

vivencia *f* experience

víveres *mpl* provisions (*pl*), supplies (*pl*)

vivero *m* (de plantas) nursery; (de peces) hatchery; (de moluscos) bed

viveza *f* **(a)** (rapidez, agilidad) liveliness; **~ de ingenio** readiness *o* sharpness of wit **(b)** (de recuerdo) vividness; **lo describió con gran ~** she described it very vividly **(c)** (de color) brightness; (de ojos, mirada) liveliness, brightness; (de emoción, deseo) strength, intensity

vividor -dora *m,f* pleasure seeker

vivienda *f*: **el problema de la ~** the housing *o* accommodation problem; **un bloque de ~s** an apartment building, a block of flats (BrE); **la construcción de 50 ~s** the construction of 50 homes *o* (frml) dwellings

vivir [I1] *vi* **1** (en general) to live; **vive solo** he lives alone *o* on his own; **~ para algo/algn** to live for sth/sb; **~ en paz** to live in peace; **la pintura no da para ~** you can't make a living from painting; **el sueldo no le alcanza para ~** his salary isn't enough (for him) to live on; **~ DE algo** ‹*de la caridad*› to live ON sth; ‹*del arte/de la pesca*› to make a living FROM sth **2** (estar vivo) to be alive **3** (*como interj*): **¡viva el Rey!** long live the King!; **¡vivan los novios!** three cheers for the bride and groom!; **¡viva!** hurray! ■ **~** *vt* **(a)** (pasar por): **~ momentos difíciles** to live in difficult times; **los que vivimos la guerra** those of us who lived through the war **(b)** ‹*personaje/música*› to live **(c)** ‹*vida*› to live

vivo -va *adj* **1 (a)** (con vida) alive; **no quedó nadie ~** no one was left alive; ***en ~*** ‹*actuación/transmisión*› live **(b)** ‹*lengua*› living (*before n*) **2 (a)** ‹*persona*› (despierto, animado) vivacious, bubbly; ‹*descripción*› vivid, graphic; ‹*relato/imaginación*› lively **(b)** ‹*color*› bright, vivid; ‹*llama/fuego*› bright; ‹*ojos/mirada*› lively, bright **(c)** ‹*sentimiento/deseo*› intense, strong **3** (avispado, astuto) sharp; **no seas tan ~** don't try to be clever ■ *m,f* (oportunista) sharp *o* smooth operator (colloq); (aprovechado) freeloader

vizconde -desa *m,f* (*m*) viscount; (*f*) viscountess

vocablo *m* (frml) word

vocabulario *m* vocabulary; **¡qué ~!** what language!

vocación *f* vocation; **tiene ~ de músico** he has a vocation for music

vocacional *adj* vocational

vocal *adj* vocal ■ *f* **1** (Ling) vowel **2 vocal** *mf* (de consejo, tribunal) member

vocalizar [A4] *vi* to vocalize

voceador *m* (Col, Méx) (de periódicos) newspaper vendor

vocear [A1] *vt* **(a)** ‹*mercancías*› to cry (dated); ‹*noticias*› to shout out **(b)** (hacer público) to spread **(c)** (corear) to shout **(d)** (Méx) ‹*persona*› to page

vocerío *m* clamor*, shouting

vocero -ra *m,f* (AmL) (*m*) spokesman, spokesperson; (*f*) spokeswoman, spokesperson

vociferar [A1] *vi* to shout, vociferate (frml)

vodevil *m* vaudeville (AmE), variety (BrE)

vodka *m* *or* *f* /'bo(ð)ka/ vodka

volado *m* **(a)** (Méx fam) (con moneda): **te lo juego a un ~** I'll toss you for it; **echar un ~** to toss *o* flip a coin **(b)** (RPl, Ven) (en costura) flounce

volador[1] **-dora** *adj* flying (*before n*)

volador[2] *m* (en pirotécnica) rocket

volanta *f* (RPl) horse-drawn carriage

volantazo *m* (Esp, Méx) swerve; **dar un ~** to swerve

volante *m* **1** (Auto) steering wheel; **ir/ponerse al ~** to be at/to take the wheel **2 (a)** (AmL) (de propaganda) leaflet, flier **(b)** (Esp) (para el médico) referral note *o* slip **3** (en costura) flounce **4** (Dep) shuttlecock

volantín *m* **1** (Chi) (cometa) kite; **encumbrar un ~** to fly a kite **2** (Per) (en gimnasia) somersault

volar [A10] *vi* **1** «*pájaro/avión*» to fly **2 (a)** «*tiempo*» to fly; **¡cómo vuela el tiempo!** doesn't time fly!; **las malas noticias vuelan** bad news travels fast **(b) volando** *ger* ‹*comer/cambiarse*› in a rush, in a hurry; **se fue volando** he/she rushed off; **sus clases se me pasan volando** her classes seem to go so quickly **3 (a)** (con el viento) «*sombrero*» to blow off; **~on todos los papeles** my papers blew all over the place **(b)** (fam) (desaparecer) «*dinero/pasteles*» to vanish, disappear ■ **~** *vt* **1** ‹*puente/edificio*› to blow up; ‹*caja fuerte*› to blow **2** (Méx, Ven fam) (robar) to swipe (colloq), to nick (BrE colloq)

■ **volarse** *v pron* **1 (a)** (Col fam) «*preso*» to escape **(b)** (Col, Méx fam) «*alumno*» to play hooky (esp AmE colloq), to skive off (school) (BrE colloq) **3 (a)** (Méx fam) (coquetear) to flirt **(b)** (Méx, Ven fam) (robar) to swipe (colloq), nick (BrE colloq)

volcán *m* volcano

volcánico -ca *adj* volcanic

volcar [A9] *vt* **1 (a)** (tumbar) to knock over **(b)** ‹*carga*› to tip, dump **(c)** (vaciar) to empty (out) **(d)** (Inf) to dump ■ **~** *vi* «*automóvil/camión*» to overturn, turn over; «*embarcación*» to capsize

■ **volcarse** *v pron* **1 (a)** «*vaso/botella*» to get knocked *o* tipped over **(b)** ⇒ VOLCAR *vi* **2** (entregarse, dedicarse) **~se** A **algo** ‹*a tarea*› to throw oneself INTO sth **3** (desvivirse) **~se** PARA *or* POR **hacer algo** to go out of one's way to do sth; **~se** CON **algn**: **se ~on conmigo** they bent over backwards to make me feel welcome

volea *f* volley

volear [A1] *vt/vi* (Dep) to volley

vóleibol, **voleibol** *m* volleyball

voleo *m*: **a** *or* **al ~** (al azar) at random; **contesté al ~** I said the first thing that came into my head

volibol *m* (Col, Méx, Ven) volleyball

voltaje *m* voltage

volteado -da *adj* (Col, Méx fam & pey) bent (pej), queer (pej)

voltear [A1] *vt* **1 (a)** ‹*mies*› to winnow; ‹*tierra*› to turn (over) **(b)** (por el aire) «*toro*» to toss; «*caballo*» to throw **2** (AmL exc CS) **(a)** ‹*tortilla/disco*› to turn over; ‹*cuadro*› to turn ... around; ‹*copa/jarrón*› (poner — boca arriba) to turn ... the right way up; (— boca abajo) to turn ... upside down **(b)** ‹*calcetín/manga*› (poner — del revés) to turn ... inside out; (— del derecho) to turn ... the right way round; **~ la página** to turn the page **3** (AmL exc CS) (dar la vuelta): **me volteó la espalda** she turned her back on me; **al oír su voz volteó la cara** when she heard his voice she turned her head **4** (CS) (tumbar, echar abajo) ‹*bolos/botella*› to knock over; ‹*puerta*› to knock down

■ **voltearse** *v pron* **(a)** (AmL exc CS) (volverse, darse la vuelta) to turn around; (cambiar de ideas) to change one's ideas **(b)** (Méx) «*vehículo*» to overturn, turn over

voltereta *f* somersault

voltio *m* volt

voluble *adj* (inconstante) changeable, fickle

volumen *m* **1** (en general) volume; **~ de ventas** volume of sales, turnover; **bajar/subir el ~** to turn the volume down/up; **a todo ~** on full volume, at full blast (colloq) **2** (tomo) volume

voluminoso -sa *adj* ‹*paquete*› sizeable, bulky

voluntad *f* **1 (a)** (facultad) will **(b)** (deseo) wish; **por expresa ~ de los familiares** by express wish of the family; **lo hizo por (su) propia ~** he did it of his own free will; **manifestó su ~ de renunciar** he expressed his wish to resign; **por causas ajenas a su ~** for reasons beyond his control **2** (firmeza de intención) *tb* **fuerza de ~** willpower **3** (disposición, intención): **con la mejor ~** with the best of intentions; **agradezco tu buena ~** I appreciate your willingness to help; **mostrar buena ~ hacia algn** to show goodwill to *o* toward(s) sb

voluntario -ria *adj* **(a)** ‹*acto/donación*› voluntary; **fue una elección voluntaria** I/he did it of my/his own free will **(b)** (*como adv*) voluntarily ■ *m,f* volunteer

voluptuoso -sa *adj* voluptuous

volver [E11] *vi* **1** (regresar — al lugar donde se está) to come back; (— a otro lugar) to go back; **no sé a qué hora ~é** I don't know what time I'll be back; **¿cómo vas a ~?** how are you getting back?; **ha vuelto con su familia** she's gone back to her family; **~** A **algo** ‹*a un lugar*› to go back TO sth; ‹*a una situación/actividad*› to return TO sth; **mañana volvemos a clases** tomorrow we go back to school; **quiere ~ al mundo del espectáculo** he wants to return to show business; **volviendo a lo que decía** ... to get *o* go back to what I was saying ...; **¿cuándo volviste de las vacaciones?** when did you get back from your vacation?; **ha vuelto de París** she's back from Paris **2** «*calma/paz*» to return; **~** A **algo** to return TO sth **3 volver en sí** to come to *o* round ■ **~** *v aux*: **~ a empezar** to start again *o* (AmE) over; **no ~á a ocurrir** it won't happen again; **lo tuve que ~ a llevar al taller** I had to take it back to the workshop ■ **~** *vt* **1** (dar la vuelta) **(a)** ‹*colchón/tortilla*› to turn (over); ‹*tierra*› to turn *o* dig over; ‹*calcetín/chaqueta*› (poner — del revés) to turn ... inside out; (— del derecho) to turn ... the right way round; ‹*cuello*› to turn; **~ la página** to turn the page **(b)** ‹*cabeza*› to turn; **volvió la mirada hacia mí** he turned his gaze toward(s) me **(c)** ‹*esquina*› to turn **2** (convertir en, poner): **la ha vuelto muy egoísta** it has made her very selfish; **me está volviendo loca** it's/he's/she's driving me mad **3** (Méx) **~ el estómago** to be sick

■ **volverse** *v pron* **1** (girar) to turn (around); **se volvió hacia él** she turned to face him; **no te vuelvas, que nos están siguiendo** don't look back, we're being followed; **se volvió de espaldas** he turned his back on me (*o* her *etc*); **~se boca arriba/abajo** to turn over onto one's back/stomach **2** (convertirse en, ponerse): **se ha vuelto muy antipático** he's become very unpleasant; **se vuelve agrio** it turns *o* goes sour; **se volvió loca** she went mad

vomitar [A1] *vi* to vomit, be sick; **tengo ganas de ~** I think I'm going to vomit *o* be sick, I feel sick ■ **~** *vt* ‹*comida*› to bring up; ‹*sangre*› to cough up

■ **vomitarse** *v pron* (Col, Méx, Ven) to vomit, be sick

vómito *m* **(a)** (acción) vomiting; **¿ha tenido ~s?** have you been vomiting *o* (BrE) sick? **(b)** (cosa vomitada) vomit

voraz *adj* ‹*persona/animal/apetito*› voracious; ‹*incendio/fuego*› fierce

vos *pron pers* [*Familiar form of address which is widely used instead of* TÚ *mainly in the River Plate area and parts of Central America*] **1** (como sujeto, en comparaciones, con preposición) you; **¿quién lo va a hacer? — vos** who's going to do it? — you (are); **che, ~** hey, you; **~ misma lo dijiste** you said so yourself; **menos que ~** less than you; **para/sin ~** for/without you **2** (uso impersonal) you; **dan tres opciones y ~ elegís** you're given three options and you choose one

vosear [A1] *vt* to address sb using the vos form

voseo *m* use of the vos form instead of TÚ

vosotros -tras *pron pers pl* [*Familiar form of address not normally used in Latin America or in certain parts of Spain, where* USTEDES *is used instead*] you; **¿quién lo va a hacer? — vosotros** who's going to do it? — you (are); **lo podéis hacer**

~ mismos you can do it yourselves; **más que ~** more than you; **para ~** for you

votación *f* (acción) voting; (método) vote; **decidir por ~** to decide by ballot; **fue elegida por ~** she was elected *o* voted in; **hagamos una ~** let's vote on it; **una ~ a mano alzada** a vote by a show of hands

votante *mf* voter

votar [A1] *vi* to vote; **~** POR **algo/algn** to vote FOR sth/sb; **~** A FAVOR DE/EN CONTRA DE **algo** to vote FOR/AGAINST sth ■ **~** *vt* ‹*candidato*› to vote for; ‹*reforma/aumento*› to approve, vote to approve

voto *m* **1** (en general) vote; **~ secreto** secret ballot *o* vote; **por ~ a mano alzada** by a show of hands; **~ de confianza/censura** vote of confidence/no confidence; **~ en blanco** blank ballot paper; **~ por correo** postal vote, absentee ballot (AmE) **2** (Relig) vow; **hacer los ~s solemnes** to take solemn vows

voy *see* IR

voyeurista /bwaɟe'rista, boɟer'ista/ *mf* voyeur

voz *f* **1** (en general) voice; **levantar la ~** to raise one's voice; **tener la ~ tomada** to be hoarse; **hablar en ~ baja** to speak quietly; **en ~ alta** ‹*hablar*› loudly; ‹*leer*› aloud, out loud; **quedarse sin ~** to lose one's voice; **una pieza a cuatro voces** (Mús) a piece for four voices, a four-part piece; **~ activa/pasiva** (Ling) active/passive voice **2 voces** *fpl* (gritos) shouting, shouts (*pl*); **hablar a voces** to talk in loud voices

vozarrón *m* booming voice

vudú *m* voodoo

vuela, vuelan, etc *see* VOLAR

vuelco *m* **1** (sobre sí mismo): **dar un ~** «*coche*» to overturn, turn over; «*embarcación*» to capsize **2** (cambio radical): **las cosas pueden dar un ~** things could change *o* alter drastically; **el mercado dio un ~ favorable** the market registered a favorable upturn **3** (Inf) dump

vuelo *m* **1 (a)** (acción): **el ~ de las gaviotas** the seagulls' flight; **remontar el ~** to soar up; ***alzar*** *or* ***levantar el ~*** «*pájaro*» to fly away *o* off; «*avión*» to take off; «*persona*» to fly *o* leave the nest; ***a ~ de pájaro*** (AmL): **un cálculo a ~ de pájaro** a rough estimate; **lo leí a ~ de pájaro** I just skimmed through it **(b)** (Aviac) flight; **son dos horas de ~** it is a two-hour flight; **~ charter/regular** charter/schedule flight; **~ internacional/nacional** international/domestic *o* internal flight; **~ sin motor** gliding, soaring (AmE) **2** (en costura) (amplitud): **la falda tiene mucho ~** it is a very full skirt

vuelo *see* VOLAR

vuelta *f* **I 1 (a)** (circunvolución): **dar ~s alrededor de algo** to go around sth; **da ~s alrededor de su eje** it spins *o* turns on its axis; **dar la ~ al mundo** to go around the world; **todo/la cabeza me da ~s** everything's/my head's spinning; **dar una ~ a la manzana** to go around the block; **dar toda la ~** to go all the way around **(b)** (Dep) (en golf) round; (en carreras) lap; **~ al ruedo** (Taur) lap of honor; **~ ciclista** cycle race, tour **(c)** (en carretera) bend; **el camino da muchas ~s** the road winds about a lot; **el autobús da muchas ~s** the bus takes a very roundabout route **2** (giro): **darle ~** A **algo** ‹*a llave/manivela*› to turn sth; **dale otra ~** give it another turn; **el coche dio una ~ de campana** the car turned (right) over; **~ (de) carnero** (CS) somersault; **~ en redondo** (vuelta completa) 360 degree turn, complete turn; (cambio radical) U-turn **3 (a) darle la ~** A **algo** ‹*a disco/colchón*› to turn ... (over); ‹*a calcetín*› (ponerlo — del derecho) to turn ... the right way out; (— del revés) to turn ... inside out; ‹*a copa*› (ponerla — boca arriba) to turn ... the right way up; (— boca abajo) to turn ... upside down; **dar la ~ a la página** to turn the page, turn over **(b)** (para cambiar de dirección, posición): **dar la ~** (Auto) to turn (around); **darse la ~** to turn (around) **4** (CS) **dar vuelta algo** ‹*disco/colchón*› to turn sth over; ‹*calcetín*› (ponerlo — del derecho) to turn sth the right way out; (— del revés) to turn sth inside out; ‹*copa*› (ponerla — boca arriba) to turn sth the right way up; (— boca abajo) to turn sth upside down; **dar ~ la página** to turn the page, turn over; **dio ~ la cara** she looked away; **¿damos ~ aquí?** (Auto) shall we turn (around) here?; **darse ~** «*persona*» to turn (around); «*vehículo*» to overturn; «*embarcación*» to capsize **5** (paseo): **dar una ~** (a pie) to go for a walk; (en coche) to go for a drive; (en bicicleta) to go for a ride **6 (a) a la vuelta (de la esquina)** (just) around the corner **(b) vuelta y vuelta** (Coc) rare **7 (a)** (regreso) return; (viaje de regreso) return journey; **a la ~ paramos para almorzar** on the way back we stopped for lunch; **a la ~ se encontró con una sorpresa** when he got back he found a surprise; **¡hasta la ~!** see you when you get back! **(b)** (a un estado anterior) **~** A **algo** return TO sth **8 (a)** (Esp) (cambio) change; **quédese con la ~** keep the change **(b) vueltas** (Col) (cambio, dinero suelto) change **9 (a)** (en elecciones) round **(b)** (de bebidas) round **10** (Per, RPl fam) (vez) time; **de ~** (de nuevo) again **11** (de collar) strand; (en labores de punto) row; (de pantalones) cuff (AmE), turn-up (BrE)

vuelto -ta *pp*: *see* VOLVER

vuelto *m* (AmL) change; **quédese con el ~** keep the change

vuelva, vuelvas, etc *see* VOLVER

vuestro -tra *adj* **(a)** (Esp) (de vosotros) your; **~s libros** your books; **un amigo ~** a friend of yours **(b)** (frml) your; **Vuestra Majestad** Your Majesty ■ *pron* (Esp): **el ~, la vuestra, etc** yours; **sabe lo ~** he knows about the two of you

vulcanizadora *f* (Chi, Méx) tire* repairshop

vulgar *adj* **(a)** (corriente, común) common; **un ~ resfríado** a common cold **(b)** (poco refinado) vulgar, coarse **(c)** (no técnico) common, popular

vulgaridad *f* (cualidad) vulgarity, coarseness

vulnerable *adj* vulnerable

Ww

W, **w** *f (read as* /ˈdoβle βe/, /ˈdoβle u/ *or* (Esp) /ˈdoβle ˈuβe/, /ˈuβe ˈðoβle/) *the letter* W, w

w. (= **watio**) w, watt

walkie-talkie /ˈwo(l)ki ˈto(l)ki/ *m* (*pl* **-kies**) walkie-talkie

walkman® *m* (*pl* **-mans**) Walkman®

wáter /ˈ(g)water *or* (Esp) ˈbater/ *m* **(a)** (inodoro) toilet; **(b)** ▶ **52** (cuarto) bathroom (esp AmE), toilet (BrE)

waterpolo /ˈ(g)waterpolo/ *m* water polo

WC /ˈbe θe, ˈuβe ˈðoβle θe/ *m* WC

weekend /ˈwiken/ *m* weekend

western *m* (*pl* **~** *or* **-terns**) western

whisky /ˈ(g)wiski/ *m* (*pl* **-kies** *or* **-kys**) whiskey*; **~ americano** bourbon

windsurf /ˈwinsurf/ *m* (deporte) windsurfing; (tabla) windsurfer, sailboard

windsurfing /ˈwinsurfin/ *m* windsurfing

windsurfista *mf* windsurfer

X, **x** *f (read as* /ˈekis/) *the letter* X, x

xenofobia *f* xenophobia

xilofón, **xilófono** *m* xylophone

Y, **y** *f (read as* /i ˈɣrjeɣa/, /je/ *or* (RPl) /ʒe/) *the letter* Y, y

y *conj* **1** (en general) and; **habla inglés y alemán** he speaks English and German; **¡yo gano el dinero y él lo gasta!** I earn the money and he spends it! **2 (a)** (en preguntas): **¿y tu padre? ¿qué tal está?** and how's your father?; **yo no oigo nada ¿y tú?** I can't hear anything, can you? **(b)** (fam) (expresando indiferencia) so (colloq); **¿y qué?** so what?; **¿y a mí qué?** so, what's it to me? **3** (esp RPl fam) (encabezando respuestas) well; **¿fuiste? — y sí, no tuve más remedio** did you go? — well yes, I had no choice; **y bueno** oh well **4** ▶ **293** (en números): **cuarenta y cinco** forty-five; **doscientos treinta y tres** two hundred and thirty-three

ya *adv* [*Both the simple past* YA TERMINÉ *and the present perfect* YA HE TERMINADO *are used to refer to the recent indefinite past. The former is the preferred form in Latin America while in Spain there is a tendency to use the latter*] **1 (a)** (en frases afirmativas o interrogativas) already; **¿~ te has gastado todo el dinero?** have you spent all the money already?; **~ terminé** I've (already) finished; **¿~ ha llegado Ernesto?** has Ernesto arrived yet?, did Ernesto arrive yet? (AmE); **aprietas este botón ¡y ~ está!** you press this button, and that's it! **(b)** (expresando que se ha comprendido) yes, sure (colloq) **2 (a)** (en frases negativas) any more; **ese color ~ no se lleva** nobody wears that color any more **(b) no ya … sino** not (just) … but **3** (enseguida, ahora) right now; **desde ~ te digo que no puede ser** (esp AmL) I can tell you right now that it's not possible; **~ mismo** (esp AmL) right away, straightaway (BrE); **¡~ voy!** coming!; **preparados listos ¡~!** on your mark(s), get set, go! **4** (con verbo en futuro): **~ te contaré** I'll tell you all about it; **~ lo entenderás** you'll understand one day **5** (uso enfático): **¡~ quisiera yo!** I should be so lucky!; **~ era hora** about time (too)!; **¡~ me tienes harta!** I'm (just about) fed up with you! **6 ya que** since, as; **~ que estás aquí** since *o* as you're here ■ *conj*: **se puede solicitar ~ sea en persona o por teléfono** it can be ordered either in person or by telephone

yacer [E5] *vi* (frml) to lie (frml)
yacimiento *m* **(a)** (de mineral) deposit; **~ petrolífero** oilfield **(b)** (Arqueol) site
yámper *m* (Per) jumper (AmE), pinafore dress (BrE)
yanqui *adj* (*pl* **-quis**) (fam) Yankee (colloq) ■ *mf* Yank (colloq), Yankee (colloq)
yapa *f* (CS, Per fam) *small amount of extra goods given free*, lagniappe (AmE); **dar algo de ~** to throw sth in (for free) (colloq)
yate *m* yacht
yayo -ya *m,f* (fam) (*m*) grandpa (colloq), granddad (colloq); (*f*) granny (colloq), grandma (colloq)
yedra *f* ivy
yegua *f* (Zool) mare
yelmo *m* helmet
yema *f* **(a)** (de huevo) yolk **(b)** (dulce) *sweet made with egg yolk and sugar* **(c)** (del dedo) fingertip **(d)** (Bot) leaf bud
yen *m* yen
yendo *see* IR
yerba *f* **(a)** *tb* **~ mate** maté **(b)** (Andes, Méx, Ven fam) (marihuana) grass (sl) **(c)** (césped) grass
yerbatero -ra *adj* maté (*before n*) ■ *m,f* (Andes) (curandero) witch doctor; (que vende hierbas medicinales) herbalist
yerga, **yergue** *see* ERGUIR
yerno *m* son-in-law
yerra, **yerras, etc** *see* ERRAR
yeso *m* **(a)** (Art, Const) plaster **(b)** (AmL) (Med) (plaster) cast; **me quitaron el ~** I had my cast taken off
yesquero *m* (Col, RPl, Ven) cigarette lighter
yo *pron pers* **(a)** (como sujeto) I; **~ que tú** if I were you; **¿quién quiere más? — ¡yo!** who wants some more? — me! *o* I do!; **soy ~** it's me; **¿quién, ~?** who, me?; **~ misma** myself; **estoy cansada — ~ también** I'm tired — so am I *o* me too **(b)** (en comparaciones, con ciertas preposiciones) me; **come más que ~** he eats more than me *o* more than I do; **llegó después que ~** she arrived after me
yodo *m* iodine
yoga *m* yoga
yogui *m* yogi
yogurt (*pl* **-gurts**, **yogur** *m* yogurt, yoghurt
yo-yo *m* (*pl* **-yos**) yo-yo
yuca *f* (tubérculo comestible) cassava, manioc; (planta ornamental) yucca
yudo *m* judo
yudoca *mf* judoka, judoist
yugo *m* yoke
Yugoslavia, **Yugoeslavia** *f* (Hist) Yugoslavia
yugoslavo -va, **yugoeslavo -va** *adj/m,f* (Hist) Yugoslavian
yugular *adj/f* jugular
yunque *m* anvil
yunta *f* (de bueyes) yoke
yute *m* jute
yuyo *m* **(a)** (Per, RPl) (hierba) herb; **té de ~s** herbal tea **(b)** (RPl) (mala hierba) weed **(c)** (Per) (alga) seaweed

Zz

Z, **z** *f* (*read as* /'seta/ *or* (Esp) /'θeta/) *the letter* Z, z
zacate *m* (AmC, Méx) **(a)** (hierba) grass; (heno) hay **(b)** (estropajo) scourer
zafar [A1] *vt* **(a)** (Chi, Méx) ‹*brazo/dedo*› to dislocate **(b)** (Col, Ven) ‹*nudo*› to untie; ‹*tuerca*› to unscrew; ‹*persona/animal*› to let … loose
■ **zafarse** *v pron* **(a)** (de compromiso) **~se DE algo** to get *o* wriggle OUT OF sth **(b)** (soltarse) «*persona/animal*» to get loose, get away **(c)** (*refl*) (Chi, Méx) (dislocarse): **~se la muñeca** to dislocate one's wrist
zafiro *m* sapphire
zaga *f* **(a)** (Dep) defense* **(b) a la zaga** ‹*ir/quedarse*› in the rear, behind
zaguán *m* hallway
zalamería *f*: *tb* **~s** sweet talk, flattery; **hacerle ~s a algn** to sweet-talk sb
zalamero -ra *adj* ‹*palabras*› flattering; **¡qué ~ estás!** you're being very nice (to me)! (iro)
zamarra *f* (chaqueta) leather/sheepskin jacket; (chaleco) leather/sheepskin jerkin
zamba *f* zamba (*South American folk dance*)
zambo -ba *adj* bowlegged ■ *m,f* (AmL) *person of mixed black and Amerindian origin*
zambomba *f* (Mús) *traditional drum-like instrument*
zambullida *f* (salto) dive, plunge; (baño) dip
zambullirse [I9] *v pron* (lanzarse) to dive (in); (sumergirse) to duck *o* dive underwater
zamuro *m* (Ven) turkey vulture
zanahoria *adj* **(a)** (RPl fam) (tonto) stupid **(b)** (Ven fam) (anticuado) square (colloq) ■ *mf* **(a)** (RPl fam) (tonto) idiot, nerd (colloq) **(b)** (Ven fam) (mojigato) straitlaced person; (anticuado) old fogey (colloq) ■ *f* (Bot, Coc) carrot
zanca *f* leg
zancada *f* stride; **bajaba la cuesta a ~s** he came striding down the hill
zancadilla *f* trip; **me hizo una ~** he tripped me (up)
zancos *mpl* stilts (*pl*)
zancuda *f* wader, wading bird
zancudo[1] -da *adj* **(a)** ‹*ave*› wading (*before n*) **(b)** (fam) ‹*persona*› long-legged

zancudo² *m* (típula) crane fly, daddy longlegs; (mosquito) (AmL) mosquito

zángano -na *m,f* **1** (fam) (persona) lazybones (colloq) **2 zángano** *m* (abeja) drone

zanja *f* (para desagüe) ditch; (para cimientos, tuberías) trench; (acequia) irrigation channel

zanjar [A1] *vt* ‹*polémica/diferencias*› to settle, resolve; ‹*deuda*› to settle, pay off

zapallito *m* (CS): *tb* ~ **largo** *or* **italiano** zucchini (AmE), courgette (BrE)

zapallo *m* (CS, Per) pumpkin

zapata *f* (Auto, Mec) brake shoe

zapatear [A1] *vi* **(a)** (en danza) to tap one's feet; (más fuerte) to stamp (*in time to the music*) **(b)** (para protestar, vitorear) to stamp (one's feet)

zapateo *m* tapping; (más fuerte) stamping

zapatería *f* **(a)** (tienda) shoe store (AmE), shoe shop (BrE) **(b)** (taller — de fabricación) shoemaker's, cobbler's; (— de reparación) shoe repairer's, cobbler's

zapatero -ra *m,f* shoemaker, cobbler

zapatilla *f* **(a)** (de lona) canvas shoe; (para deportes) sneaker (AmE), trainer (BrE); (alpargata) espadrille; (para ballet) ballet shoe; (pantufla) slipper **(b)** (Méx) (zapato de mujer) lady's shoe; ~ **de piso** flat shoe

zapato *m* shoe; **~s bajos/de tacón** low-heeled/ high-heeled shoes; ~ **de cordón** lace-up shoe; ~ **de goma** (Ven) sneaker (AmE), trainer (BrE)

zaperoco *m* (Ven fam) riot

zar *m* tsar, czar

Zaragoza *f* Saragossa

zarandear [A1] *vt* (de un lado a otro) to shake; (para arriba y para abajo) to shake *o* jog up and down ■ **zarandearse** *v pron* (esp AmL) «*tren*» to shake around; «*barco*» to toss about; **nos zarandeamos mucho durante el vuelo** we got shaken around *o* buffeted a lot during the flight

zarape *m* (en AmC, Méx) serape (*colorful blanket-like shawl worn esp by men*)

zarcillo *m* **1** (arete) earring **2** (Bot) tendril

zarina *f* czarina

zarpa *f* **(a)** (Zool) paw **(b)** (fam) (mano) paw (colloq)

zarpar [A1] *vi* to set sail, weigh anchor

zarpazo *m* (de gato, león) swipe; **me dio un** ~ it took a swipe at me (with its paw)

zarza *f* bramble, blackberry bush

zarzamora *f* (fruto) blackberry; (arbusto) bramble, blackberry bush

zarzo *m* (Col) loft, attic

zarzuela *f* (Espec, Mús) *traditional Spanish operetta*

zenit *m* zenith

zeppelin /sepe'lin, θepe'lin/, **zepelín** *m* zeppelin, airship

zeta *f*: *name of the letter* z

zigzag *m* (*pl* **-zags** *or* **-zagues**) zigzag

zigzaguear [A1] *vi* to zigzag

zinc *m* zinc; **techo de chapa de** ~ corrugated iron roof

zíper *m* (AmC, Méx, Ven) zipper (AmE), zip (BrE)

zócalo *m* **1** (rodapié) baseboard (AmE), skirting board (BrE) **2** (Méx) (plaza) main square

zodíaco *m* zodiac

zombi *mf* zombie

zona *f* **1** (área, región) area; **fue declarada** ~ **neutral** it was declared a neutral zone; Ⓢ **zona de carga y descarga** loading and unloading only; ~ **comercial** commercial district; ~ **de castigo** penalty area; ~ **industrial** industrial park; ~ **peatonal** pedestrian precinct; ~ **roja** (AmL) (zona de prostitución) red-light district; ~ **verde** park, green space **2** (en baloncesto) free-throw lane, three-second area

zonzo -za *m,f* (AmL fam) idiot, fool

zoo *m* zoo

zoología *f* zoology

zoológico *m* zoo, zoological garden (frml)

zoólogo -ga *m,f* zoologist

zoom /sum, θum/ *m* zoom (lens)

zopilote *m* (AmC, Méx) turkey vulture

zoquete *adj* (fam) dim, dense (colloq) ■ *mf* (fam) (persona) dimwit (colloq), blockhead ■ *m* (CS) (Indum) sock, ankle sock

zorra *f* (fam & pey) (prostituta) whore (colloq & pej), tart (colloq & pej); *ver tb* ZORRO 1 (a)

zorrillo *m* (AmL) (mofeta) skunk

zorro -rra *m,f* **1 (a)** (Zool) (*m*) fox; (*f*) vixen **(b)** (AmC, Méx fam) (oposum) opossum **2** (fam) (persona astuta) sly *o* crafty person; **3 zorro** *m* (piel) fox (fur) *ver tb* ZORRA

zorzal *m* thrush

zozobrar [A1] *vi* **1** «*barco*» (hundirse) to founder; (volcar) to capsize **2** «*proyecto/negocio*» to founder

zueco *m* clog

zumbar [A1] *vi* «*insecto*» to buzz; «*motor*» to hum, whirr; **pasar zumbando** «*bala/coche*» to whizz by; **me zumbaban los oídos** my ears were buzzing *o* ringing ■ ~ *vt* **1** (fam) ‹*persona*› to give ... a good hiding (colloq) **2** (Ven fam) (tirar) to chuck (colloq), to throw

zumbido *m* (de insecto) buzzing, droning; (de motor) humming, whirring

zumo *m* (esp Esp) juice

zurcir [I4] *vt* to darn, mend

zurdo -da *adj* left-handed; ‹*futbolista*› left-footed; ‹*boxeador/lanzador*› southpaw (*before n*) ■ *m,f* left-handed person; (tenista) left-hander; (boxeador) southpaw

zurra *f* (fam) (good) hiding (colloq)

zurrar [A1] *vt* (fam) to wallop (colloq), to give ... a (good) thrashing *o* hiding (colloq)

zurrón *m* (de pastor) leather bag; (de cazador) hunter's pouch

zancudo² *m* (típula) crane fly, daddy longlegs; (mosquito) (AmL) mosquito

zángano -na *m,f* **1** (fam) (persona) lazybones (colloq) **2 zángano** *m* (abeja) drone

zanja *f* (para desagüe) ditch; (para cimientos, tuberías) trench; (acequia) irrigation channel

zanjar [A1] *vt* ‹*polémica/diferencias*› to settle, resolve; ‹*deuda*› to settle, pay off

zapallito *m* (CS): *tb* **~ largo** *or* **italiano** zucchini (AmE), courgette (BrE)

zapallo *m* (CS, Per) pumpkin

zapata *f* (Auto, Mec) brake shoe

zapatear [A1] *vi* **(a)** (en danza) to tap one's feet; (más fuerte) to stamp (*in time to the music*) **(b)** (para protestar, vitorear) to stamp (one's feet)

zapateo *m* tapping; (más fuerte) stamping

zapatería *f* **(a)** (tienda) shoe store (AmE), shoe shop (BrE) **(b)** (taller — de fabricación) shoemaker's, cobbler's; (— de reparación) shoe repairer's, cobbler's

zapatero -ra *m,f* shoemaker, cobbler

zapatilla *f* **(a)** (de lona) canvas shoe; (para deportes) sneaker (AmE), trainer (BrE); (alpargata) espadrille; (para ballet) ballet shoe; (pantufla) slipper **(b)** (Méx) (zapato de mujer) lady's shoe; **~ de piso** flat shoe

zapato *m* shoe; **~s bajos/de tacón** low-heeled/high-heeled shoes; **~ de cordón** lace-up shoe; **~ de goma** (Ven) sneaker (AmE), trainer (BrE)

zaperoco *m* (Ven fam) riot

zar *m* tsar, czar

Zaragoza *f* Saragossa

zarandear [A1] *vt* (de un lado a otro) to shake; (para arriba y para abajo) to shake *o* jog up and down ■ **zarandearse** *v pron* (esp AmL) «*tren*» to shake around; «*barco*» to toss about; **nos zarandeamos mucho durante el vuelo** we got shaken around *o* buffeted a lot during the flight

zarape *m* (en AmC, Méx) serape (*colorful blanket-like shawl worn esp by men*)

zarcillo *m* **1** (arete) earring **2** (Bot) tendril

zarina *f* czarina

zarpa *f* **(a)** (Zool) paw **(b)** (fam) (mano) paw (colloq)

zarpar [A1] *vi* to set sail, weigh anchor

zarpazo *m* (de gato, león) swipe; **me dio un ~** it took a swipe at me (with its paw)

zarza *f* bramble, blackberry bush

zarzamora *f* (fruto) blackberry; (arbusto) bramble, blackberry bush

zarzo *m* (Col) loft, attic

zarzuela *f* (Espec, Mús) *traditional Spanish operetta*

zenit *m* zenith

zeppelin /sepe'lin, θepe'lin/, **zepelín** *m* zeppelin, airship

zeta *f*: *name of the letter* z

zigzag *m* (*pl* **-zags** *or* **-zagues**) zigzag

zigzaguear [A1] *vi* to zigzag

zinc *m* zinc; **techo de chapa de ~** corrugated iron roof

zíper *m* (AmC, Méx, Ven) zipper (AmE), zip (BrE)

zócalo *m* **1** (rodapié) baseboard (AmE), skirting board (BrE) **2** (Méx) (plaza) main square

zodíaco *m* zodiac

zombi *mf* zombie

zona *f* **1** (área, región) area; **fue declarada ~ neutral** it was declared a neutral zone; Ⓢ **zona de carga y descarga** loading and unloading only; **~ comercial** commercial district; **~ de castigo** penalty area; **~ industrial** industrial park; **~ peatonal** pedestrian precinct; **~ roja** (AmL) (zona de prostitución) red-light district; **~ verde** park, green space **2** (en baloncesto) free-throw lane, three-second area

zonzo -za *m,f* (AmL fam) idiot, fool

zoo *m* zoo

zoología *f* zoology

zoológico *m* zoo, zoological garden (frml)

zoólogo -ga *m,f* zoologist

zoom /sum, θum/ *m* zoom (lens)

zopilote *m* (AmC, Méx) turkey vulture

zoquete *adj* (fam) dim, dense (colloq) ■ *mf* (fam) (persona) dimwit (colloq), blockhead ■ *m* (CS) (Indum) sock, ankle sock

zorra *f* (fam & pey) (prostituta) whore (colloq & pej), tart (colloq & pej); *ver tb* ZORRO 1 (a)

zorrillo *m* (AmL) (mofeta) skunk

zorro -rra *m,f* **1 (a)** (Zool) (*m*) fox; (*f*) vixen **(b)** (AmC, Méx fam) (oposum) opossum **2** (fam) (persona astuta) sly *o* crafty person; **3 zorro** *m* (piel) fox (fur) *ver tb* ZORRA

zorzal *m* thrush

zozobrar [A1] *vi* **1** «*barco*» (hundirse) to founder; (volcar) to capsize **2** «*proyecto/negocio*» to founder

zueco *m* clog

zumbar [A1] *vi* «*insecto*» to buzz; «*motor*» to hum, whirr; **pasar zumbando** «*bala/coche*» to whizz by; **me zumbaban los oídos** my ears were buzzing *o* ringing ■ **~** *vt* **1** (fam) ‹*persona*› to give ... a good hiding (colloq) **2** (Ven fam) (tirar) to chuck (colloq), to throw

zumbido *m* (de insecto) buzzing, droning; (de motor) humming, whirring

zumo *m* (esp Esp) juice

zurcir [I4] *vt* to darn, mend

zurdo -da *adj* left-handed; ‹*futbolista*› left-footed; ‹*boxeador/lanzador*› southpaw (*before n*) ■ *m,f* left-handed person; (tenista) left-hander; (boxeador) southpaw

zurra *f* (fam) (good) hiding (colloq)

zurrar [A1] *vt* (fam) to wallop (colloq), to give ... a (good) thrashing *o* hiding (colloq)

zurrón *m* (de pastor) leather bag; (de cazador) hunter's pouch

Aa

A, a /eɪ/ *n* **(a)** (letter) A, a *f* **(b)** (Mus) la *m*

a /ə, *stressed form* eɪ/ ▶ 443 (*before vowel* **an**) *indef art* un, una; **a Mrs Smith called** llamó una tal señora Smith; **have you got a car?** ¿tienes coche?; **he didn't say a word** no dijo ni una palabra

AA *n* **1** (*no art*) = **Alcoholics Anonymous** **2** (in US) = **Associate in Arts** **3** (in UK) = **Automobile Association**

AAA *n* = **American Automobile Association**

aback /ə'bæk/ *adv see* TAKE ABACK

abacus /'æbəkəs/ *n* (*pl* **-cuses** *or* **-ci** /-saɪ/) ábaco *m*

abandon¹ /ə'bændən/ *vt* ‹*home/family*› abandonar; ‹*project/idea/search*› renunciar a; ‹*hope*› perder*; **to ~ ship** abandonar el barco

abandon² *n* [U]: **they were dancing with gay ~** bailaban desenfrenadamente

abandoned /ə'bændənd/ *adj* ‹*vehicle/cottage/wife*› abandonado

abase /ə'beɪs/ *v refl* **to ~ oneself** humillarse

abashed /ə'bæʃt/ *adj* (*pred*) avergonzado

abate /ə'beɪt/ (frml) *vi* «*storm/wind*» amainar; «*anger*» aplacarse*; «*noise/violence*» disminuir*; «*pain*» calmarse

abattoir /'æbətwɑːr ‖ 'æbətwɑː(r)/ *n* matadero *m*

abbey /'æbi/ *n* (*pl* **abbeys**) abadía *f*

abbot /'æbət/ *n* abad *m*

abbreviate /ə'briːvieɪt/ *vt* abreviar

abbreviation /ə'briːvi'eɪʃən/ *n* abreviatura *f*

ABC *n* **1** (alphabet, rudiments) abecé *m* **2** (in US) (*no art*) (= **American Broadcasting Company**) la ABC

abdicate /'æbdɪkeɪt/ *vt/i* abdicar*

abdication /'æbdɪ'keɪʃən/ *n* [U C] abdicación *f*

abdomen /'æbdəmən/ *n* abdomen *m*

abduct /æb'dʌkt ‖ əb'dʌkt/ *vt* (frml) raptar, secuestrar

abduction /æb'dʌkʃən ‖ əb'dʌkʃən/ *n* [C U] (frml) rapto *m*, secuestro *m*

abet /ə'bet/ *vt* **-tt-** ⇒ AID²

abeyance /ə'beɪəns/ *n* [U]: **to be in ~** estar* suspendido

abhor /əb'hɔːr ‖ əb'hɔː(r)/ *vt* **-rr-** (frml) detestar

abide /ə'baɪd/ *vt* tolerar, soportar

• **abide by** [*v* + *prep* + *o*] ‹*verdict/rules*› acatar

ability /ə'bɪləti/ *n* (*pl* **-ties**) capacidad *f*; **to the best of one's ~** lo mejor que uno pueda

abject /'æbdʒekt/ *adj* (frml) (*before n*) ‹*slave/flattery*› abyecto; **in ~ poverty** en la mayor miseria

ablaze /ə'bleɪz/ *adj* (*pred*): **to be ~** arder

able /'eɪbəl/ *adj* **1** (*pred*) **to be ~ to** + INF poder* + INF; (referring to particular skills) saber* + INF; **to be**

---

a

The indefinite article a *or* an *is translated by* un *before a masculine noun,* una *before a feminine noun*:

a car	=	un coche
an actress	=	una actriz

Singular feminine nouns, however, that begin with a stressed or accented a *or* ha *take the article* un *rather than* una:

an eagle	=	un águila
a fairy	=	un hada

The article is not translated in the following cases:
With jobs and professions:

she's an accountant	=	es contadora
he works as a waiter	=	trabaja de camarero

But the indefinite article is translated when there is a qualification:

he's a good dentist	=	es un buen dentista
she is an excellent teacher	=	es una profesora excelente

After what a:

what a shock!	=	¡qué susto!
what a big dog!	=	¡qué perro más grande!

After such a:

how could you do such a thing?	=	¿cómo pudiste hacer eso?
I have never said such a thing	=	nunca he dicho tal cosa
it's such a bore	=	es tan aburrido

Before a certain *when qualifying a subject noun*:

a certain man	=	cierto hombre

When expressing prices in relation to weight or length, the indefinite article is translated by el *before a masculine noun or* la *before a feminine noun*:

it costs 2 dollars a pound/3 dollars a meter	=	cuesta 2 dólares la libra/3 dólares el metro

When a *means* per, *there are various translations*:

twice a week	=	dos veces a la *or* por semana
three times a day	=	tres veces al día
50 miles an hour	=	50 millas por hora

~ to see/hear poder* ver/oír **2 abler** /'eɪblər ‖ 'eɪblə(r)/, **ablest** /'eɪbləst ‖ 'eɪblɪst/ (proficient) hábil

able-bodied /'eɪbəl'bɑːdid ‖ ˌeɪbəl'bɒdid/ *adj* sano, no discapacitado

abnormal /'æb'nɔːrməl ‖ æb'nɔːməl/ *adj* anómalo, anormal

abnormality /'æbnər'mæləti ‖ ˌæbnɔː'mæləti/ *n* [C U] (*pl* **-ties**) anomalía *f*, anormalidad *f*

aboard¹ /ə'bɔːrd ‖ ə'bɔːd/ *adv* (on ship, plane) a bordo

aboard² *prep* a bordo de; **~ the bus/train** en el autobús/tren

abode /ə'bəʊd/ *n* (liter *or* hum) morada *f* (liter *o* hum); **of no fixed ~** (Law) sin domicilio fijo

abolish /ə'bɑːlɪʃ ‖ ə'bɒlɪʃ/ *vt* abolir*

abolition /'æbə'lɪʃən/ *n* [U] abolición *f*

abominable /ə'bɑːmənəbəl ‖ ə'bɒmɪnəbəl/ *adj* **(a)** (horrible) ‹*deed*› abominable **(b)** (awful) (colloq) ‹*weather/food*› espantoso

abomination /ə'bɑːmə'neɪʃən ‖ əˌbɒmɪ'neɪʃən/ *n* [U C] abominación *f*

aboriginal¹ /'æbə'rɪdʒənl̩/ *adj* aborigen

aboriginal² *n* **(a)** (indigenous inhabitant) aborigen *mf* **(b)** ⇒ ABORIGINE

Aborigine /'æbə'rɪdʒəni/ *n* aborigen australiano, -na *m,f*

abortion /ə'bɔːrʃən ‖ ə'bɔːʃən/ *n* [C U] aborto *m* (*provocado*); **to have an ~** hacerse* un aborto, abortar

abortive /ə'bɔːrtɪv ‖ ə'bɔːtɪv/ *adj* frustrado

abound /ə'baʊnd/ *vi* abundar; **to ~ IN *o* WITH sth** abundar EN algo

about¹ /ə'baʊt/ *adv* **1** (approximately) más o menos, aproximadamente; **she must be ~ 60** debe (de) tener unos 60 años; **at ~ six o'clock** alrededor de *or* a eso de las seis; **~ a month ago** hace cosa de un mes **2 to be about to** + INF estar* a punto de + INF **3** (movement): **she can't get ~ very easily** le cuesta desplazarse; **he was waving a knife ~** blandía un cuchillo **4** (in the vicinity, in circulation) (esp BrE): **is Teresa ~?** ¿Teresa anda por aquí?; **there's a lot of flu ~** hay mucha gente con gripe

about² *prep* **1 (a)** (concerning) sobre, acerca de; **what's the play ~?** ¿de qué se trata la obra?; **he wants to see you about something** quiere verte acerca de *or* por algo; **she won — how ~ that!** ganó — ¡pues qué te parece! *or* ¡pues mira tú! **(b)** (pertaining to): **there's something ~ him that I don't like** tiene un no sé qué que no me gusta **2** (engaged in): **while you're ~ it, could you fetch my book?** ¿ya que estás me traes el libro?

aboutface /ə'baʊt'feɪs/, (BrE also) **about-turn** /-'tɜːrn ‖ -'tɜːn/ *n* cambio *m* radical de postura

above¹ /ə'bʌv/ *prep* **1 (a)** (on top of, over) encima de; **~ sea level** sobre el nivel del mar **(b)** (upstream of) más allá *or* más arriba de **2** (superior to) por encima de; ***to get ~ oneself*** (pej) subirse a la parra **3** (more than): **~ average** por encima de la media; **~ and beyond** más allá de

above² *adv* **1** (on top, higher up) arriba **2** (in text): **as shown ~** como se demostró anteriormente *or* más arriba; **see ~, page 43** véase página 43

above³ *adj* (frml) (*before n*): **for the ~ reasons** por dichas razones, por lo antedicho

above: **~board** /ə'bʌv'bɔːrd ‖ əˌbʌv'bɔːd/ *adj* (*pred*) legítimo; **open and ~board** sin tapujos; **~mentioned** /ə'bʌv'mentʃənd ‖ əˌbʌv'menʃənd/ *adj* antedicho

abrasive /ə'breɪsɪv/ *adj* ‹*powder*› abrasivo; ‹*surface*› áspero; ‹*tone/manner*› áspero

abreast /ə'brest/ *adv* **(a)** (side by side): **to march four ~** marchar en columna de cuatro en fondo **(b)** (up to date): **to keep ~ of sth** mantenerse* al día en *or* al corriente de algo

abridge /ə'brɪdʒ/ *vt* ‹*book*› compendiar; **~d edition** edición *f* condensada

abroad /ə'brɔːd/ *adv* ‹*live/work*› en el extranjero *or* el exterior; ‹*go*› al extranjero, al exterior; **I've never been ~** nunca he salido del país

abrupt /ə'brʌpt/ *adj* ‹*departure/conclusion*› repentino; ‹*rise/decline*› abrupto; ‹*manner*› brusco

abruptly /ə'brʌptli/ *adv* ‹*end/stop*› repentinamente; ‹*rise/fall*› bruscamente; ‹*speak/act*› abruptamente

abscess /'æbses/ *n* absceso *m*

abscond /æb'skɑːnd ‖ əb'skɒnd/ *vi* (frml) fugarse*

absence /'æbsəns/ *n* **(a)** [U C] (of person) ausencia *f* **(b)** [U] (lack) **~ OF sth** falta *f* DE algo

absent /'æbsənt/ *adj* ausente; **to be ~ FROM sth** faltar A algo

absentminded /'æbsənt'maɪndəd ‖ ˌæbsənt'maɪndɪd/ *adj* (temporarily) distraído; (habitually) despistado

absolute /'æbsəluːt/ *adj* **1** (complete) ‹*trust/confidence*› absoluto; **it was an ~ disaster** fue un absoluto desastre *or* un desastre total **2** ‹*right*› incuestionable; ‹*pardon/freedom*› incondicional; ‹*guarantee/monarchy/rule*› absoluto

absolutely /'æbsə'luːtli/ *adv* ‹*deny/reject*› rotundamente; ‹*impossible*› absolutamente; **I'm ~ certain** estoy segurísima *or* absolutamente segura; **you're ~ right!** ¡tienes toda la razón!

absolution /'æbsə'luːʃən/ *n* [U] absolución *f*

absolve /əb'zɑːlv ‖ əb'zɒlv/ *vt* **to ~ sb OF sth** absolver* a algn DE algo; **to ~ sb FROM sth** eximir a algn DE algo

absorb /əb'sɔːrb ‖ əb'zɔːb/ *vt* ‹*light/energy*› absorber; ‹*impact/shock*› amortiguar*; ‹*information*› asimilar; **to be ~ed IN sth** estar* absorto EN algo

absorbent /əb'sɔːrbənt ‖ əb'zɔːbənt/ *adj* absorbente

absorbent cotton *n* [U] (AmE) algodón *m* (hidrófilo)

absorption /əb'sɔːrpʃən ‖ əb'zɔːpʃən/ *n* [U] absorción *f*

abstain /əb'steɪn/ *vi* **1** (in vote) abstenerse* **2** (refrain) **to ~ FROM sth/-ING** abstenerse* DE algo/+ INF

abstract /'æbstrækt/ *adj* abstracto

absurd /əb'sɜːrd ‖ əb'sɜːd/ *adj* absurdo

absurdity /əb'sɜːrdəti ‖ əb'sɜːdəti/ *n* [C U] (*pl* **-ties**) lo absurdo

abundance /ə'bʌndəns/ *n* [U] abundancia *f*

abundant /əˈbʌndənt/ *adj* ‹*resources*› abundante; ‹*enthusiasm*› desbordante

abuse¹ /əˈbjuːs/ *n* **1** [U] (insulting language) insultos *mpl*; **a term of ~** un insulto **2** [C U] (misuse) abuso *m*; **sexual ~** abusos *mpl* deshonestos; **drug ~** consumo *m* de drogas

abuse² /əˈbjuːz/ *vt* **1 (a)** (use wrongly) ‹*power/hospitality*› abusar de **(b)** ‹*child/woman*› maltratar; (sexually) abusar de **2** (insult) insultar

abusive /əˈbjuːsɪv/ *adj* insultante

abysmal /əˈbɪzməl/ *adj* pésimo

abyss /əˈbɪs/ *n* (liter) abismo *m*

a/c (= **account**) cta.

AC /ˈeɪˈsiː/ **(a)** (= **alternating current**) CA **(b)** (esp AmE) = **air conditioning**

A/C = **air conditioning**

academic¹ /ˈækəˈdemɪk/ *adj* **1 (a)** ‹*career/record*› académico **(b)** ‹*child/student*› intelectualmente capaz **2** (abstract) ‹*question/debate*› puramente teórico

academic² *n* académico, -ca *m,f*

academy /əˈkædəmi/ *n* (*pl* **-mies**) academia *f*; (*before n*) **A~ Award** Oscar *m*

accede /əkˈsiːd/ *vi* (frml) **to ~ TO sth** (grant) acceder A algo

accelerate /əkˈseləreɪt/ *vi* «*vehicle*» acelerar; «*person*» acelerar; (Auto) apretar* el acelerador; «*process/growth*» acelerarse ■ **~** *vt* acelerar

accelerator /əkˈseləreɪtər ‖ əkˈseləreɪtə(r)/ *n* acelerador *m*

accent /ˈæksent ‖ ˈæksent, ˈæksənt/ *n* **(a)** (Ling, Mus) acento *m* **(b)** (emphasis) énfasis *m*

accentuate /əkˈsentʃueɪt/ *vt* **(a)** ‹*difference*› hacer* resaltar; ‹*fact/necessity*› subrayar; ‹*eyes/features*› realzar*, hacer* resaltar **(b)** ‹*syllable/word*› acentuar*

accept /əkˈsept/ *vt* aceptar; **do you ~ that you were wrong?** ¿reconoces que estabas equivocado?

acceptable /əkˈseptəbəl/ *adj* (satisfactory) aceptable; (tolerable) admisible

acceptance /əkˈsæptəns/ *n* **1** [U C] (of offer, responsibility) aceptación *f* **2** [U] (approval) aprobación *f*

access¹ /ˈækses/ *n* [U] acceso *m*; (*before n*) **~ road** carretera *f* de acceso

access² *vt* (Comput) obtener* acceso a, entrar a

accessible /əkˈsesəbəl/ *adj* accesible

accession /əkˈseʃən, ækˈseʃən/ *n* (frml) **(a)** [U] (to throne, power) acceso *m* **(b)** [U C] (acquisition) adquisición *f*

accessory /əkˈsesəri/ *n* (*pl* **-ries**) **1 (a)** (extra) accesorio *m* **(b)** **accessories** *pl* (Clothing) accesorios *mpl* **2** (Law) **~ (TO sth)** cómplice *mf* (EN algo)

accident /ˈæksədənt ‖ ˈæksɪdənt/ *n* **(a)** [C] (mishap) accidente *m* **(b)** [C U] (chance) casualidad *f*; **by ~** (by chance) por casualidad; (unintentionally) sin querer

accidental /ˈæksəˈdentl ‖ ˌæksɪˈdentl/ *adj* ‹*discovery/meeting*› fortuito; ‹*blow*› accidental; **~ death** muerte *f* por caso fortuito

accidentally /ˈæksəˈdentli ‖ ˌæksɪˈdentəli/ *adv* **(a)** (unintentionally) sin querer **(b)** (by chance) por casualidad, de manera fortuita

accident-prone /ˈæksədəntprəʊn ‖ ˈæksɪdənt prəʊn/ *adj* propenso a los accidentes

acclaim¹ /əˈkleɪm/ *vt* aclamar

acclaim² *n* [U] aclamación *f*

acclimate /ˈækləmeɪt/ *vt* (AmE) ⇒ ACCLIMATIZE

acclimatize /əˈklaɪmətaɪz/ *vt* aclimatar; **to become ~d TO sth** aclimatarse A algo

accolade /ˈækəleɪd/ *n* (praise) elogio *m*; (honor) honor *m*; (award) galardón *m*

accommodate /əˈkɑːmədeɪt ‖ əˈkɒmədeɪt/ *vt* **1 (a)** (provide lodging for) ‹*guests*› alojar **(b)** (have room for) tener* cabida para **2** (cater to) ‹*wish/need*› tener* en cuenta

accommodating /əˈkɑːmədeɪtɪŋ ‖ əˈkɒmədeɪtɪŋ/ *adj* complaciente

accommodation /əˈkɑːməˈdeɪʃən ‖ əˌkɒməˈdeɪʃən/ *n* **1 (a)** [U] (AmE also) **accommodations** (lodgings) alojamiento *m* **(b)** [C] (seat, berth) (AmE) plaza *f* **2** [U] (agreement, compromise) acuerdo *m*

accompaniment /əˈkʌmpənimənt/ *n* [U C] acompañamiento *m*

accompanist /əˈkʌmpənəst ‖ əˈkʌmpənɪst/ *n* acompañante *mf*

accompany /əˈkʌmpəni/ *vt* **-nies, -nying, -nied (a)** (go with) acompañar **(b)** (Mus) acompañar

accomplice /əˈkɑːmpləs ‖ əˈkʌmplɪs/ *n* cómplice *mf*

accomplish /əˈkɑːmplɪʃ ‖ əˈkʌmplɪʃ/ *vt* ‹*task*› llevar a cabo; ‹*goal*› lograr

accomplished /əˈkɑːmplɪʃt ‖ əˈkʌmplɪʃt/ *adj* ‹*performer/liar/thief*› consumado; ‹*performance*› logrado

accomplishment /əˈkɑːmplɪʃmənt ‖ əˈkʌmplɪʃmənt/ *n* **(a)** [U] (of aim) logro *m* **(b)** [C] (success) logro *m* **(c)** [C U] (skill) habilidad *f*

accord /əˈkɔːrd ‖ əˈkɔːd/ *n* [U C] acuerdo *m*; ***of one's own ~*** (de) motu proprio

accordance /əˈkɔːrdn̩s ‖ əˈkɔːdn̩s/ *n*: **in ~ with** de acuerdo con *or* a, según

according /əˈkɔːrdɪŋ ‖ əˈkɔːdɪŋ/ **according to** *prep* según

accordion /əˈkɔːrdiən ‖ əˈkɔːdiən/ *n* acordeón *m*

accost /əˈkɔːst ‖ əˈkɒst/ *vt* abordar

account /əˈkaʊnt/ *n* **I 1** (explanation) explicación *f*; (version) versión *f*; (report) informe *m*; **by all ~s** a decir de todos **2** (consideration): **to take sth into ~** tener* algo en cuenta **3** (*in phrases*) **on account of** (*as prep*) debido a; **on no account** de ningún modo, de ninguna manera; **on sb's account** por algn

II 1 (with bank, at shop) cuenta *f* **2** **accounts** (Busn, Fin) (+ *pl vb*) contabilidad *f*

● **account for** [*v* + *prep* + *o*] **1 (a)** (provide record of, justify) ‹*expenditure/time*› dar* cuentas de **(b)** (explain) explicar*; ***there's no ~ing for taste*** sobre gustos no hay nada escrito **2** (add up to): **wages ~ for 70% of the total** los sueldos representan un *or* el 70% del total

accountable /əˈkaʊntəbəl/ *adj* (*pred*) responsable; **to be ~ TO sb (FOR sth)** ser* responsable ANTE algn (DE algo)

accountancy /ə'kaʊntn̩si/ *n* [U] contabilidad *f*
accountant /ə'kaʊntn̩t/ *n* contador, -dora *m,f* (AmL), contable *mf* (Esp)
accredit /ə'kredət ‖ ə'kredɪt/ *vt* (*usu pass*) acreditar
accrue /ə'kru:/ *vi* acumularse ■ ~ *vt* acumular
accumulate /ə'kju:mjəleɪt ‖ ə'kju:mjʊleɪt/ *vt* ‹*wealth/interest*› acumular; ‹*information/evidence*› reunir* ■ ~ *vi* acumularse
accuracy /'ækjərəsi/ *n* [U] (of measurement, instrument, description, translation) exactitud *f*; (of weapon) precisión *f*; (of aim, blow) lo certero
accurate /'ækjərət/ *adj* ‹*measurement/instrument/description/translation*› exacto; ‹*weapon/aim/blow*› certero
accusation /'ækjə'zeɪʃən ‖ ˌækju:'zeɪʃən/ *n* [C U] acusación *f*
accuse /ə'kju:z/ *vt* acusar
accused /ə'kju:zd/ *n* (*pl* ~) (Law) **the** ~ el acusado, la acusada; (*pl*) los acusados, las acusadas
accusing /ə'kju:zɪŋ/ *adj* acusador
accustom /ə'kʌstəm/ *vt* **to** ~ **sb** TO **sth**/-ING acostumbrar a algn A algo/+INF
accustomed /ə'kʌstəmd/ *adj* (*pred*) **to be** ~ TO **sth**/-ING estar* acostumbrado A algo/+ INF; **to become** ~ TO **sth**/-ING acostumbrarse A algo/+ INF
AC/DC /'eɪsi:'di:si:/ *adj* (Elec) CA/CC
ace /eɪs/ *n* **(a)** (in cards, dice) as *m* **(b)** (expert, champion) as *m*
ache¹ /eɪk/ ▶ 484 *vi* **(a)** «*tooth/ear/leg*» doler*; **my back** ~**s** me duele la espalda **(b) aching** *pres p* ‹*shoulders/muscles*› dolorido
ache² ▶ 484 *n* dolor *m* (*sordo y continuo*); ~**s and pains** achaques *mpl*
achieve /ə'tʃi:v/ *vt* **(a)** (accomplish) lograr **(b)** (attain) ‹*success/victory*› conseguir*, obtener*; ‹*aim*› lograr, conseguir*; ‹*ambition*› hacer* realidad
achievement /ə'tʃi:vmənt/ *n* **(a)** [C] (feat) logro *m* **(b)** [U] (success) éxito *m*; **a sense of** ~ la satisfacción de haber logrado algo
Achilles heel /ə'kɪli:z/ *n* talón *m* de Aquiles
acid¹ /'æsəd ‖ 'æsɪd/ *n* [U C] ácido *m*
acid², **acidic** /ə'sɪdɪk/ *adj* ácido
acid rain *n* [U] lluvia *f* ácida
acknowledge /ək'nɑ:lɪdʒ ‖ ək'nɒlɪdʒ/ *vt* **1 (a)** (admit) ‹*mistake/failure*› admitir **(b)** (recognize) ‹*skill/authority/right*› reconocer*; ‹*quotations/sources*› hacer* mención de **(c)** (express appreciation of) agradecer* **2** ‹*letter/order*› acusar recibo de; ‹*greeting*› responder a; ‹*person*› saludar
acknowledgment, **acknowledgement** /ək'nɑ:lɪdʒmənt ‖ ək'nɒlɪdʒmənt/ *n* [C U] **(a)** (recognition) reconocimiento *m* **(b)** (confirmation, response): **I've had no** ~ **of my letter** no han acusado recibo de mi carta **(c) acknowledgments** *pl* (in book) lista *f* de menciones
acne /'ækni/ *n* [U] acné *m* or *f*, acne *f*‡
acorn /'eɪkɔ:rn ‖ 'eɪkɔ:n/ *n* bellota *f*
acoustic /ə'ku:stɪk/ *adj* acústico
acoustics /ə'ku:stɪks/ *n* (of room) (+ *pl vb*) acústica *f*
acquaintance /ə'kweɪntn̩s/ *n* **(a)** [C] (person) conocido, -da *m,f* **(b)** [U C] (with person) relación *f*; **to make sb's** ~ conocer* a algn **(c)** [U C] (knowledge) ~ WITH **sth** conocimiento *m* DE algo
acquainted /ə'kweɪntəd ‖ ə'kweɪntɪd/ *adj* (*pred*) **(a) to be** ~ WITH **sb** conocer* a algn **(b) to be** ~ WITH **sth** (be informed of) estar* al corriente DE algo; (be familiar with) estar* familiarizado CON algo
acquiesce /ˌækwi'es/ *vi* **to** ~ (IN **sth**/-ING) consentir* (algo/EN + INF)
acquire /ə'kwaɪr ‖ ə'kwaɪə(r)/ *vt* ‹*collection/skill*› adquirir*; ‹*reputation*› hacerse*
acquired /ə'kwaɪrd ‖ ə'kwaɪəd/ *adj* ‹*characteristic*› adquirido; **it's an** ~ **taste** es algo a lo que se le va tomando el gusto con el tiempo
acquisition /'ækwə'zɪʃən ‖ ˌækwɪ'zɪʃən/ *n* [C U] adquisición *f*
acquit /ə'kwɪt/ *vt* **-tt- to** ~ **sb** (OF **sth**) absolver* a algn (DE algo)
acre /'eɪkər ‖ 'eɪkə(r)/ *n* acre *m* (*0,405 hectáreas*)
acrid /'ækrəd ‖ 'ækrɪd/ *adj* acre
acrobat /'ækrəbæt/ *n* acróbata *mf*
acrobatic /'ækrə'bætɪk/ *adj* acrobático
across¹ /ə'krɔ:s ‖ ə'krɒs/ *adv* **(a)** (indicating movement): **the boatman ferried them** ~ el barquero los cruzó **(b)** (indicating position) del otro lado; **she sat** ~ **from me** estaba sentada frente a mí **(c)** (in width, diameter): **it is 20m** ~ tiene *or* mide 20m de ancho
across² *prep* **(a)** (from one side to other): **they ran** ~ **the road** cruzaron la calle corriendo **(b)** (on the other side of): **they live just** ~ **the road** viven justo enfrente; **it's** ~ **the river** está al otro lado del río
acrylic /ə'krɪlɪk/ *n* [U C] acrílico *m*; (*before n*) acrílico
act¹ /ækt/ *vi* **1 (a)** (take action, do sth) actuar* **(b)** «*drug/chemical*» hacer* efecto **(c)** (serve) **to** ~ AS **sth** servir* DE algo; **she will** ~ **as interpreter** hará de intérprete **(d) acting** *pres p* ‹*chairman/director*› interino **2** (behave) comportarse; **don't** ~ **dumb** ¡no te hagas el tonto! **3** (perform) actuar*; (as profession) ser* actor/actriz ■ ~ *vt* **(a)** (perform) ‹*role/part*› interpretar **(b)** (behave like, play role of) hacerse*
● **act for** [*v* + *prep* + *o*] (represent) representar
● **act on** [*v* + *prep* + *o*] **(a)** (follow) ‹*advice*› seguir*; ‹*orders*› cumplir **(b)** (affect) «*drug/chemical*» actuar* sobre
● **act out** [*v* + *o* + *adv*, *v* + *adv* + *o*] representar
act² *n* **1** (deed) acto *m*; ***to catch sb in the*** ~ agarrar *or* (esp Esp) coger* a algn con las manos en la masa **2** (Govt) ley *f* **3 (a)** (division of play) acto *m* **(b)** (routine) número *m*; ***to get one's*** ~ ***together*** organizarse* **4** (pretense): **it was all a big** ~ era puro cuento (fam)
acting /'æktɪŋ/ *n* [U] (performance) interpretación *f*; **have you done any** ~ **before?** ¿has hecho teatro/cine alguna vez?
action /'ækʃən/ *n* **1** [U] **(a)** (practical measures): **prompt** ~ **by the police saved several lives** la rápida actuación de la policía salvó varias vidas; **to take** ~ **(against sb/sth)** tomar medidas

(contra algn/algo); **~!** (Cin) ¡acción! **(b)** (*in phrases*) **to put sth into ~** poner* algo en práctica; **to be out of ~** «*car*» estar* averiado; «*person*» estar* fuera de circulación **2** [C] (deed) acto *m* **3** [U] (Mil) acción *f* (de guerra) **4** [U] **(a)** (plot of play, movie) acción *f* **(b)** (exciting activity) animación *f* **5 (a)** [C] (movement) movimiento *m* **(b)** [U] (operation) funcionamiento *m* **(c)** [U] (of drug, chemical) acción *f*

action: **~-packed** *adj* lleno de acción; **~ replay** *n* (BrE) repetición *f* de la jugada

active /'æktɪv/ *adj* **1** ‹*person/life*› activo; ‹*volcano*› en actividad **2** (Ling) activo

activist /'æktəvəst ‖ 'æktɪvɪst/ *n* activista *mf*

activity /æk'tɪvəti/ *n* (*pl* **-ties**) [C U] actividad *f*

actor /'æktər ‖ 'æktə(r)/ *n* actor, actriz *m,f*

actress /'æktrəs/ *n* actriz *f*

actual /'æktʃuəl/ *adj* (*before n*) **(a)** (real) real; **in ~ fact** en realidad **(b)** (precise, very) mismo; **on the ~ day of the election** el mismo día de las elecciones

actually /'æktʃuəli/ *adv* en realidad; **~, I'd rather not go** la verdad es que preferiría no ir

acumen /ə'kju:mən ‖ 'ækju:mən/ *n* [U] sagacidad *f*, perspicacia *f*; **business ~** visión *f* para los negocios

acupuncture /'ækjəˌpʌŋktʃər ‖ 'ækjʊˌpʌŋktʃə(r)/ *n* [U] acupuntura *f*

acute /ə'kju:t/ *adj* **1** ‹*condition/pain*› agudo; ‹*crisis/shortage*› grave; ‹*anxiety*› profundo; ‹*sense of smell*› fino; ‹*sight/hearing*› agudo **2** (Ling) ‹*accent*› agudo

ad /æd/ *n* (colloq) ⇒ ADVERTISEMENT

AD (= **Anno Domini**) después de Cristo; (written form) d. de C., d. de J.C.

Adam /'ædəm/ *n* Adán; **~'s apple** nuez *f* (de Adán)

adamant /'ædəmənt/ *adj* ‹*refusal*› firme; **she was ~ that she wouldn't go** se mantuvo firme en su decisión de no ir

adapt /ə'dæpt/ *vt* adaptar ■ **~** *vi* **to ~** (TO **sth**/ -ING) adaptarse (A algo/+ INF)

adaptable /ə'dæptəbəl/ *adj* adaptable

adaptation /'ædæp'teɪʃən/ *n* [U C] adaptación *f*

adapter, **adaptor** /ə'dæptər ‖ ə'dæptə(r)/ *n* (plug — with several sockets) enchufe *m* múltiple; (— for different sockets) adaptador *m*

add /æd/ *vt* **1** (put in in addition) añadir; **at least I think so, she ~ed** —al menos eso creo —añadió **2** (Math) sumar; **~ the numbers together** suma los números **3 added** *past p* ‹*bonus/incentive*› adicional; **with ~ed vitamins** con vitaminas

• **add to** [*v* + *prep* + *o*] ‹*building*› ampliar*; ‹*confusion/difficulties*› aumentar

• **add up 1** [*v* + *adv*] **(a)** (Math) cuadrar **(b)** (make sense) (colloq) «*story/facts*» cuadrar; **it just doesn't ~ up** no tiene sentido **2** [*v* + *o* + *adv*, *v* + *adv* + *o*] (Math) ‹*figures*› sumar; ‹*bill*› hacer*, preparar

• **add up to** [*v* + *adv* + *prep* + *o*] «*figures*» sumar en total; «*total*» ascender* a

adder /'ædər ‖ 'ædə(r)/ *n* víbora *f*

addict /'ædɪkt/ *n* adicto, -ta *m,f*; **drug ~** drogadicto, -ta *m,f*

addicted /ə'dɪktəd ‖ ə'dɪktɪd/ *adj* **to be ~** (TO **sth**) ser* adicto (A algo)

addiction /ə'dɪkʃən/ *n* [U C] adicción *f*

addictive /ə'dɪktɪv/ *adj* ‹*drug*› que crea adicción; ‹*activity*› que crea hábito

addition /ə'dɪʃən/ *n* **1 (a)** [U] (Math) suma *f*, adición *f* (frml) **(b)** [U] (adding) adición *f* **(c)** (*in phrases*) **in addition** además; **in addition to** además de **2** [C] (extra thing): **the latest ~s to our library** las últimas adquisiciones de nuestra biblioteca

additional /ə'dɪʃn̩əl ‖ ə'dɪʃənl/ *adj* ‹*cost/weight*› extra, adicional

additive /'ædətɪv ‖ 'ædɪtɪv/ *n* [C U] aditivo *m*

address[1] /'ædres ‖ ə'dres/ *n* **1 (a)** (of house, offices etc) dirección *f*, señas *fpl*; Ⓢ **address** (on form) domicilio; (*before n*) **~ book** libreta *f* de direcciones **(b)** (Comput) dirección *f* **2** [C] (speech) discurso *m* **3 form of ~** tratamiento *m*

address[2] /ə'dres/ *vt* **1** (AmE also) /'ædres/ ‹*mail*› ponerle* la dirección a **2 (a)** (speak to) ‹*person*› dirigirse* a; ‹*assembly*› pronunciar un discurso ante **(b)** (direct) (frml) ‹*question/remark*› dirigir* **3** (deal with, confront) ‹*problem/issue*› tratar ■ *v refl* **(a)** (speak to) **to ~ oneself** TO **sb** dirigirse* A algn **(b)** (turn one's attention to) (frml) **to ~ oneself** TO **sth** dedicarse* A algo

adept /ə'dept/ *adj* experto

adequate /'ædɪkwət/ *adj* ‹*help/funding*› suficiente; ‹*standard/explanation*› adecuado

adhere /æd'hɪr ‖ əd'hɪə(r)/ *vi* (frml) **(a)** (stick) **to ~** (TO **sth**) adherirse* (A algo) **(b) to ~** TO **sth** ‹*to principles/cause*› adherirse* A algo; ‹*to regulations*› observar algo

adhesive[1] /æd'hi:sɪv ‖ əd'hi:sɪv/ *adj* adhesivo

adhesive[2] *n* [C U] adhesivo *m*

ad hoc /'æd'hɑ:k ‖ ˌæd'hɒk/ *adj* ‹*arrangement/measure*› ad hoc; **~ ~ committee** comisión *f* especial *or* ad hoc

adjacent /ə'dʒeɪsn̩t/ *adj* ‹*fields*› adyacente; ‹*rooms*› contiguo; **~** TO **sth** «*field*» adyacente A algo; «*room*» contiguo A algo

adjective /'ædʒɪktɪv/ *n* adjetivo *m*

adjoin /ə'dʒɔɪn/ *vt* (frml) **(a)** (be adjacent to) lindar con **(b) adjoining** *pres p* ‹*houses*› contiguo; **the ~ing room** el cuarto de al lado

adjourn /ə'dʒɜ:rn ‖ ə'dʒɜ:n/ *vt* ‹*talks/trial*› suspender; **the meeting was ~ed** se levantó la sesión ■ **~** *vi*: **the court ~ed** el tribunal levantó la sesión

adjournment /ə'dʒɜ:rnmənt ‖ ə'dʒɜ:nmənt/ *n* [U C] suspensión *f*

adjudicate /ə'dʒu:dɪkeɪt/ *vi* (give judgment) arbitrar ■ **~** *vt* (frml) ‹*competition*› juzgar*; ‹*claim*› decidir sobre

adjust /ə'dʒʌst/ *vt* ‹*instrument/prices/wages*› ajustar; ‹*volume/temperature/speed*› regular; **he ~ed his tie** se arregló la corbata ■ **~** *vi* **to ~** (TO **sth**/ -ING) adaptarse (A algo/+ INF)

adjustable /ə'dʒʌstəbəl/ *adj* ‹*focus/temperature*› regulable

adjustment /ə'dʒʌstmənt/ *n* **1** [C] (to machine, instrument, figures) ajuste *m*; (to clothes) arreglo *m*; (to plan, system) cambio *m* **2** [U] (act, process) **(a)** (of machine, instrument) ajuste *m* **(b)** (of person) adaptación *f*

ad-lib /'æd'lɪb/ *vt/i* **-bb-** improvisar

administer /əd'mɪnəstər ‖ əd'mɪnɪstə(r)/ *vt* **(a)** (manage) administrar **(b)** (frml) ‹*punishment/drug*› administrar

administration /əd'mɪnə'streɪʃən ‖ əd,mɪnɪ'streɪʃən/ *n* **(a)** [U] (of institution, business, estate) administración *f* **(b)** [C] (managing body) administración *f*; (Pol) gobierno *m*, administración *f* **(c)** [U] (of justice, medicine) administración *f*

administrative /əd'mɪnəstreɪtɪv ‖ əd'mɪnɪstrətɪv/ *adj* administrativo

administrator /əd'mɪnəstreɪtər ‖ əd'mɪnɪstreɪtə(r)/ *n* administrador, -dora *m,f*

admirable /'ædmərəbəl/ *adj* ‹*honesty/work*› digno de admiración; ‹*plan*› excelente

admiral /'ædmərəl/ *n* almirante *mf*

admiration /'ædmə'reɪʃən/ *n* [U] admiración *f*

admire /əd'maɪr ‖ əd'maɪə(r)/ *vt* admirar

admirer /əd'maɪrər ‖ əd'maɪərə(r)/ *n* admirador, -dora *m,f*

admission /əd'mɪʃən/ *n* **1 (a)** [U] (to building, exhibition) entrada *f*; (price) (precio *m* de) entrada *f*; (into college, society) ingreso *m* **(b)** [C] (into hospital) ingreso *m* **2** [C U] (confession) admisión *f*; **he was, by his own ~, a poor father** él mismo admitía que no era un buen padre

admit /əd'mɪt/ **-tt-** *vt* **1 (a)** (allow entry) dejar entrar; ‹*light/air*› permitir entrar; Ⓢ **admit one** entrada individual **(b)** ‹*patient*› ingresar, internar (CS, Méx) **2** (confess) ‹*crime/mistake*› admitir; **to ~ sth TO sb** confesarle* algo A algn

• **admit to** [*v* + *prep* + *o*] (confess) ‹*error*› admitir; ‹*crime*› declararse culpable de

admittance /əd'mɪtn̩s/ *n* [U] (frml) **~ (TO sth)** acceso *m* (A algo); Ⓢ **no admittance** prohibida la entrada

admittedly /əd'mɪtədli ‖ əd'mɪtɪdli/ *adv* (*indep*): **~, it wasn't an easy task, but** ... hay que reconocer que no era una tarea fácil pero ...

admonish /æd'mɑːnɪʃ ‖ əd'mɒnɪʃ/ *vt* (frml) **to ~ sb (FOR sth)** amonestar a algn (POR algo)

ado /ə'duː/ *n* [U]: **without further** *o* **more ~** sin más (preámbulos)

adolescence /'ædə'lesn̩s/ *n* [U] adolescencia *f*

adolescent¹ /'ædə'lesn̩t/ *n* adolescente *mf*

adolescent² *adj* adolescente

adopt /ə'dɑːpt ‖ ə'dɒpt/ *vt* **(a)** ‹*child*› adoptar **(b)** ‹*idea/custom/title*› adoptar **(c)** ‹*recommendation*› aprobar*

adopted /ə'dɑːptəd ‖ ə'dɒptɪd/ *adj* ‹*son/country*› adoptivo; **she's ~** es adoptada

adoption /ə'dɑːpʃən ‖ ə'dɒpʃən/ *n* **(a)** [U C] (of child) adopción *f* **(b)** [U] (of approach, custom, title) adopción *f* **(c)** [U] (of report, motion) aprobación *f*

adoptive /ə'dɑːptɪv ‖ ə'dɒptɪv/ *adj* (*before n*) adoptivo

adorable /ə'dɔːrəbəl/ *adj* ‹*house/hat*› divino; ‹*child*› adorable

adoration /'ædə'reɪʃən/ *n* [U] adoración *f*

adore /ə'dɔːr ‖ ə'dɔː(r)/ *vt* **(a)** (love, worship) adorar **(b) adoring** *pres p* ‹*gaze*› lleno de adoración; ‹*mother*› amantísimo **(c)** (like, enjoy): **I ~ figs** me encantan los higos

adorn /ə'dɔːrn ‖ ə'dɔːn/ *vt* (frml *or* liter) adornar

adornment /ə'dɔːrnmənt ‖ ə'dɔːnmənt/ *n* [U C] adorno *m*

adrenaline /ə'drenl̩ən ‖ ə'drenəlɪn/ *n* [U] adrenalina *f*

Adriatic /'eɪdri'ætɪk/ *n* **the ~ (Sea)** el (mar) Adriático

adrift /ə'drɪft/ *adj* (*pred*) (Naut) a la deriva; ***to come*** *o* ***go ~*** «*plans*» fallar

adroit /ə'drɔɪt/ *adj* **(a)** ‹*answer/speaker*› hábil **(b)** ‹*movement*› ágil; ‹*player*› diestro

adulation /'ædʒə'leɪʃən ‖ ,ædjʊ'leɪʃən/ *n* [U] adulación *f*

adult¹ /ə'dʌlt, 'ædʌlt/ *n* adulto, -ta *m,f*

adult² *adj* **(a)** (physically mature) adulto **(b)** (mature) ‹*behavior/approach*› maduro, adulto **(c)** (suitable for adults) para mayores *or* adultos

adultery /ə'dʌltəri/ *n* [U] adulterio *m*

adulthood /ə'dʌlthʊd ‖ 'ædʌlthʊd/ *n* [U] edad *f* adulta, adultez *f*

advance¹ /əd'væns ‖ əd'vɑːns/ *vi* «*person/vehicle*» avanzar*; «*science/society*» avanzar*, progresar ■ **~** *vt* **1 (a)** (move forward) ‹*troops*› avanzar* **(b)** (further) ‹*knowledge*› fomentar; ‹*interests/cause*› promover* **2 (a)** ‹*date/meeting*› adelantar **(b)** ‹*money/wages*› anticipar

advance² *n* **1** [C U] (of person, army, vehicle) avance *m*; (of civilization, science) avance *m*, progreso *m* **2 advances** *pl* (overtures) insinuaciones *fpl* **3** [C] **(a)** (early payment) anticipo *m* **(b)** (loan) préstamo *m* **4 in advance**: **to pay in ~** pagar* por adelantado; **it was planned well in ~** se planeó con mucha antelación

advance³ *adj* (*before n*): **~ booking is essential** es imprescindible hacer la reserva por anticipado

advanced /əd'vænst ‖ əd'vɑːnst/ *adj* ‹*civilization/course/student*› avanzado

advantage /əd'væntɪdʒ ‖ əd'vɑːntɪdʒ/ *n* **(a)** [C] (superior factor) ventaja *f* **(b)** [U] (gain): **to take ~ of sth** aprovechar algo; (pej) aprovecharse de algo; **to take ~ of sb** (exploit) aprovecharse de algn; **to turn sth to one's ~** sacar* provecho de algo **(c)** (in tennis) (*no pl*) ventaja *f*

advantageous /,ædvæn'teɪdʒəs ‖ ,ædvən'teɪdʒəs/ *adj* ‹*arrangement*› ventajoso; ‹*position/situation*› de ventaja

advent /'ædvent/ *n* **(a)** (arrival) llegada *f* **(b) Advent** (Relig) Adviento *m*

adventure /əd'ventʃər ‖ əd'ventʃə(r)/ *n* [C U] aventura *f*; (*before n*) ‹*story/film*› de aventuras

adventurous /əd'ventʃərəs/ *adj* ‹*traveler*› intrépido; ‹*spirit/person*› aventurero

adverb /'ædvɜːrb ‖ 'ædvɜːb/ ▶ **449** *n* adverbio *m*

adversary /'ædvərseri ‖ 'ædvəsəri/ *n* (*pl* **-ries**) (frml) adversario, -ria *m,f*

Adverbs

Many English adverbs end in the suffix -ly*; in Spanish, this corresponds very broadly to the suffix* -mente, *which is added to the feminine form of the adjective to form an adverb*:

absolutely = absolutamente
deeply = profundamente
drastically = drásticamente
happily = alegremente

Where two or more adverbs ending in -mente *appear in series,* -mente *appears only at the end of the final adverb*:

quickly, economically, and efficiently done = rápida, económica y eficazmente hecho
they can't claim anything, either legally or logically = no pueden reclamar nada ni judicial ni lógicamente

Many English adverbs are translated by an adverbial phrase in Spanish, usually consisting of a preposition + noun or adjective:

delicately = con delicadeza
generally = por lo general
luckily = por suerte
seriously = en serio

Some adverbs in English, which have the meaning from the perspective of, *modify a whole sentence*:

ecologically, this is a disaster = desde el punto de vista ecológico *or* ecológicamente hablando esto es un desastre
admittedly it wasn't easy = hay que admitir que no fue fácil *or* la verdad es que no fue fácil

These are marked in the text by the label (indep)

An English adverb expressing emotion is often translated by an adjective in Spanish. In this case, the adjective agrees with the subject:

no!, he shouted angrily = – ¡no! – gritó enojado
she looked at him enviously = lo miró envidiosa
they live happily = viven felices

adverse /'ædvɜːrs, æd'vɜːrs ‖ 'ædvɜːs/ *adj* adverso

adversity /æd'vɜːrsəti ‖ əd'vɜːsəti/ *n* [U C] (*pl* **-ties**) adversidad *f*

advertise /'ædvərtaɪz ‖ 'ædvətaɪz/ *vt* ‹*product*› hacerle* publicidad a, hacerle* réclame a (AmL); **I saw it ~d on TV** lo vi anunciado en la tele ■ ~ *vi* hacer* publicidad

advertisement /'ædvər'taɪzmənt ‖ əd'vɜːtɪsmənt/ *n* anuncio *m*, aviso *m* (AmL)

advertiser /'ædvərtaɪzər ‖ 'ædvətaɪzə(r)/ *n* anunciante *mf*

advertising /'ædvərtaɪzɪŋ ‖ 'ædvətaɪzɪŋ/ *n* [U] **(a)** (action, business) publicidad *f*; (*before n*) ‹*campaign/slot*› publicitario; **~ agency** agencia *f* de publicidad **(b)** (advertisements) propaganda *f*

advice /əd'vaɪs/ *n* [U] (counsel) consejos *mpl*; (professional) asesoramiento *m*; **a piece of ~** un consejo; **to give sb ~** aconsejar a algn; **to take sb's ~** seguir* los consejos de algn

advisable /əd'vaɪzəbəl/ *adj* aconsejable

advise /əd'vaɪz/ *vt* **1 (a)** (recommend) aconsejar; **to ~ sb to + INF** aconsejar(le) A algn QUE (+ *subj*); **they ~d him against marrying so young** le aconsejaron que no se casara tan joven **(b)** (give advice to) aconsejar; (professionally) asesorar **2** (inform) (frml) informar; (in writing) notificar* (frml) ■ ~ *vi* aconsejar; (professionally) asesorar; **to ~ AGAINST sth/-ING** desaconsejar algo/+ INF

adviser, advisor /əd'vaɪzər ‖ əd'vaɪzə(r)/ *n* consejero, -ra *m,f*; (professional) asesor, -sora *m,f*

advisory /əd'vaɪzəri/ *adj* ‹*body/service*› consultivo; **in an ~ capacity** en calidad de asesor

advocate¹ /'ædvəkət/ *n* **(a)** (supporter, defender) **~ (OF sth)** defensor, -sora *m,f* (DE algo) **(b)** (in a court of law) abogado, -da *m,f*

advocate² /'ædvəkeɪt/ *vt* recomendar*, abogar* por

Aegean /ɪ'dʒiːən/ *n* **the ~ (Sea)** el (mar) Egeo

aerial¹ /'eriəl ‖ 'eəriəl/ *adj* (*before n*) aéreo; **~ photograph** aerofoto *f*

aerial² *n* (esp BrE) antena *f*

aerobics /e'rəʊbɪks, ə- ‖ eə'rəʊbɪks/ *n* (+ *sing or pl vb*) aerobic(s) *m*, aerobismo *m* (CS)

aerodynamic /'erəʊdaɪ'næmɪk ‖ ˌeərəʊdaɪ'næmɪk/ *adj* aerodinámico

aeroplane /'erəpleɪn ‖ 'eərəpleɪn/ *n* (BrE) avión *m*

aerosol /'erəsɑːl ‖ 'eərəsɒl/ *n* aerosol *m*, spray *m*

aerospace /'erəʊspeɪs ‖ 'eərəʊspeɪs/ *adj* (*before n*) ‹*research/industry*› aeroespacial

aesthetic, (AmE also) **esthetic** /es'θetɪk ‖ iːs'θetɪk/ *adj* estético

afar /ə'fɑːr ‖ ə'fɑː(r)/ *adv* (liter) lejos

affable /'æfəbəl/ *adj* afable

affair /ə'fer ‖ ə'feə(r)/ *n* **1 (a)** (case) caso *m* **(b)** (event): **the wedding was a small, family ~** la boda se celebró en la intimidad; **it was a very formal ~** fue una ocasión muy ceremoniosa **(c)** (business, concern) asunto *m* **(d) affairs** *pl* (matters) asuntos *mpl* **2** (liaison) affaire *m*

affect /ə'fekt/ *vt* (have effect on) afectar a; ‹*organ/nervous system*› comprometer

affected /ə'fektəd ‖ ə'fektɪd/ *adj* afectado

affection /ə'fekʃən/ *n* [C U] cariño *m*

affectionate /ə'fekʃṇət/ *adj* cariñoso

affiliate /ə'fɪlieɪt/ *vt* (*often pass*) afiliar

affiliation /ə'fɪli'eɪʃən/ *n* [C U] afiliación *f*; **her political ~s** su filiación política

affinity /ə'fɪnəti/ *n* (*pl* **-ties**) [C U] afinidad *f*

affirm /ə'fɜːrm ‖ ə'fɜːm/ *vt* declarar

affirmative /ə'fɜːrmətɪv ‖ ə'fɜːmətɪv/ *adj* afirmativo

affix /ə'fɪks/ *vt* (frml) ‹*stamp/seal*› poner*; ‹*notice*› fijar

afflict /ə'flɪkt/ *vt* «*disease/problem*» aquejar

affliction /ə'flɪkʃən/ *n* **(a)** [U] (suffering) aflicción *f* **(b)** [C] (cause of suffering) desgracia *f*; (ailment) mal *m*

affluence /'æfluəns/ *n* [U] prosperidad *f*

affluent /'æfluənt/ *adj* ‹*suburb/country*› próspero; ‹*person*› acomodado

afford /ə'fɔːrd ‖ ə'fɔːd/ *vt*: **I can't ~ a new car** no me alcanza el dinero para comprarme un coche nuevo; **you can't ~ to miss this opportunity** no puedes perderte esta oportunidad

affordable /ə'fɔːrdəbəl ‖ ə'fɔːdəbəl/ *adj* asequible

affront /ə'frʌnt/ *n* (frml) afrenta *f*

Afghan¹ /'æfgæn/ *adj* afgano

Afghan² *n* afgano, -na *m,f*

Afghanistan /æf'gænəstæn ‖ æf'gænɪstɑːn/ *n* Afganistán *m*

afield /ə'fiːld/ *adv*: **she travels as far ~ as China** viaja a lugares tan distantes como la China; **we had to look further ~ for help** tuvimos que buscar ayuda en otra parte

afloat /ə'fləʊt/ *adj* (*pred*) a flote; **to stay ~** mantenerse* a flote

afoot /ə'fʊt/ *adj* (*pred*): **plans are ~ to create** ... hay planes de crear ...; **what's ~?** ¿qué se está tramando?

aforementioned /ə'fɔːr'mentʃənd ‖ ə,fɔː'menʃənd/ *adj* (frml) (*before n*) ‹*clause/statement*› anteriormente mencionado, antedicho (frml); **the ~ person** el susodicho, la susodicha (frml *o* hum)

afraid /ə'freɪd/ *adj* (*pred*) **1** (scared): **to be ~ OF sb/sth** tenerle* miedo A algn/A algo; **there's nothing to be ~ of** no tienes nada que temer **2** (sorry): **she's not in, I'm ~** lo siento pero no está; **I'm ~ not** me temo que no

afresh /ə'freʃ/ *adv*: **to start ~** empezar* de nuevo, volver* a empezar

Africa /'æfrɪkə/ *n* África *f*‡

African¹ /'æfrɪkən/ *adj* africano

African² *n* africano, -na *m,f*

African-American¹ /'æfrɪkənə'merɪkən/ *adj* norteamericano de origen africano

African-American² *n* norteamericano, -na *m,f* de origen africano

Afro-American¹ /'æfrəʊə'merɪkən/ *adj* afroamericano

Afro-American² *n* afroamericano, -na *m,f*

after¹ /'æftər ‖ 'ɑːftə(r)/ *prep* **1** ▶ **884** (following in time) después de; **I'll be at home ~ eight o'clock** estaré en casa después de *or* a partir de las ocho; **it's just ~ midnight** son las doce pasadas; **it's a quarter ~ two** (AmE) son las dos y cuarto; **the day ~ the party** al día siguiente de la fiesta **2** (in sequence, rank) tras; **day ~ day** día tras día; **do go in — ~ you!** pase — ¡primero usted! **3 (a)** (behind): **shut the door ~ you** cierra la puerta al salir **(b)** (in pursuit of) tras; **he ran ~ them** corrió tras ellos; **he's ~ her money** anda a la caza de su dinero (fam); *see also* ASK AFTER **4 after all** después de todo

after² *conj*: **it happened ~ you left** ocurrió después de que tú te fuiste; **~ examining it** después de examinarlo

after³ *adv* **(a)** (afterward, following) después; **the day ~** al día siguiente **(b)** (behind) detrás

aftereffect /'æftərɪ,fekt ‖ 'ɑːftərɪ,fekt/ *n* (of drug) efecto *m* secundario; (of problem) secuela *f*

aftermath /'æftərmæθ ‖ 'ɑːftəmæθ, 'ɑːftəmɑːθ/ *n* **(a)** (subsequent period): **in the ~ of the riots** tras los disturbios **(b)** (consequences) repercusiones *fpl*

afternoon /'æftər'nuːn ‖ ,ɑːftə'nuːn/ ▶ **884** *n* **1** (time of day) tarde *f*; **on Friday ~** el viernes por *or* (AmL) en la tarde; **he came in the ~** vino por la tarde, vino en la tarde (AmL); **good ~!** ¡ buenas tardes! **2 afternoons** (*as adv*) por las tardes, en las tardes (AmL)

after: **~shave (lotion)** *n* [U] loción *f* para después de afeitarse, aftershave *m*; **~thought** *n*: **it occurred to me as an ~thought that** ... después se me ocurrió qué ...; **it was added on as an ~thought** fue una idea de último momento

afterward /'æftərwərd ‖ 'ɑːftəwəd/, (BrE also) **afterwards** /-z/ *adv* después

again /ə'gen, ə'geɪn/ *adv* otra vez, de nuevo; **to do sth ~** volver* a hacer algo, hacer* algo otra vez *or* de nuevo; **never ~!** ¡nunca más!

against /ə'genst, ə'geɪnst/ *prep* contra; **I've nothing ~ her** no tengo nada contra ella *or* en contra suya *or* en contra de ella; **he put a cross ~ my name** puso una cruz al lado de mi nombre

age¹ /eɪdʒ/ *n* **1** ▶ **451** [C U] (of person, animal, thing) edad *f*; **he is six years of ~** tiene seis años; **to be under ~** ser* menor de edad; (*before n*) **~ group** grupo *m* etario (frml) **2** [C] **(a)** (epoch, period) era *f*; **through the ~s** a través de los tiempos **(b)** (long time) (colloq): **I haven't seen her for ~s** hace siglos que no la veo (fam)

age² (*pres p* **aging** *or* **ageing**; *past p* **aged** /eɪdʒd/) *vi* «*person*» envejecer*; «*cheese*» madurar ■ **~** *vt* ‹*person*› hacer* envejecer; ‹*wine*› añejar

aged *adj* **1** /'eɪdʒəd ‖ 'eɪdʒɪd/ (elderly) anciano **2** /eɪdʒd/ (*pred*): **he was ~ 20** tenía 20 años de edad

ageing *adj/n* ⇒ AGING

ageism /'eɪdʒɪzəm/ *n* [U] discriminación *f* por razones de edad

agency /'eɪdʒənsi/ *n* (*pl* **-cies**) **(a)** (office) agencia *f* **(b)** (branch) sucursal *f* **(c)** (department) organismo *m*

agenda /ə'dʒendə/ *n* orden *m* del día, agenda *f*

agent /'eɪdʒənt/ *n* **1** [C] (person) agente *mf* **2** [C U] (substance) agente *m*

aggravate /'ægrəveɪt/ *vt* **(a)** (make worse) agravar **(b)** (annoy) (colloq) exasperar

aggression /ə'greʃən/ *n* **(a)** [U] (feeling, attitude) agresividad *f* **(b)** [C] (unprovoked attack) agresión *f*

aggressive /ə'gresɪv/ *adj* ‹*person/country*› agresivo; ‹*tactics/strategy*› de agresión

aghast /ə'gæst ‖ ə'gɑːst/ *adj* (*pred*) aterrado

agile /'ædʒəl ‖ 'ædʒaɪl/ *adj* ágil

agility /ə'dʒɪləti/ *n* [U] agilidad *f*

aging¹ /'eɪdʒɪŋ/ *adj* (*before n*) ‹*person*› envejecido

aging² *n* [U] envejecimiento *m*

agitate /'ædʒəteɪt ‖ 'ædʒɪteɪt/ *vt* **(a)** (disturb) ‹*surface/liquid*› agitar **(b)** (upset) inquietar ■ **~** *vi* **to ~ FOR/AGAINST sth** hacer* campaña A FAVOR DE/EN CONTRA DE algo

Age

Where English says to be X years old, *Spanish says* tener X años (*to have X years*):

how old are you?	=	¿cuántos años tienes?
what age is he/she?	=	¿qué edad tiene?
he's/she's fifteen *o* (more formal) he/she is fifteen years old	=	tiene quince años
he is fifteen years of age (formal)	=	tiene quince años de edad
the house is two hundred years old	=	la casa tiene doscientos años

Note the use of the verb cumplir *to express becoming a certain age and having a birthday*:

when will you be six?	=	¿cuándo cumples seis años?
she was five last week	=	cumplió cinco años la semana pasada
he's just ten	=	tiene diez años recién cumplidos *or* acaba de cumplir (los) diez años
it's my eighteenth birthday next month	=	voy a cumplir dieciocho años el mes que viene

The word años (*years*) *is always included in Spanish* (*except in certain colloquial expressions; see 'Approximate Age', below*):

a woman of fifty	=	una mujer de cincuenta años
a seventy-five-year-old man	=	un hombre de setenta y cinco años
my eight-year-old son	=	mi hijo de ocho años
a class of six-year-olds	=	una clase de niños de seis años
at (the age of) four he was reading perfectly	=	a los cuatro años (de edad) leía a la perfección
at the age of sixteen he joined the army	=	a la edad de dieciséis años se alistó en el ejército

Approximate age

he's about thirty	=	tiene *or* tendrá alrededor de *or* (less formal) unos treinta años
he's in his fifties	=	tiene cincuenta y tantos años *or* tiene entre cuarenta y cincuenta años
she's in her early twenties	=	tiene un poco más de veinte años
she's in her late twenties	=	tiene cerca de treinta años
he's in his mid-thirties	=	tiene alrededor de 35 años *or* tiene entre 34 y 37 años
he must be over sixty	=	debe de tener más de sesenta años
he's in his early/late teens	=	tendrá unos trece o catorce/unos dieciocho o diecinueve años
he's thirty-something	=	tiene treinta y tantos años *or* tiene treinta y pico años (fam)
she's just over ten	=	tiene un poco más de diez años
he's under eighteen	=	tiene menos de dieciocho años
he's pushing forty	=	ronda los cuarenta
she's going on *o* not far off fifty	=	ya va para los cincuenta (fam)

Note the following Spanish terms:

es cuarentón	=	he's in his forties
una cuarentona (pejorative)	=	a woman in her forties
un programa para cincuentones	=	a progam for people over fifty *o* (colloq) for the over-fifties

Comparison

she's older/younger than me	=	es mayor/menor que yo
he's two years older/younger than me	=	es dos años mayor/menor que yo
they're the same age	=	son de la misma edad *or* tienen la misma edad
he's twice her age	=	le dobla la edad *or* la dobla en edad

Note also the common idiomatic construction with llevar:

me lleva dos años	=	he's/she's two years older than me
le llevo tres años	=	I'm three years older than him/her

agitated /'ædʒəteɪtəd ‖ 'ædʒɪteɪtɪd/ *adj* ‹*movements/gestures*› nervioso; **to become/get ~** ponerse* nervioso

agitation /ædʒə'teɪʃən ‖ ˌædʒɪ'teɪʃən/ *n* [U] agitación *f*

AGM *n* (BrE) = **annual general meeting**

agnostic /æg'nɑːstɪk ‖ æg'nɒstɪk/ *n* agnóstico, -ca *m,f*

ago /ə'gəʊ/ *adv*: **five days ~** hace cinco días; **a long time ~** hace mucho (tiempo)

agog /ə'gɑːg ‖ ə'gɒg/ *adj* (*pred*): **I was all ~** estaba que me moría de curiosidad

agonize /'ægənaɪz/ *vi*: **stop agonizing, just do it** no le des más vueltas al asunto y hazlo; **he ~d over the decision** le costó muchísimo decidirse

agonizing /'ægənaɪzɪŋ/ *adj* ‹*experience*› angustioso; ‹*pain*› atroz; ‹*decision*› muy difícil

agony /'ægəni/ *n* [U C] (*pl* **-nies**): **he was in ~** estaba desesperado de dolor; **she's going through agonies of doubt** las dudas la están atormentando; **to prolong the ~** alargar* el martirio

agoraphobia /'ægərə'fəʊbiə/ *n* agorafobia *f*

agree /ə'griː/ *vt* **1 (a)** (be in agreement over) **to ~** (THAT) estar* de acuerdo (EN QUE); **yes, it must feel odd, he ~d** —sí, debe resultar extraño —asintió **(b)** (reach agreement over) decidir; **it was ~d that he should go on his own** se decidió que fuera él solo; **to ~** WHEN/WHAT/HOW *etc* ponerse* de acuerdo EN CUÁNDO/EN QUÉ/EN CÓMO *etc* **(c)** (decide on) ‹*price*› acordar* **2** (admit) **to ~** (THAT) reconocer* (QUE) ■ **~** *vi* **1** (be of same opinion) estar* de acuerdo; **to ~** ABOUT **sth** estar* de acuerdo EN algo **2 (a)** (get on well) congeniar **(b)** (tally) «*statements/figures*» concordar*

• **agree on** [*v* + *prep* + *o*] ‹*date/details*› acordar*; **we ~ on the color** estamos de acuerdo en el color

• **agree to** [*v* + *prep* + *o*] ‹*terms/conditions*› aceptar

• **agree with** [*v* + *prep* + *o*] **(a)** (approve of) estar* de acuerdo con **(b) to ~ with sb** «*food/heat/climate*» sentarle* bien a algn

agreeable /ə'griːəbəl/ *adj* **1** (pleasant) agradable **2** (willing) (*pred*): **bring her along, if she's ~** tráela, si quiere venir; **he seemed quite ~ to coming** parecía dispuesto a venir

agreed /ə'griːd/ *adj* **(a)** (in agreement) (*pred*) de acuerdo **(b)** (prearranged): **we met at ten, as ~** nos encontramos a las diez como habíamos quedado; (*before n*) ‹*price/terms*› acordado

agreement /ə'griːmənt/ *n* **1 (a)** [U] (shared opinion) acuerdo *m*; **to be in ~ (with sb)** estar* de acuerdo (con algn) **(b)** [C] (written arrangement) acuerdo *m*; (Busn) contrato *m* **2** [U] (consent) consentimiento *m*

agricultural /ˌægrɪ'kʌltʃərəl/ *adj* agrícola

agriculture /'ægrɪkʌltʃər ‖ 'ægrɪkʌltʃə(r)/ *n* [U] agricultura *f*

aground /ə'graʊnd/ *adv*: **to go** *o* **run ~** (ON **sth**) encallar (EN algo)

ahead /ə'hed/ *adv* **1 (a)** (indicating movement): **go straight ~** siga todo recto; **I'll go on ~** yo iré delante **(b)** (indicating position): **the post office is straight ~** la oficina de correos está siguiendo recto **(c)** (in race, competition): **our team was ~** nuestro equipo llevaba la delantera **(d)** (in time): **the months ~** los meses venideros, los próximos meses **2 ahead of (a)** (in front of) delante de **(b)** (in race, competition) por delante de; **the Japanese are way ~ of us in this field** los japoneses nos llevan mucha ventaja en este campo **(c)** (before): **she got there an hour ~ of him** llegó una hora antes que él

aid¹ /eɪd/ *n* **(a)** [U] (assistance, support) ayuda *f*; **to come/go to sb's ~** venir*/ir* en ayuda de algn **(b)** [U] (monetary) ayuda *f*, asistencia *f*; **a concert in ~ of** … un concierto a beneficio de …

aid² *vt* ayudar; **to ~ and abet sb** (Law) instigar* *or* secundar a algn (*en la comisión de un delito*)

aide /eɪd/ *n* asesor, -sora *m,f*

AIDS /eɪdz/ *n* [U] (= **acquired immune deficiency syndrome**) sida *m*, SIDA *m*

ailing /'eɪlɪŋ/ *adj* ‹*person*› enfermo; ‹*economy*› renqueante

ailment /'eɪlmənt/ *n* enfermedad *f*, dolencia *f* (frml)

aim¹ /eɪm/ *vt*: **he ~ed the gun at her** le apuntó con la pistola; **she ~ed a blow at his head** intentó darle en la cabeza; **the movie is ~ed at a young audience** la película está dirigida a un público joven ■ **~** *vi* **(a)** (point weapon) apuntar; **to ~** AT **sth/sb** apuntar(le) A algo/algn **(b)** (intend) **to ~ to** + INF querer* + INF

aim² *n* **(a)** [C] (goal, object) objetivo *m* **(b)** [U] (with weapon) puntería *f*; **to take ~** hacer* puntería, apuntar

aimless /'eɪmləs ‖ 'eɪmlɪs/ *adj* ‹*wandering*› sin rumbo (fijo); ‹*existence*› sin norte

ain't /eɪnt/ (colloq & dial) **(a)** = **am not (b)** = **is not (c)** = **are not (d)** = **has not (e)** = **have not**

air¹ /er ‖ eə(r)/ *n* **1** [U] aire *m*; **to go by ~** ir* en avión; ***to be up in the ~*** «*plans*» estar* en el aire; ***to vanish into thin ~*** esfumarse; (*before n*) ‹*route/attack*› aéreo; **~ pressure** presión *f* atmosférica **2** [U] (Rad, TV): **to be on the ~** estar* en el aire; **to come** *o* **go on the ~** salir* al aire **3 (a)** [C] (manner, look, atmosphere) aire *m* **(b) airs** *pl* (affectations) aires *mpl*

air² *vt* **1 (a)** ‹*clothes/linen*› airear, orear; ‹*bed/room*› ventilar, airear **(b)** ‹*opinion/grievance*› manifestar*; ‹*knowledge*› hacer* alarde de **2** (broadcast) (AmE) ‹*program*› transmitir, emitir

air: **~ bag** *n* (Auto) bolsa *f* de aire; **~ base** *n* base *f* aérea; **~borne** *adj* **(a)** ‹*seeds/dust*› transportado por el aire; ‹*troops/units*› aerotransportado **(b)** (off the ground): **the plane is now ~borne** el avión ha despegado; **~-conditioned** /'erkən'dɪʃənd ‖ 'eəkəndɪʃənd/ *adj* con aire acondicionado, climatizado; **~ conditioning** *n* [U] aire *m* acondicionado

aircraft /'erkræft ‖ 'eəkrɑːft/ *n* (*pl* **~**) avión *m*

aircraft carrier *n* portaaviones *m*

air: **~fare** *n* precio *m* del pasaje *or* (Esp tb) del billete de avión; **~fares are set to rise** van a subir las tarifas aéreas; **~field** *n* aeródromo *m*; **~ force** *n* (of nation) fuerza *f* aérea; **~ freshener** /'freʃnər ‖ 'freʃnə(r)/ *n* ambientador *m*, desodorante *m* ambiental *or* de ambientes (CS); **~ gun** *n* (revolver) pistola *f* de aire comprimido; (rifle) escopeta *f* *or* rifle *m* de aire comprimido; **~ hostess** *n* azafata *f*, aeromoza *f* (AmL); **~ letter** *n* aerograma *m*; **~lift** *n* puente *m* aéreo; **~line** *n* línea *f* aérea, aerolínea *f*; **~mail** *n* [U] correo *m* aéreo; **to send sth (by) ~mail** mandar algo por avión *or* por vía aérea; (*before n*) ‹*paper/envelope*› de avión; **~plane** *n* (AmE) avión *m*; **~port** *n* aeropuerto *m*; **~ raid** *n* ataque *m* aéreo; (*before n*) **~-raid shelter** refugio *m* antiaéreo; **~ship** *n* dirigible *m*, zepelín *m*; **~sick** *adj*: **to be ~sick** estar* mareado (*en un avión*); **to get ~sick** marearse (*al viajar en avión*); **~strip** *n* pista *f* de aterrizaje; **~tight** *adj* ‹*room/box*› hermético; ‹*alibi/argument*› a toda prueba; **~ traffic control** *n* [U] control *m* del tráfico aéreo; **~ traffic controller** *n* controlador aéreo, controladora aérea *m,f*; **~worthy** *adj*: **to be ~worthy** estar* en condiciones de vuelo

airy /'eri ‖ 'eəri/ *adj* **airier, airiest (a)** ‹*room/house*› espacioso y aireado **(b)** ‹*manner/reply*› displicente

aisle /aɪl/ *n* (gangway) pasillo *m*; (Archit) nave *f* lateral
ajar /ə'dʒɑːr ‖ ə'dʒɑː(r)/ *adj* (*pred*) entreabierto
AK = **Alaska**
akin /ə'kɪn/ *adj* (*pred*) **to be ~ (TO sth)** ser* similar (A algo)
AL = **Alabama**
Ala = **Alabama**
à la carte /'ɑːlə'kɑːrt ‖ ˌɑːlɑː'kɑːt/ *adj/adv* a la carta
alarm¹ /ə'lɑːrm ‖ ə'lɑːm/ *n* **1** [U] (apprehension) gran preocupación *f* **2** [C] (warning, device) alarma *f*
alarm² *vt* (worry) alarmar; (scare) asustar
alarm clock *n* (reloj *m*) despertador *m*
alarmed /ə'lɑːrmd ‖ ə'lɑːmd/ *adj* (apprehensive): **don't be ~** no te asustes; **I began to be ~** empecé a alarmarme
alarming /ə'lɑːrmɪŋ ‖ ə'lɑːmɪŋ/ *adj* alarmante
alas /ə'læs/ *interj* (liter *or* frml) ¡ay! (liter)
Albania /æl'beɪniə/ *n* Albania *f*
Albanian¹ /æl'beɪniən/ *adj* albanés
Albanian² *n* **(a)** [C] (person) albanés, -nesa *m,f* **(b)** [U] (language) albanés *m*
albeit /ɔːl'biːɪt/ *conj* (frml) aunque
albino /æl'baɪnəʊ ‖ æl'biːnəʊ/ *n* (*pl* **-nos**) albino, -na *m,f*; (*before n*) albino
album /'ælbəm/ *n* **(a)** (book) álbum *m*; **photograph ~** álbum de fotos **(b)** (Audio) álbum *m*
alchemist /'ælkəməst ‖ 'ælkəmɪst/ *n* alquimista *mf*
alcohol /'ælkəhɔːl ‖ 'ælkəhɒl/ *n* [U] alcohol *m*
alcoholic¹ /'ælkə'hɔːlɪk ‖ ˌælkə'hɒlɪk/ *adj* alcohólico
alcoholic² *n* alcohólico, -ca *m,f*
alcoholism /'ælkəhɔːlɪzəm ‖ 'ælkəhɒlɪzəm/ *n* [U] alcoholismo *m*
alcove /'ælkəʊv/ *n* (recess) hueco *m*; (niche) hornacina *f*
alderman /'ɔːldərmən ‖ 'ɔːldəmən/ *n* (*pl* **-men** /-mən/) **(a)** (in UK) regidor, -dora *m,f* **(b)** (in US) concejal *m*
alderwoman /'ɔːldərˌwʊmən ‖ 'ɔːldəˌwʊmən/ *n* (*pl* **-women**) (in US) concejala *f*
ale /eɪl/ *n* [U C] cerveza *f*
alert¹ /ə'lɜːrt ‖ ə'lɜːt/ *adj* alerta *adj inv*; **to be ~** (vigilant) estar* alerta; (lively-minded) estar* despierto
alert² *n* alerta *f*; **to be on the ~** estar* alerta
alert³ *vt* **to ~ sb (TO sth)** alertar a algn (DE algo)
A level *n* (in UK) *estudios de una asignatura a nivel de bachillerato superior*
alga /'ælgə/ *n* (*pl* **algae** /'ældʒiː, 'ælgiː/) alga *f*‡
algebra /'ældʒəbrə ‖ 'ældʒɪbrə/ *n* [U] álgebra *f*‡
Algeria /æl'dʒɪriə ‖ æl'dʒɪəriə/ *n* Argelia *f*
Algerian /æl'dʒɪriən ‖ æl'dʒɪəriən/ *adj* argelino
alias /'eɪliəs/ *adv* alias
alibi /'æləbaɪ ‖ 'ælɪbaɪ/ *n* coartada *f*
alien¹ /'eɪliən/ *n* **(a)** (foreigner) extranjero, -ra *m,f* **(b)** (in science fiction) extraterrestre *mf*
alien² *adj* **(a)** (strange, foreign) extraño; **to be ~ TO sb/sth** serle* ajeno A algn/algo **(b)** (in science fiction) (*before n*) extraterrestre
alienate /'eɪliəneɪt/ *vt* (Pol, Psych) alienar; (estrange): **he has ~d all his friends** ha hecho que todos sus amigos se alejen *or* se distancien de él
alight¹ /ə'laɪt/ *adj* (*pred*) **to be ~** estar* ardiendo; **to set sth ~** prender(le) fuego a algo
alight² *vi* (frml) «*passenger*» apearse (frml); (land) «*bird/insect*» posarse
align /ə'laɪn/ *vt* alinear
alignment /ə'laɪnmənt/ *n* **(a)** [U] (Tech) alineación *f* **(b)** [C U] (Pol) alineamiento *m*
alike¹ /ə'laɪk/ *adj* (*pred*) parecido
alike² *adv* ‹*think/act*› igual; **popular with young and old ~** popular tanto entre los jóvenes como entre los mayores
alimony /'æləməʊni ‖ 'ælɪməni/ *n* [U] pensión *f* alimenticia
alive /ə'laɪv/ *adj* (*pred*) vivo; **is he still ~?** ¿todavía vive?; **to stay ~** sobrevivir; **she's ~ and well** está sana y salva; **the place was ~ with insects** el lugar estaba plagado de insectos
alkaline /'ælkəlaɪn/ *adj* alcalino
all¹ /ɔːl/ *adj* (*before n*) todo, -da; (*pl*) todos, -das; **~ four of us went** fuimos los cuatro; **~ morning** toda la mañana; **of ~ the stupid things to do!** ¡qué estupidez!; *see also* ALL³ 3(d)
all² *pron* **1** (everything) (+ *sing vb*) todo; **will that be ~, madam?** ¿algo más señora?; **when ~ is said and done** a fin de cuentas; **for ~ I care** por lo que a mí me importa **2 all of**: **~ of the children go to school** todos los niños van al colegio; **~ of the cheese** todo el queso **3** (*after n, pron*) todo, -da; (*pl*) todos, -das; **it was ~ gone** no quedaba nada **4** (*in phrases*) **(a) all in all** en general **(b) all told** en total **(c) and all** y todo; **he ate it, skin and ~** se lo comió con la cáscara y todo **(d) at all**: **they don't like him at ~** no les gusta nada; **thank you — not at ~** gracias — de nada *or* no hay de qué; **it's not at ~ bad** no está nada mal **(e) in all** en total
all³ *adv* **1** (completely): **you've gone ~ red** te has puesto todo colorado/toda colorada; **she was ~ alone** estaba completamente sola **2** (each, apiece) (Sport): **the score was one ~** iban (empatados) uno a uno; **30 ~** 30 iguales **3** (*in phrases*) **(a) all along** desde el primer momento **(b) all but** casi; **the game had ~ but finished** ya casi había terminado el partido **(c) all that** (particularly) (*usu neg*): **I don't know her ~ that well** no la conozco tan bien; **I don't care ~ that much** no me importa demasiado **(d) all the** (+ *comp*): **~ the more reason to fire them!** ¡más razón para echarlos!; **~ the more so because** … tanto más cuanto que …
Allah /'ælə/ *n* Alá
all: **~-American** /'ɔːlə'merəkən ‖ ˌɔːlə'merɪkən/ *adj* ‹*boy/girl*› típicamente americano; **~-around** /'ɔːlə'raʊnd/ *adj* (AmE) (*before n*) **(a)** (versatile) ‹*athlete/scholar*› completo **(b)** ‹*experience/visibility*› amplio
allay /ə'leɪ/ *vt* ‹*doubt/fear*› disipar
all-clear /'ɔːl'klɪr ‖ 'ɔːl'klɪə(r)/ *n*: **to give sb/sth the ~** dar* luz verde a algn/algo

allegation /ælɪ'geɪʃən/ *n* acusación *f*

allege /ə'ledʒ/ *vt* afirmar; **she is ~d to have accepted bribes** se dice que aceptó sobornos

alleged /ə'ledʒd/ *adj* (*before n*) ‹*thief/violation*› presunto

allegedly /ə'ledʒədli ‖ ə'ledʒɪdli/ *adv* (*indep*) supuestamente

allegiance /ə'li:dʒəns/ *n* [U C] lealtad *f*; (political) filiación *f*

allergic /ə'lɜ:rdʒɪk ‖ ə'lɜ:dʒɪk/ *adj* alérgico; **to be ~** TO **sth** ser alérgico A algo

allergy /'ælərdʒi ‖ 'ælədʒi/ *n* (*pl* **-gies**) alergia *f*

alleviate /ə'li:vieɪt/ *vt* ‹*pain*› aliviar; ‹*problem*› paliar

alley /'æli/ *n* (*pl* **alleys**) callejón *m*

alleyway /'æliweɪ/ *n* callejón *m*

alliance /ə'laɪəns/ *n* alianza *f*

allied /'ælaɪd/ *adj* **(a)** (combined) (*pred*) **~** WITH *o* TO **sth** unido A algo **(b)** ‹*nations/groups*› aliado **(c)** (related) ‹*subjects/industries*› relacionado

alligator /'æləgeɪtər ‖ 'ælɪgeɪtə(r)/ *n* [C] aligátor *m*

all: **~-important** /ɔ:lɪm'pɔ:rtn̩t ‖ ˌɔ:lɪm'pɔ:tn̩t/ *adj* de suma importancia; **~-night** /'ɔ:l'naɪt/ *adj* ‹*party/show*› que dura toda la noche; ‹*café/store*› que está abierto toda la noche

allocate /'æləkeɪt/ *vt* asignar; (distribute) repartir; **$3 million has been ~d for research** se han destinado tres millones de dólares a la investigación

allot /ə'lɑ:t ‖ ə'lɒt/ *vt* **-tt-** (distribute) repartir; (assign) asignar

all: **~out** /'ɔ:l'aʊt/ *adj* ‹*attack*› con todo; ‹*opposition*› acérrimo; ‹*strike*› general; ‹*war*› total; **~ over** *adv* ‹*search*› por todas partes; **people came from ~ over** vino gente de todas partes

allow /ə'laʊ/ *vt* **1 (a)** (permit) permitir; Ⓢ **no dogs allowed** no se admiten perros **(b)** (give, grant) dar*; **they are ~ed an hour for lunch** les dan una hora para comer; **within the time ~ed** dentro del plazo concedido **2** (plan for): **~ a good two hours to reach the coast** calculen que les va a llevar por lo menos dos horas llegar a la costa; **I normally ~ about £50 for spending money** normalmente calculo unas 50 libras para gastos **3** (Sport) «*referee*» ‹*goal*› dar* por bueno

• **allow for** [*v* + *prep* + *o*] ‹*contingency*› tener* en cuenta

allowance /ə'laʊəns/ *n* **1** (from employer) complemento *m*; (from state) prestación *f*; (private) asignación *f*; (from parents) mensualidad *f*, mesada *f* (AmL) **2 to make ~(s) for sb** ser* indulgente con algn; **we've made ~(s) for delays** hemos tenido en cuenta posibles retrasos

alloy /'ælɔɪ/ *n* aleación *f*

all-powerful /'ɔ:l'paʊərfəl ‖ ˌɔ:l'paʊəfəl/ *adj* todopoderoso

all right¹ *adj* (*pred*): **are you ~?** ¿estás bien?; **the hotel looks ~ ~** el hotel no parece estar mal; **do I look ~ ~ in this dress?** ¿estoy bien con este vestido?; **I'll pay you back tomorrow: is that ~ ~?** mañana te devuelvo el dinero ¿okey? *or* (Esp) ¿vale?; **I'm sorry — that's ~ ~** lo siento — no tiene importancia; **it's ~ ~: I'm not going to hurt you** tranquilo, que no te voy a hacer daño

all right² *adv* bien

all right³ *interj* (colloq): **I won't be home till late, ~ ~?** volveré tarde ¿okey *or* (Esp) vale? (fam); **can I come too? — all right** ¿puedo ir yo también? — bueno

all: **~-round** /'ɔ:l'raʊnd/ *adj* (esp BrE) ⇒ ALL-AROUND; **A~ Saints' Day** *n* día *m* de Todos los Santos; **~-time** *adj* ‹*record*› sin precedentes; ‹*favorite*› de todos los tiempos

allude /ə'lu:d/ *vi* **to ~** TO **sth/sb** aludir A algo/algn

alluring /ə'lʊrɪŋ ‖ ə'lʊərɪŋ/ *adj* seductor

allusion /ə'lu:ʒən/ *n* alusión *f*

ally¹ /'ælaɪ/ *n* (*pl* **allies**) aliado, -da *m,f*

ally² *v refl* **allies, allying, allied**: **to ~ oneself** WITH **sb** aliarse CON algn; *see also* ALLIED

almanac /'ɔ:lmənæk/ *n* (yearbook) anuario *m*; (calendar) almanaque *m*

almighty /ɔ:l'maɪti/ *adj* todopoderoso

almond /'ɑ:mənd/ *n* almendra *f*

almost /'ɔ:lməʊst/ *adv* casi

■ **Note** Where *almost* is used with a verb in the past tense, it is translated by *casi* or *por poco*, and the verb is usually in the present tense: *I almost fell* casi me caigo; *we almost missed the train* casi *or* por poco perdemos el tren.

In some Latin American countries the preterite tense is often used: *we almost missed the train* casi *or* por poco perdimos el tren.

---

alms /ɑ:mz/ *pl n* limosnas *fpl*

aloft /ə'lɔ:ft ‖ ə'lɒft/ *adv* en el aire; **he held the cup ~** levantó la copa en alto

alone¹ /ə'ləʊn/ *adj* **(a)** (without others) solo; **I want to be ~ with you** quiero estar a solas contigo; **leave me ~** ¡déjame en paz! **(b) let alone**: **I can't afford beer, let ~ champagne** no puedo comprar ni cerveza, para qué hablar de champán; **she can't sew a button on, let ~ make a dress** no sabe ni pegar un botón menos aún hacer un vestido

alone² *adv* solo

along¹ /ə'lɔ:ŋ ‖ ə'lɒŋ/ *adv* **(a)** (forward): **a bit further ~ on the right** un poco más adelante, a mano derecha; **I was walking ~** iba caminando; *see also* COME, GET, MOVE *etc* ALONG **(b)** (with one): **why don't you come ~?** ¿por qué no vienes conmigo/con nosotros?; **she brought her brother ~** trajo a su hermano; *see also* SING ALONG **(c) along with** (junto) con

along² *prep*: **we walked ~ the shore** caminamos por la playa; **a bit further ~ the road** un poco más adelante

alongside¹ /ə'lɔ:ŋsaɪd ‖ ə'lɒŋsaɪd/ *prep* al lado de

alongside² *adv* al costado

aloof /ə'lu:f/ *adj* distante

aloud /ə'laʊd/ *adv* en alto, en voz alta

alphabet /'ælfəbet/ *n* alfabeto *m*

alphabetical /'ælfə'betɪkəl/ *adj* alfabético; **in ~ order** en *or* por orden alfabético

alpine /'ælpaɪn/ *adj* **(a)** (of high mountains) alpino **(b)** **Alpine** ‹*scenery/people*› de los Alpes, alpino

Alps /ælps/ *pl n* **the ~** los Alpes

already /ɔːl'redi/ *adv* ya; **I've ~ been there** ya he estado allí, ya estuve allí (AmL)

alright /ɔːl'raɪt/ *adj/adv/interj* ⇒ ALL RIGHT

Alsatian /æl'seɪʃən/ *n* (esp BrE) ⇒ GERMAN SHEPHERD (DOG)

also /'ɔːlsəʊ/ *adv* **(a)** (as well) también **(b)** (moreover) (*as linker*) además

altar /'ɔːltər ‖ 'ɔːltə(r)/ *n* altar *m*

alter /'ɔːltər ‖ 'ɔːltə(r)/ *vt* ‹*text/situation*› cambiar; ‹*garment*› arreglar ■ ~ *vi* cambiar

alteration /'ɔːltə'reɪʃən/ *n* [C U] (to text) cambio *m*; (to building) reforma *f*; (to garment) arreglo *m*

alternate¹ /'ɔːltərnət ‖ ɔːl'tɜːnət/ *adj* (*before n*) **(a)** (every second): **she works ~ Tuesdays** trabaja un martes sí y otro no; **write on ~ lines** escriba dejando un renglón por medio **(b)** (happening by turns) alterno **(c)** (AmE) ⇒ ALTERNATIVE¹ (a)

alternate² /'ɔːltərneɪt ‖ 'ɔːltəneɪt/ *vt/i* alternar

alternately /'ɔːltərnətli ‖ ɔːl'tɜːnətli/ *adv*: **he and she take the class ~** se turnan para dar la clase

alternating /'ɔːltərneɪtɪŋ ‖ 'ɔːltəneɪtɪŋ/ *adj* alterno

alternating current *n* [U] corriente *f* alterna

alternative¹ /ɔːl'tɜːrnətɪv ‖ ɔːl'tɜːnətɪv/ *adj* (*before n*) **(a)** (other) ‹*plan/method*› diferente **(b)** (progressive) ‹*lifestyle/medicine*› alternativo

alternative² *n* alternativa *f*

alternatively /ɔːl'tɜːrnətɪvli ‖ ɔːl'tɜːnətɪvli/ *adv* (*indep*): **~, you could stay with us** si no, te podrías quedar con nosotros

although /ɔːl'ðəʊ/ *conj* aunque

altitude /'æltətuːd ‖ 'æltɪtjuːd/ *n* [U C] altitud *f*

alto¹ /'æltəʊ/ *n* (*pl* **altos**) contralto *f*

alto² *adj* alto

altogether /'ɔːltə'geðər ‖ ˌɔːltə'geðə(r)/ *adv* **(a)** (completely) totalmente; **the decision wasn't ~ wise** la decisión no fue del todo acertada **(b)** (in total) en total **(c)** (on the whole) (*indep*) en general

aluminum /ə'luːmɪnəm/, (BrE) **aluminium** /'æljə'mɪniəm/ *n* [U] aluminio *m*

always /'ɔːlweɪz/ *adv* siempre

am¹ /æm, *weak form* əm/ *1st pers sing of* BE

am² ▶ **884** (before midday) a.m.; **at 7 ~** a las 7 de la mañana *or* 7 a.m.

amalgamate /ə'mælgəmeɪt/ *vt* ‹*collections/indexes*› unir, amalgamar; ‹*companies/departments*› fusionar ■ ~ *vi* «*companies*» fusionarse

amass /ə'mæs/ *vt* ‹*fortune*› amasar; ‹*arms/information/debts*› acumular

amateur¹ /'æmətər ‖ 'æmətə(r)/ *n* amateur *mf*

amateur² *adj* ‹*athlete/musician*› amateur; ‹*sport/competition*› para amateurs; **an ~ photographer** un aficionado a la fotografía

amaze /ə'meɪz/ *vt* asombrar

amazed /ə'meɪzd/ *adj* ‹*expression*› de asombro; **to be ~** estar* asombrado

amazement /ə'meɪzmənt/ *n* [U] asombro *m*

amazing /ə'meɪzɪŋ/ *adj* increíble

Amazon /'æməzɑːn ‖ 'æməzən/ *n* **(a)** (Myth) amazona *f* **(b)** (Geog) **the ~** el Amazonas; (*before n*) ‹*rain forest*› amazónico

ambassador /æm'bæsədər ‖ æm'bæsədə(r)/ ▶ **603** *n* embajador, -dora *m,f*

amber /'æmbər ‖ 'æmbə(r)/ *n* [U] **(a)** ▶ **515** (substance, color) ámbar *m* **(b)** (BrE Aut) amarillo

ambidextrous /'æmbɪ'dekstrəs/ *adj* ambidiestro, ambidextro

ambiguity /'æmbə'gjuːəti ‖ ˌæmbɪ'gjuːəti/ *n* [U C] (*pl* **-ties**) ambigüedad *f*

ambiguous /æm'bɪgjuəs/ *adj* ambiguo

ambition /æm'bɪʃən/ *n* [C U] ambición *f*

ambitious /æm'bɪʃəs/ *adj* **(a)** ‹*person/plan*› ambicioso **(b)** (overadventurous) (*pred*): **aren't you being a bit ~?** ¿no estás pretendiendo hacer demasiado?

ambivalent /æm'bɪvələnt/ *adj* ambivalente

amble /'æmbəl/ *vi*: **to ~ along** ir* tranquilamente

ambulance /'æmbjələns ‖ 'æmbjʊləns/ *n* ambulancia *f*

ambulanceman /'æmbjələnsmən ‖ 'æmbjʊlənsmən/ *n* (*pl* **-men** /-mən/) (BrE) ambulanciero *m*

ambush¹ /'æmbʊʃ/ *vt* tenderle* una emboscada a

ambush² *n* emboscada *f*

ameba /ə'miːbə/ (AmE) ⇒ AMOEBA

amen /'ɑː'men, 'eɪ'men/ *interj* amén

amenable /ə'miːnəbəl/ *adj* ‹*temperament*› dócil; **they proved quite ~ to the idea** se mostraron bien dispuestos frente a la idea

amend /ə'mend/ *vt* **(a)** ‹*text*› corregir* **(b)** (Law) enmendar*

amendment /ə'mendmənt/ *n* [C] **(a)** (alteration) corrección *f* **(b)** (Law) enmienda *f*

amends /ə'mendz/ *pl n*: **to make ~ to sb** desagraviar a algn; **to make ~** reparar el daño

amenity /ə'miːnəti/ *n* (*pl* **-ties**) [C] servicio *m*

America /ə'merəkə ‖ ə'merɪkə/ *n* (USA) Norteamérica *f*, Estados *mpl* Unidos, América *f*; (continent) América *f*

American¹ /ə'merəkən ‖ ə'merɪkən/ *adj* (of USA) estadounidense, norteamericano, americano

American² *n* (from USA) estadounidense *mf*, norteamericano, -na *m,f*, americano, -na *m,f*

amethyst /'æməθəst ‖ 'æməθɪst/ *n* [U C] amatista *f*

amiable /'eɪmiəbəl/ *adj* afable

amicable /'æmɪkəbəl/ *adj* ‹*person*› amigable; ‹*relations*› cordial

amid /ə'mɪd/, **amidst** /ə'mɪdst/ *prep* en medio de, entre

amiss /ə'mɪs/ *adj* (*pred*): **there was nothing ~** no había ningún problema; **there's something ~** pasa algo

ammunition /'æmjə'nɪʃən ‖ ˌæmjʊ'nɪʃən/ *n* [U] munición *f*

amnesia /æm'niːʒə ‖ æm'niːziə/ *n* [U] amnesia *f*

amnesty /'æmnəsti/ *n* (*pl* **-ties**) amnistía *f*

amoeba, (AmE also) **ameba** /ə'mi:bə/ *n* ameba *f*, amiba *f*

amok /ə'mʌk ‖ ə'mɒk/ *adv* **to run ~** «*person*» tener* un ataque de locura

among /ə'mʌŋ/, **amongst** /ə'mʌŋst/ *prep* entre

amount /ə'maʊnt/ *n* cantidad *f*

• amount to [*v* + *prep* + *o*] **(a)** (add up to) «*debt/assets*» ascender* a **(b)** (be equivalent to) equivaler* a; **it ~s to the same thing** viene a ser lo mismo

amp /æmp/ *n* **(a)** (Elec) amperio *m* **(b)** (amplifier) (colloq) amplificador *m*

amphetamine /æm'fetəmi:n/ *n* anfetamina *f*

amphibian /æm'fɪbiən/ *n* (Zool) anfibio *m*

amphibious /æm'fɪbiəs/ *adj* anfibio

amphitheater, (BrE) **amphitheatre** /'æmfɪˌθi:ətər ‖ 'æmfɪˌθɪətə(r)/ *n* anfiteatro *m*

ample /'æmpəl/ *adj* **(a)** ‹*space*› amplio; ‹*funds/resources*› abundante; ‹*helping*› generoso **(b)** (plenty) (*pred*) más que suficiente

amplifier /'æmpləfaɪər ‖ 'æmplɪfaɪə(r)/ *n* amplificador *m*

amplify /'æmpləfaɪ ‖ 'æmplɪfaɪ/ *vt* **-fies, -fying, -fied** amplificar*

amputate /'æmpjəteɪt ‖ 'æmpjʊteɪt/ *vt* amputar

Amtrak /'æmtræk/ *n* (in US) Ferrocarriles *mpl* de los EEUU

amuse /ə'mju:z/ *vt* **(a)** (entertain) entretener* **(b)** (make laugh) divertir* ■ *v refl* **to ~ oneself** (entertain oneself) entretenerse*; (have fun) divertirse*

amused /ə'mju:zd/ *adj* ‹*expression*› divertido; **she was ~ at the look on his face** le hizo gracia la cara que puso

amusement /ə'mju:zmənt/ *n* **(a)** [U] (entertainment) distracción *f*, entretención *f* (AmL) **(b)** [U] (mirth) diversión *f*; **much to our ~** para nuestro gran regocijo; (*before n*) **~ arcade** sala *f* de juegos recreativos; **~ park** parque *m* de diversiones *or* (Esp) atracciones

amusing /ə'mju:zɪŋ/ *adj* divertido

an /æn, *weak form* ən/ *indef art before vowel* ⇒ A

anachronism /ə'nækrənɪzəm/ *n* anacronismo *m*

anaemia *etc* (BrE) ⇒ ANEMIA *etc*

anaesthetic *n* (BrE) ⇒ ANESTHETIC

anagram /'ænəgræm/ *n* anagrama *m*

analogy /ə'nælədʒi/ *n* [C U] (*pl* **-gies**) analogía *f*

analyse *vt* (BrE) ⇒ ANALYZE

analysis /ə'næləsəs ‖ ə'nælɪsɪs/ *n* (*pl* **-lyses** /-lɪsi:z/) **(a)** [C U] (examination) análisis *m* **(b)** [U] (Psych) psicoanálisis *m*, análisis *m*

analyst /'ænləst ‖ 'ænəlɪst/ *n* **(a)** (of data) analista *mf* **(b)** (Psych) psicoanalista *mf*, analista *mf*

analytical /'ænə'lɪtɪkəl/ *adj* analítico

analyze, (BrE) **analyse** /'ænəlaɪz/ *vt* **(a)** ‹*data*› analizar* **(b)** (Psych) psicoanalizar*, analizar*

anarchist /'ænərkəst ‖ 'ænəkɪst/ *n* anarquista *mf*

anarchy /'ænərki ‖ 'ænəki/ *n* [U] anarquía *f*

anatomy /ə'nætəmi/ *n* [U] anatomía *f*

ancestor /'ænsestər ‖ 'ænsestə(r)/ *n* antepasado, -da *m,f*

ancestry /'ænsestri/ *n* [U] ascendencia *f*

anchor[1] /'æŋkər ‖ 'æŋkə(r)/ *n* (Naut) ancla *f*‡

anchor[2] *vt* ‹*ship*› anclar; ‹*rope/tent*› sujetar

anchor: **~man** /'æŋkərmæn ‖ 'æŋkəmæn/ *n* (*pl* **-men** /-men/) (TV) presentador *m*; **~woman** *n* (TV) presentadora *f*

anchovy /'æntʃəʊvi ‖ 'æntʃəvi/ *n* (*pl* **-vies** *or* **-vy**) anchoa *f*

ancient /'eɪnʃənt/ *adj* **(a)** ‹*civilizations/ruin*› antiguo; **A~ Greek** griego *m* clásico **(b)** (colloq) (old) ‹*car*› del año de la pera (fam)

and /ænd, *weak form* ənd/ *conj*

■ **Note** The usual translation of *and*, *y*, becomes *e* when it precedes a word beginning with *i*, *hi*, or *y*.

(a) y; **bread ~ butter** pan con mantequilla **(b)** (in numbers): **one ~ a half** uno y medio; **two hundred ~ twenty** doscientos veinte **(c)** (showing continuation, repetition): **faster ~ faster** cada vez más rápido **(d)** (*with inf*): **try ~ finish this today** trata de terminar esto hoy

Andalusia /'ændə'lu:ʒə ‖ ˌændə'lu:siə/ *n* Andalucía *f*

Andes /'ændi:z/ *pl n* **the ~** los Andes

Andorra /æn'dɔ:rə/ *n* Andorra *f*

anecdote /'ænɪkdəʊt/ *n* anécdota *f*

anemia, (BrE) **anaemia** /ə'ni:miə/ *n* [U] anemia *f*

anemic, (BrE) **anaemic** /ə'ni:mɪk/ *adj* anémico

anemone /ə'neməni/ *n* anémona *f*

anesthetic, (BrE) **anaesthetic** /'ænəs'θetɪk ‖ ˌænɪs'θetɪk/ *n* [C U] anestésico *m*; **to be under ~** estar* bajo los efectos de la anestesia

anew /ə'nu: ‖ ə'nju:/ *adv* (liter) de nuevo, otra vez

angel /'eɪndʒəl/ *n* ángel *m*

angelic /æn'dʒelɪk/ *adj* angelical

anger /'æŋgər ‖ 'æŋgə(r)/ *n* [U] ira *f*, enojo *m* (esp AmL), enfado *m* (esp Esp)

angina /æn'dʒaɪnə/ *n* [U] angina *f* (de pecho)

angle /'æŋgəl/ *n* **1** ángulo *m*; **she wore her hat at an ~** llevaba el sombrero ladeado **2** (point of view) perspectiva *f*

angler /'æŋglər ‖ 'æŋglə(r)/ *n* pescador, -dora *m,f* (de caña)

Anglican[1] /'æŋglɪkən/ *n* anglicano, -na *m,f*

Anglican[2] *adj* anglicano

angling /'æŋglɪŋ/ *n* [U] pesca *f* (con caña)

Anglo-Saxon[1] /'æŋgləʊ'sæksən/ *adj* anglosajón

Anglo-Saxon[2] *n* **(a)** [C] (person) anglosajón, -jona *m,f* **(b)** [U] (language) anglosajón *m*

Angola /æŋ'gəʊlə/ *n* Angola *f*

Angolan /æŋ'gəʊlən/ *adj* angoleño

angrily /'æŋgrəli ‖ 'æŋgrɪli/ *adv* con ira

angry /'æŋgri/ *adj* **angrier, angriest** ‹*person*› enojado (esp AmL), enfadado (esp Esp); **to get ~** enojarse (esp AmL), enfadarse (esp Esp)

anguish /'æŋgwɪʃ/ *n* [U] angustia *f*

angular /'æŋgjələr ‖ 'æŋgjʊlə(r)/ *adj* ‹*shape*› angular; ‹*features*› anguloso

animal /'ænəməl ‖ 'ænɪməl/ *n* animal *m*

animate /'ænəmeɪt ‖ 'ænɪmeɪt/ *vt* animar

animated /'ænəmeɪtəd ‖ 'ænɪmeɪtɪd/ *adj* animado

animation /ænə'meɪʃən ‖ ,ænɪ'meɪʃən/ *n* [U] animación *f*

animator /'ænəmeɪtər ‖ 'ænɪmeɪtə(r)/ *n* animador, -dora *m,f*

animosity /'ænə'mɑːsəti ‖ ,ænɪ'mɒsəti/ *n* [U C] (*pl* **-ties**) animosidad *f*

aniseed /'ænəsiːd ‖ 'ænɪsiːd/ *n* [U] anís *m*

ankle /'æŋkəl/ ▶ 484 *n* tobillo *m*; (*before n*) ~ **boot** botín *m*; ~ **sock** calcetín *m* corto, soquete *m* (CS)

annex[1] /ə'neks/ *vt* ‹*territory*› anexar

annex[2], (BrE) **annexe** /'æneks/ *n* anexo *m*, anejo *m*

annihilate /ə'naɪəleɪt/ *vt* ‹*army/city*› aniquilar

anniversary /'ænə'vɜːrsəri ‖ ,ænɪ'vɜːsəri/ *n* (*pl* **-ries**) aniversario *m*; **(wedding)** ~ aniversario *m* de boda de casados

announce /ə'naʊns/ *vt* **(a)** ‹*flight/guest/marriage*› anunciar **(b)** (declare) anunciar **(c)** (AmE Rad, TV) ‹*game/race*› comentar

announcement /ə'naʊnsmənt/ *n* anuncio *m*

announcer /ə'naʊnsər ‖ ə'naʊnsə(r)/ *n* (Rad, TV) **(a)** (commentator) (AmE) comentarista *mf* **(b)** (between programs) (BrE) locutor, -tora *m,f* de continuidad

annoy /ə'nɔɪ/ *vt* molestar, irritar

annoyance /ə'nɔɪəns/ *n* **(a)** [U] (irritation) irritación *f*; (anger) enojo *m* (esp AmL), enfado *m* (esp Esp) **(b)** [C] (cause of irritation) molestia *f*

annoyed /ə'nɔɪd/ *adj* enojado (esp AmL), enfadado (esp Esp)

annoying /ə'nɔɪɪŋ/ *adj* ‹*person*› pesado; ‹*noise/habit*› molesto; **how ~!** ¡qué rabia!

annual[1] /'ænjuəl/ *adj* (*before n*) anual

annual[2] *n* **1** (plant) planta *f* anual **2** (publication) anuario *m*

annually /'ænjuəli/ *adv* anualmente

annul /ə'nʌl/ *vt* **-ll-** anular

annulment /ə'nʌlmənt/ *n* [C U] anulación *f*

anoint /ə'nɔɪnt/ *vt* ungir*

anonymous /ə'nɑːnəməs ‖ ə'nɒnɪməs/ *adj* anónimo; **to remain ~** permanecer* en el anonimato; **~ letter** anónimo *m*

anorak /'ænəræk/ *n* (BrE) anorak *m*

anorexia (nervosa) /'ænə'reksiə (nər'vəʊsə) ‖ ,ænə'reksiə (nɜː'vəʊsə)/ *n* [U] anorexia *f* (nerviosa)

another[1] /ə'nʌðər ‖ ə'nʌðə(r)/ *adj* otro, otra; (*pl*) otros, otras

another[2] *pron* otro, otra

answer[1] /'ænsər ‖ 'ɑːnsə(r)/ *n* **1 (a)** (reply) respuesta *f*, contestación *f*; **in ~ to your question** para contestar tu pregunta **(b)** (response): **her ~ to his rudeness was to ignore it** respondió a su grosería ignorándola; **Britain's ~ to Elvis Presley** el Elvis Presley británico **2 (a)** (in exam, test, quiz) respuesta *f* **(b)** (solution) solución *f*; **~ TO sth** solución DE algo

answer[2] *vt* **1 (a)** (reply to) ‹*person/letter*› contestar **(b)** ‹*telephone*› contestar, atender* (AmL), coger* (Esp); **will you ~ the door?** ¿vas tú (a abrir)? **(c)** ‹*critic/criticism*› responder a **2** (fit): **to ~ (to) a description** responder a una descripción ■ ~ *vi* contestar, responder

● **answer back 1** [*v* + *adv*] (rudely) contestar **2** [*v* + *o* + *adv*] **to ~ sb back** contestarle mal *or* de mala manera a algn

● **answer for** [*v* + *prep* + *o*] (accept responsibility for) ‹*conduct/consequences*› responder de; **his parents have a lot to ~ for** sus padres tienen mucha culpa

answerable /'ænsərəbəl ‖'ɑːnsərəbəl/ *adj*: **she said she was not ~ for his behavior** dijo que ella no era responsable de lo que él hiciera; **I'm ~ to no one** no tengo que rendirle cuentas a nadie

answering machine /'ænsərɪŋ ‖ 'ɑːnsərɪŋ/ *n* contestador *m* (automático)

ant /ænt/ *n* hormiga *f*

antagonize /æn'tægənaɪz/ *vt* suscitar el antagonismo de

Antarctic[1] /ænt'ɑːrktɪk ‖ æn'tɑːktɪk/ *adj* antártico; **the ~ Ocean** el Océano Antártico; **the ~ Circle** el círculo polar antártico

Antarctic[2] *n* **the ~** la región antártica

Antarctica /ænt'ɑːrktɪkə ‖ æn'tɑːktɪkə/ *n* la Antártida

anteater /'ænt,iːtər ‖ 'ænt,iːtə(r)/ *n* oso *m* hormiguero

antecedent /,æntə'siːdn̩t ‖ ,æntɪ'siːdənt/ *n* antecedente *m*

antelope /'æntələʊp ‖ 'æntɪləʊp/ *n* (*pl* **~s** *or* **~**) antílope *m*

antenatal /'ænti'neɪtl/ *adj* prenatal; **~ clinic** *consulta médica para mujeres embarazadas*

antenna /æn'tenə/ *n* **(a)** (*pl* **-nae** /-niː/) (Zool) antena *f* **(b)** (*pl* **-nas**) (Rad, TV) antena *f*

anthem /'ænθəm/ *n* himno *m*; **national ~** himno nacional

anthology /æn'θɑːlədʒi ‖ æn'θɒlədʒi/ *n* (*pl* **-gies**) antología *f*

anthropologist /'ænθrə'pɑːlədʒəst ‖ ,ænθrə'pɒlədʒɪst/ *n* antropólogo, -ga *m,f*

anthropology /'ænθrə'pɑːlədʒi ‖ ,ænθrə'pɒlədʒi/ *n* [U] antropología *f*

anti- /'æntaɪ, 'ænti ‖ 'ænti/ *pref* anti-

antiaircraft /'æntaɪ'erkræft ‖ ,ænti'eəkrɑːft/ *adj* antiaéreo

antibiotic /'æntɪbaɪ'ɑːtɪk ‖ ,æntibaɪ'ɒtɪk/ *n* [C U] antibiótico *m*

antibody /'ænti,bɑːdi ‖ 'ænti,bɒdi/ *n* (*pl* **-dies**) anticuerpo *m*

anticipate /æn'tɪsəpeɪt ‖ æn'tɪsɪpeɪt/ *vt* **1 (a)** (expect) ‹*consequences*› prever*; **I don't ~ any problems** no creo que vaya a haber ningún problema **(b)** (look forward to) esperar **2 (a)** (foresee and act accordingly) ‹*movements/objections/needs*› prever* **(b)** (preempt) anticiparse a

anticipation /æn'tɪsə'peɪʃən ‖ æn,tɪsɪ'peɪʃən/ *n* [U] **(a)** (foresight) previsión *f*; **thanking you in ~** agradeciéndole de antemano su atención **(b)** (expectation) expectativa *f*

anticlimax /'æntaɪ'klaɪmæks ‖ ,ænti'klaɪmæks/ *n* [C U] *suceso caracterizado por un descenso de la tensión*; (disappointment) decepción *f*

anticlockwise /'æntɪ'klɑ:kwaɪz ‖ ,ænti'klɒk waɪz/ *adj/adv* (BrE) en sentido contrario a las agujas del reloj

antics /'æntɪks/ *pl n* (clowning) payasadas *fpl*; (of naughty children) travesuras *fpl*

antidote /'æntɪdəʊt/ *n* ~ (TO **sth**) antídoto *m* (CONTRA algo)

antifreeze /'æntɪfri:z/ *n* [U] anticongelante *m*

antipathy /æn'tɪpəθi/ *n* [C U] (*pl* **-thies**) antipatía *f*

antiperspirant /'æntɪ'pɜ:rspərənt ‖ ,ænti'pɜ: spɪrənt/ *n* [C U] antitranspirante *m*

antique¹ /æn'ti:k/ *n* antigüedad *f*; (*before n*) ~ **shop** tienda *f* de antigüedades

antique² *adj* antiguo

antiquity /æn'tɪkwəti/ *n* (*pl* **-ties**) **1** [U] (ancient times, age) antigüedad *f* **2 antiquities** *pl* antigüedades *fpl*

anti-Semitic /'æntɪsə'mɪtɪk ‖ ,æntisɪ'mɪtɪk/ *adj* antisemita

antiseptic¹ /'æntɪ'septɪk/ *n* [C U] antiséptico *m*

antiseptic² *adj* (Pharm) antiséptico

antisocial /'æntɪ'səʊʃəl/ *adj* **(a)** (offensive to society) antisocial **(b)** (unsociable) poco sociable

antithesis /æn'tɪθəsəs ‖ æn'tɪθəsɪs/ *n* (*pl* **-eses** /-əsi:z/) antítesis *f*

antler /'æntlər ‖ 'æntlə(r)/ *n* cuerno *m*, asta *f*‡; **the animal's** ~**s** la cornamenta del animal

anus /'eɪnəs/ *n* ano *m*

anvil /'ænvəl ‖ 'ænvɪl/ *n* yunque *m*

anxiety /æŋ'zaɪəti/ *n* (*pl* **-ties**) **(a)** [U] (distress, concern) preocupación *f* **(b)** [C] (problem, worry) preocupación *f* **(c)** [U] (Med, Psych) ansiedad *f*

anxious /'æŋkʃəs/ *adj* **(a)** (worried) preocupado **(b)** (worrying) ‹*time/moment*› (lleno) de preocupación **(c)** (eager) deseoso; **he's very** ~ **to please** tiene mucho afán de agradar

anxiously /'æŋkʃəsli/ *adv* **(a)** (worriedly) con preocupación **(b)** (eagerly) ansiosamente

any¹ /'eni/ *adj* **I 1** (*in questions*) **(a)** (+ *pl n*): **are there** ~ **questions?** ¿alguien tiene alguna pregunta?; **does she have** ~ **children?** ¿tiene hijos? **(b)** (+ *uncount n*): **do you need** ~ **help?** ¿necesitas ayuda?; **do you want** ~ **more coffee?** ¿quieres más café? **(c)** (+ *sing count n: as indef art*) algún, -guna; **is there** ~ **chance they'll come?** ¿existe alguna posibilidad de que vengan? **2** (*in 'if' clauses and suppositions*) **(a)** (+ *pl n*): **call me if there are** ~ **changes** llámame si hay algún cambio; **if you see** ~ **flowers, buy some** si ves flores, compra algunas **(b)** (+ *uncount n*): **let me know if you have** ~ **pain** avíseme si siente dolor; **take** ~ **money you need** toma el dinero que necesites **(c)** (+ *sing count n*): ~ **upset could kill him** cualquier disgusto podría matarlo; ~ **act of disobedience will be punished** toda desobediencia será castigada **3** ▶ **718** (*with neg and implied neg*) **(a)** (+ *pl n*): **don't buy** ~ **more eggs** no compres más huevos; **aren't there** ~ **apples left?** ¿no queda ninguna manzana? **(b)** (+ *uncount n*): **don't make** ~ **noise** no hagas ruido; **it doesn't make** ~ **sense** no tiene ningún sentido **II 1 (a)** (no matter which): **take** ~ **book you want** llévate cualquier libro; ~ **day now** cualquier día de éstos **(b)** (every, all): **in** ~ **large school, you'll find that** ... en cualquier *or* todo colegio grande, verás que ... **2** (countless, a lot): ~ **number/amount of sth** cualquier cantidad de algo

any² *pron* **1** (*in questions*) **(a)** (*referring to pl n*) alguno, -na; **those chocolates were nice, are there** ~ **left?** ¡qué ricos esos bombones! ¿queda alguno? **(b)** (*referring to uncount n*): **we need sugar; did you buy** ~**?** nos hace falta azúcar ¿compraste?; **is there** ~ **of that cake left?** ¿queda algo de ese pastel? **2** (*in if clauses and suppositions*) **(a)** (*referring to pl n*): **buy some red ones if you can find** ~ compra algunas rojas si encuentras; **if** ~ **of my friends calls, take a message** si llama alguno de mis amigos, toma el recado **(b)** (*referring to uncount n*): **help yourself to cake if you want** ~ sírvete pastel si quieres **3** ▶ **718** (*with neg and implied neg*) **(a)** (*referring to pl n*): **some children were here — I didn't see** ~ aquí había algunos niños — yo no vi (a) ninguno *or* no los vi; **you'll have to go without cigarettes; I forgot to buy** ~ te vas a tener que arreglar sin cigarrillos porque me olvidé de comprar **(b)** (*referring to uncount n*): **she offered me some wine, but I didn't want** ~ me ofreció vino, pero no quise; **I didn't understand** ~ **of that lecture** no entendí nada de esa conferencia

any³ *adv* **1** (*with comparative*): **do you feel** ~ **better now?** ¿te sientes (algo) mejor ahora?; **they don't live here** ~ **more** ya no viven aquí **2** (at all) (AmE): **have you thought about it** ~ **since then?** ¿has pensado en ello desde entonces?; **it doesn't seem to have affected him** ~ no parece haberlo afectado en absoluto

anybody /'eni,bɑ:di ‖ 'eni,bɒdi/ *pron* **1 (a)** (somebody) (*in interrog, conditional sentences*) alguien; **will** ~ **be seeing Emma today?** ¿alguno de ustedes va a ver a Emma hoy? **(b)** ▶ **718** (*with neg*) nadie; **don't tell** ~**!** ¡no se lo digas a nadie! **2 (a)** (whoever, everybody): **give it to** ~ **you like** dáselo a quien quieras; ~ **who's been to Paris knows** ... cualquier persona que haya estado en París sabe ...; **before** ~ **could stop her** antes de que nadie pudiera detenerla **(b)** (no matter who) cualquiera; ~ **could do it** cualquiera podría hacerlo

anyhow /'enihaʊ/ *adv* **1** ⇒ ANYWAY **2** (haphazardly) de cualquier manera

anyone /'eniwʌn/ ▶ **718** *pron* ⇒ ANYBODY

anyplace /'enipleɪs/ *adv* (AmE) ⇒ ANYWHERE[1] 1

anything /'eniθɪŋ/ *pron* **1 (a)** (something) (*in interrog, conditional sentences*) algo; **have you ever heard** ~ **so ridiculous?** ¡habráse oído semejante ridiculez! **(b)** ▶ **718** (a single thing) (*with neg*) nada; **don't say** ~**!** ¡no digas nada! **2 (a)** (whatever): ~ **you say!** ¡lo que tú digas!; **we'll do** ~ **we can to help** haremos todo lo que podamos para ayudar **(b)** (no matter what): ~ **is possible** todo es posible; ~ **could happen** podría pasar cualquier cosa **3**

(*used for emphasis*): **was it interesting? — ~ but!** ¿fue interesante? — ¡qué va!; **the portrait doesn't look ~ like her** el retrato no se parece en nada a ella

anyway /'eniweɪ/ *adv* **1** (in any case) de todos modos **2** (changing the subject, moving conversation on) (*as linker*) bueno; **~, to cut a long story short,** … bueno, en resumidas cuentas …

anywhere[1] /'enihwer ‖ 'eniweə(r)/ *adv* **1 (a)** (no matter where) en cualquier sitio *or* lugar; **you can sit ~ you like** te puedes sentar donde quieras **(b)** (in, to any unspecified place): **have you seen my book ~?** ¿has visto mi libro por alguna parte *or* por algún lado?; **we never go ~ together** nunca vamos juntos a ningún lado **2 anywhere near**: **is it ~ near Portland?** ¿queda cerca de Portland?; **we aren't ~ near ready yet** todavía no estamos listos ni mucho menos

anywhere[2] *pron*: **is there ~ that sells oysters?** ¿hay algún sitio donde vendan ostras?; **she hasn't ~ to stay** no tiene donde quedarse

apace /ə'peɪs/ *adv* (liter *or* journ) a paso *or* ritmo acelerado

apart /ə'pɑːrt ‖ ə'pɑːt/ *adv* **1 (a)** (separated): **they've lived ~ for some years** ya hace algunos años que viven separados; **keep them ~** manténgalos separados **(b)** (into pieces): *see* COME, FALL, PULL, TAKE *etc* APART **2** (distant): **in places as far ~ as Tokyo and Paris** en lugares tan alejados el uno del otro como Tokio y París **3** (excluded) (*after n*): **these faults ~** … aparte de estos defectos …; **joking ~** … bromas aparte … **4 apart from** (*as prep*) **(a)** (except for) excepto, aparte de **(b)** (separated from): **she always sits ~ from the rest of the group** siempre se sienta apartada del resto del grupo

apartheid /ə'pɑːrteɪt ‖ ə'pɑːteɪt/ *n* [U] apartheid *m*

apartment /ə'pɑːrtmənt ‖ ə'pɑːtmənt/ *n* (set of rooms) apartamento *m*, departamento *m* (AmL), piso *m* (Esp); (*before n*) **~ building** edificio *m* de apartamentos *or* (AmL tb) de departamentos

apathetic /'æpə'θetɪk/ *adj* apático

apathy /'æpəθi/ *n* [U] apatía *f*

ape[1] /eɪp/ *n* simio *m*, mono *m*

ape[2] *vt* remedar, imitar

aperitif /ə'perə'tiːf ‖ ə'perətif/ *n* aperitivo *m*

aperture /'æpərtʃər ‖ 'æpətʃə(r)/ *n* **(a)** (Opt, Phot) apertura *f* **(b)** (hole, opening) (frml) orificio *m*; (long and narrow) rendija *f*

apex /'eɪpeks/ *n* (*pl* **apexes** *or* **apices**) **(a)** (Math) vértice *m* **(b)** (pinnacle) cúspide *f* **(c)** (pointed end, tip) ápice *m*

APEX /'eɪpeks/ *adj* (= **advance purchase excursion**) (*before n*) ‹*ticket/booking*› Apex *adj inv*

aphid /'eɪfəd ‖ 'eɪfɪd/ *n* afídido *m*, áfido *m*

aphrodisiac /'æfrə'dɪziæk/ *n* afrodisíaco *m*

apices /'eɪpəsiːz ‖ 'eɪpɪsiːz/ *pl of* APEX

apiece /ə'piːs/ *adv* cada uno

apocalypse /ə'pɑːkəlɪps ‖ ə'pɒkəlɪps/ *n* apocalipsis *m*

apologetic /ə'pɑːlə'dʒetɪk ‖ əˌpɒlə'dʒetɪk/ *adj* ‹*letter/look*› de disculpa; **she was very ~** se deshizo en disculpas

apologize /ə'pɑːlədʒaɪz ‖ ə'pɒlədʒaɪz/ *vi* pedir* perdón, disculparse; **we ~ for the delay** rogamos disculpen el retraso; **you must ~ to her for being so rude** tienes que pedirle perdón por haber sido tan grosero

apology /ə'pɑːlədʒi ‖ ə'pɒlədʒi/ *n* (*pl* **-gies**) (*often pl*) disculpa *f*; **please accept my apologies** le ruego me disculpe

apostle /ə'pɑːsəl ‖ ə'pɒsəl/ *n* apóstol *m*

apostrophe /ə'pɑːstrəfi ‖ ə'pɒstrəfi/ *n* apóstrofo *m*

appall, (BrE) **appal** /ə'pɔːl/ *vt* (BrE) **-ll-** horrorizar*

appalling /ə'pɔːlɪŋ/ *adj* ‹*conditions*› atroz; **the play is absolutely ~** la obra es pésima

apparatus /'æpə'rætəs ‖ ˌæpə'reɪtəs/ *n* [U C] (*pl* **~**) **(a)** (equipment) aparatos *mpl*; **a piece of ~** un aparato **(b)** (Pol) aparato *m*

apparel /ə'pærəl/ *n* [U] **(a)** (finery) (liter) atavío *m* (liter) **(b)** (AmE Busn) ropa *f*

apparent /ə'pærənt/ *adj* **(a)** (evident): **for no ~ reason** sin motivo aparente; **it was ~ that** … estaba claro que …, era evidente que … **(b)** (seeming) ‹*interest/concern*› aparente

apparently /ə'pærəntli/ *adv* **(a)** (*indep*) al parecer, por lo visto, según parece **(b)** (seemingly) ‹*intelligent/happy*› aparentemente

apparition /'æpə'rɪʃən/ *n* aparición *f*

appeal[1] /ə'piːl/ *n* **1** [C] (call) llamamiento *m*, llamado *m* (AmL); (request) solicitud *f*, pedido *m* (AmL); (plea) ruego *m* **2** [C] (Law) apelación *f* **3** [C] (fund, organization) *campaña para recaudar fondos* **4** [U] (attraction) atractivo *m*

appeal[2] *vi* **1** (call) **to ~ FOR sth** ‹*for funds*› pedir* algo; **the police ~ed to witnesses to come forward** la policía hizo un llamamiento *or* (AmL tb) un llamado para que se presentaran testigos del hecho **2** (Law) apelar **3** (be attractive) **to ~ TO sb** atraerle* A algn ■ **~** *vt* (AmE) ‹*decision/verdict*› apelar contra *or* de

appealing /ə'piːlɪŋ/ *adj* atractivo

appear /ə'pɪr ‖ ə'pɪə(r)/ *vi* **1 (a)** (come into view) aparecer* **(b)** (be published): **to ~ (in print)** publicarse* **(c)** (Law) comparecer*; **to ~ in court** comparecer* **2** (seem) parecer*; **so it ~s** eso parece; **to ~ to** + INF parecer* + INF; **we ~ to be lost** parece que nos hemos perdido

appearance /ə'pɪrəns ‖ ə'pɪərəns/ *n* **1 (a)** [U C] (coming into view) aparición *f* **(b)** (Law) comparecencia *f* **(c)** [U] (of book) publicación *f* **2** [U] **(a)** (look) aspecto *m* **(b) appearances** *pl* apariencias *fpl*; **to keep up ~s** guardar las apariencias

appease /ə'piːz/ *vt* ‹*person*› apaciguar*; ‹*anger*› aplacar*

appendices /ə'pendəsiːz ‖ ə'pendɪsiːz/ *pl of* APPENDIX

appendicitis /ə'pendə'saɪtəs ‖ əˌpendɪ'saɪtɪs/ *n* [U] apendicitis *f*

appendix /ə'pendɪks/ *n* (*pl* **-dixes** *or* **-dices**) apéndice *m*

appetite /'æpətaɪt ‖ 'æpɪtaɪt/ *n* [C U] apetito *m*

appetizer /ˈæpətaɪzər ‖ ˈæpɪtaɪzə(r)/ *n* **(a)** (drink) aperitivo *m* **(b)** (snack) aperitivo *m*, tapa *f* (Esp), botana *f* (Méx)

appetizing /ˈæpətaɪzɪŋ ‖ ˈæpɪtaɪzɪŋ/ *adj* apetitoso

applaud /əˈplɔːd/ *vt/i* aplaudir

applause /əˈplɔːz/ *n* [U] aplausos *mpl*

apple /ˈæpəl/ *n* [C U] manzana *f*; (*before n*) **~ pie** pastel *m* de manzana, pay *m* de manzana (Méx); **~ tree** manzano *m*

appliance /əˈplaɪəns/ *n* aparato *m*; **electrical ~s** electrodomésticos *mpl*

applicable /ˈæplɪkəbəl, əˈplɪkəbəl/ *adj* (frml): **these regulations are only ~ to foreigners** estas normas se refieren únicamente a los extranjeros; **delete as ~** tache lo que no corresponda

applicant /ˈæpləkənt ‖ ˈæplɪkənt/ *n* (for job) candidato, -ta *m,f*, postulante *mf* (CS), aplicante *mf* (Ven)

application /ˈæpləˈkeɪʃən ‖ ˌæplɪˈkeɪʃən/ *n* **1** [C U] (request) solicitud *f*; **~ FOR sth** ‹*for loan/grant/visa*› solicitud DE algo; (*before n*) **~ form** (impreso *m* de) solicitud *f* **2 (a)** [C U] (of method, skills, theory) aplicación *f* **(b)** [U C] (of paint, ointment) aplicación *f*

applied /əˈplaɪd/ *adj* aplicado

apply /əˈplaɪ/ **applies, applying, applied** *vt* **(a)** (put on) aplicar* **(b)** ‹*method/theory/rules*› aplicar*; **to ~ the brakes** frenar; **she applied herself to her work** se puso a trabajar con diligencia ■ **~** *vi* **(a)** (make application): **please ~ in writing to** ... diríjase por escrito a ...; **to ~ FOR sth** ‹*for loan/permission*› solicitar algo; **to ~ for a job** solicitar un trabajo, aplicar* a un trabajo (Ven), postular para un trabajo (CS) **(b)** (be applicable) «*regulation/criterion*» aplicarse*

appoint /əˈpɔɪnt/ *vt* **1** (name, choose) nombrar **2** (frml) ‹*date*› designar (frml)

appointment /əˈpɔɪntmənt/ *n* **1** [C] (arrangement to meet) cita *f*; (with doctor, hairdresser) hora *f*, cita *f*; **to make an ~** pedir* hora *or* una cita **2 (a)** [U C] (act of appointing) nombramiento *m* **(b)** [C] (post) (frml) puesto *m*

appraisal /əˈpreɪzəl/ *n* (of situation, employee) evaluación *f*; (of work, novel) valoración *f*; (of property) tasación *f*

appraise /əˈpreɪz/ *vt* ‹*situation/employee*› evaluar*; ‹*novel/painting*› valorar; ‹*property*› tasar, avaluar* (AmL)

appreciable /əˈpriːʃəbəl/ *adj* ‹*change/difference*› apreciable; ‹*loss/sum*› importante

appreciate /əˈpriːʃieɪt/ *vt* **(a)** (value) ‹*food/novel*› apreciar **(b)** (be grateful for) agradecer* **(c)** (understand) ‹*danger/difficulties*› darse* cuenta de; **I ~ that, but** ... lo comprendo, pero ... ■ **~** *vi* «*shares/property*» (re)valorizarse*

appreciation /əˈpriːʃiˈeɪʃən/ *n* [U] **(a)** (gratitude) agradecimiento *m* **(b)** (discriminating enjoyment): **he showed a genuine ~ of music** demostró saber apreciar la música

appreciative /əˈpriːʃətɪv/ *adj* **(a)** (grateful) ‹*smile/gesture*› de agradecimiento **(b)** (of art, good food) apreciativo

apprehend /ˈæprɪˈhend/ *vt* (frml) apresar, detener*

apprehension /ˈæprɪˈhentʃən ‖ ˌæprɪˈhenʃən/ *n* [U] aprensión *f*

apprehensive /ˈæprɪˈhensɪv/ *adj* ‹*look*› aprensivo, de aprensión; **I'm rather ~ about the consequences** estoy algo inquieto por lo que pueda pasar

apprentice[1] /əˈprentəs ‖ əˈprentɪs/ *n* aprendiz, -diza *m,f*

apprentice[2] *vt*: **to be ~d TO sb** estar* de aprendiz CON algn

apprenticeship /əˈprentəsʃɪp ‖ əˈprentɪsʃɪp/ *n* aprendizaje *m* (*de un oficio*)

approach[1] /əˈprəʊtʃ/ *vi* acercarse*, aproximarse ■ **~** *vt* **(a)** (draw near to) aproximarse *or* acercarse* a **(b)** (talk to): **have you ~ed her about it?** ¿ya se lo ha planteado?, ¿ya ha hablado con ella del asunto?; **he ~ed me for a loan** se dirigió a mí para pedirme un préstamo **(c)** (tackle) ‹*problem/question*› enfocar*

approach[2] *n* **1** [C] (method, outlook) enfoque *m* **2** [C] (overture — offering sth) propuesta *f*; (— requesting sth) solicitud *f*, petición *f*, pedido *m* (AmL) **3** [U] (drawing near): **at the ~ of winter** al acercarse el invierno **4** [C] (means of entering) acceso *m*

approachable /əˈprəʊtʃəbəl/ *adj* ‹*person/place*› accesible

appropriate[1] /əˈprəʊpriət/ *adj* apropiado

appropriate[2] /əˈprəʊprieɪt/ *vt* ‹*possessions*› apropiarse de; ‹*money*› destinar

approval /əˈpruːvəl/ *n* [U] aprobación *f*; **on ~** a prueba

approve /əˈpruːv/ *vi* **to ~ (OF sth/sb)**: **they don't ~ of my smoking** les parece mal que fume; **mother seems to ~ of him** a mamá parece gustarle; **I don't ~ of his methods** no estoy de acuerdo con sus métodos ■ **~** *vt* ‹*decision/plan*› aprobar*

approving /əˈpruːvɪŋ/ *adj* ‹*smile/look*› de aprobación

approximate /əˈprɑːksəmət ‖ əˈprɒksɪmət/ *adj* aproximado

approximately /əˈprɑːksəmətli ‖ əˈprɒksɪmətli/ *adv* aproximadamente

approximation /əˈprɑːksəˈmeɪʃən ‖ əˌprɒksɪˈmeɪʃən/ *n* aproximación *f*

apricot /ˈæprəkɑːt ‖ ˈeɪprɪkɒt/ *n* albaricoque *m or* (Méx) chabacano *m or* (AmS) damasco *m*

April /ˈeɪprəl ‖ ˈeɪprɪl/ ▶ 540 *n* abril *m*; (*before n*) **~ Fools' Day** ≈ el día de los (Santos) Inocentes (*en EEUU y GB se celebra el 1º de abril*)

apron /ˈeɪprən/ *n* delantal *m*, mandil *m* (Esp)

apt /æpt/ *adj* **(a)** (fitting, suitable) acertado **(b)** (likely) **to be ~ to + INF** ser* propenso A + INF

aptitude /ˈæptətuːd ‖ ˈæptɪtjuːd/ *n* [C U] **~ (FOR sth)** aptitud *f* (PARA algo)

aquarium /əˈkweriəm ‖ əˈkweəriəm/ *n* (*pl* **-riums** *or* **-ria** /-riə/) acuario *m*

Aquarius /əˈkweriəs ‖ əˈkweəriəs/ *n* **(a)** (sign) (*no art*) Acuario **(b)** (person) Acuario *or* acuario *mf*, acuariano, -na *m,f*

aquatic /əˈkwætɪk, əˈkwɑːtɪk ‖ əˈkwætɪk/ *adj* acuático

AR = **Arkansas**

Arab¹ /'ærəb/ *adj* árabe

Arab² *n* árabe *mf*

Arabian /ə'reɪbiən/ *adj* árabe; **the ~ Sea** el Mar de Omán

Arabic¹ /'ærəbɪk/ *adj* árabe; **a~ numerals** números *mpl* arábigos

Arabic² *n* [U] árabe *m*

arable /'ærəbəl/ *adj* arable; **~ land** tierras *fpl* de cultivo

arbiter /'ɑːrbətər ‖ 'ɑːbɪtə(r)/ *n* árbitro, -tra *m,f*

arbitrary /'ɑːrbəˌtreri ‖ 'ɑːbɪtrəri/ *adj* arbitrario

arbitrate /'ɑːrbətreɪt ‖ 'ɑːbɪtreɪt/ *vt* ‹*dispute*› arbitrar (en) ■ ~ *vi* arbitrar

arbitration /ˌɑːrbə'treɪʃən ‖ ˌɑːbɪ'treɪʃən/ *n* [U] arbitraje *m*

arc /ɑːrk ‖ ɑːk/ *n* arco *m*

arcade /ɑːr'keɪd ‖ ɑː'keɪd/ *n* **(a)** (Archit) arcada *f*; (around square, along street) soportales *mpl*, recova *f* (Arg) **(b)** (of shops) galería *f* comercial

arch¹ /ɑːrtʃ ‖ ɑːtʃ/ *n* arco *m*

arch² *vt* ‹*eyebrows/back*› arquear ■ ~ *vi* formar un arco

archaeologist *etc* (BrE) ⇒ ARCHEOLOGIST *etc*

archaic /ɑːr'keɪɪk ‖ ɑː'keɪɪk/ *adj* arcaico

archangel /'ɑːrkˌeɪndʒəl ‖ 'ɑːkˌeɪndʒəl/ *n* arcángel *m*

archbishop /ˌɑːrtʃ'bɪʃəp ‖ ˌɑːtʃ'bɪʃəp/ ▶ **603** *n* arzobispo *m*

archenemy /ˌɑːrtʃ'enəmi ‖ ˌɑːtʃ'enəmi/ *n* (*pl* **-mies**) archienemigo, -ga *m,f*

archeologist, (BrE) **archaeologist** /ˌɑːrki'ɑːlədʒəst ‖ ˌɑːki'ɒlədʒɪst/ *n* arqueólogo, -ga *m,f*

archeology, (BrE) **archaeology** /ˌɑːrki'ɑːlədʒi ‖ ˌɑːki'ɒlədʒi/ *n* [U] arqueología *f*

archer /'ɑːrtʃər ‖ 'ɑːtʃə(r)/ *n* arquero, -ra *m,f*

archery /'ɑːrtʃəri ‖ 'ɑːtʃəri/ *n* [U] tiro *m* con *or* al arco

architect /'ɑːrkətekt ‖ 'ɑːkɪtekt/ *n* arquitecto, -ta *m,f*

architecture /'ɑːrkətektʃər ‖ 'ɑːkɪtektʃə(r)/ *n* [U] arquitectura *f*

archive /'ɑːrkaɪv ‖ 'ɑːkaɪv/ *n* (*often pl*) archivo *m*

Arctic¹ /'ɑːrktɪk ‖ 'ɑːktɪk/ *adj* ártico; **the ~ Ocean** el Océano (Glacial) Ártico, el Ártico; **the ~ Circle** el círculo polar ártico

Arctic² *n* **the ~** la región ártica, el Ártico

ardent /'ɑːrdn̩t ‖ 'ɑːdn̩t/ *adj* ‹*supporter*› apasionado; ‹*plea/desire*› ferviente

ardor, (BrE) **ardour** /'ɑːrdər ‖ 'ɑːdə(r)/ *n* [U] (liter) (zeal) fervor *m*, ardor *m*; (love) pasión *f*

arduous /'ɑːrdʒuəs ‖ 'ɑːdjuːəs/ *adj* ‹*task*› arduo; ‹*training/conditions*› duro; ‹*march/climb*› difícil

are /ɑːr ‖ ɑː(r), *weak form* ər/ *2nd pers sing, 1st, 2nd & 3rd pers pl pres of* BE

area /'eriə ‖ 'eəriə/ *n* **1** (geographical) zona *f*, área *f*‡, región *f*; (neighborhood) barrio *m*; (urban) zona *f* **2** (part of room, building) zona *f*; **play ~** zona de recreo **3** (expanse, patch): **the shaded ~ represents** … el área sombreada representa …; **the wreckage was scattered over a wide ~** los restos del siniestro quedaron esparcidos sobre une extensa zona **4** (Math) superficie *f*, área *f*‡; (of room, land) superficie *f* **5** (field, sphere) terreno *m*; (of knowledge) campo *m*

area code *n* (AmE) código *m* de la zona (AmL), prefijo *m* (local) (Esp)

arena /ə'riːnə/ *n* **(a)** (of stadium) arena *f* **(b)** (scene of activity) ruedo *m*; **the political ~** el ruedo político

aren't /ɑːrnt ‖ ɑːnt/ = **are not**

Argentina /ˌɑːrdʒən'tiːnə ‖ ˌɑːdʒən'tiːnə/ *n* Argentina *f*

Argentine /'ɑːrdʒəntaɪn ‖ 'ɑːdʒəntaɪn/ *adj* argentino

Argentinian¹ /ˌɑːrdʒən'tɪniən ‖ ˌɑːdʒən'tɪniən/ *adj* argentino

Argentinian² *n* argentino, -na *m,f*

arguably /'ɑːrgjuəbli ‖ 'ɑːgjʊəbli/ *adv* (*indep*): **this is ~ his best novel** podría decirse que ésta es su mejor novela

argue /'ɑːrgjuː ‖ 'ɑːgjuː/ *vi* **1** (quarrel) discutir; (more heatedly) pelear(se), reñir* (esp Esp); **don't ~ with me!** ¡no me discutas! **2** (reason): **she ~s convincingly** sabe expresar su punto de vista de manera muy convincente; **he ~s against changing the law** da razones en contra de que se cambie la ley ■ ~ *vt* **(a)** (put forward) ‹*case*› exponer* **(b)** (present as argument) argüir*, sostener*; **supporters of the bill ~ that** … los partidarios del proyecto arguyen *or* sostienen que …

argument /'ɑːrgjəmənt ‖ 'ɑːgjʊmənt/ *n* **1** [C U] (quarrel) discusión *f*; (more heated) pelea *f*, riña *f* (esp Esp); **to have an ~ with sb** tener* una discusión con algn; (more heatedly) pelearse *or* (esp Esp) reñir* con algn **2** [U C] (debate) polémica *f* **3** [C] **(a)** (case) **~** (FOR/AGAINST) **sth** razones *fpl or* argumentos *mpl* (A FAVOR/EN CONTRA DE) algo **(b)** (line of reasoning) razonamiento *m*

argumentative /ˌɑːrgjə'mentətɪv ‖ ˌɑːgjʊ'mentətɪv/ *adj* discutidor

arid /'ærəd ‖ 'ærɪd/ *adj* árido

Aries /'eriːz ‖ 'eəriːz/ *n* **(a)** (sign) (*no art*) Aries **(b)** [C] (person) Aries *or* aries *mf*, ariano, -na *m,f*

arise /ə'raɪz/ *vi* (*past* **arose**; *past p* **arisen** /ə'rɪzən/) «*difficulty/opportunity*» surgir*; **if the need ~s** si fuera necesario

aristocracy /ˌærə'stɑːkrəsi ‖ ˌærɪ'stɒkrəsi/ *n* (*pl* **-cies**) aristocracia *f*

aristocrat /ə'rɪstəkræt ‖ 'ærɪstəkræt/ *n* aristócrata *mf*

aristocratic /əˌrɪstə'krætɪk ‖ ˌærɪstə'krætɪk/ *adj* aristocrático

arithmetic /ə'rɪθmətɪk/ *n* [U] aritmética *f*

Ariz = **Arizona**

Ark¹ = **Arkansas**

Ark² /ɑːrk ‖ ɑːk/ *n* arca *f*‡; **Noah's ~** el arca de Noé

arm¹ /ɑːrm ‖ ɑːm/ ▶ **484** *n* **1** (Anat) brazo *m*; **they walked along ~ in ~** iban del brazo **2 (a)** (of chair, crane) brazo *m* **(b)** (of garment) manga *f* **3 arms** *pl* (weapons) armas *fpl*

arm² *vt* armar; *see also* ARMED

armament /'ɑːrməmənt ‖ 'ɑːməmənt/ *n* armamento *m*

arm: **~band** *n* (to denote rank, mourning etc) brazalete *m*; (for swimming) flotador *m* (*que se coloca en el brazo*), alita *f* (AmS); **~chair** *n* sillón *m*, butaca *f*

armed /ɑːrmd ‖ ɑːmd/ *adj* ‹*resistance/struggle*› armado; **the ~ forces** las fuerzas armadas; **~ robbery** robo *m* a mano armada

Armenia /ɑːr'miːniə ‖ ɑː'miːniə/ *n* Armenia *f*

Armenian /ɑːr'miːniən ‖ ɑː'miːniən/ *adj* armenio

armistice /'ɑːrməstəs ‖ 'ɑːmɪstɪs/ *n* armisticio *m*

armor, (BrE) **armour** /'ɑːrmər ‖ 'ɑːmə(r)/ *n* [U] armadura *f*; **suit of ~** armadura *f*

armored, (BrE) **armoured** /'ɑːrmərd ‖ 'ɑːməd/ *adj* blindado

armor-plated, (BrE) **armour-plated** /'ɑːr mər'pleɪtəd ‖ ˌɑːmə'pleɪtɪd/ *adj* blindado

armory, (BrE) **armoury** /'ɑːrməri ‖ 'ɑːməri/ *n* (*pl* **-ries**) **(a)** (storehouse) arsenal *m* **(b)** (factory) (AmE) fábrica *f* de armas

arm: **~pit** *n* axila *f*, sobaco *m*; **~rest** *n* (of chair, sofa) brazo *m*; (of car, airplane seat) apoyabrazos *m*

army /'ɑːrmi ‖ 'ɑːmi/ *n* (*pl* **armies**) ejército *m*

aroma /ə'rəʊmə/ *n* aroma *m*

aromatic /'ærə'mætɪk/ *adj* aromático

arose /ə'rəʊz/ *past of* ARISE

around¹ /ə'raʊnd/ *adv* **1 (a)** (in a circle): **~ and ~ they drove** estuvieron dando vueltas y vueltas con el coche **(b)** (so as to face in different direction): **she glanced ~** echó un vistazo a su alrededor; *see also* TURN *etc* AROUND **(c)** (on all sides): **there's nothing for miles ~** no hay nada en millas a la redonda; **everyone crowded ~** todo el mundo se apiñó alrededor **2** (in the vicinity): **is John ~?** ¿anda *or* está John por ahí?; **there's no one ~** aquí no hay nadie **3** (from one place to another): **he keeps following me ~** me sigue a todas partes; **he knows his way ~** conoce la ciudad (*or* la zona *etc*) **4** (approximately) más o menos; **he must be ~ 35** debe (de) tener unos 35; **at ~ five thirty** alrededor de *or* a eso de las cinco y media, sobre las cinco y media (Esp); **~ 1660** alrededor de 1660

around² *prep* **1** (encircling) alrededor de; **he put his arm ~ her** la rodeó con el brazo; **they sailed ~ the world** dieron la vuelta al mundo en un velero **2 (a)** (in the vicinity of) alrededor de; **do you live ~ here?** ¿vives por aquí? **(b)** (within, through): **they traveled ~ Europe** viajaron por Europa; **she took them ~ the house** les mostró la casa

arouse /ə'raʊz/ *vt* ‹*interest/suspicion*› despertar*; (sexually) excitar

arrange /ə'reɪndʒ/ *vt* **1 (a)** (put in certain order, position) ‹*furniture/flowers*› arreglar **(b)** (put in order) arreglar **2** (fix up in advance) ‹*meeting/party*› organizar*; ‹*date/fee*› fijar; ‹*deal/appointment*› concertar*; ‹*loan*› tramitar; **she had ~d to meet them for lunch** había quedado en encontrarse con ellos para comer, había quedado con ellos para comer (Esp) ■ **~** *vi:* **could you ~ for the carpets to be cleaned?** ¿podría encargarse de que alguien venga a limpiar las alfombras?; **we've ~d for you to see the specialist** le hemos pedido hora *or* una cita con el especialista

arrangement /ə'reɪndʒmənt/ *n* **1** [C U] (of furniture) disposición *f*; **a flower ~** un arreglo floral **2** [C] (agreement): **we made an ~ to meet the next day** quedamos en encontrarnos al día siguiente; **I have an ~ with the bank** tengo un acuerdo con el banco **3 arrangements** *pl* (plans) planes *mpl*; (for a funeral) preparativos *mpl*; **what are the sleeping ~s?** ¿cómo vamos (*or* van *etc*) a dormir? **4** [C] (Mus) arreglo *m*

array /ə'reɪ/ *n* selección *f*

arrears /ə'rɪrz ‖ ə'rɪəz/ *pl n* atrasos *mpl*; **to be in ~ with the rent** estar* atrasado en el pago del alquiler; **salaries are paid monthly in ~** los sueldos se pagan mensualmente, una vez cumplido cada mes de trabajo

arrest¹ /ə'rest/ *n* detención *f*, arresto *m*; **to be under ~** estar* detenido *or* arrestado

arrest² *vt* **1** (detain) detener*, arrestar **2** ‹*progress/growth*› (hinder) dificultar; (halt) detener*; ‹*decline*› atajar

arrival /ə'raɪvəl/ *n* [U C] llegada *f*, arribo *m* (esp AmL frml); **on ~** al llegar

arrive /ə'raɪv/ *vi* llegar*; **to ~** AT llegar* A

arrogance /'ærəgəns/ *n* [U] arrogancia *f*

arrogant /'ærəgənt/ *adj* arrogante

arrow /'ærəʊ/ *n* flecha *f*

arse /ɑːrs ‖ ɑːs/ *n* (BrE vulg) culo *m* (fam: en algunas regiones vulg)

arsenal /'ɑːrsn̩əl ‖ 'ɑːsənl̩/ *n* arsenal *m*

arson /'ɑːrsn̩ ‖ 'ɑːsn̩/ *n* [U] incendiarismo *m*

art /ɑːrt ‖ ɑːt/ *n* **1 (a)** [U] arte *m*; **she's studying ~** estudia Bellas Artes; (*before n*) ‹*class*› de arte; (in school) de dibujo; **~ gallery** (museum) museo *m* de arte; (commercial) galería *f* de arte; **~ school** *o* **college** escuela *f* de Bellas Artes **(b)** [U C] (artwork) trabajos *mpl* artísticos; **~s and crafts** artesanía **2 arts** *pl* **(a) the ~s** la cultura y las artes **(b)** (BrE Educ) letras *fpl*

artefact /'ɑːrtɪfækt ‖ 'ɑːtɪfækt/ *n* (BrE) artefacto *m*

artery /'ɑːrtəri ‖ 'ɑːtəri/ *n* (*pl* **-ries**) arteria *f*

arthritis /ɑːr'θraɪtəs ‖ ɑː'θraɪtɪs/ *n* [U] artritis *f*

artichoke /'ɑːrtətʃəʊk ‖ 'ɑːtɪtʃəʊk/ *n* **(a)** (*globe* ~) alcachofa *f*, alcaucil *m* (RPl) **(b)** (*Jerusalem* ~) aguaturma *f*, pataca *f*

article /'ɑːrtɪkəl ‖ 'ɑːtɪkəl/ *n* **1** (thing, item) artículo *m*; **an ~ of clothing** una prenda (de vestir) **2** (in newspaper, encyclopedia) artículo *m* **3** **▶ 443**, **878** (Ling) artículo *m*

articulate¹ /ɑːr'tɪkjəleɪt ‖ ɑː'tɪkjʊleɪt/ *vt* **(a)** ‹*idea/feeling*› expresar **(b)** ‹*word/sound*› articular

articulate² /ɑːr'tɪkjələt ‖ ɑː'tɪkjʊlət/ *adj* ‹*utterance*› articulado; **he's very ~** se expresa muy bien

articulated lorry /ɑːr'tɪkjəleɪtəd ‖ ɑː'tɪkjəleɪtɪd/ *n* (BrE) camión *m* articulado

artifact /'ɑːrtɪfækt/, (BrE) **artefact** *n* artefacto *m*

artificial /'ɑːrtə'fɪʃəl ‖ ˌɑːtɪ'fɪʃəl/ *adj* artificial; ‹*leather*› sintético; ‹*arm/leg*› ortopédico; **~ respiration** respiración *f* artificial

artillery /ɑːr'tɪləri ‖ ɑː'tɪləri/ *n* [U] artillería *f*

artisan /'ɑːrtəzən ‖ ˌɑːtɪ'zæn/ *n* artesano, -na *m,f*

artist /ɑːrtəst ‖ 'ɑːtɪst/ *n* **(a)** (writer, musician, painter, sculptor) artista *mf* **(b)** (performer) (Mus) intérprete *mf*; (Theat) actor, -triz *m,f*, artista *mf*

artistic /ɑːr'tɪstɪk ‖ ɑː'tɪstɪk/ *adj* artístico

as[1] /æz, *weak form* əz/ *conj* **1 (a)** (when, while) cuando; **~ she was eating breakfast** ... cuando *or* mientras tomaba el desayuno ... **(b)** (indicating progression) a medida que; **~ the date drew closer,** ... a medida que se acercaba la fecha, ... **2** (because, since) como **3** (though): **try ~ he might, he could not open it** por más que trató, no pudo abrirlo; **strange ~ it may seem** por extraño que parezca **4** (in accordance with) como; **~ I was saying** como iba diciendo **5 (a)** (in the way that) como; **do ~ I say** haz lo que te digo; **I'm only interested in the changes ~ they affect me** sólo me interesan los cambios en la medida en que me afectan a mí **(b)** (*in phrases*) **as it is**: **we've got too much work ~ it is** ya tenemos demasiado trabajo; **as it were** por así decirlo **6** (in comparisons of equal degree) **as** ... **as** tan ... como; **there weren't ~ many people ~ last time** no había tanta gente como la última vez **7 as if/as though** como si (+ *subj*)

as[2] *adv* **1** (equally): **it's not ~ cold today** hoy no hace tanto frío; **I can't run ~ quickly now** no puedo correr tan rápido ahora **2 as** ... **as**: **~ many ~ 400 people** hasta 400 personas; **~ long ago ~ 1960** ya en 1960

as[3] *prep* **1** (in the condition, role of): **~ a child she adored dancing** de pequeña le encantaba bailar; **~ a teacher** ... como maestro ...; **he works ~ a clerk** trabaja de oficinista **2** (*in phrases*) **as for** en cuanto a; **as of** *o* (BrE) **as from** desde, a partir de

asbestos /æs'bestəs/ *n* [U] asbesto *m*, amianto *m*

ascend /ə'send/ *vi* (frml) **(a)** «*person/rocket*» ascender* (frml) **(b) ascending** *pres p* ‹*slope/spiral/scale*› ascendente ■ **~** *vt* (frml) ‹*steps*› subir; ‹*mountain*› escalar

ascension /ə'sentʃən ‖ ə'senʃən/ *n* [U] **the A~** (Relig) la Ascensión

ascent /ə'sent/ *n* **(a)** [U C] (of mountain) escalada *f* **(b)** [U C] (rise) ascenso *m* **(c)** [C] (slope) subida *f*

ascertain /'æsər'tem/ *vt* establecer*

ASCII /'æski/ (*no art*) (= **American standard code for information interchange**) ASCII *m*

ascribe /ə'skraɪb/ *vt* **to ~ sth** TO **sth/sb** atribuirle* algo A algo/algn

aseptic /eɪ'septɪk/ *adj* aséptico

ash /æʃ/ *n* **1 (a)** (*often pl*) ceniza *f* **(b) ashes** *pl* (cremated remains) cenizas *fpl* **2** [C] **~ (tree)** fresno *m*

ashamed /ə'ʃeɪmd/ *adj* (*pred*) avergonzado, apenado (AmL exc CS); **she was ~ of what she'd done** estaba avergonzada de *or* (AmL exc CS) apenada por lo que había hecho; **to be ~** OF **sb** avergonzarse* DE algn; **he's ~ to ask** le da vergüenza *or* (AmL exc CS) pena preguntar

ashcan /'æʃkæn/ *n* (AmE) ⇒ GARBAGE CAN

ashore /ə'ʃɔːr/ *adv* en tierra; **to go ~** desembarcar*; **we swam ~** nadamos hasta la orilla

ash: **~tray** *n* cenicero *m*; **A~ Wednesday** *n* miércoles *m* de Ceniza

Asia /'eɪʒə, 'eɪʃə ‖ 'eɪʃə/ *n* Asia *f*‡

Asian[1] /'eɪʒən, 'eɪʃən ‖ 'eɪʃən/ *adj* **(a)** (of Asia) asiático **(b)** (from the Indian subcontinent) (BrE) *de India, Pakistán etc*

Asian[2] *n* **(a)** (from Asia) asiático, -ca *m,f* **(b)** (from the Indian subcontinent) (BrE) *persona proveniente de India, Pakistán etc*

aside[1] /ə'saɪd/ *adv* **1** a un lado; *see also* PUT ASIDE, SET ASIDE, STAND[2] 2(a), STEP ASIDE, TAKE ASIDE **2 aside from** (*as prep*) (esp AmE) **(a)** (except for) aparte de **(b)** (as well as) aparte de, además de

aside[2] *n* aparte *m*

ask /æsk ‖ɑːsk/ *vt* **1** (inquire) preguntar; (inquire of) preguntarle a; **to ~ sb sth** preguntarle algo A algn; **have you ~ed him about his trip?** ¿le has preguntado por el viaje? **2** (request) ‹*approval/advice/favor*› pedir*; **to ~ sb** FOR **sth** pedirle* algo A algn; **to ~ sb to** + INF pedirle* A algn QUE (+ *subj*); **I ~ed to see the manager** pedí hablar con el director **3** (invite) invitar; **to ~ sb (**TO **sth)** invitar a algn (A algo); **to ~ sb out** invitar a algn a salir ■ **~** *vi* **1** (inquire) preguntar **2** (request): **there's no harm in ~ing** con preguntar no se pierde nada; **to ~** FOR **sth** pedir* algo; **to ~** FOR **sb** preguntar POR algn

● **ask after** [*v* + *prep* + *o*] preguntar por

askance /ə'skæns/ *adv*: **to look ~ at sb** mirar a algn con recelo

askew /ə'skjuː/ *adv* torcido

asleep /ə'sliːp/ *adj* (*pred*): **to be ~** estar* dormido; **to fall ~** dormirse*

asparagus /ə'spærəgəs/ *n* [U C] espárrago *m*

ASPCA *n* = **American Society for the Prevention of Cruelty to Animals**

aspect /'æspekt/ *n* **1** (feature, facet) aspecto *m* **2** (frml) (orientation) orientación *f*

aspersions /ə'spɜːrʒənz ‖ ə'spɜːʃənz/ *pl n* (*sometimes sing*): **to cast ~ on sth/sb** poner* algo/a algn en entredicho

asphalt /'æsfɔːlt ‖ 'æsfælt/ *n* [U] asfalto *m*

asphyxiate /æs'fɪksieɪt/ *vt* asfixiar

aspiration /'æspə'reɪʃən ‖ ˌæspɪ'reɪʃən/ *n* aspiración *f*

aspire /ə'spaɪr ‖ ə'spaɪə(r)/ *vi* **(a) to ~** TO **sth** aspirar A algo **(b) aspiring** *pres p*: **aspiring writers** personas que aspiran a ser escritores

aspirin /'æsprən ‖ 'æsprɪn/ *n* [C U] (*pl* **~** *or* **-rins**) aspirina *f*

ass /æs/ *n* **1 (a)** (donkey) (liter) asno *m*, jumento *m* (liter) **(b)** (idiot) (colloq) imbécil *mf* **2** (part of body) (AmE vulg) culo *m* (fam: en algunas regiones vulg)

assailant /ə'seɪlənt/ *n* (frml) agresor, -sora *m,f*

assassin /ə'sæsn̩ ‖ ə'sæsɪn/ *n* asesino, -na *m,f* (*de un personaje importante*)

assassinate /ə'sæsn̩eɪt ‖ ə'sæsɪneɪt/ *vt* asesinar (*a un personaje importante*)

assassination /ə'sæsə'neɪʃən ‖ əˌsæsɪ'neɪʃən/ *n* [C U] asesinato *m* (*de un personaje importante*)

assault[1] /ə'sɔːlt/ *n* **1** [U C] (Law) (violence) agresión *f*; (molestation) agresión *f* sexual **2** [C] **(a)** (Mil) asalto *m* **(b)** (onslaught) **~ (ON sth)** ataque *m* (A algo)

assault[2] *vt* (use violence against) agredir*; (sexually) agredir* sexualmente

assemble /ə'sembəl/ *vt* **(a)** (construct) montar; ‹*model*› armar **(b)** (get together) reunir* **(c)** (gather) ‹*facts*› recopilar; ‹*collection*› reunir* ■ **~** *vi* (gather) reunirse*

assembly /ə'sembli/ *n* (*pl* **-blies**) **1 (a)** [U] (coming together) reunión *f* **(b)** [C] (group) concurrencia *f* **(c)** [C] (Govt) asamblea *f* **(d)** (Educ) (*no art*) *reunión de profesores y alumnos, al iniciarse la jornada escolar* **2** (Tech) [U] (process) montaje *m*; (*before n*) **~ line** cadena *f* de montaje

assent[1] /ə'sent/ *n* [U] asentimiento *m*; **to give one's ~ to sth** dar* su (*or* mi *etc*) conformidad a algo

assent[2] *vi* asentir*; **to ~ TO sth** acceder A algo

assert /ə'sɜːrt ‖ ə'sɜːt/ *vt* **(a)** (declare) afirmar **(b)** (demonstrate, enforce) ‹*superiority*› reafirmar; ‹*rights/claims*› hacer* valer ■ *v refl* **to ~ oneself** hacerse* valer

assertion /ə'sɜːrʃən ‖ ə'sɜːʃən/ *n* **(a)** [C U] (declaration) afirmación *f* **(b)** [U] (demonstration) reafirmación *f*

assertive /ə'sɜːrtɪv ‖ ə'sɜːtɪv/ *adj* ‹*tone*› autoritario; **to be ~** ser* firme y enérgico

assess /ə'ses/ *vt* ‹*value/amount*› calcular; ‹*student/performance*› evaluar*; ‹*situation*› aquilatar

assessment /ə'sesmənt/ *n* [C U] (of performance, results) evaluación *f*; (of amount) cálculo *m*

asset /'æset/ *n* **(a)** (valuable quality): **her intelligence is her greatest ~** su inteligencia es su gran baza; **she's an ~ to the company** es una empleada muy valiosa para la compañía **(b) assets** *pl* (Fin) activo *m*

asset stripping /'strɪpɪŋ/ *n* [U] vaciamiento *m*

assiduous /ə'sɪdʒuəs ‖ ə'sɪdjʊəs/ *adj* (frml) ‹*student*› diligente

assign /ə'saɪn/ *vt* **(a)** (appoint) **to ~ sb TO sth** nombrar a algn PARA algo **(b)** (allocate) asignar

assignment /ə'saɪnmənt/ *n* **1** [C] **(a)** (mission) misión *f* **(b)** (task) función *f* **(c)** (schoolwork) tarea *f* **2** [U] **(a)** (posting) nombramiento *m* **(b)** (allocation) asignación *f*

assimilate /ə'sɪməleɪt ‖ ə'sɪmɪleɪt/ *vt* asimilar

assimilation /ə'sɪmə'leɪʃən ‖ əˌsɪmɪ'leɪʃən/ *n* [U] asimilación *f*

assist /ə'sɪst/ *vt* ayudar

assistance /ə'sɪstəns/ *n* [U] ayuda *f*

assistant[1] /ə'sɪstənt/ *n* **(a)** (in shop) dependiente, -ta *m,f*, empleado, -da *m,f* (AmL) **(b)** (subordinate, helper) ayudante *mf*; **clerical ~** auxiliar administrativo, -va *m,f* **(c)** (*language ~*) (BrE) (in university) ayudante *mf or* (Esp) lector, -tora *m,f*; (in school) auxiliar *mf* de lengua

assistant[2] *adj* (*before n*): **~ manager** subdirector, -tora *m,f*

associate[1] /ə'səʊʃieɪt, -sieɪt/ *vt* **(a)** (involve, connect) (*usu pass*) vincular **(b)** (link in mind) asociar ■ **~** *vi* **to ~ (WITH sb)** relacionarse (CON algn)

associate[2] /ə'səʊʃiət, -siət/ *n* **(a)** (in business, profession) colega *mf* **(b)** (member of professional body) colegiado, -da *m,f*

associate[3] /ə'səʊʃiət, -siət/ *adj* (*before n*) ‹*member*› no numerario; ‹*editor/professor*› (AmE) adjunto

association /ə'səʊʃi'eɪʃən, -si'eɪʃən/ *n* [C U] asociación *f*; **in ~ with** (*as prep*) en asociación con

assorted /ə'sɔːrtəd ‖ ə'sɔːtɪd/ *adj* (*before n*) surtido

assortment /ə'sɔːrtmənt ‖ ə'sɔːtmənt/ *n* surtido *m*

assuage /ə'sweɪdʒ/ *vt* (liter) **(a)** (satisfy) ‹*hunger/desire*› saciar (liter) **(b)** (ease) ‹*pain/grief*› aliviar **(c)** (calm) ‹*anxiety*› calmar; ‹*fear*› disipar

assume /ə'suːm ‖ə'sjuːm/ *vt* **1** (suppose) suponer* **2** (frml) ‹*duties/command/responsibility*› asumir; **~d name** nombre *m* ficticio

assumption /ə'sʌmpʃən/ *n* **1** [C] (supposition): **the ~ was that** ... se suponía que ...; **his reasoning is based on the ~ that** ... su razonamiento se basa en el supuesto de que ... **2** [U] (frml) (of duties, leadership, responsibility) asunción *f*

assurance /ə'ʃʊrəns ‖ ə'ʃʊərəns, ə'ʃɔːrəns/ *n* **1** [C] (guarantee): **she gave me her ~ that** ... me aseguró que ... **2** [U] (self-confidence) seguridad *f* en sí mismo **3** [U] (insurance) (BrE) seguro *m*

assure /ə'ʃʊr ‖ ə'ʃʊə(r), ə'ʃɔː(r)/ *vt* **1 (a)** (guarantee) asegurar **(b)** (convince) convencer* **2** (make certain) **to ~ sb (OF) sth: this work will ~ me (of) a regular income** este trabajo me asegurará una entrada fija **3** (insure) (BrE) ‹*life*› asegurar

asterisk /'æstərɪsk/ *n* asterisco *m*

asteroid /'æstərɔɪd/ *n* asteroide *m*

asthma /'æzmə ‖ 'æsmə/ *n* [U] asma *f*‡

asthmatic /æz'mætɪk ‖ æs'mætɪk/ *adj* asmático

astonish /ə'stɑːnɪʃ ‖ ə'stɒnɪʃ/ *vt* asombrar; (more intensely) dejar pasmado

astonished /ə'stɑːnɪʃt ‖ ə'stɒnɪʃt/ *adj* asombrado; **the ~ look on their faces** la cara de asombro que pusieron; **I'm ~ (that) he got so far** me asombra que haya llegado tan lejos

astonishing /ə'stɑːnɪʃɪŋ ‖ ə'stɒnɪʃɪŋ/ *adj* asombroso; (more intensely) pasmoso

astonishment /ə'stɑːnɪʃmənt ‖ ə'stɒnɪʃmənt/ *n* [U] asombro *m*; (more intense) estupefacción *f*

astound /ə'staʊnd/ *vt* dejar estupefacto

astounded /ə'staʊndəd ‖ ə'staʊndɪd/ *adj* atónito

astounding /ə'staʊndɪŋ/ *adj* increíble

astray /ə'streɪ/ *adv*: **to go ~** (get lost) extraviarse*; (do wrong) (euph *or* hum) descarriarse*; **to lead sb ~** (euph *or* hum) llevar a algn por mal camino

astride /ə'straɪd/ *prep*: **he sat ~ the fence/horse** estaba sentado en la valla/montado en el caballo a horcajadas

astringent /ə'strɪndʒənt/ *adj* ‹*lotion*› astringente; ‹*comment*› mordaz

astrologer /ə'strɑːlədʒər ‖ ə'strɒlədʒə(r)/ *n* astrólogo, -ga *m,f*

astrology /ə'strɑːlədʒi ‖ ə'strɒlədʒi/ *n* [U] astrología *f*

astronaut /'æstrənɔːt/ *n* astronauta *mf*

astronomer /ə'strɑːnəmər ‖ ə'strɒnəmə(r)/ *n* astrónomo, -ma *m,f*

astronomical /ˌæstrə'nɑːmɪkəl ‖ ˌæstrə'nɒmɪkəl/ *adj* astronómico

astronomy /ə'strɑːnəmi ‖ ə'strɒnəmi/ *n* [U] astronomía *f*

astute /ə'stuːt ‖ə'stjuːt/ *adj* ‹*person*› sagaz; ‹*decision*› inteligente

asylum /ə'saɪləm/ *n* **(a)** [U C] (refuge) asilo *m* **(b)** [C] (*lunatic* ~) manicomio *m*

at /æt, *weak form* ət/ *prep* **1** (location) en; **she's ~ the office** está en la oficina; **he's ~ the bank** ha ido al banco **2** (direction): **to point ~ sth/sb** señalar algo/a algn; **he smiled ~ me** me sonrió **3** (time): **~ 6 o'clock** a las seis; **~ Christmas** en Navidad, por Navidades (Esp); **~ night** por la noche, de noche **4 (a)** (indicating state): **~ a disadvantage** en desventaja; **~ war/peace** en guerra/paz **(b)** (occupied with): **people ~ work** gente trabajando; **children ~ play** niños jugando **5** (with measurements, numbers, rates etc): **they sell them ~ around $80** las venden a alrededor de $80 **6** (because of): **he was surprised ~ the decision** le sorprendió la decisión

ate /eɪt/ *past of* EAT

atheist /'eɪθiəst ‖ 'eɪθiɪst/ *n* ateo, atea *m,f*

Athens /'æθənz/ *n* Atenas *f*

athlete /'æθliːt/ *n* atleta *mf*

athlete's foot *n* [U] pie *m* de atleta

athletic /æθ'letɪk/ *adj* atlético

athletics /æθ'letɪks/ *n* (+ *sing or pl vb*) **(a)** (active sports) (AmE) deportes *mpl* **(b)** (track and field) (esp BrE) atletismo *m*

Atlantic[1] /ət'læntɪk/ *adj* atlántico

Atlantic[2] *n* **the ~ (Ocean)** el (océano) Atlántico

atlas /'ætləs/ *n* atlas *m*

ATM *n* (AmE) (= **automated** *or* **automatic teller machine**) cajero *m* automático

atmosphere /'ætməsfɪr ‖ 'ætməsfɪə(r)/ *n* **(a)** (of planet) atmósfera *f* **(b)** (feeling, mood) ambiente *m*

atom /'ætəm/ *n* átomo *m*

atomic /ə'tɑːmɪk ‖ ə'tɒmɪk/ *adj* ‹*warfare/energy*› atómico; **~ bomb** bomba *f* atómica

atone /ə'təʊn/ *vi* (frml) **to ~** FOR **sth** ‹*for sins*› expiar* algo; ‹*for crime/harm*› reparar algo

atrocious /ə'trəʊʃəs/ *adj* **(a)** (very bad) (colloq) ‹*spelling/manners*› espantoso (fam) **(b)** (horrifying) ‹*injuries/conditions*› atroz

atrocity /ə'trɑːsəti ‖ ə'trɒsəti/ *n* [C U] (*pl* **-ties**) atrocidad *f*

attach /ə'tætʃ/ *vt* (fasten) sujetar; (tie) atar, amarrar (AmL exc RPl); (stick) pegar*; (to letter, document) adjuntar; **it is ~ed to the wall with screws** está sujeto a la pared con tornillos; **the ~ed form** el formulario adjunto; **to ~ importance to sth** dar(le) importancia a algo

attaché /ˌætæ'ʃeɪ ‖ ə'tæʃeɪ/ *n* agregado, -da *m,f*

attaché case *n* maletín *m*

attached /ə'tætʃt/ *adj* (*pred*) (fond) **to be ~** TO **sb/sth** tenerle* mucho cariño A algn/algo

attachment /ə'tætʃmənt/ *n* **1** [C] (part) accesorio *m* **2** [U] (fondness) **~ (**TO **sb/sth)** cariño *m* (POR algn/algo)

attack[1] /ə'tæk/ *n* **(a)** [C U] (physical, verbal) ataque *m*; **terrorist ~s** atentados *mpl* terroristas **(b)** [C] (Med) ataque *m*; **heart ~** infarto *m*

attack[2] *vt* **1** (physically, verbally) atacar* **2** ‹*task*› acometer; ‹*problem*› combatir ■ **~** *vi* (Mil, Sport) atacar*

attacker /ə'tækər ‖ ə'tækə(r)/ *n* agresor, -sora *m,f*

attain /ə'teɪn/ *vt* (frml) ‹*position/goal*› alcanzar*, lograr; ‹*ambition*› realizar*

attempt[1] /ə'tempt/ *vt* **(a)** (try) **to ~ to** + INF/-ING tratar DE *or* intentar + INF **(b)** (have a try at) «*student*» ‹*exam question*› intentar responder a (frml) **(c) attempted** *past p*: **~ed suicide/murder** intento *m* de suicidio/tentativa *f* de asesinato

attempt[2] *n* intento *m*; **I made an ~ at conversation** traté de *or* intenté entablar conversación; **to make an ~ on sb's life** atentar contra la vida de algn

attend /ə'tend/ *vt* **1** (frml) **(a)** (be present at) asistir a (frml) **(b)** (go to regularly) ‹*church/school/classes*› ir* a **2** ‹*patient*› atender* ■ **~** *vi* **1** (be present) asistir **2** (pay attention) **to ~ (**TO **sth)** atender* (A algo), poner* atención (A algo) (AmL)

• **attend to** [*v* + *prep* + *o*] ‹*patient/customer*› atender*; ‹*correspondence/filing*› ocuparse de

attendance /ə'tendəns/ *n* **(a)** [U C] (presence) asistencia *f*; **to be in ~** estar* presente **(b)** [C] (people present): **what was the ~?** ¿cuántos asistentes hubo?; **to take ~** (AmE) pasar lista

attendant /ə'tendənt/ *n* (in museum, parking lot) guarda *m*; (in pool, toilets) encargado, -da *m,f*

attention /ə'tentʃən ‖ ə'tenʃən/ *n* **1** [U] **(a)** (concentration) atención *f*; **to pay ~ to sth/sb** prestarle atención a algo/algn **(b)** (notice) atención *f*; **to catch sb's ~** atraer* la atención de algn; **it has been brought to my ~** *o* **it has come to my ~ that** ... me han informado que ... **(c)** (care) atención *f* **2** [U] (Mil): **to stand to ~** ponerse* en posición de firme(s)

attentive /ə'tentɪv/ *adj* atento

attenuate /ə'tenjueɪt/ *vt* atenuar*; **attenuating circumstances** circunstancias *fpl* atenuantes

attic /'ætɪk/ *n* desván *m*, ático *m*, altillo *m* (esp AmL)

attire /ə'taɪr ‖ ə'taɪə(r)/ *n* [U] (liter) atuendo *m* (frml), atavío *m* (liter)

attitude /'ætətuːd ‖ 'ætɪtjuːd/ *n* actitud *f*

attorney /ə'tɜːrni ‖ ə'tɜːni/ *n* (*pl* **-neys**) (AmE) abogado, -da *m,f*; *see also* POWER OF ATTORNEY

Attorney General *n* (*pl* **~ ~s** *or* **~s ~**) (in US — at national level) ≈ Ministro, -tra *m,f* de Justicia; (— at state level) ≈ Fiscal *mf* General

attract /ə'trækt/ *vt* atraer*

attraction /ə'trækʃən/ *n* **(a)** [U C] (Phys) atracción *f* **(b)** [U] (interest): **I still feel a great ~ toward the place** todavía me atrae mucho el lugar; **what's the ~?** ¿qué atractivo tiene? **(c)** [C] (attractive feature) atractivo *m*; **tourist ~** atracción *f* turística

attractive /ə'træktɪv/ *adj* atractivo

attribute¹ /'ətrɪbjət ‖ ə'trɪbjuːt/ *vt* **to ~ sth** TO **sth/sb** atribuirle* algo A algo/algn

attribute² /'ætrəbjuːt ‖ 'ætrɪbjuːt/ *n* atributo *m*

attrition /ə'trɪʃən/ *n* [U] **1** (destruction) desgaste *m*; **war of ~** guerra *f* de desgaste **2** (AmE Lab Rel) bajas *fpl* vegetativas

aubergine /'əʊbərʒiːn ‖ 'əʊbəʒiːn/ *n* (BrE) berenjena *f*

auburn /'ɔːbərn ‖ 'ɔːbən/ ▶ 515 *adj* castaño rojizo *adj inv*

auction¹ /'ɔːkʃən/ *n* [C U] subasta *f*, remate *m* (AmL)

auction² *vt* subastar, rematar (AmL)

auctioneer /'ɔːkʃə'nɪr ‖ ˌɔːkʃə'nɪə(r)/ *n* subastador, -dora *m,f*, rematador, -dora *m,f* (AmL)

audacious /ɔː'deɪʃəs/ *adj* **(a)** (daring) ‹*act/plan*› audaz **(b)** (impudent) ‹*behavior/person*› atrevido

audacity /ɔː'dæsəti/ *n* [U] (daring) audacia *f*; (impudence) atrevimiento *m*

audible /'ɔːdəbəl/ *adj* audible

audience /'ɔːdiəns/ *n* **1** (at play, film) público *m*; (at concert, lecture) auditorio *m*; (TV) audiencia *f* **2** (interview) audiencia *f*

audio- /'ɔːdiəʊ/ *pref* audio-

audiovisual /'ɔːdiəʊ'vɪʒuəl/ *adj* audiovisual

audit¹ /'ɔːdət ‖ 'ɔːdɪt/ *vt* **(a)** (Busn, Fin) ‹*accounts*› auditar **(b)** (AmE Educ) ‹*classes/course*› asistir como oyente a

audit² *n* [C U] (Busn, Fin) **(a)** (inspection) auditoría *f* **(b)** (report) (AmE) informe *m* de auditoría

audition¹ /ɔː'dɪʃən/ *vi*: **to ~** (FOR **sth**) dar* una audición (PARA algo)

audition² *n* audición *f*

auditor /'ɔːdətər ‖ 'ɔːdɪtə(r)/ *n* **(a)** (Busn, Fin) auditor, -tora *m,f* **(b)** (AmE Educ) oyente *mf*

auditorium /'ɔːdə'tɔːriəm ‖ ˌɔːdɪ'tɔːriəm/ *n* (*pl* **-riums** *or* **-ria** /-riə/) auditorio *m*

augment /ɔːg'ment/ *vt* (frml) aumentar, incrementar (frml)

augur /'ɔːgər ‖ 'ɔːgə(r)/ *vi*: **to ~ well/ill** ser* de buen/mal agüero

august /ɔː'gʌst/ *adj* augusto

August /'ɔːgəst/ ▶ 540 *n* agosto *m*

aunt /ænt ‖ ɑːnt/ *n* tía *f*

auntie, **aunty** /'ænti ‖ 'ɑːnti/ *n* (colloq) tía *f*, tiíta *f* (fam)

au pair /'əʊ'per ‖ ˌəʊ'peə(r)/ *n* au pair *mf*

aura /'ɔːrə/ *n* halo *m*, aura *m*

aural /'ɔːrəl/ *adj* auditivo

auspices /'ɔːspəsəz ‖ 'ɔːspɪsɪz/ *pl n* (frml): **under the ~ of sb/sth** bajo los auspicios de algn/algo

auspicious /ɔː'spɪʃəs/ *adj* (frml) prometedor, auspicioso (CS)

austere /ɔː'stɪr ‖ ɒ'stɪə(r), ɔː'stɪə(r)/ *adj* austero

austerity /ɔː'sterəti ‖ ɒ'sterəti, ɔː'sterəti/ *n* [U] austeridad *f*

Australasia /'ɔːstrə'leɪʒə, -'leɪʃə ‖ ˌɒstrə'leɪʒiə, -'leɪʃə/ *n* Australasia *f*

Australia /ɔː'streɪliə ‖ ɒ'streɪliə/ *n* Australia *f*

Australian¹ /ɔː'streɪliən ‖ ɒ'streɪliən/ *adj* australiano

Australian² *n* australiano, -na *m,f*

Austria /'ɔːstriə ‖ 'ɒstriə/ *n* Austria *f*

Austrian¹ /'ɔːstriən ‖ 'ɒstriən/ *adj* austriaco, austríaco

Austrian² *n* austriaco, -ca *m,f*, austríaco, -ca *m,f*

authentic /ə'θentɪk ‖ ɔː'θentɪk/ *adj* **(a)** (genuine) auténtico **(b)** (realistic) ‹*atmosphere*› realista

authenticate /ə'θentɪkeɪt ‖ ɔː'θentɪkeɪt/ *vt* **(a)** (declare genuine) autenticar* **(b)** (prove, confirm) probar*

authenticity /'ɔːθen'tɪsəti/ *n* [U] (of manuscript, painting) autenticidad *f*

author /'ɔːθər ‖ 'ɔːθə(r)/ *n* (writer) escritor, -ra *m,f*; (in relation to her/his works) autor, -tora *m,f*

authoritarian /ɔː'θɔːrə'teriən ‖ ɔːˌθɒrɪ'teəriən/ *adj* autoritario

authoritative /ə'θɔːrəteɪtɪv ‖ ɔː'θɒrətətɪv/ *adj* **1** ‹*manner/tone*› de autoridad **2** (reliable, respected) ‹*source*› fidedigno; ‹*work/study*› autorizado

authority /ə'θɔːrəti ‖ ɔː'θɒrəti/ *n* (*pl* **-ties**) **1** [U] **(a)** (power) autoridad *f* **(b)** (authorization) **~ to** + INF autorización *f* PARA + INF **2** [C] (person, body) autoridad *f*; **she was detained by the Belgian authorities** fue detenida por las autoridades belgas **3** [C] **(a)** (expert) **~** (ON **sth**) autoridad *f* (EN algo) **(b)** (source) autoridad *f*; **to have sth on good ~** saber* algo de buena fuente

authorize /'ɔːθəraɪz/ *vt* **(a)** ‹*publication/transaction*› autorizar*; ‹*funds*› aprobar* **(b)** (empower) **to ~ sb to** + INF autorizar* a algn PARA + INF

autistic /ɔː'tɪstɪk/ *adj* autista

autobiographical /'ɔːtəˌbaɪə'græfɪkəl/ *adj* autobiográfico

autobiography /'ɔːtəbaɪ'ɑːgrəfi/ *n* [U C] (*pl* **-phies**) autobiografía *f*

autocratic /'ɔːtə'krætɪk/ *adj* autocrático

autograph¹ /'ɔːtəgræf ‖ 'ɔːtəgrɑːf/ *n* autógrafo *m*

autograph² *vt* autografiar*

automata /ɔː'tɑːmətə ‖ ɔː'tɒmətə/ *pl of* AUTOMATON

automate /'ɔːtəmeɪt/ *vt* automatizar*

automatic¹ /'ɔːtə'mætɪk/ *adj* automático

automatic² *n* (car) coche *m* automático; (pistol) automática *f*

automatically /'ɔːtə'mætɪkli/ *adv* automáticamente

automation /'ɔːtə'meɪʃən/ *n* [U] automatización *f*

automaton /ɔː'tɑːmətən ‖ ɔː'tɒmətən/ *n* (*pl* **automata** *or* **-tons**) autómata *m*

automobile /'ɔːtəməbiːl/ *n* (esp AmE) coche *m*, carro *m* (AmL exc CS), auto *m* (esp CS), automóvil *m* (frml)

autonomous /ɔː'tɑːnəməs ‖ ɔː'tɒnəməs/ *adj* autónomo

autonomy /ɔː'tɑːnəmi ‖ ɔː'tɒnəmi/ *n* [U] autonomía *f*

autopsy /'ɔːtɑːpsi ‖ 'ɔːtɒpsi/ *n* (*pl* **-sies**) autopsia *f*

autumn /'ɔːtəm/ *n* (esp BrE) otoño *m*; (*before n*) ‹*day/weather*› de otoño, otoñal

auxiliary¹ /ɔːg'zɪljəri/ *adj* auxiliar

auxiliary² *n* (*pl* **-ries**) auxiliar *mf*; **nursing ~** enfermero, -ra *m,f* auxiliar

avail¹ /ə'veɪl/ *v refl* (frml) **to ~ oneself OF sth** aprovechar algo

avail² *n* [U] (liter): **to no ~** en vano

available /ə'veɪləbəl/ *adj* **(a)** (obtainable) (*pred*): **to be readily ~** ser* fácil de conseguir; **brochures are ~ on request** hay folletos a disposición de quien los solicite **(b)** (at sb's disposal) ‹*resources/manpower*› disponible; **to make sth ~ to sb** poner* algo a disposición de algn **(c)** (free, contactable) (*pred*) libre; (for work, job) disponible

avalanche /'ævəlæntʃ ‖ 'ævəlɑːnʃ/ *n* alud *m*, avalancha *f*

avant-garde /'ɑːvɑːn'gɑːrd ‖ ˌævɒn'gɑːd/ *adj* vanguardista, de vanguardia

avarice /'ævərəs ‖ 'ævərɪs/ *n* [U] (liter) codicia *f* (liter)

avaricious /'ævə'rɪʃəs/ *adj* (liter) codicioso

Ave (= **Avenue**) Avda., Av.

avenge /ə'vendʒ/ *vt* vengar*

avenue /'ævənuː ‖ 'ævənjuː/ *n* **1 (a)** (tree-lined walk) paseo *m* (*arbolado*) **(b)** (broad street) avenida *f* **2** (means, method) vía *f*

average¹ /'ævrɪdʒ, 'ævərɪdʒ/ *n* (Math) promedio *m*, media *f*

average² *adj* **(a)** (Math) ‹*time/age*› medio, promedio *adj inv*; **he is of ~ height** es de estatura mediana **(b)** (typical): **the ~ family** la familia tipo **(c)** (ordinary): **how was the movie? — average** ¿qué tal la película? — normal

• average out [*v + adv*]: **our speed ~d out at about 60mph** hicimos una media *or* un promedio de 60 millas por hora

averse /ə'vɜːrs ‖ ə'vɜːs/ *adj* (*pred*) **to be ~ TO sth** ‹*to an idea*› ser* reacio A algo

aversion /ə'vɜːrʒən, -ʃən ‖ ə'vɜːʃən/ *n* (*no pl*) aversión *f*

avert /ə'vɜːrt ‖ ə'vɜːt/ *vt* **(a)** ‹*eyes/gaze*› apartar **(b)** ‹*danger/suspicion*› evitar; ‹*accident/strike*› impedir*

aviary /'eɪvieri/ *n* (*pl* **-ries**) pajarera *f*

aviation /'eɪvi'eɪʃən/ *n* [U] aviación *f*

avid /'ævəd ‖ 'ævɪd/ *adj* ‹*reader/interest*› ávido; ‹*fan/follower*› ferviente

avocado /'ævə'kɑːdəʊ/ *n* (*pl* **-dos**) [U C] **~ (pear)** aguacate *m or* (Bol, CS, Per) palta *f*

avoid /ə'vɔɪd/ *vt* ‹*obstacle/place/topic*› evitar; ‹*blow*› esquivar; **why are you ~ing me?** ¿por qué me rehúyes?

avoidable /ə'vɔɪdəbəl/ *adj* evitable

avowed /ə'vaʊd/ *adj* (*before n*) declarado

await /ə'weɪt/ *vt* esperar

awake¹ /ə'weɪk/ *adj* (*pred*) **to be ~** estar* despierto

awake² (*past* **awoke**; *past p* **awoken**), **awaken** /ə'weɪkən/ *vt/i* despertar*

awakening /ə'weɪkənɪŋ/ *n* despertar *m*

award¹ /ə'wɔːrd ‖ ə'wɔːd/ *vt* **(a)** ‹*prize/medal/pay increase*› conceder; ‹*honor*› conferir* **(b)** (Sport) ‹*penalty/free kick*› conceder

award² *n* **(a)** (prize) galardón *m*; (medal) condecoración *f* **(b)** (sum of money) asignación *f*

award-winning /ə'wɔːrd'wɪnɪŋ ‖ ə'wɔːdˌwɪnɪŋ/ *adj* (*before n*) galardonado

aware /ə'wer ‖ ə'weə(r)/ *adj* (conscious) (*pred*) **to be ~ OF sth** ser* *or* (Chi, Méx) estar* consciente DE algo; **is your father ~ that you drink?** ¿sabe tu padre que bebes?

awareness /ə'wernəs ‖ ə'weənɪs/ *n* [U] conciencia *f*

awash /ə'wɔːʃ ‖ ə'wɒʃ/ *adj* (*pred*) **to be ~ (WITH sth)** estar* inundado (DE algo)

away /ə'weɪ/ *adv* **1** (from place, person): **I looked ~** aparté la vista; **he limped ~** se alejó cojeando **2 (a)** (in the distance): **it isn't far ~** no queda lejos; **it's 20 miles ~** queda a 20 millas; **Easter is a long way ~** falta mucho para Pascua **(b)** (absent): **she's ~ in Canada** está en Canadá; **I'll be ~ all next week** toda la semana que viene no voy a estar **(c)** (esp BrE Sport): **to play ~** jugar* fuera (de casa) **3** (continuously): **he's been painting ~ all morning** se ha pasado toda la mañana pintando; **I could hear him singing ~** lo oía cantar **4 away from** (*as prep*) **(a)** (in opposite direction to): **she pulled him ~ from the cliff edge** lo apartó del borde del acantilado **(b)** (at a distance, separated from) lejos de; **to get ~ from it all** alejarse del mundanal ruido

awe /ɔː/ *n* [U] sobrecogimiento *m*; **to be in ~ of sb** sentirse* intimidado por algn

awe-inspiring /'ɔːɪn'spaɪrɪŋ ‖ 'ɔːɪnˌspaɪərɪŋ/ *adj* impresionante

awesome /'ɔːsəm/ *adj* imponente

awestruck /'ɔːstrʌk/ *adj* atemorizado

awful /'ɔːfəl/ *adj* (colloq) ‹*journey/weather/day*› horrible; ‹*clothes*› horroroso; ‹*joke/movie*› malísimo; **I felt ~** me sentía fatal

awkward /'ɔːkwərd ‖ 'ɔːkwəd/ *adj* **1** (clumsy) ‹*movement/person*› torpe; ‹*phrase*› poco elegante **2 (a)** (difficult, inconvenient) ‹*shape/angle*› incómodo; **at a rather ~ moment** en mal momento; **she could make things very ~ for you** te podría hacer la vida imposible **(b)** (difficult to deal with) difícil **3 (a)** (embarrassing) ‹*decision/subject*› delicado; **you've put me in a very ~ position** me has puesto en una situación muy violenta **(b)** (embarrassed) ‹*silence*› incómodo; **I felt very ~** me sentí muy incómodo

awning /'ɔːnɪŋ/ *n* toldo *m*

awoke /ə'wəʊk/ *past of* AWAKE²

awoken /ə'wəʊkən/ *past p of* AWAKE²

awry /ə'raɪ/ *adj* (*pred*) torcido; **to go ~** salir* mal

ax¹, (BrE) **axe** /æks/ *n* hacha *f*‡; ***to have an ~ to grind*** tener* un interés personal

ax², (BrE) **axe** *vt* (journ) ‹*project/services/jobs*› suprimir; ‹*employee*› despedir*

axis /'æksəs ‖ 'æksɪs/ *n* (*pl* **axes** /'æksiːz/) eje *m*

axle /'æksəl/ *n* eje *m*

AZ = **Arizona**

Azerbaijan /'æzərbar'dʒɑːn ‖ˌæzəbar'dʒɑːn/ *n* Azerbaiyán *m*, Azerbaiján *m*

Azerbaijani /'æzərbar'dʒɑːni ‖ˌæzəbar'dʒɑːni/ *adj* azerbaiyaní

Aztec[1] /'æztek/ *adj* azteca

Aztec[2] *n* azteca *mf*

azure /'æʒər ‖'æzjə(r), 'æzjʊə(r)/ ▶515 *adj* (liter) azur (liter)

Bb

B, b /biː/ *n* **(a)** (letter) B, b *f* **(b)** (Mus) si *m*

b (= **born**) n.

BA *n* = **Bachelor of Arts**

babble /'bæbəl/ *vi* (talk foolishly) parlotear (fam); (talk unintelligibly) farfullar; «*baby*» balbucear; **a babbling brook** (liter) un arroyo rumoroso (liter)

baby /'beɪbi/ *n* (*pl* **babies**) **(a)** (infant) bebé *m*, niño, -ña *m,f*, bebe, -ba *m,f* (Per, RPl), guagua *f* (Andes); **to have a ~** tener* un hijo *or* un niño **(b)** (animal) cría *f* **(c)** (youngest member) benjamín, -mina *m,f*

baby: **~ buggy**, **~ carriage** *n* (AmE) cochecito *m* de bebé, carriola *f* (Méx); **~-sit** *vi* (*pres p* **-sitting**; *past & past p* **-sat**) cuidar niños, hacer* de canguro (Esp); **~-sitter** /'beɪbiˌsɪtər ‖'beɪbiˌsɪtə(r)/ *n* baby sitter *mf*, canguro *mf* (Esp)

bachelor /'bætʃələr ‖'bætʃələ(r)/ *n* **1** (single man) soltero *m* **2** (Educ) licenciado, -da *m,f*; **B~ of Arts/Science** (degree) licenciatura *f* en Filosofía y Letras/en Ciencias

back[1] /bæk/ ▶484 *n* **1** [C] (Anat) (of human) espalda *f*; (of animal) lomo *m*; **they laugh at him behind his ~** se ríen de él a sus espaldas; ***to turn one's ~ on sb*** volverle* la espalda a algn **2** [C] **(a)** (of chair) respaldo *m*; (of dress, jacket) espalda *f*; (of electrical appliance, watch) tapa *f* **(b)** (reverse side — of envelope, photo) dorso *m*; (— of head) parte *f* posterior; (— of hand) dorso *m*; **your sweater is on ~ to front** te has puesto el suéter al revés; ⇒ HAND[1] 2 **3** [C U] (rear part): **the ~ of the house** la parte de atrás de la casa; **we sat at the ~** nos sentamos al fondo; **I'll sit in the ~** (of car) yo me siento detrás *or* (en el asiento de) atrás; ***in the ~ of beyond*** quién sabe dónde, donde el diablo perdió el poncho (AmS fam), en el quinto pino (Esp fam) **4** [C] (Sport) defensa *mf*, zaguero, -ra *m,f*

back[2] *adj* (*before n, no comp*) **1** ‹*door*› trasero; ‹*garden*› de atrás **2** (of an earlier date): **~ number** *o* **issue** número *m* atrasado; **~ pay** atrasos *mpl*

back[3] *adv* **1** (indicating return, repetition): **the journey ~** el viaje de vuelta; **he's ~ from Paris** ha vuelto de París; **long hair is ~ (in fashion)** vuelve (a estar de moda) el pelo largo; **to run/fly ~** volver* corriendo/en avión; **he asked for the ring ~** pidió que le devolviera el anillo; *see also* GO, TAKE *etc* BACK **2** (in reply, reprisal): **he slapped her and she slapped him ~** él la abofeteó y ella le devolvió la bofetada **3** (backward): **take two steps ~** da dos pasos atrás **4** (in the past): **~ in 1972** (ya) en 1972 **5 back and forth** = **backward(s) and forward(s)**: *see* BACKWARD[2] (a)

back[4] *vt* **1 (a)** ‹*person/decision*› respaldar **(b)** (bet money on) ‹*horse/winner*› apostar* por **2** (reverse): **he ~ed the car out of the garage** sacó el coche del garaje dando marcha atrás *or* (Col, Méx) en reversa **3** (Mus) acompañar ■ **~** *vi* «*vehicle/driver*» dar* marcha atrás, meter reversa (Col, Méx); **he ~ed into a lamppost** se dio contra una farola al dar marcha atrás *or* al meter reversa

• **back away** [*v* + *adv*] echarse atrás

• **back down** [*v* + *adv*] volverse* atrás

• **back out** [*v* + *adv*] volverse* atrás; **they ~ed out of the deal** no cumplieron el trato

• **back up 1** [*v* + *o* + *adv, v* + *adv* + *o*] **(a)** (support) respaldar, apoyar **(b)** (Comput) ‹*file*› hacer* una copia de seguridad de **2** [*v* + *adv*] (reverse) dar* marcha atrás, meter reversa (Col, Méx)

back: **~ache** *n* [U] dolor *m* de espalda; **~bencher** /'bæk'bentʃər ‖ˌbæk'bentʃə(r)/, **~bench MP** *n* (in UK) diputado, -da *m,f* (*sin cargo específico en el gobierno o la oposición*); **~bone** *n* (Anat) columna *f* (vertebral); (main strength) columna *f* vertebral, eje *m*; **~date** /'bæk'deɪt/ *vt* ‹*wage increase*› pagar* con retroactividad; ‹*check*› ponerle* una fecha anterior a; **~drop** *n* telón *m* de fondo

backer /'bækər ‖'bækə(r)/ *n* patrocinador, -dora *m,f*

backfire /'bækfaɪr ‖bæk'faɪə(r)/ *vi* **(a)** «*car*» producir* detonaciones en el escape **(b)** (fail) fracasar

background[1] /'bækgraʊnd/ *n* **(a)** (of picture, scene) fondo *m*; **she prefers to stay in the ~** prefiere permanecer en un segundo plano **(b)** (of events) **~** (TO **sth**) antecedentes *mpl* (DE algo) **(c)** (of person — origin) origen *m*; (— education) formación *f*; (— previous activities) experiencia *f*

background[2] *adj* (*before n*) ‹*noise/music*› de fondo; **~ reading** lecturas *fpl* preparatorias (*acerca del momento histórico, antecedentes etc*)

backhand /'bækhænd/ *n* revés *m*

backing /'bækɪŋ/ *n* **(a)** [U] (support) respaldo *m* **(b)** [C] (Mus) acompañamiento *m*

backlash /'bæklæʃ/ *n* reacción *f* violenta; (Mech Eng) contragolpe *m*

backless /'bækləs ‖'bæklɪs/ *adj* sin espalda

back: **~log** *n* atraso *m*; **a ~log of work** trabajo atrasado; **~pack** *n* mochila *f*; **~ seat** *n* asiento *m* trasero *or* de atrás; **~side** /'bæk'saɪd/ *n* (colloq) trasero *m* (fam); **~stage** /'bæk'steɪdʒ/ *adj/adv* entre bastidores; **~street** *n* callejuela *f*; (*before n*) ‹*abortion*› clandestino; **~stroke** *n* [U] estilo *m* espalda; **~track** *vi* **(a)** (retrace one's steps) retroceder **(b)** (reverse opinion, plan) dar* marcha atrás; **~-up** *n* **(a)** [U] (support) respaldo *m*, apoyo *m*; (*before n*) ‹*team/equipment*› de refuerzo **(b)** [C] (Comput) copia *f* de seguridad; (*before n*) ‹*disk/file*› de reserva, de seguridad

backward[1] /'bækwərd ‖ 'bækwəd/ *adj* **1** (*before n*) ‹*movement*› hacia atrás; **a ~ glance** una mirada atrás **2** ‹*child*› retrasado; ‹*nation*› atrasado

backward[2], (esp BrE) **backwards** /'bækwərdz ‖ 'bækwədz/ *adv* **(a)** (toward rear) hacia atrás; **~ and forward(s)** para atrás y para adelante; ⇒ KNOW[1] *vt* 1(a) **(b)** (back to front, in reverse order) al revés

back yard *n* (paved) patio *m* trasero; (grassed) (AmE) jardín *m* trasero, fondo *m* (RPl)

bacon /'beɪkən/ *n* [U] tocino *m or* (Esp) bacon *m or* (RPl) panceta *f*

bacteria /bæk'tɪriə ‖ bæk'tɪəriə/ *pl n* bacterias *mpl*

bad[1] /bæd/ *adj*

■ **Note** The usual translation of *bad*, *malo*, becomes *mal* when it is used before a masculine singular noun.

(*comp* **worse**; *superl* **worst**) **1** (not good) malo; **to be ~ AT sth/-ING** ser* malo PARA algo/+ INF; **to go from ~ to worse** ir* de mal en peor; **too much food is ~ for you** comer demasiado es malo; **she's got a ~ knee** tiene problemas con la rodilla; **I feel ~ about not having written to her** me da no sé qué no haberle escrito; ***to be in a ~ way*** (colloq) estar* fatal (fam) **2** (serious) ‹*mistake/injury*› grave; ‹*headache*› fuerte **3** (rotten) ‹*egg/fruit*› podrido; **to go ~** echarse a perder

bad[2] *n* [U]: **all the ~ that he's done** todo el mal que ha hecho; **there's good and ~ in everybody** todos tenemos cosas buenas y malas

bad[3] *adv* (esp AmE colloq): **to need sth real ~** necesitar algo desesperadamente

bade /bæd, beɪd/ *past of* BID[1] *vt* 2

badge /bædʒ/ *n* (pin-on) chapa *f*, botón *m* (AmL); (sew-on) insignia *f*

badger[1] /'bædʒər ‖ 'bædʒə(r)/ *n* tejón *m*

badger[2] *vt* fastidiar

badly /'bædli/ *adv* (*comp* **worse**; *superl* **worst**) **1** (poorly) ‹*play/sing*› mal **2** (improperly) ‹*behave/treat*› mal **3** (*as intensifier*) ‹*fail*› miserablemente; **~ injured** gravemente herido

badly off *adj* (*comp* **worse off**; *superl* **worst off**) (*pred*) mal de dinero

badminton /'bædmɪntn̩/ *n* [U] bádminton *m*

bad-tempered /'bæd'tempərd ‖ ˌbæd'tempəd/ *adj* ‹*reply/tone*› malhumorado; ‹*person*› (as permanent characteristic) de mal genio; (in a bad mood) de mal humor

baffle /'bæfəl/ *vt* **(a)** (perplex) desconcertar* **(b)** (frustrate) ‹*efforts*› frustrar

baffled /'bæfəld/ *adj* perplejo; ‹*expression*› de perplejidad

bag /bæg/ *n* **1 (a)** (container, bagful) bolsa *f*; **a paper ~** una bolsa de papel; (*hand~*) (esp BrE) cartera *f or* (Esp) bolso *m or* (Méx) bolsa *f* **(b)** (piece of luggage) maleta *f*, valija *f* (RPl), petaca *f* (Méx); **to pack one's ~s** hacer* la maleta (*or* valija *etc*) **2** (of skin) bolsa *f*; **to have ~s under one's eyes** (of skin) tener* bolsas en los ojos; (dark rings) tener* ojeras

baggage /'bægɪdʒ/ *n* [U] equipaje *m*; (*before n*) **~ room** (AmE) consigna *f*

baggy /'bægi/ *adj* **-gier, -giest** ancho, guango (Méx)

bagpipes /'bægpaɪps/ *pl n* gaita *f*

Bahamas /bə'hɑːməz/ *pl n* **the ~** las Bahamas

bail /beɪl/ *n* [U] (Law) fianza *f*; **he was released on ~** fue puesto en libertad bajo fianza

● **bail out 1** [*v + o + adv, v + adv + o*] **(a)** (Law): **to ~ sb out** pagarle* la fianza a algn **(b)** (Naut) ‹*water*› achicar* **2** [*v + o + adv, v + adv + o*] (rescue) sacar* de apuros **3** [*v + adv*] (Aviat) tirarse en paracaídas

bailiff /'beɪləf ‖ 'beɪlɪf/ *n* (Law) **(a)** (in UK) alguacil *mf* **(b)** (in US) *funcionario que custodia al acusado en el juzgado*

bait[1] /beɪt/ *n* [U] cebo *m*

bait[2] *vt* **1** ‹*hook/trap*› cebar **2** (persecute) acosar

bake /beɪk/ *vt*: **~ in a hot oven** hornear en horno caliente; **she ~s her own bread** hace el pan en casa; **~d potato** papa *f or* (Esp) patata *f* asada ■ **~** *vi* hacer* pasteles (*or* pan *etc*)

baked beans /beɪkt/ *pl n* **(a)** (in can) frijoles *mpl or* (Esp) judías *fpl or* (CS) porotos *mpl* en salsa de tomate **(b)** (dish) (AmE) *el mismo plato preparado con cerdo*

baker /'beɪkər ‖ 'beɪkə(r)/ *n* panadero, -ra *m,f*; **~'s (shop)** panadería *f*

bakery /'beɪkəri/ *n* (*pl* **-ries**) panadería *f*

baking /'beɪkɪŋ/ *n* [U]: **we do a lot of ~** hacemos muchos pasteles (*or* pan *etc*); (*before n*) **~ dish** fuente *f* para el horno; **~ powder** polvo *m* de hornear, Royal® *m*, levadura *f* en polvo (Esp); **~ tin** molde *m*; **~ tray** bandeja *f* (de horno)

balance[1] /'bæləns/ *n* **1** [C] (apparatus) balanza *f* **2** [U] (equilibrium) equilibrio *m*; **to lose one's ~** perder* el equilibrio **3** [C] **(a)** (in accounting) balance *m* **(b)** (*bank ~*) saldo *m* **(c)** (difference, remainder) resto *m*; (of sum of money) saldo *m*

balance[2] *vt* **1** ‹*load*› equilibrar; ‹*object*› mantener* en equilibrio **2** (Fin) ‹*account*› hacer* el balance de

balcony /'bælkəni/ *n* (*pl* **-nies**) **(a)** (Archit) balcón *m*; (large) terraza *f* **(b)** (Theat) (in US) platea *f* alta; (in UK) galería *f*

bald /bɔːld/ *adj* **-er, -est (a)** ‹*man*› calvo, pelón (AmC, Méx), pelado (CS); **to go ~** quedarse calvo (*or* pelón *etc*) **(b)** (worn) ‹*tire*› gastado

bale /beɪl/ *n* paca *f*

● **bale out** (BrE) ⇒ BAIL OUT

Balearic Islands /ˌbæli'ærɪk/ *pl n* **the ~ ~** las (Islas) Baleares

baleful /'beɪlfəl/ *adj* torvo

Balkan /'bɔːlkən/ *adj* balcánico

Balkans /ˈbɔːlkənz/ *pl n* **the ~** los países balcánicos

ball /bɔːl/ *n* **1** [C] (in baseball, golf) pelota *f*, bola *f*; (in basketball, football) pelota *f* (esp AmL), balón *m* (esp Esp); (in billiards) bola *f*; ***to be on the ~*** (colloq) ser* muy espabilado **2** [U] **(a) to play ~ (with sb)** (lit: play game) jugar* a la pelota (con algn); (cooperate) (colloq) cooperar (con algn) **(b)** (*base~*) (AmE) béisbol *m* **3 (a)** [C] (round mass) bola *f*; (of string, wool) ovillo *m* **(b)** [C] (Anat): **the ~ of the foot** la parte anterior de la planta del pie **4** [C] (dance) baile *m*

ballad /ˈbæləd/ *n* (narrative poem, song) romance *m*; (sentimental song) balada *f*

ballast /ˈbæləst/ *n* [U] (Aviat, Naut) lastre *m*

ballerina /ˌbæləˈriːnə/ *n* bailarina *f* (de ballet)

ballet /ˈbæleɪ/ *n* [U C] ballet *m*; (*before n*) **~ dancer** bailarín, -rina *m,f* de ballet

ball game *n* juego *m* de pelota; (baseball game) (AmE) partido *m* de béisbol; (US football game) (AmE) partido *m* de fútbol *or* (AmC, Méx) futbol americano

ballistics /bəˈlɪstɪks/ *n* (+ *sing vb*) balística *f*

balloon /bəˈluːn/ *n* **(a)** (toy) globo *m*, bomba *f* (Col), chimbomba *f* (AmC) **(b)** (Aviat) globo *m*

ballot /ˈbælət/ *n* [U C] votación *f*; (*before n*) **~ box** urna *f*; **~ (paper)** papeleta *f*, boleta *f* electoral (Méx, RPl)

ball: **~park** *n* (AmE Sport) estadio *m or* (Méx) parque *m* de béisbol; (*before n*) **a ~park figure** una cifra aproximada; **~player** *n* (AmE) (in baseball) jugador, -dora *m,f* de béisbol, beisbolista *mf*; (in US football) jugador, -dora *m,f* de fútbol *or* (AmC, Méx) de futbol americano; (in basketball) jugador, -dora *m,f* de baloncesto, baloncestista *mf*, basquetbolista *mf* (AmL); **~point (pen)** *n* bolígrafo *m*, esfero(gráfico) *m* (Col), pluma *f* atómica (Méx), birome *f* (RPl), lápiz *m* de pasta (Chi); **~room** *n* sala *f or* salón *m* de baile; **~room dancing** *n* [U] baile *m* de salón

balm /bɑːm/ *n* [U C] bálsamo *m*

Baltic /ˈbɔːltɪk/ *n* **the ~ (Sea)** el (mar) Báltico

bamboo /ˈbæmˈbuː ‖ bæmˈbuː/ *n* [U C] (*pl* **-boos**) bambú *m*

ban¹ /bæn/ *vt* **-nn-** ‹*book/smoking*› prohibir*; ‹*organization*› proscribir*; **he was ~ned from the club** le prohibieron la entrada al club

ban² *n* prohibición *f*

banal /bəˈnæl, ˈbeɪnəl ‖ bəˈnɑːl/ *adj* banal

banana /bəˈnænə ‖ bəˈnɑːnə/ *n* plátano *m*, banana *f* (Per, RPl), banano *m* (AmC, Col), cambur *m* (Ven)

band /bænd/ *n* **1 (a)** (group) grupo *m*; (of thieves, youths) pandilla *f* **(b)** (Mus) (*jazz ~*) grupo *m or* conjunto *m* de jazz; (*rock ~*) grupo *m* de rock **2 (a)** (ribbon) cinta *f*; (strip — of cloth) banda *f*; (— for hat) cinta *f* **(b)** (stripe) franja *f*

• **band together** [*v* + *adv*] unirse

bandage¹ /ˈbændɪdʒ/ *n* venda *f*

bandage² *vt* vendar

Band-Aid® /ˈbændeɪd/ *n* (AmE) curita® *f*, tirita® *f* (Esp)

B & B /ˈbiːənˈbiː/ *n* = **bed and breakfast**

bandit /ˈbændət ‖ ˈbændɪt/ *n* bandido, -da *m,f*, bandolero, -ra *m,f*

band: **~stand** *n* quiosco *m* de música; **~wagon** *n*: ***to jump on the ~wagon*** subirse al carro

bandy¹ /ˈbændi/ *adj* **-dier, -diest** arqueado, torcido

bandy² **-dies, -dying, -died** *vt* ‹*remarks/jokes*› intercambiar

bane /beɪn/ *n*: **to be the ~ of sb's life** ser* la cruz de algn

bang¹ /bæŋ/ *n* **1** (loud noise) estrépito *m*; (explosion) explosión *f* **2** (blow) golpe *m*, trancazo *m* **3 bangs** *pl* (AmE) (fringe) flequillo *m*, cerquillo *m* (AmL), chasquilla *f* (Chi), capul *f* (Col), fleco *m* (Méx), pollina *f* (Ven)

bang² *vt* **(a)** (strike) golpear **(b)** (slam): **he ~ed the door** dio un portazo (fam) ■ **~** *vi* **(a)** (strike) **to ~ ON sth** golpear algo; **to ~ INTO sth** darse* CONTRA algo **(b)** (slam) «*door*» cerrarse* de un golpe

bang³ *adv* **1** : **to go ~** «*gun*» dispararse **2** (*as intensifier*) (esp BrE colloq): **~ on time** a la hora justa

banger /ˈbæŋər ‖ ˈbæŋə(r)/ *n* (BrE colloq) **(a)** (sausage) salchicha *f* **(b)** (firework) petardo *m* **(c)** (car) (*old ~*) cacharro *m* (fam)

Bangkok /ˈbæŋkɑːk ‖ ˌbæŋˈkɒk/ *n* Bangkok *m*

Bangladesh /ˈbɑːŋgləˈdeʃ ‖ ˌbæŋgləˈdeʃ/ *n* Bangladesh *m*

Bangladeshi /ˈbɑːŋgləˈdeʃi ‖ ˌbæŋgləˈdeʃi/ *adj* bangladesí

bangle /ˈbæŋgəl/ *n* pulsera *f*, brazalete *m*; (thin, of gold or silver) esclava *f*, aro *m*

banish /ˈbænɪʃ/ *vt* **(a)** (exile) desterrar*; ‹*fear/doubts*› hacer* olvidar **(b)** (prohibit) prohibir*

banister /ˈbænəstər ‖ ˈbænɪstə(r)/ *n* pasamanos *m*

bank¹ /bæŋk/ *n* **1 (a)** (Fin) banco *m*; (*before n*) **~ balance** saldo *m* **(b)** (store, supply) banco *m*; **blood ~** banco de sangre **2** (edge of river) orilla *f*, ribera *f* **3 ~ of earth/snow** montículo *m* de tierra/nieve

bank² *vt* depositar *or* (esp Esp) ingresar (en el banco) ■ **~** *vi* **1** (Fin): **I ~ with the National** tengo la cuenta en el National **2** (Aviat) ladearse

• **bank on** [*v* + *prep* + *o*] ‹*victory/help*› contar* con; **I wouldn't ~ on it** yo no me confiaría demasiado

bank: **~ account** *n* cuenta *f* bancaria; **~book** *n* libreta *f* de ahorros; **~card** *n* (AmE) tarjeta *f* de crédito (*expedida por un banco*); (BrE) tarjeta *f* bancaria

banker /ˈbæŋkər ‖ ˈbæŋkə(r)/ *n* **(a)** (Fin) banquero, -ra *m,f* **(b)** (in gambling) banca *f*

bank holiday *n* (BrE) día *m* festivo, feriado *m* (esp AmL)

banking /ˈbæŋkɪŋ/ *n* [U] banca *f*

bank: **~ note** *n* **(a)** (promissory note) (AmE) pagaré *m* **(b)** (paper money) (BrE) billete *m* de banco; **~ rate** *n* tasa *f or* (esp Esp) tipo *m* de interés

bankrupt¹ /ˈbæŋkrʌpt/ *adj* en quiebra, en bancarrota; **to be ~** estar* en quiebra *or* en bancarrota; **to go ~** quebrar*, ir* a la bancarrota

bankrupt² *vt* llevar a la quiebra *or* a la bancarrota

bankruptcy /ˈbæŋkrʌptsi/ *n* [U C] (*pl* **-cies**) quiebra *f*, bancarrota *f*

banner /ˈbænər ‖ ˈbænə(r)/ *n* (flag) estandarte *m*; (in demonstration) pancarta *f*

bannister *n* ⇒ BANISTER

banns /bænz/ *pl n* amonestaciones *fpl*

banquet /ˈbæŋkwət ‖ ˈbæŋkwɪt/ *n* banquete *m*

banter /ˈbæntər ‖ ˈbæntə(r)/ *n* [U] bromas *fpl*

baptism /ˈbæptɪzəm/ *n* [C U] bautismo *m*

Baptist /ˈbæptəst ‖ ˈbæptɪst/ *n* baptista *mf*, bautista *mf*

baptize /bæpˈtaɪz/ *vt* bautizar*

bar¹ /bɑːr ‖ bɑː(r)/ *n* **1** (rod, rail) barra *f*; (— on cage, window) barrote *m* **2** (Sport) (*cross*~) (in soccer) larguero *m*; (in rugby) travesaño *m*; (in high jump) barra *f* or (Esp) listón *m*; (*horizontal* ~) barra *f* (fija) **3** (block) barra *f*; **~ of chocolate** barra *f* de chocolate; **gold ~** lingote *m* de oro; **~ of soap** pastilla *f* or (CS) barra *f* de jabón **4** (establishment) bar *m*; (counter) barra *f*, mostrador *m* **5** (Law) **the Bar** (legal profession) (AmE) la abogacía; (barristers) (BrE) *el conjunto de* BARRISTERS **6** (Mus) compás *m*

bar² *vt* **-rr- 1** (secure) ‹*door/window*› atrancar* **2** (block) ‹*path/entrance*› bloquear **3** (prohibit) ‹*smoking/jeans*› prohibir*; ‹*person/group*› excluir*

bar³ *prep* salvo, excepto, a or con excepción de

barb /bɑːrb ‖ bɑːb/ *n* (of fishhook, arrow) lengüeta *f*

Barbados /bɑːrˈbeɪdəʊs ‖ bɑːˈbeɪdɒs/ *n* Barbados *m*

barbarian /bɑːrˈberiən ‖ bɑːˈbeəriən/ *n* bárbaro, -ra *m,f*

barbaric /bɑːrˈbærɪk ‖ bɑːˈbærɪk/ *adj* (primitive) primitivo; (brutal) brutal

barbarity /bɑːrˈbærəti ‖ bɑːˈbærəti/ *n* (*pl* **-ties**) [U C] brutalidad *f*

barbecue /ˈbɑːrbɪkjuː ‖ ˈbɑːbɪkjuː/ *n* **1** (grid and fireplace) barbacoa *f*, parrilla *f*, asador *m* (AmL) **2** (social occasion) barbacoa *f*, parrillada *f*, asado *m* (AmL)

barbed wire /bɑːrbd ‖ bɑːbd/ *n* [U] alambre *m* de púas or (Esp tb) de espino

barber /ˈbɑːrbər ‖ ˈbɑːbə(r)/ *n* peluquero *m*, barbero *m* (ant); **the ~('s)** la peluquería

barbwire /ˈbɑːrbˈwaɪr ‖ ˌbɑːbˈwaɪə(r)/ *n* [U] (AmE) ⇒ BARBED WIRE

bar code *n* código *m* de barras

bare¹ /ber ‖ beə(r)/ *adj* **barer** /ˈberər ‖ ˈbeərə(r)/, **barest** /ˈberəst ‖ ˈbeərɪst/ (uncovered) ‹*blade/flesh/walls*› desnudo; ‹*head*› descubierto; ‹*foot*› descalzo; ‹*floorboards*› sin alfombrar; ‹*tree*› pelado; ‹*wire*› pelado or (Esp) desnudo; ‹*room*› con pocos muebles; **the ~ essentials** lo estrictamente esencial; **he gave me the ~ facts** se ciñó a los hechos; **to lay sth ~** poner* or dejar algo al descubierto

bare² *vt*: **to ~ one's head** descubrirse* (la cabeza); **the dog ~d its teeth** el perro enseñó or mostró los dientes

bareback /ˈberbæk ‖ ˈbeəbæk/ *adv* ‹*ride*› a pelo

barefoot¹ /ˈberfʊt ‖ ˈbeəfʊt/ *adj* descalzo

barefoot² *adv*: **she ran ~** corrió descalza

barely /ˈberli ‖ ˈbeəli/ *adv* (hardly) apenas

bargain¹ /ˈbɑːrgən ‖ ˈbɑːgən/ *n* **1** (cheap purchase) ganga *f* **2** (deal, agreement) trato *m*, acuerdo *m*; **to strike a ~** llegar a un acuerdo; ***into*** o (AmE also) ***in the ~*** encima, por si fuera poco

bargain² *vi* **(a)** (haggle) regatear **(b)** (negotiate) negociar

● **bargain for** [*v* + *prep* + *o*]: **we hadn't ~ed for such an eventuality** no habíamos tenido en cuenta esa posibilidad; **I got more than I had ~ed for** no me esperaba algo así

bargaining /ˈbɑːrgənɪŋ ‖ ˈbɑːgənɪŋ/ *n* [U] **(a)** (haggling) regateo *m* **(b)** (negotiating) negociaciones *fpl*; (*before n*) ‹*strategy/position*› negociador

barge¹ /bɑːrdʒ ‖ bɑːdʒ/ *n* barcaza *f*

barge² *vi* (+ *adv compl*): **he ~d past (me)** me dio un empujón para pasar; **he always ~s in when we're trying to talk** siempre se entromete cuando queremos hablar

baritone /ˈbærətəʊn ‖ ˈbærɪtəʊn/ *n* barítono *m*

bark¹ /bɑːrk ‖ bɑːk/ *n* **1** [U] (on tree) corteza *f* **2** [C] (of dog) ladrido *m*

bark² *vi* ladrar; ■ **~** *vt* (shout) espetar; **to ~ (out) an order** gritar una orden

barkeep /ˈbɑːrkiːp ‖ ˈbɑːkiːp/, **barkeeper** /-ˌkiːpər ‖ -ˌkiːpə(r)/ *n* (AmE) (male) barman *m*, camarero *m* (Esp, Ven); (female) mesera *f* or (Esp, Ven) camarera *f* or (Col, CS) moza *f*

barley /ˈbɑːrli ‖ ˈbɑːli/ *n* [U] cebada *f*

bar: **~maid** *n* mesera *f* or (Esp, Ven) camarera *f* or (Col, RPl) moza *f*; **~man** /ˈbɑːrmən ‖ ˈbɑːmən/ *n* (*pl* **-men** /-mən/) (BrE) barman *m*, camarero *m* (Esp, Ven)

barn /bɑːrn ‖ bɑːn/ *n* **(a)** (for crops) granero *m*; (for livestock) establo *m* **(b)** (for vehicles) (AmE) cochera *f*

barometer /bəˈrɑːmətər ‖ bəˈrɒmɪtə(r)/ *n* barómetro *m*

baron /ˈbærən/ *n* **(a)** (nobleman) barón *m* **(b)** (magnate) magnate *m*

baroness /ˈbærəˈnes, ˈbærənes/ *n* baronesa *f*

barracks /ˈbærəks/ *n* (*pl* ~) (+ *sing or pl vb*) cuartel *m*

barrage /bəˈrɑːʒ ‖ ˈbærɑːʒ/ *n* (Mil) (action) descarga *f*; (fire) cortina *f* de fuego

barrel /ˈbærəl/ *n* **1** (container) barril *m*, tonel *m* **2** (of handgun) cañón *m*; (of cannon) tubo *m*

barren /ˈbærən/ *adj* **-er, -est** ‹*land/soil*› estéril; ‹*tree/plant/animal*› (*no comp*) estéril; ‹*woman*› (dated or liter) infecunda

barrette /bɑːˈret ‖ bəˈret/ *n* (AmE) pasador *m*, broche *m* (Méx, Ur), hebilla *f* (Arg)

barricade¹ /ˈbærəkeɪd ‖ ˌbærɪˈkeɪd/ *n* barricada *f*

barricade² *vt* cerrar* con barricadas; **they ~d themselves into the building** se atrincheraron en el edificio

barrier /ˈbæriər ‖ ˈbæriə(r)/ *n* barrera *f*; **language ~** barrera idiomática

Barrier Reef *n* **the Great ~ ~** el Gran Arrecife Coralino, la Gran Barrera Coral

barrister /ˈbærəstər ‖ ˈbærɪstə(r)/ *n* (BrE) abogado, -da *m,f* (*habilitado para alegar ante un tribunal superior*)

barrow /ˈbærəʊ/ *n* (*wheel*~) carretilla *f*

bar: **~stool** *n* taburete *m*; **~tender** *n* (esp AmE) (male) barman *m*, camarero *m* (Esp, Ven); (female) mesera *f or* (Esp, Ven) camarera *f or* (Col, CS) moza *f*

barter /'bɑːrtər || 'bɑːtə(r)/ *vt* cambiar, trocar* ■ ~ *vi* hacer* trueques

base¹ /beɪs/ *n* **1** (of column, wall) base *f*; (of mountain, tree) pie *m*; (of spine, skull) base *f*; (of lamp) pie *m* **2** (foundation, basis) base *f* **3** (of patrol, for excursion) base *f*; (of organization) sede *f* **4** (in baseball) base *f*

base² *vt* **1** (found) **to ~ sth** ON **sth** ‹*opinion/conclusion*› basar algo EN algo; **the movie is ~d on a real event** la película se basa en una historia real **2** (locate) basar; **the company is ~d in Madrid** la compañía tiene su base en Madrid

base³ *adj* **baser, basest** ‹*conduct/motive*› abyecto

baseball /'beɪsbɔːl/ *n* **(a)** [U] (game) béisbol *m*; (*before n*) **~ bat** bate *m* de béisbol **(b)** [C] (ball) pelota *f* de béisbol

basement /'beɪsmənt/ *n* sótano *m*

base pay *n* [U] (AmE) sueldo *m* base *or* básico

bases¹ /'beɪsiːz/ *pl of* BASIS

bases² /'beɪsəz || 'beɪsɪz/ *pl of* BASE¹

bash¹ /bæʃ/ *n* (colloq) **1** (blow) golpe *m*, madrazo *m* (Méx fam) **2** (party) juerga *f* (fam)

bash² *vt* (colloq) pegarle* a

bashful /'bæʃfəl/ *adj* tímido, penoso (AmL exc CS)

basic /'beɪsɪk/ *adj* **1** (fundamental) fundamental **2** (simple, rudimentary) ‹*knowledge/need*› básico; ‹*hotel/food*› sencillo **3** (Econ) ‹*pay*› básico

basically /'beɪsɪkli/ *adv* fundamentalmente

basics /'beɪsɪks/ *pl n* lo básico

basil /'beɪzəl || 'bæzəl/ *n* [U] albahaca *f*

basin /'beɪsn/ *n* **(a)** (for liquid, food) cuenco *m*, bol *m*, tazón *m* **(b)** (*hand ~*) (BrE) lavamanos *m*, lavabo *m*, pileta *f* (RPl) **(c)** (Geog, Geol) cuenca *f*

basis /'beɪsəs || 'beɪsɪs/ *n* (*pl* **bases** /'beɪsiːz/) **1** [C U] (foundation, grounds) base *f* **2** (system, level) (*no pl*): **employed on a daily ~** contratado por día; **on a regional ~** a nivel regional

bask /bæsk ||bɑːsk/ *vi*: **to ~ in the sun** disfrutar (del calor) del sol; **she ~ed in their adulation** se deleitaba *or* se regodeaba con su adulación

basket /'bæskət || 'bɑːskɪt/ *n* **1** (for shopping) canasta *f* (esp AmL), cesta *f* (esp Esp) **2** (in basketball) **(a)** (goal) canasta *f*, cesto *m* **(b)** (score) canasta *f*, enceste *m*

basketball /'bæskətbɔːl || 'bɑːskɪtbɔːl/ *n* **(a)** [U] (game) baloncesto *m*, básquetbol *m* (AmL) **(b)** [C] (ball) pelota *f* de básquetbol *or* (Esp) balón *m* de baloncesto

Basque¹ /bæsk || bæsk, bɑːsk/ *adj* vasco; **the ~ Country** el País Vasco, Euskadi *m*

Basque² *n* **(a)** [C] (person) vasco, -ca *m,f* **(b)** [U] (language) euskera *m*, vasco *m*, vascuence *m*

bass¹ *n* /beɪs/ (*pl* **~es**) (Mus) **(a)** [U C] (voice, singer) bajo *m* **(b)** [C] (double bass or bass guitar) (contra)bajo *m* **(c)** [U] (Audio) graves *mpl*

bass² *adj* ‹*voice*› de bajo

bass clef clave *f* de fa

bassoon /bə'suːn/ *n* fagot *m*

bastard /'bæstərd || 'bɑːstəd/ *n* **1** (illegitimate child) bastardo, -da *m,f* **2** (colloq *or* vulg) cabrón *m* (fam *o* vulg), hijo *m* de puta (vulg)

baste /beɪst/ *vt* **(a)** (Culin) *rociar con su jugo o con mantequilla etc durante la cocción* **(b)** (sew loosely) hilvanar

bastion /'bæstʃən || 'bæstiən/ *n* **(a)** (Archit) bastión *m* **(b)** (stronghold) baluarte *m*, bastión *m*

bat¹ /bæt/ *n* **1** (in baseball, cricket) bate *m*; (in table tennis) (BrE) paleta *f*, raqueta *f* **2** (Zool) murciélago *m*

bat² *vi* **-tt-** (Sport) batear

batch /bætʃ/ *n* (of cakes) hornada *f*; (of goods) (Busn) lote *m*; (of trainees, candidates) grupo *m*; (of mail, paperwork) pila *f*; (Comput) lote *m*

bated /'beɪtəd || 'beɪtɪd/ *adj*: **with ~ breath** con ansiedad

bath¹ /bæθ || bɑːθ/ *n* (*pl* **baths** /bæðz || bɑːðz/) **1 (a)** (wash) baño *m*; **to have** *o* (AmE also) **take a ~** bañarse, darse* un baño **(b)** (tub) bañera *f*, tina *f* (AmL) **2 baths** *pl* (*swimming ~s*) (BrE) piscina *f*, alberca *f* (Méx), pileta *f* (RPl)

bath² (BrE) *vt* bañar

bathe /beɪð/ *vt* (wash) ‹*wound/eyes*› lavar; ‹*baby/dog*› (AmE) bañar ■ ~ *vi* **(a)** (take bath) (AmE) bañarse **(b)** (go swimming) (BrE) bañarse

bathing suit, (BrE also) **bathing costume** /'beɪðɪŋ/ *n* traje *m* de baño, bañador *m* (Esp), malla *f* (de baño) (RPl), vestido *m* de baño (Col)

bath: **~mat** *n* alfombrilla *f or* tapete *m or* (Chi) piso *m* de baño; **~robe** *n* bata *f* de baño, albornoz *m* (Esp); **~room** *n* **(a)** (room with bath) (cuarto *m* de) baño *m* **(b)** (toilet) (esp AmE) baño *m*, servicio *m*; **~tub** *n* bañera *f*, tina *f* (AmL), bañadera *f* (Arg)

baton /bə'tɑːn || 'bætən/ *n* **(a)** (Mus) batuta *f* **(b)** (truncheon) (BrE) bastón *m* **(c)** (in relay race) testigo *m*

battalion /bə'tæljən/ *n* batallón *m*

batter¹ /'bætər || 'bætə(r)/ *vt* **1** (beat) ‹*victim/opponent*› apalear; ‹*child/wife*› maltratar **2** (cover with batter) rebozar*

batter² *n* **1** [U] (for fried fish, etc) rebozado *m*; (for pancakes) masa *f*; (for cake) (AmE) masa *f* **2** [C] (in baseball) bateador, -dora *m,f*

battered /'bætərd || 'bætəd/ *adj* ‹*car*› abollado; ‹*hat/suitcase*› estropeado; ‹*reputation/image*› maltrecho; ‹*baby/wife*› maltratado

battering ram /'bætərɪŋ/ *n* ariete *m*

battery /'bætəri/ *n* (*pl* **-ries**) **1** (in radio, lamp) pila *f*; (in car, motorcycle) batería *f* **2** (artillery) batería *f* **3** (Agr) batería *f* (*conjunto de jaulas instaladas para la explotación avícola intensiva*); (*before n*) ‹*eggs/hens*› de criadero, de batería; **~ farming** cría *f* intensiva

battle¹ /'bætl/ *n* [C U] batalla *f*; **to fight a losing ~** luchar por una causa perdida

battle² *vi* luchar

battle: **~field** *n* campo *m* de batalla; **~ground** *n* campo *m* de batalla

battlements /'bætlmənts/ *pl n* almenas *fpl*

battleship /'bætlʃɪp/ *n* acorazado *m*

baud /bɔːd/ *n* (Comput) baudio *m*

bawdy /'bɔːdi/ *adj* **-dier, -diest** subido de tono

bawl /bɔːl/ *vi* **(a)** (shout) vociferar **(b)** (cry noisily) berrear

bay¹ /beɪ/ *n* **1** (Geog) bahía *f* **2 (a)** (*loading* ~) muelle *m or* plataforma *f* de carga **(b)** (area, recess) espacio *m* **3** : **at ~** acorralado; **to keep** *o* **hold sth/sb at ~** mantener* algo/a algn a raya **4 ~ (tree)** laurel *m*

bay² *vi* «*hounds*» aullar*

bayleaf /ˈbeɪliːf/ *n* (*pl* **-leaves**) hoja *f* de laurel

bayonet /ˈbeɪənət/ *n* bayoneta *f*

bay window *n* ventana *f* en saliente

bazaar /bəˈzɑːr ‖ bəˈzɑː(r)/ *n* **(a)** (oriental market) bazar *m* **(b)** (charity sale) venta *f* benéfica

BBC *n* (= **British Broadcasting Corporation**) **the ~** la BBC

BC (= **before Christ**) antes de Cristo; (written form) aC, a. de C., a. de J.C.

be /biː, *weak form* bi/ (*pres* **am, are, is**; *past* **was, were**; *past p* **been**) *vi* [*See notes at* SER *and* ESTAR] **I 1** (*followed by an adjective*): **she's French** es francesa; **he's worried** está preocupado; **how are you?** ¿cómo estás?; **I'm much better** estoy *or* me encuentro mucho mejor; **she's pregnant/tired/ill** está embarazada/cansada/enferma; **I'm cold/hot/hungry/thirsty** tengo frío/calor/hambre/sed; **he's dead** está muerto; **he's blind** es *or* (Esp tb) está ciego; **he's short** es bajo; **Tony is married/divorced** Tony está *or* (esp AmL) es casado/divorciado; **these shoes are new** estos zapatos son nuevos; **she was very rude to me** estuvo *or* fue muy grosera conmigo; **she's very rude** es muy grosera; **~ good** sé bueno **2** (*followed by a noun*) ser*; **if I were you, I'd stay** yo que tú me quedaría **3 (a)** (talking about age) tener*; **how old are you?** ¿cuántos años tienes?; **I'm 31** tengo 31 años; **Paul was four last Monday** Paul cumplió cuatro años el lunes pasado; **our house is over 100 years old** nuestra casa tiene más de 100 años **(b)** (giving cost, measurement, weight): **they are $15 each** cuestan *or* valen 15 dólares cada una; **two plus two is four** dos más dos son cuatro; **how tall is he?** ¿cuánto mide?; **Jim's over six feet tall** Jim mide más de seis pies **II 1 (a)** (exist, live): **to let sth/sb ~** dejar tranquilo algo/a algn **(b)** (in expressions of time): **I'm drying my hair, I won't ~ long** me estoy secando el pelo, enseguida estoy; **the party is tomorrow** la fiesta es mañana **2** (be situated, present) estar*; **where is the library?** ¿dónde está la biblioteca? **3** (*only in perfect tenses*) (visit) estar*; **I've never been to India** nunca he estado en la India ■ **~** *v impers* **1 (a)** (talking about physical conditions, circumstances): **it's cold/hot** hace frío/calor; **it's so noisy in here!** ¡qué ruido hay aquí! **(b)** (in expressions of time) ser*; **it's three o'clock** son las tres; **it's Wednesday today** hoy es miércoles **(c)** (talking about distance) estar*; **it's 500 miles from here to Detroit** Detroit queda a 500 millas de aquí **2** (introducing person, object) ser*; **it's me/Daniel** soy yo/es Daniel ■ **~** *v aux* **1 to ~ -ING** estar* + GER; **I'm working** estoy trabajando; **how long have you been waiting?** ¿cuánto (tiempo) hace que esperas?; **when are you seeing her?** ¿cuándo la vas a ver? **2** **▶ 744** (*in the passive voice*) ser* [*The passive voice, however, is less common in Spanish than it is in English*] **it was built in 1903** fue construido en 1903, se construyó en 1903, lo construyeron en 1903; **it is known that** ... se sabe que ... **3 to ~ to** + INF **(a)** (with future reference): **the dessert is (still) to come** todavía falta el postre **(b)** (expressing possibility): **what are we to do?** ¿qué podemos hacer?; **it was nowhere to ~ found** no se lo pudo encontrar por ninguna parte **4 (a)** (*in tag questions*): **she's right, isn't she?** tiene razón, ¿no? *or* ¿verdad? **(b)** (*in elliptical uses*): **are you disappointed? — yes, I am/no, I'm not** ¿estás desilusionado? — sí (, lo estoy)/no (, no lo estoy); **she was told the news, and so was he/but I wasn't** a ella le dieron la noticia, y también a él/pero a mí no

beach /biːtʃ/ *n* playa *f*

beacon /ˈbiːkən/ *n* (light) faro *m*; (fire) almenara *f*

bead /biːd/ *n* cuenta *f*, abalorio *m*; (drop) gota *f*; **~s of sweat** gotas *fpl* de sudor

beady /ˈbiːdi/ *adj*: **~ eyes** ojos redondos y brillantes

beak /biːk/ *n* pico *m*

beaker /ˈbiːkər ‖ ˈbiːkə(r)/ *n* **(a)** (Chem) vaso *m* de precipitados **(b)** (cup) (BrE) taza *f* (*gen alta y sin asa*)

be-all and end-all /ˈbiːɔːlənˈendɔːl/ *n*: **it is the ~ ~ ~ of his life** es su razón de ser; **work isn't the ~ ~ ~** el trabajo no lo es todo

beam¹ /biːm/ *n* **1** (in building) viga *f*; (in ship) bao *m* **2** (ray) rayo *m*; (broad) haz *m* de luz; **keep the headlights on high** *o* (BrE) **full** *o* **main ~** (Auto) deja las (luces) largas *or* (Chi) altas

beam² *vi* **(a)** (shine) brillar **(b)** (smile) sonreír* (*abiertamente*) ■ **~** *vt* (broadcast) transmitir

bean /biːn/ *n* **(a)** (fresh, in pod) ⇒ GREEN BEAN **(b)** (dried) frijol *m or* (Esp) alubia *f or* judía *f or* (CS) poroto *m or* (Ven) caraota *f*; ***to be full of ~s*** (colloq) estar* lleno de vida

bean: **~ curd** *n* tofu *m*, queso *m* de soya (AmL) *or* (Esp) soja; **~shoot, ~ sprout** *n* frijol *m* germinado *or* (Esp) judía *f* germinada *or* (CS) poroto *m* germinado; (of soy bean) brote *m or* germinado *m* de soya (AmL) *or* (Esp) soja

bear¹ /ber ‖ beə(r)/ (*past* **bore**; *past p* **borne**) *vt* **1 (a)** (support) ‹*weight*› aguantar; ‹*cost*› correr con; ‹*responsibility*› cargar* con **(b)** (endure) ‹*pain/uncertainty*› soportar **(c)** (put up with, stand) (colloq) (*with can*) ‹*person*› aguantar (fam); ‹*noise*› aguantar **(d)** (stand up to): **her argument doesn't ~ close scrutiny** su razonamiento no resiste un análisis cuidadoso; **it doesn't ~ thinking about** da miedo sólo de pensarlo **2 (a)** (carry) (liter) ‹*banner/coffin*› llevar, portar (liter) **(b)** (harbor): **she's not one to ~ a grudge** no es rencorosa; **to ~ sb malice** guardarle rencor a algn **3** (have, show) ‹*title/signature*› llevar; ‹*scars*› tener*; ‹*resemblance*› tener* **4 (a)** (produce) ‹*fruit/crop*› dar*; ‹*interest*› devengar* **(b)** (give birth to) ‹*child*› dar* a luz; *see also* BORN¹ ■ **~** *vi* (turn) torcer*; **~ left** tuerza a la izquierda

• **bear out** [*v + o + adv, v + adv + o*] ‹*theory*› confirmar

● **bear up** [*v* + *adv*]: **she bore up well under the strain** sobrellevó muy bien la situación

● **bear with** [*v* + *prep* + *o*] ‹*person/mood*› tener* paciencia con; **if you'll just ~ with me for a moment,** ... (asking to wait) si tienen la bondad de esperar un momento, ...; (asking for patience) si puedo poner a prueba su paciencia, ...

bear² *n* oso, osa *m,f*

bearable /'berəbəl ‖ 'beərəbəl/ *adj* soportable

beard /bɪrd ‖ bɪəd/ *n* barba *f*

bearded /'bɪrdəd ‖ 'bɪədɪd/ *adj* con *or* de barba

bearer /'berər ‖ 'beərə(r)/ *n* **(a)** (of news) portador, -dora *m,f* **(b)** (carrier, porter) portador, -dora *m,f*, porteador, -dora *m,f* **(c)** (holder — of check) portador, -dora *m,f*; (— of passport) titular *mf*

bearing /'berɪŋ ‖ 'beərɪŋ/ *n* **1 (a)** [C] (Aviat, Naut) demora *f*; ***to get/lose one's ~s*** orientarse/desorientarse **(b)** [U C] (relevance): **that has no ~ on the subject** eso no tiene ninguna relación con el tema **2** [C] (way of standing) porte *m*

beast /bi:st/ *n* bestia *f*

beat¹ /bi:t/ (*past* **beat**; *past p* **beaten** /'bi:tn̩/) *vt* **1 (a)** (hit) golpear; ‹*carpet*› sacudir; ‹*wings*› batir; ‹*child/wife*› maltratar **(b)** (hammer) ‹*metal*› batir **(c)** (Culin) batir **2** ‹*opponent*› ganarle a; ‹*record*› batir; **our prices can't be ~en** nuestros precios son imbatibles **3** (arrive before, anticipate): **I ~ him to the telephone** llegué antes que él al teléfono; ***to ~ sb to it*** adelantársele a algn **3** (Mus) ‹*time*› marcar* ■ ~ *vi* **(a)** (strike): **he could hear them ~ing on the door** los oía golpear la puerta; **the waves were ~ing against the cliff** las olas golpeaban contra el acantilado **(b)** (pulsate) «*heart*» latir, palpitar; «*drum*» redoblar; «*wings*» batir

● **beat down 1** [*v* + *o* + *adv*, *v* + *adv* + *o*] ‹*door*› tirar abajo; ‹*crop*› aplastar **2** [*v* + *adv*] «*sun*» caer* de lleno; «*rain*» llover* con fuerza

● **beat up** [*v* + *o* + *adv*, *v* + *adv* + *o*] (colloq) darle* una paliza a (fam)

● **beat up on** [*v* + *adv* + *prep* + *o*] (AmE colloq) darle* una paliza a

beat² *n* **1** (of heart) latido *m*; (of drum) golpe *m* **2** (Mus) (rhythmic accent) tiempo *m*; (rhythm) ritmo *m* **3** (of policeman) ronda *f*

beat³ *adj* (colloq) (*pred*): **to be (dead) ~** estar* reventado (fam)

beaten /'bi:tn̩/ *past p of* BEAT¹

beating /'bi:tɪŋ/ *n* **(a)** [C] (thrashing) paliza *f* **(b)** [C] (defeat) paliza *f* (fam) **(c)** [U] (surpassing): **her time will take some ~** va a ser difícil superar su marca

beautiful /'bju:təfəl ‖ 'bju:tɪfəl/ *adj* **(a)** (in appearance) precioso, hermoso, bello (liter) **(b)** (very good) (colloq) ‹*meal/weather*› estupendo **(c)** (kind) (esp AmE) ‹*person*› encantador

beautifully /'bju:təfli ‖ 'bju:tɪfəli/ *adv* (excellently, very well) ‹*sing/dance*› maravillosamente (bien); **she was ~ dressed** iba elegantísima

beauty /'bju:ti/ *n* (*pl* **-ties**) **1** [U] (quality) belleza *f*, hermosura *f*; (*before n*) **~ contest** *o* (esp AmE) **pageant** concurso *m* de belleza; **~ queen** reina *f* de la belleza **2** [C] (woman) belleza *f*

beauty: **~ salon** *n* salón *m* de belleza; **~ shop** *n* (AmE) salón *m* de belleza; **~ spot** *n* **1** (place) lugar *m* pintoresco; **2** (on face) lunar *m*

beaver /'bi:vər ‖ 'bi:və(r)/ *n* castor *m*

became /bɪ'keɪm/ *past of* BECOME

because /bə'kɔ:z, bɪ'kɒz/ *conj* **1** porque **2 because of** (*as prep*) por, a *or* por causa de (frml)

beck /bek/ *n*: ***to be at sb's ~ and call*** estar* siempre a entera disposición de algn

beckon /'bekn̩/ *vt*: **to ~ sb over** hacerle* señas a algn para que se acerque ■ ~ *vi* hacer* una seña; **she ~ed to him to follow** le hizo señas para que la siguiera

become /bɪ'kʌm/ (*past* **became**; *past p* **become**) *vi*: **to ~ famous** hacerse* famoso; **to ~ accustomed to sth** acostumbrarse a algo; **she soon became bored** pronto se aburrió; **the heat became unbearable** el calor se hizo insoportable; **they became friends** se hicieron amigos ■ ~ *vt* **(a)** (befit) (frml) (*often neg*) ser* apropiado para **(b)** (suit) favorecer*

● **become of** (*usu interrog*) ser* de; **what's to ~ of me?** ¿qué va a ser de mí?

becoming /bɪ'kʌmɪŋ/ *adj* **(a)** (fitting) (frml) apropiado **(b)** ‹*outfit/hat*› favorecedor, sentador (AmL)

bed /bed/ *n* **1** (for sleeping) cama *f*; **to make the ~** hacer* *or* (AmL tb) tender* la cama; **to get into/out of ~** acostarse*/levantarse; **to go to ~** acostarse*; **he's in ~ with measles** está en cama con sarampión; **we put the children to ~ early** acostamos a los niños temprano **2** (for plants) arriate *m*, cantero *m* (RPl) **3** (of river) lecho *m*, cauce *m*; (of sea) fondo *m* **4** (base, support) base *f*

bed: **~ and breakfast** /'bedn̩'brekfəst/ *n* **(a)** [U] (service): **they do ~ and breakfast** dan alojamiento y desayuno **(b)** [C] (establishment) ≈ pensión *f*; **~clothes** *pl n* ropa *f* de cama

bedding /'bedɪŋ/ *n* [U] **(a)** ⇨ BEDCLOTHES **(b)** (for animals) cama *f*

bedlam /'bedləm/ *n* [U] (colloq): **there was ~ when he announced the news** se armó la de San Quintín cuando anunció la noticia (fam)

bedpan /'bedpæn/ *n* (Med) cuña *f*

bedraggled /bɪ'drægəld/ *adj* desaliñado; ‹*hair*› despeinado

bed: **~ridden** *adj* postrado en cama; **~room** *n* dormitorio *m*, cuarto *m*, pieza *f* (esp AmL), recámara *f* (esp Méx); **~side** *n*: **they sat at his ~side throughout the night** pasaron toda la noche junto a su cabecera; **~side table** mesita *f* de noche, velador *m* (AmS), mesa *f* de luz (RPl); **~sit**, **~sitter** /'bed,sɪtər ‖ ,bed'sɪtə(r)/ *n* (BrE colloq) habitación *f* amueblada (*cuyo alquiler suele incluir el uso de baño y cocina comunes*); **~sore** *n* escara *f*, úlcera *f* de decúbito (frml) (*llaga que se produce por estar mucho tiempo en cama*); **~spread** *n* cubrecama *m*, colcha *f*; **~time** *n* [U] hora *f* de acostarse

bee /bi:/ *n* **1** (Zool) abeja *f* **2** (social gathering) (esp AmE) círculo *m*

beech /bi:tʃ/ *n* **~ (tree)** haya *f*

beef /bi:f/ *n* [U] carne *f* de vaca *or* (AmC, Méx) de res, ternera *f* (Esp)

beefburger /ˈbiːfˌbɜːrgər || ˈbiːfˌbɜːgə(r)/ *n* (esp BrE) hamburguesa *f*

bee: **~hive** *n* colmena *f*; **~line** *n*: ***to make a ~line for sb/sth*** (colloq) irse* derechito a algn/algo (fam)

been /bɪn ||biːn/ **(a)** *past p of* BE **(b)** *past p of* GO[1] *vi* I 2

beep[1] /biːp/ *n* (colloq) pitido *m*

beep[2] *vt/i* (colloq) pitar

beer /bɪr || bɪə(r)/ *n* [U C] cerveza *f*

beer: **~ garden** *n*: *jardín o patio abierto de un bar*; **~ mat** *n* posavasos *m* (*de cartón*)

beeswax /ˈbiːzwæks/ *n* [U] cera *f* de abeja

beet /biːt/ *n* (*pl* **~s**) (AmE) remolacha *f or* (Méx) betabel *m or* (Chi) betarraga *f*

beetle /ˈbiːtl/ *n* escarabajo *m*

beetroot /ˈbiːtruːt/ *n* [C U] (BrE) ⇒ BEET

befall /bɪˈfɔːl/ *vt* (*past* **befell** /bɪˈfel/ *past p* **befallen** /bɪˈfɔːlən/) (liter) sucederle *or* ocurrirle a

before[1] /bɪˈfɔːr || bɪˈfɔː(r)/ *prep* **1** (preceding in time) antes de; **~ long** dentro de poco; **~ going in** antes de entrar **2 (a)** (in front of) delante de, ante (frml) **(b)** (in rank, priority): **she puts her work ~ her family** antepone el trabajo a su familia

before[2] *conj* **(a)** (earlier than) antes de que (+ *subj*), antes de (+ *inf*) **(b)** (rather than) antes que

before[3] *adv* (preceding) antes; **the day ~** el día anterior; **have you been to Canada ~?** ¿ya has estado en el Canadá?

beforehand /bɪˈfɔːrhænd || bɪˈfɔːhænd/ *adv* (earlier) antes; (in advance) de antemano

befriend /bɪˈfrend/ *vt* hacerse* amigo de

beg /beg/ **-gg-** *vt* **1** ‹*money/food*› pedir*, mendigar* **2** (frml) **(a)** (entreat) ‹*person*› suplicarle* a, rogarle* a **(b)** (ask for) ‹*forgiveness*› suplicar*, rogar* ■ **~** *vi* «*beggar*» pedir*, mendigar*; **to ~ for mercy** pedir* *or* suplicar* clemencia

began /bɪˈgæn/ *past of* BEGIN

beget /bɪˈget/ *vt* (*pres p* **begetting**; *past* **begot** *or* (arch) **begat** /bɪˈgæt/; *past p* **begotten**) (liter) engendrar

beggar /ˈbegər || ˈbegə(r)/ *n* mendigo, -ga *m,f*

begin /bɪˈgɪn/ (*pres p* **beginning**; *past* **began**; *past p* **begun**) *vt* empezar*, comenzar*; **to ~** -ING/**to** + INF empezar* *or* comenzar* A + INF ■ **~** *vi* empezar*, comenzar*; «*custom*» originarse; **to ~ with** para empezar

beginner /bɪˈgɪnər || bɪˈgɪnə(r)/ *n* principiante *mf*

beginning /bɪˈgɪnɪŋ/ *n* **(a)** (in time, place) principio *m*; **at the ~ of the year/of June** a principios del año/de junio; **I'll start again from the ~** volveré a empezar desde el principio; **from ~ to end** de principio a fin **(b)** (origin, early stage) (*often pl*) comienzo *m* **(c)** (start, debut) (*no pl*) comienzo *m*

begot /bɪˈgɑːt || bɪˈgɒt/ *past of* BEGET

begotten /bɪˈgɑːtn̩ || bɪˈgɒtn̩/ *past p of* BEGET

begrudge /bɪˈgrʌdʒ/ *vt*: **I ~ paying so much** me da rabia pagar tanto; **I don't ~ you your success** no te envidio el éxito que tienes

beguile /bɪˈgaɪl/ *vt* (charm) cautivar, seducir*

beguiling /bɪˈgaɪlɪŋ/ *adj* cautivador, seductor

begun /bɪˈgʌn/ *past p of* BEGIN

behalf /bɪˈhæf || bɪˈhɑːf/ *n*: **on** *o* (AmE also) **in ~ of sb, on** *o* (AmE also) **in sb's ~ 1** (as representative of): **I'd like to thank you on ~ of the team** quisiera darle las gracias en nombre de *or* de parte de todo el equipo; **he accepted the award on her ~** aceptó el premio en su nombre **2** (in the interest of): **he argued on her ~ that** … alegó en su defensa *or* en su favor que …

behave /bɪˈheɪv/ *vi* **(a)** (act) comportarse; (esp of children) portarse **(b)** (be good) «*child/animal*» portarse bien, comportarse ■ *v refl* **to ~ oneself** portarse bien, comportarse

behavior, (BrE) **behaviour** /bɪˈheɪvjər || bɪˈheɪvjə(r)/ *n* [U] conducta *f*, comportamiento *m*

behead /bɪˈhed/ *vt* decapitar

beheld /bɪˈheld/ *past and past p of* BEHOLD

behind[1] /bɪˈhaɪnd/ *prep* **1 (a)** (to the rear of) detrás de, atrás de (AmL); **we're ten years ~ the Japanese in microelectronics** en microelectrónica llevamos un retraso de diez años respecto a los japoneses **(b)** (on the other side of) detrás de, atrás de (AmL) **2** (responsible for) detrás de; **the motives ~ his decision** los motivos que lo llevaron a esa decisión **3** (in time): **all that is ~ us now** todo eso ha quedado atrás; **I'm ~ schedule** voy retrasado (con el trabajo *or* los preparativos *etc*)

behind[2] *adv* **(a)** (to the rear, following): **he ran along ~** iba corriendo detrás *or* (AmL tb) atrás; **I was attacked from ~** me atacaron por la espalda; **keep an eye on the car ~** no pierdas de vista al coche de atrás **(b)** (in race, competition): **England were two goals ~** Inglaterra iba perdiendo por dos goles **(c)** (in arrears): **I'm ~ with my work/payments** estoy atrasada con el trabajo/en los pagos

behind[3] *n* (colloq & euph) trasero *m* (fam)

behold /bɪˈhəʊld/ (*past and past p* **beheld**) *vt* (liter) contemplar (liter)

beige /beɪʒ/ ▶ **515** *adj* beige *adj inv*, beis *adj inv* (Esp)

Beijing /ˈbeɪˈdʒɪŋ/ *n* Beijing *m*

being /ˈbiːɪŋ/ *n* [C U] ser *m*

Belarus /ˈbeləˈruːs/ *n* Bielorrusia *f*

belated /bɪˈleɪtəd || bɪˈleɪtɪd/ *adj* tardío

belch /beltʃ/ *vi* «*person*» eructar; **flames ~ed from the cannon** la boca del cañón escupía llamas

Belgian[1] /ˈbeldʒən/ *adj* belga

Belgian[2] *n* belga *mf*

Belgium /ˈbeldʒəm/ *n* Bélgica *f*

belie /bɪˈlaɪ/ *vt* **belies, belying, belied (a)** (disguise) no dejar traslucir **(b)** (show to be false): **this ~s the notion that** … esto demuestra que no es cierto que …

belief /bəˈliːf || bɪˈliːf/ *n* **(a)** [U C] (conviction, opinion) creencia *f* **(b)** [U] (confidence) **~** IN **sb/sth** confianza *f or* fe *f* EN algn/algo **(c)** [U C] (Relig) fe *f*

believable /bəˈliːvəbəl || bɪˈliːvəbəl/ *adj* ‹*story/account*› verosímil

believe /bəˈliːv || bɪˈliːv/ *vt* **(a)** ‹*statement/story*› creer*; ‹*person*› creerle* a; **I don't ~ it!** ¡no puedo creerlo!; ***to make ~ (that)*** hacer* de cuenta que **(b)** (think) creer* ■ ~ *vi* creer*; **to ~ IN sth/sb** creer* EN algo/algn

believer /bə'li:vər || bɪ'li:və(r)/ *n* creyente *mf*

belittle /bɪ'lɪtl/ *vt* ‹*achievements*› menospreciar; ‹*person*› denigrar

bell /bel/ *n* (of church, clock) campana *f*; (on cat, toy) cascabel *m*; (on door, bicycle) timbre *m*; (of telephone, timer) timbre *m*; ***to ring a ~***: **the name rings a ~** me suena el nombre; (*before n*) **~ tower** campanario *m*

belligerent /bə'lɪdʒərənt/ *adj* agresivo

bellow /'beləʊ/ *vi* bramar; (shout) gritar

bellows /'beləʊz/ *n* (*pl* ~) (for fire) fuelle *m*

bell pepper *n* (AmE) ⇒ CAPSICUM

belly /'beli/ *n* (*pl* **-lies**) **(a)** (of person) vientre *m*, barriga *f* (fam); (of animal) panza *f*, vientre *m*; (*before n*) **~ button** (colloq) ombligo *m*; **to do a ~ flop** darse* un planchazo *or* (Andes) un guatazo (fam)

belong /bɪ'lɔ:ŋ || bɪ'lɒŋ/ *vi* **1 (a)** (be property) **to ~ TO sb** ser* DE algn, pertenecerle* A algn **(b)** (be member) **to ~ TO sth** ‹*to a club*› ser* socio DE algo; ‹*to a union/political party*› estar* afiliado A algo **2** (have as usual place) ir*; **put them back where they ~** vuélvelos a poner en su lugar

belongings /bɪ'lɔ:ŋɪŋz || bɪ'lɒŋɪŋz/ *pl n* pertenencias *fpl*

beloved /bɪ'lʌvəd || bɪ'lʌvɪd/ *adj* (*before n*) querido

below¹ /bɪ'ləʊ/ *prep* **1** (under) debajo de, abajo de (AmL) **2** (inferior, junior to) por debajo de **3** (less than) por debajo de; **~ zero** bajo cero

below² *adv* **1** (underneath) abajo; **put it on the shelf ~** ponlo en el estante de abajo **2** (in text) más abajo **3** (of temperature): **20 (degrees) ~** 20 (grados) bajo cero

belt¹ /belt/ *n* **1** (Clothing) cinturón *m* **2** (Mech Eng) correa *f*

belt² *vt* (colloq) darle* una paliza a

beltway /'beltweɪ/ *n* (AmE) carretera *f* de circunvalación

bemoan /bɪ'məʊn/ *vt* lamentarse de

bemused /bɪ'mju:zd/ *adj* de desconcierto

bench /bentʃ/ *n* **1** [C] **(a)** (seat) banco *m* **(b)** (*work~*) mesa *f* de trabajo **2** (Law) **the bench** *or* **the Bench** (judges collectively) la judicatura; (tribunal) el tribunal

bend¹ /bend/ *n* **(a)** (in road, river) curva *f* **(b) bends** *pl* **the ~s** la enfermedad del buzo

bend² (*past and past p* **bent**) *vt* ‹*wire/branch*› torcer*, curvar; ‹*back/leg*› doblar; Ⓢ **do not bend** no doblar ■ ~ *vi* **(a)** «*pipe/wire*» torcerse* **(b)** «*person*» ⇒ BEND DOWN **(c)** «*road/river*» hacer* una curva

- **bend down** [*v* + *adv*] agacharse
- **bend over** [*v* + *adv*] inclinarse

beneath¹ /bɪ'ni:θ/ *prep* **1** (under) bajo **2 (a)** (inferior to): **she married ~ her** no se casó bien **(b)** (unworthy of): **it's ~ her** es indigno de ella; **you're ~ contempt** no mereces ni desprecio

beneath² *adv*: **the floor ~** el piso de abajo; **I wondered what lay ~** me preguntaba qué habría debajo *or* abajo

benefactor /'benəfæktər || 'benɪfæktə(r)/ *n* benefactor, -tora *m,f*

beneficial /'benə'fɪʃəl || ˌbenɪ'fɪʃəl/ *adj* beneficioso

beneficiary /'benə'fɪʃieri || ˌbenɪ'fɪʃəri/ *n* (*pl* **-ries**) beneficiario, -ria *m,f*

benefit¹ /'benəfɪt || 'benɪfɪt/ *n* **1** [U C] (good) beneficio *m*, bien *m*; (advantage) provecho *m*; ***to give sb the ~ of the doubt*** darle* a algn el beneficio de la duda **2** [C U] (Soc Adm) prestación *f*; *see also* UNEMPLOYMENT **3** [C] (concert, performance) beneficio *m*; (*before n*) con fines benéficos

benefit² **-t-** *or* (AmE also) **-tt-** *vt* beneficiar ■ ~ *vi* beneficiarse; **to ~ FROM sth** beneficiarse CON algo

benevolent /bə'nevələnt/ *adj* ‹*person/smile*› benévolo; ‹*gesture*› de benevolencia

benign /bɪ'naɪn/ *adj* **(a)** ‹*person/attitude*› benévolo **(b)** (Med) benigno

bent¹ /bent/ *past and past p of* BEND[2]

bent² *adj* **1** ‹*pipe*› curvado, torcido **2** (determined) **to be ~ ON doing sth** estar* empeñado EN hacer algo

bequeath /bɪ'kwi:ð, -'kwi:θ/ *vt* **to ~ sth TO sb** legarle* algo A algn

bequest /bɪ'kwest/ *n* legado *m*

berate /bɪ'reɪt/ *vt* (frml) **to ~ sb (FOR sth)** reprender a algn (POR algo)

bereaved /bɪ'ri:vd/ *adj* desconsolado (*por la muerte de un ser querido*)

bereavement /bɪ'ri:vmənt/ *n* [C U] dolor *m* (*por la muerte de un ser querido*)

beret /bə'reɪ ||'bereɪ/ *n* boina *f*

Berlin /'bɜ:r'lɪn || bɜ:'lɪn/ *n* Berlín *m*

Bermuda /bər'mju:də || bə'mju:də/ *n* las (islas) Bermudas

berry /'beri/ *n* (*pl* **-ries**) (Bot) baya *f*; (Culin) *fresas, frambuesas, moras etc*

berserk /bər'sɜ:rk || bə'sɜ:k/ *adj*: **to go ~** ponerse* como una fiera

berth¹ /bɜ:rθ || bɜ:θ/ *n* **(a)** (bunk) litera *f*, cucheta *f* (RPl); (cabin) camarote *m* **(b)** (mooring) atracadero *m*; ***to give sb a wide ~*** eludir a algn

berth² *vt/i* atracar*

beseech /bɪ'si:tʃ/ *vt* (*past & past p* **beseeched** *or* **besought**) (liter) suplicar*, rogar*

beset /bɪ'set/ *vt* (*pres p* **besetting**; *past & past p* **beset**) «*anxieties/fears*» acuciar; **he was ~ by doubts** lo acosaban las dudas

beside¹ /bɪ'saɪd/ *prep* (at the side of) al lado de; ***to be ~ oneself***: **he was ~ himself with rage** estaba fuera de sí (de la rabia); **she's beside herself with happiness** está que no cabe en sí de la alegría **(b)** (compared with) comparado con **(c)** (extraneous to): **that's ~ the point** eso no tiene nada que ver **(d)** ⇒ BESIDES[1]

beside² *adv* **(a)** (alongside) al lado **(b)** ⇒ BESIDES[2]

besides¹ /bɪ'saɪdz/ *prep* **(a)** (in addition to) además de **(b)** (apart from) excepto, aparte de

besides² *adv* además

besiege /bɪ'si:dʒ/ *vt* sitiar, asediar; **the village was ~d by reporters** el pueblo se vio asediado por periodistas

besotted /bɪ'sɑːtəd ‖ bɪ'sɒtɪd/ *adj* (*usu pred*): **he's totally ~ with her** está perdidamente enamorado de ella

besought /bɪ'sɔːt/ *past & past p of* BESEECH

bespectacled /bɪ'spektɪkəld/ *adj* de anteojos *or* lentes (AmL), con gafas (esp Esp)

best¹ /best/ *adj* (*superl of* GOOD¹) mejor; **for the ~ part of an hour/a month** durante casi una hora/un mes; **she's not very tolerant at the ~ of times** la tolerancia no es precisamente una de sus características

best² *adv* (*superl of* WELL^1,2) mejor; **I did it as ~ I could** lo hice lo mejor que pude; **it's ~ forgotten** más vale olvidarlo

best³ *n* **1 the ~ (a)** (+ *sing vb*) lo mejor; **to do one's ~** hacer* todo lo posible; **we'll just have to make the ~ of what we've got** tendremos que arreglarnos con lo que tenemos; **(b)** (+ *pl vb*): **they're (the) ~ of friends** son de lo más amigos; **she can ski with the ~ of them** (colloq) esquía tan bien como el mejor **2 (a) at best: at ~, we'll just manage to cover costs** como mucho, podremos cubrir los gastos **(b) at/past one's best: at his ~, his singing rivals that of Caruso** en sus mejores momentos puede compararse a Caruso; **the roses were past their ~** las rosas ya no estaban en su mejor momento **3 (a)** (in greetings): **all the ~!** ¡buena suerte! **(b)** (Sport) récord *m*; **a personal ~ for Flynn** un récord para Flynn

best man *n*: *amigo que acompaña al novio el día de la boda*, ≈ padrino *m*, testigo *m*

bestow /bɪ'stəʊ/ *vt* (frml *or* liter) **to ~ sth** ON *o* UPON **sb** ‹*title/award*› conferirle* algo A algn (frml)

best-seller /'best'selər ‖ ,best'selə(r)/ *n* (book) bestseller *m*; (product) superventas *m*; (author) autor, -tora *m,f* de bestsellers

bet¹ /bet/ *n* apuesta *f*; **I had a ~ with Charlie that Brazil would win** le aposté a Charlie que ganaría Brasil; **your best ~ is to stay here** lo mejor que puedes hacer es quedarte aquí

bet² (*pres p* **betting**; *past & past p* **bet**) *vt* apostar* ■ **~** *vi* jugar*; **to ~** ON **sth/sb** apostarle* A algo/algn; **I wouldn't ~ on it if I were you** yo no estaría tan seguro, yo no me fiaría

betray /bɪ'treɪ/ *vt* ‹*ally*› traicionar; **he ~ed us to the enemy** nos vendió al enemigo; **her voice ~ed her nervousness** su voz revelaba el miedo que sentía

betrayal /bɪ'treɪəl/ *n* [C U] traición *f*

betrothal /bɪ'trəʊðəl/ *n* [U C] (frml) esponsales *mpl* (frml)

better¹ /'betər ‖ 'betə(r)/ *adj* **1** (*comp of* GOOD¹) mejor; **to get ~** mejorar; **if they can both come, so much the ~** si pueden venir los dos, mucho *or* tanto mejor **2** (*pred*) (recovered from illness): **to be ~** estar* mejor; **to get ~** recuperarse

better² *adv* **1** (*comp of* WELL^1,2) mejor **2 had better** (ought): **I'd ~ leave before it gets dark** va a ser mejor que me vaya antes de que oscurezca; **well, I'd ~ be off** bueno, me tengo que ir

better³ *n* **(a)** (superior of two): **the ~ of the two** el mejor de los/las dos; **for the ~** para bien; ***to get the ~ of sb/sth*** ganarle la batalla a algn/algo **(b) betters** *pl* (superiors) superiores *mpl*; **his elders and ~s** sus mayores

better⁴ *vt* mejorar; **to ~ oneself** superarse

better-off /,betər'ɔːf ‖ ,betər'ɒf/ *adj* (*pred* **better off**) **(a)** (financially) de mejor posición económica **(b)** (emotionally, physically) (*pred*) mejor

betting shop /'betɪŋ/ *n* (BrE) agencia *f* de apuestas

between¹ /bɪ'twiːn/ *prep* entre

between² *adv*: **the one ~** el/la de en medio

beverage /'bevərɪdʒ/ *n* bebida *f*

beware /bɪ'wer ‖ bɪ'weə(r)/ *vi* (*only in inf and imperative*): **~!** ¡(ten) cuidado!; Ⓢ **beware of the dog** cuidado con el perro

bewildered /bɪ'wɪldərd ‖ bɪ'wɪldəd/ *adj* desconcertado; (overwhelmed) apabullado

bewildering /bɪ'wɪldərɪŋ/ *adj* desconcertante; (overwhelming) apabullante

bewitch /bɪ'wɪtʃ/ *vt* (cast spell on) embrujar; (entrance, delight) cautivar

beyond¹ /bɪ'ɑːnd ‖ bɪ'jɒnd/ *prep* **1** (on other side of): **I live just ~ the station** vivo justo pasando la estación; **~ this point** de aquí en adelante **2 (a)** (further than): **try to think ~ the immediate future** trata de pensar más allá del futuro inmediato **(b)** (more than, apart from): **I can't tell you anything ~ that** no te puedo decir nada más que eso **3** (past): **it's ~ repair** ya no tiene arreglo; **circumstances ~ our control** circunstancias ajenas a nuestra voluntad; **it's ~ me what she sees in him** (colloq) no puedo entender qué es lo que ve en él; **to live ~ one's means** vivir por encima de sus (*or* mis *etc*) posibilidades

beyond² *adv* **(a)** (in space) más allá **(b)** (in time): **we're planning for the year 2000 and ~** estamos haciendo planes para el 2000 y más allá del 2000

bias /'baɪəs/ *n* [U C] parcialidad *f*; **the course has a scientific ~** el curso tiene un enfoque científico

biased, biassed /'baɪəst/ *adj* ‹*report/criticism*› tendencioso; ‹*judge*› parcial; **to be ~** AGAINST/TOWARD(S) **sth/sb** estar* predispuesto EN CONTRA DE/A FAVOR DE algo/algn

bib /bɪb/ *n* **(a)** (for baby) babero *m* **(b)** (on dungarees) peto *m*

Bible /'baɪbəl/ *n* Biblia *f*

biblical /'bɪblɪkəl/ *adj* bíblico

bibliography /'bɪbli'ɑːgrəfi ‖ ,bɪbli'ɒgrəfi/ *n* (*pl* **-phies**) bibliografía *f*

bicarbonate of soda /baɪ'kɑːrbəneɪt ‖ baɪ'kɑːbəneɪt/ *n* [U] bicarbonato *m* de sodio *or* de soda *or* (Esp) de sosa

biceps /'baɪseps/ *n* (*pl* **~**) bíceps *m*

bicker /'bɪkər ‖ 'bɪkə(r)/ *vi* pelear, discutir

bicycle /'baɪsɪkəl/ *n* bicicleta *f*

bid¹ /bɪd/ *vt* **1** (*pres p* **bidding**; *past & past p* **bid**) (at auction) ofrecer* **2** (*pres p* **bidding**; *past* **bade** *or* **bid**; *past p* **bidden** *or* **bid**) (liter) **(a)** (wish, say): **to ~ sb farewell** despedirse* de algn **(b)** (request) **to ~ sb (to)** + INF pedirle* a algn QUE + SUBJ ■ **~** *vi* (*pres p* **bidding**; *past & past p* **bid**) (at auction) hacer* ofertas, pujar; **to ~ FOR sth** pujar POR algo

bid² *n* **1** (at auction) oferta *f*, puja *f* **2** (attempt) intento *m*, tentativa *f*; (unsuccessful) intentona *f*, intento *m*; **~ to + INF** intento *m* DE + INF

bidden /ˈbɪdn̩/ *past p of* BID¹ *vt* 2

bidder /ˈbɪdər ‖ ˈbɪdə(r)/ *n* postor, -tora *m,f*

bidding /ˈbɪdɪŋ/ *n* [U] **1** (at auction): **the ~ opened at $100** la subasta abrió con una oferta de $100 **2** (wishes): **they had servants to do their ~** tenían criados para lo que se les antojara; **at his father's ~** a petición de su padre

bide /baɪd/ *vt*: ***to ~ one's time*** esperar el momento oportuno

bidet /bɪˈdeɪ ‖ ˈbiːdeɪ/ *n* bidet *m*, bidé *m*

biennial /baɪˈeniəl/ *adj* bienal

bier /bɪr ‖ bɪə(r)/ *n* andas *fpl*

bifocals /ˈbaɪˈfəʊkəlz/ *pl n* anteojos *mpl or* (esp Esp) gafas *fpl* bifocales

big /bɪg/ *adj*

■ **Note** The usual translation of *big*, *grande*, becomes *gran* when it is used before a singular noun.

-gg- grande; **a ~ garden** un jardín grande, un gran jardín; **how ~ is the table?** ¿cómo es de grande la mesa?; **a ~ hug/kiss** un abrazote/besote (fam); **a ~ decision** una gran decisión; **our ~gest customer** nuestro cliente más importante; **she's really ~ in Europe** es muy conocida en Europa; **my ~ brother** mi hermano mayor

bigamy /ˈbɪgəmi/ *n* [U] bigamia *f*

big: **~ business** *n* [U] el gran capital; **to be ~ business** ser* un gran negocio; **~-headed** /ˈbɪg ˈhedəd ‖ ˌbɪgˈhedɪd/ *adj* (colloq) creído (fam); **~ league** *n* (in US) (Sport) liga *f* mayor; (top rank) los grandes; **~mouth** *n* (colloq) (boaster) fanfarrón, -rrona *m,f*; (gossip) chismoso, -sa *m,f*, cotilla *mf* (Esp fam), hocicón, -cona *m,f* (Chi, Méx fam)

bigot /ˈbɪgət/ *n* intolerante *mf*

bigotry /ˈbɪgətri/ *n* [U] intolerancia *f*

big: **~ shot** *n* (colloq) pez *m* gordo (fam); **~ top** *n* carpa *f* de circo

bike /baɪk/ *n* (colloq) (bicycle) bici *f* (fam); (motorcycle) moto *f*

bikini /bɪˈkiːni/ *n* bikini *m or* (RPl) *f*

bilateral /ˈbaɪˈlætərəl/ *adj* bilateral

bilberry /ˈbɪlˌberi ‖ ˈbɪlbəri/ *n* (*pl* **-ries**) arándano *m*

bilingual /baɪˈlɪŋgwəl/ *adj* bilingüe

bilious /ˈbɪliəs/ *adj*: **to feel ~** sentirse* descompuesto; **~ attack** ataque *m* al *or* de hígado

bill¹ /bɪl/ *n* **1 (a)** (invoice) factura *f*, cuenta *f*; **the telephone ~** la cuenta *or* (Esp tb) el recibo del teléfono **(b)** (in restaurant) (esp BrE) cuenta *f*, adición *f* (RPl) **2** (AmE Fin) (banknote) billete *m* **3** (Govt) proyecto *m* de ley **4** (program) programa *m*; **to top the ~** encabezar* el reparto **5** (certificate): **~ of sale** contrato *m* de venta; **a clean ~ of health** (favorable report) el visto bueno **6** (beak) pico *m*

bill² *vt* **1** (invoice, charge) pasarle la cuenta *or* la factura a **2** (advertise) ‹*play/performer*› anunciar

billboard /ˈbɪlbɔːrd ‖ ˈbɪlbɔːd/ *n* (esp AmE) cartelera *f*

billet /ˈbɪlət ‖ ˈbɪlɪt/ *vt* alojar

billfold /ˈbɪlfəʊld/ *n* (AmE) billetera *f*, cartera *f*

billiards /ˈbɪljərdz ‖ ˈbɪljədz/ *n* [U] (+ *sing vb*) billar *m*

billion /ˈbɪljən/ ▶ **724** *n* **(a)** (10^9) mil millones *mpl*, millar *m* de millones **(b)** (BrE) (10^{12}) billón *m*

billow /ˈbɪləʊ/ *vi* **(a) ~ (out)** «*sail/parachute*» hincharse **(b)** «*smoke*»: **smoke ~ed from the window** nubes de humo salían de *or* por la ventana

billy /ˈbɪli/ *n* (*pl* **-lies**) **~ (goat)** macho *m* cabrío

bin /bɪn/ *n* (for kitchen refuse etc) (BrE) cubo *m or* (CS) tacho *m or* (Méx) bote *m or* (Col) caneca *f or* (Ven) tobo *m* de la basura; (wastepaper basket) (BrE) papelera *f*, papelero *m*, caneca *f* (Col); (*litter* ~) papelera *f*, basurero *m* (Chi, Méx), caneca *f* (Col)

binary /ˈbaɪnəri/ *adj* binario

bind¹ /baɪnd/ *vt* (*past & past p* **bound**) **1** (tie, fasten) ‹*person*› atar, amarrar; ⇒ BOUND⁴ 1(a) **2 (a)** (wrap) envolver* **(b) ~ (up)** ‹*wound*› vendar **3** (Law) obligar* **4** ‹*book*› encuadernar **5** (Culin) ligar*

bind² *n* (colloq) (difficult situation) aprieto *m*, apuro *m*; (nuisance) (BrE) lata *f* (fam), rollo *m* (Esp fam)

binder /ˈbaɪndər ‖ ˈbaɪndə(r)/ *n* (file, folder) carpeta *f*

binding¹ /ˈbaɪndɪŋ/ *n* **(a)** [C] (book cover) tapa *f*, cubierta *f* **(b)** [U] (tape) ribete *m*

binding² *adj* ‹*promise/commitment*› que hay que cumplir; (Law) vinculante

binge /bɪndʒ/ *n* (colloq): **to go on a ~** irse* de juerga (fam)

bingo /ˈbɪŋgəʊ/ *n* [U] bingo *m*

binliner /ˈbɪnˌlaɪnər ‖ ˈbɪnˌlaɪnə(r)/ *n* (BrE) bolsa *f* de (la) basura

binoculars /bəˈnɑːkjələrz ‖ bɪˈnɒkjʊləz/ *pl n* gemelos *mpl*, prismáticos *mpl*, anteojos *fpl* de larga vista (esp AmL)

biochemistry /ˈbaɪəʊˈkeməstri ‖ ˌbaɪəʊˈkemɪstri/ *n* [U] bioquímica *f*

biodegradable /ˈbaɪəʊdɪˈgreɪdəbəl/ *adj* biodegradable

biographer /baɪˈɑːgrəfər ‖ baɪˈɒgrəfə(r)/ *n* biógrafo, -fa *m,f*

biographical /ˈbaɪəˈgræfɪkəl/ *adj* biográfico

biography /baɪˈɑːgrəfi ‖ baɪˈɒgrəfi/ *n* [U C] (*pl* **-phies**) biografía *f*

biological /ˈbaɪəˈlɑːdʒɪkəl ‖ ˌbaɪəˈlɒdʒɪkəl/ *adj* biológico

biologist /baɪˈɑːlədʒəst ‖ baɪˈɒlədʒɪst/ *n* biólogo, -ga *m,f*

biology /baɪˈɑːlədʒi ‖ baɪˈɒlədʒi/ *n* [U] biología *f*

biopsy /ˈbaɪɑːpsi ‖ ˈbaɪɒpsi/ *n* (*pl* **-sies**) biopsia *f*

birch /bɜːrtʃ ‖ bɜːtʃ/ *n* **~ (tree)** abedul *m*

bird /bɜːrd ‖ bɜːd/ *n* (small) pájaro *m*; (large) ave *f*‡; ***to kill two ~s with one stone*** matar dos pájaros de un tiro

bird: **~cage** *n* jaula *f* de pájaros; (large) pajarera *f*; **~ of prey** *n* (*pl* **~s of prey**) ave *f*‡ rapaz *or* de rapiña *or* de presa; **~'s-eye view** *n* vista *f* aérea; **~watcher** /ˈbɜːrdˈwɑːtʃər ‖ ˈbɜːdˌwɒtʃə(r)/ *n* observador, -dora *m,f* de aves; **~watching** /ˈbɜːrdˌwɑːtʃɪŋ ‖ ˈbɜːdˌwɒtʃɪŋ/ *n* [U] observación *f* de las aves (*como hobby*)

Biro®, **biro** /ˈbaɪrəʊ ‖ ˈbaɪərəʊ/ *n* (*pl* **biros**) (BrE) bolígrafo *m*, birome *f* (RPl), esfero *m* (Col), lápiz *m* de pasta (Chi), boli *m* (Esp fam)

birth /bɜːrθ ‖ bɜːθ/ *n* [U C] nacimiento *m*; (childbirth) parto *m*; **at ~** al nacer; **date of ~** fecha *f* de nacimiento; **to give ~** dar* a luz, parir

birth: **~ certificate** *n* partida *f* or certificado *m* or (Méx) acta *f* de nacimiento; **~ control** *n* [U] control *m* de la natalidad

birthday /ˈbɜːrθdeɪ ‖ ˈbɜːθdeɪ/ *n* cumpleaños *m*; (of institution) aniversario *m*; **it'll be his fifth ~** cumple cinco años; **happy ~!** ¡feliz cumpleaños!; (*before n*) ‹*cake/card/party*› de cumpleaños

birth: **~mark** *n* mancha *f* or marca *f* de nacimiento, antojo *m*; **~place** *n* (of person) lugar *m* de nacimiento; (of movement, fashion, idea) cuna *f*

biscuit /ˈbɪskɪt/ *n* [C] (Culin) **(a)** (AmE) bollo *m*, panecillo *m*, bísquet *m* (Méx) **(b)** (cookie, cracker) (BrE) galleta *f*, galletita *f* (RPl)

bisect /baɪˈsekt/ *vt* bisecar*

bisexual /ˌbaɪˈsekʃuəl/ *adj* bisexual

bishop /ˈbɪʃəp/ **(a)** ▶603 *n* (Relig) obispo *m* **(b)** (in chess) alfil *m*

bison /ˈbaɪsn/ *n* (*pl* **~**) bisonte *m*

bit¹ /bɪt/ *past of* BITE¹

bit² *n* **1** (fragment, scrap) pedazo *m*, trozo *m*; **to smash sth to ~s** hacer* pedazos algo; ***~s and pieces*** (assorted items) cosas *fpl*; (belongings) cosas *fpl*; (broken fragments) pedazos *mpl* **2** (section, piece) parte *f* **3 a bit of** (+ *uncount noun*) un poco de; **they have quite a ~ of work to do** tienen bastante trabajo que hacer **4 a bit** (*as adv*) **(a)** (somewhat) un poco; **the town's changed a ~** la ciudad ha cambiado algo or un poco; **she hasn't changed a ~** no ha cambiado (para) nada **(b)** (a while) un momento or rato **5** (*in adv phrases*) **(a) bit by bit** poco a poco, de a poco (AmL) **(b) every bit**: **I'm every ~ as disappointed as you** estoy absolutamente tan decepcionado como tú **6** (Comput) bit *m* **7** (of bridle) freno *m*, bocado *m*

bitch /bɪtʃ/ *n* **1** (female dog) perra *f* **2** (spiteful woman) (AmE vulg, BrE sl) bruja *f* (fam), arpía *f* (fam), cabrona *f* (Esp, Méx vulg)

bite¹ /baɪt/ (*past* **bit**; *past p* **bitten**) *vt* «*person/dog*» morder*; «*bug*» picar*; ***to ~ off more than one can chew*** tratar de abarcar más de lo que se puede; ***once bitten, twice shy*** el gato escaldado del agua fría huye ■ **~** *vi* **1 (a)** «*person/dog*» morder*; «*mosquito*» picar*; «*wind/frost*» cortar; **to ~ INTO sth** darle* un mordisco A algo **(b)** (take bait) «*fish*» picar* **2** «*law/recession*» hacerse* sentir

bite² *n* **1** (act) mordisco *m*; (fierce) tarascada *f* **2** (wound — from insect) picadura *f*; (— from dog, snake) mordedura *f* **3** (snack) (colloq) (*no pl*) bocado *m*; **to have a ~ (to eat)** comer un bocado, comer algo

biting /ˈbaɪtɪŋ/ *adj* ‹*wind*› cortante; ‹*sarcasm/criticism*› mordaz

bit part *n* papel *m* pequeño

bitten /ˈbɪtn̩/ *past p of* BITE¹

bitter¹ /ˈbɪtər ‖ ˈbɪtə(r)/ *adj* **1 (a)** (in taste) amargo **(b)** (very cold) ‹*weather*› glacial; ‹*wind/frost*› cortante **2 (a)** (painful, hard) ‹*disappointment*› amargo; **they fought on to the ~ end** lucharon valientemente hasta el final **(b)** ‹*person*› resentido, amargado **(c)** ‹*enemies/hatred*› implacable; ‹*struggle*› enconado

bitter² *n* [U] (BrE) *tipo de cerveza ligeramente amarga*

bitterly /ˈbɪtərli ‖ ˈbɪtəli/ *adv* **1** ‹*cold*›: **it was ~ cold** hacía un frío glacial **2 (a)** ‹*disappointed*› tremendamente; ‹*weep/complain/say*› amargamente **(b)** (implacably) implacablemente

bitterness /ˈbɪtərnəs ‖ ˈbɪtənɪs/ *n* [U] **1** (of taste) amargor *m* **2** (of person, disappointment) amargura *f*

bittersweet /ˈbɪtərswiːt ‖ ˌbɪtəˈswiːt/ *adj* agridulce; ‹*chocolate*› (AmE) amargo

bizarre /bɪˈzɑːr ‖ bɪˈzɑː(r)/ *adj* ‹*story/coincidence*› extraño; ‹*appearance/behavior*› estrambótico

black¹ /blæk/ ▶515 *adj* **-er, -est 1** ‹*dress/hair/ink*› negro; ‹*sky*› oscuro; ‹*coffee*› negro (AmL), solo (Esp), tinto (Col), puro (Chi); ‹*tea*› solo, sin leche, puro (Chi); **~ cloud** nubarrón *m* **2** *also* **Black** ‹*person/community*› negro **3** (sad, hopeless) negro

black² ▶515 *n* **1** [U] (color) negro *m* **2** [C] *also* **Black** (person) negro, -gra *m,f* **3** (freedom from debt): ***to be in the ~*** no estar* en números rojos

● **black out 1** [*v + adv*] (lose consciousness) perder* el conocimiento **2** [*v + o + adv, v + adv + o*] (in wartime) ‹*windows*› tapar; ‹*lights*› apagar*; (by accident) ‹*town/district*› dejar sin luz

black: **~ and white** *n* (Cin, Phot, TV) blanco y negro *m*; **she sees things in ~ and white** para ella no hay términos medios; **~-and-white** /ˈblækənˈhwaɪt ‖ ˈblækənˈwaɪt/ ▶515 *adj* (*pred* **~ and white**) en blanco y negro; **~ belt** *n* cinturón *m* negro, cinta *f* negra (Méx); (person) cinturón *mf* negro, cinta *mf* negra (Méx); **~berry** /ˈblækˌberi ‖ ˈblækbəri/ *n* mora *f*; **~bird** *n* (European) mirlo *m*; (North American) totí *m*; **~board** *n* pizarra *f*, pizarrón *m* (AmL), tablero *m* (Col); **~ box** *n* (Aviat) caja *f* negra; **~currant** /ˈblækˈkɜːrənt ‖ ˌblækˈkʌrənt/ *n* grosella *f* negra

blacken /ˈblækən/ *vt* **(a)** (make black) ennegrecer* **(b)** (defame) ‹*person*› deshonrar; ‹*reputation*› manchar

black: **~ eye** *n* ojo *m* morado, ojo *m* a la funerala (Esp fam), ojo *m* en compota (CS fam), ojo *m* en tinta (Chi fam); **~head** *n* espinilla *f*; **~ hole** *n* agujero *m* negro; **~ ice** *n* [U] *capa fina de hielo en las carreteras*

blacklist¹ /ˈblæklɪst/ *n* lista *f* negra

blacklist² *vt* poner* en la lista negra

blackmail¹ /ˈblækmeɪl/ *n* [U] chantaje *m*

blackmail² *vt* chantajear, hacerle* chantaje a

black: **~ mark** *n* punto *m* en contra; **~ market** *n* mercado *m* negro; **~out** /ˈblækaʊt/ *n* **1** (loss of consciousness) desvanecimiento *m*, desmayo *m*; **2** (in wartime) *oscurecimiento de la ciudad para que ésta no sea visible desde los aviones enemigos*; **B~ Sea** *n* the B~ Sea el Mar Negro; ~ **sheep** *n* oveja *f* negra; ~**smith** *n* herrero *m*

bladder /'blædər ‖ 'blædə(r)/ *n* (Anat) vejiga *f*

blade /bleɪd/ *n* **1** (of knife, razor) hoja *f* **2** (of propeller) pala *f*, paleta *f* **3** (Bot) (of grass) brizna *f*

blame[1] /bleɪm/ *vt* echarle la culpa a, culpar; **to ~ sb** FOR **sth** culpar a algn DE algo, echarle la culpa DE algo A algn; **to be to ~ for sth** tener* la culpa de algo; **to ~ sth** ON **sb/sth** echarle la culpa DE algo A algn/algo

blame[2] *n* [U] culpa *f*; **it's always me that gets the ~** siempre me echan la culpa a mí

bland /blænd/ *adj* **-er, -est (a)** ‹*colors/music*› soso; ‹*food/taste*› insípido; ‹*statement/reply*› anodino; ‹*smile/manner*› insulso **(b)** (mild) ‹*food*› suave

blank[1] /blæŋk/ *adj* **(a)** (empty) ‹*page/space*› en blanco; ‹*tape*› virgen; **my mind went ~** me quedé en blanco; **a ~ expression** un rostro carente de expresión **(b)** (uncompromising) ‹*refusal/rejection*› rotundo **(c)** (Mil) ‹*ammunition*› de fogueo

blank[2] *n* **(a)** (empty space) espacio *m* en blanco; ***to draw a ~*** no obtener* ningún resultado **(b)** (Mil) cartucho *m* de fogueo

blank check, (BrE) **cheque** *n* cheque *m* en blanco

blanket[1] /'blæŋkət ‖ 'blæŋkɪt/ *n* manta *f*, cobija *f* (AmL), frazada *f* (AmL)

blanket[2] *adj* (*before n, no comp*) ‹*measure*› global

blare *vi* atronar*

• **blare out** [*v + adv + o*]: **the radio was blaring out music** el radio emitía música retumbante

blasphemous /'blæsfəməs/ *adj* blasfemo

blasphemy /'blæsfəmi/ *n* [U C] (*pl* **-mies**) blasfemia *f*

blast[1] /blæst ‖ blɑːst/ *n* **1** (of air, wind) ráfaga *f*; (of water) chorro *m* **2** (explosion) (journ) explosión *f* **3** (of sound) toque *m*; **he had the TV on full ~** tenía la tele a todo lo que daba (fam)

blast[2] *vt* **(a)** (blow) ‹*rock*› volar*; **they used dynamite to ~ the safe open** usaron dinamita para volar la caja fuerte **(b)** (attack) (journ) atacar*

• **blast off** [*v + adv*] despegar*

blast-off /'blæstɔːf ‖ 'blɑːstɒf/ *n* despegue *m*

blatant /'bleɪtn̩t/ *adj* ‹*prejudice/disrespect*› descarado; ‹*lie*› flagrante; ‹*incompetence*› patente

blatantly /'bleɪtn̩tli/ *adv* descaradamente; **it's ~ obvious that** ... está clarísimo que ...

blaze[1] /bleɪz/ *n* **1** [C] (in grate) fuego *m*; (bonfire) fogata *f*; (flames) llamaradas *fpl*; (dangerous fire) (journ) incendio *m* **2** (dazzling display) (*no pl*): **a ~ of color** un derroche de color; **in a ~ of glory** cubierto de gloria

blaze[2] *vi* «*fire*» arder; «*lights*» brillar; «*eyes*» centellear

blazer /'bleɪzər ‖ 'bleɪzə(r)/ *n* blazer *m*

bleach[1] /bliːtʃ/ *n* [U C] lejía *f*, blanqueador *m* (Col, Méx), lavandina *f* (Arg), agua *f*‡ Jane® (Ur), cloro *m* (AmC, Chi)

bleach[2] *vt* ‹*cloth*› (in the sun) blanquear; (with bleach) poner* en lejía (*or* blanqueador *etc*)

bleachers /'bliːtʃərz ‖ 'bliːtʃəz/ *pl n* (AmE) tribuna *f* descubierta

bleak /bliːk/ *adj* **-er, -est (a)** ‹*landscape*› inhóspito; ‹*room*› lóbrego **(b)** ‹*winter*› crudo; ‹*day*› gris y deprimente **(c)** (miserable, cheerless) ‹*prospects/news*› sombrío

bleary-eyed /'blɪri'aɪd ‖ 'blɪəri'aɪd/ *adj* con cara de sueño

bleat /bliːt/ *vi* balar

bleed /bliːd/ (*past & past p* **bled** /bled/) *vi* sangrar; **he bled to death** murió desangrado ■ ~ *vt* **(a)** (Med) sangrar; ***to ~ sb dry*** chuparle la sangre a algn (fam) **(b)** ‹*brakes/radiator*› purgar*

bleeding /'bliːdɪŋ/ *n* [U] hemorragia *f*

bleep[1] /bliːp/ *n* pitido *m*

bleep[2] *vi* (BrE) emitir un pitido

blemish /'blemɪʃ/ *n* (on skin) imperfección *f*; (on reputation) mancha *f*

blend[1] /blend/ *n* combinación *f*, mezcla *f*

blend[2] *vt* mezclar, combinar; (in blender) licuar* ■ ~ *vi* «*flavors/colors*» armonizar*

• **blend in 1** [*v + o + adv, v + adv + o*] ‹*ingredients*› añadir y mezclar **2** [*v + adv*] (merge, harmonize) armonizar*

blender /'blendər ‖ 'blendə(r)/ *n* licuadora *f*

bless /bles/ *vt* (*past* **blessed**; *past p* **blessed** *or* (arch) **blest**) **(a)** (Relig) bendecir* **(b)** (*in interj phrases*) **~ you!** (to sb who sneezes) ¡salud! *or* (Esp) ¡Jesús!; **~ my soul!** (colloq) ¡válgame Dios!

blessed /'blesəd ‖ 'blesɪd/ *adj* bienaventurado

blessing /'blesɪŋ/ *n* **1 (a)** (Relig — benediction) bendición *f*; (— of bread, wine) consagración *f* **(b)** (approval) aprobación *f* **2** (fortunate thing) bendición *f* (del cielo); ***to be a mixed ~*** tener* sus pros y sus contras

blest /blest/ (arch) *past & past pt of* BLESS

blew /bluː/ *past of* BLOW[2]

blight[1] /blaɪt/ *n* [U] (Agr, Hort) añublo *m*; (loosely) peste *f*; (curse) plaga *f*

blight[2] /blaɪt/ *vt* ‹*crop/career/health*› arruinar; ‹*region*› asolar*; ‹*hopes*› malograr

blind[1] /blaɪnd/ *adj* **1 (a)** (Med) ciego; **to go ~** quedarse ciego; **to be ~** TO **sth** no ver* algo **(b)** (Auto) ‹*corner*› de poca visibilidad **2** ‹*faith/fury*› ciego

blind[2] *vt* **(a)** (permanently) dejar ciego **(b)** «*ambition/passion*» cegar*, enceguecer* (AmL); «*light/wealth*» deslumbrar

blind[3] *n* **1** (outside window) persiana *f*; (*roller ~*) persiana *f* (de enrollar), estor *m* (Esp); (*venetian ~*) persiana *f* veneciana **2** (blind people) (*+ pl vb*) **the ~** los ciegos

blind date *n* cita *f* con un desconocido/una desconocida

blinders /'blaɪndərz ‖ 'blaɪndəz/ *n pl* (AmE) (on horse) anteojeras *fpl*

blindfold[1] /'blaɪndfəʊld/ *vt* vendarle los ojos a

blindfold[2] *n* venda *f* (*para tapar los ojos*)

blindfold[3] *adv* con los ojos vendados

blindly /'blaɪndli/ *adv* **(a)** (without seeing) ‹*grope*› a ciegas **(b)** (without reasoning) ‹*follow*› ciegamente

blindness /'blaɪndnəs ‖ 'blaɪndnɪs/ *n* [U] ceguera *f*

blind spot *n* **(a)** (weak point) punto *m* flaco **(b)** (Auto) punto *m* ciego

blink¹ /blɪŋk/ *n* parpadeo *m*, pestañeo *m*; ***to be on the ~*** (colloq) no marchar, no andar* bien (AmL)

blink² *vi* «*eye/person*» pestañear, parpadear; «*light*» parpadear

blinker /'blɪŋkər ‖ 'blɪŋkə(r)/ *n* **1 (a)** (Auto) (colloq) intermitente *m* direccional *f* (Col, Méx), señalizador *m* (de viraje) (Chi) **(b)** (AmE Transp) señal *f* intermitente **2 blinkers** *pl* (on horse) anteojeras *fpl*

blinkered /'blɪŋkərd ‖ 'blɪŋkəd/ *adj* ‹*attitude*› de miras estrechas; ‹*view/outlook*› estrecho

blip /blɪp/ *n* **(a)** (sound) bip *m*, pitidito *m* **(b)** (irregularity) accidente *m*; (problem) problema *m* pasajero

bliss /blɪs/ *n* [U] dicha *f*

blissful /'blɪsfəl/ *adj* ‹*smile*› de gozo

blissfully /'blɪsfəli/ *adv* ‹*smile/sigh*› con gran felicidad

blister¹ /'blɪstər ‖ 'blɪstə(r)/ *n* **(a)** (Med) ampolla *f* **(b)** (on paintwork) ampolla *f*, burbuja *f*

blister² *vi* ampollarse

blithely /'blaɪðli/ *adv* alegremente

blitz /blɪts/ *n* **(a)** (Aviat, Mil) bombardeo *m* aéreo **(b)** (intense attack): **this weekend we're going to have a ~ on the garden** (colloq) este fin de semana vamos a atacar el jardín

blizzard /'blɪzərd ‖ 'blɪzəd/ *n* ventisca *f*

bloated /'bləʊtəd ‖ 'bləʊtɪd/ *adj* hinchado

blob /blɑːb ‖ blɒb/ *n* **(a)** (drip) gota *f* **(b)** (indistinct shape) mancha *f*

bloc /blɑːk ‖ blɒk/ *n* (Pol) bloque *m*

block¹ /blɑːk ‖ blɒk/ *n* **1** (of stone, wood) bloque *m*; (*starting ~*) (Sport) taco *m* de salida; (of paper) bloc *m* **2 (a)** (space enclosed by streets) manzana *f*; (distance between two streets): **it's eight ~s from here** (AmE) está a ocho cuadras (AmL) *or* (Esp) calles de aquí **(b)** (building): **a ~ of flats** (BrE) un edificio de apartamentos *or* de departamentos (AmL), una casa de pisos (Esp); **an office ~** un edificio de oficinas **3** (section of text) sección *f*, bloque *m* **4** (Comput) bloque *m* **5** (blockage) obstrucción *f*, bloqueo *m*; **I have a mental ~ about physics** tengo un bloqueo mental con la física **6** (Sport) bloqueo *m*

block² *vt* **1 (a)** (obstruct) ‹*road/entrance*› bloquear; **you're ~ing my way** me estás impidiendo el paso; **that fat man is ~ing my view** ese gordo no me deja ver **(b)** ‹*drain/sink*› atascar*, tapar (AmL); **my nose is ~ed** tengo la nariz tapada **2 (a)** (prevent) ‹*progress*› obstaculizar*; ‹*funds/sale*› congelar **(b)** (Sport) bloquear ■ ~ *vi* (Sport) bloquear

• **block in** [*v + o + adv, v + adv + o*] cerrarle* el paso a

• **block off** [*v + o + adv, v + adv + o*] ‹*street*› cortar

• **block out** [*v + o + adv, v + adv + o*] **(a)** (shut out) ‹*thought*› ahuyentar **(b)** (obstruct) ‹*light*› tapar

• **block up** [*v + o + adv, v + adv + o*] **(a)** (seal) ‹*entrance/window*› tapiar **(b)** (cause obstruction in) ‹*drain/sink*› atascar*, tapar (AmL); **my nose is ~ed up** tengo la nariz tapada

blockade¹ /blɑː'keɪd ‖ blɒ'keɪd/ *n* bloqueo *m*

blockade² *vt* bloquear

blockage /'blɑːkɪdʒ ‖ 'blɒkɪdʒ/ *n* (in pipe, road) obstrucción *f*; (Med) oclusión *f*

block capitals, block letters *pl n* (letras *fpl*) mayúsculas *fpl* de imprenta

bloke /bləʊk/ *n* (BrE colloq) tipo *m* (fam), tío *m* (Esp fam)

blond /blɑːnd ‖ blɒnd/ ▶ 515 *adj* (*f* **blonde**) rubio *or* (Méx) güero *or* (Col) mono *or* (Ven) catire

blood /blʌd/ *n* [U] sangre *f*; ***in cold ~*** a sangre fría; (*before n*) **~ donor** donante *mf* de sangre; **~ group** grupo *m* sanguíneo; **~ test** análisis *m* de sangre; **~ transfusion** transfusión *f* de sangre

blood: **~ bath** *n* masacre *f*; **~curdling** /'blʌd,kɜːrdlɪŋ ‖ 'blʌd,kɜːdlɪŋ/ *adj* espeluznante, aterrador

bloodless /'blʌdləs ‖ 'blʌdlɪs/ *adj* ‹*coup*› sin derramamiento de sangre

blood: **~ pressure** *n* [U] tensión *f* *or* presión *f* (arterial); **~shed** *n* [U] derramamiento *m* de sangre; **~shot** *adj* rojo, inyectado de sangre; **~ sport** *n* deporte *m* sangriento; **~stain** *n* mancha *f* de sangre; **~-stained** /'blʌdsteɪnd/ *adj* manchado de sangre; **~stream** *n* **the ~stream** el torrente sanguíneo; **~thirsty** *adj* **(a)** (cruel) sanguinario **(b)** ‹*story/description*› sangriento; **~ vessel** *n* vaso *m* sanguíneo

bloody¹ /'blʌdi/ *adj* **-dier, -diest 1 (a)** ‹*hands/clothes*› ensangrentado; ‹*wound*› que sangra, sangrante **(b)** ‹*battle*› sangriento **2** (esp BrE vulg *or* colloq) (*no comp*) (expressing annoyance, surprise, shock etc): **where's that ~ dog?** ¿dónde está ese maldito *or* (Méx) pinche perro? (fam); **~ hell!** ¡coño! (vulg), ¡chingado! (Méx vulg), ¡hostias! (Esp vulg)

bloody² *adv* (BrE vulg *or* colloq) (*as intensifier*): **the weather was ~ awful!** ¡hizo un tiempo de mierda! (vulg)

bloom¹ /bluːm/ *n* **1 (a)** [C] (flower) flor *f* **(b)** [U] **to be in ~** estar* en flor; **to be in full ~** estar* en plena floración **2** [U] (on fruits, leaves) vello *m*

bloom² *vi* «*plant/garden*» florecer*; «*flower*» abrirse*

blossom¹ /'blɑːsəm ‖ 'blɒsəm/ *n* **(a)** [U] (mass of flowers) flores *fpl* **(b)** [C] (by single bloom) flor *f*

blossom² *vi* **(a)** (flower) «*tree*» florecer* **(b)** (flourish) «*arts*» florecer*; «*person/relationship*» alcanzar* su plenitud

blot¹ /blɑːt ‖ blɒt/ *n* **(a)** (of ink) borrón *m* **(b)** (blemish): **the factory is a ~ on the landscape** la fábrica afea el paisaje

blot² **-tt-** *vt* **(a)** (stain, smear) ‹*page/word*› emborronar **(b)** (dry) ‹*ink*› secar* (*con papel secante*)

• **blot out** [*v + o + adv, v + adv + o*] ‹*word*› tachar; ‹*view*› tapar; ‹*memory*› borrar

blotchy /'blɑːtʃi ‖ 'blɒtʃi/ *adj* **blotchier, blotchiest** ‹*skin*› lleno de manchas

blotting paper /'blɑːtɪŋ ‖ 'blɒtɪŋ/ *n* [U] papel *m* secante

blouse /blaʊs ‖ blaʊz/ *n* blusa *f*

blow¹ /bləʊ/ *n* golpe *m*; **to come to ~s** llegar* a las manos; **his death came as a ~ to us** su muerte fue un duro golpe para nosotros

blow² (*past* **blew**; *past p* **blown**) *vt* **1** (propel): **stop ~ing smoke in my face!** ¡no me eches el humo a la cara!; **a gust of wind blew the door shut** una ráfaga de viento cerró la puerta de golpe; **the plane was ~n off course** el viento sacó el avión de su curso **2 (a)** (make by blowing): **to ~ bubbles** hacer* pompas de jabón **(b)** (clear): **to ~ one's nose** sonarse* la nariz **(c)** (play) ‹*note*› tocar*; ‹*signal*› dar*; **the referee blew the whistle** el árbitro tocó el silbato *or* pito **3 (a)** (smash) ‹*bridge/safe*› volar* **(b)** (burn out) ‹*fuse*› hacer* saltar, quemar **(c)** (burst) ‹*gasket*› reventar* **4** (colloq) **(a)** (squander) ‹*money*› despilfarrar **(b)** (spoil): **I blew it** la pifié (fam); **I blew the oral test** la pifié en el oral (fam), la regué en el oral (Méx fam) ■ ~ *vi* **1 (a)** «*wind*» soplar **(b)** «*person*» soplar; **she came up the stairs, puffing and ~ing** subió las escaleras bufando y resoplando **2** (be driven by wind): **litter was ~ing everywhere** volaba basura por todas partes; **his hat blew off** se le voló el sombrero; **the door blew open** la puerta se abrió con el viento **3** (produce sound) «*whistle*» sonar* **4** (burn out) «*fuse*» saltar, quemarse

• **blow down 1** [*v* + *o* + *adv*, *v* + *adv* + *o*] tirar (abajo) **2** [*v* + *adv*] caerse* (*con el viento*)

• **blow out 1** [*v* + *o* + *adv*, *v* + *adv* + *o*] ‹*match/flame*› apagar* (*soplando*); **to ~ sb's brains out** (colloq) saltarle la tapa de los sesos a algn (fam) **2** [*v* + *adv*] «*candle*» apagarse*

• **blow over** [*v* + *adv*] «*trouble*» caer* en el olvido; «*storm*» pasar

• **blow up 1** [*v* + *adv*] **(a)** (explode) «*bomb*» estallar; «*car*» saltar por los aires **(b)** (begin) «*wind/storm*» levantarse; «*conflict*» estallar; **the affair blew up into a major scandal** el caso terminó en un gran escándalo **2** [*v* + *o* + *adv*, *v* + *adv* + *o*] **(a)** ‹*mine/car*› volar* **(b)** ‹*balloon*› inflar **(c)** (colloq) ‹*incident*› exagerar **(d)** ‹*photo*› ampliar*

blow: **~-by-~** /ˈbləʊbaɪˈbləʊ/ *adj* (*before n*) ‹*account*› con pelos y señales (fam); **~-dry** *vt* **-dries, -drying, -dries**: **to ~-dry one's hair** hacerse* un brushing (*secarse el pelo con secador de mano y cepillo*); **~gun** *n* (AmE) cerbatana *f*

blown /bləʊn/ *past p of* BLOW²

blow: **~out** *n* **(a)** (feast) (colloq) comilona *f* (fam) **(b)** (burst tire) reventón *m*; **~pipe** *n* cerbatana *f*; **~torch** *n* soplete *m*

blubber¹ /ˈblʌbər ‖ ˈblʌbə(r)/ *n* [U] grasa *f* de ballena

blubber² *vi* (colloq & pej) lloriquear

bludgeon /ˈblʌdʒən/ *vt* aporrear

blue¹ /bluː/ *adj* **bluer, bluest 1** ▶ **515** ‹*dress/sea/sky*› azul **2** (pornographic) (colloq) verde, porno *adj inv*, colorado (Méx) **3** (unhappy) (esp AmE) triste, deprimido

blue² ▶ **515** *n* azul *m*; ***out of the ~*** ‹*call/arrive*› cuando menos se (*or* me *etc*) lo esperaba

blue: **~bell** *n* jacinto *m* silvestre; **~berry** /ˈbluːˌberi ‖ ˈbluːbəri/ *n* arándano *m*; **~-blooded** /ˈbluːˈblʌdəd ‖ ˌbluːˈblʌdɪd/ *adj* de sangre azul; **~bottle** *n* mosca *f* azul; **~-collar** /ˈbluːˈkɑːlər ‖ ˌbluːˈkɒlə(r)/ *adj* ‹*union*› obrero; ‹*job*› manual; **~-collar workers** los obreros; **~print** *n* (of technical drawing) plano *m*; (plan of action) programa *m*

blues /bluːz/ *pl n* **1** (depression) (colloq): **the ~** la depre (fam) **2** (Mus) blues *m*

bluff¹ /blʌf/ *vi* hacer* un bluff *or* (Col, Méx) blof ■ ~ *vt*: **he managed to ~ his way out of it** logró salir del apuro embaucándolos

bluff² *n* [U C] (pretense) bluff *m*, blof *m* (Col, Méx); **to call sb's ~** poner* a algn en evidencia

blunder¹ /ˈblʌndər ‖ ˈblʌndə(r)/ *vi* **1** (move clumsily, stumble): **he ~ed into the table** se topó con el jefe en el pasillo; **he ~ed around in the dark** andaba dando tumbos en la oscuridad **2** (make mistake) cometer un error garrafal

blunder² *n* (mistake) error *m* garrafal; (faux pas) metedura *f or* (AmL tb) metida *f* de pata (fam)

blunt¹ /blʌnt/ *adj* **-er, -est (a)** (not sharp) ‹*pencil*› desafilado, mocho (esp AmL); ‹*tip/edge*› romo; **a ~ instrument** un objeto contundente **(b)** (straightforward) ‹*person/manner*› directo, franco; ‹*refusal*› rotundo

blunt² *vt* **(a)** ‹*pencil*› despuntar; ‹*knife/scissors*› desafilar **(b)** (make dull) ‹*senses/intellect*› embotar

bluntly /ˈblʌntli/ *adv* ‹*say*› sin rodeos; ‹*refuse*› rotundamente

blur /blɜːr ‖ blɜː(r)/ **-rr-** *vt* ‹*outline*› desdibujar; ‹*distinction*› hacer* menos claro; ‹*memory*› hacer* borroso ■ ~ *vi* «*outline*» desdibujarse

blurred /blɜːrd ‖ blɜːd/ *adj* ‹*outline/vision*› borroso

blurt out /blɜːrt ‖ blɜːt/ [*v* + *o* + *adv*, *v* + *adv* + *o*] espetar

blush /blʌʃ/ *vi* ruborizarse*, ponerse* colorado

blusher /ˈblʌʃər ‖ ˈblʌʃə(r)/ *n* [U C] colorete *m*, rubor *m* (Méx, RPl)

bluster¹ /ˈblʌstər ‖ ˈblʌstə(r)/ *vi* bravuconear

bluster² *n* [U] bravatas *fpl*, bravuconería *f*

B-movie /ˈbiːˌmuːvi/ *n* película *f* de serie B *or* de bajo presupuesto

boa /ˈbəʊə/ *n* (Zool) boa *f*; **a ~ constrictor** una boa constríctor

boar /bɔːr ‖ bɔː(r)/ *n* (*pl* **~s** *or* **~**) **(a)** (male pig) cerdo *m* macho, verraco *m* **(b)** (*wild ~*) jabalí *m*

board¹ /bɔːrd ‖ bɔːd/ *n* **1** [C] (plank) tabla *f*, tablón *m* **2** [C] **(a)** (*diving ~*) trampolín *m* **(b)** (for surfing, windsurfing) tabla *f* (de surf) **(c)** (Games) tablero *m* **3** [C] **(a)** (*notice~*) tablero *m or* (Esp) tablón *m* de anuncios, cartelera *f* (AmL), diario *m* mural (Chi) **(b)** (sign) letrero *m*, cartel *m* **(c)** (*score~*) marcador *m* **(d)** (blackboard) pizarra *f*, pizarrón *m* (AmL), tablero *m* (Col) **4** [C] **(a)** (committee) junta *f*, consejo *m* **(b)** (administrative body): **the Water/Gas B~** la compañía del agua/gas **(c)** ~ **(of directors)** (Busn) junta *f* directiva, consejo *m* de administración **(d)** (of examiners) tribunal *m* **5** [U] (provision of meals): **~ and lodging** comida y alojamiento; **full/half ~** pensión *f* completa/media pensión *f* **6** [U] (*in phrases*) **across the board**: **they have promised to reduce taxation across the ~** han prometido una reducción general de impuestos; **on board** a bordo; **on ~ the ship/plane** a bordo del barco/avión

board² *vt* **1** (go aboard): **to ~ a ship** embarcar(se)*, abordar (Méx) **2** (accommodate) hospedar ■ ~ *vi* **1** (go aboard) embarcar(se)*, abordar (Col, Méx) **2** (be

accommodated) **to ~** WITH **sb** alojarse *or* hospedarse en casa de algn
• **board up** [*v* + *o* + *adv*, *v* + *adv* + *o*] cerrar* con tablas

boarder /'bɔːrdər || 'bɔːdə(r)/ *n* **(a)** (lodger) huésped *mf* **(b)** (at boarding school) (esp BrE) interno, -na *m,f*

board game *n* juego *m* de mesa

boarding /'bɔːrdɪŋ || 'bɔːdɪŋ/: **~ card** *n* ⇒ **~** PASS; **~ house** *n* pensión *f*; **~ pass** *n* tarjeta *f* de embarque, pase *m* de abordar (Chi, Méx); **~ school** *n* internado *m*

board: **~room** *n* sala *f or* salón *m* de juntas; **~walk** *n* (AmE) *paseo marítimo entarimado*

boast¹ /bəʊst/ *vi* presumir, fanfarronear (fam); **to ~** ABOUT **sth** alardear *or* jactarse *or* vanagloriarse DE algo ■ **~** *vt* **(a)** (brag): **I won, he ~ed** —gané yo —dijo vanagloriándose **(b)** (possess) contar* con

boast² *n* alarde *m*

boastful /'bəʊstfəl/ *adj* jactancioso

boat /bəʊt/ *n* barco *m*; (small, open) bote *m*, barca *f*; **by ~** en barco

boat: **~house** *n* cobertizo *m* (*para botes*); **~man** /'bəʊtmən/ *n* (*pl* **-men** /-mən/) barquero *m*; **~ race** *n* regata *f*; **~swain** /'bəʊsn/ *n* contramaestre *m*

bob¹ /bɑːb || bɒb/ *n* **1 (a)** (movement of head) inclinación *f* **(b)** (curtsy) reverencia *f* **2** (haircut) melena *f*

bob² *vi* **-bb-** (move abruptly): **the cork ~bed up and down on the water** el corcho cabeceaba en el agua

bobbin /'bɑːbən || 'bɒbɪn/ *n* bobina *f*

bobby /'bɑːbi || 'bɒbi/: **~ pin** /'bɑːbi || 'bɒbi/ **bobby pin** *n* (AmE) horquilla *f*, pasador *m* (Méx), pinche *m* (Chi); **~ socks**, (AmE also) **~ sox** /sɑːks || sɒks/ *pl n* calcetines *mpl* cortos

bode /bəʊd/ *vi* (liter): **to ~ well/ill** ser* buena/mala señal

bodice /'bɑːdəs || 'bɒdɪs/ *n* (of dress) canesú *m*; (undergarment) corpiño *m*

bodily¹ /'bɑːdḷi || 'bɒdɪli/ *adj* (*before n*) corporal; **~ functions** funciones *fpl* fisiológicas

bodily² *adv*: **they dragged him ~ into the car** lo agarraron y lo metieron en el coche a la fuerza

body /'bɑːdi || 'bɒdi/ *n* (*pl* **bodies**) **1** [C] **(a)** (of human, animal) cuerpo *m*; (*before n*) **~ language** lenguaje *m* corporal **(b)** (trunk) cuerpo *m* **(c)** (*dead*) cadáver *m*; ***over my dead ~!*** ¡tendrán (*or* tendrá *etc*) que pasar por encima de mi cadáver! **2** [C] (main part — of plane) fuselaje *m*; (— of ship) casco *m*; (Auto) carrocería *f* **3 (a)** [C] (organization) organismo *m* **(b)** (unit) (*no pl*): **they walked out in a ~** salieron en masa **(c)** [C] (collection): **a ~ of evidence** un conjunto de pruebas; **a growing ~ of opinion** una creciente corriente de opinión **(d)** [C] (of water) masa *f* **4** [C] (object) cuerpo *m*; **heavenly ~** (poet) cuerpo *m* celeste **5** [U] (density — of wine) cuerpo *m*; (— of hair) volumen *m*, cuerpo *m*

body: **~ builder** *n* fisiculturista *mf*; **~ building** *n* [U] fisiculturismo *m*; **~guard** *n* guardaespaldas *mf*; (group) escolta *f*; **~ stocking** *n* body *m*; **~work** *n* [U] carrocería *f*

bog /bɔːg, bɑːg || bɒg/ *n* [C U] ciénaga *f*; (*peat* **~**) tremedal *m*
• **bog down**: **-gg-** [*v* + *o* + *adv*] (*usu pass*): **to be ~ged down with work** estar* inundado de trabajo; **don't get ~ged down in too much detail** no te enredes con demasiados detalles

boggle /'bɑːgəl || 'bɒgəl/ *vi*: **the mind ~s** (hum) uno se queda helado, uno alucina (Esp, Méx fam)

bogus /'bəʊgəs/ *adj* ‹*claim/name*› falso; ‹*argument*› falaz

Bohemian /bəʊ'hiːmiən/ *adj also* **bohemian** (unconventional) bohemio

boil¹ /bɔɪl/ *n* **1** (Med) furúnculo *m* **2** (boiling point): **the vegetables are on the ~** las verduras se están haciendo; **bring the water to the ~** dejar que el agua rompa el hervor

boil² *vi* «*water/vegetables*» hervir*; **the rice has ~ed dry** el arroz se ha quedado sin agua ■ **~** *vt* **1** (bring to boiling point) hervir*; (keep at boiling point) hervir*, dejar hervir; (cook in boiling water) cocer*, hervir* **2 boiled** *past p* ‹*potatoes/rice*› hervido; ‹*ham*› cocido; ‹*egg*› (soft) pasado por agua; (hard) duro
• **boil down to** [*v* + *adv* + *prep* + *o*] reducirse* a
• **boil over** [*v* + *adv*] «*milk*» irse* por el fuego; «*pan*» desbordarse; «*person*» perder* el control

boiler /'bɔɪlər || 'bɔɪlə(r)/ *n* caldera *f*

boiler suit *n* (BrE) overol *m* (AmL), mono *m* (Esp, Méx)

boiling /'bɔɪlɪŋ/ *adj* (colloq): **this coffee is ~** este café está hirviendo; **I'm ~** estoy asado (fam); **it's ~ hot today/in here** (*as adv*) hace un calor espantoso hoy/aquí

boiling point *n* punto *m* de ebullición

boisterous /'bɔɪstərəs/ *adj* bullicioso

bold /bəʊld/ *adj* **-er, -est 1** (daring) audaz **2** (impudent) ‹*smile/advances*› descarado **3** ‹*pattern*› llamativo; ‹*color*› fuerte

boldly /'bəʊldli/ *adv* **1** (daringly) con audacia, audazmente **2** (impudently) descaradamente

Bolivia /bə'lɪviə/ *n* Bolivia *f*

Bolivian /bə'lɪviən/ *adj* boliviano

bollard /'bɑːlərd || 'bɒlɑːd/ *n* **(a)** (on quay) noray *m*, bolardo *m* **(b)** (by road) (BrE) baliza *f*

bolster¹ /'bəʊlstər || 'bəʊlstə(r)/ *vt* **to ~ (up)** ‹*popularity/economy*› reforzar*; ‹*argument*› reafirmar; ‹*morale*› levantar

bolster² *n* cabezal *m* (*almohada de forma cilíndrica*)

bolt¹ /bəʊlt/ *n* **1** (Tech) tornillo *m*, perno *m* **2 (a)** (on door) pestillo *m*, pasador *m*, cerrojo *m* **(b)** (on firearm) cerrojo *m*

bolt² *vt* **1** (fasten with bolt) atornillar, sujetar con un tornillo *or* perno **2** ‹*door*› echarle el pestillo *or* el pasador *or* el cerrojo a **3 ~ (down)** ‹*food/meal*› engullir* ■ **~** *vi* «*horse*» desbocarse*; «*person*» salir* disparado

bolt³ *adv*: **~ upright** muy erguido; **he sat ~ upright in bed** se irguió en la cama

The Human Body

Whereas English uses a possessive pronoun in referring to parts of the body, Spanish uses the definite article:

she closed her eyes = cerró los ojos
he knitted his brows = frunció el ceño

Spanish often uses a reflexive verb in these cases:

I washed my face = me lavé la cara
he brushed his hair = se cepilló el pelo
she rubbed her arm = se sobó el brazo

This includes many verbs which describe accidents:

he injured his knee = se lesionó la rodilla
she broke her elbow = se rompió el codo
I burned my fingers = me quemé los dedos
I bit my tongue = me mordí la lengua

When intransitive verbs are used it is the pronouns me/te/le *etc that indicate the person being referred to*:

my arm/liver/nose hurts = me duele el brazo/el hígado/la nariz
my arm itches = me pica el brazo
his hands were shaking = le temblaban las manos
her eyes were stinging = le escocían *or* le ardían los ojos

For an action involving more than one person, Spanish uses the indirect personal pronoun (me/te/le *etc*) *with a transitive verb, in order to show who the object of the action is*:

she kissed his cheek = le besó la mejilla (*literally* she kissed to him the cheek)
she touched my arm = me tocó el brazo
she brushed her (another person's) hair = le cepilló el pelo

Note the translations of the examples below, in which the action is performed on more than one person:

he cut off their heads = les cortaba la cabeza (i.e. each individual has only one head to be cut off)

Describing People

In describing general physical features, Spanish uses:

tener + *definite article*:

he has blue eyes *o* his eyes are blue = tiene los ojos azules
she has a thin face = tiene la cara delgada
she has short hair = tiene el pelo corto

ser de:

her eyes are blue *o* he has blue eyes = es de ojos azules
her hair is blond = es de pelo rubio
she has fine features = es de rasgos finos

tener *can also be used to describe a changed or unusual appearance*:

your face is red = tienes la cara roja
his lips are swollen = tiene los labios hinchados

Expressions relating to conditions or illnesses affecting parts of the body

to have a weak heart = sufrir del corazón
to have a bad back = tener problemas de espalda
to have breast cancer = tener cáncer de mama
to have a stomach ulcer = tener una úlcera estomacal

Aches and pains are both expressed using the verb doler *or the noun* dolor:

my legs ache = me duelen las piernas
I have a pain in my leg = me duele la pierna
I have a headache = tengo dolor de cabeza *or* me duele la cabeza
I have toothache = tengo dolor de muelas *or* me duelen las muelas
I have a stomach ache = tengo dolor de estómago *or* me duele el estómago
stomach/chest pains = dolores de estómago/de pecho

bomb[1] /bɑːm ‖ bɒm/ *n* bomba *f*; (*before n*) **~ disposal** desactivación *f* de explosivas; **~ scare** amenaza *f* de bomba; **~ squad** (colloq) brigada *f* antiexplosivos

bomb[2] *vt* (from air) bombardear; (plant bomb in) colocar* una bomba en

bombard /bɑːm'bɑːrd ‖ bɒm'bɑːd/ *vt* (Mil) bombardear; **she was ~ed with questions** la acribillaron a preguntas

bomber /'bɑːmər ‖ 'bɒmə(r)/ *n* **(a)** (aircraft) bombardero *m* **(b)** (terrorist) terrorista *mf* (*que perpetra atentados colocando bombas*)

bomber jacket *n* chaqueta *f or* (Esp) cazadora *f or* (Méx) chamarra *f or* (RPl) campera *f* de aviador

bombing /'bɑːmɪŋ ‖ 'bɒmɪŋ/ *n* [C U] **(a)** (from aircraft) bombardeo *m* **(b)** (by terrorists) atentado *m* (terrorista)

bombshell /'bɑːmʃel ‖ 'bɒmʃel/ *n* (shocking news) bomba *f*

bona fide /'bəʊnəfaɪd ‖ ˌbəʊnə'faɪdi/ *adj* genuino, auténtico

bonanza /bə'nænzə/ *n* **(a)** (piece of luck) filón *m* **(b)** (plentiful supply) superabundancia *f*

bond[1] /bɑːnd ‖ bɒnd/ *n* **1** [C] **(a)** (link) vínculo *m* **(b) bonds** *pl* (fetters) cadenas *fpl* **2** [U] (adhesion) adherencia *f*

bond[2] *vi* **(a)** (stick) adherirse* **(b)** (form relationship) establecer* vínculos afectivos ■ **~** *vt* (stick) **to ~ sth TO sth** adherir* *or* pegar* algo A algo

bondage /ˈbɑːndɪdʒ ‖ ˈbɒndɪdʒ/ *n* [U] (enslavement) (liter) cautiverio *m* (liter)

bone[1] /bəʊn/ *n* **(a)** [C U] (Anat) hueso *m*; ***to have a ~ to pick with sb*** tener* que ajustar cuentas con algn **(b)** [C] (of fish) espina *f*

bone[2] *vt* ‹*meat*› deshuesar; ‹*fish*› quitarle las espinas a

bone: **~ china** *n* [U] porcelana *f* fina; **~-dry** /ˈbəʊnˈdraɪ/ (*pred* **~ dry**) *adj* completamente seco

bonfire /ˈbɑːnfaɪr ‖ ˈbɒnfaɪə(r)/ *n* hoguera *f*

bonnet /ˈbɑːnət ‖ ˈbɒnɪt/ *n* **1** (Clothing) sombrero *m*; (for baby) gorrito *m* **2** (BrE Auto) capó *m*, capote *m* (Méx)

bonus /ˈbəʊnəs/ *n* **1** (payment to employee) plus *m*, prima *f* **2** (added advantage): **(added) ~** ventaja *f*

bony /ˈbəʊni/ *adj* **bonier, boniest (a)** ‹*knee*› huesudo **(b)** (made of bone) óseo

boo[1] /buː/ *interj* ¡bu!

boo[2] *n* ≈ silba *f*

boo[3], **boos, booing, booed** *vt/i* abuchear

booby /ˈbuːbi/: **~ prize** *n* premio *m* al peor; **~ trap** *n* (Mil) trampa *f*; (bomb) bomba *f* trampa; **~-trap** *vt* **-pp-** (Mil): **his car was ~-trapped** le pusieron una bomba en el coche

book[1] /bʊk/ *n* **1** (printed work) libro *m*; **to go by the ~** ceñirse* (estrictamente) a las normas *or* reglas; ***to throw the ~ at sb*** castigar* duramente a algn **2 (a)** (*exercise* **~**) cuaderno *m* **(b)** (*note***~**) libreta *f or* cuaderno *m* (de apuntes) **3** (set — of samples) muestrario *m*; (— of matches, stamps) librito *m* **4 books** *pl* (Busn, Fin): **the ~s** los libros

book[2] *vt* (esp BrE) **1 (a)** ‹*room/seat/flight*› reservar; ‹*appointment*› concertar*; **the hotel/flight is fully ~ed** el hotel/vuelo está completo; **I'm ~ed (up) all this week** tengo toda la semana ocupada **(b)** ‹*performer*› contratar **2** (record) ‹*order*› asentar* **3 (a)** (record charge against) multar **(b)** (in soccer) (BrE) amonestar ■ **~** *vi* (esp BrE) hacer* una reserva

• **book in** [*v + o + adv, v + adv + o*] (reserve room for): **she'd ~ed us in at the Hilton** nos había reservado habitación en el Hilton

• **book up** [*v + o + adv, v + adv + o*] (reserve) (*often pass*): **the hotels are all ~ed up** los hoteles están todos completos; **tonight's performance is ~ed up** no quedan localidades para la función de esta noche

book: **~case** *n* biblioteca *f*, librería *f* (Esp), librero *m* (Méx); **~end** *n* sujetalibros *m*

booking /ˈbʊkɪŋ/ *n* (esp BrE) **(a)** [C U] (reservation) reserva *f*, reservación *f* (AmL) **(b)** [C] (engagement) compromiso *m*

booking office *n* (BrE Theat) taquilla *f*, boletería *f* (AmL)

bookkeeping /ˈbʊk,kiːpɪŋ/ *n* [U] contabilidad *f*, teneduría *f* de libros

booklet /ˈbʊklət ‖ ˈbʊklɪt/ *n* folleto *m*

book: **~maker** *n* corredor, -dora *m,f* de apuestas; **~mark** *n* señalador *m*, marcador *m*; **~seller** *n* librero, -ra *m,f*; **~shelf** *n* **(a)** (shelf) estante *m*, balda *f* (Esp) (*para libros*) **(b) ~shelves** ⇒ BOOKCASE; **~shop** *n* librería *f*; **~store** *n* (AmE) librería *f*; **~ token** *n* (BrE) cheque *m* regalo *m*, vale *m* (*canjeable por libros*)

boom[1] /buːm/ *n* **1** (Econ, Fin) boom *m* **2** (sound of guns, explosion) estruendo *m*

boom[2] *vi* **1** «*guns*» tronar*; «*voice/thunder*» retumbar **2** (*usu in -ing form*) «*market/industry*» vivir un boom

boomerang /ˈbuːməræŋ/ *n* bumerang *m*

booming /ˈbuːmɪŋ/ *adj* **(a)** ‹*sound*› retumbante **(b)** ‹*industry*› en auge

boon /buːn/ *n* gran ayuda *f*

boost[1] /buːst/ *n* [C] (uplift): **to give a ~ to sth** dar* empuje a algo; **it was a tremendous ~ to her confidence** le dio mucha más confianza en sí misma

boost[2] *vt* ‹*economy/production*› estimular; ‹*sales*› aumentar; ‹*morale*› levantar

booster /ˈbuːstər ‖ ˈbuːstə(r)/ *n* **(a)** (Rad, Telec, TV) repetidor *m* **(b)** (Med) **~ (shot)** (vacuna *f* de) refuerzo *m*

booster cable *n* (AmE) cable *m* de arranque

boot[1] /buːt/ *n* **1** (Clothing) bota *f*; (short) botín *m* **2** (kick) (colloq) (*no pl*) patada *f*, puntapié *m* **3** (BrE Auto) maletero *m*, portamaletas *m*, cajuela *f* (Méx), baúl *m* (Col, CS, Ven), maleta *f* (Chi), maletera *f* (Per) **4 to boot** (*as linker*) para rematarla

boot[2] *vt* **(a)** (kick) (colloq) darle* un puntapié a **(b)** (Comput) **~ (up)** cargar*

booth /buːθ ‖buːð, buːθ/ *n* **(a)** (cabin) cabina *f*; **photo ~** fotomatón *m* **(b)** (*polling* **~**) cabina *f* de votación **(c)** (*telephone* **~**) cabina *f* (de teléfono) **(d)** (stall — at fair) barraca *f*, caseta *f*; (— at exhibition) stand *m*

bootleg /ˈbuːtleg/ *adj* (*before n*) ‹*liquor*› de contrabando; ‹*tape*› pirata *adj inv*

booty /ˈbuːti/ *n* [U] botín *m*

booze[1] /buːz/ *n* [U] (colloq) bebida *f*, trago *m* (esp AmL fam)

booze[2] *vi* (colloq) beber, tomar (esp AmL)

border[1] /ˈbɔːrdər ‖ ˈbɔːdə(r)/ *n* **1** (Pol) frontera *f*; (*before n*) ‹*dispute/town*› fronterizo **2 (a)** (edge) borde *m* **(b)** (edging — on fabric, plate) cenefa *f*

border[2] *vt* **(a)** ‹*country/state*› limitar con; ‹*fields/lands*› lindar con **(b)** (edge — with ribbon, binding) ribetear

• **border on** [*v + prep + o*] **(a)** «*country*» limitar con **(b)** (verge on) rayar en, lindar con

borderline /ˈbɔːrdərlaɪn ‖ ˈbɔːdəlaɪn/ *adj* ‹*case/score*› dudoso; ‹*candidate*› en el límite entre el aprobado y el reprobado *or* (Esp) el suspenso

bore[1] /bɔːr ‖ bɔː(r)/ *past of* BEAR[1]

bore[2] *vt* **1** ‹*shaft/tunnel*› hacer*, abrir* **2** (weary) aburrir

bore[3] *n* **1** (person) pesado, -da *m,f* (fam); (thing) aburrimiento *m*, lata *f* (fam) **2** (of cylinder, gun barrel) calibre *m*

bored /bɔːrd ‖ bɔːd/ *adj* aburrido; **to be ~ WITH sth** estar* aburrido DE algo; **to get ~** aburrirse

boredom /ˈbɔːrdəm ‖ ˈbɔːdəm/ *n* [U] aburrimiento *m*

boring /ˈbɔːrɪŋ/ *adj* aburrido, aburridor (AmL)

born¹ /bɔːrn ‖ bɔːn/ (*past p of* BEAR¹): **to be ~** nacer*

born² *adj* (*before n*) ‹*teacher/leader*› nato; **he's a ~ loser** siempre ha sido y será un perdedor

born-again /ˈbɔːrnəˈgen ‖ ˌbɔːnəˈgen/ *adj* (*before n*): **~ Christian** *cristiano convertido, especialmente a una secta evangélica*

borne /bɔːrn ‖ bɔːn/ *past p of* BEAR¹

borough /ˈbɜːrəʊ ‖ ˈbʌrə/ *n* **(a)** (in US) distrito *m* municipal **(b)** (in UK) municipio *m*

borrow /ˈbɑːrəʊ ‖ ˈbɒrəʊ/ *vt* **1 (a)** (have on loan): **may I ~ your pencil?** ¿me prestas *or* (Esp tb) me dejas el lápiz?; **to ~ sth FROM sb** pedirle* prestado algo A algn; **I ~ed $5,000 from the bank** pedí un préstamo de 5.000 dólares al banco **(b)** (from library) sacar* **2** ‹*idea*› sacar*; ‹*word*› tomar

borrower /ˈbɑːrəʊər ‖ ˈbɒrəʊə(r)/ *n* **(a)** (Fin) prestatario, -ria *m,f* **(b)** (from library) usuario, -ria *m,f*

borrowing /ˈbɑːrəʊɪŋ ‖ ˈbɒrəʊɪŋ/ *n* [U] (Fin) préstamos *mpl*

Bosnia Herzegovina /ˈbɑːzniəˌhertsəgəʊˈviːnə ‖ ˌbɒzniəˌhɜːtsəgəʊˈviːnə/ *n* Bosnia Herzegovina *f*

Bosnian /ˈbɑːzniən ‖ ˈbɒzniən/ *adj* bosnio

bosom /ˈbʊzəm/ *n* **(a)** (breast, chest) (liter) pecho *m*; (*before n*) ‹*friend*› del alma **(b)** (of woman — bust) pecho *m*, busto *m*; (— breast) pecho *m*, seno *m* **(c)** (heart, center) (liter) seno *m*

boss /bɑːs ‖ bɒs/ *n* (colloq) **(a)** (superior) jefe, -fa *m,f*; (employer, factory owner) patrón, -trona *m,f* **(b)** (leader) dirigente *mf*

• **boss around**, (BrE also) **boss about** [*v + o + adv*] (colloq) mandonear (fam)

bossy /ˈbɑːsi ‖ ˈbɒsi/ *adj* **bossier, bossiest** (colloq) mandón (fam)

bosun /ˈbəʊsn̩/ *n* ⇒ BOATSWAIN

botanic /bəˈtænɪk/, **-ical** /-ɪkəl/ *adj* botánico

botanist /ˈbɑːtn̩əst ‖ ˈbɒtənɪst/ *n* botánico, -ca *m,f*

botany /ˈbɑːtn̩i ‖ ˈbɒtəni/ *n* [U] botánica *f*

botch /bɑːtʃ ‖ bɒtʃ/ *vt* (colloq) **~ (up)** ‹*repair*› hacer* una chapuza de (fam); ‹*plan*› estropear

both¹ /bəʊθ/ *adj* ambos, -bas, los dos, las dos

both² *pron* ambos, -bas, los dos, las dos; **we ~ like chess** a los dos nos gusta el ajedrez; **the coats are ~ too big** los dos abrigos son demasiado grandes

both³ *conj* **both ... and ...**: **~ Paul and John are in Italy** tanto Paul como John están en Italia, Paul y John están los dos en Italia; **she ~ wrote and played the music** compuso y tocó la música ella misma

bother¹ /ˈbɑːðər ‖ ˈbɒðə(r)/ *vt* **(a)** (irritate, pester) molestar; **sorry to ~ you** perdone (que lo moleste) **(b)** (trouble) preocupar; **she's very quiet, but don't let it ~ you** es muy callada, no te inquietes por ello **(c)** (make effort) **not to ~ -ING**: **don't ~ writing a long letter** no hace falta que escribas una carta larga; **to ~ to + INF** tomarse la molestia DE + INF ■ **~** *vi* **(a)** (make effort) molestarse **(b)** (worry) **to ~ ABOUT sth/sb** preocuparse POR algo/algn

bother² *n* [U] molestia *f*; (work) trabajo *m*; (problems) problemas *mpl*

bothered /ˈbɑːðərd ‖ ˈbɒðəd/ *adj* (*pred*): **I can't be ~ to go** me da pereza ir; **she yelled at him, but he wasn't a bit ~** le pegó un berrido, pero él ni se inmutó

bottle¹ /ˈbɑːtl̩ ‖ ˈbɒtl̩/ *n* (container, contents) botella *f*; (of perfume) frasco *m*; **baby's ~** biberón *m*, mamadera *f* (CS, Per), tetero *m* (Col, Ven); (*before n*) **~ opener** abrebotellas *m*, destapador *m* (AmL)

bottle² *vt* **(a)** ‹*wine/milk*› embotellar; **~d milk** leche *f* en *or* de botella; **~d water** agua *f*‡ embotellada **(b)** (BrE) ‹*fruit/vegetables*› poner* en conserva

• **bottle up** [*v + o + adv, v + adv + o*] (colloq) ‹*emotion*› reprimir

bottle: **~ bank** *n* contenedor *m* de recogida de vidrio; **~feed** *vt* (*past & past p* **-fed**) alimentar con biberón *or* (Méx) con mamila *or* (CS, Per) con mamadera *or* (Col) con tetero; **~neck** *n* (narrow stretch of road) cuello *m* de botella; (hold-up) embotellamiento *m*

bottom¹ /ˈbɑːtəm ‖ ˈbɒtəm/ *n* **1 (a)** (of box, bottle, drawer) fondo *m*; (of hill, stairs) pie *m*; (of page) final *m*, pie *m*; (of pile) parte *f* de abajo; ***to get to the ~ of sth*** llegar* al fondo de algo **(b)** (underneath — of box) parte *f* de abajo; (— of ship) fondo *m* **(c)** (of bed) pies *mpl*; (of garden) fondo *m*; (of road) final *m* **(d)** (of sea, river, lake) fondo *m* **2** (of hierarchy): **he is at the ~ of the class** es el último de la clase; **she started out at the ~** empezó desde abajo **3 (a)** (of person) trasero *m* (fam), traste *m* (CS fam) **(b)** (of pyjamas, tracksuit) (*often pl*) pantalón *m*, pantalones *mpl*; (of bikini) parte *f* de abajo

bottom² *adj* (*before n*) ‹*shelf/layer*› de más abajo; ‹*grade*› más bajo; ‹*part/edge/lip*› inferior

bottomless /ˈbɑːtəmləs ‖ ˈbɒtəmlɪs/ *adj* ‹*well/shaft*› sin fondo

bough /baʊ/ *n* rama *f*

bought /bɔːt/ *past & past p of* BUY¹

boulder /ˈbəʊldər ‖ ˈbəʊldə(r)/ *n* roca *f* (*grande, alisada por la erosión*)

boulevard /ˈbʊləvɑːrd ‖ ˈbuːləvɑːd/ *n* bulevar *m*

bounce¹ /baʊns/ *vi* **(a)** «*ball/object*» rebotar, picar* (AmL), botar (Esp, Méx); **the child was bouncing up and down on the sofa** el niño saltaba en el sofá **(b)** «*check*» (colloq) ser* devuelto, rebotar (fam) ■ **~** *vt* **(a)** ‹*ball/object*› hacer* rebotar, hacer* picar (AmL), (hacer*) botar (Esp, Méx) **(b)** ‹*check*› (colloq) devolver*

• **bounce back** [*v + adv*] (colloq) levantarse

bounce² *n* **(a)** [C] (action) rebote *m*, pique *m* (AmL) **(b)** [U] (springiness, vitality): **this shampoo puts the ~ back into your hair** este champú les da nueva vida a sus cabellos; **she's full of ~** es una persona llena de vida

bouncer /ˈbaʊnsər ‖ ˈbaʊnsə(r)/ *n* (colloq) gorila *m* (fam), sacabullas *m* (Méx fam)

bound¹ /baʊnd/ *n* **1 bounds** *pl* (limits) límites *mpl*; **within the ~s of possibility** dentro de lo posible; **the shop is out of ~s to schoolchildren** los niños tienen prohibido entrar en la tienda **2** (jump) salto *m*, brinco *m*

bound² *vi* saltar; **to ~ in/out** entrar/salir* dando saltos

bound³ *past & past p of* BIND¹

bound[4] *adj* **1 (a)** (tied up) atado, amarrado (AmL exc RPl) **(b)** (obliged): **they are ~ by law to supply the goods** están obligados por ley a suministrar los artículos; **I'm duty ~ to tell you the truth** es mi deber decirte la verdad **2** (*pred*) (certain): **it was ~ to happen sooner or later** tarde o temprano tenía que suceder; **it was ~ to go wrong** no cabía duda de que iba a salir mal **3** (headed) (*pred*): **the truck was ~ for Italy** el camión iba rumbo a Italia; **they are Moscow ~** van camino a Moscú

boundary /'baʊndri, -dəri/ *n* (*pl* **-ries**) límite *m*

bountiful /'baʊntɪfəl/ *adj* (liter) ‹*king/nature*› munificente (liter); ‹*harvest/gifts*› copioso

bounty /'baʊnti/ *n* (*pl* **-ties**) **1** [U C] (liter) (generosity) munificencia *f* (liter) **2** [C] (reward) recompensa *f*; (*before n*) **~ hunter** cazador, -dora *m,f* de recompensas

bouquet /bəʊ'keɪ, buː'keɪ ‖ bʊ'keɪ, bəʊ'keɪ/ *n* **1** (of flowers) ramo *m*; (small) ramillete *m* **2** (of wine) bouquet *m*

bourbon /'bɜːrbən ‖ 'bɜːbən/ *n* [U C] bourbon *m*

bourgeois /'bʊrʒwɑː ‖ 'bɔːʒwɑː, 'bʊəʒ-/ *adj* burgués

bout /baʊt/ *n* **1** (period, spell): **I had a ~ of flu** tuve una gripe *or* (Col, Méx) una gripa muy mala; **a drinking ~** una borrachera **2** (in boxing, wrestling) combate *m*, encuentro *m*

boutique /buː'tiːk/ *n* boutique *f*

bow[1] /baʊ/ *n* **1** (movement) reverencia *f* **2** (of ship) (*often pl*) proa *f*

bow[2] /baʊ/ *vi* hacer* una reverencia; **they ~ed to government pressure** cedieron ante la presión del gobierno ■ **~** *vt* ‹*head*› inclinar

• **bow out** [*v* + *adv*] retirarse

bow[3] /bəʊ/ *n* **1** (knot) lazo *m*, moño *m* (esp AmL) **2** (weapon) arco *m* **3** (Mus) arco *m*

bow[4] /bəʊ/ *vi* «*branch/plank*» arquearse, pandearse (esp AmL)

bowel /'baʊəl/ *n* (Anat) intestino *m* grueso; **in the ~s of the earth** (liter) en las entrañas de la tierra

bowl[1] /bəʊl/ *n* **1 (a)** (container) (Culin) bol *m*, tazón *m*, cuenco *m*; (for washing etc) palangana *f*, barreño *m*; **fruit ~** frutero *m*, frutera *f* (CS); **soup ~** sopero *m* **(b)** (contents) bol *m*, tazón *m* **(c)** (of toilet) taza *f* **2** (in game of bowls) bola *f*, bocha *f*; *see also* BOWLS

bowl[2] *vt/i* lanzar*

• **bowl over** [*v* + *o* + *adv*, *v* + *adv* + *o*] derribar; **we were ~ed over by the beauty of the island** la belleza de la isla nos dejó pasmados

bowlegged /'bəʊ'legd/ *adj* patizambo

bowler /'bəʊlər ‖ 'bəʊlə(r)/ *n* **1** (in cricket) lanzador, -dora *m,f*; (in bowling, bowls) jugador, -dora *m,f* **2 ~ (hat)** bombín *m*, sombrero *m* de hongo

bowling /'bəʊlɪŋ/ *n* [U] **(a)** (in bowling alley) bolos *mpl* **(b)** (on grass) ⇒ BOWLS

bowling: **~ alley** *n* bolera *f*, bowling *m*; **~ green** *n*: *pista donde se juega a los* BOWLS

bowls /bəʊlz/ *n* (+ *sing vb*) *juego semejante a la petanca que se juega sobre césped*

bow tie /bəʊ/ *n* corbata *f* de moño (AmL), pajarita *f* (Esp)

box[1] /bɑːks ‖ bɒks/ *n* **1** (container, contents) caja *f*; (large) cajón *m*; (for watch, pen) estuche *m* **2** (on form) casilla *f* **3 (a)** (in theater) palco *m* **(b)** (booth) cabina *f*

box[2] *vi* boxear ■ **~** *vt* poner* en una caja, embalar

• **box in** [*v* + *o* + *adv*, *v* + *adv* + *o*] **(a)** (restrict, surround) cerrarle* el paso a **(b)** (enclose) ‹*pipes*› esconder (*tapando con una tabla etc*)

boxer /'bɑːksər ‖ 'bɒksə(r)/ *n* **(a)** (person) boxeador, -dora *m,f* **(b)** (dog) bóxer *mf*

boxer shorts *pl n* calzoncillos *mpl*, calzones *mpl* (Méx), interiores *mpl* (Col, Ven)

boxing /'bɑːksɪŋ ‖ 'bɒksɪŋ/ *n* [U] boxeo *m*; (*before n*) **~ ring** ring *m*, cuadrilátero *m*

Boxing Day /'bɑːksɪŋ ‖ 'bɒksɪŋ/ *n*: *el 26 de diciembre, día festivo en Gran Bretaña*

box: **~ number** *n* (at post office) apartado *m* (de correos), apartado *m* postal (Méx), casilla *f* postal *or* de correo (CS); **~ office** *n* taquilla *f*, boletería *f* (AmL)

boy /bɔɪ/ *n* **(a)** (baby, child) niño *m*, chico *m* **(b)** (son) hijo *m*, chico *m* **(c)** (young man) (colloq) muchacho *m*, chico *m*

boycott[1] /'bɔɪkɑːt ‖ 'bɔɪkɒt/ *n* boicot *m*

boycott[2] *vt* boicotear

boyfriend /'bɔɪfrend/ *n* novio *m*, pololo *m* (Chi fam)

boyish /'bɔɪɪʃ/ *adj* ‹*enthusiasm/smile*› de chico, de niño; (used of woman) de muchacho, de chico

boy scout *n* boy scout *m*, explorador *m*

bra /brɑː/ *n* sostén *m*, sujetador *m* (Esp), brasier *m* (Col, Méx), corpiño *m* (RPl), soutien *m* (Ur)

brace[1] /breɪs/ *n* **1** (support) abrazadera *f* **2** (Dent) ⇒ 4(b) **3** (drill) berbiquí *m* **4 braces** *pl* **(a)** (BrE Clothing) tirantes *mpl*, cargaderas *fpl* (Col), tiradores *mpl* (RPl), suspensores *mpl* (Chi) **(b)** (esp AmE Dent) aparato(s) *m(pl)*, frenos *mpl* (Méx), fierros *mpl* (Méx, Per), frenillos *mpl* (Chi) **5** (*pl* **~**) (pair) (BrE) par *m*

brace[2] *vt* (support) apuntalar ■ *v refl* **to ~ oneself for sth** prepararse para algo

bracelet /'breɪslət ‖ 'breɪslɪt/ *n* pulsera *f*, brazalete *m*

bracing /'breɪsɪŋ/ *adj* vigorizante

bracken /'brækən/ *n* [U] helechos *mpl*

bracket[1] /'brækət ‖ 'brækɪt/ *n* **1 (a)** (Print) (square bracket) corchete *m* **(b)** (parenthesis) (BrE) paréntesis *m* **2** (category): **income ~** nivel *m* de ingresos; **the 25-30 age ~** el grupo etario de entre 25 y 30 años **3** (support) soporte *m*; (for shelves) escuadra *f*

bracket[2] *vt* **(a)** ‹*word/phrase*› poner* entre corchetes; (in parentheses) (BrE) poner* entre paréntesis **(b)** (categorize) catalogar*

brag /bræg/ *vi/t* **-gg-** fanfarronear (fam)

braid[1] /breɪd/ *n* **(a)** [C] (of hair) (esp AmE) trenza *f* **(b)** [U] (Tex) galón *m*

braid[2] *vt* trenzar*

braille, Braille /breɪl/ *n* [U] braille *m*, Braille *m*

brain /breɪn/ *n* cerebro *m*; (*before n*) **~ damage** lesión *f* cerebral; **~ tumor** tumor *m* cerebral

brain: **~child** *n* creación *m*; **~-dead** *adj* clínicamente muerto

brains /breɪnz/ *n* **1** (+ *pl vb*) **(a)** (substance) sesos *mpl*; (Culin) sesos *mpl* **(b)** (intelligence) inteligencia *f*

2 (+ *sing vb*) (mastermind) cerebro *m*, autor, -tora *m,f* intelectual (AmL); **he's the ~ of the family** es la lumbrera de la familia

brain: **~wash** *vt* hacerle* un lavado de cerebro a; **~wave** *n* (colloq) idea *f* genial, lamparazo *m* (Col fam)

braise /breɪz/ *vt* estofar

brake¹ /breɪk/ *n* (on vehicle) freno *m*; (*before n*) **~ lights** luces *fpl* de freno

brake² *vi/t* frenar

bramble /'bræmbəl/ *n* zarza *f*

bran /bræn/ *n* [U] salvado *m*, afrecho *m*

branch¹ /bræntʃ ‖ brɑːntʃ/ *n* (of tree) rama *f*; (of river, road, railway) ramal *m*; (of family, field of study) rama *f*; (of company, bank) sucursal *f*

branch² *vi* «*river/family*» ramificarse*; «*road*» bifurcarse*; **a path ~es (off) to the right** un sendero sale a la derecha

• **branch out** [*v* + *adv*] **(a)** (take on new activity) diversificar* sus (*or* nuestras *etc*) actividades; **the company has ~ed out into publishing** la compañía ha diversificado sus actividades lanzándose al campo editorial **(b)** (become independent): **he has ~ed out on his own** «*business partner*» se ha establecido por su cuenta

brand¹ /brænd/ *n* **1 (a)** (Busn) marca *f* **(b)** (type) tipo *m*; (style) estilo *m* **2** (identification mark) marca *f* (*hecha a fuego*)

brand² *vt* **(a)** (mark) ‹*cattle*› marcar* (*con hierro candente*) **(b)** (label) **to ~ sb AS sth** tachar a algn DE algo

brandish /'brændɪʃ/ *vt* blandir

brand: **~ name** *n* marca *f*; **~-new** /'brænd'nuː ‖ ˌbrænd'njuː/ *adj* nuevo

brandy /'brændi/ *n* [U C] (*pl* **-dies**) coñac *m*, brandy *m*

brash /bræʃ/ *adj* **-er, -est** excesivamente desenvuelto

brass /bræs ‖ brɑːs/ *n* [U] **(a)** (Metall) latón *m*; (*before n*) ‹*button*› dorado **(b)** (Mus) (+ *sing or pl vb*) bronces *mpl*, metales *mpl*

brass band *n* banda *f* de música, tambora *f* (Méx)

brassiere /brə'zɪr ‖ 'bræziə(r)/ *n* ⇒ BRA

brass knuckles *pl n* (AmE) nudilleras *fpl* de metal, manoplas *fpl* (AmL)

brat /bræt/ *n* (pej) mocoso, -sa *m,f* (pey)

bravado /brə'vɑːdəʊ/ *n* [U] bravuconadas *fpl*

brave¹ /breɪv/ *adj* **-ver, -vest** valiente

brave² *vt* ‹*peril*› afrontar; **to ~ the weather** hacerle frente al mal tiempo

brave³ *n* **1** (North American Indian) guerrero *m* piel roja **2** (liter) (+ *pl vb*) **the ~** los valientes

bravely /'breɪvli/ *adv* valientemente

bravery /'breɪvəri/ *n* [U] valentía *f*, valor *m*

bravo /'brɑːvəʊ ‖ brɑː'vəʊ/ *interj* ¡bravo!

brawl¹ /brɔːl/ *n* pelea *f*

brawl² *vi* pelearse

brawny /'brɔːni/ *adj* **-nier, -niest** musculoso

bray /breɪ/ *vi* «*donkey*» rebuznar; «*person*» cacarear

brazen /'breɪzn̩ ‖ 'breɪzən/ *adj* descarado

brazier /'breɪʒər, 'breɪziər ‖ 'breɪziə(r)/ *n* brasero *m*

Brazil /brə'zɪl/ *n* Brasil *m*

Brazilian /brə'zɪliən/ *adj* brasileño

brazil nut /brə'zɪl/ *n* coquito *m* del Brasil, castaña *f* de Pará (RPl)

breach¹ /briːtʃ/ *n* **1** [C U] (of law) infracción *f*; **~ of contract** incumplimiento *m* de contrato; **she was arrested for ~ of the peace** la detuvieron por alterar el orden público **2** [C] (gap, opening) (frml) brecha *f* **3** [C] (break) (frml) ruptura *f*

breach² *vt* **(a)** ‹*rule*› infringir*, violar; ‹*security*› poner* en peligro **(b)** (frml) ‹*defenses*› abrir* una brecha en

bread /bred/ *n* [U] pan *m*; **~ and butter** pan con mantequilla *or* (RPl) manteca

bread: **~bin** *n* (BrE) ⇒ ~BOX; **~board** *n* tabla *f* de cortar el pan; **~box** *n* (AmE) panera *f* (*para guardar el pan*); **~crumb** *n* miga *f* (de pan); **~crumbs** (Culin) pan *m* rallado *or* (Méx) molido; **~line** *n*: ***they're on the ~line*** (colloq) apenas tienen para vivir

breadth /bredθ/ *n* **(a)** [C U] (width) anchura *f*, ancho *m* **(b)** [U] (extent) amplitud *f*; **~ of vision** amplitud de miras

breadwinner /'bredˌwɪnər ‖ 'bredˌwɪnə(r)/ *n*: **she's the ~ of the family** es la que mantiene a la familia

break¹ /breɪk/ (*past* **broke**; *past p* **broken**) *vt* **1** ‹*window/plate*› romper*; ‹*stick*› partir, quebrar* (AmL); **he broke his wrist** se rompió la muñeca **2** (render useless) ‹*machine*› romper*, descomponer* (AmL) **3** (violate) ‹*rule*› infringir*; ‹*promise*› no cumplir; ‹*contract*› incumplir; ‹*strike*› romper*; ⇒ LAW (b) **4** (end) ‹*strike*› poner* fin a; ‹*drug ring*› desarticular; ‹*impasse*› salir* de; ‹*habit*› dejar **5 (a)** (ruin) ‹*person/company*› arruinar a **(b)** (crush) ‹*person*› destrozar* **6** (impart): **Sue broke the news to him** Sue le dio la noticia; **they broke it to her gently** se lo dijeron con mucho tacto **7** (exceed) ‹*record*› batir **8** (disrupt) ‹*pattern/monotony*› romper* **9** (decipher) ‹*code*› descifrar ■ **~** *vi* **1** «*window/plate*» romperse*; «*stick*» partirse, quebrarse* (AmL) **2** (give in) «*resistance*» desmoronarse; **she broke under constant interrogation** no resistió el constante interrogatorio **3 (a)** (begin) «*storm*» estallar; «*day*» romper* **(b)** (change) «*weather*» cambiar; **his voice is ~ing** le está cambiando la voz; **his voice broke** (with emotion) se le entrecortó la voz **4** «*wave/surf*» romper*

• **break away** [*v* + *adv*] **to ~ away (FROM sth)** «*piece*» desprenderse (DE algo); «*faction/region*» escindirse (DE algo)

• **break down I** [*v* + *adv*] **1** «*vehicle/machine*» estropearse, averiarse*, descomponerse* (AmL), quedarse en pana (Chi), quedarse varado (Col); «*system*» fallar; «*talks*» fracasar **2** (lose composure) perder* el control

II [*v* + *o* + *adv*, *v* + *adv* + *o*] **1** ‹*door/barrier*› echar abajo **2** (divide up) ‹*expenditure*› desglosar; ‹*sentence*› descomponer*; **the process can be broken**

down into three steps el proceso puede dividirse en tres pasos

• **break in 1** [*v* + *adv*] «*intruder*» entrar (*para robar etc*) **2** [*v* + *o* + *adv, v* + *adv* + *o*] ‹*horse*› domar

• **break into** [*v* + *prep* + *o*] ‹*building*› entrar en (*para robar etc*)

• **break off 1** [*v* + *o* + *adv, v* + *adv* + *o*] **(a)** (detach) partir **(b)** ‹*engagement/diplomatic relations*› romper* **2** [*v* + *adv*] (snap off, come free) «*piece of ice*» desprenderse; **the handle broke off** se le rompió el asa

• **break out** [*v* + *adv*] **1** (start) «*war/epidemic/rioting*» estallar **2** (escape) «*prisoner*» escaparse, fugarse*

• **break through 1** [*v* + *adv*] (penetrate) (Mil) penetrar en las defensas enemigas; «*sun*» salir* **2** [*v* + *prep* + *o*] ‹*barrier*› atravesar*, romper*; **they broke through our defenses** penetraron en nuestras defensas

• **break up I** [*v* + *o* + *adv, v* + *adv* + *o*] **1** (divide) ‹*land*› dividir; ‹*ship*› desaguazar*; ‹*sentence*› descomponer* **2 (a)** ‹*demonstration*› disolver* **(b)** (wreck, ruin) ‹*home*› deshacer*
II [*v* + *adv*] **(a)** «*lovers/band*» separarse; **their marriage broke up** su matrimonio fracasó; **to ~ up WITH sb** romper* CON algn **(b)** «*meeting*» terminar; «*crowd*» dispersarse

break² *n* **1 (a)** (Rad, TV) pausa *f* (comercial); (Theat) entreacto *m*, intermedio *m* **(b)** (rest period) descanso *m*; (at school) (BrE) recreo *m* **(c)** (short vacation) vacaciones *fpl* **(d)** (change, respite) cambio *m*; **I need a ~ from all this** necesito descansar de todo esto; (a holiday) necesito un cambio de aires **2** (gap) interrupción *f* **3** (fracture) fractura *f*, rotura *f*; **to make a clean ~** cortar por lo sano

breakable /ˈbreɪkəbəl/ *adj* frágil

breakage /ˈbreɪkɪdʒ/ *n* **(a)** [U] (action) rotura *f* **(b) breakages** *pl* (objects broken) roturas *fpl*

break: ~away *n* (separation) ruptura *f*, escisión *f*; (*before n*) ‹*faction*› disidente, escindido; **~down** *n* **1 (a)** (failure — of car, machine) avería *f*, descompostura *f* (Méx), varada *f* (Col), pana *f* (Chi); (—of service, communications) interrupción *f*; (— of negotiations) fracaso *m*; (*before n*) **~down truck** grúa *f* **(b)** (*nervous ~down*) crisis *f* nerviosa; **2** (analysis): **a ~down of expenditure** un desglose de los gastos

breaker /ˈbreɪkər ‖ ˈbreɪkə(r)/ *n* gran ola *f*

breakfast /ˈbrekfəst/ *n* desayuno *m*; **to have ~** desayunar, tomar el desayuno

break-in /ˈbreɪkɪn/ *n* robo *m* (*con escalamiento*)

breaking /ˈbreɪkɪŋ/: **~ and entering** /ˈbreɪ kɪŋəndˈentərɪŋ/ *n* [U] allanamiento *m* de morada; **~ point** *n* [U] límite *m*

break: ~through *n* gran avance *m*; **~up** *n* (of structure, family) desintegración *f*; (of empire, company) desmembramiento *m*; (of political party) disolución *f*; (of talks) fracaso *m*; **the ~up of their marriage** su separación; **~water** *n* rompeolas *m*

breast /brest/ ▶ 484 *n* **(a)** [C] (of woman) pecho *m*, seno *m*; (*before n*) **~ cancer** cáncer *m* de mama *or* de pecho **(b)** [C] (chest) (liter) pecho *m* **(c)** [C U] (Culin) (of chicken, turkey) pechuga *f*

breast: ~feed (*past & past p* **-fed**) *vt* darle* el pecho a, darle* de mamar a ■ **~** *vi* dar* el pecho, dar* de mamar; **~stroke** *n* (estilo) pecho *m* (AmL), braza *f* (Esp)

breath /breθ/ *n* [C U] aliento *m*; **to have bad ~** tener* mal aliento; **to take a ~** aspirar, inspirar; **take a deep ~** respire hondo; **out of ~** sin aliento; ***to hold one's ~*** contener* la respiración; ***to take sb's ~ away*** dejar a algn sin habla

Breathalyzer®, Breathalyser® /ˈbreθəlaɪzər ‖ ˈbreθəlaɪzə(r)/ *n* alcohómetro *m*, alcoholímetro *m*; (*before n*) **~ test** prueba *f* del alcohol *or* de la alcoholemia

breathe /briːð/ *vi* respirar ■ **~** *vt* ‹*air/fumes*› aspirar, respirar

• **breathe in 1** [*v* + *adv*] aspirar **2** [*v* + *o* + *adv, v* + *adv* + *o*] ‹*air/fumes*› aspirar, respirar

• **breathe out 1** [*v* + *adv*] espirar **2** [*v* + *o* + *adv, v* + *adv* + *o*] ‹*smoke*› expeler; ‹*air*› exhalar

breathing /ˈbriːðɪŋ/ *n* [U] respiración *f*

breathing space *n* [U] respiro *m*

breathless /ˈbreθləs ‖ ˈbreθlɪs/ *adj*: **the blow left me ~** el golpe me dejó sin aliento; **he arrived ~** llegó jadeando

breathtaking /ˈbreθˌteɪkɪŋ/ *adj* impresionante

bred /bred/ *past & past p of* BREED²

breeches /ˈbrɪtʃəz ‖ ˈbrɪtʃɪz/ *pl n* (*knee ~*) (pantalones *mpl*) bombachos *mpl*; (*riding ~*) pantalones *mpl* de montar

breed¹ /briːd/ *n* (of animals) raza *f*; (of plants) variedad *f*

breed² (*past & past p* **bred**) *vt* ‹*animals*› criar*; ‹*violence*› engendrar ■ **~** *vi* reproducirse*

breeder /ˈbriːdər ‖ ˈbriːdə(r)/ *n* (of animals) criador, -dora *m,f*; (of plants) cultivador, -dora *m,f*

breeding /ˈbriːdɪŋ/ *n* [U] **(a)** (reproduction) reproducción *f* **(b)** (raising — of animals) cría *f*; (— of plants) cultivo *m* **(c)** (upbringing): **politeness is a sign of good ~** la cortesía es señal de buena educación

breeze¹ /briːz/ ▶ 920 *n* [C U] brisa *f*

breeze² *vi* (colloq): **to ~ in/out** entrar/salir* tan campante (fam)

breezy /ˈbriːzi/ *adj* **-zier, -ziest 1** ▶ 920 (windy) ‹*spot*› ventoso; **it's a bit ~ today** hace un poco de vientecito hoy **2** (lively) (colloq) ‹*person*› dinámico

brethren /ˈbreðrən/ *pl n* (arch *or* liter) hermanos *mpl*

brevity /ˈbrevəti/ *n* [U] brevedad *f*

brew /bruː/ *vt* **(a)** ‹*beer*› fabricar* **(b)** ‹*tea*› preparar **(c)** ‹*mischief*› tramar ■ **~** *vi* **(a)** (make beer) fabricar* cerveza **(b)** «*tea*»: **the tea is ~ing** el té se está haciendo **(c)** «*storm*» avecinarse; «*trouble*» gestarse

brewer /ˈbruːər ‖ ˈbruːə(r)/ *n* cervecero, -ra *m,f*

brewery /ˈbruːəri/ *n* (*pl* **-ries**) fábrica *f* de cerveza, cervecería *f*

bribe¹ /braɪb/ *n* soborno *m*

bribe² *vt* sobornar

bribery /ˈbraɪbəri/ *n* [U] soborno *m*

bric-a-brac /ˈbrɪkəbræk/ *n* [U] baratijas *fpl*

brick /brɪk/ *n* ladrillo *m*

bricklayer /ˈbrɪkˌleɪər ‖ ˈbrɪkˌleɪə(r)/ *n* albañil *m*

bridal /ˈbraɪdl/ *adj* ‹*procession*› nupcial; ‹*shop*› para novias

bride /braɪd/ *n* novia *f*; **the ~ and groom** los novios; (after ceremony) los recién casados

bride: **~groom** *n* novio *m*; **~smaid** *n* dama *f* de honor; (child) *niña que acompaña a la novia*

bridge¹ /brɪdʒ/ *n* **1** [C] **(a)** puente *m* **(b)** (on ship) puente *m* (de mando) **(c)** (of nose) caballete *m* **2** [C] (Dent) puente *m* **3** [U] (card game) bridge *m*

bridge² *vt* ‹*river*› tender* un puente sobre; ‹*differences*› salvar

bridle /ˈbraɪdl/ *n* brida *f*

brief¹ /bri:f/ *adj* breve; **in ~** en resumen

brief² *n* **(a)** (Law) *expediente entregado por el abogado al* BARRISTER **(b)** (instructions) instrucciones *fpl* **(c)** (area of responsibility) competencia *f*

brief³ *vt* ‹*lawyer*› instruir*; ‹*pilot/spy*› darle* instrucciones a; ‹*committee*› informar

briefcase /ˈbri:fkeɪs/ *n* maletín *m*, portafolio(s) *m* (esp AmL)

briefing /ˈbri:fɪŋ/ *n* **(a)** (*~ session*) sesión *f* para dar instrucciones **(b)** (*press ~*) reunión *f* informativa (para la prensa)

briefly /ˈbri:fli/ *adv* **(a)** ‹*visit/rule*› por poco tiempo **(b)** ‹*reply/speak*› brevemente **(c)** (*indep*) en resumen

briefs /bri:fs/ *pl n* (man's) calzoncillos *mpl*, slip *m*; (woman's) calzones *mpl* (esp AmL), bragas *fpl* (Esp), bombachas *fpl* (RPl), pantaletas *fpl* (AmC, Ven)

brigade /brɪˈgeɪd/ *n* brigada *f*

bright /braɪt/ *adj* **-er, -est 1 (a)** ‹*star/light*› brillante; ‹*room*› con mucha luz **(b)** ‹*color*› fuerte **2 (a)** (cheerful) ‹*eyes*› lleno de vida **(b)** (hopeful) ‹*future*› prometedor; ***to look on the ~ side of sth*** mirar el lado bueno de algo **3** (intelligent) ‹*person*› inteligente; **whose ~ idea was it to ...?** (iro) ¿quién tuvo la brillante idea de ...? (iró)

brighten /ˈbraɪtn/ *vi* **(a)** (become brighter) «*light*» hacerse* más brillante **(b) ~ (up)** (become cheerful, hopeful) «*person*» animarse; «*situation/prospects*» mejorar ■ **~** *vt* **(a)** (make brighter) iluminar **(b) ~ (up)** ‹*room*› alegrar; ‹*occasion/party*› animar

brightly /ˈbraɪtli/ *adv* **(a)** ‹*shine*› intensamente **(b)** ‹*say/smile*› alegremente

brights /braɪts/ *pl n* (Auto) (AmE colloq) (luces *fpl*) largas *or* (Andes, Méx) altas *fpl*

brilliance /ˈbrɪljəns/ *n* [U] **(a)** (brightness) resplandor *m* **(b)** (skill, intelligence) brillantez *f*

brilliant /ˈbrɪljənt/ *adj* **(a)** ‹*light*› brillante; ‹*sunshine*› radiante; ‹*red/green*› brillante **(b)** ‹*student/performance*› brillante

brilliantly /ˈbrɪljəntli/ *adv* **(a)** ‹*shine*› intensamente **(b)** ‹*write*› con brillantez

brim¹ /brɪm/ *n* **1** (of hat) ala *f*‡ **2** (of vessel) borde *m*

brim² *vi* **-mm-**: **her eyes were ~ming with tears** tenía los ojos llenos de lágrimas; **to ~ with confidence** rebosar seguridad

brine /braɪn/ *n* [U] **(a)** (saltwater) salmuera *f* **(b)** (seawater) agua *f*‡ salada *or* de mar

bring /brɪŋ/ (*past & past p* **brought**) *vt* traer*; **I couldn't ~ myself to do it** no pude hacerlo; **it brought tears to my eyes** hizo que se me llenaran los ojos de lágrimas; ***to ~ sth to bear***: **to ~ pressure to bear on sb** ejercer* presión sobre algn

• **bring about** [*v + o + adv, v + adv + o*] dar* lugar a

• **bring along** [*v + o + adv, v + adv + o*] traer*

• **bring back** [*v + o + adv, v + adv + o*] **(a)** (return): **I'll ~ your book back tomorrow** te devolveré *or* (AmL exc CS) te regresaré el libro mañana; **to ~ sb back to life** devolverle* la vida a algn **(b)** ‹*gift/souvenir*› traer* **(c)** (reintroduce) ‹*custom*› volver* a introducir **(d)** (recall) recordar*; **it brought back memories** me (*or* le *etc*) trajo recuerdos

• **bring down** [*v + o + adv, v + adv + o*] **(a)** (lower) ‹*price*› reducir*; ‹*temperature*› hacer* bajar **(b)** (cause to fall) ‹*tree/wall*› tirar; ‹*player/opponent/plane*› derribar; ‹*government*› derrocar*

• **bring home** [*v + o + adv, v + adv + o*]: **her letter brought home to me the seriousness of the situation** su carta me hizo dar cuenta cabal de la gravedad de la situación

• **bring off** [*v + o + adv, v + adv + o*] ‹*feat/victory*› conseguir*, lograr; ‹*plan*› llevar a cabo; ‹*deal*› conseguir*

• **bring on** [*v + o + adv, v + adv + o*] ‹*attack/breakdown*› provocar*; **what brought this on?** ¿esto a qué se debe? **2** [*v + o + prep + o*] (cause to befall): **he brought it all on himself** él (mismo) se lo buscó

• **bring out** [*v + o + adv, v + adv + o*] **(a)** ‹*product/model*› sacar* (al mercado); ‹*edition/book*› publicar* **(b)** (accentuate): **children ~ out the best in her** el trato con niños hace resaltar sus mejores cualidades

• **bring together** [*v + o + adv, v + adv + o*]: **the conference will ~ together scientists from all over the world** el congreso reunirá a científicos de todo el mundo; **a tragedy like this can ~ a family together** una tragedia así puede unir a una familia

• **bring up** [*v + o + adv, v + adv + o*] **(a)** (rear) ‹*child*› criar* **(b)** (mention) ‹*subject*› sacar* **(c)** (vomit) vomitar, devolver*

brink /brɪŋk/ *n* borde *m*; **to be on the ~ of -ING** estar* a punto de + INF

brisk /brɪsk/ *adj* **(a)** (lively, quick) ‹*pace*› rápido y enérgico; ‹*walk*› a paso ligero; **ice-cream sellers did a ~ trade** los vendedores de helados vendieron muchísimo **(b)** (efficient) ‹*person/manner*› enérgico *or* dinámico y eficiente

bristle¹ /ˈbrɪsəl/ *n* [C U] (on animal) cerda *f*; (on person): **his face was covered in ~(s)** tenía la barba crecida

bristle² *vi* **(a)** (stand up) «*hair*» erizarse*, ponerse* de punta **(b)** (show annoyance) erizarse*

Britain /ˈbrɪtn ‖ ˈbrɪtən/ *n* Gran Bretaña *f*

British¹ /ˈbrɪtɪʃ/ *adj* británico

British² *pl n* **the ~** los británicos

Britisher /ˈbrɪtɪʃər ‖ ˈbrɪtɪʃə(r)/ *n* (AmE) británico, -ca *m,f*

British: ~ **Isles** *pl n* **the ~ Isles** las Islas Británicas; ~ **Summer Time** *n* [U] *hora de verano en Gran Bretaña, adelantada en una hora con respecto a la hora de Greenwich*

Briton /'brɪtn̩ || 'brɪtən/ *n* ciudadano británico, ciudadana británica *m,f*; **the ancient ~s** los antiguos britanos

Brittany /'brɪtn̩i || 'brɪtəni/ *n* Bretaña *f*

brittle /'brɪtl̩/ *adj* quebradizo

broach /brəʊtʃ/ *vt* ‹*subject*› mencionar

broad¹ /brɔːd/ *adj* **1** ‹*avenue*› ancho; ‹*valley*› grande; ‹*forehead*› despejado; ‹*grin*› de oreja a oreja **2 (a)** (extensive) ‹*syllabus*› amplio; ‹*interests*› numeroso; **in its ~est sense** en su sentido más amplio **(b)** (general) ‹*guidelines/conclusions*› general **3 (a)** **a ~ hint** una indirecta muy clara **(b)** ‹*accent*› cerrado

broad² *n* (woman) (AmE sl) tipa *f* (fam), vieja *f* (Col, Méx, Ven fam)

broad bean *n* haba *f*

broadcast¹ /'brɔːdkæst || 'brɔːdkɑːst/ *vt/i* (*past & past p* **broadcast**) transmitir, emitir

broadcast² *n* programa *m*, emisión *f* (frml)

broadcaster /'brɔːdkæstər || 'brɔːdkɑːstə(r)/ *n*: *presentador, locutor etc de radio o televisión*

broadcasting /'brɔːdkæstɪŋ || 'brɔːdkɑːstɪŋ/ *n* [U] (Rad) radiodifusión *f*; (TV) televisión *f*

broaden /'brɔːdn̩/ *vt* ‹*scope/horizons/interests*› ampliar*

broadly /'brɔːdli/ *adv*: **the two systems are ~ similar** en líneas generales, los dos sistemas son similares; **~ speaking** en líneas generales

broad: **~minded** /'brɔːd'maɪndəd || ˌbrɔːd'maɪndɪd/ *adj* de criterio amplio; **~sheet** *n*: *periódico de formato grande*

brocade /brəʊ'keɪd || brə'keɪd/ *n* [U] brocado *m*

broccoli /'brɑːkəli || 'brɒkəli/ *n* [U] brócoli *m*, brécol *m*

brochure /brəʊ'ʃʊr || 'brəʊʃə(r)/ *n* folleto *m*

brogue /brəʊg/ *n* **1** (shoe) *zapato bajo de cuero* **2** (Irish accent) (*no pl*) acento *m* irlandés

broil /brɔɪl/ (esp AmE) *vt* asar a la parrilla *or* al grill

broiler /'brɔɪlər || 'brɔɪlə(r)/ *n* (AmE) parrilla *f*, grill *m*

broke¹ /brəʊk/ *past of* BREAK¹

broke² *adj* (colloq) (*pred*): **to be ~** estar* pelado

broken¹ /'brəʊkən/ *past p of* BREAK¹

broken² *adj* **1 (a)** ‹*window/vase/chair/glass*› roto; ‹*bone*› roto, quebrado (AmL) **(b)** (not working) roto **2** ‹*voice*› quebrado; **to die of a ~ heart** morirse* de pena; **he's a ~ man** está destrozado **3** ‹*home/marriage*› deshecho **4** (imperfect): **in ~ English** en inglés chapurreado

broken-down /'brəʊkən'daʊn/ *adj* ‹*car/machine*› averiado, descompuesto (AmL), en pana (Chi), varado (Col); ‹*shed/gate*› destartalado

broker /'brəʊkər || 'brəʊkə(r)/ *n* **(a)** (agent) agente *mf*; **insurance ~** agente *mf* de seguros **(b)** (*stock~*) corredor, -dora *m,f* de bolsa

bronchitis /brɑːŋ'kaɪtəs || brɒŋ'kaɪtɪs/ *n* [U] bronquitis *f*

bronze /brɑːnz || brɒnz/ *n* [U] (Metall) bronce *m*

brooch /brəʊtʃ/ *n* prendedor *m*, broche *m*

brood¹ /bruːd/ *n* (of birds) nidada *f*; (of mammals) camada *f*; (of children) (hum) prole *f* (fam & hum)

brood² *vi* (reflect): **she sat ~ing on the unfairness of life** rumiaba lo injusta que era la vida; **stop ~ing over it** deja de darle vueltas al asunto

brook /brʊk/ *n* arroyo *m*

broom /bruːm/ *n* **1** [C] (brush) escoba *f* **2** [U] (plant) retama *f*, hiniesta *f*

broomstick /'bruːmstɪk/ *n* palo *m* de escoba; (of a witch) escoba *f*

broth /brɔːθ || brɒθ/ *n* [U] caldo *m*

brothel /'brɑːθəl || 'brɒθəl/ *n* burdel *m*

brother /'brʌðər || 'brʌðə(r)/ *n* hermano *m*; **do you have any ~s and sisters?** ¿tienes hermanos?

brotherhood /'brʌðərhʊd || 'brʌðəhʊd/ *n* **(a)** [U] (fellowship) fraternidad *f* **(b)** [C] (association) hermandad *f*; (Relig) cofradía *f*

brother-in-law /'brʌðərɪnˌlɔː/ *n* (*pl* **brothers-in-law**) cuñado *m*

brotherly /'brʌðərli || 'brʌðəli/ *adj* fraternal

brought /brɔːt/ *past & past p of* BRING

brow /braʊ/ ▶**484** *n* **(a)** (forehead) (liter) frente *f* **(b)** (*eye~*) ceja *f* **(c)** (of hill) cima *f*

browbeat /'braʊbiːt/ *vt* (*past* **browbeat**; *past p* **browbeaten** /'braʊˌbiːtn̩/) intimidar

brown¹ /braʊn/ ▶**515** *adj* **-er, -est** ‹*shoe/dress/eyes*› marrón, café *adj inv* (AmC, Chi, Méx), carmelito (Col); ‹*hair*› castaño; ‹*skin/person*› (naturally) moreno; (suntanned) bronceado; **to get ~** broncearse

brown² ▶**515** *n* [U] marrón *m*, café *m* (AmC, Chi, Méx), carmelito *m* (Col)

brown³ *vt* **(a)** (Culin) dorar **(b)** (tan) broncear

brown bread *n* pan *m* negro *or* (Esp) moreno

brownie /'braʊni/ *n* **1** (cake) *bizcocho de chocolate y nueces* **2 Brownie**, (BrE) **Brownie (Guide)** alita *f*

brown: **~ paper** *n* [U] papel *m* de estraza; **~ rice** *n* arroz *m* integral; **~ sugar** *n* [U] azúcar *m* moreno, azúcar *f* morena

browse /braʊz/ *vi* (look) mirar (*en una tienda, catálogo etc*); **she was browsing through a magazine** estaba hojeando una revista

bruise¹ /bruːz/ *n* moretón *m*, cardenal *m*, morado *m* (Esp, Ven)

bruise² *vt* ‹*body/arm*› contusionar (frml); ‹*fruit*› magullar, mallugar* (Méx, Ven)

brunch /brʌntʃ/ *n* [U C] (colloq) brunch *m* (*combinación de desayuno y almuerzo*)

brunette /bruː'net/ *n* morena *f*, morocha *f* (CS)

brunt /brʌnt/ *n*: **to bear** *o* **take the ~ of sth** sufrir algo

brush¹ /brʌʃ/ *n* **1** [C] (for cleaning) cepillo *m*; (for hair) cepillo *m*; (*paint~*) pincel *m*; (large) brocha *f* **2** [C] (of fox) cola *f* **3** [C] **(a)** (act): **I gave my hair a ~** me cepillé el pelo **(b)** (faint touch) roce *m* **(c)** (encounter) **~** WITH **sth/sb** ‹*with the law/the police*› roce *m* CON algo/algn **4** [U] (scrub) maleza *f*

brush² *vt* **(a)** (clean, groom) ‹*jacket/hair*› cepillar; **to ~ one's teeth** lavarse los dientes **(b)** (sweep): **he**

~ed the crumbs off the table quitó las migas de la mesa **(c)** (touch lightly) rozar* ■ ~ *vi* **to ~ AGAINST sth/sb** rozar* algo/a algn
• **brush off** [*v + o + adv, v + adv + o*] **(a)** ‹*mud/hair*› quitar (*cepillando*) **(b)** ‹*advances/suggestions*› no hacer* caso de
• **brush up (a)** [*v + o + adv, v + adv + o*] (colloq) darle* un repaso a **(b)** [*v + adv*] **to ~ up ON sth** darle* un repaso A algo

brusque /brʌsk ‖ brʊsk/ *adj* brusco

Brussels /'brʌsəlz/ *n* Bruselas *f*

brussels sprout, **Brussels Sprout** *n* col *f or* (AmS) repollito *m* de Bruselas

brutal /'bru:tl̩/ *adj* brutal

brutality /bru:'tæləti/ *n* [U C] (*pl* **-ties**) brutalidad *f*

brutally /'bru:tl̩i/ *adv* **(a)** (cruelly) ‹*attack/treat*› brutalmente **(b)** (mercilessly) ‹*frank*› crudamente

brute¹ /bru:t/ *n* (colloq) **(a)** (person) animal *mf* (fam) **(b)** (animal) bestia *f* (fam)

brute² *adj* (*before n*) **~ force** fuerza *f* bruta

BS *n* (AmE), **BSc** *n* (BrE) = **Bachelor of Science**

BST = **British Summer Time**

bubble¹ /'bʌbəl/ *n* (of air, gas) burbuja *f*; (of soap) pompa *f*

bubble² *vi* **1** (form bubbles) «*lava*» bullir*; «*champagne*» burbujear **2** «*person*»: **she ~s with enthusiasm** rebosa (de) entusiasmo

bubble: **~ bath** *n* [C U] baño *m* de burbujas *or* espuma; **~ gum** *n* [U] chicle *m* (de globos), chicle *m* de bomba (Col, Ven), chicle *m* globero (Ur)

bubbly /'bʌbli/ *adj* **-lier, -liest (a)** ‹*person*› lleno de vida; ‹*personality*› efervescente **(b)** (full of bubbles) burbujeante

Bucharest /'bu:kərest ‖ ˌbu:kə'rest/ *n* Bucarest *m*

buck¹ /bʌk/ *n* **1** (male deer) ciervo *m* (macho); (male rabbit) conejo *m* (macho) **2** (dollar) (esp AmE colloq) dólar *m*, verde *m* (AmL fam) **3** (responsibility): ***to pass the ~*** (colloq) pasar la pelota (fam); **the ~ stops here** la responsabilidad es mía (*or* nuestra *etc*)

buck² *vi* «*horse*» corcovear ■ ~ *vt* ‹*trend*› resistirse a
• **buck up** (colloq) **1** [*v + adv*] (become cheerful) levantar el ánimo **2** [*v + o + adv, v + adv + o*] (cheer up) ‹*person*› levantarle el ánimo a

bucket /'bʌkət ‖ 'bʌkɪt/ *n* balde *m or* (Esp) cubo *m or* (Méx) cubeta *f or* (Ven) tobo *m*

buckle¹ /'bʌkəl/ *n* hebilla *f*

buckle² *vt* abrochar ■ ~ *vi* (bend, crumple) «*wheel/metal*» torcerse*; **his knees ~d beneath him** se le doblaron las rodillas

bud /bʌd/ *n* brote *m*, yema *f*; (of flower) capullo *m*

Budapest /'bu:dəpest ‖ ˌbu:də'pest/ *n* Budapest *m*

Buddha /'bu:də ‖ 'bʊdə/ *n* Buda *m*

Buddhism /'bu:dɪzəm ‖ 'bʊdɪzəm/ *n* [U] budismo *m*

Buddhist¹ /'bu:dəst ‖ 'bʊdɪst/ *n* budista *mf*

Buddhist² *adj* budista

budding /'bʌdɪŋ/ *adj* (*before n*) ‹*artist/genius*› en ciernes

buddy /'bʌdi/ *n* (*pl* **-dies**) (AmE colloq) amigo *m*, compinche *m* (fam), cuate *m* (Méx fam)

budge /bʌdʒ/ *vi* (*usu with neg*) **(a)** (move) moverse* **(b)** (change opinion) cambiar de opinión ■ ~ *vt* **(a)** (move) correr **(b)** (persuade) convencer*

budgerigar /'bʌdʒərigɑ:r ‖ 'bʌdʒərigɑ:(r)/ *n* periquito *m*

budget¹ /'bʌdʒət ‖ 'bʌdʒɪt/ *n* presupuesto *m*

budget² *vi* administrarse; **to learn to ~** aprender a administrar el dinero; **I hadn't ~ed for staying in a hotel** no había contado con gastos de hotel

buff¹ /bʌf/ *n* (colloq) aficionado, -da *m,f*; **film ~** cinéfilo, -la *m,f*

buff² *vt* ‹*metal*› pulir; ‹*shoes*› sacar* brillo a

buffalo /'bʌfələʊ/ *n* (*pl* **-loes** *or* **-los**) **(a)** (wild ox) búfalo *m*; (*water ~*) búfalo *m* de agua, carabao *m* **(b)** (bison) (AmE) bisonte *m*

buffer /'bʌfər ‖ 'bʌfə(r)/ *n* **1 (a)** (AmE Auto) parachoques *m*, paragolpes *m* (RPl) **(b)** (BrE Rail) (on train) tope *m*; (in station) parachoques *m*; (*before n*) **~ state** estado *m* tapón **2** (Comput) memoria *f* intermedia

buffet¹ /bə'feɪ ‖ 'bʊfeɪ, 'bʌfeɪ/ *n* **1** (meal) buffet *m* **2** (BrE) **(a)** (in train) bar *m*; (*before n*) **~ car** (also AmE) coche *m* restaurante, coche *m* comedor **(b)** (cafeteria) bar *m* (*en una estación*)

buffet² /'bʌfət ‖ bʌfɪt/ *vt* zarandear, sacudir

bug¹ /bʌg/ *n* **1** (biting insect) chinche *f or m*; (any insect) (esp AmE) bicho *m* **2** (germ, disease) (colloq): **he picked up a stomach ~** se agarró algo al estómago; **she got the travel ~** le entró la fiebre de los viajes **3** (listening device) (colloq) micrófono *m* oculto

bug² *vt* **-gg-** (colloq) **1** ‹*room/telephone*› colocar* micrófonos ocultos en **2** (bother, irritate) fastidiar

bugger /'bʌgər ‖ 'bʌgə(r)/ *n* (BrE vulg) hijo, -ja *m,f* de puta (vulg)

buggy /'bʌgi/ *n* (*pl* **-gies**) **1** (horse-drawn vehicle) calesa *f* **2** (*baby ~*) (baby carriage) (AmE) cochecito *m*; (pushchair) (BrE) sillita *f* de paseo (*plegable*)

bugle /'bju:gəl/ *n* clarín *m*

build¹ /bɪld/ (*past & past p* **built**) *vt* ‹*house/road/ship/wall*› construir*; ‹*fire/nest*› hacer*
• **build up 1** [*v + o + adv, v + adv + o*] **(a)** (make bigger, stronger) fortalecer* **(b)** (accumulate) ‹*supplies/experience*› acumular; ‹*reserves*› acrecentar* **(c)** (develop) ‹*reputation*› forjarse; **to ~ up one's hopes** hacerse* ilusiones; **he built the firm up from nothing** levantó la empresa de la nada **2** [*v + adv*] (increase) «*pressure/noise*» ir* en aumento; **the tension ~s up to a climax** la tensión va en aumento hasta llegar a un punto culminante

build² *n* complexión *f*

builder /'bɪldər ‖ 'bɪldə(r)/ *n* albañil *mf*; (contractor) contratista *mf*

building /'bɪldɪŋ/ *n* **(a)** [C] (edifice) edificio *m* **(b)** [U] (construction) construcción *f*; (*before n*) **~ contractor** contratista *mf* (de obras); **~ site** obra *f*

building society *n* (in UK) sociedad *f* de crédito hipotecario

buildup /'bɪldʌp/ *n* **(a)** (accumulation) acumulación *f*; (of tension, pressure) aumento *m* **(b)** (of troops) concentración *f* **(c)** (publicity) propaganda *f*

built /bɪlt/ *past & past p of* BUILD[1]

built: **~-in** /'bɪlt'ɪn/ *adj (before n)* ‹*bookcase/desk*› empotrado; ‹*equipment*› fijo; ‹*mechanism/feature*› incorporado; **~-up** /'bɪlt'ʌp/ *adj (before n)* ‹*area*› urbanizado

bulb /bʌlb/ *n* **1** (Bot, Hort) (of flower) bulbo *m*, papa *f* (Chi); (of garlic) cabeza *f* **2** (*light* **~**) bombilla *f or* (Méx) foco *m or* (Col, Ven) bombillo *m or* (RPl) bombita *f or* lamparita *f or* (Chi) ampolleta *f or* (AmC) bujía *f*

bulbous /'bʌlbəs/ *adj* ‹*growth*› bulboso; ‹*nose*› protuberante

Bulgaria /bʌl'geriə ‖ bʌl'geəriə/ *n* Bulgaria *f*

Bulgarian[1] /bʌl'geriən ‖ bʌl'geəriən/ *adj* búlgaro

Bulgarian[2] *n* **(a)** [C] (person) búlgaro, -ra *m,f* **(b)** [U] (language) búlgaro *m*

bulge[1] /bʌldʒ/ *n* bulto *m*

bulge[2] *vi* **(a)** (protrude) sobresalir*; **the bag was bulging with books** la bolsa estaba repleta de libros **(b)** **bulging** *pres p* ‹*pocket/bag*› repleto; ‹*eyes*› saltón

bulimia (nervosa) /bju:'li:miə(nɜ:r'vəʊsə) ‖ bju:'lɪmiə(nɜ:'vəʊsə)/ *n* [U] bulimia *f* (nerviosa)

bulk /bʌlk/ *n* [U] **1 (a)** (Busn) (large quantity): **in ~** en grandes cantidades **(b)** (large mass) mole *f* **2** (largest part): **the ~ of sth** la mayor parte de algo

bulky /'bʌlki/ *adj* **-kier, -kiest** ‹*package*› voluminoso; ‹*person*› corpulento; ‹*sweater*› (AmE) grueso

bull /bʊl/ *n* toro *m*

bull: **~dog** *n* bul(l)dog *m*; **~doze** *vt* demoler*; **~dozer** /'bʊldəʊzər ‖ 'bʊldəʊzə(r)/ *n* bulldozer *m*, topadora *f* (Arg)

bullet /'bʊlət ‖ 'bʊlɪt/ *n* bala *f*

bulletin /'bʊlətn̩ ‖ 'bʊlətɪn/ *n* (notice) anuncio *m*; (newsletter) boletín *m*; (report) (Journ) boletín *m* (informativo)

bulletin board *n* (AmE) tablero *m or* (Esp) tablón *m* de anuncios, cartelera *f* (AmL), diario *m* mural (Chi)

bulletproof /'bʊlətpru:f ‖ 'bʊlɪtpru:f/ *adj* ‹*vest*› antibalas *adj inv*; ‹*vehicle*› blindado

bull: **~fight** *n* corrida *f* de toros; **~fighter** *n* torero, -ra *m,f*; **~fighting** *n* [U] (deporte *m* de) los toros; (art) tauromaquia *f*; **~frog** *n* rana *f* toro

bullion /'bʊljən ‖ 'bʊliən/ *n* [U]: **gold/silver ~** oro/plata en lingotes

bullock /'bʊlək/ *n* **(a)** (castrated bull) buey *m* **(b)** (young bull) (esp AmE) novillo *m*

bull: **~ring** *n* plaza *f* de toros; **~seye** *n* diana *f*; **~shit** /'bʊlʃɪt/ *n* [U] (vulg) sandeces *fpl* (fam), pendejadas (AmL exc CS vulg), gilipolleces *fpl* (Esp arg), huevadas *fpl* (Andes, Ven vulg), boludeces *fpl* (Col, RPl vulg), mamadas *fpl* (Méx vulg)

bully[1] /'bʊli/ *n* (*pl* **-lies**) matón, -tona *m,f*

bully[2] *vt* **-lies, -lying, -lied** intimidar

bum /bʌm/ *n* (colloq) **1 (a)** (worthless person) vago, -ga *m,f* (fam) **(b)** (vagrant) (AmE) vagabundo, -da *m,f* **2** (buttocks) (BrE) trasero *m* (fam), culo *m* (fam *o* vulg), traste *m* (CS fam), poto *m* (Chi, Per fam)

bumblebee /'bʌmbəl,bi:/ *n* abejorro *m*

bumbling /'bʌmblɪŋ/ *adj* torpe

bump[1] /bʌmp/ *n* **1** (blow) golpe *m*; (jolt) sacudida *f*; (collision) topetazo *m* **2** (lump — in surface) bulto *m*; (— on head) chichón *m*; (— on road) bache *m*

bump[2] *vt*: **I ~ed my elbow on** *o* **against the door** me di en el codo con *or* contra la puerta; **I ~ed the post as I was reversing** choqué con *or* contra el poste al dar marcha atrás ■ **~** *vi* (hit, knock) **to ~** (AGAINST **sth**) darse* *or* chocar* (CONTRA *or* CON algo)

• bump into [*v + prep + o*] **(a)** (collide with) darse* *or* chocar* contra **(b)** (meet by chance) (colloq) toparse *or* tropezarse* con

bumper[1] /'bʌmpər ‖ 'bʌmpə(r)/ *n* (Auto) parachoques *m*, paragolpes *m* (AmL)

bumper[2] *adj (before n)* ‹*crop/year*› récord *adj inv*; ‹*edition*› extra; ‹*pack*› gigante

bumper car *n* coche *m* de choque, autito *m* chocador (RPl), carro *m* loco (Andes), carrito *m* chocón (Méx, Ven)

bumpkin /'bʌmpkɪn/ *n*: **(country) ~** pueblerino, -na *m,f*, paleto, -ta *m,f* (Esp fam), pajuerano, -na *m,f* (RPl fam)

bumpy /'bʌmpi/ *adj* **-pier, -piest** ‹*surface*› desigual; ‹*road*› lleno de baches; **we had a ~ flight** el avión se movió mucho

bun /bʌn/ *n* **1 (a)** (sweetened) bollo *m* **(b)** (bread roll) panecillo *m*, pancito *m* (CS), bolillo *m* (Méx) **2** (hairstyle) moño *m*, rodete *m* (RPl), chongo *m* (Méx) **3** **buns** *pl* (AmE colloq) trasero *m* (fam), culo *m* (fam *o* vulg), traste *m* (CS fam), poto *m* (Chi, Per fam)

bunch /bʌntʃ/ *n* **(a)** (of flowers) ramo *m*, bonche *m* (Méx); (small) ramillete *m*; (of bananas) racimo *m*, penca *f* (Méx), cacho *m* (RPl); (of grapes) racimo *m*; (of keys) manojo *m* **(b)** (group) grupo *m*; **they're an odd ~** son gente de lo más rara

bundle[1] /'bʌndl̩/ *n* (of clothes) lío *m*, fardo *m*, atado *m* (AmL); (of newspapers, letters) paquete *m*; (of money) fajo *m*; (of sticks) haz *m*, atado *m* (AmL)

bundle[2] *vt* **(a)** (make into a bundle) liar*, atar **(b)** (push) (+ *adv compl*): **she ~d them off to school** los despachó al colegio; **they ~d him into the car** lo metieron a empujones en el coche

bung /bʌŋ/ *n* tapón *m*

bungalow /'bʌŋgələʊ/ *n* casa *f* de una planta

bungle /'bʌŋgəl/ *vt* echar a perder; **a ~d attempt** un intento fallido

bungling /'bʌŋglɪŋ/ *adj* (*before n, no comp*) torpe

bunion /'bʌnjən/ *n* juanete *m*

bunk /bʌŋk/ *n* litera *f*

• bunk off ⇒ SKIVE OFF

bunk bed *n* litera *f*

bunny (*pl* **-nies**), **bunny rabbit** /'bʌni/ *n* (used to or by children) conejito *m* (fam)

bunting /'bʌntɪŋ/ *n* [U] (esp AmE) *tela usada para la confección de banderas*

buoy /bɔɪ, 'bu:i ‖ bɔɪ/ *n* boya *f*

• buoy up [*v + o + adv, v + adv + o*] **(a)** ‹*boat/person*› mantener* a flote **(b)** (keep cheerful) animar

buoyant /'bɔɪənt/ *adj* **(a)** (able to float) flotante **(b)** ‹*mood/spirits*› optimista **(c)** (Fin) ‹*currency*› fuerte; ‹*market*› alcista

burble /'bɜːrbəl ‖ 'bɜːbəl/ *vi* **(a)** «*stream/spring*» borbotar, borbotear **(b)** (talk meaninglessly) parlotear (fam), cotorrear (fam); (talk excitedly) hablar atropelladamente

burden¹ /'bɜːrdn̩ ‖ 'bɜːdn̩/ *n* carga *f*

burden² *vt* cargar*; **I don't want to ~ you with my problems** no te quiero preocupar con mis problemas

bureau /'bjʊrəʊ ‖ 'bjʊərəʊ/ *n* (*pl* **bureaus** *or* **bureaux** /-z/) **1 (a)** (agency) agencia *f* **(b)** (government department) (AmE) departamento *m* **2 (a)** (chest of drawers) (AmE) cómoda *f* **(b)** (desk) (BrE) buró *m*, escritorio *m*

bureaucracy /bjʊ'rɑːkrəsi ‖ bjʊə'rɒkrəsi/ *n* [U C] (*pl* **-cies**) burocracia *f*

bureaucrat /'bjʊrəkræt ‖ 'bjʊərəkræt/ *n* burócrata *mf*

bureaucratic /'bjʊrə'krætɪk ‖ ˌbjʊərə'krætɪk/ *adj* burocrático

bureau de change /'bjʊrəʊdə'ʃɑːnʒ ‖ 'bjʊərəʊdə'ʃɑ̃ʒ/ *n* (*pl* **bureaux de change**) (casa *f* de) cambio *m*

burgeon /'bɜːrdʒən ‖ 'bɜːdʒən/ *vi* (liter) florecer*

burger /'bɜːrgər ‖ 'bɜːgə(r)/ *n* (colloq) hamburguesa *f*

burglar /'bɜːrglər ‖ 'bɜːglə(r)/ *n* ladrón, -drona *m,f*; (*before n*) **~ alarm** alarma *f* antirrobo

burglarize /'bɜːrgləraɪz ‖ 'bɜːgləraɪz/ *vt* (AmE) robar

burglary /'bɜːrgləri ‖ 'bɜːgləri/ *n* [C U] (*pl* **-ries**) robo *m* (*con allanamiento de morada o escalamiento*)

burgle /'bɜːrgəl ‖ 'bɜːgəl/ *vt* robar

burial /'beriəl/ *n* [C U] entierro *m*

Burkina Faso /bɜːr'kiːnə'fæsəʊ ‖ ˌbɜːkiːnə'fæsəʊ/ *n* Burkina Faso *m*

burlesque /bɜːr'lesk ‖ bɜː'lesk/ *n* [C U] obra *f* burlesca

burly /'bɜːrli ‖ 'bɜːli/ *adj* **-lier, -liest** fornido

Burma /'bɜːrmə ‖ 'bɜːmə/ *n* Birmania *f*

Burmese¹ /'bɜːr'miːz ‖ bɜː'miːz/ *adj* birmano

Burmese² *n* (*pl* **~**) **(a)** [C] (person) birmano, -na *m,f* **(b)** [U] (language) birmano *m*

burn¹ /bɜːrn ‖ bɜːn/ (*past & past p* **burned** *or* **burnt**) *vi* **1 (a)** «*fire/building/wood/coal*» arder; «*food*» quemarse **(b)** (in sun) «*skin*» quemarse **2** (sting) «*eyes/wound*» escocer*, arder (esp AmL); **a ~ing sensation** un escozor, un ardor (esp AmL) ■ **~** *vt* **(a)** ‹*letter/rubbish/food*› quemar; ‹*building/town*› incendiar; **I ~ed a hole in my sleeve** me quemé la manga (*con un cigarrillo etc*) **(b)** (injure) quemar

• **burn down 1** [*v + o + adv, v + adv + o*] incendiar **2** [*v + adv*] incendiarse

burn² *n* quemadura *f*

burner /'bɜːrnər ‖ 'bɜːnə(r)/ *n* quemador *m*

burning /'bɜːrnɪŋ ‖ 'bɜːnɪŋ/ *adj* (*before n*) **(a)** (hot) ‹*sand*› ardiente; ‹*sun*› abrasador **(b)** (intense) ‹*desire*› ardiente; ‹*hatred*› violento

burnt /bɜːrnt ‖ bɜːnt/ *past & past p of* BURN¹

burp *vi* eructar

burrow¹ /'bərəʊ ‖ 'bʌrəʊ/ *n* madriguera *f*; (of rabbits) conejera *f*

burrow² *vi* cavar

bursar /'bɜːrsər ‖ 'bɜːsə(r)/ *n* administrador, -dora *m,f*

burst¹ /bɜːrst ‖ bɜːst/ (*past & past p* **burst**) *vi* **1** «*balloon/tire*» reventarse*; «*pipe*» reventar*, romperse*; «*dam*» romperse*; **to ~ open** abrirse* de golpe **2** (move suddenly) (+ *adv compl*): **he ~ into the room** entró de sopetón en la habitación; **they ~ through the police cordon** rompieron el cordón policial ■ **~** *vt* ‹*balloon/bubble*› reventar*; **the river ~ its banks** el río se desbordó

• **burst into** [*v + prep + o*]: **to ~ into tears** echarse a llorar; **to ~ into song** ponerse* a cantar; **to ~ into flames** estallar en llamas

burst² *n* **1** (of applause) salva *f*; (of activity) arrebato *m*; (of gunfire) ráfaga *f* **2** (of pipe) rotura *f*

bursting /'bɜːrstɪŋ ‖ 'bɜːstɪŋ/ *adj* (*pred, no comp*) **to be ~** (WITH **sth**) estar* repleto (DE algo); **he was ~ with energy** rebosaba (de) energía

bury /'beri/ **buries, burying, buried** *vt* (inter) enterrar*; **the village was buried by the avalanche** el pueblo fue sepultado por la avalancha; **he buried his head in his hands** ocultó la cabeza entre las manos ■ *v refl* **to ~ oneself** IN **sth** ‹*in one's work/one's books*› enfrascarse* EN algo

bus /bʌs/ *n* (*pl* **buses** *or* (AmE also) **busses**) (Transp) **(a)** (local) autobús *m*, bus *m* (AmL), camión *m* (AmC, Méx), colectivo *m* (Arg), ómnibus *m* (Per, Ur), micro *f* (Chi), guagua *f* (Cu); (*before n*) **~ conductor** cobrador, -dora *m,f*, guarda *mf* (RPl) de autobuses; **~ driver** conductor, -tora *m,f* *or* chofer *mf* *or* (Esp) chófer *mf* de autobús, camionero, -ra *m,f* (AmC, Méx), colectivero, -ra *m,f* (Arg), microbusero, -ra *m,f* (Chi); **~ stop** parada *f* *or* (AmL exc RPl) paradero *m* de autobús (*or* bus *etc*) **(b)** (long-distance) autobús *m*, autocar *m* (Esp), pullman *m* (CS)

bush /bʊʃ/ *n* **1** [C] (shrub) arbusto *m*; ***to beat about the ~*** andarse* con rodeos **2** [U] (wild country) **the ~** el monte

bushy /'bʊʃi/ *adj* **bushier, bushiest** ‹*beard*› poblado; ‹*eyebrows*› tupido; ‹*undergrowth*› espeso

busily /'bɪzəli ‖ 'bɪzɪli/ *adv* ‹*work*› afanosamente

business /'bɪznəs ‖ 'bɪznɪs/ *n* **1** [U] (Busn) **(a)** (world of commerce, finance) negocios *mpl*; (*before n*) **~ studies** (ciencias *fpl*) empresariales *fpl* **(b)** (commercial activity, trading) comercio *m*; **the firm has been in ~ for 50 years** la empresa tiene 50 años de actividad comercial; **they went into ~ together** montaron un negocio juntos; **she's away on ~** está de viaje por negocios; **to go out of ~** cerrar*; ***to get down to ~*** ir* al grano; ***to mean ~*** decir* algo muy en serio; (*before n*) ‹*appointment/lunch*› de trabajo, de negocios; **~ letter** carta *f* comercial; **~ trip** viaje *m* de negocios **(c)** (custom, clients): **to lose ~** perder* clientes *or* clientela **2** [C] **(a)** (firm) negocio *m*, empresa *f* **(b)** (branch of commerce): **I'm in the antiques ~** trabajo en la compra y venta de antigüedades; **the music ~** la industria de la música **3** [U] (rightful occupation, concern) asunto *m*; **mind your own ~!** ¡no te metas en lo que no te importa!;

that's none of your ~ eso no es asunto tuyo **4** (affair, situation, activity) (colloq) (*no pl*) asunto *m*; **what's all this ~ about you leaving?** ¿qué es eso de que te vas?

business: **~like** *adj* ‹*person/manner*› (serious) formal; (efficient) eficiente; ‹*discussion*› serio; **~man** /ˈbɪznəsmæn ‖ ˈbɪznɪsmən/ *n* (*pl* **-men** /-men ‖ -mən/) empresario *m*, hombre *m* de negocios; **~woman** *n* empresaria *f*, mujer *f* de negocios

busker /ˈbʌskər ‖ ˈbʌskə(r)/ *n* (BrE) músico *m* callejero

bust¹ /ˈbʌst/ *vt* **(a)** (*past & past p* **busted** *or* (BrE also) **bust**) (break) (colloq) romper* **(b)** (*past & past p* **busted**) (raid) (sl) ‹*person*› agarrar (fam), trincar* (Esp fam); ‹*premises*› hacer* una redada en

bust² *n* **(a)** (sculpture) busto *m* **(b)** (bosom) busto *m*, pecho *m*

bust³ *adj* (bankrupt) (colloq): **to go ~** quebrar*, ir(se)* a la bancarrota, fundirse (Per, RPl fam)

bustle¹ /ˈbʌsəl/ *vi* **(a)** (move busily): **to ~ around** ir* de aquí para allá **(b)** (be crowded, lively) «*street/store*» **to ~ (WITH sth)** bullir* (DE algo)

bustle² *n* [U] ajetreo *m*

bustling /ˈbʌslɪŋ/ *adj* ‹*street/shop*› animado

bust-up /ˈbʌstʌp/ *n* (breakup) ruptura *f*

busy¹ /ˈbɪzi/ *adj* **busier, busiest 1** ‹*person*› ocupado; **the children keep me very ~** los niños me tienen muy atareada **2** ‹*street/market*› concurrido; **I've had a ~ day** he tenido un día de mucho trabajo; **a ~ road** una carretera con mucho tráfico **3** (AmE Telec) ocupado (AmL), comunicando (Esp); **the ~ signal** la señal de ocupado *or* (Esp) de comunicando

busy² *v refl* **busies, busying, busied**: **to ~ oneself WITH sth** entretenerse* CON algo

busybody /ˈbɪziˌbɑːdi ‖ ˈbɪziˌbɒdi/ *n* (*pl* **-dies**) (colloq) entrometido, -da *m,f*, metomentodo *mf* (fam), metiche *mf* (AmL fam)

but¹ /bʌt, *weak form* bət/ *conj* pero; **not … ~ …** no … sino …; **~ then you never were very ambitious, were you?** pero la verdad es que tú nunca fuiste muy ambicioso ¿no?; **not only did she hit him, ~ she also** … no sólo le pegó, sino que también …

but² *prep*: **everyone ~ me** todos menos *or* excepto yo; **the last street ~ one** la penúltima calle; **~ for them, we'd have lost everything** de no haber sido por ellos, habríamos perdido todo

but³ *adv* (frml): **we can ~ try** con intentarlo no se pierde nada

butane /ˈbjuːteɪn/ *n* [U] butano *m*

butcher¹ /ˈbʊtʃər ‖ ˈbʊtʃə(r)/ *n* **(a)** (meat dealer) carnicero, -ra *m,f*; **~'s (shop)** carnicería *f* **(b)** (murderer) asesino, -na *m,f*

butcher² *vt* **(a)** ‹*cattle/pig*› matar, carnear (CS) **(b)** ‹*people*› masacrar

butler /ˈbʌtlər ‖ ˈbʌtlə(r)/ *n* mayordomo *m*

butt¹ /bʌt/ *n* **1 (a)** (of rifle) culata *f* **(b) ~ (end)** (blunt end) extremo *m* **(c)** (of cigarette) colilla *f*, bacha *f* (Méx fam) **2** (target of jokes or criticism) blanco *m* **3 (a)** (from goat) topetazo *m* **(b)** (*head ~*) cabezazo *m* **4** (buttocks) (AmE colloq) trasero *m* (fam), culo *m* (fam *o* vulg), traste *m* (CS fam), poto *m* (Chi, Per fam)

butt² *vt* «*goat*» topetar

• butt in [*v* + *adv*] interrumpir

butter¹ /ˈbʌtər ‖ ˈbʌtə(r)/ *n* [U] mantequilla *f*, manteca *f* (RPl)

butter² *vt* ‹*bread*› untar con mantequilla *or* (RPl) manteca

butter: **~ bean** *n* **(a)** (dried bean) *tipo de frijol blanco*, poroto *m* de manteca (RPl) **(b)** (wax bean) (AmE) *tipo de frijol fresco con vaina amarilla*; **~cup** *n* ranúnculo *m*; **~fly** *n* **(a)** [C] (Zool) mariposa *f*; **to have ~flies (in one's stomach)** ponerse*/estar* nervioso **(b)** [U] (swimming stroke) estilo *m* mariposa

buttock /ˈbʌtək/ *n* nalga *f*

button¹ /ˈbʌtn/ *n* botón *m*

button² *vt* abotonar ■ **~** *vi* abotonarse

• button up [*v* + *o* + *adv*, *v* + *adv* + *o*] abotonar

buttonhole /ˈbʌtn̩həʊl/ *n* **(a)** (Clothing) ojal *m* **(b)** (flower) (BrE) *flor que se lleva en el ojal*

buttress /ˈbʌtrəs ‖ ˈbʌtrɪs/ *n* (Archit) contrafuerte *m*; **flying ~** arbotante *m*

buxom /ˈbʌksəm/ *adj* con mucho busto *or* pecho

buy¹ /baɪ/ (*past & past p* **bought**) *vt* comprar; **to ~ sb sth** comprarle algo a algn; **to ~ sth FROM sb** comprarle algo A algn; **to ~ sth FOR sb** comprar algo PARA algn ■ **~** *vi* comprar; **to ~ FROM sb** comprarle A algn

• buy off [*v* + *o* + *adv*, *v* + *adv* + *o*] sobornar

• buy out [*v* + *o* + *adv*, *v* + *adv* + *o*] ‹*partner/shareholder*› comprarle su parte a

• buy up [*v* + *adv* + *o*] comprarse todas las existencias de

buy² *n* compra *f*

buyer /ˈbaɪər ‖ ˈbaɪə(r)/ *n* **(a)** (customer) comprador, -dora *m,f* **(b)** (buying agent) encargado, -da *m,f* de compras

buzz¹ /bʌz/ *n* (of insect) zumbido *m*; (of voices) rumor *m*; (as signal) zumbido *m*

buzz² *vi* «*insect*» zumbar; «*telephone/alarm clock*» sonar*; **my ears were ~ing** me zumbaban los oídos

buzzard /ˈbʌzərd ‖ ˈbʌzəd/ *n* **(a)** (hawk) (esp BrE) águila *f*‡ ratonera **(b)** (vulture) (AmE) aura *f*‡, gallinazo *m*, zopilote *m* (AmC, Méx)

buzzer /ˈbʌzər ‖ ˈbʌzə(r)/ *n* timbre *m*

by¹ /baɪ/ *prep* **1** **▶ 744** (indicating agent, cause) (*with passive verbs*) por [*The passive voice is, however, less common in Spanish than it is in English*] **she was brought up ~ her grandmother** la crió su abuela; **a play ~ Shakespeare** una obra de Shakespeare **2 (a)** (indicating means, method): **made ~ hand** hecho a mano; **to travel ~ train** viajar en tren; **to pay ~ credit card** pagar* con tarjeta de crédito; **I'll begin ~ introducing myself** empezaré por presentarme **(b)** (owing to, from): **~ chance** por casualidad; **they have lost public support ~ being too extreme** han perdido apoyo popular por ser demasiado extremistas **3 (a)** (at the side of, near to) al lado de; **it's right ~ the door** está justo al lado de la puerta **(b)** (to hand) (AmE): **I always keep some money ~ me** siempre llevo algo de dinero encima **4 (a)** (past): **I said hello, but he walked right ~ me** lo saludé pero él pasó de largo **(b)** (via, through) por; **~ land/sea/air** por tierra/mar/avión **5 (a)** (indicating rate) por; **we are paid ~ the hour** nos pagan por hora(s) **(b)** (indicating extent of difference): **she broke the record ~ several seconds** batió el récord en *or* por varios segundos **(c)** (indicating gradual progression): **one ~ one** uno por uno **6 (a)** (not later than): **he told her to be home ~ 11** le dijo que volviera antes de las 11; **they should be there ~ now** ya deberían estar allí; **~ the time he arrived, Ann had left** cuando llegó, Ann se había ido **(b)** (during, at) **~ day/night** de día/noche **7** (according to): **~ that clock it's almost half past** según ese reloj son casi y media; **that's fine ~ me** por mí no hay problema **8** (Math) por; **multiply two ~ three** multiplica dos por tres; **a room 20ft ~ 12ft** una habitación de 20 pies por 12 **9 by oneself** (alone, without assistance) solo

by² *adv* **(a)** (past): **she rushed ~ without seeing me** pasó corriendo y no me vio; **they watched the parade march ~** vieron pasar el desfile **(b)** (to sb's residence): **call** *o* **stop ~ on your way to work** pasa por casa de camino al trabajo **(c)** (*in phrases*) **by and by**: **~ and ~ they came to the clearing** al poco rato llegaron al claro; **by and large** por lo general, en general

bye, (AmE) **'bye** /baɪ/ *interj* (colloq) ¡adiós!, ¡chao *or* chau! (esp AmL fam)

bye-bye /'baɪ'baɪ/ *interj* (colloq) ¡adiós!, ¡chaucito! (AmL fam), ¡chaíto! (Chi fam)

by: **~gone** *adj* (liter) (*before n*) ‹*age/days*› de antaño (liter); ***to let ~gones be ~gones*** olvidar el pasado; **~law** *n* (BrE) ordenanza *f* municipal

bypass¹ /'baɪpæs ‖ 'baɪpɑːs/ *n* **(a)** (road) (BrE) carretera *f* de circunvalación **(b)** (Med) bypass *m*

bypass² *vt* **(a)** (circumvent) ‹*person/difficulty*› eludir **(b)** (Transp) «*road*» circunvalar; «*driver*» evitar entrar en

by: **~-product** *n* (in manufacture) subproducto *m*; (consequence) consecuencia *f*; **~road** *n* carretera *f* secundaria; **~stander** /'baɪˌstændər ‖ 'baɪˌstændə(r)/ *n*: **they opened fire, killing innocent ~standers** abrieron fuego y mataron a varias personas inocentes *or* varios transeúntes

byte /baɪt/ *n* byte *m*, octeto *m*

by: **~way** *n* camino *m* (*apartado*); **~word** *n*: **to be a ~word** FOR **sth** ser* sinónimo DE algo; **~-your-leave** /'baɪjər'liːv ‖ ˌbaɪjɔː'liːv/ *n*: ***without so much as a ~-your-leave*** sin (ni) siquiera pedir permiso

Cc

C, **c** /siː/ *n* **(a)** (letter) C, c *f* **(b)** (Mus) re *m*

c (a) (Corresp) = **copy to (b)** (in US) (= **cent(s)**) centavo(s) *m(pl)* **(c)** (= **circa**)

C ▶ 406 (= **Celsius** *or* **centigrade**) C

ca = **circa**

CA, **Ca** = **California**

cab /kæb/ *n* **1** (taxi) taxi *m*; (*before n*) **~ driver** taxista *mf* **2** (driver's compartment) cabina *f*

cabaret /ˌkæbə'reɪ ‖ 'kæbəreɪ/ *n* [C U] cabaret *m*

cabbage /'kæbɪdʒ/ *n* [C U] repollo *m*, col *f*

cabin /'kæbən ‖ 'kæbɪn/ *n* **(a)** (hut) cabaña *f* **(b)** (Naut) camarote *m* **(c)** (Aerosp, Auto, Aviat) cabina *f*

cabinet /'kæbənət ‖ 'kæbɪnɪt/ *n* **1** (cupboard) armario *m*; (with glass front) vitrina *f* **2** *also* **Cabinet** (Govt) gabinete *m* (ministerial)

cable /'keɪbəl/ *n* **(a)** [C] (Elec, Naut) cable *m* **(b)** [C] (Telec) cable *m* **(c)** [U] ⇒ CABLE TELEVISION

cable: **~ car** *n* (suspended) teleférico *m*; (funicular) funicular *m*; (streetcar) (AmE) tranvía *m*; **~ television** *n* [U] televisión *f* por cable, cablevisión *f* (esp AmL)

caboose /kə'buːs/ *n* (AmE Rail) furgón *m* de cola

cache /kæʃ/ *n* alijo *m*

cackle /'kækəl/ *vi* «*hen*» cacarear; «*person*» reírse* socarronamente

cactus /'kæktəs/ *n* (*pl* **-ti** /-taɪ/ *or* **-tuses**) cactus *m*

caddie, **caddy** (*pl* **-dies**) /'kædi/ *n* caddie *mf*

cadet /kə'det/ *n* cadete *mf*

cadge /kædʒ/ (colloq) *vt* **to ~ sth** FROM *o* OFF **sb** gorronearle *or* gorrearle *or* (RPl) garronearle *or* (Chi) bolsearle algo A algn (fam)

Caesarean (section) /sɪ'zæriən ‖ sɪ'zeəriən/ *n* ⇒ CESAREAN (SECTION)

café, **cafe** /kæ'feɪ ‖ 'kæfeɪ/ *n* (coffee bar) café *m*, cafetería *f*; (restaurant) *restaurante económico*

cafeteria /ˌkæfə'tɪriə ‖ ˌkæfə'tɪəriə/ *n* (in hospital, college) cantina *f*, cafetería *f*; (restaurant) restaurante *m* autoservicio, self-service *m*

caffeine /kæ'fiːn ‖ 'kæfiːn/ *n* [U] cafeína *f*

cage¹ /keɪdʒ/ *n* jaula *f*; (in basketball) canasta *f*, cesta *f*; (in ice hockey) portería *f*, meta *f*, arco *m* (Col, CS)

cage² *vt* (*usu pass*) enjaular

Cairo /'kaɪrəʊ ‖ 'kaɪərəʊ/ *n* El Cairo

cajole /kə'dʒəʊl/ *vt* convencer* con zalamerías

cake¹ /keɪk/ *n* [U C] (Culin) (large) pastel *m*, tarta *f* (Esp), torta *f* (esp CS); (small, individual) pastel *m*, masa *f* (RPl); ***to be a piece of ~*** (colloq) ser* pan comido (fam)

cake² *vt* (*usu pass*): **our shoes were ~d with mud** teníamos los zapatos cubiertos de barro endurecido

cake tin *n* (BrE) (for baking) molde *m* (para pastel); (for storage) lata *f* (*para guardar pasteles*)

Cal = **California**

calamity /kə'læməti/ *n* (*pl* **-ties**) calamidad *f*

calcium /'kælsiəm/ *n* [U] calcio *m*

calculate /'kælkjəleɪt ‖ 'kælkjʊleɪt/ *vt* calcular

calculating /'kælkjəleɪtɪŋ ‖ 'kælkjʊleɪtɪŋ/ *adj* calculador

calculation /'kælkjə'leɪʃən ‖ ˌkælkjʊ'leɪʃən/ *n* [C U] cálculo *m*

calculator /'kælkjəleɪtər ‖ 'kælkjʊleɪtə(r)/ *n* calculadora *f*

calendar /'kæləndər ‖ 'kælɪndə(r)/ *n* [C] calendario *m*, almanaque *m*; (*before n*) **~ month** mes *m* (del calendario)

calf /kæf ‖ kɑːf/ *n* (*pl* **calves**) **1** (Zool) **(a)** [C] (animal) ternero, -ra *m,f*, becerro, -rra *m,f* **(b)** [U] (leather) piel *f or* cuero *m* de) becerro *m* **2** (Anat) pantorrilla *f*

caliber, (BrE) **calibre** /'kæləbər ‖ 'kælɪbə(r)/ *n* [C U] calibre *m*

Calif = **California**

calipers, (BrE) **callipers** /'kæləpərz ‖ 'kælɪpəz/ *pl n* **(a)** (for measuring) calibrador *m* **(b)** (Med) aparato *m* ortopédico (*para la pierna*)

call¹ /kɔːl/ *n* **1** (by telephone) llamada *f*; **to give sb a ~** llamar a algn (por teléfono); **2 (a)** (of person — cry) llamada *f*, llamado *m* (AmL); (— shout) grito *m* **(b)** (of animal) grito *m*; (of bird) reclamo *m* **3** (summons): **to be on ~** estar* de guardia; **beyond the ~ of duty** más de lo que el deber exigía (*or* exige *etc*) (frml) **4** (demand) llamamiento *m*, llamado *m* (AmL); **there were ~s for his resignation** pidieron su dimisión **5** (*usu with neg*) **(a)** (reason) motivo *m* **(b)** (demand) demanda *f*; **there's not much ~ for this product** no hay mucha demanda para este producto **6** (visit) visita *f* **7** (Sport) decisión *f*, cobro *m* (Chi)

call² *vt* **(a)** (shout) llamar **(b)** ‹*police/taxi/doctor*› llamar; ‹*strike*› llamar a, convocar* **(c)** (by telephone) llamar **(d)** (name, describe as) llamar; **we ~ her Betty** la llamamos *or* (esp AmL) le decimos Betty; **what are you going to ~ the baby?** ¿qué nombre le van a poner al bebé?; **what's this ~ed in Italian?** ¿cómo se llama esto en italiano? ■ **~** *vi* **(a)** «*person*» llamar **(b)** (by telephone) llamar; **who's ~ing, please?** ¿de parte de quién, por favor? **(c)** (visit) pasar

• **call around** [*v + adv*] **(a)** (Telec) llamar (*a varias personas*) **(b)** (visit) pasar (por casa)

• **call at** [*v + prep + o*]: «*train*» parar en; **I ~ed at your place yesterday** ayer pasé por tu casa

• **call back 1** (Telec) [*v + o + adv*] llamar más tarde **2** [*v + adv*] (Telec) volver* a llamar

• **call for** [*v + prep + o*] **(a)** (require) ‹*skill/courage*› requerir*, exigir* **(b)** (demand) pedir* **(c)** (collect) pasar a buscar *or* a recoger

• **call in 1** [*v + o + adv, v + adv + o*] **(a)** ‹*expert/doctor*› llamar **(b)** ‹*coin/note*› retirar de circulación **2** [*v + adv*] **to ~ in** (ON **sb**) pasar a ver a algn

• **call off** [*v + o + adv, v + adv + o*] **(a)** (cancel) suspender **(b)** ‹*dog*› llamar

• **call on** [*v + prep + o*] **(a)** (visit) pasar a ver a **(b)** ⇒ CALL UPON

• **call out** [*v + o + adv, v + adv + o*] **(a)** ‹*fire brigade/doctor*› llamar **(b)** (utter): **he ~ed out her name** la llamó

• **call round** [*v + adv*] (BrE) ⇒ CALL AROUND

• **call up** [*v + o + adv, v + adv + o*] **(a)** ‹*spirits*› invocar* **(b)** (telephone) (esp AmE) llamar **(c)** (Mil) (*often pass*) llamar (a filas)

• **call upon** [*v + prep + o*] **(a)** (invite): **to ~ upon sb to speak** dar* la palabra a algn **(b)** (appeal to) apelar a

call box *n* (BrE) cabina *f* telefónica

caller /'kɔːlər ‖ 'kɔːlə(r)/ *n*: **we didn't have many ~s** no vino mucha gente; (Telec) no tuvimos *or* no hubo muchas llamadas; **the ~ didn't leave her name** la persona que llamó no dejó su nombre

callipers *n* (BrE) ⇒ CALIPERS

callous /'kæləs/ *adj* insensible, cruel

callus /'kæləs/ *n* (*pl* **-luses**) (Med) callo *m*

calm¹ /kɑːm/ *adj* **-er, -est** ‹*sea*› en calma, calmo (esp AmL); ‹*person/voice*› tranquilo, calmo (esp AmL)

calm² *vt* tranquilizar*, calmar

• **calm down (a)** [*v + o + adv, v + adv + o*] tranquilizar*, calmar **(b)** [*v + adv*] tranquilizarse*; **~ down!** ¡tranquilízate!, ¡tranquilo!

calm³ *n* [U] calma *f*

calmly /'kɑːmli/ *adv* con calma

Calor Gas® /'kælər ‖ 'kælə(r)/ *n* [U] (BrE) (gas *m*) butano *m*, supergás® *m* (RPl)

calorie /'kæləri/ *n* (Culin) (kilo)caloría *f*

calves /kævz ‖ kɑːvz/ *pl of* CALF

camcorder /'kæmˌkɔːrdər ‖ 'kæmˌkɔːdə(r)/ *n* videocámara *f*, camcórder *m*

came /keɪm/ *past of* COME

camel /'kæməl/ *n* camello *m*

cameo /'kæmiəʊ/ *n* **1** (jewelry) camafeo *m* **2** (Cin, TV) actuación *f* especial

camera /'kæmərə/ *n* cámara *f* (fotográfica), máquina *f* fotográfica *or* de fotos

camera: **~man** /'kæmərəmæn/ *n* (*pl* **-men** /-men/) camarógrafo, -fa *m,f*, cameraman *mf* (esp AmL), cámara *mf* (Esp); **~work** *n* [U] fotografía *f*

Cameroon /'kæmə'ruːn/ *n* Camerún *m*

camomile /'kæməmaɪl/ *n* ⇒ CHAMOMILE

camouflage¹ /'kæməflɑːʒ/ *n* [C U] camuflaje *m*

camouflage² *vt* camuflar, camuflajear (AmL)

camp¹ /kæmp/ *n* (collection of tents, huts) campamento *m*; **(summer) ~** (in US) campamento *m* de verano, colonia *f* de vacaciones *or* verano

camp² *vi* acampar; **to go ~ing** ir* de camping

camp³ *adj* **(a)** (effeminate) amanerado, afeminado **(b)** ‹*performance*› afectado, exagerado

campaign¹ /kæm'peɪn/ *n* campaña *f*

campaign² *vi* (Pol, Sociol) **to ~** FOR/AGAINST **sth** hacer* una campaña A FAVOR DE/EN CONTRA DE algo

campaigner /kæm'peɪnər ‖ kæm'peɪnə(r)/ *n* (Pol, Sociol) defensor, -sora *m,f*

camper /'kæmpər ‖ 'kæmpə(r)/ *n* **(a)** (person) campista *mf* **(b)** (Transp) cámper *f*

campground /'kæmpgraʊnd/ (AmE), **campsite** /'kæmpsaɪt/ *n* camping *m*

campus /'kæmpəs/ *n* (*pl* **-puses**) campus *m*

can¹ /kæn/ *n* **(a)** (container) lata *f*, bote *m* (Esp), tarro *m* (Chi); (*before n*) **~ opener** abrelatas *m* **(b)** (for petrol, water) bidón *m*; (for garbage) (AmE) cubo *m or* (CS) tacho *m or* (Col) caneca *f*, bote *m* (Méx), tobo *m* de la basura (Ven)

can² *vt* **-nn-** (put in cans) enlatar; (bottle) (AmE) ‹*fruit*› preparar conservas de

can³ /kæn, *weak form* kən/ *v mod*

■ **Note** When *can* means *to be capable of* or *to be allowed to*, it is translated by *poder*: *he can't eat* no puede comer; *can you come out tonight?* ¿puedes salir esta noche?
When *can* means *to know how to*, it is translated by *saber*: *can you swim?* ¿sabes nadar?; *she can already read and write* ya sabe leer y escribir.
When *can* is used with a verb of perception such as *see*, *hear*, or *feel*, it is often not translated: *can you see her from here?* ¿la ves desde aquí?; *she couldn't feel anything* no sentía nada.

(*past* **could**) **1** (indicating ability) poder*; (referring to particular skills) saber*; **she couldn't answer the question** no pudo contestar la pregunta; **~ you swim?** ¿sabes nadar? **2 (a)** (with verbs of perception): **I ~'t see very well** no veo muy bien; **~ you hear me?** ¿me oyes? **(b)** (with verbs of mental activity): **I ~'t understand it** no lo entiendo; **~'t you tell he's lying?** ¿no te das cuenta de que está mintiendo? **3 (a)** (indicating, asking etc permission) poder*; **~ I come with you?** ¿puedo ir contigo? **(b)** (in requests) poder*; **~ you turn that music down, please?** ¿puedes bajar esa música, por favor? **(c)** (in offers): **~ I help you?** ¿me permite?; (in shop) ¿lo/la atienden?, ¿qué desea?; **~ I carry that for you?** ¿quieres que (te) lleve eso? **(d)** (in suggestions, advice): **~'t you give it another try?** ¿por qué no lo vuelves a intentar? **4** (indicating possibility) poder*; **it ~'t be true!** ¡no puede ser!, ¡no es posible!

Canada /'kænədə/ *n* (el) Canadá *m*

Canadian¹ /kə'neɪdiən/ *adj* canadiense

Canadian² *n* canadiense *mf*

canal /kə'næl/ *n* canal *m*

Canaries /kə'neriz ‖ kə'neəriz/ *pl n* **the ~** (las) Canarias

canary /kə'neri ‖ kə'neəri/ *n* (*pl* **-ries**) canario *m*

Canary Islands *pl n* **the ~ ~** las Islas Canarias

cancel /'kænsəl/, (BrE) **-ll-** *vt* cancelar; ‹*check*› anular

• **cancel out** [*v* + *o* + *adv*, *v* + *adv* + *o*] ‹*deficit*/*loss*› compensar; ‹*debt*› cancelar

cancellation /'kænsə'leɪʃən/ *n* [U C] cancelación *f*; (Theat) devolución *f*

cancer /'kænsər ‖ 'kænsə(r)/ *n* **1** ▶ 484 [U C] (disease) cáncer *m* **2 Cancer** (Astrol) **(a)** (sign) (*no art*) Cáncer **(b)** [C] (person) Cáncer *or* cáncer *mf*, canceriano, -na *m,f*

candid /'kændəd ‖ 'kændɪd/ *adj* franco

candidate /'kændədeɪt ‖ 'kændɪdət/ *n* candidato, -ta *m,f*

candle /'kændl̩/ *n* (for domestic use) vela *f*; (for altar) cirio *m*

candle: **~light** *n* [U]: **by ~light** a la luz de una vela/de las velas; **~stick** *n* candelero *m*; (flat) palmatoria *f*

candy /'kændi/ *n* (*pl* **-dies**) (AmE) **(a)** [U] (confectionery) golosinas *fpl*, dulces *mpl* (AmL exc RPl) **(b)** [C] (individual piece) caramelo *m*, dulce *m* (AmL exc RPl)

cane¹ /keɪn/ *n* **1** [C] [U] (for wickerwork) mimbre *m* **2** [C] (walking stick) bastón *m*; (for punishment) palmeta *f*; (for supporting plants) rodrigón *m*

cane² *vt* castigar* con la palmeta

canine¹ /'keɪnaɪn/ *n* **1** (Zool) canino *m*, cánido *m* **2 ~ (tooth)** (diente *m*) canino *m*, colmillo *m*

canine² *adj* canino

canister /'kænəstər ‖ 'kænɪstə(r)/ *n* **(a)** (for tea, coffee) lata *f*, bote *m* (Esp) **(b)** (Mil) bote *m* (*de humo, metralla etc*)

cannabis /'kænəbəs ‖ 'kænəbɪs/ *n* [U] hachís *m*, cannabis *m*

canned /kænd/ *adj* **(a)** ‹*food*› enlatado, en *or* de lata, en conserva **(b)** (pre-recorded) (colloq) ‹*music*› enlatado (fam); ‹*laughter*› grabado

cannibal /'kænəbəl ‖ 'kænɪbəl/ *n* caníbal *mf*, antropófago, -ga *m,f*

cannon /'kænən/ *n* (*pl also* **~**) cañón *m*

cannonball /'kænənbɔːl/ *n* (Mil) bala *f* de cañón

cannot /'kænɑːt ‖ 'kænɒt/ = **can not**

canoe¹ /kə'nuː/ *n* canoa *f*, piragua *f*

canoe² *vi* **-noes, -noeing, -noed** ir* en canoa *or* piragua

canoeing /kə'nuːɪŋ/ *n* [U] piragüismo *m*, canotaje *m*

canopy /'kænəpi/ *n* (*pl* **-pies**) (over bed, throne) dosel *m*, baldaquín *m*, baldaquino *m*; (over person) palio *m*, dosel *m*

can't /kænt ‖ kɑːnt/ = **can not**

canteen /kæn'tiːn/ *n* **1** (dining hall) (BrE) cantina *f*, comedor *m*, casino *m* (Chi) (*en un lugar de trabajo, colegio etc*) **2** (water bottle) cantimplora *f*

canter /'kæntər ‖ 'kæntə(r)/ *vi* ir* a medio galope

canvas /'kænvəs/ *n* **1** [U] (cloth) lona *f* **2** (Art) [C U] (for painting) lienzo *m*, tela *f*

canvass /'kænvəs/ *vt* **1** (Pol): **to ~ voters in an area** hacer* campaña entre los votantes de una zona **2** (scrutinize) (AmE): **to ~ the votes** hacer* el escrutinio de los votos ■ **~** *vi* (Pol) **to ~ (FOR sb)** hacer* campaña (A *or* EN FAVOR DE algn)

canyon /'kænjən/ *n* cañón *m*

cap¹ /kæp/ *n* **1** (hat) gorra *f*; **swimming ~** gorro *m or* (esp AmL) gorra *f* de baño; **baseball/golf ~** gorra de béisbol/golf **2** (of bottle) tapa *f*, tapón *m*; (metal) chapa *f*, tapa *f*; (of pen) capuchón *m*, tapa *f* **3** (upper limit) tope *m*

cap² *vt* **-pp- 1** ‹*bottle*/*tube*› tapar **2** (crown): **to ~ it all off** *o* (BrE) **to ~ it all** ... para colmo (de desgracias *or* de males) ..., para rematarla ... (fam) **3** ‹*expenditure*› poner* un tope a **4** (Dentistry): **to have a tooth ~ped** ponerse* una funda *or* una corona

capability /'keɪpə'bɪləti/ *n* (*pl* **-ties**) **(a)** [U] (ability) capacidad *f* **(b) capabilities** *pl* aptitudes *fpl*

capable /'keɪpəbəl/ *adj* **(a)** (competent) capaz **(b)** (*pred*) (able) **to be ~ OF -ING** ser* capaz DE + INF

capacity /kə'pæsəti/ *n* (*pl* **-ties**) **1** [U C] **(a)** (maximum content) capacidad *f*; (*before n*) **a ~ crowd** un lleno completo **(b)** (output) capacidad *f* **2** [U] (ability) capacidad *f*; **~ FOR sth** capacidad DE algo; **~ to + INF** capacidad PARA + INF; **the job was beyond her ~** el trabajo estaba por encima de su capacidad **3** [C] (role) calidad *f*; **in his ~ as union delegate** en su calidad de delegado del sindicato

cape /keɪp/ *n* **1** (Clothing) capa *f* **2** (Geog) cabo *m*

caper¹ /'keɪpər ‖ 'keɪpə(r)/ *n* **1** (jump) salto *m* **2** (prank) travesura *f* **3** (Bot, Culin) alcaparra *f*

caper² *vi* correr y brincar*, dar* saltos *or* brincos

capital¹ /'kæpətl̩ ‖ 'kæpɪtl/ *n* **(a)** [C] (city) capital *f* **(b)** [C] (letter) mayúscula *f* **(c)** [U] (Fin) capital *m*

capital² *adj* **(a)** (Law): **~ punishment** pena *f* capital **(b)** (Geog, Pol): **~ (city)** capital *f* **(c)** (Print) ‹*letter*› mayúscula

capitalism /'kæpətl̩ɪzəm ‖ 'kæpɪtəlɪzəm/ *n* [U] capitalismo *m*

capitalist¹ /'kæpətl̩əst ‖ 'kæpɪtəlɪst/ *n* capitalista *mf*

capitalist² *adj* capitalista

capitulate /kə'pɪtʃəleɪt ‖ kə'pɪtjʊleɪt/ *vi* capitular

Capricorn /'kæprɪkɔːrn ‖ 'kæprɪkɔːn/ *n* **(a)** (sign) (*no art*) Capricornio **(b)** [C] (person) Capricornio *or* capricornio *mf*, capricorniano, -na *m,f*

caps = **capital letters**

capsicum /'kæpsɪkəm/ *n* pimiento *m*, pimentón *m* (AmS exc RPl), ají *m* (RPl)

capsize /'kæpsaɪz ‖ kæp'saɪz/ *vi* volcarse*

capsule /'kæpsəl ‖ 'kæpsjuːl/ *n* cápsula *f*

captain¹ /'kæptən ‖ 'kæptɪn/ *n* **(a)** (rank) capitán *m* **(b)** (person in command) capitán, -tana *m,f*; (of airline plane) comandante *mf*

captain² *vt* (Naut, Sport) capitanear

caption /'kæpʃən/ *n* (under picture) leyenda *f*, pie *m* de foto (*or* ilustración *etc*); (headline) título *m*

captivate /'kæptəveɪt ‖ 'kæptɪveɪt/ *vt* cautivar

captive¹ /'kæptɪv/ *n* (liter) cautivo, -va *m,f*

captive² *adj*: **to take/hold sb ~** tomar prisionero/mantener* cautivo a algn; **to have a ~ audience** tener* un público que no tiene más remedio que escuchar

captivity /kæp'tɪvəti/ *n* [U] cautiverio *m*, cautividad *f*

captor /'kæptər ‖ 'kæptə(r)/ *n* captor, -tora *m,f*

capture¹ /'kæptʃər ‖ 'kæptʃə(r)/ *vt* **1** ‹*person/animal*› capturar; ‹*city*› tomar **2 (a)** ‹*attention/interest*› captar, atraer* **(b)** ‹*mood/atmosphere*› captar, reproducir*

capture² *n* [U] (of person, animal) captura *f*; (of city) conquista *f*, toma *f*

car /kɑːr ‖ kɑː(r)/ *n* **(a)** (Auto) coche *m*, automóvil *m* (frml), carro *m* (AmL exc CS), auto *m* (esp CS) **(b)** (Rail, Transp) vagón *m*, coche *m*

caramel /'kɑːrml̩ ‖ 'kærəmel, -mel/ *n* [U] caramelo *m*

carat /'kærət/ *n* **(a)** (for gold) (AmE also **karat**) quilate *m*; **18-~ gold** oro *m* de 18 quilates **(b)** (for precious stones) quilate *m*

caravan /'kærəvæn/ *n* **(a)** (group) caravana *f* **(b)** (vehicle) (BrE) caravana *f*, rulot *f* (Esp), casa *f* rodante (CS), tráiler *m* (Andes, Méx); (*before n*) **~ park** *o* **site** camping *m* para caravanas

carbohydrate /'kɑːrbəʊ'haɪdreɪt ‖ ˌkɑːbə'haɪdreɪt/ *n* [C U] hidrato *m* de carbono

car bomb *n* coche *m* bomba

carbon /'kɑːrbən ‖ 'kɑːbən/ *n* [U] carbono *m*

carbon: **~ copy** *n* copia *f* (*hecha con papel carbón*); **~ dioxide** /daɪ'ɑːksaɪd ‖ daɪ'ɒksaɪd/ *n* [U] anhídrido *m* carbónico; **~ monoxide** /mə'nɑːksaɪd ‖ mə'nɒksaɪd/*n* [U] monóxido *m* de carbono

carburetor, (BrE) **carburettor** /ˌkɑːrbə'reɪtər ‖ ˌkɑːbə'retə(r)/ *n* carburador *m*

carcass, (BrE also) **carcase** /'kɑːrkəs ‖ 'kɑːkəs/ *n* (dead animal) *cuerpo de animal muerto*; (for meat) res *f* (*muerta*)

card /kɑːrd ‖ kɑːd/ *n* **1** [C] **(a)** (for identification, access) tarjeta *f*; (*business ~*) tarjeta (de visita); (*credit ~*) tarjeta (de crédito) **(b)** (*greeting ~*) tarjeta *f* (de felicitación) **(c)** (*index ~*) ficha *f*; (*before n*) **~ index** fichero *m* **(d)** (*post~*) (tarjeta *f*) postal *f* **2** [U] (thin cardboard) cartulina *f* **3** [C] (playing card) carta *f*, naipe *m*, baraja *f* (AmC, Col, Méx, RPl); **to play ~s** jugar* a las cartas *or* (Col) jugar* cartas

cardamom /'kɑːrdəməm ‖ 'kɑːdəməm/ *n* [U] cardamomo *m*

cardboard /'kɑːrdbɔːrd ‖ 'kɑːdbɔːd/ *n* [U] (stiff) cartón *m*; (thin) cartulina *f*; (*before n*) **~ box** caja *f* de cartón

cardiac /'kɑːrdiæk ‖ 'kɑːdiæk/ *adj* cardíaco; **~ arrest** paro *m* cardíaco

cardigan /'kɑːrdɪgən ‖ 'kɑːdɪgən/ *n* cárdigan *m*, chaqueta *f* de punto, rebeca *f* (esp Esp), saco *m* (tejido) (RPl), chaleca *f* (Chi)

cardinal /'kɑːrdn̩əl ‖ 'kɑːdɪnl/ *n* **1** **▶603** (Relig) cardenal *m* **2** **▶724** **~ (number)** número *m* cardinal

care¹ /ker ‖ keə(r)/ *n* **1** [U] (attention, carefulness) cuidado *m*, atención *f*; **to take ~** tener* cuidado; **take ~!** (saying goodbye) ¡cuídate!; (as a warning) ¡ten cuidado! **2** [U] (of people): **medical ~** asistencia *f* médica; (of animals, things) cuidado *m*; **in ~ of** (AmE), **~ of** (BrE) (on letters) en casa de **3 to take ~ of sb/sth (a)** (look after) ‹*of patient*› atender* a algn, cuidar de algn; ‹*of children*› cuidar a *or* de algn, ocuparse de algn; ‹*of pet/plant/machine*› cuidar algo; **I can take ~ of myself** yo sé cuidarme **(b)** (deal with) ocuparse *or* encargarse* de algn/algo **4** [C U] (worry) preocupación *f*

care² *vi* **to ~ (ABOUT sth/sb)** preocuparse (POR algo/algn); **I don't ~** no me importa ■ **~** *vt* **(a)** (feel concern) (*usu neg, interrog*): **I couldn't ~ less what he does** me tiene sin cuidado lo que haga **(b)** (wish) (frml) **to ~ to + INF**: **would you ~ to join us for dinner?** ¿le gustaría cenar con nosotros?

● **care for** [*v* + *prep* + *o*] **(a)** (look after) ‹*patient*› cuidar (de), atender* **(b)** (be fond of) querer*, sentir* afecto *or* cariño por

career[1] /kəˈrɪr ‖ kəˈrɪə(r)/ *n* carrera *f*

career[2] *vi* ir* a toda velocidad

carefree /ˈkerfriː ‖ ˈkeəfriː/ *adj* despreocupado

careful /ˈkerfəl ‖ ˈkeəfəl/ *adj* **1** (cautious) cuidadoso, prudente; **(be) ~** (ten) cuidado; **to be ~ OF/WITH sth** tener* cuidado CON algo **2** (painstaking) ‹*planning*› cuidadoso; ‹*work*› cuidado, esmerado; ‹*worker*› meticuloso

carefully /ˈkerfli ‖ ˈkeəfəli/ *adv* ‹*handle/drive*› con cuidado; ‹*plan/examine*› cuidadosamente; ‹*designed/chosen*› con esmero

careless /ˈkerləs ‖ ˈkeəlɪs/ *adj* ‹*person*› descuidado; ‹*work*› poco cuidado; ‹*driving*› negligente; **you made some ~ mistakes** cometiste errores por descuido

carelessly /ˈkerləsli ‖ ˈkeəlɪsli/ *adv* sin cuidado, sin la debida atención

carelessness /ˈkerləsnəs ‖ ˈkeəlɪsnɪs/ *n* [U] falta *f* de atención *or* de cuidado

caress[1] /kəˈres/ *n* caricia *f*

caress[2] *vt* acariciar

caretaker /ˈkerˌteɪkər ‖ ˈkeəˌteɪkə(r)/ *n* conserje *mf*

cargo /ˈkɑːrgəʊ ‖ ˈkɑːgəʊ/ *n* (*pl* **-goes** *or* **-gos**) **(a)** [C] (load) cargamento *m* **(b)** [U] (goods) carga *f*

Caribbean[1] /ˌkærəˈbiːən, kəˈrɪbiən ‖ ˌkærɪˈbiːən/ *adj* caribeño, del Caribe

Caribbean[2] *n* **the ~ (Sea)** el (mar) Caribe; **the ~** (region) el Caribe, las Antillas

caricature /ˈkærɪkətʃʊr ‖ ˈkærɪkətʃʊə(r)/ *n* caricatura *f*

caring /ˈkerɪŋ ‖ ˈkeərɪŋ/ *adj* ‹*society/approach*› humanitario; ‹*person*› (kindly) bondadoso; (sympathetic) comprensivo

carnage /ˈkɑːrnɪdʒ ‖ ˈkɑːnɪdʒ/ *n* [U] carnicería *f*

carnation /kɑːrˈneɪʃən ‖ kɑːˈneɪʃən/ *n* clavel *m*

carnival /ˈkɑːrnəvəl ‖ ˈkɑːnɪvəl/ *n* carnaval *m*

carnivorous /kɑːrˈnɪvərəs ‖ kɑːˈnɪvərəs/ *adj* carnívoro

carol /ˈkærəl/ *n* villancico *m*

carousel /ˈkærəˈsel/ *n* **(a)** (esp AmE) ⇒ MERRY-GO-ROUND **(b)** (for baggage) cinta *f or* correa *f* transportadora **(c)** (in shops) (AmE) expositor *m* giratorio

car park *n* (BrE) (open space) ⇒ PARKING LOT; (building) ⇒ PARKING GARAGE

carpenter /ˈkɑːrpəntər ‖ ˈkɑːpəntə(r)/ *n* carpintero, -ra *m,f*

carpentry /ˈkɑːrpəntri ‖ ˈkɑːpəntri/ *n* [U] carpintería *f*

carpet /ˈkɑːrpət ‖ ˈkɑːpɪt/ *n* **(a)** [C] (rug) alfombra *f*, tapete *m* (Col, Méx, Ven); ⇒ SWEEP[2] *vt* 1(b) **(b)** [U C] (wall-to-wall) alfombra *f*, moqueta *f* (Esp), moquette *f* (RPl) **(c)** [C] (of flowers, leaves, moss) (liter) alfombra *f* (liter)

carphone /ˈkɑːrfəʊn ‖ ˈkɑːfəʊn/ *n* teléfono *m* de automóvil

carriage /ˈkærɪdʒ/ *n* **1** [C] **(a)** (horse-drawn) carruaje *m*, coche *m* **(b)** (BrE Rail) vagón *m* **(c)** (*baby* **~**) (AmE) cochecito *m*, carriola *f* (Méx) **2** [U] (transport) transporte *m* **3** [U] (bearing) (frml) porte *m*

carrier /ˈkæriər ‖ ˈkæriə(r)/ *n* **1** (company) compañía *f or* empresa *f* de transportes; (Aviat) línea *f* aérea **2** (of disease, gene) portador, -dora *m,f*

carrier bag *n* (BrE) bolsa *f* (de plástico *or* papel)

carrion /ˈkæriən/ *n* [U] carroña *f*

carrot /ˈkærət/ *n* [C U] zanahoria *f*

carry /ˈkæri/ **-ries, -rying, -ried** *vt* **1 (a)** (bear, take) llevar; **I can't ~ this, it's too heavy** no puedo cargar con esto, pesa demasiado **(b)** (have with one) llevar encima **(c)** (be provided with) ‹*guarantee*› tener* **(d)** (be pregnant with) estar* embarazada *or* encinta de **2 (a)** (convey) ‹*goods/passengers*› llevar, transportar; **she was carried along by the crowd** fue arrastrada por la multitud **(b)** (channel, transmit) ‹*oil/water/sewage*› llevar **(c)** ‹*disease*› ser* portador de **3** (support) ‹*weight*› soportar **4** (involve, entail) ‹*responsibility*› conllevar **5** (gain support for) ‹*bill/motion*› aprobar* **6** (stock) ‹*model*› tener*, vender ■ **~** *vi*: **sound carries further in the mountains** en la montaña los sonidos llegan más lejos; **her voice carries well** su voz tiene mucha proyección

● **carry away** [*v* + *o* + *adv*, *v* + *adv* + *o*] (*usu pass*): **I got carried away and painted the window as well** me entusiasmé y pinté la ventana también; **there's no need to get carried away** no te pases

● **carry off** [*v* + *o* + *adv*, *v* + *adv* + *o*] **1** (abduct) ‹*victim/hostage*› llevarse **2 (a)** (win) ‹*trophy/cup*› llevarse **(b)** (succeed with): **she tried to appear disinterested but failed to ~ it off** intentó aparentar desinterés pero no lo logró

● **carry on 1 (a)** [*v* + *o* + *adv*, *v* + *adv* + *o*] ‹*practice*› seguir* *or* continuar* con **(b)** [*v* + *adv* + *o*] ‹*conversation/correspondence*› mantener* **2** [*v* + *adv*] **(a)** (continue) seguir*, continuar* **(b)** (make a fuss) (colloq): **what a way to ~ on!** ¡qué manera de hacer escándalo, por favor!

● **carry out** [*v* + *o* + *adv*, *v* + *adv* + *o*] ‹*work/repairs/investigation*› llevar a cabo; ‹*order*› cumplir; ‹*duty*› cumplir con

carry: **~all** *n* (AmE) bolso *m* de viaje, bolsón *m* (RPl); **~cot** *n* (BrE) cuna *f* portátil; **~-on** *adj* (AmE) (*before n*) ‹*bag/baggage*› de mano; **~out** *n* (esp AmE) *comida preparada o bebida que se vende para consumir fuera del lugar de venta*

car: **~ seat** *n* asiento *m* del coche; (for infant) asiento *m* de bebé (*para el coche*); **~sick** *adj* mareado (*por viajar en coche*)

cart[1] /kɑːrt ‖ kɑːt/ *n* **(a)** (waggon) carro *m*, carreta *f* **(b)** (in supermarket, airport) (AmE) carrito *m*

cart[2] *vt* (colloq): **I had to ~ the books around all day** tuve que cargar con los libros todo el día

cartel /kɑːrˈtel ‖ kɑːˈtel/ *n* cártel *m*

carthorse /ˈkɑːrthɔːrs ‖ ˈkɑːthɔːs/ *n* caballo *m* de tiro

cartilage /ˈkɑːrtḷɪdʒ ‖ ˈkɑːtɪlɪdʒ/ *n* [U C] cartílago *m*

carton /ˈkɑːrtn̩ ‖ ˈkɑːtn̩/ *n* (of cigarettes) cartón *m*; **a ~ of milk** una leche en cartón

cartoon /kɑːrˈtuːn ‖ kɑːˈtuːn/ *n* **(a)** (humorous drawing) chiste *m* (*gráfico*), viñeta *f* (Esp), mono *m* (Chi) **(b)** (Cin) dibujos *mpl* animados

cartridge /ˈkɑːrtrɪdʒ ‖ ˈkɑːtrɪdʒ/ *n* (for gun, pen) cartucho *m*

cartwheel /ˈkɑːrthwiːl ‖ ˈkɑːtwiːl/ *n* voltereta *f* lateral, rueda *f*, rueda *f* de carro (Méx, RPl)

carve /kɑːrv ‖ kɑːv/ *vt* **1** (Art) ‹*wood/stone*› tallar; ‹*figure/bust*› esculpir, tallar; ‹*initials*› grabar **2** (Culin) ‹*meat*› cortar, trinchar

• **carve out** [*v + o + adv, v + adv + o*] ‹*reputation*› forjarse; ‹*name*› hacerse*

carving /ˈkɑːrvɪŋ ‖ ˈkɑːvɪŋ/ *n* talla *f*, escultura *f*

carving knife *n* trinchante *m*, cuchillo *m* de trinchar

car wash *n* túnel *m* *or* tren *m* de lavado

cascade¹ /kæsˈkeɪd/ *n* cascada *f*

cascade² *vi* caer* en cascada

case /keɪs/ *n* **1** (matter) caso *m*; **to lose/win a ~** (Law) perder*/ganar un pleito *or* juicio **2 (a)** (Med, Soc Adm) caso *m* **(b)** (eccentric) (colloq) caso *m* (fam) **3** (instance, situation) caso *m*; **if that's the ~** si es así; **in that ~, I'm not interested** en ese caso, no me interesa **4** (*in phrases*) **in any case** de todas maneras *or* formas; **in case** (*as conj*): **make a note in ~ you forget** apúntalo por si te olvidas; **just in case** por si acaso **5** (argument): **she has a good ~** sus argumentos son buenos; **there is a ~ for doing nothing** hay razones para no hacer nada **6 (a)** (*suit~*) maleta *f*, valija *f* (RPl) **(b)** (*attaché ~*) maletín *m* **(c)** (crate) caja *f*, cajón *m*, jaba *f* (Chi, Per); (of wine, liquor) *caja de 12 botellas* **(d)** (hard container — for small objects) estuche *f*; (— for large objects) caja *f*; (soft container) funda *f*

case: **~ history** *n* (Med) historial *m* clínico, historia *f* clínica (AmL); **~ study** *n* estudio *m*

cash¹ /kæʃ/ *n* [U] **(a)** (notes and coins) dinero *m* (en) efectivo; **(in) ~** en efectivo; **~ on delivery** entrega *f* contra reembolso; (*before n*) ‹*payment*› en efectivo; ‹*refund*› al contado **(b)** (funds) (colloq) dinero *m*, lana *f* (AmL fam), plata *f* (AmS fam), tela *f* (Esp fam)

cash² *vt* ‹*check*› cobrar

• **cash in 1** [*v + o + adv, v + adv + o*] (exchange for money) canjear **2** [*v + adv*] (profit) **to ~ in** (ON **sth**) aprovecharse (DE algo)

cash: **~ and carry** *n*: *tienda de venta al por mayor*; **~ crop** *n* cultivo *m* industrial *or* comercial; **~ desk** *n* (BrE) caja *f*; **~ dispenser** *n* (BrE) cajero *m* automático

cashew (nut) /ˈkæʃuː/ *n* anacardo *m*, castaña *f* de cajú (CS, Ven), nuez *f* de la India (Méx)

cash flow *n* flujo *m* de caja, cash-flow *m*

cashier /kæˈʃɪr ‖ kæˈʃiə(r)/ *n* cajero, -ra *m,f*

cashier's check *n* (AmE) cheque *m* bancario *or* de caja *or* de gerencia

cashmere /ˈkæʒmɪr ‖ ˌkæʃˈmɪə(r)/ *n* [U] cachemir *m*, cachemira *f*

cash: **~point** *n* (BrE) cajero *m* automático; **~ register** *n* caja *f* registradora

casing /ˈkeɪsɪŋ/ *n* (cover) cubierta *f*; (case) caja *f*

casino /kəˈsiːnəʊ/ *n* (*pl* **-nos**) casino *m*

cask /kæsk ‖ kɑːsk/ *n* barril *m*, tonel *m*

casket /ˈkæskət ‖ ˈkɑːskɪt/ *n* **(a)** (for jewels) cofre *m* **(b)** (coffin) (AmE) ataúd *m*

casserole /ˈkæsərəʊl/ *n* **(a)** [C] (dish) cazuela *f* **(b)** [C U] (food) guiso *m*, guisado *m* (Méx)

cassette /kəˈset/ *n* (Audio) cassette *f or m*; (*before n*) **~ player** pasacintas *m*, cassette *m* (Esp), pasacassettes *m* (RPl), tocacassettes *m* (Chi)

cast¹ /kæst ‖ kɑːst/ *n* **1 (a)** (molded object) (Art) vaciado *m*; (Metall) pieza *f* fundida **(b)** (mold) molde *m* **2** (Cin, Theat) (*+ sing or pl vb*) reparto *m*, elenco *m* (esp AmL)

cast² (*past & past p* **cast**) *vt* **1 (a)** ‹*stone*› arrojar, lanzar*, tirar; ‹*line*› lanzar*; ‹*net*› echar **(b)** ‹*shadow/light*› proyectar; **to ~ doubt on sth** poner* algo en duda **(c)** ‹*vote*› emitir **2** «*snake*» ‹*skin*› mudar de, mudar **3** (Cin, Theat) ‹*role*› asignar; **she was ~ as the princess** le dieron el papel de la princesa ■ **~** *vi* (in angling) lanzar*

• **cast away** [*v + o + adv*]: **they were ~ away on a desert island** llegaron a una isla desierta tras naufragar

• **cast off** [*v + adv*] **1 (a)** (in knitting) cerrar* **(b)** (Naut) soltar* amarras **2** [*v + o + adv, v + adv + o*] **(a)** (in knitting) ‹*stitch*› cerrar* **(b)** (abandon) ‹*friend/lover*› dejar

• **cast on 1** [*v + adv*] (in knitting) poner* *or* montar los puntos **2** [*v + o + adv, v + adv + o*] ‹*stitch*› montar, poner*

• **cast out** [*v + o + adv, v + adv + o*] (liter) expulsar

castanets /ˌkæstəˈnets/ *pl n* castañuelas *fpl*

castaway /ˈkæstəweɪ ‖ ˈkɑːstəweɪ/ *n* náufrago, -ga *m,f*

caste /kæst ‖ kɑːst/ *n* [C U] casta *f*

caster /ˈkæstər ‖ ˈkɑːstə(r)/ *n* ruedecita *f*, ruedita *f* (esp AmL)

caster sugar *n* (BrE) *azúcar blanca de granulado muy fino*

Castile /kæsˈtiːl ‖ kæˈstiːl/ *n* Castilla *f*

Castilian¹ /kæsˈtɪljən ‖ kəˈstɪliən/ *adj* castellano

Castilian² *n* **(a)** [C] (person) castellano, -na *m,f* **(b)** [U] (language) castellano *m*

cast: **~ iron** *n* [U] hierro *m* fundido *or* colado; **~-iron** *adj* (*before n*) ‹*guarantee*› sólido; ‹*alibi*› a toda prueba

castle /ˈkæsəl ‖ ˈkɑːsəl/ *n* **(a)** (Archit) castillo *m* **(b)** (in chess) torre *f*

castoff /ˈkæstɔːf ‖ ˈkɑːstɒf/ *n*: **she gave me her ~s** me dio la ropa que ya no quería

castrate /ˈkæstreɪt ‖ kæˈstreɪt/ *vt* castrar

casual /ˈkæʒuəl/ *adj* **1 (a)** (superficial) (*before n*) ‹*inspection*› superficial; **a ~ acquaintance** un conocido, una conocida; **~ sex** relaciones *fpl* sexuales promiscuas **(b)** (chance) (*before n*) ‹*visit/reader*› ocasional **(c)** (informal) ‹*chat*› informal; ‹*clothes*› de sport, informal **2** (unconcerned) ‹*attitude/tone*› despreocupado; ‹*remark*› hecho al pasar **3** (not regular) ‹*employment/labor*› eventual, ocasional

casually /ˈkæʒuəli/ *adv* **(a)** (informally) ‹*dressed*› de manera informal; ‹*chat*› informalmente **(b)** (with indifference) con indiferencia

casualty /kæʒuəlti/ *n* (*pl* **-ties**) **1** (injured person) herido, -da *m,f*; (dead person) víctima *f*; (Mil) baja *f* **2** (hospital department) (BrE) (*no art*) urgencias *fpl*

cat /kæt/ *n* gato, -ta *m,f*; felino *m*; ***to let the ~ out of the bag*** descubrir* el pastel, levantar la liebre *or* (RPl) la perdiz; ***to rain ~s and dogs*** llover* a cántaros

Catalan¹ /'kætlæn ‖ 'kætəlæn/ *adj* catalán

Catalan² *n* **(a)** [C] (person) catalán, -lana *m,f* **(b)** [U] (language) catalán *m*

catalog¹, **catalogue** /'kætlɔ:g ‖ 'kætəlɒg/ *n* catálogo *m*

catalog², **catalogue** *vt* catalogar*

Catalonia /'kætl'əʊniə ‖ ˌkætə'ləʊniə/ *n* Cataluña *f*

catalyst /'kætləst ‖ 'kætəlɪst/ *n* catalizador *m*

catalytic converter /ˌkætl'ɪtɪk kən'vɜ:rtər ‖ ˌkætə'lɪtɪk kən'vɜ:tə(r)/ *n* catalizador *m*

catapult¹ /'kætəpʊlt ‖ 'kætəpʌlt/ *n* (Aviat, Mil) catapulta *f*

catapult² *vt* catapultar

cataract /'kætərækt/ *n* **1** (over a precipice) catarata *f*; (in a river) rápido *m* **2** (Med) catarata *f*

catarrh /kə'tɑ:r ‖ kə'tɑ:(r)/ *n* [U] catarro *m*

catastrophe /kə'tæstrəfi/ *n* catástrofe *f*

catch¹ /kætʃ/ (*past & past p* **caught**) *vt* **1** ‹*ball/object*› agarrar, coger* (esp Esp) **2** (capture) ‹*mouse/lion*› atrapar, coger* (esp Esp); ‹*fish*› pescar*, coger* (esp Esp); ‹*thief*› atrapar **3 (a)** (take by surprise) agarrar, pillar (fam), pescar* (fam); **we got caught in the rain** nos sorprendió la lluvia **(b)** (intercept) ‹*person*› alcanzar*; **~ you later** (colloq) nos vemos **4 (a)** ‹*train/plane*› (take) tomar, coger* (esp Esp); (be in time for) alcanzar* **(b)** (manage to see, hear): **we'll just ~ the end of the game** todavía podemos pescar el final del partido (fam); **we could ~ a movie before dinner** (AmE) podríamos ir al cine antes de cenar **5** (entangle, trap): **I caught my skirt on a nail** se me enganchó *or* (Méx tb) se me atoró *or* (Chi) se me pescó la falda en un clavo; **I caught my finger in the drawer** me pillé *or* (AmL tb) me agarré el dedo en el cajón **6** (hear or understand clearly): **did you ~ what she said?** ¿oíste lo que dijo? **7** ‹*disease*› contagiarse de; **to ~ a cold** resfriarse*, agarrar *or* (esp Esp) coger* un resfriado **8** (hit): **he caught his head on the beam** se dio en la cabeza con la viga ■ **~** *vi* **1 (a)** (grasp) agarrar, coger* (esp Esp), cachar (Méx) **(b)** (become hooked) engancharse **2** (ignite) «*fire*» prender, agarrar (AmL)

• **catch on** [*v* + *adv*] (colloq) **(a)** (become popular) «*fashion/idea*» imponerse*; «*game/style*» ponerse* de moda **(b)** (understand) caer* (fam)

• **catch out** [*v* + *o* + *adv*, *v* + *adv* + *o*] **(a) to ~ sb out** pillar *or* agarrar a algn desprevenido **(b)** (trick) pillar (fam), agarrar (CS fam)

• **catch up 1** [*v* + *adv*] (with work, studies) ponerse* al día; **to ~ up** WITH **sb/sth** (physically) alcanzar* a algn/algo; **she had to ~ up with the rest of the class** tuvo que ponerse al nivel del resto de la clase **2** [*v* + *o* + *adv*] (draw level with) (BrE) alcanzar* **3** (trap, involve) **to be/get caught up in sth** ‹*in barbed wire/thorns*› estar*/quedar enganchado/atrapado en algo; ‹*in scandal/dispute*› verse* envuelto en algo; ‹*in excitement/enthusiasm*› contagiarse de algo; **I got caught up in the traffic** me agarró *or* (esp Esp) me cogió el tráfico

catch² *n* **1 (a)** (Sport) atrapada *f*, atajada *f* (CS) **(b)** (of fish) pesca *f* **2** (on door) pestillo *m*, pasador *m* (AmL); (on window, box, necklace) cierre *m* **3** (hidden drawback) trampa *f*; **I knew there'd be a ~ in it somewhere** ya sabía yo que tenía que haber gato encerrado; **it's a C~-22 situation** es una situación sin salida

catcher /'kætʃər ‖ 'kætʃə(r)/ *n* (in baseball) receptor, -tora *m,f*, catcher *mf*

catching /'kætʃɪŋ/ *adj* (*pred*) contagioso

catchment area /'kætʃmənt/ *n* zona *f* de captación (*distrito que corresponde a un hospital, colegio etc*)

catch: **~phrase** *n* (of person) latiguillo *m*; (of political party) eslogan *m*; **~word** *n* **(a)** (slogan) eslogan *m* **(b)** ⇒ ~PHRASE

catchy /'kætʃi/ *adj* **catchier, catchiest** pegadizo, pegajoso (AmL exc RPl)

categorical /'kætə'gɔ:rɪkəl ‖ ˌkætə'gɒrɪkəl/ *adj* categórico; ‹*refusal*› rotundo

categorize /'kætəgəraɪz/ *vt* ‹*things*› clasificar*; ‹*people*› catalogar*

category /'kætəgɔ:ri ‖ 'kætəgəri/ *n* (*pl* **-ries**) categoría *f*

cater /'keɪtər ‖ 'keɪtə(r)/ *vt* (AmE) encargarse* del buffet de

• **cater to**, (BrE) **cater for** [*v* + *prep* + *o*]: **to ~ to** *o* **for people of all ages** ofrecer* servicios para gente de todas las edades; **we try to ~ to** *o* **for all needs** tratamos de satisfacer todas las necesidades

caterer /'keɪtərər ‖ 'keɪtərə(r)/ *n*: *persona o firma que se encarga del servicio de comida y bebida para fiestas, cafeterías etc*

catering /'keɪtərɪŋ/ *n* [U] **(a)** (provision of food): **to do the ~** encargarse* del servicio de comida y bebida (*or* del buffet *etc*) **(b)** (trade, department) restauración *f*

caterpillar /'kætərpɪlər ‖ 'kætəpɪlə(r)/ *n* oruga *f*, azotador *m* (Méx), cuncuna *f* (Chi)

cathedral /kə'θi:drəl/ *n* catedral *f*

Catholic¹ /'kæθəlɪk/ *n* católico, -ca *m,f*

Catholic² *adj* **1** (Relig) católico; **the Roman ~ Church** la iglesia católica (apostólica romana) **2 catholic** ‹*tastes/interests*› variado

Catholicism /kə'θɑ:ləsɪzəm ‖ kə'θɒlɪsɪzəm/ *n* [U] catolicismo *m*

cat: **~nap** *n* siestecita *f*; **C~'s-eye**® *n* (Transp) catafaros *m*, ojo *m* de gato (CS), estoperol *m* (Col)

catsup /'kætsəp/ *n* [U C] (AmE) ⇒ KETCHUP

cattle /'kætl/ *pl n* ganado *m*, reses *fpl*; (*before n*) **~ breeder** ganadero, -ra *m,f*

catwalk /'kætwɔ:k/ *n* pasarela *f*

Caucasian /kɔ:'keɪʒən/ *n* (Anthrop) caucásico, -ca *m,f*; **the suspect is a male ~** el sospechoso es un hombre de raza blanca

caught /kɔ:t/ *past & past p of* CATCH¹

cauliflower /'kɑ:lɪflaʊər ‖ 'kɒlɪflaʊə(r)/ *n* [C U] coliflor *f*

cause¹ /kɔːz/ *n* **1 (a)** [C] (of accident, event, death) causa *f* **(b)** [U] (reason, grounds) motivo *m*, razón *f*; **there's no ~ for concern** no hay por qué preocuparse **2** [C] (ideal, movement) causa *f*

cause² *vt* causar; **to ~ sb problems** causarle problemas a algn; **to ~ sb/sth** TO + INF hacer* que algn/algo (+ *subj*)

causeway /ˈkɔːzweɪ/ *n* (path) paso *m* elevado; (road) carretera *f* elevada

caustic /ˈkɔːstɪk/ *adj* cáustico

caution¹ /ˈkɔːʃən/ *n* **(a)** [U] (care, prudence) cautela *f*, prudencia *f* **(b)** [C] (warning) advertencia *f*, aviso *m*; (Law, Sport) amonestación *f*

caution² *vt* **(a)** (warn) advertir* **(b)** (inform of rights) informar de sus derechos

cautious /ˈkɔːʃəs/ *adj* cauteloso, cauto

cautiously /ˈkɔːʃəsli/ *adv* cautelosamente

cavalry /ˈkævəlri/ *n* [U] caballería *f*

cave /keɪv/ *n* cueva *f*; (*before n*) **~ painting** pintura *f* rupestre

• cave in [*v* + *adv*] derrumbarse

caveman /ˈkeɪvmæn/ *n* (*pl* **-men** /-men/) hombre *m* de las cavernas

cavern /ˈkævərn ‖ ˈkævən/ *n* caverna *f*

caviar, **caviare** /ˈkæviɑːr ‖ ˈkæviɑː(r)/ *n* [U] caviar *m*

cavity /ˈkævəti/ *n* (*pl* **-ties**) cavidad *f*; (Dent) caries *f*

caw /kɔː/ *vi* graznar

CBS *n* (in US) (*no art*) (= **Columbia Broadcasting System**) la CBS

cc (= **cubic centimeter** *o* (BrE) **centimetre**) c.c.

CD *n* (= **compact disc** *or* (AmE also) **disk**) CD *m*

cease /siːs/ *vt* **(a) to ~ to** + INF/ **to ~ -ING** dejar DE + INF **(b)** ‹*production/publication*› interrumpir, suspender ■ **~** *vi* «*noise*» cesar; «*production*» interrumpirse; «*work*» detenerse*

cease-fire /ˈsiːsˈfaɪr ‖ ˈsiːsfaɪə(r)/ *n* alto *m* el fuego, cese *m* del fuego (AmL)

ceaseless /ˈsiːsləs ‖ ˈsiːslɪs/ *adj* incesante

cedar /ˈsiːdər ‖ ˈsiːdə(r)/ *n* cedro *m*

cede /siːd/ *vt* **to ~ sth** (TO **sb**) ceder(le) algo (A algn)

ceiling /ˈsiːlɪŋ/ *n* (Const) techo *m*, cielo *m* raso; (upper limit) límite *m*, tope *m*

celebrate /ˈseləbreɪt ‖ ˈselɪbreɪt/ *vt* celebrar ■ **~** *vi*: **we won: let's ~!** ¡ganamos, vamos a celebrarlo!

celebration /ˈseləˈbreɪʃən ‖ ˌselɪˈbreɪʃən/ *n* [C U] (event) fiesta *f*; **he attended the ~s** asistió a los festejos

celebrity /səˈlebrəti ‖ sɪˈlebrəti/ *n* (*pl* **-ties**) famoso, -sa *m,f*, celebridad *mf*

celery /ˈseləri/ *n* [U] apio *m*, celeri *m* (Ven)

celibate /ˈseləbət ‖ ˈselɪbət/ *adj* célibe

cell /sel/ *n* **1** (in prison) celda *f* **2** (Biol, Elec) célula *f*

cellar /ˈselər ‖ ˈselə(r)/ *n* sótano *m*; (for coal) carbonera *f*; (for wine) bodega *f*

cello /ˈtʃeləʊ/ *n* (*pl* **-los**) violoncelo *m*, violonchelo *m*, chelo *m*

cellophane, (BrE) **Cellophane®** /ˈseləfeɪn/ *n* [U] celofán *m*

cellulite /ˈseljəlaɪt ‖ ˈseljʊlaɪt/ *n* [U] celulitis *f*

celluloid /ˈseljəlɔɪd ‖ ˈseljʊlɔɪd/ *n* [U] celuloide *m*

cellulose /ˈseljələʊs ‖ ˈseljʊləʊs/ *n* [U] celulosa *f*

Celsius /ˈselsiəs/ ▶ **406** *adj*: **20 degrees ~** 20 grados centígrados *or* Celsio(s)

Celt /kelt/ *n* celta *mf*

Celtic /ˈkeltɪk/ *adj* celta

cement¹ /sɪˈment/ *n* [U] cemento *m*

cement² *vt* **(a)** (Const) unir con cemento **(b)** ‹*friendship/alliance*› consolidar, fortalecer*

cement mixer *n* hormigonera *f*

cemetery /ˈseməteri ‖ ˈsemətri/ *n* (*pl* **-ries**) cementerio *m*

censor¹ /ˈsensər ‖ ˈsensə(r)/ *n* censor, -sora *m,f*

censor² *vt* censurar

censorship /ˈsensərʃɪp ‖ ˈsensəʃɪp/ *n* [U] censura *f*

censure /ˈsentʃər ‖ ˈsensjə(r)/ *vt* censurar

census /ˈsensəs/ *n* (*pl* **-suses**) censo *m*

cent /sent/ *n* centavo *m*

centenary /senˈtenəri ‖ senˈtiːnəri/ *n* (*pl* **-ries**) centenario *m*

centennial /senˈteniəl/ *n* (esp AmE) centenario *m*

center¹, (BrE) **centre** /ˈsentər ‖ ˈsentə(r)/ *n* **1** (middle point, area) centro *m* **2** (site of activity) centro *m* **3** (Sport) (in US football, rugby) centro *mf*; (in basketball) pivot *mf*, pivote *mf* (AmL)

center², (BrE) **centre** *vt* centrar ■ **~** *vi* **(a)** (focus on) **to ~** ON *o* UPON **sth/sb** centrarse EN algo/algn **(b)** (revolve around) **to ~** ON *o* AROUND **sth/sb** girar ALREDEDOR DE algo/algn

center: **~ forward** *n* delantero *mf* centro; **~ half** (*pl* **halfs** *or* **halves**) *n* medio *mf* centro; **~piece** *n* (decoration) centro *m* (de mesa); (main feature) eje *m*

centigrade /ˈsentɪgreɪd/ ▶ **406** *adj* centígrado

centimeter, (BrE) **centimetre** /ˈsentəˌmiːtər ‖ ˈsentɪˌmiːtə(r)/ ▶ **681** *n* centímetro *m*

centipede /ˈsentəpiːd ‖ ˈsentɪpiːd/ *n* ciempiés *m*

central /ˈsentrəl/ *adj* **(a)** (main) central; ‹*problem*› fundamental **(b)** (in the center) ‹*area/street*› céntrico; **in ~ Chicago** en el centro de Chicago

central: **C~ America** *n* Centroamérica *f*, América *f* Central; **C~ American** *adj* centroamericano, de (la) América Central; **C~ Europe** *n* Europa *f* Central; **~ heating** *n* [U] calefacción *f* central

centralize /ˈsentrəlaɪz/ *vt* centralizar*

central reservation *n* (BrE) mediana *f*, bandejón *m* (central) (Chi), camellón *m* (Méx)

centre *etc* (BrE) ⇒ CENTER *etc*

century /ˈsentʃəri/ ▶ **540** *n* (*pl* **-ries**) siglo *m*; **in the 19th ~** en el siglo XIX

ceramic /səˈræmɪk ‖ sɪˈræmɪk/ *adj* ‹*pot*› de cerámica; **~ tile** (for walls) azulejo *m*; (for floors) baldosa *f* (de cerámica)

ceramics /səˈræmɪks ‖ sɪˈræmɪks/ *n* (+ *pl vb*) objetos *mpl* de cerámica, cerámicas *fpl*

cereal /ˈsɪriəl ‖ ˈsɪəriəl/ *n* [C U] **(a)** (plant, grain) cereal *m* **(b)** (*breakfast* ~) cereales *mpl*

cerebral palsy /səˈri:brəl ˈpɔ:lzi ‖ ˈserɪbrəl ˈpɔ:lzi/ *n* [U] parálisis *f*

ceremonial /ˌserəˈməʊniəl ‖ ˌserɪˈməʊniəl/ *adj* ‹*robes*› ceremonial; ‹*occasion*› solemne

ceremony /ˈserəməʊni ‖ ˈserɪməni/ *n* [C U] (*pl* **-nies**) ceremonia *f*

certain /ˈsɜ:rtn̩ ‖ ˈsɜ:tn̩/ *adj* **1 (a)** (definite) seguro; **to make ~ OF sth** asegurarse *or* cerciorarse DE algo; **for ~** con certeza **(b)** (convinced) (*pred*) **to be ~ (OF sth)** estar* seguro (DE algo); **I checked the list to make ~ (that)** ... revisé la lista para asegurarme de que ... **2** (particular) (*before n*) cierto; **he has a ~ something** tiene un no sé qué *or* (un) algo especial

certainly /ˈsɜ:rtn̩li ‖ ˈsɜ:tn̩li/ *adv* **(a)** (definitely): **we're almost ~ going to win** es casi seguro que vamos a ganar; **do you see what I mean? — certainly** ¿te das cuenta de lo que quiero decir? — desde luego **(b)** (emphatic): **I ~ won't be buying anything there again!** por cierto que no voy a volver a comprar nada allí; **may I use your phone? — certainly!** ¿puedo llamar por teléfono? — pues claro ¡(no) faltaría más!; **~ not!** ¡de ninguna manera!

certainty /ˈsɜ:rtn̩ti ‖ ˈsɜ:tn̩ti/ *n* (*pl* **-ties**) [U C] certeza *f*, seguridad *f*; **defeat is now a ~** la derrota es algo seguro

certificate /sərˈtɪfɪkət ‖ səˈtɪfɪkət/ *n* certificado *m*

certify /ˈsɜ:rtəfaɪ ‖ ˈsɜ:tɪfaɪ/ *vt* **-fies, -fying, -fied (a)** ‹*facts/claim/death*› certificar*; **this is to ~ that** ... por la presente certifico que ... **(b)** (declare insane) (*usu pass*) declarar demente **(c)** (license) (AmE): **he isn't certified to teach in this state** no está habilitado para ejercer la docencia en este estado **(d) certified** *past p* (AmE) certificado; **certified public accountant** contador público, contadora pública *m,f* (AmL), censor jurado, censora jurada *m,f* de cuentas (Esp)

cervical /ˈsɜ:rvɪkəl ‖ ˈsɜ:vɪkəl, sɜ:ˈvaɪkəl/ *adj* del cuello del útero; **~ smear** (BrE) citología *f*, Papanicolau *m* (AmL)

cervix /ˈsɜ:rvɪks ‖ ˈsɜ:vɪks/ *n* (*pl* **-vixes** *or* **-vices** /-vəsi:z/) cuello *m* del útero

Cesarean (section), **Cesarian (section)** /sɪˈzæriən ‖sɪˈzeəriən/ *n* (AmE) cesárea *f*

cesspit /ˈsespɪt/ *n* pozo *m* negro *or* séptico *or* ciego

cf (compare) cf.

CFC *n* = **chlorofluorocarbon**

ch *n* (*pl* **chs**) (= **chapter**) c.

chafe /tʃeɪf/ *vt/i* rozar*

chaff /tʃæf ‖ tʃɑ:f/ *n* [U] barcia *f*

chagrin /ʃəˈgrɪn ‖ ˈʃægrɪn/ *n* [U] (liter) disgusto *m*; **to his ~** para su disgusto

chain¹ /tʃeɪn/ *n* cadena *f*; **a ~ of events** una cadena de acontecimientos

chain² *vt* **to ~ sth/sb TO sth** encadenar algo/a algn A algo

chain: **~ reaction** *n* reacción *f* en cadena; **~smoke** *vi* fumar un cigarrillo tras otro; **~ store** *n* tienda *f* de una cadena

chair¹ /tʃer ‖ tʃeə(r)/ *n* **1** (seat) silla *f*; (*arm~*) sillón *m*, butaca *f* (esp Esp) **2 (a)** (at university) cátedra *f* **(b)** (in meeting) presidencia *f*; **to take the ~** presidir

chair² *vt* ‹*meeting*› presidir

chair: **~lift** *n* telesilla *f or* (Esp) telesquí *m*; **~man** /ˈtʃermən ‖ ˈtʃeəmən/ *n* (*pl* **-men** /-mən/) presidente, -ta *m,f*; **~woman** *n* presidenta *f*

chalet /ʃæˈleɪ/ *n* **(a)** (cabin) chalet *m* (*de montaña*) **(b)** (in motel) (BrE) bungalow *m*

chalk /tʃɔ:k/ *n* **1** [U] (Geol) creta *f*, caliza *f* **2** [C U] (for writing) tiza *f*, gis *m* (Méx)

challenge¹ /ˈtʃæləndʒ ‖ ˈtʃælɪndʒ/ *vt* **1 (a)** (summon) desafiar*, retar; **to ~ sb to + INF** desafiar* a algn A QUE (+ *subj*) **(b)** (question) ‹*authority/findings*› cuestionar **2** (stop) (Mil) darle* el alto a

challenge² *n* [C U] desafío *m*, reto *m*

challenger /ˈtʃæləndʒər ‖ ˈtʃælɪndʒə(r)/ *n* contendiente *mf*, rival *mf*

chamber /ˈtʃeɪmbər ‖ ˈtʃeɪmbə(r)/ *n* **1** (room) (arch) cámara *f* (arc) **2** (of gun) recámara *f*

chamber: **~maid** *n* camarera *f* (*en un hotel*); **~ music** *n* [U] música *f* de cámara; **~ of commerce** *n* cámara *f* de comercio; **~ pot** *n* orinal *m or* (AmL exc RPl) bacinilla *f or* (CS) escupidera *f*

chameleon /kəˈmi:liən/ *n* camaleón *m*

chamois (leather) /ˈʃæmi/ *n* gamuza *f*

chamomile /ˈkæməmaɪl/ *n* manzanilla *f*, camomila *f*; **~ tea** manzanilla *f*

champagne /ʃæmˈpeɪn/ *n* [U C] champán *m*, champaña *f or m*

champion¹ /ˈtʃæmpiən/ *n* **(a)** (Sport) campeón, -peona *m,f* **(b)** (of cause) defensor, -sora *m,f*

champion² *vt* abogar* por, defender*

championship /ˈtʃæmpiənʃɪp/ *n* (Sport) (*often pl*) campeonato *m*

chance¹ /tʃæns ‖ tʃɑ:ns/ *n* **1** [U] (fate) casualidad *f*, azar *m*; **by ~** por *or* de casualidad; (*before n*) ‹*meeting*› fortuito **2** [C] (risk) riesgo *m*; **don't take any ~s** no te arriesgues **3** [C] (opportunity) oportunidad *f* **4** [C U] (likelihood) posibilidad *f*, chance *f or m* (esp AmL); **(the) ~s are (that)** ... (colloq) lo más probable es que ...

chance² *vt*: **to ~ it** arriesgarse*

chancellor /ˈtʃænslər ‖ ˈtʃɑ:nsələ(r)/ *n* **(a) Chancellor (of the Exchequer)** (in UK) ≈ ministro, -tra *m,f* de Economía/Hacienda **(b)** (premier) canciller *mf* **(c)** (of university) rector, -tora *m,f*

chandelier /ˈʃændəˈlɪr ‖ ˌʃændəˈlɪə(r)/ *n* araña *f* (*de luces*)

change¹ /tʃeɪndʒ/ *n* **1 (a)** [U C] cambio *m*; **a ~ in temperature** un cambio de temperatura; **for a ~** para variar **(b)** (of clothes) muda *f* **2** [U] **(a)** (coins) cambio *m*, monedas *fpl*, sencillo *m* (AmL), menudo *m* (Col), dinero *m* suelto, plata *f* suelta (AmS) **(b)** (money returned) cambio *m*, vuelto *m* (AmL), vuelta *f* (Esp), vueltas *fpl* (Col)

change² *vt* cambiar; **the witch ~d her into a stone** la bruja la convirtió en una piedra; **to ~ one's clothes** cambiarse de ropa; **to ~ color** cambiar de color; **let's ~ the subject** cambiemos de tema; **I wouldn't want to ~ places with her** no quisiera estar en su lugar; **to change train(s)**

hacer* transbordo, cambiar (de tren) ■ ~ *vi* **1 (a)** (become different) cambiar; **to ~ INTO sth** convertirse* EN algo **(b) changing** *pres p* ‹*needs/role/moods*› cambiante **2 (a)** (put on different clothes) cambiarse; **she ~d into a black dress** se cambió y se puso un vestido negro; **to get ~d** cambiarse **(b)** (Transp) cambiar, hacer* transbordo

• change over [*v* + *adv*] cambiar

changeable /'tʃeɪndʒəbəl/ *adj* cambiante

change: **~over** *n* (transition) **~over (FROM sth) (TO sth)** cambio *m* (DE algo) (A algo); **~ purse** *n* (AmE) monedero *m*, portamonedas *m*

changing room /'tʃeɪndʒɪŋ/ *n* (BrE) **(a)** (Sport) vestuario *m*, vestidor *m* (Chi, Méx) **(b)** (in shop) probador *m*

channel¹ /'tʃænl/ *n* **1** (strait) canal *m*; (course of river) cauce *m*; (navigable course) canal *m*; **the (English) C~** el Canal de la Mancha **2** (for irrigation) canal *m*, acequia *f* **3** (system, method) vía *f*; **you must go through the official ~s** tiene que hacer el trámite por los conductos oficiales **4** (Comput, TV) canal *m*

channel² *vt*, (BrE) **-ll-** ‹*water/proposals/complaints*› canalizar*; ‹*efforts/energies*› encauzar*

channel: **C~ Islands** *pl n* **the C~ Islands** las Islas Anglonormandas, las islas del Canal de la Mancha; **C~ Tunnel** *n* **the C~ Tunnel** el Eurotúnel, el túnel del Canal de la Mancha

chant¹ /tʃænt ‖ tʃɑːnt/ *n* (of demonstrators) consigna *f*; (of sports fans) alirón *m*, canción *f*

chant² *vt/i* (Mus, Relig) salmodiar; «*crowd*» gritar

chaos /'keɪɑːs ‖ 'keɪɒs/ *n* [U] caos *m*

chaotic /keɪ'ɑːtɪk ‖ keɪ'ɒtɪk/ *adj* caótico

chap /tʃæp/ *n* (colloq) tipo *m* (fam)

chap. *n* (*pl* **chaps**) (= **chapter**) c., cap.

chapel /'tʃæpəl/ *n* capilla *f*

chaperon, **chaperone** /'ʃæpərəʊn/ *n* (of young lady) acompañante *f*, chaperona *f*; (for young people) (AmE) acompañante *mf*

chaplain /'tʃæplən ‖ 'tʃæplɪn/ *n* capellán *m*

chapped /tʃæpt/ *adj* ‹*lips*› agrietado

chapter /'tʃæptər ‖ 'tʃæptə(r)/ *n* capítulo *m*

char /tʃɑːr ‖ tʃɑː(r)/ *vt* **-rr-** carbonizar*

character /'kærəktər ‖ 'kærəktə(r)/ *n* **1** [U C] (of person, thing) carácter *m*; **to be in/out of ~** ser*/no ser* típico; **her face is full of ~** tiene una cara con mucha personalidad **2** [C] **(a)** (in novel, play, movie) personaje *m* **(b)** (person) tipo *m* (fam) **(c)** (eccentric person) caso *m* **3** [C] (symbol) carácter *m*

characteristic¹ /'kærəktə'rɪstɪk/ *n* característica *f*

characteristic² *adj* característico

characterize /'kærəktəraɪz/ *vt* caracterizar*

charade /ʃə'reɪd ‖ʃə'rɑːd/ *n* farsa *f*; **~s** (+ *sing vb*) (game) charada *f*

charcoal /'tʃɑːrkəʊl ‖ 'tʃɑːkəʊl/ *n* [U] carbón *m* (vegetal); (Art) carboncillo *m*, carbonilla *f* (RPl)

charge¹ /tʃɑːrdʒ ‖ tʃɑːdʒ/ *n* **1** [C] (Law) cargo *m*, acusación *f*; **to bring** *o* **press ~s against sb** formular cargos contra algn **2** [C] (price) precio *m*; (fee) honorario *m*; **free of ~** gratuitamente, gratis **3** (responsibility): **the person in ~** la persona responsable; **to be in ~ of sth/sb** tener* algo/a algn a su (*or* mi *etc*) cargo; **to take ~ of** (of situation) hacerse* cargo de; (of class, guests) hacerse* cargo de, encargarse* de; (of task) encargarse de, ocuparse de **4** [C U] (Elec, Phys) carga *f* **5** [C] (of explosive) carga *f* **6** [C] (attack) carga *f*

charge² *vt* **1** (accuse) **to ~ sb WITH sth/-ING** acusar a algn DE algo/+ INF **2** (ask payment) cobrar **3** (obtain on credit): **to ~ sth TO sb** cargar* algo a la cuenta de algn **4 (a)** (entrust) (frml) **to ~ sb WITH sth/-ING** encomendarle* A algn algo/QUE (+ *subj*) **(b)** (allege) (AmE) aducir* **5** (attack) (Mil) cargar* contra; «*animal*» embestir* *or* arremeter contra **6** (Elec) ‹*battery*› cargar* ■ ~ *vi* **to ~ (AT sth/sb)** (Mil) cargar* (CONTRA algo/algn); «*animal*» arremeter *or* embestir* (CONTRA algo/algn)

charge: **~ account** *n* cuenta *f* de crédito; **~ card** *n* tarjeta *f* de pago

charger /'tʃɑːrdʒər ‖ 'tʃɑːdʒə(r)/ *n* (*battery* ~) cargador *m* de pilas; (Auto) cargador *m* de baterías

chariot /'tʃæriət/ *n* carro *m* (de guerra)

charisma /kə'rɪzmə/ *n* [U] carisma *m*

charismatic /'kærəz'mætɪk ‖ ˌkærɪz'mætɪk/ *adj* carismático

charitable /'tʃærətəbəl ‖ 'tʃærɪtəbəl/ *adj* **(a)** (generous, giving) caritativo **(b)** (kind) ‹*person*› bueno; ‹*interpretation*› benévolo, generoso

charity /'tʃærəti/ *n* (*pl* **-ties**) **1 (a)** [C] (organization) organización *f* benéfica *or* de beneficencia **(b)** [U] (relief) obras *fpl* de beneficencia; **to raise money for ~** recaudar dinero para un fin benéfico; (*before n*) ‹*work*› de beneficencia, benéfico **2** [U] (generosity, kindness) caridad *f*

charm¹ /tʃɑːrm ‖ tʃɑːm/ *n* **1 (a)** [U] (attractiveness) encanto *m* **(b)** [C] (attractive quality, feature) encanto *m* **2** [C] (spell) hechizo *m* **3** [C] (amulet) amuleto *m*, fetiche *m*; (on bracelet) dije *m*

charm² *vt* cautivar

charming /'tʃɑːrmɪŋ ‖ 'tʃɑːmɪŋ/ *adj* ‹*person*› encantador; ‹*room/house*› precioso

chart¹ /tʃɑːrt ‖ tʃɑːt/ *n* **1** (Aviat, Naut) carta *f* de navegación; (diagram, graph) gráfico *m*; (table) tabla *f* **2 charts** *pl* (best-selling records) **the ~s** la lista de éxitos

chart² *vt* ‹*course*› trazar*; ‹*progress/changes*› (follow closely) seguir* atentamente; (record) registrar gráficamente

charter¹ /'tʃɑːrtər ‖ 'tʃɑːtə(r)/ *n* **1** [C] **(a)** (constitution) carta *f* **(b)** (guarantee of rights) fuero *m*, privilegio *m* **2** [U] (Transp) (*before n*) ‹*flight/plane*› chárter *adj inv*

charter² *vt* **1** ‹*plane/ship/bus*› fletar, alquilar **2** (BrE) **chartered** *past p* ‹*engineer/surveyor*› colegiado; **~ed accountant** contador público, contadora pública *m,f* (AmL), censor jurado, censora jurada *m,f* de cuentas (Esp)

chase¹ /tʃeɪs/ *n* persecución *f*

chase² *vt* perseguir* ■ ~ *vi*: **we ~d after the thief** fuimos tras el ladrón; **to ~ after girls** ir* detrás de las chicas

• chase up [*v* + *o* + *adv*, *v* + *adv* + *o*] (colloq):

~ up this order for me, please averíguame qué pasó con este pedido, por favor; **I'll have to ~ him up about the report** voy a tener que recordarle lo del informe

chasm /'kæzəm/ *n* sima *f*, abismo *m*

chassis /'tʃæsi ‖ 'ʃæsi/ *n* (*pl* **chassis** /'tʃæsiz ‖ 'ʃæ-/) (Auto) chasis *m*, bastidor *m* (Esp)

chastise /tʃæs'taɪz/ *vt* (frml) (verbally) reprender; (physically) castigar*

chastity /'tʃæstəti/ *n* [U] castidad *f*

chat¹ /tʃæt/ *n* charla *f*, conversación *f* (esp AmL), plática *f* (AmC, Méx)

chat² *vi* **-tt- to ~** (TO *o* WITH **sb**) charlar *or* (esp AmL) conversar *or* (AmC, Méx) platicar* (CON algn)

chat show *n* (BrE) programa *m* de entrevistas

chatter /'tʃætər ‖ 'tʃætə(r)/ *vi* «*person*» charlar; «*monkeys*» parlotear; «*birds*» cotorrear; **his teeth are ~ing** le castañetean los dientes

chatterbox /'tʃætərbɑ:ks ‖ 'tʃætəbɒks/ *n* charlatán, -tana *m,f*

chatty /'tʃæti/ *adj* **-tier, -tiest** ‹*person*› conversador; ‹*letter*› simpático y lleno de noticias

chauffeur /'ʃəʊfər ‖ 'ʃəʊfə(r)/ *n* chofer *mf* *or* (Esp) chófer *mf*

chauvinism /'ʃəʊvənɪzəm ‖ 'ʃəʊvɪnɪzəm/ *n* [U] chovinismo *m*; **male ~** machismo *m*

chauvinist /'ʃəʊvənəst ‖ 'ʃəʊvɪnɪst/ *n* chovinista *mf*; **(male) ~** machista *m*

cheap /tʃi:p/ *adj* **-er, -est 1 (a)** (inexpensive) barato; ‹*restaurant/hotel*› económico **(b)** (shoddy) ‹*merchandise/jewelry*› ordinario, de baratillo; ‹*mechanic/electrician*› (AmE) chapucero **2 (a)** (vulgar, contemptible) ‹*joke/gimmick*› de mal gusto; ‹*trick/tactics*› bajo; ‹*liar/crook*› vil **(b)** (worthless) ‹*flattery/promises*› fácil

cheapen /'tʃi:pən/ *vt* quitarle valor a, degradar

cheaply /'tʃi:pli/ *adv* ‹*buy/sell/get*› barato; ‹*dress/eat/live*› con poco dinero

cheat¹ /tʃi:t/ *vt* estafar, engañar ■ **~** *vi* **(a)** (act deceitfully) hacer* trampas **(b)** (be unfaithful) **to ~** ON **sb** engañar a algn

cheat² *n* (swindler) estafador, -dora *m,f*; (at cards, in exam) tramposo, -sa *m,f*

check¹ /tʃek/ *n* **1** [C] (stop, restraint) control *m* **2** [C] (inspection — of passport, documents) control *m*; (— of work) examen *m*, revisión *f*; (— of machine, product) inspección *f*; **to keep a ~ on sth** controlar algo **3** [C U] (*before n*) ‹*jacket/shirt*› a *or* de cuadros **4** [U] (in chess) jaque *m* **5** (Fin), (BrE) **cheque** cheque *m*, talón *m* (Esp); **to pay by ~** pagar* con cheque *or* (Esp) con talón **6** [C] (restaurant bill) (AmE) cuenta *f*, adición *f* (RPl) **7** [C] (tick) (AmE) signo *m*, tic *m*, palomita *f* (Méx), visto *m* (Esp), palomita *f* (Méx fam)

check² *vt* **1** (restrain) ‹*anger/impulse*› contener* **2 (a)** (inspect) ‹*passport/ticket*› revisar, checar* (Méx); ‹*machine/product*› inspeccionar; ‹*quality*› controlar; ‹*temperature/pressure/volume*› comprobar*, checar* (Méx) **(b)** (verify) ‹*facts/information*› comprobar*, verificar*, checar* (Méx); ‹*accounts/bill*› revisar **3** (AmE) **(a)** (in cloakroom) dejar en el guardarropa; (in baggage office) dejar *or* (frml) depositar en consigna **(b)** (Aviat) ‹*baggage*› facturar, chequear (AmL) **4** (tick) (AmE) marcar*, hacer* un tic *or* (Méx fam) una palomita en, poner* un visto en (Esp) ■ **~** *vi* comprobar*, verificar*, checar* (Méx)

• **check in 1** [*v* + *adv*] (at airport) facturar *or* (AmL tb) chequear el equipaje; (at hotel) registrarse **2** [*v* + *o* + *adv*, *v* + *adv* + *o*] (Aviat) ‹*luggage*› facturar, chequear (AmL)

• **check out 1** [*v* + *adv*] *dejar el hotel* (*or pensión etc*) (*habiendo pagado la factura etc*) **2** [*v* + *adv*] (tally) (AmE) «*story*» cuadrar **3** [*v* + *o* + *adv*, *v* + *adv* + *o*] **(a)** ‹*facts/story*› verificar*, comprobar*, checar* (Méx) **(b)** (esp AmE) ‹*shopping*› «*customer*» pagar*; «*cashier*» cobrar

• **check up** [*v* + *adv*]: **we ~ed up and found out he was lying** hicimos averiguaciones y comprobamos que mentía; **can you ~ up on that?** ¿puedes comprobarlo?

checkbook, (BrE) **chequebook** /'tʃekbʊk/ *n* chequera *f*, talonario *m* de cheques (esp Esp)

checked /tʃekt/ *adj* (*no comp*) a *or* de cuadros

checker /'tʃekər ‖ 'tʃekə(r)/ *n* (AmE) (cashier) cajero, -ra *m,f*

checkered, (BrE) **chequered** /'tʃekərd ‖ 'tʃekəd/ *adj* ‹*career/history*› accidentado

checkers /'tʃekərz ‖ 'tʃekəz/ *n* (AmE) (+ *sing vb*) damas *fpl*

check-in /'tʃekɪn/ *n* facturación *f* de equipajes

checking account /'tʃekɪŋ/ *n* (AmE) cuenta *f* corriente

check: **~list** *n* lista *f* de control; **~mate** *n* [C U] (jaque *m*) mate *m*; **~out** *n* caja *f*; **~point** *n* control *m*; **~room** *n* (AmE) guardarropa *m*; **~up** *n* (Med) chequeo *m*, revisión *f*

cheek /tʃi:k/ *n* **1** ▶ **484** [C] (of the face) mejilla *f*, cachete *m* (AmL fam) **2** [U] (colloq) (impudence) descaro *m*, cara *f* (fam)

cheekbone /'tʃi:kbəʊn/ *n* pómulo *m*

cheeky /'tʃi:ki/ *adj* **-kier, -kiest** (esp BrE) ‹*boy/girl*› fresco, descarado; ‹*grin*› pícaro

cheep /tʃi:p/ *vi* piar*

cheer¹ /tʃɪr ‖ tʃɪə(r)/ *n* **1** [C] (of encouragement, approval) ovación *f*, aclamación *f*; **three ~s for Fred!** ¡viva Fred! **2 cheers** *pl* (*as interj*) (drinking toast) ¡salud!

cheer² *vt* **(a)** (shout in approval) aclamar, vitorear **(b) ~ (on)** (shout encouragement at) animar ■ **~** *vi* aplaudir

• **cheer up 1** [*v* + *adv*] animarse **2** [*v* + *o* + *adv*, *v* + *adv* + *o*] ‹*person*› animar

cheerful /'tʃɪrfəl ‖ 'tʃɪəfəl/ *adj* alegre; ‹*news/prospect*› alentador

cheerleader /'tʃɪr,li:dər ‖ 'tʃɪə,li:də(r)/ *n* animador, -dora *m,f* (*en encuentros deportivos, mitines políticos*), porrista *mf* (Col, Méx)

cheese /tʃi:z/ *n* [U C] queso *m*

cheese: **~board** *n* tabla *f* de quesos; **~cake** *n* [U C] tarta *f* de queso; **~cloth** *n* [U] estopilla *f*, bambula *f*

cheetah /'tʃi:tə/ *n* guepardo *m*, chita *f*

chef /ʃef/ *n* chef *m*, jefe -fa *m,f* de cocina

chemical¹ /'kemɪkəl/ *n* [C U] sustancia *f* química, producto *m* químico

chemical² *adj* químico

chemist /'kemәst ‖ 'kemɪst/ *n* **(a)** (scientist) químico, -ca *m,f* **(b)** (pharmacist) (BrE) farmacéutico, -ca *m,f*; **the ~'s** la farmacia

chemistry /'kemәstri ‖ 'kemɪstri/ *n* [U] química *f*

chemotherapy /'ki:mәʊ'θerәpi/ *n* [U] quimioterapia *f*

cheque /tʃek/ *n* (BrE) ⇒ CHECK¹ 5

chequebook /'tʃekbʊk/ *n* (BrE) ⇒ CHECKBOOK

chequered /'tʃekәrd ‖ 'tʃekәd/ *adj* (BrE) ⇒ CHECKERED

cherish /'tʃerɪʃ/ *vt* **(a)** (care for, value) apreciar **(b)** (cling to) ‹*memory/hope*› conservar

cherry /'tʃeri/ *n* (*pl* **-ries**) cereza *f*; (*before n*) **~ tree** cerezo *m*

chess /tʃes/ *n* [U] ajedrez *m*

chessboard /'tʃesbɔ:rd ‖ 'tʃesbɔ:d/ *n* tablero *m* de ajedrez

chest /tʃest/ *n* **1** **▶ 484** (Anat) pecho *m*; ***to get sth off one's ~*** desahogarse* contando/confesando algo **2** (box) arcón *m* **3** (AmE) (treasury) tesorería *f*; (funds) fondos *mpl*

chestnut¹ /'tʃesnʌt/ *n* castaña *f*; **~ tree** castaño *m*

chestnut² **▶ 515** *adj* castaño

chest of drawers *n* (*pl* **~s ~ ~**) cómoda *f*

chew /tʃu:/ *vt* ‹*food*› mascar*, masticar*; ‹*gum*› mascar*

chewing gum /'tʃu:ɪŋ/ *n* [U] chicle *m*

chick /tʃɪk/ *n* (young bird) polluelo, -la *m,f*; (young chicken) pollito, -ta *m,f*

chicken /'tʃɪkәn ‖ 'tʃɪkɪn/ *n* **(a)** [C] (hen) gallina *f*; (as generic term) pollo *m* **(b)** [U] (Culin) pollo *m*

• chicken out [*v* + *adv*] (colloq) acobardarse, achicarse* (fam), rajarse (fam)

chickenpox /'tʃɪkәnpɑ:ks ‖ 'tʃɪkɪnpɒks/ *n* [U] varicela *f*, peste *f* cristal (Chi)

chickpea /'tʃɪkpi:/ *n* garbanzo *m*

chicory /'tʃɪkәri/ *n* [U] (Bot) endivia *f*; (in coffee) achicoria *f*

chief¹ /tʃi:f/ *n* jefe, -fa *m,f*, líder *mf*; **~ of police** jefe de policía

chief² *adj* (*before n, no comp*) principal

chief: **~ constable** *n* jefe, -fa *m,f* de policía; **~ justice** *n* (in US) presidente, -ta *m,f* del tribunal

chilblain /'tʃɪlbleɪn/ *n* sabañón *m*

child /tʃaɪld/ *n* (*pl* **children** /'tʃɪldrәn/) **(a)** (boy) niño *m*; (girl) niña *f* **(b)** (son) hijo *m*; (daughter) hija *f*

childbirth /'tʃaɪldbɜ:rθ ‖ 'tʃaɪldbɜ:θ/ *n* [U] parto *m*

childhood /'tʃaɪldhʊd/ *n* [U C] niñez *f*, infancia *f*

childish /'tʃaɪldɪʃ/ *adj* infantil

childlike /'tʃaɪldlaɪk/ *adj* ingenuo, de niño

children /'tʃɪldrәn/ *pl of* CHILD

Chile /'tʃɪli/ *n* Chile *m*

Chilean /'tʃɪliәn/ *adj* chileno

chili, **chilli** /'tʃɪli/ *n* (*pl* **-lies**) ají *m*, chile *m*

chill¹ /tʃɪl/ *n* **(a)** [U] (coldness — of weather) frío *m*, fresco *m* **(b)** [C] (Med) enfriamiento *m*, resfriado *m*

chill² *vt* enfriar*; ‹*wine/food*› poner* a enfriar

chilli *n* (*pl* **-lies**) ⇒ CHILI

chilly /'tʃɪli/ *adj* **-lier, -liest** frío

chime¹ /tʃaɪm/ *n* (of bells, clock) campanada *f*; (of doorbell) campanilla *f*

chime² *vi* «*bell*» sonar*; «*clock*» dar* la hora

chimney /'tʃɪmni/ *n* chimenea *f*

chimney sweep *n* deshollinador, -dora *m,f*

chimpanzee /'tʃɪmpæn'zi: ‖ ˌtʃɪmpәn'zi:/ *n* chimpancé *m*

chin /tʃɪn/ *n* barbilla *f*, mentón *m*

china /'tʃaɪnә/ *n* [U] loza *f*; (fine) porcelana *f*

China /'tʃaɪnә/ *n* China *f*

Chinese¹ /tʃaɪ'ni:z/ *adj* chino

Chinese² *n* (*pl* **~**) **(a)** [C] (person) chino, -na *m,f* **(b)** [U] (language) chino *m*

chink /tʃɪŋk/ *n* grieta *f*, abertura *f*

chip¹ /tʃɪp/ *n* **1** **(a)** (of wood) astilla *f*; (of stone) esquirla *f*; ***to have a ~ on one's shoulder*** ser* un resentido **(b)** (in cup) desportilladura *f* **2** (Culin) **(a)** (in packet) (AmE) papa *f* or (Esp) patata *f* frita, papa *f* chip (Ur) **(b)** (French fry) (BrE) papa *f* or (Esp) patata *f* frita **3** (Games) ficha *f* **4** (Comput, Electron) chip *m*

chip² **-pp-** *vt* ‹*crockery*› desportillar, cascar* (RPl), saltar (Chi); ‹*tooth*› romper* un trocito de ■ **~** *vi* «*china/cup*» desportillarse, cascarse* (RPl), saltarse (Chi); «*paint/varnish*» saltarse, desconcharse

chipboard /'tʃɪpbɔ:rd ‖ 'tʃɪpbɔ:d/ *n* [U] **(a)** (of wood) madera *f* prensada *or* aglomerada, aglomerado *m* **(b)** (of paper) (AmE) cartón *m* prensado

chipmunk /'tʃɪpmʌŋk/ *n* ardilla *f* listada

chiropodist /kә'rɑ:pәdәst ‖ kɪ'rɒpәdɪst/ *n* pedicuro, -ra *m,f*, podólogo, -ga *m,f*, callista *mf*

chirp /tʃɜ:rp ‖ tʃɜ:p/ *vi* piar*

chisel¹ /'tʃɪzәl/ *n* (for stone) cincel *m*; (for wood) formón *m*, escoplo *m*

chisel² *vt*, (BrE) **-ll-** ‹*stone*› cincelar; ‹*wood*› labrar

chivalry /'ʃɪvәlri/ *n* [U] caballerosidad *f*, cortesía *f*

chives /tʃaɪvz/ *pl n* cebollinos *mpl*, cebolletas *fpl*

chlorine /'klɔ:ri:n/ *n* [U] cloro *m*

chlorofluorocarbon /'klɔ:rәʊ'flʊrәʊ'kɑ:rbәn ‖ ˌklɔ:rәʊˌflʊәrәʊ'kɑ:bәn, -flɔ:rә-/ *n* clorofluorocarbono *m*

chloroform /'klɔ:rәfɔ:rm ‖ 'klɒrәfɔ:m/ *n* [U] cloroformo *m*

chocolate /'tʃɑ:klәt ‖ 'tʃɒklәt/ *n* **(a)** [U C] chocolate *m*; (candy, sweet) bombón *m* **(b)** [U] (*drinking* **~**) chocolate *m* en polvo; **a cup of hot ~** una taza de chocolate

choice¹ /tʃɔɪs/ *n* **(a)** [C U] (act, option) elección *f*; **I don't work here out of ~** no es por (mi) gusto que trabajo aquí **(b)** [C] (person, thing chosen): **she's a possible ~ for the job** es una de las candidatas posibles para el puesto; **it was an unfortunate ~ of words** no fue la mejor manera de decirlo **(c)** (variety) (*no pl*) surtido *m*, selección *f*

choice² *adj* **choicer, choicest** ‹*fruit/wine*› selecto; ‹*beef/veal*› (in US) de primera

choir /kwaɪr ‖ 'kwaɪә(r)/ *n* coro *m*

choke¹ /tʃəʊk/ *vt* estrangular, ahogar*, asfixiar ■ ~ *vi* ahogarse*, asfixiarse; **to ~ ON sth** atragantarse *or* (AmL tb) atorarse CON algo

choke² *n* [C U] (Auto) choke *m*, estárter *m*, cebador *m* (RPl), ahogador *m* (Chi, Méx)

cholera /'kɑːlərə ‖ 'kɒlərə/ *n* [U] cólera *m*

cholesterol /kə'lestərəʊl ‖ kə'lestərɒl/ *n* [U] colesterol *m*

choose /tʃuːz/ (*past* **chose**; *past p* **chosen**) *vt* **(a)** (select) elegir*, escoger*; ‹*candidate*› elegir* **(b)** (decide) **to ~ to** + INF decidir + INF, optar POR + INF ■ ~ *vi* elegir*, escoger*

choosy /'tʃuːzi/ *adj* **-sier, -siest** (colloq) exigente

chop¹ /tʃɑːp ‖ tʃɒp/ *n* **1** (with ax, cleaver) hachazo *m*; (with hand) manotazo *m*; (in karate) golpe *m* **2** (Culin) chuleta *f*, costilla *f* (AmS)

chop² -pp- *vt* **(a)** (cut) ‹*wood*› cortar; ‹*meat/apple*› cortar (*en trozos pequeños*); ‹*parsley/onion*› picar* **(b) chopped** *past p* ‹*onions/herbs*› picado; ‹*meat*› (AmE) molido *or* (Esp, RPl) picado

• **chop down** [*v* + *o* + *adv*, *v* + *adv* + *o*] cortar

• **chop off** [*v* + *o* + *adv*, *v* + *adv* + *o*] ‹*branch*› cortar

• **chop up** [*v* + *o* + *adv*, *v* + *adv* + *o*] ⇒ CHOP² (a)

chopper /'tʃɑːpər ‖ 'tʃɒpə(r)/ *n* **(a)** (hatchet) hacha *f*‡ pequeña **(b)** (helicopter) (colloq) helicóptero *m*

chopping board /'tʃɑːpɪŋ ‖ 'tʃɒpɪŋ/ *n* tabla *f* de picar

choppy /'tʃɑːpi ‖ 'tʃɒpi/ *adj* **-pier, -piest** ‹*sea*› picado

chopstick /'tʃɑːpstɪk ‖ 'tʃɒpstɪk/ *n* palillo *m* (*para comer comida oriental*)

chord /kɔːrd ‖ kɔːd/ *n* (Mus) acorde *m*

chore /tʃɔːr ‖ tʃɔː(r)/ *n* (routine task) tarea *f*; (tedious task) lata *f* (fam)

choreographer /'kɔːri'ɑːgrəfər ‖ ˌkɒri'ɒgrəfə(r)/ *n* coreógrafo, -fa *m,f*

choreography /'kɔːri'ɑːgrəfi ‖ ˌkɒri'ɒgrəfi/ *n* [U] coreografía *f*

chortle /'tʃɔːrtl̩ ‖ 'tʃɔːtl̩/ *vi* reírse* (*con satisfacción*)

chorus /'kɔːrəs/ *n* **1** (+ *sing o pl vb*) (in musical, opera) coro *m* **2** (refrain) estribillo *m*; (choral piece) coral *m*

chose /tʃəʊz/ *past of* CHOOSE

chosen /'tʃəʊzən/ *past p of* CHOOSE

Christ /kraɪst/ *n* **(a)** (Relig) Cristo **(b)** (*as interj*) (colloq) ¡Jesús! (fam); **for ~'s sake!** ¡por amor de Dios!

christen /'krɪsn̩/ *vt* bautizar*

christening /'krɪsn̩ɪŋ/ *n* [U C] bautismo *m*, bautizo *m*

Christian¹ /'krɪstʃən/ *n* cristiano, -na *m,f*

Christian² *adj* cristiano

Christianity /'krɪsti'ænəti, 'krɪstʃi- ‖ ˌkrɪsti'ænətɪ/ *n* [U] (faith) cristianismo *m*; (believers) los cristianos

Christian name *n* nombre *m* de pila

Christmas /'krɪsməs/ *n* Navidad *f*, Pascua *f* (Chi, Per); (**~*time***) las Navidades, la Navidad, la Pascua (Chi, Per); **merry** *o* (BrE also) **happy ~!** ¡Feliz Navidad!, ¡Felices Pascuas!; (*before n*) **~ cake** pastel *m* de Navidad (*pastel de frutas cubierto de mazapán y azúcar glaseado*); **~ card** tarjeta *f* de Navidad, tarjeta *f* de Pascua (Chi, Per), crismas *m* (Esp); **~ Day** día *m* de Navidad *or* (Chi, Per tb) de Pascua; **~ Eve** (day) la víspera de Navidad; (evening) Nochebuena *f*; **~ tree** árbol *m* de Navidad *or* (Chi, Per tb) de Pascua

chrome /krəʊm/ *n* [U] cromo *m*

chromium /'krəʊmiəm/ *n* [U] cromo *m*

chromosome /'krəʊməsəʊm/ *n* cromosoma *m*

chronic /'krɑːnɪk ‖ 'krɒnɪk/ *adj* (Med) crónico; ‹*unemployment/shortages*› crónico; ‹*smoker/liar*› empedernido

chronicle /'krɑːnɪkəl ‖ 'krɒnɪkəl/ *n* crónica *f*

chronological /'krɑːnə'lɑːdʒɪkəl ‖ ˌkrɒnə'lɒdʒɪkəl/ *adj* cronológico

chrysalis /'krɪsələs ‖ 'krɪsəlɪs/ *n* crisálida *f*

chubby /'tʃʌbi/ *adj* **-bier, -biest** (colloq) ‹*legs/cheeks/face*› regordete (fam); ‹*person*› gordinflón (fam)

chuck /tʃʌk/ *vt* (colloq) **(a)** (throw) tirar, aventar* (Méx) **(b)** (throw away) tirar, botar (AmL exc RPl) **(c)** (give up) (colloq) ‹*job*› dejar, plantar (fam); ‹*boyfriend/girlfriend*› plantar (fam), botar (AmC, Chi fam), largar* (RPl fam)

chuckle /'tʃʌkəl/ *vi* reírse*

chum /tʃʌm/ *n* (colloq) amigo, -ga *m,f*, compinche *mf* (fam), cuate *m* (Méx fam), pata *m* (Per fam), pana *mf* (Ven fam)

chunk /tʃʌŋk/ *n* pedazo *m*, trozo *m*

chunky /'tʃʌŋki/ *adj* **-kier, -kiest** ‹*person*› fornido; ‹*sweater*› grueso

church /tʃɜːrtʃ ‖ tʃɜːtʃ/ *n* iglesia *f*

churchgoer /'tʃɜːrtʃˌgəʊər ‖ 'tʃɜːtʃˌgəʊə(r)/ *n* practicante *mf*

churn¹ /tʃɜːrn ‖ tʃɜːn/ *n* mantequera *f*

churn² *vt* ‹*milk*› batir; ‹*butter*› hacer*

• **churn out** [*v* + *o* + *adv*, *v* + *adv* + *o*] (colloq) producir* como salchichas (fam)

• **churn up** [*v* + *o* + *adv*, *v* + *adv* + *o*] revolver*

chute /ʃuːt/ *n* tolva *f*, vertedor *m*; (in swimming pool, amusement park) tobogán *m*, rodadero *m* (Col)

CIA *n* (= **Central Intelligence Agency**) CIA *f*

cider /'saɪdər ‖ 'saɪdə(r)/ *n* [U C] **(a)** (alcoholic) sidra *f*; **hard ~** (AmE) sidra *f* fermentada **(b)** (non-alcoholic) (AmE): **(sweet) ~** jugo *m or* (Esp) zumo *m* de manzana

cigar /sɪ'gɑːr ‖ sɪ'gɑː(r)/ *n* cigarro *m*, puro *m*, tabaco *m* (Col)

cigarette /'sɪgə'ret/ *n* cigarrillo *m*; (*before n*) **~ end** colilla *f*; **~ holder** boquilla *f*; **~ lighter** encendedor *m*, mechero *m* (Esp)

cinch /sɪntʃ/ *n* (colloq) (*no pl*) (easy task): **it's a ~** es pan comido (fam), es tirado (Esp fam), es una papa *or* un bollo (RPl fam), es botado (Chi fam)

cinder /'sɪndər ‖ 'sɪndə(r)/ *n* **(a)** [C] (ember) carbonilla *f*, carboncillo *m*; **the dinner was burnt to a ~** la cena estaba carbonizada **(b) cinders** *pl* (ashes) ceniza *f*, rescoldo *m*

cinecamera /'sɪnɪˌkæmərə/ *n* (BrE) filmadora *f* (AmL), tomavistas *m* (Esp); (large, professional) cámara *f* cinematográfica

cinema /'sɪnəmə || 'sɪnəmɑː/ *n* [C U] cine *m*

cinnamon /'sɪnəmən/ *n* [U] canela *f*

cipher /'saɪfər || 'saɪfə(r)/ *n* [C U] clave *f*, cifra *f*

circa /'sɜːrkə || 'sɜːkə/ *prep* alrededor de, hacia

circle¹ /'sɜːrkəl || 'sɜːkəl/ *n* círculo *m*; **their ~ of friends** su círculo de amigos; ***to come/go full ~*** volver* al punto de partida

circle² *vt* **1** (move around) dar* vueltas alrededor de; (be around) rodear, cercar* **2** (draw circle around) trazar* un círculo alrededor de ■ ~ *vi* dar* vueltas; «*aircraft/bird*» volar* en círculos

circuit /'sɜːrkət || 'sɜːkɪt/ *n* **1** (passage around) recorrido *m*, vuelta *f* **2** (Elec) circuito *m*

circular¹ /'sɜːrkjələr || 'sɜːkjʊlə(r)/ *adj* circular

circular² *n* circular *f*

circulate /'sɜːrkjəleɪt || 'sɜːkjʊleɪt/ *vi* circular ■ ~ *vt* ‹*report/news*› hacer* circular, divulgar*

circulation /'sɜːrkjə'leɪʃən || ˌsɜːkjʊ'leɪʃən/ *n* [U] circulación *f*

circumcise /'sɜːrkəmsaɪz || 'sɜːkəmsaɪz/ *vt* circuncidar

circumference /sər'kʌmfərəns || sə'kʌmfərəns/ *n* circunferencia *f*

circumflex (accent) /'sɜːrkəmfleks || 'sɜːkəmfleks/ *n* (acento *m*) circunflejo *m*

circumstance /'sɜːrkəmstæns || 'sɜːkəmstəns/ *n* **1** (condition, fact) circunstancia *f*; **in** *o* **under the ~s** dadas las circunstancias; **under no ~s** bajo ningún concepto, bajo ninguna circunstancia **2 circumstances** *pl* (financial position): **a person in my ~s** una persona en mi situación económica

circumstantial /'sɜːrkəm'stæntʃəl || ˌsɜːkəm'stænʃəl/ *adj* ‹*evidence*› circunstancial

circus /'sɜːrkəs || 'sɜːkəs/ *n* circo *m*

cirrhosis /sə'rəʊsəs || sɪ'rəʊsɪs/ *n* [U] cirrosis *f*

CIS *n* (= **Commonwealth of Independent States**) CEI *f*

cistern /'sɪstərn || 'sɪstən/ *n* cisterna *f*

cite /saɪt/ *vt* citar

citizen /'sɪtəzən || 'sɪtɪzən/ *n* ciudadano, -na *m,f*

citizenship /'sɪtəzənʃɪp || 'sɪtɪzənʃɪp/ *n* [U] ciudadanía *f*

citrus /'sɪtrəs/ *adj* (*before n*) cítrico

city /'sɪti/ *n* (*pl* **cities**) ciudad *f*; (*before n*) **~ center** centro *m* de la ciudad

city: **~ hall** *n* (AmE) ayuntamiento *m*, municipio *m*; **~ planner** *n* (AmE) urbanista *mf*; **~ planning** *n* [U] (AmE) urbanismo *m*

civic /'sɪvɪk/ *adj* ‹*authorities*› civil; ‹*leader*› de la ciudad; ‹*duty/virtues*› cívico; **~ center** edificios *mpl* municipales

civil /'sɪvəl || 'sɪvl̩/ *adj* **(a)** (of society, citizens) civil **(b)** (polite) cortés

civilian /sə'vɪljən || sɪ'vɪljən/ *n* civil *mf*

civilization /'sɪvələ'zeɪʃən || ˌsɪvəlar'zeɪʃən/ *n* [U C] civilización *f*

civilized /'sɪvəlaɪzd/ *adj* ‹*society*› civilizado; ‹*person*› educado

civil: **~ liberties** *pl n* derechos *mpl* civiles; **~ rights** *pl n* derechos *mpl* civiles; **~ servant** *n* funcionario, -ria *m,f* (del Estado); **~ service** *n* **the ~ service** la administración pública; (employees) el funcionariado (del Estado); **~ war** *n* [U C] guerra *f* civil; **the C~ War** (in US) la guerra de Secesión

claim¹ /kleɪm/ *n* **1** (demand): **wage** *o* **pay ~** reivindicación *f* salarial; **insurance ~** reclamación *f* al seguro; **a ~ for expenses** una solicitud de reembolso de gastos **2** (to right, title) **~ (TO sth)** derecho *m* (A algo) **3** (allegation) afirmación *f*

claim² *vt* **1 (a)** ‹*throne/inheritance/land*› reclamar; ‹*right*› reivindicar*; ‹*diplomatic immunity*› alegar* **(b)** ‹*lost property*› reclamar **(c)** ‹*social security/benefits*› (apply for) solicitar; (receive) cobrar; **you can ~ your expenses back** puedes pedir que te reembolsen los gastos **2** (allege, profess): **he ~ed (that) he knew nothing about it** aseguraba *or* afirmaba no saber nada de ello

claimant /'kleɪmənt/ *n* **(a)** (Soc Adm) solicitante *mf* **(b)** (to throne) pretendiente, -ta *m,f*

clairvoyant /kler'vɔɪənt || kleə'vɔɪənt/ *n* clarividente *mf*

clam /klæm/ *n* almeja *f*

● **clam up**: **-mm-** [*v* + *adv*] (colloq) ponerse* muy poco comunicativo

clamber /'klæmbər || 'klæmbə(r)/ *vi* trepar; **they ~ed over the wall** treparon al muro y saltaron

clammy /'klæmi/ *adj* **-mier, -miest** ‹*handshake*› húmedo; ‹*weather*› bochornoso

clamor, (BrE) **clamour** /'klæmər || 'klæmə(r)/ *vi* gritar; **to ~ FOR sth** ‹*for war/resignation*› pedir* algo a gritos

clamp¹ /klæmp/ *n* **(a)** (Const) abrazadera *f*; (in carpentry) tornillo *m* de banco **(b)** (*wheel ~*) (BrE) cepo *m*

clamp² *vt* **(a)** (join, fasten) sujetar con abrazaderas **(b)** (BrE Auto) (colloq) ‹*car*› ponerle* el cepo a

● **clamp down** [*v* + *adv*] **to ~ down ON sth/sb** tomar medidas drásticas CONTRA algo/algn

clampdown /'klæmpdaʊn/ *n* (colloq): **a ~ on illegal immigrants** medidas *fpl* drásticas contra los inmigrantes ilegales; **there's been a ~ on loans** se ha restringido severamente la concesión de créditos

clan /klæn/ *n* clan *m*

clandestine /klæn'destən || klæn'destɪn/ *adj* clandestino

clang /klæŋ/ *vi* «*bells*» sonar*

clank /klæŋk/ *vi* hacer* ruido

clap¹ /klæp/ *n* **(a)** (applause): **to give sb a ~** aplaudir a algn **(b) a ~ of thunder** un trueno

clap² **-pp-** *vt* (applaud) aplaudir; **to ~ one's hands to the music** dar* palmadas al compás de la música ■ ~ *vi* (applaud) aplaudir; (to music etc) dar* una palmada

clapping /'klæpɪŋ/ *n* [U] aplausos *mpl*

clarify /'klærəfaɪ || 'klærɪfaɪ/ **-fies, -fying, -fied** *vt* **(a)** (explain, make clear) aclarar **(b)** (purify) ‹*butter/wine*› clarificar*

clarinet /'klærə'net/ *n* clarinete *m*

clarity /'klærəti/ *n* [U] claridad *f*

clash¹ /klæʃ/ *n* **1** (of interests) conflicto *m*; (of cultures, personalities) choque *m*; (of opinions, views) disparidad *f* **2** (between armies, factions) enfrentamiento *m*, choque *m* **3** (noise): **the ~ of the cymbals** el sonido de los platillos

clash² *vi* **(a)** «*personalities*» chocar*; «*colors/patterns*» desentonar **(b)** «*armies/factions/leaders*» chocar* **(c)** «*dates*» coincidir **(d)** «*cymbals/swords*» sonar* (*al entrechocarse*)

clasp¹ /klæsp ‖klɑ:sp/ *n* broche *m*, cierre *m*

clasp² *vt*: **she ~ed her bag firmly** sujetó firmemente el bolso; **he ~ed her in his arms** la estrechó entre sus brazos

class¹ /klæs ‖ klɑ:s/ *n* **1** [C U] (social stratum) clase *f* **2** [C] (group of students) clase *f*; (lesson) clase *f*; **the ~ of '86** la promoción del 86 **3** [C] (group, type) clase *f* **4** [U] **(a)** (Transp) clase *f* **(b)** (in UK) (Post): **send the letter first/second ~** manda la carta por correo preferente/normal **5** [U] (style) (colloq) clase *f*

class² *vt* catalogar*

classic¹ /'klæsɪk/ *adj* clásico; ‹*scene/line*› memorable

classic² *n* clásico *m*; *see also* CLASSICS

classical /'klæsɪkəl/ *adj* (of Greece, Rome) clásico; **~ music** música *f* clásica

classics /'klæsɪks/ *n* [U] (+ *sing vb*) clásicas *fpl*

classification /'klæsəfə'keɪʃən ‖ ˌklæsɪfɪ'keɪʃən/ *n* [C U] clasificación *f*

classified /'klæsəfaɪd ‖ 'klæsɪfaɪd/ *adj* **(a)** (categorized) clasificado; **~ advertising** anuncios *mpl* por palabras, avisos *mpl* clasificados (AmL) **(b)** (secret) ‹*information*› secreto

classify /'klæsəfaɪ ‖ 'klæsɪfaɪ/ *vt* **-fies, -fying, -fied** ‹*books/data*› clasificar*

class: **~mate** *n* compañero, -ra *m,f* de clase; **~room** *n* aula *f*‡, clase *f*

clatter¹ /'klætər ‖ 'klætə(r)/ *vi* «*pans*» hacer* ruido; «*typewriter*» repiquetear

clatter² *n* [U] (of trains) traqueteo *m*; (of typewriters) repiqueteo *m*; (of hooves) chacoloteo *m*

clause /klɔ:z/ *n* **(a)** (in contract) cláusula *f* **(b)** (Ling) oración *f*, cláusula *f*

claustrophobia /'klɔ:strə'fəʊbiə ‖ˌklɒstrə'fəʊbiə/ *n* [U] claustrofobia *f*

claustrophobic /'klɔ:strə'fəʊbɪk ‖ˌklɒstrə'fəʊbɪk/ *adj* claustrofóbico

claw /klɔ:/ *n* (of tiger, lion) zarpa *f*, garra *f*; (of eagle) garra *f*; (of crab, lobster) pinza *f*

clay /kleɪ/ *n* [U C] arcilla *f*; (for children) (AmE) plastilina® *f*, plasticina® *f* (CS)

clean¹ /kli:n/ *adj* **-er, -est** limpio; ‹*joke*› inocente; ‹*game/player*› limpio; ‹*driver's license*› donde no constan infracciones; ‹*stroke/features*› bien definido, nítido; **she made a ~ break with the past** cortó radicalmente con el pasado

clean² *adv* (colloq) **(a)** (completely): **I ~ forgot about it** se me olvidó por completo **(b)** (fairly) ‹*fight/play*› limpio, limpiamente

clean³ *vt* **(a)** limpiar; ‹*blackboard*› borrar; **to ~ one's teeth** lavarse los dientes; **you can ~ it off with a sponge** lo puedes quitar con una esponja **(b)** (dry-clean) limpiar en seco

• **clean out** [*v* + *o* + *adv*, *v* + *adv* + *o*] (clean thoroughly) vaciar* y limpiar (*a fondo*)

• **clean up 1** [*v* + *o* + *adv*, *v* + *adv* + *o*] (physically, morally) limpiar **2** [*v* + *adv*] (make clean) limpiar

clean-cut /'kli:n'kʌt/ *adj* ‹*outline*› bien definido; ‹*appearance*› muy cuidado

cleaner /'kli:nər ‖ 'kli:nə(r)/ *n* **(a)** (person) limpiador, -dora *m,f* **(b)** (substance) producto *m* de limpieza

cleaning /'kli:nɪŋ/ *n* [U] limpieza *f*; (*before n*) **~ fluid** líquido *m* limpiador; **the ~ lady** la señora de la limpieza

cleanliness /'klenlinəs ‖ 'klenlinɪs/ *n* [U] limpieza *f*; **personal ~** el aseo personal

cleanse /klenz/ *vt* limpiar

cleanser /'klenzər ‖ 'klenzə(r)/ *n* [C U] (for household use) producto *m* de limpieza; (for skin) leche *f* (*or* crema *f etc*) limpiadora *or* de limpieza

clean-shaven /'kli:n'ʃeɪvən/ *adj* ‹*face*› bien afeitado *or* (esp Méx) rasurado

cleansing /'klenzɪŋ/ *adj* limpiador; **~ lotion** loción *f* limpiadora *or* de limpieza

clear¹ /klɪr ‖ klɪə(r)/ *adj* **-er, -est 1** ‹*sky*› despejado; **she has very ~ skin** tiene muy buen cutis; **to keep a ~ head** mantener* la mente despejada **2** (distinct) ‹*outline/picture*› nítido, claro; ‹*voice*› claro **3 (a)** (plain, evident): **it's a ~ case of suicide** es un caso evidente de suicidio; **it became ~ that** ... se hizo evidente que ... **(b)** ‹*explanation/instructions*› claro **4** (free, unobstructed) ‹*space/road*› despejado

clear² *adv*: **stand ~ of the doors** manténganse alejados de las puertas; **the curtains should hang ~ of the radiators** las cortinas no deben tocar los radiadores; **to keep/stay ~ (of sth)** mantenerse* alejado (de algo), no acercarse* (a algo)

clear³ *vt* **1** (make free, unobstructed) ‹*room*› vaciar*; ‹*surface*› despejar; ‹*drain/pipe*› desatascar*, destapar (AmL); ‹*building*› desalojar; ‹*land*› despoblar de árboles, desmontar; **to ~ the table** levantar *or* (Esp tb) quitar la mesa; **to ~ one's throat** carraspear **2** ‹*fence/ditch*› salvar; **to ~ customs** pasar por la aduana **3** (free from suspicion) ‹*name*› limpiar; **he was ~ed of all charges** lo absolvieron de todos los cargos **4** (authorize) autorizar* **5** ‹*debt/account*› liquidar, saldar ■ **~** *vi* **1** «*sky/weather/traffic*» despejarse; «*water*» aclararse; «*fog/smoke*» levantarse **2** (Fin) «*check*» ser* compensado

• **clear off** [*v* + *adv*] (colloq) largarse* (fam)

• **clear out** [*v* + *o* + *adv*, *v* + *adv* + *o*] ‹*cupboard/drawer*› vaciar* y ordenar

• **clear up 1** [*v* + *o* + *adv*, *v* + *adv* + *o*] **(a)** ‹*crime*› esclarecer*; ‹*misunderstanding/doubts*› aclarar **(b)** ‹*rubbish/toys*› recoger* **2** [*v* + *adv*] **(a)** (tidy) ordenar **(b)** «*weather*» despejar **(c)** (get better) «*cough/cold*» mejorarse; **the rash has ~ed up** se le (*or* me *etc*) ha ido el sarpullido

clearance /'klɪrəns ‖ 'klɪərəns/ *n* [U] **1** (authorization) autorización *f*; (from customs) despacho *m* de aduana **2** (of building land) desmonte *m*, despeje *m* **3** (of stock) liquidación *f*

clear-cut /'klɪr'kʌt ‖ ˌklɪə'kʌt/ *adj* claro, bien definido

clearing /'klɪrɪŋ ‖ 'klɪərɪŋ/ *n* (in forest) claro *m*

clearly /'klɪrli ‖ 'klɪəli/ *adv* ‹*visible/marked*› claramente; ‹*speak/write/think*› con claridad, claramente; **it's ~ impossible** es a todas luces imposible, está claro que es imposible

cleavage /'kli:vɪdʒ/ *n* [C U] escote *m*

cleaver /'kli:vər ‖ 'kli:və(r)/ *n* cuchilla *f* de carnicero

clef /klef/ *n* clave *f*

cleft[1] /kleft/ *adj* ‹*chin*› partido; **~ palate** paladar *m* hendido, fisura *f* del paladar

cleft[2] *n* hendidura *f*, grieta *f*

clench /klentʃ/ *vt* **(a)** ‹*fist/jaw*› apretar* **(b)** (grip) apretar*, agarrar

clergy /'klɜ:rdʒi ‖ 'klɜ:dʒi/ *n* (+ *sing or pl vb*) clero *m*

clerical /'klerɪkəl/ *adj* **1** (Relig) clerical **2** ‹*job/work*› de oficina; **~ assistant** oficinista *mf*

clerk /klɜ:rk ‖ klɑ:k/ *n* (in office) empleado (administrativo), empleada (administrativa) *m,f*, oficinista *mf*; (in bank) empleado, -da *m,f*, bancario, -ria *m,f* (CS); (*sales* ~) (AmE) vendedor, -dora *m,f*, dependiente, -ta *m,f*; (*desk* ~) (AmE) recepcionista *mf*

clever /'klevər ‖ 'klevə(r)/ *adj* **-verer, -verest** **(a)** (intelligent) inteligente, listo **(b)** (artful) (pej) listo **(c)** (skillful, adept) ‹*player/politician*› hábil; ‹*invention/solution*› ingenioso

cliché /kli:'ʃeɪ ‖ 'kli:ʃeɪ/ *n* [C U] lugar *m* común, cliché *m*

click[1] /klɪk/ *vt* ‹*fingers*› chasquear, tronar* (Méx); ‹*tongue*› chasquear ■ ~ *vi* hacer* un ruidito seco

click[2] *n* (of fingers, tongue) chasquido *m*; (of camera, switch) clic *m*

client /'klaɪənt/ *n* cliente, -ta *m,f*

clientele /'klaɪən'tel ‖ ˌkli:ɒn'tel, ˌkli:ən'tel/ *n* (+ *sing or pl vb*) clientela *f*

cliff /klɪf/ *n* acantilado *m*; (not by sea) precipicio *m*

cliffhanger /'klɪfˌhæŋər ‖ 'klɪfˌhæŋə(r)/ *n* situación *f* de suspenso *or* (Esp) de suspense

climate /'klaɪmət ‖ 'klaɪmɪt/ *n* clima *m*

climax /'klaɪmæks/ *n* (*pl* **-maxes**) clímax *m*; (orgasm) orgasmo *m*

climb[1] /klaɪm/ *vt* ‹*mountain*› escalar, subir a; ‹*tree*› trepar a, subirse a, treparse a (esp AmL); ‹*stairs*› subir ■ ~ *vi* **(a)** (clamber) trepar, treparse; **she ~ed onto the table** se subió a la mesa, trepó *or* se trepó a la mesa **(b)** (rise) subir

• **climb down** **1** [*v* + *prep* + *o*] ‹*rope*› bajarse por; ‹*tree*› bajarse de **2** [*v* + *adv*] (concede) (colloq) ceder

climb[2] *n* **(a)** (ascent) subida *f* **(b)** (Aviat) ascenso *m*

climber /'klaɪmər ‖ 'klaɪmə(r)/ *n* **(a)** (*rock* ~) escalador, -dora *m,f*; (mountaineer) alpinista *mf*, andinista *mf* (AmL) **(b)** (Hort) enredadera *f*, trepadora *f*

climbing /'klaɪmɪŋ/ *n* [U] (Sport) alpinismo *m*, andinismo *m* (AmL)

clinch /klɪntʃ/ *vt* ‹*deal*› cerrar*; ‹*title*› ganar; ‹*argument*› resolver* de forma contundente

cling /klɪŋ/ *vi* (*past & past p* **clung**) **1** **(a)** (hold fast) **to ~ TO sth/sb** estar* aferrado A algo/algn **(b)** (be dependent) (pej) **to ~ (TO sb)** pegársele* A algn **2** (stick) **to ~ (TO sth)** pegarse* (A algo)

clingfilm /'klɪŋfɪlm/ *n* [U] (BrE) film *m* transparente (*para envolver alimentos*)

clinic /'klɪnɪk/ *n* (treatment center) centro *m* médico; (in state hospital) consultorio *m*; (private hospital) clínica *f*

clinical /'klɪnɪkəl/ *adj* **(a)** (Med) (*before n*) clínico **(b)** (unemotional) ‹*manner/detachment*› frío

clink /klɪŋk/ *vt* hacer* tintinear ■ ~ *vi* tintinear

clip[1] /klɪp/ *n* **1** (device) clip *m*, gancho *m* **2** (from film) fragmento *m*, clip *m*

clip[2] *vt* **-pp-** **1** **(a)** (cut) ‹*hair/nails/grass/hedge*› cortar; ‹*sheep*› trasquilar; ‹*dog*› recortarle el pelo a **(b)** (punch) ‹*ticket*› picar*, perforar **2** (cut out) (AmE) recortar **3** (attach) sujetar (*con un clip*)

clip-on /'klɪpɑ:n ‖ 'klɪpɒn/ *adj* (*before n*) ‹*sunglasses*› que se engancha; ‹*earrings*› de clip

clippers /'klɪpərz ‖ 'klɪpəz/ *pl n* (for nails) cortaúñas *m*; (for hair) maquinilla *f* (*para cortar el pelo*); (for hedge, lawn) podadera *f*, tijeras *fpl* de podar

clipping /'klɪpɪŋ/ *n* (from newspaper) recorte *m*

clique /kli:k/ *n* camarilla *f*

cloak[1] /kləʊk/ *n* capa *f*; (disguise) tapadera *f*

cloak[2] *vt* ‹*purpose/activities*› encubrir*; **~ed in secrecy** rodeado de un velo de misterio

cloakroom /'kləʊkru:m, -rʊm/ *n* guardarropa *m*

clock /klɑ:k ‖ klɒk/ **(a)** ▶ 884 *n* (timepiece) reloj *m*; **to work around** *o* **round the ~** trabajar las veinticuatro horas del día **(b)** (Auto) (mileometer) cuentakilómetros *m*; (speedometer) velocímetro *m*

• **clock in**, (BrE) **clock on** [*v* + *adv*] fichar, marcar* *or* (Méx) checar* tarjeta (*al entrar al trabajo*)

• **clock out**, (BrE) **clock off** [*v* + *adv*] fichar, marcar* *or* (Méx) checar* tarjeta (*al salir del trabajo*)

clockwise[1] /'klɑ:kwaɪz ‖ 'klɒkwaɪz/ *adj* ‹*direction*› de las agujas del reloj

clockwise[2] *adv* en el sentido de las agujas del reloj

clockwork /'klɑ:kwɜ:rk ‖ 'klɒkwɜ:k/ *n* [U] mecanismo *m* de relojería; **like/regular as ~** como un reloj; (*before n*) **~ toy** (esp BrE) juguete *m* de cuerda

clog[1] /klɑ:g ‖ klɒg/ *n* zueco *m*

clog[2] **-gg-** **~ (up)** *vt* ‹*pipe/filter*› obstruir*, atascar* ■ ~ *vi* «*pipe*» obstruirse*, atascarse*

cloister /'klɔɪstər ‖ 'klɔɪstə(r)/ *n* claustro *m*

clone /kləʊn/ *vt* clonar

close[1] /kləʊs/ *adj* **closer, closest** **1** **(a)** (near) próximo, cercano **(b)** ‹*shave*› al ras, apurado; ***that was a ~ shave*** (colloq) se salvó (*or* me salvé *etc*) por un pelo *or* por los pelos (fam) **2** ‹*link/connection*› estrecho; ‹*contact*› directo; ‹*relative*› cercano; **they are ~ friends** son muy amigos **3** (in similarity): **he bears a ~ resemblance to his brother** tiene un gran parecido a *or* con su hermano **4** ‹*fit*› ajustado **5** (careful) ‹*examination*› detenido; **to keep a ~ watch on sth/sb** vigilar algo/a algn de cerca **6** ‹*contest/finish*› reñido **7** ‹*weather/atmosphere*› pesado, bochornoso

close² /kləʊs/ *adv* **closer, closest 1** (in position) cerca; **to draw/get/come ~** acercarse*; **~ TO sth/sb** cerca DE algo/algn **2** (in intimacy): **the tragedy brought them ~r together** la tragedia los acercó más **3** (in approximation): **the temperature is ~ to** ... la temperatura es de casi ...; **he was ~ to tears** estaba a punto de llorar **4** (*in phrases*) **close by** cerca; **close together** (physically) juntos; **close up** de cerca

close³ /kləʊz/ *n* fin *m*; **to come/draw to a ~** llegar*/acercarse* a su fin

close⁴ /kləʊz/ *vt* cerrar* ■ ~ *vi* **1** «*door/window*» cerrar(se)*; «*gap/wound*» cerrarse* **2** «*shop/library/museum*» cerrar* **3 (a)** (finish, end) «*lecture/book*» terminar, concluir* **(b) closing** *pres p* ‹*minutes*› último; ‹*speech*› de clausura

• **close down 1** [*v + o + adv, v + adv + o*] ‹*shop/factory*› cerrar* **2** [*v + adv*] «*shop/factory*» cerrar*

• **close in** [*v + adv*] **(a)** «*pursuers/enemy*» acercarse*; **to ~ in ON sth/sb** cercar* algo/a algn **(b)** «*winter*» acercarse*

• **close off** [*v + o + adv, v + adv + o*] clausurar

• **close out** [*v + o + adv, v + adv + o*] (AmE) liquidar

• **close up 1** [*v + adv*] «*shop/museum*» cerrar*; «*wound/gash*» cerrarse* **2** [*v + o + adv, v + adv + o*] ‹*shop/museum*› cerrar*

closed /kləʊzd/ *adj* cerrado

closed circuit *n* circuito *m* cerrado; (*before n*) **closed-circuit television** televisión *f* en circuito cerrado

close /kləʊs/: **~-fitting** *adj* ajustado, ceñido; **~-knit** *adj* unido

closely /'kləʊsli/ *adv* **1** ‹*connected/associated*› estrechamente; **they worked ~ with the French** trabajaron en estrecha colaboración con los franceses **2 (a)** (at a short distance) ‹*follow/mark*› de cerca **(b)** (carefully) ‹*study/examine*› detenidamente; ‹*watch*› de cerca; ‹*question*› a fondo; **a ~ guarded secret** un secreto muy bien guardado **3** (in approximation): **somebody who resembled her ~** alguien que se le parecía mucho

closet /'klɑːzət ‖ 'klɒzɪt/ *n* (AmE) (cupboard) armario *m*, placard *m* (RPl); (for clothes) armario *m*, closet *m* (AmL exc RPl), placard *m* (RPl)

close-up /'kləʊsʌp/ *n* primer plano *m*

closing /'kləʊzɪŋ/: **~ date** *n* fecha *f* límite, fecha *f* tope; **~ time** *n* hora *f* de cierre

closure /'kləʊʒər ‖ 'kləʊʒə(r)/ *n* [U C] cierre *m*

clot¹ /klɑːt ‖ klɒt/ *n* (*blood* ~) coágulo *m*

clot² *vi* **-tt-** «*blood*» coagularse

cloth /klɔːθ ‖ klɒθ/ *n* **(a)** [U] (fabric) tela *f*, género *m*; (thick, woolen) paño *m* **(b)** [C] (for cleaning) trapo *m*

clothe /kləʊð/ *vt* vestir*

clothes /kləʊðz/ *pl n* ropa *f*; **he had no ~ on** estaba desnudo; (*before n*) **~ brush** cepillo *m* para *or* de la ropa, escobilla *f* de ropa (Chi); **~ horse** tendedero *m* (*plegable*); **~ line** cuerda *f* de tender

clothespin /'kləʊðzpɪn/ (AmE), **clothes-peg** /'kləʊðzpeg/ (BrE) *n* pinza *f or* (Arg) broche *m or* (Chi) perrito *m or* (Ur) palillo *m* (de tender la ropa)

clothing /'kləʊðɪŋ/ ▶ 401 *n* [U] ropa *f*

cloud¹ /klaʊd/ *n* **(a)** ▶ 920 [C U] (Meteo) (single) nube *f*; (mass) nubes *fpl*, nubosidad *f* **(b)** [C] (of smoke, dust) nube *f*; (of suspicion) halo *m*, nube *f*

cloud² *vt* ‹*view/vision*› nublar

• **cloud over** ▶ 920 [*v + adv*] nublarse

cloudy /'klaʊdi/ ▶ 920 *adj* **-dier, -diest** ‹*day/sky*› nublado; ‹*liquid*› turbio

clout¹ /klaʊt/ *n* (colloq) **1** [C] (blow) tortazo *m* (fam) **2** [U] (power, influence) peso *m*, influencia *f*

clout² *vt* (colloq) darle* un tortazo a (fam)

clove /kləʊv/ *n* **(a)** (spice) clavo *m* (de olor) **(b)** (of garlic) diente *m*

clover /'kləʊvər ‖ 'kləʊvə(r)/ *n* [U C] trébol *m*

clown¹ /klaʊn/ *n* payaso, -sa *m,f*

clown² *vi* **~ (around** *o* **about)** hacer* payasadas, payasear (AmL fam), hacer* el payaso (Esp)

cloying /'klɔɪɪŋ/ *adj* empalagoso

club¹ /klʌb/ *n* **1 (a)** (cudgel) garrote *m*, cachiporra *f* **(b)** (*golf* ~) palo *m* de golf **2** (society, association) club *m* **3** (Games) **clubs** *pl* (suit) (+ *sing or pl vb*) tréboles *mpl*; (in Spanish pack) bastos *mpl*

club² **-bb-** *vt* aporrear ■ ~ *vi* (visit nightclubs): **to go ~bing** ir* de nightclubs

cluck /klʌk/ *vi* «*hen*» cloquear

clue /kluː/ *n* pista *f*; (in crosswords) clave *f*; ***not to have a ~*** (colloq) no tener* ni (la más mínima *or* la menor) idea (fam)

clump /klʌmp/ *n* **(a)** (of trees) grupo *m*; (of flowers) macizo *m* **(b)** (of earth) terrón *m*

clumsily /'klʌmzəli ‖ 'klʌmzɪli/ *adv* ‹*handle/apologize*› torpemente

clumsy /'klʌmzi/ *adj* **-sier, -siest** ‹*person/movement*› torpe; ‹*tool/shape*› tosco; ‹*translation*› burdo

clung /klʌŋ/ *past & past p of* CLING

cluster¹ /'klʌstər ‖ 'klʌstə(r)/ *n* (of people, buildings, stars) grupo *m*; (of berries, bananas) racimo *m*

cluster² *vi* apiñarse, agruparse

clutch¹ /klʌtʃ/ *n* **1 clutches** *pl* garras *fpl*; **to be in/fall into sb's ~es** estar*/caer* en las garras de algn **2** (Auto) embrague *m*, clutch *m* (AmC, Col, Méx) **3** (of eggs) nidada *f*

clutch² *vt* tener* firmemente agarrado ■ ~ *vi* **to ~ AT sth** tratar de agarrarse DE algo

clutter /'klʌtər ‖ 'klʌtə(r)/ *vt* **~ (up)** abarrotar

cluttered /'klʌtərd ‖ 'klʌtəd/ *adj* abarrotado de cosas

cm ▶ 681 (= **centimeter(s)** *or* (BrE) **centimetre(s)**) cm.

c/o (= **in care of** *or* (BrE) **care of**): **John Smith, c/o Ana Mas** John Smith, en casa de Ana Mas

Co (a) /kəʊ/ (= **company**) Cía. **(b)** (Geog) = **County**

CO 1 (Geog) = **Colorado 2** (Mil) = **Commanding Officer**

coach¹ /kəʊtʃ/ *n* **1 (a)** (horse-drawn carriage) coche *m* (de caballos), carruaje *m* **(b)** (long-distance bus) (BrE) autobús *m*, autocar *m* (Esp), pullman *m* (CS) **2** (Rail) **(a)** (AmE) vagón *m* de tercera (clase) **(b)** (BrE) vagón *m* **3 (a)** (tutor) profesor, -sora *m,f* particular **(b)** (team manager) entrenador, -dora *m,f*, director técnico, directora técnica *mf* (AmL)

coach² *vt* ‹*team/player*› entrenar; ‹*pupil/student/singer*› preparar

coal /kəʊl/ *n* [U C] carbón *m*; (*before n*) **~ fire** fuego *m* de *or* a carbón

coalition /ˈkəʊəˈlɪʃən/ *n* [U C] coalición *f*

coal: **~man** /ˈkəʊlmæn/ *n* (*pl* **-men** /-men/) carbonero *m*; **~mine** *n* mina *f* de carbón; **~miner** *n* minero, -ra *m,f* de carbón

coarse /kɔːrs || kɔːs/ *adj* **coarser, coarsest (a)** ‹*sand/filter*› grueso; ‹*cloth*› basto, ordinario, burdo; ‹*features*› tosco **(b)** ‹*person/manners/language*› ordinario, basto

coast¹ /kəʊst/ *n* **(a)** (shoreline) costa *f*; ***the ~ is clear*** no hay moros en la costa **(b)** (region) costa *f*, litoral *m*

coast² *vi* «*car*» deslizarse* (*sin llevar el motor en marcha*)

coastal /ˈkəʊstl̩/ *adj* (*before n*) costero

coaster /ˈkəʊstər || ˈkəʊstə(r)/ *n* **(a)** (ship) barco *m* de cabotaje **(b)** (drink mat) posavasos *m*

coast: **~guard** *n* guardacostas *mf*; **~line** *n* [U C] costa *f*, litoral *m*; **~ to ~** *adv* (AmE) a lo largo y ancho del país; **~-to-~** /ˈkəʊsttəˈkəʊst/ *adj* (AmE) de costa a costa

coat¹ /kəʊt/ *n* **1** (Clothing) (*over~*) (for men) abrigo *m* *or* (RPl) sobretodo *m*; (for women) abrigo *m* *or* (RPl) tapado *m*; (jacket) chaqueta *f*; (heavier) chaquetón *m*; (*before n*) **~ hanger** percha *f*; **~ stand** perchero *m* **2** (of animals) pelaje *m* **3** (layer) capa *f*; (of paint) capa *f*, mano *f*

coat² *vt* cubrir*

coating /ˈkəʊtɪŋ/ *n* capa *f*

coat of arms *n* (*pl* **~s ~ ~**) escudo *m* de armas

coax /kəʊks/ *vt*: **I ~ed the animal into the cage** con paciencia logré que el animal se metiera en la jaula; **I managed to ~ the information out of her** logré sonsacarle la información

cobbled /ˈkɑːbəld || ˈkɒbəld/ *adj* adoquinado

cobbler /ˈkɑːblər || ˈkɒblə(r)/ *n* zapatero *m* (remendón)

cobblestone /ˈkɑːbəlstəʊn || ˈkɒbəlstəʊn/ *n* adoquín *m*

cobra /ˈkəʊbrə/ *n* cobra *f*

cobweb /ˈkɑːbweb || ˈkɒbweb/ *n* telaraña *f*

cocaine /kəʊˈkeɪn/ *n* [U] cocaína *f*

cock¹ /kɑːk || kɒk/ *n* (male fowl) gallo *m*; (male bird) macho *m*

cock² *vt* **1** ‹*gun*› montar **2** ‹*head*› ladear; ‹*ears*› levantar, parar (AmL)

cockerel /ˈkɑːkrəl || ˈkɒkərəl/ *n* gallito *m*

cockeyed /ˈkɑːkaɪd || ˈkɒkaɪd/ *adj* **(a)** (ridiculous) disparatado **(b)** (askew) torcido, chueco (AmL)

cockle /ˈkɑːkəl || ˈkɒkəl/ *n* berberecho *m*

Cockney, **cockney** /ˈkɑːkni || ˈkɒkni/ *n* (*pl* **-neys**) cockney *mf* (*persona nacida en el East End, tradicionalmente de clase obrera*)

cockpit /ˈkɑːkpɪt || ˈkɒkpɪt/ *n* (Aviat) cabina *f* de mando

cockroach /ˈkɑːkrəʊtʃ || ˈkɒkrəʊtʃ/ *n* cucaracha *f*

cocktail /ˈkɑːkteɪl || ˈkɒkteɪl/ *n* **(a)** [C] (drink) cóctel *m*, coctel *m*, combinado *m*; (*before n*) **~ bar** bar *m*, coctelería *f*; **~ cabinet** mueble-bar *m*; **~ party** cóctel *m*, coctel *m*; **~ stick** palillo *m*, mondadientes *m* **(b)** [C U] (food): **shrimp** *o* (BrE) **prawn ~** cóctel *m* de camarones *or* (Esp) de gambas *or* (CS) de langostinos, langostinos *mpl* con salsa golf (RPl)

cocky /ˈkɑːki || ˈkɒkɪ/ *adj* **cockier, cockiest** (colloq) gallito (fam), chulo (Esp fam)

cocoa /ˈkəʊkəʊ/ *n* [U C] (powder) cacao *m*, cocoa *f* (AmL); (drink) chocolate *m*, cocoa *f* (AmL)

coconut /ˈkəʊkənʌt/ *n* [C U] coco *m*

cocoon /kəˈkuːn/ *n* capullo *m*

cod /kɑːd || kɒd/ *n* [C U] (*pl* **~** *or* **~s**) bacalao *m*

COD *adv* (= **cash** *or* (AmE also) **collect on delivery**) contra reembolso

code¹ /kəʊd/ *n* **1 (a)** [C U] (cipher) clave *f*, código *m*; **in ~** en clave, cifrado **(b)** [C] (for identification) código *m* **(c)** [U] (Comput) código *m* **(d)** [C] (Telec) código *m*, prefijo *m* **2** [C] (social, moral) código *m*

code² *vt* **(a)** (encipher) cifrar, poner* en clave **(b)** (give identifying number, mark) codificar*

coerce /kəʊˈɜːrs || kəʊˈɜːs/ *vt* **to ~ sb** (INTO -ING) coaccionar a algn (PARA QUE (+ *subj*))

coexist /ˈkəʊɪgˈzɪst/ *vi* **to ~** (WITH **sb/sth**) coexistir (CON algn/algo)

coffee /ˈkɔːfi || ˈkɒfi/ *n* [U] (beans, granules, drink) café *m*; **black ~** café negro *or* (Esp) solo *or* (Chi) puro *or* (Col) tinto; **white ~** (BrE) café con leche; (*before n*) **~ bean** grano *m* de café; **~ break** pausa *f* del café; **~ maker** cafetera *f*; **~ mill** *o* **grinder** molinillo *m* de café

coffee: **~ klatsch** /klætʃ, klɑːtʃ/ *n* (AmE) tertulia *f*; **~pot** *n* cafetera *f*; **~ table** *n* mesa *f* de centro, mesa *f* ratona (RPl)

coffin /ˈkɔːfən || ˈkɒfɪn/ *n* ataúd *m*, féretro *m*, cajón *m* (AmL)

cog /kɑːg || kɒg/ *n* **(a)** (tooth) diente *m* **(b)** (wheel) piñón *m*, rueda *f* dentada

cognac /ˈkɑːnjæk || ˈkɒnjæk/ *n* [U C] coñac *m*, coñá *m*

cohabit /kəʊˈhæbət || kəʊˈhæbɪt/ *vi* (frml) cohabitar (frml)

coherent /kəʊˈhɪrənt || kəʊˈhɪərənt/ *adj* coherente

coil¹ /kɔɪl/ *n* **1 (a)** (series of loops — of rope, wire) rollo *m*; (— of smoke) espiral *f*, volutas *fpl* **(b)** (single loop) lazada *f*, vuelta *f* **2** (contraceptive) (BrE) espiral *f*

coil² *vt* enrollar

coin¹ /kɔɪn/ *n* moneda *f*

coin² *vt* ‹*word/expression*› acuñar; **to ~ a phrase** (set phrase) como se suele decir

coin box *n* depósito *m* de monedas

coincide /ˈkəʊənˈsaɪd || ˌkəʊɪnˈsaɪd/ *vi* **to ~** (WITH **sth**) coincidir (CON algo)

coincidence /kəʊˈɪnsədəns || kəʊˈɪnsɪdəns/ *n* [C U] casualidad *f*, coincidencia *f*

coincidental /kəʊˈɪnsəˈdentl̩ || kəʊˈɪnsɪdentl̩/ *adj* casual, fortuito

coin-operated /'kɔɪn'ɑːpəreɪtəd ‖ 'kɔɪn,ɒpəreɪtɪd/ *adj* que funciona con monedas

coke /kəʊk/ *n* [U] **1** (fuel) (carbón *m* de) coque *m* **2** (cocaine) (colloq) coca *f* (fam) **3 Coke**® (colloq) Coca-Cola® *f*

colander /'kʌləndər ‖ 'kʌləndə(r)/ *n* colador *m*, escurridor *m* (*de pasta, verduras*)

cold[1] /kəʊld/ ▶ 920 *adj* frío; **I'm ~** tengo frío; **my feet are ~** tengo los pies fríos, tengo frío en los pies; **it's ~ today** hoy hace frío; **your dinner's getting ~** se te está enfriando la comida; **I got a very ~ reception** me recibieron con mucha frialdad; **I came to the job ~** empecé el trabajo sin ninguna preparación

cold[2] *n* **1** [U] (low temperature) frío *m*; **come in out of the ~** entra, que hace frío; **to feel the ~** ser* friolento *or* (Esp) friolero, sentir* el frío **2** [C] (Med) resfriado *m*, constipado *m* (Esp), resfrío *m* (CS); **to have a ~** estar* resfriado

cold: **~-blooded** /'kəʊld'blʌdəd ‖ ,kəʊld'blʌdɪd/ *adj* **(a)** ‹*murder*› a sangre fría; ‹*killer*› despiadado, cruel **(b)** (Zool) de sangre fría; **~ cream** *n* [U] crema *f* limpiadora *or* de limpieza, cold cream *f*; **~ cuts** *pl n* (AmE) fiambres *mpl*; **~-hearted** /'kəʊld'hɑːrtəd ‖ ,kəʊld'hɑːtɪd/ *adj* frío, insensible

coldly /'kəʊldli/ *adv* con frialdad, fríamente

cold: **~ sore** *n* herpes *m* (labial), fuego *m* (AmL), pupa *f* (Esp fam); **~ storage** *n* [U] almacenamiento *m* en cámaras frigoríficas; **~ war** *n* guerra *f* fría

coleslaw /'kəʊlslɔː/ *n* [U] *ensalada de repollo, zanahoria y cebolla con mayonesa*

collaborate /kə'læbəreɪt/ *vi* colaborar

collaboration /kə'læbə'reɪʃən/ *n* [U] (cooperation) colaboración *f*; (with enemy) colaboracionismo *m*

collaborator /kə'læbəreɪtər ‖ kə'læbəreɪtə(r)/ *n* (partner) colaborador, -dora *m,f*; (with enemy) colaboracionista *mf*

collapse[1] /kə'læps/ *vi* **1** «*building*» derrumbarse, desmoronarse **2** «*person*» desplomarse; (Med) sufrir un colapso **3** (fail) fracasar **4** (fold up) «*table/chair*» plegarse*

collapse[2] *n* [C U] **(a)** (of building) derrumbe *m*, desmoronamiento *m* **(b)** (Med) colapso *m* **(c)** (of company) quiebra *f*

collapsible /kə'læpsəbəl/ *adj* plegable

collar /'kɑːlər ‖ 'kɒlə(r)/ *n* **(a)** ▶ 401 (Clothing) cuello *m* **(b)** (for animal) collar *m*

collarbone /'kɑːlərbəʊn ‖ 'kɒləbəʊn/ *n* clavícula *f*

colleague /'kɑːliːg ‖ 'kɒliːg/ *n* colega *mf*

collect[1] /kə'lekt/ *vt* **1** ‹*information/evidence/data*› reunir*; ‹*dust*› acumular **2** (as hobby) coleccionar, juntar (esp AmL) **3** (fetch, pick up) recoger* **4** (obtain payment) ‹*rent*› cobrar; ‹*taxes*› recaudar **5** (put in order): **give me some time to ~ my thoughts** déjame pensar un momento ■ **~** *vi* **1 (a)** (gather, assemble) «*people*» reunirse* **(b)** (accumulate) «*dust/water*» acumularse **2** (for charity etc) recaudar dinero

collect[2] *adj* (AmE) ‹*call*› a cobro revertido, por cobrar (Chi, Méx)

collect[3] *adv* (AmE) ‹*call*› a cobro revertido, por cobrar (Chi, Méx)

collection /kə'lekʃən/ *n* **1 (a)** [U] (of evidence) recopilación *f*; (of rent, debts) cobro *m*; (of taxes) recaudación *f* **(b)** [U] (act of fetching): **the goods are ready for ~** puede recoger *or* pasar a buscar las mercancías **(c)** [C] (of mail, refuse) recogida *f* **2** [C] (of money) colecta *f* **3** [C] (group of objects) colección *f*

collective /kə'lektɪv/ *adj* (*usu before n*) colectivo

collector /kə'lektər ‖ kə'lektə(r)/ *n* **(a)** coleccionista *mf*; **a ~'s item** una pieza de colección **(b)** (official) cobrador, -dora *m,f*

college /'kɑːlɪdʒ ‖ 'kɒlɪdʒ/ *n* **(a)** (university) (esp AmE) universidad *f* **(b)** (for vocational training) escuela *f*, instituto *m*; *see also* TEACHERS COLLEGE **(c)** (department of university) facultad *f*, departamento *m*; (in Britain) colegio *m* universitario

collegiate /kə'liːdʒət, -dʒiət/ *adj* (esp AmE) universitario

collide /kə'laɪd/ *vi* «*vehicle*» chocar*, colisionar (frml); **to ~ WITH sth/sb** chocar* CON algo/algn; **we ~ed in the corridor** nos chocamos en el pasillo

collie /'kɑːli ‖ 'kɒli/ *n* collie *mf*, pastor escocés, pastora escocesa *m,f*

collision /kə'lɪʒən/ *n* [C U] (of cars, trains) choque *m*, colisión *f* (frml); (of boats) abordaje *m*, colisión *f* (frml)

colloquial /kə'ləʊkwiəl/ *adj* coloquial

collusion /kə'luːʒən/ *n* [U] colusión *f*

Colo = **Colorado**

cologne /kə'ləʊn/ *n* [U C] (*eau de ~*) colonia *f*

Colombia /kə'lʌmbiə/ *n* Colombia *f*

Colombian /kə'lʌmbiən/ *adj* colombiano

colon /'kəʊlən/ *n* **(a)** (Anat) colon *m* **(b)** (in punctuation) dos puntos *mpl*

colonel /'kɜːrnl ‖ 'kɜːnl/ *n* coronel, -nela *m,f*

colonial /kə'ləʊniəl/ *adj* colonial

colonize /'kɑːlənaɪz ‖ 'kɒlənaɪz/ *vt* colonizar*

colony /'kɑːləni ‖ 'kɒləni/ *n* (*pl* **-nies**) colonia *f*

color[1], (BrE) **colour** /'kʌlər ‖ 'kʌlə(r)/ ▶ 515 *n* **1** [C U] color *m*; **what ~ is the ball?** ¿de qué color es la pelota?; (*before n*) ‹*photograph*› en colores *or* (Esp) en color; ‹*television*› a color(es) *or* en colores *or* (Esp) en color **2 colors** *pl* **(a)** (flag) bandera *f*; ***with flying ~s***: **he passed his exams with flying ~s** le fue estupendamente en los exámenes **(b)** (BrE Sport): **the team ~s** los colores del equipo

color[2], (BrE) **colour** *vt* **(a)** (Art) pintar, colorear; **to ~ sth blue** colorear algo de azul **(b)** (dye) teñir* **(c)** (influence, bias) ‹*atmosphere*› empañar; **you shouldn't let that ~ your judgment** no deberías dejar que eso influya en tu opinión ■ **~** *vi* (flush) ruborizarse*, sonrojarse, ponerse* colorado

color: **~-blind** *adj* daltónico, daltoniano; **~-coded** /'kʌlər'kəʊdəd ‖ ,kʌlə'kəʊdɪd/ *adj* codificado con colores

colored, (BrE) **coloured** /'kʌlərd ‖ 'kʌləd/ *adj* ‹*walls/blouse*› de color

-colored, (BrE) **-coloured** /,kʌlərd ‖ 'kʌləd/ ▶ 515 *suff*: **slate~/coral~** de color pizarra/coral

colorful, (BrE) **colourful** /'kʌlərfəl ‖ 'kʌləfəl/ *adj* ‹*clothes/plumage*› de colores muy vivos; ‹*parade/description*› lleno de color

Colors

what color is it? = ¿de qué color es?
it's yellow = es amarillo/amarillla

Note the use of the preposition de *in the following sentences*:

she always wears green = siempre se viste de verde
to paint something yellow = pintar algo de amarillo
dressed in black = vestido de negro
the woman in white = la mujer de blanco

Nouns of color

These are all masculine:

a deep red = un rojo intenso
you look good in green = el verde te queda bien
violet = el violeta (*i.e. the color; the flower is feminine —* la violeta)

They are used as in English:

we have it in red and yellow = lo tenemos en rojo y amarillo
I love green = me encanta el verde
blue is in fashion = está de moda el azul

Adjectives of color

Some of the most common of these agree in gender and number with the noun they modify:

a yellow blouse = una blusa amarilla
blue/black shoes = zapatos azules/negros

Many, however, are invariable in form:

turquoise curtains = unas cortinas turquesa

Some adjectives may be either variable or invariable in number, principally naranja, rosa, malva, *and* violeta:

pink shirts = camisas rosa *or* rosas

Note the use of the Spanish word color *in combination with adjectives of color, whether as an integral part of a compound*:

cream trousers = pantalones color crema

or as an optional addition:

strawberry-pink = (color) fresa
salmon = (color) salmón
lilac socks = calcetines (color) lila
lemon yellow paint = pintura (color) amarillo limón

de color *is also used to indicate approximation*:

flesh-colored tights = medias (de) color carne

'Combined' colors

Most of these in Spanish are compound nouns as in English:

dusty pink = rosa viejo
cherry red = rojo cereza
emerald green = verde esmeralda

Several 'combined' colors are expressed in Spanish by a single word:

bluish white = blanquiazul
greenish-white = verdiblanco
red-green = verdirrojo
red-and white = blanquirrojo
black-and-white = blanquinegro (*but note that* black-and-white TV/photos *is translated by* televisión/fotos en blanco y negro)

Shades of color

Spanish has various endings which can be used to translate the suffix -ish:

greenish = verdoso
yellowish = amarillento
reddish = rojizo
blackish = negruzco
bluish = azulado
whitish = blancuzco

It also uses the phrase tirando a *to denote tinges of color*:

a bright orangish yellow = un amarillo fuerte tirando a naranja
a blackish grey = un gris oscuro tirando a negro

Shades of color are expressed with adjectives such as light *and* dark *are always invariable in Spanish*:

a light blue skirt = una falda azul claro
dark brown shoes = zapatos marrón oscuro

Hair color

fair/blond hair = pelo rubio
brown hair = pelo marrón
light/dark brown hair = pelo marrón claro/oscuro
mousy(-colored) hair = pelo color castaño desvaído
black hair = pelo negro
white hair = pelo blanco
auburn hair = pelo castaño rojizo *or* pelo color caoba

But:

she has red hair = es pelirroja
he has gray hair = es canoso *or* tiene el pelo canoso

Eye color

blue eyes = ojos azules
brown eyes = ojos marrones *or* (*AmC, Chi, Méx*) café
light blue eyes = ojos azul claro
green eyes = ojos verdes
gray eyes = ojos grises *or* color gris
hazel eyes = ojos color avellana

coloring, (BrE) **colouring** /'kʌlərɪŋ/ *n* [U] **1** (of skin) color *m*, tono *m*; (of fur, plumage) colorido *m* **2** (*food* ~) colorante *m*

colorless, (BrE) **colourless** /'kʌlərləs ‖ 'kʌləlɪs/ *adj* incoloro, sin color; ‹*person/life*› anodino, gris

color: ~ **scheme** *n* (combinación *f* de) colores *mpl*; ~ **supplement** *n* suplemento *m* a todo color *or* en color

colossal /kə'lɑːsəl ‖ kə'lɒsəl/ *adj* (colloq) colosal

colour *etc* (BrE) ⇒ COLOR *etc*

colt /kəʊlt/ *n* potro *m*

column /'kɑːləm ‖ 'kɒləm/ *n* columna *f*

columnist /'kɑːləmnəst, 'kɑːləməst ‖ 'kɒləmnɪst, 'kɒləmɪst/ *n* columnista *mf*

coma /'kəʊmə/ *n* (*pl* ~**s**) (Med) coma *m*

comb[1] /kəʊm/ *n* (for hair) peine *m*, peinilla *f* (AmL), peineta *f* (Chi)

comb[2] *vt* **(a)** (pass a comb through): **to ~ one's hair** peinarse **(b)** (search) ‹*area/field*› peinar

combat[1] /kəm'bæt ‖ 'kɒmbæt/ *vt*, (BrE) **-tt-** combatir

combat[2] /'kɑːmbæt ‖ 'kɒmbæt/ *n* [C U] combate *m*

combination /'kɑːmbə'neɪʃən ‖ ˌkɒmbɪ'neɪʃən/ *n* [C U] combinación *f*

combine /kəm'baɪn/ *vt* ‹*elements*› combinar; ‹*ingredients*› (Culin) mezclar; ‹*efforts*› aunar* ■ ~ *vi* «*elements*» combinarse; «*ingredients*» mezclarse; «*teams/forces*» unirse

combined /kəm'baɪnd/ *adj* conjunto; **our ~ efforts led to success** la suma de nuestros esfuerzos nos condujo al éxito

combine harvester /'kɑːmbaɪn 'hɑːvəstər ‖ 'kɒmbaɪn 'hɑːvɪstə(r)/ *n* cosechadora *f*

combustion /kəm'bʌstʃən/ *n* [U] combustión *f*; (*before n*) ~ **engine** motor *m* de combustión

come /kʌm/ (*past* **came**; *past p* **come**) *vi* **1 (a)** (advance, approach, travel) venir*; **~ here** ven (aquí); **we've ~ a long way since** ... (made much progress) hemos avanzado mucho desde que ...; **can I ~ with you?** ¿puedo ir contigo?, ¿te puedo acompañar?; **after a while, you'll ~ to a crossroads** al cabo de un rato, llegarás a un cruce; **I'm coming, I won't be a moment** enseguida voy **(b)** (originate): **where do you ~ from?** ¿de dónde eres?; **it ~s from Italy** viene de Italia **(c) to come and go** ir* y venir*; **three o'clock came and went and he still hadn't arrived** pasaron las tres y no llegaba **2 (a)** (occur in time, context): **Christmas is coming** ya llega la Navidad; **it came as a complete surprise** fue una sorpresa total; **to take life as it ~s** aceptar la vida tal (y) como se presenta; **~ what may** pase lo que pase **(b)** (*as prep*) para; **I'll be tired out ~ Friday** estaré agotado para el viernes **(c) coming** *pres p*: **this coming Friday** este viernes que viene **(d) to come** (in the future) (*as adv*): **in years to ~** en años venideros; **a taste of things to ~** una muestra de lo que nos espera **3** (reach) (+ *adv compl*) llegar*; **the water came up to our knees** el agua nos llegaba a las rodillas **4** (be gained): **it'll ~, just keep practicing** ya te va a salir; sigue practicando; **driving didn't ~ easily to me** aprender a manejar *or* (Esp) conducir no me fue fácil **5** (be available, obtainable) (+ *adv compl*) venir*; **sugar ~s in half-pound bags** el azúcar viene en paquetes de media libra; **the car ~s with the job** el coche te lo dan con el trabajo **6** (+ *adv compl*) **(a)** (in sequence, list, structure): **Cancer ~s between Gemini and Leo** Cáncer está entre Géminis y Leo **(b)** (in race, competition) llegar*; **to ~ first** (in a race) llegar* el primero; (in an exam) quedar *or* salir* el primero **(c)** (be ranked) estar*; **my children ~ first** primero están mis hijos **7 (a)** (become) (+ *adj compl*): **my dream has ~ true** mi sueño se ha hecho realidad **(b)** (reach certain state) **to ~ to** + INF llegar* a + INF; **~ to think of it** ... ahora que lo pienso ... **8** (*in phrases*) **come, come!** ¡vamos, vamos!, ¡dale! (CS fam); **how come?** (colloq) ¿cómo?

• **come across 1** [*v* + *prep* + *o*] (find) encontrar(se)*; (meet) ‹*person*› encontrarse* con **2** [*v* + *adv*] (communicate, be communicated) «*meaning*» ser* comprendido; «*feelings*» transmitirse; **he came across very well in the interview** hizo muy buena impresión en la entrevista

• **come along** [*v* + *adv*] **1** (*in imperative*) **(a)** (hurry up): **~ along, children** ¡vamos, niños!, ¡apúrense, niños! (AmL), ¡órale, niños! (Méx fam) **(b)** (as encouragement, rebuke) **~ along!** ¡vamos! **2** (accompany): **can I ~ along?** ¿puedo ir (yo) también?; **~ along with me** ven conmigo, acompáñame **3** (progress) ir*, marchar

• **come apart** [*v* + *adv*] **(a)** (fall apart) deshacerse* **(b)** (have detachable parts) desmontarse

• **come around**, (BrE also) **come round 1** [*v* + *prep* + *o*] (turn) ‹*bend*› tomar; ‹*corner*› doblar **2** [*v* + *adv*] **(a)** (visit) (esp BrE) venir* (a casa) **(b)** (recover consciousness) volver* en sí **(c)** (change mind): **he'll ~ around eventually** ya se va a convencer

• **come away** [*v* + *adv*] **1** (leave, depart) **to ~ away** (FROM **sth**) ‹*from meeting/stadium*› salir* (DE algo) **2** (become detached) «*handle*» salirse*

• **come back** [*v* + *adv*] **(a)** (return) volver* **(b)** (be remembered): **it's all coming back (to me)** estoy volviendo a recordarlo todo

• **come down** [*v* + *adv*] **1 (a)** (descend) bajar **(b)** (reach) llegar* **(c)** (collapse) «*ceiling/wall*» caerse* **(d)** «*plane*» aterrizar*; (in accident) caer* **2** (decrease) «*price*» bajar

• **come down to** [*v* + *adv* + *prep* + *o*] (*impers*) ser* cuestión de

• **come forward** [*v* + *adv*] «*witness*» presentarse; «*volunteer*» ofrecerse*; «*culprit*» darse* a conocer

• **come in** [*v* + *adv*] **1** (enter) entrar; **~ in!** ¡adelante! **2 (a)** «*boat*» llegar* **(b)** «*tide*» subir **3** (be received) «*applications/reports/donations*» llegar* **4** (play useful role): **where do I ~ in?** ¿cuál es mi papel?; **that's where these boxes ~ in** para eso están las cajas

• **come in for** [*v* + *adv* + *prep* + *o*] ‹*criticism*› ser* objeto de

• **come into** [*v* + *prep* + *o*] **(a)** (enter into) entrar en, entrar a (AmL) **(b)** (inherit) heredar **(c)** (be, become relevant): **principles don't ~ into it** no es cuestión de principios

•**come off** **1 (a)** [*v* + *adv*] (detach itself) «*handle*» soltarse*; «*button*» desprenderse; «*wallpaper*» despegarse*; «*dirt/grease*» quitarse **(b)** [*v* + *prep* + *o*] (fall off) ‹*horse/motorcycle*› caerse* de **2** [*v* + *adv*] (fare, acquit oneself): **he always ~s off worst** siempre sale perdiendo **3** [*v* + *prep* + *o*] **(a)** (stop taking) ‹*drug*› dejar de tomar **(b)** (be serious): **~ *off it!*** (colloq) ¡anda! ¡no digas tonterías! (fam)

•**come on** [*v* + *adv*] **1** (urging sb) (*only in imperative*): **~ on!** ¡vamos! ¡date prisa! *or* (AmL tb) ¡apúrate!, ¡órale! (Méx fam) **2 (a)** (begin) «*night/winter*» entrar **(b)** (begin to operate) «*heating/appliance*» encenderse*, ponerse* en funcionamiento; «*light*» encenderse*

•**come out I** [*v* + *adv* (+ *prep* + *o*)] **1** (from inside) salir* **2** «*tooth/hair*» caerse*; «*stain*» salir* **II** [*v* + *adv*] **1** (appear) «*sun/stars*» salir*; «*flowers*» florecer*, salir* **2** (be said, spoken) salir*; (be revealed, emphasized) «*secret/truth*» revelarse, salir* a la luz **3 (a)** (declare oneself) declararse; **to ~ out on strike** declararse en huelga **(b)** (as being gay) destaparse (fam), declararse abiertamente homosexual **4** «*newspaper/record/product*» salir*

•**come over 1** [*v* + *adv*] (to sb's home) venir* (a casa) **2** [*v* + *prep* + *o*] (affect, afflict): **I don't know what came over me** no sé qué me pasó

•**come round** (BrE) ⇒ COME AROUND

•**come through 1** «*message/news/supplies*» llegar*; **you're coming through loud and clear** te recibimos muy bien **2** [*v* + *prep* + *o*] ‹*ordeal/illness*› salir* de; ‹*war*› sobrevivir

•**come to I** [*v* + *prep* + *o*] **1 (a)** (reach) llegar* a; **what's the world coming to!** ¡hasta dónde vamos a llegar! **(b)** (occur) «*idea/answer/name*» ocurrirse; **it came to me in a flash** se me ocurrió de repente **(c)** (be a question of): **when it ~s to** ... cuando se trata de ... **2** (amount to) «*total*» ascender* a (frml); **it ~s to $15 exactly** son 15 dólares justos; **the plan never came to anything** el plan nunca llegó a nada

II [*v* + *adv*] (recover consciousness) volver* en sí

•**come up** [*v* + *adv*] **1 (a)** (ascend, rise) «*person*» subir; «*sun/moon*» salir* **(b)** (approach) acercarse*; **to ~ up TO sb** acercársele* A algn **2 (a)** (occur, arise) «*problem*» surgir*; **something important has just ~ up** acaba de surgir algo importante **(b)** (be raised, mentioned) «*subject/point*» surgir*; «*name*» ser* mencionado

•**come up against** [*v* + *adv* + *prep* + *o*] ‹*opposition/prejudice*› enfrentarse a

•**come up for** [*v* + *adv* + *prep* + *o*]: **the car is coming up for its annual service** dentro de poco hay que hacerle la revisión anual al coche; **I should ~ up for promotion next year** me deberían considerar para un ascenso el año que viene

•**come up to** [*v* + *adv* + *prep* + *o*] **(a)** (reach as far as) llegar* a *or* hasta **(b)** (attain) ‹*standard*› alcanzar*, llegar* a

•**come up with** [*v* + *adv* + *prep* + *o*] ‹*plan/scheme*› idear; ‹*proposal*› presentar; ‹*money*› conseguir*; **if you can ~ up with a better idea** si a ti se te ocurre algo mejor

comeback /'kʌmbæk/ *n* **1** (return, revival) vuelta *f*, retorno *m*; **to make a ~** volver* a la escena (*or* a la política *etc*) **2** (redress) (*no pl*): **the trouble is that you have no ~ at all** el problema es que no puedes hacer ninguna reclamación

comedian /kə'mi:diən/ *n* humorista *mf*, cómico, -ca *m,f*

comedy /'kɑ:mədi ‖ 'kɒmədi/ *n* [C U] (*pl* **-dies**) **(a)** (play, film) comedia *f* **(b)** (comic entertainment) humorismo *m*; (*before n*) ‹*show/program*› humorístico

comet /'kɑ:mət ‖ 'kɒmɪt/ *n* cometa *m*

comfort¹ /'kʌmfərt ‖ 'kʌmfət/ *n* **1 (a)** [U] (physical, material) comodidad *f*, confort *m* **(b)** [C] (sth pleasant, luxury) comodidad *f* **2** [U] (mental) consuelo *m*; **to take ~ from sth** consolarse* con algo

comfort² *vt* ‹*child/bereaved person*› consolar*

comfortable /'kʌmftərbəl ‖ 'kʌmftəbəl/ *adj* **1** ‹*chair/clothes*› cómodo; ‹*house/room*› confortable; **a ~ lifestyle** una vida desahogada **2** ‹*margin/majority*› amplio, holgado

comfortably /'kʌmftərbli ‖ 'kʌmftəbli/ *adv* ‹*lie/sit*› cómodamente; ‹*live/win*› holgadamente

comforter /'kʌmfərtər ‖ 'kʌmfətə(r)/ *n* **(a)** (bedcover) (AmE) edredón *m* **(b)** (for baby) (BrE) ⇒ PACIFIER

comforting /'kʌmfərtɪŋ ‖ 'kʌmfətɪŋ/ *adj* ‹*words*› de consuelo; **it's a ~ thought** es reconfortante pensarlo

comic¹ /'kɑ:mɪk ‖ 'kɒmɪk/ *adj* ‹*actor/scene*› cómico; ‹*writer*› humorístico

comic² *n* **1** (comedian) cómico, -ca *m,f*, humorista *mf* **2 (a)** (BrE) (book) comic *m*, libro *m* de historietas; (magazine) ⇒ COMIC BOOK **(b) comics** *pl* (comic strips) (AmE) tiras *fpl* cómicas, historietas *fpl*, monitos *mpl* (Andes, Méx)

comical /'kɑ:mɪkəl ‖ 'kɒmɪkəl/ *adj* cómico

comic: **~ book** *n* (AmE) revista *f* de historietas, tebeo *m* (Esp), revista *f* de chistes (RPl); (for adults) comic *m*; **~ strip** *n* tira *f* cómica, historieta *f*

coming /'kʌmɪŋ/ *adj* (*before n*) ‹*week/year*› próximo; **this ~ Monday** este lunes, el lunes que viene

comma /'kɑ:mə ‖ 'kɒmə/ *n* coma *f*

command¹ /kə'mænd ‖ kə'mɑ:nd/ *vt* **1 (a)** (order) **to ~ sb to + INF** ordenarle A algn QUE (+ *subj*) **(b)** ‹*army/ship*› estar* al mando de **2** ‹*wealth/resources*› contar* con **3** ‹*respect*› imponer*; ‹*fee*› exigir*; ‹*price*› alcanzar*

command² *n* **1 (a)** [C] (order) orden *f* **(b)** [U] (authority) mando *m*; **under sb's ~** bajo las órdenes *or* el mando de algn **2** [U] (mastery) dominio *m* **3** [C] (Comput) orden *f*, comando *m*

commandant /'kɑ:məndænt ‖ 'kɒməndænt/ *n* comandante *mf*

commandeer /'kɑ:mən'dɪr ‖ ˌkɒmən'dɪə(r)/ *vt* (Mil) requisar

commander /kə'mændər ‖ kə'mɑ:ndə(r)/ *n* **(a)** (officer in command) comandante *mf* **(b)** (navy rank) ≈ capitán *m* de fragata

commanding /kə'mændɪŋ ‖ kə'mɑ:ndɪŋ/ *adj* **(a)** ‹*position*› de superioridad; ‹*lead*› considerable **(b)** ‹*presence*› que impone; ‹*tone*› autoritario

commanding officer *n* oficial *mf* al mando

commandment /kəˈmændmənt ‖ kəˈmɑːnd mənt/ *n* precepto *m*; **the Ten C~s** los diez mandamientos

commando /kəˈmændəʊ ‖ kəˈmɑːndəʊ/ *n* (*pl* **-dos** *or* **-does**) comando *m*

commemorate /kəˈmeməreɪt/ *vt* conmemorar

commence /kəˈmens/ *vi* (frml) «*session/celebration*» dar* comienzo (frml); «*person*» comenzar* ■ ~ *vt* (frml) ‹*work/discussion*› dar* comienzo a (frml)

commend /kəˈmend/ *vt* **1 (a)** (praise) elogiar **(b)** (recommend) recomendar* **2** (frml) (entrust) **to ~ sb/sth TO sb** encomendar(le)* algn/algo A algn

commendable /kəˈmendəbəl/ *adj* loable, encomiable

commendation /ˈkɑːmənˈdeɪʃən ‖ ˌkɒmenˈdeɪʃən/ *n* **(a)** [U C] (praise) (frml) encomio *m* (frml), elogios *mpl* **(b)** [C] (award) mención *f* de honor, accésit *m*

comment¹ /ˈkɑːment ‖ ˈkɒment/ *n* **(a)** [C] (remark) comentario *m* **(b)** [U] (reaction) comentarios *mpl*; **no ~** sin comentarios

comment² *vi* **to ~ (ON sth)** hacer* comentarios (SOBRE algo) ■ ~ *vt* comentar

commentary /ˈkɑːmənteri ‖ ˈkɒməntəri, -tri/ *n* (*pl* **-ries**) (Rad, Sport, TV) comentarios *mpl*, crónica *f*; (analysis) comentario *m*

commentator /ˈkɑːmənteɪtər ‖ ˈkɒmənteɪtə(r)/ *n* comentarista *mf*

commerce /ˈkɑːmərs ‖ ˈkɒmɜːs/ *n* [U] comercio *m*

commercial¹ /kəˈmɜːrʃəl ‖ kəˈmɜːʃəl/ *adj* comercial

commercial² *n* spot *m* publicitario, anuncio *m*, aviso *m* (AmL), comercial *m* (AmL)

commercialize /kəˈmɜːrʃəlaɪz ‖ kəˈmɜːʃəlaɪz/ *vt* comercializar*

commiserate /kəˈmɪzəreɪt/ *vi*: **I ~d with him about losing his job** le dije cuánto sentía que se hubiera quedado sin trabajo

commiseration /kəˈmɪzəˈreɪʃən/ *n* [U] (*often pl*) conmiseración *f*

commission¹ /kəˈmɪʃən/ *n* **1** [C] (group) comisión *f* **2** [C U] (for sales) comisión *f* **3** [C] **(a)** (for music, painting, building) encargo *m*, comisión *f* (esp AmL) **(b)** (office) (Govt) cargo *m*

commission² *vt* **1 (a) to ~ sb to** + INF ‹*artist/writer/researcher*› encargarle* a algn que (+ *subj*) **(b)** ‹*painting/novel/study*› encargar*, comisionar (esp AmL) **2 (a)** (Mil) nombrar oficial; **~ed officer** oficial *mf* (del ejército) (*con grado de teniente o superior a teniente*) **(b)** (Naut) ‹*ship*› poner* en servicio

commissioner /kəˈmɪʃənər ‖ kəˈmɪʃənə(r)/ *n* **(a)** (commission member) comisionado, -da *m,f*, miembro *mf* de la comisión **(b)** (of police) (BrE) inspector, -tora *m,f* jefe

commit /kəˈmɪt/ **-tt-** *vt* **1** (perpetrate) ‹*crime/error/sin*› cometer **2** (assign) ‹*funds/time/resources*› asignar **3** (send): **to ~ sb to an asylum** internar a algn en un manicomio ■ *v refl* **to ~ (oneself) TO -ING/+ INF** comprometerse (A + INF)

commitment /kəˈmɪtmənt/ *n* **1** [C] **(a)** (responsibility) responsabilidad *f*; (obligation) obligación *f* **(b)** (engagement) compromiso *m* **2** [U] (dedication) dedicación *f*

committed /kəˈmɪtəd ‖ kəˈmɪtɪd/ *adj* ‹*Christian/feminist*› comprometido; ‹*teacher/worker*› entregado a su trabajo

committee /kəˈmɪti/ *n* (of club, society) comité *m*, comisión *f*; (of parliament) comisión *f*

commodity /kəˈmɑːdəti ‖ kəˈmɒdəti/ *n* (*pl* **-ties**) **(a)** (product) artículo *m*, producto *m*, mercadería *f* (AmS) **(b)** (Fin) materia *f* prima

common¹ /ˈkɑːmən ‖ ˈkɒmən/ *adj* **1 (a)** (widespread, prevalent) común; **the ~ cold** el resfriado común **(b)** (average, normal) ‹*soldier*› raso; **the ~ people** la gente común y corriente **(c)** (low class, vulgar) ordinario **2 (a)** (shared, mutual) común **(b)** (public): **it's ~ knowledge** todo el mundo lo sabe

common² *n* **1** [U] (*in phrases*) **in common** en común; **to have sth in ~ (with sb)** tener* algo en común (con algn); *see also* COMMONS **2** [C] (in UK) *terreno perteneciente al municipio*

common: **~ law** *n* [U] derecho *m* consuetudinario; (*before n*) **common-law wife** concubina *f*, conviviente *f* (Chi); **C~ Market** *n* **the C~ Market** el Mercado Común; **~-or-garden** /ˈkɑːmənɔːrˈgɑːrdn̩ ‖ ˈkɒmənɔːˈgɑːdn̩/ *adj* (BrE colloq) vulgar *or* común y corriente

commonplace /ˈkɑːmənpleɪs ‖ ˈkɒmənpleɪs/ *adj* (ordinary) común; (trite) banal

Commons /ˈkɑːmənz ‖ ˈkɒmənz/ *n* (in UK) (+ *sing or pl vb*) **the ~** la Cámara de los Comunes

common sense *n* [U] sentido *m* común

Commonwealth /ˈkɑːmənwelθ ‖ ˈkɒmənwelθ/ *n* **the ~** la *or* el Commonwealth

commotion /kəˈməʊʃən/ *n* (*no pl*) **(a)** (outrage) conmoción *f*; **to cause (a) ~** producir* una conmoción **(b)** (noise) alboroto *m*

communal /kəˈmjuːnl̩ ‖ ˈkɒmjʊnl̩, kəˈmjuːnl̩/ *adj* **(a)** ‹*land/ownership*› comunal; ‹*kitchen/bathroom*› común; ‹*life*› comunitario **(b)** (between groups) ‹*violence*› interno

commune /ˈkɑːmjuːn ‖ ˈkɒmjuːn/ *n* comuna *f*

communicate /kəˈmjuːnɪkeɪt/ *vi* comunicarse* ■ ~ *vt* comunicar*

communication /kəˈmjuːnəˈkeɪʃən ‖ kəˌmjuːnɪˈkeɪʃən/ *n* **1** [U] (act) comunicación *f* **2 communications** *pl* comunicaciones *fpl*

communicative /kəˈmjuːnəkeɪtɪv ‖ kəˈmjuːnɪkətɪv/ *adj* comunicativo

communion /kəˈmjuːnjən/ *n* **1** (*Holy C~*) la Santa *or* Sagrada Comunión **2** [U] (exchange of ideas, fellowship) (frml) comunión *f*

communism, **Communism** /ˈkɑːmjənɪzəm ‖ ˈkɒmjʊnɪzəm/ *n* [U] comunismo *m*

communist¹, **Communist** /ˈkɑːmjənəst ‖ ˈkɒmjʊnɪst/ *adj* comunista

communist², **Communist** *n* comunista *mf*

community /kəˈmjuːnəti/ *n* (*pl* **-ties**) comunidad *f*; **the city's black ~** la población *or* comunidad negra de la ciudad

community: **~ center**, (BrE) **~ centre** *n* centro *m* social; **~ chest** *n* (in US) *fondos reunidos* *voluntariamente por la comunidad, destinados a beneficencia y bienestar social*

commute /kə'mju:t/ *vi* viajar todos los días (*entre el lugar de residencia y el de trabajo*) ■ ~ *vt* ‹*sentence/punishment*› conmutar

commuter /kə'mju:tər ‖ kə'mju:tə(r)/ *n*: *persona que viaja diariamente una distancia considerable entre su lugar de residencia y el de trabajo*

compact[1] /kəm'pækt/ *adj* compacto

compact[2] /'kɑ:mpækt ‖ 'kɒmpækt/ *n* **1** **(powder)** ~ polvera *f* **2** (agreement) (frml) pacto *m*

compact disc, **compact disk** /'kɑ:mpækt ‖ 'kɒmpækt/ *n* disco *m* compacto, compact-disc *m*; (*before n*) ~ ~ **player** (reproductor *m* de) compact-disc *m*

companion /kəm'pænjən/ *n* compañero, -ra *m,f*

companionship /kəm'pænjənʃɪp/ *n* [U] compañía *f*

company /'kʌmpəni/ (*pl* **-nies**) *n* **1** [U] (companionship, companions) compañía *f*; **to keep sb ~** hacerle* compañía a algn; **to part ~** separarse; **she's excellent ~** es muy agradable (*or* divertido *etc*) estar con ella; **we've got ~** tenemos visita **2** [C] (Busn) compañía *f*, empresa *f*; (*before n*) ‹*car*› de la compañía *or* empresa **3** [C] **(a)** (Theat) compañía *f* **(b)** (Mil) compañía *f* **(c)** (Naut): **ship's ~** tripulación *f*, dotación *f*

comparable /'kɑ:mpərəbəl ‖ 'kɒmpərəbəl/ *adj* comparable

comparative[1] /kəm'pærətɪv/ *adj* relativo; ‹*literature/linguistics*› comparado; ‹*analysis/study*› comparativo

comparative[2] *n* (Ling) comparativo *m*

compare /kəm'per ‖ kəm'peə(r)/ *vt* **(a)** (make comparison between) comparar; **to ~ sth/sb** TO *o* WITH **sth/sb** comparar algo/a algn CON algo/algn **(b)** (liken) **to ~ sth/sb** TO **sth/sb** comparar algo/a algn CON *or* A algo/algn ■ ~ *vi*: **how do the two models ~ for speed?** en cuanto a velocidad ¿qué diferencia hay entre los dos modelos?; **this novel ~s favorably with the previous one** esta novela no desmerece de la anterior

comparison /kəm'pærəsən ‖ kəm'pærɪsən/ *n* [U C] comparación *f*

compartment /kəm'pɑ:rtmənt ‖ kəm'pɑ:tmənt/ *n* **(a)** (of bag, desk, refrigerator) compartimento *m*, compartimiento *m* **(b)** (in train) (BrE Rail) compartimento *m*, compartimiento *m*

compass /'kʌmpəs/ *n* **(a)** (*magnetic* ~) brújula *f* **(b)** (Math) (*often pl*) compás *m*

compassion /kəm'pæʃən/ *n* [U] compasión *f*

compassionate /kəm'pæʃənət/ *adj* compasivo

compatible /kəm'pætəbəl/ *adj* **(a)** ‹*people/ideas/principles*› compatible **(b)** (Comput) compatible; **an IBM ~ computer** una computadora *or* (Esp tb) un ordenador compatible con IBM

compel /kəm'pel/ *vt* **-ll- to ~ sb to** + INF obligar* a algn A + INF

compelling /kəm'pelɪŋ/ *adj* ‹*argument*› convincente; ‹*book*› absorbente

compendium /kəm'pendiəm/ *n* (*pl* **-diums** *or* **-dia** /-dɪə/) (BrE) **(a)** (book) compendio *m* **(b)** (of games) juegos *mpl* reunidos

compensate /'kɑ:mpənseɪt ‖ 'kɒmpenseɪt/ *vt* indemnizar*, compensar; **to ~ sb** FOR **sth** indemnizar* *or* compensar a algn POR algo ■ ~ *vi* **to ~** FOR **sth** compensar algo

compensation /'kɑ:mpən'seɪʃən ‖ ˌkɒmpen'seɪʃən/ *n* **(a)** [U C] (recompense) indemnización *f*, compensación *f*; **I received $20,000 as** *o* **in ~ for the damage** me dieron 20.000 dólares de indemnización *or* en compensación por los daños **(b)** [U] (remuneration) (AmE) remuneración *f*

compete /kəm'pi:t/ *vi* competir*; **to ~** FOR **sth** competir* POR algo

competence /'kɑ:mpətəns ‖ 'kɒmpɪtəns/ *n* [U] competencia *f*

competent /'kɑ:mpətənt ‖ 'kɒmpɪtənt/ *adj* competente

competition /'kɑ:mpə'tɪʃən ‖ ˌkɒmpə'tɪʃən/ *n* **1** [U] **(a)** (competing) competencia *f*; **to be in ~ with sb/sth** competir* con algn/algo **(b)** (opposition) competencia *f* **2** [C] (contest) concurso *m*; (Sport) competencia *f* (AmL), competición *f* (Esp)

competitive /kəm'petətɪv ‖ kəm'petɪtɪv/ *adj* competitivo

competitor /kəm'petətər ‖ kəm'petɪtə(r)/ *n* **(a)** (contestant) participante *mf*, concursante *mf* **(b)** (rival) (Busn) competidor, -dora *m,f*, rival *mf*; (Sport) contrincante *mf*

compile /kəm'paɪl/ *vt* **(a)** ‹*dictionary/index*› compilar **(b)** ‹*information*› recopilar, reunir*

complacent /kəm'pleɪsn̩t/ *adj* ‹*person*› satisfecho de sí mismo; ‹*attitude*› displicente

complain /kəm'pleɪn/ *vi/t* quejarse

complaint /kəm'pleɪnt/ *n* **(a)** (grievance) queja *f*, reclamo *m* (AmL); **to make a ~** quejarse **(b)** (ailment) dolencia *f* (frml)

complement[1] /'kɑ:mpləmənt ‖ 'kɒmplɪmənt/ *n* **1** ~ (TO **sth**) complemento *m* (DE algo) **2** (full number): **the orchestra had the full ~ of strings** la orquesta contaba con una sección de cuerdas completa

complement[2] *vt* complementar

complementary /'kɑ:mplə'mentri ‖ ˌkɒmplɪ'mentri/ *adj* complementario

complete[1] /kəm'pli:t/ *adj* **1** **(a)** (entire) completo **(b)** (finished) terminado, concluido **2** (thorough, absolute) (*as intensifier*) total, completo; **it came as a ~ surprise** fue una auténtica sorpresa

complete[2] *vt* **(a)** (finish) ‹*building/education*› acabar, terminar; ‹*sentence*› cumplir; ‹*investigations*› completar, concluir* **(b)** (make whole) ‹*set/collection*› completar **(c)** (fill in) (frml) ‹*form*› llenar, rellenar

completely /kəm'pli:tli/ *adv* completamente, totalmente

completion /kəm'pli:ʃən/ *n* [U] finalización *f*, terminación *f*

complex[1] /'kɑ:mpleks ‖ 'kɒmpleks/ *adj* complejo

complex[2] *n* **1** (buildings) complejo *m* **2** (Psych) complejo *m*

complexion /kəm'plekʃən/ *n* cutis *m*; (in terms of color) tez *f*

complexity /kəm'pleksəti/ *n* [U C] (*pl* **-ties**) complejidad *f*

complicate /'kɑːmpləkeɪt ‖ 'kɒmplɪkeɪt/ *vt* complicar*

complicated /'kɑːmpləkeɪtəd ‖ 'kɒmplɪkeɪtɪd/ *adj* complicado

complication /'kɑːmplə'keɪʃən ‖ ˌkɒmplɪ'keɪʃən/ *n* complicación *f*; **~s set in** (Med) surgieron complicaciones

compliment¹ /'kɑːmpləmənt ‖ 'kɒmplɪmənt/ *n* **(a)** (expression of praise) cumplido *m*, halago *m*; **to pay sb a ~** hacerle* un cumplido a algn, halagar* a algn **(b) compliments** *pl* (best wishes) saludos *mpl*; **with the ~s of the management** gentileza de la casa

compliment² *vt* **to ~ sb (ON sth)** felicitar a algn (POR algo)

complimentary /'kɑːmplə'mentəri ‖ ˌkɒmplɪ'mentri/ *adj* **(a)** (flattering) elogioso, halagüeño **(b)** (free) ‹*copy*› de obsequio *or* regalo; **~ ticket** invitación *f*

comply /kəm'plaɪ/ *vi* **-plies, -plying, -plied**: **to ~ with a request/an order** acceder a una solicitud/cumplir una orden

component¹ /kəm'pəʊnənt/ *n* componente *m*; (Auto) pieza *f*; (Electron) componente *m*

component² *adj* componente; ‹*element*› constituyente; **~ part** componente *m*

compose /kəm'pəʊz/ *vt* **1** (constitute) (*usu pass*) **to be ~d OF sth** estar* compuesto DE algo **2** ‹*music*› componer*; ‹*letter*› redactar **3** (calm, control) (liter): **to ~ oneself** serenarse, recobrar la compostura

composed /kəm'pəʊzd/ *adj* sereno

composer /kəm'pəʊzər ‖ kəm'pəʊzə(r)/ *n* compositor, -tora *m,f*

composition /'kɑːmpə'zɪʃən ‖ ˌkɒmpə'zɪʃən/ *n* [U C] composición *f*

compost /'kɑːmpəʊst ‖ 'kɒmpɒst/ *n* [U] abono *m* orgánico

composure /kəm'pəʊʒər ‖ kəm'pəʊʒə(r)/ *n* [U] compostura *f*

compound¹ /'kɑːmpaʊnd ‖ 'kɒmpaʊnd/ *adj* ‹*number/interest*› compuesto

compound² /'kɑːmpaʊnd ‖ 'kɒmpaʊnd/ *n* **1 (a)** (Chem) compuesto *m* **(b)** (word) palabra *f* compuesta **2** (residence) complejo *m* habitacional; (for prisoners etc) barracones *mpl*

compound³ /kɑːm'paʊnd ‖ kəm'paʊnd/ *vt* ‹*problem*› agravar; ‹*risk/difficulties*› acrecentar*

comprehend /'kɑːmprɪ'hend ‖ ˌkɒmprɪ'hend/ *vt* comprender

comprehension /'kɑːmprɪ'hentʃən ‖ ˌkɒmprɪ'henʃən/ *n* **(a)** [U] (understanding) comprensión *f* **(b)** [C U] (school exercise) (BrE) ejercicio *m* de comprensión

comprehensive /'kɑːmprɪ'hensɪv ‖ ˌkɒmprɪ'hensɪv/ *adj* **(a)** ‹*survey/report*› exhaustivo, global; ‹*view*› integral, de conjunto; ‹*list/range*› completo; ‹*insurance/cover*› contra todo riesgo **(b)** (Educ) (in UK) *relativo al sistema educativo en el cual no se separa a los alumnos según su nivel de aptitud*

comprehensive (school) *n* (in UK) *instituto de segunda enseñanza para alumnos de cualquier nivel de aptitud*

compress¹ /kəm'pres/ *vt* comprimir

compress² /'kɑːmpres ‖ 'kɒmpres/ *n* compresa *f*

comprise /kəm'praɪz/ *vt* **(a)** (consist of) comprender **(b)** (constitute, make up) componer*

compromise¹ /'kɑːmprəmaɪz ‖ 'kɒmprəmaɪz/ *n* [C U] acuerdo *m* mutuo, arreglo *m*, compromiso *m*

compromise² *vi* transigir*, transar (AmL) ■ ~ *vt* **(a)** (discredit) comprometer; **to ~ oneself** ponerse* en una situación comprometida **(b)** (endanger) comprometer

compromising /'kɑːmprəmaɪzɪŋ ‖ 'kɒmprəmaɪzɪŋ/ *adj* ‹*evidence*› comprometedor; ‹*situation*› comprometido

compulsion /kəm'pʌlʃən/ *n* **(a)** [U] (force, duress) coacción *f* **(b)** [C] (obsession) compulsión *f*

compulsive /kəm'pʌlsɪv/ *adj* **(a)** (compelling): **the book is ~ reading** es uno de esos libros que se empiezan y no se pueden dejar **(b)** (obsessive) ‹*behavior*› compulsivo; **he's a ~ eater/liar** come/miente por compulsión

compulsory /kəm'pʌlsəri/ *adj* ‹*attendance*› obligatorio; ‹*retirement*› forzoso

computer /kəm'pjuːtər ‖ kəm'pjuːtə(r)/ *n* computadora *f* (esp AmL), computador *m* (esp AmL), ordenador *m* (Esp); (*before n*) ‹*society/age/revolution*› de la informática; ‹*program/game*› de computadora (*or* ordenador *etc*); **~ programmer** programador, -dora *m,f*; **~ programming** programación *f*; **~ science** informática *f*; **~ studies** informática *f*, computación *f*

computerize /kəm'pjuːtəraɪz/ *vt* computarizar*, computerizar*; ‹*company/department*› informatizar*

computing /kəm'pjuːtɪŋ/ *n* [U] informática *f*, computación *f*

comrade /'kɑːmræd ‖ 'kɒmreɪd/ *n* compañero, -ra *m,f*, camarada *mf*

con¹ /kɑːn ‖ kɒn/ *n* **1** (fraud) (colloq) timo *m* (fam), estafa *f* **2** (convict) (sl) preso, -sa *m,f* **3** (colloq) (objection) contra *m*; *see also* PRO 2

con² *vt* **-nn-** (colloq) timar (fam), estafar

concave /'kɑːnkeɪv ‖ 'kɒŋkeɪv/ *adj* cóncavo

conceal /kən'siːl/ *vt* ‹*object/facts*› ocultar; ‹*emotions*› disimular; **to ~ sth FROM sb** ocultar(le) algo A algn

concede /kən'siːd/ *vt* **(a)** (admit) reconocer* **(b)** (allow) ‹*right/privilege*› conceder **(c)** (give away) ‹*game/penalty*› conceder

conceit /kən'siːt/ *n* engreimiento *m*, presunción *f*

conceited /kən'siːtəd ‖ kən'siːtɪd/ *adj* engreído, presuntuoso

conceivable /kən'siːvəbəl/ *adj* imaginable

conceive /kən'siːv/ *vt* **1 (a)** (devise) ‹*plan*› concebir* **(b)** (imagine) imaginar; (consider) considerar **2** ‹*child*› concebir* ■ ~ *vi* concebir*

concentrate¹ /'kɑːnsəntreɪt ‖ 'kɒnsəntreɪt/ *vt* **to ~ sth (ON sth)** concentrar algo (EN algo) ■ ~ *vi* ‹‹*person*›› concentrarse; ‹‹*talks*›› centrarse; **~ on getting this finished** concéntrate en terminar esto

concentrate² *n* [U] concentrado *m*

concentrated /'kɑ:nsəntreɪtəd ‖ 'kɒnsəntreɪtɪd/ *adj* **(a)** ‹*effort*› intenso y continuado **(b)** ‹*solution/juice*› concentrado

concentration /'kɑ:nsən'treɪʃən ‖,kɒnsən'treɪʃən/ *n* [C U] concentración *f*

concentration camp *n* campo *m* de concentración

concept /'kɑ:nsept ‖ 'kɒnsept/ *n* concepto *m*

conception /kən'sepʃən/ *n* **1** [C U] (idea) noción *f* **2** [U] (of baby, plan) concepción *f*

concern¹ /kən'sɜ:rn ‖ kən'sɜ:n/ *n* **1** [C] (business, affair) asunto *m*; **that's no ~ of yours** eso no es asunto tuyo **2** [U] **(a)** (anxiety) preocupación *f*, inquietud *f* **(b)** (interest) **~ FOR sb/sth** interés *m* POR algn/algo; **to be of ~ to sb** importarle a algn **3** [C] (firm) empresa *f*; ⇒ GOING²

concern² *vt* **1** (affect, involve) concernir*, incumbir; **to be ~ed WITH sth** ocuparse DE algo; **as far as I'm ~ed** en lo que a mí respecta, por mi parte; **to whom it may ~** (frml) a quien corresponda (frml) **2 (a)** (interest) interesar **(b)** (worry, bother) preocupar, inquietar **3** (relate to): **item one ~s the new office** el primer punto trata de la nueva oficina

concerned /kən'sɜ:rnd ‖ kən'sɜ:nd/ *adj* ‹*person*› preocupado; ‹*look*› de preocupación; **to be ~ ABOUT/FOR sb/sth** estar* preocupado POR algn/algo

concerning /kən'sɜ:rnɪŋ ‖ kən'sɜ:nɪŋ/ *prep* sobre, acerca de, con respecto a

concert¹ /'kɑ:nsərt ‖ 'kɒnsət/ *n* concierto *m*; **in ~** en vivo, en concierto; (*before n*) **~ hall** sala *f* de conciertos, auditorio *m*

concert² /kən'sɜ:rt ‖ kən'sɜ:t/ *vt* (frml) concertar*, coordinar; **we made a ~ed effort to ...** coordinamos *or* concertamos nuestros esfuerzos para ...

concerto /kən'tʃertəʊ ‖ kən'tʃɜ:təʊ, kən'tʃeətəʊ/ *n* (*pl* **-tos** *or* **-ti**) concierto *m*

concession /kən'seʃən/ *n* [C U] concesión *f*

conciliation /kən'sɪli'eɪʃən/ *n* [U] conciliación *f*

conciliatory /kən'sɪliətɔ:ri ‖ kən'sɪliətəri/ *adj* conciliador, conciliatorio

concise /kən'saɪs/ *adj* conciso

conclude /kən'klu:d/ *vt* **1 (a)** (end) concluir* (frml), finalizar* **(b)** (settle) ‹*deal*› cerrar*; ‹*agreement*› llegar* a; ‹*treaty*› firmar; ‹*alliance*› pactar **2** (infer) concluir* (frml) ■ **~** *vi* concluir* (frml), terminar

conclusion /kən'klu:ʒən/ *n* **1** [C] (end) conclusión *f*; **in ~** (*as linker*) para concluir **2** [C] (decision, judgment) conclusión *f*; **to come to** *o* **reach a ~** llegar* a una conclusión; ***to jump to ~s*** precipitarse (a sacar conclusiones)

conclusive /kən'klu:sɪv/ *adj* ‹*evidence/argument*› concluyente; ‹*victory*› decisivo

concoct /kən'kɑ:kt ‖ kən'kɒkt/ *vt* ‹*meal/drink*› preparar; ‹*excuse/story*› inventarse; ‹*plan*› tramar

concrete¹ /kɑ:n'kri:t, 'kɑ:nkri:t ‖ 'kɒnkri:t/ *adj* concreto

concrete² /'kɑ:nkri:t ‖ 'kɒnkri:t/ *n* [U] hormigón *m*, concreto *m* (AmL)

concur /kən'kɜ:r ‖ kən'kɜ:(r)/ *vi* **-rr-** (frml) **to ~ (WITH sb/sth)** coincidir (CON algn/algo)

concuss /kən'kʌs/ *vt* (*usu pass*): **to be ~ed** sufrir una conmoción (cerebral) *or* una concusión

concussion /kən'kʌʃən/ *n* [U] conmoción *f* cerebral, concusión *f*

condemn /kən'dem/ *vt* **1 (a)** (sentence) condenar **(b)** (censure) condenar **2 (a)** (declare unusable) ‹*building*› declarar ruinoso **(b)** (in US: convert to public use) ‹*building*› expropiar (*por causa de utilidad pública*)

condemnation /'kɑ:ndem'neɪʃən ‖,kɒndem'neɪʃən/ *n* [U] condena *f*

condensation /'kɑ:nden'seɪʃən ‖,kɒnden'seɪʃən/ *n* [U] (process) condensación *f*; **(b)** (on windows etc) vapor *m*, vaho *m*

condense /kən'dens/ *vt* **1** (abridge) ‹*book/article*› condensar **2** (Chem) condensar

condensed /kən'densd/ *adj* condensado; **~ milk** leche *f* condensada

condescend /'kɑ:ndɪ'send ‖,kɒndɪ'send/ *vi* **to ~ to** + INF dignarse *or* condescender* A + INF

condescending /'kɑ:ndɪ'sendɪŋ ‖,kɒndɪ'sendɪŋ/ *adj* ‹*tone/smile*› condescendiente

condiment /'kɑ:ndəmənt ‖ 'kɒndɪmənt/ *n* (seasoning) condimento *m*, aliño *m*; (relish) salsa *f* (*para condimentar*)

condition¹ /kən'dɪʃən/ *n* **1** (stipulation, requirement) condición *f*; **on ~ that** con la condición de que **2 (a)** (state) (*no pl*) estado *m*, condiciones *fpl*; **in good ~** en buen estado **(b)** (state of fitness): **to be in/out of ~** estar*/no estar* en forma **(c)** (Med) afección *f* (frml), enfermedad *f* **3 conditions** *pl* **(a)** (circumstances) condiciones *fpl*; **working/housing ~s** condiciones de trabajo/vivienda **(b)** (Meteo): **weather ~s are good** el estado del tiempo es bueno

condition² *vt* **(a)** (influence, determine) condicionar **(b)** ‹*hair*› acondicionar

conditional /kən'dɪʃn̩əl ‖ kən'dɪʃənl̩/ *adj* **(a)** (provisional) condicional **(b)** (Ling) condicional

conditioner /kən'dɪʃn̩ər ‖ kən'dɪʃn̩ə(r)/ *n* (*hair ~*) acondicionador *m*, enjuague *m* (AmL), suavizante *m* (Esp), bálsamo *m* (Chi); (*fabric ~*) suavizante *m*

conditioning /kən'dɪʃn̩ɪŋ/ *n* [U] (Psych) condicionamiento *m*

condo /'kɑ:ndəʊ ‖ 'kɒndəʊ/ *n* (AmE colloq) ⇒ CONDOMINIUM

condolences /kən'dəʊlənsɪz/ *pl n* (frml) condolencias *fpl* (frml)

condom /'kɑ:ndəm ‖ 'kɒndɒm/ *n* preservativo *m*, condón *m*

condominium /'kɑ:ndə'mɪniəm ‖,kɒndə'mɪniəm/ *n* (*pl* **~s**) (AmE) apartamento *m*, piso *m* (Esp) (*en régimen de propiedad horizontal*)

condone /kən'dəʊn/ *vt* aprobar*

conduct¹ /'kɑ:ndʌkt ‖ 'kɒndʌkt/ *n* [U] conducta *f*

conduct² /kən'dʌkt/ *vt* **(a)** ‹*inquiry/experiment/business*› llevar a cabo, realizar*; ‹*conversation*› mantener* **(b)** (Mus) dirigir* **(c)** ‹*visitor/tour/party*› guiar* **(d)** ‹*heat/electricity*› conducir*

conductor /kənˈdʌktər ‖ kənˈdʌktə(r)/ *n* **1** (Mus) director, -tora *m,f* (de orquesta) **2** (on bus) cobrador, -dora *m,f*, guarda *mf* (RPl); (on train) (AmE) cobrador, -dora *m,f* **3** (Elec, Phys) conductor *m*

cone /kəʊn/ *n* **(a)** (Auto, Math) cono *m* **(b)** (*ice-cream* ~) cucurucho *m* or barquillo *m* or (Ven) barquilla *f* or (Col) cono *m*

confectionery /kənˈfekʃəneri ‖ kənˈfekʃənəri/ *n* [U] productos *mpl* de confitería

confer /kənˈfɜːr ‖ kənˈfɜː(r)/ **-rr-** *vt* (bestow) conceder, conferir* (frml); **to ~ sth** ON *o* UPON **sb/sth** concederle *or* (frml) conferirle* algo A algn/algo ■ ~ *vi* (discuss) consultar

conference /ˈkɑːnfrəns ‖ ˈkɒnfərəns/ *n* **(a)** [C] (large assembly, convention) congreso *m*, conferencia *f*; (*before n*) ~ **center** *o* (BrE) **centre** centro *m* de conferencias **(b)** [C U] (meeting, discussion) conferencia *f*; (*before n*) ~ **room** sala *f* de juntas

confess /kənˈfes/ *vt* confesar* ■ ~ *vi* **(a)** (admit) confesar* **(b)** (Relig) confesarse*

confession /kənˈfeʃən/ *n* **(a)** [C] (statement) confesión *f* **(b)** [C U] (Relig) confesión *f*

confetti /kənˈfeti/ *n* [U] confeti *m* or (Chi) chaya *f* or (RPl) papel *m* picado or (Ven) papelillos *mpl*

confide /kənˈfaɪd/ *vi* (tell secrets) **to ~** IN **sb** confiarse* A algn ■ ~ *vt* **to ~ sth** TO **sb** confiarle* algo A algn

confidence /ˈkɑːnfədəns ‖ ˈkɒnfɪdəns/ *n* **1** [U] **(a)** (trust, faith) confianza *f* **(b)** (self-confidence) confianza *f* en sí mismo **2** [U] (confidentiality): **he took her into his ~** se confió a ella; **in ~** en confianza

confidence game *n* (AmE), **confidence trick** *n* estafa *f*, timo *m* (fam)

confident /ˈkɑːnfədənt ‖ ˈkɒnfɪdənt/ *adj* **(a)** (sure) ‹*statement/forecast*› hecho con confianza; **to be ~** OF **sth** confiar* EN algo **(b)** (self-confident) ‹*person*› seguro de sí mismo

confidential /ˈkɑːnfəˈdentʃəl ‖ ˌkɒnfɪˈdenʃəl/ *adj* confidencial

confidentiality /ˈkɑːnfəˈdentʃiˈæləti ‖ ˌkɒnfɪdenʃɪˈæləti/ *n* [U] confidencialidad *f*

confine /kənˈfaɪn/ *vt* **(a)** (limit, restrict) **to ~ sth** TO **sth** limitar algo A algo **(b)** (shut in, imprison) ‹*person*› confinar, recluir*; ‹*animal*› encerrar*

confined /kənˈfaɪnd/ *adj* ‹*space*› limitado

confinement /kənˈfaɪnmənt/ *n* **(a)** [U] (act, state) reclusión *f*, confinamiento *m* **(b)** [U C] (in childbirth) parto *m*

confines /ˈkɑːnfaɪnz ‖ ˈkɒnfaɪnz/ *pl n* confines *mpl*

confirm /kənˈfɜːrm ‖ kənˈfɜːm/ *vt* **1 (a)** (substantiate) ‹*report/reservation*› confirmar **(b) confirmed** *past p* ‹*bachelor/liar*› empedernido **2** (Relig) confirmar

confirmation /ˈkɑːnfərˈmeɪʃən ‖ ˌkɒnfəˈmeɪʃən/ *n* **1** [U] **(a)** (substantiation) confirmación *f* **(b)** (ratification) (frml) ratificación *f* **2** [U C] (Relig) confirmación *f*

confiscate /ˈkɑːnfəskeɪt ‖ ˈkɒnfɪskeɪt/ *vt* confiscar*

conflict¹ /ˈkɑːnflɪkt ‖ ˈkɒnflɪkt/ *n* [C U] conflicto *m*

conflict² /kənˈflɪkt/ *vi* discrepar

conflicting /kənˈflɪktɪŋ/ *adj* ‹*interests*› opuesto; ‹*views/accounts/emotions*› contradictorio

conform /kənˈfɔːrm ‖ kənˈfɔːm/ *vi* **(a)** (be in accordance) **to ~** TO *o* WITH **sth** ajustarse A *or* cumplir CON algo **(b)** (act in a conformist way) ser* conformista; **he usually ~s to their wishes** por lo general se aviene a sus deseos

confound /kənˈfaʊnd/ *vt* **(a)** (perplex) ‹*person*› confundir **(b)** (thwart) ‹*attempt*› frustrar

confront /kənˈfrʌnt/ *vt* **(a)** (come face to face with) ‹*danger/problem*› afrontar, enfrentar; **police were ~ed by a group of demonstrators** la policía se vio enfrentada a un grupo de manifestantes **(b)** (face up to) ‹*enemy/fear/crisis*› hacer* frente a

confrontation /ˈkɑːnfrʌnˈteɪʃən ‖ ˌkɒnfrʌnˈteɪʃən/ *n* **(a)** [C U] (conflict) enfrentamiento *m*, confrontación *f* **(b)** [C] (encounter) confrontación *f*

confuse /kənˈfjuːz/ *vt* **1 (a)** (bewilder) confundir **(b)** (blur) ‹*situation*› complicar* **2** (mix up, be unable to distinguish) ‹*ideas/sounds*› confundir

confused /kənˈfjuːzd/ *adj* **(a)** (perplexed) confundido; **to get ~** confundirse **(b)** (unclear) ‹*argument*› confuso

confusing /kənˈfjuːzɪŋ/ *adj* confuso

confusion /kənˈfjuːʒən/ *n* [U] **(a)** (turmoil) confusión *f* **(b)** (disorder) desorden *m*

congeal /kənˈdʒiːl/ *vi* «*fat*» solidificarse*; **~ed blood** sangre *f* coagulada

congested /kənˈdʒestəd ‖ kənˈdʒestɪd/ *adj* **(a)** (with traffic) congestionado; (with people) abarrotado de gente **(b)** (Med) congestionado

congestion /kənˈdʒestʃən/ *n* [U] **(a)** (with traffic) congestión *f*; (with people) abarrotamiento *m* **(b)** (Med) congestión *f*

Congo /ˈkɑːŋgəʊ ‖ ˈkɒŋgəʊ/ *n* el Congo

congratulate /kənˈgrætʃəleɪt ‖ kənˈgrætjʊleɪt/ *vt* felicitar; **to ~ sb** ON **sth**/-ING felicitar *or* darle* la enhorabuena a algn POR algo/+ INF

congratulation /kənˈgrætʃəˈleɪʃən ‖ kənˌgrætjʊˈleɪʃən/ *n* **(a)** [U] (praise) felicitación *f* **(b) congratulations** *pl* enhorabuena *f*, felicitaciones *fpl*; (*as interj*) **~s!** ¡enhorabuena!, ¡felicitaciones! (AmL)

congregate /ˈkɑːŋgrɪgeɪt ‖ ˈkɒŋgrɪgeɪt/ *vi* congregarse*

congregation /ˈkɑːŋgrɪˈgeɪʃən ‖ ˌkɒŋgrɪˈgeɪʃən/ *n* (Relig) (attending service) fieles *mpl*; (parishioners) feligreses *mpl*

congress /ˈkɑːŋgrəs ‖ ˈkɒŋgres/ *n* **(a)** (conference) congreso *m* **(b) Congress** (in US) el Congreso (de los Estados Unidos)

congress: **~man** /ˈkɑːŋgrəsmən ‖ ˈkɒŋgresmən/ *n* (*pl* **-men** /-mən/) (in US) miembro *m* del Congreso; **~woman** *n* (in US) miembro *f* del Congreso

conifer /ˈkɑːnəfər ‖ ˈkɒnɪfə(r)/ *n* conífera *f*

conjecture¹ /kənˈdʒektʃər ‖ kənˈdʒektʃə(r)/ *n* [U]: **it's pure ~** no son más que conjeturas

conjecture² *vt/i* (frml) conjeturar

conjugal /ˈkɑːndʒəgəl ‖ ˈkɒndʒʊgəl/ *adj* (frml) conyugal

conjunctivitis /kən'dʒʌŋktɪ'vaɪtəs ‖ kən,dʒʌŋk tɪ'vaɪtɪs/ *n* [U] conjuntivitis *f*

conjurer /'kɑːndʒərər ‖ 'kʌndʒərə(r)/ *n* prestidigitador, -dora *m,f*, mago, -ga *m,f*

conjure up /'kɑːndʒər ‖ 'kʌndʒə(r)/ [*v* + *o* + *adv*, *v* + *adv* + *o*] (evoke) evocar*; **it ~s ~ images of** … hace pensar en …

conjuror *n* ⇒ CONJURER

con man *n* estafador *m*, timador *m*

Conn = **Connecticut**

connect /kə'nekt/ *vt* **1 (a)** (attach) **to ~ sth** (TO **sth**) conectar algo (A algo) **(b)** (link together) ‹*rooms/buildings*› comunicar*; ‹*towns*› conectar **(c)** (Telec): **I'm trying to ~ you** un momento que lo comunico *or* (Esp) le pongo con el número **(d)** ‹*phone/gas*› conectar **2** (associate) relacionar ■ **~** *vi* **1 (a)** (be joined together) «*rooms*» comunicarse*; «*pipes*» empalmar **(b)** (be fitted) **to ~** (TO **sth**) estar* conectado (a algo) **2** (Transp) **to ~** WITH **sth** «*train/flight*» enlazar* CON algo, conectar CON algo (AmL)

• **connect up 1** [*v* + *o* + *adv*, *v* + *adv* + *o*] ‹*wires/apparatus*› conectar **2** [*v* + *adv*] «*wires*» conectarse; **it all ~s up** todo está relacionado

connected /kə'nektəd ‖ kə'nektɪd/ *adj* ‹*ideas/events*› relacionado; **to be ~ed** WITH **sth** estar* relacionado CON algo

connection /kə'nekʃən/ *n* **1** [C] **(a)** (link) **~** (WITH **sth**) enlace *m* *or* conexión *f* (CON algo) **(b)** (Elec) conexión *f* **2** [C] (Transp) **~** (WITH **sth**) conexión *f* *or* enlace *m* (CON algo) **3** [C U] (relation) relación *f* *or* conexión *f* **4 connections** *pl* (links, ties) lazos *mpl*; (influential people) contactos *mpl*, conexiones *fpl* (AmL)

connive /kə'naɪv/ *vi* **(a)** (plot) **to ~** (WITH **sb**) actuar* en complicidad (CON algn) **(b)** (cooperate) **to ~** AT **sth** ser* cómplice EN algo

connoisseur /'kɑːnə'sɜːr ‖ ,kɒnə'sɜː(r)/ *n* entendido, -da *m,f*

connotation /'kɑːnə'teɪʃən ‖ ,kɒnə'teɪʃən/ *n* [U C] connotación *f*

conquer /'kɑːŋkər ‖ 'kɒŋkə(r)/ *vt* ‹*country/mountain*› conquistar; ‹*enemy/fear*› vencer

conqueror /'kɑːŋkərər ‖ 'kɒŋkərə(r)/ *n* conquistador, -dora *m,f*

conquest /'kɑːŋkwest ‖ 'kɒŋkwest/ *n* [C U] conquista *f*

conscience /'kɑːntʃəns ‖ 'kɒnʃəns/ *n* [C U] conciencia *f*; **to have a clear ~** tener* la conciencia tranquila

conscientious /'kɑːntʃi'entʃəs ‖ ,kɒnʃi'enʃəs/ *adj* ‹*work*› concienzudo; ‹*student*› aplicado

conscientious objector /əb'jektər ‖ əb 'jektə(r)/ *n* objetor, -tora *m,f* de conciencia

conscious /'kɑːntʃəs ‖ 'kɒnʃəs/ *adj* **1 (a)** (awake, alert) (*no comp*) consciente **(b)** (aware) (*pred*) **to be ~** OF **sth** ser* *or* (Chi, Méx tb) estar* consciente DE algo **2** (deliberate) ‹*decision*› deliberado; **she made a ~ effort to be nice** se esforzó por ser amable

consciousness /'kɑːntʃəsnəs ‖ 'kɒnʃəsnɪs/ *n* [U] **(a)** (state of being awake, alert) conocimiento *m* **(b)** (awareness) conciencia *f*

conscript¹ /'kɑːnskrɪpt ‖ 'kɒnskrɪpt/ *n* recluta *mf*, conscripto, -ta *m,f* (AmL)

conscript² /kən'skrɪpt/ *vt* reclutar

conscription /kən'skrɪpʃən/ *n* [U] conscripción *f* (esp AmL), reclutamiento *m* (*para el servicio militar obligatorio en casos de guerra*)

consecrate /'kɑːnsəkreɪt ‖ 'kɒnsɪkreɪt/ *vt* consagrar

consecutive /kən'sekjətɪv ‖ kən'sekjʊtɪv/ *adj* ‹*numbers*› consecutivo; **he was absent on three ~ days** faltó tres días seguidos

consensus /kən'sensəs/ *n* [C U] consenso *m*

consent¹ /kən'sent/ *vi* acceder; **to ~** TO **sth** acceder A *or* consentir* EN algo

consent² *n* [U] consentimiento *m* de común acuerdo; **age of ~** (Law) *edad a partir de la cual es válido el consentimiento que se da para tener relaciones sexuales*

consequence /'kɑːnsəkwens ‖ 'kɒnsɪkwəns/ *n* **1** [C] (result) consecuencia *f* **2** [U] (importance) trascendencia *f*

consequently /'kɑːnsəkwentli ‖ 'kɒnsɪkwentli/ *adv* consiguientemente, por consiguiente

conservation /'kɑːnsər'veɪʃən ‖ ,kɒnsə'veɪʃən/ *n* [U] protección *f* *or* conservación *f* del medio ambiente

conservationist /'kɑːnsər'veɪʃənəst ‖ ,kɒnsə 'veɪʃənɪst/ *n* conservacionista *mf*

conservative /kən'sɜːrvətɪv ‖ kən'sɜːvətɪv/ *adj* **(a)** (traditional) conservador **(b) Conservative** (in UK) (*before n*) conservador **(c)** (cautious) cauteloso; **a ~ estimate** un cálculo por lo bajo

Conservative *n* (in UK) conservador, -dora *m,f*

conservatory /kən'sɜːrvətɔːri ‖ kən'sɜːvətri/ *n* (*pl* **-ries**) **(a)** (greenhouse) jardín *m* de invierno **(b)** (school of music) conservatorio *m*

conserve /kən'sɜːrv ‖ kən'sɜːv/ *vt* **(a)** (preserve) ‹*wildlife/rivers*› proteger*, conservar **(b)** (save) ‹*energy/resources*› conservar

consider /kən'sɪdər ‖ kən'sɪdə(r)/ *vt* **(a)** (think about, of) considerar; **we're ~ing moving house** estamos pensando en mudarnos; **~ yourself lucky** puedes darle por afortunado **(b)** (take into account) tener* en cuenta, considerar; **all things ~ed, I think that** … bien considerado, creo que …

considerable /kən'sɪdərəbəl/ *adj* ‹*achievement/risk*› considerable; ‹*sum*› importante; **with ~ difficulty** con bastante dificultad

considerably /kən'sɪdərəbli/ *adv* bastante, considerablemente

considerate /kən'sɪdərət/ *adj* atento, considerado

consideration /kən'sɪdə'reɪʃən/ *n* **1 (a)** [U] (attention, thought): **their case has been given careful ~** su caso ha sido estudiado *or* considerado detenidamente; **to take sth into ~** tener* algo en cuenta **(b)** [C] (factor): **a major ~ is the cost** un factor muy a tener en cuenta es el costo **2** (thoughtfulness) consideración *f* **3** (importance): **of little/no ~** de poca/ninguna importancia

considering¹ /kən'sɪdərɪŋ/ *prep* teniendo en cuenta

considering² *conj*: **~ (that) she's only two years old** teniendo en cuenta que tiene sólo dos años

consignment /kən'saınmənt/ *n* **(a)** [C] (goods sent) envío *m*, remesa *f* **(b)** [U] (sending) envío *m*

consist /kən'sıst/ *vi* **to ~ OF sth** constar DE algo

consistency /kən'sıstənsi/ *n* (*pl* **-cies**) **(a)** [U] (regularity) regularidad *f* **(b)** [U C] (of mixture) consistencia *f*

consistent /kən'sıstənt/ *adj* **(a)** (compatible) **to be ~ (WITH sth)** «*statements/beliefs*» concordar* (CON algo) **(b)** (constant) ‹*excellence/failure*› constante; ‹*denial*› sistemático

consistently /kən'sıstəntli/ *adv* **(a)** (without change) ‹*argue*› coherentemente; ‹*behave*› consecuentemente **(b)** (constantly) ‹*claim/refuse*› sistemáticamente

consolation /ˌkɑːnsə'leıʃən ‖ˌkɒnsə'leıʃən/ *n* [C U] consuelo *m*; (*before n*) **~ prize** premio *m* de consolación, premio *m* (de) consuelo (CS)

console¹ /'kɑːnsəʊl ‖ 'kɒnsəʊl/ *n* consola *f*

console² /kən'səʊl/ *vt* consolar*

consolidate /kən'sɑːlədeıt ‖ kən'sɒlıdeıt/ *vt* **(a)** (reinforce) ‹*support/position*› consolidar **(b)** (combine) ‹*companies*› fusionar; ‹*debts*› consolidar

consonant /'kɑːnsənənt ‖ 'kɒnsənənt/ *n* consonante *f*

consort /'kɑːnsɔːrt ‖ 'kɒnsɔːt/ *n* (frml) consorte *mf* (frml)

consortium /kən'sɔːrʃiəm ‖ kən'sɔːtiəm/ *n* (*pl* **-tia** /-tiə/ *or* **-tiums**) consorcio *m*

conspicuous /kən'spıkjuəs/ *adj* ‹*hat/badge*› llamativo; ‹*differences/omissions*› manifiesto, evidente; **to make oneself ~** llamar la atención; **to be ~ by one's absence** brillar por su (*or* mi *etc*) ausencia

conspiracy /kən'spırəsi/ *n* [C U] (*pl* **-cies**) conspiración *f*

conspirator /kən'spırətər ‖ kən'spırətə(r)/ *n* conspirador, -dora *m,f*

conspire /kən'spaır ‖ kən'spaıə(r)/ *vi* conspirar; **to ~ to + INF** conspirar PARA + INF

constable /'kɑːnstəbəl ‖ 'kʌnstəbəl/ ▶ **603** *n* (BrE) agente *mf* de policía

constant /'kɑːnstənt ‖ 'kɒnstənt/ *adj* **(a)** (continual) ‹*pain/complaints*› constante **(b)** (unchanging) ‹*temperature/speed*› constante **(c)** (loyal) (liter) fiel, leal

constantly /'kɑːnstəntli ‖ 'kɒnstəntli/ *adv* constantemente

constellation /'kɑːnstə'leıʃən ‖ ˌkɒnstə'leıʃən/ *n* constelación *f*

constipated /'kɑːnstəpeıtəd ‖ 'kɒnstıpeıtıd/ *adj* estreñido

constipation /ˌkɑːnstə'peıʃən ‖ ˌkɒnstı'peıʃən/ *n* [U] estreñimiento *m*

constituency /kən'stıtʃuənsi ‖ kən'stıtjʊənsi/ *n* (*pl* **-cies**) (area) circunscripción *f or* distrito *m* electoral; (supporters) electores *mpl* potenciales (*de una circunscripción electoral*)

constituent¹ /kən'stıtʃuənt ‖ kən'stıtjʊənt/ *n* **1** (Pol) elector, -tora *m,f* **2** (component) (frml) componente *m*, elemento *m* constitutivo *or* constituyente

constituent² *adj* (*before n*) ‹*part/element*› constituyente, constitutivo

constitute /'kɑːnstətuːt ‖ 'kɒnstıtjuːt/ *vt* (frml) constituir* (frml)

constitution /'kɑːnstə'tuːʃən ‖ ˌkɒnstı'tjuːʃən/ *n* **1** (of country) constitución *f*; (of association, party) estatutos *mpl* **2** (of person) constitución *f*

constitutional /'kɑːnstə'tuːʃn̩əl ‖ ˌkɒnstı'tjuːʃənl/ *adj* constitucional

constrain /kən'streın/ *vt* (*often pass*) obligar*

constraint /kən'streınt/ *n* **(a)** [U] (compulsion) coacción *f* **(b)** [U C] (restriction) (*often pl*) restricción *f*, limitación *f*

constrict /kən'strıkt/ *vt* ‹*opening/channel*› estrechar; ‹*flow/breathing*› dificultar; ‹*freedom*› coartar

construct /kən'strʌkt/ *vt* **(a)** (build) (frml) construir* **(b)** (put together) ‹*model*› armar, montar

construction /kən'ʃtrʌkʃən/ *n* **1 (a)** [U] (of building) construcción *f*; (*before n*) ‹*industry/worker*› de la construcción **(b)** [C] (Ling, Math) construcción *f* **2** [C] (structure) estructura *f*

constructive /kən'strʌktıv/ *adj* constructivo

consul /'kɑːnsəl ‖ 'kɒnsəl/ *n* cónsul *mf*

consulate /'kɑːnsələt ‖ 'kɒnsjʊlət/ *n* consulado *m*

consult /kən'sʌlt/ *vt* consultar ■ **~** *vi*: **I ought to ~ with my wife first** primero debería consultárselo a mi mujer

consultancy /kən'sʌltənsi/ *n* [C U] (*pl* **-cies**) (Busn) asesoría *f*, consultoría *f*

consultant /kən'sʌltənt/ *n* (adviser) asesor, -sora *m,f*, consultor, -tora *m,f*; (BrE Med) especialista *mf*

consultation /'kɑːnsəl'teıʃən ‖ ˌkɒnsəl'teıʃən/ *n* [U C] **(a)** (with doctor, lawyer) consulta *f* **(b)** (of dictionary, notes) consulta *f* **(c)** (discussion): **there was no ~ with the tenants** no se consultó a los inquilinos; **in ~ with sb** en conferencia con algn

consume /kən'suːm ‖ kən'sjuːm/ *vt* consumir; **he was ~d by** *o* **with jealousy** lo consumían los celos

consumer /kən'suːmər ‖ kən'sjuːmə(r)/ *n* consumidor, -dora *m,f*; (*before n*) **~ goods** artículos *mpl or* bienes *mpl* de consumo

consummate¹ /'kɑːnˌsəmət ‖ 'kɒnsəmət/ *adj* (frml) (*before n*) ‹*actor/liar*› consumado

consummate² /'kɑːnsəmeıt ‖ 'kɒnsəmeıt/ *vt* consumar

consumption /kən'sʌmpʃən/ *n* [U] consumo *m*

contact¹ /'kɑːntækt ‖ 'kɒntækt/ *n* **(a)** [U] (physical) contacto *m*; **to come into ~ with sth** hacer* contacto con algo **(b)** [U C] (communication) contacto *m*; **to come in/into ~ with sb** tratar a algn; **to be/get in ~ with sb** estar*/ponerse* en contacto con algn

contact² *vt* ponerse* en contacto con

contact lens *n* lente *f or* (AmL) lente *m* de contacto, lentilla *f* (Esp)

contagious /kən'teıdʒəs/ *adj* contagioso

contain /kən'teın/ *vt* **1** (hold) contener* **2** ‹*enemy/fire/epidemic*› contener*; ‹*anger/laughter*› contener*; **to ~ oneself** contenerse*

container /kən'teɪnər ‖ kən'teɪnə(r)/ *n* (receptacle) recipiente *m*; (as packaging) envase *m*; (Transp) contenedor *m*, contáiner *m*; (*before n*) **~ ship** buque *m* portacontenedores

contaminate /kən'tæməneɪt ‖ kən'tæmɪneɪt/ *vt* contaminar

contamination /kən'tæmə'neɪʃən ‖ kən,tæmɪ'neɪʃən/ *n* [U] contaminación *f*

contd (= **continued**) sigue

contemplate /'kɑːntəmpleɪt ‖ 'kɒntəmpleɪt/ *vt* contemplar; **I ~d phoning her** pensé (en) llamarla

contemporary[1] /kən'tempəreri ‖ kən'tempərəri/ *adj* **(a)** (of the same period) ‹*person*› contemporáneo, coetáneo; ‹*object*› de la época **(b)** (present-day) contemporáneo, actual

contemporary[2] *n* (*pl* **-ries**) **(a)** (sb living at same time) contemporáneo, -nea *m,f*, coetáneo, -na *m,f* **(b)** (sb of same age): **he looks older than his contemporaries** parece mayor que la gente de su edad

contempt /kən'tempt/ *n* [U] desprecio *m*; **to be beneath ~** ser* despreciable; **~ (of court)** (Law) desacato *m* al tribunal

contemptible /kən'temptəbəl/ *adj* despreciable

contemptuous /kən'temptʃuəs ‖ kən'temptjʊəs/ *adj* despectivo

contend /kən'tend/ *vi* **(a)** (compete) **to ~ (WITH sb) (FOR sth)** competir* (CON algn) (POR algo) **(b)** (face) **to ~ WITH sth** lidiar CON algo ■ **~** *vt* argüir*

contender /kən'tendər ‖ kən'tendə(r)/ *n* **~ (FOR sth)** aspirante *mf* (A algo)

content[1] /'kɑːntent ‖ 'kɒntent/ *n* **1 contents** *pl* (of box, bottle) contenido *m*; **~s** (of book) índice *m* de materias; (in magazine) sumario *m* **2** [U] (amount contained) contenido *m*

content[2] /kən'tent/ *adj* (*pred*) contento

content[3] /kən'tent/ *v refl* **to ~ oneself WITH sth/-ING** contentarse CON algo/+ INF

contented /kən'tentəd ‖ kən'tentɪd/ *adj* ‹*sigh/purr*› de satisfacción; ‹*person/workforce*› satisfecho; **to be ~ WITH sth** contentarse CON algo

contention /kən'tentʃən ‖ kən'tenʃən/ *n* **1** [U] (dispute): **there is considerable ~ over** … existe un gran desacuerdo sobre … **2** [C] (assertion) opinión *f*; **it is her ~ that** … ella sostiene que …

contentious /kən'tentʃəs ‖ kən'tenʃəs/ *adj* ‹*issue*› polémico

contentment /kən'tentmənt/ *n* [U] satisfacción *f*

contest[1] /'kɑːntest ‖ 'kɒntest/ *n* **(a)** (competition) (Games) concurso *m*; (Sport) competencia *f* (AmL), competición *f* (Esp); (in boxing) combate *m* **(b)** (struggle) lucha *f*

contest[2] /kən'test/ *vt* **(a)** ‹*allegation*› refutar; ‹*will*› impugnar; ‹*decision*› protestar contra **(b)** ‹*election*› presentarse como candidato a

contestant /kən'testənt/ *n* concursante *mf*

context /'kɑːntekst ‖ 'kɒntekst/ *n* [U C] contexto *m*

continent /'kɑːntṇənt ‖ 'kɒntɪnənt/ *n* continente *m*; **the C~** Europa *f* (continental)

continental /'kɑːntṇ'entl4 ‖ ,kɒntɪ'nentḷ/ *adj* continental; **C~** (European) de Europa (continental)

continental: **~ breakfast** *n* [U] desayuno *m* continental (*desayuno de café o té y bollos con mantequilla y mermelada*); **~ quilt** *n* (BrE) ⇒ DUVET

contingency /kən'tɪndʒənsi/ *n* [C] (*pl* **-cies**) (eventuality) contingencia *f*; (*before n*) ‹*fund*› (para casos) de emergencia; **a ~ plan** un plan para prever

continual /kən'tɪnjuəl/ *adj* continuo, constante

continually /kən'tɪnjuəli/ *adv* continuamente, constantemente

continuation /kən'tɪnju'eɪʃən/ *n* [U C] continuación *f*

continue /kən'tɪnjuː/ *vi* continuar*, seguir*; **we ~d on our way** reanudamos el camino ■ **~** *vt* **(a)** (keep on) continuar*, seguir* con; **to ~ -ING/to + INF** continuar* *or* seguir* + GER **(b)** (resume) continuar*, seguir* con, proseguir* (frml); **to be ~d** continuará **(c)** (extend, prolong) prolongar*

continuity /'kɑːntṇ'uːəti ‖ ,kɒntɪ'njuːɪti/ *n* [U] continuidad *f*

continuous /kən'tɪnjuəs/ *adj* continuo; **~ assessment** (Educ) evaluación *f* continua

continuously /kən'tɪnjuəsli/ *adv* continuamente, sin interrupción

contort /kən'tɔːrt ‖ kən'tɔːt/ *vt* ‹*face*› contraer*; **to ~ oneself** contorsionarse ■ **~** *vi* crisparse

contortion /kən'tɔːrʃən ‖ kən'tɔːʃən/ *n* contorsión *f*

contour /'kɑːntʊr ‖ 'kɒntʊə(r)/ *n* contorno *m*; (*before n*) **~ line** curva *f* de nivel, cota *f*

contraband /'kɑːntrəbænd ‖ 'kɒntrəbænd/ *n* [U] contrabando *m*

contraception /'kɑːntrə'sepʃən ‖ ,kɒntrə'sepʃən/ *n* [U] anticoncepción *f*, contracepción *f*

contraceptive /'kɑːntrə'septɪv ‖ ,kɒntrə'septɪv/ *n* anticonceptivo *m*, contraconceptivo *m*

contract[1] /'kɑːntrækt ‖ 'kɒntrækt/ *n* (agreement, document) contrato *m*; (for public works) contrata *f*

contract[2] /kən'trækt/ *vt also* /'kɑːntrækt/ **(a)** (place under contract) ‹*person*› contratar **(b)**‹*debt/disease*› contraer* (frml) **(c)** ‹*muscle*› contraer* ■ **~** *vi* (become smaller tighter) contraerse*

• **contract out** /'kɑːntrækt ‖ 'kɒntrækt/ [*v + o + adv, v + adv + o*] ‹*job/work*› subcontratar

contraction /kən'trækʃən/ *n* [C U] contracción *f*

contractor /kən'træktər ‖ kən'træktə(r)/ *n* contratista *mf*

contradict /'kɑːntrə'dɪkt ‖ ,kɒntrə'dɪkt/ *vt* contradecir*

contradiction /'kɑːntrə'dɪkʃən ‖ ,kɒntrə'dɪkʃən/ *n* [C U] contradicción *f*; **a ~ in terms** un contrasentido

contradictory /'kɑːntrə'dɪktəri ‖ ,kɒntrə'dɪktəri/ *adj* contradictorio

contralto /kən'træltəʊ/ *n* (*pl* **~s**) contralto *f*

contraption /kən'træpʃən/ *n* (colloq) artilugio *m*

contrary[1] *adj* **1** /'kɑːntreri ‖'kɒntrəri/ **(a)** (opposed, opposite) contrario **(b) ~ to** (*as prep*) contrariamente a, al contrario de **2** /'kɑːntreri, kən'treri || kən'treəri/ (obstinate): **he's so ~** siempre tiene que llevar la contraria

contrary² /'kɑ:ntreri || 'kɒntrəri/ *n* (*pl* **-ries**): **the ~** lo contrario; **on the contrary** (*as linker*) al contrario

contrast¹ /'kɑ:ntræst || 'kɒntrɑ:st/ *n* [C U] contraste *m*; **by ~** (*as linker*) por contraste; **in ~ to** *o* **with** (*as prep*) en contraste con

contrast² /kən'træst || kən'trɑ:st/ *vt* contrastar ■ **~** *vi* **(a)** (differ) contrastar **(b) contrasting** *pres p* ‹*opinions/approaches*› contrastante

contribute /kən'trɪbjət, -bju:t/ *vt* **(a)** ‹*money/time*› contribuir* con, aportar, hacer* una aportación *or* (esp AmL) un aporte de; ‹*suggestions/ideas*› aportar **(b)** ‹*article/poem/paper*› escribir* ■ **~** *vi* **(a)** (play significant part) **to ~** (**TO sth**) contribuir* (A algo) **(b)** (give money) contribuir* **(c)** (participate) **to ~ TO sth** participar EN algo **(d)** (Journ) **to ~ TO sth** escribir* PARA algo

contribution /'kɑ:ntrə'bju:ʃən || ˌkɒntrɪ'bju:ʃən/ *n* **(a)** [C] (participation, part played) contribución *f* **(b)** [C U] (payment, donation) contribución *f*; (to a fund) aportación *f*, aporte *m* (esp AmL)

contributor /kən'trɪbjətər || kən'trɪbjʊtə(r)/ *n* **(a)** (writer) colaborador, -dora *m,f* **(b)** (donor) donante *mf*

contrive /kən'traɪv/ *vt* **(a)** (manage) **to ~ to** + INF lograr + INF/QUE (+ *subj*), ingeniárselas *or* arreglárselas PARA + INF/PARA QUE (+ *subj*) **(b)** (create) ‹*method/device*› idear

contrived /kən'traɪvd/ *adj* artificioso

control¹ /kən'trəʊl/ *vt* **-ll-** controlar; ‹*traffic*› dirigir*; **to ~ oneself** controlarse

control² *n* **1** [U] control *m*; **to be in ~ of sth** dominar algo; **to gain ~ of sth** hacerse* con; **circumstances beyond our ~** circunstancias ajenas a nuestra voluntad; **to be out of ~** estar* fuera de control; **to get out of ~** descontrolarse **2** [U C] **price ~(s)** control *m* de precios **3 controls** *pl* (of vehicle) mandos *mpl* **4** [U] (mastery) dominio *m*

controlled /kən'trəʊld/ *adj* ‹*voice/emotion*› contenido; ‹*response*› mesurado; ‹*conditions/experiment*› controlado

controller /kən'trəʊlər || kən'trəʊlə(r)/ *n* director, -tora *m,f*

control: **~ room** *n* (Mil, Naut) centro *m* de operaciones; (Audio, Rad, TV) sala *f* de control; **~ tower** *n* torre *f* de control

controversial /'kɑ:ntrə'vɜ:rʃəl || ˌkɒntrə'vɜ:ʃəl/ *adj* controvertido

controversy /'kɑ:ntrəvɜ:rsi || 'kɒntrevɜ:si, kən'trɒvəsi/ *n* [U C] (*pl* **-sies**) controversia *f*

conundrum /kə'nʌndrəm/ *n* adivinanza *f*

conurbation /'kɑ:nɜ:r'beɪʃən || ˌkɒnɜ:'beɪʃən/ *n* conurbación *f*

convalesce /'kɑ:nvə'les || ˌkɒnvə'les/ *vi* recuperarse, convalecer*

convene /kən'vi:n/ *vi* reunirse*

convenience /kən'vi:niəns/ *n* **(a)** [U] (comfort, practicality) conveniencia *f*; **at your ~** cuando le resulte conveniente **(b)** [C] (amenity, appliance): **with every modern ~** con todas las comodidades modernas

convenience food *n* [C U] comida *f* de preparación rápida

convenient /kən'vi:niənt/ *adj* **(a)** (opportune, suitable) conveniente **(b)** (practical) práctico; **a very ~ way of storing things** una manera muy práctica de guardar las cosas **(c)** (handy, close): **it's very ~ having the school so near** resulta muy práctico tener la escuela tan cerca

conveniently /kən'vi:niəntli/ *adv* **(a)** (handily) convenientemente **(b)** (expediently): **the government ~ forgets its election promises** le resulta muy cómodo al gobierno olvidarse de sus promesas electorales

convent /'kɑ:nvənt || 'kɒnvənt/ *n* convento *m*

convention /kən'ventʃən || kən'venʃən/ *n* **1 (a)** [U] (social code) convenciónes *fpl*, convencionalismos *mpl* **(b)** [C] (established practice) convención *f* **2** [C] (agreement) convención *f* **3** [C] (conference) convención *f*, congreso *m*

conventional /kən'ventʃn̩əl || kən'venʃənl̩/ *adj* convencional

converge /kən'vɜ:rdʒ || kən'vɜ:dʒ/ *vi* «*lines/roads*» converger*, convergir*; «*crowd/armies*» reunirse*

conversation /'kɑ:nvər'seɪʃən || ˌkɒnvə'seɪʃən/ *n* [U C] conversación *f*

conversational /'kɑ:nvər'seɪʃn̩əl || ˌkɒnvə'seɪʃənl/ *adj* familiar, coloquial

converse /kən'vɜ:rs || kən'vɜ:s/ *vi* conversar

conversion /kən'vɜ:rʒən || kən'vɜ:ʃən/ *n* **1** [U C] **(a)** (change) conversión *f* **(b)** (of house): **to do a ~** transformar una casa **(c)** (Relig) conversión *f* **2** [C U] (in rugby) conversión *f*, transformación *f*

convert¹ /'kɑ:nvɜ:rt || 'kɒnvɜ:t/ *n* converso, -sa *m,f*

convert² /kən'vɜ:rt || kən'vɜ:t/ *vt* **1** ‹*building*› remodelar; ‹*vehicle*› transformar; **to ~ sth INTO sth** convertir* algo EN algo **2** (cause to change view, religion) convertir* **3** (in rugby) transformar, convertir* ■ **~** *vi* (Pol, Relig) convertirse*

convertible¹ /kən'vɜ:rtəbəl || kən'vɜ:təbəl/ *adj* convertible

convertible² *n* (Auto) descapotable *m*, convertible *m* (AmL)

convex /'kɑ:nveks || 'kɒnveks/ *adj* convexo

convey /kən'veɪ/ *vt* ‹*goods/people*› transportar; ‹*feeling*› expresar; ‹*thanks*› hacer* llegar

conveyor (belt) /kən'veɪər || kən'veɪə(r)/ *n* cinta *f or* correa *f* transportadora, banda *f* transportadora (Méx)

convict¹ /'kɑ:nvɪkt || 'kɒnvɪkt/ *n* recluso, -sa *m,f*, presidiario, -ria *m,f*

convict² /kən'vɪkt/ *vt* (*often pass*) declarar culpable, condenar; **to be ~ed OF sth** ser* condenado POR algo

conviction /kən'vɪkʃən/ *n* [U C] **1** [C] (Law) condena *f* **2** [U C] (certainty) convicción *f*

convince /kən'vɪns/ *vt* convencer*; **to ~ sb THAT** convencer* a algn DE QUE

convinced /kən'vɪnst/ *adj* (persuaded) (*pred*): **to be ~ OF sth/THAT** estar* convencido DE algo/DE QUE

convincing /kən'vɪnsɪŋ/ *adj* convincente

convivial /kən'vɪviəl/ *adj* ‹*atmosphere*› cordial; ‹*person*› simpático

convoy /'kɑːnvɔɪ ‖ 'kɒnvɔɪ/ *n* convoy *m*

convulsion /kən'vʌlʃən/ *n* convulsión *f*

coo /kuː/ *vi* «*dove/pigeon*» arrullar

cook¹ /kʊk/ *n* cocinero, -ra *m,f*; **he's a good ~** cocina muy bien, es muy buen cocinero

cook² *vt* ‹*food/meal*› hacer*, preparar ■ **~** *vi* **(a)** (prepare food) cocinar, guisar **(b)** (become ready) «*food*» hacerse*

cookbook /'kʊkbʊk/ *n* libro *m* de cocina *or* de recetas

cooker /'kʊkər ‖ 'kʊkə(r)/ *n* (BrE) (stove) cocina *f or* (Col, Méx) estufa *f*

cookery /'kʊkəri/ *n* [U] cocina *f*; (*before n*) **~ book** (BrE) ⇒ COOKBOOK

cookie /'kʊki/ *n* (AmE Culin) galleta *f*, galletita *f* (RPl)

cooking /'kʊkɪŋ/ *n* [U]: **to do the ~** cocinar; **it is used in ~** se usa para cocinar; **home ~** la comida casera; **Spanish ~** la cocina española

cooky *n* ⇒ COOKIE

cool¹ /kuːl/ *adj* **-er, -est** ▶ **920** **1** (cold) fresco; **it's ~ today** hace *or* está fresco hoy **2** (reserved, hostile) ‹*reception/behavior*› frío **3** (calm) sereno, tranquilo; **keep ~!** ¡tranquilo!, no te pongas nervioso; **he's a very ~ customer** tiene una sangre fría impresionante **4** (sl) (trendy, laid-back): **he's really ~** es muy en la onda (fam)

cool² *n* **1** (low temperature): **let's stay here in the ~** quedémonos aquí al fresco **2** (composure) calma *f*; **to keep/lose one's ~** mantener*/perder* la calma

cool³ *vt* ‹*air/room*› refrigerar; ‹*engine/food/enthusiasm*› enfriar* ■ **~** *vi* «*air/room*» refrigerarse; «*engine/food/enthusiasm*» enfriarse*

● **cool down** [*v* + *adv*] **(a)** (become cooler) «*food/iron*» enfriarse*; «*person*» refrescarse* **(b)** (become calmer) calmarse

● **cool off** [*v* + *adv*] **(a)** (become cooler) «*person*» refrescarse* **(b)** (become calmer) calmarse

coolly /'kuːlli/ *adv* **(a)** (calmly) con serenidad *or* calma **(b)** (boldly) descaradamente, con la mayor frescura **(c)** (with reserve, hostility) fríamente, con frialdad

coop /kuːp/ *n*: **chicken/hen ~** gallinero *m*

● **coop up** [*v* + *o* + *adv*, *v* + *adv* + *o*] (*usu passive*) encerrar*

co-op /'kəʊɑːp ‖ 'kəʊɒp/ *n* cooperativa *f*

cooperate /kəʊ'ɑːpəreɪt ‖ kəʊ'ɒpəreɪt/ *vi* cooperar, colaborar

cooperation /kəʊ'ɑːpə'reɪʃən ‖ kəʊˌɒpə'reɪʃən/ *n* [U] cooperación *f*, colaboración *f*

cooperative¹ /kəʊ'ɑːpərətɪv ‖ kəʊ'ɒpərətɪv/ *adj* **(a)** ‹*attitude*› de colaboración, cooperativo **(b)** ‹*effort/venture*› conjunto

cooperative² *n* cooperativa *f*

co-opt /kəʊ'ɑːpt ‖ kəʊ'ɒpt/ *vt*: **to ~ sb onto a committee** invitar a algn a formar parte de una comisión

coordinate¹ /kəʊ'ɔːrdn̩eɪt ‖ ˌkəʊ'ɔːdɪneɪt/ *vt* coordinar

coordinate² /kəʊ'ɔːrdn̩ət ‖ kəʊ'ɔːdɪnət/ *n* **1** (Math) coordenada *f* **2 coordinates** *pl* prendas *fpl* para combinar, coordinados *mpl*

coordination /kəʊ'ɔːrdn̩'eɪʃən ‖ kəʊˌɔːdɪ'neɪʃən/ *n* [U] coordinación *f*

coordinator /kəʊ'ɔːrdn̩eɪtər ‖ kəʊ'ɔːdɪneɪtə(r)/ *n* coordinador, -dora *m,f*

coowner /'kəʊ'əʊnər ‖ kəʊ'əʊnə(r)/ *n* copropietario, -ria *m,f*

cop /kɑːp ‖ kɒp/ *n* (colloq) poli *mf* (fam), tira *mf* (Méx fam), cana *mf* (RPl arg), cachaco, -ca *m,f* (Per fam), paco, -ca *m,f* (Chi fam)

cope /kəʊp/ *vi*: **I can't ~ with all this work** no doy abasto *or* no puedo con tanto trabajo; **how do you ~ without a washing machine?** ¿cómo te las arreglas sin lavadora?; **how is he coping on his own?** ¿qué tal se las arregla solo?; **these are some of the problems they have to ~ with** éstos son algunos de los problemas a los que tienen que enfrentarse

Copenhagen /'kəʊpən'heɪgən/ *n* Copenhague *m*

copious /'kəʊpiəs/ *adj* copioso

copper /'kɑːpər ‖ 'kɒpə(r)/ *n* **1 (a)** [U] (metal) cobre *m* **(b) coppers** *pl* (coins) (colloq) peniques *mpl*, perras *fpl* (Esp fam), quintos *mpl* (Méx fam), chauchas *fpl* (Chi fam), vintenes *mpl* (Ur fam) **(c)** ▶ **515** (color) color *m* cobre; (*before n*) cobrizo **2** (police officer) (colloq) ⇒ COP

copy¹ /'kɑːpi ‖ 'kɒpi/ *n* (*pl* **copies**) **1** [C] (of painting, document) copia *f* **2** [C] (of newspaper, book) ejemplar *m* **3** [U] (text): **he/she must be able to produce clear ~** debe saber redactar con claridad

copy² **copies, copying, copied** *vt* **1 (a)** (reproduce, transcribe) copiar **(b)** (photocopy) fotocopiar **2** (imitate) ‹*painter/singer*› copiarle a; ‹*style/behavior*› copiar

copy: **~cat** *n* (colloq) copión, -piona *m,f* (fam), imitamonos *mf* (Méx fam); **~right** *n* [U] copyright *m*, derechos *mpl* de reproducción

coral /'kɔːrəl ‖ 'kɒrəl/ *n* [U] coral *m*

cord /kɔːrd ‖ kɔːd/ *n* **1** [C U] **(a)** (string, rope) cuerda *f*; (of pajamas, curtains) cordón *m* **(b)** (AmE Elec) cordón *m*, cable *m* **(c)** (Anat) ⇒ SPINAL CORD, UMBILICAL CORD, VOCAL CORDS **2** [U] (Tex) pana *f*, corderoy *m* (AmS), cotelé *m* (Chi)

cordial¹ /'kɔːrdʒəl ‖ 'kɔːdiəl/ *adj* cordial

cordial² *n* [C U] refresco *m* (*concentrado*)

cordless /'kɔːrdləs ‖ 'kɔːdlɪs/ *adj* inalámbrico

cordon /'kɔːrdn̩ ‖ 'kɔːdn̩/ *n* cordón *m*

● **cordon off** [*v* + *o* + *adv*, *v* + *adv* + *o*] acordonar

corduroy /'kɔːrdərɔɪ ‖ 'kɔːdərɔɪ/ *n* [U] pana *f*, corderoy *m* (AmS), cotelé *m* (Chi)

core¹ /kɔːr ‖ kɔː(r)/ *n* (of apple, pear) corazón *m*; (of Earth) centro *m*; (of nuclear reactor) núcleo; (of problem) meollo *m*

core² *vt* ‹*apple*› quitarle el corazón a

coriander /'kɔːriændər ‖ ˌkɒri'ændə(r)/ *n* cilantro *m*, culantro *m*

cork /kɔːrk ‖ kɔːk/ *n* [U C] corcho *m*

corkscrew /'kɔːrkskruː ‖ 'kɔːkskruː/ *n* sacacorchos *m*, tirabuzón *m*

corn /kɔːrn ‖ kɔːn/ *n* **1** [U] **(a)** (cereal crop — in general) grano *m*; (maize) (AmE) maíz *m*; (wheat) (BrE) trigo *m*; (oats) (BrE) avena *f* **(b)** (foodstuff) maíz *m*, choclo *m* (AmS); **~ on the cob** mazorca *f* de maíz *or* (AmS) de choclo, elote *f* (Méx) **2** [C] (on toe) callo *m*

corner¹ /'kɔːrnər ‖ 'kɔːnə(r)/ *n* **1 (a)** (inside angle — of room, cupboard) rincón *m*; (— of field) esquina *f*; (— of mouth) comisura *f*; (— of page) ángulo *m* **(b)** (outside angle — of street, page) esquina *f*; (— of table) esquina *f*, punta *f*; (bend in road) curva *f*; ***to cut ~s***: (financially) hacer* economías; (in a process) simplificar*; (*before n*) **~ shop** (BrE) tienda *f* de la esquina; (local shop) tienda *f* de barrio **2** (in soccer) (**~** *kick*) córner *m*, tiro *m or* saque *m* de esquina **3** (in boxing) esquina *f*

corner² *vt* **1** (trap) acorralar **2** (monopolize) acaparar ■ **~** *vi* tomar una curva; **this car ~s well** este coche tiene buen agarre en las curvas

cornerstone /'kɔːrnərstəʊn ‖ 'kɔːnəstəʊn/ *n* piedra *f* angular

corn: **~flakes** *pl n* copos *mpl or* hojuelas *fpl* de maíz; **~flour** *n* [U] (BrE) maizena® *f*

Cornish /'kɔːrnɪʃ ‖ 'kɔːnɪʃ/ *adj* de Cornualles

cornstarch /'kɔːrnstɑːrtʃ ‖ 'kɔːnstɑːtʃ/ *n* [U] (AmE) maizena® *f*

Cornwall /'kɔːrnwɔːl ‖ 'kɔːnwɔːl/ *n* Cornualles *m*

corny /'kɔːrni ‖ 'kɔːni/ *adj* **-nier, -niest** (colloq) **(a)** ‹*song/movie*› cursi, sensiblero **(b)** (BrE) ‹*joke*› malo

coronary¹ /'kɔːrəneri ‖'kɒrənri/ *adj* coronario

coronary² *n* (*pl* **-ries**) infarto *m* (de miocardio)

coronation /'kɔːrə'neɪʃən ‖ ˌkɒrə'neɪʃən/ *n* [U C] coronación *f*

coroner /'kɔːrənər ‖ 'kɒrənə(r)/ *n*: *funcionario encargado de investigar las causas de muertes violentas, repentinas o sospechosas*, ≈ juez *mf* de instrucción

corporal /'kɔːrprəl ‖ 'kɔːpərəl/ *n* cabo *m*

corporal punishment *n* [U] castigos *mpl* corporales

corporate /'kɔːrpərət ‖ 'kɔːpərət/ *adj* **1 (a)** (of a company) ‹*headquarters/lawyer*› de la empresa *or* compañía **(b)** ‹*mentality/jargon*› empresarial **2** (joint, collective) ‹*action/decision*› colectivo

corporation /'kɔːrpə'reɪʃən ‖ ˌkɔːpə'reɪʃən/ *n* (company — in US) sociedad *f* anónima; (— in UK) compañía *f*, empresa *f*, corporación *f*

corpse /kɔːrps ‖ kɔːps/ *n* cadáver *m*

corpuscle /'kɔːrpʌsəl ‖ 'kɔːpʌsəl/ *n* corpúsculo *m*

corral /kə'ræl ‖ kɒ'rɑːl/ *n* corral *m*

correct¹ /kə'rekt/ *vt* corregir*

correct² *adj* correcto

correction /kə'rekʃən/ *n* [U C] corrección *f*

correctly /kə'rektli/ *adv* correctamente

correlate /'kɔːrəleɪt ‖ 'kɒ-/ *vi* **to ~** (**WITH sth**) estar* correlacionado (CON algo)

correlation /ˌkɔːrə'leɪʃən ‖ ˌkɒrə'leɪʃən/ *n* [C U] correlación *f* (frml)

correspond /'kɔːrə'spɑːnd ‖ ˌkɒrə'spɒnd/ *vi* **1 (a)** (tally) **to ~** (**WITH sth**) corresponderse *or* concordar* (CON algo) **(b)** (be equivalent) **to ~** (**TO sth**) equivaler* *or* corresponder (A algo) **2** (communicate by letter) **to ~** (**WITH sb**) mantener* correspondencia (CON algn)

correspondence /'kɔːrə'spɑːndəns ‖ ˌkɒrə'spɒndəns/ *n* **1** [U C] (agreement) correspondencia *f* **2** [U] (letters, letter-writing) correspondencia *f*

correspondence course *n* curso *m* por correspondencia

correspondent /'kɔːrə'spɑːndənt ‖ ˌkɒrə'spɒndənt/ *n* **(a)** (letter writer) corresponsal *mf* **(b)** (Journ) corresponsal *mf*

corridor /'kɔːrədər ‖ 'kɒrɪdɔː(r)/ *n* pasillo *m*, corredor *m*

corroborate /kə'rɑːbəreɪt ‖ kə'rɒbəreɪt/ *vt* corroborar

corrode /kə'rəʊd/ *vt* corroer* ■ **~** *vi* corroerse*

corrosion /kə'rəʊʒən/ *n* [U] **(a)** (action) corrosión *f* **(b)** (substance) herrumbre *f*, orín *m*

corrosive /kə'rəʊsɪv/ *adj* corrosivo

corrugated /'kɔːrəgeɪtəd ‖ 'kɒrəgeɪtɪd/ *adj* ondulado; **~ cardboard** cartón *m* corrugado; **~ iron** chapa *f* de zinc, calamina *f* (Chi, Per)

corrupt¹ /kə'rʌpt/ *vt* (deprave) corromper; (bribe) sobornar; (Comput) corromper

corrupt² *adj* ‹*person/government*› corrompido, corrupto

corruption /kə'rʌpʃən/ *n* [U] corrupción *f*

corset /'kɔːrsət ‖ 'kɔːsɪt/ *n* (*often pl*) corsé *m*

cosmetic /kɑːz'metɪk ‖ kɒz'metɪk/ *adj* **(a)** (beautifying) (*before n*) ‹*powder/cream*› cosmético; **~ surgery** cirugía *f* estética **(b)** (superficial) ‹*reforms/changes*› superficial

cosmetics /kɑːz'metɪks ‖ kɒz'metɪks/ *pl n* cosméticos *mpl*

cosmic /'kɑːzmɪk ‖ 'kɒzmɪk/ *adj* cósmico

cosmonaut /'kɑːzmənɔːt ‖ 'kɒzmənɔːt/ *n* cosmonauta *mf*

cosmopolitan /'kɑːzmə'pɑːlətn̩ ‖ ˌkɒzmə'pɒlɪtn̩/ *adj* cosmopolita

cosmos /'kɑːzməʊs ‖ 'kɒzmɒs/ *n* **the ~** el cosmos

cost¹ /kɔːst ‖ kɒst/ *n* **1 (a)** (expense) (*often pl*) costo *m* (esp AmL), coste *m* (Esp); **to cut ~s** reducir* los gastos **(b) costs** *pl* (Law) costas *fpl* **2** [U] (loss, sacrifice): **she helped me out, at great ~ to herself** sacrificó mucho al ayudarme; **at all ~s** a toda costa

cost² *vt* **1** (*past & past p* **cost**) **(a)** «*article/service*» costar* **(b)** (cause to lose) costar*; **one slip ~ him the title** un error le costó el título **2** (*past & past p* **costed**) (calculate cost of) calcular el costo *or* (Esp) coste de

co-star /'kəʊstɑːr ‖ 'kəʊstɑː(r)/ *n* coprotagonista *mf*

Costa Rica /'kɔːstə'riːkə ‖ˌkɒstə'riːkə/ *n* Costa Rica *f*

Costa Rican /'kɔːstə'riːkən ‖ ˌkɒstə'riːkən/ *adj* costarricense

cost: **~-effective** /'kɔːstɪ'fektɪv ‖ ˌkɒstɪ'fektɪv/ *adj* rentable; **~ of living** *n* costo *m or* (Esp) coste *m* de (la) vida; ~ **price** *n* precio *m* de costo *or* (Esp) de coste

costume /'kɑ:stu:m || 'kɒstju:m/ *n* **(a)** [U] (style of dress) traje *m*; (for parties, disguise) disfraz *m* **(b)** [C] (wardrobe) (Theat) vestuario *m*; (individual outfit) traje *m* **(c)** [C] *(swimming* ~) traje *m* de baño

costume jewelry, (BrE) **costume jewellery** *n* [U] bisutería *f*, alhajas *fpl* de fantasía

cosy[1] /'kəʊzi/ *adj* **cosier, cosiest** (BrE) ⇒ cozy[1]

cosy[2] *n* (*pl* **cosies**) (BrE) ⇒ cozy[2]

cot /kɑ:t || kɒt/ *n* **(a)** (campbed) (AmE) catre *m* **(b)** (for child) (BrE) cuna *f*, cama *f* (*con barandas*)

cottage /'kɑ:tɪdʒ || 'kɒtɪdʒ/ *n* casita *f*

cottage cheese *n* [U] requesón *m*

cotton /'kɑ:tn̩ || 'kɒtn̩/ *n* [U] **(a)** (cloth) algodón *m*; (*before n*) ‹*dress/sheet/print*› de algodón **(b)** (thread) (BrE) hilo *m* (de coser) **(c)** (*absorbent* ~) (AmE) algodón *m* (hidrófilo)

cotton wool *n* [U] (BrE) algodón *m* (hidrófilo)

couch /kaʊtʃ/ *n* (sofa) sofá *m*; (doctor's, psychoanalyst's) diván *m*

cough[1] /kɔ:f || kɒf/ *n* tos *f*; (*before n*) ~ **mixture** jarabe *m* para la tos

cough[2] *vi* toser ■ ~ *vt* ~ **(up)** expectorar

● **cough up 1** [*v* + *adv* + *o*] (pay) (colloq) ‹*money*› soltar* (fam), aflojar (fam) **2** [*v* + *adv*] (pay) soltar* la plata *or* (Esp) la pasta *or* (AmL tb) la lana (fam)

could /kʊd/ *v mod* **1** *past of* CAN[3] **2** (indicating possibility) poder*; **I would help you if I** ~ te ayudaría si pudiera; **you** ~ **have killed us all!** ¡podrías *or* podías habernos matado a todos!; **you** ~ **be right** puede (ser) que tengas razón **3 (a)** (asking permission): ~ **I use your bathroom?** ¿podría *or* me permitiría pasar al baño? **(b)** (in requests): ~ **you sign here please?** ¿quiere firmar aquí, por favor? **4 (a)** (in suggestions) poder*; **you** ~ **try doing it this way** podrías tratar de hacerlo de esta manera **(b)** (indicating strong desire) poder*; **I** ~ **have killed her** la hubiera matado, la podría *or* podía haber matado

couldn't /'kʊdn̩t/ = **could not**

council /'kaʊnsəl/ *n* **(a)** (advisory group) consejo *m* **(b)** (Govt) ayuntamiento *m*, municipio *m*; ~ **housing** (BrE) *viviendas de alquiler subvencionadas por el ayuntamiento*

councillor *n* (BrE) ⇒ COUNCILOR

Council of Europe *n* **the** ~ ~ ~ el Consejo de Europa

councilor, (BrE) **councillor** /'kaʊnsələr || 'kaʊnsələ(r)/ *n* concejal, -jala *m,f*

council tax *n* (in UK) ≈contribución *f* (municipal *or* inmobiliaria)

counsel[1] /'kaʊnsəl/ *n* (*pl* ~) (*no art*) (Law) abogado, -da *m,f*; ~ **for the defense** abogado defensor, abogada defensora *m,f*; ~ **for the prosecution** fiscal *mf*

counsel[2] *vt*, (BrE) **-ll-** (frml) aconsejar

counseling, (BrE) **counselling** /'kaʊnsəlɪŋ/ *n* [U] (Educ, Psych) orientación *f* psicopedagógica

counselor, (BrE) **counsellor** /'kaʊnsələr || 'kaʊnsələ(r)/ *n* **(a)** (Educ, Psych) consejero, -ra *m,f*, orientador, -dora *m,f* **(b)** (AmE Law) abogado, -da *m,f*

count[1] /kaʊnt/ *n* **1 (a)** (act of counting) recuento *m*, cómputo *m*; (of votes) escrutinio *m*, recuento *m*, cómputo *m*, conteo *m* (Andes, Ven); **to keep/lose** ~ **of sth** llevar/perder* la cuenta de algo **(b)** (total) total *m*; **the final** ~ (of votes) el recuento *or* cómputo final **2** (point): **it has been criticized on several** ~**s** ha sido criticado por varios motivos **3** ▶ **603** (rank) conde *m*

count[2] *vt* **1** (enumerate, add up) contar* **2** (include) contar*; **not** ~**ing the driver** sin contar al conductor **3** (consider) considerar; **to** ~ **oneself lucky** darse* por afortunado ■ ~ *vi* **1** (enumerate) contar* **2** (be valid, matter) contar*; **that doesn't** ~ eso no cuenta *or* no vale; **every minute** ~**s** cada minuto cuenta

● **count for** [*v* + *prep* + *o*] contar*; **your opinion** ~**s for a great deal/won't** ~ **for much** tu opinión importa mucho/no va a contar mucho

● **count on** [*v* + *prep* + *o*] **(a)** (rely on) ‹*friend/help*› contar* con **(b)** (expect) esperar; **we hadn't** ~**ed on that happening** no esperábamos que fuera a pasar eso

● **count out 1** [*v* + *o* + *adv*]: **you can** ~ **me out** a mí no me incluyan, no cuenten conmigo **2** [*v* + *o* + *adv*, *v* + *adv* + *o*] ‹*money/objects*› contar* (*uno por uno*)

countdown /'kaʊntdaʊn/ *n* cuenta *f* atrás *or* regresiva, conteo *m* regresivo (Andes, Ven)

counter[1] /'kaʊntər || 'kaʊntə(r)/ *n* **1** (in shop) mostrador *m*; (in café) barra *f*; (in bank, post office) ventanilla *f*; (in kitchen) (AmE) encimera *f* **2** (Games) ficha *f*

counter[2] *vt* **(a)** (oppose) ‹*deficiency/trend*› contrarrestar **(b)** (in debate) ‹*idea/statement*› rebatir, refutar; **to** ~ THAT responder *or* replicar* QUE

counter[3] *adv*: **to run** *o* **go** ~ **to sth** ser* contrario a *or* oponerse* a algo

counteract /'kaʊntər'ækt/ *vt* contrarrestar

counterattack[1] /'kaʊntərə'tæk/ *n* contraataque *m*

counterattack[2] *vi* contraatacar*

counterbalance /'kaʊntər'bæləns || 'kaʊntə ˌbæləns/ *n* contrapeso *m*

counterclockwise /'kaʊntər'klɑ:kwaɪz || ˌkaʊntə'klɒkwaɪz/ *adj/adv* (AmE) en sentido contrario a las agujas del reloj

counterfeit[1] /'kaʊntərfɪt || 'kaʊntəfɪt/ *n* falsificación *f*

counterfeit[2] *adj* ‹*money*› falso

counter: ~**foil** *n* talón *m* (AmL), matriz *f* (Esp); ~**part** *n* (person) homólogo, -ga *m,f*; (thing) equivalente *m*; ~**point** *n* [U C] (Mus) contrapunto *m*; ~**productive** /'kaʊntərprə'dʌktɪv || ˌkaʊntə prə'dʌktɪv/ *adj* contraproducente

countess /'kaʊntəs || 'kaʊntes/ ▶ **603** *n* condesa *f*

countless /'kaʊntləs || 'kaʊntlɪs/ *adj* ‹*stars/hours*› incontables, innumerables

country /'kʌntri/ *n* (*pl* **-tries**) **1** [C] (nation) país *m*; (people) pueblo *m*; (native land) patria *f* **2** [U] (rural area) **the** ~ el campo; (*before n*) ‹*people*› del campo; ‹*cottage*› de campo **3** [U] (region) terreno *m* **4** [U] (Mus) (música *f*) country *m*

country: **~-and-western** /ˈkʌntriənˈwestərn ‖ˌkʌntriənˈwestən/ *n* [U] (música *f*) country *m*; **~ dancing** *n* [U] (esp BrE) danzas *fpl* folklóricas; **~ house** *n* casa *f* solariega; **~man** /ˈkʌntrimən/ *n* (*pl* **-men** /-mən/) (*fellow* ~) (liter) compatriota *m*; **~side** *n* [U] campiña *f*, campo *m*; **~wide** /ˈkʌntri ˈwaɪd/ *adj/adv* a escala nacional

county /ˈkaʊnti/ *n* (*pl* **-ties**) condado *m*

county: **~ council** *n* (in UK) *corporación de gobierno a nivel de condado*; **~ court** *n* (in US) juzgado *m* comarcal; (in UK) juzgado *m* comarcal (*que conoce de causas de derecho civil*)

coup /kuː/ *n* (*pl* **~s** /kuːz/) **1** (successful action) golpe *m* maestro **2 ~ (d'état)** /deɪtɑː/ (Pol) golpe *m* (de estado)

couple¹ /ˈkʌpəl/ *n* **1** (two people) (+ *sing o pl vb*) pareja *f*; **a married ~** un matrimonio **2** (two or small number): **a ~ (of sth)** (+ *pl vb*) un par (de algo)

couple² *vt* **(a)** (connect) (Rail) enganchar; ‹*theories/events*› asociar; **to ~ sth/sb WITH sth/sb** asociar algo/a algn CON algo/algn **(b)** (combine) (*often pass*): **the fall in demand, ~d with competition from abroad** el descenso de la demanda, unido a la competencia extranjera

coupon /ˈkuːpɑːn ‖ˈkuːpɒn/ *n* **(a)** (voucher — for discount) vale *m*; (— in rationing) cupón *m* de racionamiento **(b)** (form — in advertisement) cupón *m*; (— for competition) boleto *m*

courage /ˈkərɪdʒ ‖ˈkʌrɪdʒ/ *n* [U] valor *m*, coraje *m*

courageous /kəˈreɪdʒəs/ *adj* ‹*person*› valiente, corajudo; ‹*words*› valiente; ‹*act*› valeroso

courgette /kʊrˈʒet ‖kɔːˈʒet/ *n* [C U] (BrE) ⇒ ZUCCHINI

courier /ˈkʊriər ‖ˈkʊriə(r)/ *n* **(a)** (guide) guía *mf* **(b)** (messenger) (BrE) mensajero, -ra *m,f*, correo *mf*, rutero, -ra *m,f*

course /kɔːrs ‖kɔːs/ *n* **1 (a)** (of river) curso *m*; (of road) recorrido *m* **(b)** (way of proceeding): **the best ~ of action** las mejores medidas que se pueden tomar **(c)** (progress, direction) (*no pl*): **in the normal ~ of events** normalmente; **in due ~** a su debido tiempo; **it changed the ~ of history** cambió el curso de la historia **2 of course** claro, desde luego, por supuesto; **of ~ not** claro *or* por supuesto que no **3** (Aviat, Naut) rumbo *m*; **to go off ~** desviarse* de rumbo; **to change ~** cambiar de rumbo **4 (a)** (Educ) curso *m*; **~ IN/ON sth** curso DE/SOBRE algo; **to take a ~** hacer* un curso **(b)** (Med): **a ~ of treatment** un tratamiento **5** (part of a meal) plato *m*; **main ~** plato principal *or* fuerte; **a three-~ meal** una comida de dos platos y postre **6** (Sport) (*race~*) hipódromo *m*, pista *f* (de carreras); (*golf ~*) campo *m* or (CS tb) cancha *f* (de golf)

court¹ /kɔːrt ‖kɔːt/ *n* **1** (Law) **(a)** (tribunal) tribunal *m*; **to take sb to ~** demandar a algn, llevar a algn a juicio; (*before n*) **~ case** causa *f*, juicio *m* **(b)** (building) juzgado *m* **2** (of sovereign) corte *f* **3** (Sport) cancha *f* (AmL), pista *f* (Esp) **4** (courtyard) patio *m*

court² *vt* **(a)** ‹*girl*› (dated) cortejar (ant), hacerle* la corte a (ant) **(b)** (seek) ‹*danger/favor*› buscar*; ‹*danger*› exponerse* a

courteous /ˈkɜːrtiəs ‖ˈkɜːtiəs/ *adj* cortés

courtesy /ˈkɜːrtəsi ‖ˈkɜːtəsi/ *n* [U] cortesía *f*; **~ of** por atención de

courthouse /ˈkɔːrthaʊs ‖ˈkɔːthaʊs/ *n* juzgado *m*

courtier /ˈkɔːrtiər ‖ˈkɔːtiə(r)/ *n* cortesano, -na *m,f*

court-martial¹ /ˈkɔːrtˈmɑːrʃəl ‖ˌkɔːtˈmɑːʃəl/ *n* (*pl* **courts-martial** /ˈkɔːrts-/) consejo *m* de guerra

court-martial² *vt*, (BrE) **-ll-** formarle consejo de guerra a

court: **~room** *n* sala *f* (*de un tribunal*); **~ shoe** *n* (BrE) zapato *m* (de) salón; **~yard** *n* patio *m*

cousin /ˈkʌzn̩/ *n* primo, -ma *m,f*; **first ~** primo hermano *or* carnal, prima hermana *or* carnal; **second ~** primo segundo, prima segunda

cove /kəʊv/ *n* cala *f*, caleta *f*

covenant /ˈkʌvənənt/ *n* pacto *m*

cover¹ /ˈkʌvər ‖ˈkʌvə(r)/ *n* **1** [C] **(a)** (lid, casing) tapa *f*, cubierta *f*; (for cushion, sofa, typewriter) funda *f*; (for book) forro *m* **(b) covers** *pl* (bedclothes) **the ~s** las mantas, las cobijas (AmL), las frazadas (AmL) **2** [C] (of book) tapa *f*, cubierta *f*; (of magazine) portada *f*, carátula *f* (Andes); (*front ~*) portada *f*; **to read sth from ~ to ~** leer* algo de cabo a rabo **3 (a)** [U] (shelter, protection): **to take ~** guarecerse*, ponerse* a cubierto; **to run for ~** correr a guarecerse *or* a ponerse a cubierto; **under ~ of darkness** al abrigo de la oscuridad **(b)** [C U] (front, pretense) tapadera *f*, pantalla *f*; **to blow sb's ~** desenmascarar a algn **4** [U] (insurance) (BrE) cobertura *f*

cover² *vt* **1 (a)** (overlay) cubrir*; **to be ~ed IN sth** estar* cubierto DE algo **(b)** ‹*hole/saucepan*› tapar **(c)** ‹*cushion*› ponerle* una funda a; ‹*book*› forrar; ‹*sofa*› tapizar*, recubrir* **(d)** ‹*passage/terrace*› techar, cubrir* **2 (a)** (extend over) ‹*area/floor*› cubrir*; ‹*page*› llenar **(b)** (travel) ‹*distance*› recorrer **3 (a)** (deal with) ‹*syllabus*› cubrir*; ‹*topic*› tratar **(b)** (report on) (Journ) cubrir* **4 (a)** (hide) tapar; **to ~ one's head** cubrirse* (la cabeza) **(b)** (mask) ‹*surprise/ignorance*› disimular; ‹*mistake*› ocultar **5 (a)** (guard, protect) cubrir* **(b)** (point gun at) apuntarle a **(c)** (Sport) ‹*opponent*› marcar*; ‹*shot/base*› cubrir* **6** (Fin) **(a)** ‹*costs/expenses*› cubrir*; ‹*liabilities*› hacer* frente a; **will $100 ~ it?** ¿alcanzará con 100 dólares? **(b)** (insurance) cubrir* ■ **~** *vi* **(a)** (deputize) **to ~ FOR sb** sustituir* a algn **(b)** (conceal truth) **to ~ FOR sb** encubrir* a algn

• **cover up 1** [*v + o + adv, v + adv + o*] **(a)** (cover completely) cubrir*, tapar **(b)** (conceal) ‹*facts/truth*› ocultar; ‹*mistake*› disimular **2** [*v + adv*] (conceal error) disimular; (conceal truth) **to ~ up FOR sb** encubrir* a algn

coverage /ˈkʌvərɪdʒ/ *n* [U] (Journ) cobertura *f*

cover-alls /ˈkʌvərɔːlz/ *pl n* (AmE) overol *m* (AmL), mono *m* (Esp, Méx)

covering letter /ˈkʌvərɪŋ/ *n* carta *f* adjunta

covert /ˈkəʊvərt ‖ˈkʌvət, ˈkəʊ-/ *adj* encubierto

cover-up /ˈkʌvərʌp/ *n* (of crime) encubrimiento *m*

covet /ˈkʌvət/ *vt* codiciar

cow /kaʊ/ *n* **(a)** (Agr) vaca *f* **(b)** (female whale, elephant, seal) hembra *f*

coward /ˈkaʊərd ‖ˈkaʊəd/ *n* cobarde *mf*

cowardice /ˈkaʊərdəs ‖ˈkaʊədɪs/ *n* [U] cobardía *f*

cowardly /'kaʊərdli ‖ 'kaʊədli/ *adj* cobarde

cowboy /'kaʊbɔɪ/ *n* (in Western US) vaquero *m*; (in Wild West) vaquero *m*, cowboy *m*

cower /'kaʊər ‖ 'kaʊə(r)/ *vi* encogerse* (de miedo)

coworker /'kəʊ'wɜːrkər ‖ kəʊ'wɜːkə(r)/ *n* (esp AmE) (workmate) colega *mf*, compañero, -ra *m,f* de trabajo; (collaborator) colaborador, -dora *m,f*

coy /kɔɪ/ *adj* **coyer, coyest** (shy) tímido; (evasive) evasivo

coyote /kaɪ'əʊti ‖ kɔɪ'əʊti/ *n* (*pl* **-otes** *or* **-ote**) coyote *m*

cozy¹, (BrE) **cosy** /'kəʊzi/ *adj* **cozier, coziest** **(a)** ‹*room*› acogedor **(b)** ‹*chat*› íntimo y agradable

cozy², (BrE) **cosy** *n* (*pl* **-ies**) (*tea* ~) cubreteteras *m*

CPA *n* (in US) = **Certified Public Accountant**

crab /kræb/ *n* [C U] (animal, meat) cangrejo *m*, jaiba *f* (AmL)

crack¹ /kræk/ *n* **1** [C] **(a)** (in ice, wall, pavement) grieta *f*; (in glass, china) rajadura *f* **(b)** (chink, slit) rendija *f* **2** [C] (sound — of whip, twig) chasquido *m*; (— of rifle shot) estallido *m*; (— of thunder) estruendo *m* **3** [C] (blow) golpe *m* **4** (instant): **at the ~ of dawn** al amanecer **5** [C] (attempt) (colloq) intento *m*; **to have a ~ at sth** intentar algo **6** [C] (colloq) (wisecrack) comentario *m* socarrón **7** [U] (drug) crack *m*

crack² *adj* (*before n*) ‹*shot/troops*› de primera

crack³ *vt* **1** ‹*cup/glass*› rajar; ‹*ground/earth/skin*› agrietar; **he ~ed a rib** se fracturó una costilla **2 (a)** (break open) ‹*egg/nut*› cascar*; ‹*safe*› forzar*; ‹*drugs ring/spy ring*› desmantelar **(b)** (decipher, solve) ‹*code*› descifrar; ‹*problem*› resolver* **3** (make cracking sound with) ‹*whip*› (hacer*) chasquear; ‹*finger/knuckle*› hacer* crujir **4** (hit sharply) pegar* **5** ‹*joke*› (colloq) contar* ■ ~ *vi* **1 (a)** «*cup/glass*» rajarse; «*rock/paint/skin*» agrietarse **(b)** (make cracking sound) «*whip*» chasquear; «*bones/twigs*» crujir **(c)** «*voice*» quebrarse* **(d)** (break down): **she ~ed under the strain** sufrió una crisis nerviosa a causa de la tensión **2** (be active, busy): **to get ~ing** (colloq) poner(se)* manos a la obra

• **crack down** [*v* + *adv*] **to ~ down ON sb/sth** tomar medidas enérgicas CONTRA algn/algo

• **crack up** [*v* + *adv*] **(a)** (break down) (colloq) «*person*» sufrir un ataque de nervios, sucumbir a la presión **(b)** (burst out laughing) (colloq) soltar* una carcajada

cracked /krækt/ *adj* **(a)** ‹*cup/glass*› rajado; ‹*rib*› fracturado; ‹*wall/ceiling*› con grietas; ‹*lips*› partido; ‹*skin*› agrietado **(b)** (crazy) (colloq) ‹*person*› loco, chiflado (fam) **(c)** ‹*voice*› cascado

cracker /'krækər ‖ 'krækə(r)/ *n* **1** (biscuit) cracker *f*, galleta *f* (*salada*) **2 (a)** (*fire*~) petardo *m* **(b)** (BrE) sorpresa *f* (*que estalla al abrirla*)

crackle¹ /'krækəl/ *vi* «*fire*» crepitar; «*twigs/paper*» crujir

crackle² *n* [U] (of twigs, paper) crujido *m*; (of fire) chisporroteo *m*

cradle¹ /'kreɪdl̩/ *n* cuna *f*

cradle² *vt* ‹*baby*› acunar, mecer*

craft /kræft ‖ krɑːft/ *n* **1 (a)** [U C] (trade) oficio *m*; (skill) arte *m* **(b) crafts** *pl* artesanía *f*; *see also* ART 1(b) **2** [U] (guile, deceit) (liter) artimañas *fpl* **3** [C] (*pl* ~) (Naut) embarcación *f*; (Aerosp, Aviat) nave *f*

craftsman /'kræftsmən ‖ 'krɑːftsmən/ *n* (*pl* **-men** /mən/) artesano *m*, artífice *m*

crafty /'kræfti ‖ 'krɑːfti/ *adj* **-tier, -tiest** ‹*person*› astuto; ‹*methods/tactics*› hábil

craggy /'krægi/ *adj* **-gier, -giest** escarpado; **he had a ~, weather-beaten face** tenía un rostro curtido y de facciones bien marcadas

cram /kræm/ **-mm-** *vt* (stuff) meter; **the room was ~med with books** la habitación estaba abarrotada de libros; **I ~med three meetings into one morning** logré asistir a tres reuniones en una mañana ■ ~ *vi* (for exam) empollar (Esp fam), zambutir (Méx), tragar* (RPl fam), matearse (Chi fam), empacarse* (Col fam)

cramp¹ /kræmp/ *n* [U C] (in leg) calambre *m*, rampa *f* (Esp); **stomach ~s** retorcijones *mpl* *or* (Esp) retortijones *mpl* en el estómago

cramp² *vt* (limit) ‹*work/progress*› entorpecer*; ***to ~ sb's style*** cortarle los vuelos a algn

cramped /kræmpt/ *adj* ‹*handwriting*› apretado; **they work in ~ conditions** están muy estrechos en el trabajo; **they live in ~ conditions** viven hacinados

cranberry /'kræn,beri ‖ 'krænbəri/ *n* (*pl* **-ries**) arándano *m* (*rojo y agrio*)

crane¹ /kreɪn/ *n* **1** (for lifting) grúa *f* **2** (Zool) grulla *f*

crane² *vt*: **to ~ one's neck** estirar el cuello

crank /kræŋk/ *n* **1 (a)** (Mech Eng) cigüeñal *m* **(b)** ~ **(handle)** (Auto) manivela *f* (de arranque) **2** (colloq) **(a)** (eccentric) maniático, -ca *m,f* **(b)** (bad-tempered person) (AmE) cascarrabias *mf*

cranny /'kræni/ *n* (*pl* **-nies**) ranura *f*; ⇨ NOOK

crap /kræp/ *n* [U] **(a)** (excrement) (vulg) mierda *f* (vulg) **(b)** (nonsense) (sl) estupideces *fpl*, gilipolleces *fpl* (Esp fam *o* vulg), pendejadas *fpl* (AmL exc CS fam), huevadas *fpl* (Andes, Ven vulg), boludeces *fpl* (Col, RPl vulg)

crash¹ /kræʃ/ *n* **(a)** (loud noise) estrépito *m* **(b)** (collision, accident) accidente *m*, choque *m* **(c)** (financial failure) crac *m*, crack *m*

crash² *vt* **1** (smash): **he ~ed the car** tuvo un accidente con el coche, chocó **2** (colloq) **to ~ a party** colarse* en una fiesta (fam) ■ ~ *vi* **(a)** (collide) **to ~ (INTO sth)** estrellarse *or* chocar* (CONTRA algo) **(b)** (make loud noise) «*thunder*» retumbar; **the dishes ~ed to the floor** los platos se cayeron al suelo estrepitosamente **(c)** (Fin) «*shares*» caer* a pique

crash³ *adj* (*before n*) ‹*program/course*› intensivo; **~ diet** régimen *m* muy estricto

crash: **~ barrier** *n* barrera *f* de protección; **~ helmet** *n* casco *m* (protector); **~-landing** /'kræʃ'lændɪŋ/ *n* aterrizaje *m* forzoso

crate /kreɪt/ *n* cajón *m* (de embalaje), jaba *f* (Chi)

crater /'kreɪtər ‖ 'kreɪtə(r)/ *n* cráter *m*

cravat /krə'væt/ *n* pañuelo *m* de cuello (de caballero)

crave /kreɪv/ *vt* ‹*admiration*› ansiar*; ‹*affection*› tener* ansias de; ‹*food/drink*› morirse* por (fam)

craving /'kreɪvɪŋ/ *n* [U C] **(a)** (strong desire) ansias *fpl* **(b)** (in pregnancy) antojo *m*

crawfish /ˈkrɔːfɪʃ/ *n* (*pl* **-fish** *or* **-fishes**) ⇒ CRAYFISH

crawl¹ /krɔːl/ *vi* **1** **(a)** (creep) arrastrarse; «*baby*» gatear, ir* a gatas; «*insect*» andar* **(b)** (go slowly) «*traffic/train*» avanzar* muy lentamente **2** (teem): **the beach was ~ing with tourists** la playa estaba plagada de turistas **3** (demean oneself) (colloq) arrastrarse

crawl² *n* **1** (slow pace) (*no pl*): **to go at a ~** avanzar* muy lentamente **2** (swimming stroke) crol *m*

crayfish /ˈkreɪfɪʃ/ *n* (*pl* **-fish** *or* **-fishes**) (freshwater) ástaco *m*, cangrejo *m* de río; (marine) langosta *f* (*pequeña*), cigala *f*

crayon /ˈkreɪɑːn ‖ ˈkreɪən/ *n* (pencil) lápiz *m* de color; (*wax* ~) crayola® *f*, crayón *m* (Méx, RPl), lápiz *m* de cera (Chi)

craze /kreɪz/ *n* (fashion) moda *f*; (fad) manía *f*

crazy /ˈkreɪzi/ *adj* **-zier, -ziest** loco; **to go ~** volverse* loco; **to be ~** ABOUT *o* (AmE) FOR *o* (AmE) OVER **sb** estar* loco POR algn (fam)

creak /kriːk/ *vi* «*door*» chirriar*; «*bedsprings/floorboards/joints*» crujir

cream¹ /kriːm/ *n* **1** (Culin) crema *f* (de leche) (esp AmL), nata *f* (Esp) **2** [C U] (lotion) crema *f* **3** [U] (elite) **the ~ of society** la flor y nata de la sociedad **4** ▶515 [U] (color) color *m* crema

cream² ▶515 *adj* color crema *adj inv*

cream³ *vt* ‹*butter/sugar*› batir (*hasta obtener una consistencia cremosa*); **~ed potatoes** puré *m* de papas *or* (Esp) patatas

cream cheese *n* [U] queso *m* crema (AmL), queso *m* para untar (Esp)

creamer /ˈkriːmər ‖ ˈkriːmə(r)/ *n* **1** [C] (jug) (AmE) jarrita *f* para crema **2** [U] (powder) leche *f* en polvo

creamy /ˈkriːmi/ *adj* **-mier, -miest** (containing cream) con crema; (smooth) cremoso

crease¹ /kriːs/ *n* (in paper, clothes) arruga *f*; (in trousers) raya *f*, pliegue *m* (Méx, Ven)

crease² *vi* arrugarse* ■ ~ *vt* ‹*clothes*› arrugar*; ‹*paper*› doblar, plegar*

create /kriˈeɪt/ *vt* crear; ‹*impression*› producir*

creation /kriˈeɪʃən/ *n* [U C] creación *f*

creative /kriˈeɪtɪv/ *adj* creativo

creativity /ˈkrieɪˈtɪvəti/ *n* [U] creatividad *f*

creator /kriˈeɪtər ‖ kriˈeɪtə(r)/ *n* creador, -dora *m,f*

creature /ˈkriːtʃər ‖ ˈkriːtʃə(r)/ *n* **(a)** (animate being) criatura *f*; **sea ~** animal *m* marino **(b)** (person) ser *m*, criatura *f*

creche, crèche /kreʃ/ *n* **(a)** (hospital for foundlings) (AmE) orfanato *m*, orfelinato *m*, orfanatorio *m* **(b)** (day nursery) (BrE) guardería *f* (infantil) (*puede ser en el lugar de trabajo para los empleados etc*)

credentials /krɪˈdentʃəlz ‖ krɪˈdenʃəlz/ *pl n* (of ambassador) cartas *fpl* credenciales; (references) referencias *fpl*; (identifying papers) documentos *mpl* (de identidad)

credibility /ˈkredəˈbɪləti/ *n* [U] credibilidad *f*

credible /ˈkredəbəl/ *adj* creíble

credit¹ /ˈkredət ‖ ˈkredɪt/ *n* **1** (Fin) **(a)** [U] (in store) crédito *m*; **on ~** a crédito **(b)** [U] (in banking): **to keep one's account in ~** mantener* un saldo positivo; (*before n*) **~ balance** saldo *m* positivo; **~ limit** límite *m* de crédito **(c)** [C] (on balance sheet) saldo *m* acreedor *or* a favor **2** [U] (honor, recognition) mérito *m*; **Jim must take the ~ for the excellent organization** la excelente organización es obra de Jim; **your children are a ~ to you** puedes estar orgulloso de tus hijos **3** [C] (Educ) **(a)** (for study) crédito *m* (*unidad de valor de una asignatura dentro de un programa de estudios*) **(b)** (grade) ≈ notable *m* **4 credits** *pl* (Cin, TV, Video) créditos *mpl*

credit² *vt* **1 to ~ money to an account** abonar *or* ingresar dinero en una cuenta **2** **(a)** (ascribe to) **please, ~ me with *some* intelligence** reconóceme algo de inteligencia, por favor; **they are ~ed with having invented the game** se les atribuye la invención del juego **(b)** (believe) creer*

credit card *n* tarjeta *f* de crédito

creditor /ˈkredətər ‖ ˈkredɪtə(r)/ *n* acreedor, -dora *m,f*

creed /kriːd/ *n* credo *m*

creek /kriːk/ *n* **(a)** (stream) (AmE) arroyo *m*, riachuelo *m* **(b)** (inlet) (BrE) cala *f*

creep¹ /kriːp/ (*past & past p* **crept**) *vi* (+ *adv compl*) **(a)** (crawl) arrastrarse **(b)** (move stealthily): **to ~ into a room** entrar en un cuarto sigilosamente; **a note of suspicion crept into his voice** se empezó a notar un elemento de sospecha en su voz

creep² *n* (colloq) **(a)** (unpleasant person) asqueroso, -sa *m,f* **(b)** (favor-seeking person) adulador, -dora *m,f*, pelota *mf* (Esp fam), chupamedias *mf* (CS, Ven fam), lambiscón, -cona *m,f* (Méx fam), lambón, -bona *m,f* (Col fam)

creeper /ˈkriːpər ‖ ˈkriːpə(r)/ *n* planta *f* trepadora

cremate /ˈkriːmeɪt ‖ krɪˈmeɪt/ *vt* incinerar, cremar

cremation /krɪˈmeɪʃən/ *n* [C U] incineración *f*, cremación *f*

crematorium /ˈkriːməˈtɔːriəm ‖ ˌkreməˈtɔːriəm/ *n* (*pl* **-riums** *or* **-ria** /-riə/) crematorio *m*

crepe, crêpe /kreɪp/ *n* **1** [U] (fabric) crep *m*, crepé *m* **2** [C] (pancake) (Culin) crep *m*, crêpe *f*, panqueque *m* (AmC, CS), crepa *f* (Méx)

crepe paper *n* [U] papel *m* crepé *or* crep

crept /krept/ *past & past p of* CREEP¹

crescendo /krəˈʃendəʊ ‖ krɪˈʃendəʊ/ *n* (*pl* **-dos**) (Mus) crescendo *m*; (climax) punto *m* culminante

crescent /ˈkresn̩t/ *n* **1** (moon) creciente *m* **2** **(a)** (shape) media luna *f* **(b)** (street) *calle en forma de media luna*

cress /kres/ *n* [U] mastuerzo *m*

crest /krest/ *n* **1** (Zool) (of skin) cresta *f*; (of feathers) penacho *m* **2** (in heraldry) emblema *m*, divisa *f* **3** (of wave) cresta *f*; (of mountain) cima *f*

crestfallen /ˈkrestˌfɔːlən/ *adj* alicaído

crevice /ˈkrevəs ‖ ˈkrevɪs/ *n* grieta *f*

crew /kruː/ *n* **(a)** (Aviat, Naut) tripulación *f* **(b)** (team) equipo *m*; **film ~** (Cin) equipo *m* de rodaje **(c)** (gang, band) banda *f*, pandilla *f*

crew: **~ cut** *n* pelo *m* cortado al rape; **~ neck** *n* cuello *m* redondo

crib /krɪb/ *n* **1 (a)** (child's bed) (AmE) cuna *f* **(b)** (Nativity scene) nacimiento *m*, pesebre *m*, belén *m* (Esp) **2** (Agr) **(a)** (manger) pesebre *m* **(b)** (for storing grain) (AmE) granero *m*

crick /krɪk/ *vt*: **to ~ one's neck** hacer* un mal movimiento con el cuello

cricket /ˈkrɪkət ‖ ˈkrɪkɪt/ *n* **1** [C] (Zool) grillo *m* **2** [U] (Sport) críquet *m*

cricketer /ˈkrɪkətər ‖ ˈkrɪkɪtə(r)/ *n* jugador, -dora *m,f* de críquet

crime /kraɪm/ *n* **(a)** [C] (wrongful act) delito *m*; (murder) crimen *m* **(b)** [U] (criminal activity) delincuencia *f*; **~ wave** ola *f* delictiva

criminal¹ /ˈkrɪmənḷ ‖ ˈkrɪmɪnḷ/ *n* delincuente *mf*; (serious offender) criminal *mf*

criminal² *adj* ‹*act*› delictivo; ‹*organization/mind*› criminal; **~ court** juzgado *m* en lo penal; **~ law** derecho *m* penal; **~ offense** delito *m*

criminal record *n* antecedentes *mpl* penales, prontuario *m* (CS)

crimson¹ /ˈkrɪmzən/ ▶**515** *n* [U] carmesí *m*

crimson² ▶**515** *adj* carmesí *adj inv*

cringe /krɪndʒ/ *vi* **(a)** (shrink, cower) encogerse* **(b)** (grovel) arrastrarse

crinkle /ˈkrɪŋkəl/ **~ (up)** *vt* arrugar* ■ **~** *vi* arrugarse*

cripple¹ /ˈkrɪpəl/ *n* lisiado, -da *m,f*

cripple² *vt* **(a)** (lame, disable): **he was ~d for life** quedó lisiado de por vida; **he's ~d with arthritis** la artritis lo tiene casi inmovilizado **(b)** (make inactive, ineffective) ‹*ship/plane*› inutilizar*; ‹*industry*› paralizar*

crippling /ˈkrɪplɪŋ/ *adj* ‹*costs/debts*› agobiante; ‹*losses/strike*› de consecuencias catastróficas; ‹*pain*› atroz

crisis /ˈkraɪsəs ‖ ˈkraɪsɪs/ *n* (*pl* **-ses** /-siːz/) crisis *f*; (*before n*) **to reach ~ point** hacer* crisis

crisp¹ /krɪsp/ *adj* **-er, -est 1 (a)** (crunchy) ‹*toast/bacon*› crujiente, crocante (RPl); ‹*lettuce*› fresco; ‹*apple/snow*› crujiente **(b)** ‹*sheets*› limpio y almidonado **(c)** (cold) ‹*air*› frío y vigorizante **2** (brisk, concise) ‹*manner*› seco; ‹*style*› escueto

crisp² *n* (*potato* **~**) (BrE) papa *f or* (Esp) patata *f* frita (*de bolsa*), papa *f* chip (Ur)

crisscross¹ /ˈkrɪskrɔːs ‖ ˈkrɪskrɒs/ *adj* entrecruzado

crisscross² *vt* entrecruzar*

criterion /kraɪˈtɪriən ‖ kraɪˈtɪəriən/ *n* (*pl* **-ria** /-riə/) criterio *m*

critic /ˈkrɪtɪk/ *n* (Art, Theat, Lit) crítico, -ca *m,f*; (detractor) detractor, -tora *m,f*

critical /ˈkrɪtɪkəl/ *adj* **1** ‹*remark/report*› crítico **2 (a)** (very serious) ‹*condition/shortage*› crítico **(b)** (crucial) ‹*period*› crítico

critically /ˈkrɪtɪkli/ *adv* **1** ‹*ill*› gravemente **2 (a)** (as a critic): **she looked ~ at her reflection** miró con ojo crítico la imagen que le devolvía el espejo **(b)** (censoriously): **she spoke rather ~ of him** habló de él en tono de crítica

criticism /ˈkrɪtəsɪzəm ‖ ˈkrɪtɪsɪzəm/ *n* [C U] crítica *f*

criticize /ˈkrɪtəsaɪz ‖ ˈkrɪtɪsaɪz/ *vt* criticar*

croak¹ /krəʊk/ *n* (of frog) croar *m*; (of raven) graznido *m*; (of person) voz *f* ronca

croak² *vi* «*frog*» croar; «*raven*» graznar; «*person*» hablar con voz ronca ■ **~** *vt* decir* con voz ronca

Croat /ˈkrəʊæt/ *n* croata *mf*

Croatia /krəʊˈeɪʃə/ *n* Croacia *f*

Croatian /krəʊˈeɪʃən/ *adj* croata

crochet¹ /krəʊˈʃeɪ ‖ ˈkrəʊʃeɪ/ *vt* tejer a crochet *or* a ganchillo; (*before n*) **~ hook** aguja *f* de crochet, ganchillo *m*, crochet *m* (Chi)

crochet² *n* [U] crochet *m*, ganchillo *m*

crockery /ˈkrɑːkəri ‖ ˈkrɒkəri/ *n* [U] vajilla *f*, loza *f*

crocodile /ˈkrɑːkədaɪl ‖ ˈkrɒkədaɪl/ *n* cocodrilo *m*

crocus /ˈkrəʊkəs/ *n* (*pl* **-cuses**) azafrán *m* de primavera

crook /krʊk/ *n* sinvergüenza *mf*

crooked /ˈkrʊkəd ‖ ˈkrʊkɪd/ *adj* **(a)** ‹*line/legs*› torcido, chueco (AmL); ‹*back*› encorvado; ‹*path*› sinuoso **(b)** (dishonest) (colloq) ‹*person/deal*› deshonesto, chueco (Chi, Méx fam)

crop¹ /krɑːp ‖ krɒp/ *n* **1 (a)** (quantity of produce) cosecha *f* **(b)** (type of produce) cultivo *m* **2** (haircut) corte *m* de pelo muy corto **3** (*riding* **~**) fusta *f*, fuete *m* (AmL exc CS)

crop² **-pp-** *vt* ‹*hair*› cortar muy corto

• **crop up** [*v* + *adv*] (colloq) surgir*

croquet /krəʊˈkeɪ ‖ ˈkrəʊkeɪ/ *n* [U] croquet *m*

croquette /krəʊˈket/ *n* (*potato* **~**) *rollito de puré de papa envuelto en pan rallado y frito*

cross¹ /krɔːs ‖ krɒs/ *n* **1 (a)** (Relig) cruz *f* **(b)** (mark, sign) cruz *f* **2** (hybrid) cruce *m*, cruza *f* (AmL) **3** (Sport) **(a)** (in soccer) pase *m* cruzado **(b)** (in boxing) cruzado *m*, cross *m*

cross² *vt* **1** (go across) ‹*road/river/desert*› cruzar*; **it ~ed my mind that** ... se me ocurrió que ... **2** ‹*arms/legs*› cruzar* **3** ‹*plants/breeds*› cruzar* **4** (go against) ‹*person*› contrariar*; ‹*plans*› frustrar ■ **~** *vi* **(a)** (walk across road) cruzar* **(b)** «*paths/letters*» cruzarse* ■ *v refl* **to ~ oneself** persignarse, santiguarse*

• **cross out** [*v* + *o* + *adv*, *v* + *adv* + *o*] tachar

cross³ *adj* **-er, -est** (esp BrE) enojado (esp AmL), enfadado (esp Esp); **to get ~** enojarse (esp AmL), enfadarse (esp Esp)

cross: **~bar** *n* (on bicycle) barra *f*; (of goal) larguero *m*; **~bow** /ˈkrɔːsbəʊ ‖ ˈkrɒsbəʊ/ *n* ballesta *f*; **~breed** *vt* (*past & past p* **-bred**) cruzar*; **~-Channel** /ˈkrɔːsˈtʃænḷ ‖ ˌkrɒsˈtʃænl/ *adj* (*before n*) ‹*ferry/traffic*› que cruza el Canal de la Mancha; **~-check** /ˈkrɔːsˈtʃek ‖ ˌkrɒsˈtʃek/ *vt* ‹*facts/references*› verificar* (*consultando otras fuentes*); **to ~-check sth AGAINST sth** cotejar algo CON algo; **~-country** /ˈkrɔːsˈkʌntri ‖ krɒsˈkʌntri/ *adj* ‹*route/drive*› campo a través; **~-examination** /ˈkrɔːs ɪɡˌzæməˈneɪʃən ‖ ˌkrɒsɪɡˌzæmɪˈneɪʃən/ *n* [C U] repreguntas *fpl*, contrainterrogación *f* (Chi); **~-examine** /ˈkrɔːsɪɡˈzæmən ‖ ˈkrɒsɪɡˈzæmɪn/ *vt* ‹*witness*› repreguntar; **~-eyed** /ˈkrɔːsˈaɪd ‖ ˈkrɒs aɪd/ *adj* bizco; **~fire** *n* [U] fuego *m* cruzado

crossing /'krɔ:sɪŋ ‖ 'krɒsɪŋ/ *n* **1** (across sea) travesía *f*, cruce *m* (AmS) **2** (for pedestrians) cruce *m* peatonal *or* de peatones

cross: **~-legged** /'krɔ:s'legd‖,krɒs'legd/ *adv* con las piernas cruzadas (*en el suelo*); **~-purposes** /'krɔ:s'pɜ:rpəsəz ‖ ,krɒs'pɜ:pəsɪz/ *pl n*: **we're (talking) at ~-purposes** estamos hablando de cosas distintas; **~-question** /'krɔ:s'kwestʃən ‖ ,krɒs'kwestʃən/ *vt* interrogar*; **~-reference** /'krɔ:s'refrəns ‖ ,krɒs'refrəns/ *n* remisión *f*; **~roads** *n* (*pl* **~roads**) cruce *m*, encrucijada *f* (liter); **~ section**, (BrE) **~-section** /'krɔ:s'sekʃən ‖ ,krɒs'sekʃən/ *n* [C U] (Biol, Eng) sección *f*, corte *m* transversal; **~walk** *n* (AmE) cruce *m* peatonal *or* de peatones; **~word (puzzle)** *n* crucigrama *f*, palabras *fpl* cruzadas (CS)

crotch /krɑ:tʃ ‖ krɒtʃ/ *n* entrepierna *f*

crotchet /'krɑ:tʃət ‖ 'krɒtʃɪt/ *n* (BrE Mus) negra *f*

crouch /kraʊtʃ/ *vi* agacharse, ponerse* en cuclillas

croupier /'kru:piər ‖ 'kru:piə(r)/ *n* crupier *mf*, croupier *mf*

crow¹ /krəʊ/ *n* cuervo *m*; ***as the ~ flies*** en línea recta

crow² *vi* **(a)** «*cock*» cacarear **(b)** (exult) alardear

crowbar /'krəʊbɑ:r ‖ 'krəʊbɑ:(r)/ *n* palanca *f*

crowd¹ /kraʊd/ *n* **(a)** (gathering of people) muchedumbre *f*, multitud *f*; **the game attracted a good ~** el partido atrajo mucho público **(b)** (masses, average folk) (pej); ***to stand out from the ~*** destacar(se)* **(c)** (group, set) (colloq): **they are a nice ~** son gente simpática

crowd² *vi* aglomerarse ■ **~** *vt* ‹*hall/entrance*› llenar, abarrotar

crowded /'kraʊdəd ‖ 'kraʊdɪd/ *adj* ‹*street/room/bus*› abarrotado, atestado; **the beach gets very ~** la playa se llena de gente

crown¹ /kraʊn/ *n* **1** (of monarch) corona *f* **2** (top — of hill) cima *f*; (— of tree) copa *f*; (— of tooth) corona *f*; (— of head) coronilla *f*; (— of hat) copa *f* **3** (Fin) corona *f*

crown² *vt* **1** (make monarch) coronar **2** (be culmination of) coronar; **to ~ it all, I lost my wallet** y para rematarla, perdí la billetera

crown court *n* (in UK) juzgado *m* (*que conoce de causas de derecho penal*)

crowning /'kraʊnɪŋ/ *adj* (*before n*) ‹*success/achievement*› supremo, mayor

crown: **~ jewels** *pl n* joyas *fpl* de la corona; **~ prince** *n* príncipe *m* heredero

crow's feet *pl n* patas *fpl* de gallo

crucial /'kru:ʃəl/ *adj* crucial, decisivo

crucifixion /'kru:sə'fɪkʃən ‖ ,kru:sɪ'fɪkʃən/ *n* [U C] crucifixión *f*

crucify /'kru:səfaɪ ‖ 'kru:sɪfaɪ/ *vt* (*past & past p* **-fied**) crucificar*

crude /kru:d/ *adj* **-der, -dest (a)** (vulgar) ordinario, grosero **(b)** (unsophisticated) rudimentario, burdo **(c)** (containing impurities) (*before n*) ‹*oil*› crudo

cruel /'kru:əl/ *adj* **crueller, cruellest** cruel

cruelty /'kru:əlti/ *n* [U C] (*pl* **-ties**) crueldad *f*

cruet /'kru:ət ‖ 'kru:ɪt/ *n* (Culin) vinagrera *f*, aceitera *f*, alcuza *f* (Chi)

cruise¹ /kru:z/ *vi* **1 (a)** (Naut) hacer* un crucero **(b)** «*police car*» patrullar **2** (travel at steady speed) «*plane*» volar*; «*car*» ir* (*a una velocidad constante*)

cruise² *n* crucero *m*

cruiser /'kru:zər ‖ 'kru:zə(r)/ *n* (warship) crucero *m*; (*cabin* **~**) lancha *f*

crumb /krʌm/ *n* [C] miga *f*

crumble /'krʌmbəl/ *vi* «*cake/soil*» desmenuzarse*; «*wall*» desmoronarse; «*democracy/resolve*» desmoronarse ■ **~** *vt* ‹*earth/cake*› desmenuzar*; ‹*bread*› desmigajar

crummy /'krʌmi/ *adj* **-mier, -miest** (colloq) malo, horrible

crumpet /'krʌmpət ‖ 'krʌmpɪt/ *n* (Culin) *panecillo de levadura que se come tostado*

crumple /'krʌmpəl/ *vt* ‹*paper/clothes*› arrugar*; ‹*metal*› abollar; **she ~d the sheet of paper into a ball** hizo una bola estrujando la hoja de papel

crunch¹ /krʌntʃ/ *vt* **(a)** (eat noisily) mascar*, ronchar **(b)** (crush) aplastar (*haciendo crujir*)

crunch² *n* **1** (noise) crujido *m* **2** (crisis): **when it comes to the ~** a la hora de la verdad

crunchy /'krʌntʃi/ *adj* **-chier, -chiest** crujiente

crusade /kru:'seɪd/ *n* **(a)** (Hist) *also* **Crusade** cruzada *f* **(b)** (campaign) cruzada *f*

crush¹ /krʌʃ/ *vt* **1** (squash) ‹*box/car/person/fingers*› aplastar; ‹*grapes*› prensar; ‹*dress/suit*› arrugar* **2** (subdue) ‹*resistance/enemy*› aplastar

crush² *n* **1** (crowd) (*no pl*) aglomeración *f* **2** [C] (infatuation) (colloq) enamoramiento *m*; **to have a ~ on sb** estar* chiflado por algn (fam)

crush barrier *n* valla *f* de protección

crushing /'krʌʃɪŋ/ *adj* ‹*defeat*› aplastante; ‹*reply/contempt*› apabullante

crust /krʌst/ *n* **(a)** (on bread) corteza *f* **(b)** (thin outer layer) costra *f*, corteza *f*; **the earth's ~** la corteza terrestre

crustacean /krʌ'steɪʃən/ *n* crustáceo *m*

crusty /'krʌsti/ *adj* **-tier, -tiest (a)** (crispy) ‹*bread*› crujiente **(b)** (irascible) malhumorado

crutch /krʌtʃ/ *n* **1** (walking aid) muleta *f* **2** (BrE) ⇒ CROTCH

crux /krʌks/ *n* (*no pl*) **the ~ (of the matter)** el quid (de la cuestión)

cry¹ /kraɪ/ *n* (*pl* **cries**) **1** [C] **(a)** (exclamation) grito *m*; ***to be a far ~ from sth*** ser* muy distinto de *or* a algo **(b)** (of street vendor) pregón *m* **(c)** (*no pl*) (call of seagull) chillido *m* **2** (weep) (colloq) (*no pl*) llanto *m*; **to have a ~** llorar

cry² **cries, crying, cried** *vi* **1** (weep) llorar **2** (call) «*bird*» chillar; «*person*» gritar

• **cry out** [*v* + *adv*] **(a)** (call out) gritar **(b)** (need) **to ~ out FOR sth** pedir* algo a gritos

crypt /krɪpt/ *n* cripta *f*

cryptic /'krɪptɪk/ *adj* enigmático

crystal /'krɪstl/ *n* **(a)** [C] (Chem) cristal *m* **(b)** [U] **~ (glass)** cristal *m*

crystal: **~ ball** *n* bola *f* de cristal; **~-clear** /'krɪstl'klɪr ‖ ,krɪstl'klɪə(r)/ *adj* ‹*water*› (liter) cristalino; ‹*sound/image*› nítido, claro

crystallize /ˈkrɪstəlaɪz/ *vt* **(a)** (Chem, Geol) cristalizar*; ‹*idea/plan*› materializar* **(b)** (Culin) ‹*fruit*› confitar, escarchar, abrillantar (RPl), cristalizar* (Méx)

CS gas /ˈsiːˈes/ *n* [U] gas *m* lacrimógeno

CST (in US) = **Central Standard Time**

CT = **Connecticut**

cub /kʌb/ *n* **(a)** (young animal) cachorro *m* **(b)** **Cub (Scout)** lobato *m*

Cuba /ˈkjuːbə/ *n* Cuba *f*

Cuban /ˈkjuːbən/ *adj* cubano

cubbyhole /ˈkʌbihəʊl/ *n* cuchitril *m*

cube¹ /kjuːb/ *n* (solid, shape) cubo *m*; (of meat, cheese) dado *m*, cubito *m*; (of sugar) terrón *m*

cube² *vt* (Math) elevar al cubo, cubicar*

cubic /ˈkjuːbɪk/ *adj* (of measure, shape) cúbico; **~ capacity** volumen *m*; (of engine) cilindrada *f*, cubicaje *m*

cubicle /ˈkjuːbɪkəl/ *n* (in dormitory, toilets) cubículo *m*; (booth) cabina *f*; (in store) probador *m*

cuckoo /ˈkuːkuː ‖ ˈkʊkuː/ *n* (*pl* **cuckoos**) cuco *m*, cucú *m*, cuclillo *m*

cuckoo clock *n* reloj *m* de cuco *or* cucú

cucumber /ˈkjuːkʌmbər ‖ ˈkjuːkʌmbə(r)/ *n* [C U] pepino *m*

cud /kʌd/ *n* [U]: ***to chew the ~*** (lit) «*cow*» rumiar; «*person*» rumiar el asunto

cuddle¹ /ˈkʌdl̩/ *vt* abrazar*

cuddle² *n* abrazo *m*

cuddly /ˈkʌdli/ *adj* **-dlier, -dliest** adorable; **~ toy** muñeco *m* de peluche

cudgel /ˈkʌdʒəl/ *n* garrote *m*, porra *f*

cue /kjuː/ *n* **1** (Mus) entrada *f*; (Theat) pie *m*; **right on ~** en el momento justo **2** (in snooker) taco *m*

cuff¹ /kʌf/ *n* **1** **(a)** (of sleeve) puño *m*; (of pants) (AmE) vuelta *f or* (Chi) bastilla *f or* (Méx) valenciana *f or* (RPl) botamanga *f* **(b)** (*in phrases*) **off the cuff** (*as adv*): **he spoke off the ~** habló improvisando; (*as adj*): **an off-the-~ speech** un discurso improvisado **2** (blow — on side of head) cachete *m*, bofetón *m*, cachetada *f* (AmL); (— on head) coscorrón *m*

cuff² *vt* darle* un cachete (*or* coscorrón *etc*) a

cuff link *n* gemelo *m or* (Col) mancorna *f or* (Chi) collera *f or* (Méx) mancuernilla *or* mancuerna *f*

cuisine /kwɪˈziːn/ *n* [U C] cocina *f*

cul-de-sac /ˈkʌldɪsæk/ *n* calle *f* sin salida *or* (Col) ciega *or* (RPl) cortada

cull /kʌl/ *vt sacrificar de forma selectiva*

culminate /ˈkʌlməneɪt ‖ ˈkʌlmɪneɪt/ *vi* (reach peak) **to ~ IN sth** culminar EN algo

culprit /ˈkʌlprət ‖ ˈkʌlprɪt/ *n* culpable *mf*

cult /kʌlt/ *n* (belief, worship) culto *m*; (sect) secta *f*; (*before n*) **~ figure** ídolo *m*

cultivate /ˈkʌltəveɪt ‖ ˈkʌltɪveɪt/ *vt* cultivar

cultural /ˈkʌltʃərəl/ *adj* cultural

culture¹ /ˈkʌltʃər ‖ ˈkʌltʃə(r)/ *n* **1** [C U] (civilization) cultura *f*; (*before n*) **~ shock** choque *m* cultural *or* de culturas **2** [C U] (Agr, Biol) cultivo *m*

culture² *vt* cultivar

cultured /ˈkʌltʃərd ‖ ˈkʌltʃəd/ *adj* ‹*person/mind*› culto; ‹*tastes*› refinado

cumbersome /ˈkʌmbərsəm ‖ ˈkʌmbəsəm/ *adj* ‹*movements/gait*› pesado y torpe

cumin /ˈkʌmən ‖ ˈkʌmɪn/ *n* [U] comino *m*

cumulative /ˈkjuːmjələtɪv ‖ ˈkjuːmjʊlətɪv/ *adj* acumulativo

cunning /ˈkʌnɪŋ/ *adj* **(a)** (clever, sly) astuto; ‹*smile*› malicioso **(b)** (ingenious) ‹*device*› ingenioso

cup¹ /kʌp/ *n* **1** [C] **(a)** (container, contents, cupful) taza *f*; **paper ~** vaso *m* de papel **(b)** (goblet) copa *f* **2** [C] (trophy) copa *f*

cup² *vt* **-pp-**: **to ~ one's hands** (to drink) ahuecar* las manos; (to shout) hacer* bocina (con las manos)

cupboard /ˈkʌbərd ‖ ˈkʌbəd/ *n* **(a)** (cabinet) armario *m*; (in dining-room) aparador *m* **(b)** (full-length, built-in) (BrE) armario *m or* (AmL exc RPl) clóset *m or* (RPl) placard *m*

curable /ˈkjʊrəbəl ‖ ˈkjʊərəbəl/ *adj* curable

curate /ˈkjʊrət ‖ ˈkjʊərət/ *n* coadjutor *m*

curator /kjʊˈreɪtər ‖ kjʊəˈreɪtə(r)/ *n* (of museum, art gallery) conservador, -dora *m,f*; (of exhibition) comisario, -ria *m,f*

curb¹ /kɜːrb ‖ kɜːb/ *n* **1** (restraint) freno *m* **2** **curb**, (BrE) **kerb** (in street) bordillo *m* (de la acera), borde *m* de la banqueta (Méx), cuneta *f* (Chi), sardinel *m* (Col), cordón *m* de la vereda (RPl)

curb² *vt* (control) ‹*anger*› dominar, refrenar; ‹*spending/prices*› poner* freno a, frenar

curd /kɜːrd ‖ kɜːd/ *n* (*often pl*) cuajada *f*

curdle /ˈkɜːrdl̩ ‖ ˈkɜːdl̩/ *vi* **(a)** (go bad, separate) «*milk/sauce*» cortarse **(b)** (form curds) «*milk*» cuajarse

cure¹ /kjʊr ‖ ˈkjʊə(r)/ *vt* **1** (Med) curar **2** ‹*meat*› curar

cure² *n* cura *f*

curfew /ˈkɜːrfjuː ‖ ˈkɜːfjuː/ *n* toque *m* de queda

curiosity /ˈkjʊriˈɑːsəti ‖ ˌkjʊəriˈɒsəti/ *n* (*pl* **-ties**) [U C] curiosidad *f*

curious /ˈkjʊriəs ‖ ˈkjʊəriəs/ *adj* **(a)** (inquisitive) curioso **(b)** (strange) curioso, extraño

curiously /ˈkjʊriəsli ‖ ˈkjʊəriəsli/ *adv* (with curiosity) con curiosidad; (strangely) curiosamente; **~ enough, …** (*indep*) curiosamente, …

curl¹ /kɜːrl ‖ kɜːl/ *n* rizo *m*, rulo *m* (CS), chino *m* (Méx); (ringlet) bucle *m*, tirabuzón *m*

curl² *vt* ‹*hair*› rizar*, encrespar (CS), enchinar (Méx), enrular (RPl) ■ **~** *vi* «*hair*» rizarse*, encresparse (CS), enchinarse (Méx), enrularse (RPl); «*paper/leaf/edge*» ondularse

• **curl up** [*v* + *adv*] (twist) «*leaf/pages*» ondularse; «*cat*» hacerse* un ovillo; **to ~ up in a chair** acurrucarse* en un sillón

curler /ˈkɜːrlər ‖ ˈkɜːlə(r)/ *n* (for hair) rulo *m*, rulero *m* (RPl), marrón *m* (Col), tubo *m* (Chi, Méx)

curling irons, **curling tongs** /ˈkɜːrlɪŋ ‖ ˈkɜːlɪŋ/ *pl n* tenacillas *fpl* (*para rizar el pelo*)

curly /ˈkɜːrli ‖ ˈkɜːli/ *adj* **-lier, -liest** ‹*hair*› rizado, crespo (CS), chino (Méx); ‹*tail*› enroscado

currant /ˈkɜːrənt ‖ ˈkʌrənt/ *n* pasa *f* de Corinto

currency /'kɜːrənsi ‖ 'kʌrənsi/ *n* [C U] (*pl* **-cies**) moneda *f*; **foreign ~** moneda *f* extranjera, divisas *fpl*

current¹ /'kɜːrənt ‖ 'kʌrənt/ *adj* **1** (*before n*) **(a)** (existing) ‹*situation/prices*› actual; ‹*year*› en curso **(b)** (most recent) ‹*issue*› último **2 (a)** (valid) ‹*license/membership*› vigente **(b)** (prevailing) ‹*opinion/practice*› corriente

current² *n* [C U] (Elec) corriente *f*

current: **~ account** *n* (BrE) cuenta *f* corriente; **~ affairs** *pl n* sucesos *mpl* de actualidad

currently /'kɜːrəntli ‖ 'kʌrəntli/ *adv* **(a)** (at present) actualmente **(b)** (commonly) comúnmente

curriculum /kə'rɪkjələm ‖ kə'rɪkjʊləm/ *n* (*pl* **-lums** *or* **-la** /-lə/) **(a)** (range of courses) plan *m* de estudios **(b)** (for single course) programa *m* (de estudio), currículo *m*, curriculum *m* (AmL)

curriculum vitae /'viːtaɪ/ *n* (*pl* **curricula vitae**) (BrE) currículum *m* (vitae), historial *m* personal

curry¹ /'kɜːri ‖ 'kʌri/ *n* (*pl* **curries**) [C U] curry *m*

curry² *vt* **-ries, -rying, -ried 1** (Culin) preparar al curry; **curried chicken** pollo *m* al curry **2** ⇒ FAVOR¹ 1(a)

curse¹ /kɜːrs ‖ kɜːs/ *n* **(a)** (evil spell) maldición *f* **(b)** (oath) maldición *f*, palabrota *f*

curse² *vt/i* maldecir*

cursor /'kɜːrsər ‖ 'kɜːsə(r)/ *n* cursor *m*

cursory /'kɜːrsəri ‖ 'kɜːsəri/ *adj* ‹*glance*› rápido; ‹*description*› somero; ‹*interest*› superficial

curt /kɜːrt ‖ kɜːt/ *adj* cortante, seco

curtail /kɜːr'teɪl ‖ kɜː'teɪl/ *vt* (cut short) abreviar; (restrict) restringir*; (reduce) reducir*

curtain /'kɜːrtn̩ ‖ 'kɜːtn̩/ *n* (at window) cortina *f*; (Theat) telón *m*

curtain call *n* salida *f* a escena (*para saludar*), telón *m* (Méx)

curtsey¹ *n* (*pl* **-seys**) (esp BrE) ⇒ CURTSY¹

curtsey² *vi* **-seys, -seying, -seyed** (BrE) ⇒ CURTSY²

curtsy¹ /'kɜːrtsi ‖ 'kɜːtsi/ *n* (*pl* **-sies**) reverencia *f* (*que hacen las mujeres agachándose*)

curtsy² *vi* **-sies, -sying, -sied** hacer* una reverencia

curve¹ /kɜːrv ‖ kɜːv/ *n* curva *f*

curve² *vi* «*surface*» estar* curvado; «*river/ball*» describir* una curva

curved /kɜːrvd ‖ kɜːvd/ *adj* curvo

cushion¹ /'kʊʃən/ *n* almohadón *m*; (*before n*) **~ cover** funda *f* de almohadón

cushion² *vt* ‹*blow*› amortiguar*; (protect) **to ~ sb** AGAINST **sth** proteger* a algn CONTRA algo

cuss /kʌs/ (esp AmE colloq) *vi* **(a)** (complain) despotricar* **(b)** (swear) maldecir*

custard /'kʌstərd ‖ 'kʌstəd/ *n* **(a)** (sauce) (BrE) crema *f*; (cold, set) ≈ natillas *fpl* **(b)** (*egg ~*) *especie de flan*

custodian /kʌ'stəʊdiən/ *n* **(a)** (of morals, tradition) guardián, -diana *m,f*, custodio, -dia *m,f* **(b)** (of museum, library) conservador, -dora *m,f*

custody /'kʌstədi/ *n* [U] **1** (detention): **to be in (police) ~** estar* detenido **2** (of child) custodia *f*

custom /'kʌstəm/ *n* **1** [C U] (convention, tradition, habit) costumbre *f* **2** [U] (patronage) (esp BrE): **I'll take my ~ elsewhere** dejaré de ser su cliente **3 customs** *pl* aduana *f*

customary /'kʌstəməri/ *adj* **(a)** (traditional) tradicional; **it is ~ to** + INF es la costumbre + INF **(b)** (habitual) habitual, acostumbrado

custom-built /'kʌstəm'bɪlt/ *adj* ‹*car*› hecho de encargo; ‹*house*› construido según las especificaciones del cliente

customer /'kʌstəmər ‖ 'kʌstəmə(r)/ *n* cliente, -ta *m,f*; (*before n*) Ⓢ **customer services** información y reclamaciones

customize /'kʌstəmaɪz/ *vt* ‹*car/program*› hacer* (*or* adaptar *etc*) según los requisitos del cliente

custom-made /'kʌstəm'meɪd/ *adj* hecho de encargo; ‹*suit/shoes*› a la medida

cut¹ /kʌt/ *n* **1 (a)** (wound) tajo *m*, corte *m* **(b)** (incision) corte *m* **2 (a)** (reduction): **to make ~s in essential services** hacer* recortes en los servicios esenciales **(b)** (in text, film) corte *m* **(c)** (*power ~*) apagón *m* **3 (a)** (*hair~*) corte *m* de pelo **(b)** (of suit) corte *m* **4** (of meat — type) corte *m*; (— piece) trozo *m* **5** (share) (colloq) tajada *f* (fam), parte *f* **6** (blow — with knife) cuchillada *f*

cut² (*pres p* **cutting**; *past & past p* **cut**) *vt* **1** ‹*wood/paper/wire/rope*› cortar; **to ~ sth in half** cortar algo por la mitad; **I ~ my finger** me corté el dedo; **to cut sb's throat** degollar* a algn; *see also* SHORT² 1 **2 (a)** (trim) ‹*hair/nails*› cortar; ‹*grass/corn*› cortar, segar*; **to get one's hair ~** cortarse el pelo **(b)** (shape) ‹*glass/stone*› tallar; ‹*key*› hacer* **3** (reduce) ‹*level/number*› reducir*; ‹*budget*› recortar; ‹*price/rate*› rebajar; ‹*service/workforce*› hacer* recortes en **4 (a)** (shorten) ‹*text*› acortar **(b)** (remove) ‹*scene*› cortar **(c)** ‹*film*› (edit) editar; «*censors*» hacer* cortes en **5** (in cards) ‹*deck*› cortar **6** (colloq) (cease): **~ the jokes!** ¡basta ya de bromas! ■ **~** *vi* **1** «*knife/scissors*» cortar; **the rope ~ into her wrists** la cuerda le estaba cortando las muñecas **2** (Cin, Rad): **~!** ¡corte(n)! **3** (in cards) cortar

• **cut across** [*v* + *prep* + *o*] **(a)** (take shortcut across) cortar por **(b)** (cross boundaries of) trascender*

• **cut back 1** [*v* + *o* + *adv*, *v* + *adv* + *o*] **(a)** (prune) ‹*hedge*› podar **(b)** (reduce) ‹*spending*› recortar **2** [*v* + *adv*] (make reductions) hacer* economías; **to ~ back** ON **sth** reducir* algo

• **cut down 1** [*v* + *o* + *adv*, *v* + *adv* + *o*] **(a)** (fell) ‹*tree*› cortar, talar **(b)** (kill) matar **2** [*v* + *adv*] (make reductions): **cigarette? — no, thanks, I'm trying to ~ down** ¿un cigarrillo? — no, gracias, estoy tratando de fumar menos; **you should ~ down on carbohydrates** debería reducir el consumo de hidratos de carbono

• **cut in** [*v* + *adv*] **(a)** (interrupt) interrumpir **(b)** (Auto) atravesarse*

• **cut off 1** [*v* + *o* + *adv*, *v* + *adv* + *o*] (sever) ‹*branch/limb*› cortar **2** [*v* + *o* + *adv*, *v* + *adv* + *o*] (interrupt, block) ‹*supply/route*› cortar **3** [*v* + *o* + *adv*] **(a)** (isolate) aislar*; **to feel ~ off** sentirse* aislado;

the town was ~ off la ciudad quedó sin comunicaciones **(b)** (on telephone): **we were ~ off** se cortó la comunicación

• **cut out 1** [*v* + *o* + *adv*, *v* + *adv* + *o*] ‹*article/photograph*› recortar **2** [*v* + *o* + *adv*, *v* + *adv* + *o*] **(a)** ‹*dress/cookies*› cortar **(b)** (exclude) ‹*noise/carbohydrates*› eliminar; **he ~ me out of his will** me excluyó de su testamento; **~ it out!** (colloq) ¡basta ya! **3** (suit): **to be ~ out FOR sth** estar* hecho para algo **4** [*v* + *adv*] «*engine*» pararse

• **cut up** [*v* + *o* + *adv*, *v* + *adv* + *o*] ‹*vegetables/wood*› cortar en pedazos

cut³ *adj* (*before n*) ‹*flowers*› cortado; ‹*glass*› tallado

cutback /'kʌtbæk/ *n* recorte *m*

cute /kju:t/ *adj* **cuter, cutest (a)** (sweet) ‹*baby/face*› mono (fam), cuco (fam), rico (CS fam) **(b)** (attractive) (AmE) guapo

cut-glass /'kʌt'glæs ‖ kʌt'glɑ:s/ *adj* de cristal tallado

cuticle /'kju:tɪkəl/ *n* cutícula *f*

cutlery /'kʌtləri/ *n* [U] cubiertos *mpl*, cubertería *f*, cuchillería *f* (Chi)

cutlet /'kʌtlət ‖ 'kʌtlɪt/ *n* chuleta *f* (*pequeña*)

cut: **~off (point)** *n* límite *m*; **~-price** /'kʌt'praɪs/ *adj* (BrE) ⇒ ~-RATE; **~-rate** /'kʌt'reɪt/ *adj* (AmE) a precio rebajado; **~throat** *adj* ‹*competition*› feroz, salvaje

cutting¹ /'kʌtɪŋ/ *n* **1 (a)** (from newspaper) (BrE) recorte *m* **(b)** (from plant) esqueje *m* **2** (for road, railway) (BrE) zanja *f*

cutting² *adj* **(a)** (*before n*) ‹*tool/blade*› cortante **(b)** (cold) ‹*wind*› cortante **(c)** (hurtful) ‹*remark*› hiriente

CV *n* = **curriculum vitae**

cwt *n* = **hundredweight**

cyanide /'saɪənaɪd/ *n* [U] cianuro *m*

cyberspace /'saɪbərspeɪs ‖ 'saɪbəspeɪs/ *n* [U] ciberespacio *m*

cycle¹ /'saɪkəl/ *n* **1** (process) ciclo *m* **2** (Elec, Comput) ciclo *m* **3** (bicycle) bicicleta *f*

cycle² *vi* ir* en bicicleta

cycling /'saɪklɪŋ/ *n* [U] ciclismo *m*

cyclist /'saɪkləst ‖ 'saɪklɪst/ *n* ciclista *mf*

cyclone /'saɪkləʊn/ *n* ciclón *m*

cylinder /'sɪləndər ‖ 'sɪlɪndə(r)/ *n* **1** (Math) cilindro *m* **2** (of engine) cilindro *m*

cymbal /'sɪmbəl/ *n* platillo *m*, címbalo *m*

cynic /'sɪnɪk/ *n* cínico, -ca

cynical /'sɪnɪkəl/ *adj* cínico

cynicism /'sɪnəsɪzəm/ *n* [U] cinismo *m*

cypher *n* (esp BrE) ⇒ CIPHER

cypress /'saɪprəs/ *n* ciprés *m*

Cyprus /'saɪprəs/ *n* Chipre *f*

cyst /sɪst/ *n* quiste *m*

cystic fibrosis /'sɪstɪkfaɪ'brəʊsəs ‖ ˌsɪstɪkfaɪ'brəʊsɪs/ *n* [U] fibrosis *f* cística *or* pancreática

cystitis /sɪ'staɪtəs ‖ sɪ'staɪtɪs/ *n* [U] cistitis *f*

czar /zɑ:r ‖ zɑ:(r)/ *n* (esp AmE) ⇒ TSAR

Czech¹ /tʃek/ *adj* checo

Czech² *n* **(a)** [C] (person) checo, -ca *m,f* **(b)** [U] (language) checo *m*

Czechoslovakia /'tʃekəslə'vɑ:kiə ‖ ˌtʃekəslə'vækiə/ *n* (Hist) Checoslovaquia *f*

Czechoslovakian /'tʃekəslə'vɑ:kiən ‖ ˌtʃekəslə'vækiən/ *adj* (Hist) checoslovaco

Czech Republic *n* **the ~ ~** la Répública Checa

Dd

D, d /di:/ *n* **(a)** (letter) D, d *f* **(b)** (Mus) re *m*

d' = **do; d'you go there often?** ¿vas ahí a menudo?

'd /d/ **(a)** = **had (b)** = **would (c)** = **did**

DA *n* (in US) = **district attorney**

dab /dæb/ *vt*: **~ the stain with a damp cloth** frote suavemente la mancha con un trapo húmedo; **~ antiseptic on the cut** dese unos toques de antiséptico en la herida

dabble /'dæbəl/ *vi*: **to ~ in politics/journalism** tener* escarceos con la política/el periodismo

dad /dæd/ *n* (colloq) papá *m* (fam)

daddy /'dædi/ *n* papi *m* (fam)

daddy longlegs /'lɔ:ŋlegz ‖ 'lɒŋlegz/ *n* (*pl* **~ ~**) (colloq) **(a)** (harvestman) (AmE) segador *m*, falangio *m* **(b)** (cranefly) (BrE) típula *f*

daffodil /'dæfədɪl/ *n* narciso *m*

daft /dæft ‖ dɑ:ft/ *adj* **-er, -est** (esp BrE colloq) tonto, bobo (fam)

dagger /'dægər ‖ 'dægə(r)/ *n* daga *f*, puñal *m*

dahlia /'dæljə ‖ 'deɪliə/ *n* dalia *f*

daily¹ /'deɪli/ *adj* (*before n*) ‹*newspaper/prayers*› diario; ‹*walk/visit*› diario, cotidiano

daily² *adv* a diario, diariamente

daily³ *n* (*pl* **-lies**) diario *m*, periódico *m*

dainty /'deɪnti/ *adj* **-tier, -tiest** ‹*flowers/vase*› delicado; ‹*appearance*› delicado, refinado

dairy /'deri ‖ 'deəri/ *n* (*pl* **-ries**) **(a)** (on farm) lechería *f*; (*before n*) ‹*produce*› lácteo; ‹*butter/cream*› de granja; ‹*cow/industry*› lechero **(b)** (shop) lechería *f*; (company) central *f* lechera

daisy /'deɪzi/ *n* (*pl* **-sies**) (cultivated) margarita *f*; (wild) margarita *f* de los prados, maya *f*

dally /ˈdæli/ *vi* **-lies, -lying, -lied** perder* el tiempo

dam¹ /dæm/ *n* dique *m*, presa *f*, represa *f* (AmS)

dam² *vt* **-mm-** construir* una presa *or* (AmS) una represa en

damage¹ /ˈdæmɪdʒ/ *n* **1** [U] (to object) daño *m*; (to reputation, cause) daño *m*, perjuicio *m* **2 damages** *pl* (Law) daños y perjuicios *mpl*

damage² *vt* ‹*building/vehicle*› dañar; ‹*health*› perjudicar*, ser* perjudicial para; ‹*reputation/cause*› perjudicar*, dañar

damaging /ˈdæmɪdʒɪŋ/ *adj* perjudicial

dame /deɪm/ *n* **1 Dame** (title in UK) Dame (*título honorífico*) **2** (woman) (AmE sl) tipa *f* (fam), tía *f* (Esp fam)

damn¹ /dæm/ *vt* **(a)** (Relig) condenar **(b)** (condemn) condenar

damn² *interj* (colloq) ¡caray! (fam & euf)

damn³ *adj* (colloq) (*before n*) (*as intensifier*) condenado (fam), maldito (fam), pinche (Méx fam)

damnation /dæmˈneɪʃən/ *n* [U] condenación *f*

damned /dæmd/ ⇒ DAMN³

damning /ˈdæmɪŋ/ *adj* **(a)** (condemnatory) ‹*evidence*› condenatorio **(b)** (critical) ‹*appraisal*› crítico

damp¹ /dæmp/ *adj* **-er, -est** húmedo; **to smell ~** oler* a humedad

damp² *n* [U] humedad *f*

damp³ *vt* **~ (down)** ‹*fire*› sofocar*; ‹*enthusiasm/excitement*› apagar*, enfriar*

damp course *n* membrana *f* aislante

dampen /ˈdæmpən/ *vt* **1** (moisten) humedecer*, mojar **2** (discourage) ‹*hopes*› hacer* perder; ‹*enthusiasm*› hacer* perder, apagar*

damper /ˈdæmpər ‖ ˈdæmpə(r)/ *n* (of piano) sordina *f*; ***to put a ~ on sth*** (colloq): **the bad news put a ~ on the celebrations** la mala noticia estropeó las fiestas

damp: **~-proof** *vt* proteger* contra la humedad; **~-proof course** *n* ⇒ DAMP COURSE

damson /ˈdæmzən/ *n* ciruela *f* damascena

dance¹ /dæns ‖ dɑːns/ *n* [C U] baile *m*; (*before n*) ‹*music*› de baile, bailable

dance² *vi* **1 (a)** (to music) bailar **(b)** (skip) dar* saltos **2** «*eyes/flames*» (liter) bailar, danzar* (liter); ■ **~** *vt* ‹*waltz/tango*› bailar

dancer /ˈdænsər ‖ ˈdɑːnsə(r)/ *n* bailarín, -rina *m,f*

dancing /ˈdænsɪŋ ‖ ˈdɑːnsɪŋ/ *n* [U] baile *m*; (*before n*) ‹*lesson/shoes*› de baile

dandelion /ˈdændəlaɪən ‖ ˈdændɪlaɪən/ *n* diente *m* de león

dandruff /ˈdændrʌf/ *n* [U] caspa *f*; (*before n*) **~ shampoo** champú *m* anti-caspa

Dane /deɪn/ *n* danés, -nesa *m,f*, dinamarqués, -quesa *m,f*

danger /ˈdeɪndʒər ‖ ˈdeɪndʒə(r)/ *n* [U C] peligro *m*; **in ~** en peligro *or* en riesgo; **to be in ~ of -ING** correr peligro *or* riesgo de + INF; (*before n*) **to be on the ~ list** encontrarse* en estado grave; **~ signal** señal *f*

dangerous /ˈdeɪndʒərəs/ *adj* peligroso

dangerously /ˈdeɪndʒərəsli/ *adv* peligrosamente

dangle /ˈdæŋgəl/ *vi* colgar*, pender ■ **~** *vt* hacer* oscilar

Danish¹ /ˈdeɪnɪʃ/ *adj* danés, dinamarqués

Danish² *n* [U] danés *m*

Danish (pastry) *n*: *bollo cubierto de azúcar glaseado*

dank /dæŋk/ *adj* frío y húmedo

dapper /ˈdæpər ‖ ˈdæpə(r)/ *adj* atildado, pulcro

dare¹ /der ‖ deə(r)/ *n* reto *m*, desafío *m*

dare² *v mod* atreverse a, osar (liter); **how ~ you!** ¡cómo te atreves!; **I ~ say you've had enough** estarás harto(, me imagino) ■ **~** *vt* **1** (be so bold) **to ~ to** + INF atreverse a + INF, osar + INF (liter) **2** (challenge) **to ~ sb to** + INF retar *or* desafiar* a algn a + INF *or* A QUE (+ *subj*)

daredevil /ˈderˌdevl̩ ‖ ˈdeəˌdevl̩/ *n* corajudo, -da *m,f* (fam); (*before n*) ‹*feat/exploit*› temerario

daring¹ /ˈderɪŋ ‖ ˈdeərɪŋ/ *adj* **(a)** ‹*explorer/pilot*› osado; ‹*plan*› audaz **(b)** ‹*dress/film*› atrevido

daring² *n* [U] **(a)** (courage) arrojo *m*, coraje *m* **(b)** (audacity) audacia *f*

dark¹ /dɑːrk ‖ dɑːk/ ▶ 515 *adj* **-er, -est 1** (unlit) ‹*room/night*› oscuro; **it's getting ~** está oscureciendo, se está haciendo de noche **2 (a)** (in color) oscuro; **~ chocolate** chocolate *m* sin leche; **~ glasses** anteojos *mpl* oscuros (esp AmL), gafas *fpl* negras (Esp) **(b)** (in complexion) moreno

dark² *n* [U] (absence of light) **the ~** la oscuridad; **to wait until ~** esperar hasta que anochezca; ***to keep sb in the ~ about sth*** ocultarle algo a algn

Dark Ages *pl n* **the ~ ~** la Alta Edad Media, la Edad de las tinieblas

darken /ˈdɑːrkən ‖ ˈdɑːkən/ *vt* **(a)** (make dark) oscurecer* **(b)** (make somber) ensombrecer* ■ **~** *vi* **(a)** (grow dark) «*room/color/sky*» oscurecerse* **(b)** (grow somber) ensombrecerse*

darkness /ˈdɑːrknəs ‖ ˈdɑːknɪs/ *n* [U] oscuridad *f*

darkroom /ˈdɑːrkruːm, -rʊm ‖ ˈdɑːkruːm, -rʊm/ *n* cuarto *m* oscuro

darling¹ /ˈdɑːrlɪŋ ‖ ˈdɑːlɪŋ/ *n* (*as form of address*) cariño

darling² *adj* (*before n*) querido

darn¹ /dɑːrn ‖ dɑːn/ *vt* zurcir*

dart¹ /dɑːrt ‖ dɑːt/ *n* **(a)** (weapon) dardo *m* **(b)** (Games) dardo *m* **(c)** (Clothing) pinza *f*

dart² *vi*: **to ~ into/out of a room** entrar como una flecha en/salir* como una flecha de una habitación ■ **~** *vt* ‹*look*› lanzar*

dartboard /ˈdɑːrtbɔːrd ‖ ˈdɑːtbɔːd/ *n* diana *f*

darts /dɑːrts ‖ dɑːts/ *n* (+ *sing vb*) dardos *mpl*

dash¹ /dæʃ/ *n* **1** [C] (small amount) poquito *m*; **a ~ of milk** un chorrito de leche **2** [C] (punctuation mark) guión *m*

dash² *vt* **1** (hurl) tirar; **she ~ed the plate to pieces** hizo añicos *or* trizas el plato; **the ship was ~ed against the rocks** el barco se estrelló contra las rocas **2** (disappoint) ‹*hopes*› (*usu pass*) defraudar

■ ~ *vi:* **I ~ed to the rescue** me lancé al rescate; **she ~ed out** salió disparada
• dash off 1 [*v* + *o* + *adv*, *v* + *adv* + *o*] (write hurriedly) escribir* corriendo **2** [*v* + *adv*] (leave hastily) irse* corriendo

dashboard /'dæʃbɔːrd ‖ 'dæʃbɔːd/ *n* tablero *m* de mandos, salpicadero *m* (Esp)

data /'deɪtə/ *n* **1** (facts, information) (+ *pl vb*) datos *mpl*, información *f* **2** (Comput) (+ *sing vb*) datos *mpl*

database /'deɪtəbeɪs/ *n* base *f* de datos

date¹ /deɪt/ ▶ **540** *n* **1** (of appointment, battle) fecha *f*; **what's the ~ today?** ¿a qué fecha estamos?; **to ~** hasta la fecha, hasta el momento **2** (colloq) (appointment) cita *f*; **Greg has a ~ with Ana on Sunday** Greg sale con Ana el domingo **3** (fruit) dátil *m*

date² *vt* **1 (a)** (mark with date) fechar **(b)** (give date to) ‹*remains/pottery/fossil*› datar, determinar la antigüedad de **2** (betray age) (colloq): **that really ~s you** eso delata tu edad, eso demuestra lo viejo que eres
■ ~ *vi* **1** (originate in) datar; **his title ~s back to the 14th century** los orígenes de su título se remontan al siglo XIV **2** (become old-fashioned) pasar de moda

dated /'deɪtəd ‖ 'deɪtɪd/ *adj* ‹*fashion/word*› anticuado; **his plays are ~** sus obras han perdido actualidad

date: **~ stamp** *n* (instrument) fechador *m*; (date) fecha *f*; **~-stamp** *vt* fechar

daub /dɔːb/ *vt* (smear) **to ~ sth** WITH **sth** embadurnar algo DE algo

daughter /'dɔːtər ‖ 'dɔːtə(r)/ *n* hija *f*

daughter-in-law /'dɔːtərmlɔː/ *n* (*pl* **daughters-in-law**) nuera *f*

daunt /dɔːnt/ *vt* (*usu pass*) amilanar, intimidar

daunting /'dɔːntɪŋ/ *adj* ‹*prospect*› desalentador, sobrecogedor; ‹*task*› de enormes proporciones

dawdle /'dɔːdl/ *vi* entretenerse*

dawn¹ /dɔːn/ *n* [U C] amanecer *m*; **at ~** al amanecer, al alba (liter)

dawn² *vi* (liter) «*day*» amanecer*, clarear, alborear (liter); «*new age*» alborear (liter), nacer*
• dawn on [*v* + *prep* + *o*]: **it gradually ~ed on me that** ... fui cayendo en la cuenta de que ...

dawn chorus *n* **the ~ ~** el trino de los pájaros al amanecer

day /deɪ/ ▶ **540** *n* **1** día *m*; (working day) jornada *f*, día *m*; **twice a ~** dos veces al día; **all ~** todo el día; **every ~** todos los días; **one of these ~s** un día de éstos; **~ by ~** día a día, de día en día; **it's not my/his ~** no es mi/su día; **to take a ~ off (from work)** tomarse un día libre; **in this ~ and age** hoy (en) día, el día de hoy; **these ~s** hoy (en) día; **that'll be the ~** (colloq & iro) cuando las ranas críen cola; **have a good** *o* **nice ~!** (AmE) ¡que le vaya bien!; ***to call it a ~*** (temporarily) dejarlo para otro día; (permanently) dejar de trabajar (*or* estudiar *etc*); ***to make one's ~*** (colloq) alegrarle la vida a algn **2 days** (*as adv*): **to work ~s** trabajar durante el día

day: **~break** *n* [U] alba *f*‡ (liter), amanecer *m*; **~-care center** *n* (AmE) guardería *f* infantil

daydream¹ /'deɪdriːm/ *n* ensueño *m*, ensoñación *f*

daydream² *vi* soñar* despierto, fantasear

day: **~light** *n* [U] luz *f* (del día); **~light (saving) time** *n* [U] (AmE) hora *f* de verano; **~ release** *n* [U] (in UK) *sistema que permite a un empleado ausentarse regularmente de su trabajo para seguir estudios relacionados con el mismo*; **~room** *n*: *sala de estar comunal en hospitales, prisiones etc*; **~time** *n*: **in** *o* **during the ~time** de día *or* durante el día; **~-to-~** /'deɪtə'deɪ/ *adj* (*before n*) ‹*occurrence*› cotidiano, diario; ‹*chores/difficulties*› de cada día; ‹*existence*› diario; **~ trip** *n* excursión *f* de un día

daze /deɪz/ *n* (*no pl*) aturdimiento *m*; **to go about in a ~** estar* en las nubes

dazed /deɪzd/ *adj* aturdido

dazzle /'dæzəl/ *vt* «*light*» deslumbrar, encandilar; «*beauty/wit*» deslumbrar

dazzling /'dæzlɪŋ/ *adj* (bright) ‹*light/glare*› deslumbrante, resplandeciente, que encandila; (impressive) ‹*wit/looks*› deslumbrante, deslumbrador

DC (a) (= **direct current**) CC **(b)** = **District of Columbia**

D-day /'diːdeɪ/ *n* **(a)** (in World War II) día *m* D (*día del desembarco aliado en Normandía*) **(b)** (important day) el día señalado

DE = **Delaware**

DEA *n* (= **Drug Enforcement Administration**) DEA *f*

deacon /'diːkən/ *n* diácono *m*

deaconess /'diːkənəs ‖ ˌdiːkə'nes, 'diːkənɪs/ *n* diaconisa *f*

dead¹ /ded/ *adj* **1** (no longer alive) muerto; **he's ~** está muerto; **to drop ~** caerse* muerto; **I wouldn't be seen ~ in that dress** (colloq) yo no me pondría ese vestido ni muerta *or* ni loca; ⇒ BODY 1(c) **2** (numb) (*usu pred*) dormido; **to go ~** «*limb*» dormirse* **3** (very tired, ill) (colloq) muerto (fam) **4** (obsolete) ‹*language*› muerto; ‹*custom*› en desuso **5 (a)** (not functioning) ‹*wire/circuit*› desconectado; ‹*telephone*› desconectado, cortado; ‹*battery*› descargado **(b)** (not alight) ‹*fire/match*› apagado **(c)** (not busy) ‹*town/hotel/party*› muerto

dead² *adv* **1 (a)** (exactly) justo **(b)** (directly) justo, directamente; **~ ahead** justo delante **(c)** (suddenly): **to stop ~** parar en seco **2** (colloq) ‹*straight/level*› completamente; **~ slow** lentísimo; **to be ~ certain** estar* totalmente seguro; **it was ~ easy** estuvo regalado *or* tirado (fam)

dead³ *pl n*: **the ~** los muertos

deaden /'dedn̩/ *vt* ‹*impact*› amortiguar; ‹*noise/vibration*› reducir*; ‹*pain*› atenuar*, aliviar; ‹*nerve*› insensibilizar*; ‹*faculties*› entorpecer*

dead: **~ end** *n* callejón *m* sin salida; **~-end** /'ded'end/ *adj* ‹*street*› sin salida, ciego (Andes, Ven); **a ~-end job** (colloq) un trabajo sin porvenir *or* futuro; **~line** *n* fecha *f* tope *or* límite, plazo *m* de entrega; **~lock** *n* (*no pl*) punto *m* muerto

Dates, Days, Months and Years

The days of the week

Spanish uses lower-case letters for the names of days:

Monday	=	lunes
Tuesday	=	martes
Wednesday	=	miércoles
Thursday	=	jueves
Friday	=	viernes
Saturday	=	sábado
Sunday	=	domingo

The names of the days of the week are preceded by an article in spoken Spanish:

the course starts on Monday	=	el curso empieza el lunes
he works (on) Saturdays	=	trabaja los sábados
Monday morning	=	el lunes por la mañana *or* la mañana del lunes

The months of the year

Spanish also uses lower-case letters for the names of months:

January	=	enero
February	=	febrero
March	=	marzo
April	=	abril
May	=	mayo
June	=	junio
July	=	julio
August	=	agosto
September	=	septiembre *or* setiembre
October	=	octubre
November	=	noviembre
December	=	diciembre

in May	=	en mayo
in early March	=	a principios de marzo
in mid-October	=	a mediados de octubre
in late December	=	a fines *or* a finales de diciembre

The names of the months can be preceded by el mes de:

I spent August in London	=	pasé el mes de agosto en Londres

Years, decades and centuries

1936	=	1936 (*mil novecientos treinta y seis*)
October 12th, 1942	=	el 12 octubre de 1942 (*el doce de octubre de mil novecientos cuarenta y dos*)
in the spring of 1790/1880/1990 etc	=	en la primavera del 90 (*noventa*)
the sixties	=	los sesenta *or* los años sesenta *or* la década de los sesenta

Ordinal numbers are used for the first to the ninth centuries:

the 4th century = el siglo cuarto

For the 10th century, both cardinal and ordinal numbers are accepted:

the 10th century = el siglo décimo *or* el siglo diez

From the 11th century onward, cardinal numbers are used:

the 21st century = el siglo vientiuno

Dates

Spanish uses cardinal numbers for the date:

today is the 6th	=	hoy es seis

In most other contexts, the article el *is required*:

he died on the 10th of October	=	murió el 10 (*diez*) de octubre

If the day of the week is mentioned, the article el *is not repeated before the number*:

they met on Monday, August 4th	=	se reunieron el lunes 4 (cuatró) de agosto

When the month is not mentioned, el día *can precede the date*:

he arrives on the 20th	=	llega el veinte *or* el día veinte

However the ordinal number is preferred for the first day of the month in Latin America, whereas the cardinal number is more commonly used in Spain:

January 1st	=	1° de enero (*el primero de enero*) *or* 1 de enero (*el uno de enero*)

Asking the date

what's the date?	=	¿a cuánto estamos? *or* ¿a cómo estamos?
it's the 6th	=	estamos a 6 (*seis*)
today is November 6th	=	hoy es 6 de noviembre

deadly¹ /ˈdedli/ *adj* **-lier, -liest 1** (fatal) ‹*disease/poison*› mortal; ‹*weapon*› mortífero **2** (dull) (colloq) aburridísimo, terriblemente aburridor (AmL)

deadly² *adv* (*as intensifier*) ‹*dull*› terriblemente

dead: **~pan** *adj* ‹*expression*› de póquer *or* (fam) de palo; ‹*voice/delivery*› deliberadamente inexpresivo; **D~ Sea** *n* **the D~ Sea** el Mar Muerto; **~ weight** *n* peso *m* muerto

deaf /def/ *adj* sordo; **to go ~** quedarse sordo; **~ and dumb** sordomudo

deaf-aid /ˈdefeɪd/ *n* (BrE) audífono *m*

deafen /ˈdefən/ *vt* ensordecer*

deafening /ˈdefənɪŋ/ *adj* ensordecedor

deaf-mute /'def'mju:t/ *n* sordomudo, -da *m,f*

deafness /'defnəs || 'defnɪs/ *n* [U] sordera *f*

deal[1] /di:l/ *n* **1** (indicating amount): **it makes a great/good ~ of difference** cambia mucho/bastante las cosas; **we've seen a great ~ of her lately** la hemos visto mucho *or* muy a menudo últimamente **2** [C] **(a)** (agreement) trato *m*, acuerdo *m*; **to do a ~ with sb** llegar* a un acuerdo con algn, hacer* un trato *or* un pacto con algn; **it's no big ~** no es nada del otro mundo **(b)** (financial arrangement) acuerdo *m* **(c)** (bargain): **you'll get a better ~ if you shop around** lo conseguirás más barato si vas a otras tiendas **3** (treatment) trato *m*; **she's had a raw ~ in life** la vida la ha tratado muy mal

deal[2] (*past & past p* **dealt**) *vt/i* (Games) dar*, repartir

• **deal in** [*v + prep + o*] (Busn) dedicarse* a la compra y venta de, comerciar en

• **deal out** [*v + o + adv, v + adv + o*] ‹*gifts/money*› repartir, distribuir*

• **deal with** [*v + prep + o*] **1** (do business with) ‹*company*› tener* relaciones comerciales con; **I prefer to ~ with her** yo prefiero tratar con ella **2 (a)** (tackle, handle) ‹*complaint*› ocuparse de, atender*; ‹*situation*› manejar **(b)** (be responsible for) ocuparse *or* encargarse* de **3** ‹*issue*› (discuss, treat) tratar; (have as subject) tratar de

dealer /'di:lər || 'di:lə(r)/ *n* **1 (a)** (trader): **she's a car ~** se dedica a la compra-venta de coches; **visit your local Hoover ~** visite a su representante Hoover más próximo; **drug ~** traficante *mf* de drogas **(b)** (Fin) corredor, -dora *m,f* de bolsa *or* de valores **2** (Games): **the ~** el que da *or* reparte las cartas

dealing /'di:lɪŋ/ *n* **1 (a)** [U] (business methods): **the company has a reputation for honest/shady ~** la empresa tiene fama de honradez en los negocios/de hacer negocios turbios **(b) dealings** *pl* (contacts, relations) relaciones *fpl*, trato *m* **2** [U] (trafficking) tráfico *m*

dealt /delt/ *past & past p of* DEAL[2]

dean /di:n/ *n* **1** (Relig) deán *m* **2 (a)** (in university) decano, -na *m,f* **(b)** (in college, secondary school) (AmE) *docente a cargo del asesoramiento y de la disciplina de los estudiantes*

dear[1] /dɪr, ||dɪə(r)/ *adj* **dearer, dearest 1** (loved) querido **2** (in direct address) **(a)** (in speech): **my ~ Mrs Harper, I can assure you that** ... mi buena señora (Harper), le aseguro que ... **(b)** (in letter-writing): **D~ Mr Jones** Estimado Sr. Jones; **D~ Sir or Madam** Estimado/a Señor(a), Muy señor mío/señora mía; **D~ Jimmy** Querido Jimmy **3** (lovable) adorable **4** (expensive) caro

dear[2] *interj*: **oh ~!** ¡ay!, ¡qué cosa!

dear[3] *n* (*as form of address*) querido, -da, cariño; **(you) poor ~!** ¡pobre ángel!, ¡pobrecito!

dearly /'dɪrli || 'dɪəli/ *adv* **1** (*as intensifier*): **I love him ~** lo quiero mucho *or* de verdad; **~ beloved** (frml) (Relig) (amados) hermanos **2** (at great cost) caro *adj*

death /deθ/ *n* [U C] muerte *f*, fallecimiento *m* (frml); **to put sb to ~** ejecutar a algn; **to be worried to ~** (colloq) estar* preocupadísimo

death: **~bed** *n* lecho *m* de muerte; **~ certificate** *n* certificado *m* de defunción; **~ penalty** *n* **the ~ penalty** la pena de muerte; **~ row** /rəʊ/ *n* (*no art*) pabellón *m* de los condenados a muerte, corredor *m* de la muerte; **~ sentence** *n*: **the ~ sentence** la pena de muerte; **~ squad** *n* escuadrón *m* de la muerte; **~ toll** *n* número *m* de víctimas (mortales) *or* de muertos; **~ trap** *n*: *edificio, vehículo etc muy poco seguro*; **~ warrant** *n* sentencia *f* de muerte; **~ wish** *n* (*no pl*) (Psych) pulsión *f* de muerte

debar /dɪ'bɑ:r || dɪ'bɑ:(r)/ *vt* **-rr-** (frml) **the fact that she didn't have a degree ~red her from promotion** el hecho de no tener un título universitario le impedía ascender; **he was ~red from taking his final exam** se le prohibió rendir el examen final

debase /dɪ'beɪs/ *vt* **(a)** (devalue) ‹*ideal/principle*› degradar, envilecer*; ‹*language*› corromper, viciar **(b)** (demean) ‹*person*› degradar, rebajar

debate[1] /dɪ'beɪt/ *n* **(a)** [C] (public, parliamentary) debate *m* **(b)** [U] (discussion) debate *m*, discusión *f*

debate[2] *vt* **(a)** ‹*question/topic/motion*› debatir, discutir **(b)** (weigh up) ‹*idea/possibility*› darle* vueltas a, considerar

debauchery /dɪ'bɔ:tʃəri/ *n* [U] disipación *f*, libertinaje *m*

debenture /dɪ'bentʃər || dɪ'bentʃə(r)/ *n* **~ (bond)** (Fin) obligación *f*, bono *m*

debilitating /dɪ'bɪləteɪtɪŋ || dɪ'bɪlɪteɪtɪŋ/ *adj* ‹*disease*› debilitante; ‹*climate*› extenuante

debit[1] /'debət || 'debɪt/ *n* débito *m*, cargo *m*; (*before n*) **~ card** tarjeta *f* de cobro automático

debit[2] *vt* (Fin) debitar, cargar*

debonair /ˌdebə'ner || ˌdebə'neə(r)/ *adj* (suave) elegante y desenvuelto; (courteous) cortés, afable

debriefing /di:'bri:fɪŋ/ *n* [U C]: **they were sent for ~** los llamaron para que rindiesen informe *or* diesen parte de su misión

debris /də'bri: || 'debri:, 'deɪbri:/ *n* [U] **(a)** (rubble) escombros *mpl*; (of plane, ship) restos *mpl*; (rubbish) desechos *mpl* **(b)** (Geol) detritos *mpl*

debt /det/ *n* **(a)** [U] (indebtedness) endeudamiento *m*; **I'm $200 in ~** debo 200 dólares, tengo deudas por 200 dólares; **to be in ~ to sb** (frml) estarle* en deuda a algn, estar* en deuda con algn; **to get into ~** endeudarse, llenarse *or* cargarse* de deudas **(b)** [C] (money owing) deuda *f*; **bad ~s** deudas incobrables

debtor /'detər || 'detə(r)/ *n* deudor, -dora *m,f*

debunk /di:'bʌŋk/ *vt* (colloq) desacreditar

debut, **début** /'deɪbju:, 'de-/ (*pl* **-buts** /-bju:z/) *n* debut *m*

decade /'dekeɪd/ ▶ 540 *n* década *f*

decadence /'dekədəns/ *n* [U] decadencia *f*

decadent /'dekədənt/ *adj* decadente

decaffeinated /di:'kæfəneɪtəd || ˌdi:'kæfɪneɪtɪd/ *adj* descafeinado

decanter /dɪ'kæntər || dɪ'kæntə(r)/ *n* licorera *f*

decapitate /dɪ'kæpɪteɪt/ *vt* decapitar

decathlon /dɪ'kæθlən/ *n* decatlón *m*

decay¹ /dɪ'keɪ/ *vi* «*foodstuffs/corpse*» descomponerse*, pudrirse*; «*wood*» pudrirse*; «*tooth*» cariarse, picarse*; «*building/machine*» deteriorarse; «*empire/culture/civilization*» decaer*, declinar

decay² *n* [U] (of organic matter) descomposición *f*; (*tooth* ~) caries *f*; (of building) deterioro *m*; (of culture) decadencia *f*

deceased¹ /dɪ'si:st/ *n* (*pl* ~) (frml) **the** ~ el difunto, la difunta; (*pl*) los difuntos, las difuntas (frml)

deceased² *adj* (frml) difunto

deceit /dɪ'si:t/ *n* [U C] engaño *m*

deceitful /dɪ'si:tfəl/ *adj* ‹*person*› falso, embustero; ‹*action*› engañoso

deceive /dɪ'si:v/ *vt* engañar

deceiver /dɪ'si:vər ‖ dɪ'si:və(r)/ *n* impostor, -tora *m,f*

decelerate /'di:'seləreɪt/ *vi* (frml) «*vehicle/driver*» reducir* *or* aminorar la velocidad

December /dɪ'sembər ‖ dɪ'sembə(r)/ ▶ 540 *n* diciembre *m*

decency /'di:sn̩si/ *n* [U] **(a)** (of dress, conduct) decencia *f*, decoro *m* **(b)** (propriety) buena educación *f*, consideración *f*; **she didn't even have the ~ to ask me** ni siquiera tuvo la consideración de preguntarme

decent /'di:sn̩t/ *adj* **1** (appropriate, respectable) decente, decoroso **2** (acceptable) ‹*person*› pasable, aceptable; ‹*meal/housing*› decente, como es debido

decently /'di:sn̩tli/ *adv* **1** (respectably) ‹*dress/behave*› decentemente, con decencia **2** (acceptably) ‹*perform/cook*› bastante bien

decentralize /di:'sentrəlaɪz/ *vt* descentralizar*

deception /dɪ'sepʃən/ *n* [U C] engaño *m*

decibel /'desəbel ‖ 'desɪbel/ *n* decibelio *m*, decibel *m*

decide /dɪ'saɪd/ *vt* **1** (make up one's mind) decidir; **to ~ to** + INF decidir *or* resolver + INF **2** (settle) ‹*question/issue*› decidir; ‹*outcome*› determinar ■ ~ *vi* decidirse

decided /dɪ'saɪdəd ‖ dɪ'saɪdɪd/ *adj* **(a)** (definite) (*before n*) ‹*improvement/advantage*› claro, marcado **(b)** (determined) ‹*character/tone*› decidido

deciduous /dɪ'sɪdʒuəs ‖ dɪ'sɪdjʊəs/ *adj* de hoja caduca, caducifolio (téc)

decimal¹ /'desəməl ‖ 'desɪməl/ *adj* decimal

decimal² ▶ 543 *n* decimal *m*

decimalization /desəmələ'zeɪʃən ‖ ˌdesɪməlaɪ'zeɪʃən/ *n* decimalización *f*, conversión *f* al sistema decimal

decimal point ▶ 543 *n* ≈ coma *f* (*decimal o de los decimales*), punto *m* decimal

decimate /'desəmeɪt ‖ 'desɪmeɪt/ *vt* diezmar

decipher /dɪ'saɪfər ‖ dɪ'saɪfə(r)/ *vt* descifrar

decision /dɪ'sɪʒən/ *n* [C U] decisión *f*; **to make** *o* (BrE also) **take a ~** tomar una decisión

decision-making /dɪ'sɪʒənˌmeɪkɪŋ/ *n* [U] toma *f* de decisiones; (*before n*) ‹*body/process*› decisorio

decisive /dɪ'saɪsɪv/ *adj* **1** (conclusive) ‹*battle/factor*› decisivo; ‹*victory*› contundente **2** (purposeful) ‹*person*› decidido, resuelto; ‹*leadership/answer*› firme

deck¹ /dek/ *n* **1 (a)** (Naut) cubierta *f* **(b)** (of stadium) (AmE) nivel *m* **(c)** (*sun* ~) terraza *f* **(d)** (of bus) (BrE) piso *m* **2** (Audio) deck *m* (AmL), pletina *f* (Esp) **3** (AmE Games) ~ **(of cards)** baraja *f*, mazo *m* (de naipes *or* cartas) (esp AmL)

deck² *vt* **1** (adorn) **to ~ sth (out)** WITH **sth** engalanar *or* adornar algo CON algo; **he was all ~ed out in his Sunday best** iba muy endomingado **2** (knock down) (AmE colloq) tumbar (fam)

deckchair /'dektʃer ‖ 'dektʃeə(r)/ *n* silla *f* de playa, perezosa *f* (Col, Per), reposera *f* (RPl)

declaim /dɪ'kleɪm/ *vt/i* declamar

declaration /'deklə'reɪʃən/ *n* **1** (statement) declaración *f* **2** (Law) (finding) pronunciamiento *m* (oficial); (statement) declaración *f*

declare /dɪ'kler ‖ dɪ'kleə(r)/ *vt* **(a)** (state, announce) ‹*intention*› declarar; ‹*opinion*› manifestar*; **to ~ war** declarar la guerra; **to ~ war on sb/sth** declararle la guerra a algn/algo **(b)** (Tax) ‹*goods/income*› declarar

decline¹ /dɪ'klaɪn/ *n* (*no pl*) **(a)** (decrease) descenso *m*, disminución *f* **(b)** (downward trend) declive *m*, decadencia *f*, deterioro *m*; **to be in ~** estar* en declive *or* en decadencia

decline² *vi* **1 (a)** (decrease) «*production/strength*» disminuir*, decrecer*; «*interest*» disminuir*, decaer* **(b)** (deteriorate) «*health*» deteriorarse; «*standard*» decaer*; «*industry/region/standards*» decaer* **(c) declining** *pres p* ‹*industry/region/standards*› en declive, en decadencia **2** (refuse): **I invited him, but he ~d** lo invité, pero rehusó *or* declinó mi invitación ■ ~ *vt* ‹*offer/invitation*› rehusar, declinar

decode /'di:'kəʊd/ *vt* ‹*signal*› descodificar*; ‹*message*› descifrar

decompose /'di:kəm'pəʊz/ *vi* descomponerse*, pudrirse*

decor, décor /deɪ'kɔ:r ‖ 'deɪkɔ:(r)/ *n* [U C] (furnishings) decoración *f*

decorate /'dekəreɪt/ *vt* **(a)** ‹*room/house*› (with paint) pintar; (with wallpaper) empapelar **(b)** ‹*Christmas tree*› adornar, decorar (AmL); ‹*cake*› decorar

decoration /'dekə'reɪʃən/ *n* **1 (a)** [U] (act) decoración *f* **(b)** [U] (ornamentation) decoración *f* **(c)** [C] (ornament) adorno *m* **2** [U C] (Mil) condecoración *f*

decorative /'dekərətɪv/ *adj* ‹*object*› ornamental, de adorno

decorator /'dekəreɪtər ‖ 'dekəreɪtə(r)/ *n* **(a)** (painter) pintor, -tora *m,f*; (paperhanger) empapelador, -dora *m,f* **(b)** (designer) decorador, -dora *m,f*, interiorista *mf*

decorous /'dekərəs/ *adj* (frml) decoroso

decorum /dɪ'kɔ:rəm/ *n* [U] decoro *m*

decoy /'di:kɔɪ/ *n* (lure) señuelo *m*; (in hunting) señuelo *m*, reclamo *m*

decrease¹ /dɪ'kri:s, 'di:kri:s/ *vi* **(a)** (in quantity) «*amount/numbers*» disminuir*, decrecer*; «*prices*» bajar; «*speed*» disminuir* **(b)** (in inten-

Decimals, Fractions and Percentages

Decimals

In most Spanish-speaking countries, a comma indicates the decimal place:

0.5 (*point five*)	=	0,5 (*cero coma cinco*)
12.76 (*twelve point seven six*)	=	*12,76 (doce coma setenta y seis*)

Some Latin American countries, however, use a point as in English:

0.5 (*point five*)	=	0.5 (*cero punto cinco*)
12.76 (*twelve point seven six*)	=	*12.76 (doce punto setenta y seis*)

Fractions

1/2	=	un medio	1/8	=	un octavo
1/3	=	un tercio	1/9	=	un noveno
1/4	=	un cuarto	1/10	=	un décimo
1/5	=	un quinto	2/3	=	dos tercios
1/6	=	un sexto	3/4	=	tres cuartos
1/7	=	un séptimo			

Any fraction smaller than a tenth is formed by adding the suffix -avo to the cardinal number:

1/11	=	un onceavo	1/2	=	un veinteavo
1/12	=	un doceavo	1/3	=	un treintavo
7/16	=	siete dieciseisavos	1/4	=	un cuarentavo

But:

1/100	=	un centésimo	1/1000	=	un milésimo

The less common fractions are expressed as follows:

3/52	=	tres sobre cincuenta y dos
7/102	=	siete sobre ciento dos

When not used in a strictly mathematical context, fractions are expressed in a different way:

half an apple	=	media manzana *or* la mitad de una manzana
a third of the mixture	=	la tercera parte de la mezcla
three quarters of the population	=	las tres cuartas de la población

Percentages

The article is used before a percentage in Spanish:

10% of the population	=	el 10% (*diez por ciento*) de la población
prices have gone up by 15%	=	los precios han subido un 15% (*un quince por ciento*)

sity) «*quality*» disminuir*, bajar; «*power/effectiveness*» disminuir*, decrecer*; «*interest*» disminuir*, decaer* ■ ~ *vt* disminuir*, reducir*

decrease² /'di:kri:s, dɪ'kri:s/ *n* [C U] disminución *f*, descenso *m*

decree¹ /dɪ'kri:/ *n* decreto *m*

decree² *vt* decretar

decrepit /dɪ'krepət ‖ dɪ'krepɪt/ *adj* **(a)** (dilapidated) ‹*bus/furniture*› destartalado; ‹*house*› deteriorado, viejo y en mal estado **(b)** (infirm) ‹*person/animal*› decrépito

dedicate /'dedɪkeɪt/ *vt* **(a)** (devote) **to ~ sth TO sth/-ING** dedicar* algo A algo/+ INF **(b)** ‹*poem/book*› dedicar*

dedicated /'dedɪkeɪtəd ‖ 'dedɪkeɪtɪd/ *adj* **1** ‹*musician/nurse/teacher*› de gran dedicación, dedicado *or* entregado a su (*or* mi *etc*) trabajo **2** (Comput) (*before n*) dedicado

dedication /'dedɪ'keɪʃən/ *n* **1** [U] (devotion) dedicación *f*, entrega *f* **2** [C] (written message) dedicatoria *f*

deduce /dɪ'du:s ‖ dɪ'dju:s/ *vt* deducir*, inferir*

deduct /dɪ'dʌkt/ *vt* deducir*, descontar*

deduction /dɪ'dʌkʃən/ *n* **1** [U C] (subtraction) deducción *f*, descuento *m* **2** [U C] (reasoning, conclusion) deducción *f*

deed /di:d/ *n* **1** (action) hecho *m* **2** (Law) escritura *f*

deed poll *n* (BrE): **to change one's name by ~ ~** ≈ cambiarse el apellido oficialmente

deem /di:m/ *vt* (frml) considerar, juzgar*

deep¹ /di:p/ *adj* **-er, -est 1 (a)** ‹*water*› profundo; ‹*hole/pit*› profundo, hondo; ‹*gash*› profundo; ‹*dish*› hondo; ‹*pan*› alto; **the ditch is 6 ft ~** la zanja tiene 6 pies de profundidad **(b)** (horizontally) ‹*shelf*› profundo; **the soldiers were standing 12 ~** los soldados formaban columnas de 12 en fondo **2** ‹*sigh/groan*› profundo, hondo; **take a ~ breath** respire hondo **3 (a)** ‹*voice*› profundo, grave; ‹*note*› grave **(b)** ‹*color*› intenso, subido **4 (a)** (intense) ‹*sleep/love/impression*› profundo; **it is with ~ regret that** ... es con gran *or* profundo pesar que ... **(b)** ‹*thoughts*› profundo **(c)** ‹*mystery/secret*› profundo

deep² *adv* **-er, -est 1** (of penetration): **to dig ~** cavar hondo; **feelings run very ~ among the population** hay un sentir muy fuerte entre la población; **he looked ~ into her eyes** la miró fijamente a los ojos; **to go ~er (into sth)** ahondar *or* profundizar* más (en algo) **2** (situated far from edge): **~ in the forest** en lo profundo del bosque; **~ down you know I'm right** en el fondo sabes que tengo razón

deepen /'di:pən/ *vt* **1** ‹*canal/well*› hacer* más profundo *or* hondo **2** ‹*knowledge*› profundizar* *or* ahondar en; ‹*concern*› aumentar; ‹*friendship*› estrechar ■ ~ *vi* **1** «*gorge/river*» hacerse* *or* volverse* más hondo *or* profundo **2** «*concern/love*» hacerse* más profundo; «*friendship*» estrecharse; «*mystery*» crecer*, aumentar; «*crisis*» acentuarse*

deep: **~ end** *n* **the ~ end** (of swimming pool) la parte honda, lo hondo (fam); ***to throw sb in (at)***

the ~ end meter a algn de lleno en lo más difícil; **~ freeze** *n* congelador *m*, freezer *f* (AmL); **~-fry** /'di:p'fraɪ/ *vt* **-fries, -frying, -fried** freír* (*en abundante aceite*)

deeply /'di:pli/ *adv* **1** ‹*sigh*› profundamente; **to breathe ~** respirar hondo **2** ‹*think*› a fondo; ‹*concerned*› profundamente; ‹*interested*› sumamente

deep: **~-sea** /'di:p'si:/ *adj* (*before n*) **~-sea diving** buceo *m* de altura *or* en alta mar; **~-sea fishing** pesca *f* de altura; **~-seated** /'di:p'si:təd ‖ ˌdi:p'si:tɪd/ *adj* ‹*prejudice/conviction*› profundamente arraigado; ‹*problem*› de raíces profundas; **~-set** /'di:p'set/ *adj* ‹*eyes*› hundido

deer /dɪr ‖ dɪə(r)/ *n* (*pl* **~**) ciervo *m*, venado *m*

deface /dɪ'feɪs/ *vt* ‹*wall/notice*› pintarrajear

defamation /'defə'meɪʃən/ *n* [U] (frml) difamación *f*

default¹ /dɪ'fɔ:lt/ *n* [U] **1** (omission) omisión *f*; (on payments) mora *f*; (failure to appear) incomparecencia *f*; (Law) rebeldía *f* **2** (lack) falta *f*; **he was elected by ~** fue elegido por ausencia de otros candidatos; (*before n*) **~ option** (Comput) opción *f* por defecto

default² *vi* **(a)** (Fin) **to ~** (ON **sth**) no pagar* (algo) **(b)** (Law) estar* en rebeldía **(c)** (Sport) no presentarse

defeat¹ /dɪ'fi:t/ *n* [U C] **1** (by opponent) derrota *f* **2** (of motion, bill) (Adm, Govt) rechazo *m*

defeat² *vt* **1** ‹*opponent*› derrotar, vencer* **2** ‹*hopes/plans*› frustrar; **that would ~ the object of the exercise** eso iría en contra de lo que se pretende lograr **3** (Adm, Govt) ‹*opposition*› derrotar; ‹*bill/motion*› rechazar*

defeatist /dɪ'fi:təst ‖ dɪ'fi:tɪst/ *adj* derrotista

defect¹ /'di:fekt/ *n* defecto *m*; **a speech ~** un defecto en el habla

defect² /dɪ'fekt/ *vi* (Pol) desertar*, defeccionar (period)

defective /dɪ'fektɪv/ *adj* defectuoso

defector /dɪ'fektər ‖ dɪ'fektə(r)/ *n* desertor, -tora *m,f*

defence *etc* (BrE) ⇨ DEFENSE *etc*

defend /dɪ'fend/ *vt* defender* ■ **~** *vi* **1** (Law) actuar* por la defensa **2** (Sport): **he's better at ~ing** juega mejor como defensa

defendant /dɪ'fendənt/ *n* (Law) (in civil case) demandado, -da *m,f*; (in criminal case) acusado, -da *m,f*

defender /dɪ'fendər ‖ dɪ'fendə(r)/ *n* **(a)** (of cause, course of action, opinion) defensor, -sora *m,f* **(b)** (Sport) defensa *mf*

defending /dɪ'fendɪŋ/ *adj*: **the ~ champion** el actual campeón (*que defiende su título*)

defense, (BrE) **defence** /dɪ'fens, 'di:fens ‖ dɪ'fens/ *n* **1** [U] **(a)** (Mil) defensa *f* **(b)** (on personal level) defensa *f* **2** [C] **(a)** (protection) defensa *f*, protección *f* **(b)** (apologia) defensa *f* **3 defenses** *pl* (Mil, Med, Psych) defensas *fpl* **4** [C] (Law) defensa *f* **5 (a)** [U] (Sport) defensa *f* **(b)** [C] (in chess) defensa *f*

defenseless, (BrE) **defenceless** /dɪ'fensləs ‖ dɪ'fenslɪs/ *adj* indefenso

defensive /dɪ'fensɪv/ *adj* defensivo

defer /dɪ'fɜ:r ‖ dɪ'fɜ:(r)/ **-rr-** *vt* (frml) diferir* (frml), aplazar*, postergar* (esp AmL)

• **defer to** [*v* + *prep* + *o*] (frml) deferir* a (frml)

deference /'defərəns/ *n* [U] (frml) deferencia *f*

deferential /'defə'rentʃəl ‖ ˌdefə'renʃəl/ *adj* deferente

defiance /dɪ'faɪəns/ *n* [U] **an act of ~** un desafío, un acto de rebeldía; **in ~ of her orders** haciendo caso omiso de sus órdenes

defiant /dɪ'faɪənt/ *adj* ‹*attitude/tone*› desafiante; ‹*person*› rebelde

deficiency /dɪ'fɪʃənsi/ *n* (*pl* **-cies**) [C U] deficiencia *f*

deficient /dɪ'fɪʃənt/ *adj* (frml) deficiente, insuficiente

deficit /'defəsɪt ‖ 'defɪsɪt/ *n* déficit *m*

define /dɪ'faɪn/ *vt* **(a)** (state meaning of, describe) ‹*word/position*› definir **(b)** ‹*powers/duties*› delimitar **(c)** (characterize) distinguir*

definite /'defənət, 'defnət ‖ 'defɪnɪt/ *adj* **1 (a)** (final) ‹*date/price/offer*› definitivo, en firme **(b)** (certain) seguro, confirmado **(c)** (firm, categorical) ‹*tone*› firme, terminante **(d)** (distinct): **it's a ~ advantage/possibility** es, sin duda, una ventaja/posibilidad **2** ▶ 878 (Ling): **~ article** artículo *m* determinado *or* definido

definitely /'defənətli, 'defnətli ‖ 'defɪnɪtli/ *adv* **(a)** (without doubt): **it's ~ true** es indudablemente cierto; **he ~ said we should meet here** seguro que dijo que nos encontráramos aquí **(b)** (definitively) ‹*arrange/agree*› definitivamente

definition /'defə'nɪʃən ‖ ˌdefɪ'nɪʃən/ *n* **1** [C U] **(a)** (statement of meaning) definición *f*; **by ~** por definición **(b)** (categorization) definición *f*, delimitación *f*

definitive /dɪ'fɪnətɪv/ *adj* (*no comp*) **(a)** (final) ‹*verdict/victory*› definitivo **(b)** (authoritative) ‹*biography/study*› de mayor autoridad

deflate /dɪ'fleɪt/ *vt* **(a)** ‹*balloon/tire*› desinflar **(b)** (humble): **to ~ sb** bajarle los humos a algn **(c)** (depress) deprimir; **I felt ~d** me sentí por los suelos

deflation /dɪ'fleɪʃən/ *n* [U] deflación *f*

deflect /dɪ'flekt/ *vt* **to ~ sth** (FROM **sth**) desviar* algo (DE algo) ■ **~** *vi* desviarse*

defogger /'di:'fɔ:gər ‖ ˌdi:'fɒgə(r)/ *n* (AmE) desempañador *m*

deformed /dɪ'fɔ:rmd ‖ dɪ'fɔ:md/ *adj* deforme

deformity /dɪ'fɔ:rməti ‖ dɪ'fɔ:məti/ *n* [U C] (*pl* **-ties**) deformidad *f*

defraud /dɪ'frɔ:d/ *vt* ‹*person*› estafar

defray /dɪ'freɪ/ *vt* (frml) ‹*cost*› sufragar* (frml)

defrost /'di:'frɔ:st ‖ ˌdi:'frɒst/ *vt* ‹*food*› descongelar; ‹*refrigerator*› deshelar*, descongelar ■ **~** *vi* «*meat*» descongelarse; «*refrigerator*» deshelarse*, descongelarse

deft /deft/ *adj* **-er, -est** ‹*movement*› hábil, diestro

deftly /'deftli/ *adv* hábilmente, con destreza

defunct /dɪ'fʌŋkt/ *adj* ‹*idea/theory*› caduco; ‹*institution*› desaparecido, extinto, fenecido (frml)

defuse /'di:'fju:z/ *vt* ‹*bomb*› desactivar; ‹*situation*› distender*; ‹*crisis*› calmar

defy /dɪˈfaɪ/ *vt* **defies, defying, defied (a)** (disobey) ‹*order/authority*› desacatar, desobedecer* **(b)** (resist): **to ~ understanding/description** ser* incomprensible/indescriptible **(c)** (ignore) ‹*danger/death*› desafiar*

degenerate¹ /dɪˈdʒenəreɪt/ *vi* degenerar; «*health*» deteriorarse

degenerate² /dɪˈdʒenərət/ *adj* degenerado

degeneration /dɪˈdʒenəˈreɪʃən/ *n* [U] **(a)** (deterioration) degeneración *f*, deterioro *m* **(b)** (Med) (of tissue, organs) degeneración *f*

degrade /dɪˈgreɪd/ *vt* degradar

degrading /dɪˈgreɪdɪŋ/ *adj* degradante

degree /dɪˈgriː/ *n* **1** (level, amount) grado *m*, nivel *m*; **there's a ~ of truth in what she says** hay cierta verdad en lo que dice; ***to a ~*** (extremely) en grado sumo; (to some extent) hasta cierto punto **2** (grade, step) grado *m*; **first/third ~ burns** quemaduras *fpl* de primer/tercer grado; **first/second ~ murder** (in US) homicidio *m* en primer/segundo grado; ***by ~s*** gradualmente, paulatinamente **3** (Math, Geog, Meteo, Phys) grado *m*; **12 ~s below zero** 12 grados bajo cero; **this wine is 12 ~s proof** este vino es de *or* tiene 12 grados **4** (Educ) título *m*; **first ~** licenciatura *f*

dehydrated /ˈdiːharˈdreɪtəd ‖ ˌdiːharˈdreɪtɪd/ *adj* deshidratado; **to become ~** deshidratarse

dehydration /ˈdiːharˈdreɪʃən/ *n* [U] deshidratación *f*

deign /deɪn/ *vi* **to ~ to** + INF dignarse (A) + INF

deity /ˈdiːəti/ *n* (*pl* **-ties**) deidad *f*

dejected /dɪˈdʒektəd ‖ dɪˈdʒektɪd/ *adj* abatido, desalentado

Del = **Delaware**

delay¹ /dɪˈleɪ/ *vt* **1** (make late, hold up) retrasar, demorar (esp AmL) **2** (defer) ‹*decision/payment*› retrasar, demorar (esp AmL) ■ **~** *vi* tardar, demorar (esp AmL)

delay² *n* **(a)** [U] (waiting) tardanza *f*, dilación *f*, demora *f* (esp AmL) **(b)** [C] (holdup) retraso *m*, demora *f* (esp AmL); **~s can be expected on major roads** se puede esperar embotellamientos en las principales carreteras

delayed action /dɪˈleɪd/ *n* [U] acción *f* retardada

delectable /dɪˈlektəbəl/ *adj* **(a)** (delicious) delicioso, exquisito **(b)** (delightful) delicioso, encantador

delegate¹ /ˈdelɪgeɪt/ *vt/i* delegar*

delegate² /ˈdelɪgət/ *n* delegado, -da *m,f*

delegation /ˈdelɪˈgeɪʃən/ *n* [C U] delegación *f*

delete /dɪˈliːt/ *vt* suprimir, eliminar; (by crossing out) tachar

deliberate¹ /dɪˈlɪbərət, -brət/ *adj* **1** (intentional) ‹*act/attempt*› deliberado, intencionado **2 (a)** (considered) reflexivo **(b)** (unhurried) pausado, lento

deliberate² /dɪˈlɪbəreɪt/ *vi* (frml) **to ~ (ABOUT/ON sth)** deliberar (SOBRE algo) ■ **~** *vt* (frml) deliberar sobre

deliberately /dɪˈlɪbərətli, -brətli/ *adv* **1** (intentionally) adrede, a propósito **2** (unhurriedly) pausadamente, con parsimonia

deliberation /dɪˈlɪbəˈreɪʃən/ *n* (frml) **(a)** [U] (consideration) deliberación *f* **(b) deliberations** *pl* (decision-making) deliberaciones *fpl*

delicacy /ˈdelɪkəsi/ *n* (*pl* **-cies**) **1** [U] **(a)** (fineness, intricacy) delicadeza *f*, lo delicado; (fragility) fragilidad *f*, lo delicado **(b)** (tact) delicadeza *f* **(c)** (subtleness) lo delicado **2** [C] (choice food) manjar *m*, exquisitez *f*

delicate /ˈdelɪkət/ *adj* **1 (a)** (fine, intricate) ‹*lace/features*› delicado; ‹*workmanship*› fino, esmerado **(b)** (fragile, needing care) delicado **2 (a)** (needing skill, tact) delicado **(c)** (tactful) delicado, discreto **3** (subtle) ‹*shade/taste*› delicado

delicately /ˈdelɪkətli/ *adv* **1** ‹*carve/paint*› con delicadeza, delicadamente **2** ‹*treat*› con delicadeza **3** ‹*patterned/perfumed*› delicadamente

delicatessen /ˈdelɪkəˈtesən/ *n* charcutería *f*, rotisería *f* (CS), salsamentaria *f* (Col), salchichonería *f* (Méx)

delicious /dɪˈlɪʃəs/ *adj* delicioso

delight¹ /dɪˈlaɪt/ *n* **(a)** [U] (joy) placer *m*, deleite *m*; **to take ~ in sth** disfrutar *or* gozar* con algo **(b)** [C] (source of joy) placer *m*

delight² *vt* **(a)** (make very happy) llenar de alegría; **his success ~ed them** su éxito los llenó de alegría **(b)** (give pleasure to) deleitar; **the clown ~ed the children** el payaso hizo las delicias de *or* deleitó a los niños ■ **~** *vi* **to ~** IN **-ING** deleitarse + GER

delighted /dɪˈlaɪtəd ‖ dɪˈlaɪtɪd/ *adj* ‹*grin/look*› de alegría; **I'm ~ (that) you can come** me alegra mucho que puedas venir; **to be ~** WITH **sth/sb** estar* encantado CON algo/algn

delightful /dɪˈlaɪtfəl/ *adj* ‹*weather/evening*› muy agradable, delicioso; ‹*person*› encantador; ‹*dress*› precioso

delineate /dɪˈlɪnieɪt/ *vt* (frml) **(a)** (draw) trazar*, delinear **(b)** (describe) ‹*problem*› definir

delinquency /dɪˈlɪŋkwənsi/ *n* [U] (Law, Sociol) delincuencia *f*

delinquent /dɪˈlɪŋkwənt/ *n* delincuente *mf*

delirious /dɪˈlɪriəs/ *adj* **(a)** (Med) delirante; **to be ~** delirar, desvariar* **(b)** (wildly excited, happy) (colloq) loco de alegría (fam)

deliver /dɪˈlɪvər ‖ dɪˈlɪvə(r)/ *vt* **1 (a)** (hand over) entregar* **(b)** (distribute) repartir (*a domicilio*) **2 (a)** (administer) ‹*blow/punch*› propinar, asestar **(b)** (issue) ‹*ultimatum/lecture/sermon*› dar*; ‹*warning*› hacer*; ‹*speech*› pronunciar; ‹*judgment*› dictar, pronunciar, emitir **(c)** (produce, provide): **he promised much, but ~ed little** cumplió muy poco de lo mucho que había prometido **(d)** (Sport) ‹*ball*› lanzar* **(e)** (in elections) (AmE) ‹*state*› ganar **3** (Med): **her husband ~ed the baby** su marido la asistió en el parto ■ **~** *vi* **1** (Busn): **we ~ free of charge** hacemos reparto(s) a domicilio gratuitamente **2** (produce the necessary) (colloq) cumplir

delivery /dɪˈlɪvəri/ *n* (*pl* **-ries**) **1 (a)** [U] (act) entrega *f*; (*before n*) **~ charges** gastos *mpl* de envío *or* transporte; **~ man** repartidor *m*; **~ truck** *o* (BrE) **van** camioneta *f or* furgoneta *f* de los repartos **(b)** [C] (occasion) reparto *m*; **is there a ~ on Saturdays?** ¿hay reparto los sábados? **(c)** [C] (consignment) partida *f*, remesa *f* **2** [C] (of baby) parto *m*, alumbramiento *m* (frml) **3** [U] (manner of speaking) expresión *f* oral

delta /'deltə/ *n* delta *m*

delude /dɪ'lu:d/ *vt* engañar

deluge /'delju:dʒ/ *n* **1 (a)** (flood) inundación *f* **(b)** (downpour) diluvio *m* **2** (of protests, questions, letters) aluvión *m*, avalancha *f*

delusion /dɪ'lu:ʒən/ *n* (mistaken idea) error *m*; (vain hope) falsa ilusión *f*

deluxe /də'lʊks/ *adj* de lujo

delve /delv/ *vi* (liter) **to ~ INTO sth** ahondar EN algo; **to ~ into the past** hurgar* en el pasado

demand¹ /dɪ'mænd ‖ dɪ'mɑ:nd/ *vt* **1** «*person*» (call for, insist on) exigir*; **the unions are ~ing better conditions** los sindicatos reclaman mejores condiciones **2** (require) ‹*determination/perseverance*› exigir*, requerir*

demand² *n* **1** [C] (claim) exigencia *f*; (Lab Rel, Pol) reivindicación *f*, reclamo *m*; (request) petición *f*, pedido *m* (AmL); **the ~s of the job** las exigencias del trabajo; **abortion on ~** libre aborto *m* **2** [U] (requirement) demanda *f*; **he's in great ~** está muy solicitado, es popular

demanding /dɪ'mændɪŋ ‖ dɪ'mɑ:ndɪŋ/ *adj* ‹*job*› que exige mucho; ‹*book/music*› difícil; ‹*teacher*› exigente

demarcation /'di:mɑ:r'keɪʃən ‖ ˌdi:mɑ:'keɪʃən/ *n* [U] demarcación *f*; (*before n*) **~ line** línea *f* de demarcación

demean /dɪ'mi:n/ *vt* (frml) degradar

demeaning /dɪ'mi:nɪŋ/ *adj* degradante

demeanor, (BrE) **demeanour** /dɪ'mi:nər ‖ dɪ'mi:nə(r)/ *n* [U] (frml) **(a)** (behavior) comportamiento *m*, conducta *f* **(b)** (bearing) porte *m*

demented /dɪ'mentəd ‖ dɪ'mentɪd/ *adj* ‹*person*› demente; ‹*screams/mutterings*› enloquecido

dementia /dɪ'mentʃə ‖ dɪ'menʃə/ *n* [U] demencia *f*

demerara (sugar) /'demə'rɑ:rə ‖ ˌdemə'reərə/ *n* [U] (BrE) azúcar *f* morena, azúcar *m* moreno

demerit /di:'merət ‖ di:'merɪt/ *n* (frml) demérito *m* (frml)

demise /dɪ'maɪz/ *n* (*no pl*) (frml) **(a)** (death) fallecimiento *m* (frml), deceso *m* (AmL frml) **(b)** (end) desaparición *f*

demister /'di:'mɪstər ‖ ˌdi:'mɪstə(r)/ *n* (BrE) desempañador *m*

demo /'deməʊ/ *n* (*pl* **demos**) **1** (Mus) demostración *f*; (*before n*) **~ tape** cinta *f* de demostración **2** (protest) (BrE colloq) manifestación *f*

demobilize /'dɪ'məʊbəlaɪz ‖ di:'məʊbɪlaɪz/ *vt* desmovilizar*

democracy /dɪ'mɑ:krəsi ‖ dɪ'mɒkrəsi/ *n* [U C] (*pl* **-cies**) democracia *f*

democrat /'deməkræt/ *n* **(a)** (believer in democracy) demócrata *mf* **(b) Democrat** (in US) demócrata *mf*

democratic /'demə'krætɪk/ *adj* **(a)** ‹*country/election*› democrático **(b) Democratic** (in US) demócrata

demographic /'demə'græfɪk/ *adj* demográfico

demography /dɪ'mɑ:grəfi ‖ dɪ'mɒgrəfi/ *n* [U] demografía *f*

demolish /dɪ'mɑ:lɪʃ ‖ dɪ'mɒlɪʃ/ *vt* ‹*structure/building*› demoler*, derribar, echar abajo; ‹*argument/theory*› demoler*, echar por tierra

demolition /'demə'lɪʃən/ *n* [U C] (of building) demolición *f*, derribo *m*; (of theory) demolición *f*, destrucción *f*

demon /'di:mən/ *n* demonio *m*

demonstrate /'demənstreɪt/ *vt* **(a)** (show) ‹*need/ability*› demostrar* **(b)** (Marketing) hacer* una demostración de ■ *~ vi* (Pol) manifestarse*

demonstration /'demən'streɪʃən/ *n* **1 (a)** (expression) muestra *f*, demostración *f* **(b)** (display) demostración *f* **2** (Pol) manifestación *f*

demonstrative /dɪ'mɑ:nstrətɪv ‖ dɪ'mɒnstrətɪv/ *adj* efusivo, expresivo, demostrativo (AmL)

demonstrator /'demənstreɪtər ‖ 'demənstreɪtə(r)/ *n* manifestante *mf*

demoralize /dɪ'mɔ:rəlaɪz ‖ dɪ'mɒrəlaɪz/ *vt* desmoralizar*

demoralizing /dɪ'mɔ:rəlaɪzɪŋ ‖ dɪ'mɒrəlaɪzɪŋ/ *adj* desalentador, desmoralizante

demote /dɪ'məʊt, 'di:-/ *vt* (in organization) bajar de categoría; (Mil) degradar

demur /dɪ'mɜ:r ‖ dɪ'mɜ:(r)/ *vi* **-rr-** (frml) objetar

demure /dɪ'mjʊr ‖ dɪ'mjʊə(r)/ *adj* recatado

den /den/ *n* **1** (of animals, thieves) guarida *f* **2** (room) (colloq) cuarto *m* de estar; (for study, work) estudio *m*

denial /dɪ'naɪəl/ *n* **1** [U C] (of accusation, fact): **to issue a ~ of sth** desmentir* algo **2** [U C] (of request, rights) denegación *f* **3** [U C] (repudiation) negación *f*, rechazo *m* **4** [U] (abstinence) renuncia *f*

denier /'denjər ‖ 'denɪə(r)/ *n* denier *m*

denigrate /'denɪgreɪt/ *vt* (frml) ‹*character/person*› denigrar; ‹*effort*› menospreciar

denim /'denəm ‖ 'denɪm/ *n* [U] (Tex) tela *f* vaquera *or* de jeans, mezclilla *f* (Chi, Méx); (*before n*) ‹*jacket/skirt*› vaquero, tejano (Esp), de mezclilla (Chi, Méx)

Denmark /'denmɑ:rk ‖ 'denmɑ:k/ *n* Dinamarca *f*

denomination /dɪ'nɑ:mə'neɪʃən ‖ dɪˌnɒmɪ'neɪʃən/ *n* **1** (Relig) confesión *f* **2** (of currency) valor *m*, denominación *f* (AmL)

denominator /dɪ'nɑ:məneɪtər ‖ dɪ'nɒmɪneɪtə(r)/ *n* (Math) denominador *m*

denote /dɪ'nəʊt/ *vt* denotar

denounce /dɪ'naʊns/ *vt* denunciar

dense /dens/ *adj* **denser, densest 1 (a)** (closely spaced) ‹*forest/jungle*› espeso; ‹*population/traffic*› denso; ‹*crowd*› compacto, apretado **(b)** (thick) ‹*fog/mist/smoke*› denso, espeso **(c)** (Phys) denso **(d)** (complicated) ‹*prose/article*› denso **2** (stupid) (colloq) burro (fam), duro de entendederas (fam)

densely /'densli/ *adv* ‹*populated/forested*› densamente; ‹*packed*› apretadamente

density /'densəti/ *n* [U C] (*pl* **-ties**) densidad *f*; (of fog) lo espeso, densidad *f*

dent¹ /dent/ *n* (in metal) abolladura *f*, abollón *m*; (in wood) marca *f*

dent² *vt* ‹*metal*› abollar; ‹*wood*› hacer* una marca en; ‹*popularity*› afectar; ‹*pride*› hacer* mella en

dental /ˈdentḷ/ *adj* dental; ‹*school*› de odontología

dental floss /flɑːs ‖ flɒs/ *n* [U] hilo *m or* seda *f* dental

dentist /ˈdentəst ‖ ˈdentɪst/ *n* dentista *mf*, odontólogo, -ga *m, f* (frml)

dentistry /ˈdentəstri ‖ ˈdentɪstri/ *n* [U] odontología *f*

dentures /ˈdentʃərz ‖ ˈdentʃəz/ *pl n* dentadura *f* postiza

deny /dɪˈnaɪ/ *vt* **denies, denying, denied 1** ‹*accusation/fact*› negar*; ‹*rumors*› desmentir* **2** (refuse) ‹*request*› denegar*

deodorant /diːˈəʊdərənt/ *n* [C U] desodorante *m*

depart /dɪˈpɑːrt ‖ dɪˈpɑːt/ *vi* (Transp) salir*, partir (frml); «*person*» (frml) partir (frml), salir*

department /dɪˈpɑːrtmənt ‖ dɪˈpɑːtmənt/ *n* **1** (of store) sección *f*; (of company) departamento *m*, sección *f* **2 (a)** (Govt) ministerio *m*, secretaría *f* (Méx) **(b)** (AmE Adm): **the police/fire ~** el cuerpo de policía/bomberos **3** (Educ) departamento *m*

department store *n* (grandes) almacenes *mpl*, tienda *f* de departamentos (Méx)

departure /dɪˈpɑːrtʃər ‖ dɪˈpɑːtʃə(r)/ *n* [U C] (Transp) salida *f*, partida *f* (frml); (of person) (frml) partida *f* (frml), ida *f*; **point of ~** punto *m* de partida; **a ~ from the norm** una desviación de la norma; (*before n*) **~ lounge** sala *f* de embarque

depend /dɪˈpend/ *vi* **to ~ ON sb/sth** depender DE algn/algo

dependable /dɪˈpendəbəl/ *adj* ‹*person*› formal, digno de confianza; ‹*ally/workman*› digno de confianza

dependant, (AmE also) **dependent** /dɪˈpendənt/ *n* carga *f* familiar, familiar *mf* a su (*or* mi *etc*) cargo

dependence /dɪˈpendəns/ *n* [U] dependencia *f*

dependent¹ /dɪˈpendənt/ *adj* **(a)** (reliant) (*pred*) **to be ~ ON sth/sb** depender DE algo/algn **(b)** (conditional) (*pred*) **to be ~ ON sth** depender DE algo

dependent² *n* (AmE) ⇒ DEPENDANT

depict /dɪˈpɪkt/ *vt* (frml) **(a)** (portray) representar **(b)** (describe) describir*, pintar

depiction /dɪˈpɪkʃən/ *n* [U C] (frml) **(a)** (representation) representación *f* **(b)** (description) descripción *f*

depilatory /dɪˈpɪlətɔːri ‖ dɪˈpɪlətri/ *n* [C U] (*pl* **-ries**) depilatorio *m*

deplete /dɪˈpliːt/ *vt* (reduce) ‹*supply/stock*› reducir*; (exhaust) ‹*energy source*› agotar

deplorable /dɪˈplɔːrəbəl/ *adj* **(a)** (disgraceful) deplorable, vergonzoso **(b)** (regrettable) lamentable

deplore /dɪˈplɔːr ‖ dɪˈplɔː(r)/ *vt* (frml) **(a)** (condemn) deplorar, condenar **(b)** (regret) deplorar, lamentar

deploy /dɪˈplɔɪ/ *vt* **1** (position) (Mil) desplegar* **2** (distribute, use) (frml) utilizar*, hacer* uso de

deport /dɪˈpɔːrt ‖ dɪˈpɔːt/ *vt* deportar

deportation /ˈdiːpɔːrˈteɪʃən ‖ ˌdiːpɔːˈteɪʃən/ *n* [U C] deportación *f*

deportment /dɪˈpɔːrtmənt ‖ dɪˈpɔːtmənt/ *n* [U] (frml) **(a)** (carriage) porte *m* **(b)** (conduct) conducta *f*

depose /dɪˈpəʊz/ *vt* ‹*dictator/ruler*› deponer*, derrocar*; ‹*champion/king*› destronar

deposit¹ /dɪˈpɑːzət ‖ dɪˈpɒzɪt/ *vt* **1 (a)** (set down) depositar, poner* **(b)** (Geol) ‹*silt*› depositar **2 (a)** (leave) depositar **(b)** ‹*money*› depositar, ingresar (Esp)

deposit² *n* **1 (a)** (payment into account) depósito *m*, ingreso *m* (Esp); (*before n*) **~ account** cuenta *f* de ahorros **(b)** (down payment — on large amounts) depósito *m*, entrega *f* inicial; (— on small amounts) depósito *m*, señal *f*, seña *f* (RPl) **(c)** (security) depósito *m*, fianza *f* **2** (accumulation — of silt, mud) depósito *m*; (— of dust) capa *f* **3** (Min) (of gas) depósito *m*; (of gold, copper) yacimiento *m*

depot /ˈdiːpəʊ ‖ ˈdepəʊ/ *n* **1 (a)** (storehouse) depósito *m*, almacén *m* **(b)** (Mil) depósito *m* **2** (esp AmE) (bus station) terminal *f or* (Chi) *m*, estación *f* de autobuses; (train station) estación *f* **3** (esp BrE) (storage area) **(a)** (for buses) garage *m* (esp AmL), cochera *f* (Esp), depósito *m* (Chi) **(b)** (for trains) depósito *m* de locomotoras

depraved /dɪˈpreɪvd/ *adj* depravado

depravity /dɪˈprævəti/ *n* [U] depravación *f*

deprecating /ˈdeprɪkeɪtɪŋ/ *adj* (frml) **(a)** (disapproving) ‹*remark*› de desaprobación, reprobatorio **(b)** (belittling) ‹*smile/laugh*› de desprecio

depreciate /dɪˈpriːʃieɪt/ *vt* (Fin) depreciar ■ **~** *vi* (Fin) depreciarse

depress /dɪˈpres/ *vt* **1** (sadden) deprimir, abatir **2** (press down) (frml) ‹*lever*› bajar; ‹*button*› pulsar (frml) **3** (Econ) ‹*market*› deprimir; ‹*prices/wages*› reducir*, hacer* bajar

depressed /dɪˈprest/ *adj* **1** (dejected) deprimido, abatido; **to get ~** deprimirse, dejarse abatir **2** (Econ) ‹*economy/market/area*› deprimido

depressing /dɪˈpresɪŋ/ *adj* deprimente

depression /dɪˈpreʃən/ *n* **1** [U] (despondency) depresión *f*, abatimiento *m* **2** [C] (in flat surface) depresión *f* **3** [C] (Econ) depresión *f*, crisis *f*

deprivation /ˈdeprəˈveɪʃən ‖ ˌdeprɪˈveɪʃən/ *n* [U C] (lack, loss) privación *f*; (hardship) privaciones *fpl*, penurias *fpl*

deprive /dɪˈpraɪv/ *vt*: **to ~ sb OF sth** privar a algn DE algo

deprived /dɪˈpraɪvd/ *adj* ‹*child*› carenciado, desventajado; ‹*region*› carenciado

dept (= **department**) Dpto.

depth /depθ/ *n* **1** [U C] **(a)** (of hole, water) profundidad *f*; ***out of one's ~***: **when it comes to computers I'm out of my ~** estoy muy flojo en informática; **don't go out of your ~** (in water) no vayas donde no haces pie *or* no tocas fondo **(b)** (of shelf, cupboard) profundidad *f*, fondo *m*; (of hem) ancho *m* **2** [U C] (of emotion, knowledge) profundidad *f*; **to study sth in ~** estudiar algo a fondo *or* en profundidad **3** (of voice) profundidad *f*; (of sound) intensidad *f* **4 depths** *pl n*: **in the ~s of the ocean** en las profundidades del océano; **in the ~s of despair** en lo más hondo de la desesperación

deputation /ˈdepjəˈteɪʃən ‖ ˌdepjʊˈteɪʃən/ *n* delegación *f*

deputy /'depjəti/ *n* (*pl* **-ties**) **1 (a)** (second-in-command) segundo, -da *m,f*; (substitute) suplente *mf*, reemplazo *mf* **(b)** **~ (sheriff)** (AmE Law) ayudante *mf* del sheriff **2** (Govt) diputado, -da *m,f*

derail /dɪ'reɪl/ *vt* **(a)** ‹*train*› hacer* descarrilar **(b)** (upset) ‹*plan*› desbaratar

deranged /dɪ'reɪndʒd/ *adj* trastornado

derby /'dɜːrbi ‖'dɑːbi/ *n* (*pl* **derbies**) **1** (Sport): **the D~** (in UK) el Derby, el clásico de Epsom; **the Kentucky D~** el Derby de Kentucky **2** (hat) (AmE) bombín *m*, sombrero *m* de hongo

deregulate /'diː'regjəleɪt ‖ ,diː'regjʊleɪt/ *vt* desregular, liberalizar*

deregulation /'diː'regjə'leɪʃən ‖ diː,regjʊ'leɪʃən/ *n* [U] desregulación *f*, liberalización *f*

derelict /'derəlɪkt/ *adj* abandonado y en ruinas

deride /dɪ'raɪd/ *vt* ridiculizar*, burlarse de

derision /dɪ'rɪʒən/ *n* [U] escarnio *m* (frml), irrisión *f* (frml)

derisive /dɪ'raɪsɪv/ *adj* ‹*smile/laughter*› burlón; ‹*attitude/remark*› desdeñoso y burlón

derisory /dɪ'raɪzəri/ *adj* ‹*sum/offer*› irrisorio

derivative¹ /dɪ'rɪvətɪv/ *adj* (unoriginal) ‹*novel*› carente de originalidad; ‹*plot/theme*› manido, trillado; ‹*artist/writer*› adocenado

derivative² *n* (in industry) derivado *m*

derive /dɪ'raɪv/ *vt* **children can ~ great enjoyment from the simplest things** las cosas más simples pueden dar enorme placer a un niño; **the name is ~d from the Greek** el nombre viene *or* deriva del griego ■ **~** *vi* **to ~ FROM sth** «*attitude/problem*» provenir* DE algo; «*idea*» tener* su origen EN algo; (Ling) derivar(se) DE algo

dermatitis /'dɜːrmə'taɪtəs ‖ ,dɜːmə'taɪtɪs/ *n* [U] dermatitis *f*

derogatory /dɪ'rɑːgətɔːri ‖ dɪ'rɒgətri/ *adj* despectivo, peyorativo

descant /'deskænt/ *n* contrapunto *m*

descend /dɪ'send/ *vi* (move downwards) descender* (frml), bajar; **in ~ing order of importance** en orden decreciente *or* descendente de importancia; **don't ~ to his level** no te pongas a su nivel ■ **~** *vt* descender* (frml), bajar

descendant /dɪ'sendənt/ *n* descendiente *mf*

descended /dɪ'sendəd ‖ dɪ'sendɪd/ *adj* (*pred*) **to be ~ FROM sb** ser* descendiente DE algn, descender* DE algn

descendent *n* (AmE) ⇒ DESCENDANT

descent /dɪ'sent/ *n* **1** [U C] **(a)** (by climbers, plane) descenso *m*, bajada *f* **(b)** (in terrain) pendiente *f*, bajada *f* **2** [U] (decline) caída *f* **3** [U] (lineage) ascendencia *f*

describe /dɪ'skraɪb/ *vt* describir*; **he ~s himself as a socialist** se define como socialista

description /dɪ'skrɪpʃən/ *n* [C U] descripción *f*; **of every ~** de todo tipo, de toda clase

descriptive /dɪ'skrɪptɪv/ *adj* descriptivo

desecrate /'desɪkreɪt/ *vt* profanar

desert¹ /'dezərt ‖ 'dezət/ *n* (Geog) desierto *m*; (*before n*) ‹*region/climate*› desértico; ‹*tribe/sand*› del desierto

desert² /dɪ'zɜːrt ‖ dɪ'zɜːt/ *vt* **(a)** (frml) ‹*place*› abandonar, huir* de **(b)** ‹*family*› abandonar; ‹*cause*› desertar de ■ **~** *vi* (Mil) desertar

deserted /dɪ'zɜːrtəd ‖ dɪ'zɜːtɪd/ *adj* **(a)** ‹*streets/village*› desierto **(b)** ‹*husband/wife*› abandonado

deserter /dɪ'zɜːrtər ‖ dɪ'zɜːtə(r)/ *n* desertor, -tora *m,f*

desertion /dɪ'zɜːrʃən ‖ dɪ'zɜːʃən/ *n* [U] **(a)** (Mil) deserción *f* **(b)** (of family, place) abandono *m*

desert island *n* isla *f* desierta

deserts /dɪ'zɜːrts ‖ dɪ'zɜːts/ *pl n*: ***to get one's just ~*** recibir su (*or* tu *etc*) merecido

deserve /dɪ'zɜːrv ‖ dɪ'zɜːv/ *vt* merecer(se)*; **they got what they ~d** se llevaron su merecido

deserving /dɪ'zɜːrvɪŋ ‖ dɪ'zɜːvɪŋ/ *adj* ‹*cause/case*› meritorio; **the ~ poor** los pobres dignos de ayuda

desiccated /'desɪkeɪtəd ‖ 'desɪkeɪtɪd/ *adj* seco; **~ coconut** coco *m* rallado

design¹ /dɪ'zaɪn/ *n* **1** [C U] **(a)** (of product, car, machine) diseño *m*; (drawing) diseño *m*, boceto *m* **(b)** (pattern, decoration) diseño *m*, motivo *m*, dibujo *m* **(c)** (product, model) modelo *m* **2** [U] **(a)** (Art) diseño *m* **(b)** (style) estilo *m*, líneas *fpl* **3 (a)** [C] (plan) (liter) plan *m*; **by ~** deliberadamente **(b)** **designs** *pl n* (intentions) propósitos *mpl*, designios *mpl* (liter)

design² *vt* ‹*house/garden*› diseñar, proyectar; ‹*dress/product*› diseñar; ‹*course/program*› planear, estructurar; **a statement ~ed to reassure the public** una declaración destinada a tranquilizar al público

designate¹ /'dezɪgneɪt/ *vt* **1** (name officially) nombrar, designar **2** (call) (frml) designar

designate² /'dezɪgneɪt, -nət ‖ 'dezɪgnət/ *adj* (*after n*): **the governor ~** quien ha sido nombrado gobernador

designer /dɪ'zaɪnər ‖ dɪ'zaɪnə(r)/ *n* diseñador, -dora *m,f*; ‹*clothes/jeans*› de diseño exclusivo; ‹*furniture/pen*› de diseño

desirable /dɪ'zaɪrəbəl ‖ dɪ'zaɪərəbəl/ *adj* **(a)** ‹*property/location*› atractivo **(b)** (sexually) ‹*man/woman*› atractivo, deseable, apetecible **(c)** ‹*outcome*› deseable, conveniente; ‹*option*› conveniente, aconsejable

desire¹ /dɪ'zaɪr ‖ dɪ'zaɪə(r)/ *n* **1** [C] (wish) deseo *m*, anhelo *m* (liter) **2** [U] (lust) deseo *m*

desire² *vt* **(a)** (want) ‹*happiness/success*› desear; **to leave a lot to be ~d** dejar bastante que desear **(b)** (lust after) ‹*person*› desear

desirous /dɪ'zaɪrəs ‖ dɪ'zaɪərəs/ *adj* (frml) (*pred*): **we are ~ of your success** le deseamos éxito

desist /dɪ'zɪst/ *vi* (frml) **to ~ (FROM sth/-ING)** (cease) desistir (DE algo/+ INF); (abstain) abstenerse* (DE algo/+ INF)

desk /desk/ *n* **(a)** (table) escritorio *m*, mesa *f* de trabajo; (in school) pupitre *m*; (*before n*) ‹*lamp*› de escritorio, de (sobre)mesa; **a ~ job** un trabajo de oficina **(b)** (service counter) mostrador *m* **(c)** (Journ) sección *f*

desktop /'desktɑːp ‖ 'desktɒp/ *adj* (*before n*) ‹*calculator/computer*› de escritorio, de (sobre)mesa; **~ publishing** autoedición *f*, edición *f* electrónica

desolate /'desələt/ *adj* **1** (deserted) ‹*place/landscape*› desierto, desolado **2** ‹*person*› desconsolado, desolado; ‹*outlook/existence*› sombrío, lúgubre

despair¹ /dɪ'sper ‖ dɪ'speə(r)/ *n* [U] desesperación *f*; **to be in ~** estar* desesperado

despair² *vi* perder* las esperanzas, desesperar(se); **honestly, I ~ of you!** ¡francamente, eres un caso perdido!

despairing /dɪ'sperɪŋ ‖ dɪ'speərɪŋ/ *adj* ‹*look/cry*› de desesperación

despatch /dɪ'spætʃ/ *vt/n* ⇒ DISPATCH¹˒²

desperate /'despərət/ *adj* **1** (frantic) ‹*person/attempt*› desesperado; **to be ~** estar* desesperado **2** (critical) ‹*state/situation*› grave, desesperado; ‹*need*› apremiante

desperately /'despərətli/ *adv* ‹*struggle*› desesperadamente; ‹*need*› urgentemente, con urgencia

desperation /'despə'reɪʃən/ *n* [U] desesperación *f*

despicable /dɪ'spɪkəbəl/ *adj* vil, despreciable

despise /dɪ'spaɪz/ *vt* despreciar (profundamente)

despite /dɪ'spaɪt/ *prep* a pesar de

despondent /dɪ'spɑːndənt ‖ dɪ'spɒndənt/ *adj* abatido, descorazonado

despot /'despɑːt ‖ 'despɒt/ *n* déspota *mf*

dessert /dɪ'zɜːrt ‖ dɪ'zɜːt/ *n* [C U] postre *m*

dessertspoon /dɪ'zɜːrtspuːn ‖ dɪ'zɜːtspuːn/ *n* cuchara *f* de postre

destabilize /'diː'steɪbəlaɪz/ *vt* desestabilizar*

destination /'destə'neɪʃən ‖ ˌdestɪ'neɪʃən/ *n* **(a)** (end of journey) destino *m* **(b)** (purpose) meta *f*

destined /'destənd ‖ 'destɪnd/ *adj* (*pred*) **1** (fated) **to be ~ to + INF** estar* (pre)destinado A + INF **2 (a)** (intended) **~ FOR sth** destinado A algo **(b)** (bound, on way): **~ for the West Indies** con destino al Caribe

destiny /'destəni ‖ 'destɪni/ *n* [C U] (*pl* **-nies**) destino *m*, sino *m* (liter)

destitute /'destətuːt ‖ 'destɪtjuːt/ *adj* indigente

destroy /dɪ'strɔɪ/ *vt* **(a)** (ruin, wreck) ‹*building/forest*› destruir*; ‹*reputation/confidence*› acabar con; ‹*life*› arruinar **(b)** ‹*animal*› sacrificar* (euf)

destroyer /dɪ'strɔɪər ‖ dɪ'strɔɪə(r)/ *n* destructor *m*

destruction /dɪ'strʌkʃən/ *n* [U] **1** (of city, books, forest) destrucción *f*; (of reputation, civilization) ruina *f*, destrucción *f*; (slaughter) exterminación *f* **2** (cause of downfall) (frml) ruina *f*, perdición *f* **3** (damage) destrucción *f*, estragos *mpl*, destrozos *mpl*

destructive /dɪ'strʌktɪv/ *adj* ‹*storm/weapon*› destructor; ‹*tendency*› destructivo; ‹*child*› destrozón; ‹*criticism*› destructivo, negativo

desultory /'desəltɔːri ‖ 'dezəltəri/ *adj* ‹*effort/attempt*› desganado

detach /dɪ'tætʃ/ *vt* (separate) separar, quitar; (unstick) despegar*; **the headrest can be ~ed** el apoyacabezas se puede desmontar *or* quitar

detachable /dɪ'tætʃəbəl/ *adj* ‹*cover*› de quita y pon, de quitar y poner; ‹*lining*› desmontable

detached /dɪ'tætʃt/ *adj* **1** ‹*person/manner*› (aloof) distante, indiferente; (objective) objetivo, imparcial **2** (BrE) ‹*house*› no adosado

detachment /dɪ'tætʃmənt/ *n* **1** [U] (aloofness) distancia *f*, indiferencia *f*; (objectivity) objetividad *f*, imparcialidad *f* **2** [U] (act of detaching) (frml) desprendimiento *m* **3** [C] (Mil) destacamento *m*

detail¹ /dɪ'teɪl, 'diːteɪl ‖'diːteɪl/ *n* **1** [C] **(a)** (particular) detalle *m*, pormenor *m*; **he asked for further ~s** pidió más información *or* información más detallada **(b)** (embellishment) detalle *m* **(c)** (insignificant matter) minucia *f*, detalle *m* (sin importancia) **2** [U] (minutiae) detalles *mpl*; **to go into ~** entrar en detalles *or* pormenores; **to explain sth in ~** explicar* algo detalladamente *or* minuciosamente

detail² *vt* **1** (describe) exponer* en detalle, detallar **2** (Mil) destacar*

detailed /'diːteɪld/ *adj* ‹*description*› detallado, minucioso, pormenorizado; ‹*examination*› minucioso, detenido

detain /dɪ'teɪn/ *vt* **(a)** (delay) (frml): **don't let me ~ you** no quiero entretenerlo *or* demorarlo **(b)** (in custody) detener*

detect /dɪ'tekt/ *vt* ‹*object/substance*› detectar

detection /dɪ'tekʃən/ *n* [U] **1** (of error) descubrimiento *m*; (of act, crime, criminal): **to escape ~** pasar desapercibido *or* inadvertido **2** (of substance) detección *f*

detective /dɪ'tektɪv/ *n* (private) detective *mf*; (in police force) agente *mf*, oficial *mf*; (*before n*) **~ story** novela *f* policíaca *or* policial

detector /dɪ'tektər ‖ dɪ'tektə(r)/ *n* detector *m*

detente /deɪ'tɑːnt/ *n* [U] (Pol) distensión *f*

detention /dɪ'tentʃən ‖ dɪ'tenʃən/ *n* [U] **1** (in custody) detención *f* **2** (Educ): **to be in ~** estar* castigado

deter /dɪ'tɜːr ‖ dɪ'tɜː(r)/ *vt* **-rr-** ‹*person*› disuadir, hacer* disuadir; ‹*crime/war*› impedir*; **to ~ sb FROM sth/-ING** disuadir a algn DE algo/+ INF

detergent /dɪ'tɜːrdʒənt ‖ dɪ'tɜːdʒənt/ *n* [U C] (Chem) detergente *m*; (for clothes) detergente *m*; (for dishes) lavavajillas *m*

deteriorate /dɪ'tɪriəreɪt ‖ dɪ'tɪərieretɪt/ *vi* «*health/relationship/material*» deteriorarse; «*weather/work*» empeorar

deterioration /dɪ'tɪriə'reɪʃən ‖ dɪˌtɪəriə'reɪʃən/ *n* [U] deterioro *m*

determination /dɪ'tɜːrmə'neɪʃən ‖ dɪˌtɜːmɪ'neɪʃən/ *n* [U] determinación *f*, resolución *f*

determine /dɪ'tɜːrmən ‖ dɪ'tɜːmɪn/ *vt* **1** (ascertain) establecer*, determinar **2 (a)** (influence) determinar, condicionar **(b)** (mark) ‹*boundary/limit*› definir, demarcar* **3** (liter) (resolve) decidir; **to ~ to + INF** decidir + INF, tomar la determinación DE + INF

determined /dɪ'tɜːrmənd ‖ dɪ'tɜːmɪnd/ *adj* ‹*mood/person*› decidido, resuelto; **to be ~ to + INF** estar* decidido A + INF, estar* empeñado EN + INF; **to be ~ THAT** estar* resuelto *or* decidido A QUE (+ *subj*)

deterrent /dɪ'terənt/ *n*: **it may act as a ~ to thieves** puede servir para disuadir a los ladrones;

the nuclear ~ las armas nucleares como fuerza disuasoria

detest /dɪ'test/ *vt* detestar, odiar

dethrone /dɪ'θrəʊn/ *vt* destronar

detonate /'detəneɪt/ *vt* hacer* detonar

detour[1] /'di:tʊr ‖ 'di:tʊə(r)/ *n* **(a)** (deviation) rodeo *m*, vuelta *f*; **to make a ~** dar* un rodeo, desviarse* **(b)** (AmE Transp) desvío *m*, desviación *f*

detour[2] *vt* (AmE) ‹*traffic*› desviar*

detract /dɪ'trækt/ *vi*: **I didn't wish to ~ from her achievement** no quise quitarle méritos *or* restarle valor a su logro; **it ~s from the beauty of the painting** desmerece la belleza del cuadro

detractor /dɪ'træktər ‖ dɪ'træktə(r)/ *n* detractor, -tora *m,f*

detriment /'detrəmənt ‖ 'detrɪmənt/ *n* [U] (frml) detrimento *m*, perjuicio *m*; **to the ~ of sb/sth** en detrimento *or* perjuicio de algn/algo

devalue /'di:'vælju:/ *vt* (Fin) devaluar*

devastate /'devəsteɪt/ *vt* **(a)** (lay waste) devastar, asolar* **(b)** (overwhelm) ‹*opposition/argument*› aplastar, demoler*; **I was ~d when I heard** quedé deshecho *or* anonadado cuando me enteré

devastating /'devəsteɪtɪŋ/ *adj* **(a)** ‹*punch/shock*› devastador **(b)** ‹*accuracy/logic*› abrumador, apabullante; ‹*reply/defeat*› demoledor, aplastante; ‹*beauty*› irresistible

devastation /'devə'steɪʃən/ *n* [U] devastación *f*

develop /dɪ'veləp/ *vt* **1 (a)** (elaborate, devise) desarrollar **(b)** (improve) ‹*skill/ability/quality*› desarrollar **(c)** (exploit) ‹*land/area*› urbanizar* **(d)** (expand) ‹*business/range*› ampliar* **(e)** (create) ‹*drug/engine*› crear **2** (acquire) ‹*immunity/resistance*› desarrollar; ‹*disease*› contraer* (frml); **the machine ~ed a fault** la máquina empezó a funcionar mal **3** (Phot) revelar ■ **~** *vi* **1 (a)** (grow) «*person/industry*» desarrollarse; «*interest*» crecer*, aumentar **(b)** (evolve) **to ~ INTO sth** convertirse* *or* transformarse EN algo **2** (appear) «*problem/complication*» surgir*, aparecer*; «*crisis*» producirse*

developer /dɪ'veləpər ‖ dɪ'veləpə(r)/ *n* **1** [C] (of land, property) promotor inmobiliario, promotora inmobiliaria *m,f* **2** [U] (Phot) revelador *m*

developing /dɪ'veləpɪŋ/ *adj* ‹*country*› en vías de desarrollo

development /dɪ'veləpmənt/ *n* **1** [U] (of person, idea, situation) desarrollo *m* **2** [U] (of drug, engine) creación *f* **3** [U] (of land, area) urbanización *f* **4** [C] (*housing* ~) complejo *m* habitacional, fraccionamiento *m* (Méx), urbanización *f* (Esp) **5** [U] (Econ) desarrollo *m* **6** [C] (happening, event) acontecimiento *m*, suceso *m*

deviant /'di:viənt/ *adj* ‹*practices/conduct*› desviado, que se aparta de la norma; ‹*person/personality*› anormal

deviate /'di:vieɪt/ *vi* **to ~ FROM sth** ‹*from course*› desviarse* DE algo; ‹*from truth/norm*› apartarse DE algo

deviation /'di:vi'eɪʃən/ *n* [U C] desviación *f*

device /dɪ'vaɪs/ *n* **1** (gadget, tool) artefacto *m*, dispositivo *m*, aparato *m*; (mechanism) dispositivo *m*, mecanismo *m* **2** (stratagem) recurso *m*, estratagema *f*; *to leave sb to her/his own ~s* dejar que algn se las arregle solo

devil /'devl̩/ *n* **1 (a)** (Relig) diablo *m*, demonio *m* **(b)** (evil spirit) demonio *m* **2** (colloq) (person): **he's a little ~!** ¡es un diablillo!; **poor ~!** ¡pobre diablo!

devious /'di:viəs/ *adj* **(a)** (underhand) ‹*person*› taimado, artero **(b)** (roundabout) ‹*route/path*› tortuoso, sinuoso

devise /dɪ'vaɪz/ *vt* ‹*plan/system*› idear, crear, concebir*; ‹*machine/tool*› inventar

devoid /dɪ'vɔɪd/ *adj* (*pred*) (frml) **to be ~ OF sth** carecer* DE algo

devolution /'devə'lu:ʃən ‖ ˌdi:və'lu:ʃən/ *n* [U] **(a)** (delegation) delegación *f*, transferencia *f* **(b)** (BrE Govt) *transferencia de competencias del gobierno central a un gobierno regional*

devolve /dɪ'vɑ:lv ‖ dɪ'vɒlv/ *vt* (frml) ‹*power*› delegar*, transferir*; ‹*privilege/right*› conceder

devote /dɪ'vəʊt/ *vt* **to ~ sth TO sth/-ING** dedicar* algo A algo/+ INF ■ *v refl* **to ~ oneself TO sth/-ING** dedicarse* A algo/+ INF

devoted /dɪ'vəʊtəd ‖ dɪ'vəʊtɪd/ *adj* **(a)** (loving) ‹*couple/family*› unido; **to be ~ TO sb** sentir* devoción POR algn **(b)** (dedicated) (*before n*) ‹*follower/admirer*› ferviente, devoto; ‹*service/friendship*› leal

devotion /dɪ'vəʊʃən/ *n* [U] (love) devoción *f*; (loyalty) lealtad *f*

devour /dɪ'vaʊr ‖ dɪ'vaʊə(r)/ *vt* devorar

devout /dɪ'vaʊt/ *adj* **(a)** (Relig) devoto, piadoso **(b)** (earnest) (frml) (*before n*) ‹*supporter*› ferviente

dew /du: ‖dju:/ *n* [U] rocío *m*

dexterity /dek'sterəti/ *n* [U] (manual) destreza *f*, habilidad *f*; (skill) habilidad *f*

diabetes /'daɪə'bi:ti:z/ *n* [U] diabetes *f*

diabetic[1] /'daɪə'betɪk/ *adj* diabético; ‹*jam/chocolate*› para diabéticos

diabetic[2] *n* diabético, -ca *m,f*

diabolical /'daɪə'bɑ:lɪkəl ‖ ˌdaɪə'bɒlɪkəl/ *adj* ‹*machinations*› diabólico, satánico; ‹*cruelty*› perverso, satánico

diagnose /'daɪəgnəʊs, -əʊz ‖ 'daɪəgnəʊz/ *vt* ‹*illness*› diagnosticar*; ‹*cause/fault*› determinar

diagnosis /'daɪəg'nəʊsəs ‖ ˌdaɪəg'nəʊsɪs/ *n* (*pl* **-ses** /-si:z/) diagnóstico *m*

diagonal /daɪ'ægənl̩/ *adj* ‹*line*› diagonal; ‹*path*› en diagonal

diagram /'daɪəgræm/ *n* diagrama *m*, esquema *m*, gráfico *m*

dial[1] /'daɪl ‖ 'daɪəl/ *n* (on clock, watch) esfera *f*; (on measuring instrument) cuadrante *m*; (of telephone) disco *m*; (on radio) dial *m*

dial[2], (BrE) **-ll-** *vt/i* (Telec) marcar*, discar* (AmL)

dialect /'daɪəlekt/ *n* dialecto *m*

dialling tone /'daɪlɪŋ ‖ 'daɪəlɪŋ/ *n* (BrE) ⇒ DIAL TONE

dialogue, (AmE also) **dialog** /'daɪəlɔ:g ‖ 'daɪəlɒg/ *n* [C U] diálogo *m*

dial tone *n* tono *m* de marcar *or* (AmL) de discado

diameter /daɪ'æmətər ‖ daɪ'æmɪtə(r)/ *n* diámetro *m*

diamond /ˈdaɪəmənd/ *n* **1** [C U] (Min) diamante *m*; (cut) brillante *m*, diamante *m* **2** (shape) rombo *m* **3** (Games) **diamonds** (suit) (+ *sing or pl vb*) diamantes *mpl*

diaper /ˈdaɪpər ‖ ˈdaɪəpə(r)/ *n* (AmE) pañal *m*

diaphragm /ˈdaɪəfræm/ *n* **1** (Anat) diafragma *m* **2** (contraceptive) diafragma *m*

diarrhea, (BrE) **diarrhoea** /ˌdaɪəˈriːə ‖ ˌdaɪəˈrɪə/ *n* [U] diarrea *f*

diary /ˈdaɪəri/ *n* (*pl* **-ries**) **1** (personal record) diario *m* **2** (book for appointments) agenda *f*

dice[1] /daɪs/ *n* (*pl* ~) dado *m*

dice[2] *pl of* DIE[2] *and of* DICE[1]

dice[3] *vt* (Culin) cortar en dados *or* cubitos

dictate /ˈdɪkteɪt ‖ dɪkˈteɪt/ *vt* **1** (read out) dictar **2** (prescribe, lay down) «*law*» establecer*, dictar; «*common sense*» dictar

dictation /dɪkˈteɪʃən/ *n* [U C] (Corresp, Educ) dictado *m*

dictator /ˈdɪkteɪtər ‖ dɪkˈteɪtə(r)/ *n* dictador, -dora *m,f*

dictatorial /ˈdɪktəˈtɔːriəl/ *adj* dictatorial

dictatorship /dɪkˈteɪtərʃɪp ‖ dɪkˈteɪtəʃɪp/ *n* [C U] dictadura *f*

diction /ˈdɪkʃən/ *n* [U] dicción *f*

dictionary /ˈdɪkʃəneri ‖ ˈdɪkʃənri, ˈdɪkʃənəri/ *n* (*pl* **-ries**) diccionario *m*

did /dɪd/ *past of* DO[1]

didactic /daɪˈdæktɪk/ *adj* didáctico

diddle /ˈdɪdl/ *vt* (colloq) estafar, timar (fam)

didn't /ˈdɪdn̩t/ = **did not**

die[1] /daɪ/ **dies, dying, died** *vi* **(a)** (stop living) morir*; (violently) matarse, morir*; **to be dying** FOR **sth** (colloq) morirse* POR algo; **to be dying to** + INF (colloq) morirse* POR + INF, morirse* de ganas de + INF **(b)** (stop functioning) «*engine/motor*» apagarse*, dejar de funcionar ■ ~ *vt:* **to ~ a natural death** morir* de muerte natural; **to ~ a violent death** tener* *or* sufrir una muerte violenta

• **die away** [*v* + *adv*] «*storm/wind*» amainar; «*anger*» pasar

• **die down** [*v* + *adv*] «*fire/noise*» irse* apagando; «*storm/wind*» amainar; «*anger/excitement*» calmarse

• **die out** [*v* + *adv*] «*race/species*» extinguirse*; «*custom*» morir*, caer* en desuso

die[2] *n* (*pl* **dice**) (Games) dado *m*

diehard /ˈdaɪhɑːrd ‖ ˈdaɪhɑːd/ *n* intransigente *mf*; (*before n*) intransigente, acérrimo

diesel[1] /ˈdiːzəl/ *n* **(a)** [C] (vehicle) coche *m* (*or* camión *m etc*) diesel, diesel *m* **(b)** [U] (fuel) diesel *m*, gasóleo *m*, gas-oil *m*

diesel[2] *adj* (*before n*) diesel *adj inv*

diet[1] /ˈdaɪət/ *n* **(a)** (special food) régimen *m*, dieta *f*; **to be/go on a ~** estar*/ponerse* a régimen *or* a dieta; (*before n*) ‹*cola*› light *adj inv* **(b)** (nourishment) alimentación *f*, dieta *f* (alimenticia); **they live on a ~ of rice and fish** se alimentan de arroz y pescado

diet[2] *vi* hacer* régimen *or* dieta

differ /ˈdɪfər ‖ ˈdɪfə(r)/ *vi* **1 (a)** (be at variance) diferir*; **how do they ~?** ¿en qué difieren? **(b)** (be unlike) ser* distinto *or* diferente; **to ~** FROM **sb/sth** diferenciarse *or* diferir* DE algn/algo **2** (disagree) discrepar, diferir* (frml)

difference /ˈdɪfrəns/ *n* [C U] diferencia *f*; **to tell the ~** notar *or* ver* la diferencia; **it could make a ~ in** *o* (BrE) **to the outcome** podría influir en el resultado; **it will make no ~ to you** a ti no te va a afectar

different /ˈdɪfrənt/ *adj* **(a)** (not the same) distinto, diferente; ~ FROM *o* TO *o* (AmE also) THAN **sth/sb** distinto *or* diferente DE *or* A algo/algn **(b)** (unusual) diferente, original

differential /ˈdɪfəˈrentʃəl ‖ ˌdɪfəˈrenʃəl/ *n* diferencial *m*

differentiate /ˈdɪfəˈrentʃieɪt ‖ ˌdɪfəˈrenʃieɪt/ *vi* distinguir* ■ ~ *vt* (frml): **to ~ sth** (FROM **sth**) diferenciar *or* distinguir* algo (DE algo)

differently /ˈdɪfrəntli/ *adv*: **they think ~** no piensan igual *or* del mismo modo; **I view things ~** yo veo las cosas de otra forma *or* otro modo

difficult /ˈdɪfɪkəlt/ *adj* difícil; **the ~ part is** ... lo difícil es ..., la dificultad está en ...

difficulty /ˈdɪfɪkəlti/ *n* (*pl* **-ties**) **(a)** [U] (of situation, task) dificultad *f*; **she had great ~ walking** caminaba con mucha dificultad **(b)** [C] (problem) dificultad *f*, problema *m*; **to get into difficulties** meterse en líos

diffident /ˈdɪfədənt ‖ ˈdɪfɪdənt/ *adj* ‹*person*› poco seguro de sí mismo; ‹*smile*› tímido

diffuse[1] /dɪˈfjuːz/ *vt* ‹*heat*› difundir, esparcir*; ‹*light*› tamizar*, difuminar; ‹*knowledge*› (frml) difundir

diffuse[2] /dɪˈfjuːs/ *adj* difuso

dig[1] /dɪg/ (*pres p* **digging**; *past & past p* **dug**) *vt* **1** ‹*ground*› cavar; ‹*hole/trench*› (by hand) cavar; (by machine) excavar **2** (jab, thrust) **to ~ sth** INTO **sth** clavar algo EN algo ■ ~ *vi* **1** (excavate — by hand) cavar; (— by machine) excavar; «*dog*» escarbar; **to ~ for oil** hacer* prospecciones petrolíferas **2** (search) buscar*; **she dug in her pockets for the key** buscó la llave en los bolsillos

• **dig up** [*v* + *o* + *adv*, *v* + *adv* + *o*] **(a)** ‹*lawn*› levantar; ‹*weeds/tree*› arrancar* **(b)** ‹*body/treasure*› desenterrar* **(c)** ‹*facts*› (colloq) sacar* a la luz

dig[2] *n* **1** (Archeol) excavación *f* **2** (jab — with elbow) codazo *m*; (— with pin) pinchazo *m* **3** (critical remark) (colloq) pulla *f*; (hint) indirecta *f*; **to have a ~ at sb/sth** meterse con algn/algo

digest[1] /daɪˈdʒest, -də- ‖ daɪˈdʒest, dɪ-/ *vt* ‹*food*› digerir*; (assimilate mentally) asimilar, digerir* (fam)

digest[2] /ˈdaɪdʒest/ *n* (summary) compendio *m*; (journal) boletín *m*, revista *f*

digestible /daɪˈdʒestəbəl, də- ‖ daɪˈdʒestəbəl, dɪ-/ *adj* (Physiol) digerible; (comprehensible) fácil de asimilar *or* (fam) digerir

digestion /daɪˈdʒestʃən, də- ‖ daɪˈdʒestʃən, dɪ-/ *n* [U] digestión *f*

digestive /daɪˈdʒestɪv, də- ‖ daɪˈdʒestɪv, dɪ-/ *adj* digestivo

digger /ˈdɪgər ‖ ˈdɪgə(r)/ *n* (machine) excavadora *f*; (person) excavador, -dora *m,f*

digit /ˈdɪdʒət ‖ ˈdɪdʒɪt/ *n* **1** (Math) dígito *m* (frml) **2** (Anat) dedo *m*

digital /ˈdɪdʒətəl ‖ ˈdɪdʒɪtl/ *adj* digital

dignified /ˈdɪgnəfaɪd ‖ ˈdɪgnɪfaɪd/ *adj* **(a)** ‹*person/reply*› digno, circunspecto; ‹*silence/attitude*› digno **(b)** (stately) majestuoso

dignity /ˈdɪgnəti/ *n* [U] (of person) dignidad *f*; (of occasion) solemnidad *f*

digress /daɪˈgres/ *vi*: **but I ~** pero estoy divagando; **to ~ FROM sth** apartarse DE algo

digression /daɪˈgreʃən/ *n* [C U] digresión *f*

dike /daɪk/ *n* **1 (a)** (to keep out water) dique *m* **(b)** (causeway) terraplén *m* **(c)** (ditch) acequia *f* **2** ⇒ DYKE 2

dilapidated /dəˈlæpədeɪtəd ‖ dɪˈlæpɪdeɪtɪd/ *adj* ‹*building*› ruinoso; ‹*car*› destartalado

dilate /daɪˈleɪt/ *vi* dilatarse

dilemma /dəˈlemə, daɪ- ‖ dɪˈlemə, daɪ-/ *n* dilema *m*

diligence /ˈdɪlədʒəns ‖ ˈdɪlɪdʒəns/ *n* [U] diligencia *f*

diligent /ˈdɪlədʒənt ‖ ˈdɪlɪdʒənt/ *adj* ‹*worker*› diligente, cumplidor; ‹*student*› aplicado, diligente; ‹*work/study*› esmerado, concienzudo

dilute /daɪˈluːt ‖ daɪˈljuːt/ *vt* diluir*

dim¹ /dɪm/ *adj* **-mm- 1 (a)** (dark) ‹*room*› oscuro, poco iluminado; ‹*light*› débil, tenue **(b)** (indistinct) ‹*memory/shape*› borroso; ‹*idea*› vago **(c)** (gloomy) ‹*prospects*› nada halagüeño, nada prometedor **2** (stupid) (colloq) corto (de luces) (fam), tonto (fam)

dim² *vt* **-mm-** ‹*lights*› atenuar*; **to ~ one's headlights** (AmE) poner* las (luces) cortas *or* de cruce *or* (AmL tb) las (luces) bajas

dime /daɪm/ *n* (AmE colloq) *moneda de diez centavos*

dimension /dəˈmentʃən, daɪ- ‖ dɪˈmenʃən, daɪ-/ *n* dimensión *f*

dime store *n* (AmE) *tienda que vende artículos de bajo precio*, ≈ baratillo *m*

diminish /dəˈmɪnɪʃ ‖ dɪˈmɪnɪʃ/ *vi* «*cost/number*» disminuir*, reducirse*; «*enthusiasm*» disminuir*, apagarse* ■ ~ *vt* ‹*size/cost*› reducir*, disminuir*; ‹*enthusiasm*› disminuir*

diminutive /dəˈmɪnjətɪv ‖ dɪˈmɪnjʊtɪv/ *adj* diminuto, minúsculo

dimly /ˈdɪmli/ *adv* ‹*shine*› débilmente; **a ~ lit room** una habitación poco iluminada *or* iluminada por una luz tenue

dimmer /ˈdɪmər ‖ ˈdɪmə(r)/ *n* potenciómetro *m*, dimmer *m*

dimple /ˈdɪmpəl/ *n* (in cheeks, chin) hoyuelo *m*

dimwit /ˈdɪmwɪt/ *n* (colloq) tarado, -da (mental) *m,f* (fam)

din /dɪn/ *n* [U] (colloq) (*no pl*) (of conversation, voices) barullo *m* (fam), bulla *f* (fam); (of drill, traffic) estruendo *m*, ruido *m*

dine /daɪn/ *vi* (frml) cenar

diner /ˈdaɪnər ‖ ˈdaɪnə(r)/ *n* **1** (person) comensal *mf* **2 (a)** (restaurant) (AmE) cafetería *f* **(b)** ⇒ DINING CAR

dinghy /ˈdɪŋgi, ˈdɪŋi/ *n* (*pl* **-ghies**) (sailing boat) bote *m*; (*inflatable o rubber* ~) bote *m* neumático

dingy /ˈdɪndʒi/ *adj* **-gier, -giest** ‹*building/room*› lúgubre; ‹*furnishings*› deslucido; (dirty) sucio

dining /ˈdaɪnɪŋ/: **~ car** *n* coche *m* restaurante, coche *m* comedor; **~ room** *n* comedor *m*; **~ table** *n* mesa *f* (de comedor)

dinner /ˈdɪnər ‖ ˈdɪnə(r)/ *n* [U C] **(a)** (in evening) cena *f*, comida *f* (AmL); **to eat** *o* **have ~** cenar, comer (AmL) **(b)** (formal) cena *f* (de gala) **(c)** (at midday) almuerzo *m*, comida *f* (esp Esp, Méx); **to eat** *o* (BrE) **have ~** almorzar*, comer (esp Esp, Méx)

dinner: **~ dance** *n* cena *f* con baile, comida *f* bailable (esp AmL), cena-baile *f* (Méx); **~ jacket** *n* (esp BrE) esmoquin *m*, smoking *m*; **~ party** *n* cena *f*, comida *f* (AmL); **~ plate** *n* plato *m* llano *or* (Méx) plano *or* (RPl tb) playo *or* (Chi) bajo; **~ service** *n* vajilla *f*; **~ table** *n* mesa *f*; **~time** *n* [U C] (in evening) hora *f* de cenar *or* (esp AmL) de comer; (at midday) hora *f* de almorzar *or* (esp Esp, Méx) de comer

dinosaur /ˈdaɪnəsɔːr ‖ ˈdaɪnəsɔː(r)/ *n* dinosaurio *m*

dint /dɪnt/ *n*: **by ~ of sth** a fuerza de algo

diocese /ˈdaɪəsəs ‖ ˈdaɪəsɪs/ *n* diócesis *f*

dip¹ /dɪp/ **-pp-** *vt* **1 to ~ sth IN(TO) sth** meter algo EN algo; (into liquid) mojar algo EN algo **2** (Agr) ‹*sheep*› desinfectar (*haciendo pasar por un baño*) **3 (a)** (lower) ‹*head*› agachar, bajar **(b)** (BrE Auto): **to ~ one's headlights** poner* las (luces) cortas *or* de cruce *or* (AmL tb) las (luces) bajas ■ ~ *vi* **(a)** (decrease) «*sales/prices*» bajar **(b)** (move downward) «*aircraft/bird*» bajar en picada *or* (Esp) en picado

dip² *n* **1** (swim) (colloq) (*no pl*) chapuzón *m* (fam) **2** (Agr) baño *m* desinfectante **3** (depression, hollow) hondonada *f* **4** (in sales, production) caída *f*, descenso *m* **5** [U C] (Culin) *salsa en la que se mojan diferentes bocaditos* (*en una fiesta etc*)

diphthong /ˈdɪfθɔːŋ ‖ ˈdɪfθɒŋ/ *n* diptongo *m*

diploma /dəˈpləʊmə ‖ dɪˈpləʊmə/ *n* diploma *m*

diplomacy /dəˈpləʊməsi ‖ dɪˈpləʊməsi/ *n* [U] diplomacia *f*

diplomat /ˈdɪpləmæt/ *n* diplomático, -ca *m,f*

diplomatic /ˈdɪpləˈmætɪk/ *adj* **(a)** (Govt) (*before n*) diplomático; **~ immunity** inmunidad *f* diplomática **(b)** (tactful) diplomático

dipstick /ˈdɪpstɪk/ *n* varilla *f* (medidora) del aceite

dire /daɪr ‖ ˈdaɪə(r)/ *adj* **direr, direst 1 (a)** ‹*news/consequences*› funesto, nefasto; **to be in ~ straits** estar* en una situación desesperada **(b)** (very bad) (BrE colloq) espantoso (fam), atroz **2** (ominous) ‹*warning*› serio, grave **3** (desperate) ‹*need/misery*› extremo

direct¹ /dəˈrekt, daɪ- ‖ daɪˈrekt, dɪ-/ *adj* **1 (a)** ‹*route/flight*› directo; ‹*contact*› directo; ‹*cause/consequence*› directo **(b)** (Ling) (*before n*) ‹*question/command*› en estilo directo; **~ discourse** *o* (BrE) **speech** estilo *m* directo **2** (frank, straightforward) ‹*person/manner*› franco, directo; ‹*question*› directo

direct² *adv* **1** ‹*write/phone*› directamente; ‹*go/travel*› (BrE) directo, directamente **2** (straight) directamente; **~ from Paris** (Rad, TV) en directo desde París

Street Directions

How do I get there?

Al salir de la estación, doble a su izquierda, siga todo recto hasta llegar al semáforo, pasar el semáforo y doblar en la bocacalle inmediatamente a la izquierda. Camine hasta el final de la calle hasta donde hay una plaza, cruce la plaza y camine unos 100 metros siguiendo la misma calle. Se encontrará en frente de un edificio blanco, tome* el callejón que está a la derecha y saldrá a la Avenida Colón, atraviese la avenida hacia un espacio abierto. El hotel se encuentra a la derecha, entre un gimnasio y un edificio de oficinas.

**Peninsular Spanish prefers* coger *in this case*

direct[3] *vt* **1 (a)** (give directions to) indicarle* el camino a **(b)** (address) ‹*letter/parcel*› mandar, dirigir* **2** (aim) dirigir*; **it was ~ed at us** iba dirigido a nosotros **3** ‹*play/orchestra/traffic*› dirigir* **4** (order) (frml) ordenar; **to ~ sb to + INF** ordenarle A algn QUE (+ *subj*) ■ **~** *vi* (Cin, Theat) dirigir*

direct: **~ billing** /'bɪlɪŋ/ *n* [U C] (AmE) débito *m* bancario *or* (Esp) domiciliación *f* de pagos; **~ current** *n* [U] corriente *f* continua; **~ debit** *n* [U C] ⇒ **~** BILLING

direction /də'rekʃən, daɪ- ‖ daɪ'rekʃən, dɪ-/ *n* **1** [C] (course, compass point) dirección *f*; **sense of ~** sentido *m* de (la) orientación; **in the ~ of** en dirección a **2** [U] (purpose): **he lacks ~** no tiene un norte **3** [U] (supervision) dirección *f* **4** ▶ 553 | **directions** *pl* (for route) indicaciones *fpl*; (for task, use, assembly) instrucciones *fpl*, indicaciones *fpl*

directive /də'rektɪv, daɪ- ‖ daɪ'rektɪv, dɪ-/ *n* directriz *f*, directiva *f* (esp AmL)

directly /də'rektli, daɪ- ‖ daɪ'rektli, dɪ-/ *adv* **1 (a)** (without stopping) ‹*go/drive/fly*› directamente, directo **(b)** (without intermediaries) ‹*report/deal*› directamente; **he's ~ responsible** es el responsable directo **(c)** (exactly) ‹*opposite/above*› justo **(d)** (in genealogy) ‹*related/descended*› por línea directa **2** (frankly, straightforwardly) ‹*ask*› directamente; ‹*speak*› con franqueza **3** (now, at once) inmediatamente, ahora mismo

director /də'rektər, daɪ- ‖ daɪ'rektə(r), dɪ-/ *n* **1** (of company) directivo, -tiva *m,f*; (of department, project) director, -tora *m,f*; *see also* MANAGING DIRECTOR **2** (Cin, Theat) director, -tora *m,f*; (esp AmE Mus) director, -tora *m,f*

directory /də'rektəri, daɪ- ‖ daɪ'rektəri, dɪ-/ *n* (*pl* **-ries**) **(a)** (*telephone* **~**) guía *f* telefónica *or* de teléfonos, directorio *m* telefónico (Col, Méx) **(b)** (index, yearbook) directorio *m*, guía *f*

dirt /dɜːrt ‖ dɜːt/ *n* [U] suciedad *f*, mugre *f*

dirty[1] /'dɜːrti ‖ 'dɜːti/ *adj* **-tier, -tiest 1** (soiled) sucio; **to get ~** ensuciarse **2 (a)** (obscene) ‹*story/book*› cochino (fam), guarro (Esp fam); ‹*leer/grin*› lascivo; ‹*joke*› verde *or* (Méx) colorado; ‹*magazine*› porno *adj inv* **(b)** (shameful) ‹*job/work*› sucio; **to do sb's ~ work** hacerle* el trabajo sucio a algn

dirty[2] *vt* **dirties, dirtying, dirtied** ensuciar

disability /'dɪsə'bɪləti/ *n* (*pl* **-ties**) **(a)** [U] (state) invalidez *f*, discapacidad *f*; (*before n*) ‹*pension/allowance*› por invalidez **(b)** [C] (particular handicap) problema *m*

disable /dɪs'eɪbəl/ *vt* **(a)** «*illness/accident/injury*» dejar inválido (*or* lisiado *or* ciego *etc*) **(b)** ‹*machine/weapon*› (Mil) inutilizar*

disabled /dɪs'eɪbəld/ *adj* discapacitado, minusválido

disabuse /'dɪsə'bjuːz/ *vt* (frml) desengañar; **I tried to ~ him of the notion that** ... intenté sacarlo del error de que ...

disadvantage /'dɪsəd'væntɪdʒ ‖ ˌdɪsəd'vɑːntɪdʒ/ *n* desventaja *f*, inconveniente *m*; **to be at a ~** estar* en desventaja

disadvantageous /dɪs'ædvæn'teɪdʒəs ‖ dɪsˌædvən'teɪdʒəs/ *adj* desventajoso, desfavorable

disaffected /'dɪsə'fektəd ‖ ˌdɪsə'fektɪd/ *adj* desafecto

disagree /'dɪsə'griː/ *vi* **1 (a)** (differ in opinion) **to ~** (WITH **sb/sth**) no estar* de acuerdo (CON algn/algo), discrepar (DE algn/algo) (frml) **(b)** (conflict) «*figures/accounts*» no coincidir, discrepar **2** (cause discomfort) «*food*» **to ~** WITH **sb** sentarle* *or* caerle* mal A algn

disagreeable /'dɪsə'griːəbəl/ *adj* ‹*smell/experience/person*› desagradable; ‹*task/job*› ingrato, desagradable

disagreement /'dɪsə'griːmənt/ *n* **(a)** [U] (difference of opinion) desacuerdo *m*, disconformidad *f* **(b)** [C] (quarrel) discusión *f* **(c)** [U C] (disparity) discrepancia *f*

disallow /'dɪsə'laʊ/ *vt* (frml) ‹*claim/evidence*› (Law) rechazar*, desestimar; ‹*goal*› anular

disappear /'dɪsə'pɪr ‖ ˌdɪsə'pɪə(r)/ *vi* **(a)** (become invisible) desaparecer* **(b)** (go away) «*pain/problems*» desaparecer*, irse*; «*worries/fears*» desvanecerse*

disappearance /'dɪsə'pɪrəns ‖ ˌdɪsə'pɪərəns/ *n* desaparición *f*

disappoint /'dɪsə'pɔɪnt/ *vt* ‹*person*› decepcionar; ‹*hopes/desires*› defraudar

disappointed /'dɪsə'pɔɪntəd ‖ ˌdɪsə'pɔɪntɪd/ *adj* (*pred*) **to be ~** estar* desilusionado *or* decepcionado; **I'm ~ with the results** los resultados me han decepcionado

disappointing /'dɪsə'pɔɪntɪŋ/ *adj* decepcionante

disappointment /'dɪsə'pɔɪntmənt/ *n* **(a)** [U] (emotion) desilusión *f*, decepción *f* **(b)** [C] (letdown) decepción *f*, chasco *m*

disapproval /'dɪsə'pruːvəl/ *n* [U] desaprobación *f*

disapprove /'dɪsə'pruːv/ *vi*: **he ~s of smoking** está en contra del tabaco *or* del cigarrillo; **she ~s of her son's fiancée** no tiene buen concepto de la novia de su hijo

disapproving /'dɪsə'pruːvɪŋ/ *adj* ‹*tone/look*› de reproche

disarm /dɪs'ɑːrm ‖ dɪs'ɑːm/ *vt* **1** ‹*troops/opposition*› desarmar; ‹*bomb/mine*› desactivar; ‹*criticism*› desbaratar **2** (win confidence of) desarmar ■ **~** *vi* desarmarse

disarmament /dɪs'ɑːrməmənt ‖ dɪs'ɑːməmənt/ *n* [U] desarme *m*

disarming /dɪs'ɑːrmɪŋ ‖ dɪs'ɑːmɪŋ/ *adj* que desarma

disarray /'dɪsə'reɪ/ *n* [U] (of political party) desorganización *f*; (of appearance) desaliño *m*; **her papers were in total ~** sus papeles estaban completamente desordenados

disassociate /'dɪsə'səʊʃieɪt, -sieɪt/ *vt* ⇒ DISSOCIATE

disaster /dɪ'zæstər ‖ dɪ'zɑːstə(r)/ *n* **1** [C] (flood, earthquake) catástrofe *f*, desastre *m*; (crash, sinking) siniestro *m*, desastre *m*; (*before n*) **~ fund** fondo *m* para los damnificados **2** [C] **(a)** (fiasco) desastre *m* **(b)** (hopeless person) (colloq) desastre *m* (fam) **3** [U] (misfortune): **~ struck** ocurrió *or* se produjo una catástrofe

disaster area *n* zona *f* siniestrada, zona *f* de desastre; **my room is a real ~ ~** (colloq & hum) mi habitación está hecha un desastre (fam)

disastrous /dɪ'zæstrəs ‖ dɪ'zɑːstrəs/ *adj* desastroso, catastrófico

disband /dɪs'bænd/ *vt* ‹*organization*› disolver*; ‹*army*› licenciar ■ ~ *vi* «*organization*» disolverse*; «*group*» desbandarse

disbelief /'dɪsbə'liːf/ *n* [U] incredulidad *f*

disbelieve /'dɪsbə'liːv/ *vt* (frml) ‹*statement*› no creer*; ‹*person*› no creerle* a

disc /dɪsk/ *n* (esp BrE) ⇒ DISK

discard /dɪs'kɑːrd ‖ dɪs'kɑːd/ *vt* **(a)** (dispose of) desechar, deshacerse* de **(b)** ‹*idea/belief*› desechar **(c)** (shed) ‹*skin/leaves*› mudar **(d)** (take off) ‹*clothing*› desembarazarse* de

discern /dɪ'sɜːrn ‖ dɪ'sɜːn/ *vt* (frml) distinguir*, percibir

discerning /dɪ'sɜːrnɪŋ ‖ dɪ'sɜːnɪŋ/ *adj* ‹*reader/customer*› exigente, con criterio; ‹*palate/taste*› exigente, fino; ‹*ear/eye*› educado

discharge[1] /dɪs'tʃɑːrdʒ ‖ dɪs'tʃɑːdʒ/ *vt* **1 (a)** (release) ‹*prisoner*› liberar, poner* en libertad; ‹*patient*› dar* de alta; ‹*juror*› dispensar; ‹*bankrupt*› rehabilitar **(b)** (dismiss) (frml) despedir* **2 (a)** (send out) ‹*fumes*› despedir*; ‹*electricity*› descargar*; ‹*sewage/waste*› verter* **(b)** (unload) ‹*cargo*› descargar* **(c)** (shoot) ‹*volley/broadside*› descargar* **3 (a)** ‹*duty*› cumplir con **(b)** ‹*debt*› saldar, liquidar

discharge[2] /'dɪstʃɑːrdʒ ‖ 'dɪstʃɑːdʒ/ *n* **1** [U C] (release — from army) baja *f*; (— from hospital) alta *f*‡; (— from prison) puesta *f* en libertad **2 (a)** [C] (Med) secreción *f*; (*vaginal* ~) flujo *m* (vaginal) **(b)** [C U] (of toxic fumes, gases) emisión *f*; (of sewage, waste) vertido *m* **(c)** [C U] (Elec) descarga *f* **3** [U] (of debt, liabilities) liquidación *f*, pago *m*; (of duty) (frml) cumplimiento *m*

disciple /dɪ'saɪpəl/ *n* (Relig) discípulo, -la *m,f*; (adherent) seguidor, -dora *m,f*

disciplinary /'dɪsəpləneri ‖ ˌdɪsɪ'plɪnəri/ *adj* disciplinario

discipline[1] /'dɪsəplən ‖ 'dɪsɪplɪn/ *n* [U C] disciplina *f*

discipline[2] *vt* **(a)** (control) ‹*child/pupils*› disciplinar; ‹*emotions*› controlar **(b)** (punish) ‹*employee*› sancionar **(c)** (train) ‹*body/mind*› disciplinar

disc jockey *n* disc(-)jockey *mf*, pinchadiscos *mf* (Esp fam)

disclaim /dɪs'kleɪm/ *vt* (deny): **she ~ed all knowledge of his whereabouts** negó conocer su paradero; **he ~ed any connection with him** negó tener ninguna relación con él

disclaimer /dɪs'kleɪmər ‖ dɪs'kleɪmə(r)/ *n* (Law) descargo *m* de responsabilidad

disclose /dɪs'kləʊz/ *vt* revelar

disclosure /dɪs'kləʊʒər ‖ dɪs'kləʊʒə(r)/ *n* [U C] revelación *f*

disco /'dɪskəʊ/ *n* (*pl* **-cos**) discoteca *f*, disco *f* (fam)

discolor, (BrE) **discolour** /dɪs'kʌlər ‖ dɪs'kʌlə(r)/ *vt* (fade) decolorar; (stain) dejar amarillento, manchar

discomfort /dɪs'kʌmfərt ‖ dɪs'kʌmfət/ *n* **(a)** [U C] (lack of comfort) incomodidad *f*; (pain) molestia(s) *f(pl)*, malestar *m* **(b)** [U] (emotional, mental) inquietud *f*, desasosiego *m*

disconcert /'dɪskən'sɜːrt ‖ ˌdɪskən'sɜːt/ *vt* desconcertar*

disconcerting /'dɪskən'sɜːrtɪŋ ‖ ˌdɪskən'sɜːtɪŋ/ *adj* desconcertante

disconnect /'dɪskə'nekt/ *vt* desconectar; **I didn't pay my bills, so I was ~ed** me cortaron el teléfono (*or* el gas *etc*) por no pagar

discontent /'dɪskən'tent/ *n* [U] descontento *m*

discontented /'dɪskən'tentəd ‖ ˌdɪskən'tentɪd/ *adj* descontento

discontinue /'dɪskən'tɪnjuː/ *vt* ‹*production*› suspender; ‹*model*› discontinuar*, descontinuar*; ‹*action/suit*› (Law) desistir de

discord /'dɪskɔːrd ‖ 'dɪskɔːd/ *n* **1** [U] (conflict) discordia *f* **2** (Mus) **(a)** [U] (lack of harmony) discordancia *f*, disonancia *f* **(b)** [C] (chord) acorde *m* disonante

discotheque /'dɪskətek/ *n* ⇒ DISCO

discount[1] /'dɪskaʊnt/ *n* descuento *m*; **at a ~** ‹*sell*› con descuento, a precio reducido; (*before n*) ‹*store*› de saldos; ‹*goods*› de saldo

discount[2] /'dɪskaʊnt, dɪs'kaʊnt ‖ dɪs'kaʊnt/ *vt* **1** (Busn) **(a)** ‹*amount*› descontar* **(b)** ‹*goods*› rebajar **(c)** ‹*price*› reducir* **2** (disregard) ‹*possibility*› descartar; ‹*claim/criticism*› pasar por alto

discourage /dɪs'kɜːrɪdʒ ‖ dɪs'kʌrɪdʒ/ *vt* **(a)** (depress) desalentar*, desanimar **(b)** (deter) ‹*crime/speculation*› poner* freno a; ‹*burglar*› ahuyentar, disuadir **(c)** (dissuade) **to ~ sb** FROM -ING: **she ~d me from taking the exam** trató de convencerme de que no me presentara al examen

discouraging /dɪs'kɜːrɪdʒɪŋ ‖ dɪs'kʌrɪdʒɪŋ/ *adj* ‹*news/result*› desalentador, descorazonador

discourse /'dɪskɔːrs ‖ 'dɪskɔːs/ *n* (frml) **(a)** [C] (dissertation) disertación *f* **(b)** [U] (talk) conversación *f*

discourteous /dɪs'kɜːrtiəs/ *adj* descortés

discover /dɪs'kʌvər ‖ dɪs'kʌvə(r)/ *vt* descubrir*

discoverer /dɪs'kʌvərər ‖ dɪs'kʌvərə(r)/ *n* descubridor, -dora *m,f*

discovery /dɪs'kʌvəri/ *n* [U C] (*pl* **-ries**) descubrimiento *m*

discredit¹ /dɪs'kredət ‖ dɪs'kredɪt/ *vt* desacreditar

discredit² *n* [U] descrédito *m*

discreet /dɪs'kri:t/ *adj* **(a)** (tactful) ‹*person/inquiries*› discreto **(b)** (restrained) ‹*elegance/colors*› discreto, sobrio

discreetly /dɪs'kri:tli/ *adv* discretamente, con discreción

discrepancy /dɪs'krepənsi/ *n* [C U] (*pl* **-cies**) discrepancia *f*

discretion /dɪs'kreʃən/ *n* [U] **1** (tact) discreción *f* **2** (judgment) criterio *m*; **at the committee's ∼** a criterio *or* a discreción de la comisión

discretionary /dɪs'kreʃəneri ‖ dɪs'kreʃənəri, -ənri/ *adj* discrecional

discriminate /dɪs'krɪmənert ‖ dɪ'skrɪmɪneɪt/ *vi* **1** (act with prejudice) hacer* discriminaciones, discriminar; **to ∼ AGAINST sb** discriminar a algn **2 (a)** (distinguish) distinguir*, discriminar **(b)** (be discerning) discernir*, utilizar* el sentido crítico

discriminating /dɪs'krɪməneɪtɪŋ ‖ dɪ'skrɪmɪneɪtɪŋ/ *adj* (discerning) ‹*critic/customer*› exigente; ‹*judgment*› sagaz; ‹*taste*› refinado, educado

discrimination /dɪs'krɪmə'neɪʃən ‖ dɪˌskrɪmɪ'neɪʃən/ *n* [U] **1** (unfair treatment) discriminación *f* **2** (discernment) criterio *m*, discernimiento *m*

discus /'dɪskəs/ *n* (*pl* **-cuses**) disco *m*

discuss /dɪs'kʌs/ *vt* (talk about) ‹*person*› hablar de; ‹*topic*› hablar de, tratar; (debate) debatir; ‹*plan/problem*› discutir

discussion /dɪs'kʌʃən/ *n* [C U] discusión *f*, debate *m*

disdain /dɪs'deɪn/ *n* [U] desdén *m*

disdainful /dɪs'deɪnfəl/ *adj* ‹*manner/tone*› despectivo, desdeñoso

disease /dɪ'zi:z/ *n* enfermedad *f*, dolencia *f* (frml)

diseased /dɪ'zi:zd/ *adj* ‹*organ/tissue*› afectado; ‹*plant/animal*› enfermo

disembark /'dɪsəm'bɑ:rk ‖ ˌdɪsɪm'bɑ:k/ *vi* desembarcar*

disembodied /'dɪsəm'bɑ:did ‖ ˌdɪsɪm'bɒdid/ *adj* incorpóreo

disembowel /'dɪsəm'baʊəl ‖ ˌdɪsɪm'baʊəl/ *vt*, (BrE) **-ll-** destripar

disenchanted /'dɪsn̩'tʃæntəd ‖ ˌdɪsɪn'tʃɑ:ntɪd/ *adj* **to be ∼ WITH sb/sth** estar* desilusionado CON *or* DE algn/DE algo

disenfranchise /'dɪsn̩'fræntʃaɪz ‖ ˌdɪsɪn'fræntʃaɪz/ *vt* ‹*person*› privar del derecho al voto; ‹*place*› privar del derecho de representación

disengage /'dɪsn̩'geɪdʒ ‖ ˌdɪsɪn'geɪdʒ/ *vt* **1 (a)** (extricate) soltar* **(b)** (Mil) ‹*troops/forces*› retirar **2** (Tech) ‹*gears/mechanism*› desconectar

disentangle /'dɪsn̩'tæŋgəl ‖ ˌdɪsɪn'tæŋgəl/ *vt* ‹*rope/hair/wool*› desenredar, desenmarañar; ‹*mystery*› esclarecer*, desentrañar

disfavor, (BrE) **disfavour** /dɪs'feɪvər ‖ dɪs'feɪvə(r)/ *n* [U] (frml) desaprobación *f*

disfigure /dɪs'fɪgjər ‖ dɪs'fɪgə(r)/ *vt* ‹*face/person*› desfigurar; ‹*landscape/building*› afear, estropear

disgrace¹ /dɪs'greɪs/ *n* [U C] vergüenza *f*; **she was sent upstairs in ∼** la mandaron arriba castigada

disgrace² *vt* **(a)** (bring shame on) ‹*person/family/school*› deshonrar **(b)** (destroy reputation of) ‹*enemy/politician*› desacreditar

disgraceful /dɪs'greɪsfəl/ *adj* vergonzoso

disgruntled /dɪs'grʌntl̩d/ *adj* ‹*child/look*› contrariado; ‹*employee*› descontento

disguise¹ /dɪs'gaɪz/ *vt* **(a)** ‹*person*› disfrazar*; ‹*voice*› cambiar **(b)** (conceal) ‹*mistake*› ocultar; ‹*disapproval/contempt*› disimular

disguise² *n* [C U] disfraz *m*; **in ∼** disfrazado

disgust¹ /dɪs'gʌst/ *vt* darle* asco a

disgust² *n* [U] (revulsion) indignación *f*; (physical, stronger) asco *m*, repugnancia *f*; **she stormed out of the meeting in ∼** salió indignada *or* furiosa de la reunión

disgusted /dɪs'gʌstəd ‖ dɪs'gʌstɪd/ *adj* indignado; (stronger) asqueado

disgusting /dɪs'gʌstɪŋ/ *adj* **(a)** ‹*smell/taste/food*› asqueroso, repugnante **(b)** ‹*conduct/attitude*› vergonzoso

dish /dɪʃ/ *n* **1 (a)** (plate) plato *m*; (*serving* ∼) fuente *f*; **to wash the ∼es** lavar los platos **(b)** (amount) plato *m* **2** (Culin) plato *m* **3** (Telec, TV) antena *f* parabólica

• dish up [*v* + *o* + *adv*, *v* + *adv* + *o*] [*v* + *adv*] (Culin) servir*

dishcloth /'dɪʃklɔ:θ ‖ 'dɪʃklɒθ/ *n* **(a)** (for drying) paño *m* de cocina, repasador *m* (RPl), limpión *m* (Col) **(b)** (BrE) ⇒ DISHRAG

disheartening /dɪs'hɑ:rtn̩ɪŋ ‖ dɪs'hɑ:tn̩ɪŋ/ *adj* descorazonador, desalentador

disheveled, (BrE) **dishevelled** /dɪ'ʃevəld/ *adj* despeinado

dishonest /dɪs'ɑ:nəst ‖ dɪs'ɒnɪst/ *adj* ‹*person/answer*› deshonesto; ‹*dealings/means*› fraudulento, deshonesto

dishonesty /dɪs'ɑ:nəsti ‖ dɪs'ɒnɪsti/ *n* [U] deshonestidad *f*, falta *f* de honradez; (of statement) falsedad *f*; (of dealings) fraudulencia *f*

dishonor, (BrE) **dishonour** /dɪs'ɑ:nər ‖ dɪs'ɒnə(r)/ *n* [U] deshonra *f*, deshonor *m*

dishonorable, (BrE) **dishonourable** /dɪs'ɑ:nərəbəl ‖ dɪs'ɒnərəbəl/ *adj* deshonroso

dish: **∼rag** *n* (AmE) trapo *m*, bayeta *f*, fregón *m* (RPl); **∼ soap** *n* [U] (AmE) lavavajillas *m*, detergente *m*; **∼towel** *n* ⇒ DISHCLOTH (a); **∼washer** /'dɪʃ'wɔ:ʃər ‖ 'dɪsˌwɒʃə(r)/ *n* (machine) lavaplatos *m*, lavavajillas *m*; **∼washing liquid** /'dɪʃˌwɔ:ʃɪŋ ‖ 'diʃˌwɒʃiŋ/ *n* [U] (AmE) ⇒ ∼ SOAP; **∼water** *n* [U] agua *f*‡ de fregar *or* de lavar los platos

disillusion /'dɪsə'lu:ʒən ‖ ˌdɪsɪ'lu:ʒən/ *vt* desilusionar

disillusionment /'dɪsə'lu:ʒənmənt ‖ ˌdɪsɪ'lu:ʒənmənt/ *n* [U] desilusión *f*

disinfect /'dɪsn̩'fekt ‖ ˌdɪsɪn'fekt/ *vt* desinfectar

disinfectant /'dɪsn̩'fektənt ‖ ˌdɪsɪn'fektənt/ *n* [U C] desinfectante *m*

disinherit /'dɪsn̩'herət ‖ ˌdɪsɪn'herɪt/ *vt* desheredar

disintegrate /dɪs'ɪntəgreɪt ‖ dɪs'ɪntɪgreɪt/ *vi* desintegrarse

disintegration /dɪsˈɪntəˈgreɪʃən ‖ dɪsˌɪntɪˈgreɪʃən/ *n* desintegración *f*

disinterested /dɪsˈɪntrəstəd ‖ dɪsˈɪntrəstɪd/ *adj* ‹*decision/advice*› imparcial; ‹*action*› desinteresado

disjointed /dɪsˈdʒɔɪntəd ‖ dɪsˈdʒɔɪntɪd/ *adj* inconexo, deshilvanado

disk /dɪsk/ *n* **(a)** (flat, circular object) disco *m* **(b)** (Comput, Audio, Anat) disco *m*

disk drive *n* unidad *f* de disco

diskette /dɪsˈket/ *n* disquete *m*

dislike¹ /dɪsˈlaɪk/ *vt*: **I ∼ dogs** no me gustan los perros; **he ∼s wearing a tie** le desagrada *or* no le gusta llevar corbata

dislike² *n* **(a)** [U] (emotion) (*no pl*): **I have a strong ∼ of dogs** no me gustan nada los perros, (les) tengo aversión a los perros; **to take a ∼ to sb** tomarle antipatía a algn **(b)** [C] (sth disliked): **you'll have to tell us all your likes and ∼s** tendrás que decirnos lo que te gusta y lo que no te gusta

dislocate /ˈdɪsləkeɪt/ *vt* (Med) dislocarse*

dislodge /dɪsˈlɑːdʒ ‖ dɪsˈlɒdʒ/ *vt* (shift, remove) sacar*; **the wind ∼d some tiles** el viento causó que se soltaran varias tejas

disloyal /dɪsˈlɔɪəl/ *adj* desleal

dismal /ˈdɪzməl/ *adj* **(a)** (gloomy) ‹*place/tone*› sombrío, deprimente, lúgubre **(b)** (very bad) ‹*news/prophecy*› funesto; ‹*future*› muy negro; ‹*weather*› malísimo; ‹*results/performance*› pésimo

dismantle /dɪsˈmæntl̩/ *vt* ‹*machinery/furniture*› desmontar; ‹*organization*› desmantelar

dismay¹ /dɪsˈmeɪ/ *n* [U] consternación *f*; **they looked at him in** *o* **with ∼** lo miraron consternados; **much to my/his ∼** para mi/su desgracia

dismay² *vt* consternar

dismember /dɪsˈmembər ‖ dɪsˈmembə(r)/ *vt* ‹*animal*› descuartizar*; ‹*corpse*› desmembrar*

dismiss /dɪsˈmɪs/ *vt* **1 (a)** ‹*employee*› despedir*; ‹*executive, minister*› destituir* **(b)** (send away) ‹*class*› dejar salir **2** ‹*possibility/suggestion*› descartar, desechar; ‹*request/petition/claim*› desestimar, rechazar* **3** (Law) ‹*charge/appeal*› desestimar; **to ∼ a case** sobreseer* una causa

dismissal /dɪsˈmɪsəl/ *n* [U C] **(a)** (of employee) despido *m*; (of executive, minister) destitución *f* **(b)** (sending away) autorización *f* para retirarse **(c)** (of theory, request) rechazo *m* **(d)** (Law) desestimación *f*

dismount /dɪsˈmaʊnt/ *vi* desmontar

disobedience /ˈdɪsəˈbiːdiəns/ *n* [U] desobediencia *f*

disobedient /ˈdɪsəˈbiːdiənt/ *adj* desobediente

disobey /ˈdɪsəˈbeɪ/ *vt/i* desobedecer*

disorder /dɪsˈɔːrdər ‖ dɪsˈɔːdə(r)/ *n* **1** [U] **(a)** (confusion) desorden *m* **(b)** (unrest) desórdenes *mpl*, disturbios *mpl* **2** [C] (Med) afección *f* (frml), problema *m*

disorderly /dɪsˈɔːrdərli ‖ dɪsˈɔːdəli/ *adj* **(a)** (untidy) desordenado **(b)** (unruly) ‹*crowd*› alborotado; ‹*person*› revoltoso; **∼ conduct** alteración *f* del orden público

disorganized /dɪsˈɔːrgənaɪzd ‖ dɪsˈɔːgənaɪzd/ *adj* desorganizado

disorient /dɪsˈɔːrient/, **disorientate** /dɪsˈɔːrienteɪt/ *vt* desorientar

disown /dɪsˈəʊn/ *vt* **(a)** (repudiate) renegar* de, repudiar **(b)** (deny responsibility for) no reconocer* como propio

disparaging /dɪsˈpærədʒɪŋ/ *adj* desdeñoso, despreciativo

disparity /dɪsˈpærəti/ *n* [C U] (inequality) disparidad *f*; (difference) discrepancia *f*

dispassionate /dɪsˈpæʃənət/ *adj* ‹*account*› desapasionado, objetivo; ‹*adjudication/onlooker*› imparcial

dispatch¹ /dɪˈspætʃ/ *vt* **1** (send) despachar, enviar* **2 (a)** (carry out) (frml) ‹*task/duty*› despachar **(b)** (kill) (euph) ‹*person/animal*› despachar (euf) **(c)** (consume) (hum) ‹*food/drink*› despacharse (hum)

dispatch² *n* **1** [C] (message) despacho *m*; (Mil) parte *m* **2** [U] (sending) despacho *m*, envío *m*, expedición *f*

dispel /dɪˈspel/ *vt* **-ll- (a)** ‹*doubts/fear*› disipar, hacer* desvanecer **(b)** ‹*fog*› disipar

dispensary /dɪˈspensəri/ *n* (*pl* **-ries**) (in hospital) dispensario *m*, farmacia *f*; (in school) enfermería *f*

dispensation /ˈdɪspənˈseɪʃən/ *n* **1** [C] **(a)** (exemption) exención *f* **(b)** (Relig) dispensa *f* **2** [U] (of justice) administración *f*

dispense /dɪˈspens/ *vt* **1 (a)** ‹*grants/alms*› dar*; ‹*advice*› ofrecer*, dar*; ‹*favors*› conceder* **(b)** «*machine*» ‹*coffee/soap*› expender **2** ‹*drugs/prescription*› despachar, preparar **3** (administer) ‹*justice*› administrar

• **dispense with** [*v* + *prep* + *o*] prescindir de

dispenser /dɪˈspensər ‖ dɪˈspensə(r)/ *n* (device): **a cash ∼** un cajero automático; **a soap ∼** un dispositivo que suministra jabón

disperse /dɪˈspɜːrs ‖ dɪˈspɜːs/ *vt* dispersar ■ **∼** *vi* dispersarse

dispirited /dɪˈspɪrətəd ‖ dɪˈspɪrɪtɪd/ *adj* ‹*person*› desanimado, abatido

displace /dɪsˈpleɪs/ *vt* **(a)** (Phys) ‹*liquid/volume*› desplazar* **(b)** (replace) reemplazar* **(c)** (force from home) ‹*refugees/workers*› desplazar*

display¹ /dɪˈspleɪ/ *vt* **(a)** (put on show) ‹*exhibit*› exponer*; ‹*data/figures*› (Comput) visualizar* **(b)** (flaunt) ‹*finery/erudition*› hacer* despliegue *or* gala de; ‹*muscles*› lucir*, hacer* alarde de **(c)** (reveal) ‹*anger/interest*› demostrar*, manifestar*; ‹*feelings*› exteriorizar*, demostrar*; ‹*tendencies/symptoms*› presentar; ‹*skill/courage*› demostrar*

display² *n* **1 (a)** (exhibition) exposición *f*, muestra *f*; (show) show *m*; **to be on ∼** «*painting/wares*» estar* expuesto; (*before n*) **∼ cabinet** vitrina *f* **(b)** (of feeling) exteriorización *f*, demostración *f*; (of courage, strength, knowledge) despliegue *m*; (of ignorance) demostración *f* **2** (Comput, Electron) display *m*, visualizador *m* **3** (Journ, Print) (*before n*) **∼ advertising** anuncios *mpl* destacados

displease /dɪsˈpliːz/ *vt* desagradar, contrariar*

displeasure /dɪsˈpleʒər ‖ dɪsˈpleʒə(r)/ *n* [U] desagrado *m*

disposable /dɪˈspəʊzəbəl/ *adj* **1** ‹*cup/razor/pen*› desechable, de usar y tirar **2** ‹*income*› disponible

disposal /dɪ'spəʊzəl/ *n* **1** (removal, riddance): **the problem of the ~ of waste** el problema de cómo deshacerse de residuos; **arrangements were made for the ~ of the body** se hicieron arreglos para que el cadáver fuera inhumado (*or* trasladado al crematorio *etc*) **2** (power to use) disposición *f*; **to have sth at one's ~** disponer* de algo, tener* algo a su (*or* mi *etc*) disposición

disposed /dɪ'spəʊzd/ *adj* (*pred*) **(a)** (inclined) **to be ~ to + INF** estar* dispuesto A + INF **(b)** (liable) (frml) **to be ~ TO sth** ser* propenso A algo, tener* propensión A algo

dispose of /dɪ'spəʊz/ [*v + prep + o*] **1 (a)** (get rid of) ‹*refuse/evidence*› deshacerse* de; ‹*rival/opponent*› deshacerse* de, liquidar (fam) **(b)** (sell) ‹*house/car/land*› vender, enajenar (frml) **(c)** (deal with) ‹*problem/question/objection*› despachar **2** (have use of) (frml) ‹*funds/resources*› disponer* de

disposition /'dɪspə'zɪʃən/ *n* **1 (a)** [C] (personality) manera *f or* modo *m* de ser, temperamento *m* **(b)** (inclination) (*no pl*) (frml) **~ TO sth** predisposición *f* A algo **2** [U C] (arrangement) disposición *f*

dispossess /'dɪspə'zes/ *vt* (frml) **to ~ sb OF sth** desposeer* *or* despojar a algn DE algo (frml)

disproportionate /'dɪsprə'pɔːrʃn̩ət ‖ ˌdɪsprə'pɔːʃənət/ *adj* ‹*number/size*› desproporcionado

disprove /dɪs'pruːv/ *vt* ‹*claim/assertion/charge*› desmentir*; ‹*doctrine/theory*› rebatir, refutar

dispute¹ /dɪ'spjuːt/ *n* **(a)** [C] (controversy, clash) polémica *f*, controversia *f* **(b)** [U] (debate) discusión *f*; (quarrel) disputa *f* **(c)** [C] (Lab Rel) conflicto *m* (laboral)

dispute² *vt* **1 (a)** (contest) discutir, cuestionar **(b)** ‹*will/decision*› impugnar **(c)** (argue) ‹*point/question*› debatir, discutir **(d) disputed** *past p* ‹*decision*› discutido, polémico; ‹*territory*› en litigio **2** (fight for) ‹*possession/victory/territory*› disputarse

disqualify /dɪs'kwɑːləfaɪ ‖ dɪs'kwɒlɪfaɪ/ *vt* **-fies, -fying, -fied (a)** (make ineligible): **as a professional she was disqualified from entering the Olympics** el hecho de ser profesional le impedía participar en las Olimpiadas; **a criminal record disqualifies you from jury service** tener antecedentes penales inhabilita para ser miembro de un jurado **(b)** (debar) (Sport) descalificar*

disquiet /dɪs'kwaɪət/ *n* [U] (frml) inquietud *f*, intranquilidad *f*, desasosiego *m*

disregard¹ /'dɪsrɪ'gɑːrd ‖ ˌdɪsrɪ'gɑːd/ *vt* ‹*danger/difficulty*› ignorar, despreciar; ‹*advice*› hacer* caso omiso de, no prestar atención a; ‹*feelings/wishes*› no tener* en cuenta

disregard² *n* [U] **~ FOR sth/sb** indiferencia *f* HACIA algo/algn

disrepair /'dɪsrɪ'per ‖ ˌdɪsrɪ'peə(r)/ *n* [U] mal estado *m*; **to be in (a state of) ~** estar* en mal estado

disreputable /dɪs'repjətəbəl ‖ dɪs'repjʊtəbəl/ *adj* ‹*person/firm*› de dudosa reputación, de mala fama; ‹*nightclub/district*› de mala fama; ‹*conduct/action*› vergonzoso

disrepute /'dɪsrɪ'pjuːt/ *n* [U] (frml): **to fall into ~** caer* en descrédito; **to bring sth into ~** desacreditar algo

disrespect /'dɪsrɪ'spekt/ *n* [U] **~ (FOR sth)** falta *f* de respeto (HACIA algo); **I meant no ~** no fue mi intención ofenderlo, no quise faltarle al *or* (CS) el respeto

disrespectful /'dɪsrɪ'spektfəl/ *adj* ‹*person*› irrespetuoso; ‹*attitude*› irreverente

disrupt /dɪs'rʌpt/ *vt* ‹*meeting/class*› perturbar el desarrollo de; ‹*traffic/communications*› crear problemas de, afectar a; ‹*plans*› desbaratar, trastocar*

disruption /dɪs'rʌpʃən/ *n* [U C] trastorno *m*

disruptive /dɪs'rʌptɪv/ *adj* ‹*influence*› perjudicial, negativo; **a ~ pupil** un alumno problema

dissatisfaction /'dɪs'sætəs'fækʃən ‖ dɪsˌsætɪs'fækʃən/ *n* [U] descontento *m*, insatisfacción *f*

dissatisfied /'dɪs'sætəsfaɪd ‖ dɪ'sætɪsfaɪd/ *adj* descontento, insatisfecho

dissect /dɪ'sekt, daɪ-/ *vt* ‹*animal/body*› diseccionar, hacer* la disección de

dissent /dɪ'sent/ *n* [U] (frml) desacuerdo *m*

dissertation /'dɪsər'teɪʃən ‖ ˌdɪsə'teɪʃən/ *n* (in US: for PhD) tesis *f* (doctoral); (in UK: for lower degree) tesis *f*, tesina *f*

disservice /'dɪs'sɜːrvəs ‖ dɪs'sɜːvɪs/ *n* [U] (frml): **this report does him a ~** este informe no le hace justicia

dissident /'dɪsədənt ‖ 'dɪsɪdənt/ *n* disidente *mf*

dissimilar /dɪ'sɪmələr ‖ dɪ'sɪmɪlə(r)/ *adj* distinto, diferente

dissipate /'dɪsəpeɪt ‖ 'dɪsɪpeɪt/ *vt* (frml) **(a)** (squander) ‹*inheritance*› disipar, dilapidar; ‹*energy/talents*› desperdiciar **(b)** (dispel) ‹*anxiety*› disipar, hacer* desvanecer ■ **~** *vi* (frml) «*anger/doubts*» disiparse, desvanecerse*

dissociate /dɪ'səʊʃieɪt, -sieɪt/ *vt* **(a)** (separate) disociar **(b)** (distance) **to ~ oneself FROM sb/sth** desvincularse DE algn/algo

dissolute /'dɪsəluːt/ *adj* disoluto

dissolve /dɪ'zɑːlv ‖ dɪ'zɒlv/ *vt* disolver* ■ **~** *vi* disolverse*

dissuade /dɪ'sweɪd/ *vt* **to ~ sb (FROM sth)** disuadir a algn (DE algo); **I managed to ~ her from leaving** logré convencerla de que no se fuera

distance¹ /'dɪstəns/ *n* [C U] distancia *f*; **in the (far) ~** en la distancia *or* lejanía, a lo lejos; ***to keep one's ~*** (remain aloof) guardar las distancias; (lit: keep away) no acercarse*

distance² *v refl* **to ~ oneself (FROM sb/sth)** (emotionally) distanciarse (DE algn/algo); (deny involvement) desvincularse DE algn/algo

distant /'dɪstənt/ *adj* ‹*spot/country*› distante, lejano; ‹*relative*› lejano; **in the ~ past** en el pasado remoto

distantly /'dɪstəntli/ *adv* ‹*hear/see*› en la lejanía; **we are ~ related** somos parientes lejanos

distaste /dɪs'teɪst/ *n* [U] desagrado *m*

distasteful /dɪs'teɪstfəl/ *adj* **(a)** (unpleasant) ‹*task/chore*› desagradable **(b)** (offensive) ‹*remark/picture*› de mal gusto

distend /dɪ'stend/ *vt* dilatar, hinchar ■ **~** *vi* dilatarse, hincharse

distill, (BrE) **distil** *vt* **-ll-** /dɪ'stɪl/ destilar

distillery /dɪ'stɪləri/ *n* (*pl* **-ries**) destilería *f*

distinct /dɪ'stɪŋkt/ *adj* **1** ‹*shape/outline*› definido, claro, nítido; ‹*likeness*› obvio, marcado; ‹*improvement*› decidido, marcado; ‹*possibility*› nada desdeñable **2** (different, separate) distinto, bien diferenciado **we are talking about English people as ~ from British people** nos referimos a los ingleses en particular y no a los británicos

distinction /dɪ'stɪŋkʃən/ *n* **1 (a)** [C] (difference) distinción *f*; **we must make** *o* **draw a ~ between** ... debemos distinguir entre ... **(b)** [U] (act of differentiating) distinción *f*; **without ~ of race or creed** sin distinción de raza o credo **2 (a)** [U] (merit, excellence): **a writer of ~** un distinguido *or* destacado escritor; **a car of ~** un coche de categoría **(b)** [U] (distinguished appearance) distinción *f* **(c)** [C U] (mark of recognition) honor *m*, distinción *f* **(d)** [U C] (BrE Educ) mención *f* especial

distinctive /dɪ'stɪŋktɪv/ *adj* ‹*marking/plumage*› distintivo, característico; ‹*gesture/laugh*› personal, inconfundible; ‹*decor/dress*› particular

distinctly /dɪ'stɪŋktli/ *adv* **(a)** ‹*speak/enunciate*› con claridad **(b)** ‹*hear*› perfectamente, claramente; **I ~ remember telling you** me acuerdo perfectamente *or* muy bien de que te lo dije

distinguish /dɪ'stɪŋgwɪʃ/ *vt* **1 (a)** (differentiate) distinguir*, diferenciar **(b) distinguishing** *pres p* ‹*feature/mark*› distintivo, característico **2** (make out) distinguir* ■ **~** *vi* distinguir*

distinguished /dɪ'stɪŋgwɪʃt/ *adj* distinguido

distort /dɪ'stɔːrt ‖ dɪ'stɔːt/ *vt* **(a)** (deform) ‹*metal/object*› deformar **(b)** (Opt) ‹*image/reflection*› deformar, distorsionar **(c)** (Electron) ‹*signal/sound*› distorsionar **(d)** (misrepresent) ‹*facts/statement*› tergiversar, distorsionar

distortion /dɪ'stɔːrʃən ‖ dɪ'stɔːʃən/ *n* **(a)** [U] (of metal, object) deformación *f*; (of features) distorsión *f* **(b)** (Opt) deformación *f*, distorsión *f* **(c)** [U C] (of facts, news) tergiversación *f*, distorsión *f*

distract /dɪ'strækt/ *vt* **(a)** (divert) ‹*person*› distraer* **(b)** (amuse) entretener*, distraer*

distraction /dɪ'strækʃən/ *n* **1 (a)** [C U] (interruption) distracción *f* **(b)** [C] (entertainment) (frml) entretenimiento *m*, distracción *f* **2** [U] (madness): **to drive sb to ~** sacar* a algn de quicio

distraught /dɪ'strɔːt/ *adj* ‹*voice/person*› consternado, angustiado

distress¹ /dɪ'stres/ *n* [U] angustia *f*, aflicción *f*; **he was in great ~** sufría mucho

distress² *vt* (upset) afligir*; (grieve) consternar

distressed /dɪ'strest/ *adj* afligido

distressing /dɪ'stresɪŋ/ *adj* ‹*news/circumstance*› penoso, angustiante

distribute /dɪ'strɪbjət, -bjuːt ‖ dɪ'strɪbjuːt/ *vt* distribuir*; ‹*profits*› repartir

distribution /'dɪstrɪ'bjuːʃən/ *n* [U C] distribución *f*, reparto *m*; (of dividends) reparto *m*

distributor /dɪ'strɪbjətər ‖ dɪ'strɪbjʊtə(r)/ *n* **1** (Busn) distribuidor *m*; (Cin) distribuidora *f* **2** (Auto, Elec) distribuidor *m* (del encendido)

district /'dɪstrɪkt/ *n* **1 (a)** (region) zona *f*, región *f* **(b)** (locality) barrio *m* **2** (Govt) (in US: of state, city) distrito *m*

district: **~ attorney** *n* (in US) fiscal *mf* del distrito; **~ court** *n* (in US) tribunal *m* de distrito; **~ nurse** *n* (in UK) *enfermero que tiene a su cuidado a los pacientes de un distrito*

distrust¹ /dɪs'trʌst/ *vt* desconfiar* de, no fiarse* de

distrust² *n* [U] desconfianza *f*, recelo *m*

distrustful /dɪs'trʌstfəl/ *adj* desconfiado, receloso

disturb /dɪ'stɜːrb ‖ dɪ'stɜːb/ *vt* **1 (a)** (interrupt): **the noise ~ed my concentration** el ruido me hizo perder la concentración; **the calm was ~ed by the arrival of the tourists** la llegada de los turistas vino a perturbar la calma **(b)** (inconvenience) molestar **(c)** (burst in upon) ‹*thief*› sorprender **2** (disarrange): **she found that her papers had been ~ed** notó que alguien había tocado sus papeles **3** (trouble) perturbar, inquietar, llenar de inquietud

disturbance /dɪ'stɜːrbəns ‖ dɪ'stɜːbəns/ *n* **1** [U C] **(a)** (noisy disruption): **to cause/create a ~** provocar*/armar un alboroto **(b)** (interruption) interrupción *f* **2** [U C] (of routine) alteración *f* **3** [C] (riot) disturbio *m*

disturbed /dɪ'stɜːrbd ‖ dɪ'stɜːbd/ *adj* **1 (a)** (Psych) ‹*person/mind*› trastornado **(b)** (perturbed) (*pred*): **I was greatly ~ to hear of his misfortune** la noticia de su desgracia me impresionó *or* afectó muchísimo **2** (restless) ‹*sleep*› agitado, inquieto

disturbing /dɪ'stɜːrbɪŋ ‖ dɪ'stɜːbɪŋ/ *adj* (worrying, upsetting) inquietante, perturbador; (alarming) alarmante

disuse /dɪʃ'uːs ‖ dɪs'juːs/ *n* [U] desuso *m*

disused /dɪʃ'uːzd ‖ dɪs'juːzd/ *adj* ‹*factory/quarry*› abandonado; ‹*machinery*› en desuso

ditch¹ /dɪtʃ/ *n* zanja *f*; (at roadside) cuneta *f*; (for irrigation) acequia *f*

ditch² *vt* **1** (abandon) (colloq) ‹*girlfriend/boyfriend*› plantar (fam), botar (AmC, Chi fam); ‹*object*› deshacerse* de, botar (AmL exc RPl), tirar (Esp, RPl); ‹*plan*› abandonar, desechar **2** (Aviat): **to ~ a plane** hacer* un amaraje *or* amarizaje *or* amerizaje (forzoso)

dither /'dɪðər ‖ 'dɪðə(r)/ *vi* (colloq) **(a)** (become agitated) (AmE) ponerse* muy nervioso **(b)** (be indecisive) titubear, vacilar

ditto /'dɪtəʊ/ *adv* (colloq): **I'm fed up — ditto!** estoy harto — ¡y yo ídem de ídem! (fam)

divan /dɪ'væn/ *n* **(a)** (sofa) diván *m*, canapé *m* **(b)** **~ (bed)** cama *f* turca

dive¹ /daɪv/ *vi* (*past* **dived** *or* (AmE also) **dove**; *past p* **dived**) **(a)** (from height) zambullirse*, tirarse (al agua), tirarse *or* echarse un clavado (AmL) **(b)** (from surface) «*person/whale*» sumergirse*, zambullirse*; «*submarine*» sumergirse* **(c)** (swoop) «*plane/bird*» bajar en picada *or* (Esp) en picado

dive² *n* **1 (a)** (into water) zambullida *f*, clavado *m* (AmL); (Sport) salto *m* (de trampolín), clavado *m* (AmL) **(b)** (of submarine, whale) inmersión *f* **(c)** (swoop) descenso *m* en picada *or* (Esp) en picado **2** (lunge, sudden movement) (colloq): **he made a ~ for the gun** se abalanzó sobre la pistola **3** (disreputable club, bar) (colloq) antro *m*

dive-bomb /ˈdaɪvbɑːm ‖ ˈdaɪvbɒm/ *vt* bombardear en picada *or* (Esp) en picado

diver /ˈdaɪvər ‖ ˈdaɪvə(r)/ *n* **(a)** (from diving board *etc*) saltador, -dora *m,f*, clavadista *mf* **(b)** (deep-sea) buzo *mf*, submarinista *mf*

diverge /dəˈvɜːrdʒ ‖ daɪˈvɜːdʒ/ *vi* **(a)** «*lines/paths*» separarse **(b)** «*opinions/explanations*» divergir*

diverse /daɪˈvɜːrs ‖ daɪˈvɜːs/ *adj* **(a)** (varied) ‹*interests/tastes*› diversos, variados; **plant life in the area is extremely ~** la vegetación en la zona es muy variada **(b)** (unlike) diferentes, distintos

diversion /dəˈvɜːrʒən ‖ daɪˈvɜːʃən/ *n* **1 (a)** [U] (of river) desviación *f* **(b)** [U] (of funds) malversación *f* **(c)** [C] (BrE Transp) desvío *m*, desviación *f* **2** [C] (distraction) (Mil) diversión *f*, divertimiento *m* estratégico **3** [C U] (amusement) (frml) diversión *f*, entretenimiento *m*

diversity /dəˈvɜːrsəti ‖ daɪˈvɜːsəti/ *n* diversidad *f*

divert /dəˈvɜːrt ‖ daɪˈvɜːt/ *vt* **1 (a)** (redirect) ‹*stream/flow*› desviar*; ‹*traffic*› (BrE) desviar* **(b)** (ward off) ‹*blow/attack*› eludir, esquivar **2** (distract) ‹*attention/thoughts*› distraer* **3** (amuse) (frml) divertir*, entretener*

divest /daɪˈvest/ *vt* (frml) **to ~ sb OF sth** despojar a algn DE algo (frml)

divide /dəˈvaɪd ‖ dɪˈvaɪd/ *vt* **1 (a)** (split up) dividir; **to ~ sth INTO sth** dividir algo EN algo **(b)** (separate) **to ~ sth FROM sth** separar algo DE algo **(c)** (share) ‹*cake/money/work*› repartir **2** (cause to disagree) dividir **3** (Math) dividir; ⇒ FOUR[1] ■ ~ *vi* **1 (a)** (fork) «*road/river*» dividirse **(b)** (split) «*group/particles/cells*» dividirse **2** (Math) dividir

● **divide up 1** [*v* + *o* + *adv*, *v* + *adv* + *o*] dividir **2** [*v* + *adv*] dividirse

divided /dəˈvaɪdəd ‖ dɪˈvaɪdɪd/ *adj* ‹*opinion*› dividido

divided highway *n* (AmE) autovía *f*, carretera *f* de doble pista

dividend /ˈdɪvədend ‖ ˈdɪvɪdend/ *n* dividendo *m*; ***to pay ~s*** dar* dividendos, reportar beneficios

divider /dəˈvaɪdər ‖ dɪˈvaɪdə(r)/ *n* **(a)** (screen) mampara *f*; (in filing system) separador *m* **(b) dividers** *pl* (Math) compás *m* de puntas fijas

dividing line /dəˈvaɪdɪŋ ‖ dɪˈvaɪdɪŋ/ *n* línea *f* divisoria

divine[1] /dəˈvaɪn ‖ dɪˈvaɪn/ *adj* **1** (*before n*) ‹*intervention/inspiration*› divino **2** (wonderful) divino, precioso

divine[2] *vt* **(a)** (discover, guess) (liter) adivinar **(b)** ‹*water/minerals*› descubrir* (*con una varita de zahorí*)

diving /ˈdaɪvɪŋ/ *n* [U] **(a)** (from height) saltos *mpl* de trampolín, clavados *mpl* (AmL) **(b)** (under water) submarinismo *m*, buceo *m*

diving: **~ board** *n* trampolín *m*; **~ suit** *n* escafandra *f*, traje *m* de buzo

divinity /dəˈvɪnəti ‖ dɪˈvɪnəti/ *n* (*pl* **-ties**) (frml) **(a)** [U C] (divine nature, being) divinidad *f* **(b)** [U] (theology) teología *f*

division /dəˈvɪʒən ‖ dɪˈvɪʒən/ *n* **1 (a)** [U C] (distribution) reparto *m*, división *f* **(b)** [C] (boundary) división *f*; **class ~s** divisiones de clase **(c)** [C] (part) división *f* **2** [U] (disagreement) desacuerdo *m* **3** [C] (department) división *f*, sección *f* **4** [C] (Mil) división *f* **5** [C] (Sport) **(a)** (in boxing) categoría *f* **(b)** (in US: area) zona *f* **(c)** (in UK: by standard) división *f* **6** [U C] (Math) división *f*

divisive /dəˈvaɪsɪv ‖ dɪˈvaɪsɪv/ *adj* divisivo

divorce[1] /dəˈvɔːrs ‖ dɪˈvɔːs/ *n* [C U] divorcio *m*

divorce[2] *vt* (Law) divorciarse de; **to get ~d** divorciarse ■ ~ *vi* divorciarse

divorcee /dəˈvɔːrˈseɪ ‖ dɪˌvɔːˈsiː/ *n* divorciado, -da *m,f*

divulge /daɪˈvʌldʒ/ *vt* divulgar*; **to ~ sth TO sb** revelarle algo A algn

DIY *n* [U] (BrE) (= **do-it-yourself**) bricolaje *m*

dizzy /ˈdɪzi/ *adj* **-zier, -ziest (a)** (giddy) ‹*sensation*› de mareo; **to feel ~** estar* mareado **(b)** (causing dizziness) ‹*speed*› vertiginoso; ‹*height*› de vértigo

DJ *n* = **disc jockey**

DNA *n* [U] (= **deoxyribonucleic acid**) ADN *m*, DNA *m*

do[1] /duː, *weak form* dʊ, də/ (*3rd pers sing pres* **does**; *pres* **doing**; *past* **did**; *past p* **done**) *vt* **1** hacer*; **to have something/nothing to ~** tener* algo/no tener* nada que hacer; **it was a silly thing to ~** fue una estupidez; **can I ~ anything to help?** ¿puedo ayudar en algo? **2** (carry out) ‹*job/task*› hacer*; **to ~ the cooking** cocinar; **well done!** ¡muy bien! **3** (achieve, bring about): **she's done it: it's a new world record** lo ha logrado: es una nueva marca mundial; **it was climbing those stairs that did it** fue por subir esa escalera; **that mustache really does something for him** la verdad es que le queda muy bien el bigote **4 (a)** (fix, arrange, repair): **I have to ~ my nails** me tengo que arreglar las uñas; **she had her hair done** se hizo peinar **(b)** (clean) ‹*dishes*› lavar; ‹*brass/windows*› limpiar **5** (make, produce) ‹*meal*› preparar, hacer*; ‹*drawing/translation*› hacer* **6** (travel): **he was ~ing 100 mph** iba a 100 millas por hora; **the car has only done 4,000 miles** el coche sólo tiene 4.000 millas ■ ~ *vi* **1** (act, behave) hacer*; **~ as you're told!** ¡haz lo que se te dice!; **his concern to ~ well by his son** su preocupación por hacer todo lo posible por su hijo **2** (get along, manage): **how are you ~ing?** (colloq) ¿qué tal estás *or* andas *or* te va?; **how do you ~?** (as greeting) mucho gusto, encantado; **how are we ~ing for time?** ¿cómo *or* qué tal vamos *or* andamos de tiempo?; **she did well in her exams** le fue bien en los exámenes; **he's done well for himself** ha sabido abrirse camino **3** (go on, happen) (colloq) (*in -ing form*): **there's nothing ~ing in town** no pasa nada en el pueblo; **nothing ~ing!** ¡ni hablar!, ¡ni lo sueñes! **4** (be suitable, acceptable): **look, this won't ~!** ¡mira, esto no puede ser!; **it's not ideal, but it'll ~** no es lo ideal, pero sirve; **this box will ~ for *o* as a table** esta caja nos servirá de mesa **5** (be enough) ser* suficiente, alcanzar*, bastar; **that'll ~! shut up!** ¡basta! ¡cállate la boca! ■ ~ *v aux* [*El verbo auxiliar* DO *se usa para formar el* *negativo* (I 1) *y el interrogativo* (I 2), *para agregar énfasis* (I 3) *o para sustituir a un verbo usado anteriormente* (II)] **I 1** (*used to form negative, interrogative, exclamations*): **I ~ not** *o* **don't know** no sé; **not only does it cost more, it also** ... no sólo cuesta más, sino que también ...; **did I frighten you?** ¿te asusté?; **doesn't it make you sick!** ¡dime si no es asqueante! **2** (emphasizing): **you ~ exaggerate!** ¡cómo exageras!; **you must admit, she did look ill** tienes que reconocer que tenía mala cara

II 1 (*in elliptical uses*): **~ you live here? — yes, I ~/no, I don't** ¿vives aquí? — sí/no; **she says she understands, but she doesn't** dice que comprende, pero no es así **2** (*in tag questions*): **you know Bob, don't you?** conoces a Bob, ¿no? *or* ¿verdad? *or* ¿no es cierto?; **I told you, didn't I?** te lo dije ¿no? *or* ¿no es cierto?

• **do away with** [*v* + *adv* + *prep* + *o*] **(a)** (abolish) ‹*privilege/tax*› abolir*, suprimir; ‹*need*› eliminar, acabar con **(b)** (kill) (colloq) eliminar, liquidar (fam)

• **do up** [*v* + *o* + *adv*, *v* + *adv* + *o*] **(a)** (fasten) ‹*coat/necklace/button*› abrochar; ‹*zipper*› subir/cerrar*; **to ~ up one's shoes** atarse los cordones *or* (Méx) las agujetas *or* (Per) los pasadores (de los zapatos) **(b)** (wrap up) ‹*parcel*› envolver* **(c)** (dress up) (colloq): **she was all done up** estaba muy elegante **(d)** (colloq) ‹*house*› arreglar (*pintando, empapelando etc*)

• **do with** [*v* + *prep* + *o*] **1** (benefit from) (*with can, could*): **that door could ~ with a coat of paint** no le vendría mal una mano de pintura a esa puerta; **you could ~ with a change** te hace falta *or* te vendría bien un cambio **2** (expressing connection) **I don't want to have anything to ~ with him/this business** yo no quiero tener nada que ver con él/este asunto; **it's nothing to ~ with you!** no es nada que te concierna *or* que te importe a ti

• **do without 1** [*v* + *prep* + *o*]: **to ~ without sth/sb** prescindir de *or* arreglárselas sin algo/algn **2** [*v* + *adv*] arreglárselas

do² /duː/ *n* (*pl* **dos**) **1** (party, gathering) (colloq) fiesta *f*, reunión *f* **2 do's and don'ts** (rules) normas *fpl*

do³ /dəʊ/ *n* (*pl* **dos**) (Mus) do *m*

docile /ˈdɑːsəl ‖ ˈdəʊsaɪl/ *adj* dócil, sumiso

dock¹ /dɑːk ‖ dɒk/ *n* **1** (Naut) **(a)** [C] (wharf, quay) muelle *m*; (for cargo ships) dársena *f*; (*before n*) ‹*worker/strike*› portuario **(b) docks** *pl* puerto *m* **2** (Law) (*no pl*) **the ~** el banquillo de los acusados **3** [U] (Bot) acedera *f*

dock² *vt* **1 (a)** ‹*tail*› cortar **(b)** ‹*wages*› descontar* dinero de **2** ‹*vessel/ship*› fondear, atracar* ■ **~** *vi* **(a)** (Naut) «*ship/vessel*» atracar*, fondear **(b)** (Aerosp) acoplarse

docker /ˈdɑːkər ‖ ˈdɒkə(r)/ *n* (BrE) estibador, -dora *m,f*

dockyard /ˈdɑːkjɑːrd ‖ ˈdɒkjɑːd/ *n* (*often pl*) astillero *m*

doctor¹ /ˈdɑːktər ‖ ˈdɒktə(r)/ **▶ 603** *n* **1** (Med) médico, -ca *m,f*, doctor, -tora *m,f*, facultativo, -va *m,f* (frml); **D~ Jones** el doctor Jones **2** (Educ) doctor, -tora *m,f*

doctor² *vt* (pej) **(a)** ‹*food/drink*› adulterar **(b)** ‹*text*› arreglar **(c)** ‹*results/evidence*› falsificar*

doctorate /ˈdɑːktərət ‖ ˈdɒktərət/ *n* doctorado *m*

doctrine /ˈdɑːktrən ‖ ˈdɒktrɪn/ *n* [U C] doctrina *f*

document¹ /ˈdɑːkjəmənt ‖ ˈdɒkjʊmənt/ *n* documento *m*

document² *vt* /ˈdɑːkjəment ‖ ˈdɒkjʊment/ documentar

documentary¹ /ˌdɑːkjəˈmentəri ‖ ˌdɒkjʊˈmentri/ *adj* documental

documentary² *n* (*pl* **-ries**) documental *m*

documentation /ˌdɑːkjəmenˈteɪʃən ‖ ˌdɒkjʊmenˈteɪʃən/ *n* [U] documentación *f*

dodge /dɑːdʒ ‖ dɒdʒ/ *vt* **(a)** ‹*blow*› esquivar; ‹*pursuer*› eludir **(b)** ‹*question*› esquivar, soslayar; ‹*problem/issue*› soslayar; ‹*work/responsibility*› eludir; ‹*tax*› evadir ■ **~** *vi* echarse a un lado, apartarse; **she ~d behind the car** se escondió rápidamente detrás del coche

dodgem (car) /ˈdɑːdʒəm ‖ ˈdɒdʒəm/ *n* ⇒ BUMPER CAR

dodger /ˈdɑːdʒər ‖ ˈdɒdʒə(r)/ *n*: **tax ~** evasor, -sora *m,f* de impuestos; **fare ~** *persona que intenta viajar sin pagar en un medio de transporte público*

doe /dəʊ/ *n* (of deer) hembra *f* de gamo, gama *f*; (of rabbit) coneja *f*

does /dʌz, *weak form* dəz/ *3rd pers sing pres of* DO¹

doesn't /ˈdʌznt/ = **does not**

dog¹ /dɔːg ‖ dɒg/ *n* (Zool) perro, -rra *m,f*; (male canine) macho *m*; ***it's ~ eat ~*** hay una competencia brutal; ***to go to the ~s*** venirse* abajo; ***let sleeping ~s lie*** mejor no revolver el asunto; (*before n*) **~ show** exposición *f* canina

dog² *vt* **-gg-** (*often pass*) perseguir*

dog-eared /ˈdɔːgɪrd ‖ ˈdɒgɪəd/ *adj* sobado y con las esquinas dobladas

dogged /ˈdɔːgəd ‖ ˈdɒgɪd/ *adj* obstinado

doggedly /ˈdɔːgədli ‖ ˈdɒgɪdli/ *adv* obstinadamente

doggerel /ˈdɔːgərəl ‖ ˈdɒgərəl/ *n* [U] ripios *mpl*

doghouse /ˈdɔːghaʊs ‖ ˈdɒghaʊs/ *n* (AmE) casa *f or* casilla *f or* (Esp) caseta *f or* (Chi) casucha *f* del perro, perrera *f* (Col); ***to be in the ~*** (also BrE colloq) haber* caído en desgracia

dogma /ˈdɔːgmə ‖ ˈdɒgmə/ *n* dogma *m*

dogmatic /dɔːgˈmætɪk ‖ dɒgˈmætɪk/ *adj* dogmático

do-gooder /ˈduːˌgʊdər ‖ duːˈgʊdə(r)/ *n* (pej) hacedor, -dora *m,f* de buenas obras (hum)

dog: **~ paddle** *n* [U] estilo *m* perro *or* perrito; **~sbody** *n* (esp BrE colloq): **I'm just the general ~sbody around here** yo aquí no soy más que el botones

doh /dəʊ/ *n* (Mus) do *m*

doily /ˈdɔɪli/ *n* (*pl* **-lies**) **(a)** (on plate) blonda *f* **(b)** (under plate, ornament) tapete *m*, pañito *m*, carpeta *f* (Col, CS)

doing /ˈduːɪŋ/ *n* **1** [U] (action): **that takes some ~** eso no es nada fácil; **it was none of our ~** nosotros no tuvimos nada que ver **2 doings** *pl* (activities, events) actividades *fpl*

do-it-yourself /ˈduːətʃərˈself ‖ ˌduːɪtjɔːˈself/ *n* [U] bricolaje *m*

doldrums /ˈdəʊldrəmz, ˈdɑːl- ‖ ˈdɒldrəmz/ *pl n*: ***to be in the ~*** estar* de capa caída

dole /dəʊl/ *n* (BrE): **to be on the ~** estar* cobrando subsidio de desempleo *or* (Chi tb) de cesantía, estar* en el paro (Esp)

• **dole out** [*v + o + adv, v + adv + o*] ‹*food/money*› dar*, repartir

doleful /ˈdəʊlfəl/ *adj* ‹*face/look*› compungido, triste; ‹*sound/voice*› plañidero, lúgubre

doll /dɑːl ‖ dɒl/ *n* muñeca *f*

• **doll up** [*v + o + adv*] (colloq): **to get (all) ~ed up** emperifollarse (fam)

dollar /ˈdɑːlər ‖ ˈdɒlə(r)/ *n* dólar *m*; ***you can bet your bottom ~*** (colloq) puedes estar seguro, te lo doy firmado (fam); (*before n*) **~ bill** billete *m* de un dólar; **~ sign** signo *m* *or* símbolo *m* del dólar

dollhouse /ˈdɑːlhaus ‖ ˈdɒlhaʊs/ (AmE) *n* casa *f* de muñecas

dollop /ˈdɑːləp ‖ ˈdɒləp/ *n* (colloq) (served with a spoon) cucharada *f*; (serving, measure) porción *f*

doll's house *n* (BrE) casa *f* de muñecas

dolly /ˈdɑːli ‖ ˈdɒli/ *n* (*pl* **-lies**) (used to or by children) muñequita *f*

dolphin /ˈdɑːlfən ‖ ˈdɒlfɪn/ *n* (*pl* **~s** *or* **~**) delfín *m*

domain /dəˈmeɪn, dəʊ-/ *n* (sphere of influence, activity) campo *m*, esfera *f*; **in the public ~** de(l) dominio público

dome /dəʊm/ *n* (Archit) cúpula *f*

domestic /dəˈmestɪk/ *adj* **1 (a)** (of the home) ‹*life/problems*› doméstico; **~ violence** violencia *f* en el hogar **(b)** (home-loving) casero, hogareño **2** ‹*animal*› doméstico **3** (Econ, Pol) ‹*affairs/policy/market*› interno; ‹*produce/flight*› nacional

domesticated /dəˈmestɪkeɪtəd ‖ dəˈmestɪkeɪtɪd/ *adj* ‹*animal/species*› domesticado

domesticity /ˈdəʊmesˈtɪsəti ‖ ˌdɒmesˈtɪsəti, dəʊ-/ *n* [U] (frml *or* hum) domesticidad *f*

domestic science *n* [U] economía *f* doméstica, hogar *m* (Esp)

domicile /ˈdɑːməsaɪl ‖ ˈdɒmɪsaɪl/ *n* (frml) domicilio *m* (frml)

dominance /ˈdɑːmənəns ‖ ˈdɒmɪnəns/ *n* [U] **(a)** (supremacy) dominio *m*, dominación *f* **(b)** (predominance) predominio *m*, preponderancia *f*

dominant /ˈdɑːmənənt ‖ ˈdɒmɪnənt/ *adj* **(a)** (more powerful) ‹*nation/influence*› dominante **(b)** (predominant) ‹*crop/industry*› predominante, preponderante **(c)** (Biol, Ecol) dominante

dominate /ˈdɑːməneɪt ‖ ˈdɒmɪneɪt/ *vt* dominar

domination /ˈdɑːməˈneɪʃən ‖ ˌdɒmɪˈneɪʃən/ *n* [U] dominación *f*

domineering /ˌdɑːməˈnɪrɪŋ ‖ ˌdɒmɪˈnɪərɪŋ/ *adj* dominante

Dominican Republic /dəˈmɪnɪkən/ *n* **the ~ ~** la República Dominicana

dominion /dəˈmɪnjən/ *n* [U C] (liter) dominio *m*

domino /ˈdɑːmənəʊ ‖ ˈdɒmɪnəʊ/ *n* (*pl* **-noes**) **(a)** (counter) ficha *f* de dominó **(b) dominoes** (+ *sing vb*) dominó *m*

don /dɑːn ‖ dɒn/ *vt* **-nn-** (put on) (liter) ponerse*

donate /ˈdəʊneɪt, dəʊˈneɪt/ *vt* donar

donation /dəʊˈneɪʃən/ *n* **(a)** [C] (gift) donativo *m*, donación *f* **(b)** [U] (act) donación *f*

done¹ /dʌn/ *past p of* DO¹

done² *adj* (*no comp*) **1** (*pred*) **(a)** (finished) hecho **(b)** (cooked) cocido **2** (accepted): **it's not ~** *o* **not the ~ thing** no está bien visto

donkey /ˈdɑːŋki ‖ ˈdɒŋki/ *n* (*pl* **-keys**) burro *m*, asno *m*

donor /ˈdəʊnər ‖ ˈdəʊnə(r)/ *n* donante *mf*

don't /dəʊnt/ = **do not**

doodle /ˈduːdḷ/ *vi/t* garabatear, garrapatear

doom¹ /duːm/ *vt* (*usu pass*) condenar

doom² *n* [U] **(a)** (fate) sino *m* (liter); (death) muerte *f* **(b)** (ruin) fatalidad *f*

doomsday /ˈduːmzdeɪ/ *n* (arch) día *m* del Juicio Final

door /dɔːr ‖ dɔː(r)/ *n* puerta *f*; **double ~s** puerta de dos hojas; **there's someone at the ~** llaman a la puerta; **tickets are available at the ~** se pueden comprar las localidades en la puerta *or* a la entrada; **he's not allowed out of ~s** no le permiten salir; ***to show sb the ~*** mostrarle* *or* enseñarle la puerta a algn, echar a algn

door: **~bell** *n* timbre *m*; **~ knob** *n* pomo *m* (de la puerta); **~man** /ˈdɔːrmən ‖ ˈdɔːmən/ *n* (*pl* **-men** /-mən/) portero *m*; **~mat** *n* felpudo *m*; **~step** *n* umbral *m*; **~stop** *n* cuña *f* (*para mantener la puerta abierta*); **~-to-~** /ˈdɔːrtəˈdɔːr ‖ ˌdɔːtəˈdɔː(r)/ *adj* ‹*delivery/service*› de puerta a puerta; **a ~-to-~ salesman** un vendedor ambulante (*que va de puerta a puerta*); **~way** *n* entrada *f*

dope¹ /dəʊp/ *n* **1** [U] **(a)** (drugs) (sl) droga *f*, pichicata *f* (CS, Per fam); (cannabis) hachís *m*, chocolate *m* (Esp arg) **(b)** (Sport) estimulante *m*, droga *f*, doping *m*; (*before n*) ‹*test*› antidoping *adj inv* **2** [U] (information) (sl) información *f* **3** [C] (stupid person) (colloq) imbécil *mf*, tarugo *mf* (fam)

dope² *vt* (colloq) ‹*person/racehorse*› dopar (fam), drogar*; ‹*food/drink*› poner* droga en

dopey, **dopy** /ˈdəʊpi/ *adj* **dopier, dopiest** (colloq) **(a)** (stupid) lelo (fam), bobo (fam) **(b)** (befuddled) atontado, grogui (fam)

dormant /ˈdɔːrmənt ‖ ˈdɔːmənt/ *adj* **1 (a)** ‹*animal/plant*› aletargado **(b)** ‹*volcano*› inactivo **2** (frml) ‹*idea/emotion*› latente

dormice /ˈdɔːrmaɪs ‖ ˈdɔːmaɪs/ *pl of* DORMOUSE

dormitory /ˈdɔːrmətɔːri ‖ ˈdɔːmɪtri/ *n* (*pl* **-ries**) **(a)** (in school, hostel) dormitorio *m*; (*before n*) **~ town** (BrE) ciudad *f* dormitorio **(b)** (students' residence) (AmE) residencia *f* de estudiantes

dormouse /ˈdɔːrmaʊs ‖ ˈdɔːmaʊs/ *n* (*pl* **-mice** /-maɪs/) lirón *m*

dorsal /ˈdɔːrsəl ‖ ˈdɔːsəl/ *adj* dorsal

DOS /dɑːs ‖ dɒs/ *n* (= **disc-operating system**) DOS *m*

dosage /ˈdəʊsɪdʒ/ *n* [C U] dosis *f*

dose /dəʊs/ *n* (of medication) dosis *f*; **a bad ~ of flu** (colloq) una gripe *or* (Col, Méx) una gripa muy mala

dose² *vt*: **I'm all ~d up with painkillers** me he tomado no sé cuántos analgésicos

dossier /'dɔːsieɪ || 'dɒsiə(r), -ieɪ/ *n* dossier *m*, expediente *m*

dot¹ /dɑːt || dɒt/ *n* punto *m*; **~ ~ ~** puntos suspensivos

dot² *vt* **-tt- 1** (add dot) puntuar*; **to sign on the ~ted line** firmar la línea punteada *or* de puntos **2** (scatter) (*usu pass*) salpicar*; **her family is ~ted about all over Europe** su familia está desperdigada por toda Europa

dote /dəʊt/ *vi* **to ~** ON **sb** adorar a algn

doting /'dəʊtɪŋ/ *adj*: **his ~ mother** su madre, que lo adora

dotty /'dɑːti || 'dɒti/ *adj* **-tier, -tiest** (colloq) ‹*person*› chiflado (fam); ‹*idea*› descabellada

double¹ /'dʌbəl/ *adj* doble; ‹*bed*› de matrimonio, de dos plazas (AmL); **it's ~ that** es el doble de eso; **my number is ~ three seven ~ four eight** (esp BrE) mi número es tres tres siete, cuatro cuatro ocho; **it's spelled with a ~ 't'** se escribe con dos tes; **~ bend** curva *f* en S (*read as: curva en ese*); **inflation reached ~ figures** la inflación alcanzó/rebasó el 10%

double² *adv* ‹*pay/earn/cost*› el doble; **she spends ~ what she earns** gasta el doble de lo que gana; **to see ~** ver* doble

double³ *n* **1 (a)** (hotel room) doble *f* **(b)** (of spirits): **I'll have a ~** (deme) uno doble **2** (lookalike) doble *mf* **3** (Sport) (double win) doblete *m* **4** (pace): **at** *o* **on the ~** (Mil) a paso ligero

double⁴ *vt* **(a)** (increase twofold) ‹*earnings/profits*› doblar, duplicar*; ‹*efforts*› redoblar **(b)** (Games) ‹*stake/call/bid*› doblar ■ **~** *vi* **1** (increase twofold) «*price/amount*» duplicarse*, doblarse **2** (have dual role): **the table ~s as a desk** la mesa también se usa como escritorio; **somebody ~d for him in the dangerous scenes** alguien lo doblaba en las escenas peligrosas

● **double back** [*v* + *adv*] «*person/animal*» volver* sobre sus pasos; **the path ~d back on itself** el camino doblaba sobre sí mismo

● **double up** [*v* + *adv* (+ *o*)] **(a)** (bend): **to ~ up with laughter** morirse* *or* desternillarse de risa; **he was ~d up with pain** se retorcía de dolor **(b)** (redouble) (AmE) doblar

double: **~ act** *n*: **they are a ~ act** actúan en pareja; **~-barreled**, (BrE) **~-barrelled** /'dʌbəl 'bærəld/ *adj* **(a)** ‹*shotgun*› de dos cañones **(b)** (BrE) ‹*surname*› compuesto; **~ bass** *n* contrabajo *m*; **~-book** /'dʌbəl'bʊk/ *vt* (BrE): **the room had been ~-booked** la habitación había sido reservada para dos personas distintas; **~-breasted** /'dʌbəl'brestəd || ˌdʌbəl'brestɪd/ *adj* cruzado; **~-check** /'dʌbəl'tʃek/ *vi* volver* a mirar, verificar* dos veces ■ **~** *vt* ‹*facts/information*› volver* a revisar; **~ chin** *n* papada *f*; **~ cream** *n* (BrE) crema *f* doble, nata *f* para montar (Esp), doble crema *f* (Méx); **~-cross** /'dʌbəl'krɔːs || ˌdʌbəl 'krɒs/ *vt* traicionar; **~-decker** /'dʌbəl'dekər || ˌdʌbəl'dekə(r)/ *n* **~-decker (bus)** (esp BrE) autobús *m* de dos pisos; **~ Dutch** *n* [U] (colloq) chino *m* (fam); **~-edged** /'dʌbəl'edʒd/ *adj* ‹*knife/blade/scheme*› de doble filo; ‹*remark/comment*› de doble sentido; **~ glazing** /'gleɪzɪŋ/ *n* [U] (BrE) doble ventana *f*; **~-jointed** /'dʌbəl'dʒɔɪntəd || ˌdʌbəl'dʒɔɪntɪd/ *adj*: **he's ~-jointed** tiene articulaciones dobles

doubles /'dʌbəlz/ *pl n* dobles *mpl*

double standard *n*: **to have ~ ~s** aplicar* una ley para unos y otra para otros

doubly /'dʌbli/ *adv* ‹*difficult/dangerous/interesting*› doblemente

doubt¹ /daʊt/ *n* [U C] (uncertainty) duda *f*; **no ~ she will phone** con seguridad que llama, seguro que llama; **if in ~, don't go** si estás en (la) duda, no vayas; **I have my ~s** tengo mis dudas

doubt² *vt* **(a)** ‹*fact/truth*› dudar de **(b)** (consider unlikely) dudar; **to ~ (**THAT**)** *o* **if** *o* **whether** dudar QUE (+ *subj*)

doubtful /'daʊtfəl/ *adj* **(a)** (full of doubt) ‹*expression/tone*› de indecisión *or* duda, dubitativo; **I am ~ as to its value** tengo mis dudas acerca de su valor **(b)** (in doubt) dudoso; **the outcome remains ~** el resultado sigue siendo dudoso *or* incierto

doubtfully /'daʊtfəli/ *adv* ‹*say*› sin convicción; ‹*agree*› con reserva

doubtless /'daʊtləs || 'daʊtlɪs/ *adv* sin duda, indudablemente

dough /dəʊ/ *n* [U] **1** (Culin) masa *f* **2** (money) (sl) guita *f* (arg), lana *f* (AmL fam), plata *f* (AmS fam), pasta *f* (Esp fam)

doughnut /'dəʊnʌt/ *n* donut *m*, rosquilla *f*

dour /daʊr, dʊr || dʊə(r)/ *adj* adusto

douse /daʊs/ *vt* ‹*flames*› sofocar*

dove¹ /dʌv/ *n* paloma *f*

dove² /dəʊv/ (AmE) *past of* DIVE¹

dovetail /'dʌvteɪl/ *vi* encajar

dowager /'daʊədʒər || 'daʊədʒə(r)/ *n*: *viuda de un noble*

dowdy /'daʊdi/ *adj* **-dier, -diest** ‹*woman*› sin gracia, sin estilo

down¹ /daʊn/ *adv* **1 (a)** (in downward direction): **to go ~** bajar; **to look ~** mirar (hacia *or* para) abajo; **from the waist ~** desde la cintura para abajo; **~ with tyranny!** ¡abajo la tiranía! **(b)** (downstairs): **can you come ~?** ¿puedes bajar? **2 (a)** (of position) abajo; **two floors ~** dos pisos más abajo; **~ here/there** aquí/allí (abajo) **(b)** (downstairs): **I'm ~ in the cellar** estoy aquí abajo, en el sótano **(c)** (lowered, pointing downward) bajado; **face ~** boca abajo **(d)** (prostrate): **I was ~ with flu all last week** estuve con gripe toda la semana pasada **3** (of numbers, intensity): **my temperature is ~ to 38° C** la fiebre me ha bajado a 38° C; **they were two goals ~** iban perdiendo por dos goles **4 (a)** (in, toward the south): **to go/come ~ south** ir*/venir* al sur **(b)** (at, to another place) (esp BrE): **~ on the farm** en la granja; **I'm going ~ to the library** voy a la biblioteca **5 (a)** (dismantled, removed): **the room looks bare with the pictures ~** la habitación queda desnuda sin los cuadros; **once this wall is ~** una vez que hayan derribado esta pared **(b)** (out of action): **the telephone lines are ~** las líneas de teléfono están cortadas; **the system is ~**

(Comput) el sistema no funciona **6 down to (a)** (as far as) hasta; **~ to the present day** hasta nuestros días **(b)** (reduced to): **we're ~ to our last can of tomatoes** nos queda sólo una lata de tomates

down² *prep* **1** (in downward direction): **we ran ~ the slope** corrimos cuesta abajo; **it fell ~ a hole** se cayó por un agujero; **halfway ~ the page** hacia la mitad de la página **2** (along): **we drove on ~ the coast** seguimos por la costa; **the library is just ~ the street** la biblioteca está un poco más allá

down³ *adj* **1** (*before n*) (going downward): **the ~ escalator** la escalera mecánica de bajada *or* para bajar **2** (depressed) (colloq) (*pred*) deprimido

down⁴ *n* [U] **(a)** (on bird) plumón *m* **(b)** (on face, body) vello *m*, pelusilla *f* **(c)** (on plant, fruit) pelusa *f*

down⁵ *vt* **(a)** (drink) beberse *or* tomarse rápidamente **(b)** (knock down) ‹*person*› tumbar, derribar

down: **~ and out** *adj* (colloq) (*pred*): **to be ~ and out** estar* en la miseria; **~cast** *adj* **(a)** (dejected) alicaído, abatido **(b)** (directed downward): **with ~cast eyes** con la mirada baja; **~fall** *n* (of person) perdición *f*, ruina *f*; (of king, dictator) caída *f*; **~grade** ‹*employee/hotel*› bajar de categoría; **~hearted** /'daʊn'hɑːrtəd ‖ ˌdaʊn'hɑːtɪd/ *adj* desanimado, desmoralizado; **~hill** /'daʊn'hɪl/ *adv* ‹*walk/run*› cuesta abajo; ***to go ~hill*** ir* cuesta abajo, ir* de mal en peor

Downing Street /'daʊnɪŋ/ *n* Downing Street (*calle de Londres donde se encuentra la residencia oficial del primer ministro británico*)

download /'daʊn'ləʊd/ *vt* (Comput) trasvasar

downmarket¹ /'daʊn'mɑːrkət ‖ ˌdaʊn'mɑːkɪt/ *adv*: **the paper has gone ~** el diario ha perdido categoría; (deliberately) el diario se dirige ahora a un sector más popular del público

downmarket² *adj* ‹*newspaper*› popular; ‹*store*› barato

down: **~ payment** *n* cuota *f or* entrega *f* inicial, entrada *f* (Esp), pie *m* (Chi); **~pour** *n* aguacero *m*, chaparrón *m*

downright¹ /'daʊnraɪt/ *adj* ‹*lie/insolence*› descarado; ‹*crook/liar/rogue*› redomado, de tomo y lomo (fam); ‹*madness*› total y absoluto

downright² *adv*: **it was ~ dangerous!** ¡fue peligrosísimo!; **he was ~ rude!** ¡estuvo de lo más grosero!

downriver /'daʊn'rɪvər ‖ ˌdaʊn'rɪvə(r)/ *adv* río abajo

Down's syndrome /daʊnz/ *n* [U] síndrome *m* de Down; (*before n*) ‹*child*› afectado por el síndrome de Down

downstairs¹ /'daʊn'sterz ‖ ˌdaʊn'steəz/ *adv* abajo; **he went ~ to open the door** bajó a abrir la puerta

downstairs² *n* planta *f* baja; (*before n*) ‹*neighbor/toilet*› (del piso) de abajo

down: **~stream** /'daʊn'striːm/ *adv* río abajo; **~-to-earth** /'daʊntʊ'ɜːrθ ‖ ˌdaʊntə'ɜːθ/ *adj* (*pred* **~ to earth**) realista, práctico

downtown¹ /'daʊn'taʊn/ *n* [U] (AmE) centro *m* (*de la ciudad*); (*before n*) **~ New York** el centro de Nueva York

downtown² *adv* (AmE): **to go/live ~** ir* al/vivir en el centro

downtrodden /'daʊn'trɑːdn̩ ‖ 'daʊnˌtrɒdn̩/ *adj* oprimido

downward¹ /'daʊnwərd ‖ 'daʊnwəd/ *adj* ‹*direction/pressure*› hacia abajo; ‹*movement/spiral*› descendente; ‹*tendency*› (Fin) a la baja

downward² /'daʊnwərd ‖ 'daʊnwəd/, (esp BrE) **downwards** /-z/ *adv* hacia abajo

downwind /'daʊn'wɪnd/ *adv* en la dirección del viento

dowry /'daʊəri/ *n* (*pl* **-ries**) dote *f*

doze /dəʊz/ *vi* dormitar

• doze off [*v* + *adv*] quedarse dormido, dormirse*

dozen¹ /'dʌzn̩/ *n* (*pl* **~** *or* **~s**) docena *f*; **four dollars a** *o* **per ~** cuatro dólares la docena; **I got ~s of cards** recibí montones de tarjetas (fam)

dozen² *adj* docena *f* de; **a ~/two ~ eggs** una docena/dos docenas de huevos

dozy /'dəʊzi/ *adj* **dozier, doziest** amodorrado, adormilado

Dr /'dɑːktər ‖ 'dɒktə(r)/ (title) (= **Doctor**) Dr., Dra.

drab /dræb/ *adj* ‹*clothing/decor/appearance*› soso, sin gracia; ‹*life/occupation*› gris, monótono

draft¹ /dræft ‖ drɑːft/ *n* **1** [C] (BrE) **draught** (cold air) corriente *f* de aire **2** [C] (formulation) versión *f* **3** (Fin) cheque *m or* efecto *m* bancario **4** (AmE) **the ~** (Mil) el llamamiento *or* (AmL tb) llamado a filas

draft² *vt* **1** (formulate) ‹*document/contract/letter*› redactar el borrador de; ‹*speech*› preparar **2** (conscript) (AmE) reclutar, llamar a filas

draftproof /'dræftpruːf ‖ 'drɑːftpruːf/ *adj* hermético

draftsman, (BrE) **draughtsman** /'dræftsmən ‖ 'drɑːftsmən/ *n* (*pl* **-men** /-mən/) dibujante *mf*

drafty, (BrE) **draughty** /'dræfti ‖ 'drɑːfti/ *adj* **-tier, -tiest** con corrientes de aire

drag¹ /dræg/ **-gg-** *vt* **1** (haul) arrastrar, llevar a rastras; **I couldn't ~ myself away** (colloq) no tenía fuerzas para irme **2** (allow to trail) ‹*tail/garment/anchor*› arrastrar; ***to ~ one's feet*** *o* ***heels*** dar(le)* largas al asunto ■ **~** *vi* **1 (a)** (trail) «*anchor*» garrar; «*coat*» arrastrar **(b)** (lag) rezagarse* **2** (go on slowly) «*work/conversation*» hacerse* pesado; «*film/play*» hacerse* largo

• drag on [*v* + *adv*] alargarse* (*interminablemente*)

drag² *n* (*no pl*) **1** (tiresome thing): **what a ~!** ¡qué lata! (fam) **2** [U] (resistant force) resistencia *f* al avance **3** [U] (women's clothes): **in ~** vestido de mujer

dragon /'drægən/ *n* dragón *m*

dragonfly /'drægənflaɪ/ *n* (*pl* **-flies**) libélula *f*, caballito *m* del diablo, matapiojos *m* (Andes)

drain¹ /dreɪn/ *n* **1 (a)** (pipe) sumidero *m*, resumidero *m* (AmL); **the ~s** (of town) el alcantarillado; (of building) las tuberías de desagüe **(b)** (grid) (BrE) sumidero *m*, resumidero *m* (AmL) **2** (plughole) desagüe *m* **3** (*no pl*) (cause of depletion) **a ~ on the country's resources** una sangría para el país;

the extra work is an enormous ~ on my energy el trabajo extra me está agotando

drain² *vt* **1 (a)** ‹*container/tank*› vaciar*; ‹*land/swamp*› drenar, avenar; ‹*blood*› drenar; ‹*sap/water*› extraer* **(b)** (Culin) ‹*vegetables/pasta*› escurrir, colar* **(c)** (Med) drenar **2** (drink up) ‹*glass/cup*› vaciar*, apurar **3** (consume, exhaust) ‹*resources/strength*› agotar, consumir ■ ~ *vi* **(a)** (dry) «*dishes*» escurrir(se) **(b)** (disappear): **all the strength seemed to ~ from my limbs** los brazos y las piernas se me quedaron como sin fuerzas **(c)** (discharge) «*pipes/river*» desaguar*

drainage /'dreɪnɪdʒ/ *n* [U] **(a)** (of household waste) desagüe *m* (de aguas residuales); (of rainwater) canalización *f* (de agua de lluvia); (*before n*) **~ system** (red *f* de) alcantarillado *m* **(b)** (of fields, marshes) drenaje *m*, avenamiento *m*

drainboard /'dreɪnbɔːrd ‖'dreɪnbɔːd/ *n* (AmE) escurridero *m*

draining board /'dreɪnɪŋ/ *n* (BrE) escurridero *m*

drainpipe /'dreɪnpaɪp/ *n* tubo *m* *or* caño *m* del desagüe, bajante *f*

drake /dreɪk/ *n* pato *m* (macho)

drama /'drɑːmə/ *n* (*pl* **-mas**) **1** (Theat) **(a)** [C] (play) obra *f* dramática, drama *m* **(b)** [U] (plays collectively) teatro *m*, drama *m*; (dramatic art) arte *m* dramático **2** [U] (excitement) dramatismo *m*

dramatic /drə'mætɪk/ *adj* **1** (Theat) (*before n*) dramático, teatral **2 (a)** (striking) ‹*change/improvement*› espectacular, drástico; ‹*increase*› espectacular **(b)** (momentous) ‹*events/development*› dramático

dramatically /drə'mætɪkli/ *adv* **(a)** (exaggeratedly) ‹*pause/announce*› dramáticamente, de manera teatral *or* histriónica **(b)** (strikingly) ‹*change/improve/increase*› de manera espectacular

dramatics /drə'mætɪks/ *n* (Theat) (+ *sing vb*): **amateur ~** teatro *m* amateur *or* de aficionados

dramatist /'dræmətɪst/ *n* dramaturgo, -ga *m,f*

dramatize /'dræmətaɪz/ *vt* **1** ‹*story/novel*› (Theat) dramatizar*, hacer* una adaptación teatral de; (Cin) llevar al cine **2** (exaggerate) ‹*situation/event*› dramatizar*, exagerar

drank /dræŋk/ *past of* DRINK²

drape /dreɪp/ *vt* **(a)** (arrange): **they ~d a flag over the tomb** colocaron una bandera formando pliegues sobre la tumba; **she ~d herself over the sofa** se tendió sobre el sofá **(b)** (cover) cubrir*

drapes /dreɪps/ *pl n* (AmE) cortinas *fpl*

drastic /'dræstɪk/ *adj* drástico, radical

drastically /'dræstɪkli/ *adv* drásticamente

draught /dræft ‖drɑːft/ *n* **1** [U] (storage under pressure): **beer on ~** cerveza *f* de barril; (*before n*) ‹*beer/cider*› de barril **2** [C] (liter) (of water, beer) trago *m* **3** (BrE) ⇒ DRAFT¹ 1

draughtproof /'dræftpruːf ‖'drɑːftpruːf/ *adj* (BrE) ⇒ DRAFTPROOF

draughts /dræfts ‖drɑːfts/ *n* (BrE) (+ *sing vb*) damas *fpl*

draughtsman /'dræftsmən ‖'drɑːftsmən/ *n* (BrE) ⇒ DRAFTSMAN

draughty /'dræfti ‖'drɑːfti/ *adj* (BrE) ⇒ DRAFTY

draw¹ /drɔː/ (*past* **drew**; *past p* **drawn**) *vt* **1 (a)** (move by pulling) ‹*curtains/bolt*› (open) descorrer; (shut) correr; **he drew her to one side** la llevó a un lado, la llevó aparte **(b)** (pull along) ‹*cart/sled*› tirar de, arrastrar **2 (a)** (pull out) ‹*tooth/cork*› sacar*, extraer* (frml); ‹*gun*› desenfundar, sacar*; ‹*sword*› desenvainar, sacar* **(b)** (cause to flow) sacar*; **to ~ blood** sacar* sangre, hacer* sangrar; **to ~ breath** respirar **3 (a)** (Fin) ‹*salary/pension*› cobrar, percibir (frml); ‹*check*› girar, librar **(b)** (derive) ‹*strength/lesson*› sacar* **4** (establish) ‹*distinction/parallel*› establecer* **5 (a)** (attract) ‹*customers/crowd*› atraer*; **to be ~n to sb/sth** sentirse* atraído por algn/algo **(b)** (elicit) ‹*praise*› conseguir*; ‹*criticism/protest*› provocar*, suscitar **6** (sketch) ‹*flower/picture*› dibujar; ‹*line*› trazar* **7** (BrE Games, Sport) empatar ■ ~ *vi* **1** (move): **to ~ close to sth/sb** acercarse* a algo/algn; **to ~ to a close** terminar, finalizar* (frml); **the train drew out of/into the station** el tren salió de/entró en la estación; **to ~ ahead of sb/sth** adelantarse a algn/algo **2** (Art) dibujar **3** (BrE Games, Sport) empatar; (in chess game) hacer* tablas

• **draw back** [*v* + *adv*] **(a)** (retreat) retirarse **(b)** (recoil) retroceder

• **draw in 1** [*v* + *o* + *adv*, *v* + *adv* + *o*] **(a)** (retract) ‹*claws*› esconder, retraer* **(b)** (into quarrel, war) involucrar; (into conversation) darle* participación a **2** [*v* + *adv*] **(a)** (arrive) «*train*» llegar* **(b)** «*days/nights*» hacerse* más corto

• **draw on** [*v* + *prep* + *o*] (make use of) ‹*resources/reserves*› recurrir a, hacer* uso de; **she drew on her own experiences** se inspiró en sus propias experiencias

• **draw out 1** [*v* + *adv*] **(a)** (depart) «*train*» salir* **(b)** (become longer) hacerse* más largo **2** [*v* + *o* + *adv*, *v* + *adv* + *o*] **(a)** (prolong) alargar*, estirar **(b)** (extract, remove) ‹*tooth/thorn*› sacar*, extraer* (frml); ‹*wallet/handkerchief*› sacar*; ‹*information*› sacar*, sonsacar*; ‹*confession*› arrancar* **(c)** (withdraw) ‹*money*› sacar*

• **draw up 1** [*v* + *adv*] «*car*» detenerse*, parar **2** [*v* + *o* + *adv*, *v* + *adv* + *o*] **(a)** (prepare, draft) ‹*contract/treaty*› redactar, preparar; ‹*list/plan*› hacer* **(b)** (arrange in formation) ‹*troops/competitors*› alinear, formar **(c)** (bring near) ‹*chair*› acercar*, arrimar

draw² *n* **1** (raffle) sorteo *m* **2** (tie) (Games, Sport) empate *m*

draw: **~back** *n* inconveniente *m*, desventaja *f*; **~bridge** *n* puente *m* levadizo

drawer *n* /drɔːr ‖'drɔː(r)/ **1** (in furniture) cajón *m*, gaveta *f* (esp AmC, Méx) **2 drawers** *pl* (Clothing) calzones *mpl*

drawing /'drɔːɪŋ/ *n* [C U] dibujo *m*

drawing: **~ pin** *n* (BrE) ⇒ THUMBTACK; **~ room** *n* sala *f*, salón *m*

drawl /drɔːl/ *n*: *acento caracterizado por la longitud de las vocales*

drawn¹ /drɔːn/ *past p of* DRAW¹

drawn² *adj* ‹*features/face*› demacrado

drawstring /'drɔːstrɪŋ/ *n* cordón *m* (*del que se tira para cerrar algo*); (*before n*) ‹*bag/waist*› fruncido con un cordón o una cinta

dread¹ /dred/ *vt* tenerle* terror *or* pavor a

dread² *n* [U] terror *m*

dreadful /'dredfəl/ *adj* ‹*news/experience/weather*› espantoso, terrible; **I feel ~** me siento pésimo

dreadfully /'dredfəli/ *adv* (*as intensifier*) ‹*upset/late*› terriblemente, enormemente

dream¹ /dri:m/ *n* sueño *m*; **a ~ come true** un sueño hecho realidad; (*before n*) **he lives in a ~ world** vive de ilusiones, vive en las nubes

dream² (*past & past p* **dreamed** *or* (BrE also) **dreamt** /dremt/) *vi* soñar*; **to ~** ABOUT **sth/sb** soñar* CON algo/algn; **would you do that? — I wouldn't ~ of it!** ¿harías eso? — ¡ni pensarlo! ■ **~** *vt* soñar*; **I never ~ed he'd be so rude** nunca (me) imaginé que iba a ser tan grosero

• **dream up** [*v + o + adv, v + adv + o*] ‹*plan*› idear

dreamer /'dri:mər ‖ 'dri:mə(r)/ *n* soñador, -dora *m,f*

dreamt /dremt/ (BrE) *past & past p of* DREAM²

dreamy /'dri:mi/ *adj* **-mier, -miest** (a) (abstracted) ‹*person*› soñador, fantasioso; ‹*gaze*› distraído **(b)** ‹*music*› etéreo, sutil

dreary /'drɪri ‖ 'drɪəri/ *adj* **-rier, -riest (a)** ‹*room/landscape*› deprimente, lóbrego, sombrío; ‹*weather*› gris, deprimente **(b)** ‹*work/routine*› monótono, aburrido, aburridor (AmL)

dredge /dredʒ/ *vt* dragar*

• **dredge up** [*v + o + adv, v + adv + o*] ‹*mud/sand*› dragar*; ‹*story/scandal*› desenterrar*

dredger /'dredʒər ‖ 'dredʒə(r)/ *n* (machine) draga *f*; (vessel) dragador *m*, draga *f*

dregs /dregz/ *pl n* posos *mpl*, cunchos *mpl* (Col), conchos *mpl* (Chi); **the ~ of society** la escoria de la sociedad

drench /drentʃ/ *vt* (*usu pass*) empapar

dress¹ /dres/ *n* **1** [C] (for woman, girl) vestido *m* **2** [U] (style of dressing): **they adopted Western ~** adoptaron el modo de vestir *or* la vestimenta occidental; (*before n*) **she has no ~ sense** tiene mal gusto para vestirse

dress² *vt* **1** (put clothes on) vestir*; **to get ~ed** vestirse*; **he was ~ed in white** iba (vestido) de blanco **2** (Culin) **(a)** (prepare) ‹*chicken/fish*› preparar **(b)** (season) ‹*salad*› aliñar **3** (Med) ‹*wound*› vendar ■ **~** *vi* vestirse*

• **dress up** [*v + adv*] **(a)** (dress smartly) ponerse* elegante **(b)** (in fancy dress) disfrazarse*; **to ~ up** AS **sth** disfrazarse* DE algo

dresser /'dresər ‖ 'dresə(r)/ *n* **1** (person): **he's a stylish ~** (se) viste con mucho estilo **2 (a)** (in bedroom) (AmE) tocador *m* **(b)** (in kitchen) (BrE) aparador *m*

dressing /'dresɪŋ/ *n* **1** [C] (Med) apósito *m*, gasa *f*; (bandage) vendaje *m* **2** [U C] (Culin) (for salad) aliño *m*, aderezo *m*; (stuffing) (AmE) relleno *m*

dressing: **~ gown** *n* bata *f*, salto *m* de cama (CS); **~ room** *n* (Theat) camerino *m*; (in house) vestidor *m*; **~ table** *n* tocador *m*

dress: **~maker** *n* modista *mf*; (designer) modisto, -ta *m,f*; **~ rehearsal** *n* ensayo *m* general; **~ suit** *n* traje *m* de etiqueta

dressy /'dresi/ *adj* **-sier, -siest** elegante

drew /dru:/ *past of* DRAW¹

dribble /'drɪbəl/ *vi* **1** (drool) babear **2** (Sport) driblar, driblear

dribs and drabs /'drɪbzən'dræbz/ *pl n*: **in ~ ~** poquito a poco

dried /draɪd/ *adj* ‹*figs/flowers*› seco; ‹*fish*› salado, seco; ‹*milk/eggs*› en polvo

drier /'draɪər ‖ 'draɪə(r)/ *n* ⇒ DRYER

drift¹ /drɪft/ *vi* **1 (a)** (on water) *moverse empujado por la corriente* **(b)** (be adrift) «*boat/person*» ir* a la deriva **(c)** (in air) «*balloon*» *moverse empujado por el viento* **2** (proceed aimlessly): **the crowd began to ~ away** la muchedumbre comenzó a dispersarse; **to ~ apart** «*couple/friends*» distanciarse **3** (pile up) «*sand/snow*» amontonarse

drift² *n* **1** [C] (of sand) montón *m*; (of snow) ventisquero *m* **2** (meaning) (*no pl*) sentido *m*; **I didn't quite catch your ~** no entendí *or* capté muy bien lo que querías decir

driftwood /'drɪftwʊd/ *n* [U] *madera, tablas etc que flotan en el mar a la deriva o que arrastra el mar hasta la playa*

drill¹ /drɪl/ *n* **1** [C] (*electric o power ~*) taladradora *f*, taladro *m*; (*hand ~*) taladro *m* (manual); (Dent) torno *m*, fresa *f*; (Eng, Min) perforadora *f*, barreno *m*; (drill head) broca *f* **2 (a)** [U] (Mil) instrucción *f* **(b)** [C] (Educ) ejercicio *m*

drill² *vt* **1** ‹*hole*› hacer*, perforar; ‹*wood/metal*› taladrar, perforar, barrenar; ‹*tooth*› trabajar *or* limpiar con la fresa **2** (Mil) ‹*soldiers*› instruir* ■ **~** *vi* perforar, hacer* perforaciones; **to ~ for oil** perforar en busca de petróleo

drily /'draɪli/ *adv* secamente, con sequedad

drink¹ /drɪŋk/ *n* **1** [U] **(a)** (any liquid) bebida *f* **(b)** (alcohol) bebida *f* **2** [C] **(a)** (amount drunk, served, sold): **have a ~ of water/milk** bebe *or* (esp AmL) toma un poco de agua/leche **(b)** (alcoholic) copa *f*, trago *m* (fam); **to have a ~** tomar una copa

drink² (*past* **drank**; *past p* **drunk**) *vt/i* beber, tomar (esp AmL)

• **drink up 1** [*v + adv*] bebérselo *or* (esp AmL) tomárselo todo, terminar su (*or* mi *etc*) copa (*or* leche *etc*) **2** [*v + o + adv, v + adv + o*] beberse, tomarse (esp AmL)

drinkable /'drɪŋkəbəl/ *adj* ‹*water*› potable

drinker /'drɪŋkər ‖ 'drɪŋkə(r)/ *n*: **he's a heavy ~** es un gran bebedor *or* un bebedor empedernido; **I'm a beer ~ myself** yo prefiero la cerveza

drinking /'drɪŋkɪŋ/ *n* [U] **(a)** (of liquid) beber **(b)** (of alcohol): **his ~ is causing concern** lo mucho que bebe está causando preocupación

drinking: **~ chocolate** *n* [U] chocolate *m* en polvo; **~ water** *n* [U] agua *f*‡ potable

drip¹ /drɪp/ *vi* **-pp-** «*washing/hair*» chorrear, gotear; «*faucet/tap*» gotear; **water was ~ping from the ceiling** el techo goteaba, caían gotas del techo

drip² *n* **1** (of rainwater, tap) (*no pl*) goteo *m* **2** (Med) suero *m*, gota a gota *m* **3** (ineffectual person) (colloq) soso, -sa *m,f* (fam)

drip-dry /ˈdrɪpˈdraɪ/ *adj* ‹*fabric/garment*› de lava y pon, de lavar y poner

dripping /ˈdrɪpɪŋ/ *adj* (colloq) empapado; (*as intensifier*) **to be ~ wet** estar* chorreando *or* empapado

drive¹ /draɪv/ (*past* **drove**; *past p* **driven**) *vt* **1** (Transp) **(a)** ‹*car/bus/train*› manejar *or* (Esp) conducir* **(b)** (convey in vehicle) llevar en coche **2 (a)** (cause to move) (+ *adv compl*): **the Indians were ~n off their land** los indios fueron expulsados de sus tierras; **we drove them away with sticks** los ahuyentamos con palos **(b)** (Sport) ‹*ball*› mandar, lanzar* **(c)** (provide power for, operate) hacer* funcionar, mover* **3** (make penetrate) ‹*nail*› clavar; ‹*stake*› hincar* **4 (a)** (cause to become) volver*; **to ~ sb mad** volver* loco a algn; **he ~s me crazy with his incessant chatter** me saca de quicio con su constante cháchara **(b)** (compel to act) **to ~ sb to + INF** llevar *or* empujar a algn A + INF; **she is ~n by ambition** la impulsa *or* motiva la ambición **(c)** (overwork): **he drove them mercilessly** los hizo trabajar como esclavos; **she ~s herself too hard** se exige demasiado a sí misma ■ ~ *vi* manejar *or* (Esp) conducir*; **she ~s to work** va a trabajar en coche

• drive out [*v + o + adv, v + adv + o*] expulsar

drive² *n* **1** [C] (in vehicle): **to go for a ~** ir* a dar un paseo *or* una vuelta en coche; **it's a three-hour ~** es un viaje de tres horas en coche **2** [C] **(a)** (leading to house) camino *m*, avenida *f* (*que lleva hasta una casa*) **(b)** (in front of house) entrada *f* (*para coches*) **3** [C] (in golf, tennis) golpe *m* fuerte **4 (a)** [U] (energy) empuje *m*, dinamismo *m* **(b)** [C] (compulsion) (Psych) impulso *m*, instinto *m*; **the sex ~** el apetito sexual **5** [C] **(a)** (organized effort) campaña *f* **(b)** (attacking move) (Mil) ofensiva *f*, avanzada *f* **(c)** (in US football) ataque *m* **6 (a)** [U C] (propulsion system) transmisión *f*, propulsión *f* **(b)** [U] (Auto): **front-wheel/rear-wheel ~** tracción *f* delantera/trasera

drive-in /ˈdraɪvɪn/ *n* (AmE) (cinema) autocine *m*; (restaurant) drive in *m* (*restaurante que sirve a los clientes en el propio automóvil*)

drivel /ˈdrɪvəl/ *n* [U] tonterías *fpl*, estupideces *fpl*

driven /ˈdrɪvən/ *past p of* DRIVE¹

driver /ˈdraɪvər ‖ ˈdraɪvə(r)/ *n* (of car, truck, bus) conductor, -ra *m,f*, chofer *m or* (Esp) chófer *mf*; (of racing car) piloto *mf*; **she's a good ~** maneja *or* (Esp) conduce bien

driver's license *n* (AmE) licencia *f or* (Esp) permiso *m* de conducción; (less formally) carné *m or* permiso *m* (de conducir) (Esp), carné *m* (Chi) *or* (Ur) libreta *f or* (AmC, Méx, Ven) licencia *f or* (Col) pase *m* (de manejar), registro *m* (Arg), brevete *m* (Per)

driving¹ /ˈdraɪvɪŋ/ *n* [U] (Auto) conducción *f* (frml)

driving² *adj* **(a)** ‹*rain*› torrencial; ‹*wind*› azotador **(b)** (dynamic): **she's the ~ force behind the project** es el alma-máter *or* la impulsora del proyecto

driving: **~ instructor** *n* instructor, -tora *m,f* de autoescuela; **~ licence** *n* (BrE) ⇒ DRIVER'S LICENSE; **~ test** *n* examen *m* de conducir *or* (AmL tb) de manejar

drizzle¹ /ˈdrɪzəl/ ▶ 920 *n* llovizna *f*, garúa *f* (AmL)

drizzle² ▶ 920 *v impers* lloviznar, garuar* (AmL)

droll /drəʊl/ *adj* **(a)** (comic) gracioso, con chispa **(b)** (quaint, curious) curioso

drone¹ /drəʊn/ *n* **1** [C] (bee) zángano *m* **2** [U] (sound — of bees, traffic, aircraft) zumbido *m*; (— of voice) cantinela *f* (fam), sonsonete *m*

drone² *vi* «*bee/engine/plane*» zumbar; **she ~d (on) for hours** estuvo horas con la misma perorata (fam)

drool /druːl/ *vi* «*dog/baby*» babear; **we ~ed at the sight of the cakes** se nos hizo la boca agua *or* agua la boca al ver los pasteles

droop /druːp/ *vi* **(a)** (sag) «*flowers*» ponerse* mustio; **his shoulders ~ed** se encorvó **(b)** (flag) «*spirits*» flaquear, decaer*; «*person*» desfallecer*, decaer* **(c) drooping** *pres p* ‹*head*› gacho; ‹*flowers*› mustio

drop¹ /drɑːp ‖ drɒp/ *n* **1 (a)** (of liquid) gota *f*; **she's had a ~ too much** ha bebido más de la cuenta **(b) drops** *pl* (Med) gotas *fpl*; **nose ~s** gotas para la nariz **(d)** (candy): **acid ~s** caramelos *mpl* ácidos; **chocolate ~s** pastillas *fpl* de chocolate **2** (fall) (*no pl*) (in temperature) descenso *m*; (in prices) caída *f*, baja *f*; **a sheer ~** una caída a plomo; ***at the ~ of a hat*** en cualquier momento

drop² **-pp-** *vt* **1 (a)** (accidentally): **I/he ~ped the cup** se me/le cayó la taza; **don't ~ it!** ¡que no se te caiga! **(b)** (deliberately) ‹*cup/vase*› dejar caer, tirar; ‹*bomb/supplies*› lanzar*; **~ that gun!** ¡suelta ese revólver! **2** (lower) ‹*hem*› alargar*, bajar; ‹*eyes/voice*› bajar **3 (a)** (set down) ‹*passenger/cargo*› dejar **(b)** (deliver) pasar a dejar **4** (send) (colloq) ‹*card/letter*› mandar; **~ me a line** a ver si me mandas *or* me escribes unas líneas **5** (utter) ‹*hint/remark*› soltar*, dejar caer; **to let it ~ that ...** (inadvertently) dejar escapar que ...; (deliberately) dejar caer que ... **6 (a)** (omit) ‹*letter/syllable/word*› omitir; **to ~ sb from a team** sacar* a algn de un equipo **(b)** (give up, abandon) ‹*case*› abandonar; ‹*charges*› retirar; ‹*plan/idea*› abandonar, renunciar a; ‹*friend/associate*› dejar de ver a; **to ~ the subject** dejar el tema ■ ~ *vi* **1 (a)** (fall) «*object*» caer(se)*; «*plane*» bajar, descender*; **he ~ped to the ground** (deliberately) se tiró al suelo; (fell) cayó de un golpe **(b)** (collapse) desplomarse **2 (a)** (decrease) «*wind*» amainar; «*temperature*» bajar, descender*; «*prices*» bajar, experimentar un descenso (frml); «*voice*» bajar **(b)** (in height) «*terrain*» caer*

• drop in [*v + adv*] (colloq) pasar; **to ~ in ON sb** pasar a ver a algn, caerle* a algn (fam)

• drop off 1 [*v + adv*] **(a)** (fall off) caerse* **(b)** (fall asleep) dormirse*, quedarse dormido **(c)** (decrease) «*sales/numbers*» disminuir* **2** [*v + o + adv*] ‹*person/goods*› dejar

• drop out [*v + adv*]: **to ~ out of school** abandonar los estudios; **to ~ out (of a competition/race)** (before event) no presentarse (a un concurso/una carrera); (during event) abandonar (un curso/una carrera); **to ~ out (of society)** marginarse, convertirse* en un marginado

droplet /ˈdrɑːplət ‖ ˈdrɒplɪt/ *n* gotita *f*

dropper /ˈdrɑːpər ‖ ˈdrɒpə(r)/ *n* cuentagotas *m*, gotero *m*

droppings /'drɑːpɪŋz ‖ 'drɒpɪŋz/ *pl n* (of bird, flies) excremento *m* (frml), cagadas *fpl* (fam); (of rabbit, sheep) cagarrutas *fpl*

dross /drɑːs ‖ drɒs/ *n* [U] **(a)** (waste) basura *f* **(b)** (Metall) escoria *f*

drought /draʊt/ *n* [C U] sequía *f*

drove¹ /drəʊv/ *past of* DRIVE¹

drove² *n* **(a)** (of animals) manada *f* **(b) droves** *pl* (of people) hordas *fpl*, manadas *fpl*

drown /draʊn/ *vt* **1** ‹*person/animal*› ahogar* **2** ~ **(out)** (make inaudible) ‹*noise/cries/screams*› ahogar* ■ ~ *vi* ahogarse*, morir* ahogado

drowsy /'draʊzi/ *adj* **-sier, -siest** somnoliento, adormilado

drudge /drʌdʒ/ *n* esclavo, -va *m,f*

drudgery /'drʌdʒəri/ *n* [U]: **this job is sheer ~** este trabajo es una pesadez

drug¹ /drʌg/ *n* **(a)** (narcotic) droga *f*, estupefaciente *m* (frml); **to be on ~s** drogarse* **(b)** (medication) medicamento *m*, medicina *f*, fármaco *m* (frml)

drug² *vt* **-gg-** drogar*

drug addict *n* drogadicto, -ta *m,f*

druggist /'drʌgɪst/ *n* (AmE) farmacéutico, -ca *m,f*

drugstore /'drʌgstɔːr ‖ 'drʌgstɔː(r)/ *n* (AmE) *establecimiento que vende medicamentos, cosméticos, periódicos y una gran variedad de artículos*

drum¹ /drʌm/ *n* **1** (Mus) **(a)** tambor *m* **(b) drums** *pl* (in band) batería *f* **2 (a)** (container) bidón *m* **(b)** (machine part) tambor *m* **(c)** (spool) tambor *m*

drum² **-mm-** *vt* ‹*table/floor*› golpetear; **to ~ one's fingers** tamborilear con los dedos ■ ~ *vi* **(a)** (Mus) tocar* el tambor **(b)** (beat, tap) «*person*» dar* golpecitos, tamborilear; «*rain/hail/hooves*» repiquetear

● **drum up** [*v* + *adv* + *o*] ‹*support*› conseguir*, obtener*

drum: **~beat** *n* son *m* del tambor; **~kit** *n* batería *f*

drummer /'drʌmər ‖ 'drʌmə(r)/ *n* (pop, jazz) batería *mf*, baterista *mf* (AmL); (military) tambor *m*

drumstick /'drʌmstɪk/ *n* **1** palillo *m* (de tambor), baqueta *f* **2** (Culin) muslo *m*, pata *f*

drunk¹ /drʌŋk/ *past p of* DRINK²

drunk² *adj* (*pred*) borracho; **to get ~** emborracharse; **~ and disorderly** (Law) en estado de embriaguez y alterando el orden público (frml)

drunk³ *n* borracho, -cha *m,f*

drunkard /'drʌŋkərd ‖ 'drʌŋkəd/ *n* (frml & pej) borracho, -cha *m,f*, beodo, -da *m,f* (frml)

drunken /'drʌŋken/ *adj* (*before n*) ‹*person/mob*› borracho; ‹*orgy/brawl*› de borrachos

dry¹ /draɪ/ *adj* **drier, driest 1 (a)** (not wet) ‹*ground/washing*› seco **(b)** (lacking natural moisture) ‹*leaves/skin/hair*› seco; ‹*cough*› seco **(c)** (dried-up) ‹*well/river*› seco; **to run ~** «*river/well*» secarse* **(d)** ▶ 920 (not rainy, not humid) ‹*climate/weather/heat*› seco; **tomorrow will be ~** mañana no lloverá **2** (not sweet) ‹*wine/sherry*› seco **3** (ironic) ‹*humor/wit*› mordaz **4** (dull, boring) ‹*lecture/book*› árido

dry² dries, drying, dried *vt* secar*; **to ~ one's eyes** secarse* *or* (liter) enjugarse* las lágrimas ■ ~ *vi* secarse*

● **dry up** [*v* + *adv*] **(a)** «*stream/pond*» secarse* (*completamente*) **(b)** «*funds/resources/inspiration*» agotarse

dry: **~ clean** *vt* limpiar en seco; **~ cleaner('s)** *n* tintorería *f*; **~ dock** *n* dique *m* seco

dryer /'draɪər ‖ 'draɪə(r)/ *n* **(a)** (for clothes — machine) secadora *f*; (— rack) tendedor *m*, tendedero *m*; (*spin* ~) secadora *f* (centrífuga); (*tumble* ~) secadora *f* (de aire caliente) **(b)** ⇒ HAIRDRIER

dry: **~ goods** *pl n* **(a)** (clothing) (AmE) artículos *mpl* *or* prendas *fpl* de confección; (*before n*) **~ goods store** tienda *f* de confecciones **(b)** (groceries) (BrE) comestibles *mpl* no perecederos; **~ ice** *n* [U] hielo *m* seco

dryly *adv* ⇒ DRILY

dryness /'draɪnəs ‖ 'draɪnɪs/ *n* [U] **1** (of ground, hair, skin, climate) sequedad *f* **2** (of wine, sherry) lo seco **3** (of humor, wit) lo mordaz

dry: **~ rot** *n* [U] *putrefacción de la madera producida por un hongo*; **~ wall**, (BrE) **~-stone wall** *n* muro *m* de mampostería sin mortero

dual /'duːəl ‖'djuːəl/ *adj* (*before n*) ‹*role/function*› doble; ‹*nationality*› doble

dual: **~ carriageway** /'kærɪdʒweɪ/ *n* (BrE) autovía *f*, carretera *f* de doble pista; **~-control** /'duːəlkən'trəʊl ‖ ˌdjuːəlkən'trəʊl/ *adj* ‹*car/brakes*› de doble mando *or* control; **~-purpose** /'duːəl 'pɜːrpəs ‖ ˌdjuːəl'pɜːpəs/ *adj* ‹*utensil*› de doble uso; ‹*cleaner*› de doble acción; ‹*furniture*› de doble función *or* uso

dub /dʌb/ *vt* **-bb- 1** (nickname) apodar **2 (a)** (Cin) ‹*film*› doblar **(b)** (Audio) mezclar

dubious /'duːbiəs ‖ 'djuːbiəs/ *adj* **(a)** (questionable) ‹*honor/achievement*› dudoso, discutible; ‹*past*› turbio; ‹*motives/person*› sospechoso **(b)** (doubtful) **to be ~ (ABOUT sth/sb)** tener* reservas *or* dudas (SOBRE *or* ACERCA DE algo/algn)

duchess /'dʌtʃəs ‖ 'dʌtʃɪs/ ▶ 603 *n* duquesa *f*

duchy /'dʌtʃi/ *n* (*pl* **duchies**) ducado *m*

duck¹ /dʌk/ *n* pato, -ta *m,f*

duck² *vi* (bow down) agacharse; (hide): **I ~ed behind a pillar** me escondí rápidamente detrás de una columna ■ ~ *vt* **1** (lower) ‹*head*› agachar, bajar **2** (submerge) hundir **3** (dodge) ‹*question*› eludir, esquivar; ‹*responsibility*› evadir, eludir

duckling /'dʌklɪŋ/ *n* patito *m*, anadón *m*

duct /dʌkt/ *n* (Tech, Anat) conducto *m*

dud¹ /dʌd/ *n* (colloq) **(a)** (useless thing) birria *f* (fam), porquería *f* (fam) **(b)** (useless person) calamidad *f*, inútil *mf*

dud² *adj* (colloq) **(a)** (useless, valueless) ‹*note/coin*› falso; ‹*check*› sin fondos **(b)** (Mil) ‹*shell/bomb*› que no estalla

dude /duːd ‖ djuːd/ *n* (AmE sl) tipo *m* (fam), tío *m* (Esp fam)

dudgeon /'dʌdʒən/ *n*: **in high ~** indignadísimo, lleno de indignación

due¹ /duː ‖ djuː/ *adj* **1** (*pred*): **the rent is ~** hay que pagar el alquiler; **the respect ~ to one's elders** el respeto que se les debe a los mayores; **it's all ~ to you** todo gracias a ti, te lo debemos todo a ti; **when is the next train ~?** ¿cuándo llega el próximo tren?; **she's ~ back tomorrow** vuelve mañana, su regreso está previsto para mañana **2** (*before n*) ‹*consideration/regard*› debido; **with all ~ respect** con el debido respeto **3 due to** (*as prep*) (crit) debido a

due² *adv*: **the fort is ~ west of the town** el fuerte está justo *or* exactamente al oeste del pueblo; **we headed ~ north** nos dirigimos derecho hacia el norte

due³ *n* **1 to give him his ~, he is efficient** tienes que reconocer que es eficiente **2 dues** *pl n* (subscription) cuota *f*

duel /'du:əl || 'dju:əl/ *n* duelo *m*

duet /du:'et || dju:'et/ *n* dúo *m*

duffel bag, (BrE) **duffle bag** /'dʌfəl/ *n* talego *m*, tula *f* (Col), bolso *m* marinero (RPl)

duffel coat, (BrE) **duffle coat** /'dʌfəl/ *n* trenca *f*, montgomery *m* (CS)

dug /dʌg/ *past & past p of* DIG¹

dugout /'dʌgaʊt/ *n* **1** (Mil) refugio *m* subterráneo **2 ~ (canoe)** piragua *f* **3** (in baseball) dogaut *m*, caseta *f*

duke /du:k || dju:k/ **▶ 603** *n* duque *m*

dull¹ /dʌl/ *adj* **1 (a)** (not bright) ‹*color*› apagado; ‹*light/glow*› pálido; ‹*eyes/complexion*› sin brillo **(b)** (not shiny) ‹*finish*› mate; ‹*hair*› sin brillo **(c) ▶ 920** (overcast) ‹*day/morning*› gris, feo **2** (boring) ‹*speech/person*› aburrido **3 (a)** ‹*faculties*› torpe, lerdo; ‹*pain/ache*› sordo; ‹*sound*› sordo, amortiguado **(b)** ‹*edge/blade*› romo, embotado

dull² *vt* **(a)** (make less bright) ‹*color/surface*› quitar el brillo a, opacar* **(b)** (make less sharp) ‹*pain*› aliviar, calmar; ‹*senses*› entorpecer*, embotar

dully /'dʌlli/ *adv* **(a)** (dimly) ‹*glow/shine*› débilmente, pálidamente **(b)** (boringly) ‹*talk/write*› de manera aburrida

duly /'du:li || 'dju:li/ *adv* debidamente; **permission was ~ granted** el permiso fue concedido, como era de esperar

dumb /dʌm/ *adj* **1** (unable to speak) mudo; **to be struck ~** quedarse mudo *or* sin habla **2** (stupid) (colloq) bobo (fam)

dumb: **~bell** *n* pesa *f*, mancuerna *f*; **~found** /'dʌm'faʊnd/ *vt* (*usu pass*) anonadar; **~struck** *adj* estupefacto; **~waiter** /'dʌm'weɪtər ||,dʌm 'weɪtə(r)/ *n* (elevator) montaplatos *m*; (table) mesita *f* rodante

dummy¹ /'dʌmi/ *n* **1 (a)** (in window display, for dressmaker) maniquí *m* **(b)** (in tests, stunts) muñeco *m* **(c)** (in US football) domi *m* **2** (for baby) (BrE) ⇒ PACIFIER **3** (fool) (colloq) bobo, -ba *m,f* (fam)

dummy² *adj* ‹*gun/telephone*› de juguete

dump¹ /dʌmp/ *n* **1** (place for waste) vertedero *m* (de basura), basural *m* (AmL), tiradero *m* (Méx) **2** (temporary store) (Mil) depósito *m* **3** (unpleasant place) (colloq) lugar *m* de mala muerte **4** ***to be (down) in the ~s*** (colloq) estar* *or* andar* con la depre (fam)

dump² *vt* **1** (get rid of) ‹*waste/refuse*› tirar, botar (AmL exc RPl); ‹*boyfriend/girlfriend*› (colloq) plantar (fam), botar (AmS exc RPl fam), largar* (RPl fam) **2 (a)** (set on ground) ‹*load/sand*› descargar*, verter*; **where can I ~ my things?** (colloq) ¿dónde puedo dejar *or* poner mis cosas? **(b)** (Comput) ‹*data/disks*› volcar*

dumper (truck) /'dʌmpər || 'dʌmpə(r)/ *n* ⇒ DUMP TRUCK

dumpling /'dʌmplɪŋ/ *n*: *bola de masa que se come en sopas o guisos*

Dumpster® /'dʌmpstər || 'dʌmpstə(r)/ *n* (AmE) contenedor *m* (*para escombros*)

dump truck *n* volquete *m*, camión *m* volteador (RPl) *or* (Méx) de volteo, volqueta *f* (Col)

dumpy /'dʌmpi/ *adj* **-pier, -piest** regordete

dunce /dʌns/ *n* (pej) burro, -rra *m,f*

dune /du:n ||dju:n/ *n* duna *f*

dung /dʌŋ/ *n* [U] **(a)** (feces) boñiga *f*, bosta *f* **(b)** (manure) (esp BrE) estiércol *m*

dungarees /'dʌŋgə'ri:z/ *pl n* (workman's) overol *m*; (fashion) pantalón *m* de peto *m*

dungeon /'dʌndʒən/ *n* mazmorra *f*, calabozo *m*

duo /'du:əʊ || 'dju:əʊ/ *n* (*pl* **-os**) dúo *m*

dupe¹ /du:p || dju:p/ *vt* engañar, embaucar*

dupe² *n* inocentón, -tona *m,f*, primo, -ma *m,f* (Esp fam)

duplex /'du:pleks || 'dju:pleks/ *n* (AmE) **~ (apartment)** dúplex *m*; **~ (house)** *casa de dos viviendas adosadas*

duplicate¹ /'du:plɪkət || 'dju:plɪkət/ *adj* (*before n*): **a ~ copy** un duplicado; **a ~ key** un duplicado *or* una copia de una llave

duplicate² /'du:plɪkət || 'dju:plɪkət/ *n* duplicado *m*, copia *f*

duplicate³ /'du:plɪkeɪt || 'dju:plɪkeɪt/ *vt* **(a)** (copy) ‹*letter/document*› hacer* copias de **(b)** (repeat) ‹*work/efforts*› repetir* (*en forma innecesaria*)

durable /'dʊrəbəl || 'djʊərəbəl/ *adj* durable

duration /dʊ'reɪʃən || 'djʊə'reɪʃən/ *n* [U] duración *f*

duress /dʊ'res || djʊə'res/ *n* [U]: **under ~** bajo coacción

during /'dʊrɪŋ || 'djʊərɪŋ/ *prep* durante

dusk /dʌsk/ *n* [U] anochecer *m*

dust¹ /dʌst/ *n* [U] polvo *m*; ***to bite the ~*** «*person*» morder* el polvo

dust² *vt* **1** (remove dust from): **to ~ the furniture** quitarles el polvo a los muebles, sacudir los muebles (CS, Méx) **2** (sprinkle) **to ~ sth WITH sth** espolvorear algo CON algo

dust: **~bin** /'dʌstbɪn, 'dʌsbɪn/ *n* (BrE) cubo *m* *or* (CS, Per) tacho *m* *or* (Méx) tambo *m* *or* (Col) caneca *f* *or* (Ven) tobo *m* de la basura; **~cart** /'dʌstkɑ:rt, 'dʌskɑ:rt || 'dʌstkɑ:t, dʌskɑ:t/ *n* (BrE) camión *m* de la basura; **~ cloth** *n* (AmE) trapo *m* del polvo, trapo *m* de sacudir (CS, Méx), sacudidor *m* (Méx)

duster /'dʌstər || 'dʌstə(r)/ *n* **1** (Clothing) (housecoat) (AmE) guardapolvo *m* **2** (BrE) **(a)** (for blackboard) borrador *m* **(b)** ⇒ DUST CLOTH

dust: **~ jacket** *n* sobrecubierta *f*; **~man** /'dʌstmən, 'dʌsmən/ *n* (*pl* **-men** /-mən/) (BrE) basurero *m*; **~pan** /'dʌstpæn, 'dʌspæn/ *n* pala *f*, recogedor *m*

dusty /ˈdʌsti/ *adj* **-tier, -tiest** ‹*furniture*› cubierto de polvo; ‹*road/plain*› polvoriento

Dutch¹ /dʌtʃ/ *adj* holandés; ***to go* ~** pagar* a escote (fam), pagar* *or* ir* a la americana (AmL), pagar* *or* ir* a la inglesa (Chi fam)

Dutch² *n* **(a)** [U] (language) holandés *m* **(b)** (people) (+ *pl vb*) **the ~** los holandeses

Dutch: **~man** /ˈdʌtʃmən/ *n* (*pl* **-men** /-mən/) holandés *m*; **~woman** *n* holandesa *f*

dutiful /ˈdu:tifəl ‖ ˈdju:tifəl/ *adj* consciente de sus deberes

duty /ˈdu:ti ‖ ˈdju:ti/ *n* (*pl* **duties**) **1** [C U] (obligation) deber *m*, obligación *f* **2** [U] **(a)** (service) servicio *m*; **to do ~ as sth** hacer* las veces de algo, servir* de algo **(b)** (in phrases) **to be on/off ~** «*nurse/doctor*» estar*/no estar* de turno *or* guardia; «*policeman/fireman*» estar*/no estar* de servicio **(c) duties** *pl n* (responsibilities) (frml) funciones *fpl*, responsabilidades *fpl* **3** [C U] (Tax) (*often pl*) impuesto *m*

duty: **~-free** /ˈdu:tiˈfri: ‖ ˌdju:tiˈfri:/ *adj* libre de impuestos; **~-free shop** *n* duty free *m*, tienda *f* libre de impuestos

duvet /du:veɪ/ *n* (BrE) edredón *m* (nórdico)

dwarf¹ /dwɔ:rf ‖ dwɔ:f/ *n* (*pl* **~s** *or* **dwarves** /dwɔ:rvz/) enano, -na *m,f*; (*before n*) ‹*tree/species*› enano

dwarf² *vt* ‹*building*› hacer* parecer pequeño

dwell /dwel/ (*past & past p* **dwelt** *or* **dwelled**) *vi* (liter) morar (liter), vivir

• **dwell on** [*v* + *prep* + *o*]: **try not to ~ on the past** trata de no pensar demasiado en el pasado; **the documentary ~s excessively on** ... el documental se detiene demasiado *or* hace demasiado hincapié en ...

dwelling /ˈdwelɪŋ/ *n* **(a)** (habitation) (liter) morada *f* (liter) **(b)** (house) (frml) vivienda *f*

dwelt /dwelt/ *past & past p of* DWELL

dwindle /ˈdwɪndl/ *vi* **(a)** «*numbers/population*» disminuir*, menguar*, reducirse* **(b) dwindling** *pres p*: **dwindling resources** recursos *mpl* cada vez más limitados

dye¹ /daɪ/ *n* tintura *f*, tinte *m*

dye² **dyes, dyeing, dyed** *vt* teñir*

dying /ˈdaɪɪŋ/ *adj* (*before n*) **(a)** (near death, extinction) ‹*person/animal*› moribundo, agonizante; ‹*race/art*› en vías de extinción **(b)** (related to time of death) ‹*wish/words/breath*› último, postrero (liter)

dyke /daɪk/ *n* **1** ⇒ DIKE 1 **2** (lesbian) (sl & often pej) tortillera *f* (arg)

dynamic /daɪˈnæmɪk/ *adj* dinámico

dynamite /ˈdaɪnəmaɪt/ *n* dinamita *f*

dynamo /ˈdaɪnəməʊ/ *n* (*pl* **-mos**) dínamo *m or* dinamo *m* (AmL), dinamo *f or* dínamo *f* (Esp)

dynasty /ˈdaɪnəsti ‖ ˈdɪnəsti/ *n* (*pl* **-ties**) dinastía *f*

dysentery /ˈdɪsn̩teri ‖ ˈdɪsəntri/ *n* [U] disentería *f*

dysfunction /dɪsˈfʌŋkʃən/ *n* [U C] disfunción *f*

dysfunctional /dɪsˈfʌŋkʃnəl ‖ dɪsˈfʌŋkʃənl̩/ *adj* disfuncional

dyslexia /dɪsˈleksiə/ *n* [U] dislexia *f*

dyslexic /dɪsˈleksɪk/ *adj* disléxico

Ee

E, e /i:/ *n* **(a)** (letter) E, e *f* **(b)** (Mus) mi *m*

E (= **east**) E

each¹ /i:tʃ/ *adj* cada *adj inv*

each² *pron* **1** cada uno, cada una; **he questioned ~ of them in turn** les preguntó uno por uno **2 each other**: **they are always criticizing ~ other** siempre se están criticando el uno al otro; (if more than two people) siempre se están criticando unos a otros; **their respect for ~ other** su mutuo respeto

each³ *adv*: **we were paid $10 ~** nos pagaron 10 dólares a cada uno; **the apples are 20 cents ~** las manzanas valen 20 centavos por pieza *or* cada una

eager /ˈi:gər ‖ ˈi:gə(r)/ *adj* (excited, impatient) impaciente, ansioso; (keen) entusiasta; **she looked at their ~ faces** miró sus caras llenas de ilusión; **he's ~ to please** está deseoso de complacer; **she is ~ for change** tiene muchos deseos de cambio

eagerly /ˈi:gərli ‖ ˈi:gəli/ *adv* ‹*accept/agree*› con entusiasmo; ‹*await*› ansiosamente, con ansiedad e impaciencia; ‹*listen/read*› con avidez

eagle /ˈi:gəl/ *n* águila *f*‡

ear /ɪr ‖ ɪə(r)/ **▶000** *n* **1 (a)** (Anat) oreja *f*; (organ) oído *m* **(b)** (sense of hearing) (*no pl*) oído *m*; **to play sth by ~** tocar* algo de oído **2** (of corn) espiga *f*

ear: **~ache** *n* [U C] dolor *m* de oído; **~drum** *n* tímpano *m*

earl /ɜ:rl ‖ ɜ:l/ *n* conde *m*

early¹ /ˈɜ:rli ‖ ˈɜ:li/ *adj* **-lier, -liest 1** (before expected time) ‹*arrival/elections*› anticipado; **to be ~** «*person*» llegar* temprano; **the bus was ~** el autobús pasó (*or* salió *etc*) antes de la hora **2 (a)** (before normal time): **to have an ~ night** acostarse* temprano; **~ retirement** jubilación *f* anticipada **(b)** ‹*crop/variety*› temprano, tempranero **3** (far back in time): **~ man** el hombre primitivo; **his earliest memories** sus primeros recuerdos **4** (toward beginning of period): **it's too ~ to tell** es demasiado pronto para saber; **in ~ June** a principios de junio; **he was in his ~ twenties** tenía poco más de veinte años

early² *adv* **-lier, -liest 1** (before expected time) temprano **2** (before usual time) temprano, pronto (Esp) **3** (toward beginning of period): **~ in the morning** por la mañana temprano; **~ in the year** a principios de año; **~ (on) in her career** en los comienzos de su carrera **4** (soon) pronto; **they won't be here till nine at the earliest** por temprano que lleguen no estarán aquí antes de las nueve

ear: **~mark** *vt* ‹*money/funds*› destinar; **~muffs** *pl n* orejeras *fpl*

earn /ɜ:rn ‖ ɜ:n/ *vt* **1** ‹*money/wages*› ganar; ‹*interest*› dar* **2** ‹*respect/gratitude*› ganarse; ‹*promotion*› ganar

earnest¹ /'ɜ:rnəst ‖ 'ɜ:nɪst/ *adj* **(a)** (sincere) (frml) ‹*effort/attempt*› serio; ‹*wish*› ferviente **(b)** (serious) serio

earnest² *n* **in ~** en serio

earnings /'ɜ:rnɪŋz ‖ 'ɜ:nɪŋz/ *pl n* ingresos *mpl*

ear: **~plug** *n* tapón *m* para el oído; **~ring** *n* arete *m* (AmL), aro *m* (CS), pendiente *m* (Esp), caravana *f* (Ur); **~shot** *n*: **to be within/out of ~shot** estar*/no estar* lo suficientemente cerca como para oír

earth /ɜ:rθ ‖ ɜ:θ/ *n* **1** [U] **(a)** (Astron, Relig) tierra *f*; **the ~** *o* **E~** la Tierra **(b)** (*as intensifier*): **why on ~ didn't you warn me?** ¿por qué diablos no me avisaste? **2** [U] (land, soil) tierra *f* **3** [U] (BrE Elec) tierra *f*

earthenware /'ɜ:rθənwer ‖ 'ɜ:θənweə(r)/ *n* [U] (material) barro *m* (cocido); (dishes) vajilla *f* de barro (cocido)

earth: **~quake** *n* terremoto *m*; **~worm** *n* lombriz *f* (de tierra)

earwig /'ɪrwɪg ‖ 'ɪəwɪg/ *n* tijereta *f*, cortapicos *m*

ease¹ /i:z ‖ i:z/ *n* [U] **1** (facility) facilidad *f*; **~ of operation** facilidad de manejo; **for ~ of access** para facilitar el acceso; **with ~** fácilmente **2 (a)** (freedom from constraint): **at ~** a gusto; **to put sb at his/her ~** hacer* que algn se sienta a gusto **(b)** (Mil): **(stand) at ~!** ¡descansen!

ease² *vt* **1 (a)** (relieve) ‹*pain*› calmar, aliviar; ‹*tension*› hacer* disminuir, aliviar; ‹*burden*› aligerar; **to ~ sb's mind** tranquilizar* a algn **(b)** (make easier) ‹*situation*› paliar; ‹*transition*› facilitar; **to ~ the way for sth** preparar el terreno para algo **2 (a)** ‹*rules/restrictions*› relajar **(b)** ‹*belt/rope*› aflojar **3** (move with care) (+ *adv compl*): **they ~d him into the wheelchair** lo sentaron con cuidado en la silla de ruedas; **he ~d the key into the lock** introdujo la llave en la cerradura con cuidado ■ **~** *vi* «*pain*» aliviarse, calmarse; «*tension*» disminuir*

• **ease off** [*v* + *adv*] «*rain*» amainar; «*pain*» aliviarse, calmarse; «*pressure/traffic*» disminuir*

• **ease up** [*v* + *adv*] (slacken pace — of life) tomarse las cosas con más calma; (— of work, activity) bajar el ritmo

easel /'i:zəl/ *n* caballete *m*

easily /'i:zəli ‖ 'i:zɪli/ *adv* **1 (a)** (without difficulty) fácilmente, con facilidad **(b)** (readily) ‹*break/stain/cry*› **2** (by far) con mucho, (de) lejos (AmL fam); **there's ~ enough for everybody** hay de sobra para todos

east¹ /i:st/ *n* [U] **1** (point of the compass, direction) este *m*; **the ~, the E~** (region) el este **2 the East** (the Orient) (el) Oriente

east² *adj* (*before n*) este *adj inv*, oriental; ‹*wind*› del este

east³ *adv* al este

eastbound /'i:stbaʊnd/ *adj* que va (*or* iba *etc*) en dirección este *or* hacia el este

Easter /'i:stər ‖ 'i:stə(r)/ *n* Pascua *f* (de Resurrección); (*before n*) **~ Day** *o* **Sunday** (el) Domingo de Pascua *or* Resurrección; **~ egg** huevo *m* de Pascua

easterly /'i:stərli ‖ 'i:stəli/ *adj* ‹*wind*› del este; **in an ~ direction** hacia el este, en dirección este

eastern /'i:stərn ‖ 'i:stən/ *adj* **(a)** (Geog) (*before n*) oriental, este *adj inv*; **heavy rain over ~ England** fuertes lluvias en *or* sobre el este de Inglaterra; **the ~ states** los estados del este; **E~ Europe** Europa Oriental *or* del Este **(b)** (oriental) ‹*appearance/custom*› oriental

eastward¹ /'i:stwərd ‖ 'i:stwəd/ *adj* (*before n*): **in an ~ direction** en dirección este, hacia el este

eastward², (BrE) **eastwards** /-z/ *adv* hacia el este

easy¹ /'i:zi/ *adj* **easier, easiest 1** (not difficult) fácil; **it's ~ to see that** ... es fácil ver que ...; **she was an ~ winner** ganó sin problemas **2** (undemanding) ‹*life*› fácil; **to be ~ on the eye** ser* agradable a la vista

easy² *adv* **1** (without difficulty): **money doesn't come ~** el dinero no es fácil de conseguir; **~ *come*, ~ *go*** así como viene se va **2** (slowly, calmly) despacio, con calma; **~ does it** despacito; **to take it ~** tomárselo con calma

easy: **~ chair** *n* sillón *m*, poltrona *f*, butaca *f*; **~going** /'i:zi'gəʊɪŋ/ *adj*: **she's very ~going** es una persona de trato fácil *or* sin complicaciones

eat /i:t/ (*past* **ate**; *past p* **eaten**) *vt/i* comer

• **eat away** [*v* + *o* + *adv*, *v* + *adv* + *o*] «*rats/mice*» roer*; «*moths*» picar*, comerse; «*acid*» corroer*

• **eat into** [*v* + *prep* + *o*] «*acid/rust*» corroer*; ‹*profits/savings*› comerse

• **eat up 1** [*v* + *o* + *adv*, *v* + *adv* + *o*] (finish) ‹*meal/food*› comerse **2** [*v* + *adv*] (finish meal) terminar (de comer) **3** [*v* + *adv* + *o*] (consume) ‹*fuel/electricity*› consumir, gastar **4** [*v* + *o* + *adv*] «*curiosity/ambition*» consumir

eaten /'i:tn̩/ *past p of* EAT

eater /'i:tər ‖ 'i:tə(r)/ *n*: **he's a big ~** come mucho, es muy comelón *or* (CS, Esp) comilón (fam); **we're big meat ~s** comemos mucha carne

eaves /i:vz/ *pl n* alero *m*

eavesdrop /'ivzdrɑ:p ‖ 'i:vzdrɒp/ *vi* **-pp- to ~** (ON **sth/sb**) escuchar (algo/a algn) a escondidas

ebb¹ /eb/ *n* reflujo *m*; **the ~ and flow of the tide** el flujo y reflujo de la marea; ***to be at a low ~*** «*person*» estar* decaído; «*diplomatic relations*» estar* en un punto bajo

ebb² *vi* **(a)** «*tide*» bajar, retroceder; **to ~ and flow** fluir* y refluir* **(b)** (dwindle) decaer*

• **ebb away** [*v* + *adv*]: **his life was ~ing away**

se consumía poco a poco; **I felt my strength ~ing away** sentí que me abandonaban las fuerzas

ebb tide *n* reflujo *m*

ebony /'ebəni/ *n* [U] **(a)** (wood) ébano *m* **(b)** ▶515 (color) color *m* (de) ébano; (*before n*) ‹*hair/skin*› negro como el ébano

EC *n* (= **European Community**) CE *f*

eccentric¹ /ɪk'sentrɪk, ek-/ *adj* excéntrico

eccentric² *n* excéntrico, -ca *m,f*

eccentricity /'eksen'trɪsəti/ *n* [U C] (*pl* **-ties**) excentricidad *f*

ecclesiastical /ɪ'kli:zi'æstɪkəl/ *adj* eclesiástico

echo¹ /'ekəʊ/ *n* (*pl* **-oes**) eco *m*

echo² *vi* «*footsteps/voices*» hacer* eco

eclair /eɪ'kleə(r), ɪ'kleə(r)/ *n*: *pastel individual relleno de crema*

eclipse¹ /ɪ'klɪps/ *n* eclipse *m*

eclipse² *vt* eclipsar

ecological /'i:kə'lɑ:dʒəkəl ‖ ˌi:kə'lɒdʒɪkəl/ *adj* ecológico

ecologist /ɪ'kɑ:lədʒəst ‖ i:'kɒlədʒɪst/ *n* (student of ecology) ecólogo, -ga *m,f*; (conservationist) ecologista *mf*

ecology /ɪ'kɑ:lədʒi ‖ ɪ'kɒlədʒi/ *n* [U] ecología *f*

economic /'ekə'nɑ:mɪk, 'i:k- ‖ ˌi:kə'nɒmɪk, ˌek-/ *adj* económico

economical /'ekə'nɑ:mɪkəl, 'i:k- ‖ ˌi:kə'nɒmɪkəl, ˌek-/ *adj* económico

economics /'ekə'nɑ:mɪks, 'i:k- ‖ ˌi:kə'nɒmɪks, ˌek-/ *n* **(a)** (+ *sing vb*) economía *f* **(b)** (financial aspect) (+ *pl vb*) aspecto *m* económico

economist /ɪ'kɑ:nəməst ‖ ɪ'kɒnəmɪst/ *n* economista *mf*

economize /ɪ'kɑ:nəmaɪz ‖ ɪ'kɒnəmaɪz/ *vi* economizar*; **to ~ ON sth** economizar* algo

economy /ɪ'kɑ:nəmi, i:- ‖ ɪ'kɒnəmi/ *n* (*pl* **-mies**) **1** [C] (economic state or system of country) economía *f* **2 (a)** [C] (saving): **to make economies** economizar*, hacer* economía(s) **(b)** [U] (thrift) economía *f*; (*before n*) ‹*pack/size*› familiar; **~ class** clase *f* turista

ecstasy /'ekstəsi/ *n* (*pl* **-sies**) **(a)** [U C] (state) éxtasis *m* **(b)** [U] (drug) éxtasis *m*

ecstatic /ɪk'stætɪk/ *adj* ‹*look/expression*› extasiado, extático; ‹*applause*› clamoroso

ECU /'i:kju:, eɪ'ku:/ *n* (*pl* **ECUs**) ecu *m*

Ecuador /'ekwədɔ:r ‖ 'ekwədɔ:(r)/ *n* Ecuador *m*

Ecuadorean /'ekwə'dɔ:riən/ *adj* ecuatoriano

ecumenical /'ekjə'menɪkəl ‖ ˌi:kju:'menɪkəl, 'ek-/ *adj* ecuménico

eczema /ɪg'zi:mə, 'egzəmə ‖ 'eksɪmə/ *n* [U] eczema *m*

eddy¹ /'edi/ *n* (*pl* **eddies**) remolino *m*, torbellino *m*

eddy² *vi* **eddies, eddying, eddied** «*water*» formar remolinos; «*smoke/dust*» arremolinarse

Eden /'i:dn̩/ *n* Edén *m*

edge¹ /edʒ/ *n* **1 (a)** (*no pl*) (border, brink — of town) afueras *fpl*; (— of forest) lindero *m*, borde *m*; (— of river, lake) orilla *f*, margen *m*; (— of cliff) borde *m* **(b)** (of plate, table, chair) borde *m*; (of coin) canto *m*; (of page) margen *m* **2** (cutting part) filo *m*; ***to be on ~*** estar* nervioso, tener* los nervios de punta (fam)

edge² *vt*: **the collar was ~d with fur** el cuello estaba ribeteado de piel; **the paper was ~d in black** el papel tenía un borde negro ■ ~ *vi* (+ *adv compl*): **to ~ forward/closer/away** ir* avanzando/acercándose/alejándose (poco a poco)

edging /'edʒɪŋ/ *n* borde *m*

edgy /'edʒi/ *adj* tenso, con los nervios de punta

edible /'edəbəl/ *adj* (safe to eat) comestible; (eatable) pasable, comible

edifying /'edəfaɪɪŋ ‖ 'edɪfaɪɪŋ/ *adj* edificante

Edinburgh /'edn̩ˌbɜ:rə, -rəʊ ‖ 'edɪnbrə/ *n* Edimburgo *m*

edit /'edət ‖ 'edɪt/ *vt* **1** ‹*manuscript*› (correct) corregir*, editar; (cut) recortar, editar **2** ‹*movie/tape*› editar **3** (manage) ‹*newspaper/magazine*› dirigir*

edition /ɪ'dɪʃən/ *n* edición *f*

editor /'edətər ‖ 'edɪtə(r)/ *n* **1** (of text) redactor, -tora *m,f*, editor, -tora *m,f*; (of collected works, series) editor, -tora *m,f* **2** (of newspaper, magazine) director, -tora *m,f*, redactor, -tora *m,f* responsable **3** (of movie, radio show) editor, -tora *m,f*

editorial¹ /'edə'tɔ:riəl ‖ ˌedɪ'tɔ:riəl/ *adj* **(a)** (Publ) ‹*assistant/director*› de redacción **(b)** (Journ) ‹*comment/decision/freedom*› editorial

editorial² *n* editorial *m*

EDT (in US) = **Eastern Daylight Time**

educate /'edʒəkeɪt ‖ 'edjʊkeɪt/ *vt* **(a)** (teach, school) educar* **(b)** (make aware) concientizar* *or* (Esp) concienciar

educated /'edʒəkeɪtəd ‖ 'edjʊkeɪtɪd/ *adj* ‹*person*› culto; **to make an ~ guess** hacer* una conjetura hecha con cierta base

education /'edʒə'keɪʃən ‖ ˌedjʊ'keɪʃən/ *n* [U] educación *f*; (*before n*) ‹*system/policy*› educativo

educational /'edʒə'keɪʃn̩əl ‖ ˌedjʊ'keɪʃənl̩/ *adj* **(a)** ‹*establishment*› docente, de enseñanza; ‹*toy*› educativo **(b)** (instructive) instructivo

Edwardian /ed'wɔ:rdiən ‖ ed'wɔ:diən/ *adj* eduardiano

EEC *n* (= **European Economic Community**) CEE *f*

eel /i:l/ *n* anguila *f*

e'er /er ‖ eə(r)/ *adv* (poet & arch) ⇒ EVER

eerie /'ɪri ‖ 'ɪəri/ *adj* **eerier, eeriest** ‹*atmosphere/silence/cry*› inquietante, espeluznante; ‹*glow/place*› fantasmagórico

efface /ɪ'feɪs/ *vt* (frml) borrar

effect¹ /ɪ'fekt/ *n* **1 (a)** (consequence) efecto *m*; **to take ~** surtir efecto **(b) in effect** de hecho, realmente **(c)** (phenomenon) efecto *m* **2** (impression) impresión *f*; **he only did it for ~** lo hizo sólo para llamar la atención **3** (applicability, operation): **to come into ~, to take ~** entrar en vigor *or* en vigencia **4** (meaning): **a statement was issued to the ~ that** ... (frml) se hizo público un comunicado anunciando que ...; **he said it wasn't true, or words to that ~** dijo que no era verdad o algo de ese tenor **5 effects** *pl* **(a)** (*special ~s*) (Cin, TV) efectos *mpl* especiales **(b)** (belongings) (frml) efectos *mpl* (frml)

effect² *vt* (frml) ‹*reconciliation/cure*› lograr; ‹*escape*› llevar a cabo; ‹*repairs/payment*› efectuar* (frml)

effective /ɪ'fektɪv/ *adj* **(a)** (producing the desired result) ‹*method/treatment*› eficaz, efectivo **(b)** (striking) ‹*design/contrast*› de mucho efecto **(c)** (real) (*before n*) ‹*control/leader*› efectivo

effectively /ɪ'fektɪvli/ *adv* **(a)** ‹*manage/spend*› con eficacia, eficazmente **(b)** ‹*contrast/decorate*› con mucho gran efecto; ‹*speak*› convincentemente **(c)** (in effect) (*indep*) de hecho

effeminate /ə'femənət ‖ ɪ'femɪnət/ *adj* afeminado

effervescent /'efər'vesənt ‖ ˌefə'vesənt/ *adj* ‹*liquid/personality*› efervescente

efficiency /ɪ'fɪʃənsi/ *n* [U] (*pl* **-cies**) (of person, system) eficiencia *f*; (Mech Eng, Phys) rendimiento *m*

efficient /ɪ'fɪʃənt/ *adj* ‹*person/system*› eficiente; ‹*machine/engine*› de buen rendimiento

efficiently /ɪ'fɪʃəntli/ *adv* eficientemente

effigy /'efədʒi ‖ 'efɪdʒi/ *n* (*pl* **-gies**) efigie *f*

effluent /'efluənt/ *n* [U C] (liquid waste) vertidos *mpl*; (sewage) aguas *fpl* residuales

effort /'efərt ‖ 'efət/ *n* [C U] esfuerzo *m*; **to make an ~** hacer* un esfuerzo, esforzarse*; **it's not worth the ~** no merece *or* vale la pena

effortless /'efərtləs ‖ 'efətlɪs/ *adj* ‹*grace*› natural; ‹*prose/style*› fluido

e.g. (for example) p. ej. *or* vg. *or* e.g.; (in speech) por ejemplo

egalitarian /ɪ'gælə'teriən ‖ ɪˌgælɪ'teəriən/ *adj* igualitario

egg /eg/ *n* huevo *m*
• egg on [*v* + *o* + *adv*, *v* + *adv* + *o*] incitar

egg: **~cup** *n* huevera *f*; **~plant** *n* [C U] (AmE) berenjena *f*; **~shell** *n* [C U] cáscara *f* de huevo; **~ timer** *n* (with sand) reloj *m* de arena (*de tres minutos*); (clockwork) avisador *m*; **~ white** *n* [C U] clara *f* de huevo; **~ yolk** *n* [C U] yema *f* de huevo

ego /'i:gəʊ, 'egəʊ/ *n* (*pl* **egos**) **(a)** (Psych) **the ~** el yo, el ego **(b)** (self-regard) amor *m* propio, ego *m*

ego trip *n* (colloq): **his autobiography is simply an ~ ~** su autobiografía es un regodeo ególatra

Egypt /'i:dʒəpt ‖ 'i:dʒɪpt/ *n* Egipto *m*

Egyptian¹ /ɪ'dʒɪpʃən/ *adj* egipcio

Egyptian² *n* egipcio, -cia *m,f*

eiderdown /'aɪdərdaʊn ‖ 'aɪdədaʊn/ *n* edredón *m*

eight /eɪt/ ▶ **451**, **724**, **884** *adj/n* ocho *adj inv/m*; *see also* FOUR¹

eighteen /eɪ'ti:n/ ▶ **451**, **724**, **884** *adj/n* dieciocho *adj inv/m*; *see also* FOUR¹

eighteenth¹ /eɪ'ti:nθ/ ▶ **540**, **725** *adj* decimoctavo

eighteenth² *adv* en decimoctavo lugar

eighteenth³ ▶ **540**, **543**, **725** *n* **(a)** (Math) dieciochoavo *m*; (part) dieciochoava parte *f* **(b)** (birthday): **it's her ~ today** hoy cumple dieciocho años

eighth¹ /eɪtθ/ ▶ **540**, **725** *adj* octavo

eighth² *adv* en octavo lugar

eighth³ ▶ **540**, **543**, **725** *n* (Math) octavo *m*; (part) octava parte *f*

eighth note *n* (AmE) corchea *f*

eightieth¹ /'eɪtiəθ/ ▶ **725** *adj* octogésimo

eightieth² *adv* en octogésimo lugar

eightieth³ ▶ **543**, **725** *n* (Math) ochentavo *m*; (part) ochentava *or* octogésima parte *f*

eighty /'eɪti/ ▶ **451**, **540**, **724** *adj/n* ochenta *adj inv/m*; *see also* FOUR¹

Eire /'erə ‖ 'eərə/ *n* Eire *m*, Irlanda *f*

either¹ /'i:ðər, 'aɪðər ‖ 'i:ðə(r), 'aɪðə(r)/ ▶ **718** *conj* **either** ... **or** ... o ... o ...

■ **Note** In the usual translation of *either* ... *or*, *o* ... *o*, *o* becomes *u* when it precedes a word beginning with *o* or *ho*.

---

either² *adj*: **you can take ~ route** puedes tomar cualquiera de las dos rutas; **on ~ side of the path** a ambos lados del camino

either³ ▶ **718** *pron* (esp BrE) cualquiera; (*with neg*) ninguno, -na; (*in questions*) alguno, -na

either⁴ *adv* (*with neg*) tampoco; **she can't cook and he can't ~** ella no sabe cocinar y él tampoco

ejaculate /ɪ'dʒækjəleɪt ‖ ɪ'dʒækjʊleɪt/ *vi* (Physiol) eyacular

eject /ɪ'dʒekt/ *vt* ‹*troublemaker/cassette*› expulsar ■ **~** *vi* (Aviat) eyectarse

eke out /i:k/ [*v* + *adv* + *o*, *v* + *o* + *adv*] **(a)** (make last) ‹*resources/funds*› estirar, hacer* alcanzar **(b)** (barely obtain): **to ~ out a living** ganarse la vida a duras penas

elaborate¹ /ɪ'læbərət/ *adj* ‹*decoration/design/hairstyle*› complicado; ‹*meal*› de mucho trabajo; ‹*plan*› minucioso

elaborate² /ɪ'læbəreɪt/ *vt* elaborar ■ **~** *vi* dar* (más) detalles

elapse /ɪ'læps/ *vi* transcurrir

elastic¹ /ɪ'læstɪk/ *n* **(a)** [U] (Tex) elástico *m* **(b)** [C] (garter) (AmE) liga *f* **(c)** [C] (AmE) ⇒ ELASTIC BAND

elastic² *adj* ‹*waistband/garter*› de elástico; ‹*stocking*› elastizado; ‹*fiber/properties*› elástico

elastic band *n* (esp BrE) goma *f* (elástica), gomita *f*, liga *f* (Méx), caucho *m* (Col), elástico *m* (Chi), banda *f* elástica (Ven)

elated /ɪ'leɪtəd ‖ ɪ'leɪtɪd/ *adj* eufórico

elbow¹ /'elbəʊ/ ▶ **484** *n* codo *m*

elbow² *vt* darle* un codazo a; **they ~ed us out of the way** nos apartaron a empujones

elbow: **~ grease** *n* [U] (colloq): **put some ~ grease into it!** ¡dale con más fuerza! (fam); **~ room** *n* [U] espacio *m*

elder¹ /'eldər ‖ 'eldə(r)/ *adj* mayor

elder² *n* **1 (a)** (older person): **she's my ~ by two years** me lleva dos años, es dos años mayor que yo **(b)** (senior person): **the village/tribal ~s** los ancianos del pueblo/de la tribu **(c)** (Relig) miembro *m* del consejo **2** (Bot) saúco *m*

elderberry /'eldərˌberi ‖ 'eldəberi/ *n* (*pl* **-ries**) baya *f* del saúco

elderly /'eldərli ‖ 'eldəli/ *adj* mayor, de edad

eldest /'eldəst ‖ 'eldɪst/ *adj* (*before n*) ‹*brother/sister/child*› mayor; **the ~** (*as pron*) el/la mayor, el/la de más edad

elect¹ /ɪ'lekt/ *vt* **1** (Adm, Govt) elegir* **2** (choose) (frml) **to ~ to** + INF optar POR + INF

elect² *adj* (*after n*): **the president ~** el presidente electo, la presidenta electa

election /ɪ'lekʃən/ *n* **(a)** [C] (event) elecciones *fpl*; **to call/hold an ~** convocar*/celebrar elecciones; (*before n*) ‹*campaign/speech*› electoral; ‹*day/results*› de las elecciones **(b)** [U] (act) elección *f*

elector /ɪ'lektər ‖ ɪ'lektə(r)/ *n* elector, -tora *m,f*

electoral /ɪ'lektərəl/ *adj* (*usu before n*) ‹*system/reform*› electoral; **~ register** *o* **roll** padrón *m* (AmL) *or* (Esp) censo *m or* (Chi, Ven) registro *m or* (Col) planilla *f* electoral

electorate /ɪ'lektərət/ *n* (+ *sing or pl vb*) electorado *m*

electric /ɪ'lektrɪk/ *adj* eléctrico; ‹*fence*› electrificado; ‹*performance/atmosphere*› electrizante

electrical /ɪ'lektrɪkəl/ *adj* eléctrico

electric: **~ blanket** *n* manta *f or* (AmL exc CS) cobija *f or* (CS) frazada *f* eléctrica; **~ chair** *n* silla *f* eléctrica

electrician /ɪ,lek'trɪʃən/ *n* electricista *mf*

electricity /ɪ,lek'trɪsəti/ *n* [U] electricidad *f*

electric shock *n* [C U] descarga *f* eléctrica

electrify /ɪ'lektrəfaɪ ‖ ɪ'lektrɪfaɪ/ *vt* **-fies, -fying, -fied** electrificar*; (excite, thrill) electrizar*

electrocute /ɪ'lektrəkju:t/ *vt* electrocutar

electrode /ɪ'lektrəʊd/ *n* electrodo *m*

electrolysis /ɪ'lek'trɑ:ləsɪs ‖ ,ɪlek'trɒləsɪs/ *n* [U] electrólisis *f*

electron /ɪ'lektrɑ:n ‖ ɪ'lektrɒn/ *n* electrón *m*

electronic /ɪ'lek'trɑ:nɪk ‖ ,ɪlek'trɒnɪk/ *adj* electrónico

electronic mail *n* [U] correo *m* electrónico

electronics /ɪ'lek'trɑ:nɪks ‖ ,ɪlek'trɒnɪks/ *n* **(a)** (subject) (+ *sing vb*) electrónica *f*, (*before n*) ‹*industry*› electrónico **(b)** (circuitry) (+ *sing or pl vb*) sistema *m* electrónico

elegance /'elɪgəns/ *n* [U] elegancia *f*

elegant /'elɪgənt/ *adj* elegante

element /'eləmənt ‖ 'elɪmənt/ *n* **1 (a)** (part, group) elemento *m*; **an ~ of doubt** algo de duda; **extremist ~s in society** elementos extremistas de la sociedad **(b) elements** *pl* (rudiments): **the basic ~s of self-defense** los principios elementales de la defensa personal **2** (Chem) elemento *m* **3 elements** *pl* (weather) (liter) **the ~s** los elementos **4** (preferred environment) elemento *m*; **to be in one's ~** estar* en su (*or* mi *etc*) elemento **5** (of kettle, heater) resistencia *f*, elemento *m* (CS)

elementary /'elə'mentəri ‖ ,elɪ'mentri/ *adj* elemental

elementary: **~ school** *n* (in US) escuela *f* (de enseñanza) primaria; **~ teacher** *n* (in US) maestro, -tra *m,f* de enseñanza primaria

elephant /'eləfənt ‖ 'elɪfənt/ *n* elefante, -ta *m,f*

elevate /'eləveɪt ‖ 'elɪveɪt/ *vt* **(a)** (promote): **to ~ sb to the peerage** concederle a algn el título de lord/lady; **he's been ~d to the position of manager** (hum) lo han ascendido a director **(b)** (frml) ‹*spirit*› elevar **(c)** ‹*load/platform*› elevar (frml), subir

elevated railroad /'eləveɪtəd ‖ 'elɪveɪtɪd/ *n* [U C] (AmE) ferrocarril *m* elevado

elevation /'elə'veɪʃən ‖ ,elɪ'veɪʃən/ *n* **1** [U] (promotion) elevación *f* **2** [C] (angle) elevación *f* **3** [C] (altitude) altura *f*

elevator /'eləveɪtər ‖ 'elɪveɪtə(r)/ *n* **(a)** (for passengers) (AmE) ascensor *m*, elevador *m* (Méx) **(b)** (for goods) elevador *m*, montacargas *m*

eleven¹ /ɪ'levən/ ▶**451**, **724**, **884** *n* **(a)** (number) once *m*; *see also* FOUR¹ **(b)** (in soccer, field hockey) equipo *m*, once *m* (period)

eleven² ▶**451**, **724**, **884** *adj* once *adj inv*

eleventh¹ /ɪ'levənθ/ ▶**540**, **725** *adj* undécimo

eleventh² *adv* en undécimo lugar

eleventh³ ▶**540**, **543**, **725** *n* (Math) onceavo *m*; (part) onceava parte *f*

elf /elf/ *n* (*pl* **elves**) geniecillo *m*, elfo *m*

elicit /ɪ'lɪsət ‖ ɪ'lɪsɪt/ *vt* ‹*laughter/smile*› provocar*; **to ~ sth** (FROM **sb**) ‹*explanation/reply*› obtener* algo (DE algn)

eligible /'elədʒəbəl ‖ 'elɪdʒəbəl/ *adj* **(a)** (qualified, suitable) ‹*applicant/candidate*› que reúne los requisitos necesarios; **he's ~ for a grant** tiene derecho a solicitar una beca; **he is not ~ to compete** no reúne los requisitos necesarios para competir **(b)** (marriageable): **an ~ bachelor** un buen partido

eliminate /ɪ'lɪməneɪt ‖ ɪ'lɪmɪneɪt/ *vt* eliminar; ‹*possibility/suspect*› descartar

elimination /ɪ'lɪmə'neɪʃən ‖ ɪ,lɪmɪ'neɪʃən/ *n* [U] (getting rid of) eliminación *f*; (ruling out) descarte *m*; **by a process of ~** por (un proceso de) eliminación *or* descarte

elite¹ /eɪ'li:t, i-/ *n* (+ *sing or pl vb*) elite *f*, élite *f*

elite² *adj* (*before n*) selecto, de elite *or* élite

elitism /eɪ'li:tɪzəm, i-/ *n* [U] elitismo *m*

elitist /eɪ'li:tɪst, i-/ *adj* elitista

elixir /ɪ'lɪksər ‖ ɪ'lɪksə(r)/ *n* elixir *m*

Elizabethan /ɪ'lɪzə'bi:θən/ *adj* isabelino

elk /elk/ *n* (*pl* **~s** *or* **~**) (European animal) alce *m*; (American animal) uapití *m*

elm /elm/ *n* **~ (tree)** olmo *m*

elocution /'elə'kju:ʃən/ *n* [U] dicción *f*, elocución *f*

elongated /ɪ'lɔ:ŋgeɪtəd ‖ 'i:lɒŋgeɪtɪd/ *adj* alargado

elope /ɪ'ləʊp/ *vi* fugarse* (*con un amante, novio para casarse*)

eloquent /'eləkwənt/ *adj* elocuente

El Salvador /el'sælvədɔ:r ‖ ,el'sælvədɔ:(r)/ *n* El Salvador

else /els/ *adv* **1** (*after pron*): **somebody** *o* **someone ~** otra persona; **everybody** *o* **everyone ~** todos los demás; **everything ~** todo lo demás; **there's not much ~ we can do** no podemos hacer mucho más; **nobody ~** nadie más; **they have nowhere ~ to go** no tienen ningún otro sitio *or* lugar adonde ir; **anything ~?** ¿algo más? **2** (with interrog): **what/who ~?** ¿qué/quién más?; **what ~ can you expect from her?** ¿qué otra cosa se puede esperar de ella? **3 or else** (*as conj*) si no

elsewhere /'elshwer ‖ ˌels'weə(r)/ *adv*: **to go ~** ir* a otro sitio *or* lugar; **~ in Europe** en otras partes *or* otros lugares de Europa

elude /iː'luːd ‖ ɪ'luːd/ *vt* (avoid) eludir; (escape from) escaparse de

elusive /iː'luːsɪv ‖ i'luːsɪv/ *adj* ‹*enemy/prey*› escurridizo, difícil de aprehender; ‹*goal/agreement*› difícil de alcanzar

elves /elvz/ *pl of* ELF

emaciated /ɪ'meɪʃieɪtəd ‖ ɪ'meɪsieɪtɪd/ *adj* ‹*person/animal*› escuálido; ‹*body/face*› consumido

E-mail, e-mail /'iːmeɪl/ *n* [U] correo *m* electrónico

emanate /'emənert/ *vi* **to ~ FROM sth** «*gas/light/sound*» emanar DE algo; «*ideas/suggestions*» provenir* DE algo

emancipate /ɪ'mænsəpeɪt ‖ ɪ'mænsɪpeɪt/ *vt* (frml) emancipar

emancipated /ɪ'mænsəpeɪtəd ‖ ɪ'mænsɪpeɪtɪd/ *adj* emancipado; ‹*viewpoint/lifestyle*› independiente y progresista

embankment /ɪm'bæŋkmənt/ *n* (for road, railroad) terraplén *m*; (as protection) muro *m* de contención

embargo /ɪm'bɑːrgəʊ ‖ ɪm'bɑːgəʊ/ *n* (*pl* **-goes**) embargo *m*, prohibición *f*; **to put an ~ on sth** imponer* un embargo sobre algo

embark /ɪm'bɑːrk ‖ ɪm'bɑːk/ *vi* **(a)** (on ship, plane) embarcar(se)* **(b)** (start) **to ~ ON** *o* **UPON sth** ‹*on career/new life*› emprender algo; ‹*on adventure/undertaking*› embarcarse* EN algo

embarrass /ɪm'bærəs/ *vt* hacerle* pasar vergüenza a, avergonzar*

embarrassed /ɪm'bærəst/ *adj*: **an ~ silence** un silencio violento; **I'm ~** me da vergüenza, me da pena (AmL exc CS)

embarrassing /ɪm'bærəsɪŋ/ *adj* ‹*situation/question*› embarazoso; **how ~!** ¡qué vergüenza *or* (AmL exc CS) pena!

embarrassment /ɪm'bærəsmənt/ *n* **(a)** [U] (shame) bochorno *m*, vergüenza *f*, pena *f* (AmL exc CS) **(b)** [C] (cause of shame): **he's an ~ to his friends** les hace pasar vergüenza a sus amigos

embassy /'embəsi/ *n* (*pl* **-sies**) embajada *f*

embed /ɪm'bed/ *vt* **-dd-** (in rock, wood) enterrar*; **the bullet was ~ded in his arm** la bala quedó alojada en el brazo

ember /'embər ‖ 'embə(r)/ *n* brasa *f*, ascua *f*

embezzle /ɪm'bezəl/ *vt* desfalcar*, malversar

embittered /ɪm'bɪtərd ‖ ɪm'bɪtəd/ *adj* ‹*person*› amargado; ‹*fighting/rivalry*› enconado

emblem /'embləm/ *n* emblema *m*

embody /ɪm'bɑːdi ‖ ɪm'bɒdi/ *vt* **-dies, -dying, -died (a)** (personify) encarnar, personificar* **(b)** (express) ‹*thought/idea*› plasmar, expresar

emboss /ɪm'bɑːs, ɪm'bɔːs ‖ ɪm'bɒs/ *vt* **(a)** ‹*leather/metal*› repujar **(b) embossed** *past p* ‹*stationery*› con membrete en relieve; ‹*wallpaper*› estampado en relieve

embrace¹ /ɪm'breɪs/ *vt* **(a)** (hug) abrazar* **(b)** ‹*idea/principle*› abrazar*; ‹*lifestyle/religion*› adoptar ■ **~** *vi* abrazarse*

embrace² *n* abrazo *m*

embrocation /ˌembrə'keɪʃən/ *n* [U C] linimento *m*, embrocación *f* (ant)

embroider /ɪm'brɔɪdər ‖ ɪm'brɔɪdə(r)/ *vt* ‹*cloth/design*› bordar; ‹*story*› adornar

embroidery /ɪm'brɔɪdəri/ *n* [U C] (*pl* **-ries**) bordado *m*

embroil /ɪm'brɔɪl/ *vt*: **to be/become ~ed in sth** estar*/verse* envuelto en algo

embryo /'embriəʊ/ *n* (*pl* **-os**) embrión *m*

emend /iː'mend ‖ ɪ'mend/ *vt* (frml) enmendar*

emerald /'emərəld/ *n* **(a)** [C U] (gem) esmeralda *f*; **(b)** ▶ **515** [U] (color) verde *m* esmeralda

emerge /ɪ'mɜːrdʒ ‖ ɪ'mɜːdʒ/ *vi* **(a)** (come out) salir*, aparecer* **(b)** (become evident, known) «*problem*» surgir*; «*pattern*» dibujarse; «*truth*» revelarse; «*facts*» salir* a la luz

emergency /ɪ'mɜːrdʒənsi ‖ ɪ'mɜːdʒənsi/ *n* [C U] (*pl* **-cies**) **(a)** (serious situation) emergencia *f*; **in an ~** *o* **in case of ~** en una emergencia *or* en caso de emergencia **(b)** (Med) urgencia *f*; (*before n*) ‹*case/operation*› de urgencia **(c)** (Govt): **a state of ~ was declared** se declaró el estado de excepción

emergency: **~ exit** *n* salida *f* de emergencia; **~ landing** *n* aterrizaje *m* forzoso; **~ stop** *n* parada *f* de emergencia

emery /'eməri/: **~ board** *n* lima *f* de esmeril; **~ paper** *n* [U] papel *m* de lija

emigrant /'eməgrənt ‖ 'emɪgrənt/ *n* emigrante *mf*

emigrate /'eməgreɪt ‖ 'emɪgreɪt/ *vi* emigrar

emigration /ˌemə'greɪʃən ‖ ˌemɪ'greɪʃən/ *n* [U C] emigración *f*

eminent /'emənənt ‖ 'emɪnənt/ *adj* eminente, ilustre

emission /iː'mɪʃən ‖ ɪ'mɪʃən/ *n* [U C] emisión *f*

emit /iː'mɪt ‖ i'mɪt/ *vt* **-tt-** ‹*gas/smell/vapor*› despedir*; ‹*heat/light/radiation/sound*› emitir

emotion /ɪ'məʊʃən/ *n* **(a)** [C] (feeling) sentimiento *m* **(b)** [U] (strength of feeling) emoción *f*

emotional /ɪ'məʊʃnəl ‖ ɪ'məʊʃənl/ *adj* **(a)** ‹*disorder*› emocional **(b)** (sensitive) ‹*person/nature*› emotivo **(c)** (upset) emocionado; **to get ~** emocionarse **(d)** (moving) ‹*speech/experience/scene*› emotivo

emperor /'empərər ‖ 'empərə(r)/ *n* emperador *m*

emphasis /'emfəsəs ‖ 'emfəsɪs/ *n* (*pl* **-ses** /-siːz/) énfasis *m*; **to lay** *o* **put ~ on sth** hacer* hincapié *or* poner* énfasis en la importancia de algo

emphasize /'emfəsaɪz/ *vt* ‹*phrase/word*› enfatizar*; ‹*fact/point/warning*› recalcar*, hacer* hincapié en; ‹*fault/value*›, poner* de relieve; ‹*shape/feature*› resaltar, hacer* resaltar

emphatic /ɪm'fætɪk/ *adj* ‹*gesture/tone*› enérgico, enfático; ‹*assertion/refusal*› categórico

empire /'empaɪr ‖ 'empaɪə(r)/ *n* [U C] imperio *m*

employ /ɪm'plɔɪ/ *vt* **(a)** ‹*person*› (take on) contratar, emplear; (have working) emplear, dar* empleo a **(b)** ‹*method/tactics/tool*› emplear

employee /ɪm'plɔɪ'iː/ *n* empleado, -da *m,f*

employer /ɪm'plɔɪər ‖ ɪm'plɔɪə(r)/ *n* empleador, -dora *m,f*; (of domestic worker etc) patrón, -trona *m,f*

employment /ɪm'plɔɪmənt/ *n* [U] **(a)** (work) trabajo *m*; **to be in ~** tener* trabajo; (*before n*) **~ agency** agencia *f* de trabajo **(b)** (availability of work) empleo *m*; **full ~** pleno empleo *m*

empress /'emprəs ‖ 'emprɪs/ *n* emperatriz *f*

empty¹ /'empti/ *adj* **-tier, -tiest** ‹*container/table*› vacío; ‹*words/gesture/life*› vacío; ‹*threat/promise*› vano

empty² -ties, -tying, -tied *vt* ‹*container/warehouse*› vaciar*; **she emptied the contents all over the floor** vació la caja (*or* el bolso *etc*) en el suelo ■ **~** *vi* «*room/street*» vaciarse*; «*river/stream*» **to ~ INTO sth** desaguar* EN algo

• **empty out** [*v* + *o* + *adv*, *v* + *adv* + *o*] ‹*bag/drawer/pockets*› vaciar*; ‹*garbage*› tirar, botar (AmL exc RPl)

empty-handed /'empti'hændəd ‖ ˌempti'hændɪd/ *adv* con las manos vacías

emu /'iːmjuː/ *n* emú *m*

emulate /'emjəleɪt ‖ 'emjʊleɪt/ *vt* emular

emulsion /ɪ'mʌlʃən/ *n* [U] **~ (paint)** pintura *f* al agua

enable /ɪn'eɪbəl/ *vt* **(a)** (provide means for) **to ~ sb to + INF** permitir(le) A algn + INF **(b)** (make possible) posibilitar, permitir

enact /ɪn'ækt/ *vt* **1** (Govt, Law) ‹*law*› promulgar* **2** ‹*play/role*› representar

enamel /ɪ'næməl/ *n* [U] esmalte *m*

enamored, (BrE) **enamoured** /ɪ'næmərd ‖ ɪ'næməd/ *adj* (frml) **to be ~ OF sb** estar* enamorado *or* prendado DE algn; **I'm not very ~ of the idea** no estoy muy entusiasmado con la idea

enc (= **enclosed**) anexo

encampment /ɪn'kæmpmənt/ *n* campamento *m*

encase /ɪn'keɪs/ *vt* revestir*, recubrir*; **~d IN sth** revestido *or* recubierto DE algo

enchant /ɪn'tʃænt ‖ ɪn'tʃɑːnt/ *vt* (delight, charm) cautivar; (Occult) hechizar*

enchanting /ɪn'tʃæntɪŋ ‖ ɪn'tʃɑːntɪŋ/ *adj* encantador

encircle /ɪn'sɜːrkəl ‖ ɪn'sɜːkəl/ *vt* ‹*camp/house*› rodear; ‹*waist/wrist*› ceñir*

enclave /'enkleɪv/ *n* enclave *m*

enclose /ɪn'kləʊz/ *vt* **1 (a)** (surround) encerrar*; (fence in) cercar* **(b) enclosed** *past p* ‹*area/space*› cerrado **2** (in letter) adjuntar, acompañar

enclosure /ɪn'kləʊʒər ‖ ɪn'kləʊʒə(r)/ *n* recinto *m*; **a fenced ~** un cercado

encode /ɪn'kəʊd, en-/ *vt* codificar*, cifrar

encompass /ɪn'kʌmpəs/ *vt* (frml) abarcar*

encore /'ɑːnkɔːr ‖ 'ɒŋkɔː(r)/ *n* bis *m*; (*as interj*) ¡otra!

encounter¹ /ɪn'kaʊntər ‖ ɪn'kaʊntə(r)/ *vt* **(a)** (be faced with) ‹*danger/difficulty/opposition*› encontrar*, encontrarse* con **(b)** (come across) tropezar* *or* toparse con

encounter² *n* encuentro *m*

encourage /ɪn'kɜːrɪdʒ ‖ ɪn'kʌrɪdʒ/ *vt* **(a)** (give hope, courage to) animar, alentar*; **she/it ~d me to carry on** me animó a seguir adelante **(b)** ‹*industry/competition/growth*› fomentar

encouragement /ɪn'kɜːrɪdʒmənt ‖ ɪn'kʌrɪdʒmənt/ *n* [U C] ánimo *m*

encouraging /ɪn'kɜːrɪdʒɪŋ ‖ ɪn'kʌrɪdʒɪŋ/ *adj* alentador

encroach /ɪn'krəʊtʃ/ *vi* **to ~ ON** *o* **UPON sth** ‹*on land*› invadir algo; ‹*on rights*› cercenar algo

encumber /ɪn'kʌmbər ‖ ɪn'kʌmbə(r)/ *vt* cargar*

encyclopedia, (BrE also) **encyclopaedia** /ɪn'saɪklə'piːdiə/ *n* enciclopedia *f*

end¹ /end/ *n* **1 (a)** (extremity — of rope, stick) extremo *m*, punta *f*; (— of nose) punta *f*; (— of street) final *m*; **for weeks on ~** durante semanas y semanas, durante semanas enteras; **it measures five feet (from) ~ to ~** mide cinco pies de un lado al otro *or* de punta a punta; ***to make ~s meet*** llegar* a fin de mes **(b)** (remaining part) final *m*, resto *m* **2 (a)** (finish, close) fin *m*, final *m*; **at the ~ of January** a fines *or* a finales de enero; **in the ~** al final; **to put an ~ to sth** poner* fin *or* poner* punto final a algo **(b)** (death, destruction) final *m*, fin *m* **(c)** (outcome) final *m* **3** (purpose) fin *m*; **to this ~** (frml) con este fin (frml)

end² *vt* **(a)** (stop) ‹*argument/discussion/fight*› terminar; ‹*gossip/speculation*› acabar *or* terminar con **(b)** (conclude) terminar ■ **~** *vi* acabar, terminar

• **end up** [*v* + *adv*] terminar, acabar

endanger /ɪn'deɪndʒər ‖ ɪn'deɪndʒə(r)/ *vt* **(a)** ‹*life*› poner* en peligro; ‹*chances/reputation*› hacer* peligrar **(b) endangered** *past p* ‹*species*› en peligro

endear /ɪn'dɪr ‖ ɪn'dɪə(r)/ *vt* **to ~ oneself TO sb** granjearse el cariño de algn

endearing /ɪn'dɪrɪŋ ‖ ɪn'dɪərɪŋ/ *adj* atractivo

endearment /ɪn'dɪrmənt ‖ ɪn'dɪəmənt/ *n* [C U] expresión *f* de cariño

endeavor¹, (BrE) **endeavour** /ɪn'devər ‖ ɪn'devə(r)/ *n* (frml) esfuerzo *m*, intento *m*

endeavor², (BrE) **endeavour** *vt* (frml) **to ~ to + INF** intentar por todos los medios + INF, esforzarse* POR + INF

ending /'endɪŋ/ *n* **(a)** (conclusion) final *m*, desenlace *m* **(b)** (Ling) desinencia *f*, terminación *f*

endless /'endləs ‖ 'endlɪs/ *adj* **(a)** ‹*journey/meeting*› interminable; ‹*plain/patience*› sin límites; ‹*chatter/complaining*› continuo **(b)** (innumerable) innumerable; **the possibilities are ~** las posibilidades son infinitas

endorse /ɪn'dɔːrs ‖ ɪn'dɔːs/ *vt* **1** (approve) ‹*statement/decision*› aprobar* **2** (sign) ‹*check/bill*› endosar

endorsement /ɪn'dɔːrsmənt ‖ ɪn'dɔːsmənt/ *n* [C U] **1 (a)** (approval) aval *m*, aprobación *f* **(b)** (Pol) refrendo *m* **2** (on driving licence) (BrE) anotación *f* (*de una infracción de tráfico*)

endow /ɪn'daʊ/ *vt* **(a)** (provide) (*usu pass*) **~ed WITH sth** dotado DE algo **(b)** (provide income for) ‹*college/school/hospital*› dotar (de fondos) a

endowment /ɪn'daʊmənt/ *n* [C U] (Fin) donación *f*

end product *n* producto *m* final

endurance /ɪn'dʊrəns ‖ ɪn'djʊərəns/ *n* [U] (physical) resistencia *f*; (mental) entereza *f*; (*before n*) **~ test** prueba *f* de resistencia

endure /ɪn'dʊr ‖ ɪn'djʊə(r)/ *vt* soportar ■ ~ *vi* «*fame/friendship/memories*» perdurar

enemy /'enəmi/ *n* (*pl* **-mies**) enemigo, -ga *m,f*

energetic /'enər'dʒetɪk ‖ ˌenə'dʒetɪk/ *adj* ‹*person*› lleno de energía; ‹*exercise*› enérgico

energy /'enərdʒi ‖ 'enədʒi/ *n* [U] energía *f*; (power, effort) energías *fpl*

enforce /ɪn'fɔːrs ‖ ɪn'fɔːs/ *vt* ‹*law/regulation*› hacer* respetar *or* cumplir; ‹*claim/right*› hacer* valer

engage /ɪn'geɪdʒ/ *vt* **1** ‹*attention/interest*› captar **2** ‹*cog/wheel*› engranar con; ‹*gear*› engranar **3** (hire) ‹*staff/performer*› contratar ■ ~ *vi* (take part) **to ~ IN sth** ‹*in politics/voluntary work/study*› dedicarse* A algo; **they ~d in a variety of activities** participaron en una variedad de actividades

engaged /ɪn'geɪdʒd/ *adj* **1** (betrothed) prometido, comprometido (AmL); **to be ~ TO sb** estar* prometido A algn, estar* comprometido CON algn (AmL); **to get ~** prometerse, comprometerse (AmL) **2** (*pred*) **(a)** (occupied) (frml) ocupado; **I'm otherwise ~** tengo otro compromiso; **they are ~ in a new business venture** tienen un nuevo negocio entre manos **(b)** (BrE) ‹*toilet*› ocupado **(c)** (BrE Telec) ocupado, comunicando (Esp); **the ~ tone** *o* **signal** la señal de ocupado *or* (Esp) de comunicando

engagement /ɪn'geɪdʒmənt/ *n* **1** (pledge to marry) compromiso *m*; (period) noviazgo *m*; (*before n*) **~ ring** anillo *m* de compromiso **2** (appointment) compromiso *m*

engine /'endʒən ‖ 'endʒɪn/ *n* **(a)** (motor) motor *m* **(b)** (locomotive) locomotora *f*, máquina *f*

engine driver *n* (BrE) maquinista *mf*

engineer¹ /'endʒə'nɪr ‖ ˌendʒɪ'nɪə(r)/ *n* **1 (a)** (graduate) ingeniero, -ra *m,f* **(b)** (for maintenance) (BrE) técnico *mf*, ingeniero, -ra *m,f* (Méx) **2** (AmE Rail) maquinista *mf*

engineer² *vt* ‹*plan*› urdir, tramar; ‹*defeat/downfall*› fraguar*

engineering /'endʒə'nɪrɪŋ ‖ ˌendʒɪ'nɪərɪŋ/ *n* [U] ingeniería *f*

England /'ɪŋglənd/ *n* Inglaterra *f*

English¹ /'ɪŋglɪʃ/ *adj* inglés

English² *n* **(a)** [U] (language) inglés *m*; (*before n*) ‹*lesson/teacher*› de inglés **(b)** (people) (+ *pl vb*) **the ~** los ingleses

English: **~man** /'ɪŋglɪʃmən/ *n* (*pl* **-men** /-mən/) inglés *m*; **~woman** *n* inglesa *f*

engrave /ɪn'greɪv/ *vt* grabar

engraving /ɪn'greɪvɪŋ/ *n* [C U] grabado *m*

engross /ɪn'grəʊs/ *vt* absorber*; **to be ~ed IN sth** estar* absorto EN algo

engulf /ɪn'gʌlf/ *vt* «*flames/fire/waves*» envolver*; «*lava*» sepultar; «*feeling*» asaltar

enhance /ɪn'hæns ‖ ɪn'hɑːns/ *vt* ‹*beauty/taste*› realzar*; ‹*value*› aumentar; ‹*reputation/performance*› mejorar

enigma /ɪ'nɪgmə/ *n* (*pl* **-mas**) enigma *m*

enigmatic /'enɪg'mætɪk/ *adj* enigmático

enjoy /ɪn'dʒɔɪ/ *vt* **1** (like): **I ~ traveling/music** me gusta viajar/la música; **I ~ed the party** lo pasé bien en la fiesta **2** (have, experience) ‹*good health*› disfrutar de, gozar* de ■ *v refl* **to ~ oneself** divertirse*, pasarlo *or* pasarla bien

enjoyable /ɪn'dʒɔɪəbəl/ *adj* agradable

enjoyment /ɪn'dʒɔɪmənt/ *n* [U C] placer *m*

enlarge /ɪn'lɑːrdʒ ‖ ɪn'lɑːdʒ/ *vt* ‹*hole/area*› agrandar; ‹*gland/heart*› dilatar; ‹*room/office*› ampliar*; ‹*print/photograph*› ampliar*

enlighten /ɪn'laɪtn/ *vt* ‹*people/population*› ilustrar (frml); **would you care to ~ me?** ¿te importaría explicarme?

enlightened /ɪn'laɪtnd/ *adj* ‹*person/view*› progresista; ‹*decision*› inteligente

Enlightenment /ɪn'laɪtnmənt/ *n* [U] (Hist) **the (Age of) ~** la Ilustración, el Siglo de las Luces

enlist /ɪn'lɪst/ *vi* alistarse ■ ~ *vt* ‹*soldiers/helpers/members*› reclutar, alistar; ‹*sailors*› enrolar; ‹*support/aid*› conseguir*

enlisted man /ɪn'lɪstəd ‖ ɪn'lɪstɪd/ *n* (AmE) soldado *m* raso

en masse /ɑːn'mæs ‖ ɒn'mæs/ *adv* en masa

enmity /'enməti/ *n* [U C] (*pl* **-ties**) (frml) enemistad *f*

enormous /ɪ'nɔːrməs ‖ ɪ'nɔːməs/ *adj* enorme, inmenso

enormously /ɪ'nɔːrməsli ‖ ɪ'nɔːməsli/ *adv* ‹*enjoy/benefit*› enormemente; **he's ~ fat** es gordísimo

---

■ **Note** **enough** Where the meaning ... *enough to* ... is being translated, the translation uses the structure *lo bastante* or *lo suficiente* ... *como para* ...: *you aren't eating enough* (*to stay healthy*) no estás comiendo lo suficiente *or* lo bastante (como para mantenerte saludable).

---

enough¹ /ɪ'nʌf/ *adj* bastante, suficiente; (*pl*) bastantes, suficientes; **they had more than ~ time** tuvieron tiempo de sobra

enough² *pron*: **they don't pay us ~** no nos pagan bastante *or* lo suficiente; **I've had ~!** ¡ya estoy harto!

enough³ *adv* **you don't go out ~** no sales lo suficiente; **make sure it's big ~** asegúrate de que sea lo suficientemente grande; **curiously ~** curiosamente

enquire *etc* (BrE) /ɪn'kwaɪr ‖ ɪn'kwaɪə(r)/ ⇒ INQUIRE *etc*

enrage /ɪn'reɪdʒ/ *vt* enfurecer*

enrich /ɪn'rɪtʃ/ *vt* enriquecer*

enroll, (BrE) **enrol -ll-** /ɪn'rəʊl/ *vi* matricularse, inscribirse* ■ ~ *vt* matricular, inscribir*

enrollment, (BrE) **enrolment** /ɪn'rəʊlmənt/ *n* [U C] inscripción *f*, matrícula *f*

en route /ɑːn'ruːt ‖ ɒn'ruːt/ *adv* por el camino, de camino

ensemble /ɑːn'sɑːmbəl ‖ ɒn'sɒmbəl/ *n* **1** (group of performers) conjunto *m* **2** (Clothing) conjunto *m*

enslave /ɪn'sleɪv/ *vt* esclavizar*

ensue /ɪn'suː ‖ ɪn'sjuː/ *vi* seguir*; **in the ensuing fight** en la pelea que tuvo lugar a continuación

en suite /ˌɑːn'swiːt ‖ ˌɒn'swiːt/ *adj* adjunto, en suite

ensure /ɪn'ʃʊr ‖ ɪn'ʃʊə(r), ɪn'ʃɔː(r)/ *vt* asegurar

entail /ɪn'teɪl/ *vt* ‹*risk*› implicar*, suponer*; ‹*expense*› acarrear, suponer*; ‹*responsibility*› conllevar

entangle /ɪn'tæŋgəl/ *vt* enredar

enter /'entər ‖ 'entə(r)/ *vt* **1 (a)** ‹*room/house/country*› entrar en, entrar a (esp AmL) **(b)** (penetrate) entrar en **2** (begin) ‹*period/phase*› entrar en **3 (a)** (join) ‹*army*› alistarse en, entrar en; ‹*firm/organization*› entrar en, incorporarse a **(b)** (begin to take part in) ‹*war/negotiations*› entrar en; ‹*debate/dispute*› sumarse a **(c)** ‹*student/candidate*› presentar **(d)** ‹*race*› inscribirse* (para tomar parte) en; **to ~ a competition** presentarse a un concurso **4 (a)** (record — in register) inscribir*; (— in ledger, book) anotar **(b)** (Comput) dar* entrada a ■ ~ *vi* **1** entrar **2 to ~** (FOR **sth**) ‹*for competition/race*› inscribirse* (EN algo); ‹*for examination*› presentarse (A algo)

enterprise /'entərpraɪz ‖ 'entəpraɪz/ *n* **1 (a)** [C] (project) empresa *f* **(b)** [U] (initiative, daring) empuje *m* **2 (a)** [C] (company) empresa *f* **(b)** [U] (business activity): **free ~** la libre empresa; **private ~** la iniciativa privada; (sector) el sector privado

entertain /'entər'teɪn ‖ ,entə'teɪn/ *vt* **1** (amuse) ‹*audience*› entretener* **2** (frml) ‹*idea/suggestion*› contemplar; ‹*doubt/suspicions*› abrigar* (frml) ■ ~ *vi* **1** (provide entertainment) entretener* **2** (have guests) recibir

entertainer /'entər'teɪnər ‖ ,entə'teɪnə(r)/ *n* artista *mf* (*del mundo del espectáculo*); (presenter of program) (Rad, TV) animador, -dora *m,f*

entertaining /'entər'teɪnɪŋ ‖ ,entə'teɪnɪŋ/ *adj* ‹*book/movie/anecdote*› entretenido; ‹*person*› divertido

entertainment /'entər'teɪnmənt ‖ ,entə'teɪnmənt/ *n* **(a)** [U] (amusement) entretenimiento *m* **(b)** [C] (show) espectáculo *m*

enthrall, (BrE) **enthral** /ɪn'θrɔːl/ *vt* **-ll-** cautivar

enthusiasm /ɪn'θuːziæzəm ‖ ɪn'θjuːziæzəm/ *n* [U C] entusiasmo *m*

enthusiast /ɪn'θuːziæst ‖ ɪn'θjuːziæst/ *n* entusiasta *mf*

enthusiastic /ɪn'θuːzi'æstɪk ‖ ɪn,θjuːzi'æstɪk/ *adj* entusiasta

entice /ɪn'taɪs/ *vt* atraer*

entire /ɪn'taɪr ‖ ɪn'taɪə(r)/ *adj* **(a)** (whole) (*before n*) entero **(b)** (intact) (*pred*) intacto

entirely /ɪn'taɪrli ‖ ɪn'taɪəli/ *adv* totalmente, completamente

entirety /ɪn'taɪrəti ‖ ɪn'taɪərəti/ *n* [U]: **in its ~** íntegramente, en su totalidad

entitle /ɪn'taɪtl/ *vt* **1** (give right) **to ~ sb TO sth** darle* a algn derecho A algo; **to be ~d TO sth** tener* derecho A algo **2** (name) (frml) (*often pass*) titular

entity /'entəti/ *n* (*pl* **-ties**) entidad *f*

entourage /'ɑːntʊ'rɑːʒ ‖ ,ɒntʊ'rɑːʒ/ *n* séquito *m*

entrails /'entreɪlz/ *pl n* (of person) entrañas *fpl*; (of animal) vísceras *fpl*

entrance¹ /'entrəns/ *n* **1 (a)** [C] (way in) entrada *f* **(b)** [C] (foyer) hall *m*; (*before n*) **~ hall** hall *m*, vestíbulo *m* **(c)** [U] (access) (frml) entrada *f* **2** [U] (admission — to club, museum) entrada *f*; (— to school, university) ingreso *m*; (*before n*) **~ fee** (for entry) (precio *m* de) entrada *f*; (to join club) cuota *f* de ingreso *or* inscripción; (for exam, competition) cuota *f or* tasa *f* de inscripción **3** [C] (act of entering) entrada *f*; (Theat) entrada *f* en escena

entrance² /ɪn'træns ‖ ɪn'trɑːns/ *vt* embelesar, extasiar*

entrant /'entrənt/ *n* (in competition) participante *mf*; (for exam) candidato, -ta *m,f*

entreat /ɪn'triːt/ *vt* (liter) suplicar*, rogar*

entreaty /ɪn'triːti/ *n* (*pl* **-ties**) (liter) súplica *f*, ruego *m*

entrepreneur /'ɑːntrəprə'nɜːr ‖ ,ɒntrəprə'nɜː(r)/ *n* empresario, -ria *m,f*

entrust /ɪn'trʌst/ *vt* **to ~ sth TO sb** encomendarle* *or* confiarle* algo A algn

entry /'entri/ *n* (*pl* **entries**) **1** [U] (coming, going in) entrada *f* **2** [U] (access) entrada *f*, acceso *m*; ⊖ **no entry** (on door) prohibida la entrada; (on road sign) prohibido el paso **3** [C U] **(a)** (in accounts) entrada *f*, asiento *m* **(b)** (in diary) anotación *f*, entrada *f* **(c)** (in dictionary — headword) entrada *f*; (in encyclopedia — article) artículo *m* **4** [C] (in contest): **the winning ~ in the painting competition** el ejemplar ganador del concurso de pintura; **there were 20 entries** hubo 20 inscripciones **5** [C] (door, gate) (AmE) entrada *f*

entryphone /'entrifəʊn/ *n* (BrE) portero *m* eléctrico *or* (Esp) automático, interfón *m* (Méx), intercomunicador *m* (Ven)

entwine /ɪn'twaɪn/ *vt* (liter) entrelazar*

envelop /ɪn'veləp/ *vt* envolver*

envelope /'envələʊp/ *n* sobre *m*

enviable /'enviəbəl/ *adj* envidiable

envious /'enviəs/ *adj* envidioso; ‹*expression*› (lleno) de envidia

environment /ɪn'vaɪrənmənt ‖ ɪn'vaɪərənmənt/ *n* **(a)** (Ecol) **the ~** el medio ambiente **(b)** (surroundings): **she's studying gorillas in their natural ~** estudia a las gorilas en su entorno *or* hábitat natural; **the home ~** el ambiente del hogar

environmental /ɪn'vaɪrən'mentl̩ ‖ ɪn,vaɪərən'mentl̩/ *adj* **(a)** (Ecol) ‹*factor*› ambiental; ‹*damage*› al medio ambiente, medioambiental; **~ groups** grupos *mpl* ecologistas **(b)** (of surroundings) ‹*factor*› ambiental; ‹*influence*› del ambiente *or* entorno

environment-friendly /ɪn'vaɪrənmənt,frendli ‖ ɪn'vaɪərənmənt,frendli/ *adj*: **~ products** productos *mpl* ecológicos, productos *mpl* que no dañan al medio ambiente

environs /ɪn'vaɪrənz ‖ ɪn'vaɪərənz/ *pl n* alrededores *mpl*, entorno *m*

envisage /ɪn'vɪzɪdʒ/ *vt* **(a)** (foresee) prever* **(b)** (visualise) imaginarse

envision /ɪn'vɪʒən/ *vt* (AmE) prever*

envoy /'envɔɪ/ *n* enviado, -da *m,f*

envy¹ /'envi/ *n* [U] envidia *f*

envy² *vt* **envies, envying, envied** envidiar

enzyme /'enzaɪm/ *n* enzima *f*

epic¹ /'epɪk/ *adj* (*usu before n*) ‹*poem/poetry/film*› épico; ‹*achievement/struggle*› colosal, de epopeya

epic² *n* (poem) poema *m* épico; (film) superproducción *f*; (novel) epopeya *f*

epidemic /ˈepəˈdemɪk ‖ ˌepɪˈdemɪk/ *n* epidemia *f*

epigram /ˈepəgræm ‖ ˈepɪgræm/ *n* epigrama *m*

epilepsy /ˈepəlepsi ‖ ˈepɪlepsi/ *n* [U] epilepsia *f*

epileptic /ˈepəˈleptɪk ‖ ˌepɪˈleptɪk/ *adj* ‹*fit/attack*› epiléptico, de epilepsia; **she's ~** es epiléptica

epilogue, (AmE also) **epilog** /ˈepəlɔːg ‖ ˈepɪlɒg/ *n* epílogo *m*

Epiphany /ɪˈpɪfəni/ *n* **the ~** la Epifanía (del Señor)

episode /ˈepəsəʊd ‖ ˈepɪsəʊd/ *n* episodio *m*

epistle /ɪˈpɪsəl/ *n* epístola *f*

epitaph /ˈepətæf ‖ ˈepɪtɑːf/ *n* epitafio *m*

epitome /ɪˈpɪtəmi/ *n* (embodiment) personificación *f*; (typical example) arquetipo *m*

epitomize /ɪˈpɪtəmaɪz/ *vt* tipificar*; «*person*» ser* la personificación de

epoch /ˈepək ‖ ˈiːpɒk/ *n* era *f*, época *f*

equal¹ /ˈiːkwəl/ *adj* igual; **~ opportunities** igualdad *f* de oportunidades; **he doesn't feel ~ to the task** no se siente capaz de hacerlo

equal² *n* igual *mf*

equal³ *vt*, (BrE) **-ll- 1** (Math) ser* igual a; **three times three ~s nine** tres por tres son nueve *or* es igual a nueve **2** ‹*record/time*› igualar

equality /ɪˈkwɑːləti ‖ ɪˈkwɒləti/ *n* [U] igualdad *f*

equalize /ˈiːkwəlaɪz/ *vt* ‹*pressure/weight*› igualar; ‹*incomes*› equiparar ■ **~** *vi* (Sport) empatar

equalizer /ˈiːkwəlaɪzər ‖ ˈiːkwəlaɪzə(r)/ *n* (Sport) gol *m* de la igualada *or* del empate

equally /ˈiːkwəli/ *adv* **1 (a)** (in equal amounts) ‹*divide/share*› por igual **(b)** (without bias) ‹*treat*› de la misma manera, (por) igual **2** (to an equal degree) igualmente; **~ easily** con igual *or* con la misma facilidad **3** (*indep*) **(a)** (just as possibly) **~ (well)** de igual modo **(b)** (at the same time) (*as linker*) al mismo tiempo

equate /ɪˈkweɪt/ *vt* (compare) equiparar; (identify) identificar*

equation /ɪˈkweɪʒən/ *n* ecuación *f*

equator /ɪˈkweɪtər ‖ ɪˈkweɪtə(r)/ *n* **the ~** *o* **E~** el ecuador

equilibrium /ˈiːkwəˈlɪbriəm ‖ ˌiːkwɪˈlɪbriəm/ *n* [U] (*pl* **-riums** *or* **-ria** /-riə/) equilibrio *m*

equinox /ˈiːkwənɑːks, ˈek- ‖ ˈiːkwɪnɒks, ˈek-/ *n* equinoccio *m*

equip /ɪˈkwɪp/ *vt* **-pp- (a)** (furnish, supply) ‹*troops/laboratory*› equipar; **to ~ sth/sb** WITH **sth** proveer* algo/a algn DE algo **(b)** (prepare, make capable) preparar

equipment /ɪˈkwɪpmənt/ *n* [U] equipo *m*; **office ~** *mobiliario, máquinas y material de oficina*; **sports ~** artículos *mpl* deportivos

equity /ˈekwəti/ *n* **1** [U] (fairness) (frml) equidad *f* (frml) **2** (Busn, Fin) **(a)** [U] (shareholders' interest in company) patrimonio *m* neto **(b) equities** *pl n* (shares) valores *mpl* de renta variable

equivalent¹ /ɪˈkwɪvələnt/ *adj* **(a)** (equal) ‹*size/value*› equivalente; **to be ~ TO sth/-ING** equivaler A algo/+ INF **(b)** (corresponding) ‹*position/term*› equivalente

equivalent² *n* equivalente *m*

era /ˈirə, ˈerə ‖ ˈɪərə/ *n* era *f*, época *f*

eradicate /ɪˈrædəkeɪt ‖ ɪˈrædɪkeɪt/ *vt* erradicar*

erase /ɪˈreɪs ‖ ɪˈreɪz/ *vt* borrar

eraser /ɪˈreɪsər ‖ ɪˈreɪzə(r)/ *n* goma *f* (de borrar)

erect¹ /ɪˈrekt/ *adj* **1** ‹*bearing/posture*› erguido **2** (Physiol) erecto

erect² *vt* ‹*altar/monument*› erigir* (frml), levantar; ‹*barricade/wall*› levantar; ‹*tent*› armar

erection /ɪˈrekʃən/ *n* **1** (frml) **(a)** [U] (of building, monument) construcción *f*; (of barricade) levantamiento *m* **(b)** [C] (building) construcción *f* **2** [C] (Physiol) erección *f*

erode /ɪˈrəʊd/ *vt* «*water/wind/waves*» erosionar; «*acid*» corroer*; ‹*confidence/faith*› minar

erosion /ɪˈrəʊʒən/ *n* [U] (by water, wind, waves) erosión *f*; (by acid) corrosión *f*; (of confidence, power, rights) menoscabo *m*

erotic /ɪˈrɑːtɪk ‖ ɪˈrɒtɪk/ *adj* erótico

err /er ‖ ɜː(r)/ *vi* (frml): **to ~ IN sth** equivocarse* EN algo; **to ~ on the side of caution** pecar* de cauteloso

errand /ˈerənd/ *n* mandado *m* (esp AmL), recado *m* (Esp); **to run an ~ for sb** hacerle* un mandado *or* (Esp) recado a algn

erratic /ɪˈrætɪk/ *adj* ‹*performance/work*› desigual; ‹*person/moods*› imprevisible; ‹*course*› errático

erroneous /ɪˈrəʊniəs/ *adj* erróneo

error /ˈerər ‖ ˈerə(r)/ *n* [C U] error *m*

erstwhile /ˈɜːrsthwaɪl ‖ ˈɜːstwaɪl/ *adj* (liter) antiguo

erudite /ˈerjədaɪt ‖ ˈeruːdaɪt/ *adj* (frml) erudito

erupt /ɪˈrʌpt/ *vi* **(a)** «*volcano/geyser*» entrar en erupción **(b)** (break out) «*violence/fighting*» estallar

eruption /ɪˈrʌpʃən/ *n* [C U] **(a)** (of volcano) erupción *f* **(b)** (of violence) brote *m*; (of anger) estallido *m*

escalate /ˈeskəleɪt/ *vi* **(a)** «*fighting/violence/dispute*» intensificarse*; «*prices/claims*» aumentar **(b) escalating** *pres p* ‹*dispute/tension*› creciente

escalator /ˈeskəleɪtər ‖ ˈeskəleɪtə(r)/ *n* escalera *f* mecánica

escapade /ˈeskəpeɪd/ *n* aventura *f*

escape¹ /ɪˈskeɪp/ *vi* **1 (a)** (flee) escaparse; «*prisoner*» fugarse*; **to ~ FROM sth** ‹*from prison*› fugarse* DE algo; ‹*from cage/zoo*› escaparse DE algo; ‹*from danger/routine*› escapar DE algo **(b)** «*air/gas/water*» escaparse **2** (from accident, danger) salvarse ■ **~** *vt* ‹*pursuer/police*› escaparse de; ‹*capture*› salvarse de; ‹*responsibilities/consequences*› librarse de; **that detail had ~d my notice** se me había escapado ese detalle

escape² *n* **(a)** [C U] (from prison) fuga *f*, huida *f*; **to make one's ~** escaparse **(b)** [C U] (from accident, danger): **to have a miraculous ~** salvarse milagrosamente; **there's no ~** no hay escapatoria posible **(c)** [C] (of gas, air, water) escape *m* **(d)** [C U] (from reality) evasión *f* **(e)** [C U] (Comput): **press ~** pulse la tecla de escape

escapist /ɪˈskeɪpəst ‖ ɪˈskeɪpɪst/ *adj* escapista

escort¹ /ˈeskɔːrt ‖ ˈeskɔːt/ *n* **1** (guard) escolta *f*; **under police ~** escoltado por la policía **2** (companion) acompañante *mf*; (male companion) (frml) acompañante *m*

escort² /ɪ'skɔːrt ‖ ɪ'skɔːt/ *vt* **(a)** (accompany) acompañar; ‹*prisoner/intruder*› llevar **(b)** (for protection) ‹*politician/procession/ship*› escoltar

Eskimo *n* (*pl* **-mos**) esquimal *mf*

esoteric /ˌesə'terɪk ‖ ˌiːsəʊ'terɪk, ˌesəʊ-/ *adj* esotérico

especially /ɪ'speʃli/ *adv* especialmente; **everyone was bored, ~ me** estaba todo el mundo aburrido, sobre todo *or* especialmente yo

espionage /'espiənɑːʒ/ *n* [U] espionaje *m*

Esquire /ɪ'skwaɪr ‖ ɪ'skwaɪə(r)/ *n* (as title): **Frederick Saunders, ~** Sr. Frederick Saunders, Sr Don Frederick Saunders (esp Esp)

essay /'eseɪ/ *n* (literary composition) ensayo *m*; (academic composition) trabajo *m*, ensayo *m*; (language exercise) composición *f*, redacción *f*

essence /'esns/ *n* **1** [U] **(a)** (central feature, quality) esencia *f*; **in ~** en esencia **(b)** (personification) personificación *f* **2** [C U] (Culin): **vanilla ~** esencia *f* de vainilla

essential¹ /ɪ'sentʃəl ‖ ɪ'senʃəl/ *adj* esencial

essential² *n* **(a)** (sth indispensable) imperativo *m*, elemento *m* esencial **(b) essentials** *pl n* (fundamental features) puntos *mpl* esenciales

essentially /ɪ'sentʃəli ‖ ɪ'senʃəli/ *adv* esencialmente; (*indep*) en lo esencial

EST (in US) = **Eastern Standard Time**

establish /ɪ'stæblɪʃ/ *vt* **(a)** ‹*colony/company*› establecer*, fundar; ‹*committee/fund*› instituir*, crear **(b)** ‹*procedure/diplomatic relations*› establecer* **(c)** (prove) ‹*guilt/innocence*› establecer*; (ascertain) ‹*motive/fact/identity*› establecer*

established /ɪ'stæblɪʃt/ *adj* **1** ‹*expert/company*› de reconocido prestigio; ‹*star*› de renombre; ‹*reputation*› sólido; ‹*practice*› establecido; ‹*fact*› comprobado **2** ‹*church/religion*› oficial

establishment /ɪ'stæblɪʃmənt/ *n* **1** [U] **(a)** (of colony, business) fundación *f*; (of committee) creación *f* **(b)** (of criteria, relations) establecimiento *m* **2** [C] (club, hotel, shop) establecimiento *m* **3 the Establishment** la clase dirigente, el establishment

estate /ɪ'steɪt/ *n* **1 (a)** (land, property) finca *f*, propiedad *f* **(b)** (group of buildings): **a private ~** un complejo habitacional, una urbanización (Esp), un fraccionamiento (Méx) **2** (Law) patrimonio *m*; (of deceased person) sucesión *f* **3 ~ (car)** (BrE) ⇒ STATION WAGON

estate agent *n* (BrE) agente *mf* de la propiedad inmobiliaria

esteem /ɪ'stiːm/ *n* [U] estima *f*; **I hold him in high ~** lo aprecio mucho

esthetic /es'θetɪk ‖ 'iːsθetɪk/ *adj* estético

estimate¹ /'estəmeɪt ‖ 'estɪmeɪt/ *vt* **(a)** (calculate approximately) ‹*price/number/age*› calcular **(b) estimated** *past p* ‹*cost/speed*› aproximado; **~d time of arrival** hora *f* de llegada previsto **(c)** (form judgment of) ‹*outcome/ability*› juzgar*, valorar

estimate² /'estəmət ‖ 'estɪmət/ *n* **(a)** (rough calculation) cálculo *m* aproximado **(b)** (of costs) (Busn) presupuesto *m*

estimation /ˌestə'meɪʃən ‖ ˌestɪ'meɪʃən/ *n* **(a)** [C] (judgment, opinion) juicio *m*, valoración *f* **(b)** [U] (esteem): **to go up/down in sb's ~** ganarse/perder* la estima de algn

Estonia /es'təʊniə/ *n* Estonia *f*

Estonian /es'təʊniən/ *adj* estonio

estrange /ɪ'streɪndʒ/ *vt*: **his ~d wife** su mujer, de quien está separado

estuary /'estʃueri ‖ 'estjʊəri/ *n* (*pl* **-ries**) estuario *m*

etc (= **et cetera**) etc.

et cetera /ɪt'setrə/ *adv* etcétera

etch /etʃ/ *vt* (Art, Print) grabar

etching /'etʃɪŋ/ *n* [C U] grabado *m*

eternal /ɪ'tɜːrnl ‖ ɪ'tɜːnl/ *adj* eterno; (colloq) ‹*noise/complaints*› constante

eternity /ɪ'tɜːrnəti ‖ ɪ'tɜːnəti/ *n* [U C] (*pl* **-ties**) eternidad *f*

ethereal /ɪ'θɪriəl ‖ ɪ'θɪəriəl/ *adj* (liter) etéreo (liter)

ethical /'eθɪkəl/ *adj* ‹*dilemma*› ético; ‹*code*› de conducta

ethics /'eθɪks/ *n* **1** (Phil) (+ *sing vb*) ética *f* **2** (+ *pl vb*) (morality) ética *f*

Ethiopia /ˌiːθi'əʊpiə/ *n* Etiopía *f*

Ethiopian /ˌiːθi'əʊpiən/ *adj* etíope

ethnic /'eθnɪk/ *adj* ‹*origin/group*› étnico; ‹*culture/art/vote*› de las minorías étnicas; **an ~ minority** una minoría étnica; **~ cleansing** limpieza *f* étnica

etiquette /'etɪket/ *n* [U] etiqueta *f*

etymology /ˌetə'mɑːlədʒi ‖ ˌetɪ'mɒlədʒi/ *n* [U C] (*pl* **-gies**) etimología *f*

EU *n* = **European Union**

eucalyptus /ˌjuːkə'lɪptəs/ *n* (*pl* **-tuses**) eucalipto *m*

Eucharist /'juːkərəst ‖ 'juːkərɪst/ *n* Eucaristía *f*

eulogy /'juːlədʒi/ *n* (*pl* **-gies**) (liter) elogio *m*, loa *f* (liter)

eunuch /'juːnək/ *n* eunuco *m*

euphemism /'juːfəmɪzəm/ *n* [C U] eufemismo *m*

euphemistic /ˌjuːfə'mɪstɪk/ *adj* eufemístico

euphoria /juː'fɔːriə/ *n* [U] euforia *f*

euphoric /juː'fɔːrɪk ‖ juː'fɒrɪk/ *adj* eufórico

Europe /'jʊrəp ‖ 'jʊərəp/ *n* **(a)** (Geog) Europa *f* **(b)** (the EC) (BrE) Europa *f*

European¹ /ˌjʊrə'piːən ‖ ˌjʊərə'piən/ *adj* europeo

European² *n* europeo, -pea *m,f*

European: **~ Commission** *n* Comisión *f* Europea, Comisión *f* de las Comunidades Europeas; **~ Currency Unit** *n* unidad *f* monetaria europea; **~ (Economic) Community** *n* Comunidad *f* (Económica) Europea; **~ Union** *n* Unión *f* Europea

euthanasia /ˌjuːθə'neɪʒə ‖ ˌjuːθə'neɪziə/ *n* [U] eutanasia *f*

evacuate /ɪ'vækjueɪt/ *vt* evacuar*

evacuation /ɪˌvækju'eɪʃən/ *n* [U C] evacuación *f*

evade /ɪ'veɪd/ *vt* ‹*arrest/enemy/responsibility*› eludir, evadir; ‹*question/issue*› eludir; ‹*regulations/military service*› eludir; ‹*taxes*› evadir

evaluate /ɪ'væljueɪt/ *vt* **(a)** ‹*ability/data*› evaluar* **(b)** (value) (AmE) valorar, tasar, avaluar* (AmL)

evangelical /'iːvæn'dʒelɪkəl/ *adj* evangélico

evaporate /ɪ'væpəreɪt/ *vi* «*liquid/support/opposition*» evaporarse; «*hope/fear*» desvanecerse*; «*confidence*» esfumarse

evaporated milk /ɪ'væpəreɪtəd ‖ ɪ'væpəreɪtɪd/ *n* [U] leche *f* evaporada, leche *f* condensada (*sin azúcar*)

evasion /ɪ'veɪʒən/ *n* [U] evasión *f*

evasive /ɪ'veɪsɪv/ *adj* ‹*reply*› evasivo

eve /iːv/ *n* (day, night before) (liter *or* journ) víspera *f*

even¹ /'iːvən/ *adv* **1 (a)** hasta, incluso **(b)** (*with neg*): **he can't ~ sew a button on** no sabe ni pegar un botón; **you're not ~ trying** ni siquiera lo estás intentando **(c)** (*with comparative*) aún, todavía **2** (*in phrases*) **even if** aunque (+ *subj*); **even so** aun así; **even though** aun cuando, a pesar de que

even² *adj* **1 (a)** (flat, smooth) ‹*ground/surface*› plano; ‹*coat of paint*› uniforme **(b)** (regular, uniform) ‹*color/lighting*› uniforme, parejo (AmL); ‹*breathing*› acompasado; ‹*temperature*› constante **2** (equal) ‹*distribution*› equitativo; **to break ~** recuperar los gastos; ***to get ~*** desquitarse; **I'll get ~ with her** me las pagará **3** (divisible by two) ‹*number*› par

even³ *vt* **1** (level) ‹*surface*› allanar, nivelar **2** (make equal) ‹*score*› igualar; ‹*contest/situation*› equilibrar

• **even out 1** [*v + o + adv, v + adv + o*] compensar, nivelar **2** [*v + adv*] compensarse, nivelarse

• **even up** [*v + o + adv, v + adv + o*] ‹*numbers/amounts*› equilibrar

evening /'iːvnɪŋ/ **▶ 884** *n* **1 (a)** (after dark) noche *f*; (before dark) tarde *f*; **good ~** (early on) buenas tardes; (later) buenas noches; (*before n*) **~ meal** cena *f* **(b)** (period of entertainment) velada *f* (frml), noche *f* **2 evenings** (*as adv*) (before dark) por la tarde, en la tarde (AmL), a la tarde *or* de tarde (RPl); (after dark) por la noche, de noche, en la noche (AmL)

evening: **~ class** *n* clase *f* nocturna; **~ dress** *n* **(a)** [C] (for woman) traje *m* de noche **(b)** [U] (formal wear) traje *m* de etiqueta

evenly /'iːvənli/ *adv* **1** (equally) ‹*distribute/divide*› equitativamente; ‹*spread*› uniformemente **2 (a)** (calmly) ‹*say/speak*› sin alterar la voz **(b)** (steadily) ‹*breathe*› con regularidad

event /ɪ'vent/ *n* **1 (a)** (happening, incident) acontecimiento *m* **(b)** (Sport) prueba *f* **2** (*in phrases*) **in the event**: **in the ~ of the reactor becoming overheated** en caso de que el reactor se recalentara; **in any event** en todo caso; **at all events** de cualquier modo

eventful /ɪ'ventfəl/ *adj* ‹*week*› lleno de incidentes; ‹*life*› rico en experiencias

eventuality /ɪ'ventʃu'æləti/ *n* (*pl* **-ties**) eventualidad *f*

eventually /ɪ'ventʃuəli/ *adv* finalmente, al final

ever /'evər ‖ 'evə(r)/ **▶ 718** *adv* **1** (at any time): **have you ~ visited London?** ¿has estado en Londres (alguna vez)?; **nobody ~ comes to see me** nunca viene nadie a verme; **hardly ~** casi nunca **2** (*after comp or superl*): **these are our worst ~ results** éstos son los peores resultados que hemos tenido hasta ahora; **the situation is worse than ~** la situación está peor que nunca **3** (always, constantly) **as ever** como siempre; **ever since**: **~ since we first saw her** desde que la vimos por primera vez; **we've been friends ~ since** somos amigos desde entonces; **for ever** para siempre **4** (*as intensifier*): **when will you ~ learn?** ¿cuándo vas a aprender?; **thanks ~ so much** (esp BrE colloq) muchísimas gracias

ever: **~green** *adj* ‹*tree/shrub*› de hoja perenne; **~lasting** /'evər'læstɪŋ ‖ ˌevə'lɑːstɪŋ/ *adj* eterno

every /'evri/ *adj* **1** (each): **~ room was searched** se registraron todas las habitaciones; **~ minute is precious** cada minuto es precioso; **she comes ~ month** viene todos los meses **2** (indicating recurrence) cada; **~ three days, ~ third day** cada tres días; **~ other day** un día sí, otro no, día por medio (CS, Per); **~ so often** cada tanto, de vez en cuando **3** (very great, all possible): **they have ~ confidence in us** confían plenamente en nosotros; **she made ~ effort to satisfy him** hizo lo indecible por satisfacerlo

everybody /'evrɪˌbɑːdi ‖ 'evrɪˌbɒdi/ *pron* todos; **is that ~?** ¿están todos?, ¿está todo el mundo?

everyday /'evri'deɪ/ *adj* (*before n*) ‹*occurrence/problems/activities*› de todos los días, cotidiano; ‹*suit/clothes*› de diario; ‹*expression*› corriente, de todos los días; ‹*life*› diario , cotidiano

everyone /'evriwʌn/ *pron* ⇒ EVERYBODY

everything /'evriθɪŋ/ *pron* todo

everywhere /'evrihwer ‖ 'evriweə(r)/ *adv* ‹*be*› en todas partes; **I've looked ~ for it** lo he buscado por todas partes *or* por todos lados; **they go ~ by car** van a todos lados *or* a todas partes en coche

evict /ɪ'vɪkt/ *vt* ‹*tenant/squatter*› desahuciar, desalojar; ‹*demonstrators*› desalojar

eviction /ɪ'vɪkʃən/ *n* [U C] (of tenant, squatter) desalojo *m*, desahucio *m*

evidence /'evədəns ‖ 'evɪdəns/ *n* [U] **1** (Law) **(a)** (proof) pruebas *fpl* **(b)** (testimony) testimonio *m*; **to give ~** declarar declaración **2** (sign, indication) indicio *m*, señal *f*

evident /'evədənt ‖ 'evɪdənt/ *adj* evidente

evidently /'evədəntli ‖ 'evɪdəntli/ *adv* **(a)** ‹*embarrassed/unsuitable*› claramente, obviamente **(b)** (*indep*) aparentemente, según parece

evil¹ /'iːvəl/ *adj* ‹*demon/wizard*› malvado; ‹*deeds/thoughts/character*› de gran maldad; ‹*influence*› maléfico; ‹*plan/suggestion*› diabólico; ‹*spirit*› maligno

evil² *n* [U C] mal *m*

evildoer /'iːvəl'duːər ‖ 'iːvəlˌduːə(r)/ *n* malhechor, -chora *m,f*

evocative /ɪ'vɑːkətɪv ‖ ɪ'vɒkətɪv/ *adj* evocador

evoke /ɪ'vəʊk/ *vt* ‹*response/admiration/sympathy*› provocar*; ‹*memories/associations*› evocar*

evolution /'evə'luːʃən ‖ ˌiːvə'luːʃən/ *n* [U] evolución *f*

evolve /ɪ'vɑːlv ‖ ɪ'vɒlv/ *vi* evolucionar

ewe /juː/ *n* oveja *f* (*hembra*)

ex- /'eks/ *pref* ex(-); **~wife** ex(-)esposa

exact¹ /ɪg'zækt/ *adj* **(a)** (precise) ‹*number/size/time/date*› exacto **(b)** (accurate) ‹*description/definition*› preciso

exact² *vt* ‹*promise*› arrancar*; **he ~ed his revenge** se vengó

exacting /ɪg'zæktɪŋ/ *adj* ‹*work/job*› que exige mucho; ‹*supervisor/employer*› exigente; ‹*standards/conditions*› riguroso

exactly /ɪg'zæktli/ *adv* ‹*measure/calculate*› exactamente; **at ~ six-thirty** a las seis y media en punto

exaggerate /ɪg'zædʒəreɪt/ *vi/t* exagerar

exaggeration /ɪg'zædʒə'reɪʃən/ *n* [C U] exageración *f*

exalt /ɪg'zɔ:lt/ *vt* (frml) **(a)** (elevate) exaltar (frml), elevar **(b)** (praise) ensalzar*, exaltar (frml)

exam /ɪg'zæm/ *n* ⇒ EXAMINATION 1

examination /ɪg'zæmə'neɪʃən ‖ ɪg,zæmɪ'neɪʃən/ *n* **1** [C] (Educ) (frml) examen *m* **2** [C U] **(a)** (inspection — of accounts) revisión *f*, inspección *f*; (— of passports) control *m*; (— by doctor) reconocimiento *m*, examen *m*, revisación *f* (RPl) **(b)** (study, investigation) examen *m*; **on closer ~** al examinarlo más de cerca

examine /ɪg'zæmən ‖ ɪg'zæmɪn/ *vt* **1 (a)** (inspect) examinar; ‹*accounts*› inspeccionar, revisar; ‹*baggage*› registrar, revisar (AmL) **(b)** (Med, Dent) examinar, revisar (AmL) **(c)** (study, investigate) examinar, estudiar **2 (a)** (Educ) examinar **(b)** (Law) ‹*witness/accused*› interrogar*

examiner /ɪg'zæmənər ‖ ɪg'zæmɪnə(r)/ *n* examinador, -dora *m,f*

example /ɪg'zæmpəl ‖ ɪg'zɑ:mpəl/ *n* **1** (specimen, sample) ejemplo *m*; **for ~** por ejemplo **2 (a)** (model) ejemplo *m* **(b)** (warning): **to make an ~ of sb** darle* un castigo ejemplar a algn

exasperated /ɪg'zæspəreɪtəd ‖ ɪg'zæspəreɪtɪd/ *adj* exasperado

exasperating /ɪg'zæspəreɪtɪŋ/ *adj* exasperante

exasperation /ɪg'zæspə'reɪʃən/ *n* [U] exasperación *f*

excavate /'ekskəveɪt/ *vt/i* excavar

excavation /'ekskə'veɪʃən/ *n* [U C] excavación *f*

exceed /ɪk'si:d/ *vt* **(a)** (be greater than) exceder de **(b)** (go beyond) ‹*limit/minimum*› rebasar; ‹*expectations/hopes*› superar; ‹*powers*› (frml) excederse en

excel /ɪk'sel/ **-ll-** *vi* **to ~ AT/IN sth** destacar* EN algo ■ *v refl* **to ~ oneself** lucirse*

excellence /'eksələns/ *n* [U] excelencia *f*

excellent /'eksələnt/ *adj* excelente; (Educ) sobresaliente

except /ɪk'sept/ *prep* **(a)** (apart from): **~ (for)** menos, excepto, salvo **(b) ~ for** (if it weren't for) si no fuera por

exception /ɪk'sepʃən/ *n* **1** [C U] excepción *f* **2** (offense): **to take ~ to sth** ofenderse por algo

exceptional /ɪk'sepʃn̩əl ‖ ɪk'sepʃənl/ *adj* excepcional

excerpt /'eksɜ:rpt ‖ 'eksɜ:pt/ *n* pasaje *m*

excess¹ /ɪk'ses/ *n* **1** (*no pl*) exceso *m* **2** [U] (surplus) excedente *m*; **in ~ of** superior a

excess² /ɪk'ses ‖ 'ekses/ *adj*: **~ baggage/weight** exceso *m* de equipaje/de peso

excessive /ɪk'sesɪv/ *adj* ‹*price/charges*› excesivo; ‹*demands/pressure/interest*› exagerado

exchange¹ /ɪks'tʃeɪndʒ/ *n* **1 (a)** [C U] (of information, greetings, insults) intercambio *m*; (of prisoners, hostages) canje *m*; **in ~ for sth** a cambio de algo **(b)** [C] (of students) intercambio *m* **(c)** [C] (dialogue) intercambio *m* de palabras **(d)** [U] (of currency) cambio *m* **2** [C] (Telec) (*telephone* **~**) central *f* telefónica

exchange² *vt* **(a)** (give in place of) **to ~ sth FOR sth** cambiar algo POR algo **(b)** ‹*information/addresses*› intercambiar(se); ‹*blows*› darse*; ‹*insults*› intercambiar; ‹*prisoners/hostages*› canjear

exchange rate *n* tasa *f* or (esp Esp) tipo *m* de cambio

Exchequer /'ekstʃekər ‖ ɪks'tʃekə(r)/ *n* (in UK) **the ~** el tesoro público, el erario público; *see also* CHANCELLOR (a)

excise /'eksaɪz/ *n* impuestos *mpl* internos

excitable /ɪk'saɪtəbəl/ *adj* excitable

excite /ɪk'saɪt/ *vt* **1 (a)** (make happy, enthusiastic) entusiasmar; (make impatient, boisterous) ‹*children*› alborotar **(b)** (sexually) excitar **2** ‹*interest/admiration*› despertar*; ‹*envy/curiosity*› provocar*

excited /ɪk'saɪtəd ‖ ɪk'saɪtɪd/ *adj* **(a)** (happy, enthusiastic) ‹*person*› entusiasmado, excitado; ‹*shouts*› de excitación or entusiasmo; **to get ~** entusiasmarse **(b)** (nervous, worried) ‹*person*› excitado, agitado; ‹*voice/gesture*› vehemente, ansioso **(c)** (impatient, boisterous) ‹*children*› excitado, alborotado **(d)** (sexually) excitado

excitement /ɪk'saɪtmənt/ *n* [U] (enthusiasm, happiness) excitación *f*, entusiasmo *m*; (agitation) agitación *f*, alboroto *m*

exciting /ɪk'saɪtɪŋ/ *adj* ‹*events/experience*› emocionante; ‹*film/story*› apasionante

exclaim /ɪk'skleɪm/ *vi/t* exclamar

exclamation /'ekskla'meɪʃən/ *n* exclamación *f*

exclamation point, (BrE) **exclamation mark** *n* signo *m* de admiración

exclude /ɪk'sklu:d/ *vt* excluir*

excluding /ɪk'sklu:dɪŋ/ *prep* sin incluir, excluyendo

exclusion /ɪk'sklu:ʒən/ *n* [U] exclusión *f*

exclusive /ɪk'sklu:sɪv/ *adj* **1** ‹*rights/ownership/privileges*› exclusivo; ‹*story/interview*› en exclusiva **2** ‹*club/gathering*› selecto, exclusivo

excommunicate /'ekskə'mju:nəkeɪt ‖ ,ekskə'mju:nɪkeɪt/ *vt* excomulgar*

excrement /'ekskrəmənt ‖ 'ekskrɪmənt/ *n* [U] (frml) excremento *m* (frml)

excruciating /ɪk'skru:ʃieɪtɪŋ/ *adj* ‹*pain*› atroz; ‹*boredom/embarrassment*› espantoso

excursion /ɪk'skɜ:rʒən ‖ ɪk'skɜ:ʃən/ *n* excursión *f*

excuse¹ /ɪk'skju:z/ *vt* **1 (a)** (forgive) ‹*mistake/misconduct*› disculpar, perdonar; **~ me!** ¡perdón!; **~ me, please** (con) permiso **(b)** (justify) ‹*conduct/rudeness*› excusar, justificar* **2** (release from obligation) disculpar; **to ~ sb (FROM) sth** dispensar a algn DE algo

excuse² /ɪk'skju:s/ *n* excusa *f*; **to make ~s** poner* excusas

ex-directory /'eksdaɪ'rektəri, -də- ‖ ˌeksdaɪ'rektəri, -dɪ-/ *adj* (BrE Telec) que no figura en la guía telefónica, privado (Méx)

execute /'eksɪkju:t/ *vt* **1** (carry out, perform) ejecutar; ‹*duties*› desempeñar **2** (put to death) ejecutar

execution /'eksɪ'kju:ʃən/ *n* **1** [U] (of order, plan) ejecución *f*; (of duties) desempeño *m* **2** [U C] (putting to death) ejecución *f*

executioner /'eksɪ'kju:ʃnər ‖ ˌeksɪ'kju:ʃənə(r)/ *n* verdugo *m*

executive¹ /ɪg'zekjətɪv ‖ ɪg'zekjʊtɪv/ *adj* **1** (Adm, Busn) (managerial) ejecutivo; ‹*washroom/suite/jet*› para ejecutivos; ‹*car/briefcase*› de ejecutivo **2** (Govt) ‹*powers/branch*› ejecutivo

executive² *n* **1** (manager) ejecutivo, -va *m,f* **2 (a)** (branch of government) **the ~** el (poder) ejecutivo **(b)** (~ *committee*) (esp BrE) comisión *f* directiva

executor /ɪg'zekjətər ‖ ɪg'zekjʊtə(r)/ *n* albacea *mf*, testamentario, -ria *m,f*

exemplify /ɪg'zempləfaɪ ‖ ɪg'zemplɪfaɪ/ *vt* **-fies, -fying, -fied (a)** (give example of) ejemplificar* **(b)** (be example of) demostrar*

exempt /ɪg'zempt/ *adj*: **to be ~ FROM sth** estar* exento DE algo

exemption /ɪg'zempʃən/ *n* [U C] **~ FROM sth** exención *f or* exoneración *f* DE algo

exercise¹ /'eksərsaɪz ‖ 'eksəsaɪz/ *n* **1** [U] (physical) ejercicio *m*; **to take ~** hacer* ejercicio **2** [C] (Sport, Educ) ejercicio *m*; (Mil) ejercicios *mpl*, maniobras *fpl* **3** [C] (undertaking): **a public relations ~** una operación de relaciones públicas **4** [U] (use — of rights, power) (frml) ejercicio *m*; (— of caution, patience) uso *m*

exercise² *vt* **1** ‹*body*› ejercitar; ‹*dog*› pasear; ‹*horse*› ejercitar **2** ‹*power/control/right*› ejercer*; ‹*patience/tact*› hacer* uso de ■ **~** *vi* hacer* ejercicio

exercise book *n* cuaderno *m*

exert /ɪg'zɜ:rt ‖ ɪg'zɜ:t/ *vt* ejercer*; ‹*force*› emplear ■ *v refl* **to ~ oneself** hacer* un (gran) esfuerzo

exertion /ɪg'zɜ:rʃən ‖ ɪg'zɜ:ʃən/ *n* [U] (*often pl*) esfuerzo *m*

exhale /eks'heɪl/ *vi* espirar

exhaust¹ /ɪg'zɔ:st/ *n* **(a)** [C] (~ *pipe*) tubo *m or* (RPl) caño *m* de escape, mofle *m* (AmC, Méx), exhosto *m* (Col) **(b)** [C] (system) escape *m*, exhosto *m* (Col) **(c)** [U] (fumes) gases *mpl* del tubo de escape

exhaust² *vt* agotar

exhausted /ɪg'zɔ:stəd ‖ ɪg'zɔ:stɪd/ *adj* agotado

exhaustion /ɪg'zɔ:stʃən/ *n* [U] agotamiento *m*

exhaustive /ɪg'zɔ:stɪv/ *adj* (frml) exhaustivo

exhibit¹ /ɪg'zɪbət ‖ ɪg'zɪbɪt/ *vt* **1** ‹*goods/paintings*› exponer* **2** (frml) ‹*skill/dexterity*› demostrar*; ‹*fear/courage*› mostrar*; ‹*symptoms*› presentar

exhibit² *n* **(a)** (in gallery, museum) *objeto en exposición* **(b)** (Law) *documento u objeto que se exhibe en un juicio como prueba* **(c)** (exhibition) (AmE) exposición *f*

exhibition /'eksə'bɪʃən ‖ ˌeksɪ'bɪʃən/ *n* [C U] (of paintings, goods) exposición *f*; **to make an ~ of oneself** dar* un expectáculo

exhilarate /ɪg'zɪləreɪt/ *vt* **(a)** (make happy) llenar de júbilo **(b)** (stimulate) tonificar*

exhilarating /ɪg'zɪləreɪtɪŋ/ *adj* ‹*experience*› excitante; ‹*climate*› tonificante

exile¹ /'eksaɪl/ *n* **(a)** [C] (person — voluntary) exiliado, -da *m,f*, exilado, -da *m,f*; (— expelled) desterrado, -da *m,f*, exiliado, -da *m,f*, exilado, -da *m,f* **(b)** [U] (state) exilio *m*, destierro *m*

exile² *vt* desterrar*, exiliar, exilar

exist /ɪg'zɪst/ *vi* **1** (be real) existir **2** (survive) subsistir

existence /ɪg'zɪstəns/ *n* **1** [U] (being) existencia *f*; **this is the only copy in ~** éste es el único ejemplar existente **2** [C] (life) vida *f*, existencia *f*

existing /ɪg'zɪstɪŋ/ *adj* existente

exit /'egzət ‖ 'eksɪt/ *n* salida *f*

exodus /'eksədəs/ *n* (*no pl*) éxodo *m*

exorbitant /ɪg'zɔ:rbətənt ‖ ɪg'zɔ:bɪtənt/ *adj* (frml) ‹*price/rent*› exorbitante

exorcize /'eksɔ:rsaɪz ‖ 'eksɔ:saɪz/ *vt* exorcizar*

exotic /ɪg'zɑ:tɪk ‖ ɪg'zɒtɪk/ *adj* exótico

expand /ɪk'spænd/ *vt* **1** (enlarge) expandir; ‹*lungs*› ensanchar; ‹*chest*› desarrollar; ‹*horizons*› ampliar*; ‹*influence/role*› extender* **2** ‹*story/summary*› ampliar* ■ **~** *vi* **(a)** «*metal/gas*» expandirse; «*elastic/rubber band*» estirarse **(b)** **expanding** *pres p* ‹*industry/market*› en expansión

expanse /ɪk'spæns/ *n* [C U] extensión *f*

expansion /ɪk'spæntʃən ‖ ɪk'spænʃən/ *n* [U] expansión *f*

expatriate /eks'peɪtriət ‖ eks'pætriət/ *n* expatriado, -da *m,f*

expect /ɪk'spekt/ *vt* **1** (anticipate) esperar; **is he coming tonight? — I ~ so** ¿va a venir esta noche? — supongo que sí; **we're not ~ing any trouble** no creemos que vaya a haber problemas **2** (imagine) suponer*, imaginarse **3** (await) esperar; **I'll ~ you at eight** te espero a las ocho; **to be ~ing a baby** esperar un bebé **4** (require): **he ~ed me to pay** esperaba que yo pagara; **that's the least you'd ~** es lo menos que se puede esperar ■ **~** *vi* (colloq): **she's ~ing** está esperando (familia)

expectancy /ɪk'spektənsi/ *n* [U] expectación *f*; **life ~** esperanza *f or* expectativas *fpl* de vida

expectant /ɪk'spektənt/ *adj* expectante

expectation /'ekspek'teɪʃən/ *n* **1** [U] (anticipation): **in ~ of victory** previendo la victoria; **an atmosphere of great ~** un ambiente de gran expectación **2 expectations** *pl* (of inheritance, promotion) expectativas *fpl*

expedient¹ /ɪk'spi:diənt/ *adj* (frml) (*usu pred*) conveniente

expedient² *n* (frml) recurso *m*, expediente *m* (frml)

expedition /'ekspə'dɪʃən ‖ ˌekspɪ'dɪʃən/ *n* expedición *f*

expel /ɪk'spel/ *vt* **-ll-** expulsar

expendable /ɪk'spendəbəl/ *adj* prescindible

expenditure /ɪk'spendɪtʃər ‖ ɪk'spendɪtʃə(r)/ *n* [U] (amount) gastos *mpl*; (spending) gasto *m*

expense /ɪk'spens/ *n* **1** [U] (cost, outlay) gasto *m*; **they had a good laugh at my ~** se partieron de risa a costa mía **2 expenses** *pl* (Busn) (incidental costs) gastos *mpl*

expense account *n* cuenta *f* de gastos de representación

expensive /ɪk'spensɪv/ *adj* caro

experience¹ /ɪk'spɪriəns ‖ ɪk'spɪəriəns/ *n* [U C] experiencia *f*

experience² *vt* ‹*loss/setback/delays*› sufrir; ‹*difficulty*› tener*; ‹*change/improvement/pleasure/pain*› experimentar

experienced /ɪk'spɪriənst ‖ ɪk'spɪəriənst/ *adj* ‹*secretary/chef*› con experiencia; ‹*driver*› experimentado

experiment¹ /ɪk'sperəmənt ‖ ɪk'sperɪmənt/ *n* experimento *m*

experiment² *vi* **to ~ ON sth/sb** experimentar CON algo/algn; **to ~ WITH sth** experimentar CON algo

experimental /ɪk'sperə'mentl ‖ ɪk,sperɪ'mentl/ *adj* experimental

expert¹ /'ekspɜːrt ‖ 'ekspɜːt/ *n* experto, -ta *m,f*

expert² *adj* experto; **~ witness** perito, -ta *m,f*

expertise /'ekspɜːr'tiːz ‖ ,ekspɜː'tiːz/ *n* [U] pericia *f*

expire /ɪk'spaɪr ‖ ɪk'spaɪə(r)/ *vi* (run out) «*visa/passport/ticket*» caducar*; «*lease/contract*» vencer*

expiry /ɪk'spaɪri ‖ ɪk'spaɪəri/ *n* [U] vencimiento *m*, caducidad *f*

explain /ɪk'spleɪn/ *vt* explicar* ■ *v refl* **to ~ oneself** explicarse*

• **explain away** [*v + o + adv, v + adv + o*] ‹*fact/result*› encontrar* una explicación convincente para

explanation /'eksplə'neɪʃən/ *n* [C U] explicación *f*

explanatory /ɪk'splænətɔːri ‖ ɪk'splænətri/ *adj* explicativo

explicit /ɪk'splɪsət ‖ ɪk'splɪsɪt/ *adj* explícito; ‹*denial/refutation*› categórico

explode /ɪk'spləʊd/ *vi* **(a)** «*gunpowder/bomb*» estallar, hacer* explosión, explotar; «*vehicle*» hacer* explosión; (with emotion) explotar, estallar **(b)** «*population/costs*» dispararse ■ **~** *vt* **1** ‹*bomb/dynamite*› explosionar, hacer* explotar *or* estallar **2** (discredit) ‹*theory*› rebatir; ‹*myth*› destruir*

exploit¹ /ɪk'splɔɪt/ *vt* explotar; ‹*situation/relationship*› aprovecharse de

exploit² /'eksplɔɪt/ *n* hazaña *f*

exploitation /'eksplɔɪ'teɪʃən/ *n* [U] explotación *f*

exploration /'eksplə'reɪʃən/ *n* [U C] exploración *f*

exploratory /ɪk'splɔːrətɔːri ‖ ɪk'splɒrətəri/ *adj* ‹*talks*› preliminar; ‹*surgery*› exploratorio

explore /ɪk'splɔːr ‖ ɪk'splɔː(r)/ *vt* ‹*territory/town*› explorar; ‹*topic/possibility*› investigar*

explorer /ɪk'splɔːrər ‖ ɪk'splɔːrə(r)/ *n* **(a)** (traveler) explorador, -dora *m,f* **(b) Explorer** (in US) boy scout *m* (*mayor de 14 años*)

explosion /ɪk'spləʊʒən/ *n* (of bomb, gas) explosión *f*, estallido *m*; (of anger) estallido *m*, explosión *f*

explosive¹ /ɪk'spləʊsɪv/ *adj* explosivo

explosive² *n* [C U] explosivo *m*

exponent /ɪk'spəʊnənt/ *n* (of idea, theory) defensor, -sora *m,f*; (of art style) exponente *mf*

export¹ /ek'spɔːrt ‖ ɪk'spɔːt/ *vt* exportar

export² /'ekspɔːrt ‖ 'ekspɔːt/ *n* **(a)** [C] (item exported) artículo *m or* producto *m* de exportación **(b)** [U] (act of exporting) exportación *f*

exporter /ek'spɔːrtər ‖ ɪk'spɔːtə(r)/ *n* exportador, -dora *m,f*

expose /ɪk'spəʊz/ *vt* **1** (lay bare) ‹*nerve/wire/wound*› exponer*; **to ~ oneself to criticism** exponerse* a las críticas **2** (uncover) ‹*secret/scandal*› poner* al descubierto, sacar* a la luz; ‹*inefficiency/weaknesses*› poner* en evidencia; ‹*criminal*› desenmascarar **3** (Phot) exponer*

exposition /'ekspə'zɪʃən/ *n* [U C] exposición *f*

exposure /ɪk'spəʊʒər ‖ ɪk'spəʊʒə(r)/ *n* **1** [U] **(a)** (contact) **~ TO sth** exposición *f* A algo **(b)** (Med) congelación *f*; **to die from ~** morir* de frío **2** [U] **(a)** (unmasking): **she was threatened with public ~** amenazaron con ponerla al descubierto **(b)** (publicity) publicidad *f* **3** (Phot) exposición *f*

expound /ɪk'spaʊnd/ *vt* (frml) exponer*

express¹ /ɪk'spres/ *vt* expresar

express² *n* (train) expreso *m*, rápido *m*; (bus) directo *m*

express³ *adj* **1** (fast) ‹*train*› expreso, rápido; ‹*bus*› directo; ‹*delivery/letter*› exprés *adj inv* **2** (specific) (frml) ‹*intention/wish*› expreso

expression /ɪk'spreʃən/ *n* expresión *f*

expressive /ɪk'spresɪv/ *adj* expresivo

expressly /ɪk'spresli/ *adv* (frml) expresamente

expressway /ɪk'spresweɪ/ *n* (AmE) autopista *f*; (urban) vía *f* rápida

expropriate /eks'prəʊprieɪt/ *vt* expropiar

expulsion /ɪk'spʌlʃən/ *n* [U C] expulsión *f*

exquisite /ek'skwɪzət ‖ 'ekskwɪzɪt/ *adj* **(a)** ‹*dress/meal/taste*› exquisito; ‹*carving/brooch*› de exquisita factura; ‹*work/workmanship*› intrincado **(b)** ‹*pleasure*› infinito

ex-serviceman /'eks'sɜːrvəsmən ‖ ,eks'sɜːvɪsmən/ *n* (*pl* **-men** /-mən/) soldado (*or* marinero *etc*) *m* retirado

extend /ɪk'stend/ *vt* **1 (a)** (stretch out) ‹*limbs/wings/telescope*› extender*; ‹*rope/wire*› tender* **(b)** (lengthen) ‹*road/line/visit*› prolongar*; ‹*lease/contract/deadline*› prorrogar* **(c)** (enlarge) ‹*house/room*› ampliar*; ‹*range/scope/influence*› extender* **2** (offer) (frml): **to ~ an invitation to sb** invitar a algn; (of written invitations) cursarle invitación a algn (frml) ■ **~** *vi* **(a)** (stretch) «*fence/property/influence*» extenderse* **(b)** (in time) «*talks*» prolongarse* **(c)** (become extended) «*ladder/antenna*» extenderse*

extension /ɪk'stentʃən ‖ ɪk'stenʃən/ *n* **1 (a)** [U] (of power, meaning) extensión *f* **(b)** [U C] (lengthening) prolongación *f*; (of deadline) prórroga *f*, extensión *f* **2** [C] (to building) ampliación *f* **3** [C] (Telec) **(a)** (line) extensión *f*, interno *m* (RPl), anexo *m* (Chi) **(b)** (telephone) supletorio *m*

extension cord, (BrE) **extension lead** *n* extensión *f*, alargador *m*, alargue *m* (RPl)

extensive /ɪk'stensɪv/ *adj* ‹*area/field*› extenso; ‹*knowledge*› vasto; ‹*experience/coverage*› amplio; ‹*search/inquiries*› exhaustivo; ‹*damage/repairs*› de consideración

extensively /ɪk'stensɪvli/ *adv* **(a)** (widely): **he's traveled ~** ha viajado por todas partes; **this technique is used ~** esta técnica es de uso extendido **(b)** (thoroughly, at length) ‹*research/investigate*› exhaustivamente

extent /ɪk'stent/ *n* [U] **1** (size, area) extensión *f* **2** (range, degree — of knowledge) amplitud *f*; (— of problem) alcance *m*; **to some ~** hasta cierto punto; **to a large ~** en gran parte

extenuate /ɪk'stenjueɪt/ *vt* (frml) atenuar*; **extenuating circumstances** circunstancias *fpl* atenuantes, atentuantes *mpl or fpl*

exterior¹ /ek'stɪriər ‖ ɪk'stɪəriə(r)/ *adj* ‹*wall/surface*› exterior

exterior² *n* exterior *m*

exterminate /ɪk'stɜ:rməneɪt ‖ ɪk'stɜ:mɪneɪt/ *vt* exterminar

external /ek'stɜ:rnḷ ‖ ɪk'stɜ:nḷ/ *adj* **(a)** (exterior) ‹*appearance/sign*› externo, exterior; ‹*wall*› exterior; ‹*wound/treatment*› externo **(b)** ‹*aid/influence*› del exterior; ‹*pressure/evidence*› externo **(c)** (foreign) ‹*affairs/trade/policy*› exterior

extinct /ɪk'stɪŋkt/ *adj* ‹*animal/species*› extinto, desaparecido; ‹*volcano*› extinto, apagado

extinction /ɪk'stɪŋkʃən/ *n* [U] extinción *f*

extinguish /ɪk'stɪŋgwɪʃ/ *vt* **(a)** ‹*fire*› extinguir*; ‹*candle/cigar*› apagar* **(b)** (liter) ‹*hope/memory*› apagar* (liter); ‹*passion/life*› extinguir* (liter)

extinguisher /ɪk'stɪŋgwɪʃər ‖ ɪk'stɪŋgwɪʃə(r)/ *n* (*fire ~*) extinguidor *m* (AmL), extintor *m* (Esp)

extortion /ɪk'stɔ:rʃən ‖ ɪk'stɔ:ʃən/ *n* [U] extorsión *f*

extortionate /ɪk'stɔ:rʃənət ‖ ɪk'stɔ:ʃənət/ *adj* ‹*fee/price*› abusivo; ‹*demand*› excesivo

extra¹ /'ekstrə/ *adj* **(a)** (additional) (*before n*) de más; **we need ~ staff** necesitamos más personal; **at no ~ charge** sin cargo adicional; **they organized three ~ flights** organizaron tres vuelos adicionales; **~ time** (in soccer) prórroga *f* **(b)** (especial) (*before n*) ‹*care/caution*› especial

extra² *adv* **(a)** (*as intensifier*): **~ long** extralargo; **I worked ~ hard** trabajé más que nunca **(b)** (more): **to charge ~ for sth** cobrar algo aparte

extra³ *n* **1** (additional payment or expense) extra *m*; **optional ~s** (Auto) equipamiento *m* opcional, extras *mpl* **2** (Cin) extra *mf*

extract¹ /ɪk'strækt/ *vt* extraer*

extract² /'ekstrækt/ *n* **1** [C] (excerpt) fragmento *m* **2** [U C] (concentrate) extracto *m*

extraction /ɪk'strækʃən/ *n* **1 (a)** [C U] (Dent) extracción *f* **(b)** [U] (of mineral, juice) extracción *f* **2** [U] (ancestry) extracción *f*; **of Polish ~** de extracción polaca

extradite /'ekstrədaɪt/ *vt* extraditar

extradition /'ekstrə'dɪʃən/ *n* [U] extradición *f*; (*before n*) ‹*order/treaty*› de extradición

extraordinary /ɪk'strɔ:rdṇeri ‖ ɪk'strɔ:dṇri/ *adj* **1** (exceptional) extraordinario; (very odd) ‹*sight/appearance*› insólito; (incredible) increíble **2** (frml) (Adm, Govt) ‹*powers/meeting*› extraordinario

extrapolate /ɪk'stræpəleɪt/ *vt* (frml) extrapolar

extrasensory /'ekstrə'sensəri/ *adj* extrasensorial; **~ perception** percepción *f* extrasensorial

extravagance /ɪk'strævəgəns/ *n* **1 (a)** [U] (lavishness, wastefulness) despilfarro *m*, derroche *m* **(b)** [C] (luxury) lujo *m* **2** [U] (of gestures, dress) extravagancia *f*; (of claim, story) lo insólito

extravagant /ɪk'strævəgənt/ *adj* **(a)** (lavish, wasteful) ‹*person*› derrochador, despilfarrador; ‹*lifestyle*› de lujo **(b)** ‹*claim/notions*› insólito; ‹*praise/compliments*› exagerado; ‹*behavior/dress/gesture*› extravagante

extravaganza /ɪk'strævə'gænzə/ *n* gran espectáculo *m* (*realizado con alarde de color, fantasía y dinero*)

extreme¹ /ɪk'stri:m/ *adj* **(a)** (very great) ‹*poverty/caution/urgency*› extremo; ‹*annoyance/relief*› enorme; ‹*heat*› extremado **(b)** (not moderate) ‹*action/measure*› extremo; ‹*opinion*› extremista **(c)** (outermost) (*before n*): **in the ~ north/south** en la zona más septentrional/meridional

extreme² *n* extremo *m*; **~s of temperature** temperaturas *fpl* extremas

extremely /ɪk'stri:mli/ *adv* (*as intensifier*) sumamente; **it's ~ difficult** es dificilísimo

extremist /ɪk'stri:məst ‖ ɪk'stri:mɪst/ *n* extremista *mf*

extremity /ɪk'streməti/ *n* (*pl* **-ties**) **1 (a)** [C] (farthest point) extremo *m* **(b) extremities** *pl* (Anat) extremidades *fpl* **2** [U C] (critical degree, situation) (frml) extremo *m*

extricate /'ekstrəkeɪt ‖ 'ekstrɪkeɪt/ *vt* sacar* (*con dificultad*)

extrovert /'ekstrəvɜ:rt ‖ 'ekstrəvɜ:t/ *n* extrovertido, -da *m,f*

exude /ɪg'zu:d ‖ ɪg'zju:d/ *vt* ‹*resin/fluid*› exudar; ‹*charm/confidence*› emanar

exult /ɪg'zʌlt/ *vi* (frml) exultar (frml)

exultation /'egzʌl'teɪʃən/ *n* [U] (frml) exultación *f* (frml)

eye¹ /aɪ/ *n* **1 (a)** **▶ 484**, **515** (Anat) ojo *m*; **as far as the ~ can/could see** hasta donde alcanza/alcanzaba la vista; **I can't believe my ~s** si no lo veo, no lo creo; ***to see ~ to ~ with sb*** (*usu with neg*) estar* de acuerdo con algn; ***to be up to one's eyes in sth*** estar* hasta aquí de algo (fam) **(b)** (look, gaze) mirada *f*; **before my very ~s** ante mis propios ojos; **nothing caught my ~ in the store** no vi nada que me llamara la atención en la tienda; ***to keep an ~ on sth/sb*** vigilar *or* cuidar algo/a algn **(c)** (attention): **the company has been in the public ~ a lot recently** últimamente se ha hablado mucho de la compañía; ***to have one's ~ on sth*** echarle el ojo a algo (fam) **(d)** (ability to judge) ojo *m*; **to have an ~ for design** tener* ojo para el diseño **2 (a)** (of needle) ojo *m* **(b)** (of hurricane, storm) ojo *m* **(c)** (in potato) ojo *m*

eye² *vt* (*pres p* **eyeing** *or* (BrE) **eyeing**) mirar

eye: **~ball** /'aɪbɔːl/ *n* globo *m* ocular; **~brow** *n* ceja *f*; **to raise one's ~brows** arquear las cejas; ***to raise one's ~brows at sth*** asombrarse ante algo; **~-catching** *adj* llamativo; **~drops** *pl n* colirio *m*

eyeful /'aɪfʊl/ *n*: **I got an ~ of dust** se me llenó el ojo de polvo

eye: **~glasses** *pl n* (AmE) gafas *fpl*, anteojos *mpl* (esp AmL), lentes *mpl* (esp AmL); **~lash** *n* pestaña *f*

eyelet /'aɪlət ‖ 'aɪlɪt/ *n* ojete *m*

eye: **~lid** *n* párpado *m*; **~liner** *n* [U] delineador *m* (de ojos); **~-opener** *n* (colloq) (*no pl*) revelación *f*; **~ shadow** *n* [U C] sombra *f* de ojos; **~sight** *n* [U] vista *f*; **~sore** *n* monstruosidad *f*, adefesio *m*; **~strain** *n* [U] fatiga *f* visual; **~wash** *n* [U] colirio *m*; **it's a lot of ~wash** (colloq) es un cuento chino (fam); **~witness** /'aɪ'wɪtnəs ‖ 'aɪwɪtnɪs/ *n* testigo *mf* ocular

F, f /ef/ *n* **(a)** (letter) F, f *f* **(b)** (Mus) fa *m*

F ▶406 (= **Fahrenheit**) F

fa /fɑː/ *n* (Mus) fa *m*

FA *n* (in UK) = **Football Association**

fable /'feɪbəl/ *n* [C U] fábula *f*

fabric /'fæbrɪk/ *n* **(a)** [U C] (Tex) tela *f* **(b)** [U] (of building, society) estructura *f*

fabricate /'fæbrɪkeɪt/ *vt* **(a)** (invent) inventar(se) **(b)** (manufacture) fabricar*

fabulous /'fæbjələs ‖ 'fæbjʊləs/ *adj* **(a)** (wonderful) (colloq) magnífico **(b)** (imaginary) fabuloso

facade, façade /fə'sɑːd/ *n* fachada *f*

face[1] /feɪs/ ▶484 *n* **1** [C] (of person, animal) cara *f*, rostro *m*; **a new ~** una cara nueva; **in the ~ of stiff opposition** en medio de una fuerte oposición; ***to fall flat on one's ~*** caerse* de bruces; ***to keep a straight ~***: **I could hardly keep a straight ~** casi no podía aguantarme (de) la risa; ***to make*** *o* (BrE also) ***pull a ~*** poner* mala cara; ***to put a brave ~ on it*** poner(le)* al mal tiempo buena cara; ***to sb's ~*** a *or* en la cara **2 (a)** (appearance, nature) (*no pl*) fisonomía *f*; ***on the ~ of it*** aparentemente **(b)** [U] (dignity): **to lose ~** desprestigiarse; **to save ~** guardar las apariencias **3** [C] (of coin, medal, solid) cara *f*; (of clock, watch) esfera *f*, carátula *f* (Méx) **4** [C] (of cliff) pared *f*; ***to disappear off the ~ of the earth*** desaparecer* de la faz de la tierra

face[2] *vt* **1** (be opposite): **she turned to ~ him** se volvió hacia él; **the hotel ~s the sea** el hotel está frente al mar **2** (confront) enfrentarse a; **to be ~d with sth** estar* *or* verse* frente a algo **3 (a)** (be presented with) ‹*problem/increase*› enfrentarse a **(b)** (bear): **I can't ~ going through all that again** no podría volver a pasar por todo eso; **I can't ~ food first thing in the morning** no puedo ni oler la comida temprano por la mañana ■ ~ *vi*: **the house ~s north** la casa está orientada al norte; **I was facing the other way** miraba para el otro lado

• **face up to** [*v* + *adv* + *prep* + *o*] afrontar

face: **~cloth**, (BrE also) **~ flannel** *n* toallita *f* (*para lavarse*); **~ lift** *n* lifting *m*, estiramiento *m* (facial); **the building was given a ~ lift** remozaron el edificio; **~ pack** *n* mascarilla *f* (*de belleza*)

facet /'fæsət ‖ 'fæsɪt/ *n* faceta *f*

facetious /fə'siːʃəs/ *adj* burlón

face: **~ to ~** *adv* cara a cara; **~ value** *n* [U] valor *m* nominal; ***to take sb/sth at ~ value***: **I took her/what she said at ~ value** me fié de ella/yo me creí lo que dijo

facial /'feɪʃəl/ *adj* facial

facile /'fæsəl ‖ 'fæsaɪl/ *adj* superficial, simplista

facilitate /fə'sɪləteɪt ‖ fə'sɪlɪteɪt/ *vt* (frml) facilitar

facility /fə'sɪləti/ *n* (*pl* **-ties**) **1 facilities** *pl*: **facilities for the disabled** instalaciones *fpl* para minusválidos; **the hotel has conference facilities** el hotel dispone de sala(s) de conferencia **2** (building) (AmE) complejo *m*, centro *m*

-facing /'feɪsɪŋ/ *suff*: **north/south~** que da al norte/sur

facsimile /fæk'sɪməli/ *n* facsímil(e) *m*

fact /fækt/ *n* **1** [C] (sth true) hecho *m*; **hard ~s** datos *mpl* concretos; ***to face (the) ~s*** aceptar la realidad **2** [U] (reality): **this novel is based on ~** esta novela está basada en hechos reales; **in ~** de hecho, en realidad

fact-finding /'fækt,faɪndɪŋ/ *adj* (*before n*) de investigación, investigador

faction /'fækʃən/ *n* facción *f*

factor /'fæktər ‖ 'fæktə(r)/ *n* factor *m*

factory /'fæktri, -təri/ *n* (*pl* **-ries**) fábrica *f*

factory: **~ farming** *n* [U] (BrE) cría *f* intensiva; **~ ship** *n* buque *m* factoría

factual /'fæktʃuəl/ *adj* ‹*account*› que se atiene a los hechos

faculty /'fækəlti/ *n* (*pl* **-ties**) **1** (sense) facultad *f* **2** (Educ) **(a)** (of university, college) facultad *f* **(b)** (academic personnel) (AmE) cuerpo *m* docente

fad /fæd/ *n* moda *f* pasajera

fade /feɪd/ *vi* **1** «*color*» apagarse*; «*fabric*» perder* color, desteñirse* **2 (a)** (disappear) «*hope/memories*» desvanecerse*; «*beauty*» marchitarse; «*interest*» decaer*; «*sound*» debilitarse **(b)** «*flower/plant*» ajarse ■ ~ *vt* ‹*fabric*› desteñir*, hacer* perder el color a

• **fade away** [*v* + *adv*] irse* apagando

faded /ˈfeɪdəd ‖ ˈfeɪdɪd/ *adj* ‹*color*› apagado; ‹*fabric*› desteñido

faeces /ˈfiːsiːz/ *pl n* (BrE frml) ⇒ FECES

fag /fæg/ *n* **1** (male homosexual) (AmE sl & pej) maricón *m* (fam & pey) **2** (cigarette) (BrE colloq) cigarrillo *m*, pitillo *m* (fam)

fah /fɑː/ *n* (BrE Mus) fa *m*

Fahrenheit /ˈfærənhaɪt/ ▶**406** *adj* Fahrenheit *adj inv*

fail¹ /feɪl/ *vi* **1** (not succeed) «*marriage/business/plan*» fracasar; **if all else ~s** como último recurso; **he ~ed to live up to our expectations** no dio todo lo que se esperaba de él **2 (a)** «*brakes/lights*» fallar **(b)** «*crop*» perderse*, malograrse **(c) failing** *pres p*: **he could no longer read because of his ~ing eyesight** la vista se le había deteriorado tanto que ya no podía leer; **he retired because of ~ing health** se retiró porque su salud se había deteriorado mucho **3** (in exam) ser* reprobado (AmL), suspender (Esp) ■ **~** *vt* **1 (a)** ‹*exam*› no pasar, ser* reprobado en (AmL), suspender (Esp), reprobar* (Méx), perder* (Col, Ur), salir* mal en (Chi) **(b)** ‹*student*› reprobar* *or* (Esp) suspender **2** (let down): **his courage ~ed him** le faltó valor; **words ~ me!** ¡es el colmo!

fail² *n* **1** [C] (in exam, test) (BrE) reprobado *m or* (Esp) suspenso *m or* (RPl) aplazo *m* **2** [U] **without ~** sin falta

failing¹ /ˈfeɪlɪŋ/ *n* defecto *m*

failing² *prep*: **~ that, try bleach** si eso no resulta, prueba con lejía

fail-safe /ˈfeɪlseɪf/ *adj* ‹*mechanism*› de seguridad

failure /ˈfeɪljər ‖ ˈfeɪljə(r)/ *n* [C U] (unsuccessful thing, act, person) fracaso *m*; **engine ~** falla *f* mecánica *or* (Esp) fallo *m* mecánico; **power ~** apagón *m*; **heart ~** insuficiencia *f* cardíaca; **~ to carry out orders** el incumplimiento de las órdenes

faint¹ /feɪnt/ *adj* **-er, -est** ‹*line*› apenas visible; ‹*light*› débil; ‹*noise*› apenas perceptible; ‹*hope/smile*› ligero; **I feel ~** estoy mareado; **I haven't the ~est (idea)** (colloq) no tengo la más mínima idea

faint² *vi* desmayarse

faint³ *n* desmayo *m*

faintly /ˈfeɪntli/ *adv* **(a)** (barely perceptibly) ‹*see/hear*› apenas; ‹*shine*› débilmente **(b)** (slightly) ‹*amused*› ligeramente; ‹*amusing/ridiculous*› algo

fair¹ /fer ‖ feə(r)/ *adj* **-er, -est 1** (just) ‹*person/decision*› justo; ‹*contest/election*› limpio; **~ enough** bueno, está bien; **I've had my ~ share of problems recently** ya he tenido bastantes problemas últimamente; **~ *and square***: **he won ~ and square** ganó en buena ley **2** ▶**515** ‹*hair*› rubio, güero (Méx), mono (Col), catire (Ven); ‹*skin*› blanco **3** (beautiful) (liter) hermoso, bello **4 (a)** (quite good) ‹*work*› pasable; **we have a ~ chance of winning** tenemos bastantes posibilidades de ganar **(b)** (considerable) (*before n*) ‹*number/amount*› bueno **5** ▶**920** (Meteo): **the weather tomorrow will be ~** mañana va a hacer buen tiempo

fair² *adv* (impartially) ‹*play*› limpio, limpiamente

fair³ *n* **1** (market) feria *f*; (*trade* **~**) feria *f* industrial/comercial **2** (funfair) (BrE) feria *f*

fair: **~ground** *n* (funfair) (BrE) feria *f*; (permanent) parque *m* de diversiones *or* (Esp) atracciones; **~-haired** /ˈferˈherd ‖ ˌfeəˈheəd/ *adj* (BrE) rubio, güero (Méx), mono (Col), catire (Ven)

fairly /ˈferli ‖ ˈfeəli/ *adv* **1** (justly) ‹*play*› limpio; ‹*judge*› con imparcialidad; ‹*divide*› equitativamente **2** (moderately) bastante; **I'm ~ sure** estoy casi segura

fairness /ˈfernəs ‖ ˈfeənɪs/ *n* [U] imparcialidad *f*; **in all ~** sinceramente

fair: **~ play** *n* [U] juego *m* limpio; **~-sized** /ˈferˈsaɪzd ‖ ˌfeəˈsaɪzd/ *adj* (*before n*) bastante grande

fairy /ˈferi ‖ ˈfeəri/ *n* (*pl* **-ries**) hada *f*‡

fairy: **~ godmother** *n* hada *f*‡ madrina; **~land** *n* el país de las hadas; **~ story**, **~ tale** *n* cuento *m* de hadas

faith /feɪθ/ *n* **1** [U] (trust) confianza *f*; **to have ~ IN sb/sth** tener* confianza *or* fe EN algn/algo **2** (Relig) [U C] fe *f*

faithful /ˈfeɪθfəl/ *adj* fiel

faithfully /ˈfeɪθfəli/ *adv* **(a)** (in letters): **yours ~** (esp BrE) (le saluda) atentamente **(b)** ‹*serve/record*› fielmente

faith healer /ˈhiːlər ‖ ˈhiːlə(r)/ *n* curandero, -ra *m,f*

fake¹ /feɪk/ *n* (object) falsificación *f*; (person) farsante *mf*

fake² *adj* ‹*jewel/document*› falso; ‹*fur*› sintético

fake³ *vt* ‹*document/signature*› falsificar*; ‹*results/evidence*› falsear ■ **~** *vi* fingir*

falcon /ˈfælkən ‖ ˈfɔːlkən/ *n* halcón *m*

Falkland Islands /ˈfɔːlklənd/, **Falklands** /ˈfɔːlkləndz/ *pl n* **the ~ ~** las (Islas) Malvinas

fall¹ /fɔːl/ *n* **1** (tumble, collapse) caída *f* **2** (autumn) (AmE) otoño *m* **3** (decrease): **a ~ in temperature** un descenso de (las) temperaturas; **a ~ in prices** una bajada de precios **4** (of snow) nevada *f*; (of rocks) desprendimiento *m* **5 falls** *pl* (waterfall) cascada *f*; (higher) catarata *f*

fall² (*past* **fell**; *past p* **fallen**) *vi* **1 (a)** (tumble) caerse*; **I fell over a piece of wood** tropecé con un trozo de madera; **I fell down the stairs** me caí por la escalera **(b)** (descend) «*night/rain*» caer* **2** «*temperature/price*» bajar; **his face fell** puso cara larga **3** (be captured, defeated) **to ~ (TO sb)** «*city/country*» caer* (en manos de algn) **4** (pass into specified state): **to ~ ill** *o* (esp AmE) **sick** caer* *or* (Esp tb) ponerse* enfermo, enfermarse (AmL); **to ~ silent** callarse **5** (land): **Christmas ~s on a Thursday this year** este año Navidad cae en (un) jueves; **the burden will ~ on the poor** los pobres serán los que sufrirán la carga

● **fall apart** [*v* + *adv*] «*clothing*» deshacerse*; «*system*» venirse* abajo; «*relationship*» irse* a pique

● **fall back** [*v* + *adv*] «*troops*» replegarse*

● **fall back on** [*v* + *adv* + *prep* + *o*] ‹*one's parents*› recurrir a; ‹*resources*› echar mano de

● **fall behind** [*v* + *adv*] [*v* + *prep* + *o*] (in class,

race) rezagarse*, quedarse atrás; **to ~ behind** WITH **sth** ‹*with payments*› atrasarse EN algo
• **fall down** [*v* + *adv*] «*person/tree*» caerse*; «*house/wall*» venirse* abajo
• **fall for** [*v* + *prep* + *o*] **(a)** (be attracted to) ‹*man/woman*› enamorarse de **(b)** (be deceived by) ‹*trick/story*› tragarse* (fam)
• **fall in** [*v* + *adv*] **(a)** (tumble in) caerse* (*a un pozo, al agua etc*) **(b)** (collapse) «*roof*» venirse* abajo **(c)** (form ranks) (Mil) formar filas
• **fall off** [*v* + *adv*] **(a)** (tumble down) caerse* (*de una bicicleta, un caballo etc*) **(b)** (break off) «*button/handle*» caerse* **(c)** (decline) «*production/attendance*» decaer*
• **fall out** [*v* + *adv*] **(a)** (drop out) caerse* **(b)** (break ranks) (Mil) romper* filas **(c)** (quarrel) «*friends*» pelearse
• **fall over** [*v* + *adv*] «*person/object*» caerse*
• **fall through** [*v* + *adv*] (fail) no salir* adelante

fallacy /'fæləsi/ *n* [C U] (*pl* **-cies**) falacia *f*

fallen /'fɔːlən/ *past p of* FALL[2]

fallible /'fæləbəl/ *adj* falible

falling /'fɔːlɪŋ/: **~-off** /'fɔːlɪŋ'ɔːf ‖ ˌfɔːlɪŋ'ɒf/ *n* ⇒ FALLOFF; **~-out** /'fɔːlɪŋ'aʊt/ *n* (AmE) pelea *f*

falloff /'fɔːlɔːf ‖ 'fɔːlɒf/ *n* (*no pl*) (in speed) disminución *f*

Fallopian tube /fə'ləʊpiən/ *n* trompa *f* de Falopio

fallout /'fɔːlaʊt/ *n* [U] lluvia *f* radiactiva; (*before n*) **~ shelter** refugio *m* antinuclear

fallow /'fæləʊ/ *adj* ‹*land*› en barbecho

false /fɔːls/ *adj* ‹*statement/pride/name*› falso; ‹*belief*› erróneo; ‹*eyelashes/fingernails*› postizo; **true or ~?** ¿verdadero o falso?

false alarm *n* falsa alarma *f*

falsehood /'fɔːlshʊd/ *n* [C U] (frml) falsedad *f*

falsely /'fɔːlsli/ *adv* ‹*accuse*› falsamente

false: **~ start** *n* (Sport) salida *f* en falso; (to career, speech) intento *m* fallido; **~ teeth** *pl n* dentadura *f* postiza

falsify /'fɔːlsəfaɪ ‖ 'fɔːlsɪfai/ *vt* **-fies, -fying, -fied** ‹*accounts/evidence*› falsificar*; ‹*truth*› falsear

falter /'fɔːltər ‖ 'fɔːltə(r)/ *vi* **(a)** (speak hesitantly) titubear, balbucear **(b)** «*enthusiasm/interest*» decaer*; «*courage/resolve*» flaquear

fame /feɪm/ *n* [U] fama *f*

familiar /fə'mɪljər ‖ fə'mɪlɪə(r)/ *adj* **(a)** (well-known) ‹*sound/face*› familiar, conocido; **the name sounds ~** el nombre me suena **(b)** (having knowledge of) **to be ~** WITH **sth/sb** estar* familiarizado CON algo/algn

familiarity /fə'mɪli'ærəti/ *n* (*pl* **-ties**) **(a)** (knowledge): **she claimed extensive ~ with the method** dijo estar muy familiarizada con el método; **some ~ with computers would be an asset** se valorará la experiencia previa con computadoras **(b)** (of person, book, landscape) familiaridad *f*; **~ *breeds contempt*** lo que se tiene no se aprecia

familiarize /fə'mɪljəraɪz ‖ fə'mɪlɪəraɪz/ *vt* **to ~ oneself** WITH **sth** familiarizarse* CON algo

family /'fæmli, 'fæməli ‖ 'fæmɪli, 'fæmli/ *n* [C U] (*pl* **-lies**) (relatives) familia *f*; (*before n*) ‹*business*› familiar; ‹*fortune*› de la familia

family: **~ planning** *n* [U] planificación *f* familiar; **~ tree** *n* árbol *m* genealógico

famine /'fæmən ‖ 'fæmɪn/ *n* [C U] hambruna *f*

famished /'fæmɪʃt/ *adj* famélico; **I'm ~!** (colloq) ¡estoy muerto de hambre! (fam)

famous /'feɪməs/ *adj* famoso

fan[1] /fæn/ *n* **1** (hand-held) abanico *m*; (mechanical) ventilador *m* **2** (of group, actor) fan *mf*; (of football team) hincha *mf*

fan[2] **-nn-** *vt* ‹*person*› abanicar*; ‹*interest/curiosity*› avivar
• **fan out** [*v* + *adv*] «*searchers*» abrirse* en abanico

fanatic /fə'nætɪk/ *n* fanático, -ca *m,f*

fanatical /fə'nætɪkəl/ *adj* ‹*believer*› fanático; ‹*belief*› ciego

fan belt *n* correa *f or* (Méx) banda *f* del ventilador

fanciful /'fænsɪfəl/ *adj* **(a)** (impractical) ‹*idea*› extravagante **(b)** (elaborate) ‹*design*› imaginativo

fan club *n* club *m* de fans

fancy[1] /'fænsi/ *vt* **fancies, fancying, fancied** (esp BrE) **1** (expressing surprise) (*in interj*): **(just) ~ that!** ¡pues mira tú!; **~ meeting them here!** ¡qué casualidad encontrarnos con ellos aquí! **2** (feel desire for) (colloq): **I really ~ an ice-cream** ¡qué ganas de tomarme un helado!; **do you ~ going to see a movie?** ¿tienes ganas de ir al cine? **3**(be physically attracted to) (colloq): **I ~ her/him** me gusta mucho **4** (imagine) (frml) **to ~** (THAT): **she fancied she saw his face in the crowd** creyó ver su cara entre la multitud

fancy[2] *adj* **-cier, -ciest (a)** (elaborate) elaborado **(b)** (superior) (pej) ‹*hotel*› de campanillas; ‹*car*› lujoso; ‹*ideas*› extravagante

fancy[3] *n* (*pl* **-cies**) **1** (liking) (*no pl*): **to take a ~ to sb**: **she seems to have taken a ~ to you** parece que le has caído en gracia; ***to tickle sb's ~***: **the idea rather tickled my ~** la idea me resultó atractiva **2** [C U] (imagination) imaginación *f*

fancy: **~ dress** *n* [U] (BrE) disfraz *m*; (*before n*) **~-dress party** fiesta *f* de disfraces; **~-free** /'fænsi'friː/ *adj see* FOOTLOOSE; **~ goods** *pl n* (Busn) artículos *mpl* para regalo

fanfare /'fænfer ‖ 'fænfeə(r)/ *n* fanfarria *f*

fang /fæŋ/ *n* (of dog) colmillo *m*; (of snake) diente *m*

fan heater *n* electroconvector *m*

fanny /'fæni/ *n* (*pl* **-nies**) (buttocks) (AmE sl) culo *m* (fam: en algunas regiones vulg), traste *m* (CS fam), poto *m* (Chi, Per fam)

fantasize /'fæntəsaɪz/ *vi* fantasear

fantastic /fæn'tæstɪk/ *adj* **(a)** (wonderful) (colloq) fantástico **(b)** (incredible) ‹*story*› absurdo

fantasy /'fæntəsi/ *n* (*pl* **-sies**) **(a)** [U C] (unreality) fantasía *f* **(b)** [C] (daydream) sueño *m*

far[1] /fɑːr ‖ fɑː(r)/ *adv* **1** (*comp* **further** *or* **farther**; *superl* **furthest** *or* **farthest**) **(a)** (in distance) lejos; **how ~ is it?** ¿a qué distancia está?; **~ away in the distance** a lo lejos **(b)** (in progress): **the plans**

are now quite ~ advanced los planes están ya muy avanzados; **that girl will go ~** esa chica va a llegar lejos **(c)** (in time): **Christmas isn't ~ away** *o* **off now** ya falta poco para Navidad; **I can't remember that ~ back** no recuerdo cosas tan lejanas **(d)** (in extent, degree): **the new legislation doesn't go ~ enough** la nueva legislación no tiene el alcance necesario; **his jokes went a bit too ~** se pasó un poco con esos chistes **2** (very much): **~ better** mucho mejor **3** (*in phrases*) **as** *o* **so far as**: **as** *o* **so ~ as I know** que yo sepa; **by far**: **their team was by ~ the worst** su equipo fue con mucho el peor; **so far**: **so ~, everything has gone according to plan** hasta ahora todo ha salido de acuerdo a lo planeado

far[2] *adj* (*comp* **farther**; *superl* **farthest**) **(a)** (distant) lejano **(b)** (most distant, extreme) (*before n, no comp*): **at the ~ end of the room** en el otro extremo de la habitación; **the ~ left/right** (Pol) la extrema izquierda/derecha

faraway /ˈfɑːrəˈweɪ/ *adj* (*before n*) ‹*lands*› lejano; ‹*look*› ausente

farce /fɑːrs ‖ fɑːs/ *n* [C U] farsa *f*

farcical /ˈfɑːrsɪkəl ‖ ˈfɑːsɪkəl/ *adj* ridículo

fare /fer ‖ feə(r)/ *n* **1** (cost of travel — by air) pasaje *m or* (Esp) billete *m*; (— by bus) boleto *m or* (esp Esp) billete *m*; **~s will rise again next year** las tarifas subirán de nuevo en el próximo año **2** [U] (food and drink) comida *f*

Far East *n* **the ~ ~** el Lejano *or* Extremo Oriente

farewell[1] /ˈferˈwel ‖ ˌfeəˈwel/ *n* despedida *f*

farewell[2] *interj* (liter) adiós

far-fetched /ˈfɑːrˈfetʃt ‖ ˌfɑːˈfetʃt/ *adj* exagerado

farm[1] /fɑːrm ‖ fɑːm/ *n* (small) granja *f*, chacra *f* (CS, Per); (large) hacienda *f*, cortijo *m* (Esp), rancho *m* (Méx), estancia *f* (RPl), fundo *m* (Chi); (*before n*) ‹*machinery/worker*› agrícola

farm[2] *vt* ‹*land*› cultivar

• **farm out** [*v* + *o* + *adv*, *v* + *adv* + *o*] ‹*work*› encargar* (*a terceros*)

farmer /ˈfɑːrmər ‖ ˈfɑːmə(r)/ *n* agricultor, -tora *m, f*, granjero, -ra *m,f*, chacarero, -ra *m,f* (CS, Per); (owner of large farm) hacendado, -da *m,f*, ranchero, -ra *m,f* (Méx), estanciero, -ra *m,f* (RPl), dueño, -ña *m,f* de fundo (Chi)

farm: **~hand** *n* peón *m or* (Esp) mozo *m* de labranza; **~house** *n* casa *f* de labranza, alquería *f* (*en Esp*), ≈ casco *m* de la estancia (*en RPl*)

farming /ˈfɑːrmɪŋ ‖ ˈfɑːmɪŋ/ *n* [U] (of land) labranza *f*; (of animals) crianza *f*; (*before n*) ‹*community*› agrícola; ‹*methods*› de labranza

farm: **~land** *n* [U] tierras *fpl* de labranza; **~yard** *n* corral *m*

far: **~-off** /ˈfɑːrˈɔːf ‖ ˈfɑːrɒf/ *adj* (*pred* **~ off**) (in space) remoto; (in time) distante; **~-reaching** /ˈfɑːrˈriːtʃɪŋ ‖ ˌfɑːˈriːtʃɪŋ/ *adj* de gran alcance; **~-sighted** /ˈfɑːrˈsaɪtəd ‖ ˌfɑːˈsaɪtɪd/ *adj* **(a)** (showing foresight) con visión de futuro **(b)** (AmE Med) hipermétrope

fart[1] /fɑːrt ‖ fɑːt/ *n* (vulg) pedo *m* (fam)

fart[2] *vi* (vulg) tirarse *or* echarse un pedo (fam)

farther[1] /ˈfɑːrðər ‖ ˈfɑːðə(r)/ *adv comp of* FAR[1] 1

farther[2] *adj comp of* FAR[2]

farthest[1] /ˈfɑːrðəst ‖ ˈfɑːðɪst/ *adv superl of* FAR[1] 1

farthest[2] *adj superl of* FAR[2]

fascinate /ˈfæsn̩eɪt ‖ ˈfæsɪmeɪt/ *vt* fascinar

fascinated /ˈfæsn̩eɪtəd ‖ ˈfæsɪmeɪtɪd/ *adj* fascinado

fascinating /ˈfæsn̩eɪtɪŋ ‖ ˈfæsɪmeɪtɪŋ/ *adj* fascinante

fascination /ˈfæsn̩ˈeɪʃən ‖ ˌfæsɪˈneɪʃən/ *n* [U] fascinación *f*

fascism /ˈfæʃɪzəm/ *n* [U] fascismo *m*

fascist[1] /ˈfæʃəst ‖ ˈfæʃɪst/ *n* fascista *mf*

fascist[2] *adj* fascista

fashion[1] /ˈfæʃən/ *n* **1** [C U] (vogue) moda *f*; **to be in/out of ~** estar* de moda/estar* pasado de moda; (*before n*) **~ designer** diseñador, -dora *m,f* de modas **2** [U] (custom) costumbre *f* **3** [U] (manner) manera *f*; ***after a ~***: **can you swim? — well, after a ~** ¿sabes nadar? — bueno, a mi manera

fashion[2] *vt* crear

fashionable /ˈfæʃnəbəl/ *adj* ‹*clothes/designs*› a la moda; ‹*restaurant/people/idea*› de moda

fashionably /ˈfæʃnəbli/ *adv* a la moda

fashion show *n* desfile *m* de modas

fast[1] /fæst ‖ fɑːst/ *adj* **-er, -est 1 (a)** (speedy) rápido **(b)** (of clock, watch) (*pred*): **my watch is five minutes ~** mi reloj (se) adelanta cinco minutos **2** (permanent) ‹*color*› inalterable

fast[2] *adv* **1** (quickly) rápidamente, rápido **2** (firmly): **the car was stuck ~ in the mud** el coche estaba atascado en el barro completamente; **to be ~ asleep** estar* profundamente dormido

fast[3] *vi* ayunar

fast[4] *n* ayuno *m*

fasten /ˈfæsn̩ ‖ ˈfɑːsn̩/ *vt* **(a)** (attach) sujetar; (tie) atar **(b)** (do up, close) ‹*case*› cerrar*; ‹*coat/seat belt*› abrochar ■ **~** *vi* «*suitcase*» cerrar*; «*skirt/necklace*» abrocharse

fastener /ˈfæsn̩ər ‖ ˈfɑːsnə(r)/ *n* cierre *m*

fast: **~ food** *n* [C U] comida *f* rápida; **~-forward** /ˈfæstˈfɔːrwərd ‖ ˌfɑːstˈfɔːwəd/ *vt/i* avanzar*

fastidious /fæsˈtɪdiəs/ *adj* **(a)** (demanding) muy exigente **(b)** (fussy) maniático, mañoso (AmL)

fat[1] /fæt/ *adj* **-tt-** ‹*person/animal*› gordo; ‹*book/cigar*› grueso; **to get ~** engordar; **a ~ lot of good that'll do!** (iro) ¡para lo que va a servir!

fat[2] *n* [U C] grasa *f*

fatal /ˈfeɪtl̩/ *adj* **(a)** (causing death) mortal **(b)** (disastrous) ‹*decision/mistake*› fatídico

fatalistic /ˈfeɪtl̩ˈɪstɪk ‖ ˌfeɪtəˈlɪstɪk/ *adj* fatalista

fatality /feɪˈtæləti ‖ fəˈtæləti/ *n* (*pl* **-ties**) muerto *m*

fatally /ˈfeɪtl̩i ‖ ˈfeɪtəli/ *adv* mortalmente

fate /feɪt/ *n* **(a)** [U] (destiny) destino *m* **(b)** (*no pl*) (one's lot, end) suerte *f*

fated /ˈfeɪtəd ‖ ˈfeɪtɪd/ *adj* (destined) **to be ~ to** + INF (liter) estar* predestinado A + INF

fateful /ˈfeɪtfəl/ *adj* **(a)** (momentous) ‹*day/decision*› fatídico **(b)** (prophetic) ‹*words*› profético

father¹ /ˈfɑːðər ‖ ˈfɑːðə(r)/ *n* padre *m*

father² *vt* ‹*child*› engendrar, tener*

Father Christmas *n* (BrE) Papá *m* Noel, viejo *m* Pascuero (Chi)

fatherhood /ˈfɑːðərhʊd ‖ ˈfɑːðəhʊd/ *n* [U] paternidad *f*

father: **~-in-law** *n* (*pl* **~s-in-law**) suegro *m*; **~land** *n* patria *f*

fatherly /ˈfɑːðərli ‖ ˈfɑːðəli/ *adj* paternal

fathom¹ /ˈfæðəm/ *n* braza *f*

fathom² *vt* **~ (out)** entender*

fatigue /fəˈtiːg/ *n* [U] fatiga *f*

fatten /ˈfætn̩/ *vt* **~ (up)** ‹*animal*› cebar

fattening /ˈfætn̩ɪŋ/ *adj*: **cakes are extremely ~** los pasteles engordan muchísimo

fatty /ˈfæti/ *adj* **-tier, -tiest** ‹*food/substance*› graso, grasoso (AmL)

faucet /ˈfɔːsət/ *n* (AmE) llave *f* *or* (Esp) grifo *m* *or* (RPl) canilla *f* *or* (Per) caño *m* *or* (AmC) paja *f*, chorro *m* (AmC, Ven)

fault¹ /fɔːlt/ *n* **1** [U] (responsibility, blame) culpa *f*; **they're always finding ~ with me** todo lo que hago les parece mal **2** [C] **(a)** (failing) defecto *m*; **she is generous to a ~** es generosa en extremo **(b)** (in machine) avería *f*; (in goods) defecto *m* **3** [C] (Geol) falla *f* **4** [C] (in tennis, show jumping) falta *f*

fault² *vt* encontrarle* defectos a

faultless /ˈfɔːltləs ‖ ˈfɔːltlɪs/ *adj* impecable

faulty /ˈfɔːlti/ *adj* **-tier, -tiest** ‹*goods/design*› defectuoso; ‹*workmanship*› imperfecto

faux pas /ˈfəʊˈpɑː/ *n* (*pl* **~ ~** /-z/) metedura *f* *or* (AmL tb) metida *f* de pata (fam)

favor¹, (BrE) **favour** /ˈfeɪvər ‖ ˈfeɪvə(r)/ *n* **1** [U] (approval): **to find ~ with sb** (frml) tener* buena acogida por parte de algn (frml); ***to curry ~ with sb*** tratar de congraciarse con algn **2 in ~** a favor; **to be in ~ of sth** estar* a favor de algo **3** [C] (act of kindness) favor *m*; **to do/ask sb a ~** hacerle*/pedirle* un favor a algn

favor², (BrE) **favour** *vt* **(a)** (be in favor of) estar* a favor de **(b)** (benefit) favorecer* **(c)** (treat preferentially) favorecer*

favorable, (BrE) **favourable** /ˈfeɪvrəbəl/ *adj* favorable; **to be ~ TO sth** favorecer* algo

favorite¹, (BrE) **favourite** /ˈfeɪvrət ‖ ˈfeɪvərɪt/ *adj* preferido

favorite², (BrE) **favourite** *n* **(a)** (person, thing) preferido, -da *m,f*; (Sport) favorito, -ta *m,f* **(b)** (of teacher, ruler) favorito, -ta *m,f*

favoritism, (BrE) **favouritism** /ˈfeɪvrətɪzəm ‖ ˈfeɪvərɪtɪzəm/ *n* [U] favoritismo *m*

fawn¹ /fɔːn/ *n* **1** [C] (young deer) cervato *m* **2** **▶ 515** [U] (color) beige *m*, beis *m* (Esp); (*before n*) ‹*sweater/coat*› beige *adj inv*, beis *adj inv* (Esp)

fawn² *vi* (flatter) **to ~ ON sb** «*person*» (pej) adular a algn

fax¹ /fæks/ *n* fax *m*; (*before n*) **~ machine** fax *m*

fax² *vt* faxear

faze /feɪz/ *vt* (colloq) perturbar

FBI *n* (in US) (= **Federal Bureau of Investigation**) FBI *m*

FDA *n* (in US) = **Food and Drug Administration**

fear¹ /fɪr ‖ fɪə(r)/ *n* [U C] miedo *m*, temor *m*; **~ of heights** miedo a las alturas; **no ~!** (*as interj*) (colloq) ¡ni loco! *or* ¡ni muerto!

fear² *vt* **(a)** (dread) temer **(b)** (suspect) **to ~ (THAT)** temerse QUE ■ **~** *vi* temer; **to ~ FOR sb/sth** temer POR algn/algo

fearful /ˈfɪrfəl ‖ ˈfɪəfəl/ *adj* **1** (frightening) aterrador **2** (timid) miedoso

fearless /ˈfɪrləs ‖ ˈfɪəlɪs/ *adj* intrépido

fearsome /ˈfɪrsəm ‖ ˈfɪəsəm/ *adj* ‹*enemy*› aterrador; ‹*task*› tremendo

feasibility /ˈfiːzəˈbɪləti/ *n* [U] viabilidad *f*; (*before n*) **~ study** estudio *m* de viabilidad

feasible /ˈfiːzəbəl/ *adj* (practicable) viable; (possible) posible

feast¹ /fiːst/ *n* **1** (banquet) banquete *m* **2** (Relig) fiesta *f*; (*before n*) **~ day** día *m* festivo

feast² *vi* festejar ■ **~** *vt* **to ~ one's eyes ON sth** regalarse los ojos CON algo

feat /fiːt/ *n* hazaña *f*

feather /ˈfeðər ‖ ˈfeðə(r)/ *n* pluma *f*; ***as light as a ~*** ligero *or* (esp AmL) liviano como una pluma; (*before n*) **~ bed** colchón *m* de plumas; **~ duster** plumero *m*

feature¹ /ˈfiːtʃər ‖ ˈfiːtʃə(r)/ *n* **1 (a)** (of face) rasgo *m* **(b)** (of character, landscape, machine, style) característica *f* **2 (a) ~ (film)** película *f* **(b)** (Journ) artículo *m* **(c)** (Rad, TV) documental *m*

feature² *vt* **1** (Journ, Cin): **he was ~d in 'The Globe' recently** 'The Globe' publicó un artículo sobre él hace poco; **featuring John Ball** con la actuación de John Ball **2 (a)** (have as feature) «*hotel/house*» ofrecer* **(b)** (depict) mostrar* ■ **~** *vi* figurar; **rice ~s prominently in their diet** el arroz ocupa un lugar importante en su alimentación

February /ˈfebrueri ‖ ˈfebrʊəri/ **▶ 540** *n* febrero *m*

feces, (BrE) **faeces** /ˈfiːsiːz/ *pl n* (frml) heces *fpl* (frml)

fed /fed/ *past & past p of* FEED¹

federal /ˈfedərəl/ *adj* federal

federal: **F~ Republic of Germany** *n* **the F~ Republic of Germany** la República Federal de Alemania; **F~ Reserve Board** *n* (in US) la Junta de Gobernadores de la Reserva Federal

federation /ˈfedəˈreɪʃən/ *n* [C U] federación *f*

fed up *adj* (colloq) (*usu pred*) **to be ~ ~ (WITH sb/sth/-ING)** estar* harto (DE algn/algo/+ INF)

fee /fiː/ *n* **(a)** (payment — to doctor, lawyer) honorarios *mpl*; (— to actor, singer) caché *m* **(b)** (charge) (*often pl*): **on payment of a small ~** por una módica suma; **membership ~(s)** cuota *f* (de socio)

feeble /ˈfiːbəl/ *adj* **-bler** /-blər ‖ -blə(r)/, **-blest** /-bləst ‖ -blɪst/ **(a)** (weak) débil **(b)** (poor) ‹*joke*› flojo; ‹*excuse*› pobre

feed¹ /fiːd/ (*past & past p* **fed**) *vt* **1 (a)** (give food to) dar* de comer a; ‹*baby*› (breastfeed) darle* el pecho a; (with a bottle) darle* el biberón *or* (CS, Per) la mamadera *or* (Col, Ven) el tetero a **(b)** (provide food for) alimentar **(c)** (give as food) **to ~ sth TO sb** dar* algo (de comer) A algn **2** (insert) **to ~ sth INTO sth** ‹*into a machine*› introducir* algo EN algo **3** (sustain) ‹*imagination/rumor*› avivar; ‹*hope/fire*› alimentar ■ ~ *vi* comer; **to ~ ON sth** alimentarse DE algo

feed² *n* **(a)** [C] (act of feeding): **it's time for the baby's ~** es hora de darle de comer al niño **(b)** [U] (food) alimento *m*; (for cattle) pienso *m*

feedback /ˈfiːdbæk/ *n* [U] (reaction) reacción *f*; (Audio, Electron) retroalimentación *f*

feeding bottle /ˈfiːdɪŋ/ *n* (BrE) biberón *m*, mamadera *f* (CS, Per), tetero *m* (Col, Ven)

feel¹ /fiːl/ (*past & past p* **felt**) *vi* **1** (physically, emotionally) sentirse*; **to ~ hot/cold/hungry/thirsty** tener* calor/frío/hambre/sed **2** (have opinion): **it's something I ~ strongly about** es algo que me parece muy importante; **how do you ~ about these changes?** ¿qué opinas de estos cambios? **3 to ~ like -ING** (be in the mood for) tener* ganas DE + INF **4** (seem): **your hands ~ cold** tienes las manos frías; **how does that ~? — it's still too tight** ¿cómo lo sientes? — todavía me queda apretado **5** (grope) **to ~ FOR sth** buscar* algo a tientas ■ ~ *vt* **1** (touch) tocar*; ***to ~ one's way*** ir* a tientas **2** ‹*sensation/movement/shame*› sentir*; **I couldn't ~ my fingers** no sentía los dedos **3** (consider) considerar; **I ~ that** ... me parece que ...

feel² *n* (*no pl*) **1 (a)** (sensation) sensación *f* **(b)** (sense of touch) tacto *m* **2 (a)** (atmosphere — of house, room) ambiente *m* **(b)** (instinct): **to have a ~ for sth** tener* sensibilidad para algo; **to get the ~ of sth** acostumbrarse a algo

feeler /ˈfiːlər ‖ ˈfiːlə(r)/ *n* **(a)** (Zool) (antenna) antena *f*; (tentacle) tentáculo *m* **(b)** (tentative approach): **to put out ~s** tantear el terreno

feeling /ˈfiːlɪŋ/ *n* **1 (a)** [U] (physical sensitivity) sensibilidad *f* **(b)** [C] (physical, emotional sensation) sensación *f* **2 (a)** [U] (sincere emotion) sentimiento *m* **(b) feelings** *pl* (sensitivity) sentimientos *mpl* **3** [C U] (opinion) opinión *f* **4** (*no pl*) (impression) impresión *f*; **I've a ~ that he knows already** tengo *or* me da la sensación de que ya lo sabe

feet /fiːt/ *n pl of* FOOT[1]

feign /feɪn/ *vt* fingir*

feline /ˈfiːlaɪn/ *adj* felino

fell¹ /fel/ *past of* FALL[2]

fell² *vt* ‹*tree*› talar; ‹*person*› derribar

fellow¹ /ˈfeləʊ/ *n* **1** (man) tipo *m* (fam), hombre *m* **2** (member — of college) *miembro del cuerpo docente y de la junta rectora de una universidad*; (— of learned society) miembro *mf* de número

fellow² *adj* (*before n*): **~ worker/traveler** compañero, -ra *m,f* de trabajo/viaje; **~ citizen** conciudadano, -na *m,f*; **he has no love for his ~ men** no le tiene amor al prójimo

fellow feeling *n* [U] camaradería *f*

fellowship /ˈfeləʊʃɪp/ *n* **1** [C] (Educ) **(a)** (at university) título *m* de FELLOW[1] 2 **(b)** (endowment) beca *f* de investigación **2 (a)** [U] (companionship) (liter) hermandad *f* (liter) **(b)** [C] (fraternity) fraternidad *f*

felon /ˈfelən/ *n* (in US law) delincuente *mf* (*que ha cometido un delito grave*)

felony /ˈfeləni/ *n* [C U] (*pl* **-nies**) (in US Law) delito *m* grave

felt¹ /felt/ *n* [U] fieltro *m*

felt² *past & past p of* FEEL[1]

felt pen, **felt-tip (pen)** /ˈfelttɪp/ *n* rotulador *m*, marcador *m* (AmL)

female¹ /ˈfiːmeɪl/ *adj* ‹*sex*› femenino; ‹*animal/plant*› hembra; **the victim was ~** la víctima era una mujer

female² *n* hembra *f*; (woman, girl) mujer *f*

feminine /ˈfemənən ‖ ˈfemɪnɪn/ *adj* femenino

feminism /ˈfemənəzəm ‖ ˈfemɪnɪzəm/ *n* [U] feminismo *m*

feminist¹ /ˈfemənəst ‖ ˈfemɪnɪst/ *n* feminista *mf*

feminist² *adj* feminista

fence¹ /fens/ *n* **1 (a)** (barrier) cerca *f*, cerco *m* (AmL); ***to sit on the ~*** nadar entre dos aguas **(b)** (in showjumping) valla *f* **2** (receiver of stolen goods) (colloq) *persona que comercia con objetos robados*, reducidor, -dora *m,f* (AmS)

fence² *vt* cercar* ■ ~ *vi* (Sport) practicar* la esgrima

• **fence in** [*v + adv + o, v + o + adv*] cercar*

• **fence off** [*v + adv + o, v + o + adv*] separar con una cerca

fencer /ˈfensər ‖ ˈfensə(r)/ *n* esgrimista *mf*

fencing /ˈfensɪŋ/ *n* [U] **1** (Sport) esgrima *f* **2 (a)** (material) *materiales para cercos o vallas* **(b)** (fence) cerca *f*

fend /fend/ *vi*: **to ~ for oneself** valerse* por sí mismo

• **fend off** [*v + o + adv, v + adv + o*] ‹*attack/enemy*› rechazar*; ‹*blow*› esquivar; ‹*questions*› eludir

fender /ˈfendər ‖ ˈfendə(r)/ *n* **1** (around fireplace) rejilla *f* **2** (on car) (AmE) guardabarros *m or* (Méx) salpicadera *f or* (Chi, Per) tapabarro(s) *m*; (on boat) defensa *f*

fennel /ˈfenl̩/ *n* [U] hinojo *m*

ferment /fərˈment ‖ fəˈment/ *vi* fermentar

fern /fɜːrn ‖ fɜːn/ *n* [C U] helecho *m*

ferocious /fəˈrəʊʃəs/ *adj* feroz

ferocity /fəˈrɑːsəti ‖ fəˈrɒsəti/ *n* [U] ferocidad *f*

ferret /ˈferət ‖ ˈferɪt/ *n* hurón *m*

• **ferret around** , **ferret about** [*v + adv*] husmear

• **ferret out** [*v + o + adv, v + adv + o*] (colloq) descubrir*

ferry¹ /ˈferi/ *n* (*pl* **-ries**) (boat) transbordador *m*, ferry *m*; (smaller) balsa *f*

ferry² *vt* **-ries, -rying, -ried** llevar; **we ~ the children to and from school in the car** llevamos a los niños al colegio y los vamos a buscar en coche

fertile /ˈfɜːrtl̩ ‖ ˈfɜːtaɪl/ *adj* ‹*woman/animal/plant/soil*› fértil; ‹*seed/egg*› fecundado; ‹*imagination*› fértil

fertility /fərˈtɪləti ‖ fəˈtɪləti/ *n* [U] fertilidad *f*

fertilize /ˈfɜːrtl̩aɪz ‖ ˈfɜːtɪlaɪz/ *vt* ‹*egg/plant/cell*› fecundar; ‹*soil/crop*› abonar

fertilizer /ˈfɜːrtl̩aɪzər ‖ ˈfɜːtɪlaɪzə(r)/ *n* [U C] fertilizante *m*

fervent /'fɜ:rvənt ‖ 'fɜ:vənt/ *adj* ferviente

fervor, (BrE) **fervour** /'fɜ:rvər ‖ 'fɜ:və(r)/ *n* [U] fervor *m*

fester /'festər ‖ 'festə(r)/ *vi* enconarse

festival /'festəvəl ‖ 'festɪvəl/ *n* **(a)** (Relig) fiesta *f* **(b)** (Cin, Mus, Theat) festival *m* **(c)** (celebration) fiesta *f*

festive /'festɪv/ *adj* festivo; **the ~ season** (set phrase) las Navidades

festivity /fes'tɪvəti/ *n* (*usu pl*) celebración *f*

festoon /fe'stu:n/ *vt* **to ~ sth/sb** (WITH **sth**) adornar algo/a algn (CON algo)

fetch /fetʃ/ *vt* **1** (bring) traer*, ir* a por (Esp) **2** (sell for) (colloq): **the car ~ed $4,000** el coche se vendió en 4.000 dólares ■ ~ *vi*: ***to ~ and carry*** ser* el recadero/la recadera

fetching /'fetʃɪŋ/ *adj* ‹*smile*› atractivo; ‹*dress*/*hat*› sentador, que sienta bien (Esp)

fete, **fête** /feɪt/ *n* **(a)** (fund-raising event) (BrE) feria *f* (*benéfica*), kermesse *f* (CS, Méx), bazar *m* (Col) **(b)** (party) (AmE) fiesta *f* (*en un jardín*)

fetish /'fetɪʃ/ *n* fetiche *m*

fetter /'fetər ‖ 'fetə(r)/ *vt* (liter) encadenar; **he felt ~ed by convention** se sentía prisionero de los convencionalismos

fetters /'fetərz ‖ 'fetəz/ *pl n* (liter) grillos *mpl*

fettle /'fetl̩/ *n*: ***to be in fine ~*** estar* en (buena) forma

fetus, (BrE) **foetus** /'fi:təs/ *n* feto *m*

feud[1] /fju:d/ *n* contienda *f* (frml)

feud[2] *vi* contender* (frml)

feudal /'fju:dl/ *adj* feudal

fever /'fi:vər ‖ 'fi:və(r)/ *n* [C U] fiebre *f*

feverish /'fi:vərɪʃ/ *adj* (Med) con fiebre; (frantic) febril

fever pitch *n*: ***to reach ~ ~*** llegar* al paroxismo

few[1] /fju:/ *adj* **-er, -est** pocos, -cas; **the last ~ days have been difficult** estos últimos días han sido difíciles; **there were ~er people than usual** había menos gente que de costumbre; **I've been there a ~ times** he estado allí unas cuantas veces

few[2] *pron* **-er, -est** pocos, -cas; **the privileged ~** la minoría privilegiada; **a ~ of us complained** algunos (de nosotros) nos quejamos

fiancé /'fi:ɑ:n'seɪ, fi:'ɑ:nseɪ ‖ fi:'ɒnseɪ/ *n* prometido *m*

fiancée /'fi:ɑ:n'seɪ, fi:'ɑ:nseɪ ‖ fi:'ɒnseɪ/ *n* prometida *f*

fiasco /fi'æskəʊ/ *n* (*pl* **-cos** *or* **-coes**) fracaso *m*

fib[1] /fɪb/ *n* (colloq) mentirilla *f*, bola *f* (fam)

fib[2] *vi* **-bb-** (colloq) mentir*, decir* mentirillas *or* (fam) bolas

fiber, (BrE) **fibre** /'faɪbər ‖ 'faɪbə(r)/ *n* [C U] fibra *f*

fiberglass /'faɪbərglæs ‖ 'faɪbəglɑ:s/ *n* [U] fibra *f* de vidrio

fickle /'fɪkəl/ *adj* veleidoso

fiction /'fɪkʃən/ *n* [U C] ficción *f*

fictional /'fɪkʃn̩əl ‖ 'fɪkʃənl/ *adj* ficticio

fictitious /fɪk'tɪʃəs/ *adj* **(a)** (false) ‹*name*› ficticio **(b)** (imaginary) imaginario

fiddle[1] /'fɪdl̩/ *n* **1** (violin) violín *m*; ***as fit as a ~*** rebosante de salud **2** (cheat) (BrE colloq) chanchullo *m* (fam)

fiddle[2] *vt* (BrE colloq) ‹*accounts*› hacer* chanchullos con (fam); ‹*results*› amañar ■ ~ *vi* (fidget) **to ~** WITH **sth** juguetear CON algo

fiddler /'fɪdlər ‖ 'fɪdlə(r)/ *n* violinista *mf*

fidelity /fə'deləti ‖ fɪ'deləti/ *n* [U] fidelidad *f*

fidget /'fɪdʒət ‖ 'fɪdʒɪt/ *vi*: **stop ~ing** ¡estáte quieto!

field[1] /fi:ld/ *n* **1** (Agr) campo *m* **2** (Sport) **(a)** (area of play) campo *m*, cancha *f* (AmL) **(b)** (competitors) (+ *sing o pl vb*): **to lead the ~** llevar la delantera; **our products lead the ~** nuestros productos son los líderes del mercado **3** (of study, work) campo *m*; (of activities) esfera *f* **4** (Opt, Phot, Phys) campo *m*; **~ of vision** campo visual

field[2] *vt* (Sport) fildear

field: **~ day** *n*: ***to have a ~ day*** hacer* su agosto; **~ glasses** *pl n* gemelos *mpl*, prismáticos *mpl*; **~ hockey** *n* [U] (AmE) hockey *m* (sobre hierba); **~ marshal** *n* mariscal *m* de campo; **~ trip** *n* viaje *m* de estudio; **~work** *n* [U] trabajo *m* de campo

fiend /fi:nd/ *n* **(a)** (demon) demonio *m* **(b)** (cruel person) (journ *or* hum) desalmado, -da *m,f*

fiendish /'fi:ndɪʃ/ *adj* **(a)** (wicked) diabólico **(b)** (very difficult) (colloq) endemoniado (fam)

fierce /fɪrs ‖ 'fɪəs/ *adj* **fiercer, fiercest (a)** ‹*dog*/*lion*› fiero; ‹*temper*› feroz **(b)** ‹*hatred*/*love*› intenso; ‹*fighting*› encarnizado; ‹*criticism*/*opposition*› violento **(c)** ‹*storm*› violento; ‹*wind*› fortísimo; **the ~ tropical sun** el implacable sol del trópico

fiercely /'fɪrsli ‖ 'fɪəsli/ *adv* **(a)** ‹*growl*› con ferocidad **(b)** ‹*fight*› con fiereza; ‹*criticize*› duramente; ‹*competitive*/*independent*› extremadamente

fiery /'faɪri ‖ 'faɪəri/ *adj* **-rier, -riest** ‹*glow*› ardiente; ‹*red*› encendido; ‹*heat*/*sun*› abrasador; ‹*liquor*› muy fuerte; ‹*temper*› exaltado; ‹*speech*› fogoso

FIFA /'fi:fə/ *n* (*no art*) la FIFA

fifteen /'fɪf'ti:n/ ▶ **451**, **724**, **884** *adj*/*n* quince *adj inv*/*m*; *see also* FOUR[1]

fifteenth[1] /'fɪf'ti:nθ/ ▶ **540**, **725** *adj* decimoquinto

fifteenth[2] *adv* en decimoquinto lugar

fifteenth[3] ▶ **540**, **543**, **725** *n* (Math) quinceavo *m*; (part) quinceava parte *f*

fifth[1] /fɪfθ/ ▶ **540**, **725** *adj* quinto

fifth[2] *adv* en quinto lugar

fifth[3] ▶ **540**, **543**, **725** *n* **1 (a)** (Math) quinto *m*; (part) quinta parte *f*, quinto *m* **(b)** (Mus) quinta *f* **(c)** (in competition): **he finished a disappointing ~** llegó en un deslucido quinto lugar **2 ~ (gear)** (*no art*) quinta *f*

fiftieth[1] /'fɪftiəθ/ ▶ **725** *adj* quincuagésimo

fiftieth[2] *adv* en quincuagésimo lugar

fiftieth[3] ▶ **543**, **725** *n* (Math) cincuentavo *m*; (part) cincuentava *or* quincuagésima parte *f*

fifty /'fɪfti/ ▶ **451**, **540**, **724**, **884** *adj*/*n* cincuenta *adj inv*/*m*; *see also* FOUR[1]

fifty-fifty[1] /'fɪfti'fɪfti/ *adv* (colloq) a medias

fifty-fifty[2] *adj* (colloq): **a ~ chance** un 50% de posibilidades; **on a ~ basis** a medias

fig /fɪg/ *n* higo *m*; (*before n*) **~ tree** higuera *f*

fight[1] /faɪt/ (*past & past p* **fought**) *vi* «*army/country/animal*» luchar; «*person*» pelear; **to ~ FOR/AGAINST sb/sth** luchar POR/CONTRA algn/algo; **to ~ OVER sth** pelearse POR algo ■ **~** *vt* **1 (a)** ‹*army/country*› luchar contra **(b)** ‹*fire/disease/measure*› combatir **2 (a)** (conduct): **they fought a long war against the rebels** lucharon contra los rebeldes durante largo tiempo **(b)** (contest) ‹*election*› presentarse a; **we intend to ~ the case** (Law) pensamos llevar el caso a los tribunales (*or* defendernos *etc*)

•fight back 1 [*v + adv*] defenderse*; **to ~ back AGAINST sb/sth** luchar CONTRA algn/algo **2** [*v + o + adv, v + adv + o*] ‹*tears*› contener*; ‹*anger*› reprimir

•fight off [*v + o + adv, v + adv + o*] ‹*attack/enemy*› rechazar*; ‹*cold*› combatir

•fight out [*v + o + adv*]: **you'll have to ~ it out among yourselves** tendrán que resolverlo entre ustedes

fight[2] *n* **1 (a)** (between persons) pelea *f*; (between armies, companies) lucha *f* **(b)** (boxing match) pelea *f* **2 (a)** (struggle) lucha *f* **(b)** (quarrel) pelea *f*

fighter /'faɪtər ‖ 'faɪtə(r)/ *n* **1 (a)** (person) luchador, -dora *m,f* **(b)** (boxer) boxeador, -dora *m,f* **2** (plane) caza *m*; (*before n*) **~ pilot** piloto *m* de caza

fighting /'faɪtɪŋ/ *n* [U] (Mil) enfrentamientos *mpl*; (brawling, arguing) peleas *fpl*

figment /'fɪgmənt/ *n*: **a ~ of the imagination** (un) producto de la imaginación

figurative /'fɪgjərətɪv ‖ 'fɪgərətɪv/ *adj* figurado

figure[1] /'fɪgjər ‖ 'fɪgə(r)/ *n* **1** (digit) cifra *f*; **recent ~s show that** ... estadísticas recientes muestran que ... **2 (a)** (person) figura *f*; **a public ~** un personaje público **(b)** (body shape) figura *f* **3** (Art, Math, Mus) figura *f*

figure[2] *vi* **1** (feature) figurar; **to ~ prominently** destacarse* **2** (make sense) (colloq): **it just doesn't ~** no me lo explico ■ **~** *vt* (reckon) (AmE colloq) calcular

•figure on [*v + prep + o*] (AmE colloq) contar* con

•figure out [*v + o + adv, v + adv + o*] **(a)** (understand) entender* **(b)** (calculate) ‹*sum/result*› calcular; ‹*problem*› resolver*

figure: **~head** *n* (Naut) mascarón *m* de proa; **he's merely a ~head** no es más que una figura decorativa; **~ of speech** *n* figura *f* retórica; **~ skating** *n* [U] patinaje *m* artístico

Fiji /'fiːdʒiː/ *n* Fiji

filament /'fɪləmənt/ *n* filamento *m*

filch /fɪltʃ/ *vt* (colloq) birlar (fam)

file[1] /faɪl/ *n* **1** (tool) lima *f* **2 (a)** (folder) carpeta *f*; (*box ~*) clasificador *m*; (for card index) fichero *m* **(b)** (collection of documents) archivo *m*; (of a particular case) expediente *m* **(c)** (Comput) archivo *m*

file[2] *vt* **1** (sort) ‹*papers*› archivar **2** ‹*application/suit*› presentar **3** ‹*metal*› limar; **to ~ one's nails** limarse las uñas ■ **~** *vi* **1** (walk in line) (+ *adv compl*): **they ~d into the room** entraron en la habitación en fila; **the crowd ~d past the tomb** la multitud desfiló ante la tumba **2** (Law): **to ~ for divorce** presentar una demanda de divorcio

file: **~ card** *n* (AmE) ficha *f*; **~ clerk** *n* (AmE) administrativo, -va *m,f* (*encargado de archivar*)

filing /'faɪlɪŋ/ *n*: **there's a lot of ~ to do** hay mucho que archivar

filing: **~ cabinet** *n* archivador *m*; **~ clerk** *n* (BrE) ⇒ FILE CLERK

Filipino /fɪlə'piːnəʊ ‖ ˌfɪlɪ'piːnəʊ/ *adj* filipino

fill[1] /fɪl/ *vt* **1 (a)** (make full) **to ~ sth (WITH sth)** llenar algo (DE algo); ‹*cake/sandwich*› rellenar algo (DE algo) **(b)** (plug) ‹*hole/crack*› rellenar; ‹*tooth*› empastar, tapar (Andes), emplomar (RPl), calzar* (Col) **2** ‹*vacancy*› cubrir* ■ **~** *vi* «*bath/auditorium*» **to ~ (WITH sth)** llenarse (DE algo)

•fill in 1 [*v + o + adv, v + adv + o*] **(a)** ‹*hole/outline*› rellenar **(b)** ‹*form*› rellenar **2** [*v + o + adv*] (inform) (colloq) **to ~ sb in (ON sth)** poner* a algn al corriente (DE algo) **3** [*v + adv*] (deputize) **to ~ in FOR sb** sustituir* a algn

•fill out [*v + o + adv, v + adv + o*] ‹*form*› rellenar

•fill up 1 [*v + o + adv, v + adv + o*] **(a)** (make full) llenar **(b)** (Auto) : **~ her up!** ¡llénelo! **2** [*v + adv*] **(a)** (become full) llenarse **(b)** (buy fuel) echar gasolina

fill[2] *n*: **to eat one's ~ of sth** (liter) comer algo hasta saciarse; **to have had one's ~ of sth** estar* harto de algo

filler /'fɪlər ‖ 'fɪlə(r)/ *n* [U C] (for cracks) masilla *f*

fillet[1] /'fɪlət ‖ 'fɪlɪt/ *n* [U C] (of beef) filete *m*, solomillo *m* (Esp), lomo *m* (AmS); (of pork) lomo *m*; (of fish) filete *m*; (*before n*) **a ~ steak** un filete, un solomillo de ternera (Esp), un bife de lomo (RPl)

fillet[2] *vt* ‹*meat*› cortar en filetes; ‹*fish*› quitarle la espina a

filling[1] /'fɪlɪŋ/ *n* **1** [C] (Dent) empaste *m*, tapadura *f* (Chi, Méx), emplomadura *f* (RPl), calza *f* (Col) **2** [U C] (Culin) relleno *m*

filling[2] *adj*: **pasta's very ~** la pasta llena mucho

filling station *n* ⇒ GAS STATION

filly /'fɪli/ (*pl* **-lies**) *n* potra *f*

film[1] /fɪlm/ *n* **1 (a)** [C U] (Phot) película *f* (fotográfica) **(b)** [C] (movie) película *f*, film(e) *m* (period); (*before n*) **~ star** estrella *f* de cine **2 (a)** [C] (thin covering) película *f* **(b)** [U] (wrap) film *m* transparente

film[2] *vt* ‹*scene*› filmar; ‹*novel/play*› llevar al cine ■ **~** *vi* rodar*

filmstrip /'fɪlmstrɪp/ *n*: *película o serie de filminas para proyección fija*

Filofax® /'faɪləfæks/ *n* filofax® *m*

filter[1] /'fɪltər ‖ 'fɪltə(r)/ *n* **1** (device) filtro *m*; (*before n*) **~ coffee** café *m* americano **2** (BrE Transp) flecha *f* (*que autoriza el giro a derecha o izquierda en algunos semáforos*); (*before n*) **~ lane** carril *m* de giro

filter[2] *vt* filtrar ■ **~** *vi* «*gas/light/sound*» filtrarse

filter-tipped /'fɪltər'tɪpt ‖ ˌfɪltə'tɪpt/ *adj* con filtro

filth /fɪlθ/ *n* [U] mugre *f*

filthy /'fɪlθi/ *adj* **-thier, -thiest (a)** (dirty) mugriento **(b)** (obscene) ‹*language*› obsceno **(c)**

(unpleasant) (BrE colloq) ‹*weather/habit*› asqueroso (fam)

fin /fɪn/ *n* aleta *f*

final[1] /ˈfaɪnl/ *adj* **1** (last) (*before n*) último; **a ~ demand (for payment)** (Busn) un último aviso de pago **2** (definitive) final; **the judges' decision is ~** (frml) la decisión del jurado es inapelable

final[2] *n* **1** (Games, Sport) (*often pl*) final *f* **2 finals** *pl* (Educ) exámenes *mpl* finales

finale /fəˈnæli ‖ fɪˈnɑːli/ *n* **(a)** (Mus) final *m* **(b)** (Theat) apoteosis *f*

finalist /ˈfaɪnl̩əst ‖ ˈfaɪnəlɪst/ *n* finalista *mf*

finalize /ˈfaɪnl̩aɪz ‖ ˈfaɪnəlaɪz/ *vt* ultimar

finally /ˈfaɪnl̩i ‖ ˈfaɪnəli/ *adv* **(a)** (lastly) (*indep*) por último **(b)** (at last) por fin

finance[1] /fəˈnæns, faɪ- ‖ ˈfaɪnæns, faɪˈnæns/ *n* **(a)** [U] (banking, business) finanzas *fpl* **(b) finances** *pl* recursos *mpl* financieros **(c)** [U] (funding) financiación *f*, financiamiento *m* (esp AmL)

finance[2] *vt* financiar

financial /fəˈnæntʃəl ‖ faɪˈnænʃəl/ *adj* ‹*system/risk*› financiero; ‹*difficulties/independence*› económico; ‹*news*› de economía, de negocios; **~ advice** asesoría *f* económica; **~ management** gestión *f* financiera

financial year *n* (BrE) (of company) ejercicio *m*; (of government) año *m* fiscal

financier /ˈfɪnənˈsɪr ‖ faɪˈnænsɪə(r)/ *n* financiero, -ra *m,f*

find[1] /faɪnd/ (*past & past p* **found**) *vt* encontrar*; **I can't ~ it** no lo encuentro; **I found (that) it was easier to do it this way** descubrí que era más fácil hacerlo así; **I ~ that hard to believe!** ¡me cuesta creerlo!; **to ~ sb guilty/not guilty** (Law) declarar a algn culpable/inocente ■ *v refl* **to ~ oneself** encontrarse* a sí (*or* mí *etc*) mismo

● **find out 1** [*v + o + adv, v + adv + o*] (discover) ‹*truth*› descubrir*; ‹*information*› (by making enquiries) averiguar* **2** [*v + adv*] **(a)** (learn) enterarse; **to ~ out** ABOUT **sth** enterarse DE algo **(b)** (make inquiries) averiguar*

find[2] *n* hallazgo *m*

findings /ˈfaɪndɪŋz/ *pl n* conclusiones *fpl*

fine[1] /faɪn/ *adj* **finer, finest 1** (*usu before n*) **(a)** (excellent) ‹*house/speech/example*› magnífico; ‹*wine/ingredients*› de primera calidad **(b)** (fair) ‹*weather*› bueno **2** (colloq) (*pred*) **(a)** (in good health) muy bien **(b)** (OK) bien; (perfect) perfecto **3** (thin, delicate) ‹*hair/china/point*› fino **4** (subtle) ‹*distinction/nuance*› sutil; ‹*balance*› delicado; ‹*adjustment*› preciso

fine[2] *adv* (adequately) bien; (very well) muy bien

fine[3] *n* multa *f*

fine[4] *vt* multar

fine art *n* [U C] arte *m*; ***to have (got) sth down to a ~ ~*** hacer* algo a la perfección

finely /ˈfaɪnli/ *adv* **(a)** (in small pieces): **to chop sth ~** picar* algo muy fino **(b)** (subtly) ‹*adjust*› con precisión

fine print *n* (AmE) **the ~ ~** la letra pequeña *or* menuda, la letra chica (AmL)

finery /ˈfaɪnəri/ *n* [U]: **in all their ~** con sus mejores galas

finesse /fəˈnes ‖ fɪˈnes/ *n* [U] **(a)** (refinement) finura *f* **(b)** (tact) diplomacia *f*

fine-tooth(ed) comb /ˈfaɪnˈtuːθ(t)/ *n*: ***to go over sth with a ~-tooth(ed) comb*** mirar algo con lupa

finger[1] /ˈfɪŋgər ‖ ˈfɪŋgə(r)/ ▶ **484** *n* (of hand, glove) dedo *m*; **index ~** (dedo) índice *m*; **middle ~** (dedo) corazón *m or* medio *m*; **ring ~** (dedo) anular *m*; **little ~** (dedo) meñique *m*; ***to cross one's ~s***: **I'll keep my ~s crossed for you** ojalá (que) tengas suerte; ***to snap one's ~s*** chasquear *or* (Méx) tronar* los dedos

finger[2] *vt* toquetear, tentalear (Méx)

finger: **~nail** *n* uña *f*; **~print** *n* huella *f* digital; **~tip** *n* yema *f* del dedo

finish[1] /ˈfɪnɪʃ/ *vt* **1 (a)** (complete) terminar, acabar; **we ~ work at four o'clock today** hoy salimos a las cuatro; **to ~ -ING** terminar *or* acabar DE + INF **(b)** (consume) ‹*drink/rations*› terminar, acabar **2** ‹*cloth/porcelain*› terminar; ‹*wood*› pulir **3** (destroy) (colloq) acabar con ■ **~** *vi* terminar, acabar

● **finish off 1** [*v + o + adv, v + adv + o*] **(a)** (complete) terminar, acabar **(b)** (exhaust) dejar agotado **(c)** (consume) terminar **(d)** (kill) matar **2** [*v + adv*] (conclude) terminar, acabar

● **finish up 1** [*v + o + adv, v + adv + o*] ‹*food/paint*› terminar **2** [*v + adv*] (end up) acabar

finish[2] *n* **1** (*no pl*) (end) fin *m*, final *m*; (of race) llegada *f* **2** (surface texture) acabado *m*

finished /ˈfɪnɪʃt/ *adj* (*pred*) **(a)** (complete, achieved): **to get sth ~** terminar *or* acabar algo; **I'm ~ with the scissors** no necesito más la tijera **(b)** (ruined) acabado

finishing /ˈfɪnɪʃɪŋ/: **~ line** *n* (BrE) ⇒ FINISH LINE; **~ school** *n*: *colegio privado para señoritas donde se aprende a comportarse en sociedad*; **~ touch** *n*: **to put the ~ touch(es) to sth** darle* los últimos toques a algo

finish line, (BrE) **finishing line** *n* meta *f*, línea *f* de llegada

finite /ˈfaɪnaɪt/ *adj* finito

Finland /ˈfɪnlənd/ *n* Finlandia *f*

Finn /fɪn/ *n* finlandés, -desa *m,f*, finés, -nesa *m,f*

Finnish[1] /ˈfɪnɪʃ/ *adj* finlandés, finés

Finnish[2] *n* [U] finlandés *m*

fiord /fiˈɔːrd ‖ fiˈɔːd/ *n* fiordo *m*

fir /fɜːr ‖ fɜː(r)/ *n* abeto *m*

fire[1] /faɪr ‖ ˈfaɪə(r)/ *n* **1 (a)** [U] (flames) fuego *m*; **to be on ~** estar* en llamas; **to set sth on ~** *o* **to set ~ to sth** prenderle fuego a algo; **to catch ~** prender fuego **(b)** [C] (outdoors) hoguera *f*; (in hearth) fuego *m* **2** [C] (blaze which destroys a building) incendio *m*; (*as interj*) **~!** ¡fuego!; (*before n*) **~ curtain** telón *m* contra incendios; **this is a ~ hazard** esto podría causar un incendio **3** [C] (heater) (BrE) estufa *f* **4** [U] (of guns) fuego *m*; **to open ~ on sb/sth** abrir* fuego sobre algn/algo

fire[2] *vt* **1** ‹*gun/shot*› disparar; ‹*rocket*› lanzar*; **to ~ questions at sb** hacerle* preguntas a algn **2** (dismiss) (colloq) echar, despedir* **3** ‹*imagination*› avivar ■ **~** *vi* (shoot) disparar; **to ~** AT **sb/sth**

disparar CONTRA algn/algo; **ready, aim, ~!** apunten ¡fuego!

fire: ~ **alarm** *n* (apparatus) alarma *f* contra incendios; (signal) alarma *f*; ~**arm** *n* arma *f*‡ de fuego; ~ **department**, (BrE) ~ **brigade** *n* cuerpo *m* de bomberos; ~ **door** *n* puerta *f* contra incendios; ~ **drill** *n* simulacro *m* de incendio; ~ **engine** *n* (BrE) ⇒ ~ TRUCK; ~ **escape** *n* escalera *f* de incendios; ~ **extinguisher** *n* extinguidor *m* (de incendios) (AmL), extintor *m* (Esp); ~**fighter** *n* bombero *mf*; ~ **guard** *n* rejilla *f* (*de chimenea*); ~**lighter** *n*: *líquido o pastilla utilizados para facilitar el encendido del fuego de leña o carbón*; ~**man** /'faɪrmən ‖ 'faɪəmən/ (*pl* **-men** /-mən/) *n* bombero *m*; ~**place** *n* chimenea *f*; ~**proof** *adj* ignífugo; ~**side** *n* [U] hogar *m*; ~ **station** *n* estación *f or* (Esp) parque *m or* (RPl) cuartel *m* de bomberos, bomba *f* (Chi); ~ **truck** *n* (AmE) carro *m or* (Esp) coche *m* de bomberos, autobomba *m* (RPl), bomba *f* (Chi); ~**wood** *n* [U] leña *f*; ~**works** *pl n* fuegos *mpl* artificiales

firing /'faɪrɪŋ ‖ 'faɪərɪŋ/: ~ **line** *n*: ***to be on*** *o* (BrE) ***in the ~ line*** (exposed to criticism) estar* expuesto a las críticas; (Mil) estar* en la línea de combate; ~ **squad** *n* pelotón *m* de fusilamiento

firm[1] /fɜːrm ‖ fɜːm/ *adj* **1 (a)** (secure) ‹*grasp*› firme **(b)** (not yielding) ‹*surface/muscles*› firme; ‹*mattress*› duro; ‹*foundation*› sólido **2 (a)** (steadfast) ‹*friendship*› sólido; ‹*support*› firme **(b)** (strict) estricto **3** (definite) ‹*offer/date*› en firme

firm[2] *n* empresa *f*, firma *f*

firmly /'fɜːrmli ‖ 'fɜːmli/ *adv* ‹*grasp/believe*› con firmeza; ‹*fixed/supported*› firmemente

first[1] /fɜːrst ‖ fɜːst/ ▶ **540**, **725** *adj*

> ■ **Note** The usual translation of *first*, *primero*, becomes *primer* when it precedes a masculine singular noun.

1 (initial) primero; **the ~ president of the USA** el primer presidente de los EE UU; **who's going to be ~?** ¿quién va a ser el primero?; ~ **things ~** primero lo más importante **2** (elliptical use): **he'll be arriving on the ~ (of the month)** llegará el primero *or* (Esp tb) el uno (del mes); **she was the ~ to arrive** fue la primera en llegar **3** (*in phrases*) **at first** al principio; **from first to last** de(l) principio a(l) fin

first[2] *adv* **1 (a)** (ahead of others) primero; **he came ~ in the exam** sacó la mejor nota en el examen; **I always put my children ~** para mí antes que nada están mis hijos; **ladies ~** primero las damas **(b)** (before other actions, events) primero **(c)** (beforehand) antes **(d)** (for the first time) por primera vez **2** (*in phrases*) **first and foremost** ante todo; **first and last** por encima de todo; **first of all** en primer lugar

first[3] ▶ **540**, **725** *n* **(a)** ~ **(gear)** (Auto) (*no art*) primera *f* **(b)** (original idea, accomplishment) primicia *f*

first: ~ **aid** *n* [U] primeros auxilios *mpl*; (*before n*) ~**-aid kit** botiquín *m* (de primeros auxilios); ~**-aid station** *o* (BrE) **post** puesto *m* de primeros auxilios; ~ **class** *adv* ‹*travel*› en primera (clase); ~**-class** /'fɜːrst'klæs ‖ ˌfɜːst'klɑːs/ *adj* (*pred* ~ **class**) **(a)** (of highest grade) ‹*hotel/ticket*› de primera clase; ‹*travel*› en primera (clase) **(b)** (excellent) de primera **(c)** (BrE Corresp) ~**-class mail** *correspondencia enviada a una tarifa superior, que garantiza una rápida entrega*; ~**-hand** /'fɜːrst 'hænd ‖ ˌfɜːst'hænd/ *adj* ‹*news*› de primera mano; ~ **lady** *n* primera dama *f*

firstly /'fɜːrstli ‖ 'fɜːstli/ *adv* (*as linker*) en primer lugar

first: ~ **name** *n* nombre *m* de pila; ~**-rate** /'fɜːrst'reɪt ‖ ˌfɜːst'reɪt/ *adj* de primera; ~**-time buyer** *n*: *persona que compra algo, gen una vivienda, por primera vez*

fiscal /'fɪskəl/ *adj* fiscal

fiscal year *n* (AmE) año *m* fiscal

fish[1] /fɪʃ/ *n* (*pl* **fish** *or* **fishes**) **(a)** [C] (Zool) pez *m*; (*before n*) ~ **pond** estanque *m*; ~ **tank** pecera *f* **(b)** [U] (Culin) pescado *m*; ~ **and chips** (esp BrE) pescado *m* frito con papas *or* (Esp) patatas fritas

fish[2] *vi* pescar*; **to go ~ing** ir* de pesca; **to ~** FOR **sth** ‹*for trout*› pescar* algo; ‹*for compliments*› andar* a la caza de algo; **to ~ (around) in one's pockets/bag** rebuscar* en los bolsillos/la bolsa
• **fish out** [*v* + *o* + *adv*, *v* + *adv* + *o*] sacar*

fish: ~**bone** *n* espina *f* (*de pez*); ~**cake** *n* ≈ croqueta *f* (*de pescado y papas*)

fisherman /'fɪʃərmən ‖ 'fɪʃəmən/ *n* (*pl* **-men** /-mən/) pescador *m*

fishery /'fɪʃəri/ *n* (*pl* **-eries**) **1** ⇒ FISH FARM **2 fisheries** *pl* (industry) industria *f* pesquera, pesca *f*

fish: ~ **farm** *n* piscifactoría *f*; ~ **finger** *n* (BrE) ⇒ FISH STICK; ~**hook** *n* anzuelo *m*

fishing /'fɪʃɪŋ/ *n* [U] pesca *f*; (*before n*) ‹*industry/port*› pesquero

fishing: ~ **net** *n* red *f* de pesca; ~ **pole** (AmE), ~ **rod** *n* caña *f* de pescar

fish: ~**monger** /'fɪʃˌmɑːŋgər ‖ 'fɪʃˌmʌŋgə(r)/ *n* (BrE) pescadero, -ra *m,f*; **at the ~monger('s)** en la pescadería; ~**net** *n* **(a)** [C] (AmE) ⇒ FISHING NET **(b)** [U] (Tex) red *f*; (*before n*) ‹*stockings*› de malla gruesa *or* de red; ~ **slice** *n* (BrE) espumadera *f*; ~ **stick** *n* (AmE) palito *m* de bacalao (*or* merluza *etc*) (*trozo de pescado rebozado y frito*)

fishy /'fɪʃi/ *adj* **-fishier, -fishiest 1** ‹*smell/taste*› a pescado **2** (suspicious) (colloq) sospechoso

fission /'fɪʃən/ *n* [U] fisión *f*

fist /fɪst/ *n* puño *m*

fistfight /'fɪstfaɪt/ *n* pelea *f* (*a puñetazos*)

fit[1] /fɪt/ *adj* **-tt- 1** (healthy) en forma; **to keep ~** mantenerse* en forma; **to be ~ to** + INF ‹*to play/travel*› estar* en condiciones DE + INF **2** (suitable) ‹*person/conduct*› adecuado; **this isn't ~ to eat** (harmful) esto no está en buenas condiciones; (unappetizing) esto está incomible; **he's not ~ to be a father** no es digno de ser padre; **he did not see ~ to reply to our letter** ni se dignó contestar a nuestra carta

fit[2] **-tt-** *vt* **1 (a)** (Clothing): **the dress ~s you perfectly** el vestido te queda perfecto; **the jacket doesn't ~ me** la chaqueta no me queda bien **(b)** (be right size, shape for) ‹*socket*› encajar en **(c)** (correspond to) ‹*theory*› concordar* con; **to ~ a**

description responder a una descripción **2** (install) (esp BrE) ‹*carpet/lock*› poner*; ‹*double glazing*› instalar **3** (accommodate) **to ~ sth** INTO **sth** meter algo EN algo ■ **~** *vi* **(a)** (Clothing): **these shoes don't ~** estos zapatos no me quedan bien; **to make sth ~** ajustar algo **(b)** (be right size, shape) «*lid*» ajustar; «*key/peg*» encajar **(c)** (correspond) «*facts/description*» encajar

• **fit in 1** [*v* + *adv*] **(a)** (have enough room) caber* **(b)** (accord) «*detail/event*» **to ~ in** (WITH **sth**) concordar* (CON algo) **(c)** (belong): **she doesn't ~ in here** esto no es para ella **(d)** (conform to): **he'll have to ~ in with our plans** tendrá que amoldarse a nuestros planes **2** [*v* + *o* + *adv*, *v* + *adv* + *o*] **(a)** (find space for) acomodar **(b)** (find time for): **I can ~ you in at ten o'clock** puedo atenderla a las diez; **she hoped to ~ in some sightseeing** esperaba tener un poco de tiempo para salir a conocer el lugar

• **fit out** [*v* + *o* + *adv*, *v* + *adv* + *o*] equipar; **to ~ sb out** WITH **sth** ‹*with boots/equipment*› equipar a algn CON algo; ‹*with uniform*› proveer* a algn DE algo

fit³ *n* **1 (a)** (attack) ataque *m*; **epileptic ~** ataque epiléptico; ***to have a ~*** (colloq): **I nearly had a ~** casi me da un ataque (fam) **(b)** (short burst): **a ~ of coughing** un acceso de tos; ***in ~s and starts*** a los tropezones **2** (of clothes) (*no pl*): **my new jacket is a good ~** la chaqueta nueva me queda bien; **it's a tight ~** es muy entallado

fitful /ˈfɪtfəl/ *adj* ‹*progress/sunshine*› intermitente; ‹*sleep*› irregular

fitfully /ˈfɪtfəli/ *adv* de manera irregular

fitness /ˈfɪtnəs ‖ ˈfɪtnɪs/ *n* [U] **1** (healthiness) salud *f*; **(physical) ~** (buena) forma *f* física **2** (suitability) aptitud *f*

fitted /ˈfɪtəd ‖ ˈfɪtɪd/ *adj* **(a)** ‹*cupboard*› empotrado; ‹*shelves*› hecho a medida; ‹*sheet*› ajustable, de cajón (Méx); **~ carpet** (esp BrE) alfombra *f* de pared a pared, moqueta *f* (Esp) **(b)** ‹*kitchen*› integral

fitter /ˈfɪtər ‖ ˈfɪtə(r)/ *n* **1** (Clothing) probador, -dora *m,f* **2** (mechanic — in garage) mecánico, -ca *m,f*; (— in car industry, shipbuilding) operario, -ria *m,f*

fitting¹ /ˈfɪtɪŋ/ *adj* ‹*conclusion*› adecuado; ‹*tribute*› digno

fitting² *n* **1** (Clothing) **(a)** (trying on) prueba *f* **(b)** (BrE) (size — of clothes) medida *f*; (— of shoe) horma *f* **2 (a)** (accessory) accesorio *m* **(b) fittings** *pl* (esp BrE Const) accesorios *mpl*; **electrical ~s** instalaciones *fpl* eléctricas; **bathroom ~s** grifería *f* y accesorios *mpl* de baño

fitting room *n* probador *m*

five /faɪv/ ▶ 451, 724, 884 *adj/n* cinco *adj inv/m*; *see also* FOUR¹

fiver /ˈfaɪvər ‖ ˈfaɪvə(r)/ *n* **(a)** ($5) (AmE sl) cinco dólares *mpl* **(b)** (£5) (BrE colloq) cinco libras *fpl*

fix¹ /fɪks/ *vt* **I 1** ‹*plank/shelf*› sujetar; **to ~ a notice on a door** poner* un anuncio en una puerta; **to ~ sth in one's memory** grabar algo en la memoria **2** (direct steadily): **his eyes were ~ed on the road ahead** tenía la mirada fija en la carretera; **he ~ed her with a stony gaze** clavó en ella una mirada glacial

II 1 ‹*date/time/price*› fijar **2** (repair) (colloq) arreglar **3** (prepare) (esp AmE colloq) preparar **4** (colloq) ‹*election/contest*› amañar (fam) ■ **~** *vi* (make plans) (AmE): **we're ~ing to go fishing on Sunday** estamos planeando ir de pesca el domingo

• **fix up** [*v* + *o* + *adv*, *v* + *adv* + *o*] **(a)** (provide for): **I need somewhere to stay: can you ~ me up?** necesito alojamiento ¿me lo puedes arreglar?; **she ~ed me up with a job** me encontró un trabajo **(b)** (repair) ‹*house/room*› (AmE) arreglar

fix² *n* (predicament) (colloq) aprieto *m*, apuro *m*

fixation /fɪkˈseɪʃən/ *n* obsesión *f*

fixed /fɪkst/ *adj* **1** ‹*price/rate/ideas*› fijo; ‹*principles/position*› rígido; **a ~-term contract** un contrato a plazo fijo **2** ‹*gaze*› fijo; ‹*smile*› petrificado

fixed: **~ assets** *pl n* activo *m* fijo; **~-rate** /ˈfɪkstˈreɪt/ *adj* a una tasa de interés fija *or* (esp Esp) a tipo de interés fijo

fixture /ˈfɪkstʃər ‖ ˈfɪkstʃə(r)/ *n* **1 (a)** (in building) *elemento de la instalación, como los artefactos del baño, cocina etc* **(b)** (permanent feature) parte *f* integrante **2** (BrE Sport) encuentro *m*

fizz /fɪz/ *vi* «*champagne/cola*» burbujear

fizzle out /ˈfɪzəl/ [*v* + *adv*] «*fire/firework*» apagarse*; «*excitement*» esfumarse

fizzy /ˈfɪzi/ *adj* **-zier, -ziest** gaseoso, efervescente

fjord /fiˈɔːrd ‖ fiˈɔːd/ *n* fiordo *m*

FL, **Fla** = **Florida**

flabbergasted /ˈflæbərˌgæstəd ‖ ˈflæbəˌgɑːstɪd/ *adj* estupefacto

flabby /ˈflæbi/ *adj* **-bier, -biest** ‹*stomach*› fofo; ‹*muscle*› flojo

flag¹ /flæg/ *n* bandera *f*

flag² **-gg-** *vi* «*person/animal*» desfallecer*; «*interest/conversation/spirits*» decaer*; «*attendance*» disminuir* ■ **~** *vt* **(a)** (mark with flags) marcar* con banderas **(b)** (mark for special attention) marcar*

• **flag down** [*v* + *o* + *adv*, *v* + *adv* + *o*] parar (*haciendo señas*)

flagpole /ˈflægpəʊl/ *n* asta *f*‡ de (la) bandera

flagrant /ˈfleɪgrənt/ *adj* flagrante

flag: **~ship** *n* (Naut) buque *m* insignia; (showpiece) producto *m* (*or* programa *m etc*) bandera; **~stone** *n* losa *f*

flair /fler ‖ ˈfleə(r)/ *n* **(a)** (natural aptitude) (*no pl*): **a ~ for languages/business** facilidad *f* para los idiomas/olfato *m* para los negocios **(b)** [U] (stylishness) estilo *m*

flak /flæk/ *n* [U] **(a)** (Aviat, Mil) fuego *m* antiaéreo **(b)** (criticism) críticas *fpl*

flake¹ /fleɪk/ *n* (of snow, cereals) copo *m*; (of paint, rust, skin) escama *f*

flake² *vi* «*paint/plaster*» descascararse

flaky, **flakey** /ˈfleɪki/ *adj* **-kier, -kiest** ‹*piecrust*› hojaldrado; ‹*paint/plaster*› que se desconcha; **~ pastry** *masa tipo hojaldre*

flamboyant /flæmˈbɔɪənt/ *adj* **(a)** (dashing) ‹*style/person*› exuberante; ‹*gesture*› ampuloso **(b)** (brilliant) ‹*color*› vistoso; ‹*hat/dress*› llamativo

flame /fleɪm/ *n* [C U] **(a)** llama *f*; **to be in ~s** estar* (envuelto) en llamas; **to go up in ~s** incendiarse **(b)** (lover): **he's an old ~ of mine** es un antiguo enamorado mío

flame: **~proof** *adj* ‹*fabric*› ininflamable; ‹*dish*› resistente al fuego; **~thrower** /'fleɪm'θrəʊər ‖ 'fleɪm,θrəʊə(r)/*n* lanzallamas *m*

flamingo /flə'mɪŋgəʊ/ *n* (*pl* **-gos** *or* **-goes**) flamenco *m*

flammable /'flæməbəl/ *adj* inflamable, flamable (Méx)

flan /flæn/ *n* [C U] (sweet) tarta *f*, kuchen *m* (Chi); (individual) tartaleta *f*, tarteleta *f* (RPl)

flank¹ /flæŋk/ *n* **(a)** (of animal) ijada *f*, ijar *m*; (of person) costado *m* **(b)** (Mil, Sport) flanco *m*

flank² *vt* (*often pass*) flanquear

flannel /'flænl/ *n* **1 (a)** [U] (fabric) franela *f*; (*before n*) ‹*shirt/nightgown*› de franela **(b) flannels** *pl* (trousers) pantalón *m* de franela **2** [C] (*face ~*) (BrE) toallita *f* (*para lavarse*)

flap¹ /flæp/ *n* **1 (a)** (cover) tapa *f*; (of pocket, envelope) solapa *f*; (of table) hoja *f*; (of jacket, coat) faldón *m*; (of tent) portezuela *f*; (*ear ~*) orejera *f*; **a cat ~** una gatera **(b)** (Aviat) alerón *m* **2** (motion) aletazo *m* **3** (commotion, agitation) (colloq): **to be in/get into a ~** estar*/ponerse* como loco (fam)

flap² -pp- *vi* «*sail/curtain*» agitarse; «*flag*» ondear ■ ~ *vt* ‹*wings*› batir; ‹*arms*› agitar

flapjack /'flæpdʒæk/ *n* **1** (pancake) (esp AmE) *crepe o panqueque pequeño y grueso* **2** (cookie) (BrE) *tipo de galleta dulce de avena*

flare /fler ‖ fleə(r)/ *n* **1 (a)** (marker light) bengala *f*; (on runway, road) baliza *f* **(b)** (sudden light) destello *m*; (flame) llamarada *f* **2** (Clothing) **(a)** (on jacket) vuelo *m* **(b) flares** (BrE) pantalones *mpl* acampanados
• flare up [*v* + *adv*] **(a)** «*fire*» llamear; «*fighting*» estallar **(b)** «*infection/disease*» recrudecer* **(c)** (lose temper) explotar

flared /flerd ‖ fleəd/ *adj* ‹*skirt*› con mucho vuelo, evasé (RPl); ‹*trousers*› acampanado

flare-up /'flerʌp ‖ 'fleərʌp/ *n* (of violence) brote *m*

flash¹ /flæʃ/ *n* **1** [C] **(a)** (of light) destello *m*; (from explosion) fogonazo *m*; **a ~ of inspiration** un ramalazo de inspiración; **(*as*) *quick as a* ~** como un rayo; ***in a* ~**: **it came to me in a ~** de repente lo vi claro **(b)** (Phot) flash *m* **2** [C] (*news ~*) avance *m* informativo

flash² *vt* **1** (direct): **they ~ed a light in my face** me enfocaron la cara con una luz; **to ~ one's headlights at sb** hacerle* una señal con los faros a algn **2** (show) ‹*card*› mostrar*, enseñar (esp Esp); **she loves ~ing her money around** le encanta ir por ahí haciendo ostentación de su dinero ■ ~ *vi* **1 (a)** (emit sudden light) destellar **(b)** (Auto) hacer* una señal con los faros **(c) flashing** *pres p* ‹*sign/light*› intermitente; ‹*eyes/smile*› brillante **2** (move fast) (+ *adv compl*): **a message ~ed across the screen** un mensaje apareció fugazmente en la pantalla; **to ~ by** *o* **past** «*train/car/person*» pasar como una bala

flash: **~back** *n* (Cin, Lit) flashback *m*; **~bulb** *n* (Phot) lámpara *f* de flash; **~cube** *n* (Phot) cubo *m* (de) flash; **~ gun** *n* flash *m* electrónico; **~light** *n* (AmE) linterna *f*

flashy /'flæʃi/ *adj* **-shier, -shiest** llamativo

flask /flæsk ‖ flɑːsk/ *n* (bottle) frasco *m*; (in laboratory) matraz *m*; (*hip ~*) petaca *f*, nalguera *f* (Méx); (*vacuum ~*) (BrE) termo *m*

flat¹ /flæt/ *adj* **-tt- 1 (a)** ‹*surface*› plano; ‹*countryside*› llano; **~ feet** pies *mpl* planos; **I was ~ on my back for two months** (me) pasé dos meses en cama **(b)** ‹*dish*› llano, bajo (Chi), playo (RPl); **~ shoes** zapatos *mpl* bajos, zapatillas *fpl* de piso (Méx) **(c)** (deflated) ‹*ball*› desinflado, ponchado (Méx); **you have a ~ tire** *o* (BrE) **tyre** tienes un neumático desinflado *or* (Méx) una llanta ponchada **2 (a)** ‹*lemonade/beer*› sin efervescencia **(b)** ‹*battery*› descargado **3** (dull, uninteresting) ‹*conversation/party*› soso (fam); ‹*joke*› sin gracia; ‹*voice*› monótono; ***to fall* ~** «*play/project*» fracasar*; **the joke fell very ~** el chiste no hizo ni pizca de gracia **4** (total, firm) ‹*denial/refusal*› rotundo **5** (Mus) (referring to key) bemol; **A ~** la *m* bemol **6** (fixed) (*before n*) ‹*rate*› fijo

flat² *adv* **1 (a)** ‹*refuse/turn down*› de plano **(b)** (exactly): **it took him two hours ~** tardó dos horas justas **2** (Mus) demasiado bajo

flat³ *n* **1** (apartment) (BrE) apartamento *m*, departamento *m* (AmL), piso *m* (Esp) **2 (a)** (surface — of sword) cara *f* de la hoja; (— of hand) palma *f* **(b)** (level ground) llano *m* **3** (Mus) bemol *m*

flatly /'flætli/ *adv* de plano

flatmate /'flætmeɪt/ *n* (BrE) compañero, -ra *m,f* de apartamento *or* (Esp) de piso

flat out¹ *adj* (colloq) (*pred*) (prostrate) tirado

flat out² *adv* (at full speed) (colloq) a toda máquina

flat-rate /'flæt'reɪt/ *adj* (BrE) a una tasa de interés fija *or* (esp Esp) a tipo de interés fijo

flatten /'flætn̩/ *vt* ‹*surface*› aplanar; ‹*path/lawn*› allanar; ‹*city*› arrasar

flatter /'flætər ‖ 'flætə(r)/ *vt* **(a)** (gratify) halagar* **(b)** favorecer*

flattering /'flætərɪŋ/ *adj* **(a)** ‹*words/speech*› halagador **(b)** ‹*clothes/hairstyle*› favorecedor

flattery /'flætəri/ *n* [U] halagos *mpl*

flaunt /flɔːnt/ *vt* ‹*possessions*› hacer* ostentación de; ‹*knowledge*› alardear de

flavor¹, (BrE) **flavour** /'fleɪvər ‖ 'fleɪvə(r)/ *n* [C U] sabor *m*, gusto *m*

flavor², (BrE) **flavour** *vt* sazonar; **chocolate-~ed** con sabor *or* gusto a chocolate

flavoring, (BrE) **flavouring** /'fleɪvərɪŋ/ *n* [C U] condimento *m*

flaw /flɔː/ *n* (in material, character) defecto *m*; (in argument) error *m*

flawless /'flɔːləs ‖ 'flɔːlɪs/ *adj* ‹*performance/logic*› impecable; ‹*conduct*› intachable; ‹*complexion/gem*› perfecto

flax /flæks/ *n* [U] lino *m*

flay /fleɪ/ *vt* desollar*

flea /fliː/ *n* pulga *f*; (*before n*) ‹*collar/powder*› antipulgas *adj inv*

flea market *n* mercado *m* de las pulgas *or* (CS) de pulgas, rastro *m* (Esp)

fleck¹ /flek/ *n* (of dust) mota *f*; (of paint, mud) salpicadura *f*

fleck² *vt* (with mud) salpicar*; **beige ~ed with brown** beige moteado de marrón

fled /fled/ *past & past p of* FLEE

fledgling, **fledgeling** /ˈfledʒlɪŋ/ *n* polluelo *m*; (*before n*) **a ~ democracy** una democracia en ciernes

flee /fliː/ (*past & past p* **fled**) *vi* huir* ■ ~ *vt* huir* de

fleece¹ /fliːs/ *n* [C U] (on sheep) lana *f*; (from sheep) vellón *m*

fleece² *vt* (colloq) desplumar (fam)

fleet /fliːt/ *n* **(a)** (naval unit, body of shipping) flota *f* **(b)** (navy) armada *f* **(c)** (of cars) parque *m* móvil, flota *f*

fleeting /ˈfliːtɪŋ/ *adj* (*usu before n*) fugaz

Flemish¹ /ˈflemɪʃ/ *adj* flamenco

Flemish² *n* [U] flamenco *m*

flesh /fleʃ/ *n* [U] carne *f*; **in the ~** en persona; **~ *and blood*: after all, I'm only ~ and blood** después de todo, soy de carne y hueso

fleshy /ˈfleʃi/ *adj* **-shier, -shiest** *adj* ‹*arms*/*person*› rollizo; ‹*plant*/*leaf*› carnoso

flew /fluː/ *past of* FLY²

flex¹ /fleks/ *vt* ‹*arm*/*knees*/*body*› doblar; **to ~ one's muscles** (to warm up) hacer* ejercicios de calentamiento; (in body building) mostrar* los músculos; «*regime*» mostrar* su poderío

flex² *n* [U C] (BrE) cable *m* (eléctrico)

flexible /ˈfleksəbəl/ *adj* flexible

flextime /ˈflekstaɪm/, (BrE) **flexitime** /ˈfleksɪtaɪm/ *n* [U] horario *m* flexible

flick¹ /flɪk/ *vt* **(a)** (strike lightly): **she ~ed a piece of bread at me** me tiró un pedazo de pan **(b)** (remove): **he ~ed the ash off his lapel** se sacudió la ceniza de la solapa

• flick through [*v* + *prep* + *o*] ‹*book*› hojear; ‹*pages*› pasar

flick² *n* (of tail) coletazo *m*; (of wrist) giro *m*

flicker¹ /ˈflɪkər ‖ ˈflɪkə(r)/ *vi* parpadear

flicker² *n* [U C] parpadeo *m*

flier /ˈflaɪər ‖ ˈflaɪə(r)/ *n* **1 (a)** (pilot) aviador, -dora *m,f* **(b)** (passenger) usuario -ria *m,f* (regular) del avion **2** (handbill) (AmE) folleto *m* (publicitario), volante *m* (AmL)

flight /flaɪt/ *n* **1 (a)** [U] (of bird, aircraft) vuelo *m*; (of ball, projectile) trayectoria *f*; **in ~** en vuelo **(b)** [C] (air journey) vuelo *m*; (*before n*) **~ path** ruta *f*; **~ recorder** caja *f* negra **2** [C] (group of birds) bandada *f* **3** [C] (of stairs) tramo *m* **4** [U] (act of fleeing) huida *f*; **to take ~** darse* a la fuga

flight: **~ attendant** *n* auxiliar *mf* de vuelo; **~ deck** *n* (on plane) cabina *f* de mando; (on aircraft carrier) cubierta *f* de vuelo

flimsy /ˈflɪmzi/ *adj* **-sier, -siest (a)** ‹*material*/*garment*› ligerísimo **(b)** ‹*construction*/*object*› endeble **(c)** ‹*excuse*› pobre; ‹*argument*/*evidence*› poco sólido

flinch /flɪntʃ/ *vi* estremecerse*

fling¹ /flɪŋ/ *vt* (*past & past p* **flung**) lanzar*, aventar* (Col, Méx, Per)

fling² *n* (colloq) **(a)** (love affair) aventura *f* **(b)** (wild time) juerga *f* (fam)

flint /flɪnt/ *n* **(a)** [U C] (Geol) sílex *m*, pedernal *m*; (piece of stone) pedernal *m* **(b)** [C] (for cigarette lighter) piedra *f*

flip /flɪp/ **-pp-** *vt* tirar, aventar* (Méx); **we'll ~ a coin to decide** vamos a echarlo a cara o cruz *or* (Andes, Ven) a cara o sello *or* (Arg) a cara o ceca, vamos a echar un volado (Méx) ■ ~ *vi* (sl) (lose self-control) perder* la chaveta (fam)

flip-flop /ˈflɪpflɑːp ‖ ˈflɪpflɒp/ *n* (BrE) ⇒ THONG (b)

flippant /ˈflɪpənt/ *adj* ‹*remark*› frívolo; ‹*attitude*› displicente

flipper /ˈflɪpər ‖ ˈflɪpə(r)/ *n* aleta *f*

flip side *n* **the ~ ~** (Audio) la cara B; (of a situation) (colloq) la otra cara de la moneda (fam)

flirt¹ /flɜːrt ‖ flɜːt/ *vi* flirtear

flirt² *n*: **he is a terrible ~** le encanta flirtear

flirtation /flɜːrˈteɪʃən ‖ ˌflɜːˈteɪʃən/ *n* **(a)** [C] (relationship) flirt *m* **(b)** [U] (coquetry) flirteo *m*

flit /flɪt/ *vi* **-tt-** «*bird*/*butterfly*/*bat*» revolotear

float¹ /fləʊt/ *vi* **(a)** (on water) flotar; **to ~ (up) to the surface** salir* a flote **(b)** «*cloud*/*smoke*» flotar en el aire ■ ~ *vt* **1** ‹*ship*/*boat*› poner* a flote; ‹*raft*/*logs*› llevar **2** (Fin) **(a)** (establish): **to ~ a company** introducir* una compañía en Bolsa **(b)** ‹*shares*/*stock*› emitir **(c)** ‹*currency*› dejar flotar **3** (circulate) ‹*idea*› presentar

float² *n* **1 (a)** (for fishing, for buoyancy) flotador *m* **(b)** (in cistern, carburetor) flotador *m* **(c)** (raft, platform) plataforma *f* (flotante) **2 (a)** (in parade) carroza *f*, carro *m* alegórico (CS, Méx) **(b)** (*milk ~*) (BrE) furgoneta *f* (*del reparto de leche*) **3** (ready cash) caja *f* chica; (Busn, Fin) fondo *m* fijo

floating /ˈfləʊtɪŋ/ *adj* (*before n*) **1** ‹*harbor*/*restaurant*› flotante **2** (Fin) ‹*currency*› flotante; ‹*assets*› circulante **3** ‹*population*› flotante; ‹*voter*› (BrE) indeciso

flock¹ /flɑːk ‖ flɒk/ *n* (+ *sing or pl vb*) (of sheep) rebaño *m*; (of birds) bandada *f*; (of people) (*often pl*) tropel *m*, multitud *f*

flock² *vi* acudir (*en gran número, en masa*)

floe /fləʊ/ *n* témpano *m* de hielo

flog /flɑːg ‖ flɒg/ *vt* **-gg- 1** (beat) azotar **2** (sell) (BrE sl) vender

flood¹ /flʌd/ *n* (of water) inundación *f*; (of complaints, calls) avalancha *f*; **she was in ~s of tears** estaba hecha un mar de lágrimas

flood² *vt* inundar; ‹*engine*› ahogar*; **to ~ the market with imports** (Busn) inundar el mercado de productos importados ■ ~ *vi* «*river*/*sewers*» desbordarse; «*mine*/*basement*» inundarse; (Auto) ahogarse*; **to ~ in** «*sunshine*» entrar a raudales; **donations came ~ing in** llovieron los donativos

flooding /ˈflʌdɪŋ/ *n* [U] inundación *f*

floodlight¹ /ˈflʌdlaɪt/ *n* [C U] reflector *m*, foco *m*

floodlight² *vt* (*past & past p* **floodlit** /ˈflʌdlɪt/) **(a)** iluminar (*con reflectores o focos*) **(b) floodlit** *past p* ‹*arena*/*building*› iluminado; ‹*game*› que se juega con luz artificial

flood: **~ tide** *n* pleamar *f*; **~water** *n* [U] (*often pl*) crecida *f*

floor¹ /flɔːr ‖ flɔː(r)/ *n* **1 (a)** (of room, vehicle) suelo *m*, piso *m* (AmL) **(b)** (for dancing) pista *f* (de baile) **(c)** (of ocean, valley, forest) fondo *m* **2** (storey) piso *m*; **we live on the first/second ~** (AmE) vivimos en la planta baja/el primer piso *or* (Chi) en el primer/segundo piso; (BrE) vivimos en el primer/segundo piso *or* (Chi) en el segundo/tercer piso

floor² *vt* **(a)** (knock down) derribar **(b)** (nonplus) (colloq) dejar helado (fam)

floorboard /'flɔːrbɔːrd ‖ 'flɔːbɔːd/ *n* tabla *f* del suelo, duela *f* (Méx)

flooring /'flɔːrɪŋ/ *n* [U] revestimiento *m* para suelos

floor show *n* espectáculo *m* (*de cabaret*)

flop¹ /flɑːp ‖ flɒp/ *vi* **-pp- 1** (fall, move slackly) (+ *adv compl*): **she ~ped down into a chair** se dejó caer en un sillón; **he ~ped down exhausted onto the bed** se desplomó en la cama muerto de cansancio **2** (fail) (colloq) fracasar estrepitosamente

flop² *n* (colloq) fracaso *m*

floppy¹ /'flɑːpi ‖ 'flɒpi/ *adj* ‹*hat/bag*› flexible; ‹*ears/tail*› caído

floppy² *n* (*pl* **-pies**) (colloq) ⇒ FLOPPY DISK

floppy disk *n* disquete *m*, floppy (disk) *m*

floral /'flɔːrəl/ *adj* ‹*fabric/dress*› floreado; **a ~ print** un estampado de flores

florid /'flɔːrəd ‖ 'flɒrɪd/ *adj* **(a)** (red) ‹*complexion*› rubicundo **(b)** (ornate) ‹*decoration/style*› recargado; ‹*language*› florido

florist /'flɔːrəst ‖ 'flɒrɪst/ *n* (person) florista *mf*; **is there a ~'s near here?** ¿hay una floristería *or* (AmL tb) florería cerca de aquí?

flotation /fləʊ'teɪʃən/ *n* (of company) salida *f* a Bolsa; (of shares) emisión *f*

flotsam /'flɑːtsəm ‖ 'flɒtsəm/ *n* [U] restos *mpl* flotantes (*de un naufragio*); **~ and jetsam** desechos *mpl*

flounce¹ /flaʊns/ *vi* (+ *adv compl*): **to ~ in/out** entrar/salir* indignado (*or* airado *etc*)

flounce² *n* (ruffle) volante *m*, elán *m* (Méx), volado *m* (RPl), vuelo *m* (Chi)

flounder /'flaʊndər ‖ 'flaʊndə(r)/ *vi* **(a)** (in water) luchar para mantenerse a flote **(b)** «*speaker*» quedarse sin saber qué decir

flour /flaʊər ‖ 'flaʊə(r)/ *n* [U] harina *f*

flourish¹ /'flɜːrɪʃ ‖ 'flʌrɪʃ/ *vi* «*arts/trade*» florecer*; «*business*» prosperar; «*plant*» darse* *or* crecer* bien ■ ~ *vt* ‹*stick/letter*› blandir

flourish² *n* **(a)** (showy gesture) floreo *m* **(b)** (embellishment) floritura *f*, firulete *m* (AmL); (in signature) rúbrica *f*

flourishing /'flɜːrɪʃɪŋ ‖ 'flʌrɪʃɪŋ/ *adj* ‹*business*› próspero

flout /flaʊt/ *vt* desobedecer* abiertamente

flow¹ /fləʊ/ *vi* **(a)** «*liquid/electric current*» fluir*; «*tide*» subir; «*blood*» correr; (from wound) manar **(b)** (run smoothly, continuously) «*traffic*» circular con fluidez; «*music/words*» fluir*

flow² *n* **1** [U] **(a)** (of liquid, current) flujo *m* **(b)** (of traffic, information) circulación *f*; (of capital, money) movimiento *m* **2** [C] (stream — of water, lava) corriente *f*

flow chart, **flow diagram** *n* organigrama *m*

flower¹ /flaʊər ‖ 'flaʊə(r)/ *n* flor *f*

flower² *vi* florecer*, florear (Chi, Méx)

flower: **~bed** *n* arriate *m* (Esp, Méx), parterre *m* (Esp), cantero *m* (Cu, RPl); **~pot** *n* maceta *f*, tiesto *m* (Esp), macetero *m* (AmS)

flowery /'flaʊri ‖ 'flaʊəri/ *adj* ‹*pattern*› floreado; ‹*meadow*› florido; ‹*style/prose*› florido

flowing /'fləʊɪŋ/ *adj* **(a)** ‹*beard/robe*› largo y suelto **(b)** ‹*handwriting/movement*› fluido

flown /fləʊn/ *past p of* FLY²

flu /fluː/ *n* [U] gripe *f*, gripa *f* (Col, Méx)

fluctuate /'flʌktʃueɪt ‖ 'flʌktjʊeɪt/ *vi* fluctuar*

fluctuation /'flʌktʃu'eɪʃən ‖ ˌflʌktjʊ'eɪʃən/ *n* [U C] fluctuación *f*

flue /fluː/ *n* tiro *m*

fluency /'fluːənsi/ *n* [U] fluidez *f*

fluent /'fluːənt/ *adj*: **to speak ~ Italian** hablar italiano con fluidez

fluently /'fluːəntli/ *adv* con fluidez

fluff /flʌf/ *n* [U] pelusa *f*

fluffy /'flʌfi/ *adj* **-fier, -fiest** ‹*fabric/garment*› suave y esponjoso; ‹*fur/hair*› suave y sedoso

fluid¹ /'fluːəd ‖ 'fluːɪd/ *n* [U C] fluido *m*

fluid² *adj* fluido

fluke /fluːk/ *n* (colloq) chiripa *f* (fam)

flummox /'flʌməks/ *vt* (colloq) desconcertar*

flung /flʌŋ/ *past & past p of* FLING¹

fluorescent /flʊ'resənt ‖ flʊə'resənt, flɔː-/ *adj* fluorescente; **~ light** tubo *m* fluorescente, tubolux® *m* (RPl)

fluoride /'flʊraɪd ‖ 'flɔːraɪd/ *n* [C U] (Chem) fluoruro *m*; (Dent) flúor *m*; (*before n*) **~ toothpaste** dentífrico *m* con flúor

flurry /'flɜːri ‖ 'flʌri/ *n* (*pl* **-ries**) **1** (of snow, wind) ráfaga *f*; (of rain) chaparrón *m* **2** (sudden burst): **a ~ of excitement/activity** una oleada de emoción/un frenesí de actividad

flush¹ /flʌʃ/ *n* **1 (a)** (blush) rubor *m* **(b)** (of anger, passion) arrebato *m*; **in the first ~ of success** con la euforia del triunfo **2** (in cards) flor *f*

flush² *vt* **1** ‹*toilet*›: **to ~ the toilet** tirar de la cadena, jalarle (a la cadena) (AmL exc CS) **2** (drive out) **~ (out)** ‹*person/criminal*› hacer* salir ■ ~ *vi* **1** «*toilet*» funcionar **2** (blush) «*person/face*» (with anger) enrojecer*; (with embarrassment) ruborizarse*

flush³ *adj* alineado

flushed /flʌʃt/ *adj* ‹*cheeks*› colorado; **~ with success** exaltado por el éxito

fluster /'flʌstər ‖ 'flʌstə(r)/ *vt* poner* nervioso; **to get ~ed** ponerse* nervioso

flute /fluːt/ *n* flauta *f*

flutter¹ /'flʌtər ‖ 'flʌtə(r)/ *vi* «*bird/butterfly*» revolotear; «*flag*» ondear, agitarse; «*heart*» latir con fuerza ■ ~ *vt* ‹*wings*› batir, sacudir

flutter² *n* **~ (of wings)** (*no pl*) aleteo *m*

flux /flʌks/ *n* [U]: **to be in (a state of) ~** estar* en un estado de cambio

fly¹ /flaɪ/ *n* (*pl* **flies**) **1** (insect) mosca *f* **2** (on trousers) (*often pl in BrE*) bragueta *f*, marrueco *m* (Chi)

fly² (*3rd pers sing pres* **flies**; *pres p* **flying**; *past* **flew**; *past p* **flown**) *vi* **1 (a)** volar*; «*passenger*» ir* en avión; **to ~ away** irse* volando; **to ~ in/out** «*bird/bee*» entrar/salir* volando; «*plane/pilot*» llegar*/salir* (*en avión*) **(b)** «*flag*» ondear **2 (a)** (rush) «*person*» correr, ir* (*or* salir* *etc*) volando; **to ~ AT sb** lanzarse* SOBRE algn; **to ~ into a rage** ponerse* hecho una furia **(b)** (move, be thrown) volar*; **I tripped and went ~ing** tropecé y salí volando **(c)** (pass quickly) «*time*» pasar volando ■ **~** *vt* **1 (a)** (control) ‹*plane/glider/balloon*› pilotar; ‹*kite*› hacer* volar *or* encumbrar (Andes), remontar (RPl) **(b)** (carry) ‹*cargo*› transportar (*en avión*); ‹*person*› llevar (*en avión*) **(c)** (travel over) ‹*distance*› recorrer (*en avión*) **2** ‹*flag*› izar*, enarbolar

flyer /'flaɪər || 'flaɪə(r)/ *n* ⇒ FLIER

flying¹ /'flaɪɪŋ/ *adj* (*before n*) **(a)** (hurried): **a ~ visit** una visita relámpago **(b)** ‹*glass/debris*› que vuela (por los aires)

flying² *n* [U] **(a)** (as pilot) pilotaje *m*; (*before n*) ‹*time/lesson*› de vuelo; ‹*helmet/jacket*› de piloto **(b)** (as passenger): **I hate ~** odio viajar en avión

flying: **~ saucer** *n* platillo *m* volador *or* (Esp) volante; **~ start** *n* salida *f* lanzada; ***to get off to a ~ start*** «*person/business*» empezar* con muy buen pie

fly: **~leaf** *n* guarda *f*; **~over** *n* (BrE Transp) paso *m* elevado, paso *m* a desnivel (Méx); **~ spray** *n* [U C] insecticida *m* (*en aerosol*); **~swatter** /'flaɪˌswɑːtər || 'flaɪˌswɒtə(r)/ *n* matamoscas *m*; **~wheel** *n* volante *m*

FM *n* (= **frequency modulation**) FM *f*

foal /fəʊl/ *n* (male) potro *m*, potrillo *m*; (female) potranca *f*, potra *f*

foam¹ /fəʊm/ *n* [U C] espuma *f*

foam² *vi* «*sea/waves*» hacer* espuma; **to ~ at the mouth** echar espuma por la boca

foam rubber *n* [U] goma espuma *f*, hule *m* espuma (Méx)

fob /fɑːb || fɒb/ *n* (watchchain) leontina *f*; (*before n*) **~ watch** reloj *m* de bolsillo

• **fob off**: **-bb-** [*v* + *o* + *adv*] (placate) **to ~ sb off** (WITH **sth**) engatusar a algn (CON algo)

focal /'fəʊkəl/ *adj* (*before n*) **(a)** (Opt) focal **(b)** ‹*issue*› central

focal point *n* **(a)** (Opt) foco *m* **(b)** (of attention, activity) centro *m*

focus¹ /'fəʊkəs/ *n* (*pl* **-cuses** *or* **foci** /'fəʊsaɪ/) **1** [U] (Opt, Phot) foco *m*; **to be in/out of ~** estar* enfocado **2** [C] (central point) centro *m*

focus² **-s-** *or* **-ss-** *vt* **(a)** (Opt, Phot) enfocar* **(b)** (concentrate) **to ~ sth** (ON **sth**) ‹*attention*› centrar algo (EN algo) ■ **~** *vi* **(a)** «*camera/eyes*» enfocar* **(b)** «*lecturer/chapter/attention*» **to ~ ON sth/sb** centrarse EN algo/algn

fodder /'fɑːdər || 'fɒdə(r)/ *n* [U] forraje *m*

foe /fəʊ/ *n* (liter) enemigo, -ga *m,f*

foetus /'fiːtəs/ *n* (BrE) ⇒ FETUS

fog /fɔːg || fɒg/ **▶920** *n* [U C] (Meteo) niebla *f*

fogbound /'fɔːgbaʊnd || 'fɒgbaʊnd/ *adj* ‹*airport/road*› afectado por la niebla; ‹*plane/ferry*› retenido a causa de la niebla

foggy /'fɔːgi || 'fɒgi/ **▶920** *adj* **-gier, -giest (a)** ‹*day*› de niebla; ‹*weather*› nebuloso; **it's ~** hay niebla **(b)** (confused) confuso

fog: **~horn** *n* sirena *f* (*de niebla*); **~ light**, (BrE) **~ lamp** *n* faro *m* antiniebla

foible /'fɔɪbəl/ *n* debilidad *f*

foil¹ /fɔɪl/ *n* [U] **(a)** (metal sheet) lámina *f* de metal **(b)** (Culin) (*kitchen ~*) papel *m* de aluminio *or* de plata

foil² *vt* ‹*plan/attempt*› frustrar

foist /fɔɪst/ *vt* **to ~ sth** (OFF) ON *o* ONTO **sb** endilgarle* algo a algn

fold¹ /fəʊld/ *vt* **1 (a)** (bend, bring together) ‹*paper/sheet*› doblar; **to ~ one's arms** cruzar* los brazos **2** (Culin) **to ~ sth** INTO **sth** incorporar algo A algo ■ **~** *vi* **1 (a)** «*chair/table*» plegarse*; «*map/poster*» doblarse **(b) folding** *pres p* ‹*chair/table*› plegable **2** (fail) «*project*» venirse* abajo; «*play*» bajar de cartel; «*business*» cerrar* (sus puertas)

• **fold up** [*v* + *o* + *adv*, *v* + *adv* + *o*] ‹*sheet/newspaper*› doblar; ‹*chair/table*› plegar*

fold² *n* **1** (crease) doblez *m* **2** (sheep pen) redil *m*

-fold /fəʊld/ *suff*: **his income increased five~** sus ingresos se multiplicaron por cinco *or* se quintuplicaron; **the problem is three~** el problema tiene tres aspectos

folder /'fəʊldər || 'fəʊldə(r)/ *n* carpeta *f*

foliage /'fəʊliɪdʒ/ *n* [U] follaje *m*

folio /'fəʊliəʊ/ *n* (*pl* **folios**) (sheet) pliego *m*; (numbered leaf) folio *m*

folk /fəʊk/ *n* **1 (a)** *also* **folks** *pl* (people) (colloq) gente *f* **(b) folks** *pl* (esp AmE colloq) (relatives) familia *f*; (parents) padres *mpl*, viejos *mpl* (fam) **2** (+ *pl vb*) (Anthrop) pueblo *m*; (*before n*) ‹*art/medicine*› popular; ‹*dancing*› folklórico

folk: **~lore** *n* [U] folklore *m*; **~ music** *n* [U] (traditional) música *f* folklórica; (modern) música *f* folk; **~ song** *n* [C U] (traditional) canción *f* popular; (modern) canción *f* folk

follow /'fɑːləʊ || 'fɒləʊ/ *vt* **1** (go, come after) seguir*; **the lecture was ~ed by a discussion** después de la conferencia hubo un debate **2** (keep to, conform to) ‹*road*› seguir* (por); ‹*trail*› seguir*; ‹*instructions*› seguir*; ‹*order*› cumplir; ‹*fashion/example*› seguir* **3** (pay close attention to) ‹*movement/progress*› seguir* de cerca; ‹*news*› mantenerse* al tanto de; ‹*TV serial*› seguir* **4** ‹*argument/reasoning*› entender* ■ **~** *vi* **1** (come after): **you go first, and I'll ~** tú ve delante que yo te sigo; **the winners were as ~s** ... los ganadores fueron ... **2** (be logical consequence) deducirse*; **that doesn't necessarily ~** una cosa no implica la otra **3** (understand) entender*

• **follow up** [*v* + *o* + *adv*, *v* + *adv* + *o*] seguir*

follower /'fɑːləʊər || 'fɒləʊə(r)/ *n* seguidor, -dora *m,f*

following¹ /'fɑːləʊɪŋ || 'fɒləʊɪŋ/ *adj* (*before n*) (next) siguiente; **(on) the ~ day** al día siguiente

following² *n* **1** (followers) seguidores *mpl*; (admirers) admiradores *mpl* **2** (what, who comes next) **the ~**: **the ~ are to play in tomorrow's game** ... los siguientes jugarán en el partido de mañana ...; **the letter said the ~** ... la carta decía lo siguiente ...

follow-up /ˈfɑːləʊʌp ‖ ˈfɒləʊʌp/ *n* [C] (sequel) continuación *f*; (*before n*): **she sent a ~ letter** mandó una segunda (*or* tercera *etc*) carta

folly /ˈfɑːli ‖ ˈfɒli/ *n* (*pl* **-lies**) [U C] locura *f*

fond /fɑːnd ‖ fɒnd/ *adj* **-er, -est 1** (*pred*): **she's very ~ of Sue** le tiene mucho cariño a Sue; **he was ~ of chocolate** le gustaba el chocolate **2** (*before n*) (loving) ‹*gesture/look*› cariñoso

fondle /ˈfɑːndl̩ ‖ ˈfɒndl̩/ *vt* acariciar

fondly /ˈfɑːndli ‖ ˈfɒndli/ *adv* **(a)** (lovingly) cariñosamente; ‹*remember*› con cariño **(b)** (foolishly) ingenuamente

fondness /ˈfɑːndnəs ‖ ˈfɒndnɪs/ *n* [U] (love) cariño *m*; (liking) afición *f*

font /fɑːnt ‖ fɒnt/ *n* pila *f* bautismal

food /fuːd/ *n* **(a)** [U] (in general) comida *f*; (*before n*) ‹*shortage/exports*› de alimentos **(b)** [C] (specific kind) alimento *m*

food: **~ poisoning** *n* [U] intoxicación *f* (*por alimentos*); **~ processor** /ˈprɑːsesər, ˈprəʊ- ‖ ˈprəʊsesə(r)/ *n* robot *m* de cocina; **~stuffs** *pl n* productos *mpl* alimenticios

fool¹ /fuːl/ *n* idiota *mf*; **to make a ~ of oneself** hacer* el ridículo

fool² *vt* engañar

• **fool around**, (BrE also) **fool about** [*v* + *adv*] hacer* payasadas, hacer* el tonto (Esp)

foolhardy /ˈfuːlˈhɑːrdi ‖ ˈfuːlhɑːdi/ *adj* imprudente

foolish /ˈfuːlɪʃ/ *adj* ‹*person/prank*› tonto; ‹*look/grin*› de tonto; ‹*decision/plan*› insensato

fool: **~proof** *adj* ‹*idea/plan*› infalible; ‹*machine*› sencillo de manejar; **~scap** /ˈfuːlskæp/ *n* [U] *pliego de aprox 43 x 35 cm*

foot¹ /fʊt/ *n* (*pl* **feet**) **1** ▶ **484** [C] (of person) pie *m*; (of animal) pata *f*; (on sewing machine) pie *m*; **to be on one's feet** estar* de pie, estar* parado (AmL); **to go/come on ~** ir*/venir* a pie; ***to find one's feet***: **it didn't take him long to find his feet in his new school** no tardó en habituarse a la nueva escuela; ***to put one's ~ down*** (be firm) imponerse*; (accelerate vehicle) (colloq) apretar* el acelerador, meterle (AmL fam); ***to put one's ~ in it*** (colloq) meter la pata (fam); ***under sb's feet***: **the cat keeps getting under my feet** el gato siempre me anda alrededor **2** (lower end) (*no pl*) pie *m*; **the ~ of the bed** los pies de la cama **3** ▶ **681** [C] (measure) (*pl* **foot** *or* **feet**) pie *m*

foot² *vt*: **to ~ the bill** pagar*

footage /ˈfʊtɪdʒ/ *n* [U] (Cin) secuencias *fpl* (filmadas)

foot-and-mouth (disease) /ˈfʊtn̩ˈmaʊθ/ *n* [U] fiebre *f* aftosa, glosopeda *f*

football /ˈfʊtbɔːl/ *n* **1** [U] **(a)** (*American ~*) fútbol *m or* (AmC, Méx) futbol *m* americano **(b)** (soccer) fútbol *m or* (AmC, Méx) futbol *m*; (*before n*) **~ match** partido *m* de fútbol *or* (Méx) futbol; **~ player** ⇨ FOOTBALLER **2** [C] (ball) balón *m or* (esp AmL) pelota *f* de fútbol *or* (AmC, Méx) futbol

footballer /ˈfʊtbɔːlər ‖ ˈfʊtbɔːlə(r)/ *n* (BrE) futbolista *mf*, jugador, -dora *m,f* de fútbol *or* (AmC, Méx) futbol

football: **~ pool** *n* (AmE) apuesta *f* colectiva, polla *f* (AmL); **~ pools** *pl n* (BrE) **the ~ pools** *juego de apuestas en que se trata de acertar los resultados de los partidos de la liga de fútbol*, ≈ el pronóstico deportivo (*en Méx*), ≈ las quinielas (*en Esp*), ≈ el prode (*en Arg*), ≈ el totogol (*en Col*), ≈ la polla-gol (*en Chi*), ≈ la polla (*en Per*)

-footed /ˈfʊtəd ‖ ˈfʊtɪd/ *suff*: **four~** de cuatro patas; **light~** ligero de pies

foot: **~hills** *pl n* estribaciones *fpl*; **~hold** *n* punto *m* de apoyo (*para el pie*); **to gain a ~hold** «*ideology*» prender*

footing /ˈfʊtɪŋ/ *n* (*no pl*) **1** (balance) equilibrio *m*; **to miss one's ~** resbalar **2** (basis): **on an equal ~** en igualdad de condiciones

foot: **~lights** *pl n* candilejas *fpl*; **~loose** *adj* libre y sin compromiso; **~loose and fancy-free** libre como el viento; **~man** /ˈfʊtmən/ *n* (*pl* **-men** /-mən/) lacayo *m*; **~note** *n* nota *f* a pie de página; **~path** *n* (path) sendero *m*; (pavement) (BrE) acera *f*, banqueta *f* (Méx), vereda *f* (CS, Per); **~print** *n* huella *f*; **~step** *n* paso *m*; **~wear** *n* [U] calzado *m*

for¹ /fɔːr ‖ fɔː(r), *weak form* fər ‖ fə(r)/ *prep* **I 1** (intended for) para; **is there a letter ~ me?** ¿hay carta para mí?; **my love ~ her** mi amor por ella **2 (a)** (on behalf of, representing): **I did it ~ you** lo hice por ti; **he plays ~ England** forma parte de *or* juega en la selección inglesa; **D ~ David** D de David **(b)**(as): **we're having chicken ~ dinner** vamos a cenar pollo; **I can see him now ~ what he is** ahora me doy cuenta de cómo es en realidad **(c)** (in favor of) a favor de **3** (indicating purpose): **what's that ~?** ¿para qué es eso?; **it's ~ decoration** es de adorno; **it's ~ your own good!** ¡es por tu (propio) bien! **4** (giving reason) por; **~ that reason** por esa razón; **if it weren't ~ Joe** ... si no fuera por Joe ... **5** (in exchange for) por; **I bought the book ~ $10** compré el libro por 10 dólares; **she left him ~ somebody else** lo dejó por otro **6** (as concerns) para; **it's too cold ~ me here** aquí hace demasiado frío para mí **7 (a)** (in spite of): **~ all her faults, she's been very kind to us** tendrá sus defectos, pero con nosotros ha sido muy buena **(b)** (*with infinitive clause*): **it's unusual ~ me to forget a name** es raro que se me olvide un nombre; **it's not ~ me to decide** no me corresponde a mí decidir

II 1 (in the direction of) para; **the plane ~ New York** el avión para *or* de Nueva York **2 (a)** (indicating duration): **he spoke ~ half an hour** habló (durante) media hora; **I've only been here ~ a day** sólo llevo un día aquí; **how long are you going ~?** ¿por cuánto tiempo vas? **(b)** (on the occasion of) para; **he gave it to me ~ my birthday** me lo regaló para mi cumpleaños **(c)** (by, before) para; **we have to be there ~ six o'clock** tenemos que estar allí a las seis **3** (indicating distance): **we drove ~ 20 miles** hicimos 20 millas; **we could see ~ miles** se podía ver hasta muy lejos

for² *conj* (liter) pues (liter), puesto que (frml)

forage /ˈfɔːrɪdʒ ‖ ˈfɒrɪdʒ/ *vi* **(a)** «*animal*» forrajear **(b)** (for supplies) **to ~ FOR sth** buscar* algo

foray /ˈfɔːreɪ ‖ ˈfɒreɪ/ *n* (Mil) incursión *f*

forbid /fər'bɪd ‖fə'bɪd/ *vt* (*past* **forbad(e)** /fər'bæd, -'beɪd ‖fə'bæd, -'beɪd/; *past p* **forbidden**) /fər'bɪdn̩ ‖fəbɪdn̩/ **1** (not allow) prohibir*; **to ~ sb to** + INF prohibirle* A algn + INF, prohibirle* A algn QUE (+ *subj*)

force¹ /fɔːrs ‖fɔːs/ *n* [C U] fuerza *f*; **the (armed) ~s** las fuerzas armadas; **a ~ eight gale** vientos de fuerza ocho; **to join ~s with sb** unirse a algn; **to come into ~** entrar en vigor *or* vigencia; **to be in ~** estar* en vigor *or* vigencia

force² *vt* **1** (compel) **to ~ sb to** + INF obligar* a algn A + INF **2**(push, drive) ‹*door/link*› forzar*; **they ~d their way in** entraron por la fuerza

• **force down** [*v + o + adv, v + adv + o*] **(a)** ‹*aircraft/pilot*› obligar* a aterrizar **(b)** ‹*food*› tragar* (*a duras penas*)

forced /fɔːrst ‖fɔːst/ *adj* (*before n*) ‹*labor/smile*› forzado; ‹*landing/stopover*› forzoso

force-feed /'fɔːrs'fiːd ‖'fɔːsfiːd/ *vt* (*past & past p* **-fed**) alimentar por la fuerza

forceful /'fɔːrsfəl ‖'fɔːsfəl/ *adj* **(a)** (vigorous) ‹*person*› con carácter; ‹*personality*› fuerte **(b)** (persuasive) ‹*words/argument*› convincente

forceps /'fɔːrsəps ‖'fɔːseps/ *pl n* fórceps *m*

forcible /'fɔːrsəbəl ‖'fɔːsəbəl/ *adj* forzoso

ford /fɔːrd ‖fɔːd/ *n* vado *m*

fore /fɔːr ‖fɔː(r)/ *n*: **to come to the ~** «*issue*» saltar a primera plana

forearm /'fɔːrɑːrm ‖'fɔːrɑːm/ *n* antebrazo *m*

foreboding /fɔːr'bəʊdɪŋ ‖fɔː'bəʊdɪŋ/ *n* **(a)** [U] (apprehension) aprensión *f* **(b)** [C] (presentiment) premonición *f*

forecast¹ /'fɔːrkæst ‖'fɔːkɑːst/ *n* (*weather* ~) pronóstico *m* del tiempo; (prediction) previsión *f*

forecast² *vt* (*past & past p* **forecast** *or* **forecasted**) ‹*weather*› pronosticar*; ‹*result/trend*› prever*

forecourt /'fɔːrkɔːrt ‖'fɔːkɔːt/ *n* patio *m* delantero

forefathers /'fɔːr,fɑːðərz ‖'fɔːfɑːðəz/ *pl n* (liter) antepasados *mpl*

forefinger /'fɔːr,fɪŋgər ‖'fɔː,fɪŋgə(r)/ *n* índice *m*

forefront /'fɔːrfrʌnt ‖'fɔːfrʌnt/ *n*: **in** *o* **at the ~ of sth** al frente de algo; (in the vanguard) a la vanguardia de algo

forego /fɔːr'gəʊ ‖fɔː'gəʊ/ *vt* (*3rd pers sing pres* **-goes**; *pres p* **-going**; *past* **-went**; *past p* **-gone**) ⇒ FORGO

foregone /'fɔːrgɑːn ‖'fɔːgɒn/ *adj*: **the result was a ~ conclusion** el resultado era de prever

foreground /'fɔːrgraʊnd ‖'fɔːgraʊnd/ *n*: **in the ~** en primer plano

forehand /'fɔːrhænd ‖'fɔːhænd/ *n* golpe *m* de derecho

forehead /'fɑːrəd, 'fɔːrhed ‖'fɒrɪd, 'fɔːhəd/ *n* frente *f*

foreign /'fɔːrən, 'fɑː- ‖'fɒrən/ *adj* **1 (a)** ‹*custom/country/language*› extranjero **(b)** ‹*policy/trade/relations*› exterior; **~ debt** deuda *f* externa **2** (Med) extraño; **a ~ body** un cuerpo extraño

foreigner /'fɔːrənər, 'fɑː- ‖'fɒrənə(r)/ *n* extranjero, -ra *m,f*

foreign: **~ exchange** *n* [U] divisas *fpl*; **F~ minister** *n* ministro, -tra *or* (Méx) secretario, -ria *m,f* de relaciones *or* (Esp) asuntos exteriores, canciller *mf* (AmS); **F~ Office** *n* (in UK) **the F~ Office** el Foreign Office, el ministerio de relaciones exteriores de Gran Bretaña; **F~ Secretary** *n* (in UK) ⇒ F~ MINISTER

foreleg /'fɔːrleg ‖'fɔːleg/ *n* pata *f* delantera

foreman /'fɔːrmən ‖'fɔːmən/ *n* (*pl* **-men** /-mən/) **(a)** (supervisor) capataz *m* **(b)** (of jury) presidente *m* del jurado

foremost¹ /'fɔːrməʊst ‖'fɔːməʊst/ *adj* más importante

foremost² *adv* en primer lugar

forename /'fɔːrneɪm ‖'fɔːneɪm/ *n* nombre *m* (de pila)

forensic /fə'rensɪk/ *adj* (*before n*) forense

forerunner /'fɔːr,rʌnər ‖'fɔː,rʌnə(r)/ *n* precursor, -sora *m,f*

foresee /fɔːr'siː ‖fɔː'siː/ *vt* (*past* **foresaw**; *past p* **foreseen**) prever*

foreshore /'fɔːrʃɔːr ‖'fɔːʃɔː(r)/ *n*: *parte de la playa entre la pleamar y la bajamar*

foresight /'fɔːrsaɪt ‖'fɔːsaɪt/ *n* [U] previsión *f*

foreskin /'fɔːrskɪn ‖'fɔːskɪn/ *n* prepucio *m*

forest /'fɔːrəst ‖'fɒrɪst/ *n* [U C] (wood) bosque *m*; (tropical) selva *f*; (*before n*) forestal

forestall /fɔːr'stɔːl ‖fɔː'stɔːl/ *vt* **(a)** (prevent) prevenir* **(b)** (preempt) adelantarse a

forestry /'fɔːrəstri ‖'fɒrɪstri/ *n* [U] silvicultura *f*

foretaste /'fɔːrteɪst ‖'fɔːteɪst/ *n* anticipo *m*

foretell /fɔːr'tel ‖fɔː'tel/ *vt* (*past & past p* **foretold**) predecir*

forever /fə'revər ‖fə'revə(r)/ *adv*: **those days are gone ~** esos días no volverán; **nothing lasts ~** nada dura eternamente

forewarn /fɔːr'wɔːrn ‖fɔː'wɔːn/ *vt* **to ~ sb OF sth** advertir* A algn DE algo

forewent /fɔːr'went ‖fɔː'went/ *past of* FOREGO

foreword /'fɔːrwɜːrd ‖'fɔːwɜːd/ *n* prólogo *m*

forfeit¹ /'fɔːrfət ‖'fɔːfɪt/ *vt* ‹*property*› perder* el derecho a; ‹*rights/respect/game*› perder*

forfeit² *n* **(a)** (penalty) multa *f* **(b)** (Games) prenda *f*

forgave /fər'geɪv ‖fə'geɪv/ *past of* FORGIVE

forge¹ /fɔːrdʒ ‖fɔːdʒ/ *vt* **1** ‹*metal/bond*› forjar **2** (counterfeit) falsificar*

forge² *n* **(a)** (smithy) forja *f* **(b)** (furnace) fragua *f*

forger /'fɔːrdʒər ‖'fɔːdʒə(r)/ *n* falsificador, -dora *m,f*

forgery /'fɔːrdʒəri ‖'fɔːdʒəri/ *n* [U C] (*pl* **-ries**) falsificación *f*

forget /fər'get ‖fə'get/ (*pres p* **forgetting**; *past* **forgot**; *past p* **forgotten**) *vt* olvidarse de, olvidar ■ ~ *vi*: **to ~ (ABOUT sth)** olvidarse (DE algo)

forgetful /fər'getfəl ‖fə'getfəl/ *adj* olvidadizo

forget-me-not /fər'getmi'nɑːt ‖fə'getminɒt/ *n* nomeolvides *f*

forgive /fər'gɪv ‖fə'gɪv/ *vt* (*past* **forgave**; *past p* **forgiven**) perdonar; **to ~ sb FOR sth** perdonarle algo a algn

forgiveness /fərˈgɪvnəs ‖ fəˈgɪvnɪs/ *n* [U] (quality) clemencia *f*; **to ask sb's ~ for sth** pedirle* perdón a algn por algo

forgo /fɔːrˈgəʊ ‖ fɔːˈgəʊ/ *vt* (*3rd pers sing pres* **-goes**; *pres p* **-going**; *past* **-went**; *past p* **-gone**) (fml) privarse de

forgot /fəːrˈgɑːt ‖ fəˈgɒt/ *past of* FORGET

forgotten /fəːrˈgɑːtn ‖ fəˈgɒtn̩/ *past p of* FORGET

fork[1] /fɔːrk ‖ fɔːk/ *n* (Culin) tenedor *m*; (for gardening) horca *f*

fork[2] *vi* **(a)** (split) «*branch/road/river*» bifurcarse* **(b)** (turn): **to ~ (to the) right** desviarse* a la derecha

forklift (truck) /ˈfɔːrkˈlɪft ‖ ˈfɔːklɪft/ *n* carretilla *f* elevadora (*de horquilla*)

forlorn /fərˈlɔːrn ‖ fəˈlɔːn/ *adj* **(a)** ‹*glance/smile*› triste; ‹*appearance*› de tristeza y desamparo **(b)** ‹*attempt*› desesperado

form[1] /fɔːrm ‖ fɔːm/ *n* **1** [C U] (shape, manner) forma *f* **2** [C U] (type, kind) tipo; **other ~s of life** otras formas de vida **3** [U] (fitness, ability) forma *f*; **to be on ~** estar* en forma **4** [C] (document) formulario *m*, forma *f* (Méx) **5** [C] (BrE Educ) (class) clase *f*; (year) curso *m*

form[2] *vt* ‹*character/shape/company/basis*› formar; ‹*opinion*› formarse; ‹*habit*› adquirir* ■ ~ *vi* «*idea/plan*» tomar forma; «*ice/fog*» formarse

formal /ˈfɔːrməl ‖ ˈfɔːməl/ *adj* ‹*reception/dinner/language*› formal; ‹*manner/person*› ceremonioso; **~ dress** traje *m* de etiqueta

formality /fɔːrˈmæləti ‖ fɔːˈmæləti/ *n* (*pl* **-ties**) **1** [U] (formal quality) ceremonia *f* **2** [C] (convention) formalidad *f*

formalize /ˈfɔːrməlaɪz ‖ ˈfɔːməlaɪz/ *vt* formalizar*

formally /ˈfɔːrməli ‖ ˈfɔːməli/ *adv* ‹*invite/reprimand*› formalmente

format[1] /ˈfɔːrmæt ‖ ˈfɔːmæt/ *n* [C U] formato *m*

format[2] *vt* **-tt-** formatear

formation /fɔːrˈmeɪʃən ‖ fɔːˈmeɪʃən/ *n* [U C] formación *f*

former[1] /ˈfɔːrmər ‖ ˈfɔːmə(r)/ *adj* **1** (previous) antiguo **2** (first-mentioned) primero

former[2] *n* **the ~** el primero, la primera; (*pl*) los primeros, las primeras

formerly /ˈfɔːrmərli ‖ ˈfɔːməli/ *adv* antes

formidable /ˈfɔːrmədəbəl ‖ ˈfɔːmɪdəbəl, fɔːˈmɪdəbəl/ *adj* ‹*task*› imponente; ‹*problem/obstacle*› tremendo; ‹*opponent*› temible

formula /ˈfɔːrmjələ ‖ ˈfɔːmjʊlə/ *n* (*pl* **-las** *o* (fml) **-lae** /-liː/) fórmula *f*; **~ one** (motor racing) fórmula uno

formulate /ˈfɔːrmjəleɪt ‖ ˈfɔːmjʊleɪt/ *vt* formular

fornication /ˈfɔːrnəˈkeɪʃən ‖ ˌfɔːnɪˈkeɪʃən/ *n* [U] (fml) fornicación *f* (fml)

for-profit /fərˈprɑːfət ‖ fəˈprɒfɪt/ *adj* comercial, con fines de lucro

forsake /fərˈseɪk ‖ fəˈseɪk/ *vt* (*past* **forsook** /fərˈsʊk ‖ fəˈsʊk/; *past p* **forsaken** /fərˈseɪkən ‖ fəˈseɪkən/) (liter) **(a)** (abandon) abandonar **(b)** (relinquish) ‹*pleasure/habits*› renunciar a

fort /fɔːrt ‖ fɔːt/ *n* fuerte *m*; (small) fortín *m*

forte /ˈfɔːrteɪ ‖ ˈfɔːteɪ/ *n* fuerte *m*

forth /fɔːrθ ‖ fɔːθ/ *adv* (liter) **(a)** (out): **~ he went to battle with his enemy** marchó a luchar con su enemigo **(b)** (in time): **from this day ~** de hoy en adelante

forthcoming /ˈfɔːrθˈkʌmɪŋ ‖ ˌfɔːθˈkʌmɪŋ/ *adj* **1 (a)** (approaching) (*usu before n*) ‹*event*› próximo **(b)** (about to appear) ‹*article/record*› de próxima aparición; ‹*film*› a estrenarse próximamente **2** (available) (*pred*): **no explanation was ~** no dieron (*or* dio *etc*) ninguna explicación **3** (open, helpful): **he was not very ~** no estuvo muy comunicativo

forthright /ˈfɔːrθraɪt ‖ ˈfɔːθraɪt/ *adj* directo

forthwith /ˈfɔːrθˈwɪð ‖ fɔːθˈwɪθ/ *adv* (fml *or* liter) inmediatamente

fortieth[1] /ˈfɔːrtiəθ ‖ ˈfɔːtiəθ/ ▶ 725 *adj* cuadragésimo

fortieth[2] *adv* en cuadragésimo lugar

fortieth[3] ▶ 543, 725 *n* (Math) cuarentavo *m*; (part) cuarentava *or* cuadragésima parte *f*

fortification /ˈfɔːrtəfəˈkeɪʃən ‖ ˌfɔːtɪfɪˈkeɪʃən/ *n* [C U] (Mil) fortificación *f*

fortify /ˈfɔːrtəfaɪ ‖ ˈfɔːtɪfaɪ/ *vt* **-fies, -fying, -fied** ‹*town/building*› fortificar*; ‹*person/determination*› fortalecer*; ‹*argument*› reforzar*; **fortified wine** vino *m* fortificado

fortnight /ˈfɔːrtnaɪt ‖ ˈfɔːtnaɪt/ *n* (esp BrE) quince días, dos semanas

fortnightly[1] /ˈfɔːrtnaɪtli ‖ ˈfɔːtnaɪtli/ *adv* (esp BrE) cada dos semanas

fortnightly[2] *adj* (esp BrE) quincenal

fortress /ˈfɔːrtrəs ‖ ˈfɔːtrɪs/ *n* fortaleza *f*

fortuitous /fɔːrˈtuːɪtəs ‖ fɔːˈtjuːɪtəs/ *adj* fortuito

fortunate /ˈfɔːrtʃnət ‖ ˈfɔːtʃənət/ *adj* afortunado; **it was ~ that he came** fue una suerte que viniera

fortunately /ˈfɔːrtʃnətli ‖ ˈfɔːtʃənətli/ *adv* (*indep*) afortunadamente

fortune /ˈfɔːrtʃən ‖ ˈfɔːtʃən, ˈfɔːtʃuːn/ *n* **1** [C] (money, prosperity) fortuna *f*; (a lot of money) (colloq) (*no pl*) dineral *m*, platal *m* (AmL fam), pastón *m* (Esp fam) **2** [C U] (destiny) destino *m*; **to tell sb's ~** decirle* la buenaventura a algn **3** [U] (luck) **good ~** suerte *f*

fortune-teller /ˈfɔːrtʃənˌtelər ‖ ˈfɔːtʃənˌtelə(r), ˈfɔːtʃuːn-/ *n* adivino, -na *m,f*

forty /ˈfɔːrti ‖ ˈfɔːti/ ▶ 451, 540, 724, 884 *adj/n* cuarenta *adj inv/m*; *see also* FOUR[1]

forum /ˈfɔːrəm/ *n* foro *m*

forward[1] /ˈfɔːrwərd ‖ ˈfɔːwəd/, (esp BrE) **forwards** /ˈfɔːrwərdz ‖ ˈfɔːwədz/ *adv* **(a)** ‹*bend/slope/lean*› hacia adelante **(b)** (in time) (fml) en adelante; **from this day ~** desde hoy en adelante

forward[2] *adj* **1** (*before n*) ‹*movement*› hacia adelante **2** (advance): **~ planning** planificación *f* **3** (assertive) atrevido

forward[3] *vt* (send) (Busn) enviar*; Ⓢ **please forward** hacer* seguir

forward[4] *n* (Sport) delantero *mf*

forwent /fɔːrˈwent ‖ fɔːˈwent/ *past of* FORGO

fossil /ˈfɑːsəl ‖ ˈfɒsəl/ *n* fósil *m*

foster[1] /ˈfɔːstər ‖ ˈfɒstə(r)/ *vt* **1** ‹*child*› (BrE) *acoger en el hogar sin adoptarlo legalmente* **2** ‹*suspicion/talent*› fomentar; ‹*reconciliation*› promover*

Forms of address

For ways of saying you, *see separate box* **You 1** *(p. 935).*

Señor/señora/señorita

Forms of address used with surnames are señor *(for a man),* señora *(for a married or older woman), and* señorita *(for an unmarried woman)*:

buenos días, señor Gómez
pase por favor, señora Lozano
señorita Abreu, la esperan en recepción

When talking about someone, these forms are preceded by the definite article and the first name may also be included:

hará uso de la palabra el señor Antonio Gómez
permítame presentarle a la señorita Lucía Jiménez

Señorita *is also used with the first name when talking to or about a teacher*:

¿puedo salir un momento, señorita Raquel?
me lo dijo la señorita Ana

Señor, señora *and* señorita *are also used without a name, for example, to address a stranger*:

buenos días, señorita
pase, señora
¿esto es suyo, señor?

In restaurants, stores, etc they are heard more frequently than the English Sir, Madam, or Miss:

¿la atienden, señora?
¿me permite su abrigo, señor?

The customer is sometimes addressed in the third person:

¿qué desea la señora?
¿qué va a beber el señor?

Don/doña

The forms don *(for a man) and* doña *(for a woman) are used as a sign of respect, particularly to older people with a certain social status. They are commonly heard when addressing doctors, priests, teachers, etc. They are used with first names*:

buenas tardes, Don Carlos
¿cómo está, Doña Susana?

When talking about someone the surname may also be included:

Don Carlos Valenzuela
Doña Susana Salvador

However, don *and* doña *cannot be used with surnames only*

Addressing people and referring to them by their professions or titles

Titles like doctor, profesor, ingeniero, *etc, and their feminine forms, are used with the surname*:

doctora Bonino
ingeniero Soto

Padre *can be used with a priest's surname or with his first name*:

Padre Martín
Padre Garese

Nuns are addressed by using hermana, madre *or* sor *with their Christian name*:

hermana Angélica

Some titles, like doctor, profesor, padre, *and* hermana *are often heard without the surname*:

¿puedo salir, profesor?
¿qué me recomienda, doctor?

Ingeniero, licenciado, *and their feminine forms, are also used in this way, but mainly in certain Latin American countries*:

a sus órdenes, licenciado
como usted diga, ingeniero

To refer to someone by their profession or title requires the use of the definite article:

el príncipe Felipe
el doctor Tercedor
el catedrático Jiménez López

As a mark of respect people can be referred to in the following way:

el señor doctor
la señora abogada
el señor alcalde

---

foster² *adj ‹child›* ≈ adoptivo; **~ home** casa *f* de acogida de menores

fought /fɔːt/ *past & past p of* FIGHT¹

foul¹ /faʊl/ *adj* **-er, -est 1** (offensive) *‹smell›* nauseabundo; *‹taste›* repugnante **2** (horrible) (colloq) *‹person›* asqueroso (fam); *‹weather›* pésimo **3** (obscene) *‹language/gesture›* ordinario

foul² *n* falta *f*, faul *m or* foul *m* (AmL)

foul³ *vt* **1** (pollute) contaminar **2 (a)** (block) *‹drain/chimney›* obstruir* **(b)** (entangle) *‹rope/chain›* enredar **3** (Sport) cometer una falta *or* (AmL tb) un foul *or* faul contra, faulear (AmL)

foul: **~-mouthed** /'faʊl'maʊðd/ *adj* malhablado; **~ play** *n* [U] **(a)** (Law): **they suspect ~ play** sospechan que se trata de un crimen **(b)** (Sport) juego *m* sucio

found¹ /faʊnd/ *past & past p of* FIND¹

found² *vt* **1 (a)** (establish) fundar **(b) founding** *pres p* fundador **2** (base) **to ~ sth** ON **sth** fundar algo EN algo

foundation /faʊn'deɪʃən/ *n* **1 (a)** [U] (establishing) fundación *f* **(b)** [C] (institution) fundación *f* **2** [C] *(often pl)* **(a)** (Const) cimientos *mpl* **(b)** (groundwork, basis) fundamentos *mpl*; *(before n)* **~ course** curso *m* preparatorio **3** [U] (grounds) fundamento *m* **4** [C U] (cosmetic) base *f* de maquillaje

founder¹ /'faʊndər ‖ 'faʊndə(r)/ *n* fundador, -dora *m,f*

founder² *vi* «*ship*» hundirse; «*plan/project*» irse* a pique

foundry /'faʊndri/ *n (pl* **-ries**) foundición *f*

fountain /ˈfaʊntn̩ ‖ ˈfaʊntɪn/ *n* **(a)** (ornamental) fuente *f* **(b)** (*drinking* ~) fuente *f*, bebedero *m* (CS, Méx)

fountain pen *n* pluma *f* (estilográfica), pluma *f* fuente (AmL), estilográfica *f*, lapicera *f* fuente (CS)

four[1] /fɔːr ‖ fɔː(r)/ ▶ 451, 724, 884 *n* cuatro *m*; 4 + 1 = 5 (*léase: four plus one equals* o *is five*) 4 + 1 = 5 (*read as: cuatro más uno es igual a cinco*); 4 − 1 = 3 (*léase: four minus one equals* o *is three*) 4 − 1 = 3 (*read as: cuatro menos uno es igual a tres*); 3 × 4 = 12 (*léase: three times four equals* o *is twelve*, o *three fours are twelve*) 3 × 4 = 12 (*read as: tres (multiplicado) por cuatro (son) doce*); 4 ÷ 2 = 2 (*léase: four divided by two equals* o *is two*) 4 ÷ 2 = 2 (*read as: cuatro dividido por dos es (igual a) dos*); ***on all* ~*s*** en *or* a cuatro patas, a gatas

four[2] ▶ 451, 724, 884 *adj* cuatro *adj inv*

four: **~-poster (bed)** /ˈfɔːrˈpəʊstər ‖ ˌfɔːˈpəʊstə(r)/ *n*: *cama con cuatro columnas, gen con dosel*; **~-seater** /ˈfɔːrˈsiːtər ‖ ˈfɔːˌsiːtə(r)/ *n* coche *m*/avión *m* de cuatro plazas

foursome /ˈfɔːrsəm ‖ ˈfɔːsɒm/ *n*: *grupo de cuatro personas*

fourteen /ˈfɔːrˈtiːn ‖ ˌfɔːˈtiːn/ ▶ 451, 724, 884 *adj/n* catorce *adj inv/m*; *see also* FOUR[1]

fourteenth[1] /ˈfɔːrˈtiːnθ ‖ ˌfɔːˈtiːnθ/ ▶ 540, 725 *adj* decimocuarto

fourteenth[2] *adv* en decimocuarto lugar

fourteenth[3] ▶ 540, 543, 725 *n* (Math) catorceavo *m*; (part) catorceava parte *f*

fourth[1] /fɔːrθ ‖ fɔːθ/ ▶ 540, 725 *adj* cuarto

fourth[2] *adv* **(a)** (in position, time, order) en cuarto lugar **(b)** (fourthly) en cuarto lugar

fourth[3] ▶ 540, 725 *n* **1** (part) cuarto *m* **2** ~ **(gear)** (Auto) (*no art*) cuarta *f*

fourthly /ˈfɔːrθli ‖ ˈfɔːθli/ *adv* (*indep*) en cuarto lugar

four-wheel drive /ˈfɔːrhwiːl ‖ ˈfɔːwiːl/ *n* [U] tracción *f* integral

fowl /faʊl/ *n* (*pl* **~s** *or* **~**) ave *f*‡ (de corral)

fox[1] /fɑːks ‖ fɒks/ *n* zorro *m*

fox[2] *vt* (colloq) confundir

fox: **~glove** *n* [C U] dedalera *f*, digital *f*; **~-hunting** *n* [U] caza *f* del zorro

foyer /ˈfɔɪeɪ/ *n* (of theatre) foyer *m*; (of hotel) vestíbulo *m*

fracas /ˈfreɪkəs, ˈfrækəs ‖ ˈfrækɑː/ *n* (*pl* **fracases** *or* (BrE) **fracas** /-z/) (liter) altercado *m*

fraction /ˈfrækʃən/ ▶ 543 *n* fracción *f*

fracture[1] /ˈfræktʃər ‖ ˈfræktʃə(r)/ *n* fractura *f*

fracture[2] *vt* fracturar

fragile /ˈfrædʒəl ‖ˈfrædʒaɪl/ *adj* **(a)** ‹*object/china/glass*› frágil; ‹*relationship/link/agreement*› precario **(b)** ‹*person*› débil; ‹*health*› delicado

fragment /ˈfrægmənt/ *n* fragmento *m*

fragrance /ˈfreɪgrəns/ *n* (smell) fragancia *f*; (perfume) perfume *m*

fragrant /ˈfreɪgrənt/ *adj* fragante

frail /freɪl/ *adj* **-er, -est (a)** (physically delicate) ‹*person*› débil; ‹*health*› delicado **(b)** (morally weak) débil **(c)** (fragile) precario

frame[1] /freɪm/ *n* **(a)** (structure — of building, ship, plane) armazón *m or f*; (— of car, motorcycle, bed, door) bastidor *m*; (— of bicycle) cuadro *m*, marco *m* (Chi, Col) **(b)** (edge — of picture, window, door) marco *m* **(c) frames** *pl* (for spectacles) montura *f*

frame[2] *vt* **1** ‹*picture/photograph*› enmarcar*; ‹*plan/policy/question*› formular, elaborar **2** (incriminate unjustly) (colloq): **I was ~d** me tendieron una trampa para incriminarme

frame: **~ of mind** *n* (*pl* **~s of mind**) estado *m* de ánimo; **~work** *n* (basis) marco *m*; (plan) esquema *m*; (Eng) armazón *m or f*

franc /fræŋk/ *n* franco *m*

France /fræns ‖ frɑːns/ *n* Francia *f*

franchise /ˈfræntʃaɪz/ *n* **1** (Busn) **(a)** [U C] (right — to operate retail outlet) franquicia *f*; (— to market product, service) concesión *f* **(b)** [C] (retail outlet) franquicia *f* **2** (Pol frml) **the ~** el derecho de *or* al voto

frank[1] /fræŋk/ *adj* **-er, -est (a)** (candid) sincero **(b)** (outspoken) franco

frank[2] *vt* **(a)** ‹*letter/parcel/envelope*› franquear **(b)** (postmark) ‹*stamp/letter*› matasellar

frankfurter /ˈfræŋkfɜːrtər ‖ ˈfræŋkfɜːtə(r)/ *n* salchicha *f* de Frankfurt *or* (Arg, Col) de Viena, frankfurter *m* (Ur), vienesa *f* (Chi), salchicha *f* alemana (Ven)

frankincense /ˈfræŋkənsens ‖ ˈfræŋkɪnsens/ *n* [U] incienso *m*

frankly /ˈfræŋkli/ *adv* francamente

frantic /ˈfræntɪk/ *adj* **(a)** (very worried) desesperado **(b)** (frenzied) ‹*activity*› frenético

fraternal /frəˈtɜːrnl̩ ‖ frəˈtɜːnl/ *adj* ‹*love*› fraternal, fraterno; ‹*jealousy*› entre hermanos

fraternity /frəˈtɜːrnəti ‖ frəˈtɜːnəti/ *n* (*pl* **-ties**) **1** [U] (virtue of brotherhood) fraternidad *f* **2** [C] **(a)** (Relig) hermandad *f* **(b)** (university club) asociación *f* estudiantil

fraternize /ˈfrætərnaɪz ‖ ˈfrætənaɪz/ *vi* confraternizar*

fraud /frɔːd/ *n* **1** [U C] (deception) fraude *m* **2** [C] (person) farsante *mf*

fraudulent /ˈfrɔːdʒələnt ‖ ˈfrɔːdjʊlənt/ *adj* fraudulento

fraught /frɔːt/ *adj* **(a)** (*pred*) **to be ~ WITH sth** ‹*with danger/problems*› estar* lleno DE algo **(b)** (tense) ‹*atmosphere/relationship*› tirante

fray[1] /freɪ/ *vi* «*cloth/collar/rope*» deshilacharse; «*wire*» pelarse

fray[2] *n* refriega *f*

frayed /freɪd/ *adj* **(a)** ‹*collar/cloth*› deshilachado; ‹*rope/wire*› desgastado **(b)** ‹*nerves*› crispado; **tempers were getting ~** se estaban exaltando los ánimos

freak[1] /friːk/ *n* **(a)** (abnormal specimen) fenómeno *m*; (monster) monstruo *m* **(b)** (unnatural event) fenómeno *m*

freak[2] *adj* (*before n*) ‹*weather*› inusitado; ‹*happening*› inesperado

• **freak out** (sl) **1** [*v* + *adv*] flipar (arg), friquear(se) (Méx arg) **2** [*v* + *o* + *adv*] alucinar (fam), friquear (Méx arg)

freckle /ˈfrekəl/ *n* peca *f*

free¹ /fri:/ *adj* **freer** /ˈfri:ər ‖ ˈfri:ə(r)/, **freest** /ˈfri:əst ‖ ˈfri:ɪst/ **1 (a)** (at liberty) (*usu pred*) libre; **to set sb ~** dejar *or* poner* a algn en libertad **(b)** ‹*country/people/press*› libre; **the right of ~ speech** la libertad de expresión **(c)** (loose) suelto; **to work ~** soltarse* **2** (*pred*) (without, rid of) **~ FROM** *o* **OF sth** libre DE algo; **~ of** *o* **from additives** sin aditivos; **~ of charge** gratis **3** (costing nothing) ‹*ticket/sample*› gratis *adj inv*; ‹*schooling/health care*› gratuito **4** (not occupied) ‹*table/time*› libre

free² *adv* **(a)** (without payment) gratuitamente; **I got in for ~** (colloq) entré gratis **(b)** (without restriction) ‹*roam/run*› a su (*or* mi *etc*) antojo

free³ *vt* **1** (liberate) ‹*prisoner/hostage*› poner* *or* dejar en libertad; ‹*animal*› soltar*; ‹*nation/slave*› liberar **2 (a)** (release) ‹*bound person*› soltar*; ‹*trapped person*› rescatar **(b)** (loose, clear) ‹*sth stuck or caught*› desenganchar

-free /fri:/ *suff* **trouble~** sin problemas; **nuclear~ zone** zona *f* desnuclearizada

freedom /ˈfri:dəm/ *n* [U C] libertad *f*

freedom fighter *n* guerrillero, -ra *m,f*

free: **~-for-all** /ˈfri:fərˈɔ:l/ *n* gresca *f*; **~hold** *adj* (esp BrE): **~hold property** bien *m* raíz (*que se compra o vende en plena propiedad junto con el suelo sobre el que está edificado*); **~ kick** *n* (in soccer) tiro *m* libre; (in rugby) patada *f* libre

freelance¹ /ˈfri:læns ‖ ˈfri:lɑ:ns/ *adj* por cuenta propia, por libre (Esp)

freelance² *adv* por cuenta propia, por libre (Esp)

freely /ˈfri:li/ *adv* **1 (a)** (without restriction) libremente **(b)** (openly) ‹*speak/write*› con libertad **(c)** (willingly) ‹*offer*› de buen grado **2 (a)** (generously) ‹*spend/give*› a manos llenas **(b)** (copiously) ‹*flow/pour*› profusamente

free: **~mason** /ˈfri:ˈmeɪsən ‖ ˈfri:meɪsən/ *n* masón, -sona *m,f*, francmasón, -sona *m,f*; **~-range** /ˈfri:ˈreɪndʒ/ *adj* (BrE) ‹*chicken/eggs*› de granja; **~style** *n* estilo *m* libre; **~ trade** *n* [U] libre comercio *m*; **~way** *n* [C U] (AmE) autopista *f* (*sin peaje*); **~wheel** /ˈfri:ˈhwi:l ‖ ˌfri:ˈwi:l/ *vi*: **he ~wheeled down the hill** (on bike) bajó la cuesta sin pedalear; (in car) bajó la cuesta en punto muerto; **~ will** *n* [U]: **of one's own ~ will** por su (*or* mi *etc*) propia voluntad

freeze¹ /fri:z/ (*past* **froze**; *past p* **frozen**) *vi* **1** «*pipe/lock/ground/person*» helarse*; **I'm freezing!** ¡estoy helado! **2** (stand still) quedarse inmóvil ■ **~** *vt* ‹*water/stream/pipe*› helar*; ‹*food*› congelar **2** (Fin) ‹*assets/account/prices*› congelar ■ **~** *v impers* **▶920** helar*

• **freeze over** [*v* + *adv*] helarse*

• **freeze up** [*v* + *adv*] helarse*

freeze² *n* congelación *f*; **a wage/price ~** una congelación salarial/de precios

freezer /ˈfri:zər ‖ ˈfri:zə(r)/ *n* (deep freeze) freezer *m*; (freezing compartment) congelador *m*

freezing¹ /ˈfri:zɪŋ/ **▶920** *adj* ‹*temperatures*› bajo cero; ‹*weather*› con temperaturas bajo cero; ‹*hands/feet*› helado; **it's ~ (cold) in here** aquí hace un frío que pela (fam)

freezing² *n* [U] **1 ~ (point)** punto *m* de congelación; **three degrees below ~** tres grados sobre/bajo cero **2** (process) congelación *f*

freight /freɪt/ *n* **(a)** [U] (goods transported) carga *f* **(b)** [U] (transportation) transporte *m*, flete *m* (AmL)

freighter /ˈfreɪtər ‖ ˈfreɪtə(r)/ *n* buque *m* de carga

freight train *n* tren *m* de carga

French¹ /frentʃ/ *adj* francés

French² *n* **(a)** [U] (language) francés *m* **(b)** (people) (+ *pl vb*) **the ~** los franceses

French: **~ bean** *pl n* (BrE) ⇒ GREEN BEAN; **~ doors** *pl n* (AmE) ⇒ **~** WINDOWS; **~ dressing** *n* [U] *aliño para ensaladas a base de aceite, vinagre y mostaza*; (AmE) *aderezo (para ensaladas) a base de aceite, vinagre y tomate*; **~ fries** *pl n* papas *fpl or* (Esp) patatas *fpl* fritas, papas *fpl* a la francesa (Col, Méx); **~man** /ˈfrentʃmən/ *n* (*pl* **-men** /-mən/) francés *m*; **~ windows** *pl n* puerta *f* ventana, cristalera *f* (Esp); **~woman** *n* francesa *f*

frenetic /frəˈnetɪk/ *adj* ‹*activity*› frenético; ‹*attempt*› desesperado

frenzy /ˈfrenzi/ *n* (*no pl*) frenesí *m*

frequency /ˈfri:kwənsi/ *n* [U C] (*pl* **-cies**) frecuencia *f*

frequent¹ /ˈfri:kwənt/ *adj* ‹*attempts/journeys*› frecuente; ‹*visitor*› asiduo

frequent² /fri:ˈkwent/ *vt* frecuentar

frequently /ˈfri:kwəntli/ *adv* con frecuencia, a menudo

fresh /freʃ/ *adj* **-er, -est 1 (a)** (not stale, frozen or canned) ‹*food*› fresco; **to get some ~ air** tomar el fresco **(b)** (not tired) ‹*complexion/appearance*› fresco **2** (not salty): **~ water** agua *f*‡ *dulce* **3 (a)** (new, clean) ‹*clothes/linen*› limpio **(b)** (new, additional) ‹*supplies/initiative*› nuevo

freshen /ˈfreʃən/ *vt* refrescar*

• **freshen up** [*v* + *adv*] lavarse

fresher /ˈfreʃər ‖ ˈfreʃə(r)/ *n* (BrE colloq) ⇒ FRESHMAN

freshly /ˈfreʃli/ *adv* recién

freshman /ˈfreʃmən/ *n* (*pl* **-men** /-mən/) (Educ) estudiante *mf* de primer año, mechón, -chona *m,f* (Chi fam)

freshness /ˈfreʃnəs ‖ ˈfreʃnɪs/ *n* [U] frescura *f*

freshwater /ˈfreʃˈwɔ:tər ‖ ˈfreʃˌwɔ:tə(r)/ *adj* (*before n*) de agua dulce

fret /fret/ *vi* **-tt-** preocuparse

fretful /ˈfretfəl/ *adj* **(a)** (querulous) quejoso **(b)** (anxious) inquieto

friar /ˈfraɪər ‖ ˈfraɪə(r)/ *n* fraile *m*

friction /ˈfrɪkʃən/ *n* [U] **1** (Phys, Tech) rozamiento *m*, fricción *f* **2** (discord) tirantez *f*

Friday /ˈfraɪdeɪ, -di/ **▶540** *n* viernes *m*; *see also* MONDAY

fridge /frɪdʒ/ *n* (colloq) nevera *f*, refrigerador *m*, frigorífico *m* (Esp), heladera *f* (RPl), refrigeradora *f* (Col, Per)

fried /fraɪd/ *adj* frito; **a ~ egg** un huevo frito *or* (Méx) estrellado

friend /frend/ *n* amigo, -ga *m,f*; **he soon made ~s with her** en poco tiempo se hizo amigo suyo

friendly /'frendli/ *adj* **-lier, -liest (a)** ‹*person/pet*› simpático; ‹*place/atmosphere*› agradable; ‹*welcome*› cordial; **to be ~ WITH sb** ser* amigo, -ga DE algn **(b)** (good-natured) ‹*rivalry/match*› amistoso

friendship /'frendʃɪp/ *n* [U C] amistad *f*

frieze /friːz/ *n* (on building, wall) friso *m*; (on wallpaper) greca *f*

frigate /'frɪgət ‖ 'frɪgɪt/ *n* fragata *f*

fright /fraɪt/ *n* **(a)** [U] (fear) miedo *m*; **to take ~ at sth** asustarse por algo **(b)** [C] (shock) susto *m*

frighten /'fraɪtn̩/ *vt* asustar

• **frighten away, frighten off** [*v + o + adv, v + adv + o*] espantar

frightened /'fraɪtn̩d/ *adj* ‹*person/animal*› asustado; **to be ~ OF sb/sth** tenerle* miedo A algn/algo

frightening /'fraɪtn̩ɪŋ/ *adj* ‹*experience*› espantoso; (stronger) aterrador

frightful /'fraɪtfəl/ *adj* **1** (horrific) aterrador **2** (BrE colloq) (very unpleasant) horroroso

frigid /'frɪdʒəd ‖ 'frɪdʒɪd/ *adj* frígido

frill /frɪl/ *n* volante *m or* (RPl) volado *m or* (Méx) olán *m or* (Chi) vuelo *m*; **a ceremony with no ~s** una ceremonia sencilla

frilly /'frɪli/ *adj* **-lier, -liest** ‹*dress/petticoat*› de volantes *or* (RPl) de volados *or* (Méx) de olanes *or* (Chi) de vuelos

fringe /frɪndʒ/ *n* **1** (on shawl, carpet, tablecloth) fleco *m* **2** (of hair) (BrE) flequillo *m*, cerquillo *m* (AmL), fleco *m* (Méx), chasquilla *f* (Chi), capul *m* (Col), pollina *f* (Ven) **3** (periphery) (*often pl*): **to live on the ~(s) of society** vivir al margen de la sociedad; (*before n*) ‹*area/group*› marginal; ‹*music/medicine*› alternativo

fringe benefit *n* **(a)** (Lab Rel) incentivo *m* **(b)** (incidental advantage) ventaja *f* adicional

frisk /frɪsk/ *vt* cachear, catear (Méx)

frisky /'frɪski/ *adj* **-kier, -kiest** retozón

fritter /'frɪtər ‖ 'frɪtə(r)/ *n* buñuelo *m*, fruta *f* de sartén (Esp)

• **fritter away** [*v + o + adv, v + adv + o*] ‹*money*› malgastar; ‹*fortune*› dilapidar; ‹*time*› desperdiciar

frivolous /'frɪvələs/ *adj* frívolo

frizzy /'frɪzi/ *adj* **-zier, -ziest** crespo, chino (Méx), como mota (CS)

frock /frɑːk ‖ frɒk/ *n* vestido *m*

frog /frɔːg ‖ frɒg/ *n* rana *f*; ***to have a ~ in the*** *o* ***one's throat*** tener* carraspera

frog: **~man** /'frɔːgmən ‖ 'frɒgmən/ *n* (*pl* **-men** /-mən/) hombre *m* rana; **~spawn** *n* [U] (BrE) huevos *mpl* de rana

frolic /'frɑːlɪk ‖ 'frɒlɪk/ *vi* **-ck-** retozar*

from /frɑːm ‖ frɒm, *weak form* frəm/ *prep* **1** (indicating starting point) desde; **~ the beginning** desde el principio **2** (indicating distance): **2cm ~ the edge** a 2cm del borde; **we're still three hours ~ Tulsa** todavía faltan tres horas para llegar a Tulsa **3** (after): **~ today** a partir de hoy; **50 years ~ now** dentro de 50 años **4** (indicating origin) de; **I'm ~ Texas** soy de Texas; **the flight ~ Madrid** el vuelo procedente de Madrid; **a letter ~ my lawyer** una carta de mi abogado **5 from ... to ...**; **they flew ~ New York to Lima** volaron de Nueva York a Lima; **they stretch ~ Derbyshire to the borders of Scotland** se extienden desde el condado de Derbyshire hasta el sur de Escocia; **we work ~ nine to five** trabajamos de nueve a cinco; **~ $50 to $100** entre 50 y 100 dólares **6** (as a result of) de; **his eyes were red ~ crying** tenía los ojos rojos de tanto llorar; **~ experience I would say that** ... según mi experiencia diría que ... **7** (out of, off) de; **~ the cupboard/shelf** del armario/estante; **if you take 5 ~ 10** si le restas 5 a 10 **8** (with preps & advs): **~ above/below** desde arriba/abajo; **he crawled out ~ under the table** salió gateando de debajo de la mesa

frond /frɑːnd ‖ frɒnd/ *n* (of fern) fronda *f*; (of palm) hoja *f*

front¹ /frʌnt/ *n* **1** (forward part) frente *m*; (of building) frente *m*, fachada *f*; (of dress) delantera *f*; **you sit in the ~** tú siéntate delante *or* (esp AmL) adelante **2** (*in phrases*) **in front** (*as adv*) delante, adelante (esp AmL); **in front of sb/sth** delante *or* (esp AmL) adelante de algn/algo; (facing) enfrente de algn/algo **3** (Meteo, Mil, Pol) frente *m* **4** (outward show) fachada *f*; (— for illegal activity) pantalla *f* **5** (overlooking sea) paseo *m* marítimo, malecón *m* (AmL), rambla *f* (RPl)

front² *adj* (at front) ‹*seat/wheel/leg*› delantero, de delante *or* (esp AmL) de adelante; **the ~ door** la puerta de (la) calle; **the ~ yard** *o* (BrE) **garden** el jardín del frente; **a ~-row seat** un asiento en primera fila

frontbencher /'frʌnt'bentʃər ‖ ˌfrʌnt'bentʃə(r)/ *n* (BrE) *diputado con cargo ministerial en el gobierno o en el gabinete fantasma*

frontier /frʌn'tɪr ‖ 'frʌntɪə(r)/ *n* frontera *f*; (*before n*) ‹*guard/zone*› fronterizo

frontispiece /'frʌntɪspiːs/ *n* frontispicio *m*

front room *n* salón *m*, living *m* (esp AmL)

frost¹ /frɔːst ‖ frɒst/ ▶ 920 *n* **(a)** [U C] (sub-zero temperature) helada *f* **(b)** [U] (frozen dew) escarcha *f*

frost² *vt* **1** (Meteo) helar*; ‹*plant*› quemar **2** (AmE Culin) bañar

frostbite /'frɔːstbaɪt ‖ 'frɒstbaɪt/ *n* [U] congelación *f*

frosting /'frɔːstɪŋ ‖ 'frɒstɪŋ/ *n* [U] (AmE Culin) baño *m*

frosty /'frɔːsti ‖ 'frɒsti/ ▶ 920 *adj* **-tier, -tiest** ‹*weather/air*› helado; ‹*night*› de helada; ‹*manner/reception*› glacial

froth /frɔːθ ‖ frɒθ/ *n* [U] espuma *f*

frothy /'frɔːθi ‖ 'frɒθi/ *adj* **frothier, frothiest** espumoso

frown¹ /fraʊn/ *vi* fruncir* el ceño; **to ~ AT sb** mirar a algn con el ceño fruncido

• **frown on, frown upon** [*v + prep + o*]: **that sort of thing is ~ed upon** eso está muy mal visto

frown² *n* ceño *m* fruncido

froze /frəʊz/ *past of* FREEZE¹

frozen¹ /'frəʊzn̩/ *past p of* FREEZE¹

frozen² *adj* **1 (a)** ‹*water/lock/pipe/food*› congelado; ‹*region*› helado; **my feet are ~** (colloq) tengo los pies helados **(b)** (Fin) ‹*prices/incomes*› congelado **2** (motionless): **I stood there ~ (to the spot)** me quedé allí clavado, paralizado por el terror

frugal /'fru:gəl/ *adj* frugal

fruit /fru:t/ *n* **1 (a)** [U] (collectively) fruta *f*; **dried ~** (BrE) fruta *f* seca; **~ juice** jugo *m* *or* (Esp) zumo *m* de frutas **(b)** [C] (type — as food) fruta *f*; (Bot) fruto *m* **2** [U C] (product) fruto *m* ***to bear ~*** dar* (su) fruto

fruit: **~cake** *n* [U C] plum-cake *m*, ponqué *m* de frutas (Col), fruit cake *m* (Méx), budín *m* inglés (RPl); **~ cocktail** *n* [U C] (dish) ensalada *f* *or* macedonia *f* *or* cóctel *m* de frutas; **~ cup** *n* [U C] (AmE) ⇒ ~ COCKTAIL

fruitful /'fru:tfəl/ *adj* provechoso, fructífero

fruition /fru:'ɪʃən/ *n* [U] (frml): **their plan never came to ~** su plan nunca cristalizó

fruitless /'fru:tləs ‖ 'fru:tlɪs/ *adj* infructuoso

fruit: **~ machine** *n* (BrE) máquina *f* tragamonedas *or* (Esp tb) tragaperras; **~ salad** *n* [U C] **(a)** (AmE) *ensalada de frutas, gen en gelatina* **(b)** (BrE) ⇒ FRUIT COCKTAIL

frustrate /'frʌstreɪt ‖ frʌs'treɪt/ *vt* frustrar

frustrated /'frʌstreɪtəd ‖ frʌs'treɪtɪd/ *adj* **(a)** (thwarted) frustrado **(b)** (dissatisfied) descontento; **(sexually) ~** sexualmente frustrado

frustrating /'frʌstreɪtɪŋ ‖ frʌs'treɪtɪŋ/ *adj* frustrante

frustration /frʌs'treɪʃən/ *n* [U C] frustración *f*

fry¹ /fraɪ/ **fries, frying, fried** *vt* freír* ■ **~** *vi* freírse*

fry² *n* (*pl* **fries**) **1 fries** *pl* (*French fries*) papas *or* (Esp) patatas fritas, papas *fpl* a la francesa (Col, Méx) **2** [U] **(a)** (+ *pl vb*) (Zool) alevines *mpl*, majuga *f* (Ur) **(b)** (people): **small ~** gente *f* de poca monta

frying pan /'fraɪɪŋ/, (AmE also) **fry pan** *n* sartén *f*, sartén *m* *or* *f* (AmL)

ft = **foot/feet**

fuchsia /'fju:ʃə/ *n* [C U] (Bot) fucsia *f*, aljaba *f* (RPl)

fuck /fʌk/ *vt* (vulg) (copulate with) joder (vulg), tirarse (vulg), follarse (Esp vulg), coger* (Méx, RPl, Ven vulg) ■ **~** *vi* (vulg) joder (vulg), tirar (vulg), coger* (Méx, RPl, Ven vulg), follar (Esp vulg), cachar (Chi, Per vulg)

• **fuck off** [*v* + *adv*] (vulg): **~ off!** ¡vete a la mierda! (vulg), ¡vete a tomar por (el) culo! (Esp vulg), ¡vete a la chingada! (Méx vulg), ¡andá a cagar! (RPl vulg)

fucking /'fʌkɪŋ/ *adj* (vulg) (*before n*): **~ hell!** ¡puta madre! (vulg)

fudge¹ /fʌdʒ/ *n* [U] (Culin) *especie de caramelo de dulce de leche*

fudge² *vt* (colloq) **(a)** (falsify) ‹*figures*› amañar **(b)** (evade) ‹*issue*› esquivar

fuel¹ /'fju:əl/ *n* [U C] combustible *m*

fuel² *vt* (BrE) **-ll- 1** ‹*ship/plane*› abastecer* de combustible; ‹*stove/furnace*› alimentar **2** ‹*hope/passion*› alimentar; ‹*debate*› avivar; ‹*fear*› exacerbar

fuel oil *n* [U] fuel-oil *m*

fugitive /'fju:dʒətɪv/ *n* fugitivo, -va *m,f*

fulfill, (BrE) **fulfil** /fʊl'fɪl/ **-ll-** *vt* **1 (a)** (carry out) ‹*duty*› cumplir con; ‹*task*› llevar a cabo **(b)** (obey, keep) ‹*order/promise/contract*› cumplir **(c)** (serve) ‹*need*› satisfacer* **(d)** (meet) ‹*requirements*› satisfacer* **2** (realize) ‹*ambition*› hacer* realidad; ‹*potential*› alcanzar* **3** (make content) ‹*person*› satisfacer*

fulfilled /fʊl'fɪld/ *adj* (*usu pred*) realizado

fulfillment, (BrE) **fulfilment** /fʊl'fɪlmənt/ *n* [U] **(a)** (of duty, promise) cumplimiento *m* **(b)** (satisfaction): **her family gave her a sense of ~** su familia la hacía sentirse realizada

full¹ /fʊl/ *adj* **-er, -est 1** (filled) lleno; **I'm ~ (up)** estoy lleno; **~ OF sth** lleno DE algo **2 (a)** (complete) ‹*report/description*› detallado; ‹*name/answer*› completo; **you have my ~ support** tienes todo mi apoyo; **to lead a very ~ life** llevar una vida muy activa **(b)** (maximum): **at ~ speed** a toda velocidad; **~ employment** (Econ) pleno empleo *m* **3** ‹*figure*› regordete

full² *adv* **1** (*as intensifier*) **~ well** muy bien **2** (directly): **the sun was shining ~ in my face** el sol me daba de lleno en la cara **3 in full**: **write your name in ~** escriba su nombre completo; **it will be paid in ~** será pagado en su totalidad

full: **~-blown** /'fʊl'bləʊn/ *adj* (*before n*) verdadero; **~-fledged** /'fʊl'fledʒd/ *adj* (AmE) **1** ‹*chick*› capaz de volar; **2** ‹*lawyer/nurse*› hecho y derecho; **~-grown** /'fʊl'grəʊn/ *adj* (*before n*) totalmente desarrollado; **~-length** /'fʊl'leŋθ/ *adj* ‹*portrait/mirror*› de cuerpo entero; ‹*dress/skirt*› largo

fullness /'fʊlnəs ‖ 'fʊlnɪs/ *n* [U] plenitud *f*; ***in the ~ of time*** con el tiempo

full: **~-scale** /'fʊl'skeɪl/ *adj* **1** (actual size) a escala natural; **2** (major) ‹*work*› de envergadura; ‹*investigation*› a fondo; ‹*test*› a escala real; ‹*war*› declarado; **~-size** /'fʊl'saɪz/, **~-sized** /-d/ *adj* **(a)** (life-size) de tamaño natural **(b)** (of adult size) ‹*bicycle/bed*› de adulto; **~ stop** *n* (BrE) punto *m*

full-time¹ /'fʊltaɪm/ *adj* ‹*student/soldier*› de tiempo completo; ‹*employment/post*› de jornada completa

full-time² /fʊl'taɪm/ *adv* a tiempo completo

fully /'fʊli/ *adv* **1 (a)** (completely): **I ~ understand** comprendo muy bien; **she's a ~ trained nurse** es una enfermera diplomada **(b)** (in full) enteramente **2** (at least) por lo menos, como poco

fully-fledged /'fʊli'fledʒd/ *adj* (BrE) ⇒ FULL-FLEDGED

fulsome /'fʊlsəm/ *adj* ‹*praise*› empalagoso; ‹*manner*› excesivamente efusivo

fumble /'fʌmbəl/ *vi*: **she ~d in her pockets** revolvió en sus bolsillos; **he ~d for the right words** tartamudeó, tratando de encontrar las palabras adecuadas; **she ~d with her buttons** intentó torpemente abrocharse/desabrocharse

fume /fju:m/ *vi* **1** (smoke) (Chem) despedir* gases **2** (be angry) (colloq): **she was absolutely fuming** estaba que echaba humo

fumes /fju:mz/ *pl n* gases *mpl*

fumigate /'fju:məgeɪt ‖ 'fju:mɪgeɪt/ *vt* fumigar*

fun /fʌn/ *n* [U] diversión *f*; **to have ~** divertirse*; **he's good ~** es muy divertido; **to do sth for ~** hacer* algo por gusto; ***to make ~ of sb/sth*** reírse* de algn/algo

function[1] /ˈfʌŋkʃən/ *n* **1** (of tool, organ, person) función *f*; **to carry out/perform a ~** cumplir/desempeñar una función **2** (reception, party) recepción *f* **3** (Comput, Math) función *f*

function[2] *vi* **(a)** (operate) «*machine/organ*» funcionar **(b)** (serve) **to ~ AS sth** «*object/building*» hacer* (las veces) DE algo

functional /ˈfʌŋkʃnəl ‖ ˈfʌŋkʃənl/ *adj* **(a)** (functioning) ‹*machine/part*› en buen estado (de funcionamiento) **(b)** (practical) ‹*furniture/design*› funcional

fund[1] /fʌnd/ *n* **(a)** (money reserve) fondo *m* **(b) funds** *pl* (resources, money) fondos *mpl*

fund[2] *vt* **(a)** (finance) ‹*research/organization*› financiar **(b)** (Fin) ‹*debt*› consolidar

fundamental /ˈfʌndəˈmentl/ *adj* **(a)** (basic) ‹*principle/error*› fundamental **(b)** (essential) ‹*skill/constituent*› esencial **(c)** (intrinsic) ‹*absurdity/truth*› intrínseco

fundamentalism /ˈfʌndəˈmentəlɪzəm/ *n* [U] integrismo *m*, fundamentalismo *m*

fundamentalist /ˈfʌndəˈmentləst ‖ ˈfʌndəˈmentəlɪst/ *n* integrista *mf*, fundamentalista *mf*

fundamentally /ˈfʌndəˈmentli ‖ ˌfʌndəˈmentəli/ *adv* **(a)** (radically) ‹*different/mistaken*› fundamentalmente **(b)** (in essence) ‹*correct/justified*› esencialmente

fundamentals /ˈfʌndəˈmentlz/ *pl n* fundamentos *mpl*

funding /ˈfʌndɪŋ/ *n* [U] (act) financiación *f*; (resources) fondos *mpl*

fund-raising /ˈfʌndˈreɪzɪŋ ‖ ˈfʌndˌreɪzɪŋ/ *n* [U] recaudación *f* de fondos

funeral /ˈfjuːnərəl/ *n* funerales *mpl*

funeral: **~ director** *n* (frml) director, -tora *m,f* de una funeraria; **~ home** (AmE), **~ parlour** (BrE) *n* funeraria *f*

funfair /ˈfʌnfer ‖ ˈfʌnfeə(r)/ *n* (BrE) (traveling) feria *f*; (permanent) parque *m* de diversiones *or* (Esp) de atracciones

fungus /ˈfʌŋgəs/ *n* [C U] (*pl* **fungi** /ˈfʌŋgaɪ/) hongo *m*

funnel /ˈfʌnl/ *n* **(a)** (for pouring) embudo *m* **(b)** (on steamship, steam engine) (BrE) chimenea *f*

funnily /ˈfʌnli ‖ ˈfʌnɪli/ *adv* **(a)** (strangely) (esp BrE) de modo extraño **(b) ~ enough** (*indep*) casualmente

funny /ˈfʌni/ *adj* **-nier, -niest 1** (amusing) ‹*joke*› gracioso; ‹*person*› divertido **2** (strange) raro; **(it's) ~ (that) you should mention it** es curioso que lo menciones; **to taste/smell ~** saber*/oler* raro **3** (colloq) (unwell): **I feel a bit ~** me siento medio mal

fur /fɜːr ‖ fɜː(r)/ *n* **(a)** [U] (of animal) (Zool) pelo *m*, pelaje *m*; (Clothing) piel *f*; (*before n*) **~ coat** abrigo *m* de piel *or* (Esp tb) de pieles **(b)** [C] (pelt) piel *f*

furious /ˈfjʊriəs ‖ ˈfjʊəriəs/ *adj* **(a)** (angry) furioso **(b)** (violent, intense) ‹*struggle*› feroz; ‹*speed*› vertiginoso; ‹*storm*› violento; ‹*activity*› febril

furlough /ˈfɜːrləʊ ‖ ˈfɜːləʊ/ *n* [U C] (AmE) permiso *m*, licencia *f*; **on ~** de permiso, con licencia

furnace /ˈfɜːrnəs ‖ ˈfɜːnɪs/ *n* (in industry) horno *m*; (for heating) caldera *f*

furnish /ˈfɜːrnɪʃ ‖ ˈfɜːnɪʃ/ *vt* **1 (a)** ‹*house/room*› amueblar, amoblar* (AmL) **(b) furnished** *past p* ‹*room/apartment*› amueblado, amoblado (AmL) **2** (supply) (frml) proporcionar; **to ~ sb WITH sth** ‹*with information*› proporcionarle algo a algn

furnishings /ˈfɜːrnɪʃɪŋz ‖ ˈfɜːnɪʃɪŋz/ *pl n*: *mobiliario, cortinas, alfombras, etc*

furniture /ˈfɜːrnɪtʃər ‖ ˈfɜːnɪtʃə(r)/ *n* [U] (in home, office) muebles *mpl*, mobiliario *m*; **a piece of ~** un mueble; (*before n*) **~ mover** *o* (BrE) **remover** empresa *f* de mudanzas; **~ polish** cera *f* para muebles

furor /ˈfjʊrɔːr ‖ ˈfjʊərɔː(r)/, (BrE) **furore** /fjʊˈrɔːri ‖ fjʊəˈrɔːri/ *n* escándalo *m*

furrow /ˈfɜːrəʊ ‖ ˈfʌrəʊ/ *n* surco *m*

furry /ˈfɜːri/ *adj* **-rier, -riest** ‹*animal*› peludo; ‹*toy*› de peluche; ‹*covering/lining*› afelpado

further[1] /ˈfɜːrðər ‖ ˈfɜːðə(r)/ *adv* **1** *comp of* FAR[1] 1 **(a)** (in distance): **they live even ~ away** ellos viven aún más lejos; **how much ~ is it?** ¿cuánto camino nos queda por hacer?; **~ on, there's another set of traffic lights** más adelante, hay otro semáforo **(b)** (in progress): **the legislation should have gone ~** la legislación debería haber ido más lejos; **have you got any ~ with that essay?** ¿has adelantado ese trabajo? **(c)** (in time): **we must look back even ~** tenemos que retroceder aún más en el tiempo; **this vase dates back even ~** este jarrón es aún más antiguo **(d)** (in extent, degree): **I'll look ~ into that possibility** voy a estudiar esa posibilidad más a fondo; **the situation is ~ complicated by her absence** el hecho de que ella no esté complica aún más la situación **2 further to** (Corresp) (*as prep*): **~ to your letter of June 6, ...** con relación a su carta del 6 de junio, ... **3** (furthermore) (*as linker*) además

further[2] *adj* más; **have you any ~ questions?** ¿tienen más preguntas?; **until ~ notice** hasta nuevo aviso

further[3] *vt* ‹*cause/aims*› promover*; ‹*career/interests*› favorecer*

further education *n* [U] (BrE) *programa de cursos de extensión cultural para adultos*

furthermore /ˈfɜːrðərmɔːr ‖ ˌfɜːðəˈmɔː(r)/ *adv* además

furthest /ˈfɜːrðəst ‖ ˈfɜːðɪst/ *adv superl of* FAR[1] 1

furtive /ˈfɜːrtɪv ‖ ˈfɜːtɪv/ *adj* **(a)** (stealthy) ‹*movement/look*› furtivo; ‹*person*› solapado **(b)** (suspicious, shifty) ‹*appearance*› sospechoso; ‹*manner*› solapado

furtively /ˈfɜːrtɪvli ‖ ˈfɜːtɪvli/ *adv* ‹*creep*› sigilosamente; ‹*peep/listen*› a hurtadillas

fury /ˈfjʊri ‖ ˈfjʊəri/ *n* [U C] (*pl* **furies**) ira *f*

fuse[1] /fjuːz/ *n* **1** (Elec) fusible *m*, plomo *m* (Esp), tapón *m* (CS) **2** (for explosives) mecha *f*

fuse[2] *vt* **1** (Elec) **(a)** (short-circuit) (BrE): **to ~ the lights** hacer* saltar los fusibles *or* (CS tb) los tapones, fundir los plomos (Esp) **(b) fused** *past p* con fusible **2 (a)** (melt together) alear **(b)** (merge) fusionar

fuse box *n* caja *f* de fusibles *or* (Esp tb) de plomos *or* (CS tb) de tapones

fuselage /ˈfjuːzəlɑːʒ/ *n* fuselaje *m*

fusion /ˈfjuːʒən/ *n* [U C] fusión *f*

fuss¹ /fʌs/ *n* [U] alboroto *m*; ***to kick up a ~*** armar un lío, montar un número (Esp fam); ***to make*** *o* (AmE also) ***raise a ~*** hacer* un escándalo

fuss² *vi* preocuparse

fussbudget /'fʌs'bʌdʒɪt/, (BrE also) **fusspot** /'fʌspɑ:t ‖ 'fʌspɒt/ *n* maniático, -ca *m,f*, mañoso, -sa *m,f* (AmL)

fussy /'fʌsi/ *adj* **-sier, -siest** exigente; **I'm a ~ eater** soy muy maniático *or* (AmL tb) mañoso para comer

futile /'fju:tl̩ ‖ 'fju:taɪl/ *adj* ‹*attempt*› inútil; ‹*suggestion/question*› trivial

futility /fjʊ'tɪləti/ *n* [U] inutilidad *f*

future¹ /'fju:tʃər ‖ 'fju:tʃə(r)/ *n* **1** (time ahead) **the ~** el futuro; **in ~** de ahora en adelante **2** [C U] (prospects) futuro *m*; **a job with a ~** un trabajo con futuro **3** (Ling) futuro *m* **4 futures** *pl* (Fin) futuros *mpl*

future² *adj* (*before n*) **(a)** ‹*husband/home*› futuro **(b)** (Ling): **the ~ tense** el futuro

futuristic /'fju:tʃə'rɪstɪk/ *adj* futurista

fuze /fju:z/ *n* (AmE) ⇒ FUSE¹ 2

fuzzy /'fʌzi/ *adj* **-zier, -ziest 1** ‹*hair*› muy rizado; ‹*beard*› enmarañado **2** (blurred) ‹*sound*› confuso; ‹*picture/outline*› borroso

Gg

G, g /dʒi:/ *n* **(a)** (letter) G, g *f* **(b)** (Mus) sol *m*

g ▶ 322 (= **gram(s)**) g., gr.

G (in US) (Cin) (= **general**) apta para todo público

GA, Ga = **Georgia**

gab /gæb/ *vi* **-bb-** (colloq) charlar (fam)

gabble /'gæbəl/ *vi* (speak incoherently) hablar atropelladamente, farfullar; (speak quickly) parlotear (fam)

gable /'geɪbəl/ *n* gablete *m*; **~ (end)** hastial *m*

gadget /'gædʒət ‖ 'gædʒɪt/ *n* (colloq) aparato *m*, chisme *m* (Esp fam)

Gaelic /'geɪlɪk/ *n* [U] gaélico *m*

gaffe /gæf/ *n* metedura *f or* (AmL tb) metida *f* de pata (fam)

gag¹ /gæg/ *n* **1** (for mouth) mordaza *f* **2** (joke) (colloq) chiste *m*, gag *m*

gag² **-gg-** *vt* amordazar* ■ **~** *vi* hacer* arcadas

gage /geɪdʒ/ *vt/n* (AmE) ⇒ GAUGE[1,2]

gaggle /'gægəl/ *n* (of geese) bandada *f*

gain¹ /geɪn/ *vt* **1** (acquire) ‹*control*› conseguir*; ‹*experience*› adquirir*; ‹*recognition*› obtener* **2** (increase) ‹*strength/speed*› ganar **3** ‹*time*› ganar; **my watch is ~ing ten minutes a day** mi reloj (se) adelanta diez minutos por día ■ **~** *vi* **1 (a)** (improve) **to ~ in value** subir *or* aumentar de valor; **she's gradually ~ing in confidence** poco a poco va adquiriendo confianza en sí misma **(b)** (benefit) beneficiarse **2 (a)** (go fast) «*clock/watch*» adelantar(se) **(b)** (move nearer) **to ~ ON sb** acortar (las) distancias con respecto a algn

gain² *n* **1** [U C] (profit) ganancia *f* **2** [C U] (increase) aumento *m*

gainful /'geɪnfəl/ *adj* retribuido

gait /geɪt/ *n* (*no pl*) modo *m* de andar

gala /'gælə, 'geɪlə ‖ 'gɑ:lə/ *n* fiesta *f*

Galapagos Islands /gə'lɑ:pəgəs ‖ gə'læpəgəs/ *pl n* **the ~ ~** las Islas Galápagos

galaxy /'gæləksi/ *n* (*pl* **-xies**) galaxia *f*

gale /geɪl/ ▶ 920 *n* vendaval *f*; (*before n*) **~-force winds** vientos *mpl* (huracanados)

Galicia /gə'lɪʃiə, gə'lɪsiə/ *n* Galicia *f*

Galician¹ /gə'lɪʃiən, gə'lɪsiən/ *n* **(a)** [C] (person) gallego, -ga *m,f* **(b)** [U] (language) gallego *m*

Galician² *adj* gallego

gallant *adj* **(a)** /'gælənt/ (brave) (liter) aguerrido (liter) **(b)** /gə'lænt/ (chivalrous) galante

gall bladder /gɔ:l/ *n* vesícula *f* (biliar)

galleon /'gæliən/ *n* galeón *m*

gallery /'gæləri/ *n* (*pl* **-ries**) **1** (Art) museo *m* (de Bellas Artes); (commercial) galería *f* (de arte) **2** (Archit) galería *f*; (for press, spectators) tribuna *f*

galley /'gæli/ *n* **1** (ship) galera *f* **2** (kitchen on boat, plane) cocina *f*

gallon /'gælən/ *n* galón *m* (*EEUU: 3,78 litros, RU: 4,55 litros*)

gallop¹ /'gæləp/ *n* galope *m*

gallop² *vi* galopar

gallows /'gæləʊz/ *n* (*pl* **~**) (+ *sing o pl vb*) horca *f*

gallstone /'gɔ:lstəʊn/ *n* cálculo *m* biliar

galore /gə'lɔ:r ‖ gə'lɔ:(r)/ *adj* (*after n*) en abundancia

galvanize /'gælvənaɪz/ *vt* **1** (rouse) **to ~ sb** (INTO sth/-ING) impulsar a algn (A algo /+ INF) **2 galvanized** *past p* ‹*iron/steel*› galvanizado

Gambia /'gæmbiə/ *n* Gambia *f*

gambit /'gæmbət ‖ 'gæmbɪt/ *n* (stratagem) táctica *f*; (in chess) gambito *m*

gamble¹ /'gæmbəl/ *vi* jugar*; **to ~ on a horse** apostar* a un caballo ■ **~** *vt* jugarse*

gamble² *n* (*no pl*) **(a)** (bet) apuesta *f* **(b)** (risk): **to take a ~** arriesgarse*

gambler /'gæmblər ‖ 'gæmblə(r)/ *n* jugador, -dora *m,f*

gambling /'gæmblɪŋ/ *n* [U] juego *m*

gambol /'gæmbəl/ *vi*, (BrE) **-ll-** retozar*

game¹ /geɪm/ *n* **1** [C] **(a)** (amusement) juego *m* **(b)** (type of sport) deporte *m* **2** [C] **(a)** (complete match) (Sport) partido *m*; (in board games, cards) partida *f* **(b)** [C] (part of tennis, squash match) juego *m* **3** [C] (underhand scheme, ploy) juego *m* **4** [U] (in hunting) caza *f*; **big ~** caza mayor **5** [U] (Culin) caza *f*

game² *adj* **we're going swimming, are you ~?** vamos a nadar ¿te apuntas?; **she's ~ for anything** se apunta a todo

game: **~keeper** *n* guardabosque(s) *mf*; **~ reserve** *n* coto *m* de caza; **~ show** *n* programa *m* concurso

gammon /'gæmən/ *n* [U] (esp BrE) jamón *m* fresco

gamut /'gæmət/ *n* gama *f*; **to run the (whole) ~ of sth** cubrir* toda la gama de algo

gander /'gændər ‖'gændə(r)/ *n* (Zool) ganso *m* (*macho*)

gang /gæŋ/ *n* (of criminals) banda *f*; (of youths, children) pandilla *f*

• **gang up** [*v* + *adv*] (colloq) **to ~ up** AGAINST *o* ON **sb** ponerse*/estar* en contra de algn

gang: **~land** *n* (journ) hampa *f*‡, mundo *m* del crimen organizado; **~plank** *n* plancha *f*

gangrene /'gæŋgri:n/ *n* [U] gangrena *f*

gangster /'gæŋstər ‖'gæŋstə(r)/ *n* gángster *mf*

gangway /'gæŋweɪ/ *n* **1** (walkway) pasarela *f* **2** (between rows of seats) (BrE) pasillo *m*

gantlet /'gɔ:ntlət/ *n* (AmE) ⇒ GAUNTLET

gaol /dʒeɪl/ *n/vt* (esp BrE) ⇒ JAIL[1,2]

gap /gæp/ *n* **1** (space) espacio *m*; (in fence, hedge) hueco *m* **2 (a)** (in knowledge) laguna *f* **(b)** (in time) intervalo *m*, interrupción *f* **(c)** (disparity) distancia *f*, brecha *f* **(d)** (void) vacío *m*

gape /geɪp/ *vi* **1** (stare) mirar boquiabierto **2** (be open) estar* abierto

gaping /'geɪpɪŋ/ *adj* ‹*wound*› abierto; ‹*hole*› enorme

garage /gə'rɑ:ʒ ‖'gærɑ:dʒ, -ɪdʒ/ *n* **1** (for parking) garaje *m*, garage *m* (esp AmL) **2 (a)** (for repairs) taller *m* (mecánico), garaje *m*, garage *m* (esp AmL) **(b)** (for fuel) (BrE) ⇒ GAS STATION

garb /gɑ:rb ‖gɑ:b/ *n* [U] (liter *or* hum) atuendo *m* (liter *o* hum)

garbage /'gɑ:rbɪdʒ ‖'gɑ:bɪdʒ/ *n* [U] **(a)** (AmE) (refuse) basura *f*; (*before n*) **~ dump** vertedero *m* (de basuras), basurero *m*, basural *m* (AmL) **(b)** (junk) (colloq) trastos *mpl*, cachivaches *mpl* (fam), porquerías *fpl* (fam); **this book is absolute ~** este libro es una auténtica porquería

garbage: **~ bag** *n* AmE bolsa *f* de la basura; **~ can** *n* (AmE) cubo *m or* (CS) tacho *m or* (Col) caneca *f or* (Méx) bote *m or* (Ven) tobo *m* de la basura; **~man** /'gɑ:rbɪdʒ'mæn/ *n* (*pl* **-men** /-men/) (AmE) basurero *m*; **~ truck** *n* (AmE) camión *m* de la basura

garbled /'gɑ:bəld ‖'gɑ:bəld/ *adj* ‹*account*› confuso; ‹*message*› incomprensible

garden¹ /'gɑ:rdn̩ ‖'gɑ:dn̩/ *n* **(a)** (for ornamental plants) jardín *m*; (for vegetables) huerta *f*, huerto *m* **(b) gardens** *pl* (public, on private estate) jardines *mpl*, parque *m*

garden² *vi* trabajar en el jardín

garden center, (BrE) **garden centre** *n* vivero *m*, centro *m* de jardinería

gardener /'gɑ:rdnər ‖'gɑ:dnə(r)/ *n* jardinero, -ra *m,f*

gardening /'gɑ:rdnɪŋ ‖'gɑ:dnɪŋ/ *n* [U] jardinería *f*; (vegetable growing) horticultura *f*; **he does the ~** él se encarga del jardín

garden: **~ party** *n* recepción *f* al aire libre; **~-variety** *adj* (AmE colloq) (*before n*) vulgar *or* común y corriente

gargle /'gɑ:rgəl ‖'gɑ:gəl/ *vi* hacer* gárgaras

gargoyle /'gɑ:rgɔɪl ‖'gɑ:gɔɪl/ *n* gárgola *f*

garish /'gerɪʃ ‖'geərɪʃ/ *adj* ‹*color*› chillón, charro (AmL fam); ‹*garment*› estridente, charro (AmL fam)

garland /'gɑ:rlənd ‖'gɑ:lənd/ *n* guirnalda *f*

garlic /'gɑ:rlɪk ‖'gɑ:lɪk/ *n* [U] ajo *m*

garment /'gɑ:rmənt ‖'gɑ:mənt/ *n* prenda *f* (de ropa)

garnet /'gɑ:rnət ‖'gɑ:nɪt/ *n* [U C] granate *m*

garnish¹ /'gɑ:rnɪʃ ‖'gɑ:nɪʃ/ *vt* adornar

garnish² *n* [C U] adorno *m*, aderezo *m*; (more substantial) guarnición *f*

garret /'gærət/ *n* buhardilla *f*

garrison /'gærəsən ‖'gærɪsən/ *n* **(a)** (place) plaza *f* fuerte *or* de armas **(b)** (troops) guarnición *f*

garrulous /'gærələs/ *adj* charlatán

garter /'gɑ:rtər ‖'gɑ:tə(r)/ *n* liga *f*

gas¹ /gæs/ *n* (*pl* **gases** *or* **gasses**) **1** [U C] (Phys) gas *m* **2** [U] **(a)** (fuel) gas *m*; (*before n*) ‹*ring/heater*› de *or* a gas **(b)** (anesthetic) gas *m* **3** [U] (gasoline) (AmE) ⇒ GASOLINE **4** [U] (flatulence) (AmE) gases *mpl*

gas² *vt* **-ss-** (Mil) gasear; (kill) asfixiar con gas; (in gas chamber) ejecutar en la cámara de gas

gas chamber *n* cámara *f* de gas

gaseous /'gæsiəs/ *adj* gaseoso

gash¹ /gæʃ/ *n* tajo *m*, corte *m* profundo

gash² *vt* hacer* un tajo en, cortar (*profundamente*)

gasket /'gæskət ‖'gæskɪt/ *n* junta *f*

gas: **~light** *n* [U] (illumination) luz *f* de gas; **~ mask** *n* máscara *f* antigás

gasoline /'gæsəli:n/ *n* [U] (AmE) gasolina *f*, nafta *f* (RPl), bencina *f* (Andes)

gasp¹ /gæsp ‖gɑ:sp/ *vi* **(a)** (inhale sharply) dar* un grito ahogado **(b)** (pant) respirar entrecortadamente, jadear ■ **~** *vt* decir* jadeando

gasp² *n* exclamación *f*, grito *m* (*entrecortado o ahogado*)

gas: **~ pedal** *n* (esp AmE) acelerador *m*; **~ pump** *n* [C] (AmE) (in service station) surtidor *m*, bomba *f* bencinera (Andes); **~ station** *n* (AmE) estación *f* de servicio *or* (RPl tb) de nafta, gasolinera *f*, bomba *f* (Andes, Ven), grifo *m* (Per); **~ tank** *n* [C] (AmE) depósito *m or* tanque *m* de gasolina *or* (RPl) de nafta *or* (Andes) de bencina

gastric /'gæstrɪk/ *adj* gástrico

gastroenteritis /'gæstrəʊ,entə'raɪtəs ‖,gæstrəʊ,entə'raɪtɪs/ *n* [U] gastroenteritis *f*

gasworks /'gæswɜ:rks ‖'gæswɜ:ks/ *n* (*pl* **~**) (+ *sing o pl vb*) fábrica *f* de gas

gate /geɪt/ *n* **(a)** (to garden — wooden) puerta *f* (del jardín); (— wrought-iron) verja *f*, cancela *f* (Esp); (to field) tranquera *f* (AmL), portillo *m* (Esp) **(b)** (to castle, city) (*usu pl*) puerta *f* **(c)** (controlling admission) entrada *f* **(d)** (at airport) puerta *f* (de embarque)

gate: **~crash** *vi* colarse*; **~way** *n* verja *f*, portalón *m*

gather¹ /ˈgæðər ‖ ˈgæðə(r)/ *vi* congregarse*, reunirse* ■ **~** *vt* **1 (a)** (collect) ‹*wood/berries*› recoger*, coger* (esp Esp); ‹*information*› reunir*, juntar; ‹*people*› reunir*; **to ~ dust** juntar *or* acumular polvo **(b)** ‹*thoughts*› poner* en orden; ‹*strength*› juntar, hacer* acopio de **(c)** ‹*speed*› ir* adquiriendo **2** (conclude) deducir*; **I ~ you're moving** tengo entendido que te mudas (de casa) **3** (by sewing) fruncir*

• **gather in** [*v + o + adv, v + adv + o*] recoger*

gather² *n* fruncido *m*, frunce *m*

gathering¹ /ˈgæðərɪŋ/ *n* (meeting) reunión *f*; (group of people) concurrencia *f*

gathering² *adj* (*before n*) creciente; **the ~ storm** la tormenta que se avecinaba

gaudy /ˈgɔːdi/ *adj* chillón, charro (AmL fam)

gauge¹, (AmE also) **gage** /geɪdʒ/ *vt* **(a)** (estimate) ‹*size*› calcular **(b)** (judge) ‹*effects*› evaluar* **(c)** (measure) medir*

gauge², (AmE also) **gage** *n* **1** (instrument) indicador *m* **2** (measure, indication) indicio *m* **3** (Rail): **narrow ~** vía *f* estrecha, trocha *f* angosta (CS)

gaunt /gɔːnt/ *adj* ‹*person*› descarnado, delgado y adusto; (from illness, tiredness) demacrado

gauntlet /ˈgɔːntlət ‖ ˈgɔːntlɪt/ *n* guante *m* (*con el puño largo*); (of suit of armor) guantelete *m*, manopla *f*

gauze /gɔːz/ *n* [U] (Tex, Med) gasa *f*; (fine mesh) malla *f*

gave /geɪv/ *past of* GIVE¹

gavel /ˈgævəl/ *n* mazo *m or* martillo *m* (*usado por jueces, subastadores etc*)

gay /geɪ/ *adj* **1** (homosexual) gay *adj inv* **2** (dated) (merry) alegre

gaze¹ /geɪz/ *vi* mirar (larga y fijamente); **to ~** AT **sth/sb** mirar algo/a algn

gaze² *n* mirada *f* (*larga y fija*)

gazelle /gəˈzel/ *n* (*pl* **~s** *or* **~**) gacela *f*

gazette /gəˈzet/ *n* gaceta *f*

gazetteer /ˈgæzəˈtɪr ‖ ˌgæzəˈtɪə(r)/ *n* índice *m* geográfico

GB = **Great Britain**

GCSE *n* [C U] (in UK) = **General Certificate of Secondary Education** ≈ bachillerato *m* elemental (*exámenes que se toman en diferentes asignaturas alrededor de los 16 años*)

gear¹ /gɪr ‖ ˈgɪə(r)/ *n* **1** (Mech Eng) engranaje *m*; (Auto) marcha *f*, velocidad *f*, cambio *m*; **to shift** *o* (BrE) **change ~** cambiar de marcha, cambiar de velocidad, hacer* un cambio **2** [U] **(a)** (equipment) equipo *m*; (tools) herramientas *fpl*; (*fishing* **~**) aparejo(s) *m(pl)* de pesca **(b)** (miscellaneous items) (colloq) cosas *fpl*

gear² *vt* orientar; **(to be) ~ed** TO/TOWARD **sth/sb** (estar*) dirigido A algo/algn

• **gear up 1** [*v + adv*] (prepare) prepararse **2** [*v + o + adv, v + adv + o*] preparar

gearbox /ˈgɪrbɑːks ‖ ˈgɪəbɒks/ *n* (Auto) caja *f* de cambios *or* velocidades

gee /dʒiː/ *interj* (AmE colloq): **~, I'm sorry to hear that** oye, lo siento; **~, thanks!** ¡pero ... gracias!

geese /giːs/ *pl of* GOOSE

gel¹ /dʒel/ *n* [U] gel *m*

gel² *vi* **-ll- (a)** «*liquid*» gelificarse* **(b)** (BrE) «*plans/ideas*» cuajar

gelatin /ˈdʒelətn̩ ‖ ˈdʒelətɪn/, **gelatine** /ˈdʒelətiːn/ *n* [U] gelatina *f*

gem /dʒem/ *n* **(a)** (stone) gema *f*, piedra *f* preciosa/semipreciosa **(b)** (wonderful example) joya *f*

Gemini /ˈdʒemənaɪ, -niː ‖ ˈdʒemɪnaɪ, -niː/ *n* **(a)** (sign) (*no art*) Géminis **(b)** [C] (person) Géminis *or* géminis *mf*, geminiano, -na *m,f*

gender /ˈdʒendər ‖ ˈdʒendə(r)/ *n* **(a)** [U C] (Ling) género *m* **(b)** [U] (sex) sexo *m*

gene /dʒiːn/ *n* gen *m*, gene *m*

genealogy /ˈdʒiːniˈælədʒi/ *n* [U] genealogía *f*

general¹ /ˈdʒenrəl/ *adj* **1** (not detailed or specific) general; **in ~** en general **2** (widespread) ‹*tendency*› generalizado **3** (usual) general; **as a ~ rule** por lo general, por regla general **4** (chief) ‹*manager*› general **5** (Med) ‹*anesthetic*› general

general² *n* (Mil) general *mf*

general: **~ delivery** *n* [U] (AmE) lista *f* de correos, poste *f* restante (AmL); **~ election** *n* elecciones *fpl* generales

generalization /ˈdʒenrələˈzeɪʃən ‖ ˌdʒenrəlaɪˈzeɪʃən/ *n* generalización *f*

generalize /ˈdʒenrəlaɪz/ *vi/t* generalizar*

general knowledge *n* [U] cultura *f* general

generally /ˈdʒenrəli/ *adv* **(a)** (usually, as a rule) generalmente, por lo general **(b)** (broadly) (*indep*) **~ (speaking)** por lo general, en general **(c)** (as a whole) en general

general: **~ practitioner** *n* médico, -ca *m,f* de medicina general; **~ public** *n* **the ~ public** el público en general, el gran público; **~-purpose** *adj* ‹*tool*› para todo uso; ‹*dictionary*› de uso general; **~ store** *n* (AmE) tienda *f* (*que vende todo tipo de artículos en una comunidad pequeña*), almacén *m* (CS); **~ strike** *n* huelga *f* general, paro *m* general (AmL)

generate /ˈdʒenəreɪt/ *vt* generar

generation /ˈdʒenəˈreɪʃən/ *n* **1** [C] generación *f*; **the older ~** la gente de más edad; **first-~ computers** computadoras *fpl or* (Esp tb) ordenadores *mpl* de primera generación **2** [U] (act of generating) generación *f*

generation gap *n* brecha *f* generacional

generator /ˈdʒenəreɪtər ‖ ˈdʒenəreɪtə(r)/ *n* generador *m*, grupo *m* electrógeno

generic /dʒəˈnerɪk/ *adj* ‹*term*› genérico

generosity /ˈdʒenəˈrɑːsəti ‖ ˌdʒenəˈrɒsəti/ *n* [U] generosidad *f*

generous /ˈdʒenrəs ‖ ˈdʒenərəs/ *adj* **(a)** (openhanded) generoso **(b)** (ample, large) abundante, generoso

genetic /dʒəˈnetɪk ‖ dʒɪˈnetɪk/ *adj* genético

genetics /dʒə'netɪks ‖ dʒɪ'netɪks/ *n* (+ *sing vb*) genética *f*

genial /'dʒi:njəl ‖ 'dʒi:niəl/ *adj* ‹*person*› simpático; ‹*welcome/smile*› cordial

genie /'dʒi:ni/ *n* genio *m*

genitals /'dʒenətḷz ‖ 'dʒenɪtḷz/ *pl n* genitales *mpl*

genius /'dʒi:niəs/ *n* **1** [C] (clever person) genio *m* **2** [U] (brilliance) genialidad *f*

genre /'ʒɑ:nrə/ *n* género *m*

gent /dʒent/ *n* (BrE colloq) caballero *m*; Ⓢ **Gents** Caballeros

gentle /'dʒentl/ *adj* **gentler** /dʒentlər ‖ 'dʒen tlə(r)/, **gentlest** /'dʒentləst ‖ 'dʒentlɪst/ **1 (a)** ‹*person*› dulce; ‹*character*› suave **(b)** (of voice): **in a ~ voice** en un tono suave *or* dulce **2** ‹*murmur/breeze*› suave; ‹*exercise*› moderado; ‹*slope*› poco empinado; ‹*reminder*› discreto

gentleman /'dʒentlmən/ *n* (*pl* **-men** /-mən/) **(a)** (man) caballero *m*, señor *m* **(b)** (well-bred man) caballero *m*

gently /'dʒentli/ *adv* **(a)** (not roughly or violently) ‹*handle*› con cuidado; ‹*tap*› ligeramente; ‹*hint*› con tacto **(b)** (tenderly) dulcemente; (tactfully) con delicadeza

gentry /'dʒentri/ *n* (+ *sing o pl vb*) alta burguesía *f*, pequeña nobleza *f*

genuine /'dʒenjuən ‖ 'dʒenjʊɪn/ *adj* **(a)** ‹*interest/person*› genuino, sincero; ‹*inquiry/buyer/mistake*› serio; **it was a ~ mistake** fue realmente un error **(b)** ‹*antique*› auténtico; ‹*leather*› legítimo

genuinely /'dʒenjuənli ‖ 'dʒenjʊɪnli/ *adv* **(a)** (sincerely) sinceramente **(b)** (really) realmente

geographical /'dʒi:ə'græfɪkəl/ *adj* geográfico

geography /dʒi'ɑ:grəfi ‖ dʒɪ'ɒgrəfi/ *n* [U] geografía *f*

geological /'dʒi:ə'lɑ:dʒɪkəl ‖ ˌdʒiə'lɒdʒɪkəl/ *adj* geológico

geologist /dʒi'ɑ:lədʒəst ‖ dʒi'ɒlədʒɪst/ *n* geólogo, -ga *m,f*

geology /dʒi'ɑ:lədʒi ‖ dʒi'ɒlədʒi/ *n* [U] geología *f*

geometrical /'dʒi:ə'metrɪkəl ‖ ˌdʒiə'metrɪkəl/ *adj* geométrico

geometry /dʒi:'ɑ:mətri ‖ dʒi'ɒmətri/ *n* [U] geometría *f*

Georgia /'dʒɔ:rdʒə ‖ 'dʒɔ:dʒə/ *n* **(a)** (republic in the Caucasus) Georgia *f* **(b)** (US state) Georgia *f*

Georgian¹ /'dʒɔ:rdʒən ‖ 'dʒɔ:dʒən/ *adj* **(a)** (of Georgia in the Caucasus) georgiano **(b)** (of Georgia in USA) georgiano **(c)** (in architecture, UK history) georgiano

Georgian² *n* **(a)** [C] (from the Caucasus) georgiano, -na *m,f* **(b)** [U] (language) georgiano *m* **(c)** [C] (from USA) georgiano, -na *m,f*

geriatric /dʒeri'ætrɪk/ *adj* (Med) ‹*patient*› anciano; ‹*ward*› de geriatría

germ /dʒɜ:rm ‖ dʒɜ:m/ *n* **1** (Med) microbio *m*, germen *m* **2** (Biol, Bot) germen *m*

German¹ /'dʒɜ:rmən ‖ 'dʒɜ:mən/ *adj* alemán

German² *n* **(a)** [U] (language) alemán *m* **(b)** [C] (person) alemán, -mana *m,f*

German: **~ measles** *n* [U] (+ *sing vb*) rubéola *f*, rubeola *f*; **~ shepherd (dog)** *n* pastor *m or* (CS) ovejero *m* alemán

Germany /'dʒɜ:rməni ‖ 'dʒɜ:məni/ *n* Alemania *f*

germinate /'dʒɜ:rməneɪt ‖ 'dʒɜ:mɪneɪt/ *vi* germinar

gerund /'dʒerənd/ *n* gerundio *m*

gestation /dʒe'steɪʃən/ *n* [U] gestación *f*

gesticulate /dʒe'stɪkjəleɪt ‖ dʒe'stɪkjʊleɪt/ *vi* gesticular

gesture¹ /'dʒestʃər ‖ 'dʒestʃə(r)/ *n* **(a)** (of body) gesto *m*, ademán *m* **(b)** (token, expression) gesto *m*; **a ~ of good will** un gesto de buena voluntad; **it was a nice ~** fue todo un detalle

gesture² *vi* hacer* gestos

get /get/ (*pres p* **getting**; *past* **got**; *past p* **got** *or* (AmE also) **gotten**) *vt* **I 1 (a)** (obtain) conseguir*, obtener*; ‹*job/staff*› conseguir*; ‹*idea*› sacar*; **where did you ~ that beautiful rug?** ¿dónde conseguiste esa alfombra tan preciosa? **(b)** (buy) comprar; **I got it from Harrods** lo compré en Harrods **(c)** (achieve, win) ‹*prize/grade*› sacar*, obtener* (frml) **(d)** (on the telephone) ‹*person*› lograr comunicarse con; **you've got the wrong number** se ha equivocado de número **2 (a)** (receive) ‹*letter/reward/reprimand*› recibir; **I got a stereo for my birthday** me regalaron un estéreo para mi cumpleaños **(b)** (be paid) ‹*salary/pay*› ganar; **I got £200 for the piano** me dieron 200 libras por el piano **(c)** (experience) ‹*shock/surprise*› llevarse; **I ~ the feeling that** ... tengo la sensación de que ... **(d)** (suffer): **how did you ~ that bump on your head?** ¿cómo te hiciste ese chichón en la cabeza? **3** (fetch) ‹*hammer/scissors*› traer*, ir* a buscar; ‹*doctor/plumber*› llamar; **~ your coat** anda *or* vete a buscar tu abrigo **4 (a)** (take hold of) agarrar, coger* (esp Esp) **(b)** (catch, trap) pillar (fam), agarrar (AmL), coger* (esp Esp) **5** (contract) ‹*cold/flu*› agarrar, pescar* (fam), pillar (fam), coger* (esp Esp) **6** (catch) ‹*bus/train*› tomar, coger* (Esp) **7** (colloq) **(a)** (irritate) fastidiar **(b)** (puzzle): **what ~s me is how** ... lo que no entiendo es cómo ... **8 (a)** (understand) (colloq) entender*; **don't ~ me wrong** no me malentiendas **(b)** (take note of): **did you ~ the number?** ¿tomaste nota del número? **9** (possess) **to have got** *see* HAVE *vt*

II 1 (bring, move, put) (+ *adv compl*): **we'll ~ it there by two o'clock** lo tendremos allí antes de las dos; **they couldn't ~ it up the stairs** no lo pudieron subir por las escaleras **2** (cause to be) (+ *adj compl*): **he got the children ready** preparó a los niños; **I can't ~ the window open** no puedo abrir la ventana; **they got their feet wet** se mojaron los pies **3 to ~ sb/sth + pp (a)** (with action carried out by subject): **we must ~ some work done** tenemos que trabajar un poco; **to ~ oneself organized** organizarse* **(b)** (with action carried out by somebody else): **he got the house painted** hizo pintar la casa; **I must ~ this watch fixed** tengo que llevar a *or* (AmL tb) mandar (a) arreglar este reloj **4** (arrange, persuade, force) **to ~ sb/sth to + INF**: **I'll ~ him to help you** (order) le diré que te ayude; (ask) le pediré que te ayude; (persuade) lo convenceré de que te ayude; **I can't ~ it to work** no puedo hacerlo funcionar ■ **~** *vi* **1** (reach) (+ *adv compl*) llegar*; **can you ~ there by train?** ¿se puede ir en tren? **2** (become): **to ~ tired** cansarse; **to ~ dressed**

vestirse*; **he got very angry** se puso furioso; *see* MARRIED, COLD *etc* **3 to ~ to** + INF **(a)** (come to) llegar* a + INF; **I never really got to know him** nunca llegué a conocerlo de verdad **(b)** (have opportunity to): **in this job you ~ to meet many interesting people** en este trabajo uno tiene la oportunidad de conocer a mucha gente interesante; **when do we ~ to open the presents?** ¿cuándo podemos abrir los regalos? **4** (start) **to ~ -ING** empezar* a + INF, ponerse* a + INF

• **get about** [*v* + *adv*] [*v* + *prep* + *o*] (BrE) ⇒ GET AROUND I 1

• **get above** [*v* + *prep* + *o*]: ***to ~ above oneself*** llenarse de infulas

• **get across 1** [*v* + *prep* + *o*] [*v* + *adv*] (cross) ‹*river*› atravesar*, cruzar*; ‹*road*› cruzar* **2** [*v* + *o* + *adv, v* + *adv* + *o*] ‹*meaning/concept*› hacer* entender **3** [*v* + *adv*] (be understood) «*teacher/speaker*» hacerse* entender

• **get ahead** [*v* + *adv*] **(a)** (get in front) «*student/worker*» adelantar **(b)** (progress, succeed) progresar

• **get along** [*v* + *adv*] **1** (manage, cope) arreglárselas **2** (progress) «*work/patient*» marchar, andar*; **he's ~ting along just fine at school** le va muy bien en el colegio **3** (be on good terms) **to ~ along (WITH sb)** llevarse bien (CON algn)

• **get around I 1** [*v* + *adv*] **(a)** (walk, move about) caminar, andar*; (using transport, car) desplazarse* **(b)** (travel) viajar **(c)** (circulate): **it** *o* **word got around that** ... pronto corrió el rumor de que ... **2** [*v* + *prep* + *o*] (gather in circle): **we can't all ~ around this table** no cabemos todos alrededor de esta mesa

II [*v* + *prep* + *o*] **(a)** (avoid, circumvent) ‹*difficulty/obstacle*› sortear, evitar; ‹*rule/law*› eludir el cumplimiento de **(b)** (persuade) ‹*person*› engatusar

III [*v* + *adv*] (go) ir*; (come) venir*

• **get around to** [*v* + *adv* + *prep* + *o*]: **I meant to write to you, I just never got around to it** tenía intenciones de escribirte pero nunca llegué a hacerlo; **I must ~ around to writing those letters** debo ponerme a escribir esas cartas

• **get at** [*v* + *prep* + *o*] **1 (a)** (reach) ‹*pipe/wire*› llegar* a **(b)** (ascertain) ‹*facts/truth*› establecer* **2** (nag, criticize) (colloq) criticar*, meterse con (fam) **3** (hint at, mean) (colloq): **what are you ~ting at?** ¿qué quieres decir?

• **get away** [*v* + *adv*] **1** (escape) escaparse **2 (a)** (leave) salir* **(b)** (go on vacation) irse* de vacaciones; ***to ~ away from it all*** alejarse del mundanal ruido

• **get away with** [*v* + *adv* + *prep* + *o*] **1** (make off with) llevarse, escaparse con **2 (a)** (go unpunished for): **you won't ~ away with this** esto no va a quedar así; **don't let them ~ away with it** no dejes que se salgan con la suya **(b)** (be let off with) ‹*fine/warning*› escaparse *or* librarse con

• **get back 1** [*v* + *adv*] **(a)** (return) volver*, regresar; (arrive home) llegar* (a casa) **(b)** (retreat): **~ back!** ¡atrás! **2** [*v* + *o* + *adv, v* + *adv* + *o*] (regain possession of) ‹*property*› recuperar; ‹*health*› recobrar; **we never got our money back** nos devolvieron el dinero

• **get behind 1** [*v* + *adv*] (fall behind) **to ~ behind (WITH sth)** atrasarse (CON algo) **2** [*v* + *prep* + *o*] (move to rear of) ponerse* detrás de; (fall behind) rezagarse*, quedarse atrás

• **get by** [*v* + *adv*] (manage) arreglárselas; **I speak enough French to ~ by** me defiendo en francés; **to ~ by ON sth** arreglárselas CON algo

• **get down 1** [*v* + *adv*] **(a)** (descend) bajar **(b)** (crouch) agacharse **2** [*v* + *o* + *adv, v* + *adv* + *o*] **(a)** (take, lift, bring down) bajar **(b)** (write down) anotar, tomar nota de **3** [*v* + *o* + *adv*] **(a)** (reduce) ‹*costs/inflation*› reducir*; ‹*blood pressure*› bajar **(b)** (depress) deprimir **4** [*v* + *prep* + *o*] (descend) ‹*stairs*› bajar; ‹*ladder*› bajarse de; ‹*rope*› bajar por

• **get down to** [*v* + *adv* + *prep* + *o*] (start work on) ponerse* a

• **get in 1 (a)** [*v* + *adv*] (enter) entrar **(b)** [*v* + *prep* + *o*] ⇒ GET INTO 1(a) **2** [*v* + *adv*] **(a)** (arrive) «*person/train*» llegar* **(b)** (gain admission to, be selected for) entrar, ser* admitido **(c)** (be elected) (Pol) ganar, resultar elegido **3** [*v* + *o* + *adv, v* + *adv* + *o*] **(a)** (bring in, collect up) ‹*washing/chairs*› entrar; ‹*harvest*› recoger* **(b)** (buy, obtain) (BrE) ‹*wood/coal/food*› aprovisionarse de **(c)** (call out) ‹*doctor/plumber*› llamar **(d)** (interpose) ‹*blow/kick*› dar*; ‹*remark*› hacer*

• **get into 1** [*v* + *prep* + *o*] **(a)** (enter) ‹*house*› entrar en *or* (AmL tb) a; ‹*car*› subir a; ‹*hole*› meterse en **(b)** (arrive at) ‹*station/office*› llegar* a **(c)** (be selected for, elected to) ‹*college/club/Congress*› entrar en *or* (AmL tb) a **(d)** (put on) ‹*coat/robe*› ponerse*; (fit into) **I can't ~ into this dress any more** este vestido ya no me entra **(e)** (into a given state): **to ~ into a rage/a mess** ponerse* furioso/meterse en un lío **(f)** (affect): **I don't know what's got into him lately** no sé qué le pasa últimamente **2** [*v* + *o* + *prep* + *o*] **(a)** (bring, take, put in) meter **(b)** (involve): **you got me into this** tú me metiste en esto

• **get off 1** [*v* + *adv*] [*v* + *prep* + *o*] **(a)** (alight, dismount) bajarse; **to ~ off a train/horse/bicycle** bajarse de un tren/de un caballo/de una bicicleta **(b)** (remove oneself from) ‹*flowerbed/lawn*› salir* de **(c)** (finish) ‹*work/school*› salir* de **2** [*v* + *adv*] **(a)** (leave) «*person/letter*» salir* **(b)** (escape unpunished) «*person accused*» salir* libre; **he got off lightly** *o* (AmE also) **easy** no recibió el castigo que se merecía; **he got off with a fine** se escapó con sólo una multa **3** [*v* + *prep* + *o*] **(a)** (get up from) ‹*floor*› levantarse de **(b)** (deviate from) ‹*track/tourist routes*› salir* *or* alejarse de; ‹*point*› desviarse* *or* irse* de; **I tried to ~ him off the subject** intenté hacerlo cambiar de tema **(c)** (evade) ‹*duty*› librarse *or* salvarse de **4** [*v* + *o* + *adv*] (remove) ‹*lid/top/stain*› quitar **5** [*v* + *o* + *adv*] (send, see off): **we got the children off to school** mandamos a los niños a la escuela **6** (save from punishment) salvar

• **get on I** [*v* + *adv*] **1** (move on) seguir* adelante; **to ~ on TO sth** pasar A algo; **~ on with what you're doing** sigue con lo que estás haciendo **2 (a)** (fare): **how's Joe ~ting on nowadays?** ¿qué tal anda Joe?; **how did he ~ on at the interview?** ¿cómo le fue en la entrevista? **(b)** (succeed) tener* éxito; **to ~ on in life** tener éxito en la vida **3** (be friends, agree) **to ~ on (WITH sb)** llevarse bien (CON algn) **4** (*in -ing form*) **(a)** (in time) **it's ~ting on** se

está haciendo tarde **(b)** (in age): **she's ~ting on (in years)** está vieja, ya no es joven
II [*v* + *adv*] [*v* + *prep* + *o*] (climb on, board) subirse; **to ~ on the bus/a horse** subirse al autobús/ subirse a un caballo
III [*v* + *o* + *adv*] [*v* + *o* + *prep* + *o*] (place, fix on) poner; **I can't ~ the top on (it)** no puedo ponerle la tapa
IV [*v* + *o* + *adv*] (put on) ‹*clothes*› ponerse*

● **get on for** [*v* + *adv* + *prep* + *o*] (approach) (BrE) (*usu in -ing form*): **it's ~ting on for six o'clock** van a ser las seis; **he must be ~ting on for 40** debe (de) andar rondando los 40

● **get onto** [*v* + *prep* + *o*] **1 (a)** (contact) ‹*person/ department*› ponerse* en contacto con **(b)** (begin discussing) ‹*subject*› empezar* a hablar de **2** (mount, board) ‹*table/bus/train*› subirse a; ‹*horse/bicycle*› montarse en

● **get out I** [*v* + *adv*] **1 (a)** (of car, bus, train) bajar(se); (of hole) salir*; (of bath) salir*; **to ~ out of bed** levantarse (de la cama) **(b)** (of room, country) salir*; **~ out!** ¡fuera (de aquí)! **2 (a)** (escape) «*animal/prisoner*» escaparse **(b)** (become known) «*news/ truth*» saberse*
II [*v* + *o* + *adv, v* + *adv* + *o*] **(a)** (remove, extract) ‹*stopper/nail*› sacar*; ‹*stain*› quitar, sacar* (esp AmL) **(b)** (take out) ‹*knife/map*› sacar* **(c)** (withdraw) ‹*money*› sacar* **(d)** (borrow) ‹*library book*› sacar*
III [*v* + *o* + *adv*] **1** (remove) ‹*tenant*› echar; **~ that dog out of here!** ¡saquen (a) ese perro de aquí!; **I can't ~ you out of this mess** no te puedo sacar de este lío **2** (send for) ‹*doctor/repairman*› llamar

● **get out of 1** [*v* + *adv* + *prep* + *o*] **(a)** (avoid) ‹*obligation*› librarse *or* salvarse de; **to ~ out of** -ING librarse *or* salvarse de + INF **(b)** (give up): **you must ~ out of that bad habit** tienes que sacarte esa mala costumbre; **I'd got out of the habit of setting my alarm clock** había perdido la costumbre de poner el despertador **2** [*v* + *o* + *adv* + *prep* + *o*] **(a)** (extract) ‹*information/truth*› sonsacar*, sacar* **(b)** (derive, gain) ‹*money/profit*› sacar*

● **get over 1** [*v* + *prep* + *o*] ‹*river/chasm*› cruzar*; ‹*wall/fence*› pasar por encima de; ‹*hill/ridge*› atravesar*; ‹*obstacle*› superar **2** [*v* + *prep* + *o*] ‹*loss/tragedy/difficulty*› superar; ‹*illness/shock*› reponerse* de; **he's very disappointed — he'll ~ over it** ha quedado muy decepcionado — ya se le pasará **3** [*v* + *o* + *adv*] (cause to come, take): **~ those documents over to Wall Street right away** manda esos documentos a Wall Street enseguida; ***to ~ sth over with*: I'd like to ~ it over with as quickly as possible** quisiera salir de eso *or* quitarme eso de encima lo más pronto posible **4** [*v* + *o* + *adv*] (communicate) ‹*emotion*› comunicar*

● **get past 1** [*v* + *adv*] (move past) pasar **2** [*v* + *prep* + *o*] **(a)** (move past) ‹*vehicle*› pasar, adelantarse a; ‹*opponent/attacker*› eludir **(b)** (get beyond) ‹*obstacle*› superar; ‹*semifinals*› pasar

● **get round** (esp BrE) ⇒ GET AROUND

● **get through I** [*v* + *prep* + *o*] [*v* + *adv*] **(a)** (pass through) ‹*gap/hole*› pasar por **(b)** ‹*ordeal*› superar; ‹*winter/difficult time*› pasar **(c)** (Sport) ‹*heat*› pasar
II [*v* + *adv*] **1 (a)** (reach destination) «*supplies/messenger*» llegar* a destino; «*news/report*» llegar* **(b)** (on the telephone) **to ~ through** (TO *sb/sth*) comunicarse* (CON algn/algo) **(c)** (make understand): **am I ~ting through to you?** ¿me entiendes?; **I can't ~ through to him** no logro hacerme entender con él **2** (finish) (AmE) terminar, acabar
III [*v* + *prep* + *o*] **(a)** (use up) (BrE) ‹*money*› gastarse; ‹*materials*› usar; ‹*shoes*› destrozar* **(b)** (deal with): **I've only got ten more pages to ~ through** me quedan sólo diez páginas por leer (*or* estudiar *etc*)
IV [*v* + *o* + *adv*] [*v* + *o* + *prep* + *o*] (bring through) pasar; **to ~ sth through customs** pasar algo por la aduana
V [*v* + *o* + *adv*] **(a)** (send) ‹*supplies/message*› hacer* llegar **(b)** (make understood) hacer* entender

● **get together 1** [*v* + *adv*] **(a)** (meet up) reunirse*, quedar (Esp); (have a family reunion) juntarse, reunirse* **(b)** (join forces) «*nations/unions*» unirse **(c)** (become couple, team) (colloq) juntarse **2** [*v* + *o* + *adv, v* + *adv* + *o*] (assemble) ‹*people/money*› reunir*; **~ your things together** junta *or* recoge tus cosas

● **get up 1** [*v* + *prep* + *o*] [*v* + *adv*] (climb up) subir; **to ~ up** ON **sth** subir(se) A algo **2** [*v* + *adv*] **(a)** (out of bed) levantarse **(b)** (stand up) levantarse **3** [*v* + *o* + *adv*] (raise, lift) ‹*person*› levantar **4** [*v* + *o* + *adv, v* + *adv* + *o*] (develop, arouse) ‹*appetite/ enthusiasm*› despertar*; ‹*speed*› agarrar, coger* (esp Esp); **she didn't want to ~ their hopes up** no quería esperanzarlos

● **get up to** [*v* + *adv* + *prep* + *o*] **1** (reach): **when he got up to them** ... cuando los alcanzó ...; **we got up to page 161** llegamos hasta la página 161 **2** (be involved in) (colloq) hacer*; **to ~ up to mischief** hacer* travesuras *or* de las suyas

get: **~away** *n* huida *f*, fuga *f*; **to make one's ~away** escaparse, huir*; **~-together** *n* (colloq) reunión *f*

geyser /'gaɪzər ‖ 'gi:zə(r)/ *n* (Geog) géiser *m*

Ghana /'gɑ:nə/ *n* Ghana *f*

Ghanaian /gɑ:'neɪən/ *adj* ghanés

ghastly /'gæstli ‖ 'gɑ:stli/ *adj* **(a)** (very bad, awful) (colloq) espantoso, horrendo (fam) **(b)** (horrible, hideous) horrible, espantoso

gherkin /'gɜ:rkən ‖ 'gɜ:kɪn/ *n* pepinillo *m*

ghetto /'getəʊ/ *n* (*pl* **-tos** *or* **-toes**) gueto *m*

ghost /gəʊst/ *n* fantasma *m*, espíritu *m*

ghostly /'gəʊstli/ *adj* **-lier, -liest** fantasmal, fantasmagórico

ghoul /gu:l/ *n* **(a)** (person) morboso, -sa *m,f* **(b)** (evil spirit) demonio *m* necrófago

GI *n* (colloq) soldado *m* estadounidense

giant[1] /'dʒaɪənt/ *n* gigante, -ta *m,f*

giant[2] *adj* (*before n*) ‹*organization*› gigantesco; ‹*insect*› gigante; ‹*stride*› gigantesco

gibber /'dʒɪbər ‖ 'dʒɪbə(r)/ *vi* farfullar

gibberish /'dʒɪbərɪʃ/ *n* [U] galimatías *m*; **to talk ~** decir* sandeces (fam)

gibe /dʒaɪb/ *n* pulla *f*

giblets /'dʒɪbləts ‖ 'dʒɪblɪts/ *pl n* menudillos *mpl*, menudos *mpl*

Gibraltar /dʒəˈbrɔːltər || dʒɪˈbrɔːltə(r)/ *n* Gibraltar

giddy /ˈgɪdi/ *adj* **-dier, -diest** ‹*sensation*› de mareo *or* aturdimiento; **to feel ~** sentirse* mareado

gift /gɪft/ *n* **1** (present) regalo *m*; **it was a ~** me lo regalaron, es un regalo **2** (talent) don *m*; **she has a ~ for poetry** tiene talento para la poesía

gift certificate *n* (AmE) vale *m* (*canjeable por artículos en una tienda*), cheque regalo *m*

gifted /ˈgɪftəd || ˈgɪftɪd/ *adj* ‹*person*› de talento, talentoso

gift: **~ token**, **~ voucher** *n* (BrE) ⇒ GIFT CERTIFICATE; **~-wrap** *vt* **-pp-** envolver* para regalo *or* (frml) obsequio

gig /gɪg/ *n* (sl) actuación *f*

gigantic /dʒaɪˈgæntɪk/ *adj* gigantesco; ‹*success/appetite*› enorme; ‹*effort*› titánico

giggle[1] /ˈgɪgəl/ *vi* reírse* tontamente

giggle[2] *n* risita *f*

gild /gɪld/ *vt* dorar

gill *n* **1** /dʒɪl/ *medida para líquidos equivalente a la cuarta parte de una pinta o 0,142 l* **2** /gɪl/ (Zool) agalla *f*, branquia *f*

gilt /gɪlt/ *n* [U] dorado *m*

gimmick /ˈgɪmɪk/ *n* **(a)** (ingenious idea, device) truco *m* **(b)** (catch, snag) (AmE) trampa *f*

gin /dʒɪn/ *n* [U] ginebra *f*, gin *m*

ginger[1] /ˈdʒɪndʒər || ˈdʒɪndʒə(r)/ *n* [U] jengibre *m*

ginger[2] ▶ 515 *adj* ‹*hair*› color zanahoria; ‹*cat*› rojizo

ginger: **~ ale** *n* [U C] ginger ale *m*, refresco *m* de jengibre; **~ beer** *n* [U C] cerveza *f* de jengibre; **~bread** *n* [U] (cake) pan *m* de jengibre; (cookie) galleta *f* de jengibre

gipsy, **Gipsy** /ˈdʒɪpsi/ *n* ⇒ GYPSY

giraffe /dʒəˈræf || dʒɪˈrɑːf/ *n* jirafa *f*

girder /ˈgɜːrdər || ˈgɜːdə(r)/ *n* viga *f* (*de metal*)

girdle /ˈgɜːrdl || ˈgɜːdl/ *n* faja *f*

girl /gɜːrl || gɜːl/ *n* **1 (a)** (baby, child) niña *f*, nena *f* (esp RPl) **(b)** (young woman) chica *f*, muchacha *f* **2** (daughter) hija *f*, niña *f*

girl: **~friend** *n* **(a)** (of man) novia *f* **(b)** (of woman) (esp AmE) amiga *f*; (in lesbian couple) compañera *f*; **~ guide** (BrE) ⇒ GIRL SCOUT

girlish /ˈgɜːrlɪʃ || ˈgɜːlɪʃ/ *adj* de niña

girl scout *n* (AmE) guía *f* (*de los scouts*), exploradora *f*

giro /ˈdʒaɪrəʊ/ *n* (*pl* **-ros**) (in UK) (system) transferencia *f*, giro *m*

girth /gɜːrθ || gɜːθ/ *n* **1** [C U] (of person, object) circunferencia *f* **2** [C] (Equ) cincha *f*

gist /dʒɪst/ *n* lo esencial; **to get the ~ of sth** captar lo esencial de algo

give[1] /gɪv/ (*past* **gave**; *past p* **given**) *vt* **I 1 (a)** (hand, pass) dar*; **~ her/me/them a glass of water** dale/dame/dales un vaso de agua **(b)** (as gift) regalar; **to ~ sb a present** hacerle* un regalo a algn, regalarle algo a algn **(c)** (donate) dar*, donar **(d)** (dedicate, devote) ‹*love/affection*› dar*; ‹*attention*› prestar; **I'll ~ it some thought** lo pensaré **(e)** (sacrifice) ‹*life*› dar*, entregar* **(f)** ‹*injection/sedative*› dar*, administrar (frml) **2 (a)** (supply, grant) ‹*help*› dar*, brindar; ‹*idea*› dar* **(b)** (allow, concede) ‹*opportunity/permission*› dar*, conceder (frml) **3 (a)** (cause) ‹*pleasure/shock*› dar*; ‹*cough*› dar* **(b)** (yield) ‹*results/fruit*› dar* **4 (a)** (award, allot) ‹*title/authority/right*› dar*, otorgar* (frml); ‹*contract*› dar*, adjudicar*; ‹*mark*› dar*, poner* **(b)** (entrust) ‹*task/responsibility*› dar*, confiar* **5** (pay, exchange) dar*; **I'd ~ anything for a cigarette** no sé qué daría por un cigarrillo **6** (care) (colloq): **I don't ~ a damn** me importa un bledo (fam)

II 1 (convey, state) ‹*apologies/information*› dar*; **she gave a detailed description of the place** describió el lugar detalladamente **2** (make sound, movement) ‹*cry/jump*› dar*; ‹*laugh*› soltar* **3** (indicate) ‹*speed/temperature*› señalar **4** (hold) ‹*party/dinner*› dar*, ofrecer* (frml); ‹*concert*› dar*; ‹*speech*› decir*

■ **~** *vi* **1 (a)** (yield under pressure) ceder, dar* de sí **(b)** (break, give way) ‹‹*planks/branch*›› romperse* **2** (make gift) dar*; **to ~ to charity** dar* dinero a organizaciones de caridad

● **give away** [*v + o + adv, v + adv + o*] **1 (a)** (free of charge) regalar **(b)** ‹*prizes*› hacer* entrega de **2 (a)** (disclose) revelar; **he didn't ~ anything away** no dejó entrever nada **(b)** (betray) delatar **3** ‹*bride*› entregar* en matrimonio

● **give back** [*v + o + adv, v + adv + o*] devolver*

● **give in** [*v + adv*] (surrender, succumb) ceder; (in guessing games) rendirse*; **we will not ~ in to terrorists** no vamos a ceder frente a los terroristas

● **give off** [*v + adv + o*] ‹*smell/fumes*› despedir*, largar* (RPl fam); ‹*heat*› dar*; ‹*radiation*› emitir

● **give out 1** [*v + o + adv, v + adv + o*] ‹*leaflets*› repartir, distribuir* **2** [*v + adv + o*] **(a)** (let out) ‹*cry/yell*› dar* **(b)** (emit) ‹*heat*› dar*; ‹*signal*› emitir

● **give up I** [*v + o + adv, v + adv + o*] **1 (a)** (renounce, cease from) ‹*alcohol*› dejar; ‹*fight*› abandonar; **to ~ up hope** perder* las esperanzas; **to ~ up** -ING dejar DE + INF **(b)** (relinquish, hand over) ‹*territory/position*› ceder; **to ~ up one's seat for sb** cederle el asiento a algn **2** (surrender): **to ~ oneself up** entregarse*

II [*v + adv*] **(a)** (cease fighting, trying) rendirse*; **I've ~n up on them** yo con ellos no insisto más, no pierdo más tiempo **(b)** (stop doing sth) dejar

III [*v + o + adv*] (abandon hope for): **to ~ sb up for lost** dar* a algn por desaparecido

give[2] *n* [U] elasticidad *f*

give: **~-and-take** /ˈgɪvənˈteɪk/ *n* [U] concesiones *fpl* mutuas, toma y daca *m*; **~away** *n* **1** (evidence): **her accent is a real ~away** el acento la delata *or* (fam) la vende; **2 (a)** (free gift) regalo *m*; (*before n*) **at ~away prices** a precio de regalo **(b)** (sth easily done, obtained): **the last question was a ~away** la última pregunta estaba regalada *or* tirada (fam)

given[1] /ˈgɪvən/ *past p of* GIVE[1]

given[2] *adj* ‹*amount/time*› determinado, dado

given[3] *prep* **1** (in view of) dado **2** (*as conj*) **~** (THAT) dado que

given name *n* (AmE) nombre *m* de pila

glacé /glæˈseɪ || ˈglæseɪ/ *adj* (*before n*) glaseado

glacier /ˈgleɪʃər || ˈglæsɪə(r), ˈgleɪsɪə(r)/ *n* glaciar *m*

glad /glæd/ *adj* **-dd-** (*pred*) **to be ~ (ABOUT sth)** alegrarse DE algo; **to be ~ (THAT)** alegrarse DE QUE (+ *subj*); **I'm only too ~ to help** es un placer poder ser útil

gladden /'glædn/ *vt* (liter) llenar de alegría *or* (liter) de gozo

gladly /'glædli/ *adv* con mucho gusto

glamor /'glæmər ‖ 'glæmə(r)/ *n* (AmE) ⇒ GLAMOUR

glamorous /'glæmərəs/ *adj* ‹*person/dress*› glamoroso; ‹*lifestyle*› sofisticado; ‹*job*› rodeado de glamour

glamour, (AmE also) **glamor** /'glæmər ‖ 'glæmə(r)/ *n* [U] glamour *m*

glance¹ /glæns ‖ glɑːns/ *n* mirada *f*; **to take a ~ at sth** echarle un vistazo *or* una ojeada a algo; **at first ~** a primera vista

glance² *vi* mirar; **to ~ AT sth** echarle una ojeada *or* un vistazo A algo; **to ~ AT sb** echarle una mirada A algn

glancing /'glænsɪŋ ‖ 'glɑːnsɪŋ/ *adj* (*before n*): **to strike sb a ~ blow** pegarle* a algn de refilón

gland /glænd/ *n* **(a)** (organ) glándula *f* **(b)** (lymph node) ganglio *m*

glandular fever /'glændjələr ‖ 'glændjʊlə(r)/ *n* [U] mononucleosis *f* (infecciosa)

glare¹ /gler ‖ gleə(r)/ *n* **1** [C] (stare) mirada *f* (*hostil, feroz, de odio etc*) **2** [U] (light) resplandor *m*

glare² *vi* **1** (stare) **to ~ AT sb** fulminar a algn con la mirada **2** (shine) brillar

glaring /'glerɪŋ ‖ 'gleərɪŋ/ *adj* **(a)** ‹*light*› deslumbrante **(b)** (flagrant) (*before n*) ‹*error*› mayúsculo

glass /glæs ‖ glɑːs/ *n* **1** [U] (material) vidrio *m*, cristal *m* (Esp) **2** [C] (vessel) vaso *m*; (with stem) copa *f*; **a ~ of wine** una copa de vino **3 glasses** *pl* (spectacles) gafas *fpl*, lentes *mpl* (esp AmL), anteojos *mpl* (esp AmL) **4** [C] (*magnifying ~*) lupa *f*, lente *f* de aumento

glassblowing /'glæs,bləʊɪŋ ‖ 'glɑːs,bləʊɪŋ/ *n* [U] soplado *m* del vidrio

glassy /'glæsi ‖ 'glɑːsi/ *adj* **(a)** (like glass) vítreo **(b)** (dull, lifeless) ‹*stare*› vidrioso

glaze¹ /gleɪz/ *n* [C U] **(a)** (on pottery) vidriado *m* **(b)** (Culin) glaseado *m*

glaze² *vt* **1** (fit with glass) ‹*window/door*› acristalar; **to ~ a window** ponerle* vidrio(s) *or* (Esp) cristal(es) a **2** (make shiny, glossy) **(a)** ‹*pottery*› vidriar **(b)** (Culin) glasear ■ **~** *vi* **~ (over)** «*eyes*» vidriarse

glazed /gleɪzd/ *adj* **1** (fitted with glass) ‹*window/door*› con vidrio *or* (Esp) cristal **2 (a)** (Culin) glaseado **(b)** ‹*expression*› vidrioso

glazier /'gleɪʒər ‖ 'gleɪziə(r)/ *n* vidriero, -ra *m,f*, cristalero, -ra *m,f* (Esp)

gleam¹ /gliːm/ *vi* «*metal*» relucir*

gleam² *n* (on metal, water) reflejo *m*; **he had a wicked ~ in his eyes** sus ojos despedían un destello maleficioso

gleaming /'gliːmɪŋ/ *adj* reluciente

glean /gliːn/ *vt* ‹*information*› recoger*

glee /gliː/ *n* [U] regocijo *m*

gleeful /'gliːfəl/ *adj* lleno de alegría

glen /glen/ *n* cañada *f*

glib /glɪb/ *adj* **-bb-** ‹*remark/answer*› simplista; ‹*salesman/politician*› con mucha labia

glide /glaɪd/ *vi* **1** (move smoothly over a surface) deslizarse* **2** «*bird/plane*» planear

glider /'glaɪdər ‖ 'glaɪdə(r)/ *n* planeador *m*

glimmer¹ /'glɪmər ‖ 'glɪmə(r)/ *vi* brillar con luz trémula

glimmer² *n* luz *f* débil; **a ~ of hope** un rayo de esperanza

glimpse¹ /glɪmps/ *n*: **I caught a ~ of the room** pude ver brevemente la habitación; **a ~ of life in rural England** una visión de la vida en la Inglaterra rural

glimpse² *vt* alcanzar* a ver

glint¹ /glɪnt/ *vi* destellar

glint² *n* (of metal, light) destello *m*; (in eye) (*no pl*) chispa *f*, brillo *m*

glisten /'glɪsən/ *vi* brillar

glitter¹ /'glɪtər ‖ 'glɪtə(r)/ *vi* relumbrar

glitter² *n* **(a)** (sparkle) (*no pl*) destello *m* **(b)** [U] (superficial attractiveness) oropel *m* **(c)** [U] (decoration) purpurina *f*, brillantes *mpl* (Arg), brillantina *f* (Ur, Ven), brillo *m* (Chi)

gloat /gləʊt/ *vi* **to ~ (OVER sth)** regodearse (CON algo)

global /'gləʊbəl/ *adj* **(a)** (worldwide) a escala mundial, global; **~ warming** calentamiento *m* global **(b)** (overall, comprehensive) global

globe /gləʊb/ *n* **(a)** (world) **the ~** el globo **(b)** (model) globo *m* terráqueo

globe: **~ artichoke** *n* alcachofa *f*, alcaucil *m* (RPl); **~trotter** /'gləʊb,trɑːtər ‖ 'gləʊb,trɒtə(r)/ *n* trotamundos *mf*

globule /'glɑːbjuːl ‖ 'glɒbjuːl/ *n* glóbulo *m*

gloom /gluːm/ *n* [U] **(a)** (darkness) penumbra *f*, oscuridad *f* **(b)** (melancholy) melancolía *f*

gloomily /'gluːməli ‖ 'gluːmɪli/ *adv* ‹*sigh/stare*› tristemente; ‹*predict*› con pesimismo

gloomy /'gluːmi/ *adj* **-mier, -miest (a)** (dark) ‹*day/place*› sombrío **(b)** (dismal) ‹*person*› lúgubre, fúnebre; ‹*prospect*› nada halagüeño; ‹*prediction*› pesimista

glorify /'glɔːrəfaɪ ‖ 'glɔːrɪfaɪ/ *vt* **-fies, -fying, -fied** ‹*person*› ensalzar*; ‹*violence/war*› exaltar

glorious /'glɔːriəs/ *adj* **(a)** (deserving glory) glorioso **(b)** (wonderful) ‹*view/weather*› maravilloso

glory¹ /'glɔːri/ *n* (*pl* **-ries**) **(a)** [U] (fame) gloria *f* **(b)** [U C] (beauty, magnificence) esplendor *m*

glory² *vi* **-ries, -rying, -ried**: **to ~ IN sth** (take pleasure) disfrutar DE algo; (in unpleasant way) regodearse CON algo

gloss /glɑːs ‖ glɒs/ *n* [U] **(a)** (shine) brillo *m*; (*before n*) **~ finish** acabado *m* brillante **(b) ~ (paint)** (pintura *f* al *or* de) esmalte *m*

• **gloss over** [*v* + *adv* + *o*] (make light of) quitarle importancia a; (ignore) pasar por alto

glossary /'glɑːsəri ‖ 'glɒsəri/ *n* (*pl* **-ries**) glosario *m*

glossy /'glɑːsi ‖ 'glɒsi/ *adj* **-sier, -siest** ‹*coat of animal*› brillante, lustroso; ‹*hair*› brillante, brilloso (AmL); ‹*photograph*› brillante; **~ magazine** revista *f* ilustrada (*impresa en papel satinado*)

glove /glʌv/ *n* guante *m*

glove compartment *n* guantera *f*

glow[1] /gləʊ/ *vi* «*fire*» brillar; «*metal*» estar* al rojo vivo; **to ~ with health** rebosar (de) salud; **to be ~ing with happiness** estar* radiante de felicidad

glow[2] *n* (*no pl*) brillo *m*; **he felt a ~ of pride** sintió una oleada de orgullo

glower /ˈglaʊər ‖ ˈglaʊə(r)/ *vi* tener* el ceño fruncido; **to ~ AT sb** lanzarle* miradas fulminantes/una mirada fulminante A algn

glowing /ˈgləʊɪŋ/ *adj* **(a)** (shining) (*before n*) ‹*cheeks*› encendido; **the ~ embers** las brasas **(b)** (expressing praise) ‹*report*› elogioso

glucose /ˈgluːkəʊs, -kəʊz/ *n* [U] glucosa *f*

glue[1] /gluː/ *n* [U C] goma *f* de pegar, pegamento *m*

glue[2] *vt* **glues, glueing, glued (a)** (stick) pegar* **(b)** (fix): **he was ~d to the television** estaba pegado a la televisión

glum /glʌm/ *adj* **-mm-** apesadumbrado

glut /glʌt/ *n* superabundancia *f*

glutton /ˈglʌtn̩/ *n* glotón, -tona *m,f*

gluttony /ˈglʌtn̩i ‖ ˈglʌtəni/ *n* [U] glotonería *f*

glycerin /ˈglɪsərən ‖ ˈglɪsərm/, **glycerine** /ˈglɪsərən ‖ˈglɪsəriːn/ *n* [U] glicerina *f*

GMT (= **Greenwich Mean Time**) GMT

gnarled /nɑːrld ‖ nɑːld/ *adj* ‹*wood/fingers*› nudoso; ‹*tree*› retorcido

gnash /næʃ/ *vt*: **to ~ one's teeth** hacer* rechinar los dientes

gnat /næt/ *n* jején *m*; (general usage) mosquito *m*

gnaw /nɔː/ *vt* roer* ■ ~ *vi* **to ~ AT sth** roer* algo

gnome /nəʊm/ *n* gnomo *m*

go[1] /gəʊ/ (*3rd pers sing pres* **goes**; *past* **went**; *past p* **gone**) *vi* **I 1 (a)** (move, travel) ir*; **where do we ~ from here?** ¿y ahora qué hacemos? **(b)** (start moving, acting): **ready, (get) set, ~!** preparados *or* en sus marcas, listos ¡ya!; **let's ~!** ¡vamos!; **here ~es!** ¡allá vamos (*or* voy *etc*)! **2** (*past p* **gone/been**) **(a)** (travel to) ir*; **she's gone to France** se ha ido a Francia; **I have never been abroad** no he estado nunca en el extranjero; **to ~ by car/bus** ir* en coche/autobús; **to ~ on foot** ir* a pie; **to ~ for a walk** ir* a dar un paseo; **~ and see what she wants** anda *or* vete a ver qué quiere **(b)** (attend) ir*; **to ~ on a course** hacer* un curso; **to ~ -ING** ir* A + INF; **to ~ swimming** ir* a nadar **3** (attempt, make as if to) **to ~ to + INF** ir* A + INF

II 1 (leave, depart) «*visitor*» irse*, marcharse (esp Esp); «*bus/train*» salir*; ⇒ LET 1(c) **2 (a)** (pass) «*time*» pasar; **the time ~es quickly** el tiempo pasa volando **(b)** (disappear) «*headache/pain/fear*» pasarse *or* irse* (+ *me/te/le etc*) **(c)** «*money*» (be spent) irse*; (be used up) acabarse **3 (a)** (be disposed of): **that sofa will have to ~** nos vamos (*or* se van *etc*) a tener que deshacer de ese sofá **(b)** (be sold) venderse; **the painting went for £1,000** el cuadro se vendió en 1.000 libras **4 (a)** (cease to function, wear out) «*bulb/fuse*» fundirse; «*thermostat/fan/exhaust*» estropearse; **her memory/eyesight is ~ing** está fallándole la memoria/la vista; **my legs went (from under me)** me fallaron las piernas **(b)** (die) (colloq) morir* **5 to go (a)** (remaining): **only two weeks to ~ till he comes** sólo faltan dos semanas para que llegue; **I still have 50 pages to ~** todavía me faltan *or* me quedan 50 páginas **(b)** (take away) (AmE): **two burgers to ~** dos hamburguesas para llevar

III 1 (a) (lead) «*path/road*» ir*, llevar **(b)** (extend, range) «*road/railway line*» ir*; **it only ~es as far as Croydon** sólo va hasta Croydon **2** (have place) ir*; (fit) caber*; *see also* GO IN, GO INTO

IV 1 (a) (become): **to ~ blind** quedarse ciego; **to ~ crazy** volverse* loco; **her face went red** se puso colorada **(b)** (be, remain): **to ~ barefoot** ir* *or* andar* descalzo; **to ~ hungry** pasar hambre **2** (turn out, proceed, progress) ir*; **how are things ~ing?** ¿cómo van *or* andan las cosas? **3 (a)** (be available) (*only in -ing form*): **I'll take any job that's ~ing** estoy dispuesto a aceptar el trabajo que sea **(b)** (be in general): **it's not expensive as dishwashers ~** no es caro, para lo que cuestan los lavavajillas

V 1 (a) (function, work) «*heater/engine/clock*» funcionar **(b) to get going**: **the car's OK once it gets ~ing** el coche marcha bien una vez que arranca; **we'd better get ~ing** más vale que nos vayamos; **we tried to get a fire ~ing** tratamos de hacer fuego **(c) to keep going** (continue to function) aguantar; (not stop) seguir*; **to keep a project ~ing** mantener* a flote un proyecto **2** (continue, last out) seguir*; **the club's been ~ing for 12 years now** el club lleva 12 años funcionando **3 (a)** (sound) «*bell/siren*» sonar* **(b)** (make sound, movement) hacer* **4 (a)** (contribute): **everything that ~es to make a good school** todo lo que contribuye a que una escuela sea buena; **it just ~es to show: we can't leave them on their own** está visto que no los podemos dejar solos **(b)** (be used) **all their savings are ~ing toward the trip** van a gastar todos sus ahorros en el viaje; **the money will ~ to pay the workmen** el dinero se usará para pagar a los obreros **5** (run, be worded) decir*; **how does the song ~?** ¿cómo es la (letra/música de la) canción? **6 (a)** (be permitted): **anything ~es** todo vale **(b)** (be necessarily obeyed, believed): **what the boss says ~es** lo que dice el jefe, va a misa **(c)** (match, suit) pegar*, ir* ■ ~ *v aux* (*only in -ing form*) **to be ~ing to + INF** (expressing intention, prediction) ir* A + INF

• go about [*v + prep + o*] **(a)** (tackle) ‹*task*› acometer; **how would you ~ about solving this equation?** ¿cómo harías para resolver esta ecuación? **(b)** (occupy oneself with): **to ~ about one's business** ocuparse de sus (*or* mis *etc*) cosas

• go after [*v + prep + o*] (pursue, chase) perseguir*, dar* caza a

• go against [*v + prep + o*] **(a)** (oppose, resist) ‹*instructions/policy/person*› oponerse* a, ir* en contra de **(b)** (be unfavorable to): **the decision went against them** la decisión les fue desfavorable

• go ahead [*v + adv*] (proceed, begin) **to ~ ahead** (WITH **sth**) seguir* adelante (CON algo); **may I ask you a question? — ~ ahead!** ¿le puedo hacer una pregunta? — por supuesto *or* (AmL tb) pregunte nomás

• **go along** [*v* + *adv*] **(a)** (accompany, be present) ir* **(b)** (proceed, progress) ir*; **I usually make corrections as I ~ along** normalmente hago correcciones sobre la marcha **(c)** (acquiesce): **to ~ along with a proposal** secundar una propuesta

• **go around**, (BrE also) **go round I** [*v* + *prep* + *o*] **1 (a)** (turn) ‹*corner*› doblar, dar* la vuelta a, dar* vuelta (CS); ‹*bend*› tomar **(b)** (make detour) ‹*obstacle*› rodear **2** (visit, move through) ‹*country/city*› recorrer; ‹*museum/castle*› visitar; **to ~ around the world** dar* la vuelta al mundo

II [*v* + *adv*] **1 (a)** (move, travel, be outdoors) andar*; **to ~ around -ING** ir* por ahí + GER **(b)** (circulate) «*joke/rumor*» correr **(c)** (be sufficient for everybody): **there aren't enough to ~ round** no alcanzan **2** (revolve) «*wheel/world*» dar* vueltas **3** (visit) ir*; **I'll ~ around and see him** iré a verlo

• **go away** [*v* + *adv*] **(a)** (depart, leave) irse* **(b)** (from home): **I'm ~ing away this weekend** voy a salir este fin de semana; **to ~ away on vacation** irse* de vacaciones **(c)** (disappear, fade away) «*smell*» irse*; «*pain*» pasarse *or* irse* (+ *me/te/le etc*)

• **go back** [*v* + *adv*] **1** (return) volver*; **~ back!** ¡vuelve atrás!, ¡retrocede! **2 (a)** (date, originate) «*tradition/dynasty*» remontarse; **we ~ back a long way** (colloq) nos conocemos desde hace mucho **(b)** «*clocks*» atrasarse

• **go back on** [*v* + *adv* + *prep* + *o*] ‹*one's promise*› dejar de cumplir; ‹*one's word*› faltar a

• **go before** [*v* + *prep* + *o*] ‹*court/committee*› presentarse ante

• **go by 1** [*v* + *adv*] **(a)** (move past) pasar; **to let an opportunity ~ by** dejar pasar una oportunidad **(b)** (elapse) «*days/years*» pasar; **as time goes by** con el tiempo **2** [*v* + *prep* + *o*] **(a)** (be guided by) ‹*instinct*› dejarse llevar por; ‹*rules*› seguir* **(b)** (base judgment on) ‹*appearances*› guiarse* *or* dejarse llevar por; **if previous experience is anything to ~ by** a juzgar por lo que ha sucedido en otras ocasiones

• **go down** [*v* + *adv*] **1 (a)** (descend) «*person*» bajar; «*sun*» ponerse*; «*curtain*» (Theat) caer* **(b)** (fall) «*boxer/horse*» caerse*; «*plane*» caer*, estrellarse **(c)** (sink) «*ship*» hundirse **(d)** «*computer*» dejar de funcionar, descomponerse* (AmL) **(e)** (be defeated) (Sport) perder*; **to ~ down fighting** caer* luchando **2 (a)** (decrease) «*temperature/exchange rate*» bajar; «*population/unemployment*» disminuir*; **to ~ down in value** perder* valor **(b)** (decline) «*standard/quality*» empeorar **(c)** (abate) «*wind/storm*» amainar; «*floods/swelling*» bajar; **his temperature's gone down** le ha bajado la fiebre **(d)** (deflate) «*tire*» perder* aire **3** (extend): **this road ~es down to the beach** este camino baja a *or* hasta la playa; **the skirt ~es down to her ankles** la falda le llega a los tobillos **4 (a)** (be swallowed): **it just won't ~ down** no lo puedo tragar; **it went down the wrong way** se me fue por el otro camino **(b)** «*present/proposal/remarks*»: **how did the announcement ~ down?** ¿qué tipo de acogida tuvo el anuncio?; **that won't ~ down too well with your father** eso no le va a caer muy bien a tu padre **5** (be recorded, written): **all these absences will ~ down on your record** va a quedar constancia de estas faltas en tu ficha; **to ~ down in history as sth** pasar a la historia como algo

• **go down with** [*v* + *adv* + *prep* + *o*] (BrE): **to ~ down with flu/hepatitis** caer* en cama con gripe/caer* enfermo de hepatitis

• **go for** [*v* + *prep* + *o*] **1 (a)** (head toward, reach for): **he went for his gun** fue a echar mano de la pistola **(b)** (attack): **he went for Bill** se le echó encima a Bill **2** (choose) decidirse por **3** (aim at): **~ for it!** ¡haz la tentativa!, ¡a por ello! (Esp)

• **go in** [*v* + *adv*] **1 (a)** (enter) entrar **(b)** «*screw/key*» entrar; **the big case won't ~ in** la maleta grande no cabe **(c)** (go to work) ir* a trabajar **2** (be obscured) «*sun/moon*» ocultarse

• **go in for** [*v* + *adv* + *prep* + *o*] **(a)** (enter) ‹*competition*› participar en; ‹*exam/test*› presentarse a **(b)** (take up, practice): **he'd thought of ~ing in for teaching** había pensado dedicarse a la enseñanza

• **go into** [*v* + *prep* + *o*] **1 (a)** (enter) ‹*room/building*› entrar en, entrar a (AmL) **(b)** (crash into) ‹*car/wall*› chocar* contra **(c)** (fit into) entrar en **2 (a)** (start, embark on) ‹*phase/era*› entrar en **(b)** (enter certain state) ‹*coma/trance*› entrar en **(c)** (enter profession) ‹*television/Parliament*› entrar en **3 (a)** (discuss, explain) entrar en; **I don't want to ~ into that** no quiero entrar en ese tema **(b)** (investigate, analyze) ‹*problem/motives*› analizar* **4** (be devoted to): **after all the money/work that has gone into this!** ¡después de todo el dinero/trabajo que se ha metido en esto!

• **go off I** [*v* + *adv*] **1** (depart) irse*, marcharse (esp Esp); **to ~ off WITH sth** llevarse algo **2** «*milk/meat/fish*» echarse a perder **3 (a)** «*bomb/firework*» estallar; «*gun*» dispararse **(b)** «*alarm*» sonar* **4** (stop operating) «*heating/lights*» apagarse*

II [*v* + *prep* + *o*] (lose liking for) (BrE): **to ~ off one's food** perder* el apetito; **I've gone off the idea** ya no me atrae la idea

• **go on** [*v* + *adv*] **1 (a)** (go further) seguir*; **I can't ~ on** no puedo más **(b)** (go ahead): **you ~ on, we'll follow** tú vete que nosotros ya iremos; **he went on ahead to look for a hotel** él fue antes para buscar hotel **2** (continue) «*fight/struggle*» continuar*; **we can't ~ on like this** no podemos seguir así; **the discussion went on for hours** la discusión duró horas; **to ~ on -ING** seguir* + GER; **he went on to become President** llegó a ser presidente; **to ~ on WITH sth** seguir* CON algo; **~ on!** (encouraging, urging) ¡dale!, ¡vamos!, ¡ándale! (Méx), ¡ándele! (Col), ¡venga! (Esp) **3 (a)** (continue speaking) seguir*, continuar* **(b)** (talk irritatingly) (pej): **he went on and on** siguió dale que dale; **to ~ on ABOUT sth** hablar insistentemente DE algo **4** (happen): **what's ~ing on?** ¿qué pasa?; **is there anything ~ing on between them?** ¿hay algo entre ellos?; **how long has this been ~ing on?** ¿desde cuándo viene sucediendo esto? **5 (a)** (onto stage) salir* a escena; (onto field of play) salir* al campo **(b)** (fit, be placed): **the lid won't ~ on** no le puedo (*or* podemos *etc*) poner la tapa

• **go out** [*v* + *adv*] **1 (a)** (leave, exit) salir*; **to ~ out hunting/shopping** salir* de caza/de compras **(b)** (socially, for entertainment) salir*; **to ~ out for a**

meal salir* a comer fuera **(c)** (as boyfriend, girlfriend) **to ~ out** (WITH **sb**) salir* (CON algn) **2 (a)** (be broadcast) «*TV, radio program*» emitirse **(b)** (be issued, distributed): **a warrant has gone out for her arrest** se ha ordenado su detención; **the invitations have already gone out** ya se han mandado las invitaciones **3** (be extinguished) «*fire/cigarette/light*» apagarse* **4** «*tide*» bajar **5** (become outmoded) «*clothes/style*» pasar de moda

• go over I [*v + prep + o*] **1** (check) ‹*text/figures/work*› revisar; ‹*car*› revisar; ‹*house/premises*› inspeccionar **2** (revise, review) ‹*notes/chapter*› repasar **II** [*v + adv*] **1** (make one's way, travel) ir*; **she went over to Jack and took his hand** se acercó a Jack y le tomó la mano **2** (change sides) pasarse

• go past [*v + adv*] [*v + prep + o*] pasar

• go round (BrE) ⇒ GO AROUND

• go through I [*v + prep + o*] **1 (a)** (pass through) ‹*process/stage*› pasar por **(b)** (perform): **let's ~ through the procedure once more** repitamos otra vez todos los pasos del procedimiento **(c)** (endure) ‹*ordeal/hard times*› pasar por **2 (a)** (search) ‹*attic/suitcase*› registrar, revisar (AmL); ‹*drawers/desk*› hurgar* en; **to ~ through sb's mail** abrirle* las cartas a algn **(b)** ⇒ GO OVER I 2 **3** (consume, use up) ‹*money/fortune*› gastarse; **he ~es through ten shirts a week** ensucia diez camisas por semana **II** [*v + adv*] **(a)** (be carried out) «*changes/legislation*» ser* aprobado; «*business deal*» llevarse a cabo; **when his divorce ~es through** cuando obtenga el divorcio **(b)** (Sport): **to ~ through to the next round** pasar a la siguiente etapa

• go through with [*v + adv + prep + o*] ‹*threat/plans*› llevar a cabo

• go together [*v + adv*] «*colors*» combinar; **lamb and mint sauce ~ well together** el cordero queda muy bien con salsa de menta

• go under [*v + adv*] **(a)** (sink) «*ship*» hundirse; «*submarine/diver*» sumergirse* **(b)** (fail, go bankrupt) hundirse

• go up [*v + adv*] **1 (a)** (ascend) «*person*» subir; «*balloon/plane*» subir; «*curtain*» (Theat) levantarse **(b)** (approach) **to ~ up** TO **sb/sth** acercarse* A algn/algo **2 (a)** (increase) «*temperature/price/cost*» subir, aumentar; «*population/unemployment*» aumentar; **to ~ up in price** subir *or* aumentar de precio **(b)** (improve) «*standard*» mejorar **3** (burst into flames) prenderse fuego; (explode) estallar; **to ~ up in flames** incendiarse

• go with [*v + prep + o*] **(a)** (be compatible with): **this sauce ~es well with hamburgers** esta salsa queda muy bien con hamburguesas; **choose a tie to ~ with your shirt** elija una corbata que quede bien con su camisa **(b)** (accompany, be associated with): **the house ~es with the job** la casa va con el puesto

• go without (a) [*v + prep + o*] (do without) pasar sin; **she often went without food** a menudo pasaba sin comer; **they went without food/sleep for days** (not by choice) no comieron nada/no durmieron durante días **(b)** [*v + adv*]: **in order to feed her children she herself often went without** para darles de comer a los niños a menudo pasaba privaciones; **there's no coffee left, you'll just have to ~ without** no queda café, así que tendrás que pasar sin él

go² *n* (*pl* **goes**) **1** [C] **(a)** (attempt): **at one ~** (AmE), **in one ~** (BrE) ‹*empty/eat*› de un tirón (fam); ‹*drink*› de un trago; **she succeeded in lifting it at the third ~** consiguió levantarlo al tercer intento; **I want to have a ~ at learning Arabic** quiero intentar aprender árabe; **have a ~** prueba a ver, inténtalo; ***to have a ~ at sb*** (colloq): **she had a ~ at me for not having told her** se la agarró conmigo por no habérselo dicho (fam) **(b)** (turn): **whose ~ is it?** ¿a quién le toca?; **it's my ~** me toca a mí **2** [U] (energy, drive) empuje *m*; ***(to be) on the ~***: **I've been on the ~ all morning** no he parado en toda la mañana

goad /gəʊd/ *vt* ‹*person*› acosar; ‹*animal*› aguijonear

go-ahead /'gəʊəhed/ *n*: **to give sb/sth the ~** darle* luz verde a algn/algo

goal /gəʊl/ *n* **1** (Sport) **(a)** (structure) portería *f*, arco *m* (AmL) **(b)** (point) gol *m* **2** (aim) meta *f*

goal: **~keeper** *n* portero, -ra *m,f*, guardameta *mf*, arquero, -ra *m,f* (AmL); **~post** *n* poste *m* de la portería *or* (AmL tb) del arco; **~tender** *n* (AmE) ⇒ ~KEEPER

goat /gəʊt/ *n* (Zool) cabra *f*

gobble /'gɑːbəl || 'gɒbəl/ *vt* engullirse*

• gobble up [*v + o + adv, v + adv + o*] tragarse*

gobbledygook /'gɑːbəldi'guːk || 'gɒbəldi,guːk/ *n* [U] (colloq & pej) jerigonza *f*

go-between /'gəʊbɪtwiːn/ *n* (intermediary) intermediario, -ria *m,f*; (messenger) mensajero, -ra *m,f*

goblet /'gɑːblət || 'gɒblɪt/ *n* copa *f*

goblin /'gɑːblən || 'gɒblɪn/ *n* duende *m* travieso, trasgo *m*

god /gɑːd || gɒd/ *n* **1 God** Dios *m*; **G~ bless (you)** que Dios te bendiga; **G~!** ¡Dios (santo)! **2** (deity, idol) dios *m*

god: **~child** *n* ahijado, -da *m,f*; **~dam**, **~damn** *adj* (AmE sl) (*before n*) condenado (fam); **~daughter** /'gɑːd'dɔːtər || 'gɒd,dɔːtə(r)/ *n* ahijada *f*

goddess /'gɑːdəs || 'gɒdɪs/ *n* diosa *f*

god: **~father** /'gɑːd'fɑːðər || 'gɒd,fɑːðə(r)/ *n* padrino *m*; **~mother** /'gɑːd'mʌðər || 'gɒd,mʌðə(r)/ *n* madrina *f*; **~parent** /'gɑːd'perənt || 'gɒd,peərənt/ *n* (man) padrino *m*; (woman) madrina *f*; **my ~parents** mis padrinos; **~send** *n* bendición *f* (del cielo); **~son** *n* ahijado *m*

goggle /'gɑːgəl || 'gɒgəl/ *vi* (pej) **to ~** AT **sth/sb** mirar algo/a algn con los ojos desorbitados

goggles /'gɑːgəlz || 'gɒgəlz/ *pl n* (Sport) gafas *fpl or* anteojos *mpl* (esp AmL) de esquí (*or* natación *etc*); (for welders) gafas *fpl* protectoras, anteojos *mpl* protectores (esp AmL)

going¹ /'gəʊɪŋ/ *n* (*no pl*) **1** (progress): **once at the top, the ~ was easier** una vez en la cima, la marcha fue más fácil; **I found that lecture hard ~** me resultó difícil seguir la conferencia; **the novel was heavy ~** la novela era pesada **2** (departure) partida *f* **3** (situation) situación *f*; **if I were you,**

I'd buy it while the ~ is good yo que tú lo compraría ahora, aprovechando el buen momento; **when the ~ got tough** cuando las cosas se pusieron difíciles

going² *adj* (*before n*) **(a)** (in operation) en marcha; **a ~ concern** (Busn) un negocio *or* una empresa en marcha **(b)** (present, current): **that's the ~ rate** es lo que se suele cobrar/pagar

gold /gəʊld/ *n* **1** [U] (metal) oro *m*; (money) (monedas *fpl* de) oro *m*; (*before n*) ‹*ring/medal*› de oro **2** ▶ **515** [U] (color) dorado *m*, color *m* (de) oro

gold dust *n* [U] oro *m* en polvo

golden /ˈgəʊldən/ *adj* **1 (a)** (made of gold) de oro **(b)** ▶ **515** (in color) dorado **2 (a)** (happy, prosperous) ‹*years*› dorado **(b)** (excellent): **a ~ opportunity** una excelente oportunidad

golden: **~ age** *n* época *f* dorada, edad *f* de oro; **~ wedding (anniversary)** *n* bodas *fpl* de oro

gold: **~fish** *n* (*pl* **-fish** *or* **-fishes**) pececito *m* (rojo); (plural) peces *mpl* de colores; **~ leaf** *n* [U] oro *m* batido, pan *m* de oro; **~ mine** *n* mina *f* de oro; **~-plated** /ˈgəʊldˈpleɪtəd ‖ ˌgəʊldˈpleɪtɪd/ *adj* chapado en oro; **~ rush** *n* fiebre *f* del oro; **~smith** *n* orfebre *mf*

golf /gɑːlf ‖ gɒlf/ *n* [U] golf *m*

golf: **~ ball** *n* (Sport) pelota *f* de golf; **~ club** *n* **(a)** (stick) palo *m* de golf **(b)** (place) club *m* de golf; **~ course** *n* campo *m* *or* (AmL tb) cancha *f* de golf

golfer /ˈgɑːlfər ‖ ˈgɒlfə(r)/ *n* golfista *mf*

gone¹ /gɔːn ‖ gɒn/ *past p of* GO¹

gone² *adj* (*pred*) **(a)** (not here): **my briefcase is ~!** ¡se me ha desaparecido la cartera!; **how long has she been ~?** ¿cuánto hace que se fue? **(b)** (past): **those days are (long) ~** de eso hace ya mucho, ha llovido mucho desde entonces **(c)** (used up): **the money is all ~** se ha acabado el dinero, no queda nada de dinero

gone³ ▶ **884** *prep* (BrE): **it's just ~ five** acaban de dar las cinco

gong /gɑːŋ ‖ gɒŋ/ *n* gong *m*

gonna /gənə ‖ ˈgɒnə/ (colloq) (= **going to**) *see* GO¹ *v aux*

gonorrhea, (BrE) **gonorrhoea** /ˈgɑːnəˈriːə ‖ ˌgɒnəˈrɪə/ *n* [U] gonorrea *f*

goo /guː/ *n* [U] (colloq) mugre *f*

good¹ /gʊd/ *adj*

■ **Note** The usual translation of *good*, *bueno*, becomes *buen* when it precedes a masculine singular noun.

(*comp* **better**; *superl* **best**) **1** ‹*food/quality/book/work/reputation*› bueno; **it smells ~** huele bien; **her French is very ~** habla muy bien (el) francés; **is this a ~ time to phone?** ¿es buena hora para llamar?; **it's ~ to be back home** ¡qué alegría estar otra vez en casa!; **I had a ~ night's sleep** dormí bien **2** (advantageous, useful) ‹*deal/offer/advice*› bueno; **burn it; that's all it's ~ for** quémalo, no sirve para otra cosa; **~ idea!, ~ thinking!** ¡buena idea! **3** (healthy) ‹*diet/habit/exercise*› bueno; **I'm not feeling too ~** (colloq) no me siento bien; **spinach is ~ for you** las espinacas son buenas para la salud **4** (attractive): **it looks ~** tiene buen aspecto; **that dress looks really ~ on her** ese vestido le queda *or* le sienta muy bien **5 (a)** (in interj phrases): **~! now to the next question** bien, pasemos ahora a la siguiente pregunta; **~ for you!** bien hecho **(b)** (for emphasis) (colloq): **I'll do it when I'm ~ and ready** lo haré cuando me parezca; **the water's ~ and hot** el agua está bien caliente **(c) as good as**: **it's as ~ as new** está como nuevo; **he as ~ as admitted it** prácticamente lo admitió **6** (skilled, competent) bueno; **he's no ~ in emergencies** en situaciones de emergencia no sabe qué hacer; **to be ~ at languages** tener* facilidad para los idiomas; **he is ~ with children** tiene buena mano con los niños; **she is ~ with her hands** es muy habilidosa **7** (well-behaved, virtuous) bueno; **~ boy!** ¡muy bien! **8** (kind) bueno; **she was very ~ to me** fue muy amable conmigo **9** (valid) ‹*argument/excuse*› bueno; **this ticket is ~ for another week** este billete vale para una semana más; **it's simply not ~ enough!** ¡esto no puede ser! **10** (substantial, considerable) ‹*meal/salary/distance*› bueno; **there were a ~ many people there** había bastante gente allí **11** (not less than): **it'll take a ~ hour** va a llevar su buena hora *or* una hora larga; **a ~ half of all the people interviewed** más de la mitad de los entrevistados

good² *n* **1** [U] (moral right) bien *m*; **to do ~** hacer* el bien; **there is some ~ in everyone** todos tenemos algo bueno; **to be up to no ~** (colloq) estar* tramando algo, traerse* algo entre manos **2** [U] **(a)** (benefit) bien *m*; **no ~ will come of it** nada bueno saldrá de ello; **to do sb ~** hacerle* bien a algn **(b)** (use): **this knife is no ~ (at all)** este cuchillo no sirve (para nada); **this book is no ~** este libro no vale nada **(c) for good** para siempre **3 goods** *pl* **(a)** (merchandise) artículos *mpl*, mercancías *fpl*, mercaderías *fpl* (AmS); **manufactured ~s** productos *mpl* manufacturados, manufacturas *fpl* **(b)** (property) (frml) bienes *mpl*

goodbye¹ /ˈgʊdˈbaɪ/ *interj* ¡adiós!, ¡chao! *or* ¡chau! (esp AmL)

goodbye² *n*: **to say ~ to sb** decirle* adiós a algn

good: **G~ Friday** *n* Viernes *m* Santo; **~-humored**, (BrE) **~-humoured** /ˈgʊdˈhjuːmərd ‖ ˌgʊdˈhjuːməd/ *adj* ‹*person*› (permanent characteristic) alegre, jovial; (in good mood) de buen humor; ‹*joke*› sin mala intención; **~-looking** /ˈgʊdˈlʊkɪŋ/ *adj* ‹*man*› buen mozo (esp AmL), guapo (esp Esp); **a ~looking woman** una mujer bonita *or* (esp Esp) guapa; **~-natured** /ˈgʊdˈneɪtʃərd ‖ ˌgʊdˈneɪtʃəd/ *adj* (as permanent characteristic) bueno, de natural bondadoso

goodness /ˈgʊdnəs ‖ ˈgʊdnɪs/ *n* [U] **1 (a)** (moral worth) bondad *f* **(b)** (of food) valor *m* nutritivo **2** (*in interj phrases, as intensifier*): **(my) ~!** ¡Dios (mío)!; **~ me!** ¡Dios mío!, ¡válgame Dios!; ⇒ THANK

goodwill /ˈgʊdˈwɪl/ *n* [U] **(a)** (benevolence) buena voluntad *f* **(b)** (Busn, Fin) fondo *m* de comercio, llave *f* (CS)

goofy /ˈguːfi/ *adj* **-fier, -fiest** (AmE sl) ‹*person*› memo (fam); ‹*smile*› bobalicón (fam)

goose /guːs/ *n* (*pl* **geese**) **(a)** [C] (Zool) oca *f*, ganso *m* **(b)** [U] (Culin) ganso *m*

goose: **~berry** /'gu:s,beri ‖ 'gʊzbəri/ *n* **1** (Bot) grosella *f* espinosa, uva *f* espina; **2** (unwanted third person) (BrE colloq) carabina *f* (fam), chaperón, -rona *m,f*, violinista *mf* (Chi fam); **to play ~berry** hacer* de carabina (Esp fam), tocar* el violín (Chi fam); **~bumps** *pl n* (AmE colloq), **~flesh** *n*, **~ pimples** *pl n* carne *f* de gallina

gore /gɔ:r ‖ gɔ:(r)/ *vt* cornear

gorge¹ /gɔ:rdʒ ‖ gɔ:dʒ/ *n* (Geog) desfiladero *m*, cañón *m*

gorge² *v refl* **to ~ oneself** atiborrarse de comida

gorgeous /'gɔ:rdʒəs ‖ 'gɔ:dʒəs/ *adj* **(a)** (lovely) (colloq) ‹*girl*› precioso, guapísimo; ‹*dress*› precioso, divino; ‹*day*› maravilloso, espléndido **(b)** (splendid) ‹*color*› magnífico

gorilla /gə'rɪlə/ *n* gorila *m*

gorse /gɔ:rs ‖ 'gɔ:s/ *n* [U] aulaga *f*, tojo *m*

gory /'gɔ:ri/ *adj* **gorier, goriest** (colloq) sangriento

gosh /gɑ:ʃ ‖ gɒʃ/ *interj* (colloq) ¡(mi) Dios!, ¡Dios mío!

gospel /'gɑ:spəl ‖ 'gɒspəl/ *n* **(a)** [C] **Gospel** (in New Testament) evangelio *m* **(b)** (Christian teaching) (*no pl*) Evangelio *m*; (*before n*) **it's ~ (truth)** es la pura verdad **(c)** [U] **~ (music)** (Mus) gospel *m*

gossamer /'gɑ:səmər ‖ 'gɒsəmə(r)/ *n* [U] (liter) telaraña *f*; (*before n*) ‹*threads*› tenue

gossip¹ /'gɑ:səp ‖ 'gɒsɪp/ *n* **(a)** [U] (speculation, scandal) chismorreo *m* (fam), cotilleo *m* (Esp fam); **an interesting piece of ~** un chisme interesante; (*before n*) **~ column** crónica *f* de sociedad **(b)** [C U] (chat): **to have a ~ with sb** chismorrear (fam) *or* (Esp tb) cotillear con algn **(c)** [C] (person) chismoso, -sa *m,f* (fam), cotilla *mf* (Esp fam)

gossip² *vi* **(a)** (chatter) chismorrear (fam), cotillear (Esp fam) **(b)** (spread tales) contar* chismes

got /gɑ:t ‖ gɒt/ **1** *past & past p of* GET **2** (crit) *pres of* HAVE

Gothic /'gɑ:θɪk ‖ 'gɒθɪk/ *adj* (Archit, Lit) gótico

gotta /'gɑ:tə ‖ 'gɒtə/ (sl) = **have got to**

gotten /'gɑ:tn ‖ 'gɒtn/ (AmE) *past p of* GET

gouge /gaʊdʒ/ *vt* ‹*hole*› abrir*

• **gouge out** [*v + o + adv, v + adv + o*] sacar*

gourd /gʊrd, gɔ:rd ‖ gʊəd/ *n* (Bot) calabaza *f*, jícaro *m* (AmC, Col, Méx)

gourmet /'gʊrmeɪ ‖ 'gʊəmeɪ/ *n* gourmet *mf*, gastrónomo, -ma *m,f*

gout /gaʊt/ *n* [U] gota *f*

govern /'gʌvərn ‖ 'gʌvən/ *vt* **(a)** (rule) gobernar* **(b)** (determine) determinar **(c) governing** *pres p* ‹*party*› de gobierno; ‹*principle*› rector; **~ing body** organismo *m* rector ■ **~** *vi* gobernar*

governess /'gʌvərnəs ‖ 'gʌvənɪs/ *n* institutriz *f*

government /'gʌvərnmənt ‖ 'gʌvənmənt/ *n* [U C] gobierno *m*; (*before n*) **~ policy** política *f* gubernamental

governor /'gʌvənər ‖ 'gʌvənə(r)/ *n* **1** (of state, province, colony) gobernador, -dora *m,f* **2** (of institution): **prison ~** (BrE) director, -tora *m,f* de una cárcel; **school ~** (BrE) *miembro de un consejo escolar*

gown /gaʊn/ *n* **1 (a)** (dress) vestido *m*; **evening ~** traje *m* de fiesta **(b)** (*night~*) (AmE) camisón *m* **2 (a)** (Educ, Law) toga *f* **(b)** (Med) bata *f*

GP *n* (= **general practitioner**) médico, -ca *m,f* de medicina general; **my ~** mi médico de cabecera

gr ▶ **322** (= **gram(s)**) gr., g.

grab /græb/ **-bb-** *vt* **(a)** (seize) ‹*rope/hand*› agarrar; ‹*chance*› aprovechar **(b)** (appropriate) ‹*land*› apropiarse de; ‹*money*› llevarse **(c)** (appeal to) (colloq) «*idea*» atraer*; **how does that ~ you?** ¿qué te parece? ■ **~** *vi*: **to ~ AT sth**: **she ~bed at the rope** trató de agarrar la cuerda

grace /greɪs/ *n* **1** [U] (elegance — of movement) gracia *f*, garbo *m*; (— of expression, form) elegancia *f* **2 (a)** [U] (courtesy) cortesía *f*, gentileza *f* **(b)** [U] (good nature): **to do sth with good/bad ~** hacer* algo de buen talante/a regañadientes **(c)** [C] (good quality): **her saving ~ is her sense of humor** lo que la salva es que tiene sentido del humor; **social ~s** modales *mpl* **3** [U] (Relig) **(a)** (mercy) gracia *f*; **by the ~ of God** ... gracias a Dios ... **(b)** (prayer): **to say ~** (before a meal) bendecir* la mesa **4** [U] (respite) gracia *f*; **16 days' ~** (BrE Law) 16 días de gracia

graceful /'greɪsfəl/ *adj* ‹*dancer/movement*› lleno de gracia, grácil (liter); ‹*style*› elegante

gracefully /'greɪsfəli/ *adv* con gracia *or* garbo

gracious¹ /'greɪʃəs/ *adj* **(a)** ‹*smile/act*› gentil, cortés **(b)** (merciful) misericordioso

gracious² *interj*: **(good** *o* **goodness) ~!** (expressing surprise) ¡Dios Santo!; (expressing exasperation) ¡por favor!

graciously /'greɪʃəsli/ *adv* ‹*smile/apologize*› gentilmente

grade¹ /greɪd/ *n* **1 (a)** (quality) calidad *f*; **~ A tomatoes** tomates *mpl* de la mejor calidad **(b)** (degree, level): **it divides hotels into four ~s** divide a los hoteles en cuatro categorías **(c)** (in seniority) grado *m* (*del escalafón*); (Mil) rango *m* **2** (Educ) **(a)** (class) (AmE) grado *m*, año *m*, curso *m* **(b)** (in exam) nota *f*

grade² *vt* **1 (a)** (classify) clasificar* **(b)** (order in ascending scale) ‹*exercise/questions*› ordenar por grado de dificultad **(c)** (mark) (AmE) ‹*test/exercise*› corregir* y calificar* **(d) graded** *past p* ‹*produce*› clasificado **2** (make more level) ‹*surface/soil*› (AmE) nivelar

grade: **~ crossing** *n* (AmE) paso *m* a nivel, crucero *m* (Méx); **~ school** *n* (AmE) escuela *f* primaria

gradient /'greɪdiənt/ *n* (slope) pendiente *f*, gradiente *f* (AmL)

gradual /'grædʒuəl/ *adj* ‹*improvement*› gradual; ‹*slope*› no muy empinado

gradually /'grædʒuəli/ *adv* ‹*improve*› gradualmente, poco a poco; ‹*rise/slope*› suavemente

graduate¹ /'grædʒueɪt/ *vi* **1** (Educ) **(a)** (from a college, university) terminar la carrera, recibirse (AmL), graduarse*; (obtain bachelor's degree) licenciarse **(b)** (from high school) (AmE) terminar el bachillerato, recibirse de bachiller (AmL) **2** (progress) **to ~ (FROM sth) TO sth** pasar (DE algo) A algo

graduate² /'grædʒuət/ *n* **(a)** (from higher education) *persona con título universitario*; (with a bachelor's degree) licenciado, -da *m,f*; (*before n*) ‹*course/student*› de posgrado *or* postgrado; **he went to ~ school** (AmE) hizo un curso de posgrado **(b)** (from high school) (AmE) bachiller *mf*

graduated /'grædʒueɪtəd ‖ 'grædʒueɪtɪd/ *adj* **(a)** (progressive) ‹*scale*› graduado; ‹*payments*› escalonado **(b)** (calibrated) ‹*flask/test tube*› graduado

graduation /'grædʒu'eɪʃən/ *n* [U] (Educ) graduación *f*

graffiti /grə'fiːti/ *n* (+ *sing o pl vb*) graffiti *mpl*

graft¹ /græft ‖ grɑːft/ *vt* (Hort) injertar

graft² *n* **1** [C] (Hort, Med) injerto *m* **2** [U] (bribery, corruption) (AmE colloq) chanchullos *mpl* (fam)

grain /greɪn/ *n* **1** [C] (of cereal, salt, sugar, sand) grano *m* **2** [U] (Agr) grano *m*, cereal *m* **3** [U] (of wood — pattern) veta *f*, veteado *m*; (— texture) grano *m*; ***to go against the* ~**: **it goes against the ~ for me to support them** apoyarlos va en contra de mis principios

gram, (BrE also) **gramme** /græm/ ▶ 322 *n* gramo *m*

grammar /'græmər ‖ 'græmə(r)/ *n* [U C] gramática *f*

grammar school *n* **(a)** (in US) ⇒ ELEMENTARY SCHOOL **(b)** (in UK) *colegio de enseñanza secundaria para ingresar al cual hay que aprobar un examen de aptitud*

grammatical /grə'mætɪkəl/ *adj* **(a)** (of grammar) gramatical **(b)** (correct) gramaticalmente correcto

gramme /græm/ *n* (BrE) ⇒ GRAM

granary /'greɪnəri, 'grænəri ‖ 'grænəri/ *n* (*pl* **-ries**) granero *m*

grand /grænd/ *adj* **-er, -est 1 (a)** (impressive) magnífico **(b)** (ostentatious) ‹*gesture*› grandilocuente; ‹*entrance*› triunfal **(c)** (ambitious, lofty) ‹*vision*› grandioso; ‹*ideal*› elevado **(d)** (overall) (*before n, no comp*) global; **the ~ total** el total **2** (formal, ceremonial) ‹*opening/occasion*› solemne **3** (very good) (colloq) ‹*day/weather*› espléndido

grandad /'grændæd/ *n* abuelo *m*

grand: **G~ Canyon** *n* **the G~ Canyon** el Cañón del Colorado; **~child** /'græntʃaɪld/ *n* nieto, -ta *m,f*; **~dad** /'grændæd/ *n* abuelo *m*; **~daughter** /'græn,dɔːtər ‖ 'græn,dɔːtə(r)/ *n* nieta *f*

grandeur /'grændʒər ‖ 'grændʒə(r)/ *n* [U] grandiosidad *f*

grandfather /'græn,fɑːðər ‖ 'græn,fɑːðə(r)/ *n* abuelo *m*; (*before n*) **~ clock** reloj *m* de pie

grandiose /'grændiəʊs/ *adj* ‹*claim/scheme/notion*› fatuo; ‹*speech*› altisonante

grand: **~ jury** *n* (in US) jurado *m* de acusación (*jurado que decide si hay suficientes pruebas para procesar*); **~ma** /'grænmɑː/ *n* (colloq) abuela *f*; **~mother** /'græn,mʌðər ‖ 'græn,mʌðə(r)/ *n* abuela *f*; **~pa** /'grænpɑː/ *n* abuelo *m*; **~parent** /'græn,perənt ‖ 'græn,peərənt/ *n* abuelo, -la *m,f*; **my ~parents** mis abuelos; **~ piano** *n* piano *m* de cola; **~son** /'grænsʌn/ *n* nieto *m*; **~stand** *n* tribuna *f*; (*before n*) ‹*ticket/seat*› de tribuna

granite /'grænət ‖ 'grænɪt/ *n* [U] granito *m*

granny, **grannie** /'græni/ *n* (*pl* **-nies**) abuelita *f* (fam)

grant¹ /grænt ‖ grɑːnt/ *vt* **1 (a)** ‹*desire/request*› conceder **(b)** ‹*interview/asylum*› conceder **(c)** ‹*land/pension*› otorgar* **2** (admit) reconocer* **3**

granted *past p* (admittedly): **~ed, it's very expensive, but** ... de acuerdo, es muy caro, pero ...; ***to take sth for ~ed*** dar* algo por sentado

grant² *n* (subsidy — to body, individual) subvención *f*, subsidio *m* (AmL); (— to student) (esp BrE) beca *f*

granulated /'grænjəleɪtəd ‖ 'grænjʊleɪtɪd/ *adj*: **~ sugar** azúcar *f* granulada, azúcar *m* granulado

granule /'grænjuːl/ *n* gránulo *m*

grape /greɪp/ *n* (fruit) uva *f*; **it's sour ~s** (set phrase) las uvas están verdes (fr hecha)

grape: **~fruit** *n* (*pl* **-fruit** *or* **-fruits**) toronja *f* (AmL exc CS), pomelo *m* (CS, Esp); **~vine** *n* **(a)** (Agr, Bot) parra *f* **(b)** (source of information) (colloq): **I heard it on** *o* **through the ~vine** me lo dijo un pajarito (fam), lo he escuchado en radio macuto (Esp fam)

graph /græf ‖ grɑːf/ *n* gráfico *m*, gráfica *f*

graphic /'græfɪk/ *adj* **1** (vivid) ‹*account/description*› muy gráfico; **in ~ detail** con todo lujo de detalles **2** (Art) gráfico; **~ design** diseño *m* gráfico

graphics /'græfɪks/ *pl n* **1** (graphic design) diseño *m* gráfico **2** (Comput) gráficos *mpl*

graph paper *n* [U] papel *m* milimetrado *or* (Méx) cuadriculado

grapple /'græpl/ *vi* **to ~** (WITH **sb/sth**) forcejear (CON algn/algo); **to ~ with one's conscience** tener* escrúpulos de conciencia

grasp¹ /græsp ‖ grɑːsp/ *vt* **1 (a)** (seize) ‹*object/person*› agarrar; ‹*opportunity/offer*› aprovechar **(b)** (hold tightly) tener* agarrado **2** (understand) ‹*concept*› captar ■ **~** *vi* **to ~** AT **sth** tratar de agarrar algo; ‹*opportunity*› aprovechar

grasp² *n* (*no pl*) **1 (a)** (grip): **he tightened his ~ on my arm** me apretó más el brazo **(b)** (reach) alcance *m* **2** (understanding) comprensión *f*; (knowledge) conocimientos *mpl*

grasping /'græspɪŋ ‖ 'grɑːspɪŋ/ *adj* avaricioso

grass /græs ‖ grɑːs/ *n* **(a)** [U] (as pasture) pasto *m*, zacate *m* (Méx); (lawn) césped *m*, hierba *f*, pasto *m* (AmL), grama (AmC, Ven); ***the ~ is always greener on the other side*** nadie está contento con su suerte **(b)** [C U] (Bot) hierba *f*

grass: **~hopper** /'græs,hɑːpər ‖ 'grɑːs,hɒpə(r)/ *n* saltamontes *m*; **~ roots** *pl n* (ordinary members) (*before n*) ‹*support/opinion*› de las bases

grassy /'græsi ‖ 'grɑːsi/ *adj* **-sier, -siest** cubierto de hierba

grate¹ /greɪt/ *vt* (Culin) rallar; **~d cheese** queso *m* rallado ■ **~** *vi* **(a)** (irritate) ser* crispante **(b)** (make harsh noise) chirriar*

grate² *n* (metal frame in fireplace) rejilla *f*; (fireplace) chimenea *f*

grateful /'greɪtfəl/ *adj* agradecido; **I'm very ~ to you for your advice** le agradezco mucho sus consejos

grater /'greɪtər ‖ 'greɪtə(r)/ *n* rallador *m*

gratify /'grætəfaɪ ‖ 'grætɪfaɪ/ *vt* **-fies, -fying, -fied (a)** (fulfill) satisfacer* **(b)** (give satisfaction) complacer*

grating¹ /'greɪtɪŋ/ *adj* **(a)** (harsh) ‹*noise/sound*› chirriante **(b)** (irritating) crispante

grating² *n* rejilla *f*

gratitude /'grætətu:d ‖ 'grætɪtju:d/ *n* [U] gratitud *f*

gratuitous /grə'tu:ətəs ‖ grə'tju:ɪtəs/ *adj* (pej) gratuito

grave[1] /greɪv/ *adj* **graver, gravest 1** ‹*error/danger/voice*› grave **2** /grɑ:v/ (Ling) ‹*accent*› grave

grave[2] *n* tumba *f*, sepultura *f*

gravedigger /'greɪv,dɪgər ‖ 'greɪv,dɪgə(r)/ *n* sepulturero, -ra *m,f*

gravel /'grævəl/ *n* [U] grava *f*; (finer) gravilla *f*

gravely /'greɪvli/ *adv* **(a)** (seriously) gravemente **(b)** (solemnly) con gravedad

grave: **~stone** *n* lápida *f*; **~yard** *n* cementerio *m*, panteón *m* (Méx)

gravitate /'grævəteɪt ‖ 'grævɪteɪt/ *vi*: **people of similar interests naturally ~ toward each other** uno tiende a acercarse a gente con intereses afines; **young people tend to ~ toward the big cities** las grandes ciudades son un polo de atracción para los jóvenes

gravity /'grævəti/ *n* [U] **1** (Phys) gravedad *f* **2** (seriousness) gravedad *f*

gravy /'greɪvi/ *n* [U] (Culin) *salsa hecha con el jugo de la carne asada*

gray[1], (BrE) **grey** /greɪ/ ▶ **515** *adj* **-er, -est** gris; ‹*outlook/future*› poco prometedor; **a ~ hair** una cana; **she has ~ hair** es canosa

gray[2], (BrE) **grey** ▶ **515** *n* [U] gris *m*

graze[1] /greɪz/ *vt* **(a)** (cut, injure) rasguñarse **(b)** (touch, brush) rozar* ■ ~ *vi* (Agr) pastar

graze[2] *n* rasguño *m*

grease[1] /gri:s/ *n* [U] grasa *f*

grease[2] *vt* **(a)** (lubricate) ‹*machinery/hinge*› engrasar **(b)** (Culin): **to ~ (with butter)** enmantequillar, enmantecar* (RPl); **to ~ (with oil)** aceitar

grease: **~paint** *n* [U] maquillaje *m* teatral; **~proof paper** *n* [U] (BrE) papel *m* encerado *or* (Esp) parafinado, papel *m* manteca (RPl), papel *m* mantequilla (Chi)

greasy /'gri:si/ *adj* **-sier, -siest (a)** (soiled) ‹*hands*› grasiento; ‹*overalls*› cubierto de grasa **(b)** (containing grease) ‹*food*› graso; (pej) grasiento **(c)** ‹*hair/skin*› graso, grasoso (esp AmL)

great[1] /greɪt/ *adj* **1** (*before n*) (large in size, number, quantity) (*sing*) gran (*delante del n*); (*pl*) grandes (*delante del n*); **a ~ many people** muchísima gente **2** (*before n*) **(a)** (important) ‹*landowner/occasion*› (*sing*) gran (*delante del n*); (*pl*) grandes (*delante del n*); **Catherine the G~** Catalina la Grande **(b)** (genuine, real) (*before n*) ‹*friend/rival*› (*sing*) gran (*delante del n*); (*pl*) grandes (*delante del n*) **3** (excellent) (colloq) ‹*goal/movie/meal*› sensacional; **he's a really ~ guy** es un tipo *or* (Esp tb) tío sensacional (fam); (*as interj*) **(that's) ~!** ¡fenomenal!, ¡estupendo! (fam)

great[2] *adv* (esp AmE colloq) fenomenal (fam)

great: **~-aunt** /'greɪt'ænt ‖ ,greɪt'ɑ:nt/ *n* tía *f* abuela; **G~ Britain** *n* Gran Bretaña *f*; **G~ Dane** *n* gran danés *m*; **~-granddaughter** /'greɪt'græn,dɔ:tər ‖ ,greɪt'græn,dɔ:tə(r)/ *n* bisnieta *f*, biznieta *f*; **~-grandfather** /'greɪt 'græn,fɑ:ðer ‖ ,greɪt'græn,fɑ:ðə(r)/ *n* bisabuelo *m*; **~-grandmother** /'greɪt'græn,mʌðər ‖ ,greɪt 'græn,mʌðə(r)/ *n* bisabuela *f*; **~-grandson** /'greɪt'grænsʌn/ *n* bisnieto *m*, biznieto *m*

greatly /'greɪtli/ *adv* (*as intensifier*) ‹*admire/improve*› enormemente

great-uncle /'greɪt'ʌŋkəl/ *n* tío *m* abuelo

Greece /gri:s/ *n* Grecia *f*

greed /gri:d/ *n* [U] **(a)** (for food) gula *f*, angurria *f* (CS) **(b)** (for power, money) codicia *f*

greedy /'gri:di/ *adj* **-dier, -diest (a)** (for food, drink) glotón, angurriento (CS) **(b)** (for power, wealth) **to be ~ FOR sth** tener* ansias DE algo

Greek[1] /gri:k/ *adj* griego

Greek[2] *n* **(a)** [U] (language) griego *m* **(b)** [C] (person) griego, -ga *m,f*

green[1] /gri:n/ ▶ **515** *adj* **-er, -est 1** (in color) verde; **he was ~ with envy** se moría de envidia; ***to have a ~ thumb*** *o* (BrE) ***~ fingers*** tener* mano para las plantas **2 (a)** (unripe) verde **(b)** (colloq) (*pred*) (inexperienced) verde (fam) **3** (Pol) verde, ecologista

green[2] ▶ **515** *n* **1** [U] (color) verde *m* **2** [C] (in village, town) ≈ plaza *f* (*con césped*) **3 greens** *pl* (vegetables) verdura *f* (*de hoja verde*)

green: **~back** *n* (AmE colloq) dólar *m*, verde *m* (esp AmL fam); **~ bean** *n* habichuela *f or* (Esp) judía *f* verde *or* (Méx) ejote *m or* (RPl) chaucha *f or* (Chi) poroto *m* verde *or* (Ven) vainita *f*; **~ card** *n* (in US) permiso *m* de residencia y trabajo; **~fly** *n* (*pl* **-flies** *or* **-fly**) (BrE) pulgón *m*; **~grocer** *n* (BrE) verdulero, -ra *m,f*; **the ~grocer('s)** la verdulería; **~house** *n* invernadero *m*; (*before n*) **the ~house effect** (Ecol) el efecto invernadero; **G~land** /'gri:nlənd/ *n* Groenlandia *f*; **~ onion** *n* (AmE) cebolleta *f*, cebollino *m*; **~ pepper** *n see* PEPPER[1] 2

Greenwich Mean Time /'grenɪdʒ, 'grenɪtʃ/ *n* [U] hora *f* de Greenwich

greet /gri:t/ *vt* **1 (a)** (welcome, receive) ‹*guest/client*› recibir **(b)** (say hello to) saludar **2** (react to) acoger* **3** (meet): **a strange sight ~ed our eyes** un extraño espectáculo se ofreció a nuestra vista

greeting /'gri:tɪŋ/ ▶ **624** *n* **(a)** (spoken) saludo *m*; (*as interj*) **~s!** (arch *or* hum) ¡buenas! (fam) **(b)** (message) (*usu pl*): Ⓢ **birthday/Christmas greetings** feliz cumpleaños/Navidad; (*before n*) **a ~** *o* (BrE also) **~s card** una tarjeta de felicitación

gregarious /grɪ'geriəs ‖ grɪ'geəriəs/ *adj* ‹*person*› sociable; (Zool) gregario

Grenada /grə'neɪdə/ *n* Granada *f*

grenade /grə'neɪd/ *n* granada *f*

grew /gru:/ *past of* GROW

grey *adj/n* (BrE) ⇨ GRAY[1,2]

greyhound /'greɪhaʊnd/ *n* galgo *m*

grid /grɪd/ *n* **1** (grating over opening) rejilla *f* **2** (on map) (Geog) cuadriculado *m*; (*before n*) **~ reference** coordenadas *fpl* cartográficas

griddle /'grɪdl/ *n* plancha *f*

grid: **~iron** /'grid'aɪərn ‖ 'grɪdaɪən/ *n* **1** (Culin) parrilla *f*; **2** (in US football) campo *m*, cancha *f* (AmL), emparrillado *m* (Méx); **~lock** *n* [U] (esp AmE) paralización *f* total del tráfico

Greetings and Introductions

Hello *o* (colloq) hi. How are you?	=	hola, ¿qué tal (estas)?
very well, thanks	=	muy bien, gracias
fine thanks, and you?	=	muy bien, gracias ¿y tú?
hi, how are things? *o* (AmE) what's up?	=	hola ¿qué hay?
not too bad	=	aquí ando, tirando

Other possible replies:

all right *o* OK, thanks	=	bien, gracias
so-so	=	más o menos
the same as ever	=	igual que siempre *or* nada nuevo
what have you been doing?	=	¿qué has estado haciendo?
what have you been up to?	=	¿en qué has andado últimamente?
how are things? *o* what's up?	=	¿qué cuentas (de nuevo)?

Introductions

Jane, this is my brother Tim *o* Tim, this is Jane	=	Jane, te presento a mi hermano Tim
Hello *o* (fam) hi. Nice to meet you	=	hola ¿qué tal?

In a more formal situation

John, I'd like you to meet Rowland *o* I'd like to introduce you to Mr Rowland *o* meet Mr Rowland	=	John, le presento a Mr Rowland *or* permítame presentarle *or* que le presente a Mr Rowland
How do you do? Pleased to meet you	=	¿cómo está? encantado (de conocerlo) *or* mucho gusto

General conversation on meeting people

what's your name?	=	¿cómo te llamas/cómo se llama usted?
John *o* I'm John	=	John
where are you from? *o* where do you come from?	=	¿de dónde eres/es usted?
I'm from Newcastle/ New Zealand	=	soy de Newcastle/ Nueva Zelandia
I'm Portuguese	=	soy portugués
where do you live?	=	¿dónde vives/vive?
what do you do?	=	¿qué haces/hace usted? *or* ¿en qué trabajas/ trabaja?
I'm a teacher/ a student	=	soy profesor/estudiante
I'm married/single	=	soy *or* (*esp Esp*) estoy casado/soltero
do you have (any) children?	=	¿tienes/tiene usted hijos?
no, I don't	=	no
I have three children, two boys and a girl	=	tengo tres hijos, dos niños y una niña

grief /gri:f/ *n* [U] dolor *m*, profunda pena *f*; ***to come to ~*** «*plans*» fracasar, irse* al traste (fam); **he'll come to ~ one day** va a acabar mal

grievance /'gri:vəns/ *n* **(a)** (ground for complaint) motivo *m* de queja; **to air one's ~s** quejarse **(b)** (Lab Rel) queja *f* formal; (*before n*) **~ procedure** procedimiento *m* conciliatorio

grieve /gri:v/ *vi* sufrir; **to ~ FOR sb** llorar a algn ■ **~** *vt* apenar

grievous /'gri:vəs/ *adj* (liter) ‹*loss*› doloroso; ‹*wound/injury*› de extrema gravedad; **~ bodily harm** (Law) lesiones *fpl* (corporales) graves

grill¹ /grɪl/ *vt* **1** (BrE Culin) (in electric, gas grill) hacer* al grill; (over hot fire) hacer* a la parrilla **2** (interrogate) (colloq) interrogar*

grill² *n* **(a)** (on stove) (esp BrE) grill *m*, gratinador *m* **(b)** (on barbecue) parrilla *f*

grille /grɪl/ *n* **(a)** (partition) reja *f* **(b)** (protective covering) (Tech) rejilla *f*; (Auto) calandra *f*

grim /grɪm/ *adj* **-mm-** ‹*person/expression*› adusto; (gloomy) ‹*outlook/situation*› nefasto; **she carried on with ~ determination** siguió adelante, resuelta a no dejarse vencer

grimace¹ /'grɪməs, grɪ'meɪs/ *n* mueca *f*

grimace² *vi* hacer* una mueca

grime /graɪm/ *n* [U] mugre *f*

grimy /'graɪmi/ *adj* **-mier, -miest** mugriento

grin¹ /grɪn/ *vi* **-nn-** sonreír* (*abiertamente o burlonamente*); ***to ~ and bear it*** aguantarse

grin² *n* sonrisa *f*

grind¹ /graɪnd/ (*past & past p* **ground**) *vt* ‹*coffee/wheat*› moler*; (in mortar) machacar*; ‹*meat*› (AmE) moler* *or* (Esp, RPl) picar*; ‹*crystals/ore*› triturar; **he ~s his teeth in his sleep** le rechinan los dientes cuando duerme ■ **~** *vi* (move with friction) rechinar, chirriar*; ***to ~ to a halt** o **standstill*** «*vehicle*» pararse *or* detenerse* con un chirrido; «*negotiations*» llegar* a un punto muerto

grind² *n* **(a)** (drudgery) (colloq) (*no pl*): **the daily ~** el monótono trajín diario **(b)** (over-conscientious worker) (AmE colloq): **she's the office ~** es la niña aplicada de la oficina (iró)

grinder /'graɪndər ‖ 'graɪndə(r)/ *n* (machine) molinillo *m*; **a coffee ~** un molinillo de café

grindstone /'graɪnstəʊn, 'graɪndstəʊn ‖ 'graɪnd stəʊn/ *n* muela *f*, piedra *f* de afilar; **back to the ~!** ¡de vuelta al yugo!

grip¹ /grɪp/ *n* **1 (a)** (hold): **she held his arm in a strong ~** lo tenía agarrado *or* asido fuertemente del brazo; **he kept a firm ~ on expenses** llevaba un rígido control de los gastos; **get a ~ on yourself!** ¡contrólate!; **the region is in the ~ of an epidemic** una epidemia asola la región; ***to come to ~s with sth*** ‹*idea/situation*› aceptar *or* asumir algo; ***to get to ~s with sth*** ‹*subject*› entender* algo; ‹*new system*› aprender **(b)** (of tires) adherencia *f* **2** (on handle) empuñadura *f* **3** (*hair ~*) (BrE) horquilla *f*, pinche *m* (Chi), pasador *m* (Méx)

grip² *vt* **-pp- 1** (take hold of) agarrar; (have hold of) tener* agarrado **2** (of feelings, attention): **the audience was ~ped by the play** la obra captó la atención del público

gripping /'grɪpɪŋ/ *adj* apasionante

grisly /'grɪzli/ *adj* **-lier, -liest** truculento

gristle /'grɪsəl/ *n* [U] cartílago *m*

grit¹ /grɪt/ *n* [U] **1 (a)** (dirt) polvo *m* **(b)** (gravel) arenilla *f* **2** (courage) (colloq) agallas *fpl* (fam) **3 grits** *pl* (*hominy ~s*) (AmE Culin) sémola *f* de maíz

grit² *vt* **-tt- (a)** (BrE) ‹*road*› echar arenilla en **(b)** ⇒ TOOTH (a)

grizzly /'grɪzli/ *n* (*pl* **-lies**), **grizzly bear** oso *m* pardo

groan¹ /grəʊn/ *vi* **1 (a)** (with pain, suffering) gemir* **(b)** (with dismay) gruñir* **(c)** (creak) «*door/timber*» crujir **2** (grumble) (colloq) refunfuñar (fam)

groan² *n* **(a)** (of pain, suffering) quejido *m* **(b)** (of dismay) gruñido *m* **(c)** (creak) crujido *m*

grocer /'grəʊsər ‖ 'grəʊsə(r)/ *n* tendero, -ra *m,f*, almacenero, -ra *m,f* (esp CS); **the ~'s** (BrE) la tienda de comestibles *or* de ultramarinos, la bodega (Cu, Per, Ven), la tienda de abarrotes (AmC, Andes, Méx), el almacén (esp CS)

grocery /'grəʊsəri/ *n* (*pl* **-ries**) **(a)** (shop) tienda *f* de comestibles *or* de ultramarinos, bodega *f* (Cu, Per, Ven), tienda *f* de abarrotes (AmC, Andes, Méx), almacén *m* (esp CS) **(b) groceries** *pl* (provisions) comestibles *mpl*, provisiones *fpl*

groggy /'grɑːgi ‖ 'grɒgi/ *adj* **-gier, -giest** (colloq) grogui (fam)

groin /grɔɪn/ ▶ 484 *n* (Anat) ingle *f*

groom¹ /gruːm/ *vt* **(a)** ‹*dog*› cepillar; ‹*horse*› cepillar, almohazar* **(b)** (make neat, attractive) (*usu pass*): **well ~ed** bien arreglado **(c)** (prepare) preparar; **to ~ sb for sth** preparar a algn para algo

groom² *n* **1** (Equ) mozo *m* de cuadra **2** (*bride~*) novio *m*

groove /gruːv/ *n* ranura *f*; (Audio) surco *m*

grope /grəʊp/ *vi* andar* a tientas; **to ~ FOR sth** buscar* algo a tientas ■ *~ vt* ‹*person*› (colloq) manosear, meterle mano a (fam)

gross¹ /grəʊs/ *adj* **1** (extreme, flagrant) (*before n*) ‹*disregard/injustice*› flagrante; ‹*exaggeration*› burdo **2** (total) ‹*weight/profit/income*› bruto; **~ national product** (Econ) producto *m* nacional bruto **3 (a)** (fat) obeso **(b)** (disgusting) ‹*person*› asqueroso; ‹*language/joke*› soez

gross² *vt* «*worker/earner*» tener* una entrada bruta de; **their profits ~ed 2 million** tuvieron beneficios brutos de 2 millones

gross³ *n* **1** (*pl ~*) (144) gruesa *f* **2** (*pl* **grosses**) (gross profit) (AmE) ingresos *mpl* brutos

grossly /'grəʊsli/ *adv* ‹*exaggerated/unfair*› terriblemente

grotesque /grəʊ'tesk/ *adj* grotesco

grotto /'grɑːtəʊ ‖ 'grɒtəʊ/ *n* (*pl* **-toes** *or* **-tos**) gruta *f*

ground¹ /graʊnd/ *n* **1** [U] (land, terrain) terreno *m*; ***to gain/lose ~*** ganar/perder* terreno; ***to stand one's ~*** (in argument) mantenerse* firme; (in battle) no ceder terreno **2 grounds** *pl* (premises) terreno *m*; (gardens) jardines *mpl* **3** [U] (surface of the earth) suelo *m*; (soil) tierra *f*; ***to break new ~*** abrir* nuevos caminos; ***to get off the ~*** «*plan/project*» llegar* a concretarse; «*talks*» empezar* a encaminarse; ***to get sth off the ~*** ‹*project*› poner* algo en marcha; ***to suit sb down to the ~*** (colloq) «*arrangement*» venirle* de perlas a algn (fam); «*hat*» quedarle que ni pintado a algn (fam) **4** [U] (matter, subject): **we covered a lot of ~ in our discussions** tratamos muchos puntos en nuestras conversaciones **5** [C] (outdoor site): **football ~** (BrE) campo *m* de fútbol, cancha *f* de fútbol (AmL); **recreation ~** parque *m* (*donde se practican deportes*) **6** [U] (AmE Elec) tierra *f* **7** (justification) (*usu pl*) motivo *m*; **~s for divorce** causal *f* de divorcio; **on ~s of ill health** por motivos de salud; **they refused, on the ~s that** ... se negaron, alegando que ... **8 grounds** *pl* (dregs): **coffee ~s** posos *mpl* de café

ground² *vt* **1** (*usu pass*) **(a)** (base) ‹*argument/theory*› fundar **(b)** (instruct): **we were well ~ed in German** se nos dio una sólida base en alemán **2 (a)** ‹*plane*› retirar del servicio **(b)** ‹*child/teenager*› (esp AmE colloq): **I can't go out tonight; I'm ~ed** no puedo salir esta noche, estoy castigado *or* no me dejan **3** (Naut) ‹*ship*› hacer* encallar

ground³ *past & past p of* GRIND¹

ground⁴ *adj* ‹*coffee/pepper*› molido; **~ beef** (AmE) carne *f* molida *or* (Esp, RPl) picada

ground: **~cloth**, (BrE) **~sheet** *n* suelo *m* impermeable (*de una tienda de campaña*); **~ control** *n* [U] control *m* de tierra; **~ floor** *n* (BrE) **the ~ floor** la planta baja, el primer piso (Chi)

grounding /'graʊndɪŋ/ *n* (*no pl*) base *f*

groundless /'graʊndləs ‖ 'graʊndlɪs/ *adj* infundado

ground: **~ level** *n* [U]: **at ~ level** a ras del suelo; **above ~ level** sobre el nivel del suelo; **below ~ level** bajo tierra; **~ rule** *n* **1** (guiding principle) directriz *f*; **2** (AmE Sport) regla *f* de terreno *or* de campo, regla local (Ven); **~sheet** *n* (BrE) ⇒ GROUNDCLOTH; **~work** *n* [U] trabajo *m* preliminar *or* de base

group¹ /gruːp/ *n* **1** (+ *sing o pl vb*) **(a)** (of people) grupo *m*; **a women's/gay ~** una agrupación de mujeres/gay; (*before n*) ‹*discussion/visit*› en grupo; ‹*portrait*› de conjunto **(b)** (Mus) grupo *m*, conjunto *m* **2** (Busn, Chem, Math) grupo *m*

group² *vt* agrupar ■ *~ vi*: **to ~ together** agruparse

grouse¹ /graʊs/ *n* (*pl ~*) (bird) urogallo *m*

grouse² *vi* (colloq) gruñir* (fam); **to ~ ABOUT sb/sth** quejarse DE algn/algo

grout /graʊt/ *vt* ‹*tiles*› enlechar

grove /grəʊv/ *n* (of trees) bosquecillo *m*; **an orange ~** un naranjal

grovel /'grɑːvəl || 'grɒvəl/ *vi*, (BrE) **-ll-** (physically) postrarse; (abase oneself) arrastrarse

grow /grəʊ/ (*past* **grew**; *past p* **grown**) *vi* **1** (get bigger) crecer*; (develop emotionally) madurar; (expand, increase) «*city/company/influence*» crecer*; «*quantity/population/membership*» aumentar; **his hair has ~n** le creció el pelo; **the economy is ~ing again** la economía vuelve a experimentar un período de crecimiento *or* expansión **2 (a)** (become): **to ~ careless** volverse* descuidado; **to ~ old** envejecer* **(b)** (get) **to ~ to + INF**: **she grew to love him** llegó a quererlo ■ **~** *vt* ‹*flowers/plants/crops*› cultivar; **to ~ a beard** dejarse (crecer) la barba; **to ~ one's hair (long)** dejarse crecer el pelo

● **grow into** [*v + prep + o*] **(a)** (become) convertirse* en **(b)** (grow to fit): **she will soon ~ into these dresses** pronto podrá usar estos vestidos

● **grow on** [*v + prep + o*] (colloq): **it ~s on you** «*music/place*» llega a gustar con el tiempo

● **grow out of** [*v + adv + prep + o*] **(a)** ‹*habit*› perder*, quitarse (*con el tiempo o la edad*); **it's just a phase, she'll ~ out of it** son cosas de la edad, ya se le pasará **(b)** ‹*clothes*›: **she's ~n out of those shoes already** esos zapatos ya le quedan chicos *or* (Esp) le están pequeños

● **grow up** [*v + adv*] **(a)** (spend childhood) criarse*, crecer* **(b)** (become adult) hacerse* mayor; **when I ~ up** cuando sea grande ...; **~ up!** ¡no seas infantil! **(c)** (arise) «*friendship/custom/feeling*» surgir*; «*settlement/town*» desarrollarse

grower /'grəʊər || 'grəʊə(r)/ *n* cultivador, -dora *m,f*

growing /'grəʊɪŋ/ *adj* (*before n*) **(a)** ‹*quantity/reputation*› cada vez mayor; ‹*influence*› creciente **(b)** ‹*child*›: **you need a lot to eat; you're a ~ boy** tienes que comer mucho, estás creciendo **(c)** ‹*plant/stem/vegetable*› que está creciendo

growl[1] /graʊl/ *vi* gruñir*

growl[2] *n* gruñido *m*

grown[1] /grəʊn/ *past p of* GROW

grown[2] *adj*: **he's a ~ man** es un hombre hecho y derecho; **when the young are fully ~** (Zool) cuando las crías han alcanzado su pleno desarrollo

grown-up[1] /'grəʊnʌp/ *n* persona *f* mayor

grown-up[2] *adj* **(a)** (adult) mayor **(b)** (mature) (colloq) maduro, adulto

growth /grəʊθ/ *n* **1** [U] (of animals, plants, humans) crecimiento *m* **2** [U C] (of population, city, business) crecimiento *m*; (of quantity, profits) aumento *m*; (in popularity) aumento *m* **3 (a)** [U] (what grows): **new ~** brotes *mpl* nuevos; **several days' ~ of beard** una barba de varios días **(b)** [C] (Med) bulto *m*, tumor *m*

grub /grʌb/ *n* **1** [C] (Zool) larva *f* **2** [U] (food) (colloq) comida *f*, papeo *m* (Esp arg), morfe *m* (CS arg)

grubby /'grʌbi/ *adj* **-bier, -biest** mugriento

grudge[1] /grʌdʒ/ *n* rencilla *f*; **to bear sb a ~** tenerle* *or* guardarle rencor a algn

grudge[2] *vt* ⇒ BEGRUDGE

grueling, (BrE) **gruelling** /'gruːəlɪŋ/ *adj* ‹*journey*› extenuante; ‹*experience/ordeal*› penoso

gruesome /'gruːsəm/ *adj* truculento

gruff /grʌf/ *adj* **-er, -est** ‹*voice*› áspero; ‹*manner/reply*› brusco

grumble /'grʌmbəl/ *vi* refunfuñar (fam), rezongar*; **to ~ ABOUT sth/sb** quejarse DE algo/algn

grumpy /'grʌmpi/ *adj* **-pier, -piest** ‹*person*› gruñón; ‹*remark/voice*› malhumorado

grunt[1] /grʌnt/ *vi* gruñir*

grunt[2] *n* gruñido *m*

guarantee[1] /'gærən'tiː/ *n* garantía *f*

guarantee[2] *vt* garantizar*

guarantor /'gærən'tɔːr || ˌgærən'tɔː(r)/ *n* garante *mf*

guard[1] /gɑːrd || gɑːd/ *vt* **(a)** ‹*building/prisoner*› vigilar; ‹*person/reputation*› proteger*; ‹*secret*› guardar **(b)** (AmE Sport) marcar*

● **guard against** [*v + prep + o*] ‹*injury/temptation*› evitar; ‹*risk*› protegerse* contra

guard[2] *n* **1 (a)** [C] (sentry, soldier) guardia *mf*; **security ~** guarda *mf* de seguridad; **prison ~** (AmE) carcelero, -ra *m,f*, oficial *mf* de prisiones **(b)** (squad) (*no pl*) guardia *f* **(c)** [C] (Sport) (in US football) defensa *mf*; (in basketball) escolta *mf* **2** [U] (surveillance) guardia *f*; **to be on ~** estar* de guardia; (*before n*) **~ duty** guardia *f*, posta *f* (AmC) **3** [U] (in boxing, fencing) guardia *f*; ***to be on/off (one's) ~*** estar* alerta/desprevenido **4** [C] **(a)** (*fire ~*) guardallama(s) *m* **(b)** (on machinery) cubierta *f* (*or* dispositivo *m etc*) de seguridad **5** [C] (BrE Rail) jefe, -fa *m,f* de tren

guard dog *n* perro *m* guardián

guarded /'gɑːrdəd || 'gɑːdɪd/ *adj* ‹*reply/admission*› cauteloso; ‹*optimism*› cauto

guardian /'gɑːrdiən || 'gɑːdiən/ *n* **(a)** (of child) tutor, -tora *m,f* **(b)** (protector) defensor, -sora *m,f*, custodio, -dia *m,f*

guardian angel *n* ángel *m* de la guarda, ángel *m* custodio

guard: **~rail** *n* (in staircase) barandilla *f*; (in roads etc) barrera *f* de seguridad; **~'s van** *n* (BrE Rail) furgón *m* de cola

Guatemala /'gwɑːtə'mɑːlə/ *n* Guatemala *f*

Guatemalan /'gwɑːtə'mɑːlən/ *adj* guatemalteco

Guernsey /'gɜːrnzi || 'gɜːnzi/ *n* (*pl* **-seys**) Guernesey

guerrilla /gə'rɪlə/ *n* guerrillero, -ra *m,f*; (*before n*) ‹*tactics/leader*› guerrillero; **~ warfare** guerrilla *f*

guess[1] /ges/ *n*: **have a ~!** ¡a ver si adivinas!; **your ~ is as good as mine** quién sabe, vete tú a saber

guess[2] *vt* **(a)** (conjecture, estimate) adivinar; **~ what!** ¿sabes qué?; **you'll never ~ what he said** no te puedes imaginar lo que dijo **(b)** (suppose) (esp AmE colloq) suponer*; **I ~ so** supongo (que sí) ■ **~** *vi*: **how did you ~?** ¿cómo adivinaste? *or* (Esp) ¿cómo lo has adivinado?; **to ~ right** acertar*, adivinar, atinar(le) (Méx)

guesswork /'geswɜːrk || 'geswɜːk/ *n* [U] conjeturas *fpl*

guest /gest/ *n* (visitor) invitado, -da *m,f*; (in hotel) huésped *mf*, cliente, -ta *m,f*; (*before n*) **~ list** lista *f* de invitados; ~ **speaker** conferenciante invitado, -da *m,f*; ~ **star** estrella *f* invitada

guest: ~**house** *n* **(a)** (in US, attached to mansion) pabellón *m* de huéspedes **(b)** (Tourism) (in UK) casa *f* de huéspedes, pensión *f*; ~**room** *n* cuarto *m* de huéspedes *or* (Chi) de alojados

guffaw[1] /gʌ'fɔː/ *n* risotada *f*

guffaw[2] *vi* reírse* a carcajadas

guidance /'gaɪdns/ *n* [U] orientación *f*; **he needs** ~ necesita que lo orienten; (*before n*) ~ **counselor** (AmE) orientador, -dora *m,f* vocacional

guide[1] /gaɪd/ *n* **1 (a)** (Tourism) (person) guía *mf*; (publication) guía *f* **(b)** (adviser) consejero, -ra *m,f* **2 Guide** (BrE) exploradora *f*, guía *f* **3** (indicator) guía *f*; **to use** *o* **take sth as a** ~ guiarse* por algo

guide[2] *vt* **(a)** ‹*tourist/stranger*› guiar*; **a priest** ~**d them round the cathedral** un sacerdote les hizo de guía en la catedral **(b)** (help, advise) guiar*, aconsejar **(c)** (steer, manipulate) (+ *adv compl*): **the captain** ~**d the ship between the rocks** el capitán condujo *or* guió el barco por entre las rocas

guide: ~**book** *n* guía *f*; ~ **dog** *n* perro *m* guía, perro *m* lazarillo

guided tour /'gaɪdəd || 'gaɪdɪd/ *n* visita *f* guiada

guideline /'gaɪdlaɪn/ *n* pauta *f*

guild /gɪld/ *n* **(a)** (of workers) gremio *m* **(b)** (club, society) asociación *f*

guile /gaɪl/ *n* [U] astucia *f*

guillotine /'gɪlətiːn/ *n* guillotina *f*

guilt /gɪlt/ *n* [U] **(a)** (blame) culpa *f*; (Law) culpabilidad *f* **(b)** (Psych) culpa *f*

guilty /'gɪlti/ *adj* **-tier, -tiest (a)** (Law) (*no comp*) culpable; **to be** ~ **OF sth** ser* culpable DE algo **(b)** (ashamed, remorseful) culpable **(c)** (shameful) (*before n*) ‹*secret*› vergonzoso

guinea /'gɪni/ *n* guinea *f*

guinea pig *n* **(a)** (Zool) cobayo *m*, cobaya *f*, conejillo *m* de Indias, cuy *m* (AmS) **(b)** (person) conejillo *m* de Indias

guise /gaɪz/ *n*: **under the** ~ **of friendship** bajo una apariencia de amistad; **in many different** ~**s** de muchas formas distintas

guitar /gə'tɑːr || gɪ'tɑː(r)/ *n* guitarra *f*

guitarist /gə'tɑːrəst || gɪ'tɑːrɪst/ *n* guitarrista *mf*

gulf /gʌlf/ *n* **(a)** (Geog) golfo *m* **(b)** (gap) abismo *m*

gull /gʌl/ *n* (Zool) gaviota *f*

gullet /'gʌlət || 'gʌlɪt/ *n* garganta *f*

gulley /'gʌli/ *n* (*pl* **-leys**) ⇒ GULLY

gullible /'gʌləbəl/ *adj* crédulo

gully /'gʌli/ *n* (*pl* **-lies**) **(a)** (small valley) barranco *m* **(b)** (channel) surco *m*, cauce *m*

gulp[1] /gʌlp/ *vi* tragar* saliva ■ ~ *vt* ~ **(down)** ‹*food*› engullir*; ‹*drink/medicine*› beberse de un trago

gulp[2] *n* (of liquid) trago *m*; (of air) bocanada *f*: **in one** ~ de un trago

gum /gʌm/ *n* **1** [C] (Anat) encía *f* **2** [U] (*chewing* ~) chicle *m*, goma *f* de mascar **3 (a)** [U] (glue) (BrE) goma *f* de pegar **(b)** [U] (from plant) resina *f*

gun /gʌn/ *n* (pistol) pistola *f*, revólver *m*; (shotgun, rifle) escopeta *f*, fusil *m*, rifle *m*; (artillery piece) cañón *m*

• **gun down** [*v* + *o* + *adv*, *v* + *adv* + *o*] abatir a tiros

gun: ~**dog** *n* perro *m* de caza; ~**fight** *n* tiroteo *m*, balacera *f* (AmL); ~**fire** *n* [U] disparos *mpl*; (from heavy artillery) cañoneo *m*, cañonazos *mpl*; ~**man** /'gʌnmən/ *n* (*pl* **-men** /-mən/) pistolero *m*, gatillero *m* (Méx); ~**point** *n*: **at** ~**point** a punta de pistola; ~**powder** *n* [U] pólvora *f*; ~**running** *n* [U] tráfico *m* de armas; ~**shot** *n* disparo *m*; (*before n*) ~**shot wound** herida *f* de bala; ~**smith** *n* armero, -ra *m,f*

gurgle[1] /'gɜːrgəl || 'gɜːgəl/ *vi* «*water/brook*» borbotar; «*baby*» gorjear

gurgle[2] *n* (of water, liquid) borboteo *m*; (of delight) gorjeo *m*

gush /gʌʃ/ *vi* «*liquid*» salir* a borbotones

gushing /'gʌʃɪŋ/ *adj* (pej) demasiado efusivo

gusset /'gʌsət || 'gʌsɪt/ *n* entretela *f*

gust /gʌst/ **▶920** *n* ráfaga *f*

gusto /'gʌstəʊ/ *n* [U] entusiasmo *m*; **with** ~ ‹*eat*› con ganas; ‹*sing/play*› con brío

gusty /'gʌsti/ **▶920** *adj* **-tier, -tiest** ‹*wind*› racheado; ‹*weather/day*› ventoso

gut[1] /gʌt/ *n* **(a)** [C] (intestine) intestino *m* **(b)** [C] (belly) (colloq) barriga *f* (fam); (*before n*) ‹*reaction*› instintivo

gut[2] *vt* **-tt- (a)** ‹*fish/chicken/rabbit*› limpiar **(b)** ‹*building*› destruir* el interior de

guts /gʌts/ *n* **1** (+ *pl vb*) (colloq) (bowels) tripas *fpl* (fam) **2** (+ *sing o pl vb*) (courage) (colloq) agallas *fpl* (fam)

gutter /'gʌtər || 'gʌtə(r)/ *n* **(a)** (on roof) canaleta *f*, canalón *m* (Esp) **(b)** (in street) alcantarilla *f* **(c)** (lowest section of society) **the** ~ el arroyo; (*before n*) **the** ~ **press** la prensa sensacionalista

guttural /'gʌtərəl/ *adj* gutural

guy /gaɪ/ *n* (colloq) **(a)** (man) tipo *m* (fam), tío *m* (Esp fam), chavo *m* (Méx fam) **(b) guys** *pl* (people) (AmE) gente *f*

Guyana /gaɪ'ænə/ *n* Guyana *f*, Guayana *f*

Guyanese /,gaɪə'niːz/ *adj* guyanés, guayanés

guzzle /'gʌzəl/ *vt* **(a)** (drink greedily) chupar (fam) **(b)** (eat greedily) (BrE) engullirse*, tragarse*

gym /dʒɪm/ *n* **(a)** [C] (gymnasium) gimnasio *m* **(b)** [U] (gymnastics) gimnasia *f*

gymnasium /dʒɪm'neɪziəm/ *n* (*pl* **-siums** *or* **-sia** /-ziə/) gimnasio *m*

gymnast /'dʒɪmnæst/ *n* gimnasta *mf*

gymnastics /dʒɪm'næstɪks/ *n* **(a)** (activity) (+ *sing vb*) gimnasia *f* **(b)** (exercises) (+ *pl vb*) gimnasia *f*

gynecologist, (BrE) **gynaecologist** /'gaɪnə'kɑːlədʒəst || ,gaɪnə'kɒlədʒɪst/ *n* ginecólogo, -ga *m,f*

gynecology, (BrE) **gynaecology** /'gaɪnə'kɑːlədʒi || ,gaɪnə'kɒlədʒi/ *n* [U] ginecología *f*

gypsy, **Gypsy** /'dʒɪpsi/ *n* (*pl* **-sies**) gitano, -na *m,f*

gyrate /'dʒaɪreɪt || dʒaɪ'reɪt/ *vi* girar

Hh

H, **h** /eɪtʃ/ *n* H, h *f*

haberdashery /ˈhæbərˌdæʃəri ‖ ˈhæbəˌdæʃəri/ *n* (*pl* **-ries**) [U] **(a)** (clothes) (AmE) ropa *f* y accesorios *mpl* para caballeros **(b)** (sewing materials) (BrE) (artículos *mpl* de) mercería *f*

habit /ˈhæbət ‖ ˈhæbɪt/ *n* **1 (a)** [C] (usual piece of behavior) costumbre *f*, hábito *m*; (bad) vicio *m*, mala costumbre *f*, mal hábito *m*; **to get out of/into the ~ of doing sth** perder*/tomar la costumbre de hacer algo **(b)** [U] (customary behavior) costumbre *f*; **by** *or* **out of** *or* **from force of ~** por fuerza *f* de la costumbre **2** [C] (Clothing) hábito *m*

habitat /ˈhæbətæt ‖ ˈhæbɪtæt/ *n* hábitat *m*

habitation /ˈhæbəˈteɪʃən ‖ ˌhæbɪˈteɪʃən/ *n* (frml): **unfit for human ~** inhabitable

habitual /həˈbɪtʃuəl/ *adj* **(a)** (usual) habitual, acostumbrado **(b)** (compulsive) ‹*liar/gambler*› empedernido

hack¹ /hæk/ *vt* cortar a tajos, tajear (Andes) ■ ~ *vi* **1** (to cut): **to ~ at sth** darle* (golpes) a algo; **we ~ed through the undergrowth** nos abrimos paso a machetazos (*or* hachazos *etc*) a través de la espesura **2** (Comput colloq) **to ~ into** ‹*system*› piratear

hack² *n* **1** (pej *or* hum) (writer) escritorzuelo, -la *m,f* (pey); (journalist) gacetillero, -ra *m,f* (pey) **2** (horse — for hire) caballo *m* de alquiler; (— worn-out) jaco *m*, jamelgo *m* **3** (AmE colloq) **(a)** (taxi driver) taxista *mf*, tachero, -ra *m,f* (RPl fam), ruletero, -ra *m,f* (Méx fam) **(b)** (taxi) taxi *m*, tacho *m* (RPl fam)

hacker /ˈhækər ‖ ˈhækə(r)/ *n* (Comput colloq) pirata informático, -ca *m,f*

hacking /ˈhækɪŋ/ *adj* ‹*cough*› áspero

hackles /ˈhækəlz/ *pl n* **to make sb's ~ rise** poner* furioso a algn; **his ~ rose** se enfureció

hackneyed /ˈhæknid/ *adj* manido, trillado

hacksaw /ˈhæksɔː/ *n* sierra *f* de arco (*para metales*)

had /hæd, *weak form* həd, əd/ *past & past p of* HAVE

haddock /ˈhædək/ *n* (*pl* ~) **(a)** [C] (Zool) eglefino *m* **(b)** [U] (Culin) abadejo *m*

hadn't /ˈhædn̩t/ = **had not**

haem- *etc* (BrE) ⇒ HEM- *etc*

hag /hæg/ *n* bruja *f*, arpía *f*

haggard /ˈhægərd ‖ ˈhægəd/ *adj* demacrado

haggis /ˈhægəs ‖ ˈhægɪs/ *n* [C U] (*pl* **-gis** *or* **-gises**) *plato escocés hecho con vísceras de cordero y avena*

haggle /ˈhægəl/ *vi* regatear

Hague /heɪg/ *n* **The ~** La Haya

hail¹ /heɪl/ ▶ 920 *n* **(a)** [U] (Meteo) granizo *m*, pedrisco *m* **(b)** (of bullets, insults) (*no pl*) lluvia *f*

hail² ▶ 920 *v impers* (Meteo) granizar* ■ ~ *vt* **1** (call to) ‹*person*› llamar; ‹*ship*› saludar; ‹*taxi*› hacerle* señas a **2** (acclaim, welcome) ‹*king/leader*› aclamar; **it was ~ed as a major breakthrough** fue acogido como un importantísimo avance ■ ~ *vi* **to ~** FROM «*person*» ser* DE

hail: **H~ Mary** /ˈmeri ‖ ˈmeəri/ *n* Avemaría *m*; **~stone** *n* granizo *m*, piedra *f* (de granizo)

hair /her ‖ heə(r)/ ▶ 484, 515 *n* **(a)** [U] (on human head) pelo *m*, cabello *m* (frml *o* liter); **to have one's ~ done** peinarse (*en la peluquería*); *before n*) ‹*gel/lacquer/oil*› para el pelo; ‹*transplant*› capilar **(b)** [U] (on human body) vello *m*; (on animal, plant) pelo *m* **(c)** [C] (single strand) pelo *m*

hair: **~-band** *n* (elastic) cinta *f*, huincha *f* (Bol, Chi, Per), balaca *f* (Col), banda *f* (Méx), vincha *f* (RPl, Ven); (rigid) diadema *f*, cintillo *m*, vincha *f* (RPl, Ven); **~brush** *n* cepillo *m* (*del pelo*); **~clip** *n* (BrE) horquilla *f*, pinche *m* (Chi), pasador *m* (Méx); **~cut** *n* corte *m* de pelo; **~do** *n* (colloq) peinado *m*; **~dresser** *n* peluquero, -ra *m,f*; **the ~dresser's** la peluquería; **~drier**, **~dryer** *n* secador *m or* (Méx) secadora *f*; **~grip** *n* (BrE) horquilla *f*, pinche *m* (Chi), pasador *m* (Méx); **~line** *n* **(a)** (where hair begins) nacimiento *m* del pelo **(b)** (fine line) línea *f* delgada; (*before n*) **a ~line fracture** una pequeña fisura; **~net** *n* redecilla *f*; **~piece** *n* postizo *m*; **~pin** *n* horquilla *f* (de moño); (*before n*) **~pin turn** *o* (BrE) **bend** curva *f* muy cerrada; **~-raising** /ˈherˌreɪzɪŋ ‖ ˈheəˌreɪzɪŋ/ *adj* espeluznante; **~'s breadth**, **~sbreadth** *n* (*no pl*): **by a ~'s breadth** por un pelo (fam); **~slide** *n* (BrE) ⇒ BARRETTE; **~spray** *n* laca *f*, fijador *m* (*para el pelo*); **~style** *n* peinado *m*, corte *m* de pelo

hairy /ˈheri ‖ ˈheəri/ *adj* **-rier, -riest** ‹*legs/chest*› peludo, velludo

Haiti /ˈheɪti/ *n* Haití *m*

Haitian /ˈheɪʃən/ *adj* haitiano

halal /hɑːˈlɑːl/ *adj* (Culin) ‹*meat*› de animales faenados *or* (Esp) sacrificados según la ley musulmana

hale /heɪl/ *adj* (liter): **~ and hearty** (fuerte) como un roble

half¹ /hæf ‖ hɑːf/ ▶ 543 *n* (*pl* **halves**) **1 (a)** (part) mitad *f*; **to break sth in ~** romper* algo por la mitad *or* en dos; ***to go halves*** (colloq) pagar* a medias **(b)** (Math) medio *m* **(c)** ▶ 884 (elliptical use): **an hour and a ~** una hora y media; **it's ~ past ten** son las diez y media **2** (Sport) **(a)** (period) tiempo *m* **(b)** (of pitch) campo *m* **(c)** (interval) (AmE) descanso *m*, medio tiempo *m* (AmL)

half² ▶ 543 *pron* la mitad

half³ ▶ 543 *adj* medio, -dia; **~ a pint of milk** media pinta de leche; **one and a ~ hours** una hora y media

half⁴ *adv* medio; **she was ~ asleep** estaba medio dormida *or* semidormida; **the work is only ~ done** el trabajo está a medio hacer; **she is ~ Italian, ~ Greek** es hija de italianos y griegos; **they are paid ~ as much as we are** les pagan la mitad que a nosotros

half- /hæf ‖ hɑːf/ *pref*: **~closed/~open** entreabierto; **~starved** medio muerto de hambre

half: **~ a dozen** *n* (*no pl*) media docena *f*; **~ a dozen eggs** media docena de huevos; **~ an hour** ▶ 884 *n* [U] media hora *f*; **~ brother** *n* hermanastro *m*, medio hermano *m*; **~hearted** /'hæf'hɑːrtəd ‖ ˌhɑːf'hɑːtɪd/ *adj* poco entusiasta; **~-hour** /'hæf'aʊr ‖ ˌhɑːf'aʊə(r)/ ▶ 884 *n* media hora *f*; **~-light** *n* [U] penumbra *f*; **~-mast** /'hæf'mæst ‖ ˌhɑːf'mɑːst/ *n* [U]: **at ~-mast** a media asta; **~ measures** *pl n* medias tintas *fpl*; **~-moon** /'hæf'muːn ‖ ˌhɑːf'muːn/ *n* media luna *f*; **~ note** *n* (AmE) blanca *f*; **~penny** /'heɪpni/ *n* (Hist) **(a)** (*pl* **-pennies**) (coin) medio penique *m* **(b)** (*pl* **-pence** /'heɪpəns/) (value) medio penique *m*; **~ price** *n* [U] mitad *f* de precio; **~ sister** *n* hermanastra *f*, media hermana *f*; **~-staff** *n* (AmE) ⇒ ~-MAST; **~ term** *n* (in UK) vacaciones *fpl* de mitad de trimestre; **~-time** *n* [U] **(a)** (Sport) descanso *m*, medio tiempo *m* (AmL); **(b)** (Busn, Lab Rel) media jornada *f*

half-way¹ /'hæf'weɪ ‖ ˌhɑːf'weɪ/ *adv* (at, to mid point) a mitad de camino; **I'm about ~ through** voy por la mitad; ***to meet sb ~*** (compromise) llegar* a una solución intermedia con algn; (lit: on journey) encontrarse* con algn a mitad de camino

half-way² *adj* (*before n*) ‹*point*› medio; ‹*stage*› intermedio; **the ~ mark** el punto medio, la mitad

half-yearly /'hæf'jɪrli ‖ ˌhɑːf'jɪəli/ *adj* semestral

hall /hɔːl/ *n* **1 (a)** (vestibule) vestíbulo *m*, entrada *f* **(b)** (corridor) (AmE) pasillo *m*, corredor *m* **2 (a)** (for gatherings) salón *m* **(b)** (in castle, mansion) sala *f* **3** (student residence) (BrE) *or* de estudiantes residencia *f* universitaria, colegio *m* mayor (Esp) **4** (large country house) (BrE) casa *f* solariega

halleluja /'hælə'luːjə ‖ ˌhælɪ'luːjə/ *interj* ¡aleluya!

hallmark /'hɔːlmɑːrk ‖ 'hɔːlmɑːk/ *n* **(a)** (on gold, silver) contraste *m*, sello *m* (de contraste) **(b)** (distinguishing characteristic) distintivo *m*, sello *m*

hallo /hə'ləʊ/ *interj* ⇒ HELLO

hall of residence *n* (*pl* **~s of residence**) (BrE) ⇒ HALL 3

Halloween, Hallowe'en /'hæləʊ'iːn/ *n* víspera *f* del día de Todos los Santos

hallucination /hə'luːsṇ'eɪʃən ‖ hə'luːsɪ'neɪʃən/ *n* [U C] alucinación *f*

hallway /'hɔːlweɪ/ *n* ⇒ HALL 1

halo /'heɪləʊ/ *n* (*pl* **-los** *or* **-loes**) **(a)** (Art, Relig) aureola *f*, halo *m* **(b)** (Astron, Opt) halo *m*

halt¹ /hɔːlt ‖ hɒlt, hɔːlt/ *n*: **to come to a ~** pararse

halt² *vi* detenerse* (frml); **~!** (Mil) ¡alto! ■ **~** *vt* ‹*vehicle/troops*› detener* (frml); ‹*process*› atajar, detener* (frml); ‹*work/production*› interrumpir

halter /'hɔːltər ‖ 'hɒltə(r), 'hɔː-/ *n* cabestro *m*, ronzal *m*

halve /hæv ‖ hɑːv/ *vt* **(a)** (reduce by half) ‹*expense/time/length*› reducir* a la mitad *or* en un 50%; ‹*number*› dividir por dos **(b)** (divide into halves) partir por la mitad ■ **~** *vi* reducirse* a la mitad *or* en un 50%

halves /hævz ‖ hɑːvz/ *pl of* HALF¹

ham /hæm/ *n* **1** (Culin) (cured) jamón *m* (crudo), jamón *m* serrano (Esp); (cooked) jamón *m* (cocido), jamón *m* (de) York (Esp) **2** (Theat) *actor extravagantemente histriónico*

hamburger /'hæmbɜːrgər ‖ 'hæmbɜːgə(r)/ *n* hamburguesa *f*

hamlet /'hæmlət ‖ 'hæmlɪt/ *n* aldea *f*, caserío *m*

hammer¹ /'hæmər ‖ 'hæmə(r)/ *n* martillo *m*

hammer² *vt* ‹*nail*› clavar (*con un martillo*); ‹*metal*› martillar, batir ■ **~** *vi* (strike) dar* golpes; (with hammer) dar* martillazos; **to ~ at** *or* **on the door** golpear la puerta

• **hammer home** [*v* + *o* + *adv*, *v* + *adv* + *o*] ‹*nail*› remachar; ‹*point*› recalcar*, machacar*

• **hammer out** [*v* + *o* + *adv*, *v* + *adv* + *o*] ‹*metal/dent*› alisar a martillazos; ‹*compromise/deal*› negociar (*con mucho toma y daca*)

hammock /'hæmək/ *n* hamaca *f*, hamaca *f* paraguaya (RPl); (Naut) coy *m*

hamper¹ /'hæmpər ‖ 'hæmpə(r)/ *vt* dificultar

hamper² *n* cesta *f*, canasta *f*

hamster /'hæmstər ‖ 'hæmstə(r)/ *n* hámster *m*

hamstring /'hæmstrɪŋ/ *n* (of person) ligamento *m* de la corva; (of horse) tendón *m* del corvejón *or* jarrete

hand¹ /hænd/ *n* **1** ▶ 484 (Anat) mano *f*; **~s off!** ¡quita las manos de ahí!; **~s up all those in favor** que levanten la mano los que estén a favor; **~s up!** ¡manos arriba! **2** (in phrases) **at hand**: **help was at ~** la ayuda estaba en camino; **by hand** ‹*make/write/wash*› a mano; ‹*deliver*› en mano; **hand in hand** (tomados *or* agarrados *or* (esp Esp) cogidos) de la mano; **poverty and disease go ~ in ~** la pobreza y la enfermedad van de la mano; **on hand**: **the police were on ~** la policía estaba cerca; **to have sth on ~** tener* algo a mano; **out of hand**: **the situation is getting out of ~** la situación se nos (*or* les *etc*) va de las manos; **to reject sth out of ~** rechazar* algo de plano; **to hand** (BrE) (within reach) al alcance de la mano, a (la) mano; (available) disponible; ***to beat sb/win ~s down*** ganarle a algn/ganar sin problemas; ***to get one's ~s on sb/sth***: **just wait till I get my ~s on him!** ¡vas a ver cuando lo agarre!; **she can't wait to get her ~s on the new computer** se muere por usar la computadora nueva; ***to give sb/have a free ~*** darle* a algn/tener* carta blanca; ***to know a place like the back of one's ~*** conocer* un sitio al dedillo; ***to try one's ~ (at sth)*** probar* (a hacer algo) **3 (a)** (agency) mano *f*; **to have a ~ in sth** tener* parte en algo; **the town had suffered at the ~s of invaders** la ciudad había sufrido a manos de los invasores **(b)** (assistance) (colloq): **to give sb a ~** echarle *or* darle* una mano a algn; **if you need a ~** si necesitas ayuda **(c) hands** *pl* (possession, control, care): **to change ~s** cambiar de dueño; **in good/capable ~s** en buenas manos; **my life is in your ~s** mi vida depende de ti; **we've got a problem on our ~s** tenemos un problema; **the matter is out of my ~s** el asunto no está en mis manos **4** (side): **on sb's right/left**

~ a la derecha/izquierda de algn; **on the one ~ … on the other (~)** … por un lado … por otro (lado) … **5** (Games) **(a)** (set of cards) mano *f*, cartas *fpl* **(b)** (round of card game) mano *f* **6 (a)** (worker) obrero, -ra *m,f*; (*farm ~*) peón *m* **(b)** (Naut) marinero *m* **(c)** (experienced person): **an old ~** un veterano, una veterana **7** (applause) (colloq) (*no pl*): **a big ~ for …** un gran aplauso para … **8** (handwriting) (liter) letra *f* **9** (on clock) manecilla *f*, aguja *f*, puntero *m* (Andes)

hand[2] *vt* **to ~ sb sth, to ~ sth TO sb** pasarle algo A algn

• **hand around,** (BrE also) **hand round** [*v + o + adv, v + adv + o*] (distribute) repartir, distribuir*; (offer round) ‹*cakes*› ofrecer*

• **hand down** [*v + o + adv, v + adv + o*] (pass down) ‹*custom/heirloom/story*› transmitir; ‹*clothes*› pasar

• **hand in** [*v + o + adv, v + adv + o*] ‹*homework/form/ticket*› entregar*; ‹*resignation*› presentar

• **hand on** [*v + o + adv, v + adv + o*] ‹*skills/knowledge*› transmitir, pasar; ‹*object/photograph*› pasar

• **hand out** [*v + o + adv, v + adv + o*] repartir, distribuir*; ‹*advice*› dar*

• **hand over** [*v + o + adv, v + adv + o*] **(a)** (relinquish) entregar* **(b)** (transfer) transferir*

• **hand round** (BrE) ⇒ HAND AROUND

hand: **~bag** *n* (used by women) cartera *f* *or* (Esp) bolso *m* *or* (Méx) bolsa *f*; (small suitcase) (AmE) maletín *m*; **~ baggage**, (BrE) **~ luggage** *n* [U] equipaje *m* de mano; **~ball** *n* **(a)** [U] (game — in US) frontón *m*, pelota *f*; (— in Europe) balonmano *m*, handball *m* (AmL) **(b)** [U C] (in soccer) mano *f*; **~book** *n* manual *m*; **~brake** *n* (on bicycle) (AmE) freno *m* (de pastilla); (BrE Auto) freno *m* de mano; **~craft** *n* ⇒ HANDICRAFT; **~ cream** *n* [U C] crema *f* de manos *or* para las manos; **~cuff** *vt* esposar, ponerle* esposas a; **~cuffs** *pl n* esposas *fpl*

handful /'hændfʊl/ *n* **(a)** (amount) puñado *m* **(b)** (small number) (+ *sing o pl vb*) puñado *m*; **a ~ of people** unas cuantas personas **(c)** (troublesome person or people) (*no pl*): **that child is a real ~** ese niño da mucho trabajo

hand grenade *n* granada *f* (de mano)

handicap[1] /'hændɪkæp/ *n* **1 (a)** (disability): **physical ~** impedimento *m* físico; **mental ~** retraso *m* mental **(b)** (disadvantage) desventaja *f* **2** (Sport) (in golf, polo) hándicap *m*; (penalty) desventaja *f*

handicap[2] *vt* **-pp-** ‹*person/chances*› perjudicar*

handicapped /'hændɪkæpt/ *adj* disminuido, discapacitado, minusválido; **mentally/physically ~** disminuido *or* discapacitado *or* minusválido psíquico/físico

handicraft /'hændɪkræft ‖ 'hændɪkrɑːft/, **handcraft** *n* **(a)** [U] (skill) artesanía *f*, trabajo *m* artesanal **(b)** [C] (product) producto *m* de artesanía

handiwork /'hændiwɜːrk ‖ 'hændiwɜːk/ *n* [U] **(a)** (craftsmanship) trabajo *m* **(b)** (product) artesanías *fpl*, objetos *mpl* artesanales **(c)** (doing) (pej) obra *f*; **it looks like Laura's ~ to me** a mí me parece obra de Laura

handkerchief /'hæŋkərtʃəf, -tʃiːf ‖ 'hæŋkətʃɪf, -tʃiːf/ *n* (*pl* **-chieves** /-tʃiːvz/ *or* **-chiefs**) pañuelo *m*

handle[1] /'hændl̩/ *n* (of cup, jug, bag) asa *f*‡; (of door) picaporte *m*; (knob) pomo *m*; (of drawer) tirador *m*, manija *f*; (of broom, knife, spade) mango *m*; (of wheelbarrow) brazo *m*; (of pump) manivela *f*

handle[2] *vt* **1 (a)** (touch) tocar*; Ⓢ **handle with care** frágil **(b)** (manipulate, manage) ‹*vehicle/weapon*› manejar; ‹*chemicals*› manipular **2** (deal with) ‹*people*› tratar; ‹*situation/affair*› manejar; **he can't ~ the job** (colloq) no puede con el trabajo **3 (a)** (be responsible for) ‹*business/financial matters*› encargarse* *or* ocuparse de, llevar **(b)** (do business in) ‹*goods/commodities*› comerciar con **(c)** «*computer*» ‹*data*› procesar

handlebar /'hændlbɑːr ‖ 'hændlbɑː(r)/ *n* (*often pl*) **~(s)** manillar *m*, manubrio *m* (AmL)

handling /'hændlɪŋ/ *n* [U] **1** (treatment — of situation) manejo *m*; (— of subject) tratamiento *m* **2 (a)** (Busn) porte *m* **(b)** (Aviat) handling *m* **(c)** (Auto) manejo *m*

hand: **~ luggage** *n* [U] (BrE) equipaje *m* de mano; **~made** /'hænd'meɪd/ *adj* hecho a mano; **~-me-down** *n*: *prenda usada o heredada*; **~out** *n* **(a)** (of money, food) dádiva *f* **(b)** (advertising leaflet) folleto *m* **(c)** (at lecture, in class) notas *fpl* (*que se distribuyen a los asistentes*); **~-picked** /'hænd'pɪkt/ *adj* cuidadosamente seleccionado; **~rail** *n* (on stairs, slope) pasamanos *m*; (on bridge, ship) baranda *f*, barandilla *f*; **~set** *n* auricular *m*, tubo *m* (RPl); **~shake** *n* apretón *m* de manos; **~ signal** *n* (Auto) seña *f* (*hecha con la mano*); (by referee, coach) (AmE) señal *f*

handsome /'hænsəm/ **handsomer, handsomest** *adj* **(a)** (attractive) ‹*man*› apuesto, buen mozo (AmL), guapo (esp Esp, Méx) **(b)** ‹*gift/offer*› generoso

hand: **~s-on** /'hændz'ɑːn ‖ 'hændz,ɒn/ *adj* (*before n*) **(a)** ‹*instruction/experience*› práctico **(b)** (Comput) manual; **~stand** *n*: **to do a ~stand** hacer* la vertical *or* (Esp) el pino, pararse de manos (AmL); **~-to-mouth** /'hændtə'maʊθ/ *adj* pobre, precario; **~-wash** /'hænd'wɔːʃ ‖ 'hænd,wɒʃ/ *vt* lavar a mano; **~writing** *n* [U] letra *f*; **~written** /'hænd'rɪtn̩/ *adj* manuscrito, escrito a mano

handy /'hændi/ *adj* **-dier, -diest** (colloq) **1** (*pred*) **(a)** (readily accessible) a mano **(b)** (conveniently situated) cerca, a mano **2** (useful) práctico; **to come in ~** venir* bien, resultar útil **3** ‹*person*› hábil, habilidoso

handyman /'hændimæn/ *n* (*pl* **-men** /-men/) *hombre habilidoso para trabajos de carpintería, albañilería etc*

hang[1] /hæŋ/ *vt* **1** (*past & past p* **hung**) **(a)** (suspend) ‹*coat/picture*› colgar* **(b)** (put in position) ‹*door/gate*› colocar* **(c) to ~ one's head** bajar la cabeza **2** (*past & past p* **hanged** *or* **hung**) (execute) ahorcar* ■ **~** *vi* **1** (*past p* **hung**) **(a)** (be suspended) colgar*, estar* colgado; **to ~ BY/FROM/ON sth** colgar* DE algo; **it's ~ing on the wall** está colgado en la pared **(b)** (hover) «*fog/smoke*» flotar; «*bird*» planear, cernerse*; **he still has the court case ~ing over him** todavía tiene el juicio pendiente **(c)** «*clothing/fabric*» caer* **2** (*past & past p* **hanged** *or* **hung**) (be executed): **he should ~ for his crime** debería ir a la horca por este crimen

• **hang about** [*v + adv*] ⇒ HANG AROUND

• **hang around** (colloq) [*v* + *adv*] **(a)** (wait) esperar **(b)** (stay) quedarse **(c)** (spend time idly): **they just ~ around on street corners** pasan el tiempo en la calle, holgazaneando; **to ~ around** WITH **sb** andar* *or* juntarse CON algn

• **hang on 1** [*v* + *adv*] **(a)** (wait) esperar **(b)** (keep hold) **to ~ on** TO **sth**: **you ~ on to this end of the rope** tú sostén esta punta de la cuerda **(c)** (keep) (colloq) **to ~ on** TO **sth** conservar *or* guardar algo **(d)** (in a crisis) aguantar, resistir **2** [*v* + *prep* + *o*] (depend on) ‹‹*outcome/decision*›› depender de

• **hang out 1** [*v* + *o* + *adv*, *v* + *adv* + *o*] ‹*washing*› tender*, colgar*; ‹*flag*› poner* **2** [*v* + *adv*] (dangle) ‹‹*wires*›› estar* suelto; **with his shirt/tongue ~ing out** con la camisa/la lengua afuera

• **hang up 1** [*v* + *adv*] (put down receiver) colgar*, cortar (CS) **2** [*v* + *o* + *adv*, *v* + *adv* + *o*] ‹*coat*› colgar*

hang² *n* (*no pl*) ***to get the ~ of sth*** (colloq) agarrarle la onda a algo (AmL fam), cogerle* el tranquillo a algo (Esp fam), agarrarle la mano a algo (CS fam)

hangar /'hæŋər ‖ 'hæŋə(r)/ *n* hangar *m*

hanger /'hæŋər ‖ 'hæŋə(r)/ *n* (*clothes or coat ~*) percha *f*, gancho *m* (para la ropa) (AmL)

hang: **~ glider** *n* ala *f*‡ delta, deslizador *m* (Méx); **~ gliding** /'glaɪdɪŋ/ *n* [U] vuelo *m* con ala delta *or* (Méx) en deslizador

hanging /'hæŋɪŋ/ *n* **1** (execution) ejecución *f* (*en la horca*) **2** (*wall ~*) tapiz *m*

hanging basket *n*: *cesto colgante para plantas*

hang: **~man** *n* (*pl* **-men** /-mən/) verdugo *m*; **~-over** *n* **(a)** (from drinking) resaca *f*, cruda *f* (AmC, Méx fam), guayabo *m* (Col fam), ratón *m* (Ven fam) **(b)** (something surviving) vestigio *m*, reliquia *f*; **~-up** *n* (colloq) complejo *m*, trauma *m*

hanker /'hæŋkər ‖ 'hæŋkə(r)/ *vi* **to ~** AFTER *o* FOR **sth** anhelar *or* ansiar* algo

hanky, **hankie** /'hæŋki/ *n* (*pl* **-kies**) (colloq) pañuelo *m*

Hanukkah, **Hanukah** /'hɑːnəkə/ *n* Janucá *m*, Hanukkah *m* (*fiesta judía de la dedicación del Templo*)

haphazard /'hæp'hæzərd ‖ ˌhæp'hæzəd/ *adj* **(a)** (random): **they promote people in a very ~ way** ascienden a la gente caprichosamente *or* al azar **(b)** (without order): **his approach is very ~** no es coherente en su enfoque

hapless /'hæpləs ‖ 'hæplɪs/ *adj* (*before n*) (liter *or* journ) desafortunado, desventurado (liter)

happen /'hæpən/ *vi* **1 (a)** (occur) pasar, suceder, ocurrir **(b)** (befall, become of) **to ~** TO **sb** pasarle A algn **2 to ~ to** + INF: **she ~ed to be there** dio la casualidad de que estaba ahí; **if you ~ to see her** ... si por casualidad la ves ... ■ **~** *v impers:* **it (just) so ~s that** ... da la casualidad de que ...

happening /'hæpənɪŋ/ *n* suceso *m*

happily /'hæpəli ‖ 'hæpɪli/ *adv* **1 (a)** ‹*smile/laugh*› alegremente; **to be ~ married** ser* feliz en el matrimonio **(b)** (gladly) (*usu before vb*) ‹*help*› con mucho gusto **2** (fortunately) (*indep*) por suerte, afortunadamente

happiness /'hæpines ‖ 'hæpinɪs/ *n* [U] felicidad *f*

happy /'hæpi/ *adj* **-pier, -piest 1 (a)** (joyful, content) ‹*person/home*› feliz; ‹*smile*› de felicidad, alegre **(b)** (pleased) (*pred*) **to be ~** alegrarse **(c)** (satisfied) (*pred*) **to be ~** (WITH **sth**) estar* contento (CON algo) **2** ‹*days/occasion*› feliz; **~ birthday** feliz cumpleaños

happy-go-lucky /'hæpigəʊ'lʌki/ *adj* despreocupado

harangue /hə'ræŋ/ *vt* arengar*

harass /'hærəs, hə'ræs/ *vt* **(a)** (persistently annoy) acosar **(b)** (Mil) hostigar*

harassment /'hærəsmənt, hə'ræs-/ *n* [U] acoso *m*; **racial ~** hostilidad *f* racial; **sexual ~** acoso *m* sexual

harbor¹, (BrE) **harbour** /'hɑːrbər ‖ 'hɑːbə(r)/ *n* puerto *m*

harbor², (BrE) **harbour** *vt* **(a)** (shelter) ‹*fugitive*› albergar*, dar* refugio a **(b)** ‹*desire/suspicion*› albergar* (liter); **to ~ a grudge** guardar rencor

hard¹ /hɑːrd ‖ hɑːd/ *adj* **-er, -est 1 (a)** (firm, solid) ‹*object/surface*› duro **(b)** (forceful) ‹*push/knock*› fuerte **2 (a)** (difficult) ‹*question/subject*› difícil; ‹*task*› arduo; **I find that ~ to believe** me cuesta creerlo; **to learn sth the ~ way** aprender algo a base de cometer errores **(b)** (severe) ‹*winter/climate/master*› duro, severo; **to give sb a ~ time** hacérselas* pasar mal a algn; **don't be too ~ on him** no seas demasiado duro con él; **~ luck** mala suerte **(c)** (tough, cynical) ‹*person/attitude*› duro **3** (concentrated, strenuous) ‹*work*› duro; **children are very ~ work** los niños dan mucho trabajo; **he's a ~ worker** es muy trabajador **4** (definite) ‹*evidence*› concluyente **5** (sharp, harsh) ‹*light/voice*› fuerte **6 (a)** (in strongest form): **~ drugs** drogas *fpl* duras; **~ liquor** bebidas *fpl* (alcohólicas) fuertes; **~ porn** porno *m* duro **(b)** ‹*water*› duro

hard² *adv* **-er, -est 1 (a)** (with force) ‹*pull/push*› con fuerza; ‹*hit*› fuerte **(b)** (strenuously) ‹*work*› mucho, duro, **(c)** (intently) ‹*listen*› atentamente **2** (heavily) ‹*rain/snow*› fuerte, mucho; ‹*pant/breathe*› pesadamente **3** (severely): **to be ~ hit** ser* muy afectado; ***to feel ~ done by***: **she feels ~ done by** piensa que la han tratado injustamente

hard: **~-and-fast** /'hɑːrdn̩'fæst ‖ 'hɑːdən'fɑːst/ *adj* (*no comp, usu before n*) absoluto; **~back** *n* [C] (book) libro *m* de tapa dura *or* en cartoné; **~ball** *n* [U] (AmE) béisbol *m*; **~board** *n* [U] cartón *m* madera; **~-boiled** /'hɑːrd'bɔɪld ‖ ˌhɑːd'bɔɪld/ *adj* **(a)** ‹*egg*› duro **(b)** (unsentimental) endurecido; **~ disk** *n* disco *m* duro; **~-earned** /'hɑːrd'ɜːrnd ‖ 'hɑːdˌɜːnd/ *adj* (*usu before n*) ‹*cash*› ganado con el sudor de la frente

harden /'hɑːrdn̩ ‖ 'hɑːdn̩/ *vt* **(a)** (make hard) ‹*clay/cement/skin*› endurecer*; ‹*steel/glass*› templar **(b)** (make tough, unfeeling) ‹*person*› endurecer*; **you must ~ your heart and tell him to go** tienes que hacerte fuerte y decirle que se vaya ■ **~** *vi* **(a)** (become hard, rigid) endurecerse* **(b)** (become inflexible) ‹‹*attitude*›› volverse* inflexible

hardened /'hɑːrdn̩d ‖ 'hɑːdn̩d/ *adj* (*before n*) ‹*sinner/drinker*› empedernido; ‹*criminal*› habitual

hard: **~ hat** *n* (Clothing, Const) casco *m*; **~-headed** /'hɑːrd'hedəd ‖ ˌhɑːd'hedɪd/ *adj* **(a)**

(practical, realistic) práctico, realista **(b)** (stubborn) (AmE) testarudo, cabezota (fam); **~-hearted** /'hɑːrd'hɑːrtəd ‖ ˌhɑːd'hɑːtɪd/ *adj* duro de corazón; **~-hitting** /'hɑːrd'hɪtɪŋ ‖ ˌhɑːd'hɪtɪŋ/ *adj* implacable, feroz; **~ labor**, (BrE) **~ labour** *n* [U] trabajos *mpl* forzados; **~-liner** /'hɑːrd'lamər ‖ ˌhɑːd 'lamə(r)/ *n* partidario, -ria *m,f* de la línea dura

hardly /'hɑːrdli ‖ 'hɑːdli/ *adv* **(a)** (scarcely): **~ anyone/anything** casi nadie/nada; **~ ever** casi nunca; **he ~ knew her** apenas la conocía **(b)** (surely not): **it's ~ what you'd call a masterpiece** no es precisamente una obra maestra

hardness /'hɑːrdnəs ‖ 'hɑːdnɪs/ *n* [U] dureza *f*

hard: **~ of hearing** *adj* duro de oído; **~-pressed** /'hɑːrd'prest ‖ ˌhɑːd'prest/ *adj* (*pred* **~ pressed**) ‹*industry/nation/staff*› en apuros; **~ sell** *n* (*no pl*) venta *f* agresiva

hardship /'hɑːrdʃɪp ‖ 'hɑːdʃɪp/ *n* [U C]: **to experience** *o* **suffer great ~** pasar muchos apuros; **the ~s of the journey** las penurias del viaje

hard: **~ shoulder** *n* (BrE) arcén *m*, berma *f* (Andes), acotamiento *m* (Méx), banquina *f* (RPl), hombrillo *m* (Ven); **~ up** *adj* (colloq) (*pred*) **to be ~ up** estar* mal de dinero; **~ware** /'hɑːrdwer ‖ 'hɑːdweə(r)/ *n* [U] **(a)** (ironmongery) ferretería *f*; (*before n*) **~ware store** ferretería *f* **(b)** (Mil): **military ~ware** armamento *m* **(c)** (Comput) hardware *m*, soporte *m* físico, equipo *m*; **~-wearing** /'hɑːrd'werɪŋ ‖ ˌhɑːd'weərɪŋ/ *adj* (BrE) resistente; **~-working** /'hɑːrd'wɜːrkɪŋ ‖ ˌhɑːd'wɜːkɪŋ/ *adj* trabajador

hardy /'hɑːrdi ‖ 'hɑːdi/ *adj* **-dier, -diest** ‹*person/animal*› fuerte; ‹*plant*› resistente (*a las heladas etc*)

hare /her ‖ heə(r)/ *n* liebre *f*

haricot (bean) /'hærɪkəʊ/ *n* frijol *m* *or* (Esp) alubia *f* *or* judía *f* *or* (CS) poroto *m* (*de color blanco*)

hark back /hɑːrk ‖ hɑːk/ *vi* **to ~ ~ TO sth** «*person*» rememorar algo; «*book*» evocar* algo

harm¹ /hɑːrm ‖ hɑːm/ *n* [U] daño *m*; **to do ~ to sb/sth** hacerle* daño a algn/algo; **there's no ~ in asking** con preguntar no se pierde nada; **he won't come to any ~** no le va a pasar nada; ***to be out of ~'s way*** estar* a salvo

harm² *vt* ‹*person/object*› hacerle* daño a; ‹*reputation/career*› perjudicar*

harmful /'hɑːrmfəl ‖ 'hɑːmfəl/ *adj* ‹*substance*› nocivo; ‹*influence*› pernicioso, dañino; ‹*effect*› perjudicial

harmless /'hɑːrmləs ‖ 'hɑːmlɪs/ *adj* ‹*animal/person*› inofensivo; ‹*substance*› inocuo; ‹*joke/suggestion/fun*› inocente

harmonica /hɑːr'mɑːnɪkə ‖ hɑː'mɒnɪkə/ *n* armónica *f*

harmonious /hɑːr'məʊniəs ‖ hɑː'məʊniəs/ *adj* armonioso

harmonize /'hɑːrmənaɪz ‖ 'hɑːmənaɪz/ *vi* (Mus) cantar en armonía; (be in accord) «*colors/ideas*» armonizar* ■ **~** *vt* ‹*policies/plans*› armonizar

harmony /'hɑːrməni ‖ 'hɑːməni/ *n* [U C] (*pl* **-nies**) (Mus) armonía *f*; **in ~** en armonía

harness¹ /'hɑːrnəs ‖ 'hɑːnɪs/ *n* **(a)** (for horse) arnés *m*, arreos *mpl* **(b)** (for baby, on parachute) arnés *m* **(c)** (*safety ~*) arnés *m* de seguridad

harness² *vt* **(a)** (put harness on) ‹*horse*› enjaezar*, ponerle* los arreos *or* el arnés a **(b)** (utilize) ‹*energy/resources*› aprovechar, utilizar*

harp /hɑːrp ‖ hɑːp/ *n* arpa *f*‡

• **harp on** [*v* + *adv*] (colloq) **to ~ on ABOUT sth** insistir SOBRE algo

harpoon¹ /hɑːr'puːn ‖ hɑː'puːn/ *n* arpón *m*

harpoon² *vt* arponear

harrowing /'hærəʊɪŋ/ *adj* ‹*experience*› angustioso, terrible; ‹*tale*› desgarrador

harry /'hæri/ *vt* **-ries, -rying, -ried (a)** (raid) ‹*enemy*› hostilizar* **(b)** (pester) hostigar*, acosar

harsh /hɑːrʃ ‖ hɑːʃ/ *adj* ‹*punishment*› duro, severo; ‹*words/conditions*› duro; ‹*light*› fuerte; ‹*climate*› riguroso; ‹*contrast*› violento; ‹*color*› chillón; ‹*sound*› discordante; ‹*tone/texture*› áspero

harshly /'hɑːrʃli ‖ 'hɑːʃli/ *adv* ‹*judge/punish/speak*› severamente, con severidad

harvest¹ /'hɑːrvəst ‖ 'hɑːvɪst/ *n* **(a)** [C U] (of grain) cosecha *f*, siega *f*; (of fruit, vegetables) cosecha *f*, recolección *f*; (of grapes) vendimia *f* **(b)** [C] (yield) cosecha *f*

harvest² *vt* ‹*crop/wheat*› cosechar; ‹*grapes*› vendimiar; ‹*field*› realizar* la cosecha en

harvester /'hɑːrvəstər ‖ 'hɑːvɪstə(r)/ *n* **(a)** (machine) cosechadora *f* **(b)** (person) segador, -dora *m,f*

has /hæz, *weak form* həz, əz/ *3rd pers sing pres of* HAVE

has-been /'hæzbɪn ‖ 'hæzbiːn/ *n* (colloq & pej) nombre *m* del pasado

hash /hæʃ/ *n* **(a)** [U C] (Culin) *plato de carne y verduras picadas y doradas* **(b)** [C] (muddle): **to make a ~ of sth** (colloq) hacer* algo muy mal

hash browns *pl n* (AmE colloq) *papas y cebolla doradas en la sartén*

hashish /'hæʃiːʃ/ *n* [U] hachís *m*

hasn't /'hæznt/ = **has not**

hassle¹ /'hæsəl/ *n* [C U] (colloq) lío *m* (fam), rollo *m* (fam)

hassle² *vt* (colloq) fastidiar, jorobar (fam)

haste /heɪst/ *n* [U] prisa *f*, apuro *m* (AmL)

hasten /'heɪsn/ *vt* ‹*process*› acelerar; ‹*defeat/death*› adelantar ■ **~** *vi* apresurarse, apurarse (AmL)

hastily /'heɪstəli ‖ 'heɪstɪli/ *adv* **(a)** (quickly) ‹*built/thought up*› a toda prisa, apresuradamente **(b)** (rashly) ‹*speak/act*› con precipitación, precipitadamente

hasty /'heɪsti/ *adj* **-tier, -tiest (a)** (quick) ‹*glance/meal*› rápido **(b)** (rash) ‹*move/decision/judgment*› precipitado; **I think you're being rather ~** creo que te precipitas

hat /hæt/ *n* sombrero *m*

hatch¹ /hætʃ/ *vt* **(a)** ‹*egg*› incubar **(b) ~ (out)** ‹*chick*› empollar **(c)** (devise) (pej) ‹*plot/scheme*› tramar, urdir ■ **~** *vi* **(a)** «*egg*» romperse* **(b) ~ (out)** «*chick*» salir* del cascarón, nacer*

hatch² *n* **(a)** (opening, cover) trampilla *f*; (Aviat, Naut) escotilla *f* **(b)** (*serving ~*) ventanilla *f* (*que comunica cocina y comedor*)

hatchback /'hætʃbæk/ *n* (car) coche *m* con tres/cinco puertas; (door) puerta *f* trasera

hatchet /'hætʃət ‖ 'hætʃɪt/ *n* hacha *f*‡, hachuela *f*; ***to bury the ~*** enterrar* el hacha de guerra

hate¹ /heɪt/ *vt* odiar, detestar

hate² *n* **(a)** [U] (hatred) odio *m* **(b)** [C] (object of hatred) ⇒ PET² (b)

hatred /'heɪtrəd ‖ 'heɪtrɪd/ *n* [U] odio *m*

hat trick *n*: **to score a ~ ~** marcar* tres goles (*or* tantos *etc*) en un partido

haughty /'hɔːti/ *adj* **-tier, -tiest** altivo, altanero

haul¹ /hɔːl/ *vt* **(a)** (drag) ‹*logs/load*› llevar arrastrando; **the fishermen ~ed in their nets** los pescadores cobraron las redes **(b)** (Transp) transportar

haul² *n* **1** (catch — of fish) redada *f*; (— of stolen goods) botín *m* **2** (distance) (Transp) recorrido *m*, trayecto *m*

haulage /'hɔːlɪdʒ/ *n* [U] **(a)** (activity) transporte *m*; (*before n*) **~ contractor** transportista *mf* **(b)** (charge) (gastos *mpl* de) transporte *m*

hauler /'hɔːlər ‖ 'hɔːlə(r)/, (BrE) **haulier** /'hɔːljə(r)/ *n* (person) transportista *mf*; (business) empresa *f* de transportes

haunch /hɔːntʃ/ *n* (*usu pl*) (of animal) anca *f*‡; (of horse) grupa *f*, anca *f*‡; (of person) cadera *f*

haunt¹ /hɔːnt/ *vt* «*ghost*» rondar; «*memory/idea*» perseguir*

haunt² *n*: **we went to all her old ~s** fuimos a todos los sitios a los que solía ir

haunted /'hɔːntəd ‖ 'hɔːntɪd/ *adj* ‹*house*› embrujado; ‹*look*› angustiado

haunting /'hɔːntɪŋ/ *adj* evocador e inquietante

Havana /hə'vænə/ *n* La Habana

have /hæv, *weak forms* həv, əv/ (*3rd pers sing pres* **has**; *past & past p* **had**) *vt* **I 1** (possess) tener*; **I ~** *o* (esp BrE) **I've got two cats** tengo dos gatos **2** (hold, have at one's disposal) tener*; **can I ~ a sheet of paper?** ¿me das una hoja de papel?; **I've (got) a lot to do** tengo mucho que hacer **3 (a)** (receive) ‹*letter/news*› tener*, recibir; ***to ~ had it*** (colloq): **I've had it** (I'm in trouble) estoy frito (AmL), me la he cargado (Esp fam); (I've lost my chance) la he fastidiado (fam); ***to ~ it in for sb*** (colloq) tenerle* manía *or* tirria a algn (fam) **(b)** (obtain) conseguir*; **they were the only seats to be had** eran los únicos asientos que había **4** (consume) ‹*steak/spaghetti*› comer, tomar (Esp); ‹*champagne/beer*› tomar; ‹*cigarette*› fumar(se); **to ~ sth to eat/drink** comer/beber algo; **to ~ breakfast** desayunar; **to ~ lunch** almorzar* *or* (esp Esp, Méx) comer; **to ~ dinner** cenar, comer (AmL) **5 (a)** (experience, undergo) ‹*accident*› tener*; **~ a nice day!** ¡adiós! ¡que le (*or* te *etc*) vaya bien!; **we had a very pleasant evening** pasamos una noche muy agradable; **she had a heart attack** le dio un ataque al corazón **(b)** (organize) ‹*party*› hacer*, dar*; ‹*meeting*› tener* **(c)** (suffer from) ‹*cancer/diabetes/flu*› tener*; **to ~ a cold** estar* resfriado **6** (give birth to) ‹*baby*› tener* **7** (colloq) (swindle, dupe): **you've been had!** ¡te han timado *or* engañado!

II 1 (*causative use*): **we'll ~ it clean in no time** enseguida lo limpiamos *or* lo dejamos limpio; **he had them all in tears** los hizo llorar a todos; **you had me worried** me tenías preocupado; **to ~ sth + PAST P**: **we had it repaired** lo hicimos arreglar, lo mandamos (a) arreglar (AmL); **to ~ one's hair cut** cortarse el pelo **2** (indicating what happens to sb): **to have sth + PAST P**: **he had his bicycle stolen** le robaron la bicicleta **3 (a)** (allow) (*with neg*) tolerar, consentir*; **I won't ~ it!** ¡no lo consentiré *or* toleraré! **(b)** (accept, believe) aceptar, creer*; **she wouldn't ~ it** no lo quiso aceptar *or* creer **4** (indicating state, position) tener*; **I had the radio on** tenía la radio puesta ■ **~** *v aux* **I 1** (*used to form perfect tenses*) haber*; **I ~/had seen her** la he/había visto; **~ you been waiting long?** ¿hace mucho que esperas?; **if I'd known that** … si hubiera sabido que …; **when he had finished, she** … cuando terminó *or* (liter) cuando hubo terminado, ella … **2 (a)** (in tags): **you've met Joe, ~n't you?** conoces a Joe ¿no? *or* ¿no es cierto? *or* ¿no es verdad?; **you ~n't lost the key, ~ you?** ¡no habrás perdido la llave …! **(b)** (elliptical use): **you may ~ forgiven him, but I ~n't** puede que tú lo hayas perdonado, pero yo no; **the clock has stopped — so it has!** el reloj se ha parado — ¡es verdad! *or* ¡es cierto!; **you've forgotten something — ~ I?** te has olvidado de algo — ¿sí?

II (expressing obligation): **to ~ to + INF** tener* QUE + INF; **you don't ~ to be an expert to realize that** no hay que *or* no se necesita ser un experto para darse cuenta de eso

• have back 1 [*v + o + adv, v + adv + o*] (receive back): **can I ~ the ring back?** ¿me devuelves el anillo? **2** [*v + o + adv*] ‹*guests*› **to ~ sb back** (invite again) volver* a invitar a algn; (reciprocate invitation) devolverle* a algn una invitación

• have on [*v + o + adv*] (tease) (colloq) **to ~ sb on** tomarle el pelo a algn (fam)

• have out [*v + o + adv*] **(a)** (have removed): **to ~ a tooth out** sacarse* una muela; **she had her tonsils out** la operaron de las amígdalas **(b)** (discuss forcefully) **to ~ it out WITH sb** ponerle* las cosas claras A algn

haven /'heɪvən/ *n* **(a)** (refuge) refugio *m* **(b)** (port) (liter) puerto *m*

haven't /'hævənt/ = **have not**

haversack /'hævərsæk ‖ 'hævəsæk/ *n* mochila *f*, morral *m*

haves /hævz/ *pl n* **the ~ and the have-nots** los ricos y los pobres *or* los desposeídos

havoc /'hævək/ *n* [U]: **the accident caused ~** el accidente creó gran confusión; **the children created ~** los niños armaron un lío tremendo (fam); **to play ~ with sth** trastocar* *or* desbaratar algo

Hawaii /hə'waiː/ *n* Hawai *m*

Hawaiian /hə'waɪən/ *adj* hawaiano

hawk¹ /hɔːk/ *n* halcón *m*

hawk² *vt* ‹*goods/wares*› vocear, pregonar

hawthorn /'hɔːθɔːrn ‖ 'hɔːθɔːn/ *n* [C U] espino *m*

hay /heɪ/ *n* [U] heno *m*

hay: **~ fever** *n* [U] fiebre *f* del heno; **~rick** /'heɪrɪk/ *n* almiar *m*; **~seed** *n* (AmE sl) ⇒ YOKEL; **~stack** *n* almiar *m*; **~wire** *adj* (colloq) (*pred*):

to go ~wire «*person*» perder* la chaveta (fam); «*machine*» estropearse, descomponerse* (AmL)

hazard¹ /ˈhæzərd ‖ ˈhæzəd/ *n* peligro *m*, riesgo *m*

hazard² *vt* (frml) ‹*remark/question*› aventurar; **to ~ a guess** aventurar una respuesta

hazard lights, (BrE also) **hazard warning lights** *pl n* (Auto) luces *fpl* de emergencia

hazardous /ˈhæzərdəs ‖ ˈhæzədəs/ *adj* peligroso, arriesgado

haze /heɪz/ *n* (*no pl*) (due to humidity) neblina *f*, bruma *f*; (due to heat) calima *f*

hazel /ˈheɪzəl/ *n* **(a)** [C] (plant) avellano *m* **(b)** [U] (wood) (madera *f* de) avellano *m* **(c)** ▶ 515 [U] (color) color *m* avellana; (*before n*) ‹*eyes*› color avellana *adj inv*

hazelnut /ˈheɪzəlnʌt/ *n* avellana *f*

hazy /ˈheɪzi/ *adj* **hazier, haziest (a)** ‹*day*› (due to humidity) neblinoso, brumoso; (due to heat) de calima **(b)** ‹*memory/idea/distinction*› vago, confuso

he /hiː, *weak form* i/ *pron* él

■ **Note** Although *él* is given as the main translation of *he*, it is in practice used only for emphasis, or to avoid ambiguity: *he went to the theater* fue al teatro; *she went to the theater, he went to the cinema* ella fue al teatro y él fue al cine; ***he** did it* él lo hizo.

head¹ /hed/ *n* **1** ▶ 484 (Anat) cabeza *f*; **a fine ~ of hair** una buena cabellera; **from ~ to foot** *o* **toe** de pies a cabeza, de arriba (a) abajo; ***~ over heels***: **she tripped and went ~ over heels down the steps** tropezó y cayó rodando escaleras abajo; **to be ~ over heels in love** estar* locamente enamorado; ***to go to sb's ~*** subírsele a la cabeza a algn; ***to make ~ or tail*** *o* (AmE also) ***~s or tails of sth*** entender* algo **2** (mind, brain) cabeza *f*; **I said the first thing that came into my ~** dije lo primero que se me ocurrió; **she added it up in her ~** hizo la suma mentalmente; **she has a good ~ for business** tiene cabeza para los negocios; **I've no ~ for heights** sufro de vértigo; **it never entered my ~ that** ... ni se me pasó por la cabeza que ...; ***to keep/lose one's ~*** mantener*/perder* la calma **3 (a)** (of nail, tack, pin) cabeza *f*; (of spear, arrow) punta *f*; (of hammer) cabeza *f*; (on beer) espuma *f* **(b)** (top end — of bed, table) cabecera *f*; (— of page, letter) encabezamiento *m*; (— of procession, line) cabeza *f* **4 (a)** (chief) director, -tora *m,f*; **~ of state** jefe, -fa *m,f* de Estado; **the ~ of the household** el/la cabeza de familia; (*before n*) **~ waiter** maître *m*, capitán *m* de meseros (Méx) **(b)** (*~ teacher*) (esp BrE) director, -tora *m,f* (de colegio) **5** (person): **$15 per ~** 15 dólares por cabeza *or* persona **6** (crisis): **to come to a ~** hacer* crisis **7 (a)** (magnetic device) (Audio, Comput) cabeza *f*, cabezal *m* **(b)** (of drill) cabezal *m* **8** (Geog) cabo *m*

head² *vt* **1 (a)** ‹*march/procession*› encabezar*, ir* a la cabeza de **(b)** ‹*revolt*› acaudillar; ‹*team*› capitanear; ‹*expedition/department*› dirigir* **2** (direct) (+ *adv compl*) ‹*vehicle/ship*› dirigir* **3** (in soccer) ‹*ball*› cabecear **4** ‹*page/chapter*› encabezar* ■ **~** *vi*: **to ~ west/north** ir* en dirección oeste/norte

● **head for** [*v* + *prep* + *o*] **(a)** (go toward) «*ship*» ir* con rumbo a; **to ~ for home** ponerse* en camino a casa; **the car was ~ing straight for me** el coche venía derecho hacia mí **(b)** (be in danger of): **to be ~ed** *o* **~ing for sth** ir* camino de algo

● **head off 1** [*v* + *adv*] (set out) salir* **2** [*v* + *o* + *adv*, *v* + *adv* + *o*] **(a)** (get in front of) atajar, cortarle el paso a **(b)** (prevent, forestall) ‹*criticism/threat*› prevenir*

head: **~ache** ▶ 484 *n* dolor *m* de cabeza; **~band** *n* cinta *f* del pelo, vincha *f* (AmS), huincha *f* (Bol, Chi, Per); **~board** *n* cabecera *f*; **~dress** *n* tocado *m*

headed /ˈhedəd ‖ ˈhedɪd/ *adj* ‹*notepaper*› con membrete, membretado, membreteado (Andes)

header /ˈhedər ‖ ˈhedə(r)/ *n* (in soccer) cabezazo *m*

head: **~first** /ˈhedˈfɜːrst ‖ ˌhedˈfɜːst/ *adv* **(a)** (with head foremost) de cabeza **(b)** (over-hastily) precipitadamente; **~hunt** *vt* ofrecerle* un puesto a; **~hunter** *n* (Busn) cazatalentos *m*

heading /ˈhedɪŋ/ *n* (title) encabezamiento *m*, título *m*, acápite *m* (AmL); (letterhead) membrete *m*

head: **~lamp** *n* faro *m*; **~land** /ˈhedlənd/ *n* cabo *m*; **~light** *n* faro *m*; **~line** *n* titular *m*; **the news ~lines** el resumen informativo *or* de noticias; **~long** *adv* **(a)** (hastily) precipitadamente **(b)** (with head foremost) de cabeza; **~master** /ˈhedˈmæstər ‖ ˌhedˈmɑːstə(r)/ *n* director *m* (de colegio); **~mistress** /ˈhedˈmɪstrəs ‖ ˌhedˈmɪstrɪs/ *n* directora *f* (de colegio); **~ office** *n* (oficina *f*) central *f*; **~-on** /ˈhedˈɑːn ‖ ˌhedˈɒn/ *adj* ‹*crash/collision*› frontal, de frente; **~phones** *pl n* auriculares *mpl*, cascos *mpl*; **~quarters** /ˈhedˈkwɔːrtərz ‖ ˌhedˈkwɔːtəz/ *n* (*pl* **~quarters**) (+ *sing or pl vb*) oficina *f* central; (Mil) cuartel *m* general; **~rest** *n* reposacabezas *m*, apoyacabezas *m*; **~room** *n* [U] altura *f*

heads /hedz/ *adv* (on coin) cara *f*, águila *f*† (Méx); **~ or tails?** ¿cara o cruz, ¿águila o sol? (Méx), ¿cara o sello? (Andes, Ven), ¿cara o ceca? (Arg)

head: **~scarf** *n* pañuelo *m* (de cabeza); **~set** *n* auriculares *mpl*, cascos *mpl*; **~stand** *n*: **to do a ~stand** pararse de cabeza (AmL), hacer* el pino (Esp); **~ start** *n* ventaja *f*; **~stone** *n* lápida *f*; **~strong** *adj* testarudo, obstinado; **~teacher** /ˈhedˈtiːtʃər ‖ ˌhedˈtiːtʃə(r)/ *n* (BrE) director, -tora *m,f* (de colegio); **~way** *n* [U]: **to make ~way** hacer* progresos, avanzar*

heady /ˈhedi/ *adj* **-dier, -diest** ‹*scent*› embriagador; ‹*wine*› que se sube a la cabeza

heal /hiːl/ *vt* curar ■ **~** *vi* cicatrizar*, cerrarse*

health /helθ/ *n* [U] salud *f*; **to be in good/poor ~** estar* bien/mal de salud; **your (good) ~!** (proposing a toast) ¡salud!; (*before n*) ‹*policy/services*› sanitario, de salud pública; ‹*inspector/regulations*› de sanidad

health: **~ care** *n* [U] asistencia *f* sanitaria *or* médica; **~ centre** *n* (BrE) centro *m* médico *or* de salud; **~ food** *n* [U C] alimentos *mpl* naturales; **~ insurance** *n* [U] seguro *m* de enfermedad; **~ service** *n* (in UK) ⇒ NATIONAL HEALTH (SERVICE)

healthy /ˈhelθi/ *adj* **-thier, -thiest 1 (a)** (in good health) ‹*person/animal/complexion*› sano; **she has a ~ appetite** tiene buen apetito **(b)** (promoting good health) ‹*diet/living/environment*› sano, saludable **(c)**

(sound) ‹*respect*› sano **2** ‹*economy/finances*› próspero

heap¹ /hiːp/ *n* **(a)** (pile) montón *m*, pila *f* **(b)** (car) (colloq) cacharro *m* (fam)

heap² *vt* **(a)** (make pile) amontonar, apilar **(b)** (supply liberally): **she ~ed his plate with food** le llenó el plato de comida; **a ~ing** (AmE) *o* (BrE) **~ed spoonful** (Culin) una cucharada colmada

hear /hɪr ‖ hɪə(r)/ (*past & past p* **heard** /hɜːrd ‖ hɜːd/) *vt* **1** ‹*sound*› oír* **2** (get to know) oír*; **I've ~d so much about you** me han hablado tanto de ti, he oído hablar tanto de ti; **he's very ill, I ~** me han dicho que está muy enfermo **3** (listen to) **(a)** ‹*lecture/broadcast/views*› escuchar, oír* **(b)** (Law) ‹*case*› ver*; ‹*charge*› oír* ■ ~ *vi* **1** (perceive) oír*; **~, ~!** ¡eso, eso!, ¡bien dicho! **2** (get news): **have you ~d?** ¿te has enterado?; **to ~ ABOUT sth** enterarse DE algo; **I haven't ~d from them for months** hace meses que no sé nada de ellos *or* que no tengo noticias suyas

● **hear of** [*v + prep + o*] **(a)** (encounter, come to know of): **I've ~d of him** he oído hablar de él; **if you ~ of anything interesting, let me know** si te enteras de algo interesante, me lo dices **(b)** (have news of) tener* noticias *or* saber* de **(c)** (allow): **I won't ~ of it!** ¡ni hablar!

● **hear out** [*v + o + adv, v + adv + o*] escuchar (*hasta el final*)

hearing /ˈhɪrɪŋ ‖ ˈhɪərɪŋ/ *n* **1** [U] (sense) oído *m* **2** [C] **(a)** (consideration) **to give sb a ~** escuchar a algn **(b)** (trial) vista *f*

hearing aid *n* audífono *m*

hearsay /ˈhɪrseɪ ‖ ˈhɪəseɪ/ *n* [U] habladurías *fpl*

hearse /hɜːrs ‖ hɜːs/ *n* coche *m* fúnebre

heart /hɑːrt ‖ hɑːt/ ▶ 484 *n* **1** (Anat) corazón *m*; (*before n*) ‹*disease*› del corazón, cardíaco **2** (seat of emotions): **to have a kind ~** tener* buen corazón, ser* de buen corazón; **to have sb's interests at ~** preocuparse por algn; ***to learn/know sth by ~*** aprender/saber* algo de memoria; ***my/her/his ~ wasn't in it*** lo hacía sin ganas; ***to take sth to ~*** tomarse algo a pecho **3** (courage, morale) ánimos *mpl*; **to lose ~** descorazonarse, desanimarse; **to take ~** animarse; ***not to have the ~ to do sth***: **I didn't have the ~ to tell him** no tuve valor para decírselo **4 (a)** (central part): **the ~ of the city/country** el corazón *or* centro de la ciudad/del país; **the ~ of the matter** el meollo del asunto **(b)** (of cabbage, lettuce) cogollo *m* **5** (Games) **hearts** (suit) (+ *sing or pl vb*) corazones *mpl*

heart: **~ache** *n* [U] pena *f*, dolor *m*; **~ attack** *n* ataque *m* al corazón, infarto *m*; **~beat** *n* latido *m* (del corazón); **~break** *n* **(a)** [U] (grief) congoja *f*, sufrimiento *m* **(b)** [C] (cause of grief) desengaño *m*; **~breaking** *adj* desgarrador; **~broken** *adj* ‹*look/sobs*› desconsolado; **she was ~broken when he died** su muerte la dejó destrozada; **~burn** *n* [U] ardor *m* de estómago; **~felt** *adj* sincero

hearth /hɑːrθ ‖ hɑːθ/ *n* chimenea *f*, hogar *m*

heartily /ˈhɑːrtḷi ‖ ˈhɑːtɪli/ *adv* **(a)** (warmly) ‹*congratulate/greet*› efusivamente **(b)** (with enthusiasm) ‹*laugh/eat*› con ganas

heartless /ˈhɑːrtləs ‖ ˈhɑːtlɪs/ *adj* ‹*person*› sin corazón; ‹*refusal*› cruel

heart: **~-shaped** *adj* ‹*card/cake*› con forma de corazón; ‹*face*› en forma de corazón; **~-to-~** *n* (colloq) charla *f* íntima

hearty /ˈhɑːrti ‖ ˈhɑːti/ *adj* **-tier, -tiest** ‹*person*› campechano; ‹*welcome*› caluroso; ‹*appetite*› bueno

heat¹ /hiːt/ *n* **1** [U] **(a)** (warmth) calor *m* **(b)** (for cooking) fuego *m* **2** [U] **in the ~ of the moment** en un momento de enojo (*or* exaltación *etc*) **3** [U] (estrus) celo *m*; **to be in** *o* (BrE) **on ~** estar* en celo **4** [C] (Sport) (prueba) eliminatoria *f*

heat² *vt* calentar*; ‹*house*› calentar*, calefaccionar (CS)

● **heat up 1** [*v + adv*] calentarse* **2** [*v + o + adv, v + adv + o*] calentar*

heated /ˈhiːtəd ‖ ˈhiːtɪd/ *adj* **(a)** (warmed) ‹*pool*› climatizado; ‹*seat/rear window*› térmico **(b)** (impassioned) ‹*argument*› acalorado; **to get ~** acalorarse

heater /ˈhiːtər ‖ ˈhiːtə(r)/ *n* calentador *m*, estufa *f*; (*water ~*) calentador *m* (de agua)

heath /hiːθ/ *n* [C U] brezal *m*, monte *m*

heathen /ˈhiːðən/ *n* pagano, -na *m,f*

heather /ˈheðər ‖ ˈheðə(r)/ *n* [U] brezo *m*

heating /ˈhiːtɪŋ/ *n* [U] calefacción *f*

heat wave *n* ola *f* de calor

heave¹ /hiːv/ *vt* **1 (a)** (move with effort): **we ~d the box onto the shelf** con esfuerzo logramos subir la caja al estante; **they ~d it into place** lo colocaron empujando/levantándolo **(b)** (throw) (colloq) tirar **2** (utter): **to ~ a sigh** suspirar ■ ~ *vi* **1** (pull) tirar, jalar (AmL exc CS) **2** (rise and fall): **his chest ~d** respiraba agitadamente

heave² *n* (pull) tirón *m*, jalón *m* (AmL exc CS); (push) empujón *m*

heaven /ˈhevən/ *n* cielo *m*; **(good) ~s!** ¡Dios mío!; **thank ~** gracias a Dios

heavenly /ˈhevənli/ *adj* **(a)** (Relig) celestial **(b)** (Astron) celeste **(c)** (superb) (colloq) divino (fam)

heavily /ˈhevəli ‖ ˈhevɪli/ *adv* **1 (a)** ‹*tread/fall*› pesadamente; **to be ~ built** ser* corpulento; **to breathe ~** jadear **(b)** (thickly) ‹*underlined*› con trazo grueso; **she was ~ made-up** iba muy maquillada **2 (a)** (copiously) ‹*rain/snow*› mucho **(b)** (immoderately) ‹*drink/smoke*› en exceso **(c)** (greatly): **to borrow ~** contraer* considerables deudas; **~ pregnant** en avanzado estado de gravidez (frml) *or* (period) de gestación

heavy¹ /ˈhevi/ *adj* **-vier, -viest 1 (a)** (weighty) ‹*load/suitcase/weight*› pesado; ‹*fabric/garment*› grueso, pesado; ‹*saucepan*› de fondo grueso; ‹*boots*› fuerte; ‹*work*› pesado; **it's very ~** es muy pesado, pesa mucho **(b)** (large-scale) (*before n*) ‹*artillery/machinery*› pesado **2 (a)** (ponderous) ‹*tread/footstep/fall*› pesado; ‹*thud*› sordo **(b)** ‹*features*› tosco; ‹*irony*› poco sutil **3 (a)** (oppressive) ‹*clouds/sky*› pesado **(b)** (loud) ‹*sigh*› profundo **4 (a)** (bigger than usual) ‹*expenditure*› cuantioso **(b)** (intense) ‹*book*› pesado, denso; ‹*rain*› fuerte; ‹*traffic*› denso; ‹*schedule*› apretado; **to be a ~ drinker/smoker** beber/fumar mucho **(c)** (severe) ‹*sentence*› severo; ‹*casualties*› numeroso; ‹*blow*› duro, fuerte

heavy² *n* (*pl* **-vies**) (colloq) matón *m* (fam)

heavy: **~ cream** *n* (AmE) crema *f* doble, nata *f* para montar (Esp), doble crema *f* (Méx); **~-duty** /'hevi'du:ti ‖ ˌhevɪ'dju:ti/ *adj* ‹*material/sacks*› muy resistente; ‹*machine*› para uso industrial; ‹*clothing/overalls*› de trabajo; **~-handed** /'hevi 'hændəd ‖ ˌhevi'hændɪd/ *adj* torpe; **~ metal** *n* [U] (Mus) heavy *m* (metal), rock *m* duro

heavyweight¹ /'heviweɪt/ *n* (Sport) peso *mf* pesado; **a political ~** un peso pesado de la política

heavyweight² *adj* **(a)** (Sport) (*before n*) ‹*boxer/wrestler*› de la categoría de los pesos pesados; ‹*title*› de los pesos pesados **(b)** (Tex) ‹*cotton/denim*› grueso y resistente

Hebrew¹ /'hi:bru:/ *adj* hebreo

Hebrew² *n* [U] hebreo *m*

Hebrides /'hebrədi:z ‖ 'hebrɪdi:z/ *pl n* **the ~** las (islas) Hébridas

heck /hek/ *n* (colloq & euph): **~!** ¡caray! (fam & euf); **what the ~!** ¡qué diablos! (fam)

heckle /'hekl/ *vt* interrumpir (*con preguntas o comentarios molestos*)

heckler /'heklər ‖ 'heklə(r)/ *n*: *persona que interrumpe a un orador para molestar*

hectare /'hekter ‖ 'hekteə(r)/ *n* hectárea *f*

hectic /'hektɪk/ *adj* ‹*day/week*› ajetreado, agitado; ‹*journey/pace*› agotador; ‹*activity*› frenético, febril

he'd /hi:d/ **(a)** = **he had (b)** = **he would**

hedge¹ /hedʒ/ *n* seto *m* (verde *or* vivo)

hedge² *vt* ‹*field/garden*› cercar* (*con seto*); ■ **~** *vi* (evade the issue) dar* rodeos

hedgehog /'hedʒhɔ:g ‖ 'hedʒhɒg/ *n* erizo *m*

hedgerow /'hedʒrəʊ/ *n* [C U] (*usu pl*) seto *m* (verde *or* vivo)

hedonism /'hi:dnɪzəm ‖ 'hi:dənɪzəm/ *n* [U] hedonismo *m*

hedonist /'hi:dnəst ‖ 'hi:dənɪst/ *n* hedonista *mf*

heed¹ /hi:d/ *n* [U]: **to take ~** tener* cuidado

heed² *vt* prestar atención a, hacer* caso de

heedless /'hi:dləs ‖ 'hi:dlɪs/ *adj* (frml) **~ OF sth**: **~ of the danger** ... haciendo caso omiso del peligro ...

heel¹ /hi:l/ *n* **(a)** (Anat) talón *m* **(b)** (of shoe) tacón *m*, taco *m* (CS)

heel² *vt* ‹*shoes*› ponerles* tacones *or* (CS) tacos nuevos a; ‹*high-heeled shoes*› ponerles* tapas *or* (Chi) tapillas a

hefty /'hefti/ *adj* **-tier, -tiest** (colloq) **(a)** (large and heavy) ‹*person*› robusto, fornido, corpulento; ‹*load/case*› pesado **(b)** (strong) fuerte **(c)** (substantial) ‹*price/salary*› alto; ‹*fine*› considerable

heifer /'hefər ‖ 'hefə(r)/ *n* vaquilla *f*, novilla *f*

height /haɪt/ *n* **1** [U C] **(a)** (tallness — of object) altura *f*; (— of person) estatura *f*, talla *f*; **what ~ are you?** ¿cuánto mides? **(b)** (Aviat) altura *f*; **to gain/lose ~** ganar/perder* altura **2** (peak) (*no pl*): **to be at the ~ of one's power** estar* en la cima *or* en la cumbre *or* en la cúspide de su (*or* mi etc) poder; **at the ~ of the season** en plena temporada; **it's the ~ of stupidity** es el colmo de la estupidez **3 heights** *pl* **(a)** (high ground) cerros *mpl*, cumbres *fpl* **(b) to be afraid of ~s** sufrir de vértigo

heighten /'haɪtn̩/ *vt* ‹*effect/impression*› destacar*, realzar*; ‹*suspense/admiration/respect*› aumentar

heinous /'heɪnəs/ *adj* (frml) atroz, abyecto

heir /er ‖ eə(r)/ *n* heredero, -ra *m,f*; **~ TO sth** (to fortune, title) heredero DE algo; (to throne) heredero A algo

heiress /'erəs ‖ 'eəres/ *n* heredera *f*

heirloom /'erlu:m ‖ 'eəlu:m/ *n* reliquia *f*

heist /haɪst/ *n* (AmE colloq) golpe *m* (fam), atraco *m*

held /held/ *past and past p of* HOLD¹

helicopter /'heləkɑ:ptər ‖ 'helɪkɒptə(r)/ *n* helicóptero *m*

heliport /'heləpɔ:rt ‖ 'helɪpɔ:t/ *n* helipuerto *m*

helium /'hi:liəm/ *n* helio *m*

hell /hel/ *n* **1** (Relig) infierno *m*; **three months of sheer ~** tres meses infernales; ***to make sb's life ~*** (colloq) hacerle* la vida imposible a algn **2** (colloq) (*as intensifier*): **how/why the ~ ...?** ¿cómo/por qué demonios *or* diablos ...? (fam); **he's a** *o* **one ~ of a guy** es un tipo sensacional (fam); **to run like ~** correr como un loco (fam); **oh, well, what the ~!** bueno ¿qué importa? (fam)

he'll /hi:l/ **(a)** = **he will (b)** = **he shall**

hello /hə'ləʊ/ *interj* **(a)** (greeting) ¡hola! **(b)** (answering the telephone) sí, aló (AmS), diga *or* dígame (Esp), bueno (Méx), olá (RPl)

helm /helm/ *n* (Naut) timón *m*

helmet /'helmət ‖ 'helmɪt/ *n* (headgear) casco *m*; (armor) yelmo *m*

help¹ /help/ *vt* **1** (assist) ayudar; **to ~ sb (to) +** INF ayudar a algn A + INF **2** (avoid, prevent) (*usu neg or interrog*): **I can't ~ it** no lo puedo remediar; **they can't ~ being poor** no tienen la culpa de ser pobres ■ **~** *vi* «*person/remark*» ayudar; «*tool*» servir* ■ *v refl* **to ~ oneself 1** (assist) ayudarse (a sí mismo) **2** (resist impulse) (*usu neg*) controlarse; **I can't ~ myself** no me puedo controlar **3** (take) **to ~ oneself (TO sth)** ‹*to food/a drink*› servirse* (algo)

• **help out 1** [*v + o + adv, v + adv + o*] ayudar **2** [*v + adv*] ayudar

help² *n* [U] **(a)** (rescue) ayuda *f*; (*as interj*) **~!** ¡socorro!, ¡auxilio! **(b)** (assistance) ayuda *f*; **can I be of (any) ~ to you?** ¿la/lo puedo ayudar (en algo)?

helper /'helpər ‖ 'helpə(r)/ *n* ayudante, -ta *m,f*

helpful /'helpfəl/ *adj* **(a)** (obliging) ‹*person/attitude*› servicial, amable **(b)** (useful) ‹*advice*› útil

helping /'helpɪŋ/ *n* porción *f* (esp AmL), ración *f* (esp Esp)

helpless /'helpləs ‖ 'helplɪs/ *adj* **(a)** (defenseless) ‹*prey/victim*› indefenso **(b)** (powerless) ‹*look/expression*› de impotencia; **to be ~ to +** INF ser* incapaz DE + INF **(c)** (incapacitated): **to leave sb ~** dejar a algn sin recursos

helplessly /'helpləsli ‖ 'helplɪsli/ *adv* ‹*look on/stand by*› sin poder hacer nada; ‹*struggle/try*› en vano, inútilmente

helter-skelter /'heltər'skeltər ‖ ˌheltə'skeltə(r)/ *adv* atropelladamente, a la desbanda

hem /hem/ *n* dobladillo *m*, basta *f* (Chi)
• **hem in**: **-mm-** [*v* + *o* + *adv*, *v* + *adv* + *o*] encerrar*

hemisphere /'heməsfɪr ‖ 'hemɪsfiə(r)/ *n* (Geog) hemisferio *m*

hemline /'hemlaɪn/ *n* bajo *m*, ruedo *m*

hemoglobin, (BrE) **haemoglobin** /'hi:mə,gləʊbən ‖ ,hi:mə'gləʊbɪn/ *n* [U] hemoglobina *f*

hemophilia, (BrE) **haemophilia** /'hi:mə'fɪliə/ *n* [U] hemofilia *f*

hemorrhage[1], (BrE) **haemorrhage** /'hemərɪdʒ/ *n* (Med) hemorragia *f*

hemorrhage[2], (BrE) **haemorrhage** *vi* «*patient*» tener* *or* (frml) sufrir una hemorragia; «*wound/blood vessel*» sangrar mucho

hemorrhoids, (BrE) **haemorrhoids** /'hemərɔɪdz/ *pl n* hemorroides *fpl*, almorranas *fpl*

hemp /hemp/ *n* [U] (fiber) cáñamo *m*; (drug) marihuana *f*, cannabis *m*; (plant) cannabis *m*, cáñamo *m* índico *or* de la India

hen /hen/ *n* (chicken) gallina *f*; (female bird) hembra *f*

hence /hens/ *adv* **1 (a)** (that is the reason for) de ahí **(b)** (therefore) por lo tanto, por consiguiente **2** (from now) (frml): **a few years ~** dentro de algunos años

henceforth /'hens'fɔːrθ ‖ ,hens'fɔːθ/ *adv* (liter) a partir de ahora, de ahora en adelante

henchman /'hentʃmən/ *n* (*pl* **-men** /-mən/) secuaz *m*

henna /'henə/ *n* henna *f*

hen: **~ night**, **hen party** *n* **(a)** (all-female celebration) fiesta *f* de mujeres **(b)** (before wedding) despedida *f* de soltera; **~pecked** /'henpekt/ *adj* (colloq): **a ~pecked husband** un marido dominado por su mujer, un mandilón (Méx fam), un calzonazos (Esp fam)

hepatitis /'hepə'taɪtəs ‖ ,hepə'taɪtɪs/ *n* [U] hepatitis *f*

her[1] /hɜːr ‖ hɜː(r), *weak form* ər ‖ ə(r)/ ▶ 638 *pron* **1 (a)** (as direct object) la; **I can't stand ~** no la soporto; **call ~** llámala **(b)** (as indirect object) le; (with direct object pronoun present) se; **I wrote ~ a letter** le escribí una carta **(c)** (after preposition) ella **2** (emphatic use) ella; **it's ~** es ella

her[2] ▶ 638 *adj* (*sing*) su; (*pl*) sus; **she took ~ hat off** se quitó el sombrero

herald[1] /'herəld/ *n* (Hist) heraldo *m*

herald[2] *vt* anunciar

heraldry /'herəldri/ *n* [U] heráldica *f*

herb /ɜːrb, hɜːrb ‖ hɜːb/ *n* hierba *f*, yuyo *m* (Per, RPl)

herbal /'ɜːrbəl, 'hɜːrbəl‖'hɜːbəl/ *adj* ‹*shampoo*› de hierbas; **~ tea** (esp BrE) ⇒ HERB TEA

herb tea *n* infusión *f*, agua *f*‡ (AmC, Andes), té *m* de yuyos (Per, RPl)

herd[1] /hɜːrd ‖ hɜːd/ *n* **(a)** (of cattle) manada *f*, vacada *f*; (of goats) rebaño *m*; (of pigs) piara *f*, manada *f*; (of wild animals) manada *f* **(b)** (of people) (pej) tropel *m*

herd[2] *vt* ‹*animals*› arrear, arriar (RPl); **the refugees were ~ed into trucks** metieron a los refugiados en camiones como si fueran ganado

here /hɪr ‖ hɪə(r)/ *adv* **1 (a)** (at, to this place) aquí, acá (esp AmL); (less precise) acá **(b)** (*in phrases*) **here and there** aquí y allá; **here, there and everywhere** por todas partes **2** (calling attention to sth, sb): **~'s £20** toma 20 libras; **~ he is** aquí está **3 (a)** (present): **he isn't ~ today** hoy no está **(b)** (arrived): **they're ~!** ¡ya llegaron!, ¡ya están aquí! **4** (*as interj*): **~, let me do it** trae, deja que lo haga yo

hereabouts /'hɪrə'baʊts ‖ ,hɪərə'baʊts/ *adv* por aquí, por acá

hereafter /,hɪr'æftər ‖ ,hɪər'ɑːftə(r)/ *adv* (frml: used esp in legal texts) (from now on) de aquí en adelante; (in the future) en el futuro, en lo sucesivo

hereditary /hə'redəteri ‖ hɪ'redɪtri/ *adj* hereditario

heredity /hə'redəti ‖ hɪ'redəti/ *n* [U] herencia *f*

heresy /'herəsi/ *n* [U C] (*pl* **-sies**) herejía *f*

heretic /'herətɪk/ *n* hereje *mf*

heritage /'herətɪdʒ ‖ 'herɪtɪdʒ/ *n* (*no pl*) patrimonio *m*

hermetically /hɜːr'metɪkli ‖ hɜː'metɪkli/ *adv*: **~ sealed** herméticamente cerrado

hermit /'hɜːrmət ‖ 'hɜːmɪt/ *n* ermitaño, -ña *m, f*, eremita *mf*

hernia /'hɜːrniə ‖ 'hɜːniə/ *n* hernia *f*

hero /'hiːrəʊ ‖ 'hɪərəʊ/ *n* (*pl* **heroes**) héroe *m*; (of novel, film) protagonista *mf*

heroic /hɪ'rəʊɪk/ *adj* heroico

heroin /'herəʊɪn/ *n* [U] heroína *f*

heroine /'herəʊɪn/ *n* (brave, admirable woman) heroína *f*; (of novel, film) protagonista *f*

heroism /'herəʊɪzəm/ *n* [U] heroísmo *m*

heron /'herən/ *n* garza *f* (real)

hero worship *n* [U] adoración *f* (*de alguien a quien se tiene como ídolo*)

herpes /'hɜːrpiːz ‖ 'hɜːpiːz/ *n* [U] herpes *m*, herpe *f*

herring /'herɪŋ/ *n* [C U] (*pl* **herrings** *or* **herring**) arenque *m*

hers /hɜːrz ‖ hɜːz/ *pron*

■ **Note** The translation *suyo* reflects the gender and number of the noun it is standing for; *her* is translated by *el suyo*, *la suya*, *los suyos*, *las suyas*, depending on what is being referred to.

(*sing*) suyo, -ya; (*pl*) suyos, -yas, de ella; **they're ~** son suyos/suyas, son de ella; **~ is blue** el suyo/la suya es azul, el/la de ella es azul; **a friend of ~** un amigo suyo *or* de ella

herself /hər'self ‖ hə'self/ *pron* **(a)** (reflexive): **she cut ~** se cortó; **she bought ~ a hat** se compró un sombrero; **she only thinks of ~** sólo piensa en sí misma; **by ~** sola; **she was talking to ~** estaba hablando sola **(b)** (emphatic use) ella misma; **she told me so ~** me lo dijo ella misma **(c)** (normal self): **she's not ~** no es la de siempre

he's /hiːz/ **(a)** = **he is (b)** = **he has**

hesitant /'hezətənt ‖ 'hezɪtənt/ *adj* ‹*voice*› vacilante; ‹*manner*› inseguro; ‹*steps*› vacilante; **he seemed a little ~** parecía un poco indeciso

hesitate /'hezəteɪt ‖ 'hezɪteɪt/ *vi* vacilar, titubear

hesitation /'hezə'teɪʃən ‖ ,hezɪ'teɪʃən/ *n* [U C] vacilación *f*

Her

Note that the points given below on the position of her *as a direct and indirect object pronoun also apply to the other object pronouns* me, you, him, it, us, them

As a pronoun

◆ *When used as a direct object pronoun,* her *is translated by* la, *and usually precedes the verb*:

I know/don't know her = la conozco/no la conozco
I've already seen her = ya la he visto

In imperatives, her *is translated by* la, *and is attached to the end of the verb*:

look at her! = ¡mírala! (*with tú*)
kill her! = ¡mátela! (*with usted*)

In negative commands, however, la *comes before the verb*:

don't touch her! = ¡no la toques!

◆ *When used as an indirect object pronoun,* her *is translated by* le, *and usually precedes the verb; a* ella *may be added to avoid ambiguity*:

I gave her the book *o* I gave the book to her = le di el libro (a ella)

Where a direct object pronoun is also used, her *is translated by* se *to avoid two pronouns beginning with* l *appearing together. The order is* se + direct object pronoun + verb:

I said it to her = se lo dije (a ella) (*and not* le lo dije)

In imperatives, her *as indirect object is translated by* le, *and is attached to the end of the verb*:

buy her the book! = ¡cómprale el libro!

Where a direct object pronoun is also used, her *is translated by* se. *It is attached to the end of the verb, followed by the direct object pronoun*:

give it to her! = ¡dáselo (a ella)!

In negative imperatives, the order is se + direct object pronoun + verb:

don't give it to her! = ¡no se lo des!

With the infinitive

When her *as direct or indirect object follows an infinitive, the translation can always be attached to the infinitive. Note that, in some of the examples below,* her *can also be placed before the finite verb preceding the infinitive*:

I want to see her = quiero verla *or* la quiero ver
he wants to give her a book = quiere darle un libro *or* le quiero dar un libro
we ought to explain it to her = deberíamos explicárselo *or* se lo deberíamos explicar

With the gerund

When her *as direct or indirect object follows a gerund, the translation is attached to the gerund*:

he stood there staring at her = se quedó allí mirándola fijamente

When used with continuous tenses, however, it may precede the auxiliary verb:

why are you looking at her = ¿por qué estás mirándola *or* la estás mirando?
I've been talking with her about it for two hours = llevo dos horas hablándole del asunto

Accentuation

Note that the addition of a pronoun or pronouns to the end of an imperative, infinitive, or gerund does not alter the stress on the word to which it is added. An accent is therefore required if the stressed syllable is no longer in the penultimate position:

search for her! = ¡búsquela!
looking at = mirando
looking at her = mirándola
to communicate = comunicar
to communicate it to her = comunicárselo

This applies to imperatives with vos *with reverse effect; in the example below, the addition of the pronoun means that the stress now follows the usual pattern by falling on the penultimate syllable*:

look! = ¡mirá!
look at her! = ¡mirala!

The different forms of the imperative with pronoun are:

look at her! = ¡mírala! (*with* tú — *basic form* mira)
= ¡mirala! (*with* vos — *basic form* mirá)
= ¡miradla! (*with* vosotros/vosotras — *basic form* mirad)
= ¡mírela! (*with* usted — *basic form* mire)
= ¡mírenla! (*with* ustedes — *basic form* miren)

In the case of a single-syllable 'root' word, stress still falls on that word:

to give = dar
to give it to her = dárselo

After prepositions and the verb **to be**

The translation of her *after prepositions and* to be *is* ella:

he did it for her = lo hizo por ella
it's her = es ella

As an adjective

When translating her *as an adjective, the translation* su *agrees in number with the noun which it modifies*:

her father/mother = su padre/madre
her books/magazines = sus libros/revistas

For her *used with parts of the body, see* **▶ 484**

heterosexual[1] /'hetərəʊ'sekʃuəl/ *adj* heterosexual

heterosexual[2] *n* heterosexual *mf*

heterosexuality /'hetərəʊ'sekʃu'æləti/ *n* [U] heterosexualidad *f*

hew /hju:/ *vt* (*past* **hewed**; *past p* **hewed** *or* **hewn** /hju:n/) (extract) extraer*; (fashion) ‹*stone*› labrar

hexagon /'heksəgɑ:n ‖ 'heksəgən/ *n* hexágono *m*

hey /heɪ/ *interj* **(a)** (calling attention) ¡eh! **(b)** (expressing dismay, protest, indignation) ¡oye!, ¡oiga(n)!

heyday /'heɪdeɪ/ *n* apogeo *m*, auge *m*; **in his ~** en sus buenos tiempos

HGV *n* (BrE) (= **heavy goods vehicle**) vehículo *m* pesado

hi /haɪ/ *interj* (colloq) hola (fam)

HI = **Hawaii**

hiatus /haɪ'eɪtəs/ *n* (*pl* **-tuses**) (frml) paréntesis *m* (frml)

hibernate /'haɪbərneɪt ‖ 'haɪbəneɪt/ *vi* hibernar

hibernation /'haɪbər'neɪʃən ‖ ˌhaɪbə'neɪʃən/ *n* [U] hibernación *f*; **to go into ~** entrar en estado de hibernación

hiccough /'hɪkʌp/ *n*/*vi* ⇒ HICCUP[1,2]

hiccup[1] /'hɪkʌp/ *n* **(a)** hipo *m*; **to have (the) ~s** tener* hipo **(b)** (brief interruption) dificultad *f*

hiccup[2] *vi*, (BrE also) **-pp-** hipar

hick /hɪk/ *n* (AmE colloq & pej) pueblerino, -na *m,f*, paleto, -ta *m,f* (Esp fam & pey), pajuerano, -na *m,f* (RPl fam & pey)

hid /hɪd/ **(a)** *past of* HIDE[1] **(b)** (arch) *past p of* HIDE[1]

hidden[1] /'hɪdn/ *adj* ‹*entrance/camera/reserves*› oculto; ‹*cost*› no aparente

hidden[2] *past p of* HIDE[1]

hide[1] /haɪd/ (*past* **hid** /hɪd/; *past p* **hidden**) *or* (arch) **hid**) *vt* **(a)** (conceal) esconder; **she hid the money from the police** escondió el dinero para que no lo encontrara la policía; **to ~ oneself** esconderse **(b)** (keep secret) ‹*feelings/thoughts*› ocultar; **to ~ sth** FROM **sb** ocultarle algo A algn **(c)** (mask, screen) tapar ■ **~** *vi* esconderse

• **hide away 1** [*v* + *adv*] esconderse **2** [*v* + *o* + *adv, v* + *adv* + *o*] esconder

hide[2] *n* [C U] (raw) piel *f*; (tanned) cuero *m*

hide: **~-and-seek** /'haɪdn'si:k/, (AmE & Scot also) **~-and-go-seek** /'haɪdngəʊ'si:k/ *n* [U]: **to play ~-and-seek** jugar* al escondite, jugar* a las escondidas (AmL); **~away** *n* **(a)** (hiding place) (AmE) escondite *m* **(b)** (secluded spot) rincón *m*

hideous /'hɪdiəs/ *adj* ‹*monster/sight*› horroroso, horrible; ‹*crime/fate*› espantoso; ‹*color/furniture*› (colloq) horrendo, espantoso

hideout /'haɪdaʊt/ *n* guarida *f*

hiding /'haɪdɪŋ/ *n* **1** [U] (concealment): **to be in ~/go into ~** estar* escondido/esconderse; (*before n*) **~ place** escondite *m*, escondrijo *m* **2** [C] (beating) (colloq) paliza *f*, tunda *f*

hierarchy /'haɪərɑ:rki ‖ 'haɪərɑ:ki/ *n* (*pl* **-chies**) jerarquía *f*

hieroglyphics /'haɪərə'glɪfɪks/ *pl n* jeroglíficos *mpl*

hi-fi /'haɪfaɪ/ *n* **(a)** [U] (equipment) alta fidelidad *f* **(b)** [C] (set) equipo *m* de alta fidelidad, hi-fi *m*

higgledy-piggledy /'hɪgəldi'pɪgəldi/ *adv* (colloq) sin orden ni concierto, de cualquier manera

high[1] /haɪ/ *adj* **-er, -est 1 (a)** (tall) ‹*wall/mountain*› alto; **how ~ is it?** ¿qué altura tiene?; **the tower is 40 m ~** la torre tiene 40 m de alto *or* de altura **(b)** (high up) ‹*window/balcony*› alto; ‹*plateau*› elevado; **at a ~ altitude** a gran altitud; **~ cheekbones** pómulos *mpl* salientes **(c)** (in status) ‹*office/rank*› alto; **he has friends in ~ places** tiene amigos muy bien situados; **~ society** la alta sociedad **(d)** (morally, ethically) ‹*ideals/principles*› elevado **(e)** (in pitch) ‹*voice*› agudo; ‹*note*› alto **2** (greater than usual) ‹*temperature/speed/pressure*› alto; ‹*wind*› fuerte; **unemployment is very ~** hay mucho desempleo; **to be ~ in vitamins** ser* rico en vitaminas **3** (climactic) culminante; **the ~ point** el punto culminante **4 (a)** (happy, excited): **she was in ~ spirits** estaba muy animada **(b)** (intoxicated) (colloq) drogado, colocado (Esp fam) **5** (of time): **~ noon** mediodía *m*; **in ~ summer** en pleno verano **6** ‹*meat*› pasado; ‹*game*› que tiene un olor fuerte

high[2] *adv* **-er, -est 1** ‹*fly*› alto; **~ up** arriba, en lo alto; ***to search ~ and low (for sth)*** remover* cielo y tierra (para encontrar algo) **2** (in pitch) ‹*sing*› alto

high[3] *n* **1** [C] (level) récord *m* **2** [C] (Meteo) (anticyclone) zona *f* de altas presiones; (high temperature) máxima *f* **3** [U] (top gear) (AmE Auto) (*no art*) directa *f*

high- /'haɪ/ *pref*: **~quality** de alta calidad, de gran calidad; **~speed** ‹*train*› de alta velocidad

high: **~brow** *adj* (colloq) ‹*tastes*› de intelectual; ‹*art/music*› para intelectuales; **~chair** *n* silla *f* alta (*para niño*); **~-class** /'haɪ'klæs ‖ ˌhaɪ'klɑ:s/ *adj* ‹*restaurant/hotel*› de lujo; ‹*merchandise*› de primera calidad; **H~ Court** *n* (in England and Wales) *una de las dos ramas del Tribunal Supremo, con competencia para conocer de causas civiles cuyo coste excede cierta cuantía*

higher /'haɪər ‖ 'haɪə(r)/ *adj* **(a)** *comp of* HIGH[1] **(b)** (*before n*) ‹*mammals/organs*› superior

higher education *n* [U] enseñanza *f* superior

high: **~ finance** *n* [U] altas finanzas *fpl*; **~flier**, **~flyer** /'haɪ'flaɪər ‖ ˌhaɪ'flaɪə(r)/ *n* persona *f* muy prometedora; **~flown** *adj* altisonante; **~-frequency** /'haɪ'fri:kwənsi/ *adj* de alta frecuencia; **~-grade** *adj* de calidad superior; **~-handed** /'haɪ'hændəd ‖ ˌhaɪ'hændɪd/ *adj* arbitrario; **~-heeled** /'haɪ'hi:ld/ *adj* de tacón *or* (CS) de taco alto; **~ jump** *n* salto *m* de altura, salto *m* alto (AmL); **~lands** /'haɪləndz/ *pl n* **(a)** (uplands) tierras *fpl* altas, altiplanicie *f* **(b)** (in Scotland) **the H~lands** las *or* los Highlands, las tierras altas; **~-level** /'haɪ'levəl/ *adj* **(a)** ‹*talks/delegation*› de alto nivel **(b)** ‹*bridge/road*› elevado **(c)** (Comput) de alto nivel

highlight[1] /'haɪlaɪt/ *vt* (*past & past p* **-lighted**) **1** (call attention to) ‹*problem/question*› destacar*, poner* de relieve **2** (Art, Phot) realzar*, dar* realce a

highlight[2] *n* **1** (most memorable part) lo más destacado; **her performance was the ~ of the evening** su actuación fue el plato fuerte de la velada

2 (a) (Art, Phot) toque *m* de luz **(b) highlights** *pl* (in hair) reflejos *mpl*, claritos *mpl* (RPl), visos *mpl* (Chi), luces *fpl* (Méx), mechones *mpl* (Col)

highlighter /'haɪlaɪtər ‖ 'haɪlaɪtə(r)/ *n* [U C] **(a)** (makeup) sombra *f* clara de ojos **(b)** (pen) rotulador *m*, marcador *m* (AmL)

highly /'haɪli/ *adv* **(a)** (to a high degree): **~ unlikely** muy poco probable; **~ intelligent** inteligentísimo; **~ trained** altamente capacitado **(b)** (favorably): **his boss speaks/thinks very ~ of him** su jefe habla muy bien/tiene muy buena opinión de él **(c)** (at a high rate): **a ~ paid job** un trabajo muy bien pagado

highly-strung /'haɪli'strʌŋ/ *adj* (BrE) ⇒ HIGH-STRUNG

Highness /'haməs ‖ 'haɪnɪs/ ▶603 *n*: **Her/His/Your (Royal) ~** Su Alteza (Real)

high: **~-pitched** /'haɪ'pɪtʃt/ *adj* ‹*voice/sound*› agudo; ‹*instrument*› de tono agudo *or* alto; **~-powered** /'haɪ'paʊərd ‖ ˌhaɪ'paʊəd/ *adj* ‹*car/machine*› muy potente, de gran potencia; ‹*executive/campaign*› dinámico, enérgico; ‹*job*› de alto(s) vuelo(s); **~-profile** /'haɪ'prəʊfaɪl/ *adj* prominente; **~-ranking** /'haɪ'ræŋkɪŋ/ *adj* ‹*officer*› de alto rango; ‹*official*› alto, de alta jerarquía; **~ rise** *n* (esp AmE) torre *f* (de apartamentos *or* (Esp) pisos); **~-rise** /'haɪ'raɪz/ *adj* (*before n*) ‹*building/block*› alto, de muchas plantas; ‹*apartment*› de una torre, de un edificio alto; **~-risk** /'haɪ'rɪsk/ *adj* de alto riesgo; **~road** *n* carretera *f*; **~ school** *n* colegio *m* secundario, ≈ instituto *m* (*en Esp*), ≈ liceo *m* (*en CS, Ven*); **~ season** *n* [U] temporada *f* alta; **~-spirited** /'haɪ'spɪrətəd ‖ ˌhaɪ'spɪrɪtɪd/ *adj* lleno de vida, brioso; **~ street** *n* (BrE) calle *f* principal, calle *f* mayor (Esp); **~-strung** /'haɪ'strʌŋ/, (BrE) **highly-strung** *adj* ‹*person*› nervioso; ‹*dog/horse*› muy excitable; **~-tech** /'haɪ'tek/ *adj* de alta tecnología; ‹*era*› high tech *adj inv*; **~-up** *n* (esp AmE colloq) gerifalte *mf*, capo, -pa *m,f* (fam); **~way** *n* (main road) carretera *f*; (public way) vía *f* pública; (*before n*) ‹*patrol/patrolman*› (AmE) de carretera; **H~way Code** *n* (in UK) Código *m* de la Circulación; **~wayman** /'haɪweɪmən/ *n* (*pl* **-men** /-mən/) salteador *m* de caminos, bandolero *m*; **~ wire** *n* cuerda *f* floja

hijack¹ *vt* /'haɪdʒæk/ secuestrar

hijack² *n* secuestro *m*

hijacker /'haɪdʒækər ‖ 'haɪdʒækə(r)/ *n* secuestrador, -dora *m,f*; (of planes) pirata aéreo, -rea *m,f*

hike¹ /haɪk/ *n* **1** (long walk) caminata *f*, excursión *f* **2** (increase) subida *f*

hike² *vi* (walk) ir* de caminata *or* de excursión; **to go hiking** hacer* excursionismo

hiker /'haɪkər ‖ 'haɪkə(r)/ *n* excursionista *mf*

hilarious /hɪ'leriəs ‖ hɪ'leəriəs/ *adj* divertidísimo, comiquísimo

hill /hɪl/ *n* (low) colina *f*, cerro *m*, collado *m*; (higher) montaña *f*; (slope, incline) cuesta *f*

hill: **~billy** *n* (AmE colloq) rústico, -ca *m,f*, paleto, -ta *m,f* (Esp fam & pey), pajuerano, -na *m,f* (RPl fam & pey); **~side** *n* ladera *f*; **~top** *n* cima *f*, cumbre *f*

hilly /'hɪli/ *adj* **-lier, -liest** accidentado

hilt /hɪlt/ *n* empuñadura *f*, puño *m*

him /hɪm, *weak form* ɪm/ ▶638 *pron* **1 (a)** (as direct object) lo, le (Esp); **I saw ~** lo *or* (Esp tb) le vi; **call ~** llámalo, llámale (Esp) **(b)** (as indirect object) le; (with direct object pronoun present) se; **I sent ~ a card** le mandé una tarjeta **(c)** (after preposition) él **2** (emphatic use) él; **it's ~** es él

Himalayas /'hɪmə'leɪəz/ *pl n* **the ~** el Himalaya

himself /hɪm'self/ *pron* **(a)** (reflexive): **he cut/hurt ~** se cortó/lastimó; **he bought ~ a hat** se compró un sombrero; **he only thinks of ~** sólo piensa en sí mismo; **by ~** solo; **he was talking to ~** estaba hablando solo **(b)** (emphatic use) él mismo; **he told me so ~** me lo dijo él mismo **(c)** (normal self): **he's not ~** no es el de siempre

hind /haɪnd/ *adj* (*before n, no comp*) ‹*legs*› trasero

hinder /'hɪndər ‖ 'hɪndə(r)/ *vt* dificultar

Hindi /'hɪndi/ *n* [U] indi *m*, hindi *m*

hindrance /'hɪndrəns/ *n* estorbo *m*

hindsight /'haɪndsaɪt/ *n* [U]: **with (the benefit of) ~** a posteriori, en retrospectiva

Hindu¹ /'hɪndu:/ *n* hindú *mf*

Hindu² *adj* hindú

Hinduism /'hɪndu:ɪzəm/ *n* [U] hinduismo *m*

hinge¹ /hɪndʒ/ *n* (of door, window, gate) bisagra *f*, gozne *m*; (of box, lid) bisagra *f*

hinge² hinges, hinging, hinged *vi* **to ~ ON sth** (turn) girar SOBRE algo; (be fixed) ir* asegurado con bisagras A algo; (depend) depender DE algo

hint¹ /hɪnt/ *n* **1 (a)** (oblique reference) insinuación *f*, indirecta *f*; (clue) pista *f*; **to drop a ~ to sb** lanzarle* una indirecta a algn; **to take the ~** captar *or* (Esp tb) coger* la indirecta **(b)** (trace – of bitterness, sadness) dejo *m*; (– of color) toque *m*, matiz *m*; (– of garlic, lemon) dejo *m*, gusto *m* **2** (tip) consejo *m*

hint² *vt* insinuar*, dar* a entender ■ **~** *vi* lanzar* indirectas; **to ~ AT sth** insinuar* *or* dar* a entender algo

hip¹ /hɪp/ ▶484 *n* cadera *f*

hip² *interj*: **~, ~, hooray** *o* **hurrah!** ¡hurra!, ¡viva!

hippie /'hɪpi/ *n* ⇒ HIPPY

hippo /'hɪpəʊ/ *n* (*pl* **-pos**) (colloq) hipopótamo *m*

hippopotamus /'hɪpə'pɑ:təməs ‖ ˌhɪpə'pɒtəməs/ *n* (*pl* **-muses** *or* **-mi** /-maɪ/) hipopótamo *m*

hippy, hippie /'hɪpi/ *n* (*pl* **-pies**) hippy *mf*

hire¹ /haɪr ‖ 'haɪə(r)/ *vt* **1 (a)** ‹*hall/boat/suit*› alquilar, arrendar* **(b)** (Busn, Lab Rel) ‹*staff/person*› contratar **(c) hired** *past p* ‹*car*› alquilado **2** ⇒ HIRE OUT

• **hire out** [*v* + *o* + *adv*, *v* + *adv* + *o*] (BrE) alquilar, arrendar*

hire² *n* [U] **1** (of hall/car/suit) alquiler *m*, arriendo *m*; Ⓢ **for hire** se alquila *or* se arrienda; (on taxis) libre **2** (payment) alquiler *m*, arriendo *m*

hire purchase *n* [U] (BrE) compra *f* a plazos; **to buy sth on ~ ~** comprar algo a plazos, comprar algo en cuotas (esp AmL)

his¹ /hɪz, *weak form* ɪz/ *adj* (*sing*) su; (*pl*) sus

■ **Note** The translation *su* agrees in number with the noun which it modifies; *his* is translated by *su, sus*, depending on what follows: *his father/mother* su padre/madre; *his books/magazines* sus libros/revistas. For *his* used with parts of the body, *see* ▶ **484**

his² *pron*

■ **Note** The translation *suyo* reflects the gender and number of the noun it is standing for; *his* is translated by *el suyo, la suya, los suyos, las suyas*, depending on what is being referred to.

(*sing*) suyo, -ya; (*pl*) suyos, -yas, de él; **they're ~** son suyos/suyas, son de él; **~ is blue** el suyo/la suya es azul, el/la de él es azul; **a friend of ~** un amigo suyo *or* de él

Hispanic¹ /hɪ'spænɪk/ *adj* hispánico, hispano; ‹*community/voter*› (in US) hispano

Hispanic² *n* (esp AmE) hispano, -na *m,f*

hiss¹ /hɪs/ *vi* silbar; «*cat*» bufar ■ **~** *vt* decir* entre dientes

hiss² *n* (of snake, audience) silbido *m*; (of cat) bufido *m*

historian /hɪ'stɔːriən/ *n* historiador, -dora *m,f*

historic /hɪ'stɔːrɪk ‖ hɪ'stɒrɪk/ *adj* **(a)** (momentous) ‹*event/moment*› memorable **(b)** (old) ‹*house/building*› histórico

historical /hɪ'stɔːrɪkəl ‖ hɪ'stɒrɪkəl/ *adj* **(a)** (relating to history) histórico **(b)** (crit) ⇒ HISTORIC

history /'hɪstəri/ *n* (*pl* **-ries**) **1** [U C] historia *f*; **the worst earthquake in ~** el peor terremoto de la historia **2** [C] (record, background) historial *m*

hit¹ /hɪt/ (*pres p* **hitting**; *past & past p* **hit**) *vt* **1 (a)** (deal blow to) ‹*door/table*› dar* un golpe en, golpear; ‹*person*› pegarle* a **(b)** (strike) golpear; **the truck ~ a tree** el camión chocó con *or* contra un árbol; **the house was ~ by a bomb** una bomba cayó sobre la casa; **the bullet ~ him in the leg** la bala le dio *or* lo alcanzó en la pierna; **to ~ one's head on sth** darse* un golpe en la cabeza contra algo; ***to ~ it off with sb*** congeniar con algn **2 (a)** (strike accurately) ‹*target*› dar* en **(b)** (attack) ‹*opponent/enemy*› atacar* **(c)** (score) (Sport) anotarse, marcar* **3** (affect adversely) afectar (a) **4 (a)** (meet with, run into) ‹*difficulty/problem*› toparse con **(b)** (reach) llegar* a, alcanzar* **5** (occur to): **suddenly it ~ me: why had he ... ?** de repente se me ocurrió: ¿por qué había ... ?

● **hit back (a)** [*v* + *adv*] (strike in return) devolver* el golpe; **she ~ back at her critics** arremetió contra sus detractores **(b)** [*v* + *o* + *adv*] devolverle* el golpe a

● **hit on** [*v* + *prep* + *o*] ‹*solution*› dar* con

● **hit out** [*v* + *adv*] **(a)** (strike) **to ~ out** (AT **sb**) (once) lanzar*(le) un golpe (A algn); (repeatedly) tirar(le) golpes (A algn) **(b)** (attack verbally) **to ~ out** AT *o* AGAINST **sth/sb** atacar* algo/a algn

● **hit upon** ⇒ HIT ON

hit² *n* **1 (a)** (blow, stroke) (Sport) golpe *m* **(b)** (in shooting) blanco *m* **2** (success) (colloq) éxito *m*

hit: **~-and-miss** /'hɪtən'mɪs/ *adj* (*pred* **~ and miss**) ⇒ HIT-OR-MISS; **~-and-run** /'hɪtən'rʌn/ *adj* (*before n*) ‹*driver*› *que se da a la fuga tras atropellar a algn*

hitch¹ /hɪtʃ/ *n* **1** (difficulty) complicación *f*, problema *m*, pega *f* (Esp fam); **a technical ~** un problema técnico **2** (limp) (AmE) cojera *f*, renguera *f* (AmL)

hitch² *vt* **1** (attach) **to ~ sth** TO **sth** enganchar algo A algo **2** (thumb) (colloq): **to ~ a ride** *o* (BrE also) **a lift** hacer* dedo (fam), hacer* autostop, ir* de aventón (Col, Méx fam), pedir* cola (Ven fam) ■ **~** *vi* ⇒ HITCHHIKE

hitch: **~hike** *vi* hacer* autostop, hacer* dedo (fam), ir* de aventón (Col, Méx fam), pedir* cola (Ven fam); **~hiker** *n* autoestopista *mf*

hi-tech /'haɪ'tek/ *adj* ⇒ HIGH-TECH

hitherto /'hɪðər'tuː ‖ ˌhɪðə'tuː/ *adv* (frml) hasta ahora, hasta la fecha

hit: **~ list** *n* (colloq) (murder list) lista *f* de sentenciados; (blacklist) lista *f* negra; **~ man** *n* (colloq) (assassin) asesino *m* a sueldo, sicario *m*; **~-or-miss** /'hɪtər'mɪs ‖ ˌhɪtɔː'mɪs/ *adj* (*pred* **~ or miss**) ‹*method/approach*› poco científico

hitter /'hɪtər ‖ 'hɪtə(r)/ *n* (in baseball) bateador, -dora *m,f*; (in US football) liniero, -ra *m,f*

HIV *n* (= **Human Immunodeficiency Virus**) VIH *m*, virus *m* del sida; **he's ~ positive** es seropositivo

hive /haɪv/ *n* (home of bees) colmena *f*; (bee colony) enjambre *m*

hives /haɪvz/ *n* (Med) urticaria *f*

HM (= **Her/His Majesty**) S.M.

HMS (in UK) = **Her/His Majesty's Ship**

hoard¹ /hɔːrd ‖ hɔːd/ *n* (of food) reserva *f*; **a ~ of treasure** un tesoro escondido

hoard² *vt* acumular, juntar; (anticipating a shortage) acaparar

hoarding /'hɔːrdɪŋ ‖ 'hɔːdɪŋ/ *n* **1** [U] (anticipating a shortage) acaparamiento *m* **2** [C] (billboard) (BrE) valla *f* publicitaria, barda *f* de anuncios (Méx)

hoarse /hɔːrs ‖ hɔːs/ *adj* **hoarser, hoarsest** ronco

hoax /həʊks/ *n* (deception) engaño *m*; (joke) broma *f*; (tall story) patraña *f*

hob /hɑːb ‖ hɒb/ *n* **(a)** (beside open fire) placa *f* **(b)** (of cooker) (BrE) hornillas *fpl* (AmL exc CS), hornillos *mpl* (Esp), hornallas *fpl* (RPl), platos *mpl* (Chi)

hobble /'hɑːbəl ‖ 'hɒbəl/ *vi* cojear, renguear (AmL)

hobby /'hɑːbi ‖ 'hɒbi/ *n* (*pl* **-bies**) hobby *m*, pasatiempo *m*, afición *f*

hobnailed /'hɑːbneɪld ‖ 'hɒbneɪld/ *adj* con tachuelas

hobo /'həʊbəʊ/ *n* (*pl* **-boes** *or* **-bos**) (AmE colloq) vagabundo, -da *m,f*, linyera *mf* (CS fam)

hockey /'hɑːki ‖ 'hɒki/ *n* **(a)** (*ice* **~**) (AmE) hockey *m* sobre hielo **(b)** (played on grass) (BrE) hockey *m* (sobre hierba)

hod /hɑːd ‖ hɒd/ *n* (for bricks) capacho *m* (*para acarrear ladrillos*)

hoe¹ /həʊ/ *n* azada *f*, azadón *m*

hoe² *vt* azadonar, pasar la azada por

hog¹ /hɔːg ‖ hɒg/ *n* **1** (AmE Agr, Zool) cerdo, -da *m,f*, puerco, -ca *m,f*, chancho, -cha *m,f* (AmL) **2** (person) (colloq) tragón, -gona *m,f* (fam), angurriento, -ta *m,f* (CS fam)

hog² *vt* **-gg-** (colloq) ‹*food/bathroom/limelight*› acaparar; ‹*discussion*› monopolizar*

Hogmanay /ˈhɑːgməneɪ ‖ ˈhɒgməneɪ/ *n* (Scot) Nochevieja *f*, noche *f* de fin de año

hoist¹ /hɔɪst/ *vt* (lift) levantar, alzar*; ‹*sail/flag*› izar*

hoist² *n* (elevator) montacargas *m*; (crane, derrick) grúa *f*

hokum /ˈhəʊkəm/ *n* (colloq) **(a)** (nonsense) paparruchas *fpl* (fam) **(b)** (corny material) (AmE) *recursos efectistas de tipo melodramático o cómico*

hold¹ /həʊld/ (*past & past p* **held**) *vt* **1 (a)** (have in one's hand(s)) tener* (en la mano); **will you ~ this for me?** ¿me puedes tener *or* (esp AmL) agarrar esto por favor? **(b)** (clasp): **~ it with both hands** sujétalo *or* (esp AmL) agárralo con las dos manos; **he was ~ing her hand** la tenía agarrada *or* (esp Esp) cogida de la mano **(c)** (grip) (Auto) agarrar, adherirse* **2** (have room for) «*cup/jug*» tener* una capacidad de; «*stadium*» tener* capacidad *or* cabida para; **this report ~s all the answers to** ... este informe contiene todas las respuestas a ...; **who knows what the future ~s** quién sabe qué nos deparará el futuro **3 (a)** (keep in position) ‹*ladder*› sujetar, sostener* **(b)** (maintain) ‹*attention/interest*› mantener*; **she held the lead throughout the race** se mantuvo a la cabeza durante toda la carrera **4 (a)** (keep) ‹*tickets/room*› reservar, guardar **(b)** (detain, imprison): **she is being held at the police station for questioning** está detenida en la comisaría para ser interrogada **(c)** (restrain) detener* **(d)** (control) «*troops/rebels*» ocupar **5 (a)** (have) ‹*passport/permit*› tener*, estar* en posesión de (frml); ‹*degree/shares*› tener*; ‹*record*› ostentar, tener*; ‹*post/position*› tener*, ocupar; **he ~s the view that** ... sostiene *or* mantiene que ... **(b)** (consider) considerar; (assert) sostener*, mantener*; **to ~ sb responsible for sth** responsabilizar* a algn de algo **(c)** (conduct) ‹*meeting/elections*› celebrar; ‹*demonstration*› hacer*; ‹*party*› dar*; ‹*conversation*› mantener* **6** (stop): **~ it!** ¡espera! ■ **~** *vi* **1** (clasp, grip): **~ tight!** ¡agárrate fuerte! **2 (a)** (stay firm) «*rope/door*» aguantar, resistir **(b)** (continue) «*weather*» seguir* *or* continuar* bueno; **if our luck ~s** si nos sigue acompañando la suerte

• **hold against** [*v + o + prep + o*]: **I won't ~ that against him** no se lo voy a tomar en cuenta

• **hold back 1** [*v + o + adv, v + adv + o*] **(a)** (restrain) ‹*crowds/water/tears*› contener* **(b)** (withhold, delay) ‹*information*› no revelar; ‹*payment*› retrasar **2** [*v + adv*] (restrain oneself) contenerse*, frenarse

• **hold down** [*v + o + adv, v + adv + o*] **(a)** (force, press down) ‹*lid/papers*› sujetar; ‹*person*› inmovilizar **(b)** ‹*job*›: **he can't ~ down a job** es incapaz de tener un trabajo y cumplir con él **(c)** (limit) ‹*price/increase*› moderar, contener*

• **hold in** [*v + o + adv, v + adv + o*] ‹*stomach*› meter; ‹*feelings/laughter*› contener*

• **hold off 1** [*v + o + adv, v + adv + o*] **(a)** (resist) ‹*attack/enemy*› resistir **(b)** (defeat) ‹*challenger/rival*› derrotar **2** [*v + adv*] (be delayed): **if the rain ~s off** si no empieza a llover

• **hold on** [*v + adv*] **(a)** (wait) esperar **(b)** (survive) resistir, aguantar **(c)** (clasp, grip) agarrarse; **to ~ on TO sth/sb** agarrarse A *or* DE algo/algn **(d)** (keep) **to ~ on TO sth** ‹*receipt/photo*› conservar *or* guardar algo

• **hold out 1** [*v + o + adv, v + adv + o*] (extend) ‹*hands/arms*› tender*, alargar* **2** [*v + adv + o*] **(a)** (offer) ‹*possibility*› ofrecer*; ‹*hope*› dar* **(b)** (have, retain) ‹*hope*› tener*; **I don't ~ out much hope of getting the job** no tengo muchas esperanzas de que me den el trabajo **3** [*v + adv*] **(a)** (survive, last) «*person*» aguantar **(b)** (resist, make a stand) «*army/town*» resistir

• **hold over** [*v + o + adv, v + adv + o*] (postpone) ‹*meeting/decision*› aplazar*, postergar* (esp AmL)

• **hold together 1** [*v + adv*] «*arguments*» tener* lógica *or* solidez; «*people*» mantenerse* unidos **2** [*v + o + adv*] (keep united) ‹*family/group*› mantener* unido

• **hold up 1** [*v + o + adv, v + adv + o*] **(a)** (raise) ‹*hand/banner*› levantar; ‹*head*› mantener* erguido **(b)** (support) ‹*roof/walls*› sostener* **(c)** (delay) ‹*person/arrival*› retrasar; ‹*progress*› entorpecer* **(d)** (rob) atracar*, asaltar **2** [*v + adv*] «*theory/argument*» resultar válido

• **hold with** [*v + prep + o*] estar* de acuerdo con

hold² *n* **1** [U] **(a)** (grip, grasp): **to catch** *o* **grab** *o* **take ~ of sth** agarrar *or* (esp Esp) coger* algo; (so as not to fall etc) agarrarse *or* asirse de *or* a algo; **to get ~ of sb** (find) localizar* *or* (AmL tb) ubicar* a algn; **to get ~ of sth** (manage to get) conseguir* algo **(b)** (control): **the ~ they have over the members of the sect** el dominio que ejercen sobre los miembros de la secta **2** [C] **(a)** (in wrestling, judo) llave *f*; ***with no ~s barred*** sin ningún tipo de restricciones **(b)** (in mountaineering) asidero *m* **3** [C] (delay, pause) demora *f*; **I've got Mr Brown on ~** (Telec) el Sr Brown está esperando para hablar con usted; **to put sth on ~** ‹*project*› dejar algo aparcado **4** [C] (of ship, aircraft) bodega *f*

holdall /ˈhəʊldɔːl/ *n* (BrE) bolso *m*, de viaje, bolsón *m* (RPl)

holder /ˈhəʊldər ‖ ˈhəʊldə(r)/ *n* **1** (of permit, passport, job) titular *mf*; (of ticket) poseedor, -dora *m,f*; (of bonds etc) titular *mf*, tenedor, -dora *m,f*; (of title, cup) poseedor, -dora *m,f* **2** (wallet) funda *f*

holdup /ˈhəʊldʌp/ *n* **(a)** (delay) demora *f*, retraso *m*; (in traffic) atasco *m*, embotellamiento *m* **(b)** (armed robbery) atraco *m*

hole /həʊl/ *n* **1 (a)** (in belt, material, clothing) agujero *m*; (in ground) hoyo *m*, agujero *m*; (in road) bache *m*; (in wall) boquete *m*; **to make a ~ in sth** hacer* un agujero en algo, agujerear algo **(b)** (in argument, proposal) punto *m* débil; ***to pick ~s in sth*** encontrarle* defectos *or* faltas a algo **(c)** (of animal) madriguera *f* **2** (in golf) hoyo *m* **3** (unpleasant place) (colloq): **this town is a real ~!** ¡qué pueblo de mala muerte! (fam)

holiday /ˈhɑːlədeɪ ‖ ˈhɒlədeɪ/ *n* **(a)** (day) fiesta *f*, día *m* festivo, (día *m*) feriado *m* (AmL) **(b)** (period away from work) (esp BrE) (*often pl*) vacaciones *fpl*, licencia *f* (Col, Méx, RPl); **to go/be on ~** irse*/estar* de vacaciones; (*before n*) ‹*mood/spirit*› festivo; ‹*cottage*› de vacaciones **(c)** (BrE Educ) (*often pl*) vacaciones *fpl*

holiday: **~ camp** *n* (BrE) colonia *f* de vacaciones; **~maker** *n* (BrE) turista *mf*; (on summer holidays) veraneante *mf*; **~ resort** *n* centro *m* turístico

Holland /'hɑːlənd ‖ 'hɒlənd/ *n* Holanda *f*

holler /'hɑːlər ‖ 'hɒlə(r)/ (AmE colloq) *vt/i* gritar

hollow[1] /'hɑːləʊ ‖ 'hɒləʊ/ *adj* **1** ‹*tree/tooth/wall*› hueco; ‹*sound*› hueco; ‹*voice*› apagado; ‹*cheeks/eyes*› hundido **2** ‹*success/triumph*› vacío; ‹*person*› vacío, vacuo; ‹*promises/threats*› vano, falso; ‹*words*› hueco, vacío

hollow[2] *n* **(a)** (empty space) hueco *m*; (depression) hoyo *m*, depresión *f* **(b)** (dell, valley) hondonada *f*

• **hollow out** [*v + o + adv, v + adv + o*] vaciar*, ahuecar*

holly /'hɑːli ‖ 'hɒli/ *n* [C U] acebo *m*

holocaust /'həʊləkɔːst, 'hɑː- ‖ 'hɒləkɔːst/ *n* hecatombe *f*, desastre *m*; **nuclear ~** holocausto *m* nuclear; **the H~** el Holocausto

hologram /'həʊləgræm, 'hɑː- ‖ 'hɒləgræm/ *n* holograma *m*

holster /'həʊlstər ‖ 'həʊlstə(r)/ *n* pistolera *f*, funda *f* de pistola (*or* revólver *etc*)

holy /'həʊli/ *adj* **-lier, -liest** ‹*ground/place*› sagrado, santo; ‹*day*› de precepto, de guardar; ‹*water*› bendito; ‹*person/life/virtue*› santo; **the H~ Bible** la Sagrada *or* Santa Biblia

holy: **H~ Ghost** *n* **the H~ Ghost** el Espíritu Santo; **H~ Spirit** *n* **the H~ Spirit** el Espíritu Santo

homage /'hɑːmɪdʒ ‖ 'hɒmɪdʒ/ *n* [U] (frml) homenaje *m*; **to pay ~ to sb/sth** rendir* homenaje a algn/algo

home[1] /həʊm/ *n* **1** [U C] (of person) **(a)** (dwelling) casa *f* **(b)** (in wider sense): **New York is my ~ now** Nueva York es donde vivo ahora; **~ sweet ~** hogar dulce hogar; **to leave ~** irse* de casa **(c)** (family environment) hogar *m* **2** [C] (of animal, plant) (Bot, Zool) hábitat *m* **3 at home (a)** (in house) en casa **(b)** (at ease): **make yourself at ~** ponte cómodo, estás en tu casa **(c)** (not abroad): **at ~ and abroad** dentro y fuera del país **(d)** (Sport) en casa **4** [C] (institution) (for children) asilo *m* (AmL), orfanatorio *m* (Méx), centro *m* de acogida de menores (Esp); (for old people) residencia *f* de ancianos; **dogs' ~** (BrE) perrera *f*

• **home in** [*v + adv*] **to ~ in ON sth** localizar* y dirigirse* HACIA algo

home[2] *adv* **1** (where one lives) ‹*come/arrive*› a casa; **I'll be ~ at five** estaré en casa a las cinco **2** (to desired place): **to hit ~** dar* en el blanco; ***to drive sth ~ (to sb)*** hacer(le)* entender algo (a algn)

home[3] *adj* (*before n*) **(a)** ‹*address/telephone number*› particular; ‹*background/environment*› familiar; ‹*cooking/perm*› casero; **~ visit** (by doctor) (BrE) visita *f* a domicilio **(b)** (of origin): **~ state** (in US) estado *m* natal *or* de procedencia **(c)** (not foreign) ‹*affairs/market*› nacional **(d)** (Sport) ‹*team*› de casa, local; ‹*game*› en casa

home: **~ base** *n* (AmE) **(a)** (Busn, Mil) base *f* de operaciones **(b)** (in baseball) ⇒ HOME PLATE; **~boy** *n* (AmE sl) compinche *m* (fam), cuate *m* (Méx fam); **~ brew** *n* [U] *cerveza hecha en casa*; **~coming** *n* **(a)** (return home) regreso *m*, vuelta *f* (*a casa, a la patria etc*) **(b)** (at school, college) (AmE) *fiesta estudiantil al comienzo del año académico con asistencia de ex-alumnos*; **H~ Counties** *pl n* (in UK) **the H~ Counties** *los condados de los alrededores de Londres*; **~-grown** /'həʊm'grəʊn/ *adj* (from one's own garden) de la huerta propia; (not foreign) del país, local, nacional; **~ help** *n* (BrE) auxiliar *mf*; **~land** *n* patria *f*, tierra *f* natal

homeless /'həʊmləs ‖ 'həʊmlɪs/ *adj* sin hogar, sin techo

homely /'həʊmli/ *adj* **-lier, -liest (a)** (characteristic of home) ‹*meal/food*› casero; ‹*atmosphere/room*› acogedor, hogareño **(b)** (plain) (AmE) feo

home: **~-made** /'həʊm'meɪd/ *adj* ‹*clothes*› hecho en casa; ‹*food*› casero; **~-maker** *n* ama *f*‡ de casa; **~ movie** *n* película *f* casera; **~ office** *n* (AmE) oficina *f* central; **H~ Office** *n* (in UK) **the H~ Office** el Home Office, el Ministerio del Interior británico

homeopathic, (BrE) **homoeopathic** /'həʊmiə'pæθɪk/ *adj* homeopático

home: **~ owner** *n* propietario, -ria *m,f* (*de una vivienda*); **~ plate** *n* home *m*, pentágono *m* (Méx)

homer /'həʊmər ‖ 'həʊmə(r)/ *n* (AmE colloq) ⇒ HOME RUN

home: **~room** *n* (AmE Educ) clase *f or* aula *f*‡ del curso; **~ rule** *n* [U] autogobierno *m*; **~ run** *n* cuadrangular *m*, jonrón *m* (AmL); **H~ Secretary** *n* (in UK) ministro, -tra *m,f* del Interior; **~sick** *adj*: **I am** *o* **feel ~sick** echo de menos *or* (AmL tb) extraño a mi familia (*or* mi país *etc*)

homestead /'həʊmsted/ *n* (AmE) casa *f* (*en una granja, hacienda etc*)

home: **~ straight**, **~ stretch** *n* (Sport) recta *f* final *or* de llegada; **~town** /'həʊm'taʊn/ *n* ciudad *f*/pueblo *m* natal; **~ truth** *n* (*usu pl*) verdad *f* (*desagradable*)

homeward[1] /'həʊmwərd ‖ 'həʊmwəd/ **(a)** (BrE also) **homewards** /-z/ *adv* ‹*travel/journey/sail*› de vuelta a casa **(b) to be ~ bound** ir* de camino *or* de vuelta a casa

homeward[2] *adj* (*before n*) ‹*journey*› de vuelta *or* de regreso

homework /'həʊmwɜːrk ‖ 'həʊmwɜːk/ *n* [U] deberes *mpl*, tarea *f*

homey /'həʊmi/ *adj* **homier, homiest** (AmE colloq) ‹*atmosphere/place*› hogareño, acogedor; ‹*manner*› campechano

homicidal /'hɑːmə'saɪdl̩ ‖ ˌhɒmɪ'saɪdl/ *adj* ‹*tendency*› homicida; ‹*rage*› asesino

homicide /'hɑːməsaɪd ‖ 'hɒmɪsaɪd/ *n* **(a)** [U C] (crime, act) homicidio *m* **(b)** [C] (murderer) (frml) homicida *mf*

homing /'həʊmɪŋ/ *adj* (*before n*) ‹*instinct*› de volver al hogar; ‹*device/missile*› buscador; **~ pigeon** paloma *f* mensajera

homoeopathic /'həʊmiə'pæθɪk/ *adj* (BrE) ⇒ HOMEOPATHIC

homogeneous /'həʊmə'dʒiːniəs ‖ˌhɒmə'dʒiːniəs/ *adj* homogéneo

homosexual[1] /'həʊmə'sekʃuəl ‖ˌhəʊmə'sekʃʊəl, ˌhɒmə-/ *adj* homosexual

homosexual[2] *n* homosexual *mf*

homosexuality /'həʊmə'sekʃu'æləti ‖ˌhəʊmə sekʃʊ'æləti, ˌhɒmə-/ *n* [U] homosexualidad *f*

Hon /ɑːn ‖ ɒn/ (in UK) = **Honourable**

Honduran /hɑːn'dʊrən ‖ hɒn'djʊərən/ *adj* hondureño

Honduras /hɑːn'dʊrəs ‖ hɒn'djʊərəs/ *n* Honduras *f*

hone /həʊn/ *vt* ‹*blade/edge*› afilar; ‹*style/skill*› afinar

honest /'ɑːnəst ‖ 'ɒnɪst/ *adj* **(a)** (trustworthy, upright) ‹*person/action*› honrado, honesto; ‹*face*› de persona honrada *or* honesta **(b)** (sincere) ‹*appraisal/opinion*› sincero; **to be ~ with you** … si quieres que te diga la verdad …

honestly /'ɑːnəstli ‖'ɒnɪstli/ *adv* **(a)** (sincerely) ‹*answer/say/think*› sinceramente, francamente **(b)** (*indep*) en serio, de verdad **(c)** (*as interj*) (expressing exasperation) ¡por favor! **(d)** (legitimately) ‹*act/earn*› con honradez, honradamente

honesty /'ɑːnəsti ‖ 'ɒnɪsti/ *n* [U] **(a)** (probity) honradez *f*, honestidad *f*, rectitud *f* **(b)** (truthfulness) franqueza *f*, sinceridad *f*; **in all ~** … para ser sincero …

honey /'hʌni/ *n* (*pl* **honeys**) **1** [U] miel *f* **2** [C] (*as form of address*) (colloq) cariño (fam)

honey: **~ bee** *n* abeja *f*; **~comb** *n* [C U] panal *m*; **~moon** *n* luna *f* de miel; **~suckle** *n* [C U] madreselva *f*

Hong Kong /'hɑːŋ'kɑːŋ ‖ˌhɒŋ'kɒŋ/ *n* Hong-Kong *m*

honk *vi* (hoot) «*goose*» graznar; «*driver*» tocar* el claxon, pitar

honor[1], (BrE) **honour** /'ɑːnər ‖ 'ɒnə(r)/ *n* **1** [U] (good name) honor *m* **2** [C U] (privilege, mark of distinction) honor *m*; **to have the ~ to** + INF *o* **of -ING** (frml) tener* el honor DE + INF (frml); **a reception in ~ of the delegates** una recepción en honor de los delegados **3 ▶ 603 | Honor** (as title) **Your/His H~** Su Señoría **4 honors** *pl* **(a)** (special mention) (*before n*) **~s list** (AmE) cuadro *m* de honor **(b)** (Educ): **to graduate with ~s** licenciarse con matrícula (de honor) *or* con honores; (*before n*) **an honours degree** (BrE) ≈ una licenciatura

honor[2], (BrE) **honour** *vt* **1** (show respect) honrar **2 (a)** (keep to) ‹*agreement/obligation*› cumplir (con) **(b)** (Fin) ‹*bill/debt*› satisfacer* (frml), pagar*; ‹*check/draft*› pagar*, aceptar

honorable, (BrE) **honourable** /'ɑːnərəbəl ‖ 'ɒnərəbəl/ *adj* **1 (a)** (honest, respectable) ‹*person/action*› honorable **(b)** (creditable) ‹*peace/settlement*› honroso **2 ▶ 603 | Honourable** (in UK) *tratamiento dado a representantes parlamentarios y a hijos de vizcondes, barones y condes*

honorary /'ɑːnəreri ‖'ɒnərəri/ *adj* honorario; ‹*doctorate*› honoris causa

honour *etc* (BrE) ⇒ HONOR *etc*

hood /hʊd/ *n* **1** (on coat, jacket) capucha *f*; (pointed) capirote *m*; (of monk) capucha *f*, capuchón *m* **2 (a)** (on chimney, cooker) campana *f*; (on machine) cubierta *f* **(b)** (AmE Auto) capó *m* **(c)** (folding cover) (BrE) capota *f*

hoodlum /'huːdləm/ *n* **(a)** (thug) (AmE) matón, -tona *m,f* (fam), gorila *mf* **(b)** (rowdy youth) vándalo, -la *m,f*, gamberro, -rra *m,f* (Esp)

hoodwink /'hʊdwɪŋk/ *vt* engañar; **to ~ sb** INTO -ING engañar a algn PARA QUE (+ *subj*)

hoof /hʊf ‖ huːf/ *n* (*pl* **hoofs** *or* **hooves**) (of horse) casco *m*, vaso *m* (RPl), pezuña *f* (Méx); (of cow) pezuña *f*

hoof-and-mouth disease /'hʊfən'maʊθ ‖ˌhuːfən'maʊθ/ *n* [U] (AmE) fiebre *f* aftosa, glosopeda *f* (téc)

hook[1] /hʊk/ *n* **1 (a)** gancho *m*; (for hanging clothes) percha *f*, gancho *m*; (for fishing) anzuelo *m*; **to take the phone off the ~** descolgar* el teléfono; ***to let sb off the ~*** dejar salir a algn del atolladero **(b)** (Clothing) corchete *m*, ganchito *m*; **~s and eyes** corchetes (*macho y hembra*) **2** (in boxing) gancho *m*

hook[2] *vt* (grasp, secure) enganchar

• hook up 1 [*v* + *o* + *adv*, *v* + *adv* + *o*] **(a)** (fasten) ‹*dress/bra*› abrochar **(b)** (connect, link) enganchar **2** [*v* + *adv*] **(a)** (Rad, TV) conectarse, transmitir en cadena **(b)** (fasten) «*dress*» abrocharse

hooked /hʊkt/ *adj* **1** (hook-shaped) ‹*tool*› en forma de gancho; ‹*beak*› ganchudo; ‹*nose*› aguileño **2** (addicted) (colloq) **to be/get ~** ON **sth** estar* enviciado/enviciarse CON algo, estar enganchado/engancharse A algo (Esp)

hooker /'hʊkər ‖ 'hʊkə(r)/ *n* (esp AmE colloq) prostituta *f*, puta *f* (vulg)

hooky, **hookey** /'hʊki/ *n*: **to play ~** (esp AmE colloq) faltar a clase, hacer* novillos *or* (Méx) irse* de pinta *or* (RPl) hacerse* la rata *or* la rabona *or* (Per) la vaca *or* (Chi) hacer* la cimarra *or* (Col) capar clase *or* (Ven) jubilarse (fam)

hooligan /'huːlɪgən/ *n* vándalo, -la *m,f*, gamberro, -rra *m,f* (Esp)

hoop /huːp/ *n* aro *m*

hooray /hʊ'reɪ/ *interj* ¡hurra!

hoot[1] /huːt/ *n* (of owl) grito *m*, ululato *m*; **~s of laughter** risotadas *fpl*, carcajadas *fpl*

hoot[2] *vi* «*owl*» ulular; «*car/driver*» tocar* el claxon, pitar

hooter /'huːtər ‖ 'huːtə(r)/ *n* (BrE) **(a)** (siren) sirena *f* **(b)** (horn) claxon *m*, bocina *f*

hoover /'huːvər ‖ 'huːvə(r)/ (BrE) *vt* pasar la aspiradora *or* el aspirador por, aspirar (AmL)

Hoover®, **hoover** /'huːvər ‖'huːvə(r)/ *n* (BrE) aspiradora *f*, aspirador *m*

hooves /hʊvz ‖ huːvz/ *pl of* HOOF

hop[1] /hɑːp ‖ hɒp/ *n* **1** (jump — of person) salto *m* a la pata coja, brinco *m* de cojito (Méx); (— of rabbit) salto *m*, brinco *m*; (— of bird) saltito *m* **2** (Bot, Culin) (*usu pl*) lúpulo *m*

hop[2] **-pp-** *vi* **(a)** «*frog/rabbit*» brincar*, saltar; «*bird*» dar* saltitos **(b)** «*person/child*» saltar a la pata coja, brincar* de cojito (Méx) **(c)** (move quickly) (colloq): **~ in, I'll take you to the station** súbete, que te llevo a la estación; **to ~ on a bus** tomarse un autobús ■ ~ *vt* (AmE colloq) ‹*flight/train*› tomar, pillar (fam)

hope¹ /həʊp/ *n* [U C] esperanza *f*; **she did it in the ~ of a reward** lo hizo con la esperanza de obtener una recompensa

hope² *vi* esperar; **I ~ so/not** espero que sí/que no; **we're hoping for good weather** esperamos tener buen tiempo ■ ~ *vt* **to ~** (THAT) esperar QUE (+ *subj*); **to ~ to** + INF esperar + INF

hope chest *n* (AmE) baúl *m or* arcón *m* del ajuar

hopeful¹ /'həʊpfəl/ *adj* **(a)** ‹*person*› esperanzado, optimista **(b)** (promising) esperanzador, prometedor

hopeful² *n* aspirante *mf*, candidato, -ta *m,f*

hopefully /'həʊpfəli/ *adv* **(a)** (in hopeful way): **can you pay me in dollars? she asked ~** —¿puedes pagarme en dólares? —preguntó esperanzada **(b)** (crit) (*indep*): **when do you leave? — ~, on Friday** ¿cuándo te vas? — el viernes, espero

hopeless /'həʊpləs ‖ 'həʊplɪs/ *adj* **1** (allowing no hope) ‹*situation*› desesperado; ‹*task*› imposible; **he's a ~ case** «*patient*» está desahuciado; (colloq) «*pupil*» no tiene remedio **2** (incompetent, inadequate) (colloq): **you're ~!** ¡eres un inútil!; **the train service on this line is ~** el servicio de trenes en esta línea es desastroso *or* es un desastre; **to be ~** AT **sth** ser* negado PARA algo

hopelessly /'həʊpləsli ‖ 'həʊplɪsli/ *adv* **(a)** (irredeemably) (*as intensifier*): **to be ~ lost/in love** estar* completamente perdido/perdidamente enamorado **(b)** (without hope) sin esperanzas

hopscotch /'hɑːpskɑːtʃ ‖ 'hɒpskɒtʃ/ *n* [U]: **to play ~** jugar* al tejo *or* (Méx) al avión *or* (RPl) a la rayuela *or* (Col) a la golosa *or* (Chi) al luche

horde /hɔːrd ‖ hɔːd/ *n* (colloq) multitud *f*, horda *f*

horizon /hə'raɪzən/ *n* (Geog) **the ~** el horizonte

horizontal /'hɔːrə'zɑːntl ‖ ˌhɒrɪ'zɒntl/ *adj* horizontal

hormone /'hɔːrməʊn ‖ 'hɔːməʊn/ *n* hormona *f*; (*before n*) **~ replacement therapy** terapia *f* hormonal sustitiva

horn /hɔːrn ‖ hɔːn/ *n* **1** [C U] (Zool) (of animal) cuerno *m*, asta *f*‡, cacho *m* (AmS), guampa *f* (CS) **2** [C] (Mus) **(a)** (wind instrument) cuerno *m* **(b)** (*French ~*) trompa *f* **3** [C] (Auto) claxon *m*, bocina *f*; (Naut) sirena *f*

hornet /'hɔːrnət ‖ 'hɔːnɪt/ *n* avispón *m*

horoscope /'hɔːrəskəʊp ‖ 'hɒrəskəʊp/ *n* horóscopo *m*

horrendous /hɔː'rendəs ‖ hɒ'rendəs/ *adj* **(a)** (horrifying) ‹*crime/account*› horrendo, horroroso **(b)** (dreadful) (colloq) ‹*price/mistake*› terrible

horrible /'hɔːrəbəl ‖ 'hɒrɪbəl/ *adj* horrible, horroroso

horrid /'hɔːrəd ‖ 'hɒrɪd/ *adj* (esp BrE colloq) ‹*weather/taste*› horroroso

horrific /hɔː'rɪfɪk ‖ hɒ'rɪfɪk, hə-/ *adj* horroroso, espantoso

horrify /'hɔːrəfaɪ ‖ 'hɒrɪfaɪ/ *vt* **-fies, -fying, -fied** horrorizar*

horrifying /'hɔːrəfaɪɪŋ ‖ 'hɒrɪfaɪɪŋ/ *adj* horroroso, horrendo, horripilante

horror /'hɔːrər ‖ 'hɒrə(r)/ *n* [U C] horror *m*; (*before n*) ‹*movie/story*› de terror

horror-struck /'hɔːrərstrʌk ‖ 'hɒrəstrʌk/ *adj* horrorizado

hors d'oeuvre /ɔːr'dɜːrv ‖ ɔː'dɜːvrə/ *n* (*pl* **hors d'oeuvres** /-'dɜːrv ‖ -'dɜːvrə/) entremés *m*, botana *f* (Méx)

horse /hɔːrs ‖ hɔːs/ *n* **1** [C] (Zool) caballo *m*; ***I could eat a ~*** tengo un hambre canina; (*before n*) **~ riding** (BrE) equitación *f* **2** [C] (vaulting-block) potro *m*, caballo *m* (Méx)

horse: **~back** *n*: **on ~back** a caballo; (*before n*) **~back riding** (AmE) equitación *f*; **~box** *n* (BrE) ⇒ ~CAR; **~car** *n* (AmE) (for transporting horses) remolque *m or* trailer *m* (*para transportar caballos*); **~ chestnut** *n* **(a)** (tree) castaño *m* de Indias **(b)** (fruit) castaña *f* de Indias; **~-drawn** *adj* tirado por caballos; **~fly** *n* tábano *m*; **~man** /'hɔːrsmən ‖ 'hɔːsmən/ *n* (*pl* **-men** /-mən/) jinete *m*; **~power** *n* [U] caballo *m* (de fuerza); **~ racing** *n* [U] carreras *fpl* de caballos, hípica *f*; **~radish** /'hɔːrs'rædɪʃ ‖ 'hɔːsrædɪʃ/ *n* [C U] rábano *m* picante; **~shoe** *n* herradura *f*; **~ show** *n* concurso *m* hípico

horticulture /'hɔːrtəˌkʌltʃər ‖ 'hɔːtɪˌkʌltʃə(r)/ *n* [U] horticultura *f*

hose /həʊz/ *n* **1** [C U] (*~pipe*) manguera *f*, manga *f*; (Auto) manguito *m* **2** (Clothing) (+ *pl vb*) **(a)** (tights) (Hist, Theat) calzas *fpl*, malla *f* **(b)** (AmE) ⇒ PANTYHOSE

● **hose down** [*v* + *o* + *adv*, *v* + *adv* + *o*] lavar (*con manguera*)

hosepipe /'həʊzpaɪp/ *n* (esp BrE) ⇒ HOSE 1

hosiery /'həʊʒəri ‖ 'həʊzɪəri/ *n* [U] (frml) calcetería *f*

hospice /'hɑːspəs ‖ 'hɒspɪs/ *n*: *residencia para enfermos desahuciados*

hospitable /hɑː'spɪtəbəl ‖ hɒ'spɪtəbəl/ *adj* hospitalario

hospital /'hɑːspɪtl ‖ 'hɒspɪtl/ *n* hospital *m*

hospitality /ˌhɑːspə'tæləti ‖ ˌhɒspɪ'tæləti/ *n* [U] hospitalidad *f*

hospitalize /'hɑːspɪtlaɪz ‖ 'hɒspɪtlaɪz/ *vt* hospitalizar*, internar (CS, Méx)

host¹ /həʊst/ *n* **1 (a)** (person dispensing hospitality) anfitrión, -triona *m,f* **(b)** (Rad, TV) presentador, -dora *m,f* **2** (of parasite) huésped *m* **3** (multitude) gran cantidad *f* **4 the Host** (Relig) la Sagrada Hostia

host² *vt* **(a)** (be the venue for) ‹*conference/event*› ser* la sede de **(b)** (Rad, TV) ‹*program*› presentar

hostage /'hɑːstɪdʒ ‖ 'hɒstɪdʒ/ *n* rehén *m*

hostel /'hɑːstl ‖ 'hɒstl/ *n* **(a)** (*youth ~*) albergue *m* juvenil *or* de juventud **(b)** (for students) (BrE) residencia *f*; (for homeless people, battered wives etc) hogar *m*

hostess /'həʊstəs ‖ 'həʊstes/ *n* **(a)** (in private capacity) anfitriona *f* **(b)** (*air ~*) (esp BrE) ⇒ STEWARDESS (b) **(c)** (on TV show) (presenter) presentadora *f*; (assistant) azafata *f*

hostile /'hɑːstl ‖ 'hɒstaɪl/ *adj* hostil

hostility /hɑː'stɪləti ‖ hɒ'stɪləti/ *n* [U C] hostilidad *f*

hot /hɑːt ‖ hɒt/ *adj* **-tt- 1 (a)** ▶ 920 ‹*food/water*› caliente; ‹*weather/day/country*› caluroso; ‹*climate*› cálido; **it's ~ today** hoy hace calor; **I'm ~** tengo calor; **to be ~** «*object*» estar* caliente; **to get ~**

«*oven/iron/radiator*» calentarse* **(b)** (spicy) picante, picoso (Méx) **2 (a)** (fresh) ‹*news/scent*› reciente, fresco **(b)** (current) ‹*story/issue*› de plena actualidad **(c)** (popular, in demand) ‹*product*› de gran aceptación; ‹*play/movie*› taquillero **3** (colloq) (knowledgeable, keen): **he's very ~ on current affairs** está muy al tanto en temas de actualidad; **she's ~ on punctuality** le da mucha importancia a la puntualidad

hot: **~ air** *n* [U] palabrería *f*; **~-air balloon** /'hɑːt'er ‖ ˌhɒt'eə/ *n* globo *m* de aire caliente; **~bed** *n* (of crime, unrest) semillero *m*; **~-blooded** /'hɑːt'blʌdəd ‖ ˌhɒt'blʌdɪd/ *adj* apasionado; **~ dog** *n* perro *m or* perrito *m* caliente, pancho *m* (RPl)

hotel /həʊ'tel/ *n* hotel *m*

hotelier /həʊ'teljər ‖ həʊ'teliə(r)/ *n* hotelero, -ra *m,f*

hot: **~ flush**, (AmE) **~ flash** *n* sofoco *m*, bochorno *m*, calor *m* (RPl fam); **~headed** /'hɑːt'hedəd ‖ ˌhɒt'hedɪd/ *adj* exaltado; **~house** *n* invernadero *m*; (*before n*) ‹*plant/flowers*› de invernadero; **~ line** *n* (Pol) teléfono *m* rojo; (for public) línea *f* directa

hotly /'hɑːtli ‖ 'hɒtli/ *adv* ‹*dispute/deny*› con vehemencia; ‹*debated*› acaloradamente

hot: **~ pepper** *n* [U C] (AmE) pimiento *m* picante, ají *m* picante (AmS), chile *m* (Méx); **~plate** *n* (for cooking) placa *f*, hornilla *f* (AmL exc CS), hornalla *f* (RPl), plato *m* (Chi); (for keeping food warm) calientaplatos *m*; **~ seat** *n* (colloq): **to be in the ~ seat** estar* en la línea de fuego; **~shot** *n* personaje *m*; **~ spot** *n* (colloq) **(a)** (Pol) punto *m* conflictivo **(b)** (night club) club *m* nocturno; **~ spring** *n* fuente *f* termal; **~-tempered** /'hɑːt'tempərd ‖ ˌhɒt'tempəd/ *adj* irascible; **~-water bottle** /'hɑːt'wɔːtər ‖ ˌhɒt'wɔːtə/ *n* bolsa *f* de agua caliente

hound[1] /haʊnd/ *n* perro *m* de caza, sabueso *m*

hound[2] *vt* acosar

hour /aʊr ‖ aʊə(r)/ ▶ **884** *n* **(a)** (60 minutes) hora *f* **(b)** (time of day) hora *f*; **on the ~** a la hora en punto; **at 1600 ~s** a las 16:00 horas **(c)** (particular moment) momento *m*; **her finest ~** su mejor momento

hourly[1] /'aʊrli ‖ 'aʊəli/ *adj* ‹*rate/wage*› por hora

hourly[2] *adv* **(a)** (every hour) ‹*run/broadcast*› cada hora **(b)** (by the hour) ‹*pay/charge*› por hora(s)

house[1] /haʊs/ *n* (*pl* **houses** /'haʊzəz ‖ 'haʊzɪz/) **1** (dwelling, household) casa *f*; ***to put one's (own) ~ in order*** poner* sus (*or* mis *etc*) asuntos en orden; ***to set up ~*** poner* casa **2** (Govt) Cámara *f*; **the H~ of Representatives** (in US) la Cámara de Representantes *or* de Diputados; **the H~ of Commons/of Lords** (in UK) la Cámara de los Comunes/de los Lores; **the H~s of Parliament** (in UK) el Parlamento **3** (Busn) casa *f*, empresa *f*; **publishing ~** editorial *f*; **drinks are on the ~** invita la casa; (*before n*) **~ wine** vino *m* de la casa **4** (Theat) **(a)** (auditorium) sala *f* **(b)** (audience) público *m*

house[2] /haʊz/ *vt* **(a)** (accommodate) ‹*person/family*› alojar **(b)** (contain) ‹*office/museum*› albergar*

house /haʊs/: **~ arrest** *n* arresto *m* domiciliario; **~boat** *n* casa *f* flotante; **~bound** *adj*: **she's 85 and completely ~bound** tiene 85 años y está completamente confinado a su casa; **~broken** *adj* (AmE) ‹*pet*› enseñado; **~fly** *n* mosca *f* común *or* doméstica

household /'haʊshəʊld/ *n* casa *f*; **~s with more than one wage earner** las familias *or* (frml) los hogares donde trabajan dos o más personas; (*before n*) **a ~ name** un nombre muy conocido

householder /'haʊshəʊldər ‖ 'haʊshəʊldə(r)/ *n* dueño, -ña *m,f* de casa

house /haʊs/: **~-hunt** *vi* (*usu in -ing form*) buscar* casa (*para comprar o alquilar*); **~keeper** *n* (woman) ama *f*‡ de llaves; (in hotel) gobernanta *f*; (man) encargado *m* de la casa; **~keeping** *n* [U] **(a)** (running of home) gobierno *m* de la casa **(b) ~keeping (money)** dinero *m* (para los gastos) de la casa; **~maid** *n* criada *f*, mucama *f* (AmL); **~plant** *n* planta *f* de interior; **~-proud** *adj* (esp BrE) muy meticuloso (*en la limpieza y el arreglo de la casa*); **~-to-~** /'haʊstə'haʊs/ *adj* ‹*inquiries/search*› puerta a puerta; **~-trained** *adj* (BrE) ‹*pet*› enseñado; **~warming (party)** /'haʊsˌwɔːrmɪŋ ‖ 'haʊsˌwɔːmɪŋ/ *n*: *fiesta de inauguración de una casa*; **~wife** *n* ama *f*‡ de casa; **~work** *n* [U] tareas *fpl* domésticas, trabajo *m* de la casa

housing /'haʊzɪŋ/ *n* [U] **(a)** (dwellings) viviendas *fpl* **(b)** (provision of houses): **the government's policy on ~** la política del gobierno en cuanto al problema de la vivienda

housing: **~ association** *n* (in UK) *asociación que construye o renueva viviendas para alquilarlas a precios módicos*; **~ development** *n* (AmE) complejo *m* habitacional, urbanización *f* (Esp), fraccionamiento *m* (Méx); **~ estate** *n* (BrE) **(a)** (council estate) *urbanización de viviendas de alquiler subvencionadas por el ayuntamiento* **(b)** (privately owned) ⇒ ~ DEVELOPMENT; **~ project** *n* (in US) complejo *m* de viviendas subvencionadas

hovel /'hʌvəl ‖ 'hɒvəl/ *n* casucha *f*, rancho *m* (RPl)

hover /'hʌvər ‖ 'hɒvə(r)/ *vi* «*helicopter*» sostenerse* en el aire (*sin avanzar*); «*bird*» cernerse*; **the temperature ~ed around 20°** la temperatura rondaba los 20°; **the waiter ~ed around, waiting for a tip** el mesero estuvo rondando la mesa, esperando una propina

hovercraft /'hʌvərkræft ‖ 'hɒvəkrɑːft/ *n* (*pl* **-craft** *or* **-crafts**) aerodeslizador *m*

how /haʊ/ *adv* **1** (in questions) cómo; **~ are you?** ¿cómo estás? **2** (*with adjs, advs*) **(a)** (in questions): **~ wide is it?** ¿cuánto mide *or* tiene de ancho?, ¿qué tan ancho es? (AmL exc CS); **~ heavy is it?** ¿cuánto pesa?; **~ often do you meet?** ¿con qué frecuencia se reúnen?; **~ old are you?** ¿cuántos años tienes? **(b)** (in exclamations) qué; **~ strange/rude!** ¡qué raro/grosero! **3** (*in phrases*) **how about** *o* (colloq) **how's about sth**: **Thursday's no good; ~ about Friday?** el jueves no puede ser ¿qué te parece el viernes?; **I'd love to go; ~ about you?** me encantaría ir ¿y a ti?; **how come** (colloq): **~ come the door's locked?** ¿cómo es que la puerta está cerrada con llave?

however /haʊ'evər ‖ haʊ'evə(r)/ *adv* **1** (*as linker*) sin embargo, no obstante (frml) **2** (*used before adj or adv*) (no matter how): **~ hard she tried** … por más que trataba … **3** (interrog) cómo

howl¹ /haʊl/ *vi* **(a)** «*dog/wolf*» aullar*; «*person*» dar* alaridos; «*wind/gale*» aullar*, bramar **(b)** (weep noisily) (colloq) berrear (fam)

howl² *n* (of dog, wolf) aullido *m*; (of person) alarido *m*, aullido *m*

hp (= **horsepower**) CV, HP

HP *n* [U] (BrE) = **hire purchase**

HQ *n* = **headquarters**

hr ▶ 884 (= **hour**) h.

HRH (in UK) (= **Her/His Royal Highness**) S.A.R.

HRT *n* = **hormone replacement therapy**

hub /'hʌb/ *n* **(a)** (of wheel) cubo *m* **(b)** (focal point) centro *m*

hub cap *n* tapacubos *m*, taza *f* (RPl)

huddle¹ /'hʌdl/ *vi* **(a)** ~ **(together)** (crowd together) apiñarse **(b)** ~ **(up)** (curl up) acurrucarse*

huddle² *n* (tight group) grupo *m*, corrillo *m*; (in US football) timbac *m*, jol *m*

hue /hju:/ *n* (liter) (color) color *m*; (shade) tono *m*

hue and cry *n* (*no pl*) revuelo *m*

huff /hʌf/ *n* (*no pl*): **to be in a** ~ estar* enfurruñado, estar* con mufa (RPl fam)

hug¹ /hʌg/ *vt* **-gg- (a)** (embrace) abrazar* **(b)** (keep close to) ir* pegado a

hug² *n* abrazo *m*

huge /'hju:dʒ/ *adj* enorme

hull /hʌl/ *n* (of ship, plane, tank) casco *m*

hullo /hə'ləʊ ‖ hʌ'ləʊ/ (esp BrE) ⇒ HELLO

hum¹ /hʌm/ **-mm-** *vi* «*machinery/bee/wire*» zumbar; «*person*» tararear (*con la boca cerrada*) ■ ~ *vt* ‹*tune*› tararear (*con la boca cerrada*)

hum² *n* (*no pl*) (of bees, machinery) zumbido *m*; (of voices, traffic) murmullo *m*

human¹ /'hju:mən/ *adj* humano

human² *n* ser* *m* humano

human being *n* ser *m* humano

humane /hju:'meɪn/ *adj* humanitario, humano

humanism /'hju:mənɪzəm/ *n* [U] humanismo *m*

humanist /'hju:mənəst ‖ 'hju:mənɪst/ *n* humanista *mf*

humanitarian /hju:'mænə'teriən ‖ hju:ˌmænɪ'teəriən/ *adj* humanitario

humanities /hju:'mænətiz/ *n* **(a)** (+ *pl vb*) **the** ~ las humanidades, las artes y las letras **(b)** (discipline) (+ *sing vb*) humanidades *fpl*

humanity /hju:'mænəti/ *n* humanidad *f*

human: ~ **nature** *n* [U] naturaleza *f* humana; ~ **rights** *pl n* derechos *mpl* humanos

humble /'hʌmbəl/ *adj* humilde

humbly /'hʌmbli/ *adv* humildemente

humdrum /'hʌmdrʌm/ *adj* monótono, rutinario

humid /'hju:məd ‖ 'hju:mɪd/ ▶ 920 *adj* húmedo

humidity /hju:'mɪdəti/ *n* [U] humedad *f*

humiliate /hju:'mɪlieɪt/ *vt* humillar

humiliating /hju:'mɪlieɪtɪŋ/ *adj* humillante

humiliation /hju:'mɪli'eɪʃən/ *n* humillación *f*

humility /hju:'mɪləti/ *n* [U] humildad *f*

humor¹, (BrE) **humour** /'hju:mər ‖ 'hju:mə(r)/ *n* [U C] humor *m*

humor², (BrE) **humour** *vt* seguirle* la corriente a

humorless, (BrE) **humourless** /'hju:mərləs ‖ 'hju:məlɪs/ *adj* ‹*person*› sin sentido del humor

humorous /'hju:mərəs/ *adj* ‹*novel/play/speech*› humorístico; ‹*situation*› cómico, gracioso

humour *n/vt* (BrE) ⇒ HUMOR[1,2]

hump /hʌmp/ *n* **(a)** (of camel) joroba *f*, giba *f*; (of person) joroba *f* **(b)** (in ground) montículo *m*

hunch¹ /hʌntʃ/ *vt* ‹*back/shoulders*› encorvar

hunch² *n* (intuitive feeling) (colloq) presentimiento *m*, pálpito *m*, corazonada *f*

hunch: ~**back** *n* (person) jorobado, -da *m,f*; (hump) joroba *f*; ~**backed** /'hʌntʃbækt/ *adj* jorobado

hundred /'hʌndrəd/ ▶ 451, 724 *n* cien *m*; **a/one** ~ cien; **a/one** ~ **and one** ciento uno; **two** ~ doscientos; **five** ~ quinientos; **five** ~ **pages** quinientas páginas; **in (the year) fifteen** ~ en el (año) mil quinientos; **she lived in the seventeen** ~**s** vivió en el siglo XVIII; **ten** ~**s are a thousand** diez centenas son un millar; **they are sold by the** ~ *o* **in** ~**s** se venden de a cien *or* (Esp) de cien en cien; **a/one** ~ **thousand/million** cien mil/millones; ~**s of times** cientos de veces

hundredfold /'hʌndrədfəʊld/ *adj/adv see* -FOLD

hundredth¹ /'hʌndrədθ/ ▶ 725 *adj* centésimo

hundredth² *adv* en centésimo lugar

hundredth³ ▶ 543, 725 *n* (Math) centésimo *m*; (part) centésima parte *f*

hundredweight /'hʌndrədweɪt/ ▶ 322 *n* (*pl* ~) *unidad de peso equivalente a 45,36kg. en EEUU y a 50,80kg. en RU*

hung /hʌŋ/ *past & past p of* HANG[1]

Hungarian¹ /hʌŋ'geriən ‖ hʌŋ'geəriən/ *adj* húngaro

Hungarian² *n* **(a)** [U] (language) húngaro *m* **(b)** [C] (person) húngaro, -ra *m,f*

Hungary /'hʌŋgəri/ *n* Hungría *f*

hunger /'hʌŋgər ‖ 'hʌŋgə(r)/ *n* **(a)** [U] (physical) hambre *f*‡ **(b)** (strong desire) (*no pl*): **a** ~ **for adventure** un ansia *f*‡ *or* (liter) hambre de aventura

hunger strike *n* huelga *f* de hambre

hung: ~ **jury** *n*: *jurado que se disuelve al no ponerse de acuerdo sus miembros*; ~**over** /hʌŋ'əʊvər ‖ hʌŋ'əʊvə(r)/ *adj* **to be** ~**over** tener* resaca *or* (Col fam) guayabo *or* (AmL, Méx fam) cruda *or* (Ven fam) ratón

hungrily /'hʌŋgrəli ‖ 'hʌŋgrɪli/ *adv* ávidamente

hungry /'hʌŋgri/ *adj* **-grier, -griest** hambriento; **to be** ~ tener* hambre; **to be** ~ FOR **sth** estar* ávido DE algo

hunk /hʌŋk/ *n* **(a)** (chunk) trozo *m*, pedazo *m* **(b)** (man) (colloq): **he's a real** ~ está buenísimo (fam)

hunt¹ /hʌnt/ *vt* **1** ‹*game/fox*› cazar* **2** (search for) buscar* ■ ~ *vi* **(a)** (pursue game) cazar*; **to go** ~**ing** ir* de caza *or* de cacería **(b)** (search) **to** ~ (FOR **sth**) buscar* (algo)

hunt² *n* **1 (a)** (chase) caza *f*, cacería *f* **(b)** (hunters) partida *f* de caza, cacería *f* **2** (search) búsqueda *f*

hunter /'hʌntər ‖ 'hʌntə(r)/ *n* (person) cazador, -dora *m,f*; (horse) caballo *m* de caza

hunting /'hʌntɪŋ/ *n* [U] (Sport) caza *f*, cacería *f*

hurdle /'hɜːrdl̩ ‖ 'hɜːdl/ *n* **(a)** (Sport) (obstacle) obstáculo *m*, valla *f*; *see also* HURDLES **(b)** (problem) obstáculo *m*

hurdles /'hɜːrdl̩z ‖ 'hɜːdl̩z/ *n* (+ *sing vb*) vallas *fpl*

hurl /hɜːrl ‖ hɜːl/ *vt* tirar, arrojar, lanzar*

hurrah /hʊ'rɑː/, **hurray** /hʊ'reɪ/ *interj* ⇨ HOORAY

hurricane /'hɜːrəkeɪn ‖ 'hʌrɪkən, -keɪn/ *n* huracán *m*

hurry¹ /'hɜːri ‖ 'hʌri/ *n* (*no pl*) prisa *f*, apuro *m* (AmL); **I'm in a ~** tengo prisa, estoy apurado (AmL); **he wrote it in a ~** lo escribió deprisa (fam)

hurry² **-ries, -rying, -ried** *vi* **(a)** (make haste) darse* prisa, apurarse (AmL) **(b)** (move hastily) (+ *adv compl*): **she hurried after him** corrió tras él; **he hurried back/in/out** volvió/entró/salió corriendo ■ ~ *vt* **(a)** ‹*person*› meterle prisa a, apurar (AmL) **(b)** ‹*work*› hacer* apresuradamente

• **hurry away**, **hurry off** [*v* + *adv*] alejarse rápidamente

• **hurry up** **1** [*v* + *adv*] darse* prisa, apurarse (AmL) **2** [*v* + *o* + *adv*, *v* + *adv* + *o*] ‹*person*› meterle prisa a, apurar (AmL); ‹*work*› acelerar, apurar (AmL)

hurt¹ /hɜːrt ‖ hɜːt/ ▶ **484** (*past & past p* **hurt**) *vt* **1 (a)** (cause pain): **you're ~ing her/me!** ¡le/me estás haciendo daño!, ¡la/me estás lastimando! (esp AmL) **(b)** (injure): **I ~ my ankle** me hice daño en el tobillo, me lastimé el tobillo (esp AmL); **to ~ oneself, to get ~** hacerse* daño, lastimarse (esp AmL) **2** (distress emotionally): **I've been ~ too often** me han hecho sufrir demasiadas veces; **to ~ sb's feelings** herir* los sentimientos de algn ■ ~ *vi* **1** (be source of pain) doler*; **my leg ~s** me duele la pierna **2** (have adverse effects): **it won't ~ to postpone it for a while** no pasa nada si lo dejamos por el momento **3** (suffer adverse effects) (AmE colloq): **to be ~ing** estar* pasándola *or* pasándolo mal (fam)

hurt² *n* [U] (emotional) dolor *m*, pena *f*

hurt³ *adj* **(a)** (physically) ‹*finger/foot*› lastimado; **she was badly ~** estaba gravemente herida **(b)** (emotionally) ‹*feelings/pride*› herido; ‹*tone/expression*› dolido; **to feel/be ~** sentirse*/estar* dolido

hurtful /'hɜːrtfəl ‖ 'hɜːtfəl/ *adj* hiriente

hurtle /'hɜːrtl̩ ‖ 'hɜːtl/ *vi* (+ *adv compl*): **to ~ along/past** ir*/pasar volando *or* a toda velocidad

husband /'hʌzbənd/ *n* marido *m*, esposo *m*

hush¹ /hʌʃ/ *n* (*no pl*) silencio *m*

hush² *vt* (quieten) hacer* callar; (calm down) calmar

• **hush up** **1** [*v* + *o* + *adv*, *v* + *adv* + *o*] ‹*scandal/story*› acallar **2** [*v* + *adv*] (be quiet) (AmE colloq) callarse

hush³ *interj*: **~!** ¡shh!, ¡chitón!

hushed /hʌʃt/ *adj* (*before n*) silencioso; **in ~ tones** en voz muy baja, en murmullos

hush-hush *adj* (colloq) super secreto (fam)

husk /hʌsk/ *n* (of wheat, rice) cáscara *f*, cascarilla *f*; (of maize) chala *f* *or* (Esp) farfolla *f*

husky¹ /'hʌski/ *adj* **-kier, -kiest** ronco

husky² *n* (*pl* **-kies**) husky *mf*, perro, -rra *m,f* esquimal

hustings /'hʌstɪŋz/ *pl n* **the ~** la campaña electoral

hustle¹ /'hʌsəl/ *vt* **1 (a)** (move hurriedly) (+ *adv compl*): **she was ~d into the car** la metieron en el coche a empujones; **he was ~d away by his bodyguards** sus guardaespaldas se lo llevaron precipitadamente **(b)** (pressure) apremiar, meterle prisa a, apurar (AmL) **2** (AmE colloq) **(a)** (obtain aggressively) hacerse* con **(b)** (hawk, sell) vender

hustle² *n* **1** [U] (hurry) ajetreo *m*; **the ~ and bustle of the big city** el ajetreo y bullicio de la gran ciudad **2** [C] (trick, swindle) (AmE colloq) chanchullo *m* (fam)

hustler /'hʌslər ‖ 'hʌslə(r)/ *n* (AmE) **(a)** (hard worker) (colloq) persona *f* trabajadora **(b)** (swindler) (sl) estafador, -dora *m,f* **(c)** (prostitute) (sl) puto, -ta *m,f* (vulg)

hut /hʌt/ *n* **(a)** (cabin) cabaña *f*; (of mud, straw) choza *f* **(b)** (hovel) casucha *f*

hutch /hʌtʃ/ *n* (*rabbit* ~) conejera *f*

hyaena /haɪ'iːnə/ *n* ⇨ HYENA

hybrid /'haɪbrəd ‖ 'haɪbrɪd/ *n* híbrido *m*

hydrant /'haɪdrənt/ *n* boca *f* de riego, toma *f* de agua, hidrante *m* (AmC, Col); (*fire* ~) boca *f* de incendios *or* (Esp) de riego, toma *f* de agua, hidrante *m* de incendios (AmC, Col), grifo *m* (Chi)

hydraulic /haɪ'drɔːlɪk ‖ haɪ'drɔːlɪk, haɪ'drɒlɪk/ *adj* hidráulico

hydroelectric /'haɪdrəʊɪ'lektrɪk/ *adj* hidroeléctrico

hydrofoil /'haɪdrəfɔɪl/ *n* (vessel) hidrodeslizador *m*, aliscafo *m*

hydrogen /'haɪdrədʒən/ *n* [U] hidrógeno *m*

hyena /haɪ'iːnə/ *n* hiena *f*

hygiene /'haɪdʒiːn/ *n* higiene *f*

hygienic /haɪ'dʒiːnɪk/ *adj* higiénico

hymn /hɪm/ *n* (Relig) cántico *m*, himno *m*

hype¹ /haɪp/ *n* [U] (colloq) despliegue *m* *or* bombo *m* publicitario

hype² *vt* (colloq) promocionar con bombos y platillos *or* (Esp) a bombo y platillo

• **hype up** [*v* + *adv* + *o*, *v* + *o* + *adv*] (colloq) ‹*movie*› promocionar con bombos y platillos *or* (Esp) a bombo y platillo; ‹*person*› poner* nervioso

hyperactive /'haɪpər'æktɪv/ *adj* hiperactivo

hypermarket /'haɪpər,mɑːrkət ‖ 'haɪpəmɑːkɪt/ *n* (BrE) hipermercado *m*

hypertension /'haɪpər'tentʃən ‖ ,haɪpə'tenʃən/ *n* [U] hipertensión *f*

hyperventilate /'haɪpər'ventl̩eɪt ‖ ,haɪpə'ventɪleɪt/ *vi* hiperventilarse

hyphen /'haɪfən/ *n* guión *m*

hypnosis /hɪp'nəʊsəs ‖ hɪp'nəʊsɪs/ *n* [U] hipnosis *f*

hypnotic /hɪp'nɑːtɪk ‖ hɪp'nɒtɪk/ *adj* ‹*suggestion/state*› hipnótico; ‹*voice/eyes/rhythm*› hipnotizador, hipnotizante

hypnotism /'hɪpnətɪzəm/ *n* [U] hipnotismo *m*

hypnotist /'hɪpnətəst ‖ 'hɪpnətɪst/ *n* hipnotizador, -dora *m,f*

hypnotize /'hɪpnətaɪz/ *vt* hipnotizar*

hypoallergenic /'haɪpəʊ,ælər'dʒenɪk ‖ ,haɪpəʊ,ælə'dʒenɪk/ *adj* hipoalérgeno

hypochondriac /ˈhaɪpəˈkɑːndriæk ‖ ˌhaɪpə ˈkɒndriæk/ *n* hipocondríaco, -ca *m,f*

hypocrisy /hɪˈpɑːkrəsi ‖ hɪˈpɒkrəsi/ *n* [U C] (*pl* **-sies**) hipocresía *f*

hypocrite /ˈhɪpəkrɪt/ *n* hipócrita *mf*

hypocritical /ˈhɪpəˈkrɪtɪkəl/ *adj* hipócrita

hypodermic¹ /ˈhaɪpəˈdɜːrmɪk ‖ ˌhaɪpəˈdɜːmɪk/ *adj* hipodérmico

hypodermic² *n* (aguja *f*) hipodérmica *f*

hypothermia /ˈhaɪpəˈθɜːrmiə ‖ ˌhaɪpəˈθɜːmiə/ *n* [U] hipotermia *f*

hypothesis /haɪˈpɑːθəsəs ‖ haɪˈpɒθəsɪs/ *n* (*pl* **-ses** /-siːz/) hipótesis *f*

hypothetical /ˈhaɪpəˈθetɪkəl/ *adj* hipotético

hysterectomy /ˈhɪstəˈrektəmi/ *n* (*pl* **-mies**) histerectomía *f*

hysteria /hɪˈstɪriə ‖ hɪˈstɪəriə/ *n* [U] histerismo *m*, histeria *f*

hysterical /hɪˈsterɪkəl/ *adj* **(a)** (Psych) histérico **(b)** (very funny) (colloq) para morirse de (la) risa

hysterics /hɪˈsterɪks/ *pl n* **(a)** (nervous agitation) histeria *f*, histerismo *m*; **to go into** *or* **have ~** ponerse* histérico **(b)** (laughter) (colloq) **to be in ~** estar* como loco

Ii

I, i /aɪ/ *n* I, i *f*

I /aɪ/ *pron* yo

■ **Note** Although *yo* is given as the main translation of *I*, it is in practice used only for emphasis, or to avoid ambiguity: *I went to the theater* fui al teatro; *I was singing, he was playing the piano* yo cantaba y él tocaba el piano; ***I** did it* yo lo hice.

IA = **Iowa**

IBA *n* (in UK) = **Independent Broadcasting Authority**

Iberian /aɪˈbɪriən ‖ aɪˈbɪəriən/ *adj* ibérico

ice¹ /aɪs/ *n* **1** [U] (frozen water) hielo *m*; ***to break the ~*** (overcome reserve) romper* el hielo; (make a start) (AmE) dar* los primeros pasos **2** [C U] (sherbet) (AmE) sorbete *m*, helado *m* de agua (AmL), nieve *f* (Méx)

ice² *vt* ‹*cake*› bañar (*con fondant*)

Ice Age *n*: **the ~ ~** la edad de hielo

iceberg /ˈaɪsbɜːrg ‖ ˈaɪsbɜːg/ *n* iceberg *m*

ice: **~box** *n* **(a)** (refrigerator) (AmE colloq & dated) refrigerador *m*, nevera *f*, heladera *f* (RPl) **(b)** (freezing compartment) (BrE) congelador *m*; **~ cream** *n* [U C] helado *m*; **~ cube** *n* cubito *m* de hielo

iced /aɪst/ *adj* **1** (chilled) helado **2** (Culin) glaseado

ice hockey *n* [U] hockey *m* sobre hielo

Iceland /ˈaɪslənd/ *n* Islandia *f*

Icelandic¹ /aɪsˈlændɪk/ *adj* islandés

Icelandic² *n* [U] islandés *m*

ice: **~ lolly** *n* (BrE) paleta *f* helada *or* (Esp) polo *m* *or* (RPl) palito *m* helado *or* (CS) chupete *m* helado; **~ rink** *n* (BrE) pista *f* de (patinaje sobre) hielo; **~ skating** *n* [U] patinaje *m* sobre hielo

icicle /ˈaɪsɪkəl/ *n* carámbano *m* (de hielo)

icing /ˈaɪsɪŋ/ *n* (Culin) glaseado *m*

icing sugar *n* [U] (BrE) azúcar *m* *or* *f* glas(é) *or* (RPl) impalpable *or* (Chi) flor *or* (Col) en polvo

icon /ˈaɪkɑːn ‖ ˈaɪkɒn/ *n* icono *m*, ícono *m*

icy /ˈaɪsi/ *adj* **icier, iciest (a)** ‹*wind/rain*› helado, glacial; ‹*feet/hands*› helado; (*as adv*) **~ cold** helado **(b)** ‹*stare/reception*› glacial **(c)** ‹*roads/ground*› cubierto de hielo

ID (a) = **identification (b)** = **Idaho**

idea /aɪˈdiːə ‖ aɪˈdiə/ *n* idea *f*; **I had an ~** se me ocurrió una idea; **that's the general ~** de eso se trata; **that's not my ~ of fun** eso no es lo que yo entiendo por diversión; **where is he? — (I've) no ~!** ¿dónde está? — (no tengo) ni idea

ideal¹ /aɪˈdiːəl/ *adj* ideal

ideal² *n* [U C] ideal *m*

idealism /aɪˈdiːəlɪzəm/ *n* [U] idealismo *m*

idealistic /aɪˈdiːəˈlɪstɪk ‖ ˌaɪdiəˈlɪstɪk/ *adj* idealista

idealize /aɪˈdiːəlaɪz ‖ aɪˈdiəlaɪz/ *vt* idealizar*

ideally /aɪˈdiːəli ‖ aɪˈdiəli/ *adv* ‹*located/placed/equipped*› inmejorablemente; **they are ~ suited** están hechos el uno para el otro; **~, no one would have to do it** (*indep*) lo ideal sería que nadie tuviera que hacerlo

identical /aɪˈdentɪkəl/ *adj* idéntico; **~ twins** gemelos *mpl* univitelinos (téc), gemelos *mpl* (AmL), gemelos *mpl* idénticos (Esp); **to be ~ TO *o* WITH sth** ser* idéntico A algo

identification /aɪˈdentəfəˈkeɪʃən ‖ aɪˌdentɪfɪˈkeɪʃən/ *n* [U] **(a)** (act of identifying) identificación *f* **(b)** (evidence of identity): **have you got any ~?** ¿tiene algún documento que acredite su identidad?

identification parade *n* (BrE) rueda *f* de identificación *or* de sospechosos

identify /aɪˈdentəfaɪ ‖ aɪˈdentɪfaɪ/ **-fies, -fying, -fied** *vt* identificar* ■ *v refl* (reveal identity) **to ~ oneself** identificarse* ■ **~** *vi* **to ~ WITH sb/sth** identificarse* CON algn/algo

Identikit® /aɪˈdentəkɪt ‖ aɪˈdentɪkɪt/ *n* [U]: **~ picture** Identikit® *m*, retrato *m* hablado (AmS) *or* (Méx) reconstruido *or* (Esp) robot

identity /aɪˈdentəti/ *n* (*pl* **-ties**) identidad *f*; (*before n*) **~ card** carné *m* *or* (AmL tb) cédula *f* de identidad

ideological /ˌaɪdiəˈlɑːdʒɪkəl ‖ ˌaɪdiəˈlɒdʒɪkəl/ *adj* ideológico

ideology /ˈaɪdiˈɑːlədʒi ‖ ˌaɪdiˈɒlədʒi/ *n* [U C] (*pl* **-gies**) ideología *f*

idiom /ˈɪdiəm/ *n* modismo *m*

idiomatic /ˈɪdiəˈmætɪk/ *adj* idiomático

idiosyncrasy /ˈɪdiəˈsɪŋkrəsi/ *n* [C U] (*pl* **-sies**) idiosincrasia *f*

idiosyncratic /ˈɪdiəsɪnˈkrætɪk ‖ ˌɪdiəsɪŋˈkrætɪk/ *adj* idiosincrásico

idiot /ˈɪdiət/ *n* idiota *mf*

idiotic /ˈɪdiˈɑːtɪk ‖ ˌɪdiˈɒtɪk/ *adj* idiota

idle¹ /ˈaɪdḷ/ *adj* **idler** /ˈaɪdlər ‖ ˈaɪdlə(r)/, **idlest** /ˈaɪdləst ‖ ˈaɪdlɪst/ **1 (a)** (not in use or employment): **to be ~** «*worker*» no tener* trabajo; «*machine/factory*» estar* parado **(b)** (unoccupied) ‹*hours/moment*› de ocio **2** (lazy) holgazán **3** (frivolous): **it was ~ curiosity** era pura curiosidad; **~ speculation** conjeturas *fpl* inútiles

idle² *vi* **(a)** (be lazy) holgazanear **(b)** (Auto) «*engine*» andar* al ralentí

idleness /ˈaɪdlnəs ‖ ˈaɪdḷnɪs/ *n* **(a)** (involuntary inactivity) inactividad *f* **(b)** (laziness) holgazanería *f*

idol /ˈaɪdḷ/ *n* ídolo *m*

idolize /ˈaɪdlaɪz/ *vt* idolatrar

idyll /ˈaɪdl ‖ ˈɪdɪl/ *n* idilio *m*

idyllic /aɪˈdɪlɪk ‖ ɪˈdɪlɪk/ *adj* idílico

i.e. /ˈaɪˈiː/ (that is) (in writing) i.e.; (in speech) esto es

if /ɪf/ *conj* **1** (on condition that) si; **~ I were you, I wouldn't do it it** yo en tu lugar *or* yo que tú, no lo haría; **she was very offhand, ~ not downright rude** estuvo muy brusca, por no decir verdaderamente grosera; **~ nothing else** aunque no sea más que eso; **~ so** (*as linker*) si es así **2** (whether) si **3** (though) aunque, si bien

igloo /ˈɪgluː/ *n* iglú *m*

ignite /ɪgˈnaɪt/ *vt* prenderle fuego a ■ **~** *vi* «*fuel/paper*» prenderse fuego

ignition /ɪgˈnɪʃən/ *n* **(a)** [U] (act) encendido *m* **(b)** (mechanism) (Auto) encendido *m*; (*before n*) **~ key** llave *f* de contacto *or* (AmL tb) del arranque

ignorance /ˈɪgnərəns/ *n* [U] ignorancia *f*

ignorant /ˈɪgnərənt/ *adj* (lacking knowledge) ignorante; **to be ~ OF sth** ignorar algo

ignore /ɪgˈnɔːr ‖ ɪgˈnɔː(r)/ *vt* ‹*person/remark*› ignorar; ‹*warning*› hacer* caso omiso de; **we can't ~ the fact that** … no podemos dejar de tener en cuenta el hecho de que …

IL = **Illinois**

ilk /ɪlk/ *n* tipo *m*

ill¹ /ɪl/ *adj* **1 -er, -est** (unwell) enfermo; **to feel ~** sentirse* mal **2** (bad) (*before n*): **~ effects** efectos *mpl* negativos; **his ~ health** su mala salud

ill² *adv* (*no comp*) **(a)** (hardly): **I can ~ afford to buy a new car** mal puedo yo permitirme comprar un coche nuevo **(b)** (badly) (frml) mal; **to speak ~ of sb** hablar mal de algn

ill³ *n* mal *m*

Ill = **Illinois**

I'll /aɪl/ = **I will, I shall**

ill: **~-advised** /ˈɪlədˈvaɪzd/ *adj* ‹*action*› desacertado; **you would be ~-advised to go** no sería aconsejable que fueras; **~ at ease** *adj* (*pred*) (uncomfortable) incómodo; (anxious) inquieto; **~-bred** /ˈɪlˈbred/ *adj* sin educación

illegal /ɪˈliːgəl/ *adj* **(a)** (unlawful) ilegal **(b)** (AmE Sport) antirreglamentario

illegible /ɪˈledʒəbəl/ *adj* ilegible

illegitimate /ˈɪlɪˈdʒɪtəmət ‖ ˌɪlɪˈdʒɪtɪmət/ *adj* ilegítimo

ill: **~-fated** /ˈɪlˈfeɪtəd ‖ ˌɪlˈfeɪtɪd/ *adj* infortunado; **~ feeling** *n* resentimiento *m*, rencor *m*; **~-gotten** /ˈɪlˈgɑːtn ‖ ˌɪlˈgɒtn/ *adj*: **~-gotten gains** dinero *m* mal habido

illicit /ɪˈlɪsət ‖ ɪˈlɪsɪt/ *adj* ilícito

ill-informed /ˈɪlɪnˈfɔːrmd ‖ ˌɪlɪnˈfɔːmd/ *adj* mal informado

illiteracy /ɪˈlɪtərəsi/ *n* [U] analfabetismo *m*

illiterate /ɪˈlɪtərət/ *adj* analfabeto

illness /ˈɪlnəs ‖ ˈɪlnɪs/ ▶ 484 *n* [U C] enfermedad *f*

illogical /ɪˈlɑːdʒɪkəl ‖ ɪˈlɒdʒɪkəl/ *adj* ilógico

ill: **~-treat** /ˈɪlˈtriːt/ *vt* maltratar; **~-treatment** /ˈɪlˈtriːtmənt/ *n* [U] malos tratos *mpl*

illuminate /ɪˈluːməneɪt ‖ ɪˈluːmɪneɪt/ *vt* iluminar

illumination /ɪˈluːməˈneɪʃən ‖ ɪˌluːmɪˈneɪʃən/ *n* [U] iluminación *f*

illusion /ɪˈluːʒən/ *n* **(a)** [C U] (false appearance): **to give** *o* **create an ~ of sth** dar* la impresión de algo; (Art) crear la ilusión de algo; **an optical ~** una ilusión óptica **(b)** [C] (false idea) ilusión *f*

illustrate /ˈɪləstreɪt/ *vt* **1** ‹*book/magazine*› ilustrar **2 (a)** (explain by examples) ilustrar **(b)** (show) poner* de manifiesto

illustration /ˈɪləˈstreɪʃən/ *n* **1** [C U] (picture, technique) ilustración *f* **2** [C] (example) ejemplo *m*

illustrator /ˈɪləstreɪtər ‖ ˈɪləstreɪtə(r)/ *n* ilustrador, -dora *m,f*

illustrious /ɪˈlʌstriəs/ *adj* (liter) ilustre

ill will *n* [U] **(a)** (hostility) animadversión *f* **(b)** (spite) rencor *m*

I'm /aɪm/ = **I am**

image /ˈɪmɪdʒ/ *n* imagen *f*; ***to be the (spitting) ~*** *o* ***spit and ~ of sb*** ser* la viva imagen de algn

imagery /ˈɪmɪdʒəri/ *n* [U] imaginería *f*, imágenes *fpl*

imaginable /ɪˈmædʒənəbəl ‖ ɪˈmædʒɪnəbəl/ *adj* imaginable

imaginary /ɪˈmædʒəneri ‖ ɪˈmædʒɪnəri/ *adj* imaginario

imagination /ɪˈmædʒəˈneɪʃən ‖ ɪˌmædʒɪˈneɪʃən/ *n* [U C] imaginación *f*

imaginative /ɪˈmædʒənətɪv ‖ ɪˈmædʒɪnətɪv/ *adj* imaginativo

imagine /ɪˈmædʒən ‖ ɪˈmædʒɪn/ *vt* **(a)** (picture to oneself) imaginarse; **I can just ~ her saying that** ya me la imagino diciendo eso **(b)** (fancy mistakenly): **you're imagining things** son imaginaciones *or* figuraciones tuyas **(c)** (assume) imaginarse; **I ~ she's very tired** me imagino que estará muy cansada

imbalance /ɪmˈbæləns/ *n* [C U] desequilibrio *m*

imbecile /ˈɪmbəsəl ‖ ˈɪmbəsiːl/ *n* imbécil *mf*
imbed /ɪmˈbed/ *vt* **-dd-** (AmE) ⇒ EMBED
IMF *n* (= **International Monetary Fund**) FMI *m*
imitate /ˈɪməteɪt ‖ ˈɪmɪteɪt/ *vt* imitar
imitation¹ /ˈɪməˈteɪʃən ‖ ˌɪmɪˈteɪʃən/ *n* [U C] imitación *f*
imitation² *adj* ‹*gold/pearls*› de imitación
immaculate /ɪˈmækjələt ‖ ɪˈmækjʊlət/ *adj* impecable
immaterial /ˈɪməˈtɪriəl ‖ ˌɪməˈtɪəriəl/ *adj* irrelevante
immature /ˈɪməˈtʊr ‖ ˌɪməˈtjʊə(r)/ *adj* **(a)** ‹*tree/animal*› joven; ‹*fruit*› verde, inmaduro **(b)** (childish) ‹*person/attitude*› inmaduro
immaturity /ˈɪməˈtʊrəti ‖ ˌɪməˈtjʊərəti/ *n* [U] inmadurez *f*
immediate /ɪˈmiːdiət/ *adj* **1 (a)** (instant, prompt) inmediato **(b)** ‹*problem/need*› urgente, apremiante **2** (*before n*) (close): **in the ~ future** en el futuro inmediato; **in the ~ vicinity** en las inmediaciones
immediately /ɪˈmiːdiətli/ *adv* **1** (at once) inmediatamente **2** ‹*before/after/above/below*› justo
immemorial /ˈɪməˈmɔːriəl/ *adj* (liter) inmemorial (liter)
immense /ɪˈmens/ *adj* inmenso, enorme
immensely /ɪˈmensli/ *adv* ‹*enjoy/like*› enormemente; ‹*popular/powerful*› inmensamente
immerse /ɪˈmɜːrs ‖ ɪˈmɜːs/ *vt* **(a)** (submerge) **to ~ sth/sb** (IN **sth**) sumergir* algo/a algn (EN algo) **(b)** (absorb, involve) **to be ~d** IN **sth** estar* absorto EN algo
immersion heater /ɪˈmɜːrʒən ‖ ɪˈmɜːʃən/ *n* calentador *m* eléctrico (*de agua*), termo *m* (Chi), termofón *m* (RPl)
immigrant /ˈɪməgrənt ‖ ˈɪmɪgrənt/ *n* inmigrante *mf*; (*before n*) ‹*worker/population*› inmigrante
immigration /ˈɪməˈgreɪʃən ‖ ˌɪmɪˈgreɪʃən/ *n* [U] inmigración *f*
imminent /ˈɪmənənt ‖ ˈɪmɪnənt/ *adj* inminente
immobile /ɪˈməʊbəl ‖ ɪˈməʊbaɪl/ *adj* inmóvil
immobilize /ɪˈməʊbəlaɪz ‖ ɪˈməʊbɪlaɪz/ *vt* inmovilizar*
immoderate /ɪˈmɑːdərət ‖ ɪˈmɒdərət/ *adj* ‹*demands/appetite*› desmedido
immodest /ɪˈmɑːdəst ‖ ɪˈmɒdɪst/ *adj* **(a)** (conceited) presuntuoso, inmodesto **(b)** (indecent) ‹*behavior/suggestion*› impúdico, inmodesto
immoral /ɪˈmɔːrəl ‖ ɪˈmɒrəl/ *adj* inmoral
immorality /ˈɪmɔːˈræləti ‖ ˌɪməˈræləti/ *n* [U] inmoralidad *f*
immortal /ɪˈmɔːrtl ‖ ɪˈmɔːtl/ *adj* inmortal
immortality /ˈɪmɔːrˈtæləti ‖ ˌɪmɔːˈtæləti/ *n* [U] inmortalidad *f*
immortalize /ɪˈmɔːrtḷaɪz ‖ ɪˈmɔːtḷaɪz/ *vt* inmortalizar*
immune /ɪˈmjuːn/ *adj* **(a)** (not susceptible) **to be ~** TO **sth** ser* inmune A algo **(b)** (*before n*) ‹*system/response*› inmunológico
immunity /ɪˈmjuːnəti/ *n* [U] inmunidad *f*
immunization /ˈɪmjənəˈzeɪʃən ‖ ˌɪmjʊnaɪˈzeɪʃən/ *n* [U C] inmunización *f*
immunize /ˈɪmjənaɪz ‖ ˈɪmjʊnaɪz/ *vt* inmunizar*
imp /ɪmp/ *n* diablillo *m* (fam)
impact /ˈɪmpækt/ *n* [U C] impacto *m*
impair /ɪmˈper ‖ ɪmˈpeə(r)/ *vt* afectar; **~ed vision/hearing** problemas *mpl* de vista/audición
impale /ɪmˈpeɪl/ *vt* **to ~ sth/sb** ON **sth** atravesar* algo/a algn CON algo
impart /ɪmˈpɑːrt ‖ ɪmˈpɑːt/ *vt* (frml) ‹*news*› comunicar*; ‹*knowledge*› impartir; ‹*feeling/quality*› conferir* (frml)
impartial /ɪmˈpɑːrʃəl ‖ ɪmˈpɑːʃəl/ *adj* imparcial
impassable /ɪmˈpæsəbəl ‖ ɪmˈpɑːsəbəl/ *adj* ‹*river/barrier*› infranqueable; ‹*road*› intransitable
impasse /ˈɪmpæs ‖ ˈæmpæs/ *n* impasse *m*
impassioned /ɪmˈpæʃənd/ *adj* apasionado
impassive /ɪmˈpæsɪv/ *adj* impasible
impatience /ɪmˈpeɪʃəns/ *n* [U] impaciencia *f*
impatient /ɪmˈpeɪʃənt/ *adj* ‹*person*› impaciente; ‹*gesture/voice*› de impaciencia
impatiently /ɪmˈpeɪʃəntli/ *adv* con impaciencia
impeach /ɪmˈpiːtʃ/ *vt* (Law) *acusar a un alto cargo de delitos cometidos en el desempeño de sus funciones*
impeccable /ɪmˈpekəbəl/ *adj* impecable
impecunious /ˈɪmpɪˈkjuːniəs/ *adj* (liter *or* hum) sin peculio (liter *o* hum)
impede /ɪmˈpiːd/ *vt* dificultar
impediment /ɪmˈpedəmənt ‖ ɪmˈpedɪmənt/ *n* **(a)** (hindrance) impedimento *m* **(b)** (physical defect) defecto *m*; **a speech ~** un defecto del habla
impel /ɪmˈpel/ *vt* **-ll-** impeler
impending /ɪmˈpendɪŋ/ *adj* (*before n*) inminente
impenetrable /ɪmˈpenətrəbəl/ *adj* impenetrable
imperative¹ /ɪmˈperətɪv/ *adj* **1 (a)** (essential) imprescindible, fundamental **(b)** ‹*need*› imperioso, imperativo **2** (Ling) ‹*mood*› imperativo; ‹*sentence*› en imperativo
imperative² *n* imperativo *m*
imperceptible /ˈɪmpərˈseptəbəl ‖ ˌɪmpəˈseptəbəl/ *adj* imperceptible
imperfect¹ /ɪmˈpɜːrfɪkt ‖ ɪmˈpɜːfɪkt/ *adj* imperfecto
imperfect² *n* imperfecto *m*
imperfection /ˈɪmpərˈfekʃən ‖ ˌɪmpəˈfekʃən/ *n* [C U] imperfección *f*
imperial /ɪmˈpɪriəl ‖ ɪmˈpɪəriəl/ *adj* (of empire) (*before n*) imperial, del imperio
imperialism /ɪmˈpɪriəlɪzəm ‖ ɪmˈpɪəriəlɪzəm/ *n* [U] imperialismo *m*
imperialist /ɪmˈpɪriələst ‖ ɪmˈpɪəriəlɪst/ *n* imperialista *mf*
imperil /ɪmˈperəl ‖ ɪmˈperɪl, ɪmˈperəl/ *vt*, (BrE) **-ll-** poner* en peligro
imperious /ɪmˈpɪriəs ‖ ɪmˈpɪəriəs/ *adj* imperioso
impermeable /ɪmˈpɜːrmiəbəl ‖ ɪmˈpɜːmiəbəl/ *adj* impermeable

impersonal /ɪm'pɜːrsn̩əl ‖ ɪm'pɜːsənl̩/ *adj* impersonal

impersonate /ɪm'pɜːrsəneɪt ‖ ɪm'pɜːsəneɪt/ *vt* **(a)** (pretend to be) hacerse* pasar por **(b)** (mimic) imitar, impersonar (Méx)

impersonator /ɪm'pɜːrsəneɪtər ‖ ɪm'pɜːsəneɪtə(r)/ *n* imitador, -dora *m,f*, impersonador, -dora *m,f* (Méx)

impertinent /ɪm'pɜːrtn̩ənt ‖ ɪm'pɜːtɪnənt/ *adj* impertinente

impervious /ɪm'pɜːrviəs ‖ ɪm'pɜːviəs/ *adj* **(a)** ‹*rock/material*› impermeable **(b)** (unaffected) **to be ~ TO sth** ‹*to criticism/doubt*› ser* impermeable A algo

impetuous /ɪm'petʃuəs/ *adj* ‹*person*› impetuoso; ‹*action/decision*› impulsivo

impetus /'ɪmpətəs ‖ 'ɪmpɪtəs/ *n* [U] ímpetu *m*

impinge /ɪm'pɪndʒ/ *vi* **to ~ ON** *o* **UPON sth** ‹*privacy/freedom*› vulnerar algo

implacable /ɪm'plækəbəl/ *adj* implacable

implant /ɪm'plænt ‖ ɪm'plɑːnt/ *vt* **(a)** ‹*idea/ideal*› inculcar* **(b)** ‹*embryo/hair*› implantar

implausible /ɪm'plɔːzəbəl/ *adj* inverosímil

implement¹ /'ɪmpləment ‖ 'ɪmplɪment/ *vt* implementar

implement² /'ɪmpləmənt ‖ 'ɪmplɪmənt/ *n* instrumento *m*, implemento *m* (AmL)

implicate /'ɪmpləkeɪt ‖ 'ɪmplɪkeɪt/ *vt* implicar*

implication /'ɪmplə'keɪʃən ‖ ˌɪmplɪ'keɪʃən/ *n* **1** [C U] (consequence, significance) repercusión *f*, implicación *f* **2** [U] (involvement) implicación *f*

implicit /ɪm'plɪsət ‖ ɪm'plɪsɪt/ *adj* **(a)** ‹*threat*› implícito **(b)** ‹*confidence/trust*› incondicional, total

implode /ɪm'pləʊd/ *vi* implosionar

implore /ɪm'plɔːr ‖ ɪm'plɔː(r)/ *vt* implorar

imply /ɪm'plaɪ/ *vt* **implies, implying, implied** **1** (suggest, hint) dar* a entender, insinuar* **2** (involve) implicar*, suponer*

impolite /'ɪmpə'laɪt/ *adj* maleducado, descortés

import¹ /'ɪmpɔːrt ‖ 'ɪmpɔːt/ *n* **1** (Busn) **(a)** [U] (act) importación *f* **(b)** [C] (article): **a foreign ~** un artículo de importación **2** [U] (significance) (frml) importancia *f*

import² /ɪm'pɔːrt ‖ ɪm'pɔːt/ *vt* importar

importance /ɪm'pɔːrtn̩s ‖ ɪm'pɔːtn̩s/ *n* [U] importancia *f*

important /ɪm'pɔːrtn̩t ‖ ɪm'pɔːtn̩t/ *adj* importante

importer /ɪm'pɔːrtər ‖ ɪm'pɔːtə(r)/ *n* importador, -dora *m,f*

impose /ɪm'pəʊz/ *vt* imponer* ■ ~ *vi* molestar; **to ~ on sb's goodwill** abusar de la buena voluntad de algn

imposing /ɪm'pəʊzɪŋ/ *adj* imponente

imposition /'ɪmpə'zɪʃən/ *n* **(a)** [U] (enforcement) imposición *f* **(b)** [C] (taking unfair advantage) abuso *m*

impossibility /ɪm'pɑːsə'bɪləti ‖ ɪmˌpɒsə'bɪləti/ *n* [U] imposibilidad *f*

impossible¹ /ɪm'pɑːsəbəl ‖ ɪm'pɒsəbəl/ *adj* **(a)** ‹*job/request*› imposible; **it's ~ for me to arrive by twelve** me es imposible llegar para las doce **(b)** (intolerable) intolerable

impossible² *n* **to ask/attempt the ~** pedir*/intentar lo imposible

impostor /ɪm'pɑːstər ‖ ɪm'pɒstə(r)/ *n* impostor, -tora *m,f*

impotence /'ɪmpətəns/ *n* [U] impotencia *f*

impotent /'ɪmpətənt/ *adj* impotente

impound /ɪm'paʊnd/ *vt* **(a)** ‹*possessions/assets*› incautar(se de) **(b)** ‹*vehicle*› llevar al depósito municipal

impoverished /ɪm'pɑːvərɪʃt ‖ ɪm'pɒvərɪʃt/ *adj* (financially, spiritually) empobrecido; ‹*soil/diet*› pobre

impractical /ɪm'præktɪkəl/ *adj* poco práctico

impregnable /ɪm'pregnəbəl/ *adj* ‹*fortress*› inexpugnable; ‹*organization*› impenetrable

impregnate /ɪm'pregneɪt ‖ 'ɪmpregneɪt/ *vt* **1** (saturate) **to ~ sth WITH sth** impregnar algo CON *or* DE algo **2** (make pregnant) (frml) fecundar

impresario /'ɪmprə'sɑːriəʊ ‖ ˌɪmprɪ'sɑːriəʊ/ (*pl* **-os**) *n* empresario, -ria *m,f* teatral

impress /ɪm'pres/ *vt* **1** (make impression on): **we were ~ed by your work** tu trabajo nos causó muy buena impresión; **he only did it to ~ her** lo hizo sólo para impactarla **2** (emphasize) **to ~ sth ON** *o* **UPON sb** recalcarle* algo a algn ■ ~ *vi* impresionar

impression /ɪm'preʃən/ *n* **1 (a)** (idea, image) impresión *f*; **to be under the ~ (that)** ... creer* *or* pensar* que ... **(b)** (effect) impresión *f*; **to make** *o* **create a good/bad ~ on sb** causarle a algn una buena/mala impresión **2** (imprint) impresión *f*, huella *f* **3** (impersonation) imitación *f*

impressionable /ɪm'preʃn̩əbəl/ *adj* **(a)** (easily influenced) influenciable **(b)** (easily frightened, upset) impresionable

impressionism /ɪm'preʃənɪzəm/ *n* [U] impresionismo *m*

impressionist /ɪm'preʃənəst ‖ ɪm'preʃənɪst/ *n* **(a)** (Art) impresionista *mf* **(b)** (impersonator) imitador, -dora *m,f*

impressive /ɪm'presɪv/ *adj* ‹*record/work*› admirable; ‹*building/ceremony*› imponente

imprint¹ /'ɪmprɪnt/ *n* marca *f*, huella *f*

imprint² /ɪm'prɪnt/ *vt* (physically) imprimir*; (on mind) grabar

imprison /ɪm'prɪzən/ *vt* (Law) encarcelar

imprisonment /ɪm'prɪzənmənt/ *n* [U] (act) encarcelamiento *m*; (state) prisión *f*; **life ~** cadena *f* perpetua

improbable /ɪm'prɑːbəbəl ‖ ɪm'prɒbəbəl/ *adj* **(a)** (unlikely) improbable **(b)** (implausible) inverosímil

impromptu /ɪm'prɑːmptu ‖ ɪm'prɒmptjuː/ *adj* improvisado

improper /ɪm'prɑːpər ‖ ɪm'prɒpə(r)/ *adj* **1** ‹*behavior/language*› indecoroso; ‹*suggestion*› deshonesto **2** (incorrect) (frml) ‹*use*› indebido; ‹*term*› incorrecto

improve /ɪm'pruːv/ *vt* **(a)** ‹*design/results*› mejorar; ‹*chances*› aumentar; **to ~ one's mind** cultivarse **(b)** ‹*property*› hacer* mejoras en ■ ~ *vi* «*situation/weather/health*» mejorar; «*chances*» aumentar

improvement /ɪm'pruːvmənt/ *n* [U C] (in design, situation) mejora *f*; (in health) mejoría *f*

improvise /ˈɪmprəvaɪz/ *vi/t* improvisar

imprudent /ɪmˈpruːdn̩t/ *adj* (frml) imprudente

impudence /ˈɪmpjədəns ‖ ˈɪmpjʊdəns/ *n* [U] insolencia *f*

impudent /ˈɪmpjədənt ‖ ˈɪmpjʊdənt/ *adj* insolente

impulse /ˈɪmpʌls/ *n* impulso *m*; **I did it on ~** lo hice sin pensarlo

impulsive /ɪmˈpʌlsɪv/ *adj* impulsivo

impunity /ɪmˈpjuːnəti/ (frml) *n* [U] impunidad *f*

impure /ˈɪmˈpjʊr ‖ ɪmˈpjʊə(r)/ *adj* impuro

impurity /ɪmˈpjʊrəti ‖ ɪmˈpjʊərəti/ *n* [U C] (*pl* **-ties**) impureza *f*

in¹ /ɪn/ *prep* **1 (a)** (indicating place, location) en; **~ Japan** en (el) Japón; **he went ~ the shop** entró en la tienda; **who's that ~ the photo?** ¿quién es ése de la foto?; **~ here/there** aquí/allí dentro *or* (esp AmL) adentro; **~ the rain** bajo la lluvia **(b)** (*with superl*) de; **the highest mountain ~ Italy** la montaña más alta de Italia; **the worst storm ~ living memory** la peor tormenta que se recuerda **2** (indicating time) en; **~ spring/January/1924** en primavera/enero/1924; **at four o'clock ~ the morning** a las cuatro de la mañana; **she did it ~ three hours** lo hizo en tres horas; **~ two months' time** dentro de dos meses **3 (a)** (indicating manner) en; **~ dollars** en dólares; **~ French** en francés; **~ twos** de dos en dos, de a dos (AmL); **cut it ~ half** córtalo por la mitad; **they came ~ their thousands** vinieron miles y miles **(b)** (wearing): **he turned up ~ a suit** apareció de traje; **are you going ~ that dress?** ¿vas a ir con ese vestido? **4** (indicating circumstances, state): **the company is ~ difficulties** la empresa está pasando dificultades; **to be ~ a good mood** estar* de buen humor; **he's ~ pain** está dolorido; **low ~ calories** bajo en calorías **5** (indicating ratio): **one ~ four** uno de cada cuatro; **she's one ~ a million** es única **6 (a)** (+ *gerund*): **~ so doing, they set a precedent** al hacerlo, sentaron precedente **(b) in that** (*as conj*): **the case is unusual ~ that** ... el caso es poco común en el sentido de que ...

in² *adv* **1 (a)** (inside): **is the cat ~?** ¿el gato está dentro *or* (esp AmL) adentro?; **~ you go!** ¡entra! **(b)** (at home, work): **is Lisa ~?** ¿está Lisa?; **there was nobody ~** no había nadie **2 (a)** (in position): **she had her curlers ~** llevaba *or* tenía los rulos puestos **(b)** (at destination): **the train isn't ~ yet** el tren no ha llegado todavía; **application forms must be ~ by October 5** las solicitudes deben entregarse antes del 5 de octubre **3** (involved): **we were ~ on the planning stage** participamos en la planificación; ***to be ~ for sth***: **it looks like we're ~ for some rain** parece que va a llover; **you're ~ for a big surprise** te vas a llevar una buena sorpresa

in³ *adj* **1 (a)** (fashionable) (colloq) (*no comp*): **black is ~ this season** el negro está de moda esta temporada; **the ~ place** el lugar in (fam) **(b)** (exclusive, private) (*before n*): **an ~ joke** un chiste para iniciados **2** (*pred*) (in tennis, badminton, etc): **the ball was ~** la pelota fue buena *or* cayó dentro *or* (esp AmL) adentro

in⁴ *n*: **the ~s and outs (of sth)** los pormenores (de algo)

in⁵ ▶ 681 (*pl* **in** *or* **ins**) = **inch(es)**

IN = **Indiana**

inability /ˈɪnəˈbɪləti/ *n* [U] incapacidad *f*; **~ to +** INF incapacidad PARA + INF

inaccessible /ˈɪnəkˈsesəbəl ‖ ˌɪnækˈsesəbəl/ *adj* inaccesible

inaccurate /ɪnˈækjərət/ *adj* **(a)** ‹*translation/estimate*› inexacto **(b)** ‹*aim/shot*› impreciso

inactive /ɪnˈæktɪv/ *adj* inactivo

inactivity /ˈɪnækˈtɪvəti/ *n* [U] inactividad *f*

inadequate /ɪnˈædɪkwət/ *adj* **(a)** ‹*resources/measures*› insuficiente **(b)** ‹*person*› inepto

inadvertently /ˈɪnədˈvɜːrtn̩tli ‖ ˌɪnədˈvɜːtn̩tli/ *adv* sin querer

inadvisable /ˈɪnədˈvaɪzəbəl/ *adj* desaconsejable

inane /ɪˈneɪn/ *adj* estúpido, idiota

inanimate /ɪnˈænəmət ‖ ɪnˈænɪmət/ *adj* inanimado

inapplicable /ɪnˈæplɪkəbəl, ˌɪnəˈplɪkəbəl/ *adj* inaplicable, no aplicable

inappropriate /ˈɪnəˈprəʊpriət/ *adj* ‹*measure/dress*› inadecuado; ‹*moment*› inoportuno

inarticulate /ˈɪnɑːrˈtɪkjələt ‖ ˌɪnɑːˈtɪkjʊlət/ *adj* ‹*babbling/grunt*› inarticulado; ‹*person*› con dificultad para expresarse

inasmuch as /ˈɪnəzˈmʌtʃ/ *conj* (frml) **(a)** (since, seeing that) ya que, puesto que **(b)** ⇒ INSOFAR AS

inattentive /ˈɪnəˈtentɪv/ *adj* ‹*pupil/listener*› distraído, poco atento

inaudible /ɪnˈɔːdəbəl/ *adj* inaudible

inaugural /ɪnˈɔːgjərəl ‖ ɪˈnɔːgjʊrəl/ *adj* **(a)** ‹*speech/lecture*› inaugural **(b)** (of official) ‹*speech*› de toma de posesión; ‹*ceremony*› de investidura

inaugurate /ɪnˈɔːgjəreɪt ‖ ɪˈnɔːgjʊreɪt/ *vt* **(a)** (begin, open) inaugurar **(b)** (frml) ‹*president*› investir*

inauguration /ɪnˈɔːgjəˈreɪʃən ‖ ɪˌnɔːgjʊˈreɪʃən/ *n* **(a)** (investiture) investidura *f*; (*before n*) **I~ Day** (in US) *día de la toma de posesión del presidente de los EEUU* **(b)** (opening) inauguración *f*

inbreeding /ˈɪnˌbriːdɪŋ/ *n* [U] endogamia *f*

Inc /ɪnk/ (AmE) = **Incorporated**

Inca¹ /ˈɪŋkə/ *adj* incaico, inca

Inca² *n* inca *mf*

incapable /ɪnˈkeɪpəbəl/ *adj* (*pred*) **(a)** (not able) **to be ~** OF -ING ser* incapaz DE + INF **(b)** (helpless) inútil, incapaz

incapacitate /ˈɪnkəˈpæsəteɪt ‖ ˌɪnkəˈpæsɪteɪt/ *vt* **(a)** (disable) incapacitar **(b)** (Law) inhabilitar

incarcerate /ɪnˈkɑːrsəreɪt ‖ ɪnˈkɑːsəreɪt/ *vt* encarcelar

incarnate /ɪnˈkɑːrnət ‖ ɪnˈkɑːnət/ *adj* (liter) (*usu pred*) encarnado

incarnation /ˈɪnkɑːrˈneɪʃən ‖ ˌɪnkɑːˈneɪʃən/ *n* encarnación *f*

incendiary /ɪnˈsendieri ‖ ɪnˈsendiəri/ *adj* incendiario

incense¹ /ˈɪnsens/ *n* [U] incienso *m*

incense² /ɪnˈsens/ *vt* indignar

incentive /ɪn'sentɪv/ *n* [C U] incentivo *m*
inception /ɪn'sepʃən/ *n* (frml) inicio *m*
incessant /ɪn'sesn̩t/ *adj* incesante
incessantly /ɪn'sesn̩tli/ *adv* sin cesar
incest /'ɪnsest/ *n* [U] incesto *m*
incestuous /ɪn'sestʃuəs ‖ ɪn'sestjʊəs/ *adj* incestuoso
inch[1] /ɪntʃ/ ▶ 681 *n* pulgada *f* (*2,54 centímetros*); **I've searched every ~ of the house** he buscado hasta en el último rincón de la casa; **she wouldn't budge** *o* **give an ~** no cedió ni un ápice
inch[2] *vi*: **to ~ forward** avanzar* lentamente
incidence /'ɪnsədəns ‖ 'ɪnsɪdəns/ *n* [U] **1** (frequency) índice *m* **2** (Opt, Phys) incidencia *f*
incident /'ɪnsədənt ‖ 'ɪnsɪdənt/ *n* incidente *m*
incidental /'ɪnsə'dentl̩ ‖ ˌɪnsɪ'dentl̩/ *adj* **(a)** (accompanying) ‹*effect*› secundario; ‹*advantage/benefit*› adicional; ‹*expenses*› imprevisto **(b)** (minor) incidental
incidentally /'ɪnsə'dentl̩i ‖ ˌɪnsɪ'dentl̩i/ *adv* (*indep*) a propósito
incinerate /ɪn'sɪnəreɪt/ *vt* incinerar
incinerator /ɪn'sɪnəreɪtər ‖ ɪn'sɪnəreɪtə(r)/ *n* incinerador *m*
incision /ɪn'sɪʒən/ *n* [C U] incisión *f*
incisor /ɪn'saɪzər ‖ ɪn'saɪzə(r)/ *n* incisivo *m*
incite /ɪn'saɪt/ *vt* ‹*hatred/violence*› instigar* a, incitar a; ‹*person*› **to ~ sb TO sth/+INF** instigar* *or* incitar a algn A algo/+ INF
inclination /'ɪnklə'neɪʃən ‖ ˌɪnklɪ'neɪʃən/ *n* [U C] **(a)** (leaning) tendencia *f* **(b)** (desire) **to have an/no ~ to + INF** tener*/no tener* deseos de + INF
incline[1] /ɪn'klaɪn/ *vt* (frml) ‹*head*› inclinar
incline[2] /'ɪnklaɪn/ *n* (frml) pendiente *f*
inclined /ɪn'klaɪnd/ *adj* (disposed) **~ to + INF**: **I'm ~ to agree** yo me inclino a pensar lo mismo; **she's ~ to be irritable in the morning** tiende a estar de mal humor por la mañana
include /ɪn'klu:d/ *vt* incluir*; (with letter) adjuntar; **service isn't ~d** el servicio no está incluido
including /ɪn'klu:dɪŋ/ *prep*: **up to and ~ page 25** hasta la página 25 inclusive; **not ~ insurance** sin incluir el seguro
inclusion /ɪn'klu:ʒən/ *n* [U] inclusión *f*
inclusive /ɪn'klu:sɪv/ *adj* ‹*price/charge*› global; **to be ~ OF sth** incluir* algo
incognito /ˌɪnkɑ:g'ni:təʊ ‖ ˌɪnkɒg'ni:təʊ/ *adv* de incógnito
incoherent /'ɪnkəʊ'hɪrənt ‖ ˌɪnkəʊ'hɪərənt/ *adj* incoherente
income /'ɪnkʌm/ *n* [U C] ingresos *mpl*
income: **~ support** *n* [U] (in UK) *subsidio otorgado a personas de bajos ingresos*; **~ tax** *n* [U] impuesto *m* sobre *or* a la renta, impuesto *m* a los réditos (Arg)
incoming /'ɪn'kʌmɪŋ/ *adj* (*before n*) **(a)** (inbound): **the area has been closed to ~ traffic** no se permite la entrada de vehículos a la zona; **the secretary takes all ~ calls** la secretaria atiende todas las llamadas **(b)** (about to take office) ‹*president*› entrante
incommunicado /'ɪnkə'mju:nə'kɑ:dəʊ ‖ ˌɪnkəˌmju:nɪ'kɑ:dəʊ/ *adj* (*pred*) **to be ~** estar* incomunicado
incomparable /ɪn'kɑ:mpərəbəl ‖ ɪn'kɒmpərəbəl/ *adj* (liter) incomparable
incompatible /'ɪnkəm'pætəbəl/ *adj* incompatible
incompetence /ɪn'kɑ:mpətəns ‖ ɪn'kɒmpɪtəns/ *n* [U] incompetencia *f*
incompetent /ɪn'kɑ:mpətənt ‖ ɪn'kɒmpɪtənt/ *adj* ‹*person*› incompetente; ‹*work*› deficiente
incomplete /'ɪnkəm'pli:t/ *adj* **(a)** (with sth or sb missing) incompleto **(b)** (unfinished) inacabado
incomprehensible /ɪn'kɑ:mprə'hensəbəl ‖ ɪnˌkɒmprɪ'hensəbəl/ *adj* incomprensible
incomprehension /ɪn'kɑ:mprɪ'hentʃən ‖ ɪnˌkɒmprɪ'henʃən/ *n* [U] incomprensión *f*
inconceivable /'ɪnkən'si:vəbəl/ *adj* inconcebible
inconclusive /'ɪnkən'klu:sɪv/ *adj* ‹*evidence/findings*› no concluyente
incongruous /ɪn'kɑ:ŋgruəs ‖ ɪn'kɒŋgrʊəs/ *adj* ‹*behavior/remark*› fuera de lugar, inapropiado; ‹*appearance*› extraño, raro
inconsequential /ɪn'kɑ:nsə'kwentʃəl ‖ ɪnˌkɒnsɪ'kwenʃəl/ *adj* intrascendente
inconsiderate /'ɪnkən'sɪdərət/ *adj* desconsiderado
inconsistent /'ɪnkən'sɪstənt/ *adj* **(a)** (contradictory) contradictorio; **to be ~ WITH sth** no concordar* CON algo; ‹*with principles/ideas*› no compadecerse* CON algo **(b)** (changeable) ‹*person/attitude*› inconsecuente
inconspicuous /'ɪnkən'spɪkjuəs/ *adj* que no llama la atención
incontinent /ɪn'kɑ:ntn̩ənt ‖ ɪn'kɒntɪnənt/ *adj* (Med) incontinente
inconvenience[1] /'ɪnkən'vi:niəns/ *n* **(a)** [U] (unsuitability, troublesomeness) inconveniencia *f* **(b)** [U] (trouble) molestias *fpl* **(c)** [C] (drawback, nuisance) inconveniente *m*
inconvenience[2] *vt* causarle molestias a
inconvenient /'ɪnkən'vi:niənt/ *adj* ‹*moment*› poco conveniente; ‹*position*› poco práctico
incorporate /ɪn'kɔ:rpəreɪt ‖ ɪn'kɔ:pəreɪt/ *vt* **1 (a)** (take in) ‹*idea/plan*› incorporar; **to ~ sth INTO sth** incorporar algo A algo **(b)** (include, contain) incluir* **2** (Busn, Law) ‹*business/enterprise*› constituir* (en sociedad)
incorrect /'ɪnkə'rekt/ *adj* ‹*answer/spelling*› incorrecto; ‹*statement/belief*› equivocado
incorrigible /ɪn'kɔ:rədʒəbəl ‖ ɪn'kɒrɪdʒəbəl/ *adj* incorregible
increase[1] /ɪn'kri:s/ *vi* «*number/size/prices/output*» aumentar; «*influence/popularity*» crecer*; **to ~ in size** aumentar de tamaño; **to ~ in number** crecer* en número; **to ~ in value** aumentar de valor ■ **~** *vt* aumentar
increase[2] /'ɪnkri:s/ *n* aumento *m*; **to be on the ~** estar* *or* ir* en aumento
increasing /ɪn'kri:sɪŋ/ *adj* (*before n*) creciente

increasingly /ɪn'kri:sɪŋli/ *adv*: **~ difficult** cada vez más difícil; **it is becoming ~ clear that ...** resulta cada vez más claro que ...

incredible /ɪn'kredəbəl/ *adj* increíble

incredibly /ɪn'kredəbli/ *adv* (colloq) (*as intensifier*) increíblemente

incredulous /ɪn'kredʒələs ‖ ɪn'kredjʊləs/ *adj* de incredulidad

increment /'ɪŋkrəmənt/ *n* (in salary) incremento *m* (salarial) (frml)

incriminate /ɪn'krɪməneɪt ‖ ɪn'krɪmɪneɪt/ *vt* incriminar (frml)

incriminating /ɪn'krɪməneɪtɪŋ ‖ ɪn'krɪmɪneɪtɪŋ/ *adj* ‹*evidence/document*› comprometedor

incubate /'ɪŋkjəbeɪt ‖ 'ɪŋkjʊbeɪt/ *vt* incubar ■ **~** *vi* «*bird*» empollar; «*egg/bacteria*» incubarse

incubation /'ɪŋkjə'beɪʃən ‖ ˌɪŋkjʊ'beɪʃən/ *n* [U] incubación *f*

incubator /'ɪŋkjəbeɪtər ‖ 'ɪŋkjʊbeɪtə(r)/ *n* incubadora *f*

inculcate /'ɪnkʌlkeɪt/ *vt* (frml) **to ~ sth IN(TO) sb, to ~ sb WITH sth** inculcarle* algo A algn, inculcar* algo EN algn

incumbent[1] /ɪn'kʌmbənt/ *adj* (frml) **to be ~ ON** *o* **UPON sb** incumbirle A algn

incumbent[2] *n* titular *mf* del cargo

incur /ɪn'kɜ:r ‖ ɪn'kɜ:(r)/ *vt* **-rr-** (frml) ‹*anger*› provocar*, incurrir en (frml); ‹*penalty*› acarrear; ‹*damage/loss*› sufrir; ‹*debt/liability*› contraer*; ‹*expense*› incurrir en (frml)

incurable /ɪn'kjʊrəbəl ‖ ɪn'kjʊərəbəl/ *adj* ‹*illness*› incurable; ‹*optimist/romantic*› empedernido

incursion /ɪn'kɜ:rʒən ‖ ɪn'kɜ:ʃən/ *n* [C U] incursión *f*

Ind = **Indiana**

indebted /ɪn'detəd ‖ ɪn'detɪd/ *adj* **to be ~ TO sb (FOR sth)** estar* en deuda CON algn (POR algo)

indecency /ɪn'di:sṇsi/ *n* [U] indecencia *f*

indecent /ɪn'di:sṇt/ *adj* indecente

indecipherable /'ɪndɪ'saɪfərəbəl/ *adj* indescifrable

indecision /'ɪndɪ'sɪʒən/ *n* [U] indecisión *f*

indecisive /'ɪndɪ'saɪsɪv/ *adj* **(a)** (hesitant) indeciso **(b)** (inconclusive) no decisivo

indeed /ɪn'di:d/ *adv* **1** (*as intensifier*): **thank you very much ~** muchísimas gracias; **this is ~ a great privilege** éste es un auténtico *or* verdadero privilegio **2** (in fact): **the wheel was ~ loose** en efecto, la rueda estaba suelta; **if ~ he is right** si es que tiene razón

indefensible /ˌɪndɪ'fensəbəl/ *adj* inexcusable

indefinite /ɪn'defənət ‖ ɪn'defɪnət/ *adj* **1 (a)** ‹*number/period/outline*› indefinido **2** ▶ 443 (Ling): **~ article** artículo *m* indefinido

indelible /ɪn'deləbəl/ *adj* indeleble

indelicate /ɪn'deləkət ‖ ɪn'delɪkət/ *adj* **(a)** (vulgar) indelicado **(b)** (tactless) indiscreto

indemnify /ɪn'demnəfaɪ ‖ ɪn'demnɪfaɪ/ *vt* **-fies, -fying, -fied (a)** (insure) asegurar **(b)** (compensate) indemnizar*

indemnity /ɪn'demnəti/ *n* (*pl* **-ties**) **(a)** [U] (insurance) indemnidad *f* **(b)** [C] (compensation) indemnización *f*

indent /ɪn'dent/ *vt* **(a)** ‹*line/paragraph*› sangrar **(b)** ‹*surface/edge*› marcar*

independence /'ɪndɪ'pendəns/ *n* [U] independencia *f*

Independence Day *n* día *m* de la Independencia

independent /'ɪndɪ'pendənt/ *adj* independiente

in-depth /'ɪn'depθ/ *adj* (*before n*) a fondo

indescribable /'ɪndɪ'skraɪbəbəl/ *adj* indescriptible

indestructible /'ɪndɪ'strʌktəbəl/ *adj* indestructible

indeterminate /'ɪndɪ'tɜ:rmənət ‖ ˌɪndɪ'tɜ:mɪnət/ *adj* indeterminado

index[1] /'ɪndeks/ *n* **1** (*pl* **indexes**) **(a)** (in book, journal) índice *m* **(b)** (list) lista *f*; (*before n*) **~ card** ficha *f* **2** (*pl* **indexes** *o* **indices**) (Econ, Fin) índice *m* **3** (*pl* **indices**) (Math) índice *m*

index[2] *vt* **1** (Publ) **(a)** (provide with index) ponerle* un índice a **(b)** (enter in index) incluir* en un índice **2** (Econ, Fin) ‹*prices/wages*› indexar

index: **~ finger** *n* (dedo *m*) índice *m*; **~-linked** /'ɪndeks'lɪŋkt/ *adj* (esp BrE) indexado

India /'ɪndiə/ *n* la India

Indian[1] /'ɪndiən/ *adj* **1** (of India) indio **2** (of America) indígena, indio

Indian[2] *n* **1** (person from India) indio, -dia *m,f* **2** (*American* ~) indígena *mf*, indio, -dia *m,f*

Indian: **~ Ocean** *n* **the ~ Ocean** el (Océano) Índico; **~ summer** *n* (in northern hemisphere) ≈ veranillo *m* de San Martín *or* de San Miguel; (in southern hemisphere) ≈ veranillo *m* de San Juan

indicate /'ɪndəkeɪt ‖ 'ɪndɪkeɪt/ *vt* **1 (a)** (point out) señalar **(b)** (Auto) indicar* **2 (a)** (show) ‹*change/condition*› ser* indicio de **(b)** (state) señalar ■ **~** *vi* (BrE Auto) indicar*, señalizar*, poner* el intermitente *or* (Col, Méx) las direccionales *or* (Chi) el señalizador

indication /'ɪndə'keɪʃən ‖ ˌɪndɪ'keɪʃən/ *n* **(a)** [C U] (sign, hint) indicio *m* **(b)** [C] (Med) indicación *f*

indicative[1] /ɪn'dɪkətɪv/ *adj* **1** (revealing) (frml) **to be ~ OF sth** ser* indicio DE algo **2** (Ling) ‹*mood/form*› indicativo

indicative[2] *n* (Ling) indicativo *m*

indicator /'ɪndəkeɪtər ‖ 'ɪndɪkeɪtə(r)/ *n* **1 (a)** (pointer) indicador *m* **(b)** (instrument) indicador *m* **2** (Auto) intermitente *m*, direccional *f* (Col, Méx), señalizador *m* (de viraje) (Chi) **3** (sign) indicador *m*

indices /'ɪndəsi:z ‖ 'ɪndɪsi:z/ *pl of* INDEX[1] 2,3

indict /ɪn'daɪt/ *vt* (Law) acusar

indictment /ɪn'daɪtmənt/ *n* **1** (Law) [C U] acusación *f* **2** [C] (criticism): **the report was an ~ of his management** el informe censuraba su gestión

indifference /ɪn'dɪfrəns/ *n* [U] indiferencia *f*

indifferent /ɪn'dɪfrənt/ *adj* **1** (uninterested) indiferente **2** (mediocre) mediocre

indigenous /ɪn'dɪdʒənəs/ *adj* ‹*population/language*› indígena, autóctono; ‹*species*› autóctono

indigestible /ˈɪndarˈdʒestəbəl, -də- ‖ˌɪndɪˈdʒest əbəl/ *adj* (impossible to digest) no digerible; (hard to digest) indigesto

indigestion /ˈɪndarˈdʒestʃən, -də- ‖ˌɪndɪˈdʒes tʃən/ *n* [U] indigestión *f*

indignant /ɪnˈdɪgnənt/ *adj* indignado

indignation /ˈɪndɪgˈneɪʃən/ *n* [U] indignación *f*

indignity /ɪnˈdɪgnəti/ *n* [U C] (*pl* **-ties**) humillación *f*

indigo /ˈɪndɪgəʊ/ ▶ 515 *n* [U] índigo *m*, añil *m*; (*before n*) ‹*ink/sea*› color añil *adj inv*

indirect /ˈɪndəˈrekt, -daɪ- ‖ˌɪndɪˈrekt, -daɪ-/ *adj* **1 (a)** ‹*route/method*› indirecto; ‹*result/benefit*› indirecto **(b)** (Ling) ‹*statement/question*› indirecto; **~ discourse** *o* (BrE) **speech** estilo *m* indirecto **2** (Fin) ‹*costs/taxes*› indirecto

indirectly /ˈɪndəˈrektli, -daɪ- ‖ˌɪndɪˈrektli, -daɪ-/ *adv* indirectamente

indiscreet /ˈɪndɪsˈkriːt/ *adj* indiscreto

indiscretion /ˈɪndɪsˈkreʃən/ *n* [C U] indiscreción *f*

indiscriminate /ˈɪndɪsˈkrɪmənət ‖ˌɪndɪˈskrɪ mɪnət/ *adj* indiscriminado

indispensable /ˈɪndɪsˈpensəbəl/ *adj* indispensable

indisposed /ˈɪndɪˈspəʊzd/ *adj* (frml) (*pred*) (ill) **to be ~** estar* indispuesto (frml)

indisputable /ˈɪndɪˈspjuːtəbəl/ *adj* ‹*evidence/proof*› irrefutable; ‹*leader/winner*› indiscutible

indistinct /ˈɪndɪˈstɪŋkt/ *adj* ‹*sound/shape*› poco definido; ‹*speech*› poco claro

indistinguishable /ˈɪndɪˈstɪŋgwɪʃəbəl/ *adj* **~ (FROM sth)** indistinguible (DE algo)

individual¹ /ˈɪndəˈvɪdʒuəl ‖ˌɪndɪˈvɪdjʊəl/ *adj* **1** (*before n*) (*no comp*) **(a)** (for one person) ‹*portion*› individual; ‹*tuition*› personal **(b)** (single, separate): **you can purchase the whole set or ~ items** se puede comprar el juego o cada pieza por separado **(c)** (particular, personal) ‹*style*› personal **2** (distinctive) personal

individual² *n* **(a)** (single person, animal) individuo *m* **(b)** (person) (colloq) individuo, -dua *m,f*

indivisible /ˈɪndəˈvɪzəbəl ‖ˌɪndɪˈvɪzəbəl/ *adj* indivisible

indoctrinate /ɪnˈdɑːktrəneɪt ‖ɪnˈdɒktrɪneɪt/ *vt* adoctrinar

indolent /ˈɪndələnt/ *adj* (frml) indolente

Indonesia /ˈɪndəˈniːʒə ‖ˌɪndəˈniːziə/ *n* Indonesia *f*

Indonesian¹ /ˈɪndəˈniːʒən ‖ˌɪndəˈniːziən/ *adj* indonesio

Indonesian² *n* **(a)** [C] (person) indonesio, -sia *m,f* **(b)** [U] (language) indonesio *m*

indoor /ˈɪndɔːr ‖ˈɪndɔː(r)/ *adj* (*before n*) ‹*clothes/shoes*› para estar en casa; ‹*plants*› de interior(es); ‹*swimming pool*› cubierto, techado

indoors /ˈɪnˈdɔːrz ‖ˌɪnˈdɔːz/ *adv* dentro, adentro (esp AmL)

induce /ɪnˈduːs ‖ɪnˈdjuːs/ *vt* **1** (persuade) **to ~ sb to + INF** inducir* a algn A + INF **2** (Med) ‹*sleep/labor*› inducir*

inducement /ɪnˈduːsmənt ‖ɪnˈdjuːsmənt/ *n* incentivo *m*

induction /ɪnˈdʌkʃən/ *n* [U] **1** (introduction) **~ (INTO sth)** iniciación *f* (EN algo); (*before n*) ‹*course/period*› introductorio **2** (Med) (of labor) inducción *f*

indulge /ɪnˈdʌldʒ/ *vt* ‹*child*› consentir*, mimar; ‹*desire*› satisfacer*; **it doesn't hurt to ~ oneself every now and again** es bueno darse algún gusto de vez en cuando ■ **~** *vi* **to ~ IN sth** permitirse algo

indulgence /ɪnˈdʌldʒəns/ *n* **(a)** [C] (extravagance): **an occasional cigar is my only ~** un puro de vez en cuando es el único lujo que me permito **(b)** [U] (partaking): **too much ~ in anything is bad** es malo abusar de cualquier placer

indulgent /ɪnˈdʌldʒənt/ *adj* indulgente

industrial /ɪnˈdʌstriəl/ *adj* ‹*town/production/engineering*› industrial; **~ dispute** conflicto *m* laboral

industrial estate *n* (BrE) zona *f* industrial, polígono *m* industrial (Esp)

industrialist /ɪnˈdʌstriələst ‖ɪnˈdʌstriəlɪst/ *n* industrial *mf*

industrialize /ɪnˈdʌstriəlaɪz/ *vt* industrializar*

industrial: **~ park** *n* (AmE) zona *f* industrial, polígono *m* industrial (Esp); **I~ Revolution** *n* **the I~ Revolution** la Revolución Industrial

industrious /ɪnˈdʌstriəs/ *adj* ‹*worker*› trabajador; ‹*student*› aplicado

industry /ˈɪndəstri/ *n* (*pl* **-tries**) [U C] industria *f*; **the steel ~** la industria siderúrgica; **the tourist ~** el turismo

inebriated /ɪnˈiːbrieɪtəd ‖ɪnˈiːbrieɪtɪd/ *adj* (frml) ‹*person*› beodo (frml), ebrio (frml); ‹*state*› de embriaguez (frml)

inedible /ɪnˈedəbəl/ *adj* (impossible to eat) no comestible; (unpalatable) incomible

ineffective /ˈɪnəˈfektɪv ‖ˌɪnɪˈfektɪv/ *adj* ‹*measure*› ineficaz; ‹*attempt*› infructuoso; ‹*person*› incompetente

inefficiency /ˈɪnəˈfɪʃənsi ‖ˌɪnɪˈfɪʃənsi/ *n* [U] (of machinery) falta *f* de eficiencia; (of persons, method) ineficiencia *f*

inefficient /ˈɪnəˈfɪʃənt ‖ˌɪnɪˈfɪʃənt/ *adj* ineficiente

ineligible /ɪnˈelədʒəbəl ‖ɪnˈelɪdʒəbəl/ *adj* (*usu pred*) ‹*candidate*› inelegible; **she was ~ to vote** no tenía derecho a votar

inept /ɪˈnept/ *adj* ‹*person*› inepto; ‹*conduct*› torpe

inequality /ˈɪnɪˈkwɑːləti ‖ˌɪnɪˈkwɒləti/ *n* (*pl* **-ties**) desigualdad *f*

inert /ɪˈnɜːrt ‖ɪˈnɜːt/ *adj* inerte

inertia /ɪˈnɜːrʃə ‖ɪˈnɜːʃə/ *n* [U] inercia *f*

inevitable¹ /ɪnˈevətəbəl ‖ɪnˈevɪtəbəl/ *adj* inevitable

inevitable² *n* **the ~** lo inevitable

inevitably /ɪnˈevətəbli ‖ɪnˈevɪtəbli/ *adv* inevitablemente

inexact /ˈɪnɪgˈzækt/ *adj* inexacto

inexcusable /ˈɪnɪkˈskjuːzəbəl/ *adj* imperdonable

inexpensive /ˈɪnɪkˈspensɪv/ *adj* económico

inexperience /ˈɪnɪkˈspɪriəns ‖ˌɪnɪkˈspɪəriəns/ *n* [U] inexperiencia *f*, falta *f* de experiencia

inexperienced /ˈɪnɪkˈspɪriənst ‖ˌɪnɪkˈspɪəriənst/ *adj* ‹*nurse/pilot*› sin experiencia; ‹*swimmer/driver*› inexperto, novato

inexpert /ɪnˈekspɜːrt ‖ ɪnˈekspɜːt/ *adj* inexperto

inexplicable /ˈɪnɪkˈsplɪkəbəl/ *adj* inexplicable

inextricably /ˈɪnɪkˈstrɪkəbli/ *adv* inextricablemente

infallible /ɪnˈfæləbəl/ *adj* infalible

infamous /ˈɪnfəməs/ *adj* **(a)** (notorious) de triste fama **(b)** (shameful) infame

infancy /ˈɪnfənsi/ *n* [U] primera infancia *f*

infant /ˈɪnfənt/ *n* **(a)** (baby) bebé *m*, niño, -ña *m,f* **(b)** (BrE Educ) niño, -ña *m,f* (*entre cinco y siete años de edad*); (*before n*) **~ school** (in UK) *escuela para niños de entre cinco y siete años de edad*

infantile /ˈɪnfəntaɪl/ *adj* pueril, infantil

infantry /ˈɪnfəntri/ *n* [U] (+ *sing or pl vb*) infantería *f*

infatuated /ɪnˈfætʃueɪtəd ‖ ɪnˈfætjʊeɪtɪd/ *adj* **to be ~ WITH sb** estar* encaprichado CON *or* (Esp tb) DE algn

infatuation /ɪnˈfætʃuˈeɪʃən ‖ɪnˌfætjʊˈeɪʃən/ *n* [U C] encaprichamiento *m*

infect /ɪnˈfekt/ *vt* ‹*wound/cut*› infectar; ‹*person/animal*› contagiar; **the wound became ~ed** la herida se infectó

infection /ɪnˈfekʃən/ *n* **(a)** [C] (disease) infección *f* **(b)** [U] (of wound) infección *f*; (of person) contagio *m*

infectious /ɪnˈfekʃəs/ *adj* ‹*disease*› infeccioso, contagioso; ‹*laughter/enthusiasm*› contagioso

infer /ɪnˈfɜːr ‖ ɪnˈfɜː(r)/ *vt* **-rr-** (deduce) **to ~ sth** (**FROM sth**) inferir* *or* deducir* algo (DE algo)

inferior¹ /ɪnˈfɪriər ‖ ɪnˈfɪəriə(r)/ *adj* (*no comp*) ‹*product*› (de calidad) inferior; ‹*workmanship/rank*› inferior

inferior² *n* inferior *mf*

inferiority /ɪnˈfɪriˈɔːrəti ‖ ɪnˌfɪərɪˈɒrəti/ *n* [U] inferioridad *f*; (*before n*) **~ complex** complejo *m* de inferioridad

inferno /ɪnˈfɜːrnəʊ ‖ ɪnˈfɜːnəʊ/ *n* (*pl* **-noes**) (journ): **the building was a blazing ~** el edificio estaba totalmente envuelto en llamas

infertile /ɪnˈfɜːrtl̩ ‖ ɪnˈfɜːtaɪl/ *adj* ‹*land*› estéril, infecundo; ‹*woman/man/animal*› estéril

infertility /ˈɪnfərˈtɪləti ‖ˌɪnfəˈtɪləti/ *n* [U] (Agr) infecundidad *f*; (Biol) esterilidad *f*

infest /ɪnˈfest/ *vt* infestar

infidelity /ˈɪnfəˈdeləti ‖ˌɪnfɪˈdeləti/ *n* [U C] (*pl* **-ties**) infidelidad *f*

infighting /ˈɪnˌfaɪtɪŋ/ *n* [U] luchas *fpl* internas

infiltrate /ɪnˈfɪltreɪt ‖ ˈɪnfɪltreɪt/ *vt* infiltrarse en

infiltrator /ɪnˈfɪltreɪtər ‖ ˈɪnfɪltreɪtə(r)/ *n* infiltrado, -da *m,f*

infinite /ˈɪnfənət ‖ ˈɪnfɪnət/ *adj* infinito

infinitesimal /ˈɪnfɪnəˈtesɪml̩ ‖ˌɪnfɪnɪˈtesɪml̩/ *adj* infinitesimal

infinitive /ɪnˈfɪnətɪv/ *n* infinitivo *m*

infinity /ɪnˈfɪnəti/ *n* **(a)** [U] (Math) infinito *m* **(b)** [U] (endless space) infinito *m* **(c)** (vast number, quantity) (liter) (*no pl*) infinidad *f*

infirm /ɪnˈfɜːrm ‖ ɪnˈfɜːm/ *adj* (weak) endeble; (ill) enfermo

infirmary /ɪnˈfɜːrməri ‖ ɪnˈfɜːməri/ *n* (*pl* **-ries**) (used in titles) hospital *m*

infirmity /ɪnˈfɜːrməti ‖ ɪnˈfɜːməti/ *n* [C U] (*pl* **-ties**) dolencia *f* (frml), padecimiento *m*

inflame /ɪnˈfleɪm/ *vt* ‹*person/passion*› encender*; ‹*situation*› exacerbar

inflamed /ɪnˈfleɪmd/ *adj* inflamado; **to become ~** inflamarse

inflammable /ɪnˈflæməbəl/ *adj* inflamable, flamable (Méx)

inflammation /ˈɪnfləˈmeɪʃən/ *n* [U C] inflamación *f*

inflate /ɪnˈfleɪt/ *vt* (with air, gas) inflar, hinchar (Esp)

inflation /ɪnˈfleɪʃən/ *n* [U] inflación *f*

inflexible /ɪnˈfleksəbəl/ *adj* ‹*personality/regulations*› inflexible; ‹*material*› rígido

inflict /ɪnˈflɪkt/ *vt* ‹*pain/damage*› causar; ‹*punishment*› imponer*; **to ~ sth ON sb**: **the suffering which he ~ed on his family** el sufrimiento que le causó a su familia

influence¹ /ˈɪnfluəns/ *n* [C U] influencia *f*: **she's a good/bad ~ on him** ejerce buena/mala influencia sobre él

influence² *vt* influir* en, influenciar

influential /ˈɪnfluˈentʃəl ‖ˌɪnflʊˈenʃəl/ *adj* influyente

influenza /ˈɪnfluˈenzə/ *n* [U] (Med) gripe *f* *or* (Chi tb) influenza *f* *or* (Col, Méx) gripa *f*

influx /ˈɪnflʌks/ *n* [U C] (of people) afluencia *f*; (of goods) entrada *f*; (of ideas) llegada *f*

inform /ɪnˈfɔːrm ‖ ɪnˈfɔːm/ *vt* informar; **to keep sb ~ed** mantener* a algn informado *or* al corriente ■ **~** *vi* **to ~ ON sb** delatar *or* denunciar a algn

informal /ɪnˈfɔːrməl ‖ ɪnˈfɔːməl/ *adj* informal

informality /ˈɪnfɔːrˈmæləti ‖ˌɪnfɔːˈmæləti/ *n* [U] falta *f* de ceremonia, informalidad *f*

informally /ɪnˈfɔːrməli ‖ ɪnˈfɔːməli/ *adv* **(a)** (casually) ‹*talk/dress*› de manera informal **(b)** (unofficially) ‹*meet/discuss*› informalmente

informant /ɪnˈfɔːrmənt ‖ ɪnˈfɔːmənt/ *n* informante *mf*

information /ˈɪnfərˈmeɪʃən ‖ˌɪnfəˈmeɪʃən/ *n* [U] información *f*; **a piece of ~** un dato; (*before n*) **~ desk** información *f*

information technology *n* informática *f*

informative /ɪnˈfɔːrmətɪv ‖ ɪnˈfɔːmətɪv/ *adj* ‹*article/lecture*› instructivo, informativo; ‹*guidebook*› lleno de información, informativo

informed /ɪnˈfɔːrmd ‖ ɪnˈfɔːmd/ *adj* ‹*source*› bien informado; ‹*criticism/approach*› bien fundado

informer /ɪnˈfɔːrmər ‖ ɪnˈfɔːmə(r)/ *n* informante *mf*

infrared /ˈɪnfrəˈred/ *adj* infrarrojo

infrastructure /ˈɪnfrəˈstrʌktʃər ‖ ˈɪnfrəˌstrʌktʃə(r)/ *n* infraestructura *f*

infrequent /ɪnˈfriːkwənt/ *adj* poco frecuente

infringe /ɪn'frɪndʒ/ *vt* ‹*contract*› no cumplir (con); ‹*treaty/rule*› infringir* ■ ~ *vi* **to ~ ON** *o* **UPON sth** violar algo

infringement /ɪn'frɪndʒmənt/ *n* [C U] (of law) contravención *f*, violación *f*; (of contract) incumplimiento *m*; (Sport) falta *f*; (of rights) violación *f*

infuriate /ɪn'fjʊrieɪt ‖ ɪn'fjʊərieɪt/ *vt* enfurecer*

infuriating /ɪn'fjʊrieɪtɪŋ ‖ ɪn'fjʊərieɪtɪŋ/ *adj* exasperante

infuse /ɪn'fju:z/ *vt* ‹*tea/herb*› hacer* una infusión de

infusion /ɪn'fju:ʒən/ *n* [C U] infusión *f*

ingenious /ɪn'dʒi:njəs ‖ ɪn'dʒi:niəs/ *adj* ingenioso

ingenuity /ˌɪndʒə'nu:əti ‖ ˌɪndʒə'nju:əti/ *n* [U] (of person) ingenio *m*; (of gadget, idea) lo ingenioso

ingenuous /ɪn'dʒenjuəs/ *adj* ingenuo

ingot /'ɪŋgət/ *n* lingote *m*

ingrained /'ɪn'greɪnd/ *adj* **(a)** ‹*belief/habit*› arraigado **(b)** ‹*dirt*› incrustado

ingratiate /ɪn'greɪʃieɪt/ *v refl* **to ~ oneself** (WITH **sb**) congraciarse (CON algn)

ingratitude /ɪn'grætətu:d ‖ ɪn'grætɪtju:d/ *n* [U] ingratitud *f*

ingredient /ɪn'gri:diənt/ *n* **(a)** (Culin) ingrediente *m* **(b)** (Pharm) componente *m* **(c)** (element) elemento *m*

ingrowing /'ɪn'grəʊɪŋ/ *adj* (BrE) ‹*toenail*› encarnado

ingrown /'ɪngrəʊn/ *adj* ‹*toenail*› encarnado

inhabit /ɪn'hæbət ‖ ɪn'hæbɪt/ *vt* habitar (frml), vivir en

inhabitant /ɪn'hæbətənt ‖ ɪn'hæbɪtənt/ *n* habitante *mf*

inhale /ɪn'heɪl/ *vi* aspirar

inhaler /ɪn'heɪlər ‖ ɪn'heɪlə(r)/ *n* inhalador *m*

inherent /ɪn'hɪrənt, -'her- ‖ ɪn'hɪərənt, -'her-/ *adj* inherente; **to be ~ IN sth** ser* inherente A algo

inherit /ɪn'herət ‖ ɪn'herɪt/ *vt* heredar

inheritance /ɪn'herətəns ‖ ɪn'herɪtəns/ *n* **(a)** [C] (sth inherited) herencia *f* **(b)** [U] (act) sucesión *f*

inhibit /ɪn'hɪbət ‖ ɪn'hɪbɪt/ *vt* (frml) inhibir

inhibited /ɪn'hɪbətəd ‖ ɪn'hɪbɪtɪd/ *adj* inhibido

inhibition /'ɪnə'bɪʃən ‖ ˌɪnhɪ'bɪʃən/ *n* inhibición *f*

inhospitable /ˌɪnhɑ:'spɪtəbəl ‖ ˌɪnhɒ'spɪtəbəl/ *adj* ‹*person*› poco hospitalario; ‹*climate/region*› inhóspito

in-house /'ɪnhaʊs/ *adj* ‹*training*› en la empresa (*or* organización *etc*); ‹*staff*› interno

inhuman /ɪn'hju:mən/ *adj* inhumano

inhumane /'ɪnhju:'meɪn/ *adj* ‹*treatment*› inhumano; ‹*person*› cruel

inhumanity /'ɪnhju:'mænəti/ *n* (*pl* **-ties**) **(a)** [U] (cruelty) crueldad *f* **(b)** [C] (cruel act) atrocidad *f*

inimitable /ɪn'ɪmətəbəl ‖ ɪ'nɪmɪtəbəl/ *adj* inimitable

initial¹ /ɪ'nɪʃəl/ *adj* inicial

initial² *n* inicial *f*

initial³ *vt*, (BrE) **-ll-** inicialar

initially /ɪ'nɪʃəli/ *adv* inicialmente

initiate /ɪ'nɪʃieɪt/ *vt* **1** (start) (frml) ‹*talks*› iniciar (frml); ‹*reform/plan*› poner* en marcha **2** (admit, introduce) **to ~ sb** (INTO **sth**) iniciar a algn (EN algo)

initiation /ɪ'nɪʃi'eɪʃən/ *n* **1** [C U] (admission) iniciación *f*; (*before n*) **~ ceremony** ceremonia *f* iniciática **2** [U] (of plan, talks) inicio *m* (frml)

initiative /ɪ'nɪʃətɪv/ *n* [C U] iniciativa *f*; **on one's own ~** por iniciativa propia; **to take the ~** tomar la iniciativa

inject /ɪn'dʒekt/ *vt* ‹*drug*› inyectar; **to ~ sth** (INTO **sth**) ‹*capital/resources*› inyectarle algo (A algo)

injection /ɪn'dʒekʃən/ *n* [C U] inyección *f*

injunction /ɪn'dʒʌŋkʃən/ *n* (Law) mandamiento *m* judicial

injure /'ɪndʒər ‖ 'ɪndʒə(r)/ *vt* **(a)** ▶ **484** ‹*person/feelings*› herir* **(b) injured** *past p*: **she gave me an ~d look** me miró con expresión ofendida; **I am the ~d party** soy yo quien sufrió el agravio

injurious /ɪn'dʒʊriəs ‖ ɪn'dʒʊəriəs/ *adj* (frml) perjudicial

injury /'ɪndʒəri/ *n* [C U] (*pl* **-ries**) herida *f*; (*before n*) **~ time** (BrE Sport) tiempo *m* de descuento

injustice /ɪn'dʒʌstəs ‖ ɪn'dʒʌstɪs/ *n* [U C] injusticia *f*; **to do sb an ~** cometer una injusticia con algn

ink /ɪŋk/ *n* [U C] tinta *f*

inkling /'ɪŋklɪŋ/ *n* [U]: **I had an ~ something had gone wrong** tuve el presentimiento *or* (CS, Per tb) el pálpito de que algo había salido mal

inkwell /'ɪŋkwel/ *n* tintero *m* (*empotrado en un escritorio*)

inlaid¹ /'ɪn'leɪd/ *past & past p of* INLAY²

inlaid² *adj* ‹*design*› de marquetería; ‹*box/lid*› con incrustaciones

inland¹ /'ɪnlənd/ *adj* (*before n*) ‹*town*› del interior; ‹*sea*› interior

inland² /'ɪn'lænd/ *adv* tierra adentro

Inland Revenue /'ɪnlənd/ *n* (in UK) **the ~ ~** ≈Hacienda, ≈la Dirección General Impositiva (*en RPl*), ≈Impuestos Internos (*en Chi*)

in-laws /'ɪnlɔ:z/ *pl n* (colloq) (spouse's parents) suegros *mpl*; (spouse's family) parientes *mpl* políticos

inlay¹ /'ɪnleɪ/ *n* [U C] (of wood, metal, ivory) incrustación *f*

inlay² /'ɪn'leɪ/ *vt* (*past & past p* **inlaid**) **to ~ sth** WITH **sth** hacer* incrustaciones de algo EN algo

inlet /'ɪnlet/ *n* (in coastline) ensenada *f*, entrada *f*; (of river, sea) brazo *m*

inmate /'ɪnmeɪt/ *n* (of asylum) interno, -na *m,f*; (of prison) preso, -sa *m,f*; (of hospital) paciente hospitalizado, -da *m,f*

inmost /'ɪnməʊst/ *adj* ⇒ INNERMOST

inn /ɪn/ *n* (tavern) taberna *f*; (hotel) hostal *m*

innards /'ɪnərdz ‖ 'ɪnədz/ *pl n* tripas *fpl* (fam)

innate /ɪ'neɪt/ *adj* innato

inner /'ɪnər ‖ 'ɪnə(r)/ *adj* (*before n, no comp*) **(a)** ‹*room/part*› interior; **the ~ city** *la zona del centro urbano habitada por familias de escasos ingresos, caracterizada por problemas sociales etc* **(b)** (of person) ‹*life*› interior; ‹*thoughts*› íntimo

innermost /'ɪnərməʊst ‖ 'ɪnəməʊst/ *adj* ‹*part/chamber*› más recóndito; ‹*thoughts*› más íntimo

inner tube *n* cámara *f*

inning /'ɪnɪŋ/ *n* (in baseball) entrada *f*, manga *f*

innings /'ɪnɪŋz/ *n* (*pl* ~) (in cricket) entrada *f*

innkeeper /'ɪnˌki:pər ‖ 'ɪnˌki:pə(r)/ *n* posadero, -ra *m,f*

innocence /'ɪnəsəns/ *n* [U] inocencia *f*

innocent /'ɪnəsənt/ *adj* inocente

innocuous /ɪ'nɑ:kjuəs ‖ ɪ'nɒkjʊəs/ *adj* ‹*drug*› inocuo; ‹*person/comment*› inofensivo

innovation /'ɪnə'veɪʃən/ *n* [C U] innovación *f*

innovative /'ɪnəveɪtɪv ‖ 'ɪnəvətɪv/ *adj* innovador

innuendo /'ɪnju'endəʊ/ *n* [C U] (*pl* **-dos** *or* **-does**) indirecta *f*, insinuación *f*

innumerable /ɪ'nu:mərəbəl ‖ ɪ'nju:mərəbəl/ *adj* innumerable

inoculate /ɪ'nɑ:kjəleɪt ‖ ɪ'nɒkjʊleɪt/ *vt* inocular

inoculation /ɪ'nɑ:kjə'leɪʃən ‖ ɪˌnɒkjʊ'leɪʃən/ *n* [C U] inoculación *f*

inoffensive /'ɪnə'fensɪv/ *adj* inofensivo

inordinate /ɪ'nɔ:rdṇət ‖ ɪn'ɔ:dɪnət/ *adj*: **an ~ amount of money** una cantidad exorbitante de dinero; **they are making ~ demands** lo que piden es excesivo

inpatient /'ɪnˌpeɪʃənt/ *n* paciente hospitalizado, -da *m,f*

input[1] /'ɪnpʊt/ *n* **1** [U C] **(a)** (of resources) aportación *f*, aporte *m* (esp AmL) **(b)** (contribution) aportación *f*, aporte *m* (esp AmL) **2** [U C] (Comput) entrada *f*

input[2] *vt* (*pres p* **inputting**; *past & past p* **input** *or* **inputted**) ‹*data*› entrar

inquest /'ɪnkwest/ *n* investigación *f*

inquire, (BrE) **enquire** /ɪn'kwaɪr ‖ ɪn'kwaɪə(r)/ *vt* preguntar ■ ~ *vi* preguntar; **to ~** ABOUT **sth** informarse ACERCA DE algo

inquiring, (BrE) **enquiring** /ɪn'kwaɪrɪŋ ‖ ɪn'kwaɪərɪŋ/ *adj* (*before n*) ‹*mind*› curioso; ‹*look*› inquisitivo

inquiry, (BrE) **enquiry** /ɪn'kwaɪri, 'ɪnkwəri ‖ ɪn'kwaɪəri/ *n* (*pl* **-ries**) **(a)** (question): **we made inquiries about** *o* **into his past** hicimos averiguaciones sobre su pasado; **all inquiries to …** para cualquier información dirigirse a … **(b)** (investigation) investigación *f*

inquisition /'ɪnkwə'zɪʃən ‖ˌɪnkwɪ'zɪʃən/ *n* **(a)** (severe questioning) interrogatorio *m* **(b) the Spanish I~** la (Santa) Inquisición, el Santo Oficio

inquisitive /ɪn'kwɪzətɪv/ *adj* ‹*mind*› inquisitivo; ‹*person/animal*› muy curioso

inroads /'ɪnrəʊdz/ *pl n*: **we are making ~ into the Japanese market** estamos haciendo avances en el mercado japonés; **this made substantial ~ into her savings** esto le comió buena parte de los ahorros

INS *n* (in US) = **Immigration and Naturalization Service**

insane /ɪn'seɪn/ *adj* (mad) demente; (foolish) insensato

insanitary /ɪn'sænəteri ‖ ɪn'sænɪtəri/ *adj* malsano, insanitorio

insanity /ɪn'sænəti/ *n* [U] demencia *f*

insatiable /ɪn'seɪʃəbəl/ *adj* insaciable

inscribe /ɪn'skraɪb/ *vt* **to ~ sth** (ON **sth**) ‹*letters*› inscribir* algo (EN algo); ‹*design*› grabar algo (EN algo)

inscription /ɪn'skrɪpʃən/ *n* inscripción *f*

insect /'ɪnsekt/ *n* insecto *m*

insecticide /ɪn'sektəsaɪd ‖ ɪn'sektɪsaɪd/ *n* [C U] insecticida *m*

insecure /'ɪnsɪ'kjʊr ‖ˌɪnsɪ'kjʊə(r)/ *adj* **(a)** (unsafe, exposed) inseguro **(b)** (not firmly fixed) poco seguro **(c)** (not confident) inseguro

insecurity /'ɪnsɪ'kjʊrəti ‖ˌɪnsɪ'kjʊərəti/ *n* [U C] (*pl* **-ties**) inseguridad *f*

insemination /ɪn'semə'neɪʃən ‖ ɪnˌsemɪ'neɪʃən/ *n* [U C] inseminación *f*

insensible /ɪn'sensəbəl/ *adj* (frml) **(a)** (unconscious) inconsciente **(b)** (without sensation) insensible

insensitive /ɪn'sensətɪv/ *adj* ‹*person*› insensible; ‹*behavior*› falto de sensibilidad

insensitivity /ɪn'sensə'tɪvəti/ *n* [U] falta *f* de sensibilidad

inseparable /ɪn'seprəbəl/ *adj* inseparable

insert /ɪn'sɜ:rt ‖ ɪn'sɜ:t/ *vt* ‹*coin/token*› introducir*; ‹*zipper*› poner*; ‹*word/paragraph*› insertar

insertion /ɪn'sɜ:rʃən ‖ ɪn'sɜ:ʃən/ *n* introducción *f*

inshore[1] /'ɪn'ʃɔ:r ‖ˌɪn'ʃɔ:(r)/ *adj* costero

inshore[2] *adv* hacia la costa

inside[1] /'ɪn'saɪd/ *n* **1** (interior part) interior *m*; (inner side, surface) parte *f* de dentro *or* (esp AmL) de adentro **2 insides** *pl* (internal organs) (colloq) tripas *fpl* (fam) **3 inside out** *adv*: **turn it ~ out** ponlo de adentro para fuera; **you've got your socks on ~ out** llevas los calcetines del *or* al revés

inside[2] *prep* **(a)** (within) dentro de; **we did the journey ~ 3 hours** (colloq) hicimos el viaje en menos de 3 horas **(b)** (into): **he followed her ~ the bar** la siguió al interior del bar

inside[3] *adv* **(a)** (within, indoors) dentro, adentro (esp AmL); **come ~** entra, pasa **(b)** (in prison) (colloq) entre rejas (fam), a la sombra (fam)

inside[4] *adj* (*before n*) **(a)** ‹*pages*› interior; ‹*pocket*› interior, de adentro (esp AmL) **(b) the ~ lane** (Auto) el carril de la derecha; (in UK etc) el carril de la izquierda; (Sport) el carril (AmL) *or* (Esp) la calle número uno **(c)** (from within group) ‹*information*› de dentro, de adentro (esp AmL)

insider /ɪn'saɪdər ‖ ɪn'saɪdə(r)/ *n*: *persona que pertenece a una organización determinada o que tiene acceso a información confidencial*

insidious /ɪn'sɪdiəs/ *adj* insidioso

insight /'ɪnsaɪt/ *n* **(a)** [U] (perceptiveness) perspicacia *f* **(b)** [C] (comprehension): **to gain an ~ into sth** llegar* a comprender bien algo

insignia /ɪn'sɪgniə/ *n* (*pl* **~** *or* **~s**) insignia *f*

insignificant /'ɪnsɪg'nɪfɪkənt/ *adj* ‹*person/amount*› insignificante; ‹*detail*› nimio

insincere /'ɪnsɪn'sɪr ‖ˌɪnsɪn'sɪə(r)/ *adj* ‹*offer*› poco sincero; ‹*person/smile*› falso

insincerity /'ɪnsɪn'serəti/ *n* [U] falta *f* de sinceridad

insinuate /ɪn'sɪnjueɪt/ *vt* insinuar*

insinuation /ɪn'sɪnju'eɪʃən/ *n* [C U] insinuación *f*

insipid /ɪn'sɪpəd ‖ ɪn'sɪpɪd/ *adj* ‹*food/drink*› insípido; ‹*person/novel*› insulso

insist /ɪn'sɪst/ *vt* **(a)** (demand) **to ~ (THAT)** insistir EN QUE (+ *subj*) **(b)** (maintain) **to ~ (THAT)** insistir EN QUE ■ ~ *vi* insistir

● **insist on** [*v* + *prep* + *o*] **to ~ on -ING** insistir EN + INF/EN QUE (+ *subj*)

insistence /ɪn'sɪstəns/ *n* [U] insistencia *f*

insistent /ɪn'sɪstənt/ *adj* **(a)** (persistent) insistente; **to be ~ THAT** insistir EN QUE **(b)** (pressing) ‹*need*› apremiante

insofar as /'ɪnsə'fɑːr ‖ ˌɪnsə'fɑː(r)/ *conj* (frml) en la medida en que

insole /'ɪnsəʊl/ *n* plantilla *f*

insolence /'ɪnsələns/ *n* [U] insolencia *f*

insolent /'ɪnsələnt/ *adj* insolente

insolvent /ɪn'sɑːlvənt ‖ ɪn'sɒlvənt/ *adj* insolvente

insomnia /ɪn'sɑːmniə ‖ ɪn'sɒmniə/ *n* [U] insomnio *m*

insomniac /ɪn'sɑːmniæk ‖ ɪn'sɒmniæk/ *n* insomne *mf*

inspect /ɪn'spekt/ *vt* **(a)** (look closely at) ‹*car/camera*› revisar, examinar; (examine officially) ‹*school/restaurant/equipment*› inspeccionar **(b)** ‹*troops*› pasar revista a

inspection /ɪn'spekʃən/ *n* [C U] **(a)** (official examination) inspección *f* **(b)** (of troops) revista *f* **(c)** (scrutiny) examen *m*, revisión *f*

inspector /ɪn'spektər ‖ ɪn'spektə(r)/ *n* **(a)** (official) inspector, -tora *m,f* **(b)** (police officer) inspector, -tora *m,f* (de policía)

inspiration /'ɪnspə'reɪʃən/ *n* [U] inspiración *f*

inspire /ɪn'spaɪr ‖ ɪn'spaɪə(r)/ *vt* inspirar; ‹*hope/courage*› infundir; **what ~d you to do that?** ¿qué te movió *or* te llevó a hacer eso?

inspired /ɪn'spaɪrd ‖ ɪn'spaɪəd/ *adj* inspirado

inspiring /ɪn'spaɪrɪŋ ‖ ɪn'spaɪərɪŋ/ *adj* inspirador

instability /'ɪnstə'bɪləti/ *n* [U] inestabilidad *f*

install, **instal** /ɪn'stɔːl/ *vt* **-ll-** instalar

installation /'ɪnstə'leɪʃən/ *n* [U C] instalación *f*

installment, (BrE) **instalment** /ɪn'stɔːlmənt/ *n* **1** (payment) plazo *m*, cuota *f* (esp AmL); **to pay in *o* by ~s** pagar* a plazos, pagar* en cuotas (esp AmL) **2** (of publication) entrega *f*; (of TV, radio serial) episodio *m*

installment plan *n* (AmE) plan *m* de financiación; **to buy sth on an ~ ~** comprar algo a plazos, comprar algo en cuotas (esp AmL)

instance /'ɪnstəns/ *n* **(a)** (example) ejemplo *m*; **for ~** por ejemplo **(b)** (case) caso *m*; **in this ~** en este caso

instant¹ /'ɪnstənt/ *adj* instantáneo

instant² *n* **(a)** (precise moment) instante *m* **(b)** (short time) momento *m*

instantaneous /'ɪnstən'teɪniəs/ *adj* instantáneo

instantly /'ɪnstəntli/ *adv* al instante

instant replay *n* [C U] repetición *f* (de la jugada)

instead /ɪn'sted/ *adv*: **I couldn't go, so she went ~** no pude ir, así que fue ella (en vez de mí); **~ of** (*as prep*) en vez de, en lugar de

instep /'ɪnstep/ *n* (of foot — arch) arco *m* (del pie); (— upper surface) empeine *m*

instigate /'ɪnstəgeɪt ‖ 'ɪnstɪgeɪt/ *vt* ‹*rebellion/mutiny*› instigar* a

instigation /'ɪnstə'geɪʃən ‖ ˌɪnstɪ'geɪʃən/ *n* [U] instigación *f*; **it was carried out at the director's ~** se llevó a cabo a instancias del director

instill, **instil** /ɪn'stɪl/ *vt* **-ll-**: **to ~ sth IN/INTO sb** ‹*habit/attitude*› inculcarle* algo A algn; ‹*courage/fear*› infundirle algo A algn

instinct /'ɪnstɪŋkt/ *n* [C U] instinto *m*

instinctive /ɪn'stɪŋktɪv/ *adj* instintivo

institute¹ /'ɪnstətuːt ‖ 'ɪnstɪtjuːt/ *vt* (frml) ‹*search/inquiry*› iniciar; ‹*proceedings*› entablar

institute² *n* instituto *m*

institution /'ɪnstə'tuːʃən ‖ ˌɪnstɪ'tjuːʃən/ *n* **1** (established practice) institución *f* **2 (a)** (organization) organismo *m*; (building) institución *f* **(b)** (hospital, asylum, home) *establecimiento sanitario, penitenciario o de asistencia social*

institutional /'ɪnstə'tuːʃnəl ‖ ˌɪnstɪ'tjuːʃənl/ *adj* institucional

instruct /ɪn'strʌkt/ *vt* **1** (command) **to ~ sb to + INF** ordenar a algn QUE (+ *subj*) **2** (frml) (teach) **to ~ sb IN sth** enseñarle algo a algn

instruction /ɪn'strʌkʃən/ *n* [C U] instrucción *f*; ❸ **instructions (for use)** instrucciones; **they were acting on the ~s of the chief of police** cumplían órdenes del jefe de policía

instructive /ɪn'strʌktɪv/ *adj* instructivo

instructor /ɪn'strʌktər ‖ ɪn'strʌktə(r)/ *n* **(a)** (teacher) (Mil) instructor, -tora *m,f* **(b)** (in US colleges) profesor, -sora *m,f* auxiliar

instrument /'ɪnstrəmənt ‖ 'ɪnstrʊmənt/ *n* **1** (*musical ~*) instrumento *m* (musical) **2 (a)** (piece of equipment) instrumento *m* **(b) instruments** *pl n* (Aviat) instrumentos *mpl*; (Auto) instrumentación *f*

instrumental /'ɪnstrə'mentl ‖ ˌɪnstrʊ'mentl/ *adj* **1** (serving as a means) **to be ~ IN sth** jugar* un papel decisivo EN algo **2** (Mus) instrumental

instrument panel *n* (Auto) tablero *m* de mandos, salpicadero *m* (Esp); (Aviat) tablero *m* de mandos

insubordination /'ɪnsə'bɔːrdn̩'eɪʃən ‖ ˌɪnsəbɔːdɪ'neɪʃən/ *n* [U] insubordinación *f*

insubstantial /'ɪnsəb'stæntʃəl ‖ ˌɪnsəb'stænʃəl/ *adj* ‹*structure/object*› frágil; ‹*evidence/argument*› inconsistente

insufferable /ɪn'sʌfrəbəl/ *adj* (frml) ‹*person/rudeness*› insufrible; ‹*heat/noise*› insoportable

insufficient /'ɪnsə'fɪʃənt/ *adj* insuficiente

insular /'ɪnsələr ‖ 'ɪnsjʊlə(r)/ *adj* ‹*mentality*› cerrado; ‹*person*› estrecho de miras

insulate /'ɪnsəleɪt ‖ 'ɪnsjʊleɪt/ *vt* aislar*

insulation /'ɪnsə'leɪʃən ‖ ˌɪnsjʊ'leɪʃən/ *n* [U] aislamiento *m*

insulin /'ɪnsələn ‖ 'ɪnsjʊlɪn/ *n* [U] insulina *f*

insult¹ /ɪn'sʌlt/ *vt* insultar

insult² /'ɪnsʌlt/ *n* insulto *m*

insulting /ɪn'sʌltɪŋ/ *adj* insultante

insurance /ɪn'ʃʊrəns ‖ ɪn'ʃʊərəns, ɪn'ʃɔːrəns/ *n* seguro *m*; **to take out ~** hacerse* un seguro; (*before n*) **~ company** compañía *f* de seguros

insure /ɪn'ʃʊr ‖ ɪn'ʃʊə(r), ɪn'ʃɔː(r)/ *vt* **1** (Fin) asegurar **2** (AmE) ⇒ ENSURE

insurer /ɪn'ʃʊrər ‖ ɪn'ʃʊərə(r), ɪn'ʃɔːrə(r)/ *n* (company) compañía *f* de seguros; (person) asegurador, -dora *m,f*

insurgent /ɪn'sɜːrdʒənt ‖ ɪn'sɜːdʒənt/ *adj* (frml) insurgente (frml)

insurmountable /'ɪnsər'maʊntəbəl ‖ ˌɪnsə'maʊntəbəl/ *adj* (frml) ‹*difficulty*› insalvable

insurrection /'ɪnsə'rekʃən/ *n* [C U] (frml) insurrección *f* (frml)

intact /ɪn'tækt/ *adj* (*usu pred*) intacto

intake /'ɪnteɪk/ *n* **1** (of water, air) entrada *f*; (of calories, protein) consumo *m* **2** (Tech) (pipe, vent) toma *f* (de aire, agua *etc*)

intangible /ɪn'tændʒəbəl/ *adj* intangible

integral /'ɪntɪgrəl/ *adj* ‹*part/feature*› integral

integrate /'ɪntəgreɪt ‖ 'ɪntɪgreɪt/ *vt* integrar ■ **~** *vi* integrarse

integrated /'ɪntəgreɪtəd ‖ 'ɪntɪgreɪtɪd/ *adj* **(a)** ‹*system/network*› integrado **(b)** (not separate) ‹*component/feature*› incorporado **(c)** (nonsegregated) no segregacionista

integration /'ɪntə'greɪʃən ‖ ˌɪntɪ'greɪʃən/ *n* [U] integración *f*

integrity /ɪn'tegrəti/ *n* [U] integridad *f*

intellect /'ɪntḷekt ‖ 'ɪntəlekt/ *n* intelecto *m*

intellectual¹ /'ɪntə'lektʃuəl/ *adj* intelectual

intellectual² *n* intelectual *mf*

intelligence /ɪn'telədʒəns ‖ ɪn'telɪdʒəns/ *n* **1** (mental capacity) inteligencia *f* **2** [U] (Govt, Mil) **(a)** (information) inteligencia *f* **(b)** (department) servicio *m* de información

intelligent /ɪn'telədʒənt ‖ ɪn'telɪdʒənt/ *adj* inteligente

intelligible /ɪn'telədʒəbəl ‖ ɪn'telɪdʒəbəl/ *adj* inteligible

intemperate /ɪn'tempərət/ *adj* ‹*climate*› inclemente, riguroso

intend /ɪn'tend/ *vt*: **no insult was ~ed** no fue mi intención ofender; **to ~ -ING** *o* **to ~ to + INF** pensar* + INF; **to ~ sb/sth to + INF** querer* QUE algn/algo (+ *subj*)

intense /ɪn'tens/ *adj* intenso

intensely /ɪn'tensli/ *adv* (*as intensifier*) ‹*moving*› profundamente, sumamente; **I dislike him ~** siento una profunda antipatía hacia él

intensify /ɪn'tensəfaɪ ‖ ɪn'tensɪfaɪ/ **-fies, -fying, -fied** *vt* ‹*search*› intensificar*; ‹*efforts*› redoblar ■ **~** *vi* «*pain*» agudizarse*; «*search*» intensificarse*; «*fighting*» recrudecer*

intensity /ɪn'tensəti/ *n* intensidad *f*

intensive /ɪn'tensɪv/ *adj* intensivo

intensive care *n* [U] cuidados *mpl* intensivos, terapia *f* intensiva (Méx, RPl)

intent¹ /ɪn'tent/ *adj* **(a)** (determined) (*pred*) **to be ~ ON sth/-ING** estar* decidido *or* resuelto A + INF **(b)** (attentive, concentrated) ‹*expression*› de viva atención; ‹*look*› penetrante, fijo; **to be ~ ON sth** estar* abstraído EN algo

intent² *n* [U C] propósito *m*; ***to all ~s and purposes*** a efectos prácticos

intention /ɪn'tentʃən ‖ ɪn'tenʃən/ *n* [U C] intención *f*

intentional /ɪn'tentʃṇəl ‖ ɪn'tenʃənḷ/ *adj* ‹*destruction*› intencional; ‹*insult/cruelty*› deliberado

intently /ɪn'tentli/ *adv* ‹*listen*› atentamente; **he was staring ~ at them** tenía la mirada fija en ellos

inter /ɪn'tɜːr ‖ ɪn'tɜː(r)/ *vt* **-rr-** (frml *or* liter) inhumar (frml)

interact /'ɪntər'ækt/ *vi* «*people/organizations*» relacionarse

interaction /'ɪntər'ækʃən/ *n* [U C] interacción *f*

interactive /'ɪntər'æktɪv/ *adj* interactivo

intercede /'ɪntər'siːd ‖ ˌɪntə'siːd/ *vi* interceder

intercept /'ɪntər'sept ‖ ˌɪntə'sept/ *vt* interceptar; **they were ~ed before they reached the building** les cerraron el paso antes de llegar al edificio

interchange¹ /'ɪntər'tʃeɪndʒ ‖ ˌɪntə'tʃeɪndʒ/ *vt* intercambiar

interchange² /'ɪntərtʃeɪndʒ ‖ 'ɪntətʃeɪndʒ/ *n* **1** [U C] (exchange) intercambio *m* **2** [C] (on road system) enlace *m*, intercambiador *m* (Esp)

interchangeable /'ɪntər'tʃeɪndʒəbəl ‖ ˌɪntə'tʃeɪndʒəbəl/ *adj* intercambiable

intercity /'ɪntər'sɪti ‖ ˌɪntə'sɪti/ *adj* rápido interurbano

intercom /'ɪntərkɑːm ‖ 'ɪntəkɒm/ *n* **(a)** (on plane, ship, in office) interfono *m* **(b)** (at building entrance) (AmE) portero *m* eléctrico *or* (Esp) automático, interfón *m* (Méx), intercomunicador *m* (Ven)

intercourse /'ɪntərkɔːrs ‖ 'ɪntəkɔːs/ *n* [U] (*sexual* **~**) coito *m* (frml), acto *m* sexual; **to have ~ with sb** tener* relaciones sexuales con algn

interest¹ /'ɪntrəst/ *n* **1 (a)** [U] (enthusiasm) interés *m*; **to take (an) ~ IN sth/sb** interesarse POR algo/algn **(b)** [C] (hobby) interés *m* **2** [C] **(a)** (stake) participación *f*; **he has a number of business ~s abroad** tiene varios negocios en el extranjero **(b)** (advantage) (*often pl*) interés *m*; **it was not in our ~(s) to intervene** no nos convenía intervenir **3** [U] (Fin) interés *m*; (*before n*) **~ rate** tasa *f or* (esp Esp) tipo *m* de interés

interest² *vt* interesar

interested /'ɪntrəstəd ‖ 'ɪntrəstɪd/ *adj* interesado; **I am ~ in astronomy** me interesa la astronomía; **~ party** parte *f* interesada

interesting /'ɪntrəstɪŋ/ *adj* interesante

interface /'ɪntərfeɪs ‖ 'ɪntəfeɪs/ *n* (Comput) interface *f or m*, interfaz *f or m*, interfase *f or m*

interfere /'ɪntər'fɪr ‖ ˌɪntə'fɪə(r)/ *vi* **1** (get involved) **to ~ (IN sth)** entrometerse (EN algo) **2 (a)** (disrupt) **to ~ WITH sth** afectar (A) algo **(b)** (tamper) **to ~ WITH sth** tocar* algo

interference /'ɪntər'fɪrəns ‖ ˌɪntə'fɪərəns/ *n* [U] **(a)** (interfering) intromisión *f* **(b)** (Phys, Rad, Telec) interferencia *f*

interfering /'ɪntər'fɪrɪŋ ‖ ˌɪntə'fɪərɪŋ/ *adj* entrometido

interim¹ /ˈɪntərəm ‖ ˈɪntərɪm/ *adj* (*before n*) ‹*measure*› provisional, provisorio (AmS); **an ∼ period** un período intermedio

interim² *n*: **in** *o* **during the ∼** en el interín *or* ínterin

interior¹ /ɪnˈtɪriər ‖ ɪnˈtɪəriə(r)/ *n* **1 (a)** (of building) interior *m* **(b)** (Cin) interior *m* **2 (a)** (Geog) **the ∼** el interior **(b)** (Govt) **the Ministry/Department of the I∼** el Ministerio/Departamento del Interior

interior² *adj* **1 (a)** (inside) ‹*walls*› interior **(b)** (mental) interior **2** (inland) del interior

interior: **∼ decorator** *n* (painter) pintor, -tora *m, f*; (designer) interiorista *mf*, decorador, -dora *m,f* (de interiores); **∼ design** *n* [U] interiorismo *m*

interjection /ˈɪntərˈdʒekʃən ‖ ˌɪntəˈdʒekʃən/ *n* (Ling) interjección *f*; (exclamation) exclamación *f*

interloper /ˈɪntərləʊpər ‖ ˈɪntələʊpə(r)/ *n* intruso, -sa *m,f*

interlude /ˈɪntərluːd ‖ ˈɪntəluːd/ *n* **1** (intervening period) intervalo *m* **2 (a)** (Theat) (intermission) entreacto *m* **(b)** (Mus) interludio *m*

intermediary /ˈɪntərˈmidieri ‖ ˌɪntəˈmiːdiəri/ *n* (*pl* **-ries**) (frml) intermediario, -ria *m,f*

intermediate /ˈɪntərˈmiːdiət ‖ ˌɪntəˈmiːdiət/ *adj* ‹*stage/step*› intermedio; ‹*size/weight/level*› medio; ‹*course*› de nivel medio *or* intermedio

intermediate school *n* [C U] (in US) **(a)** (secondary) *escuela donde se cursa el primer ciclo de la enseñanza secundaria* **(b)** (primary) *escuela donde se cursa segundo ciclo de la enseñanza primaria*

interminable /ɪnˈtɜːrmənəbəl ‖ ɪnˈtɜːmɪnəbəl/ *adj* interminable

intermission /ˈɪntərˈmɪʃən ‖ ˌɪntəˈmɪʃən/ *n* intermedio *m*

intermittent /ˈɪntərˈmɪtn̩t ‖ ˌɪntəˈmɪtənt/ *adj* intermitente

intern¹ /ɪnˈtɜːrn ‖ ɪnˈtɜːn/ *vt* recluir*, confinar

intern² /ˈɪntɜːrn ‖ ˈɪntɜːn/ *n* (AmE) **(a)** (Med) interno, -na *m,f* **(b)** (Educ) profesor, -sora *m,f* en prácticas

internal /ɪnˈtɜːrnl̩ ‖ ɪnˈtɜːnl/ *adj* interno

Internal Revenue Service *n* (in US) **the ∼ ∼ ∼** ≈ Hacienda, ≈ la Dirección General Impositiva (*en RPl*), ≈ Impuestos Internos (*en Chi*)

international¹ /ˈɪntərˈnæʃnəl ‖ ˌɪntəˈnæʃənl/ *adj* internacional

international² *n* (Sport) **(a)** (event) partido *m* internacional **(b)** (player) internacional *mf*

internationally /ˈɪntərˈnæʃn̩əli ‖ ˌɪntəˈnæʃn̩əli/ *adv* **(a)** ‹*expand/trade*› internacionalmente **(b)** ‹*famous/known*› mundialmente

International Monetary Fund *n* **the ∼ ∼ ∼** el Fondo Monetario Internacional

Internet /ˈɪntərnet ‖ ˈɪntənet/ *n* **the ∼** el Internet

internment /ɪnˈtɜːrnmənt ‖ ɪnˈtɜːnmənt/ *n* [U] internamiento *m*

interpret /ɪnˈtɜːrprət ‖ ɪnˈtɜːprɪt/ *vt* interpretar ■ **∼** *vi* (Ling) (translate) traducir* (*oralmente*), interpretar

interpretation /ɪnˈtɜːrprəˈteɪʃən ‖ ɪnˌtɜːprɪˈteɪʃən/ *n* [C U] interpretación *f*

interpreter /ɪnˈtɜːrprətər ‖ ɪnˈtɜːprɪtə(r)/ *n* intérprete *mf*

interrogate /ɪnˈterəgeɪt/ *vt* interrogar*

interrogation /ɪnˈterəˈgeɪʃən/ *n* [U C] interrogatorio *m*

interrogation point *n* (AmE frml) signo *m* de interrogación

interrogative /ˈɪntəˈrɑːgətɪv ‖ ˌɪntəˈrɒgətɪv/ *adj* interrogativo

interrupt /ˈɪntəˈrʌpt/ *vt/i* interrumpir

interruption /ˈɪntəˈrʌpʃən/ *n* [C U] interrupción *f*

intersect /ˈɪntərˈsekt ‖ ˌɪntəˈsekt/ *vi* «*roads/paths*» cruzarse*

intersection /ˈɪntərˈsekʃən ‖ ˌɪntəˈsekʃən/ *n* **(a)** (Transp) cruce *m* **(b)** (Geog, Math) intersección *f*

intersperse /ˈɪntərˈspɜːrs ‖ ˌɪntəˈspɜːs/ *vt* intercalar

interstate (highway) /ˈɪntərsteɪt ‖ ˈɪntəsteɪt/ *n* (AmE) carretera *f* interestatal

intertwine /ˈɪntərˈtwaɪn ‖ ˌɪntəˈtwaɪn/ *vi* «*fingers/plants*» entrelazarse*; «*paths/destinies*» entrecruzarse* ■ **∼** *vt* ‹*fingers*› entrelazar*

interval /ˈɪntərvəl ‖ ˈɪntəvəl/ *n* **1** (time, distance) intervalo *m* **2** (pause) (BrE Cin, Mus) intermedio *m*; (BrE Theat) entreacto *m*; (Sport) descanso *m*, entretiempo *m* (Chi) **3** (Mus) intervalo *m*

intervene /ˈɪntərˈviːn ‖ ˌɪntəˈviːn/ *vi* **(a)** (interpose oneself) intervenir* **(b) intervening** *pres p*: **in the intervening period** en el interín *or* ínterin

intervention /ˈɪntərˈventʃən ‖ ˌɪntəˈvenʃən/ *n* intervención *f*

interview¹ /ˈɪntərvjuː ‖ ˈɪntəvjuː/ *n* entrevista *f*

interview² *vt* entrevistar

interviewee /ˈɪntərvjuːˈiː ‖ ˌɪntəvjuːˈiː/ *n* entrevistado, -da *m,f*

interviewer /ˈɪntərvjuːər ‖ ˈɪntəvjuːə(r)/ *n* entrevistador, -dora *m,f*

interweave /ˈɪntərˈwiːv ‖ ˌɪntəˈwiːv/ *vt* (*past* **-wove** *or* **-weaved**; *past p* **-woven** *or* **-weaved**) entretejer; **their lives were interwoven** sus vidas estaban inextricablemente unidas

intestate /ɪnˈtesteɪt/ *adj* intestado

intestine /ɪnˈtestən ‖ ɪnˈtestɪn/ *n* (*often pl*) intestino *m*; **the small/large ∼** el intestino delgado/grueso

intimacy /ˈɪntəməsi ‖ ˈɪntɪməsi/ *n* (*pl* **-cies**) [U] intimidad *f*

intimate /ˈɪntəmət ‖ ˈɪntɪmət/ *adj* ‹*friend/atmosphere*› íntimo; ‹*talk*› de carácter íntimo; ‹*knowledge*› profundo; **to be on ∼ terms with sb** ser* íntimo de algn

intimation /ˈɪntəˈmeɪʃən ‖ ˌɪntɪˈmeɪʃən/ *n* (sign) indicio *m*; (inkling) presentimiento *m*

intimidate /ɪnˈtɪmədeɪt ‖ ɪnˈtɪmɪdeɪt/ *vt* intimidar

intimidating /ɪnˈtɪmədeɪtɪŋ ‖ ɪnˈtɪmɪdeɪtɪŋ/ *adj* intimidante

intimidation /ɪnˈtɪməˈdeɪʃən ‖ ɪnˌtɪmɪˈdeɪʃən/ *n* [U] intimidación *f*

into /ˈɪntu, *before consonant* ˈɪntə/ *prep* **1 (a)** (indicating motion, direction): **to walk ∼ a building**

entrar en *or* (esp AmL) a un edificio; **they helped him ~ the chair** lo ayudaron a sentarse en el sillón; **she sat staring ~ space** estaba sentada mirando al vacío; **to translate sth ~ Spanish** traducir* algo al español **(b)** (against): **she walked ~ a tree** se dio contra un árbol; **he drove ~ the other car** chocó con el otro coche **2** (in time, distance): **ten minutes ~ the game** a los diez minutos de empezar el partido; **they penetrated deep ~ the jungle** entraron en el corazón de la selva **3** (indicating result of action): **we split ~ two groups** nos dividimos en dos grupos; **roll the dough ~ a ball** haga una bola con la masa **4** (involved in) (colloq) **they're ~ drugs** se drogan; **at two, children are ~ everything** a los dos años, los niños son muy inquietos

intolerable /ɪn'tɑːlərəbəl ‖ ɪn'tɒlərəbəl/ *adj* intolerable

intolerance /ɪn'tɑːlərəns ‖ ɪn'tɒlərəns/ *n* [U] intolerancia *f*

intolerant /ɪn'tɑːlərənt ‖ ɪn'tɒlərənt/ *adj* intolerante

intonation /'ɪntə'neɪʃən/ *n* [U C] entonación *f*

intone /ɪn'təʊn/ *vt* ‹*psalm/Gloria*› entonar

intoxicated /ɪn'tɑːksəkeɪtəd ‖ ɪn'tɒksɪkeɪtɪd/ *adj* (frml) en estado de embriaguez (frml)

intoxicating /ɪn'tɑːksəkeɪtɪŋ ‖ ɪn'tɒksɪkeɪtɪŋ/ *adj* (frml) ‹*substance*› estupefaciente; **~ liquor** bebida *f* alcohólica

intractable /ɪn'træktəbəl/ *adj* (frml) **(a)** ‹*temperament*› obstinado; ‹*child*› incorregible **(b)** ‹*problem/dilemma*› inextricable (frml)

intransigent /ɪn'trænsədʒənt ‖ ɪn'trænsɪdʒənt/ *adj* intransigente

intransitive /ɪn'trænsətɪv/ *adj* intransitivo

intrauterine device /'ɪntrə'juːtərən ‖ ˌɪntrə'juːtəraɪn/ *n* dispositivo *m* intrauterino; (in the shape of a coil) espiral *f*

intravenous /'ɪntrə'viːnəs/ *adj* intravenoso

intrepid /ɪn'trepəd ‖ ɪn'trepɪd/ *adj* intrépido

intricacy /'ɪntrɪkəsi/ *n* **(a)** [U] (of pattern, embroidery) lo intrincado **(b) intricacies** *pl* (complexities) complejidades *fpl*

intricate /'ɪntrɪkət/ *adj* complicado

intrigue¹ /'ɪntriːg/ *n* intriga *f*

intrigue² /ɪn'triːg/ *vt* intrigar*

intriguing /ɪn'triːgɪŋ/ *adj* ‹*problem/text*› intrigante; ‹*possibility*› fascinante; ‹*person*› interesante

intrinsic /ɪn'trɪnzɪk/ *adj* intrínseco

introduce /'ɪntrə'duːs ‖ ˌɪntrə'djuːs/ *vt* **1 (a)** (acquaint) presentar; **to ~ sb** TO **sb** presentarle a algn A algn **(b)** (initiate) **to ~ sb** TO **sth** introducir* a algn A algo, iniciar a algn EN algo **(c)** (present) ‹*speaker/program*› presentar; ‹*meeting/article*› iniciar **2** (bring in) ‹*subject/custom/legislation*› introducir*; ‹*product*› lanzar*, sacar*

introduction /'ɪntrə'dʌkʃən/ *n* **1** **▶ 624** [U C] **(a)** (to person) presentación *f* **(b)** (to activity, experience) **~** TO **sth** introducción *f* A algo **(c)** (of speaker, performer) presentación *f* **2** [U] (of species, practice, legislation) introducción *f* **3** [U] (insertion, entry) (frml) introducción *f* **4** [C] **(a)** (to meeting, lecture) presentación *f* **(b)** (in book) introducción *f* **(c)** (Mus) introducción *f* **5** [C] (elementary instruction) introducción *f*, iniciación *f*

introductory /'ɪntrə'dʌktəri/ *adj* **(a)** (opening) ‹*notes/remarks*› preliminar; ‹*lecture/chapter*› de introducción; ‹*offer*› (Busn) de lanzamiento **(b)** (elementary) ‹*course/lesson*› de introducción

introspective /'ɪntrə'spektɪv/ *adj* introspectivo

introvert /'ɪntrəvɜːrt ‖ 'ɪntrəvɜːt/ *n* introvertido, -da *m,f*

intrude /ɪn'truːd/ *vi* (disturb) importunar; (interfere) inmiscuirse*; **to ~ on sb's privacy** inmiscuirse* en la vida privada de algn

intruder /ɪn'truːdər ‖ ɪn'truːdə(r)/ *n* intruso, -sa *m,f*

intrusion /ɪn'truːʒən/ *n* [U C] intrusión *f*

intrusive /ɪn'truːsɪv/ *adj* **(a)** ‹*noise/smell*› molesto **(b)** ‹*questioning/reporter*› impertinente

intuition /'ɪntuː'ɪʃən ‖ ˌɪntjuː'ɪʃən/ *n* [U C] intuición *f*

intuitive /ɪn'tuːətɪv ‖ ɪn'tjuːɪtɪv/ *adj* intuitivo

Inuit /'ɪnuɪt ‖ 'ɪnjuːɪt/ *n* (*pl* **~** *or* **~s**) **(a)** [C] (person) esquimal *mf* **(b)** [U] (Ling) esquimal *m*

inundate /'ɪnʌndeɪt/ *vt* inundar

invade /ɪn'veɪd/ *vt/i* invadir

invader /ɪn'veɪdər ‖ ɪn'veɪdə(r)/ *n* invasor, -sora *m,f*

invalid¹ /ɪn'væləd ‖ ɪn'vælɪd/ *adj* inválido

invalid² /'ɪnvəlɪd ‖ 'ɪnvəliːd, 'ɪnvəlɪd/ *n* inválido, -da *m,f*

invalidate /ɪn'vælədeɪt ‖ ɪn'vælɪdeɪt/ *vt* (frml) invalidar

invalidity /'ɪnvə'lɪdəti/ *n* [U] (frml) invalidez *f*

invaluable /ɪn'væljuəbəl/ *adj* inapreciable, invalorable (AmL)

invariable /ɪn'veriəbəl ‖ ɪn'veəriəbəl/ *adj* invariable

invariably /ɪn'veriəbli ‖ ɪn'veəriəbli/ *adv* invariablemente, siempre

invasion /ɪn'veɪʒən/ *n* invasión *f*

invective /ɪn'vektɪv/ *n* [U C] **(a)** (abuse) invectivas *fpl* (frml) **(b)** (condemnation) invectiva *f* (frml)

invent /ɪn'vent/ *vt* inventar

invention /ɪn'ventʃən ‖ ɪn'venʃən/ *n* **1 (a)** [C] (device) invento *m* **(b)** [U] (action) invención *f* **2** [U] (imagination): **(powers of) ~** inventiva *f*

inventive /ɪn'ventɪv/ *adj* ingenioso

inventor /ɪn'ventər ‖ ɪn'ventə(r)/ *n* inventor, -tora *m,f*

inventory /'ɪnvəntɔːri ‖'ɪnvəntri/ *n* (*pl* **-ries**) inventario *m*

inverse /'ɪn'vɜːrs, 'ɪnvɜːrs ‖ ˌɪn'vɜːs, 'ɪnvɜːs/ *adj* (*usu before n*) inverso; **in ~ proportion to sth** en proporción inversa a algo

inversion /ɪn'vɜːrʒən ‖ ɪn'vɜːʃən/ *n* inversión *f*

invert /ɪn'vɜːrt ‖ ɪn'vɜːt/ *vt* invertir*

invertebrate /ɪn'vɜːrtəbrət ‖ ɪn'vɜːtɪbrət/ *n* invertebrado, -da *m,f*

inverted commas /ɪn'vɜːrtəd ‖ ɪn'vɜːtɪd/ *pl n* (BrE) comillas *fpl*

invest /ɪn'vest/ *vt* **to ∼ sth** (IN **sth**) ‹*money/time*› invertir* algo (EN algo) ■ ∼ *vi* **to ∼** (IN **sth**) invertir* (EN algo)

investigate /ɪn'vestəgeɪt ‖ ɪn'vestɪgeɪt/ *vt* **(a)** ‹*crime/cause*› investigar*; ‹*complaint/possibility*› estudiar **(b)** (do research on) hacer* una investigación sobre ■ ∼ *vi* investigar*

investigation /ɪn'vestə'geɪʃən ‖ ɪn,vestɪ'geɪʃən/ *n* [U C] **(a)** (detailed examination) estudio *m* **(b)** (official, scientific) investigación *f*

investigator /ɪn'vestəgeɪtər ‖ ɪn'vestɪgeɪtə(r)/ *n* **(a)** (*private* ∼) investigador privado, investigadora privada *m,f* **(b)** (official) inspector, -tora *m,f*

investiture /ɪn'vestətʃʊr ‖ ɪn'vestɪtʃə(r)/ *n* [U C] investidura *f*

investment /ɪn'vestmənt/ *n* [U C] inversión *f*

investor /ɪn'vestər ‖ ɪn'vestə(r)/ *n* inversor, -sora *m,f*, inversionista *mf*

inveterate /ɪn'vetərət/ *adj* (frml) (*usu before n*) ‹*thief/liar*› empedernido

invigorating /ɪn'vɪgəreɪtɪŋ/ *adj* ‹*weather/walk*› vigorizante; ‹*environment/change*› estimulante

invisible /ɪn'vɪzəbəl/ *adj* invisible

invitation /'ɪnvə'teɪʃən ‖ ,ɪnvɪ'teɪʃən/ *n* [C U] invitación *f*; **at the ∼ of** invitado por, por invitación de

invite /ɪn'vaɪt/ *vt* **to ∼ sb** (TO **sth**)/**to** + INF invitar a algn (A algo)/A + INF *or* A QUE (+ *subj*); **to ∼ sb in/out** invitar a algn a pasar/a salir; **his work ∼s comparison with the classics** su obra sugiere comparación con los clásicos

inviting /ɪn'vaɪtɪŋ/ *adj* ‹*prospect/offer*› atractivo

in vitro /ɪn'vi:trəʊ/ *adj* in vitro *adj inv*

invoice¹ /'ɪnvɔɪs/ *n* factura *f*

invoice² *vt* **to ∼ sb** (FOR **sth**) pasarle A algn factura (POR algo)

invoke /ɪn'vəʊk/ *vt* invocar*

involuntary /ɪn'vɑ:lənteri ‖ ɪn'vɒləntri/ *adj* involuntario

involve /ɪn'vɑ:lv ‖ ɪn'vɒlv/ *vt* **1 (a)** (entail, comprise) suponer*; **what exactly does your work ∼?** ¿en qué consiste exactamente tu trabajo? **(b)** (affect, concern): **where national security is ∼d** ... cuando se trata de la seguridad nacional ...; **it's my reputation that's ∼d here** es mi reputación lo que está en juego **2 to ∼ sb** IN **sth**/-ING (implicate) implicar* *or* involucrar a algn EN algo; (allow to participate) darle* participación a algn EN algo **3 involved** *past p* **(a)** (implicated): **I was ∼d in an accident last year** el año pasado me vi envuelto en un accidente; **several high-ranking officials were ∼d in the affair** había varios oficiales de alto rango implicados en el asunto; **the people you're ∼d with** la gente con la que andas metido **(b) to be ∼d** IN **sth** (engrossed) estar* absorto EN algo; (busy) estar* ocupado CON algo **(c)** (emotionally): **she doesn't want to get too ∼d with him** no quiere llegar a una relación muy seria con él

involved /ɪn'vɑ:lvd ‖ ɪn'vɒlvd/ *adj* enrevesado, complicado

involvement /ɪn'vɑ:lvmənt ‖ ɪn'vɒlvmənt/ *n* [U C] **(a)** *n* (entanglement) participación *f*; **they deny any ∼ in terrorist attacks** niegan estar implicados en ningún ataque terrorista **(b)** (relationship) relación *f* (sentimental)

inward¹ /'ɪnwərd ‖ 'ɪnwəd/ *adj* **(a)** (toward inside) ‹*curve*› hacia adentro **(b)** (private, mental) ‹*torment/serenity*› interior

inward², (BrE also) **inwards** *adv* **(a)** (toward inside) ‹*move/bend*› hacia adentro; ‹*travel*› hacia el interior **(b)** (toward mind, spirit): **meditation involves looking ∼** la meditación exige introspección

iodine /'aɪədaɪn ‖ 'aɪədi:n/ *n* [U] yodo *m*

ion /'aɪən, 'aɪɑ:n ‖ 'aɪən/ *n* ión *m*

iota /aɪ'əʊtə/ *n* (*usu with neg*) pizca *f*, ápice *m*

IOU *n* (= **I owe you**) pagaré *m*

IQ *n* (= **intelligence quotient**) CI *m*

IRA *n* (= **Irish Republican Army**) IRA *m*

Iran /ɪ'rɑ:n, ɪ'ræn/ *n* Irán *m*

Iranian¹ /ɪ'remiən/ *adj* iraní

Iranian² *n* iraní *mf*

Iraq /ɪ'rɑ:k, ɪ'ræk/ *n* Irak *m*

Iraqi¹ /ɪ'rɑ:ki, ɪ'ræki/ *adj* iraquí

Iraqi² *n* iraquí *mf*

irascible /ɪ'ræsəbəl/ *adj* irascible

irate /aɪ'reɪt/ *adj* airado

ire /aɪr ‖ 'aɪə(r)/ *n* [U] (liter) ira *f*, cólera *f*

Ireland /'aɪrlənd ‖ 'aɪələnd/ *n* (the island) Irlanda *f*; (the Republic) Irlanda *f*, (el) Eire

iris /'aɪrəs ‖ 'aɪərɪs/ *n* (Bot) lirio *m*

Irish¹ /'aɪrɪʃ ‖ 'aɪərɪʃ/ *adj* irlandés; **the ∼ Sea** el Mar de Irlanda

Irish² *n* **(a)** (people) (+ *pl vb*) **the ∼** los irlandeses **(b)** [U] (language) irlandés *m*

Irish: **∼man** /'aɪrɪʃmən ‖ 'aɪərɪʃmən/ *n* (*pl* **-men** /-mən/) irlandés *m*; **∼woman** *n* irlandesa *f*

irk /ɜ:rk ‖ ɜ:k/ *vt* fastidiar, irritar

iron¹ /'aɪərn ‖ 'aɪən/ *n* **1** [U] **(a)** (metal) hierro *m*, fierro *m* (AmL) **(b)** (in food) hierro *m* **2** [C] (for clothes) plancha *f* **3** [C] (golf club) hierro *m* **4 irons** *pl* (fetters) grilletes *mpl*, grillos *mpl*

iron² *adj* **(a)** (made of iron) de hierro **(b)** (strong) (*before n*) ‹*constitution*› de hierro; ‹*will/resolve*› férreo, de hierro

iron³ *vt/i* planchar

• **iron out** [*v* + *o* + *adv*, *v* + *adv* + *o*] ‹*problems*› resolver*; ‹*difficulties*› allanar

Iron Curtain *n* **the ∼** la cortina de hierro (AmL), el telón de acero (Esp)

ironic /aɪ'rɑ:nɪk ‖ aɪ'rɒnɪk/ *adj* irónico

ironically /aɪ'rɑ:nɪkli ‖ aɪ'rɒnɪkli/ *adv* irónicamente

ironing /'aɪərnɪŋ ‖ 'aɪənɪŋ/ *n* [U] **to do the ∼** planchar

ironing board *n* tabla *f or* (Méx) burro *m* de planchar

ironmonger /'aɪərn,mɑ:ŋgər ‖ 'aɪən,mʌŋgə(r)/ *n* (BrE) ferretero, -ra *m,f*; **at the ∼'s** en la ferretería

irony /'aɪrəni/ *n* [C U] (*pl* **-nies**) ironía *f*

irrational /ɪ'ræʃnəl ‖ ɪ'ræʃənl/ *adj* irracional

irreconcilable /ɪ'rekən'saɪləbəl/ *adj* irreconciliable

irrefutable /ɪ'refjətəbəl, 'ɪrɪ'fju:- ‖ ˌɪrɪ'fju:təbəl/ *adj* irrefutable

irregular /ɪ'regjələr ‖ ɪ'regjʊlə(r)/ *adj* **1** (in shape, positioning, time) irregular **2** (contrary to rules) inadmisible, contrario a las normas **3** (Ling) irregular

irregularity /ɪ'regjə'lærəti ‖ ɪˌregjʊ'lærəti/ *n* [U C] (*pl* **-ties**) **1** (in shape, positioning, time) irregularidad *f* **2** (of action) lo inadmisible; **several irregularities** varias contravenciones de las normas

irrelevant /ɪ'reləvənt/ *adj* ‹*fact/detail*› irrelevante; **to be ~ TO sth** no tener* relación *or* no tener* que ver CON algo

irreparable /ɪ'reprəbəl/ *adj* irreparable

irreplaceable /'ɪrɪ'pleɪsəbəl/ *adj* irreemplazable

irrepressible /'ɪrɪ'presəbəl/ *adj* ‹*laughter*› incontenible; ‹*desire*› irreprimible

irresistible /'ɪrɪ'zɪstəbəl/ *adj* irresistible

irrespective /'ɪrɪ'spektɪv/ *adv* **~ OF sth**: **~ of what you say** independientemente de lo que usted diga; **~ of age or sex** sin distinción de edad o sexo

irresponsible /'ɪrɪ'spɑ:nsəbəl ‖ ˌɪrɪ'spɒnsəbəl/ *adj* irresponsable

irreverent /ɪ'revrənt, ɪ'revərənt/ *adj* irreverente

irrigate /'ɪrəgeɪt ‖ 'ɪrɪgeɪt/ *vt* irrigar*, regar*

irrigation /'ɪrə'geɪʃən ‖ ˌɪrɪ'geɪʃən/ *n* [U] irrigación *f*, riego *m*

irritable /'ɪrətəbəl ‖ 'ɪrɪtəbəl/ *adj* **1** (bad-tempered) ‹*person/mood*› irritable; ‹*reply*› irritado **2** (sensitive) ‹*skin/scalp*› sensible

irritant /'ɪrətənt ‖ 'ɪrɪtənt/ *n* **(a)** (Med) agente *m* irritante **(b)** (person, thing) fastidio *m*

irritate /'ɪrəteɪt ‖ 'ɪrɪteɪt/ *vt* irritar

irritated /'ɪrəteɪtəd ‖ 'ɪrɪteɪtɪd/ *adj* **1** ‹*look/frown*› de impaciencia; **to be ~ WITH** *o* **AT sth/WITH sb** estar* irritado POR algo/CON algn **2** ‹*skin/hands*› irritado

irritating /'ɪrəteɪtɪŋ ‖ 'ɪrɪteɪtɪŋ/ *adj* irritante

irritation /'ɪrə'teɪʃən ‖ ˌɪrɪ'teɪʃən/ *n* [U C] irritación *f*

IRS *n* (in US) = **Internal Revenue Service**

is /ɪz/ *3rd pers sing pres of* BE

ISBN *n* (= **International Standard Book Number**) ISBN *m*

-ish /ɪʃ/ ▶**515** *suff*: **long~** más bien largo; **green~** verdoso; **tenn~** a eso de las diez

Islam /'ɪzlɑ:m, ɪz'lɑ:m/ *n* [U] el Islam

Islamic /ɪz'læmɪk, ɪz'lɑ:mɪk/ *adj* islámico

island /'aɪlənd/ *n* isla *f*

islander /'aɪləndər ‖ 'aɪləndə(r)/ *n* isleño, -ña *m,f*

isle /aɪl/ *n* **(a)** (poet) isla *f*, ínsula *f* (liter) **(b)** (in place names): **the I~ of Wight** la Isla de Wight

Isles of Scilly /'aɪlzəv'sɪli/ *pl n* **the ~ ~ ~** las islas Scilly *or* Sorlingas

isn't /'ɪznt/ = **is not**

isolate /'aɪsəleɪt/ *vt* aislar*

isolated /'aɪsəleɪtəd ‖ 'aɪsəleɪtɪd/ *adj* aislado

isolation /'aɪsə'leɪʃən/ *n* [U] aislamiento *m*

Israel /'ɪzreɪəl/ *n* Israel *m*

Israeli¹ /ɪz'reɪli/ *adj* israelí

Israeli² *n* israelí *mf*

issue¹ /'ɪʃu: ‖ 'ɪʃju:, ɪsju:/ *n* **1** [C] (subject discussed) tema *m*, cuestión *f*, asunto *m*; ***to take ~ with sb/sth*** discrepar de *or* con algn/en *or* de algo **2 (a)** [U] (of documents) expedición *f*; (of library books) préstamo *m*; (of tickets) venta *f* **(b)** [U C] (of stamps, shares, bank notes) emisión *f* **(c)** [C] (of newspaper, magazine) número *m*

issue² *vt* (give out) ‹*statement/report*› hacer* público; ‹*instructions*› dar*; ‹*guidelines*› establecer*; ‹*tickets/visas*› expedir*; ‹*library books*› prestar; ‹*bank notes/stamps/shares*› emitir; ‹*summons*› dictar; **we can ~ you with the necessary documents** le podemos proporcionar los documentos necesarios ■ **~** *vi* (frml) **1** (result) **to ~ FROM sth** derivar(se) DE algo (frml) **2** (emerge) salir*; «*liquid*» fluir*

it /ɪt/ ▶**638** *pron* **1** (replacing noun — as direct object) lo, la; (— as indirect object) le; (— as subject, after prep) *gen not translated*; **~'s enormous** es enorme; **there's nothing behind ~** no hay nada detrás **2** (introducing person, thing, event): **who is ~?** ¿quién es?; **~'s me** soy yo; **I'll see to ~** yo me encargo (de ello); **~'s his attitude that I don't like** su actitud es lo que no me gusta; **a little higher up ... that's ~!** un poco más arriba ... ¡ahí está! *or* ¡eso es!; **one more and that's ~** uno más y ya está *or* se acabó **3** (in impersonal constructions): **~'s raining** está lloviendo; **~'s two o'clock** son las dos; **~ says here that** ... aquí dice que ...; **~ is known that** ... se sabe que ...

Italian¹ /ɪ'tæljən/ *adj* italiano

Italian² *n* **(a)** [C] (person) italiano, -na *m,f* **(b)** [U] (language) italiano *m*

italics /ɪ'tælɪks/ *pl n* (letra *f*) cursiva *f*

Italy /'ɪtl̩i ‖ 'ɪtəli/ *n* Italia *f*

itch¹ /ɪtʃ/ *vi* **1 (a)** «*scalp/toe*» picar* (+ *me/te/le etc*) **(b)** (be impatient, eager) (colloq) **to be ~ing to** + INF: **he was ~ing to tell her** estaba que se moría por decírselo (fam) **2** «*wool/underwear*» (cause irritation) picar*

itch² *n* **(a)** (irritation) picor *m*, picazón *f* **(b)** (desire) ansia *f*‡

itchy /'ɪtʃi/ *adj* **itchier, itchiest (a)** (feeling irritation): **I've got an ~ nose/scalp** me pica la nariz/la cabeza **(b)** (causing irritation) ‹*garment/material*› que pica

it'd /'ɪtəd/ **(a)** = **it had (b)** = **it would**

item /'aɪtəm/ *n* **(a)** (article) (Busn) artículo *m*; (in collection) pieza *f*; (on agenda) punto *m*: **~s of clothing** prendas *fpl* de vestir **(b)** (in newspaper) artículo *m*; **news ~** noticia *f*

itemize /'aɪtəmaɪz/ *vt* (break down) detallar; (list) hacer* una lista de

itinerant /aɪ'tɪnərənt/ *adj* (frml) ‹*worker/judge*› itinerante (frml); ‹*salesman/musician*› ambulante

itinerary /aɪ'tɪnəreri ‖ aɪ'tɪnərəri/ *n* (*pl* **-ries**) itinerario *m*

it'll /'ɪtl̩/ = **it will**

its /ɪts/ *adj* (*sing*) su; (*pl*) sus

■ **Note** The translation *su* agrees in number with the noun which it modifies; *its* is translated by *su, sus*, depending on what follows: *its snout/head* su hocico/cabeza; *its problems/difficulties* sus problemas/dificultades.

it's /ɪts/ **(a)** = **it is (b)** = **it has**

itself /ɪt'self/ *pron* **(a)** (reflexive): **it has earned ~ a reputation** se ha hecho fama; **another problem presented ~** se presentó otro problema **(b)** (emphatic use): **the town ~ is small** la ciudad en sí *or* propiamente dicha es pequeña

ITV *n* (in UK) (*no art*) = **Independent Television**

IUD *n* (= **intrauterine device**) DIU *m*

I've /aɪv/ = **I have**

ivory /'aɪvəri/ *n* (*pl* **-ries**) **(a)** (material) marfil *m* **(b)** ▶ **515** (color) (color *m*) marfil *m*

Ivory Coast *n* Costa *f* de Marfil

ivy /'aɪvi/ *n* [U] hiedra *f*

Ivy League *n* (AmE) **the ~ ~** *grupo de ocho universidades prestigiosas de EEUU*

Jj

J, j /dʒeɪ/ *n* J, j *f*

jab¹ /dʒæb/ *vt* **-bb-**: **I ~bed myself with the needle** me pinché con la aguja, me piqué con la aguja (Méx); **she ~bed me with her fork** me clavó con el tenedor

jab² *n* **(a)** (prick) pinchazo *m*; (blow) golpe *m*; (with elbow) codazo *m* **(b)** (in boxing) jab *m*, corto *m* **(c)** (injection) (BrE colloq) inyección *f*

jabber /'dʒæbər ‖ 'dʒæbə(r)/ *vi/t* farfullar

jack /dʒæk/ *n* **(a)** (lifting device) gato *m* **(b)** (socket) enchufe *m* hembra **(c)** (in French pack of cards) jota *f*, valet *m*; (in Spanish pack) sota *f*

•jack up [*v* + *o* + *adv, v* + *adv* + *o*] ‹*car*› levantar (*con el gato*)

jackal /'dʒækəl/ *n* chacal *m*

jackdaw /'dʒækdɔː/ *n* grajilla *f*

jacket /'dʒækət ‖ 'dʒækɪt/ *n* **1** (Clothing) chaqueta *f*; (*sports* ~) americana *f*, saco *m* (sport) (AmL) **2** (of book) sobrecubierta *f*; (of record) (AmE) funda *f*, carátula *f* **3** (of potato) (BrE): **~ potatoes** papas *fpl* asadas (*con la cáscara*) (AmL), patatas *fpl* asadas (*con la piel*) (Esp)

jack: **~hammer** *n* martillo *m* neumático; **~-in-the-box** /'dʒækənðə'bɑːks ‖ 'dʒækɪnðə,bɒks/ *n* caja *f* de sorpresas (*con muñeco a resorte*); **~knife** *vi* «*truck*» plegarse*; **~ of all trades** /'dʒækəv'ɔːltreɪdz/ *n* (*pl* **~s of all trades**) hombre *m or* mujer *f* orquesta, manitas *mf* (Esp, Méx fam); **~pot** *n* (in bingo, lottery) bote *m*, pozo *m*; **~rabbit** *n*: *tipo de liebre de Norteamérica*

Jacuzzi®, jacuzzi /dʒə'kuːzi/ *n* Jacuzzi® *m*

jade /dʒeɪd/ *n* [U] **(a)** (Min) jade *m* **(b)** ▶ **515** (color) verde *m* jade

jaded /'dʒeɪdəd ‖ 'dʒeɪdɪd/ *adj* hastiado

jagged /'dʒægəd ‖ 'dʒægɪd/ *adj* ‹*edge/cut*› irregular; ‹*rock/cliff*› recortado, con picos

jaguar /'dʒægwɑːr ‖ 'dʒægjʊə(r)/ *n* jaguar *m*

jail¹ /dʒeɪl/ *n* cárcel *f*, prisión *f*; **he went to ~** lo metieron preso

jail² *vt* encarcelar

jailer, jailor /'dʒeɪlər ‖ 'dʒeɪlə(r)/ *n* carcelero, -ra *m,f*

jailhouse /'dʒeɪlhaʊs/ *n* (AmE) cárcel *f*

jam¹ /dʒæm/ *n* **1** [U C] (Culin) mermelada *f*, dulce *m* (RPl) **2** [C] (difficult situation) (colloq) aprieto *m*

jam² **-mm-** *vt* **1 (a)** (cram) **to ~ sth INTO sth** meter algo a la fuerza EN algo **(b)** (congest, block) ‹*road*› atestar; **the switchboard was ~med with calls** la centralita estaba saturada de llamadas **2** (wedge firmly): **he ~med his foot in the door** metió el pie entre la puerta y el marco **3** (Rad) interferir*

■ **~** *vi* «*brakes*» bloquearse; «*machine*» trancarse*; «*switch/lock*» trabarse; «*gun*» encasquillarse

•jam on [*v* + *o* + *adv, v* + *adv* + *o*]: **to ~ on the brakes** dar* un frenazo

Jamaica /dʒə'meɪkə/ *n* Jamaica *f*

Jamaican /dʒə'meɪkən/ *adj* jamaicano

jamb /dʒæm/ *n* jamba *f*

jam: **~ jar** *n* (BrE) tarro *m or* bote *m* para mermelada; **~-packed** /'dʒæm'pækt/ *adj* (colloq) repleto, atestado (de gente); **~ session** *n*: *sesión de un grupo de músicos de jazz o rock que se reúnen para improvisar*

jangle /'dʒæŋgəl/ **~** *vi* hacer* ruido (*metálico*)

janitor /'dʒænətər ‖ 'dʒænɪtə(r)/ *n* conserje *m*

January ▶ **540** /'dʒænjueri ‖ 'dʒænjʊəri/ *n* enero *m*

Japan /dʒə'pæn/ *n* (el) Japón *m*

Japanese¹ /'dʒæpə'niːz/ *adj* japonés

Japanese² *n* (*pl* **~**) **(a)** [U] (language) japonés *m* **(b)** [C] (person) japonés, -nesa *m,f*

jar¹ /dʒɑːr ‖ dʒɑː(r)/ *n* **1** (container) tarro *m*, bote *m* **2** (jolt) sacudida *f*

jar² **-rr-** *vi* **(a)** (clash) desentonar **(b)** (irritate): **it ~s on my nerves** me crispa los nervios, me enerva

■ **~** *vt* sacudir

jargon /'dʒɑːrgən ‖ 'dʒɑːgən/ *n* [U] jerga *f*

jarring /'dʒɑːrɪŋ/ *adj* ‹*sound*› discordante

jasmine /'dʒæzmən ‖ 'dʒæsmɪn/ *n* [C U] jazmín *m*

jaundice /'dʒɔːndəs || 'dʒɔːndɪs/ *n* [U] ictericia *f*

jaundiced /'dʒɔːndəst || 'dʒɔːndɪst/ *adj* **(a)** (Med) ‹*skin/baby*› ictérico **(b)** ‹*view/opinion*› negativo

jaunt /dʒɔːnt/ *n* excursión *f*

jaunty /'dʒɔːnti/ *adj* **-tier, -tiest** (*usu before n*) ‹*air*› garboso; ‹*tune*› alegre

javelin /'dʒævlən || 'dʒævlɪn/ *n* jabalina *f*

jaw /dʒɔː/ ▶ 484 *n* **(a)** (of person, animal) mandíbula *f*; (esp of animal) quijada *f*; **his ~ dropped** se quedó boquiabierto **(b) jaws** *pl* fauces *fpl*

jawbone /'dʒɔːbəʊn/ *n* mandíbula *f*, maxilar *m*; (of an animal) quijada *f*

jay /dʒeɪ/ *n* arrendajo *m*

jay: **~walk** *vi* cruzar* la calzada imprudentemente; **~walker** *n* peatón *m* imprudente

jazz /dʒæz/ *n* [U] (Mus) jazz *m*

• jazz up [*v* + *o* + *adv, v* + *adv* + *o*] (colloq) **(a)** ‹*music*› tocar* con ritmo sincopado **(b)** ‹*room*› alegrar, darle* vida a

jazzy /'dʒæzi/ *adj* **jazzier, jazziest 1** (flashy) (colloq) llamativo **2** (Mus) ‹*rhythm*› de jazz

jealous /'dʒeləs/ *adj* **(a)** ‹*husband/wife*› celoso; **to be ~** estar* celoso, tener* celos **(b)** (envious) envidioso; **to be ~ OF sb** tenerle* envidia A algn

jealousy /'dʒeləsi/ *n* (*pl* **-sies**) **(a)** [U] (fear of rivalry) celos *mpl* **(b)** [U C] (envy) envidia *f*

jeans /dʒiːnz/ *pl n* vaqueros *mpl*, jeans *mpl*, bluyines *mpl* (Andes)

Jeep®, jeep /dʒiːp/ *n* Jeep® *m*

jeer /dʒɪr || dʒɪə(r)/ *vi*: **to ~ AT sth/sb** (boo) abuchear (algo/a algn); (mock) burlarse (DE algo/algn)

Jehovah /dʒə'həʊvə/ *n* Jehová

Jehovah's Witness *n* testigo *mf* de Jehová

jell /dʒel/ *vi* ⇒ GEL²

Jell-O® /'dʒeləʊ/ *n* [U] (AmE) gelatina *f* (*con sabor a frutas*)

jelly /'dʒeli/ *n* [U C] (*pl* **-lies**) **1** (Culin) **(a)** (clear jam) jalea *f* **(b)** (as dessert) (BrE) gelatina *f* (*con sabor a frutas*) **2** (gelatinous substance) gelatina *f*

jellyfish /'dʒeliˌfɪʃ/ *n* (*pl* **-fish** *or* **-fishes**) medusa *f*, malagua *f* (Per), aguaviva *f* (RPl), aguamala *f* (Col, Méx)

jeopardize /'dʒepərdaɪz || 'dʒepədaɪz/ *vt* poner* en peligro, hacer* peligrar

jeopardy /'dʒepərdi || 'dʒepədi/ *n* [U]: **in ~** en peligro

jerk¹ /dʒɜːrk || dʒɜːk/ *vi* «*leg/arm*» hacer* un movimiento brusco; (repeatedly) «*legs/arms*» agitarse; **the train ~ed to a stop** el tren se detuvo con una sacudida ■ **~** *vt*: **the impact ~ed him forward** el impacto lo propulsó hacia adelante

jerk² *n* **1 (a)** (tug) tirón *m* **(b)** (sudden movement) sacudida *f* **2** (contemptible person) (colloq) estúpido, -da *m,f*, pendejo, -ja *m,f* (AmL exc CS fam), gilipollas *mf* (Esp fam), huevón, -ona *m,f* (Andes, Ven fam)

jerky /'dʒɜːrki || 'dʒɜːki/ *adj* **-kier, -kiest** ‹*speech*› entrecortado; **it was a ~ ride** fuimos (*or* fueron *etc*) dando botes por el camino

jerry /'dʒeri/: **~-built** *adj* mal construido; **~ can** *n* bidón *m*

jersey /'dʒərzi || 'dʒɜːzi/ *n* (*pl* **-seys**) **1 (a)** [C] (sports shirt) camiseta *f* **(b)** [U] (Tex) jersey *m* **(c)** [C] (BrE) ⇒ SWEATER **2 Jersey** (la isla de) Jersey

Jerusalem /dʒə'ruːsələm/ *n* Jerusalén *m*

jest /dʒest/ *n* (arch) broma *f*, chanza *f* (arc); **in ~** en broma

jester /'dʒestər || 'dʒestə(r)/ *n* bufón *m*

Jesuit /'dʒeʒuət || 'dʒezjʊɪt/ *n* jesuita *m*

Jesus /'dʒiːzəs/ *n* Jesús; **~ Christ** Jesucristo

jet¹ /dʒet/ *n* **1** [C] (Aviat) avión *m* (*con motor a reacción*) **2** [C] (of water, air, gas) chorro *m* **3** [U] (Min) azabache *m*

jet² *vi* **-tt-** (fly) (colloq) volar*

jet: **~-black** /'dʒet'blæk/ ▶ 515 *adj* (*pred* **~ black**) negro azabache *adj inv*; **~ lag** *n* [U] jet lag *m*, desfase *m* horario

jetsam /'dʒetsəm/ *n* [U] echazón *f*; *see also* FLOTSAM

jet set *n* **the ~ ~** el jet set (AmL), la jet set (Esp)

jettison /'dʒetəsən || 'dʒetɪsən/ *vt* (Naut) echar por la borda; (Aviat) deshacerse* de

jetty /'dʒeti/ *n* (*pl* **-ties**) embarcadero *m*, malecón *m*

Jew /dʒuː/ *n* judío, -día *m,f*

jewel /'dʒuːəl/ *n* (gem) piedra *f* preciosa; (piece of jewelry) alhaja *f*, joya *f*; (in watch) rubí *m*; (sb, sth wonderful) joya *f*

jeweler, (BrE) **jeweller** /'dʒuːələr || 'dʒuːələ(r)/ *n* joyero, -ra *m,f*; **a ~'s (shop)** una joyería

jewelry, (BrE) **jewellery** /'dʒuːəlri/ *n* [U] joyas *fpl*, alhajas *fpl*; (*before n*) **~ box** joyero *m*; **~ store** (AmE) joyería *f*

Jewish /'dʒuːɪʃ/ *adj* judío

jibe /dʒaɪb/ *n* pulla *f*

jiffy /'dʒɪfi/ *n* (colloq) (*no pl*) segundo *m*

jig /dʒɪg/ *n* **1** (dance) giga *f* **2** (Tech) plantilla *f* de guía

jiggle /'dʒɪgəl/ *vt* mover*, sacudir

jigsaw /'dʒɪgsɔː/ *n* **1 ~ (puzzle)** rompecabezas *m*, puzzle *m* **2** (saw) sierra *f* de vaivén *or* de puñal

jilt /dʒɪlt/ *vt* dejar plantado

jingle¹ /'dʒɪŋgəl/ *n* **1** (sound) (*no pl*) tintineo *m*; (of harness bells) cascabeleo *m*, tintineo *m* **2** [C] (Marketing) jingle *m* (publicitario)

jingle² *vi* tintinear

jingoism /'dʒɪŋgəʊɪzəm/ *n* [U] patriotería *f*, jingoísmo *m*

jinx¹ /dʒɪŋks/ *n*: **there's a ~ on this project** a este proyecto le han echado una maldición

jinx² *vt* traer* mala suerte a

jitters /'dʒɪtərz || 'dʒɪtəz/ *pl n* (colloq): **he got the ~** se puso nervioso, le dio el tembleque (fam)

jittery /'dʒɪtəri/ *adj* nervioso

Jnr (BrE) (= **Junior**) (h), Jr.

job /dʒɑːb || dʒɒb/ *n* **1 (a)** (occupation, post) trabajo *m*, empleo *m*; **is he the right person for the ~?** ¿es la persona idónea para el puesto?; (*before n*) **~ creation** creación *f* de empleo **(b)** (duty, responsibility): **it's your ~ to make the tea** tú eres el encargado de hacer el té; **I'm only doing my ~** sólo cumplo con mi deber **2 (a)** (task, piece of work) trabajo *m*; (Comput) trabajo *m*; **you're doing a fine ~** lo estás haciendo muy bien; ***a good* ~** (BrE colloq) menos mal; **it's a good ~ I did it yesterday** menos mal que lo hice ayer; ***to give sth up as a bad* ~** dejar algo por imposible; ***to make the best of a bad* ~** apechugar* y hacer* lo que se pueda **(b)** (difficult task) (colloq): **I had a (terrible) ~ getting that nail out** me dio mucho trabajo sacar ese clavo

job: **~ description** *n* descripción *f* del puesto; **~-hunt** *vi* (*usu in -ing form*) buscar* trabajo

jobless /'dʒɑːbləs || 'dʒɒblɪs/ *adj* (journ) desempleado, en paro (Esp), cesante (Chi)

job: **~ lot** *n* lote *m*; **~ sharing** /'ʃerɪŋ || 'ʃeərɪŋ/ *n* [U] *sistema en el cual dos personas comparten un puesto de trabajo*

jockey /'dʒɑːki || 'dʒɒki/ *n* (*pl* **~s**) jockey *mf*, jinete *mf*

Jockey shorts® /'dʒɑːki || 'dʒɒki/ *pl n* (AmE) calzoncillos *mpl*, calzones *mpl* (Méx), interiores *mpl* (Col, Ven)

jockstrap /'dʒɑːkstræp || 'dʒɒkstræp/ *n* suspensorio *m*, suspensor *m* (Per, RPl)

jocular /'dʒɑːkjələr || 'dʒɒkjʊlə(r)/ *adj* jocoso

jodhpurs /'dʒɑːdpərz || 'dʒɒdpəz/ *pl n* pantalones *mpl* de montar, breeches *mpl* (Col, RPl)

jog¹ /dʒɑːg || dʒɒg/ **-gg-** *vt* ‹*table*› mover*; **she ~ged his elbow** le dio en el codo; **to ~ sb's memory** refrescarle* la memoria a algn ■ **~** *vi* **(a)** (run) correr **(b)** (Leisure) hacer* footing *or* jogging; **to go ~ging** salir* a hacer jogging *or* footing

jog² *n* (*no pl*) (Leisure): **to go for a ~** hacer* footing *or* jogging

jogger /'dʒɑːgər || 'dʒɒgə(r)/ *n*: *persona que hace footing*

jogging /'dʒɑːgɪŋ || 'dʒɒgɪŋ/ *n* [U] footing *m*, jogging *m*

john /dʒɑːn || dʒɒn/ *n* **1** (toilet) (AmE colloq) baño *m*, váter *m* (Esp fam) **2 John Doe** (AmE) (Law) persona *f* inidentificada; (colloq) el típico americano

join¹ /dʒɔɪn/ *vt* **1** (fasten, link) ‹*ropes/wires*› unir; (put together) ‹*tables*› juntar; **to ~ two things together** unir dos cosas; **to ~ hands** tomarse *or* (esp Esp) cogerse* de la mano **2** (meet, keep company with): **we're going for a drink, will you ~ us?** vamos a tomar algo ¿nos acompañas?; **you go ahead, I'll ~ you later** ustedes vayan que ya iré yo luego; **may I ~ you?** ¿le importa si me siento aquí? **3 (a)** (become part of) unirse a, sumarse a; **I ~ed the line** me puse en la cola **(b)** (become member of) ‹*club*› hacerse* socio de; ‹*union*› afiliarse a; ‹*army*› alistarse en; ‹*firm*› entrar en *or* (AmL tb) entrar a ■ **~** *vi* **1 to ~ (together)** «*parts/groups*» unirse **2** (merge) «*streams*» confluir*; «*roads*» empalmar

●**join in 1** [*v + adv*] participar, tomar parte **2** [*v + adv + o*] ‹*celebrations*› participar *or* tomar parte en

●**join up** [*v + adv*] **(a)** (enlist) alistarse **(b)** (fit together) «*pieces/parts*» encajar **(c)** (team up) «*people*» unirse

join² *n* juntura *f*, unión *f*

joiner /'dʒɔɪnər || 'dʒɔɪnə(r)/ *n* carpintero, -ra *m,f* (de obra)

joint¹ /dʒɔɪnt/ *n* **1** (Anat) articulación *f* **2** (Const) (point of joining) unión *f*, junta *f*; (in woodwork) ensambladura *f* **3** (Culin) trozo *m* de carne (*para asar*)

joint² *adj* (*before n*) ‹*action*› conjunto; **~ owner** copropietario, -ria *m,f*; **it was a ~ effort** fue un trabajo realizado en conjunto

joint account *n* cuenta *f* conjunta

jointly /'dʒɔɪntli/ *adv* ‹*decide/act*› conjuntamente

joint: **~ stock company** *n* sociedad *f* por acciones; **~ venture** *n* empresa *f* conjunta

joist /dʒɔɪst/ *n* viga *f*

joke¹ /dʒəʊk/ *n* **(a)** (verbal) chiste *m*; (directed at sb) broma *f*; **he can't take a ~** no sabe aceptar una broma **(b)** (*practical* **~**) broma *f*

joke² *vi* bromear; **you must be joking!** ¡tú debes estar loco!; **I was only joking** lo dije en broma

joker /'dʒəʊkər || 'dʒəʊkə(r)/ *n* **1** (cards) comodín *m* **2** (prankster) bromista *mf*; (contemptible person) (colloq) tipo, -pa *m,f* (fam)

jokey /'dʒəʊki/ *adj* ⇒ JOKY

joky /'dʒəʊki/ *adj* **jokier, jokiest** jocoso

jolly¹ /'dʒɑːli || 'dʒɒli/ *adj* **-lier, -liest** ‹*person*› jovial; ‹*laugh/tune*› alegre

jolly² *adv* (BrE colloq) (*as intensifier*): **you were ~ lucky!** ¡qué suerte tuviste!; **~ good!** ¡muy bien!

jolly³ *vt* **-lies, -lying, -lied** (colloq): **to ~ sb along** animar a algn

jolt¹ /dʒəʊlt/ *vi* «*train/bus*» dar* *or* pegar* una sacudida; (repeatedly) dar* tumbos ■ **~** *vt*: **she ~ed his arm** le movió el brazo

jolt² *n* sacudida *f*

Jordan /'dʒɔːrdn̩ || 'dʒɔːdn̩/ *n* **(a)** (country) Jordania *f* **(b) the ~, the ~ River** (AmE), **the River ~** (BrE) el Jordán

Jordanian /dʒɔːr'deɪniən || dʒɔː'deɪniən/ *adj* jordano

jostle /'dʒɑːsəl || 'dʒɒsəl/ *vt* empujar ■ **~** *vi*: **people were jostling trying to get out** la gente se empujaba tratando de salir

jot /dʒɑːt || dʒɒt/ *n* (*no pl, usu with neg*): **it doesn't make a** *o* **one ~ of difference** da exactamente igual

●**jot down**: **-tt-** [*v + o + adv, v + adv + o*] apuntar *or* anotar (*rápidamente*)

journal /'dʒɜːrnl̩ || 'dʒɜːnl/ *n* **(a)** (periodical) revista *f*, publicación *f*; (newspaper) periódico *m* **(b)** (diary) (frml) diario *m*

journalism /'dʒɜːrnl̩ɪzəm || 'dʒɜːnəlɪzəm/ *n* [U] periodismo *m*

journalist /'dʒɜːrnl̩əst || 'dʒɜːnl̩ɪst/ *n* periodista *mf*

journey /'dʒɜːrni || 'dʒɜːni/ *n* (*pl* **-neys**) viaje *m*; **to go on** *o* **to make a ~** hacer* un viaje

joust /dʒaʊst/ *vi* justar

jovial /'dʒəʊviəl/ *adj* jovial

jowls /dʒaʊlz/ *pl n* (*sometimes sing*) *parte inferior de los carrillos, que a veces cuelga de la mandíbula*

joy /dʒɔɪ/ *n* **(a)** [U] (emotion) alegría *f*, dicha *f*; **to jump for ~** saltar de alegría **(b)** [C U] (source of pleasure): **she's a ~ to teach** es un verdadero placer *or* da gusto tenerla como alumna

joyful /ˈdʒɔɪfəl/ *adj* ‹*event*› feliz; ‹*dance/news*› alegre

joyless /ˈdʒɔɪləs ‖ ˈdʒɔɪlɪs/ *adj* ‹*occasion*› falto de alegría; ‹*existence*› sombrío

joyous /ˈdʒɔɪəs/ *adj* ‹*expression*› de dicha; ‹*occasion*› feliz

joy: **~rider** *n*: *joven que roba un coche para dar una vuelta*; **~stick** *n* (Aviat) palanca *f* de mando; (Electron, Comput) mando *m*, joystick *m*

Jr (esp AmE) (= **Junior**) (h), Jr.

jubilant /ˈdʒu:bələnt ‖ ˈdʒu:bɪlənt/ *adj* ‹*expression*› de júbilo (liter); ‹*speech*› exultante (liter); **to be ~** estar* radiante de alegría

jubilee /ˈdʒu:bəli: ‖ ˈdʒu:bɪli:/ *n*: **the Queen's silver ~** el vigésimo quinto aniversario de la reina

Judaism /ˈdʒu:dəɪzəm ‖ ˈdʒu:deɪɪzəm/ *n* [U] judaísmo *m*

judge¹ /dʒʌdʒ/ *n* **1 ▶ 603** (Law) juez *mf*, juez, jueza *m,f*; (of competition) juez *mf*; (Sport) juez *mf* **2** (appraiser): **he's a good ~ of character** es muy buen psicólogo; **let me be the ~ of that** eso lo decidiré yo

judge² *vt* **1** (Law) ‹*case/person*› juzgar*; ‹*contest*› ser* el juez de **2 (a)** (estimate) ‹*size/speed*› calcular **(b)** (assess) ‹*situation/position*› evaluar*; ‹*person*› juzgar* **(c)** (deem) juzgar* **3** (censure, condemn) juzgar* ■ ~ *vi* juzgar*; **judging by** a juzgar por

judgment, **judgement** /ˈdʒʌdʒmənt/ *n* **1** [U C] (Law) fallo *m*, sentencia *f*; (in arbitration) fallo *m*; **to pass ~ on sth/sb** juzgar* algo/a algn **2** [U C] **(a)** (estimation) cálculo *m* **(b)** (view) opinión *f* **3** [U] (sense, discernment): **an error of ~** una equivocación; **I lent him the money against my better ~** le presté el dinero sabiendo que era un error

judgmental, **judgemental** /dʒʌdʒˈmentl/ *adj* ‹*attitude/assessment*› sentencioso

judicial /dʒu:ˈdɪʃəl/ *adj* judicial

judiciary /dʒu:ˈdɪʃieri ‖ dʒu:ˈdɪʃəri/ *n* (judges) judicatura *f*; (arm of government) poder *m* judicial

judicious /dʒu:ˈdɪʃəs/ *adj* ‹*decision*› acertado; ‹*historian*› de criterio

judo /ˈdʒu:dəʊ/ *n* [U] judo *m*

jug /dʒʌg/ *n* (large) jarra *f*; (for milk, cream) jarrita *f*

juggernaut /ˈdʒʌgərnɔ:t ‖ ˈdʒʌgənɔ:t/ *n* (BrE) camión *m* grande

juggle /ˈdʒʌgəl/ *vi* hacer* malabarismos ■ ~ *vt* hacer* malabarismos con

juggler /ˈdʒʌglər ‖ ˈdʒʌglə(r)/ *n* malabarista *mf*

Jugoslavia /ˈju:gəʊˈslɑ:viə, ˈju:gəˈslɑ:viə/ *etc* ⇒ YUGOSLAVIA *etc*

jugular /ˈdʒʌgjələr ‖ ˈdʒʌgjʊlə(r)/ *n* (vena *f*) yugular *f*

juice /dʒu:s/ *n* [U C] (fruit drink) jugo *m*, zumo *m*; (from fruit, meat) jugo *m*; (Physiol) jugo *m*

juicer /ˈdʒu:sər ‖ ˈdʒu:sə(r)/ *n* exprimidor *m* (*gen eléctrico*), juguera *f* (CS)

juicy /ˈdʒu:si/ *adj* **-cier, -ciest (a)** (Culin) jugoso **(b)** (colloq) ‹*gossip/details*› sabroso (fam)

jukebox /ˈdʒu:kbɑ:ks ‖ ˈdʒu:kbɒks/ *n* máquina *f* de discos, rocola *f* (AmL)

July /dʒʊˈlaɪ/ **▶ 540** *n* julio *m*

jumble¹ /ˈdʒʌmbəl/ *vt* ~ **(up)** ‹*cards/pieces*› mezclar; **the clothes were all ~d up in the drawer** la ropa estaba toda revuelta en el cajón

jumble² *n* (*no pl*) (of clothes, papers) revoltijo *m*; (of facts, data) embrollo *m*

jumble sale *n* (BrE) *mercadillo de beneficencia donde se venden artículos de segunda mano*

jumbo /ˈdʒʌmbəʊ/ *adj* (*before n*) ‹*packet/size*› gigante

jumbo (jet) *n* jumbo *m*

jump¹ /dʒʌmp/ *vi* **1 (a)** (leap) saltar; **the horse ~ed over the gate** el caballo saltó la verja **(b)** (move quickly): **I ~ed out of bed** me levanté (de la cama) de un salto; **they'll ~ at the chance** no van a dejar pasar la oportunidad **2 (a)** (change, skip) saltar **(b)** (increase, advance suddenly) subir de un golpe **3 (a)** (jerk) saltar **(b)** (in alarm) sobresaltarse; **you made me ~!** ¡qué susto me diste! ■ ~ *vt* **1** (leap over) ‹*hurdle*› saltar, brincar* (Méx); **to ~ rope** (AmE) saltar a la cuerda *or* (Esp tb) a la comba *or* (Chi) al cordel, brincar* la reata (Méx) **2 (a)** (spring out of) ‹*rails/tracks*› salirse* de **(b)** (disregard) saltarse; **to ~ the lights** pasar el semáforo en rojo, pasarse el alto (Méx); **to ~ the line** *o* (BrE) **queue** colarse* **3** (ambush, attack) (colloq) asaltar, atacar*

jump² *n* **1 (a)** (leap) salto *m*; **I sat up with a ~** me incorporé sobresaltado **(b)** (fence) valla *f* **2 (a)** (sudden transition) salto *m* **(b)** (increase, advance) aumento *m*

jumper /ˈdʒʌmpər ‖ ˈdʒʌmpə(r)/ *n* **(a)** (dress) (AmE) jumper *m or f* (AmL), pichi *m* (Esp) **(b)** (BrE) ⇒ SWEATER

jumper cables *pl n* (AmE) cables *mpl* de arranque

jump: **~ jet** *n* avión *m* de despegue vertical; **~ leads** /li:dz/ *pl n* (BrE) ⇒ JUMPER CABLES; **~ rope** *n* (AmE) cuerda *f or* (Méx) reata *f or* (Chi) cordel *m* (de saltar), comba *f* (Esp); **~-start** *vt*: *hacer arrancar un coche ya sea empujándolo o haciendo un puente*; **~ suit** *n* mono *m*, enterito *m* (RPl)

jumpy /ˈdʒʌmpi/ *adj* **-pier, -piest** nervioso

junction /ˈdʒʌŋkʃən/ *n* **(a)** (meeting point — of roads, rails) cruce *m*; (— of rivers) confluencia *f* **(b)** (Elec) empalme *m*

juncture /ˈdʒʌŋktʃər ‖ ˈdʒʌŋktʃə(r)/ *n* coyuntura *f*; **at this ~** en este momento

June /dʒu:n/ **▶ 540** *n* junio *m*

jungle /ˈdʒʌŋgəl/ *n* [C U] selva *f*, jungla *f*

junior¹ /ˈdʒu:njər ‖ ˈdʒu:niə(r)/ *adj* **1 (a)** (lower in rank) ‹*official*› subalterno; ‹*position*› de subalterno **(b)** (younger) más joven; **James D. Clark J~** (AmE) James D. Clark, hijo *or* junior **2** (AmE Educ) (*before n*) de tercer año

junior² *n* **1 (a)** (younger person): **he is two years my ~** tiene dos años menos que yo **(b)** (person of lower rank) subalterno, -na *m,f* **2** (Educ) (in US) *estudiante de tercer año de colegio secundario o universidad*; (in UK) *alumno de primaria o de los primeros años de secundaria*

junior: **~ college** *n* (in US) *establecimiento universitario donde se estudian los dos primeros años de la carrera*; **~ high (school)** *n* (in US) *colegio en* *el que se imparten los dos o tres primeros años de la enseñanza secundaria*; ~ **school** *n* (in UK) escuela *f* primaria (*para niños de 7 a 11 años*)

junk /dʒʌŋk/ *n* **1** [U] **(a)** (discarded items) trastos *mpl* (viejos); (*before n*) ~ **shop** tienda *f* de viejo **(b)** (worthless stuff) (colloq) basura *f* (fam); (*before n*) ~ **mail** propaganda *f* que se recibe por correo **2** [C] (boat) junco *m*

junk food *n* [U] comida *f* basura, alimento *m* chatarra (Méx)

junkie /'dʒʌŋki/ *n* (colloq) yonqui *mf* (fam), drogadicto, -ta *m,f*, pichicatero, -ra (CS, Per fam)

junkyard /'dzʌŋk,jɑːrd ‖ 'dʒʌŋk,jɑːd/ *n* depósito *m* de chatarra, deshuesadero *m* (Méx)

junta /'hʊntə ‖ 'dʒʌntə/ *n* junta *f* militar

Jupiter /'dʒuːpətər ‖ 'dʒuːpɪtə(r)/ *n* Júpiter *m*

jurisdiction /'dʒʊrəs'dɪkʃən ‖ ,dʒʊərɪs'dɪkʃən/ *n* [U C] jurisdicción *f*

juror /'dʒʊrər ‖ 'dʒʊərə(r)/ *n* jurado *mf*

jury /'dʒʊri ‖ 'dʒʊəri/ *n* (*pl* **-ries**) jurado *m*

just¹ /dʒʌst/ *adj* justo

just² *adv* **1 (a)** (in recent past): **she's ~ left** se acaba de ir, recién se fue (AmL) **(b)** (at the moment): **I was ~ about to leave when he called** estaba a punto de salir cuando llamó **2 (a)** (barely) justo; **I arrived ~ in time** llegué justo a tiempo; **I ~ missed him** no lo vi por poco *or* por apenas unos minutos **(b)** (a little): **~ above the knee** justo *or* apenas encima de la rodilla **3 (a)** (only) sólo; **she was ~ three when her father died** tenía apenas *or* sólo tres años cuando murió su padre; **would you like some more? — ~ a little, please** ¿quieres más? — bueno, un poquito **(b)** (simply): **I ~ stopped by to say hello** pasé para saludarte; **that's ~ gossip** no son más que chismes; **~ because he's famous doesn't mean he can be rude** (colloq) el hecho de que sea famoso no le da derecho a ser grosero **4 (a)** (exactly, precisely): **it's ~ what I wanted** es justo *or* precisamente *or* exactamente lo que quería; **the temperature was ~ right** la temperatura era la perfecta **(b)** (equally): **the desserts were ~ as good as the rest of the meal** los postres estuvieron tan buenos como el resto de la comida; **it's ~ as well you're leaving** menos mal que te vas **5** (emphatic use): **I ~ can't understand it** simplemente no lo entiendo; **~ leave it here** déjelo aquí, déjelo aquí nomás (AmL)

justice /'dʒʌstəs ‖ 'dʒʌstɪs/ *n* [U] justicia *f*; **to do sb/sth ~: the photo doesn't do her ~** la foto no le hace justicia; **he couldn't do ~ to the meal** no pudo hacerle honor a la comida; **she didn't do herself ~ in the exam** no rindió a la altura de su capacidad en el examen

Justice of the Peace *n* (*pl* **~s ~ ~ ~**) juez *mf* de paz, juez, jueza *m,f* de paz

justifiable /'dʒʌstəfaɪəbəl ‖ 'dʒʌstɪfaɪəbəl/ *adj* justificable

justification /'dʒʌstəfə'keɪʃən ‖ ,dʒʌstɪfɪ'keɪʃən/ *n* [U] justificación *f*

justified /'dʒʌstəfaɪd ‖ 'dʒʌstɪfaɪd/ *adj* justificado

justify /'dʒʌstəfaɪ ‖ 'dʒʌstɪfaɪ/ *vt* **-fies, -fying, -fied** justificar*

jut /dʒʌt/ **-tt-** *vi* sobresalir*

• **jut out** [*v* + *adv*] sobresalir*

jute /dʒuːt/ *n* [U] yute *m*

juvenile¹ /'dʒuːvənaɪl, -vənl ‖ 'dʒuːvənaɪl/ *adj* **(a)** (Law) (*before n*) ‹*court*› de menores; ‹*delinquent*› juvenil **(b)** (childish) (pej) infantil **(c)** ‹*literature*› (AmE) infantil y juvenil

juvenile² *n* (Law) menor *mf*

juxtapose /'dʒʌkstəpəʊz ‖ ,dʒʌkstə'pəʊz/ *vt* yuxtaponer*

K, k /keɪ/ *n* K, k *f*

K (Comput) (= **kilobyte**) K

kale /keɪl/ *n* [U] col *f* rizada

kaleidoscope /kə'laɪdəskəʊp/ *n* caleidoscopio *m*

Kampuchea /,kæmpuː'tʃiə/ *n* Kampuchea *f*

kangaroo /'kæŋgə'ruː/ *n* (*pl* **-roos**) canguro *m*

Kans = **Kansas**

karaoke /'kæri'əʊki/ *n* karaoke *m*

karat *n* (AmE) ⇒ CARAT (a)

karate /kə'rɑːti/ *n* [U] kárate *m*, karate *m* (AmL)

kayak /'kaɪæk/ *n* kayak *m*

Kazakhstan /,kɑːzɑːk'stɑːn/ *n* Kazajstán *m*

kebab /'kəbɑːb ‖ kɪ'bæb/ *n* pincho *m*, anticucho *m* (Bol, Chi, Per), brocheta *f* (Esp, Méx)

keel /kiːl/ *n* quilla *f*

• **keel over** [*v* + *adv*] **(a)** (capsize) «*ship*» volcar(se)* **(b)** (collapse) (colloq) «*person*» caer* redondo (fam)

keen /kiːn/ *adj* **-er, -est 1** (enthusiastic) ‹*photographer*› entusiasta; ‹*student*› aplicado; **he was ~ to start work** tenía muchas ganas de empezar a trabajar; **he's ~ to take part** tiene mucho interés en participar; **to be ~ ON sth/sb/-ING** (BrE): **I'm ~ on golf** me encanta el golf; **she's very ~ on him** le gusta muchísimo; **they're ~ on joining the club** tienen muchas ganas de hacerse socios del club **2 (a)** (sharp) ‹*blade*› afilado, filoso (AmL), filudo (Chi, Per) **(b)** (acute) ‹*hearing*› muy fino; ‹*sight/sense of smell/intelligence*› agudo **(c)** (intense) ‹*competition*› muy reñido; ‹*interest*› vivo

keep¹ /kiːp/ *n* **1** (living) sustento *m* **2** *for* **~s** (colloq) para siempre **3** (in castle, fortress) torre *f* del homenaje

keep² (*past & past p* **kept**) *vt* **1 (a)** (not throw away) ‹*receipt/ticket*› guardar; (not give back) quedarse con; (not lose) conservar; **~ the change** quédese (con) el cambio **(b)** (look after, reserve) **to ~ sth (FOR sb)** guardar(le) algo (A algn) **2** (store) guardar; **I always ~ a first-aid kit in the car** me gusta tener un botiquín en el coche **3** (reserve for future use) guardar **4 (a)** (raise) ‹*pigs/bees*› criar* **(b)** (manage, run) ‹*stall/guesthouse*› tener* **5 (a)** (support) mantener* **(b)** (maintain): **I've kept a note** *o* **record of everything** he tomado nota de todo **6 (a)** (cause to remain, continue) mantener*; **try and ~ it clean** trata de mantenerlo limpio; **the noise kept me awake** el ruido no me dejó dormir **(b)** (detain): **don't let me ~ you** no te quiero entretener; **what kept you?** ¿qué te retuvo?; **they kept her in hospital** la dejaron ingresada *or* (CS, Méx tb) internada **7** (adhere to, fulfil) ‹*promise/vow*› cumplir; ‹*secret*› guardar ■ **~** *vi* **1** (remain) mantenerse*: **to ~ fit** mantenerse* en forma; **to ~ awake** mantenerse* despierto; **~ still!** ¡estáte quieto! **2 (a)** (continue) seguir*; **~ left** siga por la izquierda; **to ~ -ING** seguir* + GER; **to ~ at it** seguir* dándole (fam) **(b)** (repeatedly): **he ~s interfering** está continuamente entrometiéndose; **I ~ forgetting to bring it** nunca me acuerdo de traerlo **3** «*food*» conservarse (fresco) **4** (be in certain state of health) (colloq): **how are you ~ing?** ¿qué tal estás? (fam)

● **keep away** [*v + adv*] **to ~ away (FROM sb/sth)** no acercarse* (A algn/algo)

● **keep back I** [*v + adv*]: **~ back!** ¡atrás!; **~ well back from the edge** mantente bien alejado del borde

II [*v + o + adv, v + adv + o*] **1 (a)** ‹*crowd/floodwaters*› contener* **(b)** ‹*tears/sobs*› contener* **2** (not reveal) ‹*information/facts*› ocultar

● **keep down 1** [*v + o + adv*] **(a)** (not raise): **~ your head/voice down** no levantes la cabeza/la voz **(b)** ‹*food*› retener* **2** [*v + o + adv, v + adv + o*] (not allow to increase) ‹*prices*› mantener* al mismo nivel; ‹*weeds*› contener*

● **keep from** [*v + o + prep + o*] **1** (restrain, prevent): **I don't want to ~ you from your work** no quiero distraerte de tu trabajo; **I managed to ~ myself from laughing** pude aguantar la risa **2** (not reveal to) ocultar; **he kept vital information from them/us** les/nos ocultó información vital

● **keep in** [*v + o + adv, v + adv + o*] **(a)** (detain): **the teacher kept me in after school** el maestro me hizo quedar después de clase; **he was kept in for observation** lo dejaron ingresado *or* (CS, Méx tb) internado en observación **(b)** ‹*anger/feelings*› contener*

● **keep off 1** [*v + prep + o*] **(a)** (stay away from) ‹*land/property*› mantenerse* alejado de; Ⓢ **keep off the grass** prohibido pisar el césped **(b)** (avoid) ‹*cigarettes/subject*› evitar **2** [*v + o + prep + o*] **~ your hands off me!** ¡quítame las manos de encima!

● **keep on 1** [*v + adv*] **(a)** (continue) seguir*; **to ~ on -ING** seguir* + GER **(b)** (repeatedly): **I ~ on forgetting to tell him** siempre me olvido de decírselo; **she kept on interrupting him** lo interrumpía constantemente **(c)** (talk incessantly): **she ~s on at me about my weight** me está siempre encima con que estoy muy gordo **2** [*v + o + adv, v + adv + o*] (continue to employ) no despedir* **3** [*v + o + adv*] (continue to wear): **~ your coat on** no te quites el abrigo

● **keep out 1** [*v + adv*] (not enter): Ⓢ **keep out** prohibido el paso; **~ out of the kitchen** no entres en la cocina **2** [*v + o + adv, v + adv + o*] (prevent from entering, exclude) ‹*rain/sun*› impedir* que entre

● **keep out of** [*v + adv + prep + o*] ‹*danger*› no exponerse* a; ‹*trouble/argument*› no meterse en

● **keep to 1** [*v + prep + o*] **(a)** (adhere to, fulfil) ‹*plan*› ceñirse* a; ‹*promise*› cumplir **(b)** (not deviate from) ‹*path*› seguir* por; ‹*script*› ceñirse* a **(c)** (stay on): **~ to the right** (Auto) mantenga su derecha **2** [*v + o + prep + o*] (not divulge): **to ~ sth to oneself** guardarse algo **3** [*v + prep + o*] [*v + o + prep + o*]: **to ~ (oneself) to oneself** no ser* muy sociable

● **keep up I** [*v + adv*] **1** (not stop) «*rain/noise*» seguir*, continuar*; **to ~ up WITH sth** seguir* *or* continuar* CON algo **2 (a)** (maintain pace) **to ~ up WITH sb** seguirle* el ritmo A algn; **he's finding it difficult to ~ up in class** le está resultando difícil mantenerse al nivel de la clase **(b)** (remain informed) **to ~ up WITH sth** mantenerse* al tanto *or* al corriente DE algo

II [*v + o + adv, v + adv + o*] **1** (maintain at present level) mantener* **2** (continue, not stop) ‹*payments*› mantenerse* al día con; ‹*friendship*› mantener*

III [*v + o + adv*] **1** ‹*trousers/socks*› sujetar **2** (prevent from sleeping): **I hope we're not ~ing you up** espero que no te estemos quitando el sueño; **the baby kept me up all night** el niño me tuvo toda la noche en vela

keeper /ˈkiːpər ‖ ˈkiːpə(r)/ *n* (in zoo) guarda *mf*, cuidador, -dora *m,f*; (in museum) (BrE) conservador, -dora *m,f*

keep-fit /ˈkiːpˈfɪt/ *n* [U] (BrE) gimnasia *f* (de mantenimiento)

keeping /ˈkiːpɪŋ/ *n* [U] **(a)** (conformity): **in ~ with** ‹*with law/tradition*› en conformidad con **(b)** (trust, care): **to leave sth in sb's ~** dejar algo al cuidado de algn

keepsake /ˈkiːpseɪk/ *n* recuerdo *m*

keg /keg/ *n* barril *m*

kennel /ˈkenl̩/ *n* **(a)** (AmE) (for boarding) residencia *f* canina; (for breeding) criadero *m* de perros **(b)** (BrE) (hut) casa *f* del perro

kennels /ˈkenlz/ *n* (*pl* **~**) (BrE) (+ *sing vb*) ⇒ KENNEL (a)

Kenya /ˈkenjə, ˈkiː-/ *n* Kenia *f*

Kenyan /ˈkenjən, ˈkiː-/ *adj* keniano

kept /kept/ *past & past p of* KEEP²

kerb /kɜːrb ‖ kɜːb/ *n* (BrE) ⇒ CURB¹ 2

kernel /ˈkɜːrnl̩ ‖ ˈkɜːnl̩/ *n* (of nut, fruit) almendra *f*; (of corn, wheat) grano *m*

kerosene /ˈkerəsiːn/ *n* [U] queroseno *m*, kerosene *m*

kestrel /ˈkestrəl/ *n* cernícalo *m*

ketchup /ˈketʃəp ‖ ˈketʃʌp/ *n* [U] salsa *f* de tomate, ketchup *m*, catsup *m*

kettle /'ketl̩/ *n* pava *f or* (Bol, Ur) caldera *f or* (Andes, Méx) tetera *f*

kettledrum /'ketl̩drʌm/ *n* timbal *m*

key¹ /kiː/ *n* (*pl* **~s**) **1** (for lock) llave *f*; (on can) llave *f*, abridor *m*; (*before n*) **~ ring** llavero *m* **2 (a)** (to puzzle, code etc) clave *f* **(b)** (to map) explicación *f* de los signos convencionales **(c)** (answers) soluciones *fpl* **3** (crucial element) clave *f*; **patience is the ~** la paciencia es el factor clave *or* la clave **4** (of typewriter, piano) tecla *f*; (of wind instrument) llave *f* **5** (Mus) tono *m*; **to be off ~** no estar* en el tono

key² *adj* ‹*man/question*› clave *adj inv*

● **key in** [*v* + *o* + *adv*, *v* + *adv* + *o*] ‹*text/data*› teclear

key: **~board** *n* teclado *m*; **~hole** *n* ojo *m* de la cerradura; **~note** *n* (Mus) tónica *f*; (central idea) tónica *f*; **~pad** *n* (Comput, Telec, TV) teclado *m* numérico; **~word** *n* palabra *f* clave

kg ▶ 322 (= **kilo(s)** *o* **kilogram(s)**) Kg.

khaki /'kæki ‖ 'kɑːki/ ▶ 515 *adj* caqui *or* kaki *adj inv*

kibbutz /kɪ'bʊts/ *n* (*pl* **-butzim** /-bʊtsɪm/) kibbutz *m*

kick¹ /kɪk/ *n* **1** (by person) patada *f*, puntapié *m*; (by horse) coz *f* **2** (colloq) (thrill, excitement): **to get a ~ out of doing sth** deleitarse haciendo algo; **just for ~s** nada más que por divertirse

kick² *vi* «*person*» dar* patadas; «*swimmer*» patalear; «*horse*» cocear ■ **~** *vt* **1** ‹*ball*› patear, darle* una patada *or* un puntapié a; ‹*person*› pegarle* una patada a algn **2** (stop) (colloq) ‹*habit*› dejar

● **kick around**, (BrE also) **kick about** (colloq) [*v* + *o* + *adv*] **(a)** (treat badly) maltratar **(b)** ‹*idea*› estudiar **(c) to ~ a ball around** pelotear

● **kick down** [*v* + *o* + *adv*, *v* + *adv* + *o*] ‹*door*› echar abajo (*a patadas*)

● **kick off 1** [*v* + *adv*] **(a)** (in football): **they ~ off at three** el partido empieza a las tres **(b)** (begin) (colloq) «*person/meeting*» empezar* **2** [*v* + *adv* + *o*] (begin) ‹*discussion*› iniciar, empezar*

● **kick out** [*v* + *o* + *adv*] echar

● **kick up 1** [*v* + *o* + *adv*, *v* + *adv* + *o*] ‹*leaves/dust*› levantar **2** [*v* + *adv* + *o*]: **to ~ up a fuss** *o* **row** armar una bronca (fam); **to ~ up a din** armar un escándalo

kick: **~off** *n* (Sport) saque *m or* puntapié *m* inicial, patada *f* de inicio; **~start** *vt* ‹*engine*› arrancar* (*con el pedal de arranque*)

kid¹ /kɪd/ *n* **1** [C] (colloq) **(a)** (child) niño, -ña *m,f*, chaval, -vala *m,f* (Esp fam), chavalo, -vala *m,f* (AmC, Méx fam), escuincle, -cla (Méx fam), pibe, -ba *m,f* (RPl fam), cabro, -bra *m,f* (Chi fam) **(b)** (young person) chico, -ca *m,f* **2 (a)** [C] (goat) cabrito, -ta *m,f*, choto, -ta *m,f* **(b)** [U] (leather) cabritilla *f*

kid² **-dd-** *vi* (colloq) bromear ■ **~** *vt* **(a)** (tease) **to ~ sb** (ABOUT **sth**) tomarle el pelo a algn (CON algo) **(b)** (deceive) engañar; **don't ~ yourself!** ¡no te hagas ilusiones!

kidnap /'kɪdnæp/ *vt* **-pp-** *or* (AmE) **-p-** secuestrar, raptar

kidnapper, (AmE also) **kidnaper** /'kɪdnæpər ‖ 'kɪdnæpə(r)/ *n* secuestrador, -dora *m,f*, raptor, -tora *m,f*

kidnapping, (AmE also) **kidnaping** /'kɪdnæpɪŋ/ *n* secuestro *m*, rapto *m*

kidney /'kɪdni/ ▶ 484 *n* (*pl* **-neys**) (Anat, Culin) riñón *m*; (*before n*) ‹*disease/stone*› renal; **~ machine** riñón *m* artificial

kidney bean *n* frijol *m or* (Esp) judía *f or* (CS) poroto *m* (*con forma de riñón*)

kill¹ /kɪl/ *vt* **1** (cause death of) ‹*person/animal*› matar; **she was ~ed in a car crash** se mató *or* murió en un accidente de coche **2 (a)** (destroy) ‹*hopes*› acabar con **(b)** (spoil) ‹*flavor/taste*› estropear **(c)** (deaden) ‹*pain*› calmar **(d)** (use up): **to ~ time** matar el tiempo ■ **~** *vi* matar

● **kill off** [*v* + *o* + *adv*, *v* + *adv* + *o*] matar

kill² *n* **(a)** [C] (act): **he went in for the ~** entró a matar **(b)** [U] (animal, animals killed) presa *f*

killer /'kɪlər ‖ 'kɪlə(r)/ *n* (person) asesino, -na *m,f*; (*before n*) ‹*shark*› asesino; ‹*disease*› mortal

killer whale *n* orca *f*

killing /'kɪlɪŋ/ *n* [C U] (of person) asesinato *m*; (of animal) matanza *f*; ***to make a ~*** hacer* un gran negocio, forrarse (fam)

killjoy /'kɪldʒɔɪ/ *n* aguafiestas *mf*

kiln /kɪln/ *n* horno *m*

kilo /'kiːləʊ/ ▶ 322 *n* (*pl* **-los**) kilo *m*

kilobyte /'kɪləbaɪt/ *n* kilobyte *m*, kiloocteto *m*

kilogram, (BrE also) **kilogramme** /'kɪləgræm/ ▶ 322 *n* kilogramo *m*

kilometer, (BrE) **kilometre** /'kɪləmiːtər ‖ kɪ'lɒmɪtə(r), 'kɪləmiːtə(r)/ ▶ 681 *n* kilómetro *m*

kilowatt /'kɪləwɑːt ‖ 'kɪləwɒt/ *n* kilovatio *m*

kilt /kɪlt/ *n* falda *f or* (CS) pollera *f* escocesa

kimono /kə'məʊnəʊ ‖ kɪ'məʊnəʊ/ *n* (*pl* **-nos**) kimono *m*, quimono *m*

kin /kɪn/ *n* (+ *pl vb*) familiares *mpl*, parientes *mpl*

kind¹ /kaɪnd/ *n* **1** (sort, type) **(a)** (of things) tipo *m*, clase *f*; **of all ~s** de todo tipo, de toda clase **(b)** (of people) clase *f*, tipo *m* **2** (sth approximating to) especie *f*; **she was overcome by a ~ of yearning** la invadió una especie de añoranza **3** (*in phrases*) **in kind** ‹*pay*› en especie; **kind of** (colloq): **he seemed ~ of stupid** parecía como tonto (fam); **of a kind**: **they served a meal, of a ~** sirvieron una especie de comida, si se le puede llamar así; **they're two of a ~** son tal para cual

kind² *adj* **-er, -est** ‹*offer*› amable; **he's very ~** es muy buena persona; **she's always been ~ to me** siempre ha sido muy amable conmigo; **it's very ~ to your skin** no daña la piel; **would you be ~ enough to accompany me?** ¿tendría la amabilidad de acompañarme?

kindergarten /'kɪndər,gɑːrtn̩ ‖ 'kɪndəgɑːtn̩/ *n* jardín *m* de infancia *or* de niños

kind-hearted /'kaɪnd'hɑːrtəd ‖ ,kaɪnd'hɑːtɪd/ *adj* de buen corazón

kindle /'kɪndl̩/ *vt* ‹*fire*› encender*; ‹*interest*› despertar*; ‹*passion*› encender*

kindly¹ /'kaɪndli/ *adv* **1 (a)** (generously) amablemente **(b)** (adding polite emphasis) (fml): **passengers are ~ requested to** ... se ruega a los pasajeros tengan la amabilidad de ... **2** (favorably): **they didn't**

take ~ to my suggestions no recibieron demasiado bien mis sugerencias; she doesn't take ~ to being contradicted no le hace ninguna gracia que la contradigan

kindly² *adj* **-lier, -liest** bondadoso

kindness /'kaɪndnəs ‖ 'kaɪndnɪs/ *n* **(a)** [U] (quality) ~ (TO *o* TOWARD **sb**) amabilidad *f* (PARA CON algn) **(b)** [C] (act) favor *m*

kindred /'kɪndrəd ‖ 'kɪndrɪd/ *adj* (*before n*) (similar) similar; ~ **spirits** almas *fpl* gemelas

king /kɪŋ/ ▶603 *n* rey *m*

kingdom /'kɪŋdəm/ *n* reino *m*; **the animal ~** el reino animal

king: **~fisher** /'kɪŋˌfɪʃər ‖ 'kɪŋˌfɪʃə(r)/ *n* martín *m* pescador; **~-size**, **~-sized** /'kɪŋsaɪzd/ *adj* ‹*cigarette*› extralargo; ‹*bed*› de matrimonio (*extragrande*)

kink /kɪŋk/ *n* (in rope, wire) vuelta *f*, curva *f*; (in hair) onda *f*

kinky /'kɪŋki/ *adj* **-kier, -kiest** (colloq) pervertidillo (fam)

kinship /'kɪnʃɪp/ *n* [U] parentesco *m*

kiosk /'kiːɑːsk ‖ 'kiːɒsk/ *n* (stall) quiosco *m*

kipper /'kɪpər ‖ 'kɪpə(r)/ *n* arenque *m* salado y ahumado

Kirghizia /kɪr'giːziə ‖ kiə'gɪziə/, **Kirghizstan** /ˌkɪrgiː'stɑːn ‖ kɪəgɪ'stɑːn/ *n* Kirguizistán *m*

kiss¹ /kɪs/ *vt* ‹*person*› besar; **to ~ sb goodbye/goodnight** darle* un beso de despedida/de buenas noches a algn ■ ~ *vi* besarse

kiss² *n* beso *m*; **to give sb a ~** darle* un beso a algn; **she gave him the ~ of life** le hizo (la) respiración artificial

kit /kɪt/ *n* **1** [C] **(a)** (set of items): **first-aid ~** botiquín *m* de primeros auxilios; **tool ~** caja *f* de herramientas **(b)** (parts for assembly) kit *m* **2** [U] **(a)** (personal effects) cosas *fpl*; (Mil) petate *m* **(b)** (Clothing) (esp BrE) **gym ~** (Sport) equipo *m* de gimnasia

kitchen /'kɪtʃən ‖ 'kɪtʃɪn/ *n* cocina *f*

kitchen garden *n* huerto *m*

kite /kaɪt/ *n* cometa *f* *or* (RPl tb) barrilete *m* *or* (AmC, Méx) papalote *m* *or* (Ven) papagayo *m* *or* (Chi) volantín *m*

kitten /'kɪtn̩/ *n* gatito, -ta *m,f*

kitty /'kɪti/ *n* (*pl* **-ties**) (colloq) bote *m*, fondo *m* común

kiwi /'kiːwiː/ *n* **(a)** (Zool) kiwi *m* **(b)** ~ **(fruit)** kiwi *m*

kleptomaniac /'kleptə'meɪniæk/ *n* cleptómano, -na *m,f*

klutz /klʌts/ *n* (AmE colloq) torpe *mf*, patoso, -sa *m,f* (Esp fam)

km ▶681 (= **kilometer(s)** *o* (BrE) **kilometre(s)**) Km.

knack /næk/ *n*: **there's a ~ to making omelettes** hacer tortillas tiene su truco *or* (Méx) su chiste; **I'll never get the ~ of this!** ¡nunca le voy a agarrar la onda (AmL fam) *or* (Esp) coger el tranquillo a esto!

knapsack /'næpsæk/ *n* mochila *f*

knave /neɪv/ *n* **(a)** (rogue) (arch) truhán *m* (ant) **(b)** (in French pack of cards) jota *f*; (in Spanish pack) sota *f*

knead /niːd/ *vt* (Culin) amasar

knee¹ /niː/ ▶484 *n* (Anat, Clothing) rodilla *f*; **to be on one's ~s** estar* arrodillado; **to go** *o* **get down on one's ~s** ponerse* de rodillas

knee² *vt* darle* *or* pegarle* un rodillazo a

knee: **~cap** *n* rótula *f*; **~-deep** /'niː'diːp/ *adj* (*pred*): **the water is ~-deep** el agua llega hasta la(s) rodilla(s); **they were ~-deep in mud** estaban con el barro hasta las rodillas; **~-high** /'niː'haɪ/ *adj* ‹*sock*› largo

kneel /niːl/ *vi* (*past & past p* **kneeled** *or* **knelt**) (get down on one's knees) arrodillarse; (be on one's knees) estar* arrodillado; **to ~ down** arrodillarse

knee-length /'niːleŋθ/ *adj* ‹*sock*› largo; ‹*skirt*› hasta la rodilla; ‹*boot*› alto

knelt /nelt/ *past & past p of* KNEEL

knew /nuː ‖ njuː/ *past of* KNOW

knickerbockers /'nɪkərbɑːkərz ‖ 'nɪkəbɒkəz/ *pl n* pantalones *mpl* bombachos

knickers /'nɪkərz ‖ 'nɪkəz/ *pl n* **1** (AmE) ⇨ KNICKERBOCKERS **2** (BrE) (undergarment) calzones *mpl* (AmS), bragas *fpl* (Esp), pantaletas *fpl* (AmC, Ven), bombacha *f* (RPl)

knickknack /'nɪknæk/ *n* chuchería *f*

knife¹ /naɪf/ *n* (*pl* **knives**) cuchillo *m*; (penknife) navaja *f*, cortaplumas *m* *or f*; (dagger) puñal *m*

knife² *vt* acuchillar

knife: ~ **edge** *n* filo *m* (*de cuchillo, navaja etc*); ***to be on a ~ edge*** pender de un hilo; **~-point** *n*: **he was robbed at ~-point** le robaron amenazándolo con un cuchillo

knight¹ /naɪt/ *n* **(a)** (Hist) caballero *m* **(b)** (holder of title) sir *m* **(c)** (in chess) caballo *m*

knight² *vt* conceder el título de sir a

knighthood /'naɪthʊd/ *n* título *m* de sir

knit /nɪt/ (*pres p* **knitting**; *past & past p* **knitted** *or* **knit**) *vt* **1** ‹*sweater*› (by hand) hacer*, tejer; (with machine) tejer, tricotar (Esp) **2** (join, unite): ‹*bones*› soldar*; **a tightly ~ family** una familia muy unida ■ ~ *vi* (by hand) tejer, hacer* punto *or* calceta (Esp); (with machine) tejer, tricotar (Esp)

knitting /'nɪtɪŋ/ *n* [U] **(a)** (piece of work) tejido *m*, punto *m* (Esp) **(b)** (activity): **I like ~** me gusta tejer, me gusta hacer* punto *or* calceta (Esp)

knitting: ~ **machine** *n* máquina *f* de tejer, tricotosa *f* (Esp); ~ **needle** *n* aguja *f* de tejer *or* (Esp) de hacer punto, palillo *m* (Chi)

knives /naɪvz/ *pl of* KNIFE¹

knob /nɑːb ‖ nɒb/ *n* **(a)** (on door) pomo *m*, perilla *f* (AmL); (on drawer) tirador *m*, perilla *f* (AmL); (on walking stick) puño *m*; (on radio, TV) botón *m* **(b)** (lump) bulto *m* **(c)** (small piece) (esp BrE): **a ~ of butter** un trocito *or* una nuez de mantequilla

knobbly /'nɑːbli ‖ 'nɒbli/ *adj* **-lier, -liest** ‹*tree/fingers*› nudoso; ‹*knees*› huesudo

knock¹ /nɑːk ‖ nɒk/ *n* (sound) golpe *m*; (blow to head, on door) golpe *m*

knock² *vt* **1** (strike, push): **to ~ one's head on/against sth** darse* (un golpe) en la cabeza con/contra algo; **she ~ed the vase off the shelf** tiró el jarrón de la repisa; **they ~ed a large hole in**

the wall hicieron un gran boquete en la pared **2** (criticize) (colloq) criticar* ■ ~ *vi* **(a)** (on door) llamar, golpear (AmL), tocar* (AmL) **(b)** (collide) **to ~ AGAINST/INTO sb/sth** darse* *or* chocar* CONTRA algn/algo

• knock about, knock around (colloq) [*v + o + adv*] pegarle* a

• knock back [*v + o + adv, v + adv + o*] (colloq) ‹*drink*› beberse, tomarse

• knock down [*v + o + adv, v + adv + o*] **1 (a)** (cause to fall) ‹*door/fence*› tirar abajo; ‹*obstacle*› derribar; **he ran into her and ~ed her down** chocó con ella y la hizo caer **(b)** «*vehicle/driver*» atropellar **(c)** (demolish) echar abajo **2** (colloq) (reduce) ‹*price/charge*› rebajar

• knock off 1 [*v + adv*] [*v + prep + o*] (stop work) (colloq): **when do you ~ off (work)?** ¿a qué hora sales del trabajo?, ¿hasta qué hora trabajas?; **let's ~ off for lunch** vamos a parar para comer **2** [*v + o + adv, v + adv + o*] (stop) (colloq) dejar de; **~ it off, will you!** ¡déjala ya! (fam) **3** [*v + o + adv, v + adv + o*] (deduct, eliminate) (colloq) rebajar; **I'll ~ off 25% for you** le hago un descuento del 25%

• knock out 1 [*v + o + adv, v + adv + o*] (make unconscious) dejar sin sentido, hacer* perder el conocimiento; (in boxing) dejar K.O., noquear; **she hit her head and ~ed herself out** se dio un golpe en la cabeza y perdió el conocimiento **2** [*v + o + adv, v + adv + o*] (of competition) eliminar

• knock over [*v + o + adv, v + adv + o*] **(a)** (cause to fall) tirar **(b)** «*vehicle*» atropellar

• knock up [*v + o + adv, v + adv + o*] (colloq) (assemble hurriedly) improvisar

knocker /'nɑ:kər ‖ 'nɒkə(r)/ *n* aldaba *f*, llamador *m*

knocking /'nɑ:kɪŋ ‖ 'nɒkɪŋ/ *n* **(a)** (noise) (*no pl*) golpes *mpl* **(b)** [U] (Auto) golpeteo *m*, cascabeleo *m* (AmL)

knock: **~-kneed** /'nɑ:k'ni:d ‖ ˌnɒk'ni:d/ *adj* patizambo; **~-on effect** /'nɑ:k'ɑ:n ‖ nɒk'ɒn/ *n* repercusiones *fpl*; **~out** *n* (in boxing) nocaut *m*, K.O. *m* (*read as: nocaut or* (Esp) cao)

knoll /nəʊl/ *n* loma *f*, montículo *m*

knot¹ /nɑ:t ‖ nɒt/ *n* **1** (in string, hair, wood) nudo *m*; (in muscles) nódulo *m* **2** (measure of speed) nudo *m*

knot² *vt* **-tt-** hacer* un nudo en

know¹ /nəʊ/ (*past* **knew**; *past p* **known**) *vt* **1 (a)** (have knowledge of, be aware of) saber*; **I don't ~ his name/how old he is** no sé cómo se llama/cuántos años tiene; **it is well ~n that** ... todo el mundo sabe que ...; **to let sb ~ sth** decirle* algo a algn; (warn) avisarle algo a algn; **without our ~ing it** sin saberlo nosotros; **there's no ~ing what he might do** quién sabe qué hará; **I ~ what: let's go skating!** ¡tengo una idea: vayamos a patinar!; ***to ~ sth backwards*** ‹*part/play*› saber* algo al dedillo *or* al revés y al derecho **(b)** (have skill, ability) **to ~ how to** + INF saber* + INF **2** (be acquainted with) ‹*person/place*› conocer*; **how did they get to ~ each other?** ¿cómo se conocieron?; **to get to ~ sth** ‹*subject/job*› familiarizarse* con algo **3 (a)** (recognize, identify) reconocer*; **to ~ sth/sb BY sth** reconocer* algo/a algn POR algo **(b)** (distinguish) **to ~ sth/sb FROM sth/sb** distinguir* algo/a algn DE algo/algn ■ ~ *vi* saber*; **how do you ~?** ¿cómo lo sabes?; **I ~!** ¡ya sé!, ¡tengo una idea!; **you never ~** nunca se sabe; **I'm not stupid, you ~!** oye, que no soy tonto ¿eh? *or* ¿sabes?; **did you ~ about John?** ¿sabías lo de John?; **to get to ~ about sth** enterarse de algo; **she knew of their activities** tenía conocimiento *or* estaba enterada de sus actividades; **not that I ~ of** que yo sepa, no; **do you ~ of a good carpenter?** ¿conoces a *or* sabes de algún carpintero bueno?

know² *n*: ***to be in the ~*** estar* enterado

know: **~-all** *n* (BrE) ⇒ KNOW-IT-ALL; **~how** *n* [U] know-how *m*, conocimientos *mpl* y experiencia

knowing /'nəʊɪŋ/ *adj* ‹*smile*› de complicidad; **she gave me a ~ look** me miró dándome a entender que ya lo sabía

knowingly /'nəʊɪŋli/ *adv* **(a)** ‹*smile/nod*› de manera cómplice **(b)** (deliberately) ‹*hurt/lie*› a sabiendas

know-it-all /'nəʊɪtɔ:l/ *n* (colloq) sabelotodo *mf* (fam)

knowledge /'nɑ:lɪdʒ ‖ 'nɒlɪdʒ/ *n* [U] **1** (awareness) conocimiento *m*; **to the best of my ~** que yo sepa; **it is common ~ that** ... todo el mundo sabe que ... **2** (facts known) saber *m*; (by particular person) conocimientos *mpl*

knowledgeable /'nɑ:lɪdʒəbəl ‖ 'nɒlɪdʒəbəl/ *adj* (about current affairs) informado; (about given subject) entendido; (in general) culto

known¹ /nəʊn/ *past p of* KNOW

known² *adj* ‹*fact*› conocido, sabido; **a little-~ artist** un artista poco conocido; **to be ~ AS sth** (have reputation) tener* fama DE algo; **better ~ as** ... más conocido como ...; **for reasons best ~ to herself** por motivos que ella conocerá; **he's better ~ for his work in films** se le conoce mejor por su trabajo cinematográfico

knuckle /'nʌkəl/ *n* **(a)** (finger joint) nudillo *m* **(b)** (of pork) codillo *m*; (of veal) morcillo *m*, jarrete *m*

• knuckle down [*v + adv*] ponerse* a trabajar en serio

• knuckle under [*v + adv*] ceder*, pasar por el aro

knuckleduster /'nʌkəlˌdʌstər ‖ 'nʌkəlˌdʌstə(r)/ *n* (BrE) ⇒ BRASS KNUCKLES

koala /kəʊ'ɑ:lə/ *n* **~ (bear)** koala *m*

kooky /'ku:ki/ *adj* **-kier, -kiest** (AmE colloq) chiflado (fam)

Koran /kə'rɑ:n/ *n* **the ~** el Corán

Korea /kə'ri:ə/ *n* Corea *f*

Korean¹ /kə'ri:ən/ *adj* coreano

Korean² *n* **(a)** [C] (person) coreano, -na *m,f* **(b)** [U] (language) coreano *m*

kosher /'kəʊʃər ‖ 'kəʊʃə(r)/ *adj* ‹*food/butcher*› kosher *adj inv*

kowtow /'kaʊ'taʊ/ *vi* **to ~ TO sb** doblar la cerviz ANTE algn

kph (= **kilometers** *o* (BrE) **kilometres per hour**) Km/h.

KS = **Kansas**

kung fu /'kʌŋ'fu:/ *n* [U] kung fu *m*
Kurd /kɜ:rd || kɜ:d/ *n* kurdo, -da *m,f*
Kurdish /'kɜ:rdɪʃ || 'kɜ:dɪʃ/ *adj* kurdo
Kuwait /kə'weɪt || kʊ'weɪt/ *n* Kuwait *m*
Kuwaiti /kə'weɪti || kʊ'weɪti/ *adj* kuwaití
KY, **Ky** = **Kentucky**

L, **l** /el/ *n* L, l *f*
l (= **liter(s)** *or* (BrE) **litre(s)**) l.
L **(a)** (BrE Auto) Ⓢ L (= **learner**) L (*conductor en aprendizaje*) **(b)** (Clothing) (= **large**) G (*talla grande*)
la /lɑ:/ *n* (Mus) la *m*
La = **Louisiana**
LA (a) = **Los Angeles** (b) = **Louisiana**
lab /læb/ *n* (colloq) laboratorio *m*
label¹ /'leɪbəl/ *n* etiqueta *f*
label² *vt*, (BrE) **-ll-** **(a)** ‹*bottle/luggage*› ponerle* una etiqueta a **(b)** (categorize) **to ~ sth/sb (AS) sth** catalogar* algo/a algn DE algo
labor¹, (BrE) **labour** /'leɪbər || 'leɪbə(r)/ *n* **1** [U] **(a)** (work) trabajo *m*; (*before n*) ‹*dispute/laws*› laboral **(b)** (workers) mano *f* de obra **2** **Labour** (in UK) (Pol) (*no art, + sing or pl vb*) los laboristas, el Partido Laborista **3** **(a)** [U C] (effort) esfuerzos *mpl*, trabajo *m* **(b)** [C] (task) labor *f*, tarea *f* **4** [U] (Med) parto *m*; **to be in ~** estar* de parto; (*before n*) **~ pains** dolores *mpl* *or* contracciones *fpl* del parto
labor², (BrE) **labour** *vt*: **to ~ a point** insistir excesivamente sobre un punto ■ **~** *vi* (toil) trabajar; **he ~ed up the hill** subió trabajosamente *or* penosamente la cuesta
laboratory /'læbərətɔ:ri || lə'bɒrətri/ *n* (*pl* **-ries**) laboratorio *m*
Labor Day *n* Día *m* del Trabajo *or* de los trabajadores
labored, (BrE) **laboured** /'leɪbərd || 'leɪbəd/ *adj* ‹*breathing*› dificultoso, fatigoso; ‹*metaphor/joke*› forzado, torpe
laborer, (BrE) **labourer** /'leɪbərər || 'leɪbərə(r)/ *n* peón *m*; **farm ~** peón *m*, trabajador *m* agrícola
laborious /lə'bɔ:riəs/ *adj* ‹*task/process*› laborioso; ‹*style*› farragoso
labor union *n* (AmE) sindicato *m*
labour *etc* (BrE) ⇒ LABOR *etc*
labrador /'læbrədɔ:r || 'læbrədɔ:(r)/ *n* labrador *m*
labyrinth /'læbərɪnθ/ *n* laberinto *m*
lace¹ /leɪs/ *n* **1** [U] (fabric) encaje *m*; (as border) puntilla *f* **2** [C] (*shoe~*) cordón *m* (de zapato), agujeta *f* (Méx), pasador *m* (Per)
lace² *vt* **1** ‹*shoes/boots*› ponerles* los cordones *or* (Méx) las agujetas *or* (Per) los pasadores a **2** (fortify): **he ~d my drink with vodka** me echó un chorro de vodka en la bebida
lacerate /'læsəreɪt/ *vt* lacerar
lack¹ /læk/ *n* **~ OF sth** falta *f* *or* (frml) carencia *f* DE algo
lack² *vt* no tener*, carecer* de (frml); **it ~s originality** le falta *or* no tiene originalidad, carece de originalidad (frml)
lacking /'lækɪŋ/ *adj* (*pred*) **(a)** (absent): **the necessary resources are ~** faltan los recursos necesarios **(b)** (deficient) **to be ~ IN sth** no tener* algo, carecer DE algo (frml)
lackluster, (BrE) **lacklustre** /'læk,lʌstər || 'læk,lʌstə(r)/ *adj* **(a)** ‹*eyes*› apagado; ‹*hair*› opaco **(b)** (mediocre) ‹*performance/campaign*› deslucido; ‹*candidate*› mediocre
laconic /lə'kɑ:nɪk || lə'kɒnɪk/ *adj* lacónico
lacquer /'lækər || 'lækə(r)/ *n* [U C] **(a)** (varnish) laca *f* **(b)** (*hair ~*) laca *f* *or* fijador *m* (para el pelo)
lad /læd/ *n* muchacho *m*, chaval *m* (Esp fam), pibe *m* (RPl fam), chavo *m* (Méx, Ven fam), chavalo *m* (AmC, Méx fam), cabro *m* (Chi fam)
ladder /'lædər || 'lædə(r)/ *n* **1** (Const) escalera *f* (de mano) **2** (in stocking, tights) (BrE) carrera *f*
laden /'leɪdn/ *adj* **~ WITH sth** cargado DE algo
ladies /'leɪdiz/ *n* (BrE) ⇒ LADIES' ROOM
ladies' room *n* (AmE) baño *m* *or* (esp Esp) servicio *m* de señoras; Ⓢ **Ladies (Room)** Señoras, Damas
ladle /'leɪdl/ *n* cucharón *m*
lady /'leɪdi/ *n* (*pl* **ladies**) **1** **(a)** (woman) señora *f*; **ladies and gentlemen** señoras y señores, damas y caballeros **(b)** (refined woman) señora *f*, dama *f* **2** ▶**603** (noblewoman or wife of a knight) lady *f*
lady: **~bug** (AmE), **~bird** (BrE) *n* mariquita *f*, catarina *f* (Méx), petaca *f* (Col), chinita *f* (Chi), San Antonio *m* (Ur), vaca *f* de San Antón (Arg); **~-in-waiting** /'leɪdim'weɪtɪŋ/ *n* (*pl* **ladies-in-waiting**) dama *f* de honor; **~like** *adj* fino
ladyship /'leɪdiʃɪp/ ▶**603** *n*: **Her/Your L~** la señora
lag¹ /læg/ *n* (interval) lapso *m*, intervalo *m*; (delay) retraso *m*, demora *f* (esp AmL)
lag² **-gg-** *vi* **to ~ (behind)** quedarse atrás; **to ~ behind sb/sth** ir* a la zaga de algn/algo ■ **~** *vt* ‹*pipes*› revestir* con aislantes
lager /'lɑ:gər || 'lɑ:gə(r)/ *n* [U C] cerveza *f* (rubia)
lagoon /lə'gu:n/ *n* laguna *f*
lah /lɑ:/ *n* (BrE Mus) la *m*
laid /leɪd/ *past & past p of* LAY²
laid-back /'leɪd'bæk/ *adj* (colloq) ‹*person*› tranquilo y relajado; ‹*atmosphere*› relajado

lain /leɪn/ *past p of* LIE² II
lair /ler ‖ leə(r)/ *n* guarida *f*
lake /leɪk/ *n* lago *m*
lamb /læm/ *n* [C] cordero *m*
lame¹ /leɪm/ *adj* **1** (in foot, leg) cojo, rengo (AmL); **to go ~** quedarse cojo *or* (AmL tb) rengo **2** (weak) ‹*excuse*› pobre, malo
lame² *vt* lisiar
lament¹ /lə'ment/ *n* lamento *m*
lament² *vt* **(a)** ‹*misfortune/failure*› lamentar **(b)** (liter) ‹*death/loss*› llorar
lamentable /'læməntəbəl/ *adj* lamentable
lamp /læmp/ *n* lámpara *f*; (Auto) luz *f*
lamplight /'læmplaɪt/ *n* [U] (of table lamp) luz *f* de (la) lámpara; (of streetlamp) luz *f* de(l) farol
lampoon /læm'pu:n/ *vt* satirizar*
lamp: **~post** *n* farol *m*; **~shade** *n* pantalla *f* (*de lámpara*)
lance¹ /læns ‖ lɑ:ns/ *n* lanza *f*
lance² *vt* abrir* con lanceta
lancet /'lænsət ‖ 'lɑ:nsɪt/ *n* lanceta *f*
land¹ /lænd/ *n* **1** [U] (Geog, Agr) tierra *f*; (*before n*) ‹*animal/defenses*› de tierra; **~ reform** reforma *f* agraria **2** [C] (country, realm) (liter) país *m*; (kingdom) reino *m*
land² *vi* **1 (a)** (Aerosp, Aviat) aterrizar*; (on the moon) alunizar* **(b)** (fall) caer* **2** (arrive, end up) (colloq) ir* a parar (fam) **3** (Naut) «*ship*» atracar*; «*traveler/troops*» desembarcar* ■ **~** *vt* **1 (a)** (from sea) ‹*passengers*› desembarcar*; ‹*cargo*› descargar* **(b)** (from air) ‹*plane*› hacer* aterrizar; ‹*troops*› desembarcar*; ‹*supplies*› descargar* **2** ‹*fish*› sacar* del agua; ‹*contract/job*› conseguir* **3** (burden) (colloq) **to ~ sb** WITH **sth/sb, to ~ sth/sb** ON **sb** endilgarle* algo/a algn A algn (fam)
landing /'lændɪŋ/ *n* **1 (a)** [U C] (Aerosp, Aviat) aterrizaje *m*; (on moon) alunizaje *m*; (*before n*) **~ strip** pista *f* de aterrizaje **(b)** [C] (Mil, Naut) desembarco *m* **(c)** [U] (of cargo) descarga *f*; (of troops) desembarco *m* **2** [C] (on staircase) rellano *m*, descanso *m* (Col, CS)
land: **~lady** *n* **(a)** (of rented dwelling) casera *f* **(b)** (of small hotel) dueña *f* **(c)** (BrE) (of pub — owner) dueña *f*; (— manager) encargada *f*; **~locked** /'lændlɑ:kt ‖ 'lændlɒkt/ *adj* sin salida al mar; **~lord** *n* **(a)** (of landed estate) terrateniente *m* **(b)** (of rented dwelling) casero *m*, dueño *m* **(c)** (BrE) (of pub — owner) dueño *m*; (— manager) encargado *m*; **~mark** *n* monumento *m* (*or* edificio *m etc*) famoso; **~ mine** *n* mina *f* (de tierra); **~owner** *n* terrateniente *mf*; **~scape** /'lændskeɪp/ *n* [U C] paisaje *m*; (*before n*) **~scape gardener** jardinero, -ra *m,f* paisajista; **~slide** *n* **(a)** (Geog) derrumbamiento *m or* desprendimiento *m* de tierras **(b)** (Pol) victoria *f* aplastante
lane /leɪn/ *n* **1** (in countryside) camino *m*, sendero *m*; (alleyway) callejón *m* **2** (Transp) **(a)** (for road traffic) carril *m or* (Chi) pista *f or* (RPl) senda *f*; **bus/bicycle ~** carril *m* de autobuses/bicicletas **(b)** (for ships) ruta *f* **3** (in athletics) carril *m* (Andes, Ven), calle *f* (Esp)
language /'læŋgwɪdʒ/ *n* **1** [C U] (means of communication, style of speech) lenguaje *m*; **bad ~** palabrotas *fpl* **2** [C] **(a)** (particular tongue) idioma *m*, lengua *f* **(b)** (Comput) lenguaje *m*
languid /'læŋgwəd ‖ 'læŋgwɪd/ *adj* lánguido
languish /'læŋgwɪʃ/ *vi* (liter) languidecer*; (in prison) pudrirse*
lank /læŋk/ *adj* lacio
lanky /'læŋki/ *adj* **-kier, -kiest** desgarbado
lantern /'læntərn ‖ 'læntən/ *n* farol *m*
Laos /laʊs ‖ 'lɑ:ɒs, laʊs/ *n* Laos *m*
lap¹ /læp/ *n* **1** (of body) rodillas *fpl* **2 (a)** (Sport) vuelta *f* **(b)** (stage) etapa *f*
lap² **-pp-** *vt* **1** (Sport) sacarle* una vuelta de ventaja a **2** ‹*water/milk*› beber a lengüetazos ■ **~** *vi* chapalear; **to ~** AGAINST **sth** lamer *or* besar algo (liter)
• **lap up** [*v + o + adv, v + adv + o*] beber a lengüetazos
lapel /lə'pel/ *n* solapa *f*
Lapland /'læplænd/ *n* Laponia *f*
lapse¹ /læps/ *n* **1** (fault, error) falla *f*, fallo *m* (Esp) **2** (interval) lapso *m*, período *m*
lapse² *vi* **1** (fall, slip): **standards have ~d** el nivel ha decaído; **to ~ into bad habits** adquirir* malos hábitos **2 (a)** (cease) «*project*» cancelarse; «*practice*» perderse* **(b)** «*membership/contract*» caducar*, vencer* **3** «*time*» transcurrir
laptop /'læptɑ:p ‖ 'læptɒp/ *n* (**~** *computer*) laptop *f or* (Esp) *m*
lapwing /'læpwɪŋ/ *n* avefría *f*‡
larceny /'lɑ:rsəni ‖ 'lɑ:səni/ *n* [U] (in US) robo *m*
larch /lɑ:rtʃ ‖ lɑ:tʃ/ *n* alerce *m*
lard /lɑ:rd ‖ lɑ:d/ *n* [U] manteca *f or* (RPl) grasa *f* de cerdo
larder /'lɑ:rdər ‖ 'lɑ:də(r)/ *n* despensa *f*
large¹ /lɑ:rdʒ ‖ lɑ:dʒ/ *adj*

■ **Note** The usual translation of *large*, *grande*, becomes *gran* when it precedes a singular noun.

larger, largest grande; **the ~st collection of stamps in the world** la mayor colección de sellos del mundo
large² *n* **at large (a)** (as a whole) en general; **the public at ~** el público en general **(b)** (at liberty): **to be at ~** andar* suelto
largely /'lɑ:rdʒli ‖ 'lɑ:dʒli/ *adv* en gran parte
lark /lɑ:rk ‖ lɑ:k/ *n* alondra *f*
larva /'lɑ:rvə ‖ 'lɑ:və/ *n* (*pl* **-vae** /-vi:/) larva *f*
laryngitis /'lærən'dʒaɪtəs ‖ ˌlærɪn'dʒaɪtɪs/ *n* [U] laringitis *f*
larynx /'lærɪŋks/ *n* (*pl* **larynxes** *or* **larynges** /lə'rɪndʒi:s/) laringe *f*
laser /'leɪzər ‖ 'leɪzə(r)/ *n* láser *m*; (*before n*) **~ beam** rayo *m* láser; **~ printer** impresora *f* láser
lash¹ /læʃ/ *n* **1** (*eye~*) pestaña *f* **2** (whip) látigo *m*
lash² *vt* **1 (a)** (whip) ‹*person*› azotar; ‹*horse*› fustigar* **(b)** (beat against) azotar **2** (bind) **to ~ sth/sb** TO **sth** amarrar algo/a algn A algo
• **lash out** [*v + adv* (*+ prep + o*)] atacar*; **to ~ out** AT/AGAINST **sb** (physically) emprenderla a golpes (*or* patadas *etc*) CON algn; (verbally) arremeter CONTRA algn
lass /læs/ *n* (liter *or* dial) muchacha *f*
lasso /'læsəʊ, læ'su: ‖ læ'su:/ *n* (*pl* **-sos** *or* **-soes**) lazo *m*

last¹ /læst ‖ lɑːst/ *adj* **1 (a)** (in series) último; **the ~ door but one** la penúltima puerta; **to be ~** (in race, on arrival) ser* el último (en llegar); **to be ~ to + INF** ser* el último EN + INF **(b)** (final, ultimate) ‹*chance/day*› último; **at the very ~ minute** en el último momento, a última hora **(c)** (only remaining) último; **I'm down to my ~ few dollars** sólo me quedan unos pocos dólares **2** (previous, most recent) (*before n*): **~ Tuesday** el martes pasado; **in my ~ letter** en mi última carta **3** (least likely): **that was the ~ thing I expected to hear from you** es lo que menos me esperaba que me dijeras; **that's the ~ thing I'd do!** ¡no se me ocurriría hacer eso!

last² *pron* **1 (a)** (in series) último, -ma *m,f*; **the ~ to + INF** el último/la última/los últimos/las últimas EN + INF; **the ~ I remember** lo último que recuerdo **(b)** (only remaining): **the ~ of its kind** el último de su clase; **that's the ~ of the jam** esa es toda la mermelada que queda **(c)** (*in phrases*) (liter) **at the last** al final; **to the ~** hasta el último momento **2** (preceding one): **the night before ~** anteanoche, antenoche (AmL); **each hill seemed steeper than the ~** cada colina parecía más empinada que la anterior

last³ *adv* **1 (a)** (at the end): **I went in ~** fui el último en entrar; **our team finished ~** nuestro equipo quedó en último lugar **(b)** (finally): **~ of all** por último; **and ~ but not least** y por último, pero no por eso menos importante **(c)** (*in phrases*) **at last** por fin, al fin; **at long last** por fin, finalmente **2** (most recently): **she was ~ seen a year ago** la última vez que se la vio fue hace un año; **when did you ~ see him?** ¿cuándo fue la última vez que lo viste?

last⁴ *vi/t* durar

last-ditch /læst'dɪtʃ ‖ 'lɑːst'dɪtʃ/ *adj* (*before n*) desesperado

lasting /læstɪŋ ‖ 'lɑːstɪŋ/ *adj* duradero

lastly /læstli ‖ 'lɑːstli/ *adv* (*as linker*) por último

last-minute /læst'mɪnət ‖ ˌlɑːst'mɪnɪt/ *adj* (*before n*) de última hora

latch /lætʃ/ *n* pasador *m*, pestillo *m*; (on lock) seguro *m*

• latch on [*v* + *adv* (+ *prep* + *o*)] (understand) (colloq) agarrar *or* (Esp) coger* la onda; **to ~ on TO sth** entender* algo; (realize) darse* cuenta DE algo

late¹ /leɪt/ *adj* **later, latest 1** (after correct, scheduled time): **the ~ arrival of the train** el retraso en la llegada del tren; **to be ~** «*person*» llegar* tarde; **the train was an hour ~** el tren llegó con una hora de retraso; **you'll be ~ for work** vas a llegar tarde al trabajo **2 (a)** (after usual time): **to have a ~ night** acostarse* tarde; **Spring is ~ this year** la primavera se ha atrasado este año **(b)** ‹*chrysanthemum/potatoes*› tardío **3 (a)** (far on in time): **it's ~** es tarde; **it's getting ~** se está haciendo tarde **(b)** (*before n*) ‹*shift/bus*› último; **at this ~ stage** a estas alturas; **in ~ April** a finales de abril; **she's in her ~ forties** tiene cerca de cincuenta años **4** (*before n*) (deceased) difunto (frml); **the ~ John Doe** el difunto John Doe

late² *adv* **later, latest 1** (after correct, scheduled time) tarde; **the trains are running 20 minutes ~** los trenes llevan 20 minutos de retraso; ***better ~ than never*** más vale tarde que nunca **2** (after usual time) ‹*work/sleep*› hasta tarde; ‹*mature*› tarde **3** (recently): **as ~ as the thirteenth century** aún en el siglo trece; **of ~** últimamente **4** (toward end of period): **~ in the afternoon** a última hora de la tarde; **~ in the year** a finales del año; **~ in her career** hacia el final de su carrera **5** (far on in time) tarde; **don't leave it too ~** no lo dejes para muy tarde; **we stayed up ~** nos quedamos levantados hasta tarde

lately /'leɪtli/ *adv* últimamente

latent /'leɪtn̩t/ *adj* latente

later¹ /'leɪtər ‖ 'leɪtə(r)/ *adj* posterior

later² *adv* después, más tarde; **~ that day** más tarde *or* posteriormente ese día; **not *o* no ~ than May 14** a más tardar el 14 de mayo; **~ on** más tarde, después; **see you ~!** ¡hasta luego!

lateral /'lætərəl/ *adj* lateral

latest /'leɪtəst ‖ 'leɪtɪst/ *adj* **(a)** (*superl of* LATE¹) último **(b)** (most up to date) (*before n*) último

latex /'leɪteks/ *n* [U] látex *m*

lathe /leɪð/ *n* torno *m*

lather¹ /'læðər ‖ 'lɑːðə(r), læðə(r)/ *n* (*no pl*) espuma

lather² *vt* enjabonar

Latin¹ /'lætn̩ ‖ 'lætɪn/ *adj* latino

Latin² *n* **(a)** [U] (language) latín *m* **(b)** [C] (person) latino, -na *m,f*

Latin America *n* América *f* Latina, Latinoamérica *f*

Latin American¹ *adj* latinoamericano

Latin American² *n* latinoamericano, -na *m,f*

latitude /'lætətuːd ‖ 'lætɪtjuːd/ *n* **(a)** [C U] (Geog) latitud *f* **(b)** [U] (freedom to choose) libertad *f*

latter¹ /'lætər ‖ 'lætə(r)/ *n* (*pl* ~) **the ~** éste, -ta; (*pl*) éstos, -tas

latter² *adj* (*before n*) **(a)** (second of two) segundo, último **(b)** (later, last): **in the ~ part of the season** hacia el final de la temporada; **in his ~ years** (frml) en sus últimos años

lattice /'lætəs ‖ 'lætɪs/ *n* entramado *m*, enrejado *m*

Latvia /'lætviə/ *n* Letonia *f*

Latvian /'lætviən/ *adj* letón

laugh¹ /læf ‖ lɑːf/ *n* risa *f*; ; **she's a good ~** es muy divertida; **to do/say sth for a ~** hacer*/decir* algo por divertirse; **to have a ~ (about/at sth)** reírse* (de algo)

laugh² *vi* reír(se)*; **to burst out ~ing** soltar* una carcajada; **to ~ AT sb/sth** reírse* DE algn/algo

• laugh off [*v* + *o* + *adv*, *v* + *adv* + *o*] tomar a broma

laughing /'læfɪŋ ‖ 'lɑːfɪŋ/ *adj* risueño; **this is no ~ matter** no es motivo de risa

laughingstock /'læfɪŋstɑːk ‖ 'lɑːfɪŋstɒk/ *n* hazmerreír *m*; **he made a ~ of his opponent** dejó *or* puso a su contrincante en ridículo

laughter /'læftər ‖ 'lɑːftə(r)/ *n* [U] risas *fpl*

launch¹ /lɔːntʃ/ *vt* **1 (a)** ‹*new vessel*› botar; ‹*lifeboat*› echar al agua **(b)** ‹*satellite/missile*› lanzar*; ‹*attack*› emprender **2** ‹*product/campaign*› lanzar*; ‹*company*› fundar*

launch² *n* **1** (motorboat) lancha *f* (a motor) **2 (a)** (of new vessel) botadura *f*; (of lifeboat) lanzamiento *m* (*al agua*) **(b)** (of rocket, missile) lanzamiento *m* **3** (of product, campaign) lanzamiento *m*

launching pad /'lɔːntʃɪŋ/, **launchpad** /'lɔːntʃ pæd/ *n* **(a)** (Aerosp) rampa *f* de lanzamiento **(b)** (for ideas, career) trampolín *m*

launder /'lɔːndər ‖ 'lɔːndə(r)/ *vt* **(a)** (wash and iron) (frml) lavar y planchar **(b)** ‹*money*› blanquear, lavar (AmL)

launderette /lɔːndə'ret ‖ lɔːn'dret/ *n* lavandería *f* automática

Laundromat®, **laundromat** /'lɔːndrəmæt/ *n* (AmE) lavandería *f* automática

laundry /'lɔːndri/ *n* (*pl* **-dries**) **(a)** [C] (commercial) lavandería *f*, lavadero *m* (RPl); (in home) lavadero *m* **(b)** [U] (dirty clothes) ropa *f* sucia *or* para lavar; (washed clothes) ropa *f* limpia *or* lavada; (*before n*) **~ basket** canasto *m or* cesto *m* de la ropa sucia

laurel /'lɔːrəl ‖ 'lɒrəl/ *n* laurel *m*

lava /'lɑːvə/ *n* [U] lava *f*

lavatory /'lævətɔːri ‖ 'lævətri/ *n* (*pl* **-ries**) **(a)** (room in house) (cuarto *m* de) baño *m* **(b)** (public) (*often pl*) baños *mpl*, servicios *mpl* (Esp) **(c)** (receptacle) taza *f*, inodoro *m*

lavender /'lævəndər ‖ 'lævəndə(r)/ *n* [U] lavanda *f*, espliego *m*

lavish¹ /'lævɪʃ/ *adj* ‹*lifestyle*› de derroche; ‹*gift/meal*› espléndido; ‹*production*› fastuoso

lavish² *vt* **to ~ sth ON sb** prodigar(le)* algo A algn

lavishly /'lævɪʃli/ *adv* ‹*give*› con esplendidez; ‹*decorated/illustrated*› magníficamente

law /lɔː/ *n* **(a)** [C] (rule, principle) ley *f* **(b)** [U] (collectively): **the ~** la ley; **to break the ~** violar *or* contravenir* *or* infringir* la ley; **it is against the ~** es ilegal; **under French ~** según la ley francesa; ***to lay down the ~*** dar* órdenes **(c)** [U] (as field, discipline) derecho *m*; (profession) abogacía *f*; (*before n*) **~ school** facultad *f* de Derecho

law: **~-abiding** /'lɔː əˌbaɪdɪŋ/ *adj* respetuoso de la ley; **~ and order** *n* [U] (+ *sing o pl vb*) el orden público

lawful /'lɔːfəl/ *adj* ‹*ruler/heir*› legítimo; ‹*contract*› válido, legal; ‹*conduct*› lícito

lawless /'lɔːləs ‖ 'lɔːlɪs/ *adj* ‹*mob*› desmandado; ‹*region*› anárquico, donde no rige la ley

lawn /lɔːn/ *n* césped *m*, pasto *m* (AmL), grama *f* (AmC, Ven)

lawnmower /'lɔːnˌməʊər ‖ 'lɔːnˌməʊə(r)/*n* máquina *f* de cortar el césped *or* (AmL tb) el pasto, cortadora *f* de césped *or* (AmL tb) de pasto, cortacésped *m* (Esp), cortagrama *m* (AmC, Ven)

lawsuit /'lɔːsuːt/ *n* juicio *m*

lawyer /'lɔːjər ‖ 'lɔːjə(r)/ *n* abogado, -da *m,f*

lax /læks/ *adj* ‹*discipline/supervision*› poco estricto; ‹*standards*› laxo

laxative /'læksətɪv/ *n* [C U] laxante *m*

lay¹ /leɪ/ *past of* LIE² II

lay² (*past & past p* **laid**) *vt* **1** (put) poner*; **~ the cloth flat on the table** extiende la tela sobre la mesa **2** (put in position) ‹*bricks/carpet*› poner*, colocar*; ‹*cable/pipes*› tender*; ‹*mines*› sembrar* **3** (prepare) ‹*trap*› tender*; ‹*plans*› hacer*; **to ~ the table** poner* la mesa **4** (cause to be): **one blow laid him flat on his back** de un golpe quedó tendido de espaldas en el suelo; ***to ~ sb low***: **he was laid low by malaria** estuvo postrado con malaria **5** (Zool): **to ~ eggs** «*bird/reptile*» poner* huevos; «*fish/insects*» desovar* ■ **~** *vi* **1** «*hen*» poner* huevos **2** (crit) ⇒ LIE² II

● **lay down** [*v + o + adv, v + adv + o*] **(a)** ‹*tools/weapons*› dejar (a un lado) **(b)** ‹*guidelines/procedure*› establecer*

● **lay off** [*v + adv + o, v + o + adv*] (AmE) despedir*; (BrE) *suspender temporalmente por falta de trabajo*

● **lay on** [*v + adv + o, v + o + adv*] ‹*transport/food*› hacerse* cargo de; ‹*entertainment*› ofrecer*

● **lay out** [*v + o + adv, v + adv + o*] **1 (a)** ‹*park/garden*› diseñar; ‹*town*› hacer* el trazado de; ‹*objects*› disponer* **(b)** ‹*page*› diseñar **2** (spend) gastar; (invest) invertir* **3** (knock unconscious) dejar sin sentido **4** ‹*dead body*› amortajar

lay³ *adj* (*before n*) **(a)** (secular) laico; **~ preacher** predicador, -dora *m,f* seglar **(b)** (not expert): **the ~ reader** el lector profano en la materia

lay-by /'leɪbaɪ/ *n* (BrE) área *f*‡ de reposo

layer¹ /'leɪər ‖ 'leɪə(r)/ *n* (of dust, paint, snow) capa *f*; (of rock, sediment) capa *f*, estrato *m*

layer² *vt*: **I had my hair ~ed** me corté el pelo en *or* (Esp) a capas, me rebajé el pelo (RPl)

lay: **~man** /'leɪmən/ *n* (*pl* **-men** /-mən/) (non-expert): **a book written for the ~man** un libro dirigido al gran público; **in ~man's terms** en lenguaje accesible; **~out** *n* **(a)** (of house) distribución *f*; (of town, garden) trazado *m* **(b)** (in magazine, newspaper) diseño *m*

laze /leɪz/ *vi* haraganear

lazily /'leɪzəli ‖ 'leɪzɪli/ *adv* perezosamente

lazy /'leɪzi/ *adj* **lazier, laziest** perezoso

lazybones /'leɪzibəʊnz/ *n* (*pl* **~**) (colloq) haragán, -gana *m,f*

lb = **pound(s)**

LCD *n* = **liquid crystal display**

lead¹ *n* **I** /led/ **1** [U] (metal) plomo *m*; (*before n*) **~ poisoning** intoxicación *f* por plomo; (chronic disease) saturnismo *m* **2** [C U] (in pencil) mina *f*
II /liːd/ **1**(in competition) (*no pl*): **to be in/take the ~** llevar/tomar la delantera **2** (example, leadership) (*no pl*) ejemplo *m*; **to follow sb's ~** seguir* el ejemplo de algn **3** [C] (clue) pista *f* **4** [C] **(a)** (for dog) (BrE) correa *f* **(b)** (Elec) cable *m* **5** [C] **(a)** (main role) papel *m* principal **(b)** (Mus) solista *mf*; (*before n*) ‹*guitar/singer*› principal

lead² /liːd/ (*past & past p* **led**) *vt* **1** (conduct) ‹*person/animal*› llevar, guiar*; **to ~ sb TO sth/sb** conducir* *or* llevar a algn A algo/ANTE algn; **to ~ sb away** llevarse a algn; **I was led to believe that** … me dieron a entender que …; **he's easily led** se deja llevar fácilmente **2** (head, have charge of) ‹*discussion*› conducir*; **the expedition was led by Smith** la expedición iba al mando de Smith **3 (a)** (be at front of) ‹*parade/attack*› encabezar* **(b)** (in race, competition) aventajar **4** ‹*life*› llevar ■ **~** *vi* **1 to ~ TO sth** «*road/steps*» llevar *or* conducir* *or* dar* A algo; «*door*» dar* A algo **2 (a)** (be leader): **you ~, we'll follow** ve delante *or* (esp AmL) adelante, que te seguimos **(b)** (in race, competition) ir* a la cabeza, puntear (AmL); **they are ~ing by three goals** van ganando por tres goles

• **lead on 1** [*v* + *adv*]: **~ on!** ¡adelante! (¡te seguimos!) **2** [*v* + *o* + *adv*] (raise false hopes) engañar

• **lead to** [*v* + *prep* + *o*] llevar *or* conducir* a

leaded /'ledəd ‖ 'ledɪd/ *adj* ‹*fuel*› con plomo

leader /'li:dər ‖ 'li:də(r)/ *n* **(a)** (of group, political party) líder *mf*; (of expedition) jefe, -fa *m,f*; (of gang) cabecilla *mf* **(b)** (in race, competition) primero, -ra *m,f*; (in league) líder *m*

leadership /'li:dərʃɪp ‖ 'li:dəʃɪp/ *n* **(a)** [U] (direction, control — of party) liderazgo *m*; (— of country) conducción *f* **(b)** [U] (quality) autoridad *f*, dotes *fpl* de mando **(c)** (leaders) (+ *sing o pl vb*) dirigentes *mpl*

lead-free /'led'fri:/ *adj* ‹*fuel*› sin plomo

leading /'li:dɪŋ/ *adj* (*before n*) **(a)** (principal) ‹*scientist/playwright*› destacado; ‹*brand/company*› líder *adj inv* **(b)** (in front) ‹*runner/horse/driver*› que va a la cabeza

leading: **~ lady** *n* (Cin) protagonista *f*; (Theat) primera actriz *f*; **~ light** *n* estrella *f*

leaf /li:f/ *n* (*pl* **leaves**) **1** (of plant) hoja *f* **2** (page, sheet) hoja *f*; ***to turn (over) a new ~*** reformarse **3** (of table) ala *f*‡; (of door, shutter) hoja *f*

• **leaf through** [*v* + *prep* + *o*] hojear

leaflet /'li:flət ‖ 'li:flɪt/ *n* (Print) folleto *m*; (Pol) panfleto *m*

leafy /'li:fi/ *adj* **-fier, -fiest** ‹*boughs*› frondoso; ‹*lane*› arbolado

league /li:g/ *n* **1** (alliance) liga *f*; ***to be in ~ (with sb)*** estar* aliado (con algn) **2 (a)** (Sport) liga *f* **(b)** (level, category): **not to be in the same ~ as sb/sth** no estar* a la misma altura que algn/algo **3** (measure of distance) legua *f*

leak¹ /li:k/ *vi* **(a)** «*bucket/tank*» gotear, perder* (RPl), salirse* (Chi, Méx); «*shoes/tent*» dejar pasar el agua; «*faucet*» gotear; «*pen*» perder* tinta; **the roof is ~ing** hay una gotera/hay goteras en el techo **(b)** (escape) «*liquid*» escaparse ■ **~** *vt* **(a)** ‹*liquid/gas*› perder*, botar (AmL exc RPl) **(b)** ‹*information*› filtrar

leak² *n* **(a)** (in bucket, boat, pipe) agujero *m*; (in roof) gotera *f* **(b)** (escaping liquid, gas) escape *m* **(c)** (of information) filtración *f*

leakage /'li:kɪdʒ/ *n* [C U] escape *m*

leaky /'li:ki/ *adj* **-kier, -kiest** agujereado

lean¹ /li:n/ (*past & past p* **leaned** *or* (BrE also) **leant** /lent/) *vi* **(a)** (bend, incline): **she ~ed back in her chair** se echó hacia atrás en la silla; **don't ~ out of the window** no te asomes por la ventana **(b)** (support oneself) apoyarse; **to ~ AGAINST sth** apoyarse CONTRA algo; **to ~ ON sth/sb** apoyarse EN algo/algn ■ **~** *vt* apoyar

lean² *adj* **(a)** ‹*person*› delgado; ‹*animal*› flaco **(b)** ‹*meat*› magro

leant /lent/ (BrE) *past & past p of* LEAN¹

leap¹ /li:p/ *vi/t* (*past & past p* **leaped** *or* (BrE also) **leapt** /lept/) saltar

leap² *n* salto *m*, brinco *m*; ***by ~s and bounds*** a pasos agigantados

leapfrog /'li:pfrɔ:g ‖ 'li:pfrɒg/ *n* [U]: **to play ~** jugar* a la pídola, brincar* al burro (Méx), jugar* al rango (RPl)

leapt /lept/ (BrE) *past & past p of* LEAP¹

leap year *n* año *m* bisiesto

learn /lɜ:rn ‖ lɜ:n/ (*past & past p* **learned** *or* (BrE also) **learnt**) *vt* **1 (a)** (gain knowledge of) aprender; **to ~ to + INF** aprender A + INF **(b)** (memorize) aprender de memoria **2** (become informed about) enterarse de ■ **~** *vi* **1** (gain knowledge) aprender **2** (become informed) **to ~ ABOUT *o* OF sth** enterarse DE algo

learned /'lɜ:rnəd ‖ 'lɜ:nɪd/ *adj* docto

learner /'lɜ:rnər ‖ 'lɜ:nə(r)/ *n*: **he's a fast/slow ~** aprende con mucha rapidez/tiene dificultades de aprendizaje; (*before n*) **~ (driver)** (esp BrE) *persona que está aprendiendo a conducir*

learning /'lɜ:rnɪŋ ‖ 'lɜ:nɪŋ/ *n* [U] **(a)** (knowledge) saber *m*; (education) educación *f*; **a man of ~** un erudito **(b)** (act) aprendizaje *m*; (*before n*) **~ difficulties** dificultades *fpl* de aprendizaje

learnt /lɜ:rnt ‖ lɜ:nt/ (BrE) *past & past p of* LEARN

lease¹ /li:s/ *n* ≈ contrato *m* de arrendamiento; (of real estate) ≈ usufructo *m*

lease² *vt* **(a) ~ (out)** (grant use of) arrendar*; ‹*real estate*› dar* en usufructo **(b)** (hold under lease) arrendar*; ‹*real estate*› tener* el usufructo de

leasehold /'li:shəʊld/ *n* [U C] arrendamiento *m*

leash /li:ʃ/ *n* correa *f*

least¹ /li:st/ *adj* **1** (*superl of* LITTLE¹ II): **she has the ~ money** es quien menos dinero tiene **2** (smallest, slightest) más mínimo; **that's the ~ of my worries** eso es lo que menos me preocupa

least² *pron* **1** (*superl of* LITTLE²): **to say the ~** por no decir más; **it's the ~ I can do** es lo menos que puedo hacer **2** (in adv phrases) **at least** por lo menos; **in the least** en lo más mínimo

least³ *adv* **1** (*superl of* LITTLE³): **~ of all you** tú menos que nadie; **when you ~ expect it** cuando menos te lo esperas **2** (*before adj, adv*) menos

leather /'leðər ‖ 'leðə(r)/ *n* [U] cuero *m*, piel *f* (Esp, Méx)

leave¹ /li:v/ *n* **1** [U C] (authorized absence) permiso *m*, licencia *f* (esp AmL); (Mil) licencia *f*; **to be/go on ~** estar*/salir* de permiso *or* (esp AmL) de licencia **2** [U] (permission) (frml) permiso *m* **3** [U] (departure) (frml): **to take ~ of sb** despedirse* de algn; **have you taken ~ of your senses?** ¿te has vuelto loco?

leave² (*past & past p* **left**) *vt* **1 (a)** (go away from): **she ~s home at 6** sale de casa a las 6; **I left her reading a book** la dejé leyendo un libro; **to ~ school** terminar el colegio; **she left home at the age of 17** se fue de casa a los 17 años **(b)** (withdraw from) ‹*profession/organization/politics*› dejar **2** (abandon) dejar; **she left her husband for another man** dejó a su marido por otro (hombre) **3 (a)** (deposit in specified place) dejar; **to ~ sth FOR sb** dejarle algo A algn **(b)** (not take — deliberately) dejar; (— inadvertently) olvidarse de, dejarse **(c)** (not eat) ‹*food*› dejar **4** (allow, cause to remain) dejar; **please ~ the window open** por favor dejen la ventana abierta **5** (have as aftereffect) ‹*stain/scar*› dejar **6 (a)** (not attend to) dejar **(b)** (not disturb) dejar; **~ her to finish on her own** déjala terminar sola **7** (entrust): **~ it to me!** ¡déjalo por mi cuenta!; **we must ~ nothing to chance** no debemos dejar nada (librado) al azar **8** (after deduction, elimination): **6 from 10 ~s 4** si a 10 le quitamos 6, quedan 4; **there isn't much time left** no queda mucho tiempo **9** (bequeath) **to ~ sth TO sb/sth** dejar(le) algo A algn/algo ■ **~** *vi* irse*, marcharse (esp Esp); **the train ~s at 5 o'clock** el tren sale a las 5 en punto

• **leave behind** [*v* + *o* + *adv, v* + *adv* + *o*] **(a)** (not take or bring — deliberately) dejar; (— inadvertently) olvidarse de, dejarse **(b)** ‹*worries/cares*› dejar atrás

• **leave on** [*v* + *o* + *adv, v* + *adv* + *o*] **(a)** ‹*light/machine/television*› dejar encendido *or* (AmL tb) prendido **(b)** (keep wearing) no quitarse

• **leave out 1** [*v* + *o* + *adv, v* + *adv* + *o*] [*v* + *o* + *adv* (+ *prep* + *o*)] **(a)** (omit) omitir **(b)** (exclude) excluir* **2** [*v* + *o* + *adv*] **(a)** (leave outside) dejar fuera *or* (esp AmL) afuera **(b)** (not put away) ‹*clothes/toys*› no guardar **(c)** (leave available) dejar preparado

leaves /liːvz/ *pl of* LEAF

leaving /ˈliːvɪŋ/ *adj* (*before n*) ‹*present*› de despedida; **~ party** despedida *f*

Lebanese /ˈlebəˈniːz/ *adj* libanés

Lebanon /ˈlebənɑːn ‖ ˈlebənən/ *n* (el) Líbano

lecherous /ˈletʃərəs/ *adj* libidinoso

lectern /ˈlektərn ‖ ˈlektɜːn/ *n* atril *m*; (in church) facistol *m*

lecture[1] /ˈlektʃər ‖ ˈlektʃə(r)/ *n* (public address) conferencia *f*; (Educ) clase *f*; (*before n*) **~ theater** auditorio *m*

lecture[2] *vi* (Educ) dar* clase, dictar clase (AmL frml), hacer* clase (Chi) ■ **~** *vt* (scold) sermonear

lecturer /ˈlektʃərər ‖ ˈlektʃərə(r)/ *n* **(a)** (speaker) conferenciante *mf*, conferencista *mf* (AmL) **(b)** (esp BrE Educ) profesor universitario, profesora universitaria *m,f*

led /led/ *past & past p of* LEAD[2]

ledge /ledʒ/ *n* **(a)** (on wall) cornisa *f*; (*window* **~**) (exterior) alféizar *m* (de la ventana); (interior) repisa *f* (de la ventana) **(b)** (on cliff) saliente *m or f*

ledger /ˈledʒər ‖ ˈledʒə(r)/ *n* libro *m* de contabilidad

leech /liːtʃ/ *n* sanguijuela *f*

leek /liːk/ *n* puerro *m*

leer /lɪr ‖ lɪə(r)/ *vi* **to ~ AT sb** lanzarle* una mirada lasciva a algn

leeway /ˈliːweɪ/ *n* [U]: **I am given a lot of ~** me dan mucha libertad de acción; **there isn't much ~ in the budget** el presupuesto tiene poco margen de flexibilidad

left[1] /left/ *past & past p of* LEAVE[2]

left[2] *n* **1 (a)** (left side) izquierda *f*; **on the ~** a la izquierda; **to drive on the ~** manejar *or* (esp Esp) conducir* por la izquierda **(b)** (left turn): **to make** *o* (BrE) **take a ~** girar a la izquierda **(c)** (Sport) (hand) izquierda *f* **2** (Pol) **the ~** la izquierda

left[3] *adj* (*before n*) izquierdo

left[4] ▶ 553 *adv* a *or* hacia la izquierda

left: **~-hand** *adj* (*before n*) de la izquierda; **on the ~-hand side** a mano izquierda; **~-handed** /ˈleftˈhændəd ‖ ˌleftˈhændɪd/ *adj* ‹*person*› zurdo; ‹*tool*› para zurdos; **~-luggage (office)** /ˈleftˈlʌgɪdʒ/ *n* (BrE) consigna *f*; **~over** *adj* (*before n*) sobrante; **~overs** /ˈleftˌəʊvərz ‖ ˈleftˌəʊvəz/ *pl n* sobras *fpl*; **~ wing** *n* **(a)** (Pol) (+ *sing or pl vb*) (ala *f*‡) izquierda *f* **(b)** (Sport) ala *f*‡ izquierda; **~-wing** /ˈleftˈwɪŋ/ *adj* (Pol) izquierdista

leg /leg/ *n* **1** ▶ 484 (Anat) (of person) pierna *f*; (of animal, bird) pata *f*; ***to pull sb's ~*** (colloq) tomarle el pelo a algn (fam) **2 (a)** (Culin) (of lamb, pork) pierna *f*; (of chicken) pata *f*, muslo *m* **(b)** (Clothing) pierna *f* **(c)** (of chair, table) pata *f* **3** (stage — of competition, race) manga *f*; (— of journey) etapa *f*

legacy /ˈlegəsi/ *n* (*pl* **-cies**) legado *m*

legal /ˈliːgəl/ *adj* **1 (a)** (allowed) legal; ‹*tackle/move*› reglamentario **(b)** (founded upon law) ‹*contract/requirement*› legal **2** (relating to legal system, profession) (*before n*) jurídico; **we will be forced to take ~ action** nos veremos obligados a poner el asunto en manos de nuestro(s) abogado(s)

legal holiday *n* (AmE) día *m* festivo oficial, feriado *m* oficial (esp AmL)

legalize /ˈliːgəlaɪz/ *vt* legalizar*

legally /ˈliːgəli/ *adv* legalmente

legal tender *n* [U] moneda *f* de curso legal

legend /ˈledʒənd/ *n* [C U] leyenda *f*

legendary /ˈledʒənderi ‖ ˈledʒəndri/ *adj* legendario

leggings /ˈlegɪŋz/ *pl n* **(a)** (pants, trousers) leggings *mpl*, mallas *fpl*, calzas *fpl* (RPl) **(b)** (for lower leg) polainas *fpl*

legible /ˈledʒəbəl/ *adj* legible

legion /ˈliːdʒən/ *n* legión *f*

legislate /ˈledʒəsleɪt ‖ ˈledʒɪsleɪt/ *vi* legislar

legislation /ˈledʒəsˈleɪʃən ‖ ˌledʒɪsˈleɪʃən/ *n* [U] legislación *f*

legislative /ˈledʒəsleɪtɪv ‖ ˈledʒɪslətɪv/ *adj* (*before n*) legislativo

legislator /ˈledʒəsleɪtər ‖ ˈledʒɪsleɪtə(r)/ *n* legislador, -dora *m,f*

legislature /ˈledʒɪsleɪtʃər ‖ ˈledʒɪsleɪtʃə(r)/ *n* asamblea *f* legislativa

legitimate /lɪˈdʒɪtəmət ‖ lɪˈdʒɪtɪmət/ *adj* legítimo

legitimize /lɪˈdʒɪtəmaɪz ‖ lɪˈdʒɪtɪmaɪz/ *vt* legitimar

legroom /ˈlegruːm, -rʊm/ *n* [U] espacio *m* para las piernas

leisure /ˈliːʒər ‖ˈleʒə(r)/ *n* [U] tiempo *m* libre; **read it at your ~** léalo cuando le venga bien; (*before n*) ‹*activity*› de tiempo libre; **~ center** (AmE) centro *m* recreativo; **~ centre** (BrE) centro *m* deportivo

leisurely /ˈliːʒərli ‖ˈleʒəli/ *adj* lento, pausado; **at a ~ pace** sin prisas

lemon /ˈlemən/ *n* **(a)** [C U] (fruit) limón *m*, limón *m* francés (Méx, Ven); (*before n*) **~ squeezer** (BrE) exprimelimones *m*, exprimidor *m*; **~ tea** té *m* con limón **(b)** [C] **~ (tree)** limonero *m* **(c)** [U] ▶ 515 (color) amarillo *m* limón; (*before n*) amarillo limón *adj inv*

Length/Longitud

Conversion/Conversión

Miles to kilometers
Divide by 5 and multiply by 8

Millas a kilómetros
Dividir por 5 y multiplicar por 8

Kilometers to miles
Divide by 8 and multiply by 5

Kilómetros a millas
Dividir por 8 y multiplicar por 5

Metric system *Sistema métrico*				**US/UK system** *Sistema estadounidense y británico*
10 millimeters	=	1 centimeter	=	0.394 inch
10 milímetros	=	1 centímetro		
10 centimeters	=	1 decimeter	=	3.94 inches
10 centímetros	=	1 decímetro		
100 centimeters	=	1 meter	=	39.4 inches/ 1.094 yards
100 centímetros	=	1 metro		
10 meters	=	1 dekameter	=	10.94 yards
10 metros	=	1 decámetro		
1,000 meters	=	1 kilometer	=	0.6214 mile
1.000 metros	=	1 kilómetro	=	⅝ mile

US/UK system *Sistema estadounidense y británico*				**Metric system** *Sistema métrico*
		1 inch	=	25.4 mm
		1 pulgada		
12 inches	=	1 foot	=	30.48 cm
	=	1 pie		
3 feet	=	1 yard	=	0.914 m
	=	1 yarda		
220 yards	=	1 furlong	=	201.17 m
	=	1 estadio		
8 furlongs	=	1 mile	=	1.609 km
	=	1 milla		
1,760 yards	=	1 mile	=	1.609 km
	=	1 milla		

lemonade /ˈlemәˈneɪd/ *n* [C U] **(a)** (with fresh lemons) limonada *f* **(b)** (fizzy drink) (BrE) (bebida *f*) gaseosa *f*

lemon cheese, **lemon curd** *n* [U] crema *f* de limón (*en conserva*)

lend /lend/ *vt* (*past & past p* **lent**) prestar; **this ~s an air of mystery to the scene** esto le da un aire de misterio a la escena

lender /ˈlendәr ‖ ˈlendә(r)/ *n* (institution) entidad *f* crediticia; (person) prestamista *mf*

length /leŋθ/ ▶ 681 *n* **1** [U] **(a)** (of line, surface) longitud *f*; (of sleeve, coat) largo *m*; **it's 5m in ~** mide 5 metros de largo; **he traveled the ~ and breadth of the country** viajó a lo largo y (a lo) ancho del país; **he'd go to any ~s to get what he wants** es capaz de hacer cualquier cosa con tal de obtener lo que se propone **(b)** (of book, list) extensión *f* **2** [U] **(a)** (duration) (of movie, play) duración *f*; **after a considerable ~ of time** después de mucho tiempo **(b) at length** (finally) finalmente; (for a long time) extensamente; (in detail) detenidamente; **to talk at ~** hablar largo y tendido **3** [C] (section — of wood, pipe) trozo *m*; (— of river, road) tramo *m* **4** [C] **(a)** (in swimming) largo *m* **(b)** (in horse, dog racing) cuerpo *m*; (in rowing) largo *m*

lengthen /ˈleŋθәn/ *vt* ‹*skirt/novel*› alargar*; ‹*line/visit*› alargar*

lengthwise /ˈleŋθwaɪz/, (esp BrE) **lengthways** /-weɪz/ *adv* a lo largo

lengthy /ˈleŋθi/ *adj* **-thier -thiest** (long) largo; (tedious) largo y pesado

lenient /ˈliːniәnt/ *adj* ‹*attitude/view*› indulgente; ‹*sentence*› poco severo

lens /lenz/ *n* (*pl* **lenses**) **(a)** (Opt) lente *f* **(b)** (for magnifying) lupa *f* **(c)** (in spectacles) cristal *m* **(d)** ⇒ CONTACT LENS **(e)** (Phot) lente *f*

lent /lent/ *past & past p of* LEND

Lent /lent/ *n* Cuaresma *f*

lentil /ˈlentl̩/ *n* lenteja *f*

Leo /ˈliːәʊ/ *n* (*pl* **-os**) **(a)** (sign) (*no art*) Leo **(b)** [C] (person) Leo *or* leo *mf*

leopard /ˈlepәrd ‖ ˈlepәd/ *n* leopardo *m*

leotard /ˈliːәtɑːrd ‖ ˈliːәtɑːd/ *n* malla *f*

leper /ˈlepәr ‖ ˈlepә(r)/ *n* leproso, -sa *m,f*

leprosy /ˈleprәsi/ *n* [U] lepra *f*

lesbian /ˈlezbiәn/ *n* lesbiana *f*

lesion /ˈliːʒәn/ *n* lesión *f*

less[1] /les/ *adj* (*comp of* LITTLE[1] II) menos; **~ and ~ money** cada vez menos dinero

less[2] *pron* (*comp of* LITTLE[2]) menos; **a sum of ~ than $1,000** una suma inferior a los 1.000 dólares

less[3] *adv* (*comp of* LITTLE[3]) menos; **the situation is no ~ serious than it was** la situación sigue siendo tan grave como antes

-less /lәs ‖ lɪs/ *suff* sin; **hat~** sin sombrero

lessen /ˈlesn̩/ *vt* ‹*pain*› aliviar; ‹*cost/risk*› reducir* ■ **~** *vi* «*noise*» disminuir*; «*pain*» aliviarse; «*interest*» decrecer*

lesser /ˈlesәr ‖ ˈlesә(r)/ *adj* (*before n*) menor; **to a ~ extent** en menor grado

lesson /ˈlesn̩/ *n* **1** (Educ) **(a)** (class) clase *f* **(b)** (in textbook) lección *f* **2** (from experience) lección *f*; **to learn one's ~** aprender la lección

lest /lest/ *conj* (liter) no sea que (+ *subj*); **~ we forget** para que no olvidemos

let /let/ (*pres p* **letting**; *past & past p* **let**) *vt* **1** (*no pass*) **(a)** (allow to) dejar; **he ~ his hair grow** se dejó crecer el pelo; **~ me help you** deja que te ayude; **~ me see** ¿a ver?; **don't ~ me catch you**

here again! ¡que no te vuelva a pescar por aquí! **(b)** (cause to, make): **~ me know if there are any problems** avísame si hay algún problema; **he ~ it be known that** ... hizo saber que ... **(c) to ~ go** soltar*; **~ go of my hand!** ¡suéltame la mano!; *to ~ oneself go* (enjoy oneself) soltarse*; (neglect oneself) abandonarse **2** (+ *adv compl*): **to ~ sth/sb by** *o* **past** dejar pasar algo/a algn; **she ~ herself into the house** abrió la puerta y entró en la casa **3** [*Used to form 1st pers pl imperative*] **~'s go** vamos, vámonos; **~'s ask Chris** vamos a preguntarle a Chris, preguntémosle a Chris; **don't ~'s** *o* **~'s not argue** no discutamos; **~ us pray** (frml) oremos **4** [*Used to form 3rd pers imperative, gen translated by* QUE + SUBJ *in Spanish*] **~ that be a lesson to you** que te sirva de lección; **just ~ them try!** ¡que se atrevan! **5** (rent) (esp BrE) alquilar; Ⓢ **to let** se alquila

• let down [*v + o + adv, v + adv + o*] **1 (a)** (lower) ‹*rope/bucket*› bajar **(b)** (lengthen) ‹*skirt*› alargar*; (lower) ‹*hem*› bajar, sacar **(c)** ‹*tire/balloon*› desinflar **2** (disappoint) fallar; **her spelling ~s her down** su ortografía no le hace justicia a su trabajo

• let in [*v + o + adv, v + adv + o*] dejar entrar

• let off **I 1 (a)** [*v + o + adv*] (not punish, forgive) perdonar; **she was ~ off with a reprimand** sólo le hicieron una amonestación **(b)** [*v + o + adv*] [*v + o + prep + o*] (excuse from) perdonar **2** [*v + o + adv*] (allow to go) dejar salir

II [*v + o + adv, v + adv + o*] ‹*fireworks*› hacer* estallar; ‹*rocket/cracker*› tirar

• let on [*v + adv*] [*v + adv + o*]: **you mustn't ~ on about this to Jim** no le vayas a decir nada de esto a Jim; **don't ~ on (that) you know me!** no digas que me conoces

• let out **I** [*v + o + adv, v + adv + o*] **1** (disclose) ‹*secret*› revelar **2** (rent out) (esp BrE) alquilar **3** (make wider) ‹*skirt/dress*› ensanchar, agrandar

II [*v + o + adv, v + adv + o*] [*v + o + adv* (+ *prep + o*)] (allow to leave) dejar salir; **someone ~ the air out of my tires** alguien me desinfló los neumáticos

III [*v + adv + o*] ‹*scream/yell*› soltar*

• let up [*v + adv*] «*wind/storm*» amainar; «*pressure/work*» disminuir*

letdown /'letdaʊn/ *n* decepción *f*

lethal /'li:θəl/ *adj* mortal, letal; ‹*weapon*› mortífero

lethargic /lə'θɑ:rdʒɪk ‖ lɪ'θɑ:dʒɪk/ *adj* aletargado

let's /lets/ (= **let us**) *see* LET[2] 3

letter /'letər ‖ 'letə(r)/ *n* **1** (written message) carta *f* **2** (of alphabet) letra *f*

letter: **~ bomb** *n* carta *f* bomba; **~ box** *n* buzón *m*

lettuce /'letəs ‖ 'letɪs/ *n* [U C] lechuga *f*

let-up /'letʌp/ *n* interrupción *f*

leukemia, (esp BrE) **leukaemia** /lu:'ki:miə/ *n* [U] leucemia *f*

level[1] /'levəl/ *n* nivel *m*; **at eye ~** a la altura de los ojos; **a top-~ meeting** una reunión de *or* a alto nivel

level[2] *adj* **1** ‹*ground/surface*› plano, llano; **a ~ spoonful** una cucharada rasa; **to do one's ~ best** hacer* todo lo posible **2 (a)** (at same height) **to be ~** (WITH **sth**) estar* al nivel (DE algo) **(b)** (abreast, equal): **the two teams were ~ at half-time** al medio tiempo los dos equipos iban empatados; **to draw ~ with sb** (in a race) alcanzar* a algn **3** (unemotional, calm) desapasionado

level[3], (BrE) **-ll-** *vt* **1 (a)** (make flat) ‹*ground/surface*› nivelar **(b)** (raze) ‹*building/town*› arrasar **2** (make equal) igualar **3** (direct) **to ~ sth** AT **sb/sth** ‹*weapon*› apuntarle A algn/A algo CON algo; **to ~ an accusation at sb** acusar a algn ■ **~** *vi* (be honest) (colloq) **to ~** WITH **sb** ser* franco CON algn

• level off [*v + adv*] **(a)** «*aircraft*» nivelarse, enderezarse* **(b)** «*prices/growth/inflation*» estabilizarse*

level: **~ crossing** *n* (BrE) paso *m* a nivel, crucero *m* (Méx); **~-headed** /'levəl'hedəd ‖ ˌlevəl'hedɪd/ *adj* sensato

lever[1] /'levər ‖'li:və(r)/ *n* palanca *f*

lever[2] *vt* (+ *adv compl*): **to ~ sth open** abrir* algo haciendo palanca

levy[1] /'levi/ *vt* **levies, levying, levied (a)** ‹*tax/duty*› (impose) imponer*; (collect) recaudar **(b)** ‹*fee/charge*› cobrar **(c)** ‹*fine*› imponer*

levy[2] *n* (*pl* **levies**) **(a)** [U] (raising of tax, contributions): **the strike was funded by a ~ on all members** la huelga se financió mediante el cobro de una cuota a todos los miembros **(b)** [C] (tax) impuesto *m*

lewd /lu:d ‖ lju:d/ *adj* **-er, -est** lascivo

liability /'laɪə'bɪləti/ *n* (*pl* **-ties**) **1** [U] (responsibility) responsabilidad *f* **2 liabilities** *pl* (debt) (Fin) pasivo *m* **3** (disadvantage) (*no pl*): **she's a positive ~** es un verdadero lastre; **the car turned out to be a ~** el coche terminó dándonos más problemas que otra cosa

liable /'laɪəbəl/ *adj* (*pred*) **1** (responsible) reponsable; **to be ~** FOR **sth** ser* responsable DE algo **2**(likely): **I'm ~ to forget** es probable que me olvide; **the earlier model was ~ to overheat** el modelo anterior tenía tendencia a recalentarse

liaise /li'eɪz/ *vi* (esp BrE) **to ~** (WITH **sb**) actuar* de enlace (CON algn); **the departments will ~ closely** los departamentos mantendrán un estrecho contacto

liaison /li'eɪzɑ:n ‖ li'eɪzn/ *n* **1** [U] (coordination) enlace *m* **2** [C] (affair) (liter) affaire *m*

liar /'laɪər ‖ 'laɪə(r)/ *n* mentiroso, -sa *m,f*

libel[1] /'laɪbəl/ *n* [U C] (defamation) difamación *f*; (where a crime is implied) calumnia *f*

libel[2] *vt*, (BrE) **-ll-** (defame) difamar; (where a crime is implied) calumniar

liberal[1] /'lɪbərəl/ *adj* **1 (a)** (tolerant) ‹*ideas*› liberal; ‹*interpretation*› libre **(b) Liberal** (Pol) del Partido Liberal; **L~ Democrat** (in UK) demócrata *mf* liberal **2** (generous) generoso

liberal[2] *n* **(a)** (progressive thinker) liberal *mf* **(b) Liberal** (party member) liberal *mf*

liberalism /'lɪbərəlɪzəm/ *n* [U] liberalismo *m*

liberalize /'lɪbərəlaɪz/ *vt* liberalizar*

liberally /'lɪbərəli/ *adv* **(a)** (generously) generosamente **(b)** (not strictly) libremente

liberate /'lɪbəreɪt/ *vt* liberar

liberation /'lɪbə'reɪʃən/ *n* [U] liberación *f*

Liberia /laɪˈbɪriə ‖ laɪˈbɪəriə/ *n* Liberia *f*

Liberian /laɪˈbɪriən ‖ laɪˈbɪəriən/ *adj* liberiano

liberty /ˈlɪbərti ‖ ˈlɪbəti/ *n* (*pl* **-ties**) [U C] libertad *f*; **I'm not at ~ to tell you** no se lo puedo decir; **to take the ~ of -ING** (esp BrE) tomarse la libertad DE + INF

Libra /ˈliːbrə, ˈlaɪbrə ‖ ˈliːbrə/ *n* **(a)** (sign) (*no art*) Libra **(b)** [C] (person) Libra *or* libra *mf*

librarian /laɪˈbreriən ‖ laɪˈbreəriən/ *n* bibliotecario, -ria *m,f*

library /ˈlaɪbreri ‖ ˈlaɪbrəri/ *n* (*pl* **-ries**) biblioteca *f*

libretto /ləˈbretəʊ ‖ lɪˈbretəʊ/ *n* (*pl* **-tos** *or* **-ti** /-tiː/) libreto *m*

Libya /ˈlɪbiə/ *n* Libia *f*

Libyan /ˈlɪbiən/ *adj* libio

lice /laɪs/ *pl of* LOUSE

license¹, (BrE) **licence** /ˈlaɪsns/ *n* **1** [C] **(a)** (permit) permiso *m*; **import/export ~** permiso de importación/exportación; (*before n*) **~ number** (AmE Auto) número *m* de matrícula *or* (CS) de patente; **~ plate** matrícula *f*, placa *f* (AmL), patente *f* (CS), chapa *f* (RPl) **(b)** ⇒ DRIVER'S LICENSE **2** [U] **(a)** (freedom): **poetic ~** licencia *f* poética **(b)** (excessive freedom) (frml) libertinaje *m*

license² /ˈlaɪsns/ *vt* otorgarle* un permiso a

licensed /ˈlaɪsnst/ *adj* ‹*practitioner*› autorizado para ejercer; ‹*premises*› (BrE) autorizado para vender bebidas alcohólicas

licentious /laɪˈsentʃəs ‖ laɪˈsenʃəs/ *adj* licencioso

lichen /ˈlaɪkən, ˈlɪtʃən/ *n* [U C] liquen *m*

lick /lɪk/ *vt* lamer; ‹*stamp*› pasarle la lengua a

licorice, (BrE) **liquorice** /ˈlɪkərɪʃ, -ɪs/ *n* [U] regaliz *f*, orozuz *m*

lid /lɪd/ *n* **1** (of container) tapa *f* **2** (*eye ~*) párpado *m*

lie¹ /laɪ/ *n* (untruth) mentira *f*; **to tell ~s** decir* mentiras, mentir*

lie² *vi* **I** (*3rd pers sing pres* **lies**; *pres p* **lying**; *past & past p* **lied**) (tell untruths) mentir* **II** (*3rd pers sing pres* **lies**; *pres p* **lying**; *past* **lay**; *past p* **lain**) **1 (a)** (lie down) echarse, tenderse* **(b)** (be in lying position) estar* tendido; **I lay awake for hours** estuve horas sin poder dormir **(c)** (be buried) yacer* (liter); Ⓢ **here lies John Brown** aquí yacen los restos de John Brown **2** (be) «*object*» estar*; **the snow lay two feet deep** la nieve tenía dos pies de espesor **3** (be located) «*building/city*» encontrarse*; **a group of islands lying off the west coast** un conjunto de islas situadas cerca de la costa occidental **4** «*problem/difference*» radicar*; «*answer*» estar*

● **lie down** [*v* + *adv*] **(a)** (adopt lying position) echarse, tenderse* **(b)** (be lying) estar* tendido

lie detector *n* detector *m* de mentiras

lieu /luː ‖ ljuː/ *n* (frml): **in ~ of** en lugar de, en vez de; **time off in ~** horas *fpl*/días *mpl* libres a cambio

lieutenant /luːˈtenənt ‖lefˈtenənt/ *n* **(a)** (in navy) teniente *mf* de navío, teniente *mf* primero (*en Chi*) **(b)** (in other services) teniente *mf*

life /laɪf/ *n* (*pl* **lives**) **1** [C U] vida *f*; **animal/plant ~** vida animal/vegetal; **in later ~** más tarde *or* más adelante; **it brings the history of this period to ~** hace cobrar vida a este período de la historia; **to bring sb back to ~** resucitar a algn; **to come to ~** «*party*» animarse; «*puppet*» cobrar vida; **he was fighting for his life** se debatía entre la vida y la muerte; **to have the time of one's ~** divertirse* como nunca; **run for your lives!** ¡sálvese quien pueda!; **to save sb's ~** salvarle la vida a algn; ***to be the ~*** *o* (esp BrE) ***the ~ and soul of the party*** ser* el alma de la fiesta; ***to live the ~ of Riley*** darse* la gran vida; ***to take one's ~ in one's hands*** jugarse* la vida; (*before n*) ‹*member/president*› vitalicio; **his ~ story** la historia de su vida **2** [U] (duration — of battery) duración *f*; (— of agreement) vigencia *f* **3** [U] (imprisonment) (colloq) cadena *f* perpetua

life: **~ assurance** *n* [U] (BrE) ⇒ **~** INSURANCE; **~ belt** *n* (BrE) salvavidas *m*; **~boat** *n* (on ship) bote *m* salvavidas; (shore-based) lancha *f* de salvamento; **~ buoy** *n* salvavidas *m*; **~ cycle** *n* ciclo *m* vital; **~guard** *n* salvavidas *mf*, socorrista *mf*; **~ insurance** *n* seguro *m* de vida; **~ jacket** *n* chaleco *m* salvavidas

lifeless /ˈlaɪfləs ‖ ˈlaɪflɪs/ *adj* (dead) sin vida, inánime (frml), exánime (liter); (unconscious) inerte

life: **~like** *adj* verosímil; **~line** *n* (rope) cuerda *f* de salvamento; **his letters were my ~line** sus cartas eran lo único que me mantenía viva; **~long** *adj* (*before n*): **a ~long friend** un amigo de toda la vida; **~ preserver** /prɪˈzɜːrvər ‖ prɪˈzɜːvə(r)/ *n* (AmE) **(a)** ⇒ LIFE BUOY **(b)** ⇒ LIFE JACKET; **~ raft** *n* balsa *f* salvavidas; **~ ring** *n* (AmE) salvavidas *m*; **~saver** /ˈlaɪfˌseɪvər ‖ ˈlaɪfˌseɪvə(r)/ *n* **(a)** ⇒ LIFEGUARD **(b)** (from bad situation) salvación *f*; **~-saving** *adj* (*before n*) que salva vidas; **~-size** /ˈlaɪfˈsaɪz/, **~-sized** /-d/ *adj* (de) tamaño natural; **~ span** *n* (of living creature) vida *f*; (of project) duración *f*; (of equipment) vida *f* útil; **~style** *n* estilo *m* de vida; **~time** *n* vida *f*; **the chance of a ~time** la oportunidad de su (*or* mi *etc*) vida; (*before n*) ‹*appointment/post*› vitalicio; **~time guarantee** garantía *f* para toda la vida; **~ vest** *n* (AmE) chaleco *m* salvavidas

lift¹ /lɪft/ *n* **1** [U C] (boost) impulso *m* **2** [C] (ride): **can I give you a ~?** ¿quieres que te lleve *or* (Per fam) jale?, ¿quieres que te dé un aventón (Méx) *or* (Col fam) una palomita? **3** [C] (elevator) (BrE) ascensor *m*

lift² *vt* **1** (raise) levantar **2** (end) ‹*ban/siege*› levantar ■ **~** *vi* **(a)** (rise) «*curtain*» levantarse **(b)** (clear) «*mist*» disiparse

● **lift off** [*v* + *adv*] «*rocket*» despegar*

● **lift up** [*v* + *o* + *adv*, *v* + *adv* + *o*] levantar

lift-off /ˈlɪftɔːf ‖ ˈlɪftɒf/ *n* (Aerosp) despegue *m*

ligament /ˈlɪgəmənt/ *n* ligamento *m*

ligature /ˈlɪgətʃʊr ‖ ˈlɪgətʃə(r)/ *n* ligadura *f*

light¹ /laɪt/ *n* **1** [U] luz *f*; **by the ~ of the moon** a la luz de la luna; ***to come to ~*** salir* a la luz; ***to see the ~*** abrir* los ojos **2** [C] **(a)** (source of light) luz *f*; (lamp) lámpara *f*; (*before n*) **~ switch** interruptor *m* **(b)** (of car, bicycle) luz *f* **(c)** (*traffic ~*) semáforo *m* **3 (a)** (aspect) (*no pl*): **to see sth/sb in a good/bad/new** *o* **different ~** ver* algo/a algn con buenos/malos/otros ojos **(b) in the ~ of** *o* (AmE also) **in ~**

of (*as prep*) a la luz de, en vista de **4** [C] (for igniting): **have you got a ~?** ¿tienes fuego?; **to set ~ to sth** prender fuego a algo

light² *adj* **-er, -est I 1** (not heavy) ligero, liviano (esp AmL); ‹*voice*› suave **2 (a)** (Meteo) ‹*breeze/wind*› suave; **~ rain** llovizna *f* **(b)** (sparse): **the losses were fairly ~** las pérdidas fueron de poca consideración **(c)** (not strenuous) ‹*work/duties*› ligero, liviano (esp AmL) **3** (not serious) ‹*music/comedy/reading*› ligero; ***to make ~ of sth*** quitarle *or* restarle importancia a algo

II (a) ▶ 515 (pale) ‹*green/brown*› claro **(b)** (bright): **it gets ~ very early these days** ahora amanece muy temprano; **it's already ~** ya es de día

light³ *adv*: **to travel ~** viajar con el mínimo de equipaje

light⁴ *vt* **1** (*past & past p* **lighted** *or* **lit**) (set alight) encender* **2** (*past & past p* **lit**) (illuminate) iluminar ■ **~** *vi* (*past & past p* **lighted** *or* **lit**) encenderse*
• **light up** (*past & past p* **lit**) **1** [*v + adv*] **(a)** «*eyes/face*» iluminarse **(b)** «*smoker*» encender* un cigarrillo (*or* un puro *etc*) **2** [*v + o + adv, v + adv + o*] **(a)** ‹*street/square*› iluminar **(b)** ‹*cigar/pipe*› encender*

light: **~ bulb** *n* ⇒ BULB 2; **~ cream** *n* (AmE) crema *f* líquida, nata *f* líquida (Esp)

lighten /'laɪtn̩/ *vt* **1** ‹*load/workload*› aligerar; ‹*responsibility/conscience*› descargar* **2 (a)** ‹*room*› dar* más luz a; ‹*sky*› iluminar **(b)** ‹*color/hair*› aclarar ■ **~** *vi* **1** «*load/weight*» hacerse* más ligero *or* (esp AmL) liviano, aligerarse **2** «*sky*» despejarse; «*face*» iluminarse; «*atmosphere*» relajarse

lighter /'laɪtər ‖ 'laɪtə(r)/ *n* (*cigarette ~*) encendedor *m*, mechero *m* (Esp)

light: **~-fingered** /'laɪt'fɪŋgərd ‖ ˌlaɪt'fɪŋgəd/ *adj* (colloq): **to be ~-fingered** tener* (la) mano larga (fam); **~-hearted** /'laɪt'hɑːrtəd ‖ ˌlaɪt'hɑːtɪd/ *adj* alegre, desenfadado; **~house** *n* faro *m*

lighting /'laɪtɪŋ/ *n* [U] iluminación *f*; (on streets) alumbrado *m*

lightly /'laɪtli/ *adv* **1 (a)** ‹*touch*› suavemente; ‹*snow*› ligeramente **(b)** ‹*grill/beat*› ligeramente **2 (a)** (frivolously) a la ligera **(b)** (not severely): **they were let off ~** los trataron con indulgencia

lightning¹ /'laɪtnɪŋ/ *n* [U]: **a bolt of ~** un relámpago; **a flash of ~** un relámpago; **a streak of ~** un rayo; ***like greased ~*** como un relámpago; (*before n*) **~ conductor** *o* **rod** pararrayos *m*

lightning² *adj* relámpago *adj inv*; **with ~ speed** como un rayo

lightweight¹ /'laɪtweɪt/ *adj* ligero, liviano (esp AmL); ‹*writer/performance*› de poco peso

lightweight² *n* (in boxing, wrestling) peso *m* ligero; (minor figure) persona *f* de poco peso

light year *n* año *m* luz

likable /'laɪkəbəl/ *adj* agradable, simpático

like¹ /laɪk/ *vt* **1** ▶ 685 (enjoy, be fond of): **I ~ tennis** me gusta el tenis; **she ~s him, but she doesn't love him** le resulta simpático pero no lo quiere; **do as** *o* **what you ~** haz lo que quieras; **I ~ dancing** me gusta bailar; **I don't ~ to mention it, but** ... no me gusta (tener que) decírtelo pero ... **2** (in requests, wishes) querer*; **we would just ~ to say how grateful we are** queríamos decirle lo agradecidos que estamos; **would you ~ a cup of tea?** ¿quieres una taza de té? ■ **~** *vi* querer*; **if you ~** si quieres

like² *n* **1** (sth liked): **her/his ~s and dislikes** sus preferencias **2** (similar thing, person) **the ~: judges, lawyers and the ~** jueces, abogados y (otra) gente por el estilo; **I've never heard the ~ (of this)** nunca he oído cosa igual

like³ *adj* (dated *or* frml) parecido

like⁴ *prep* **1 (a)** (similar to) como; **what's she ~?** ¿cómo es?; **she's very ~ her mother** se parece mucho a su madre **(b)** (typical of): **that's not ~ her** es muy raro en ella; **it's just ~ you to think of food** ¡típico! *or* ¡cuándo no! ¡tú pensando en comida! **2** (indicating manner): **~ this/that** así; **to run ~ mad** correr como un loco **3** (such as, for example) como

like⁵ *conj* (crit) **(a)** (as if): **she looks ~ she knows what she's doing** parece que sabe lo que hace; **they stared at him ~ he was crazy** se quedaron mirándolo como si estuviera loco **(b)** (as, in same way) como

-like /laɪk/ *suff*: **prison~** parecido a una prisión; **snake~** ‹*appearance*› (como) de serpiente; ‹*movement*› serpenteante

likeable *adj* ⇒ LIKABLE

likelihood /'laɪklihʊd/ *n* [U] probabilidad *f*, posibilidad *f*; **there is every ~ that she'll agree** es muy probable que acepte

likely /'laɪkli/ *adj* **-lier, -liest (a)** (probable) ‹*outcome/winner*› probable; **it's more than ~ that she's out** lo más seguro es que no esté; **a ~ story!** (iro) ¡cuéntame otra! (iró); **it is ~ to be a tough match** lo más probable es que sea un partido difícil **(b)** (promising): **she's the most ~ applicant** es la candidata con más posibilidades; **this is a ~ place to find a telephone** aquí tiene que haber un teléfono

liken /'laɪkən/ *vt* **to ~ sth/sb** TO **sth/sb** comparar algo/a algn CON *or* A algo/algn

likeness /'laɪknəs ‖ 'laɪknɪs/ *n* **(a)** [U C] (resemblance) parecido *m* **(b)** [C] (referring to a portrait): **it's a good ~** es un buen retrato

likewise /'laɪkwaɪz/ *adv* **(a)** (in the same way) asimismo **(b)** (the same): **to do ~** hacer* lo mismo

liking /'laɪkɪŋ/ *n* **(a)** (fondness) **~ (FOR sth)** afición *f* (A algo); **to take a ~ to sb/sth** tomarle *or* (esp Esp) cogerle* simpatía a algn/gusto a algo **(b)** (satisfaction) gusto *m*; **to be to sb's ~** ser* del gusto de algn

lilac /'laɪlək/ *n* **(a) ~ (bush)** lila *f*, lilo *m*; (*before n*) **~ flower** lila *f* **(b)** ▶ 515 (color) lila *m*; (*before n*) lila *adj inv*

lilt /lɪlt/ *n* (of song, tune) cadencia *f*; **to speak with a ~** hablar con un tono cantarín

lilting /'lɪltɪŋ/ *adj* ‹*voice*› cantarín, musical; ‹*melody*› cadencioso

lily /'lɪli/ *n* (*pl* **lilies**) (Bot) liliácea *f*; (*white ~*) azucena *f*, lirio *m* blanco

lily-of-the-valley /'lɪliəvðə'væli/ *n* (*pl* **lilies-of-the-valley**) lirio *m* de los valles, muguete *m*

Like[1]

The transitive verb to like *is most commonly translated using the intransitive verb* gustar + an indirect personal pronoun:

English		Spanish
I like wine	=	me gusta el vino
we like the house	=	nos gusta la casa
I like apples	=	me gustan las manzanas
we like apples	=	nos gustan las manzanas

If the full indirect object is mentioned, the indirect object pronoun must still be included:

my father doesn't like traveling	=	a mi padre no le gusta viajar

The translation of do you like it? *is simply* ¿te gusta?

limb /lɪm/ *n* **(a)** (Anat) miembro *m*; **to tear sb ~ from ~** despedazar* a algn **(b)** (of tree) rama *f* (*principal*); ***to go out on a ~*** aventurarse

limber up /ˈlɪmbər ‖ ˈlɪmbə(r)/ [*v* + *adv*] hacer* ejercicios de calentamiento

lime /laɪm/ *n* **1** [U] (calcium oxide) cal *f* **2 (a)** [C] (fruit) lima *f* **(b)** [C] (tree) limero *m*, lima *f* **(c)** ▶**515** [U] (color) verde *m* lima; (*before n*) verde lima *adj inv* **3** [C] (linden) (BrE) tilo *m*

lime: **~-green** /ˈlaɪmˈgriːn/ ▶**515** *adj* (*pred* **~ green**) verde lima *adj inv*; **~light** *n*: **to be in the ~light** estar* en primer plano; **to steal the ~light** acaparar la atención del público

limerick /ˈlɪmərɪk/ *n*: *poema humorístico de cinco versos*

limestone /ˈlaɪmstəʊn/ *n* [U] (piedra *f*) caliza *f*

limit[1] /ˈlɪmət ‖ ˈlɪmɪt/ *n* **1 (a)** [C U] (boundary) límite *m* **(b)** [C U] (furthest extent): **she pushes herself to the ~** se esfuerza al máximo; **that's the ~!** (colloq) ¡es el colmo! (fam) **2** [C U] (restriction, maximum) límite *m*

limit[2] *vt* limitar; **to ~ oneself TO sth/-ING** limitarse A algo/+ INF

limitation /ˈlɪməˈteɪʃən ‖ ˌlɪmɪˈteɪʃən/ *n* [U C] limitación *f*

limited /ˈlɪmətəd ‖ ˈlɪmɪtɪd/ *adj* **(a)** ‹*number/experience/scope*› limitado **(b)** (AmE Transp) ‹*express/train/bus*› semi-directo **(c)** (Busn) ‹*liability*› limitado; **public ~ company** (BrE) sociedad *f* anónima

limitless /ˈlɪmətləs ‖ ˈlɪmɪtlɪs/ *adj* ilimitado, sin límites

limousine /ˈlɪməziːn, lɪməˈziːn/ *n* limusina *f*

limp[1] /lɪmp/ *vi* cojear, renguear (AmL)

limp[2] *n* cojera *f*, renguera *f* (AmL); **she walks with a ~** cojea *or* (AmL tb) renguea

limp[3] *adj* ‹*handshake*› flojo; ‹*lettuce*› mustio; ‹*hair*› lacio y sin vida

limpet /ˈlɪmpət ‖ ˈlɪmpɪt/ *n* lapa *f*

linden /ˈlɪndən/ *n* (AmE) tilo *m*

line[1] /laɪn/ *n* **1** [C] **(a)** (mark, trace) línea *f*; (Math) recta *f*; ***to be on the ~*** (colloq) estar* en peligro, peligrar; (*before n*) **~ drawing** dibujo *m* lineal **(b)** (on face, palm) línea *f*; (wrinkle) arruga *f* **2 (a)** [C] (boundary, border) línea *f*; **the county/state ~** (AmE) (la línea de) la frontera del condado/estado **(b)** [C] (Sport) línea *f*; (*before n*) **~ judge** juez *mf* de línea **(c)** [C U] (contour) línea *f* **3 (a)** [C U] (cable, rope) cuerda *f*; (*clothes o washing ~*) cuerda (de tender la ropa); (*fishing ~*) sedal *m*; **power ~** cable *m* eléctrico **(b)** [C] (Telec) línea *f*; **hold the ~, please** no cuelgue *or* (CS tb) no corte, por favor; **it's a very bad ~** se oye muy mal **4** [C] (Transp) **(a)** (company, service) línea *f*; **shipping ~** línea de transportes marítimos **(b)** (Rail) línea *f*; (track) (BrE) vía *f* **5** [U C] **(a)** (path) línea *f*; **it was right in my ~ of vision** me obstruía la visual **(b)** (attitude, policy) postura *f*, línea *f*; **to take a hard ~ (with sb/on sth)** adoptar una postura *or* línea dura (con algn/con respecto a algo) **(c)** (method, style): **~ of inquiry** línea *f* de investigación; **I was thinking of something along the ~s of** ... pensaba en algo del tipo de ... **6** [C] **(a)** (row) fila *f*; (queue) (AmE) cola *f*; **to wait in ~** (AmE) hacer* cola; **to get in ~** (AmE) ponerse* en la cola; **to cut in ~** (AmE) colarse* (fam), brincarse* *or* saltarse la cola (Méx fam); ***in/into (~) with sth***: **the new measures are in ~ with government policy** las nuevas medidas siguen la línea de la política del gobierno; **he needs to be brought into ~** hay que llamarlo al orden **(b)** (series) serie *f*; **he's the latest in a long ~ of radical leaders** es el último de una larga serie de dirigentes radicales **(c)** (succession) línea *f*; **he's next in ~ to the throne** es el siguiente en la línea de sucesión al trono **7** [C] (Mil) línea *f* **8 (a)** [C] (of text) línea *f*, renglón *m*; (of poem) verso *m*; ***to read between the ~s*** leer* entre líneas **(b) lines** *pl* (Theat): **to learn one's ~s** aprenderse el papel; **he forgot his ~s** se olvidó de lo que le tocaba decir **(c)** (note): **to drop sb a ~** escribirle* a algn unas líneas

line[2] *vt* **1 (a)** ‹*skirt/box*› forrar **(b)** (form lining along) cubrir* **2** (border): **the avenue is ~d with trees** la avenida está bordeada de árboles; **crowds ~d the route** cientos de personas estaban alineadas a ambos lados del camino

• **line up 1** [*v* + *adv*] (form line, row) ponerse* en fila; (queue up) (AmE) hacer* cola **2** [*v* + *o* + *adv*, *v* + *adv* + *o*] **(a)** (form into line) ‹*soldiers/prisoners*› poner* en fila **(b)** (arrange): **we've a busy program ~d up for you** le tenemos preparada una apretada agenda **(c)** (align) alinear

lineage /ˈlɪniɪdʒ/ *n* [U] linaje *m*

linear /ˈlɪniər ‖ ˈlɪniə(r)/ *adj* lineal

lined /laɪnd/ *adj* **(a)** ‹*paper*› con renglones *or* (Chi) reglones **(b)** ‹*jacket/boots/curtains*› forrado **(c)** (Tech) revestido **(d)** ‹*face/skin*› arrugado

linen /'lɪnən/ *n* [U] **1** (cloth) hilo *m*, lino *m* **2** (*bed* ~) ropa *f* blanca *or* de cama; (*table* ~) mantelerías *fpl*; (*before n*) ~ **basket** canasto *m or* cesto *m* de la ropa sucia

liner /'laɪnər ‖ 'laɪnə(r)/ *n* **1** [C] (ship) buque *m* (de pasaje *or* pasajeros); (*ocean* ~) transatlántico *m* **2** [C] **(a)** (lining) forro *m*; **(dust)bin** ~ (BrE) bolsa *f* de la basura **(b)** (of record) (AmE) funda *f*, carátula *f*

line: ~**sman** /'laɪnzmən/ *n* (*pl* **-men** /-mən/) (Sport) juez *m* de línea; ~**up** *n* **(a)** (Sport) alineación *f*; **the band's original** ~**up** la integración original del grupo **(b)** (of suspects) (AmE) rueda *f* de identificación *or* de sospechosos

linger /'lɪŋgər ‖ 'lɪŋgə(r)/ *vi* **(a)** (delay leaving) quedarse (un rato) **(b)** ~ **(on)** «*aftertaste/smell*» persistir; «*tradition*» perdurar, sobrevivir **(c)** **lingering** *pres p* persistente, que no desaparece **(d)** (take one's time): **her eyes** ~**ed on the child** se quedó largo rato mirando al niño; **they** ~**ed over their coffee** se entretuvieron tomando el café

lingerie /'lɑːnʒə'reɪ ‖ 'læ̃nʒəri/ *n* [U] lencería *f*

linguist /'lɪŋgwəst ‖ 'lɪŋgwɪst/ *n* lingüista *mf*

linguistic /lɪŋ'gwɪstɪk/ *adj* lingüístico

linguistics /lɪŋ'gwɪstɪks/ *n* [U] (+ *sing vb*) lingüística *f*

lining /'laɪnɪŋ/ *n* forro *m*

link¹ /lɪŋk/ *n* **1** **(a)** (in chain) eslabón *m* **(b)** ⇒ CUFF LINK **2** **(a)** (connection) conexión *f* **(b)** (tie, bond) vínculo *m*, lazo *m* **(c)** (Telec, Transp) conexión *f*, enlace *m*

link² *vt* **(a)** ‹*components*› unir; ‹*terminals*› conectar; **to** ~ **arms** tomarse *or* (esp Esp) cogerse* del brazo **(b)** ‹*buildings/towns*› unir, conectar **(c)** ‹*facts/events*› relacionar

• **link up** **1** [*v* + *adv*] conectar; «*spacecraft*» acoplarse **2** [*v* + *o* + *adv*, *v* + *adv* + *o*] conectar

links /lɪŋks/ *n* (*pl* ~) (+ *sing o pl vb*) campo *m* de golf (*esp a orillas del mar*)

linkup /'lɪŋkʌp/ *n* **(a)** [C U] (connection) conexión *f*; (of spacecraft) acoplamiento *m* **(b)** [C] (Rad, TV) conexión *f*, enlace *m*

linoleum /lɪ'nəʊliəm/ *n* [U] linóleo *m*

linseed /'lɪnsiːd/ *n* [U] linaza *f*; (*before n*) ~ **oil** aceite *m* de linaza

lint /lɪnt/ *n* [U] hilas *fpl*

lion /'laɪən/ *n* león *m*

lioness /'laɪənəs ‖ 'laɪənes/ *n* leona *f*

lion tamer /'teɪmər ‖ 'teɪmə(r)/ *n* domador, -dora *m,f* de leones

lip /lɪp/ *n* **(a)** ▶ **484** (Anat) labio *m* **(b)** (of cup, tray) borde *m*

lip: ~ **gloss** *n* [U] brillo *m* de labias; ~**read** (*past & past p* **-read** *vi* /-red/) leer* los labios; ~ **salve** *n* bálsamo *m* labial; ~ **service** *n*: **he just pays** ~ **service to feminism** es feminista de los dientes para afuera; ~**stick** *n* **(a)** [C] (stick) lápiz *m or* barra *f* de labios, lápiz *m* labial (AmL), pintalabios *m* (Esp fam) **(b)** [U] (substance) rouge *m*

liquefy /'lɪkwəfaɪ ‖ 'lɪkwɪfaɪ/ **-fies, -fying, -fied** *vi* licuarse* ■ ~ *vt* licuar*

liqueur /lɪ'kɜːr ‖ lɪ'kjʊə(r)/ *n* [U C] licor *m*

liquid¹ /'lɪkwəd ‖ 'lɪkwɪd/ *n* [U C] líquido *m*

liquid² *adj* líquido

liquidation /'lɪkwə'deɪʃən ‖ ˌlɪkwɪ'deɪʃən/ *n* [U C] liquidación *f*

liquid crystal display *n* pantalla *f* de cristal líquido

liquidize /'lɪkwədaɪz ‖ 'lɪkwɪdaɪz/ *vt* licuar*

liquidizer /'lɪkwədaɪzər ‖ 'lɪkwɪdaɪzə(r)/ *n* (BrE) licuadora *f*

liquor /'lɪkər ‖ 'lɪkə(r)/ *n* [U] alcohol *m*, bebidas *fpl* alcohólicas; (*before n*) ~ **cabinet** (AmE) mueblebar *m*

liquorice (BrE) ⇒ LICORICE

liquor store *n* (AmE) ≈ tienda *f* de vinos y licores, botillería *f* (Chi)

Lisbon /'lɪzbən/ *n* Lisboa *f*

lisp¹ /lɪsp/ *n* ceceo *m*

lisp² *vi* cecear

list¹ /lɪst/ *n* lista *f*

list² *vt* **(a)** (enumerate) hacer* una lista de; (verbally) enumerar **(b)** ‹*securities/stocks*› cotizar* ■ ~ *vi* (Naut) escorar

listen /'lɪsn̩/ *vi* escuchar; **to** ~ TO **sth/sb** escuchar algo/a algn

listener /'lɪsnər ‖ 'lɪsn̩ə(r)/ *n* **(a)** (Rad) oyente *mf*, radioyente *mf* **(b)** (in conversation): **he's a good** ~ es una persona que sabe escuchar

listing /'lɪstɪŋ/ *n* lista *f*; ~**s magazine** guía *f* de espectáculos, ≈ guía *f* del ocio (*en Esp*)

listless /'lɪstləs ‖ 'lɪstlɪs/ *adj* (lacking enthusiasm) apático; (lacking energy) lánguido

lit /lɪt/ *past & past p of* LIGHT⁴

litany /'lɪtəni/ *n* (*pl* **-nies**) letanía *f*

liter, (BrE) **litre** /'liːtər ‖ 'liːtə(r)/ *n* litro *m*

literacy /'lɪtərəsi/ *n* [U] alfabetismo *m*

literal /'lɪtərəl/ *adj* literal

literally /'lɪtərəli/ *adv* literalmente; **I didn't mean it** ~ no lo decía en sentido literal

literary /'lɪtəreri ‖ 'lɪtərəri/ *adj* literario

literate /'lɪtərət/ *adj* alfabetizado

literature /'lɪtərətʃʊr ‖ 'lɪtrətʃə(r)/ *n* [U] **(a)** (art) literatura *f* **(b)** [U] (promotional material) folletos *mpl*

lithe /laɪð/ *adj* **lither, lithest** ágil

lithograph /'lɪθəgræf ‖ 'lɪθəgrɑːf/ *n* litografía *f*

Lithuania /'lɪθju'eɪniə/ *n* Lituania *f*

Lithuanian /'lɪθju'eɪniən/ *adj* lituano

litigation /'lɪtə'geɪʃən ‖ ˌlɪtɪ'geɪʃən/ *n* [U] litigio *m*

litmus /'lɪtməs/: ~ **paper** *n* papel *m* (de) tornasol; ~ **test** *n* (Chem) prueba *f* de acidez *or* de tornasol

litre /'liːtər ‖ 'liːtə(r)/ *n* (BrE) ⇒ LITER

litter¹ /'lɪtər ‖ 'lɪtə(r)/ *n* **1** [U] (refuse) basura *f* **2** [C] (offspring) (Zool) camada *f*, cría *f* **3** [U] (for horses, cows) lecho *m* de paja; (for cats) arena *f* higiénica

litter² *vt*: **newspapers** ~**ed the floor** el suelo estaba cubierto de papeles; **to be** ~**ed** WITH **sth** estar* lleno DE algo

litter: ~ **bin** *n* (BrE) papelera *f or* (AmL tb) papelero *m or* (Col) caneca *f*; ~**bug** *n*: *persona que tira basura en lugares públicos*; ~ **lout** *n* (BrE) ⇒ ~BUG

little¹ /ˈlɪtl̩/ *adj* **I** (*comp* **littler** /ˈlɪtl̩ər ‖ ˈlɪtl̩ə(r)/; *superl* **littlest** /ˈlɪtl̩əst ‖ ˈlɪtlɪst/) (small, young) pequeño, chico (esp AmL); **a ~ while** un ratito; **my ~ sister/brother** mi hermanita/hermanito
II (*comp* **less**; *superl* **least**) **(a)** (not much) poco; **there is very ~ bread left** queda muy poco pan **(b) a little** (some) un poco de

little² *pron* (*comp* **less**; *superl* **least**) **(a)** (not much) poco, -ca; **~ by ~** poco a poco **(b) a little** (some) un poco, algo

little³ *adv* (*comp* **less**; *superl* **least**) poco; **~ did he know that** ... lo que menos se imaginaba era que ...; **a little** (somewhat) un poco; **I'm feeling a ~ tired** estoy algo *or* un poco cansado

live¹ /lɪv/ *vi* vivir; **she ~d to be 100** llegó a cumplir 100 años; **she had three months to ~** le quedaban tres meses de vida; **where do you ~?** ¿donde vives?; **long ~ the king!** ¡viva el rey!; **~ and let ~** (set phrase) vive y deja vivir a los demás ■ **~** *vt* vivir; **she ~s a happy life** lleva una vida feliz, vive feliz; **to ~ life to the full** vivir la vida al máximo

• **live down** [*v + o + adv, v + adv + o*]: **if they see you wearing that, you'll never ~ it down** si te ven con eso no lo van a olvidar nunca

• **live for** [*v + prep + o*]: **she ~s for her work** vive para su trabajo; **I've nothing left to ~ for** ya no tengo nada por lo que vivir

• **live off** [*v + prep + o*] **(a)** (be supported by) ‹*family/friends*› vivir a costa de; ‹*crime/the land*› vivir de **(b)** (feed on) ‹*fruits/seeds*› alimentarse de

• **live on 1** [*v + adv*] «*memory*» seguir* presente; «*tradition*» seguir* existiendo **2** [*v + prep + o*] **(a)** (feed on) alimentarse de **(b)** (support oneself with): **she ~s on $75 a week** vive con 75 dólares a la semana

• **live through** [*v + prep + o*] ‹*war/experience*› vivir

• **live together** [*v + adv*] **(a)** (cohabit) vivir juntos **(b)** (coexist) convivir

• **live up** [*v + o + adv*]: *to ~ it up* (colloq) darse* la gran vida (fam)

• **live up to** [*v + adv + prep + o*]: **it didn't ~ up to its reputation** no estuvo a la altura de su reputación; **they ~ up to their name** hacen honor a su nombre

live² /laɪv/ *adj* **1** (alive) vivo **2** (of current interest) ‹*issue*› candente **3** (Rad, TV): **the show was ~** el programa era en directo; **the program is recorded before a ~ audience** el programa se graba con público en la sala

live³ /laɪv/ *adv* ‹*broadcast*› en directo

live-in /ˈlɪvˈɪn/ *adj* (*before n*) ‹*staff*› residente; ‹*nanny/maid*› con cama, de planta (Méx), puertas adentro (Chi); **she has a ~ lover** su amante vive con ella

livelihood /ˈlaɪvlihʊd/ *n* (*no pl*): **farming is their ~** viven de la agricultura; **to earn one's ~** ganarse la vida

lively /ˈlaɪvli/ *adj* **-lier, -liest** ‹*place/debate*› animado; ‹*music*› alegre; ‹*account*› vívido

liven up /ˈlaɪvən/ **1** [*v + adv*] animarse **2** [*v + o + adv, v + adv + o*] animar

liver /ˈlɪvər ‖ ˈlɪvə(r)/ **▶ 484** *n* hígado *m*

lives /laɪvz/ *pl of* LIFE

livestock /ˈlaɪvstɑːk ‖ ˈlaɪvstɒk/ *n* [U] (+ *sing or pl vb*) animales *mpl* (de cría); (cattle) ganado *m*

livid /ˈlɪvəd ‖ ˈlɪvɪd/ *adj* **1** (furious) (colloq) furioso **2** ‹*bruise*› amoratado; ‹*face*› lívido

living¹ /ˈlɪvɪŋ/ *n* **1** (livelihood) (*no pl*): **to earn** *o* **make one's/a ~** ganarse la vida; **to work for a ~** trabajar para vivir; **what does he do for a ~?** ¿en qué trabaja? **2** [U] (style of life) vida *f*; (*before n*) ‹*space/area*› destinado a vivienda; **~ standards** nivel *m* de vida

living² *adj* (*before n*) vivo

living room *n* sala *f* (de estar), living *m* (esp AmS), salón *m* (esp Esp)

lizard /ˈlɪzərd ‖ ˈlɪzəd/ *n* lagarto *m*; (*wall ~*) lagartija *f*

'll /l̩/ **(a)** = **will (b)** = **shall**

llama /ˈlɑːmə/ *n* llama *f*

LLB *n* = **Bachelor of Laws**

lo /ləʊ/ *interj* (arch *or* hum): **~ and behold** ¡y quién lo iba a decir!

load¹ /ləʊd/ *n* **1** [C] (cargo, burden) carga *f*; **four ~s of washing** cuatro lavados *or* (Esp) coladas **2** (*often pl*) (colloq) (much, many) cantidad *f*, montón *m* (fam); **the play is a ~ of rubbish** la obra es una porquería (fam) **3** (Civil Eng) carga *f*; **Ⓢ maximum load 15 tons** peso máximo: 15 toneladas

load² *vt/i* cargar*

• **load up 1** [*v + o + adv, v + adv + o*] cargar* **2** [*v + adv*] cargar*

loaded /ˈləʊdəd ‖ ˈləʊdɪd/ *adj* **(a)** ‹*vehicle/gun/camera*› cargado **(b)** (richly provided) (*pred*) **to be ~** WITH **sth** estar* repleto DE algo **(c)** (weighted) ‹*dice*› cargado; ‹*question*› tendencioso

loaf¹ /ləʊf/ *n* (*pl* **loaves**): **a ~ (of bread)** un pan; (of French bread) una barra de pan, una flauta (CS); (baked in tin) un pan de molde

loaf² *vi* (colloq): **to ~ (around** *o* **about)** holgazanear

loan¹ /ləʊn/ *n* préstamo *m*

loan² *vt* prestar

loath /ləʊθ/ *adj* (*pred*) **to be ~ to** + INF resistirse A + INF

loathe /ləʊð/ *vt* odiar, detestar

loathsome /ˈləʊðsəm/ *adj* repugnante

loaves /ləʊvz/ *pl of* LOAF¹

lob¹ /lɑːb ‖ lɒb/ *vt* **-bb-** lanzar* por lo alto

lob² *n* globo *m*, lob *m*

lobby¹ /ˈlɑːbi ‖ ˈlɒbi/ *n* (*pl* **-bies**) **1** (entrance hall) vestíbulo *m*; (in theater) foyer *m* **2** (pressure group) grupo *m* de presión

lobby², **-bies, -bying, -bied** *vt* ejercer* presión sobre ■ **~** *vi* **to ~** FOR **sth** ejercer* presión para obtener algo

lobe /ləʊb/ *n* (*ear~*) lóbulo *m* (de la oreja)

lobster /ˈlɑːbstər ‖ ˈlɒbstə(r)/ *n* langosta *f*, bogavante *m* (Esp)

local¹ /ˈləʊkəl/ *adj* **1** ‹*dialect/newspaper*› local; ‹*council/election*› ≈municipal; **a ~ call** una llamada urbana; **he's a ~ man** es de aquí (*or* de allí) **2** (Med) ‹*anesthetic*› local; ‹*infection*› localizado

local² *n* **(a)** (inhabitant): **he's not a ~** no es de aquí (*or* de allí); **the ~s say it's true** los (vecinos) del lugar dicen que es verdad **(b)** (pub) (BrE colloq): **our ~** el bar de nuestro barrio (*or* de nuestra zona *etc*)

locale /ləʊ'kæl ‖ ləʊ'kɑːl/ *n* escenario *m*

local government *n* [U] ≈ administración *f* municipal; (*before n*) ‹*elections*› ≈ municipal

locality /ləʊ'kæləti/ *n* (*pl* **-ties**) (frml) localidad *f*

localize /'ləʊkəlaɪz/ *vt* localizar*

locally /'ləʊkəli/ *adv* ‹*live/work*› en la zona

locate /'ləʊkeɪt ‖ ləʊ'keɪt/ *vt* **1** (find) ‹*fault/leak*› localizar*, ubicar* (esp AmL) **2** (position) ‹*building/business*› situar*, ubicar* (esp AmL)

location /ləʊ'keɪʃən/ *n* **1** [C] (position) posición *f*, ubicación *f* (esp AmL) **2** [C U] (Cin) lugar *m* de filmación; **we were filming on ~ in Italy** estábamos rodando los exteriores en Italia

loch /lɑːk, lɑːx ‖ lɒk, lɒx/ *n* lago

lock¹ /lɑːk ‖ lɒk/ *n* **1** [C] (device) cerradura *f*, chapa *f* (AmL) **2** [C] (on canal) esclusa *f* **3** [C] (of hair) mechón *m*

lock² *vt* ‹*door/car*› cerrar* (con llave); **to ~ sb in a room** encerrar* a algn en una habitación

• **lock in** [*v + o + adv, v + adv + o*] encerrar*

• **lock out** [*v + o + adv, v + adv + o*]: **I ~ed myself out (of the house)** me quedé afuera sin llaves

• **lock up** [*v + o + adv, v + adv + o*] **(a)** ‹*valuables*› guardar bajo llave; ‹*person*› encerrar* **(b)** ‹*house/shop*› cerrar* con llave

locker /'lɑːkər ‖ 'lɒkə(r)/ *n* armario *m*, locker *m* (AmL); (at bus, railway station) (casilla *f* de la) consigna *f* automática

locker room *n* (esp AmE) vestuario *m*

locket /'lɑːkət ‖ 'lɒkɪt/ *n* relicario *m*

lock: **~out** *n* cierre *m* patronal, paro *m* patronal (AmL); **~smith** *n* cerrajero, -ra *m,f*

locomotive /'ləʊkə'məʊtɪv/ *n* locomotora *f*

locust /'ləʊkəst/ *n* langosta *f*

lode /ləʊd/ *n* veta *f*, filón *m*

lodge¹ /lɑːdʒ ‖ lɒdʒ/ *n* **1 (a)** (for gatekeeper) (BrE) casa *f* del guarda **(b)** (for porter) portería *f* **(c)** (on private estate) pabellón *m* **(d)** (at resort) (AmE) hotel *m* **2** (branch, meeting place) logia *f*

lodge² *vt* **1** ‹*appeal*› interponer*; ‹*complaint*› presentar **2** (deposit) depositar ■ **~** *vi* **1** (become stuck): **the bullet had ~d in his spine** la bala se le había alojado en la columna **2** (live as lodger) alojarse, hospedarse

lodger /'lɑːdʒər ‖ 'lɒdʒə(r)/ *n* inquilino, -na *m,f* (*de una habitación en una casa particular*)

lodging /'lɑːdʒɪŋ ‖ 'lɒdʒɪŋ/ *n* **(a)** [U] (accommodations) alojamiento *m* **(b) lodgings** *pl* (rented): **to live in ~s** vivir en una habitación alquilada (*or* en una pensión *etc*)

loft /lɔːft ‖ lɒft/ *n* (BrE) desván *m*, altillo *m* (esp AmL), zarzo *m* (Col)

loftily /'lɔːftəli ‖ 'lɒftɪli/ *adv* con altivez, altaneramente

lofty /'lɔːfti ‖ 'lɒfti/ *adj* **-tier, -tiest (a)** (elevated) ‹*ideals/sentiments*› noble, elevado **(b)** (haughty) altivo, altanero **(c)** (high) (liter) alto, majestuoso (liter)

log¹ /lɔːg ‖ lɒg/ *n* **1** (wood) tronco *m*; (as fuel) leño *m*; ***to sleep like a ~*** dormir* como un tronco (fam) **2** (record) diario *m* **3** (Math) logaritmo *m*

log² **-gg-** *vt* ‹*speed/position/time*› registrar, anotar; ‹*call*› registrar

• **log in**, **log on** [*v + adv*] (Comput) entrar (al sistema)

• **log off**, **log out** [*v + adv*] (Comput) salir* (del sistema)

loganberry /'ləʊgən,beri ‖ 'ləʊgənbəri/ *n* (*pl* **-ries**) frambuesa *f* de Logan

logarithm /'lɔːgərɪðəm ‖ 'lɒgərɪðəm/ *n* logaritmo *m*

logbook /'lɔːgbʊk ‖ 'lɒgbʊk/ *n* (register) diario *m*; (Naut) diario *m* de navegación *or* de a bordo; (Aviat) diario *m* de vuelo

loggerheads /'lɔːgərhedz ‖ 'lɒgəhedz/ *pl n*: **they were constantly at ~** siempre estaban en desacuerdo

logic /'lɑːdʒɪk ‖ 'lɒdʒɪk/ *n* [U] lógica *f*

logical /'lɑːdʒɪkəl ‖ 'lɒdʒɪkəl/ *adj* lógico

logistics /lə'dʒɪstɪks/ *n* **(a)** (Mil) (+ *sing vb*) logística *f* **(b)** (practicalities) (+ *pl vb*) problemas *mpl* logísticos

logo /'ləʊgəʊ, 'lɑː- ‖ 'ləʊgəʊ/ *n* (*pl* **logos**) logo *m*

loin /lɔɪn/ *n* **(a)** (meat) lomo *m* **(b) loins** *pl* (Anat) (liter) entrañas *fpl* (liter)

loincloth /'lɔɪnklɔːθ ‖ 'lɔɪnklɒθ/ *n* taparrabos *m*

loiter /'lɔɪtər ‖ 'lɔɪtə(r)/ *vi* perder* el tiempo

lollipop /'lɑːlipɑːp ‖ 'lɒlipɒp/ *n* piruleta *f* *or* (Esp) chupachup(s)® *m* *or* (Andes, Méx) paleta *f* *or* (RPl) chupetín *m* *or* (Col) colombina *f* *or* (Chi, Per) chupete *m*

lolly /'lɑːli ‖ 'lɒli/ *n* (*pl* **-lies**) (BrE) (*ice ~*) paleta *f* (helada) *or* (Esp) polo *m* *or* (RPl) palito *m* *or* (CS) chupete *m* helado

London /'lʌndən/ *n* Londres; (*before n*) londinense

lone /ləʊn/ *adj* solitario; ‹*explorer/sailor*› en solitario

loneliness /'ləʊnlinəs ‖ 'ləʊnlinɪs/ *n* [U] soledad *f*

lonely /'ləʊnli/ *adj* **-lier, -liest (a)** (feeling alone): **to feel ~** sentirse* solo **(b)** (isolated) solitario, aislado

loner /'ləʊnər ‖ 'ləʊnə(r)/ *n*: **she's a bit of a ~** le gusta estar sola

lonesome /'ləʊnsəm/ *adj* (esp AmE) ⇒ LONELY

long¹ /lɔːŋ ‖ lɒŋ/ *adj* **longer** /'lɔːŋgər ‖ 'lɒŋgə(r)/, **longest** /'lɔːŋgəst ‖ 'lɒŋgɪst/ **1** (in space) ‹*distance/hair/list*› largo; **how ~ do you want the skirt?** ¿cómo quieres la falda de larga?; **the wall is 200 m ~** el muro mide 200 m de largo; **the book is over 300 pages ~** el libro tiene más de 300 páginas **2** (in time) largo; **two months isn't ~ enough** dos meses no son suficientes; **she's been gone a ~ time** hace tiempo que se fue

long² *adv* **-er, -est 1** (in time): **how ~ have you been living here?** ¿cuánto hace que vives aquí?; **people live ~er now** ahora la gente vive más (años); **it won't be ~ before they get here** no tardarán en llegar; **not ~ afterwards** poco después; **not ~ ago** no hace mucho **2 (a)** (*in phrases*) **before long**: **you'll be an aunt before ~** dentro de poco serás tía; **for long**: **she wasn't gone for ~** no estuvo fuera mucho tiempo; **no longer, not any longer**: **I can't stand it any ~er** ya no aguanto más; **they no ~er live here** ya no viven aquí **(b) as long as, so long as** (*as conj*) (for the period) mientras; (providing that) con tal de que (+ *subj*); **for as ~ as I can remember** desde que tengo memoria

long[3] *vi* **to ~ to** + INF estar* deseando + INF

• long for [*v* + *prep* + *o*] ‹*mother/friend*› echar de menos, extrañar (esp AmL); **she ~ed for Friday to arrive** estaba deseando que llegara el viernes

long-distance[1] /ˈlɔːŋˈdɪstəns ‖ ˌlɒŋˈdɪstəns/ *adj* ‹*truck driver*› que hace largos recorridos; ‹*train*› de largo recorrido; ‹*race/runner*› de fondo; **a ~ telephone call** una llamada de larga distancia, una conferencia (interurbana) (Esp)

long-distance[2] *adv* (esp AmE): **to call ~** hacer* una llamada de larga distancia, poner* una conferencia (Esp)

longevity /lɑːnˈdʒevəti ‖ lɒnˈdʒevəti/ *n* [U] (frml) longevidad *f*

long: **~-haired** /ˈlɔːŋˈherd ‖ ˌlɒŋˈheəd/ *adj* de pelo largo; **~hand** *n* [U]: **in ~hand** en escritura normal (*no en taquigrafía*); **~-haul** /ˈlɔːŋˈhɔːl ‖ ˌlɒŋˈhɔːl/ *adj* (*before n*) de larga distancia

longing /ˈlɔːŋɪŋ ‖ ˈlɒŋɪŋ/ *n* [U C] (nostalgia) añoranza *f*; (desire) vivo deseo *m*

longitude /ˈlɑːndʒətuːd ‖ ˈlɒŋgɪtjuːd, ˈlɒndʒɪtjuːd/ *n* [U] longitud *f*

long: **~ johns** /dʒɑːnz ‖ dʒɒnz/ *pl n* calzoncillos *mpl* largos; **~ jump** *n* [U C] salto *m* de longitud, salto *m* (en) largo (AmL); **~-lost** /ˈlɔːŋˈlɔːst ‖ ˈlɒŋlɒst/ *adj* (*before n*): **she had a ~-lost uncle in Australia** tenía un tío en Australia a quien había perdido de vista hacía mucho tiempo; **~-playing record** /ˈlɔːŋˈpleɪɪŋ ‖ ˈlɒŋˌpleɪɪŋ/ *n* disco *m* de larga duración; **~-range** /ˈlɔːŋˈreɪndʒ ‖ ˈlɒŋreɪndʒ/ *adj* (*before n*) ‹*missile*› de largo alcance; ‹*aircraft*› para vuelos largos; **~-running** /ˈlɔːŋˈrʌnɪŋ ‖ ˈlɒŋˌrʌnɪŋ/ *adj* ‹*musical/farce*› que lleva tiempo en cartelera; ‹*feud/controversy*› que viene (*or* venía *etc*) de largo; **~shoreman** /ˈlɔːŋˈʃɔːrmən ‖ ˈlɒŋˌʃɔːmən/ *n* (*pl* **-men** /-mən/) (AmE) estibador *m*, changador *m* (RPl); **~sighted** /ˈlɔːŋˈsaɪtəd ‖ ˌlɒŋˈsaɪtɪd/ *adj* hipermétrope; **~-sleeved** /ˈlɔːŋˈsliːvd ‖ ˈlɒŋsliːvd/ *adj* de manga larga; **~standing** /ˈlɔːŋˈstændɪŋ ‖ ˌlɒŋˈstændɪŋ/ *adj* antiguo, que viene (*or* venía *etc*) de largo; **~-suffering** /ˈlɔːŋˈsʌfərɪŋ ‖ ˌlɒŋˈsʌfərɪŋ/ *adj* sufrido; **~-term** /ˈlɔːŋˈtɜːrm ‖ ˈlɒŋtɜːm/ *adj* (*usu before n*) **(a)** (in the future) ‹*effects/benefits*› a largo plazo **(b)** (for a long period) ‹*solution*› duradero; ‹*effects*› prolongado; ‹*unemployment*› de larga duración; **~ wave** *n* onda *f* larga; **~-winded** /ˈlɔːŋ ˈwɪndəd ‖ ˌlɒŋˈwɪndɪd/ *adj* ‹*speech/article*› denso, prolijo

loo /luː/ *n* (BrE colloq) baño *m* (esp AmL), váter *m* (Esp fam)

look[1] /lʊk/ *n* **1** (glance) mirada *f*; **to have** *o* **take a ~ at sth/sb** echarle un vistazo a algo/algn **2** (search, examination): **have a ~ for my pipe, will you?** mira a ver si me encuentras la pipa, por favor; **do you mind if I take a ~ around?** ¿le importa si echo un vistazo? **3 (a)** (expression) cara *f* **(b)** (appearance) aire *m*; **I don't like the ~ of his friend** no me gusta el aspecto *or* (fam) la pinta de su amigo **(c)** (Clothing) moda *f*, look *m* **(d) looks** *pl* (beauty) belleza *f*; **she was attracted by his good ~s** la atrajo lo guapo *or* (AmL tb) lo buen mozo que era

look[2] *vi* **I 1** (see, glance) mirar; **I ~ed around** (behind) me volví a mirar *or* miré hacia atrás; (all around) miré a mi alrededor; **to ~ away** apartar la vista; **to ~ down** (lower eyes) bajar la vista; (from tower, clifftop) mirar hacia abajo; **~ out (of) the window** mira por la ventana; **to ~ up** (raise eyes) levantar la vista; (toward ceiling, sky) mirar hacia arriba; ***to ~ on the bright side of sth*** ver* el lado bueno *or* positivo de algo **2** (search, investigate) mirar, buscar*

II (seem, appear): **he ~s well** tiene buena cara; **he ~s like his father** se parece a su padre; **I wanted to ~ my best** quería estar lo mejor posible ■ **~** *vt* mirar; **to ~ sb up and down** mirar a algn de arriba (a) abajo; **~ where you're going!** ¡mira por dónde vas!

• look after [*v* + *prep* + *o*] **(a)** (care for) ‹*invalid/child/animal*› cuidar (de); ‹*guest*› atender* **(b)** (keep watch on) cuidar **(c)** (be responsible for) encargarse* de

• look ahead [*v* + *adv*] (in space) mirar hacia adelante; (into the future) mirar hacia el futuro

• look at [*v* + *prep* + *o*] **1** ‹*person/picture*› mirar **2** (consider) considerar; **~ at it from my point of view** míralo desde mi punto de vista; **the program ~s at university life** el programa enfoca la vida universitaria **3** (check) ‹*patient/arm*› examinar; ‹*car/pump*› revisar

• look back [*v* + *adv*] **(a)** (in space) mirar (hacia) atrás **(b)** (into the past): **~ing back, it seems foolish** mirándolo ahora, parece una locura; **the program ~s back over the last 20 years** el programa es una retrospectiva de los últimos veinte años

• look down on [*v* + *adv* + *prep* + *o*] mirar por encima del hombro a

• look for [*v* + *prep* + *o*] buscar*

• look forward to [*v* + *adv* + *prep* + *o*]: **I'm ~ing forward to my birthday** estoy deseando que llegue mi cumpleaños; **I'm really ~ing forward to the trip** tengo muchas ganas de hacer el viaje; **I ~ forward to hearing from you soon** (Corresp) esperando tener pronto noticias suyas

• look into [*v* + *prep* + *o*] ‹*matter/case*› investigar*; ‹*possibility*› estudiar

• look on [*v* + *adv*] mirar

• look out [*v* + *adv*] **(a)** (be careful) tener* cuidado; **~ out!** ¡cuidado! **(b)** (overlook) **to ~ out** ON *o* OVER **sth** dar* A algo

• look out for [*v* + *adv* + *prep* + *o*]: **~ out for her at the station** fíjate a ver si la ves en la estación; **we were warned to ~ out for thieves** nos advirtieron que tuviéramos cuidado con los ladrones

• look over [*v* + *o* + *adv*, *v* + *adv* + *o*] ‹*work/contract*› revisar; ‹*building*› inspeccionar

• **look to** [*v* + *prep* + *o*] (rely on): **they are ~ing to you for guidance** esperan que tú los guíes
• **look up 1** [*v* + *o* + *adv*, *v* + *adv* + *o*] **(a)** ‹*word*› buscar* (*en el diccionario*) **(b)** ‹*person*› ir* a ver **2** [*v* + *adv*] (improve) mejorar
• **look up to** [*v* + *adv* + *prep* + *o*] admirar

look-alike /'lʊkə,laɪk/ *n* (colloq) (person) doble *mf*

looking glass /'lʊkɪŋ,glæs ‖ 'lʊkɪŋ,glɑːs/ *n* (dated) espejo *m*

lookout /'lʊkaʊt/ *n* **(a)** (watch) (*no pl*): **to be on the ~ for sth/sb** andar* a la caza de algo/algn **(b)** (person) (Mil) vigía *mf*

loom¹ /luːm/ *n* telar *m*

loom² *vi* **(a)** (be imminent) avecinarse **(b)** (look threatening): **the mountain ~ed high above them** la montaña surgió imponente ante ellos; **the problem ~ed large in his mind** el problema dominaba sus pensamientos
• **loom up** [*v* + *adv*]: **a figure ~ed up in the mist** una figura surgió de entre las tinieblas

loop¹ /luːp/ *n* **1 (a)** (shape) curva *f*; (in river) meandro *m* **(b)** (in string) lazada *f* **(c)** (in sewing) presilla *f* **(d)** (Aviat): **to loop the ~** rizar* el rizo **2 (a)** (circuit) circuito *m* cerrado **(b)** (Comput) bucle *m*

loop² *vt*: **~ the wool** haz una lazada con la lana; **I ~ed the dog's lead over the post** enganché la correa del perro en el poste ■ **~** *vi* «*road*» serpentear

loophole /'luːphəʊl/ *n*: **a legal ~** una laguna jurídica (*que se presta a trampas*)

loose¹ /luːs/ *adj* **looser, loosest 1 (a)** (not tight) ‹*garment*› suelto **(b)** (not secure) ‹*screw*/*knot*› flojo; ‹*thread*/*end*› suelto; ‹*hair*› suelto; ***to be at a ~ end*** no tener* nada que hacer **(c)** (separate, not packaged) ‹*cigarettes*› suelto; ‹*tea*/*lentils*› a granel, suelto; **~ change** calderilla *f* **2** (free) (*pred*) suelto; **to let** *o* **set** *o* **turn sb ~** soltar* a algn; ***to be on the ~*** andar* suelto **3** ‹*definition*› poco preciso; ‹*translation*› libre

loose² *vt* (liter) **(a)** ‹*prisoner*› poner* en libertad; ‹*horse*› soltar* **(b)** ‹*arrow*› lanzar*; ‹*violence*/*wrath*› desatar

loose: **~-fitting** /'luːs'fɪtɪŋ/ *adj* suelto; ‹*clothes*› holgado; **~-leaf** /'luːs'liːf/ *adj* ‹*binder*› de anillas

loosely /'luːsli/ *adv* **1** (not tightly) ‹*tie*/*bandage*› sin apretar; **the dress fits ~** el vestido no es entallado **2** (not precisely) ‹*define*› sin excesivo rigor; ‹*translate*› libremente; **~ speaking** (*indep*) (hablando) en términos generales

loosen /'luːsn̩/ *vt* **(a)** ‹*tooth*› aflojar **(b)** ‹*collar*/*knot*/*bolt*› aflojar, soltar*; **she ~ed her grip on the steering wheel** dejó de apretar con tanta fuerza el volante ■ **~** *vi* «*knot*/*bolt*» aflojarse

loot¹ /luːt/ *n* [U] **(a)** (plunder) botín *m* **(b)** (money) (sl) guita *f* (arg), lana *f* (AmL fam), pasta *f* (Esp fam)

loot² *vt*/*i* saquear

looter /'luːtər ‖ 'luːtə(r)/ *n* saqueador, -dora *m,f*

looting /'luːtɪŋ/ *n* [U] saqueo *m*

lop /lɑːp ‖ lɒp/ *vt* **-pp- (a)** ‹*tree*› podar **(b) ~ (off)** ‹*branch*› cortar

lope /ləʊp/ *vi* «*wolf*/*dog*» trotar

lopsided /'lɑːp'saɪdəd ‖ ,lɒp'saɪdɪd/ *adj* **(a)** (not straight) torcido, chueco (AmL) **(b)** (asymmetric) ‹*face*/*smile*› torcido; ‹*shape*› asimétrico

lord /lɔːrd ‖ lɔːd/ *n* **1** **▶ 603** **(a)** (nobleman) señor *m*, noble *m* **(b) Lord** (in UK) lord *m*; **the (House of) L~s** la cámara de los lores **(c) my L~** (addressing judge) (BrE) (su) señoría **2 Lord** (God): **the L~** el Señor; **the L~'s Prayer** el Padrenuestro

lordship /'lɔːrdʃɪp ‖ 'lɔːdʃɪp/ **▶ 603** *n*: **His/Your L~** (of or to peers, judges) (su) señoría; (of or to bishops) (su) Ilustrísima

lore /lɔːr ‖ lɔː(r)/ *n* [U]: **French peasant ~** las tradiciones rurales francesas

lorry /'lɔːri ‖ 'lɒri/ *n* (*pl* **-ries**) (BrE) camión *m*; (*before n*) **~ driver** camionero, -ra *m,f*

lose /luːz/ *vt* (*past & past p* **lost**) **I 1** (mislay) perder* **2** (be deprived of) ‹*sight*/*territory*/*right*› perder*; **to ~ one's voice** quedarse afónico **3** (rid oneself of) ‹*inhibitions*› perder*; **to ~ weight** adelgazar*, perder* peso **4** (cause to lose) costar*; **their hesitation lost them the contract** la falta de decisión les costó *or* les hizo perder el contrato **5** (let pass) ‹*time*/*opportunity*› perder*; **my watch ~s three minutes every day** mi reloj (se) atrasa tres minutos por día
II (fail to win) ‹*game*/*battle*/*election*› perder* ■ **~** *vi* **1 (a)** (be beaten) «*team*/*contestant*/*party*» perder*; **they're losing 3-1** van perdiendo 3 a 1; **to ~ TO sb** perder* FRENTE A algn **(b) losing** *pres p* ‹*team*/*party*› perdedor **2** (suffer losses) perder* **3** «*watch*/*clock*» atrasar, atrasarse

loser /'luːzər ‖ 'luːzə(r)/ *n* perdedor, -dora *m,f*

loss /lɔːs ‖ lɒs/ *n* pérdida *f*; ***to be a dead ~*** (colloq): **this typewriter is a dead ~** esta máquina de escribir no sirve para nada *or* (fam) es una porquería; ***to be at a ~***: **I was at a ~ for words** no supe qué decir; ***to cut one's ~es*** cortar por lo sano; (Fin) reducir* las pérdidas

lost¹ /lɔːst ‖ lɒst/ *past & past p of* LOSE

lost² *adj* **I 1** (mislaid, missing) perdido; **to get ~** perderse*, extraviarse* (frml); **get ~!** (sl) ¡vete al diablo! (fam), ¡andá a pasear! (RPl fam) **2** (wasted) ‹*time*› perdido; ‹*opportunity*› desperdiciado, perdido; ***to be ~ on sb***: **these subtleties are ~ on him** se le escapan estas sutilezas **4** (*pred*) (absorbed) **to be ~ IN sth** estar* ensimismado EN algo; **to be ~ in thought** estar* absorto *or* ensimismado
II (not won) ‹*battle*/*election*› perdido

lost: **~ and found** /'lɔːstən'faʊnd ‖ ,lɒstən'faʊnd/ *n* [U] (AmE) objetos *mpl* perdidos; **~ property** *n* [U] (esp BrE) objetos *mpl* perdidos

lot /lɑːt ‖ lɒt/ *n* **1** (large number, quantity) **(a)** (*no pl*): **a ~ of wine** mucho vino; **I've seen a ~ of her recently** la he visto mucho últimamente; **what a ~ of books you've got!** ¡cuántos libros tienes! **(b) a ~** (*as adv*) mucho **(c) lots** *pl* (colloq): **how many seats are there left? — lots** ¿cuántos asientos quedan? — muchos *or* (fam) montones; **~s of people liked it** a mucha gente le gustó **2 (a)** (group, mass of things) montón *m*, pila *f* **(b)** (group of people) (colloq): **they're a funny ~** son raros, son gente rara; **come on, you ~!** ¡vamos, ustedes *or* (Esp) vosotros! **(c) the ~** (esp BrE): **they ate the ~**

se lo comieron todo (*or* se las comieron todas *etc*) **3** (at auction) lote *m*

loth /ləʊθ/ *adj* ⇒ LOATH

lotion /ˈləʊʃən/ *n* [C U] loción *f*

lottery /ˈlɑːtəri ‖ ˈlɒtəri/ *n* (*pl* **-ries**) lotería *f*

lotus /ˈləʊtəs/ *n* (*pl* **~es**) loto *m*

loud¹ /laʊd/ *adj* **-er, -est** **(a)** ‹*noise*› fuerte; **he said it in a ~ voice** lo dijo en voz alta **(b)** (vigorous) ‹*protests*› enérgico **(c)** (ostentatious) ‹*color*› llamativo, chillón

loud² *adv* **-er, -est** ‹*speak*› alto; **she laughed (the) ~est of all** fue la que se rió más fuerte

loudly /ˈlaʊdli/ *adv* **(a)** ‹*shout*› fuerte; ‹*speak*› alto, en voz alta **(b)** ‹*complain*› a voz en grito

loud: **~mouth** *n* (colloq) gritón, -tona *m,f*; **~speaker** /ˈlaʊdˈspiːkər ‖ ˌlaʊdˈspiːkə(r)/ *n* altavoz *m*, altoparlante *m* (AmL)

lounge¹ /laʊndʒ/ *n* (on ship, in hotel) salón *m*; (in house) (BrE) sala *f* (de estar), living *m* (esp AmS), salón *m* (esp Esp)

lounge² *vi*: **to ~ around** *o* **about** no hacer* nada

louse /laʊs/ *n* (*pl* **lice**) (Zool) piojo *m*

lousy /ˈlaʊzi/ *adj* **-sier, -siest** (colloq) ‹*food/weather*› asqueroso (fam); **a ~ movie** una película malísima

lout /laʊt/ *n* patán *m* (fam), gandalla *m* (Méx fam), jallán *m* (AmC)

louver, (BrE) **louvre** /ˈluːvər ‖ ˈluːvə(r)/ *n* lama *f*, listón *m* (*de persiana*); (*before n*) ‹*door/window*› de lamas, tipo persiana

lovable /ˈlʌvəbəl/ *adj* adorable, amoroso (AmL)

love¹ /lʌv/ *n* **1** **(a)** (emotional attachment) amor *m*; **to fall/be in ~ with sb/sth** enamorarse/estar* enamorado de algn/algo; **to make ~ to sb** hacer* el amor con algn **(b)** (enthusiasm, interest) **~ OF sth** amor *m* A *or* POR algo **2** **(a)** (greetings, regards): **give my ~ to your parents** (dale) recuerdos a tus padres (de mi parte) **(b)** (in letters) **~ from John** *o* **~, John** un abrazo, John **3** (person loved) amor *m*; (thing loved) pasión *f* **4** (colloq) (*as form of address*) cariño **5** (in tennis) cero *m*

love² *vt* querer*, amar (liter); **I ~ music/reading** me encanta la música/leer; **I'd ~ a cup of tea** una taza de té me vendría de maravilla

loveable *adj* ⇒ LOVABLE

loveless /ˈlʌvləs ‖ ˈlʌvlɪs/ *adj* sin amor

lovely /ˈlʌvli/ *adj* **-lier, liest** ‹*appearance*› precioso, lindo (esp AmL); ‹*person/nature*› encantador, amoroso (AmL); ‹*meal/taste*› (BrE) riquísimo; **the weather was ~** hacía un tiempo buenísimo

lover /ˈlʌvər ‖ ˈlʌvə(r)/ *n* **1** (partner in love) amante *mf* **2** (fan) **~ OF sth** amante *mf* DE algo

loving /ˈlʌvɪŋ/ *adj* cariñoso; **with ~ care** con tierno cuidado

lovingly /ˈlʌvɪŋli/ *adv* ‹*gaze/whisper*› tiernamente; ‹*handwritten/prepared*› con amor *or* cariño; ‹*restored*› con el mayor cuidado

low¹ /ləʊ/ *adj* **-er, -est** **1** (in height) bajo; **the dress had a very ~ back** el vestido era muy escotado por la espalda **2** **(a)** (in volume) ‹*voice*› bajo; ‹*sound/whisper*› débil; **turn the radio down ~** bájale al radio (AmL exc CS), baja la radio (CS, Esp) **(b)** ‹*key/note/pitch*› grave **3** (in intensity, amount, quality) bajo; ‹*proportion*› pequeño; **cook on a ~ flame** *o* **heat** cocinar a fuego lento; **he has a ~ opinion of doctors** no tiene muy buena opinión de los médicos; **a ~ point in his career** un momento bajo en su carrera **4** (in short supply): **stocks are running ~** se están agotando las existencias

low² *adv* **-er, -est** **1** bajo; **to fly ~** volar* bajo *or* a poca altura **2** (in volume, pitch) bajo

low³ *n* punto *m* más bajo; **relations between the two countries are at an all-time ~** las relaciones entre los dos países nunca han sido peores

low⁴ *vi* mugir*

low- /ləʊ/ *pref*: **~priced** de bajo precio; **~income** de bajos ingresos

low: **~-calorie** /ˈləʊˈkæləri/ *adj* bajo en calorías; **~-class** /ˈləʊˈklæs ‖ ˌləʊˈklɑːs/ *adj* ‹*place*› de mala muerte (fam); ‹*clientele*› de poca categoría; **~-cut** /ˈləʊˈkʌt/ *adj* escotado; **~down** *n* [U] (colloq): **to give sb the ~down (on sth)** poner* a algn al tanto (de algo)

lower¹ /ˈləʊər ‖ ˈləʊə(r)/ *adj* **1** **(a)** (spatially, numerically) ‹*jaw/lip*› inferior; **~ age limit** edad *f* mínima **(b)** (in rank, importance) inferior, más bajo **(c)** ‹*life form*› inferior **2** (Geog) bajo; **the ~ reaches of the Nile** el curso bajo del Nilo

lower² /ˈləʊər ‖ ˈləʊə(r)/ *vt* **1** ‹*blind/flag*› bajar; **he ~ed himself into his chair** se sentó en el sillón **2** ‹*temperature/volume/price/voice*› bajar ■ *v refl* **to ~ oneself** rebajarse

lowest common denominator /ˈləʊəst ‖ ˈləʊɪst/ *n* (Math) mínimo común denominador *m*; **a series aimed at the ~ ~ ~** una serie dirigida al público de nivel más bajo

low: **~-fat** /ˈləʊˈfæt/ *adj* de bajo contenido graso; **~-flying** /ˈləʊˈflaɪɪŋ/ *adj* ‹*aircraft*› que vuela bajo; **~-grade** /ˈləʊˈgreɪd/ *adj* ‹*oil*› de baja calidad; ‹*ore*› pobre; **~-key** /ˈləʊˈkiː/ *adj* ‹*speech*› mesurado; ‹*ceremony*› sencillo; **~land** /ˈləʊlənd/ *adj* (*before n*) de las tierras bajas; (in tropical countries) de tierra caliente; **~lands** /ˈləʊləndz/ *pl n* tierras *fpl* bajas; (in tropical countries) tierras *fpl* calientes; **~-level** /ˈləʊˈlevəl/ *adj* **(a)** ‹*talks*› a bajo nivel **(b)** ‹*radiation*› de baja intensidad **(c)** (Comput): **~-level language** lenguaje *m* de bajo nivel

lowly /ˈləʊli/ *adj* **-lier, -liest** humilde

low: **~-lying** /ˈləʊˈlaɪɪŋ/ *adj* bajo; **~-necked** /ˈləʊˈnekt/ *adj* escotado; **~-paid** /ˈləʊˈpeɪd/ *adj* mal remunerado; **~-profile** /ˈləʊˈprəʊfaɪl/ *adj* poco prominente; **~-rise** /ˈləʊˈraɪz/ *adj* de poca altura; **~-risk** /ˈləʊˈrɪsk/ *adj* ‹*business*› poco arriesgado; ‹*investment*› de poco *or* bajo riesgo; **~ season** *n* [U] (BrE) temporada *f* baja

loyal /ˈlɔɪəl/ *adj* ‹*friend/customer*› fiel; **to be ~ TO sth** ‹*to the state/party*› ser* leal A algo; ‹*to one's ideals*› ser* fiel A algo; **he is ~ to his friends** es un amigo leal *or* fiel

loyalist /ˈlɔɪələst ‖ ˈlɔɪəlɪst/ *n* partidario, -ria *m,f* del régimen

loyalty /ˈlɔɪəlti/ *n* (*pl* **-ties**) [U C] lealtad *f*

lozenge /ˈlɑːzn̩dʒ ‖ ˈlɒzɪndʒ/ *n* (Med) pastilla *f*

LP *n* (= **long-playing record**) LP *m*, elepé *m*

L-plate /'elpleɪt/ *n* (in UK) placa *f* de la L *or* de prácticas (*placa que se debe exhibir en el coche cuando se aprende a conducir*)

LSD *n* (= **lysergic acid diethylamide**) LSD *m*

LST (in US) = **Local Standard Time**

Ltd (= **Limited**) Ltda., S.A.

lubricant /'lu:brɪkənt/ *n* [U C] lubricante *m*

lubricate /'lu:brɪkeɪt/ *vt* lubricar*

lucid /'lu:səd || 'lu:sɪd/ *adj* lúcido

luck /lʌk/ *n* [U] suerte *f*; **a piece** *o* **stroke of ~** un golpe de suerte; ***to be down on one's ~*** estar* de mala racha; ***to push one's ~*** desafiar* a la suerte

luckily /'lʌkəli || 'lʌkɪli/ *adv* (*indep*) por suerte

lucky /'lʌki/ *adj* **luckier, luckiest (a)** ‹*person*› con suerte, suertudo (AmL fam); **he's ~ to be alive** tuvo suerte de no matarse; **~ you!** (colloq) ¡qué suerte (tienes)! **(b)** (fortuitous): **he had a ~ escape** se salvó de milagro; **it was ~ you were there** fue una suerte que estuvieras ahí **(c)** (bringing luck): **~ charm** amuleto *m* (de la suerte); **seven is my ~ number** el siete es mi número de la suerte

lucrative /'lu:krətɪv/ *adj* lucrativo

ludicrous /'lu:dɪkrəs/ *adj* ridículo

lug /lʌg/ *vt* **-gg-** (colloq) arrastrar

luggage /'lʌgɪdʒ/ *n* [U] equipaje *m*

luggage: **~ checkroom** /'tʃekru:m, -rum/ *n* (AmE) consigna *f* (de equipajes); **~ rack** *n* **(a)** (Rail) rejilla *f* (portaequipajes) **(b)** (Auto) baca *f*, parrilla *f* (Andes)

lugubrious /lʊ'gu:briəs/ *adj* lúgubre

lukewarm /'lu:k'wɔ:rm || ˌlu:k'wɔ:m/ *adj* **(a)** ‹*water/milk*› tibio **(b)** ‹*support/reaction*› poco entusiasta

lull¹ /lʌl/ *vt* **(a)** ‹*baby*›: **to ~ a baby to sleep** arrullar a un niño hasta dormirlo **(b)** ‹*fears*› calmar; ‹*suspicions*› desvanecer **(c)** (deceive): **we were ~ed into a false sense of security** nos confiamos demasiado

lull² *n* (in activity) período *m* de calma; (in fighting) tregua *f*; (in conversation) pausa *f*

lullaby /'lʌləbaɪ/ *n* (*pl* **-bies**) canción *f* de cuna

lumbago /lʌm'beɪgəʊ/ *n* [U] lumbago *m*

lumber¹ /'lʌmbər || 'lʌmbə(r)/ *n* [U] **(a)** (timber) (AmE) madera *f* **(b)** (junk) cachivaches *mpl*

lumber² *vt* (colloq) **to ~ sb** WITH **sth** enjaretarle algo A algn (fam) ■ **~** *vi* **(a)** (move awkwardly) avanzar* pesadamente **(b) lumbering** *pres p* ‹*gait*› torpe

lumber: **~jack** *n* leñador *m*; **~yard** *n* (AmE) almacén *m* de maderas, barraca *f* (CS)

luminous /'lu:mənəs || 'lu:mɪnəs/ *adj* luminoso

lump¹ /lʌmp/ *n* **1** (swelling, protuberance) bulto *m*; (as result of knock) chichón *m*; ***a ~ in one's throat*** un nudo en la garganta **2** (piece — of coal, iron, clay, cheese) trozo *m*, pedazo *m*; (— of sugar) terrón *m*

lump² *vt* **(a)** (put up with) (colloq): ***to ~ it*** aguantarse (fam); **if you don't like it, (you can) ~ it** si no te gusta, te aguantas **(b)** (place together): **to ~ sth together**: **you can ~ all those items together under one heading** todo eso puede ir junto bajo el mismo epígrafe; **they can't all be ~ed together as reactionaries** no se puede tachar a todos indiscriminadamente de reaccionarios

lump sum *n* cantidad *f* global (*que se paga o recibe para saldar totalmente una obligación*)

lumpy /'lʌmpi/ *adj* **-pier, -piest (a)** ‹*sauce*› lleno de grumos **(b)** ‹*mattress/cushion*› lleno de bultos

lunacy /'lu:nəsi/ *n* (*pl* **-cies**) locura *f*

lunar /'lu:nər || 'lu:nə(r)/ *adj* lunar

lunatic /'lu:nətɪk/ *n* loco, -ca *m,f*

lunch /lʌntʃ/ *n* [U C] almuerzo *m*, comida *f* (esp Esp, Méx); **to have ~** almorzar*, comer (esp Esp, Méx)

lunchbox /'lʌntʃbɑ:ks || 'lʌntʃbɒks/ *n* lonchera *f* (AmL), fiambrera *f* (Esp)

luncheon /'lʌntʃən/ *n* (frml) almuerzo *m*

lunchtime /'lʌntʃtaɪm/ *n* hora *f* de almorzar, hora *f* de comer (esp Esp, Méx)

lung /lʌŋ/ **▶ 484** *n* (*often pl*) pulmón *m*; (*before n*) **~ cancer** cáncer *m* de pulmón

lunge¹ /lʌndʒ/ *vi* embestir*; **to ~** AT **sb/sth** arremeter CONTRA algn/algo

lunge² *n* arremetida *f*

lurch¹ /lɜ:rtʃ || lɜ:tʃ/ *vi* «*vehicle*» dar* bandazos; «*person*» tambalearse

lurch² *n* bandazo *m*; ***to leave sb in the ~*** (colloq) dejar a algn plantado

lure /lʊr || ljʊə(r), lʊə(r)/ *vt* atraer*

lurid /'lʊrəd || 'lʊərɪd/ *adj* **(a)** (sensational) ‹*details/imagination*› morboso **(b)** (garish) ‹*color/garment*› chillón

lurk /lɜ:rk || lɜ:k/ *vi* merodear

luscious /'lʌʃəs/ *adj* **(a)** ‹*girl*› seductor **(b)** ‹*scent/sweetness*› exquisito

lush /lʌʃ/ *adj* **-er, -est** ‹*vegetation*› exuberante

lust¹ /lʌst/ *n* **(a)** [U] (sexual) lujuria *f* **(b)** [C] (craving) deseo *m*

lust² *vi* **to ~** AFTER **sb** desear a algn; **to ~** AFTER **sth** codiciar algo

luster, (BrE) **lustre** /'lʌstər || 'lʌstə(r)/ *n* [U] (liter) lustre *m*

lustful /'lʌstfəl/ *adj* lujurioso

lustre /'lʌstər || 'lʌstə(r)/ *n* (BrE) ⇒ LUSTER

lusty /'lʌsti/ *adj* **-tier, tiest** sano

Luxembourg, **Luxemburg** /'lʌksəmbɜ:rg || 'lʌksəmbɜ:g/ *n* Luxemburgo *m*

luxuriant /lʌg'ʒʊriənt || lʌg'zjʊəriənt/ *adj* ‹*vegetation/growth*› exuberante; ‹*hair*› hermoso y abundante

luxuriate /lʌg'ʒʊrieɪt || lʌg'zjʊərieɪt/ *vi* (revel) **to ~** IN **sth** deleitarse CON algo

luxurious /lʌg'ʒʊriəs || lʌg'zjʊəriəs/ *adj* lujoso

luxury /'lʌkʃəri/ *n* (*pl* **-ries**) [U C] lujo *m*; (*before n*) ‹*car/hotel*› de lujo

lying¹ /'laɪɪŋ/ *n* [U] mentiras *fpl*

lying² *adj* (*before n*) mentiroso

lymph /lɪmf/ *n* [U] linfa *f*; (*before n*) **~ gland** glándula *f* linfática

lynch /lɪntʃ/ *vt* linchar

lynx /lɪŋks/ *n* (*pl* **~es** *or* **~**) lince *m*

lyre /'laɪr ‖ 'laɪə(r)/ *n* lira *f*

lyric /'lɪrɪk/ *n* **(a)** (poem) poema *m* lírico **(b) lyrics** *pl n* (Mus) letra *f*

lyrical /'lɪrɪkəl/ *adj* (Lit) lleno de lirismo

M, m /em/ *n* M, m *f*

m (a) (= **million(s)**) m **(b)** ▶ 681 (= **meter(s)** *o* (BrE) **metre(s)**) m **(c)** (= **male**) de sexo masculino **(d)** (Ling) (= **masculine**) m

M (a) (Clothing) (= **medium**) M, talla *f* mediana *or* (RPl) talle *m* mediano **(b)** (in UK) (Transp) (= **motorway**) *indicador de autopista*

ma /mɑː/ *n* (colloq) mamá *f*

MA /'em'eɪ/ *n* **(a)** = **Master of Arts (b)** = **Massachusetts**

macabre /mə'kɑːbrə/ *adj* macabro

macaroni /'mækə'rəʊni/ *n* [U] macarrones *mpl*

mace /meɪs/ *n* **1** (Art, Hist, Mil) maza *f* **2** (Culin) macis *f* **3 Mace®** (tear gas) (AmE) *gas para defensa personal*

machete /mə'ʃeti, mə'tʃeti/ *n* machete *m*

machinations /'mækə'neɪʃənz, 'mæʃ- ‖ ,mækɪ'neɪʃənz, ,mæʃ-/ *pl n* (liter) maquinaciones *fpl*

machine /mə'ʃiːn/ *n* máquina *f*; (*washing* **~**) lavadora *f*, máquina *f* (de lavar), lavarropas *m* (RPl)

machine gun *n* ametralladora *f*

machinery /mə'ʃiːnəri/ *n* [U] (machines) maquinaria *f*; (working parts) mecanismo *m*

macho /'mɑːtʃəʊ ‖ 'mætʃəʊ/ *adj* ‹*behavior/attitude*› machista; ‹*image*› de macho

macintosh *n* ⇒ MACKINTOSH

mackerel /'mækrəl/ *n* [C U] (*pl* **~** *or* **~s**) caballa *f*

mackintosh /'mækəntɑːʃ ‖ 'mækɪntɒʃ/ *n* impermeable *m*

macro /'mækrəʊ/ *n* (*pl* **-ros**) (Comput) macro *m*

mad /mæd/ *adj* **-dd- 1 (a)** (insane) loco; **to go ~** volverse* loco; **to work/run like ~** trabajar/correr como un loco **(b)** ‹*rush*› loco; **we made a ~ dash for the airport** salimos como locos para el aeropuerto **(c)** ‹*scheme/idea*› disparatado **2** (angry) (esp AmE) (*pred*) **to be ~ (WITH/AT sb)** estar* furioso *or* (esp AmL) enojadísimo *or* (esp Esp) enfadadísimo (CON algn); **to get ~** ponerse* furioso **3** (very enthusiastic) (colloq) (*pred*) **to be ~ ABOUT sb** estar* loco POR algn; **she's ~ about** *o* **on African music** la música africana la vuelve loca

Madagascar /'mædə'gæskər ‖ ,mædə'gæskə(r)/ *n* Madagascar *m*

madam /'mædəm/ ▶ 603 *n* (as title) señora *f*

madden /'mædn̩/ *vt* (make angry) enfurecer*; (drive mad) enloquecer*

made¹ /meɪd/ *past & past p of* MAKE¹

made² *adj* (*pred*) **(a)** (assured of success) ***to have it* ~** tener* el éxito asegurado **(b)** (ideally suited): **they were ~ for each other** estaban hechos el uno para el otro

Madeira /mə'dɪrə ‖ mə'dɪərə/ *n* Madeira *f*, Madera *f*

made-to-measure /'meɪdtə'meʒər ‖ ,meɪdtə'meʒə(r)/ *adj* (*pred* **made to measure**) hecho a (la) medida

madly /'mædli/ *adv* **(a)** (frantically) ‹*rush/work*› como un loco; ‹*love*› locamente **(b)** (very) (*as intensifier*): **~ in love** locamente enamorado

madman /'mædmən/ *n* (*pl* **-men** /-mən/) loco *m*

madness /'mædnəs ‖ 'mædnɪs/ *n* [U] locura *f*

Madrid /mə'drɪd/ *n* Madrid *m*; (*before n*) madrileño

Mafia /'mɑːfiə, 'mæ- ‖ 'mæfiə/ *n* Mafia *f*

magazine /'mægə'ziːn/ *n* **1 (a)** (Publ) revista *f*; (*before n*) **~ rack** revistero *m* **(b) ~ (program)** (Rad, TV) programa *m* de entrevistas y variedades **2** (on gun — compartment) recámara *f*; (— bullet case) cargador *m*

maggot /'mægət/ *n* gusano *m*

magic¹ /'mædʒɪk/ *n* [U] magia *f*

magic² *adj* **(a)** ‹*power/potion*› mágico; ‹*trick*› de magia **(b)** (enchanting) ‹*moment/beauty*› mágico

magical /'mædʒɪkəl/ *adj* mágico

magician /mə'dʒɪʃən/ *n* (sorcerer) mago *m*; (conjurer) mago, -ga *m,f*, prestidigitador, -dora *m,f*

magistrate /'mædʒəstreɪt ‖ 'mædʒɪstreɪt/ *n* (in UK) *juez que conoce de faltas y asuntos civiles de menor importancia*

magnanimous /mæg'nænəməs ‖ mæg'nænɪməs/ *adj* magnánimo

magnesium /mæg'niːziəm/ *n* [U] magnesio *m*

magnet /'mægnət ‖ 'mægnɪt/ *n* imán *m*

magnetic /mæg'netɪk/ *adj* magnético; ‹*personality*› lleno de magnetismo

magnetism /'mægnətɪzəm ‖ 'mægnɪtɪzəm/ *n* [U] magnetismo *m*

magnificent /mæg'nɪfəsənt ‖ mæg'nɪfɪsənt/ *adj* magnífico

magnify /'mægnəfaɪ ‖ 'mægnɪfaɪ/ *vt* **-fies, -fying, -fied** ‹*image*› ampliar*, aumentar de tamaño; ‹*problem/difficulty*› exagerar

magnifying glass /'mægnəfaɪɪŋ ‖ 'mægnɪfaɪɪŋ/ *n* lupa *f*

magnitude /'mægnətu:d ‖ 'mægnɪtju:d/ *n* (size) magnitud *f*; (importance) envergadura *f*

magpie /'mægpaɪ/ *n* urraca *f*, picaza *f*

mahogany /mə'hɑ:gəni ‖ mə'hɒgəni/ *n* [U] caoba *f*

maid /meɪd/ *n* **1 (a)** (servant) sirvienta *f*, criada *f*, mucama *f* (AmL); (*parlor/lady's* ~) (primera) doncella *f* **(b)** (in hotel) camarera *f*, mucama *f* (AmL) **(c)** (occasional housekeeper) (AmE) señora *f* de la limpieza, limpiadora *f* **2** (young woman) (arch *or* liter) doncella *f* (arc *o* liter)

maiden¹ /'meɪdn/ *n* (arch *or* liter) doncella *f* (arc *o* liter)

maiden² *adj* (*before n*) ‹*flight/speech*› inaugural

maiden name *n* apellido *m* de soltera

mail¹ /meɪl/ *n* [U] **1 (a)** (system) correo *m*; **by ~** por correo **(b)** (letters, parcels) correspondencia *f*, correo *m* **2** (armor) malla *f*

mail² *vt* (esp AmE): ‹*letter/parcel*› echar al correo; (drop in mailbox) echar al buzón; **to ~ sth TO sb** mandarle *or* enviarle* algo por correo A algn

mail: **~box** *n* **(a)** (for receiving mail) (AmE) buzón *m*, casillero *m* (Ven) **(b)** (for sending mail) (AmE) buzón *m* (de correos) **(c)** (electronic) buzón *m*; **~ carrier** *n* (AmE) cartero, -ra *m,f*

mailing list /'meɪlɪŋ/ *n* (Marketing) banco *m or* lista *f* de direcciones

mail: **~man** /'meɪlmæn/ *n* (*pl* **-men** /-men/) (AmE) cartero *m*; **~ order** *n* [U] venta *f* por correo; (*before n*) **~-order catalog** catálogo *m* de venta por correo

maim /meɪm/ *vt* (cripple) lisiar; (mutilate) mutilar

main¹ /meɪn/ *adj* (*before n, no comp*) principal; **the ~ thing** lo principal; **~ course** plato *m* principal *or* fuerte; **~ street** calle *f* principal

main² *n* **(a)** [C] (pipe) cañería *f or* tubería *f* principal; (cable) cable *m* principal **(b)** (supply) **the ~** *o* (BrE) **the ~s** la red de suministro; **to turn the water/gas off at the ~** *o* (BrE) **the ~s** cerrar la llave (principal) del agua/del gas

main: **~frame** *n* unidad *f* central, computadora *f or* (Esp tb) ordenador *m* central; **~land** /'meɪnlənd, -lænd/ *n*: **the ~land** *la masa territorial de un país o continente excluyendo sus islas*; (*before n*) **~land China** (la) China continental; **~ line** *n* (Rail) línea *f* principal

mainly /'meɪnli/ *adv* principalmente

main: **~ road** *n* (BrE) carretera *f* principal; **~stream** *adj* ‹*culture*› establecido; **~stream politics** la política a nivel de los partidos mayoritarios

maintain /meɪn'teɪn/ *vt* **1 (a)** ‹*speed/lead*› mantener*; ‹*silence*› guardar **(b)** ‹*house/machine*› ocuparse del mantenimiento de; ‹*aircraft*› mantener* **(c)** ‹*family/dependents*› mantener* **2** (claim) mantener*

maintenance /'meɪntṇəns ‖ 'meɪntənəns/ *n* [U] **1** (repairs) mantenimiento *m* **2** (money) (BrE Law) pensión *f* alimenticia

maisonette /'meɪzṇ'et ‖ ˌmeɪzə'net/ *n* (BrE) (apartment) dúplex *m*; (house) *vivienda independiente de dos pisos que forma parte de una casa*

maize /meɪz/ *n* [U] **(a)** (plant) maíz *m* **(b)** (grains) maíz *m*, choclo *m* (CS, Per), elote *m* (Méx)

majestic /mə'dʒestɪk/ *adj* majestuoso

majesty /'mædʒəsti/ *n* (*pl* **-ties**) **(a)** [U] (of appearance, landscape) majestuosidad *f* **(b)** ▶ **603** [C] (as title) **Her/Your M~** su Majestad

major¹ /'meɪdʒər ‖ 'meɪdʒə(r)/ *adj* **1** ‹*change/client*› muy importante; ‹*setback*› serio; ‹*revision*› a fondo **2** (Mus) mayor

major² *n* **1** (Mil) mayor *mf* (*en AmL*), comandante *mf* (*en Esp*) **2** (AmE Educ) asignatura *f* principal

major³ *vi* (AmE Educ) **to ~ IN sth** especializarse* EN algo

Majorca /mə'jɔ:rkə ‖ mə'jɔ:kə, mə'dʒɔ:kə/ *n* Mallorca *f*

majority /mə'dʒɔ:rəti ‖ mə'dʒɒrəti/ *n* (*pl* **-ties**) (greater number) (+ *sing o pl vb*) mayoría *f*; (*before n*) ‹*decision/party*› mayoritario

major league *n* (Sport) liga *f* nacional

make¹ /meɪk/ (*past & past p* **made**) *vt* **I 1** (create, produce) hacer*; **to ~ a note of sth** anotar algo; **she made the dress out of an old sheet** se hizo el vestido con una sábana vieja; **it's made of wood** es de madera; *see also* DIFFERENCE, FUSS¹, MESS 1 *etc* **2 (a)** (carry out) ‹*repairs/payment/journey*› hacer*; **~ a left (turn) here** (AmE) dobla a la izquierda aquí **(b)** ‹*remark/announcement*› hacer*

II 1 (cause to be): **I'll ~ you happy** te haré feliz; **that made me sad** eso me entristeció; **the work made me thirsty** el trabajo me dio sed; **what ~s me angry is** ... lo que me da rabia es ...; **they've made him supervisor** lo han nombrado supervisor; **if nine o'clock is too early, ~ it later** si las nueve es muy temprano, podemos reunirnos (*or* encontrarnos *etc*) más tarde **2 (a)** (cause to) hacer*; **whatever made you do it?** ¿por qué lo hiciste? **(b)** (compel) obligar* a, hacer*; **she was made to apologize** la obligaron a *or* la hicieron pedir perdón **(c)** (*in phrases*) **to make believe**: **you can't just ~ believe it never happened** no puedes hacer como si no hubiera sucedido; **to make do (with sth)** arreglárselas con algo

III 1 (a) (constitute, be) ser*; **it would ~ a nice change** sería un cambio agradable; **they ~ a nice couple** hacen buena pareja **(b)** (amount to) ser*; **five plus five ~s ten** cinco y *or* más cinco son diez **2** (calculate): **I ~ it 253** (a mí) me da 253; **what time do you ~ it?** ¿qué hora tienes? **3 (a)** (understand): **I could ~ nothing of the message** no entendí el mensaje; **~ of that what you will** tú saca tus propias conclusiones **(b)** (think) **to ~ sth OF sb/sth**: **what did you ~ of him?** ¿qué te pareció?; **I don't know what to ~ of it** no sé qué pensar

IV 1 (a) (gain, earn) ‹*money*› hacer* **(b)** (acquire) ‹*friends*› hacer*; **to ~ a name for oneself** hacerse* un nombre **2** (colloq) (manage to attend, reach): **we just made the 3 o'clock train** llegamos justo a tiempo para el tren de las tres; ***to ~ it***: **he'll never ~ it as a doctor** nunca será un buen médico **3** (assure success of): ***to ~ or break sth/sb*** ser* el éxito o la ruina de algo/algn

● **make for** [*v* + *prep* + *o*] **1** (head toward) dirigirse* hacia/a **2** (encourage, promote) contribuir* a

• **make out** I [*v* + *o* + *adv*, *v* + *adv* + *o*] **1 (a)** (discern) ‹*object/outline*› distinguir*; (from a distance) divisar; ‹*sound*› distinguir*; ‹*writing*› descifrar **(b)** (figure out) (colloq) entender* **2** (write) ‹*list/invoice/receipt*› hacer*; **~ the check out to P. Jones** haga el cheque pagadero a P. Jones
II (claim, pretend) [*v* + *adv* + *o*]: **she made out it was her own work** dio a entender que lo había hecho ella misma; **you're not as ill as you ~ out** no estás tan enfermo como pretendes

• **make up** I [*v* + *o* + *adv*, *v* + *adv* + *o*] **1** ‹*story/excuse*› inventar **2** (prepare) ‹*prescription/food parcel*› preparar; ‹*agenda/list*› hacer* **3 (a)** (complete, add) completar; **she came along to ~ up the numbers** vino para completar el grupo **(b)** (compensate for): **I'll take the afternoon off, and ~ up the time later** me tomaré la tarde libre y ya recuperaré el tiempo más tarde
II [*v* + *adv* + *o*] (constitute) formar; **it is made up of three parts** está compuesto de tres partes
III [*v* + *adv*, *v* + *o* + *adv*] (achieve reconciliation) **to ~ (it) up** (WITH **sb**) hacer* las paces (CON algn)

make² *n* marca *f*

make: **~-believe** *n* [U] fantasía *f*; **don't be frightened, it's only ~-believe** no te asustes, es de mentira; **~over** *n* (AmE) maquillaje *m*; **to have a (cosmetic) ~over** maquillarse

maker /'meɪkər ‖ 'meɪkə(r)/ *n* fabricante *mf*

make: **~shift** *adj* ‹*repair*› provisional, provisorio (AmS); ‹*bed*› improvisado; **~up** *n* **1** [U] (cosmetics) maquillaje *m*; **to put on one's ~up** maquillarse, pintarse; (*before n*) **~up remover** desmaquillador *m*; **2** (*no pl*) (of person) carácter *m*; **3** [C] (AmE Educ) examen *m* de recuperación

making /'meɪkɪŋ/ *n* [U] **(a)** (production, creation): **a book about the ~ of the TV series** un libro que trata de cómo se hizo la serie de televisión; **this is history in the ~** esto va a pasar a la historia **(b) makings** *pl*: **you have the ~s of a good story there** allí tienes material para una buena historia; **she has the ~s of a great actress** es una gran actriz en ciernes

malaria /mə'leriə ‖ mə'leəriə/ *n* [U] malaria *f*, paludismo *m*

Malawi /mə'lɑːwi/ *n* Malaui *m*, Malawi *m*

Malawian /mə'lɑːwiən/ *adj* malauiano

Malaysia /mə'leɪʒə ‖ mə'leɪziə/ *n* Malaisia *f*; (continental part) Malasia *f*

Malaysian¹ /mə'leɪʒən ‖ mə'leɪziən/ *adj* malaisio; (from continental part) malasio

Malaysian² *n* malaisio, -sia *m,f*; (from continental part) malasio, -sia *m,f*

Maldive Islands /'mɔːldiːv, -daɪv/, **Maldives** /-z/ *pl n* **the ~ ~** las (islas) Maldivas

male¹ /meɪl/ *adj* ‹*animal/plant*› macho; ‹*attitude*› masculino; **there were several ~ applicants** se presentaron varios candidatos varones

male² *n* (animal) macho *m*; (person) varón *m*

malevolent /mə'levələnt/ *adj* ‹*grin*› malévolo; ‹*deity*› maligno

malfunction¹ /'mæl'fʌŋkʃən/ *n* **(a)** [U] (defective functioning) mal funcionamiento *m* **(b)** [C] (failure) falla *f or* (Esp) fallo *m*

malfunction² *vi* (Med, Tech) fallar, funcionar mal

malice /'mæləs ‖ 'mælɪs/ *n* [U] mala intención *f*

malicious /mə'lɪʃəs/ *adj* ‹*person/gossip*› malicioso; ‹*damage*› doloso

malignant /mə'lɪgnənt/ *adj* maligno

malinger /mə'lɪŋgər ‖ mə'lɪŋgə(r)/ *vi* hacerse* el enfermo

mall /mɔːl ‖ mæl, mɔːl/ *n* **(a)** (for shopping) centro *m* comercial **(b)** (avenue) paseo *m*

mallet /'mælət ‖ 'mælɪt/ *n* mazo *m*

malnutrition /'mælnuː'trɪʃən ‖ ˌmælnjuː'trɪʃən/ *n* [U] desnutrición *f*

malpractice /'mæl'præktəs ‖ ˌmæl'præktɪs/ *n* [U] mala práctica *f* (*en el ejercicio de la profesión*)

malt /mɔːlt/ *n* **(a)** [U] (grain) malta *f* **(b)** [U C] **~ (whisky)** whisky *m* de malta

Malta /'mɔːltə/ *n* Malta *f*

Maltese¹ /'mɔːl'tiːz/ *adj* maltés

Maltese² *n* (*pl* **~**) **(a)** [C] (person) maltés, -tesa *m,f* **(b)** [U] (language) maltés *m*

mamma *n* ⇒ MOMMA

mammal /'mæməl/ *n* mamífero *m*

mammoth¹ /'mæməθ/ *n* mamut *m*

mammoth² *adj* ‹*building/cost*› gigantesco; ‹*task*› de titanes

man¹ /mæn/ *n* (*pl* **men** /men/) **1 (a)** (adult male) hombre *m* **(b)** (husband/boyfriend): **her new ~** su nueva pareja (*or* su nuevo compañero *etc*); **to live together as ~ and wife** vivir como marido y mujer **(c)** (type): **he's a local ~** es del lugar; **he's a family ~** es un padre de familia **2 (a)** (person) persona *f*; **every ~ for himself** (set phrase) sálvese quien pueda (fr hecha) **(b)** *also* **Man** (mankind) (*no art*) el hombre **3 men** *pl*: **the men** (troops) los soldados; (employees) los trabajadores **4** (in chess) pieza *f*; (in draughts) ficha *f* **5** (*as form of address*) (colloq): **hey, ~!** ¡oiga, amigo!, ¡oye, tío (Esp) *or* (AmL exc CS) mano *or* (Chi) gallo! (fam), ¡oíme, che! (RPl fam)

man² *vt* **-nn-** ‹*switchboard*› encargarse* de; ‹*ship*› tripular; **soldiers ~ned the barricades** había soldados apostados en las barricadas

manacles /'mænəkəlz/ *pl n* (for wrists) esposas *fpl*; (for legs) grillos *mpl*

manage /'mænɪdʒ/ *vt* **1** (Busn) ‹*company/bank*› dirigir*, administrar, gerenciar (AmL); ‹*staff/team*› dirigir*; ‹*land/finances*› administrar **2** (handle, cope with) ‹*children*› manejar; ‹*household*› llevar; **she can't ~ the stairs** no puede subir la escalera **3** (achieve): **he ~d a smile** esbozó una sonrisa forzada; **I can't ~ the meeting** no puedo ir a la reunión; **to ~ to** + INF lograr + INF ■ **~** *vi* **1** (Busn) dirigir*, administrar **2** (cope): **can I help you? — thank you, I can ~** ¿me permite que la ayude? — gracias, yo puedo sola; **they have to ~ on $300 a week** tienen que arreglarse con 300 dólares a la semana

manageable /'mænɪdʒəbəl/ *adj* ‹*child/animal/hair*› dócil; ‹*task/goal*› posible de alcanzar; ‹*size/amount*› razonable

management /'mænɪdʒmənt/ *n* **1** [U] (act) **(a)** (Busn) dirección *f*, administración *f* **(b)** (handling, control) manejo *m* **2** (managers) **(a)** (as group) (*no art*, +

sing o pl vb) directivos *mpl*; **senior ~** altos cargos *mpl* **(b)** [C] (of particular company) dirección *f*, gerencia *f*

manager /'mænɪdʒər ‖ 'mænɪdʒə(r)/ *n* (Busn) (of company, department) director, -tora *m,f*, gerente *mf*; (of store, restaurant) gerente *mf*, encargado, -da *m,f*; (of estate, fund) administrador, -dora *m,f*; (of pop group, boxer) manager *mf*; (Sport) agente *mf*; (in soccer) entrenador, -dora *m,f*, director técnico, directora técnica *m,f* (AmL)

manageress /'mænɪdʒərəs ‖ ˌmænɪdʒə'res/ *n* (esp BrE) encargada *f*

managerial /'mænə'dʒɪriəl ‖ ˌmænɪ'dʒɪəriəl/ *adj* directivo, gerencial (AmL)

managing director /'mænɪdʒɪŋ/ *n* (esp BrE) /'mænədʒɪŋ/ director ejecutivo, directora ejecutiva *m,f*

mandarin /'mændərən ‖ 'mændərɪn/ *n* [C] **~ (orange)** mandarina *f*

mandate /'mændeɪt/ *n* mandato *m*

mandatory /'mændətɔːri ‖ 'mændətəri/ *adj* (frml) obligatorio

mane /meɪn/ *n* (of horse) crin(es) *f(pl)*; (of lion) melena *f*

maneuver¹, (BrE) **manoeuvre** /mə'nuːvər ‖ mə'nuːvə(r)/ *n* maniobra *f*

maneuver², (BrE) **manoeuvre** *vt* **they ~ed the piano up the stairs** subieron trabajosamente el piano por la escalera; **she ~ed the car out of the garage** sacó el coche del garaje maniobrando ■ **~** *vi* «*vehicle/driver*» maniobrar, hacer* una maniobra; **to have room to ~** «*driver*» tener* espacio para maniobrar; «*diplomat*» tener* libertad de acción

manger /'meɪndʒər ‖ 'meɪndʒə(r)/ *n* pesebre *m*

mangle¹ /'mæŋgəl/ *vt* destrozar*

mangle² *n* rodillo *m* (escurridor)

mango /'mæŋgəʊ/ *n* (*pl* **-goes** *or* **-gos**) mango *m*

mangy /'meɪndʒi/ *adj* **-gier, -giest** ‹*cat*› sarnoso

man: **~handle** *vt* (move by hand) mover* a pulso; (treat roughly) maltratar; **~hole** *n* registro *m*, pozo *m* de inspección; (into sewer) boca *f* de alcantarilla

manhood /'mænhʊd/ *n* [U] **(a)** (adulthood) madurez *f* **(b)** (virility) hombría *f*

man: **~-hour** *n* hora *f* hombre; **~hunt** *n* persecución *f*

mania /'meɪniə/ *n* (*pl* **-nias**) [U C] manía *f*

maniac /'meɪniæk/ *n* maniaco, -ca *m,f*, maníaco, -ca *m,f*

manic /'mænɪk/ *adj* ‹*behavior*› maniaco, maníaco; ‹*activity*› frenético

manic-depressive /'mænɪkdɪ'presɪv/ *n* maniacodepresivo, -va *m,f*

manicure¹ /'mænəkjʊr ‖ 'mænɪkjʊə(r)/ *n* [U C] manicura *f*, manicure *f* (AmL exc RPl)

manicure² *vt* arreglarle las manos *or* las uñas a

manifest¹ /'mænəfest ‖ 'mænɪfest/ *v refl* (frml) **to ~ itself** «*ghost*» aparecerse*; «*disease/fear*» manifestarse* ■ **~** *vt* (express) manifestar*

manifest² *adj* manifiesto

manifestation /'mænəfə'steɪʃən ‖ ˌmænɪfə'steɪʃən/ *n* manifestación *f*; (of ghost) aparición *f*

manifesto /'mænə'festəʊ ‖ ˌmænɪ'festəʊ/ *n* (*pl* **-toes** *or* **-tos**) manifiesto *m*; (for a specific election) (esp BrE) plataforma *f* electoral

manifold¹ /'mænəfəʊld ‖ 'mænɪfəʊld/ *adj* (frml) múltiples

manifold² *n* colector *m*

manipulate /mə'nɪpjəleɪt ‖ mə'nɪpjʊleɪt/ *vt* manipular

manipulative /mə'nɪpjələtɪv ‖ mə'nɪpjʊlətɪv/ *adj* manipulador

mankind /mæn'kaɪnd/ *n* [U] humanidad *f*, género *m* humano

manly /'mænli/ *adj* **-lier, -liest** ‹*physique/pursuits*› varonil, masculino

man-made /'mæn'meɪd/ *adj* ‹*lake*› artificial; ‹*material*› sintético

manna /'mænə/ *n* [U] maná *m*

manner /'mænər ‖ 'mænə(r)/ *n* **1** (way, fashion) forma *f*, modo *m*, manera *f*; **in a ~ of speaking** en cierto modo **2** (bearing, demeanor) actitud *f*; **a good telephone ~ is essential** es imprescindible tener buen trato por teléfono **3** (variety) tipo *m*, suerte *f*, clase *f*; **all ~ of things** todo tipo *or* toda suerte *or* toda clase de cosas **4 manners** *pl* (personal conduct) modales *mpl*, educación *f*

mannerism /'mænərɪzəm/ *n* (peculiarity, habit) peculiaridad *f*; (gesture) gesto *m*

manoeuvre *n/vt/vi* (BrE) ⇒ MANEUVER[1,2]

manor /'mænər ‖ 'mænə(r)/ *n* **~ (house)** casa *f* solariega

manpower /'mænpaʊər ‖ 'mænpaʊə(r)/ *n* [U] (workers) personal *m*; (blue-collar) mano *f* de obra

mansion /'mænʃən/ *n* mansión *f*

manslaughter /'mænˌslɔːtər ‖ 'mænˌslɔːtə(r)/ *n* [U] homicidio *m* sin premeditación

mantelpiece /'mæntlpiːs/ *n* repisa *f* de la chimenea

mantle /'mæntl/ *n* **1** (covering) (liter) manto *m* (liter) **2** (Geol) manto *m*, sima *f*

manual¹ /'mænjuəl/ *adj* manual

manual² *n* manual *m*

manufacture¹ /'mænjə'fæktʃər ‖ ˌmænjʊ'fæktʃə(r)/ *vt* ‹*cars/toys*› fabricar*; ‹*clothes*› confeccionar; ‹*foodstuffs*› elaborar

manufacture² *n* [U] (act) fabricación *f*; (of clothes) confección *f*; (of foodstuffs) elaboración *f*

manufacturer /'mænjə'fæktʃərər ‖ ˌmænjʊ'fæktʃərə(r)/ *n* fabricante *mf*

manufacturing /'mænjə'fæktʃərɪŋ ‖ ˌmænjʊ'fæktʃərɪŋ/ *adj* ‹*sector/town*› manufacturero; ‹*output/capacity*› industrial; **~ industry** industria *f* manufacturera

manure /mə'nʊr ‖ mə'njʊə(r)/ *n* [U C] estiércol *m*

manuscript /'mænjəskrɪpt ‖ 'mænjʊskrɪpt/ *n* manuscrito *m*

Manx /mæŋks/ *adj* manés, de la isla de Man

many¹ /'meni/ *adj* muchos, -chas; **how ~ plates/cups?** ¿cuántos platos/cuántas tazas?; **I've had as**

~ **jobs as you** he tenido tantos trabajos como tú; **too ~ problems** demasiados problemas

many² *pron* muchos, -chas; **how ~ of you smoke?** ¿cuántos/cuántas de ustedes fuman?; **would ten be too ~?** ¿diez serían demasiados?

Maori /'maʊri/ *n* maorí *mf*

map¹ /mæp/ *n* (of country, region) mapa *m*; (of town, subway, building) plano *m*

map² **-pp-** *vt* trazar* el mapa de

• **map out** [*v + o + adv, v + adv + o*] ‹*itinerary/holiday*› planear

maple /'meɪpəl/ *n* ~ (**tree**) arce *m*; (*before n*) ~ **syrup** jarabe *m or* sirope *m* de arce

mar /mɑːr ‖ mɑː(r)/ *vt* **-rr-** estropear

marathon /'mærəθɑːn ‖ 'mærəθən/ *n* maratón *m or f*

marauder /mə'rɔːdər ‖ mə'rɔːdə(r)/ *n* (criminal) maleante *mf*; (prowler) merodeador, -dora *m,f*

marble /'mɑːrbəl ‖ 'mɑːbəl/ *n* **1** [U] (Min) mármol *m* **2** [C] (Games) canica *f or* (AmS) bolita *f*

march¹ /mɑːrtʃ ‖ mɑːtʃ/ *n* **1** **(a)** (Mil, Mus) marcha *f* **(b)** (demonstration) marcha *f* (de protesta) **2** (of time) paso *m*; (of science, technology) avance *m*

march² *vi* «*troops*» marchar; **when Saddam ~ed on Kuwait** cuando Saddam invadió Kuwait; **she ~ed into the office** entró con paso firme en *or* (esp AmL) a la oficina ■ ~ *vt* hacer* marchar; **the prisoner was ~ed in** hicieron entrar al prisionero

March /mɑːrtʃ ‖ mɑːtʃ/ ▶ 540 *n* marzo *m*

mare /mer ‖ meə(r)/ *n* yegua *f*

margarine /'mɑːrdʒərən ‖ ˌmɑːdʒə'riːn/ *n* [U] margarina *f*

margin /'mɑːrdʒən ‖ 'mɑːdʒɪn/ *n* **1** (on page, typewriter) margen *m* **2** **(a)** [C U] (leeway) margen *m* **(b)** (Busn) (of profit) margen *m* (de ganancia) **3** (fringe — of lake) (*often pl*) margen *f*; (— of society) margen *m*

marginal /'mɑːrdʒənəl ‖ 'mɑːdʒɪnl/ *adj* ‹*difference*› mínimo; ‹*role*› menor

marginally /'mɑːrdʒənəli ‖ 'mɑːdʒɪnəli/ *adv* ligeramente

marigold /'mærəgəʊld ‖ 'mærɪgəʊld/ *n* caléndula *f*, maravilla *f*

marijuana, **marihuana** /ˌmærə'wɑːnə, -'hwɑː- ‖ ˌmæri'wɑːnə/ *n* [U] marihuana *f*

marinade, **marinate** /'mærəneɪd, -eɪt ‖ 'mærɪneɪd, -eɪt/ *vt* dejar en adobo

marine¹ /mə'riːn/ *n also* **Marine** (Mil) ≈ infante *m* de marina

marine² *adj* (*before n*) ‹*biology*› marino; ‹*engineering*› naval; ‹*insurance*› marítimo

marital /'mærətl ‖ 'mærɪtl/ *adj* ‹*problems*› matrimonial; ‹*bliss*› conyugal; ~ **status** estado *m* civil

marjoram /'mɑːrdʒərəm ‖ 'mɑːdʒərəm/ *n* [U] mejorana *f*

mark¹ /mɑːrk ‖ mɑːk/ *n* **1** (sign, symbol) marca *f*; (stain) mancha *f*; (imprint) huella *f*; (on body) marca *f*; **as a ~ of respect** en señal de respeto; ***to make one's ~*** dejar su impronta **2** (Educ) nota *f*; (Sport) punto *m* **3** **(a)** (indicator): **the cost has reached the $100,000 ~** el costo ha llegado a los 100.000 dólares; ***to overstep the ~*** pasarse de la raya **(b)** (for race) línea *f* de salida; **on your ~s!** ¡a sus marcas! **4** (target) blanco *m*; ***to be wide of the ~***: **his estimate was wide of the ~** erró por mucho en su cálculo **5** *also* **Mark** (type, version) modelo *m* **6** (Fin) marco *m*

mark² *vt* **1** (stain, scar) manchar **2** (indicate) señalar, marcar* **3** ‹*anniversary*› celebrar; ‹*beginning*› marcar*, señalar **4** ‹*exam*› (make corrections in) corregir*; (grade) poner(le)* nota a **5** (BrE Sport) ‹*opponent*› marcar*

• **mark down** [*v + o + adv, v + adv + o*] **(a)** (Busn) ‹*goods*› rebajar **(b)** (BrE Educ) ‹*person/work*› bajarle la nota a

• **mark out** [*v + o + adv, v + adv + o*] **(a)** ‹*sports ground*› marcar* **(b)** (select) señalar **(c)** (distinguish) distinguir*

marked /mɑːrkt ‖ mɑːkt/ *adj* ‹*improvement*› marcado; ‹*contrast*› acusado

marker /'mɑːrkər ‖ 'mɑːkə(r)/ *n* **(a)** (to show position) indicador *m* **(b)** ~ (**pen**) rotulador *m*

market¹ /'mɑːrkət ‖ 'mɑːkɪt/ *n* mercado *m*; (*street ~*) mercado *m or* mercadillo *m or* (CS, Per) feria *f*; **to come on (to) the ~** salir* a la venta; **we put the house on the ~ at $320,000** pusimos la casa en venta en $320.000; (*before n*) ~ **forces** fuerzas *fpl* del mercado **2** (Fin) (*stock ~*) bolsa *f* (de valores); ***to corner the ~ (in sth)*** hacerse* con el mercado (de algo)

market² *vt* comercializar*

market garden *n* (BrE) huerta *f*

marketing /'mɑːrkətɪŋ ‖ 'mɑːkɪtɪŋ/ *n* [U] marketing *m*

market: **~place** *n* (in town) mercado *m*, plaza *f* del mercado; (Busn) mercado *m*; **~ research** *n* [U] estudio *m or* investigación *f* de mercado

marking /'mɑːrkɪŋ ‖ 'mɑːkɪŋ/ *n* **(a)** (on animal, plant) mancha *f* **(b)** (manmade) marca *f*; **road ~s** líneas *fpl* de señalización vial

marksman /'mɑːrksmən ‖ 'mɑːksmən/ *n* (*pl* **-men** /-mən/) tirador *m*

marmalade /'mɑːrməleɪd ‖ 'mɑːməleɪd/ *n* [U C] mermelada *f* (*de cítricos*)

maroon¹ /mə'ruːn/ ▶ 515 *adj* granate *adj inv*

maroon² *vt* (*usu pass*) ‹*castaway*› abandonar (*en una isla desierta*)

marquee /mɑːr'kiː ‖ mɑː'kiː/ *n* **(a)** (canopy) (AmE) marquesina *f* **(b)** (tent) (BrE) entoldado *m*

marriage /'mærɪdʒ/ *n* **1** **(a)** [U] (act) casamiento *m*, matrimonio *m*; (*before n*) ~ **certificate** certificado *m* de matrimonio **(b)** [U C] (relationship) matrimonio *m*; **her ~ to the poet lasted two years** estuvo dos años casada con el poeta **2** (union) (liter) (*no pl*) maridaje *m*, unión *f*

married /'mærid/ *adj* ‹*man/woman*› casado; **a ~ couple** un matrimonio; **they have been ~ for two years** llevan dos años casados; **to get ~ (to sb)** casarse (con algn)

marrow /'mærəʊ/ *n* **1** [U] (*bone ~*) médula *f* **2** [C] ~ **squash** *o* (BrE) ~ (Culin) *tipo de calabaza alargada y de cáscara verde*

marry /'mæri/ **-ries, -rying, -ried** *vt* **(a)** (get married to) casarse con **(b)** (perform ceremony) casar **(c)** (unite, combine) unir ■ ~ *vi* casarse

● **marry off** [*v + o + adv, v + adv + o*] casar

Mars /mɑːrz ‖ mɑːz/ *n* Marte *m*

marsh /mɑːrʃ ‖ mɑːʃ/ *n* [C U] (*often pl*) pantano *m*; (on coast) marisma *f*

marshal¹ /'mɑːrʃəl ‖ 'mɑːʃəl/ *n* **1** (as title) (Mil) mariscal *m* **2** (as title) (AmE) **(a)** (police chief) jefe, -fa *m,f* de policía **(b)** (Law) *supervisor de los tribunales de un distrito judicial* **3** (at public gathering) miembro *m* del servicio de vigilancia

marshal² *vt*, (BrE) **-ll-** ‹*troops/crowd*› reunir*; ‹*thoughts*› poner* en orden; ‹*evidence*› reunir*

martial /'mɑːrʃəl ‖ 'mɑːʃəl/ *adj* marcial

martial: ~ **arts** *pl n* artes *fpl* marciales; ~ **law** *n* [U] ley *f* marcial

martyr /'mɑːrtər ‖ 'mɑːtə(r)/ *n* mártir *mf*

martyrdom /'mɑːrtərdəm ‖ 'mɑːtədəm/ *n* martirio *m*

marvel¹ /'mɑːrvəl ‖ 'mɑːvəl/ *n* maravilla *f*

marvel², (BrE) **-ll-** *vi* **to ~ (AT sth)** maravillarse (DE algo)

marvelous, (BrE) **marvellous** /'mɑːrvləs ‖ 'mɑːvələs/ *adj* maravilloso

Marxism /'mɑːrksɪzəm ‖ 'mɑːksɪzəm/ *n* [U] marxismo *m*

Marxist¹ /'mɑːrksəst ‖ 'mɑːksɪst/ *n* marxista *mf*

Marxist² *adj* marxista

marzipan /'mɑːrzəpɑːn ‖ 'mɑːzɪpæn, ˌmɑːzɪ'pæn/ *n* [U] mazapán *m*

mascara /mæ'skærə ‖ mæ'skɑːrə/ *n* [U C] rímel® *m*

mascot /'mæskɑːt ‖ 'mæskət, -skɒt/ *n* mascota *f*

masculine /'mæskjələn ‖ 'mæskjʊlɪn/ *adj* masculino

mash¹ /mæʃ/ *n* [U] (BrE colloq) puré *m* de papas *or* (Esp) de patatas

mash² *vt* hacer* puré de, moler* (Chi, Méx), pisar (RPl, Ven), espichar (Col); **~ed potato(es)** puré *m* de papas *or* (Esp) de patatas

mask¹ /mæsk ‖ mɑːsk/ *n* (for disguise, ritual) máscara *f*; (in fencing, ice-hockey) careta *f*; (used by doctors) mascarilla *f*, barbijo *m*; (for diving) gafas *fpl or* anteojos *mpl* de bucear; (against dust, fumes) mascarilla *f*

mask² *vt* **(a)** (conceal) ocultar **(b)** (cover) cubrir*

masking tape /'mæskɪŋ ‖'mɑːskɪŋ/ *n* cinta *f* adhesiva protectora, cinta *f* de enmascarar (Col), tirro *m* (Ven)

masochist /'mæsəkəst ‖ 'mæsəkɪst/ *n* masoquista *mf*

mason /'meɪsn/ *n* **(a)** (Const) albañil *mf*; (*stone ~*) mampostero *m* **(b)** *also* **Mason** (*Free~*) masón *m*, francmasón *m*

masquerade¹ /'mæskə'reɪd ‖ ˌmɑːskə'reɪd, ˌmæ-/ *n* mascarada *f*

masquerade² *vi* **to ~ AS sb** hacerse* pasar POR algn

mass¹ /mæs/ *n* **1** (bulk, body) masa *f*; **her hair was a ~ of curls** tenía la cabeza cubierta de rizos **2** **masses** *pl* **(a)** (great quantity) (BrE colloq): **we received ~es of complaints** recibimos montones de quejas (fam) **(b) the ~es** las masas **3** [U] (Phys) masa *f* **4** [C] *also* **Mass** (Mus, Relig) misa *f*

mass² *vi* «*crowd/clouds*» concentrarse

mass³ *adj* (*before n*) ‹*culture/market*› de masas; ‹*hysteria/suicide*› colectivo; ‹*protest*› masivo; ‹*unemployment*› generalizado; **a ~ meeting** una reunión de todo el personal (*or* el estudiantado *etc*); **~ transit** (AmE) transporte *m* público

Mass = **Massachusetts**

massacre¹ /'mæsəkər ‖ 'mæsəkə(r)/ *vt* masacrar

massacre² *n* [C U] matanza *f*, masacre *f*

massage¹ /mə'sɑːʒ ‖ 'mæsɑːʒ/ *vt* masajear

massage² *n* [C U] masaje *m*

massive /'mæsɪv/ *adj* ‹*wall*› sólido; ‹*support/task*› enorme; ‹*heart attack/overdose*› masivo

mass: ~ **media** *pl n* **the ~ media** los medios de comunicación (de masas); **~-produce** /'mæsprə'duːs ‖ ˌmæsprə'djuːs/ *vt* fabricar* en serie

mast /mæst ‖ mɑːst/ *n* **(a)** (Naut) mástil *m* **(b)** (flagpole) mástil *m* **(c)** (*relay ~*) antena *f* repetidora, repetidor *m*

mastectomy /mæ'stektəmi/ *n* [U C] (*pl* **-mies**) mastectomía *f*

master¹ /'mæstər ‖ 'mɑːstə(r)/ *n* **1** (of household) señor *m*, amo *m*; (of animal) amo *m*, dueño *m*; (of servant) amo *m*, patrón *m* **2** (expert) **~ OF sth** maestro, -tra *m,f* DE algo **3** (Educ) **(a)** (degree) **~'s (degree)** master *m*, maestría *f*; **M~ of Arts/Science** *poseedor de una maestría en Humanidades/Ciencias* **(b)** (BrE) (in secondary school) profesor *m* **4** (Naut) capitán *m* **5** (*~ copy*) (Audio, Comput, Print) original *m*

master² *vt* ‹*technique/subject*› llegar* a dominar

master³ *adj* (*before n, no comp*) **(a)** (expert): **~ baker/builder** maestro *m* panadero/de obras **(b)** (main) ‹*switch/key*› maestro **(c)** (original) ‹*tape*› original, matriz; **~ plan** plan *m* general

mastermind¹ /'mæstərmaɪnd ‖ 'mɑːstəmaɪnd/ *n* cerebro *m*

mastermind² *vt* planear y organizar*

master: ~ **of ceremonies** *n* maestro, -tra *m,f* de ceremonias; **~piece** *n* obra *f* maestra

mastery /'mæstəri ‖ 'mɑːstəri/ *n* [U] **(a)** (expertise, skill) maestría *f*; (of language, technique) dominio *m* **(b)** (control) dominio *m*

masturbate /'mæstərbeɪt ‖ 'mæstəbeɪt/ *vi* masturbarse

mat¹ /mæt/ *n* (of rushes, straw) estera *f*, esterilla *f*; (*door ~*) felpudo *m*, tapete *m* (Col, Méx); (*table~*) (individual) (mantel *m*) individual *m*; (in center of table) salvamanteles *m*, posafuentes *m* (CS)

mat² *adj* (AmE) ⇒ MATT

match¹ /mætʃ/ *n* **1** (for fire) fósforo *m*, cerilla *f* (Esp), cerillo *m* (esp AmC, Méx) **2** (Sport): **boxing ~** combate *m* de boxeo; **tennis ~** partido *m* de tenis; **football ~** (BrE) partido *m* de fútbol **3** (equal) (*no pl*): **to be a/no ~ for sb** estar*/no estar* a la altura de algn

match² *vt* **1** (equal) igualar **2 (a)** (correspond to) ‹*description*› ajustarse a, corresponder a **(b)**

(harmonize with) hacer* juego con **(c)** (make correspond, find equivalent for): **~ the words with the pictures** encuentra la palabra que corresponda a cada dibujo; **to be well ~ed** «*competitors*» ser* del mismo nivel, ser* muy parejos (esp AmL); «*couple*» hacer* buena pareja **(d) matching** *pres p* haciendo juego, a juego (Esp) ■ ~ *vi* **(a)** (go together) «*clothes/colors*» hacer* juego; **a demanding job with a salary to ~** un trabajo que exige mucho con un salario acorde **(b)** (tally) coincidir

match: **~book** *n* (AmE) librito *m* de fósforos *or* (Esp) de cerillas *or* (AmC, Méx tb) de cerillos; **~box** *n* caja *f* de fósforos *or* (Esp) de cerillas *or* (AmC, Méx tb) de cerillos; **~maker** *n* casamentero, -ra *m,f*; **~ point** *n* punto *m* de partido; **~stick** *n* **(a)** ⇒ MATCH[1] **(b)** (stick) palillo *m*

mate[1] /meɪt/ *n* **1 (a)** (assistant) ayudante *mf* **(b)** (Naut) oficial *mf* de cubierta; **first ~** primer oficial *m* **2 (a)** (Zool) (male) macho *m*; (female) hembra *f* **(b)** (of person) pareja *f* **3** (BrE colloq) amigo, -ga *m,f*, cuate, -ta *m,f* (Méx fam) **4** (*check~*) (jaque *m*) mate *m*

mate[2] *vi* aparearse

material[1] /mə'tɪriəl ‖ mə'tɪəriəl/ *n* **1 (a)** [C U] (used in manufacturing etc) material *m* **(b) materials** *pl* (equipment) material *m* **2** [U C] (cloth) tela *f*, género *m*, tejido *m* **3** [U] **(a)** (for book, show etc) material *m* **(b)** (potential, quality): **this is bestseller ~** éste es un bestseller en potencia; **she's champion ~** tiene madera de campeona

material[2] *adj* material

materialistic /mə'tɪriə'lɪstɪk ‖ məˌtɪəriə'lɪstɪk/ *adj* materialista

materialize /mə'tɪriəlaɪz ‖ mə'tɪəriəlaɪz/ *vi* «*object/ghost*» aparecer*; «*hope/idea*» hacerse* realidad

maternal /mə'tɜːrnl̩ ‖ mə'tɜːnl̩/ *adj* **(a)** (motherly) maternal **(b)** (on mother's side) (*before n*) ‹*grandfather*› materno

maternity /mə'tɜːrnəti ‖ mə'tɜːnəti/ *n* [U] maternidad *f*; (*before n*) ‹*clinic/ward*› de obstetricia; ‹*dress/clothes*› de embarazada, premamá *adj inv* (Esp); ‹*pay/leave*› por maternidad; **~ hospital** maternidad *f*

math /mæθ/ *n* [U] (AmE) matemática(s) *f(pl)*

mathematical /'mæθə'mætɪkəl/ *adj* matemático

mathematician /'mæθəmə'tɪʃən/ *n* matemático, -ca *m,f*

mathematics /'mæθə'mætɪks/ *n* (+ *sing vb*) matemática(s) *f(pl)*

maths /mæθs/ *n* [U] (BrE) (+ *sing vb*) matemática(s) *f(pl)*

matinee, matinée /'mætn̩'eɪ ‖ 'mætɪneɪ/ *n* (Cin) primera sesión *f* (*de la tarde*), matiné(e) *f* (AmS); (Theat) función *f* de tarde, matiné(e) *f* (AmS)

matrices /'meɪtrəsiːz, 'mæt- ‖ 'meɪtrɪsiːz/ *pl of* MATRIX

matriculate /mə'trɪkjəleɪt ‖ mə'trɪkjʊleɪt/ *vi* (frml) matricularse

matrimony /'mætrəməʊni ‖ 'mætrɪməni/ *n* [U] (frml) matrimonio *m*

matrix /'meɪtrɪks/ *n* (*pl* **matrices** *or* **~es**) matriz *f*

matron /'meɪtrən/ *n* **(a)** (dignified woman) matrona *f* **(b)** (in prison) (AmE) matrona *f* **(c)** (in hospital) (BrE dated) enfermera *f* jefe *or* jefa **(d)** (in school) ≈ enfermera *f*

matt, (AmE also) **matte, mat** /mæt/ *adj* mate; **a ~ finish** un acabado mate

matted /'mætəd ‖ 'mætɪd/ *adj* enmarañado y apelmazado

matter[1] /'mætər ‖ 'mætə(r)/ *n* **1** [U] **(a)** (substance) (Phil, Phys) materia *f* **(b)** (discharge) (Med) pus *m*, materia *f* **(c)** (*subject ~*) temática *f*, tema *m* **(d)** (written, printed material): **printed ~** impresos *mpl*; **reading ~** material *m* de lectura **2** [C] **(a)** (question, affair) asunto *m*, cuestión *f*; **it's only a ~ of time** sólo es cuestión de tiempo; **that's a ~ of opinion** eso es discutible **(b) matters** *pl*: **to make ~s worse** para colmo (de males); **that didn't help ~s** aquello no ayudó a mejorar la situación **(c)** (*in phrases*) **as a matter of fact**: **as a ~ of fact, I've never been to Spain** la verdad es que nunca he estado en España; **for that matter** en realidad; **no matter** (*as interj*) no importa; (*as conj*): **no ~ how hard I try** por mucho que me esfuerce **3** [C] (problem, trouble): **what's the ~?** ¿qué pasa?; **what's the ~ with Jane?** ¿qué le pasa a Jane?

matter[2] *vi* importar

matter-of-fact /'mætərəv'fækt/ *adj* ‹*person*› práctico; **he explained it in a very ~ way** lo explicó con total naturalidad

mattress /'mætrəs ‖ 'mætrɪs/ *n* colchón *m*

mature[1] /mə'tʊr ‖ mə'tjʊə(r)/ *adj* **(a)** (developed) ‹*animal/tree*› adulto; ‹*fruit/artist/ideas*› maduro **(b)** (sensible) maduro

mature[2] *vi* **(a)** (develop) «*plant/animal/person*» desarrollarse; «*artist/work*» madurar; «*wine*» añejarse **(b)** (become sensible) madurar **(c)** (Fin) «*bond/policy*» vencer*

maturity /mə'tʊrəti ‖ mə'tjʊərəti/ *n* [U] madurez *f*

maudlin /'mɔːdlən ‖ 'mɔːdlɪn/ *adj* llorón

maul /mɔːl/ *vt* atacar* (y herir*)

mausoleum /'mɔːsə'liːəm/ *n* (*pl* **-ums**) mausoleo *m*

mauve /məʊv/ ▶**515** *adj* malva *adj inv*

maverick /'mævərɪk/ *n* inconformista *mf*; (Pol) disidente *mf*

maxim /'mæksəm ‖ 'mæksɪm/ *n* máxima *f*

maximize /'mæksəmaɪz ‖ 'mæksɪmaɪz/ *vt* maximizar*

maximum[1] /'mæksəməm ‖ 'mæksɪməm/ *n* máximo *m*

maximum[2] *adj* (*before n*) máximo

may /meɪ/ *v mod* (*past* **might**) **1** (asking, granting permission) poder*; **~ I smoke?** ¿puedo fumar?; **~ I have your name and address, please?** ¿quiere darme su nombre y dirección, por favor? **2** (indicating probability) [*El grado de probabilidad que indica* MAY *es mayor que el que expresan* MIGHT *o* COULD]: **we ~ increase the price** quizás aumentemos el precio; **it ~ or ~ not be true** puede o no ser cierto **3** (indicating sth is natural): **you ~ well ask!** ¡buena pregunta! **4** (conceding): **he ~ not be clever, but he's very hard-working** no será inteligente, pero es muy trabajador; **that's as ~ be** puede ser

May /meɪ/ ▶540 *n* mayo *m*

maybe /'meɪbi:/ *adv* quizá(s), tal vez; **~ I'll come later** quizá(s) *or* tal vez venga luego

May: **~ Day** *n* el primero de mayo; (in some countries) el día del trabajo; **mayfly** *n* efímera *f*, cachipolla *f*

mayhem /'meɪhem/ *n* [U] caos *m*

mayonnaise /'meɪə'neɪz, 'meɪəneɪz ‖ ˌmeɪə'neɪz/ *n* [U] mayonesa *f*, mahonesa *f*

mayor /'meɪər ‖ meə(r)/ ▶603 *n* alcalde, -desa *m,f*, intendente *mf* (municipal) (RPl)

mayoress /'meɪərəs ‖ 'meəres/ ▶603 *n* (BrE) (female mayor) alcaldesa *f*, intendente *f* (RPl); (mayor's wife) alcaldesa *f*

maze /meɪz/ *n* laberinto *m*

MB (= **megabyte(s)**) Mb.

MBA *n* = **Master of Business Administration**

MC *n* = **master of ceremonies**

Md = **Maryland**

me¹ /mi:, *weak form* mi/ ▶638 *pron* **1 (a)** (as direct object) me; **she helped ~** me ayudó; **help ~** ayúdame **(b)** (as indirect object) me; **he bought ~ flowers** me compró flores **(c)** (after prep) mí; **for/behind ~** para mí/detrás de mí; **come with ~** ven conmigo; **she's older than ~** es mayor que yo **2** (emphatic use) yo; **it's ~** soy yo

me² /mi:/ *n* (Mus) mi *m*

ME 1 (Geog) = **Maine 2** = **myalgic encephalomyelitis**

meadow /'medəʊ/ *n* [C U] prado *m*, pradera *f*

meager, (BrE) **meagre** /'mi:gər ‖ 'mi:gə(r)/ *adj* ‹*portion/salary*› escaso; ‹*existence*› precario

meal /mi:l/ *n* **1** [C] (Culin) comida *f* **2** [U] (Agr, Culin) harina *f* (*de avena, maíz etc*)

mealtime /'mi:ltaɪm/ *n* hora *f* de comer

mean¹ /mi:n/ *vt* (*past & past p* **meant**) **1** (represent, signify) «*word/symbol*» significar*, querer* decir; **that ~s trouble** eso quiere decir que va a haber problemas; **does the number 0296 ~ anything to you?** ¿el número 0296 te dice algo?; **fame ~s nothing to her** la fama la tiene sin cuidado **2 (a)** (refer to, intend to say) «*person*» querer* decir; **what do you ~?** ¿qué quieres decir (con eso)?; **do you know what I ~?** ¿me entiendes?; **I know who you ~** ya sé de quién hablas **(b)** (be serious about) decir* en serio **3** (equal, entail) significar*; **that would ~ repainting the kitchen** eso supondría volver a pintar la cocina **4 (a)** (intend): **he didn't ~ (you) any harm** no quiso hacerte daño; **to ~ to + INF**: **I ~ to succeed** mi intención es triunfar; **I ~t to do it but I forgot** tenía toda la intención de hacerlo pero me olvidé **(b) to be ~t to + INF** (supposed, intended): **you weren't ~t to hear that** no pensaron (*or* pensé *etc*) que tú estarías escuchando; **I was never ~t to be a teacher** yo no estoy hecho para enseñar

mean² *adj* **1** (miserly) ‹*person*› tacaño; ‹*portion*› mezquino **2 (a)** (unkind, nasty) malo; **it was really ~ of you** fue una maldad (de tu parte) **(b)** (excellent) (esp AmE sl) genial **3** (inferior, humble) (liter) humilde; **that's no ~ feat** no es poca cosa **4** (Math) (*before n*) medio

mean³ *n* media *f*, promedio *m*; *see also* MEANS

meander /mi'ændər ‖ mi'ændə(r)/ *vi* «*river*» serpentear; «*person*» deambular, vagar*

meaning /'mi:nɪŋ/ *n* [C U] significado *m*

meaningful /'mi:nɪŋfəl/ *adj* ‹*look/experience/relationship*› significativo; ‹*explanation*› con sentido; ‹*discussions*› positivo

meaningless /'mi:nɪŋləs ‖ 'mi:nɪŋlɪs/ *adj* sin sentido

means /mi:nz/ *n* (*pl* **~**) **1** (+ *sing vb*) **(a)** (method) medio *m*; **a ~ to an end** un medio para lograr un fin; **~ of transport** medio de transporte; *see also* WAYS AND MEANS **(b)** (*in phrases*) **by all means** por supuesto, ¡cómo no! (esp AmL); **by no means, not by any means**: **we are by no ~ rich** no somos ricos ni mucho menos: **it's not a perfect film by any ~** de ninguna manera es una película perfecta; **by means of** (*as prep*) por medio de, mediante **2** (frml) (+ *pl vb*) (wealth) medios *mpl* (económicos); (income) ingresos *mpl*

means test *n*: *investigación de los ingresos de una persona para determinar si tiene derecho o no a ciertas prestaciones*

meant /ment/ *past & past p of* MEAN¹

meantime /'mi:ntaɪm/ *n*: **in the ~** (while sth else happens) mientras tanto, entretanto; (in the intervening period) en el ínterin *or* interín; **for the ~** por ahora

meanwhile /'mi:nhwaɪl ‖ 'mi:nwaɪl/ *adv* mientras tanto, entretanto

measles /'mi:zəlz/ *n* (+ *sing or pl vb*) (Med) sarampión *m*

measure¹ /'meʒər ‖ 'meʒə(r)/ *n* **1 (a)** [U] (system) medida *f* **(b)** [C] (unit) medida *f* **(c)** [C U] (amount) cantidad *f*; **with a (certain) ~ of success** con cierto éxito **2** [C] (device) medida *f* **3** [C] (step) medida *f*; **to take ~s to + INF** tomar medidas para + INF **4** (AmE Mus) compás *m*

measure² *vt* **1** ‹*length/speed/waist*› medir*; ‹*weight*› pesar **2** (assess) calcular; **to ~ sth AGAINST sth** comparar algo CON algo ■ **~** *vi* medir*

• **measure out** [*v* + *o* + *adv*, *v* + *adv* + *o*] ‹*length*› medir*; ‹*weight*› pesar

• **measure up** [*v* + *adv*] estar* a la altura de las circunstancias; **to ~ up TO sth** estar* a la altura DE algo

measurement /'meʒərmənt ‖ 'meʒəmənt/ *n* **(a)** [U C] (act) medición *f* **(b)** [C] (dimension) medida *f*

measuring /'meʒərɪŋ/: **~ cup**, (BrE) **~ jug** *n* jarra *f* graduada; **~ spoon** *n* cuchara *f* de medir

meat /mi:t/ *n* **(a)** [U C] carne *f*; (*before n*) ‹*product*› cárnico **(b)** [U] (substance) sustancia *f*

meat: **~ball** *n* albóndiga *f*; **~loaf** *n* [U C] pan *m* de carne

meaty /'mi:ti/ *adj* **-tier, -tiest** ‹*taste/smell*› a carne; ‹*soup/stew*› con mucha carne

Mecca /'mekə/ *n* **(a)** La Meca **(b)** *also* **mecca** (center of attraction) meca *f*

mechanic /mə'kænɪk ‖ mɪ'kænɪk/ *n* mecánico, -ca *m,f; see also* MECHANICS

mechanical /mə'kænɪkəl ‖ mɪ'kænɪkəl/ *adj* mecánico, maquinal; ‹*action/reply*› mecánico

mechanics /mə'kænɪks ‖ mɪ'kænɪks/ *n* **1** (+ *sing vb*) (Phys, Mech Eng) mecánica *f* **2** (+ *pl vb*) **the ~** (practical details) los aspectos prácticos; (mechanical parts) el mecanismo

mechanism /'mekənɪzəm/ *n* mecanismo *m*

mechanize /'mekənaɪz/ *vt* mecanizar*

medal /'medḷ/ *n* medalla *f*

medalist, (BrE) **medallist** /'medḷəst ‖ 'medəlɪst/ *n* medallista *mf*; **gold/silver ~** medalla *mf* de oro/plata

medallion /mə'dæljən/ *n* medallón *m*

medallist (BrE) ⇒ MEDALIST

meddle /'medḷ/ *vi* **(a)** (interfere) **to ~ (IN/WITH sth)** meterse *or* entrometerse (EN algo) **(b)** (tamper) **to ~ WITH sth** toquetear algo

media[1] /'mi:diə/ *n*: **the ~** (+ *pl or* (crit) *sing vb*) los medios de comunicación

media[2] *pl of* MEDIUM[2] 1,2

mediaeval /'mi:di'i:vəl, 'me- ‖ ,medi'i:vəl/ ⇒ MEDIEVAL

median[1] /'mi:diən/ *adj* (Math) medio

median[2] *n* **1** (Math) mediana *f* **2 ~ (strip)** (AmE) mediana *f*, bandejón *m* (central) (Chi), camellón *m* (Méx)

mediate /'mi:dieɪt/ *vi* mediar

mediator /'mi:dieɪtər ‖ 'mi:dieɪtə(r)/ *n* mediador, -dora *m,f*

Medicaid /'medɪkeɪd/ *n* (in US) *organismo y programa estatal de asistencia sanitaria a personas de bajos ingresos*

medical[1] /'medɪkəl/ *adj* ‹*care/examination/insurance*› médico; ‹*student*› de medicina; **~ school** facultad *f* de medicina

medical[2] *n* revisión *f* médica

Medicare /'medɪker ‖ 'medɪkeə(r)/ *n* (in US) *organismo y programa estatal de asistencia sanitaria a personas mayores de 65 años*

medicated /'medəkeɪtəd ‖ 'medɪkeɪtɪd/ *adj* medicinal

medication /'medə'keɪʃən ‖ ,medɪ'keɪʃən/ *n* **(a)** [U C] (substance) medicamento *m* **(b)** [U] (drugs) medicación *f*

medicinal /mə'dɪsnəl ‖ mɪ'dɪsnḷ/ *adj* medicinal

medicine /'medəsən ‖ 'medsən, 'medəsən/ *n* **1** [C U] (substance) medicamento *m*, medicina *f*, remedio *m* (esp AmL) **2** [U] (science) medicina *f*

medieval /'mi:di'i:vəl, 'me- ‖ ,medi'i:vəl/ *adj* medieval, medioeval

mediocre /'mi:di'əʊkər ‖ ,mi:dɪ'əʊkə(r)/ *adj* mediocre

mediocrity /'mi:di'ɑ:krəti ‖ ,mi:di'ɒkrəti/ *n* (*pl* **-ties**) **(a)** [U] (quality) mediocridad *f* **(b)** [C] (person) mediocre *mf*

meditate /'medəteɪt ‖ 'medɪteɪt/ *vi* meditar

meditation /'medə'teɪʃən ‖ ,medɪ'teɪʃən/ *n* [U C] meditación *f*

Mediterranean[1] /'medətə'remiən ‖ ,medɪtə'remiən/ *adj* mediterráneo

Mediterranean[2] *n* **the ~ (Sea)** el (mar) Mediterráneo

medium[1] /'mi:diəm/ *adj* **1** (intermediate) ‹*size*› mediano **2** (Culin) **(a)** ‹*steak*› a punto, término medio (Méx) **(b)** (*as adv*): **~ rare** ‹*steak*› poco hecho, a la inglesa (Méx); **~ dry** ‹*wine*› semi-seco

medium[2] *n* **1** [C] (*pl* **media**) (means, vehicle) medio *m* **2** (*pl* **media**) [C] (environment) medio *m* (ambiente) **3** (middle position) (*no pl*) punto *m* medio; **to strike a happy ~** lograr un término medio **4** [C] (*pl* **mediums**) (Occult) médium *mf*

medium: **~-size** /'mi:diəm'saɪz/, (BrE also) **~-sized** /-d/ *adj* ‹*book/house*› de tamaño mediano; ‹*person*› de talla media *or* mediana; **~-term** /'mi:diəm'tɜ:rm ‖ ,mi:diəm'tɜ:m/ *adj* (*before n*) a medio plazo; **~ wave** *n* (BrE) (*no pl*) onda *f* media

medley /'medli/ *n* **(a)** (mixture) mezcla *f* **(b)** (Mus) popurrí *m*

meek /mi:k/ *adj* **-er, -est** dócil, sumiso

meet[1] /mi:t/ (*past & past p* **met**) *vt* **1 (a)** (encounter) encontrarse* con **(b)** (welcome) recibir; (collect on arrival) ir* a buscar; **she ran to ~ me** corrió a mi encuentro **2** (make acquaintance of) conocer*; **pleased to ~ you** encantado de conocerlo **3** (come up against, experience) encontrar*; **there's more to this than ~s the eye** esto es más complicado de lo que parece **4** ‹*demands/wishes/debt*› satisfacer*; ‹*deadline/quota/obligation*› cumplir con; ‹*requirements*› reunir*; ‹*cost*› hacerse* cargo de ■ **~** *vi* **1 (a)** (encounter each other) encontrarse* **(b)** (hold meeting) ‹‹*club*›› reunirse*; ‹‹*heads of state/ministers*›› entrevistarse **(c)** (make acquaintance) conocerse*; **have you two already met?** ¿ya se conocen? **2** (come into contact): **the vehicles met head on** los vehículos chocaron de frente; **their eyes met** sus miradas se cruzaron

● **meet up** [*v* + *adv*] **to ~ up (WITH sb)** encontrarse* (CON algn)

● **meet with** [*v* + *prep* + *o*] **(a)** ‹*opposition/hostility*› ser* recibido con; **she met with an unfortunate accident** le ocurrió un lamentable accidente **(b)** (meet) (AmE) encontrarse* con

meet[2] *n* **(a)** (AmE Sport) encuentro *m* **(b)** (in hunting) partida *f* (de caza)

meeting /'mi:tɪŋ/ *n* **1** (assembly) reunión *f*; **to call/hold a ~** convocar*/celebrar una reunión; **political ~** mitin *m*, mítin *m* **2** (encounter) encuentro *m*; (between presidents) entrevista *f* **3** (BrE Sport) encuentro *m*

megabyte /'megəbaɪt/ *n* megabyte *m*, megaocteto *m*

megalomaniac /'megələʊ'memiæk/ *n* megalómano, -na *m,f*

megaphone /'megəfəʊn/ *n* megáfono *m*

melancholy /'melənkɑ:li ‖ 'melənkəli/ *adj* ‹*person/mood*› melancólico; ‹*sound*› triste

mellow[1] /'meləʊ/ *adj* **-er, -est (a)** ‹*fruit*› maduro; ‹*wine*› añejo; ‹*sound/voice*› dulce; ‹*light/color*› tenue **(b)** ‹*person/mood*› apacible

mellow² *vt* suavizar* ■ ~ *vi* «*color/voice*» suavizarse*; **he has ~ed with age** se le ha suavizado el carácter con los años

melodrama /'melədrɑːmə/ *n* [C U] melodrama *m*

melodramatic /'melədrə'mætɪk/ *adj* melodramático

melody /'melədi/ *n* (*pl* **-dies**) melodía *f*

melon /'melən/ *n* [C U] melón *m*

melt /melt/ *vi* «*ice/butter*» derretirse*; «*metal/wax*» fundirse; «*anger*» desaparecer*; **they ~ed into the crowd** se perdieron en la muchedumbre ■ ~ *vt* ‹*snow/butter*› derretir*; **their cries ~ed her heart** su llanto la conmovió

• **melt away** [*v* + *adv*] «*ice/snow*» derretirse*; «*mist/fog*» levantarse; «*fear/suspicion*» disiparse; «*confidence*» desvanecerse*; «*resistance/opposition*» desaparecer*; **they ~ed away into the woods** desaparecieron ocultándose en el bosque

• **melt down** [*v* + *o* + *adv*, *v* + *adv* + *o*] ‹*gold/coins*› fundir

member /'membər ‖ 'membə(r)/ *n* **1** (of committee, board) miembro *mf*; (of club) socio, -cia *m,f*; **~ of staff** empleado, -da *m,f*; **a ~ of the audience** un espectador; **the offer is open to any ~ of the public** la oferta está abierta al público en general; (*before n*) **~ states** países *mpl* miembros **2** (limb) (arch) miembro *m*

member: **M~ of Congress** *n* (in US) miembro *mf* del Congreso; **M~ of Parliament** ▶ 603 *n* (in UK etc) diputado, -da *m,f*, parlamentario, -ria *m,f*

membership /'membərʃɪp ‖ 'membəʃɪp/ *n* **(a)** [U] (being a member): **~ of the club is restricted to residents** sólo los residentes pueden hacerse socios del club; **to apply for ~** solicitar el ingreso en un club (*or* partido *etc*); (*before n*) **~ card** carné *m* de socio **(b)** [C] (members) (+ *sing or pl vb*) socios *mpl* (*or* afiliados *mpl etc*); (number of members) número *m* de socios (*or* afiliados *etc*)

membrane /'membreɪn/ *n* membrana *f*

memento /mə'mentəʊ ‖ mɪ'mentəʊ/ *n* (*pl* **-tos** *or* **-toes**) recuerdo *m*

memo /'meməʊ/ *n* (*pl* **-os**) memorándum *m*

memoirs /'memwɑːrz ‖ 'memwɑːz/ *pl n* memorias *fpl*

memorabilia /'memərə'bɪliə/ *pl n* objetos *mpl* de interés

memorable /'memərəbəl/ *adj* memorable

memorandum /'memə'rændəm/ *n* (*pl* **-dums** *or* **-da** /-də/) memorándum *m*

memorial¹ /mə'mɔːriəl/ *n* monumento *m*

memorial² *adj* conmemorativo

Memorial Day *n* (in US) *el último lunes de mayo, día en que se recuerda a los caídos en la guerra*

memorize /'meməraɪz/ *vt* memorizar*

memory /'meməri/ *n* (*pl* **-ries**) **1 (a)** [U C] (faculty) memoria *f* **(b)** [U] (period): **the worst storm in living ~** la peor tormenta que se recuerde **2 (a)** [C] (recollection) recuerdo *m*; **his ~ will live on** su recuerdo permanecerá vivo **(b)** [U] (remembrance) memoria *f*; **in ~ of sb/sth** a la memoria de algn/en conmemoración de algo **3** [C U] (Comput) memoria *f*

men /men/ *pl of* MAN¹

menace /'menəs ‖ 'menɪs/ *n* **1 (a)** [U] (threatening quality): **the ~ in his voice** el tono amenazador de su voz **(b)** [C] (threat) amenaza *f* **2** [C] (danger) amenaza *f*

menacing /'menəsɪŋ ‖ 'menɪsɪŋ/ *adj* amenazador

menagerie /mə'nædʒəri/ *n* colección *f* de animales salvajes

mend¹ /mend/ *vt* ‹*garment*› coser; ‹*shoe/clock/roof*› arreglar, reparar; **to ~ one's ways** enmendarse* ■ ~ *vi* (heal) «*injury*» curarse; «*fracture/bone*» soldarse*

mend² *n* remiendo *m*; ***to be on the ~*** (colloq) ir* mejorando

menial /'miːniəl/ *adj* de ínfima importancia

meningitis /'menən'dʒaɪtəs ‖ ,menɪn'dʒaɪtɪs/ *n* [U] meningitis *f*

menopause /'menəpɔːz/ *n* **the ~** la menopausia

men's room *n* (AmE) baño *m or* servicios *mpl* de caballeros

menstruate /'menstrueɪt/ *vi* menstruar*

menswear /'menzwer ‖ 'menzweə(r)/ *n* [U] ropa *f* de caballero

mental /'mentl/ *adj* (*before n*) ‹*powers/illness*› mental; ‹*hospital/patient*› psiquiátrico

mental arithmetic *n* [U] cálculos *mpl* mentales

mentality /men'tæləti/ *n* (*pl* **-ties**) mentalidad *f*

mentally /'mentəli/ *adv* mentalmente; **he's ~ ill/handicapped** es un enfermo mental/un disminuido psíquico

menthol /'menθɔːl ‖ 'menθɒl/ *n* [U] mentol *m*; (*before n*) ‹*cigarettes*› mentolado

mentholated /'menθəleɪtəd ‖ 'menθəleɪtɪd/ *adj* mentolado

mention¹ /'mentʃən ‖ 'menʃən/ *vt* mencionar; **I won't ~ any names** no daré nombres; **there's the problem of time, not to ~ the cost** está el problema del tiempo y no digamos ya el costo; **don't ~ it** (on being thanked) no hay de qué, de nada

mention² *n* mención *f*

mentor /'mentɔːr ‖ 'mentɔː(r)/ *n* (liter) mentor, -tora *m,f* (liter)

menu /'menjuː/ *n* **(a)** (in restaurant) carta *f*, menú *m* (esp AmL) **(b)** (Comput) menú *m*

meow¹ /mi'aʊ/ *n* maullido *m*

meow² *vi* maullar*

MEP *n* (= **Member of the European Parliament**) eurodiputado, -da *m,f*

mercenary /'mɜːrsṇeri ‖ 'mɜːsɪnəri/ *n* (*pl* **-ries**) mercenario, -ria *m,f*

merchandise /'mɜːrtʃəndaɪz ‖ 'mɜːtʃəndaɪz/ *n* [U] mercancía *f*, mercadería *f* (AmS)

merchant /'mɜːrtʃənt ‖ 'mɜːtʃənt/ *n* **(a)** (retailer) comerciante *mf* **(b)** (Hist) mercader *m*

merchant marine, (BrE also) **merchant navy** *n* marina *f* mercante

merciful /'mɜːrsɪfəl ‖ 'mɜːsɪfəl/ *adj* misericordioso

merciless /'mɜːrsɪləs ‖ 'mɜːsɪlɪs/ *adj* despiadado

mercury /'mɜːrkjəri ‖ 'mɜːkjʊri/ *n* [U] mercurio *m*

Mercury /'mɜːrkjəri ‖ 'mɜːkjʊri/ *n* Mercurio *m*

mercy /'mɜːrsi ‖ 'mɜːsi/ *n* (*pl* **-cies**) **(a)** [U] (clemency) misericordia *f*; **to have ~ (on sb)** tener* misericordia (de algn), apiadarse (de algn); **at the ~ of the elements** a merced de los elementos **(b)** [C] (blessing) bendición *f*; **it's a ~ that** ... (colloq) es una suerte que ...; **let's be thankful for small mercies** (set phrase) seamos positivos, podría haber sido peor

mere /mɪr ‖ mɪə(r)/ *adj* (*superl* **merest**) (*before n*) simple, mero

merely /'mɪrli ‖ 'mɪəli/ *adv* simplemente

merge /mɜːrdʒ ‖ mɜːdʒ/ *vi* «*roads/rivers*» confluir*; «*colors*» fundirse; «*companies*» fusionarse; **he ~d into the crowd** se perdió entre el gentío ■ ~ *vt* ‹*companies/organizations*› fusionar; ‹*colors*› combinar

merger /'mɜːrdʒər ‖ 'mɜːdʒə(r)/ *n* **(a)** (Busn) fusión *f* **(b)** (of organizations etc) fusión *f*

meringue /mə'ræŋ/ *n* [C U] merengue *m*

merit¹ /'merət ‖ 'merɪt/ *n* [U C] mérito *m*; **each case is judged on its (own) ~s** se juzga cada caso individualmente

merit² *vt* merecer*

mermaid /'mɜːrmeɪd ‖ 'mɜːmeɪd/ *n* sirena *f*

merrily /'merəli ‖ 'merɪli/ *adv* **(a)** (joyfully) alegremente **(b)** (unconcernedly) tranquilamente

merriment /'merɪmənt/ *n* [U] (joy) alegría *f*; (laughter) risas *fpl*

merry /'meri/ *adj* **-rier, -riest** alegre; **~ Christmas!** ¡feliz Navidad!, ¡felices Pascuas!

merry-go-round /'merigəʊ,raʊnd/ *n* carrusel *m*, tiovivo *m* (Esp), calesita *f* (Per, RPl)

mesh /meʃ/ *n* [C U] malla *f*

mesmerize /'mezməraɪz/ *vt* **(a)** (fascinate) cautivar **(b)** (hypnotize) (dated) hipnotizar*

mess /mes/ *n* **1 (a)** (*no pl*) (untidiness) desorden *m*; **the bedroom was (in) a ~** el dormitorio estaba todo desordenado; **my hair is a ~** (colloq) tengo el pelo hecho un desastre **(b)** (dirt): **what a ~!** ¡qué desastre *or* (RPl tb) enchastre! (fam); **they made a ~ on the carpet** dejaron la alfombra hecha un asco (fam) **2** (*no pl*) (confused, troubled state): **the country is (in) a complete ~** la situación del país es caótica; **my life's a ~** mi vida es un desastre; **to make a ~ of sth**: **you made a real ~ of this job** hiciste muy mal este trabajo **3** [C] (Mil): **officers' ~** casino *m or* comedor *m* de oficiales

● **mess around**, (BrE also) **mess about** (colloq) [*v* + *adv*] **(a)** (misbehave) «*children*» hacer* travesuras **(b)** (interfere): **stop ~ing around with my things!** ¡deja mis cosas tranquilas!; **don't ~ around with me** no juegues conmigo

● **mess up** [*v* + *o* + *adv*, *v* + *adv* + *o*] **(a)** (make untidy) desordenar **(b)** (make dirty) ensuciar **(c)** (spoil) ‹*plans*› estropear

message /'mesɪdʒ/ *n* mensaje *m*; **would you like to leave a ~?** ¿quiere dejar algún recado *or* (esp AmL) mensaje?, ¿quiere dejar algo dicho? (CS); ***to get the ~*** (colloq) entender*, darse* cuenta

messenger /'mesn̩dʒər ‖ 'mesɪndʒə(r)/ *n* mensajero, -ra *m,f*

Messiah /mə'saɪə/ *n* Mesías *m*

Messrs /'mesərz ‖ 'mesəz/ *pl of* **Mr** Sres.

messy /'mesi/ *adj* **-sier, -siest (a)** (untidy) ‹*room*› desordenado; ‹*writing*› sucio y descuidado, desprolijo (CS) **(b)** (dirty) sucio; **he's a ~ eater** no sabe comer **(c)** (unpleasant, confused) ‹*business*› turbio

met /met/ *past & past p of* MEET¹

metabolism /mə'tæbəlɪzəm ‖ mə'tæbəlɪzəm/ *n* metabolismo *m*

metal /'metl/ *n* [U C] (Chem, Metall) metal *m*; (*before n*) ‹*box*› metálico

metallic /mə'tælɪk/ *adj* metálico

metamorphosis /'metə'mɔːrfəsəs ‖ ,metə'mɔːfəsɪs/ *n* [C U] (*pl* **-phoses** /-fəsiːz/) metamorfosis *f*

metaphor /'metəfɔːr, -fər ‖ 'metəfɔː(r), -fə(r)/ *n* [C U] metáfora *f*

metaphorical /'metə'fɔːrɪkəl ‖ ,metə'fɒrɪkəl/ *adj* metafórico

mete /miːt/ *see* METE OUT

meteor /'miːtiər, -ɔːr ‖ 'miːtiə(r), -ɔː(r)/ *n* meteorito *m*

meteoric /'miːti'ɔːrɪk ‖ ,miːtɪ'ɒrɪk/ *adj* ‹*rise/progress*› meteórico; **~ rock** piedra *f* meteórica

meteorite /'miːtiəraɪt/ *n* meteorito *m*

meteorology /'miːtiə'rɑːlədʒi ‖ ,miːtiə'rɒlədʒi/ *n* [U] meteorología *f*

mete out [*v* + *o* + *adv*, *v* + *adv* + *o*] ‹*fine/punishment*› imponer*

meter¹ /'miːtər ‖ 'miːtə(r)/ *n* **1** [C] **(a)** (measuring device): **gas/electricity/water ~** contador *m or* (AmL tb) medidor *m* de gas/electricidad/agua **(b)** (*parking ~*) parquímetro *m* **2** [U C] (AmE Mus) compás *m* **3** **▶ 681** [C] (BrE) **metre** (measure) metro *m*

meter² *vt* medir* (*con contador*)

method /'meθəd/ *n* [C U] método *m*

methodical /mə'θɑːdɪkəl ‖ mɪ'θɒdɪkəl/ *adj* metódico

Methodism /'meθədɪzəm/ *n* [U] metodismo *m*

Methodist /'meθədəst ‖ 'meθədɪst/ *n* metodista *mf*

methylated spirit(s) /'meθəleɪtəd ‖ 'meθəleɪtɪd/ *n* [U] (+ *sing vb*) alcohol *m* desnaturalizado

meticulous /mə'tɪkjələs ‖ mə'tɪkjʊləs/ *adj* meticuloso

metre (BrE) ⇒ METER¹ 3

metric /'metrɪk/ *adj* métrico

metro /'metrəʊ/ *n* (*pl* **-ros**) (Rail, Transp) metro *m*, subterráneo *m* (RPl)

metropolitan /'metrə'pɑːlətn̩ ‖ ,metrə'pɒlɪtən/ *adj* (frml) metropolitano

mettle /'metl̩/ *n* [U] temple *m*; ***to be on one's ~*** estar* dispuesto a dar lo mejor de sí

mew /mjuː/ *vi* maullar*

Mexican¹ /'meksɪkən/ *adj* mexicano, mejicano

Mexican² *n* mexicano, -na *m,f*, mejicano, -na *m,f*

Mexico /'meksɪkəʊ/ *n* México *m*, Méjico *m*

Mexico City *n* (ciudad *f* de) México *m or* Méjico *m*

mezzanine /'mezəni:n/ *n* **(a)** ~ **(floor)** entresuelo *m*, mezzanine *f or m* (AmL) **(b)** (AmE Theat) platea *f* alta

mi /mi:/ *n* (Mus) mi *m*

MI = **Michigan**

miaow /mi'aʊ/ *n/vi* ⇒ MEOW[1,2]

mice /maɪs/ *pl of* MOUSE

Mich = **Michigan**

microbe /'maɪkrəʊb/ *n* microbio *m*

microchip /'maɪkrəʊtʃɪp/ *n* (micro)chip *m*, pastilla *f* de silicio

microfilm /'maɪkrəʊfɪlm/ *n* [C U] microfilm *m*, microfilme *m*

microphone /'maɪkrəfəʊn/ *n* micrófono *m*

microscope /'maɪkrəskəʊp/ *n* microscopio *m*

microscopic /'maɪkrə'skɑ:pɪk ‖ ˌmaɪkrə'skɒpɪk/ *adj* microscópico, al microscopio

microwave /'maɪkrəʊweɪv, 'maɪkrə-/ *n* ~ **(oven)** (horno *m* de) microondas *m*

mid- /mɪd/ *pref*: **in ~January** a mediados de enero; **~morning** a media mañana; **she was in her ~forties** tenía alrededor de 45 años

midair /'mɪd'er ‖ ˌmɪd'eə(r)/ *n*: **in ~** en el aire

midday /'mɪd'deɪ/ ▶ **884** *n* mediodía *m*

middle¹ /'mɪdl/ *n* **1** (of object, place — center) centro *m*, medio *m*; (— half-way line) mitad *f*; **in the ~ of nowhere** quién sabe dónde, en el quinto pino (Esp fam), donde el diablo perdió el poncho (AmS fam) **2** (of period, activity): **in the ~ of the week/January** a mediados de semana/de enero; **it's the ~ of winter** estamos en pleno invierno; **in the ~ of the night** en la mitad de la noche; **I'm in the ~ of a really exciting novel at the moment** en este momento estoy leyendo una novela muy interesante; **I'm in the ~ of cooking dinner** estoy preparando la cena **3** (waist) cintura *f*

middle² *adj* (*before n*): **the ~ house of the three** de las tres, la casa de en medio *or* del medio

middle: **~-aged** /'mɪdl'eɪdʒd/ *adj* de mediana edad; **M~ Ages** *pl n* **the M~ Ages** la Edad Media; **~ class** *n* [C U] (*often pl*) clase *f* media; **~-class** /'mɪdl'klæs ‖ ˌmɪdl'klɑ:s/ *adj* de clase media; **~-distance** /'mɪdl'dɪstəns/ *adj* (*before n*) ‹*running/race*› de medio fondo; **~-distance runner** mediofondista *mf*; **M~ East** *n* **the M~ East** el Oriente Medio, el Medio Oriente; **~man** /'mɪdlmæn/ *n* (*pl* **-men** /-men/) intermediario *m*; **~ management** *n* mandos *mpl* (inter)medios; **~ name** *n* segundo nombre *m*; **~-of-the-road** /'mɪdləvðə'rəʊd/ *adj* ‹*politician/views*› moderado; ‹*artist*› del montón; **~ school** *n* (in US) *colegio para niños de 12 a 14 años*; (in UK) *colegio para niños de 9 a 13 años*

midge /mɪdʒ/ *n*: *especie de mosquito pequeño*

midget /'mɪdʒət ‖ 'mɪdʒɪt/ *n* enano, -na *m,f* (*de proporciones normales*)

midnight /'mɪdnaɪt/ ▶ **884** *n* medianoche *f*

midst /mɪdst/ *n*: **in the ~ of sth** en medio de algo; **in our ~** entre nosotros

midsummer /'mɪd'sʌmər ‖ ˌmɪd'sʌmə(r)/ *n* [U] pleno verano *m*; **M~'s Day** el solsticio estival *or* vernal; (in the Northern hemisphere) el día de San Juan

midtown /'mɪd'taʊn/ *n* casco *m*, centro *m*; (*before n*) ‹*apartment/hotel*› de la periferia del centro

midway /'mɪd'weɪ/ *adv* ‹*stop*› a mitad de camino; **~ through the morning** a media mañana

midweek¹ /'mɪd'wi:k/ *n*: **around ~** a mediados de semana; (*before n*) ‹*concert/flight*› de entre semana

midweek² *adv* entre semana

Midwest /'mɪd'west/ *n* **the ~** *la región central de los EEUU*

midwife /'mɪdwaɪf/ *n* (*pl* **-wives**) partera *f*

midwinter /'mɪd'wɪntər ‖ ˌmɪd'wɪntə(r)/ *n* [U] pleno invierno *m*

might¹ /maɪt/ *v mod* **1** *past of* MAY **2 (a)** (asking permission) (esp BrE) podría (*or* podríamos *etc*); **~ I make a suggestion?** si se me permite (hacer) una sugerencia ... **(b)** (in suggestions, expressing annoyance, regret) poder*; **you ~ at least listen** al menos podrías escuchar **3** (indicating possibility) [*La posibilidad que indica* MIGHT *es más remota que la que expresan* MAY *o* COULD]: **somebody ~ have found it** pudiera ser que alguien lo hubiera encontrado; **it ~ (well) have been disastrous if the police hadn't arrived** podría haber sido catastrófico si no hubiera llegado la policía **4** (indicating sth is natural): **he rang to apologize — and well he ~!** llamó para pedir perdón — ¡era lo menos que podía hacer! **5** (conceding): **the house ~ not be big, but** ... la casa no será grande pero ...

might² *n* [U] poder *m*

mighty¹ /'maɪti/ *adj* **-tier, -tiest (a)** (powerful) ‹*empire/ruler*› poderoso; ‹*kick/blow*› fortísimo **(b)** (imposing) ‹*ocean/river*› imponente

mighty² *adv* (colloq) (*as intensifier*) muy

migraine /'maɪgreɪn ‖ 'mi:greɪn, 'maɪ-/ *n* [C U] jaqueca *f*, migraña *f*

migrant¹ /'maɪgrənt/ *n* **(a)** (Zool) (species) especie *f* migratoria; (bird) ave *f*‡ migratoria **(b)** (person) trabajador, -dora *m,f* itinerante

migrant² *adj* **(a)** (Zool) migratorio **(b)** (*before n*) ‹*worker*› itinerante; (foreign) extranjero

migrate /'maɪgreɪt ‖ maɪ'greɪt/ *vi* emigrar

migration /maɪ'greɪʃən/ *n* [U C] migración *f*

mike /maɪk/ *n* (colloq) micro *m* (fam)

milage *n* ⇒ MILEAGE

mild /maɪld/ *adj* **-er, -est 1 (a)** (gentle) ‹*person*› afable; ‹*manner/criticism*› suave **(b)** (not serious or potent) ‹*attack/form*› ligero, leve; ‹*discomfort*› ligero **2** ‹*climate*› templado; ‹*winter*› no muy frío **3** ‹*cheese/tobacco/detergent/sedative*› suave

mildew /'mɪldu: ‖ 'mɪldju:/ *n* [U] (on plants) mildeu *m*, mildiu *m*; (on wall, fabric) moho *m*

mildly /maɪldli/ *adv* **(a)** (gently) ‹*rebuke*› suavemente; **to put it ~** por no decir algo peor **(b)** (slightly) ligeramente

mile /maɪl/ ▶ **681** *n* milla *f* (*1.609 metros*); **that's ~s away from here** (colloq) eso está lejísimos de aquí; ***it sticks*** *o* ***stands out a ~*** se ve a la legua

mileage /'maɪlɪdʒ/ *n* **1** (Auto) [C U] distancia *f* recorrida (*en millas*), ≈ kilometraje *m* **2** [U] (advantage, profit): **they want to extract maximum ~ from the Pope's visit** quieren explotar al máximo la visita del Papa

mileometer /maɪ'lɑːmətər ‖ maɪ'lɒmɪtə(r)/ *n* (BrE) ≈ cuentakilómetros *m*

milestone /'maɪlstəʊn/ *n* (on road) mojón *m*; (significant event) hito *m*, jalón *m*

militant[1] /'mɪlɪtənt/ *adj* militante

militant[2] *n* militante *mf*

military[1] /'mɪləteri ‖ 'mɪlɪtri/ *adj* militar; **~ academy** (in US) escuela *f* militar; **to do ~ service** hacer* el servicio militar

military[2] *n* **the ~** los militares

military police *n* [U] policía *f* militar

militia /mə'lɪʃə ‖ mɪ'lɪʃə/ *n* (+ *sing or pl vb*) milicia *f*

milk[1] /mɪlk/ *n* [U] **(a)** leche *f*; (*before n*) ‹*production/bottle*› de leche; ‹*product*› lácteo; **~ chocolate** chocolate *m* con leche **(b)** (lotion) (BrE) leche *f*

milk[2] *vt* **(a)** ‹*cow/herd*› ordeñar **(b)** (exploit) explotar

milk: **~man** /'mɪlkmən/ *n* (*pl* **-men** /-mən/) lechero *m*; **~ shake** *n* batido *m*, (leche *f*) malteada *f* (AmL), licuado *m* con leche (AmL)

milky /'mɪlki/ *adj* **-kier, -kiest** lechoso; ‹*coffee/tea*› con mucha leche

Milky Way *n* **the ~ ~** la Vía Láctea

mill[1] /mɪl/ *n* **1 (a)** (building, machine) molino *m* **(b)** (for pepper etc) molinillo *m* **2** (*cotton ~*) fábrica *f* de tejidos de algodón

mill[2] *vt* ‹*flour*› moler*

• **mill about**, **mill around** [*v* + *adv*] «*crowd*» dar* vueltas

millennium /mɪ'leniəm/ *n* (*pl* **-niums** *or* **-nia** /-niə/) milenio *m*

miller /'mɪlər ‖ 'mɪlə(r)/ *n* molinero, -ra *m,f*

milligram /'mɪləgræm ‖ 'mɪlɪgræm/ ▶**322** *n* miligramo *m*

millimeter, (BrE) **millimetre** /'mɪləˌmiːtər ‖ 'mɪlɪmiːtə(r)/ ▶**681** *n* milímetro *m*

milliner /'mɪlənər ‖ 'mɪlɪnə(r)/ *n* sombrerero, -ra *m,f* de señoras

million /'mɪljən/ ▶**451**, **774** *n* millón *m*; **a ~ people** un millón de personas

millionaire /'mɪljə'ner ‖ ˌmɪljə'neə(r)/ *n* millonario, -ria *m,f*

milometer /maɪ'lɑːmətər ‖ maɪ'lɒmɪtə(r)/ *n* ⇒ MILEOMETER

mime[1] /maɪm/ *n* **(a)** [U] (technique) mímica *f* **(b)** [C] **~ (artist)** mimo *mf* **(c)** [C] (performance) pantomima *f*

mime[2] *vt* imitar, hacer* la mímica de ■ **~** *vi* hacer* la mímica

mimic /'mɪmɪk/ *vt* **-ck-** imitar

mince[1] /mɪns/ *vt* ‹*onions*› picar* (*en trozos menudos*); ‹*meat*› moler* *or* (Esp, RPl) picar*; ***not to ~ (one's) words*** no andar(se)* con rodeos ■ **~** *vi* caminar con afectación

mince[2] *n* [U] (BrE) carne *f* molida *or* (Esp, RPl) picada

mincemeat /'mɪnsmiːt/ *n* [U] *picadillo de frutos secos, grasa y especias usado en pastelería*

mind[1] /maɪnd/ *n* **1 (a)** (Psych) mente *f*; **to bear** *o* **keep sth/sb in ~** tener* algo/a algn en cuenta; **to bring** *o* **call sth to ~** recordar(le)* algo (a algn); **to have sth/sb in ~** tener* algo/a algn en mente; **with that in ~** pensando en eso; **what's on your ~?** ¿qué es lo que te preocupa?; **that put my ~ at rest** con eso me tranquilicé; **put it out of your ~!** ¡no pienses más en eso!; **I can't get him/the thought out of my ~** no puedo quitármelo de la cabeza; ***to read sb's ~*** adivinarle *or* leerle* el pensamiento a algn **(b)** (mentality) mentalidad *f* **2** (attention): **my ~ was on other things** tenía la cabeza en otras cosas; **he needs something to take his ~ off it** necesita algo que lo distraiga **3 (a)** (opinion): **to change one's ~** cambiar de opinión; **to make up one's ~** decidirse; **to my ~** a mi parecer **(b)** (will, intention): **he has a ~ of his own** (he is obstinate) es muy empecinado; (he knows his own mind) sabe muy bien lo que quiere; **I've a good ~ to complain to the manager** tengo ganas de ir a quejarme al gerente **4** (mental faculties) juicio *m*, razón *f*; **to be/go out of one's ~** estar*/volverse* loco

mind[2] *vt* **1** (look after) ‹*children*› cuidar, cuidar de; ‹*seat/place*› guardar; ‹*shop/office*› atender* **2** (*usu in imperative*) **(a)** (be careful about): **~ your head!** ¡ojo *or* cuidado con la cabeza!; **~ (that) you don't forget!** procura no olvidarte **(b)** (concern oneself about) preocuparse por; **never ~ him!** ¡no le hagas caso! **3** (object to) (*usu neg or interrog*): **I don't ~ the noise** no me molesta *or* no me importa el ruido; **I don't ~ him, but I can't stand her** él no me disgusta, pero a ella no la soporto; **I don't ~ what you do** me da igual lo que hagas; **would you ~ waiting?** ¿le importaría esperar? ■ **~** *vi* **1** (*in imperative*) (concern oneself) **never ~** no importa, no te preocupes (*or* no se preocupen *etc*); **never you ~!** ¡(a ti) qué te importa! **2** (object) (*usu neg or interrog*): **I don't ~** me da igual; **do you ~ if I smoke? — yes, I do ~!** ¿te importa si fumo? — ¡sí que me importa!

-minded /'maɪndəd ‖ 'maɪndɪd/ *suff*: **business~** con mentalidad para los negocios; **liberal~** liberal

mindless /'maɪndləs ‖ 'maɪndlɪs/ *adj* ‹*activity*› mecánico; ‹*violence/obedience*› ciego

mine[1] /maɪn/ *n* **1** (Min) mina *f*; ***to be a ~ of information*** ser* una mina de información **2** (Mil) mina *f*

mine[2] *pron*

> ■ **Note** The translation *mío* reflects the gender and number of the noun it is standing for; *mine* is translated by *el mío*, *la mía*, *los míos*, *las mías*, depending on what is being referred to.

(*sing*) mío, mía; (*pl*) míos, mías; **~ is here** el mío/la mía está aquí; **a friend of ~** un amigo mío; **it's a hobby of ~** es uno de mis hobbies

mine[3] *vt* **1** (Min) ‹*gold/coal*› extraer* **2** (Mil) minar

minefield /'maɪnfiːld/ *n* campo *m* minado

miner /'maɪnər ‖ 'maɪnə(r)/ *n* minero, -ra *m,f*

mineral /'mɪnərəl/ *n* mineral *m*

mineral water *n* [U] agua *f*‡ mineral

mingle /'mɪŋgəl/ *vi* **(a)** «*people*» mezclarse; (at a party etc) circular **(b)** «*liquids*» mezclarse; «*sounds*» fundirse ■ ~ *vt* **to ~ sth WITH sth** mezclar algo CON algo

miniature¹ /'mɪnɪtʃʊr ‖ 'mɪnɪtʃə(r)/ *n* miniatura *f*

miniature² *adj* (*before n*) ‹*portrait*› en miniatura; ‹*poodle*› enano

minibus /'mɪnibʌs/ *n* microbús *m*, micro *m*

minicab /'mɪnikæb/ *n* (BrE) taxi *m* (*que se pide por teléfono*)

minim /'mɪnəm ‖ 'mɪnɪm/ *n* (BrE) blanca *f*

minimal /'mɪnəməl ‖ 'mɪnɪməl/ *adj* mínimo

minimize /'mɪnəmaɪz ‖ 'mɪnɪmaɪz/ *vt* ‹*risk/cost*› reducir* (al mínimo)

minimum¹ /'mɪnəməm ‖ 'mɪnɪməm/ *n* mínimo *m*

minimum² *adj* (*before n*) mínimo

mining /'maɪnɪŋ/ *n* [U] minería *f*; (*before n*) ‹*company/town*› minero

miniskirt /'mɪniskɜːrt ‖ 'mɪniskɜːt/ *n* minifalda *f*

minister¹ /'mɪnəstər ‖ 'mɪnɪstə(r)/ ▶ **603** *n* **1** (Relig) pastor, -tora *m,f* **2** (Pol) ministro, -tra *m,f*, secretario, -ria *m,f* (Méx)

minister² *vi* **to ~ TO sb** cuidar DE algn

ministry /'mɪnəstri ‖ 'mɪnɪstri/ *n* (*pl* **-tries**) (Pol) ministerio *m*, secretaría *f* (Méx)

mink /mɪŋk/ *n* (*pl* **~s** *or* **~**) **(a)** [C] (animal) visón *m* **(b)** [U] (fur) visón *m*

Minn = **Minnesota**

minor¹ /'maɪnər ‖ 'maɪnə(r)/ *adj* **1** (unimportant) ‹*poet/work*› menor; ‹*role*› secundario; ‹*operation*› de poca importancia *or* gravedad **2** (Mus) menor

minor² *n* **1** (Law) menor *mf* (de edad) **2** (AmE Educ) asignatura *f* secundaria

Minorca /mə'nɔːrkə ‖ mɪ'nɔːkə/ *n* Menorca *f*

minority /mə'nɔːrəti ‖ maɪ'nɒrɪti/ *n* (*pl* **-ties**) **(a)** (smaller number) (+ *sing o pl vb*) minoría *f*; (*before n*) ‹*group/vote*› minoritario **(b)** (in US) (Govt) oposición *f*

minor league *n* (in US) (Sport) liga *f* menor

minstrel /'mɪnstrəl/ *n* trovador *m*

mint¹ /mɪnt/ *n* **1** (Bot, Culin) **(a)** [U] (*spear~*) menta *f* (verde) **(b)** [U] (*pepper~*) menta *f*, hierbabuena *f* **(c)** [C] (confection) pastilla *f* de menta **2** [C] (Fin) casa *f* de la moneda

mint² *vt* ‹*coin*› acuñar

mint³ *adj* (*before n*) ‹*coin/stamp*› sin usar; **in ~ condition** en perfecto estado

minus¹ /'maɪnəs/ *n* (*pl* **-nuses** *or* **-nusses**) **(a)** **~ (sign)** (signo *m* de) menos *m* **(b)** (disadvantage) (colloq) desventaja *f*

minus² *adj* **(a)** (disadvantageous) (colloq) (*before n*) **on the ~ side,** ... un factor negativo es que ... **(b)** (negative) (*before n*) ‹*number*› negativo

minus³ *prep* **(a)** (Math) menos ⇒ FOUR¹ **(b)** (without, missing) (colloq) sin

minuscule /'mɪnəskjuːl/ *adj* minúsculo

minute¹ /'mɪnət ‖ 'mɪnɪt/ *n* **1** ▶ **884** **(a)** (unit of time) minuto *m*; (*before n*) **~ hand** minutero *m* **(b)** (short period) minuto *m*, momento *m* **(c)** (instant) minuto *m*; **any ~ (now)** de un momento a otro **2 (a)** (memorandum) acta *f* **(b)** (of meeting): **the ~s** el acta

minute² /maɪ'nuːt ‖ maɪ'njuːt/ *adj* ‹*amount*› mínimo; ‹*object*› diminuto

miracle /'mɪrɪkəl ‖ 'mɪrəkəl/ *n* milagro *m*; (*before n*) ‹*drug/cure*› milagroso

miraculous /mə'rækjələs ‖ mɪ'rækjʊləs/ *adj* milagroso

mirage /mə'rɑːʒ ‖ 'mɪrɑːʒ, mɪ'rɑːʒ/ *n* espejismo *m*

mirror¹ /'mɪrər ‖ 'mɪrə(r)/ *n* espejo *m*; (*driving ~*) (espejo *m*) retrovisor *m*

mirror² *vt* reflejar

mirth /mɜːrθ ‖ mɜːθ/ *n* [U] (liter) regocijo *m* (liter)

misadventure /'mɪsəd'ventʃər ‖ ˌmɪsəd'ventʃə(r)/ *n* desventura *f*

misapprehension /mɪs'æprɪ'hentʃən ‖ ˌmɪsæprɪ'henʃən/ *n* [C U] (frml) malentendido *m*

misappropriate /'mɪsə'prəʊprieɪt/ *vt* malversar

misbehave /'mɪsbɪ'heɪv/ *vi* portarse mal

miscalculation /'mɪskælkjə'leɪʃən ‖ ˌmɪskælkjʊ'leɪʃən/ *n* [C U] error *m* de cálculo

miscarriage /'mɪs'kærɪdʒ/ *n* **1** (Med) aborto *m* espontáneo *or* no provocado; **to have a ~** tener* un aborto **2 a ~ of justice** una injusticia

miscarry /'mɪs'kæri/ *vi* **-ries, -rying, -ried (a)** (Med) abortar (*espontáneamente*), tener* un aborto **(b)** (liter) «*plan*» malograrse (liter)

miscellaneous /'mɪsə'leɪniəs/ *adj* ‹*collection/crowd*› heterogéneo; ‹*assortment*› variado

mischance /'mɪs'tʃæns ‖ ˌmɪs'tʃɑːns/ *n* [U C] infortunio *m*

mischief /'mɪstʃəf ‖ 'mɪstʃɪf/ *n* **(a)** [U] (naughtiness): **to get up to ~** hacer* travesuras **(b)** [U C] (trouble, harm) daño *m*; **to make ~** causar daños

mischievous /'mɪstʃəvəs ‖ 'mɪstʃɪvəs/ *adj* ‹*child*› travieso; ‹*grin*› pícaro

misconception /'mɪskən'sepʃən/ *n* error *m*

misconduct /'mɪs'kɑːndʌkt ‖ ˌmɪs'kɒndʌkt/ *n* [U] (frml) mala conducta *f*

misconstrue /'mɪskən'struː/ *vt* (frml) malinterpretar

misdemeanor, (BrE) **misdemeanour** /'mɪsdɪ'miːnər ‖ ˌmɪsdɪ'miːnə(r)/ *n* (Law) delito *m* menor

miser /'maɪzər ‖ 'maɪzə(r)/ *n* avaro, -ra *m,f*

miserable /'mɪzərəbəl/ *adj* **1 (a)** (in low spirits) abatido **(b)** (depressing) ‹*weather*› deprimente; ‹*prospect*› triste **2 (a)** (mean-spirited) miserable **(b)** (wretched, poor) mísero **(c)** ‹*episode/failure*› lamentable

miserably /'mɪzərəbli/ *adv* **(a)** (unhappily) con abatimiento **(b)** ‹*fail*› de manera lamentable

miserly /'maɪzərli ‖ 'maɪzəli/ *adj* mezquino

misery /'mɪzəri/ *n* [U] sufrimiento *m*; **to make sb's life a ~** amargarle* la vida a algn

misfire /'mɪs'faɪr ‖ ˌmɪs'faɪə(r)/ *vi* «*gun/engine/plan*» fallar

misfit /'mɪsfɪt/ *n*: **a social ~** un inadaptado social

misfortune /mɪs'fɔːrtʃən ‖ ˌmɪs'fɔːtʃən, ˌmɪs'fɔːtʃuːn/ *n* [C U] (frml) desgracia *f*; **to have the ~ to + INF** tener* la desgracia DE + INF

misgiving /mɪs'gɪvɪŋ/ *n* [C U] recelo *m*

misguided /mɪs'gaɪdəd ‖ ,mɪs'gaɪdɪd/ *adj* equivocado

mishandle /mɪs'hændḷ/ *vt* (deal with ineptly) llevar mal

mishap /mɪshæp/ *n* percance *m*

mishear /'mɪs'hɪr ‖ ,mɪs'hɪə(r)/ (*past & past p* **-heard**) *vt/i* entender* mal

misinform /'mɪsṇ'fɔ:rm ‖ ,mɪsɪn'fɔ:m/ *vt* (frml) informar mal, malinformar (CS frml)

misinterpret /'mɪsṇ'tɜ:rprət ‖ ,mɪsɪn'tɜ:prɪt/ *vt* ‹*statement/action*› interpretar mal; (deliberately) tergiversar

misjudge /'mɪs'dʒʌdʒ/ *vt* **(a)** (judge unfairly) juzgar* mal **(b)** (miscalculate) calcular mal

mislay /'mɪs'leɪ/ *vt* (*past & past p* **-laid**) perder* (*momentáneamente*)

mislead /'mɪs'li:d/ *vt* (*past & past p* **-led**) engañar; ‹*court/parliament*› inducir* a error

mismanage /'mɪs'mænɪdʒ/ *vt* ‹*affair*› llevar mal; ‹*company*› administrar mal

misogynist /mɪ'sɑ:dʒənəst ‖ mɪ'sɒdʒmɪst/ *n* misógino *m*

misplace /'mɪs'pleɪs/ *vt* perder* (*momentáneamente*)

misprint /'mɪsprɪnt/ *n* errata *f*

misrepresent /'mɪsreprɪ'zent/ *vt* ‹*event*› deformar; ‹*remarks/views*› tergiversar

miss¹ /mɪs/ *n* **1** ▶603 **Miss** (as title) señorita *f*; **M~ Jane Smith** la señorita Jane Smith; (in correspondence) Sra Jane Smith **2** (failure to hit) fallo *m*; ***to give sth a ~*** (colloq): **I think I'll give swimming a ~ this afternoon** creo que esta tarde no voy a ir a nadar

miss² *vt* **I 1 (a)** (fail to hit): **the bomb ~ed its target** la bomba no cayó en el blanco; **the bullet just ~ed him** la bala le pasó rozando **(b)** (overlook, fail to notice): **you ~ed three mistakes** se te pasaron (por alto) tres errores; **you can't ~ it** lo va a ver enseguida, no tiene pérdida (Esp) **(c)** (fail to hear, understand) no oír*; **he's ~ed the point** no ha entendido **(d)** ‹*chance*› perder* **2** (fail to catch) ‹*bus/flight*› perder*; **sorry, you've just ~ed him** lo siento, acaba de irse **3 (a)** (fail to experience) perderse*; **you didn't ~ much** no te perdiste nada **(b)** (fail to attend) ‹*meeting*› faltar a; ‹*party/show*› perderse*

II (a) (regret absence of) ‹*friend/country/activity*› echar de menos, extrañar (esp AmL) **(b)** (notice absence of) echar en falta; **when did you first ~ the necklace?** ¿cuándo echaste en falta el collar? ■ ~ *vi* «*marksman*» errar* el tiro, fallar; «*bullet*» no dar* en el blanco

• **miss out 1** [*v + o + adv, v + adv + o*] ‹*line/paragraph*› saltarse **2** [*v + adv*] **to ~ out ON sth** perderse* algo

Miss = **Mississippi**

misshapen /mɪs'ʃeɪpən/ *adj* deforme

missile /'mɪsəl ‖ 'mɪsaɪl/ *n* (Mil) misil *m*; (sth thrown) proyectil *m*

missing /'mɪsɪŋ/ *adj*: **the ~ papers** los papeles que faltan; **~ person** desaparecido, -da *m,f*; **to be ~** faltar; **to go ~** (BrE) desaparecer*

mission /'mɪʃən/ *n* misión *f*

missionary /'mɪʃəneri ‖ 'mɪʃənəri/ *n* misionero, -ra *m,f*

misspent /'mɪs'spent/ *adj* (*before n*) ‹*money*› malgastado; ‹*hours*› perdido; **a ~ youth** (set phrase) una juventud disipada

mist /mɪst/ *n* **(a)** ▶920 [U C] (Meteo) neblina *f*; **sea ~** bruma *f* **(b)** [U] (condensation) vaho *m* **(c)** [U] (spray) vaporización *f*

• **mist over** [*v + adv*] «*eyes*» empañarse; «*glass/mirror*» empañarse

• **mist up** [*v + adv*] «*glass/mirror*» empañarse

mistake¹ /mə'steɪk ‖ mɪ'steɪk/ *n* error *m*; **to make a ~** cometer un error; **by ~** por equivocación, por error

mistake² *vt* (*past* **-took**; *past p* **-taken**) confundir; **to ~ sth/sb FOR sth/sb** confundir algo/a algn CON algo/algn

mistaken /mə'steɪkən ‖ mɪ'steɪkən/ *adj* ‹*impression/idea*› equivocado; **unless I'm (very) much ~** si no me equivoco

mistletoe /'mɪsəltəʊ/ *n* [U] muérdago *m*

mistook /mɪ'stʊk/ *past of* MISTAKE²

mistreat /'mɪs'tri:t/ *vt* maltratar

mistress /'mɪstrəs ‖ 'mɪstrɪs/ *n* **(a)** (of dog) dueña *f*, ama *f*‡; (of servant) señora *f* **(b)** (lover) amante *f*

mistrust¹ /'mɪs'trʌst/ *vt* desconfiar* de, recelar de

mistrust² *n* [U] desconfianza *f*, recelo *m*

mistrustful /'mɪs'trʌstfəl/ *adj* desconfiado, receloso

misty /'mɪsti/ ▶920 *adj* **-tier, -tiest** ‹*day/morning*› neblinoso; **it's ~** hay neblina; (it's drizzling) (AmE) está lloviznando

misunderstand /'mɪsʌndər'stænd ‖ ,mɪs,ʌndə'stænd/ (*past & past p* **-stood**) *vt* ‹*idea/instructions*› entender* *or* comprender mal; ‹*remark/motives*› malinterpretar; ‹*artist/work*› interpretar mal

misunderstanding /'mɪsʌndər'stændɪŋ ‖ ,mɪs,ʌndə'stændɪŋ/ *n* [U C] malentendido *m*

misunderstood /'mɪsʌndər'stʊd ‖ ,mɪs,ʌndə'stʊd/ *past & past p of* MISUNDERSTAND

misuse¹ /'mɪs'ju:s/ *n* [U] (of word) mal uso *m*; (of power) abuso *m*; (of funds) malversación *f*; (of resources) despilfarro *m*

misuse² /'mɪs'ju:z/ *vt* ‹*language/tool*› utilizar* *or* emplear mal; ‹*resources*› despilfarrar; ‹*funds*› malversar

mite /maɪt/ *n* (Zool) ácaro *m*

miter, (BrE) **mitre** /'maɪtər ‖ 'maɪtə(r)/ *n* mitra *f*

mitigate /'mɪtəgeɪt ‖ 'mɪtɪgeɪt/ *vt* (frml) **(a)** (soften, lessen) mitigar* (frml) **(b) mitigating** *pres p* ‹*factor*› atenuante; **mitigating circumstances** (circunstancias *fpl*) atenuantes *fpl or mpl*

mitre /'maɪtər ‖ 'maɪtə(r)/ *n* (BrE) ⇒ MITER

mitt /mɪt/ *n* **(a)** (mitten) mitón *m* **(b)** (in baseball) manopla *f*, guante *m* (de béisbol)

mitten /'mɪtṇ/ *n* mitón *m*

mix¹ /mɪks/ *n* **(a)** (mixture, ingredients) mezcla *f*; **cake ~** *preparado comercial para hacer pasteles* **(b)** (Audio) mezcla *f*

mix² *vt* **(a)** ‹*ingredients/paint*› mezclar; ‹*cocktail*› preparar **(b)** (Audio) mezclar ■ ~ *vi* **(a)** (combine) «*substances*» mezclarse **(b)** (go together) «*foods/colors*» combinar (bien) **(c)** (socially): **she doesn't ~ well at parties** le cuesta entablar conversación con la gente en una reunión; **to ~ WITH sb** tratarse CON algn

• **mix up** I [*v + o + adv, v + adv + o*] **1** (throw into confusion) desordenar **2** (confuse) confundir
II (*usu pass*) **(a)** (involve) **to get ~ed up IN sth** meterse EN algo **(b)** (confuse): **to get ~ed up** confundirse

mixed /mɪkst/ *adj* **(a)** (various) mezclado; **~ spice** mezcla *f* de especias **(b)** (male and female) ‹*sauna/bathing*› mixto **(c)** (ambivalent) ‹*fortunes*› desigual; **I have ~ feelings about it** no sé muy bien qué pensar sobre el asunto

mixer /ˈmɪksər ‖ ˈmɪksə(r)/ *n* **(a)** [C] (Culin) batidora *f* **(b)** [C] (Audio, Cin, TV) (person) operador, -dora *m,f* de sonido; (machine) mezcladora *f* **(c)** [C] (sociable person) persona *f* sociable **(d)** [C] (dance) (AmE) baile *m* **(e)** [U C] (drink) refresco *m* (*para mezclar con alcohol*)

mixing bowl /ˈmɪksɪŋ/ *n* bol *m* (*grande, para mezclar ingredientes*)

mixture /ˈmɪkstʃər ‖ ˈmɪkstʃə(r)/ *n* [C U] mezcla *f*

mix-up /ˈmɪksʌp/ *n* (colloq) lío *m* (fam)

mm ▶ 681 (= **millimeter(s)** *o* (BrE) **millimetre(s)**) mm.

MN = **Minnesota**

MO = **Missouri**

moan¹ /məʊn/ *vi* **(a)** (make sound) «*person/wind*» gemir* **(b)** (complain) (pej) **to ~ (ABOUT sth)** quejarse (DE algo)

moan² *n* **(a)** (sound) gemido *m* **(b)** (complaint) (colloq) (*no pl*) queja *f*

moat /məʊt/ *n* foso *m*

mob¹ /mɑːb ‖ mɒb/ *n* turba *f*; (*before n*) **~ rule** la ley de la calle

mob² *vt* **-bb-** atacar* en grupo

mobile¹ /ˈməʊbəl ‖ ˈməʊbaɪl/ *adj* **(a)** ‹*library/shop*› ambulante **(b)** (able to move): **we try and get the patient ~ as soon as possible** tratamos de que el paciente recupere su movilidad lo más pronto posible

mobile² *n* móvil *m*

mobile: **~ home** *n* trailer *m* (AmL), caravana *f* fija (Esp); **~ phone** *n* (teléfono *m*) celular *m* (AmL), (teléfono *m*) móvil *m* (Esp)

mobilize /ˈməʊbəlaɪz ‖ ˈməʊbɪlaɪz/ *vt* movilizar*

mock¹ /mɑːk ‖ mɒk/ *vt* burlarse de

mock² *adj* (*before n*) ‹*examination/interview*› de práctica; ‹*anger/outrage*› fingido

mockery /ˈmɑːkəri ‖ ˈmɒkəri/ *n* **(a)** [U] (ridicule) burla *f* **(b)** (travesty) (*no pl*) farsa *f*; **to make a ~ of sth** ridiculizar* algo

mocking /ˈmɑːkɪŋ ‖ ˈmɒkɪŋ/ *adj* burlón

mod cons /ˈmɑːdˈkɑːnz ‖ ˌmɒdˈkɒnz/ *pl n* (= **modern conveniences**) (BrE colloq & journ) comodidades *fpl*

mode /məʊd/ *n* **1 (a)** (means) medio *m*; (kind) modo *m* **(b)** (operating method) (Comput, Tech) modalidad *f* **2** (Math) modo *m* **3** (Clothing) moda *f*

model¹ /ˈmɑːdl̩ ‖ ˈmɒdl̩/ *n* **1** (reproduction) maqueta *f*, modelo *m* **2** (paragon, example) modelo *m* **3** (design) modelo *m* **4** (person) modelo *mf*

model², (BrE) **-ll-** *vt* **1** ‹*clay/shape*› modelar **2** (base): **their education system was ~ed on that of France** su sistema educativo se inspiró en el francés; **to ~ oneself on sb** tomar a algn como modelo **3** ‹*garment*›: **she ~s sportswear** es modelo de ropa sport

model³ *adj* (*before n, no comp*) **1** (miniature) ‹*railway/village*› en miniatura **2** (ideal) ‹*citizen/husband/pupil*› modelo *adj inv*; ‹*answer*› tipo *adj inv*

modem /ˈməʊdem/ *n* módem *m*

moderate¹ /ˈmɑːdərət ‖ ˈmɒdərət/ *adj* moderado

moderate² /ˈmɑːdəreɪt ‖ ˈmɒdəreɪt/ *vt* moderar

moderate³ /ˈmɑːdərət ‖ ˈmɒdərət/ *n* moderado, -da *m,f*

moderation /ˈmɑːdəˈreɪʃən ‖ ˌmɒdəˈreɪʃən/ *n* [U] moderación *f*; **drinking is not harmful, in ~** beber no es nocivo, si se hace con moderación

modern /ˈmɑːdərn ‖ ˈmɒdn̩/ *adj* moderno

modernize /ˈmɑːdərnaɪz ‖ ˈmɒdənaɪz/ *vt* modernizar*

modest /ˈmɑːdəst ‖ ˈmɒdɪst/ *adj* **(a)** (not boastful) ‹*person/remark*› modesto **(b)** ‹*income/gift*› modesto; ‹*improvement/success*› moderado **(c)** (chaste) pudoroso

modesty /ˈmɑːdəsti ‖ ˈmɒdɪsti/ *n* [U] **(a)** (absence of conceit) modestia *f* **(b)** (propriety) recato *m*, pudor *m*

modicum /ˈmɑːdɪkəm ‖ ˈmɒdɪkəm/ *n* (*no pl*) (frml) **a ~ OF sth** un atisbo DE algo (frml), un mínimo DE algo

modification /ˈmɑːdəfəˈkeɪʃən ‖ ˌmɒdɪfɪˈkeɪʃən/ *n* [C U] modificación *f*

modify /ˈmɑːdəfaɪ ‖ ˈmɒdɪfaɪ/ *vt* **-fies, -fying, -fied** modificar*

modulate /ˈmɑːdʒəleɪt ‖ ˈmɒdjʊleɪt/ *vt* modular

modulation /ˈmɑːdʒəˈleɪʃən ‖ ˌmɒdjʊˈleɪʃən/ *n* modulación *f*; **frequency ~** frecuencia *f* modulada

module /ˈmɑːdʒuːl ‖ ˈmɒdjuːl/ *n* módulo *m*

Mohammed /məʊˈhæməd ‖ məʊˈhæmɪd/ *n* Mahoma

moist /mɔɪst/ *adj* ‹*climate/soil*› húmedo; ‹*cake*› no seco

moisten /ˈmɔɪsn̩/ *vt* humedecer*

moisture /ˈmɔɪstʃər ‖ ˈmɔɪstʃə(r)/ *n* [U] humedad *f*

moisturize /ˈmɔɪstʃəraɪz/ *vt* hidratar

moisturizer /ˈmɔɪstʃəraɪzər ‖ ˈmɔɪstʃəraɪzə(r)/, **moisturizing cream** /ˈmɔɪstʃəraɪzɪŋ/ *n* [U C] crema *f* hidratante

molar /ˈməʊlər ‖ ˈməʊlə(r)/ *n* muela *f*

molasses /məˈlæsəz ‖ məˈlæsɪz/ *n* [U] (+ *sing vb*) melaza *f*

mold¹, (BrE) **mould** /məʊld/ *n* **1 (a)** [C] (hollow vessel) molde *m* **(b)** [C U] (dish) timbal *m* **2** [U C] (fungus) moho *m*

mold², (BrE) **mould** *vt* ‹*steel/plastic*› moldear; ‹*character/attitudes*› formar

Moldavia /mɑːl'deɪvjə ‖ mɒl'deɪviə/ *n* Moldavia *f*

Moldova /mɑːl'dəʊvə ‖ mɒl'dəʊvə/ *n* Moldova *f*

moldy, (BrE) **mouldy** /'məʊldi/ *adj* mohoso; **to become** *o* (BrE) **go ~** enmohecerse*

mole /məʊl/ *n* **1** (Zool) topo *m* **2** (on skin) lunar *m*

molecule /'mɑːlɪkjuːl ‖ 'mɒlɪkjuːl/ *n* molécula *f*

molest /mə'lest/ *vt* **(a)** (sexually) abusar (sexualmente) de **(b)** (harass) importunar

mollusk, **mollusc** /'mɑːləsk ‖ 'mɒləsk/ *n* molusco *m*

mollycoddle /'mɑːlikɑːdḷ ‖ 'mɒlɪkɒdḷ/ *vt* (colloq & pej) mimar

molt, (BrE) **moult** /məʊlt/ *vi* «*snake*» mudar de piel; «*bird*» mudar de plumas; «*dog/cat*» pelechar, mudar de pelo

molten /'məʊltən/ *adj* ‹*rock/metal*› fundido; ‹*lava*› líquido

mom /mɑːm ‖ mɒm/ *n* (AmE colloq) mamá *f* (fam)

moment /'məʊmənt/ *n* momento *m*; **at the ~** en este momento; **for the ~** de momento; ***to have one's ~s*** tener* sus (*or* mis *etc*) buenos momentos

momentary /'məʊmənteri ‖ 'məʊməntri/ *adj* ‹*feeling/glimpse*› momentáneo

momentous /məʊ'mentəs/ *adj* ‹*occasion/decision*› trascendental; ‹*day*› memorable

momentum /məʊ'mentəm/ *n* [U C] (*pl* **-ta** /-tə/ *or* **-tums**) **(a)** (Phys) momento *m* **(b)** (speed) velocidad *f*; **to gather ~** ir* adquiriendo velocidad

momma /'mɑːmə ‖ 'mɒmə/ *n* (AmE) (colloq) mamá *f* (fam)

mommy /'mɑːmi ‖ 'mɒmi/ *n* (*pl* **-mies**) (AmE colloq) mami *f* (fam), mamita *f* (fam)

Monaco /'mɑːnəkəʊ, mə'nɑː- ‖ 'mɒnəkəʊ/ *n* Mónaco *m*

monarch /'mɑːnərk ‖ 'mɒnək/ *n* monarca *mf*

monarchist /'mɑːnərkəst ‖ 'mɒnəkɪst/ *n* monárquico, -ca *m,f*

monarchy /'mɑːnərki ‖ 'mɒnəki/ *n* [C U] monarquía *f*

monastery /'mɑːnəsteri ‖ 'mɒnəstri/ *n* (*pl* **-ries**) monasterio *m*

Monday /'mʌndeɪ, -di/ **▶540** *n* **1** (day) lunes *m*; **on ~** el lunes; **next ~** el próximo lunes *or* el lunes que viene; **(on) ~s** los lunes; **the ~ after next** el lunes que viene no, el siguiente; (*before n*) **~ afternoon/morning** el lunes por la tarde/mañana, la tarde/mañana del lunes **2 Mondays** (*as adv*) los lunes

monetarism /'mɑːnətərɪzəm ‖ 'mʌnɪtərɪzəm/ *n* [U] monetarismo *m*

monetary /'mɑːnəteri ‖ 'mʌnɪtəri/ *adj* monetario

money /'mʌni/ *n* [U] (*pl* **-nies** *or* **-neys**) dinero *m*; (currency) moneda *f*, dinero *m*; **their European operation is making a lot of ~** su operación europea está dando mucho; **to put ~ into sth** invertir* dinero en algo; **~ *talks*** poderoso caballero es don Dinero

money: **~ belt** *n* faltriquera *f*; **~box** *n* alcancía *f* (AmL), hucha *f* (Esp); **~lender** *n* prestamista *mf*; **~-making** *adj* lucrativo; **~ order** *n* ≈ giro *m* postal; **~ supply** *n* **the ~ supply** la masa monetaria

Mongolia /mɑːn'gəʊliə ‖ mɒŋ'gəʊliə/ *n* Mongolia *f*

Mongolian /mɑːn'gəʊliən ‖ mɒŋ'gəʊliən/ *adj* mongol

mongrel /'mɑːŋgrəl ‖ 'mʌŋgrəl/ *n*: *perro mestizo*, chucho, -cha *m,f* (fam), gozque *mf* (Col), quiltro, -tra *m,f* (Chi fam)

monitor¹ /'mɑːnətər ‖ 'mɒnɪtə(r)/ *n* **1 (a)** (screen) monitor *m* **(b)** (for measuring) monitor *m* **2** (listener) escucha *mf* **3** (Educ) encargado, -da *m,f*, monitor, -tora *m,f* (CS)

monitor² *vt* **(a)** ‹*elections*› observar; ‹*process/progress*› seguir*; (esp electronically) monitorizar* **(b)** ‹*radio station*› escuchar

monk /mʌŋk/ *n* monje *m*

monkey /'mʌŋki/ *n* mono, -na *m,f*

monkey wrench *n* llave *f* inglesa; ***to throw a ~ ~ in the works*** *o* ***the machinery*** (AmE) fastidiarlo todo

mono /'mɑːnəʊ ‖ 'mɒnəʊ/ *n* [U] (Audio) monofonía *f*

monochrome /'mɑːnəkrəʊm ‖ 'mɒnəkrəʊm/ *adj* ‹*picture*› monocromático, monocromo

monogamy /mə'nɑːgəmi ‖ mə'nɒgəmi/ *n* [U] monogamía *f*

monologue, (AmE also) **monolog** /'mɑːnəlɔːg ‖ 'mɒnəlɒg/ *n* monólogo *m*

monopolize /mə'nɑːpəlaɪz ‖ mə'nɒpəlaɪz/ *vt* ‹*market/industry*› monopolizar*; ‹*conversation/television*› acaparar

monopoly /mə'nɑːpəli ‖ mə'nɒpəli/ *n* [C U] (*pl* **-lies**) monopolio *m*

monosyllable /'mɑːnəˌsɪləbəl ‖ 'mɒnəsɪləbəl/ *n* monosílabo *m*

monotone /'mɑːnətəʊn ‖ 'mɒnətəʊn/ *n* tono *m* monocorde

monotonous /mə'nɑːtṇəs ‖ mə'nɒtənəs/ *adj* monótono

monotony /mə'nɑːtṇi ‖ mə'nɒtəni/ *n* [U] monotonía *f*

monsoon /mɑːn'suːn ‖ mɒn'suːn/ *n* monzón *m*

monster /'mɑːnstər ‖ 'mɒnstə(r)/ *n* monstruo *m*

monstrous /'mɑːnstrəs ‖ 'mɒnstrəs/ *adj* **(a)** (huge) gigantesco **(b)** (shocking) monstruoso

Mont = **Montana**

month /mʌnθ/ **▶540** *n* mes *m*; **$900 a ~** 900 dólares mensuales *or* por mes *or* al mes; **in a ~'s time** dentro de un mes

monthly¹ /'mʌnθli/ *adj* ‹*journal/event*› mensual; **~ payment** mensualidad *f*, cuota *f* mensual (esp AmL)

monthly² *adv* mensualmente, una vez al *or* por mes

monthly³ *n* (*pl* **-lies**) publicación *f* mensual

monument /'mɑːnjəmənt ‖ 'mɒnjʊmənt/ *n* monumento *m*

monumental /ˈmɑːnjəˈmentl̩ || ˌmɒnjʊˈmentl̩/ *adj* monumental

moo /muː/ *vi* **moos, mooing, mooed** mugir*

mood /muːd/ *n* **1 (a)** (state of mind) humor *m*; **to be in a good/bad ~** estar* de buen/de mal humor; **I'm not in the ~** no tengo ganas; **I'm not in the ~ for dancing** no tengo ganas de bailar **(b)** (atmosphere) atmósfera *f* **2** (Ling) modo *m*

moody /ˈmuːdi/ *adj* **-dier, -diest (a)** (irritable, sulky) de mal humor; (gloomy) deprimido **(b)** (changeable) ‹*person*› temperamental

moon /muːn/ *n* luna *f*; ***once in a blue ~*** muy de vez en cuando

moonbeam /ˈmuːnbiːm/ *n* rayo *m* de luna

moonlight¹ /ˈmuːnlaɪt/ *n* [U] luz *f* de la luna

moonlight² *vi* tener* un segundo empleo; **he ~s as a cab driver** trabaja además como taxista

moon: **~lighting** *n* [U] pluriempleo *m*; **~lit** *adj* iluminado por la luna

moor¹ /mʊr || mʊə(r), mɔː(r)/ *n* **(a)** (boggy area) llanura *f* anegadiza **(b)** (high exposed area) (esp BrE) páramo *m*; (covered with heather) brezal *m*

moor² *vt* amarrar ■ ~ *vi* echar amarras

mooring /ˈmʊrɪŋ || ˈmʊərɪŋ, ˈmɔːrɪŋ/ *n* **(a)** (place) amarradero *m* **(b) moorings** *pl* (ropes) amarras *fpl*

moose /muːs/ *n* (*pl* **moose**) alce *m* americano *or* de América

mop¹ /mɑːp || mɒp/ *n* **(a)** (for floor) trapeador *m* (AmL), fregona *f* (Esp) **(b) ~ of hair** mata *f* de pelo

mop² **-pp-** *vt* ‹*floor/room*› limpiar, trapear (AmL), pasarle la fregona a (Esp); **to ~ one's brow** secarse* la frente

• **mop up** [*v* + *o* + *adv*, *v* + *adv* + *o*] ‹*water*› secar*; ‹*mess*› limpiar

mope /məʊp/ *vi* (colloq) estar* deprimido

moped /ˈməʊped/ *n* ciclomotor *m*

moral¹ /ˈmɔːrəl || ˈmɒrəl/ *adj* moral

moral² *n* **1** (message) moraleja *f* **2 morals** *pl* (principles) moralidad *f*

morale /məˈræl || məˈrɑːl/ *n* [U] moral *f*

morality /məˈræləti/ *n* [U C] (*pl* **-ties**) moralidad *f*

morally /ˈmɔːrəli || ˈmɒrəli/ *adv* moralmente

morbid /ˈmɔːrbəd || ˈmɔːbɪd/ *adj* morboso

more¹ /mɔːr || mɔː(r)/ *adj* más; **there'll be no ~ talking** se acabó la charla; **how much ~ flour?** ¿cuánta harina más?; **for ~ information call 387351** para mayor información llamar al 38-73-51; **~ and ~ people** cada vez más gente; **I eat ~ meat than you** yo como más carne que tú

more² *pron* más; **let's say no ~ about it** no hablemos más del asunto; **the ~ she eats, the thinner she gets** cuanto más come, más adelgaza; **you eat ~ than me** tú comes más que yo

more³ *adv* más; **you watch television ~ than I do** tú ves más televisión que yo; **~ or less** más o menos; **could you please speak ~ clearly?** ¿podría hacer el favor de hablar más claro?; **~ often** con más frecuencia; **I don't eat meat any ~** ya no como carne

moreover /mɔːrˈəʊvər || mɔːˈrəʊvə(r)/ *adv* (frml) (*as linker*) además

morgue /mɔːrg || mɔːg/ *n* depósito *m* de cadáveres, morgue *f* (AmL)

Mormon /ˈmɔːrmən || ˈmɔːmən/ *n* mormón, -mona *m,f*

morning /ˈmɔːrnɪŋ || ˈmɔːnɪŋ/ ▶ **884** *n* **1** (time of day) mañana *f*; **yesterday/tomorrow ~** ayer/mañana por la mañana *or* (AmL tb) en la mañana *or* (RPl tb) a la mañana *or* de mañana; **(good) ~!** ¡buenos días!, ¡buen día! (RPl) **2 mornings** (*as adv*) por las mañanas, en las mañanas (AmL), a la *or* de mañana (RPl)

morning: **~ coat** *n* chaqué *m*, frac *m*; **~ sickness** *n* [U] náuseas *fpl* (matinales) (*del embarazo*)

Moroccan /məˈrɑːkən || məˈrɒkən/ *adj* marroquí

Morocco /məˈrɑːkəʊ || məˈrɒkəʊ/ *n* Marruecos *m*

moron /ˈmɔːrɑːn || ˈmɔːrɒn/ *n* (colloq & pej) imbécil *mf*, tarado, -da *m,f* (fam)

morose /məˈrəʊs/ *adj* taciturno

morphine /ˈmɔːrfiːn || ˈmɔːfiːn/ *n* [U] morfina *f*

Morse /mɔːrs || mɔːs/ *n* [U] morse *m*; **in ~ (code)** en (código) morse

morsel /ˈmɔːrsəl || ˈmɔːsəl/ *n* bocado *m*

mortal¹ /ˈmɔːrtl̩ || ˈmɔːtl̩/ *adj* **(a)** (subject to death) mortal **(b)** (liter) ‹*blow/injury/sin*› mortal

mortal² *n* mortal *mf*

mortality /mɔːrˈtæləti || mɔːˈtæləti/ *n* [U] **(a)** (death rate) mortalidad *f* **(b)** (loss of life) mortandad *f* **(c)** (condition) mortalidad *f*

mortar /ˈmɔːrtər || ˈmɔːtə(r)/ *n* **1** [U] (cement) argamasa *f*, mortero *m* **2** [C] (weapon) mortero *m* **3** [C] (bowl) mortero *m*, molcajete *m* (Méx)

mortgage¹ /ˈmɔːrgɪdʒ || ˈmɔːgɪdʒ/ *n* (charge) hipoteca *f*; (loan) préstamo *m* hipotecario, hipoteca *f*; **to take out a ~ on a property** hipotecar* una propiedad

mortgage² *vt* hipotecar*

mortician /mɔːrˈtɪʃən || mɔːˈtɪʃən/ *n* (AmE) (employee) *persona que trabaja en una funeraria*; (funeral director) director, -tora *m,f* de pompas fúnebres

mortified /ˈmɔːrtəfaɪd || ˈmɔːtɪfaɪd/ *adj*: **I was ~** me dio mucha vergüenza, me dio mucha pena (AmL exc CS)

mortuary /ˈmɔːrtʃueri || ˈmɔːtjʊəri/ *n* (*pl* **-ries**) depósito *m* de cadáveres, morgue *f* (AmL)

mosaic /məʊˈzeɪɪk/ *n* mosaico *m*

Moscow /ˈmɑːskaʊ || ˈmɒskəʊ/ *n* Moscú *m*

Moslem /ˈmɑːzləm || ˈmɒzləm/ *n/adj* ⇒ MUSLIM[1,2]

mosque /mɑːsk || mɒsk/ *n* mezquita *f*

mosquito /məˈskiːtəʊ || mɒsˈkiːtəʊ/ *n* (*pl* **-toes** *or* **-tos**) mosquito *m*, zancudo *m* (AmL)

moss /mɔːs || mɒs/ *n* [U C] musgo *m*

most¹ /məʊst/ *adj* **(a)** (nearly all) la mayoría de, la mayor parte de; **~ days** casi todos los días **(b)** (*as superl*) más; **who eats (the) ~ meat in your family?** ¿quién es el que come más carne de tu familia?

most² *pron* **(a)** (nearly all) la mayoría, la mayor parte; **I read ~ of it** lo leí casi todo **(b)** (*as superl*): **she ate the ~** fue la que más comió; **at (the) ~**

como máximo; ***to make the ~ of sth*** sacar* el mejor provecho posible de algo **(c)** (people) la mayoría

most³ *adv* **1 (a)** (to greatest extent) más; **I enjoyed the last act ~ of all** el último acto fue el que más me gustó **(b)** (*before adj, adv*) más; **which is the ~ expensive?** ¿cuál es el más caro? **2** (*as intensifier*): **what happened was ~ interesting** lo que sucedió fue de lo más interesante; **~ likely** muy probablemente **3** (almost) (AmE colloq) casi

mostly /'məʊstli/ *adv*: **her friends are ~ students** la mayoría de sus amigos son estudiantes; **the land is ~ flat** el terreno es en su mayor parte llano

motel /məʊ'tel/ *n* motel *m*

moth /mɔːθ ‖ mɒθ/ *n* mariposa *f* de la luz, palomilla *f*; (*clothes ~*) polilla *f*

mother¹ /'mʌðər ‖ 'mʌðə(r)/ *n* madre *f*; (*before n*) **~ country** madre patria *f*

mother² *vt* mimar

motherhood /'mʌðərhʊd ‖ 'mʌðəhʊd/ *n* [U] maternidad *f*

Mothering Sunday /'mʌðərɪŋ/ *n* (BrE) ⇒ MOTHER'S DAY

mother: **~-in-law** *n* (*pl* **~s-in-law**) suegra *f*; **~land** *n* patria *f*

motherly /'mʌðərli ‖ 'mʌðəli/ *adj* maternal

mother: **~-of-pearl** /'mʌðərəv'pɜːrl ‖ ˌmʌðərəv'pɜːl/ *n* [U] nácar *m*, madreperla *f*, concha *f* nácar (Méx), concha *f* de perla (Chi); **M~'s Day** *n* el día de la Madre (*el segundo domingo de mayo en EEUU y el cuarto domingo de Cuaresma en GB*); **M~ Superior** *n* Madre *f* Superiora; **~-to-be** /'mʌðərtə'biː ‖ ˌmʌðətə'biː/ *n* (*pl* **~s-to-be**) futura madre *f*, futura mamá *f*; **~ tongue** *n* lengua *f* materna

motif /məʊ'tiːf/ *n* **(a)** (theme) tema *m* **(b)** (design) motivo *m*

motion¹ /'məʊʃən/ *n* **1 (a)** [U] (movement) movimiento *m*; **to be in ~** estar* en movimiento; **to set** *o* **put sth in ~** ‹*wheel*› poner* algo en movimiento; ‹*project/plan*› poner* algo en marcha **(b)** [C] (action, gesture) gesto *m*; ***to go through the ~s***: **he went through the ~s of interviewing them** los entrevistó por pura fórmula **2** (for vote) moción *f*

motion² *vi*: **she ~ed to her assistant** le hizo una señal a su ayudante; **they ~ed to us to sit down** nos hicieron señas para que nos sentáramos

motionless /'məʊʃənləs ‖ 'məʊʃənlɪs/ *adj* inmóvil

motion picture *n* película *f*

motivate /'məʊtəveɪt ‖ 'məʊtɪveɪt/ *vt* motivar

motivation /ˌməʊtə'veɪʃən ‖ ˌməʊtɪ'veɪʃən/ *n* **(a)** [U] (drive) motivación *f* **(b)** [C] (motive) motivo *m*

motive /'məʊtɪv/ *n* motivo *m*

motley /'mɑːtli ‖ 'mɒtli/ *adj* variopinto

motor¹ /'məʊtər ‖ 'məʊtə(r)/ *n* motor *m*

motor² *adj* (*before n*) **1** (Auto, Mech Eng) ‹*parts*› de automóvil; ‹*mechanic*› de automóviles; **~ show** salón *m* del automóvil; **~ vehicle** (vehículo *m*) automóvil *m* (frml) **2** (Physiol) ‹*neuron/nerve*› motor [*The feminine of* MOTOR *is* MOTRIZ *or* MOTORA]

motor: **~bike** *n* moto *f*; **~boat** *n* lancha *f* a motor; **~car** *n* (frml) automóvil *m* (frml); **~cycle** *n* motocicleta *f*; **~cyclist** *n* motociclista *mf*, motorista *mf*

motoring /'məʊtərɪŋ/ *n* [U] automovilismo *m*

motorist /'məʊtərəst ‖ 'məʊtərɪst/ *n* automovilista *mf*, conductor, -tora *m,f*

motorway /'məʊtərweɪ ‖ 'məʊtəweɪ/ *n* (BrE) autopista *f*

mottled /'mɑːtḷd ‖ 'mɒtḷd/ *adj* ‹*skin*› manchado; ‹*marble*› veteado

motto /'mɑːtəʊ ‖ 'mɒtəʊ/ *n* (*pl* **-toes**) (of family, school) lema *m*

mould *etc* (BrE) ⇒ MOLD *etc*

moult *vi* (BrE) ⇒ MOLT

mound /maʊnd/ *n* (hillock) montículo *m*; (man-made) túmulo *m*; **burial ~** túmulo funerario **(c)** (heap) montón *m*

mount¹ /maʊnt/ *n* **1** (mountain) (liter) monte *m* **2** (Equ) montura *f* **3** (for machine, gun) soporte *m*; (for picture — surround) paspartú *m*, marialuisa *f* (Méx); (— backing) fondo *m*; (for slide) marco *m*; (for stamp) fijasellos *m*; (for jewel) montura *f*, engaste *m*

mount² *vt* **1 (a)** ‹*horse*› montar, montarse en **(b)** ‹*platform/throne*› subir a **2** ‹*gun/picture*› montar; ‹*stamp/butterfly*› fijar; ‹*gem*› engarzar*, montar **3** ‹*attack/offensive*› preparar; ‹*campaign/event*› organizar* ■ **~** *vi* **1 (a)** «*cost/temperature*» subir; «*excitement/alarm*» crecer* **(b) mounting** *pres p* ‹*cost/fears/tension*› cada vez mayor, creciente **2** (climb onto horse) montar

● **mount up** [*v + adv*] «*bills*» irse* acumulando

mountain /'maʊntn̩ ‖ 'maʊntɪn/ *n* (Geog) montaña *f*; (*before n*) ‹*stream/path*› de montaña; ‹*scenery*› montañoso; **~ range** cordillera *f*; (shorter) sierra *f*

mountain bike *n* bicicleta *f* de montaña

mountaineer /'maʊntn̩'ɪr ‖ ˌmaʊntɪ'nɪə(r)/ *n* alpinista *mf*, andinista *mf* (AmL)

mountaineering /'maʊntn̩'ɪrɪŋ ‖ ˌmaʊntɪ'nɪərɪŋ/ *n* [U] alpinismo *m*, andinismo *m* (AmL)

mountainous /'maʊntnəs ‖ 'maʊntɪnəs/ *adj* montañoso

mountaintop /'maʊntnˌtɑːp ‖ 'maʊntɪnˌtɒp/ *n* cima *f* *or* cumbre *f* (de la montaña)

mounted /'maʊntəd ‖ 'maʊntɪd/ *adj* montado: **~ police** policía *f* montada

mourn /mɔːrn ‖ mɔːn/ *vt* ‹*loss/tragedy*› llorar ■ **~** *vi* **to ~** FOR **sb** llorar a algn

mourner /'mɔːrnər ‖ 'mɔːnə(r)/ *n* doliente *mf*

mournful /'mɔːrnfəl ‖ 'mɔːnfəl/ *adj* ‹*expression/glance*› de profunda tristeza; ‹*sigh/cry*› lastimero

mourning /'mɔːrnɪŋ ‖ 'mɔːnɪŋ/ *n* [U] (action, period) duelo *m*, luto *m*; **to be in ~ for sb** estar* de luto por algn

mouse /maʊs/ *n* (*pl* **mice**) **1** (animal) ratón *m*, laucha *f* (CS) **2** (Comput) ratón *m*

mousey *adj* ⇒ MOUSY

mousse /muːs/ *n* [U C] **(a)** (Culin) mousse *f or m* **(b)** (for hair) mousse *f*

moustache *n* (BrE) ⇒ MUSTACHE

mousy /'maʊsi/ ▶515 *adj* **-sier, -siest** ‹*hair*› castaño desvaído *adj inv*

mouth¹ /maʊθ/ *n* (*pl* **mouths** /maʊðz/) **1** (of person, animal) boca *f*; ***down in the ~*** alicaído; ***to make sb's ~ water***: **it made my ~ water** se me hizo agua la boca *or* (Esp) se me hizo la boca agua **2** (of bottle) boca *f*; (of tunnel, cave) entrada *f*; (of river) desembocadura *f*

mouth² /maʊð/ *vt* (silently): **it's him, she ~ed** —es él —me/le dijo articulando para que le leyera los labios

mouthful /'maʊθfʊl/ *n* (of food) bocado *m*; (of drink) trago *m*; (of air) bocanada *f*

mouth: **~ organ** *n* armónica *f*; **~piece** *n* **1** (of telephone) micrófono *m*; (Mus) boquilla *f*; **2** (spokesperson) portavoz *mf*; **~-to-~** /'maʊθtə'maʊθ/ *adj* (*before n*) boca a boca; **~wash** *n* [U C] enjuague *m* (bucal); **~-watering** /'maʊθ,wɔ:tərɪŋ/ *adj* delicioso

move¹ /mu:v/ *n* **1** (movement) movimiento *m*; ***on the ~***: **she's always on the ~** siempre está de un lado para otro **2** (change — of residence) mudanza *f*, trasteo *m* (Col); (— of premises) traslado *m* **3 (a)** (action, step) paso *m*; (measure) medida *f*; **what's the next ~?** ¿cuál es el siguiente paso? **(b)** (in profession, occupation): **it would be a good career ~** sería un cambio muy provechoso para mi (*or* su *etc*) carrera profesional **4** (Games) movimiento *m*; **whose ~ is it?** ¿a quién le toca mover?

move² *vi* **1 (a)** (change place): **he ~d nearer the fire** se acercó al fuego; **to ~ to a new job** cambiar de trabajo **(b)** (change location, residence) mudarse **2** (change position) moverse* **3** (proceed, go): **the vehicle began to ~** el vehículo se puso en marcha; **the police kept the crowds moving** la policía hacía circular a la multitud; **the earth ~s around the sun** la Tierra gira alrededor del sol; **we ~d to one side** nos apartamos, nos hicimos a un lado **4** (advance, develop): **events ~d rapidly** los acontecimientos se desarrollaron rápidamente; **to ~ with the times** mantenerse* al día; **to ~ into the lead** pasar a ocupar el primer lugar **5** (carry oneself) moverse* **6** (go fast) (colloq) correr **7** (take steps, act): **we must ~ now** tenemos que actuar ahora; **she ~d quickly to scotch rumors** inmediatamente tomó medidas para acallar los rumores ■ **~** *vt* **1** (transfer, shift position of): **~ your chair a little** corre un poco la silla; **ask him to ~ the boxes out of the way** dile que quite las cajas de en medio; **I can't ~ my leg** no puedo mover la pierna **2 (a)** (transport) transportar **(b)** (relocate, transfer) trasladar **(c)** (change residence, location): **the firm that ~d us** la compañía que nos hizo la mudanza; **to ~ house** (BrE) mudarse de casa **3 (a)** (arouse emotionally) conmover*; **to ~ sb to tears** hacer* llorar a algn de la emoción **(b)** (prompt) **to ~ sb to** + INF: **this ~d her to remonstrate** esto la indujo a protestar **4** (propose) (Adm, Govt) proponer*

• **move along 1** [*v* + *adv*] **(a)** (go further along) correrse **(b)** (disperse) circular **2** [*v* + *o* + *adv*] (cause to disperse) hacer* circular

• **move around,** (BrE also) **move about** [*v* + *adv*] **(a)** (walk) andar* **(b)** (change residence) mudarse (*a menudo*); (change job) cambiar de trabajo (*a menudo*)

• **move away** [*v* + *adv*] **(a)** (move house) mudarse (*de la ciudad, el barrio etc*) **(b)** ⇒ MOVE OFF

• **move down 1** [*v* + *adv*] bajar **2** [*v* + *o* + *adv*] bajar

• **move in** [*v* + *adv*] **(a)** (set up home) mudarse (*a una casa etc*); **to ~ in WITH sb** irse* a vivir CON algn **(b)** (draw closer) acercarse* **(c)** (go into action) «*police*» intervenir*; (Mil) atacar*

• **move off** [*v* + *adv*] «*procession*» ponerse* en marcha; «*car*» arrancar*

• **move on I** [*v* + *adv*] **1** (walk further) seguir* adelante; (continue journey) continuar* el viaje **2 (a)** (proceed) pasar **(b)** (progress) progresar **II** [*v* + *o* + *adv*] (cause to disperse) hacer* circular

• **move out** [*v* + *adv*] irse* (*de una casa etc*)

• **move over** [*v* + *adv*] (make room) correrse

• **move up 1** [*v* + *adv*] **(a)** (rise) subir **(b)** (make room) correrse **2** [*v* + *o* + *adv*] ‹*picture/shelf*› subir; **they ~d him up a class** lo pusieron en la clase inmediatamente superior

movement /'mu:vmənt/ *n* **1 (a)** [U C] (motion) movimiento *m* **(b) movements** *pl* (activities, whereabouts) desplazamientos *mpl*, movimientos *mpl* **2** [U] **(a)** (transportation) movimiento *m* **(b)** (travel) desplazamiento *m* **3** [C] (Art, Pol, Relig) movimiento *m*

mover /'mu:vər ‖ 'mu:və(r)/ *n* (of furniture, belongings) (AmE): **a firm of ~s** una compañía de mudanzas

movie /'mu:vi/ *n* (esp AmE) **1** (film) película *f*, film(e) *m* (period); (*before n*) ‹*actor/director*› de cine **2 movies** *pl* (esp AmE) **the ~s** el cine

movie camera *n* (esp AmE) filmadora *f or* (Esp) tomavistas *m*; (large, professional) cámara *f* cinematográfica

moving /'mu:vɪŋ/ *adj* **1** (emotionally) emotivo, conmovedor **2** (in motion) (*before n*) **~ part** pieza *f* movible **3** (AmE) (*before n*) ‹*van/company*› de mudanzas

mow /məʊ/ *vt* (*past* **mowed**; *past p* **mown** *or* **mowed**) ‹*hay*› segar*; ‹*lawn*› cortar

• **mow down** [*v* + *o* + *adv*, *v* + *adv* + *o*] acribillar

mower /'məʊər ‖ 'məʊə(r)/ *n* **(a)** (Hort) ⇒ LAWNMOWER **(b)** (on farm) segadora *f*

mown /məʊn/ *past p of* MOW

Mozambique /'məʊzəm'bi:k ‖ ,məʊzæm'bi:k/ *n* Mozambique *m*

MP *n* **(a)** ▶603 (in UK) (Govt) = **Member of Parliament (b)** (= **military police**) PM *f*

mph = **miles per hour**

Mr /'mɪstər ‖ 'mɪstə(r)/ ▶603 (= **Mister**) Sr.

Mrs /'mɪsəs ‖ 'mɪsɪz/ ▶603 Sra.

Ms /mɪz ‖ məz/ ▶603 ≈ Sra. (*tratamiento que se da a las mujeres y que no indica su estado civil*)

MS *n* **(a)** [C] *also* **ms** (*pl* **MSS** *or* **mss**) (= **manuscript**) ms. **(b)** [U] (= **multiple sclerosis**) E.M. *f* **(c)** [C] (AmE) = **Master of Science (d)** = **Mississippi**

MSc *n* (BrE) = **Master of Science**

MST (in US) = **Mountain Standard Time**

Mt (= **Mount**) **~ Rushmore** el monte Rushmore

MT = **Montana**

much¹ /mʌtʃ/ *adj* mucho, -cha; **how ~ coffee/milk?** ¿cuánto café/cuánta leche?; **I do as ~ work as anybody** trabajo tanto como cualquiera; **too ~ coffee** demasiado café

much² *pron* mucho, -cha; **do you see ~ of the Smiths?** ¿ves mucho a los Smith?; **how ~ does it cost?** ¿cuánto cuesta?; **I've done as ~ as I can** he hecho todo lo que he podido; **and as ~ again** y otro tanto; **you've drunk too ~** has bebido demasiado

much³ *adv* mucho; **I'd very ~ like to meet her** me gustaría mucho conocerla; **you deserve the prize just as ~ as I do** te mereces el premio tanto como yo; **so ~ the better** tanto mejor; **you talk too ~** hablas demasiado; **this church is ~ the larger of the two** de las dos iglesias ésta es, con mucho, la más grande; **I'm ~ too busy to do it** estoy demasiado ocupada para hacerlo

muck /mʌk/ *n* [U] (dung) estiércol *m*; (dirt) mugre *f*
• **muck out** [*v + o + adv, v + adv + o*] limpiar

mucus /'mju:kəs/ *n* [U] mucosidad *f*

mud /mʌd/ *n* [U] barro *m*, fango *m*, lodo *m*; (*before n*) ‹*brick/hut*› de barro, de adobe

muddle¹ /'mʌdl̩/ *n* lío *m*, follón *m* (Esp fam); **to be in a ~** «*papers*» estar* (todo) revuelto; «*person*» estar* liado *or* hecho un lío (fam)

muddle² *vt* ⇒ MUDDLE UP
• **muddle up** [*v + o + adv, v + adv + o*] **(a)** ‹*papers*› entreverar **(b)** (mix up) confundir **(c)** (bewilder) confundir; **to get ~d up** confundirse

muddled /'mʌdl̩d/ *adj* confuso; **to get ~** hacerse* un lío (fam)

muddy /'mʌdi/ *adj* **-dier, -diest** ‹*boots/hands/road*› lleno *or* cubierto de barro *or* de lodo; ‹*water*› turbio

mudguard /'mʌdgɑ:rd ‖'mʌdgɑ:d/ *n* guardabarros *m*, salpicadera *f* (Méx), tapabarros *m* (Chi, Per)

muesli /'mju:zli, 'mu:- ‖ 'mju:zli/ *n* [U] (esp BrE) musli *m*, muesli *m*

muff¹ /mʌf/ *vt* (colloq) ‹*shot*› errar*; ‹*chance*› desperdiciar

muff² *n* (Clothing) manguito *m*

muffin /'mʌfən ‖ 'mʌfɪn/ *n* (AmE) mollete *m* (*bollo dulce hecho con huevos*); (BrE) *bollo de pan que suele servirse tostado*

muffle /'mʌfl̩/ *vt* **1** ‹*sound*› amortiguar* **2 ~ (up)**: **her face was ~d (up) in a scarf** una bufanda casi le tapaba la cara

muffler /'mʌflər ‖'mʌflə(r)/ *n* **1** (scarf) bufanda *f* **2 (a)** (Mus) sordina *f* **(b)** (AmE Auto) silenciador *m*, mofle *m* (AmC, Méx)

mug¹ /mʌg/ *n* **1** (cup) taza *f* (*alta y sin platillo*), tarro *m* (Méx, Ven) **2** (gullible person) (BrE colloq) idiota *mf* **3** (face) (sl) cara *f*, jeta *f* (arg), careto *m* (Esp arg)

mug² *vt* **-gg-** atracar*

mugger /'mʌgər ‖'mʌgə(r)/ *n* atracador, -dora *m,f*

muggy /'mʌgi/ ▶ 920 *adj* **-gier, -giest** ‹*weather/day*› pesado

mug shot *n* (colloq) foto *f* (*de archivo policial*)

Muhammad /mə'hæməd ‖mə'hæmɪd/ *n* Mahoma

mulberry /'mʌl,beri ‖ 'mʌlbəri/ *n* (*pl* **-ries**) (tree) morera *f*; (fruit) mora *f* (de morera)

mule /mju:l/ *n* mula *f* (*cruce de burro y yegua*); ***stubborn as a ~*** más terco que una mula

mull /mʌl/ *vt* **(a)** (Culin): **~ed wine** *ponche caliente de vino y especias* **(b)** (AmE) ⇒ MULL OVER
• **mull over** [*v + o + adv, v + adv + o*] reflexionar sobre

multicolored, (BrE) **multi-coloured** /'mʌlti ,kʌlərd ‖ ,mʌltɪ'kʌləd/ *adj* multicolor

multilevel /'mʌlti'levl̩/ *adj* (AmE) de varias plantas, de varios pisos

multinational¹ /'mʌlti'næʃn̩əl ‖,mʌlti'næʃənl̩/ *adj* multinacional

multinational² *n* multinacional *f*

multiple¹ /'mʌltəpəl ‖ 'mʌltɪpəl/ *adj* **(a)** (involving many elements) múltiple **(b)** (many) múltiples

multiple² *n* múltiplo *m*

multiple: **~-choice** /'mʌltəpəl'tʃɔɪs ‖,mʌltɪpəl 'tʃɔɪs/ *adj* de opción múltiple, tipo test; **~ sclerosis** /sklə'rəʊsəs/ *n* [U] esclerosis *f* múltiple

multiplication /'mʌltəplə'keɪʃən ‖,mʌltɪplɪ'keɪʃən/ *n* [U] multiplicación *f*

multiply /'mʌltəplaɪ ‖'mʌltɪplaɪ/ **-plies, -plying, -plied** *vt* **(a)** (Math) **to ~ sth (BY sth)** multiplicar* algo (POR algo) **(b)** (increase) multiplicar* ■ **~** *vi* **(a)** (Math) multiplicar* **(b)** (increase, reproduce) multiplicarse*

multipurpose /'mʌlti'pɜ:rpəs ‖,mʌlti'pɜ:pəs/ *adj* ‹*tool/appliance*› multiuso *adj inv*

multistory, (BrE) **multistorey** /'mʌlti'stɔ:ri/ *adj* de varias plantas, de varios pisos

multitude /'mʌltətu:d ‖ 'mʌltɪtju:d/ *n* **(a)** (large number) (frml) (*no pl*) **a ~ OF sth**: **a ~ of problems** innumerables *or* múltiples problemas **(b)** [C] (crowd) (arch *or* liter) multitud *f*

mum /mʌm/ *n* **1** (mother) (BrE colloq) mamá *f* (fam) **2** (silence) (colloq): ***~'s the word*** ¡punto en boca! (fam); ***to keep ~*** no decir* ni pío (fam)

mumble /'mʌmbəl/ *vi* hablar entre dientes ■ **~** *vt* mascullar

mumbo jumbo /'mʌmbəʊ'dʒʌmbəʊ/ *n* [U] (pej): **religion, he said, was a lot of ~ ~** dijo que la religión no era más que supercherías

mummy /'mʌmi/ *n* (*pl* **-mies**) **1** (mother) (BrE colloq: esp used by children) mami *f* (fam), mamita *f* (fam) **2** (Archeol) momia *f*

mumps /mʌmps/ *n* [U] paperas *fpl*

munch /mʌntʃ/ *vt/i* mascar*

mundane /mʌn'deɪn/ *adj* ‹*existence*› prosaico; ‹*activity*› rutinario

municipal /mjʊ'nɪsəpəl ‖ mju:'nɪsɪpəl/ *adj* (*usu before n*) municipal

munitions /mjʊ'nɪʃənz ‖ mju:'nɪʃənz/ *pl n* municiones *fpl*

mural /'mjʊrəl ‖ 'mjʊərəl/ *n* mural *m*

murder¹ /'mɜ:rdər ‖ 'mɜ:də(r)/ *n* [U C] asesinato *m*; (Law) homicidio *m*; ***to get away with ~***: **she lets**

them get away with ~ les permite cualquier cosa

murder² *vt* **(a)** (kill) asesinar **(b)** (ruin) ‹*music/play*› destrozar* ■ ~ *vi* matar

murderer /'mɜːrdərər ‖ 'mɜːdərə(r)/ *n* asesino, -na *m,f*

murderous /'mɜːrdərəs ‖ 'mɜːdərəs/ *adj* ‹*instinct/look*› asesino; ‹*individual*› de instintos asesinos

murky /'mɜːrki ‖ 'mɜːki/ *adj* **-kier, -kiest** ‹*water*› turbio; ‹*green/brown*› sucio; ‹*past*› turbio

murmur¹ /'mɜːrmər ‖ 'mɜːmə(r)/ *n* murmullo *m*

murmur² *vt* murmurar

muscle /'mʌsəl/ *n* **(a)** [C U] (Anat) músculo *m* **(b)** [U] (power) fuerza *f*

● **muscle in** [*v* + *adv*] (colloq) meterse por medio (*con prepotencia*); **a rival company ~d in on their market** una compañía de la competencia se introdujo en su sector del mercado

muscular /'mʌskjələr ‖ 'mʌskjʊlə(r)/ *adj* **(a)** ‹*arms/build*› musculoso **(b)** ‹*strain/contraction*› muscular

muscular dystrophy /'dɪstrəfi/ *n* [U] distrofia *f* muscular

muse¹ /mjuːz/ *vi* **to ~ (ON** *o* **UPON sth)** cavilar *or* reflexionar (SOBRE algo)

muse², **Muse** *n* musa *f*

museum /mjʊ'ziːəm/ *n* museo *m*

mush /mʌʃ/ *n* [U] papilla *f*, pasta *f*

mushroom¹ /'mʌʃrʊm, -ruːm/ *n* hongo *m* (esp AmL), seta *f* (esp Esp), callampa *f* (Chi); (rounded, white) champiñón *m*

mushroom² *vi* «*town/population*» crecer* rápidamente; «*companies/buildings*» aparecer* como hongos *or* (Chi) como callampas, multiplicarse*

mushy /'mʌʃi/ *adj* **mushier, mushiest** ‹*vegetables/fruit*› blando

music /'mjuːzɪk/ *n* [U] **(a)** (art form) música *f*; ***to face the ~*** afrontar las consecuencias **(b)** (written notes) partitura *f*, música *f*

musical¹ /'mjuːzɪkəl/ *adj* **(a)** (Mus) (*before n*) ‹*ability/tradition*› musical **(b)** (musically gifted) con aptitudes para la música **(c)** (melodious) ‹*voice/laugh*› musical

musical² *n* musical *m*

musical chairs *n* (+ *sing vb*): **to play ~ ~** jugar* a las sillitas

music: **~ box** *n* caja *f* de música; **~ hall** *n* **(a)** [U] (entertainment) music hall *m*, ≈revista *f* de variedades **(b)** [C] (building) teatro *m* de variedades

musician /mjʊ'zɪʃən/ *n* músico, -ca *m,f*

musk /mʌsk/ *n* [U] almizcle *m*

musket /'mʌskət ‖ 'mʌskɪt/ *n* mosquete *m*

Muslim¹ /'mʊzləm ‖ 'mʊzlɪm/ *n* musulmán, -mana *m,f*, mahometano, -na *m,f*

Muslim² *adj* musulmán

muslin /'mʌzlən ‖ 'mʌzlɪn/ *n* [U] muselina *f* (*de algodón*)

muss /mʌs/ *vt* **~ (up)** (AmE colloq) ‹*room*› desordenar; **she ~ed her hair** se despeinó

mussel /'mʌsəl/ *n* mejillón *m*

must¹ /mʌst, *weak form* məst/ *v mod* **1** (expressing obligation) tener* que *or* deber; **it ~ be remembered that** ... hay que recordar que ..., tenemos que *or* debemos recordar que ...; **she ~ not know that I am here** no debe enterarse de que estoy aquí, que no se entere de que estoy aquí; **I ~ say, everywhere looks very tidy** tengo que reconocer que está todo muy ordenado **2** (expressing certainty, supposition) deber (de) *or* (esp AmL) haber* de; **it ~ be six o'clock** deben (de) ser *or* (esp AmL) han de ser las seis, serán las seis

must² /mʌst/ *n* (essential thing, activity): **a car is a ~ here** aquí es indispensable tener coche; **this book is a ~** éste es un libro que hay que leer

mustache /'mʌstæʃ/, (BrE) **moustache** /mə'stɑːʃ/ *n* bigote(s) *m(pl)*; **to grow a ~** dejarse bigote(s) *or* el bigote

mustard /'mʌstərd ‖ 'mʌstəd/ *n* [U] mostaza *f*

muster /'mʌstər ‖ 'mʌstə(r)/ *vt* **(a)** (Mil) ‹*soldiers*› reunir*, llamar a asamblea **(b)** (succeed in raising) **to ~ (up)** ‹*team/army*› lograr formar; **if they can ~ enough support** si logran el apoyo que necesitan

mustn't /'mʌsn̩t/ = **must not**

musty /'mʌsti/ *adj* **-tier, tiest** que huele a humedad *or* a moho

mutate /'mjuːteɪt ‖ mjuː'teɪt/ *vi* **(a)** (Biol, Ling) mutar **(b)** (change) (frml) sufrir una transformación/transformaciones

mutation /mjuː'teɪʃən/ *n* [U C] **(a)** (Biol, Ling) mutación *f* **(b)** (change) (frml) transformación *f*

mute /mjuːt/ *adj* mudo

muted /'mjuːtəd ‖ 'mjuːtɪd/ *adj* ‹*sound*› sordo; ‹*voice*› apagado; ‹*trumpet*› con sordina; ‹*shade*› apagado; ‹*protest/reaction*› débil

mutilate /'mjuːtl̩eɪt ‖ 'mjuːtɪleɪt/ *vt* mutilar

mutiny¹ /'mjuːtn̩i ‖ 'mjuːtɪni/ *n* (*pl* **-nies**) **(a)** [C] (instance) motín *m*, amotinamiento *m* **(b)** [U] (offense) amotinamiento *m*

mutiny² *vi* **-nies, -nying, -nied** amotinarse

mutt /mʌt/ *n* (AmE colloq) (dog) chucho *m* (fam), gozque *m* (Col fam), quiltro *m* (Chi fam), pichicho *m* (RPl fam)

mutter /'mʌtər ‖ 'mʌtə(r)/ *vi* hablar entre dientes ■ ~ *vt* mascullar

mutton /'mʌtn̩/ *n* [U] carne *f* de ovino (*de más de un año*), añojo *m* (Esp), capón *m* (RPl)

mutual /'mjuːtʃuəl/ *adj* **(a)** (reciprocal) mutuo **(b)** (shared, common) (*before n*) ‹*friend/enemy*› común

muzzle /'mʌzəl/ *n* **(a)** (snout) hocico *m* **(b)** (for dog) bozal *m* **(c)** (of gun) boca *f*

my /maɪ/ *adj*

■ **Note** The translation *mi* agrees in number with the noun which it modifies; *my* is translated by *mi*, *mis*, depending on what follows: *my father/mother* mi padre/madre; *my books/magazines* mis libros/revistas. For *my* used with parts of the body, *see* ▶ **484**

(*sing*) mi; (*pl*) mis; **I put ~ hat on** me puse el sombrero; **I broke ~ arm** me rompí el brazo

myalgic encephalomyelitis /maɪ'ældʒɪk en,sefələʊmaɪə'laɪtəs ‖ maɪ,ældʒɪken,sefələʊ,maɪə'laɪtɪs/ *n* encefalomielitis *f* miálgica

myriad /'mɪriəd/ *adj* (liter): **the ~ varieties of butterfly** los miles tipos de mariposas

myrrh /mɜːr ‖ mɜː(r)/ *n* [U] mirra *f*

myself /maɪ'self/ *pron* **(a)** (reflexive): **I cut/hurt ~** me corté/lastimé; **I was talking to ~** estaba hablando solo/sola; **I was by ~** estaba solo/sola **(b)** (*emphatic use*) yo mismo, yo misma; **I made it ~** lo hice yo mismo/misma **(c)** (normal self): **I haven't been feeling ~ lately** no me encuentro muy bien últimamente

mysterious /mɪ'stɪriəs ‖ mɪ'stɪəriəs/ *adj* misterioso

mystery /'mɪstəri/ *n* (*pl* **-ries**) **1 (a)** [C] (puzzle) misterio *m* **(b)** [U] (quality) misterio *m*; (*before n*) ‹*guest/tour*› sorpresa *adj inv* **2** [C] (Cin, Lit, Theat) película *f* (*or* novela *f etc*) de misterio *or* de suspenso *or* (Esp) de suspense

mystical /'mɪstɪkəl/ *adj* místico

mystify /'mɪstəfaɪ ‖ 'mɪstɪfaɪ/ *vt* **-fies, -fying, -fied** desconcertar*

myth /mɪθ/ *n* mito *m*

mythology /mɪ'θɑːlədʒi ‖ mɪ'θɒlədʒi/ *n* (*pl* **-gies**) mitología *f*

Nn

N, n /en/ *n* **(a)** (letter) N, n *f* **(b)** (indeterminate number) (Math) (número *m*) n

'n' /ən/ = **and**

N (= **north**) N

NAACP /'endʌbəl'eɪsiː'piː/ *n* (in US) = **National Association for the Advancement of Colored People**

nab /næb/ *vt* **-bb-** (colloq) **(a)** (catch) ‹*person*› pescar* (fam) **(b)** (snatch) agarrar *or* (esp Esp) coger*

nadir /'neɪdɪr ‖ 'neɪdiə(r)/ *n* (Astron) nadir *m*; (lowest point) punto *m* más bajo

nag /næg/ **-gg-** *vt* **(a)** (pester) fastidiar **(b)** (criticize): **he's always ~ging her for being untidy** siempre le está encima con que es desordenada ■ ~ *vi* **1 (a)** (pester) fastidiar **(b)** (criticize) rezongar* **2 nagging** *pres p* ‹*doubt/worry*› persistente; ‹*husband/wife*› rezongón (fam)

nail¹ /neɪl/ *n* **1** (Const) clavo *m*; (smaller) puntilla *f*; ***to be as hard as ~s*** ser* muy duro (de corazón) **2** (Anat) uña *f*; (*before n*) **~ polish** *o* (BrE also) **varnish** esmalte *m* de uñas

nail² *vt* **1** (fix) clavar **2** (colloq) (apprehend) agarrar *or* (esp Esp) coger

• **nail down** [*v* + *o* + *adv*, *v* + *adv* + *o*] clavar, asegurar con clavos

nail: **~brush** *n* cepillo *m* de uñas; **~ clippers** *pl n* cortaúñas *m*; **~ file** *n* lima *f* (de uñas)

naive, naïve /nɑː'iːv, naɪ'iːv/ *adj* ingenuo

naked /'neɪkəd ‖ 'neɪkɪd/ *adj* **(a)** (unclothed) desnudo **(b)** ‹*sword/blade*› desenvainado; **visible/invisible to the ~ eye** que se puede ver/invisible a simple vista

name¹ /neɪm/ *n* **1** (of person, thing) nombre *m*; (surname) apellido *m*; **what's your ~?** ¿cómo te llamas?, ¿cómo se llama (Ud)?; **my ~ is John Baker** me llamo John Baker; **he knows them all by ~** los conoce a todos por su nombre; **in ~ only** sólo de nombre; **mentioning no ~s** sin mencionar a nadie; ***to call sb ~s*** insultar a algn; (*before n*) **~ tag** etiqueta *f* de identificación **2 (a)** (reputation) fama *f*; **to give sb/sth a bad ~** darle* mala fama a algn/algo **(b)** (person) figura *f*; (company) nombre *m*; ***to drop ~s*** mencionar a gente importante (*para darse tono*)

name² *vt* **1** (give name to) ‹*company/town*› ponerle* nombre a; ‹*boat*› bautizar*; **a man ~d Smith** un hombre llamado Smith; **they ~d her after** *o* (AmE also) **for Ann's mother** le pusieron el nombre de la madre de Ann **2** (identify, mention): **police have ~d the suspect** la policía ha dado el nombre del sospechoso; **to ~ but a few** por mencionar a unos pocos; **you ~ it, she's done it** ha hecho de todo lo habido y por haber **3** (appoint) nombrar

nameless /'neɪmləs ‖ 'neɪmlɪs/ *adj* **1** (not specified) anónimo **2** ‹*fear/yearning*› indescriptible

namely /'neɪmli/ *adv* (frml) a saber (frml)

namesake /'neɪmseɪk/ *n* tocayo, -ya *m,f*

nanny /'næni/ *n* (*pl* **-nies**) **1** (nursemaid) (esp BrE) niñera *f* **2** (granny) (used to or by children) abuelita *f* (fam) **3 ~ goat** cabra *f*

nap /næp/ *n* sueñecito *m* (fam), sueñito *m* (esp AmL fam); (esp in the afternoon) siesta *f*

nape /neɪp/ *n* nuca *f*

napkin /'næpkɪn/ *n* servilleta *f*

nappy /'næpi/ *n* (*pl* **-pies**) (BrE) pañal *m*

narcotic /nɑːr'kɑːtɪk ‖ nɑː'kɒtɪk/ *n* estupefaciente *m*, narcótico *m*

narrate /'næreɪt ‖ nə'reɪt/ *vt* **(a)** (Lit frml) ‹*story/events*› narrar **(b)** ‹*film/documentary*› hacer* el comentario de

narrative¹ /'nærətɪv/ *adj* narrativo

narrative² *n* **(a)** [C] (story) (frml) narración *f* **(b)** [U] (Lit) (narrated part) narración *f*

narrator /'næreɪtər ‖ nə'reɪtə(r)/ *n* **(a)** (Lit) narrador, -dora *m,f* **(b)** (Cin, Theat, TV) comentarista *mf*

narrow¹ /'nærəʊ/ *adj* **1 (a)** (not wide) ‹*path/opening/hips*› estrecho, angosto (esp AmL) **(b)** (slender) ‹*margin*› escaso; ‹*win/victory*› conseguido por un escaso margen; **to have a ~ escape** salvarse de milagro **2** (restricted) ‹*range/view*› limitado; ‹*attitude/ideas*› cerrado

narrow² *vt* **(a)** (reduce width of) estrechar, angostar (esp AmL) **(b)** (restrict) ‹*range/field*› restringir* ■ ~ *vi* **(a)** «*road/river/valley*» estrecharse, angostarse (esp AmL) **(b)** «*options/odds*» reducirse*

• **narrow down** [*v + o + adv, v + adv + o*]: **they've ~ed their investigation down to this area** han restringido su investigación a esta área; **we ~ed it down to only three candidates** fuimos descartando candidatos hasta quedar con sólo tres

narrowly /'nærəʊli/ *adv* por poco

narrow-minded /'nærəʊ'maɪndəd ‖ ˌnærəʊ 'maɪndɪd/ *adj* de mentalidad cerrada

NASA /'næsə/ *n* (in US) (*no art*) (= **National Aeronautics and Space Administration**) la NASA

nasal /'neɪzəl/ *adj* (Anat, Ling) nasal; ‹*voice/accent*› gangoso, (de timbre) nasal

nasty /'næsti ‖ 'nɑːsti/ *adj* **-tier, -tiest 1** ‹*taste/smell/medicine*› asqueroso; ‹*habit*› feo **2** (spiteful) ‹*person*› malo **3 (a)** (severe) ‹*cut/injury/cough*› feo; ‹*accident*› serio; (stronger) horrible **(b)** (unpleasant) ‹*situation/experience*› desagradable

nation /'neɪʃn̩/ *n* nación *f*

national¹ /'næʃnəl ‖ 'næʃənl̩/ *adj* nacional

national² *n* ciudadano, -na *m,f*

national: **N~ Health (Service)** *n* [U] (in UK) **the N~ Health (Service)** *servicio de asistencia sanitaria de la Seguridad Social*; **N~ Insurance** *n* [U] (in UK) Seguridad *f* Social

nationalism /'næʃnəlɪzəm ‖ 'næʃnəlɪzəm/ *n* [U] nacionalismo *m*

nationalist¹ /'næʃn̩ələst ‖ 'næʃn̩əlɪst/ *adj* nacionalista

nationalist² *n* nacionalista *mf*

nationality /'næʃə'næləti/ *n* (*pl* **-ties**) [U C] nacionalidad *f*

nationalize /'næʃn̩əlaɪz ‖ 'næʃnəlaɪz/ *vt* nacionalizar*

nationally /'næʃn̩əli ‖ 'næʃn̩əli/ *adv* a escala nacional

national park *n* parque *m* nacional

nationwide¹ /'neɪʃənwaɪd/ *adj* ‹*campaign*› a escala nacional; ‹*appeal*› a toda la nación

nationwide² *adv* ‹*distribute/operate*› a escala nacional

native¹ /'neɪtɪv/ *adj* **1 (a)** (of or by birth) ‹*country/town*› natal; ‹*customs*› nativo; ‹*language*› materno; **his ~ land** su patria, su tierra natal; **a ~ speaker of** ... un hablante nativo de ... **(b)** (innate) ‹*ability/wit/charm*› innato **2** (indigenous) ‹*plant/animal*› autóctono

native² *n* **(a)** (Anthrop) nativo, -va *m,f*, indígena *mf* **(b)** (plant, animal): **the dingo is a ~ of Australia** el dingo es originario de Australia

Native American *n* indio americano, india americana *m,f*

nativity /nə'tɪvəti/ *n*: **The N~** (Relig) la Natividad

NATO /'neɪtəʊ/ *n* (*no art*) (= **North Atlantic Treaty Organization**) la OTAN

natural /'nætʃrəl/ *adj* **1** (as in nature) natural **2 (a)** ‹*talent/propensity*› innato; ‹*leader*› nato **(b)** ‹*reaction/response*› natural; ‹*successor*› lógico **3** (not forced) ‹*warmth/style*› natural

natural history *n* [U] historia *f* natural

naturalist /'nætʃrələst ‖ 'nætʃrəlɪst/ *n* naturalista *mf*

naturalized /'nætʃrəlaɪzd/ *adj* **(a)** ‹*citizen/American*› naturalizado **(b)** (Bot, Zool) aclimatado

naturally /'nætʃrəli/ *adv* **1 (a)** (inherently) ‹*shy/tidy*› por naturaleza **(b)** (unaffectedly) ‹*smile/behave/speak*› con naturalidad **2** (without artifice) ‹*form/heal*› de manera natural **3** (*indep*) (of course) naturalmente, por supuesto

nature /'neɪtʃər ‖ 'neɪtʃə(r)/ *n* **1** [U] (universe, way of things) naturaleza *f* **2 (a)** [U C] (of people) carácter *m*; **by ~** por naturaleza **(b)** [U] (of things, concepts) naturaleza *f*

nature reserve *n* reserva *f* natural

naturist /'neɪtʃərəst ‖ 'neɪtʃərɪst/ *n* (esp BrE) nudista *mf*; (*before n*) ‹*beach/camp*› nudista

naught /nɔːt/ *n* (esp AmE) cero *m*

naughty /'nɔːti/ *adj* **-tier, -tiest** malo, travieso

nausea /'nɔːsiə, -ziə/ *n* [U] náusea *f*

nauseating /'nɔːsieɪtɪŋ, 'nɔːz-/ *adj* ‹*violence/brutality*› repugnante; ‹*smell*› nauseabundo

nauseous /'nɔːʃəs, 'nɔːziəs ‖ 'nɔːsiəs, nɔːz-/ *adj* (bilious): **to feel ~** sentir* náuseas

nautical /'nɔːtɪkl̩ ‖ 'nɔːtɪkəl/ *adj* náutico, marítimo; **~ mile** milla *f* marina

naval /'neɪvəl/ *adj* naval; ‹*officer*› de marina

nave /neɪv/ *n* nave *f*

navel /'neɪvəl/ *n* ombligo *m*

navigable /'nævɪgəbəl/ *adj* navegable

navigate /'nævəgeɪt ‖ 'nævɪgeɪt/ *vi* **(a)** (Aviat, Naut) navegar* **(b)** (in car) hacer* de copiloto ■ ~ *vt* **(a)** (steer) ‹*ship/plane*› conducir*, llevar **(b)** (travel across, along) ‹*sea/river*› navegar* por

navigation /'nævə'geɪʃən ‖ ˌnævɪ'geɪʃən/ *n* [U] navegación *f*; (in car) dirección *f*

navigator /'nævəgeɪtər ‖ 'nævɪgeɪtə(r)/ *n* **1** (crew member) (Naut) oficial *mf* de derrota; (Aviat) navegante *mf* **2** (explorer) navegante *m*

navy¹ /'neɪvi/ *n* (*pl* **navies**) **1** [C] (Mil, Naut) marina *f* de guerra **2** ▶ **515** [U] **~ (blue)** azul *m* marino

navy², navy-blue /'neɪvi'bluː/ ▶ **515** (*pred* **navy blue**) *adj* azul marino *adj inv*

Nazi¹ /'nɑːtsi/ *n* nazi *mf*, nazista *mf*

Nazi² *adj* nazi, nazista

NB (= **nota bene**) NB

NBC *n* (in US) (*no art*) (= **National Broadcasting Company**) la NBC

NC = **North Carolina**

NCO *n* = **noncommissioned officer**

ND, N Dak = **North Dakota**

NE (a) (= **northeast**) NE **(b)** = **Nebraska**

near¹ /nɪr ‖ nɪə(r)/ *adj* **-er, -est 1 (a)** (in position, time) cercano, próximo **(b)** ‹*relative*› cercano **2** (virtual) (*before n*): **there was ~ panic when the alarms sounded** casi se produjo el pánico cuando sonaron las alarmas; **in a state of ~ exhaustion** prácticamente en estado de agotamiento

near² *adv* **-er, -est 1** (in position) cerca; **from ~ and far** de todas partes **2** (nearly) casi

near³ *prep* **-er, -est (a)** (in position) cerca de; **don't go too ~ the fire** no te acerques demasiado al fuego **(b)** (in time): **we're getting very ~ Christmas** falta muy poco para Navidad **(c)** (in approximation): **I'd say he's ~er 70 than 60** yo diría que está más cerca de los 70 que de los 60

near⁴ *vt* acercarse* a; **the project is ~ing completion** el proyecto se está por acabar

near- /'nɪr ‖ 'nɪə(r)/ *pref* casi

nearby¹ /'nɪrbaɪ ‖ nɪə'baɪ/ *adj* cercano

nearby² *adv* cerca

nearly /'nɪrli ‖ 'nɪəli/ *adv* casi; **she very ~ died** por poco *or* casi se muere

nearsighted /'nɪr'saɪtəd ‖ ˌnɪə'saɪtɪd/ *adj* miope, corto de vista

neat /ni:t/ *adj* **-er, -est 1** (tidy, orderly) ‹*appearance*› arreglado, cuidado, prolijo (RPl); ‹*person*› pulcro, prolijo (RPl); ‹*garden*› muy cuidado **2** (good, nice) (AmE colloq) fantástico (fam), padre (Méx fam), chévere (AmL exc CS fam), chulo (Esp fam), encachado (Chi fam) **3** (BrE) ‹*brandy/alcohol*› solo

neatly /'ni:tli/ *adv* **(a)** (tidily): **the papers were ~ organized into piles** los papeles estaban cuidadosamente apilados; **she was ~ dressed** iba bien arreglada **(b)** (snugly): **the table fits ~ into the alcove** la mesa cabe perfectamente en el hueco **(c)** ‹*explain/evade*› hábilmente

Neb, **Nebr** = **Nebraska**

necessarily /'nesə'serəli ‖ ˌnesə'serɪli/ *adv* forzosamente, necesariamente

necessary /'nesəseri ‖ 'nesəsəri / *adj* necesario

necessitate /nə'sesɪteɪt ‖ nɪ'sesɪteɪt/ *vt* (frml) exigir*

necessity /nə'sesəti ‖ nɪ'sesəti/ *n* (*pl* **-ties**) **1** (imperative need) (*no pl*) necesidad *f*; **~ FOR sth** necesidad DE algo; **out of ~** por necesidad **2** [C] (necessary item): **the bare necessities** lo indispensable; **a car is a ~ for me** para mí tener coche es una necesidad

neck /nek/ *n* **1** ▶ **484** (Anat) (of person) cuello *m*; (of animal) cuello *m*, pescuezo *m*; **they were ~ and ~** iban a la par, iban parejos (esp AmL); ***to be up to one's ~ in sth*** (colloq): **she's up to her ~ in work** está hasta aquí de trabajo (fam); **they're up to their ~s in debt** deben hasta la camisa (fam) **2** (Clothing) cuello *m*, escote *m*; (measurement) cuello *m* **3** (of pork, beef, lamb) (esp BrE) cuello *m* **4** (of bottle, vase) cuello *m*; (of guitar, violin) mástil *m*; **a ~ of land** un istmo

necklace /'nekləs ‖ 'neklɪs/ *n* collar *m*

neck: **~line** *n* escote *m*; **~tie** *n* (AmE) corbata *f*

nectar /'nektər ‖ 'nektə(r)/ *n* [U] néctar *m*

nectarine /'nektəri:n ‖ 'nektərɪn, -ri:n/ *n* nectarina *f*, pelón *m* (RPl), durazno *m* pelado (Chi)

née /neɪ/ *adj* de soltera

need¹ /ni:d/ *n* **1** [C U] (requirement, necessity) necesidad *f*; **~ FOR sth/to + INF** necesidad DE algo/DE + INF; **there's no ~ to tell her** no hay ninguna necesidad de decírselo; **if ~ be** si hace falta; **the house is badly in ~ of renovation** a la casa le hacen muchísima falta unos arreglos **2** [U] **(a)** (emergency): **he abandoned them in their hour of ~** los abandonó cuando más falta les hacía **(b)** (poverty) necesidad *f*; **those in ~** los necesitados

need² *vt* necesitar; **the plants ~ watering** hay que regar las plantas; **to ~ to + INF** tener* QUE + INF ■ **~** *v mod* (*usu with neg or interrog*) (be obliged to): **you ~n't come if you don't want to** no hay necesidad de que vengas si no tienes ganas; **that ~n't mean that** ... eso no significa necesariamente que ...

needle¹ /'ni:dl/ *n* [C] **(a)** (for sewing, on syringe) aguja *f*; (on record player) aguja *f*, púa *f* (RPl); (*knitting* **~**) aguja *f* de tejer *or* (Esp) de hacer punto, palillo *m* (Chi); ***to look for a ~ in a haystack*** buscar* una aguja en un pajar **(b)** (on gauge) aguja *f* **(c)** (Bot) aguja *f*

needle² *vt* pinchar (fam)

needless /'ni:dləs ‖ 'ni:dlɪs/ *adj* innecesario; **~ to say, no one asked me** de más está decir que nadie me preguntó

needlework /'ni:dlwɜ:rk ‖ 'ni:dlwɜ:k/ *n* [U] (activity, skill) labores *fpl* de aguja

needn't /'ni:dn̩t/ = **need not**

needy /'ni:di/ *adj* **-dier, -diest** necesitado

negative¹ /'negətɪv/ *adj* negativo

negative² *n* **1** ▶ **718** **(a)** (word, particle) negación *f* **(b)** (no) negativa *f* **2** (Phot) negativo *m*

neglect¹ /nɪ'glekt/ *vt* **(a)** (leave uncared-for) ‹*family/child*› desatender*; ‹*house/health*› descuidar **(b)** (not carry out) ‹*duty/obligations*› desatender*; ‹*studies/business*› descuidar

neglect² *n* [U] (lack of care) abandono *m*; (negligence) negligencia *f*

neglected /nɪ'glektəd ‖ nɪ'glektɪd/ *adj* ‹*building/garden*› abandonado, descuidado; ‹*appearance*› dejado, abandonado

neglectful /nɪ'glektfəl/ *adj* negligente

negligee /'neglə'ʒeɪ ‖ 'neglɪʒeɪ/ *n* negligé *m*

negligence /'neglɪdʒəns/ *n* [U] negligencia *f*

negligent /'neglɪdʒənt/ *adj* negligente

negligible /'neglɪdʒəbəl/ *adj* insignificante

negotiable /nɪ'gəʊʃəbəl/ *adj* **(a)** (subject to negotiation) ‹*contract/claim/salary*› negociable **(b)** (passable) ‹*road*› transitable; ‹*obstacle*› superable

negotiate /nɪ'gəʊʃieɪt/ *vi* negociar ■ **~** *vt* **1** (obtain by discussion) ‹*contract/treaty*› negociar; ‹*loan*› gestionar **2** (pass, deal with) ‹*obstacle*› sortear; ‹*difficulty*› superar

negotiation /nɪ'gəʊʃi'eɪʃən/ *n* [U] (*sometimes pl*) negociación *f*

negotiator /nɪ'gəʊʃɪeɪtər ‖ nɪ'gəʊʃɪeɪtə(r)/ *n* negociador, -dora *m,f*

Negro /'ni:grəʊ/ *n* (*pl* **Negroes**) (often offensive) negro, -gra *m,f*

neigh /neɪ/ *vi* relinchar

neighbor, (BrE) **neighbour** /'neɪbər ‖ 'neɪbə(r)/ *n* vecino, -na *m,f*

Negatives

Not

The translation of not *is* no, *which precedes the word it is negating*:

he's not *or* he isn't at home = no está en casa
not one but two = no uno sino dos

Where the Spanish has a pronoun or pronouns preceding a verb, they are placed between no *and the verb*:

I didn't see him = no lo vi
she didn't give it to me = no me lo dio

Never, Nobody, No one, Nothing, Neither, No

Spanish uses the double negative structure of no + verb + negative:

he never comes *o* he doesn't ever come = no viene nunca or jamás
nobody *o* no one spoke to him = no le habló nadie
there was nothing *o* there wasn't anything in the box = no había nada en la caja
she speaks neither French nor German *o* she doesn't speak (either) French or German = no habla ni francés ni alemán *or* no habla francés ni alemán
neither of them came = no vino ninguno de los dos
he paid no attention *o* he didn't pay any attention = no prestó ninguna atención

The double negative is not used when a negative precedes a verb in Spanish:

he never comes = nunca *or* jamás viene
nobody *o* no one saw him = nadie lo vio
I liked nothing I saw *o* I didn't like anything I saw = nada de lo que vi me gustó
neither he nor his mother did it = ni él ni su madre lo hicieron
neither of them came = ninguno de los dos vino
no country has criticized him = ningún país lo ha criticado

neighborhood, (BrE) **neighbourhood** /'neɪbərhʊd ‖ 'neɪbəhʊd/ *n* **(a)** (residential area) barrio *m*; (*before n*) ‹*school/policeman*› del barrio **(b)** (inhabitants) vecindario *m* **(c)** (vicinity) zona *f*; **in the ~** en los alrededores

neighboring, (BrE) **neighbouring** /'neɪbərɪŋ/ *adj* ‹*country*› vecino; **the town and the ~ villages** la ciudad y los pueblos de los alrededores

neither[1] /'ni:ðər, 'naɪ- ‖ 'naɪðə(r), 'ni:ð-/ **▶ 718** *conj* **1 neither … nor** … ni … ni … **2** (nor) tampoco; **I don't want to go — ~ do I** *o* (colloq) **me ~** no quiero ir — yo tampoco *or* ni yo

neither[2] *adj*: **~ proposal was accepted** no se aceptó ninguna de las (dos) propuestas

neither[3] **▶ 718** *pron* ninguno, -na

neon /'ni:ɑ:n ‖ 'ni:ɒn/ *n* [U] neón *m*; (*before n*) ‹*glow/lighting/sign*› de neón

Nepal /nə'pɔ:l ‖ nɪpɔ:l/ *n* Nepal *m*

Nepalese /,nepə'li:z/ *adj* nepalés

nephew /'nefju: ‖ 'nevju:, 'nef-/ *n* sobrino *m*

nepotism /'nepətɪzəm/ *n* [U] nepotismo *m*

Neptune /'neptu:n ‖ 'neptju:n/ *n* Neptuno *m*

nerve /nɜ:rv ‖ nɜ:v/ *n* **1** [C] (Anat, Bot) nervio *m*; (*before n*) ‹*fiber/ending*› nervioso **2 nerves** *pl* **(a)** (emotional constitution) nervios *mpl*; ***to get on sb's ~s*** (colloq) ponerle* los nervios de punta a algn **(b)** (anxiety) nervios *mpl* **3 (a)** [U] (resolve) valor *m*; **to lose one's ~** perder* el valor **(b)** (effrontery) (colloq) (*no pl*) frescura *f* (fam); **to have the ~ to + INF** tener* la frescura de + INF (fam)

nerve-racking /'nɜ:rv'rækɪŋ ‖ 'nɜ:v,rækɪŋ/ *adj* que destroza los nervios

nervous /'nɜ:rvəs ‖ 'nɜ:vəs/ *adj* **1** (apprehensive, tense) nervioso; **to feel/get ~** estar*/ponerse* nervioso; **to make sb ~** poner* nervioso a algn **2** ‹*system/tissue/tension*› nervioso; **she's a ~ wreck** (colloq) es un manojo de nervios

nervously /'nɜ:rvəsli ‖ 'nɜ:vəsli/ *adv* nerviosamente

nest[1] /nest/ *n* nido *m*

nest[2] *vi* anidar

nest egg *n* (colloq) ahorros *mpl*

nestle /'nesəl/ *vi* (snuggle) acurrucarse*; **the village ~s at the foot of the hill** el pueblo está enclavado al pie de la montaña

net[1] /net/ *n* **1** [C] red *f* **2** [C] (Sport) red *f* **3** [U] (fabric) tela *f* de visillos; (*before n*) **~ curtains** visillos *mpl*

net[2] *vt* **-tt- 1** (catch) ‹*butterfly*› cazar* (*con red*); ‹*fish*› pescar* (*con red*) **2** (earn) «*company/sale*» producir*; **he ~ted $50,000** se embolsó 50.000 dólares limpios (fam)

net[3] *adj* ‹*income/profit*› neto; ‹*effect/result*› global

netball /'netbɔ:l/ *n* [U] (in UK) *deporte similar al baloncesto jugado esp por mujeres*

Netherlands /'neðərləndz ‖ 'neðələndz/ *n* (+ *sing or pl vb*) **the ~** los Países Bajos

nett *adj* (BrE) ⇒ NET[3]

netting /'netɪŋ/ *n* [U] redes *fpl*; **wire ~** tela *f* metálica, tejido *m* metálico (RPl), anjeo *m* (Col)

nettle /'netḷ/ *n* ortiga *f*; (*stinging ~*) ortiga *f* (romana)

network[1] /'netwɜ:rk ‖ 'netwɜ:k/ *n* **(a)** (system) red *f* **(b)** (Elec) red *f* **(c)** (Rad, TV) cadena *f*; (*before*) **~ television** (in US) emisiones *fpl* televisivas en cadena

network[2] *vt* **1** (BrE Rad, TV) transmitir en cadena **2** (link together) (Comput) interconectar

neuralgia /nʊ'rældʒə ‖ njʊə'rældʒə/ *n* [U] neuralgia *f*

neurosis /nʊ'rəʊsəs ‖njʊə'rəʊsɪs/ *n* [C U] (*pl* **-roses** /-'rəʊsi:z/) neurosis *f*

neurotic /nʊ'rɑ:tɪk ‖ njʊə'rɒtɪk/ *adj* neurótico

neuter[1] /'nu:tər ‖ 'nju:tə(r)/ *adj* neutro

neuter[2] *vt* castrar

neutral[1] /'nu:trəl ‖ 'nju:trəl/ *adj* **(a)** (impartial) neutral **(b)** (not bright) ‹*shade/tone*› neutro **(c)** (Chem, Elec, Ling) neutro

neutral[2] *n* (Auto): **to be in ~** estar* en punto muerto

neutralize /'nu:trəlaɪz ‖ 'nju:trəlaɪz/ *vt* neutralizar*

neutron /'nu:trɑ:n ‖ 'nju:trɒn/ *n* neutrón *m*

Nev = **Nevada**

never /'nevər ‖ 'nevə(r)/ ▶**718** *adv* nunca; (more emphatic) jamás; **as ~ before** como nunca; **she said she'd call but she ~ did** dijo que llamaría pero no llamó; **this will ~ do!** ¡esto no puede ser!

never: **~-ending** /'never'endɪŋ/ *adj* (*pred* **~ ending**) ‹*dispute/saga*› interminable; ‹*devotion/supply*› inagotable; **~theless** /ˌnevərðə'les ‖ ˌnevəðə'les/ *adv* sin embargo, no obstante (frml)

new[1] /nu: ‖nju:/ *adj* **-er, -est** nuevo; **after the shower I felt like a ~ man** la ducha me dejó como nuevo

new[2] *adv* recién

new: **~born** /'nu:bɔ:n ‖ 'nju:bɔ:n/ *adj* recién nacido; **~comer** /'nu:kʌmər ‖ 'nju:kʌmə(r)/ *n* recién llegado, -da *m,f*; **~fangled** /'nu:'fæŋgəld ‖ 'nju:'fæŋgəld/ *adj* (*before n*) (pej) moderno; **~found** /'nju:ˌfaʊnd/ *adj* nuevo, recién descubierto

newlyweds /'nu:liwedz ‖ 'nju:liwedz/ *pl n* recién casados *mpl*

news /nu:z ‖nju:z/ *n* [U] **1** (fresh information): **a piece of ~** una noticia; **I have (some) good/bad ~** tengo buenas/malas noticias **2** (Journ, Rad, TV) noticias *fpl*; (*before n*) **~ bulletin** boletín *m* informativo

news: **~agent** *n* (BrE) *dueño o empleado de una tienda que vende prensa, caramelos etc*; **~caster** *n* locutor, -tora *m,f*, presentador, -dora *m,f* (*de un informativo*); **~ flash** *n* (BrE) información *f* de última hora; **~letter** *n* boletín *m* informativo

newspaper /'nu:zˌpeɪpər ‖ 'nju:sˌpeɪpə(r)/ *n* periódico *m*, diario *m*

news: **~print** *n* [U] papel *m* de prensa; **~reel** *n* [C U] noticiario *m* *or* (AmL tb) noticiero *m* (cinematográfico), nodo *m* (Esp); **~stand** *n* kiosco *m* de periódicos

newt /nu:t ‖ nju:t/ *n* tritón *m*

new: **N~ Year** *n* Año *m* Nuevo; **N~ Year's Day** *n* día *m* de Año Nuevo; **N~ Year's Eve** *n* la noche de Fin de Año, la Nochevieja (Esp); **N~ York** /jɔ:rk ‖ jɔ:k/ *n* Nueva York *f*; (*before n*) neoyorquino; **N~ Zealand** /'zi:lənd/ *n* Nueva Zelanda; (*before n*) neocelandés

next[1] /nekst/ *adj* **(a)** (in time — talking about the future) próximo; (— talking about the past) siguiente; **I'll see you ~ Thursday** nos vemos el jueves que viene *or* el jueves próximo; **the matter was discussed at the ~ meeting** el asunto se trató en la reunión siguiente; **the week after ~** la semana que viene no, la otra *or* la siguiente **(b)** (in position) siguiente; **take the ~ turning on the right** tome la próxima *or* la siguiente a la derecha **(c)** (in sequence): **who's ~?** ¿quién sigue?; **you're the ~ to speak** luego te toca a ti hablar

next[2] *adv* **1 (a)** (then) luego, después **(b)** (now): **what shall we do ~?** ¿y ahora qué hacemos?; **what comes ~?** ¿qué sigue (ahora)?; **whatever ~!** ¡adónde vamos (a ir) a parar! **2** (second): **Tom is the tallest in the class, Bob the ~ tallest** Tom es el más alto de la clase y (a Tom) le sigue Bob; **it's the ~ best thing to champagne** después del champán, es lo mejor que hay **3 next to (a)** (beside) al lado de; **come and sit ~ to me** ven y siéntate a mi lado **(b)** (compared with) al lado de **(c)** (second): **the ~ to last page** la penúltima página **(d)** (almost, virtually); **I bought it for ~ to nothing** lo compré por poquísimo dinero; **I'll have it ready in ~ to no time** lo termino en un segundo

next: **~ door** *adv* al lado; **~ door TO sb/sth** al lado DE algn/algo; **~-door** /'neks'dɔ:r ‖ 'neks'dɔ:(r)/ *adj* (*before n*) de al lado; **~ of kin** *n* (*pl* **~ of kin**) familiar(es) *m(pl)* más cercano(s)

NH = **New Hampshire**

NHS *n* (in UK) = **National Health Service**

nib /nɪb/ *n* plumín *m*, pluma *f*

nibble /'nɪbəl/ *vt* **(a)** (bite) mordisquear **(b)** (eat, pick at) picar* ■ **~** *vi* **(a)** (bite, gnaw) **to ~ AT/ON sth** mordisquear algo **(b)** (eat) picar*

Nicaragua /'nɪkə'rɑ:gwə ‖ ˌnɪkə'rægjʊə/ *n* Nicaragua *f*

Nicaraguan /'nɪkə'rɑ:gwən ‖ ˌnɪkə'rægjʊən/ *adj* nicaragüense

nice /naɪs/ *adj* **nicer, nicest 1 (a)** (kind, amiable) amable; (kind-hearted) bueno; (friendly) simpático; **to be ~ TO sb** ser* amable CON algn **(b)** (attractive, appealing) ‹*place/dress/face*› bonito, lindo (esp AmL); ‹*food*› bueno, rico; **the soup smells ~** la sopa huele bien **(c)** (enjoyable) ‹*walk/surprise*› agradable, lindo (esp AmL) **2** (*as intensifier*): **I had a ~ hot shower** me di una buena ducha caliente; **her apartment is ~ and sunny** tiene un apartamento muy *or* de lo más soleado **3** (respectable, decent): **he seemed such a ~ boy** parecía tan buen chico; **it isn't a very ~ area** es un barrio bastante feo

nicely /'naɪsli/ *adv* **1 (a)** (amiably) ‹*treat/smile*› amablemente **(b)** (politely, respectably) con buenos modales **2** (attractively) ‹*presented/dressed*› bien

niceties /'naɪsətiz/ *pl n* sutilezas *fpl*

niche /nɪtʃ, ni:ʃ/ *n* nicho *m*, hornacina *f*

nick[1] /nɪk/ *n* (in wood) muesca *f*; (in blade) mella *f*; **did you cut yourself? — it's just a little ~** ¿te cortaste? — es sólo un rasguño; ***in the ~ of time*** justo a tiempo

nick[2] *vt* **1** (notch) hacer* una muesca en; **I ~ed myself shaving** me corté al afeitarme **2** (steal) (BrE colloq) afanar (arg), volar* (Méx, Ven fam), robar

nickel /'nɪkəl/ **1** *n* [U] (Chem, Metall) níquel *m* **2** [C] (US coin) *moneda de cinco centavos*

nickname[1] /'nɪkneɪm/ *n* apodo *m*; (relating to personal characteristics) mote *m*

nickname[2] *vt* apodar

nicotine /ˈnɪkəti:n/ *n* [U] nicotina *f*

niece /ni:s/ *n* sobrina *f*

Nigeria /naɪˈdʒɪriə ‖ naɪˈdʒɪəriə/ *n* Nigeria *f*

Nigerian /naɪˈdʒɪriən ‖ naɪˈdʒɪəriən/ *adj* nigeriano

niggle /ˈnɪgəl/ *vt*: **something's niggling him** algo le preocupa

niggling /ˈnɪglɪŋ/ *adj* ‹*doubt/worry*› constante

night /naɪt/ ▶884 *n* **1** [C U] noche *f*; **at ~** por la noche, de noche; **~ and day** día y noche; **last ~** anoche; **the ~ before last** anteanoche, antenoche (AmL); **we stayed (for) the ~** nos quedamos a dormir; **we haven't had a ~ out for ages** hace muchísimo que no salimos por la noche; **good ~** buenas noches; (*before n*) ‹*flight/patrol*› nocturno **2 nights** (*as adv*) por las noches

night: **~cap** *n* **(a)** (Clothing) gorro *m* de dormir **(b)** (drink) *bebida alcohólica o caliente tomada antes de acostarse*; **~clothes** *pl n* ropa *f* de dormir; **~club** *n* club *m* nocturno; **~dress** *n* camisón *m*; **~fall** *n* [U] anochecer *m*; **at ~fall** al anochecer; **~gown** *n* camisón *m*

nightingale /ˈnaɪtn̩geɪl ‖ ˈnaɪtɪŋgeɪl/ *n* ruiseñor *m*

nightlife /ˈnaɪtlaɪf/ *n* [U] vida *f* nocturna

nightly¹ /ˈnaɪtli/ *adj* diario, de todas las noches

nightly² *adv* todas las noches

nightmare /ˈnaɪtmer ‖ ˈnaɪtmeə(r)/ *n* pesadilla *f*

night: **~ school** *n* clases *fpl* nocturnas; **~time** *n* noche *f*; **~ watchman** /ˈwɑ:tʃmən ‖ ˈwɒtʃmən/ *n* sereno *m*

nil /nɪl/ *n* **(a)** (nothing): **its food value is virtually ~** su valor nutritivo es casi nulo **(b)** (BrE Sport) cero *m*

Nile /naɪl/ *n* **the ~** el Nilo

nimble /ˈnɪmbəl/ *adj* **-bler** /-blər/, **-blest** /-bləst/ ‹*person/step/mind*› ágil; ‹*fingers*› diestro

nine¹ /naɪn/ ▶451, 724, 884 *n* nueve *m*; *see also* FOUR¹

nine² ▶451, 724, 884 *adj* nueve *adj inv*; **~ times out of ten he's late/right** casi siempre llega tarde/tiene razón

ninefold /ˈnaɪnfəʊld/ *adj/adv see* -FOLD

nineteen *adj/n* diecinueve /ˈnaɪnˈti:n/ ▶451, 724, 884 *adj inv/m*; ***to talk ~ to the dozen*** hablar (hasta) por los codos *or* como una cotorra (fam); *see also* FOUR¹

nineteenth¹ /ˈnaɪnˈti:nθ/ ▶540, 725 *adj* decimonoveno

nineteenth² *adv* en decimonoveno lugar

nineteenth³ ▶540, 543, 725 *n* (Math) diecinueveavo *m*; (part) diecinueveava parte *f*

ninetieth¹ /ˈnaɪntiəθ/ ▶725 *adj* nonagésimo

ninetieth² *adv* en nonagésimo lugar

ninetieth³ ▶543, 725 *n* (Math) noventavo *m*; (part) noventava *or* nonagésima parte *f*

nine-to-five /ˈnaɪntəˈfaɪv/ *adj* ‹*job/worker*› de oficina (*con horario de nueve a cinco*)

ninety /ˈnaɪnti/ ▶451, 540, 724 *adj/n* noventa *adj inv/m*; *see also* FOUR¹

ninth¹ /naɪnθ/ ▶540, 725 *adj* noveno

ninth² *adv* en noveno lugar

ninth³ ▶540, 543, 725 *n* (Math) noveno *m*; (part) novena parte *f*

nip¹ /nɪp/ *n* **(a)** (pinch) pellizco *m*; (bite) mordisco *m* **(b)** (chill): **there's a ~ in the air** hace bastante fresco

nip² *vt* **-pp-** (pinch) pellizcar*; (bite) mordisquear

nipple /ˈnɪpəl/ *n* **(a)** (on breast — of woman) pezón *m*; (— of man) tetilla *f* **(b)** (on bottle) (AmE) tetina *f*, chupón *m* (Méx)

nippy /ˈnɪpi/ *adj* **-pier, -piest** (colloq) frío; **it's ~** hace frío

nit /nɪt/ *n* (Zool) liendre *f*

nit: **~pick** *vi* encontrarle* defectos a todo; **~picking** *adj* quisquilloso

nitrate /ˈnaɪtreɪt/ *n* [C U] nitrato *m*

nitrogen /ˈnaɪtrədʒən/ *n* [U] nitrógeno *m*

NJ = **New Jersey**

NM, **N Mex** = **New Mexico**

no¹ /nəʊ/ ▶718 *adj* **1 (a)** (+ *pl n*): **they have ~ children** no tienen hijos; **the room has ~ windows** la habitación no tiene ninguna ventana *or* no tiene ventanas **(b)** (+ *uncount n*): **there's ~ food left** no queda nada de comida; **there's ~ time for that now** no tenemos tiempo para eso ahora; **I'll be finished in ~ time (at all)** termino enseguida **(c)** (+ *sing count n*): **this cup has ~ handle** esta taza no tiene asa; **~ intelligent person would do that** ninguna persona inteligente haría eso **2** (in understatements): **I'm ~ expert, but ...** no soy ningún experto, pero ...; **she told him what she thought in ~ uncertain terms** le dijo lo que pensaba muy claramente **3 (a)** (prohibiting, demanding): Ⓢ **no smoking** prohibido fumar **(b)** (*with -ing form*): **there's ~ pleasing some people** no hay manera de complacer a cierta gente; **there'll be ~ stopping them now** ahora no hay quien los pare

no² *adv* (*before adj or adv*): **my house is ~ larger than yours** mi casa no es más grande que la tuya; **~ fewer than 200 guests are expected** se espera nada menos que a unos 200 invitados

no³ *interj* no; **to say ~** decir* que no; **have you seen John? — ~, I haven't** ¿has visto a John? — no

no⁴ *n* (*pl* **noes**) no *m*

no⁵ (*pl* **nos**) (= **number**) nº, Nº

Nobel Prize /nəʊˈbel/ *n* **the ~ ~** el Premio Nobel

nobility /nəʊˈbɪləti/ *n* [U] nobleza *f*; **the ~** la nobleza

noble¹ /ˈnəʊbəl/ *adj* **nobler** /-blər/, **noblest** /-bləst/ noble

noble² *n* noble *mf*

nobleman /ˈnəʊbəlmən/ *n* (*pl* **-men** /-mən/) noble *m*

nobody¹ /ˈnəʊˌbɑ:di ‖ ˈnəʊbədi/ ▶718 *pron* nadie

nobody² *n* (*pl* **-dies**): **to be (a) ~** ser* un don nadie

nocturnal /nɑ:kˈtɜ:rnl̩ ‖ nɒkˈtɜ:nl̩/ *adj* nocturno

nod¹ /nɑːd ‖ nɒd/ *n*: **he greeted her with a ~** la saludó con un movimiento de cabeza; ***to give sb/sth the ~*** darle* luz verde a algn/algo

nod² -dd- *vt*: **he ~ded his head (in agreement)** asintió con la cabeza ■ **~** *vi*: **she smiled at me and I ~ed to her** me sonrió y la saludé con la cabeza; **they ~ded in assent** asintieron con la cabeza

● **nod off** [*v* + *adv*] (colloq) dormirse*

nodule /'nɑːdʒuːl ‖ 'nɒdjuːl/ *n* nódulo *m*

no-good /nəʊ'gʊd/ *adj* (AmE colloq) maldito (fam)

noise /nɔɪz/ *n* [C U] ruido *m*

noisily /'nɔɪzəli ‖ 'nɔɪzɪli/ *adv* ruidosamente

noisy /'nɔɪzi/ *adj* **-sier, -siest** ‹*machine/office/street*› ruidoso; ‹*person/child/party*› bullicioso

nomad /'nəʊmæd/ *n* nómada *mf*, nómade *mf* (CS)

no-man's land /'nəʊmænzlænd/ *n* [U C] tierra *f* de nadie

nominal /'nɑːmənl̩ ‖ 'nɒmɪnl̩/ *adj* **(a)** (in name) nominal **(b)** (token) ‹*fee/rent*› simbólico

nominate /'nɑːməneɪt ‖ 'nɒmɪneɪt/ *vt* **(a)** (propose) **to ~ sb** (FOR **sth**) ‹*for a post*› proponer* *or* (AmL tb) postular a algn (PARA algo) **(b)** (appoint, choose) nombrar; ‹*candidate*› (AmE Pol) proclamar

nomination /'nɑːmə'neɪʃən ‖ ˌnɒmɪ'neɪʃən/ *n* [C U] **(a)** (choice, appointment) nombramiento *m*; (of candidate) (AmE Pol) proclamación *f* **(b)** (proposal) propuesta *f*, postulación *f* (AmL)

nominee /'nɑːmə'niː ‖ ˌnɒmɪ'niː/ *n* **(a)** (person proposed) candidato, -ta *m,f* **(b)** (person appointed) persona *f* nombrada; (candidate) (AmE Pol) candidato, -ta *m,f*

non- /nɑːn ‖ nɒn/ *pref* no; **~swimmers must** ... las personas que no saben nadar deben ...

nonchalant /'nɑːnʃə'lɑːnt ‖ 'nɒnʃələnt/ *adj* (casual) despreocupado; (indifferent) indiferente

noncommissioned officer /ˌnɑːnkə'mɪʃənd ‖ ˌnɒnkə'mɪʃənd/ *n* ≈ suboficial *mf*

noncommittal /ˌnɑːnkə'mɪtl̩ ‖ ˌnɒnkə'mɪtl̩/ *adj* ‹*reply*› evasivo

nondescript /'nɑːndɪ'skrɪpt ‖ 'nɒndɪskrɪpt/ *adj* (not unusual or outstanding) anodino; (dull) insulso

none¹ /nʌn/ *pron* **1** (not any, not one) (*referring to count n*) ninguno, ninguna; **I tried to get tickets, but there were ~ left** traté de comprar entradas pero no quedaba ninguna *or* ni una; **~ of us know** *o* **knows her** ninguno de nosotros la conoce **2** (no amount or part) (*referring to uncount n*): **did you buy any milk? there's ~ left** ¿compraste leche? no hay más

none² *adv* **(a) none the** (not, in no way) (*with comp*): **I was ~ the wiser after his explanation** su explicación no me aclaró nada **(b) none too** (not very) (*with adj or adv*): **she was ~ too pleased to see me** no le hizo demasiada gracia verme

nonentity /nɑː'nentəti ‖ nɒ'nentəti/ *n* (*pl* **-ties**) persona *f* insignificante

nonetheless /'nʌnðə'les/ *adv* ⇨ NEVERTHELESS

non-existent /ˌnɑːnɪg'zɪstənt ‖ ˌnɒnɪg'zɪstənt/ *adj* inexistente

nonfiction /'nɑːn'fɪkʃən ‖ ˌnɒn'fɪkʃən/ *n* [U] no ficción *f* (*ensayos, biografías, obras de divulgación etc*)

no-nonsense /'nəʊ'nɑːnsens ‖ ˌnəʊ'nɒnsəns/ *adj* (*before n*) ‹*approach/attitude*› sensato

nonplused, **nonplussed** /nɑːn'plʌst ‖ ˌnɒn'plʌst/ *adj* desconcertado

nonprofit /'nɑːn'prɑːfət ‖ ˌnɒn'prɒfɪt/, (BrE) **non-profitmaking** /'nɑːn'prɑːfətˌmeɪkɪŋ ‖ ˌnɒn'prɒfɪt meɪkɪŋ/ *adj* sin fines lucrativos

nonsense /'nɑːnsens ‖ 'nɒnsəns/ *n* [U] tonterías *fpl*

nonsensical /nɑːn'sensɪkəl ‖ nɒn'sensɪkəl/ *adj* disparatado

nonsmoker /'nɑːn'sməʊkər ‖ ˌnɒn'sməʊkə(r)/ *n* no fumador, -dora *m,f*

nonstick /'nɑːn'stɪk ‖ ˌnɒn'stɪk/ *adj* antiadherente, de teflón®, de tefal®

nonstop /'nɑːn'stɑːp ‖ ˌnɒn'stɒp/ *adv* **(a)** ‹*work/talk*› sin parar **(b)** ‹*sail/fly*› sin hacer escalas

noodle /'nuːdl̩/ *n* fideo *m*

nook /nʊk/ *n* rincón *m*; ***to search every ~ and cranny*** mirar/buscar* hasta en el último rincón

noon /nuːn/ *n* mediodía *m*; **at ~** a mediodía

no one ▶ 718 *pron* ⇨ NOBODY¹

noose /nuːs/ *n* soga *f*, dogal *m*

noplace /'nəʊpleɪs/ *adv* (AmE) ⇨ NOWHERE¹ 1

nor /nər, nɔːr ‖ nɔː(r)/ *conj* **(a)** ▶ 718 **neither** ... **nor** ... *see* NEITHER¹ 1 **(b)** (*usu with neg*) tampoco

norm /nɔːrm ‖ nɔːm/ *n* norma *f*

normal /'nɔːrməl ‖ 'nɔːməl/ *adj* normal; **when things get back to ~** cuando todo vuelva a la normalidad

normality /nɔːr'mæləti ‖ nɔːmæləti/ *n* [U] normalidad *f*

normally /'nɔːrməli ‖ 'nɔːməli/ *adv* normalmente

north¹ /nɔːrθ ‖ nɔːθ/ *n* [U] (point of the compass, direction) norte *m*; **the ~, the N~** (region) el norte

north² *adj* (*before n*) norte *adj inv*, septentrional; ‹*wind*› norte *adj inv*

north³ *adv* al norte

north: **N~ America** *n* Norteamérica *f*, América *f* del Norte; **N~ American** *adj* de América del Norte, norteamericano; **~bound** *adj* ‹*traffic/train*› que va (*or* iba *etc*) en dirección norte

northeast¹, **Northeast** /'nɔːrθ'iːst ‖ ˌnɔːθ'iːst/ *n* [U] **the ~** el nor(d)este, el Nor(d)este

northeast² *adj* nor(d)este *adj inv*, del nor(d)este, nororiental

northeast³ *adv* hacia el nor(d)este, en dirección nor(d)este

northeasterly /'nɔːrθ'iːstərli ‖ ˌnɔːθ'iːstəli/ *adj* ‹*wind*› del nor(d)este

northeastern /'nɔːrθ'iːstərn ‖ ˌnɔːθ'iːstən/ *adj* nor(d)este *adj inv*, del nor(d)este, nororiental

northerly /'nɔːrðərli ‖ 'nɔːðəli/ *adj* ‹*wind*› del norte; ‹*latitude*› norte *adj inv*; **in a ~ direction** hacia el *or* en dirección norte

northern /'nɔːrðərn ‖ 'nɔːðən/ *adj* ‹*region/country*› del norte, septentrional, norteño, nortino

(Chi, Per); ~ **England** el norte de Inglaterra; **the ~ states** (in US) los estados del norte

Northern Ireland *n* Irlanda *f* del Norte

north: **N~ Sea** *n* Mar *m* del Norte; **N~ Star** *n* estrella *f* polar

northward¹ /ˈnɔːrθwərd ˈnɔːθwəd/ *adj (before n)*: **in a ~ direction** en dirección norte, hacia el norte

northward², (BrE) **northwards** /-z/ *adv* hacia el norte

northwest¹, **Northwest** /ˈnɔːrθˈwest ‖ˌnɔːθ ˈwest/ *n* [U] **the ~** el noroeste *or* Noroeste

northwest² *adj* noroeste *adj inv*, del noroeste

northwest³ *adv* hacia el noroeste, en dirección noroeste

northwesterly /ˈnɔːrθˈwestərli ‖ˌnɔːθˈwestəli/ *adj* ‹*wind*› del noroeste

northwestern /ˈnɔːrθˈwestərn ‖ˌnɔːθˈwestən/ *adj* noroccidental, noroeste *adj inv*, del noroeste

Norway /ˈnɔːrweɪ ‖ ˈnɔːweɪ/ *n* Noruega *f*

Norwegian¹ /nɔːrˈwiːdʒən ‖ nɔːˈwiːdʒən/ *adj* noruego

Norwegian² *n* **(a)** [C] (person) noruego, -ga *m,f* **(b)** [U] (language) noruego *m*

nose¹ /nəʊz/ *n* ▶ **484** **1** (of person, animal) nariz *f*; ***to look down one's ~ at sb*** mirar a algn por encima del hombro; ***to turn one's ~ up at sth/sb*** (colloq) despreciar algo/a algn **2** (of plane, car) parte *f* delantera, trompa *f* (RPl)

nose² *vi* (rummage, pry) entrometerse; **to ~ around** *o* **about in sth** husmear en algo

nose: **~bleed** *n* hemorragia *f* nasal (frml); **I've got a ~bleed** me sangra la nariz; **~dive** *vi* **(a)** (Aviat) «*plane/pilot*» descender* *or* bajar en picada *or* (Esp) en picado **(b)** (drop sharply) «*prices*» caer* en picada *or* (Esp) en picado

nosey /ˈnəʊzi/ *adj* (BrE) ⇒ NOSY

no-smoking /ˈnəʊˈsməʊkɪŋ/ *adj* ‹*compartment/section*› para no fumadores

nostalgia /nɑːˈstældʒə ‖ nɒˈstældʒə/ *n* [U] nostalgia *f*

nostalgic /nɑːˈstældʒɪk ‖ nɒˈstældʒɪk/ *adj* nostálgico

nostril /ˈnɑːstrəl ‖ ˈnɒstrɪl/ *n* ventana *f* de la nariz

nosy, (BrE also) **nosey** /ˈnəʊzi/ *adj* **nosier, nosiest** (colloq) ‹*person*› entrometido, metiche (AmL fam), metido (AmL fam); ‹*question*› impertinente

not /nɑːt ‖ nɒt/ ▶ **718** *adv* **(a)** no; **I asked them ~ to tell anyone** les pedí que no se lo dijeran a nadie **(b) not that** (*as conj*): **I'm going to London, ~ that it's any business of yours** voy a Londres, no es que a ti te importe, pero ... **(c)** (emphatic) ni; **~ a penny more** ni un penique más **(d)** (replacing clause): **I hope ~** — espero que no; **are you going to help me or ~?** ¿me vas a ayudar o no?

notable /ˈnəʊtəbəl/ *adj* ‹*author/actor*› distinguido; ‹*success*› señalado; ‹*improvement/difference*› notable

notably /ˈnəʊtəbli/ *adv* **(a)** (noticeably) notablemente **(b)** (in particular) particularmente, en particular

notch /nɑːtʃ ‖ nɒtʃ/ *n* (in wood, metal) muesca *f*; (on belt) agujero *m*

• **notch up** [*v* + *adv* + *o*] (colloq) apuntarse

note¹ /nəʊt/ *n* **1** [C] (record, reminder) nota *f*; **to make a ~ of sth** anotar *or* apuntar algo; **to make ~s** hacer* anotaciones; **to take ~s** tomar apuntes *or* notas; **to compare ~s** cambiar impresiones **2** [C] (message) nota *f* **3** [C] **(a)** (Mus) nota *f* **(b)** (tone): **I detected a ~ of sarcasm in his voice** percibí un tono de sarcasmo en su voz; **the evening ended on a sad ~** la velada terminó con una nota triste **4** [C] (esp BrE) (*bank~*) billete *m* **5** [U] (attention): **take ~ of what he says** toma nota de *or* presta atención a lo que dice

note² *vt* **(a)** (observe, notice) observar **(b)** (record) ‹*information*› apuntar, anotar

• **note down** [*v* + *adv* + *o*, *v* + *o* + *adv*] apuntar

notebook /ˈnəʊtbʊk/ *n* cuaderno *m*

noted /ˈnəʊtəd ‖ ˈnəʊtɪd/ *adj* ‹*historian/surgeon*› renombrado, de nota

note: **~pad** *n* bloc *m*; **~paper** *n* [U] papel *m* de carta(s)

nothing /ˈnʌθɪŋ/ *pron* ▶ **718** **1** nada; **there's ~ to eat** no hay nada de comer **2** (*in phrases*) **for nothing**: **she gave it to me for ~** me lo dio gratis; **it was all for ~** todo fue en vano; **if nothing else** al menos, por lo menos; **nothing but**: **she's caused ~ but trouble** no ha causado (nada) más que problemas; **nothing like**: **there's ~ like a shower to freshen you up** no hay (nada) como una ducha para refrescarse; **nothing much**: **~ much happened** no pasó gran cosa

notice¹ /ˈnəʊtəs ‖ ˈnəʊtɪs/ *n* **1** [C] **(a)** (written sign) letrero *m* **(b)** (item of information) anuncio *m* **2** [U] (attention): **it has come/been brought to my ~ that** ... (frml) ha llegado a mi conocimiento que .../se me ha señalado que ... (frml); **she took no ~** no hizo caso; **don't take any ~ of him** no le hagas caso **3** [U] **(a)** (notification) aviso *m*; **until further ~** hasta nuevo aviso; **it's impossible to do it at such short ~** es imposible hacerlo a tan corto plazo **(b)** (of termination of employment) preaviso *m*; **I have to give (the company) a month's ~** tengo que dar un mes de preaviso; **to give** *o* **hand in one's ~** presentar su (*or* mi *etc*) renuncia

notice² *vt* notar; **nobody ~d him put it in his pocket** nadie lo vio ponérselo en el bolsillo ■ **~** *vi* (realize, observe) darse* cuenta

noticeable /ˈnəʊtəsəbəl ‖ ˈnəʊtɪsəbəl/ *adj* perceptible

noticeboard /ˈnəʊtəsbɔːrd ‖ ˈnəʊtɪsbɔːd/ *n* (esp BrE) tablero *m or* (Esp) tablón *m* de anuncios, cartelera *f* (AmL), diario *m* mural (Chi)

notification /ˈnəʊtəfəˈkeɪʃən ‖ˌnəʊtɪfɪˈkeɪʃən/ *n* [U] notificación *f*

notify /ˈnəʊtəfaɪ ‖ ˈnəʊtɪfaɪ/ *vt* **-fies, -fying, -fied** (inform) informar; (in writing) notificar*; **to ~ sb** OF **sth** comunicarle* algo A algn

notion /ˈnəʊʃən/ *n* **1** [C] (idea) idea *f* **2** [C] (concept) concepto *m* **3 notions** *pl* **(a)** (in sewing) artículos *mpl* de mercería **(b)** (AmE): **household/gift ~s** artículos *mpl* para el hogar/de regalo

notorious /nəʊ'tɔːriəs/ *adj* ‹*thief/womanizer/gossip*› (bien) conocido; ‹*place*› de mala fama

notwithstanding[1] /'nɑːtwɪð'stændɪŋ ‖ ˌnɒtwɪθ'stændɪŋ/ *prep* (frml) a pesar de, no obstante (frml)

notwithstanding[2] *adv* (frml) no obstante (frml)

nought /nɔːt/ *n* (esp BrE) cero *m*

noun /naʊn/ *n* sustantivo *m*, nombre *m*

nourish /'nɜːrɪʃ ‖ 'nʌrɪʃ/ *vt* nutrir

nourishing /'nɜːrɪʃɪŋ ‖ 'nʌrɪʃɪŋ/ *adj* nutritivo

nourishment /'nɜːrɪʃmənt ‖ 'nʌrɪʃmənt/ *n* [U] alimento *m*

nouveau riche /'nuːvəʊ'riːʃ/ *n* (*pl* **~x ~s** /'nuːvəʊ'riːʃ/) (pej) nuevo rico, nueva rica *m,f* (pey)

novel[1] /'nɑːvəl ‖ 'nɒvəl/ *n* novela *f*

novel[2] *adj* original, novedoso (esp AmL)

novelist /'nɑːvələst ‖ 'nɒvəlɪst/ *n* novelista *mf*

novelty /'nɑːvəlti ‖ 'nɒvəlti/ *n* (*pl* **-ties**) **(a)** [U] (newness): **the ~ will soon wear off** pronto dejará de ser novedad *or* (esp AmL) novedoso **(b)** [C] (new thing, situation) novedad *f*

November /nəʊ'vembər ‖ nəʊ'vembə(r)/ ▶ **540** *n* noviembre *m*

novice /'nɑːvəs ‖ 'nɒvɪs/ *n* principiante *mf*, novato, -ta *m,f*

now[1] /naʊ/ *adv* **1 (a)** (at this time) ahora; **you can come in ~** ya puedes entrar; **any minute ~** en cualquier momento; **~'s your chance** ésta es tu oportunidad **(b)** (at that time): **it was ~ time to say goodbye** había llegado el momento de decir adiós **(c)** (nowadays) hoy en día, actualmente **(d)** (*in phrases*) **(every) now and then** *o* **again** de vez en cuando; **for now** por ahora **2 (a)** (at once, immediately) ahora (mismo); **it's ~ or never!** ¡ahora o nunca! **(b)** (*in phrases*) **just now**: **he's talking to a client just ~** en este momento está hablando con un cliente; **right now** (immediately) ahora mismo, inmediatamente; (at present) ahora mismo, en este momento **3 (a)** (showing length of time) ya; **we've been living here for 40 years ~** ya hace 40 años que vivimos aquí **(b)** (*after prep*): **between ~ and Friday** de aquí al viernes; **she should be here by ~** ya debería estar aquí; **(up) until** *o* **till ~, up to ~** hasta ahora **4 (a)** (indicating pause, transition): **~, who's next?** bueno ¿(ahora) a quién le toca? **(b)** (emphasizing command, request, warning, advice): **~ look here!** ¡espera un momento! **(c)** (*in phrases*) **now, now** ¡vamos, vamos!; **now then** … a ver …

now[2] *conj* **~ (that)** ahora que

nowadays /'naʊədeɪz/ *adv* hoy (en) día, actualmente

nowhere[1] /'nəʊhwer ‖ 'nəʊweə(r)/ *adv* **1** : **where did you go last night? — nowhere** ¿adónde fuiste anoche? — a ningún lado *or* a ninguna parte; **she was ~ to be found/seen** no se la encontraba/se la veía por ningún lado *or* por ninguna parte; ***to get* ~** no conseguir* nada **2 nowhere near**: **Warsaw is ~ near Moscow** Varsovia está lejísimos de Moscú; **I'm ~ near finished** me falta mucho para terminar

nowhere[2] *pron*: **he had ~ to go** no tenía dónde ir; **the car just appeared from ~** el coche apareció de la nada

noxious /'nɑːkʃəs ‖ 'nɒkʃəs/ *adj* (frml) nocivo

nozzle /'nɑːzəl ‖ 'nɒzəl/ *n* (on hose) boca *f*; (on fire extinguisher) boquilla *f*

NSPCC *n* (in UK) (= **National Society for the Prevention of Cruelty to Children**) ≈ Asociación *f* de protección a la infancia

nuance /'nuːɑːns ‖'njuːɑːns/ *n* matiz *m*

nuclear /'nuːkliər ‖'njuːkliə(r)/ *adj* nuclear; **~ power** energía *f* nuclear; **~ power station** central *f* nuclear

nuclear: **~ family** *n* familia *f* nuclear; **~-powered** /'nuːkliər'paʊərd ‖ 'njuːklɪə'paʊəd/ *adj* nuclear

nucleus /'nuːkliəs ‖ 'njuːkliəs/ *n* (*pl* **-clei** /-kliaɪ/) núcleo *m*

nude[1] /nuːd ‖njuːd/ *n* (Art) desnudo *m*; **in the ~** desnudo

nude[2] *adj* desnudo

nudge[1] /nʌdʒ/ *vt* codear (ligeramente)

nudge[2] *n* golpe *m* (suave) con el codo

nudist /'nuːdəst ‖ 'njuːdɪst/ *n* nudista *mf*; (*before n*) ‹*beach/camp*› nudista

nudity /'nuːdəti ‖ 'njuːdəti/ *n* [U] desnudez *f*

nugget /'nʌgət ‖ 'nʌgɪt/ *n* (Min) pepita *f*

nuisance /'nuːsns ‖ 'njuːsns/ *n* **(a)** (occurrence, thing): **to be a ~** ser* una molestia, ser* un incordio (Esp) **(b)** (person) pesado, -da *m,f*, incordio *m* (Esp fam)

null /nʌl/ *adj* (Law): **to declare sth ~ and void** declarar nulo algo

numb[1] /nʌm/ *adj* **-er, -est** (with cold) entumecido; **the injection made my gums go ~** la inyección me durmió las encías

numb[2] *vt* «*cold*» entumecer*; «*drug*» dormir*

number[1] /'nʌmbər ‖ 'nʌmbə(r)/ ▶ **724**, **725** *n* número *m*; (*telephone* **~**) número de teléfono; **student ~s** el número de estudiantes; **on a ~ of occasions** en varias ocasiones

number[2] *vt* **(a)** (assign number to) ‹*houses/pages/items*› numerar **(b)** (amount to): **the spectators ~ed 50,000** había (un total de) 50.000 espectadores **(c)** (count) contar*; **his days are ~ed** tiene los días contados

numberplate /'nʌmbəpleɪt/ *n* (BrE) matrícula *f*, placa *f* (AmL), patente *f* (CS), chapa *f* (RPl)

numeral /'nuːmərəl ‖ 'njuːmərəl/ *n* número *m*

numerical /nʊ'merɪkəl ‖ njuː'merɪkəl/ *adj* numérico

numerous /'nuːmərəs ‖ 'njuːmərəs/ *adj* numeroso

nun /nʌn/ ▶ **603** *n* monja *f*, religiosa *f* (frml)

nurse[1] /nɜːrs ‖ nɜːs/ *n* **(a)** (Med) enfermero, -ra *m,f* **(b)** (nanny) niñera *f*

nurse[2] *vt* **1** (Med) ‹*patient*› atender*; **he ~d her back to health** la atendió hasta que se repuso **2** (cradle) ‹*baby*› arrullar **3** (suckle) ‹*baby*› amamantar

nursery /'nɜːrsri ‖ 'nɜːsəri/ *n* (*pl* **-ries**) **(a)** (*day* **~**) guardería *f* **(b)** (room in house) cuarto *m or* habitación *f* de los niños **(c)** (Agr, Hort) vivero *m*

nursery: **~ rhyme** *n* canción *f* infantil; **~ school** *n* jardín *m* de infancia, jardín *m* infantil

Numbers 1

Cardinal numbers

1 = uno	21 = vientiuno	101 = ciento uno
2 = dos	22 = vientidós	102 = ciento dos
3 = tres	23 = vientitrés	200 = doscientos
4 = cuatro	24 = vienticuatro	300 = trescientos
5 = cinco	25 = vienticinco	400 = cuatrocientos
6 = seis	26 = vientiséis	500 = quinientos
7 = siete	27 = vientisiete	600 = seiscientos
8 = ocho	28 = vientiocho	700 = setecientos
9 = nueve	29 = vientinueve	800 = ochocientos
10 = diez	30 = treinta	900 = novecientos
11 = once	31 = treinta y uno	1000 = mil
12 = doce	32 = treinta y dos	1001 = mil uno
13 = trece	40 = cuarenta	10 000 = diez mil
14 = catorce	50 = cincuenta	100 000 = cien mil
15 = quince	60 = sesenta	1 000 000 = un millón
16 = dieciséis	70 = setenta	
17 = diecisiete	80 = ochenta	
18 = dieciocho	90 = noventa	
19 = diecinueve	100 = cien	
20 = veinte		

In numbers after 30 the conjunction y *is used between the tens and the units, but not between the hundreds and the tens*:

46 = cuarenta y seis
432 = cuatrocientos treinta y dos

millón *requires the use of* de:

a million people = un millón de personas
three million votes = tres millones de votos

In most Spanish-speaking countries a point is used for writing figures over one thousand:

1,000 (*one thousand*) = 1.000 (*mil*)
1,000,000 (*one million*) = 1.000.000 (*un millón*)

Some Latin American countries, however, use the comma as in English:

1,000 (*one thousand*) = 1,000 (*mil*)
1,000,000 (*one million*) = 1,000,000 (*un millón*)

Gender and Agreement

Numbers in Spanish are masculine when used as nouns, and require an article:

there's a zero missing = le falta un cero
the prize went to number 21344 = el premio correspondió al vientiún mil trescientos cuarenta y cuatro

When a number refers to a noun which does not appear in the sentence, thearticle will agree with that noun:

which is your office? — 603 = ¿cuál es tu oficina? — la 603

When used as adjectives, numbers are invariable, except uno *and* ciento, *any number ending in* uno *and* ciento, *and* quinientos:

40 pesetas = cuarenta pesetas
300 pesetas = trescientas pesetas

Un/uno/una

uno *becomes* un *before a masculine noun*:

one *o* a peso = un peso
21 *pesos* = veintiún pesos

una *is used before a feminine noun*:

one *o* a peseta = una peseta
21 pesetas = vientiuna pesetas

uno *and* una *are used as pronouns*:

I have only one left = sólo me queda uno
I asked him for one = le pedí una

Cien/ciento

The form cien *is used*:

◆ *When the word is used alone*:

How many are there? – 100 = ¿cuántos hay? – cien

◆ *When modifying another larger number*:

100 000 people = cien mil personas
100 000 000 pesos = cien millones de pesos

◆ *Before a noun*:

100 tickets = cien entradas
100 pupils = cien alumnos

ciento *is used to express numbers between 100 and 199*:

100 = ciento cinco
198 = ciento noventa y ocho

Numbers 2

Ordinal numbers

1st	=	primero	1º
2nd	=	segundo	2º
3rd	=	tercero	3º
4th	=	cuarto	4º
5th	=	quinto	5º
6th	=	sexto	6º
7th	=	séptimo	7º
8th	=	octavo	8º
9th	=	noveno	9º
10th	=	décimo	10º
11th	=	undécimo *or* decimoprimero	11º
12th	=	duodécimo *or* decimosegundo	12º
13th	=	decimotercero	13º
14th	=	decimocuarto	14º
15th	=	decimoquinto	15º
16th	=	decimosexto	16º
17th	=	decimoséptimo	17º
18th	=	decimoctavo	18º
19th	=	decimonoveno *or* decimonono	19º
20th	=	vigésimo	20º
21st	=	vigesimoprimero	21º
22nd	=	vigesimosegundo	22º
23rd	=	vigesimotercero	23º
30th	=	trigésimo	30º
40th	=	cuadragésimo	40º
50th	=	quincuagésimo	50º
60th	=	sexagésimo	60º
70th	=	septuagésimo	70º
80th	=	octogésimo	80º
90th	=	nonagésimo	90º
100th	=	centésimo	100º
1,000th	=	milésimo	1,000º
1,000,000th	=	millonésimo	1,000.000º

Ordinals above décimo *(10th) are often replaced by the corresponding cardinal number, especially in less formal speech*:

the 40th anniversary = el cuarenta *or* el cuadragésimo aniversario

Cardinal numbers are also used in titles where the number is above ten:

Carlos V	=	Carlos quinto
Isabel II	=	Isabel segundo
Alfonso XIII	=	Alfonso trece
Juan XXIII	=	Juan vientitrés

Gender and agreement

Spanish ordinal numbers agree with the noun they are qualifying, as do their abbreviated forms:

the 2nd volume	=	el segundo tomo *or* el 2º tomo
the 5th installment	=	la quinta entrega *or* la 5ª entrega

primero *and* tercero *become* primer *and* tercer *when they precede a masculine singular noun, even if there is an intervening adjective*:

his third attempt	=	su tercer intento
the first great scholar of the subject	=	el primer gran estudioso del tema

The abbreviated forms of primer *and* tercer *are* 1er *and* 3er

(AmL), kindergarten *m* (AmL); (preschool) pre-escolar *m*

nursing /'nɜːrsɪŋ ‖ 'nɜːsɪŋ/ *n* [U] **(a)** (profession) enfermería *f* **(b)** (care) atención *f*

nursing home *n* (for the aged) residencia *f* de ancianos (*con mayor nivel de asistencia médica*); (for convalescence) clínica *f*, casa *f* de reposo *or* (Ur) de salud

nurture /'nɜːrtʃər ‖ 'nɜːtʃə(r)/ *vt* ‹*child/person*› criar*; ‹*plant/crop*› cuidar; ‹*friendship*› cultivar

nut /nʌt/ *n* **1** (Agr, Bot, Culin) fruto *m* seco (*nuez, almendra, avellana etc*) **2** (Tech) tuerca *f*

nut: **~case** *n* (colloq) chiflado, -da *m,f* (fam); **~crackers** *pl n* (BrE) cascanueces *m*

nutmeg /'nʌtmeg/ *n* [U C] nuez *f* moscada

nutrient /'nuːtriənt ‖ 'njuːtriənt/ *n* nutriente *m*

nutrition /nʊ'trɪʃən ‖ njuː'trɪʃən/ *n* [U] nutrición *f*

nutritious /nʊ'trɪʃəs ‖ njuː'trɪʃəs/ *adj* nutritivo

nuts /nʌts/ *adj* (colloq) (*pred*) chiflado (fam)

nutshell /'nʌtʃel/ *n* cáscara *f* de nuez; ***in a ~*** en dos *or* en pocas palabras

nutty /'nʌti/ *adj* **-tier, -tiest 1** ‹*taste*› a nueces (*or* almendras *etc*) **2** (colloq) (eccentric) ‹*professor*› chiflado (fam); ‹*idea*› de loco

NW (= **northwest**) NO

NY = **New York**

nylon /'naɪlɑːn ‖ 'naɪlɒn/ *n* [U] nylon *m*

nymph /nɪmf/ *n* (Myth, Zool) ninfa *f*

Oo

O, o /əʊ/ *n* O, o *f*

oaf /əʊf/ *n* zoquete *mf* (fam)

oak /əʊk/ *n* **(a)** [C] **~ (tree)** roble *m* **(b)** [U] (wood) roble *m*

OAP *n* (BrE) = **old age pensioner**

oar /ɔːr ‖ ɔː(r)/ *n* remo *m*

OAS *n* (= **Organization of American States**) OEA *f*

oasis /əʊ'eɪsɪs/ *n* (*pl* **oases** /əʊ'eɪsiːz/) oasis *m*

oat /əʊt/ *n* **(a)** (plant) avena *f* **(b) oats** *pl* (cereal) avena *f*, copos *mpl* de avena

oath /əʊθ/ *n* (*pl* **~s** /əʊðz/) **(a)** (promise) juramento *m*; **under** *o* (BrE also) **on ~** (Law) bajo juramento **(b)** (curse) (liter) juramento *m* (liter)

oatmeal /'əʊtmiːl/ *n* [U] (Culin) (flour) harina *f* de avena; (flakes) (AmE) avena *f* (*en copos*)

obedience /ə'biːdiəns, əʊ-/ *n* [U] obediencia *f*

obedient /ə'biːdiənt, əʊ-/ *adj* obediente

obese /əʊ'biːs/ *adj* obeso

obesity /əʊ'biːsəti/ *n* [U] obesidad *f*

obey /ə'beɪ, əʊ-/ *vt/i* obedecer*

obituary /ə'bɪtʃueri ‖ ə'bɪtʃʊəri/ *n* (*pl* **-ries**) obituario *m*, nota *f* necrológica

object¹ /'ɑːbdʒɪkt ‖ 'ɒbdʒɪkt/ *n* **1 (a)** (thing) objeto *m* **(b)** ***no* ~**: **money's no ~ for them** el dinero no les preocupa **(c)** (of actions, feelings) objeto *m* **2** (aim, purpose) objetivo *m* **3** (Ling) complemento *m*

object² /əb'dʒekt/ *vi* **to ~** (TO STH) oponerse* (A algo); **I ~!** ¡protesto!; **if you don't ~** si no le molesta ■ **~** *vt* objetar

objection /əb'dʒekʃən/ *n* **(a)** [C] (argument against) objeción *f* **(b)** [C] (Law) protesta *f*; **~!** ¡protesto! **(c)** [U] (disapproval, dislike): **I have no ~ to her** no tengo nada en contra de ella

objectionable /əb'dʒekʃnəbəl ‖ əb'dʒekʃnəbəl/ *adj* ‹*attitude/remark*› censurable; ‹*person/tone*› desagradable

objective¹ /ɑːb'dʒektɪv ‖ əb'dʒektɪv/ *adj* objetivo

objective² *n* objetivo *m*

objectively /ɑːb'dʒektɪvli ‖ əb'dʒektɪvli/ *adv* objetivamente

obligate /'ɑːbləgeɪt ‖ 'ɒblɪgeɪt/ *vt* (esp AmE frml) **to ~ sb to + INF** obligar* a algn A + INF; **to be/feel ~d (to + INF)** estar*/sentirse* obligado (A + INF)

obligation /'ɑːblə'geɪʃən ‖ ˌɒblɪ'geɪʃən/ *n* [C U] obligación *f*; **~ to + INF** obligación DE + INF; **I understand that I am under no ~** entiendo que no contraigo ninguna obligación

obligatory /ə'blɪgətɔːri ‖ ə'blɪgətri/ *adj* obligatorio

oblige /ə'blaɪdʒ/ *vt* **1** (require, compel) **to ~ sb to + INF** obligar* a algn A + INF; **to be ~d to + INF** estar* obligado A + INF **2** (do favor for): **I'd be much ~d if you could help me** le quedaría muy agradecido si pudiera ayudarme ■ **~** *vi*: **he's always willing to ~** siempre está dispuesto a hacer un favor

obliging /ə'blaɪdʒɪŋ/ *adj* atento

oblique /ə'bliːk, əʊ- ‖ ə'bliːk/ *adj* ‹*line/angle*› oblicuo; ‹*reply/reference*› indirecto

obliterate /ə'blɪtəreɪt/ *vt* **(a)** (destroy) arrasar **(b)** (obscure, erase) borrar

oblivion /ə'blɪviən/ *n* [U] **(a)** (obscurity) olvido *m* **(b)** (unconsciousness) inconsciencia *f*

oblivious /ə'blɪviəs/ *adj* (*pred*): **she was quite ~ of** *o* **to her surroundings** estaba totalmente ajena a lo que la rodeaba; **~ of** *o* **to the danger** (unaware of) ignorante del peligro; (not mindful of) haciendo caso omiso del peligro

oblong¹ /'ɑːblɔːŋ ‖ 'ɒblɒŋ/ *adj* alargado

oblong² *n* rectángulo *m*

obnoxious /ɑː'bnɑːkʃəs ‖ əb'nɒkʃəs/ *adj* detestable

oboe /'əʊbəʊ/ *n* oboe *m*

obscene /ɑːb'siːn ‖ əb'siːn/ *adj* obsceno

obscenity /ɑːb'senəti ‖ əb'senəti/ *n* (*pl* **-ties**) [U C] obscenidad *f*

obscure¹ /əb'skjʊr ‖ əb'skjʊə(r)/ *adj* **obscurer, obscurest (a)** (not easily understood) ‹*meaning*› oscuro; ‹*message/reference*› críptico **(b)** (little known) ‹*writer/journal*› oscuro

obscure² *vt* ‹*object/beauty/sun*› ocultar; ‹*sky*› oscurecer*; ‹*issue*› impedir* ver claramente

obscurity /əb'skjʊrəti ‖ əb'skjʊərəti/ *n* [U C] (*pl* **-ties**) oscuridad *f*

obsequious /əb'siːkwiəs/ *adj* servil

observant /əb'zɜːrvənt ‖ əb'zɜːvənt/ *adj* observador

observation /'ɑːbzər'veɪʃən ‖ ˌɒbzə'veɪʃən/ *n* [U C] (all senses) observación *f*

observatory /əb'zɜːrvətɔːri ‖ əb'zɜːvətri/ *n* (*pl* **-ries**) observatorio *m*

observe /əb'zɜːrv ‖ əb'zɜːv/ *vt* **1** (watch, notice) observar; ‹*patient*› observar **2** (comment) (liter) observar

observer /əb'zɜːrvər ‖ əb'zɜːvə(r)/ *n* observador, -dora *m,f*

obsess /əb'ses/ *vt* obsesionar

obsessed /əb'sest/ *adj* (*pred*) obsesionado

obsession /əb'seʃən/ *n* obsesión *f*

obsessive /əb'sesɪv/ *adj* obsesivo

obsolete /'ɑːbsəliːt ‖ 'ɒbsəliːt/ *adj* obsoleto

obstacle /'ɑːbstɪkəl ‖ 'ɒbstəkəl/ *n* obstáculo *m*

obstetrics /əb'stetrɪks/ *n* (+ *sing vb*) obstetricia *f*, tocología *f*

obstinate /'ɑːbstənət ‖ 'ɒbstɪnət/ *adj* obstinado

obstinately /'ɑːbstənətli ‖ 'ɒbstɪnətli/ *adv* (stubbornly) obstinadamente; (determinedly) tenazmente

obstruct /əb'strʌkt/ *vt* **(a)** (block) obstruir* **(b)** (impede, hinder) ‹*traffic*› bloquear **(c)** (Sport) obstruir*

obstruction /əb'strʌkʃən/ *n* **(a)** [U C] (in traffic, pipeline) obstrucción *f*; (Med) obstrucción *f*, oclusión *f* **(b)** [U] (Sport) obstrucción *f*

obtain /əb'teɪn/ *vt* conseguir*, obtener* (frml)

obtrusive /əb'truːsɪv/ *adj* ‹*presence/building*› demasiado prominente; ‹*noise*› molesto; ‹*smell*› penetrante

obtuse /ɑː'buːs ‖ ɒb'tjuːs/ *adj* **1** (Math) ‹*angle*› obtuso **2** (frml) (stupid) obtuso

obvious /'ɑːbviəs ‖ 'ɒbviəs/ *adj* **(a)** (evident) ‹*answer/advantage/difference*› obvio **(b)** (unmistakable) (*before n*) ‹*candidate/choice*› indiscutible

obviously /'ɑːbviəsli ‖ 'ɒbviəsli/ *adv* obviamente; **they're ~ not coming** está visto que no van a venir; **the two ideas are ~ not related** es evidente que las dos ideas no tienen relación; **~, I'm sad, but what can I do?** (*indep*) como es lógico estoy triste pero ¿qué puedo hacer?

OCAS (= **Organization of Central American States**) *n* ODECA *f*

occasion /ə'keɪʒən/ *n* ocasión *f*

occasional /ə'keɪʒnəl ‖ ə'keɪʒənḷ/ *adj* ‹*showers/sunny spells*› aislado; **I like an** *o* **the ~ glass of wine** de tanto en tanto me gusta tomarme un vaso de vino

occasionally /ə'keɪʒnəli/ *adv* de vez en cuando

occult¹ /ə'kʌlt ‖ ɒ'kʌlt/ *n* **the ~** las ciencias ocultas

occult² *adj* ‹*arts/powers*› oculto; ‹*ritual*› ocultista

occupant /'ɑːkjəpənt ‖ 'ɒkjʊpənt/ *n* (of building, room, vehicle) ocupante *mf*; (tenant) inquilino, -na *m,f*

occupation /ˌɑːkjə'peɪʃən ‖ ˌɒkjʊ'peɪʃən/ *n* **(a)** [C] (profession, activity) ocupación *f* **(b)** [U C] (Mil) ocupación *f* **(c)** [U] (of accommodations) ocupación *f*

occupational /ˌɑːkjə'peɪʃnəl ‖ ˌɒkjʊ'peɪʃənḷ/ *adj* ‹*training*› ocupacional; ‹*disease*› profesional; **it's an ~ hazard** son riesgos de la profesión/del oficio

occupational therapy *n* terapia *f* ocupacional

occupier /'ɑːkjəpaɪər ‖ 'ɒkjʊpaɪə(r)/ *n* (BrE) ocupante *mf*

occupy /'ɑːkjəpaɪ ‖ 'ɒkjʊpaɪ/ *vt* **-pies, -pying, -pied** ocupar; **to keep sb occupied** mantener* a algn ocupado

occur /ə'kɜːr ‖ ə'kɜː(r)/ *vi* **-rr- 1 (a)** (take place) (frml) «*event/incident*» tener* lugar (frml); «*change*» producirse* (frml) **(b)** (appear, be found) «*disease/species*» darse*, encontrarse* **2** (come to mind) **to ~ TO sb (to + INF)** ocurrírsele A algn (+ INF)

occurrence /ə'kɜːrəns ‖ ə'kʌrəns/ *n* **(a)** [C] (event, instance): **it is a rare ~** no es algo frecuente **(b)** [U] (incidence) incidencia *f*

ocean /'əʊʃən/ *n* océano *m*

ocean-going /'əʊʃənˌgəʊɪŋ/ *adj* ‹*vessel*› transatlántico

o'clock /ə'klɑːk ‖ ə'klɒk/ **▶ 884** *adv*: **it's four ~** son las cuatro; **it's one ~** es la una

octagon /'ɑːktəgɑːn ‖ 'ɒktəgən/ *n* octágono *m*, octógono *m*

octane /'ɑːkteɪn ‖ 'ɒkteɪn/ *n* octano *m*

octave /'ɑːktɪv ‖ 'ɒktɪv/ *n* (Lit, Mus) octava *f*

October /ɑːk'təʊbər ‖ ɒk'təʊbə(r)/ **▶ 540** *n* octubre *m*

octopus /'ɑːktəpəs ‖ 'ɒktəpəs/ *n* (*pl* **-puses**) pulpo *m*

odd /ɑːd ‖ ɒd/ *adj* **-er, -est 1** (strange) raro, extraño **2** (occasional, random) (*no comp*): **she smokes the ~ cigarette** se fuma algún *or* alguno que otro cigarrillo **3** (*no comp*) **(a)** (unmatched, single) desparejado, sin pareja; **the ~ one out** la excepción **(b)** (Math) ‹*number*› impar

oddball /'ɑːdbɔːl ‖ 'ɒdbɔːl/ *n* (colloq) bicho *m* raro (fam)

oddity /'ɑːdəti ‖ 'ɒdɪti/ *n* (*pl* **-ties**) rareza *f*

odd-job man /ˌɑːd'dʒɑːbmæn ‖ ˌɒd'dʒɒbmæn/ *n* (*pl* **-men** /-men/) *hombre que hace pequeños trabajos o arreglos*

oddly /'ɑːdli ‖ 'ɒdli/ *adv* ‹*dress/behave*› de una manera rara *or* extraña

oddment /'ɑːdmənt ‖ 'ɒdmənt/ *n*: **~s of fabric** *o* **material** retazos *mpl or* (Esp) retales *mpl*

odds /ɑːdz ‖ ɒdz/ *pl n* **1** (in betting) *proporción en que se ofrece pagar una apuesta, que refleja las posibilidades de acierto de la misma* **2** (likelihood, chances) probabilidades *fpl*, posibilidades *fpl*; **the ~ are against her winning** tiene pocas probabilidades *or* posibilidades de ganar; **the pilot survived against all (the) ~** aunque parezca increíble, el piloto sobrevivió **3** (variance): **those two are always at ~ with each other** esos dos siempre están en desacuerdo; **that's at ~ with the official version** eso no concuerda con la versión oficial

odds and ends /'ɑdzən'endz ‖ ˌɒdzən'endz/ *pl n* (colloq) cosas *fpl* sueltas; (trinkets) chucherías *fpl*; (junk) cachivaches *mpl*

odious /'əʊdiəs/ *adj* (frml) detestable

odometer /əʊ'dɑːmətər ‖ ɒ'dɒmɪtə(r), əʊ-/ *n* (AmE) cuentarrevoluciones *m*

odor, (BrE) **odour** /'əʊdər ‖ 'əʊdə(r)/ *n* olor *m*; (pleasant) aroma *m*

of /ɑːv ‖ ɒv, *weak form* əv/ *prep* **1** (indicating relationship, material, content) de; **it's made ~ wood** es de madera; **a colleague ~ mine/his** un colega mío/suyo **2** (descriptive use): **a boy ~ ten** un niño de diez años; **a woman ~ courage** una mujer valiente **3 (a)** (partitive use): **there were eight ~ us** éramos ocho; **six ~ them survived** seis de ellos sobrevivieron **(b)** (with superl) de; **the wisest ~ men** el más sabio de los hombres; **most ~ all** más que nada **4 (a)** **▶ 540** (indicating date) de; **the sixth ~ October** el seis de octubre **(b)** **▶ 884** (indicating time): **it's ten (minutes) ~ five** (AmE) son las cinco menos diez, son diez para las cinco (AmL exc RPl); **Jane, his wife**

~ **six months** … Jane, con la que lleva/llevaba casado seis meses … **5** (on the part of): **it was very kind ~ you** fue muy amable de su parte **6** (indicating cause): **it's a problem ~ their own making** es un problema que ellos mismos se han creado; **what did he die ~?** ¿de qué murió?

off¹ /ɔːf ‖ ɒf/ *prep* **1** (from) de; **she picked it up ~** *o* (crit) **~ of the floor** lo recogió del suelo; **he bought it ~ a friend** (colloq) se lo compró a un amigo **2 (a)** (distant from): **3 ft ~ the ground** a 3 pies del suelo; **just ~ the coast of Florida** a poca distancia de la costa de Florida **(b)** (leading from): **it's just ~ Oxford Street** está en una bocacalle de Oxford Street; **the bathroom's ~ the bedroom** el baño da al dormitorio **3 (a)** (absent from): **I've been ~ work for a week** hace una semana que no voy a trabajar **(b)** (indicating dislike, abstinence) (BrE): **he's ~ his food** anda sin apetito; **is he ~ drugs now?** ¿ha dejado las drogas?

off² *adv* **1 (a)** (removed): **the lid was ~** la tapa no estaba puesta; **20% ~** 20% de descuento **(b) off and on** ⇒ ON² 2(c) **2** (indicating departure): **I must be ~** me tengo que ir **3** (distant): **some way ~** a cierta distancia; **my birthday is a long way ~** falta mucho para mi cumpleaños

off³ *adj* **1** (*pred*) **(a)** (not turned on): **to be ~** «*TV/light*» estar* apagado **(b)** (canceled): **the game/wedding is ~** el partido/la boda se ha suspendido; **the deal is ~** ya no hay trato **2** (absent, not on duty) libre; **a day ~** *o* (AmE also) **an ~ day** un día libre **3** (poor, unsatisfactory) (*before n*) malo; **to have an ~ day** tener* un mal día **4** (Culin) (*pred*) **to be ~** «*meat/fish*» estar* malo *or* pasado; «*milk*» estar* cortado; «*butter/cheese*» estar* rancio

offal /'ɔːfəl ‖ 'ɒfəl/ *n* [U] (Culin) despojos *mpl*, achuras *fpl* (RPl), interiores *mpl* (Chi)

off: **~beat** *adj* poco convencional; **~-chance** *n*: **on the ~-chance** por si acaso; **~-color**, (BrE) **~-colour** /'ɔːf'kʌlər ‖ ,ɒf'kʌlə(r)/ *adj* (*pred* **~ color**) **(a)** (unwell) (*pred*): **to feel ~ color** no encontrarse* muy bien **(b)** (risqué) (esp AmE) ‹*joke*› subido de tono; **~cut** *n* (of leather fabric, paper, wood) recorte *m*; (of meat) resto *m*

offence /ə'fens/ *n* (BrE) ⇒ OFFENSE

offend /ə'fend/ *vt* ofender ■ **~** *vi* **(a)** (cause displeasure) «*person/action/remark*» ofender **(b) offending** *pres p*: **he rewrote it omitting the ~ing paragraph** volvió a escribirlo omitiendo el párrafo que había causado controversia **(c)** (Law frml) infringir* la ley (*or* el reglamento *etc*); (criminally) cometer un delito

offender /ə'fendər ‖ ə'fendə(r)/ *n* (against regulations) infractor, -tora *m,f*; (criminal) delincuente *mf*; **young ~** menor *mf* (*que ha cometido un delito*)

offense, (BrE) **offence** /ə'fens/ *n* **1** [C] (breach of law, regulations) infracción *f*; (*criminal* **~**) delito *m* **2 (a)** (cause of outrage) (*no pl*) atentado *m* **(b)** (resentment, displeasure): **to take ~ at sth** ofenderse *or* sentirse* ofendido por algo **3** (AmE) *also* /'ɑːfens/ **(a)** [U] (attack) ataque *m* **(b)** [U C] (Sport) (línea *f* de) ataque *m*

offensive¹ /ə'fensɪv/ *adj* **1** ‹*language/gesture*› ofensivo; ‹*sight/smell*› desagradable **2 (a)** ‹*strategy*› ofensivo **(b)** (AmE Sport) ‹*play/tactics*› de ataque

offensive² *n* ofensiva *f*

offer¹ /'ɔːfər ‖ 'ɒfə(r)/ *vt* **1 (a)** (proffer) ofrecer* **(b)** (show willingness) **to ~ to** + INF ofrecerse* A + INF **2** (put forward) ‹*idea/solution*› proponer* **3** (provide) ‹*reward*› ofrecer*; ‹*opportunity*› brindar ■ **~** *vi* (show willingness) ofrecerse*

offer² *n* **1 (a)** (proposal— of job, money) oferta *f*; (— of help, mediation) ofrecimiento *m* **(b)** (bid) oferta *f*; **$650 or nearest ~** 650 dólares negociables **2** (bargain, reduced price) oferta *f*; **on ~** (BrE) (at reduced price) de oferta

offering /'ɔːfərɪŋ ‖ 'ɒfərɪŋ/ *n* ofrenda *f*

offhand¹ /'ɔːf'hænd ‖ ,ɒf'hænd/ *adj*: **to say sth in a very ~ way** *o* **manner** decir* algo muy a la ligera; **she was very ~ with me** estuvo muy brusca conmigo

offhand² *adv* así de pronto, en este momento

office /'ɑːfəs ‖ 'ɒfɪs/ *n* **1** [C] (room) oficina *f*, despacho *m*; (building, set of rooms) oficina *f*, oficinas *fpl*; (staff) oficina *f*; (*doctor's* **~**) (AmE) consultorio *m*, consulta *f*; (*before n*) ‹*work/furniture*› de oficina; ‹*block/building*› de oficinas; **during ~ hours** en horas de oficina; **~ worker** oficinista *mf*, empleado, -da *m,f* de oficina **2** [U] (post, position) cargo *m*; **he was in ~ for three years** ocupó el cargo durante tres años

officer /'ɑːfəsər ‖ 'ɒfɪsə(r)/ *n* **(a)** (Mil, Naut) oficial *mf* **(b)** (*police* **~**) policía *mf*, agente *mf* de policía; (*as form of address*) agente

official¹ /ə'fɪʃəl/ *adj* oficial

official² *n* (*government* **~**) funcionario, -ria *m,f* del Estado *or* gobierno; (*party/union* **~**) dirigente *mf* (del partido/sindicato)

officially /ə'fɪʃəli/ *adv* oficialmente

officiate /ə'fɪʃieɪt/ *vi* **to ~ AT sth** ‹*at mass/at a wedding*› oficiar (EN) *or* celebrar algo

officious /ə'fɪʃəs/ *adj* oficioso

offing /'ɔːfɪŋ ‖ 'ɒfɪŋ/ *n*: **in the ~** en perspectiva

off: **~ key** *adv*: **to play/sing ~ key** desafinar; **~-licence** *n* (in UK) ≈ tienda *f* de vinos y licores, botillería *f* (Chi); **~ limits** /'lɪməts ‖ 'lɪmɪts/ *adv*: **to go/be ~ limits** entrar/estar* en zona prohibida; **~-line** /'ɔːf'laɪn ‖ ,ɒf'laɪn/ *adj* (*pred* **~ line**) ‹*storage/printer*› autónomo; **~-putting** /'ɔːf'pʊtɪŋ ‖ ,ɒf'pʊtɪŋ/ *adj* (BrE) (disagreeable) desagradable; (discouraging) desmoralizador; **~set** /'ɔːf'set ‖ 'ɒfset/ *vt* (*pres* **-sets**; *pres p* **-setting**; *past & past p* **-set**) compensar; **~shoot** *n* **(a)** (of plant, tree) retoño *m* **(b)** (of company, organization) filial *f*; **~shore** /'ɔːf'ʃɔːr ‖ ,ɒf'ʃɔː(r)/ *adj* ‹*oilfield/pipeline*› submarino; ‹*exploration/drilling*› off-shore *adj inv*; **~side** *adj* (Sport) ‹*player*› en fuera de juego *or* (AmL tb) de lugar; **~spring** *n* (*pl* **~spring**) **(a)** (animal) cría *f* **(b)** (hum) (child) hijo, -ja *m,f*, crío, cría *m,f* (fam); (children) prole *f* (fam & hum), críos *mpl* (fam); **~stage** /'ɔːf 'steɪdʒ ‖ ,ɒf'steɪdʒ/ *adv* fuera del escenario; **~-the-peg** /'ɔːfðə'peg ‖ ,ɔfðə'peg/ *adj* (*pred* **~ the peg**) (esp BrE) ⇒ ~-THE-RACK; **~-the-rack** /'ɔːfðə'ræk ‖ ,ɔfðə'ræk/ *adj* (*pred* **~ the rack**) (AmE) ‹*suit*› de confección; **~-white** /'ɔːf'hwaɪt ‖ ˌɒf'waɪt/ *adj* color hueso *adj inv*

often /'ɔːfən, 'ɔːftən ‖ 'ɒfən, 'ɒftən/ *adv* a menudo; **how ~ do you see her?** ¿con qué frecuencia la ves?

ogle /'əʊgəl/ *vt* comerse con los ojos

ogre /'əʊgər ‖ 'əʊgə(r)/ *n* ogro *m*

oh /əʊ/ *interj*: **~, it's you** ah, eres tú; **~ no, not him again!** ¡ay no, es él otra vez!

OH = **Ohio**

oil[1] /ɔɪl/ *n* **1** [U] **(a)** (petroleum) petróleo *m*; (*before n*) **~ refinery** refinería *f* de petróleo; **~ tanker** (ship) petrolero *m*; (truck) camión *m* cisterna (*para petróleo*) **(b)** (lubricant) aceite *m* **(c)** (*fuel* ~) fuel-oil *m* **2** [U C] (Culin) aceite *m* **3 oils** *pl* (paints): **he paints in ~s** pinta al óleo

oil[2] *vt* lubricar*, aceitar

oil: **~can** *n* aceitera *f*; **~cloth** *n* [U] hule *m*; **~field** *n* yacimiento *m* petrolífero; **~ paint** *n* [U C] óleo *m*; **~ painting** *n* óleo *m*; **~ rig** *n* plataforma *f* petrolífera; (derrick) torre *f* de perforación; **~ slick** *n* marea *f* negra; **~ well** *n* pozo *m* petrolero

oily /'ɔɪli/ *adj* **oilier, oiliest** ‹*substance*› oleaginoso; ‹*food*› aceitoso; ‹*skin/hair*› graso (AmL)

ointment /'ɔɪntmənt/ *n* [U C] pomada *f*

OK[1], **okay** /'əʊ'keɪ/ *interj* (colloq) ¡bueno!, ¡okey! (esp AmL fam), ¡vale! (Esp fam), ¡vaya (pues)! (AmC)

OK[2], **okay** *adj* (all right) (colloq) (*pred*): **how are you? — ~, thanks** ¿qué tal estás? — bien, gracias; **the job's ~, but** ... el trabajo no está mal, pero ...

OK[3], **okay** *vt* (*pres* **OK's**; *pres p* **OK'ing**; *past & past p* **OK' ed**) (colloq) darle* el visto bueno a

OK[4], **Okla** = **Oklahoma**

old /əʊld/ *adj* **1** ▶ **451** (of certain age): **he's 10 years ~** tiene 10 años; **how ~ are you?** ¿cuántos años tienes?; **she's two years ~er than me** me lleva dos años **2** (not young) mayor; (less polite) viejo; **~** *o* **~er people** los ancianos, las personas mayores *or* de edad; **to get** *o* **grow ~/~er** envejecer* **3 (a)** (not new) ‹*clothes/car/custom*› viejo; ‹*city/civilization*› antiguo **(b)** (longstanding, familiar) (*before n*) ‹*friend/enemy/rivalry*› viejo; ‹*injury/problem*› antiguo **4** (former, previous) (*before n*) antiguo **5** (colloq) (*before n*) (*as intensifier*): **just wear any ~ thing** ponte cualquier cosa; **this book is a load of ~ rubbish** este libro es una porquería (fam)

old: **~ age** *n* [U] vejez *f*; **~ age pensioner** *n* (BrE) pensionista *mf* (de la tercera edad)

olden /'əʊldən/ *adj* (liter): **in ~ days** *o* **times** antaño (liter)

old: **~-fashioned** /'əʊld'fæʃənd/ *adj* (outdated) anticuado; (traditional) tradicional; **~ people's home** *n* residencia *f* de ancianos; **~ wives' tale** *n* cuento *m* de viejas

olive[1] /'ɑːlɪv ‖ 'ɒlɪv/ *n* **(a)** (Culin) aceituna *f*; (*before n*) **~ oil** aceite *m* de oliva **(b) ~ tree** olivo *m*

olive[2] ▶ **515** *adj* color aceituna *adj inv*; ‹*skin*› aceitunado

Olympic /ə'lɪmpɪk/ *adj* olímpico

Olympic Games *pl n* **the ~ ~** los juegos Olímpicos

Olympics /ə'lɪmpɪks/ *pl n* **the ~** las Olimpíadas *or* Olimpiadas

ombudsman /'ɑːmbʊdzmən ‖ 'ɒmbʊdzmən/ *n* (*pl* **-men** /-mən/) defensor *m* del pueblo, ombudsman *m*

omelet, (BrE) **omelette** /'ɑːmlət ‖ 'ɒmlɪt/ *n* omelette *f or* (Esp) tortilla *f* francesa

omen /'əʊmən/ *n* presagio *m*; **it's a good/bad ~** es un buen/mal augurio

ominous /'ɑːmənəs ‖ 'ɒmɪnəs/ *adj*: **there was an ~ silence** se hizo un silencio que no presagiaba nada bueno; **there are some ~ clouds on the horizon** hay nubes que no auguran nada bueno

omission /əʊ'mɪʃən ‖ ə'mɪʃən/ *n* [U C] omisión *f*

omit /əʊ'mɪt ‖ ə'mɪt/ *vt* **-tt-** (leave out) omitir; (accidentally) olvidar incluir

omnibus /'ɑːmnɪbəs ‖ 'ɒmnɪbəs/ *n* (*pl* **-buses**) **1** (Publ) antología *f* **2** (Transp dated) ómnibus *m* (ant exc en Per y RPl)

omnipotent /ɑːm'nɪpətənt ‖ ɒm'nɪpətənt/ *adj* (frml) omnipotente

omnivorous /ɑːm'nɪvərəs ‖ ɒm'nɪvərəs/ *adj* omnívoro

on[1] /ɑːn ‖ ɒn/ *prep* **1 (a)** (indicating position) en; **put it ~ the table** ponlo en *or* sobre la mesa; **~ the ground** en el suelo; **he hung it ~ a hook** lo colgó de un gancho **(b)** (belonging to) de; **the handle ~ the cup** el asa de la taza **(c)** (against): **I hit my head ~ the shelf** me di con la cabeza contra el estante; **he cut his hand ~ the glass** se cortó la mano con el vidrio **2 (a)** (of clothing): **it looks better ~ you than me** te queda mejor a ti que a mí **(b)** (about one's person): **I didn't have any cash ~ me** no llevaba dinero encima **3** (indicating means of transport): **I went ~ the bus** fui en autobús; **~ a bicycle/horse** en bicicleta/a caballo; **~ foot** a pie **4 (a)** (playing instrument) a; **George Smith ~ drums** George Smith a la *or* en la batería **(b)** (Rad, TV): **I heard it ~ the radio** lo oí por la radio; **I was ~ TV last night** anoche salí por televisión; **the play's ~ channel** 4 la obra la dan en el canal 4 **5 (a)** (using equipment): **who's ~ the computer?** ¿quién está usando la computadora?; **you've been ~ the phone an hour!** ¡hace una hora que estás hablando por teléfono! **(b)** (contactable via): **call us ~ 800 7777** llámenos al 800 7777 **6** (a member of): **she's ~ the committee** está en la comisión; **~ a team** (AmE) en un equipo **7** (indicating time): **~ Monday** el lunes; **~ Wednesdays** los miércoles; **~ -ING** al + INF; **~ hearing the news** al enterarse de la noticia **8** (about, concerning) sobre **9** (working on, studying): **we're ~ page 45** vamos por la página 45; **I'm still ~ question 1** todavía estoy con la pregunta número 1 **10** (taking, consuming): **she's ~ antibiotics** está tomando antibióticos; **he's ~ heroin** es heroinómano **11** (talking about income, available funds): **I manage ~ less than that** yo me las arreglo con menos de eso **12** (at the expense of): **this round's ~ me** a esta ronda invito yo **13** (in comparison with): **profits are up ~ last year** los beneficios han aumentado respecto al año pasado

on[2] *adv* **1 (a)** (worn): **she had a blue dress ~** llevaba (puesto) un vestido azul; **I had nothing**

~ estaba desnudo **(b)** (in place): **the lid's not ~ properly** la tapa no está bien puesta **2** (indicating progression) **(a)** (in space): **further ~** un poco más allá; **go ~ up; I'll follow in a minute** tú ve subiendo que yo ya voy **(b)** (in time, activity): **from then ~** a partir de ese momento; **from now ~** de ahora en adelante **(c) on and off, off and on**: **we still see each other ~ and off** todavía nos vemos de vez en cuando; **it rained ~ and off** *o* **off and ~ all week** estuvo lloviendo y parando toda la semana

on³ *adj* **1** (*pred*) **(a)** (functioning): **to be ~** ‹‹*light/TV/radio*›› estar* encendido, estar* prendido (AmL); ‹‹*faucet*›› estar* abierto; **the electricity/water isn't ~ yet** la electricidad/el agua todavía no está conectada **(b)** (on duty): **we work four hours ~, four hours off** trabajamos cuatro horas y tenemos otras cuatro de descanso **2** (*pred*) **(a)** (taking place): **there's a lecture ~ in there** hay una conferencia allí; **while the conference is ~** mientras dure el congreso **(b)** (due to take place): **the party's definitely ~ for Friday** la fiesta es el viernes seguro; **I don't have anything ~ that day** no tengo ningún compromiso ese día **(c)** (being presented): **what's ~ at the Renoir?** (Cin, Rad, Theat, TV) ¿qué dan *or* (Esp tb) ponen en el Renoir?; **the exhibition is still ~** la exposición sigue abierta **3** (indicating agreement, acceptance) (colloq): **you teach me Spanish and I'll teach you French — you're ~!** tú me enseñas español y yo te enseño francés — ¡trato hecho!; **that sort of thing just isn't ~** (esp BrE) ese tipo de cosa no se puede tolerar

once¹ /wʌns/ *adv* **1 (a)** (one time, on one occasion) una vez; **~ a week** una vez por semana **(b)** (formerly): **a health care system which was ~ the pride of the nation** un sistema de asistencia sanitaria que antes era el orgullo de la nación; **~ upon a time there was** ... érase una vez ... **2** (*in phrases*) **at once**: **come here at ~!** ¡ven aquí inmediatamente!; **don't all shout at ~** no griten todos al mismo tiempo; **for once** por una vez; **once again** *o* **once more** otra vez; **once (and) for all** de una vez por todas; **(every) once in a while** de vez en cuando; **once or twice** una o dos veces

once² *conj* una vez que; (with verb omitted) una vez

once- /'wʌns/ *pref* otrora (liter)

oncoming /'ɑːn,kʌmɪŋ ‖ 'ɒnkʌmɪŋ/ *adj* (*before n*) ‹*vehicle*› que viene (*or* venía) en dirección contraria

one¹ /wʌn/ **▶451**, **724**, **884** *n* **1 (a)** (number) uno *m*; *see also* FOUR¹ **(b)** (elliptical use): **he's nearly ~** tiene casi un año; **it was interesting in more ways than ~** fue interesante en más de un sentido **2** (*in phrases*) **as one**: **they rose as ~** se pusieron de pie todos a la vez; **for one** por lo pronto; **one by one** uno a *or* por uno

one² **▶451**, **774**, **884** *adj* **1** (stating number) un, una; **~ button/pear** un botón/una pera; **~ window looks out over the park** una de las ventanas da al parque **2** (single): **she was the ~ person I trusted** era la única persona en quien confiaba; **there is not ~ shred of evidence** no existe ni la más mínima prueba; **the ~ and only Frank Sinatra** el incomparable Frank Sinatra **3** (unspecified) un, una; **you must come over ~ evening** tienes que venir una noche **4** (with names): **in the name of ~ John Smith/Sarah Brown** a nombre de un tal John Smith/una tal Sarah Brown

one³ *pron* **1** (thing): **this ~** éste/ésta; **that ~** ése/ésa; **which ~?** ¿cuál?; **the ~ on the right/left** el/la de la derecha/izquierda; **the ~s on the table** los/las que están en la mesa; **the blue ~s** los/las azules; **I want the big ~** quiero el/la grande; **~ of the oldest cities in Europe** una de las ciudades más antiguas de Europa **2** (person): **the ~ on the right's my cousin** el/la de la derecha es mi primo/prima; **I'm not ~ to gossip, but** ... no me gustan los chismes pero ...; **~ after another** *o* **the other** uno tras otro *or* detrás de otro

one⁴ *pron* uno, una; **~ simply never knows** realmente nunca se sabe; **~ another** ⇒ EACH OTHER, *see* EACH² 2

one: **~-armed** /'wʌn'ɑːrmd ‖ 'wʌn,ɑːmd/ *adj* manco; **~-man** /'wʌn'mæn/ *adj* (*before n*) ‹*business*› unipersonal; ‹*operation*› dirigido por una sola persona; **~-off** /'wʌn'ɔːf ‖ ,wʌn'ɒf/ *n* (BrE colloq): **this payment is strictly a ~-off** este pago es una excepción; **~ on ~** *adv* (AmE) uno a uno; **~-piece** /'wʌnpiːs/ *adj* ‹*swimsuit*› entero

onerous /'əʊnərəs/ *adj* ‹*task*› pesado

one: **~self** /wʌn'self/ *pron* (frml) (reflexive) se; (after prep) sí mismo; (emphatic use) uno mismo; **to cut ~self** cortarse; **~-sided** /'wʌn'saɪdəd ‖ ,wʌn'saɪdɪd/ *adj* ‹*account/version*› parcial; ‹*game/contest*› desigual; **~-time** *adj* antiguo; **~-to-~** /'wʌn tə'wʌn/ *adj* ‹*teaching/attention*› individualizado; ‹*discussion*› mano a mano; **on a ~-to-~ basis** de uno a uno

one-upmanship /'wʌn'ʌpmənʃɪp/ *n* [U] (colloq) *arte de colocarse siempre en una situación de superioridad con respecto a los demás*

one-way /'wʌn'weɪ/ *adj* **(a)** ‹*street*› de sentido único **(b)** (for one journey): **~ or round trip?** ¿ida sólo o ida y vuelta?, ¿sencillo o redondo? (Méx)

ongoing /'ɑːn,gəʊɪŋ ‖ 'ɒngəʊɪŋ/ *adj*: **the ~ talks** las conversaciones en curso; **the investigations have been ~ for several months** se están llevando a cabo investigaciones desde hace meses

onion /'ʌnjən/ *n* [C U] cebolla *f*

on: **~ line** *adv*: **to edit/work ~ line** (Comput) editar/trabajar en línea; **~-line** /'ɑːn'laɪn ‖ ,ɒn'laɪn/ *adj* (*pred* **~ line**) (Comput) conectado, en línea; **~looker** /'ɑːnlʊkər ‖ 'ɒnlʊkə(r)/ *n* espectador, -dora *m,f*

only¹ /'əʊnli/ *adv* **(a)** (merely, no more than) sólo, solamente; **you'll ~ make matters worse** lo único que vas a lograr es empeorar las cosas **(b)** (exclusively) sólo, solamente, únicamente **(c)** (no longer ago than): **~ last week the very same problem came up** la semana pasada, sin ir más lejos, surgió el mismo problema **(d)** (*in phrases*) **if only**: **if ~ I were rich!** ¡ojalá fuera rico!; **if ~ I'd known** si lo hubiera sabido; **only just**: **they've ~ just arrived** ahora mismo acaban de llegar; **will it fit in? — ~ just** ¿cabrá? — apenas *or* (fam) justito; **not only** ... , **but also** ... no sólo ... , sino también ...

only² *adj* (*before n*) único; **she's an ~ child** es hija única

only³ *conj* (colloq) pero

-only /ˈəʊnli/ *suff*: **a men~/women~ session** una sesión sólo *or* exclusivamente para hombres/mujeres

on: **~set** *n* (of winter, rains) llegada *f*; (of disease) aparición *f*; **~shore** /ˈɑːnˈʃɔːr ‖ ˈɒnʃɔː(r)/ *adj* **(a)** ‹*wind*› que sopla desde el mar **(b)** (on land) ‹*oil terminal/location*› en tierra

onslaught /ˈɑːnslɔːt ‖ ˈɒnslɔːt/ *n* ataque *m*

onstage /ˈɑːnˈsteɪdʒ ‖ ˌɒnˈsteɪdʒ/ *adv*: **to come ~** salir* a escena

onto /ˈɑːntuː ‖ ˈɒntuː, *before consonant* ˈɑːntə ‖ ˈɒntə/ *prep* **1** (on): **it fell ~ the table** cayó sobre la mesa; **he climbed ~ the cart** se subió al carro **2** (aware of) (colloq) **the police are ~ her** la policía anda tras ella; **I think we're ~ something big** creo que hemos dado con algo gordo (fam)

onus /ˈəʊnəs/ *n* (frml) responsabilidad *f*; **the ~ is on him to prove his theory** le corresponde a él probar su teoría

onward¹ /ˈɑːnwərd ‖ ˈɒnwəd/ *adj* (*before n*) hacia adelante

onward², (BrE also) **onwards** /-z/ *adv* (hacia) adelante; **from now ~** de ahora en adelante

ooh /uː/ *interj*: **~, what a beautiful sunset!** ¡ah, qué puesta de sol tan bonita!; **~, that hurt** ¡ay, eso me dolió!

oops /ʊps ‖ uːps/ *interj* (colloq) ¡uy! (fam)

ooze /uːz/ *vi*: **blood ~d from his wound** le salía sangre de la herida; **to ~ WITH sth**: **the walls were oozing with damp** las paredes rezumaban humedad ■ **~** *vt*: **the wound ~d pus** la herida (le) supuraba; **he ~s charm** irradia simpatía

opal /ˈəʊpəl/ *n* [U C] ópalo *m*

opaque /əʊˈpeɪk/ *adj* opaco

OPEC /ˈəʊpek/ *n* (*no art*) (= **Organization of Petroleum Exporting Countries**) la OPEC *or* la OPEP

open¹ /ˈəʊpən/ *adj* **1 (a)** (not shut, sealed, fastened) abierto; **he pushed the door ~** abrió la puerta de un empujón **(b)** (not folded) ‹*flower/newspaper/book*› abierto **2** (not enclosed) abierto; **~ prison** cárcel *f* en régimen abierto; **on the ~ seas** en alta mar **3 (a)** (not covered) ‹*carriage*› abierto; ‹*sewer*› a cielo abierto; **an ~ fire** una chimenea, un hogar **(b)** (exposed, vulnerable) **~ TO sth** ‹*to elements/enemy attack*› expuesto A algo **4** (*pred*) (ready for business) **to be ~** «*shop/museum*» estar* abierto **5** (unrestricted) ‹*membership*› abierto al público en general; ‹*meeting*› a puertas abiertas; ‹*ticket/reservation*› abierto **6** (not decided): **let's leave things ~ for the time being** no descartemos ninguna posibilidad de momento; **~ verdict** *veredicto que se emite cuando no se puede establecer la causa de la muerte de una persona* **7 (a)** (receptive) abierto; **I'm ~ to suggestions** estoy abierto a todo tipo de sugerencias **(b)** (frank, candid): **to be ~ WITH sb** ser* sincero *or* franco CON algn **8** (not concealed) ‹*resentment/hostility*› abierto

open² *vt* **1 (a)** ‹*door/box/bottle*› abrir*; **to ~ one's mouth/eyes** abrir* la boca/los ojos **(b)** (unfold) ‹*newspaper/book*› abrir* **2** (clear) ‹*road/channel*› abrir* **3** (set up, start) ‹*shop*› abrir* **4** (begin) ‹*debate/meeting*› abrir*; ‹*bidding*› iniciar; ‹*talks*› entablar ■ **~** *vi* **1 (a)** «*door/window/wound*» abrirse* **(b)** (unfold) «*flower/parachute*» abrirse* **2** (give access) **to ~ ONTO/INTO sth** dar* A algo **3** (for business) «*shop/museum*» abrir* **4** (begin) «*play/book*» comenzar*, empezar*

• **open up I** [*v + o + adv, v + adv + o*] abrir* **II** [*v + adv*] **1** (become open) abrirse* **2** (become accessible, available) «*country/market*» abrirse* **3** (start up) «*business/factory/store*» abrir*

open³ *n*: **in the ~** (in open space or country) al aire libre; (Mil) al descubierto; **I feel better now it's all out in the ~** me siento mejor ahora que todo el mundo lo sabe

open: **~ air** *n*: **in the ~ air** al aire libre; **~-and-shut** /ˈəʊpənənˈʃʌt/ *adj*: **an ~-and-shut case** un caso clarísimo; **~ day** *n* (BrE) *día en que un establecimiento educativo, científico etc puede ser visitado por el público*; **~-ended** /ˈəʊpənˈendəd ‖ ˌəʊpənˈendɪd/ *adj* ‹*contract/lease*› de duración indefinida; ‹*discussion*› abierto

opener /ˈəʊpnər ‖ ˌəʊpnə(r)/ *n* (for bottle) abridor *m*, abrebotellas *m*, destapador *m* (AmL); (for can) abrelatas *m*

open house *n* **1** [U] (*no art*): **to keep ~ ~** tener* las puertas siempre abiertas a todos; **2** [C] (AmE) *día en que un establecimiento educativo, científico etc puede ser visitado por el público*

opening /ˈəʊpnɪŋ/ *n* **1** [C] (in hedge, fence) abertura *f* **2** [U C] (beginning, initial stage) apertura *f* **3** [C U] (of exhibition, building) inauguración *f*; (Cin, Theat) estreno *m*; (*before n*) ‹*speech*› inaugural; **~ night** noche *f* del estreno **4** [U] (period when open): **hours of ~** (of shop) horario *m* comercial; (of bank, office) horario *m* de atención al público **5** [C] (favorable opportunity) oportunidad *f*

openly /ˈəʊpənli/ *adv* abiertamente

open: **~-minded** /ˈəʊpənˈmaɪndəd ‖ ˌəʊpənˈmaɪndɪd/ *adj* ‹*person*› de actitud abierta; ‹*approach*› imparcial; **~-mouthed** /ˈəʊpənˈmaʊðd/ *adj* boquiabierto; **~-plan** /ˈəʊpənˈplæn/ *adj* abierto, de planta abierta

opera /ˈɑːprə ‖ ˈɒprə/ *n* [C U] (*pl* **-ras**) ópera *f*

operate /ˈɑːpəreɪt ‖ ˈɒpəreɪt/ *vi* **1** «*machine/mechanism*» funcionar **2** (be applicable) «*rules/laws*» regir* **3** (pursue one's business) «*company/airline/gang*» operar **4** (Med) operar, intervenir* (frml); **to ~ ON sb (FOR sth)** operar A algn (DE algo) ■ **~** *vt* **1** ‹*machine/controls*› manejar **2** (manage, run) ‹*business*› llevar; ‹*bus service*› tener*

operatic /ˈɑːpəˈrætɪk ‖ ˌɒpəˈrætɪk/ *adj* operístico

operating /ˈɑːpəreɪtɪŋ ‖ ˈɒpəreɪtɪŋ/ *adj* (*before n*) **1** (Busn) ‹*profit/loss/costs*› de explotación **2** (Med): **~ room** *o* (BrE) **theatre** quirófano *m*, sala *f* de operaciones; **~ table** mesa *f* de operaciones

operation /ˈɑːpəˈreɪʃən ‖ ˌɒpəˈreɪʃən/ *n* **1** [U] (functioning) funcionamiento *m*; **to be in ~** «*machine*» estar* en funcionamiento; «*system*» regir* **2** [U] (using, running of machine) manejo *m* **3** [C] (activity, series of activities) operación *f* **4** [C] (Med) operación *f*, intervención *f* quirúrgica (frml)

operative /'ɑːpərətɪv ‖ 'ɒpərətɪv/ *adj* **to be ~** «*rules/measures*» estar* en vigor; **the ~ word** la palabra clave

operator /'ɑːpəreɪtər ‖ 'ɒpəreɪtə(r)/ *n* **(a)** (Telec) operador, -dora *m,f* **(b)** (of equipment) operario, -ria *m,f*; (Comput) operador, -dora *m,f*

ophthalmic optician /ɑːp'θælmɪk, ɑːf- ‖ ɒf'θælmɪk/ *n* ≈ oculista *mf*

opinion /ə'pɪnjən/ *n* [C U] opinión *f*; **in my ~** en mi opinión, a mi parecer; **I'd like a second ~** me gustaría consultarlo con otro especialista

opinionated /ə'pɪnjəneɪtəd ‖ ə'pɪnjə,neɪtɪd/ *adj* dogmático, aferrado a sus (*or* tus *etc*) opiniones

opinion poll *n* sondeo *m* or encuesta *f* de opinión

opium /'əʊpiəm/ *n* [U] opio *m*

opponent /ə'pəʊnənt/ *n* **(a)** (of a regime, policy) opositor, -tora *m,f*; (in debate) adversario, -ria *m,f* **(b)** (Games, Sport) contrincante *mf*, rival *mf*

opportune /'ɑːpər'tuːn ‖ 'ɒpətjuːn/ *adj* (frml) oportuno

opportunist¹ /'ɑːpər'tuːnəst ‖ ,ɒpə'tjuːnɪst/ *n* oportunista *mf*

opportunist², opportunistic /-tuː'nɪstɪk ‖ -tjuː-/ *adj* oportunista

opportunity /'ɑːpər'tuːnəti ‖ ,ɒpə'tjuːnəti/ *n* [C U] (*pl* **-ties**) oportunidad *f*, ocasión *f*; **~ to** + INF/OF -ING oportunidad DE + INF; **there was little ~ for sightseeing** hubo poco tiempo para hacer turismo

oppose /ə'pəʊz/ *vt* **(a)** (be against) ‹*measure/policy/actions*› oponerse* a **(b)** (resist) ‹*decision/plan*› combatir

opposed /ə'pəʊzd/ *adj* **1** (against, in disagreement with) (*pred*) **to be ~ TO sth** oponerse* A algo **2 as opposed to** a diferencia de

opposing /ə'pəʊzɪŋ/ *adj* (*before n*) ‹*viewpoint/faction/team*› contrario; ‹*army*› enemigo

opposite¹ /'ɑːpəzət ‖ 'ɒpəzɪt/ *adj* **1** (facing) ‹*side/wall/page*› de enfrente **2** (contrary) ‹*opinions/news*› opuesto; **we set off in ~ directions** partimos en direcciones opuestas; **it was coming in the ~ direction** venía en dirección contraria; **the ~ sex** el sexo opuesto

opposite² *adv* enfrente

opposite³ *prep* enfrente de, frente a

opposite⁴ *n*: **the ~** lo contrario

opposite number *n* homólogo, -ga *m,f*

opposition /'ɑːpə'zɪʃən ‖ ,ɒpə'zɪʃən/ *n* **1** [U] (antagonism, resistance) oposición *f* **2** (+ *sing or pl vb*) **(a)** (rivals, competitors) (Busn) competencia *f*; (Sport) adversarios *mpl* **(b)** (Pol) oposición *f*

oppress /ə'pres/ *vt* oprimir

oppression /ə'preʃən/ *n* [U] (Pol) opresión *f*; (feeling) agobio *m*

oppressive /ə'presɪv/ *adj* (Pol) opresivo; ‹*heat/humidity*› agobiante

opt /ɑːpt ‖ ɒpt/ *vi* optar; **to ~ FOR sth** optar POR algo; **to ~ to** + INF optar POR + INF

• opt out [*v* + *adv*] **to ~ out (OF sth)** decidir no tomar parte (EN algo); (when already involved) dejar de tomar parte (EN algo)

optical /'ɑːptɪkəl ‖ 'ɒptɪkəl/ *adj* óptico

optician /ɑːp'tɪʃən ‖ ɒp'tɪʃən/ *n* óptico, -ca *m,f*; (esp in UK) ≈ oculista *mf*

optics /'ɑːptɪks ‖ 'ɒptɪks/ *n* (+ *sing vb*) óptica *f*

optimism /'ɑːptəmɪzəm ‖ 'ɒptɪmɪzəm/ *n* [U] optimismo *m*

optimist /'ɑːptəməst ‖ 'ɒptɪmɪst/ *n* optimista *mf*

optimistic /'ɑːptə'mɪstɪk ‖ ,ɒptɪ'mɪstɪk/ *adj* optimista

optimum /'ɑːptəməm ‖ 'ɒptɪməm/ *adj* (*before n*) óptimo

option /'ɑːpʃən ‖ 'ɒpʃən/ *n* opción *f*; (Educ) (asignatura *f*) optativa *f*

optional /'ɑːpʃn̩l ‖ 'ɒpʃn̩l/ *adj* ‹*accessories/features*› opcional; ‹*course/subject*› optativo

opulence /'ɑːpjələns ‖ 'ɒpjʊləns/ *n* [U] opulencia *f*

opulent /'ɑːpjələnt ‖ 'ɒpjʊlənt/ *adj* opulento

opus /'əʊpəs/ *n* obra *f*; (Mus) opus *m*

or /ər, ɔːr ‖ ɔː(r)/ *conj*

■ **Note** The usual translation of *or*, *o*, becomes *u* when it precedes a word beginning with *o* or *ho*.

---

o; **either ... or ...** *see* EITHER¹; **five minutes ~ so** unos cinco minutos; **do as I say, ~ else!** ¡haz lo que digo o vas a ver!

OR = **Oregon**

oracle /'ɔːrəkəl ‖ 'ɒrəkəl/ *n* oráculo *m*

oral¹ /'ɔːrəl/ *adj* (*usu before n*) oral

oral² *n* (examen *m*) oral *m*

orange¹ /'ɑːrɪndʒ ‖ 'ɒrɪndʒ/ *n* **(a)** [C U] (fruit) naranja *f*; (*before n*) **~ juice** jugo *m* or (Esp) zumo *m* de naranja **(b) ~ (tree)** naranjo *m* **(c) ▶515** [U] (color) naranja *m*

orange² ▶515 *adj* naranja *adj inv*, de color naranja

orangeade /'ɑːrɪndʒ'eɪd ‖ ,ɒrɪndʒ'eɪd/ *n* [U] naranjada *f*

orator /'ɔːrətər ‖ 'ɒrətə(r)/ *n* orador, -dora *m,f*

orbit¹ /'ɔːrbət ‖ 'ɔːbɪt/ *n* órbita *f*

orbit² *vt* girar *or* orbitar alrededor de ■ **~** *vi* orbitar

orchard /'ɔːrtʃərd ‖ 'ɔːtʃəd/ *n* huerto *m* (*de árboles frutales*)

orchestra /'ɔːrkəstrə ‖ 'ɔːkɪstrə/ *n* **1** (Mus) orquesta *f* **2** (AmE Theat) platea *f*, patio *m* de butacas

orchestral /ɔːr'kestrəl ‖ ɔː'kestrəl/ *adj* ‹*music*› orquestal; ‹*piece*› para orquesta

orchestrate /'ɔːrkəstreɪt ‖ 'ɔːkɪstreɪt/ *vt* orquestar

orchid /'ɔːrkəd ‖ 'ɔːkɪd/ *n* orquídea *f*

ordain /ɔːr'deɪn ‖ ɔː'deɪn/ *vt* **1** (Relig) ordenar **2 (a)** (decree) (frml) **to ~ THAT** decretar QUE (+ *subj*) **(b)** (predestine) predestinar

ordeal /ɔːr'diːl ‖ ɔː'diːl/ *n* terrible experiencia *f*

order¹ /'ɔːrdər ‖ 'ɔːdə(r)/ *n* **I** [C] **1** (command) orden *f*; **~ to** + INF orden DE + inf **2** (request, goods requested) pedido *m*; **the books are on ~** los libros están pedidos; **we make them to ~** los hacemos por encargo; **the waiter took my ~** el camarero tomó nota de lo que quería

II [U] **1** (sequence) orden *m*; **to put sth in(to) ~** poner* algo en orden **2** (satisfactory condition) orden *m*; **I'm trying to put my affairs in ~** estoy tratando de poner mis asuntos en orden; **the car was in perfect working ~** el coche funcionaba perfectamente bien **3** (harmony, discipline) orden *m*; **to keep ~** mantener* el orden **4** (in phrases) **(a) in order**: **are her papers in ~?** ¿tiene los papeles en regla?; **an apology would seem to be in ~** parecería que lo indicado sería disculparse **(b) in order to** para **(c) in order that** para que (+ *subj*) **(d) out of order** (not in sequence) desordenado; (not working) averiado, descompuesto (AmL); Ⓢ **out of order** no funciona

III [C] **1** (Biol) orden *m* **2** (of monks, nuns) orden *f*

order² *vt* **1 (a)** (command) ordenar; **to ~ sb to** + INF ordenarle a algn QUE (+ *subj*) **(b)** (Med) mandar **2** (request) pedir*; ‹*goods*› encargar* **3** (put in order) ordenar ■ ~ *vi* (in restaurant): **are you ready to ~?** ¿ya han decidido qué van a tomar?

order book *n* libro *m* de pedidos

ordered /'ɔːrdərd ‖ 'ɔːdəd/ *adj* ordenado

orderly¹ /'ɔːrdərli ‖ 'ɔːdəli/ *adj* **(a)** ‹*life/mind*› ordenado **(b)** ‹*crowd*› disciplinado

orderly² *n* (*pl* **-lies**) **(a)** (in hospital) camillero *m* **(b)** (Mil) ordenanza *m*

ordinal (number) /'ɔːrdṇəl ‖ 'ɔːdɪnəl/ ▶ 725 *n* (número *m*) ordinal *m*

ordinarily /'ɔːrdṇ'erəli ‖ 'ɔːdənrəli/ *adv* **(a)** (usually) normalmente **(b)** (averagely) medianamente

ordinary¹ /'ɔːrdṇeri ‖ 'ɔːdənri/ *adj* **(a)** (average, normal) normal, corriente **(b)** (usual) normal

ordinary² *n* (average): **out of the ~** fuera de lo común

ore /ɔːr ‖ ɔː(r)/ *n* mena *f*, mineral *m* metalífero

Ore, **Oreg** = **Oregon**

oregano /ə'regənəʊ ‖ ˌɒrɪ'gɑːnəʊ/ *n* [U] orégano *m*

organ /'ɔːrgən ‖ 'ɔːgən/ *n* **1** (Anat) órgano *m* **2** (Mus) órgano *m*

organic /ɔːr'gænɪk ‖ ɔː'gænɪk/ *adj* orgánico; ‹*farming*› ecológico; ‹*vegetable*› biológico, cultivado sin pesticidas ni fertilizantes artificiales

organism /'ɔːrgənɪzəm ‖ 'ɔːgənɪzəm/ *n* organismo *m*

organization /'ɔːrgənə'zeɪʃən ‖ ˌɔːgənaɪ'zeɪʃən/ *n* **(a)** [C] (group) organización *f*; (*before n*) **~ chart** organigrama *m* **(b)** [U] (organizing) organización *f*

organize /'ɔːrgənaɪz ‖ 'ɔːgənaɪz/ *vt* **1** (arrange, set up) organizar* **2** (systematize) ‹*ideas/life*› ordenar; **to get oneself ~d** organizarse* **3** (Lab Rels) sindicalizar* (esp AmL), sindicar* (esp Esp)

organized /'ɔːrgənaɪzd ‖ 'ɔːgənaɪzd/ *adj* **1** (methodical) organizado **2** (Lab Rels) sindicalizado (esp AmL), sindicado (esp Esp) **3** ‹*crime*› organizado

organizer /'ɔːrgənaɪzər ‖ 'ɔːgənaɪzə(r)/ *n* organizador, -dora *m,f*

orgasm /'ɔːrgæzəm ‖ 'ɔːgæzəm/ *n* orgasmo *m*

orgy /'ɔːrdʒi ‖ 'ɔːdʒi/ *n* (*pl* **orgies**) orgía *f*

orient¹, **Orient** /'ɔːriənt/ *n* **the ~** (el) Oriente

orient² *vt* (esp AmE) orientar

oriental /ˌɔːri'entl/ *adj* oriental

orientate /'ɔːrienteɪt/ *vt* (esp BrE) ⇒ ORIENT²

orientation /ˌɔːrien'teɪʃən/ *n* [U] **(a)** (leanings, preference) tendencia *f* **(b)** (guidance) orientación *f*

orienteering /ˌɔːrien'tɪrɪŋ ‖ ˌɔːriən'tɪərɪŋ/ *n* [U] orientación *f*

orifice /'ɔːrəfəs ‖ 'ɒrɪfɪs/ *n* orificio *m*

origin /'ɔːrədʒən ‖ 'ɒrɪdʒɪn/ *n* origen *m*

original¹ /ə'rɪdʒənl/ *adj* **1** (first) original; **the ~ inhabitants** los primeros habitantes **2 (a)** (not copied) original **(b)** (unusual) original

original² *n* (document, painting) original *m*

originality /əˌrɪdʒə'næləti/ *n* [U] originalidad *f*

originally /ə'rɪdʒənḷi/ *adv* **(a)** (in the beginning) originariamente **(b)** (unusually) con originalidad

originate /ə'rɪdʒəneɪt ‖ ə'rɪdʒɪneɪt/ *vi* **(a)** (begin) «*custom*» originarse; «*fire*» empezar* **(b) to ~ from sth** (develop from) tener* su origen en algo **(c)** (AmE Transp) salir* de

originator /ə'rɪdʒəneɪtər ‖ ə'rɪdʒɪneɪtə(r)/ *n* creador, -dora *m,f*

Orkney Islands /'ɔːrkni ‖ 'ɔːkni/, **Orkneys** /-z/ *pl n* (Islas *fpl*) Órcadas *fpl*

ornament /'ɔːrnəmənt ‖ 'ɔːnəmənt/ *n* adorno *m*

ornamental /ˌɔːrnə'mentḷ ‖ ˌɔːnə'mentḷ/ *adj* ornamental

ornate /ɔːr'neɪt ‖ ɔː'neɪt/ *adj* ornamentado; (pej) recargado

ornithologist /ˌɔːrnə'θɑːlədʒəst ‖ ˌɔːnɪ'θɒlədʒɪst/ *n* ornitólogo, -ga *m,f*

ornithology /ˌɔːrnə'θɑːlədʒi ‖ ˌɔːnɪ'θɒlədʒi/ *n* [U] ornitología *f*

orphan¹ /'ɔːrfən ‖ 'ɔːfən/ *n* huérfano, -na *m,f*

orphan² *vt* (*usu pass*): **she was ~ed at the age of two** quedó huérfana a los dos años

orphanage /'ɔːrfənɪdʒ ‖ 'ɔːfənɪdʒ/ *n* orfanato *m*

orthodox /'ɔːrθədɑːks ‖ 'ɔːθədɒks/ *adj* ortodoxo

orthopedic, **orthopaedic** /ˌɔːrθə'piːdɪk ‖ ˌɔːθə'piːdɪk/ *adj* ortopédico

Oscar /'ɑːskər ‖ 'ɒskə(r)/ *n* oscar *m*

oscillate /'ɑːsəleɪt ‖ 'ɒsɪleɪt/ *vi* (Elec, Phys) oscilar

ostensible /ɑːs'tensəbəl ‖ ɒ'stensəbəl/ *adj* aparente

ostensibly /ɑːs'tensəbli ‖ ɒ'stensəbli/ *adv* aparentemente

ostentatious /ˌɑːstən'teɪʃəs ‖ ˌɒsten'teɪʃəs/ *adj* ostentoso

osteopath /'ɑːstiəpæθ ‖ 'ɒstiəpæθ/ *n* osteópata *mf*

ostracize /'ɑːstrəsaɪz ‖ 'ɒstrəsaɪz/ *vt* hacerle* el vacío a

ostrich /'ɑːstrɪtʃ ‖ 'ɒstrɪtʃ/ *n* avestruz *m*

other¹ /'ʌðər ‖ 'ʌðə(r)/ *adj* otro, otra; (*pl*) otros, otras; **he doesn't relate easily to ~ people** no se relaciona fácilmente con los demás; **the ~ day** el otro día

other² *pron* (*pl* **others**) **1 (a)** (different, alternative one or ones) otro, otra; **~s** otros, otras; **I'll think of some excuse or ~** ya me inventaré alguna excusa (u otra); **he was called Richard something or ~** se llamaba Richard no sé cuánto (fam) **(b)** (the remaining one or ones) otro, otra; **~s** otros, otras; **what do the ~s think?** ¿qué piensan los demás?; (additional one or ones) otro, otra; **~s** otros, otras; **answer the first three questions and one ~** conteste las tres primeras preguntas y otra más **2 other than** (apart from) aparte de; (different from) distinto (*or* distinta *etc*) de *or* a; **it was none ~ than Bob** no era ni más ni menos que Bob

other[3] *adv*: **somehow or ~** de alguna manera; **somewhere or ~** en algún sitio; **where would you like to live? — anywhere ~ than London** ¿dónde te gustaría vivir? — en cualquier (otro) sitio menos en Londres

otherwise /ˈʌðərwaɪz ‖ ˈʌðəwaɪz/ *adv* **1** (if not) (*as linker*) si no **2** (in other respects) por lo demás **3 (a)** (in a different way): **he could not have done ~** no podía haber hecho otra cosa; **unless ~ agreed, payments** ... a menos que se convenga otra cosa, los pagos ... **(b)** (other, different): **there are many problems, legal and ~** hay muchos problemas, legales y de otro tipo

otter /ˈɑːtər ‖ ˈɒtə(r)/ *n* nutria *f*

ouch /aʊtʃ/ *interj* (colloq) ¡ay!

ought /ɔːt/ *v mod* **~ to** + INF debería (*or* deberías *etc*) + INF, debiera (*or* debieras *etc*) + INF; **she ~ not to have said that** no debería haber dicho eso

ounce /aʊns/ *n* **(a)** ▶ **322** (unit) onza *f* (*28,35 gramos*) **(b)** (small quantity) (*no pl*): **if you had an ~ of decency/sense** ... si tuvieras una pizca de vergüenza/sentido común ...

our /aʊr ‖ ˈaʊə(r)/ *adj*

■ **Note** The translation *nuestro* agrees in number and gender with the noun which it modifies; *our* is translated by *nuestro*, *nuestra*, *nuestros*, *nuestras*, according to what follows: *our father/mother* nuestro padre/nuestra madre; *our books/magazines* nuestros libros/nuestras revistas. For *our* used with parts of the body, ▶ **484**

(*sing*) nuestro, -tra; (*pl*) nuestros, -tras

ours /aʊrz ‖ ˈaʊəz/ *pron*

■ **Note** The translation *nuestro* reflects the gender and number of the noun it is standing for; *ours* is translated by *el nuestro*, *la nuestra*, *los nuestros*, *las nuestras*, depending on what is being referred to.

(*sing*) nuestro, -tra; (*pl*) nuestros, -tras; **~ is blue** el nuestro/la nuestra es azul; **a friend of ~** un amigo nuestro

ourselves /aʊrˈselvz ‖ aʊəˈselvz, ɑː-/ *pron* **(a)** (reflexive): **we behaved ~** nos portamos bien; **we thought only of ~** sólo pensamos en nosotros mismos/nosotras mismas; **we were by ~** estábamos solos/solas **(b)** (emphatic use): **we did it ~** lo hicimos nosotros mismos/nosotras mismas

oust /aʊst/ *vt* ‹*rival/leader*› desbancar*; ‹*government*› derrocar*

out[1] /aʊt/ *adv* **I 1 (a)** (outside) fuera, afuera (esp AmL) **(b)** (not at home, work): **tell him I'm ~** dile que no estoy; **I was ~ most of the day** estuve (a)fuera casi todo el día; **to eat ~** cenar/comer fuera *or* (esp AmL) afuera; **~ and about**: **you must get ~ and about more** tienes que salir más **2** (removed): **I'm having my stitches ~ next week** la semana que viene me sacan los puntos **3 (a)** (indicating movement, direction): **~!** ¡fuera!; Ⓢ **out** salida; **she went over to the window and looked ~** se acercó a la ventana y miró para afuera **(b)** (outstretched, projecting): **the dog had its tongue ~** el perro tenía la lengua fuera *or* (esp AmL) afuera **4** (indicating distance): **~ here in Japan** aquí en Japón; **we live ~ Brampton way** vivimos en la dirección de Brampton **5** (from hospital, jail): **he's been ~ for a month now** ya hace un mes que salió **6** (in phrases) **out for**: **Lewis was ~ for revenge** Lewis quería vengarse; **out to** + INF: **she's ~ to beat the record** está decidida a batir el récord; **they're only ~ to make money** su único objetivo es hacer dinero; *see also* OUT OF

II 1 (a) (displayed, not put away): **are the plates ~ yet?** ¿están puestos ya los platos? **(b)** (in blossom) en flor **(c)** (shining): **when the sun's ~** cuando hay *or* hace sol **2** (published, produced): **a report ~ today points out that** ... un informe publicado hoy señala que ...; **their new album will be ~ by April** sacarán el nuevo disco para abril

out[2] *adj* **1** (*pred*) **(a)** (extinguished) **to be ~** «*fire/light/pipe*» estar* apagado **(b)** (unconscious) inconsciente **2** (*pred*) **(a)** (at an end): **before the month/year is ~** antes de que acabe el mes/año **(b)** (out of fashion) pasado de moda **3** (Sport) **(a)** (eliminated) **to be ~** ‹*batter/batsman*› quedar out; ‹*team*› quedar eliminado **(b)** (outside limit) (*pred*) fuera; **~!** ¡out!

out[3] *prep*: **he looked ~ the window** miró (hacia afuera) por la ventana; *see also* OUT OF 1

out: **~-and-~** /ˈaʊtn̩ˈaʊt/ *adj* (*as intensifier*) ‹*villain/liar*› consumado; ‹*radical/feminist*› acérrimo; ‹*defeat/disgrace*› total; **~back** *n* **the ~back** el interior (*zona despoblada de Australia*); **~bid** /ˈaʊtˈbɪd/ *vt* (*pres p* **-bidding**; *past* **-bid**; *past p* **-bid** *or* (AmE also) **-bidden**) **to ~bid sb** (FOR **sth**) pujar más que algn (POR algo); **~board** (**motor**) *n* motor *m* fuera de borda, fueraborda *m*; **~break** *n* (of war) estallido *m*; (of hostilities) comienzo *m*; (of cholera, influenza, violence) brote *m*; **~building** *n* edificación *f* anexa; **~burst** *n* (of emotion) arrebato *m*; **~cast** *n* paria *mf*; **~come** *n* (result) resultado *m*; (consequences) consecuencias *fpl*; **~crop** *n* afloramiento *m*; **~cry** *n* [U C] protesta *f* (*enérgica*); **there was a public ~cry** hubo protestas generalizadas; **~dated** /ˈaʊtˈdeɪtəd ‖ ˌaʊtˈdeɪtɪd/ *adj* ‹*style/custom*› pasado de moda; ‹*idea/theory*› anticuado; **~did** /ˈaʊtˈdɪd/ *past of* **~**DO; **~distance** /ˈaʊtˈdɪstəns/ *vt* dejar atrás; **~do** /ˈaʊtˈduː/ *vt* (*3rd pers sing pres* **-does**; *past* **-did**; *past p* **-done**) ‹*person/team*› superar; ‹*result/achievement*› mejorar; **~door** /ˈaʊtdɔːr ‖ ˈaʊtdɔː(r)/ *adj* (*before n*) ‹*clothes*› de calle; ‹*plants*› de exterior; ‹*swimming pool*› descubierto; **~doors** /ˈaʊtˈdɔːrz ‖ ˌaʊtˈdɔːz/ *adv* al aire libre

outer /ˈaʊtər ‖ ˈaʊtə(r)/ *adj* (*before n*) exterior; **~ space** el espacio sideral

out: **~fit** *n* **(a)** (clothes) conjunto *m*, tenida *f* (Chi) **(b)** (equipment) equipo *m*; **~flow** *n* (of water) desagüe *m*, flujo *m*; **~go** *n* [U C] (AmE) salida *f*; **~going** *adj* **1** (sociable) sociable; **2** ‹*president/administration*› saliente; **~goings** *pl n* (esp BrE) gastos *mpl*;

~grow /aʊt'grəʊ/ *vt* (*past* **-grew**; *past p* **-grown**): **he's already ~grown his new shoes** los zapatos nuevos ya le han quedado chicos *or* (Esp) ya se le han quedado pequeños; **she's ~grown these toys** ya está grande para jugar con esos juguetes; **~house** *n* **(a)** (building) (BrE) edificación *f* anexa **(b)** (outdoor privy) (AmE) excusado *m* exterior

outing /'aʊtɪŋ/ *n* excursión *f*

outlandish /aʊt'lændɪʃ/ *adj* ‹*clothes*› extravagante; ‹*idea/suggestion*› descabellado

outlast /'aʊt'læst ‖ ˌaʊt'lɑːst/ *vt* **(a)** (last longer than) durar más que **(b)** (survive) sobrevivir a

outlaw¹ /'aʊtlɔː/ *n* forajido, -da *m,f*, bandido, -da *m,f*

outlaw² *vt* ‹*activity/product*› prohibir*, declarar ilegal; ‹*organization*› proscribir*; ‹*person*› declarar fuera de la ley

out: **~lay** *n* desembolso *m*; **~let** *n* **1 (a)** (for liquid, gas) salida *f* **(b)** (AmE Elec) toma *f* de corriente, tomacorriente *m* (AmL); **2** (means of expression): **she found an ~let for her feelings** encontró una manera de canalizar sus sentimientos; **3** (Busn, Marketing) punto *m* de venta; **retail ~let** tienda *f* al por menor

outline¹ /'aʊtlaɪn/ *n* **1 (a)** (contour) contorno *m* **(b)** (shape) perfil *m* **2** (summary) resumen *m*; (plan of project, article) esquema *m*

outline² *vt* **(a)** (sketch) ‹*shape*› bosquejar; ‹*map*› trazar* **(b)** (summarize) esbozar*

out: **~live** /aʊt'lɪv/ *vt* sobrevivir a; **~look** *n* **(a)** (attitude) punto *m* de vista **(b)** (prospects) perspectivas *fpl*; **~lying** *adj* (*before n*) ‹*villages/islands*› alejado; ‹*area/hills/suburbs*› de la periferia; **~number** /aʊt'nʌmbər ‖ ˌaʊt'nʌmbə(r)/ *vt* superar en número a

out of *prep* **1** (from inside): **it fell ~ ~ her hand** se le cayó de la mano; **(come) ~ ~ there!** ¡salgan de ahí!; **to look ~ ~ the window** mirar (hacia afuera) por la ventana **2** (outside): **I was ~ ~ the room for two minutes** estuve dos minutos fuera *or* (AmL tb) afuera de la habitación **3** (eliminated, excluded): **Korea is ~ ~ the tournament** Corea ha quedado eliminada; **he was left ~ ~ the team** no lo incluyeron en el equipo **4 (a)** (indicating substance, makeup) de; **made ~ ~ steel** hecho de acero **(b)** (indicating motive) por; **~ ~ charity** por caridad **5** (from among) de; **eight ~ ~ ten people** ocho de cada diez personas **6** (indicating lack): **we're ~ ~ bread** nos hemos quedado sin pan

out: **~-of-date** /aʊtəv'deɪt/ *adj* (*pred* **~ of date**) ‹*ideas/technology*› desfasado, perimido (RPl); ‹*ticket/check*› caducado, vencido (AmL); ‹*clothes*› pasado de moda; **~-of-the-way** /əʊtəvðə'weɪ/ *adj* ‹*place*› apartado; **~patient** *n* paciente externo, -na *m,f*; **~post** *n* **(a)** (Mil) avanzada *f* **(b)** (settlement) puesto *m* de avanzada; **~put** *n* [U C] (of factory, writer, artist) producción *f*; (of worker, machine) rendimiento *m*; (Comput) salida *f*; (Elec) salida *f*

outrage¹ /'aʊtreɪdʒ/ *n* **(a)** [C] (cruel act) atrocidad *f* **(b)** [C] (scandal) escándalo *m* **(c)** [U] (feeling) **~** (AT **sth**) indignación *f* (ANTE algo)

outrage² *vt* (scandalize) escandalizar*

outrageous /aʊt'reɪdʒəs/ *adj* **(a)** (scandalous) ‹*behavior/state of affairs*› vergonzoso; ‹*demands/price*› escandaloso; **how dare you! this is ~!** ¡cómo te atreves! ¡esto es intolerable! **(b)** (unconventional) ‹*clothes*› extravagante

outran /aʊt'ræn/ *past of* OUTRUN

outright¹ /'aʊtraɪt/ *adj* (*before n*) ‹*refusal/opposition*› rotundo; ‹*hostility*› declarado; ‹*winner*› indiscutido; ‹*lie*› descarado

outright² *adv* **(a)** (completely) ‹*refuse/reject*› rotundamente; ‹*win*› indiscutiblemente **(b)** (directly, frankly) ‹*ask/say*› abiertamente **(c)** (instantly) ‹*kill*› en el acto

out: **~run** /aʊt'rʌn/ *vt* (*pres p* **-running**; *past* **-ran**; *past p* **-run**) dejar atrás; **~set** *n*: **from the ~set** desde el principio; **~shine** /aʊt'ʃaɪn/ *vt* (*past & past p* **-shone**) eclipsar

outside¹ /'aʊt'saɪd/ *n* (exterior part) exterior *m*; (surface) parte *f* de fuera *or* (esp AmL) de afuera; **at the (very) ~** como máximo

outside² *adv* fuera, afuera (esp AmL); **to run ~** salir* corriendo

outside³ *prep* fuera de; **it's just ~ London** está en las afueras de Londres; **it's ~ my responsibilities** no está dentro de mis responsabilidades

outside⁴ *adj* (*before n*) **(a)** (exterior, outward) exterior **(b)** (outdoor) ‹*toilet*› fuera de la vivienda, exterior **(c)** (outer) exterior; **the ~ lane** (Auto) el carril de la izquierda; (in UK etc) el carril de la derecha; (Sport) el carril (AmL) *or* (Esp) la calle número ocho (*or* seis *etc*) **(d)** (external) ‹*interference/pressure*› externo

outsider /aʊt'saɪdər ‖ ˌaʊt'saɪdə(r)/ *n* **(a)** (person not belonging) persona *f* de fuera, afuerano, -na *m,f* **(b)** (in competition): **he was beaten by an ~** fue derrotado por un desconocido (*un competidor que se consideraba tenía pocas probabilidades de ganar*)

out: **~size** /'aʊt'saɪz/, (esp AmE) **~-sized** /-d/ *adj* (Clothing) de talla *or* (RPl) talle gigante; (very large) gigantesco; **~skirts** *pl n* afueras *fpl*, alrededores *mpl*; **~smart** /aʊt'smɑːrt ‖ ˌaʊt'smɑːt/ *vt* (esp AmE colloq) burlar; **~spoken** /aʊt'spəʊkən/ *adj* directo, franco; **~spread** /aʊt'spred/ *adj* ‹*wings*› extendido; **~standing** /aʊt'stændɪŋ/ *adj* **1 (a)** (excellent) ‹*ability/beauty*› extraordinario; ‹*achievement/performer*› destacado **(b)** (prominent) (*before n*) ‹*feature*› destacado; **2** ‹*debt*› pendiente (de pago); **~stay** /aʊt'steɪ/ *vt*: **I think we've ~stayed our welcome** creo que nos hemos quedado más de la cuenta; **~stretched** /aʊt'stretʃt/ *adj* extendido; **~strip** /aʊt'strɪp/ *vt* **-pp-** (run faster than) tomarle la delantera a; (exceed) sobrepasar; **~vote** /aʊt'vəʊt/ *vt*: **to be ~voted** perder* la votación

outward¹ /'aʊtwərd ‖ 'aʊtwəd/ *adj* (*before n*) **(a)** ‹*appearance*› exterior; ‹*sign*› externo **(b)** ‹*journey/flight*› de ida

outward², (BrE also) **outwards** /-z/ *adv* hacia afuera

outwardly /'aʊtwərdli ‖ 'aʊtwədli/ *adv* en apariencia

out: **~weigh** /aʊt'weɪ/ *vt* ser* mayor que; **~wit** /aʊt'wɪt/ *vt* **-tt-** burlar

oval¹ /'əʊvəl/ *n* óvalo *m*

oval² *adj* ovalado, oval

ovary /'əʊvəri/ *n* (*pl* **-ries**) ovario *m*

ovation /əʊ'veɪʃən/ *n* (frml) ovación *f* (frml); **he got a standing ~** los delegados se pusieron de pie para aplaudirlo

oven /'ʌvən/ *n* horno *m*; (*before n*) **~ glove** guante *m* para el horno

oven: **~proof** *adj* refractario; **~-ready** /'ʌvən'redi/ *adj* listo para el horno

over¹ /'əʊvər ‖ 'əʊvə(r)/ *adv* **I 1 (a)** (across): **come ~ here!** ¡ven aquí!; **look ~ there!** ¡mira allí!; **she called me ~** me llamó (desde el otro lado); **he reached ~ and took the money** se estiró y tomó el dinero **(b)** (overhead) por encima **2 (a)** (in another place): **she was sitting ~ there** estaba sentada allí; **how long are you ~ (here) for?** ¿cuánto tiempo te vas a quedar (aquí)? **(b)** (on other page, TV station etc): **see ~** véase al dorso; **for the latest news, ~ to New York** para las últimas noticias, conectamos ahora con Nueva York **(c)** (Rad, Telec) corto; **~ and out!** corto y fuera **3** (out of upright position): **to knock sth ~** tirar *or* (AmL exc RPl) botar algo (de un golpe); **to tip sth ~** volcar* algo
II 1 (finished): **the film was ~ by 11 o'clock** la película terminó antes de las 11; **it's all ~ between us** lo nuestro se ha acabado; ***to be ~ (and done) with*** haber* terminado **2** (remaining): **if you have any material ~** si te sobra tela; **3 into 10 goes 3 and 1 ~** 10 dividido (por) 3 cabe a 3 y sobra 1 **3 (a)** (*as intensifier*): **twice/ten times ~** dos/diez veces **(b)** (again) (AmE) otra vez; **we had to start ~** tuvimos que volver a empezar **4** (more) más **5** (excessively) demasiado
III (*in phrases*) **1 all over** (everywhere) por todas partes; **I'm aching all ~** me duele todo (el cuerpo); **that's her all ~** (colloq) eso es típico de ella **2 (all) over again**: **to start (all) ~ again** volver* a empezar (desde cero) **3 over and over** (repeatedly) una y otra vez

over² *prep* **I 1** (across): **he jumped ~ the fence** saltó (por encima de) la valla; **they built a bridge ~ the river** construyeron un puente sobre el río; **she peered ~ his shoulder** atisbó por encima de su hombro **2** (above) encima de **3** (covering, on): **snow was falling ~ the countryside** nevaba sobre la campiña; **my room looks out ~ the square** mi habitación da a la plaza; **he put a coat on ~ his pajamas** se puso un abrigo encima del pijama; **she hit me ~ the head with her stick** me dio con el bastón en la cabeza **4 (a)** (through, all around): **~ an area of 50km²** en un área de 50km²; **I've been ~ the details with her** he repasado los detalles con ella **(b)** (referring to experiences, illnesses): **is she ~ her measles yet?** ¿ya se ha repuesto del sarampión?; **we're ~ the worst now** ya hemos pasado lo peor **5** (during, in the course of): **~ the past/next few years** en los últimos/próximos años; **we can discuss it ~ lunch** podemos hablarlo mientras comemos **6** (by the medium of) por; **~ the loudspeaker** por el altavoz **7** (about, on account of): **to cry ~ sth** llorar por algo; **they argued ~ money** discutieron por asuntos de dinero **8 all over**: **there are black marks all ~ the floor** hay marcas negras por todo el suelo; **all ~ town** por toda la ciudad
II 1 (a) (more than) más de **(b) over and above** (in addition to) además de **2 (a)** (senior to) por encima de **(b)** (indicating superiority) sobre; **to have control ~ sb/sth** tener* control sobre algn/algo

over³ *n* (in cricket) over *m* (*serie de seis lanzamientos*)

over- /'əʊvər ‖ 'əʊvə(r)/ *pref* **(a)** (excessively) demasiado **(b)** (in deliberate understatement): **she wasn't ~enthusiastic** no demostró mucho entusiasmo que digamos

overact /'əʊvər'ækt/ *vi* sobreactuar*

overall¹ /'əʊvərɔ:l/ *adj* (*before n*) ‹*length*› total; ‹*result/cost*› global; **the ~ impression** la impresión general

overall² 1 (protective garment) (esp BrE) bata *f* **2 overalls** *pl* **(a)** (dungarees) (AmE) overol *m* (AmL), (pantalones *mpl* de) peto *m* (Esp), mameluco *m* (CS) **(b)** (boiler suit) (BrE) overol *m* (AmL), mono *m* (Esp, Méx)

over: **~arm** *adv* (esp BrE) por encima de la cabeza; **~ate** /'əʊvər'eɪt/ *past of* ~EAT; **~awe** /'əʊvər'ɔ:/ *vt* intimidar; **~balance** /'əʊvər'bæləns ‖ ˌəʊvə'bæləns/ *vi* perder* el equilibrio; **~board** *adv*: **they threw him ~board** lo echaron por la borda; ***to go ~board*** (colloq — exaggerate) exagerar; (— be excessively enthusiastic, generous) pasarse (fam); **~came** /'əʊvər'keɪm ‖ ˌəʊvə'keɪm/ *past of* ~COME; **~cast** *adj* ▶ **920** ‹*sky*› cubierto; ‹*day*› nublado; **~charge** /'əʊvər'tʃɑ:rdʒ ‖ ˌəʊvə'tʃɑ:dʒ/ *vt* **to ~charge sb (FOR sth)** cobrarle de más a algn (POR algo); **~coat** *n* abrigo *m*, sobretodo *m* (esp RPl); **~come** /'əʊvər'kʌm ‖ ˌəʊvə'kʌm/ (*past* **-came**; *past p* **-come**) *vt* **(a)** ‹*opponent*› reducir*; ‹*fear*› superar; ‹*inhibitions*› vencer* **(b)** (overwhelm) invadir; **he was ~come by fatigue** lo venció la fatiga; **to be ~come WITH sth** ‹*with guilt/remorse*› sentirse* abrumado POR algo ■ ~ *vi:* **we shall ~come** venceremos; **~crowded** /'əʊvər'kraʊdəd ‖ ˌəʊvə'kraʊdɪd/ *adj* abarrotado (de gente); ‹*country*› superpoblado; **~crowding** /'əʊvər'kraʊdɪŋ ‖ ˌəʊvə'kraʊdɪŋ/ *n* [U]: **they complained about the ~crowding on the trains** se quejaron de lo abarrotados que iban los trenes; **the severe ~crowding in our prisons** el hacinamiento en nuestras cárceles; **~do** /'əʊvər'du: ‖ ˌəʊvə'du:/ *vt* (*3rd pers sing pres* **-does**; *past* **-did**; *past p* **-done**) **1** (exaggerate) exagerar; ***to ~do it*** (go too far) írsele la mano a algn; (overexert oneself) exigir* demasiado; **2** (Culin) cocinar demasiado, recocer*; **~dose** *n* sobredosis *f*; **~draft** *n* descubierto *m*; **~draw** /'əʊvər'drɔ: ‖ ˌəʊvə'drɔ:/ *vt* (*past* **-drew**; *past p* **-drawn**) (Fin): **I'm ~drawn** tengo un descubierto; **~drive** /'əʊvərdraɪv ‖ 'əʊvədraɪv/ *n* superdirecta *f*; **~due** /'əʊvər'du: ‖ ˌəʊvə'dju:/ *adj*: **the book is a month ~due** el plazo de devolución del libro venció hace un mes; **such measures are long ~due** tales medidas deberían haberse adoptado mucho antes; **~eat** /'əʊvər'i:t/ *vi* (*past* **-ate**; *past p* **-eaten**) comer demasiado; **~excited** /'əʊvərɪk'saɪtəd ‖ ˌəʊvərɪk'saɪtɪd/ *adj* sobreexcitado; **~feed** /'əʊvər'fi:d ‖ ˌəʊvə'fi:d/ *vt* (*past & past p* **-fed**) sobrealimentar

overflow¹ /'əʊvər'fləʊ ‖ ˌəʊvə'fləʊ/ *vi* «*liquid*» derramarse; «*bucket/bath/river*» desbordarse; **the**

house is ~ing with junk la casa está hasta el techo de cachivaches

overflow² /'əʊvərfləʊ ‖ 'əʊvəfləʊ/ *n* **(a)** [U C] (excess): **we put a bowl there to catch the ~** pusimos un bol para recoger el líquido que se derramaba **(b)** [C] (outlet) rebosadero *m*

over: **~grown** /'əʊvər'grəʊn ‖ ,əʊvə'grəʊn/ *adj* **(a)** ‹*garden*› lleno de maleza **(b)** (too big) demasiado grande; **~hand** *adv* (AmE) por encima de la cabeza; **~hang** /'əʊvər'hæŋ ‖ ,əʊvə'hæŋ/ (*past & past p* **-hung**) *vt* sobresalir* por encima de ■ **~** *vi* sobresalir*

overhaul¹ /'əʊvər'hɔːl ‖ ,əʊvə'hɔːl/ *vt* revisar

overhaul² /'əʊvərhɔːl ‖ 'əʊvəhɔːl/ *n* revisión *f* (general), overjol *m* (AmC)

overhead¹ /'əʊvər'hed ‖ ,əʊvə'hed/ *adv*: **the sun was directly ~** el sol caía de pleno; **a plane flew ~** pasó un avión

overhead² /'əʊvərhed ‖ 'əʊvəhed/ *adj* ‹*cable*› aéreo; ‹*railway*› elevado

overhead³ /'əʊvərhed ‖ 'əʊvəhed/ *n* [C U] (AmE) gastos *mpl* indirectos

over: **~heads** /'əʊvərhedz ‖ 'əʊvəhedz/ *pl n* (BrE) ⇒ OVERHEAD³; **~hear** /'əʊvər'hɪr ‖ ,əʊvə'hɪə(r)/ *vt* (*past & past p* **-heard**) oír* (*por casualidad*); **~heat** /'əʊvər'hiːt ‖ ,əʊvə'hiːt/ *vi* recalentarse*; **~hung** *past & past p of* OVERHANG; **~joyed** /'əʊvər'dʒɔɪd ‖ ,əʊvə'dʒɔɪd/ *adj* encantado; **~kill** *n* [U] exageración *f*; **~land** *adj/adv* por tierra; **~lap** /'əʊvər'læp ‖ ,əʊvə'læp/ *vi* **-pp- (a)** «*tiles/planks*» estar* montados unos sobre otros, traslaparse **(b)** «*responsibilities*» coincidir en parte; **~leaf** /'əʊvər'liːf ‖ ,əʊvə'liːf/ *adv* al dorso; **~load** /'əʊvər'ləʊd ‖ ,əʊvə'ləʊd/ *vt* sobrecargar*; **~look** /'əʊvər'lʊk ‖ ,əʊvə'lʊk/ *vt* **1 (a)** (not notice) pasar por alto **(b)** (disregard) disculpar; **2** (have view over): **a room ~looking the sea** una habitación con vista al mar *or* que da al mar

overly /'əʊvərli ‖ 'əʊvəli/ *adv* demasiado

overnight¹ /'əʊvər'naɪt ‖ ,əʊvə'naɪt/ *adv* **(a)** (through the night): **to stay ~** quedarse a pasar la noche; **there had been a heavy fall of snow ~** durante la noche había nevado mucho; **soak the chickpeas ~** ponga los garbanzos en remojo la noche anterior **(b)** (suddenly) ‹*change/disappear*› de la noche a la mañana

overnight² /'əʊvərnaɪt ‖ 'əʊvənaɪt/*adj* **(a)** (through the night) ‹*journey*› de noche; ‹*stay*› de una noche **(b)** (sudden) ‹*change/success*› repentino

over: **~paid** /'əʊvər'peɪd ‖ ,əʊvə'peɪd/ *adj*: **she's ~ paid** le pagan demasiado; **~pass** *n* paso *m* elevado, paso *m* a desnivel (Méx); **~power** /'əʊvər'paʊər ‖ ,əʊvə'paʊə(r)/ *vt* **(a)** (render helpless) dominar **(b)** (affect greatly) «*smell*» marear; «*heat*» sofocar*; «*emotion*» abrumar; **~powering** /'əʊvər'paʊrɪŋ ‖ ,əʊvə'paʊərɪŋ/ *adj* **(a)** ‹*smell*› muy fuerte; ‹*heat*› aplastante; ‹*desire*› irresistible **(b)** ‹*personality*› apabullante; **~priced** /'əʊvər'praɪst ‖ ,əʊvə'praɪst/ *vt*: **it's ~priced** es caro para lo que es; **~ran** /'əʊvər'ræn ‖ ,əʊvə'ræn/ *past of* ~RUN; **~rated** /'əʊvər'reɪtəd ‖ ,əʊvə'reɪtɪd/ *adj* sobrevalorado; **~reach** /'əʊvər'riːtʃ ‖ ,əʊvə'riːtʃ/ *v refl*: **to ~reach oneself** intentar hacer demasiado; **~react** /'əʊvərri'ækt ‖ ,əʊvəri'ækt/ *vi* reaccionar en forma exagerada; **~ride** /'əʊvər'raɪd ‖ ,əʊvə'raɪd/ *vt* (*past* **-rode**; *past p* **-ridden**) ‹*decision/recommendation*› invalidar; ‹*wishes/advice*› hacer* caso omiso de; **~ripe** /'əʊvər'raɪp ‖ ,əʊvə'raɪp/ *adj* demasiado maduro; **~rode** /'əʊvər'rəʊd ‖ ,əʊvə'rəʊd/ *past of* ~RIDE; **~rule** /'əʊvər'ruːl ‖ ,əʊvə'ruːl/ *vt* ‹*decision/verdict*› anular; ‹*objection*› rechazar*; **~run** /'əʊvər'rʌn ‖ ,əʊvə'rʌn/ *vt* (*past* **-ran**; *past p* **-run**) **(a)** (invade, swarm over) invadir; **to be ~run WITH sth** estar* plagado DE algo **(b)** (exceed) exceder; **~saw** /'əʊvər'sɔː ‖ ,əʊvə'sɔː/ *past of* OVERSEE

overseas¹ /'əʊvər'siːz ‖ 'əʊvə,siːz/ *adj* (*before n*) ‹*trade*› exterior; ‹*investments/branches*› en el exterior; ‹*student/visitor*› extranjero; ‹*news*› del exterior

overseas² /'əʊvər'siːz ‖ ,əʊvə'siːz/ *adv* ‹*live*› en el extranjero; ‹*travel/send*› al extranjero

over: **~see** /'əʊvər'siː ‖ ,əʊvə'siː/ *vt* (*past* **-saw**; *past p* **-seen**) supervisar; **~seer** /'əʊvər'sɪr, -'siːər ‖ 'əʊvəsiːə(r)/ *n* capataz *mf*; **~shadow** /'əʊvər'ʃædəʊ ‖ ,əʊvə'ʃædəʊ/ *vt* eclipsar; **~shoot** /'əʊvər'ʃuːt ‖ ,əʊvə'ʃuːt/ *vt* (*past & past p* **-shot**) ‹*runway*› salirse* de; ‹*turning*› pasarse de; ‹*target/budget*› exceder; **~sight** /'əʊvərsaɪt ‖ 'əʊvəsaɪt/ *n* [U C] descuido *m*; **~sleep** /'əʊvər'sliːp ‖ ,əʊvə'sliːp/ *vi* (*past & past p* **-slept**) quedarse dormido; **~spend** /'əʊvər'spend ‖ ,əʊvə'spend/ *vi* (*past & past p* **-spent**) gastar más de la cuenta; **~spill** *n* [U] excedente *m* de población; **~staffed** /'əʊvər'stæft ‖ ,əʊvə'stɑːft/ *adj* con exceso de personal *or* (Esp tb) de plantilla; **~state** /'əʊvər'steɪt ‖ ,əʊvə'steɪt/ *vt* exagerar; **~stay** /'əʊvər'steɪ ‖ ,əʊvə'steɪ/ *vt* ⇒ OUTSTAY; **~step** /'əʊvər'step ‖ ,əʊvə'step/ *vt* **-pp-** sobrepasar

overt /əʊ'vɜːrt ‖ 'əʊvɜːt/ *adj* ‹*hostility*› declarado; ‹*criticism*› abierto

over: **~take** /'əʊvər'teɪk ‖ ,əʊvə'teɪk/ (*past* **-took**; *past p* **-taken**) *vt* **(a)** (go past) adelantar, rebasar (Méx) **(b)** (surpass) superar ■ **~** *vi* (BrE) adelantar, rebasar (Méx); **~tax** /'əʊvər'tæks ‖ ,əʊvə'tæks/ *vt* **(a)** (strain) poner* a prueba **(b)** (Tax) gravar en exceso (*con impuestos*); **~throw** /'əʊvər'θrəʊ ‖ ,əʊvə'θrəʊ/ *vt* (*past* **-threw**; *past p* **-thrown**) ‹*government*› derrocar*; **~time** *n* [U] **1** (extra work hours) horas *fpl* extra(s), sobretiempo *m* (Chi, Per); **2** (AmE Sport) prórroga *f*; **~tone** *n* (suggestion, hint) (*usu pl*) dejo *m*, deje *m* (Esp); **~took** /'əʊvər'tʊk ‖ ,əʊvə'tʊk/ *past of* ~TAKE

overture /'əʊvərtʃʊr ‖ 'əʊvətjʊə(r)/ *n* **1** (Mus) obertura *f* **2 overtures** *pl* (approaches) (frml) intento *m* de acercamiento; (sexual) insinuación *f*

over: **~turn** /'əʊvər'tɜːrn ‖ ,əʊvə'tɜːn/ *vt* **(a)** (tip over) ‹*table/boat*› darle* la vuelta a, dar* vuelta (CS) **(b)** (depose) ‹*government*› derrocar* ■ **~** *vi* «*vehicle*» volcar*; **~weight** /'əʊvər'weɪt ‖ ,əʊvə'weɪt/ *adj* ‹*person*› demasiado gordo; **I am 10lb ~weight** peso 10 libras de más, tengo un sobrepeso de 10 libras (Chi, Méx)

overwhelm /'əʊvər'hwelm ‖ ,əʊvə'welm/ *vt* **(a)** (emotionally) abrumar **(b)** (defeat) aplastar **(c)** (swamp): **they've been ~ed with applications/complaints** han recibido infinidad de solicitudes/quejas

overwhelming /ˈəʊvərˈhwelmɪŋ ‖ˌəʊvəˈwelmɪŋ/ *adj* ‹*grief*› inconsolable; ‹*urge*› irresistible; ‹*anger*› incontenible; ‹*boredom*› insoportable; ‹*defeat*› aplastante

overwind /ˈəʊvərˈwaɪnd ‖ˌəʊvəˈwaɪnd/ *vt* (*past & past p* **-wound** /-waʊnd/) dar* demasiada cuerda a

overwork¹ /ˈəʊvərˈwɜːrk ‖ˌəʊvəˈwɜːk/ *vt* hacer* trabajar demasiado

overwork² *n* [U] agotamiento *m*

ovulate /ˈɑːvjəleɪt ‖ˈɒvjʊleɪt/ *vi* ovular

ovulation /ˈɑːvjəˈleɪʃən ‖ˌɒvjʊˈleɪʃən/ *n* [U] ovulación *f*

owe /əʊ/ *vt* **(a)** (financially) deber; **to ~ sb sth, ~ sth TO sb** deberle algo A algn **(b)** (be obliged to give, do) ‹*explanation/apology/favor*› deber

owing /ˈəʊɪŋ/ *adj* **1** (*pred*): **the money still ~** el dinero que aún se debe **2 owing to** (*as prep*) debido a

owl /aʊl/ *n* búho *m*, tecolote *m* (Méx); (*barn* ~) lechuza *f*

own¹ /əʊn/ *vt* ‹*property*› tener*

• **own up** [*v* + *adv*]: **no one ~ed up** nadie reconoció tener la culpa; **no one would ~ up to having left the window open** nadie quiso reconocer que había sido quien dejó la ventana abierta

own² *adj* **my/her/your** *etc* **~: in our ~ house** en nuestra propia casa; **she makes her ~ clothes** se hace la ropa ella misma

own³ *pron* **my/her/your** *etc* **~: it isn't a company car, it's her ~** no es un coche de la empresa, es suyo (propio); **she wanted a room of her ~** quería una habitación para ella sola; **on one's ~** solo; ***to get one's ~ back*** (BrE colloq) desquitarse

owner /ˈəʊnər ‖ˈəʊnə(r)/ *n* (of house, car) dueño, -ña *m,f*, propietario, -ria *m,f*; (of pet) dueño, -ña *m,f*

ownership /ˈəʊnərʃɪp ‖ˈəʊnəʃɪp/ *n* [U] propiedad *f*

own goal *n* autogol *m*, gol *m* en contra (CS)

ox /ɑːks ‖ɒks/ *n* (*pl* **oxen**) buey *m*

oxen /ˈɑːksən ‖ˈɒksən/ *pl of* ox

oxide /ˈɑːksaɪd ‖ˈɒksaɪd/ *n* [U C] óxido *m*

oxtail /ˈɑːksteɪl ‖ˈɒksteɪl/ *n* [U C] rabo *m* de buey

oxygen /ˈɑːksədʒən ‖ˈɒksɪdʒən/ *n* [U] oxígeno *m*; (*before n*) **~ mask** (Aviat, Med) mascarilla *f* de oxígeno

oyster /ˈɔɪstər ‖ˈɔɪstə(r)/ *n* ostra *f*, ostión *m* (Méx)

oz ▶ **322** = **ounce(s)**

ozone /ˈəʊzəʊn/ *n* [U] (Chem) ozono *m*; (*before n*) **the ~ layer** la capa de ozono

Pp

P, **p** /piː/ *n* P, p *f*

p (in UK) (= **penny/pence**) penique(s) *m(pl)*

p. (*pl* **pp.**) (= **page**) pág., p.; **pp. 12–48** págs. 12 a 48

pa¹ /pɑː/ *n* (colloq) papá *m*

pa², **p.a.** /ˈpiːˈeɪ/ = **per annum**

PA *n* **(a)** /ˈpiːˈeɪ/ **~ (system)** = **public-address system (b)** /ˈpiːˈeɪ/ (BrE) = **personal assistant (c)** *also* **Pa** = **Pennsylvania**

pace¹ /peɪs/ *n* **1** (stride) paso *m*; ***to put sb through her/his ~s*** poner* a algn a prueba **2** (speed) (*no pl*) ritmo *m*; **to keep ~ with sb** seguirle* el ritmo lento a algn; **to set the ~** marcar* la pauta

pace² *vi*: **to ~ up and down** caminar *or* (esp Esp) andar de un lado para otro

pace: **~maker** *n* (Sport) liebre *f*; (Med) marcapasos *m*; **~setter** /ˈpeɪsˈsetə(r) ‖ˈpeɪsˌsetə(r)/ *n* (Sport) liebre *f*; (pioneer) líder *mf*

Pacific /pəˈsɪfɪk/ *n* **the ~ (Ocean)** el (Océano) Pacífico

pacifier /ˈpæsəfaɪər ‖ˈpæsɪfaɪə(r)/ *n* (AmE) chupete *m*, chupón *m* (AmL exc CS), chupo *m* (Col), chupa *f* (Ven)

pacifist /ˈpæsəfəst ‖ˈpæsɪfɪst/ *n* pacifista *mf*

pacify /ˈpæsəfaɪ ‖ˈpæsɪfaɪ/ *vt* **-fies, -fying, -fied (a)** (calm, satisfy) apaciguar* **(b)** (restore to peace) pacificar*

pack¹ /pæk/ *n* **1** (bundle, load) fardo *m*; (rucksack) mochila *f* **2 (a)** (package) paquete *m*; (of cigarettes) paquete *m*, cajetilla *f* **(b)** (of cards) (BrE) baraja *f*, mazo *m* (esp AmL) **3 (a)** (of wolves) manada *f*; **a ~ of hounds** (Sport) una jauría **(b)** (in race) pelotón *m* **4** (of thieves, fools) (pej) partida *f* (pey); **a ~ of lies** una sarta de mentiras

pack² *vt* **1 (a)** (Busn) ‹*goods/products*› (put into container) envasar; (make packets with) empaquetar; (for transport) embalar **(b)** (put into suitcase, bag): **have you ~ed your toothbrush?** ¿llevas el cepillo de dientes?; **to ~ one's suitcase** hacer* la maleta *or* (RPl) la valija, empacar (AmL); **she takes a ~ed lunch to work** se lleva el almuerzo *or* (esp Esp, Méx) la comida al trabajo **2 (a)** (press tightly together): **~ the soil (down) firmly** apisone bien la tierra **(b)** (cram): **the book is ~ed with useful information** el libro está lleno de información útil; **we ~ed a lot into a short time** hicimos un montón de cosas en poco tiempo (fam) ■ **~** *vi* (fill suitcase) hacer* la(s) maleta(s) *or* (RPl) la(s) valija(s), empacar* (AmL)

• **pack in** [*v* + *o* + *adv*, *v* + *adv* + *o*] **1** (quit) (colloq) ‹*job/course*› dejar **2** (cram in): **we managed to ~ in 50 people** pudimos meter a 50 personas

• pack off [*v + o + adv, v + adv + o*] despachar, mandar; **she ~ed the children off to school** mandó a los niños al colegio

• pack up 1 [*v + adv*] **(a)** (assemble belongings) liar* el petate, hacer* su itacate (Méx) **(b)** (stop) (colloq): **let's ~ up for the day** dejémoslo por hoy **(c)** (break down) (colloq) «*motor/radio*» dejar de funcionar, descomponerse* (esp AmL), tronarse* (Méx fam) **2** [*v + o + adv, v + adv + o*] **(a)** ‹*tools/belongings*› recoger* **(b)** ⇨ PACK IN 1

package /'pækɪdʒ/ *n* paquete *m*

package: **~ holiday** (BrE) ⇨ **~** VACATION; **~ store** *n* (AmE) tienda *f* de bebidas alcohólicas; **~ tour** *n* viaje *m* organizado (*en el que se recorren diferentes localidades*); **~ vacation** *n* (AmE) vacaciones *fpl* organizadas

packaging /'pækɪdʒɪŋ/ *n* [U] **(a)** (packing) embalaje *m* **(b)** (wrapping) envoltorio *m* **(c)** (Marketing) presentación *f*

packed /pækt/ *adj* ‹*hall/restaurant*› lleno de gente, repleto

packet /'pækət ‖ 'pækɪt/ *n* (esp BrE) paquete *m*; (*before n*) ‹*soup/cake mix*› de sobre

packing /'pækɪŋ/ *n* [U] **(a)** (of suitcase): **to do one's ~** hacer* la(s) maleta(s) *or* (RPl) la(s) valija(s), empacar* (AmL) **(b)** (in factory) embalaje *m*

packing case *n* caja *f* de embalaje

pact /pækt/ *n* pacto *m*

pad¹ /pæd/ *n* **1** (cushioning) almohadilla *f*; **shoulder ~s** hombreras *fpl*; **knee ~s** rodilleras *fpl* **2** (of paper) bloc *m*

pad² *vt* **-dd- 1 (a)** (line) ‹*seat/panel*› acolchar, enguatar (Esp) **(b) padded** *past p* ‹*jacket*› acolchado, enguatado (Esp); ‹*bra*› con relleno; ‹*envelope*› acolchado; **~ded cell** celda *f* de aislamiento **2 ~ (out)** ‹*essay*› rellenar, meter* paja en (fam)

padding /'pædɪŋ/ *n* [U] (material) relleno *m*, guata *f* (Esp); (for protection) almohadillas *fpl*

paddle¹ /'pædl/ *n* **1** [C] (oar) zagual *m*, pala *f* **2** (*no pl*): **to go for a ~** ir* a mojarse los pies

paddle² *vi* **1** (wet feet) mojarse los pies (*en la orilla*) **2 (a)** (in canoe) remar (*con pala or zagual*) **(b)** (swim) «*duck/dog*» chapotear ■ **~** *vt* ‹*boat/canoe*› llevar (*remando con pala or zagual*)

paddling pool /'pædlɪŋ/ *n* (BrE) (in park) estanque *m*; (inflatable) piscina *f or* (Méx) alberca *f* inflable (*para niños*)

paddock /'pædək/ *n* prado *m*

paddy /'pædi/ *n* (*pl* **-dies**) **~ (field)** arrozal *m*

padlock¹ /'pædlɑːk ‖ 'pædlɒk/ *n* candado *m*

padlock² *vt* cerrar* con candado

paediatric *etc* (BrE) ⇨ PEDIATRIC *etc*

paedophile *n* (BrE) ⇨ PEDOPHILE

pagan¹ /'peɪgən/ *n* pagano, -na *m,f*

pagan² *adj* pagano

page¹ /peɪdʒ/ *n* **1** (of book, newspaper) página *f*; **on ~ four** en la página cuatro **2** (attendant) paje *m*; (in hotel) botones *m*

page² *vt* (over loudspeaker) llamar por megafonía; (by beeper) llamar por buscapersonas *or* (Méx) bip *or* (Chi) bíper

pageant /'pædʒənt/ *n* **(a)** (show, ceremony) festividades *fpl* **(b)** (historical show) *espectáculo histórico al aire libre*

pageboy /'peɪdʒbɔɪ/ *n* ⇨ PAGE¹ 2

pager /'peɪdʒər ‖ 'peɪdʒə(r)/ *n* buscapersonas *m*, bip *m* (Méx), bíper *m* (Chi)

paid¹ /peɪd/ *past & past p of* PAY¹

paid² *adj* ‹*employment*› remunerado; ‹*worker*› asalariado; ‹*vacation*› pagado; ‹*leave*› con goce de sueldo

pail /peɪl/ *n* balde *m*, cubo *m* (Esp), cubeta *f* (Méx)

pain /peɪn/ *n* **1 (a)** ▶ **484** [U C] (physical) dolor *m*; **she was in great ~** estaba muy dolorida *or* (AmL tb) adolorida; ***to be a ~ in the neck*** ser* un pesado **(b)** [C] (annoying person or thing) (colloq) lata *f* (fam) **2 pains** *pl* (effort): **that's all you get for your ~s** así te pagan la molestia; **I went to great ~s to explain it to them carefully** puse mucho esmero en explicárselo

painful /'peɪnfəl/ *adj* **(a)** (physically) doloroso; **it's very ~** duele mucho **(b)** (mentally) ‹*task*› desagradable; ‹*reminder*› doloroso

painfully /'peɪnfəli/ *adv*: **she dragged herself ~ along** se iba arrastrando con mucho dolor; **she's ~ shy** es tan tímida que da pena

painkiller /'peɪnˌkɪlər ‖ 'peɪnˌkɪlə(r)/ *n* [U C] analgésico *m*

painless /'peɪnləs ‖ 'peɪnlɪs/ *adj* **(a)** (causing no pain) indoloro; **~ childbirth** parto *m* sin dolor **(b)** (easy, pleasant) (colloq) ‹*method*› sencillo

painstaking /'peɪnzˌteɪkɪŋ/ *adj* ‹*research/efforts*› concienzudo; ‹*person/personality*› meticuloso

paint¹ /peɪnt/ *n* [U C] pintura *f*

paint² *vt/i* pintar

paint: **~box** *n* caja *f* de acuarelas; **~brush** *n* pincel *m*; (large, for walls) brocha *f*

painter /'peɪntər ‖ 'peɪntə(r)/ *n* (Art, Const) pintor, -tora *m,f*

painting /'peɪntɪŋ/ *n* **(a)** [C] (picture) cuadro *m*, pintura *f* **(b)** [U] (Art) pintura *f*

paintwork /'peɪntwɜːrk ‖ 'peɪntwɜːk/ *n* [U] pintura *f*

pair /per ‖ peə(r)/ *n* **1 (a)** (of shoes, socks, gloves) par *m*; **a ~ of trousers** unos pantalones; **a ~ of scissors** unas tijeras **(b)** (in cards) pareja *f*, par *m* **2** (couple) pareja *f*

• pair up [*v + adv*] formar parejas

pajamas, (BrE) **pyjamas** /pə'dʒɑːməz/ *pl n* pijama *m*, piyama *m or f* (AmL)

Pakistan /'pækɪ'stæn ‖ ˌpɑːkɪ'stɑːn, ˌpækɪ-/ *n* Pakistán *m*, Paquistán *m*

Pakistani¹ /'pækɪ'stæni ‖ ˌpɑːkɪ'stɑːnɪ, ˌpækɪ-/ *adj* pakistaní, paquistaní

Pakistani² *n* pakistaní *mf*, paquistaní *mf*

pal /pæl/ *n* (colloq) amigo *m*, compinche *m* (fam), cuate *m* (Méx fam)

palace /'pæləs ‖ 'pælɪs/ *n* palacio *m*

palatable /'pælətəbəl/ *adj* agradable

palate /'pælət/ *n* paladar *m*

pale¹ /peɪl/ *adj* **(a)** ‹*skin/person*› (naturally) blanco; (pallid) pálido **(b)** ‹*blue/pink*› pálido

pale² *vi* **(a)** «*person*» palidecer* **(b)** (seem minor) **to ~** BESIDE *o* BEFORE **sb/sth** palidecer* JUNTO A algn/algo

pale³ *n*: ***to be beyond the ~*** ser* intolerable

Palestine /'pæləstaɪn/ *n* Palestina *f*

Palestinian¹ /'pælə'stɪniən/ *adj* palestino

Palestinian² *n* palestino, -na *m,f*

palette /'pælət ‖ 'pælɪt/ *n* paleta *f*

pall¹ /pɔːl/ *n*: ***to cast a ~ on*** *o* ***over sth*** empañar algo

pall² *vi* hacerse* pesado

pallid /'pæləd ‖ 'pælɪd/ *adj* pálido

palm /pɑːm/ *n* **1 (a) ~ (tree)** palmera *f* **(b)** (leaf, branch) palma *f* **2** (Anat) palma *f*

• **palm off** [*v + o + adv*] **to ~ sth off** ON *o* ONTO **sb** encajarle algo a algn (fam); **to ~ sb off** WITH **sth** quitarse a algn de encima CON algo

palmistry /'pɑːməstri ‖ 'pɑːmɪstri/ *n* [U] quiromancia *f*

Palm Sunday *n* Domingo *m* de Ramos

palpable /'pælpəbəl/ *adj* (frml) palmario, palpable

palpitate /'pælpəteɪt ‖ 'pælpɪteɪt/ *vi* palpitar

palpitation /'pælpə'teɪʃən ‖ ˌpælpɪ'teɪʃən/ *n* [U C] (Med) palpitación *f*

paltry /'pɔːltri/ *adj* **-trier -triest** ‹*sum/amount*› mísero; ‹*excuse*› malo

pamper /'pæmpər ‖ 'pæmpə(r)/ *vt* mimar

pamphlet /'pæmflət ‖ 'pæmflɪt/ *n* (informative) folleto *m*; (political) panfleto *m*

pan¹ /pæn/ *n* **1** (Culin) cacerola *f*; (large, with two handles) olla *f*; (small) cacerola *f*, cazo *m* (Esp); (*frying ~*) sartén *f* **2** (of toilet) (BrE) taza *f*

pan² *vi* **-nn- 1** (Min): **to ~ for gold** lavar oro **2** (Cin): **the camera ~s across to the two figures** la cámara recorre hasta enfocar en las dos figuras

panacea /'pænə'siːə/ *n* (frml) panacea *f*

panache /pə'næʃ/ *n* [U] garbo *m*

Panama /'pænəmɑː/ *n* Panamá *m*; (*before n*) **~ Canal** el Canal de Panamá

Panamanian /'pænə'meɪniən/ *adj* panameño

pancake /'pænkeɪk/ *n* [C] (Culin) crep(e) *m*, panqueque *m* (AmL), crepa *f* (Méx), panqué *m* (AmC, Col), panqueca *f* (Ven)

pancreas /'pæŋkriəs/ *n* páncreas *m*

panda /'pændə/ *n* (oso, osa *m,f*) panda *mf*

pandemonium /'pændə'məʊniəm/ *n* [U] pandemonio *m*, pandemónium *m*

pander /'pændər ‖ 'pændə(r)/ *vi*: **to ~ to sb's whims** consentirle* los caprichos a algn

pane /peɪn/ *n* (hoja *f* de) vidrio *m*, cristal *m* (Esp)

panel¹ /'pænl/ *n* **1 (a)** (of door, car body, plane wing) panel *m*; (of garment) pieza *f* **(b)** (*instrument ~*) tablero *m* (de instrumentos); (*control ~*) tablero *m* (de control) **2** (in discussion, interview) panel *m* *or* (Col, Ven) pánel *m*; (in quiz, contest) equipo *m*; (in exam) mesa *f*, comisión *f* (Chi)

panel² *vt*, (BrE) **-ll- (a)** ‹*room/wall*› revestir* con paneles **(b) paneled**, (BrE) **panelled** *past p* ‹*door*› de paneles

pang /pæŋ/ *n* punzada *f*; **~s of hunger** retorcijones *mpl* *or* (Esp) retortijones *mpl* de hambre

panhandler /'pænˌhændlər ‖ 'pænˌhændlə(r)/ *n* (AmE colloq) mendigo *m*

panic¹ /'pænɪk/ *n* [U C] (fear, anxiety) pánico *m*; (*before n*) **~ button** botón *m* de alarma

panic² *vi* **-ck-** dejarse llevar por el pánico; **don't ~!** ¡tranquilo!

panicky /'pænɪki/ *adj* ‹*person*› muy nervioso; ‹*behavior/decision*› precipitado

panic-stricken /'pænɪkˌstrɪkən/ *adj* aterrorizado

pannier /'pæniər ‖ 'pæniə(r)/ *n* alforja *f*; (on cycle) maletero *m*

panorama /'pænə'ræmə ‖ ˌpænə'rɑːmə/ *n* panorama *m*

panoramic /'pænə'ræmɪk/ *adj* panorámico

pansy /'pænzi/ *n* (*pl* **-sies**) (Bot) pensamiento *m*

pant¹ /pænt/ *vi* jadear

pant² *n* jadeo *m*; *see also* PANTS

pantheon /'pænθiːɑːn ‖ 'pænθiən/ *n* panteón *m*

panther /'pænθər ‖ 'pænθə(r)/ *n* pantera *f*

panties /'pæntiz/ *pl n* calzones *mpl* (AmL), bragas *fpl* (Esp), pantaletas *fpl* (Méx, Ven), bombacha *f* (RPl), calzoneta *f* (AmC)

pantihose /'pæntihəʊz/ *pl n* ⇒ PANTYHOSE

pantomime /'pæntəmaɪm/ *n* [C U] **(a)** (mime) pantomima *f* **(b)** (in UK) *comedia musical navideña, basada en cuentos de hadas*

pantry /'pæntri/ *n* (*pl* **-tries**) despensa *f*

pants /pænts/ *pl n* **1** (trousers) (AmE) pantalón *m*, pantalones *mpl* **2** (underwear) (BrE) **(a)** (men's) calzoncillos *mpl*, calzones *mpl* (Méx), interiores *mpl* (Col, Ven) **(b)** (women's) ⇒ PANTIES

pantsuit /'pæntsuːt/, **pants suit** *n* (AmE) traje *m* pantalón

pantyhose /'pæntihəʊz/ *pl n* (AmE) medias *fpl*, pantimedias *fpl* (Méx), medias *fpl* bombacha (RPl) *or* (Col) pantalón *or* (Ven) panty

papa *n* **(a)** /'pɑːpə/ (AmE) papá *m* **(b)** /pə'pɑː/ (BrE dated) padre *m* (ant)

paper¹ /'peɪpər ‖ 'peɪpə(r)/ *n* **1 (a)** [U] (material) papel *m*; (*before n*) ‹*towel/handkerchief/bag*› de papel **(b)** [C] (wrapper) (esp BrE) envoltorio *m* **2** [C] (newspaper) diario *m*, periódico *m* **3** [C] (for journal) trabajo *m*; (at conference) ponencia *f* **4** [C] (*exam ~*) (BrE) examen *m*; (part) parte *f* **5 papers** *pl* (documents) documentos *mpl*

paper² *vt* ‹*wall/room*› empapelar *or* (Méx tb) tapizar*

paper: **~back** *n* libro *m* en rústica *or* (Méx) de pasta blanda; **~clip** *n* clip *m*, sujetapapeles *m*; **~weight** *n* pisapapeles *m*; **~work** *n* [U] papeleo *m* (fam), trabajo *m* administrativo

paprika /pə'priːkə ‖ 'pæprɪkə/ *n* [U] pimentón *m* dulce, paprika *f*

Pap smear, **Pap test** /pæp/ *n* (AmE) citología *f*, frotis *m*, Papanicolau *m* (AmL)

Papua New Guinea /'pɑːpuə ‖ 'pæpjʊə/ *n* Papua Nueva Guinea *f*

papyrus /pə'paɪrəs/ *n* (*pl* **-ruses** *or* **-ri** /-raɪ/) papiro *m*

par /pɑːr ‖ pɑː(r)/ *n* [U] **1 (a)** (equal level) **on a ~: the two athletes are on a ~** los dos atletas son del mismo nivel; **this puts us on a ~ with workers in other countries** esto nos pone en igualdad de condiciones con los trabajadores de otros países **(b)** (accepted standard): **your work is below** *o* **not up to ~** tu trabajo no está a la altura de lo que se esperaba; **to feel below** *o* **under~** no sentirse* del todo bien **2** (in golf) par *m*

parable /'pærəbəl/ *n* parábola *f*

parachute¹ /'pærəʃuːt/ *n* paracaídas *m*

parachute² *vi* saltar en *or* con paracaídas

parachutist /'pærəʃuːtəst ‖ 'pærəʃuːtɪst/ *n* paracaidista *mf*

parade¹ /pə'reɪd/ *n* **(a)** (procession) desfile *m* **(b)** (assembly) (Mil) formación *f*

parade² *vt* **(a)** (display) ‹*wealth*› hacer* ostentación de **(b)** (march, walk) ‹*streets*› desfilar por **(c)** (assemble) ‹*troops*› hacer* formar ■ **~** *vi* **(a)** (march, walk) desfilar **(b)** (assemble) (Mil) formar

paradise /'pærədaɪs/ *n* [U] **(a)** (heaven) paraíso *m* **(b) Paradise** (Garden of Eden) Paraíso *m* (Terrenal)

paradox /'pærədɑːks ‖ 'pærədɒks/ *n* [C U] paradoja *f*

paraffin /'pærəfən ‖ 'pærəfɪn/ *n* [U] **(a) ~ (wax)** parafina *f* **(b) ~ (oil)** (BrE) queroseno *m*, kerosene *m*, parafina *f* (Chi)

paragon /'pærəgɑːn ‖ 'pærəgən/ *n*: **a ~ of virtue** (set phrase) un dechado de virtudes (fr hecha)

paragraph /'pærəgræf ‖ 'pærəgrɑːf/ *n* párrafo *m*

Paraguay /'pærəgwaɪ/ *n* Paraguay *m*

Paraguayan /'pærə'gwaɪən/ *adj* paraguayo

parallel¹ /'pærəlel/ *adj* paralelo

parallel² *n* **1** (Math) (line) paralela *f* **2** (similarity) paralelismo *m*, paralelo *m*; **without ~** sin parangón

parallel³ *vt* **-l-** *or* (BrE also) **-ll-** (frml) ser* análogo *or* paralelo a

parallel bars *pl n* (barras *fpl*) paralelas *fpl*

paralysis /pə'ræləsəs ‖ pə'ræləsɪs/ *n* (*pl* **-ses** /-siːz/) [U C] (Med) parálisis *f*

paralyze /'pærəlaɪz/ *vt* paralizar*

paramedic /'pærə'medɪk/ *n*: *profesional conectado con la medicina, como enfermero, kinesiólogo etc*

parameter /pə'ræmətər ‖ pə'ræmɪtə(r)/ *n* parámetro *m*

paramilitary /'pærə'mɪləteri ‖ ˌpærə'mɪlɪtəri/ *adj* paramilitar

paramount /'pærəmaʊnt/ *adj* (frml) primordial

paranoia /'pærə'nɔɪə/ *n* [U] paranoia *f*

paranoid /'pærənɔɪd/ *adj* paranoico

parapet /'pærəpət ‖ 'pærəpɪt/ *n* parapeto *m*

paraphernalia /'pærəfər'neɪljə ‖ ˌpærəfə'neɪliə/ *n* [U] parafernalia *f*

paraphrase /'pærəfreɪz/ *vt* parafrasear

paraplegic *n* parapléjico, -ca *m,f*

parasite /'pærəsaɪt/ *n* parásito *m*

parasol /'pærəsɔːl ‖ 'pærəsɒl/ *n* sombrilla *f*, quitasol *m*

paratrooper /'pærəˌtruːpər ‖ 'pærəˌtruːpə(r)/ *n* (Mil) paracaidista *mf* (*del ejército*)

parcel /'pɑːrsəl ‖ 'pɑːsəl/ *n* (BrE) paquete *m*

parched /pɑːrtʃt ‖ pɑːtʃt/ *adj* **(a)** (very dry) reseco **(b)** (very thirsty) (colloq) (*pred*) muerto de sed (fam)

parchment /'pɑːrtʃmənt ‖ 'pɑːtʃmənt/ *n* pergamino *m*

pardon¹ /'pɑːrdn̩ ‖ 'pɑːdn̩/ *n* **1 (a)** [U] (forgiveness) perdón *m* **(b)** (*as interj*): **~?** *o* (frml) **I beg your ~?** (requesting repetition) ¿cómo?, ¿mande? (Méx); **I beg your ~** (apologizing) perdón **2** [C] (Law) indulto *m*

pardon² *vt* **1** (forgive) perdonar; **~ me!** (apologizing) ¡perdón!; **~ me?** (requesting repetition) (esp AmE) ¿cómo? **2** (Law) ‹*offender*› indultar

pare /per ‖ peə(r)/ *vt* **(a)** (peel) pelar **(b)** ‹*nails*› cortar

● **pare down** [*v* + *o* + *adv*, *v* + *adv* + *o*] reducir*

parent /'perənt ‖ 'peərənt/ *n*: **my/his ~s** mis/sus padres; **the responsibility of being a ~** las responsabilidades que conlleva el ser padre/madre; (*before n*) **~ company** sociedad *f* matriz

parental /pə'rentl/ *adj* de los padres

parenthesis /pə'renθəsəs ‖ pə'renθəsɪs/ *n* (*pl* **-theses** /-θəsiːz/) paréntesis *m*; **in parentheses** entre paréntesis

parenthood /'perənthʊd ‖ 'peərənthʊd/ *n* [U] el ser padre/madre

parenting /'perəntɪŋ ‖ 'peərəntɪŋ/ *n* [U] crianza *f* de los hijos

Paris /'pærəs ‖ 'pærɪs/ *n* París *m*

parish /'pærɪʃ/ *n* **1** (Relig) parroquia *f*; (*before n*) **~ church** parroquia *f*, iglesia *f* parroquial **2** (Govt) distrito *m*

parishioner /pə'rɪʃənər ‖ pə'rɪʃənə(r)/ *n* feligrés, -gresa *m,f* (*de una parroquia*)

Parisian /pə'rɪʒən ‖ pə'rɪziən/ *n* parisino, -na *m,f*, parisiense *mf*, parisién *mf*

parity /'pærəti/ *n* (*pl* **-ties**) [U] (equality) (frml) igualdad *f*, paridad *f*

park¹ /pɑːrk ‖ pɑːk/ *n* parque *m*; (*before n*) **~ bench** banco *m* *or* (Méx) banca *f* (de plaza)

park² *vt* ‹*car*› estacionar (esp AmL), aparcar* (Esp), parquear (AmL) ■ **~** *vi* (Auto) estacionar (esp AmL), aparcar* (Esp), parquear (AmL), estacionarse (Chi, Méx)

parking /'pɑːrkɪŋ ‖ 'pɑːkɪŋ/ *n* [U] estacionamiento *m* (esp AmL), aparcamiento *m* (Esp); Ⓢ **no parking** prohibido estacionar (esp AmL) *or* (Esp) aparcar *or* (AmL) parquear; (*before n*) **a ~ place** *o* **space** un lugar para estacionar (*or* aparcar *etc*); **~ ticket** multa *f* (por estacionamiento indebido)

parking: **~ garage** *n* (AmE) estacionamiento *m* (esp AmL), aparcamiento *m* (Esp), parking *m* (Esp); **~ lot** *n* (AmE) estacionamiento *m* (esp AmL), aparcamiento *m* (Esp), parking *m* (Esp), parqueadero *m* (Col); **~ meter** *n* parquímetro *m*

Parkinson's Disease /'pɑːrkənsənz ‖ 'pɑːkɪnsənz/ *n* [U] enfermedad *f* de Parkinson, Parkinson *m*

parkway /'pɑːrkweɪ || 'pɑːkweɪ/ *n* (AmE) carretera *f*/avenida *f* ajardinada

parliament /'pɑːrləmənt || 'pɑːləmənt/ *n* **(a)** (assembly) parlamento *m* **(b) Parliament** (in UK etc) Parlamento *m*

parliamentary /'pɑːrlə'mentəri ||,pɑːlə'mentri/ *adj* parlamentario

parlor, (BrE) **parlour** /'pɑːrlər || 'pɑːlə(r)/ *n* **1** (dated in BrE) (in house) salón *m* (esp Esp), sala *f* (de estar) **2** (for business) (AmE) sala *f*; **ice-cream ~** heladería *f*

Parmesan (cheese) /'pɑːrməzɑːn || 'pɑːmɪzæn/ *n* [U C] (queso *m*) parmesano *m*

parochial /pə'rəʊkiəl/ *adj* **(a)** (pej) ‹*person/attitude/outlook*› provinciano **(b)** (Relig) parroquial

parody¹ /'pærədi/ *n* (*pl* **-dies**) parodia *f*

parody² *vt* **-dies, -dying, -died** parodiar

parole /pə'rəʊl/ *n* [U] libertad *f* condicional

paroxysm /'pærəksɪzəm/ *n* (Med) paroxismo *m*; **the news sent them into ~s of laughter** la noticia los hizo desternillarse de risa

parquet /pɑːr'keɪ || 'pɑːkeɪ/ *n* [U] **1** (Const) parqué *m*, parquet *m* **2** (AmE Theat) platea *f*

parrot /'pærət/ *n* loro *m*, papagayo *m*

parry /'pæri/ *vt* **-ries, -rying, -ried** ‹*blow/thrust*› parar; ‹*attack*› rechazar*; ‹*question*› eludir

parsley /'pɑːrsli || 'pɑːsli/ *n* [U] perejil *m*

parsnip /'pɑːrsnəp || 'pɑːsnɪp/ *n* [C U] chirivía *f*, pastinaca *f*

parson /'pɑːrsn̩ || 'pɑːsn̩/ *n* clérigo *m*; (vicar) ≈ (cura *m*) párroco *m*

part¹ /pɑːrt || pɑːt/ *n* **1 (a)** [C] (section) parte *f* **(b)** (*in phrases*) **in part** en parte; **for the most part** en su mayor parte; **for my part** por mi parte, por mi lado **2** [C] (component) pieza *f*; (*spare* ~) repuesto *m* *or* (Méx) refacción *f* **3** [C] **(a)** (in play) papel *m* **(b)** (role, share) papel *m*; **she had** *o* **played a major ~ in** ... tuvo *or* desempeñó un papel fundamental en ...; **to take ~ in sth** tomar parte en algo **4** (episode of TV, radio serial) episodio *m*; (Publ) fascículo *m* **5** [C] (Mus) (vocal, instrumental line) parte *f* **6** [C] (in hair) (AmE) raya *f*, carrera *f* (Col, Ven), partidura *f* (Chi) **7 parts** *pl* (area): **in/around these ~s** por aquí; **in foreign ~s** en el extranjero

part² *vt* (separate) separar ■ ~ *vi* **(a)** (separate) «*lovers*» separarse; **they ~ed on bad terms** quedaron disgustados **(b)** «*curtains/lips*» (open up) abrirse*

• **part with** [*v* + *prep* + *o*] desprenderse de

part³ *adv* en parte

part⁴ *adj* (*before n*) ‹*payment*› parcial

part exchange *n* [U] (esp BrE): **in ~ ~** a cuenta *or* como parte del pago

partial /'pɑːrʃəl || 'pɑːʃəl/ *adj* **1** (not complete) parcial **2 (a)** (fond) (*pred*) **to be ~ TO sth** tener* debilidad POR algo **(b)** (biased) (frml) parcial

partially /'pɑːrʃəli || 'pɑːʃəli/ *adv* **(a)** (partly) parcialmente **(b)** (with bias) con parcialidad

participant /pər'tɪsəpənt, pɑːr- || pɑː'tɪsɪpənt/ *n* participante *mf*

participate /pər'tɪsəpeɪt, pɑːr- || pɑː'tɪsɪpeɪt/ *vi* **to ~ (IN sth)** participar (EN algo)

participation /pər'tɪsə'peɪʃən, pɑːr- || pɑː,tɪsɪ'peɪʃən/ *n* [U] participación *f*

participle /'pɑːrtəsɪpəl || 'pɑːtɪsɪpəl/ *n* participio *m*

particle /'pɑːrtɪkəl || 'pɑːtɪkəl/ *n* partícula *f*

particular¹ /pər'tɪkjələr || pə'tɪkjʊlə(r)/ *adj* **1** (specific, precise): **this ~ one** éste en especial; **is there any ~ style you'd prefer?** ¿tiene preferencia por algún estilo determinado?; **for no ~ reason** por nada en especial **2** (special) ‹*interest/concern*› especial **3** (fastidious) (*pred*) **to be ~ (ABOUT sth)**: **she's very ~ about what she eats** es muy especial con la comida

particular² *n* **(a)** (detail) (frml) (*usu pl*) detalle *m* **2 in particular** en particular

particularly /pər'tɪkjələrli || pə'tɪkjʊləli/ *adv* **(a)** (specifically) específicamente **(b)** (especially) particularmente

parting¹ /'pɑːrtɪŋ || 'pɑːtɪŋ/ *n* **1** [U] (separation) despedida *f* **2** [C] (in hair) (BrE) raya *f*, carrera *f* (Col, Ven), partidura *f* (Chi)

parting² *adj* (*before n*) ‹*kiss/words*› de despedida

partisan¹ /'pɑːrtəzən || 'pɑːtɪzæn/ *n* **(a)** (guerrilla) partisano, -na *m,f* **(b)** (supporter) partidario, -ria *m,f*

partisan² *adj* ‹*crowd/decision*› partidista

partition¹ /pər'tɪʃən, pɑːr- || pɑː'tɪʃən/ *n* **1** [C] **(a)** (screen) tabique *m*; **a glass ~** una mampara de vidrio *or* (Esp) de cristal **(b)** (divider) separador *m* **2** [U C] (of country, territory) división *f*

partition² *vt* **(a)** ‹*country/territory*› dividir **(b)** ‹*room*› dividir con un tabique/con una mampara

partly /'pɑːrtli || 'pɑːtli/ *adv* en parte

partner¹ /'pɑːrtnər || 'pɑːtnə(r)/ *n* **(a)** (in an activity) compañero, -ra *m,f*; (in dancing, tennis) pareja *f* **(b)** (Busn) socio, -cia *m,f*; **~s in crime** cómplices *mpl* *or fpl* **(c)** (in personal relationship) pareja *f*, compañero, -ra *m,f*

partner² *vt* bailar (*or* jugar* etc) en pareja con

partnership /'pɑːrtnərʃɪp || 'pɑːtnəʃɪp/ *n* [U C] **(a)** (relationship) asociación *f* **(b)** (Busn) sociedad *f* (colectiva)

part of speech *n* (*pl* **~s ~ ~**) categoría *f* gramatical

partridge /'pɑːrtrɪdʒ || 'pɑːtrɪdʒ/ *n* (*pl* **~s** *or* **~**) perdiz *f*

part-time¹ /'pɑːrt'taɪm ||,pɑːt'taɪm/ *adj* de medio tiempo (AmL), a tiempo parcial (Esp)

part-time² *adv* de medio tiempo (AmL), a tiempo parcial (Esp)

party¹ /'pɑːrti || 'pɑːti/ *n* **1** (event) fiesta *f*; **I was invited to a tea ~** me invitaron a un té **2** (Pol) partido *m* **3** (group) grupo *m*; (in hunting) partida *f* **4** (person or body involved) parte *f*; **the guilty/innocent ~** el culpable/inocente

party² *vi* (esp AmE colloq) (go to parties) ir* a fiestas; (have fun) divertirse*

party line *n* (Pol) **the ~ ~** la línea del partido

pass¹ /pæs || pɑːs/ *n* **1** (document, permit) pase *m*; (ticket) abono *m* **2** (Geog) paso *m*; (narrow) desfiladero *m* **3** (in test, examination) (BrE) aprobado *m* **4** (Sport) pase *m* **5** (sexual advance): **to make a ~ at sb** intentar besar a algn

pass² *vt* **I 1 (a)** (go by, past) ‹*shop/house*› pasar por; **I ~ed him in the street** me crucé con él en la calle **(b)** (overtake) pasar, rebasar (Méx) **2 (a)** (cross, go beyond) ‹*limit*› pasar; ‹*frontier*› pasar, cruzar* **(b)** (surpass) sobrepasar **3** (spend) ‹*time*› pasar; **to ~ the time** pasar el rato

II (a) (convey, hand over) **to ~ sb sth, to ~ sth TO sb** pasarle algo A algn **(b)** (Sport) ‹*ball*› pasar

III (a) (succeed in) ‹*exam/test*› aprobar*, salvar (Ur) **(b)** (approve) ‹*candidate/work*› aprobar* **(c)** ‹*law/motion*› aprobar* ■ ~ *vi* **I 1** (move, travel) pasar **2 (a)** (go, move past) pasar; **I was just ~ing** pasaba por aquí; **they ~ed on the stairs** se cruzaron en la escalera **(b)** (overtake) adelantarse, rebasar (Méx) **3 (a)** (elapse) «*time*» pasar **(b)** (disappear) «*feeling/pain*» pasarse **4** (be transferred) «*title/estate/crown*» pasar **5** (decline chance to play) pasar; (*as interj*) ¡paso! **6** (Sport) **to ~ (TO sb)** pasar(le) la pelota (*or* el balón *etc*) (A algn)

II (a) (be acceptable) pasar **(b)** (in an exam) aprobar*

• **pass away** [*v* + *adv*] (frml & euph) fallecer* (frml)

• **pass by 1** [*v* + *adv*] (go past) pasar **2** [*v* + *o* + *adv*] (not affect): **he felt life had ~ed him by** sentía que no había vivido

• **pass down** [*v* + *o* + *adv*, *v* + *adv* + *o*] (*often pass*) ‹*heirloom*› pasar; ‹*story/tradition*› transmitir

• **pass for** [*v* + *prep* + *o*] pasar por

• **pass off** [*v* + *o* + *adv*, *v* + *adv* + *o*] (represent falsely) hacer* pasar; **she ~ed herself off as a journalist** se hizo pasar por periodista

• **pass on 1** [*v* + *o* + *adv*, *v* + *adv* + *o*] ‹*information*› pasar; ‹*infection*› contagiar **2** [*v* + *adv*] **(a) to ~ on TO sth** pasar A algo **(b)** ⇒ PASS AWAY

• **pass out 1** [*v* + *adv*] (become unconscious) desmayarse, perder* el conocimiento **2** [*v* + *o* + *adv*, *v* + *adv* + *o*] (distribute) repartir

• **pass over 1** [*v* + *adv* + *o*] (omit) ‹*fact/detail*› pasar por alto **2** [*v* + *o* + *adv*] (disregard for promotion) (*usu pass*) pasarle por encima a

• **pass through (a)** [*v* + *adv*] pasar; **we're just ~ing through** estamos sólo de paso **(b)** [*v* + *prep* + *o*] ‹*town/area*› pasar por

• **pass up** [*v* + *o* + *adv*, *v* + *adv* + *o*] (colloq) ‹*opportunity*› dejar pasar

passable /'pæsəbəl ‖ 'pɑːsəbəl/ *adj* **(a)** (adequate) pasable **(b)** ‹*road/route*› transitable

passage /'pæsɪdʒ/ *n* **1** [C] **(a)** (alleyway) callejón *m*, pasaje *m*; (narrow) pasadizo *m* **(b)** (corridor) (esp BrE) pasillo *m* **(c)** (Anat) conducto *m* **2** [U] (lapse): **the ~ of time** el paso del tiempo **3** [C] (voyage) viaje *m*; (fare) pasaje *m* **4** [C] (extract) pasaje *m*

passageway /'pæsɪdʒweɪ/ *n* pasillo *m*

passenger /'pæsn̩dʒər ‖ 'pæsɪndʒə(r)/ *n* pasajero, -ra *m,f*

passer-by /'pæsər'baɪ ‖ ˌpɑːsə'baɪ/ *n* (*pl* **passers-by**) transeúnte *mf*

passing¹ /'pæsɪŋ ‖ 'pɑːsɪŋ/ *adj* (*before n*) **1** (going past): **she hailed a ~ taxi** llamó a un taxi que pasaba **2 (a)** ‹*fad/fashion*› pasajero; ‹*glance*› rápido **(b)** (casual): **it was only a ~ thought** simplemente fue algo que se me ocurrió

passing² *n* [U] **in passing** al pasar, de pasada

passing lane *n* (AmE) carril *m* de adelantamiento

passion /'pæʃən/ *n* [C U] pasión *f*

passionate /'pæʃənət/ *adj* ‹*love*› apasionado; ‹*hatred*› mortal; ‹*admirer*› ardiente; ‹*speech*› vehemente

passionately /'pæʃənətli/ *adv* ‹*love*› apasionadamente; ‹*believe*› fervientemente; ‹*desire*› ardientemente

passion fruit *n* granadilla *f*, maracuyá *m*, parchita *f* (Ven)

passive¹ /'pæsɪv/ *adj* pasivo

passive² ▶ 744 *n* voz *f* pasiva

pass: **~key** *n* llave *f* maestra; **P~over** *n* Pascua *f* (*judía*); **~port** *n* pasaporte *m*; **~word** *n* contraseña *f*

past¹ /pæst ‖pɑːst/ *adj* **1 (a)** (former) anterior; ‹*life*› pasado; (old) antiguo **(b)** (most recent) ‹*week/month/year*› último **(c)** (finished, gone) (*pred*): **what's ~ is ~** lo pasado, pasado **2** (Ling): **the ~ tense** el pasado, el pretérito

past² *n* **1 (a)** [U] (former times) pasado *m*; **steam trains are a thing of the ~** las locomotoras de vapor han pasado a la historia; **in the ~, women** … antes *or* antiguamente las mujeres …; **that's all in the ~** eso forma parte del pasado **(b)** [C] (of person) pasado *m*; (of place) historia *f* **2** [U] (Ling) pasado *m*, pretérito *m*

past³ *prep* **1 (a)** (by the side of): **I go ~ their house every morning** paso por (delante de) su casa todas las mañanas; **she walked straight ~ him** pasó de largo por su lado **(b)** (beyond): **it's just ~ the school** queda un poco más allá de la escuela **2 (a)** ▶ 884 (after) (esp BrE): **it's ten ~ six/half ~ two** son las seis y diez/las dos y media; **it was ~ eleven** eran las once pasadas; **it's ~ your bedtime** ya deberías estar acostado **(b)** (older than): **I'm ~ the age/stage when** … ya he pasado la edad/superado la etapa en que … **3** (outside, beyond): **to be ~ -ING**: **I'm ~ caring** ya no me importa; **I wouldn't put it ~ her** no me extrañaría que lo hiciera; ***to be ~ it*** (colloq) estar* para el arrastre (fam)

past⁴ *adv* **(a)** (with verbs of motion): **to fly/cycle/drive ~** pasar volando/en bicicleta/en coche; **he hurried ~** pasó a toda prisa **(b)** (giving time) (esp BrE): **it's twenty-five ~** son y veinticinco

pasta /'pɑːstə ‖ 'pæstə/ *n* [U] pasta(s) *f(pl)*

paste /peɪst/ *n* **(a)** [U C] (thick mixture) pasta *f* **(b)** [U] (glue) engrudo *m*; (*wallpaper ~*) pegamento *m*, cola *f* **(c)** [U] (imitation gem) estrás *m*

pastel /pæs'tel ‖ 'pæstl̩/ *n* **(a)** (Art) (crayon) pastel *m* **(b)** (pale shade) tono *m* pastel; (*before n*) ‹*shades/color*› pastel *adj inv*

pasteurize /'pæstʃəraɪz ‖ 'pɑːstʃəraɪz/ *vt* pasteurizar*, pasterizar

pastille /pæs'tiːl ‖ 'pæstɪl/ *n* pastilla *f*

pastime /'pæstaɪm ‖ 'pɑːstaɪm/ *n* pasatiempo *m*

pastor /'pæstər ‖ 'pɑːstə(r)/ *n* pastor, -tora *m,f*

pastoral /'pæstərəl ‖ 'pɑːstərəl/ *adj* **(a)** ‹*painting/scene*› pastoril **(b)** (Relig) ‹*care/duties*› pastoral

The Passive

Spanish has the same passive form as English, ser + past participle, *which agrees in gender and number with the subject*:

the houses were destroyed = las casas fueron destruidas

However, use of the passive is much less common than in English and it is used more in written than in spoken language (although it does have broader use in Latin America than in Spain)

Spanish also uses the following to express the English passive:

◆ *the personal pronoun*
This is used either in the so-called pasiva refleja:

it was published in 1933 = se publicó en 1933

or in the impersonal form:

she was informed that . . . = se le comunicó que . . .
it is known that . . . = se sabe que . . .

This impersonal use frequently occurs when describing processes:

the pulp is then extracted = luego se extrae la pulpa

Note however that if the agent of the passive construction is mentioned, the reflexive construction cannot be used:

it was written by a monk = fue escrito por un monje (*but not* se escribió por un monje)

◆ *the third person plural*:

he was robbed = le robaron

This sense of an unknown agent cannot be expressed by the third person plural in English, where the statement they robbed him *would prompt the question* who?

◆ *the active*
This works in two ways. A phrase can simply be reworded in active form, e.g. the sentence the novel was completed by her sister *might equally be expressed as* la novela fue terminada por su hermana *or* su hermana terminó la novela

Alternatively, it works by keeping the subject the same but adding an 'extra' pronoun before the verb:

this expression is used a lot by Americans = esta expresión la usan mucho los americanos

Some phrases may therefore be translated by a number of structures:

it was built in 1903 = fue construido en 1903 *or* se construyó en 1903 *or* lo construyeron en 1903

Nonetheless, the English speaker of Spanish needs to acquire a feel for which means of expressing the passive is most apt for the context being translated

Note also:

◆ *the use of relative clauses in Spanish to keep the sentence active rather than passive*:

the context being translated = el contexto que se traduce

◆ *the use of relative clauses in the subjunctive that switch subject*:

she deserves to be promoted = merece que la asciendan

◆ *the flexibility Spanish has in its use of infinitives, especially after* por, sin, para, *and* a:

lo que queda por hacer = what remains to be done
la carta está sin contestar = the letter is unanswered
está listo para pintar = it's ready to be painted
horario a convenir = hours to be arranged

Where English requires a passive construction in the above examples, Spanish can use the normal infinitive

pastry /'peɪstri/ *n* (*pl* **-tries**) **(a)** [U] (substance) masa *f* **(b)** [C] (cake) pastelito *m or* (RPl) masa *f*

pasture¹ /'pæstʃər ‖ 'pɑːstʃə(r)/ *n* [U] **(a)** (grazing land) pastos *mpl* **(b)** (grass) pasto *m*, pastura *f*

pasture² *vt* apacentar*, pastar

pasty /'pæsti/ *n* (*pl* **-ties**) (esp BrE) empanada *f* (AmL), empanadilla *f* (Esp)

pat¹ /pæt/ *vt* **-tt-** darle* palmaditas a

pat² *n* **1** (tap) palmadita *f*; (touch) toque *m* **2** (of butter) porción *f*

pat³ *adj* (pej) ‹*answer*› fácil

pat⁴ *adv* (by heart): **to have** *o* **know sth down** (AmE) *o* (BrE) **off ~** saberse* algo al dedillo

patch¹ /pætʃ/ *n* **1 (a)** (for mending clothes) remiendo *m*, parche *m*; (for reinforcing) refuerzo *m*; (on knee) rodillera *f*; (on elbow) codera *f* **(b)** (*eye* ~) parche *m* (*en el ojo*) **2 (a)** (area): **she slipped on a ~ of ice/oil** resbaló en el hielo/en una mancha de aceite; **a damp ~** una mancha de humedad; ***to go through a bad*** *o* ***rough*** *o* ***sticky ~*** (BrE) pasar por una mala racha **(b)** (of land): **a ~ of ground** un área de terreno; **a vegetable ~** un huerto **(c)** (territory) (BrE colloq): **my/his ~** mi/su territorio

patch² *vt* remendar*, parchar (esp AmL)

• patch up [*v + o + adv, v + adv + o*] **(a)** (mend) ‹*roof/furniture*› hacerle* un arreglo a (*provisionalmente*); ‹*clothes*› remendar*, parchar (esp AmL); ‹*hole*› ponerle* un parche a **(b)** (resolve, settle): **I tried to help ~ things up betweem them** quise ayudar para que hicieran las paces

patchwork /'pætʃwɜːrk ‖ 'pætʃwɜːk/ *n* [U] patchwork *m*, labor *f* de retazos *or* (Esp) retales; (*before n*) ‹*quilt*› de patchwork, de retazos *or* (Esp) retales

patchy /'pætʃi/ *adj* **-chier, -chiest** ‹*paintwork/color*› disparejo; ‹*coverage*› incompleto; ‹*descrip-*

tion› fragmentario; ‹*performance/work*› irregular; **~ fog** zonas *fpl* de niebla

pâté /pɑː'teɪ ‖ 'pæteɪ/ *n* [U C] paté *m*

patent¹ /'pætn̩t ‖ 'peɪtn̩t, 'pætn̩t/ *n* patente *f*

patent² /'pætn̩t ‖ 'peɪtn̩t, 'pætn̩t/ *vt* patentar

patent³ *adj* /'peɪtn̩t, 'pæt- ‖ 'peɪtn̩t/ (frml) patente

patent leather /'pætn̩t ‖ 'peɪtn̩t, 'pæt-/ *n* [U] charol *m*

patently /'peɪtn̩tli, 'pæt- ‖ 'peɪtn̩tli/ *adv*: **it's ~ clear** *o* **obvious that** ... salta a la vista que ...

paternal /pə'tɜːrnl̩ ‖ pə'tɜːnl̩/ *adj* **(a)** (fatherly) ‹*affection*› paternal; ‹*pride*› de padre; ‹*trait/inheritance*› paterno **(b)** (on father's side) (*before n*) por parte de padre

paternity /pə'tɜːrnəti ‖ pə'tɜːnəti/ *n* [U] (frml) paternidad *f*

path /pæθ ‖ pɑːθ/ *n* **(a)** (track, walkway) sendero *m*, senda *f* **(b)** (of missile) trayectoria *f*; (of the sun) recorrido *m*

pathetic /pə'θetɪk/ *adj* **(a)** (pitiful) patético **(b)** (feeble) (colloq): **what a ~ excuse!** ¡qué excusa más pobre!; **don't be so ~** no seas tan pusilánime

pathological /'pæθə'lɑːdʒɪkəl ‖ ˌpæθə'lɒdʒɪkəl/ *adj* patológico

pathologist /pə'θɑːlədʒəst ‖ pə'θɒlədʒɪst/ *n* patólogo, -ga *m,f*

pathology /pə'θɑːlədʒi ‖ pə'θɒlədʒi/ *n* [U] patología *f*

pathos /'peɪθɑːs ‖ 'peɪθɒs/ *n* [U] patetismo *m*

pathway /'pæθweɪ ‖ 'pɑːθweɪ/ *n* camino *m*, sendero *m*

patience /'peɪʃəns/ *n* [U] **(a)** (quality) paciencia *f* **(b)** (cards) (BrE) solitario *m*

patient¹ /'peɪʃənt/ *adj* paciente; **to be ~ WITH sb** tener* paciencia CON algn

patient² *n* paciente *mf*

patiently /'peɪʃəntli/ *adv* pacientemente

patio /'pætiəʊ/ *n* patio *m*

patriot /'peɪtriət ‖ 'pætriət, 'peɪ-/ *n* patriota *mf*

patriotic /ˌpeɪtri'ɑːtɪk ‖ ˌpætri'ɒtɪk, 'peɪ-/ *adj* patriótico

patriotism /'peɪtriətɪzəm ‖ 'pætriətɪzəm, 'peɪ-/ *n* [U] patriotismo *m*

patrol¹ /pə'trəʊl/ *n* **(a)** [U C] (act) patrulla *f*; **to be on ~** estar* patrullando, estar* de patrulla; (*before n*) **~ car** coche *m* patrulla, patrullero *m* (RPl), auto *m* patrulla (Chi) **(b)** (group) patrulla *f*

patrol² *vt/i* **-ll-** patrullar

patron /'peɪtrən/ *n* **(a)** (sponsor) patrocinador, -dora *m,f*; **a ~ of the arts** un mecenas **(b)** (customer) (frml) cliente, -ta *m,f*

patronize /'peɪtrənaɪz ‖ 'pætrənaɪz/ *vt* **1** (condescend to) tratar con condescendencia **2** (frequent) (frml) ‹*shop/hotel*› ser* cliente de; ‹*theater/cinema*› frecuentar

patronizing /'peɪtrənaɪzɪŋ ‖ 'pætrənaɪzɪŋ/ *adj* condescendiente

patter¹ /'pætər ‖ 'pætə(r)/ *vi* golpetear

patter² *n* [U] **1** (of rain) golpeteo *m* **2** (talk): **he has a good sales ~** tiene mucha labia para vender

pattern /'pætərn ‖ 'pætən/ *n* **1 (a)** (decoration) diseño *m*, dibujo *m*; (on fabric) diseño *m*, estampado *m* **(b)** (order, arrangement): **it follows the normal ~** sigue las pautas normales; **the murders all seem to follow a ~** todos los asesinatos parecen responder al mismo patrón **2 (a)** (model) modelo *m* **(b)** (in dressmaking) patrón *m*, molde *m* (CS) **(c)** (sample) muestra *f*

patterned /'pætərnd ‖ 'pætənd/ *adj* con dibujos; ‹*fabric*› estampado

paunch /pɔːntʃ/ *n* panza *f* (fam)

pauper /'pɔːpər ‖ 'pɔːpə(r)/ *n* pobre *mf*

pause¹ /pɔːz/ *n* pausa *f*; **without ~** sin interrupción

pause² *vi* (in speech) hacer* una pausa; (in movement) detenerse*

pave /peɪv/ *vt* (with concrete) pavimentar; (with flagstones) enlosar; (with stones) empedrar*

pavement /'peɪvmənt/ *n* **(a)** [C U] (paved area) pavimento *m* **(b)** [C] (beside road) (BrE) ⇒ SIDEWALK

pavilion /pə'vɪljən/ *n* **(a)** (tent, stand) pabellón *m* **(b)** (BrE Sport) caseta *f*

paving /'peɪvɪŋ/ *n* [U] pavimento *m*; (of flagstones) enlosado *m*, (of stones) empedrado *m*; (*before n*) **~stone** losa *f*

paw¹ /pɔː/ *n* pata *f*

paw² *vt* «*animal*» tocar* con la pata; **to ~ the ground** «*horse*» piafar

pawn¹ /pɔːn/ *n* **(a)** (in chess) peón *m* **(b)** (manipulated person) títere *m*

pawn² *vt* empeñar

pawnbroker /'pɔːnˌbrəʊkər ‖ 'pɔːnˌbrəʊkə(r)/ *n* prestamista *mf*

pay¹ /peɪ/ (*past & past p* **paid**) *vt* **1 (a)** ‹*tax/rent/sum/debt*› pagar*; **how much did you ~ for the painting?** ¿cuánto te costó el cuadro? **(b)** ‹*employee/creditor/tradesperson*› pagarle* a; **to ~ sb FOR sth** pagarle* algo A algn **2** ‹*respects*› presentar; ‹*attention*› prestar ■ **~** *vi* pagar*; **he paid for the mistake with his life** el error le costó la vida ■ **~** *v impers* convenir*

• **pay back** [*v + o + adv, v + adv + o*] **1** (repay) ‹*money*› devolver*, regresar (AmL exc CS); ‹*loan/mortgage*› pagar*; **to ~ sb back** devolverle *or* (AmL exc CS) regresarle el dinero a algn **2** (take revenge on): **I'll ~ you back!** ¡ya me las vas a pagar!

• **pay in** [*v + o + adv, v + adv + o*] (BrE) ‹*money*› depositar *or* (Esp) ingresar *or* (Col) consignar

• **pay off 1** [*v + o + adv, v + adv + o*] ‹*debt*› cancelar, saldar; ‹*worker*› liquidarle el sueldo (*or* jornal *etc*) a (*al despedirlo*) **2** [*v + adv*] (prove worthwhile) valer* la pena; «*gamble*» resultar

• **pay out** [*v + o + adv, v + adv + o*] pagar*

• **pay up** [*v + adv*] pagar*

pay² *n* [U] (of manual worker) paga *f*; (of employee) sueldo *m*; **equal ~** igualdad *f* salarial; (*before n*) **~ increase** aumento *m* salarial

payable /'peɪəbəl/ *adj* (frml) (*pred*) pagadero; **the rent becomes ~ on the first of the month** el alquiler vence el primero de mes; **make the check ~ to** ... extienda el cheque a nombre de ...

pay: **~check**, (BrE) **~ cheque** *n* cheque *m* del sueldo; (salary) sueldo *m*; **~day** *n* día *m* de paga

payee /peɪ'i:/ *n* beneficiario, -ria *m,f*

payment /'peɪmənt/ *n* **(a)** [U] (of debt, money, wage) pago *m*; **he received no ~ for what he did** no recibió remuneración por lo que hizo (frml) **(b)** [C] (installment) plazo *m*, cuota *f* (AmL)

pay: **~ phone** *n* teléfono *m* público, monedero *m* (público) (Ur); **~roll** *n* **(a)** (list) nómina *f*, planilla *f* (de sueldos) (AmL), plantilla *f* (Esp) **(b)** (wages) nómina *f*; **~ slip** *n* nómina *f*, recibo *m* del sueldo

PC¹ *n* **1** = **personal computer 2** (in UK) = **police constable**

PC² *adj* = **politically correct**

PD *n* (in US) = **Police Department**

PE *n* [U] = **physical education**

pea /pi:/ *n* arveja *f* or (Esp) guisante *m* or (AmC, Méx) chícharo *m*

peace /pi:s/ *n* **1** [U] paz *f*; **in** *o* **at ~** en paz; (*before n*) para la paz; ‹*proposal/initiative/treaty*› de paz; ‹*talks/march/campaign*› por la paz; **the ~ movement** el movimiento pacifista; **as a ~ offering** en señal de reconciliación **2** (Law): **to keep the ~** mantener* el orden **3** (tranquillity) paz *f*; **I went to the library for some ~ and quiet** me fui a la biblioteca para poder estar tranquilo; **I turned off the gas for my own ~ of mind** apagué el gas para quedarme tranquilo

peaceful /'pi:sfəl/ *adj* **(a)** (calm, quiet) ‹*place*› tranquilo **(b)** (non-violent) ‹*protest*› pacífico; **they are a ~ people** son un pueblo amante de la paz

peacefully /'pi:sfəli/ *adv* ‹*sleep*› plácidamente; ‹*read/sit*› tranquilamente

peace: **~keeping** *adj* (*before n*): **~keeping forces** fuerzas *fpl* de paz; **~maker** *n* conciliador, -dora *m,f*; **~time** *n* [U] época *f* de paz

peach /pi:tʃ/ *n* durazno *m* (esp AmL), melocotón *m* (Esp); (*before n*) **~ tree** duraznero *m* (esp AmL), melocotonero *m* (Esp)

peacock /'pi:kɑ:k ‖ 'pi:kɒk/ *n* pavo *m* real

peak¹ /pi:k/ *n* **(a)** (of mountain) cima *f*, cumbre *f*; (mountain) pico *m*; (of cap) visera *f* **(b)** (highest point): **at the ~ of her career** en el apogeo de su carrera

peak² *adj* (*before n*) **(a)** (maximum) ‹*level/power*› máximo; **to be in ~ condition** «*athlete/horse*» estar* en plena forma **(b)** (busiest): **during ~ hours** durante las horas de mayor demanda (*or* consumo *etc*); **~ rate** tarifa *f* alta

peal /pi:l/ *n*: **~ of bells** (sound) repique *m* de campanas; (set) carillón *m*; **~s of laughter** carcajadas *fpl*; **a ~ of thunder** un trueno

peanut /'pi:nʌt/ *n* **(a)** (Agr, Culin) maní *m* or (Esp) cacahuete *m* or (Méx) cacahuate *m* **(b) peanuts** *pl* (small sum) (colloq) una miseria (fam)

peanut butter *n* [U] mantequilla *f* de maní *or* (Esp) de cacahuete *or* (Méx) de cacahuate, manteca *f* de maní (RPl)

pear /per ‖ peə(r)/ *n* pera *f*; **~ (tree)** peral *m*

pearl /pɜ:rl ‖ pɜ:l/ *n* **(a)** [C] perla *f*; **~s of wisdom** sabias palabras *fpl*; (iro) joyitas *fpl* (iró) **(b)** [U] (*mother-of-~*) nácar *m*, madreperla *f*, concha *f* nácar (Méx), concha *f* de perla (Chi)

peasant /'peznt/ *n* campesino, -na *m,f*

peat /pi:t/ *n* [U] turba *f*

pebble /'pebəl/ *n* guijarro *m*

pecan /pɪ'kæn ‖ 'pi:kən/ *n* pacana *f*, nuez *f* (Méx)

peck¹ /pek/ *n* **(a)** (of bird) picotazo *m* **(b)** (kiss) beso *m*

peck² *vt* picotear

pecking order /'pekɪŋ/ *n* jerarquía *f*

peckish /'pekɪʃ/ *adj* (esp BrE colloq) (*pred*) **to be** *o* **feel ~** tener* un poco de hambre

peculiar /pɪ'kju:ljər ‖ pɪ'kju:liə(r)/ *adj* **(a)** (strange) raro, extraño **(b)** (particular, exclusive) peculiar, característico

peculiarity /pɪ'kju:l'jærəti ‖ pɪ,kju:li'ærəti/ *n* (*pl* **-ties**) (sth unusual) rasgo *m* singular; (oddity) rareza *f*

pedal¹ /'pedl̩/ *n* pedal *m*

pedal² *vi*, (BrE) **-ll-** pedalear

pedal bin *n* (BrE) cubo *m* or (Méx) bote *m* or (CS) tacho *m* or (Ven) tobo *m* or (Col) caneca *f* de la basura (*con pedal*)

pedantic /pɪ'dæntɪk/ *adj* pedante

peddle /'pedl̩/ *vt* vender (*en las calles o de puerta en puerta*); **to ~ drugs** traficar* con drogas

peddler /'pedlər ‖ 'pedlə(r)/ *n* vendedor, -dora ambulante *m,f*; (in former times) buhonero *m*; **a drug ~** un traficante de drogas

pedestal /'pedəstl̩ ‖ 'pedɪstl̩/ *n* pedestal *m*

pedestrian¹ /pə'destriən ‖ pɪ'destriən/ *n* peatón, -tona *m,f*; (*before n*) **~ crossing** cruce *m* peatonal *or* de peatones

pedestrian² *adj* pedestre

pediatric, (BrE also) **paediatric** /'pi:di'ætrɪk/ *adj* ‹*hospital*› pediátrico; ‹*specialist*› en pediatría

pediatrician, (BrE also) **paediatrician** /'pi:diə'trɪʃən/ *n* pediatra *mf*

pedicure /'pedɪkjʊr ‖ 'pedɪkjʊə(r)/ *n* [U C]: **to have a ~** arreglarse/hacerse* arreglar los pies

pedigree /'pedəgri: ‖ 'pedɪgri:/ *n* **(a)** (ancestry — of animal) pedigrí *m*; (— of person) linaje *m*; (*before n*) ‹*bull/dog*› de raza **(b)** (certificate, document) pedigrí *m*

pedlar /'pedlər ‖ 'pedlə(r)/ *n* (BrE) ⇒ PEDDLER

pedophile, (BrE) **paedophile** /'pi:dəfaɪl/ *n* pedófilo, -la *m,f*

pee¹ /pi:/ *vi* (*past & past p* **peed**) (colloq) hacer* pis *or* pipí (fam), hacer* del uno (Méx, Per fam & euf)

pee² *n* (colloq) (*no pl*) pis *m* (fam), pipí *m* (fam)

peek¹ /pi:k/ *vi* **~ (AT sth/sb)** mirar (algo/a algn) (*a hurtadillas*), vichar (algo/a algn) (RPl fam)

peek² *n* **to take** *o* **have a ~ at sth** echar(le) una miradita a algo, vichar algo (RPl fam)

peel¹ /pi:l/ *vt* ‹*apple/potato*› pelar ■ *~ vi* «*person*» pelarse; «*paint*» desconcharse; «*wallpaper*» despegarse*

● **peel off 1** [*v + adv*] «*wallpaper/label*» despegarse*; ‹*paint*› desconcharse **2** [*v + o + adv, v + adv + o*] ‹*stamp/sticker*› despegar*; ‹*paint/bark*› quitar

peel² *n* [U] (of potato, apple) piel *f*, cáscara *f* (esp AmL); (of orange, lemon) cáscara *f*

peelings /'pi:lɪŋz/ *pl n* cáscaras *fpl*, peladuras *fpl*

peep¹ /pi:p/ *vi* **(a)** (watch) espiar*, vichar (RPl fam); (look quickly) mirar (*a hurtadillas*), vichar (RPl fam) **(b)** (show, stick out) **~ (out)** asomar ■ **~** *vt* (colloq): **I ~ed the horn** toqué la bocina *or* el claxon

peep² *n* **1** (quick or furtive look) vistazo *m*; **to have a ~ AT sth** echarle un vistazo A algo **2** (of bird) pío *m*; (of car horn) pitido *m*

peephole /'pi:phəʊl/ *n* mirilla *f*

peer¹ /pɪr ‖ pɪə(r)/ *n* **1 (a)** (equal) par *mf* **(b)** (contemporary) coetáneo, -nea *m,f* **2** (lord) (in UK) par *m*

peer² *vi*: **to ~ AT sth/sb** (with difficulty) mirar algo/a algn con ojos de miope; (closely) mirar algo/a algn detenidamente

peerage /'pɪrɪdʒ ‖ 'pɪərɪdʒ/ *n* **the ~** la nobleza

peer group *n* grupo *m* paritario (frml)

peeved /pi:vd/ *adj* ‹*expression/look*› de fastidio; **to be** *o* **feel ~** estar* molesto

peevish /'pi:vɪʃ/ *adj* ‹*remark*› desagradable, malhumorado; **to be ~** estar* fastidioso

peg¹ /peg/ *n* **1 (a)** (in ground) estaca *f*; (on violin, guitar) clavija *f*; (*tent* **~**) estaquilla *f*; (on board game) *pieza o ficha que encaja en un tablero* **(b)** (*clothes-***~**) (BrE) *see* CLOTHESPIN **2** (hook, hanger) colgador *m*, perchero *m*, gancho *m*

peg² *vt* **-gg-** (attach, secure) sujetar, asegurar (*con estaquillas etc*)

pejorative /pɪ'dʒɔ:rətɪv ‖ pɪ'dʒɒrətɪv/ *adj* peyorativo

Peking /pi:'kɪŋ/ *n* Pekín *m*

pelican /'pelɪkən/ *n* pelícano *m*

pellet /'pelət ‖ 'pelɪt/ *n* **(a)** (of bread, paper) bolita *f* **(b)** (ammunition) perdigón *m*

pelt¹ /pelt/ *vt*: **to ~ sb with tomatoes** lanzarle* tomates a algn ■ **~** *vi* (colloq) **1** (rush): **they came ~ing down the hill** bajaron la cuesta (corriendo) a toda velocidad **2** (fall heavily): **it was ~ing with rain** llovía a cántaros

pelt² *n* (animal skin) piel *f*; (stripped) cuero *m*

pelvis /'pelvəs ‖ 'pelvɪs/ *n* (*pl* **-vises**) pelvis *f*

pen /pen/ *n* **1** (*fountain* **~**) pluma *f* estilográfica, pluma *f* fuente (AmL); (*ballpoint* **~**) bolígrafo *m*, boli *m* (Esp fam), birome *f* (RPl), pluma *f* atómica (Méx), lápiz *m* de pasta (Chi); (*felt* **~**) rotulador *m* **2** (Agr) (*sheep* **~**) redil *m*; (*cattle* **~**) corral *m*

penal /'pi:nl/ *adj* penal

penalize /'pi:nḷaɪz ‖ 'pi:nəlaɪz/ *vt* **(a)** ‹*player*› sancionar **(b)** (make punishable, illegal) penalizar*

penalty /'penlti/ *n* (*pl* **-ties**) **1** (punishment) pena *f*; (fine) multa *f*; **to pay the ~** pagar* las consecuencias **2** (Sport) (in rugby) penalty *m*; (in US football) castigo *m*; **~ (kick)** (in soccer) penalty *m*, penalti *m*, penal *m* (AmL), pénal *m* (Andes); (*before n*) **~ area** (in soccer) área *f*‡ de penalty

penance /'penəns/ *n* [U C] **(a)** (Relig) penitencia *f* **(b)** (punishment) (hum) castigo *m*

pence /pens/ *n pl of* PENNY 1(a)

penchant /'pentʃənt ‖ 'pɒŋʃɒŋ/ *n* (frml) **~ (FOR sth)** inclinación *f* (POR algo)

pencil /'pensəl/ *n* lápiz *m*; **in ~** con lápiz

pencil: **~ case** *n* estuche *m* (para lápices), plumier *m* (Esp), chuspa *f* (Col), cartuchera *f* (RPl); **~ sharpener** *n* sacapuntas *m*, tajalápiz *m* (Col)

pendant /'pendənt/ *n* colgante *m*

pending¹ /'pendɪŋ/ *adj* **(a)** (awaiting action) (*pred*): **to be ~** estar* pendiente **(b)** (imminent) próximo

pending² *prep* (frml) en espera de

pendulum /'pendʒələm ‖ 'pendjʊləm/ *n* (*pl* **-lums**) péndulo *m*

penetrate /'penətreɪt ‖ 'penɪtreɪt/ *vt* **(a)** ‹*membrane/defenses*› penetrar (en); ‹*armor*› atravesar*; ‹*enemy lines*› adentrarse en; ‹*territory*› penetrar en; ‹*organization*› infiltrarse en; ‹*market*› introducirse* en **(b)** «*liquid*» penetrar (en) ■ **~** *vi* **(a)** «*arrow/water/light*» penetrar **(b)** (sink in mentally): **it took a long time to ~** tardé (*or* tardó *etc*) en entenderlo

penetrating /'penətreɪtɪŋ ‖ 'penɪtreɪtɪŋ/ *adj* penetrante

penetration /'penə'treɪʃən ‖ ˌpenɪ'treɪʃən/ *n* [U] penetración *f*

pen friend *n* (esp BrE) ⇒ PEN PAL

penguin /'peŋgwən ‖ 'peŋgwɪn/ *n* pingüino *m*

penicillin /'penə'sɪlən ‖ ˌpenɪ'sɪlm/ *n* [U] penicilina *f*

peninsula /pə'nɪnsələ ‖ pə'nɪnsjʊlə/ *n* península *f*

penis /'pi:nəs ‖ 'pi:nɪs/ *n* pene *m*

penitent /'penətənt ‖ 'penɪtənt/ *adj* arrepentido

penitentiary /'penə'tentʃəri ‖ ˌpenɪ'tenʃəri/ *n* (*pl* **-ries**) (AmE) prisión *f*

penknife /'pennaɪf/ *n* (*pl* **-knives**) navaja *f*

Penn, **Penna** = **Pennsylvania**

pen name *n* seudónimo *m*

penniless /'peniləs ‖ 'penilɪs/ *adj* pobre, sin un céntimo

penny /'peni/ *n* **1** (in UK) **(a)** (*pl* **pence**) penique *m* **(b)** (*pl* **pennies**) (coin) penique *m* **2** (*pl* **pennies**) (cent coin) (in US, Canada) (colloq) (moneda *f* de un) centavo *m*

penny-pinching /'peniˌpɪntʃɪŋ/ *adj* cicatero (fam)

pen pal /'penpæl/ *n* (esp AmE) amigo, -ga *m,f* por correspondencia

pension /'pentʃən ‖ 'penʃən/ *n* pensión *f*; (*retirement* **~**) pensión de jubilación

pensioner /'pentʃənər ‖ 'penʃənə(r)/ *n* pensionado, -da *m,f*, pensionista *mf*; (retired person) jubilado, -da *m,f*

pensive /'pensɪv/ *adj* pensativo

pentagon /'pentəgɑ:n ‖ 'pentəgən/ *n* **(a)** (Math) pentágono *m* **(b)** (in US) **the Pentagon** el Pentágono

pentathlon /pen'tæθlən/ *n* pentatlón *m*

Pentecost /'pentəkɔ:st ‖ 'pentɪkɒst/ *n* Pentecostés *m*

penthouse /'penthaʊs/ *n* penthouse *m*

pent-up /'pent'ʌp/ *adj* (*pred* **pent up**) ‹*emotions*› contenido; ‹*energy*› acumulado

penultimate /pɪ'nʌltəmət ‖ pen'ʌltɪmət/ *adj* (*before n*) penúltimo

people¹ /'pi:pəl/ *n* **1** (+ *pl vb, no art*) **(a)** (in general) gente *f*; **~ say that** ... dicen que ..., se dice que ...; **some ~ don't like it** a algunos no les gusta **(b)** (individuals) personas *fpl* **(c)** (specific group): **tall/rich ~** la gente alta/rica, los altos/ricos; **young ~** los jóvenes **2 (a)** (inhabitants) (+ *pl vb*): **the ~ of this country** la gente de este país; **the country and its ~** el país y su(s) gente(s) **(b)** (citizens, nation) (+ *pl vb*) **the ~** el pueblo **(c)** (race) (+ *sing vb*) pueblo *m*

people² *vt* poblar*

pepper¹ /'pepər ‖ 'pepə(r)/ *n* **1** [U] (spice) pimienta *f*; **black/white ~** pimienta negra/blanca **2** [C U] (capsicum fruit, plant) pimiento *m*, pimentón *m* (AmS exc RPl), ají *m* (RPl); **green ~** pimiento (*or* pimentón *etc*) verde; **red ~** pimiento (*or* pimentón *etc*) rojo *or* colorado, ají *m* morrón (RPl)

pepper² *vt* (intersperse) **to ~ sth WITH sth** salpicar* algo DE algo

pepper: **~box** *n* (AmE) pimentero *m*; **~mint** *n* **(a)** [U] (plant) menta *f*; (*before n*) ‹*tea/oil*› de menta; ‹*flavor*› a menta **(b)** [C] (sweet) caramelo *m* de menta; **~pot** *n* (BrE) pimentero *m*

pep /pep/: **~ talk** *n*: **he gave them a ~ talk** les habló para levantarles la moral/infundirles ánimo; **~ up**: **-pp-** [*v* + *o* + *adv, v* + *adv* + *o*] (colloq) ‹*person*› animar; (physically) darle* energía a

per /pɜːr ‖ pɜː(r)/ *prep* (for each) por; **£10 ~ head** 10 libras por cabeza; **at $25 ~ kilo** a 25 dólares el kilo; **30 miles ~ hour** 30 millas por hora

per: **~ annum** /pər'ænəm/ *adv* al año, por año; **~ capita** /pər'kæpətə ‖ pə'kæpɪtə/ *adv* per cápita

perceive /pər'siːv ‖ pə'siːv/ *vt* **(a)** ‹*object/sound*› percibir **(b)** (realize) percatarse de **(c)** (regard) ver*

percent¹, per cent /pər'sent ‖ pə'sent/ **▶ 543** *n* (*no pl*) porcentaje *m*

percent², per cent *adv* por ciento

percentage /pər'sentɪdʒ ‖ pə'sentɪdʒ/ **▶ 543** *n* porcentaje *m*

perceptible /pər'septəbəl ‖ pə'septəbəl/ *adj* perceptible

perception /pər'sepʃən ‖ pə'sepʃən/ *n* **(a)** [U] (faculty) percepción *f* **(b)** [C] (idea) idea *f*; (image) imagen *f* **(c)** [U] (insight) perspicacia *f*

perceptive /pər'septɪv ‖ pə'septɪv/ *adj* perspicaz

perch¹ /pɜːrtʃ ‖ pɜːtʃ/ *n* **1** (in birdcage) percha *f* **2** (*pl* **~** *or* **~es**) (fish) perca *f*

perch² *vi* «*bird*» posarse; **he ~ed on the edge of the table** se sentó en el borde de la mesa

percolate /'pɜːrkəleɪt ‖ 'pɜːkəleɪt/ *vi* **(a)** (filter) filtrarse **(b)** (Culin) «*coffee*» hacerse*

percolator /'pɜːrkəleɪtər ‖ 'pɜːkəleɪtə(r)/ *n* cafetera *f* eléctrica

percussion /pər'kʌʃən ‖ pə'kʌʃən/ *n* [U] percusión *f*

perennial¹ /pə'reniəl/ *adj* **(a)** (Bot) perenne **(b)** (recurring) perenne, perpetuo

perennial² *n* planta *f* perenne *or* vivaz

perfect¹ /'pɜːrfɪkt ‖ 'pɜːfɪkt/ *adj* **1** (flawless, ideal) perfecto; ‹*day/opportunity*› ideal; **he speaks ~ French** habla francés perfectamente **2** (complete) (*before n*): **he's a ~ stranger to me** me es totalmente desconocido

perfect² /pər'fekt ‖ pə'fekt/ *vt* perfeccionar

perfect³ /'pɜːrfɪkt ‖ 'pɜːfɪkt/ *n*: **the future/present ~** el futuro/pretérito perfecto; **the past ~** el pluscuamperfecto

perfection /pər'fekʃən ‖ pə'fekʃən/ *n* [U] **(a)** (state, quality) perfección *f* **(b)** (act) perfeccionamiento *m*

perfectionist /pər'fekʃənəst ‖ pə'fekʃənɪst/ *n* perfeccionista *mf*

perfectly /'pɜːrfɪktli ‖ 'pɜːfɪktli/ *adv* **1 (a)** (exactly) ‹*round/straight*› totalmente; ‹*fit/match*› perfectamente **(b)** (faultlessly, ideally) perfectamente **2** (completely, utterly) ‹*safe/ridiculous*› totalmente; **he knows ~ well that** ... sabe perfectamente que ...

perforate /'pɜːrfəreɪt ‖ 'pɜːfəreɪt/ *vt* perforar

perforation /'pɜːrfə'reɪʃən ‖ ˌpɜːfə'reɪʃən/ *n* [C U] perforación *f*; **~s** (on sheet of stamps etc) perforado *m*

perform /pər'fɔːrm ‖ pə'fɔːm/ *vi* **1** (Mus, Theat) «*actor/comedian*» actuar*; «*singer*» cantar; «*musician*» tocar*; «*dancer*» bailar **2** (work, produce results) «*student/worker*» rendir*, trabajar; «*team/athlete/vehicle*» responder; «*company/stocks*» rendir* ■ **~** *vt* **1** (Mus, Theat) ‹*play*› representar; ‹*symphony*› tocar* **2** (carry out, fulfill) ‹*function*› desempeñar; ‹*role*› desempeñar; ‹*task*› ejecutar; ‹*experiment*› realizar*; ‹*ceremony*› celebrar; ‹*rites*› practicar*

performance /pər'fɔːrməns ‖ pə'fɔːməns/ *n* **1** [C] (Cin, Mus, Theat) **(a)** (session) (Theat) representación *f*, función *f*; (Cin) función *f* **(b)** (of symphony, song) interpretación *f*; (of play) representación *f* **(c)** (of actor) interpretación *f*; (of pianist, tenor) interpretación *f*; (of entertainer) actuación *f* **2** [C U] (of employee) rendimiento *m*, desempeño *m* (AmL); (of student) rendimiento *m*; (of team, athlete) actuación *f*, performance *f* (AmL period); (of machine, vehicle) comportamiento *m*, performance *f* (AmL); (of company) resultados *mpl*

performer /pər'fɔːrmər ‖ pə'fɔːmə(r)/ *n* (Theat, Cin) actor, -triz *m,f*; (entertainer) artista *mf*

performing /pər'fɔːrmɪŋ ‖ pə'fɔːmɪŋ/ *adj* (*before n*) **(a)** (Mus, Theat): **the ~ arts** las artes interpretativas **(b)** ‹*seal/dog*› amaestrado

perfume¹ /'pɜːrfjuːm ‖ 'pɜːfjuːm/ *n* perfume *m*

perfume² /pər'fjuːm ‖ 'pɜːfjuːm/ *vt* perfumar

perfunctory /pər'fʌŋktəri ‖ pə'fʌŋktəri/ *adj* ‹*inspection/description*› somero; ‹*greeting*› mecánico

perhaps /pər'hæps ‖ pə'hæps/ *adv* quizá(s), tal vez; **~ they'll come later** tal vez *or* quizá(s) vengan más tarde

peril /'perəl ‖ 'perɪl, 'perəl/ *n* [C U] peligro *m*

perilous /'perələs ‖ 'perɪləs, 'perələs/ *adj* peligroso

perimeter /pə'rɪmətər ‖ pə'rɪmɪtə(r)/ *n* perímetro *m*

period¹ /'pɪriəd ‖ 'pɪəriəd/ *n* [*the forms* PERÍODO *and* PERIODO *are equally acceptable in Spanish where this translation applies*] **1 (a)** (interval, length of time) período *m*; (when specifying a time limit) plazo *m*; **for a ~ of five hours/12 months** por un espacio de cinco horas/período de 12 meses **(b)** (epoch) época *f* **2** (menstruation) periodo *m*, regla *f* **3** (in school) hora *f* (*de clase*) **4** (in punctuation) (AmE) punto *m*

period² *adj* ‹*costume/furniture*› de época

periodic /ˈpɪriˈɑːdɪk ‖ ˌpɪəriˈɒdɪk/ *adj* periódico

periodical¹ /ˈpɪriˈɑːdɪkəl ‖ ˌpɪəriˈɒdɪkəl/ *n* publicación *f* periódica

periodical² *adj* ⇒ PERIODIC

peripheral /pəˈrɪfərəl/ *adj* **(a)** (minor, secondary) secundario **(b)** (Comput) ‹*device/unit*› periférico

periphery /pəˈrɪfəri/ *n* (*pl* **-ries**) (frml) (of city) periferia *f*; (of society) margen *m*

periscope /ˈperəskəʊp ‖ ˈperɪskəʊp/ *n* periscopio *m*

perish /ˈperɪʃ/ *vi* **(a)** (die) (liter) perecer* (liter) **(b)** (decay) «*rubber/leather*» deteriorarse; «*foodstuffs*» echarse a perder

perishable /ˈperɪʃəbəl/ *adj* perecedero

perjure /ˈpɜːrdʒər ‖ ˈpɜːdʒə(r)/ *v refl* (Law) **to ~ oneself** perjurar(se), cometer perjurio

perjury /ˈpɜːrdʒəri ‖ ˈpɜːdʒəri/ *n* [U] perjurio *m*

perk /pɜːrk ‖ pɜːk/ *n* (colloq) (of job) (beneficio *m*) extra *m*; (particular advantage) ventaja *f*

• **perk up** [*v* + *adv*] «*person*» animarse; «*business/weather*» mejorar

perky /ˈpɜːrki ‖ ˈpɜːki/ *adj* **-kier, -kiest** alegre

perm¹ /pɜːrm ‖ pɜːm/ *n* permanente *f or* (Méx) *m*

perm² *vt*: **to have one's hair ~ed** hacerse* la *or* (Méx) un permanente

permanent¹ /ˈpɜːrmənənt ‖ ˈpɜːmənənt/ *adj* permanente; ‹*address/job*› fijo, permanente; ‹*dye/ink*› indeleble

permanent² *n* (AmE) ⇒ PERM¹

permanently /ˈpɜːrmənəntli ‖ ˈpɜːmənəntli/ *adv* ‹*work/settle*› permanentemente; ‹*marked/disfigured*› para siempre

permeate /ˈpɜːrmieɪt ‖ ˈpɜːmieɪt/ *vt* «*liquid*» calar; «*smoke/smell*» impregnar

permissible /pərˈmɪsəbəl ‖ pəˈmɪsəbəl/ *adj* (permitted) permisible; (acceptable) tolerable

permission /pərˈmɪʃən ‖ pəˈmɪʃən/ *n* [U] permiso *m*; **she gave me ~** me dio (su) permiso

permissive /pərˈmɪsɪv ‖ pəˈmɪsɪv/ *adj* permisivo

permit¹ /pərˈmɪt ‖ pəˈmɪt/ **-tt-** *vt* permitir; **photography is not ~ted** no se permite tomar fotografías; **to ~ sb to** + INF permitirle a algn que (+ *subj*) ■ **~** *vi*: **weather ~ting** si hace buen tiempo

permit² /ˈpɜːrmɪt ‖ ˈpɜːmɪt/ *n* permiso *m* (*por escrito*); **work/residence ~** permiso de trabajo/de residencia; **gun ~** (AmE) licencia *f* de armas

permutation /ˈpɜːrmjʊˈteɪʃən ‖ ˌpɜːmjʊˈteɪʃən/ *n* **(a)** [C] (arrangement) variante *f* **(b)** [U C] (Math) permutación *f*

peroxide /pərˈɑːksaɪd ‖ pəˈrɒksaɪd/ *n* [U] peróxido *m*

perpendicular /ˈpɜːrpənˈdɪkjələr ‖ ˌpɜːpənˈdɪkjʊlə(r)/ *adj* **(a)** ‹*wall/surface*› perpendicular al horizonte **(b)** (Math) **~ TO sth** perpendicular A algo

perpetrate /ˈpɜːrpətreɪt ‖ ˈpɜːpɪtreɪt/ *vt* (frml) perpetrar

perpetrator /ˈpɜːrpətreɪtər ‖ ˈpɜːpɪtreɪtə(r)/ *n* (frml *or* hum) autor, -tora *m,f* (*de un crimen etc*)

perpetual /pərˈpetʃuəl ‖ pəˈpetjʊəl/ *adj* eterno, perpetuo

perpetuate /pərˈpetʃueɪt ‖ pəˈpetjʊeɪt/ *vt* perpetuar*

perplex /pərˈpleks ‖ pəˈpleks/ *vt* dejar perplejo

perplexed /pərˈplekst ‖ pəˈplekst/ *adj* perplejo

per se /ˈpɜːrˈseɪ ‖ ˌpɜːˈseɪ/ *adv* en sí, per se

persecute /ˈpɜːrsɪkjuːt ‖ ˈpɜːsɪkjuːt/ *vt* perseguir*

persecution /ˈpɜːrsɪˈkjuːʃən ‖ ˌpɜːsɪˈkjuːʃən/ *n* [U C] persecución *f*

perseverance /ˈpɜːrsəˈvɪrəns ‖ ˌpɜːsɪˈvɪərəns/ *n* [U] perseverancia *f*

persevere /ˈpɜːrsəˈvɪr ‖ ˌpɜːsɪˈvɪə(r)/ *vi* perseverar

Persia /ˈpɜːrʒə ‖ ˈpɜːʃə/ *n* Persia *f*

Persian /ˈpɜːrʒən ‖ ˈpɜːʃən/ *adj* persa; **the ~ Gulf** el Golfo Pérsico

persist /pərˈsɪst ‖ pəˈsɪst/ *vi* persistir

persistence /pərˈsɪstəns ‖ pəˈsɪstəns/ *n* [U] perseverancia *f*

persistent /pərˈsɪstənt ‖ pəˈsɪstənt/ *adj* **(a)** (unceasing) ‹*demands/warnings*› continuo, constante; ‹*cough/fog*› persistente; ‹*rain*› continuo **(b)** (undaunted) ‹*salesman/suitor*› insistente

person /ˈpɜːrsn̩ ‖ ˈpɜːsn̩/ *n* **1** (*pl* **people** *o* (frml) **persons**) persona *f*; **Sue's the ~ to ask** a quien hay que preguntarle es a Sue; **in ~** en persona **2** (Ling) (*pl* **persons**) persona *f*

personable /ˈpɜːrsn̩əbəl ‖ ˈpɜːsn̩əbəl/ *adj* agradable

personal /ˈpɜːrsnəl ‖ ˈpɜːsənl/ *adj* **1 (a)** (own) ‹*experience/preference*› personal; ‹*property*› privado **(b)** (private) personal; **a ~ call** una llamada particular; **don't ask ~ questions** no hagas preguntas indiscretas **(c)** (individual) ‹*account/loan*› personal **2 (a)** (in person) ‹*appearance*› en persona **(b)** (physical) ‹*hygiene*› íntimo; ‹*appearance*› personal **(c)** (directed against individual): **it's nothing ~, but** ... no tengo nada contra ti (*or* ella *etc*), pero ...

personal: **~ assistant** *n* (Busn) secretario, -ria *m,f* personal; **~ computer** *n* computadora *f or* (Esp tb) ordenador *m* personal

personality /ˈpɜːrsn̩ˈæləti ‖ ˌpɜːsəˈnæləti/ *n* (*pl* **-ties**) [C U] personalidad *f*

personally /ˈpɜːrsn̩əli ‖ ˈpɜːsn̩əli/ *adv* personalmente

personal organizer *n* agenda *f* de uso múltiple, Filofax® *m*

personification /pərˈsɑːnəfəˈkeɪʃən ‖ pəˌsɒnɪfɪˈkeɪʃən/ *n* [U C] personificación *f*

personify /pərˈsɑːnəfaɪ ‖ pəˈsɒnɪfaɪ/ *vt* **-fies, -fying, -fied** personificar*

personnel /ˈpɜːrsn̩ˈel ‖ ˌpɜːsəˈnel/ *n* **(a)** (staff) (+ *pl vb*) personal *m*; (*before n*) **~ manager** jefe *m,f* de personal **(b) Personnel** (department) (+ *sing vb*) sección *f* de personal

perspective /pərˈspektɪv ‖ pəˈspektɪv/ *n* [U C] perspectiva *f*; **you have to keep things in ~** no tienes que perder de vista la verdadera dimensión de las cosas

Perspex® /ˈpɜːrspeks ‖ ˈpɜːspeks/ *n* [U] (BrE) acrílico *m*, Plexiglas® *m* (Esp)

perspiration /ˈpɜːrspəˈreɪʃən ‖ˌpɜːspɪˈreɪʃən/ *n* [U] transpiración *f*

perspire /pərˈspaɪr ‖ pəˈspaɪə(r)/ *vi* transpirar

persuade /pərˈsweɪd ‖pəˈsweɪd/ *vt* ‹*person*› convencer*, persuadir; **to ~ sb to** + INF convencer* *or* persuadir a algn DE QUE *or* PARA QUE (+ *subj*)

persuasion /pərˈsweɪʒən ‖pəˈsweɪʒən/ *n* **(a)** [U] (act) persuasión *f* **(b)** [C] (Relig) (frml): **people of all ~s** gente de todas las creencias

persuasive /pərˈsweɪsɪv ‖pəˈsweɪsɪv/ *adj* ‹*person/manner*› persuasivo; ‹*argument*› convincente

pert /pɜːrt ‖ pɜːt/ *adj* ‹*reply*› descarado; ‹*hat/dress*› coqueto

pertinent /ˈpɜːrtn̩ənt ‖ˈpɜːtɪnənt/ *adj* (frml) pertinente; **to be ~ TO sth** guardar relación CON algo

perturb /pərˈtɜːrb ‖ pəˈtɜːb/ *vt* (*usu pass*) perturbar

Peru /pəˈruː/ *n* (el) Perú *m*

peruse /pəˈruːz/ *vt* **(a)** (read through) (frml or hum) leer* detenidamente **(b)** (examine, study) (frml) examinar

Peruvian /pəˈruːviən/ *adj* peruano

pervade /pərˈveɪd ‖pəˈveɪd/ *vt* «*idea/mood*» dominar; «*smell*» llenar

pervasive /pərˈveɪsɪv ‖pəˈveɪsɪv/ *adj* ‹*smell*› penetrante; ‹*idea/mood*› dominante; ‹*influence*› omnipresente

perverse /pərˈvɜːrs ‖pəˈvɜːs/ *adj* (stubborn) obstinado; (wayward, contrary) retorcido

perversion /pərˈvɜːrʒən ‖pəˈvɜːʃən/ *n* [C U] **(a)** (distortion): **a ~ of justice** una deformación de la justicia **(b)** (Psych) perversión *f*

pervert¹ /pərˈvɜːrt ‖ pəˈvɜːt/ *vt* pervertir*

pervert² /ˈpɜːrvɜːrt ‖ˈpɜːvɜːt/ *n* pervertido, -da *m,f*

peseta /pəˈseɪtə/ *n* peseta *f*

pesky /ˈpeski/ *adj* **-kier, -kiest** (AmE colloq) latoso (fam)

peso /ˈpeɪsəʊ/ *n* (*pl* **~s**) peso *m*

pessimism /ˈpesəmɪzəm ‖ˈpesɪmɪzəm/ *n* [U] pesimismo *m*

pessimist /ˈpesəməst ‖ˈpesɪmɪst/ *n* pesimista *mf*

pessimistic /ˈpesəˈmɪstɪk ‖ˌpesɪˈmɪstɪk/ *adj* pesimista

pest /pest/ *n* **(a)** (Agr, Hort) plaga *f* **(b)** (person, thing) (colloq) peste *f* (fam)

pester /ˈpestər ‖ˈpestə(r)/ *vt* molestar

pesticide /ˈpestəsaɪd ‖ˈpestɪsaɪd/ *n* [U C] pesticida *m*

pestle /ˈpesəl/ *n* mano *f* de mortero

pet¹ /pet/ *n* **(a)** (animal) animal *m* doméstico *or* de compañía; (*before n*) **~ food** comida *f* para animales; **~ shop** ≈ pajarería *f* **(b)** (favorite): **he's teacher's ~** es el niño mimado de la maestra

pet² *adj* (*before n*) **(a)** (kept as pet): **his ~ budgie** su periquito **(b)** (favorite) ‹*subject/theory*› favorito; **my ~ hate** lo que más odio

pet³ -tt- *vt* ‹*animal*› acariciar ■ **~** *vi* acariciarse, manosearse (pey)

petal /ˈpetl̩/ *n* pétalo *m*

peter out /ˈpiːtər/ [*v* + *adv*] «*supplies*» irse* agotando; «*conversation*» apagarse*

petition /pəˈtɪʃən/ *n* **(a)** (written document) petición *f* **(b)** (Law) demanda *f*

pet name *n* apodo *m*

petrified /ˈpetrɪfaɪd/ *adj* **(a)** (terrified) muerto de miedo **(b)** (Geol) petrificado

petrochemical /ˈpetrəʊˈkemɪkəl/ *n* producto *m* petroquímico; (*before n*) ‹*industry/plant*› petroquímico

petrol /ˈpetrəl/ *n* [U] (BrE) gasolina *f*, bencina *f* (Andes) nafta *f* (RPl); (*before n*) **~ pump** surtidor *m*; **~ station** estación *f* de servicio, gasolinera *f*, bomba *f* (Andes, Ven), estación *f* de nafta (RPl), bencinera *f* (Andes), grifo *m* (Per)

petroleum /pəˈtrəʊliəm/ *n* [U] petróleo *m*; (*before n*) **~ jelly** vaselina *f*

petticoat /ˈpetikəʊt/ *n* **(a)** (underskirt) enagua *f or* (Méx) fondo *m* **(b)** (slip) (BrE) combinación *f*, viso *m*

petty /ˈpeti/ *adj* **-tier, -tiest (a)** (unimportant) ‹*details*› insignificante, nimio; **~ thief** ladronzuelo, -la *m,f* **(b)** (small-minded) mezquino

petty cash *n* [U] caja *f* chica, dinero *m* para gastos menores

petulant /ˈpetʃələnt ‖ˈpetjʊlənt/ *adj* de mal genio

pew /pjuː/ *n* banco *m* (*de iglesia*)

pewter /ˈpjuːtər ‖ˈpjuːtə(r)/ *n* [U] peltre *m*

PG (= **parental guidance**) menores acompañados

PG-13 (in US) mayores de 13 años o menores acompañados

phantom¹ /ˈfæntəm/ *n* (liter) fantasma *m*

phantom² *adj* **(a)** (ghostly) (liter) (*before n*) ‹*shape*› fantasmal; ‹*horseman*› fantasma *adj inv* **(b)** (imaginary) ilusorio

Pharaoh /ˈferəʊ ‖ˈfeərəʊ/ *n* faraón *m*

pharmaceutical /ˈfɑːrməˈsuːtɪkəl ‖ˌfɑːməˈsjuːtɪkəl/ *adj* farmacéutico

pharmacist /ˈfɑːrməsəst ‖ˈfɑːməsɪst/ *n* farmacéutico, -ca *m,f*, farmaceuta *mf* (Col, Ven)

pharmacy /ˈfɑːrməsi ‖ˈfɑːməsi/ *n* (*pl* **-cies**) **(a)** [U] (discipline) química *f* farmacéutica, farmacia *f* **(b)** [C] (dispensary) farmacia *f*

phase /feɪz/ *n* fase *f*

• **phase out** [*v* + *o* + *adv*, *v* + *adv* + *o*] ‹*service*› retirar paulatinamente; ‹*old model*› dejar de producir

PhD *n* (= **Doctor of Philosophy**) (award) doctorado *m*; (person) Dr., Dra.

pheasant /ˈfezn̩t/ *n* (*pl* **~s** *or* **~**) faisán *m*

phenomena /fɪˈnɑːmənə ‖fəˈnɒmɪnə/ *pl of* PHENOMENON

phenomenal /fɪˈnɑːmənl̩ ‖fəˈnɒmɪnl/ *adj* (colloq) ‹*success/achievement*› espectacular; ‹*strength*› increíble

phenomenon /fɪˈnɑːmənɑːn ‖fəˈnɒmɪnən/ *n* (*pl* **-mena**) fenómeno *m*

phew /fjuː/ *interj* (colloq) ¡uf!

philanderer /fəˈlændərər ‖fɪˈlændərə(r)/ *n* (pej) mujeriego *m* (pey)

philanthropic /ˈfɪlənˈθrɑːpɪk ‖ˌfɪlənˈθrɒpɪk/ *adj* filantrópico

philanthropist /fə'lænθrəpəst ‖ fɪ'lænθrəpɪst/ *n* filántropo, -pa *m,f*

philately /fə'lætḷi ‖ fɪ'lætəli/ *n* [U] (fml) filatelia *f*

Philippine /'fɪləpi:n ‖ 'fɪlɪpi:n/ *adj* filipino

Philippines /'fɪləpi:nz ‖ 'fɪlɪpi:nz/ *pl n* **the ~** (las) Filipinas

philistine /'fɪləsti:n, -aɪn ‖ 'fɪlɪstaɪn/ *n* ignorante *mf*

philosopher /fə'lɑ:səfər ‖ fɪ'lɒsəfə(r)/ *n* filósofo, -fa *m,f*

philosophic /'fɪlə'sɑ:fɪk ‖ ˌfɪlə'sɒfɪk/, **-ical** /-ɪkəl/ *adj* filosófico; **to be ~ ABOUT sth** tomarse algo con filosofía

philosophy /fə'lɑ:səfi ‖ fɪ'lɒsəfi/ *n* [U C] filosofía *f*

phlegm /flem/ *n* [U] flema *f*

phobia /'fəʊbiə/ *n* fobia *f*

phoenix /'fi:nɪks/ *n* Ave *f*‡ Fénix, fénix *m or f*

phone¹ /fəʊn/ ▶875 *n* teléfono *m*; **to be on the ~** (be speaking) estar* hablando por teléfono; (subscribe) (BrE) tener* teléfono; (*before n*) **~ call** llamada *f* (telefónica); **~ number** (número *m* de) teléfono *m*

phone² *vt* ‹*person*› llamar (por teléfono), telefonear, hablar (Méx); ‹*place/number*› llamar (por teléfono) a

• **phone up** [*v + adv + o, v + o + adv*] llamar, telefonear

phone: **~ book** *n* (colloq) guía *f* (telefónica *or* de teléfonos) *or* (Col, Méx) directorio *m*; **~ booth**, (BrE) **~ box** *n* cabina *f* telefónica; **~card** *n* tarjeta *f* telefónica

phonetics /fə'netɪks/ *n* (+ *sing vb*) fonética *f*

phoney¹, (AmE also) **phony** /'fəʊni/ *adj* **-nier, -niest** (colloq & pej) falso

phoney², (AmE also) **phony** *n* (*pl* **-neys** *or* **-nies**) (colloq & pej) (person) farsante *mf* (fam); (thing) falsificación *f*

phosphate /'fɑ:sfeɪt ‖ 'fɒsfeɪt/ *n* fosfato *m*

phosphorus /'fɑ:sfərəs ‖ 'fɒsfərəs/ *n* [U] fósforo *m*

photo /'fəʊtəʊ/ *n* (*pl* **-tos**) (colloq) foto *f*; **to take a ~ (of sb/sth)** sacar(le)* *or* (Esp tb) hacer(le)* una foto (a algn/algo)

photocopier /'fəʊtəʊˌkɑ:piər ‖ 'fəʊtəʊˌkɒpiə(r)/ *n* fotocopiadora *f*

photocopy¹ /'fəʊtəʊˌkɑ:pi ‖ 'fəʊtəʊˌkɒpi/ *n* (*pl* **-copies**) fotocopia *f*

photocopy² *vt* **-copies, -copying, -copied** fotocopiar

photo: **~ finish** *n* foto(-)finish *f*; **~fit®** *n* (BrE): **P~fit (picture)** retrato *m* hablado (AmS) *or* (Esp) robot *or* (Méx) reconstruido

photogenic /'fəʊtə'dʒenɪk/ *adj* fotogénico

photograph¹ /'fəʊtəgræf ‖ 'fəʊtəgrɑ:f/ *n* fotografía *f*, foto *f*; **to take a ~ (of sb/sth)** sacar(le)* *or* (Esp tb) hacer(le)* una foto *or* una fotografía (a algn/algo)

photograph² *vt* fotografiar*, sacarle* *or* (Esp tb) hacerle* una foto *or* una fotografía a

photographer /fə'tɑ:grəfər ‖ fə'tɒgrəfə(r)/ *n* fotógrafo, -fa *m,f*

photographic /'fəʊtə'græfɪk/ *adj* ‹*copy/evidence/memory*› fotográfico; ‹*shop/equipment*› de fotografía

photography /fə'tɑ:grəfi ‖ fə'tɒgrəfi/ *n* [U] fotografía *f*

photosynthesis /'fəʊtəʊ'sɪnθəsəs ‖ ˌfəʊtəʊ'sɪnθəsɪs/ *n* [U] fotosíntesis *f*

phrasal verb /'freɪzḷ/ *n* verbo *m* con partícula(s)

phrase¹ /freɪz/ *n* frase *f*

phrase² *vt* expresar

phrase book *n* manual *m* de conversación, ≈ guía *m* de bolsillo para el viajero

physical¹ /'fɪzɪkəl/ *adj* **1** (bodily) físico; ‹*illness*› orgánico; **~ education** educación *f* física **2** (material) ‹*world*› material

physical² *n* reconocimiento *m* médico

physically /'fɪzɪkli/ *adv* ‹*attractive*› físicamente; ‹*demanding*› desde el punto de vista físico; **it's ~ impossible** es materialmente imposible

physical therapy *n* [U] (AmE) ⇒ PHYSIOTHERAPY

physician /fə'zɪʃən ‖ fɪ'zɪʃən/ *n* (fml) médico, -ca *m,f*

physicist /'fɪzəsəst ‖ 'fɪzɪsɪst/ *n* físico, -ca *m,f*

physics /'fɪzɪks/ *n* (+ *sing vb*) física *f*

physiological /'fɪziə'lɑ:dʒɪkəl ‖ ˌfɪziə'lɒdʒɪkəl/ *adj* fisiológico

physiology /'fɪzi'ɑ:lədʒi ‖ ˌfɪzi'ɒlədʒi/ *n* [U] fisiología *f*

physiotherapy /'fɪziəʊ'θerəpi/ *n* [U] (discipline) kinesiología *f*; (treatment) fisioterapia *f*, kinesiterapia *f*

physique /fə'zi:k ‖ fɪ'zi:k/ *n* físico *m*

pianist /pi'ænəst ‖ 'piənɪst/ *n* pianista *mf*

piano /pi'ænəʊ/ *n* (*pl* **-os**) piano *m*

pick¹ /pɪk/ *n* **1 (a)** ⇒ PICKAX **(b)** (*ice* **~**) piolet *m* **(c)** (plectrum) púa *f*, plectro *m*, uñeta *f* (CS), uña *f* (Méx, Ven) **2** (choice) (*no pl*): **take your ~** elige *or* escoge el (*or* los *etc*) que quieras

pick² *vt* **1 (a)** (choose, select) ‹*number/color*› elegir*, escoger*; ‹*team/crew*› seleccionar **(b)** (provoke): **to ~ a fight with sb** meterse con algn **2** (gather) ‹*flower*› cortar, coger* (esp Esp); ‹*fruit/cotton/tea*› recoger*, coger* (esp Esp), pizcar* (Méx) **3 (a)** (remove matter from): **to ~ one's nose** meterse el dedo en la nariz, hurgarse* la nariz; **don't ~ your spots** no te toques los granitos; **to ~ sb's pocket** robarle la billetera (*or* las llaves *etc*) a algn del bolsillo, bolsear a algn (Mex fam), carterear a algn (Chi fam) **(b)** (open) ‹*lock*› abrir* con una ganzúa (*or* una horquilla *etc*) ■ **~** *vi* **(a)** : **to ~ and choose** ser exigente **(b)** (take bits): **he was ~ing at his dinner** comía desganado

• **pick on** [*v + prep + o*] (colloq) meterse con, agarrársela(s) con (AmL fam)

• **pick out** [*v + o + adv, v + adv + o*] **1** (choose, select) elegir*, escoger* **2 (a)** (recognize, identify) reconocer* **(b)** (discern) distinguir*

• **pick up I** [*v + o + adv, v + adv + o*] **1** (gather off floor, ground) recoger*; (take) tomar, agarrar (esp AmL), coger* (esp Esp); (lift up) levantar **2** (learn) ‹*language*› aprender; ‹*habit*› adquirir, agarrar (esp AmL), coger* (esp Esp) **3 (a)** (collect, fetch) recoger* **(b)** (take on board) ‹*passenger*› recoger* **(c)** (colloq) ‹*man/woman*› ligarse* (fam), levantar (AmS fam) **4** (receive) ‹*signal*› captar

II [*v* + *adv* + *o*] (gain) ‹*speed*› agarrar, coger* (esp Esp)

III [*v* + *o* + *adv*] **(a)** (revive) reanimar **(b)** (correct) corregir*

IV [*v* + *adv*] (improve) «*prices/sales*» subir; «*economy/business*» repuntar; «*invalid*» mejorar; «*weather*» mejorar

pickax, (BrE) **pickaxe** /'pɪkæks/ *n* pico *m*, piqueta *f*

picket¹ /'pɪkət ‖ 'pɪkɪt/ *n* (group) piquete *m*; (*before n*) **~ line** piquete *m*

picket² *vt* ‹*factory/workplace*› formar un piquete frente a, piquetear (esp AmL)

pickings /'pɪkɪŋz/ *pl n* **(a)** (profits) ganancias *fpl* **(b)** (food) sobras *fpl*

pickle¹ /'pɪkəl/ *n* **(a)** [C] (*dill* ~) (AmE) pepinillo *m* en vinagre al eneldo **(b)** [C] **~s** (vegetables) encurtidos *mpl*, pickles *mpl* (CS) **(c)** [U] (relish) (BrE) *condimento a base de encurtidos en una salsa*

pickle² *vt* conservar en vinagre *or* (Chi tb) en escabeche, encurtir

pick: **~-me-up** *n* (colloq) estimulante *m*; **~pocket** *n* carterista *mf*, bolsista *mf* (Méx); **~up (truck)** *n* camioneta *f* (de reparto)

picky /'pɪki/ *adj* **pickier, pickiest** (colloq) quisquilloso

picnic /'pɪknɪk/ *n* picnic *m*; **to go for** *o* **on a ~** ir* de picnic

pictorial /pɪk'tɔːriəl/ *adj* ‹*representation*› pictórico; ‹*account/history*› en imágenes; ‹*magazine*› ilustrado

picture¹ /'pɪktʃər ‖ 'pɪktʃə(r)/ *n* **1 (a)** (illustration) ilustración *f*; (drawing) dibujo *m*; (painting) cuadro *m*, pintura *f*; (print) cuadro *m*, lámina *f*; (portrait) retrato *m* **(b)** (photo) foto *f*; **to take a ~ of sth/sb** sacarle* *or* (Esp tb) hacerle* una foto a algo/algn **2** (situation) panorama *m*; ***to put sb in the ~*** poner* a algn al tanto (de la situación) **3** (idea) idea *f* **4** (TV) imagen *f* **5** (Cin) **(a)** (movie) película *f* **(b) pictures** *pl* (cinema) (BrE dated) **the ~s** el cine

picture² *vt* imaginarse

picturesque /'pɪktʃə'resk/ *adj* pintoresco

pie /paɪ/ *n* [U C] (savory) empanada *f*; (sweet) pastel *m*, pay *m* (AmC, Méx)

piece /piːs/ *n* **1 (a)** (part of sth broken, torn, cut, divided) pedazo *m*, trozo *m*; **she ripped the letter into ~s** rompió la carta en pedacitos; **to come** *o* **fall to ~s** hacerse* pedazos; **a ~ of land** un terreno, una parcela; ***in one ~*** (safe) sano y salvo; (unbroken) intacto; ***to go to ~s*** perder* el control; ***to pull sth/sb to ~s*** destrozar* algo/a algn; ***to say one's ~*** dar* su (*or* mi *etc*) opinión **(b)** (component) pieza *f*, parte *f*; **to take sth to ~s** desarmar algo **2** (item): **a ~ of advice** un consejo; **a ~ of furniture** un mueble; **a ~ of paper** un papel; **an excellent ~ of work** un trabajo excelente; ***to give sb a ~ of one's mind*** cantarle las cuarenta a algn **3 (a)** (Mus): **a ~ (of music)** una pieza (de música) **(b)** (Journ) artículo *m* **4** (coin) moneda *f* **5** (in board games) ficha *f*; (in chess) figura *f*

• **piece together** [*v* + *o* + *adv*, *v* + *adv* + *o*] ‹*fragments*› juntar*; ‹*events/facts*› reconstruir*

piecemeal¹ /'piːsmiːl/ *adj* poco sistemático

piecemeal² *adv* (gradually) poco a poco; (unsystematically) de manera poco sistemática

piecework /'piːswɜːrk ‖ 'piːswɜːk/ *n* [U] trabajo *m* a destajo

pier /pɪr ‖ pɪə(r)/ *n* **(a)** (landing place) embarcadero *m*, muelle *m* **(b)** (with amusements) *paseo con juegos y atracciones sobre un muelle*

pierce /pɪrs ‖ pɪəs/ *vt* **(a)** (make a hole in) agujerear; (go through) atravesar*; **she's had her ears ~d** se ha hecho hacer agujeros en las orejas **(b)** «*sound/light*» (liter) rasgar* (liter)

piercing /'pɪrsɪŋ ‖ 'pɪəsɪŋ/ *adj* ‹*eyes/look*› penetrante; ‹*scream*› desgarrador

piety /'paɪəti/ *n* [U] piedad *f*

pig¹ /pɪg/ *n* **1** (Agr, Zool) cerdo *m*, chancho *m* (AmL) **2 (a)** (obnoxious person) (colloq) cerdo, -da *m,f* (fam) **(b)** (glutton) (colloq) glotón, -tona *m,f*, angurriento, -ta *m,f* (CS fam)

pigeon /'pɪdʒən ‖ 'pɪdʒɪn, 'pɪdʒən/ *n* [C U] (Zool) paloma *f*; (Culin) pichón *m*

pigeonhole /'pɪdʒənhəʊl ‖ 'pɪdʒɪnhəʊl, 'pɪdʒən-/ *n* **(a)** (on wall, desk) casillero *m* **(b)** (category) casilla *f*

piggy /'pɪgi/ *n* (*pl* **-gies**) (used to or by children) cerdito *m*, chanchito *m* (AmL)

piggy: **~back** *n*: **to give sb a ~back** llevar a algn a caballo; **~bank** *n* alcancía *f* (AmL), hucha *f* (Esp) (*en forma de cerdito*)

pigheaded /pɪg'hedəd ‖ ˌpɪg'hedɪd/ *adj* terco

piglet /'pɪglət ‖ 'pɪglɪt/ *n* cochinillo *m*, lechón *m*, chanchito *m* (AmL)

pigment /'pɪgmənt/ *n* [C U] pigmento *m*

pigmy /'pɪgmi/ *n* ⇒ PYGMY

pig: **~-pen** *n* (AmE) ⇒ ~ STY; **~sty** *n* pocilga *f*, chiquero *m* (AmL); **~tail** *n* (bunch) coleta *f*, chape *m* (Chi); (plait) trenza *f*

pike /paɪk/ *n* **(a)** (*pl* ~) (Zool) lucio *m* **(b)** (*turn*~) (AmE) carretera *f*

pilchard /'pɪltʃərd ‖ 'pɪltʃəd/ *n* sardina *f* (*grande*)

pile¹ /paɪl/ *n* **1** [C] (stack, heap) montón *m* **2** [C U] (Tex) pelo *m* **3 piles** *pl* (BrE Med) hemorroides *fpl*, almorranas *fpl*

pile² *vt* amontonar

• **pile in** [*v* + *adv*] (colloq) meterse

• **pile into** [*v* + *prep* + *o*] (colloq) **(a)** (squeeze into) ‹*car*› meterse en **(b)** (attack) arremeter contra **(c)** (crash into) «*vehicle*» estrellarse contra

• **pile up 1** [*v* + *adv*] (accumulate) amontonarse **2** [*v* + *o* + *adv*, *v* + *adv* + *o*] (form into pile) apilar

pileup /'paɪlʌp/ *n* choque *m* múltiple

pilfering /'pɪlfərɪŋ/ *n* [U] robos *mpl*, hurtos *mpl*

pilgrim /'pɪlgrəm ‖ 'pɪlgrɪm/ *n* peregrino, -na *m,f*; (*before n*) **the P~ Fathers** *los primeros colonizadores de Nueva Inglaterra*

pilgrimage /'pɪlgrəmɪdʒ ‖ 'pɪlgrɪmɪdʒ/ *n* peregrinación *f*

pill /pɪl/ *n* **(a)** (tablet) pastilla *f*, píldora *f* **(b)** (contraceptive) **the P~** la píldora (anticonceptiva); **to be on the P~** tomar la píldora

pillage¹ /ˈpɪlɪdʒ/ *n* [U] pillaje *m*

pillage² *vt/i* saquear

pillar /ˈpɪlər ‖ ˈpɪlə(r)/ *n* pilar *m*; **he is a ~ of the community** es uno de los pilares *or* baluartes de la comunidad

pillar box *n* (BrE) buzón *m*

pillion¹ /ˈpɪljən ‖ ˈpɪliən/ *n* (Auto) asiento *m* trasero (*de una moto*)

pillion² *adv* ‹*ride*› en el asiento trasero

pillory /ˈpɪləri/ *n* (*pl* **-ries**) picota *f*

pillow /ˈpɪləʊ/ *n* almohada *f*

pillowcase /ˈpɪləʊkeɪs/, (BrE also) **pillow slip** *n* funda *f*, almohadón *m* (Esp)

pilot¹ /ˈpaɪlət/ *n* **1** (Aerosp, Aviat) piloto *mf* **2** (Naut) práctico *mf* (de puerto) **3** (Rad, TV) programa *m* piloto

pilot² *adj* (*before n*) piloto *adj inv*

pilot³ *vt* **1** (Aviat, Naut) pilotar, pilotear (AmL) **2** (test) poner* a prueba

pilot light *n* piloto *m*

pimple /ˈpɪmpəl/ *n* grano *m*, espinilla *f* (AmL)

pin¹ /pɪn/ *n* **1** (for cloth, paper) alfiler *m* **2** (brooch, badge) (AmE) insignia *f* **3 (a)** (on plug) (BrE Elec) clavija *f*, borne *m* **(b)** (peg) (Tech) perno *m*

pin² **-nn-** *vt* **1** (fasten, attach) ‹*dress/seam*› prender con alfileres; **I ~ned the papers together** sujeté los papeles con un alfiler; **she had ~ned her hopes on getting a scholarship** había depositado sus esperanzas en conseguir una beca; **they tried to ~ the blame on him** trataron de hacerle cargar con la culpa **2** (hold motionless) inmovilizar*

• pin down [*v + o + adv, v + adv + o*] **1** (prevent from moving): **they ~ned him down** (se echaron sobre él y) lo inmovilizaron **2 (a)** (define) ‹*cause/identity*› definir; **something's wrong with me, but I can't ~ it down** algo tengo, pero no sabría decir exactamente qué **(b)** (force to state position): **I managed to ~ him down to a definite date** conseguí que se comprometiera para una fecha concreta

PIN /pɪn/ *n* (= **personal identification number**) PIN *m*

pinafore /ˈpɪnəfɔːr ‖ ˈpɪnəfɔː(r)/ *n* **(a)** ~ **(dress)** (sleeveless dress) jumper *m* *or* (Esp) pichi *m* **(b)** (apron) (BrE) delantal *m* *or* (esp Méx) mandil *m* (*con peto*) **(c)** (protective overdress) delantal *m*

pinball /ˈpɪnbɔːl/ *n* (*before n*) **~ machine** flipper *m*

pincer /ˈpɪnsər ‖ ˈpɪnsə(r)/ *n* **(a)** (Zool) pinza *f* **(b) pincers** *pl* (tool) tenaza(s) *f(pl)*

pinch¹ /pɪntʃ/ *n* **(a)** (act) pellizco *m*; ***in*** *o* (BrE) ***at a ~*** si fuera necesario **(b)** (small quantity) pizca *f*

pinch² *vt* **1** «*person*» pellizcar*; «*shoes*» apretar* **2** (BrE colloq) (steal) robar

pinched /pɪntʃt/ *adj*: **faces ~ with grief** caras transidas de dolor

pincushion /ˈpɪnˌkʊʃən/ *n* alfiletero *m*

pine¹ /paɪn/ *n* **(a)** [C] **~ (tree)** pino *m*; (*before n*) **~ cone** piña *f*; **~ needle** hoja *f* de pino **(b)** [U] (wood) (madera *f* de) pino *m*

pine² *vi* estar* triste; **to ~ FOR sth** suspirar POR algo

• pine away [*v + adv*] languidecer* de añoranza

pineapple /ˈpaɪnˌæpəl/ *n* piña *f* *or* (esp RPl) ananá *f*

Ping-Pong®, ping-pong /ˈpɪŋpɑːŋ ‖ ˈpɪŋpɒŋ/ *n* [U] ping-pong *m*

pinion /ˈpɪnjən/ *vt* ‹*person*› inmovilizar* (*esp sujetándole los brazos*)

pink¹ /pɪŋk/ ▶ 515 *adj* **-er, -est** rosa *adj inv*, rosado (AmL); ‹*cheeks*› sonrosado

pink² ▶ 515 *n* [U] rosa *m*, rosado *m* (AmL)

pinking shears /ˈpɪŋkɪŋ/ *pl n* tijeras *fpl* dentadas

pin money *n* [U] *dinero para gastos personales*

pinnacle /ˈpɪnɪkəl ‖ ˈpɪnəkəl/ *n* **(a)** (Archit) pináculo *m* **(b)** (mountain peak) cumbre *f*, cima *f*

pin: **~point** *vt* ‹*position*› localizar* *or* (AmL tb) ubicar* con exactitud; **to ~point the causes of the problem** establecer* con exactitud cuáles son las causas del problema; **~prick** *n* pinchazo *m*; **~s and needles** *pl n* hormigueo *m*; **~stripe, ~striped** *adj*: **~stripe(d) suit** traje *m* oscuro de raya diplomática

pint /paɪnt/ *n* pinta *f* (*EEUU: 0,47 litros, RU: 0,57 litros*)

pinup /ˈpɪnʌp/ *n* foto *f* (*de chica atractiva, actor famoso etc*); (person) pin-up *mf*

pioneer¹ /ˈpaɪəˈnɪr ‖ ˌpaɪəˈnɪə(r)/ *n* pionero, -ra *m,f*

pioneer² *vt* **(a)** ‹*policy*› promover*; ‹*technique*› ser* el primero (*or* la primera *etc*) en aplicar **(b) pioneering** *pres p* ‹*research*› pionero

pious /ˈpaɪəs/ *adj* piadoso; (sanctimonious) beato

pip /pɪp/ *n* **1** (seed) pepita *f* **2** (BrE Rad, Telec) pitido *m*

pipe¹ /paɪp/ *n* **1** (for liquid, gas) caño *m* **2** (for tobacco) pipa *f* **3** (Mus) **(a)** (wind instrument) caramillo *m* **(b)** (of organ) tubo *m* **(c) pipes** *pl* gaita *f*

pipe² *vt* (transport by pipe) (+ *adv compl*) llevar (*por tuberías, gasoducto, oleoducto*)

• pipe down [*v + adv*] (colloq) (*usu in imperative*) callarse la boca (fam)

piped music /paɪpt/ *n* [U] música *f* ambiental, hilo *m* musical (Esp)

pipe: **~ dream** *n* quimera *f*, sueño *m* guajiro (Méx); **~line** *n* conducto *m*, ducto *m* (Méx); ***it's in the ~line*** está proyectado

piper /ˈpaɪpər ‖ ˈpaɪpə(r)/ *n* gaitero, -ra *m,f*

piping¹ /ˈpaɪpɪŋ/ *n* [U] cañería *f*, tubería *f*

piping² *adv* (*as intensifier*): **~ hot** bien caliente

pique¹ /piːk/ *n* [U] despecho *m*

pique² *vt*: **he was ~d by her lack of interest** se resintió por su falta de interés

piracy /ˈpaɪrəsi/ *n* [U] piratería *f*

pirate /ˈpaɪrət/ *n* **(a)** (at sea) pirata *mf* **(b)** (*before n*) ‹*tape/video/radio station*› pirata *adj inv*

pirouette¹ /ˈpɪruˈet/ *n* giro *m*; (in ballet) pirueta *f*

pirouette² *vi* girar

Pisces /ˈpaɪsiːz/ *n* **(a)** (sign) (*no art*) Piscis **(b)** [C] (person) Piscis *or* piscis *mf*

piss¹ /pɪs/ *n* (sl) **(a)** (act) (*no pl*) meada *f* (vulg) **(b)** [U] (urine) meados *mpl* (vulg)

piss² *vi* (sl) mear (vulg)

• **piss off** (sl) **1** [*v* + *adv*] (go away) (BrE): **~ off!** ¡vete a la mierda! (vulg) **2** [*v* + *o* + *adv*] (anger): **it ~es me off** me revienta (fam), me encabrona (Esp, Méx vulg)

pissed /pɪst/ *adj* (sl) **(a)** (AmE) (fed up) cabreado (fam), encabronado (Esp, Méx vulg), choreado (Chi fam) **(b)** (drunk) (BrE) como una cuba (fam), tomado (AmL fam)

pistachio /pɪˈstæʃiəʊ/ *n* **~ (nut)** pistacho *m*, pistache *m* (Méx)

pistol /ˈpɪstl/ *n* pistola *f*

piston /ˈpɪstən/ *n* émbolo *m*, pistón *m*

pit¹ /pɪt/ *n* **1** (hole — in ground) hoyo *m*; (— for burying) fosa *f*; (— as trap) trampa *f*; **(inspection) ~** (Auto) foso *m* *or* (RPl) fosa *f* **2** (coalmine) mina *f* (*de carbón*); (quarry) cantera *f* **3** (*orchestra* **~**) foso *m* orquestal *or* de la orquesta **4 pits** *pl* (the very worst) (sl) **the ~s** lo peor que hay (fam) **5** (in fruit) (AmE) hueso *m*, carozo *m* (CS), pepa *f* (Col)

pit² **-tt-** *vt* ‹*surface/metal*› picar*

• **pit against** [*v* + *o* + *prep* + *o*] enfrentar a; **to ~ oneself against sb** enfrentarse a algn

pitch¹ /pɪtʃ/ *n* **(a)** (level, degree) (*no pl*) punto *m*, extremo *m* **(b)** [U C] (Mus) tono *m* **(c)** [C] (in baseball) lanzamiento *m* **(d)** [C] (Sport) (playing area) (BrE) campo *m*, cancha *f* (AmL) **(e)** [C] (position, site) (BrE) lugar *m*, sitio *m*; (in market, fair) puesto *m* **(f)** [U] (substance) brea *f*

pitch² *vt* **1** (set up) ‹*tent*› armar, montar; ‹*camp*› montar, hacer* **2** (Sport) ‹*ball*› lanzar*, pichear **3** (aim, set, address): **she doesn't know at what level to ~ her talk** no sabe qué nivel darle a la charla ■ **~** *vi* **(a)** (fall) (+ *adv compl*) caerse* **(b)** (lurch) «*ship/plane*» cabecear

• **pitch in** [*v* + *adv*] (colloq) arrimar el hombro

pitch-black /ˈpɪtʃˈblæk/, **pitch-dark** /ˈpɪtʃ ˈdɑːrk ‖ ˌpɪtʃˈdɑːk/ *adj* ▶ **515** ‹*night*› (oscuro) como boca de lobo (fam), muy oscuro; ‹*surface*› negro como el azabache

pitched battle /pɪtʃt/ *n* batalla *f* campal

pitcher /ˈpɪtʃər ‖ ˈpɪtʃə(r)/ *n* **1** (for pouring) jarra *f*, pichel *m* (AmC); (of clay) (BrE) cántaro *m* **2** (in baseball) lanzador, -dora *m,f*, pítcher *mf*

pitchfork /ˈpɪtʃfɔːrk ‖ ˈpɪtʃfɔːk/ *n* horca *f*, horquilla *f*, horqueta *f* (Chi)

pitfall /ˈpɪtfɔːl/ *n* (difficulty) dificultad *f*; (risk) riesgo *m*

pith /pɪθ/ *n* [U] *tejido blanco fibroso que recubre el interior de la cáscara de los cítricos*

pithy /ˈpɪθi/ *adj* **pithier, pithiest** ‹*remark/reply*› sucinto *or* conciso y expresivo

pitiful /ˈpɪtɪfəl/ *adj* **(a)** (arousing pity) ‹*cry/moan*› lastimero; ‹*sight*› lastimoso **(b)** (wretched, inadequate) lamentable

pittance /ˈpɪtn̩s/ *n* miseria *f*

pituitary gland /pəˈtuːəteri ‖ pɪˈtjuːɪtəri/ *n* glándula pituitaria *f*

pity¹ /ˈpɪti/ *n* **1** (*no pl*) (cause of regret) lástima *f*, pena *f*; **it's a ~** (THAT) es una lástima *or* una pena QUE (+ *subj*); **what a ~!** ¡qué lástima!, ¡que pena! **2** [U] (compassion) piedad *f*; **to take ~ on sb/sth** apiadarse de algn/algo

pity² *vt* **pities, pitying, pitied** tenerle* lástima a

pivot /ˈpɪvət/ *vi* (Mech Eng) pivotar; **he ~ed on his heel** giró sobre sus talones

pixie /ˈpɪksi/ *n* (elf) duendecillo *m*; (fairy) hadita *f*

pizza /ˈpiːtsə/ *n* pizza *f*

pizzeria /ˈpiːtsəˈriːə/ *n* pizzería *f*

placard /ˈplækɑːrd ‖ ˈplækɑːd/ *n* letrero *m*; (at demonstration) pancarta *f*

placate /ˈpleɪkeɪt ‖ pləˈkeɪt/ *vt* apaciguar*

place¹ /pleɪs/ *n* **1 (a)** [C] (spot, position, area) lugar *m*, sitio *m*; **to have friends in high ~s** tener* amigos influyentes; ***all over the* ~** por todas partes; ***to fall into* ~** aclararse **(b)** (specific location) lugar *m*; **~ of birth** lugar de nacimiento **(c)** (*in phrases*) **in place**: **to hold sth in ~** sujetar algo; **out of place**: **to look out of ~** «*furniture*» quedar mal; **to feel out of ~** sentirse* fuera de lugar **2** [C] **(a)** (building, shop, restaurant etc) sitio *m*, lugar *m* **(b)** (home): **my/his ~** mi/su casa **3** [C] **(a)** (position, role) lugar *m*; **I wouldn't change ~s with her for anything** no me cambiaría por ella por nada; **nobody can ever take your ~** nadie podrá jamás ocupar tu lugar **(b) in place of** (*as prep*) en lugar de **(c) to take place** (occur) ocurrir; «*meeting/concert/wedding*» tener* lugar **4** [C] **(a)** (seat): **save me a ~** guárdame un asiento **(b)** (at table) cubierto *m*; **to lay/set a ~ for sb** poner* un cubierto para algn **5** [C] (in contest, league) puesto *m*; **your social life will have to take second ~** tu vida social va a tener que pasar a un segundo plano **6** [C] (in book, sequence): **you've made me lose my ~** me has hecho perder la página (*or* la línea *etc*) por donde iba **7** [C] **(a)** (job) puesto *m* **(b)** (BrE Educ) plaza *f* **(c)** (on team) puesto *m*

place² *vt* **1** (put, position) ‹*object*› poner*; (carefully, precisely) colocar* **2** (in race): **this victory ~s her among the top three** este triunfo la sitúa entre las tres primeras **3 (a)** (find a home, job for) colocar* **(b)** ‹*advertisement*› poner*; ‹*phone call*› pedir*; **we ~d an order with Acme Corp** hicimos un pedido a Acme Corp **4** (identify) ‹*tune*› identificar*, ubicar* (AmL); **her face is familiar, but I can't quite ~ her** su cara me resulta conocida pero no sé de dónde *or* (AmL tb) pero no la ubico

placebo /pləˈsiːbəʊ/ *n* (*pl* **~s** *or* **~es**) placebo *m*

place mat *n* (mantel *m*) individual *m*

placement /ˈpleɪsmənt/ *n* **(a)** [C] (in employment) colocación *f* **(b)** [C U] (positioning) colocación *f*, ubicación *f* (esp AmL)

place name *n* topónimo *m*

placenta /pləˈsentə/ *n* (*pl* **~s** *or* **~e** /-tiː/) placenta *f*

placid /ˈplæsəd ‖ ˈplæsɪd/ *adj* plácido

plagiarism /ˈpleɪdʒərɪzəm/ *n* [U C] plagio *m*

plagiarize /ˈpleɪdʒəraɪz/ *vt* plagiar

plague¹ /pleɪg/ *n* **(a)** [U C] (disease) peste *f* **(b)** [C] (horde — of locusts, tourists) plaga *f*

plague² *vt* **(a)** (afflict): **a country ~d by strikes** un país asolado por constantes huelgas; **~d with problems** plagado de problemas **(b)** (pester) acosar

plaice /pleɪs/ *n* [C U] (*pl* ~) platija *f*

plaid /plæd/ *n* [U] (pattern) cuadros *mpl* escoceses; (material) tela *f* escocesa

plain¹ /pleɪn/ *adj* **-er, -est 1 (a)** (unadorned) ‹*decor/cooking/language*› sencillo; ‹*fabric*› liso **(b)** (Culin): **~ chocolate** (BrE) chocolate *m* sin leche; **~ flour** harina *f* común **2 (a)** (clear) claro; **the reasons are ~ to see** las razones saltan a la vista **(b)** (blunt): **the ~ truth** la pura verdad **3** (not good-looking) feo, poco agraciado

plain² *adv* (*as intensifier*) totalmente; **that's just ~ stupid** eso es una completa estupidez

plain³ *n* llanura *f*

plain clothes *pl n*: **in ~ ~** de civil *or* (Esp tb) de paisano

plainly /ˈpleɪnli/ *adv* **(a)** (obviously, visibly) claramente **(b)** (clearly) ‹*explain*› claramente; ‹*remember*› perfectamente **(c)** (bluntly) ‹*speak*› claramente **(d)** ‹*dress*› con sencillez

plaintiff /ˈpleɪntəf ‖ ˈpleɪntɪf/ *n* demandante *mf*

plaintive /ˈpleɪntɪv/ *adj* lastimero

plait¹ /plæt/ *n* trenza *f*

plait² *vt* trenzar*

plan¹ /plæn/ *n* **1 (a)** (diagram, map) plano *m* **(b)** (of book, essay) esquema *m* **2** (arrangement, scheme) plan *m*; **do you have any ~s for tonight?** ¿tienes algún plan para esta noche?

plan² **-nn-** *vt* ‹*journey/raid*› planear; ‹*garden/house*› diseñar; ‹*economy/strategies*› planificar*; ‹*essay*› hacer* un esquema de; ‹*surprise*› preparar; **as ~ned** según lo planeado; **to ~ to** + INF: **where are you ~ning to spend Christmas?** ¿dónde tienes pensado pasar las Navidades? ■ **~** *vi*: **to ~ ahead** planear las cosas de antemano

● **plan on** [*v* + *prep* + *o*] **(a)** (intend) pensar* **(b)** (expect, count on) contar* con

plane¹ /pleɪn/ *n* **1** (aircraft) avión *m* **2 ~ (tree)** plátano *m* **3** (tool) cepillo *m* de carpintero; (longer) garlopa *f* **4** (surface) plano *m*

plane² *vt* ‹*wood/surface*› cepillar

planet /ˈplænət ‖ ˈplænɪt/ *n* planeta *m*

planetary /ˈplænəteri ‖ ˈplænɪtəri/ *adj* (*before n*) planetario

plank /plæŋk/ *n* tabla *f*, tablón *m*

plankton /ˈplæŋktən/ *n* [U] plancton *m*

planned /plænd/ *adj* planeado; **~ parenthood** (AmE) planificación *f* familiar

planner /ˈplænər ‖ ˈplænə(r)/ *n* **(a)** (of project) planificador, -dora *m,f* **(b)** (*town* ~) urbanista *mf*

planning /ˈplænɪŋ/ *n* [U] **(a)** (of project) planificación *f* **(b)** (*town* ~) urbanismo *m*; (*before n*) **~ permission** (BrE) permiso *m* de obras

plant¹ /plænt ‖ plɑːnt/ *n* **1** [C] (Bot) planta *f* **2 (a)** [C] (factory, installation) planta *f* **(b)** [U] (equipment) maquinaria *f*

plant² *vt* **1** ‹*flower/trees*› plantar; ‹*seeds*› sembrar* **2** (place) ‹*bomb*› colocar*; ‹*kiss*› dar*, plantar (fam); **she ~ed herself right next to me** se me plantó justo al lado (fam) **3** ‹*drugs/evidence*› colocar*; ‹*agent/informer*› infiltrar

plantain /ˈplæntn̩ ‖ ˈplæntɪn/ *n* plátano *m* grande (*para cocinar*), plátano *m* (Col, Ven), plátano *m* macho (Méx)

plantation /plænˈteɪʃən ‖ plænˈteɪʃən, plɑːn-/ *n* plantación *f*

plaque /plæk/ *n* **1** [C] (tablet) placa *f* **2** [U] (Dent) sarro *m*, placa *f* (dental)

plasma /ˈplæzmə/ *n* [U] plasma *m*

plaster¹ /ˈplæstər ‖ ˈplɑːstə(r)/ *n* **1** [U] **(a)** (Const) (powder, mixture) yeso *m*; (on walls) revoque *m* **(b) ~ (of Paris)** (Art, Med) yeso *m*, escayola *f* (Esp); **to have one's leg in ~** tener* la pierna enyesada *or* (Esp) escayolada **2** [C] (*sticking* ~) (BrE) ⇒ BAND-AID

plaster² *vt* (Const) ‹*wall/room*› revocar*; ‹*cracks*› rellenar con yeso

plaster cast *n* **(a)** (Med) yeso *m or* (Esp) escayola *f* **(b)** (Art) molde *m* de yeso, escayola *f*

plastic¹ /ˈplæstɪk/ *n* [U C] plástico *m*; (*before n*) de plástico

plastic² *adj* **1** (artificial) (pej) ‹*smile/people*› de plástico (pey) **2 (a)** (malleable) (Tech) plástico, moldeable **(b)** (Art) plástico

plastic: **~ bullet** *n* bala *f* de plástico; **~ explosive** *n* [C U] explosivo *m* plástico, goma(-) dos *f*

Plasticine® /ˈplæstəsiːn/ *n* [U] plastilina® *f*, plasticina® *f* (CS)

plastic: **~ surgeon** *n* cirujano plástico, cirujana plástica *m,f* (AmL), especialista *mf* en cirugía estética *or* plástica; **~ surgery** *n* [U] cirugía *f* estética *or* plástica

plate¹ /pleɪt/ *n* **1 (a)** [C] (dish) plato *m* **(b)** [U] (dishes) vajilla *f* (*de plata u oro*) **2** [C] (of metal) chapa *f*; (thin) lámina *f*; (of glass) placa *f* **3** [C] **(a)** (Phot) placa *f* **(b)** (Art, Print) plancha *f* **(c)** (illustration) ilustración *f*, lámina *f*

plate² *vt* (Metall) **to ~ sth WITH sth** recubrir* algo DE algo

plateau /plæˈtəʊ ‖ ˈplætəʊ/ *n* (*pl* **-teaus** *or* **-teaux** /-z/) meseta *f*

platform /ˈplætfɔːrm ‖ ˈplætfɔːm/ *n* **(a)** (raised structure) plataforma *f*; (for orator) estrado *m*, tribuna *f* **(b)** (Rail) andén *m* **(c)** (Pol) (opportunity to air views) plataforma *f*, tribuna *f*

platinum /ˈplætn̩əm ‖ ˈplætɪnəm/ *n* [U] platino *m*

platitude /ˈplætətuːd ‖ ˈplætɪtjuːd/ *n* lugar *m* común

platonic /pləˈtɑːnɪk ‖ pləˈtɒnɪk/ *adj* platónico

platoon /pləˈtuːn/ *n* (Mil) sección *f*

platter /ˈplætər ‖ ˈplætə(r)/ *n* fuente *f*

platypus /ˈplætɪpəs/ *n* (*pl* **~es**) (*duck-billed* ~) ornitorrinco *m*

plausible /ˈplɔːzəbəl/ *adj* ‹*argument/story*› verosímil; ‹*liar*› convincente

play¹ /pleɪ/ *n* **1 (a)** [U] (recreation) juego *m* **(b)** [U] (Sport) juego *m* **2** [U] (interplay) juego *m* **3** [U] (slack)

(Tech) juego *m* **4** [C] (Theat) obra *f* (de teatro), pieza *f* (teatral), comedia *f* **5** [C] (pun): **a ~ on words** un juego de palabras, un albur (Méx)

play² *vt* **I 1 (a)** ‹*cards/hopscotch*› jugar* a; **to ~ a joke/trick on sb** hacerle* *or* gastarle una broma/ una jugarreta a algn **(b)** ‹*football/chess*› jugar* (AmL exc RPl), jugar* a (Esp, RPl) **2 (a)** (compete against) ‹*opponent*› jugar* contra **(b)** ‹*card*› tirar, jugar*; ‹*piece*› mover* **(c)** (in particular position) jugar* de
II 1 (Theat) **(a)** ‹*villain/Hamlet*› representar el papel de; **to ~ the innocent** hacerse* el inocente **(b)** ‹*theater/town*› actuar* en **2** (Mus) ‹*instrument/note/ piece*› tocar* **3** (Audio) ‹*tape/record*› poner* ■ ~ *vi* **I 1** (amuse oneself) «*children*» jugar*; **to ~ AT sth** jugar* A algo **2** (Games, Sport) jugar*
II 1 (a) (Theat) «*cast*» actuar*; «*show*» ser* representado **(b)** (pretend): **to ~ dead** hacerse* el muerto; ***to ~ hard to get*** hacerse* el (*or* la *etc*) interesante **2** (Mus) «*musician*» tocar*; **music was ~ing in the background** se escuchaba una música de fondo

• **play along 1** [*v* + *adv*] (cooperate): **I refuse to ~ along with him/his schemes** me niego a hacerle el juego/a tener nada que ver con sus enjuagues (fam) **2** [*v* + *o* + *adv*] (deceive, manipulate) manipular

• **play around** [*v* + *adv*] jugar*, juguetear (fam & pey)

• **play back** [*v* + *o* + *adv*, *v* + *adv* + *o*] poner* (*una grabación*)

• **play down** [*v* + *o* + *adv*, *v* + *adv* + *o*] ‹*importance*› minimizar*; ‹*risk/achievement*› quitarle importancia a

• **play off** [*v* + *o* + *adv*] oponer*; ***to ~ sb off against sb***: **she ~s her parents off against each other** hace pelear a sus padres para lograr sus propósitos

• **play up 1** [*v* + *adv*] (BrE) (cause trouble) (colloq) «*child*» dar* guerra (fam); «*car/TV*» no funcionar bien **2** [*v* + *o* + *adv*] (cause trouble) (BrE colloq) «*child*» darle* guerra a (fam); «*shoulder/back*» darle* problemas a (fam)

play: **~back** *n* play-back *m*; **~boy** *n* playboy *m*; **~-by-~** /ˈpleɪbaɪˈpleɪ/ *adj* (AmE Sport) (*before n*) jugada a jugada

player /ˈpleɪər ‖ ˈpleɪə(r)/ *n* **1** (Games, Sport) jugador, -dora *m,f* **2** (Mus) músico *mf*, músico, -ca *m,f*

playful /ˈpleɪfəl/ *adj* **(a)** (boisterous) juguetón **(b)** (not serious) pícaro

playfully /ˈpleɪfəli/ *adv* **(a)** (boisterously) juguetonamente **(b)** (humorously) ‹*remark/slap*› en broma

play: **~ground** *n* (BrE) patio *m* (de recreo); **~group** *n*: *grupo de actividades lúdico-educativas para niños de edad preescolar*

playing /ˈpleɪɪŋ/: **~ card** *n* naipe *m*, carta *f*; **~ field** *n* (BrE) (*often pl*) campo *m* de juego, cancha *f* de deportes (esp AmL)

play: **~mate** *n* compañero, -ra *m,f* de juegos; **~off** *n* desempate *m*; **~pen** *n* corral *m*, parque *m* (Esp); **~room** *n* cuarto *m* de los juguetes; **~thing** *n* juguete *m*; **~time** *n* [U] (*no art*) (BrE) recreo *m*; **~wright** /ˈpleɪraɪt/ *n* dramaturgo, -ga *m,f*

plaza /ˈplæzə ‖ ˈplɑːzə/ *n* **(a)** (square) plaza *f*; (in front of large building) explanada *f* **(b)** (complex) (AmE) centro *m* comercial

plc, **Plc** (in UK) (= **public limited company**) ≈ S.A.

plea /pliː/ *n* **1** (appeal) (frml) petición *f*; (in supplication) ruego *m* **2** (Law): **to enter a ~ of guilty/not guilty** declararse culpable/inocente

plead /pliːd/ (*past & past p* **pleaded** *or* (AmE also) **pled**) *vt* alegar*; **she's not coming, she ~ed poverty** no viene, dijo que no tenía dinero ■ ~ *vi* **(a)** (implore, beg) suplicar*; **to ~ FOR sth** suplicar* algo; **to ~ WITH sb to** + INF suplicarle* a algn QUE (+ *subj*) **(b)** (Law): **to ~ guilty/not guilty** declararse culpable/inocente

pleasant /ˈpleznt/ *adj* **-er, -est** agradable; ‹*person*› simpático, agradable

pleasantly /ˈplezntli/ *adv* ‹*say/speak*› en tono agradable; ‹*smile*› con simpatía; **I was ~ surprised by the changes** los cambios me causaron una grata sorpresa

pleasantry /ˈplezntri/ *n* (*pl* **-ries**) cortesía *f*

please¹ /pliːz/ *interj* por favor; **yes, ~** sí, gracias

please² *vt* (make happy) complacer*; (satisfy) contentar ■ ~ *vi* **(a)** (satisfy): **we do our best to ~** hacemos todo lo posible por complacer al cliente (*or* a todo el mundo *etc*) **(b)** (choose) querer*; **do as you ~** haz lo que quieras ■ *v refl* **to ~ oneself**: **~ yourself** haz lo que quieras

pleased /pliːzd/ *adj* (satisfied) satisfecho; (happy) contento; **I'm very ~ for you!** me alegro mucho por ti; **she was very ~ with herself** estaba muy ufana; **I am ~ to inform you that** ... (frml) tengo el placer de comunicarle que ... (frml); **~ to meet you** encantado (de conocerlo), mucho gusto

pleasing /ˈpliːzɪŋ/ *adj* **(a)** (pleasant) agradable **(b)** (gratifying) ‹*news*› grato

pleasurable /ˈpleʒərəbəl/ *adj* placentero

pleasure /ˈpleʒər ‖ ˈpleʒə(r)/ *n* **1** [U] (happiness, satisfaction) placer *m*; **it's a ~ to listen to her** es un placer escucharla; **it gives me great ~ to introduce** ... es un placer para mí presentarles ...; **to take ~ in sth** disfrutar con algo **2 (a)** [U] (recreation) placer *m*; **I play just for ~** toco sólo porque me gusta **(b)** [C] (source of happiness) placer *m*; **Jane is a real ~ to teach** da gusto darle clases a Jane

pleasure boat *n* (steamer) barco *m* de recreo; (small craft) bote *m* de recreo

pleat /pliːt/ *n* pliegue *m*; (wide) tabla *f*

plectrum /ˈplektrəm/ *n* (*pl* **-trums** *or* **-tra** /-trə/) púa *f*, plectro *m*, uñeta *f* (CS), uña *f* (Méx, Ven)

pled /pled/ (AmE) *past & past p of* PLEAD

pledge¹ /pledʒ/ *vt* ‹*support/funds*› prometer

pledge² *n* **(a)** (promise) promesa *f*; **to make a ~ to** + INF prometer + INF **(b)** (of money) cantidad *f* prometida

plentiful /ˈplentɪfəl/ *adj* abundante

plenty¹ /ˈplenti/ *n* [U] abundancia *f*

plenty² *pron* **1 (a)** (large, sufficient number) muchos, -chas **(b) plenty of** muchos, -chas **2 (a)** (large, sufficient quantity) mucho, -cha; **$50 is ~** 50 dólares es más que suficiente **(b) plenty of** mucho, -cha; **~ of time** tiempo de sobra

plethora /'pleθərə/ *n* (*no pl*) **a ~ OF sth** una plétora DE algo

Plexiglas® /'pleksɪglæs ‖ 'pleksɪglɑ:s/ *n* [U] (AmE) acrílico *m*, plexiglás® *m* (Esp)

pliable /'plaɪəbəl/, **pliant** /'plaɪənt/ *adj* ‹*material/substance*› maleable; ‹*person/attitude*› flexible

pliers /'plaɪərz ‖ 'plaɪəz/ *pl n* alicate(s) *m(pl)*, pinza(s) *f(pl)* (Méx, RPl)

plight /plaɪt/ *n* (*no pl*) situación *f* difícil

plimsoll /'plɪmsəl/ *n* (BrE) zapatilla *f* de lona, tenis *m*, playera *f* (Esp)

plinth /plɪnθ/ *n* (of pillar, column) plinto *m*; (of statue) pedestal *m*

plod /plɑ:d ‖ plɒd/ *vi* **-dd- (a)** (walk) caminar lenta y pesadamente **(b)** (work): **she's still ~ding away at her thesis** sigue lidiando con la tesis

plonk¹ /plɑ:ŋk ‖ plɒŋk/ *vt* (BrE colloq) ⇒ PLUNK

plonk² *n* [U] (colloq) vino *m* peleón (fam)

plot¹ /plɑ:t ‖ plɒt/ *n* **1** (conspiracy) complot *m* **2** (story) argumento *m* **3** (piece of land) terreno *m*, solar *m*, parcela *f*

plot² **-tt-** *vt* **1** (mark out) ‹*curve/graph*› trazar*; ‹*position*› determinar **2** (plan) ‹*rebellion/revenge*› tramar ■ **~** *vi* **to ~ (AGAINST sb)** conspirar (CONTRA algn)

plotter /'plɑ:tər ‖ 'plɒtə(r)/ *n* **1** (conspirator) conspirador, -dora *m,f* **2** (Comput, Tech) trazador *m* de gráficos

plough *etc* /plaʊ/ (BrE) ⇒ PLOW *etc*

plow¹, (BrE) **plough** /plaʊ/ *n* (Agr) arado *m*

plow², (BrE) **plough** *vt* arar ■ **~** *vi* arar la tierra

• **plow back,** (BrE) **plough back** [*v + o + adv, v + adv + o*] ‹*profits*› reinvertir*

• **plow into**, (BrE) **plough into** [*v + prep + o*] ‹*vehicle/wall*› estrellarse contra

• **plow through**, (BrE) **plough through** [*v + prep + o*] ‹*mud/snow*› abrirse* camino a través de; **I'm still ~ing through the book** todavía estoy tratanto de leer el libro, pero me cuesta

plowman, (BrE) **ploughman** /'plaʊmən/ *n* (*pl* **-men** /-mən/) labrador *m*

ploy /plɔɪ/ *n* treta *f*

pluck¹ /plʌk/ *vt* **(a)** ‹*chicken*› desplumar; **to ~ one's eyebrows** depilarse las cejas **(b)** ‹*fruit/flower*› arrancar*; **to ~ up (the) courage to +** INF armarse de valor para + INF **(c)** (Mus) ‹*string/guitar*› puntear

pluck² *n* [U] valor *m*

plucky /'plʌki/ *adj* **pluckier, pluckiest** valiente

plug¹ /plʌg/ *n* **1** (stopper) tapón *m* **2** (Elec) **(a)** (attached to lead) enchufe *m*; (socket) toma *f* de corriente, enchufe *m*, tomacorriente(s) *m* (AmL) **(b)** (*spark ~*) bujía *f*

plug² **-gg-** *vt* **1** ‹*hole/gap*› tapar **2** (promote) ‹*record/book*› hacerle* propaganda a

• **plug in 1** [*v + o + adv, v + adv + o*] enchufar **2** [*v + adv*] enchufarse

plughole /'plʌghəʊl/ *n* (BrE) desagüe *m*

plum /plʌm/ *n* ciruela *f*

plumage /'plu:mɪdʒ/ *n* [U] plumaje *m*

plumb¹ /plʌm/ *adv* (colloq) justo

plumb² *vt* **1** (fathom) ‹*mystery*› dilucidar **2** (Naut) sondar, sondear

plumber /'plʌmər ‖ 'plʌmə(r)/ *n* plomero, -ra *m,f or* (AmC, Esp) fontanero, -ra *m,f or* (Per) gasfitero, -ra *m,f or* (Chi) gásfiter *mf*

plumbing /'plʌmɪŋ/ *n* [U] (pipes) cañerías *fpl*, tuberías *fpl*; (installation) instalación *f* de agua

plume /plu:m/ *n* pluma *f*; (cluster of feathers) penacho *m*

plummet /'plʌmət ‖ 'plʌmɪt/ *vi* caer* en picada *or* (Esp) en picado

plump /plʌmp/ *adj* **-er, -est** ‹*person/face*› (re)llenito; ‹*chicken/rabbit*› gordo

• **plump for** [*v + prep + o*] (colloq) decidirse por

• **plump up** [*v + o + adv, v + adv + o*] ‹*pillow/cushion*› ahuecar*

plunder¹ /'plʌndər ‖ 'plʌndə(r)/ *vt* **(a)** (steal from) ‹*village*› saquear **(b)** (steal) ‹*treasure/wealth*› robar

plunder² *n* [U] **(a)** (objects) botín *m* **(b)** (action) saqueo *m*

plunge¹ /plʌndʒ/ *vt* **to ~ sth INTO sth (a)** (immerse, thrust) ‹*into liquid*› sumergir* algo EN algo; **she ~d the knife into his heart** le hundió el cuchillo en el corazón **(b)** (into state, condition) sumir algo/a algn EN algo ■ **~** *vi* **1** (dive) zambullirse*; (fall) caer* **2 (a)** (slope downward steeply) «*road/path*» descender* bruscamente **(b)** (drop) «*price/temperature/popularity*» caer* en picada *or* (Esp) en picado

plunge² *n* (in water) zambullida *f*; ***to take the ~*** (take a risk) arriesgarse*, jugarse* el todo por todo; (get married) casarse, darse* el paso

plunger /'plʌndʒər ‖ 'plʌndʒə(r)/ *n* **(a)** (for unblocking drain) desatascador *m*, chupona *f* (Esp), destapador *m* (de caño) (Méx), sopapa *f* (RPl), sopapo *m* (Chi), chupa *f* (Col), goma *f* (Ven) **(b)** (in syringe) émbolo *m*

plunk /plʌŋk/ *vt* (AmE) poner*, plantificar* (fam)

pluperfect /'plu:'pɜ:rfɪkt ‖ ˌplu:'pɜ:fɪkt/ *n* pluscuamperfecto *m*

plural¹ /'plʊrəl ‖ 'plʊərəl/ *adj* (Ling) en plural

plural² *n* plural *m*; **in the ~** en plural

plus¹ /plʌs/ *n* (*pl* **~es** *or* **~ses**) **(a) ~ (sign)** (signo *m* de) más *m* **(b)** (advantage, bonus) (colloq) ventaja *f*

plus² *adj* **(a)** (advantageous) (colloq) (*before n*) ‹*point*› positivo **(b)** (and more) (*pred*): **children aged 13 ~** niños de 13 años para arriba

plus³ *prep* más; **~ the fact that** … aparte de que …; ⇒ FOUR¹

plush /plʌʃ/ *adj* lujoso

Pluto /'plu:təʊ/ *n* Plutón *m*

plutonium /plu:'təʊniəm/ *n* [U] plutonio *m*

ply¹ /plaɪ/ *n* (*pl* **plies**) **(a)** (of wood) chapa *f* **(b)** (of wool, yarn) cabo *m*; **three-~ wool** lana *f* de tres cabos

ply² **plies, plying, plied** *vt* **(a)** (carry out): **to ~ one's trade** ejercer* su oficio **(b)** ‹*oar*› mover*; ‹*tools*› manejar **(c)** «*ship*» ‹*sea*› navegar* por ■ **~** *vi* (frml) «*ship/plane/bus*» hacer* el trayecto

• **ply with** [*v + o + prep + o*]: **he kept ~ing**

me with whiskey estaba constantemente sirviéndome whisky

plywood /'plaɪwʊd/ *n* [U] contrachapado *m* (*tablero en varias capas*)

pm ▶ 884 (after midday) p.m.; **at 2 ~** a las 2 de la tarde, a las 2 p.m.

PM (BrE) *n* = **prime minister**

PMS *n* [U] = **premenstrual syndrome**

PMT *n* [U] (BrE) = **premenstrual tension**

pneumatic drill /nʊ'mætɪk ‖ njuː'mætɪk/ *n* martillo *m* neumático

pneumonia /nʊ'məʊnjə ‖ njuː'məʊniə/ *n* [U] pulmonía *f*, neumonía *f*

poach /pəʊtʃ/ *vt* **1** (Culin) ‹*egg*› escalfar; ‹*fish*› cocer* a fuego lento **2** (steal) ‹*game*› cazar* furtivamente; ‹*staff/ideas*› robar ■ ~ *vi* (hunt game) cazar* furtivamente

poacher /'pəʊtʃər ‖ 'pəʊtʃə(r)/ *n* cazador furtivo, cazadora furtiva *m,f*

PO box *n* Apdo. postal, Apdo. de correos, C.C. (CS)

pocket¹ /'pɑːkət ‖ 'pɒkɪt/ *n* **1 (a)** (in garment) bolsillo *m* **(b)** (on billiard, snooker, pool table) tronera *f* **2** (small area) bolsa *f*; **~s of resistance** bolsas *fpl* de resistencia

pocket² *vt* **(a)** (put in pocket) meterse en el bolsillo **(b)** (steal, gain) (colloq) embolsarse (fam)

pocket³ *adj* (*before n*) de bolsillo

pocket: **~book** /'pɑːkətbʊk ‖ 'pɒkɪtbʊk/ *n* **(a)** (handbag) (AmE) cartera *f or* (Esp) bolso *m or* (Méx) bolsa *f* **(b)** (wallet) (AmE) cartera *f*, billetera *f* **(c)** (paperback) (AmE) libro *m* en rústica **(d)** (notebook) (BrE) cuaderno *m*; **~ money** *n* [U] (spending money) dinero *m* para gastos personales; (for children) (BrE) dinero *m* de bolsillo, ≈ mesada *f* (AmL), domingo *m* (Méx), propina *f* (Per)

pod /pɑːd ‖ pɒd/ *n* (of peas, beans) vaina *f*

podiatrist /pə'daɪətrəst ‖ pə'daɪətrɪst/ *n* (AmE) pedicuro, -ra *m,f*, podólogo, -ga, *m,f* (frml)

podium /'pəʊdiəm/ *n* estrado *m*

poem /'pəʊəm ‖ 'pəʊɪm/ *n* poema *m*

poet /'pəʊət ‖ 'pəʊɪt/ *n* poeta *mf*

poetic /pəʊ'etɪk/ *adj* poético

poet laureate, **Poet Laureate** /'lɔːriət ‖ 'lɒriət/ *n* (*pl* **~s ~**) poeta laureado, poeta laureada *m,f*

poetry /'pəʊətri ‖ 'pəʊɪtri/ *n* [U] poesía *f*

poignant /'pɔɪnjənt/ *adj* ‹*story/moment*› conmovedor; ‹*look/plea*› patético; ‹*reminder*› doloroso

point¹ /pɔɪnt/ *n* **I 1** [C] **(a)** (dot) punto *m* **(b)** ▶ 543 (*decimal* **~**) ≈ coma *f*, punto *m* decimal (AmL) (*the point is used instead of the comma in some Latin American countries*) **2 (a)** (in space) punto *m*; **the ~s of the compass** los puntos cardinales; ***the ~ of no return***: **we've reached the ~ of no return** ahora ya no nos podemos echar atrás **(b)** (on scale) punto *m*; **you're right, up to a ~** hasta cierto punto tienes razón **3** (in time) momento *m*; **at this ~ in time** en este momento; **to be on the ~ of** -ING estar* a punto de + INF **4** (in contest, exam) punto *m*

II 1 [C] **(a)** (item, matter) punto *m*; **to bring up** *o* **raise a ~** plantear una cuestión; ***to make a ~ of*** -ING: **I'll make a ~ of watching them closely** me encargaré de vigilarlos de cerca **(b)** (argument): **yes, that's a ~** sí, ese es un punto interesante; **to make a ~: that was a very interesting ~ you made** lo que señalaste es muy interesante; **all right, you've made your ~!** sí, bueno, ya has dicho lo que querías decir; **~ taken** de acuerdo **2** (*no pl*) (central issue, meaning): **to come/get to the ~** ir* al grano; **she was brief and to the ~** fue breve y concisa; **that's beside the ~** eso no tiene nada que ver, eso no viene al caso; **the ~ is that** ... el hecho es que ...; **that's not the ~** no se trata de eso **3** [U] (purpose): **what's the ~ of going on?** ¿qué sentido tiene seguir?; **there's no ~** *o* **there isn't any ~ (in) feeling sorry for yourself** no sirve de nada compadecerse **4** [C] (feature, quality): **strong ~** fuerte *m*; **bad ~s** defectos *mpl*; **he has many good ~s** tiene muchos puntos a su favor

III 1 [C] **(a)** (sharp end, tip) punta *f* **(b)** (promontory) (Geog) punta *f* **2 points** *pl* (BrE Rail) agujas *fpl* **3** [C] (socket) (BrE) **(electrical** *o* **power) ~** toma *f* de corriente, tomacorriente *m* (AmL)

point² *vt* (aim, direct) señalar, indicar*; **to ~ sth** AT **sb/sth: he ~ed his finger at me** me señaló con el dedo; **she ~ed the gun at him** le apuntó con la pistola ■ ~ *vi* **(a)** (with finger, stick etc) señalar; **it's rude to ~** es de mala educación señalar con el dedo; **to ~** AT/TO **sth/sb** señalar algo/a algn **(b)** (call attention) **to ~** TO **sth** señalar algo **(c)** (indicate) **to ~** TO **sth** «*facts/symptoms*» indicar* algo

● **point out** [*v + o + adv, v + adv + o*] **1** (show) señalar; **I'll ~ it/her out to you** te/lo la señalaré **2** (make aware of) ‹*problem/advantage*› señalar

point: **~ blank** *adv* ‹*shoot*› a quemarropa; **~-blank** /'pɔɪnt'blæŋk/ *adj*: **at ~-blank range** a quemarropa

pointed /'pɔɪntəd ‖ 'pɔɪntɪd/ *adj* **1** (with a point) ‹*stick/leaf*› acabado en punta, puntudo (Andes); ‹*arch*› ojival; ‹*chin/nose*› puntiagudo, puntudo (Andes); ‹*shoe*› de punta, puntudo (Andes); ‹*hat*› de pico **2** (deliberate) ‹*remark/comment*› mordaz

pointer /'pɔɪntər ‖ 'pɔɪntə(r)/ *n* **1** (on dial, gage) aguja *f* **2 (a)** (clue, signal) pista *f*; **~** TO **sth** indicador *m* DE algo **(b)** (tip) idea *f*

pointless /'pɔɪntləs ‖ 'pɔɪntlɪs/ *adj* ‹*attempt*› vano, inútil; ‹*existence*› sin sentido; **it's ~ arguing with him** no tiene sentido discutir con él

point of view *n* (*pl* **~s ~ ~**) punto *m* de vista

poise /pɔɪz/ *n* [U] **(a)** (bearing) porte *m* **(b)** (composure) desenvoltura *f*

poised /pɔɪzd/ *adj* **1 (a)** (balanced, suspended): **~ in the air** suspendido en el aire; **they were waiting with pencils ~** esperaban, lápiz en mano **(b)** (ready) listo **2** (self-assured): **she is very ~** tiene mucho aplomo

poison¹ /'pɔɪzn̩/ *n* [C U] veneno *m*

poison² *vt* **(a)** (with poison) envenenar; (make ill) intoxicar*; ‹*river/soil*› contaminar **(b)** (corrupt) ‹*mind/society*› corromper; ‹*relationship/atmosphere*› dañar

poisoning /'pɔɪznɪŋ/ *n* [U C] envenenamiento *m*

poisonous /'pɔɪznəs/ *adj* venenoso

poison-pen letter /'pɔɪzn̩'pen/ *n* anónimo *m* ponzoñoso

poke¹ /pəʊk/ *vt* **(a)** (jab): **to ~ sb's eye out** sacarle* un ojo a algn; **she ~d him in the ribs** le dio en el costado; (with elbow) le dio un codazo en el costado **(b)** (thrust): **she ~d her head around the door** asomó la cabeza por la puerta; **he ~d his finger through the crack** metió el dedo por la ranura ■ ~ *vi* (project) asomar; **her feet were poking out of the sheets** los pies le asomaban por entre las sábanas; **a few shoots were poking up out of the soil** unos cuantos brotes asomaban en la tierra

• **poke about**, **poke around** [*v* + *adv*] fisgonear

poke² *n* golpe *m*; (with elbow) codazo *m*

poker /'pəʊkər ‖ 'pəʊkə(r)/ *n* **1** [C] (for fire) atizador *m* **2** [U] (game) póker *m*, póquer *m*

poky /'pəʊki/ *adj* **pokier, pokiest** (colloq) **(a)** (cramped) diminuto **(b)** (slow) (AmE) lerdo

Poland /'pəʊlənd/ *n* Polonia *f*

polar /'pəʊlər ‖ 'pəʊlə(r)/ *adj* polar

polar bear *n* oso *m* polar

polarize /'pəʊləraɪz/ *vt* polarizar*

pole /pəʊl/ *n* **1** (fixed support) poste *m*; (*flag*~) mástil *m*; (*tent* ~) palo *m* **2 (a)** (Geog) polo *m*; **the North/South P~** el Polo Norte/Sur **(b)** (Phys) polo *m*

Pole *n* polaco, -ca *m,f*

polecat *n* **(a)** (of weasel family) turón *m* **(b)** (AmE) ⇨ SKUNK

polemical /pə'lemɪkəl/ *adj* polémico

pole: **~star**, (BrE) **P~ Star** *n* estrella *f* polar; **~-vault** *n* salto *m* con garrocha *or* (Esp) con pértiga

police¹ /pə'li:s/ *n* (force) (+ *sing or pl vb*) **the ~** la policía; (*before n*) ‹*escort*/*patrol*› policial; **~ car** coche *m* patrulla *or* de policía; **~ constable** (in UK) agente *mf*; **~ department** (in US) distrito *m* policial; **the ~ force** la policía; **~ officer** agente *mf*, policía *mf*; **to have a ~ record** estar* fichado *or* (CS tb) prontuariado

police² *vt* (keep order in) ‹*streets*› patrullar; ‹*region*/*area*› mantener* una fuerza policial en

police: **~ dog** *n* perro *m* policía; **~man** /pə'li:smən/ *n* (*pl* **-men** /-mən/) policía *m*, agente *m*; **~ state** *n* estado *m* policía; **~ station** *n* comisaría *f*; **~woman** *n* agente *f*, policía *f*, mujer *f* policía

policy /'pɑ:ləsi ‖ 'pɒləsi/ *n* (*pl* **-cies**) **1** [U C] **(a)** (Pol) política *f* **(b)** (standard practice, plan) (Busn) política *f*; **it is good/bad ~** es/no es recomendable **2** [C] (*insurance* ~) (contract) seguro *m*; (document) póliza *f* de seguros

policyholder /'pɑ:ləsi'həʊldər ‖ 'pɒləsi,həʊldə(r)/ *n* asegurado, -da *m,f*

polio /'pəʊliəʊ/ *n* [U] polio *f*

poliomyelitis /'pəʊliəʊ'maɪə'laɪtəs ‖ ,pəʊliəʊ,maɪə'laɪtɪs/ *n* [U] poliomielitis *f*

polish¹ /'pɑ:lɪʃ ‖ 'pɒlɪʃ/ *n* **(a)** [U C] (*shoe* ~) betún *m*, pomada *f* (RPl), pasta *f* (Chi); (*furniture* ~) cera *f* para muebles, lustramuebles *m* (CS); (*metal* ~) limpiametales *m*; (*floor* ~) (esp BrE) abrillantador *m* (de suelos); (*wax* ~) cera *f* (abrillantadora) **(b)** [C] (sheen) brillo *m* **(c)** [U] (refinement): **he lacks ~** tiene que pulir su estilo

polish² *vt* **(a)** ‹*floor*/*table*/*car*/*brass*› darle* *or* sacarle* brillo a; ‹*shoes*› limpiar, lustrar (esp AmL), bolear (Méx), embolar (Col); ‹*lens*/*mirror*› limpiar; ‹*stone*› (by abrasion) pulir **(b)** (refine) pulir

• **polish off** [*v* + *o* + *adv*, *v* + *adv* + *o*] (colloq) ‹*food*› liquidarse (fam)

Polish¹ /'pəʊlɪʃ/ *adj* polaco

Polish² *n* [U] polaco *m*

polished /'pɑ:lɪʃt ‖ 'pɒlɪʃt/ *adj* **(a)** (shiny) ‹*metal*/*marble*› pulido; ‹*wood*› brillante, lustrado (esp AmL) **(b)** (refined) ‹*manners*/*accent*› refinado; ‹*performance*/*translation*› pulido

polite /pə'laɪt/ *adj* **politer, politest** ‹*manner*/*person*› cortés; **they were making ~ conversation** conversaban tratando de ser agradables; **it's not ~ to shout** gritar es una falta de educación

politely /pə'laɪtli/ *adv* ‹*behave*› correctamente; ‹*ask*/*refuse*› con buenos modales

politeness /pə'laɪtnəs ‖ pə'laɪtnɪs/ *n* cortesía *f*

political /pə'lɪtɪkəl/ *adj* político

politically correct /pə'lɪtɪkli/ *adj* ‹*term*› usado por gente de ideología progresista

politician /'pɑ:lə'tɪʃən ‖ ,pɒlɪ'tɪʃən/ *n* político, -ca *m,f*

politics /'pɑ:lətɪks ‖ 'pɒlətɪks/ *n* **1** (+ *sing vb*) (science, activity) política *f* **2** (+ *pl vb*) (political relations) política *f*

polka /'pəʊlkə ‖ 'pɒlkə, 'pəʊlkə/ *n* polca *f*, polka *f*

polka dot /'pəʊkə, pəʊlkə ‖ 'pɒlkə, 'pəʊlkə/ *n* lunar *m*, topo *m* (Esp)

poll¹ /pəʊl/ *n* **(a)** (ballot) votación *f* **(b)** (*opinion* ~) encuesta *f or* sondeo *m* (de opinión)

poll² *vt* (Pol) ‹*votes*› (obtain) obtener*; (cast) emitir

pollen /'pɑ:lən ‖ 'pɒlən/ *n* [U] polen *m*

pollinate /'pɑ:ləneɪt ‖ 'pɒləneɪt/ *vt* polinizar*

polling /'pəʊlɪŋ/ *n* [U] votación *f*; **~ place** *o* (BrE) **station** centro *m* electoral

pollute /pə'lu:t/ *vt* (Ecol) contaminar

pollution /pə'lu:ʃən/ *n* [U] contaminación *f*

polo /'pəʊləʊ/ *n* [U] polo *m*

polo: **~ neck** *n* (BrE) **(a)** (style of neck) cuello *m* alto **(b)** ⇨ ~ NECK SWEATER; **~ neck sweater** *n* (BrE) suéter *m* de cuello alto, polera *f* (RPl)

poly- /'pɑ:li ‖ 'pɒli/ *pref* poli-

polyester /'pɑ:li'estər ‖ ,pɒli'estə(r)/ *n* [U C] poliéster *m*

polyethylene /'pɑ:li'eθəli:n ‖ ,pɒli'eθəli:n/ *n* [U] (esp AmE) polietileno *m*

polygamy /pə'lɪgəmi/ *n* [U] poligamia *f*

Polynesia /'pɑ:lə'ni:ʒə ‖ ,pɒlɪ'ni:ʒə/ *n* (la) Polinesia

Polynesian /'pɑ:lə'ni:ʒən ‖ ,pɒlɪ'ni:ʒən/ *adj* polinesio

polystyrene /'pɑ:li'staɪri:n ‖ ,pɒli'staɪri:n/ *n* [U C] poliestireno *m*

polythene /'pɑ:ləθi:n ‖ 'pɒlɪθi:n/ *n* [U] (BrE) plástico *m*, polietileno *m* (téc)

pomegranate /'pɑ:məgrænət ‖ 'pɒmɪgrænɪt/ *n* granada *f*

pomp /pɑːmp ‖ pɒmp/ *n* [U] pompa *f*, fausto *m*

pompom /ˈpɑːmpɑːm ‖ ˈpɒmpɒm/ *n* (on hat) borla *f*, pompón *m*

pompous /ˈpɑːmpəs ‖ ˈpɒmpəs/ *adj* pomposo

pond /pɑːnd ‖ pɒnd/ *n* (man-made) estanque *m*; (natural) laguna *f*

ponder /ˈpɑːndər ‖ ˈpɒndə(r)/ *vt* considerar

ponderous /ˈpɑːndərəs ‖ ˈpɒndərəs/ *adj* ‹*movement*› lento y pesado; ‹*explanation/speech*› pesado

pong¹ /pɑːŋ ‖ pɒŋ/ *n* [C U] (BrE colloq) peste *f* (fam)

pong² *vi* (BrE colloq) apestar (fam)

pontiff /ˈpɑːntəf ‖ ˈpɒntɪf/ *n* pontífice *m*

pony /ˈpəʊni/ *n* (*pl* **ponies**) poni *m*

ponytail /ˈpəʊniteɪl/ *n* cola *f* de caballo

poodle /ˈpuːdl/ *n* caniche *m*

pooh-pooh /ˈpuːˈpuː/ *vt* (colloq) reírse* de

pool¹ /puːl/ *n* **1** [C] **(a)** (collection of water) charca *f* **(b)** (*swimming* ~) piscina *f*, pileta *f* (RPl), alberca *f* (esp Méx) **(c)** (puddle) charco *m* **2** [C] (common reserve of money) fondo *m* común **3 pools** *pl* (BrE) ⇒ FOOTBALL POOLS **4** [U] (billiards) billar *m* americano, pool *m*

pool² *vt* hacer* un fondo común de

pooped (out) /puːpt/ *adj* (AmE sl) (*pred*) reventado (fam)

poor /pɔːr ‖ pɔːr, pʊə(r)/ *adj* **-er, -est 1** (not wealthy) pobre **2** (unsatisfactory, bad) ‹*harvest*› pobre, escaso; ‹*diet/quality*› malo; ‹*imitation*› burdo **3** (unfortunate) (*before n*) pobre; **you ~ thing!** ¡pobrecito!

poorly¹ /ˈpʊrli ‖ ˈpɔːli, ˈpʊəli/ *adj* (*pred*) (esp BrE) mal

poorly² *adv* ‹*perform/play*› mal

pop¹ /pɑːp ‖ pɒp/ *n* **1** (noise): **to go ~** hacer 'pum'; (burst) reventar* **2** [U] (Mus) música *f* pop **3** [U] (Culin) gaseosa *f* **4** [C] (father) (AmE colloq) papá *m* (fam)

pop² -pp- *vi* **1** «*balloon*» estallar, reventar(se)*; «*cork*» saltar; **my ears ~ped** se me destaparon los oídos **2** (spring) saltar; **his eyes were ~ping (out of his head)** los ojos se le salían de las órbitas **3** (go casually) (colloq): **to ~ out** salir* un momento; **he just ~ped in to say hello** pasó un minuto a saludar ■ ~ *vt* **1** (burst) ‹*balloon*› reventar*, hacer* estallar **2** (put quickly, casually): **she ~ped her head around the door** asomó la cabeza por la puerta; **~ it into your pocket** métetelo en el bolsillo
• **pop up** [*v* + *adv*] (colloq) **(a)** (rise) «*toast*» saltar; **his head ~ped up from behind the wall** asomó la cabeza por encima del muro **(b)** (appear) aparecer*

pop³ *adj* **(a)** (popular) ‹*sociology/culture*› popular; ‹*music/singer*› (AmE) popular **(b)** (BrE Mus) pop *adj inv*

popcorn /ˈpɑːpkɔːrn ‖ ˈpɒpkɔːn/ *n* [U] palomitas *fpl* (de maíz), cabritas *fpl* (de maíz) (Chi), pororó *m* (RPl), maíz *m* pira *or* tote (Col)

pope /pəʊp/ *n* papa *m*

poplar /ˈpɑːplər ‖ ˈpɒplə(r)/ *n* álamo *m* (blanco)

poppa /ˈpɑːpə ‖ ˈpɒpə/ *n* (AmE) papá *m* (fam)

poppy /ˈpɑːpi ‖ ˈpɒpi/ *n* (*pl* **-pies**) amapola *f*, adormidera *f*

Popsicle® /ˈpɑːpsɪkəl ‖ ˈpɒpsɪkəl/ *n* (AmE) paleta *f* (helada) *or* (Esp) polo *m or* (RPl) palito *m or* (CS) chupete *m* helado

populace /ˈpɑːpjələs ‖ ˈpɒpjʊləs/ *n* (+ *sing o pl vb*) **the ~** (common people) el pueblo; (population) la población

popular /ˈpɑːpjʊlər ‖ ˈpɒpjʊlə(r)/ *adj* **1 (a)** (well-liked) popular; **she is ~ with her students** goza de popularidad entre sus alumnos **(b)** ‹*resort/restaurant*› muy frecuentado; ‹*brand/product*› popular **2 (a)** (not highbrow, specialist) ‹*music/literature*› popular **(b)** (of populace) ‹*feeling*› popular; ‹*rebellion*› del pueblo, popular; **by ~ demand/request** a petición *or* (AmL tb) a pedido del público **(c)** (widespread) ‹*belief/notion*› generalizado

popularity /ˌpɑːpjəˈlærəti ‖ ˌpɒpjʊˈlærəti/ *n* [U] popularidad *f*

popularize /ˈpɑːpjələraɪz ‖ ˈpɒpjʊləraɪz/ *vt* **(a)** (make popular) popularizar* **(b)** (make accessible) divulgar*

populate /ˈpɑːpjəleɪt ‖ ˈpɒpjʊleit/ *vt* poblar*

population /ˌpɑːpjəˈleɪʃən ‖ ˌpɒpjʊˈleɪʃən/ *n* población *f*; (*before n*) **~ explosion** explosión *f* demográfica

porcelain /ˈpɔːrsələn ‖ ˈpɔːsəlɪn/ *n* [U] porcelana *f*

porch /pɔːrtʃ ‖ pɔːtʃ/ *n* **(a)** (covered entrance) porche *m* **(b)** (veranda) (AmE) porche *m*, galería *f*

porcupine /ˈpɔːrkjəpaɪn ‖ ˈpɔːkjʊpaɪn/ *n* puercoespín *m*

pore /pɔːr ‖ pɔː(r)/ *n* poro *m*
• **pore over** [*v* + *prep* + *o*] estudiar minuciosamente

pork /pɔːrk ‖ pɔːk/ *n* [U] (carne *f* de) cerdo *m*, (carne *f* de) puerco *m* (Méx), chancho *m* (Chi, Per), marrano *m* (Col)

pornographic /ˈpɔːrnəˈgræfɪk ‖ ˌpɔːnəˈgræfɪk/ *adj* pornográfico

pornography /pɔːrˈnɑːgrəfi ‖ pɔːˈnɒgræfi/ *n* [U] pornografía *f*

porous /ˈpɔːrəs/ *adj* poroso

porpoise /ˈpɔːrpəs ‖ ˈpɔːpəs/ *n* marsopa *f*

porridge /ˈpɔːrɪdʒ ‖ ˈpɒrɪdʒ/ *n* [U] avena *f* (*cocida*), gachas *fpl* (*de avena*) (Esp); (*before n*) **~ oats** copos *mpl* de avena

port¹ /pɔːrt ‖ pɔːt/ *n* **1** [C] (for ships) puerto *m*; (*before n*) ‹*authority/tax/regulation*› portuario **2** [U] (left side) babor *m* **3** [C] **(a)** (for loading) (Aviat, Naut) porta *f* **(b)** (Comput) puerto *m* **4** [U] (Culin) oporto *m*, vino *m* de Oporto

port² *adj* (*before n*) ‹*lights*› de babor

portable /ˈpɔːrtəbəl ‖ ˈpɔːtəbəl/ *adj* portátil

portcullis /pɔːrtˈkʌləs ‖ ˌpɔːtˈkʌlɪs/ *n* rastrillo *m*

portend /pɔːrˈtend ‖ pɔːˈtend/ *vt* (liter) augurar

portent /ˈpɔːrtent ‖ ˈpɔːtent/ *n* augurio *m*, presagio *m*

porter /ˈpɔːrtər ‖ ˈpɔːtə(r)/ *n* **1** (at station, airport) maletero *m*, changador *m* (RPl); (on expedition) porteador *m*; (in hospital) (BrE) camillero *m* **2** (in hotel, apartment block) portero *m*

portfolio /pɔːrtˈfəʊliəʊ ‖ pɔːtˈfəʊliəʊ/ *n* (*pl* **-lios**) **1 (a)** (case) portafolio(s) *m* **(b)** (samples of work) carpeta *f* de trabajos **2** (Pol) cartera *f*

porthole /ˈpɔːrthəʊl ‖ ˈpɔːthəʊl/ *n* (Naut) ojo *m* de buey, portilla *f*

portion /ˈpɔːrʃən ‖ ˈpɔːʃən/ *n* **(a)** (of food) porción *f* (esp AmL), ración *f* (esp Esp) **(b)** (share, part) parte *f*

portrait /ˈpɔːrtrət, -treɪt ‖ ˈpɔːtrɪt, -treɪt/ *n* retrato *m*

portray /pɔːrˈtreɪ ‖ pɔːˈtreɪ/ *vt* **(a)** (depict) «*picture*» representar **(b)** (describe, represent) ‹*person/scene*› describir*

portrayal /pɔːrˈtreɪəl ‖ pɔːˈtreɪəl/ *n* [U C] (Art) representación *f*; (Lit) descripción *f*; (Theat) interpretación *f*

Portugal /ˈpɔːrtʃɪgəl ‖ ˈpɔːtjʊgl/ *n* Portugal *m*

Portuguese¹ /ˈpɔːrtʃəˈgiːz ‖ ˌpɔːtjʊˈgiːz/ *adj* portugués

Portuguese² *n* (*pl* ~) **(a)** [U] (language) portugués *m* **(b)** [C] (person) portugués, -guesa *m,f*

pose¹ /pəʊz/ *vt* ‹*threat*› representar; ‹*problem/question*› plantear ■ ~ *vi* **(a)** (Art, Phot) posar **(b)** (put on an act) hacerse* el interesante **(c)** (pretend to be) **to ~ AS sb/sth** hacerse* pasar POR algn/algo

pose² *n* **(a)** (position of body) pose *f*, postura *f* **(b)** (assumed manner) pose *f*, afectación *f*

poser /ˈpəʊzər ‖ ˈpəʊzə(r)/ *n* **(a)** (question) pregunta *f* difícil; (problem) dilema *m* **(b)** (person) (BrE colloq) ⇒ POSEUR

poseur /pəʊˈzɜːr ‖ pəʊˈzɜː(r)/ *n*: **he's a real ~** todo en él es pura pose *or* afectación

posh /pɑːʃ ‖ pɒʃ/ *adj* **-er, -est** (esp BrE colloq) elegante, pijo (Esp fam), posudo (Col fam), pituco (CS fam), cheto (RPl fam), sifrino (Ven fam), popoff (Méx fam)

position¹ /pəˈzɪʃən/ *n* **1 (a)** (location) posición *f*, ubicación *f* (esp AmL) **(b)** (Sport) posición *f* **2 (a)** (posture) posición *f* **(b)** (stance, point of view) postura *f* **3 (a)** (in league) puesto *m* **(b)** (job, post) (frml) puesto *m* **4** (situation, circumstances) situación *f*; **I'm not in a ~ to help them** no estoy en condiciones de prestarles ayuda

position² *vt* colocar*, poner*

positive /ˈpɑːzətɪv ‖ ˈpɒzətɪv/ *adj* **1** ‹*number/quantity*› positivo; ‹*electrode*› positivo; **the test was ~** (Med) el análisis dio positivo **2** (constructive) ‹*attitude*› positivo; ‹*criticism*› constructivo **3** (definite): **there is no ~ evidence** no hay pruebas concluyentes **4** (absolute) (*before n*) ‹*disgrace/outrage*› auténtico **5** (sure) (colloq) (*pred*): **are you sure? — positive** ¿estás seguro? — segurísimo

positively /ˈpɑːzətɪvli ‖ ˈpɒzətɪvli/ *adv* **1** (constructively): **to think ~** ser* positivo; **they reacted ~** tuvieron una reacción/respuesta positiva **2 (a)** (definitely) ‹*prove*› de forma concluyente **(b)** (absolutely) ‹*delighted/furious*› verdaderamente

posse /ˈpɑːsi ‖ ˈpɒsi/ *n* (in US) partida *f* (*al mando de un sheriff*)

possess /pəˈzes/ *vt* **1** (own) tener*, poseer* (frml) **2** (influence) «*anger/fear*» apoderarse de; **whatever can gave ~ed him to say such a thing?** ¿qué lo habrá llevado a decir semejante cosa?

possessed /pəˈzest/ *adj* (*pred*) **to be ~ (by the devil)** estar* endemoniado

possession /pəˈzeʃən/ *n* **(a)** [C] (sth owned) bien *m* **(b)** [U] (ownership) posesión *f*; (of arms) tenencia *f*

possessive /pəˈzesɪv/ *adj* posesivo

possessor /pəˈzesər ‖ pəˈzesə(r)/ *n* dueño, -ña *m,f*, poseedor, -dora *m,f*

possibility /ˈpɑːsəˈbɪləti ‖ ˌpɒsəˈbɪləti/ *n* [U C] posibilidad *f*

possible /ˈpɑːsəbəl ‖ ˈpɒsəbəl/ *adj* posible; **get here by eight if ~** llega antes de las ocho, si es posible; **as little as ~** lo menos posible

possibly /ˈpɑːsəbli ‖ ˈpɒsəbli/ *adv* **(a)** (conceivably): **I couldn't ~ eat any more** me es totalmente imposible comer nada más; **could you ~ give me a hand with this?** ¿sería tan amable de ayudarme con esto? **(b)** (perhaps) (*indep*) posiblemente

post¹ /pəʊst/ *n* [U] **1** [C] (pole) poste *m* **2** [U] (mail) (esp BrE) correo *m*; **to send sth by ~** *o* **through the ~** mandar *or* enviar* algo por correo; **it's in the ~** ya ha sido enviado; **the first/second ~** (delivery) el primer/segundo reparto; (collection) la primera/segunda recogida **3** [C] (job) puesto *m*

post² *vt* **1 (a)** (position) ‹*policeman/soldier*› apostar **(b)** (send) ‹*employee/diplomat*› destinar **2** (mail) (esp BrE) ‹*letter/parcel*› echar al correo; (drop in postbox) echar al buzón; **to ~ sth to sb** mandarle *or* enviarle* algo a algn (por correo)

post- /pəʊst/ *pref* post-, pos-

postage /ˈpəʊstɪdʒ/ *n* [U] franqueo *m*; **~ and handling** (AmE), **~ and packing** (BrE) gastos *mpl* de envío

postage: **~ paid** *adv* con franqueo pagado; **~ stamp** *n* (frml) sello *m* (de correos), estampilla *f* (AmL), timbre *m* (Méx)

postal /ˈpəʊstl̩/ *adj* (*before n*) postal

postal order *n* (BrE) ≈ giro *m* postal

post: **~box** *n* (BrE) buzón *m*; **~card** *n* tarjeta *f* postal, postal *f*; **~code** *n* (BrE) código *m* postal

postdate /ˈpəʊstˈdeɪt/ *vt* ‹*contract/check*› posfechar, diferir* (RPl)

poster /ˈpəʊstər ‖ ˈpəʊstə(r)/ *n* cartel *m*, póster *m*

posterity /pɑːˈsterəti ‖ pɒˈsterəti/ *n* [U] posteridad *f*

postgraduate /pəʊstˈgrædʒuət/ *n* estudiante *mf* de postgrado; (*before n*) ‹*student/research*› de postgrado

posthumous /ˈpɑːstʃəməs ‖ ˈpɒstjʊməs/ *adj* póstumo

posting /ˈpəʊstɪŋ/ *n* destino *m*

postman /ˈpəʊstmən/ *n* (*pl* **-men** /-mən/) (esp BrE) cartero *m*

postmark¹ /ˈpəʊstmɑːrk ‖ ˈpəʊstmɑːk/ *n* matasellos *m*

postmark² *vt* matasellar

postmortem /ˈpəʊstˈmɔːrtəm ‖ ˌpəʊstˈmɔːtəm/ *n* (esp BrE Med) autopsia *f*

postnatal /ˈpəʊstˈneɪtl̩/ *adj* postnatal

post office *n* oficina *f* de correos, correo *m* (AmL), estafeta *f* de correos (Esp)

postpone /pəʊsˈpəʊn ‖ pəˈspəʊn/ *vt* aplazar*, posponer*, postergar* (esp AmL)

postponement /pəʊsˈpəʊnmənt ‖ pəˈspəʊnmənt/ *n* [U C] aplazamiento *m*, postergación *f* (esp AmL)

postscript /'pəʊstskrɪpt/ *n* (to letter) postdata *f*; (to book) epílogo *m*

posture /'pɑːstʃər ‖ 'pɒstʃə(r)/ *n* [U C] postura *f*

postwar /'pəʊst'wɔːr ‖ ˌpəʊst'wɔː(r)/ *adj* (*before n*) de la posguerra

posy /'pəʊzi/ *n* (*pl* **posies**) ramillete *m*

pot¹ /pɑːt ‖ pɒt/ *n* **1** [C] **(a)** (*cooking* ~) olla *f*; **~s and pans** cacharros *mpl* (fam), trastes *mpl* (Méx); ***to go to*** **~** (colloq) echarse a perder **(b)** (for jam, honey etc) tarro *m*, bote *m* (Esp) **(c)** (*tea*~) tetera *f*; (*coffee*~) cafetera *f* **(d)** (in pottery) vasija *f* **2** [C] (*flower*~) maceta *f*, tiesto *m* (Esp)

pot² *vt* **-tt-** ‹*plant*› plantar (*en una maceta*)

potash /'pɑːtæʃ ‖ 'pɒtæʃ/ *n* [U] potasa *f*

potassium /pə'tæsiəm/ *n* [U] potasio *m*

potato /pə'teɪtəʊ/ *n* [U C] (*pl* **-toes**) papa *f or* (Esp) patata *f*; (*before n*) **~ chips** *o* (BrE) **crisps** papas *fpl or* (Esp) patatas *fpl* fritas; **~ peeler** pelapapas *m or* (Esp) pelapatatas *m*

potbelly /'pɑːt'beli ‖ ˌpɒt'beli/ *n* barriga *f* (fam), panza *f* (fam), guata *f* (Chi fam)

potency /'pəʊtn̩si/ *n* [U] **(a)** (of drink) lo fuerte **(b)** (*sexual* ~) potencia *f* sexual

potent /'pəʊtn̩t/ *adj* **1** ‹*drink/drug/medicine*› fuerte **2** (Physiol) potente

potential¹ /pə'tentʃəl ‖ pə'tenʃəl/ *n* [U] (capacity) potencial *m*; (possibilities) posibilidades *fpl*

potential² *adj* (*before n*) ‹*danger*› potencial; ‹*leader*› en potencia

potentially /pə'tentʃəli ‖ pə'tenʃəli/ *adv* potencialmente

pot: **~hole** *n* **(a)** (cave) cueva *f* subterránea; (hole) sima *f* **(b)** (in road) bache *m*; **~holing** /'pɑːtˌhəʊlɪŋ ‖ 'pɒtˌhəʊlɪŋ/ *n* [U] (BrE) espeleología *f*

potion /'pəʊʃən/ *n* poción *f*, pócima *f*

pot: **~luck** /'pɑːt'lʌk ‖ ˌpɒt'lʌk/ *n* [U]: **to take ~luck** conformarse con lo que haya; **~ plant** *n* planta *f* (*cultivada en una maceta*), mata *f* (Col, Ven); **~shot** *n* (Dep) tiro *m* al azar

potted /'pɑːtəd ‖ 'pɒtɪd/ *adj* (*before n*) **(a)** ‹*plant*› en maceta *or* tiesto **(b)** ‹*account/version*› resumido

potter¹ /'pɑːtər ‖ 'pɒtə(r)/ *n* alfarero, -ra *m,f*

potter² *vi* (BrE) (+ *adv compl*) ⇨ PUTTER²

pottery /'pɑːtəri ‖ 'pɒtəri/ *n* (*pl* **-ries**) **(a)** [U] (vessels) cerámica *f* **(b)** [C] (workshop) alfarería *f* **(c)** [U] (craft) alfarería *f*

potty¹ /'pɑːti ‖ 'pɒti/ *n* (*pl* **-ties**) (colloq) orinal *m* (*para niños*) (fam), bacinica *f* (AmL exc RPl), pelela *f* (CS fam); **he's ~-trained** ya no usa pañales

potty² *adj* **-tier, -tiest** (BrE colloq) chiflado (fam)

pouch /paʊtʃ/ *n* **1 (a)** (small bag) bolsa *f* **(b)** (for correspondence) (AmE) valija *f* **2** (Anat, Zool) bolsa *f*

poultice /'pəʊltəs ‖ 'pəʊltɪs/ *n* cataplasma *f*

poultry /'pəʊltri/ *n* [U] **(a)** (birds) (+ *pl vb*) aves *fpl* de corral **(b)** (meat) carne *f* de ave

pounce /paʊns/ *vi* saltar; **to ~ ON/UPON sb/sth** abalanzarse* SOBRE algn/algo

pound¹ /paʊnd/ *n* **1** ▶ **322** (measure) libra *f* (*454 gramos*) **2** (Fin) libra *f*; (*before n*) **a ~ coin** una moneda de (una) libra **3** (enclosure — for cars) depósito *m*; (— for dogs) perrera *f*

pound² *vt* **(a)** ‹*corn/spices*› machacar*; ‹*garlic/chili*› majar **(b)** ‹*table/door*› aporrear; **the waves ~ed the wall** las olas batían contra el muro ■ **~** *vi* **(a)** (strike, beat) aporrear **(b)** «*heart*» palpitar; «*sound*» retumbar; **my head is ~ing** tengo la cabeza a punto de reventar

pour /pɔːr ‖ pɔː(r)/ *vt* **(a)** (+ *adv compl*) ‹*liquid*› verter*, echar; ‹*salt/powder*› echar; **he ~ed the tea down the sink** tiró el té por el fregadero **(b)** **~ (out)** (serve) ‹*drink*› servir* ■ **~** *vi* (+ *adv compl*) «*blood*» manar; «*water/sweat*» salir* ■ **~** *v impers* ▶ **920** diluviar, llover* a cántaros

• **pour out 1** [*v* + *o* + *adv*, *v* + *adv* + *o*] **(a)** ⇨ POUR *vt* (b) **(b)** (emotionally): **he ~ed out his feelings** reveló sus sentimientos; **she ~ed her heart out to him** se desahogó con él **2** [*v* + *adv*] salir*

pouring /'pɔːrɪŋ/ *adj*: **he went out in the ~ rain** salió en medio de una lluvia torrencial

pout /paʊt/ *vi* hacer* un mohín

poverty /'pɑːvərti ‖ 'pɒvəti/ *n* [U] pobreza *f*

poverty-stricken /'pɑːvərtiˌstrɪkən ‖ 'pɒvətiˌstrɪkən/ *adj* pobrísimo

POW *n* = **prisoner of war**

powder¹ /'paʊdər ‖ 'paʊdə(r)/ *n* [U] **(a)** polvo *m* **(b)** (*face* ~) polvo(s) *m*(*pl*) (de tocador); (*before n*) **~ puff** borla *f*, cisne *m* (RPl)

powder² *vt* **1** (cover) empolvar; **to ~ one's nose** retocarse* el maquillaje; (euph) lavarse las manos (euf) **2 powdered** *past p* ‹*milk/eggs*› en polvo; **~ed sugar** (AmE) azúcar *m or f* glas, azúcar *m or f* flor (Chi), azúcar *m or f* impalpable (RPl), azúcar *m or f* en polvo (Col)

powdery /'paʊdəri/ *adj* como polvo

power¹ /'paʊər ‖ 'paʊə(r)/ *n* **1 (a)** [U] (control, influence) poder *m*; (of country) poderío *m*, poder *m*; **to be in ~** estar* en el poder **(b)** [U C] (official authority) poder *m*; **~ to** + INF poder PARA + INF **2** [C] **(a)** (nation) potencia *f* **(b)** (person, group): **the ~s that be** los que mandan; **the ~s of darkness** las fuerzas del mal **3** [U] **(a)** (physical strength, force) fuerza *f* **(b)** (of engine, loudspeaker, transmitter) potencia *f* **4 (a)** [U] (ability, capacity): **I did everything in my ~** hice todo lo que estaba en mi(s) mano(s) **(b)** (specific faculty) (*often pl*): **he lost the ~ of speech** perdió el habla; **~(s) of concentration** capacidad *f* de concentración **5** [U] **(a)** (Eng, Phys) potencia *f*; (particular source of energy) energía *f* **(b)** (electricity) electricidad *f*; (*before n*) **~ lines** cables *mpl* de alta tensión; **~ point** (BrE) toma *f* de corriente, enchufe *m*, tomacorriente *m* (AmL) **6** (a lot) (colloq): **to do sb a ~ of good** hacerle* a algn mucho bien

power² *vt*: **the plane is ~ed by four engines** el avión está propulsado por cuatro motores

power: **~boat** *n* lancha *f* de motor, lancha *f* motora (Esp); **~ cut** *n* apagón *m*

powerful /'paʊərfəl ‖ 'paʊəfəl/ *adj* **(a)** ‹*country*› poderoso **(b)** ‹*shoulders/arms*› fuerte **(c)** ‹*performance/image*› impactante; ‹*argument*› poderoso; ‹*incentive*› poderoso **(d)** ‹*engine/weapon/drug*› potente; ‹*smell/current*› fuerte

powerless /'paʊərləs ‖ 'paʊəlɪs/ *adj* impotente; **they were ~ to prevent it** no pudieron hacer nada para impedirlo

power: ~ **of attorney** *n* (*pl* **~s of attorney**) (Law) poder *m* (notarial); ~ **plant** *n* (AmE) ⇒ ~ STATION; ~ **station** *n* central *f* eléctrica, usina *f* eléctrica (AmS)

pp. (= **pages**) págs.

PR¹ *n* [U] **(a)** = **public relations (b)** = **proportional representation**

PR² = **Puerto Rico**

practicable /'præktɪkəbəl/ *adj* factible

practical¹ /'præktɪkəl/ *adj* **(a)** práctico; **for all ~ purposes** a efectos prácticos **(b)** (feasible) factible

practical² *n* (Educ) práctica *f*

practicality /'præktɪ'kæləti/ *n* **1** [U] (of scheme/idea) lo práctico **2 practicalities** *pl* aspectos *mpl* prácticos

practical joke *n* broma *f*

practically /'præktɪkli/ *adv* **1** (virtually) casi, prácticamente **2** (in a practical way) ‹*consider/think*› con sentido práctico

practice¹ /'præktəs ‖ 'præktɪs/ *n* **1** [U] (training, repetition) práctica *f*; **he's out of ~** le falta práctica; **piano ~** ejercicios *mpl* de piano; ~ **teaching** *o* (BrE) **teaching ~** prácticas *fpl* de magisterio; ~ ***makes perfect*** la práctica hace al maestro **2** [U] **(a)** (carrying out, implementing) práctica *f*; **to put sth into ~** llevar algo a la práctica; **in ~** en la práctica **(b)** (exercise of profession) ejercicio *m* **3** [C U] (custom, procedure) costumbre *f* **4** [C] (Med) consultorio *m*

practice², (BrE) **practise** *vt* **1** (rehearse) practicar*; ‹*song/act*› ensayar **2** «*doctor/lawyer*» ejercer* **3 practicing** *pres p* **(a)** ‹*doctor/lawyer*› en ejercicio (de su profesión) **(b)** ‹*Catholic*› practicante ■ ~ *vi* **1** (rehearse, train) practicar* **2** (professionally) ejercer*

practitioner /præk'tɪʃn̩ər ‖ præk'tɪʃn̩ə(r)/ *n* médico, -ca *m,f*

pragmatic /præg'mætɪk/ *adj* pragmático

pragmatism /'prægmətɪzəm/ *n* [U] pragmatismo *m*

Prague /prɑːg/ *n* Praga *f*

prairie /'preri ‖ 'preəri/ *n* [C U] pradera *f*; **the ~(s)** (in US) la Pradera

prairie dog *n* perro *m* de las praderas

praise¹ /preɪz/ *n* [U] **(a)** (credit, applause) elogios *mpl*; ***to sing sth's/sb's ~s*** poner* algo/a algn por las nubes **(b)** (Relig) alabanza *f*

praise² *vt* **(a)** (compliment) elogiar **(b)** (Relig) alabar

praiseworthy /'preɪz,wɜːrði ‖ 'preɪz,wɜːði/ *adj* digno de elogio

pram /præm/ *n* (BrE) cochecito *m*

prance /præns ‖ prɑːns/ *vi* **(a)** «*horse*» brincar* **(b)** (pej) «*person*»: **she ~d into the room wearing her new dress** entró meneándose con el vestido nuevo

• **prance about** [*v* + *adv*] brincar*

prank /præŋk/ *n* broma *f*; (of child) travesura *f*

prat /præt/ *n* (BrE sl) imbécil *mf*

prattle /'prætl̩/ *vi* «*adult*» cotorrear (fam); «*child*» balbucear

prawn /prɔːn/ *n* (large) langostino *m*, camarón *m* (AmL); (medium) camarón *m* (AmL), gamba *f* (esp Esp), langostino *m* (CS); (small) camarón *m*, quisquilla *f* (Esp)

pray /preɪ/ *vi* rezar*, orar (frml)

prayer /prer ‖ preə(r)/ *n* [U C] oración *f*

pre- /'priː/ *pref* **(a)** (in advance): **~planned** planeado de antemano **(b)** (before): **a ~dinner drink** una copa antes de cenar

preach /priːtʃ/ *vt* **(a)** (Relig) predicar*; ‹*sermon*› dar* **(b)** (advocate) ‹*doctrine/ideas*› preconizar* ■ ~ *vi* predicar*

preacher /'priːtʃər ‖ 'priːtʃə(r)/ *n* **(a)** (one who preaches) predicador, -dora *m,f* **(b)** (minister) (AmE) pastor, -tora *m,f*

prearrange /'priːə'reɪndʒ/ *vt* **(a)** (arrange in advance) concertar* de antemano **(b) prearranged** *past p* ‹*meeting*› concertado de antemano; ‹*signal/place/time*› convenido

precarious /prɪ'keriəs ‖ prɪ'keəriəs/ *adj* precario

precaution /prɪ'kɔːʃən/ *n* precaución *f*; **as a ~** por *or* como precaución

precautionary /prɪ'kɔːʃəneri ‖ prɪ'kɔːʃənəri/ *adj* preventivo

precede /prɪ'siːd/ *vt* (frml) preceder a ■ ~ *vi* **(a)** (come before) preceder **(b) preceding** *pres p* anterior

precedence /'presədəns/ *n* [U] precedencia *f*

precedent /'presədənt/ *n* [C U] precedente *m*; **to set a ~ (for sth)** sentar* precedente (para algo)

precept /'priːsept/ *n* precepto *m*

precinct /'priːsɪŋkt/ *n* **1 (a)** (delimited zone) (BrE): **shopping ~** centro *m*/zona *f* comercial **(b)** (AmE) (police district) distrito *m* policial; (police station) comisaría *f* **(c)** (voting district) (AmE) circunscripción *f*, distrito *m* electoral **2 precincts** *pl* (of city) límites *mpl*; (of cathedral, castle, hospital) recinto *m*, predio(s) *m(pl)* (esp AmL)

precious¹ /'preʃəs/ *adj* **1 (a)** (valuable) ‹*jewel/object*› precioso; **~ metal** metal *m* precioso; **~ stone** piedra *f* preciosa **(b)** (dear) querido **(c)** (iro): **her ~ son** su queridísimo hijo (iró) **2** (affected) preciosista

precious² *adv* (colloq) (*as intensifier*): **~ few** muy pocos; **she's done ~ little to help** bien poco ha hecho para ayudar

precipice /'presəpəs ‖ 'presɪpɪs/ *n* precipicio *m*

precipitate /prɪ'sɪpəteɪt ‖ prɪ'sɪpɪteɪt/ *vt* (frml) precipitar

precipitation /prɪ'sɪpə'teɪʃən ‖ prɪ,sɪpɪ'teɪʃən/ *n* [U] **(a)** (Meteo) precipitaciones *fpl* **(b)** (Chem) precipitación *f*

precis, **précis** /preɪ'siː, 'preɪsiː ‖ 'preɪsiː/ *n* (*pl* ~ /-z/) resumen *m*

precise /prɪ'saɪs/ *adj* **(a)** (accurate) ‹*calculations/measurements*› exacto; ‹*description/instructions*› preciso **(b)** (specific) preciso; **there were about 60, 59 to be ~** había unos 60, 59 para ser exacto *or* preciso **(c)** (meticulous) minucioso

precisely /prɪ'saɪsli/ *adv* **(a)** (accurately) ‹*calculate/measure/describe*› con precisión **(b)** (exactly): **we have ~ one hour** tenemos exactamente una hora; **at two o'clock ~** a las dos en punto; **precisely!** ¡exacto!, ¡justamente!

precision /prɪ'sɪʒən/ *n* [U] precisión *f*; (*before n*) ‹*instrument/tool*› de precisión

preclude /prɪ'klu:d/ *vt* (frml) ‹*possibility*› excluir*

precocious /prɪ'kəʊʃəs/ *adj* precoz

preconceived /'pri:kən'si:vd/ *adj* (*before n*) preconcebido

preconception /'pri:kən'sepʃən/ *n* idea *f* preconcebida

precondition /'pri:kən'dɪʃən/ *n* condición *f* previa

precursor /prɪ'kɜ:rsər ‖ prɪ'kɜ:sə(r)/ *n* (frml) precursor, -sora *m,f*

predate /'pri:'deɪt/ *vt* (frml) **(a)** (precede) ser* anterior a **(b)** ‹*document/letter*› antedatar (frml)

predator /'predətər ‖ 'predətə(r)/ *n* depredador *m*, predador *m*

predatory /'predətɔ:ri ‖ 'predətri/ *adj* ‹*animal*› predador, depredador; ‹*person*› rapaz

predecessor /'predəsesər ‖ 'pri:dɪsesə(r)/ *n* predecesor, -sora *m,f*

predestine /'pri:'destən ‖ ,pri:'destɪn/ *vt* predestinar

predetermine /'pri:dɪ'tɜ:rmən ‖ ,pri:dɪ'tɜ:mɪn/ *vt* predeterminar

predicament /prɪ'dɪkəmənt/ *n* aprieto *m*

predicative /prɪ'dɪkətɪv/ *adj* predicativo

predict /prɪ'dɪkt/ *vt* predecir*

predictable /prɪ'dɪktəbəl/ *adj* ‹*result/outcome*› previsible; **you're so ~** siempre sales con lo mismo

predictably /prɪ'dɪktəbli/ *adv* de manera previsible

prediction /prɪ'dɪkʃən/ *n* (forecast) pronóstico *m*, predicción *f*; (prophecy) profecía *f*

predispose /'pri:dɪs'pəʊz/ *vt* (frml) predisponer*

predominance /prɪ'dɑ:mənəns ‖ prɪ'dɒmɪnəns/ *n* [U] predominio *m*

predominant /prɪ'dɑ:mənənt ‖ prɪ'dɒmɪnənt/ *adj* predominante

predominantly /prɪ'dɑ:mənəntli ‖ prɪ'dɒmɪnəntli/ *adv* predominantemente

predominate /prɪ'dɑ:məneɪt ‖ prɪ'dɒmɪneɪt/ *vi* predominar

pre-eminent /pri:'emənənt ‖ pri:'emɪnənt/ *adj* (frml) preeminente

pre-empt /pri:'empt/ *vt* ‹*attack/move*› adelantarse a

pre-emptive /pri:'emptɪv/ *adj* ‹*strike/attack*› preventivo

preen /pri:n/ *vt* ‹*feathers*› arreglar con el pico ■ *v refl* **to ~ oneself** «*bird*» arreglarse las plumas con el pico; «*person*» acicalarse

pre-exist /'pri:ɪg'zɪst/ *vi* (frml) **(a)** preexistir **(b)** **pre-existing** *pres p* preexistente

prefab /'pri:fæb/ *n* (colloq) vivienda *f* prefabricada

prefabricated /'pri:'fæbrɪkeɪtɪd/ *adj* prefabricado

preface /'prefəs ‖ 'prefɪs/ *n* (to book, speech) prefacio *m*; (to event) prólogo *m*

prefect /'pri:fekt/ *n* **1** (BrE Educ) *alumno encargado de la disciplina*, ≈ monitor, -tora *m,f* **2** (official) prefecto *m*

prefer /prɪ'fɜ:r ‖ prɪ'fɜ:(r)/ *vt* **-rr-** preferir*; **to ~ sth** TO **sth** preferir* algo A algo; **to ~ to** + INF preferir* + INF

preferable /'prefərəbəl/ *adj* preferible

preferably /'prefərəbli/ *adv* (*indep*) preferentemente; **I'd like a size 10, ~ in red** quisiera la talla 10, de ser posible en rojo

preference /'prefərəns/ *n* [C U] preferencia *f*; **~** FOR **sth** preferencia POR algo

preferential /'prefə'rentʃəl ‖ ,prefə'renʃəl/ *adj* (*before n*) preferente, preferencial; **to give ~ treatment to sb** dar* trato preferente *or* preferencial a algn

prefix /'pri:fɪks/ *n* prefijo *m*

pregnancy /'pregnənsi/ *n* [U C] (*pl* **-cies**) (of woman) embarazo *m*; (of animal) preñez *f*

pregnant /'pregnənt/ *adj* **1** ‹*woman*› embarazada; ‹*cow/mare*› preñada **2** (liter) (meaningful) ‹*pause/silence*› elocuente, preñado de significado (liter)

preheat /'pri:'hi:t/ *vt* precalentar*

prehistoric /'pri:hɪ'stɔ:rɪk ‖ ,pri:hɪ'stɒrɪk/ *adj* prehistórico

prejudge /'pri:'dʒʌdʒ/ *vt* prejuzgar*

prejudice[1] /'predʒədəs ‖ 'predʒʊdɪs/ *n* [U C] prejuicio *m*

prejudice[2] *vt* **1** (influence) predisponer* **2** (harm) ‹*case/claim*› perjudicar*

prejudiced /'predʒədəst ‖ 'predʒʊdɪst/ *adj* lleno de prejuicios, prejuiciado (AmL)

preliminary[1] /prɪ'lɪməneri ‖ prɪ'lɪmɪnəri/ *adj* preliminar

preliminary[2] *n* (*pl* **-ries**) **(a)** (preamble) prolegómeno *m* **(b)** **preliminaries** *pl* (Sport) etapa *f* de clasificación previa, preliminares *mpl or fpl*

prelude /'prelju:d/ *n* **(a)** (introduction) **~** (TO **sth**) preludio *m* (DE algo) **(b)** (Mus) preludio *m*

premature /'pri:mə'tʊr ‖ 'premətjʊə(r)/ *adj* prematuro

prematurely /'pri:mə'tʊrli ‖ 'premətjʊəli/ *adv* prematuramente

premeditated /pri:'medəteɪtəd ‖ pri:'medɪteɪtɪd/ *adj* premeditado

premenstrual /'pri:'menstruəl/ *adj* premenstrual; **~ syndrome/tension** síndrome *m*/tensión *f* premenstrual

premier /prɪ'mɪr ‖ 'premiə(r)/ *n* primer ministro, primera ministra *m,f*, premier *mf*

premiere, première /prɪ'mɪr ‖ 'premɪeə(r)/ *n* estreno *m*

premise /'preməs ‖ 'premɪs/ *n* **1** (Phil) premisa *f* **2** **premises** *pl* (building, site) local *m*; **they've moved to new ~s** se han mudado a un nuevo local (*or* a nuevas oficinas *etc*); **meals are cooked on the ~s** las comidas se preparan en el mismo establecimiento

premium /'pri:miəm/ *n* (Fin) **(a)** (*insurance ~*) prima *f* (de seguro) **(b)** (surcharge) recargo *m*; ***to be***

at a **~** (in short supply) escasear; (lit: above par) estar* por encima de la par **(c)** (bonus) prima *f*

Premium Bond *n* (in UK) *bono del Estado que permite ganar dinero participando en sorteos mensuales*

premonition /ˈpriːməˈnɪʃən, ˈprem-/ *n* premonición *f*

prenatal /ˈpriːˈneɪtl̩/ *adj* (esp AmE) ⇒ ANTENATAL

preoccupation /priːˈɑːkjəˈpeɪʃən ‖ ˌpriːɒkjʊˈpeɪʃən/ *n* [C U] **1** (obsession) obsesión *f* **2** (concern): **my main ~ was not to offend my parents** mi mayor preocupación/lo que más me importaba era no ofender a mis padres

preoccupied /priːˈɑːkjəpaɪd ‖ ˌpriːˈɒkjʊpaɪd/ *adj* (absorbed) absorto; (worried) preocupado

preoccupy /priːˈɑːkjəpaɪ ‖ ˌpriːˈɒkjʊpaɪ/ *vt* **-pies, -pying, -pied** preocupar

prepaid /ˈpriːˈpeɪd/ *adj* ‹*envelope*› con franqueo pagado; ‹*advertisement/insertion*› pagado por adelantado

preparation /ˈprepəˈreɪʃən/ *n* **1 (a)** [U] (act) preparación *f* **(b)** [C] **preparations** *pl* (arrangements) preparativos *mpl* **2** [C U] (substance) preparado *m*

preparatory /prɪˈpærətɔːri ‖ prɪˈpærətri/ *adj* preparatorio

preparatory school *n* (frml) **(a)** (in US) *colegio secundario privado* **(b)** (in UK) *colegio primario privado*

prepare /prɪˈper ‖ prɪˈpeə(r)/ *vt* preparar ■ ~ *vi* **to ~ (FOR sth)** prepararse (PARA algo)

prepared /prɪˈperd ‖ prɪˈpeəd/ *adj* **(a)** (ready in advance) ‹*speech/statement*› preparado; **I wasn't ~ for this** no contaba con esto **(b)** (willing) (*pred*) **to be ~ to** + INF estar* dispuesto A + INF

preposition /ˈprepəˈzɪʃən/ *n* preposición *f*

prepossessing /ˈpriːpəˈzesɪŋ/ *adj* (frml) (*usu neg*) atractivo

preposterous /prɪˈpɑːstərəs/ *adj* absurdo

prep school /prep/ *n* ⇒ PREPARATORY SCHOOL (b)

prerequisite /ˈpriːˈrekwəzət ‖ ˌpriːˈrekwɪzɪt/ *n* requisito *m* esencial

prerogative /prɪˈrɑːgətɪv ‖ prɪˈrɒgətɪv/ *n* prerrogativa *f*; **that's your ~** estás en todo tu derecho

Pres (title) = **President**

Presbyterian[1] /ˈprezbəˈtɪriən ‖ ˌprezbɪˈtɪəriən/ *n* presbiteriano, -na *m,f*

Presbyterian[2] *adj* presbiteriano

preschool[1] /ˈpriːˈskuːl/ *adj* (*before n*) ‹*child*› de edad preescolar; ‹*education*› preescolar

preschool[2] *n* [C U] (AmE) jardín *m* de infancia, kindergarten *m* (AmL), jardín *m* de niños (Méx), jardín *m* de infantes (RPl), jardín *m* infantil (Chi)

prescribe /prɪˈskraɪb/ *vt* **(a)** ‹*drug*› recetar; ‹*rest*› recomendar* **(b)** (order) (frml) prescribir* (frml); **~d reading** libros *mpl* de lectura obligatoria

prescription /prɪˈskrɪpʃən/ *n* receta *f*; **available on ~ only** en venta solamente bajo receta

presence /ˈprezn̩s/ *n* [U] presencia *f*; **to make one's ~ felt** hacerse* sentir

presence of mind *n* [U] presencia *f* de ánimo

present[1] /prɪˈzent/ *vt* **1 (a)** (give, hand over) **to ~ sth TO sb** entregarle* algo A algn; **to ~ sb WITH sth** obsequiar a algn CON algo (frml), obsequiarle algo A algn (esp AmL frml) **(b)** (confront): **we were ~ed with a very difficult situation** nos vimos frente a una situación muy difícil **2** ‹*ticket/passport/account/ideas*› presentar **3** (Cin, Theat, Rad, TV) presentar **4** (introduce) (frml) presentar

present[2] /ˈprezn̩t/ *adj* **1** (at scene) (*pred*) **to be ~** estar* presente **2** (*before n*) **(a)** (current) actual; **at the ~ time** en este momento **(b)** (Ling): **the ~ tense** el presente

present[3] /ˈprezn̩t/ *n* **1** [U] **(a)** (current time): **the ~** el presente; **at ~** en este momento **(b)** (Ling) **the ~** el presente **2** [C] (gift) regalo *m*

presentable /prɪˈzentəbəl/ *adj* presentable

presentation /ˈpriːzenˈteɪʃən, ˈprezənˈteɪʃən ‖ ˌprezənˈteɪʃən/ *n* **1** [U C] (of gift, prize) entrega *f* **2 (a)** [U] (of document, bill, proposal) presentación *f* **(b)** [C] (display) (Busn) presentación *f* **3** [U] (manner of presenting) presentación *f*

present-day /ˈprezn̩tˈdeɪ/ *adj* (*before n*) actual

presenter /prɪˈzentər ‖ prɪˈzentə(r)/ *n* (BrE) presentador, -dora *m,f*

presently /ˈprezn̩tli/ *adv* **(a)** (now) en este momento **(b)** (soon afterwards, in past) pronto **(c)** (soon, in future) poco después

preservation /ˈprezərˈveɪʃən ‖ ˌprezəˈveɪʃən/ *n* [U] conservación *f*

preservative /prɪˈzɜːrvətɪv ‖ prɪˈzɜːvətɪv/ *n* [U C] conservante *m*

preserve[1] /prɪˈzɜːrv ‖ prɪˈzɜːv/ *vt* **(a)** ‹*food/specimen*› conservar **(b)** (Culin) ‹*fruit/vegetables*› hacer* conserva de **(c)** ‹*building/traditions*› conservar

preserve[2] *n* **1** [C] **(a)** (exclusive privilege, sphere): **to be a male ~** ser* terreno exclusivamente masculino **(b)** (restricted area): **game ~** coto *m* de caza; **wildlife ~** (AmE) reserva *f* de animales **2** (Culin) [U C] (jam, jelly) confitura *f*, mermelada *f*

preside /prɪˈzaɪd/ *vi* presidir; **to ~ over a meeting** presidir una reunión

presidency /ˈprezədənsi ‖ ˈprezɪdənsi/ *n* presidencia *f*

president /ˈprezədənt ‖ ˈprezɪdənt/ ▶ 603 *n* **(a)** (of state, society) presidente, -ta *m,f* **(b)** (of bank, corporation) (esp AmE) director, -tora *m,f*, presidente, -ta *m,f* **(c)** (of university) (AmE) rector, -tora *m,f*

presidential /ˈprezəˈdentʃəl ‖ ˌprezɪˈdenʃəl/ *adj* (*before n*) presidencial

press[1] /pres/ *n* **1** [U] (newspapers, journalists) prensa *f*; **the ~** la prensa; (*before n*) **~ agency** (BrE) agencia *f* de prensa; **~ photographer** reportero gráfico, reportera gráfica *m,f*; **~ release** comunicado *m* de prensa **2** [C] **(a)** (*printing ~*) prensa *f*, imprenta *f*; **to go to ~** entrar en prensa **(b)** (publishing house) editorial *f* **3** [C] (for pressing — grapes, flowers, machine parts) prensa *f*; (— trousers) prensa *f* planchapantalones

press[2] *vt* **1** (push) ‹*button/doorbell*› apretar*; ‹*pedal/footbrake*› pisar **2 (a)** (squeeze) apretar* **(b)** (in press) ‹*grapes/olives/flowers*› prensar **(c)** ‹*disk/album*› imprimir* **(d)** ‹*clothes*› planchar **3 (a)** (put pressure on) presionar **(b)** (pursue): **to ~ charges against sb** presentar cargos en contra de algn ■ ~ *vi* **1** (exert pressure): **~ firmly** presione con fuerza **2** (urge, pressurize) presionar

● **press on** [*v* + *adv*] **to ~ on** (WITH **sth**) seguir* adelante (CON algo)

press conference *n* rueda *f* de prensa

pressed /prest/ *adj* (*pred*): **to be ~ for time** estar* *or* andar* escaso de tiempo

pressing /'presɪŋ/ *adj* ‹*engagements/concerns*› urgente; ‹*need/desire*› apremiante

press: **~ stud** *n* (BrE) broche *m* *or* botón *m* de presión (AmL), (cierre *m*) automático *m* (Esp); **~-up** *n* (BrE) flexión *f* (de brazos *or* de pecho), fondo *m*, lagartija *f* (Méx)

pressure[1] /'preʃər ‖ 'preʃə(r)/ *n* [U C] presión *f*; **to put ~ on sth/sb** hacer* presión sobre algo/presionar a algn; **the ~s of city life** las presiones a las que somete la vida urbana; **I've been under a lot of ~ recently** últimamente he estado muy agobiado

pressure[2] *vt* presionar; **to ~ sb to** + INF presionar a algn PARA QUE (+ *subj*)

pressure: **~ cooker** *n* olla *f* a presión *or* (Esp tb) olla *f* exprés *or* (Méx) olla *f* presto; **~ group** *n* grupo *m* de presión; **~ pan** *n* (AmE) ⇒ ~ COOKER

pressurize /'preʃəraɪz/ *vt* **(a)** (Aerosp, Aviat) presurizar* **(b)** (urge) (BrE) ⇒ PRESSURE[2]

prestige /pre'sti:ʒ/ *n* [U] prestigio *m*

prestigious /pre'stɪdʒəs/ *adj* prestigioso

presumably /prɪ'zu:məbli ‖ prɪ'zju:məbli/ *adv* (*indep*): **you've taken the necessary steps, ~** supongo *or* me imagino que habrás tomado las medidas pertinentes

presume /prɪ'zu:m ‖ prɪ'zju:m/ *vt* **(a)** (assume) suponer*; **I ~ so** supongo *or* me imagino que sí **(b)** (dare) **to ~ to** + INF atreverse A + INF

presumption /prɪ'zʌmpʃən/ *n* **(a)** [U] (boldness) atrevimiento *m* **(b)** [C U] (assumption) suposición *f*

presumptuous /prɪ'zʌmptʃəs ‖ prɪ'zʌmptʃʊəs/ *adj* impertinente

presuppose /'pri:sə'pəʊz/ *vt* presuponer*

pretence *n* (BrE) ⇒ PRETENSE

pretend[1] /prɪ'tend/ *vt/i* fingir*

pretend[2] *adj* (*used to or by children*) ‹*money/gun*› de mentira (fam)

pretender /prɪ'tendər ‖ prɪ'tendə(r)/ *n* **~** (TO **sth**) pretendiente *mf* (A algo)

pretense, (BrE) **pretence** /'pri:tens, prɪ'tens ‖ prɪ'tens/ *n* [C U]: **her air of confidence is a ~** ese aire de seguridad suyo es fingido; **let's drop this ~!** ¡vamos a dejarnos de fingir!; **under false ~s** de manera fraudulenta

pretension /prɪ'tentʃən ‖ prɪ'tenʃən/ *n* (*often pl*) pretensión *f*

pretentious /prɪ'tentʃəs ‖ prɪ'tenʃəs/ *adj* ‹*person/language/film*› pretencioso; ‹*house/decor*› presuntuoso

pretext /'pri:tekst/ *n* pretexto *m*; **on** *o* **under the ~ of** con el pretexto de

pretty[1] /'prɪti/ *adj* **-tier, -tiest** bonito, lindo (AmL)

pretty[2] *adv* (rather, quite) bastante; (emphatic) bien

prevail /prɪ'veɪl/ *vi* **1** (triumph) «*justice/common sense*» prevalecer*; «*enemy*» imponerse* **2** (predominate) «*attitude/pessimism*» preponderar; «*situation*» reinar

prevailing /prɪ'veɪlɪŋ/ *adj* (*before n*) ‹*wind*› preponderante; ‹*trend/view*› imperante; ‹*uncertainty*› reinante

prevalence /'prevələns/ *n* [U] **(a)** (widespread occurrence) preponderancia *f* **(b)** (predominance) predominio *m*

prevalent /'prevələnt/ *adj* frecuente, corriente; ‹*disease*› común

prevaricate /prɪ'værəkeɪt ‖ prɪ'værɪkeɪt/ *vi* **(a)** (not answer directly) andarse* con rodeos **(b)** (lie) (AmE) mentir*

prevent /prɪ'vent/ *vt* **(a)** (hinder) impedir*; **to ~ sb/sth** (FROM) -ING impedir* QUE algn/algo (+ *subj*) **(b)** (forestall) ‹*crime/disease/accident*› prevenir*, evitar

preventative /prɪ'ventətɪv/ *adj* ⇒ PREVENTIVE

prevention /prɪ'ventʃən ‖ prɪ'venʃən/ *n* [U] prevención *f*

preventive /prɪ'ventɪv/ *adj* preventivo

preview /'pri:vju:/ *n* **(a)** (advance showing) preestreno *m* **(b)** (trailer) avance *m*, trailer *m* (Esp), sinopsis *f* (CS)

previous /'pri:viəs/ *adj* (earlier) (*before n*) ‹*occasion/attempt/page*› anterior; ‹*experience/knowledge*› previo; **on the ~ day** el día anterior; **I had a ~ engagement** ya tenía un compromiso

previously /'pri:viəsli/ *adv* antes

prewar /'pri:'wɔ:r ‖ ,pri:'wɔ:(r)/ *adj* de antes de la guerra

prey /preɪ/ *n* [U] presa *f*

● **prey on**, **prey upon** [*v* + *prep* + *o*] **(a)** ‹*animal*› (hunt) cazar*; (feed on) alimentarse de; **it's been ~ing on my mind** me ha estado preocupando **(b)** (exploit) explotar

price[1] /praɪs/ *n* **1** (cost) precio *m*; **to go up/down in ~** subir/bajar de precio; ***to pay a/the ~ for sth*** pagar* algo caro; (*before n*) **~ list** lista *f* de precios; **it's out of my ~ range** cuesta más de lo que puedo pagar **2** (value) (liter) precio *m*; **one cannot put a ~ on freedom** la libertad no tiene precio

price[2] *vt* **(a)** (fix price of) (*often pass*): **their products are reasonably ~d** sus productos tienen precios razonables; **they have ~d themselves out of the market** han subido tanto los precios que se han quedado sin compradores (*or clientes etc*) **(b)** (mark price on) ponerle* el precio a

priceless /'praɪsləs ‖ 'praɪslɪs/ *adj* inestimable, invalorable (CS)

price tag *n* etiqueta *f* (*del precio*), precio *m*

pricey, **pricy** /'praɪsi/ *adj* **pricier, priciest** (colloq) ‹*item*› carito (fam); ‹*store*› carero (fam)

prick[1] /prɪk/ *vt* **1** (pierce, wound) pinchar, picar* (Méx); **that ~ed his conscience** eso hizo que le remordiera la conciencia **2 ~ up** ‹*ears*› «*dog*» levantar, parar (AmL); **she ~ed up her ears at the mention of France** aguzó el oído *or* (AmL fam) paró la oreja al oír hablar de Francia ■ ~ *vi* pinchar

prick² *n* **(a)** (act) pinchazo *m*, piquete *m* (Méx) **(b)** (mark) agujero *m*

prickle¹ /ˈprɪkəl/ *n* **(a)** [C] (thorn) espina *f* **(b)** [U] (sensation) picor *m*

prickle² *vi* «*wool*» picar*; «*beard*» pinchar, picar* (Méx); «*skin/scalp*» picar*

prickly /ˈprɪkli/ *adj* **-lier, -liest (a)** (with prickles) ‹*plant*› espinoso; ‹*animal*› con púas **(b)** (scratchy) ‹*wool*› que pica; ‹*beard*› que pincha *or* (Méx) pica

pride¹ /praɪd/ *n* **1** [U] **(a)** (self-respect) orgullo *m*; **false ~** vanidad *f*; **she takes great ~ in her work** se toma muy en serio su trabajo; ***to swallow one's ~*** tragarse* el orgullo **(b)** (conceit) orgullo *m* **2** [C] (source of pride) orgullo *m*; **she is her mother's ~ and joy** es el orgullo de su madre **3** [C] (of lions) manada *f*

pride² *v refl* **to ~ oneself** ON **sth**/-ING enorgullecerse* DE algo/+ INF

priest /priːst/ ▶ 603 *n* sacerdote *m*; (*parish* ~) cura *m* (párroco), párroco *m*

priestess /ˈpriːstəs ‖ ˈpriːstes/ *n* sacerdotisa *f*

priesthood /ˈpriːsthʊd/ *n* [U] **(a)** (office) sacerdocio *m* **(b)** (clergy) clero *m*

prig /prɪg/ *n* mojigato, -ta *m,f*

prim /prɪm/ *adj* **-mer, -mest (a)** (prudish) mojigato; (affected) remilgado, repipi (Esp fam); **she's so ~ and proper!** es tan correcta y formal **(b)** (neat) cuidado

primaeval *adj* (BrE) ⇒ PRIMEVAL

primarily /praɪˈmerəli ‖ˈpraɪmərɪli/ *adv* fundamentalmente

primary /ˈpraɪmeri ‖ ˈpraɪməri/ *adj* **1** (principal) ‹*purpose/role/aim*› primordial **2 (a)** (first, basic) ‹*source/energy*› primario; ‹*industry*› de base **(b)** ‹*education*› primario

primary: **~ color**, (BrE) **colour** *n* color *m* primario; **~ school** *n* escuela *f* (de enseñanza) primaria

primate *n* **1** /ˈpraɪmeɪt/ (Zool) primate *m* **2** /ˈpraɪmeɪt, -ət/ (Relig) primado *m*

prime¹ /praɪm/ *adj* (*no comp*) **(a)** (major) principal **(b)** (first-rate) ‹*example/location*› excelente; ‹*cut*› de primera (calidad)

prime² *n* [U] (best time): **to be in one's ~** *o* **in the ~ of life** estar* en la flor de la vida

prime³ *vt* **(a)** (prepare for painting) ‹*wood/metal*› aplicar* una capa de imprimación a; ‹*canvas*› preparar **(b)** ‹*pump/gun*› cebar **(c)** (brief) preparar

prime minister ▶ 603 *n* primer ministro, primera ministra *m,f*

primer /ˈpraɪmər ‖ ˈpraɪmə(r)/ *n* **1** [C U] **(a)** (paint) imprimación *f* **(b)** (explosive) cebo *m* **2** [C] (textbook) manual *m*

prime time *n* horas *fpl* de máxima audiencia

primeval, (BrE) **primaeval** /praɪˈmiːvəl/ *adj* primigenio

primitive /ˈprɪmətɪv ‖ ˈprɪmɪtɪv/ *adj* primitivo; ‹*urges/instincts*› primario

primrose /ˈprɪmrəʊz/ *n* primavera *f*, prímula *f*

prince /prɪns/ ▶ 603 *n* príncipe *m*

princess /ˈprɪnsəs ‖ ˈprɪnses/ ▶ 603 *n* princesa *f*

principal¹ /ˈprɪnsəpəl/ *adj* (*before n*) principal

principal² *n* (of school) director, -tora *m,f*; (of university) rector, -tora *m,f*

principally /ˈprɪnsəpli/ *adv* principalmente

principle /ˈprɪnsəpəl/ *n* **1** [C] (basic fact, law) principio *m*; **in ~** en principio **2** [C U] (rule of conduct) principio *m*; **I never borrow money, on ~** nunca pido dinero prestado, por principio; **it is against my ~s** va contra mis principios

print¹ /prɪnt/ *n* **1** [U] (Print) **(a)** (lettering) letra *f* **(b)** (text): **in ~** (published) publicado; (available) a la venta; **out of ~** agotado **2** [C] **(a)** (Art, Print) grabado *m* **(b)** (Phot) copia *f* **3** [C] (of foot, finger) huella *f* **4** [C U] (fabric) estampado *m*

print² *vt* **1 (a)** ‹*letter/text/design*› imprimir* **(b)** ‹*fabric*› estampar **(c)** (publish) publicar* **(d)** **printed** *past p* impreso **2** (write clearly) escribir* con letra de imprenta **3** (Phot) ‹*negative*› imprimir* ■ ~ *vi* **(a)** (Print) imprimir* **(b)** (write without joining the letters) escribir* con letra de imprenta *or* de molde

• **print out** [*v* + *adv* + *o*, *v* + *o* + *adv*] imprimir*

printer /ˈprɪntər ‖ ˈprɪntə(r)/ *n* **(a)** (worker) tipógrafo, -fa *m,f*, impresor, -sora *m,f* **(b)** (business) imprenta *f* **(c)** (machine) impresora *f*

printing /ˈprɪntɪŋ/ *n* **(a)** [U] (act, process, result) impresión *f* **(b)** [C] (quantity printed) edición *f* **(c)** [U] (trade) imprenta *f*

printing press *n* imprenta *f*, prensa *f*

printout /ˈprɪntaʊt/ *n* [U C] listado *m*

prior¹ /ˈpraɪər ‖ ˈpraɪə(r)/ *adj* (*before n*) ‹*knowledge/warning*› previo; **I had a ~ engagement** ya tenía un compromiso; **prior to** (*as prep*) antes de

prior² *n* prior *m*

priority /praɪˈɔːrəti ‖ praɪˈɒrɪti/ *n* (*pl* **-ties**) **(a)** [U] (precedence) prioridad *f*; **to have/take ~ (over sth)** tener* prioridad (sobre algo) **(b)** [C] (important matter, aim): **you have to get your priorities right** tienes que saber decidir qué es lo más importante

priory /ˈpraɪəri/ *n* (*pl* **-ries**) priorato *m*

prise /praɪz/ *vt* (BrE) ⇒ PRIZE³ 2

prism /ˈprɪzəm/ *n* prisma *m*

prison /ˈprɪzn̩/ *n* prisión *f*, cárcel *f*; (*before n*) ‹*system/reform*› carcelario, penitenciario; **~ officer** (BrE) funcionario, -ria *m,f* de prisiones

prison camp *n* campo *m* de prisioneros

prisoner /ˈprɪznər ‖ ˈprɪzn̩ə(r)/ *n* **(a)** (captive) prisionero, -ra *m,f*; **to take sb ~** tomar *or* (esp Esp) coger* a algn prisionero **(b)** (in jail) preso, -sa *m,f* **(c)** (person arrested) detenido, -da *m,f* **(d)** (accused) reo *mf*, acusado, -da *m,f*

prisoner of war *n* (*pl* **~s ~ ~**) prisionero, -ra *m,f* de guerra

prissy /ˈprɪsi/ *adj* **-sier, -siest** (colloq) remilgado, repipi (Esp fam)

pristine /ˈprɪstiːn, -taɪn/ *adj* (frml & liter) inmaculado, prístino (liter)

privacy /ˈpraɪvəsi ‖ˈprɪvəsi/ *n* [U] privacidad *f*

private¹ /ˈpraɪvət ‖ ˈpraɪvɪt/ *adj* **1 (a)** (confidential) ‹*conversation/matter*› privado; ‹*letter*› personal **(b)**

in private: **she told me in ~** me lo dijo confidencialmente; **can we talk in ~?** ¿podemos hablar en privado? **2** (for own use, in own possession) ‹*road/lesson/secretary*› particular; ‹*income*› personal; **~ property** propiedad *f* privada; **~ income** rentas *fpl* **3 (a)** (not official) ‹*visit/correspondence*› privado; **their ~ life** su vida privada **(b)** (unconnected to the state) ‹*school*› privado, de pago (Esp); ‹*ward*› reservado; ‹*patient*› particular; **~ enterprise** la empresa privada; **the ~ sector** el sector privado **4 (a)** ‹*thoughts/doubts*› íntimo; **it's a ~ joke** es un chiste que los dos entendemos/entienden **(b)** ‹*person*› reservado

private² *n* soldado *mf* raso

private: **~ detective** *n* detective *mf* privado; **~ eye** *n* (esp AmE colloq) sabueso *mf*

privately /'praɪvətli ‖ 'praɪvɪtli/ *adv* **1** (in private) en privado **2** (not by state): **she had the operation done ~** (BrE) la operaron en una clínica privada; **this land is ~ owned** esta tierra es de particulares

private parts *pl n* (euph & hum) partes *fpl* pudendas (euf & hum)

privation /praɪ'veɪʃən/ *n* [U C] (frml) privación *f*

privatization /'praɪvətə'zeɪʃən ‖ ,praɪvɪtaɪ'zeɪʃən/ *n* [U] privatización *f*

privatize /'praɪvətaɪz ‖ 'praɪvɪtaɪz/ *vt* privatizar*

privilege /'prɪvəlɪdʒ/ *n* [C U] privilegio *m*

privileged /'prɪvəlɪdʒd/ *adj* **(a)** (having advantages) ‹*position*› privilegiado **(b)** (honored) (*pred*) **to be ~ to** + INF tener* el privilegio *or* el honor DE + INF

privy /'prɪvi/ *adj* (frml) (*pred*) **to be ~ TO sth** tener* conocimiento DE algo

prize¹ /praɪz/ *n* premio *m*

prize² *adj* (*before n*) premiado

prize³ *vt* **1** (value) valorar (mucho) **2** (BrE) **prise**: **to ~ information out of sb** arrancarle* información a algn; **he ~d the lid off the crate** le arrancó la tapa a la caja haciendo palanca

prize: **~ money** *n* [U] premio *m* (*en metálico*); **~winner** *n* ganador, -dora *m,f* (*de un premio*)

pro /prəʊ/ *n* **1** (professional) (colloq) profesional *mf* **2 pros** *pl* (advantages): **the ~s and cons** los pros y los contras

pro- /'prəʊ/ *pref* pro(-)

probability /'prɑːbə'bɪləti ‖ ,prɒbə'bɪlɪti/ *n* [U C] (*pl* **-ties**) probabilidad *f*

probable /'prɑːbəbəl ‖ 'prɒbəbəl/ *adj* probable; ‹*reason*› posible

probably /'prɑːbəbli ‖ 'prɒbəbli/ *adv* (*indep*) probablemente (+ *subj*)

probation /prəʊ'beɪʃən ‖ prə'beɪʃən/ *n* [U] **1** (Law) libertad *f* condicional; **to be on ~** estar* en libertad condicional **2** (trial period) período *m* de prueba

probe¹ /prəʊb/ *vt* **(a)** (physically) sondar **(b)** (investigate) investigar*; ‹*mind/subconscious*› explorar ■ **~** *vi* investigar*

probe² *n* **(a)** (Med, Elec) sonda *f* **(b)** (investigation) investigación *f*

probing /'prəʊbɪŋ/ *adj* ‹*question*› sagaz; ‹*study*› a fondo

problem /'prɑːbləm ‖ 'prɒbləm/ *n* problema *m*; **no ~!** (colloq) ¡no hay problema!; **what's the ~?** ¿qué pasa?; (*before n*) ‹*family/child*› difícil

problematic /'prɑːblə'mætɪk ‖ ,prɒblə'mætɪk/, **-ical** /-ɪkəl/ *adj* problemático

procedure /prə'siːdʒər ‖ prə'siːdjə(r), prə'siːdʒə(r)/ *n* [U C] (practice) procedimiento *m*; (step) trámite *m*

proceed /prəʊ'siːd, prə- ‖ prə'siːd, prəʊ-/ *vi* **(a)** (move forward) (frml) «*person/vehicle*» avanzar* **(b)** (continue) continuar*; **to ~ to** + INF: **she ~ed to tell us why** pasó a explicarnos por qué **(c)** (act) (frml) proceder **(d)** (progress) marchar

proceedings /prəʊ'siːdɪŋz, prə-/ *pl n* **(a)** (events): **~ began late** la reunión (*or* el acto *etc*) empezó tarde **(b)** (measures) medidas *fpl*; (Law) juicio *m*

proceeds /'prəʊsiːdz/ *pl n*: **the ~** (from charity sale, function) lo recaudado

process¹ /'prɑːses, 'prəʊ- ‖ 'prəʊses/ *n* **(a)** (series of actions, changes) proceso *m*; **the ~ of obtaining a permit** el trámite para obtener un permiso; **I am in the ~ of writing to him right now** en este preciso momento le estoy escribiendo **(b)** (method) proceso *m*, procedimiento *m*

process² *vt* ‹*raw materials/waste*› procesar, tratar; ‹*film*› revelar; ‹*applications*› dar* curso a; ‹*order*› tramitar; ‹*data*› procesar

process cheese (AmE), **processed cheese** /'prɑːsest ‖ 'prəʊsest/ (BrE) *n* [U] queso *m* fundido

processing /'prɑːsesɪŋ, 'prəʊ- ‖ 'prəʊsesɪŋ/ *n* [U] **(a)** (of materials, waste) tratamiento *m*, procesamiento *m*; (of film) revelado *m* **(b)** (of an order, an application) tramitación *f* **(c)** (Comput) procesamiento *m*

procession /prə'seʃən/ *n* desfile *m*; (Relig) procesión *f*; **a funeral ~** un cortejo fúnebre

proclaim /prəʊ'kleɪm, prə- ‖ prə'kleɪm/ *vt* (frml) ‹*independence*› proclamar; ‹*love*› declarar

proclamation /'prɑːklə'meɪʃən ‖ ,prɒklə'meɪʃən/ *n* [C U] (frml) proclamación *f*

procrastinate /prəʊ'kræstəneɪt ‖ prəʊ'kræstɪneɪt/ *vi* dejar las cosas para más tarde

procreation /'prəʊkri'eɪʃən/ *n* [U] (frml) procreación *f*

procure /prə'kjʊr ‖ prə'kjʊə(r)/ *vt* (frml) procurar (frml)

prod¹ /prɑːd ‖ prɒd/ *vt* **-dd-** (with elbow) darle* un codazo a; (with sth sharp) pinchar

prod² *n* (with elbow) codazo *m*; (with sth sharp) pinchazo *m*

prodigal /'prɑːdɪgəl ‖ 'prɒdɪgəl/ *adj* pródigo

prodigious /prə'dɪdʒəs/ *adj* ‹*amount/cost*› enorme; ‹*efforts/strength*› prodigioso

prodigy /'prɑːdədʒi ‖ 'prɒdɪdʒi/ *n* (*pl* **-gies**) prodigio *m*; **child ~** niño, -ña *m,f* prodigio

produce¹ /prə'duːs ‖ prə'djuːs/ *vt* **1 (a)** (manufacture, yield) ‹*cars/cloth*› producir*, fabricar*; ‹*coal/grain/beef*› producir*; ‹*fruit*› «*country/region*» producir*; «*tree/bush*» dar*, producir* **(b)** (create, give) ‹*energy/sound*› producir* **(c)** (cause) ‹*effect*› surtir, producir* **(d)** (give birth to) ‹*young*› tener* **2** (show, bring out) ‹*ticket/document/evidence*› presentar, aportar; ‹*gun/knife*› sacar* **3 (a)** (Cin, TV) producir*; (Theat) ‹*play*› poner* en escena; ‹*show*› montar **(b)** (Rad, Theat) (direct) dirigir*

produce² /'prɑːduːs ‖ 'prɒdjuːs/ *n* [U] productos *mpl* (alimenticios)

producer /prə'duːsər ‖ prə'djuːsə(r)/ *n* **1** (manufacturer) fabricante *mf* **2 (a)** (Cin, TV, Theat) productor, -tora *m,f* **(b)** (Rad, Theat) (director) director, -tora *m,f*

product /'prɑːdəkt ‖ 'prɒdʌkt/ *n* producto *m*

production /prə'dʌkʃən/ *n* **1** [U] **(a)** (manufacture) fabricación *f* **(b)** (output) producción *f* **2** [U] (showing) presentación *f* **3** [C] (staging, version) (Theat, Cin) producción *f* **4** [U] **(a)** (act of producing) (Cin, TV) producción *f*; (Theat) puesta *f* en escena **(b)** (direction) (Rad, Theat) dirección *f*

production line *n* cadena *f* de fabricación

productive /prə'dʌktɪv/ *adj* ‹*land/factory/mine*› productivo; ‹*meeting*› fructífero

productively /prə'dʌktɪvli/ *adv* productivamente; **I didn't spend my time very ~** no saqué buen partido del tiempo

productivity /'prəʊdʌk'tɪvəti ‖ ˌprɒdʌk'tɪvəti/ *n* [U] productividad *f*

profane /prə'feɪn/ *adj* **(a)** (blasphemous) irreverente **(b)** (secular) profano

profanity /prə'fænəti/ *n* (*pl* **-ties**) **(a)** [U] (blasphemy, vulgarity) irreverencia *f* **(b)** [C] (swear word) blasfemia *f*

profess /prə'fes/ *vt* **(a)** (claim) (frml) ‹*desire/belief*› manifestar*; **he ~ed to be an expert** se preciaba de ser un experto **(b)** (Relig) profesar

profession /prə'feʃən/ *n* **1 (a)** [C] (occupation) profesión *f*; **by ~** de profesión **(b)** (members) (*no pl*): **the medical ~** el cuerpo médico; **the teaching ~** la enseñanza **2** [U C] (declaration) (frml) profesión *f*

professional¹ /prə'feʃnəl ‖ prə'feʃənl/ *adj* (*before n*) ‹*musician/golfer*› profesional; ‹*soldier*› de carrera; **to take ~ advice** asesorarse con un profesional (*or* un experto, técnico *etc*)

professional² *n* profesional *mf*; (competent person) experto, -ta *m,f*

professionalism /prə'feʃnəlɪzəm ‖ prə'feʃənlɪzəm/ *n* [U] profesionalidad *f*

professionally /prə'feʃnəli/ *adv* **(a)** (as livelihood) ‹*sing/act*› profesionalmente **(b)** (by qualified person): **we had the job done ~** hicimos hacer el trabajo por un experto (*or* por un pintor, albañil *etc*) **(c)** (in a professional way) con profesionalidad

professor /prə'fesər ‖ prə'fesə(r)/ ▶ 603 *n* (of the highest academic rank) catedrático, -ca *m,f*; (any university teacher) (AmE) profesor universitario, profesora universitaria *m,f*

proffer /'prɑːfər ‖ 'prɒfə(r)/ *vt* (frml) ofrecer*

proficiency /prə'fɪʃənsi/ *n* [U] competencia *f*

proficient /prə'fɪʃənt/ *adj* muy competente

profile¹ /'prəʊfaɪl/ *n* perfil *m*; ***to keep a low ~*** tratar de pasar desapercibido

profile² *vt* ‹*situation*› hacer* un esbozo de; **to ~ sb's life** hacer* una reseña biográfica de algn

profit¹ /'prɑːfət ‖ 'prɒfɪt/ *n* [C U] (Busn, Econ) ganancias *fpl*, utilidades *fpl* (AmL); **to sell sth at a ~** vender algo con ganancia

profit² *vi* **to ~ FROM sth** sacar* provecho DE algo

profitable /'prɑːfətəbəl ‖ 'prɒfɪtəbəl/ *adj* **(a)** (Busn) ‹*company/investment/crop*› rentable **(b)** ‹*day/journey*› provechoso

profitably /'prɑːfətəbli ‖ 'prɒfɪtəbli/ *adv* **(a)** (Busn) ‹*trade/operate*› de manera rentable; ‹*sell*› con ganancia **(b)** (fruitfully) provechosamente

profiteer /'prɑːfə'tɪr ‖ ˌprɒfɪ'tɪə(r)/ *n* especulador, -dora *m,f*

profiteering /'prɑːfə'tɪrɪŋ ‖ ˌprɒfɪ'tɪərɪŋ/ *n* [U] especulación *f*

profit-making /'prɑːfət,meɪkɪŋ ‖ 'prɒfɪt,meɪkɪŋ/ *adj* (profitable) rentable; (which aims to make a profit) con fines lucrativos

profound /prə'faʊnd/ *adj* **-er, -est** profundo

profoundly /prə'faʊndli/ *adv* profundamente

profuse /prə'fjuːs/ *adj* abundante; ‹*bleeding*› intenso

profusely /prə'fjuːsli/ *adv* ‹*bleed*› profusamente; ‹*thank*› efusivamente; **he apologized ~** se deshizo en disculpas

profusion /prə'fjuːʒən/ *n* [U C] profusión *f*

prognosis /prɑːg'nəʊsəs ‖ prɒg'nəʊsɪs/ *n* [C U] (*pl* **-ses** /-siːz/) pronóstico *m*

program¹, (BrE) **programme** /'prəʊgræm/ *n* **1 (a)** (schedule, plan) programa *m* **(b)** (for concert, performance) programa *m* **(c)** (esp AmE Educ) (course) curso *m* **2** (Rad, TV) programa *m* **3 program** (Comput) programa *m*

program² *vt* **-mm-** *or* **-m- 1** (BrE also) **programme (a)** (schedule) ‹*activities*› programar, planear **(b)** (instruct) programar **2** (Comput) programar

programmer, (AmE also) **programer** /'prəʊgræmər ‖ 'prəʊgræmə(r)/ *n* (Comput) programador, -dora *m,f*

progress¹ /'prɑːgrəs ‖ 'prəʊgres/ *n* [U] **1** (advancement) progreso *m*; (of situation, events) desarrollo *m*; **to make ~** «*pupil*» adelantar, hacer* progresos; «*patient*» mejorar **2 in progress**: **talks are in ~ between the two parties** los dos partidos están manteniendo conversaciones; **while the examination is in ~** mientras dure el examen **3** (forward movement) avance *m*

progress² /prə'gres/ *vi* «*work/science/technology*» progresar; «*patient*» mejorar

progression /prə'greʃən/ *n* **(a)** [U C] (advance) evolución *f* **(b)** [C] (Math, Mus) progresión *f*

progressive /prə'gresɪv/ *adj* **1** ‹*attitude/thinker/measure*› progresista **2** ‹*illness/deterioration/improvement*› progresivo

prohibit /prəʊ'hɪbɪt ‖ prə'hɪbɪt/ *vt* **(a)** (forbid) prohibir* **(b)** (prevent) impedir*

prohibition /'prəʊə'bɪʃən ‖ ˌprəʊhɪ'bɪʃən/ *n* **(a)** [U C] prohibición *f* **(b) Prohibition** (in US history) (*no art*) la Ley seca, la Prohibición

prohibitive /prəʊ'hɪbətɪv ‖ prə'hɪbətɪv/ *adj* ‹*price/cost*› prohibitivo

project¹ /'prɑːdʒekt ‖ 'prɒdʒekt/ *n* **(a)** (scheme) proyecto *m* **(b)** (Educ) trabajo *m* **(c)** (*housing* ~) (in US) complejo *m* de viviendas subvencionadas

project² /prə'dʒekt/ *vt* **1 (a)** ‹*beam/shadow/image*› proyectar **(b)** (convey) ‹*personality/image/voice*› proyectar **2** (frml) ‹*missile*› lanzar* **3** (forecast) pronosticar*; ‹*costs/trends*› hacer* una proyección de; **the ~ed figure** la cifra prevista ■ ~ *vi* (jut out) sobresalir*

projection /prə'dʒekʃən/ *n* **1** [U] (of image, slide) proyección *f* **2** [C] (forecast) proyección *f*, pronóstico *m* **3** [C] (protuberance) saliente *f or m*

projector /prə'dʒektər ‖ prə'dʒektə(r)/ *n* proyector *m*

proletarian /'prəʊlə'teriən ‖ ˌprəʊlə'teəriən/ *adj* proletario

proliferate /prə'lɪfəreɪt/ *vi* proliferar

prolific /prə'lɪfɪk/ *adj* prolífico

prologue, (AmE also) **prolog** /'prəʊlɔːg ‖ 'prəʊlɒg/ *n* prólogo *m*

prolong /prə'lɔːŋ ‖ prə'lɒŋ/ *vt* prolongar*

prom /prɑːm ‖ prɒm/ *n* **(a)** (ball) (in US) (colloq) baile *m* del colegio (*or* de la facultad *etc*) **(b)** (esplanade) (BrE colloq) ⇒ PROMENADE¹

promenade¹ /prɑːmə'neɪd ‖'prɒmənɑːd/ *n* (at seaside) (esp BrE) paseo *m* marítimo, malecón *m* (AmL), costanera *f* (CS)

promenade² *vi* pasear(se)

prominence /'prɑːmənəns ‖ 'prɒmɪnəns/ *n* [U] (conspicuousness) prominencia *f*; (eminence, importance) importancia *f*

prominent /'prɑːmənənt ‖ 'prɒmɪnənt/ *adj* **(a)** ‹*position*› destacado; ‹*role/politician*› prominente, destacado **(b)** ‹*jaw/nose*› prominente

prominently /'prɑːmənəntli ‖ 'prɒmɪnəntli/ *adv*: **it was ~ displayed** ocupaba un lugar prominente *or* destacado; **he figured ~ in the negotiations** desempeñó un papel prominente *or* destacado en las negociaciones

promiscuity /'prɑːməs'kjuːəti ‖ ˌprɒmɪ'skjuːəti/ *n* [U] promiscuidad *f*

promiscuous /prə'mɪskjuəs/ *adj* promiscuo

promise¹ /'prɑːməs ‖ 'prɒmɪs/ *n* **1** [C] (pledge) promesa *f* **2** [U] (potential): **his work showed great** *o* **a lot of ~** su trabajo prometía mucho

promise² *vt/i* prometer; **to ~ to + INF** prometer + INF

promising /'prɑːməsɪŋ ‖ 'prɒmɪsɪŋ/ *adj* ‹*pupil/writer/career*› prometedor; ‹*future*› halagüeño

promote /prə'məʊt/ *vt* **1 (a)** (raise in rank) ‹*employee*› ascender* **(b)** (AmE Educ) promover* **2 (a)** (encourage) promover*; ‹*growth*› estimular **(b)** (advocate) promover* **3** ‹*product/service*› promocionar

promoter /prə'məʊtər ‖ prə'məʊtə(r)/ *n* **(a)** (Busn) promotor, -tora *m,f* **(b)** (Sport) empresario, -ria *m,f*

promotion /prə'məʊʃən/ *n* **1** [U C] (advancement in rank) ascenso *m*; **she got (a) ~** la ascendieron **2** [U] **(a)** (of research, peace, trade) promoción *f* **(b)** (advocacy) promoción *f* **3** [U] (publicity) promoción *f*

prompt¹ /prɑːmpt ‖ prɒmpt/ *vt* **1** ‹*response/outcry*› provocar*; **to ~ sb to + INF** mover* a algn A + INF **2** ‹*actor/orator*› apuntarle a

prompt² *adj* **-er, -est** rápido

prompt³ *adv* (BrE): **at ten o'clock ~** a las diez en punto

prompt⁴ *n* **(a)** (reminder) apunte *m* **(b)** (Comput) presto *m*

prompter /'prɑːmptər ‖ 'prɒmptə(r)/ *n* apuntador, -dora *m,f*

promptly /'prɑːmptli ‖ 'prɒmptli/ *adv* **(a)** (on time) puntualmente **(b)** (speedily) ‹*pay/deliver*› sin demora **(c)** (instantly) de inmediato

prone /prəʊn/ *adj* **1** (liable, disposed) (*pred*) **to be ~ TO sth** ser* propenso A algo; **to be ~ to + INF** ser* propenso a + INF **2** (face downward) (tendido) boca abajo

prong /prɔːŋ ‖ prɒŋ/ *n* diente *m*

pronoun /'prəʊnaʊn/ *n* pronombre *m*

pronounce /prə'naʊns/ *vt* **(a)** ‹*sound/word/syllable*› pronunciar **(b)** ‹*judgment/sentence*› pronunciar **(c)** (declare) (frml): **the doctor ~d him dead** el médico dictaminó que estaba muerto

pronounced /prə'naʊnst/ *adj* pronunciado

pronouncement /prə'naʊnsmənt/ *n* declaración *f*

pronunciation /prə'nʌnsi'eɪʃən/ *n* [U] pronunciación *f*

proof¹ /pruːf/ *n* **1** [U C] (conclusive evidence) prueba *f* **2** [C] (Print) prueba *f* (de imprenta) **3** [U] (alcoholic strength) graduación *f* alcohólica

proof² *adj* (*pred*) **to be ~ AGAINST sth** ser* a prueba DE algo

proof: **~read** (*past & past p* **-read** /-red/) *vt* corregir* ■ ~ *vi* corregir* pruebas; **~reader** *n* corrector, -tora *m,f* de pruebas

prop¹ /prɑːp ‖ prɒp/ *n* **1** (holding up roof etc) puntal *m* **2** (Cin, Theat) accesorio *m*, objeto *m* de utilería *or* (Esp, Méx) del attrezzo

prop² **-pp-** *vt* **to ~ sth AGAINST sth** apoyar algo EN *or* CONTRA algo

• **prop up** [*v + o + adv, v + adv + o*] **(a)** (support) ‹*wall/building*› sostener* **(b)** (lean) apoyar

propaganda /ˌprɑːpə'gændə ‖ ˌprɒpə'gændə/ *n* [U] propaganda *f*

propagate /'prɑːpəgeɪt ‖ 'prɒpəgeɪt/ *vt* propagar*

propel /prə'pel/ *vt* **-ll-** ‹*plane/ship*› propulsar

propeller /prə'pelər ‖ prə'pelə(r)/ *n* hélice *f*

proper /'prɑːpər ‖ 'prɒpə(r)/ *adj* **1** (correct) (*before n, no comp*) ‹*treatment/procedure*› apropiado; ‹*pronunciation*› correcto **2** (*before n, no comp*) (genuine) ‹*chance*› verdadero; ‹*meal*› como Dios manda; ‹*vacation*› de verdad **3 (a)** ‹*behavior/person*› correcto **(b)** (overly decorous) recatado **4** (in the strict sense) (*after n*) propiamente dicho

properly /'prɑːpərlɪ ‖ 'prɒpəli/ *adv* **(a)** ‹*write/spell/fit*› correctamente; ‹*work/concentrate/eat*› bien **(b)** (appropriately) apropiadamente

proper name, **proper noun** *n* nombre *m* propio

property /'prɑːpərti ‖ 'prɒpəti/ *n* (*pl* **-ties**) **1** [U] (possessions) propiedad *f* **2** **(a)** [U] (buildings, land) propiedades *fpl*, bienes *mpl* raíces (frml); (*before n*) **~ developer** promotor inmobiliario, promotora inmobiliaria *m,f*; **~ tax** (in US) impuesto *m* sobre la propiedad inmobiliaria **(b)** [C] (building) inmueble *m* (frml); (piece of land) terreno *m*, solar *m*, parcela *f* **3** [C] (quality) propiedad *f*

prophecy /'prɑːfəsi ‖ 'prɒfəsi/ *n* [C U] (*pl* **-cies**) profecía *f*

prophesy /'prɑːfəsaɪ ‖ 'prɒfəsaɪ/ *vt* **-sies, -sying, -sied** predecir*; (Relig) profetizar*

prophet /'prɑːfət ‖ 'prɒfɪt/ *n* profeta, -tisa *m,f*

prophetic /prə'fetɪk/ *adj* profético

proportion /prə'pɔːrʃən ‖ prə'pɔːʃən/ *n* **1** (part) (*no pl*) parte *f* **2** [C U] (ratio) proporción *f*; **in equal ~s** por partes iguales; **in ~ to sth** en proporción a algo **3** [U] (proper relation) proporción *f*; **let's keep things in ~** no exageremos; **to blow sth up out of all ~** exagerar algo desmesuradamente **4** **proportions** *pl* (size) proporciones *fpl*

proportional /prə'pɔːrʃn̩əl ‖ prə'pɔːʃənl/ *adj* proporcional; **~ representation** representación *f* proporcional

proportionate /prə'pɔːrʃn̩ət ‖ prə'pɔːʃənət/ *adj* proporcional

proposal /prə'pəʊzəl/ *n* **(a)** (suggestion) propuesta *f* **(b)** (of marriage) proposición *f* matrimonial

propose /prə'pəʊz/ *vt* **1** **(a)** (suggest) proponer*; **to ~ -ING/(THAT)** proponer* QUE (+ *subj*) **(b)** **proposed** *past p*: **the ~d cuts** los recortes que se proponen implementar **(c)** (in meeting) ‹*amendment*› proponer*; ‹*motion*› presentar **2** (intend) **to ~ to + INF, to ~ -ING** pensar* + INF ■ **~** *vi* **to ~ TO sb** proponerle* matrimonio a algn

proposition¹ /ˌprɑːpə'zɪʃən ‖ ˌprɒpə'zɪʃən/ *n* **1** (suggestion) propuesta *f*; (offer) oferta *f* **2** (prospect): **it's not a viable ~** no es viable

proposition² *vt* hacerle* proposiciones deshonestas a (euf)

proprietary /prə'praɪəteri ‖ prə'praɪətri/ *adj* ‹*device/software/drug*› de marca registrada

proprietor /prə'praɪətər ‖ prə'praɪətə(r)/ *n* propietario, -ria *m,f*, dueño, -ña *m,f*

propulsion /prə'pʌlʃən/ *n* [U] propulsión *f*

pro rata /ˌprəʊ'rɑːtə/ *adv* a prorrata

prosaic /prəʊ'zeɪɪk/ *adj* prosaico

proscribe /prəʊ'skraɪb ‖ prə'skraɪb/ *vt* proscribir*

prose /prəʊz/ *n* [U] (Lit) prosa *f*

prosecute /'prɑːsɪkjuːt ‖ 'prɒsɪkjuːt/ *vt* (Law) **to ~ sb FOR sth** procesar a algn POR algo ■ **~** *vi* iniciar procedimiento criminal; **prosecuting attorney** (in US) fiscal *mf*

prosecution /ˌprɑːsɪ'kjuːʃən ‖ ˌprɒsɪ'kjuːʃən/ *n* (Law) **(a)** [U] (bringing to trial) interposición *f* de una acción judicial **(b)** (prosecuting side) **the ~** la acusación

prosecutor /'prɑːsɪkjuːtər ‖ 'prɒsɪkjuːtə(r)/ *n* fiscal *mf*; (in private prosecutions) abogado, -da *m,f* de *or* por la acusación

prospect¹ /'prɑːspekt ‖ 'prɒspekt/ *n* **1** **(a)** [U] (possibility) posibilidad *f*; **~ OF sth** posibilidades *fpl* DE algo **(b)** [C] (situation envisaged) perspectiva *f* **(c)** **prospects** *pl* (chances) perspectivas *fpl*; **a job with no ~s** un trabajo sin futuro **2** [C] (potential customer) posible cliente, -ta *m,f*

prospect² /'prɑːspekt ‖ prə'spekt/ *vi* **to ~ FOR sth** buscar* algo

prospective /prə'spektɪv/ *adj* (*before n*) ‹*customer*› posible; ‹*husband*› futuro

prospector /'prɑːspektər ‖ prə'spektə(r)/ *n* prospector, -tora *m,f*, cateador, -dora *m,f* (AmS)

prospectus /prə'spektəs/ *n* (*pl* **~es**) (Educ) folleto *m* informativo

prosper /'prɑːspər ‖ 'prɒspə(r)/ *vi* prosperar

prosperity /prɑː'sperəti ‖ prɒ'sperəti/ *n* [U] prosperidad *f*

prosperous /'prɑːspərəs ‖ 'prɒspərəs/ *adj* próspero

prostate (gland) /'prɑːsteɪt ‖ 'prɒsteɪt/ *n* próstata *f*

prostitute¹ /'prɑːstətuːt ‖ 'prɒstɪtjuːt/ *n* prostituta *f*; **male ~** prostituto *m*

prostitute² *vt* prostituir*; **to ~ oneself** prostituirse*

prostitution /ˌprɑːstə'tuːʃən ‖ ˌprɒstɪ'tjuːʃən/ *n* [U] prostitución *f*

prostrate /'prɑːstreɪt ‖ 'prɒstreɪt/ *adj* postrado

protagonist /prəʊ'tægənəst ‖ prə'tægənɪst/ *n* (Lit) protagonista *mf*

protect /prə'tekt/ *vt* proteger*

protection /prə'tekʃən/ *n* [U] protección *f*; (*before n*) **~ racket** chantaje *m* (*que se practica a propietarios de comercios*)

protective /prə'tektɪv/ *adj* **(a)** ‹*headgear/covering*› protector; ‹*clothing*› de protección **(b)** ‹*attitude/feelings*› protector

protector /prə'tektər ‖ prə'tektə(r)/ *n* protector, -tora *m,f*

protein /'prəʊtiːn/ *n* [C U] proteína *f*

protest¹ /'prəʊtest/ *n* **(a)** [U] (expression of disagreement) protesta *f*; **in ~ (against sth)** en señal de protesta (contra algo); **under ~** bajo protesta **(b)** [C] (complaint) protesta *f* **(c)** [C] (demonstration) manifestación *f* de protesta

protest² /prə'test/ *vi* protestar; **to ~ AGAINST/ABOUT sth** protestar CONTRA/ACERCA DE algo ■ **~** *vt* **1** **(a)** (complain) **to ~ THAT** quejarse DE QUE, protestar QUE **(b)** (object to) (AmE) ‹*decision/action*› protestar (contra) **2** (assert) ‹*love*› declarar; ‹*innocence/loyalty*› hacer* protestas de

Protestant¹ /'prɑːtəstənt ‖ 'prɒtɪstənt/ *n* protestante *mf*

Protestant² *adj* protestante

protester /prə'testər ‖ prə'testə(r)/ *n* manifestante *mf*

protocol /'prəʊtəkɔːl ‖ 'prəʊtəkɒl/ *n* [U C] protocolo *m*

prototype /'prəʊtətaɪp/ *n* prototipo *m*

protracted /prə'træktəd ‖ prə'træktɪd/ *adj* prolongado

protrude /prə'tru:d/ *vi* (frml) **(a)** «*nail/ledge*» sobresalir* **(b) protruding** *pres p* ‹*chin*› prominente; ‹*teeth*› salido; ‹*nail*› que sobresale; **protruding eyes** ojos *mpl* saltones

proud /praʊd/ *adj* **-er, -est (a)** (pleased) ‹*parent/winner*› orgulloso; ‹*smile/moment*› de orgullo; **to be ~ OF sb/sth** estar* orgulloso DE algn/algo **(b)** (having self-respect) ‹*nation/race*› digno **(c)** (arrogant, haughty) orgulloso

proudly /'praʊdli/ *adv* **(a)** (with pleasure, satisfaction) con orgullo **(b)** (arrogantly) orgullosamente

prove /pru:v/ (*past* **proved**; *past p* **proved** *or* **proven**) *vt* ‹*theory/statement/innocence*› probar*, demostrar*; ‹*loyalty/courage*› demostrar* ■ *v refl* **to ~ oneself**: **he was given three months to ~ himself** le dieron tres meses para que demostrara su valía; **to ~ oneself to be sth** demostrarse* ser algo ■ **~** *vi* resultar

proven /'pru:vən/ *adj* ‹*experience/ability*› probado; ‹*method*› de probada eficacia

proverb /'prɑ:vɜ:rb ‖ 'prɒvɜ:b/ *n* refrán *m*, proverbio *m*

proverbial /prə'vɜ:rbiəl ‖ prə'vɜ:biəl/ *adj* proverbial

provide /prə'vaɪd/ *vt* (supply) proporcionar; ‹*accomodation*› dar*; **to ~ sb WITH sth** proveer* a algn DE algo

• **provide for** [*v* + *prep* + *o*] **(a)** (support) ‹*family*› mantener* **(b)** (make arrangements for): **I have to ~ for my old age** tengo que asegurarme el bienestar en la vejez

provided /prə'vaɪdəd ‖ prə'vaɪdɪd/ *conj* **~ (that)** siempre que (+ *subj*)

providence /'prɑ:vədəns ‖ 'prɒvɪdəns/ *n* [U] **(a)** (Relig) providencia *f* **(b)** (fate, chance): **it was sheer ~ that** ... fue providencial que ...

providing /prə'vaɪdɪŋ/ *conj* ⇒ PROVIDED

province /'prɑ:vəns ‖ 'prɒvɪns/ *n* **1** (administrative unit) provincia *f* **2 (a)** (area of knowledge, activity) terreno *m* **(b)** (area of responsibility) competencia *f*

provincial /prə'vɪntʃəl ‖ prə'vɪnʃəl/ *adj* **1** (Govt) provincial **2 (a)** ‹*town*› de provincia(s) **(b)** (pej) ‹*outlook*› provinciano

provision /'prə'vɪʒən/ *n* **1** [U] (of funding) provisión *f*; (of food, supplies) suministro *m* **2** [U] (preparatory arrangements) previsiones *fpl* **3** [C] (stipulation) (Govt, Law) disposición *f* **4 provisions** *pl* provisiones *fpl*, víveres *mpl*

provisional /prə'vɪʒnəl ‖ prə'vɪʒənl/ *adj* provisional, provisorio (AmS)

proviso /prə'vaɪzəʊ/ *n* (*pl* **-sos**) condición *f*

provocation /'prɑ:və'keɪʃən ‖ ˌprɒvə'keɪʃən/ *n* [U C] provocación *f*

provocative /prə'vɑ:kətɪv ‖ prə'vɒkətɪv/ *adj* **1** (causing trouble) provocador **2** (seductive) provocativo

provoke /prə'vəʊk/ *vt* **1** ‹*person/animal*› provocar*; **I was ~d into hitting him** tanto me provocó, que le pegué **2** ‹*argument/revolt/criticism*› provocar*; ‹*discussion/debate*› motivar; ‹*interest/curiosity*› despertar*

prow /praʊ/ *n* proa *f*

prowess /'praʊəs ‖ 'praʊɪs/ *n* [U] destreza *f*

prowl /praʊl/ *vi* merodear

proximity /prɑ:k'sɪməti ‖ prɒk'sɪməti/ *n* [U] (frml) proximidad *f*

proxy /'prɑ:ksi ‖ 'prɒksi/ *n* (*pl* **-xies**) **(a)** [C] (person) representante *mf* **(b)** [U] (authorization) poder *m*; **by ~** por poder *or* (Esp) por poderes

prude /pru:d/ *n* mojigato, -ta *m,f*

prudence /'pru:dn̩s/ *n* [U] prudencia *f*

prudent /'pru:dn̩t/ *adj* prudente

prudish /'pru:dɪʃ/ *adj* mojigato

prune[1] /pru:n/ *n* ciruela *f* pasa *or* (CS) seca

prune[2] *vt* **(a)** (Hort) podar **(b)** ‹*costs/workforce*› reducir*

pry /praɪ/ **pries, prying, pried** *vi* curiosear; **to ~ INTO sth** entrometerse EN algo ■ **~** *vt* (esp AmE) (+ *adv compl*): **she pried the lid off** levantó la tapa (haciendo palanca)

PS *n* (postscript) P.D.

psalm /sɑ:m/ *n* salmo *m*

pseudonym /'su:dn̩ɪm ‖'sju:dənɪm/ *n* (p)seudónimo *m*

PST (in US) = **Pacific Standard Time**

psychiatric /'saɪki'ætrɪk/ *adj* (p)siquiátrico

psychiatrist /sə'kaɪətrəst ‖ saɪ'kaɪətrɪst/ *n* (p)siquiatra *mf*

psychiatry /sə'kaɪətri ‖ saɪ'kaɪətri/ *n* [U] (p)siquiatría *f*

psychic /'saɪkɪk/ *adj* **(a)** (Occult) para(p)sicológico **(b)** (Psych) (p)síquico

psychoanalysis /'saɪkəʊə'næləsəs ‖ ˌsaɪkəʊə'næləsɪs/ *n* [U] (p)sicoanálisis *m*

psychological /'saɪkə'lɑ:dʒɪkəl ‖ ˌsaɪkə'lɒdʒɪkəl/ *adj* (p)sicológico

psychologist /saɪ'kɑ:lədʒəst ‖ saɪ'kɒlədʒɪst/ *n* (p)sicólogo, -ga *m,f*

psychology /saɪ'kɑ:lədʒi ‖ saɪ'kɒlədʒi/ *n* (*pl* **-gies**) (p)sicología *f*

psychopath /'saɪkəpæθ ‖ 'saɪkəʊpæθ/ *n* (p)sicópata *mf*

psychosis /saɪ'kəʊsəs ‖ saɪ'kəʊsɪs/ *n* (*pl* **-ses** /-si:z/) (p)sicosis *f*

psychosomatic /'saɪkəsə'mætɪk ‖ ˌsaɪkəʊsə'mætɪk/ *adj* (p)sicosomático

psychotherapy /'saɪkəʊ'θerəpi/ *n* [U] (p)sicoterapia *f*

psychotic /saɪ'kɑ:tɪk ‖ saɪ'kɒtɪk/ *adj* (p)sicótico

PTO (= **please turn over**) sigue al dorso

pub /pʌb/ *n* (BrE) ≈ bar *m*

puberty /'pju:bərti ‖ 'pju:bəti/ *n* [U] pubertad *f*

pubic /'pju:bɪk/ *adj* ‹*hair*› púbico, pubiano; ‹*region/bone*› pubiano

public[1] /'pʌblɪk/ *adj* público; **it is ~ knowledge** es de dominio público; **at ~ expense** con fondos públicos; **the ~ sector** el sector público; **~ speaking** oratoria *f*

public[2] *n* (+ *sing or pl vb*) **(a)** [U] (people in general) **the ~** el público **(b)** [C] (audience) público *m* **(c) in public** en público

public-address system /'pʌblɪkə'dres/ *n* (sistema *m* de) megafonía *f*, altoparlantes *mpl* (AmL)

publican /'pʌblɪkən/ *n* (BrE) dueño, -ña *m,f* de un bar

public assistance *n* [U] (AmE) *ayuda estatal a los sectores más necesitados de la población*; **to be on ~ ~** recibir ayuda estatal

publication /'pʌblə'keɪʃən ‖ ,pʌblɪ'keɪʃən/ *n* [C U] publicación *f*

public: **~ health** *n* [U] salud *f or* sanidad *f* pública; **~ holiday** *n* fiesta *f* oficial, (día *m*) feriado *m* (AmL); **~ house** *n* (BrE) ≈ bar *m*

publicity /pʌb'lɪsəti/ *n* [U] publicidad *f*

publicize /'pʌbləsaɪz ‖ 'pʌblɪsaɪz/ *vt* hacer* público

publicly /'pʌblɪkli/ *adv* **(a)** públicamente **(b)** (Govt) ‹*funded/maintained*› con fondos públicos

public: **~ relations** *n* relaciones *fpl* públicas; **~ school** *n* (in US) escuela *f* pública; (in UK) colegio *m* privado; (— boarding school) internado *m* privado; **~ service** *n* (communal provision) servicio *m* público; **~-spirited** /'pʌblɪk'spɪrətəd ‖ ,pʌblɪk 'spɪrɪtɪd/ *adj* solidario; **~ transportation** (AmE), **~ transport** (BrE) *n* [U] transporte *m* público

publish /'pʌblɪʃ/ *vt* **(a)** ‹*book/newspaper/article*› publicar* **(b)** (make known) hacer* público

publisher /'pʌblɪʃər ‖ 'pʌblɪʃə(r)/ *n* **(a)** (company) editorial *f* **(b)** (job title) editor, -tora *m,f*

publishing /'pʌblɪʃɪŋ/ *n* [U] mundo *m* editorial; (*before n*) **~ house** editorial *f*

pucker /'pʌkər ‖ 'pʌkə(r)/ *vt* fruncir*

pudding /'pʊdɪŋ/ *n* [C U] **(a)** (baked, steamed) budín *m*, pudín *m* **(b)** (dessert) (BrE) postre *m*

puddle /'pʌdl̩/ *n* charco *m*

Puerto Rican /'pwertə'ri:kən ‖ ,pwɜ:təʊ'ri:kən/ *adj* portorriqueño, puertorriqueño

Puerto Rico /'pwertə'ri:kəʊ ‖ ,pwɜ:təʊ'ri:kəʊ/ *n* Puerto Rico *m*

puff¹ /pʌf/ *n* **(a)** (of wind, air) ráfaga *f*; **a ~ of smoke** una nube de humo **(b)** (action) soplo *m*; (on cigarette) chupada *f*, pitada *f* (AmL), calada *f* (Esp) **(c)** (sound) resoplido *m*

puff² *vt* **(a)** (blow) soplar **(b)** (smoke) ‹*cigarette/cigar/pipe*› dar* chupadas *or* (AmL tb) pitadas *or* (Esp tb) caladas a ■ **~** *vi* **1 (a)** (blow) soplar **(b)** (smoke) **to ~ ON *o* AT sth** ‹*on cigarette/cigar/pipe*› dar* chupadas *or* (AmL tb) pitadas *or* (Esp tb) caladas A algo **2** (pant) resoplar

• **puff out** [*v* + *o* + *adv*, *v* + *adv* + *o*] ‹*cheeks*› inflar, hinchar (Esp); ‹*feathers*› erizar*

• **puff up** [*v* + *adv*] hincharse

puffed /pʌft/ *adj* ‹*sleeve*› abombado

puffed-up /'pʌft'ʌp/ *adj* (*pred* **puffed up**) **(a)** (swollen) hinchado **(b)** (conceited) engreído

puffin /'pʌfən ‖ 'pʌfɪn/ *n* frailecillo *m*

puff paste, (BrE) **puff pastry** *n* [U] hojaldre *m*

puffy /'pʌfi/ *adj* **-fier, -fiest** hinchado

puke /pju:k/ *vi* (colloq) vomitar, devolver*

pull¹ /pʊl/ *vt* **1 (a)** (draw) tirar de, jalar (AmL exc CS); (drag) arrastrar **(b)** (in specified direction) (+ *adv compl*): **he was ~ed from the rubble alive** lo sacaron vivo de entre los escombros; **the current ~ed him under** la corriente lo arrastró al fondo **2 (a)** (tug) tirar de, jalar (AmL exc CS) **(b)** (tear, detach): **he ~ed the toy to bits** rompió el juguete **3 (a)** ‹*tooth*› sacar* **(b)** ‹*gun*› sacar* **4** (colloq) ‹*crowd/audience*› atraer* **5** (Med) ‹*muscle/tendon*› desgarrarse ■ **~** *vi* **1** (drag, tug) tirar, jalar (AmL exc CS) **2** «*vehicle*» (move) (+ *adv compl*): **to ~ off the road** salir* de la carretera; **to ~ into the station** entrar en la estación

• **pull apart** [*v* + *o* + *adv*] **(a)** (separate) separar **(b)** (pull to pieces) destrozar*, hacer* pedazos

• **pull away** [*v* + *adv*] **(a)** (free oneself) soltarse* **(b)** (move off) «*train/bus*» arrancar*

• **pull back** [*v* + *adv*] **(a)** (retreat) «*troops/enemy*» retirarse **(b)** (withdraw) echarse atrás

• **pull down** [*v* + *o* + *adv*, *v* + *adv* + *o*] **(a)** (lower) ‹*blind*› bajar **(b)** (demolish) ‹*building*› echar, tumbar (Méx)

• **pull in I** [*v* + *o* + *adv*, *v* + *adv* + *o*] **1** (draw in) ‹*nets/rope*› recoger*; ‹*claws*› retraer* **2** (attract) ‹*customers*› atraer*

II [*v* + *adv*] **1** (arrive) «*train/bus*» llegar* **2 (a)** (move over) «*ship/car*» arrimarse **(b)** (stop) (BrE) «*car/truck*» parar

• **pull off** [*v* + *o* + *adv*, *v* + *adv* + *o*] **1** (remove) ‹*cover/lid*› quitar **2** (achieve) (colloq) conseguir*

• **pull out I** [*v* + *adv*] **1** «*vehicle/driver*» **(a)** (depart) arrancar* **(b)** (enter traffic): **he ~ed out right in front of me** se me metió justo delante **2** (withdraw) «*troops/partner*» retirarse

II [*v* + *o* + *adv*, *v* + *adv* + *o*] **1 (a)** (extract, remove) ‹*tooth/nail/plug*› sacar*; ‹*weeds/page*› arrancar* **(b)** (produce) ‹*wallet/gun*› sacar* **2** (withdraw) ‹*team/troops*› retirar

• **pull over (a)** [*v* + *adv*] «*driver/car*» hacerse* a un lado; (to stop) acercarse* a la acera (*or* al arcén *etc*) y parar **(b)** [*v* + *o* + *adv*] parar

• **pull through** [*v* + *adv*] **(a)** (recover) reponerse* **(b)** [*v* + *adv*] (survive) salir* adelante

• **pull together 1** [*v* + *adv*] (cooperate) trabajar codo con codo **2** [*v* + *o* + *adv*] (control oneself): **to ~ oneself together** calmarse

• **pull up 1** [*v* + *o* + *adv*, *v* + *adv* + *o*] **(a)** (draw up) levantar, subir; **to ~ one's socks up** subirse los calcetines **(b)** (uproot) ‹*plant*› arrancar* **2** [*v* + *o* + *adv*] (reprimand) **to ~ sb up (ON sth)** regañar *or* (CS) retar a algn (POR algo) **3** [*v* + *adv*] (stop) «*car/driver*» parar

pull² *n* **1** [C] (tug) tirón *m*, jalón *m* (AmL exc CS) **2** [U] **(a)** (pulling force) fuerza *f* **(b)** (influence) influencia *f*

pulley /'pʊli/ *n* (*pl* **~s**) polea *f*

pull: **~-out** *n* **(a)** (withdrawal) retirada *f* **(b)** (Journ) suplemento *m*; **~over**, (AmE also) **~over sweater** *n* ⇒ SWEATER

pulp /pʌlp/ *n* [U] **(a)** (of fruit, vegetable) pulpa *f*, carne *f*; (of wood, paper) pasta *f* (de papel) **(b)** (crushed material) pasta *f*

pulpit /'pʊlpɪt/ *n* púlpito *m*

pulsate /'pʌlseɪt ‖ pʌl'seɪt/ *vi* «*heart*» latir; «*light/current*» oscilar

pulse¹ /pʌls/ *n* **1 (a)** (Physiol) pulso *m*; (*before n*) **~ rate** número *m* de pulsaciones **(b)** (throbbing) cadencia *f* **(c)** (Phys) pulsación *f* **2** (Agr, Culin) legumbre *f* (*como los garbanzos, las lentejas etc*)

pulse² *vi* latir
pulverize /'pʌlvəraɪz/ *vt* pulverizar*
puma /'puːmə || 'pjuːmə/ *n* puma *m*, león *m* (Chi, Méx)
pummel /'pʌməl/ *vt*, (BrE) **-ll-** darle* una paliza a
pump¹ /pʌmp/ *n* **1** bomba *f*; (*gasoline o* (BrE) *petrol* ~) surtidor *m* **2** (AmE Clothing) zapato *m* (de) salón
pump² *vt* **(a)** (supply) bombear; **to ~ sth** INTO **sth** ‹*water/oil*› bombear algo A algo **(b)** (drain) **to ~ sth** OUT OF **sth** sacar* algo de algo con una bomba; **to ~ sb's stomach out** hacerle* un lavado de estómago a algn **(c)** (ask) (colloq): **he was ~ing me for information** me estaba tratando de (son)sacar información ■ ~ *vi* «*machine/heart*» bombear
●**pump up** [*v + o + adv, v + adv + o*] (inflate) ‹*tire*› inflar, hinchar (Esp)
pumpkin /'pʌmpkən || 'pʌmpkɪn/ *n* [C U] calabaza *f*, zapallo *m* (CS, Per)
pun /pʌn/ *n* juego *m* de palabras, albur *m* (Méx)
punch¹ /pʌntʃ/ *n* **1 (a)** [C] (blow) puñetazo *m* **(b)** [U] (vigor) garra *f* (fam), fuerza *f* **2** [C] (for paper) perforadora *f*; (for metal, leather) sacabocados *m* **3** [U] (Culin) **(a)** ponche *m*; (*before n*) ~ **bowl** ponchera *f* **(b)** (in US) refresco *m* de frutas
punch² *vt* **1** (hit) pegarle* a **2** (perforate) ‹*ticket*› picar*, ponchar (Méx); ‹*leather/metal*› perforar; **to ~ a hole in sth** hacerle* un agujero a algo
●**punch in** [*v + adv*] (AmE) fichar, marcar* *or* (Méx) checar* tarjeta (*al entrar al trabajo*)
●**punch out** [*v + adv*] (AmE) fichar, marcar* *or* (Méx) checar* tarjeta (*al salir del trabajo*)
punch: **~-drunk** *adj* grogui (fam), atontado; **~ line** *n* remate *m* (*de un chiste*); **~-up** *n* (BrE colloq) bronca *f* (fam)
punctual /'pʌŋktʃuəl || 'pʌŋktjuəl, 'pʌŋktʃuəl/ *adj* puntual
punctuality /'pʌŋktʃu'æləti || ˌpʌŋktjʊ'æləti, ˌpʌŋktʃʊ'æləti/ *n* puntualidad *f*
punctually /'pʌŋktʃuəli || 'pʌŋktjʊəli, 'pʌŋktʃʊəli/ *adv* puntualmente
punctuate /'pʌŋktʃueɪt || 'pʌŋktjʊeɪt, 'pʌŋktʃʊeɪt/ *vt* **(a)** ‹*writing/text*› puntuar* **(b)** (intersperse) salpicar*
punctuation /'pʌŋktʃu'eɪʃən || ˌpʌŋktjʊ'eɪʃən, ˌpʌŋktʃʊ'eɪʃən/ *n* [U] puntuación *f*; (*before n*) ~ **mark** signo *m* de puntuación
puncture¹ /'pʌŋktʃər || 'pʌŋktʃə(r)/ *n* (in tire, ball) pinchazo *m*, pinchadura *f* (AmL), ponchadura *f* (Méx); **we had a ~ on the way there** pinchamos por el camino, se nos ponchó una llanta en el camino (Méx)
puncture² *vt* ‹*tire/ball*› pinchar, ponchar (Méx)
pungent /'pʌndʒənt/ *adj* ‹*taste/smell*› acre
punish /'pʌnɪʃ/ *vt* castigar*
punishing /'pʌnɪʃɪŋ/ *adj* ‹*schedule/treatment*› duro; ‹*pace*› agotador, extenuante
punishment /'pʌnɪʃmənt/ *n* **(a)** [C U] (chastisement) castigo *m* **(b)** [U] (rough treatment): **it's taken a lot of ~** ha sido muy maltratado
punk /pʌŋk/ *n* **1 (a)** [C] (person) ~ **(rocker)** punk *mf*, punki *mf* **(b)** [U] ~ **(rock)** punk *m* **2** [C] (young hoodlum) (AmE colloq) vándalo, -la *m,f*, gamberro, -rra *m,f* (Esp)
punt¹ /pʊnt/ *n* (Fin) libra *f* (irlandesa)
punt² /pʌnt/ *vi* (in boat): **to go ~ing** salir* de paseo en batea
puny /'pjuːni/ *adj* **punier, puniest** (pej) ‹*person*› enclenque; ‹*effort*› lastimoso
pup /pʌp/ *n* cría *f*; (of dog) cachorro, -rra *m,f*
pupil /'pjuːpəl || 'pjuːpɪl/ *n* **1** (Educ) alumno, -na *m,f*, educando, -da *m,f* (frml) **2** (of eye) pupila *f*
puppet /'pʌpət || 'pʌpɪt/ *n* **1 (a)** (marionette) marioneta *f*, títere *m* **(b)** (glove puppet) títere *m* **2** (stooge) títere *m*; (*before n*) ‹*regime/leader*› títere
puppy /'pʌpi/ *n* (*pl* **-pies**) cachorro, -rra *m,f*
purchase¹ /'pɜːrtʃəs || 'pɜːtʃəs/ *n* [C U] (frml) adquisición *f* (frml)
purchase² *vt* (frml) adquirir (frml)
pure /pjʊr || pjʊə(r)/ *adj* **purer** , **purest** puro
puree, **purée** /pjʊ'reɪ || 'pjʊəreɪ/ *n* [U C] puré *m*; **tomato ~** concentrado *m* de tomate
purely /'pjʊrli || 'pjʊəli/ *adv* ‹*decorative*› puramente; **~ by chance** por pura casualidad
purgatory /'pɜːrgətɔːri || 'pɜːgətəri/ *n* [U] purgatorio *m*
purge¹ /pɜːrdʒ/ *vt* **(a)** (cleanse) purgar* **(b)** (Pol) ‹*party/government/committee*› hacer* una purga en
purge² *n* (Med, Pol) purga *f*
purify /'pjʊrəfaɪ || 'pjʊərɪfaɪ/ *vt* **-fies, -fying, -fied** purificar*; ‹*water*› depurar
purist /'pjʊrəst || 'pjʊərɪst/ *n* purista *mf*
puritan /'pjʊrətn̩ || 'pjʊərɪtən/ *n* puritano, -na *m,f*
puritanical /ˌpjʊrə'tænɪkəl || ˌpjʊərɪ'tænɪkəl/ *adj* puritano
purity /'pjʊrəti || 'pjʊərəti/ *n* [U] pureza *f*
purl¹ /pɜːrl || pɜːl/ *n* [U] punto *m* (al *or* del) revés
purl² *vt* tejer al *or* del revés
purple¹ /'pɜːrpəl || 'pɜːpəl/ ▶ **515** *adj* (bluish) morado; (reddish) púrpura
purple² ▶ **515** *n* [U] (bluish) morado *m*, violeta *m*; (reddish) púrpura *m*
purport /pər'pɔːrt || pə'pɔːt/ *vt* (frml) **to ~ to** + INF pretender + INF
purpose /'pɜːrpəs || 'pɜːpəs/ *n* **1** [C] **(a)** (intention, reason) propósito *m*; **for one's own ~s** por su (*or* mi *etc*) propio interés; **the machine is good enough for our ~s** la máquina sirve para lo que nos proponemos hacer con ella; **on ~** a propósito **(b)** (use): **to serve a (useful) ~** servir* de algo **2** [U] (resolution) determinación *f*
purposeful /'pɜːrpəsfəl || 'pɜːpəsfəl/ *adj* ‹*person/stride*› resuelto; ‹*expression*› de determinación
purposely /'pɜːrpəsli || 'pɜːpəsli/ *adv* ‹*facetious/hurtful*› deliberadamente; ‹*say/do*› a propósito
purr¹ /pɜːr || pɜː(r)/ *vi* ronronear
purr² *n* ronroneo *m*
purse¹ /pɜːrs || pɜːs/ *n* **1 (a)** (for money) monedero *m*, portamonedas *m* **(b)** (funds) fondos *mpl* **2** (handbag) (AmE) cartera *f or* (Esp) bolso *m or* (Méx) bolsa *f*
purse² *vt* **to ~ one's lips** fruncir* la boca
purser /'pɜːrsər || 'pɜːsə(r)/ *n* sobrecargo *mf*
pursue /pər'suː || pə'sjuː/ *vt* **1** (chase) perseguir*; ‹*pleasure/happiness*› buscar* **2** ‹*policy/course of action*› continuar* con; ‹*research/study*› continuar* con; ‹*profession*› ejercer*

pursuer /pər'su:ər ‖ pə'sju:ə(r)/ *n* perseguidor, -dora *m,f*

pursuit /pər'su:t ‖ pə'sju:t/ *n* **1** [U C] (chase) persecución *f*; **she set off in ~ of the thief** salió en persecución del ladrón; **the ~ of happiness** la búsqueda de la felicidad **2** [C] (pastime) actividad *f*

pus /pʌs/ *n* [U] pus *m*

push¹ /pʊʃ/ *n* empujoncito *m*; (violent) empujón *m*; **she gave the door a ~** empujó la puerta; **at the ~ of a button** con sólo apretar un botón; ***at a ~*** (colloq): **at a ~, I could finish it by Friday** si me apuras, podría terminarlo para el viernes

push² *vt* **1 (a)** ‹*person/car/table*› empujar; **I ~ed the door to *o* shut** cerré la puerta empujándola **(b)** (press) ‹*button*› apretar* **(c)** (force): **to ~ prices up/down** hacer* que suban/bajen los precios; **I tried to ~ the thought to the back of my mind** traté de no pensar en ello **2** (put pressure on): **you're ~ing him/yourself too hard** le/te exiges demasiado; **to be ~ed for time/money** (colloq) andar* corto de tiempo/de dinero (fam) **3 (a)** (promote) promocionar **(b)** (sell) (colloq) ‹*drugs*› pasar (fam), transar (CS arg) **4** (approach) (colloq) (*only in -ing form*): **to be ~ing forty** rondar los cuarenta ■ ~ *vi* **1** (give a push) empujar **2** (apply pressure) presionar

● **push back** [*v + o + adv, v + adv + o*] **(a)** (force back) ‹*person/object*› empujar hacia atrás; ‹*crowd/army*› hacer* retroceder **(b)** (extend) ‹*limits*› ampliar*

● **push in** [*v + adv*] colarse* (fam)

● **push off** [*v + adv*] **(a)** (in boat) desatracar* **(b)** (leave, go) (colloq) largarse* (fam)

● **push on** [*v + adv*] **(a)** (continue journey) seguir* el viaje **(b)** (continue working) seguir* adelante

● **push through** [*v + o + adv, v + adv + o*] ‹*legislation*› hacer* aprobar

push: **~-bike** *n* (BrE) bicicleta *f*; **~-button** *adj* (*before n*) ‹*controls/telephone*› de botones; **~chair** *n* (BrE) sillita *f* (*de paseo*), carreola *f* (Méx)

pusher /'pʊʃər ‖ 'pʊʃə(r)/ *n* (colloq) camello *mf* (arg), jíbaro *mf* (Col, Ven arg), conecte *m,f* (Mex arg)

push: **~over** *n*: **to be a ~over** «*task/game*» ser* pan comido (fam), estar* chupado (Esp fam); «*person*» ser* un incauto; **~-start** /'pʊʃ'stɑ:rt ‖ ,pʊʃ'stɑ:t/ *vt* ‹*car*› arrancar* empujando; **~-up** *n* flexión *f* (de brazos *or* de pecho), fondo *m*, lagartija *f* (Méx)

pushy /'pʊʃi/ *adj* **pushier, pushiest** (colloq) prepotente

pussy /'pʊsi/ (*pl* **-sies**), **pussycat** /'pʊsikæt/ *n* (colloq) minino, -na *m,f* (fam), gatito, -ta *m,f* (fam)

put /pʊt/ (*pres p* **putting**; *past & past p* **put**) *vt* **I 1** (place) poner*; (with care, precision etc) colocar*; (inside sth) meter; **he ~ it in his mouth** se lo puso en la boca **2 (a)** (thrust): **he ~ his arms around her** la abrazó; **she ~ her head out of the window** asomó la cabeza por la ventana **(b)** (Sport) **to ~ the shot** lanzar* el peso **3 (a)** (rank) poner*; **she ~s herself first** se pone ella primero; **he ~s his art before everything else** antepone su arte a todo **(b)** (in competition, league): **this victory ~s them in *o* into the lead** con esta victoria pasan a ocupar la delantera

II 1 (cause to be) poner*; **the doctor ~ me on a diet** el doctor me puso a régimen **2** (make undergo) **to ~ sb TO sth**: **I don't want to ~ you to any trouble** no quiero causarle ninguna molestia

III 1 (a) (attribute, assign): **I ~ a high value on our friendship** valoro mucho nuestra amistad **(b)** (impose) **to ~ sth ON sth/sb**: **to ~ the blame on sb** echarle la culpa a algn; **it ~ a great strain on their relationship** eso sometió su relación a una gran tensión **2 (a)** (invest) **to ~ sth INTO sth** ‹*money*› invertir* algo EN algo; **she had ~ a lot of thought into it** lo había pensado mucho **(b)** (bet, stake) **to ~ sth ON sth** ‹*money*› apostar* algo A algo **(c)** (contribute) **to ~ sth TOWARD sth** contribuir* CON algo A algo

IV 1 (present) ‹*views/case*› exponer*; ‹*proposal*› presentar **2** (write, indicate, mark) poner* **3** (express) decir*; **~ it this way: I wouldn't invite him again** te digo lo siguiente: no lo volvería a invitar; **to ~ sth well/badly** expresar algo bien/mal

● **put about** [*v + o + adv*] (colloq) ‹*story/rumor*› hacer* correr

● **put across** [*v + o + adv, v + adv + o*] ‹*idea/message*› comunicar*

● **put aside** [*v + o + adv, v + adv + o*] **(a)** (lay to one side) dejar a un lado **(b)** (reserve) ‹*money*› guardar; ‹*goods/time*› reservar **(c)** ‹*differences*› dejar de lado

● **put away** [*v + o + adv, v + adv + o*] **(a)** (put in cupboard, drawer) ‹*dishes/tools/clothes*› guardar **(b)** (save) ‹*money*› guardar, ahorrar **(c)** (consume) (colloq) ‹*food/drink*› zamparse (fam) **(d)** (confine) (colloq) ‹*criminal/lunatic*› encerrar* **(e)** (destroy) (AmE euph) ‹*animal*› sacrificar* (euf)

● **put back** [*v + o + adv, v + adv + o*] **(a)** (replace) volver* a poner **(b)** (reset) ‹*clocks*› atrasar **(c)** (delay, retard) ‹*project*› retrasar **(d)** (postpone) posponer*, aplazar*, postergar* (AmL)

● **put by** [*v + o + adv, v + adv + o*] ‹*money*› ahorrar

● **put down I** [*v + o + adv, v + adv + o*] **1 (a)** (set down) ‹*bag/pen*› dejar; ‹*telephone*› colgar* **(b)** (lay) ‹*tiles/carpet*› poner*, colocar* **(c)** (lower) bajar **(d)** ‹*passenger*› dejar **2 (a)** (suppress) ‹*rebellion*› sofocar* **(b)** (destroy) (BrE euph) ‹*animal*› sacrificar* (euf) **3 (a)** (write down) ‹*thoughts*› anotar, escribir*; ‹*name*› poner*, escribir* **(b)** (attribute) **to ~ sth down TO sth** atribuirle* algo A algo **4** (in part payment) ‹*sum*› entregar*; ‹*deposit*› dejar

II [*v + o + adv*] (belittle) rebajar

● **put forward** [*v + o + adv, v + adv + o*] **1 (a)** ‹*theory/plan*› presentar; ‹*suggestion*› hacer* **(b)** ‹*candidate*› proponer*, postular (AmL) **2 (a)** ‹*clocks*› adelantar **(b)** ‹*trip/meeting*› adelantar

● **put in I** [*v + o + adv, v + adv + o*] **1** (install) ‹*central heating/shower unit*› poner*, instalar **2** (enter, submit) ‹*claim/request/tender*› presentar **3** (invest): **how much time can you put in?** ¿cuánto tiempo puedes dedicarle? **4** (insert, add) ‹*word/chapter/scene*› poner*

II [*v + adv*] **1** (Naut) hacer* escala **2** (apply) **to ~ in FOR sth** solicitar algo

● **put off I** [*v + o + adv, v + adv + o*] **1 (a)**

(postpone) ‹*meeting/visit/decision*› aplazar*, posponer*, postergar* (AmL); **I keep ~ting off going to the dentist** siempre estoy aplazando ir al dentista **(b)** (stall) ‹*visitor/creditor*›: **if Saturday isn't convenient, I can ~ them off** si el sábado no es conveniente, puedo decirles que lo dejen para más adelante **2** (turn off) (BrE) ‹*light*› apagar*
II [*v + o + adv, v + adv + o*] **1** (discourage): **the thought of the journey ~s me off going to see them** pensar en el viaje me quita las ganas de ir a visitarlos **2** (distract) distraer*; (disconcert) desconcertar*

• **put on I** [*v + o + adv, v + adv + o*] **1** ‹*jacket/sweater*› ponerse*; **to put one's clothes on** vestirse*, ponerse* la ropa; **to ~ one's shoes on** ponerse* los zapatos, calzarse* **2** ‹*light/radio/oven*› encender*, prender (AmL); ‹*music*› poner* **3** (gain): **I've ~ on four pounds** he engordado cuatro libras; **to ~ on weight** engordar **4** ‹*exhibition*› organizar*; ‹*play/show*› presentar **5** (assume) ‹*expression*› adoptar; **he's just ~ting it on** está haciendo teatro
II [*v + o + adv*] **1 (a)** (alert) **to ~ sb on TO sb**: **somebody had ~ the police on to them** alguien había puesto a la policía sobre su pista **(b)** (introduce) **to ~ sb on TO sb**: **I can ~ you on to someone who ...** puedo ponerte en contacto con una persona que ... **2** (tease) (AmE colloq) tomarle el pelo a (fam)

• **put out I** [*v + o + adv, v + adv + o*] **1 (a)** (put outside) ‹*washing/cat*› sacar* **(b)** (set out) disponer* **(c)** (extend) ‹*arm/tongue*› sacar* **(d)** (dislocate) dislocarse*, zafarse (Chi, Méx) **2 (a)** (extinguish) ‹*fire/light/cigarette*› apagar* **(b)** (anesthetize) (colloq) dormir* **3** (offend, inconvenience) molestar **4 (a)** (issue, publish) ‹*statement*› publicar* **(b)** (broadcast) transmitir
II [*v + adv*] (Naut) salir*; **to ~ out to sea** hacerse* a la mar

• **put over (a)** ⇒ PUT ACROSS **(b)** (AmE) ⇒ PUT OFF I 1(a)

• **put past** [*v + o + prep + o*]: ***not to ~ it past sb***: **I wouldn't ~ it past her** no me extrañaría nada *or* la creo muy capaz

• **put through 1** [*v + o + prep + o*] (make undergo) someter a **2** [*v + o + adv, v + adv + o*] (Telec): **to ~ sb through** (**TO sb**) pasar *or* (AmL) comunicar* *or* (Esp) poner* a algn CON algn

• **put together** [*v + o + adv, v + adv + o*] **1 (a)** (assemble) armar; ‹*collection*› reunir* **(b)** (create) ‹*team*› formar; ‹*magazine*› producir*; ‹*meal*› preparar; (quickly) improvisar **2** (combine) juntar, reunir*; **more than everything else ~ together** más que todo lo demás junto

• **put up I** [*v + o + adv, v + adv + o*] **1 (a)** ‹*hotel*› levantar; ‹*tent*› armar **(b)** ‹*decorations/curtains/notice*› poner* **(c)** ‹*umbrella*› abrir* **(d)** ‹*hand*› levantar **2** ‹*price/fare*› aumentar **3** ‹*candidate*› proponer*, postular (AmL) **4** (in accommodation) alojar; **they ~ us up for the night** nos quedamos a dormir en su casa
II [*v + adv + o*] **(a)** (present): **to ~ up resistance/a struggle/a fight** ofrecer* resistencia **(b)** ‹*money/capital*› poner*
III [*v + adv*] (stay) quedarse

• **put up to** [*v + o + adv + prep + o*]: **somebody must have ~ them up to it** alguien debe haberlos empujado a ello

• **put up with** [*v + adv + prep + o*] aguantar

put: **~-down** *n* (colloq) desprecio *m*; **~ out** *adj* (*pred*) **to be ~ out** estar* molesto

putrid /'pju:trəd ‖ 'pju:trɪd/ *adj* putrefacto, pútrido

putt /pʌt/ *vi* golpear la bola, potear (AmL) ■ **~** *vt* golpear

putter¹ /'pʌtər ‖ 'pʌtə(r)/ *n* (club) putter *m*

putter² *vi* (AmE) (+ *adv compl*): **to ~ around** *o* **about in the garden** entretenerse trabajando en el jardín; **I've been ~ing around the house all day** me he pasado el día haciendo un poco de esto y un poco de aquello en la casa

putting green /'pʌtɪŋ/ *n* putting green *m*

putty /'pʌti/ *n* [U] masilla *f*

puzzle¹ /'pʌzəl/ *n* **(a)** (game,toy) rompecabezas *m*; (riddle) adivinanza *f* **(b)** (mystery) misterio *m*

puzzle² *vt*: **one thing ~s me** hay algo que no entiendo

puzzled /'pʌzəld/ *adj* ‹*expression/tone*› de desconcierto; **I'm ~ about it** me tiene perplejo

PVC *n* [U] PVC *m*

pygmy /'pɪgmi/ *n* (*pl* **-mies**) **(a)** (Anthrop) *also* **Pygmy** pigmeo, -mea *m,f* **(b)** (Zool) (*before n*) enano

pyjamas /pə'dʒɑ:məz/ *n* (BrE) ⇒ PAJAMAS

pylon /'paɪlɑ:n, -lən ‖ 'paɪlɒn, -lən/ *n* torre *f* de alta tensión

pyramid /'pɪrəmɪd/ *n* pirámide *f*

pyre /paɪr ‖ 'paɪə(r)/ *n* pira *f*

Pyrenees /'pɪrə'ni:z ‖ ,pɪrə'ni:z/ *pl n* **the ~** los Pirineos

Pyrex® /'paɪreks/ *n* [U] pyrex® *m*, arcopal® *m*

python /'paɪθɑ:n ‖ 'paɪθən/ *n* (serpiente *f*) pitón *f*

Qq

Q, q /kjuː/ *n* Q, q *f*

QC *n* (in UK) (= **Queen's Counsel**) *título conferido a ciertos abogados de prestigio*

QED (= **quod erat demonstrandum**) Q.E.D. (frml), que es lo que había que demostrar

quack¹ /kwæk/ *vi* graznar

quack² *n* (pej) **1** (charlatan) charlatán, -tana *m,f*; (professing medical skill) (~ *doctor*) curandero, -ra *m,f* **2** (of duck) graznido *m*

quad /kwɑːd ‖ kwɒd/ *n* (colloq) **1** (quadruplet) cuatrillizo, -za *m,f* **2** (of college) ⇒ QUADRANGLE 1

quadrangle /ˈkwɑːdræŋgəl ‖ ˈkwɒdræŋgəl/ *n* **1** (BrE Archit) patio *m* interior **2** (Math) ⇒ QUADRILATERAL

quadrant /ˈkwɑːdrənt ‖ ˈkwɒdrənt/ *n* cuadrante *m*

quadrilateral /ˈkwɑːdrəˈlætərəl ‖ ˌkwɒdrɪˈlætərəl/ *n* cuadrilátero *m*

quadruped /ˈkwɑːdrəped ‖ ˈkwɒdrʊped/ *n* cuadrúpedo *m*

quadruple¹ /kwɑːˈdruːpl̩ ‖ ˈkwɒdrʊpl̩/ *adj* cuádruple, cuádruplo

quadruple² /kwɑːˈdruːpl̩ ‖ kwɒˈdruːpl̩/ *vi* cuadruplicarse*

quadruplet /kwɑːˈdruːplət ‖ ˈkwɒdrʊplət/ *n* cuatrillizo, -za *m,f*

quaff /kwɑːf ‖ kwɒf/ *vt* (hum) beberse, zamparse (fam)

quagmire /ˈkwægmaɪr, ˈkwɑːg- ‖ ˈkwɒgmaɪə(r), ˈkwæg-/ *n* **(a)** (bog) lodazal *m*, barrial *m* (AmL) **(b)** (situation) atolladero *m*

quail¹ /kweɪl/ *vi* temblar*; **she ~ed at the idea** la idea le daba pavor

quail² *n* [C U] (*pl* **quails** *or* **quail**) codorniz *f*

quaint /kweɪnt/ *adj* **-er, -est (a)** (charming, picturesque) pintoresco **(b)** (odd) extraño

quake¹ /kweɪk/ *vi* temblar*

quake² *n* (colloq) (earthquake) temblor *m*; (more violent) terremoto *m*

Quaker /ˈkweɪkər ‖ ˈkweɪkə(r)/ *n* cuáquero, -ra *m,f*

qualification /ˈkwɑːləfəˈkeɪʃən ‖ ˌkwɒlɪfɪˈkeɪʃən/ *n* **1** [C] **(a)** (Educ): **she has a teaching ~** tiene título de maestra/profesora; **his ~s are very good** está muy bien calificado *or* (Esp) cualificado **(b)** (skill, necessary attribute) requisito *m* **2** [U] **(a)** (eligibility) derecho *m* **(b)** (being accepted) clasificación *f* **3** [U C] (reservation) reserva *f*

qualified /ˈkwɑːləfaɪd ‖ ˈkwɒlɪfaɪd/ *adj* **(a)** (trained) titulado; **to be ~ to + INF** tener* la titulación necesaria PARA + INF **(b)** (competent) (*pred*) capacitado; **to be ~ to + INF** estar* capacitado PARA + INF **(c)** (eligible) (*pred*) **to be ~ to + INF** reunir* los requisitos necesarios PARA + INF

qualify /ˈkwɑːləfaɪ ‖ ˈkwɒlɪfaɪ/ **-fies, -fying, -fied** *vt* **1** (equip, entitle): **this degree qualifies you to practice anywhere in Europe** este título te habilita para ejercer en cualquier parte de Europa; **their low income qualifies them for some benefits** sus bajos ingresos les dan derecho a recibir ciertas prestaciones **2 (a)** (limit): **I'd like to ~ the statement I made earlier** quisiera matizar lo que expresé anteriormente haciendo algunas salvedades (*or* puntualizaciones *etc*) **(b)** (Ling) calificar* ■ **~** *vi* **(a)** (gain professional qualification) titularse, recibirse (AmL) **(b)** (Sport) clasificarse* **(c)** (be entitled) **to ~** (FOR **sth**) tener* derecho (A algo)

quality /ˈkwɑːləti ‖ ˈkwɒləti/ *n* (*pl* **-ties**) [U C] calidad *f*

qualm /kwɑːm/ *n* (*often pl*) **(a)** (scruple) reparo *m*; **to have no ~s about sth** no tener* ningún reparo en algo **(b)** (misgiving) duda *f*

quandary /ˈkwɑːndri ‖ ˈkwɒndri/ *n* (*pl* **-ries**) (*usu sing*) dilema *m*

quango /ˈkwæŋgəʊ/ *n* (*pl* **-gos**) (BrE) (= **quasi-autonomous non-governmental organization**) organismo *m or* ente *m* semi-autónomo

quantify /ˈkwɑːntəfaɪ ‖ ˈkwɒntɪfaɪ/ *vt* **-fies, -fying, -fied** cuantificar*

quantity /ˈkwɑːntəti ‖ ˈkwɒntəti/ *n* (*pl* **-ties**) [C U] cantidad *f*

quantity surveyor *n*: *ingeniero o técnico que se ocupa de mediciones y cálculo de materiales*

quarantine¹ /ˈkwɔːrəntiːn ‖ ˈkwɒrəntiːn/ *n* [U] cuarentena *f*

quarantine² *vt* poner* en cuarentena

quarrel¹ /ˈkwɔːrəl ‖ ˈkwɒrəl/ *n* **(a)** (argument) pelea *f*, riña *f*; **to have a ~ with sb** pelearse con algn **(b)** (disagreement) discrepancia *f*

quarrel² *vi*, (BrE) **-ll-** (argue) pelearse, discutir

quarrelsome /ˈkwɔːrəlsəm ‖ ˈkwɒrəlsəm/ *adj* peleador, peleón (Esp fam)

quarry¹ /ˈkwɔːri ‖ ˈkwɒri/ *n* (*pl* **-ries**) **1** (excavation) cantera *f* **2** (prey) presa *f*

quarry² *vt* **-ries, -rying, -ried** ‹*stone/slate*› extraer* (*de una cantera*); ‹*land/hillside*› abrir* una cantera en

quart /kwɔːrt ‖ kwɔːt/ *n* cuarto *m* de galón (*EEUU: 0,94 litros, RU: 1,14 litros*)

quarter /ˈkwɔːrtər ‖ ˈkwɔːtə(r)/ *n* **1** ▶**543** [C] (fourth part) cuarta parte *f*, cuarto *m*; **a ~ of a mile** un cuarto de milla **2** [C] (US, Canadian coin) moneda *f* de 25 centavos **3** ▶**884** [C] **(a)** (in telling time) cuarto *m*; **a ~ of an hour** un cuarto de hora; **it's a ~ of** *o*

(BrE) **to one** es la una menos cuarto *or* (AmL exc RPl) un cuarto para la una; **a ~ after** *o* (BrE) **past one** la una y cuarto **(b)** (three months) trimestre *m* **4** [C] **(a)** (district of town) barrio *m* **(b)** (area) parte *f*; ***at close ~s*** de cerca **5 quarters** *pl* (accommodations): **the servants' ~s** las habitaciones de la servidumbre

quarterfinal /ˈkwɔːrtərˈfaɪnl̩ ‖ˌkwɔːtəˈfaɪnl/ *n* cuarto *m* de final

quarterly¹ /ˈkwɔːrtərli ‖ˈkwɔːtəli/ *adj* trimestral

quarterly² *adv* trimestralmente

quarter note *n* (AmE) negra *f*

quartet /kwɔːrˈtet ‖ kwɔːˈtet/ *n* cuarteto *m*

quartz /kwɔːrts ‖ kwɔːts/ *n* [U] cuarzo *m*

quash /ˈkwɑːʃ ‖kwɒʃ/ *vt* **(a)** (Law) ‹*verdict/sentence*› anular **(b)** (suppress) ‹*revolt*› sofocar*; ‹*protest*› acallar

quaver¹ /ˈkweɪvər ‖ ˈkweɪvə(r)/ *n* **(a)** (in voice) temblor *m* **(b)** (BrE Mus) corchea *f*

quaver² *vi* «*voice*» (in singing) vibrar; (in speech) temblar*

quay /kiː/ *n* muelle *m*

quayside /ˈkiːsaɪd/ *n* muelle *m*

queasy /ˈkwiːzi/ *adj* **-sier, -siest** mareado

queen /kwiːn/ ▶ 603 *n* reina *f*

queen: **~ bee** *n* (Zool) abeja *f* reina; **~ mother** *n* reina *f* madre

queer¹ /kwɪr ‖ kwɪə(r)/ *adj* **1** (odd) raro, extraño **2** (male homosexual) (colloq & sometimes pej) maricón (fam & pey), gay

queer² *n* (colloq & sometimes pej) maricón *m* (fam & pey), gay *m*

quell /kwel/ *vt* ‹*revolt*› sofocar*; ‹*criticism*› acallar

quench /kwentʃ/ *vt* **(a)** ‹*thirst*› quitar, saciar (liter) **(b)** ‹*flames*› sofocar*

querulous /ˈkwerələs ‖ˈkwerʊləs/ *adj* quejumbroso

query¹ /ˈkwɪri ‖ ˈkwɪəri/ *n* (*pl* **-ries**) (doubt) duda *f*; (question) pregunta *f*

query² *vt* **-ries, -rying, -ried** cuestionar

quest /kwest/ *n* búsqueda *f*; **~ FOR sth** búsqueda DE algo

question¹ /ˈkwestʃən/ *n* **(a)** [C] (inquiry) pregunta *f*; **to ask a ~** hacer* una pregunta **(b)** [C] (in quiz, exam) pregunta *f* **(c)** [C] (issue, problem) cuestión *f*, asunto *m*; **the person in ~** la persona en cuestión; **if it's a ~ of money** ... si es cuestión *or* se trata de dinero ... **(d)** [U] (doubt) duda *f*; **beyond ~** fuera de duda **(e)** [U] (possibility) posibilidad *f*; **it is completely out of the ~** es totalmente imposible

question² *vt* **(a)** ‹*person*› hacerle* preguntas a; ‹*suspect/student*› interrogar* **(b)** (doubt) ‹*integrity/motives*› poner* en duda

questionable /ˈkwestʃənəbəl/ *adj* cuestionable

questioner /ˈkwestʃənər ‖ ˈkwestʃənə(r)/ *n* interrogador, -dora *m,f*

questioning¹ /ˈkwestʃənɪŋ/ *adj* ‹*expression/voice*› inquisidor; ‹*mind*› inquisitivo

questioning² *n* [U] interrogatorio *m*

question mark *n* signo *m* de interrogación

questionnaire /ˈkwestʃəˈner ‖ˌkwestʃəˈneə(r)/ *n* cuestionario *m*

queue¹ /kjuː/ *n* (BrE) cola *f*; **to form a ~** hacer* cola; **to jump the ~** colarse* (fam), brincarse* *or* saltarse la cola (Méx fam)

queue² *vi* **queues, queueing, queued ~ (up)** (BrE) hacer* cola

quibble¹ /ˈkwɪbəl/ *n* objeción *f* (*de poca monta*)

quibble² *vi* hacer* problemas por nimiedades

quick¹ /kwɪk/ *adj* **quicker, quickest (a)** (speedy) ‹*action/movement*› rápido; **I'll be as ~ as I can** volveré (*or* lo haré *etc*) lo más rápido que pueda; **that was ~!** ¡qué rapidez! **(b)** (brief) (*before n, no comp*) ‹*calculation/question*› rápido; ‹*nod*› breve; **he'd like a ~ word with you** quiere hablar contigo un momento **(c)** (easily roused): **she has a ~ temper** tiene mucho genio **(d)** (prompt): **he's ~ to take offense** se ofende por lo más mínimo

quick² *adv* **quicker, quickest** rápido, rápidamente

quick³ *n* **the ~**: **her nails were bitten to the ~** tenía las uñas en carne viva de mordérselas; ***to cut sb to the ~*** herir* a algn en lo más vivo

quicken /ˈkwɪkən/ *vt* acelerar ■ **~** *vi* acelerarse

quickly /ˈkwɪkli/ *adv* **(a)** (speedily) ‹*move/recover*› rápidamente, rápido **(b)** (promptly) ‹*understand/reply*› pronto

quickness /ˈkwɪknəs ‖ ˈkwɪknɪs/ *n* [U] rapidez *f*

quick: **~sand** *n* (*often pl*) arenas *fpl* movedizas; **~-tempered** /ˈkwɪkˈtempərd ‖ˌkwɪkˈtempəd/ *adj* ‹*person*› de genio vivo, irascible; **~-witted** /ˈkwɪkˈwɪtəd ‖ˌkwɪkˈwɪtɪd/ *adj* agudo

quid /kwɪd/ *n* (*pl* **~**) (pound) (BrE colloq) libra *f*

quiet¹ /ˈkwaɪət/ *adj* **1 (a)** (silent) ‹*street*› silencioso; **be ~!** (to one person) ¡cállate!; (to more than one person) ¡cállense! *or* (Esp tb) ¡callaros *or* callaos!, ¡silencio!; **I kept ~ about the bill** no dije nada de lo de la factura **(b)** (not loud) ‹*engine*› silencioso; **he has a very ~ voice** habla muy bajo **(c)** (not boisterous) ‹*manner*› tranquilo; **you're very ~ today** hoy estás muy callada **2 (a)** (peaceful) tranquilo; **they had a ~ wedding** la boda se celebró en la intimidad **(b)** (not busy) ‹*day*› tranquilo

quiet² *n* [U] **(a)** (silence) silencio *m* **(b)** (peace, tranquillity) tranquilidad *f*

quiet³ (AmE) *vt* **(a)** (silence) ‹*uproar/protests*› acallar; ‹*class*› hacer* callar **(b)** (calm) ‹*horse/person*› tranquilizar*; ‹*fear/suspicion*› disipar

● **quiet down** (AmE) ⇒ QUIETEN DOWN

quieten /ˈkwaɪətn̩/ *vt* (esp BrE) ⇒ QUIET³

● **quieten down 1** [*v* + *o* + *adv*, *v* + *adv* + *o*] ‹*person*› calmar; ‹*rumors/clamor*› acallar **2** [*v* + *adv*] «*person*» calmarse; (with maturity) sentar* la cabeza; «*rumors*» acallarse

quietly /ˈkwaɪətli/ *adv* **1** (silently, not loudly) ‹*move*› silenciosamente; ‹*say/speak*› en voz baja **2 (a)** (peacefully) ‹*sleep/rest*› tranquilamente **(b)** (unobtrusively) ‹*dress/mention/slip away*› discretamente

quill /kwɪl/ *n* pluma *f* (de oca *or* ganso)

quilt /kwɪlt/ *n* edredón *m*, acolchado *m* (RPl), cobija *f* (Méx)

quilted /'kwɪltəd ‖ 'kwɪltɪd/ *adj* acolchado, guateado (Esp)

quin /kwɪn/ *n* (BrE colloq) ⇒ QUINTUPLET

quince /kwɪns/ *n* membrillo *m*

quint /kwɪnt/ *n* (AmE colloq) ⇒ QUINTUPLET

quintessential /'kwɪntə'sentʃəl ‖ ,kwɪntɪ'senʃəl/ *adj* (*usu before n*) por excelencia

quintet /kwɪn'tet/ *n* quinteto *m*

quintuplet /kwɪn'tu:plət ‖ 'kwɪntjʊplət/ *n* quintillizo, -za *m,f*, quíntuple *mf* (Chi, Ven)

quip¹ /kwɪp/ *n* ocurrencia *f*, salida *f*

quip² *vt* **-pp-** decir* bromeando

quirk /kwɜ:rk ‖ kwɜ:k/ *n* **(a)** (of circumstance) singularidad *f* **(b)** (of person) rareza *f*

quit /kwɪt/ (*pres p* **quitting**; *past & past p* **quit** *or* **quitted**) *vt* (esp AmE) ‹*job/habit*› dejar; ‹*contest*› abandonar; **to ~ -ING** dejar DE + INF ■ **~** *vi* **(a)** (stop) (esp AmE) parar **(b)** (give in) abandonar **(c)** (leave): **notice to ~** notificación *f* de desahucio

quite /kwaɪt/ *adv* **1 (a)** (completely, absolutely) completamente, totalmente; **is this what you wanted? — not ~** ¿es esto lo que buscaba? — no exactamente; **there isn't ~ enough** falta un poquito; **there's nothing ~ like champagne** realmente no hay como el champán; **~ the opposite** todo lo contrario **(b)** (*as intensifier*): **it makes ~ a difference** hace bastante diferencia; **~ a few of them** muchos de ellos; **that was ~ a game!** ¡fue un partidazo! (fam), ¡fue flor de partido! (CS fam) **2** (fairly) (BrE) bastante; **it's ~ warm today** hoy hace bastante calor; **there were ~ a few** había bastantes, había unos cuantos

quits /kwɪts/ *adj* **to be ~** estar* en paz *or* (AmL) a mano; ***to call it ~***: **take the money and call it ~** toma el dinero y dejémoslo de una vez

quiver¹ /'kwɪvər ‖ 'kwɪvə(r)/ *vi* «*person/lips*» temblar*; «*leaves*» agitarse

quiver² *n* **1** (for arrows) carcaj *m*, aljaba *f* **2** (movement) temblor *m*

quiz¹ /kwɪz/ *n* (*pl* **~es**) **(a)** (competition) concurso *m*; (*before n*) **~ show** programa *m* concurso **(b)** (test) (AmE) prueba *f*

quiz² *vt* **-zz- (a)** (question) ‹*suspect*› interrogar* **(b)** (test) (AmE) ‹*students*› poner* *or* hacer* una prueba a

quizzical /'kwɪzɪkəl/ *adj* socarrón, burlón

quorum /'kwɔ:rəm/ *n* [U] quórum *m*

quota /'kwəʊtə/ *n* (*pl* **~s**) (EC, Econ) cuota *f*

quotation /kwəʊ'teɪʃən/ *n* **1** (passage) cita *f* **2** (estimate) presupuesto *m*

quotation marks *pl n* comillas *fpl*

quote¹ /kwəʊt/ *vt* **1 (a)** ‹*writer/passage*› citar; ‹*reference number*› indicar* **(b)** ‹*example*› dar*; ‹*instance*› citar **2 (a)** (Busn) ‹*price*› dar*, ofrecer* **(b)** (Fin) cotizar* ■ **~** *vi* (repeat, recite): **he was quoting from the Bible** citaba de la Biblia; **she said, and I ~** ... dijo, y lo repito textualmente ..., sus palabras textuales fueron ...

quote² *n* (colloq) **1** (passage) cita *f* **2** (estimate) presupuesto *m*

quotient /'kwəʊʃənt/ *n* (Math) cociente *m*

Rr

R, r /ɑ:r ‖ ɑ:(r)/ *n* R, r *f*

R (in US) (Cin) (= **restricted**) menores acompañados

rabbi /'ræbaɪ/ *n* (*pl* **-bis**) rabino, -na *m,f*; (as title) rabí *mf*

rabbit /'ræbət ‖ 'ræbɪt/ *n* **(a)** [C] (Zool) conejo, -ja *m,f* **(b)** [U] (meat) conejo *m*

rabble /'ræbəl/ *n* [U] **(a)** (mob) muchedumbre *f* **(b)** (common people) (pej) **the ~** la chusma (pey)

rabid /'ræbəd ‖ 'ræbɪd/ *adj* rabioso

rabies /'reɪbi:z/ *n* [U] rabia *f*

RAC *n* (in UK) = **Royal Automobile Club**

raccoon /ræ'ku:n ‖ rə'ku:n/ *n* mapache *m*

race¹ /reɪs/ *n* **1** [C] (contest) carrera *f* **2** [C U] (Anthrop) raza *f*; **the human ~** el género humano; (*before n*) **~ relations** *pl n* relaciones *fpl* raciales

race² *vi* **(a)** (rush) (+ *adv compl*): **she ~d down the hill on her bike** bajó la cuesta en bicicleta a toda velocidad **(b)** (in competition) correr, competir* **(c)** «*pulse/heart*» latir aceleradamente ■ **~** *vt* ‹*person*› echarle *or* (RPl) jugarle* una carrera a

race: **~course** *n* (stadium) hipódromo *m*; (track) pista *f* (de carreras); **~horse** *n* caballo *m* de carrera(s)

racial /'reɪʃəl/ *adj* racial

racing¹ /'reɪsɪŋ/ *n* [U] **(a)** (*horse ~*) carreras *fpl* de caballos **(b)** (sport, pastime) carreras *fpl*

racing² *adj* (*before n*) ‹*bicycle/car*› de carrera(s)

racism /'reɪsɪzəm/ *n* [U] racismo *m*

racist¹ /'reɪsəst ‖ 'reɪsɪst/ *n* racista *mf*

racist² *adj* racista

rack¹ /ræk/ *n* **1** (shelf) estante *m*; (for baggage) rejilla *f*; (*clothes ~*) perchero *m*; (*drying ~*) tendedero *m* **2** (for torture) potro *m* (de tortura); ***to go to ~ and ruin*** venirse* abajo

rack² *vt* (shake): **to be ~ed with pain** sufrir dolores atroces; **to be ~ed with guilt** estar* atormentado por el remordimiento

racket /'rækət ‖ 'rækɪt/ *n* **1** (Sport) raqueta *f* **2** (noise) (colloq) jaleo *m* (fam) **3** (business) (colloq) tinglado *m* (fam)

racketeer /'rækə'tɪr ‖ ˌrækə'tiə(r)/ *n* mafioso, -sa *m,f*

racquet /'rækət ‖ 'rækɪt/ *n* ⇨ RACKET 1

racy /'reɪsi/ *adj* **racier, raciest (a)** (lively) animado **(b)** (risqué) ‹*story/joke*› subido de tono

radar /'reɪdɑːr ‖ 'reɪdɑː(r)/ *n* [U] radar *m*

radiant /'reɪdiənt/ *adj* ‹*smile/look*› radiante; ‹*sun/blue*› resplandeciente

radiate /'reɪdieɪt/ *vt* irradiar

radiation /'reɪdi'eɪʃən/ *n* [U] radiación *f*; (*before n*) ~ **sickness** radiotoxemia *f*

radiator /'reɪdieɪtər ‖ 'reɪdieɪtə(r)/ *n* radiador *m*

radical /'rædɪkəl/ *adj* radical; ‹*writer*› de ideas radicales

radically /'rædɪkli/ *adv* radicalmente

radii /'reɪdiaɪ/ *pl of* RADIUS

radio¹ /'reɪdiəʊ/ *n* (*pl* **-os**) **(a)** [C] (receiver) radio *m* (AmL exc CS), radio *f* (CS, Esp) **(b)** [U] (medium) radio *f*

radio² (*3rd pers sing pres* **radios**; *pres p* **radioing**; *past & past p* **radioed**) *vt* ‹*person*› llamar por radio; ‹*message*› transmitir por radio

radio: **~active** /'reɪdiəʊ'æktɪv/ *adj* radiactivo; **~activity** /'reɪdiəʊæk'tɪvəti/ *n* [U] radiactividad *f*; **~-controlled** /'reɪdiəʊkən'trəʊld/ *adj* teledirigido

radiographer /'reɪdi'ɑːgrəfər ‖ ˌreɪdi'ɒgrəfə(r)/ *n* radiógrafo, -fa *m,f*

radiologist /'reɪdi'ɑːlədʒəst ‖ ˌreɪdi'ɒlədʒɪst/ *n* radiólogo, -ga *m,f*

radiotherapy /'reɪdiəʊ'θerəpi/ *n* [U] radioterapia *f*

radish /'rædɪʃ/ *n* rabanito *m*, rábano *m*

radius /'reɪdiəs/ *n* (*pl* **radiuses** *or* **radii**) radio *m*

RAF /'ɑːreɪ'ef/ (in UK) (= **Royal Air Force**) **the** ~ la Fuerza Aérea británica

raffle¹ /'ræfəl/ *n* rifa *f*

raffle² *vt* rifar, sortear

raft /ræft ‖ rɑːft/ *n* balsa *f*

rafter /'ræftər ‖ 'rɑːftə(r)/ *n* viga *f*

rag /ræg/ *n* **1 (a)** [C] (piece of cloth) trapo *m* **(b) rags** *pl* (tattered clothes) harapos *mpl*, andrajos *mpl*; **dressed in ~s** harapiento, andrajoso **2** [C] (newspaper) (colloq & pej) periodicucho *m* (pey)

ragamuffin /'rægəˌmʌfən ‖ 'rægəˌmʌfɪn/ *n* pilluelo, -la *m,f*

rag doll *n* muñeca *f* de trapo

rage¹ /reɪdʒ/ *n* **1 (a)** [U] (violent anger) furia *f* **(b)** [C] (fit of fury): **to be in a ~** estar* furioso **2** [U] (fashion) (colloq): **to be (all) the ~** hacer* furor

rage² *vi* **(a)** «*storm/sea*» rugir*; «*fire*» arder furiosamente **(b)** «*person*» rabiar **(c) raging** *pres p* ‹*storm*› rugiente; ‹*sea*› embravecido; ‹*headache*› enloquecedor; ‹*argument*› enconado

ragged /'rægəd ‖ 'rægɪd/ *adj* ‹*clothes/appearance*› harapiento, andrajoso; ‹*edge*› irregular

raid¹ /reɪd/ *n* **(a)** (Mil) asalto *m* **(b)** (*air* ~) bombardeo *m* aéreo **(c)** (by thieves) atraco *m* **(d)** (by police) redada *f*, allanamiento *m* (AmL)

raid² *vt* **(a)** (Mil) asaltar **(b)** ‹*bank*› asaltar **(c)** «*police*» ‹*house/building*› hacer* una redada en, allanar (AmL)

raider /'reɪdər ‖ 'reɪdə(r)/ *n* asaltante *mf*

rail /reɪl/ *n* **1** [C] **(a)** (bar) riel *m* **(b)** (*hand* ~) pasamanos *m* **(c)** (barrier) baranda *f* **2 (a)** [C] (for trains, trams) riel *m*, raíl *m* (Esp) **(b)** [U] (railroad) ferrocarril *m*; **by ~** en *or* por ferrocarril

railing /'reɪlɪŋ/ *n* (*often pl*) reja *f*

rail: **~road** *n* (AmE) **(a)** (system) ferrocarril *m* **(b)** (track) vía *f* férrea; **~way** *n* (BrE) ⇨ ~ROAD

rain¹ /reɪn/ ▶ 920 *n* [U C] lluvia *f*

rain² ▶ 920 *v impers* llover*

rainbow /'reɪmbəʊ/ *n* arco *m* iris

rain: **~coat** *n* impermeable *m*; **~drop** *n* gota *f* de lluvia; **~fall** *n* [U] precipitaciones *fpl*, lluvia *f*; **~ forest** *n* selva *f* tropical (húmeda); **~water** *n* [U] agua *f*‡ de lluvia

rainy /'reɪni/ ▶ 920 *adj* **-nier, -niest** lluvioso

raise¹ /reɪz/ *vt* **I 1 (a)** ‹*head/hand*› levantar, alzar*; ‹*eyebrows*› arquear; ‹*flag*› izar* **(b)** (make higher) ‹*shelf/level*› subir **2 (a)** (set upright) levantar **(b)** (erect) ‹*monument/building*› levantar, erigir* (frml) **3 (a)** ‹*pressure/temperature*› aumentar, elevar; ‹*price/salary*› subir, aumentar; **to ~ one's voice** levantar la voz **(b)** ‹*consciousness*› aumentar **II 1 (a)** ‹*money/funds*› recaudar **(b)** ‹*army*› reclutar **2** ‹*fears/doubt*› suscitar; **he managed to ~ a smile** pudo sonreír; **to ~ the alarm** dar* la alarma **3** ‹*subject*› sacar*; ‹*question*› formular; **to ~ an objection** poner* una objeción **4 (a)** ‹*family*› criar* **(b)** ‹*cattle*› dedicarse* a la cría de

raise² *n* (AmE) aumento *m or* subida *f* de sueldo

raisin /'reɪzn̩/ *n* (uva *f*) pasa *f*, pasa *f* (de uva)

rake¹ /reɪk/ *n* (tool) rastrillo *m*

rake² *vt* rastrillar

rakish /'reɪkɪʃ/ *adj* (casual, jaunty) desenfadado

rally¹ /'ræli/ *n* (*pl* **-lies**) **1** (mass meeting) concentración *f*; **political ~** mitin *m*, mítin *m* **2** (Auto) rally *m* **3** (in tennis, badminton) peloteo *m*

rally² **-lies, -lying, -lied** *vi* **1** (unite) unirse; (gather) congregarse* **2 (a)** (recover) «*person*» recuperarse, reponerse* **(b)** (Fin) «*currency/price*» repuntar, recuperarse ■ ~ *vt* **1** ‹*support/vote*› conseguir* **2** ‹*strength/spirits*› recobrar

• **rally round** [*v* + *adv*]: **all the neighbors rallied round to help** todos los vecinos se juntaron para ayudar

ram¹ /ræm/ *n* (Zool) carnero *m*

ram² **-mm-** *vt* **(a)** (force) (+ *adv compl*): **he ~med the stake into the ground** hincó la estaca en la tierra; **he ~med his fist through the door** atravesó la puerta de un puñetazo **(b)** (crash into) chocar* con; (deliberately) embestir* contra

• **ram home** [*v* + *o* + *adv*, *v* + *adv* + *o*] ‹*point/message*› hacer* entender a la fuerza

RAM /ræm/ *n* [U] (Comput) (= **random access memory**) RAM *f*

Ramadan /'rɑːmədɑːn ‖ ˌræmə'dæn/ *n* Ramadán *m*

ramble¹ /'ræmbəl/ *n* paseo *m*; (BrE Sport) excursión *f* (*a pie*)

ramble² *vi* **(a)** (walk) pasear; **to go rambling** (BrE) hacer* excursionismo **(b)** (in speech, writing) irse* por las ramas
• ramble on [*v* + *adv*] divagar*

rambler /'ræmblər ‖ 'ræmblə(r)/ *n* excursionista *mf*

rambling /'ræmblɪŋ/ *adj* **(a)** ‹*essay/lecture*› que se va por las ramas **(b)** ‹*streets*› laberíntico; **a ~ old house** una vieja casona llena de recovecos **(c)** ‹*rose*› trepador

ramp /ræmp/ *n* **(a)** (slope) rampa *f*; **entrance** *o* **on ~** (AmE) vía *f* de acceso; **exit** *o* **off ~** (AmE) vía *f* de salida **(b)** (on ship, aircraft) (for passengers) escalerilla *f*; (for vehicles) rampa *f* **(c)** (platform) elevador *m* **(d)** (hump) (BrE) desnivel *m*

rampage /'ræmpeɪdʒ/ *n*: **to be/go on the ~** empezar* a arrasarlo todo

rampant /'ræmpənt/ *adj* ‹*inflation*› galopante; ‹*growth*› desenfrenado; ‹*crime*› endémico

rampart /'ræmpɑːrt ‖ 'ræmpɑːt/ *n* (bank) terraplén *m*; (wall) muralla *f*

ramshackle /'ræm,ʃækəl/ *adj* destartalado

ran /ræn/ *past of* RUN¹

ranch /ræntʃ ‖rɑːntʃ/ *n*: **cattle ~** finca *f* (ganadera), hacienda *f* (ganadera) (esp AmL), rancho *m* ganadero (Méx), estancia *f* (CS)

rancher /'ræntʃər ‖ 'rɑːntʃə(r)/ *n* hacendado, -da *m,f*, estanciero, -ra *m,f* (CS), ranchero, -ra *m,f* (Méx); **cattle ~** ganadero, -ra *m,f*

rancid /'rænsəd ‖ 'rænsɪd/ *adj* rancio

rancor, (BrE) **rancour** /'ræŋkər ‖ 'ræŋkə(r)/ *n* [U] rencor *m*

rand /rænd/ *n* (*pl* **~**) rand *m*

random /'rændəm/ *adj* **(a)** ‹*testing/choice*› al azar; ‹*sample*› aleatorio **(b) at random** (*as adv*) al azar

rang /ræŋ/ *past of* RING²

range¹ /reɪndʒ/ *n* **1 (a)** (scope) ámbito *m* **(b)** (Mus) registro *m* **(c)** (bracket): **within/out of our price ~** dentro de/fuera de nuestras posibilidades **2 (a)** (variety) gama *f* **(b)** (selection) línea *f* **3 (a)** (of gun, transmitter) alcance *m*; **at close/long ~** de cerca/lejos; **to be within ~** ponerse*/estar* a tiro **(b)** (of vehicle, missile) autonomía *f* **4** (for shooting) campo *m* de tiro **5** (chain) cadena *f*; **a mountain ~** una cordillera **6** (stove) cocina *f* económica, estufa *f* (Col, Méx)

range² *vi*: **their ages ~ from 12 to 20** tienen entre 12 y 20 años

ranger /'reɪndʒər ‖'reɪndʒə(r)/ *n* guarda *mf* forestal, guardabosques *mf*

rank¹ /ræŋk/ *n* **1** [C] (line) fila *f* **2** [C U] (status) categoría *f*; (Mil) grado *m*, rango *m* **3** [C] (*taxi ~*) (BrE) parada *f* de taxis, sitio *m* (Méx)

rank² *vt*: **he's ~ed fourth** está clasificado cuarto ■ **~** *vi* **(a)** (be classed) estar*; **it ~s among the best** está entre los mejores **(b)** (hold rank): **to ~ above/below sb** estar* por encima/por debajo de algn

rank³ *adj* **1** (*before n*) (complete) ‹*beginner*› absoluto; ‹*injustice*› flagrante **2** ‹*smell*› fétido

rank and file *n* (Mil) (+ *pl vb*) tropa *f*; **the ~ ~ ~ of the union** las bases del sindicato

rankle /'ræŋkəl/ *vi* doler*

ransack /'rænsæk/ *vt* ‹*room/drawer*› revolver*; ‹*house/premises*› (search) registrar (*de arriba a abajo*); (pillage) saquear

ransom /'rænsəm/ *n* rescate *m*; **to hold sb to** *o* (AmE also) **for ~** exigir* un rescate por algn

rant /rænt/ *vi* despotricar*

rap¹ /ræp/ *n* **1** [C] (blow) golpe *m* **2 to take the ~ for sth** (esp AmE colloq) cargar* con la culpa de algo **3 (a)** [U] (chat) (colloq) cháchara *f* (fam) **(b)** [C U] (Mus) rap *m*

rap² -pp- *vi* dar* un golpe ■ **~** *vt*: **he ~ped my knuckles** me pegó en los nudillos

rape¹ /reɪp/ *n* **1 (a)** [U C] (sexual violation) violación *f*; (of a minor) estupro *m* **(b)** [U] (of the countryside) (liter) expoliación *f* (liter) **2** [U] (plant) colza *f*

rape² *vt* ‹*person*› violar

rapid /'ræpəd ‖ 'ræpɪd/ *adj* rápido

rapidly /'ræpədli ‖ 'ræpɪdli/ *adv* rápidamente

rapids /'ræpədz ‖ 'ræpɪdz/ *pl n* rápidos *mpl*

rapist /'reɪpəst ‖ 'reɪpɪst/ *n* violador, -dora *m,f*

rapport /ræ'pɔːr ‖ ræ'pɔː(r)/ *n* [U] relación *f* de comunicación

rapt /ræpt/ *adj* (liter) ‹*expression/smile*› embelesado

rapture /'ræptʃər ‖ 'ræptʃə(r)/ *n* [U C] éxtasis *m*, arrobamiento *m* (liter)

rapturous /'ræptʃərəs/ *adj* ‹*applause/welcome*› calurosísimo

rare /rer ‖reə(r)/ *adj* **rarer** /'rerər/, **rarest** /'rerəst/ **1 (a)** (uncommon) raro **(b)** (liter) ‹*talent/beauty*› excepcional **2** (Culin) ‹*steak*› vuelta y vuelta

rarely /'rerli ‖ 'reəli/ *adv* rara vez

raring /'rerɪŋ ‖ 'reərɪŋ/ *adj*: ***to be ~ to go***: **he's ~ to go** está que ya no se aguanta

rarity /'rerəti ‖ 'reərɪti/ *n* (*pl* **-ties**) algo poco común

rascal /'ræskəl ‖ 'rɑːskəl/ *n* granuja *mf*

rash¹ /ræʃ/ *n* sarpullido *m*

rash² *adj* **-er, -est** precipitado

rasher /'ræʃər ‖ 'ræʃə(r)/ *n* loncha *f*, lonja *f*

rashly /'ræʃli/ *adv* ‹*act*› precipitadamente

rasp¹ /ræsp ‖ rɑːsp/ *n* escofina *f*

rasp² *vt* ‹*wood*› raspar, escofinar

raspberry /'ræz,beri ‖ 'rɑːzbəri/ *n* (*pl* **-ries**) frambuesa *f*

rasping /'ræspɪŋ ‖ 'rɑːspɪŋ/ *adj* ‹*sound/voice*› áspero

Rastafarian /'ræstə'feriən ‖ ,ræstə'feəriən/ *n* rastafari *mf*

rat /ræt/ *n* **(a)** (Zool) rata *f*; (*before n*) **~ poison** raticida *m* **(b)** (person) (colloq) rata *f* de alcantarilla (fam)

rate¹ /reɪt/ *n* **1 (a)** (speed) velocidad; (rhythm) ritmo *m*; **at this ~** a este paso; ***at any ~*** (at least) por lo menos; (in any case) en todo caso **(b)** (level, ratio): **birth ~** índice *m* de natalidad; **death ~** mortalidad *f*; **~ of inflation** tasa *f* de inflación; **interest ~** tasa *f* *or* (esp Esp) tipo *m* de interés; **~ of exchange** tipo *m* de cambio **(c)** (price, charge) tarifa *f*; **that's the going ~** eso es lo que se suele pagar **2** (local tax) (formerly, in UK) (*often pl*) ≈ contribución *f* (municipal *or* inmobiliaria)

rate² *vt* **1** (rank, consider): **I ~ her work very highly** tengo una excelente opinión de su trabajo; **I ~ her as the best woman tennis player** yo la considero la mejor tenista **2** (deserve) merecer*

rather /'ræðər ‖ 'rɑːðə(r)/ *adv* **1 (a)** (stating preference): **I'd ~ walk than go by bus** prefiero andar a ir en autobús; **~ you than me!** ¡menos mal que eres tú y no yo! **(b)** (more precisely): **or ~** o mejor dicho **2** (fairly) bastante; (somewhat) algo

ratify /'rætəfaɪ ‖ 'rætɪfaɪ/ *vt* **-fies, -fying, -fied** (frml) ratificar*

rating /'reɪtɪŋ/ *n* **(a)** [C U] (evaluation): **credit ~** clasificación *f* crediticia **(b) ratings** *pl* (Rad, TV) índice *m* de audiencia

ratio /'reɪʃəʊ, -ʃiəʊ ‖ 'reɪʃiəʊ/ *n* (*pl* **ratios**) proporción *f*, ratio *m* (téc); **in a ~ of two to one** en una proporción de dos a uno

ration¹ /'ræʃən/ *n* **(a)** (allowance) ración *f* **(b) rations** *pl* víveres *mpl*

ration² *vt* racionar

rational /'ræʃnəl ‖ 'ræʃənl/ *adj* **(a)** (able to reason) ‹*being*› racional **(b)** (sane, lucid) **to be ~** estar* en su (*or* mi *etc*) sano juicio **(c)** (sensible) ‹*suggestion*› razonable

rationale /'ræʃə'næl ‖ ˌræʃə'nɑːl/ *n* (*no pl*) base *f*, razones *fpl*

rationalize /'ræʃnəlaɪz/ *vt* racionalizar*

rationally /'ræʃnəli/ *adv* ‹*think*› racionalmente; ‹*behave*› con sensatez

rationing /'ræʃənɪŋ/ *n* [U] racionamiento *m*

rattle¹ /'rætl/ *n* **1** (*no pl*) (noise) ruido *m*; (of train, carriage) traqueteo *m* **2** [C] **(baby's) ~** sonajero *m*, sonaja *f* (Méx)

rattle² *vi* **(a)** (make noise) «*chains/bottles/keys*» repiquetear; «*window/engine*» vibrar **(b)** (move) (+ *adv compl*) traquetear ■ **~** *vt* ‹*keys/chain*› hacer* repiquetear; ‹*door/window*› «*wind*» hacer* vibrar

• **rattle off** [*v + o + adv, v + adv + o*] recitar

• **rattle on** [*v + adv*] hablar *or* (fam) parlotear sin parar

rattlesnake /'rætlsneɪk/ *n* serpiente *f* (de) cascabel, cascabel *f*

raucous /'rɔːkəs/ *adj* (loud) estentóreo; (shrill) estridente

raunchy /'rɔːntʃi/ *adj* **-chier, -chiest** (colloq) ‹*humor*› picante; ‹*joke*› escabroso

ravage /'rævɪdʒ/ *vt* (plunder) saquear; **a country ~d by war** un país asolado por la guerra

ravages /'rævɪdʒəz ‖ 'rævɪdʒɪz/ *pl n* estragos *mpl*

rave¹ /reɪv/ *vi* **(a)** (talk deliriously) delirar **(b)** (talk, write enthusiastically): **to ~ about sth** poner* a algo por las nubes **(c)** (talk angrily) despotricar*

rave² *n* (colloq) **1** (*before n*) (full of praise) **~ reviews** críticas *fpl* muy favorables **2** (BrE) (party) *fiesta con música acid*

raven /'reɪvən/ *n* cuervo *m*

ravenous /'rævənəs/ *adj* hambriento; **to be ~** (colloq) tener* un hambre canina (fam)

ravine /rə'viːn/ *n* barranco *m*, quebrada *f*

raving¹ /'reɪvɪŋ/ *adj* (colloq) (*before n, as intensifier*): **he's a ~ lunatic** está loco de atar (fam); (*as adv*) **he's ~ mad** está como una cabra (fam)

raving² *n* [U C] (*often pl*) desvarío *m*

ravish /'rævɪʃ/ *vt* (liter) violar

ravishing /'rævɪʃɪŋ/ *adj* deslumbrante

raw /rɔː/ *adj* **1 (a)** ‹*meat/vegetables*› crudo **(b)** ‹*silk*› crudo; ‹*sugar*› sin refinar; ‹*sewage*› sin tratar **2** (sore): **my fingers were ~** tenía los dedos en carne viva **3** (inexperienced) verde (fam); ‹*recruit*› novato

raw material *n* [U C] materia *f* prima

ray /reɪ/ *n* **1** (beam) rayo *m* **2** (Mus) re *m* **3** (Zool) raya *f*

rayon /'reɪɑːn ‖ 'reɪɒn/ *n* [U] rayón *m*

raze /reɪz/ *vt*: **to ~ sth (to the ground)** arrasar algo

razor /'reɪzər ‖ 'reɪzə(r)/ *n* **(a)** (*safety ~*) cuchilla *f* *or* máquina *f* *or* maquinilla *f* de afeitar, rastrillo *m* (Méx); (*before n*) **~ blade** cuchilla *f*, hoja *f* de afeitar **(b)** (electric) máquina *f* *or* maquinilla *f* de afeitar, máquina *f* de rasurar (esp Méx)

razzmatazz /'ræzmə'tæz/ *n* [U] (colloq) bulla *f*; (publicity) alarde *m* publicitario

Rd = **Road**

re¹ /reɪ/ *n* (Mus) re *m*

re² /riː/ *prep* con relación a, con referencia a

re- /'riː/ *pref* re-

reach¹ /riːtʃ/ *n* **1 (a)** [C] (distance) alcance *m* **(b)** (*in phrases*) **within reach** a mi (*or* tu *etc*) alcance; **out of reach** fuera de su (*or* mi *etc*) alcance **2** [C] (of river) tramo *m*

reach² *vt* **1 (a)** (with hand) alcanzar* **(b)** (extend to) llegar* a **2** ‹*destination/limit/age*› llegar* a; ‹*stage/agreement*› llegar* a, alcanzar* **3** (contact) ponerse* en contacto con ■ **~** *vi* **(a)** (extend hand, arm): **he ~ed for his gun** echó mano a la pistola; **she ~ed across the table for the salt** agarró *or* (esp Esp) cogió la sal, que estaba al otro lado de la mesa **(b)** (stretch far enough) alcanzar*; **I can't ~!** ¡no alcanzo! **(c)** (extend) extenderse*

• **reach out** [*v + adv*] alargar* la mano

react /ri'ækt/ *vi* reaccionar

reaction /ri'ækʃən/ *n* [C U] reacción *f*

reactionary /ri'ækʃəneri ‖ ri'ækʃənri/ *adj* (pej) reaccionario (pey)

reactor /ri'æktər ‖ ri'æktə(r)/ *n* (*nuclear ~*) reactor *m* (nuclear)

read¹ /riːd/ (*past & past p* **read** /red/) *vt* **1 (a)** ‹*book/map/music/meter*› leer* **(b)** (interpret) ‹*sign/mood/situation*› interpretar **2 (a)** «*sign/notice*» decir* **(b)** (indicate) «*thermometer/gauge*» marcar* ■ **~** *vi* leer*

• **read out** [*v + o + adv, v + adv + o*] leer* (*en voz alta*)

• **read over, read through** [*v + o + adv*] leer* (*por entero*)

• **read up** [*v + adv*] **to ~ up (ON sth)** estudiar (algo)

read² /red/ *adj*: **to be well ~** ser* muy leído

readable /'riːdəbəl/ *adj* ‹*book/style*› ameno; ‹*writing*› legible

reader /'riːdər ‖ 'riːdə(r)/ *n* **1** (person) lector, -tora *m,f*; **she's a fast/slow ~** lee muy rápido/lento **2** (Educ, Publ) libro *m* de lectura

readership /'riːdərʃɪp ‖ 'riːdəʃɪp/ *n* lectores *mpl*; **it has a ~ of over 10 million** tiene una tirada de 10 millones

readily /'redḷi ‖ 'redɪli/ *adv* **(a)** (willingly): **she ~ agreed** accedió de buena gana **(b)** (easily) ‹*understand*› fácilmente; **they are ~ available** se pueden conseguir fácilmente

reading /'riːdɪŋ/ *n* **1 (a)** [U] (activity, skill) lectura *f*; (*before n*) ‹*glasses*› para leer; **~ list** lista *f* de lecturas recomendadas; **~ room** sala *f* de lectura **(b)** [C] (event): **poetry ~** recital *m* de poesía **2** [C] (on dial, gauge) lectura *f*

readjust /'riːə'dʒʌst/ *vt* reajustar ■ **~** *vi* «*person*» **to ~** (**TO sth**) readaptarse (A algo)

ready¹ /'redi/ *adj* **-dier, -diest 1 (a)** (having completed preparations) (*pred*) **to be ~** estar* listo, estar* pronto (RPl); **to be ~ to + INF** estar* listo PARA + INF; **to get ~** (prepare oneself) prepararse, aprontarse (CS); (get dressed, made up etc) arreglarse, aprontarse (CS) **(b)** (mentally prepared) (*pred*) **to be ~ FOR sth/to + INF** estar* preparado PARA algo/PARA + INF **2** (willing) dispuesto **3** (easy, available): **~ money** *o* **cash** dinero *m* (en efectivo)

ready² *n* (*pl* **-dies**) **at the ~** listo

ready³ *vt* **-dies, -dying, -died** preparar

ready: **~-made** /'redi'meɪd/ *adj* ‹*suit*› de confección; ‹*soup/sauce*› preparado; **~-to-wear** /'reditə 'wer ‖ ,reditə'weə(r)/ *adj* (*before n*) ‹*clothes*› de confección

real¹ /riːl, rɪl ‖ riːl, rɪəl/ *adj* **(a)** (actual, not imaginary) real, verdadero **(b)** (actual, true) (*before n*) ‹*reason/name*› verdadero **(c)** (genuine, not fake) ‹*fur/leather*› auténtico; ‹*gold*› de ley **(d)** (*as intensifier*) auténtico

real² *adv* (AmE colloq) (*as intensifier*) muy

real estate *n* [U] (esp AmE) bienes *mpl* raíces *or* inmuebles, propiedad *f* inmobiliaria; (*before n*) **~ ~ agent** ⇒ REALTOR

realism /'riːəlɪzəm/ *n* [U] realismo *m*

realist /'riːələst ‖ 'riːəlɪst/ *n* realista *mf*

realistic /'riːə'lɪstɪk ‖ ,rɪə'lɪstɪk/ *adj* realista

reality /ri'æləti/ *n* [C U] (*pl* **-ties**) realidad *f*; **in ~** en realidad

realization /'riːələ'zeɪʃən ‖ ,rɪəlaɪ'zeɪʃən/ *n* [U] **1** (understanding) comprensión *f* **2** (of plan) realización *f*

realize /'riːəlaɪz/ *vt* **1 (a)** (become aware of) darse* cuenta de, comprender, caer* en la cuenta de **(b)** (know, be aware of) saber* **2** (achieve) ‹*ambition*› hacer* realidad; ‹*potential*› desarrollar ■ **~** *vi* darse* cuenta

really /'riːəli ‖ 'riːəli, 'rɪəli/ *adv* **(a)** (in fact): **I ~ did see him!** ¡de verdad que lo vi!; **the tomato is ~ a fruit** el tomate en realidad es una fruta **(b)** (*as intensifier*): **it's ~ good/old** es buenísimo/viejísimo **(c)** (*as interj*): **(oh,) ~?** (expressing interest) ¿ah sí?; **really?** (expressing surprise) ¿de verdad?

realm /relm/ *n* **(a)** (kingdom) (frml) reino *m* **(b)** (sphere) (*often pl*) mundo *m*

realtor /'riːəltər ‖ 'rɪəltə(r)/ *n* (AmE) agente inmobiliario, -ria *m,f*

ream /riːm/ *n* (Print) resma *f*

reamer /'riːmər ‖ 'riːmə(r)/ *n* (AmE) exprimelimones *m*, exprimidor *m*

reap /riːp/ *vt* (Agr) cosechar, recoger*; **to ~ the benefits of sth** cosechar los beneficios de algo

reappear /'riə'pɪr ‖ ,riə'pɪə(r)/ *vi* volver* a aparecer

rear¹ /rɪr ‖ rɪə(r)/ *n* **(a)** (back part) (*no pl*) parte *f* trasera *or* de atrás **(b)** (of column, procession) (*no pl*) **the ~** la retaguardia **(c)** [C] (buttocks) (colloq) trasero *m* (fam)

rear² *adj* ‹*window/wheel*› de atrás, trasero

rear³ *vt* ‹*child/cattle*› criar* ■ **~** *vi* **~ (up)** «*horse*» encabritarse

rearguard /'rɪrgɑːrd ‖ 'rɪəgɑːd/ *n* retaguardia *f*

rearm /'riː'ɑːrm ‖ ,riː'ɑːm/ *vt* rearmar ■ **~** *vi* rearmarse

rearrange /'riːə'remdʒ/ *vt* **(a)** ‹*furniture*› cambiar de lugar **(b)** (change time of) ‹*appointment*› cambiar la fecha/la hora de

rear-view mirror /'rɪrvjuː ‖ 'rɪəvjuː/ *n* (espejo *m*) retrovisor *m*

reason¹ /'riːzṇ/ *n* **1** [C U] (cause) razón *f*, motivo *m*; **~ FOR sth** razón *or* motivo DE algo; **I left it there for a ~** por algo lo dejé ahí **2** [U] (faculty) razón *f* **3** [U] (good sense): **to listen to ~** atender* a razones; ***it stands to ~*** es lógico

reason² *vt* pensar* ■ **~** *vi* razonar, discurrir

reasonable /'riːznəbəl/ *adj* **(a)** ‹*offer/request/person*› razonable **(b)** ‹*price/sum*› razonable, moderado

reasonably /'riːznəbli/ *adv* **(a)** ‹*behave/argue*› razonablemente **(b)** (fairly): **I'm ~ certain** estoy casi seguro

reasoning /'riːzṇɪŋ/ *n* [U] razonamiento *m*

reassemble /'riːə'sembəl/ *vt* **(a)** ‹*people/group*› volver* a reunir, reunir* **(b)** ‹*parts/engine*› reensamblar ■ **~** *vi* «*meeting/group*» volverse* a reunir, reunirse*

reassurance /'riːə'ʃʊrəns ‖ ,riːə'ʃʊərəns, ,riːə'ʃɔːrəns/ *n* **(a)** [U] (feeling): **he drew ~ from his wife's words** lo que le dijo su mujer lo confortó *or* lo tranquilizó **(b)** [C U] (words, support): **he gave us countless ~s that** ... nos tranquilizó asegurándonos repetidamente que ...

reassure /'riːə'ʃʊr ‖ ,riːə'ʃʊə(r), ,riːə'ʃɔː(r)/ *vt* tranquilizar*

reassuring /'riːə'ʃʊrɪŋ ‖ ,riːə'ʃʊərɪŋ, ,riːə'ʃɔːrɪŋ/ *adj* ‹*voice/manner/answer*› tranquilizador; **it's ~ to know that** ... tranquiliza saber que ...

rebate /'riːbeɪt/ *n* (repayment) reembolso *m*; (discount) descuento *m*

rebel¹ /'rebəl/ *n* rebelde *mf*

rebel² /rɪ'bel/ *vi* **-ll-** rebelarse, sublevarse

rebellion /rɪ'beljən/ *n* [C U] rebelión *f*

rebellious /rɪ'beljəs/ *adj* rebelde

rebirth /'riː'bɜːrθ ‖ ,riː'bɜːθ/ *n* [U C] renacimiento *m*

rebound¹ /'riːbaʊnd/ *n*: **she married him on the ~** se casó con él por despecho

rebound² /rɪ'baʊnd/ *vi* «*ball*» rebotar

rebuff¹ /rɪ'bʌf/ *n*: **to meet with/receive a ~** ser* rechazado

rebuff² *vt* rechazar*

rebuild /riː'bɪld/ *vt* (*past & past p* **rebuilt**) ‹*building/economy*› reconstruir*; **he tried to ~ his life** intentó rehacer su vida

rebuke[1] /rɪ'bjuːk/ *vt* reprender

rebuke[2] *n* reprimenda *f*

rebut /rɪ'bʌt/ *vt* **-tt-** (frml) rebatir

recall[1] /rɪ'kɔːl, 'riːkɔːl/ *n* **1** [U] (memory) memoria *f*; **to have total ~** tener* una memoria excelente **2** [U C] (of goods, ambassador) retirada *f*

recall[2] /rɪ'kɔːl/ *vt* **1** (remember) recordar* **2 (a)** ‹*faulty goods*› retirar (*del mercado*) **(b)** ‹*ambassador*› retirar; (temporarily) llamar; ‹*troops*› llamar

recant /rɪ'kænt/ *vi* retractarse; (Relig) abjurar

recap[1] /'riːkæp/ *n* (colloq) resumen *m*

recap[2] /'riː'kæp/ **-pp-** *vt* **1** (summarize) (colloq) resumir, recapitular **2** (AmE Auto) ⇒ RETREAD[1] ■ **~** *vi* (colloq) resumir

recapitulate /'riːkə'pɪtʃəleɪt ‖ ˌriːkə'pɪtjʊleɪt/ *vt/i* (frml) recapitular, resumir

recapture *vt* ‹*convict/animal*› capturar; ‹*youth/beauty*› recuperar

recede /rɪ'siːd/ *vi* **(a)** (move back) «*tide*» retirarse; **to ~ into the distance** perderse en la distancia **(b)** «*danger*» alejarse; «*prospect*» desvanecerse* **(c) receding** *pres p* ‹*chin*› hundido; **he has a receding hairline** tiene entradas

receipt /rɪ'siːt/ *n* **(a)** [C] (paper) recibo *m* **(b)** [U] (act) recibo *m*, recepción *f*

receive /rɪ'siːv/ *vt* **1 (a)** ‹*letter/award/visit*› recibir; ‹*payment*› recibir, cobrar, percibir (frml); ‹*stolen goods*› comerciar con, reducir* (AmS); ‹*serve/ball*› recibir; ‹*injuries*› sufrir; ‹*blow*› recibir **(b)** (react to) ‹*news/idea*› recibir **2** (welcome, admit) (frml) ‹*person*› recibir, acoger* **3** (Rad, TV) ‹*signal*› recibir, captar

receiver /rɪ'siːvər ‖ rɪ'siːvə(r)/ *n* **1** (Telec) auricular *m* **2** (Rad, TV) receptor *m* **3** (of stolen goods) comerciante *mf* de mercancía robada

receivership /rɪ'siːvərʃɪp ‖ rɪ'siːvəʃɪp/ *n* [U] **to go into/be in ~** ≈ser* declarado/estar* en suspensión *or* en cesación de pagos

recent /'riːsn̩t/ *adj* reciente; **in ~ years/months** en los últimos años/meses; **in the ~ past** en los últimos tiempos

recently /'riːsn̩tli/ *adv* recientemente; **until quite ~** hasta hace bien poco

receptacle /rɪ'septɪkəl/ *n* (frml) recipiente *m*, receptáculo *m*

reception /rɪ'sepʃən/ *n* **(a)** (reaction) (*no pl*) recibimiento *m*, acogida *f* **(b)** (in hotel, office) (*no art*) recepción *f*; (*before n*) **~ desk** recepción *f* **(c)** [C] (social event) recepción *f* **(d)** [U] (Rad, TV) recepción *f*

receptionist /rɪ'sepʃənəst ‖ rɪ'sepʃənɪst/ *n* recepcionista *mf*

receptive /rɪ'septɪv/ *adj* receptivo

recess /'riːses/ *n* **1** [U] **(a)** (of legislative body) receso *m* (AmL), suspensión *f* de actividades (Esp); (of committee etc) intermedio *m* **(b)** (AmE Educ) recreo *m* **2** [C] (alcove) hueco *m*, entrada *f*

recession /rɪ'seʃn̩ ‖ rɪ'seʃən/ *n* [C U] (Econ) recesión *f*

recharge /'riː'tʃɑːrdʒ ‖ ˌriː'tʃɑːdʒ/ *vt* volver* a cargar, recargar*

rechargeable /'riː'tʃɑːrdʒəbəl ‖ ˌriː'tʃɑːdʒəbəl/ *adj* recargable

recipe /'resəpi/ *n* receta *f*; (*before n*) **~ book** libro *m* de cocina; (personal) cuaderno *m* de recetas (de cocina)

recipient /rɪ'sɪpiənt/ *n* (frml) (of letter) destinatario, -ria *m,f*; (of an organ) (Med) receptor, -tora *m,f*

reciprocal /rɪ'sɪprəkəl/ *adj* recíproco

reciprocate /rɪ'sɪprəkeɪt/ *vt* corresponder a, reciprocar* (AmL) ■ **~** *vi* corresponder, reciprocar* (AmL)

recital /rɪ'saɪtl/ *n* (Mus) recital *m*

recite /rɪ'saɪt/ *vt* **(a)** (declaim) ‹*poem*› recitar **(b)** (list) ‹*names*› enumerar

reckless /'rekləs ‖ 'reklɪs/ *adj* imprudente, temerario

reckon /'rekən/ *vt* **(a)** (calculate) calcular **(b)** (consider) considerar **(c)** (think) (colloq) creer*; **what do you ~?** ¿tú qué opinas?, ¿y a ti qué te parece?
• reckon on [*v* + *prep* + *o*] contar con

reckoning /'rekənɪŋ/ *n* [U] cálculos *mpl*

reclaim /rɪ'kleɪm/ *vt* **(a)** (claim back): **I filled in a form to ~ tax** llené un formulario para que me devolvieran parte de los impuestos; **to ~ one's luggage** (Aviat) recoger* el equipaje; (at left luggage) (pasar a) retirar el equipaje **(b)** (recover) recuperar; **~ed land** terreno *m* ganado al mar

recline /rɪ'klaɪn/ *vi* **(a)** (lean back) recostarse*, reclinarse; (rest) apoyarse **(b)** «*chair*» reclinarse **(c) reclining** *pres p* ‹*chair/seat*› reclinable, abatible; ‹*figure*› yacente (liter), recostado

recluse /rɪ'kluːs/ *n* ermitaño, -ña *m,f*

reclusive /rɪ'kluːsɪv/ *adj* dado a recluirse

recognition /'rekəg'nɪʃən/ *n* [U] reconocimiento *m*; **in ~ of** (frml) en reconocimiento a *or* por (frml)

recognizable /'rekəgnaɪzəbəl/ *adj* reconocible; ‹*difference*› apreciable

recognize /'rekəgnaɪz/ *vt* **(a)** ‹*voice/person*› reconocer* **(b)** (acknowledge) reconocer*, admitir

recoil[1] /rɪ'kɔɪl/ *vi* (shrink back) retroceder; **to ~ FROM sth** rehuir* algo

recoil[2] /'riːkɔɪl/ *n* [U] retroceso *m*

recollect /'rekə'lekt/ *vt* recordar*

recollection /'rekə'lekʃən/ *n* [U C] recuerdo *m*

recommend /'rekə'mend/ *vt* **(a)** (praise, declare acceptable) recomendar* **(b)** (advise) **to ~ sth/-ING** aconsejar *or* recomendar* algo/+ INF; **~ed (retail) price** precio *m* de venta recomendado

recommendation /'rekəmen'deɪʃən/ *n* [U C] recomendación *f*

recompense /'rekəmpens/ *n* [U] (frml) recompensa *f*

reconcile /'rekənsaɪl/ *vt* **(a)** ‹*enemies*› reconciliar **(b)** ‹*theories/ideals*› conciliar **(c) to become ~d TO sth** resignarse A algo

reconciliation /'rekənsɪli'eɪʃən/ *n* reconciliación *f*

recondition /'riːkən'dɪʃən/ *vt* reacondicionar

reconnaissance /rə'kɑːnəzəns, -səns ‖ rɪ'kɒnɪsəns/ *n* [U C] (Mil) reconocimiento *m*

reconnoiter, (BrE) **reconnoitre** /ˈriːkəˈnɔɪtər, ˈre- ‖ ˌrekəˈnɔɪtə(r)/ *vt* reconocer*

reconquer /ˈriːˈkɑːŋkər ‖ ˌriːˈkɒŋkə(r)/ *vt* reconquistar

reconsider /ˈriːkənˈsɪdər ‖ ˌriːkənˈsɪdə(r)/ *vt* reconsiderar

reconstruct /ˈriːkənˈstrʌkt/ *vt* reconstruir*

reconstruction /ˈriːkənˈstrʌkʃən/ *n* **(a)** [U] (rebuilding) reconstrucción *f* **(b)** [C] (re-creation) reconstitución *f*

record¹ /ˈrekərd ‖ ˈrekɔːd/ *n* **1 (a)** [C] (document) documento *m*; (of attendances etc) registro *m*; (file) archivo *m*; (minutes) acta *f*‡; (note) nota *f*; **medical ~s** historial *m* médico; **keep a ~ of your expenses** anote sus gastos; **according to our ~s** según nuestros datos **(b)** (*in phrases*) **off the record** extraoficialmente; **on record**: **the hottest summer on ~** el verano más caluroso del que se tienen datos **2** [C] **(a)** (of performance, behavior): **he has a good academic ~** tiene un buen currículum académico; **our products have an excellent safety ~** nuestros productos son de probada seguridad **(b)** (*criminal ~*) antecedentes *mpl* (penales) **3** [C] (highest, lowest, best, worst) récord *m*, marca *f* **4** [C] (Audio, Mus) disco *m*

record² /rɪˈkɔːrd ‖ rɪˈkɔːd/ *vt* **1 (a)** «*person*» (write down) anotar; (in minutes) hacer* constar **(b)** (register) «*instrument*» registrar **2** ‹*song/program/album*› grabar

record³ /ˈrekərd ‖ ˈrekɔːd/ *adj* (*before n, no comp*) récord *adj inv*

record card *n* ficha *f*

recorded /rɪˈkɔːrdəd ‖ rɪˈkɔːdɪd/ *adj* **(a)** ‹*music*› grabado **(b)** ‹*history*› escrito, documentado

recorder /rɪˈkɔːrdər ‖ rɪˈkɔːdə(r)/ *n* (Mus) flauta *f* dulce

recording /rɪˈkɔːrdɪŋ ‖ rɪˈkɔːdɪŋ/ *n* [C U] grabación *f*

record player *n* tocadiscos *m*

recount /rɪˈkaʊnt/ *vt* narrar, contar*

re-count /ˈriːˈkaʊnt/ *vt* volver* a contar; ‹*votes*› hacer* un segundo escrutinio de, recontar*

recoup /rɪˈkuːp/ *vt* ‹*costs*› recuperar; ‹*losses*› resarcirse* de

recourse /ˈriːkɔːrs ‖ rɪˈkɔːs/ *n* [U] **to have ~ to sth/sb** recurrir a algo/algn

recover /rɪˈkʌvər ‖ rɪˈkʌvə(r)/ *vt* **(a)** ‹*consciousness/strength*› recuperar, recobrar; ‹*investment/lead*› recuperar **(b)** (retrieve) rescatar ■ ~ *vi* **(a)** «*person*» reponerse*, restablecerse*, recuperarse **(b)** «*economy*» recuperarse, repuntar

recovery /rɪˈkʌvəri/ *n* (*pl* **-ries**) **1** [C U] **(a)** (return to health) recuperación *f*, restablecimiento *m* (frml) **(b)** (of economy) recuperación *f* **2** [U] (of stolen goods, missing documents) recuperación *f*; (retrieval) rescate *m*

re-create /ˈriːkriˈeɪt/ *vt* recrear

recreation /ˈrekriˈeɪʃən/ *n* [U] **(a)** (leisure) esparcimiento *m* **(b)** (in school, prison) (BrE) recreo *m*

recreational /ˈrekriˈeɪʃn̩əl ‖ ˌrekriˈeɪʃənl/ *adj* recreativo

recrimination /rɪˈkrɪməˈneɪʃən/ *n* [C U] (*often pl*) recriminación *f*

recruit¹ /rɪˈkruːt/ *n* (Mil) recluta *mf*

recruit² *vt* reclutar; ‹*staff*› contratar

recruitment /rɪˈkruːtmənt/ *n* [U] reclutamiento *m*

rectangle /ˈrektæŋgəl/ *n* rectángulo *m*

rectangular /rekˈtæŋgjələr ‖ rekˈtæŋgjʊlə(r)/ *adj* rectangular

rectify /ˈrektəfaɪ ‖ ˈrektɪfaɪ/ *vt* **-fies, -fying, -fied** rectificar*

rector /ˈrektər ‖ ˈrektə(r)/ *n* **(a)** (Relig) rector, -tora *m,f*, ≈ párroco *m* **(b)** (in US) (Educ) rector, -ra *m,f*

rectum /ˈrektəm/ *n* (*pl* **rectums** *or* **recta** /ˈrektə/) recto *m*

recuperate /rɪˈkuːpəreɪt/ *vi* recuperarse, reponerse*

recuperation /rɪˈkuːpəˈreɪʃən/ *n* [U] recuperación *f*, restablecimiento *m*

recur /rɪˈkɜːr ‖ rɪˈkɜː(r)/ *vi* **-rr- (a)** «*phenomenon*» volver* a ocurrir *or* a suceder, repetirse*; «*symptom*» volver* a presentarse **(b) recurring** *pres p* recurrente

recurrence /rɪˈkɜːrəns ‖ rɪˈkʌrəns/ *n* [C U] (of symptoms) reaparición *f*; (of incident) repetición *f*

recurrent /rɪˈkɜːrənt ‖ rɪˈkʌrənt/ *adj* recurrente

recycle /ˈriːˈsaɪkəl/ *vt* reciclar

red¹ /red/ ▶515 *adj* **redder, reddest** ‹*rose/dress*› rojo, colorado; ‹*flag/signal*› rojo; ‹*meat*› rojo; ‹*wine*› tinto; **her eyes were ~** tenía los ojos enrojecidos *or* rojos

red² ▶515 *n* [U] rojo *m*, colorado *m*; ***to see ~*** ponerse* hecho una furia *or* un basilisco; ***to be in the ~*** estar* en números rojos

red: **~ admiral** *n* vanesa *f* roja; **~ carpet** *n*: **to roll out the ~ carpet for sb** recibir* a algn con bombos y platillos *or* (Esp) a bombo y platillo

redden /ˈredn̩/ *vi* enrojecerse*

redecorate /ˈriːˈdekəreɪt/ *vt/i* pintar (y empapelar)

redeem /rɪˈdiːm/ *vt* **1 (a)** ‹*good name*› rescatar **(b)** ‹*sinners*› redimir **(c) redeeming** *pres p*: **he has no ~ing features** no tiene ningún punto a su favor **2** (from pawnshop) desempeñar

redefine /ˈriːdɪˈfaɪn/ *vt* redefinir

redemption /rɪˈdempʃən/ *n* [U] (saving) salvación *f*; (Relig) redención *f*

redeploy /ˈriːdɪˈplɔɪ/ *vt* ‹*resources*› reorientar; ‹*staff*› asignar un nuevo destino a, reubicar* (AmL); ‹*troops*› cambiar la disposición de

redevelop /ˈriːdɪˈveləp/ *vt* reurbanizar*

red: **~-haired** /ˈredˈherd ‖ ˌredˈheəd/ *adj* pelirrojo; **~-handed** /ˈredˈhændəd ‖ ˌredˈhændɪd/ *adj*: ***to catch sb ~-handed*** agarrar *or* (esp Esp) coger* a algn con las manos en la masa; **~head** *n* pelirrojo, -ja *m,f*; **~ herring** *n* (in detective story) pista *f* falsa; **~-hot** /ˈredˈhɑːt ‖ ˌredˈhɒt/ *adj* (*pred* **~ hot**) al rojo vivo

redial /ˈriːˈdaɪl ‖ ˌriːˈdaɪəl/ *vi/t*, (BrE) **-ll-** volver* a marcar *or* (AmS tb) a discar

redirect /ˈriːdəˈrekt, -daɪ- ‖ ˌriːdaɪˈrekt, -də-/ *vt* (*often pass*) ‹*mail*› enviar* a una nueva dirección; ‹*traffic*› desviar*

rediscover /ˈriːdɪˈskʌvər ‖ ˌriːdɪˈskʌvə(r)/ *vt* redescubrir*, volver* a distribuir

redistribute /ˈriːdɪˈstrɪbjət ‖ ˌriːdɪˈstrɪbjuːt/ *vt* redistribuir*

red: ~ **light** *n* luz *f* roja, semáforo *m* en rojo, alto *m* (Méx); ~**-light district** /ˈredˈlaɪt/ *n* zona *f* de tolerancia, zona *f* roja (AmL); ~**neck** *n* (in US) (pej) *sureño reaccionario de la clase baja rural*

redo /ˈriːˈduː/ *vt* (*3rd pers sing pres* **redoes**; *past* **redid**; *past p* **redone**) rehacer*, volver* a hacer

redouble /ˈriːˈdʌbəl/ *vt* ‹*efforts*› redoblar

red pepper *n* [C U] (capsicum) *see* PEPPER[1] 2

redraft /ˈriːˈdræft ‖ riːˈdrɑːft/ *vt* volver* a redactar

redress¹ /rɪˈdres/ *n* [U] reparación *f*

redress² *vt* ‹*wrong*› reparar; ‹*imbalance*› corregir*

red: **R~ Sea** *n* **the R~ Sea** el Mar Rojo; ~ **tape** *n* [U] (bureaucracy) trámites *mpl* burocráticos, papeleo *m* (fam)

reduce /rɪˈduːs ‖ rɪˈdjuːs/ *vt* **1** ‹*number/amount*› reducir*; ‹*pressure/speed*› disminuir*, reducir*; ‹*price/taxes*› reducir*, rebajar; ‹*pain*› aliviar **2** (break down, simplify) **to ~ sth TO sth** reducir* algo A algo **3 to ~ sb to tears** hacer* llorar a algn

reduced /rɪˈduːst ‖ rɪˈdjuːst/ *adj* reducido

reduction /rɪˈdʌkʃən/ *n* [C U] reducción *f*; (in prices, charges) rebaja *f*

redundancy /rɪˈdʌndənsi/ *n* [U C] (*pl* **-cies**) (BrE Lab Rel) despido *m*, cese *m*; (*before n*) ~ **money** *o* **pay** indemnización *f* (por despido *or* cese)

redundant /rɪˈdʌndənt/ *adj* **(a)** (superfluous) superfluo **(b)** (esp BrE Lab Rel): **she was made ~** la despidieron por reducción de planilla *or* (Esp) de plantilla

reed /riːd/ *n* **(a)** (Bot) carrizo *m*, junco *m* **(b)** (Mus) lengüeta *f*

reeducate /ˈriːˈedʒəkeɪt ‖ ˌriːˈedjʊkeɪt/ *vt* reeducar*

reef /riːf/ *n* (Geog) arrecife *m*; (seen as hazard) escollo *m*, arrecife *m*

reek /riːk/ *vi* **(a)** (stink) **to ~ (OF sth)** apestar *or* heder* (A algo) **(b)** (have air of) **to ~ OF sth** ‹*of corruption/fraud*› oler* A algo

reel¹ /riːl/ *n* **(a)** (for wire, thread, tape) carrete *m* **(b)** (of film) rollo *m*, carrete *m* (esp Esp) **(c)** (fishing) carrete *m*, carretel *m*

reel² *vi* tambalearse; **my head was ~ing** todo me daba vueltas

• **reel in** [*v* + *o* + *adv*, *v* + *adv* + *o*] ‹*line*› enrollar

• **reel off** [*v* + *o* + *adv*, *v* + *adv* + *o*] recitar de un tirón

reelect /ˈriːəˈlekt ‖ ˌriːɪˈlekt/ *vt* reelegir*

reemerge /ˈriːəˈmɜːrdʒ ‖ ˌriːɪˈmɜːdʒ/ *vi* **(a)** (reappear) volver* a salir **(b)** (regain prominence) resurgir*

reenact /ˈriːəˈnækt ‖ ˌriːɪˈnækt/ *vt* ‹*historical event*› recrear; ‹*crime*› reconstruir*

reenter /ˈriːˈentər ‖ ˌriːˈentə(r)/ *vt* volver* a entrar en *or* (esp AmL) a

reexamine /ˈriːɪgˈzæmən ‖ ˌriːɪgˈzæmɪn/ *vt* volver* a examinar

ref¹ /ref/ *n* (colloq) (= **referee**) árbitro, -tra *m,f*, réferi *mf* (AmL)

ref² /ref/ (= **reference**) ref.

refectory /rɪˈfektəri/ *n* (*pl* **-ries**) comedor *m*

refer /rɪˈfɜːr ‖ rɪˈfɜː(r)/ **-rr-** *vt* remitir; **to ~ sb to a specialist** (Med) mandar *or* (AmL) derivar a algn a un especialista

• **refer to** [*v* + *prep* + *o*] **(a)** (mention) hacer* referencia a, aludir a **(b)** (allude to) referirse* a **(c)** ‹*dictionary/notes*› consultar

referee¹ /ˈrefəˈriː/ *n* **1 (a)** (Sport) árbitro, -tra *m,f*, réferi *mf* (AmL) **(b)** (in dispute) árbitro -tra *m,f* **2** (for job candidate) (BrE): **you need two ~s** necesitas el aval de dos personas

referee² *vt/i* arbitrar

reference /ˈrefrəns, ˈrefərəns/ *n* **1** [C U] (allusion) alusión *f*, referencia *f*; **with ~ to** con referencia *or* relación a **2 (a)** [U] (consultation) consulta *f*; (*before n*) ~ **book/library** obra *f*/biblioteca *f* de consulta *or* de referencia **(b)** [C] (indicator) referencia *f*; (*before n*) ~ **number** número *m* de referencia **3** [C] (for job candidate — testimonial) referencia *f*, informe *m*; (— person giving testimonial) (AmE): **you need two ~s** necesitas el aval de dos personas

referendum /ˈrefəˈrendəm/ *n* (*pl* **-dums** *or* **-da** /-də/) referéndum *m*, referendo *m*

refill¹ /ˈriːfɪl/ *n* (for pen) repuesto *m*, recambio *m*; (for lighter) carga *f*

refill² /ˈriːˈfɪl/ *vt* volver* a llenar, rellenar

refine /rɪˈfaɪn/ *vt* **(a)** ‹*sugar/oil*› refinar **(b)** (improve) ‹*design/style*› pulir, perfeccionar

refined /rɪˈfaɪnd/ *adj* **(a)** ‹*person/manners*› refinado, fino **(b)** ‹*sugar/oil*› refinado

refinement /rɪˈfaɪnmənt/ *n* **(a)** [U] (gentility, elegance) refinamiento *m*, finura *f* **(b)** [C U] (improvement) mejora *f*

refinery /rɪˈfaɪnəri/ *n* (*pl* **-ries**) refinería *f*

reflect /rɪˈflekt/ *vt* reflejar ■ ~ *vi* **1** (think) **to ~ (ON sth)** reflexionar *or* meditar (SOBRE algo) **2** «*light/heat*» reflejarse

• **reflect on**, **reflect upon** [*v* + *prep* + *o*] repercutir en; **to ~ badly on sth/sb** perjudicar* algo/a algn

reflection /rɪˈflekʃən/ *n* **1 (a)** [U] (Opt, Phys) reflexión *f* **(b)** [C] (image) reflejo *m*; (of situation, feeling) reflejo *m* **2 (a)** [U] (contemplation) reflexión *f*; **on** *o* **upon ~** ... pensándolo bien ... **(b)** [C] (comment) observación *f*

reflector /rɪˈflektər ‖ rɪˈflektə(r)/ *n* (of light, heat) reflector *m*; (Auto) catafaros *m*

reflex /ˈriːfleks/ *n* reflejo *m*

reflexive /rɪˈfleksɪv/ *adj* reflexivo

reform¹ /rɪˈfɔːrm ‖ rɪˈfɔːm/ *n* [U C] reforma *f*

reform² *vt* reformar

reformation /ˈrefərˈmeɪʃən ‖ ˌrefəˈmeɪʃən/ *n* reforma *f*; **the Reformation** (Relig) la Reforma

reformatory /rɪˈfɔːrmətɔːri ‖ rɪˈfɔːmətəri/ *n* (*pl* **-ries**) (in US) reformatorio *m*

refrain¹ /rɪˈfreɪn/ *vi* (frml) **to ~ (FROM sth/-ING)** abstenerse* (DE algo/+ INF)

refrain² *n* (Lit, Mus) estribillo *m*

refresh /rɪ'freʃ/ *vt* refrescar*

refreshing /rɪ'freʃɪŋ/ *adj* ‹*drink/bath*› refrescante; ‹*sleep*› reparador; ‹*enthusiasm*› reconfortante

refreshments /rɪ'freʃmənts/ *pl n* refrigerio *m*

refrigerate /rɪ'frɪdʒəreɪt/ *vt* refrigerar

refrigerator /rɪ'frɪdʒəreɪtər ‖ rɪ'frɪdʒəreɪtə(r)/ *n* nevera *f*, refrigerador *m*, frigorífico *m* (Esp), heladera *f* (RPl), refrigeradora *f* (Col, Per)

refuel /ri:'fju:əl/, (BrE) **-ll-** *vt* reabastecer* de combustible ■ ~ *vi* repostar, reabastecerse* de combustible

refuge /'refju:dʒ/ *n* [U C] refugio *m*; **to take ~** refugiarse

refugee /'refjʊ'dʒi:/ *n* refugiado, -da *m,f*; (*before n*) **~ camp** campamento *m* de refugiados

refund¹ /rɪ'fʌnd/ *vt* ‹*expenses/postage*› reembolsar

refund² /'ri:fʌnd/ *n* reembolso *m*

refurbish /rɪ:'fɜ:rbɪʃ ‖ ,ri':'fɜ:bɪʃ/ *vt* renovar*, hacer* reformas en; (restore) restaurar

refusal /rɪ'fju:zəl/ *n* (of permission, request) denegación *f*; (of offer) rechazo *m*; (to do sth) negativa *f*

refuse¹ /rɪ'fju:z/ *vt* ‹*offer/gift*› rechazar*, no aceptar, rehusar*; **to ~ to** + INF negarse* A + INF ■ ~ *vi* negarse*

refuse² /'refju:s/ *n* [U] residuos *mpl*

refute /rɪ'fju:t/ *vt* refutar, rebatir

regain /rɪ'geɪn, 'ri:-/ *vt* recuperar, recobrar

regal /'ri:gəl/ *adj* majestuoso, regio

regalia /rɪ'geɪljə ‖ rɪ'geɪliə/ *pl n* ropajes *mpl*

regard¹ /rɪ'gɑ:rd ‖ rɪ'gɑ:d/ *vt* **1 (a)** (consider) considerar; **he is very highly ~ed within the profession** está muy bien considerado en esa profesión **(b) as regards** en lo que se refiere a, en lo que atañe a **2** (look at) (liter) contemplar

regard² *n* **1** [U] **(a)** (esteem): **to have a high ~ for sb** tener* muy buena opinión de algn, tener* a algn en gran estima **(b)** (consideration) consideración *f* **2 regards** *pl* (greeting) saludos *mpl*, recuerdos *mpl* **3** (*in phrases*) **with regard to** (con) respecto a, con relación a, en relación con

regarding /rɪ'gɑ:rdɪŋ ‖ rɪ'gɑ:dɪŋ/ *prep* (frml) en lo que concierne *or* respecta a, en lo que se refiere a

regardless /rɪ'gɑ:rdləs ‖ rɪ'gɑ:dlɪs/ *adv* **(a)** (in spite of everything): **to carry on ~** seguir* como si no pasara nada *or* (fam) como si tal cosa **(b) regardless of** (*prep*): **~ of the cost** cueste lo que cueste

regatta /rɪ'gætə/ *n* regata *f*

regenerate /rɪ'dʒenəreɪt/ *vt* (revive) revitalizar*; (Biol) regenerar

regent /'ri:dʒənt/ *n* (ruler) regente *mf*

reggae /'regeɪ/ *n* [U] reggae *m*

regime, régime /reɪ'ʒi:m/ *n* **(a)** (rule) régimen *m* **(b)** (system) sistema *m*

regiment /'redʒəmənt ‖ 'redʒɪmənt/ *n* regimiento *m*

regimental /'redʒə'mentl̩ ‖ ,redʒɪ'mentl̩/ *adj* (*before n*) ‹*mascot/band*› del regimiento

region /'ri:dʒən/ *n* **(a)** (Anat, Geog) (area) región *f*, zona *f* **(b) in the region of** alrededor de

regional /'ri:dʒənl̩/ *adj* regional

register¹ /'redʒəstər ‖ 'redʒɪstə(r)/ *n* **(a)** (record, list) registro *m*; (in school) (BrE) lista *f* **(b)** (Mus) registro *m*

register² *vt* **1** (record) ‹*death/birth*› inscribir*, registrar; ‹*ship/car*› matricular **2** (Post) mandar certificado *or* (Méx) registrado **3 registered** *past p*: **~ed trademark** marca *f* registrada; **~ed nurse** enfermero titulado, enfermera titulada *m,f* **4 (a)** (make known) ‹*complaint*› presentar **(b)** «*dial*» registrar, marcar* ■ ~ *vi* **1** (enroll) inscribirse*; (Educ) matricularse, inscribirse*; (at a hotel) registrarse **2** (show, be revealed) ser* detectado **3** (be understood, remembered): **eventually it ~ed who he was** al final caí en la cuenta de quién era

registrar /'redʒəstrɑ:r ‖ ,redʒɪs'trɑ:(r), 'redʒɪstrɑ:(r)/ *n* **(a)** (Soc Adm) *funcionario encargado de llevar los registros de nacimientos, defunciones, etc* **(b)** (in university, college) secretario, -ria *m,f* de admisiones

registration /'redʒə'streɪʃən ‖ ,redʒɪs'treɪʃən/ *n* **(a)** [U C] (enrollment) inscripción *f*, matrícula *f*; (Educ) inscripción *f*, matriculación *f* **(b)** [U C] (BrE Auto) (*before n*) **~ number** (número *m* de) matrícula *f*

registry /'redʒəstri ‖ 'redʒɪstri/ *n* (*pl* **-tries**) registro *m*; (at university) secretaría *f*; (at church) ≈ sacristía *f*

registry office *n* (in UK) ≈ juzgado *m* (de paz)

regret¹ /rɪ'gret/ *vt* **-tt-** arrepentirse* de, lamentar; **we ~ to inform you that** ... lamentamos comunicarle *or* informarle que ...

regret² *n* [U C] (sadness) pesar *m*; (remorse) arrepentimiento *m*

regretful /rɪ'gretfəl/ *adj* ‹*expression*› de pesar

regretfully /rɪ'gretfəli/ *adv* con pesar; (*indep*) muy a mi (*or* nuestro etc) pesar, lamentablemente

regrettable /rɪ'gretəbəl/ *adj* lamentable

regrettably /rɪ'gretəbli/ *adv* lamentablemente

regroup /ri:'gru:p/ *vi* reagruparse

regular¹ /'regjələr ‖ 'regjʊlə(r)/ *adj* **1 (a)** ‹*pulse*› regular; ‹*breathing*› acompasado; **at ~ intervals** (in time) con regularidad; (in space) a intervalos regulares **(b)** ‹*customer/reader*› habitual, asiduo; **a ~ income** una fuente regular de ingresos; **on a ~ basis** con regularidad **(c)** (customary) habitual **2** (even, symmetrical) ‹*shape*› regular **3** (Ling) ‹*verb/plural*› regular **4** (colloq) (*as intensifier*) verdadero

regular² *n* cliente *mf* habitual, asiduo, -dua *m,f*

regularity /'regjə'lærəti ‖ ,regjʊ'lærəti/ *n* [U] regularidad *f*

regularly /'regjələrli ‖ 'regjʊləli/ *adv* con regularidad, regularmente; (frequently) con frecuencia

regulate /'regjəleɪt ‖ 'regjʊleɪt/ *vt* regular

regulation /'regjə'leɪʃən ‖ ,regjʊ'leɪʃən/ *n* **1** [C] (rule) norma *f*, regla *f*; (*before n*) ‹*dress/haircut*› reglamentario **2** [U] (control, adjustment) regulación *f*

regurgitate /rɪ'gɜ:rdʒəteɪt ‖ rɪ'gɜ:dʒɪteɪt/ *vt* ‹*food*› regurgitar; ‹*information*› repetir* mecánicamente

rehabilitate /'ri:hə'bɪləteɪt, 'ri:ə- ‖ ,ri:hə'bɪlɪteɪt, ,ri:ə-/ *vt* rehabilitar

rehabilitation /'ri:hə'bɪlə'teɪʃən, 'ri:ə- ‖ ,ri:hə,bɪlɪ'teɪʃən, ,ri:ə-/ *n* [U] rehabilitación *f*

rehearsal /rɪ'hɜːrsəl || rɪ'hɜːsəl/ *n* [C U] ensayo *m*
rehearse /rɪ'hɜːrs || rɪ'hɜːs/ *vt/i* ensayar
reheat /'riː'hiːt/ *vt* recalentar*
rehouse /'riː'haʊz/ *vt* realojar
reign¹ /reɪn/ *n* reinado *m*
reign² *vi* **(a)** «*monarch*» reinar **(b) reigning** *pres p* ‹*monarch*› reinante; ‹*champion*› actual
reimburse /'riːɪm'bɜːrs ||ˌriːɪm'bɜːs/ *vt* reembolsar
rein /reɪn/ *n* (Equ) rienda *f*; ***to give free ~ to sb*** darle* carta blanca a algn
reincarnation /'riːɪnkɑːr'neɪʃən ||ˌriːɪnkɑː'neɪʃən/ *n* [U C] reencarnación *f*
reindeer /'reɪndɪr || 'reɪndɪə(r)/ *n* (*pl* ~) reno *m*
reinforce /'riːɪn'fɔːrs ||ˌriːɪn'fɔːs/ *vt* reforzar*
reinforcement /'riːɪn'fɔːrsmənt ||ˌriːɪn'fɔːsmənt/ *n* **(a)** [U] (strengthening) refuerzo *m* **(b) reinforcements** *pl* refuerzos *mpl*
reinstate /'riːɪn'steɪt/ *vt* ‹*worker*› reintegrar, reincorporar; ‹*official*› restituir* en el cargo
reissue /'riː'ɪʃuː/ *vt* ‹*book/record*› reeditar; ‹*document*› reexpedir*
reiterate /riː'ɪtəreɪt/ *vt* (frml) reiterar, repetir*
reject¹ /rɪ'dʒekt/ *vt* rechazar*
reject² /'riːdʒekt/ *n* (flawed product) artículo *m* (*or* producto *m etc*) defectuoso
rejection /rɪ'dʒekʃən/ *n* [U C] rechazo *m*; (following job application) respuesta *f* negativa
rejoice /rɪ'dʒɔɪs/ *vi* alegrarse mucho, regocijarse (liter)
rejoin /'riː'dʒɔɪn/ *vt* ‹*regiment/team*› reincorporarse a; ‹*firm*› reincorporarse a, reintegrarse a
rejuvenate /rɪ'dʒuːvəneɪt/ *vt* rejuvenecer*
rekindle /'riː'kɪndl/ *vt* ‹*fire*› reavivar; ‹*desire*› reavivar
relapse¹ /'riːlæps/ *n* recaída *f*
relapse² /rɪ'læps/ *vi* recaer*, tener* *or* sufrir una recaída
relate /rɪ'leɪt/ *vt* **1** (link) **to ~ sth TO sth** relacionar algo CON algo **2** (tell) (frml) ‹*story*› relatar, referir* (liter) ■ ~ *vi* **1 (a)** (be connected with) **to ~ TO sth** estar* relacionado CON algo **(b) relating to** (*as prep*) relativo a, relacionado con **2** (understand, sympathise with) **to ~ TO sb** sintonizar* CON algn; **to ~ TO sth** identificarse* CON algo
related /rɪ'leɪtəd || rɪ'leɪtɪd/ *adj* **(a)** (of same family) (*pred*) **to be ~ (TO sb)** ser* pariente (DE algn), estar* emparentado (CON algn) **(b)** ‹*ideas/questions/subjects*› relacionado, afín
relation /rɪ'leɪʃən/ *n* **1** [C] (relative) pariente *mf*, pariente, -ta *m,f*, familiar *m* **2 (a)** [U C] (connection) relación *f* **(b) in relation to** (*as prep*) en relación con, con relación a **3 relations** *pl* relaciones *fpl*; **sexual ~s** relaciones sexuales
relationship /rɪ'leɪʃənʃɪp/ *n* **1** [C] (between people) relación *f* **2** [C U] (between things, events) relación *f* **3** [U] (kinship) **~ (TO sb)** parentesco *m* (CON algn)
relative¹ /'relətɪv/ *n* pariente *mf*, pariente, -ta *m,f*, familiar *m*
relative² *adj* **(a)** (comparative): **the ~ merits of** los pros y los contras de **(b)** (not absolute) relativo; **it's all ~** (set phrase) todo es relativo (fr hecha) **(c) relative to** (compared to) en comparación con
relatively /'relətɪvli/ *adv* relativamente
relax /rɪ'læks/ *vi* relajarse ■ ~ *vt* relajar; **she ~ed her grip** sujetó con menos fuerza
relaxation /'riːlæk'seɪʃən/ *n* [U C] (rest) relax *m*; (recreation) esparcimiento *m*, distracción *f*
relaxed /rɪ'lækst/ *adj* ‹*manner/person*› relajado; ‹*atmosphere/party*› informal
relaxing /rɪ'læksɪŋ/ *adj* relajante
relay¹ /'riːleɪ/ *n* **(a)** (team) relevo *m*; **to work in ~s** trabajar en *or* por relevos **(b) ~ (race)** (Sport) carrera *f* de relevos *or* (AmL) de postas
relay² /'riːleɪ, rɪ'leɪ/ *vt* transmitir
release¹ /rɪ'liːs/ *vt* **1** ‹*prisoner/hostage*› poner* en libertad, liberar **2** ‹*information*› hacer* público; ‹*record/book*› sacar* (a la venta); ‹*movie*› estrenar **3** (emit) ‹*gas*› despedir* **4** ‹*brake/clutch*› soltar*
release² *n* [U] **1** (from prison, captivity) puesta *f* en libertad, liberación *f* **2** (of record) salida *f* al mercado; (of movie) estreno *m*; **in** *o* (BrE) **on general ~** en todos los cines
relegate /'reləgeɪt || 'relɪgeɪt/ *vt* **(a)** (consign, demote) relegar* **(b)** (BrE Sport) (*usu pass*): **the team was ~d to the third division** el equipo descendió *or* bajó a tercera división
relent /rɪ'lent/ *vi* «*person*» transigir*, ceder
relentless /rɪ'lentləs || rɪ'lentlɪs/ *adj* ‹*enemy/pursuer*› implacable; ‹*pursuit*› incesante
relentlessly /rɪ'lentləsli || rɪ'lentlɪsli/ *adv* implacablemente
relevance /'reləvəns/ *n* [U] (connection) relación *f*; (importance) relevancia *f*
relevant /'reləvənt/ *adj* ‹*document/facts*› pertinente, relevante
reliability /rɪ'laɪə'bɪləti/ *n* [U] (of worker) formalidad *f*, responsabilidad *f*; (of sources) fiabilidad *f*; (of vehicle) fiabilidad *f*
reliable /rɪ'laɪəbəl/ *adj* **(a)** ‹*information/source*› fidedigno; ‹*witness*› fiable, confiable (esp AmL) **(b)** ‹*worker*› responsable, de confianza; ‹*vehicle*› fiable
reliably /rɪ'laɪəbli/ *adv*: **I am ~ informed that** … sé de fuentes fidedignas que …, sé de buena fuente que …
reliant /rɪ'laɪənt/ *adj* (*pred*) **to be ~ ON sth/sb** depender DE algo/algn
relic /'relɪk/ *n* reliquia *f*
relief /rɪ'liːf/ *n* **1** [U] (from worry, pain) alivio *m*; **it's a ~ that the rain's stopped at last** menos mal que ha parado de llover **2** [U] (aid) ayuda *f*, auxilio *m* (*de emergencia*); **to be on ~** (AmE) recibir prestaciones de la seguridad social **3** [C] (replacement) relevo *m* **4** [U C] (Art, Geog) relieve *m*
relieve /rɪ'liːv/ *vt* **(a)** ‹*pain*› calmar, aliviar; ‹*suffering*› mitigar*, aliviar; ‹*tension*› aliviar; **to ~ sb of his/her duties** relevar a algn de su cargo **(b)** ‹*town/fortress*› liberar **(c)** ‹*guard/driver*› relevar ■ *v refl* **to ~ oneself** (euph) orinar
relieved /rɪ'liːvd/ *adj* aliviado; **to feel ~** sentir* un gran alivio, sentirse* aliviado
religion /rɪ'lɪdʒən/ *n* [C U] religión *f*

religious /rɪˈlɪdʒəs/ *adj* religioso
religiously /rɪˈlɪdʒəsli/ *adv* religiosamente
relinquish /rɪˈlɪŋkwɪʃ/ *vt* renunciar a
relish¹ /ˈrelɪʃ/ *vt* ‹*meal/joke/success*› saborear; **I don't ~ the prospect of** … no me entusiasma *or* no me hace ninguna gracia la perspectiva de …
relish² *n* **1** [C U] (Culin) *salsa o conserva que se come con carnes* **2** [U] (enjoyment): **with ~** ‹*eat/drink*› con gusto, con fruición; ‹*read/listen to*› con placer, con deleite
relive /ˈriːˈlɪv/ *vt* revivir
relocate /ˈriːləʊˈkeɪt/ *vt* trasladar ■ **~** *vi* «*company*» trasladarse; «*employee*» mudarse *or* trasladarse de domicilio
reluctance /rɪˈlʌktəns/ *n* [U] renuencia *f* (frml)
reluctant /rɪˈlʌktənt/ *adj* reacio, renuente
reluctantly /rɪˈlʌktəntli/ *adv* a su (*or* mi *etc*) pesar, a regañadientes
rely /rɪˈlaɪ/ *vi* **relies, relying, relied (a)** (have confidence) **to ~** ON *or* UPON **sb/sth** contar* CON algn/algo; **you can ~ on me** puedes contar conmigo; **she can't be relied (up)on to help** no se puede contar con *or* confiar en que vaya a ayudar **(b)** (be dependent) **to ~ on sb/sth** FOR **sth** depender* DE algn/algo (PARA algo)
remain /rɪˈmeɪn/ *vi* **1 (a)** (+ *adj or adv compl*) (continue to be) seguir*, continuar*; **her condition ~s critical** su estado sigue siendo crítico; **he ~ed silent** se mantuvo en silencio **(b)** (stay) quedarse, permanecer* (frml); **to ~ behind** quedarse **2 (a)** (be left) quedar; **what still ~s to be done?** ¿qué queda por hacer?; **that ~s to be seen** eso está por verse **(b) remaining** *pres p*: **the ~ing ten pounds** las diez libras restantes *or* que quedan
remainder /rɪˈmeɪndər ‖ rɪˈmeɪndə(r)/ *n* **the ~** el resto
remains /rɪˈmeɪnz/ *pl n* restos *mpl*; (of meal) sobras *fpl*, restos *mpl*
remake¹ /ˈriːmeɪk/ *n* nueva versión *f*
remake² /ˈriːˈmeɪk/ *vt* (*past & past p* **remade**) volver* a hacer, rehacer*
remand¹ /rɪˈmænd ‖ rɪˈmɑːnd/ *vt*: **to be ~ed on bail** quedar en libertad bajo fianza; **he was ~ed in custody** se decretó su prisión preventiva
remand² *n*: **to be on ~** (in detention) estar* en prisión preventiva
remand centre, **remand home** *n* (in UK) *centro para menores en prisión preventiva*
remark¹ /rɪˈmɑːrk ‖ rɪˈmɑːk/ *n* comentario *m*, observación *f*
remark² *vi* **to ~** ON *o* UPON **sth** hacer* un comentario/comentarios ACERCA DE algo ■ **~** *vt* observar, comentar
remarkable /rɪˈmɑːrkəbəl ‖ rɪˈmɑːkəbəl/ *adj* ‹*ability/likeness*› notable; ‹*achievement*› sorprendente; ‹*coincidence*› extraordinario; ‹*person*› excepcional
remarkably /rɪˈmɑːrkəbli ‖ rɪˈmɑːkəbli/ *adv* **(a)** (surprisingly) sorprendentemente **(b)** (exceptionally) ‹*stupid*› increíblemente
remarry /ˈriːˈmæri/ *vi* **-ries, -rying, -ried** volver* a casarse
remedial /rɪˈmiːdiəl/ *adj* de recuperación
remedy¹ /ˈremədi/ *n* (*pl* **-dies**) remedio *m*
remedy² *vt* **-dies, -dying, -died** ‹*mistake/situation*› remediar; ‹*injustice/evil*› reparar
remember /rɪˈmembər ‖ rɪˈmembə(r)/ *vt* **1** (recall) acordarse* de, recordar*; **I ~ him saying something about** … me acuerdo de *or* recuerdo que dijo algo de … **2 (a)** (be mindful of, not forget): **to ~ to** + INF acordarse* DE + INF **(b)** (commemorate) ‹*dead*› recordar* **(c)** (send regards): **~ me to your mother** dale recuerdos *or* saludos a tu madre (de mi parte) ■ **~** *vi* **(a)** (recall) acordarse*, recordar*; **try to ~!** ¡haz memoria! **(b)** (be mindful, not forget) no olvidarse
remembrance /rɪˈmembrəns/ *n* [U C] (liter *or* frml) recuerdo *m*, remembranza *f* (liter); **in ~ of sth/sb** en memoria de algo/algn; (*before n*) **R~ Sunday** (in UK) *domingo de noviembre en que se conmemora a los caídos en las dos guerras mundiales*
remind /rɪˈmaɪnd/ *vt* recordarle* a; **oh, that ~s me** ¡ah! por cierto …, y a propósito …; **to ~ sb to** + INF recordarle* A algn QUE (+ *subj*); **he ~s me of my grandfather** me recuerda a mi abuelo
reminder /rɪˈmaɪndər ‖ rɪˈmaɪndə(r)/ *n* **(a) to serve as a ~ of sth** recordar* algo **(b)** (requesting payment) recordatorio *m* de pago
reminisce /ˈreməˈnɪs ‖ ˌremɪˈnɪs/ *vi* rememorar los viejos tiempos; **to ~** ABOUT **sth** rememorar algo
reminiscences /ˈreməˈnɪsn̩sɪz ‖ ˌremɪˈnɪsn̩sɪz/ *n pl* [C U] recuerdos *mpl*, memorias *fpl*
reminiscent /ˈreməˈnɪsnt ‖ ˌremɪˈnɪsn̩t/ *adj* (*pred*) **to be ~** OF **sb/sth** recordar* a algn/(a) algo
remiss /rɪˈmɪs/ *adj* (frml) (*pred*) negligente
remission /rɪˈmɪʃən/ *n* [U] remisión *f*
remit /rɪˈmɪt/ *vt* **-tt-** (frml) **1** (send) remitir (frml) **2** (Law) ‹*sentence*› perdonar, condonar (frml)
remnant /ˈremnənt/ *n* **(a)** (left-over): **a ~ of the past** una reliquia del pasado; **the ~s of a meal** los restos de una comida **(b)** (Tex) retazo *m*, retal *m* (Esp)
remonstrate /rɪˈmɑːnstreɪt, ˈremən- ‖ ˈremənstreɪt/ *vi* protestar, quejarse; **to ~ with sb about sth** reprocharle algo a algn
remorse /rɪˈmɔːrs ‖ rɪˈmɔːs/ *n* [U] remordimiento *m*
remorseful /rɪˈmɔːrsfəl ‖ rɪˈmɔːsfəl/ *adj* arrepentido
remorseless /rɪˈmɔːrsləs ‖ rɪˈmɔːslɪs/ *adj* despiadado
remote /rɪˈməʊt/ *adj* **-ter, -test** remoto
remote: **~ control** *n* [U C] mando *m* a distancia, control *m* remoto; **~-controlled** /rɪˈməʊt kənˈtrəʊld/ *adj* (*pred* **~ controlled**) ‹*TV/hi-fi*› con mando a distancia *or* con control remoto; ‹*model/toy*› de control remoto
remotely /rɪˈməʊtli/ *adv* (at all, in the least) (*usu with neg*) remotamente
remould¹ /ˈriːˈməʊld/ *vt* (BrE Auto) ⇒ RETREAD¹
remould² /ˈriːməʊld/ *n* (BrE Auto) ⇒ RETREAD²
removable /rɪˈmuːvəbəl/ *adj* ‹*hood/lining*› de quita y pon; ‹*handle/shelf*› desmontable

removal /rɪ'mu:vəl/ *n* **1** [U] (of contents) extracción *f*; (of appendix, tonsils) extirpación *f* **2** [U] (of stain, unwanted hair) eliminación *f* **3 (a)** [U] (moving, taking away) traslado *m* **(b)** [U C] (from house to house) (BrE) mudanza *f*

remove /rɪ'mu:v/ *vt* **1 (a)** (take off) quitar, sacar* **(b)** (take out) ‹*contents*› sacar*; ‹*tonsils/appendix*› extirpar (frml); ‹*bullet*› extraer* (frml) **2 (a)** (get rid of) ‹*stain/grease*› quitar; ‹*unwanted hair*› eliminar **(b)** ‹*doubt*› disipar; ‹*threat*› eliminar **3** (take away, move) ‹*object*› quitar; ‹*person*› sacar* **4** (dismiss from post, position) destituir*

remover /rɪ'mu:vər ‖ rɪ'mu:və(r)/ *n* [U] (substance): **makeup ~** desmaquillador *m*; **nail polish** *o* (BrE also) **nail varnish ~** quitaesmalte *m*

remuneration /rɪ'mju:nə'reɪʃən/ *n* [U] (frml) remuneración *f*

renaissance /'renə'sɑ:ns ‖ rɪ'neɪsəns/ *n* **(a) Renaissance** Renacimiento *m* **(b)** (revival) (liter) renacimiento *m*

rename /'ri:'neɪm/ *vt* dar* un nuevo nombre a

render /'rendər ‖ 'rendə(r)/ *vt* **1** (make): **to ~ sth useless** hacer* que algo resulte inútil/obsoleto **2** (give, proffer) (frml) ‹*thanks*› dar*; ‹*assistance*› prestar; **for services ~ed** por servicios prestados **3** (translate) traducir*

rendezvous /'rɑ:ndeɪvu: ‖ 'rɒndɪvu:, -deɪvu:/ *n* (*pl* **~** /-z/) (meeting) encuentro *m*, cita *f*; (place) lugar *m* señalado para un encuentro *or* una cita

rendition /ren'dɪʃən/ *n* interpretación *f*

renegade /'renɪgeɪd/ *n* renegado, -da *m,f*

renew /rɪ'nu: ‖ rɪ'nju:/ *vt* **(a)** ‹*hope/promise*› renovar*; ‹*efforts/friendship*› reanudar; ‹*library book*› renovar **(b) renewed** *past p* renovado

renewal /rɪ'nu:əl ‖ rɪ'nju:əl/ *n* [U C] renovación *f*

renounce /rɪ'naʊns/ *vt* **(a)** (cede) (frml) ‹*claim/title*› renunciar a **(b)** (reject) ‹*religion*› renunciar a

renovate /'renəveɪt/ *vt* renovar*

renovation /'renə'veɪʃən/ *n* [U C] renovación *f*

renown /rɪ'naʊn/ *n* [U] renombre *m*, fama *f*

renowned /rɪ'naʊnd/ *adj* de renombre

rent¹ /rent/ *n* [U C] **(a)** (for accommodations, office) alquiler *m*, arrendamiento *m*, arriendo *m*, renta *f* (esp Méx) **(b)** (for boat, suit) (esp AmE) alquiler *m*, arriendo *m* (esp Andes), renta *f* (Méx)

rent² *vt* **(a)** (pay for) **to ~ sth** (FROM **sb**) alquilarle *or* arrendarle* *or* (Méx tb) rentarle algo (A algn) **(b)** ⇨ RENT OUT

• **rent out** [*v + o + adv, v + adv + o*] alquilar, arrendar*

rental /'rentl/ *n* **(a)** [U C] (act of renting) alquiler *m*, arriendo *m* **(b)** [C] (charge) alquiler, renta *f* (Méx), arriendo *m* (esp Andes)

renunciation /rɪ'nʌnsi'eɪʃən/ *n* [U] (frml) **(a)** (of faith) rechazo *m* **(b)** (of claim, right, title) renuncia *f*

reopen /'ri:'əʊpən ‖ ˌri:'əʊpən/ *vt* ‹*book/road*› volver* a abrir; ‹*negotiations/hostilities*› reanudar; ‹*criminal case*› reabrir* ■ **~** *vi* abrir* de nuevo

reorganize /'ri:'ɔ:rgənaɪz ‖ ˌri:'ɔ:gənaɪz/ *vt* reorganizar*

rep /rep/ *n* (*sales* **~**) representante *mf or* agente *mf* (comercial); **a union ~** un/una representante *or* (Esp) un/una enlace sindical

repair¹ /rɪ'per ‖ rɪ'peə(r)/ *vt* ‹*machinery/roof*› arreglar, reparar; ‹*shoes/clothes*› arreglar

repair² *n* [U C] arreglo *m*, reparación *f*; **the museum is closed for ~s** el museo está cerrado por obras; **in a good/bad state of ~, in good/bad ~** en buen/mal estado

repairer /rɪ'perər ‖ rɪ'peərə(r)/ *n* técnico, -ca *m,f*; **watch ~** (BrE) relojero, -ra *m,f*

repairman /rɪ'permæn ‖ rɪ'peəmæn/ *n* (*pl* **-men** /-men/) técnico *m*

repatriate /'ri:'peɪtrieɪt ‖ ˌri:'pætrɪeɪt/ *vt* repatriar

repay /'ri:'peɪ/ *vt* (*past & past p* **repaid**) **(a)** ‹*money/loan*› devolver*; ‹*debt*› pagar*, cancelar **(b)** ‹*kindness/favor*› pagar*, corresponder a

repayment /'ri:'peɪmənt/ *n* **(a)** [U] (act of repaying) pago *m* **(b)** [C] (installment) plazo *m*, cuota *f* (AmL)

repeal¹ /rɪ'pi:l/ *vt* (Govt, Law) revocar*

repeal² *n* [U] revocación *f*

repeat¹ /rɪ'pi:t/ *vt* **1 (a)** (say again) repetir* **(b)** (divulge) contar* **2** (do again) repetir* ■ *v refl* **to ~ oneself** repetirse* ■ **~** *vi* repetir*

repeat² *n* repetición *f*

repeated /rɪ'pi:təd ‖ rɪ'pi:tɪd/ *adj* (*before n*) ‹*attempts*› repetido, reiterado; ‹*requests*› reiterado

repeatedly /rɪ'pi:tədli ‖ rɪ'pi:tɪdli/ *adv* repetidamente, reiteradamente

repel /rɪ'pel/ *vt* **-ll- (a)** ‹*enemy/army*› repeler; ‹*attack*› repeler, rechazar* **(b)** ‹*insects*› repeler, ahuyentar **(c)** (disgust) repeler, repugnar

repellant /rɪ'pelənt/ *n* [U C]: **insect ~** repelente *m* para insectos

repellent /rɪ'pelənt/ *adj* repelente

repent /rɪ'pent/ *vi* arrepentirse*

repentance /rɪ'pentṇs/ *n* [U] arrepentimiento *m*

repentant /rɪ'pentṇt/ *adj* arrepentido

repercussions /'ri:pər'kʌʃənz ‖ ˌri:pə'kʌʃənz/ *npl* repercusiones *fpl*

repertoire /'repərtwɑ:r ‖ 'repətwɑ:(r)/ *n* repertorio *m*

repertory /'repərtɔ:ri ‖ 'repətəri/ *n* [U]: **to be/act/work in ~** trabajar en una compañía de repertorio

repetition /'repə'tɪʃən/ *n* [U C] repetición *f*

repetitious /'repə'tɪʃəs/ *adj* repetitivo

repetitive /rɪ'petətɪv/ *adj* repetitivo

rephrase /'ri:'freɪz/ *vt* expresar de otra manera

replace /rɪ'pleɪs/ *vt* **1 (a)** (take the place of) sustituir*, reemplazar* **(b)** ‹*lost item*› reponer*; ‹*broken window/battery*› cambiar **2** (put back in its place) volver* a poner *or* colocar; ‹*lid*› volver* a poner; ‹*receiver*› colgar*

replacement /rɪ'pleɪsmənt/ *n* **(a)** [U] (act) sustitución *f*, reemplazo *m* **(b)** [C] (person) sustituto, -ta *m,f* **(c)** [C] (object): **I'll buy you a ~** te compraré uno nuevo

replay¹ /'ri:'pleɪ/ *vt* **(a)** (Sport) ‹*game/match*› volver* a jugar, repetir* **(b)** (Audio, Video) volver* a poner

replay² /ˈri:pleɪ/ *n* (Sport) repetición *f* (de la jugada)

replenish /rɪˈplenɪʃ/ *vt* ‹*stock*› reponer*

replete /rɪˈpli:t/ *adj* (liter) **~ WITH sth** repleto DE algo

replica /ˈreplɪkə/ *n* (*pl* **-cas**) réplica *f*, reproducción *f*

reply¹ /rɪˈplaɪ/ *n* (*pl* **replies**) (spoken, written) respuesta *f*, contestación *f*; **in ~ to your letter** en respuesta a su carta

reply² replies, replying, replied *vi* responder, contestar ■ **~** *vt* responder, contestar

report¹ /rɪˈpɔ:rt ‖ rɪˈpɔ:t/ *n* **1 (a)** (account) informe *m*; (piece of news) noticia *f*; (in newspaper) reportaje *m*, crónica *f* **(b)** (evaluation) informe *m*, reporte *m* (Méx); **medical ~** parte *m* médico; **(school) ~** boletín *m* or (Méx) boleta *f* de calificaciones **2** (sound) estallido *m*

report² *vt* **1 (a)** (relate, announce): **several people ~ed seeing the tiger** varias personas dijeron haber visto al tigre; **he is ~ed to be very rich** se dice que es muy rico **(b)** (Journ) «*reporter/media*» informar sobre **2 (a)** (notify) ‹*accident*› informar de, dar* parte de; ‹*crime*› denunciar, dar* parte de, reportar (AmL); **to ~ sth TO sb** dar* parte DE algo A algn **(b)** (denounce) denunciar, reportar (AmL) ■ **~** *vi* **1** (Journ) «*reporter*» informar **2** (present oneself) presentarse, reportarse (AmL); **to ~ sick** dar* parte de enfermo

• **report back** [*v* + *adv*] **(a)** (return): **to ~ back (to base)** regresar a la base **(b)** (give report) **to ~ back (TO sb)** presentar un informe (A algn)

report card *n* (AmE Educ) boletín *m* or (Méx) boleta *f* de calificaciones

reported speech /rɪˈpɔ:rtəd ‖ rɪˈpɔ:tɪd/ *n* [U] estilo *m* indirecto

reporter /rɪˈpɔ:rtər ‖ rɪˈpɔ:tə(r)/ *n* periodista *mf*, reportero, -tera *m,f*

repose /rɪˈpəʊz/ *n* [U] (liter) reposo *m*

repossess /ˈri:pəˈzes/ *vt* ‹*car/house*› recuperar la posesión de (*por falta de pago*)

reprehensible /ˈreprɪˈhensəbəl/ *n* reprensible

represent /ˈreprɪˈzent/ *vt* **1 (a)** (stand for) representar **(b)** (constitute) representar, constituir* **2** (act as representative for) ‹*client*› representar **3** (frml) (describe) presentar

representation /ˈreprɪzenˈteɪʃən/ *n* [U C] representación *f*

representative¹ /ˈreprɪˈzentətɪv/ *n* **(a)** representante *mf* **(b)** (in US) (Govt) representante *mf*, diputado, -da *m,f* **(c)** (*sales* **~**) representante *mf* or agente *mf* comercial

representative² *adj* representativo

repress /rɪˈpres/ *vt* reprimir

repression /rɪˈpreʃən/ *n* [U] represión *f*

repressive /rɪˈpresɪv/ *adj* represivo

reprieve¹ /rɪˈpri:v/ *n* (Law) indulto *m*

reprieve² *vt* indultar

reprimand¹ /ˈreprəmænd ‖ ˈreprɪmɑ:nd/ *n* reprimenda *f*

reprimand² *vt* reprender

reprint¹ /ˈri:prɪnt/ *n* (Publ) reimpresión *f*; (Phot) copia *f*

reprint² /ˈri:ˈprɪnt/ *vt* (Publ) reimprimir*

reprisal /rɪˈpraɪzəl/ *n* represalia *f*

reproach¹ /rɪˈprəʊtʃ/ *vt* **to ~ sb FOR -ING**: **he ~ed her for not having written to him** le reprochó que no le hubiera escrito

reproach² *n* [U C] reproche *m*; **above** *o* **beyond ~** irreprochable, intachable

reproachful /rɪˈprəʊtʃfəl/ *adj* (lleno) de reproche

reproduce /ˈri:prəˈdu:s ‖ ˌri:prəˈdju:s/ *vt* reproducir* ■ **~** *vi* (Biol) reproducirse*

reproduction /ˈri:prəˈdʌkʃən/ *n* [U C] reproducción *f*

reproductive /ˈri:prəˈdʌktɪv/ *adj* reproductor

reproof /rɪˈpru:f/ *n* [U C] (frml) reprobación *f*

reprove /rɪˈpru:v/ *vt* (frml) **to ~ sb (FOR sth)** reprender or (frml) reconvenir* a algn (POR algo)

reptile /ˈreptḷ, -taɪl ‖ ˈreptaɪl/ *n* reptil *m*

republic /rɪˈpʌblɪk/ *n* república *f*

republican¹ /rɪˈpʌblɪkən/ *adj* **(a)** (of a republic) republicano **(b) Republican** (in US) republicano

republican² *n* **(a)** (supporter of republic) republicano, -na *m,f* **(b) Republican** (in US) republicano, -na *m,f*

repudiate /rɪˈpju:dieɪt/ *vt* **(a)** (deny) ‹*accusation*› rechazar*, negar* **(b)** ‹*violence/family*› repudiar

repugnance /rɪˈpʌgnəns/ *n* [U] repugnancia *f*

repugnant /rɪˈpʌgnənt/ *adj* repugnante

repulse /rɪˈpʌls/ *vt* repeler, rechazar*

repulsion /rɪˈpʌlʃən/ *n* [U] (frml) repulsión *f*

repulsive /rɪˈpʌlsɪv/ *adj* repulsivo, repugnante

reputable /ˈrepjətəbəl ‖ ˈrepjʊtəbəl/ *adj* acreditado (frml), reputado (frml)

reputation /ˈrepjəˈteɪʃən ‖ ˈrepjʊˈteɪʃən/ *n* reputación *f*; **good/bad ~** buena/mala reputación or fama; **a ~ FOR sth** fama DE algo

repute /rɪˈpju:t/ *n* [U] (frml) reputación *f*, fama *f*; **of ~** de renombre

reputed /rɪˈpju:təd ‖ rɪˈpju:tɪd/ *adj* presunto, supuesto; **she is ~ to be the best in the world** está considerada como la mejor del mundo

reputedly /rɪˈpju:tədli ‖ rɪˈpjʊtɪdli/ *adv* (*indep*) según se dice or cree

request¹ /rɪˈkwest/ *n* **(a)** (polite demand) petición *f*, pedido *m* (esp AmL), solicitud *f* (frml); **~ FOR sth** petición (or pedido *etc*) DE algo **(b)** (for song) petición *f*, pedido *m* (esp AmL)

request² *vt* pedir*, solicitar (frml)

requiem /ˈrekwiəm/ *n* réquiem *m*

require /rɪˈkwaɪr ‖ rɪˈkwaɪə(r)/ *vt* **1 (a)** (need) necesitar; (call for) ‹*patience/dedication*› requerir*, exigir* **(b)** (demand) **to ~ sb/sth to** + INF requerir* que algn/algo (+ *subj*); **I shall do all that is ~d of me** haré todo lo que me corresponda **2 required** *past p* **(a)** ‹*dose/amount*› necesario **(b)** (compulsory) ‹*reading/viewing*› obligado

requirement /rɪˈkwaɪrmənt ‖ rɪˈkwaɪəmənt/ *n* **(a)** (*usu pl*) (need) necesidad *f* **(b)** (condition) requisito *m*

requisite /'rekwəzət ‖ 'rekwɪzɪt/ *adj* (frml) necesario, requerido

requisition /'rekwə'zɪʃən ‖ ˌrekwɪ'zɪʃən/ *vt* requisar

reroute /'ri:'ru:t/ *vt* desviar*

reschedule /'ri:'skedʒu:l ‖ ˌri:'ʃedju:l/ *vt* ‹*meeting*› cambiar la hora/fecha de

rescind /rɪ'sɪnd/ *vt* (frml) ‹*contract*› rescindir; ‹*order/ruling*› revocar*; ‹*law*› derogar*

rescue¹ /'reskju:/ *n* [U C] rescate *m*; **they went to his ~** acudieron a socorrerlo (liter), fueron *or* (liter) acudieron en su auxilio

rescue² *vt* rescatar, salvar

rescuer /'reskjuər ‖ 'reskju:ə(r)/ *n* salvador, -dora *m,f*

research¹ /rɪ'sɜ:rtʃ, 'ri:sɜ:rtʃ ‖ rɪ'sɜ:tʃ/ *n* [U] investigación *f*; **~ INTO/ON sth** investigación SOBRE algo

research² *vi* investigar* ■ **~** *vt* ‹*causes/problem*› investigar*, estudiar; **this article is well ~ed** este artículo está bien documentado

researcher /rɪ'sɜ:rtʃər ‖ rɪ'sɜ:tʃə(r)/ *n* investigador, -dora *m,f*

resemblance /rɪ'zembləns/ *n* [U] parecido *m*, semejanza *f*; **~ TO sb/sth** parecido CON algn/algo

resemble /rɪ'zembəl/ *vt* parecerse* a

resent /rɪ'zent/ *vt* ‹*person*› guardarle rencor a; **he ~ed her success** le molestaba que ella tuviera éxito; **I ~ having to help him** me molesta tener que ayudarle

resentful /rɪ'zentfəl/ *adj* ‹*person*› resentido, rencoroso; ‹*air/look*› de resentimiento

resentment /rɪ'zentmənt/ *n* [U] resentimiento *m*, rencor *m*

reservation /'rezər'veɪʃən ‖ ˌrezə'veɪʃən/ *n* **(a)** [C U] (booking) reserva *f*, reservación *f* (AmL) **(b)** [C] (doubt, qualification) reserva *f*; **without ~** sin reservas **(c)** [C] (land) (in US) reserva *f*, reservación *f* (AmL)

reserve¹ /rɪ'zɜ:rv ‖ rɪ'zɜ:v/ *n* **1** [C] (stock) reserva *f*; **to keep sth in ~** ‹*money/food*› tener* algo reservado **2** [C] (Sport) reserva *mf* **3 reserves** *pl* (Mil) reservas *fpl* **4** [C] (land) coto *m*, reserva *f* **5** [U] (self-restraint) reserva *f*, cautela *f*

reserve² *vt* **(a)** (book) ‹*room/table*› reservar **(b)** (keep, save) reservar, guardar; **to ~ (one's) judgment** reservarse la opinión

reserved /rɪ'zɜ:rvd ‖ rɪ'zɜ:vd/ *adj* reservado

reservoir /'rezərvwɑ:r ‖ 'rezəvwɑ:(r)/ *n* embalse *m*, presa *f*, represa *f* (AmS)

reset /'ri:'set/ *vt* (*pres p* **resetting**; *past & past p* **reset**) **(a)** ‹*alarm clock*› (volver* a) poner*; ‹*counter/dial*› volver* a cero **(b)** (Med) ‹*bone*› colocar*

reshuffle /'ri:'ʃʌfəl/ *n* reorganización *f*; **cabinet ~** remodelación *f* del gabinete

reside /rɪ'zaɪd/ *vi* (frml) residir (frml)

residence /'rezədəns ‖ 'rezɪdəns/ *n* **1 (a)** [U] (in a country) residencia *f* **(b)** [U] (in building) (frml) residencia *f*; **to take up ~** instalarse **(c) ~ hall** (AmE) residencia *f* universitaria *or* de estudiantes, colegio *m* mayor (Esp) **2** [C] (home) residencia *f*

resident¹ /'rezədənt ‖ 'rezɪdənt/ *n* **(a)** (in country) residente *mf* **(b)** (of district) vecino, -na *m,f*

resident² *adj* residente

residential /'rezə'dentʃəl ‖ ˌrezɪ'denʃəl/ *adj* ‹*area/suburb*› residencial; ‹*course*› con alojamiento para los asistentes

residue /'rezədu: ‖ 'rezɪdju:/ *n* residuo *m*

resign /rɪ'zaɪn/ *vi* renunciar, dimitir; **to ~ FROM sth** renunciar A algo, dimitir algo ■ *v refl* **to ~ oneself (TO sth/-ING)** resignarse (A algo)

resignation /'rezɪg'neɪʃən/ *n* **1** [C U] (from job, position) renuncia *f*, dimisión *f* **2** [U] (acceptance, submission) resignación *f*

resigned /rɪ'zaɪnd/ *adj* resignado

resilience /rɪ'zɪljəns ‖ rɪ'zɪliəns/ *n* [U] **(a)** (of person) capacidad *f* de recuperación, resistencia *f* **(b)** (of material) elasticidad *f*

resilient /rɪ'zɪljənt ‖ rɪ'zɪliənt/ *adj* **(a)** ‹*person*› fuerte, con capacidad de recuperación **(b)** ‹*material*› elástico

resin /'rezn ‖ 'rezɪn/ *n* [U] resina *f*

resist /rɪ'zɪst/ *vt* resistir; ‹*change/plan*› oponer* resistencia a; **I can't ~ chocolate** el chocolate me vuelve loco; **to ~ -ING** resistirse A + INF

resistance /rɪ'zɪstəns/ *n* resistencia *f*; **the ~** la resistencia

resistant /rɪ'zɪstənt/ *adj* resistente

resit /'ri:'sɪt/ *vt* (*pres p* **resitting**; *past & past p* **resat** /'ri:'sæt/) (BrE) ‹*examination*› volver* a presentarse a

resolute /'rezəlu:t/ *adj* resuelto, decidido

resolution /'rezə'lu:ʃən/ *n* **(a)** (decision) determinación *f*, propósito *m*; **New Year's ~s** buenos propósitos de Año Nuevo **(b)** (in US, passed by legislature) resolución *f*

resolve¹ /rɪ'zɑ:lv ‖ rɪ'zɒlv/ *n* [U] resolución *f*

resolve² *vt* **(a)** (clear up) ‹*difficulty*› resolver*; ‹*differences*› saldar, resolver **(b)** (decide) **to ~ (to + INF)** resolver* *or* decidir (+ INF)

resonance /'reznəns ‖ 'rezənəns/ *n* resonancia *f*

resonant /'reznənt ‖ 'rezənənt/ *adj* resonante

resort /rɪ'zɔ:rt ‖ rɪ'zɔ:t/ *n* **1** (for vacations) centro *m* turístico *or* vacacional; **a seaside ~** un centro turístico costero, un balneario (AmL); **a ski ~** una estación de esquí **2** (recourse) recurso *m*; **as a/the last ~** como último recurso

• **resort to** [*v* + *prep* + *o*]: **to ~ to force/violence** recurrir a la fuerza/violencia; **they had to ~ to strike action** no les quedó más remedio que ir a la huelga

resound /rɪ'zaʊnd/ *vi* retumbar, resonar*

resounding /rɪ'zaʊndɪŋ/ *adj* (*before n*) **(a)** ‹*cheers/explosion*› retumbante, resonante **(b)** ‹*success/failure*› rotundo

resource /'ri:sɔ:rs ‖ rɪ'sɔ:s/ *n* recurso *m*; **natural/human ~s** recursos naturales/humanos

resourceful /rɪ'sɔ:rsfəl ‖ rɪ'sɔ:sfəl/ *adj* de recursos

respect¹ /rɪ'spekt/ *n* **1 (a)** [U] (esteem) respeto *m*; **to have ~ for sb** respetar algn **(b)** [U] (consideration) consideración *f*, respeto *m* **(c) respects** *pl* respetos *mpl* **2 (a)** [C] (way, aspect) sentido *m*, respecto *m*; **in this ~** en cuanto a esto, en este sentido **(b) with respect to** (frml) (introducing subject) en lo que concierne a (frml); (in relation to) con respecto a

respect² *vt* respetar

respectable /rɪ'spektəbəl/ *adj* **1** (socially acceptable) ‹*person/conduct*› decente, respetable **2 (a)** (quite large) ‹*amount/salary*› respetable **(b)** (reasonably good) ‹*performance/score*› digno, aceptable

respectful /rɪ'spektfəl/ *adj* respetuoso

respecting /rɪ'spektɪŋ/ *prep* (frml) en lo que concierne a (frml)

respective /rɪ'spektɪv/ *adj* (*before n*) respectivo

respiration /'respə'reɪʃən ‖ ˌrespɪ'reɪʃən/ *n* [U] respiración *f*

respirator /'respəreɪtər ‖ 'respɪreɪtə(r)/ *n* **(a)** (Med) respirador *m* **(b)** (mask) máscara *f* de oxígeno

respiratory /'respərətɔːri ‖ rɪ'spɪrətəri/ *adj* respiratorio

respite /'respət ‖ 'respaɪt/ *n* [C U] (*no pl*) respiro *m*, descanso *m*; **without ~** sin respiro

resplendent /rɪ'splendənt/ *adj* resplandeciente

respond /rɪ'spɑːnd ‖ rɪ'spɒnd/ *vi* **(a)** (reply) responder, contestar **(b)** (react) responder, reaccionar

response /rɪ'spɑːns ‖ rɪ'spɒns/ *n* **(a)** (reply) respuesta *f* **(b)** (reaction) respuesta *f*; (to news) reacción *f*

responsibility /rɪˈspɑːnsə'bɪləti ‖ rɪˌspɒnsə'bɪləti/ *n* (*pl* **-ties**) **(a)** [C] (task, duty) responsabilidad *f* **(b)** [U] (authority, accountability) responsabilidad *f*; **to take ~ for sth** responsabilizarse* *or* encargarse* de algo **(c)** [U] (liability, blame) responsabilidad *f*; **they took full ~ for the disaster** aceptaron ser responsables del desastre

responsible /rɪ'spɑːnsəbəl ‖ rɪ'spɒnsəbəl/ *adj* **(a)** (accountable) (*pred*) **to be ~ (FOR sth)**: **who's ~?** ¿quién es el responsable?; **a build-up of gas was ~ for the explosion** una acumulación de gas fue la causa de la explosión; **to hold sb ~ for sth** responsabilizar* *or* hacer* responsable a algn de algo **(b)** (in charge) (*pred*) **to be ~ FOR sth** ser* responsable DE algo **(c)** (trustworthy) responsable, formal **(d)** (*before n*) ‹*post*› de responsabilidad

responsibly /rɪ'spɑːnsəbli ‖ rɪ'spɒnsɪbli/ *adv* con responsabilidad, responsablemente

responsive /rɪ'spɑːnsɪv ‖ rɪ'spɒnsɪv/ *adj* ‹*brakes/engine*› sensible; ‹*person/audience*› receptivo

rest¹ /rest/ *n* **I 1 (a)** [C] (break) descanso *m*; **to have a ~** tomarse un descanso **(b)** [U] (relaxation) descanso *m*, reposo *m*; **try to get some ~** trata de descansar un poco **2** [U] (motionlessness) **to come to ~** detenerse* **3** [C] (support) apoyo *m* **4** [C] (Mus) silencio *m*

II (remainder) **the ~**: **the ~ of the money** el resto del dinero; **the ~ of the children** los demás niños

rest² *vi* **1** (relax) descansar **2 (a)** (be supported) **to ~ ON sth** (Const) descansar *or* apoyarse EN *or* SOBRE algo **(b)** (be based, depend) **to ~ ON sth** «*argument/theory*» descansar SOBRE algo **(c)** (stop) **to ~ ON sth/sb** «*eyes/gaze*» detenerse* SOBRE algo/algn **3** (be responsibility of) **to ~ WITH sb** «*responsibility*» recaer* SOBRE algn ■ **~** *vt* **1** (relax) descansar **2** (place for support) apoyar

• **rest up** [*v* + *adv*] (AmE) descansar

rest area *n* (AmE) área *f*‡ de reposo

restaurant /'restərɑːnt ‖ 'restrɒnt/ *n* restaurante *m*, restorán *m*

restful /'restfəl/ *adj* tranquilo, apacible

restless /'restləs ‖ 'restlɪs/ *adj* ‹*person/manner*› inquieto; ‹*waves/wind*› (liter) agitado

restoration /'restə'reɪʃən/ *n* **1** [U] **(a)** (of order, peace) restablecimiento *m* **(b)** (to throne, power) restauración *f*, reinstauración *f* **2** [U C] (of building, painting) restauración *f*

restore /rɪ'stɔːr ‖ rɪ'stɔː(r)/ *vt* **1 (a)** (re-establish) ‹*order/peace*› restablecer*; ‹*confidence/health/energy*› devolver*; ‹*monarchy/king*› restaurar, reinstaurar **(b)** (give back) (frml) restituir* (frml) **2** ‹*building/painting*› restaurar

restrain /rɪ'streɪn/ *vt* contener* ■ *v refl* **to ~ oneself** contenerse*, refrenarse

restrained /rɪ'streɪnd/ *adj* ‹*person/behavior*› moderado, comedido; ‹*colors/style*› sobrio

restraint /rɪ'streɪnt/ *n* **(a)** [U] (self-control) compostura *f*, circunspección *f* **(b)** [C] (restriction) limitación *f*, restricción *f*

restrict /rɪ'strɪkt/ *vt* ‹*power/freedom/access*› restringir*, limitar; ‹*imports/movements*› restringir*

restricted /rɪ'strɪktəd ‖ rɪ'strɪktɪd/ *adj* **(a)** ‹*number/space*› limitado **(b)** ‹*information*› confidencial

restriction /rɪ'strɪkʃən/ *n* [C U] restricción *f*

restrictive /rɪ'strɪktɪv/ *adj* restrictivo

rest room *n* (AmE) baño *m*, servicio(s) *m(pl)*

restructure /'riː'strʌktʃər ‖ ˌriː'strʌktʃə(r)/ *vt* reestructurar

rest stop *n* (AmE) ⇒ REST AREA

result¹ /rɪ'zʌlt/ *n* **1** [C U] **(a)** (consequence) resultado *m*; **the company collapsed, with the ~ that** ... la compañía quebró, y como consecuencia ... **(b)** (of calculation, exam, contest) resultado *m* **2 (a) as a result** (*as linker*) por consiguiente, por ende (frml) **(b) as a result of** (*as prep*) a raíz de

result² *vi*: **to ~ in** traer* como consecuencia, resultar en; **it could ~ in his dismissal** podría ocasionar *or* acarrear su despido

resultant /rɪ'zʌltənt/, **resulting** /rɪ'zʌltɪŋ/ *adj* (*before n*) consiguiente, resultante

resume /rɪ'zuːm ‖ rɪ'zjuːm/ *vt* ‹*work/journey*› reanudar ■ **~** *vi* «*negotiations/work*» reanudarse, continuar*

resumé /'rezəmeɪ, 'rezə'meɪ ‖ 'rezjʊmeɪ/ *n* **(a)** (summary) resumen *m* **(b)** (of career) (AmE) currículum *m* (vitae), historial *m* personal

resurgence /rɪ'sɜːrdʒəns ‖ rɪ'sɜːdʒəns/ *n* [U] resurgimiento *m*, renacer *m*

resurrect /'rezə'rekt/ *vt* desenterrar*, resucitar

resurrection /'rezə'rekʃən/ *n* [U] resurrección *f*

resuscitate /rɪ'sʌsəteɪt ‖ rɪ'sʌsɪteɪt/ *vt* (Med) resucitar

resuscitation /rɪ'sʌsə'teɪʃən ‖ rɪˌsʌsɪ'teɪʃən/ *n* [U] (Med) resucitación *f*

retail¹ /'ri:teɪl/ *vt* vender al por menor *or* al detalle ■ ~ *vi* venderse al por menor

retail² *n* [U] venta *f* al por menor *or* al detalle; (*before n*) **~ price** precio *m* de venta al público, precio *m* al por menor

retailer /'ri:teɪlər ‖ 'ri:teɪlə(r)/ *n* minorista *mf*, detallista *mf*

retail price index *n* (BrE) índice *m* de precios al consumo

retain /rɪ'teɪn/ *vt* ‹*property/money*› quedarse con; ‹*authority/power*› retener*; ‹*heat*› conservar; ‹*moisture/water*› retener*; ‹*information*› retener*

retake /'ri:'teɪk/ *vt* (*past* **retook**; *past p* **retaken**) (Educ) volver* a presentarse a, volver* a presentar

retaliate /rɪ'tælieɪt/ *vi* (Mil) tomar represalias

retaliation /rɪ'tæli'eɪʃən/ *n* [U] represalias *fpl*

retarded /rɪ'tɑ:rdəd ‖ rɪ'tɑ:dɪd/ *adj* (sometimes offensive) retrasado

retch /retʃ/ *vi* hacer* arcadas

retention /rɪ'tentʃən ‖ rɪ'tenʃən/ *n* [U] retención *f*

retentive /rɪ'tentɪv/ *adj* ‹*memory*› retentivo

rethink /'ri:'θɪŋk/ *vt* (*past & past p* **rethought**) reconsiderar, replantearse

reticence /'retəsəns ‖ 'retɪsəns/ *n* [U] reticencia *f*

reticent /'retəsənt ‖ 'retɪsənt/ *adj* reticente

retina /'retṇə ‖ 'retɪnə/ *n* (*pl* **-nas** *or* **-nae** /-ni:/) retina *f*

retinue /'retṇu: ‖ 'retɪnju:/ *n* séquito *m*, comitiva *f*

retire /rɪ'taɪr ‖ rɪ'taɪə(r)/ *vi* **1** (from occupation) jubilarse, retirarse; «*soldier/athlete*» retirarse **2 (a)** (retreat, withdraw) (frml) retirarse **(b)** (go to bed) (frml *or* hum) retirarse a sus (*or* mis *etc*) aposentos (frml *o* hum)

retired /rɪ'taɪrd ‖ rɪ'taɪəd/ *adj* jubilado, retirado

retirement /rɪ'taɪrmənt ‖ rɪ'taɪəmənt/ *n* [U C] (from job) jubilación *f*, retiro *m*

retiring /rɪ'taɪrɪŋ ‖ rɪ'taɪərɪŋ/ *adj* (shy) retraído

retort¹ /rɪ'tɔ:rt ‖ rɪ'tɔ:t/ *vt* replicar* (liter), contestar

retort² *n* réplica *f* (liter), contestación *f*

retrace /'ri:'treɪs/ *vt* **to ~ one's steps** volver* sobre sus (*or* mis *etc*) pasos

retract /rɪ'trækt/ *vt* **(a)** ‹*allegation/statement*› retirar **(b)** ‹*undercarriage*› replegar*, levantar

retrain /'ri:'treɪn/ *vi* hacer* un curso de reciclaje *or* recapacitación

retread¹ /'ri:'tred/ *vt* (*past and past p* **~ed**) ‹*tire*› recauchutar, recauchar, reencauchar (AmC, Méx)

retread² /'ri:tred/ *n* neumático *m* recauchutado *or* recauchado *or* (AmC, Ven) reencauchado, llanta *f* vulcanizada (AmL)

retreat¹ /rɪ'tri:t/ *vi* retirarse

retreat² *n* **1** (Mil) retirada *f*, repliegue *m* **2 (a)** (place) refugio *m* **(b)** (Relig) retiro *m* espiritual

retrial /'ri:'traɪəl/ *n* nuevo juicio *m*

retribution /'retrə'bju:ʃən ‖ ˌretrɪ'bju:ʃən/ *n* [U] castigo *m*

retrieve /rɪ'tri:v/ *vt* ‹*object/data*› recuperar

retriever /rɪ'tri:vər ‖ rɪ'tri:və(r)/ *n* perro *m* cobrador

retrograde /'retrəgreɪd/ *adj* retrógrado

retrospect /'retrəspekt/ *n*: **in ~** mirando hacia atrás, en retrospectiva

retrospective /'retrə'spektɪv/ *adj* retrospectivo

return¹ /rɪ'tɜ:rn ‖ rɪ'tɜ:n/ *vi* **(a)** (to place) volver*, regresar; **to ~ TO sth** (to former activity, state) volver* A algo **(b)** (reaapear) «*symptom*» volver* a aparecer; «*doubts/suspicions*» resurgir* ■ **~** *vt* **1 (a)** (give back) devolver*, regresar (AmL exc CS), restituir* (frml) **(b)** (reciprocate) ‹*affection*› corresponder a; ‹*blow/favor*› devolver*; ‹*greeting*› devolver*, corresponder a; **to ~ sb's call** devolverle* la llamada a algn **(c)** (Sport) ‹*ball*› devolver* **2** (Law) ‹*verdict*› emitir

return² *n* **1** [U] **(a)** (to place) regreso *m*, vuelta *f*, retorno *m* (frml *o* liter) **(b)** (reappearance) reaparición *f*; **many happy ~s of the day!** ¡que cumplas muchos más! **2** [U C] (to owner) devolución *f*, regreso *m* (AmL) **3** (*in phrases*) **in ~** (**FOR sth**) a cambio (DE algo) **4** [U C] (profit) rendimiento *m* **5** [C] (*tax* ~) declaración *f* (de la renta *or* de impuestos)

return³ *adj* (*before n*) ‹*journey/flight*› de vuelta, de regreso; ‹*ticket/fare*› (BrE) de ida y vuelta

returnable /rɪ'tɜ:rnəbəl ‖ rɪ'tɜ:nəbəl/ *adj* ‹*deposit*› reembolsable, reintegrable; ‹*bottle*› retornable

reunion /ri:'ju:njən/ *n* [C U] reunión *f*, reencuentro *m*; **a family ~** una reunión familiar

reunite /'ri:jʊ'naɪt/ *vt* ‹*family/party*› volver* a unir; **to be ~d with sb** reencontrarse* con algn

reuse /'ri:'ju:z/ *vt* reutilizar*, volver* a usar

rev¹ /rev/ *n* revolución *f*

rev² *vt* **-vv- ~ (up)** ‹*engine/car*› acelerar (*sin desplazarse*)

revalue /'ri:'vælju:/, (AmE also) **revaluate** /-jueɪt/ *vt* ‹*currency*› revalorizar*, revaluar* (esp AmL); ‹*house*› reevaluar*, revalorar

revamp /'ri:'væmp/ *vt* ‹*kitchen/interior*› reformar; (modernize) modernizar*; ‹*image*› cambiar; ‹*organization*› modernizar*

reveal /rɪ'vi:l/ *vt* **(a)** (disclose) revelar, develar (AmL), desvelar (Esp) **(b)** (bring to view) dejar ver

revealing /rɪ'vi:lɪŋ/ *adj* revelador

revel /'revəl/ *vi*, (BrE) **-ll-** (enjoy greatly) **to ~ IN sth** deleitarse CON *or* EN algo

revelation /'revə'leɪʃən/ *n* [C U] **(a)** (disclosure) revelación *f* **(b)** (Bib): **(the Book of) Revelations** el Apocalipsis

reveler, (BrE) **reveller** /'revələr ‖ 'revələ(r)/ *n* (liter) juerguista *mf* (fam)

revelry /'revəlri/ *n* (*pl* **-ries**) jolgorio *m*

revenge¹ /rɪ'vendʒ/ *n* [U] venganza *f*; **to take ~** vengarse*, desquitarse

revenge² *vt* vengar*

revenue /'revənu: ‖ 'revənju:/ *n* **(a)** [U] (Tax) rentas *fpl* públicas **(b) revenues** *pl* ingresos *mpl*

reverberate /rɪ'vɜ:rbəreɪt ‖ rɪ'vɜ:bəreɪt/ *vi* retumbar

revere /rɪ'vɪr ‖ rɪ'vɪə(r)/ *vt* (frml) reverenciar (frml)

reverence /'revrəns, 'revərəns/ *n* [U] reverencia *f*

Reverend ▶ 603 *adj* (in titles) reverendo

reverent /'revrənt, 'revərənt/ *adj* reverente

reverie /'revəri/ *n* [U C] ensueño *m*

reversal /rɪ'vɜ:rsəl ‖ rɪ'vɜ:səl/ *n* [C U] **(a)** (inversion) inversión *f* **(b)** (of trend, policy) cambio *m* completo *or* total **(c)** (setback) (frml) revés *m*

reverse¹ /rɪ'vɜ:rs ‖ rɪ'vɜ:s/ *n* **1** [C] (of picture, paper) reverso *m*, dorso *m*; (of cloth, garment) revés *m*; (of coin) reverso *m* **2** (*no pl*) (opposite) **the ~** lo contrario **3 ~ (gear)** (*no art*) marcha *f* atrás, reversa *f* (Col, Méx) **4** [C U] (setback) (frml) revés *m*

reverse² *vt* **1 (a)** (transpose) ‹*roles/positions*› invertir*; **to ~ the charges** (BrE Telec) llamar a cobro revertido *or* (Chi, Méx) por cobrar **(b)** (invert) ‹*order/process*› invertir* **2** (undo, negate) ‹*policy*› cambiar radicalmente; ‹*trend*› invertir* el sentido de; ‹*ruling*› revocar* **3** ‹*vehicle*›: **she ~d her car around the corner** dobló la esquina dando marcha atrás *or* (Col, Méx) en reversa ■ ~ *vi* «*vehicle/driver*» dar* marcha atrás, meter reversa (Col, Méx)

reverse³ *adj* (*before n*) **(a)** (backward, opposite) ‹*movement/direction/trend*› contrario, inverso; **in ~ order** en orden inverso **(b)** (back): **the ~ side** (of cloth) el revés; (of paper) el reverso, el dorso

reverse-charge call /rɪ'vɜ:rs'tʃɑ:rdʒ ‖ rɪˌvɜ:s'tʃɑ:dʒ/ *n* (BrE) llamada *f* a cobro revertido *or* (Chi, Méx) por cobrar

reversible /rɪ'vɜ:rsəbəl ‖ rɪ'vɜ:səbəl/ *adj* reversible

reversion /rɪ'vɜ:rʒən ‖ rɪ'vɜ:ʃən/ *n* [U C] (to former state, practice) vuelta *f*, reversión *f* (frml)

revert /rɪ'vɜ:rt ‖ rɪ'vɜ:t/ **to ~ to** volver* a

review¹ /rɪ'vju:/ *n* **1** [C] **(a)** (of book, film) crítica *f*, reseña *f* **(b)** (report, summary) resumen *m*, reseña *f* **2 (a)** [C U] (reconsideration) revisión *f* **(b)** [C] (for exam) (AmE) repaso *m*

review² *vt* **1 (a)** (consider) ‹*situation*› examinar, estudiar **(b)** (reconsider) ‹*policy/case*› reconsiderar; ‹*salary*› reajustar **2 (a)** (summarize) ‹*news/events*› resumir, reseñar **(b)** ‹*book/play*› hacer* (*or* escribir* *etc*) la crítica de, reseñar **3** (for exam) (AmE) repasar

revise /rɪ'vaɪz/ *vt* **(a)** (alter) modificar* **(b)** (for exam) (BrE) repasar ■ ~ *vi* (BrE) repasar

revision /rɪ'vɪʒən/ *n* **1 (a)** [U C] (alteration) modificación *f* **(b)** [C] (text) edición *f* corregida **2** [U] (for exam) (BrE) repaso *m*

revitalize /ri:'vaɪtl̩aɪz/ *vt* vigorizar*, darle* vitalidad a; ‹*economy*› estimular, reactivar

revival /rɪ'vaɪvəl/ *n* [C U] **(a)** (renewal, upsurge): **a ~ of interest in** … un renovado interés por …; **economic ~** reactivación *f* económica; **a religious ~** un renacer *or* un renacimiento religioso **(b)** (Med) reanimación *f*

revive /rɪ'vaɪv/ *vt* **(a)** (Med) reanimar, resucitar **(b)** (revitalize) ‹*economy*› reactivar, estimular; ‹*interest/friendship*› hacer* renacer, reavivar **(c)** ‹*custom/practice*› restablecer* ■ ~ *vi* «*trade*» reactivarse, repuntar; «*hope/interest*» renacer*, resurgir*; «*patient*» reanimarse; «*plant*» revivir

revoke /rɪ'vəʊk/ *vt* revocar*

revolt¹ /rɪ'vəʊlt/ *n* [U C] revuelta *f*, sublevación *f*

revolt² *vi* sublevarse ■ ~ *vt* darle* asco a

revolting /rɪ'vəʊltɪŋ/ *adj* (nauseating) repugnante; (horrible) (colloq) asqueroso, horrible

revolution /ˈrevə'lu:ʃən/ *n* [C U] revolución *f*

revolutionary¹ /ˈrevə'lu:ʃəneri ‖ ˌrevə'lu:ʃənəri/ *adj* revolucionario

revolutionary² *n* (*pl* **-ries**) revolucionario, -ria *m,f*

revolutionize /ˈrevə'lu:ʃənaɪz/ *vt* revolucionar

revolve /rɪ'vɑ:lv ‖ rɪ'vɒlv/ *vi* **(a)** (rotate) girar **(b)** **revolving** *pres p* ‹*chair/door*› giratorio

revolver /rɪ'vɑ:lvər ‖ rɪ'vɒlvə(r)/ *n* revólver *m*

revue /rɪ'vju:/ *n* [C U] revista *f*

revulsion /rɪ'vʌlʃən/ *n* [U] repugnancia *f*, asco *m*

reward¹ /rɪ'wɔ:rd ‖ rɪ'wɔ:d/ *n* [C U] recompensa *f*

reward² *vt* premiar, recompensar

rewarding /rɪ'wɔ:rdɪŋ ‖ rɪ'wɔ:dɪŋ/ *adj* gratificante

rewind /ri:'waɪnd/ *vt* (*past & past p* **rewound**) rebobinar

rewire /ri:'waɪr ‖ ˌri:'waɪə(r)/ *vt* ‹*house*› renovar* la instalación eléctrica de

reword /ri:'wɜ:rd ‖ ˌri:'wɜ:d/ *vt* ‹*question*› formular de otra manera; ‹*statement*› volver* a redactar

rewound /ri:'waʊnd/ *past & past p of* REWIND

rewrite /'ri:'raɪt/ *vt* (*past* **rewrote**; *past p* **rewritten**) volver* a escribir *or* redactar

rhapsody /'ræpsədi/ *n* (*pl* **-dies**) rapsodia *f*

rhetoric /'retərɪk/ *n* [U] retórica *f*

rhetorical /rɪ'tɔ:rɪkəl ‖ rɪ'tɒrɪkəl/ *adj* retórico

rheumatic /ru:'mætɪk/ *adj* reumático

rheumatism /'ru:mətɪzəm/ *n* [U] reumatismo *m*

Rhine /raɪn/ *n* **the ~** el Rin

rhino /'raɪnəʊ/ *n* (*pl* **~** *or* **~s**) rinoceronte *m*

rhinoceros /raɪ'nɑ:srəs, -sərəs ‖ raɪ'nɒsərəs, -srəs/ *n* (*pl* **-oses** *or* **~**) rinoceronte *m*

rhubarb /'ru:bɑ:rb ‖ 'ru:bɑ:b/ *n* [C U] ruibarbo *m*

rhyme¹ /raɪm/ *n* **(a)** [U C] (correspondence of sound) rima *f* **(b)** [C] (poem) rima *f*, poema *m*

rhyme² *vi/t* rimar

rhythm /'rɪðəm/ *n* [U C] ritmo *m*

rhythmic /'rɪðmɪk/, **-mical** /-mɪkəl/ *adj* rítmico

RI = **Rhode Island**

rib /rɪb/ *n* [C U] (Anat, Culin) costilla *f*

ribald /'rɪbəld/ *adj* ‹*comments/humor*› procaz, picaresco

ribbed /rɪbd/ *adj* ‹*neck/sleeves*› en punto elástico, en canalé, en resorte (AmC, Col, Méx)

ribbon /'rɪbən/ *n* **(a)** [U C] (strip of fabric) cinta *f*, listón *m* (Méx) **(b)** [C] (as insignia, award) galón *m* **(c)** [C] (of typewriter, printer etc) cinta *f* **(d)** **ribbons** *pl* (shreds) jirones *mpl*

ribcage /'rɪbkeɪdʒ/ *n* caja *f* torácica

rice /raɪs/ *n* [U] arroz *m*; (*before n*) **~ pudding** arroz con leche

rice: **~field** *n* arrozal *m*; **~ paper** *n* [U] papel *m* de arroz

rich /rɪtʃ/ *adj* **-er, -est 1 (a)** (wealthy) rico **(b)** (opulent) ‹*banquet*› suntuoso; ‹*furnishings*› lujoso, suntuoso **(c)** (abundant) ‹*harvest/supply*› abundante; ‹*reward*› generoso; ‹*history/experience*› rico **2 (a)** ‹*food*› *con alto contenido de grasas, huevos, azúcar etc* **(b)** ‹*soil*› rico; ‹*color*› cálido e intenso

riches /ˈrɪtʃəz ‖ ˈrɪtʃɪz/ *pl n* riquezas *fpl*

richness /ˈrɪtʃnəs ‖ ˈrɪtʃnɪs/ *n* [U] riqueza *f*

rickety /ˈrɪkəti/ *adj* desvencijado

rickshaw /ˈrɪkʃɔː/ *n*: *calesa oriental de dos ruedas tirada por un hombre*

ricochet /ˈrɪkəʃeɪ/ *vi* **-chets** /-ʃeɪz/, **-cheting** /-ʃeɪɪŋ/, **-cheted** /-ʃeɪd/ **to ~** (OFF **sth**) rebotar (EN algo)

rid /rɪd/ *vt* (*pres p* **ridding**; *past & past p* **rid**): **they ~ the country of corruption** libraron al país de la corrupción; **to get ~ of** (of unwanted object) deshacerse* de; (of person, cold) quitarse de encima; ‹*smell*› quitar

riddance /ˈrɪdn̩s/ *n* [U]: **good ~!** (colloq) ¡adiós y buen viaje! (fam & iró)

ridden /ˈrɪdn̩/ *past p of* RIDE[1]

riddle¹ /ˈrɪdl̩/ *n* **(a)** (puzzle) adivinanza *f*, acertijo *m* **(b)** (mystery) enigma *m*, misterio *m*

riddle² *vt* (perforate) (*often pass*) **to be ~d** WITH **sth**: **his body was ~d with bullets** lo habían acribillado a balazos; **she was ~d with cancer** tenía cáncer por todo el cuerpo

ride¹ /raɪd/ (*past* **rode**; *past p* **ridden**) *vt* **1 (a) to ~ a horse** montar a caballo; **to ~ a bicycle/motorbike** montar *or* (AmL tb) andar* en bicicleta/moto **(b)** (AmE) ‹*bus/subway/train*› ir* en **2** (be carried upon) ‹*waves/wind*› dejarse llevar por ■ **~** *vi* **(a)** (on horse) montar *or* (AmL tb) andar* a caballo **(b)** (on bicycle, in vehicle) ir*; **we rode into town** fuimos al centro en bicicleta (*or* en moto *etc*)

• **ride out** [*v + o + adv, v + adv + o*] aguantar, sobrellevar

• **ride up** [*v + adv*] subirse

ride² *n* (on horse, in vehicle etc): **let's go for a ~ on our bikes/in your car** vamos a dar una vuelta *or* un paseo en bicicleta/en tu coche; **it was a long ~** fue un viaje largo; **to give sb a ~** (esp AmE) llevar a algn en coche, darle* un aventón (Méx) *or* (Col fam) una palomita a algn; ***to take sb for a ~*** (colloq) tomarle el pelo a algn (fam)

rider /ˈraɪdər ‖ ˈraɪdə(r)/ *n* **1 (a)** (on horseback) jinete *mf*; (on bicycle) ciclista *mf*; (on motorbike) motociclista *mf*, motorista *mf* **(b)** (of subway, bus) (AmE) pasajero, -ra *m,f* **2** (appended statement) cláusula *f* adicional; (condition) condición *f*

ridge /rɪdʒ/ *n* (of hills) cadena *f*; (hilltop) cresta *f*

ridicule¹ /ˈrɪdəkjuːl ‖ ˈrɪdɪkjuːl/ *n* [U] burlas *fpl*

ridicule² *vt* ridiculizar*, burlarse de

ridiculous /rɪˈdɪkjələs ‖ rɪˈdɪkjʊləs/ *adj* ridículo

riding /ˈraɪdɪŋ/ *n* [U] equitación *f*; (*before n*) ‹*school/lesson*› de equitación; ‹*breeches/boots*› de montar

rife /raɪf/ *adj* (*pred*) extendido; **disease is ~** cunden las enfermedades; **corruption is ~** reina la corrupción

riffraff /ˈrɪfræf/ *n* [U] (*+ sing or pl vb*) chusma *f*

rifle¹ /ˈraɪfəl/ *n* rifle *m*, fusil *m*

rifle² *vi* **to ~** THROUGH **sth** hojear algo

rift /rɪft/ *n* **(a)** (in rock) fisura *f* **(b)** (within party) escisión *f*; (between people) distanciamiento *m*; (between countries) ruptura *f*

rig¹ /rɪg/ *n* (*oil ~*) plataforma *f* petrolífera *or* petrolera; (derrick) torre *f* de perforación

rig² **-gg-** *vt* ‹*election/contest*› amañar; ‹*fight*› arreglar

• **rig out** [*v + o + adv, v + adv + o*] (colloq) equipar

• **rig up** [*v + o + adv, v + adv + o*] (set up) instalar

rigging /ˈrɪgɪŋ/ *n* [U] (Naut) jarcia(s) *f(pl)*

right¹ /raɪt/ *adj* **1** (correct) ‹*answer/interpretation*› correcto; **are we going in the ~ direction?** ¿vamos bien?; **did you press the ~ button?** ¿apretaste el botón que debías?; **do you have the ~ change?** ¿tienes el cambio justo?; **do you have the ~ time?** ¿tienes hora (buena)? **2** (not mistaken): **to be ~** «*person*» tener* razón, estar* en lo cierto; «*clock*» estar* bien; **you got two answers ~** acertaste dos respuestas; **to be ~ to** + INF hacer* bien en + INF **3** (good, suitable) adecuado, apropiado; **if the price is ~** si está bien de precio; **just ~** perfecto; **the ~ person for the job** la persona indicada para el puesto **4** (just, moral) (*pred*) **to be ~** ser* justo **5** (*pred*) (in order): **to put sth ~** arreglar algo **6** (opposite of left) (*before n*) ‹*side/ear/shoe*› derecho

right² *adv* **1** (correctly, well) bien, correctamente; **nothing goes ~ for them** todo les sale mal, nada les sale bien; ⇒ SERVE[1] *vt* 2 **2 (a)** (all the way, completely): **the road goes ~ along the coast** la carretera bordea toda la costa; **~ from the start** desde el principio **(b)** (directly): **it's ~ in front of you** lo tienes allí delante; **he was ~ here/there** estaba aquí mismo/allí mismo; **~ now** ahora mismo **(c)** (immediately): **~ after lunch** inmediatamente después de comer; **I'll be ~ back** vuelvo enseguida **3** ▶ **553** ‹*turn/look*› a la derecha

right³ *n* **1 (a)** [C U] (entitlement) derecho *m*; **~ to sth/+** INF derecho A algo/+ INF; **the title is his by ~** el título le corresponde a él **(b) rights** *pl* derechos *mpl* **2** [U C] (what is correct): **to know ~ from wrong** saber* distinguir entre el bien y el mal; **to be in the ~** tener* razón, llevar la razón, estar* en lo cierto; **to put** *o* **set sth to ~s** (esp BrE) arreglar algo **3 (a)** [U] (opposite the left) derecha *f*; **on the ~** a la derecha; **to drive on the ~** manejar *or* (Esp) conducir* por la derecha **(b)** (right turn): **to make** *o* (BrE) **take a ~** girar a la derecha **(c)** (Sport) (hand) derecha *f* **4** [U] (Pol) **the ~** la derecha

right⁴ *vt* **(a)** (set upright) enderezar* **(b)** (redress) reparar; **to ~ a wrong** reparar un daño

right⁵ *interj* (colloq) ¡bueno!, ¡vale! (Esp fam)

right: **~ angle** *n* ángulo *m* recto; **~ away** *adv* enseguida

righteous /ˈraɪtʃəs/ *adj* **(a)** ‹*indignation*› justificado **(b)** ‹*person*› recto, honrado

rightful /ˈraɪtfəl/ *adj* (*before n*) ‹*owner/heir*› legítimo; ‹*share/reward*› justo

right: **~-hand** /ˈraɪtˈhænd/ *adj* (*before n*) de la derecha; **on the ~-hand side** a la derecha, a mano derecha; **~-handed** /ˈraɪtˈhændəd ‖ ˌraɪtˈhændɪd/ *adj* ‹*person*› diestro; **~-hand man** /ˈraɪtˈhænd/ *n* brazo *m* derecho

rightly /ˈraɪtli/ *adv* **(a)** (correctly, accurately): **if I remember ~** si mal no recuerdo; **I can't ~ say** (colloq) no sabría decir exactamente **(b)** (justly) con toda la razón; **~ or wrongly** justa o injustamente

right: **~ of way** *n* (*pl* **~s of way**) [U] (precedence in traffic) preferencia *f*; **~ on** *adj* (AmE colloq) (*pred*): **his analysis was ~ on** su análisis era muy acertado *or* (fam) daba justo en el clavo; **~-on** /'raɪt'ɑːn ‖ ˌraɪt'ɒn/ *adj* (BrE colloq & hum) progre (fam); **~ wing** *n* **(a)** (Pol) (ala *f*‡) derecha *f* **(b)** (Sport) ala *f*‡ derecha; **~-wing** /'raɪt'wɪŋ/ *adj* derechista

rigid /'rɪdʒəd ‖ 'rɪdʒɪd/ *adj* **(a)** (stiff) rígido **(b)** ‹*discipline*› estricto; ‹*person/principles*› inflexible

rigmarole /'rɪgmərəʊl/ *n* (colloq) lío *m* (fam)

rigor, (BrE) **rigour** /'rɪgər ‖ 'rɪgə(r)/ *n* [U C] rigor *m*

rigor mortis /'rɪgər'mɔːrtəs ‖ˌrɪgə'mɔːtɪs/ *n* [U] rigidez *f* cadavérica; **~ ~ had set in** el cuerpo ya estaba rígido

rigorous /'rɪgərəs/ *adj* riguroso

rigour *n* (BrE) ⇒ RIGOR

rile /raɪl/ *vt* (colloq) irritar

rim /rɪm/ *n* (of cup, bowl) borde *m*; (of spectacles) montura *f*, armazón *m or f*; (of wheel) (Auto) llanta *f*, rin *m* (Col, Méx); (of bicycle wheel) aro *m*

rind /raɪnd/ *n* [U C] (of lemon, orange) cáscara *f*, corteza *f*; (of cheese) corteza *f*; (of bacon) piel *f*

ring¹ /rɪŋ/ *n* **1** [C] **(a)** (on finger) anillo *m*; (woman's) anillo *m*, sortija *f* **(b)** (circle) círculo *m*; **to stand in a ~** hacer* un corro, formar un círculo **(d)** (burner) (BrE) quemador *m*, hornilla *f* (AmL exc CS), hornillo *m* (Esp) **2** [C] **(a)** (in boxing, wrestling) cuadrilátero *m*, ring *m* **(b)** (in circus) pista *f* **(c)** (*bull* ~) ruedo *m* **3** [C] (of criminals) red *f*, banda *f* **4 (a)** [C] (sound of bell) (of phone) timbrazo *m*; **there was a ~ at the door** sonó el timbre de la puerta **(b)** (telephone call) (BrE) (*no pl*): **to give sb a ~** llamar (por teléfono) a algn

ring² (*past* **rang**; *past p* **rung**) *vi* **1 (a)** (make sound) sonar* **(b)** (operate bell) «*person*» tocar* el timbre, llamar al timbre **2** (telephone) (BrE) llamar (por teléfono), telefonear **3 (a)** (resound) resonar*; **to ~ true** ser* *or* sonar* convincente **(b)** «*ears*» zumbar ■ **~** *vt* **1 (a)** ‹*bell*› tocar* **(b)** (telephone) ‹*person*› (BrE) llamar (por teléfono) **2** (*past & past p* **ringed**) **(a)** (surround) cercar*, rodear **(b)** (with pen, pencil) marcar* con un círculo

• **ring back** (BrE) **1** [*v* + *adv*] volver* a llamar **2** [*v* + *o* + *adv*] (ring again) volver* a llamar; (return call) llamar

• **ring off** [*v* + *adv*] (BrE) colgar*, cortar (CS)

• **ring out** [*v* + *adv*] «*shot/voice*» oírse*, resonar*; «*bells*» sonar*, resonar*

• **ring up 1** [*v* + *o* + *adv*, *v* + *adv* + *o*] (BrE) ⇒ RING² *vt* 1(b) **2** [*v* + *adv*] (BrE) ⇒ RING² *vi* 2

ring binder *n* archivador *m*, carpeta *f* de anillos *or* (Esp) de anillas

ringing /'rɪŋɪŋ/ *n* [U] **(a)** (of bell) repique *m*, toque *m* **(b)** (of doorbell, telephone) timbre *m* **(c)** (in ears) zumbido *m*

ringleader /'rɪŋˌliːdər ‖ 'rɪŋˌliːdə(r)/ *n* cabecilla *mf*

ringlet /'rɪŋlət/ *n* tirabuzón *m*, rizo *m*

ring road *n* (BrE) carretera *f* de circunvalación

rink /rɪŋk/ *n* (*ice* ~) pista *f* de hielo; (*skating* ~) pista *f* de patinaje

rinse¹ /rɪns/ *vt* **(a)** (wash) ‹*cutlery/hands*› enjuagar*; ‹*rice/mushrooms*› lavar **(b)** (to remove soap) ‹*clothes/hair*› enjuagar*, aclarar (Esp); ‹*dishes*› enjuagar*

rinse² *n* **(a)** (wash) enjuague *m* **(b)** (to remove soap — from clothes) enjuague *m*, aclarado *m* (Esp); (— from dishes) enjuague *m* **(c)** (tint) tintura *f* (*no permanente*)

riot¹ /'raɪət/ *n* **(a)** (disorder) disturbio *m*; (mutiny) motín *m*; ***to run ~*** «*fans*» descontrolarse, desmadrarse (fam); **she let her imagination run ~** dio rienda suelta a su imaginación; (*before n*) ‹*gear/shield*› antidisturbios *adj inv*; **the ~ squad** la brigada antidisturbios **(b)** (profusion): **a ~ of color** un derroche *or* una profusión de color

riot² *vi* causar disturbios *or* desórdenes; «*prisoners*» amotinarse

rioter /'raɪətər ‖ 'raɪətə(r)/ *n* alborotador, -dora *m,f*

rioting /'raɪətɪŋ/ *n* [U] disturbios *mpl*

riotous /'raɪətəs/ *adj* **(a)** ‹*crowd/behavior*› descontrolado, desenfrenado **(b)** ‹*occasion*› desenfrenado

rip¹ /rɪp/ **-pp-** *vt* ‹*cloth*› rasgar*, romper*; ‹*skirt/trousers*› hacerse* un rasgón en; **she ~ped the letter open** abrió la carta de un rasgón ■ **~** *vi* rasgarse*

• **rip off** [*v* + *o* + *adv*, *v* + *adv* + *o*] **1** (remove) arrancar* **2** (sl) **(a)** (cheat) timar, estafar, tracalear (Méx, Ven fam) **(b)** (steal) afanar (arg), robar

• **rip up** [*v* + *o* + *adv*, *v* + *adv* + *o*] romper*, hacer* pedazos

rip² *n* rasgón *m*, desgarrón *m*

RIP (= **rest in peace**) R.I.P.

rip cord *n* cordón *m* de apertura

ripe /raɪp/ *adj* ‹*fruit*› maduro; ‹*cheese*› a punto

ripen /'raɪpən/ *vi* madurar ■ **~** *vt* hacer* madurar

rip-off /'rɪpɔːf ‖ 'rɪpɒf/ *n* (colloq) (con) timo *m*, estafa *f*; (theft) robo *m*; (copy) plagio *m*

ripple¹ /'rɪpəl/ *n* [C] (on water) onda *f*; **a ~ of applause** un breve aplauso

ripple² *vi* **(a)** «*water*» rizarse*; «*wheat/grass*» mecerse* **(b) rippling** *pres p* ‹*muscles*› tensado

rise¹ /raɪz/ *n* **1 (a)** (upward movement — of tide, level) subida *f*; (— in pitch) elevación *f* **(b)** (increase — in prices, interest rates) subida *f*, aumento *m*, alza *f*‡ (frml); (— in pressure, temperature) aumento *m*, subida *f*; (— in number, amount) aumento *m* **(c)** (in pay) (BrE) aumento *m*, incremento *m* (frml); **a pay ~** un aumento *or* (frml) un incremento salarial **2** (advance) (to fame, power) ascenso *m*, ascensión *f*; (of movement, ideology) surgimiento *m*; ***to give ~ to sth*** ‹*to belief*› dar* origen *or* lugar a algo; ‹*to dispute*› ocasionar *or* causar algo; ‹*to ideas*› suscitar algo **3** (slope) subida *f*, cuesta *f*

rise² (*past* **rose**; *past p* **risen** /'rɪzn̩/) *vi* **1 (a)** (come, go up) subir; «*sun/moon*» salir*; «*river*» crecer*; «*cake*» subir; **to ~ to the surface** salir* *or* subir a la superficie **(b)** (increase) «*price/temperature/pressure*» subir, aumentar; «*wind*» arreciar; «*wage/amount*» aumentar; «*tension*» crecer*, aumentar **(c)** «*sound*» (become louder) aumentar de volumen; (become higher) subir de tono **(d)** (improve) «*standard*» mejorar; **their spirits rose** se les levantó el ánimo, se animaron **2 (a)** (slope upward) «*ground/land*» elevarse **(b)** (extend upwards) «*building/hill*» levantarse, alzarse* **3 (a)** (stand up) «*person/audience*» (frml) ponerse* de pie, levantarse, pararse (AmL) **(b)** (out of bed) levantarse **4** (in rank): **she has ~n in my estimation** ha ganado en mi estima **5** (revolt) **to ~ (up)** levantarse, alzarse* **6** (originate) «*river*» (frml) nacer*

• **rise above** [*v + prep + o*] ‹*disability*› sobreponerse* a; ‹*difficulty*› superar

• **rise to** [*v + prep + o*] (respond to): **to ~ to the challenge** aceptar el reto; **to ~ to the occasion** estar* a la altura de las circunstancias

rising¹ /'raɪzɪŋ/ *n* (rebellion) levantamiento *m*

rising² *adj* (*before n*) **(a)** ‹*tide/level*› creciente; **the ~ sun** el sol naciente **(b)** (increasing) ‹*number*› creciente; ‹*temperature*› creciente, en aumento; ‹*prices/interest rates*› en alza *or* en aumento **(c)** (sloping) en pendiente

rising damp *n* [U] humedad *f* (*que sube de los cimientos por las paredes*)

risk¹ /rɪsk/ *n* [C U] riesgo *m*; **those most at ~ from the disease** los que corren mayor riesgo *or* peligro de contraer la enfermedad; **at the ~ of** -ING a riesgo de + INF; **to take a ~** correr un riesgo; **to take ~s** arriesgarse, correr riesgos

risk² *vt* **(a)** (put in danger) arriesgar*, poner* en peligro **(b)** (expose oneself to) arriesgarse* a; **to ~** -ING arriesgarse* A *or* correr el riesgo DE + INF

risky /'rɪski/ *adj* **-kier, -kiest** arriesgado, riesgoso (AmL)

risqué /rɪ'skeɪ, 'rɪskeɪ/ *adj* atrevido, subido de tono

rite /raɪt/ *n* rito *m*

ritual¹ /'rɪtʃuəl/ *n* [U C] ritual *m*

ritual² *adj* ritual

rival¹ /'raɪvəl/ *n* rival *mf*

rival² *adj* (*before n*) ‹*company*› rival, competidor

rival³ *vt*, (BrE) **-ll-**: **his voice ~s that of the lead singer** su voz no tiene nada que envidiarle a la del cantante principal

rivalry /'raɪvəlri/ *n* [U C] (*pl* **-ries**) rivalidad *f*, competencia *f*

river /'rɪvər || 'rɪvə(r)/ *n* río *m*; (*before n*) ‹*traffic/port*› fluvial; ‹*mouth/basin*› del río

river: **~bank** *n* ribera *f*, margen *f* (*de un río*); **~bed** *n* lecho *m* (*de un río*); **R~ Plate** *n* Río *m* de la Plata; **~side** *n* ribera *f*, margen *f* (*de un río*); (*before n*) ‹*café*› a orillas del río

rivet¹ /'rɪvət || 'rɪvɪt/ *n* remache *m*, roblón *m*

rivet² *vt* **(a)** (attach) remachar **(b)** (fix) (*usu pass*): **my eyes were ~ed to the screen** estaba absorto, con los ojos clavados en la pantalla; **their eyes were ~ed on her** no le quitaban los ojos de encima **(c)** (fascinate) (*usu pass*) fascinar

riveting /'rɪvətɪŋ/ *adj* fascinante

Riviera /rɪvi'erə || ˌrɪvi'eərə/ *n*: **the (French) ~** la Costa Azul; **the Italian ~** la Riviera

RN *n* (in UK) = **Royal Navy**

RNA *n* [U] (= **ribonucleic acid**) RNA *m*, ARN *m*

road /rəʊd/ *n* **1** (for vehicles — in town) calle *f*; (— out of town) carretera *f*; (— minor) camino *m*; **by ~** por carretera, por tierra; (*before n*) ‹*accident*› de tráfico *or* (AmL tb) de tránsito; **~ safety** seguridad *f* en la carretera; **~ sign** señal *f* vial *or* de tráfico *or* (AmL tb) de tránsito; **~ tax** impuesto *m* de rodaje **2** (route, way) camino *m*; **the economy is on the ~ to recovery** la economía está en vías de recuperación **3 to be on the road** «*car*» estar* en circulación; **we've been on the ~ for four days** llevamos cuatro días viajando

road: **~block** *n* control *m* (de carretera); **~ hog** *n* (colloq) loco, -ca *m,f* del volante; **~map** *n* mapa *m* de carreteras; **~side** *n* borde *m* de la carretera/del camino; **~ sweeper** *n* (person) barrendero, -ra *m,f*; (machine) barredera *f*, barredora *f*; **~works** *pl n* (BrE) obras *fpl* (de vialidad); **~worthy** *adj* **-thier, -thiest** apto para circular

roam /rəʊm/ *vt* vagar* *or* deambular por ■ **~** *vi* vagar*, errar* (liter)

roar¹ /rɔːr || rɔː(r)/ *vi* «*lion/engine*» rugir*; «*sea/wind/fire*» bramar, rugir*; **to ~ with laughter** reírse* a carcajadas

roar² *n* [C U] (of lion, tiger) rugido *m*; (of person) rugido *m*, bramido *m*; (of thunder) estruendo *m*; (of traffic, engine, guns) estruendo *m*; (of crowd) clamor *m*

roaring /'rɔːrɪŋ/ *adj* (*before n*) ‹*waves*› rugiente; ‹*traffic*› estruendoso

roast¹ /rəʊst/ *adj* asado; **~ beef** rosbif *m*, rosbeef *m*

roast² *n* asado *m* (*al horno*)

roast³ *vt* ‹*meat/potatoes*› asar; ‹*coffee beans*› tostar*, torrefaccionar; ‹*peanuts*› tostar* ■ **~** *vi* asarse

roasting /'rəʊstɪŋ/ *adj* (colloq): **it's absolutely ~** hace un calor que te asas (fam)

rob /rɑːb || rɒb/ *vt* **-bb- (a)** (steal from) ‹*person*› robarle a; ‹*bank*› asaltar, atracar*, robar **(b)** (deprive) **to ~ sb/sth** OF **sth** privar a algn/algo DE algo

robber /'rɑːbər || 'rɒbə(r)/ *n* ladrón, -drona *m,f*; **bank ~** atracador, -dora *m,f or* asaltante *mf* de bancos

robbery /'rɑːbəri || 'rɒbəri/ *n* [U C] (*pl* **-ries**) robo *m*, asalto *m*; **bank ~** asalto *m or* atraco *m* a un banco

robe /rəʊb/ *n* **(a)** (worn by magistrates) (*often pl*) toga *f* **(b)** (worn in house) bata *f*, salto *m* de cama (CS)

robin /'rɑːbən || 'rɒbɪn/ *n* (European) petirrojo *m*; (N. American) ceón *m*, tordo *m* norteamericano

robot /'rəʊbɑːt || 'rəʊbɒt/ *n* robot *m*

robust /rəʊ'bʌst/ *adj* ‹*person/animal*› robusto; ‹*health*› de hierro; ‹*material*› resistente, sólido

rock¹ /rɑːk || rɒk/ *n* **1** [U] (substance) roca *f* **2** [C] **(a)** (crag, cliff) peñasco *m*, peñón *m* **(b)** (in sea) roca *f*, escollo *m*; ***on the ~s*** ‹*whisky*› con hielo; **their marriage is on the ~s** su matrimonio anda muy mal **(c)** (boulder) roca *f* **(d)** (stone) (esp AmE) piedra *f* **3** [U] (music) rock *m*

rock² *vt* **(a)** (gently) ‹*cradle*› mecer*; ‹*child*› acunar **(b)** (violently) sacudir, estremecer*; «*scandal*» convulsionar, conmocionar ■ **~** *vi* (gently) mecerse*, balancearse

rock: **~ and roll** *n* [U] ⇒ ROCK'N'ROLL; **~bottom** /'rɑːk'bɑːtəm || ˌrɒk'bɒtəm/ *n*: **to hit/reach ~bottom** tocar* fondo; **~ climbing** /'rɑːk'klaɪmɪŋ || 'rɒkˌklaɪmɪŋ/ *n* [U] escalada *f* en roca

rocket¹ /'rɑːkət ‖ 'rɒkɪt/ *n* **(a)** (spacecraft) cohete *m* espacial **(b)** (missile) cohete *m*, misil *m*; (*before n*) ~ **launcher** lanzacohetes *m*, lanzamisiles *m*

rocket² *vi* «*price*» dispararse, ponerse* por las nubes

rock: ~**face** *n* pared *f* rocosa; ~**-hard** /'rɑːk 'hɑːrd ‖ ˌrɒk'hɑːd/ *adj* (duro) como una piedra

rocking /'rɑːkɪŋ ‖ 'rɒkɪŋ/: ~ **chair** *n* mecedora *f*; ~ **horse** *n* caballito *m* mecedor *or* de balancín

rock'n'roll /'rɑːkən'rəʊl ‖ ˌrɒkən'rəʊl/ *n* [U] rocanrol *m*, rock and roll *m*

rocky /'rɑːki ‖ 'rɒki/ *adj* **rockier, rockiest 1** ‹*ground*› rocoso; ‹*path*› pedregoso **2** (unsteady) ‹*period*› de incertidumbre; ‹*base*› nada sólido, tambaleante

Rocky Mountains *pl n* **the** ~ ~ las Montañas Rocallosas *or* Rocosas

rod /rɑːd ‖ rɒd/ *n* **(a)** (bar) varilla *f*, barra *f* **(b)** (*fishing* ~) caña *f* (de pescar) **(c)** (for punishment) vara *f*

rode /rəʊd/ *past of* RIDE¹

rodent /'rəʊdn̩t/ *n* roedor *m*

rodeo /'rəʊdiəʊ, rə'deɪəʊ/ *n* (*pl* **-os**) rodeo *m*

roe /rəʊ/ *n* **1** [U C] (of fish) hueva *f* **2** [C] ~ **deer** corzo, -za *m,f*

rogue /rəʊg/ *n* pícaro, -ra *m,f*, pillo, -lla *m,f*

roguish /'rəʊgɪʃ/ *adj* pícaro

role, **rôle** /rəʊl/ *n* **(a)** (Cin, Theat) papel *m* **(b)** (function) papel *m*, rol *m*; (*before n*) ~ **model** modelo *m* de conducta

role-play /'rəʊlpleɪ/ *n* [C U] teatro *m* improvisado; (Psych) psicodrama *m*

roll¹ /rəʊl/ *n* **1** (Culin) (**bread**) ~ pancito *m or* (Esp) panecillo *m or* (Méx) bolillo *m* **2** (of paper, wire, fabric) rollo *m*; (of banknotes) fajo *m*; **a ~ of film** un rollo *or* un carrete (de fotos) **3** (sound — of drum) redoble *m*; (— of thunder) retumbo *m* **4** (list) lista *f*; **to call the ~** pasar lista

roll² *vi* **1 (a)** (rotate) «*ball/barrel*» rodar* **(b)** (turn over): **the car ~ed over three times** el coche dio tres vueltas de campana; **~ (over) onto your back** ponte boca arriba, date la vuelta *or* (CS) date vuelta; ***to be ~ing in money*** *o* ***in it*** (colloq) estar* forrado (de oro) (fam) **(c)** (sway) «*ship*» bambolearse **2** (move) (+ *adv compl*): **the car began to ~ down the hill** el coche empezó a deslizarse cuesta abajo; **tears ~ed down his cheeks** las lágrimas le corrían por las mejillas **3** (begin operating) «*camera*» empezar* a rodar **4** (make noise) «*drum*» redoblar; «*thunder*» retumbar **5 rolling** *pres p* ‹*countryside/hills*› ondulado ■ ~ *vt* **1 (a)** ‹*ball/barrel*› hacer* rodar; ‹*dice*› tirar **(b) to ~ one's eyes** poner* los ojos en blanco **2** ‹*cigarette*› liar*; **it ~ed itself into a ball** se hizo un ovillo; **to ~ up one's sleeves** arremangarse **3** ‹*dough/pastry*› estirar **4** (Ling): **to ~ one's 'r's** hacer* vibrar las erres

• **roll in** [*v* + *adv*] (arrive in large quantities) llover*

• **roll on** [*v* + *adv*] **(a)** (pass) «*time/months*» pasar **(b)** (arrive) (colloq): **~ on vacation time!** ¡que lleguen pronto las vacaciones!

• **roll out** [*v* + *o* + *adv*, *v* + *adv* + *o*] ‹*dough/pastry*› estirar

• **roll up** [*v* + *adv*] (arrive) (colloq) aparecer*

roll call *n* **(a)** (calling of roll): **~ ~ is 9 a.m.** pasan lista a las nueve de la mañana **(b)** (list) lista *f*

rolled gold /rəʊld/ *n* metal *m* (en)chapado en oro

roller /'rəʊlər ‖ 'rəʊlə(r)/ *n* **1** (for lawn, in machine, for applying paint) rodillo *m* **2** (for hair) rulo *m* **3** (caster) ruedecita *f*, ruedita *f* (esp AmL) **4** (wave) ola *f* grande

roller: ~ **blind** *n* persiana *f or* cortina *f* de enrollar; ~ **coaster** *n* montaña *f* rusa; ~ **skate** *n* patín *m* (de ruedas); ~**-skate** /'rəʊlərskeɪt ‖ 'rəʊləskeɪt/ *vi* patinar (*sobre ruedas*)

rolling pin /'rəʊlɪŋ/ *n* rodillo *m*, rollo *m* pastelero (Esp)

roll-on /'rəʊlɑːn ‖ 'rəʊlɒn/ *adj* (*before n*) ‹*deodorant*› de bola

ROM /rɑːm ‖ rɒm/ *n* [U] (= **read-only memory**) ROM *f*

Roman¹ /'rəʊmən/ *adj* **(a)** (of, from Rome) romano **(b) roman** ‹*numeral*› romano; ‹*alphabet*› latino

Roman² *n* romano, -na *m,f*

Roman Catholic¹ *n* católico, -ca *m,f*

Roman Catholic² *adj* católico

romance /rə'mæns, 'rəʊmæns ‖ rəʊ'mæns/ *n* **1 (a)** [C] (affair) romance *m*, idilio *m* **(b)** [U] (feeling) romanticismo *m* **2** [C U] (Lit) (love story) novela *f* romántica

Romance /rə'mæns, 'rəʊmæns ‖ rəʊ'mæns/ *adj* ‹*languages*› romance, románico

Romania /rəʊ'meɪniə/ *n* Rumania *f*, Rumanía *f*

Romanian¹ /rəʊ'meɪniən/ *adj* rumano

Romanian² *n* **(a)** [U] (language) rumano *m* **(b)** [C] (person) rumano, -na *m,f*

romantic¹ /rəʊ'mæntɪk, rə-/ *adj* romántico

romantic² *n* romántico, -ca *m,f*

romanticize /rəʊ'mæntəsaɪz, rə- ‖ rəʊ'mæntɪsaɪz/ *vt* idealizar*

Romany /'rɑːməni, 'rəʊ- ‖ 'rɒməni, 'rəʊ-/ *n* (*pl* **-nies**) **(a)** [C] (person) gitano, -na *m,f* **(b)** [U] (language) romaní *m*

Rome /rəʊm/ *n* Roma *f*

romp¹ /rɑːmp ‖ rɒmp/ *n* **(a)** (frolic) retozo *m* **(b)** (sexual) revolcón *m* (fam)

romp² *vi* (frolic) retozar*

rompers /'rɑːmpərz ‖ 'rɒmpəz/ *pl n*, (BrE also) **romper suit** /'rɑːmpər ‖ 'rɒmpə(r)/ *n* mameluco *m* (AmL), pelele *m* (Esp)

roof¹ /ruːf/ *n* (*pl* **~s** /ruːfs, ruːvz/) **(a)** (of building) tejado *m*, techo *m* (AmL); (*before n*) ~ **garden** terraza *f or* azotea *f* ajardinada **(b)** (of car) techo *m*; (*before n*) ~ **rack** baca *f*, portaequipajes *m*, parrilla *f* (AmL) **(c) the ~ of the mouth** el paladar

roof² *vt* techar

roofing /'ruːfɪŋ/ *n* [U] materiales *mpl* para techar

rooftop /ruːftɑːp ‖ 'ruːftɒp/ *n* tejado *m*, techo *m* (AmL)

rook /rʊk/ *n* **(a)** (Zool) grajo *m* **(b)** (in chess) torre *f*

rookie /'rʊki/ *n* (colloq) **(a)** (novice) novato, -ta *m,f* **(b)** (military recruit) recluta *m*

room /ruːm, rʊm/ *n* **1** [C] (in house, building) habitación *f*, pieza *f* (esp AmL); (bedroom) habitación *f*, dormitorio *m*, cuarto *m*, pieza *f* (esp AmL), recámara *f* (Méx); (for meeting) sala *f*; (*before n*) ~ **temperature** temperatura *f* ambiente **2** [U] (space) espacio *m*, lugar *m*; **there's ~ for improvement** se puede mejorar

room: ~ **clerk** *n* (AmE) recepcionista *mf*; ~**mate** *n* (sharing apartment) compañero, -ra *m,f* de apartamento *or* (Esp) de piso; ~ **service** *n* [U] servicio *m* a las habitaciones

roomy /'ru:mi, 'rʊmi/ *adj* **-mier, -miest** amplio

roost /ru:st/ *vi* posarse (*para pasar la noche*)

rooster /'ru:stər ‖ 'ru:stə(r)/ *n* (esp AmE) gallo *m*

root[1] /ru:t/ *n* **(a)** raíz *f*; **to take ~** «*plant*» echar raíces, arraigar*; «*idea*» arraigarse* **(b) roots** *pl* (background) raíces *fpl*

root[2] *vi* **1** «*pig*» hozar* **2** (Bot) echar raíces, arraigar*

• **root for** [*v + prep + o*] (encourage) animar, alentar; (support) apoyar

• **root out** [*v + o + adv, v + adv + o*] (remove) arrancar* de raíz, erradicar*

root beer *n* [U C] *refresco hecho con distintas raíces*

rooted /'ru:təd ‖ 'ru:tɪd/ *adj*: **a deeply ~ prejudice** un prejuicio profundamente arraigado; **he stood ~ to the spot** se quedó como clavado donde estaba

rope[1] /rəʊp/ *n* [C U] cuerda *f*, soga *f*; (Naut) cabo *m*; ***to show sb the ~s***: **Mike will show you the ~s** Mike te enseñará cómo funciona todo

rope[2] *vt* **(a)** (tie) atar, amarrar (AmL exc RPl) (*con una cuerda*) **(b)** (lasso) (AmE) ‹*steer/cattle*› enlazar* *or* (Méx) lazar* *or* (CS) lacear

• **rope in** [*v + o + adv, v + adv + o*] (colloq) (*usu pass*) agarrar (fam)

rope ladder *n* escala *f or* escalera *f* de cuerda *or* de soga

ropey, ropy /'rəʊpi/ *adj* **ropier, ropiest** (BrE colloq) ‹*wine*› malo, chungo (Esp arg); **I feel a bit ~** me siento bastante mal, estoy bastante pachucho (Esp fam)

rosary /'rəʊzəri/ *n* (*pl* **-ries**) rosario *m*

rose[1] /rəʊz/ *past of* RISE[2]

rose[2] *n* **1** (Bot) (flower) rosa *f*; (plant) rosal *m*; (*before n*) ~ **bush** rosal *m* **2** (on watering can) roseta *f*

rosé /rəʊ'zeɪ ‖ 'rəʊzeɪ/ *n* [U C] (vino *m*) rosado *m*

rose: ~**bud** *n* capullo *m or* pimpollo *m* de rosa; ~**hip** *n* escaramujo *m*

rosemary /'rəʊz,meri ‖ 'rəʊzməri/ *n* [U] romero *m*

rosette /rəʊ'zet/ *n* escarapela *f*

roster /'rɑ:stər ‖ 'rɒstə(r)/ *n* **(a)** (*duty* ~) lista *f* de turnos **(b)** (list) lista *f*

rostrum /'rɑ:strəm ‖ 'rɒstrəm/ *n* (*pl* **-trums** *or* **-tra** /-trə/) (for public speaking) tribuna *f*, estrado *m*; (for orchestra conductor) podio *m*

rosy /'rəʊzi/ *adj* **rosier, rosiest** ‹*cheeks*› sonrosado; ‹*outlook*› halagüeño, optimista

rot[1] /rɑ:t ‖ rɒt/ *n* [U] (Biol) podredumbre *f*, putrefacción *f*; **the ~ set in** las cosas empezaron a decaer *or* a venirse abajo

rot[2] **-tt-** *vi* pudrirse*; **to ~ away** pudrirse* ■ ~ *vt* ‹*wood/tree*› pudrir*, ‹*teeth*› picar*

rota /'rəʊtə/ *n* (BrE) lista *f* (de turnos)

rotary /'rəʊtəri/ *adj* rotatorio, rotativo

rotate /'rəʊteɪt ‖ rəʊ'teɪt/ *vi* girar, rotar ■ ~ *vt* **(a)** (turn, spin) (hacer*) girar, dar* vueltas a **(b)** (alternate) ‹*crops*› alternar, rotar

rotation /rəʊ'teɪʃən/ *n* [U C] rotación *f*

rote /rəʊt/ *n*: **by ~** de memoria

rotten /'rɑ:tn̩ ‖ 'rɒtn̩/ *adj* **(a)** (decayed) podrido; ‹*tooth*› picado **(b)** (bad) (colloq) ‹*weather*› horrible; ‹*food*› pésimo; **to feel ~** (ill) sentirse* mal *or* pésimo *or* (Esp fam) fatal

rotund /rəʊ'tʌnd/ *adj* (hum & euph) voluminoso

rouble /'ru:bəl/ *n* (BrE) rublo *m*

rouge /ru:ʒ/ *n* [U] colorete *m*

rough[1] /rʌf/ *adj* **-er, -est** **1 (a)** (not smooth) ‹*surface/texture/skin*› áspero, rugoso; ‹*cloth*› basto; ‹*hands*› áspero, basto **(b)** (uneven) ‹*ground/road*› desigual; ‹*terrain*› agreste, escabroso **(c)** ‹*sea*› agitado, picado **2** (colloq) **(a)** (unpleasant, hard) ‹*life*› duro **(b)** (ill): **I feel a bit ~** no estoy muy bien, me siento bastante mal **3** (not gentle) brusco; ‹*neighborhood*› peligroso **4 (a)** (crude, unpolished) tosco, rudo; **a ~ draft** un borrador **(b)** (approximate) aproximado

rough[2] *adv* ‹*sleep*› a la intemperie

rough[3] *vt*: ***to ~ it*** (colloq) pasar sin comodidades

roughage /'rʌfɪdʒ/ *n* [U] fibra *f* (*de los alimentos*)

rough-and-ready /'rʌfən'redi/ *adj* improvisado

roughen /'rʌfən/ *vt* poner* áspero

roughly /'rʌfli/ *adv* **(a)** (approximately) aproximadamente **(b)** (not gently) ‹*play*› bruscamente, de manera violenta **(c)** (crudely) toscamente

roughshod /'rʌf'ʃɑ:d ‖ 'rʌfʃɒd/ *adv*: ***to ride ~ over sth***: **he rides ~ over other people's feelings** no tiene la menor consideración para con los sentimientos de los demás; **to ride ~ over sb** llevarse por delante a algn

roulette /ru:'let/ *n* [U] ruleta *f*

Roumania /ru:'memiə/ *etc* ⇒ ROMANIA *etc*

round[1] /raʊnd/ *adj* redondo

round[2] *n* **1** [C] (circle) círculo *m*, redondel *m* **2** [C] **(a)** (series) serie *f*; **~ of talks** ronda *f* de conversaciones **(b)** (burst): **let's have a ~ of applause for** ... un aplauso para ... **3** [C] (Sport, Games) (of tournament, quiz) vuelta *f*; (in boxing, wrestling) round *m*, asalto *m*; (in golf) vuelta *f*, recorrido *m*; (in showjumping) recorrido *m*; (in card games) partida *f* **4 (a)** (of visits) (*often pl*): **the doctor is off making his ~s** *o* (BrE) **is on his ~s** el doctor está haciendo visitas a domicilio *or* visitando pacientes **(b)** [C] (of watchman) ronda *f*; (of postman, milkman) (BrE) recorrido *m* **5** [C] (of drinks) ronda *f*, vuelta *f* **6** [C] (shot) disparo *m*; (bullet) bala *f* **7** [C] (of bread) (BrE): **a ~ of toast** una tostada *or* (Méx) un pan tostado; **a ~ of sandwiches** un sándwich **8** [C] (Mus) canon *m*

round[3] *vt* ‹*corner*› doblar

• **round off** **1** [*v + o + adv, v + adv + o*] **(a)** ‹*sharp edge*› redondear **(b)** (end suitably) ‹*day/meal*› terminar, rematar **(c)** ‹*number*› redondear **2** [*v + adv*] concluir*, terminar

• **round on** [*v + prep + o*] volverse* contra

• round up [*v + o + adv, v + adv + o*] ‹*sheep/cattle*› rodear; ‹*criminals*› hacer* una redada de

round[4] *adv* (esp BrE) **1 (a)** (in a circle): **we walked all the way ~** dimos toda la vuelta; **all year ~** durante todo el año **(b)** (so as to face in different direction): **she spun ~** dio media vuelta; *see also* TURN ROUND **(c)** (on all sides) alrededor **2 (a)** (from one place, person to another): **the curator took us ~** el conservador nos mostró *or* nos enseñó el museo (*or* la colección *etc*); **a list was handed ~** se hizo circular una lista **(b) all round** (in every respect) en todos los sentidos; (for everybody) a todos

round[5] *prep* (esp BrE) **1** (encircling) alrededor de; **the wall ~ the garden** el muro que rodea el jardín; **~ the corner** a la vuelta (de la esquina) **2 (a)** (in the vicinity of) cerca de, en los alrededores de; **she lives ~ here** vive por aquí **(b)** (within, through): **he does odd jobs ~ the house** hace arreglitos en la casa; **we had a look ~ the cathedral** (le) echamos un vistazo a la catedral

round- /'raʊnd/ *pref*: **~faced** de cara redonda; **~shouldered** cargado de espaldas, encorvado

roundabout[1] /'raʊndəbaʊt/ *n* (BrE) **(a)** ⇒ MERRY-GO-ROUND **(b)** (Transp) rotonda *f*, glorieta *f*

roundabout[2] *adj* ‹*route*› indirecto; **he said it in a very ~ way** lo dijo con muchos rodeos *or* circunloquios

rounded /'raʊndəd ‖ 'raʊndɪd/ *adj* redondeado

rounders /'raʊndərz ‖ 'raʊndəz/ *n* (in UK) (+ *sing vb*) *juego parecido al béisbol*

round: **~ table** *n* mesa *f* redonda; **~ the clock** *adv* las 24 horas, día y noche; **~ trip** *n* **(a)** (there and back) (viaje *m* de) ida *f* y vuelta, viaje *m* redondo (Méx) **(b)** (return fare) (AmE) tarifa *f* de ida y vuelta *or* (Méx) de viaje redondo; **~-up** *n* **(a)** (of livestock) rodeo *m* **(b)** (summary) resumen *m*

rouse /raʊz/ *vt* despertar*

rousing /'raʊzɪŋ/ *adj* ‹*speech*› enardecedor

rout[1] /raʊt/ *n* derrota *f* aplastante

rout[2] *vt* (defeat) derrotar *or* vencer* de forma aplastante; (put to flight) poner* en fuga

route /ruːt, raʊt ‖ ruːt/ *n* **(a)** (way) camino *m*, ruta *f*; (of bus) ruta *f*, recorrido *m*; **air/sea ~** ruta aérea/marítima **(b)** (highway) (AmE) carretera *f*

routine[1] /ruː'tiːn/ *n* **1** [C U] (regular pattern) rutina *f* **2** [C] (of skater, comedian) número *m*

routine[2] *adj* **(a)** (usual) ‹*procedure/inquiries*› de rutina **(b)** (ordinary, dull) rutinario

roving /'rəʊvɪŋ/ *adj* (*before n*) errante

row[1] *n* **I** /rəʊ/ **1 (a)**(straight line) hilera *f*; (of people, seats) fila *f* **(b)** (in knitting) vuelta *f* **2** (succession) serie *f*; **four times in a ~** cuatro veces seguidas
II /raʊ/ **(a)**(noisy argument) pelea *f*, riña *f*; **to have a ~ with sb** pelearse *or* reñir* con algn **(b)** (about a public matter) disputa *f* **(c)** (noise) (*no pl*) bulla *f* (fam)

row[2] *vt* /rəʊ/: **he ~ed the boat towards the shore** remó hacia la orilla ■ **~** *vi* **I** /rəʊ/ remar; **to go ~ing** salir* *or* ir* a remar
II /raʊ/ pelearse, reñir*

rowboat /'rəʊbəʊt/, (BrE) **rowing boat** /'rəʊɪŋ/ *n* bote *m* a remo *or* de remos

rowdy /'raʊdi/ *adj* **-dier, -diest** ‹*person*› escandaloso, alborotador; (quarrelsome) pendenciero

row house /'rəʊ/ *n* (AmE) *casa adosada en una hilera de casas idénticas*

rowing /'rəʊɪŋ/ *n* [U] /'rəʊɪŋ/ (Sport) remo *m*

rowing boat *n* (BrE) ⇒ ROWBOAT

royal /'rɔɪəl/ *adj* **(a)** (monarchic) real **(b)** (magnificent) espléndido, regio

royal: **~-blue** /'rɔɪəl'bluː/ **▶515** *adj* (*pred* **~ blue**) azul real *adj inv*; **R~ Highness ▶603** *n*: **Her/Your R~ Highness** Su/Vuestra Alteza Real

royalist /'rɔɪəlɪst/ *adj* monárquico

royalty /'rɔɪəlti/ *n* (*pl* **-ties**) **1** [U] (status) realeza *f* **2 royalties** *mpl* derechos *mpl* de autor, regalías *fpl*

rpm (= **revolutions per minute**) r.p.m.

RSPCA *n* (in UK) (= **Royal Society for the Prevention of Cruelty to Animals**) ≈ Asociación *f* protectora de animales

RSVP (please reply) s.r.c., se ruega contestación

rub /rʌb/ **-bb-** *vt* **(a)** (with hand, finger) frotar; (firmly) restregar*; (massage) masajear, friccionar; **to ~ one's eyes** restregarse* *or* refregarse* *or* (Méx) tallarse los ojos **(b)** (with a cloth) frotar
• rub down [*v + o + adv, v + adv + o*] **(a)** ‹*horse*› almohazar* **(b)** (using sandpaper) lijar
• rub in [*v + o + adv, v + adv + o*] ‹*cream/lotion*› aplicar* frotando
• rub off [*v + o + adv, v + adv + o*] ‹*dirt/marks*› quitar frotando *or* restregando *or* refregando; (from blackboard) (BrE) borrar
• rub out [*v + o + adv, v + adv + o*] borrar
• rub up [*v + o + adv, v + adv + o*]: ***to ~ sb up the wrong way*** caerle* mal a algn

rubber /'rʌbər ‖ 'rʌbə(r)/ *n* **(a)** [U] (substance) goma *f*, caucho *m*, hule *m* (Méx); (*before n*) **~ ring** flotador *m* **(b)** [C] (eraser) (BrE) goma *f* (de borrar)

rubber: **~ band** *n* goma *f* (elástica), gomita *f* (RPl); **~ bullet** *n* bala *f* de goma *or* caucho; **~ plant** *n* ficus *m*, gomero *m* (CS); **~ stamp** *n* (device) sello *m*; (approval) visto *m* bueno; **~ tree** *n* árbol *m* del caucho, hule *m* (Méx)

rubbery /'rʌbəri/ *adj* ‹*texture*› gomoso; ‹*material*› parecido a la goma *or* al caucho *or* (Méx) al hule

rubbish /'rʌbɪʃ/ *n* [U] **(a)** (refuse) basura *f*; (*before n*) **~ bag** bolsa *f* de la basura; **~ bin** (BrE) cubo *m* *or* (CS) tacho *m* *or* (Méx) bote *m* *or* (Col) caneca *f* *or* (Ven) tobo *m* de la basura **(b)** (junk) (colloq) porquerías *fpl* (fam) **(c)** (nonsense) (colloq) tonterías *fpl*

rubble /rʌbəl/ *n* [U] escombros *mpl*

ruble, (BrE) **rouble** /'ruːbəl/ *n* rublo *m*

ruby /'ruːbi/ *n* (*pl* **rubies**) rubí *m*

rucksack /'rʌksæk, 'rʊk-/ *n* mochila *f*, morral *m*

ructions /'rʌkʃənz/ *pl n* (colloq) jaleo *m* (fam)

rudder /'rʌdər ‖ 'rʌdə(r)/ *n* timón *m*

ruddy /'rʌdi/ *adj* **-dier, -diest** ‹*cheeks*› rubicundo

rude /ruːd/ *adj* **(a)** (bad-mannered) ‹*person*› maleducado, grosero; ‹*remark*› grosero, descortés; **to be ~ TO sb** ser* grosero CON algn **(b)** (vulgar) (esp BrE) grosero

rudely /'ruːdli/ *adv* groseramente

rudeness /'ru:dnəs ‖ 'ru:dnɪs/ *n* [U] grosería *f*, mala educación *f*
rudimentary /'ru:də'mentri ‖ ,ru:dɪ'mentri/ *adj* rudimentario
rudiments /ru:dəmənts ‖ 'ru:dɪmənts/ *pl n* rudimentos *mpl*, nociones *fpl* elementales
rue /ru:/ *vt* lamentar, arrepentirse* de
rueful /'ru:fəl/ *adj* atribulado, compungido
ruff /rʌf/ *n* (collar) gorguera *f*; (on animal, bird) collar *m*
ruffian /'rʌfiən/ *n* rufián *m*, villano *m*
ruffle[1] /'rʌfəl/ *n* (frill) volante *m* *or* (RPl) volado *m* *or* (Chi) vuelo *m*
ruffle[2] *vt* **(a)** ‹*hair*› alborotar; ‹*feathers*› erizar*; ‹*clothes*› arrugar* **(b)** ‹*person*› alterar, contrariar
rug /rʌg/ *n* **(a)** (small carpet) alfombra *f*, alfombrilla *f*, tapete *m* (Col, Méx) **(b)** (blanket) manta *f* de viaje
rugby /'rʌgbi/ *n* [U] rugby *m*
rugged /'rʌgəd ‖ 'rʌgɪd/ *adj* **(a)** ‹*rocks/coast*› escarpado; ‹*terrain*› escabroso **(b)** ‹*face*› de facciones duras
ruin[1] /'ru:ən ‖ 'ru:ɪn/ *n* **(a)** (sth ruined) (*often pl*) ruina *f*; **his career was in ~s** su carrera estaba arruinada **(b)** (cause) (*no pl*) ruina *f*, perdición *f* **(c)** [U] (state) ruina *f*
ruin[2] *vt* **1** (destroy) ‹*city/building*› destruir*; ‹*career/plans*› arruinar; ‹*person*› (financially) arruinar **2** (spoil) ‹*dress/carpet/toy*› estropear; ‹*party/surprise*› echar a perder, estropear, arruinar
rule[1] /ru:l/ *n* **1** [C] (regulation, principle) regla *f*, norma *f*; **it's against the ~s** está prohibido; **~s and regulations** reglamento *m*; **to work to ~** (Lab Rel) hacer* huelga de celo **2 as a ~** por lo general, generalmente **3** [U] (government) gobierno *m*; (of monarch) reinado *m*; **to be under foreign ~** estar* bajo dominio extranjero
rule[2] *vt* **1** (govern, control) ‹*country*› gobernar*, administrar; ‹*person*› dominar **2** (pronounce) dictaminar **3** (draw) ‹*line*› trazar* con una regla ■ **~** *vi* **1** (govern) gobernar*; «*monarch*» reinar **2** (pronounce) **to ~** (ON sth) fallar *or* resolver* (EN algo)
• **rule out** [*v + o + adv, v + adv + o*] ‹*possibility*› descartar; ‹*course of action*› hacer* imposible
ruler /'ru:lər ‖ 'ru:lə(r)/ *n* **1** (leader) gobernante *mf*; (sovereign) soberano, -na *m,f* **2** (measure) regla *f*
ruling[1] /'ru:lɪŋ/ *n* fallo *m*, resolución *f*
ruling[2] *adj* (*before n*) ‹*monarch*› reinante; **the ~ classes** las clases dirigentes
rum /rʌm/ *n* [C U] ron *m*
Rumania /ru:'memiə/ *etc* ⇒ ROMANIA *etc*
rumble[1] /'rʌmbəl/ *n* (sound) ruido *m* sordo; (of thunder) estruendo *m*; (of stomach) ruido *m* de tripas (fam)
rumble[2] *vi* «*guns/drums*» hacer* un ruido sordo; «*thunder*» retumbar; **my stomach's rumbling** me suenan las tripas (fam)
ruminate /'ru:məneɪt ‖ 'ru:mɪneɪt/ *vi* **(a)** (Zool) rumiar **(b)** (ponder) **to ~ ON/ABOUT sth** cavilar SOBRE algo, rumiar algo
rummage /'rʌmɪdʒ/ *vi* hurgar*
rumor[1], (BrE) **rumour** /'ru:mər ‖ 'ru:mə(r)/ *n* rumor *m*
rumor[2], (BrE) **rumour** *vt* (*usu pass*) rumorear; **it is ~ed that** ... se rumorea que ...
rump /rʌmp/ *n* **(a)** [U] (Culin) cadera *f*; (*before n*) **~ steak** filete *m* de cadera, churrasco *m* de cuadril (RPl) **(b)** [C] (bottom) (colloq & hum) traste *m* (fam)
rumpus /'rʌmpəs/ *n* (*pl* **~es**) lío *m*, escándalo *m*
run[1] /rʌn/ (*pres p* **running**; *past* **ran**; *past p* **run**) *vi* **I 1** correr; **he ran downstairs/indoors** bajó/entró corriendo **2** (colloq) (drive) ir* (*en coche*) **3** (Transp): **the trains ~ every half hour** hay trenes cada media hora **4** (flow) «*water/oil*» correr; **she left the water ~ning** dejó la llave abierta (AmL) *or* (Esp) el grifo abierto; **my nose is ~ning** me gotea la nariz **5** (Pol) «*candidate*» presentarse, postularse (AmL)
II (operate, function): **with the engine ~ning** con el motor encendido *or* en marcha *or* (AmL tb) prendido; **it ~s off batteries** funciona con pilas *or* a pila(s)
III 1 (extend) **(a)** (in space): **the streets ~ parallel to each other** las calles corren paralelas; **the path ~s across the field** el sendero atraviesa el campo **(b)** «*show*» estar* en cartel **2 (a)** (be, stand): **feelings are ~ning high** los ánimos están caldeados; **inflation is ~ning at 4%** la tasa de inflación es del 4%; **it ~s in the family** es de familia **(b)** (become): **stocks are ~ning low** se están agotando las existencias; *see also* DRY[1] 1(c) **3** (melt, merge) «*paint/makeup*» correrse; «*color*» desteñir*, despintarse (Méx) ■ **~** *vt* **I 1** ‹*race/marathon*› correr, tomar parte en **2 (a)** (push, move) pasar **(b)** (drive) ‹*person*› (colloq) llevar (*en coche*) **3 to ~ a bath** preparar un baño **4 (a)** (extend) ‹*cable/wire*› tender* **(b)** (pass) (hacer*) pasar
II 1 (operate) ‹*engine*› hacer* funcionar; ‹*program*› (Comput) pasar, ejecutar **2** (manage) ‹*business*› dirigir*, llevar **3** ‹*course*› organizar*; ‹*article*› publicar*; ⇒ TEMPERATURE (b)
• **run about** ⇒ RUN AROUND
• **run across** [*v + prep + o*] **(a)** (meet) ‹*person*› encontrarse* *or* toparse con **(b)** (find) ‹*object*› encontrar*
• **run after** [*v + prep + o*] (pursue) correr detrás de *or* tras; (romantically) andar* detrás de, perseguir*
• **run along** [*v + adv*] irse*
• **run around** [*v + adv*] «*children*» corretear
• **run away** [*v + adv*] huir*, escaparse, fugarse*; (run off) salir* corriendo; **she ran away from home** se escapó de casa
• **run away with** [*v + adv + prep + o*] **1 (a)** ‹*race/contest*› ganar fácilmente **(b)** (take over): **she lets her imagination ~ away with her** se deja llevar por la imaginación **2** (elope with) escaparse *or* fugarse* *or* irse* con
• **run down I** [*v + o + adv, v + adv + o*] **1** (disparage) (colloq) criticar*, hablar mal de **2** ‹*pedestrian*› atropellar
II [*v + adv*] **(a)** «*battery*» (Auto) descargarse* **(b)** «*business/factory*» venirse* abajo **(c)** «*stocks*» agotarse
• **run in** [*v + o + adv*] (BrE Auto) ‹*car/engine*› hacer* el rodaje de
• **run into** [*v + prep + o*] **(a)** ‹*vehicle*› chocar* con **(b)** ‹*person/table*› toparse con
• **run off 1** [*v + o + adv, v + adv + o*] (produce)

‹*copies*› tirar; ‹*photocopies*› sacar* **2** [*v* + *adv*] (depart) salir* corriendo

• **run off with** [*v* + *adv* + *prep* + *o*] ⇒ RUN AWAY WITH 2

• **run out** [*v* + *adv*] **(a)** (exhaust supplies): **to ~ out OF sth** quedarse SIN algo **(b)** «*money*» acabarse; «*supplies/stock*» acabarse, agotarse; «*lease/policy*» vencer*, caducar*

• **run over 1** [*v* + *o* + *adv*, *v* + *adv* + *o*] ‹*pedestrian*› atropellar **2** [*v* + *prep* + *o*] (review) ‹*details/plan*› repasar; (rehearse) ‹*scene*› ensayar

• **run through** [*v* + *prep* + *o*] ⇒ RUN OVER 2

• **run up 1** [*v* + *adv* + *o*] **(a)** ‹*total/debts*› ir* acumulando **(b)** ‹*flag*› izar* **2** [*v* + *o* + *adv*, *v* + *adv* + *o*] ‹*dress*› hacer* (*rápidamente*)

• **run up against** [*v* + *adv* + *prep* + *o*] ‹*difficulty/obstacle*› toparse *or* tropezar* con

run² *n* **1** (on foot): **to go for a ~** salir* a correr; ***on the ~***: **he's on the run** está prófugo; **after seven years on the ~** después de estar siete años huyendo de la justicia; ***to make a ~ for it*** escaparse **2 (a)** (trip, outing) vuelta *f*, paseo *m* (*en coche*) **(b)** (journey): **it's only a short ~** está muy cerca **3 (a)** (sequence): **a ~ of good/bad luck** una racha de buena/mala suerte, una buena/mala racha **(b)** (period of time): **in the long ~** a la larga **4** (heavy demand) **~ ON sth**: **there's been a ~ on these watches** estos relojes han estado muy solicitados **5** (Cin, Theat) temporada *f* **6** (track) pista *f*; **ski ~** pista de esquí **7** (in stocking, knitted garment) carrera *f* **8** (in baseball, cricket) carrera *f*

runaway¹ /'rʌnəweɪ/ *n* fugitivo, -va *m,f*

runaway² *adj* (*before n*) ‹*slave/prisoner*› fugitivo

run: **~down** *n* resumen *m*; **~-down** /'rʌn'daʊn/ *adj* (*pred* **~ down**) **(a)** (tired, sickly) (*usu pred*) **to be/feel ~down** estar*/sentirse* cansado *or* débil **(b)** (dilapidated) ‹*district/hotel*› venido a menos

rung¹ /rʌŋ/ *past p of* RING²

rung² *n* **(a)** (of ladder, chair) travesaño *m* **(b)** (in career, organization) peldaño *m*

runner /'rʌnər ‖ 'rʌnə(r)/ *n* **1** (in race, baseball) corredor, -dora *m,f*; (taking messages) mensajero, -ra *m,f* **2 (a)** (on sled) patín *m* **(b)** (for drawer) riel *m*, guía *f*

runner: **~ bean** *n* (esp BrE) habichuela *f* (Col) *or* (Esp) judía *f* verde *or* (Chi) poroto *m* verde *or* (RPl) chaucha *f or* (Ven) vainita *f or* (Méx) ejote *m*; **~-up** /'rʌnər'ʌp/ *n* (*pl* **~s-up**): **to be ~-up** quedar en segundo lugar *or* puesto

running¹ /'rʌnɪŋ/ *n* [U] **(a)** (exercise): **~ is a good form of exercise** correr es muy buen ejercicio; **there are five candidates in the ~ for the post** hay cinco candidatos compitiendo *or* en liza por el puesto **(b)** (of machine) funcionamiento *m*, marcha *f* **(c)** (management) gestión *f*

running² *adj* (*before n, no comp*) **1(a) to take a ~ jump** saltar tomando carrera *or* (Esp) carrerilla **(b)** (continuous) ‹*joke*› continuo; **~ water** agua *f*‡ corriente **2** (discharging) ‹*sore*› supurante

running³ *adv*: **the third day ~** el tercer día consecutivo *or* seguido

running costs *pl n* (of car) gastos *mpl* de mantenimiento; (of company) costos *mpl or* (Esp) costes *mpl* corrientes

runny /'rʌni/ *adj* **-nier, -niest (a)** ‹*eyes*› lloroso; **I've got a ~ nose** me gotea la nariz **(b)** ‹*sauce*› líquido

run-of-the-mill /'rʌnəvðə'mɪl/ *adj* (*pred* **run of the mill**) ‹*job/car*› común *or* normal y corriente

runt /rʌnt/ *n* (Agr) *animal más pequeño de una camada*

run: **~-up** *n* (preparatory period) **~-up TO sth** período *m* previo A algo; **~way** *n* (Aviat) pista *f*; (at fashion show) (AmE) pasarela *f*

rupee /ru:pi:, ru:'pi:/ *n* rupia *f*

rupture¹ /'rʌptʃər ‖ 'rʌptʃə(r)/ *n* [U C] ruptura *f*

rupture² *vt* romper*

rural /'rʊrəl ‖ 'rʊərəl/ *adj* rural

ruse /ru:s, ru:z ‖ ru:z/ *n* artimaña *f*, treta *f*

rush¹ /rʌʃ/ *n* **1 (a)** (haste) (*no pl*) prisa *f*, apuro *m* (AmL); **I'm in a ~** tengo prisa, ando *or* estoy apurado (AmL) **(b)** [C] (movement): **a ~ of air** una ráfaga de aire; **there was a ~ for the exit** todo el mundo se precipitó hacia la salida **2** [C U] (Bot) junco *m*

rush² *vi* **(a)** (hurry) darse* prisa, apurarse (AmL); **she ~ed through the first course** se comió el primer plato a todo correr *or* a la carrera **(b)** (run) (+ *adv compl*): **he ~ed in/out** entró/salió corriendo; **to ~ around** ir* de acá para allá, correr de un lado para otro **(c)** (surge, flow): **blood ~ed to his face** (from anger) se le subió la sangre a la cabeza ■ **~** *vt* **(a)** ‹*job*› hacer* a todo correr *or* a la carrera, hacer* deprisa y corriendo; ‹*person*› meterle prisa a, apurar (AmL) **(b)** (take hastily): **she was ~ed to hospital** la llevaron rápidamente al hospital

• **rush into** [*v* + *prep* + *o*]: **she ~ed into marriage** se precipitó al casarse; **don't ~ into anything** no te precipites

rush: **~ hour** *n* hora *f* pico (AmL), hora *f* punta (Esp); **~ job** *n* (colloq) (urgent) trabajo *m* urgente; (hastily done): **it was a ~ job** se hizo a todo correr *or* deprisa y corriendo *or* a la(s) carrera(s)

rusk /rʌsk/ *n* galleta *f* (*dura, para bebés*)

Russia /'rʌʃə/ *n* Rusia *f*

Russian¹ /'rʌʃən/ *adj* ruso

Russian² *n* **(a)** [U] (language) ruso *m* **(b)** [C] (person) ruso, -sa *m,f*

Russian roulette *n* [U] ruleta *f* rusa

rust¹ /rʌst/ *n* [U] óxido *m*, herrumbre *f*, orín *m*

rust² *vi* oxidarse, herrumbrarse

rustic /'rʌstɪk/ *adj* rústico

rustle¹ /rʌsəl/ *vi* «*leaves*» susurrar; «*paper*» crujir ■ **~** *vt* **1** «*wind*» ‹*leaves*› hacer* susurrar **2** (steal) ‹*cattle/horses*› robar

rustle² *n* (of leaves) susurro *m*; (of paper) crujido *m*; (of silk) frufrú *m*

rustler /'rʌslər ‖ 'rʌslə(r)/ *n* ladrón, -drona *m,f* de ganado

rustproof /'rʌstpru:f/ *adj* ‹*surface/metal*› inoxidable; ‹*coating*› anticorrosivo, antioxidante

rusty /'rʌsti/ *adj* **-tier, -tiest** oxidado, herrumbrado; **to get** *o* (BrE also) **go ~** oxidarse, herrumbrarse; **my German is a bit ~** tengo muy olvidado el alemán

rut /rʌt/ *n* **1** [C] (groove) surco *m*, rodada *f*; ***to be in a ~*** estar* anquilosado; ***to get into a ~*** anquilosarse **2** [U] (Zool) celo *m*

rutabaga /ˈruːtəˈbeɪgə ‖ ˌruːtəˈbeɪgə/ *n* [U] (AmE) nabo *m* sueco

ruthless /ˈruːθləs ‖ ˈruːθlɪs/ *adj* ‹*person*› despiadado; ‹*persecution*› implacable, inexorable

Rwanda /rʊˈændə/ *n* Ruanda *f*

Rwandan /rʊˈændən/ *adj* ruandés

rye /raɪ/ *n* [U] **(a)** (plant, grain) centeno *m* **(b)** ~ **(bread)** pan *m* de centeno

Ss

S, s /es/ *n* S, s *f*

S (a) (Geog) (= **south**) S **(b)** (Clothing) (= **small**) P

Sabbath /ˈsæbəθ/ *n* (Jewish) sábado *m*; (Christian) domingo *m*

sabbatical /səˈbætɪkəl/ *n* (year) año *m* sabático; (period) período *m* sabático

saber, (BrE) **sabre** /ˈseɪbər ‖ ˈseɪbə(r)/ *n* sable *m*

sabotage¹ /ˈsæbətɑːʒ/ *n* [U] sabotaje *m*

sabotage² *vt* sabotear

saboteur /ˈsæbəˈtɜːr ‖ ˌsæbəˈtɜː(r)/ *n* saboteador, -dora *m,f*

sabre *n* (BrE) ⇒ SABER

saccharin /ˈsækərən ‖ ˈsækərɪn/ *n* [U] sacarina *f*

sachet /sæˈʃeɪ ‖ ˈsæʃeɪ/ *n* (of shampoo, cream) sachet *m*; (of powder, sugar) (BrE) sobrecito *m*

sack¹ /sæk/ *n* **1** [C] **(a)** (large bag) saco *m* **(b)** (paper bag) (AmE) bolsa *f* (de papel) **2** (dismissal) (BrE colloq): **to give sb the ~** echar a algn (del trabajo), botar a algn (del trabajo) (AmL fam)

sack² *vt* **1** (dismiss) (BrE colloq) ‹*person/employee*› echar (del trabajo), botar (del trabajo) (AmL fam) **2** (destroy) ‹*town/city*› saquear

sacrament /ˈsækrəmənt/ *n* sacramento *m*

sacred /ˈseɪkrəd ‖ ˈseɪkrɪd/ *adj* sagrado

sacrifice¹ /ˈsækrəfaɪs ‖ ˈsækrɪfaɪs/ *n* **1** (Occult, Relig) **(a)** [U] (practice, act) sacrificio *m* **(b)** [C] (offering) ofrenda *f* **2** [U C] (giving up) sacrificio *m*; **to make ~s** sacrificarse*

sacrifice² *vt* sacrificar*

sacrilege /ˈsækrəlɪdʒ ‖ ˈsækrɪlɪdʒ/ *n* [U] sacrilegio *m*

sad /sæd/ *adj* **-dd-** triste; **~ to say** lamentablemente

sadden /ˈsædn̩/ *vt* entristecer*

saddle¹ /ˈsædl̩/ *n* (on horse) silla *f* (de montar); (on bicycle) sillín *m*

saddle² *vt* **(a)** ~ **(up)** ‹*horse*› ensillar **(b)** (burden) (colloq) **to ~ sb** WITH **sth** endilgarle* *or* (esp AmL) encajarle algo A algn

saddle-bag /ˈsædl̩bæg/ *n* (on horse) alforja *f*; (on bicycle) maletero *m*

sadist /ˈseɪdəst ‖ ˈseɪdɪst/ *n* sádico, -ca *m,f*

sadly /ˈsædli/ *adv* **(a)** (sorrowfully) ‹*smile/speak*› tristemente, con tristeza **(b)** (regrettably): **you are ~ mistaken** estás totalmente equivocado **(c)** (unfortunately) (*indep*) lamentablemente

sadness /ˈsædnəs ‖ ˈsædnɪs/ *n* [U] tristeza *f*

sae, SAE *n* (BrE) (= **stamped, addressed envelope**) ⇒ SASE

safari /səˈfɑːri/ *n* [C U] safari *m*; (*before n*) **~ park** safari-park *m*

safe¹ /seɪf/ *adj* **safer, safest 1** (secure from danger) seguro; ‹*haven/place*› seguro; **you are not ~ here** corres peligro aquí; **keep these documents ~** guarda estos documentos en un lugar seguro; **they're ~** están a salvo; **they were found ~ and well** *o* **~ and sound** los encontraron sanos y salvos **2** (not dangerous) ‹*ladder*› seguro **3** (not risky) ‹*investment/sex/method*› seguro; **to be on the ~ side** por si acaso; ***better (to be) ~ than sorry*** más vale prevenir que curar

safe² *n* caja *f* fuerte, caja *f* de caudales

safe: **~-conduct** /ˈseɪfˈkɑːndʌkt ‖ ˌseɪfˈkɒndʌkt/ *n* [U] protección *f*; **~-deposit (box)** /ˈseɪfdɪˈpɑːzət ‖ ˈseɪfdɪˈpɒzɪt/ *n* caja *f* de seguridad

safeguard¹ /ˈseɪfgɑːrd ‖ ˈseɪfgɑːd/ *n* salvaguarda *f*

safeguard² *vt* salvaguardar

safe: **~ house** *n* piso *m* franco; **~keeping** *n* [U]: **he gave her the watch for ~keeping** le dio el reloj para que lo guardara en lugar seguro *or* (esp Esp frml) para que lo pusiera a buen recaudo

safely /ˈseɪfli/ *adv* **1 (a)** (without mishap, unharmed): **we got home ~** llegamos a casa sin novedad **(b)** (without danger) sin peligro; **drive ~** conduzca con prudencia *or* cuidado **2** (with certainty) ‹*say/assume*› sin temor a equivocarse (*or* equivocarnos *etc*)

safety /ˈseɪfti/ *n* (*pl* **-ties**) [U] (security, freedom from risk) seguridad *f*; (*before n*) ‹*device/precautions/regulations*› de seguridad

safety: **~ belt** *n* cinturón *m* de seguridad; **~ catch** (on gun) seguro *m*; **~ net** *n* (for acrobats) red *f* de seguridad; (protection) protección *f*; **~ pin** *n* imperdible *m*, gancho *m* (Andes), alfiler *m* de gancho (CS, Ven), gancho *m* de nodriza (Col), seguro *m* (Méx)

saffron /ˈsæfrən/ *n* [U] azafrán *m*

sag /sæg/ *vi* **-gg- (a)** «*beams/ceiling*» combarse; «*bed*» hundirse **(b)** (hang down, droop): **~ging breasts** pechos *mpl* caídos

saga /'sɑːgə/ *n* (Lit) saga *f*; (long story) historia *f*, saga *f*

sage /seɪdʒ/ *n* **1** [U] (Bot, Culin) salvia *f* **2** [C] (wise man) sabio *m*

Sagittarius /'sædʒə'teriəs ‖ ˌsædʒɪ'teəriəs/ *n* **(a)** (sign) (*no art*) Sagitario **(b)** [C] (person) Sagitario *or* sagitario *mf*, sagitariano, -na *m,f*

Sahara /sə'hærə ‖ sə'hɑːrə/ *n* **the ~** el Sahara *or* (Esp) el Sáhara

said /sed/ *past & past p of* SAY[1]

sail[1] /seɪl/ *n* [C U] (of ship, boat) vela *f*; **to set ~** (start journey) zarpar, hacerse* a la mar; «*yacht/galleon*» hacerse* a la vela

sail[2] *vt* ‹*boat/ship*› gobernar* ■ **~** *vi* **(a)** (travel) «*ship/boat*» navegar*; «*person/passenger*» ir* en barco; **to go ~ing** salir a navegar **(b)** (depart) «*person/ship*» zarpar, salir*

• **sail through** [*v* + *prep* + *o*]: **you'll ~ through the exam** aprobarás el examen con los ojos cerrados

sailboat /'seɪlbəʊt/ *n* (AmE) velero *m*, barco *m* de vela

sailing /'seɪlɪŋ/ *n* [U] **(a)** (skill) navegación *f* **(b)** (Sport) vela *f*

sailing: **~ boat** *n* (BrE) ⇒ SAILBOAT; **~ ship** *n* velero *m*, barco *m* de vela

sailor /'seɪlər ‖ 'seɪlə(r)/ *n* **(a)** (seaman) marinero *m* **(b)** (Sport) navegante *mf*

saint /seɪnt/ *n*

■ **Note** Although the usual translation for *saint* as a title is *san* for a man or *santa* for a woman, *santo* is used before *Domingo*, *Tomás*, *Tomé*, and *Toribio*.

(a) (canonized person) santo, -ta *m,f* **(b) Saint** /seɪnt ‖ sənt/ (*before name*) san, santa

sake /seɪk/ *n* **(a)** (benefit, account): **for my/their ~** por mí/ellos; **for your own ~** por tu propio bien **(b)** (purpose, end): **art for art's ~** el arte por el arte; **for argument's ~** pongamos por caso **(c)** (*in interj phrases*): **for goodness'** *o* **heaven's ~!** ¡por Dios!; **for God's ~!** ¡por el amor de Dios!

salad /'sæləd/ *n* [U C] ensalada *f*; (*before n*) **~ bowl** ensaladera *f*; **~ dressing** aliño *m* para ensalada

salad cream *n* [U] (BrE) *aliño para ensalada parecido a la mayonesa*

salami /sə'lɑːmi/ *n* [U C] (*pl* **-mis**) salami *or* (CS) salame *m*

salary /'sæləri/ *n* (*pl* **-ries**) sueldo *m*

sale /seɪl/ *n* **1 (a)** [U] (act of selling) venta *f* **(b)** [C] (individual transaction) venta *f* **(c)** [C] (auction) subasta *f*, remate *m* (AmL) **2** (*in phrases*) **for sale**: Ⓢ **for sale** se vende; **on sale** (at reduced price) (AmE): **toys are on ~ this week** esta semana los juguetes están rebajados; (offered for sale) (BrE): **on ~ now at leading stores** ya está a la venta en los principales comercios **3** (clearance) liquidación *f*; (seasonal reductions) rebajas *fpl*; (*before n*) ‹*price*› de liquidación **4 sales (a)** *pl* (volume sold) (*sometimes sing*) (volumen *m* de) ventas *fpl* **(b)** (department) (+ *sing o pl vb*) ventas (+ *sing vb*)

saleroom /'seɪlruːm, -rʊm/ *n* (BrE) ⇒ SALESROOM (a)

sales /seɪlz/: **~clerk** *n* (AmE) vendedor, -dora *m,f*, dependiente, -ta *m,f*; **~man** /'seɪlzmən/ *n* (*pl* **-men** /-mən/) (in shop) vendedor *m*; (representative) representante *m*, corredor *m* (RPl); **~room** *n* (AmE) **(a)** (for auctions) sala *f* de subastas, sala *f* de remates (AmL) **(b)** (showroom) salón *m* de exposición (y ventas); **~ slip** *n* (AmE) recibo *m*; **~woman** *n* (in shop) vendedora *f*; (representative) representante *f*, corredora *f* (RPl)

saliva /sə'laɪvə/ *n* [U] saliva *f*

sallow /'sæləʊ/ *adj* **-er, -est** cetrino

salmon /'sæmən/ *n* [C U] (*pl* **~**) salmón *m*

salon /sə'lɑːn ‖ 'sælɒn/ *n* (business): **hairdressing ~** peluquería *f*; **beauty ~** salón *m* de belleza

saloon /sə'luːn/ *n* **1** (bar) (AmE) bar *m* (*del Lejano Oeste*) **2 ~ (car)** (BrE) sedán *m*

salt[1] /sɔːlt/ *n* [U C] sal *f*

salt[2] *vt* **(a)** (put salt on) ‹*vegetables/meat*› salar, ponerle* *or* echarle sal a; ‹*road*› echar sal en **(b) salted** *past p* salado

salt: **~ cellar** *n* salero *m*; **~water** *adj* ‹*lake*› de agua salada; ‹*fish*› de mar, de agua salada

salty /'sɔːlti/ *adj* **-tier, -tiest** salado

salubrious /sə'luːbriəs/ *adj* **(a)** (healthy) (frml) saludable, salubre **(b)** (wholesome) (*usu neg*): **not a very ~ district** un barrio muy poco recomendable

salutary /'sæljəteri ‖ 'sæljʊtri/ *adj* saludable

salute[1] /sə'luːt/ *n* **(a)** [C] (gesture) saludo *m*, venia *f* (RPl) **(b)** [C] (firing of guns) salva *f* **(c)** (tribute) homenaje *m*

salute[2] *vt* **(a)** (Mil) ‹*officer*› saludar **(b)** (acknowledge, pay tribute) (frml) ‹*courage/achievement*› rendir* homenaje a ■ **~** *vi* (Mil) **to ~ (TO sb)** hacerle* el saludo *or* (RPl) la venia (A algn)

Salvadorean, **Salvadorian** /'sælvə'dɔːriən/ *adj* salvadoreño

salvage /'sælvɪdʒ/ *vt* rescatar

salvation /sæl'veɪʃən/ *n* [U] salvación *f*

Salvation Army *n* Ejército *m* de Salvación

salve[1] /sæv ‖ sælv/ *n* [U C] (ointment) bálsamo *m*, ungüento *m*

salve[2] *vt*: **to ~ one's conscience** acallar la voz de su (*or* mi *etc*) conciencia

Samaritan /sə'mærətn ‖ sə'mærɪtən/ *n* (Bib) samaritano, -na *m,f*; **the good ~** el buen samaritano

same[1] /seɪm/ *adj* (*before n*) mismo, misma; **the ~ address/mistake** la misma dirección/el mismo error; **the two boxes are exactly the ~** las dos cajas son exactamente iguales; **that dress is the ~ as mine** ese vestido es igual al mío; **the ~ thing happened to me** a mí me pasó lo mismo; **on that very ~ day** ese mismísimo día

same[2] *pron* **(a)** : **the ~** lo mismo; **have a nice vacation!— ~ to you!** ¡felices vacaciones! — ¡igualmente! **(b) all the same, just the same** igual; (*as linker*) de todas formas *or* maneras; ***it's all the ~ to me/you/them*** me/te/les da lo mismo, me/te/les da igual

same[3] *adv*: **the ~** igual

sample[1] /'sæmpəl ‖ 'sɑːmpəl/ *n* muestra *f*

sample[2] *vt* ‹*food*› degustar

sanatorium /ˈsænəˈtɔːriəm/ *n* (*pl* **-riums** *or* **-ria** /-riə/) sanatorio *m* (*para convalecientes*)

sanctify /ˈsæŋktəfaɪ ‖ ˈsæŋktɪfaɪ/ *vt* **-fies, -fying, -fied** santificar*

sanctimonious /ˈsæŋktəˈməʊniəs ‖ ˌsæŋktɪˈməʊniəs/ *adj* (fml) moralista, gazmoño, mojigato

sanction[1] /ˈsæŋkʃən/ *n* **1** [U] (authorization) autorización *f*, sanción *f* **2 sanctions** *pl* (coercive measures) sanciones *fpl*

sanction[2] *vt* ‹*act/initiative*› sancionar (fml), aprobar*; ‹*injustice*› consentir*

sanctity /ˈsæŋktəti/ *n* [U] **(a)** (inviolability) inviolabilidad *f* **(b)** (holiness) santidad *f*

sanctuary /ˈsæŋktʃueri ‖ ˈsæŋktjʊəri/ *n* (*pl* **-ries**) **(a)** [U] (protection, safety) asilo *m*, refugio *m* **(b)** [C] (place of refuge) santuario *m*

sand[1] /sænd/ *n* [U] arena *f*

sand[2] *vt* **~ (down)** ‹*wood/furniture*› lijar; ‹*floor*› pulir

sandal /ˈsændl/ *n* sandalia *f*

sand: **~bank** *n* banco *m* de arena; **~box** *n* (AmE) cajón *m* de arena (*en parques y jardines*); **~castle** *n* castillo *m* de arena; **~paper** *n* [U] papel *m* de lija; **~pit** *n* (BrE) ⇒ SANDBOX; **~stone** *n* [U] arenisca *f*; **~storm** *n* tormenta *f* de arena

sandwich[1] /ˈsænwɪtʃ ‖ ˈsændwɪdʒ/ *n* (*pl* **-wiches**) sándwich *m*, emparedado *m*, ≈ bocadillo *m* (Esp)

sandwich[2] *vt* (*usu pass*): **I was ~ed between two fat men** estaba apretujado entre dos gordos

sandy /ˈsændi/ *adj* **-dier, -diest (a)** ‹*beach/path*› de arena; ‹*soil*› arenoso **(b)** **▶ 515** (in color) ‹*hair*› rubio rojizo *adj inv*

sane /seɪn/ *adj* **saner, sanest (a)** (not mad) cuerdo **(b)** (sensible) sensato

sang /sæŋ/ *past of* SING

sanitarium /ˈsænəˈteriəm ‖ ˌsænɪˈteəriəm/ *n* (AmE) ⇒ SANATORIUM

sanitary /ˈsænəteri ‖ ˈsænɪtri/ *adj* **(a)** (concerning health) (*before n*) ‹*conditions/regulations*› sanitario; ‹*inspector*› de sanidad **(b)** (hygienic) higiénico

sanitary napkin, (BrE) **sanitary towel** *n* compresa *f*, paño *m* higiénico

sanitation /ˈsænəˈteɪʃən ‖ ˌsænɪˈteɪʃən/ *n* [U] **(a)** (hygiene) condiciones *fpl* de salubridad **(b)** (waste disposal system) servicios *mpl* sanitarios

sanitize /ˈsænətaɪz ‖ ˈsænɪtaɪz/ *vt* **(a)** (disinfect) desinfectar **(b)** (make inoffensive) (pej) hacer* potable; **a ~d version** una versión aséptica

sanity /ˈsænəti/ *n* [U] **(a)** (mental health) razón *f*, cordura *f* **(b)** (good sense) sensatez *f*

sank /sæŋk/ *past of* SINK[1]

Santa Claus /ˈsæntəklɔːz/ *n* Papá Noel, San Nicolás, Santa Claus, Viejo *m* Pascuero (Chi)

sap[1] /sæp/ *n* [U] savia *f*

sap[2] *vt* **-pp-** minar

sapling /ˈsæplɪŋ/ *n* árbol *m* joven

sapphire /ˈsæfaɪr ‖ ˈsæfaɪə(r)/ *n* [U C] zafiro *m*

sarcasm /ˈsɑːrkæzəm ‖ ˈsɑːkæzəm/ *n* [U] sarcasmo *m*

sarcastic /sɑːrˈkæstɪk ‖ sɑːˈkæstɪk/ *adj* sarcástico

sardine /sɑːrˈdiːn ‖ sɑːˈdiːn/ *n* sardina *f*

sardonic /sɑːrˈdɑːnɪk ‖ sɑːˈdɒnɪk/ *adj* sardónico

sari /ˈsɑːri/ *n* (*pl* **~s**) sari *m*

SASE *n* (AmE) (= **self-addressed stamped envelope**): **I enclose an ~** adjunto sobre franqueado (a mi nombre)

sash /sæʃ/ *n* **1** (on dress) faja *f*; (on uniform — around waist) fajín *m*; (— over shoulder) banda *f* **2** (of window) marco *m*

sassy /ˈsæsi/ *adj* **-sier, -siest** (AmE colloq) **(a)** (impertinent) caradura (fam) **(b)** (brash) ‹*hat/style*› llamativo y atrevido

sat /sæt/ *past & past p of* SIT

Satan /ˈseɪtn/ *n* Satanás

satanic /səˈtænɪk/ *adj* satánico

satchel /ˈsætʃəl/ *n* cartera *f* (*de colegial*)

sate /seɪt/ *vt* (liter) (*usu pass*) ‹*appetite/lust*› saciar (liter)

satellite /ˈsætl̩aɪt ‖ ˈsætəlaɪt/ *n* **1 (a)** (Aerosp) satélite *m* (artificial); (*before n*) **~ TV** televisión *f* por *or* vía satélite **(b)** (Astron) satélite *m* **2** (dependent body, state) satélite *m*; (*before n*) **a ~ town** una ciudad satélite

satin /ˈsætn ‖ ˈsætɪn/ *n* [U C] satén *m*, satín *m* (AmL)

satire /ˈsætaɪr ‖ ˈsætaɪə(r)/ *n* [U C] sátira *f*

satirical /səˈtɪrɪkəl/ *adj* satírico

satirize /ˈsætəraɪz/ *vt* satirizar*

satisfaction /ˈsætəsˈfækʃən ‖ ˌsætɪsˈfækʃən/ *n* [U] satisfacción *f*

satisfactory /ˈsætəsˈfæktri ‖ ˌsætɪsˈfæktəri/ *adj* satisfactorio

satisfied /ˈsætəsfaɪd ‖ ˈsætɪsfaɪd/ *adj* ‹*expression/customer*› satisfecho; ‹*smile*› de satisfacción

satisfy /ˈsætəsfaɪ ‖ ˈsætɪsfaɪ/ *vt* **-fies, -fying, -fied 1 (a)** (please) satisfacer* **(b)** (meet) ‹*requirements*› llenar; ‹*demand*› satisfacer* **2** (convince) (*often pass*) **to ~ sb OF sth** convencer* a algn DE algo

satisfying /ˈsætəsfaɪɪŋ ‖ ˈsætɪsfaɪɪŋ/ *adj* **(a)** (pleasing) ‹*result/job*› satisfactorio **(b)** (filling) ‹*meal*› que llena

satsuma /sætˈsuːmə/ *n* satsuma *f* (*tipo de mandarina*)

saturate /ˈsætʃəreɪt/ *vt* **1** (drench) empapar **2** (fill) ‹*market/mind/place*› saturar **3** (Chem, Phys) saturar

saturation /ˈsætʃəˈreɪʃən/ *n* [U] **1** (Busn, Marketing) saturación *f* **2** (Chem, Phys) saturación *f*

Saturday /ˈsætərdeɪ, -di ‖ ˈsætədeɪ, -di/ **▶ 540** *n* sábado *m*; *see also* MONDAY

Saturn /ˈsætərn ‖ ˈsætən/ *n* Saturno *m*

sauce /sɔːs/ *n* [C U] salsa *f*

saucepan /ˈsɔːspæn ‖ ˈsɔːspən/ *n* cacerola *f*, cazo *m* (Esp); (large) olla *f*

saucer /ˈsɔːsər ‖ ˈsɔːsə(r)/ *n* platillo *m*

saucy /ˈsæsi, ˈsɔːsi ‖ ˈsɔːsi/ *adj* **-cier, -ciest** insolente, fresco (fam)

Saudi[1] /ˈsaudi/ *adj* saudita, saudí

Saudi[2] *n* saudita *mf*, saudí *mf*

Saudi Arabia /ə'reɪbiə/ *n* Arabia *f* Saudita, Arabia *f* Saudí

sauna /'sɔːnə/ *n* sauna *f*, sauna *m* (AmL)

saunter /'sɔːntər ‖ 'sɔːntə(r)/ *vi* pasear; **she ~ed in/out** entró/salió andando despacio

sausage /'sɔːsɪdʒ ‖ 'sɒsɪdʒ/ *n* [C U] (for cooking) salchicha *f*; (cold, cured) embutido *m*

sauté /sɔː'teɪ ‖ 'səʊteɪ/ *vt* **-tés, -téeing** *or* **-téing, -téed** *or* **-téd** saltear

savage¹ /'sævɪdʒ/ *adj* **(a)** (fierce, wild) ‹*beast/attack*› salvaje; ‹*blow*› violento **(b)** (uncivilized) ‹*tribe/people*› salvaje

savage² *n* salvaje *mf*

savage³ *vt* atacar* salvajemente a

savagely /'sævɪdʒli/ *adv* salvajemente

savagery /'sævɪdʒri/ *n* [U] ferocidad *f*

save¹ /seɪv/ *vt* **1 (a)** (preserve) ‹*life/person/job*› salvar; ‹*possessions*› rescatar; **firefighters ~d 20 people** bomberos rescataron a 20 personas **(b)** (redeem) ‹*soul/sinner*› salvar **2 (a)** (be economical with) ‹*money/fuel/space/time*› ahorrar **(b)** (spare, avoid) ‹*trouble/expense/embarrassment*› ahorrar, evitar **3 (a)** (keep, put aside) guardar; ‹*money*› ahorrar; **don't eat it now; ~ it for later** no te lo comas ahora; déjalo para luego; **to ~ one's energy** guardarse las energías **(b)** (Comput) guardar **4** (Sport) ‹*shot/penalty*› salvar ■ ~ *vi* ahorrar

• **save up 1** [*v* + *adv*] ahorrar **2** [*v* + *o* + *adv*, *v* + *adv* + *o*] ahorrar

save² *n* parada *f*

save³ *prep* (frml) (apart from) ~ **(for)** salvo, excepto

saving¹ /'seɪvɪŋ/ *n* **(a)** [C] (economy) ahorro *m* **(b) savings** *pl* ahorros *mpl*; (*before n*) **~s account** cuenta *f* de ahorros

saving² *adj* (*before n*) *see* GRACE 2(c)

savings /'seɪvɪŋz/: ~ **and loan** *n* ~ ~ ~ **(association/company)** (AmE) sociedad *f* de ahorro y préstamos; ~ **bank** *n* caja *f* de ahorros

savior, (BrE) **saviour** /'seɪvjər ‖ 'seɪvjə(r)/ *n* salvador, -dora *m,f*

savor¹, (BrE) **savour** /'seɪvər ‖ 'seɪvə(r)/ *vt* saborear

savor², (BrE) **savour** *n* (taste) sabor *m*; (hint, trace) dejo *m*

savory, (BrE) **savoury** /'seɪvəri/ *adj* (tasty) sabroso; (wholesome) (*usu with neg*) limpio

savour *vt/n* (BrE) ⇒ SAVOR[1,2]

savoury /'seɪvəri/ *adj* (BrE) **(a)** ⇒ SAVORY² **(b)** (not sweet) salado

saw¹ /sɔː/ *past of* SEE

saw² *n* (manual) sierra *f*; (— with one handle) serrucho *m*; (power-driven) sierra *f* mecánica

saw³ *vt* (*past p* **sawed** *or* (esp BrE) **sawn**) (with handsaw) cortar (*con serrucho*), serruchar (AmL); (with a larger saw) cortar (*con sierra*), serrar*, aserrar*

sawdust /'sɔːdʌst/ *n* [U] serrín *m*, aserrín *m* (esp AmL)

sawed-off /'sɔːd'ɔːf ‖ 'sɔːdɒf/, (BrE) **sawn-off** /'sɔːnɔːf ‖ 'sɔːnɒf/ *adj*: ~ **shotgun** escopeta *f* recortada

sawn /sɔːn/ *past p of* SAW³

sawn-off *adj* (BrE) ⇒ SAWED-OFF

saxophone /'sæksəfəʊn/ *n* saxofón *m*, saxófono *m*

say¹ /seɪ/ (*pres* **says** /sez/; *past & past p* **said** /sed/) *vt* **1** (utter, express in speech) ‹*word/sentence*› decir*; ‹*prayer*› rezar*; **I said yes/no** dije que sí/no; **to ~ sth TO sb** decirle* algo A algn; **why didn't you ~ so before?** haberlo dicho antes; **that's to ~** es decir; **to ~ the least** como mínimo; **what have you got to ~ for yourself?** a ver, explícate; **~ no more** no me digas más; **you can ~ that again!** ¡y que lo digas!; **it goes without ~ing that** … huelga decir que …; **that's easier said than done** del dicho al hecho hay mucho trecho; **no sooner said than done** dicho y hecho; **when all's said and done** al fin y al cabo **2** «*watch/dial*» marcar* **3** (suppose) (colloq) suponer*; **(let's) ~ that** … supongamos que … **4** (allege) decir*; …, **or so he ~s** …, al menos eso es lo que dice ■ ~ *vi* decir*; **I'd rather not ~** prefiero no decirlo; **it's hard to ~** es difícil decirlo

say² *interj* (AmE colloq) ¡oye! (fam)

say³ *n* (*no pl*) **(a)** (statement of view): **to have one's ~** dar* su (*or* mi *etc*) opinión **(b)** (power): **I have no ~ in the matter** yo no tengo ni voz ni voto en el asunto

saying /'seɪɪŋ/ *n* refrán *m*, dicho *m*

SC = **South Carolina**

scab /skæb/ *n* **1** (on wound) costra *f* **2** (strike breaker) (pej) esquirol *mf* (pey), carnero, -ra *m,f* (RPl fam & pey)

scaffold /'skæfəld, -fəʊld/ *n* (for execution) patíbulo *m*, cadalso *m*

scaffolding /'skæfəldɪŋ, '-fəʊldɪŋ/ *n* [U] andamiaje *m*

scald /skɔːld/ *vt* escaldar

scale¹ /skeɪl/ *n* **I 1** (*no pl*) **(a)** (extent, size) escala *f*; **on a large/small ~** en gran/pequeña escala **(b)** (of map, diagram) escala *f*; (*before n*) ‹*model/drawing*› a escala **2** [C] (on measuring instrument) escala *f* **3** [C] (Mus) escala *f* **4** [C] (for weighing) (*usu pl*) balanza *f*, pesa *f*; **bathroom ~s** una báscula *or* pesa (de baño) **II 1** [C] (on fish) escama *f* **2** [U] (deposit in kettle, pipes) sarro *m*

scale² *vt* ‹*mountain/wall*› escalar; ‹*ladder*› subir

• **scale down** [*v* + *o* + *adv*, *v* + *adv* + *o*] ‹*drawing*› reducir* (a escala); ‹*operation*› recortar

scallion /'skæljən/ *n* (AmE) **(a)** (young onion) cebolleta *f*, cebollino *m* **(b)** (shallot) chalote *m*, chalota *f*

scallop /'skæləp/ *n* vieira *f*, ostión *m* (CS)

scalp¹ /skælp/ *n* (Anat) cuero *m* cabelludo

scalp² *vt*: **to ~ sb** arrancarle* la cabellera a algn

scalpel /'skælpəl/ *n* bisturí *m*, escalpelo *m*

scaly /'skeɪli/ *adj* **-lier, -liest** ‹*skin*› escamoso

scamper /'skæmpər ‖ 'skæmpə(r)/ *vi* corretear; **she ~ed off** se fue correteando

scampi /'skæmpi/ *pl n* langostinos *mpl* (*gen rebozados*)

scan¹ /skæn/ *vt* **-nn- 1 (a)** ‹*horizon*› escudriñar **(b)** ‹*noticeboard/newspaper*› recorrer con la vista; ‹*report*› echarle un vistazo a **2** (Med) ‹*body/brain*› hacer* un escáner de; (with ultrasound scanner) hacer* una ecografía de

scan² *n* (Med) escáner *m* (ultrasound) ecografía *f*

scandal /'skændl/ *n* **(a)** [C] (outrage) escándalo *m* **(b)** [U] (gossip) chismorreo *m*

scandalize /'skændlaɪz/ *vt* escandalizar*

scandalous /'skændləs/ *adj* escandaloso

Scandinavia /'skændə'neɪviə ‖ ˌskændɪ'neɪviə/ *n* Escandinavia *f*

Scandinavian¹ /'skændə'neɪviən ‖ ˌskændɪ'neɪviən/ *adj* escandinavo

Scandinavian² *n* escandinavo, -va *m,f*

scanner /'skænər ‖ 'skænə(r)/ *n* (Med) escáner *m*, scanner *m*

scanty /'skænti/ *adj* **-tier, -tiest** ‹*information*› insuficiente; ‹*meal*› poco abundante, frugal; ‹*costume*› breve

scapegoat /'skeɪpgəʊt/ *n* chivo *m* expiatorio

scar¹ /skɑːr ‖ skɑː(r)/ *n* cicatriz *f*

scar² *vt* **-rr-**: **his face was badly ~red** le quedó una enorme cicatriz en el rostro; **she'll be ~red for life** (physically) le va a quedar (la) cicatriz; (emotionally) va a quedar marcada

scarce /skers ‖ skeəs/ *adj* escaso; **to be ~** escasear

scarcely /'skersli ‖ 'skeəsli/ *adv* apenas

scarcity /'skersəti ‖ 'skeəsəti/ *n* [C U] (*pl* **-ties**) escasez *f*

scare¹ /sker ‖ skeə(r)/ *vt* asustar
• **scare away, scare off** [*v + o + adv, v + adv + o*] espantar

scare² *n* **(a)** (fright, shock) susto *m* **(b)** (panic) (Journ): **bomb ~** amenaza *f* de bomba

scarecrow /'skerkrəʊ ‖ 'skeəkrəʊ/ *n* espantapájaros *m*

scared /skerd ‖ skeəd/ *adj* asustado; **I'm ~** tengo miedo; **to be ~ OF sth/sb** tenerle* miedo A algo/algn

scarf /skɑːrf ‖ skɑːf/ *n* (*pl* **~s** *or* **scarves**) **(a)** (muffler) bufanda *f* **(b)** (square) pañuelo *m*

scarlet /'skɑːrlət ‖ 'skɑːlət/ ▶515 *adj* (rojo) escarlata *adj inv*

scarlet fever *n* [U] escarlatina *f*

scarves /skɑːrvz ‖ skɑːvz/ *pl of* SCARF

scathing /'skeɪðɪŋ/ *adj* mordaz

scatter /'skætər ‖ 'skætə(r)/ *vt* **1** ‹*salt/grit*› esparcir*; ‹*seeds*› sembrar* (a voleo) **2** (disperse) ‹*crowd/group*› dispersar; **they are ~ed all over the country** están desperdigados por todo el país ■ **~** *vi* «*crowd/light*» dispersarse

scatterbrained /'skætər'breɪnd ‖ 'skætəbreɪnd/ *adj* atolondrado, despistado

scattered /'skætərd ‖ 'skætəd/ *adj* (*before n*) ‹*fighting/applause/outbreak*› aislado; ‹*community*› diseminado; **~ showers** chubascos *mpl* aislados

scavenge /'skævəndʒ ‖ 'skævɪndʒ/ *vi* **to ~ FOR sth** escarbar *or* hurgar* en busca de algo

scavenger /'skævəndʒər ‖ 'skævɪndʒə(r)/ *n* **(a)** (animal, bird) carroñero, -ra *m,f* **(b)** (person) *persona que busca comida etc hurgando en los desperdicios*

scenario /sə'neriəʊ, -'næ- ‖ sɪ'nɑːriəʊ/ *n* (*pl* **-os**) **(a)** (Cin, TV) guión *m* **(b)** (of future) perspectiva *f*, escenario *m* (period)

scene /siːn/ *n* **1 (a)** (view, situation) escena *f* **(b)** (of incident, crime) escena *f*; **it was the ~ of violent demonstrations** fue el escenario de violentas manifestaciones; **to appear on the ~** aparecer*; **to set the ~ (for sth)** situar* la escena (de algo) **2** (in play, book etc) escena *f* **3** (stage setting) decorado *m*; ***behind the ~s*** entre bastidores **4** (fuss, row) escena *f* **5** (sphere) ámbito *m*; **it's not my ~** (colloq) no es lo mío

scenery /'siːnəri/ *n* [U] **(a)** (surroundings) paisaje *m* **(b)** (Theat) escenografía *f*

scenic /'siːnɪk/ *adj* pintoresco

scent¹ /sent/ *n* **(a)** [C U] (fragrance) perfume *m* **(b)** [C U] (perfume) (BrE) perfume *m* **(c)** (trail) rastro *m*; **to put** *o* **throw sb off the ~** despistar a algn

scent² *vt* **(a)** (sense) ‹*danger/victory*› intuir* **(b)** (perfume) ‹*air/room/skin*› perfumar **(c) scented** *past p* ‹*writing paper*› perfumado; ‹*rose*› fragante

scepter, (BrE) **sceptre** /'septər ‖ 'septə(r)/ *n* cetro *m*

sceptic *etc* (BrE) ⇒ SKEPTIC *etc*

sceptre *n* (BrE) ⇒ SCEPTER

schedule¹ /'skedʒuːl ‖ 'ʃedjuːl/ *n* **1** (plan) programa *m*; **the flight is due to arrive on ~** el vuelo llegará a la hora prevista; **to be ahead of/behind ~** estar* adelantado/ atrasado con respecto al programa **2 (a)** (list) (frml) lista *f* **(b)** (AmE) (timetable — for transport) horario *m*; (— for classes) horario *m* (de clases)

schedule² *vt* (timetable, plan) (*usu pass*) programar; **the conference is ~d to take place in August** la conferencia está planeada para el mes de agosto

scheduled /'skedʒuːld ‖ 'ʃedjuːld/ *adj* (*before n*) **(a)** (planned) ‹*meeting/visit*› previsto, programado **(b)** ‹*flight/service*› regular

scheme¹ /skiːm/ *n* (plan) plan *m*; (underhand) ardid *m*; (plot) confabulación *f*, conspiración *f*

scheme² *vi* intrigar*; (plot) conspirar

scheming¹ /'skiːmɪŋ/ *adj* intrigante

scheming² *n* [U] maquinaciones *fpl*, intrigas *fpl*

schism /'sɪzəm, 'skɪzəm/ *n* [U C] cisma *m*

schizophrenia /'skɪtsə'friːniə ‖ ˌskɪtsə'friːniə/ *n* [U] esquizofrenia *f*

schizophrenic /'skɪtsə'frenɪk, -'friːnɪk ‖ ˌskɪtsəʊ'frenɪk, 'friːnɪk/ *adj* esquizofrénico

schmaltz /ʃmɔːlts/ *n* [U] (colloq) sensiblería *f*

schmaltzy /'ʃmɔːltsi/ *adj* **-zier, -ziest** (colloq) sensiblero

scholar /'skɑːlər ‖ 'skɒlə(r)/ *n* **(a)** (learned person) erudito, -ta *m,f* **(b)** (holder of scholarship) becario, -ria *m,f*

scholarly /'skɑːlərli ‖ 'skɒləli/ *adj* ‹*person*› erudito, docto; ‹*attainments*› en el campo académico

scholarship /'skɑːlərʃɪp ‖ 'skɒləʃɪp/ *n* **1** [C] (grant) beca *f* **2** [U] (scholarliness) erudición *f*

school¹ /skuːl/ *n* **1** [C U] **(a)** (in primary, secondary education) colegio *m*, escuela *f*; **to go to ~** ir* al colegio *or* a la escuela; (*before n*) ‹*uniform/rules*› del colegio; ‹*bus*› escolar; **~ fees** *cuotas que se pagan en un colegio particular*, colegiatura *f* (Méx); **~ year** año *m* escolar *or* lectivo **(b)** (college, university) (AmE) universidad *f* **(c)** (department) facultad *f* **2** [C U] (other training establishment) academia *f*, escuela *f* **3** [C] (of fish) cardumen *m*, banco *m*; (of dolphins, whales) grupo *m*

school² *vt* ‹*person*› instruir*; (train) capacitar

school: **~boy** *n* colegial *m*, escolar *m*; **~child** *n* colegial, -giala *m,f*, escolar *mf*; **~girl** *n* colegiala *f*, escolar *f*; **~-leaver** /ˈliːvər ‖ ˈliːvə(r)/ *n* (BrE) joven *mf* que termina el colegio; **~master** *n* (BrE frml) (in primary school) maestro *m*; (in secondary school) profesor *m*; **~mistress** *n* (BrE frml) (in primary school) maestra; (in secondary school) profesora *f*; **~teacher** *n* (in primary school) maestro, -tra *m,f*; (in secondary school) profesor, -sora *m,f*

science /ˈsaɪəns/ *n* [U C] ciencia *f*

science fiction *n* [U] ciencia ficción *f*

scientific /ˈsaɪənˈtɪfɪk/ *adj* científico

scientist /ˈsaɪəntəst ‖ ˈsaɪəntɪst/ *n* científico, -ca *m,f*

Scillies /ˈsɪliz/ *pl n* ⇒ ISLES OF SCILLY

scintillating /ˈsɪntl̩eɪtɪŋ ‖ ˈsɪntɪleɪtɪŋ/ *adj* ‹*wit/conversation*› chispeante

scissors /ˈsɪzərz ‖ ˈsɪzəz/ *n* (+ *pl vb*) tijeras *fpl*, tijera *f*

scoff /skɑːf ‖ skɒf/ *vi* **to ~ (AT sb/sth)** burlarse (DE algn/algo) ■ **~** *vt* (eat greedily) (BrE colloq) engullirse*

scold /skəʊld/ *vt* reprender, regañar, retar (CS)

scone /skəʊn, skɑːn ‖ skɒn, skəʊn/ *n* (in UK) *bollito que se come untado de mantequilla, mermelada etc*, scone *m* (CS), bísquet *m* (Méx)

scoop /skuːp/ *n* **1 (a)** (for grain, ice-cream) pala *f* **(b)** (measure — of ice-cream) bola *f* **2** (Journ) primicia *f*

• scoop out 1 [*v* + *o* + *adv*, *v* + *adv* + *o*] ‹*flour/rice/soil*› sacar* (*con pala, cuchara etc*) **2** [*v* + *adv* + *o*] (hollow) ‹*hole/tunnel*› excavar

• scoop up [*v* + *o* + *adv*, *v* + *adv* + *o*] recoger* (*con pala, cuchara etc*)

scooter /ˈskuːtər ‖ ˈskuːtə(r)/ *n* **(a)** (*motor* ~) escúter *m*, Vespa® *f* **(b)** (toy) patinete *m*

scope /skəʊp/ *n* [U] (of law, regulations) alcance *m*; (of influence) ámbito *m*; (of investigation) campo *m*

scorch /skɔːrtʃ ‖ skɔːtʃ/ *vt* ‹*fabric*› chamuscar*; «*sun*» ‹*plant*› quemar, abrasar

score¹ /skɔːr ‖ skɔː(r)/ *n* **1 (a)** (in game): **the final ~** el resultado final; **what's the ~?** ¿cómo van? **(b)** (in competition, test etc) puntuación *f*, puntaje *m* (AmL) **2 (a)** (account): **I have no worries on that ~** en lo que a eso se refiere, no me preocupo; **to have a ~ to settle with sb** tener* que arreglar cuentas con algn **(b)** (situation) (colloq): **to know the ~** saber cómo son las cosas **3** (Mus) **(a)** (notation) partitura *f* **(b)** (music for show, movie) música *f* **4** (twenty) veintena *f*; **there were ~s of people there** había muchísima gente

score² *vt* **1 (a)** (Sport) ‹*goal*› marcar*, anotar(se) (AmL); **you ~ 20 points for that** eso te da *or* (AmL tb) con eso te anotas 20 puntos **(b)** (in competition, test) «*person*» sacar* **(c)** (win) ‹*success*› lograr, conseguir* **2** (cut, mark) ‹*surface/paper*› marcar* ■ **~** *vi* (Sport) marcar*, anotar(se) un tanto (AmL)

scoreboard /ˈskɔːrbɔːrd ‖ ˈskɔːbɔːd/ *n* marcador *m*

scorn¹ /skɔːrn ‖ ˈskɔːn/ *n* [U] desdén *m*; **to pour ~ on sth** desdeñar algo

scorn² *vt* (reject, despise) desdeñar

scornful /ˈskɔːrnfəl ‖ ˈskɔːnfəl/ *adj* desdeñoso; **to be ~ of sth** desdeñar algo

Scorpio /ˈskɔːrpiəʊ ‖ ˈskɔːpiəʊ/ *n* (*pl* **-os**) **(a)** (sign) (*no art*) Escorpio, Escorpión **(b)** [C] (person) Escorpio *or* escorpio *mf*, Escorpión *or* escorpión *mf*, escorpión -na *m,f*

scorpion /ˈskɔːrpiən ‖ ˈskɔːpiən/ *n* escorpión *m*, alacrán *m*

Scot /skɑːt ‖ skɒt/ *n* escocés, -cesa *m,f*

scotch¹ /skɑːtʃ ‖ skɒtʃ/ *vt* ‹*plan/efforts*› echar por tierra; ‹*rumors*› acallar

scotch², **Scotch** *n* [U C] whisky *m* *or* güisqui *m* (escocés)

Scotch: **~ egg** *n*: *huevo duro envuelto en carne de salchicha y rebozado*; **~ tape®** *n* [U] (AmE) cinta *f* Scotch®, cel(l)o® *m* (Esp), (cinta *f*) durex® *m* (AmL)

scot-free /ˈskɑːtˈfriː ‖ ˌskɒtˈfriː/ *adj* (*pred*): **to get away ~** quedar impune

Scotland /ˈskɑːtlənd ‖ ˈskɒtlənd/ *n* Escocia *f*

Scots /skɑːts ‖ skɒts/ *adj* (*before n*) escocés

Scots: **~man** /ˈskɑːtsmən ‖ ˈskɒtsmən/ *n* (*pl* **-men** /-mən/) escocés *m*; **~woman** *n* escocesa *f*

Scottish /ˈskɑːtɪʃ ‖ ˈskɒtɪʃ/ *adj* escocés

scoundrel /ˈskaʊndrəl/ *n* (dated) sinvergüenza *mf*

scour /skaʊr ‖ ˈskaʊə(r)/ *vt* **1** (rub hard) fregar* **2** (search thoroughly) registrar

scourge /skɜːrdʒ ‖ skɜːdʒ/ *n* azote *m*

scouring powder /ˈskaʊrɪŋ ‖ ˈskaʊərɪŋ/ *n* [C U] polvo *m* limpiador, limpiador *m* en polvo, pulidor *m* (RPl)

scout /skaʊt/ *n* **1** (person) explorador, -dora *m,f* **2** *also* **Scout** (*boy* ~) explorador *m*, (boy) scout *m*; (*girl* ~) exploradora *f*, (girl) scout *f*

• scout around [*v* + *adv*] **to ~ around (FOR sth)** buscar* (algo)

scowl¹ /skaʊl/ *n* ceño *m* fruncido

scowl² *vi* fruncir* el ceño; **to ~ AT sb** mirar a algn con el ceño fruncido

scrabble /ˈskræbəl/ *vi* «*dog/chicken*» escarbar; **he was scrabbling about in the drawers of the desk** estaba hurgando en los cajones del escritorio

scraggy /ˈskrægi/ *adj* **-gier, -giest (a)** (scrawny) esmirriado **(b)** (tough) ‹*meat*› duro

scram /skræm/ *vi* **-mm-** (colloq): **go on, ~!** ¡fuera *or* largo de aquí! (fam)

scramble¹ /ˈskræmbəl/ *n* (*no pl*) **(a)** (chaotic rush): barullo *m*; **there was a last-minute ~ for tickets** a último momento hubo una rebatiña para conseguir entradas **(b)** (difficult climb) subida *f* difícil

scramble² *vi* (+ *adv compl*): **we ~d through the bushes** nos abrimos paso con dificultad a través de los arbustos ■ **~** *vt* **(a)** (mix) mezclar **(b)** ‹*message*› codificar*

scrambled egg /ˈskræmbəld/ *n* [C U] (Culin) huevos *mpl* revueltos

scrap¹ /skræp/ *n* **1 (a)** [C] (of paper, cloth, leather) pedacito *m*, trocito *m* **(b)** (single bit) (*with neg, no pl*): **it doesn't make a ~ of difference what you think** lo que tú pienses no importa en lo más mínimo **2 scraps** *pl* sobras *fpl*, sobros *mpl* (AmC) **3** [U] (reusable waste) chatarra *f*; (*before n*) **~ paper** papel *m* para borrador

scrap² *vt* **-pp- (a)** (abandon) ‹*idea*› desechar; ‹*plan*› abandonar **(b)** (throw away) tirar a la basura, botar (AmL exc RPl)

scrapbook /'skræpbʊk/ *n* álbum *m* de recortes

scrape¹ /skreɪp/ *n* (colloq) lío *m* (fam)

scrape² *vt* **1 (a)** (rub against) rozar*; (grate against) rascar* **(b)** (damage, graze) ‹*paintwork*› rayar; ‹*knee/elbow*› rasparse, rasguñarse **2 (a)** (clean) ‹*carrot/potato*› pelar; ‹*woodwork*› raspar, rascar*; **to ~ sth off** ‹*paint/wallpaper*› quitar algo (*con una rasqueta/un cuchillo*); **~ the mud off your boots** quítales el barro a las botas (*con un cuchillo, contra una piedra etc*) **(b)** ‹*bowl/pan*› fregar*

• scrape through [*v* + *adv*] [*v* + *prep* + *o*] ‹*exam*› aprobar* raspando *or* (fam) por los pelos

scraper /'skreɪpər ‖ 'skreɪpə(r)/ *n* (tool) rasqueta *f*, espátula *f*

scrap: **~heap** *n*: **to throw sth on the ~heap** desechar algo; **at 50 he found himself on the ~heap** a los 50 años se vio sin trabajo y sin perspectivas de futuro; **~yard** *n* chatarrería *f*; (for cars) cementerio *m* de automóviles, desguace *m or* (Méx) deshuesadero *m*

scratch¹ /skrætʃ/ *n* [C] **1** rasguño *m*, arañazo *m*; (on paint, record, furniture) rayón *m* **2** (*in phrases*) **from scratch**: **to start from ~** empezar* desde cero; **to be up to ~** (colloq) dar* la talla

scratch² *vt* **(a)** ‹*paint/record/furniture*› rayar **(b)** (with claws, nails) arañar **(c)** ‹*name/initials*› marcar* **(d)** (to relieve itch) rascarse* ■ **~** *vi* **(a)** (damage, wound) arañar **(b)** (to relieve itching) rascarse*

• scratch out [*v* + *o* + *adv*, *v* + *adv* + *o*] **(a)** (gouge): **to ~ sb's eyes out** sacarle* los ojos a algn **(b)** (strike out) ‹*name/sentence*› tachar; (on ticket) rascar*

scratch pad *n* [U] (AmE) bloc *m* (*para borrador o apuntes*)

scrawl¹ /skrɔːl/ *n* [U] garabatos *mpl*

scrawl² *vt/i* garabatear

scrawny /'skrɔːni/ *adj* **-nier, -niest** ‹*person*› escuálido; ‹*arms/legs*› esquelético

scream¹ /skriːm/ *n* grito *m*, chillido *m*; (louder) alarido *m*

scream² *vi* gritar, chillar; «*baby*» llorar a gritos ■ **~** *vt* ‹*insult*› gritar, soltar*; ‹*command*› dar* a voces *or* a gritos

screech¹ /skriːtʃ/ *n* (of terror, pain) alarido *m*; (of joy) chillido *m*; (of brakes) chirrido *m*; (of bird) chillido *m*

screech² *vi* «*person/animal*» chillar; «*brakes/tires*» chirriar*

screen¹ /skriːn/ *n* **1** (folding) biombo *m*; (as partition) mampara *f*; (protective, defensive) cortina *f* **2** (Cin, Comput, Phot, TV) pantalla *f*

screen² *vt* **1 (a)** (conceal) ocultar, tapar **(b)** (protect) proteger* **2** ‹*TV program*› emitir; ‹*film*› proyectar **3** (check, examine) ‹*blood donor*› someter a una revisión (médica); ‹*applicants*› someter a una investigación de antecedentes

• screen off [*v* + *o* + *adv*, *v* + *adv* + *o*] aislar*, separar (*con un biombo o una mampara*)

screen: **~ door** *n* puerta *f* mosquitera; **~play** *n* guión *m*; **~ test** *n* prueba *f* (cinematográfica)

screw¹ /skruː/ *n* (Const, Tech) tornillo *m*

screw² *vt* (Const, Tech) atornillar; **to ~ sth down (securely)** atornillar (bien) algo; **~ the lid on tight** enrosca bien la tapa

• screw up [*v* + *o* + *adv*, *v* + *adv* + *o*] **1** (tighten) ‹*bolt*› apretar* **2** (crumple) ‹*letter/paper*› arrugar* **3** (spoil, botch) (sl) fastidiar (fam)

screw: **~ball** *n* (eccentric person) (AmE colloq) excéntrico, -ca *mf*, chiflado, -da *m,f* (fam); **~driver** *n* destornillador *m*, desarmador *m* (Méx), desatornillador *m* (AmC, Chi); **~-top** *adj* ‹*bottle*› con tapón de rosca; ‹*jar*› con tapa de rosca

scribble¹ /'skrɪbəl/ *n* [C U] garabato *m*

scribble² *vt* garabatear; **to ~ sth down** anotar algo rápidamente ■ **~** *vi* garabatear

scrimp /skrɪmp/ *vi*: **to ~ ON sth** escatimar EN algo; **to ~ and save** cuidar mucho el dinero

script /skrɪpt/ *n* **1 (a)** [U] (handwriting) letra *f* **(b)** [C] (style of writing) caligrafía *f* **(c)** [C] (alphabet) escritura *f* **2** [C] (text of film, broadcast) guión *m*

scripture /'skrɪptʃər ‖ 'skrɪptʃə(r)/ *n*: **the (Holy) S~s** las (Sagradas) Escrituras

scriptwriter /'skrɪpt,raɪtər ‖ 'skrɪpt,raɪtə(r)/ *n* guionista *mf*

scroll¹ /skrəʊl/ *n* rollo *m*

scroll² *vi* (Comput): **to ~ up/down** hacer* avanzar/retroceder el texto que aparece en pantalla

scrounge /skraʊndʒ/ (colloq) *vt* **to ~ sth FROM/OFF sb** gorronearle *or* gorrearle *or* (RPl) garronearle *or* (Chi) bolsearle algo A algn (fam) ■ **~** *vi* gorronear *or* gorrear *or* (RPl) garronear *or* (Chi) bolsear (fam)

scrub¹ /skrʌb/ *n* **1** [U] (vegetation) matorrales *mpl* **2** (act) (*no pl*): **to give sth a good ~** fregar* *or* (Méx) tallar algo bien (*con cepillo*); (*before n*) **~ brush** (AmE) cepillo *m* de fregar

scrub² *vt* **-bb-** ‹*floor/table*› fregar*; ‹*knees/hands*› restregar*

scrubbing brush /'skrʌbɪŋ/ *n* cepillo *m* de fregar

scruff /skrʌf/ *n*: **by the ~ of the neck** por el pescuezo

scruffy /'skrʌfi/ *adj* **-fier, -fiest** (colloq) ‹*person*› dejado, desaliñado; **a ~-looking building** un edificio de aspecto destartalado

scrum /skrʌm/, **scrummage** /'skrʌmɪdz/ *n* (in rugby) melé *f* (ordenada), scrum *m*

scrumptious /'skrʌmpʃəs/ *adj* (colloq) ‹*meal*› para chuparse los dedos (fam)

scruple /'skruːpəl/ *n* (*usu pl*) escrúpulo *m*

scrupulous /'skruːpjələs ‖ 'skruːpjʊləs/ *adj* escrupuloso

scrupulously /'skruːpjələsli ‖ 'skruːpjʊləsli/ *adv* escrupulosamente; **~ clean** impecable

scrutinize /'skru:tṇaɪz ‖ 'skru:tɪnaɪz/ *vt* ‹*document*› inspeccionar; ‹*face*› escudriñar

scrutiny /'skru:tṇi ‖ 'skru:tɪni/ *n* [C U] (*pl* **-nies**) examen *m*

scuba diving /'sku:bə/ *n* [U] buceo *m*, submarinismo *m*

scuff /skʌf/ *vt* ‹*floor*› dejar marcas en; ‹*leather*› raspar

scuffle /'skʌfəl/ *n* refriega *f*

scullery /'skʌləri/ *n* (*pl* **-ries**) *habitación anexa a la cocina donde se fregaba, se preparaban las verduras etc*

sculpt /skʌlpt/ *vt/i* esculpir

sculptor /'skʌlptər ‖ 'skʌlptə(r)/ *n* escultor, -tora *m,f*

sculpture¹ /'skʌlptʃər ‖ 'skʌlptʃə(r)/ *n* [C U] escultura *f*

sculpture² *vt* esculpir

scum /skʌm/ *n* [U] **1** (on liquid) capa *f* de suciedad **2** (colloq) (people) escoria *f*; **the ~ of the earth** la escoria de la sociedad

scupper /'skʌpər ‖ 'skʌpə(r)/ *vt* (BrE) ‹*ship*› hundir; ‹*plan/talks*› echar por tierra

scurry /'skɜ:ri ‖ 'skʌri/ *vi*: **he scurried away** *o* **off** salió disparado; **to ~ around** «*mice*» corretear

scuttle¹ /'skʌtl/ *n* (*coal* ~) cubo *m* para el carbón

scuttle² *vt* ‹*ship*› hundir; ‹*plans/talks*› echar por tierra ■ ~ *vi*: **the children ~d away** *o* **off** los niños se escabulleron rápidamente

scythe /saɪð/ *n* guadaña *f*

SD, **S Dak** = **South Dakota**

SE (= **southeast**) SE

sea /si:/ *n* **1** [C] (*often pl*) (ocean) mar *m* [*The noun* MAR *is feminine in literary language and in some set idiomatic expressions*]; **to go/travel by ~** ir*/viajar en barco; (*before n*) ‹*route/transport*› marítimo; ‹*battle*› naval; **the ~ breeze** la brisa del mar; **~ crossing** travesía *f* **2** (large mass, quantity) (*no pl*): **a ~ of faces** una multitud de rostros

sea: **~ anemone** *n* anémona *f or* ortiga *f* de mar; **~bed** *n* **the ~bed** el lecho marino; **~ bird** *n* ave *f*‡ marina; **~food** *n* [U] mariscos *mpl*, marisco *m* (Esp); **~front** *n* paseo *m* marítimo, malecón *m* (AmL), costanera *f* (CS); **~gull** *n* gaviota *f*; **~horse** *n* caballito *m* de mar

seal¹ /si:l/ *n* **1** (implement, impression) sello *m*; **he gave the plan his ~ of approval** dio su aprobación al plan **2 (a)** (security device) precinto *m* **(b)** (airtight closure) cierre *m* hermético; (on glass jar) aro *m* de goma **3** (Zool) foca *f*

seal² *vt* **1 (a)** ‹*envelope/parcel*› cerrar*; (with tape) precintar; (with wax) lacrar; **my lips are ~ed** (set phrase) soy una tumba **(b)** ‹*jar/container*› cerrar* herméticamente; ‹*tomb/door*› precintar; ‹*wood*› sellar **2** (affix seal to) ‹*document/treaty*› sellar **3** (decide, determine) ‹*victory/outcome*› decidir; **their fate was ~ed** su destino estaba escrito

• **seal off** [*v + o + adv, v + adv + o*] ‹*area/road/building*› acordonar; ‹*exit*› cerrar*

sea level *n* nivel *m* del mar

sealing wax /'si:lɪŋ/ *n* [U] lacre *m*

sea lion *n* león *m* marino

seam /si:m/ *n* **1** (stitching) costura *f* **2** (of coal, gold) veta *f*, filón *m*

seaman /'si:mən/ *n* (*pl* **-men** /-mən/) (sailor) marinero *m*; (officer) marino *m*

seamy /'si:mi/ *adj* **-mier, -miest** sórdido

seance /'seɪɑ:ns/ *n* sesión *f* de espiritismo

sear /sɪr ‖ sɪə(r)/ *vt* **(a)** ‹*flesh*› quemar; ‹*meat*› (Culin) *dorar rápidamente a fuego muy vivo* **(b)** (wither) «*heat*» secar*, abrasar

search¹ /sɜ:rtʃ ‖ sɜ:tʃ/ *vt* ‹*building*› registrar, esculcar* (AmL exc CS); ‹*person*› registrar, cachear, catear (Méx); ‹*luggage*› registrar, revisar (AmL), esculcar* (AmL exc CS); ‹*records/files*› buscar* en ■ ~ *vi* buscar*; **to ~ FOR sth/sb** buscar* algo/a algn

search² *n* **(a)** (hunt, quest) **~** (FOR **sth/sb**) búsqueda *f* (DE algo/algn) **(b)** (of building, pockets) registro *m*, esculque *m* (Col, Méx); (of records, documents) inspección *f* **(c)** (Comput) búsqueda *f*

searching /'sɜ:rtʃɪŋ ‖ 'sɜ:tʃɪŋ/ *adj* ‹*look*› inquisitivo; ‹*question*› perspicaz

search: **~light** *n* reflector *m*; **~ party** *n* partida *f* de rescate

sea: **~scape** /'si:skeɪp/ *n* marina *f*; **~shell** *n* concha *f* (de mar); **~shore** *n* [U] orilla *f* del mar; **~sick** *adj* mareado; **~side** *n* [U] costa *f*, playa *f*

season¹ /'si:zn/ *n* **1** (division of year) estación *f* **2** (for specific activity, event, crop) temporada *f* **3** (*in phrases*) **in season** (of female animal) en celo; (of fresh food, game): **cherries are in ~** es época *or* temporada de cerezas; **out of season** fuera de temporada

season² *vt* **1** (Culin) condimentar, sazonar; (with salt and pepper) salpimentar* **2** ‹*wood*› secar*, curar

seasonal /'si:znəl ‖ 'si:zənl/ *adj* ‹*variations/fluctuations*› estacional; ‹*vegetables*› del tiempo; ‹*demand*› de estación

seasoned /'si:zṇd/ *adj* **1** (experienced) ‹*troops/traveler*› avezado, experimentado **2** ‹*food*› condimentado, sazonado **3** ‹*wood*› seco, curado

seasoning /'si:zṇɪŋ/ *n* [U C] (Culin) condimento *m*, sazón *f*

season ticket *n* abono *m* (de temporada)

seat¹ /si:t/ *n* **1** (place to sit) asiento *m*; **please have** *o* **take a ~** tome asiento, por favor (frml), siéntese, por favor; **there aren't any ~s left** (in cinema) no quedan localidades **2** (of chair) asiento *m* **3 (a)** (Govt) escaño *m*, banca *f* (RPl), curul *m* (Col, Méx) **(b)** (constituency) (BrE) distrito *m* electoral **4** (center) sede *f*; **the ~ of government** la sede del gobierno

seat² *vt* **(a)** ‹*child*› sentar*; **to remain ~ed** permanecer* sentado **(b)** (have room for) «*auditorium*» tener* cabida *or* capacidad para

seat belt *n* cinturón *m* de seguridad

seating /'si:tɪŋ/ *n* [U] número *m* de asientos; (*before n*) **~ capacity** aforo *m*

sea: **~ urchin** *n* erizo *m* de mar; **~water** *n* [U] agua *f*‡ de mar, agua *f*‡ salada; **~way** *n* ruta *f* marítima; **~weed** *n* [U] alga *f*‡ marina; **~worthy** *adj* ‹*ship*› en condiciones de navegar

secluded /sɪ'klu:dəd ‖ sɪ'klu:dɪd/ *adj* ‹*house/area*› apartado, aislado; ‹*life/existence*› solitario

seclusion /sɪ'klu:ʒən/ *n* [U] aislamiento *m*

second¹ /'sekənd/ ▶ 540 |, 725 | *adj* **1** segundo; **~ language** segundo idioma *m*; **our service is ~ to none** nuestro servicio es insuperable **2** (elliptical use): **I leave on the ~ (of the month)** me voy el (día) dos

second² *adv* **(a)** (in position, time, order) en segundo lugar **(b)** (secondly) en segundo lugar **(c)** (with superl): **the ~ highest building** el segundo edificio en altura

second³ ▶ 540 |, 725 |, 884 | *n* **1** (of time) segundo *m*; **it doesn't take a ~** no lleva ni un segundo; (*before n*) **~ hand** segundero *m* **2 (a) ~ (gear)** (Auto) (*no art*) segunda *f* **(b)** (in competition): **he finished a good/poor ~** quedó en un honroso/deslucido segundo lugar **3** (substandard product) artículo *m* con defectos de fábrica **4 seconds** *pl* (second helping) (colloq): **to have ~s** repetir*

second⁴ *vt* **1** (support) ‹*motion/candidate*› secundar **2** /sɪ'kɒnd/ (attach) (BrE) **to ~ sb (TO sth)** trasladar a algn temporalmente (A algo)

secondary /'sekənderi ‖ 'sekəndri/ *adj* **1 (a)** (subordinate) ‹*matter*› de interés secundario; ‹*road*› secundario **(b)** (not primary, original) ‹*source*› de segunda mano; ‹*industry*› derivado **2** ‹*teacher/pupils*› de enseñanza secundaria

secondary school *n* instituto *m* *or* colegio *m* de enseñanza secundaria, liceo *m* (CS, Ven)

second: **~ best** *n* [U]: **he won't accept ~ best** sólo se conforma con lo mejor; **~ class** *adv* ‹*travel/go*› en segunda (clase); **~-class** /'sekənd'klæs ‖ ,sekənd'klɑːs/ *adj* (*pred* **~ class**) **(a)** (inferior) ‹*goods/service*› de segunda (clase *or* categoría), de calidad inferior **(b)** (Post): **~-class mail** (in UK) *servicio regular de correos, que tarda más en llegar a destino que el de primera clase* **(c)** (in UK) (Transp) ‹*travel/ticket/compartment*› de segunda (clase)

second-hand¹ /'sekənd'hænd/ *adj* (*pred* **second hand**) ‹*car/clothes*› de segunda mano, usado; ‹*bookstore*› de viejo; ‹*shop*› de artículos de segunda mano; ‹*information*› de segunda mano

second-hand² *adv*: **to buy sth ~** comprar algo de segunda mano

second-in-command /'sekəndɪnkə'mænd ‖ ,sekəndɪnkə'mɑːnd/ *n* (*pl* **seconds-in-command**) número dos *mf* (*persona directamente por debajo de la autoridad máxima de una organización, departamento etc*)

secondly /'sekəndli/ *adv* (*indep*) en segundo lugar

second-rate /'sekənd'reɪt/ *adj* mediocre

secrecy /'siːkrəsi/ *n* [U] secreto *m*

secret¹ /'siːkrət ‖ 'siːkrɪt/ *n* secreto *m*; **in ~** en secreto; **to make no ~ of sth** no esconder algo

secret² *adj* secreto

secretarial /'sekrə'teriəl ‖ ,sekrə'teəriəl/ *adj* ‹*job*› de oficina, de secretaria/secretario; ‹*course*› de secretariado

secretary /'sekrəteri ‖ 'sekrətri/ *n* (*pl* **-ries**) **1** (in office, of committee, of society) secretario, -ria *m,f* **2** (Govt) ministro, -tra *m,f*, secretario, -ria *m,f* (Méx)

Secretary of State *n* (*pl* **Secretaries of State**) (Govt) **(a)** (in US) secretario, -ria *m,f* de Estado (de los Estados Unidos) **(b)** (in UK) ministro, -tra *m,f*, secretario, -ria *m,f* (Méx)

secrete /sɪ'kriːt/ *vt* **1** (Biol, Physiol) segregar*, secretar **2** (hide) (frml) ocultar

secretive /'siːkrətɪv/ *adj* reservado

secret: **~ police** *n* [U] policía *f* secreta; **~ service** *n* (intelligence service) servicio *m* secreto

sect /sekt/ *n* secta *f*

sectarian /sek'teriən ‖ sek'teəriən/ *adj* ‹*views/violence*› sectario; ‹*schooling/school*› confesional

section /'sekʃən/ *n* **1** (of object, newspaper, orchestra) sección *f*; (of machine, piece of furniture) parte *f*; (of road) tramo *m*; (of city, population) sector *m* **2** (department) sección *f* **3** (in geometry, drawing) sección *f*

sector /'sektər ‖ 'sektə(r)/ *n* sector *m*

secular /'sekjələr ‖ 'sekjʊlə(r)/ *adj* ‹*education*› laico; ‹*society/art*› secular

secure¹ /sɪ'kjʊr ‖ sɪ'kjʊə(r)/ *adj* **1 (a)** (safe) ‹*fortress/hideaway*› seguro **(b)** (emotionally) ‹*childhood/home*› estable **(c)** (assured) ‹*job/investment*› seguro **2** ‹*foothold/shelf*› firme; ‹*foundation*› sólido

secure² *vt* **1** (obtain) ‹*job/votes/support*› conseguir* **2** (fasten, fix firmly) ‹*door/shelf*› asegurar

security /sɪ'kjʊrəti ‖ sɪ'kjʊərəti/ *n* (*pl* **-ties**) **1** [U] (against crime, espionage etc) seguridad *f*; (*before n*) **~ guard** guarda jurado, guarda jurada *m,f* **2** [U] **(a)** (safety, certainty) seguridad *f* **(b)** (protection) seguro *m* **3** (Fin) **(a)** [U] (guarantee) garantía *f* **(b) securities** *pl* (Fin) valores *mpl*, títulos *mpl*

Security Council *n* **the (United Nations) ~** el Consejo de Seguridad (de las Naciones Unidas)

sedan /sɪ'dæn/ *n* **1** (car) (AmE) sedán *m* **2 ~ (chair)** palanquín *m*, silla *f* de manos

sedate¹ /sɪ'deɪt/ *adj* reposado, tranquilo

sedate² *vt* (Med) sedar

sedation /sɪ'deɪʃən/ *n* [U] sedación *f*; **to be under ~** estar* bajo el efecto de los sedantes

sedative /'sedətɪv/ *n* sedante *m*

sediment /'sedəmənt ‖ 'sedɪmənt/ *n* [U] **(a)** (in wine, coffee) poso *m*, asiento *m* **(b)** (Geol) sedimento *m*

seduce /sɪ'duːs ‖ sɪ'djuːs/ *vt* seducir*

seduction /sɪ'dʌkʃən/ *n* [U C] seducción *f*

seductive /sɪ'dʌktɪv/ *adj* seductor

see /siː/ (*past* **saw**; *past p* **seen**) *vt* **1** (regard, perceive) ver*; **I can't see a thing!** ¡no veo nada!; **I saw her cross the street** la vi cruzar la calle; **I thought I was ~ing things** pensé que estaba viendo visiones; **~ page 20** ver página 20; **I don't know what she ~s in him** no sé qué es lo que le ve; **anyone can ~ she's upset** cualquiera se da cuenta de que está disgustada; **the way I ~ it, as I ~ it** a mi modo de ver; **can you ~ him as a teacher?** ¿te lo imaginas de profesor?; **I'll ~ what I can do** veré qué puedo hacer; **that remains to be ~n** eso está por verse **2** (understand) ver*; **do you ~ what I mean?** ¿entiendes? **3** (ensure) **to ~ THAT** asegurarse DE QUE; **~ that it doesn't happen again** que no vuelva a suceder **4 (a)** (meet, visit) ver*; **I'm ~ing him on Tuesday** lo voy a ver el martes **(b)** (go out with) (colloq) salir* con **(c)** (saying goodbye) (colloq): **~ you!** ¡hasta luego!, ¡hasta la vista!; **~ you later/soon!** ¡hasta luego/pronto!

5 (a) (consult) ‹*doctor/manager*› ver* **(b)** (receive) ver*, atender*; **the doctor will ~ you now** el doctor lo verá *or* lo atenderá ahora **6** (escort, accompany) acompañar; **to ~ sb to the door** acompañar a algn a la puerta ■ **~** *vi* ver*; **~ for yourself!** ¡compruébalo tú mismo!; **as far as I can ~** por lo que yo veo; **I ~** (expressing realization) ya veo; (accepting explanation) entiendo; **let's ~** vamos a ver, veamos; **will it work? — try it and ~** ¿funcionará? — prueba a ver; ***~ing is believing*** ver para creer

● **see off** [*v + o + adv, v + adv + o*] **1** (say goodbye to) despedir*, despedirse* de **2** (get rid of) deshacerse* de

● **see out** [*v + o + adv, v + adv + o*] ‹*person*› acompañar (hasta la puerta); **I can ~ myself out** no hace falta que me acompañes

● **see through 1** [*v + prep + o*] (not be deceived by) calar **2** [*v + o + adv*] [*v + o + prep + o*] (last): **make sure this ~s you through** con esto te tienes que alcanzar; **$20 should ~ me through the week** con 20 dólares me alcanza hasta el fin de semana **3** [*v + o + adv*] (carry to completion) terminar

● **see to** [*v + prep + o*] (attend to) ocuparse de

seed /siːd/ *n* **1** [C] (of plant) semilla *f*; (of orange, grape) (AmE) pepita *f*, semilla *f*; ***to go to ~*** estar* en decadencia **2** [C] (Sport) cabeza *mf* de serie, sembrado, -da *m,f* (Méx)

seedless /'siːdləs ‖ 'siːdlɪs/ *adj* sin pepitas *or* semillas

seedling /'siːdlɪŋ/ *n* planta *f* de semillero

seedy /'siːdi/ *adj* **-dier, -diest** ‹*nightclub/bar*› sórdido, de mala muerte (fam), cutre (Esp fam); ‹*appearance*› desastrado

seeing /'siːɪŋ/ *conj* (colloq) **~ (that)** *o* **~ as** ya que

seek /siːk/ (*past & past p* **sought**) *vt* **(a)** (search for) (frml) ‹*person/object*› buscar* **(b)** (try to obtain) ‹*work/companionship*› buscar*; ‹*solution/explanation*› tratar de encontrar **(c)** (request) ‹*approval/help*› pedir* **(d)** (try to bring about) (frml) ‹*reconciliation*› buscar*

● **seek out** [*v + o + adv, v + adv + o*] ‹*person*› buscar*; ‹*opinion*› pedir*

seem /siːm/ *vi* parecer*; **strange as it may ~** por raro que parezca; **she ~s to like you** parece que le caes bien; **so it ~s, so it would ~** eso parece, así parece; **I ~ to remember that you** … creo recordar que tú …; **it ~s to me/him/them that** … me/le/les parece que …; **I can't ~ to remember where I put it** no logro acordarme de dónde lo puse

seen /siːn/ *past p of* SEE

seep /siːp/ *vi* «*liquid/moisture*» filtrarse

seesaw /'siːsɔː/ *n* balancín *m*, subibaja *m*

seethe /siːð/ *vi* **(a)** (be agitated) bullir*; **the town was seething with tourists** la ciudad estaba plagada de turistas **(b)** (be angry) estar* furioso; **I was absolutely seething** me hervía la sangre

see-through /'siːθruː/ *adj* transparente

segment /'segmənt/ *n* **(a)** (Math) (of circle, sphere, line) segmento *m* **(b)** (of citrus fruit) gajo *m*; **(c)** (section) sector *m*

segregate /'segrɪgeɪt/ *vt* ‹*races/sexes*› segregar*; ‹*rival groups*› mantener* aparte

segregation /'segrɪ'geɪʃən/ *n* [U] segregación *f*

seize /siːz/ *vt* **1** (grab, snatch) ‹*hand/object*› agarrar; ‹*opportunity*› aprovechar; ‹*power*› tomar **2 (a)** (capture) ‹*town/fortress*› tomar; ‹*person*› detener* **(b)** ‹*assets/property*› (confiscate) confiscar*; (impound) embargar*; ‹*cargo/contraband*› confiscar*; ‹*drugs/arms*› incautar

● **seize on, seize upon** [*v + prep + o*] ‹*chance*› aprovechar

● **seize up** [*v + adv*] «*engine*» agarrotarse, fundirse (AmL); «*muscles*» agarrotarse; «*traffic*» paralizarse*

seizure /'siːʒər ‖ 'siːʒə(r)/ *n* **1** [U C] (of property, contraband) confiscación *f* **2** [C] (Med) ataque *m*

seldom /'seldəm/ *adv* rara vez, pocas veces

select¹ /sɪ'lekt/ *vt* ‹*gift/book/wine*› elegir*, escoger*; ‹*candidate/team member*› seleccionar

select² *adj* **(a)** (exclusive) ‹*school*› de élite; ‹*district*› distinguido **(b)** (choice) ‹*fruit/wine*› selecto **(c)** (especially chosen) ‹*group*› selecto

selection /sɪ'lekʃən/ *n* **1** [U C] (act, thing chosen) selección *f* **2** [U C] (Busn) (of chocolates, buttons, yarns) surtido *m*; **a wide ~ of new and used cars** una amplia gama de coches nuevos y usados

selective /sɪ'lektɪv/ *adj* **(a)** ‹*control/recruitment*› selectivo; ‹*reporting*› parcial **(b)** (discriminating): **he's fairly ~ about who he mixes with** elige *or* escoge mucho sus amistades

self /self/ *n* (*pl* **selves**): **she's her old ~ again** vuelve a ser la de antes; **you're not your usual cheerful ~** no estás tan alegre como de costumbre

self- /'self/ *pref* **(a)** (concerning the self): **~doubt** duda *f* de sí mismo **(b)** (with no outside agency) auto; **~financing** autofinanciado

self: **~-addressed** /'selfə'drest/ *adj*: *con el nombre y la dirección del remitente*; **send a ~-addressed envelope to** … envíe un sobre con su nombre y dirección a …; **~-adhesive** /'selfəd'hiːsɪv/ *adj* autoadhesivo; **~-assured** /'selfə'ʃʊrd ‖ ˌselfə'ʃʊəd, ˌselfə'ʃɔːd/ *adj* seguro de sí mismo; **~-catering** /'self'keɪtərɪŋ/ *adj* (BrE) ‹*accommodation*› equipado con cocina; **~-centered**, (BrE) **~-centred** /'self'sentərd ‖ ˌself'sentəd/ *adj* egocéntrico; **~-confessed** /'selfkən'fest/ *adj* (*before n*) confeso; **~-confidence** /'self'kɑːnfədəns ‖ ˌself'kɒnfɪdəns/ *n* [U] confianza *f* en sí mismo; **~-confident** /'self'kɑːnfədənt ‖ ˌself'kɒnfɪdənt/ *adj* seguro de sí mismo; **~-conscious** /'self'kɑːntʃəs ‖ ˌself'kɒnʃəs/ *adj* **1** (shy, embarrassed) ‹*person/manner*› tímido; **to feel ~-conscious** sentirse* cohibido; **2** (unspontaneous, unnatural) (pej) afectado; **~-contained** /selfkən'teɪnd/ *adj* **(a)** ‹*flat*› (BrE) *con cocina y cuarto de baño propios* **(b)** ‹*person*› independiente; **~-control** /'selfkən'trəʊl/ *n* [U] dominio *m* de sí mismo; **~-defense**, (BrE) **~-defence** /'selfdɪ'fens/ *n* [U] **(a)** (Law): **to act in ~-defense** actuar* en defensa propia **(b)** (fighting technique) defensa *f* personal; **~-destruct** /'selfdɪ'strʌkt/ *vi* autodestruirse*; **~-destructive** /'selfdɪ'strʌktɪv/ *adj* autodestructivo; **~-discipline** /'self'dɪsəplɪn ‖ ˌself'dɪsɪplɪn/ *n* [U] autodisciplina *f*; **~-employed** /'self ɪm'plɔɪd/ *adj* autónomo, por cuenta propia; **~-esteem** /'selfɪ'stiːm/ *n* [U] autoestima *f*; **~-evident** /'self'evədənt ‖ ˌself'evɪdənt/ *adj* ‹*truth*› manifiesto; ‹*conclusion*› evidente; **~-explanatory** /'selfɪk'splænətɔːri ‖ ˌselfɪk'splænətri/ *adj*: **the instructions are ~-explanatory** las instrucciones son muy claras; **~-help** /'self 'help/ *n* [U] autoayuda *f*; **~-image** /'self'ɪmɪdʒ/ *n* imagen *f* de sí mismo; **-important** /'selfɪm'pɔːrtn̩t ‖ ˌselfɪm'pɔːtn̩t/ *adj* engreído, presumido; **~-imposed** /'selfɪm'pəʊzd/ *adj* voluntario, autoimpuesto; **~-indulgent** /'selfɪn'dʌldʒənt/ *adj* demasiado indulgente consigo mismo; **~-interest** /'self'ɪntrəst ‖ ˌself'ɪntrɪst/ *n* [U] interés *m* (personal)

selfish /'selfɪʃ/ *adj* egoísta

selfishly /'selfɪʃli/ *adv* egoístamente

selfishness /'selfɪʃnəs ‖ 'selfɪʃnɪs/ *n* [U] egoísmo *m*

self: **~-made** /'self'meɪd/ *adj* (*before n*) ‹*man/woman*› que ha alcanzado su posición gracias a sus propios esfuerzos; **~-pity** /'self'pɪti/ *n* [U] autocompasión *f*; **~-portrait** /'self'pɔːrtrət ‖ ˌself'pɔːtrɪt/ *n* autorretrato *m*; **~-preservation** /'self 'prezər'veɪʃən ‖ ˌselfprezə'veɪʃən/ *n* [U]: **the instinct of ~-preservation** el instinto de conservación; **~-raising** /'self'reɪzɪŋ/ *adj* (BrE) ⇒ ~-RISING; **~-reliant** /'selfrɪ'laɪənt/ *adj* independiente; **~-respect** /'selfrɪ'spekt/ *n* [U] dignidad *f*, amor *m* propio; **~-respecting** /'selfrɪ 'spektɪŋ/ *adj* (*before n*): **no ~-respecting editor would work for them** ningún editor que se precie trabajaría para ellos; **~-righteous** /'self'raɪtʃəs/ *adj* ‹*person*› con pretensiones de superioridad moral; **~-rising** /'self'raɪzɪŋ/ *adj* (AmE) ‹*flour*› con polvos de hornear (AmL), con levadura (Esp), leudante (RPl); **~same** *adj* (*before n*) mismísimo; **~-satisfied** /'self'sætəsfaɪd ‖ ˌself 'sætɪsfaɪd/ *adj* ufano, satisfecho de sí mismo; ‹*expression/grin*› de (auto)suficiencia; **~-service** /'self'sɜːrvəs ‖ ˌself'sɜːvɪs/, (esp AmE) **self-serve** /-'sɜːrv/ *adj*: **~-service restaurant** autoservicio *m*, self-service *m*; **~-sufficient**/'selfsə'fɪʃənt/ *adj* ‹*person*› independiente; ‹*country*› autosuficiente; **~-taught** /'self'tɔːt/ *adj* autodidacta, autodidacto

sell /sel/ (*past & past p* **sold**) *vt* vender; **to ~ sth TO sb, to ~ sb sth** venderle algo A algn; **to ~ sth FOR sth** vender algo EN *or* POR algo ■ **~** *vi* **(a)** «*person/company*» vender **(b)** (be sold) «*product*» venderse; **to ~ AT/FOR sth** venderse A/POR algo

• **sell off** [*v* + *o* + *adv*, *v* + *adv* + *o*] vender; (cheaply) liquidar

• **sell out 1** [*v* + *adv* + *o*] (sell all of) ‹*stock*› agotar; ‹*article*› agotar las existencias de **2** [*v* + *adv*] **(a)** (sell all stock) «*shop*» **to ~ out** (OF **sth**): **we've** *o* **we're sold out of umbrellas** los paraguas están agotados, se agotaron los paraguas **(b)** (be sold) «*stock/tickets*» agotarse **(c)** (be traitor) «*leader/artist*» venderse

sell-by date /'selbaɪ/ *n* (BrE) fecha *f* límite de venta

seller /'selər ‖ 'selə(r)/ *n* vendedor, -dora *m,f*

selling /'selɪŋ/ *n* [U] ventas *fpl*; (*before n*) **~ price** precio *m* de venta

Sellotape® /'seləteɪp/ *n* [U] (BrE) ⇒ SCOTCH TAPE

sell-out /'selaʊt/ *n* **1** (performance) éxito *m* de taquilla **2** (betrayal) capitulación *f*

selves /selvz/ *pl of* SELF

semaphore /'seməfɔːr ‖ 'seməfɔː(r)/ *n* [U] código *m* de señales

semblance /'sembləns/ *n* [U] (frml) **~ OF sth** apariencia *f* DE algo

semen /'siːmən/ *n* [U] semen *m*

semester /sə'mestər ‖ sɪ'mestə(r)/ *n* (in US) semestre *m* (*lectivo*)

semi- /'semi, 'semaɪ ‖ 'semi/ *pref* semi-

semibreve /'semibriːv/ *n* (BrE) redonda *f*, semibreve *f*

semicircle /'semiˌsɜːrkəl ‖ 'semiˌsɜːkəl/ *n* semicírculo *m*

semicolon /'semi'kəʊlən/ *n* punto y coma *m*

semiconscious /'semi'kɑːntʃəs ‖ ˌsemi'kɒnʃəs/ *adj* semiconsciente

semidetached /'semidɪ'tætʃt/ *adj*: **a ~ house** una casa pareada *or* adosada

semifinal /'semi'faɪnl/ *n* semifinal *f*

seminar /'semənɑːr ‖ 'semɪnɑː(r)/ *n* seminario *m*

semiquaver /'semiˌkweɪvər ‖ 'semiˌkweɪvə(r)/ *n* (BrE) semicorchea *f*

semiskilled /'semi'skɪld/ *adj* semicalificado *or* (Esp) semicualificado

semitone /'semitəʊn/ *n* semitono *m*

semitrailer /'semiˌtreɪlər ‖ 'semiˌtreɪlə(r)/ *n* (AmE) camión *m* con remolque *or* (CS tb) con acoplado, tráiler *m* (Esp), trailer *m* (Méx)

senate /'senət ‖ 'senɪt/ *n* **the Senate** (Govt) el senado *or* Senado

senator /'senətər ‖ 'senətə(r)/ ▶ **603** *n* senador, -dora *m,f*

send /send/ (*past & past p* **sent**) *vt* mandar, enviar*; **to ~ sb to prison** mandar a algn a la cárcel; **the blow sent him reeling** el golpe lo dejó tambaleándose; **she sent everything flying** lo hizo saltar todo por los aires; **to ~ sb to sleep** dormir* a algn

• **send away 1** [*v* + *o* + *adv*, *v* + *adv* + *o*] **(a)** (dismiss) despachar; **don't ~ me away** no me digas que me vaya **(b)** (send elsewhere) mandar, enviar* **2** [*v* + *adv*] ⇒ SEND OFF 3

• **send for** [*v* + *prep* + *o*] **(a)** (ask to come) ‹*doctor/ambulance*› mandar a buscar, mandar llamar (AmL) **(b)** (order) ‹*catalog/application form*› pedir*; ‹*books/tapes/clothes*› encargar*

• **send in** [*v* + *o* + *adv*, *v* + *adv* + *o*] **(a)** ‹*troops*› enviar*, mandar **(b)** (by post) ‹*entry/coupon/application*› mandar, enviar* **(c)** (into room) ‹*person*› hacer* pasar; **~ him in** hágalo pasar

• **send off 1** [*v* + *o* + *adv*, *v* + *adv* + *o*] (dispatch) ‹*letter/parcel/goods*› despachar, mandar; ‹*person*› mandar **2** [*v* + *o* + *adv*, *v* + *adv* + *o*] (BrE Sport) expulsar **3** [*v* + *adv*] **to ~ off FOR sth**: **I sent off for a brochure** escribí pidiendo un folleto, mandé pedir un folleto (AmL)

• **send on** [*v* + *o* + *adv*, *v* + *adv* + *o*] ‹*luggage*› enviar* *or* mandar por adelantado; ‹*mail*› hacer* seguir

• **send out** [*v + o + adv, v + adv + o*] **(a)** (emit) ‹*heat*› despedir*, irradiar; ‹*signal/radio waves*› emitir **(b)** (on errand) mandar **(c)** ‹*invitations*› mandar, enviar*
• **send up** [*v + o + adv, v + adv + o*] **1** (to prison) (AmE) meter preso **2** (satirize) (BrE colloq) parodiar

sender /ˈsendər ‖ ˈsendə(r)/ *n* remitente *mf*

send: **~-off** *n* (colloq) despedida *f*; **~-up** *n* (esp BrE colloq) parodia *f*

Senegal /ˌsenɪˈgɔːl/ *n* (el) Senegal

Senegalese /ˌsenɪgəˈliːz/ *adj* senegalés

senile /ˈsiːnaɪl/ *adj* senil

senile dementia *n* [U] demencia *f* senil

senior¹ /ˈsiːnjər ‖ ˈsiːniə(r)/ *adj* **(a)** (superior in rank): **a ~ officer in the Army** un oficial de alto rango del Ejército; **~ lecturer** (BrE) ≈ profesor adjunto, profesora adjunta *m,f*; **she's ~ to him** es su superior **(b)** (older): **the ~ members of a club** los socios más antiguos de un club; **Robert King, S~** (esp AmE) Robert King, padre *or* sénior

senior² *n* **1 (a)** (older person): **he's five years my ~** me lleva cinco años **(b)** (person of higher rank) superior *m* **(c)** (AmE) ⇒ SENIOR CITIZEN **2** (Educ) estudiante *mf* del último año *or* curso

senior: **~ citizen** *n* persona *f* de la tercera edad; **~ high (school)** *n* (in US) *colegio donde se imparten los tres últimos años de la enseñanza secundaria*

seniority /siːnˈjɔːrəti ‖ ˌsiːniˈɒrəti/ *n* [U] **(a)** (in rank) jerarquía *f* **(b)** (in length of service) antigüedad *f*

sensation /senˈseɪʃən/ *n* **1** [C U] (feeling, impression) sensación *f* **2** [C] **(a)** (furor) sensación *f* **(b)** (success): **to be a ~** «*play/show*» ser* todo un éxito

sensational /senˈseɪʃn̩əl ‖ senˈseɪʃənl/ *adj* **(a)** (causing furor) que causa sensación **(b)** (sensationalist) sensacionalista **(c)** (very good) (colloq) sensacional (fam)

sensationalist /senˈseɪʃənələst ‖ senˈseɪʃənəlɪst/ *adj* sensacionalista

sense¹ /sens/ *n* **1 (a)** [C] (physical faculty) sentido *m*; **the ~ of hearing/smell/taste/touch** el (sentido del) oído/olfato/gusto/tacto **(b) senses** *pl* (rational state): **to come to one's ~s** entrar en razón **2 (a)** (impression) (*no pl*) sensación *f* **(b)** [C U] (awareness) sentido *m*; **~ of direction/humor** sentido de la orientación/del humor; **I lost all ~ of time** perdí completamente la noción del tiempo **3** [U] (*common ~*) sentido *m* común; **she had the (good) ~ to leave her phone number** tuvo la sensatez de dejar su número de teléfono; **I can't make him see ~** no puedo hacerlo entrar en razón **4** [C] **(a)** (meaning) sentido *m*; **in every ~ of the word** en todo sentido **(b)** (aspect, way): **in a ~ they're both correct** en cierto modo ambos tienen razón **5 to make ~ (a)** (be comprehensible) tener* sentido **(b)** (be sensible): **what he said made a lot of ~** lo que dijo era muy razonable; ***to make ~ of sth*** entender* algo

sense² *vt* **(a)** (be aware of) sentir*, notar **(b)** (detect) (Tech) detectar

senseless /ˈsensləs ‖ ˈsenslɪs/ *adj* **1** (pointless) ‹*act/destruction*› sin sentido **2** (unconscious) inconsciente

sensible /ˈsensəbəl/ *adj* ‹*person/approach*› sensato; ‹*decision*› prudente; ‹*clothes/shoes*› cómodo y práctico

sensitive /ˈsensətɪv/ *adj* **1 (a)** (emotionally responsive) ‹*person*› sensible; ‹*performance*› lleno de sensibilidad **(b)** (touchy) ‹*person*› susceptible **2** (physically responsive) ‹*skin/instrument*› sensible **3** (requiring tact) ‹*topic/issue*› delicado

sensor /ˈsensər ‖ ˈsensə(r)/ *n* sensor *m*

sensual /ˈsentʃuəl ‖ ˈsenʃʊəl/ *adj* sensual

sensuous /ˈsentʃuəs ‖ ˈsensjʊəs/ *adj* sensual

sent /sent/ *past & past p of* SEND

sentence¹ /ˈsentn̩s ‖ ˈsentəns/ *n* **1** (Ling) oración *f*, frase *f* **2** (Law) (judgment) sentencia *f*; (punishment) pena *f*; **to pass ~ (on sb)** dictar *or* pronunciar sentencia (contra algn); **a life ~** una condena a cadena perpetua

sentence² *vt* **to ~ sb (TO sth)** condenar *or* sentenciar a algn (A algo)

sentiment /ˈsentɪmənt/ *n* **(a)** [U] (feeling) sentir *m*, sentimiento *m* **(b)** [C] (view) opinión *f*; **my ~s exactly** *o* **entirely** estoy totalmente de acuerdo

sentimental /ˌsentɪˈmentl̩/ *adj* sentimental

sentry /ˈsentri/ *n* (*pl* **-tries**) centinela *m*

Seoul /səʊl/ *n* Seúl *m*

separate¹ /ˈsepərət/ *adj* **(a)** (individual) separado **(b)** (physically apart) aparte *adj inv*; **~ FROM sth** separado DE algo **(c)** (distinct, different): **it has three ~ meanings** tiene tres significados distintos; **answer each question on a ~ sheet of paper** conteste cada pregunta en una hoja aparte

separate² /ˈsepəreɪt/ *vt* **(a)** (set apart) separar **(b)** (distinguish) distinguir*; **to ~ sth FROM sth** distinguir* algo DE algo ■ **~** *vi* separarse

separately /ˈseprətli, ˈsepərətli/ *adv* **(a)** (apart) por separado **(b)** (individually) separadamente

separation /ˌsepəˈreɪʃən/ *n* [C U] separación *f*

September /sepˈtembər ‖ sepˈtembə(r)/ **▶ 540** *n* septiembre *m*, setiembre *m*

septic /ˈseptɪk/ *adj* séptico; **to go ~** infectarse

sequel /ˈsiːkwəl/ *n* **(a)** (Cin, Lit, TV) continuación *f* **(b)** (later events) secuela *f*

sequence /ˈsiːkwəns/ *n* **1** (order): **the police established the ~ of events** la policía estableció cómo se sucedieron los hechos; **it's better to look at the pictures in ~** es mejor ver las fotos en *or* por orden **2 (a)** (series) serie *f* **(b)** (Math, Mus) secuencia *f* **3** (Cin, TV) secuencia *f*

sequin /ˈsiːkwən ‖ ˈsiːkwɪn/ *n* lentejuela *f*

Serb /sɜːrb ‖ sɜːb/ *adj/n* ⇒ SERBIAN[1,2]

Serbia /ˈsɜːrbiə ‖ ˈsɜːbiə/ *n* Serbia *f*, Servia *f*

Serbian¹ /ˈsɜːrbiən ‖ ˈsɜːbiən/ *adj* serbio, servio

Serbian² *n* serbio, -bia *m,f*, servio, -via *m,f*

Serbo-Croat /ˈsɜːrbəʊˈkrəʊæt ‖ ˌsɜːbəʊˈkrəʊæt/ *n* [U] serbocroata *m*

serenade¹ /ˌserəˈneɪd/ *n* serenata *f*

serenade² *vt* darle* (una) serenata a

serene /səˈriːn ‖ sɪˈriːn/ *adj* sereno

sergeant /ˈsɑːrdʒənt ‖ ˈsɑːdʒənt/ *n* sargento *mf*

sergeant major *n* ≈ brigada *mf*

serial /'sɪriəl ‖ 'sɪəriəl/ *n* **(a)** (Rad, TV) serie *f*, serial *m or* (CS) serial *f* **(b)** (Publ): **it was published as a ~** se publicó por entregas

serialize /'sɪriəlaɪz ‖ 'sɪəriəlaɪz/ *vt* serializar*

serial: **~ killer** *n* asesino, -na *m,f* en serie; **~ number** *n* número *m* de serie

series /'sɪri:z ‖ 'sɪəri:z/ *n* (*pl* **~**) **(a)** (succession) serie *f* **(b)** (TV, Rad) serie *f*, serial *m or* (CS) *f*

serious /'sɪriəs ‖ 'sɪəriəs/ *adj* **1 (a)** (in earnest, sincere) serio; **I'm ~** lo digo en serio **(b)** (committed) (*before n*) ‹*student/worker*› dedicado **(c)** (not lightweight) (*before n*) ‹*newspaper/play/music*› serio **2** (grave) ‹*injury/illness*› grave; **I have ~ doubts about him** tengo mis serias dudas acerca de él

seriously /'sɪriəsli ‖ 'sɪəriəsli/ *adv* **1 (a)** (not frivolously) seriamente; **to take sth/sb ~** tomar(se) algo/a algn en serio **(b)** (genuinely, sincerely): **you can't ~ mean that** no lo puedes estar diciendo en serio **2** (gravely) ‹*ill/injured*› gravemente

seriousness /'sɪriəsnəs ‖ 'sɪəriəsnɪs/ *n* [U] seriedad *f*; **he said it in all ~** lo dijo muy en serio

sermon /'sɜ:rmən ‖ 'sɜ:mən/ *n* sermón *m*

serpent /'sɜ:rpənt ‖ 'sɜ:pənt/ *n* (liter) sierpe *f* (liter)

serrated /'səreɪtəd ‖ sə'reɪtɪd/ *adj* ‹*edge/knife*› serrado

serum /'sɪrəm ‖ 'sɪərəm/ *n* [U C] suero *m*

servant /'sɜ:rvənt ‖ 'sɜ:vənt/ *n* criado, -da *m,f*, sirviente, -ta *m,f*

serve¹ /sɜ:rv ‖ sɜ:v/ *vt* **1** (work for) ‹*God/country*› servir* a **2** (help, be useful to) servir*; **it ~s no useful purpose** no sirve para nada (útil); ***to ~ sb right*** (colloq): **it ~s her right!** ¡se lo merece!, ¡le está bien empleado! (Esp) **3 (a)** (Culin) ‹*food/drink*› servir* **(b)** (in shop) (BrE) atender* **4** (Law) ‹*summons/notice/order*› entregar* **5** (complete) ‹*apprenticeship*› hacer*; ‹*sentence*› cumplir ■ **~** *vi* **1 (a)** (be servant) (liter) servir* **(b)** (in shop) (BrE) atender* **(c)** (distribute food) servir* **2** (spend time, do duty): **to ~ in the army** servir* en el ejército **3** (have effect, function) **to ~ to** + INF servir* PARA + INF **4** (Sport) sacar*, servir*

serve² *n* servicio *m*, saque *m*

server /'sɜ:rvər ‖ 'sɜ:və(r)/ *n* **1** (Sport) *jugador que tiene el saque* **2** (Comput) servidor *m*

service¹ /'sɜ:rvəs ‖ 'sɜ:vɪs/ *n* **1** [U] **(a)** (duty, work) servicio *m* **(b)** given by a tool, machine): **you'll get years of ~ from this iron** esta plancha le durará años **2** [U C] (of professional, tradesman, company) servicio *m*; **we no longer require your ~s** ya no precisamos sus servicios **3** [C U] (assistance) servicio *m*; **she has done us all a ~** nos ha hecho a todos un favor *or* servicio; **how can I be of ~ to you?** ¿en qué puedo ayudarlo *or* servirlo? **4** [C] (organization, system) servicio *m*; **telephone/postal ~** servicio telefónico/postal **5** (Mil): **the ~s** las fuerzas armadas **6** [U] (in shop, restaurant) servicio *m* **7** [C U] (overhaul, maintenance) revisión *f*, servicio *m* (AmL), service *m* (RPl) **8** [C] (Relig) oficio *m* religioso **9** [C] (in tennis) servicio *m*, saque *m* **10** [C] (*dinner ~*) vajilla *f*

service² *vt* ‹*car*› hacerle* una revisión *or* (AmL) un servicio a; ‹*machine/appliance*› hacerle* el mantenimiento a

service: **~ charge** *n* **(a)** (in restaurant) servicio *m* **(b)** (for maintenance — of apartment) gastos *mpl* comunes *or* (Esp) de comunidad; (— of office) gastos *mpl* de mantenimiento; **~ industry** *n* sector *m* (de) servicios; **~man** /'sɜ:rvəsmən ‖ 'sɜ:vɪsmən/ *n* (*pl* **-men** /-mən/) militar *m*, soldado *m*; **~ station** *n* estación *f* de servicio

serviette /'sɜ:rvi'et ‖ ˌsɜ:vi'et/ *n* (BrE) servilleta *f*

serving /'sɜ:rvɪŋ ‖ 'sɜ:vɪŋ/ *n* porción *f*, ración *f*; (*before n*) **~ dish** fuente *f*; **~ spoon** cuchara *f* de servir

session /'seʃən/ *n* **1** (Adm, Govt, Law) **(a)** (single meeting) sesión *f*; **to be in ~** estar* en sesión, estar* sesionando (esp AmL) **(b)** sesión *f* **2** (period of time) sesión *f*; **a recording ~** una sesión de grabación

set¹ /set/ *n* **1** (of tools, golf clubs, pens, keys) juego *m*; (of books, records) colección *f*; (of stamps) serie *f*; **a matching ~ of sheets and pillowcases** un juego de cama **2** (TV) aparato *m*, televisor *m*; (Rad) aparato *m*, receptor *m* **3** (in tennis, squash) set *m* **4 (a)** (Theat) (stage) escenario *m*; (scenery) decorado *m* **(b)** (Cin) plató *m* **5** (in hairdressing) marcado *m*

set² *adj* **1** (established, prescribed) ‹*wage/price*› fijo; **there are no ~ times for visiting** no hay horas de visita establecidas; **a ~ phrase** una frase hecha; **we ordered the ~ menu** (BrE) pedimos el menú del día **2** (*pred*) **(a)** (ready, prepared): **to be ~** estar* listo, estar* pronto (RPl) **(b)** (likely, about to) (journ) **to be ~ to** + INF llevar camino de + INF **(c)** (determined, resolute): **she's absolutely ~ on that bicycle** está empeñada en que tiene que ser esa bicicleta; **he's dead ~ on going to college** está resuelto a ir a la universidad sea como sea **3** (rigid, inflexible): **to be ~ in one's ways** tener* costumbres muy arraigadas

set³ (*pres p* **setting**; *past & past p* **set**) *vt* **1** (put, place) poner*, colocar* **2** (cause to be, become): **to ~ sb free** poner* en libertad a algn; **to ~ fire to sth, to ~ sth on fire** prenderle fuego a algo **3 (a)** (prepare) ‹*trap*› tender*; ‹*table*› poner* **(b)** (Med) ‹*bone*› encajar, componer* (AmL) **(c)** ‹*hair*› marcar* **4** (adjust) ‹*oven/alarm clock/watch*› poner* **5 (a)** (arrange, agree on) ‹*date/time*› fijar **(b)** (impose, prescribe) ‹*target*› establecer* **(c)** (allot) ‹*task*› asignar; ‹*homework*› mandar; ‹*exam/test/problem*› poner*; ‹*text*› prescribir* **(d)** (establish) ‹*precedent*› sentar*; ‹*record/standard*› establecer*; **to ~ a good example** dar* buen ejemplo **6** (cause to do, start): **she ~ them to work in the garden** los puso a trabajar en el jardín; **to ~ sth going** poner* algo en marcha **7** (*usu pass*) ‹*book/film*› ambientar; **the novel is ~ in Japan** la novela está ambientada en el Japón **8** (mount, insert) ‹*gem*› engarzar*, engastar; ‹*stake*› hincar*, clavar; **the posts are ~ in concrete** los postes están puestos en hormigón ■ **~** *vi* **1** (go down) «*sun/moon*» ponerse* **2 (a)** (become solid, rigid) «*jelly*» cuajar(se); «*cement*» fraguar* **(b)** «*bone*» soldarse*

• **set about** [*v* + *prep* + *o*] **(a)** ‹*task*› (begin) emprender; (tackle) acometer **(b) to ~ about** -ING ponerse* a + INF **(c)** (attack) atacar*

• **set apart** [*v* + *o* + *adv*] distinguir*

• **set aside** [*v* + *o* + *adv*, *v* + *adv* + *o*] **(a)** (save, reserve) ‹*food/goods*› guardar, apartar; ‹*time*› dejar;

‹*money*› guardar, ahorrar **(b)** (put to one side, shelve) ‹*book/project*› dejar (de lado) **(c)** (disregard) ‹*hostility*› dejar de lado; ‹*rules/formality*› prescindir de
● **set back** [*v + o + adv, v + adv + o*] ‹*progress*› retrasar, atrasar; ‹*clock*› atrasar
● **set in** [*v + adv*] «*infection*» declararse
● **set off 1** [*v + adv*] (begin journey) salir* **2** [*v + o + adv, v + adv + o*] **(a)** (activate) ‹*bomb/mine*› hacer* explotar; ‹*alarm*› hacer* sonar; ‹*firework*› lanzar*, tirar **(b)** (enhance) hacer* resaltar
● **set out 1** [*v + adv*] **(a)** (begin journey) salir* **(b)** (begin, intend): **I didn't ~ out with that intention** no empecé con esa intención; **she had failed in what she had ~ out to achieve** no había logrado lo que se había propuesto **2** [*v + o + adv, v + adv + o*] **(a)** ‹*argument/theory*› exponer* **(b)** ‹*goods*› exponer*; ‹*chess pieces*› colocar*
● **set to** [*v + adv*] ponerse* a trabajar
● **set up** [*v + o + adv, v + adv + o*] **1 (a)** (erect, assemble) ‹*monument*› levantar; ‹*machine/tent*› montar, armar; **they ~ up camp near the river** acamparon cerca del río **(b)** (arrange, plan) ‹*meeting*› convocar* a **2** (institute, found) ‹*committee/commission*› crear; ‹*inquiry*› abrir*; ‹*business*› montar **3** (establish): **she ~ herself up as a photographer** se estableció como fotógrafa **4** (colloq) **(a)** (frame) tenderle* una trampa a **(b)** (rig) arreglar

set: **~back** *n* revés *m*; **~ square** *n* escuadra *f*; (with two equal sides) cartabón *m*

settee /se'tiː/ *n* sofá *m*

setting /'setɪŋ/ *n* **1** (of dial, switch) posición *f* **2 (a)** (of novel, movie) escenario *m* **(b)** (surroundings) marco *m*, entorno *m* **(c)** (for gem) engarce *m*, engaste *m*, montura *f* **3** (*place* ~) cubierto *m*

settle /'setl̩/ *vt* **1 (a)** ‹*price/terms/time*› acordar*; **it's all been ~d, we're going to Miami** ya está (todo) decidido, nos vamos a Miami; **that ~s it: I never want to see him again** ya no me cabe duda: no lo quiero volver a ver **(b)** (resolve) ‹*dispute/differences*› resolver* **2** ‹*bill/account*› pagar*; ‹*debt*› saldar, liquidar **3** ‹*country/region*› colonizar* **4** (make comfortable) ‹*patient/child*› poner* cómodo **5** (make calm) ‹*child*› calmar; ‹*doubts*› disipar; ‹*stomach*› asentar* ■ ~ *vi* **1** (come to live) establecerse* **2** (become calm) «*person*» tranquilizarse* **3 (a)** (make oneself comfortable) ponerse* cómodo **(b)** «*bird*» posarse **4 (a)** «*dust*» asentarse*; «*snow*» cuajar **(b)** (sink) «*soil/foundations*» asentarse*; «*sediment*» depositarse **5 (a)** (pay) saldar la cuenta (*or* la deuda *etc*) **(b)** (Law): **to ~ out of court** resolver* una disputa extrajudicialmente
● **settle down 1** [*v + adv*] **(a)** (become calm): **things have ~ down now** las cosas ya se han apaciguado; **~ down please, children** niños, por favor, tranquilos **(b)** (get comfortable): **we ~d down for the night** nos acomodamos para pasar la noche **(c)** (in place, activity): **she's settling down well in her new school** se está adaptando bien a su nueva escuela; **you should get a job and ~ down** deberías conseguirte un trabajo y establecerte *or* echar raíces en algún sitio **(d)** (become more responsible) sentar* (la) cabeza **2** [*v + o + adv*] (make calm) calmar, tranquilizar*
● **settle for** [*v + prep + o*] conformarse con
● **settle in** [*v + adv*]: **I'll come and see you when you've ~d in** te vendré a ver cuando estés instalado; **she's settling in well in her new job** se está adaptando bien a su nuevo trabajo
● **settle into** [*v + prep + o*] ‹*school/job*› adaptarse a; ‹*routine*› acostumbrarse a
● **settle on** [*v + prep + o*] ‹*date/place*› decidirse por
● **settle up** [*v + adv*] (colloq) arreglar (las) cuentas

settled /'setld/ *adj* **(a)** (established) ‹*habits/life*› ordenado; ‹*order*› estable **(b)** ‹*weather*› estable

settlement /'setlmənt/ *n* **1** [C] (agreement) acuerdo *m*, convenio *m*; **wage ~** (agreement) convenio *m* (laboral), acuerdo *m* salarial; (increase) aumento *m* (salarial) **2 (a)** [U] (of account, bill) pago *m*; (of debt) liquidación *f*, satisfacción *f* **(b)** [C] (payment) pago *m* **3** [U] (of dispute) resolución *f* **4** [C] (village) asentamiento *m*

settler /'setlər ‖ 'setlə(r)/ *n* colono, -na *m,f*

set-up /'setʌp/ *n* (colloq) (situation, arrangement) sistema *f*; (pej) tinglado *m* (fam & pey)

seven /'sevən/ **▶451**, **724**, **884** *adj/n* siete *adj inv/m*; *see also* FOUR[1]

sevenfold /'sevənfəʊld/ *adj/adv see* -FOLD

seventeen /'sevən'tiːn/ **▶451**, **724**, **884** *adj/n* diecisiete *adj inv/m*; *see also* FOUR[1]

seventeenth[1] /'sevən'tiːnθ/ **▶540**, **725** *adj* decimoséptimo

seventeenth[2] *adv* en decimoséptimo lugar

seventeenth[3] **▶540**, **543**, **725** *n* (Math) diecisieteavo *m*; (part) diecisieteava parte *f*

seventh[1] /'sevənθ/ **▶540**, **725** *adj* séptimo

seventh[2] *adv* en séptimo lugar

seventh[3] **▶540**, **543**, **725** *n* (Math) séptimo *m*; (part) séptima parte *f*

seventieth[1] /'sevəntiəθ/ **▶725** *adj* septuagésimo

seventieth[2] *adv* en septuagésimo lugar

seventieth[3] **▶543**, **725** *n* (Math) setentavo *m*; (part) setentava *or* septuagésima parte *f*

seventy /'sevənti/ **▶451**, **540**, **724** *adj/n* setenta *adj inv/m*; *see also* FOUR[1]

sever /'sevər ‖ 'sevə(r)/ *vt* **(a)** (cut) ‹*rope/chain*› cortar; **the saw ~ed his finger** la sierra le cortó *or* le amputó el dedo **(b)** (break off) ‹*communications*› cortar; ‹*relations*› romper*

several[1] /'sevrəl/ *adj* varios, -rias

several[2] *pron* varios, varias

severance /'sevərəns/ *n* [U] **(a)** (of relations, links) ruptura *f* **(b)** (Lab Rel) cese *m*; (*before n*) **~ pay** indemnización *f* por cese

severe /sə'vɪr ‖ sɪ'vɪə(r)/ *adj* **severer, severest** **1 (a)** (strict, harsh) ‹*punishment/judge*› severo; ‹*discipline*› riguroso **(b)** (austere) ‹*style/colors*› austero **2 (a)** (serious, bad) ‹*illness/injury*› grave; ‹*pain*› fuerte; ‹*winter*› severo; ‹*weather conditions*› muy malo **(b)** (difficult, rigorous) ‹*conditions*› estricto

severely /sə'vɪrli ‖ sɪ'vɪəli/ *adv* con severidad, severamente

severity /sə'verəti ‖ sɪ'verəti/ *n* [U] severidad *f*; (of illness, injury) gravedad *f*; (of pain) intensidad *f*

sew /səʊ/ (*past* **sewed**; *past p* **sewn** *or* **sewed**) *vt* coser; ‹*seam/hem*› hacer*; **to ~ sth on** coser algo ■ ~ *vi* coser

• **sew up** [*v + o + adv, v + adv + o*] coser

sewage /'suːɪdʒ ‖ 'suːɪdʒ, 'sjuːɪdʒ/ *n* [U] aguas *fpl* negras *or* residuales, aguas *fpl* servidas (CS)

sewer /'suːər ‖ 'suːə(r), 'sjuːə(r)/ *n* **(a)** (underground) alcantarilla *f*, cloaca *f* **(b)** (drain) (AmE) boca *f* de (la) alcantarilla, sumidero *m*

sewing /'səʊɪŋ/ *n* [U] costura *f*

sewing machine *n* máquina *f* de coser

sewn /səʊn/ *past p of* SEW

sex /seks/ *n* **1** [U] **(a)** (sexual matters) sexo *m*; (*before n*) **~ education** educación *f* sexual; **~ symbol** sex symbol *mf* **(b)** (intercourse) relaciones *fpl* sexuales **2 (a)** [C U] (gender) sexo *m* **(b)** [C] (men, women collectively) sexo *m*; (*before n*) **~ discrimination** discriminación *f* sexual

sexism /'seksɪzəm/ *n* [U] sexismo *m*

sexist¹ /'seksəst ‖ 'seksɪst/ *n* sexista *mf*

sexist² *adj* sexista

sextet /seks'tet/ *n* sexteto *m*

sexual /'sekʃuəl/ *adj* sexual

sexuality /'sekʃu'æləti/ *n* [U] sexualidad *f*

sexually /'sekʃuəli/ *adv* sexualmente; **a ~ transmitted disease** una enfermedad de transmisión sexual

sexy /'seksi/ *adj* **sexier, sexiest (a)** (sexually attractive) sexy **(b)** (erotic) ‹*book/film/talk*› erótico

sh /ʃ/ *interj* ¡sh!

shabby /'ʃæbi/ *adj* **-bier, -biest (a)** ‹*carpet/sofa/jacket*› gastado; (threadbare) raído **(b)** (bad, unfair): **what a ~ way to treat him** qué manera más fea de tratarlo

shack /ʃæk/ *n* choza *f*, casucha *f*, rancho *m* (AmL), jacal *m* (Méx), bohío *m* (AmC, Col)

shackles /'ʃækəlz/ *pl n* grilletes *mpl*

shade¹ /ʃeɪd/ *n* **1** [U] (dark place) sombra *f*; **in the ~** a la sombra **2** [C] (over window) (AmE) persiana *f*, estor *m* (Esp) **3 (a)** [C] (of color) tono *m* **(b)** [C] (degree of difference, nuance) matiz *m*

shade² *vt* ‹*eyes/face*› proteger* del sol/de la luz; **her seat was ~d from the sun** su asiento estaba resguardado del sol

shadow¹ /'ʃædəʊ/ *n* [C U] sombra *f*; **she was a ~ of her former self** no era ni sombra de lo que había sido; **without a ~ of (a) doubt** sin la más mínima duda

shadow² *vt* seguir* de cerca a

shadowy /'ʃædəʊi/ *adj* **(a)** (indistinct) ‹*form*› impreciso **(b)** (full of shadows) ‹*place/forest*› oscuro

shady /'ʃeɪdi/ *adj* **-dier, -diest (a)** (giving shade) ‹*place/garden*› sombreado; ‹*tree*› que da mucha sombra **(b)** (disreputable) (colloq) ‹*deal/business*› turbio; ‹*character*› sospechoso

shaft /ʃæft ‖ʃɑːft/ *n* **1 (a)** (of arrow, spear) asta *f*‡, astil *m*; (of hammer, ax) mango *m* **(b)** (of light) rayo *m* **2** (Mech Eng) eje *m* **3** (of elevator) hueco *m*; (of mine) pozo *m*, tiro *m*

shaggy /'ʃægi/ *adj* **-gier, -giest** ‹*dog*› lanudo, peludo; ‹*beard/hair*› enmarañado, greñudo

shake¹ /ʃeɪk/ (*past* **shook**; *past p* **shaken**) *vt* **1 (a)** (cause to move, agitate) ‹*bottle/cocktail*› agitar; ‹*person/building*› sacudir; ‹*dice*› agitar, revolver* (AmL); **she shook the sand out of the towel** sacudió la toalla para quitarle la arena; **to ~ hands with sb, to ~ sb's hand** darle* *or* estrecharle la mano a algn; **they shook hands** se dieron la mano; **to ~ one's head** negar* con la cabeza; (meaning yes) (AmE) asentir* con la cabeza **(b)** (brandish) ‹*sword/stick*› agitar; **to ~ one's fist at sb** amenazar* a algn con el puño **2 (a)** (undermine, impair) ‹*courage/nerve*› hacer* flaquear; ‹*faith*› debilitar **(b)** (shock, surprise) ‹*person*› impresionar ■ ~ *vi* **1** (move, tremble) «*earth/hand/voice*» temblar*; **he was shaking with fear/cold/rage** estaba temblando de miedo/frío/rabia **2** (shake hands) (colloq): **they shook on it** sellaron el acuerdo con un apretón de manos

• **shake off** [*v + o + adv, v + adv + o*] ‹*pursuer/reporter*› deshacerse* de; ‹*habit*› quitarse; ‹*cold*› quitarse de encima

• **shake up** [*v + o + adv, v + adv + o*] **1** ‹*liquid*› agitar **2** (colloq) ‹*industry/personnel*› reorganizar* totalmente **3** (disturb, shock) (colloq): **he's a bit ~n up** está un poco alterado

shake² *n* **1** (act) sacudida *f*; (violent) sacudida *m* violenta, sacudón *m* (AmL); **he replied with a ~ of the head** contestó negando con la cabeza **2** (*milk* ~) (AmE) batido *m*, (leche *f*) malteada *f* (AmL), licuado *m* con leche (AmL)

shaken /'ʃeɪkən/ *past p of* SHAKE¹

shaker /'ʃeɪkər ‖ 'ʃeɪkə(r)/ *n* **(a)** (for cocktails) coctelera *f* **(b)** (for salt) salero *m*; (for pepper) pimentero *m*; (for sugar) azucarero *m* **(c)** (for dice) cubilete *m*, cacho *m* (Andes)

shaky /'ʃeɪki/ *adj* **-kier, -kiest (a)** (trembling) ‹*hands/voice*› tembloroso; ‹*writing*› de trazo poco firme **(b)** (unsteady) ‹*table*› poco firme; ‹*structure*› tambaleante; ‹*health*› delicado; ‹*currency/government*› débil; ‹*theory/start*› flojo

shale /ʃeɪl/ *n* [U] esquisto *m*, pizarra *f*

shall /ʃæl, *weak forms* ʃl, ʃəl/ *v mod* (*past* **should**) **1** (*with 1st person*) **(a)** (in statements about the future): **I ~ be very interested to see what happens** tendré mucho interés en ver qué sucede; **we shan't be able to come** (BrE) no podremos venir **(b)** (making suggestions, asking for assent) [*The present tense is used in this type of question in Spanish*] **~ I open the window?** ¿abro la ventana?; **~ we go out tonight?** ¿qué te (*or* le *etc*) parece si salimos esta noche? **2** (*with 2nd and 3rd persons*) (in commands, promises etc): **they ~ not pass** no pasarán

shallot /ʃə'lɑːt ‖ ʃə'lɒt/ *n* chalote *m*, chalota *f*

shallow /'ʃæləʊ/ *adj* **-er, -est (a)** (not deep) ‹*water/pond/river*› poco profundo; ‹*dish*› llano, plano; ‹*breathing*› superficial **(b)** (superficial) ‹*person*› superficial

shallows /'ʃæləʊz/ *pl n* bajío *m*

sham¹ /ʃæm/ *n* [C U] farsa *f*

sham² *adj* (pej) (*no comp*) fingido

sham³ *vt/i* **-mm-** fingir*

shambles /'ʃæmbəlz/ *n* (*+ sing vb*) caos *m*, desquicio *m* (RPl); (fiasco) desastre *m*

shame¹ /ʃeɪm/ *n* **1** [U] (feeling) vergüenza *f*, pena *f* (AmL exc CS); **~ on you!** ¡qué vergüenza!; ***to put sb to ~***: **she's such a good hostess, she puts me to ~** es tan buena anfitriona que me hace sentir culpable **2** (pity) (*no pl*) lástima *f*, pena *f*; **what a ~!** ¡qué lástima!; **it's a ~ you can't go** es una pena que no puedas ir

shame² *vt* avergonzar*, apenar (AmL exc CS); **they ~d us into paying** nos hicieron avergonzarnos de tal manera que al final pagamos

shamefaced /'ʃeɪm'feɪst/ *adj* avergonzado

shameful /'ʃeɪmfəl/ *adj* vergonzoso

shameless /'ʃeɪmləs ‖ 'ʃeɪmlɪs/ *adj* ‹*lie/exploitation*› descarado; ‹*liar/cheat*› desvergonzado

shampoo¹ /ʃæm'puː/ *n* (*pl* **-poos**) champú *m*

shampoo² *vt* **-poos, -pooing, -pooed** ‹*hair*› lavar; ‹*carpet/upholstery*› limpiar

shan't /ʃænt ‖ ʃɑːnt/ = **shall not**

shantytown /'ʃænti͵taʊn/ *n* barriada *f* (AmL), chabolas *fpl* (Esp), población *f* callampa (Chi), villa *f* miseria (Arg), ciudad *f* perdida (Méx), cantegril *m* (Ur), ranchos *mpl* (Ven)

shape¹ /ʃeɪp/ *n* **1 (a)** [C] (visible form) forma *f*; **it is triangular in ~** tiene forma triangular; **in the ~ of a cross** en forma de cruz; **to take ~** tomar forma **(b)** [U] (general nature, outline) conformación *f*; **the ~ of things to come** lo que nos espera **2** [U] (guise): **assistance in the ~ of food stamps** ayuda consistente en vales canjeables por comida; **I won't tolerate bribery in any ~ or form** no pienso tolerar sobornos de ningún tipo **3** [U] (condition, order): **she's in pretty good/bad ~** está bastante bien/mal (de salud); **to keep in ~** mantenerse* en forma

shape² *vt* **(a)** ‹*object/material*› darle* forma a **(b)** (influence) ‹*events*› determinar; ‹*character/ideas*› formar ■ **~** *vi* «*project*» tomar forma; «*plan*» desarrollarse

• **shape up** [*v* + *adv*] **(a)** ⇒ SHAPE² *vi* **(b)** (improve, pull oneself together) entrar en vereda (fam)

-shaped /ʃeɪpt/ *suff*: **L~/heart~** con *or* en forma de L/corazón

shapeless /'ʃeɪpləs ‖ 'ʃeɪplɪs/ *adj* informe, sin forma

shapely /'ʃeɪpli/ *adj* **-lier, -liest** ‹*figure*› bien modulado, hermoso; ‹*legs*› torneado

share¹ /ʃer ‖ ʃeə(r)/ *n* **1** (portion) parte *f*; **she must take her ~ of the blame** debe aceptar que tiene parte de la culpa **2** (Busn, Fin) **(a)** (held by partner) (*no pl*) participación *f* **(b)** (held by shareholder) acción *f*

share² *vt* **1 (a)** (use jointly) **to ~ sth (WITH sb)** compartir algo (CON algn) **(b)** (have in common) ‹*interest/opinion*› compartir; ‹*characteristics*› tener* en común **2 (a)** (divide) dividir **(b)** (communicate) ‹*experience/knowledge*› intercambiar ■ **~** *vi* **(a)** (use jointly) compartir; **to ~ and ~ alike** compartir las cosas **(b)** (have a part) **to ~ IN sth** compartir algo, participar DE algo

• **share out** [*v* + *o* + *adv*, *v* + *adv* + *o*] repartir, distribuir*

shareholder /'ʃerhəʊldər ‖ 'ʃeəhəʊldə(r)/ *n* accionista *mf*

shark /ʃɑːrk ‖ ʃɑːk/ *n* (Zool) tiburón *m*

sharp¹ /ʃɑːrp ‖ ʃɑːp/ *adj* **-er, -est** **1 (a)** ‹*knife/edge/scissors*› afilado, filoso (AmL), filudo (Chi, Per); ‹*features*› anguloso; ‹*pencil*› con punta; **it has a ~ point** es muy puntiagudo **(b)** ‹*pain*› agudo **(c)** ‹*wind*› cortante; ‹*frost*› crudo, fuerte **(d)** ‹*taste*› ácido **2 (a)** (abrupt, steep) ‹*bend/angle*› cerrado; ‹*turn*› brusco; ‹*rise/fall*› brusco **(b)** (sudden) repentino, súbito **3 (a)** (keen) ‹*eyesight*› agudo; ‹*hearing*› fino, agudo **(b)** (acute) ‹*wit/mind*› agudo **4** (clear, unblurred) ‹*photo/TV picture*› nítido, ‹*outline*› definido; ‹*contrast*› marcado **5** (harsh) ‹*retort*› cortante; **to have a ~ tongue** ser* muy mordaz*, tener* una lengua muy afilada **6** (clever, shrewd) ‹*person*› listo, astuto; ‹*move*› astuto **7** (Mus) (referring to key) sostenido; **C ~** do *m* sostenido

sharp² *adv* **1** (exactly): **at six o'clock ~** a las seis en punto **2** (abruptly): **turn ~ right** gire a la derecha en curva cerrada **3** (Mus) ‹*play*› demasiado alto

sharp³ *n* (Mus) sostenido *m*

sharpen /'ʃɑːrpən ‖ 'ʃɑːpən/ *vt* ‹*knife/claws*› afilar; ‹*pencil*› sacarle* punta a

sharpener /'ʃɑːrpn̩ər ‖ 'ʃɑːpn̩ə(r)/ *n* (*knife ~*) afilador *m*; (*pencil ~*) sacapuntas *m*

sharply /'ʃɑːrpli ‖ 'ʃɑːpli/ *adv* **1 (a)** (steeply, abruptly) ‹*drop/fall/increase*› bruscamente; ‹*bend*› repentinamente **(b)** (suddenly, swiftly) de repente **2** ‹*outlined/defined*› claramente, nítidamente **3** (harshly) ‹*answer*› con dureza

shat /ʃæt/ *past and past p of* SHIT²

shatter /'ʃætər ‖ 'ʃætə(r)/ *vt* ‹*window/plate*› hacer* añicos *or* pedazos; ‹*health/nerves*› destrozar*; ‹*confidence/hopes*› destruir*; ‹*silence*› romper*; **she was ~ed by the news** la noticia la dejó destrozada ■ **~** *vi* hacerse* añicos *or* pedazos

shave¹ /ʃeɪv/ *vt* **1** ‹*person*› afeitar *or* (esp Méx) rasurar **2** (touch in passing) rozar* ■ **~** *vi* «*person*» afeitarse *or* (esp Méx) rasurarse

shave² *n* afeitada *f or* (esp Méx) rasurada *f*; **to have a ~** afeitarse *or* (esp Méx) rasurarse; ***a close ~*** (colloq): **we won in the end, but it was a pretty close ~** al final ganamos, pero por los pelos *or* por un pelo (fam)

shaven /'ʃeɪvən/ *adj* ‹*head*› rapado

shaver /'ʃeɪvər ‖ 'ʃeɪvə(r)/ *n* (*electric ~*) máquina *f* de afeitar, afeitadora *f or* (esp Méx) rasuradora *f*

shaving /'ʃeɪvɪŋ/ *n* **(a)** (*before n*) ‹*cream/soap*› de afeitar *or* (esp Méx) de rasurar; **~ brush** brocha *f* de afeitar **(b)** [C] **shavings** *pl* (pieces) virutas *fpl*

shawl /ʃɔːl/ *n* chal *m*

she /ʃiː, *weak form* ʃi/ *pron* ella

■ **Note** Although *ella* is given as the main translation of *she*, it is in practice used only for emphasis, or to avoid ambiguity: *she went to the theater* fue al teatro; *she went to the theater, he went to the cinema* ella fue al teatro y él fue al cine; ***she*** did it ella lo hizo.

sheaf /ʃiːf/ *n* (*pl* **sheaves**) **(a)** (Agr) gavilla *f* **(b)** (of notes) fajo *m*; (of arrows) haz *m*

shear /ʃɪr ‖ ʃɪə(r)/ *vt* (*past* **sheared**; *past p* **shorn**) ‹*sheep*› esquilar

shears /ʃɪrz ‖ ʃɪəz/ *pl n* (for grass, hedge) tijeras *fpl*; (for shearing sheep) tijeras *fpl* de esquilar

sheath /ʃiːθ/ *n* (*pl* **~s** /ʃiːðz/) (for sword, knife) funda *f*, vaina *f*

sheaves /ʃiːvz/ *pl of* SHEAF

shed¹ /ʃed/ *vt* (*pres p* **shedding**; *past & past p* **shed**) **1 (a)** ‹*tears/blood*› derramar **(b)** ‹*leaves/skin*› mudar; ‹*clothing*› despojarse de (frml) **2** (send out) ‹*light*› emitir

shed² *n* **(a)** (hut) cabaña *f*; (*garden* **~**) cobertizo *m* **(b)** (larger building) nave *f*

she'd /ʃiːd/ **(a)** = **she would (b)** = **she had**

sheen /ʃiːn/ *n* [U] brillo *m*, lustre *m*

sheep /ʃiːp/ *n* (*pl* **~**) oveja *f*

sheepdog /ˈʃiːpdɔːg ‖ ˈʃiːpdɒg/ *n* perro *m* pastor

sheepish /ˈʃiːpɪʃ/ *adj* avergonzado

sheepskin /ˈʃiːpskɪn/ *n* [C U] piel *f* de borrego *or* de cordero

sheer /ʃɪr ‖ ʃɪə(r)/ *adj* **sheerer, sheerest 1** (pure, absolute) (*as intensifier*) puro; **the ~ size of the problem** la mera magnitud del problema **2** (vertical) ‹*drop*› a pique; ‹*cliff*› escarpado **3** (fine) ‹*stockings/fabric*› muy fino

sheet /ʃiːt/ *n* **1** (on bed) sábana *f* **2** (of paper) hoja *f*; (of wrapping paper) pliego *m*, hoja *f*; (of stamps) pliego *m* **3 (a)** (of metal) chapa *f*, plancha *f*, lámina *f*; **a ~ of glass** un vidrio **(b)** (of ice) capa *f*; (*before n*) **~ lightning** relámpagos *mpl* difusos

sheet: **~ metal** *n* [U] metal *m* en planchas *or* chapas; **~ music** *n* [U] partituras *fpl*

sheik, sheikh /ʃiːk ‖ ʃeɪk/ *n* jeque *m*

shelf /ʃelf/ *n* (*pl* **shelves**) **1** (in cupboard, bookcase) estante *m*, balda *f* (Esp); **a set of shelves** unos estantes, una estantería **2** (Geol): **continental ~** plataforma *f* continental

shell¹ /ʃel/ *n* **1 (a)** (of egg, nut) cáscara *f*; (of sea mollusk) concha *f*; (of tortoise, turtle, snail, crustacean) caparazón *m or f* **(b)** (of building, vehicle) armazón *m or f* **2** (Mil) proyectil *m*, obús *m*

shell² *vt* **1** (Culin) ‹*peas/nuts/eggs*› pelar; ‹*mussel/clam*› quitarle la concha a **2** (Mil) ‹*position/troops/city*› bombardear

she'll /ʃiːl, *weak form* ʃɪl/ = **she will**

shell: **~fish** *n* (*pl* **~fish**) **(a)** [C] (creature) marisco *m* **(b)** [U] (collectively) mariscos *mpl*, marisco *m* (Esp); **~shock** *n* [U] neurosis *f* de guerra

shelter¹ /ˈʃeltər ‖ ˈʃeltə(r)/ *n* **1** [C] (building) refugio *m* **2** [U] **(a)** (protection): **to take ~** refugiarse **(b)** (accommodations): **they need food and ~** necesitan alimentos y albergue

shelter² *vt* **(a)** (protect from weather) resguardar **(b)** ‹*criminal/fugitive*› darle* cobijo a ■ **~** *vi* **to ~** (FROM **sth**) refugiarse *or* resguardarse (DE algo)

sheltered /ˈʃeltərd ‖ ˈʃeltəd/ *adj* ‹*valley/harbor*› abrigado; ‹*life*› protegido

shelve /ʃelv/ *vt* ‹*plan/project*› archivar

shelves /ʃelvz/ *pl of* SHELF

shelving /ˈʃelvɪŋ/ *n* [U] estantería *f*

shepherd /ˈʃepərd ‖ ˈʃepəd/ *n* pastor *m*

sherbet /ˈʃɜːrbət ‖ ˈʃɜːbət/ *n* **(a)** (sorbet) (AmE) sorbete *m* **(b)** (powder) (BrE) *polvos efervescentes con sabor a frutas*, sidral® *m* (Esp)

sheriff /ˈʃerəf ‖ ˈʃerɪf/ *n* (in US) sheriff *mf*

sherry /ˈʃeri/ *n* [U C] (*pl* **-ries**) jerez *m*

she's /ʃiːz, *weak form* ʃɪz/ **(a)** = **she is (b)** = **she has**

shield¹ /ʃiːld/ *n* **1** (Hist, Mil) escudo *m* **2** (protective cover on machine) revestimiento *m*

shield² *vt* **to ~ sth/sb** (FROM **sb/sth**) proteger* algo/a algn (DE algn/algo)

shift¹ /ʃɪft/ *vt* **(a)** (change position of) ‹*object/furniture*› correr, mover* **(b)** (transfer): **they tried to ~ the responsibility onto us** trataron de cargarnos la responsabilidad ■ **~** *vi* **1** (change position, direction) «*cargo*» correrse; «*wind*» cambiar; **he ~ed uneasily in his chair** se movía intranquilo en la silla; **the focus of attention has ~ed to Europe** el foco de atención ha pasado a Europa **2** (change gear) (AmE) cambiar de marcha *or* de velocidad

shift² *n* **1** (change in position) cambio *m* **2** (work period) turno *m*; **to work the day/night ~** hacer* el turno de día/de noche; (*before n*) **~ work** trabajo *m* por turnos **3** (AmE Auto) palanca *m* de cambio *or* (Méx) de velocidades

shift key *n* tecla *f* de las mayúsculas

shifty /ˈʃɪfti/ *adj* **-tier, -tiest** ‹*expression/eyes*› furtivo; ‹*appearance*› sospechoso

shilling /ˈʃɪlɪŋ/ *n* chelín *m*

shimmer /ˈʃɪmər ‖ ˈʃɪmə(r)/ *vi* «*water/silk*» brillar; «*lights*» titilar; (in water) rielar (liter)

shin /ʃɪn/ *n* espinilla *f*, canilla *f*

shine¹ /ʃaɪn/ *n* [U] brillo *m*

shine² (*past & past p* **shone**) *vi* **(a)** (gleam, glow) «*star/sun/eyes*» brillar; «*metal/shoes*» relucir*, brillar **(b)** (excel) **to ~** (AT **sth**) destacar(se*) (EN algo) ■ **~** *vt* (+ *adv compl*): **to ~ a light on sth** alumbrar algo con una luz

shingle /ˈʃɪŋgəl/ *n* [U] guijarros *mpl*

shingles /ˈʃɪŋgəlz/ *n* (Med) (+ *sing vb*) herpes *m*, culebrilla *f*

shining /ˈʃaɪnɪŋ/ *adj* ‹*eyes*› brillante, luminoso; ‹*hair/metal*› brillante, reluciente

shiny /ˈʃaɪni/ *adj* **-nier, -niest** ‹*hair/fabric/shoe*› brillante; ‹*coin*› reluciente

ship¹ /ʃɪp/ *n* barco *m*, buque *m*

ship² *vt* **-pp- (a)** (send by sea) enviar* *or* mandar por barco **(b)** (send) enviar*, despachar

ship: **~building** *n* [U] construcción *f* naval; **~load** *n* cargamento *m*

shipment /ˈʃɪpmənt/ *n* (goods) envío *m*, remesa *f*

shipping /ˈʃɪpɪŋ/ *n* [U] **(a)** (ships) barcos *mpl*, embarcaciones *fpl* (frml); (*before n*) ‹*lane/route*› de navegación **(b)** (transportation of freight) transporte *m*

shipshape /ˈʃɪpʃeɪp/ *adj* (*pred*) limpio y ordenado

shipwreck¹ /ˈʃɪprek/ *n* naufragio *m*

shipwreck² *vt* (*usu pass*): **to be ~ed** naufragar*

shipyard /ˈʃɪpjɑːrd ‖ ˈʃɪpjɑːd/ *n* (*often pl*) astillero *m*

shirk /ʃɜːrk ‖ ʃɜːk/ *vt* ‹*task/duty*› eludir, rehuir*

shirt /ʃɜːrt ‖ ʃɜːt/ *n* camisa *f*

shirtsleeve /'ʃɜːrtsliːv ‖ 'ʃɜːtsliːv/ *n* manga *f* de camisa; **in (one's) ~s** en mangas de camisa

shit[1] /ʃɪt/ *n* [U] (vulg) mierda *f* (vulg)

shit[2] *vi* (*pres p* **shitting**; *past & past p* **shit** *or* **shat**) (vulg) cagar* (vulg)

shit[3] *interj* (vulg) ¡carajo! (vulg), ¡mierda! (vulg)

shiver[1] /'ʃɪvər ‖ 'ʃɪvə(r)/ *n* escalofrío *m*; **the scream sent ~s** *o* **a ~ down my spine** el grito me produjo escalofríos

shiver[2] *vi* (with cold) temblar*; (with fear) temblar*; (with anticipation) estremecerse*

shivery /'ʃɪvəri/ *adj*: **to feel ~** tener* escalofríos

shmaltz, **shmalz** *etc* ⇒ SCHMALTZ *etc*

shoal /ʃəʊl/ *n* **1** (of fish) cardumen *m*, banco *m* **2** (sandbank) bajío *m*, banco *m* de arena

shock[1] /ʃɑːk ‖ ʃɒk/ *n* **1** [C] **(a)** (of impact) choque *m*; (of earthquake, explosion) sacudida *f* **(b)** (*electric* ~) descarga *f* (eléctrica) **2 (a)** [U] (Med) shock *m*; **to be in (a state of) ~** estar* en estado de shock **(b)** [U C] (distress, surprise) shock *m*; **to get a ~** llevarse un shock; **the news came as a great ~ to us** la noticia nos conmocionó **(c)** [C] (scare) susto *m*; **to get a ~** llevarse un susto **3** [C] (bushy mass): **a ~ of hair** una mata de pelo

shock[2] *vt* (stun, appal) horrorizar*; (scandalize) escandalizar*

shock absorber /əb'sɔːrbər ‖ əb'zɔːbə(r)/ *n* amortiguador *m*

shocked /ʃɑːkt ‖ ʃɒkt/ *adj* **(a)** (appalled) horrorizado **(b)** (scandalized): **I was ~ to hear that** ... me indigné cuando me enteré de que ...

shocking /'ʃɑːkɪŋ ‖ 'ʃɒkɪŋ/ *adj* **(a)** ‹*news/report*› espeluznante **(b)** ‹*behavior/language*› escandaloso

shock wave *n* (Phys) onda *f* expansiva

shod /ʃɑːd ‖ ʃɒd/ *past & past p of* SHOE[2]

shoddy /'ʃɑːdi ‖ 'ʃɒdi/ *adj* **-dier, -diest** ‹*goods/workmanship*› de muy mala calidad

shoe[1] /ʃuː/ **▶ 401** *n* **(a)** (Clothing) zapato *m*; (*before n*) **~ polish** betún *m*; **~ repairer** zapatero, -ra *m,f* **(b)** (for horse) herradura *f* **(c)** (*brake* ~) zapata *f*

shoe[2] *vt* (*pres* **shoes**; *pres p* **shoeing**; *past & past p* **shod**) ‹*horse*› herrar*

shoe: **~brush** *n* cepillo *m* de los zapatos; **~horn** *n* calzador *m*; **~lace** *n* cordón *m* (de zapato), agujeta *f* (Méx), pasador *m* (Per)

shone /ʃəʊn, ʃɑːn ‖ ʃɒn/ *past & past p of* SHINE[2]

shoo[1] /ʃuː/ *interj* ¡fuera!, ¡úscale! (Méx)

shoo[2] *vt* **shoos, shooing, shooed**: **I ~ed the birds off** *o* **away** espanté a los pájaros

shook /ʃʊk/ *past of* SHAKE[1]

shoot[1] /ʃuːt/ *n* **1** (Bot) brote *m* **2** (shooting expedition) cacería *f* **3** (Cin) rodaje *m*

shoot[2] (*past & past p* **shot**) *vt* **1 (a)** ‹*person/animal*› pegarle* un tiro a; **they shot him dead, they shot him to death** (AmE) lo mataron a tiros/de un tiro; **to ~ oneself** pegarse* un tiro **(b)** (hunt) ‹*duck/deer*› cazar* **2** (fire) ‹*bullet*› disparar, tirar; ‹*arrow/missile*› lanzar*, arrojar; ‹*glance*› lanzar* **3** (pass swiftly): **to ~ the rapids** salvar los rápidos **4** (Cin) rodar* ■ **~** *vi* **1 (a)** (fire weapon) disparar; **to ~ AT sb/sth** dispararle A algn/A algo **(b)** (hunt) cazar* **2** (move swiftly): **she ~ past** pasó como una bala (fam); **he shot out of his seat** saltó del asiento **3** (Sport) tirar, disparar

● **shoot down** [*v + o + adv, v + adv + o*] ‹*plane*› derribar, abatir

● **shoot out** [*v + adv*] (emerge quickly) salir* disparado *or* (fam) como un bólido

● **shoot up** [*v + adv*] **(a)** (grow tall) crecer* mucho **(b)** (go up quickly) «*prices/temperature*» dispararse; «*flames*» alzarse*

shoot[3] *interj* (AmE colloq) ¡miércoles! (fam & euf)

shooting /'ʃuːtɪŋ/ *n* **(a)** [U] (exchange of fire) tiroteo *m*, balacera *f* (AmL); (shots) tiros *mpl*, disparos *mpl* **(b)** [U C] (killing) asesinato *m*

shooting star *n* estrella *f* fugaz

shoot-out /'ʃuːtaʊt/ *n* tiroteo *m*, balacera *f* (AmL), baleo *m* (Chi)

shop[1] /ʃɑːp ‖ ʃɒp/ *n* **(a)** [C] (retail outlet) tienda *f*, negocio *m* (CS), comercio *m* (frml); **to go to the ~s** ir* de compras **(b)** [U] (business) (colloq): ***to talk ~*** hablar del trabajo

shop[2] **-pp-** *vi* hacer* compras; **to go ~ping** ir* de compras

shop: **~ assistant** *n* (BrE) dependiente, -ta *m,f*, empleado, -da *m,f* (de tienda) (AmL), vendedor, -dora *m,f* (CS); **~ floor** *n* (part of factory) taller *m*; (workers) obreros *mpl*, trabajadores *mpl*; (as union members) bases *fpl* sindicales; **~keeper** *n* comerciante *mf*, tendero, -ra *m,f*; **~lifter** /'ʃɑːpˌlɪftər ‖ 'ʃɒpˌlɪftə(r)/ *n* ladrón, -drona *m,f* (*que roba en las tiendas*); **~lifting** /'ʃɑːpˌlɪftɪŋ ‖ 'ʃɒpˌlɪftɪŋ/ *n* [U] hurto *m* (*en las tiendas*)

shopper /'ʃɑːpər ‖ 'ʃɒpə(r)/ *n* comprador, -dora *m,f*

shopping /'ʃɑːpɪŋ ‖ 'ʃɒpɪŋ/ *n* [U] **(a)** (act): **to do the ~** hacer* la compra *or* (AmS) las compras, hacer* el mercado (Col, Ven), hacer* el mandado (Méx); (*before n*) ‹*basket*› de la compra *or* (AmS) de las compras **(b)** (purchases) compras *fpl*

shopping: **~ bag** *n* **(a)** (given by store) (AmE) bolsa *f* (*de plástico, papel etc*) **(b)** (owned by customer) (BrE) bolsa *f* (de la compra *or* (AmS) de las compras); **~ cart** *n* (AmE) carrito *m* (de la compra *or* (AmS) de las compras); **~ center**, (BrE) **~ centre** ⇒ **~** MALL; **~ list** *n* lista *f* de la compra *or* (AmS) de las compras *or* (Col, Ven) del mercado *or* (Méx) del mandado; **~ mall** *n* (esp AmE) centro *m* comercial; **~ trolley** *n* (BrE) **(a)** ⇒ **~** CART **(b)** (bag on wheels) carrito *m*, changuito *m* (RPl)

shop: **~-soiled** *adj* ‹*goods*› deteriorado; **~ window** *n* escaparate *m*, vitrina *f* (AmL), aparador *m* (AmC, Col, Méx); **~worn** *adj* (AmE) ⇒ **~**-SOILED

shore /ʃɔːr ‖ ʃɔː(r)/ *n* **1** [C] **(a)** (of sea, lake) orilla *f* **(b)** (coast) costa *f*, ribera *f* **2** [U] (land): **to go on ~** bajar a tierra (firme)

● **shore up** [*v + o + adv, v + adv + o*] apuntalar

shorn /ʃɔːrn ‖ ʃɔːn/ *past p of* SHEAR

short[1] /ʃɔːrt ‖ ʃɔːt/ *adj* **-er, -est 1** (of length, height, distance) corto; ‹*person*› bajo **2 (a)** (brief) ‹*visit/trip*› corto; **the days are getting ~er** los días van acortándose; **a ~ time ago** hace poco (tiempo); **we call him Rob for ~** lo llamamos Rob para abreviar **(b) in short** (briefly) (*as linker*) en resumen **3** (brusque) ‹*manner*› brusco; **she has a ~ temper** tiene muy mal genio **4** (inadequate, deficient) escaso; **to be in ~ supply** escasear; **we're six people ~** todavía nos faltan seis personas; **(to be) ~** OF **sth/sb**: **we're very ~ of time** estamos muy cortos de tiempo; **they were ~ of staff** no tenían suficiente personal

short² *adv* **1** (suddenly, abruptly): **he cut ~ his vacation** interrumpió sus vacaciones; **he stopped ~ when he saw me** se paró en seco cuando me vio **2** (below target, requirement): **to fall ~** «*shell/arrow*» quedarse corto; **we never went ~ of food** nunca nos faltó la comida

short³ *n* **1** (Cin) cortometraje *m*, corto *m* **2** (drink) (BrE) *copa de bebida alcohólica de las que se sirven en pequeñas cantidades, como el whisky o el coñac* **3 shorts** *pl* **(a)** (short trousers) shorts *mpl*, pantalones *mpl* cortos **(b)** (men's underwear) (AmE) calzoncillos *mpl*

short⁴ *vi* (Elec) hacer* un cortocircuito

• **short out** (AmE Elec) [*v* + *adv*] «*fuse*» fundirse; «*iron/hairdryer*» hacer* (un) cortocircuito

shortage /ˈʃɔːrtɪdʒ ‖ ˈʃɔːtɪdʒ/ *n* [C U] **~ (**OF **sth/sb)** falta *f or* escasez *f* (DE algo/algn)

short: **~bread** *n* [U] *galleta dulce de mantequilla*; **~-change** /ˈʃɔːrtˈtʃeɪndʒ ‖ ˌʃɔːtˈtʃeɪndʒ/ *vt* (in shop): **he ~-changed me** me dio mal el cambio *or* (AmL tb) el vuelto; **~ circuit** *n* cortocircuito *m*; **~-circuit** /ˈʃɔːrtˈsɜːrkət ‖ ˌʃɔːtˈsɜːkɪt/ *vt* (Elec) provocar* un cortocircuito en ■ **~** *vi* (Elec) hacer* (un) cortocircuito; **~coming** *n* defecto *m*, deficiencia *f*; **~crust (pastry)** *n* [U] (BrE) pasta *f* quebradiza (*tipo de masa para empanadas, tartas etc*); **~ cut** *n* atajo *m*; **there are no ~ cuts to success** no hay fórmulas mágicas para el éxito

shorten /ˈʃɔːrtn̩ ‖ ˈʃɔːtn̩/ *vt* ‹*skirt/sleeves*› acortar; ‹*text/report*› acortar, abreviar

short: **~fall** *n* **~fall (**IN **sth)**: **a ~fall of 7% in revenues** un déficit de 7% en los ingresos; **~-haired** /ˈʃɔːrtherd ‖ ˌʃɔːtˈheəd/ *adj* de pelo corto; **~hand** *n* [U] taquigrafía *f*; **~ list** *n* lista *f* de candidatos preseleccionados; **~-list** *vt* preseleccionar; **~-lived** /ˈʃɔːrtˈlɪvd ‖ ˌʃɔːtˈlɪvd/ *adj* ‹*success/enthusiasm*› efímero; ‹*recovery*› pasajero

shortly /ˈʃɔːrtli ‖ ˈʃɔːtli/ *adv* dentro de poco; **~ before/after midnight** poco antes/después de la medianoche

short: **~sighted** /ˈʃɔːrtˈsaɪtəd ‖ ˌʃɔːtˈsaɪtɪd/ *adj* **(a)** (esp BrE Med) miope, corto de vista **(b)** ‹*attitude/policy*› corto de miras; **~-sleeved** /ˈʃɔːrtˈsliːvd ‖ ˌʃɔːtˈsliːvd/ *adj* de manga corta; **~-staffed** /ˈʃɔːrtˈstæft ‖ ˌʃɔːtˈstɑːft/ *adj*: **they/we were ~-staffed** les/nos faltaba personal; **~ story** *n* cuento *m*, relato *m* breve; **~-tempered** /ˈʃɔːrtˈtempərd ‖ ˌʃɔːtˈtempəd/ *adj* de mal genio; **~-term** /ˈʃɔːrt ˈtɜːrm ‖ ˌʃɔːtˈtɜːm/ *adj* a corto plazo; **~wave** /ˈʃɔːrt ˈweɪv ‖ ˌʃɔːtˈweɪv/ *n* [U] onda *f* corta

shot¹ /ʃɑːt ‖ ʃɒt/ *past & past p of* SHOOT²

shot² *n* **1** [C] **(a)** (from gun, rifle) disparo *m*, tiro *m*; (from cannon) cañonazo *m*; **she fired three ~s** disparó tres veces; **she was off like a ~** salió disparada **(b)** (marksman): **a good/poor ~** un buen/mal tirador **2** (colloq) [C] (attempt, try): **it costs $50 a ~** son 50 dólares por vez; **I'd like another ~ at it** me gustaría volver a intentarlo **3** [C] (Phot) foto *f*; (Cin) toma *f* **4** [U] (pellets): **(lead) ~** perdigones *mpl* **5** [C] (used in shotput) bala *f*, peso *m* (Esp) **6** [C] (in soccer) disparo *m*, tiro *m*; (in basketball) tiro *m*, tirada *f*; (in golf, tennis) tiro *m* **7** [C] (injection) inyección *f*

shot: **~gun** *n* escopeta *f*; **~put** *n* (event) lanzamiento *m* de bala *or* (Esp) de peso

should¹ /ʃʊd/ *past of* SHALL

should² *v mod* **1** (expressing desirability) debería (*or* deberías *etc*), debiera (*or* debieras *etc*); **you ~ have thought of that before** deberías *or* debieras haber pensado en eso antes **2** (indicating probability, logical expectation) debería (*or* deberías *etc*) (de), debiera (*or* debieras *etc*) (de); **it ~ add up to 100** debería (de) *or* debiera (de) dar 100 **3** (*with first person only*) **(a)** (conditional use) (BrE frml): **I ~ like to see her** me gustaría verla **(b)** (venturing a guess) (BrE): **I ~ think she must be over 80** yo diría que debe tener más de 80 **(c)** (expressing indignation): **I ~ think so too!** ¡(no) faltaría más! **4** (subjunctive use) (*with all persons*): **it's natural that he ~ want to go with her** es natural que quiera ir con ella; **if you ~ happen to pass a bookshop** ... si pasaras por una librería ...

shoulder¹ /ˈʃəʊldər ‖ ˈʃəʊldə(r)/ *n* **1** ▶ 484 (Anat, Clothing) hombro *m* **2** (of road) arcén *m*, berma *f* (Andes), acotamiento *m* (Méx), banquina *f* (RPl), hombrillo *m* (Ven)

shoulder² *vt* ‹*knapsack*› ponerse* *or* echarse al hombro; ‹*blame/responsibility*› cargar* con

shoulder: **~ bag** *n* bolso *m or* (CS) cartera *f or* (Méx) bolsa *f* (*con correa larga para colgar del hombro*); **~ blade** *n* omóplato *m*; **~-length** /ˈʃəʊl dərˈleŋθ ‖ ˌʃəʊldəˈleŋθ/ *adj*: **~-length hair** pelo *m* hasta los hombros; **~ strap** *n* (of garment) tirante *m or* (CS) bretel *m*; (of bag) correa *f*

shouldn't /ˈʃʊdn̩t/ = **should not**

shout¹ /ʃaʊt/ *n* grito *m*

shout² *vi* gritar; **to ~** AT **sb** gritarle A algn ■ **~** *vt* gritar

• **shout out 1** [*v* + *o* + *adv*, *v* + *adv* + *o*] ‹*answer*› gritar **2** [*v* + *adv*] dar* un grito

shouting /ˈʃaʊtɪŋ/ *n* [U] griterío *m*

shove¹ /ʃʌv/ *vt* **(a)** (push roughly) empujar; **they ~d her out of the way** la quitaron de en medio a empellones *or* a empujones **(b)** (put) (colloq) poner*, meter ■ **~** *vi* empujar

shove² *n* empujón *m*, empellón *m*

shovel¹ /ˈʃʌvəl/ *n* pala *f*

shovel² *vt*, (BrE) **-ll-** ‹*coal*› palear; ‹*snow*› espalar

show¹ /ʃəʊ/ (*past* **showed**; *past p* **shown** *or* **showed**) *vt* **1 (a)** ‹*photograph/passport*› mostrar*, enseñar; **to ~ sb sth, to ~ sth** TO **sb** mostrarle* algo A algn **(b)** ‹*feelings*› demostrar*; ‹*interest/enthusiasm*› demostrar*, mostrar*; ‹*courage*› demostrar* (tener); **could you ~ me the way?** ¿me podría indicar el camino? **(c)** (allow to be seen): **this carpet ~s every mark** en esta alfombra se notan todas las marcas; **he's started**

to ~ **his age** se le han empezado a notar los años **2** (record, register) «*barometer/dial/indicator*» marcar*, señalar, indicar*; ‹*profit/loss*› arrojar **3** **(a)** (demonstrate) ‹*truth/importance*› demostrar*; **it just goes to ~ how wrong you can be** eso te demuestra lo equivocado que puedes estar **(b)** (teach) enseñar; **I ~ed her how to do it** le enseñé cómo se hacía **4** (by accompanying) (+ *adv compl*): **he ~ed us to our seats** nos llevó hasta nuestros asientos; **to ~ sb in** hacer* pasar a algn; **to ~ sb out** acompañar a algn a la puerta **5** **(a)** (screen) ‹*movie*› dar*, pasar, poner* (Esp); ‹*program*› dar*, poner* (Esp); ‹*slides*› pasar **(b)** (exhibit) ‹*paintings/sculpture*› exponer*; ‹*horse/dog*› presentar ■ ~ *vi* **1** (be visible) «*dirt/stain*» verse*; «*emotion/scar*» notarse; **your petticoat is ~ing** se te ve la enagua **2** (be screened) (Cin): **it's ~ing at the Trocadero** la están dando en el Trocadero, la ponen en el Trocadero (Esp) ■ *v refl* **to ~ oneself** **(a)** (become visible) «*person*» asomarse **(b)** (prove to be) demostrar* ser; (turn out to be) resultar ser

• **show off** **1** [*v* + *adv*] lucirse*; **stop ~ing off** déjate de hacer tonterías **2** [*v* + *o* + *adv*, *v* + *adv* + *o*] **(a)** (display for admiration) ‹*car/girlfriend*› lucir*, presumir de (Esp); ‹*wealth/knowledge*› presumir de **(b)** (display to advantage) ‹*beauty/complexion*› hacer* resaltar

• **show up** **1** [*v* + *o* + *adv*, *v* + *adv* + *o*] **(a)** (reveal) ‹*mistake/deception*› poner* de manifiesto (frml) **(b)** (embarrass) ‹*parents/friends*› hacer* quedar mal **2** [*v* + *adv*] **(a)** (be visible) «*imperfection*» notarse **(b)** (arrive) (colloq) aparecer* (fam)

show² *n* **1** [C] (exhibition) (Art) exposición *f*; **to be on ~** estar* expuesto; **to put sth on ~** exponer* algo **2** [C] **(a)** (stage production) espectáculo *m*; ***to steal the ~*** robarse el espectáculo **(b)** (on television, radio) programa *m* **3** (*no pl*) **(a)** (display) muestra *f*, demostración *f*; **a ~ of force** un despliegue de fuerza **(b)** (outward appearance): **I made a ~ of enthusiasm** fingí estar entusiasmado; **their plush office is simply for ~** su elegante oficina es sólo para darse tono **4** (colloq) (*no pl*) (activity, organization) asunto *m*; **to run the ~** llevar la voz cantante (fam)

show: **~ business** (colloq) *n* [U] mundo *m* del espectáculo; **~case** *n* **(a)** (cabinet) vitrina *f* **(b)** (for products, ideologies) escaparate *m*; **~down** *n* enfrentamiento *m*

shower¹ /ˈʃaʊər ‖ ˈʃaʊə(r)/ *n* **1** (in bathroom) ducha *f*, regadera *f* (Méx); **to take** *o* (BrE) **have a ~** ducharse; (*before n*) **~ cap** gorro *m* de ducha **2** ▶ 920 (Meteo) chaparrón *m*, chubasco *m* **3** (party) (AmE) *fiesta en la que los invitados obsequian a la homenajeada con motivo de su próxima boda, el nacimiento de su niño etc*

shower² *vt* **(a)** (spray) regar*; **to ~ sb** WITH **sth** tirarle algo A algn **(b)** (bestow lavishly) **to ~ sb** WITH **sth**: **he ~ed her with gifts** la llenó de regalos; **the country ~ed him with honors** el país lo colmó de honores ■ ~ *vi* **(a)** (wash) ducharse **(b)** (be sprayed) «*water/leaves/stones*» caer*; «*letters/congratulations/protests*» llover*

show jumping /ˌdʒʌmpɪŋ/ *n* [U] concursos *mpl* hípicos

shown /ʃəʊn/ *past p of* SHOW¹

show: **~-off** *n* (colloq) fanfarrón, -rrona *m,f*, fantasma *mf* (Esp fam); **~room** *n* (*often pl*) salón *m* de exposición (y ventas)

showy /ˈʃəʊi/ *adj* **showier, showiest** **(a)** (gaudy) llamativo **(b)** (attractive) vistoso

shrank /ʃræŋk/ *past of* SHRINK

shrapnel /ˈʃræpnl̩/ *n* [U] metralla *f*

shred¹ /ʃred/ *n* (of paper, fabric) tira *f*, trozo *m*; **not a (single) ~ of evidence** ni una (sola) prueba; **not a ~ of truth** ni pizca de verdad; **to be in ~s** «*clothes/fabric*» estar* hecho jirones *or* tiras; «*argument/reputation*» estar* destrozado

shred² *vt* **-dd-** cortar en tiras; ‹*documents*› destruir*, triturar

shredder /ˈʃredər ‖ ˈʃredə(r)/ *n* (for paper) trituradora *f*; (for vegetables) cortadora *f*

shrew /ʃru:/ *n* (Zool) musaraña *f*

shrewd /ʃru:d/ *adj* **-er, -est** ‹*person*› astuto; ‹*move/investment/assessment*› hábil

shriek¹ /ʃri:k/ *n* (of delight, terror) grito *m*, chillido *m*; (of pain) grito *m*, alarido *m*; **we could hear ~s of laughter** oíamos risotadas

shriek² *vi/t* gritar, chillar

shrift /ʃrɪft/ *n* [U]: **to give sth short ~** ‹*idea/suggestion*› desestimar algo de plano; **to give sb short ~** echar a algn con cajas destempladas

shrill /ʃrɪl/ *adj* **-er, -est** ‹*whistle/laugh*› agudo, estridente; ‹*voice*› agudo, chillón

shrimp /ʃrɪmp/ *n* (*pl* ~ *or* (BrE also) **~s**) (large) (AmE) langostino *m*; (medium) camarón *m* (AmL), gamba *f* (esp Esp); (small) (BrE) camarón *m*, quisquilla *f* (Esp)

shrine /ʃraɪn/ *n* (holy place) santuario *m*; (in out-of-the-way place) ermita *f*

shrink /ʃrɪŋk/ (*past* **shrank** *or* **shrunk**; *past p* **shrunk** *or* **shrunken**) *vi* **1** (diminish in size) «*clothes/fabric*» encoger(se)*; «*meat*» achicarse*; «*wood*» contraerse*; «*area/amount*» reducirse* **2** (recoil) retroceder; **to ~ back** *o* **away from sth/sb** echarse atrás *or* retroceder ante algo/algn ■ ~ *vt* ‹*clothes/fabric*› encoger*

shrinkage /ˈʃrɪŋkɪdʒ/ *n* [U] (of clothes, fabric) encogimiento *m*; (of wood, metal) contracción *f*

shrivel /ˈʃrɪvəl/, (BrE) **-ll-** ~ **(up)** *vi* «*leaf/plant*» marchitarse, secarse*; «*fruit/vegetables*» resecarse* y arrugarse*; «*skin*» ajarse ■ *vt* ‹*leaf/plant*› secar*, marchitar

shroud¹ /ʃraʊd/ *n* mortaja *f*

shroud² *vt* envolver*; **a case ~ed in mystery** (journ) un caso envuelto en un velo de misterio

Shrove Tuesday /ʃrəʊv/ *n* martes *m* de Carnaval

shrub /ʃrʌb/ *n* arbusto *m*, mata *f*

shrubbery /ˈʃrʌbəri/ *n* [U] arbustos *mpl*, matas *fpl*

shrug¹ /ʃrʌg/ *n*: **with a ~ (of her shoulders)** encogiéndose de hombros

shrug² **-gg-** *vi* encogerse* de hombros ■ ~ *vt*: **to ~ one's shoulders** encogerse* de hombros

• **shrug off** [*v* + *o* + *adv*, *v* + *adv* + *o*] ‹*misfortune/disappointment*› superar; ‹*criticism*› hacer* caso omiso de

shrunk /ʃrʌŋk/ *past & past p of* SHRINK

shrunken¹ /ʃrʌnkən/ *past p of* SHRINK

shrunken² *adj* ‹*body*› consumido

shudder¹ /'ʃʌdər ‖ 'ʃʌdə(r)/ *vi* **(a)** «*person*» estremecerse* **(b)** «*bus/train/plane*» dar* sacudidas; **to ~ to a halt** pararse abruptamente

shudder² *n* **(a)** (of person) estremecimiento *m* **(b)** (of vehicle, engine) sacudida *f*

shuffle /'ʃʌfəl/ *vt* **1 to ~ one's feet** arrastrar los pies **2** ‹*cards/papers*› barajar ■ **~** *vi* caminar *or* andar* arrastrando los pies

shun /ʃʌn/ *vt* **-nn-** ‹*person/society*› rechazar*, rehuir*; ‹*publicity/limelight*› evitar, rehuir*

shunt /ʃʌnt/ *vt* (Rail) cambiar de vía

shush¹ /ʃʊʃ/ *vt* acallar

shush² *interj*: **~!** ¡chitón!, ¡silencio!

shut¹ /ʃʌt/ (*pres p* **shutting**; *past & past p* **shut**) *vt* **1 (a)** ‹*window/book/eyes*› cerrar* **(b)** ‹*store/business*› cerrar* **2** (confine) **to ~ sb IN sth** encerrar* a algn EN algo; **he ~ himself in his room** se encerró en su cuarto ■ **~** *vi* **1** «*door/window*» cerrar(se)* **2** (esp BrE) (cease business — for day) cerrar*; (— permanently) cerrar* (sus puertas)

● **shut down 1** [*v* + *adv*] «*factory/business*» cerrar*; «*machinery*» apagarse* **2** [*v* + *o* + *adv, v* + *adv* + *o*] ‹*factory/business*› cerrar*; ‹*machinery*› apagar*

● **shut in** [*v* + *o* + *adv, v* + *adv* + *o*] encerrar*

● **shut off** [*v* + *o* + *adv, v* + *adv* + *o*] **(a)** ‹*water/electricity*› cortar; ‹*engine*› apagar* **(b)** (isolate) (*often pass*) ‹*place/person*› aislar*

● **shut out** [*v* + *o* + *adv, v* + *adv* + *o*] **(a)** ‹*person/animal*› dejar (a)fuera; ‹*light/heat*› no dejar entrar; **to ~ oneself out** quedarse (a)fuera **(b)** (AmE Sport) ‹*team/pitcher*› ganarle a (*sin conceder ni un gol o carrera etc*)

● **shut up 1** [*v* + *o* + *adv, v* + *adv* + *o*] **(a)** (close) ‹*house/office*› cerrar* **(b)** (confine) ‹*dog*› encerrar* **2** [*v* + *o* + *adv*] (silence) (colloq) hacer* callar **3** [*v* + *adv*] **(a)** (close business) cerrar* **(b)** (stop talking) (colloq) callarse

shut² *adj* (*pred*) cerrado

shutdown /'ʃʌtdaʊn/ *n* (of hospital, college) cierre *m*; (of power) corte *m*; (of services) paralización *f*

shutter /'ʃʌtər ‖ 'ʃʌtə(r)/ *n* **1** (on window) postigo *m* **2** (Phot) obturador *m*

shuttle¹ /'ʃʌtl/ *n* **1** (in loom, sewing machine) lanzadera *f* **2 (a)** (Aviat) puente *m* aéreo; (bus, train service) servicio *m* (regular) de enlace **(b)** (*space ~*) transbordador *m or* lanzadera *f* espacial

shuttle² *vi*: **to ~ back and forth** ir* y venir* ■ **~** *vt* ‹*passengers*› transportar, llevar

shuttlecock /'ʃʌtlkɑːk ‖ 'ʃʌtlkɒk/ *n* volante *m*, plumilla *f*, rehilete *m*, gallito *m* (Col, Méx)

shy¹ /ʃaɪ/ *adj* **shyer, shyest** ‹*person*› tímido; ‹*animal*› huraño

shy² *vi* **shies, shying, shied** «*horse*» respingar*

shyly /'ʃaɪli/ *adv* tímidamente, con timidez

shyness /'ʃaɪnəs ‖ 'ʃaɪnɪs/ *n* [U] timidez *f*

Siamese /'saɪə'miːz/ *n* (*pl* **~**) **~ (cat)** gato *m* siamés

Siamese twins *pl n* (hermanos) siameses *mpl*, (hermanas) siamesas *fpl*

sibling /'sɪblɪŋ/ *n* (frml) (brother) hermano *m*; (sister) hermana *f*

sick /sɪk/ *adj* **-er, -est 1** (ill) enfermo; **to be off ~** estar* ausente por enfermedad **2** (nauseated) (*pred*): **to feel ~** (dizzy, unwell) estar* mareado; (about to vomit) tener* ganas de vomitar; **to be ~** vomitar; **he makes me ~** me da asco **3 (a)** (disturbed, sickened) (*pred*): **to be ~ with fear/worry** estar* muerto de miedo/preocupación **(b)** (weary, fed up) **to be ~ OF sth/-ING** estar* harto DE algo/+ INF; **I'm ~ and tired of hearing that** estoy absolutamente harto de oír eso **4** (gruesome) ‹*person/mind*› morboso; ‹*humor/joke*› de muy mal gusto

sick: **~ bay** *n* enfermería *f*; **~bed** *n* (liter) lecho *m* de enfermo (liter)

sicken /'sɪkən/ *vt* dar* rabia, enfermar (AmL); (stronger) asquear ■ **~** *vi* (BrE) **to be ~ing FOR sth** estar* incubando algo

sickening /'sɪkənɪŋ/ *adj* **(a)** (appalling): **it's ~, isn't it?** da mucha rabia ¿no?; (stronger) da asco ¿no? **(b)** ‹*smell/sight*› nauseabundo

sickle /'sɪkəl/ *n* hoz *f*

sick leave *n* [U] permiso *m or* (Esp) baja *f or* (RPl) licencia *f* por enfermedad

sickly¹ /'sɪkli/ *adj* **-lier, -liest (a)** ‹*complexion/child*› enfermizo **(b)** ‹*taste/smell*› empalagoso; ‹*color*› horrible, asqueroso

sickly² *adv*: **~ sweet** demasiado empalagoso

sickness /'sɪknəs ‖ 'sɪknɪs/ *n* **(a)** [C] (disease) (liter) enfermedad *f* **(b)** [U] (nausea) náuseas *fpl*; (vomiting) vómitos *mpl*

sick pay *n* [U] *salario que se percibe mientras se está con permiso por enfermedad*

side¹ /saɪd/ *n* **1** (surface — of cube, record, coin, piece of paper) lado *m*, cara *f*; (— of building, cupboard) lado *m*, costado *m*; (— of mountain, hill) ladera *f*, falda *f* **2** (boundary, edge): **they were playing by the ~ of the pool** estaban jugando junto a *or* al lado de la piscina **3 (a)** (of person) costado *m*; (of animal) ijada *f*, ijar *m*; **Roy stood at her ~** Roy estaba a su lado; **they sat ~ by ~** estaban sentados uno junto al otro **(b)** (Culin) **a ~ of beef** media res *f* **4** (contrasted area, part, half) lado *m*; **from ~ to ~** de un lado al otro; ***on the ~***: **he repairs cars on the ~** arregla coches como trabajo extra **5 (a)** (faction): **to take ~s** tomar partido; **whose ~ are you on?** ¿tú de parte de quién estás? **(b)** (Sport) equipo *m* **6** (area, aspect) lado *m*, aspecto *m*; **you must listen to both ~s of the story** hay que oír las dos versiones; **it's a little on the short ~** es un poco corto

● **side with** [*v* + *prep* + *o*] ponerse* de parte de

side² *adj* (*before n, no comp*) **(a)** ‹*door/entrance/wall*› lateral; **a ~ street** una calle lateral, una lateral **(b)** (incidental, secondary) ‹*issue*› secundario **(c)** (Culin): **~ dish** acompañamiento *m*; **a ~ salad** una ensalada (*como acompañamiento*)

side: **~board** *n* **1** (piece of furniture) aparador *m*, seibó *m* (Ven); **2 ~boards** *pl* (BrE) ~BURNS; **~burns** *pl n* patillas *fpl*; **~car** *n* sidecar *m*; **~ effect** *n* (of drug, treatment) efecto *m* secundario; (incidental result) consecuencia *f* indirecta; **~kick** *n* (colloq) adlátere *mf*; **~line** *n* **1** (Sport) línea *f* de banda; **2** (subsidiary activity) actividad *f* suplementaria; **~long** *adj* (*before n*) ‹*glance*› de reojo, de soslayo; **~saddle** *adv* a mujeriegas (*con las dos piernas hacia el mismo lado*); **~show** *n* (at fair) puesto *m*; **~step** *vt* **-pp-** ‹*blow/opponent*› esquivar; ‹*problem/question*› eludir; **~track** *vt* **(a)** (from subject) hacer* desviar del tema **(b)** (from purpose): **sorry, I got ~tracked** perdón, me entretuve haciendo otra cosa; **~walk** *n* (AmE) acera *f*, banqueta *f* (Méx), andén *m* (AmC, Col), vereda *f* (CS, Per)

sideways¹ /'saɪdweɪz/ *adv* **(a)** ‹*glance*› de reojo, de soslayo; ‹*walk*› de lado/de costado **(b)** (with side part forward) de lado

sideways² *adj* ‹*look*› de reojo, de soslayo; ‹*movement*› lateral, de lado

siding /'saɪdɪŋ/ *n* (Rail) apartadero *m*

sidle /'saɪdl̩/ *vi* **to ~ up to sb** acercársele* sigilosamente a algn

siege /si:dʒ/ *n* sitio *m*; **the city was under ~** la ciudad estaba sitiada

Sierra Leone /si'erəli'əʊn/ *n* Sierra Leona *f*

siesta /si'estə/ *n* siesta *f*; **to have a ~** dormir* *or* echarse una siesta

sieve¹ /sɪv/ *n* (Culin) (for flour etc) tamiz *m*, cedazo *m*, cernidor *m*

sieve² *vt* ‹*flour*› (BrE) tamizar*, cernir*, cerner*

sift /sɪft/ *vt* **(a)** ‹*sugar/flour*› tamizar*, cernir*, cerner*; (sprinkle) espolvorear **(b)** ‹*facts/evidence*› pasar por el tamiz *or* la criba

sigh¹ /saɪ/ *vi* suspirar; **he ~ed with relief/contentment** suspiró aliviado/satisfecho

sigh² *n* suspiro *m*; **she breathed** *o* **heaved a ~ of relief** dio un suspiro de alivio

sight¹ /saɪt/ *n* **1** [U] (*eye~*) vista *f* **2** [U] (range of vision): **to come into ~** aparecer*; **to lose ~ of sth/sb** perder* algo/a algn de vista; **the finishing line was now in ~** ya se veía la meta; **she watched until they were out of ~** los siguió con la mirada hasta que los perdió de vista **3** (act of seeing, view) (*no pl*): **at first ~** a primera vista; **it was love at first ~** fue amor a primera vista; **to catch ~ of sth/sb** ver* algo/ a algn; (in distance) avistar algo/a algn; **to know sb by ~** conocer* a algn de vista; **to play at** *o* **by ~** (Mus) tocar* a primera vista; **I can't stand the ~ of him** (colloq) no lo puedo ver (fam) **4** [C] **(a)** (thing seen): **the sparrow is a familiar ~ in our gardens** el gorrión se ve con frecuencia en nuestros jardines; **it's not a pretty ~** (colloq) no es muy agradable de ver **(b)** **sights** *pl* (famous places): **to see the ~s** visitar los lugares de interés **5 (a)** [C] (of gun) mira *f* **(b)** **sights** *pl* (ambition): **to have sth in one's ~s** tener* la mira puesta en algo

sight² *vt* ‹*land/ship*› divisar; ‹*person/animal*› ver*

sighted /'saɪtəd ‖ 'saɪtɪd/ *adj* vidente; **he's partially ~** tiene visión parcial

sight: **~seeing** /'saɪt,si:ɪŋ/ *n* [U]: **to go ~seeing** ir* a visitar los lugares de interés; **~seer** /'saɪt,si:ər/ *n* turista *mf*, visitante *mf*

sign¹ /saɪn/ *n* **1 (a)** [C U] (indication) señal *f*, indicio *m*; **it's a ~ of the times** es un indicio de los tiempos que corren **(b)** [C] (omen) presagio *m* **2** [C] (gesture) seña *f*, señal *f* **3** [C] **(a)** (notice, board) letrero *m*, cartel *m*; (in demonstration) pancarta *f* **(b)** (*road ~*) señal *f* (vial) **4** [C] **(a)** (symbol) símbolo *m*; (Math) signo *m* **(b)** (Astrol) signo *m*

sign² *vt* **(a)** (write signature on) firmar **(b)** (hire) ‹*actor*› contratar; ‹*player*› fichar ■ *~ vi* firmar

● **sign for** [*v + prep + o*] ‹*goods/parcel*› firmar el recibo de

● **sign on** [*v + adv*] **(a)** (enlist) «*recruit*» alistarse, enlistarse (AmC, Col, Ven) **(b)** (in UK) (Soc Adm) *anotarse para recibir el seguro de desempleo*, apuntarse al paro (Esp)

● **sign up 1** [*v + adv*] (for a course) inscribirse*, matricularse; (to join the army) alistarse, enlistarse (AmC, Col, Ven) **2** [*v + o + adv, v + adv + o*] ‹*soldiers*› reclutar; ‹*player*› fichar

signal¹ /'sɪgnl̩/ *n* señal *f*

signal², (BrE) **-ll-** *vt* señalar ■ *~ vi* **(a)** (gesture) **to ~ (TO sb)** hacer(le)* señas/una seña (a algn) **(b)** (Auto) señalizar*, poner* el intermitente *or* (Col, Méx) la direccional *or* (CS) el señalizador

signature /'sɪgnətʃʊr ‖ 'sɪgnətʃə(r)/ *n* **1** (written name) firma *f* **2** (Mus): **time ~** compás *m*, tiempo *m*

signature tune *n* (BrE) sintonía *f* (del programa), cortina *f* musical (CS)

significance /sɪg'nɪfɪkəns/ *n* [U] importancia *f*

significant /sɪg'nɪfɪkənt/ *adj* **(a)** (important) importante **(b)** (meaningful) ‹*look/smile*› expresivo; ‹*fact/remark*› significativo

significantly /sɪg'nɪfɪkəntli/ *adv* considerablemente

signify /'sɪgnəfaɪ ‖ 'sɪgnɪfaɪ/ *vt* **-fies, -fying, -fied** significar*

sign language *n* [U C] lenguaje *m* gestual

signpost¹ /'saɪnpəʊst/ *n* señal *f*, poste *m* indicador

signpost² *vt* (BrE Auto) ‹*way/route*› señalizar*

Sikh¹ /si:k/ *n* sij *mf*

Sikh² *adj* sij *adj inv*

silage /'saɪlɪdʒ/ *n* [U] ensilaje *m*, ensilado *m* (*forraje fermentado en silos*)

silence¹ /'saɪləns/ *n* silencio *m*; **in ~** en silencio

silence² *vt* ‹*cries/voice*› acallar; ‹*child/animal*› hacer* callar; ‹*opposition/criticism*› silenciar

silencer /'saɪlənsər ‖ 'saɪlənsə(r)/ *n* **(a)** (on gun) silenciador *m* **(b)** (on car) (BrE) silenciador *m*, mofle *m* (AmC, Méx)

silent /'saɪlənt/ *adj* **(a)** (noiseless, still) ‹*night/forest*› silencioso **(b)** (not speaking) ‹*gesture/protest/movie*› mudo; **the 'h' is ~** la hache es muda

silently /'saɪləntli/ *adv* **(a)** (noiselessly) ‹*creep/glide/enter*› silenciosamente **(b)** (without speaking) ‹*pray/stand/listen*› en silencio, calladamente

silent partner *n* socio, -cia *m,f* capitalista

silhouette /'sɪlu'et/ *n* silueta *f*

silicon /'sɪləkən ‖ 'sɪlɪkən/ *n* [U] silicio *m*; (*before n*) **~ chip** (Comput) pastilla *f* de silicio

silk /sɪlk/ *n* [U] seda *f*

silky /'sɪlki/ **-kier, -kiest** *adj* ‹*fabric/fur*› sedoso

sill /sɪl/ *n* (*window~*) alféizar *m*, antepecho *m*

silly /'sɪli/ *adj* **-lier, -liest** ‹*person/idea/mistake*› tonto; ‹*name/hat*› ridículo

silo /'saɪləʊ/ *n* (*pl* **-los**) silo *m*

silt /sɪlt/ *n* [U] cieno *m*, limo *m*

silver[1] /'sɪlvər ‖ 'sɪlvə(r)/ *n* [U] **1** (metal) plata *f* **2 (a)** (household items) platería *f*, plata *f* **(b)** (coins) monedas *fpl* (*de plata, aluminio etc*)

silver[2] *adj* **(a)** (made of silver) de plata **(b)** ▶ **515** (in color) plateado **(c)** (representing 25 years) (*before n*): **~ jubilee** el vigésimo quinto aniversario; **~ wedding** (BrE) bodas *fpl* de plata

silver: **~ foil** *n* [U] (BrE Culin) papel *m* de aluminio *or* de plata; **~-plate** /'sɪlvər'pleɪt ‖ ˌsɪlvə'pleɪt/ *vt* dar*(le) un baño de plata a, platear; **~smith** *n* platero, -ra *m,f*, orfebre *mf*; **~ware** /'sɪlvərwer ‖ 'sɪlvəweə(r)/ *n* [U] platería *f*, plata *f*

similar /'sɪmələr ‖ 'sɪmɪlə(r)/ *adj* similar, parecido, semejante; **to be ~ TO sth** parecerse* A algo

similarity /'sɪmə'lærəti ‖ ˌsɪmɪ'lærəti/ *n* (*pl* **-ties**) **(a)** [U] (likeness — between things) similitud *f*, parecido *m*, semejanza *f*; (— between persons) parecido *m* **(b)** [C] (common feature) semejanza *f*, similitud *f*

similarly /'sɪmələrli ‖ 'sɪmɪləli/ *adv* **(a)** (in a similar way) de modo parecido *or* similar **(b)** (equally) igualmente **(c)** (*as linker*) asimismo

simile /'sɪməli ‖ 'sɪmɪli/ *n* [C U] símil *m*

simmer /'sɪmər ‖ 'sɪmə(r)/ *vt/i* hervir* a fuego lento

simple /'sɪmpəl/ *adj* **simpler** /-plər/, **simplest** /-pləst/ **1** (uncomplicated) ‹*task/problem*› sencillo, simple **2** (plain, unpretentious) ‹*dress/food*› sencillo, simple **3 (a)** (unsophisticated, humble) simple **(b)** (backward) simple

simplicity /sɪm'plɪsəti/ *n* [U] simplicidad *f*, sencillez *f*

simplify /'sɪmpləfaɪ ‖ 'sɪmplɪfaɪ/ *vt* **-fies, -fying, -fied** simplificar*

simplistic /sɪm'plɪstɪk/ *adj* simplista

simply /'sɪmpli/ *adv* **1** (only, merely) simplemente, sencillamente **2 (a)** (plainly) con sencillez, sencillamente **(b)** (in simple language) simplemente, sencillamente

simulate /'sɪmjəleɪt ‖ 'sɪmjʊleɪt/ *vt* simular

simultaneous /'saɪməl'teɪniəs ‖ ˌsɪməl'teɪniəs/ *adj* simultáneo

simultaneously /'saɪməl'teɪniəsli ‖ ˌsɪməl'teɪniəsli/ *adv* simultáneamente, a la vez

sin[1] /sɪn/ *n* [C U] pecado *m*

sin[2] *vi* **-nn-** pecar*

since[1] /sɪns/ *conj* **1** (in time) desde que; **~ coming to London** desde que vino (*or* vine *etc*) a Londres **2** (introducing a reason) ya que; **~ you can't go, can I have your ticket?** ya que no puedes ir ¿me das tu entrada?

since[2] *prep* desde; **they've worked there ~ 1970** han trabajado allí desde 1970; **how long is it ~ your operation?** ¿cuánto (tiempo) hace de tu operación?

since[3] *adv* desde entonces; **she has lived here ever ~** desde entonces que vive aquí

sincere /sɪn'sɪr ‖ sɪn'sɪə(r)/, **sincerer, sincerest** *adj* sincero

sincerely /sɪn'sɪrli ‖ sɪn'sɪəli/ *adv* sinceramente; **~ (yours)** *o* (BrE) **yours ~** (in letters) (saluda) a usted atentamente

sincerity /sɪn'serəti/ *n* [U] sinceridad *f*

sinew /'sɪnju:/ *n* tendón *m*; (in meat) nervio *m*

sinful /'sɪnfəl/ *adj* ‹*person*› pecador; ‹*act*› pecaminoso

sing /sɪŋ/ (*past* **sang**; *past p* **sung**) *vt/i* cantar
• **sing along** [*v + adv*] **to ~ along (WITH sb)** cantar (CON algn)

Singapore /'sɪŋgə'pɔ:r ‖ ˌsɪŋə'pɔ:(r)/ *n* Singapur *m*

singe /sɪndʒ/ *vt* **singes, singeing, singed** chamuscar*

singer /'sɪŋər ‖ 'sɪŋə(r)/ *n* cantante *mf*

singing /'sɪŋɪŋ/ *n* [U] canto *m*; (*before n*) **a good ~ voice** una buena voz (para el canto)

single[1] /'sɪŋgəl/ *adj* **1** (just one) (*before n*) solo; **the largest ~ shareholder** el mayor accionista individual; **every ~ day** todos los días sin excepción; (*with neg*) **not a ~ house was left standing** no quedó ni una sola casa en pie **2** (*before n*) **(a)** (for one person) ‹*room*› individual; ‹*bed/sheet*› individual, de una plaza (AmL) **(b)** (not double): **in ~ file** en fila india **(c)** (BrE Transp) ‹*fare/ticket*› de ida, sencillo **3** (unmarried) soltero
• **single out** [*v + o + adv, v + adv + o*]: **to ~ sb out** (select) escoger* a algn en particular; (identify) señalar a algn en particular; **she was ~d out for criticism/praise** se la criticó/elogió a ella en particular

single[2] *n* **1** (Mus) single *m*, (disco *m*) sencillo *m* **2** (ticket) (BrE) boleto *m or* (Esp) billete *m* de ida

single: **~-breasted** /'sɪŋgəl'brestəd ‖ ˌsɪŋgəl 'brestɪd/ *adj* de una fila de botones, derecho (AmL); **~ cream** *n* (BrE) crema *f* líquida, nata *f* líquida (Esp); **~-handed** /'sɪŋgəl'hændəd ‖ ˌsɪŋgəl 'hændɪd/ *adv* sin (la) ayuda de nadie; **~-minded** /'sɪŋgəl'maɪndəd ‖ ˌsɪŋgəl'maɪndɪd/ *adj* decidido, resuelto; **~ parent** *n*: **he's/she's a ~ parent** es un padre/una madre que cría a su(s) hijo(s) sin pareja

singles /'sɪŋgəlz/ *pl n* (Sport) individuales *mpl*, singles *mpl* (AmL)

singsong /'sɪŋsɔ:ŋ ‖ 'sɪŋsɒŋ/ *adj* ‹*voice/accent*› cantarín

singular[1] /'sɪŋgjələr ‖ 'sɪŋgjʊlə(r)/ *adj* singular

singular[2] *n* [U C] singular *m*; **in the ~** en singular

sinister /'sɪnɪstər ‖ 'sɪnɪstə(r)/ *adj* siniestro

sink[1] /sɪŋk/ (*past* **sank**; *past p* **sunk**) *vi* **1 (a)** «*ship/stone*» hundirse **(b)** (subside) **to ~ (INTO sth)** «*building/foundations*» hundirse (EN algo); **he sank back into the chair** se arrellanó en el sillón **2** (fall, drop) «*water/level*» descender*, bajar; «*price/value*» caer* a pique; «*attendance/output*» decaer*; **my heart sank** se me cayó el alma a los pies **3** degenerate) degradarse; **I'd never ~ so low** nunca caería tan bajo ■ **~** *vt* **1** ‹*ship*› hundir **2** (bury, hide) ‹*pipe/cable*› enterrar* **3 (a)** (drive in): **the dog sank its teeth into my thigh** el perro me clavó los dientes en el muslo **(b)** (excavate) ‹*shaft*› abrir*; ‹*well*› perforar

• **sink in** [*v* + *adv*] (colloq): **it finally sank in that** ... finalmente nos dimos cuenta de que ...

sink² *n* **(a)** (in kitchen) fregadero *m*, lavaplatos *m* (Andes) **(b)** (washbasin) (AmE) lavabo *m*, lavamanos *m*, lavatorio *m* (CS), pileta *f* (RPl)

sinner /ˈsɪnər ‖ ˈsɪnə(r)/ *n* pecador, -dora *m,f*

sinus /ˈsaɪnəs/ *n* (*pl* **-nuses**) seno *m*

sip¹ /sɪp/ *vt* **-pp-** sorber, beber *or* tomar a sorbos

sip² *n* sorbo *m*

siphon /ˈsaɪfən/ *n* sifón *m*

• **siphon off** [*v* + *o* + *adv*, *v* + *adv* + *o*] ‹*liquid/fuel*› sacar* con sifón; ‹*money*› desviar*

sir /sɜːr ‖ sɜː/ *n* **1 (a)** ▶ **603** (as form of address — to male customer) señor, caballero; (— to male teacher) (BrE) profesor, señor **(b)** (Corresp): **Dear Sir** De mi mayor consideración:, Muy señor mío: **2 Sir** (as title) sir *m*

siren /ˈsaɪrən/ *n* sirena *f*

sirloin /ˈsɜːrlɔɪn ‖ ˈsɜːlɔɪn/ *n* [U C] *preciado corte de carne vacuna del cuarto trasero*

sirup *n* (AmE) ⇒ SYRUP

sister /ˈsɪstər ‖ ˈsɪstə(r)/ *n* **1** (sibling) hermana *f*; (*before n*) ‹*company*› afiliado; **~ ship** buque *m* gemelo **2 (a)** (nun) hermana *f*, monja *f* **(b)** (nurse) (BrE) enfermera *f* jefe *or* jefa (*a cargo de una o más salas*)

sisterhood /ˈsɪstərhʊd ‖ ˈsɪstəhʊd/ *n* **(a)** [C] (association of women) asociación *f* de mujeres **(b)** [C] (Relig) congregación *f* **(c)** [U] (sisterly relationship) solidaridad *f* (*entre mujeres*)

sister-in-law /ˈsɪstərənlɔː ‖ ˈsɪstərɪnlɔː/ *n* (*pl* **sisters-in-law**) cuñada *f*

sisterly /ˈsɪstərli ‖ ˈsɪstəli/ *adj* (propio) de hermana

sit /sɪt/ (*pres p* **sitting**; *past & past p* **sat**) *vi* **1 (a)** (sit down) sentarse* **(b)** (be seated) estar* sentado **2** (be in session) «*committee/court*» reunirse* en sesión, sesionar (esp AmL) **3 sitting** *pres p* ‹*figure*› sentado ■ **~** *vt* **1** (cause to be seated) ‹*person*› sentar*; ‹*object*› poner*, colocar* (*en posición vertical*) **2** (BrE Educ): **to ~ an exam** hacer* *or* dar* *or* (CS) rendir* *or* (Méx) tomar un examen, examinarse

• **sit around** [*v* + *adv*]: **he ~s around all day doing nothing** se pasa el día sentado sin hacer nada

• **sit back** [*v* + *adv*] (colloq) recostarse*

• **sit down** [*v* + *adv*] sentarse*

• **sit in** [*v* + *adv*] **to ~ in on a class** asistir a una clase como oyente (*or* observador *etc*)

• **sit out** [*v* + *o* + *adv*, *v* + *adv* + *o*] **(a)** (wait until end of) ‹*siege*› aguantar; ***to ~ it out*** aguantarse **(b)** (not participate in) ‹*dance*› no bailar; ‹*game*› no tomar parte en

• **sit up** [*v* + *adv*] **(a)** (in upright position) «*person/patient*» incorporarse; «*dog*» sentarse* sobre las patas traseras; **that should make them ~ up and take notice** eso debería alertarlos **(b)** (with straight back) ponerse* derecho, enderezarse* **(c)** (not go to bed): **we sat up talking** nos quedamos (levantados) conversando

sitcom /ˈsɪtkɑːm ‖ ˈsɪtkɒm/ *n* (colloq) ⇒ SITUATION COMEDY

site /saɪt/ *n* **(a)** (location) emplazamiento *m* (frml); (piece of land) terreno *m*, solar *m* **(b)** (*building* **~**) obra *f* **(c)** (*archeological* **~**) yacimiento *m* (arqueológico) **(d)** (*camp***~**) camping *m*

sit-in /ˈsɪtɪn/ *n* (demonstration) sentada *f*, sitin *m* (Méx); (strike) encierro *m*, ocupación *f* *or* toma *f* (*del lugar de trabajo*)

sitting /ˈsɪtɪŋ/ *n* **(a)** (for meal etc) turno *m*; **I watched three movies in a single ~** vi tres películas de una sentada (fam) **(b)** (of committee, parliament) sesión *f*

sitting: **~ duck** *n* (colloq) presa *f* fácil, blanco *m* seguro; **~ room** *n* (BrE) sala *f* de estar, living *m* (esp AmL), salón *m* (esp Esp)

situate /ˈsɪtʃueɪt ‖ ˈsɪtjʊeɪt/ *vt* (locate) (*often pass*) ‹*building/town*› situar*, ubicar* (esp AmL)

situation /ˈsɪtʃuˈeɪʃən ‖ ˌsɪtjʊˈeɪʃən/ *n* **1** (circumstances, position) situación *f* **2** (job) (frml) empleo *m*; Ⓢ **situations vacant** ofertas de empleo

situation comedy *n* [C U] comedia *f* (*acerca de situaciones de la vida diaria*)

sit-up /ˈsɪtʌp/ *n* (ejercicio *m*) abdominal *m* (*levantando el torso del suelo*)

six¹ /sɪks/ ▶ **451**, **724**, **884** *n* seis *m*; ***it's ~ of one and half a dozen of the other*** (colloq) (it makes no difference) da lo mismo; (both parties are to blame) los dos tienen parte de la culpa; *see also* FOUR¹

six² ▶ **451**, **724**, **884** *adj* seis *adj inv*

sixteen /ˈsɪksˈtiːn/ ▶ **451**, **724**, **884** *adj/n* dieciséis *adj inv/m*; *see also* FOUR¹

sixteenth¹ /ˈsɪksˈtiːnθ/ ▶ **540**, **725** *adj* decimosexto

sixteenth² *adv* en decimosexto lugar

sixteenth³ ▶ **540**, **543**, **725** *n* dieciseisavo *m*; (part) dieciseisava parte *f*

sixteenth note *n* (AmE) semicorchea *f*

sixth¹ /sɪksθ/ ▶ **540**, **725** *adj* sexto

sixth² *adv* en sexto lugar

sixth³ ▶ **540**, **543**, **725** *n* (Math) sexto *m*; (part) sexta parte *f*, sexto *m*

sixth: **~ form** *n* (in UK) *los dos últimos años de la enseñanza secundaria*; **~ sense** *n* sexto sentido *m*

sixtieth¹ /ˈsɪkstiəθ/ ▶ **725** *adj* sexagésimo

sixtieth² *adv* en sexagésimo lugar

sixtieth³ ▶ **543**, **725** *n* (Math) sesentavo *m*; (part) sesentava *or* sexagésima parte *f*

sixty /ˈsɪksti/ ▶ **451**, **540**, **724** *adj/n* sesenta *adj inv/m*; *see also* FOUR¹

sizable /ˈsaɪzəbəl/ *adj* ‹*fortune*› considerable; ‹*property*› de proporciones considerables

size /saɪz/ *n* **1** (dimensions) tamaño *m*; (of problem, task) magnitud *f*; **what ~ is it?** ¿de qué tamaño es?; ***to cut sb down to ~*** poner* a algn en su sitio, bajarle los humos a algn (fam) **2** ▶ **401** (of clothes) talla *f* *or* (RPl) talle *m*; (of shoes, gloves) número *m*; **what ~ do you take?** ¿qué talla *or* (RPl) talle tiene *or* usa?; **I take (a) ~ 10 in shoes** calzo *or* (Esp tb) gasto el número 10

• **size up** [*v* + *o* + *adv*, *v* + *adv* + *o*] (colloq) ‹*problem*› evaluar*; **she ~d him up immediately** enseguida lo caló

sizeable *adj* ⇒ SIZABLE

sizzle /'sɪzəl/ *vi* chisporrotear

skate¹ /skeɪt/ *n* **1** [C] (*ice* ~) patín *m* (*para patinaje sobre hielo*); (*roller* ~) patín *m* (*de ruedas*) **2** [U C] (*pl* ~ *or* ~**s**) (Culin, Zool) raya *f*

skate² *vi* patinar

skateboard /'skeɪtbɔ:rd ‖ 'skeɪtbɔ:d/ *n* monopatín *m or* (CS, Méx, Ven) patineta *f*

skater /'skeɪtər ‖ 'skeɪtə(r)/ *n* patinador, -dora *m,f*

skating /'skeɪtɪŋ/ *n* [U] (*ice* ~) patinaje *m* sobre hielo; (*roller* ~) patinaje *m* sobre ruedas; (*before n*) ~ **rink** pista *f* de patinaje

skeleton /'skelətn̩ ‖ 'skelɪtn̩/ *n* **(a)** (Anat) esqueleto *m* **(b)** (of building, vehicle) armazón *m or f*

skeleton key *n* llave *f* maestra

skeptic, (BrE) **sceptic** /'skeptɪk/ *n* escéptico, -ca *m,f*

skeptical, (BrE) **sceptical** /'skeptɪkəl/ *adj* ‹*person/attitude*› escéptico

skepticism, (BrE) **scepticism** /'skeptɪsɪzəm/ *n* [U] escepticismo *m*

sketch¹ /sketʃ/ *n* **1** (drawing) bosquejo *m*, esbozo *m* **2** (Theat, TV) sketch *m*, apunte *m*

sketch² *vt* hacer* un bosquejo de, bosquejar ■ ~ *vi* hacer* bosquejos *or* bocetos

sketch: ~**book** *n* cuaderno *m* de bocetos; ~**pad** *n* bloc *m* de dibujo

sketchy /'sketʃi/ *adj* **-chier, -chiest** ‹*account/treatment*› muy superficial; ‹*knowledge*› muy básico

skewer /'skju:ər ‖ 'skju:ə(r)/ *n* pincho *m*, brocheta *f*

ski¹ /ski:/ *n* esquí *m*

ski² *vi* **skis, skiing, skied** esquiar*; **to go** ~**ing** ir* a esquiar

skid¹ /skɪd/ *n* (Auto) patinazo *m*, patinada *f* (AmL)

skid² *vi* **-dd-** «*car/plane/wheels*» patinar; «*person*» resbalarse; «*object*» deslizarse*

skier /'ski:ər ‖ 'skiə(r)/ *n* esquiador, -dora *m,f*

skiing /'ski:ɪŋ/ *n* [U] esquí *m*

skilful *adj* (BrE) ⇒ SKILLFUL

skilift /'ski:lɪft/ *n* telesquí *m*

skill /skɪl/ *n* **(a)** [U] (ability) habilidad *f*; **technical** ~ destreza *f* **(b)** [C] (technique): **typing is a very useful** ~ **to have** saber escribir a máquina es muy útil; **social** ~**s** don *m* de gente

skilled /skɪld/ *adj* ‹*negotiator*› hábil; ‹*pilot*› diestro; ‹*worker/labor*› calificado *or* (Esp) cualificado; ‹*work*› de especialista

skillful, (BrE) **skilful** /'skɪlfəl/ *adj* ‹*liar/play*› hábil; ‹*surgeon/mechanic*› diestro; (at sewing, craftwork) habilidoso

skim /skɪm/ **-mm-** *vt* **1** (Culin) ‹*milk*› descremar, desnatar (Esp); ‹*soup*› espumar **2 (a)** ‹*water/treetops*› pasar casi rozando **(b)** (throw): **to** ~ **stones** hacer* cabrillas **3** (read quickly) leer* por encima ■ ~ *vi* **1** (glide): **the speedboat** ~**med over the sea** la lancha apenas rozaba la superficie del mar **2** (read quickly) leer* por encima

skim milk, (BrE) **skimmed milk** /skɪmd/ *n* [U] leche *f* descremada *or* (Esp tb) desnatada

skimp /skɪmp/ *vi* (colloq) **to** ~ (ON **sth**) escatimar (algo)

skimpy /'skɪmpi/ *adj* **-pier, -piest** ‹*meal/portion*› mezquino, pobre; ‹*funds*› escaso; ‹*nightdress/bikini*› brevísimo

skin¹ /skɪn/ *n* **(a)** [U] (of person) piel *f*; (esp of face; in terms of quality, condition) cutis *m*, piel *f*; (in terms of color) tez *f*, piel *f*; ***to have a thick/thin*** ~ ser* insensible/muy sensible a las críticas **(b)** [U C] (of animal, bird, fish) piel *f* **(c)** [U C] (of tomatoes, plums, sausage) piel *f*; (of potatoes, bananas) piel *f*, cáscara *f* **(d)** [U] (on milk, custard) nata *f*; (on paint) capa *f* dura

skin² *vt* **-nn-** ‹*animal*› despellejar, desollar*

skin: ~**deep** /'skɪn'di:p/ *adj* (*pred*) superficial; ~**diver** *n* buzo *m*, submarinista *mf*; ~**diving** *n* [U] submarinismo *m*, buceo *m*

skinny /'skɪni/ *adj* **-nier, -niest** flaco, flacucho (fam)

skintight /'skɪn'taɪt/ *adj* muy ceñido, muy ajustado

skip¹ /skɪp/ *n* **1** (jump) brinco *m*, saltito *m* **2** (BrE) (container) contenedor *m* (*para escombros, basura etc*)

skip² **-pp-** *vi* **(a)** (move lightly and quickly) brincar, dar* saltitos **(b)** (with rope) (BrE) ⇒ *vt* 2 ■ ~ *vt* **1 (a)** (omit) ‹*page/chapter*› saltarse **(b)** (not attend) ‹*class/meeting*› faltar a **2** (jump) (AmE): **to** ~ **rope** saltar a la cuerda *or* (Esp tb) a la comba

skipper /'skɪpər ‖ 'skɪpə(r)/ *n* (colloq) **(a)** (of boat) patrón, -trona *m,f*, capitán, -tana *m,f*; (of plane) capitán, -tana *m,f* **(b)** (Sport) (coach) entrenador, -dora *m,f*; (captain) capitán, -tana *m,f*

skip rope, (BrE) **skipping rope** /'skɪpɪŋ/ *n* ⇒ JUMP ROPE

skirmish /'skɜ:rmɪʃ ‖ 'skɜ:mɪʃ/ *n* escaramuza *f*

skirt¹ /skɜ:rt ‖ skɜ:t/ *n* falda *f*, pollera *f* (CS)

skirt² *vt* **(a)** (run alongside) bordear **(b)** ⇒ SKIRT AROUND

• **skirt around**, (BrE also) **skirt round** [*v* + *prep* + *o*] **(a)** ‹*mountain/lake*› bordear **(b)** ‹*issue/problem*› eludir

skittle /'skɪtl̩/ *n* bolo *m*

skittles /'skɪtl̩z/ *n* (+ *sing vb*) bolos *mpl*

skive off /skaɪv/ [*v* + *adv*] (BrE colloq) **(a)** (disappear) escurrir el bulto (fam), escaparse, pirarse (Esp fam) **(b)** (stay away — from school) hacer* novillos (fam); (— from work) no ir* a trabajar, capear (Chi) *or* (Col) capar trabajo (fam)

skulk /skʌlk/ *vi*: **I saw him** ~**ing in the background** lo vi al fondo, tratando de pasar desapercibido; **to** ~ **around** merodear

skull /skʌl/ *n* cráneo *m*

skullcap /'skʌlkæp/ *n* casquete *m*; (Relig) solideo *m*

skunk /skʌŋk/ *n* mofeta *f*, zorrillo *m* (AmL), zorrino *m* (CS), mapurite *m* (AmC, Ven)

sky /skaɪ/ *n* [U C] (*pl* **skies**) cielo *m*

sky: ~**diving** *n* [U] paracaidismo *m* (*en la modalidad de caída libre*); ~**high** /'skaɪ'haɪ/ *adj*: **prices are** ~**high** los precios están por las nubes; ~**lark** *n* alondra *f*; ~**light** *n* tragaluz *m*, claraboya *f*; ~**line** *n* **(a)** (horizon) (línea *f* del) horizonte *m* **(b)**

(of city): **the Manhattan ~line** los edificios de Manhattan recortados contra el horizonte; **~scraper** *n* rascacielos *m*

slab /slæb/ *n* (of stone) losa *f*; (of concrete) bloque *m*; (of wood) tabla *f*; (of cake, bread) pedazo *m*, trozo *m* (*grueso*)

slack¹ /slæk/ *adj* **-er, -est 1** (loose) ‹*rope/cable*› flojo **2** (lax, negligent) ‹*student*› poco aplicado; ‹*piece of work*› flojo **3** (not busy) ‹*period*› de poca actividad

slack² *n* [U]: **there's too much ~ in the rope** la cuerda está demasiado floja; ***to take up the ~ in sth*** tensar algo

slack³ *vi* (colloq) haraganear, flojear (fam)

slacken /ˈslækən/ *vi* **(a)** (become looser) «*rope/wire*» aflojarse **(b)** (diminish) ⇒ SLACKEN OFF 1 ■ ~ *vt* **(a)** (loosen) ⇒ SLACKEN OFF 2 **(b)** (reduce) ‹*speed*› reducir*; ‹*pace*› aflojar

• **slacken off 1** [*v* + *adv*] «*wind*» amainar, aflojar; «*student*» aflojar el ritmo de trabajo; «*speed/rate*» disminuir*; «*trade/demand*» decaer*, disminuir* **2** [*v* + *o* + *adv*, *v* + *adv* + *o*] ‹*rope/wire*› aflojar

slacks /slæks/ *n* pantalones *mpl* (de sport)

slag /slæg/ *n* [U] (Metall) escoria *f*; (Min) escombro *m*, escoria *f*; (*before n*) **~ heap** escorial *m*, escombrera *f*

slain /sleɪn/ *past p of* SLAY

slake /sleɪk/ *vt* (liter) ‹*thirst*› saciar

slalom /ˈslɑːləm/ *n* slalom *m*

slam /slæm/ **-mm-** *vt* **1 (a)** (close violently): **to ~ the door** dar* un portazo **(b)** (put with force): **he ~med the book down on the table** tiró el libro sobre la mesa **2** (criticize) (journ) atacar* violentamente ■ ~ *vi* «*door*» cerrarse* de un portazo

slander¹ /ˈslændər ‖ ˈslɑːndə(r)/ *n* [U C] calumnia *f*, difamación *f*

slander² *vt* calumniar, difamar

slang /slæŋ/ *n* [U] argot *m*

slant¹ /slænt ‖ slɑːnt/ *n* **1** [U] (slope) inclinación *f*; (of roof, floor) pendiente *f* **2** [C] (point of view) enfoque *m*; (bias) sesgo *m*

slant² *vi* **(a)** inclinarse **(b) slanting** *pres p* inclinado; ‹*eyes*› rasgado

slap¹ /slæp/ *vt* **-pp- 1** (hit): **to ~ sb** (on face) pegarle* *or* darle* una bofetada *or* (AmL tb) una cachetada a algn; (on arm, leg) pegarle* *or* darle* una palmada a algn **2 (a)** (put with force) tirar **(b)** (put, apply carelessly): **he ~ped some paint on it** le dio una mano de pintura rápidamente; **she ~ped on some makeup** se maquilló de cualquier manera

slap² *n* (on face) bofetada *f*, cachetada *f* (AmL); (on back, leg) palmada *f*

slap: **~dash** *adj* ‹*work*› chapucero (fam); **~stick** *n* [U] bufonadas *fpl*; (*before n*) **~stick comedy** astracanada *f*

slash¹ /slæʃ/ *n* **1** (cut — on body) cuchillada *f*, tajo *m*; (— in tire, cloth) raja *f*, corte *m* **2** (oblique) barra *f* (oblicua)

slash² *vt* **1** ‹*person/face*› acuchillar, tajear (AmL); ‹*tires/coat*› rajar; **he ~ed his wrists** se cortó las venas **2** (reduce) ‹*prices/taxes*› rebajar drásticamente

slat /slæt/ *n* (of wood) listón *m*, tablilla *f*; (of other material) tira *f*

slate¹ /sleɪt/ *n* [C U] pizarra *f*

slate² *vt* **1** ‹*roof*› empizarrar **2** (criticize) ‹*book/film/writer*› poner* por los suelos

slaughter¹ /ˈslɔːtər ‖ ˈslɔːtə(r)/ *n* [U] (of animals) matanza *f*; (massacre) matanza *f*, carnicería *f*

slaughter² *vt* ‹*animal*› matar, carnear (CS); ‹*people*› matar salvajemente

slaughterhouse /ˈslɔːtərhaʊs ‖ ˈslɔːtəhaʊs/ *n* matadero *m*

Slav /slɑːv/ *n* eslavo, -va *m,f*

slave¹ /sleɪv/ *n* esclavo, -va *m,f*

slave² *vi* (colloq): **I've been slaving away all day** he estado trabajando como un negro todo el día (fam)

slave: **~ driver** *n* (colloq) negrero, -ra *m,f* (fam); **~ labor**, (BrE) **~ labour** *n* [U] el trabajo de los esclavos

slaver /ˈslævər ‖ ˈslævə(r)/ *vi* babear

slavery /ˈsleɪvəri/ *n* [U] esclavitud *f*

slaw /slɔː/ *n* [U] (AmE) *ensalada de repollo, zanahoria y cebolla con mayonesa*

slay /sleɪ/ *vt* (*past* **slew**; *past p* **slain**) (liter *or* journ) dar* muerte a

sleazy /ˈsliːzi/ *adj* **-zier, -ziest** ‹*district/bar*› sórdido; ‹*character/type*› de mala pinta

sled¹ /sled/ *n* (AmE) trineo *m*

sled² *vi* **-dd-** (AmE) ir* en trineo

sledge /sledʒ/ *n/vi* ⇒ SLED[1,2]

sledgehammer /ˈsledʒˌhæmər ‖ ˈsledʒˌhæmə(r)/ *n* mazo *m*, almádena *f*

sleek /sliːk/ *adj* **-er, -est (a)** (glossy) ‹*hair/fur*› lacio y brillante **(b)** (well-groomed) acicalado

sleep¹ /sliːp/ *n* **1** [U C] sueño *m*; **to go to ~** dormirse*; **my foot has gone to ~** se me ha dormido el pie; **the cat had to be put to ~** (euph) hubo que sacrificar al gato (euf); **to talk in one's ~** hablar dormido **2** [U] (in eyes) lagañas *fpl*, legañas *fpl*

sleep² (*past & past p* **slept**) *vi* dormir* ■ ~ *vt*: **the hotel ~s 200 guests** el hotel tiene 200 camas

• **sleep around** [*v* + *adv*] (colloq & pej) acostarse* con cualquiera

• **sleep in** [*v* + *adv*] **(a)** (sleep late) dormir* hasta tarde **(b)** «*servant/nurse*» vivir en (la) casa (*or* hospital *etc*)

• **sleep on** [*v* + *prep* + *o*] ‹*decision/problem*› consultar con la almohada

• **sleep through** [*v* + *prep* + *o*]: **he slept through the alarm clock** no oyó el despertador y siguió durmiendo; **she slept through the whole film** durmió durante toda la película

• **sleep together** [*v* + *adv*] (euph) tener* relaciones (sexuales)

• **sleep with** [*v* + *prep* + *o*] (euph) acostarse* con (euf)

sleeper /ˈsliːpər ‖ ˈsliːpə(r)/ *n* **1** (person): **to be a heavy/light ~** tener* el sueño pesado/ligero **2** (Rail) **(a)** (berth) litera *f* **(b)** (train) tren *m* con coches camas *or* (CS) coches dormitorio **3** (on track) (Rail) durmiente *m or* (Esp) traviesa *f*

sleeping /ˈsliːpɪŋ/: ~ **bag** /ˈsliːpɪŋ/ *n* saco *m* de dormir; ~ **car** *n* (Rail) coche *m* cama, coche *m* dormitorio (CS); ~ **partner** *n* (BrE) socio, -cia *m,f* capitalista; ~ **pill**, ~ **tablet** (BrE) *n* somnífero *m*

sleepless /ˈsliːpləs ‖ ˈsliːplɪs/ *adj*: **to have a ~ night** pasar la noche en blanco

sleepwalk /ˈsliːpwɔːk/ *vi* caminar dormido

sleepy /ˈsliːpi/ *adj* **-pier, -piest** ‹*expression*› adormilado, somnoliento; **to be/feel ~** tener* sueño

sleet /sliːt/ ▶ 920 *n* [U] aguanieve *f*

sleeve /sliːv/ *n* **(a)** (of garment) manga *f*; ***to have sth up one's ~*** (colloq) tener* algo planeado **(b)** (of record) (BrE) funda *f*, carátula *f*

sleeveless /ˈsliːvləs ‖ ˈsliːvlɪs/ *adj* sin mangas

sleigh /sleɪ/ *n* trineo *m*

sleight of hand /slaɪt/ *n* [U] prestidigitación *f*

slender /ˈslendər ‖ ˈslendə(r)/ *adj* **-derer, -derest (a)** ‹*person/figure*› delgado, esbelto; ‹*waist/neck*› fino, delgado **(b)** ‹*means*› escaso; ‹*majority*› estrecho

slept /slept/ *past & past p of* SLEEP[2]

sleuth /sluːθ/ *n* sabueso *mf*

slew /sluː/ *past of* SLAY

slice[1] /slaɪs/ *n* (piece — of bread, cheese) rebanada *f*; (— of cake) trozo *m*; (— of lemon, cucumber) rodaja *f*; (— of meat) tajada *f*; (— of ham) loncha *f*, lonja *f*; (— of melon) raja *f*

slice[2] *vt* ‹*bread*› cortar (en rebanadas); ‹*meat*› cortar (en tajadas); ‹*cake*› cortar (en trozos); ‹*lemon/cucumber*› cortar (en rodajas); ‹*ham*› cortar (en lonchas)

slick[1] /slɪk/ *adj* **-er, -est 1 (a)** ‹*book/program*› ingenioso pero insustancial **(b)** ‹*person*› (glib) de mucha labia; (clever) hábil; ‹*reply*› fácil **(c)** ‹*performance/production*› muy logrado *or* pulido **2** (slippery) (AmE) ‹*surface*› resbaladizo

slick[2] *n* (*oil* ~) marea *f* negra

slide[1] /slaɪd/ (*past & past p* **slid** /slɪd/) *vi* deslizarse* ■ ~ *vt* (+ *adv compl*): **she slid the book across the table to him** le pasó el libro deslizándolo por la mesa; **to ~ the bolt back** correr el cerrojo

slide[2] *n* **1** (in playground) tobogán *m* **2** (action — accidental) resbalón *m*, resbalada *f*; (— deliberate) deslizamiento *m* **3 (a)** (Phot) diapositiva *f*; (*before n*) ~ **projector** proyector *m* de diapositivas **(b)** (for microscope — glass plate) portaobjetos *m*; (— specimen) muestra *f* **4** (for hair) (BrE) ⇒ BARRETTE

slide rule *n* regla *f* de cálculo

sliding /ˈslaɪdɪŋ/: ~ **door** puerta *f* corrediza; ~ **scale** *n* escala *f* móvil

slight[1] /slaɪt/ *adj* **-er, -est 1 (a)** ‹*improvement/accent*› ligero, leve; **she has a ~ temperature** tiene un poco de fiebre; **I haven't the ~est idea** no tengo (ni) la menor idea; **he's not the ~est bit interested** no le interesa en lo más mínimo **(b)** (minimal) ‹*chance/hope*› escaso **2** (slim) delgado, menudo

slight[2] *vt* (frml) desairar

slight[3] *n* (frml) desaire *m*

slightly /ˈslaɪtli/ *adv* ligeramente

slim[1] /slɪm/ *adj* **-mm-** ‹*person/figure*› esbelto, delgado; ‹*waist*› fino; ‹*chance*› escaso; ‹*majority*› estrecho

slim[2] *vi* **-mm- (a)** (become slimmer) adelgazar*, bajar de peso **(b)** (BrE) (diet) hacer* régimen

slime /slaɪm/ *n* [U] (thin mud) limo *m*, cieno *m*; (of snail, slug etc) baba *f*

slimmer /ˈslɪmər ‖ ˈslɪmə(r)/ *n* (BrE) *persona que está a régimen*

slimy /ˈslaɪmi/ *adj* **-mier, -miest (a)** ‹*substance/surface*› viscoso **(b)** ‹*person*› excesivamente obsequioso, falso

sling[1] /slɪŋ/ *n* **(a)** (Med) cabestrillo *m* **(b)** (for carrying a baby) canguro *m* **(c)** (for lifting) eslinga *f*

sling[2] *vt* (*past & past p* **slung**) (colloq) tirar, lanzar*, aventar* (Col, Méx, Per)

slink /slɪŋk/ *vi* (*past & past p* **slunk**) (+ *adv compl*): **to ~ off** *o* **away** escabullirse*

slip[1] /slɪp/ *n* **1** (slide) resbalón *m*, resbalada *f* (AmL); ***to give sb the ~*** (colloq) lograr zafarse de algn **2** (mistake) error *m*; **a ~ of the tongue/pen** un lapsus (linguae/cálami) **3 a ~ of paper** un papelito, un papel **4** [C] (undergarment) (full-length) combinación *f*; (half-length) enagua *f*, fondo *m* (Méx)

slip[2] **-pp-** *vi* **1 (a)** (slide, shift position) «*person*» resbalar(se); «*clutch*» patinar; **it just ~ped out of my hands** se me resbaló de las manos **(b)** «*standards/service*» decaer* **2 (a)** (move unobtrusively) (+ *adv compl*): **he ~ped out the back door** se deslizó por la puerta trasera; **we managed to ~ past the guards** logramos pasar sin que nos vieran las guardias **(b)** (escape, be lost): **to let ~ an opportunity** dejar escapar una oportunidad; **to ~ through one's fingers** escapársele a algn de las manos; **I didn't mean to say that: it just ~ped out** no quería decirlo, pero se me escapó ■ ~ *vt* **1 (a)** (put unobtrusively) (+ *adv compl*) poner*, meter, deslizar*; **she ~ped a coin into his hand** le pasó disimuladamente una moneda **(b)** (pass) **to ~ sth** TO **sb** pasarle algo A algn con disimulo **2** ***to ~ sb's mind***: **it ~ped my mind** me olvidé, se me olvidó

• **slip away** «*person/opportunity*» escabullirse*; «*hours/time*» pasar

• **slip in** [*v* + *o* + *adv*, *v* + *adv* + *o*] ‹*comment/reference*› incluir*

• **slip off 1** [*v* + *o* + *adv*, *v* + *adv* + *o*] ‹*clothes/shoes*› quitarse **2** [*v* + *adv*] escabullirse*

• **slip on** [*v* + *o* + *adv*, *v* + *adv* + *o*] ‹*clothes/shoes*› ponerse*

• **slip up** [*v* + *adv*] equivocarse*

slipped disc /slɪpt/ *n* hernia *f* de disco

slipper /ˈslɪpər ‖ ˈslɪpə(r)/ *n* zapatilla *f*, pantufla *f* (esp AmL)

slippery /ˈslɪpəri/ *adj* **(a)** ‹*surface/soap*› resbaladizo, resbaloso (AmL) **(b)** ‹*person*› (elusive) escurridizo; (untrustworthy) que no es de fiar

slip: **~-road** *n* (BrE) vía *f* de acceso; **~-up** *n* error *m*

slit[1] /slɪt/ *n* (opening) rendija *f*; (cut) raja *f*

slit² *vt* (*pres p* **sitting**; *past & past p* **slit**) cortar, rajar (Méx); **to ~ sb's throat** degollar a algn

slither /'slɪðər || 'slɪðə(r)/ *vi* «*snake*» deslizarse*

sliver /'slɪvər || 'slɪvə(r)/ *n* **(a)** (of glass, wood) astilla *f* **(b)** (thin slice) tajada *f* (*or* rodaja *f etc*) fina; *see also* SLICE¹

slob /slɑ:b || slɒb/ *n* (colloq) vago, -ga *m,f* (fam)

slobber /'slɑ:bər || 'slɒbə(r)/ *vi* babear

slog /slɑ:g || slɒg/ *n* (colloq) (*no pl*): **we've got a long ~ ahead of us** tenemos un largo y arduo camino por delante

• **slog away**: **-gg-** [*v* + *adv*] (BrE colloq) sudar tinta (fam), trabajar duro (esp AmL)

slogan /'sləʊgən/ *n* (Busn) slogan *m*, eslogan *m*; (Pol) lema *m*, consigna *f*

slop /slɑ:p || slɒp/ *vi* **-pp-** (colloq) (spill) derramarse, volcarse*

slope¹ /sləʊp/ *n* **(a)** (sloping ground) cuesta *f*, pendiente *f*, barranca *f* (RPl) **(b)** (of mountain) ladera *f*, falda *f* **(c)** (for skiing) pista *f* de esquí, cancha *f* de esquí (CS)

slope² *vi*: **to ~ down** «*hill/road*» tener* un declive; **her handwriting ~s backward/forward** tiene la letra inclinada hacia atrás/adelante

sloping /'sləʊpɪŋ/ *adj* ‹*field/floor*› en declive; ‹*roof/handwriting*› inclinado

sloppy /'slɑ:pi || 'slɒpi/ *adj* **-pier, -piest 1** (careless) ‹*manners/work*› descuidado; ‹*presentation*› descuidado, desprolijo (CS) **2** ‹*kiss*› baboso

slosh /slɑ:ʃ || slɒʃ/ *vt* (splash) echar ■ ~ *vi* **to ~ around** *o* **about** «*person*» chapotear; «*liquid*» agitarse haciendo ruido

slot¹ /slɑ:t || slɒt/ *n* **1** (opening, groove) ranura *f* **2** (Rad, TV) espacio *m*

slot² **-tt-** *vt* (insert) **to ~ sth INTO sth** encajar algo EN algo

• **slot in 1** [*v* + *adv*] «*shelf/part*» encajar **2** [*v* + *o* + *adv*, *v* + *adv* + *o*] ‹*component*› hacer* encajar

sloth /sləʊθ/ *n* (Zool) perezoso *m*

slot machine *n* **(a)** (vending machine) distribuidor *m* automático, máquina *f* expendedora **(b)** (for gambling) máquina *f* tragamonedas *or* (Esp tb) tragaperras

slouch /slaʊtʃ/ *vi* **(a)** (droop shoulders) encorvarse; **don't ~!** ¡ponte derecho! **(b)** (walk) (+ *adv compl*): **he ~ed out of the room** salió de la habitación arrastrando los pies

Slovak /'sləʊvæk/ *n* **(a)** [C] (person) eslovaco, -ca *m,f* **(b)** [U] (language) eslovaco *m*

Slovakia /sləʊ'vɑ:ki:ə || sləʊ'vækiə/ *n* Eslovaquia *f*

Slovene /'sləʊvi:n/ *n* **(a)** [C] (person) esloveno, -na *m,f* **(b)** [U] (language) esloveno *m*

Slovenia /sləʊ'vi:njə/ *n* Eslovenia *f*

slovenly /'slʌvənli/ *adj* **-lier, -liest** ‹*work*› descuidado; ‹*person*› desaliñado

slow¹ /sləʊ/ *adj* **-er, -est 1** ‹*speed/rate/reactions*› lento; **to be ~ to + INF** tardar EN + INF **2 (a)** (not lively) ‹*novel/plot*› lento **(b)** (stupid) (euph) poco despierto (euf) **3** (of clock, watch) (*pred*): **my watch is five minutes ~** mi reloj está cinco minutos atrasado

slow² *vi*: **the train ~ed to a stop** el tren fue disminuyendo la velocidad hasta detenerse ■ ~ *vt*: **bad weather ~ed their progress** el mal tiempo los retrasó

• **slow down 1** [*v* + *adv*] **(a)** (go more slowly) «*runner*» aflojar el paso; «*vehicle/driver*» reducir* la velocidad; «*speaker*» hablar más despacio **(b)** (be less active) (colloq) tomarse las cosas con más calma **2** [*v* + *o* + *adv*, *v* + *adv* + *o*] **(a)** ‹*process*› hacer* más lento **(b)** ‹*vehicle/engine*› reducir* la velocidad de

• **slow up** ⇒ SLOW DOWN

slow³ *adv* lentamente, despacio

slowly /'sləʊli/ *adv* lentamente, despacio

slow motion *n* [U] cámara *f* lenta; **in ~ ~** en *or* (Esp) a cámara lenta

sludge /slʌdʒ/ *n* lodo *m*, fango *m*

slug /slʌg/ *n* (Zool) babosa *f*

sluggish /'slʌgɪʃ/ *adj* **(a)** (slow-moving) lento; ‹*stream/river*› de aguas mansas **(b)** ‹*growth*› lento

sluice /slu:s/ *n* **(a)** (channel) canal *m*, conducto *m* (de esclusa) **(b)** (sluicegate) compuerta *f*

sluicegate /'slu:sgeɪt/ *n* compuerta *f* (de esclusa)

slum /slʌm/ *n* **(a)** (poor urban area) (*often pl*) barrio *m* bajo, barriada *f* (AmL exc CS), barrio *m* de conventillos (CS) **(b)** (filthy place) (colloq & pej) pocilga *f*

slumber¹ /'slʌmbər || 'slʌmbə(r)/ *n* (liter) (*often pl*) sueño *m*

slumber² *vi* (liter) dormir*

slump¹ /slʌmp/ *n* **(a)** (economic depression) depresión *f* **(b)** (in prices, sales) caída *f or* baja *f* repentina; (in attendance, interest) disminución *f*

slump² *vi* **1** (collapse) (+ *adv compl*) desplomarse; **they found her ~ed over her desk** la encontraron desplomada sobre su escritorio **2** «*prices/output/sales*» caer* *or* bajar repentinamente

slung /slʌŋ/ *past & past p of* SLING²

slunk /slʌŋk/ *past & past p of* SLINK

slur¹ /slɜ:r || slɜ:(r)/ *n* **1** (insult): **a racist ~** un comentario racista; **to cast a ~ on sb** injuriar a algn **2** (Mus) ligado *m*

slur² *vt* **-rr- 1** (pronounce unclearly): **to ~ one's words** arrastrar las palabras **2** (Mus) ligar*

slurp /slɜ:rp || slɜ:p/ *vt* sorber (*haciendo ruido*)

slurred /slɜ:rd || slɜ:d/ *adj*: **her speech was ~** arrastraba las palabras

slush /slʌʃ/ *n* [U] **(a)** (snow) nieve *f* fangosa *or* medio derretida **(b)** (sentimental trash) sensiblería *f*

sly /slaɪ/ *adj* **-er, -est** ‹*person*› astuto; ‹*look/grin*› malicioso; ***on the ~*** a hurtadillas

smack¹ /smæk/ *n* manotazo *m*, palmada *f* (AmL)

smack² *vt* **(a)** (slap) ‹*child*› pegarle* a (*con la mano*) **(b) to ~ one's lips** relamerse ■ ~ *vi* **to ~ OF sth** oler* A algo

smack³ *adv* (colloq): **~ in the middle** justo en el medio; **he went ~ into a tree** se dio contra un árbol

small¹ /smɔ:l/ *adj* **-er, -est** pequeño, chico (esp AmL); ‹*sum/price*› módico, reducido; ‹ *mistake/problem*› pequeño, de poca importancia; **to feel ~** sentirse* insignificante

small² *n* **the ~ of the back** *región baja de la espalda, que corresponde al segmento dorsal de la columna vertebral*

small: **~ ad** *n* (BrE) anuncio *m* (clasificado), aviso *m* (clasificado) (AmL); **~ change** *n* [U] cambio *m*, (dinero *m*) suelto *m*, sencillo *m* (AmL), feria *f* (Méx fam); **~ hours** *pl n* **the ~ hours (of the morning)** la madrugada; **~-minded** /'smɔ:l'maɪndəd ‖ ˌsmɔ:l'maɪndɪd/ *adj* cerrado, de miras estrechas; **~pox** /'smɔ:lpɑ:ks ‖ 'smɔ:lpɒks/ *n* [U] viruela *f*; **~ print** *n* [U] (BrE) **the ~ print** la letra pequeña *or* menuda, la letra chica (esp AmL); **~ talk** *n* [U] charla *f* sobre temas triviales; **~-time** /'smɔ:l 'taɪm/ *adj* de poca monta; **~-town** /'smɔ:l'taʊn/ *adj* pueblerino

smart¹ /smɑ:rt ‖ smɑ:t/ *adj* **-er, -est 1** (esp BrE) (neat, stylish) ‹*appearance/dress/hotel/neighborhood*› elegante **2** (clever, shrewd) ‹*child*› listo; ‹*answer*› inteligente **3 (a)** (brisk, prompt) ‹*pace*› rápido **(b)** (forceful) ‹*blow/tap*› seco, fuerte

smart² *vi* «*eyes/wound*» escocer*

smarten up /'smɑ:rtən ‖ 'smɑ:tən/ **(a)** [*v* + *o* + *adv, v* + *adv* + *o*] ‹*house/town*› arreglar **(b)** [*v* + *adv*] «*person*» mejorar su (*or* mi *etc*) aspecto

smash¹ /smæʃ/ *n* **1 (a)** (sound) estrépito *m*, estruendo *m* **(b)** (collision) (BrE) choque *m* **2 (a)** (blow) golpe *m* **(b)** (Sport) smash *m*, remate *m*, remache *m* **3** (success) (colloq) exitazo *m* (fam)

smash² *vt* **1** (break) ‹*furniture*› romper*; ‹*car*› destrozar*; ‹*glass*› romper*; (into small pieces) hacer* añicos **2** (destroy) ‹*rebellion*› aplastar; ‹*drug racket/spy ring*› acabar con **3** (Sport) rematar, remachar ■ **~** *vi* (shatter) hacerse* pedazos

• smash up [*v* + *o* + *adv*] (colloq) destrozar*

smash: **~ hit** *n* (colloq) exitazo *m* (fam); **~up** *n* (colloq) choque *m* violento

smattering /'smætərɪŋ/ *n* (*no pl*) nociones *fpl*

smear¹ /smɪr ‖ smɪə(r)/ *n* **1** (stain) mancha *f* **2** (slander, slur) calumnia *f*; (*before n*) **~ campaign** campaña *f* difamatoria **3** (Med) **~ (test)** citología *f*, frotis *m* cervical, Papanicolau *m* (AmL)

smear² *vt* **1 to ~ sth** ON(TO)/OVER **sth** ‹*paint/grease*› embadurnar algo de algo; ‹*butter*› untar algo con algo **2** (slander, libel) difamar ■ **~** *vi* «*ink/lipstick*» correrse

smell¹ /smel/ *n* **(a)** [C] (odor) olor *m* **(b)** [U] (sense of smell) olfato *m*

smell² (*past & past p* **smelled** *or* (BrE also) **smelt**) *vt* **(a)** (sense) oler*; **we could ~ gas/burning** olía a gas/quemado; **to ~ danger** olfatear el peligro **(b)** (sniff at) «*person*» oler*; «*animal*» olfatear ■ **~** *vi* oler*; **to ~** OF **sth** oler* A algo

smelling salts /'smelɪŋ/ *pl n* sales *fpl* (aromáticas)

smelly /'smeli/ *adj* **-lier, -liest** que huele mal

smelt¹ /smelt/ (BrE) *past & past p of* SMELL²

smelt² *vt* fundir

smile¹ /smaɪl/ *n* sonrisa *f*

smile² *vi* sonreír*; **to ~** AT **sb** sonreírle* A algn

smirk¹ /smɜ:rk ‖ smɜ:k/ *n* sonrisita *f* (*de suficiencia, de complicidad, etc*)

smirk² *vi* sonreírse* (*con suficiencia, complicidad etc*)

smith /smɪθ/ *n* herrero, -ra *m,f*

smithereens /'smɪðə'ri:nz/ *pl n*: **to smash sth to ~** hacer* algo pedazos *or* añicos

smock /smɑ:k ‖ smɒk/ *n* **(a)** (of fisherman, artist) blusón *m*, bata *f* **(b)** (dress) vestido *m* amplio

smog /smɑ:g ‖ smɒg/ *n* [U] smog *m*

smoke¹ /sməʊk/ *n* [U] humo *m*; **to go up in ~** «*books/papers*» quemarse; «*hopes*» esfumarse; «*ambitions/plans*» quedar en agua de borrajas

smoke² *vi* **1** «*person*» fumar **2** (give off smoke) echar humo ■ **~** *vt* **1** ‹*cigarettes/tobacco*› fumar; **he ~s a pipe** fuma en pipa **2** (cure) ‹*fish/cheese*› ahumar*

smoke-bomb /'sməʊkbɑ:m ‖ 'sməʊkbɒm/ *n* bomba *f* de humo

smoked /sməʊkt/ *adj* ahumado

smoke detector *n* detector *m* de humo

smokeless /'sməʊkləs ‖ 'sməʊklɪs/ *adj* ‹*fuel*› que arde sin humo; **~ zone** (in UK) *zona donde está prohibido usar combustibles que produzcan humo*

smoker /'sməʊkər ‖ 'sməʊkə(r)/ *n* fumador, -dora *m,f*; **he's a heavy smoker** fuma mucho

smoke: **~screen** *n* cortina *f* de humo; **~ signal** *n* señal *f* de humo

smoking /'sməʊkɪŋ/ *n* [U] Ⓢ **no smoking** prohibido fumar; **to give up ~** dejar de fumar

smoking: **~ car** *n* (AmE) vagón *m or* (Chi, Méx) carro *m* de fumadores; **~ compartment** *n* compartimento *m* de fumadores

smoky /'sməʊki/ *adj* **-kier, -kiest** ‹*fire/chimney*› que echa humo; ‹*room*› lleno de humo; ‹*atmosphere*› cargado de humo

smolder, (BrE) **smoulder** /'sməʊldər ‖ 'sməʊldə(r)/ *vi* «*fire*» arder (*sin llama*); «*eyes*» arder

smooth¹ /smu:ð/ *adj* **-er, -est 1 (a)** ‹*texture/stone*› liso, suave; ‹*skin*› suave, terso; ‹*sea*› tranquilo **(b)** (of consistency) ‹*sauce*› sin grumos **(c)** (of taste) ‹*wine*› suave **2 (a)** (of movement) ‹*take-off*› suave; ‹*flight*› cómodo **(b)** (trouble-free) ‹*journey*› sin complicaciones **3 (a)** (easy, polished) ‹*performance*› fluido **(b)** (glib, suave) (pej) poco sincero, falso; **he's a ~ talker** tiene mucha labia

smooth² *vt* **(a)** ‹*dress/sheets/hair*› alisar, arreglar **(b)** (polish) pulir

• smooth out [*v* + *o* + *adv, v* + *adv* + *o*] **(a)** ‹*sheets/creases*› alisar **(b)** ‹*difficulties/problems*› allanar

• smooth over [*v* + *o* + *adv, v* + *adv* + *o*] ‹*differences*› dejar de lado

smoothly /'smu:ðli/ *adv* **1 (a)** (of movement) ‹*take off/drive*› suavemente **(b)** (without problems) sin problemas **2** (glibly, suavely) (pej) ‹*talk*› con mucha labia

smother /'smʌðər ‖ 'smʌðə(r)/ *vt* **(a)** (stifle) ‹*person*› asfixiar, ahogar*; ‹*flames*› sofocar* **(b)** (suppress) ‹*yawn/giggle*› reprimir **(c)** (cover profusely): **she ~ed him with kisses** lo cubrió de besos

smoulder *vi* (BrE) ⇒ SMOLDER

smudge¹ /smʌdʒ/ *n* mancha *f*

smudge² *vt* correr; (deliberately) difuminar

smug /smʌg/ *adj* **-gg-** ‹*expression*› de suficiencia, petulante; ‹*person*› pagado de sí mismo, petulante

smuggle /'smʌgəl/ *vt* ‹*tobacco/drugs*› contrabandear, pasar de contrabando; **I ~d her into my room** la hice entrar a mi habitación a escondidas

smuggler /'smʌglər ‖ 'smʌglə(r)/ *n* contrabandista *mf*

smuggling /'smʌglɪŋ/ *n* [U] contrabando *m*

snack /snæk/ *n* tentempié *m*

snack bar *n* bar *m*, cafetería *f*

snag[1] /snæg/ *n* **(a)** (difficulty) inconveniente *m*, pega *f* (Esp fam) **(b)** (in fabric, stocking) enganchón *m*

snag[2] *vt* **-gg-** enganchar

snail /sneɪl/ *n* caracol *m*; **at a ~'s pace** a paso de tortuga

snake /sneɪk/ *n* culebra *f*, serpiente *f*; (poisonous) víbora *f*

snake: **~bite** *n* [C U] mordedura *f* de serpiente; **~ charmer** /'tʃɑ:rmər ‖ 'tʃɑ:mə(r)/ *n* encantador, -dora *m,f* de serpientes

snap[1] /snæp/ *n* **1** [C] (sound) chasquido *m* **2 ~ (fastener)** (AmE) (on clothes) broche *m* or botón *m* de presión (AmL), (cierre *m*) automático *m* (Esp) **3** [C] (photo) (colloq) foto *f*, instantánea *f* **4** [C] (Meteo): **a cold ~** una ola de frío

snap[2] **-pp-** *vt* **1 (a)** (break) partir **(b)** (cause to make sharp sound): **she ~ped the lid/book shut** cerró la tapa/el libro de un golpe; ⇒ FINGER[1] **2** (utter sharply) decir* bruscamente **3** (photograph) ‹*person/thing*› sacarle* una foto a ■ **~** *vi* **1** (bite) **to ~ AT sth** intentar morder algo **2 (a)** (break) «*twigs/branch*» romperse*, quebrarse* (esp AmL); «*elastic*» romperse* **(b)** (click): **to ~ shut** cerrarse* (con un clic) **3** (speak sharply) hablar con brusquedad **4** (move quickly): ***to ~ out of it*** (of depression) animarse; (of lethargy, inertia) espabilarse

• **snap up** [*v* + *o* + *adv*, *v* + *adv* + *o*] ‹*offer*› no dejar escapar

snap[3] *adj* ‹*decision*› precipitado, repentino

snappy /'snæpi/ *adj* **-pier, -piest (a)** ‹*person*› irascible; ‹*retort*› brusco **(b)** ‹*pace*› (colloq) ágil

snapshot /'snæpʃɑ:t ‖ 'snæpʃɒt/ *n* foto *f*, instantánea *f*

snare[1] /sner ‖ sneə(r)/ *n* trampa *f*

snare[2] *vt* atrapar

snarl[1] /snɑ:rl ‖ snɑ:l/ *n* gruñido *m*

snarl[2] *vi/t* gruñir*

• **snarl up** [*v* + *adv* + *o*] (*usu pass*) ‹*ball of wool*› enmarañar, enredar; ‹*traffic*› atascar*

snatch[1] /snætʃ/ *vt* **1 (a)** (grab) **to ~ sth FROM sb** arrebatarle algo A algn; **she ~ed the letter out of my hand** me arrancó la carta de las manos **(b)** (steal) (colloq & journ) robar (*arrebatando*) **(c)** (kidnap) (journ) secuestrar, raptar **2** (take hurriedly) ‹*opportunity*› no dejar pasar

snatch[2] *n* **1** (robbery) (BrE journ) robo *m* **2 (a)** (fragment) fragmento *m* **(b)** (brief spell) rato *m*; **to sleep in ~es** dormir* (de) a ratos

sneak /sni:k/ (*past & past p* **sneaked** or (AmE also) **snuck**) *vt* **(a)** (smuggle) (+ *adv compl*): **he ~ed the files out of the office** sacó los archivos de la oficina a escondidas; **she tried to ~ him in without paying** trató de colarlo sin pagar **(b)** (take furtively): **to ~ a look at sth/sb** mirar algo/a algn con disimulo ■ **~** *vi* (+ *adv compl*): **to ~ in** entrar a hurtadillas; **to ~ away** escabullirse*

• **sneak up** [*v* + *adv*] **to ~ up (ON sb)** acercarse* sigilosamente (A algn)

sneakers /'sni:kərz ‖ 'sni:kəz/ *pl n* zapatillas *fpl* (de deporte), tenis *mpl*, playeras *fpl* (Esp)

sneak: **~ preview** *n* (Cin, TV) preestreno *m*; **~ thief** *n* ratero, -ra *m,f*

sneaky /'sni:ki/ *adj* **-kier, -kiest** (colloq) ‹*person*› artero, taimado; ‹*behavior*› solapado

sneer[1] /snɪr ‖ snɪə(r)/ *vi* adoptar un aire despectivo; (with facial expression) hacer* una mueca de desprecio

sneer[2] *n* expresión *f* desdeñosa

sneeze[1] /sni:z/ *vi* estornudar

sneeze[2] *n* estornudo *m*

snide /snaɪd/ *adj* insidioso

sniff /snɪf/ *vt* **(a)** (smell) «*person*» oler*; «*animal*» olfatear **(b)** ‹*glue*› inhalar, esnifar ■ **~** *vi* «*animal*» husmear, olfatear; «*person*» sorberse la nariz

sniffer dog /'snɪfər ‖ 'snɪfə(r)/ *n* (BrE) perro *m* rastreador

sniffle /'snɪfəl/ *vi* (due to cold) sorberse la nariz; (when crying) gimotear

snigger[1] /'snɪgər ‖ 'snɪgə(r)/ *n* risilla *f*, risita *f*

snigger[2] *vi* reírse* (*por lo bajo*)

snip[1] /snɪp/ *n* (act) tijeretazo *m*; (sound) tijereteo *m*

snip[2] *vt* **-pp-** cortar (*con tijera*)

sniper /'snaɪpər ‖ 'snaɪpə(r)/ *n* francotirador, -dora *m,f*

snippet /'snɪpət ‖ 'snɪpɪt/ *n* (of conversation) trozo *m*; **~s of information** (algunos) datos aislados

snivel /'snɪvəl/ *vi*, (BrE) **-ll-** lloriquear

snob /snɑ:b ‖ snɒb/ *n* (e)snob *mf*

snobbery /'snɑ:bəri ‖ 'snɒbəri/ *n* [U] (e)snobismo *m*

snobbish /'snɑ:bɪʃ ‖ 'snɒbɪʃ/ *adj* (e)snob

snooker /'snʊkər ‖ 'snu:kə(r)/ *n* snooker *m* (*modalidad de billar que se juega con 15 bolas rojas y 6 de otro color*)

snoop /snu:p/ *vi* (colloq) husmear, fisgonear

snooper /'snu:pər ‖ 'snu:pə(r)/ *n* (colloq) fisgón, -gona *m,f*

snooze[1] /snu:z/ *vi* (colloq) dormitar

snooze[2] *n* (colloq) sueñecito *m* (fam), sueñito *m* (esp AmL fam); **to have a ~** echar una cabezada (fam)

snore[1] /snɔ:r ‖ snɔ:(r)/ *vi* roncar*

snore[2] *n* ronquido *m*

snoring /'snɔ:rɪŋ/ *n* [U] ronquidos *mpl*

snorkel /'snɔ:rkəl ‖ 'snɔ:kəl/ *n* esnórkel *m*

snort[1] /snɔ:rt ‖ snɔ:t/ *vi* bufar, resoplar ■ **~** *vt* (utter) bramar, gruñir*

snort[2] *n* bufido *m*, resoplido *m*

snout /snaʊt/ *n* hocico *m*, morro *m*

snow[1] /snəʊ/ **▶ 920** *n* **(a)** [U] nieve *f* **(b)** [C] (snowfall) nevada *f*

snow² ▶ 920 *v impers* nevar*
•snow in [*v + o + adv*]: **to be ∼ed in** estar* aislado por la nieve
•snow under [*v + o + adv*]: **I'm ∼ed under with work** estoy agobiada *or* desbordada de trabajo
snowball¹ /'snəʊbɔːl/ *n* (Meteo) bola *f* de nieve
snowball² *vi* «*problems*» agravarse
snow: **∼bound** *adj* bloqueado por la nieve; **∼drift** *n*: *nieve acumulada durante una ventisca*; **∼drop** *n* campanilla *f* de invierno; **∼fall** *n* [C U] nevada *f*; **∼flake** *n* copo *m* de nieve; **∼man** /'snəʊmæn/ *n* (*pl* **-men** /-men/) muñeco *m* de nieve; **∼plow**, (BrE) **∼plough** *n* quitanieves *m*; **∼shoe** *n* raqueta *f*; **∼storm** *n* tormenta *f* de nieve
snub¹ /snʌb/ *vt* **-bb- (a)** ‹*person*› desairar; (ignore) ignorar; (treat coldly) tratar fríamente (CS) **(b)** (reject) ‹*offer*› desdeñar, rechazar*
snub² *n* desaire *m*
snub³ *adj* ‹*nose*› respingón, respingado (AmL)
snub-nosed /'snʌb'nəʊzd/ *adj* de nariz respingona *or* (AmL tb) respingada
snuck /snək/ (AmE colloq) *past and past p of* SNEAK
snuff /snʌf/ *n* [U] rapé *m*
•snuff out [*v + o + adv, v + adv + o*] ‹*candle*› apagar*
snuffbox /'snʌfbɑːks ‖ 'snʌfbɒks/ *n* caja *f* de rapé
snug /snʌg/ *adj* **(a)** (cosy) cómodo y acogedor **(b)** (close-fitting) ceñido, ajustado
snuggle /'snʌgəl/ *vi* acurrucarse*; **he ∼d up against her** se le arrimó
so¹ /səʊ/ *adv* **1 (a)** (very) tan; **she's ∼ tall** es tan alta; **he did it ∼ quickly** lo hizo tan rápido; **thank you ∼ much** muchísimas gracias **(b) so much/many** (*as adj*) tanto, -ta/tantos, -tas; **∼ much space/food** tanto espacio/tanta comida; **∼ many things** tantas cosas **(c) so much** (*as pronoun*) tanto; **he eats ∼ much** come tanto **2 or so** más o menos **3** (with clauses of result or purpose) **∼ ... (that)** tan ... que; **he was ∼ rude (that) she slapped him** fue tan grosero, que le dio una bofetada **4 (a)** (thus, in this way): **the street was ∼ named because ...** se le puso ese nombre a la calle porque ...; **hold the bat like ∼** agarra el bate así **(b)** (as stated) así; **that is ∼** (frml) así es; **if ∼, they're lying** si es así *or* de ser así, están mintiendo **(c) and so on (and so forth)** etcétera (etcétera) **5** (*replacing clause, phrase, word*): **I expect ∼** me imagino que sí; **I got a bit dirty — ∼ I see** me ensucié un poco — sí, ya veo; **I told you ∼** ¿no te lo dije? **6** (*with v aux*) **(a)** (also, equally): **Peter agrees and ∼ does Bill** Peter está de acuerdo y Bill también **(b)** (indeed): **you promised — ∼ I did!** lo prometiste — ¡es verdad! *or* ¡tienes razón! **7 (a)** (indicating pause or transition) bueno; **∼ here we are again** bueno, aquí estamos otra vez **(b)** (querying, eliciting information): **∼ now what do we do?** ¿y ahora qué hacemos? **(c)** (summarizing, concluding) así que; **∼ now you know** así que ya sabes **(d)** (expressing surprised reaction) así que, conque; **∼ that's what he's after!** ¡así que *or* conque eso es lo que quiere! **(e)** (challenging): **∼ what?** ¿y qué?
so² *conj* **1** (*in clauses of purpose or result*) **(a) so (that)** (expressing purpose) para que (+ *subj*); (*expressing result*) así que *or* de manera que (+ *indic*); **she said it slowly, ∼ (that) we'd all understand** lo dijo despacio, para que todos entendiéramos; **she said it slowly, ∼ (that) we all understood** lo dijo despacio, así que *or* de manera que todos entendimos **(b) so as to** + INF para + INF **2** (therefore, consequently) así que, de manera que
so³ *n* (Mus) sol *m*
soak /səʊk/ *vt* **(a)** ‹*lentils/clothes*› (immerse) poner* en *or* a remojo; (leave immersed) dejar en *or* a remojo **(b)** (drench) empapar; **to be ∼ed (to the skin)** estar* empapado, estar* calado hasta los huesos
■ **∼** *vi* **(a)** (lie in liquid): **to leave sth to ∼** dejar algo en *or* a remojo **(b)** (penetrate) (+ *adv compl*): **to ∼ into/through sth** calar algo
•soak up [*v + o + adv, v + adv + o*] ‹*liquid/information*› absorber; ‹*sun*› empaparse de
soaking /'səʊkɪŋ/ *adj* empapado; (*as adv*) **it's ∼ wet** está empapado
so-and-so /'səʊənsəʊ/ *n* [U] (colloq) (unspecified person) (*no art*) fulano, -na *m,f*
soap /səʊp/ *n* **1** [U C] jabón *m*; (*before n*) **∼ dish** jabonera *f* **2** ⇒ SOAP OPERA
soap: **∼flakes** *pl n* jabón *m* en escamas; **∼ opera** *n* [C U] (TV) telenovela *f*, culebrón *m*; (Rad) radionovela *f*, comedia *f* (AmL); **∼ powder** *n* [U C] (BrE) jabón *m* en polvo, detergente *m* (*en polvo*); **∼suds** *pl n* espuma *f* (*de jabón*)
soapy /'səʊpi/ *adj* **-pier, -piest (a)** ‹*water*› jabonoso; ‹*cloth/hands*› enjabonado **(b)** ‹*smell/taste*› a jabón
soar /sɔːr ‖ sɔː(r)/ *vi* **1 (a)** (fly) «*bird/glider*» planear **(b)** (rise) «*bird/kite*» elevarse; «*prices/costs*» dispararse; «*hopes*» aumentar; «*popularity*» aumentar **(c)** (tower) «*skyscraper/mountain*» alzarse* **2 soaring** *pres p* ‹*inflation*› galopante, de ritmo vertiginoso; ‹*popularity*› en alza; **caused by ∼ temperatures** causado por una subida vertiginosa de las temperaturas
sob¹ /sɑːb ‖ sɒb/ *vi* **-bb-** sollozar*
sob² *n* sollozo *m*
sober /'səʊbər ‖ 'səʊbə(r)/ *adj* **1** (not drunk) sobrio **2 (a)** (serious) ‹*expression*› grave; ‹*young man*› serio; ‹*occasion*› formal **(b)** (subdued) ‹*dress/colors*› sobrio
•sober up 1 [*v + adv*]: **he's ∼ed up now** ya está sobrio **2** [*v + o + adv, v + adv + o*] despejar
sobriety /səʊ'braɪəti, sə- ‖ sə'braɪəti/ *n* [U] seriedad *f*, sensatez *f*; (*before n*) **∼ test** (AmE) prueba *f* del alcohol *or* de la alcoholemia
so-called /'səʊ'kɔːld/ *adj* (*usu before n*) **(a)** (commonly named) (así) llamado **(b)** (indicating skeptical attitude) ‹*expert*› supuesto, presunto
soccer /'sɑːkər ‖ 'sɒkə(r)/ *n* [U] fútbol *m or* (AmC, Méx) futbol *m*
sociable /'səʊʃəbəl/ *adj* sociable
social /'səʊʃəl/ *adj* social; **he has no ∼ graces** no sabe cómo comportarse; **∼ life** vida *f* social
social democrat *n* socialdemócrata *mf*
socialism /'səʊʃəlɪzəm/ *n* [U] socialismo *m*
socialist¹, Socialist /'səʊʃələst ‖ 'səʊʃəlɪst/ *adj* socialista
socialist², Socialist *n* socialista *mf*

socialize /'səʊʃəlaɪz/ *vi* alternar; (at party) circular

socially /'səʊʃəli/ *adv* **(a)** (relating to the community) ‹*divisive/useful*› socialmente; (*indep*) desde el punto de vista social **(b)** (in social situations): **it's not ~ acceptable** está mal visto, no se considera correcto

social: **~ science** *n* [U C] ciencia *f* social; **~ security** *n* [U] (BrE) seguridad *f* social; **~ service** *n* **(a)** [U] (welfare work) (AmE) asistencia *f or* trabajo *m* social **(b)** [C] (in UK) servicio *m* social; **~ work** *n* [U] asistencia *f* social; **~ worker** *n* (Soc Adm) asistente, -ta *m,f* social, trabajador, -dora *m,f* social (Méx), visitador, -dora *m,f* social (Chi)

society /sə'saɪəti/ *n* (*pl* **-ties**) **1 (a)** [U C] (community) sociedad *f*; **in polite ~** entre la gente educada **(b)** [U] (fashionable elite) (alta) sociedad *f* **2** [C] (association, club) sociedad *f*

sociologist /'səʊsi'ɑːlədʒəst, -ʃi- ‖ ˌsəʊsi'ɒlədʒɪst, -ʃi-/ *n* sociólogo, -ga *m,f*

sociology /'səʊsi'ɑːlədʒi, -ʃi- ‖ ˌsəʊsi'ɒlədʒi, -ʃi-/ *n* [U] sociología *f*

sociopath /'səʊsiəpæθ, -ʃi-/ *n* (p)sicópata *mf*

sock /sɑːk ‖ sɒk/ *n* calcetín *m*, media *f* (AmL)

socket /'sɑːkət ‖ 'sɒkɪt/ *n* **(a)** (Anat) (of eye) cuenca *f*, órbita *f*; (of joint) fosa *f*, hueco *m* **(b)** (Elec) (for plug) enchufe *m*, toma *f* de corriente, tomacorriente *m* (AmL) **(c)** (Tech) encaje *m*

sod /sɑːd ‖ sɒd/ *n* **1** (piece of turf) tepe *m*, champa *f* (Andes) **2** (BrE vulg) (obnoxious person) cabrón, -brona *m,f* (vulg)

soda /'səʊdə/ *n* **1 (a)** [U] (soda water) soda *f*, agua *f*‡ de seltz **(b)** [C U] (flavored) (AmE) refresco *m*, fresco *m* (AmL) **(c)** [C] (ice-cream soda) (AmE) ice-cream soda *m* (AmL) (*refresco con helado*) **2** [U] (Chem) soda *f*, sosa *f*

soda: **~ pop** *n* (AmE) refresco *m*; **~ water** *n* [U] soda *f*, agua *f*‡ de seltz

sodden /'sɑːdn̩ ‖ 'sɒdn̩/ *adj* empapado

sodium /'səʊdiəm/ *n* [U] sodio *m*

sodium bicarbonate *n* [U] bicarbonato *m* sódico *or* de sodio

sofa /'səʊfə/ *n* sofá *m*

soft /sɔːft ‖ sɒft/ *adj* **-er, -est 1 (a)** (not hard) blando; ‹*metal*› maleable; **to go ~** ablandarse **(b)** (smooth) ‹*fur/fabric/skin*› suave **2** (mild, subdued) ‹*light/color/music*› suave **3** (lenient) blando, indulgente **4** ‹*drugs/pornography*› blando **5** (Chem) ‹*water*› blando

soft: **~ball** *n* [U] softball *m* (*especie de béisbol que se juega con pelota blanda*); **~ drink** *n* [C U] refresco *m* (*bebida no alcohólica*)

soften /'sɔːfən ‖ 'sɒfən/ *vt* **(a)** ‹*butter/leather*› ablandar; ‹*skin*› suavizar*; ‹*light/color*› suavizar*; ‹*contours*› difuminar **(b)** (mitigate) ‹*effect*› atenuar*, mitigar*; **to ~ the blow** suavizar* el golpe **(c)** ‹*water*› ablandar, descalcificar* ■ **~** *vi* **(a)** «*butter/leather*» ablandarse; «*skin*» suavizarse* **(b)** (become gentler) ablandarse; (become more moderate) volverse* menos intransigente

• **soften up** [*v + o + adv, v + adv + o*] ablandar

softener /'sɔːfn̩ər ‖ 'sɒfn̩ə(r)/ *n* **(a)** (for water) descalcificador *m* **(b)** (for fabric) suavizante *m*

softly /'sɔːftli ‖ 'sɒftli/ *adv* **(a)** (gently) ‹*touch*› suavemente **(b)** (quietly) ‹*speak*› bajito

soft: **~-spoken** /'sɔːft'spəʊkən ‖ ˌsɒft'spəʊkən/ *adj* de voz suave; **~ top** *n* (AmE) (car) descapotable *m*, convertible *m* (AmL); (roof) capota *f*; **~ware** /'sɔːftwer ‖ 'sɒftweə(r)/ *n* software *m*

soggy /'sɑːgi ‖ 'sɒgi/ *adj* **-gier, -giest** ‹*ground/grass*› empapado; ‹*vegetables*› pasado

soh /səʊ/ *n* (Mus) sol *m*

soil¹ /sɔɪl/ *n* **(a)** [U C] (earth) tierra *f* **(b)** [U] (filth, dirt) (AmE) suciedad *f*

soil² *vt* ensuciar

soiled /sɔɪld/ *adj* ‹*linen*› sucio; ‹*goods*› dañado

sol /səʊl ‖ sɒl/ *n* (Mus) sol *m*

solace /'sɑːləs ‖ 'sɒlɪs/ *n* [U C] (liter) consuelo *m*

solar /'səʊlər ‖ 'səʊlə(r)/ *adj* solar

solar system *n* **the ~ ~** el sistema solar

sold /səʊld/ *past & past p of* SELL

solder /'sɑːdər ‖ 'səʊldə(r)/ *vt* soldar*

soldier /'səʊldʒər ‖ 'səʊldʒə(r)/ *n* soldado *mf*; (officer) militar *mf*

• **soldier on** [*v + adv*] (BrE colloq) seguir* al pie del cañon

sole¹ /səʊl/ *n* **1** (of foot) planta *f*; (of shoe) suela *f* **2** (fish) (*pl* **~** *or* **~s**) lenguado *m*

sole² *adj* (*before n*) **(a)** (only) único **(b)** (exclusive) ‹*rights*› exclusivo

sole³ *vt* (*usu pass*): **to have one's shoes ~d and heeled** hacerles* poner suelas y tacones *or* (CS, Per) tacos a los zapatos

solely /'səʊlli/ *adv* **(a)** (wholly) únicamente, exclusivamente **(b)** (only, simply) sólo, solamente, únicamente

solemn /'sɑːləm ‖ 'sɒləm/ *adj* **(a)** (serious, formal) ‹*occasion/silence*› solemne **(b)** (grave) ‹*person*› serio; ‹*face*› solemne

solicit /sə'lɪsət ‖ sə'lɪsɪt/ *vt* (frml) ‹*information/help*› solicitar (frml) ■ **~** *vi* «*prostitute*» ejercer la prostitución callejera (*abordando a posibles clientes*)

solicitor /sə'lɪsətər ‖ sə'lɪsɪtə(r)/ *n* **(a)** (in US and in UK) *abogado responsable de los asuntos legales de un municipio o de un departamento gubernamental* **(b)** (in UK) abogado, -da *m,f* (*que prepara causas legales y desempeña también funciones de notario*)

solid¹ /'sɑːləd ‖ 'sɒlɪd/ *adj* **-er, -est 1 (a)** (not liquid or gaseous) sólido **(b)** (not hollow) ‹*rubber ball/tire*› macizo **2 (a)** (unbroken) ‹*line/row*› continuo, ininterrumpido **(b)** (continuous) (colloq) ‹*month/year*› seguido **3 (a)** (physically sturdy) ‹*furniture/house*› sólido; ‹*meal*› consistente **(b)** (substantial) ‹*reason*› sólido **4** (pure) ‹*metal/wood*› macizo, puro; ‹*rock*› vivo

solid² *n* **1** (Chem, Phys) sólido *m* **2 solids** *pl* (food) alimentos *mpl* sólidos

solid³ *adv*: **to be packed/jammed ~** estar* lleno hasta el tope *or* hasta los topes

solidarity /'sɑːlə'dærəti ‖ ˌsɒlɪ'dærəti/ *n* [U] solidaridad *f*

solidify /sə'lɪdəfaɪ/ *vi* **-fies, -fying, -fied** solidificarse*

solidly /'sɑːlədli ‖ 'sɒlɪdli/ *adv* **(a)** (sturdily) ‹*fixed/grounded*› firmemente; ‹*made*› sólidamente **(b)** (unanimously) unánimemente

solitaire /ˈsɑːləˌter ‖ ˈsɒlɪˌteə(r)/ *n* **1** [C] ~ (**diamond**) solitario *m* **2** [U] (Games) solitario *m*

solitary /ˈsɑːləteri ‖ˈsɒlɪtəri/ *adj* **(a)** (alone) ‹*person/life/place*› solitario **(b)** (single) (*before n*) solo

solitary confinement *n* [U] incomunicación *f*; **he's in ~ ~** lo han incomunicado

solitude /ˈsɑːlətuːd ‖ ˈsɒlɪtjuːd/ *n* [U] soledad *f*

solo[1] /ˈsəʊləʊ/ *n* (*pl* **-los**) solo *m*

solo[2] *adj* **(a)** (Mus) ‹*violin/voices*› solista; ‹*album*› en solitario **(b)** ‹*flight*› en solitario

solo[3] *adv* en solitario

soloist /ˈsəʊləʊəst ‖ ˈsəʊləʊɪst/ *n* solista *mf*

so long *interj* (colloq) hasta luego, hasta la vista

solstice /ˈsɑːlstəs ‖ ˈsɒlstɪs/ *n* solsticio *m*

soluble /ˈsɑːljəbəl ‖ ˈsɒljʊbəl/ *adj* soluble

solution /səˈluːʃən/ *n* [C U] solución *f*

solve /sɑːlv ‖ sɒlv/ *vt* ‹*mystery/equation*› resolver*; ‹*crossword puzzle*› sacar*; ‹*crime*› esclarecer*; ‹*riddle*› encontrar* la solución a

solvent[1] /ˈsɑːlvənt ‖ ˈsɒlvənt/ *adj* solvente

solvent[2] *n* disolvente *m*, solvente *m*

Somali /səˈmɑːli/ *adj* somalí

Somalia /səˈmɑːliə/ *n* Somalia *f*

somber, (BrE) **sombre** /ˈsɑːmbər ‖ ˈsɒmbə(r)/ *adj* **(a)** (dark) sombrío **(b)** (melancholy) ‹*mood/thought*› sombrío; ‹*music*› lúgubre

some[1] /sʌm, *weak form* səm/ *adj* **1 (a)** (unstated number or type) (+ *pl n*) unos, unas; **there were ~ children in the park** había unos niños en el parque; **would you like ~ cherries?** ¿quieres (unas) cerezas? **(b)** (unstated quantity or type) (+ *uncount n*): **~ paint fell on my head** me cayó (un poco de) pintura en la cabeza; **would you like ~ coffee?** ¿quieres café? **2** (a, one) (+ *sing count noun*) algún, -guna; **~ day I'll get my revenge** ya me vengaré algún día **3** (particular, not all) (+ *pl n*) algunos, -nas; **I like ~ modern artists** algunos artistas modernos me gustan; **in ~ ways** en cierto modo **4 (a)** (not many, a few) ‹*lemons/apples*› algunos, -nas **(b)** (not much, a little) ‹*meat/rice*› un poco de **5 (a)** (several, many): **she's been bed-ridden for ~ years now** hace algunos años que está postrada en cama **(b)** (large amount of): **we've known each other for quite ~ time now** ya hace mucho (tiempo) que nos conocemos **6** (colloq) **(a)** (expressing appreciation): **that's ~ car you've got!** ¡vaya coche que tienes! **(b)** (stressing remarkable, ridiculous nature): **that was ~ exam!** ¡vaya examen! **(c)** (expressing irony): **~ friend you are!** ¡qué buen amigo eres! (iró)

some[2] *pron* **1 (a)** (a number of things or people) algunos, -nas **(b)** (an amount): **there's no salt left; we'll have to buy ~** no queda sal; vamos a tener que comprar; **the coffee's ready: would you like ~?** el café está listo: ¿quieres? **2** (certain people) algunos, -nas; **~ say that** ... algunos dicen que ...

some[3] *adv* (approximately) unos, unas, alrededor de

somebody[1] /ˈsʌmˌbɑːdi ‖ ˈsʌmbədi/ *pron* alguien; **~'s coming** viene alguien; **who was it? — John ~** ¿quién era? — John algo *or* John no sé cuánto (fam)

somebody[2] *n* (*no pl*): **to be ~** ser* alguien

somehow /ˈsʌmhaʊ/ *adv* **(a)** (by some means) de algún modo, de alguna manera; **~ or other** de algún modo u otro **(b)** (in some way, for some reason): **it isn't the same, ~** no sé por qué, pero no es lo mismo

someone /ˈsʌmwʌn/ *pron* ⇒ SOMEBODY[1]

someplace /ˈsʌmpleɪs/ *adv* (AmE) ⇒ SOMEWHERE[1] 1

somersault[1] /ˈsʌmərsɔːlt ‖ ˈsʌməsɒlt, -sɔːlt/ *n* (on ground) voltereta *f*, vuelta *f* (de) carnero (CS); (in air) (salto *m*) mortal *m*

somersault[2] *vi* (on ground) hacer* volteretas, dar* vueltas (de) carnero (CS); (in air) dar* un (salto) mortal

something /ˈsʌmθɪŋ/ *pron* **1** algo; **have ~ to eat/drink** come/bebe algo; **it's not ~ to be proud of** no es como para estar orgulloso; **that was ~ I hadn't expected** eso no me lo esperaba; **is it ~ I said?** ¿qué pasa? ¿qué he dicho? **2 (a)** (in vague statements or approximations): **she's 30 ~** tiene treinta y pico años (fam); **he said it was because of the traffic or ~** dijo que era por el tráfico o qué se yo **(b) something like**: **~ like 200 spectators** alrededor de *or* unos 200 espectadores **(c) something of** (rather): **she's ~ of an eccentric** es algo excéntrica; **it came as ~ of a surprise** me (*or* nos *etc*) sorprendió un poco **3** (sth special): **it was quite ~ for him to reach that position** era todo un logro que él alcanzara esa posición

sometime[1] /ˈsʌmtaɪm/ *adv* (at unspecified time): **I'll get around to it ~** ya lo haré en algún momento; **we'll have to finish it ~ or another** algún día habrá que terminarlo; **~ next week** un día de la semana que viene

sometime[2] *adj* (*before n*) (frml) ex, antiguo

sometimes /ˈsʌmtaɪmz/ *adv* a veces, algunas veces

someway /ˈsʌmweɪ/ *adv* (AmE) ⇒ SOMEHOW

somewhat /ˈsʌmhwɑːt ‖ ˈsʌmwɒt/ *adv* algo, un tanto

somewhere[1] /ˈsʌmhwer ‖ ˈsʌmweə(r)/ *adv* **1** (in, at a place) en algún lado *or* sitio *or* lugar; (to a place) a algún lado *or* sitio *or* lugar; ***to get* ~** avanzar*, adelantar **2** (in approximations): **~ around $10,000** cerca de *or* alrededor de 10.000 dólares

somewhere[2] *pron*: **will there be ~ open?** ¿habrá algo (*or* algún sitio *etc*) abierto?; **she's found ~ to live** ha encontrado casa (*or* habitación *etc*)

son /sʌn/ *n* hijo *m*

sonata /səˈnɑːtə/ *n* (*pl* **-tas**) (Mus) sonata *f*

song /sɔːŋ ‖ sɒŋ/ *n* **(a)** [C] (piece) canción *f* **(b)** [U] (of bird) canto *m*

song: **~bird** *n* pájaro *m* cantor; **~writer** *n* compositor, -tora *m,f* (*de canciones*)

sonic /ˈsɑːnɪk ‖ ˈsɒnɪk/ *adj* sónico

son-in-law /ˈsʌnɪnlɔː/ *n* (*pl* **sons-in-law**) yerno *m*, hijo *m* político

sonnet /ˈsɑːnət ‖ ˈsɒnɪt/ *n* soneto *m*

son of a bitch *n* (*pl* **sons of bitches**) (esp AmE sl) hijo *m* de puta, hijo *m* de la chingada (Méx vulg)

soon /suːn/ *adv* **-er, -est 1** (shortly, after a while) pronto, dentro de poco; **~ afterward** poco después; **it'll ~ be spring** ya falta poco para (que empiece) la primavera; **~er or later** tarde o temprano **2 (a)** (early, quickly) pronto; **how ~ can you be here?** ¿cuándo puedes llegar?, ¿qué tan pronto puedes llegar? (AmL); **I finished ~er than I expected** terminé antes de lo que esperaba; **not a minute** *o* **moment too ~** no antes de tiempo; **to speak too ~** hablar antes de tiempo; **as ~ as possible** lo antes posible, cuanto antes; **the ~er the better** cuanto antes mejor **(b)** (*as conj*): **as ~ as** en cuanto, tan pronto como; **as ~ as you've finished, you can go** en cuanto hayas terminado *or* tan pronto como hayas terminado, te puedes ir; **no ~er had we set out than it began to rain** apenas nos habíamos puesto en camino cuando empezó a llover; **no ~er said than done** dicho y hecho **3** (*in phrases*) **as soon … (as): I'd just as ~ stay at home (as go out)** no me importaría quedarme en casa, tanto me da quedarme en casa (como salir)

soot /sʊt/ *n* [U] hollín *m*

soothe /suːð/ *vt* ‹*person/nerves*› calmar; ‹*pain/cough*› aliviar

soothing /'suːðɪŋ/ *adj* **(a)** ‹*voice/words*› tranquilizador; ‹*music/bath*› relajante **(b)** ‹*ointment/syrup*› balsámico; ‹*medicine*› calmante

sophisticated /sə'fɪstəkeɪtəd ‖ sə'fɪstɪkeɪtɪd/ *adj* **(a)** ‹*appearance/person*› sofisticado **(b)** ‹*machine/technique*› complejo, altamente desarrollado

sophomore /'sɑːfəmɔːr ‖ 'sɒfəmɔː(r)/ *n* (AmE) estudiante *mf* de segundo curso (*en una universidad o colegio secundario estadounidense*)

sopping¹ /'sɑːpɪŋ ‖ 'sɒpɪŋ/ *adj* empapado

sopping² *adv* (*as intensifier*) **~ wet** (of people) calado hasta los huesos; (of clothes) chorreando

soprano¹ /sə'prænəʊ ‖ sə'prɑːnəʊ/ *n* (*pl* **-nos**) soprano *mf*

soprano² *adj* ‹*voice/recorder*› soprano; ‹*part/role*› de soprano

sorbet /sɔːr'beɪ, 'sɔːrbət ‖ 'sɔːbeɪ/ *n* [U C] sorbete *m*

sorcerer /'sɔːrsərər ‖ 'sɔːsərə(r)/ *n* (liter) hechicero *m*, brujo *m*

sordid /'sɔːrdəd ‖ 'sɔːdɪd/ *adj* **(a)** (base) ‹*method/deal*› vergonzoso **(b)** (squalid) ‹*hotel/conditions*› sórdido

sore¹ /sɔːr ‖ sɔː(r)/ *adj* **sorer** /'sɔːrər ‖ 'sɔːrə(r)/, **sorest** /'sɔːrəst ‖ 'sɔːrɪst/ **(a)** (painful) ‹*finger/foot*› dolorido; ‹*eye*› irritado; ‹*lips*› reseco; **she has a ~ throat** le duele la garganta; ***a ~ point/subject*** un punto/tema delicado **(b)** (angry) (AmE colloq) **to be ~ AT** *o* **WITH sb** estar* picado CON algn (fam)

sore² *n* llaga *f*, úlcera *f*

sorority /sə'rɔːrəti ‖ sə'rɒrəti/ *n* (*pl* **-ties**) (in US) hermandad *f* femenina de estudiantes (*en universidades norteamericanas*)

sorrow /'sɑːrəʊ ‖ 'sɒrəʊ/ *n* [U C] pesar *m*, pena *f*

sorrowful /'sɑːrəʊfəl ‖ 'sɒrəʊfəl/ *adj* afligido, triste

sorry /'sɑːri ‖ 'sɒri/ *adj* **-rier, -riest 1** (*pred*) **(a)** (grieved, sad): **I'm ~** lo siento; **to feel** *o* **be ~ FOR sb**: **I feel so ~ for you/him** te/lo compadezco; **to feel ~ for oneself** lamentarse de su (*or* tu *etc*) suerte; **I'm ~ to have to tell you that …** siento tener que decirte que …; **to be ~ (THAT)** sentir* QUE (+ *subj*) **(b)** (apologetic, repentant): **to say ~** pedir* perdón, disculparse; **I'm ~, I didn't mean to …** perdóname *or* lo siento *or* disculpa, no fue mi intención …; **to be ~ ABOUT sth** arrepentirse* DE algo; **I'm ~ I didn't make it to your party** siento no haber podido ir a tu fiesta **2** (*as interj*) perdón, lo siento **3** (pitiful, miserable) (*before n*) ‹*tale*› lamentable; **he was a ~ sight** tenía un aspecto lamentable

sort¹ /sɔːrt ‖ sɔːt/ *n* **1** (kind, type) tipo *m*, clase *f*; **what ~ of car is it?** ¿qué tipo *or* clase de coche es?: **she's not the ~ to let you down** no es de las que te fallan; **a ~ of** *o* **~ of a** una especie de; **I didn't say anything of the ~** no dije nada semejante **2** (*in phrases*) **sort of** (colloq): **it's ~ of sad to think of him all alone** da como pena pensar que está solo (fam); **do you want to go? — well, ~ of** ¿quieres ir? — bueno, en cierto modo sí

sort² *vt* **(a)** (classify) ‹*papers/letters*› clasificar* **(b)** (mend) arreglar

• sort out [*v + o + adv, v + adv + o*] **1 (a)** (put in order) ‹*books/photos/desk/room*› ordenar; ‹*finances*› organizar* **(b)** (separate out) separar **2 (a)** (arrange) (BrE) ‹*date*› fijar; ‹*deal*› llegar* a **(b)** (resolve) ‹*problem/dispute*› solucionar; ‹*misunderstanding*› aclarar

• sort through [*v + prep + o*] ‹*papers/files*› revisar

SOS *n* S.O.S. *m*

so-so /'səʊsəʊ/ *adj* (colloq) así así (fam)

soufflé /suː'fleɪ ‖ 'suːfleɪ/ *n* [U C] suflé *m*

sought /sɔːt/ *past & past p of* SEEK

sought-after /'sɔːtæftər ‖ 'sɔːt,ɑːftə(r)/ *adj* (*pred* **sought after**) ‹*product*› solicitado, en demanda; ‹*prize*› codiciado; ‹*area*› en demanda

soul /səʊl/ *n* **1** [C] (Relig) alma *f*‡ **2** [C] (person): **I won't tell a (living) ~** no se lo diré a nadie; **poor old ~!** ¡pobrecilla!, ¡pobrecita! **3** [U] **~ (music)** soul *m*

soul-destroying /'səʊldɪ'strɔɪɪŋ/ *adj* desmoralizador

soulful /'səʊlfəl/ *adj* enternecedor, conmovedor

soul: **~mate** *n* alma *f*‡ gemela; **~-searching** /'səʊl'sɜːrtʃɪŋ ‖ 'səʊl,sɜːtʃɪŋ/ *n* [U] introspección *f*

sound¹ /saʊnd/ *n* **1** [U C] (noise) sonido *m*; (unpleasant, disturbing) ruido *m*; (*before n*) **the ~ barrier** la barrera del sonido; **~ effects** efectos *mpl* sonoros **2** (impression conveyed) (colloq) (*no pl*): **I don't like the ~ of that at all** eso no me huele nada bien; **by** *o* **from the ~ of it, everything's going very well** parece que *or* por lo visto todo marcha muy bien

sound² *vi* **1 (a)** (give impression) sonar*; **you ~ as if** *o* **as though you could do with a rest** me da la impresión de que no te vendría mal un descanso; **that ~s like Susan now** ésa debe (de) ser Susan **(b)** (seem) parecer*; **how does that ~ to you?** ¿qué te parece?; **it ~s as if** *o* **as though you had a great time** parece que lo pasaste fenomenal **2**

(make noise, resound) «*bell/alarm*» sonar* ■ ~ *vt* ‹*trumpet/horn*› tocar*, hacer* sonar

• **sound out** [*v* + *o* + *adv*, *v* + *adv* + *o*] tantear, sondear

sound³ *adj* **-er, -est 1 (a)** (healthy) sano; **being of ~ mind** (estando) en pleno uso de sus facultades **(b)** (in good condition) ‹*basis/foundation*› sólido, firme; ‹*timber*› en buenas condiciones **2** (valid) ‹*reasoning/knowledge*› sólido; ‹*advice/decision*› sensato

sound⁴ *adv* **-er, -est**: **~ asleep** profundamente dormido

soundly /'saʊndli/ *adv* **1** ‹*sleep*› profundamente **2** (solidly, validly) sólidamente

soundproof¹ /'saʊndpru:f/ *adj* insonorizado

soundproof² *vt* insonorizar*

sound: **~ system** *n* equipo *m* de sonido; **~track** *n* banda *f* sonora

soup /su:p/ *n* sopa *f*; **clear ~** caldo *m*, consomé *m*

sour¹ /saʊər ‖ 'saʊə(r)/ *adj* **sourer**, **sourest (a)** (sharp, acid) ácido, agrio **(b)** (spoiled) ‹*milk*› agrio, cortado **(c)** (bad-tempered, disagreeable) agrio, avinagrado

sour² *vt* ‹*relationship/occasion*› amargar*

source /sɔ:rs ‖ sɔ:s/ *n* **1** (origin, supply) fuente *f*; (of river) nacimiento *m*; **~ of income** fuente de ingresos **2** (providing information) **(a)** (person) (journ) fuente *f* **(b)** (text, document) fuente *f*

sourdough /'saʊərdəʊ ‖ 'saʊədəʊ/ *n* [U] (AmE) masa *f* fermentada (*para hacer pan*)

south¹ /saʊθ/ *n* [U] (point of the compass, direction) sur *m*; **the ~**, **the S~** (region) el sur

south² *adj* (*before n*) sur *adj inv*, meridional; ‹*wind*› del sur

south³ *adv* al sur

South Africa *n* Sudáfrica *f*, Suráfrica *f*

South African *adj* sudafricano, surafricano

South America *n* América *f* del Sur *or* del Sud, Sudamérica *f*, Suramérica *f*

South American¹ *adj* sudamericano, suramericano

South American² *n* sudamericano, -na *m,f*, suramericano, -na *m,f*

southbound /'saʊθbaʊnd/ *adj* ‹*traffic/train*› que va (*or* iba *etc*) hacia el sur *or* en dirección sur

southeast¹, **Southeast** /'saʊθ'i:st/ *n* [U] **the ~** el sudeste *or* Sudeste, el sureste *or* Sureste

southeast² *adj* sudeste *adj inv*, sureste *adj inv*, del sudeste *or* sureste, sudoriental

southeast³ *adv* hacia el sudeste *or* sureste, en dirección sudeste *or* sureste

south: **~easterly** /'saʊθ'i:stərli ‖ ˌsaʊθ'i:stəli/ *adj* ‹*wind*› del sudeste *or* sureste; **~eastern** /'saʊθ'i:stərn ‖ ˌsaʊθ'i:stən/ *adj* sudeste *adj inv*, sureste *adj inv*, del sudeste *or* sureste, sudoriental

southerly /'sʌðərli ‖ 'sʌðəli/ *adj* ‹*wind*› del sur; ‹*latitude*› sur *adj inv*; **in a ~ direction** hacia el sur, en dirección sur

southern /'sʌðərn ‖ 'sʌðən/ *adj* ‹*region*› del sur, meridional, sur *adj inv*; ‹*country*› del sur, meridional; **~ Italy** el sur de Italia; **the ~ states** (in US) los estados del sur

southward¹ /'saʊθwərd ‖ 'saʊθwəd/ *adj* (*before n*): **in a ~ direction** hacia el sur, en dirección sur

southward², (BrE also) **southwards** /-z/ *adv* hacia el sur

southwest¹, **Southwest** /'saʊθ'west/ *n* [U] **the ~** el sudoeste *or* Sudoeste, el suroeste *or* Suroeste

southwest² *adj* sudoeste *adj inv*, suroeste *adj inv*, del sudoeste *or* suroeste

southwest³ *adv* hacia el sudoeste *or* suroeste, en dirección sudoeste *or* suroeste

south: **~westerly** /'saʊθ'westərli ‖ ˌsaʊθ'westəli/ *adj* ‹*wind*› del sudoeste *or* suroeste; **~western** /'saʊθ'westərn ‖ ˌsaʊθ'westən/ *adj* sudoccidental, sudoeste *adj inv*, suroeste *adj inv*, del sudoeste *or* suroeste

souvenir /'su:vənɪr ‖ ˌsu:və'nɪə(r)/ *n* recuerdo *m*, souvenir *m*

sovereign¹ /'sɑ:vrən ‖ 'sɒvrɪn/ *n* **1** (monarch) soberano, -na *m,f* **2** (coin) soberano *m*, libra *f* (de oro)

sovereign² *adj* soberano

Soviet /'səʊviet, 'sɑ:viət 'səʊviət/ *adj* (Hist) soviético

Soviet Union *n* (Hist) **the ~ ~** la Unión Soviética

sow¹ /səʊ/ *vt/i* (*past* **sowed**; *past p* **sowed** *or* **sown**) sembrar*

sow² /saʊ/ *n* cerda *f*, puerca *f*

sown /səʊn/ *past p of* sow¹

soy /sɔɪ/, (BrE) **soya** /'sɔɪə/ *n* [U] soya *f* (AmL), soja *f* (Esp)

soy: **~ bean**, (BrE) **soya bean** *n* soya *f* (AmL), soja *f* (Esp); **~ sauce** *n* [U] salsa *f* de soya (AmL) *or* (Esp) soja

spa /spɑ:/ *n* **(a)** (resort) balneario *m* **(b)** (spring) manantial *m* (*de agua mineral*) **(c)** (health club) (AmE) gimnasio *m*

space¹ /speɪs/ *n* **1** [U] **(a)** (Phys) espacio *m* **(b)** (Aerosp) espacio *m*; (*before n*) ‹*station/program*› espacial **2 (a)** [U] (room) espacio *m*, lugar *m* **(b)** [C] (empty area) espacio *m*; **let's clear a ~ for it first** hagámosle (un) sitio primero **3** (of time) (*no pl*) espacio *m*; **in the ~ of one hour** en el espacio *or* lapso de una hora **4** [C] (Print) espacio *m*

space² *vt* **~ (out)** espaciar

space: **~-age** *adj* ‹*technology*› futurista, espacial; **~craft** *n* (*pl* **~craft**) nave *f* espacial; **~man** /'speɪsmæn/ *n* (*pl* **-men** /-men/) astronauta *m*, cosmonauta *m*; **~ship** *n* nave *f* espacial, astronave *f*

spacing /'speɪsɪŋ/ *n* [U] (Print) espaciado *m*

spacious /'speɪʃəs/ *adj* ‹*house/room*› amplio, espacioso; ‹*park*› grande, extenso

spade /speɪd/ *n* **1** (tool) pala *f*; ***to call a ~ a ~*** llamar al pan, pan y al vino, vino **2** (Games) **spades** *pl* (suit) (+ *sing or pl vb*) picas *fpl*

spaghetti /spə'geti/ *n* [U] espaguetis *mpl*, spaghetti *mpl*

Spain /speɪn/ *n* España *f*

span¹ /spæn/ *n* **(a)** (of hand) palmo *m*; (of wing) envergadura *f*; (of bridge, arch) luz *f* **(b)** (part of bridge) arco *m* **(c)** (of time) lapso *m*, ⇒ LIFE SPAN

span² *vt* **-nn- (a)** (extend over) abarcar* **(b)** (cross) «*bridge*» ‹*river*› extenderse* sobre

Spaniard /'spænjərd ‖ 'spænjəd/ *n* español, -ñola *m,f*

spaniel /'spænjəl/ *n* spaniel *m*

Spanish¹ /'spænɪʃ/ *adj* español; ‹*language*› castellano, español

Spanish² *n* **(a)** [U] (language) castellano *m*, español *m* **(b)** (people) (+ *pl vb*) **the ~** los españoles

Spanish omelet, (BrE) **Spanish omelette** *n* tortilla *f* de papas *or* (Esp) patatas, tortilla *f* española

spank /'spæŋk/ *vt* pegarle* a (*en las nalgas*)

spanner /'spænər ‖ 'spænə(r)/ *n* (BrE) (*adjustable* ~) llave *f* inglesa; (*box* ~) llave *f* de tubo; ***to throw a ~ in the works*** fastidiarlo todo

spar¹ /spɑːr ‖ spɑː(r)/ *n* (Naut) palo *m*

spar² *vi* **-rr-** (in boxing) entrenarse; (argue) discutir

spare¹ /sper ‖ speə(r)/ *adj* **(a)** (not in use) ‹*umbrella/pen*› de más; **have you got any ~ paper?** ¿tienes un poco de papel que no te haga falta? **(b)** (*before n*) ‹*key/cartridge*› de repuesto **(c)** (free) libre; **if you've got a ~ minute** si tienes un minuto (libre)

spare² *n*: **I'll take a ~ just in case** llevaré uno de repuesto por si acaso

spare³ *vt* **1 (a)** (do without): **can you ~ your dictionary for a moment?** ¿me permites el diccionario un momento, si no lo necesitas?; **if you can ~ the time** si tienes *or* dispones de tiempo **(b)** (give) **to ~ (sb) sth**: **can you ~ me a pound?** ¿tienes una libra que me prestes/des?; **can you ~ me a few minutes?** ¿tienes unos minutos? **(c) to spare** (*as adj*): **there's food to ~** hay comida de sobra; **have you got a few minutes to ~?** ¿tienes unos minutos?; **have you got a few minutes to ~?** ¿tienes unos minutos? **2 (a)** (keep from using, stint) (*usu neg*): **to ~ no effort** no escatimar esfuerzos; **to ~ no expense** no reparar en gastos **(b)** (save, relieve) **to ~ sb sth** ‹*trouble/embarrassment*› ahorrarle algo A algn **(c)** (show mercy, consideration toward) perdonar

spare: **~ part** *n* repuesto *m* *or* (Méx) refacción *f*; **~ room** *n* cuarto *m* de huéspedes *or* (Esp) de los invitados, recámara *f* de visitas (Méx); **~ time** *n* [U] tiempo *m* libre; **~ tire**, (BrE) **~ tyre** *n* rueda *f* de repuesto *or* (Esp tb) de recambio, llanta *f* de refacción (Méx)

sparingly /'sperɪŋli ‖ 'speərɪŋli/ *adv* ‹*use*› con moderación

spark¹ /spɑːrk ‖ spɑːk/ *n* chispa *f*

spark² *vt*, (BrE also) **spark off** ‹*rioting/revolution*› hacer* estallar; ‹*interest*› suscitar; ‹*criticism*› provocar*

sparking plug /'spɑːrkɪŋ ‖ 'spɑːkɪŋ/ *n* (BrE) ⇒ SPARK PLUG

sparkle¹ /'spɑːrkəl ‖ 'spɑːkəl/ *vi* «*gem/glass*» centellear, destellar, brillar; «*eyes*» brillar

sparkle² *n* **(a)** (*no pl*) (of gem, glass) destello *m*, brillo *m*; (of eyes) brillo *m* **(b)** [U] (animation) chispa *f*, brillo *m*

sparkler /'spɑːrklər ‖ 'spɑːklə(r)/ *n* (firework) luz *f* de Bengala, bengala *f*

sparkling /'spɑːrklɪŋ ‖ 'spɑːklɪŋ/ *adj* **(a)** (shining) ‹*gems/stars*› centelleante; ‹*eyes*› chispeante **(b)** ‹*wit/conversation*› chispeante **(c)** (effervescent) ‹*wine*› espumoso

spark plug *n* bujía *f*, chispero *m* (AmC)

sparrow /'spærəʊ/ *n* gorrión *m*

sparse /spɑːrs ‖ spɑːs/ *adj* ‹*population/vegetation/furniture*› escaso; ‹*beard/hair*› ralo

sparsely /'spɑːrsli ‖ 'spɑːsli/ *adv*: **the area was ~ populated** la zona estaba escasamente poblada; **the room is ~ furnished** la habitación tiene pocos muebles

spartan /'spɑːrtn̩ ‖ 'spɑːtn̩/ *adj* espartano

spasm /'spæzəm/ *n* espasmo *m*

spasmodic /spæz'mɑːdɪk ‖ spæz'mɒdɪk/ *adj* **(a)** ‹*growth/activity*› irregular **(b)** (Med) ‹*pain/cough*› espasmódico

spat /spæt/ *past & past p of* SPIT²

spate /speɪt/ *n* racha *f*, serie *f*; ***to be in (full) ~*** (BrE) «*river*» estar* crecido

spatial /'speɪʃəl/ *adj* (*before n*) espacial

spatter /'spætər ‖ 'spætə(r)/ *vt/i* salpicar*

spatula /'spætʃələ ‖ 'spætjʊlə/ *n* **(a)** (Culin) (for turning, serving) pala *f* (de servir); (for scraping out bowls) espátula *f* **(b)** (Pharm, Med) espátula *f*

spawn¹ /spɔːn/ *n* [U] (of fish) hueva(s) *f(pl)*; (of frogs) huevas *fpl*

spawn² *vt* (journ) generar, producir* ■ **~** *vi* «*frogs/fish*» desovar

SPCA *n* (in US) (= **Society for the Prevention of Cruelty to Animals**) ≈ Asociación *f* protectora de animales

SPCC *n* (in US) (= **Society for the Prevention of Cruelty to Children**) ≈ Asociación *f* de proteccíon a la infancia

speak /spiːk/ (*past* **spoke**; *past p* **spoken**) *vi* **1 (a)** (say sth) hablar; **to ~ TO *o*** (esp AmE) **WITH sb** hablar CON algn, hablarle A algn; **they are not ~ing (to each other)** no se hablan; **to ~ OF sth/sb/-ING** hablar DE algo/algn/+ INF; **so to ~** por así decirlo **(b)** (on telephone): **hello, Barbara Mason ~ing** ... buenas tardes, habla *or* (Esp tb) soy Barbara Mason; **could I ~ to Mrs Hodges, please? — ~ing!** ¿podría hablar con la Sra. Hodges, por favor? — con ella (habla) *or* (Esp tb) soy yo **2** (make speech) hablar; **to ~ ON *o* ABOUT sth** hablar ACERCA DE *or* SOBRE algo ■ **~** *vt* **(a)** (say, declare): **nobody spoke a word** nadie dijo nada; **to ~ one's mind** hablar claro; **to ~ the truth** decir* la verdad **(b)** ‹*language*› hablar

• **speak for** [*v + prep + o*] hablar por; **we'd love to meet him — ~ for yourself!** nos encantaría conocerlo — ¡eso lo dirás por ti!; **the facts ~ for themselves** los hechos son elocuentes

• **speak out** [*v + adv*]: **to ~ out AGAINST sth** denunciar algo

• **speak up** [*v + adv*] **(a)** (speak loudly, clearly) hablar más fuerte *or* más alto **(b)** (speak boldly) decir* lo que se piensa; **to ~ up FOR sb** defender* a algn

speaker /'spiːkər ‖ 'spiːkə(r)/ *n* **1 (a)** (in public) orador, -dora *m,f* **(b)** (of language) hablante *mf* **(c)** (Govt) presidente, -ta *m,f* **2** (Audio) **(a)** (loudspeaker) altavoz *m*, (alto)parlante *m* (AmS) **(b)** (of hi-fi) baf(f)le *m*, parlante *m* (AmS)

speaking /'spi:kɪŋ/ *n* [U] (*before n*): **a good ~ voice** una voz muy clara (*or* potente *etc*); **to be on ~ terms with sb** estar* en buenas relaciones con algn

-speaking /ˌspi:kɪŋ/ *suff* -hablante, -parlante; **Spanish~** hispanohablante, hispanoparlante; **French~** francófono; **English~** de habla inglesa

spear¹ /spɪr ‖ 'spɪə(r)/ *n* **(a)** (weapon) lanza *f* **(b)** (for fishing) arpón *m*

spear² *vt* ‹*fish*› arponear

spear: **~head** *vt* (Mil) encabezar*; **~mint** *n* [U] menta *f* verde

spec /spek/ *n*: **on ~** (colloq) por si acaso

special /'speʃəl/ *adj* **(a)** (exceptional) (*before n*) ‹*favor/request*› especial **(b)** (for specific purpose) (*before n*) ‹*arrangements/fund*› especial **(c)** (particular, individual) especial, particular; **children with ~ needs** (Educ) niños que requieren una atención diferenciada

special: **~ delivery** *n* [U] correo *m* exprés *or* expreso; **~ effects** *pl n* efectos *mpl* especiales

specialist /'speʃələst ‖ 'speʃəlɪst/ *n* especialista *mf*; (*before n*) ‹*knowledge/shop*› especializado

speciality /'speʃi'æləti/ *n* (*pl* **-ties**) (BrE) ⇒ SPECIALTY¹

specialize /'speʃəlaɪz/ *vi* **to ~** (IN **sth**) especializarse* (EN algo)

specialized /'speʃəlaɪzd/ *adj* especializado

specially /'speʃəli/ *adv* **(a)** (specifically) especialmente, expresamente **(b)** (especially) ‹*long/difficult*› particularmente

specialty¹ /'speʃəlti/ *n* (*pl* **-ties**) (AmE) especialidad *f*

specialty² *adj* (AmE) (*before n: no comp*) ‹*merchandise/store*› especializado

species /'spi:ʃi:z/ *n* (*pl* **~**) especie *f*

specific /spɪ'sɪfɪk ‖ spə'sɪfɪk/ *adj* **(a)** (particular, individual) específico; ‹*example*› concreto **(b)** (exact, precise) preciso

specifically /spɪ'sɪfɪkli ‖ spə'sɪfɪkli/ *adv* **(a)** (explicitly) ‹*state/mention*› explícitamente **(b)** (specially, particularly) ‹*built/designed*› específicamente

specification /'spesəfə'keɪʃn ‖ ˌspesɪfɪ'keɪʃən/ *n* (*often pl*) especificación *f*

specify /'spesəfaɪ ‖ 'spesɪfaɪ/ *vt* **-fies, -fying, -fied** especificar*

specimen /'spesəmən ‖ 'spesɪmən/ *n* **(a)** (sample — of rock, plant, tissue) muestra *f*, espécimen *m*; (— of blood, urine) muestra *f*; (— of work, handwriting) muestra *f* **(b)** (individual example) ejemplar *m*, espécimen *m*

speck /spek/ *n* (of dust) mota *f*; (in distance) punto *m*; (dirt stain) manchita *f*

speckle *vt* (*usu pass*) motear; **a ~d hen** una gallina pinta *or* (RPl) bataraza

spectacle /'spektɪkəl ‖ 'spektəkəl/ *n* **1** (show, sight) espectáculo *m* **2 spectacles** *pl* gafas *fpl*, anteojos *mpl* (esp AmL), lentes *mpl* (esp AmL)

spectacular /spek'tækjələr ‖ spek'tækjʊlə(r)/ *adj* espectacular

spectator /'spekteɪtər ‖ spek'teɪtə(r)/ *n* espectador, -dora *m,f*

specter, (BrE) **spectre** /'spektər ‖ 'spektə(r)/ *n* (liter) espectro *m*

spectra /'spektrə/ *pl of* SPECTRUM

spectre /'spektər/ *n* (BrE) ⇒ SPECTER

spectrum /'spektrəm/ *n* (*pl* **-tra**) **1** (Opt, Phys) espectro *m* **2** (range) espectro *m*, gama *f*; **the political ~** el espectro político

speculate /'spekjəleɪt ‖ 'spekjʊleɪt/ *vi* **1** (Fin) especular **2** (guess, conjecture) **to ~** (ON *o* ABOUT **sth**) hacer* conjeturas *or* especular (SOBRE algo)

speculation /'spekjə'leɪʃən ‖ ˌspekjʊ'leɪʃən/ *n* [U C] especulación *f*

speculative /'spekjələtɪv ‖ 'spekjʊlətɪv/ *adj* especulativo

sped /sped/ *past & past p of* SPEED²

speech /spi:tʃ/ *n* **1 (a)** [U] (act, faculty) habla *f*‡ **(b)** [U] (manner of speaking) forma *f* de hablar **(c)** [U C] (language, dialect) habla *f*‡ **2** [C] **(a)** (oration) discurso *m*; **to make a ~** dar* un discurso **(b)** (Theat) parlamento *m*

speechless /'spi:tʃləs ‖ 'spi:tʃlɪs/ *adj*: **she was ~ with rage** enmudeció de rabia; **I'm ~!** no sé qué decir

speech therapy *n* [U] foniatría *f*, logopedia *f*

speed¹ /spi:d/ *n* **1 (a)** [C U] (rate of movement, progress) velocidad *f* **(b)** (relative quickness) rapidez *f* **2** [C] (Phot): **film ~** sensibilidad *f* de la película; **shutter ~** tiempo *m* de exposición **3** [C] (gear) velocidad *f*, marcha *f* **4** [U] (amphetamine) (sl) anfetas *fpl* (fam) ■ **~** *vt* (*past & past p* **speeded**) (hasten) acelerar

speed² *vi* **(a)** (*past & past p* **sped**) (go, pass quickly) (+ *adv compl*): **to ~ off** *o* **away** alejarse a toda velocidad; **he sped by** *o* **past in his new sports car** nos pasó a toda velocidad con su nuevo coche deportivo; **the hours sped by** las horas pasaron volando **(b)** (*past & past p* **speeded**) (drive too fast) ir* a velocidad excesiva

● **speed up** (*past & past p* **speeded**) **1** [*v* + *adv*] **(a)** (move faster) «*vehicle/driver*» acelerar; «*walker*» apretar* el paso **(b)** «*process/production*» acelerarse **2** [*v* + *o* + *adv*, *v* + *adv* + *o*] **(a)** ‹*vehicle*› acelerar **(b)** ‹*work/production*› acelerar

speed: **~boat** *n* (lancha *f*) motora *f*; **~ bump** *n* badén *m*, guardia *m* tumbado (Esp), tope *m* (Méx), policía *m* acostado (Col), lomo *m* de burro (RPl), baden *m* (Chi); **~ limit** *n* velocidad *f* máxima, límite *m* de velocidad

speedometer /spɪ'dɑ:mətər ‖ spi:'dɒmɪtə(r)/ *n* velocímetro *m*, indicador *m* de velocidad

speedway /'spi:dweɪ/ *n* **(a)** [U] (sport) carreras *fpl* de motocicletas **(b)** [C] (AmE Transp) autopista *f*

speedy /'spi:di/ *adj* **-dier, -diest** ‹*reply/delivery*› rápido; ‹*solution*› pronto, rápido

spell¹ /spel/ *n* **1** (*magic* **~**) encanto *m*, hechizo *m*, encantamiento *m*; **evil ~** maleficio *m*; **to cast a ~ over** *o* **to put a ~ on sth/sb** hechizar* *or* embrujar algo/a algn **2 (a)** (of weather) período *m* **(b)** (of work, activity) período *m*, temporada *f*; **a bad ~** una mala racha

spell² (*past & past p* **spelled** *or* (BrE also) **spelt**) *vt* **1** (write) escribir*; (orally) deletrear **2** (mean) significar*; (foretell) anunciar, augurar ■ ~ *vi*: **he can't ~** tiene mala ortografía
• spell out [*v + o + adv, v + adv + o*] **(a)** ‹*word*› deletrear **(b)** (explain) explicar* en detalle

spell: **~binding** *adj* ‹*speech/film*› fascinante; **~bound** *adj* embelesado, maravillado

spelling /'spelɪŋ/ *n* **(a)** [U] (system, ability) ortografía *f*; **to be good/bad at ~** tener* buena/mala ortografía; (*before n*) **~ mistake** falta *f* de ortografía, error *m* ortográfico **(b)** [C] (of a word) grafía *f*, ortografía *f*

spelt /spelt/ (BrE) *past & past p of* SPELL²

spelunking /spɪ'lʌŋkɪŋ/ [U] (AmE) *n* espeleología *f*

spend /spend/ *vt* (*past & past p* **spent**) **1 (a)** ‹*money*› gastar **(b)** (expend) **to ~ sth (ON sth)** dedicarle* algo A algo; **don't ~ too long on each question** no le dediquen mucho tiempo a cada pregunta **2** (pass) ‹*period of time*› pasar **3** (exhaust) agotar

spending /'spendɪŋ/ *n* [U] gastos *mpl*; **public ~** el gasto público; (*before n*) **~ power** poder *m* adquisitivo

spending money *n* [U] dinero *m* para gastos personales

spendthrift /'spendθrɪft/ *n* despilfarrador, -dora *m,f*

spent /spent/ *past & past p of* SPEND

sperm /spɜːrm ‖ spɜːm/ *n* (*pl* **~** *or* **~s**) **(a)** [U] (seminal liquid) esperma *m or f* **(b)** [C] (gamete) espermatozoide *m*, espermatozoo *m*

spew /spjuː/ *vi* **(a)** «*water*» salir* a borbotones **(b)** (vomit) (BrE sl) vomitar, lanzar* (fam) ■ **~** *vt* ‹*lava/flames*› arrojar

sphere /sfɪr ‖ sfɪə(r)/ *n* esfera *f*

spherical /'sfɪrɪkəl ‖ 'sferɪkəl/ *adj* esférico

Sphinx /sfɪŋks/ *n* **the ~** la Esfinge

spice¹ /spaɪs/ *n* **(a)** [C U] (seasoning) especia *f* **(b)** [U] (zest, interest) sabor *m*

spice² *vt* **(a)** (Culin) (*often pass*) condimentar, sazonar* **(b)** (add excitement to): **to ~ up a story** darle* más sabor a un relato

spick-and-span /'spɪkən'spæn/ *adj* (colloq) (*pred*) limpio y ordenado

spicy /'spaɪsi/ *adj* **-cier, -ciest (a)** ‹*sauce/food*› (with spices) con muchas especias; (hot, peppery) picante **(b)** (racy) ‹*story/account*› sabroso; (with sexual connotations) picante

spider /'spaɪdər ‖ 'spaɪdə(r)/ *n* araña *f*

spike¹ /spaɪk/ *n* **1** (pointed object) punta *f*, púa *f*, pincho *m or* (Arg) pinche *m*; (on track shoes) clavo *m or* (Chi, Ven) púa *f or* (Col) carramplón *m* **2 spikes** *pl* (running shoes) zapatillas *fpl* de clavos *or* (Chi, Ven) de púas *or* (Col) con carramplones, picos *mpl* (Méx)

spike² *vt* **1** (pierce) pinchar, clavar **2** (add sth to) (colloq): **they ~d his lemonade with vodka** le echaron vodka en la limonada

spiky /'spaɪki/ *adj* **-kier, -kiest (a)** (having spikes) con puntas *or* púas *or* pinchos **(b)** (sharp, pointed) puntiagudo, puntudo (Col, CS) **(c)** ‹*hair*› de punta

spill /spɪl/ (*past & past p* **spilled** *or* **spilt**) *vt* ‹*liquid*› derramar, verter*; (knock over) volcar* ■ **~** *vi* «*liquid*» derramarse; **people ~ed (out) into the streets** la gente se volcó *or* se echó a las calles
• spill over [*v + adv*] «*container*» desbordarse; «*liquid*» rebosar; «*fighting/conflict*» extenderse*

spillage /'spɪlɪdʒ/ *n* [U C] vertido *m*, derrame *m*

spin¹ /spɪn/ *n* **1** [U] (on ball) (Sport) efecto *m*, chanfle *m* (AmL) **2** [C] **(a)** (of aircraft) barrena *f* **(b)** (Auto) trompo *m* **3** [C] (ride) (colloq): **to go for a ~** ir* a dar un paseo en coche (*or* en moto *etc*), ir* a dar un garbeo (Esp fam)

spin² (*pres p* **spinning**; *past* **spun**; *past p* **spun**) *vt* **1** ‹*wheel/top*› hacer* girar **2 (a)** ‹*wool/cotton*› hilar **(b)** ‹*web*› tejer ■ **~** *vi* **1 (a)** (rotate) «*wheel/top*» girar; **my head is ~ning** la cabeza me da vueltas **(b)** «*washing machine*» centrifugar* **(c)** (move rapidly) (+ *adv compl*): **the car spun out of control** el coche giró fuera de control **2** (Tex) hilar
• spin out [*v + o + adv, v + adv + o*] ‹*money*› estirar; ‹*vacation/story*› alargar*, prolongar*

spina bifida /'spaɪnə'bɪfədə ‖ ˌspaɪnə'bɪfɪdə/ *n* [U] espina *f* bífida

spinach /'spɪnɪtʃ ‖ 'spɪnɪdʒ, -ɪtʃ/ *n* [U] (Bot) espinaca *f*; (Culin) espinaca(s) *f(pl)*

spinal /'spaɪnḷ/ *adj* de la columna vertebral

spinal: **~ column** *n* columna *f* vertebral; **~ cord** *n* médula *f* espinal

spindle /'spɪndḷ/ *n* **(a)** (Mech Eng) eje *m* **(b)** (Tex) huso *m*

spindly /'spɪndli/ *adj* **-dlier, -dliest** ‹*legs*› largo y flaco; ‹*plant*› alto y débil

spin: **~ drier** *n* centrifugadora *f* (*de ropa*); **~-dry** /'spɪn'draɪ/ *vt* **-dries, -drying, -dried** centrifugar*; **~ dryer** *n* ⇒ **~** DRIER

spine /spaɪn/ *n* **1 (a)** (Anat) columna *f* (vertebral) **(b)** (of book) lomo *m* **2** (on animal) púa *f*; (on plant) espina *f*

spine-chilling /'spaɪnˌtʃɪlɪŋ/ *adj* espeluznante

spineless /'spaɪnləs ‖ 'spaɪnlɪs/ *adj* **(a)** (cowardly, weak) débil, sin carácter **(b)** (Zool) invertebrado

spinning /'spɪnɪŋ/ *n* [U] (Tex) hilado *m*

spinning wheel *n* rueca *f*

spin-off /'spɪnɔːf ‖ 'spɪnɒf/ *n* (product) producto *m* derivado; (result) resultado *m* indirecto

spinster /'spɪnstər ‖ 'spɪnstə(r)/ *n* soltera *f*

spiral¹ /'spaɪrəl ‖ 'spaɪərəl/ *n* **(a)** (shape, movement) espiral *f* **(b)** (of smoke) voluta *f*, espiral *f*

spiral² *adj* ‹*shape*› de espiral, acaracolado; **~ staircase** escalera *f* de caracol

spiral³ *vi*, (BrE) **-ll-** «*unemployment*» escalar; «*prices*» dispararse

spire /spaɪr ‖ 'spaɪə(r)/ *n* aguja *f*, chapitel *m*

spirit /'spɪrət ‖ 'spɪrɪt/ *n* **1 (a)** [U] (life force, soul) espíritu *m* **(b)** [C] (Occult) espíritu *m* **2** [U] (vigor, courage) espíritu *m*, temple *m*; **to break sb's ~** quebrantarle el espíritu a algn **3** (mental attitude, mood) (*no pl*) espíritu *m*; **the party/Christmas ~** el espíritu festivo/navideño **4 spirits** *pl* (emotional state): **to be in good ~s** estar* animado; **keep**

your ~s up ¡arriba ese ánimo! **5 spirits** *pl* (alcohol) bebidas *fpl* alcohólicas (*de alta graduación*), licores *mpl*

spirited /'spɪrətəd ‖ 'spɪrɪtɪd/ *adj* ‹*horse/child*› brioso; ‹*reply*› enérgico; ‹*defense*› ardiente

spirit level *n* nivel *m* (de burbuja *or* de aire)

spiritual¹ /'spɪrɪtʃuəl ‖ 'spɪrɪtjʊəl/ *adj* espiritual

spiritual² *n* (*negro* ~) espiritual *m* (negro)

spiritualism /'spɪrɪtʃuəlɪzəm ‖ 'spɪrɪtjʊəlɪzəm/ *n* [U] (Occult) espiritismo *m*; (Phil) espiritualismo *m*

spit¹ /spɪt/ *n* **1** [U] (saliva) saliva *f* **2** [C] (for roasting) asador *m* (*en forma de varilla*), espetón *m*

spit² *vi* (*pres p* **spitting**; *past & past p* **spat** *or* (AmE esp) **spit**) **(a)** «*person/animal*» escupir; **to ~ AT sb** escupirle A algn; ⇒ IMAGE **(b)** «*fire/fat*» chisporrotear **(c)** «*cat*» bufar ■ ~ *vt* (*past & past p* **spat**) ‹*food/blood*› escupir ■ ~ *v impers* ▶ **920** (colloq): **it's ~ting** caen algunas gotas (de lluvia), está chispeando (fam)

• **spit out** [*v + o + adv, v + adv + o*] escupir

spite¹ /spaɪt/ *n* [U] **1** (malice) maldad *f*; (resentment) rencor *m*, resentimiento *m* **2 in spite of** (*as prep*) a pesar de

spite² *vt* molestar, fastidiar

spiteful /'spaɪtfəl/ *adj* ‹*remark*› malicioso; ‹*person*› malo; (resentful) rencoroso

spittle /'spɪtl̩/ *n* [U] baba *f*

splash¹ /splæʃ/ *n* **1 (a)** [C U] (spray) salpicadura *f* **(b)** [C] (sound): **we heard a ~** oímos el ruido de algo al caer al agua **(c)** (paddle, swim) (*no pl*) chapuzón *m* **2 (a)** (of milk, paint) (*no pl*) **a ~** un poco **(b)** [C] (mark, patch) salpicadura *f*, manchón *m*

splash² *vt* salpicar*; **to ~ sth/sb WITH sth** salpicar* algo/a algn DE algo ■ ~ *vi* **(a)** «*water/paint*» salpicar* **(b)** «*person/animal*» chapotear

• **splash out** (BrE colloq) [*v + adv*] darse* un lujo; **to ~ out ON sth** gastar(se) un dineral EN algo (fam)

splashguard /'splæʃgɑːrd ‖ 'splæʃgɑːd/ *n* (AmE) guardabarros *m*, salpicadera *f* (Méx), tapabarros *m* (Chi, Per)

splatter /'splætər ‖ 'splætə(r)/ *vt/i* ⇒ SPATTER

splay /spleɪ/ *vt* ~ **(out)** ‹*fingers*› abrir*, separar; **to ~ one's legs** abrirse* de piernas

spleen /spliːn/ *n* [C U] (Anat) bazo *m*

splendid /'splendəd ‖ 'splendɪd/ *adj* **(a)** (very good) ‹*idea/opportunity/meal*› espléndido **(b)** (imposing) ‹*clothes/building*› magnífico; ‹*ceremony*› lleno de esplendor

splendor, (BrE) **splendour** /'splendər ‖ 'splendə(r)/ *n* [U] esplendor *m*

splice /splaɪs/ *vt* ~ **(together)** ‹*ropes*› coser; ‹*tape/film*› unir

splint /splɪnt/ *n* tablilla *f*

splinter¹ /'splɪntər ‖ 'splɪntə(r)/ *n* (of wood) astilla *f*; (of glass, bone, metal) esquirla *f*, astilla *f*; (*before n*) **~ group** grupo *m* escindido

splinter² *vi* **(a)** (break into pieces) «*wood/bone*» astillarse **(b)** «*political party/society*» escindirse ■ ~ *vt* ‹*wood/bone*› astillar

split¹ /splɪt/ *n* **1 (a)** (in garment, cloth — in seam) descosido *m*; (— part of design) abertura *f*, raja *f* **(b)** (in wood, glass) rajadura *f*, grieta *f* **2 (a)** (Pol) escisión *f*; (Relig) cisma *m*, escisión *f* **(b)** (breakup) ruptura *f*, separación *f* **3 splits** *pl*: **to do the ~s** abrirse* completamente de piernas, hacer* el spagat (Esp)

split² *adj* **1** (damaged) ‹*wood*› rajado, partido; ‹*lip*› partido **2 (a)** (divided): **~ personality** doble personalidad *f*; **~ shift** horario *m* (de trabajo) partido **(b)** (in factions) dividido

split³ (*pres p* **splitting**; *past & past p* **split**) *vt* **1 (a)** (break) ‹*wood/stone*› partir; **to ~ the atom** fisionar el átomo **(b)** (burst) ‹*pants/trousers*› reventar* **(c)** (divide into factions) ‹*nation/church*› dividir **2** (divide, share) ‹*cost/food*› dividir ■ ~ *vi* **1** (crack, burst) «*wood/rock*» partirse, rajarse; «*leather/seam*» abrirse*, romperse*; **I've got a ~ting headache** tengo un dolor de cabeza espantoso **2** «*political party/church*» dividirse, escindirse **3** (leave) (sl) abrirse* (arg), largarse* (fam)

• **split away, split off** [*v + adv*] **to ~ away** *o* **off FROM sth** escindirse *or* separarse DE algo

• **split up 1** [*v + adv*] «*couple/band*» separarse; «*crowd*» dispersarse **2** [*v + o + adv, v + adv + o*] ‹*wrestlers/boxers*› separar; ‹*lovers*› hacer* que se separen; **~ them up into groups** divídelos en grupos

split: **~ end** *n* (of hair): **I've got ~ ends** tengo las puntas abiertas *or* (CS) florecidas, tengo horquillas (Col) *or* (Méx) orzuela *or* (Ven) horquetillas; **~-level** /'splɪt'levəl/ *adj* ‹*apartment*› en dos niveles; **~ second** *n* fracción *f* de segundo; (*before n*) **~-second timing** sincronización *f* perfecta

splutter /'splʌtər ‖ 'splʌtə(r)/ *vi* **(a)** «*fire/fat*» chisporrotear; «*engine*» resoplar **(b)** «*person*» resoplar; (in anger, embarrassment etc) farfullar

spoil /spɔɪl/ (*past & past p* **spoiled** *or* (BrE also) **spoilt**) *vt* **1** ‹*party/surprise*› echar a perder, estropear; **I don't want to ~ your fun but ...** no les quiero aguar la fiesta pero ...; **it will ~ your appetite** te quitará el apetito **2** (overindulge) ‹*child*› consentir*, malcriar*; **to be ~ed for choice** tener* mucho de donde elegir ■ ~ *vi* **1** «*food/meal*» echarse a perder, estropearse **2** (be eager) (colloq): **to be ~ing for a fight** estar* *or* andar* buscando pelea

spoiled /spɔɪld/, (BrE also) **spoilt** /spɔɪlt/ *adj* mimado

spoils /spɔɪlz/ *npl* botín *m*

spoilsport /'spɔɪlspɔːrt ‖ 'spɔɪlspɔːt/ *n* (colloq) aguafiestas *mf* (fam)

spoilt¹ /spɔɪlt/ (BrE) *past & past p of* SPOIL

spoilt² *adj* (BrE) ⇒ SPOILED

spoke¹ /spəʊk/ *n* rayo *m* (*de una rueda*)

spoke² *past of* SPEAK

spoken¹ /'spəʊkən/ *past p of* SPEAK

spoken² *adj* (*before n*) hablado, oral

spokesman /'spəʊksmən/ *n* (*pl* **-men** /-mən/) portavoz *m*, vocero *m* (esp AmL)

spokesperson /'spəʊks,pɜːrsn̩ ‖ 'spəʊks,pɜːsn̩/ *n* portavoz *mf*, vocero, -ra *m,f* (esp AmL)

spokeswoman /'spəʊks,wʊmən/ (*pl* **-women**) *n* portavoz *f*, vocera *f* (esp AmL)

sponge¹ /spʌndʒ/ *n* **1** [C] **(a)** (Zool) esponja *f* **(b)** (for bath) esponja *f* **2** [C U] (Culin) ~ **(cake)** bizcocho *m*, bizcochuelo *m* (CS)

sponge² *vt* pasar una esponja por ■ ~ *vi*: **he lives by sponging on** *o* **off his relatives** vive a costillas de sus parientes

sponsor¹ /'spɑːnsər ‖ 'spɒnsə(r)/ *n* **(a)** (of program, show, sporting event) patrocinador, -dora *m,f*, espónsor *mf*; (for the arts) mecenas *mf* **(b)** (for membership): **you need two members to act as ~s** te tienen que presentar dos socios **(c)** (of bill, motion) proponente *mf*

sponsor² *vt* **(a)** ‹*event/festival*› patrocinar; ‹*research/expedition*› subvencionar **(b)** ‹*applicant/application*› apoyar **(c)** ‹*bill/motion*› (present) presentar, proponer*; (support) apoyar

sponsorship /'spɑːnsərʃɪp ‖ 'spɒnsəʃɪp/ *n* patrocinio *m*; (of the arts) mecenazgo *m*

spontaneous /spɑːn'teɪniəs ‖ spɒn'teɪniəs/ *adj* espontáneo

spontaneously /spɑːn'teɪniəsli ‖ spɒn'teɪniəsli/ *adv* espontáneamente

spoof /spuːf/ *n* (colloq) parodia *f*, burla *f*

spooky /'spuːki/ *adj* **-kier, -kiest** (colloq) espeluznante

spool /spuːl/ *n* carrete *m*, carretel *m* (AmL)

spoon /spuːn/ *n* cuchara *f*; (small) cucharita *f*

spoonfeed /'spuːnfiːd/ *vt* (*past & past p* **-fed**) ‹*baby*› darle* de comer en la boca a; **she ~s her students** se lo da todo mascado a sus alumnos

spoonful /'spuːnfʊl/ *n* (*pl* **~s** *or* **spoonsful**) cucharada *f*; (small) cucharadita *f*

sporadic /spə'rædɪk/ *adj* esporádico

sport¹ /spɔːrt ‖ spɔːt/ *n* **1** [C U] deporte *m* **2** (person): **to be a good ~** (to be sporting) tener* espíritu deportivo; (to be understanding) ser* comprensivo

sport² *vt* ‹*clothes/hairstyle*› lucir*

sport³ *adj* (AmE) **(a)** (Sport) ‹*equipment*› de deportes **(b)** (casual) ‹*clothes*› sport *adj inv*, de sport

sporting /'spɔːrtɪŋ ‖ 'spɔːtɪŋ/ *adj* **1** (fair) ‹*spirit*› deportivo; **it's very ~ of you** es muy amable de tu parte **2** (*no comp*) (relating to sport) ‹*press/interests*› deportivo

sports /spɔːrts ‖ spɔːts/ *adj* **(a)** (Sport) (page/program) de deportes **(b)** (casual) ‹*clothes/shirt*› sport *adj inv*

sports: **~ car** *n* coche *m* deportivo, carro *m* sport (AmL exc CS), auto *m* sport *or* deportivo (CS); **~man** /'spɔːrtsmən ‖ 'spɔːtsmən/ *n* (*pl* **-men** /-mən/) deportista *m*

sportsmanship /'spɔːrtsmənʃɪp ‖ 'spɔːtsmənʃɪp/ *n* [U] espíritu *m* deportivo

sportswoman /'spɔːrtswʊmən ‖ 'spɔːtswʊmən/ *n* deportista *f*

sporty /'spɔːrti ‖ 'spɔːti/ *adj* **-tier, -tiest** **(a)** ‹*person*› deportista **(b)** (Auto) deportivo

spot¹ /spɑːt ‖ spɒt/ *n* **1** **(a)** (dot — on material) lunar *m*, mota *f*; (— on animal's skin) mancha *f* **(b)** (blemish, stain) mancha *f* **(c)** (pimple) (BrE) grano *m*, espinilla *f* (AmL) **2** **(a)** (location, place) lugar *m*, sitio *m*; ***on the ~***: **he had to decide on the ~** tuvo que decidir en ese mismo momento; **they were killed on the ~** los mataron allí mismo; **on-the-~ fine** *multa que se paga en el acto* **(b)** (difficult situation): **to be in a (tight) ~** estar* en apuros **3** **(a)** (drop) gota *f* **(b)** (small amount) (BrE colloq) (*no pl*): **do you fancy a ~ of supper?** ¿quieres cenar algo?

spot² *vt* **-tt-** **1** ‹*error*› descubrir*; ‹*bargain*› encontrar*; **he ~ted her in the crowd** la vio *or* (AmL tb) la ubicó entre el gentío **2** (mark) (*usu pass*) manchar

spot check *n*: *control o inspección realizada al azar*

spotless /'spɑːtləs ‖ 'spɒtlɪs/ *adj* ‹*clothes*› impecable; ‹*house*› limpísimo; ‹*reputation/record*› intachable

spotlight /'spɑːtlaɪt ‖ 'spɒtlaɪt/ *n* (in theater) foco *m*; (on building) reflector *m*

spotted /'spɑːtəd ‖ 'spɒtɪd/ *adj* ‹*tie/material*› de *or* a lunares *or* motas

spotty /'spɑːti ‖ 'spɒti/ *adj* **-tier, -tiest** (BrE) ‹*skin*› lleno de granos; ‹*youth*› con la cara llena de granos

spouse /spaʊs/ *n* (frml *or* hum) cónyuge *mf* (frml)

spout¹ /spaʊt/ *n* **(a)** (of teapot, kettle) pico *m*, pitorro *m* (Esp) **(b)** (pipe — on gutter) canalón *m*; (— on fountain, gargoyle) caño *m* **(c)** (jet) chorro *m*

spout² *vt* ‹*oil/liquid*› arrojar *or* expulsar chorros de ■ ~ *vi* «*liquid*» salir* a chorros; «*whale*» expulsar chorros de agua

sprain¹ /spreɪn/ *n* esguince *m*, distensión *f*

sprain² *vt* hacerse* un esguince en, distenderse*

sprang /spræŋ/ *past of* SPRING¹

sprawl¹ /sprɔːl/ *vi* «*person*» sentarse* (*or* tumbarse *etc*) de forma poco elegante

sprawl² *n* [U] (of built up area) expansión *f*

spray¹ /spreɪ/ *vt* **(a)** ‹*liquid*› pulverizar*, aplicar* con atomizador; ‹*paint*› aplicar* con pistola pulverizadora **(b)** ‹*plants*› rociar* (*con atomizador*)

spray² *n* **1** **(a)** [U C] (fine drops) rocío *m* **(b)** [C] (liquid in spray form) espray *m*; (*before n*) ‹*deodorant/polish*› en aerosol, en espray, en atomizador **(c)** [C] (implement) rociador *m* **2** [C] (bunch) ramillete *m*

spread¹ /spred/ (*past & past p* **spread**) *vt* **1** (extend) ‹*arms/legs*› extender*; ‹*map/sails/wings*› desplegar*; **you can ~ the cost over five years** se puede pagar el costo a lo largo de cinco años **2** **(a)** ‹*paint/glue*› extender*; ‹*seeds/sand*› esparcir*; **to ~ butter on a piece of toast** untar una tostada con mantequilla **(b)** ‹*knowledge/news*› difundir; ‹*influence*› extender*; ‹*rumor*› hacer* correr; ‹*disease*› propagar*; ‹*fear*› sembrar*; ‹*ideas/culture*› diseminar ■ ~ *vi* **1** «*disease*» propagarse*; «*liquid/fire*» extenderse*; «*ideas/culture*» diseminarse; «*panic/fear*» cundir; «*influence/revolt*» extenderse* **2** (extend in space, time) extenderse* **3** «*paint*» extenderse*; «*butter*» untarse

• **spread out** [*v* + *adv*] **(a)** (move apart) «*troops*» desplegarse* **(b)** (extend) extenderse*

spread² *n* **1** [U] (diffusion — of disease) propagación *f*; (— of ideas) difusión *f*, diseminación *f*; (— of fire) propagación *f* **2** [U] (of wings, sails) envergadura *f* **3** [C] (Culin) **(a)** (meal) (colloq) festín *m*, banquete *m* **(b)** (paste) *pasta para extender sobre pan, tostadas etc* **4**

[C] (Journ, Print): **it was advertised in a full-page ~** venía anunciado a plana entera

spread: **~-eagled** /'spred'i:gəld/ *adj* con los brazos y piernas abiertos; **~sheet** *n* hoja *f* de cálculo

spree /spri:/ *n*: **to go on a shopping ~** ir* de expedición a las tiendas

sprig /sprɪg/ *n* ramito *m*

sprightly /'spraɪtli/ *adj* **-lier, -liest** ‹*person*› lleno de brío; ‹*walk/step*› ágil

spring¹ /sprɪŋ/ (*past* **sprang** *or* (esp AmE) **sprung**; *past p* **sprung**) *vi* **1** (leap) saltar; **to ~ into action** entrar en acción **2 (a)** (liter) «*stream*» surgir*, nacer*; «*shoots*» brotar **(b) to ~ FROM sth** «*ideas/doubts*» surgir* DE algo; «*problem*» provenir* DE algo ■ **~** *vt* **(a)** (produce suddenly): **to ~ a surprise on sb** darle* una sorpresa a algn **(b) to ~ a leak** empezar* a hacer agua
• spring up [*v* + *adv*] «*stores/housing estates*» surgir*; «*plant*» brotar; «*wind*» levantarse

spring² *n* **1** [U C] (season) primavera *f*; **in (the) ~** en primavera; (*before n*) ‹*weather/showers*› primaveral **2** [C] (Geog) manantial *m*, fuente *f* **3** [C] (jump) salto *m*, brinco *m* **4 (a)** [C] (in watch, toy) resorte *m*; (in mattress) muelle *m*, resorte *m* (AmL) **(b)** (elasticity) (*no pl*) elasticidad *f*

spring: **~board** *n* trampolín *m*; **~clean** /'sprɪŋ 'kli:n/ *vi* hacer* limpieza general; **~cleaning** /'sprɪŋ'kli:nɪŋ/ *n* (*no pl*) limpieza *f* general; **~ onion** *n* (BrE) cebolleta *f*, cebollino *m*; **~time** *n* primavera *f*

springy /'sprɪŋi/ *adj* **-gier, -giest** ‹*mattress/grass*› mullido; ‹*floor*› elástico

sprinkle /'sprɪŋkəl/ *vt* **(a)** (scatter) **to ~ sth ON sth**: **to ~ water on the plants** rociar* las plantas con agua; **to ~ sugar on sth** espolvorear algo con azúcar **(b)** (cover) **to ~ sth WITH sth**: **~ the board with flour** espolvoree la tabla con harina

sprinkler /'sprɪŋklər ‖ 'sprɪŋklə(r)/ *n* **(a)** (*garden ~*) aspersor *m* **(b)** (for firefighting) (*usu pl*) rociador *m*; (*before n*) **~ system** sistema *m* de rociadores

sprint¹ /sprɪnt/ *n* **(a)** (fast run) (e)sprint *m* **(b)** (short race) (Sport) carrera *f* corta

sprint² *vi* **(a)** (Sport) (e)sprintar **(b)** (run fast): **I ~ed after him** salí corriendo tras él a toda velocidad

sprout¹ /spraʊt/ *vt* ‹*leaves/shoots*› echar ■ **~** *vi* «*plant*» echar retoños, retoñar; «*leaf*» brotar, salir*; «*seeds*» germinar

sprout² *n* **(a)** (*Brussels ~*) col *f or* (AmS) repollito *m* de Bruselas **(b)** (shoot) brote *m*

spruce¹ /spru:s/ *n* (tree) picea *f*, abeto *m* falso

spruce² *adj* **sprucer, sprucest** ‹*appearance*› cuidado, acicalado; ‹*garden*› cuidado, arreglado
• spruce up [*v* + *o* + *adv*, *v* + *adv* + *o*] ‹*garden/room*› arreglar

sprung /sprʌŋ/ *past p* & (esp AmE) *past of* SPRING¹

spry /spraɪ/ *adj* **-er, -est** lleno de vida, dinámico

spud /spʌd/ *n* (colloq) papa *f or* (Esp) patata *f*

spun¹ /spʌn/ *past & past p of* SPIN²

spun² *adj* ‹*silk/cotton*› hilado

spur¹ /spɜ:r ‖ spɜ:(r)/ *n* **(a)** espuela *f*; ***on the ~ of the moment*** sin pensarlo **(b)** (stimulus) acicate *m*

spur² *vt* **-rr- (a)** (Equ) ‹*horse*› espolear **(b) ~ (on)** ‹*person/team*› estimular

spurious /'spjʊriəs ‖ 'spjʊəriəs/ *adj* ‹*document*› falso, espurio; ‹*argument*› falaz, espurio

spurn /spɜ:rn ‖ spɜ:n/ *vt* desdeñar, rechazar*

spurt¹ /spɜ:rt ‖ spɜ:t/ *n* **(a)** (of speed, activity) racha *f*; **to put on a ~** acelerar **(b)** (jet) chorro *m*

spurt² *vi* «*liquid/steam*» salir* a chorros

spy¹ /spaɪ/ *n* (*pl* **spies**) espía *mf*; (*before n*) ‹*story*› de espías, de espionaje; **~ ring** red *f* de espionaje

spy² **spies, spying, spied** *vi* espiar*; **to ~ ON sb** espiar* a algn ■ **~** *vt* descubrir*, ver*

sq *adj* (= **square**): **220 ~ m** 220 m²

Sq (= **Square**) Pza.

squabble /'skwɑ:bəl ‖ 'skwɒbəl/ *vi* pelear(se), reñir*

squad /skwɑ:d ‖ skwɒd/ *n* **(a)** (Mil) pelotón *m*; (of workmen) cuadrilla *f* **(b)** (of policemen) brigada *f*; **drug ~** brigada *f* antidroga **(c)** (Sport) equipo *m*

squad car *n* (AmE) coche *m or* (AmL tb) auto *m* patrulla, patrullero *m* (CS, Per)

squadron /'skwɑ:drən ‖ 'skwɒdrən/ *n* (Mil, Aviat) escuadrón *m*; (Naut) escuadra *f*

squalid /'skwɑ:ləd ‖ 'skwɒlɪd/ *adj* **(a)** (dirty) ‹*existence/house*› miserable **(b)** (sordid) ‹*story/business*› sórdido

squall /skwɔ:l/ *n* borrasca *f*, turbión *m*

squalor /'skwɑ:lər ‖ 'skwɒlə(r)/ *n* [U] miseria *f*

squander /'skwɑ:ndər ‖ 'skwɒndə(r)/ *vt* ‹*money*› despilfarrar; ‹*opportunity*› desaprovechar

square¹ /skwer ‖ skweə(r)/ *n* **1 (a)** (shape) cuadrado *m*; (in fabric design) cuadro *m* **(b)** (on chessboard) casilla *f*, escaque *m*; (in crossword) casilla *f*; ***to go back to ~ one*** volver* a empezar desde cero **2** (in town, city) plaza *f* **3** (Math) cuadrado *m*

square² *adj* **squarer, squarest 1 (a)** ‹*box/table/block*› cuadrado; **the room is 15 feet ~** la habitación mide 15 (pies) por 15 (pies) **(b)** (having right angles) ‹*corner/edges*› en ángulo recto **(c)** ‹*face*› cuadrado; ‹*jaw*› angular **2** (Math) (*before n*) ‹*yard/mile*› cuadrado **3 (a)** (fair, honest): **he'll give you a ~ deal** no te va a engañar **(b)** (large and wholesome) (*before n*) ‹*meal*› decente

square³ *vt* **1** (make square) ‹*angle/side*› cuadrar **2** (Math) elevar al cuadrado **3 (a)** (settle, make even) ‹*debts/accounts*› pagar*, saldar **(b)** (reconcile) ‹*facts/principles*› conciliar ■ **~** *vi* «*ideas/arguments*» concordar*
• square up [*v* + *adv*] (settle debts) (colloq) **to ~ up (WITH sb)** arreglar cuentas (CON algn)

square root *n* raíz *f* cuadrada

squash¹ /skwɑ:ʃ ‖ skwɒʃ/ *n* **1** [U] (Sport) squash *m* **2** [U] (drink) (BrE) *refresco a base de extractos*; **orange ~** naranjada *f* **3** [C U] (Bot, Culin) *nombre genérico de varios tipos de calabaza y zapallo*

squash² *vt* **1 (a)** (crush) ‹*fruit/insect*› aplastar **(b)** (squeeze): **to ~ sth/sb in** meter algo/a algn (*apretando*) **2** (suppress, silence) (colloq) ‹*protests/rumors*› acallar ■ **~** *vi* (+ *adv compl*): **we all ~ed into his study** nos metimos todos en su despacho

squashy /'skwɑ:ʃi ‖ 'skwɒʃi/ *adj* **-shier, -shiest** ‹*fruit*› blando; ‹*ground*› húmedo y mullido

squat¹ /skwɑːt ‖ skwɒt/ *vi* **-tt- 1** (crouch) agacharse, ponerse* en cuclillas **2** (in building, on land) *ocupar un inmueble ajeno sin autorización*

squat² *adj* **-tt-** ‹*person*› rechoncho y bajo; ‹*building/church*› achaparrado

squatter /'skwɑːtər ‖ 'skwɒtə(r)/ *n* (in building) ocupante *mf* ilegal, ocupa *or* okupa *mf* (Esp), paracaidista *mf* (Méx)

squawk¹ /skwɔːk/ *n* (of bird) graznido *m*

squawk² *vi* «*bird*» graznar; «*person*» chillar

squeak¹ /skwiːk/ *n* (of animal, person) chillido *m*; (of hinge) chirrido *m*; (of shoes) crujido *m*

squeak² *vi* «*animal/person*» chillar; «*hinge*» chirriar*; «*shoes*» crujir

squeaky /'skwiːki/ *adj* **-kier, kiest** ‹*hinge/pen*› chirriante; ‹*voice*› chillón, de pito

squeal¹ /skwiːl/ *vi* **(a)** (make noise) «*person/animal*» chillar; «*brakes/tires*» chirriar* **(b)** (inform) (colloq) cantar (fam), chivarse (Esp fam), sapear (Ven fam)

squeal² *n* (of animal) chillido *m*; (of person) grito *m*, chillido *m*; (of brakes, tires) chirrido *m*

squeamish /'skwiːmɪʃ/ *adj* impresionable, aprensivo

squeeze¹ /skwiːz/ *n* **1** [C] **(a)** (application of pressure) apretón *m*; **he gave her hand a ~** le dio un apretón de manos **(b)** (restrictions): **a credit ~** una restricción crediticia **(c)** (hug) apretón *m* **2** (confined, restricted condition) (colloq) (*no pl*): **it will be a (tight) ~** vamos (*or* van *etc*) a estar apretados

squeeze² *vt* **(a)** (press) ‹*tube/pimple*› apretar*, espichar (Col); ‹*lemon*› exprimir; **to ~ a cloth (out)** retorcer* un trapo **(b)** (extract) ‹*liquid/juice*› extraer*, sacar*; **he tried to ~ more money out of them** trató de sacarles más dinero **(c)** (force, fit) meter; **I can ~ you in tomorrow morning** le puedo hacer un huequito mañana por la mañana ■ **~** *vi:* **he ~d in through the hole** se metió por el agujero

squelch /skweltʃ/ *vi* «*shoes/hooves*» *hacer* un ruido como de succión*

squid /skwɪd/ *n* (*pl* **~**) calamar *m*

squiggle /'skwɪgəl/ *n* garabato *m*

squint¹ /skwɪnt/ *n* bizquera *f*, estrabismo *m*

squint² *vi* **(a)** (attempting to see) entrecerrar* los ojos **(b)** (be cross-eyed) bizquear, torcer* la vista

squire /skwaɪr ‖ 'skwaɪə(r)/ *n* **(a)** (Hist, Mil) escudero *m* **(b)** (in UK: landowner) señor *m*

squirm /skwɜːrm ‖ skwɜːm/ *vi* retorcerse*; **she ~ed with embarrassment** le dio mucha vergüenza, no sabía dónde meterse de la vergüenza

squirrel /skwɜːrl ‖ 'skwɪrəl/ *n* ardilla *f*

squirt¹ /skwɜːrt ‖ skwɜːt/ *n* **1** (stream) chorrito *m* **2** (person) (colloq) mequetrefe *m* (fam)

squirt² *vt* ‹*liquid*› echar un chorro de ■ **~** *vi* «*liquid*» salir* a chorros

Sr (= **Senior**) Sr.

Sri Lanka /sriː'lɑːŋkə, ʃriː- ‖ srɪ'læŋkə, ʃrɪ-/ *n* Sri Lanka *m*

St (a) (= **Saint**) S(an), Sta.; **~ Thomas** Sto. Tomás **(b)** (= **Street**) c/

stab¹ /stæb/ *n* **(a)** (with knife) puñalada *f*, cuchillada *f*; ***to have a ~ at sth*** intentar algo **(b)** (sudden sensation): **a ~ of pain** una punzada de dolor

stab² *vt* **-bb-** apuñalar, acuchillar; **he had been ~bed to death** había muerto apuñalado *or* acuchillado

stabbing¹ /'stæbɪŋ/ *n* apuñalamiento *m*

stabbing² *adj* ‹*pain/sensation*› punzante

stability /stə'bɪləti/ *n* [U] estabilidad *f*

stabilize /'steɪbəlaɪz/ *vt* estabilizar* ■ **~** *vi* estabilizarse*

stable¹ /'steɪbəl/ *adj* **-bler, -blest (a)** (firm, steady) estable **(b)** (Psych) equilibrado

stable² *n* (*often pl*) (for horses) caballeriza *f*, cuadra *f*; (for other livestock) establo *m*

staccato /stə'kɑːtəʊ/ *adj* (Mus) staccato

stack¹ /stæk/ *n* **(a)** (pile) montón *m*, pila *f* **(b)** (many, much) (colloq) (*often pl*) montón *m* (fam), pila *f* (AmS fam)

stack² *vt* **~ (up)** amontonar, apilar

stadium /'steɪdiəm/ *n* (*pl* **-diums** *or* **-dia** /-diə/) estadio *m*

staff¹ /stæf ‖ stɑːf/ *n* **1 (a)** (as group) (+ *sing o pl vb*) personal *m*; **the teaching ~** el personal docente; **a member of ~** un empleado **(b)** (as individuals) (BrE) (*pl* **~**) (+ *pl vb*) empleados *mpl* **2** (*pl* **staffs** *or* **staves** /steɪvz/) (stick) bastón *m*; (of bishop) báculo *m*, cayado *m* **3** (Mus) ⇒ STAVE 2

staff² *vt* proveer* de personal

stag /stæg/ *n* ciervo *m*, venado *m*

stage¹ /steɪdʒ/ *n* **1 (a)** (platform) tablado *m*; (in theater) escenario *m*; (*before n*) **~ door** entrada *f* de artistas **(b)** (medium, profession) **the ~** el teatro; (*before n*) **~ name** nombre *m* artístico **2** (in development, activity) fase *f*, etapa *f*; **at some ~** en algún momento

stage² *vt* **1 (a)** ‹*event*› organizar*, montar; ‹*strike/demonstration*› hacer*; ‹*attack*› llevar a cabo; ‹*coup*› dar* **(b)** (engineer, arrange) arreglar, orquestar **2** (Theat) ‹*play*› poner* en escena

stage: **~coach** *n* diligencia *f*; **~ fright** *n* [U] miedo *m* a salir a escena; **~hand** *n* tramoyista *mf*; **~manage** *vt* ‹*event*› orquestar, arreglar; **~ manager** *n* director, -tora *m,f* de escena

stagger /'stægər ‖ 'stægə(r)/ *vi* tambalearse ■ **~** *vt* **1** (amaze) dejar estupefacto **2** ‹*shifts/payments*› escalonar

staggering /'stægərɪŋ/ *adj* asombroso

stagnant /'stægnənt/ *adj* estancado

stagnate /'stægneɪt ‖ stæg'neɪt/ *vi* «*water/economy*» estancarse*; «*person*» anquilosarse

stag: **~ night** *n* (for men only) ⇒ **~** PARTY (a); **~ party** *n* **(a)** (before wedding) despedida *f* de soltero **(b)** (all-male celebration) fiesta *f* para hombres, noche *f* de cuates (Méx)

staid /steɪd/ *adj* **-er, -est** serio, formal; ‹*clothes*› serio, sobrio; (pej) aburrido

stain¹ /steɪn/ *n* **(a)** (dirty mark) mancha *f* **(b)** (dye) tintura *f*, tinte *m* **(c)** (on character) mancha *f*

stain² *vt* **(a)** ‹*clothes/skin*› manchar **(b)** (dye) ‹*wood*› teñir* ■ **~** *vi* manchar

stained glass /steɪnd/ *n* [U] vidrio *m* or cristal *m* de colores; (*before n*) ~ **~ window** vitral *m*, vidriera *f* (de colores)

stainless steel /ˈsteɪnləs ‖ ˈsteɪnlɪs/ *n* [U] acero *m* inoxidable

stain remover *n* [C U] quitamanchas *m*

stair /ster ‖ steə(r)/ *n* **(a)** **stairs** *pl* (flight of stairs, stairway) escalera(s) *f(pl)* **(b)** (single step) escalón *m*, peldaño *m*

stair: **~case**, **~way** *n* escalera(s) *f(pl)*; **~well** *n* caja *f* or hueco *m* or (Méx) cubo *m* de la escalera

stake¹ /steɪk/ *n* **1** (pole) estaca *f* **2 (a)** (bet) apuesta *f*; **to be at ~** estar* en juego **(b)** (interest): **to have a ~ in a company** tener* participación or intereses en una compañía

stake² *vt* **1** (risk) ‹*money/reputation*› jugarse* **2 (a)** (mark with stakes) marcar* con estacas, estacar*; **the government was quick to ~ its claim** el gobierno se apresuró a reclamar su parte **(b)** ‹*tree/plant*› arrodrigar*

stalactite /stəˈlæktaɪt ‖ ˈstæləktaɪt/ *n* estalactita *f*

stalagmite /stəˈlægmaɪt ‖ ˈstæləgmaɪt/ *n* estalagmita *f*

stale /steɪl/ *adj* **staler, stalest** ‹*bread*› no fresco; ‹*butter/cheese*› rancio; ‹*beer*› pasado; ‹*air*› viciado; ‹*joke*› añejo, viejo; ‹*ideas*› trasnochado

stalemate /ˈsteɪlmeɪt/ *n* [U C] (in chess) tablas *fpl* (*por ahogar al rey*); **to be at a ~** estar* en un punto muerto

stalk¹ /stɔːk/ *n* (of plant) tallo *m*; (of leaf, flower) pedúnculo *m*, tallo *m*; (of fruit) rabillo *m*

stalk² *vt* acechar ■ ~ *vi*: **to ~ off** irse* ofendido/indignado

stall¹ /stɔːl/ *n* **1** (in market) puesto *m*, tenderete *m* **2** **stalls** *pl* (in theater, movie house) (BrE) platea *f*, patio *m* de butacas **3** (in stable) compartimiento *m*

stall² *vi* **1** «*engine/car*» pararse, calarse (Esp), atascarse* (Méx) **2** (play for time) (colloq): **quit ~ing** no andes con rodeos or con evasivas ■ ~ *vt* **1** ‹*engine/car*› parar, calar (Esp), atascar* (Méx) **2** (delay) (colloq) entretener*

stallion /ˈstæljən/ *n* semental *m*

stalwart /ˈstɔːlwərt ‖ ˈstɔːlwət/ *adj* ‹*supporter*› incondicional, fiel

stamina /ˈstæmənə ‖ ˈstæmɪnə/ *n* [U] resistencia *f*

stammer¹ /ˈstæmər ‖ ˈstæmə(r)/ *n* tartamudeo *m*

stammer² *vi* tartamudear

stamp¹ /stæmp/ *n* **1** (*postage* ~) sello *m*, estampilla *f* (AmL), timbre *m* (Méx); (*before n*) **~ collecting** filatelia *f*; **~ collector** coleccionista *mf* de sellos (*or* estampillas *etc*), filatelista *mf* **2 (a)** (instrument) sello *m* **(b)** (printed mark) sello *m* **3** (character) impronta *f*; **she left her ~ on the institute** dejó su impronta en el instituto

stamp² *vt* **1** (with foot) ‹*ground*› dar* una patada en; **to ~ one's foot** dar* una patada en el suelo **2** ‹*letter/parcel*› franquear, ponerle* sellos (*or* estampillas *etc*) a, estampillar (AmL), timbrar (Méx); **a ~ed addressed envelope** un sobre franqueado or (AmL tb) estampillado or (Méx) timbrado con su dirección **3 (a)** ‹*passport/ticket*› sellar **(b)** ‹*coin*› acuñar ■ ~ *vi* «*person*» dar* patadas en el suelo; «*horse*» piafar; **he ~ed on the spider** le dio un pisotón a la araña

• **stamp out** [*v + o + adv, v + adv + o*] **(a)** ‹*fire*› apagar* (con los pies) **(b)** (suppress) ‹*resistance*› aplastar; ‹*rebellion*› sofocar*; ‹*crime*› erradicar*

stampede¹ /stæmˈpiːd/ *n* estampida *f*

stampede² *vi* salir* en estampida

stance /stæns ‖ stɑːns/ *n* postura *f*

stand¹ /stænd/ *n* **1 (a)** (position) lugar *m* **(b)** (attitude) postura *f* **(c)** (resistance) resistencia *f*; **to make a ~ against sth** oponer* resistencia a algo **2 (a)** (base) pie *m*, base *f* **(b)** (for coats, hats) perchero *m* **3** (at fair, exhibition) stand *m*, caseta *f*; **newspaper ~** puesto *m* de periódicos; **a hot-dog ~** (esp AmE) un puesto de perritos calientes **4** (for spectators) (*often pl*) tribuna *f* **5** (witness box) (AmE) estrado *m*

stand² (*past & past p* **stood**) *vi* **1 (a)** (be, remain upright) «*person*» estar* de pie, estar* parado (AmL) **(b)** (rise) levantarse, ponerse* de pie, pararse (AmL); **her hair stood on end** se le pusieron los pelos de punta, se le pararon los pelos (AmL); *see also* STAND UP **2** (move, take up position) ponerse*, pararse (AmL); **~ over there** ponte or (AmL tb) párate allí; **to ~ aside** hacerse* a un lado; **to ~ on one's head** pararse de cabeza (AmL), hacer el pino (Esp) **3 (a)** (be situated, located): **a church stood here long ago** hace mucho tiempo aquí había una iglesia; **I won't ~ in your way** no seré yo quien te lo impida **(b)** (hold position): **where do you ~ on this issue?** ¿cuál es tu posición en cuanto a este problema?; **you never know where you ~ with him** con él uno nunca sabe a qué atenerse **(c)** (be mounted, fixed): **a hut ~ing on wooden piles** una choza construida sobre pilotes de madera **4 (a)** (stop, remain still) «*person*»: **they stood and stared** se quedaron mirando; **time stood still** el tiempo se detuvo **(b)** (Culin) «*batter/water*»: **leave to ~** dejar reposar **(c)** (survive, last): **the tower is still ~ing** la torre sigue en pie **5** (remain unchanged, valid) «*law/agreement*» seguir* vigente; **the offer still ~s** la oferta sigue en pie **6 (a)** (be currently): **as things ~** tal (y) como están las cosas **(b)** (be likely to) **to ~ to** + INF: **he ~s to lose a fortune** puede llegar a perder una fortuna; **what does she ~ to gain out of this?** ¿qué es lo que puede ganar con esto ? **7** (for office, election) (BrE) presentarse (como candidato) ■ ~ *vt* **1** (place) poner*; (carefully, precisely) colocar* **2 (a)** (tolerate, bear) (*with* CAN, CAN'T, WON'T) ‹*pain/noise*› aguantar, soportar; **I can't ~ him** no lo aguanto or soporto; **I can't ~ it any longer!** ¡no puedo más!; **she can't ~ being interrupted** no soporta que la interrumpan **(b)** (withstand) ‹*heat/strain*› soportar

• **stand back** [*v + adv*] (move away) **to ~ back** (FROM **sth**) apartarse (DE algo)

• **stand by 1** [*v + adv*] **(a)** (remain uninvolved) mantenerse* al margen; **people just stood by and did nothing** la gente estaba allí mirando sin hacer nada **(b)** (be at readiness) «*army/troops*» estar* en estado de alerta **2** [*v + prep + o*] **(a)** ‹*promise*› mantener*; ‹*decision*› atenerse* a **(b)** (support) ‹*friend*› apoyar

• **stand down** [*v* + *adv*] (relinquish position) retirarse; (resign) renunciar, dimitir
• **stand for** [*v* + *prep* + *o*] **(a)** (represent) «*initials/symbol*» significar*; **CTI ~s for** ... CTI son las siglas de ...; **he has betrayed everything he once stood for** ha traicionado todo aquello con lo que solía identificar **(b)** (put up with) (*usu with neg*) consentir*
• **stand in** [*v* + *adv*] **to ~ in** FOR **sb** sustituir* a algn
• **stand out** [*v* + *adv*] **(a)** (project) **to ~ out** (FROM **sth**) sobresalir* (DE algo) **(b)** (be conspicuous, contrast) sobresalir*, destacar(se)*; «*color*» resaltar
• **stand up 1** [*v* + *adv*] **(a)** (get up) ponerse* de pie, levantarse, pararse (AmL) **(b)** (be, remain standing): **~ up straight** ponte derecho **(c)** (endure, withstand wear) resistir; **to ~ up** TO **sth** ‹*to cold/pressure*› resistir *or* soportar algo; *see also* STAND UP TO **2** [*v* + *o* + *adv*] **(a)** (set upright) poner* de pie, levantar **(b)** (not keep appointment with) (colloq) dejar plantado a (fam)
• **stand up for** [*v* + *adv* + *prep* + *o*] defender*; **I can ~ up for myself** me puedo defender solo
• **stand up to** [*v* + *adv* + *prep* + *o*] ‹*person/threats*› hacerle* frente a; *see also* STAND UP 1(c)

standard¹ /ˈstændərd ‖ ˈstændəd/ *n* **1 (a)** (level) nivel *m*; (quality) calidad *f*; **~ of living** nivel *m or* estándar *m* de vida **(b)** (norm): **she sets very high ~s** exige un estándar *or* nivel muy alto; **the product was below ~** el producto no era de la calidad requerida **(c)** (official measure) estándar *m* **2 (a)** (yardstick) criterio *m*, parámetro *m* **(b) standards** *pl* (moral principles) principios *mpl* **3** (flag, emblem) estandarte *m*

standard² *adj* **1** (normal) ‹*size*› estándar *adj inv*, normal; ‹*model*› (Auto) estándar *adj inv*, de serie; ‹*procedure*› habitual; ‹*reaction*› típico; **~ rate** tarifa *f* normal **2** (officially established) ‹*weight/measure*› estándar *adj inv*, oficial; **~ time** hora *f* oficial

standardize /ˈstændərdaɪz ‖ ˈstændədaɪz/ *vt* estandarizar*

standard lamp *n* (BrE) lámpara *f* de pie

standby¹ /ˈstændbaɪ/ *n* (*pl* **-bys**) **(a)** (thing, one can turn to): **frozen meals are a useful ~** las comidas congeladas son muy socorridas **(b)** (state of readiness): **to be on ~** «*police/squadron*» estar* en estado de alerta **(c)** (Aviat) stand-by *m*

standby² *adj* (*before n*) **(a)** (ready for emergency) de emergencia; **to be on ~ duty** estar* de guardia **(b)** (Aviat) ‹*passenger/ticket/fare*› stand-by *adj inv*

stand-in /ˈstændɪn/ *n* suplente *mf*; (Cin) doble *mf*

standing¹ /ˈstændɪŋ/ *n* [U] **(a)** (position) posición *f*; (prestige) prestigio *m* **(b)** (duration): **friends of more than 20 years' ~** amigos desde hace más de 20 años

standing² *adj* (*before n, no comp*) **(a)** (permanent) permanente; **~ charge** cuota *f* fija; (for utilities) cuota *f* abono; **it's a ~ joke that he never pays for a single drink** tiene fama de no invitar nunca a una copa **(b)** (upright, not seated) ‹*passenger*› de pie, parado (AmL)

standing order *n* **(a)** (with bank) (BrE) orden *f* permanente de pago **(b)** (with supplier) pedido *m* fijo

stand: **~off** *n* (AmE) **(a)** (tie, draw) empate *m* **(b)** (deadlock) callejón *m* sin salida; **~point** *n* punto *m* de vista; **~still** *n* (*no pl*): **to be at a ~still** «*traffic*» estar* paralizado; **to come to a ~still** «*vehicle*» parar; «*city/factory*» quedar paralizado

stank /stæŋk/ *past of* STINK²

staple¹ /ˈsteɪpəl/ *n* **1** (for fastening paper, cloth etc) grapa *f*, ganchito *m*, corchete *m* (Chi) **2 (a)** (basic food) alimento *m* básico **(b)** (principal product) producto *m* principal

staple² *adj* ‹*food/ingredient*› básico; ‹*industry*› principal; **rice is their ~ diet** se alimentan principalmente a base de arroz

staple³ *vt* grapar, engrapar (AmL), corchetear (Chi)

stapler /ˈsteɪplər ‖ ˈsteɪplə(r)/ *n* grapadora *f*, engrapadora *f* (AmL), corchetera *f* (Chi)

star¹ /stɑːr ‖ stɑː(r)/ *n* **1** (in sky) estrella *f*; (Astrol, Astron) astro *m*; (*before n*) **~ sign** signo *m* del zodíaco **2** (symbol) estrella *f*; (asterisk) asterisco *m*; **a four-~ hotel** un hotel de cuatro estrellas **3** (celebrity) estrella *f*

star² **-rr-** *vt*: **the famous film which ~red Bogart and Bergman** la famosa película que tuvo como protagonistas a Bogart y Bergman; **'2005', ~ring Mike Kirnon** '2005', con (la actuación estelar de) Mike Kirnon ■ **~** *vi*: **to ~ in a film** protagonizar* una película

starboard¹ /ˈstɑːrbərd ‖ ˈstɑːbəd/ *n* [U] estribor *m*

starboard² *adj* (*before n*) de estribor

starch /stɑːrtʃ ‖ stɑːtʃ/ *n* **(a)** [U] almidón *m* **(b)** (starchy food) fécula *f*, almidón *m*

starchy /ˈstɑːrtʃi ‖ ˈstɑːtʃi/ *adj* **-chier, -chiest** ‹*diet*› a base de féculas *or* de almidones

stardom /ˈstɑːrdəm ‖ ˈstɑːdəm/ *n* [U] estrellato *m*

stare¹ /ster ‖ steə(r)/ *vi* mirar (*fijamente*); **to ~** AT **sth/sb** mirar algo/a algn fijamente

stare² *n* mirada *f* (*fija*)

starfish /ˈstɑːrfɪʃ ‖ ˈstɑːfɪʃ/ *n* (*pl* **-fish**) estrella *f* de mar

stark¹ /stɑːrk ‖ stɑːk/ *adj* **-er, -est** ‹*landscape*› agreste; ‹*truth*› escueto; ‹*realism*› descarnado

stark² *adv*: **~ naked** completamente desnudo

starlet /ˈstɑːrlət ‖ ˈstɑːlɪt/ *n* starlet(te) *f* (*joven actriz que aspira al estrellato*)

starling /ˈstɑːrlɪŋ ‖ ˈstɑːlɪŋ/ *n* estornino *m*

starry /ˈstɑːri/ *adj* **-rier, -riest** estrellado

starry-eyed /ˈstɑːriˈaɪd/ *adj* **(a)** (full of illusions) ‹*person*› iluso, soñador **(b)** (dreamy): **she gazed at him all ~** lo miraba arrobada

star: **S~s and Stripes** *n* **the S~s and Stripes** la bandera de las barras y las estrellas; **~-spangled** /ˈstɑːrˌspæŋgəld ‖ ˈstɑːˌspæŋgəld/ *adj* (liter) ‹*sky/heavens*› tachonado de estrellas (liter); **S~-Spangled Banner** *n* **the S~ Spangled Banner** el himno de las barras y las estrellas (*himno nacional de EEUU*)

start¹ /stɑːrt ‖ stɑːt/ *n* **1 (a)** (beginning) principio *m*, comienzo *m*; **from ~ to finish** del principio al fin; **to make a ~** (ON **sth**) empezar* algo; **to make an early ~** empezar* temprano; (on a journey) salir* temprano **(b) for a ~** (*as linker*) para empezar **2** (Sport) **(a)** (of race) salida *f* **(b)** (lead, advantage) ventaja *f* **3** (jump): **to give sb a ~** darle* *or* pegarle* un susto a algn; **I woke up with a ~** me desperté sobresaltado

start² *vt* **1** (begin) empezar*, comenzar*; **I ~ work at eight** empiezo a trabajar a las ocho; **to ~ -ING, to ~ to + INF** empezar* A + INF **2** (cause to begin) ‹*race*› dar* comienzo a, largar* (CS, Méx); ‹*fire/epidemic*› provocar*; ‹*argument/fight*› empezar*; ‹*war*› «*incident*» desencadenar **3** (establish) ‹*business*› abrir*; ‹*organization*› fundar **4** (cause to operate) ‹*engine/dishwasher*› encender*, prender (AmL); ‹*car*› arrancar* ■ **~** *vi* **I 1 (a)** (begin) empezar*, comenzar*; **to get ~ed** empezar*, comenzar*; **to ~ BY -ING** empezar* POR + INF; **~ing (from) next January** a partir del próximo mes de enero **(b) to ~ with** (*as linker*): primero *or* para empezar **2** (originate) empezar*, originarse **3** (set out) (+ *adv compl*): **to ~ back** emprender el regreso; **we ~ from the hotel at six** salimos del hotel a las seis **4** (begin to operate) «*car*» arrancar*

II (move suddenly) dar* un respingo; (be frightened) asustarse, sobresaltarse

• **start off 1** [*v* + *adv*] **(a)** ⇒ START OUT (a) **(b)** (begin moving) arrancar* **(c)** (begin) empezar* **2** [*v* + *o* + *adv*, *v* + *adv* + *o*] (begin) ‹*discussion/concert*› empezar* **3** [*v* + *o* + *adv*] (get sb started): **I'll do the first one, just to ~ you off** yo haré el primero, para ayudarte a empezar

• **start out** [*v* + *adv*] **(a)** (set out) salir* **(b)** (in life, career) empezar* **(c)** (begin) **to ~ out (BY) -ING: we ~ed out (by) thinking it would be easy** empezamos pensando que sería fácil

• **start over** (AmE) [*v* + *adv*] [*v* + *o* + *adv*] volver* a empezar

• **start up 1** [*v* + *adv*] **(a)** ⇒ START *vi* I 4 **(b)** (begin business) empezar* **2** [*v* + *o* + *adv*, *v* + *adv* + *o*] **(a)** ‹*engine/car/machinery*› arrancar*, poner* en marcha **(b)** ‹*business*› montar **(c)** ‹*conversation*› entablar; ‹*discussion*› empezar*

starter /'stɑːrtər ‖ 'stɑːtə(r)/ *n* **1** (Culin) entrada *f*, primer plato *m*, entrante *m* (Esp) **2** (Auto) (**~** *motor*) motor *m* de arranque

starting /'stɑːrtɪŋ ‖ 'stɑːtɪŋ/: **~ line** *n* línea *f* de salida; **~ point** *n* **~ point (FOR sth)** punto *m* de partida (DE/PARA algo)

startle /'stɑːrtl̩ ‖ 'stɑːtl̩/ *vt* sobresaltar, asustar

startling /'stɑːrtlɪŋ ‖ 'stɑːtlɪŋ/ *adj* **(a)** (surprising) asombroso; ‹*similarity/coincidence*› extraordinario **(b)** (alarming) ‹*report/increase*› alarmante

starvation /stɑːr'veɪʃən ‖ stɑː'veɪʃən/ *n* [U] hambre *f*‡, inanición *f*

starve /stɑːrv ‖ stɑːv/ *vt* **(a)** (deny food) privar de comida a; **I'm ~d** (AmE colloq) me muero de hambre **(b)** (deprive) **to ~ sth/sb OF sth** privar algo/A algn DE algo ■ **~** *vi* (die) morirse* de hambre *or* de inanición; (feel hungry) pasar hambre; **I'm starving** (BrE colloq) me muero de hambre

starving /'stɑːrvɪŋ ‖ 'stɑːvɪŋ/ *adj* hambriento, famélico

stash /stæʃ/ *vt* **~ (away)** (colloq) (hide) esconder; (save) ir* ahorrando

state¹ /steɪt/ *n* **I 1 (a)** [C] (nation) estado *m*; (*before n*) **~ visit** visita *f* oficial **(b)** [C] (division of country) estado *m*; **the S~s** los Estados Unidos **2** [U C] (Govt) estado *m*; (*before n*) (esp BrE) ‹*control/funding*› estatal; **~ school** escuela *f* pública *or* estatal **3** [U] (pomp): **to lie in ~** yacer* en capilla ardiente

II [C] (condition) estado *m*; **~ of war/emergency** estado de guerra/emergencia; **~ of mind** estado de ánimo; **I was in no (fit) ~ to make a decision** no estaba en condiciones de tomar una decisión; **the kitchen is in a ~** (colloq) la cocina está hecha un asco (fam)

state² *vt* «*person*» ‹*facts/case*› exponer*; ‹*problem*› plantear; ‹*name/address*› (in writing) escribir*; (orally) decir*; «*law/document*» establecer*; **he ~d that he had seen her there earlier** afirmó haberla visto antes allí

State Department *n* (in US) **the ~ ~** el Departamento de Estado de los EEUU, ≈ el Ministerio de Asuntos Exteriores *or* de Relaciones Exteriores

stately /'steɪtli/ *adj* **-lier, -liest** majestuoso

stately home *n* (in UK) casa *f* solariega

statement /'steɪtmənt/ *n* **1 (a)** (declaration) declaración *f*, afirmación *f*; **official ~** comunicado *m* oficial **(b)** (to police, in court) declaración *f* **2** (*bank* **~**) estado *m* *or* extracto *m* de cuenta

state: **~-of-the-art** /'steɪtəvði'ɑːrt ‖ ˌsteɪtəvði'ɑːt/ *adj* último modelo *adj inv*; **~side, S~side** *adv* (AmE colloq) en/a/hacia los Estados Unidos

statesman /'steɪtsmən/ *n* (*pl* **-men** /-mən/) estadista *m*, hombre *m* de estado

static¹ /'stætɪk/ *adj* **1** ‹*situation*› estacionario **2** ‹*electricity*› estático

static² *n* [U] **(a)** (electricity) electricidad *f* estática **(b)** (interference) estática *f*

station¹ /'steɪʃən/ *n* **1 (a)** (Rail) estación *f* **(b)** (*bus* **~**) estación *f* *or* terminal *f* de autobuses **2** (place of operations) **research ~** centro *m* de investigación; *see also* FIRE STATION, POLICE STATION *etc* **3** (TV) canal *m*; (Rad) emisora *f* *or* (AmL tb) estación *f* (de radio)

station² *vt* **(a)** (position) ‹*sentries*› apostar* **(b)** (post) (*usu pass*) ‹*personnel*› destinar; ‹*fleet/troops*› emplazar*

stationary /'steɪʃəneri ‖ 'steɪʃənri/ *adj* ‹*object/vehicle*› estacionario

stationery /'steɪʃəneri ‖ 'steɪʃənəri/ *n* [U] **(a)** (writing materials) artículos *mpl* de papelería *or* de escritorio **(b)** (writing paper) papel *m* y sobres *mpl* de carta

station: **~ house** *n* (AmE) **(a)** (police station) comisaría *f* **(b)** ⇒ FIRE STATION; **~master** *n* jefe, -fa *m,f* de estación; **~ wagon** *n* (AmE) ranchera *f*, (coche *m*) familiar *m*, camioneta *f* (AmL)

statistic /stə'tɪstɪk/ *n* estadística *f*

statistical /stə'tɪstɪkəl/ *adj* estadístico

statistics /stə'tɪstɪks/ *n* (+ *sing vb*) estadística *f*

statue /'stætʃuː ‖ 'stætjuː, 'stætʃuː/ *n* estatua *f*

stature /'stætʃər ‖ 'stætʃə(r)/ *n* **(a)** (status) talla *f* **(b)** (height) (frml) estatura *f*, talla *f*

status /'stætəs ‖ 'steɪtəs/ *n* (*pl* **-tuses**) **(a)** [U C] (category, situation): **the group has no official ~** el grupo no está oficialmente reconocido como tal;

financial ~ situación *f* económica **(b)** [U] (*social* ~) posición *f* social, estatus *m* **(c)** [U] (kudos) estatus *m*; (*before n*) ~ **symbol** símbolo *m* de estatus

status quo /kwəʊ/ *n* statu quo *m*

statute /'stætʃuːt ‖ 'stætjuːt, 'stætʃuːt/ *n* ley *f*

statutory /'stætʃuːtɔːri ‖ 'stætjʊtəri, 'stætʃuːtəri/ *adj* ‹*right/obligation*› legal; ‹*penalty*› establecido por la ley

staunch /stɔːntʃ/ *adj* **-er, -est** ‹*supporter*› incondicional; ‹*Protestant*› acérrimo

stave /steɪv/ *n* **1** (of barrel, hull) duela *f* **2** (Mus) pentagrama *m*

• **stave off** [*v + o + adv, v + adv + o*] ‹*defeat/disaster*› evitar; ‹*danger*› conjurar

staves (a) *pl of* STAFF[1] 2(a) **(b)** *pl of* STAVE

stay[1] /steɪ/ *vi* **1 (a)** (in specified place, position) quedarse; ~ **there** quédate ahí; ***to ~ put*** quedarse **(b)** (in specified state): ~ **still** quédate quieto; **we ~ed friends** seguimos siendo amigos **2 (a)** (remain, not leave) quedarse **(b)** (reside temporarily) quedarse; (in a hotel etc) hospedarse, alojarse, quedarse; **he's ~ing with us over Easter** va a pasar la Semana Santa con nosotros

• **stay away** [*v + adv*] **to ~ away** FROM **sth/sb** no acercarse* A algo/algn

• **stay in** [*v + adv*] (remain in position) quedarse en su sitio; (remain indoors) quedarse en casa

• **stay on** [*v + adv*] **(a)** (remain in position) «*hat/top*» quedarse en su sitio **(b)** (at school, in job) quedarse

• **stay out** [*v + adv*] **(a)** (not come home): **to ~ out late** quedarse fuera hasta tarde; **he usually ~s out late** normalmente no vuelve hasta tarde **(b)** (out of doors) quedarse fuera

• **stay out of** [*v + adv + prep + o*] **(a)** (avoid) ‹*trouble*› no meterse en; ~ **out of the sun** quédate a la sombra **(b)** (not get involved in) ‹*argument*› no meterse en

• **stay up** [*v + adv*] **(a)** (not fall or sink) «*tent/pole*» sostenerse* **(b)** (not go to bed) quedarse levantado

stay[2] *n* **1** (time) estadía *f* (AmL), estancia *f* (Esp, Méx); **during her ~ in hospital** mientras estuvo en el hospital **2** (Law): ~ **of execution** suspensión *f* del cumplimiento de la sentencia

staying power /'steɪɪŋ/ *n* [U] resistencia *f*, aguante *m*

stead /sted/ *n*: **in sb's ~** (liter) en lugar de algn; ***to stand sb in good ~*** resultarle muy útil a algn

steadfast /'stedfæst ‖ 'stedfɑːst/ *adj* (liter) ‹*refusal*› firme, categórico; ‹*resolve*› inquebrantable

steadily /'stedi̥ ‖ 'stedɪli/ *adv* **(a)** (constantly, gradually) ‹*breathe/beat/work*› regularmente **(b)** (incessantly) ‹*rain/work*› sin cesar, sin parar **(c)** (not shaking) ‹*gaze*› fijamente; ‹*walk*› con paso seguro

steady[1] /'stedi/ *adj* **-dier, -diest 1** (not shaky) ‹*gaze*› fijo; ‹*chair/table/ladder*› firme, seguro; **with a ~ hand** con pulso firme; **hold the camera ~** no muevas la cámara **2 (a)** (constant) ‹*rain/speed/pace*› constante; ‹*flow/stream*› continuo **(b)** (regular) (*before n*) ‹*job*› fijo; ‹*income*› regular; ~ **boyfriend** novio *m*; ~ **girlfriend** novia *f* **(c)** (dependable) ‹*person/worker*› serio, formal

steady[2] *vt* **-dies, -dying, -died (a)** (make stable) ‹*table/ladder*› (by holding) sujetar (para que no se mueva) **(b)** (make calm) calmar, tranquilizar*

steak /steɪk/ *n* **(a)** [C] bistec *m*, filete *m*, churrasco *m* (CS), bife *m* (RPl, Bol) **(b)** [U] (cut) carne *f* para filete (*or* bistec *etc*)

steal /stiːl/ (*past* **stole**; *past p* **stolen**) *vt* **1** ‹*object/idea*› robar; **to ~ sth** FROM **sb** robarle algo A algn; **to ~ a glance at sth/sb** (liter) echar una mirada furtiva a algo/algn **2 stolen** *past p* ‹*money/property*› robado ■ ~ *vi* **1** robar **2** (go stealthily) (+ *adv compl*): **to ~ away** *o* **off** escabullirse*; **they stole into the room** entraron en la habitación a hurtadillas

stealth /stelθ/ *n* [U] sigilo *m*

stealthy /'stelθi/ *adj* **-thier, -thiest** ‹*movement/departure*› furtivo; ‹*footsteps*› sigiloso

steam[1] /stiːm/ *n* [U] vapor *m*; ***to let off ~*** desahogarse*; ***to run out of ~*** perder* ímpetu

steam[2] *vt* (Culin) ‹*vegetables/rice*› cocinar *or* cocer* al vapor; ‹*pudding*› cocinar *or* cocer* al baño (de) María ■ ~ *vi* (give off steam) echar vapor; «*hot food*» humear

• **steam up** [*v + adv*] «*window/glass*» empañarse

steam: **~boat** *n* vapor *m*, barco *m* de *or* a vapor; **~ engine** *n* **(a)** (Mech Eng) motor *m* de *or* a vapor **(b)** (esp BrE Rail) locomotora *f or* máquina *f* de *or* a vapor

steamer /'stiːmər ‖ 'stiːmə(r)/ *n* **1** (Naut) vapor *m*, buque *m or* barco *m* de *or* a vapor **2** (cooking vessel) vaporera *f*

steam: **~roller** *n* apisonadora *f*, aplanadora *f* (AmL); **~ship** *n* STEAMER 1

steamy /'stiːmi/ *adj* **-mier, -miest** ‹*room/atmosphere*› lleno de vapor; ‹*window/glass*› empañado

steel[1] /stiːl/ *n* [U] (Metall) acero *m*

steel[2] *v refl* **to ~ oneself** FOR **sth/to** + INF armarse de valor PARA algo/PARA + INF

steel wool *n* [U] lana *f* de acero, virulana® *f* (Arg), fibra *f* metálica (Méx)

steely /'stiːli/ *adj* **-lier, -liest** ‹*gaze/expression*› duro; ‹*determination*› férreo

steep[1] /stiːp/ *adj* **-er, -est 1 (a)** ‹*slope*› empinado; ‹*drop*› brusco; ‹*descent*› en picada *or* (Esp) en picado **(b)** (large) ‹*increase/decline*› considerable **2** (of prices) (colloq) alto, excesivo

steep[2] *vt* (to soften, clean) remojar; (to flavor) macerar

steeple /'stiːpəl/ *n* aguja *f*, campanario *m*

steeple: **~chase** *n* carrera *f* de obstáculos; **~jack** *n*: *persona que repara chimeneas, torres etc*

steeply /'stiːpli/ *adv* **(a)** ‹*slope/rise/fall*› abruptamente **(b)** ‹*increase/decline*› considerablemente

steer[1] /stɪr ‖ stɪə(r)/ *n* **(a)** (castrated bull) buey *m* **(b)** (young bull) novillo *m*

steer[2] *vt* **(a)** ‹*vehicle/plane*› dirigir*, conducir*; ‹*ship*› gobernar* **(b)** (guide) llevar, conducir* ■ ~ *vi* (Naut) estar* *or* ir* al timón; (Auto) ir* al volante; ***to ~ clear of sth/sb*** evitar algo/a algn

steering /'stɪrɪŋ ‖ 'stɪərɪŋ/ *n* [U] dirección *f*

steering wheel *n* (Auto) volante *m*

stem¹ /stem/ *n* **1** (of plant) tallo *m*; (of leaf) peciolo *m*, pecíolo *m*; (of fruit) pedúnculo *m* **2** (of glass) pie *m*

stem² **-mm-** *vt* ‹*flow/bleeding*› contener*; ‹*outbreak/decline*› detener* ■ ~ *vi* **to ~** FROM **sth** provenir* DE algo

stench /stentʃ/ *n* fetidez *f*

stencil¹ /'stensəl ‖ 'stensɪl/ *n* **(a)** (for lettering, decoration) plantilla *f*, troquel *m* **(b)** (for duplicating) stencil *m*, cliché *m* (Esp)

stencil² *vt*, (BrE) **-ll-** ‹*design/pattern*› *escribir, dibujar o pintar utilizando una plantilla*

stenographer /stə'nɑːgrəfər ‖ ste'nɒgrəfə(r)/ *n* (esp AmE) taquígrafo, -fa *m,f*, estenógrafo, -fa *m,f*

stenography /stə'nɑːgrəfi ‖ ste'nɒgrəfi/ *n* [U] (AmE) taquigrafía *f*, estenografía *f*

step¹ /step/ *n* **1** [C] (footstep, pace) paso *m*; **to take a ~ forward** dar* un paso adelante; ***to watch one's ~*** andarse* con cuidado **2 (a)** [C] (of dance) paso *m* **(b)** [U] (in marching, walking) paso *m*; **to be in/out of ~** llevar/no llevar el paso **3** [C] (measure) medida *f*; **to take ~s (to** + INF**)** tomar medidas (PARA + INF) **4** [C] (on stair) escalón *m*, peldaño *m*; (on ladder) travesaño *m*, escalón *m* **5** [C] (AmE Mus): **whole ~** tono *m*; **half ~** semitono *m*

step² **-pp-** *vi*: **would you ~ inside/outside for a moment?** ¿quiere pasar/salir un momento?; **to ~ off a plane** bajarse de un avión; **to ~** IN/ON **sth** pisar algo

• **step aside** [*v* + *adv*] hacerse* a un lado

• **step back** [*v* + *adv*] **(a)** (move back) dar* un paso atrás **(b)** (become detached) **to ~ back (**FROM **sth)** distanciarse (DE algo)

• **step down** [*v* + *adv*] **(a)** (get down) bajar **(b)** (resign) renunciar, dimitir

• **step forward** [*v* + *adv*] **(a)** (move forward) dar* un paso adelante **(b)** (present oneself) ofrecerse*

• **step in** [*v* + *adv*] intervenir*

• **step up** [*v* + *o* + *adv*, *v* + *adv* + *o*] ‹*production/campaign*› intensificar*; ‹*efforts/security/attacks*› redoblar

step: **~brother** *n* hermanastro *m*; **~ by ~** *adv* (one stage at a time) paso a paso; (gradually) poco a poco; **~-by-~** /'stepbaɪ'step/ *adj* ‹*instructions*› detallado, paso a paso; **~child** *n* (son) hijastro *m*; (daughter) hijastra *f*; **~daughter** *n* hijastra *f*; **~father** *n* padrastro *m*; **~ladder** *n* escalera *f* de mano *or* de tijera; **~mother** *n* madrastra *f*

stepping-stone /'stepɪŋstəʊn/ *n*: *cada una de las piedras que se colocan para cruzar un arroyo, un pantano etc*; **a ~ to success** un peldaño en el camino del éxito

step: **~sister** *n* hermanastra *f*; **~son** *n* hijastro *m*

stereo¹ /'steriəʊ/ *n* (*pl* **-os**) **(a)** [C] (player) estéreo *m* **(b)** [U] (sound) estéreo *m*

stereo² *adj* estéreo *adj inv*

stereotype¹ /'steriətaɪp/ *n* estereotipo *m*

stereotype² *vt* catalogar*, estereotipar

sterile /'sterəl ‖ 'steraɪl/ *adj* estéril

sterility /stə'rɪləti/ *n* [U] esterilidad *f*

sterilize /'sterəlaɪz/ *vt* esterilizar*

sterling¹ /'stɜːrlɪŋ ‖ 'stɜːlɪŋ/ *n* [U] la libra (esterlina)

sterling² *adj*: **the pound ~** la libra esterlina

stern¹ /stɜːrn ‖ stɜːn/ *n* popa *f*

stern² *adj* **-er, -est** severo

steroid /'stɪrɔɪd, 'ste- ‖ 'stɪərɔɪd, 'ste-/ *n* esteroide *m*

stethoscope /'steθəskəʊp/ *n* estetoscopio *m*

stevedore /'stiːvədɔːr ‖ 'stiːvədɔː(r)/ *n* estibador, -dora *m,f*

stew¹ /stuː ‖ stjuː/ *n* estofado *m*, guiso *m*

stew² *vt* ‹*meat*› estofar, guisar; ‹*fruit*› hacer* compota de

steward /'stuːərd ‖ 'stjuːəd/ *n* **1 (a)** (on ship) camarero *m* **(b)** (on plane) auxiliar *m* de vuelo, sobrecargo *m*, aeromozo *m* (AmL) **2 (a)** (manager of estate) administrador, -dora *m,f* **(b)** (at public gatherings) (BrE) *persona encargada de supervisar al público en manifestaciones*

stewardess /'stuːərdəs ‖ 'stjuːədes/ *n* **(a)** (on ship) camarera *f* **(b)** (on plane) auxiliar *f* de vuelo, azafata *f*, sobrecargo *f*, aeromoza *f* (AmL)

stick¹ /stɪk/ *n* **1** (of wood) palo *m*, vara *f*; (twig) ramita *f*; (for fire) astilla *f* **2 (a)** (*walking ~*) bastón *m* **(b)** (*hockey ~*) palo *m* **3** (of celery, rhubarb) rama *f*, penca *f*; (of dynamite) cartucho *m*; (of rock, candy) palo *m*; **a ~ of chalk** una tiza; **a ~ of chewing gum** un chicle **4 sticks** *pl* **the ~s** (colloq): **to live out in the ~s** vivir en la Cochinchina *or* (Esp tb) en las Batuecas

stick² (*past & past p* **stuck**²) *vt* **1** (attach, glue) pegar* **2 (a)** (thrust) ‹*needle/knife/sword*› clavar **(b)** (impale) **to ~ sth** ON **sth** clavar algo EN algo **3** (put, place) (colloq) poner* **4** (tolerate) (esp BrE colloq) aguantar, soportar ■ **~** *vi* **1** (adhere) «*glue*» pegar*; «*food*» pegarse*; **to ~** TO **sth** pegarse* *or* (frml) adherirse* A algo; **the two pages have stuck together** las dos páginas se han pegado; **the song stuck in my mind** la canción se me quedó grabada **2** (become jammed) atascarse*; *see also* STUCK²

• **stick at** [*v* + *prep* + *o*] (colloq) seguir* con; **~ at it** sigue así

• **stick by** [*v* + *prep* + *o*] ‹*friend*› no abandonar; ‹*promise*› mantener* en pie

• **stick out 1** [*v* + *adv*] **(a)** (protrude) sobresalir* **(b)** (be obvious) resaltar; **he really ~s out in a crowd** uno enseguida lo nota en un grupo de gente **2** [*v* + *o* + *adv*, *v* + *adv* + *o*] (stretch out) (colloq) ‹*hand*› extender*; ‹*tongue*› sacar*

• **stick to** [*v* + *prep* + *o*] **(a)** (hold to) ‹*road/path*› seguir* por; ‹*principles*› mantener*; ‹*rules*› ceñirse* a, atenerse* a; **I'll ~ to my original plan** seguiré con mi plan original **(b)** (not digress from) ‹*subject/facts*› ceñirse* a **(c)** (restrict oneself to) limitarse a

• **stick together** [*v* + *adv*] no separarse; (support each other) mantenerse* unidos

• **stick up 1** [*v* + *o* + *adv*, *v* + *adv* + *o*] **(a)** (on wall) ‹*notice*› colocar*, poner* **(b)** (raise) ‹*hand*› levantar **2** [*v* + *adv*] (project): **something was ~ing up out of the ground** algo sobresalía del suelo; **her hair was ~ing up** tenía el pelo de punta, tenía el pelo parado (AmL)

• **stick up for** [*v* + *adv* + *prep* + *o*] ‹*person*›

sacar* la cara por, defender*; **to ~ up for oneself** hacerse* valer

sticker /'stɪkər ‖ 'stɪkə(r)/ *n* (label) etiqueta *f*; (with slogan etc) pegatina *f*, adhesivo *m*

sticking plaster /'stɪkɪŋ/ *n* (BrE) **(a)** [C] (individual strip) curita® *f* (AmL), tirita® *f* (Esp) **(b)** [U] (tape) esparadrapo *m*, cinta *f* adhesiva

stick: **~ insect** *n* insecto *m* palo; **~-in-the-mud** *n* (colloq): **don't be such a ~-in-the-mud** no seas tan rutinario e inflexible

stickler /'stɪklər ‖ 'stɪklə(r)/ *n*: **he's a ~ for discipline** insiste mucho en la disciplina

stick: **~-on** *adj* adhesivo; **~ shift** *n* (AmE) **(a)** (lever) palanca *f* de cambio(s) *or* (Méx) de velocidades **(b)** (car) coche *m* (de transmisión) estándar *or* manual; **~up** *n* (colloq) atraco *m*, asalto *m*

sticky /'stɪki/ *adj* **stickier, stickiest 1 (a)** ‹*label*› engomado, autoadhesivo; ‹*surface*› pegajoso **(b)** ‹*weather*› bochornoso **2** (difficult) (colloq) ‹*problem/issue*› peliagudo; ‹*situation*› violento

stiff¹ /stɪf/ *adj* **-er, -est 1 (a)** ‹*collar/bristles*› duro; ‹*fabric*› tieso, duro; ‹*corpse*› rígido; ‹*muscles*› entumecido, agarrotado; **to have a ~ neck** tener* tortícolis; **I'm ~ after that walk** estoy dolorido *or* (esp AmL) adolorido despues de la caminata **(b)** ‹*paste/dough*› consistente; ‹*egg white*› firme **2** ‹*test/climb*› difícil, duro; ‹*resistance*› férreo; ‹*penalty*› fuerte; ‹*breeze/drink*› fuerte **3** ‹*person/manner*› estirado; ‹*bow/smile*› forzado

stiff² *adv* (colloq): **I'm frozen ~** estoy helado hasta los huesos (fam); **we were bored ~** nos aburrimos como ostras (fam); **scared ~** muerto de miedo

stiffen /'stɪfən/ *vt* **(a)** (with starch) almidonar; (with fabric underneath) armar **(b) ~ (up)** ‹*resolve*› fortalecer* ■ **~** *vi* **(a) ~ (up)** (become rigid) «*person/muscles/joint*» agarrotarse **(b)** (become firm) endurecerse* **(c)** (in manner, reaction) ponerse* tenso

stiffly /'stɪfli/ *adv* **(a)** ‹*walk/move*› rígidamente, con rigidez **(b)** ‹*greet*› fríamente; ‹*bow*› con fría formalidad

stifle /'staɪfəl/ *vt* **1** (suffocate) (*often pass*) ‹*person*› sofocar* **2** (suppress) ‹*flames*› sofocar*; ‹*yawn/anger*› contener*; ‹*noise*› ahogar*

stifling /'staɪflɪŋ/ *adj* ‹*heat*› sofocante

stigma /'stɪgmə/ *n* (*pl* **-mas**) estigma *m*

stile /staɪl/ *n*: *escalones que permiten pasar por encima de una cerca*

stiletto /stɪ'letəʊ/ *n* (*pl* **-tos** *or* **-toes**) **~ (heel)** tacón *m* de aguja, taco *m* aguja *or* alfiler (CS)

still¹ /stɪl/ *adv*

> ■ **Note** Spanish has two words for *still*: *todavía* and *aún*. Both can go at the beginning or end of the sentence: *I still haven't seen him* todavía *or* aún no lo he visto *or* no lo he visto todavía *or* aún.
> The distinction in English between *he hasn't arrived yet* and *he still hasn't arrived* is not expressed verbally in Spanish. Both can be translated by *todavía* or *aún no ha llegado*, or *no ha llegado todavía* or *aún*. The degree of intensity, surprise, or annoyance is often expressed by intonation.
> Note that the verb seguir can be used to express continuation: *I still don't understand why* sigo sin entender por qué; *he's still looking for a job* sigue buscando trabajo.

1 (even now, even then) todavía, aún; **there's ~ plenty left** todavía *or* aún queda mucho; **are we ~ friends?** ¿seguimos siendo amigos? **2** (*as intensifier*) aún, todavía; **the risk is greater ~** el riesgo es aún *or* todavía mayor **3** (*as linker*): **they say it's safe, but I'm ~ scared** dicen que no hay peligro pero igual *or* aun así tengo miedo; **~, it could have been worse** de todos modos, podría haber sido peor

still² *adj* **(a)** (motionless) ‹*lake/air*› en calma, quieto, tranquilo; **sit/stand ~** quédate quieto; **her heart stood ~ for a moment** el corazón se le paró un momento **(b)** ‹*drink*› sin gas, no efervescente

still³ *n* **1** (Cin, Phot) fotograma *m* **2** (distillery) destilería *f*; (distilling apparatus) alambique *m*

still: **~born** /'stɪl'bɔːrn ‖ 'stɪlbɔːn/ *adj* nacido muerto; **~ life** *n* (*pl* **~ lifes**) naturaleza *f* muerta

stilt /stɪlt/ *n* zanco *m*

stilted /'stɪltəd ‖ 'stɪltɪd/ *adj* **(a)** ‹*conversation/manner*› forzado **(b)** ‹*language/writing*› rebuscado; ‹*acting*› acartonado

stimulate /'stɪmjəleɪt ‖ 'stɪmjʊleɪt/ *vt* estimular

stimulating /'stɪmjəleɪtɪŋ ‖ 'stɪmjʊleɪtɪŋ/ *adj* estimulante

stimulation /'stɪmjə'leɪʃən ‖ ˌstɪmjʊ'leɪʃən/ *n* [U] estímulo *m*

stimulus /'stɪmjələs ‖ 'stɪmjʊləs/ *n* [C U] (*pl* **-li** /-laɪ/) estímulo *m*

sting¹ /stɪŋ/ *n* **1** [C] **(a)** (of bee, wasp) aguijón *m* **(b)** (action, wound) picadura *f* **2** (*no pl*) (pain) escozor *m*, ardor *m* (CS)

sting² (*past & past p* **stung**) *vt* **1** «*bee/nettle*» picar* **2** (cause pain) hacer* escocer, hacer* arder (CS) ■ **~** *vi* **1** «*insect/nettle*» picar* **2** (hurt physically) «*ointment*» hacer* escocer, hacer* arder (CS); «*cut*» escocer*, arder (CS)

stinging nettle /'stɪŋɪŋ/ *n* ortiga *f*

stingy /'stɪndʒi/ *adj* **-gier -giest** ‹*person*› tacaño; ‹*portion*› mezquino

stink¹ /stɪŋk/ *n* [U] **(a)** (bad smell) hediondez *f*, mal olor *m*, peste *f* (fam) **(b)** (fuss) (colloq) escándalo *m*, lío *m* (fam), follón *m* (Esp fam); **to make** *o* **kick up a ~** armar un lío (*or* un escándalo *etc*)

stink² *vi* (*past* **stank** *or* **stunk**; *past p* **stunk**) «*person/place/breath*» apestar; **the whole business ~s** (colloq) todo el asunto da asco

stink bomb *n* bomba *f* fétida

stinking /'stɪŋkɪŋ/ *adj* (*before n*) hediondo, fétido, apestoso; **I've got a ~ cold** (colloq) tengo un resfriado espantoso

stint¹ /stɪnt/ *n* **(a)** (fixed amount, share): **I've done my ~ for today** hoy ya he hecho mi parte **(b)** (period) período *m*; **he did a five-year ~ in the army** pasó (un período de) cinco años en el ejército

stint² *vi* **to ~** ON **sth** escatimar algo

stipulate /'stɪpjəleɪt ‖ 'stɪpjʊleɪt/ *vt* estipular

stipulation /'stɪpjə'leɪʃən ‖ ˌstɪpjʊ'leɪʃən/ *n* condición *f*, estipulación *f*

stir¹ /stɜːr ‖ stɜː(r)/ *n* **(a)** [C] (action) **to give sth a ~** revolver* *or* (Esp) remover* algo **(b)** [U] (excitement) revuelo *m*, conmoción *f*

stir² **-rr-** *vt* **1** (mix) ‹*liquid/mixture*› revolver*, remover* (Esp) **2 (a)** (move slightly) agitar, mover* **(b)** (get moving) (colloq) mover* **(c)** (waken) despertar* **3 (a)** (arouse) ‹*imagination*› estimular **(b)** (move, affect) conmover* **(c)** (provoke, incite) **to ~ sb into action** empujar *or* incitar a algn a la acción ■ **~** *vi* **(a)** (change position) moverse*, agitarse **(b)** (venture out) moverse*, salir* **(c)** (wake up) despertarse*; (get up) levantarse

• **stir up** [*v + o + adv, v + adv + o*] ‹*mud/waters*› revolver*, remover* (Esp); ‹*hatred/unrest/revolt*› provocar*; ‹*discontent*› promover*; **to ~ up trouble** armar lío (fam)

stir-fry /'stɜːr'fraɪ ‖ 'stɜːfraɪ/ *vt* **-fries, -frying, -fried** *freír en poco aceite y revolviendo constantemente*

stirring /'stɜːrɪŋ/ *adj* conmovedor

stirrup /'stərəp ‖ 'stɪrəp/ *n* estribo *m*

stitch¹ /stɪtʃ/ *n* **1 (a)** (in sewing) puntada *f* **(b)** (in knitting) punto *m* **(c)** (Med) punto *m* **2** (pain) (*no pl*) punzada *f or* (CS) puntada *f* (en el costado), flato *m* (Esp)

stitch² *vt* **(a)** (sew) coser **(b)** (embroider) bordar **(c)** (Med) suturar

stoat /stəʊt/ *n* armiño *m*

stock¹ /stɑːk ‖ stɒk/ *n* **1 (a)** (supply) (*often pl*) reserva *f* **(b)** [U] (of shop, business) existencias *fpl*, estoc *m*; **we're out of ~ of green ones** las verdes se han agotado; **to take ~ of sth** hacer* un balance de algo **2** (Fin) **(a)** [U] (shares) acciones *fpl*, valores *mpl*; (government securities) bonos *mpl or* papel *m* del Estado **(b) ~s and bonds** *o* (BrE) **~s and shares** acciones *fpl* **3** [U] (livestock) ganado *m* **4** [U] (descent) linaje *m*, estirpe *f* **5** [U] (Culin) caldo *m* **6 stocks** *pl* (Hist) **the ~s** el cepo **7** [U] (Am Theat) repertorio *m*

stock² *vt* **1** (Busn) vender **2** (fill) ‹*store*› surtir, abastecer*; ‹*larder/freezer*› llenar

• **stock up** [*v + adv*] abastecerse*; (Busn) hacer* un estoc; **we'd better ~ up on coffee before it goes up** más vale que compremos bastante café antes de que suba

stock³ *adj* (*before n*) ‹*size*› estándar *adj inv*; ‹*model*› de serie

stock: **~broker** *n* corredor, -dora *m,f* de valores *or* de Bolsa, agente *mf* de Bolsa; **~ company** *n* (AmE) **(a)** (Fin) sociedad *f* anónima **(b)** (Theat) compañía *f* de repertorio; **~ cube** *n* cubito *m* de caldo; **~ exchange** *n* bolsa *f* (de valores), Bolsa *f*; **~holder** *n* accionista *mf*

Stockholm /'stɑːkhəʊlm ‖ 'stɒkhəʊm/ *n* Estocolmo

stocking /'stɑːkɪŋ ‖ 'stɒkɪŋ/ *n* media *f*

stock-in-trade /'stɑːkɪn'treɪd ‖ ˌstɒkɪn'treɪd/ *n* especialidad *f*

stockist /'stɑːkəst ‖ 'stɒkɪst/ *n* (BrE) proveedor, -dora *m,f*, distribuidor, -dora *m,f*

stock market *n* mercado *m* de valores, mercado *m* (bursátil)

stockpile¹ /'stɑːkpaɪl ‖ 'stɒkpaɪl/ *n* reservas *fpl*

stockpile² *vt* almacenar

stock: **~room** *n* almacén *m*, depósito *m*, bodega *f* (Méx); **~-still** /'stɑːk'stɪl ‖ ˌstɒk'stɪl/ *adj* inmóvil; **~taking** /'stɑːkˌteɪkɪŋ ‖ 'stɒkˌteɪkɪŋ/ *n* [U] (esp BrE Busn): Ⓢ **closed for stocktaking** cerrado por inventario

stocky /'stɑːki ‖ 'stɒki/ *adj* **stockier, stockiest** bajo y fornido

stockyard /'stɑːkjɑːrd ‖ 'stɒkjɑːd/ *n* (AmE) corral *m*

stodgy /'stɑːdʒi ‖ 'stɒdʒi/ *adj* **-dgier, -dgiest** (BrE) ‹*food*› feculento, pesado

stoical /'stəʊɪkəl/ *adj* estoico

stoke /stəʊk/ *vt* echarle carbón (*or* leña *etc*) a

stole¹ /stəʊl/ *past of* STEAL

stole² *n* estola *f*

stolen /'stəʊlən/ *past p of* STEAL

stolid /'stɑːləd ‖ 'stɒlɪd/ *adj* impasible

stomach¹ /'stʌmək/ ▶ 484 *n* **(a)** (organ) estómago *m*; **on an empty ~** con el estómago vacío, en ayunas **(b)** (belly) barriga (fam), panza *f* (fam)

stomach² *vt* (*usu neg*) ‹*insults/insolence/person*› soportar, aguantar

stomach: **~ache** *n* [C U] dolor *m* de estómago; (in lower abdomen) dolor *m* de barriga *or* (frml) de vientre; **~ pump** *n* bomba *f* estomacal

stomp /stɑːmp ‖ stɒmp/ *vi* (*+ adv compl*): **to ~ in/out** entrar/salir* pisando fuerte

stone¹ /stəʊn/ *n* **1** [U C] piedra *f* **2** [C] **(a)** (gem) piedra *f* **(b)** (in kidney) cálculo *m*, piedra *f* **(c)** (of fruit) hueso *m*, cuesco *m* **3** ▶ 322 [C] (*pl* **~** *or* **~s**) (in UK) *unidad de peso equivalente a 14 libras o 6,35kg*

stone² *vt* apedrear, lapidar

stone: **S~ Age** *n* Edad *f* de Piedra; **~-cold** /'stəʊn'kəʊld/ *adj* (colloq) helado

stoned /stəʊnd/ *adj* (colloq) (*usu pred*) (from drugs) volado, pacheco (Méx), colocado (Esp fam); **to get ~** volarse*, ponerse* pacheco (Méx), colocarse* (Esp fam)

stone: **~-deaf** /'stəʊn'def/ *adj* (colloq) sordo como una tapia (fam); **~mason** *n* picapedrero *m*, cantero *m*; **~wall** /'stəʊn'wɔːl/ *vi* (be evasive) andarse* con evasivas; (be obstructive) utilizar* tácticas obstruccionistas

stony /'stəʊni/ *adj* **-nier, -niest 1** ‹*ground/path*› pedregoso **2** ‹*look/person*› frío, glacial; ‹*silence*› sepulcral

stood /stʊd/ *past & past p of* STAND²

stool /stuːl/ *n* taburete *m*, banco *m*

stoop¹ /stuːp/ *vi* **1** (have a stoop): **he ~s a little** es un poco cargado de espaldas *or* encorvado **2** (bend over) agacharse **3** (demean oneself): **how could he ~ so low?** ¿cómo pudo llegar tan bajo?; **to ~ TO sth** rebajarse A algo

stoop² *n* (*no pl*): **she walks with a ~** camina encorvada

stop¹ /stɑːp ‖ stɒp/ *n* **1** (halt): **to come to a ~** «*vehicle/aircraft*» detenerse*; «*production/conversation*» interrumpirse; **to put a ~ to sth** ‹*to mischief/malpractice*› poner* fin a algo **2 (a)** (break on journey) parada *f* **(b)** (stopping place) parada *f*, paradero *m* (AmL exc RPl)

stop² **-pp-** *vt* **1 (a)** (halt) ‹*taxi/bus*› parar; ‹*person*› parar, detener* **(b)** (switch off) ‹*machine/engine*› parar **2 (a)** (bring to an end, interrupt) ‹*decline/inflation*› detener*, parar; ‹*discussion/abuse*› poner* fin a, acabar con; **~ that noise!** ¡deja de hacer ruido! **(b)** (cease): **~ what you're doing and listen to me** deja lo que estás haciendo y escúchame; **~ it!** ¡basta ya!; **to ~** -ING dejar DE + INF **3** (prevent): **what's ~ping you?** ¿qué te lo impide?; **I had to tell him, I couldn't ~ myself** tuve que decírselo, no pude contenerme; **to ~ sb** (FROM) -ING (esp BrE) impedirle* a algn + INF, impedir* QUE algn (+ *subj*); **to ~ sth happening** impedir* que ocurra algo **4** (cancel, withhold) ‹*subscription*› cancelar; ‹*payment*› suspender **5** (block) ‹*hole*› tapar; ‹*gap*› rellenar **6** (parry) ‹*blow/punch*› parar, detener* ■ **~** *vi* **1 (a)** (halt) «*vehicle/driver*» parar, detenerse*; **~ or I'll shoot!** ¡alto o disparo! **(b)** (interrupt journey) «*train/bus*» parar **(c)** (cease operating) «*watch/clock/machine*» pararse **2 (a)** (cease): **the rain has ~ped** ha dejado *or* parado de llover, ya no llueve; **the pain/bleeding has ~ped** ya no le (*or* me *etc*) duele/sale sangre **(b)** (interrupt activity) parar; **I didn't ~ to think** no me detuve a pensar **3** (colloq) (stay) quedarse

• **stop by** [*v* + *adv*] [*v* + *prep* + *o*]: **I ~ped by (at) the store for some milk** pasé por la tienda para comprar leche

• **stop off** [*v* + *adv*]: **I ~ped off at home to change** pasé por casa para cambiarme; **we ~ped off in San Juan for a few hours** paramos unas horas en San Juan

• **stop over** [*v* + *adv*] **(a)** (overnight) hacer* noche **(b)** (Aviat) «*plane*» hacer* escala

• **stop up** [*v* + *o* + *adv*, *v* + *adv* + *o*] (fill) ‹*hole/crack*› tapar, rellenar

stop: **~gap** *n* recurso *m* provisional *or* (AmS tb) provisorio; **~over** *n* (break in journey) parada *f*; (Aviat) escala *f*

stoppage /ˈstɑːpɪdʒ ‖ ˈstɒpɪdʒ/ *n* **1 (a)** (in play, production) interrupción *f* **(b)** (strike) huelga *f*, paro *m* (AmL) **(c)** (cancellation) suspensión *f* **2** (blockage) obstrucción *f*

stopper /ˈstɑːpər ‖ ˈstɒpə(r)/ *n* tapón *m*

stop: **~ press** *n* noticias *fpl* de última hora; **~watch** *n* cronómetro *m*

storage /ˈstɔːrɪdʒ/ *n* [U] **(a)** (of goods) depósito *m*, almacenamiento *m*, almacenaje *m*; (*before n*) **~ space** lugar *m or* espacio *m* para guardar cosas **(b)** (Comput) almacenamiento *m*

store¹ /stɔːr ‖ stɔː(r)/ *n* **1 (a)** [C U] (stock, supply) reserva *f*, provisión *f*; ***in ~***: **there's a surprise in ~ for her** la espera una sorpresa; **who knows what the future has in ~?** ¿quién sabe lo que nos deparará el futuro?; ***to set great/little ~ by sth*** dar* mucho/poco valor a algo **(b) stores** *pl* (Mil, Naut) pertrechos *mpl* **2** (warehouse, storage place) (*often pl*) almacén *m*, depósito *m*, bodega *f* (Méx) **3** [C] **(a)** (shop) (esp AmE) tienda *f* **(b)** (*department ~*) grandes almacenes *mpl*, tienda *f*

store² *vt* **(a)** (keep) ‹*food/drink/supplies*› guardar; (Busn) almacenar; ‹*information*› almacenar; ‹*electricity*› acumular **(b)** (Comput) ‹*data/program*› almacenar

• **store up** [*v* + *o* + *adv*, *v* + *adv* + *o*] **(a)** ‹*supplies*› almacenar **(b)** ‹*resentment*› ir* acumulando

store: **~house** *n* **(a)** (warehouse) almacén *m*, depósito *m*, bodega *f* (Méx) **(b)** (source) mina *f*; **~keeper** *n* tendero, -ra *m,f*; **~room** *n* almacén *m*, depósito *m*, bodega *f* (Méx); (for food) despensa *f*

storey /ˈstɔːri/ *n* (BrE) ⇒ STORY II

stork /stɔːrk ‖ stɔːk/ *n* cigüeña *f*

storm¹ /stɔːrm ‖ stɔːm/ *n* **1** ▶ **920** (Meteo) tormenta *f*; **a ~ at sea** una tempestad; ***to take sth by ~*** ‹*city/fortress*› tomar algo por asalto; **she took New York's audiences by ~** cautivó al público neoyorquino **2** (of protest) ola *f*, tempestad *f*

storm² *vi* **1** (move violently) (+ *adv compl*): **she ~ed into the office** irrumpió en la oficina **2** (express anger) despotricar*, vociferar ■ **~** *vt* ‹*city/fortress*› tomar por asalto; ‹*house*› irrumpir en

stormy /ˈstɔːrmi ‖ ˈstɔːmi/ *adj* **-mier, -miest** **(a)** ▶ **920** (Meteo) tormentoso; ‹*sea*› tempestuoso **(b)** (turbulent) ‹*relationship*› tempestuoso

story /ˈstɔːri/ *n* (*pl* **-ries**) **I 1 (a)** (account) historia *f*, relato *m*; (genre) cuento *m*; **to cut a long ~ short** en pocas palabras **(b)** (anecdote) anécdota *f* **2** (plot) argumento *m*, trama *f* **3** (Journ) artículo *m* **4** (lie) (colloq) cuento *m* (fam), mentira *f*
II (BrE) **storey** (of building) piso *m*, planta *f*

story: **~book** *n* libro *m* de cuentos; **~ line** *n* argumento *m*; **~teller** *n* narrador, -dora *m,f*

stout¹ /staʊt/ *adj* **-er, -est** ‹*person/figure*› robusto, corpulento; ‹*door*› sólido

stout² *n* [U] cerveza *f* negra

stove /stəʊv/ *n* **(a)** (for cooking) cocina *f*, estufa *f* (Col, Méx) **(b)** (for warmth) estufa *f*

stow /stəʊ/ *vt* (put away) guardar, poner*; (hide) esconder; (Naut) estibar

• **stow away** [*v* + *adv*] viajar de polizón

stowaway /ˈstəʊəˌweɪ/ *n* polizón *mf*

straddle /ˈstrædl̩/ *vt* ‹*horse*› sentarse* a horcajadas sobre; **he ~d the chair** se sentó a caballo *or* a horcajadas en la silla

straggle /ˈstrægəl/ *vi* **1** (spread untidily) «*plant*» crecer* desordenadamente **2** (lag behind, fall away) rezagarse*

straggler /ˈstræglər ‖ ˈstræglə(r)/ *n* rezagado, -da *m,f*

straggly /ˈstrægli/ *adj* **-glier, -gliest** ‹*hair*› desordenado, desgreñado; ‹*beard*› descuidado

straight¹ /streɪt/ *adj* **-er, -est** **1 (a)** (not curved or wavy) recto; ‹*hair*› lacio, liso **(b)** (level, upright, vertical) (*pred*) **to be ~** estar* derecho; **is my tie ~?** ¿tengo la corbata derecha *or* bien puesta? **2** (in order) (*pred*): **I have to put my room ~** tengo que ordenar mi cuarto; **let's get this ~** a ver si nos entendemos; **to set the record ~** dejar las cosas en claro **3 (a)** (direct, clear) ‹*denial/refusal*› rotundo, categórico **(b)** (unmixed) ‹*gin/vodka*› solo **4** (honest, frank) ‹*question*› directo; ‹*answer*› claro **5** (successive): **he won in ~ sets** (Sport) ganó sin conceder *or* sin perder ningún set; **she's had five ~ wins** ha ganado cinco veces seguidas **6 (a)** (serious) ‹*play/actor*› dramático, serio **(b)**

(conventional) (colloq) convencional **(c)** (heterosexual) (colloq) heterosexual

straight² *adv* **1 (a)** (in a straight line) ‹*walk*› en línea recta; **she looked ~ ahead** miró al frente; **the truck was coming ~ at me** el camión venía derecho hacia mí; **he made ~ for the bar** se fue derecho al bar; **keep ~ on until you come to the lights** sigue derecho hasta llegar al semáforo **(b)** (erect) ‹*sit/stand*› derecho; **sit up ~** ponte derecho **2 (a)** (directly) directamente; **I came ~ home from work** vine directamente *or* derecho a casa después del trabajo **(b)** (immediately): **~ after dinner** inmediatamente después de cenar; **I'll bring it ~ back** enseguida lo devuelvo; **I'll come ~ to the point** iré derecho al grano; **~ away** ⇒ STRAIGHTAWAY **3** (colloq) (frankly) con franqueza; **she told him ~ out** se lo dijo sin rodeos **4** (clearly) ‹*see/think*› con claridad

straight: **~ and narrow** *n* [U] **the ~ and narrow** el buen camino, el camino recto; **~away** /ˈstreɪtəˈweɪ/, **~ away** *adv* enseguida, inmediatamente

straighten /ˈstreɪtn̩/ *vt* **(a)** ‹*nail/wire/picture*› enderezar*; ‹*hair*› alisar; **he ~ed his tie** se enderezó la corbata **(b)** (tidy) ‹*room/papers*› arreglar, ordenar

• straighten out [*v + o + adv, v + adv + o*] ‹*confusion/misunderstanding*› aclarar; ‹*problem*› resolver*

• straighten up 1 [*v + o + adv, v + adv + o*] (tidy) ‹*room/papers*› ordenar, arreglar; ‹*bed*› arreglar **2** [*v + adv*] (stand up straight) ponerse* derecho

straight: **~faced** /ˈstreɪtˈfeɪst/ *adj*: **he said it completely ~faced** lo dijo muy serio; **~forward** /ˈstreɪtˈfɔːrwərd ‖ ˌstreɪtˈfɔːwəd/ *adj* **(a)** (honest, frank) ‹*person/answer*› franco **(b)** (uncomplicated) ‹*problem/question*› sencillo; **~jacket** *n* ⇒ STRAITJACKET

strain¹ /streɪn/ *n* **1** [U C] (tension) tensión *f*; (pressure) presión *f*; **it puts ~ on the spine** ejerce presión sobre la columna vertebral; **the incident put a ~ on Franco-German relations** las relaciones franco-alemanes se volvieron tirantes a raíz del incidente **2** [C U] (Med) (resulting from wrench, twist) torcedura *f*; (on a muscle) esguince *m* **3 strains** *pl* (tune): **the ~s of** el sonido de; **to the ~s of the violin** al son del violín **4 (a)** [C] (type — of plant) variedad *f*; (— of virus) cepa *f*; (— of animal) raza *f* **(b)** (streak) (*no pl*) veta *f*

strain² *vt* **1** (exert): **to ~ one's eyes/voice** forzar* la vista/voz; **he ~ed every muscle to lift the weight** usó todas sus fuerzas para levantar el peso **2 (a)** (overburden) ‹*beam/support*› ejercer* demasiada presión sobre **(b)** (injure): **to ~ one's back** hacerse* daño en la espalda; **to ~ a muscle** hacerse* un esguince **(c)** (overtax, stretch) ‹*relations*› someter a demasiada tensión; ‹*patience*› poner* a prueba **3** (filter) filtrar; (Culin) colar*; ‹*vegetables/rice*› escurrir ■ **~** *vi*: **to ~ AT sth** tirar DE algo; **to ~ to + INF** hacer* un gran esfuerzo PARA + INF

strained /streɪnd/ *adj* **1** (tense) ‹*relations/atmosphere*› tenso, tirante; ‹*expression*› tenso, crispado; ‹*voice*› forzado **2** (Med) **a ~ muscle** un esguince

strainer /ˈstreɪnər ‖ ˈstreɪnə(r)/ *n* (Culin) colador *m*

strait /streɪt/ *n* **1** (Geog) (*often pl*) estrecho *m* **2 straits** *pl* (difficulties, difficult position): **to be in dire ~s** estar* en grandes apuros

strait: **~jacket** *n* camisa *f* de fuerza, chaleco *m* de fuerza (CS); **~laced** /ˈstreɪtˈleɪst/ *adj* puritano

strand¹ /strænd/ *n* (of rope, string) ramal *m*; (of thread, wool) hebra *f*; (of wire) filamento *m*; **a ~ of hair** un pelo

strand² *vt* (*usu pass*): **to be ~ed** «*ship*» quedar encallado; «*whale*» quedar varado; **they left me ~ed** me abandonaron a mi suerte, me dejaron tirado *or* (AmL exc RPl) botado (fam)

strange /streɪndʒ/ *adj* **stranger, strangest 1** (odd) raro, extraño; **it is ~ (THAT)** es raro QUE (+ *subj*) **2 (a)** (unfamiliar, unaccustomed) ‹*faces/handwriting*› desconocido **(b)** (alien) (liter): **in a ~ land** en tierras extrañas

strangely /ˈstreɪndʒli/ *adv* ‹*behave/act*› de una manera rara *or* extraña; **~ enough** (*indep*) aunque parezca mentira

stranger /ˈstreɪndʒər ‖ ˈstreɪndʒə(r)/ *n* desconocido, -da *m,f*; (from another place) forastero, -ra *m,f*; **I'm a ~ here myself** yo tampoco soy de aquí

strangle /ˈstræŋgəl/ *vt* **(a)** ‹*person*› estrangular **(b) strangled** *past p* ‹*cry/voice*› ahogado

stranglehold /ˈstræŋgəlhəʊld/ *n* **(a)** (Sport) llave *f* al cuello **(b)** (absolute control) poder *m*, dominio *m*

strap¹ /stræp/ *n* **(a)** (of leather) correa *f*; (of canvas) asa *f*‡ **(b)** (*shoulder ~*) tirante *m*, bretel *m* (CS)

strap² *vt* **-pp-** (tie) atar *or* sujetar con una correa, amarrar con una correa (AmL exc RPl)

strapless /ˈstræpləs ‖ ˈstræplɪs/ *adj* sin tirantes, sin breteles (CS)

strapping /ˈstræpɪŋ/ *adj* robusto, fornido

Strasbourg /ˈstrɑːsbʊrg ‖ ˈstræzbɜːg/ *n* Estrasburgo *m*

strata /ˈstreɪtə, ˈstrætə ‖ ˈstrɑːtə, ˈstreɪtə/ *pl of* STRATUM

stratagem /ˈstrætədʒəm/ *n* [C U] estratagema *f*

strategic /strəˈtiːdʒɪk/ *adj* estratégico

strategy /ˈstrætədʒi/ *n* [C U] (*pl* **-gies**) estrategia *f*

stratify /ˈstrætəfaɪ ‖ ˈstrætɪfaɪ/ *vt* **-fies, -fying, -fied** (*usu pass*) estratificar*

stratum /ˈstreɪtəm, ˈstræ- ‖ ˈstrɑːtəm, ˈstreɪ-/ *n* (*pl* **-ta**) estrato *m*

straw /strɔː/ *n* **(a)** [U C] paja *f*; ***to be the last*** *o* ***final ~*** ser* el colmo; ***to clutch*** *o* ***grasp at ~s*** aferrarse desesperadamente a una esperanza **(b)** [C] (for drinking) pajita *f*, paja *f*, caña *f* (Esp), pitillo *m* (Col), popote *m* (Méx)

strawberry /ˈstrɔːˌberi ‖ ˈstrɔːbəri/ *n* (*pl* **-ries**) fresa *f*, frutilla *f* (Bol, CS); (large) fresón *m*

stray¹ /streɪ/ *vi* **(a)** (wander away) apartarse, alejarse; (get lost) extraviarse*, perderse* **(b)** (digress) apartarse, desviarse*

stray² *adj* **(a)** ‹*dog*› (ownerless) callejero; (lost) perdido; ‹*sheep*› descarriado **(b)** (random, scattered) ‹*bullet*› perdido; ‹*hair*› suelto

stray³ *n* (ownerless animal) perro *m*/gato *m* callejero; (lost animal) perro *m*/gato *m* perdido

streak¹ /striːk/ *n* **1 (a)** (line, band) lista *f*, raya *f*; (in hair) reflejo *m*, mechón *m*; (in marble) veta *f*; (of ore) veta *f*, filón *m* **(b)** (in personality) veta *f* **2** (spell) racha *f*; **to be on a winning ~** tener* una buena racha

streak² *vi* (+ *adv compl*): **to ~ past** pasar como una centella ▪ ~ *vt*: **tears ~ed her face** tenía el rostro surcado de lágrimas; **to have one's hair ~ed** hacerse* mechas *or* reflejos *or* (RPl) claritos *or* (Méx) luces *or* (Chi) visos (en el pelo)

streaky /ˈstriːki/ *adj* **-kier, -kiest (a)** (uneven) ‹*paint*› no uniforme, disparejo (AmL) **(b)** (BrE Culin): **~ bacon** tocino *m or* (Esp) bacon *m or* (RPl) panceta *f*

stream¹ /striːm/ *n* **1 (a)** (small river) arroyo *m*, riachuelo *m* **(b)** (current) corriente *f* **2** (flow): **a thin ~ of water** un chorrito de agua; **a ~ of abuse** una sarta de insultos; **there is a continuous ~ of traffic** pasan vehículos continuamente

stream² *vi* **1** (flow) (+ *adv compl*): **blood ~ed from the wound** salía *or* manaba mucha sangre de la herida; **tears were ~ing down her cheeks** lloraba a lágrima viva; **the sunlight was ~ing in through the window** el sol entraba a raudales por la ventana; **I've got a ~ing cold** tengo un resfriado muy fuerte **2** (wave) «*flag/hair*» ondear ▪ ~ *vt* (BrE Educ) *dividir (a los alumnos) en grupos según su aptitud para una asignatura*

streamer /ˈstriːmər ‖ ˈstriːmə(r)/ *n* **(a)** (banner) banderín *m* **(b)** (of paper) serpentina *f*

stream: **~line** *vt* ‹*car/plane*› hacer* más aerodinámico el diseño de, aerodinamizar*; ‹*organization/production*› racionalizar*; **~lined** *adj* ‹*car/plane*› aerodinámico; ‹*methods/production*› racionalizado

street /striːt/ *n* calle *f*; **it's on** *o* (BrE) **in Elm S~** queda en la calle Elm; (*before n*) ‹*musician/theater*› callejero; **~ corner** esquina *f*; **~ map** *o* **plan** plano *m* de la ciudad, callejero *m* (Esp); **~ market** mercado *m* al aire libre, feria *f* (CS)

street: **~car** *n* (AmE) tranvía *m*; **~ cleaner** *n* (AmE) barrendero, -ra *m,f*; **~ lamp** *n* farol *m*; **~ level** *n*: **at ~ level** a nivel de la calle; **~ light** *n* ⇒ ~ LAMP; **~ sweeper** *n* (person) barrendero, -ra *m,f*; (machine) (máquina *f*) barredora *f*

strength /streŋθ/ *n* **1** [U] (of persons) **(a)** (physical energy) fuerza(s) *f(pl)*; (health) fortaleza *f* física; **to get one's ~ back** recobrar las fuerzas **(b)** (emotional, mental) fortaleza *f* **2** [U] (of economy, currency) solidez *f* **3** [U] **(a)** (of materials) resistencia *f*; (of wind, current) fuerza *f*; (of drug, solution) concentración *f*; (of alcoholic drink) graduación *f* **(b)** (of sound, light) potencia *f*; (of emotions) intensidad *f* **(c)** (of argument, evidence) lo convincente; (of protests) lo enérgico **4** [C] (strong point) virtud *f*, punto *m* fuerte **5** [U C] (force in numbers): **their fans were there in ~** sus hinchas estaban allí en bloque *or* en masa

strengthen /ˈstreŋθən/ *vt* ‹*muscle/limb*› fortalecer*; ‹*wall/furniture/glass*› reforzar*; ‹*support*› aumentar ▪ ~ *vi* «*limb/muscle*» fortalecerse*; «*opposition/support*» aumentar

strenuous /ˈstrenjuəs/ *adj* **(a)** ‹*activity*› agotador **(b)** ‹*denial*› vigoroso; ‹*opposition*› tenaz

stress¹ /stres/ *n* **1 (a)** [U C] (tension) tensión *f*; (Med) estrés *m*, tensión, f; **she's under a lot of ~** está sometida a muchas presiones **(b)** [U] (Phys, Tech) tensión *f* **2 (a)** [U] (emphasis) énfasis *m*, hincapié *m* **(b)** [C U] (Ling, Lit) acento *m* (tónico)

stress² *vt* **(a)** (emphasize) poner* enfásis *or* hacer* hincapié en, enfatizar* **(b)** (Ling) acentuar*

stressful /ˈstresfəl/ *adj* ‹*life/job*› estresante

stretch¹ /stretʃ/ *vt* **1** ‹*arm/leg*› estirar, extender*; ‹*wing*› extender*, desplegar* **2** ‹*sheet/canvas*› extender* **3** (eke out) ‹*money/resources*› estirar **4 (a)** (make demands on) exigirle* a; **she's not being ~ed at school** en el colegio no le exigen de acuerdo a su capacidad **(b)** (strain): **our resources are ~ed to the limit** nuestros recursos están empleados al máximo **5** ‹*truth/meaning*› forzar*; ‹*rules*› apartarse un poco de ▪ ~ *vi* **1** «*person*» estirarse; (when sleepy) desperezarse* **2 (a)** (reach, extend) «*sea/influence/power*» extenderse* **(b)** (in time): **to ~ over a period** alargarse* *or* prolongarse* durante un período **3 (a)** (be elastic) «*elastic/rope*» estirarse **(b)** (become loose, longer) «*garment*» estirarse **4** (be enough) «*money/resources/supply*» alcanzar*, llegar* ▪ *v refl* **to ~ oneself** (physically) estirarse; (when sleepy) desperezarse*

• **stretch out 1** [*v* + *o* + *adv*, *v* + *adv* + *o*] (extend) estirar **2** [*v* + *adv*] **(a)** (lie full length) tenderse* **(b)** (extend — in space) extenderse*; (— in time) alargarse*

stretch² *n* **1** (act of stretching) (*no pl*): **to have a ~** estirarse; (when sleepy) desperezarse* **2** [C] **(a)** (expanse — of road, river) tramo *m*, trecho *m* **(b)** (period) período *m*; ***at a ~*** (without a break) sin parar **3** [U] (elasticity) elasticidad *f*

stretch³ *adj* (*before n, no comp*) ‹*fabric/pants*› elástico; **~ limo** (colloq) limusina *f* (*grande*)

stretcher /ˈstretʃər ‖ ˈstretʃə(r)/ *n* (Med) camilla *f*

stretch marks *pl n* estrías *fpl*

stretchy /ˈstretʃi/ *adj* **-chier, -chiest** elástico

strew /struː/ *vt* (*past* **strewn** /struːn/ *past p* **strewn** *or* **strewed** /-d/) ‹*gravel/seeds*› esparcir*; ‹*objects*› (untidily) desparramar

stricken /ˈstrɪkən/ *adj* **(a)** (afflicted) **~** WITH **sth**: **a country ~ with famine** un país asolado por el hambre; **I was suddenly ~ with remorse** de pronto me empezó a remorder la conciencia **(b)** ‹*vessel*› siniestrado (frml), dañado; ‹*area*› damnificado, afectado

strict /strɪkt/ *adj* **-er, -est (a)** (severe) estricto, severo **(b)** (rigorous) ‹*vegetarian*› estricto, riguroso **(c)** (exact) (*before n*) estricto, riguroso; **in the ~ sense of the word** en el sentido estricto *or* riguroso de la palabra **(d)** (completo) (*before n*) absoluto; **in ~est secrecy** en el más absoluto secreto

strictly /ˈstrɪktli/ *adv* **(a)** (severely) con severidad, severamente, rigurosamente **(b)** (rigorously): **smoking is ~ prohibited** fumar está terminantemente prohibido; **~ (speaking)** (*indep*) en rigor, en sentido estricto **(c)** (exactly) totalmente; **that's not ~ true** eso no es totalmente cierto **(d)** (exclusively) exclusivamente; **this is ~ between ourselves** que quede entre nosotros

stride¹ /straɪd/ *vi* (*past* **strode**; *past p* **stridden** /'strɪdn̩/) (+ *adv compl*): **he strode across the room** cruzó la habitación a grandes zancadas

stride² *n* zancada *f*, tranco *m*; ***to take sth in one's ~*** tomarse algo con calma

strident /'straɪdn̩t/ *adj* estridente

strife /straɪf/ *n* [U] (journ *or* frml) conflictos *mpl*; (armed) luchas *fpl*

strike¹ /straɪk/ (*past & past p* **struck**) *vt* **1 (a)** (hit) ‹*person*› pegarle* a, golpear; ‹*blow*› dar*, pegar*; ‹*key*› pulsar **(b)** (collide with, fall on) «*vehicle*» chocar* *or* dar* contra; «*stone/ball*» pegar* *or* dar* contra; «*lightning/bullet*» alcanzar*; **I struck my head on the beam** me di (un golpe) en la cabeza contra la viga; **he was struck by lightning** le cayó un rayo **2 (a)** (cause to become): **to be struck blind/dumb** quedarse ciego/mudo; **to ~ sb dead** matar a algn **(b)** (introduce): **to ~ fear into sb** infundirle miedo a algn **3 (a)** (occur to) ocurrirse (+ *me/te/le etc*); **it ~s me (that)** ... me da la impresión de que ..., se me ocurre que ... **(b)** (impress) parecerle* a; **it ~s me as odd** me parece raro; **I was struck by his changed appearance** me llamó la atención lo cambiado que estaba **4** ‹*oil/gold*› encontrar*, dar* con **5** ‹*match/light*› encender* **6 (a)** (Mus) ‹*note*› dar* **(b)** «*clock*» dar*; **the clock struck five** el reloj dio las cinco **7** (enter into, arrive at): **to ~ a deal** llegar* a un acuerdo, cerrar* un trato; **to ~ a balance between** ... encontrar* el justo equilibrio entre ... **8** (adopt) ‹*pose/attitude*› adoptar **9** (delete) suprimir; **his name was struck off the register** se borró su nombre del registro; *see also* STRIKE OFF ■ ~ *vi* **1** (hit) «*person*» golpear; «*lightning*» caer* **2 (a)** (attack) atacar* **(b)** (happen suddenly) «*illness/misfortune*» sobrevenir*; «*disaster*» ocurrir **3** (withdraw labor) hacer* huelga, declararse en huelga *or* (esp AmL) en paro **4** «*clock*» dar* la hora

• **strike back** [*v* + *adv*] (Mil) contraatacar*; **he struck back at his critics** devolvió el golpe a sus detractores

• **strike down** [*v* + *o* + *adv*, *v* + *adv* + *o*] (liter): **she was struck down with cholera** fue abatida por el cólera (liter)

• **strike off** [*v* + *o* + *adv*, *v* + *adv* + *o*] **(a)** (delete) tachar **(b)** (disqualify) (BrE) ‹*doctor/lawyer*› prohibirle* el ejercicio de la profesión a

• **strike out I** [*v* + *adv*] **to ~ out** (AT **sb/sth**) arremeter (CONTRA algn/algo)
II [*v* + *o* + *adv*, *v* + *adv* + *o*] (remove from list) tachar

• **strike up 1** [*v* + *adv* + *o*] **(a)** (begin) ‹*conversation*› entablar; ‹*friendship*› trabar, entablar **(b)** (start to play) ‹*tune*› empezar* a tocar **2** [*v* + *adv*] «*band*» empezar* a tocar

strike² *n* **1** (stoppage) huelga *f*, paro *m* (esp AmL); **to be on ~** estar* en *or* de huelga, estar* en *or* de paro (esp AmL); **to come out** *o* **go (out) on ~** ir* a la huelga, declararse en huelga, ir* al paro (esp AmL), declararse en paro (esp AmL); **hunger ~** huelga de hambre **2** (find) descubrimiento *m* **3** (attack) ataque *m*

strikebreaker /'straɪk,breɪkər ‖ 'straɪk,breɪkə(r)/ *n* rompehuelgas *mf*

striker /'straɪkər ‖ 'straɪkə(r)/ *n* **1** (Lab Rel) huelguista *mf* **2** (in soccer) artillero, -ra *m,f*, ariete *mf*

striking /'straɪkɪŋ/ *adj* ‹*resemblance/similarity*› sorprendente, asombroso; ‹*color*› llamativo; **a ~ woman** una mujer muy atractiva

string¹ /strɪŋ/ *n* **1 (a)** [U C] (cord, length of cord) cordel *m*, bramante *m* (Esp), mecate *m* (AmC, Méx, Ven), pita *f* (Andes), cáñamo *m* (Andes), piolín *m* (RPl) **(b)** [C] (on apron) cinta *f*; (on puppet) hilo *m*; ***no ~s attached*** sin compromisos, sin condiciones **2** [C] **(a)** (on instrument) cuerda *f* **(b)** (on racket) cuerda *f* **(c) strings** *pl* (Mus) cuerdas *fpl* **3** [C] **(a)** (set — of pearls, beads) sarta *f*, hilo *m*; (— of onions, garlic) ristra *f* **(b)** (series — of people) sucesión *f*; (— of vehicles) fila *f*; (— of events) serie *f*; (— of curses, complaints, lies) sarta *f*

string² (*past & past p* **strung**) *vt* **1** (suspend) colgar* **2** ‹*guitar/racket/bow*› encordar*, ponerle* (las) cuerdas a; ‹*beads/pearls*› ensartar, enhebrar

• **string along** (colloq) [*v* + *o* + *adv*] (mislead) tomarle el pelo a (fam) (*dando esperanzas falsas*)

• **string together** [*v* + *o* + *adv*, *v* + *adv* + *o*] ‹*thoughts*› coordinar, hilar; **she could barely ~ a sentence together** apenas podía hilar una frase

string bean *n* ⇒ RUNNER BEAN

stringed /strɪŋd/ *adj* ‹*instrument*› de cuerda

stringent /'strɪndʒənt/ *adj* riguroso, estricto

strip¹ /strɪp/ **-pp-** *vt* **1 (a)** (remove covering from) ‹*bed*› deshacer*, quitar la ropa de; ‹*wood/furniture*› quitarle la pintura (*or* el barniz *etc*) a, decapar; **to ~ sb (naked)** desnudar a algn **(b)** (remove contents from) ‹*room/house*› vaciar* **2** (Auto, Tech) **~ (down)** desmontar ■ ~ *vi* desnudarse, desvestirse*

• **strip off** [*v* + *o* + *adv*, *v* + *adv* + *o*] ‹*wallpaper/paint*› quitar; ‹*leaves*› arrancar*

strip² *n* **1** [C] (of leather, cloth, paper) tira *f*; (of metal) tira *f*, cinta *f*; (of land) franja *f* **2** (BrE Sport) (*no pl*) equipo *m*

strip cartoon *n* (BrE) historieta *f*, tira *f* cómica

stripe /straɪp/ *n* raya *f*, lista *f*

striped /straɪpt/ *adj* a *or* de rayas, rayado, listado

strip: **~ lighting** *n* [U] (BrE) luz *f* fluorescente; **~search** /'strɪp'sɜːrtʃ ‖ 'strɪp,sɜːtʃ/ *vt* hacer* desnudar y registrar

strive /straɪv/ *vi* (*past* **strove** *or* **strived**; *past p* **striven** /'strɪvən/) **to ~ FOR** *o* **AFTER sth** luchar *or* esforzarse* por alcanzar algo; **to ~ to + INF** esforzarse* POR + INF

strobe (light) /strəʊb/ *n* luz *f* estroboscópica

strode /strəʊd/ *past of* STRIDE¹

stroke¹ /strəʊk/ *n* **1** (Sport) **(a)** (in ball games) golpe *m* **(b)** (in swimming — movement) brazada *f*; (— style) estilo *m* **(c)** (in rowing — movement) palada *f*, remada *f* **2 (a)** (blow) golpe *m* **(b)** (of clock) campanada *f* **3 (a)** (of thin brush) pincelada *f*; (of thick brush) brochazo *m*; (of pen, pencil) trazo *m* **(b)** (oblique, slash) barra *f*, diagonal *f* **4 (a)** (action, feat) golpe *m*; ***not to do a ~ of work*** no hacer* absolutamente nada **(b)** (instance): **a ~ of luck** un golpe de suerte **5** (Med) ataque *m* de apoplejía, derrame *m* cerebral **6** (caress) caricia *f*

stroke[2] *vt* acariciar

stroll[1] /strəʊl/ *vi* pasear(se), dar* un paseo

stroll[2] *n* paseo *m*; **to have** *o* **go for a ~** dar* un paseo

stroller /ˈstrəʊlər ‖ˈstrəʊlə(r)/ *n* **1** (person) paseante *mf* **2** (pushchair) (esp AmE) sillita *f* (de paseo), cochecito *m*, carreola *f* (Méx)

strong[1] /strɔːŋ ‖strɒŋ/ *adj* **stronger** /ˈstrɔːŋgər ‖ˈstrɒŋgə(r)/, **strongest** /ˈstrɔːŋgəst ‖ˈstrɒŋgɪst/ **1 (a)** (physically powerful) ‹*person/arm*› fuerte **(b)** (healthy, sound) ‹*heart/lungs*› fuerte, sano; ‹*constitution*› robusto **(c)** (firm) ‹*character/leader*› fuerte **2 (a)** (solid) ‹*material/construction*› fuerte **(b)** (powerful) ‹*army/economy*› fuerte **(c)** ‹*current/wind*› fuerte **3 (a)** (deeply held) ‹*views/faith/support*› firme **(b)** (forceful) ‹*protest*› enérgico; ‹*argument/evidence*› de peso **4** (definite) **(a)** ‹*tendency/resemblance*› marcado; ‹*candidate*› con muchas posibilidades **(b)** ‹*features*› marcado **5** (good) ‹*team*› fuerte; ‹*cast*› sólido; **~ point** punto *m* fuerte; **she's a ~ swimmer** es una buena nadadora **6 (a)** (concentrated) ‹*color/light*› fuerte, intenso; ‹*tea/coffee*› cargado; ‹*solution*› concentrado **(b)** (pungent) ‹*smell/flavor*› fuerte **(c)** (unacceptable) ‹*language*› fuerte **7** (in number) (*no comp*): **an army ten thousand ~** un ejército de diez mil hombres

strong[2] *adv*: **to be going ~** «*car/machine*» marchar bien; «*organization*» ir* *or* marchar viento en popa; **he's still going ~** «*old person*» sigue (estando) en plena forma

strong: **~box** *n* caja *f* fuerte *or* de caudales; **~hold** *n* (fortress) fortaleza *f*, bastión *m*; (center of support) bastión *m*, baluarte *m*

strongly /ˈstrɔːŋli ‖ˈstrɒŋli/ *adv* **1 (a)** (powerfully) fuerte, con fuerza **(b)** (sturdily) ‹*made/welded*› sólidamente **2 (a)** (deeply, ardently) totalmente; **it's something I feel very ~ about** es algo que me parece sumamente importante **(b)** (forcefully) ‹*protest/criticize*› enérgicamente; **I ~ advise you not to sell** te recomiendo con insistencia que no vendas

strong: **~ room** *n* cámara *f* acorazada; **~-willed** /ˈstrɔːŋˈwɪld ‖ˌstrɒŋˈwɪld/ *adj* (determined) tenaz; (obstinate) terco, tozudo

strove /strəʊv/ *past of* STRIVE

struck /strʌk/ *past & past p of* STRIKE[1]

structural /ˈstrʌktʃərəl/ *adj* estructural

structure[1] /ˈstrʌktʃər ‖ˈstrʌktʃə(r)/ *n* **(a)** [U C] (composition, organization) estructura *f* **(b)** [C] (thing constructed) construcción *f*

structure[2] *vt* estructurar

struggle[1] /ˈstrʌgəl/ *n* **(a)** (against opponent) lucha *f*; (physical) refriega *f*; **to put up a ~** luchar, oponer* resistencia **(b)** (against difficulties) lucha *f*; **it's a ~ to make ends meet** cuesta mucho llegar a fin de mes

struggle[2] *vi* **1 (a)** (thrash around) forcejear **(b)** (contend, strive) luchar; **to ~ (AGAINST/WITH sth)** luchar (CONTRA algo) **(c)** (be in difficulties) pasar apuros **2** (move with difficulty) (+ *adv compl*): **he ~d up the hill** subió penosamente la cuesta; **he ~d to his feet** se levantó con gran dificultad

strum /strʌm/ *vt* **-mm-** ‹*guitar/tune*› rasguear

strung /strʌŋ/ *past & past p of* STRING[2]

strut[1] /strʌt/ *vi* **-tt-** (+ *adv compl*): **to ~ around** *o* **about** pavonearse

strut[2] *n* (Const) tornapunta *f*, puntal *m*

stub[1] /stʌb/ *n* **(a)** (of candle, pencil) cabo *m*; (of cigarette) colilla *f*, pucho *m* (AmL fam) **(b)** (of check) talón *m* (AmL), matriz *f* (Esp); (of ticket) contraseña *f*, resguardo *m* (Esp)

stub[2] **-bb-** *vt*: **to ~ one's toe** darse* en el dedo (*del pie*)

• **stub out** [*v* + *o* + *adv*, *v* + *adv* + *o*] ‹*cigarette*› apagar*

stubble /ˈstʌbəl/ *n* [U] **(a)** (Agr) rastrojo *m* **(b)** (of beard): **he had three days' ~ on his chin** tenía una barba de tres días

stubborn /ˈstʌbərn ‖ˈstʌbən/ *adj* **(a)** ‹*person/nature*› (obstinate) terco, testarudo; (resolute) tenaz, tesonero; ‹*refusal/insistence*› pertinaz **(b)** ‹*cold/weeds*› pertinaz, persistente; ‹*stain*› rebelde

stuck[1] /stʌk/ *past & past p of* STICK[2]

stuck[2] *adj* (*pred*) **(a)** (unable to move): **the drawer is ~** el cajón se ha atascado; **the door is ~** la puerta se ha atrancado; **she's ~ at home with the kids all day** está todo el día metida en la casa con los niños **(b)** (at a loss) atascado; **I got ~ on the second question** me quedé atascado en la segunda pregunta **(c)** (burdened) (colloq): **I was ~ with the bill** me tocó pagar la cuenta, me cargaron el muerto (fam); **I got ~ with Bob all evening** tuve que aguantar a Bob toda la noche

stuck-up /ˈstʌkˈʌp/ *adj* (colloq) estirado (fam)

stud[1] /stʌd/ *n* **1 (a)** (nail, knob) tachuela *f* **(b)** (earring) arete *m or* (Esp) pendiente *m* (*en forma de bolita*) **(c)** (for collar, shirtfront) gemelo *m* (*para cuello o pechera de camisa*) **2** (male animal) semental *m*

stud[2] *vt* **-dd-** (*usu pass*) (with studs) tachonar; **the sky was ~ded with stars** el cielo estaba tachonado de estrellas (liter)

student /ˈstuːdn̩t ‖ˈstjuːdn̩t/ *n* (at university) estudiante *mf*; (at school) (esp AmE) alumno, -na *m,f*; **a medical ~** un/una estudiante de medicina; (*before n*) **~ driver** (AmE) *persona que está aprendiendo a conducir*; **~ nurse** estudiante *mf* de enfermería

student union *n* (association) asociación *f* de estudiantes; (building) *centro estudiantil en el campus*

studio /ˈstuːdiəʊ ‖ˈstjuːdiəʊ/ *n* **(a)** (Art, Mus, Phot) estudio *m* **(b)** (Cin, Rad, TV) estudio *m* **(c) ~ (apartment** *o* (BrE also) **flat)** estudio *m*

studious /ˈstuːdiəs ‖ˈstjuːdiəs/ *adj* estudioso, aplicado

study[1] /ˈstʌdi/ *n* (*pl* **-dies**) **1** [U] (act, process of learning) estudio *m* **2 studies** *pl* **(a)** (work of student) estudios *mpl* **(b)** (academic discipline): **business studies** empresariado *m or* (Esp) empresariales *fpl*; **social studies** *estudios vinculados a las relaciones sociales que comprenden cursos de historia, sociología y otras asignaturas afines* **3** [C] (room) estudio *m* **4** [C] (investigation, examination) estudio *m* **5** [C] (Art, Liter, Mus) estudio *m*

study² **-dies, -dying, -died** *vt* **(a)** (at school, university) estudiar **(b)** (investigate, research into) estudiar **(c)** (examine, scrutinize) estudiar ■ **~** *vi* estudiar; **she's ~ing to be a doctor/lawyer** estudia medicina/derecho

stuff¹ /stʌf/ *n* [U] **1** (colloq) **(a)** (substance, matter): **what's this ~ called?** ¿cómo se llama esto *or* (fam) esta cosa? **(b)** (miscellaneous items) cosas *fpl*; (personal items) cosas *fpl*, bártulos *mpl*; (junk, rubbish) cachivaches *mpl*; **and ~ like that** y cosas de ésas; **what sort of ~ does he write?** ¿qué tipo de cosa(s) escribe? **2** (nonsense, excuse) (colloq): **surely you don't believe all that ~ he tells you?** tú no te creerás todo lo que te cuenta ¿no?

stuff² *vt* **1 (a)** (fill) ‹*quilt/mattress/toy*› rellenar; ‹*hole*› tapar; **the drawer as ~ed with clothes** el cajón estaba atiborrado de ropa; ***to ~ oneself/one's face*** (colloq) darse* un atracón (fam), ponerse* morado *or* ciego (Esp fam) **(b)** (Culin) rellenar **(c)** (in taxidermy) disecar* **2 (a)** (thrust) **to ~ sth** INTO **sth** meter algo EN algo **(b)** (put) (colloq) poner*

stuffed /stʌft/ *adj* **(a)** (in taxidermy) disecado; (toy) de peluche **(b)** ‹*pepper/tomatoes*› relleno

stuffing /'stʌfɪŋ/ *n* [U] relleno *m*

stuffy /'stʌfi/ *adj* **-fier, -fiest 1 (a)** ‹*air*› viciado; **it's ~ in here** está muy cargado el ambiente **(b)** ‹*nose*› tapado **2** (staid) (colloq) ‹*person*› acartonado, estirado (fam); ‹*organization*› convencional

stumble /'stʌmbəl/ *vi* **(a)** (trip) tropezar*, dar* un traspié **(b)** (in speech) atrancarse*; **he ~d over the long words** se atrancaba la lengua con las palabras largas

• **stumble across** ⇒ STUMBLE ON

• **stumble on**, **stumble upon** [*v* + *prep* + *o*] dar* con, encontrar*

stumbling block /'stʌmblɪŋ/ *n* escollo *m*

stump¹ /stʌmp/ *n* (of tree) tocón *m*, cepa *f*; (of limb) muñón *m*; (of pencil, candle) cabo *m*

stump² *vt* (colloq) (*often pass*): **the problem has me ~ed** el problema me tiene perplejo; **to be ~ed for an answer** no saber qué contestar

stun /stʌn/ *vt* **-nn- (a)** (make unconscious) dejar sin sentido; (daze) aturdir **(b)** (amaze) dejar atónito *or* (fam) helado; (shock) dejar anonadado

stung /stʌŋ/ *past & past p of* STING²

stunk /stʌŋk/ *past p of* STINK²

stunned /stʌnd/ *adj* **(a)** (unconscious) sin sentido; (dazed) aturdido **(b)** (shocked, amazed) ‹*expression*› de asombro; **he was ~ when they told him** se quedó atónito *or* (fam) helado cuando se lo dijeron

stunning /'stʌnɪŋ/ *adj* ‹*success/performance*› sensacional; ‹*person/dress*› despampanante

stunt¹ /stʌnt/ *n* **1** (feat of daring) proeza *f*; **she does all her own ~s** (Cin, TV) hace todas las escenas peligrosas ella misma; (*before n*) **~ man/woman** especialista *mf* **2** (hoax, trick) truco *m*, maniobra *f*; (*publicity ~*) ardid *m* publicitario

stunt² *vt* detener*, atrofiar

stunted /'stʌntəd ‖ 'stʌntɪd/ *adj* ‹*growth/development*› atrofiado; ‹*tree/body*› raquítico

stupefy /'stu:pəfaɪ ‖ 'stju:pɪfaɪ/ *vt* **-fies, -fying, -fied** (*usu pass*) dejar estupefacto

stupendous /stu:'pendəs ‖ stju:'pendəs/ *adj* (colloq) ‹*effort/strength*› tremendo; ‹*success*› formidable

stupid /'stu:pəd ‖ 'stju:pɪd/ *adj* (foolish) tonto (fam); (unintelligent) estúpido

stupidity /stu:'pɪdəti ‖ stju:'pɪdəti/ *n* [U] estupidez *f*, tontería *f*

stupor /'stu:pər ‖ 'stju:pə(r)/ *n* [U] (Med) estupor *m*; (lethargy) aletargamiento *m*; **in a drunken ~** en un sopor etílico (frml *o* hum)

sturdy /'stɜ:rdi ‖ 'stɜ:di/ *adj* **-dier, -diest** ‹*build/legs/figure*› robusto, macizo; ‹*furniture/bicycle*› sólido y resistente

stutter¹ /'stʌtər ‖ 'stʌtə(r)/ *n* tartamudeo *m*

stutter² *vi* tartamudear ■ **~** *vt* balbucear, decir* tartamudeando

St Valentine's Day ⇒ VALENTINE'S DAY

sty /staɪ/ *n* (*pl* **sties**) **(a)** (*pig~*) pocilga *f*, chiquero *m* (AmL) **(b)** ⇒ STYE

stye /staɪ/ *n* (*pl* **sties** *or* **styes**) orzuelo *m*

style /staɪl/ *n* **1** [C U] **(a)** (manner of acting) estilo *m*; **telling lies is not my ~** decir mentiras no va conmigo **(b)** (Art, Lit, Mus) estilo *m* **2** [U] (elegance) estilo *m*; **to live/travel in ~** vivir/viajar a lo grande **3 (a)** [C] (type, model) diseño *m*, modelo *m* **(b)** [U C] (fashion) moda *f*; **to be in ~** estar* de moda **(c)** [C] (*hair ~*) peinado *m*

-style /staɪl/ *suff*: **American~** al estilo americano, a la americana

stylish /'staɪlɪʃ/ *adj* ‹*furniture/clothes/decor*› con mucho estilo; ‹*person*› con clase *or* estilo, estiloso (AmL fam); ‹*resort/restaurant*› elegante

stylist /'staɪləst ‖ 'staɪlɪst/ *n* (*hair ~*) estilista *mf*

stylistic /staɪ'lɪstɪk/ *adj* estilístico

stylized /'staɪlaɪzd/ *adj* estilizado

stylus /'staɪləs/ *n* (*pl* **-li** *or* **-luses**) aguja *f*, púa *f* (RPl)

Styrofoam® /'staɪrəfəʊm/ *n* [U] (AmE) espuma *f* de poliestireno

suave /swɑ:v/ *adj* **suaver, suavest** ‹*voice*› engolado; ‹*man*› elegante y desenvuelto

sub /sʌb/ *n* (colloq) **(a)** (substitute) suplente *mf*, sustituto, -ta *m,f* **(b)** (submarine) submarino *m* **(c) subs** *pl* (subscription) cuota *f*

subconscious¹ /'sʌb'kɑ:ntʃəs ‖ sʌb'kɒnʃəs/ *adj* subconsciente

subconscious² *n* **the ~** el subconsciente

subcontract /ˌsʌb'kɑ:ntrækt ‖ ˌsʌbkən'trækt/ *vt* subcontratar

subcontractor /sʌb'kɑ:ntræktər ‖ ˌsʌbkən'træktə(r)/ *n* subcontratista *mf*

subdivide /'sʌbdə'vaɪd ‖ ˌsʌbdɪ'vaɪd/ *vt* subdividir

subdivision /'sʌbdə'vɪʒən ‖ ˌsʌbdɪ'vɪʒən/ *n* [U C] subdivisión *f*

subdue /səb'du: ‖ səb'dju:/ *vt* **(a)** (bring under control) ‹*person*› someter, dominar **(b)** (vanquish) (liter) sojuzgar* (liter)

subdued /səb'du:d ‖ səb'dju:d/ *adj* ‹*lighting/color*› tenue, apagado; ‹*person/atmosphere*› apagado

subheading /'sʌb,hedɪŋ/ *n* subtítulo *m*

subject¹ /'sʌbdʒɪkt/ *n* **1** (topic) tema *m*; **to change the ~** cambiar de tema **2** (discipline) asignatura *f*, materia *f* (esp AmL), ramo *m* (Chi) **3** (Pol) súbdito, -ta *m,f* **4** (Ling) sujeto *m*

subject² /'sʌbdʒɪkt/ *adj* **1** (owing obedience) ‹*people/nation*› sometido **2 (a)** (liable, prone) **to be ~ TO sth** ‹*to change/delay*› estar* sujeto A algo, ser* susceptible DE algo; ‹*to flooding*› estar* expuesto A algo **(b)** (conditional upon) **to be ~ TO sth** estar* sujeto A algo

subject³ /səb'dʒekt/ *vt* **to ~ sth/sb TO sth** someter algo/a algn A algo

subject index *n* índice *m* de materias

subjective /səb'dʒektɪv/ *adj* subjetivo

subject matter *n* [U] (theme) tema *m*; (content) contenido *m*

subjugate /'sʌbdʒəgeɪt ‖ 'sʌbdʒʊgeɪt/ *vt* subyugar*

subjunctive¹ /səb'dʒʌŋktɪv/ *n* subjuntivo *m*

subjunctive² *adj* subjuntivo

sublet /'sʌb'let/ *vt/i* (*pres p* **-letting**; *past & past p* **-let**) subarrendar*

sublime /sə'blaɪm/ *adj* sublime

submachine gun /'sʌbmə'ʃi:n/ *n* metralleta *f*

submarine /'sʌbmə'ri:n/ *n* submarino *m*

submerge /səb'mɜ:rdʒ ‖ səb'mɜ:dʒ/ *vt* **(a)** (cover, flood) sumergir* **(b)** (plunge) **to ~ sth IN sth** sumergir* algo EN algo ■ **~** *vi* sumergirse*

submission /səb'mɪʃən/ *n* **1** [U] (surrender) sumisión *f* **2** [C] (plan, proposal) propuesta *f*

submissive /səb'mɪsɪv/ *adj* sumiso

submit /səb'mɪt/ **-tt-** *vt* **1** ‹*claim/report/application*› presentar **2** (subject) **to ~ sb TO sth** someter a algn A algo **3** (contend) sostener* ■ **~** *vi* rendirse*

subnormal /'sʌb'nɔ:rməl ‖ sʌb'nɔ:məl/ *adj* por debajo de lo normal; ‹*person*› retrasado, subnormal

subordinate¹ /sə'bɔ:rdn̩ət ‖ sə'bɔ:dɪnət/ *adj* subordinado

subordinate² *n* subordinado, -da *m,f*

subscribe /səb'skraɪb/ *vi* **1** (buy) **to ~ (TO sth)** ‹*to magazine/newspaper*› suscribirse* (A algo) **2** (support) **to ~ TO sth** suscribir* algo (frml); **I ~ to the view that** ... yo soy de la opinión de que ...

subscriber /səb'skraɪbər ‖ səb'skraɪbə(r)/*n* (to paper, magazine) suscriptor, -tora *m,f*

subscription /səb'skrɪpʃən/ *n* **(a)** (to magazine) suscripción *f*; (for theatrical events) abono *m* **(b)** (membership fees) (BrE) cuota *f*

subsequent /'sʌbsɪkwənt/ *adj* (*before n*) posterior, subsiguiente

subsequently /'sʌbsɪkwəntli/ *adv* posteriormente

subservient /səb'sɜ:rviənt ‖ səb'sɜ:viənt/ *adj* servil

subside /səb'saɪd/ *vi* **1** «*land/road/foundations*» hundirse **2** (abate) «*storm/wind*» amainar; «*floods/swelling*» decrecer*, bajar; «*excitement*» decaer*; «*anger*» calmarse, pasarse

subsidence /səb'saɪdn̩s, 'sʌbsədn̩s ‖ səb'saɪdn̩s, 'sʌbsɪdəns/ *n* [U] hundimiento *m*

subsidiary¹ /səb'sɪdieri ‖ səb'sɪdiəri/ *adj* ‹*role/interest*› secundario; **~ subject** materia *f* complementaria

subsidiary² *n* (*pl* **-ries**) (Busn) filial *f*

subsidize /'sʌbsədaɪz ‖ 'sʌbsɪdaɪz/ *vt* subvencionar, subsidiar (AmL)

subsidy /'sʌbsədi ‖ 'sʌbsɪdi/ *n* (*pl* **-dies**) subvención *f*, subsidio *m*

subsist /səb'sɪst/ *vi* subsistir

subsistence /səb'sɪstəns/ *n* [U] subsistencia *f*; (*before n*) ‹*farming*› de subsistencia; **~ wage** sueldo *m* de hambre; **to live at ~ level** vivir con lo justo para subsistir

substance /'sʌbstəns/ *n* **1** [C] (type of matter) sustancia *f* **2** [U] **(a)** (solid quality, content) sustancia *f*; (of book) enjundia *f*, sustancia *f* **(b)** (foundation) fundamento *m* **(c) in ~** en lo esencial

substandard /'sʌb'stændərd ‖ ,sʌb'stændəd/ *adj* ‹*goods/clothes*› de calidad inferior

substantial /səb'stæntʃəl ‖ səb'stænʃəl/ *adj* **1 (a)** ‹*amount/income/loan*› considerable, importante **(b)** ‹*changes/difference*› sustancial; ‹*contribution*› importante **2 (a)** (sturdy, solid) ‹*furniture/building*› sólido **(b)** (nourishing, filling) ‹*meal*› sustancioso

substantiate /səb'stæntʃieɪt ‖ səb'stænʃieɪt/ *vt* ‹*rumors/story/statement*› confirmar, corroborar; **can you ~ these accusations?** ¿puede probar estas acusaciones?

substation /'sʌbsteɪʃən/ *n* (AmE) estafeta *f* de correos

substitute¹ /'sʌbstətu:t ‖ 'sʌbstɪtju:t/ *n* **(a)** (thing) **~ (FOR sth)** sucedáneo *m* (DE algo); **sugar ~** sucedáneo *m* del azúcar; **there's no ~ for experience** nada puede sustituir a la experiencia **(b)** (person) sustituto, -ta *m,f*, reemplazo *m*, suplente *mf*

substitute² *vt* sustituir*, reemplazar*

substitute teacher *n* (AmE) (profesor, -sora *m,f*) suplente *mf*

substitution /'sʌbstə'tu:ʃən ‖ ,sʌbstɪ'tju:ʃən/ *n* [U C] sustitución *f*

subterfuge /'sʌbtərfju:dʒ ‖ 'sʌbtəfju:dʒ/ *n* [C U] subterfugio *m*

subterranean /'sʌbtə'remiən/ *adj* subterráneo

subtitle¹ /'sʌb,taɪtl̩/ *n* subtítulo *m*

subtitle² *vt* (*usu pass*) subtitular

subtle /'sʌtl̩/ *adj* **subtler** /'sʌtl̩ər ‖ 'sʌtl̩ə(r)/, **subtlest** /'sʌtl̩əst ‖ 'sʌtlɪst/ **(a)** (delicate, elusive) ‹*fragrance*› sutil **(b)** (not obvious) ‹*difference/distinction/hint*› sutil; ‹*change*› imperceptible **(c)** (tactful) (colloq) delicado

subtlety /'sʌtl̩ti/ *n* (*pl* **-ties**) **(a)** [U C] (delicacy, elusiveness) sutileza *f* **(b)** [U] (tact, finesse) delicadeza *f*; **to lack ~** ser* poco delicado

subtly /'sʌtli/ *adv* **(a)** (delicately, elusively) sutilmente **(b)** (tactfully) con delicadeza

subtotal /'sʌbtəʊtl̩/ *n* subtotal *m*, total *m* parcial

subtract /səb'trækt/ *vt* **to ~ sth (FROM sth)** restar algo (DE algo)

subtraction /səb'trækʃən/ *n* [U C] resta *f*, sustracción *f* (frml)

suburb /'sʌbɜːrb ‖ 'sʌbɜːb/ *n* barrio *m* *or* (Méx) colonia *f* residencial de las afueras; **the ~s** los barrios periféricos *or* de las afueras (de la ciudad)

suburban /sə'bɜːrbən ‖ sə'bɜːbən/ *adj* ‹*area*› suburbano; ‹*shopping mall*› de las afueras

suburbia /sə'bɜːrbiə ‖ sə'bɜːbiə/ *n* [U] *zonas residenciales de las afueras de una ciudad*

subversive /səb'vɜːrsɪv ‖ səb'vɜːsɪv/ *adj* subversivo

subway /'sʌbweɪ/ *n* **1** [C U] (AmE Rail) metro *m*, subterráneo *m* (RPl) **2** [C] (BrE) (for pedestrians) pasaje *m* subterráneo

succeed /sək'siːd/ *vi* **1** (have success) «*plan*» dar* resultado, surtir efecto; **she tried to persuade him, but did not ~** intentó convencerlo pero no lo consiguió; **he's ~ed in all that he's done** ha tenido éxito en todo lo que ha hecho; **to ~ in life** triunfar en la vida; **he finally ~ed in passing the exam** al final logró aprobar el examen **2** **to ~** (TO **sth**): **he ~ed to the throne** subió al trono; **to ~ to a title** heredar un título ■ **~** *vt* suceder; **who ~ed him?** ¿quién lo sucedió?

succeeding /sək'siːdɪŋ/ *adj* (*before n*) subsiguiente

success /sək'ses/ *n* [C U] éxito *m*; **to be a ~** ser* un éxito; **without ~** sin (ningún) éxito

successful /sək'sesfəl/ *adj* ‹*person*› de éxito, exitoso (AmL); **the ~ applicant for the job** el candidato que obtenga el puesto; **to be ~ in life** triunfar en la vida

successfully /sək'sesfəli/ *adv* satisfactoriamente

succession /sək'seʃən/ *n* **1** **(a)** [U] (act of following) sucesión *f*; **for 6 years in ~** durante seis años consecutivos; **in rapid ~** uno tras otro **(b)** [C] (series) sucesión *f* **2** [U] (to office, rank) sucesión *f*

successive /sək'sesɪv/ *adj* (*before n*) consecutivo

successor /sək'sesər ‖ sək'sesə(r)/ *n* sucesor, -sora *m,f*

succinct /sək'sɪŋkt/ *adj* sucinto, conciso

succulent /'sʌkjələnt ‖ 'sʌkjʊlənt/ *adj* suculento

succumb /sə'kʌm/ *vi* **to ~** (TO **sth**) sucumbir (A algo)

such[1] /sʌtʃ/ *adj* **1** **(a)** (emphasizing degree, extent) tal (+ *noun*); tan (+ *adj*); **I woke up with ~ a headache** me levanté con tal dolor de cabeza ...; **I've got ~ a lot of work to do** tengo tanto (trabajo) que hacer; **I've never heard ~ nonsense** nunca he oído semejante estupidez **(b)** (*with clauses of result or purpose*) **such** ... **(that)** tal/tan ... que **(c)** (*in comparisons*) **such** ... **as** tan ... como **2** **(a)** (of this, that kind) tal; **~ children are known as** ... a dichos *or* a tales niños se los conoce como ...; **there's no ~ thing as the perfect crime** el crimen perfecto no existe; **I said no ~ thing!** ¡yo no dije tal cosa! **(b)** (unspecified) tal; **the letter tells you to go to ~ a house on ~ a date** la carta te dice que vayas a tal casa en tal fecha

such[2] *pron* **1** **(a)** (of the indicated kind) tal; **~ were her last words** tales fueron sus últimas palabras **(b)** **such as** como; **many modern inventions, ~ as radar** ... muchos inventos modernos, (tales) como el radar ... **(c)** **as such** como tal/tales **2** (indicating lack of quantity, quality): **the evidence, ~ as it is, seems to** ... las pocas pruebas que hay parecen ... **3** (of such a kind, extent, degree) **such that** tal ... que

such: **~-and-~** *adj* tal (o cual); **we were told to get ~-and-~ a book** nos dijeron que compráramos tal (o cual) libro; **~like** *pron* (colloq) (of things) cosas por el estilo; (of people) gente por el estilo

suck /sʌk/ *vt* **(a)** «*person*» ‹*thumb/candy*› chupar; ‹*liquid*› (through a straw) sorber; «*vacuum cleaner*» aspirar; «*pump*» succionar, aspirar; «*insect*» ‹*blood/nectar*› chupar **(b)** (pull, draw) (+ *adv compl*) arrastrar; **she was ~ed under by the current** la corriente se la tragó ■ **~** *vi* **1** «*person*» chupar; **to ~** AT/ON **sth** chupar algo **2** (be objectionable) (AmE sl): **the movie really ~s** la película es una mierda (vulg)

• **suck in** [*v* + *o* + *adv*, *v* + *adv* + *o*] ‹*air/breath*› tomar

sucker /'sʌkər ‖ 'sʌkə(r)/ *n* **1** (colloq) (fool) (pej) imbécil *mf*; ***to be a ~ for punishment*** ser* un masoquista **2** (suction device — on animal, plant) ventosa *f*; (— made of rubber) (BrE) ventosa *f* **3** (Bot) (shoot) chupón *m*, mamón *m*

suckle /'sʌkəl/ *vt* amamantar, darle* de mamar a ■ **~** *vi* mamar

suction /'sʌkʃən/ *n* [U] succión *f*; (*before n*) **~ cup** ventosa *f*

Sudan /suː'dɑːn/ *n* **(the) ~** (el) Sudán

Sudanese /'suːdn̩'iːz ‖ ˌsuːdə'niːz/ *adj* sudanés

sudden /'sʌdn̩/ *adj* **(a)** (rushed) repentino, súbito; (unexpected) imprevisto, inesperado; ***all of a ~*** de repente, de pronto **(b)** (abrupt) ‹*movement*› brusco

suddenly /'sʌdn̩li/ *adv* **(a)** (unexpectedly) de repente, de pronto **(b)** (abruptly) bruscamente

suds /sʌdz/ *pl n* espuma *f* de jabón

sue /suː ‖ suː, sjuː/ *vt* **to ~ sb** (FOR **sth**) demandar a algn (POR algo) ■ **~** *vi* (Law) entablar una demanda, poner* pleito (Esp)

suede /sweɪd/ *n* [U] ante *m*, gamuza *f*

suet /'suːət ‖ 'suːɪt, 'sjuːɪt/ *n* [U] sebo *m*, grasa *f* de pella

suffer /'sʌfər ‖ 'sʌfə(r)/ *vt* **(a)** (undergo) ‹*injury/damage/loss*› sufrir; ‹*pain*› padecer*, sufrir **(b)** (endure) aguantar, tolerar ■ **~** *vi* **(a)** (experience pain, difficulty) sufrir **(b)** (be affected, deteriorate) «*health/eyesight*» resentirse*; «*business/relationship*» verse* afectado, resentirse* **(c)** (be afflicted) **to ~** FROM **sth** sufrir *or* (frml) padecer* DE algo

sufferer /'sʌfərər ‖ 'sʌfərə(r)/ *n* **~s from arthritis, arthritis ~s** quienes sufren de artritis, los artríticos

suffering /'sʌfərɪŋ/ *n* [U] sufrimiento *m*

suffice /sə'faɪs/ *vi* (frml) bastar, ser* suficiente

sufficient /sə'fɪʃənt/ *adj* suficiente, bastante

sufficiently /sə'fɪʃəntli/ *adv* lo suficientemente

suffix /'sʌfɪks/ *n* sufijo *m*

suffocate /'sʌfəkeɪt/ *vt* asfixiar, ahogar* ■ ~ *vi* asfixiarse, ahogarse*

suffocating /'sʌfəkeɪtɪŋ/ *adj* ‹*smoke/routine*› asfixiante; ‹*heat*› sofocante

suffocation /'sʌfə'keɪʃən/ *n* [U] asfixia *f*

suffrage /'sʌfrɪdʒ/ *n* sufragio *m*

sugar /'ʃʊgər ‖ 'ʃʊgə(r)/ *n* [U C] azúcar *m or f*; (*before n*) **~ bowl** azucarero *m*, azucarera *f* (esp AmL); **~ cube** *o* **lump** terrón *m* de azúcar

sugar: **~ beet** *n* [C U] remolacha *f* azucarera *or* (Méx) betabel *m* blanco; **~ cane** *n* [C U] caña *f* de azúcar

sugary /'ʃʊgəri/ *adj* **(a)** ‹*drink/taste*› dulce, azucarado **(b)** ‹*tones/smile*› meloso, almibarado

suggest /səg'dʒest ‖ sə'dʒest/ *vt* **1 (a)** (propose) sugerir*; **to ~ sth** TO **sb** sugerirle* algo A algn; **to ~** -ING sugerir* + INF, sugerir* QUE (+ *subj*); **to ~** TO **sb** THAT sugerirle* a algn QUE (+ *subj*) **(b)** (offer for consideration): **can you ~ a possible source for this rumor?** ¿se le ocurre quién puede haber empezado este rumor? **(c)** (imply, insinuate) insinuar*; **are you ~ing (that) my son is a thief?** ¿insinúa usted que mi hijo es un ladrón? **2** (indicate, point to) indicar* **3** (evoke, bring to mind) sugerir*

suggestion /səg'dʒestʃən ‖ sə'dʒestʃən/ *n* **1 (a)** [C U] (proposal) sugerencia *f*; **to make a ~** hacer* una sugerencia; **have you any ~s for speeding up the process?** ¿se le ocurre algo para acelerar el proceso? **(b)** [C] (explanation, theory) teoría *f* **(c)** [C] (insinuation) insinuación *f* **2** [C U] (indication, hint) indicio *m* **3** [U] (Psych) sugestión *f*

suggestive /səg'dʒestɪv ‖ sə'dʒestɪv/ *adj* **1** ‹*gesture/laugh*› insinuante, provocativo **2** (*pred*) **to be ~** OF **sth (a)** (indicative) parecer* indicar algo **(b)** (reminiscent) hacer* pensar EN algo, evocar* algo

suicidal /'su:ə'saɪdl ‖ ˌsu:ɪ'saɪdl, ˌsju:-/ *adj* suicida

suicide /'su:əsaɪd ‖ 'su:ɪsaɪd, 'sju:-/ *n* [U C] (act) suicidio *m*; **to commit ~** suicidarse; (*before n*) ‹*attempt/pact*› de suicidio; ‹*mission/bombing*› suicida; **~ note** carta *f* de despedida de un suicida

suit[1] /su:t ‖ su:t, sju:t/ *n* **1** (Clothing) (male) traje *m*, terno (AmS); (female) traje *m* (de chaqueta), traje *m* sastre **2** (Law) juicio *m*, pleito *m* **3** (in cards) palo *m*; ***to follow ~*** seguir* su (*or* nuestro *etc*) ejemplo

suit[2] *vt* **1** (be convenient to, please) venirle* bien a, convenirle* a; ***to ~ oneself*** hacer* lo que uno quiere; **~ yourself!** ¡haz lo que quieras! **2 (a)** (be appropriate, good for): **the job doesn't ~ him** el trabajo no es para él *or* no le va **(b)** (look good on) «*hairstyle/dress*» quedarle *or* (esp Esp) irle* bien a; *see also* SUITED **3** (adapt) **to ~ sth** TO **sth/sb** adaptar algo A algo/algn

suitable /'su:təbəl ‖ 'su:təbəl, 'sju:-/ *adj* **(a)** (appropriate) apropiado, adecuado; **(to be) ~** FOR **sb/sth/-ING** (ser*) apropiado *or* adecuado PARA algn/algo/+ INF **(b)** (acceptable, proper) apropiado **(c)** (convenient) conveniente

suitably /'su:təbli ‖ 'su:təbli, 'sju:-/ *adv* ‹*qualified*› adecuadamente; ‹*dressed/equipped*› apropiadamente

suitcase /'su:tkeɪs ‖ 'su:tkeɪs, 'sju:-/ *n* maleta *f*, valija *f* (RPl), petaca *f* (Méx)

suite /swi:t/ *n* **(a)** (of rooms) suite *f* **(b)** (of furniture) juego *m* **(c)** (Mus) suite *f*

suited /'su:təd ‖ 'su:tɪd, 'sju:/ *adj* (*pred*) **to be ~** TO **sth** «*thing*» ser* apropiado *or* adecuado PARA algo; **I'm not ~ to this type of work** no sirvo para este tipo de trabajo; **they are very well ~ (to each other)** están hechos el uno para el otro

suitor /'su:tər ‖ 'su:tə(r), 'sju:-/ *n* (dated) pretendiente *m*

sulfur, (BrE) **sulphur** /'sʌlfər ‖ 'sʌlfə(r)/ *n* [U] azufre *m*

sulk /sʌlk/ *vi* enfurruñarse

sulky /'sʌlki/ *adj* **-kier, -kiest** ‹*child*› con tendencia a enfurruñarse; ‹*look/reply*› malhumorado

sullen /'sʌlən/ *adj* hosco, huraño

sultan /'sʌltn̩/ *n* sultán *m*

sultana /sʌl'tænə ‖ sʌl'tɑ:nə/ *n* (Culin) pasa *f* sultana *or* de Esmirna

sultry /'sʌltri/ *adj* **-trier, -triest (a)** ‹*climate/day*› bochornoso **(b)** ‹*voice/smile/person*› seductor

sum /sʌm/ *n* **1** (calculation — in general) cuenta *f*; (— addition) suma *f*, adición *f* (frml) **2** (total, aggregate) suma *f*, total *m* **3** (of money) suma *f or* cantidad *f* (de dinero)

• sum up: **-mm- 1** [*v* + *o* + *adv*, *v* + *adv* + *o*] **(a)** (summarize) ‹*discussion/report*› resumir **(b)** (assess) ‹*person*› catalogar*; **she quickly ~med up the situation** enseguida se hizo una composición de lugar **2** [*v* + *adv*] **(a)** (summarize) recapitular; **to ~ up** (*as linker*) resumiendo, en resumen **(b)** (Law) recapitular

summarize /'sʌməraɪz/ *vt* resumir

summary[1] /'sʌməri/ *n* (*pl* **-ries**) resumen *m*

summary[2] *adj* ‹*dismissal*› inmediato; ‹*trial/judgment*› sumario

summer /'sʌmər ‖ 'sʌmə(r)/ *n* verano *m*; **in (the) ~** en (el) verano; (*before n*) ‹*weather/clothes/vacation*› de verano; **~ camp** (in US) colonia *f* de vacaciones

summer: **~house** *n* cenador *m*; **~ school** *n* (in US) clases *fpl* de verano (*gen de repaso*); (in UK) curso *m* de verano; **~time** *n* verano *m*, estío *m* (liter); **~ time** *n* [U] (BrE) horario *m* de verano

summery /'sʌməri/ *adj* veraniego, de verano

summing-up /'sʌmɪŋ'ʌp/ *n* (*pl* **summings-up**) recapitulación *f*

summit /'sʌmət ‖ 'sʌmɪt/ *n* **1** (of mountain, career) cumbre *f*, cima *f* **2 ~ (conference)** (conferencia *f*) cumbre *f*

summon /'sʌmən/ *vt* **(a)** (send for) ‹*servant/waiter*› llamar, mandar llamar (AmL); ‹*police/doctor*› llamar; ‹*help/reinforcements*› pedir*; ‹*meeting/parliament*› convocar* **(b)** (Law) ‹*witness/defendant*› citar, emplazar* **(c)** ⇒ SUMMON UP

• summon up [*v* + *adv* + *o*] **(a)** (gather): **he ~ed up the courage to ask her** se armó de valor para preguntárselo; **I couldn't even ~ up the strength to get up the stairs** ni siquiera pude reunir fuerzas para subir la escalera **(b)** (call up) ‹*thoughts/memories*› evocar*

summons¹ /'sʌmənz/ *n* (*pl* **-monses**) **(a)** (Law) citación *f*, citatorio *m* (Méx) **(b)** (for help etc) llamamiento *m*, llamado *m* (AmL)

summons² *vt* (Law) citar, emplazar*

sumptuous /'sʌmptʃuəs ‖ 'sʌmptjʊəs/ *adj* ‹*fabric/color*› suntuoso; ‹*mansion/decor*› lujoso

sun¹ /sʌn/ *n* [C U] sol *m*; ***under the ~*: I've tried everything under the ~** he probado de todo

sun² *v refl* **-nn-**: **to ~ oneself** tomar el sol *or* (CS tb) tomar sol, asolearse (AmL)

sun: **~bathe** *vi* tomar el sol *or* (CS tb) tomar sol, asolearse (AmL); **~beam** *n* rayo *m* de sol; **~bed** *n* cama *f* solar; **~burn** *n* [U] quemadura *f* de sol; **~burned** /'sʌnbɜ:rnd ‖ 'sʌnbɜ:nd/, (BrE also) **~burnt** /'sʌnbɜ:rnt ‖ 'sʌnbɜ:nt/ *adj* **(a)** (painfully) quemado por el sol **(b)** (brown) bronceado, tostado, quemado (AmL), moreno (Esp), asoleado (Méx)

sundae /'sʌndeɪ/ *n* sundae *m* (*helado con fruta, crema, jarabe etc*)

Sunday /'sʌndeɪ, '-di/ **▶ 540** *n* domingo *m*; (*before n*) **~ school** *sesiones dominicales de catequesis para niños*; *see also* MONDAY

sun: **~dial** *n* reloj *m* de sol; **~down** *n* (*no art*) puesta *f* de(l) sol; **~dress** *n* vestido *m* de tirantes, solera *f* (CS)

sundries /'sʌndriz/ *pl n* **(a)** (goods) artículos *mpl* diversos **(b)** (expenses) gastos *mpl* varios

sundry¹ /'sʌndri/ *adj* varios, diversos

sundry² *pron*: **all and ~** todos sin excepción, todo el mundo

sunflower /'sʌnflaʊr ‖ 'sʌnflaʊə(r)/ *n* girasol *m*; (*before n*) **~ oil** aceite *m* de girasol; **~ seed** semilla *f* de girasol, pipa *f* (Esp)

sung /sʌŋ/ *past p of* SING

sunglasses /'sʌn,glæsəz ‖ 'sʌn,glɑ:sɪz/ *pl n* gafas *fpl or* (esp AmL) lentes *mpl or* anteojos *mpl* de sol

sunk¹ /sʌŋk/ *past p of* SINK¹

sunk² *adj* (*pred*) **(a)** (in trouble) (colloq) **to be ~** estar* perdido **(b)** (immersed) **to be ~ IN sth** ‹*in depression/gloom*› estar* sumido EN algo (liter)

sunken /'sʌŋkən/ *adj* **(a)** (*before n*) ‹*ship/treasure*› hundido, sumergido **(b)** (*before n*) ‹*garden/patio*› a nivel más bajo **(c)** (hollow) ‹*eyes/cheeks*› hundido

sun: **~ lamp** *n* lámpara *f* de rayos ultravioletas; **~light** *n* [U] sol *m*, luz *f* del sol; **~lit** *adj* soleado

sunny /'sʌni/ *adj* **-nier, -niest (a) ▶ 920** ‹*day*› de sol; ‹*room/garden*› soleado; **it's ~ today** hoy hace sol **(b)** (good-humored) alegre

sun: **~rise** *n* salida *f* del sol; **~roof** *n* techo *m* corredizo; **~screen** *n* filtro *m* solar; **~set** *n* puesta *f* de(l) sol; **at ~set** al atardecer, a la caída de la tarde; **~shine** *n* [U] sol *m*; **~spot** *n* **(a)** (Astron) mancha *f* solar **(b)** (resort) (colloq) *lugar de veraneo con mucho sol*; **~stroke** *n* [U] insolación *f*; **~tan** *n* [U C] bronceado *m*, moreno *m* (Esp); **to get a ~tan** broncearse, tostarse*, quemarse (AmL); (*before n*) ‹*lotion*› bronceador; **~trap** *n*: *lugar muy soleado y resguardado*

super /'su:pər ‖ 'su:pə(r)/ *adj* (colloq) genial (fam), súper *adj inv* (fam)

superb /sʊ'pɜ:rb ‖ su:'pɜ:b/ *adj* magnífico, espléndido

supercilious /'su:pər'sɪliəs ‖ ,su:pə'sɪliəs/ *adj* desdeñoso

superficial /'su:pər'fɪʃəl ‖ ,su:pə'fɪʃəl/ *adj* superficial

superfluous /su:'pɜ:rfluəs ‖ su:'pɜ:flʊəs/ *adj* superfluo

superhighway /'su:pər'haɪweɪ ‖ 'su:pə,haɪweɪ/ *n* **(a)** (AmE Auto) autopista *f* **(b)** (Comput): **the information ~** la autopista de la comunicación

superhuman /'su:pər'hju:mən ‖ ,su:pə'hju:mən/ *adj* sobrehumano

superimpose /'su:pərɪm'pəʊz/ *vt* superponer*

superintend /'su:pərɪn'tend/ *vt* supervisar

superintendent /'su:pərɪn'tendənt/ *n* **(a)** (person in charge — of maintenance, hostel, swimming pool) encargado, -da *m,f*; (— of building) (AmE) portero, -ra *m,f*; (— of institution) director, -tora *m,f* **(b)** (police officer) (in US) superintendente *mf* (*jefe de un departamento de policía*); (in UK) comisario, -ria *m,f* de policía

superior¹ /sʊ'pɪriər ‖ su:'pɪəriə(r)/ *adj* **1 (a)** (better) **to be ~ (TO sth/sb)** ser* superior (A algo/algn), ser* mejor (QUE algo/algn) **(b)** (above average) ‹*workmanship/writer*› de gran calidad **2** (arrogant) ‹*tone/smile*› de superioridad; **he's so ~** se da unos aires de superioridad **3** ‹*rank*› superior; **his ~ officer** su superior

superior² *n* superior *m*

superiority /sʊ'pɪri'ɔ:rəti ‖ su:,pɪəri'ɒrəti/ *n* [U] superioridad *f*

superlative¹ /sʊ'pɜ:rlətɪv ‖ su:'pɜ:lətɪv/ *adj* inigualable, excepcional

superlative² *n* superlativo *m*

superman /'su:pərmæn ‖ 'su:pəmæn/ *n* (*pl* **-men** /-men/) superhombre *m*

supermarket /'su:pər,mɑ:rkət ‖ 'su:pə,mɑ:kɪt/ *n* supermercado *m*, autoservicio *m*

supernatural /'su:pər'nætʃərəl ‖ ,su:pə'nætʃərəl/ *adj* sobrenatural

superpower /'su:pərpaʊər ‖ 'su:pəpaʊə(r)/ *n* superpotencia *f*

supersede /'su:pər'si:d ‖ ,su:pə'si:d/ *vt* (*often pass*) reemplazar*, sustituir*

supersonic /'su:pər'sɑ:nɪk ‖ ,su:pə'sɒnɪk/ *adj* supersónico

superstar /'su:pərstɑ:r ‖ 'su:pəstɑ:(r)/ *n* superestrella *f*, gran estrella *f*

superstition /'su:pər'stɪʃən ‖ ,su:pə'stɪʃən/ *n* [U C] superstición *f*

superstitious /'su:pər'stɪʃəs ‖ ,su:pə'stɪʃəs/ *adj* supersticioso

superstore /'su:pərstɔ:r ‖ 'su:pəstɔ:(r)/ *n* (BrE) hipermercado *m*

supervise /'su:pərvaɪz ‖ 'su:pəvaɪz/ *vt* **(a)** ‹*project/staff*› supervisar **(b)** (watch over) vigilar

supervision /'su:pər'vɪʒən ‖ ,su:pə'vɪʒən/ *n* [U] supervisión *f*

supervisor /'su:pərvaɪzər ‖ 'su:pəvaɪzə(r)/ *n* supervisor, -sora *m,f*

supper /'sʌpər ‖ 'sʌpə(r)/ *n* [U C] cena *f* (*ligera*), comida *f* (*ligera*) (esp AmL); **to have ~** cenar, comer (esp AmL)

supplant /sə'plænt ‖ sə'plɑːnt/ *vt* sustituir*, reemplazar*

supple /'sʌpəl/ *adj* **-pler** /-plər ‖ -plə(r)/, **-plest** /-pləst ‖ -plɪst/ ‹*body/fingers*› ágil; ‹*leather*› fino y flexible, suave

supplement¹ /'sʌpləmənt ‖ 'sʌplɪmənt/ *n* **1** (addition to diet, income) complemento *m* **2 (a)** (additional part published separately) suplemento *m* **(b)** (section of newspaper — separate) suplemento *m*; (— inserted) separata *f*

supplement² /'sʌpləment ‖ 'sʌplɪment/ *vt* ‹*diet/income*› complementar; ‹*report*› completar

supplementary /'sʌplə'mentəri ‖ ˌsʌplɪ'mentəri/ *adj* suplementario

supplier /sə'plaɪər ‖ sə'plaɪə(r)/ *n* (Busn) proveedor, -dora *m,f*, abastecedor, -dora *m,f*

supply¹ /sə'plaɪ/ *n* (*pl* **-plies**) **1** [U] (provision) suministro *m*; **the water/electricity ~** el suministro de agua/electricidad; **the law of ~ and demand** la ley de la oferta y la demanda **2** (stock, store): **food supplies are running low** se están agotando las provisiones *or* los víveres *or* (Mil) los pertrechos; **we only have a month's ~ of coal left** sólo nos queda carbón para un mes; (Busn) las existencias de carbón sólo van a durar un mes; **to be in short ~** escasear

supply² *vt* **-plies, -plying, -plied 1 (a)** (provide, furnish) ‹*electricity/gas*› suministrar; ‹*goods*› suministrar, abastecer* *or* proveer* de; ‹*evidence/information*› proporcionar, facilitar **(b)** ‹*retailer/manufacturer*› abastecer*; **to ~ sb WITH sth** ‹*with equipment*› proveer* a algn DE algo; (Busn) abastecer* a algn DE algo, suministrarle algo A algn; ‹*with information*› facilitarle *or* proporcionarle algo A algn **2** (meet) (frml) ‹*demand/need*› satisfacer*

supply teacher *n* (BrE) (profesor, -sora *m,f*) suplente *mf*

support¹ /sə'pɔːrt ‖ sə'pɔːt/ *vt* **1** (hold up) ‹*bridge/structure*› sostener*; **the chair couldn't ~ his weight** la silla no pudo aguantar *or* resistir su peso **2 (a)** (maintain, sustain) ‹*family*› mantener*; **to ~ oneself** ganarse la vida **(b)** (Comput) admitir **3 (a)** (back) ‹*cause/motion*› apoyar; **what team do you ~?** ¿de qué equipo eres (hincha)? **(b)** (back up) apoyar **4** (corroborate) ‹*theory*› respaldar, confirmar

support² *n* **1 (a)** [C] (of structure) soporte *m* **(b)** [U] (physical): **to lean on sb for ~** apoyarse en algn (para sostenerse) **2 (a)** [U] (financial) ayuda *f* (económica), apoyo *m* (económico) **(b)** [C] (person) sostén *m* **3** [U] (backing, encouragement) apoyo *m* **4** [U] (Mil) apoyo *m*, refuerzo *m* **5 in support of** (*as prep*) en apoyo de

support band *n* grupo *m* telonero

supporter /sə'pɔːrtər ‖ sə'pɔːtə(r)/ *n* **(a)** (adherent) partidario, -ria *m,f* **(b)** (Sport) hincha *mf*

supporting /sə'pɔːrtɪŋ ‖ sə'pɔːtɪŋ/ *adj* (*before n*) ‹*role/actor*› secundario; **~ act** número *m* telonero

supportive /sə'pɔːrtɪv ‖ sə'pɔːtɪv/ *adj*: **she's been very ~** me (*or* lo *etc*) ha apoyado mucho

suppose /sə'pəʊz/ *vt* **1 (a)** (assume, imagine) suponer*, imaginarse; **~ he phones and you're not in** ¿y si llama y tú no estás?; **I ~ so** supongo *or* me imagino que sí; **I ~ not** supongo que no *or* no creo **(b)** (believe, think) creer*; **what do you ~ he'll do?** ¿tú qué crees que hará? **2 to be supposed to** + INF **(a)** (indicating obligation, expectation): **I'm ~d to start work at nine** se supone que tengo que empezar a trabajar a las nueve; **aren't you ~d to be at home?** ¿tú no tendrías que estar en casa? **(b)** (indicating intention): **what's that ~d to be?** ¿y eso qué se supone que es?; **what's that ~d to mean?** ¿y qué quieres (*or* quieren *etc*) decir con eso, (si se puede saber)? **(c)** (indicating general opinion): **it's ~d to be a very interesting book** dicen que es un libro muy interesante

supposing /sə'pəʊzɪŋ/ *conj* **(a)** (expressing hypothesis) suponiendo que; **~ she agrees, will they let us go?** suponiendo que ella esté de acuerdo ¿nos dejarán ir? **(b)** (introducing suggestion) ¿y si ... ?

supposition /'sʌpə'zɪʃən/ *n* [U C] suposición *f*

suppress /sə'pres/ *vt* **(a)** ‹*anger/laughter*› contener*; ‹*feelings*› reprimir **(b)** ‹*facts/evidence/truth*› ocultar **(c)** ‹*revolt*› sofocar*; ‹*organization*› suprimir

suppression /sə'preʃən/ *n* [U] **(a)** (of feelings) represión *f* **(b)** (of evidence) ocultación *f* **(c)** (of revolt) represión *f*

supremacy /sə'preməsi ‖ suː'preməsi, sjuː-/ *n* [U] supremacía *f*

supreme /suː'priːm ‖ suː'priːm, sjuː-/ *adj* supremo

Supreme Court *n* **the ~ ~** el Tribunal Supremo *or* (esp AmL) la Corte Suprema (de Justicia)

surcharge /'sɜːrtʃɑːrdʒ ‖ 'sɜːtʃɑːdʒ/ *n* recargo *m*

sure¹ /ʃʊr ‖ ʃʊə(r), ʃɔː(r)/ *adj* **surer**, **surest 1** (convinced) (*pred*) seguro; **to be ~ ABOUT sth** estar* seguro DE algo; **I'm not ~ I agree with you** no sé si estoy de acuerdo contigo; **I'm not ~ who/why/what** ... no sé muy bien quién/por qué/qué ...; **to be ~ OF sth/sb** estar* seguro DE algo/algn; **I want to be ~ of getting there on time** quiero asegurarme de que voy a llegar a tiempo; **to be ~ of oneself** (convinced one is right) estar* seguro; (self-confident) ser* seguro de sí mismo **2** (certain): **one thing is ~: he's lying** lo que está claro *or* lo que es seguro es que está mintiendo; **it's ~ to rain** seguro que llueve; **to make ~ of sth** asegurarse de algo; **make ~ (that) you're not late** no vayas a llegar tarde **3** (accurate, reliable) ‹*remedy/method*› seguro; ‹*judgment/aim*› certero; ‹*indication*› claro; ‹*ground*› seguro **4** (*in phrases*) **for sure**: **we don't know anything for ~** no sabemos nada seguro *or* con seguridad; **we'll win for ~** seguro que ganamos; **to be sure** (admittedly) (*indep*) por cierto

sure² *adv* **1** (colloq) (*as intensifier*): **she ~ is clever, she's ~ clever** ¡qué lista es!, ¡si será lista!; **do you like it? — I ~ do!** ¿te gusta? — ¡ya lo creo! **2** (of course) por supuesto, claro **3 sure enough** efectivamente, en efecto

sure: **~fire** *adj* (*before n*) ‹*method*› segurísimo, infalible; **~footed** /'ʃʊr'fʊtəd ‖ ˌʃʊə'fʊtɪd, ʃɔː'fʊtɪd/ *adj* ‹*goat/cat*› de pie firme

surely /'ʃʊrli ‖ 'ʃʊəli, 'ʃɔːli/ *adv* **1 (a)** (expressing conviction): **~ the real problem is** ... el verdadero problema, digo yo *or* me parece a mí, es ...; **~ she doesn't mean that!** ¡no puede ser que lo diga en serio! **(b)** (expressing uncertainty): **he must be mistaken, ~?** tiene que estar equivocado ¿no? **(c)** (expressing disbelief): **~ you don't believe that!** ¡no te creerás eso!; **~ not!** ¡no es posible! *or* ¡no puede ser! **2** (undoubtedly, certainly) seguramente, sin duda **3** (gladly, willingly) por supuesto, desde luego

surf¹ /sɜːrf ‖ sɜːf/ *n* [U] **(a)** (waves) olas *fpl* (*rompientes*); (swell) oleaje *m* **(b)** (foam) espuma *f*

surf² *vi* hacer* surf *or* surfing

surface¹ /ˈsɜːrfəs ‖ ˈsɜːfəs/ *n* **1 (a)** (of solid, land) superficie *f*; (*before n*) ‹*wound/mark*› superficial; ‹*resemblance*› superficial **(b)** (of liquid, sea) superficie *f* **(c) on the surface** (superficially) en apariencia **2** (Math) **~ (area)** superficie *f*, área *f*‡

surface² *vi* «*diver/submarine*» salir* a la superficie; «*problems/difficulties*» aflorar, aparecer* ■ ~ *vt* ‹*road*› revestir*, recubrir*; (with asphalt) asfaltar

surfboard /ˈsɜːrfbɔːrd ‖ ˈsɜːfbɔːd/ *n* tabla *f* de surf *or* de surfing

surfeit /ˈsɜːrfət ‖ ˈsɜːfɪt/ *n* (liter) **a ~ OF sth** un exceso *or* (liter) una plétora DE algo

surfer /ˈsɜːrfər ‖ ˈsɜːfə(r)/ *n* surfista *mf*

surfing /ˈsɜːrfɪŋ ‖ ˈsɜːfɪŋ/ *n* [U] surf *m*, surfing *m*

surge¹ /sɜːrdʒ ‖ sɜːdʒ/ *n* (in demand, sales) aumento *m*; **a ~ of people** una oleada de gente; **we felt a new ~ of hope** sentimos renacer nuestras esperanzas

surge² *vi* «*wave*» levantarse; «*sea*» hincharse; **the crowd ~d out through the gates** la gente salió en tropel por las puertas; **anger/hatred ~d up inside her** la ira/el odio la invadió; **to ~ ahead of sb** adelantársele a algn

surgeon /ˈsɜːrdʒən ‖ ˈsɜːdʒən/ *n* cirujano, -na *m,f*

surgery /ˈsɜːrdʒəri ‖ ˈsɜːdʒəri/ *n* (*pl* **-ries**) **1** [U] (science) cirugía *f* **2** (BrE) **(a)** [C] (room) consultorio *m*, consulta *f* **(b)** [C U] (consultation period of doctor) consulta *f*; (*before n*) ‹*times/hours*› de consulta

surgical /ˈsɜːrdʒɪkəl ‖ ˈsɜːdʒɪkəl/ *adj* ‹*instruments/treatment*› quirúrgico; ‹*stocking/appliance*› ortopédico

surgical spirit *n* [U] (BrE) alcohol *m* (*de 90°*)

surly /ˈsɜːrli ‖ ˈsɜːli/ *adj* **-lier, -liest** hosco

surmise /sərˈmaɪz ‖ səˈmaɪz/ *vt* (frml) conjeturar (frml)

surmount /sərˈmaʊnt ‖ səˈmaʊnt/ *vt* superar

surname /ˈsɜːrneɪm ‖ ˈsɜːneɪm/ ▶ 864 *n* apellido *m*

surpass /sərˈpæs ‖ səˈpɑːs/ *vt* superar

surplus¹ /ˈsɜːrpləs ‖ ˈsɜːpləs/ *n* (*pl* **~es**) (of produce, stock) excedente *m*; (of funds) superávit *m*

surplus² *adj* ‹*goods/stocks*› excedente

surprise¹ /səˈpraɪz/ *n* [U C] sorpresa *f*; **to my ~** para mi sorpresa; **to take sb by ~** sorprender a algn, pillar *or* (esp Esp) coger* a algn desprevenido; (*before n*) ‹*gift/visit/attack*› sorpresa *adj inv*

surprise² *vt* **(a)** (astonish) sorprender **(b)** (catch unawares) sorprender, pillar *or* agarrar *or* (esp Esp) coger* desprevenido

surprised /səˈpraɪzd/ *adj* ‹*look*› sorprendido, de sorpresa; **I was so ~** me quedé tan sorprendido; **I'm ~ about** *o* **at that** eso me sorprende mucho; **I'm ~ (THAT)** ... me sorprende *or* me extraña QUE ... (+ *subj*)

surprising /səˈpraɪzɪŋ/ *adj* sorprendente

surprisingly /səˈpraɪzɪŋli/ *adv* **(a)** ‹*quiet/near/good*› sorprendentemente **(b)** (*indep*): **~, she feels no resentment** no está resentida, lo cual es sorprendente

surreal /səˈriːəl/ *adj* surrealista

surrealism /səˈriːəlɪzəm/ *n* [U] surrealismo *m*

surrealist /səˈriːələst ‖ səˈriːəlɪst/ *n* surrealista *mf*; (*before n*) ‹*painter/poem*› surrealista

surrender¹ /səˈrendər ‖ səˈrendə(r)/ *vt* **(a)** (Mil) rendir*, entregar* **(b)** (frml) ‹*document/ticket*› entregar* **(c)** (relinquish) ‹*right/claim*› renunciar a ■ ~ *vi* rendirse*; **to ~ TO sb** entregarse* A algn

surrender² *n* **(a)** [U C] (capitulation) rendición *f*, capitulación *f* **(b)** (frml) (*no pl*) (of passport, document) entrega *f*

surreptitious /ˈsʌrəpˈtɪʃəs/ *adj* furtivo, subrepticio

surrogate¹ /ˈsʌrəgət/ *n* (frml) sustituto *m*

surrogate² *adj* ‹*material*› sucedáneo; **~ mother** madre *f* suplente *or* de alquiler

surround¹ /səˈraʊnd/ *vt* **(a)** (encircle) ‹*place/person*› rodear; **the house is ~ed by trees** la casa está rodeada de árboles **(b)** (Mil) rodear, cercar*

surround² *n* marco *m*

surrounding /səˈraʊndɪŋ/ *adj* (*before n*) ‹*countryside/area*› de alrededor

surroundings /səˈraʊndɪŋz/ *pl n* **(a)** (of town, village) alrededores *mpl* **(b)** (environment) ambiente *m*

surveillance /sərˈveɪləns ‖ ˈsəˈveɪləns/ *n* [U] vigilancia *f*

survey¹ /ˈsɜːrveɪ ‖ ˈsɜːveɪ/ *n* **1 (a)** (of land) inspección *f*, reconocimiento *m*; (for mapping) medición *f* **(b)** (of building) inspección *f*, peritaje *m*, peritación *f*; (written report) informe *m* del perito, peritaje *m*, peritación *f* **2** (overall view) visión *f* general **3** (investigation) estudio *m*; (poll) encuesta *f*, sondeo *m*

survey² /sərˈveɪ ‖ səˈveɪ/ *vt* **1 (a)** ‹*land/region*› (measure) medir*; (inspect) inspeccionar, reconocer*

Spanish surnames

In Spanish-speaking countries people generally use two surnames. The first is the father's surname, the second is the mother's. Thus if Alberto García Rubio and Carmen Haro Santillana have a son called Alejandro, he will be called Alejandro García Haro.

A married woman may choose to keep her maiden name or to use her husband's, preceded by 'de', after her own. Thus Carmen Haro Santillana could be known as:

Carmen Haro Santillana
Carmen Haro de García
Carmen Haro Santillana de García
Señora de García
Señora de García Rubio

(b) ‹*building*› inspeccionar, llevar a cabo un peritaje de **2 (a)** (look at) contemplar, mirar **(b)** (view, consider) ‹*situation/plan/prospects*› examinar, analizar* **3** (question) ‹*group*› encuestar, hacer* un sondeo de

surveyor /sər'veɪər ‖ sə'veɪə(r)/ *n* **(a)** (of land) agrimensor, -sora *m,f*, topógrafo, -fa *m,f* **(b)** (of building) perito, -ta *m,f*

survival /sər'vaɪvəl ‖ sə'vaɪvəl/ *n* [U] (continued existence) sobrevivencia *f*, supervivencia *f*

survive /sər'vaɪv ‖ sə'vaɪv/ *vi* sobrevivir; **her last surviving descendant** su último descendiente vivo; **I can just ~ on $100 a week** con 100 dólares semanales apenas me alcanza para vivir ■ ~ *vt* **1** ‹*accident/crash*› salir* con vida de; ‹*war/earthquake*› sobrevivir a; ‹*experience*› superar **2** (outlive) ‹*person*› sobrevivir

survivor /sər'vaɪvər ‖ sə'vaɪvə(r)/ *n* superviviente *mf*, sobreviviente *mf*

susceptible /sə'septəbəl/ *adj* **~ TO sth** ‹*to colds/infections*› propenso A algo; **he's ~ to a bit of flattery** se le puede persuadir halagándolo

suspect¹ /sə'spekt/ *vt* **1 (a)** (believe guilty) ‹*person*› sospechar de; **we ~ him of lying** sospechamos que miente **(b)** (doubt, mistrust) ‹*sincerity/probity*› dudar de, tener* dudas acerca de **2 (a)** (believe to exist): **they ~ nothing** no sospechan nada; **arson is not ~ed** no existen sospechas de que el incendio haya sido provocado **(b) suspected** *past p*: **a ~ed fracture** una posible fractura; **the ~ed murderer** el presunto asesino **3** (think probable) **to ~ (THAT)** imaginarse QUE

suspect² /'sʌspekt/ *n* sospechoso, -sa *m,f*

suspect³ /'sʌspekt/ *adj* ‹*package/behavior*› sospechoso; ‹*document/evidence*› de dudosa autenticidad

suspend /sə'spend/ *vt* **1** ‹*payment/work*› suspender **2** (debar, ban) suspender; ‹*student*› expulsar temporariamente, suspender (AmL) **3** (hang) (*often pass*) suspender

suspended sentence *n*: *pena de prisión que no se cumple a menos que el delincuente reincida*

suspenders /sə'spendərz ‖ sə'spendəz/ *pl n* (*sometimes sing*) **1** (braces) (AmE) tirantes *mpl or* (RPl) tiradores *mpl or* (Chi) suspensores *mpl or* (Col) cargaderas *fpl* **2** (for stockings, socks) (BrE) ligas *fpl*

suspense /sə'spens/ *n* [U] (in literary work, movie) suspenso *m or* (Esp) suspense *m*; **to keep sb in ~** mantener* a algn sobre ascuas

suspension /sə'spenʃən/ *n* **1** [U C] (cessation) suspensión *f* **2** [C U] (banning, withdrawal) suspensión *f*; (of student) expulsión *f* temporaria, suspensión *f* (AmL) **3** [U] (hanging, being hung) suspensión *f* **4** [U] (Auto) suspensión *f*

suspension: **~ bridge** *n* puente *m* colgante; **~ points** *pl n* (AmE) puntos *mpl* suspensivos

suspicion /sə'spɪʃən/ *n* [C U] (belief) sospecha *f*; (mistrust) desconfianza *f*, recelo *m*; **he's under ~** está bajo sospecha

suspicious /sə'spɪʃəs/ *adj* **(a)** (mistrustful) desconfiado, suspicaz; **to be ~ OF/ABOUT sb/sth** desconfiar* DE algn/algo **(b)** (arousing suspicion) ‹*actions/movements*› sospechoso

suspiciously /sə'spɪʃəsli/ *adv* **(a)** (mistrustfully) ‹*regard/watch*› con desconfianza, con recelo **(b)** (arousing suspicion) ‹*act*› sospechosamente

sustain /sə'steɪn/ *vt* **(a)** ‹*life*› preservar, sustentar; ‹*hope/interest*› mantener*; ‹*pretense/conversation*› mantener*; ‹*effort*› sostener* **(b)** (suffer) ‹*injury/loss/defeat*› sufrir

sustainable /sə'steɪnəbəl/ *adj* sostenible

sustained /sə'steɪnd/ *adj* ‹*efforts*› sostenido

sustenance /'sʌstənəns/ *n* [U] alimento *m*, sustento *m*

SW (= **southwest**) SO

swab¹ /swɑːb ‖ swɒb/ *n* **(a)** (of cotton, gauze) hisopo *m* húmedo **(b)** (specimen) muestra *f*, frotis *m*

swab² *vt* **-bb- to ~ (down)** ‹*deck*› lavar, limpiar

swagger /'swægər ‖ 'swægə(r)/ *vi* caminar *or* andar* con aire arrogante

Swahili /swɑː'hiːli ‖ swə'hiːli/ *n* [U] swahili *m*, suajili *m*

swallow¹ /'swɑːləʊ ‖ 'swɒləʊ/ *n* **1** (Zool) golondrina *f* **2** (gulp) trago *m*

swallow² *vt* **1** ‹*food/drink*› tragar* **2** ‹*insult/taunts*› tragarse* (fam); **that's a bit hard to ~** eso no hay quien se lo trague (fam) **3** ⇨ SWALLOW UP ■ ~ *vi* tragar*

• **swallow up** [*v + o + adv, v + adv + o*] **(a)** (use up) ‹*money/time*› consumir, tragarse* (fam), comerse (fam) **(b)** (cause to disappear) tragarse*

swam /swæm/ *past of* SWIM¹

swamp¹ /swɑːmp ‖ swɒmp/ *n* pantano *m*, ciénaga *f*; (of sea water) marisma *f*, ciénaga *f*

swamp² *vt* **(a)** (with water) ‹*land*› anegar*, inundar **(b)** (overwhelm) (*often pass*): **they were ~ed by offers of help** los abrumaron con ofertas de ayuda; **I'm absolutely ~ed with work** estoy inundada de trabajo

swan /swɑːn ‖ swɒn/ *n* cisne *m*

swanky /'swæŋki/ *adj* **-kier, -kiest** (colloq) **(a)** (boastful) (pej) ‹*person*› fanfarrón (fam) **(b)** (classy) chic *adj inv*, pijo (Esp fam), pituco (CS fam), posudo (Col fam), popoff *adj inv* (Méx fam)

swap¹ /swɑːp ‖ swɒp/ *n* (colloq) cambio *m*, trueque *m*

swap² *vt* **-pp-** ‹*possessions/ideas*› intercambiar; **to ~ sth FOR sth** cambiar algo POR algo

swarm¹ /swɔːrm ‖ swɔːm/ *n* enjambre *m*

swarm² *vi* «*bees*» enjambrar; **the flies ~ed around the meat** las moscas revoloteaban alrededor de la carne; **the beaches were ~ing with tourists** las playas eran un hormiguero de turistas

swarthy /'swɔːrði ‖ 'swɔːði/ *adj* **-thier, -thiest** moreno

swastika /'swɑːstɪkə ‖ 'swɒstɪkə/ *n* svástica *f*, esvástica *f*, suástica *f*, cruz *f* gamada

swat /swɑːt ‖ swɒt/ *vt* **-tt-** ‹*insect*› matar (*con matamoscas, periódico etc*)

sway¹ /sweɪ/ *n* [U] **to hold ~** «*ideas*» prevalecer*; «*leader*» ejercer* dominio

sway² *vi* «*branch/tree*» balancearse; (gently) mecerse*; «*tower/building*» bambolearse ■ ~ *vt* **1** (influence) ‹*person/crowd*› influir* en **2** (move) ‹*hips*› menear, bambolear

swear /swer ‖sweə(r)/ (*past* **swore**; *past p* **sworn**) *vt* ‹*allegiance/fidelity/revenge*› jurar; **I could have sworn I left it there** hubiera jurado que lo dejé ahí ■ ~ *vi* **(a)** (vow) jurar; **but I couldn't ~ to it** pero no podría jurarlo **(b)** (curse) decir* palabrotas, soltar* tacos (Esp fam), mentar* madres (Méx fam); **to ~** AT **sb** insultar a algn (*usando palabrotas*)

• **swear by** [*v* + *prep* + *o*] ‹*gadget*› ser* un entusiasta de; ‹*remedy*› tenerle* una fe ciega a

• **swear in** [*v* + *o* + *adv, v* + *adv* + *o*] ‹*jury/witness/president*› tomarle juramento a, juramentar

swearword /'swerwɜ:rd‖'sweəwɜ:d/ *n* palabrota *f*, mala palabra *f*, taco *m* (Esp)

sweat¹ /swet/ *n* [U C] (perspiration) sudor *m*, transpiración *f*; **I broke out in a cold ~** me vino un sudor frío

sweat² *vi* (*past & past p* **sweated** *or* (AmE also) **sweat**) sudar, transpirar

sweater /'swetər ‖'swetə(r)/ *n* suéter *m*, pulóver *m*, jersey *m* (Esp), chompa *f* (Per)

sweat: **~shirt** *n* sudadera *f*, camiseta *f* gruesa; **~shop** *n*: *fábrica donde se explota a los trabajadores*; **~suit** *n* (AmE) equipo *m* (de deportes), chándal *m* (Esp), pants *mpl* (Méx)

sweaty /'sweti/ *adj* **-tier, -tiest** sudado, transpirado

swede /swi:d/ *n* (esp BrE) nabo *m* sueco

Swede /swi:d/ *n* sueco, -ca *m,f*

Sweden /'swi:dn̩/ *n* Suecia *f*

Swedish¹ /'swi:dɪʃ/ *adj* sueco

Swedish² *n* **(a)** [U] (language) sueco *m* **(b)** (people) (+ *pl vb*) **the ~** los suecos

sweep¹ /swi:p/ *n* **1 (a)** [C] (movement): **with a ~ of his arm** con un amplio movimiento del brazo **(b)** [C] (curve — of road, river) curva *f* **(c)** (range) (*no pl*) alcance *m*, extensión *f* **2** [C] (*chimney ~*) deshollinador, -dora *m,f*

sweep² (*past & pp* **swept**) *vt* **1 (a)** (clean) ‹*floor/path*› barrer; ‹*chimney*› deshollinar **(b)** (remove) ‹*leaves/dirt*› barrer; ‹*mines*› barrer; ***to ~ sth under the rug*** *o* (BrE) ***carpet*** correr un velo sobre algo **2** (touch lightly, brush) ‹*surface*› rozar* **3 (a)** (pass over, across) «*storm*» azotar, barrer; **the epidemic is ~ing the country** la epidemia se extiende como un reguero de pólvora por el país **(b)** (remove by force) «*sea/tide*» arrastrar **4 (a)** (scan) recorrer **(b)** (search) ‹*area*› peinar ■ ~ *vi* **1** (+ *adv compl*) (move proudly): **she swept into the room** entró majestuosamente en la habitación **2** (+ *adv compl*) **(a)** (spread): **fire swept through the hotel** el fuego se propagó por todo el hotel **(b)** (extend): **the path ~s down to the road** el sendero baja describiendo una curva hasta la carretera

• **sweep aside** [*v* + *o* + *adv, v* + *adv* + *o*] ‹*object*› apartar; ‹*opposition/doubts*› desechar

• **sweep away** [*v* + *o* + *adv, v* + *adv* + *o*] **(a)** (carry away) «*flood/storm*» arrastrar **(b)** (abolish) erradicar*

• **sweep up 1** [*v* + *adv*] (clear up) barrer, limpiar **2** [*v* + *o* + *adv, v* + *adv* + *o*] **(a)** (clear up) ‹*dust/leaves*› barrer y recoger* **(b)** (gather up) ‹*belongings/bags*› recoger*

sweeper /'swi:pər ‖'swi:pə(r)/ *n* **(a)** (*road~*) barrendero, -ra *m,f*, barredor, -dora *m,f* (Per) **(b)** (*carpet ~*) cepillo *m* mecánico

sweeping /'swi:pɪŋ/ *adj* **(a)** ‹*movement*› amplio; ‹*gesture*› dramático, histriónico **(b)** (indiscriminate) (pej): **that's rather a ~ statement, isn't it?** ¿no estás generalizando demasiado? **(c)** (far-reaching) ‹*reforms/changes*› radical; ‹*powers*› amplio

sweet¹ /swi:t/ *adj* **-er, -est 1** ‹*taste*› dulce **2** ‹*wine/sherry*› dulce **3** (fresh, wholesome) ‹*smell*› agradable **4 (a)** (pleasant, gratifying) ‹*sounds/voice/music*› dulce, melodioso **(b)** (kind, lovable) ‹*nature/temper/smile*› dulce; **she's a very ~ person** es un encanto (de persona); **it was very ~ of her to offer** fue un detalle que se ofreciese **(c)** (attractive) ‹*baby/puppy*› rico (fam), mono (fam), amoroso (AmL fam)

sweet² *n* **1** [C] (item of confectionery) (BrE) caramelo *m* *or* (AmL exc RPl) dulce *m* **2** [U C] (dessert) (BrE) postre *m* **3 sweets** *pl* (sugary food) (AmE) dulces *mpl*

sweet: **~-and-sour** /'swi:tn̩'saʊr ‖ˌswi:tn̩'saʊə(r)/ *adj* (*before n*) agridulce; **~corn** *n* [U] maíz *m* tierno, elote *m* (Méx), choclo *m* (AmS), jojoto *m* (Ven)

sweeten /'swi:tn̩/ *vt* **(a)** ‹*drink/dish*› endulzar* **(b)** ‹*air/breath*› refrescar*

sweetener /'swi:tnər ‖'swi:tnə(r)/ *n* (Culin) endulzante *m*; (artificial) edulcorante *m*

sweet: **~heart** /'swi:thɑ:rt ‖'swi:thɑ:t/ *n* **(a)** (lover, darling) novio, -via *m,f*, enamorado, -da *m,f* **(b)** (colloq) (*as form of address*) (mi) amor; **~ potato** *n* boniato *m*, batata *f*, camote *m* (Andes, Méx); **~-talk** *vt* (colloq) engatusar (fam), camelar (Esp fam)

swell¹ /swel/ (*past p* **swollen** *or* (AmE esp) **swelled**) *vi* **1** «*wood/sails/ankles*» hincharse; «*river/stream*» crecer*, subir **2** (increase) «*population/crowd*» crecer*, aumentar ■ ~ *vt* **1** (increase in size) ‹*body/joint/features*› hinchar; ‹*sails*› hinchar; ‹*river*› hacer* crecer *or* subir **2** (increase in number, volume) ‹*population/total/funds*› aumentar

• **swell up** [*v* + *adv*] hincharse

swell² *n* **(a)** (of sea) oleaje *m* **(b)** (surge, movement) oleada *f*

swell³ *adj* (fine, excellent) (AmE colloq) fenomenal (fam), bárbaro (fam)

swelling /'swelɪŋ/ *n* [C U] hinchazón *f*

sweltering /'sweltərɪŋ/ *adj* sofocante

swept /swept/ *past & past p of* SWEEP²

swerve /swɜ:rv ‖swɜ:v/ *vi* «*vehicle/driver/horse*» virar bruscamente

swift¹ /swɪft/ *adj* **-er, -est** ‹*runner/movement/animal*› veloz, rápido; ‹*reply/reaction/denial*› rápido

swift² *n* vencejo *m*

swiftly /'swɪftli/ *adv* (rapidly) rápidamente, con rapidez; (promptly) con prontitud *or* rapidez

swig[1] /swɪg/ *n* (colloq) trago *m*

swig[2] *vt* **-gg-** (colloq) tomar, beber

swill[1] /swɪl/ *n* [U] comida *f* para cerdos

swill[2] *vt* **1** (wash, rinse) **to ~ sth out** ‹*cups/pans*› lavar/enjuagar* algo **2** (drink) (colloq & pej) ‹*beer*› tomar *or* beber (*a grandes tragos*)

swim[1] /swɪm/ (*pres p* **swimming**; *past* **swam**; *past p* **swum**) *vi* **1** «*person/animal/fish*» nadar; **to go ~ming** ir* a nadar; **he swam across the river** cruzó el río nadando *or* a nado **2** (be immersed, overflowing) (*usu in -ing form*) **to ~ IN sth** nadar *or* flotar EN algo **3** (of blurred, confused perceptions) dar* vueltas; **my head was ~ming** la cabeza me daba vueltas ■ **~** *vt* ‹*length*› nadar, hacer*; ‹*river*› cruzar* a nado

swim[2] *n*: **to go for a ~** ir* a nadar; **to have a ~** nadar, bañarse, darse* un baño

swimmer /ˈswɪmər ‖ ˈswɪmə(r)/ *n* nadador, -dora *m,f*

swimming /ˈswɪmɪŋ/ *n* [U] natación *f*; (*before n*) **~ cap** gorro *m or* gorra *f* (de baño)

swimming: **~ bath** *n*, **~ baths** *pl n* (BrE) piscina *f* cubierta, alberca *f* techada (Méx), pileta *f* cubierta (RPl); **~ costume** *n* (BrE) ⇒ SWIMSUIT; **~ pool** *n* piscina *f*, alberca *f* (Méx), pileta *f* (RPl); **~ trunks** *pl n* ⇒ TRUNK (4)

swimsuit /ˈswɪmsuːt ‖ ˈswɪmsuːt, -sjuːt/ *n* traje *m* de baño, bañador *m* (Esp), malla *f* (de baño) (RPl)

swindle[1] /ˈswɪndl/ *n* estafa *f*, timo *m* (fam)

swindle[2] *vt* estafar, timar

swindler /ˈswɪndlər ‖ ˈswɪndlə(r)/ *n* estafador, -dora *m,f*, timador, -dora *m,f*

swine /swaɪn/ *n* **(a)** (*pl* **~**) (pig, hog) cerdo *m* **(b)** (*pl* **~s**) (contemptible person) (colloq) cerdo, -da *m,f* (fam), canalla *mf*

swing[1] /swɪŋ/ (*past & past p* **swung**) *vi* **1** (hang, dangle) balancearse; (on a swing) columpiarse *or* (RPl) hamacarse*; «*pendulum*» oscilar **2 (a)** (move on pivot) mecerse*; **the door swung open/shut** la puerta se abrió/se cerró **(b)** (turn) girar *or* doblar (*describiendo una curva*); **the ball swung away** la pelota salió desviada **3** (shift, change) «*opinion/mood*» cambiar, oscilar ■ **~** *vt* **1** (move to and fro) ‹*arms/legs*› balancear; ‹*object on rope*› hacer* oscilar; **to ~ one's hips** contonearse, contonear *or* menear las caderas **2** (wave, brandish) ‹*club/hammer*› blandir **3** (shift) ‹*vote*› inclinar

● **swing around,** (BrE also) **swing round 1** [*v + adv*] «*vehicle*» dar* un viraje, girar *or* virar (en redondo); **she swung around to face me** giró sobre sus talones para darme la cara **2** [*v + o + adv*] ‹*car/boat*› hacer* girar en redondo

swing[2] *n* **1 (a)** [C U] (movement) oscilación *f*, vaivén *m* **(b)** [C] (blow, stroke) golpe *m*; (in golf, boxing) swing *m*; **to take a ~ at sb/sth** intentar darle a algn/algo **2** [C] **(a)** (shift) cambio *m*; **a ~ in public opinion** un cambio en la opinión pública **(b)** (Pol) viraje *m* **3 (a)** [U C] (rhythm, vitality): ***to be in full ~*** estar* en pleno desarrollo; **the party was in full ~** la fiesta estaba ya muy animada; ***to get into the ~ of sth*** agarrarle el ritmo *or* (Esp) cogerle* el tranquillo a algo **(b)** [U] (Mus) swing *m* **4** [C] (Leisure) columpio *m or* (RPl) hamaca *f*

swing: **~ bin** *n* cubo *m or* (CS) tacho *m or* (Méx) bote *m or* (Col) caneca *f or* (Ven) tobo *m* de la basura (*con tapa de vaivén*); **~ bridge** *n* puente *m* giratorio; **~ door** *n* puerta *f* (de) vaivén

swinging door /ˈswɪŋɪŋ/ *n* (AmE) ⇒ SWING DOOR

swipe[1] /swaɪp/ *n* (colloq) golpe *m*

swipe[2] *vt* (colloq) **1** (hit) darle* (un golpe) a **2** (steal) afanarse (arg), volarse* (Méx fam)

swirl[1] /swɜːrl ‖ swɜːl/ *n* (of water, dust, people) remolino *m*; (of smoke) voluta *f*, espiral *f*

swirl[2] *vi* «*water/dust/paper*» arremolinarse; «*dancers/skirts*» girar

swish /swɪʃ/ *n* **(a)** (of cane) silbido *m* **(b)** (of water) rumor *m*, susurro *m* **(c)** (of skirt) frufrú *m*

Swiss[1] /swɪs/ *adj* suizo

Swiss[2] *n* (*pl* **~**) suizo, -za *m,f*

switch[1] /swɪtʃ/ *vt* **1 (a)** (change) cambiar de; **to ~ channels** cambiar de canal; **my appointment has been ~ed to Tuesday** me cambiaron la cita al martes **(b)** (exchange) ‹*suitcases/roles*› intercambiar **2** (shunt) (AmE Rail) cambiar de vía ■ **~** *vi* cambiar; **I ~ed to Channel Four** cambié al Canal Cuatro; **we've ~ed from electricity to gas** hemos empezado a usar gas en lugar de electricidad

● **switch off 1** [*v + o + adv, v + adv + o*] ‹*light/TV/heating*› apagar*; ‹*gas/electricity/water*› cortar, desconectar **2** [*v + adv*] «*light/machine/heating*» apagarse*

● **switch on 1** [*v + o + adv, v + adv + o*] (esp BrE) ‹*light/heating/television*› encender*, prender (AmL) **2** [*v + adv*] «*light/heating/machine*» encenderse*, prenderse (AmL)

● **switch over** [*v + adv*] **(a)** (change) **to ~ over TO sth** cambiar A algo **(b)** (change channels) cambiar de canal **(c)** (exchange positions, roles) cambiar

switch[2] *n* **1 (a)** (Elec) interruptor *m*, llave *f* (de encendido/de la luz) **(b)** (AmE Rail) agujas *fpl* **2** (exchange) intercambio *m*, trueque *m*

switchboard *n* centralita *f*, conmutador *m* (AmL); (*before n*) **~ operator** telefonista *mf*

Switzerland /ˈswɪtsərlənd ‖ ˈswɪtsələnd/ *n* Suiza *f*

swivel /ˈswɪvəl/, (BrE) **-ll-** *vi* girar ■ **~** *vt* hacer* girar

swivel chair *n* silla *f* giratoria

swollen[1] /ˈswəʊlən/ *past p of* SWELL[1]

swollen[2] *adj* ‹*ankle/knee/joints*› hinchado; ‹*gland*› inflamado; **~ with pride** henchido de orgullo; **the river was ~** el río iba crecido

swoon /swuːn/ *vi* **(a)** (show rapture) **to ~ (OVER sb)** derretirse* (POR algn) **(b)** (faint) (arch *or* liter) desvanecerse*

swoop[1] /swuːp/ *vi* «*bird of prey*» abatirse; «*police*» llevar a cabo una redada

swoop[2] *n* (of bird, aircraft) descenso *m* en picada *or* (Esp) en picado; (by police) redada *f*; ***in one fell ~*** de una sola vez, de un tirón (fam)

swop /swɑːp ‖ swɒp/ *vt/n* ⇒ SWAP[1,2]

sword /sɔːrd ‖ sɔːd/ *n* espada *f*

sword: **~fish** *n* (*pl* **~fish** *or* **~fishes**) pez *m* espada; **~sman** /'sɔ:rdzmən ‖'sɔ:dzmən/ *n* (*pl* **-men** /-mən/) espadachín *m*, espada *m*

swore /swɔ:r ‖ swɔ:(r)/ *past of* SWEAR

sworn[1] /swɔ:rn ‖ swɔ:n/ *past p of* SWEAR

sworn[2] *adj* (*before n*) **1** ‹*enemy*› declarado, acérrimo **2** ‹*statement*› jurado

swot[1] /swɑ:t ‖ swɒt/ *n* (BrE colloq & pej) matado, -da *m,f or* (Col) pilo, -la *m,f or* (Chi) mateo, -tea *m,f or* (Per) chancón, -cona *m,f or* (RPl) traga *mf or* (Esp) empollón, -llona *m,f* (fam & pey)

swot[2] *vi* **-tt-** (BrE colloq) estudiar como loco (fam), empollar (Esp fam), matearse (Chi fam), chancar* (Per arg), tragar* (RPl fam)

swum /swʌm/ *past p of* SWIM[1]

swung /swʌŋ/ *past & past p of* SWING[1]

sycamore /'sɪkəmɔ:r ‖ 'sɪkəmɔ:(r)/ *n* **~ (maple)** plátano *m* (falso), sicómoro *m*, sicomoro *m*

sycophantic /'sɪkə'fæntɪk/ *adj* adulador

syllable /'sɪləbəl/ *n* sílaba *f*

syllabus /'sɪləbəs/ *n* (*pl* **-buses**) plan *m* de estudios; (of a particular subject) programa *m*

symbol /'sɪmbəl/ *n* símbolo *m*

symbolic /sɪm'bɑ:lɪk ‖ sɪm'bɒlɪk/ *adj* simbólico; **to be ~ OF sth** simbolizar* algo

symbolism /'sɪmbəlɪzəm/ *n* [U] simbolismo *m*

symbolize /'sɪmbəlaɪz/ *vt* simbolizar*

symmetrical /sə'metrɪkəl ‖ sɪ'metrɪkəl/ *adj* simétrico

symmetry /'sɪmətri/ *n* [U] simetría *f*

sympathetic /'sɪmpə'θetɪk/ *adj* **1** (understanding) comprensivo; **he was most ~ to** *o* **toward me when my wife died** me dio todo su apoyo y comprensión cuando murió mi mujer **2** (approving) ‹*response/view*› favorable; ‹*audience*› bien dispuesto, receptivo

sympathetically /'sɪmpə'θetɪkli/ *adv* **(a)** (with understanding) ‹*listen/consider/respond*› con comprensión **(b)** (showing pity) con compasión

sympathize /'sɪmpəθaɪz/ *vi* **(a)** (commiserate): **I ~ with him** lo compadezco **(b)** (understand) **to ~ (WITH sth/sb)** comprender *or* entender* (algo/a algn)

sympathizer /'sɪmpəθaɪzər ‖ 'sɪmpəθaɪzə(r)/ *n* simpatizante *m,f*, partidario, -ria *m,f*

sympathy /'sɪmpəθi/ *n* (*pl* **-thies**) **1 (a)** [U] (pity) compasión *f*, lástima *f* **(b)** (condolences) (*often pl*): **you have my deepest ~** lo acompaño en el sentimiento (fr hecha), mi más sentido pésame (fr hecha) **2 (a)** [U] (support, approval): **to come out in ~ with sb** (Lab Rel) declararse en huelga en solidaridad con algn **(b) sympathies** *pl* (loyalty, leanings) (*often pl*) simpatías *fpl*

symphony /'sɪmfəni/ *n* (*pl* **-nies**) sinfonía *f*; (*before n*) **~ orchestra** orquesta *f* sinfónica

symptom /'sɪmptəm/ *n* síntoma *m*

symptomatic /'sɪmptə'mætɪk/ *adj* **~ (OF sth)** sintomático (DE algo)

synagogue /'sɪnəgɑ:g ‖ 'sɪnəgɒg/ *n* sinagoga *f*

synchronize /'sɪŋkrənaɪz/ *vt* sincronizar*

syndicate /'sɪndəkət ‖ 'sɪndɪkət/ *n* **(a)** (group, cartel) agrupación *f*; **a crime ~** una organización mafiosa **(b)** (in US) (Journ, TV) agencia *f* de distribución periodística

syndrome /'sɪndrəʊm/ *n* síndrome *m*

synonymous /sə'nɑ:nəməs ‖ sɪ'nɒnɪməs/ *adj* ‹*terms/phrases*› sinónimo; ‹*ideas*› análogo; **to be ~ WITH sth** ser* sinónimo DE algo

synopsis /sə'nɑ:psəs ‖ sɪ'nɒpsɪs/ *n* (*pl* **-opses** /-si:z/) sinopsis *f*

syntax /'sɪntæks/ *n* [U] sintaxis *f*

synthesis /'sɪnθəsəs ‖ 'sɪnθəsɪs/ *n* [C U] (*pl* **-theses** /-θəsi:z/) síntesis *f*

synthesize /'sɪnθəsaɪz/ *vt* sintetizar*

synthesizer /'sɪnθəsaɪzər ‖ 'sɪnθəsaɪzə(r)/ *n* sintetizador *m*

synthetic[1] /sɪn'θetɪk/ *adj* sintético

synthetic[2] *n* fibra *f* sintética, tejido *m* sintético

syphilis /'sɪfələs ‖ 'sɪfɪlɪs/ *n* [U] sífilis *f*

syphon *n/vt* /'saɪfən/ ⇒ SIPHON

Syria /'sɪriə/ *n* Siria *f*

Syrian /'sɪriən/ *adj* sirio

syringe /sə'rɪndʒ ‖ sɪ'rɪndʒ/ *n* jeringa *f*, jeringuilla *f*

syrup /'sɜ:rəp, 'sɪ- ‖ 'sɪrəp/ *n* [U] **(a)** (Culin) (sugar solution) almíbar *m*; (with other ingredients) jarabe *m*, sirope *m* **(b)** (medicine) jarabe *m*

system /'sɪstəm/ *n* **1** [U C] (ordered structure) sistema *m*, método *m* **2** [C] **(a)** (technical, mechanical) sistema *m* **(b)** (Comput) sistema *m* **3** [C] (Anat, Physiol): **the digestive ~** el aparato digestivo; **the nervous ~** el sistema nervioso; ***to get sth out of one's ~*** desahogarse* **4** [C] (establishment, status quo): **the ~** el sistema

systematic /'sɪstə'mætɪk/ *adj* sistemático

systematically /'sɪstə'mætɪkli/ *adv* sistemáticamente

systems analyst *n* analista *mf* de sistemas

Tt

T, t /tiː/ *n* T, t *f*

tab /tæb/ *n* **1 (a)** (flap) lengüeta *f* **(b)** (label on clothing) etiqueta *f* **2** (account, bill) (colloq) cuenta *f*; ***to keep ~s on sth/sb*** tener* algo/a algn controlado

tabby /'tæbi/ (*pl* **-bies**), **tabby cat** *n* gato atigrado, gata atigrada *m,f*

table /'teɪbəl/ *n* **1** (piece of furniture) mesa *f*; (*before n*); **~ mat** (mantelito *m*) individual *m* **2** (list) tabla *f*; **multiplication** *o* (used by children) **times ~s** tablas de multiplicar

table: **~cloth** *n* mantel *m*; **~spoon** *n* (utensil) cuchara *f* grande *or* de servir; (measure) cucharada *f* (grande)

tablet /'tæblət ‖ 'tæblɪt/ *n* **(a)** (pill) pastilla *f*, comprimido *m* **(b)** (commemorative, of stone) lápida *f*

table tennis *n* [U] ping-pong *m*, tenis *m* de mesa

tabloid /'tæblɔɪd/ *n* tabloide *m* (*formato de periódicos utilizado por la prensa popular*)

taboo /tə'buː/ *adj* tabú *adj inv*

tabulate /'tæbjəleɪt ‖ 'tæbjʊleɪt/ *vt* tabular

tacit /'tæsət ‖ 'tæsɪt/ *adj* tácito

taciturn /'tæsətɜːrn ‖ 'tæsɪtɜːn/ *adj* taciturno

tack¹ /tæk/ *n* **(a)** [C] (nail) tachuela *f* **(b)** [C] (Naut) bordada *f* **(c)** [C] (stitch) (BrE) puntada *f*; (seam) hilván *m* **(d)** [U] (Equ) arreos *mpl*, aperos *mpl* (AmL)

tack² *vt* **1** (nail) ‹*carpet*› **~ down** clavar con tachuelas **2** (stitch) (BrE) hilvanar ■ **~** *vi* (Naut) dar* bordadas

• tack on [*v + o + adv, v + adv + o*] agregar*, añadir

tackle¹ /'tækəl/ *n* **1** [U] (equipment): **sports ~** equipo *m* de deporte; **fishing ~** aparejo *m* *or* avíos *mpl* de pesca **2** [C] (Sport) (in rugby, US football) placaje *m*, tacle *m* (AmL); (in soccer) entrada *f* fuerte **3** [U] (Naut) aparejo *m*, polea *f*

tackle² *vt* **1 (a)** (come to grips with) ‹*problem*› enfrentar, abordar; ‹*subject*› tratar; ‹*task*› abordar **(b)** (confront) ‹*intruder/colleague*› enfrentar, enfrentarse con **2** (Sport) (in rugby, US football) placar*, taclear (AmL); (in soccer) entrarle a

tacky /'tæki/ *adj* **tackier, tackiest 1** (cheap, tawdry) chabacano, hortera (Esp fam), naco (Méx fam), lobo (Col fam), rasca (Chi fam), mersa (RPl fam) **2** (sticky) pegajoso

tact /tækt/ *n* [U] tacto *m*

tactful /'tæktfəl/ *adj* ‹*person*› de mucho tacto; ‹*question/reply*› diplomático

tactfully /'tæktfəli/ *adv* con mucho tacto

tactic /'tæktɪk/ *n* táctica *f*

tactical /'tæktɪkəl/ *adj* táctico

tactics /'tæktɪks/ *n* (Mil) (+ *sing or pl vb*) táctica *f*

tactless /'tæktləs ‖ 'tæktlɪs/ *adj* poco diplomático

tadpole /'tædpəʊl/ *n* renacuajo *m*

Tadzhikistan /tɑː,dʒiːkɪ'stɑːn// *n* Tayiquistán *m*

taffeta /'tæfətə ‖ 'tæfɪtə/ *n* [U C] tafetán *m*

taffy /'tæfi/ *n* [C U] (AmE) caramelo *m* masticable

tag /tæg/ *n* **1** (label) etiqueta *f* (*atada*) **2** (Ling) coletilla *f*; (*before n*) **~ question** coletilla interrogativa

• tag on: **-gg-** [*v + o + adv, v + adv + o*] agregar*, añadir

Tahiti /tə'hiːti/ *n* Tahití *m*

tail¹ /teɪl/ *n* **(a)** (of horse, fish, bird) cola *f*; (of dog, pig) rabo *m*, cola *f* **(b)** (of plane, kite) cola *f*; (of shirt, coat) faldón *m*; *see also* TAILS 1

tail² *vt* (follow) ‹*suspect*› seguir*

• tail off [*v + adv*] **(a)** «*demand*» disminuir*, mermar **(b)** «*sound/words*» apagarse*

tail: **~back** *n* (BrE) caravana *f*, cola *f* (*debido a un embotellamiento*); **~coat** *n* frac *m*; **~ end** *n*: **the ~ end** (of film, concert) el final, los últimos minutos; (of procession) la cola; **~light** *n* luz *f* trasera

tailor¹ /'teɪlər ‖ 'teɪlə(r)/ *n* sastre *m*

tailor² *vt* **1** (Clothing) **(a)** (make) confeccionar **(b) tailored** *past p* (*before n*) (fitted) entallado; (lined, structured etc) armado **2** (adapt) adaptar

tailor-made /'teɪlər'meɪd ‖ ,teɪlə'meɪd/ *adj* **(a)** ‹*suit*› hecho a (la) medida **(b)** ‹*product/plan*› a la medida de sus (*or* nuestras *etc*) necesidades

tailpipe /'teɪlpaɪp/ *n* (AmE Auto) tubo *m* *or* (RPl) caño *m* de escape

tails /teɪlz/ *n* **1** (tailcoat) (+ *pl vb*) frac *m* **2** (on coin) (+ *sing vb*) cruz *f*, sello *m* (Andes, Ven), sol *m* (Méx), ceca *f* (Arg)

taint /teɪnt/ *vt* **(a)** ‹*meat/water*› contaminar **(b)** ‹*name/reputation*› mancillar (liter), deshonrar

Taiwan /taɪ'wɑːn/ *n* Taiwan *m*

take¹ /teɪk/ (*past* **took**; *past p* **taken**) *vt* **I** (carry, lead, drive) llevar; **~ an umbrella** lleva un paraguas

II 1 (a) ‹*train/plane/bus/taxi/elevator*› tomar, coger* (esp Esp) **(b)** ‹*road/turning*› tomar, agarrar (esp AmL), coger* (esp Esp); **~ a left (turn)** (BrE) dobla a la izquierda **(c)** ‹*bend*› tomar, coger* (esp Esp); ‹*fence*› saltar **2 (a)** (grasp, seize) tomar, agarrar (esp AmL), coger* (esp Esp); ‹*opportunity*› aprovechar; **she took the knife from him** le quitó el cuchillo **(b)** (take charge of): **may I ~ your coat?** ¿me permite el abrigo? **(c)** (occupy): **~ a seat** siéntese, tome asiento (frml); **this chair is ~n** esta silla está ocupada **3** (remove, steal) ‹*wallet/purse*› llevarse **4**: **to be ~n ill** caer* enfermo **5 (a)** (capture) ‹*town/position*› tomar; ‹*pawn/piece*› comer **(b)** (win) ‹*prize/title*› llevarse, hacerse* con; ‹*game/set*› ganar **(c)** (receive as profit) hacer*, sacar* **6** ‹*medicine/drugs*› tomar; **I don't ~ sugar in my coffee** no le pongo azúcar al café **7 (a)** (buy, order) llevar(se); **I'll ~ this pair** (me) llevo este par **(b)** (rent) alquilar, coger* (Esp)

III 1 (of time) «*job/task*» llevar; «*process*» tardar; «*person/letter*» tardar, demorar(se) (AmL); **the flight ~s two hours** el vuelo dura dos horas; **it took me a long time to do it** me llevó mucho tiempo hacerlo **2** (need): **it ~s courage to do a thing like that** hay que tener *or* hace falta valor para hacer algo así; **it took four men to lift it** se necesitaron cuatro hombres para levantarlo **3 (a)** (wear): **what size shoes do you ~?** ¿qué número calzas?; **she ~s a 14** usa la talla *or* (RPl) el talle 14 **(b)** (Ling) construirse* con, regir*

IV 1 (accept) ‹*money/bribes/job*› aceptar; **do you ~ checks?** ¿aceptan cheques?; **~ it from me** hazme caso **2 (a)** (hold, accommodate): **it ~s/will ~ 42 liters** tiene una capacidad de 42 litros; **we can ~ up to 50 passengers** tenemos cabida para un máximo de 50 pasajeros **(b)** ‹*patients/pupils*› admitir, tomar **3 (a)** (withstand, suffer) ‹*strain/weight*› aguantar; ‹*beating*› recibir **(b)** (tolerate, endure) aguantar; **he can't ~ a joke** no sabe aceptar una broma **(c)** (bear): **she's ~n it very badly/well** lo lleva muy mal/bien; *see also* HEART 2, 3 **4 (a)** (understand, interpret) tomarse; **don't ~ it personally** no te lo tomes como algo personal; **I ~ it you didn't like him much** por lo que veo no te cayó muy bien **(b)** (consider) (*in imperative*) mirar; **~ Japan, for example** mira el caso del Japón, por ejemplo

V 1 ‹*steps/measures*› tomar; ‹*exercise*› hacer*; **to ~ a step forward** dar* un paso adelante **2** (Educ) **(a)** (teach) (BrE) darle* clase a **(b)** (learn) ‹*subject*› estudiar, hacer*; ‹*course*› hacer*; **to ~ an exam** hacer* *or* dar* *or* (CS) rendir* *or* (Méx) tomar un examen, examinarse (Esp) **3 (a)** (record) ‹*measurements/temperature*› tomar **(b)** (write down) ‹*notes*› tomar **4** (adopt): **he ~s the view that** ... opina que ..., es de la opinión de que ...; *see also* LIKING (a), OFFENSE 2(b), SHAPE[1] 1(a) *etc* ■ **~** *vi* **(a)** «*cutting*» prender **(b)** «*dye*» agarrar (esp AmL), coger* (esp Esp)

• take aback [*v* + *o* + *adv*] (*usu pass*) sorprender

• take after [*v* + *prep* + *o*] salir* a, parecerse* a; **he ~s after his father** salió a su padre, se parece a su padre

• take along [*v* + *o* + *adv*, *v* + *adv* + *o*] llevar

• take apart [*v* + *o* + *adv*] **(a)** (dismantle) desmontar **(b)** (show weakness of) ‹*argument*› desbaratar

• take around, (BrE) **take round** [*v* + *o* + *prep* + *o*] ‹*house/estate*› mostrar*, enseñar (esp Esp)

• take aside [*v* + *o* + *adv*] llevar aparte *or* a un lado

• take away I [*v* + *o* + *adv*, *v* + *adv* + *o*] **(a)** (carry, lead away) ‹*person/object*› llevarse **(b)** (remove, confiscate) ‹*possession*› quitar; **to ~ sth away FROM sb** quitarle algo A algn **(c)** (erase, obliterate): **this will ~ the pain away** con esto se te pasará el dolor; **this will ~ the taste away** esto te quitará el sabor de la boca

II [*v* + *adv* + *o*] (BrE) ‹*food*› llevar

• take back 1 [*v* + *o* + *adv*, *v* + *adv* + *o*] **(a)** (return) devolver* **(b)** (repossess) llevarse **(c)** (accept back): **she wouldn't ~ back the money she'd lent me** no quiso que le devolviera el dinero que me había prestado **(d)** (withdraw, retract) ‹*statement*› retirar **2** [*v* + *o* + *adv*] (in time): **it ~s me back to my childhood** me transporta a mi niñez

• take down [*v* + *o* + *adv*, *v* + *adv* + *o*] **(a)** ‹*decorations/notice*› quitar **(b)** (dismantle) desmontar **(c)** ‹*name/address*› apuntar, anotar

• take home [*v* + *adv* + *o*]: **she ~s home less than £600** su sueldo neto *or* líquido es de menos de 600 libras

• take in I [*v* + *o* + *adv*, *v* + *adv* + *o*] **1** (move indoors) meter (dentro), entrar (esp AmS) **2** (give home to) ‹*orphan*› recoger*; ‹*lodger*› alojar **3** (grasp) ‹*information*› asimilar **4** (make narrower) ‹*dress/waist*› meterle *or* tomarle a

II [*v* + *o* + *adv*] (deceive) engañar

III [*v* + *adv* + *o*] **(a)** (include) ‹*areas/topics*› incluir*, abarcar* **(b)** (visit) visitar, incluir* (*en el recorrido*)

• take off I [*v* + *o* + *adv*, *v* + *adv* + *o*] [*v* + *o* + *prep* + *o*] **1** (detach, remove) quitar, sacar*; **to ~ off one's clothes** quitarse *or* (esp AmL) sacarse* la ropa **2 (a)** (cut off) cortar **(b)** (deduct) descontar* **3** (have free): **she's ~n the morning off (from) work** se ha tomado la mañana libre

II [*v* + *adv*] **(a)** «*aircraft/pilot*» despegar*, decolar (AmL); «*flight*» salir* **(b)** (succeed) «*career*» tomar vuelo **(c)** (depart) largarse* (fam), irse*

III [*v* + *o* + *adv*] [*v* + *o* + *prep* + *o*] **1** (remove) quitar, sacar* (esp AmL); **~ your hands off me!** ¡quítame las manos de encima! **2** (take away from) (colloq) quitar, sacar* (CS)

• take on 1 [*v* + *o* + *adv*, *v* + *adv* + *o*] **(a)** (employ) ‹*staff*› contratar, tomar (esp AmL) **(b)** (undertake) ‹*work*› encargarse* de, hacerse* cargo de; ‹*responsibility*› asumir **(c)** (tackle) ‹*opponent*› enfrentarse a **2** [*v* + *adv* + *o*] (acquire) ‹*expression*› adoptar; ‹*appearance*› adquirir*

• take out I [*v* + *o* + *adv*, *v* + *adv* + *o*] **1 (a)** (remove physically) sacar*; ***to ~ it out of sb*** «*fight/race*» dejar a algn rendido **(b)** (exclude) eliminar **(c)** (transport) sacar* **(d)** (AmE) ‹*food*› llevar **2** (withdraw) ‹*money*› sacar* **3** (produce) ‹*gun/wallet*› sacar*

II [*v* + *o* + *adv*, *v* + *adv* + *o*] **(a)** (extract) ‹*tooth/appendix*› sacar* **(b)** (obtain) ‹*insurance/permit*› sacar*

III [*v* + *o* + *adv*] (accompany, conduct): **he'd like to ~ her out** le gustaría invitarla a salir; **she took me out to dinner** me invitó a cenar

• take out on [*v* + *o* + *adv* + *prep* + *o*]: **to ~ it out on sb** desquitarse con algn

• take over 1 [*v* + *adv*] **(a)** (assume control) «*political party*» asumir el poder; **he will ~ over as managing director** asumirá el cargo de director ejecutivo; **to ~ over FROM sb** sustituir* a algn; (in shift work) relevar a algn **(b)** (seize control) hacerse* con el poder **2** [*v* + *o* + *adv*, *v* + *adv* + *o*] ‹*responsibility/role*› asumir; ‹*job*› hacerse* cargo de; ‹*company*› absorber

• take round (BrE) ⇒ TAKE AROUND

• take to [*v* + *prep* + *o*] **(a)** (develop liking for): **she took to teaching immediately** enseguida le tomó gusto a la enseñanza; **I didn't ~ to him** no me cayó muy bien **(b)** (form habit of): **to ~ to drink** darse* a la bebida; **to ~ to** -ING darle* a algn POR + INF

• **take up I** [*v + o + adv, v + adv + o*] **1 (a)** (pick up) tomar **(b)** (accept) ‹*offer/challenge*› aceptar **(c)** (adopt) ‹*cause*› hacer* suyo (*or* mío *etc*) **(d)** (begin): **he's ~n up pottery** ha empezado a hacer cerámica **2** (lift) ‹*carpet/floorboards*› levantar **3 (a)** (continue) ‹*story*› seguir*, continuar*; ‹*conversation*› reanudar **(b)** ‹*issue/point*› tratar; (pursue) volver* a **4** (shorten) ‹*skirt*› acortar; ‹*hem*› subir

II [*v + adv + o*] **1** (use up) ‹*time*› llevar; ‹*space*› ocupar **2** (move into) ‹*position*› tomar

• **take up on** [*v + o + adv + prep + o*] **(a)** (take person at word): **I may well ~ you up on that** a lo mejor te tomo la palabra *or* te acepto el ofrecimiento **(b)** (challenge): **I must ~ you up on that** sobre eso discrepo con usted

take² *n* (Cin) toma *f*

takeaway¹ /'teɪkəweɪ/ *adj* (BrE) ‹*meal/pizza*› para llevar; ‹*restaurant*› de comida para llevar

takeaway² *n* (BrE) **(a)** (restaurant) restaurante *m* de comida para llevar **(b)** (meal) comida *f* preparada

take-home pay /'teɪkhəʊm/ *n* [U] sueldo *m* neto

taken¹ /'teɪkən/ *past p of* TAKE¹

taken² *adj* (*pred*) **to be ~** WITH **sth/sb**: **I was quite ~ with him** me cayó muy bien; **they were very ~ with the house** quedaron encantados con la casa

takeoff /'teɪkɔːf ‖ 'teɪkɒf/ *n* **(a)** (Aviat) despegue *m*, decolaje *m* (AmL) **(b)** (imitation) (colloq) parodia *f*

takeout¹ /'teɪkaʊt/ *adj* (AmE) ‹*meal*› para llevar; ‹*restaurant*› de comida para llevar

takeout² *n* [U] (AmE) comida *f* preparada

takeover /'teɪkəʊvər ‖ 'teɪkəʊvə(r)/ *n* **(a)** (Govt) toma *f* del poder **(b)** (Busn) absorción *f*, adquisición *f* (*de una empresa por otra*); (*before n*) **~ bid** oferta *f* pública de adquisición *or* de compra, OPA *f*

takings /'teɪkɪŋz/ *n pl* (BrE Busn) recaudación *f*; (at box office) taquilla *f*, entrada *f*

talc /tælk/ *n* [U] polvos *mpl* de talco, talco *m* (AmL)

talcum powder /'tælkəm/ *n* [U] polvos *mpl* de talco

tale /teɪl/ *n* cuento *m*, relato *m*; ***to tell ~s*** contar* chismes *or* cuentos

talent /'tælənt/ *n* **(a)** [U C] (aptitude, skill) talento *m* **(b)** [U] (talented people) gente *f* con talento

talented /'tæləntəd ‖ 'tæləntɪd/ *adj* talentoso, de talento

talisman /'tæləsmən ‖ 'tælɪzmən/ *n* (*pl* **~s**) talismán *m*

talk¹ /tɔːk/ *vi* **1** (speak) hablar; (converse) hablar, platicar* (esp AmC, Méx); **to ~** ABOUT **sb/sth** hablar DE algn/algo; **to ~** OF **sth**/-ING hablar DE algo/DE + INF; **to ~** TO **sb** hablar CON algn; **he was ~ing to Jane** estaba hablando con Jane; **are you ~ing to me ?** ¿me hablas a mí?; **we're not ~ing to each other** no nos hablamos; **to ~** WITH **sb** hablar CON algn **2 (a)** (have discussion) hablar; **we need to ~** tenemos que hablar; **to ~** ABOUT **sth** discutir algo **(b)** (give talk) **to ~** ABOUT/ON **sth** hablar DE/SOBRE algo ■ **~** *vt* **1** (speak) (colloq): **to ~ business** hablar de negocios; **don't ~ nonsense!** ¡no digas tonterías! **2** (argue, persuade) **to ~ sb** INTO/OUT OF **sth**/-ING convencer* a algn DE QUE/DE QUE NO (+ *subj*)

• **talk down to** [*v + adv + prep + o*] hablarle en tono condescendiente a

• **talk over** [*v + o + adv, v + adv + o*] discutir

talk² *n* **1** [C] **(a)** (conversation) conversación *f*; **I had a long ~ with him** estuve hablando *or* (AmC, Méx tb) platicando un rato largo con él **(b)** (lecture) charla *f* **(c) talks** *pl* (negotiations) conversaciones *fpl* **2** [U] (words) (colloq & pej) palabrería *f* (fam & pey)

talkative /'tɔːkətɪv/ *adj* conversador, hablador

talker /'tɔːkər ‖ 'tɔːkə(r)/ *n* hablador, -dora *m,f*

talking /'tɔːkɪŋ/: **~ point** *n* tema *m* de conversación; **~-to** *n* (*pl* **-tos**) (colloq): **to give sb a good ~-to** leerle* la cartilla a algn (fam)

talk show *n* programa *m* de entrevistas

tall /tɔːl/ *adj* **-er, -est** alto; **how ~ are you?** ¿cuánto mides?; **he's nearly 6 feet ~** mide casi 6 pies

tall story, **tall tale** *n* cuento *m* chino (fam)

tally¹ /'tæli/ *n* (*pl* **-lies**) cuenta *f*

tally² *vi* **-lies, -lying, -lied** coincidir, cuadrar

Talmud /'tælmʊd/ *n* **the ~** el Talmud

talon /'tælən/ *n* garra *f*

tambourine /tæmbə'riːn/ *n* pandereta *f*

tame¹ /teɪm/ *adj* **tamer, tamest (a)** ‹*animal*› (by nature) manso, dócil; (tamed) domado, domesticado **(b)** (unexciting) ‹*show/story*› insulso, insípido

tame² *vt* ‹*wild animal*› domar; ‹*stray*› domesticar*

Tamil /'tæməl ‖ 'tæmɪl/ *n* **(a)** [C] (person) tamil *mf*, tamul *mf* **(b)** [U] (language) tamul *m*

tamper with /'tæmpər ‖ 'tæmpə(r)/ [*v + prep + o*] ‹*engine/controls*› tocar*; ‹*figures*› alterar

tampon /'tæmpɑːn ‖ 'tæmpɒn/ *n* tampón *m*

tan¹ /tæn/ **-nn-** *vt* **1** ‹*leather/hide*› curtir **2** «*sun*» ‹*body/skin*› broncear, tostar* ■ **~** *vi* broncearse, quemarse (AmL)

tan² *n* (on skin) bronceado *m*, moreno *m* (esp Esp)

tan³ ▶ 515 *adj* habano

tandem /'tændəm/ *n* tándem *m*

tang /tæŋ/ *n* [C U] (strong taste) sabor *m* fuerte; (sharp taste) acidez *f*; (smell) olor *m* penetrante

tangent /'tændʒənt/ *n* tangente *f*; ***to go o fly off at o on a ~*** irse* por las ramas

tangerine /'tændʒə'riːn/ *n* mandarina *f*, tangerina *f*

tangible /'tændʒəbəl/ *adj* tangible

tangle¹ /'tæŋgəl/ *vt* enredar, enmarañar; **to get ~d (up)** enredarse

• **tangle up** [*v + o + adv, v + adv + o*] enredar, enmarañar

tangle² *n* (of threads, hair) enredo *m*, maraña *f*, embrollo *m*; (of weeds) maraña *f*

tangled /'tæŋgəld/ *adj* enredado

tango /'tæŋgəʊ/ *n* (*pl* **-gos**) tango *m*

tank /tæŋk/ *n* **1** (for liquid, gas) depósito *m*, tanque *m*; (on trucks, rail wagons) cisterna *f*; (Auto) tanque *m*, depósito *m* **2** (Mil) tanque *m*, carro *m* de combate

tankard /'tæŋkərd ‖ 'tæŋkəd/ *n* jarra *f*

tanker /'tæŋkər ‖ 'tæŋkə(r)/ *n* **(a)** (ship) buque *m* cisterna *or* tanque **(b)** (truck) camión *m* cisterna

tanned /tænd/ *adj* bronceado, moreno

Tannoy® /'tænɔɪ/ *n* (BrE) sistema *m* de megafonía

tantalizing /'tæntḷaɪzɪŋ ‖ 'tæntəlaɪzɪŋ/ *adj* tentador

tantamount /'tæntəmaʊnt/ *adj* **to be ~ TO sth** equivaler* A algo

tantrum /'tæntrəm/ *n* berrinche *m*, rabieta *f*; **Jack had** *o* **threw a ~** a Jack le dio un berrinche, Jack hizo un berrinche (Méx)

Tanzania /'tænzə'ni:ə/ *n* Tanzania *f*, Tanzanía *f*

Tanzanian /'tænzə'ni:ən/ *adj* tanzano

tap¹ /tæp/ *n* **1** [C] **(a)** (for water) (BrE) llave *f or* (Esp) grifo *m or* (RPl) canilla *f or* (Per) caño *m or* (AmC) paja *f or* (AmC, Ven) chorro *m* **(b)** (*gas ~*) llave *f* del gas **(c)** (on barrel) espita *f* **2** [C] (light blow) toque *m*, golpecito *m* **3** [U] ⇒ TAP DANCING

tap² **-pp-** *vt* **1** (strike lightly) dar* un toque *or* golpecito en **2 (a)** ‹*tree*› sangrar **(b)** ‹*resources/reserves*› explotar **3** ‹*telephone*› intervenir*, pinchar (fam); ‹*conversation*› interceptar ■ ~ *vi* **(a)** (strike lightly) **to ~ AT/ON sth** dar* toques *or* golpecitos EN algo **(b)** (make tapping sound) dar* golpecitos, tamborilear

tap dancing *n* [U] claqué *m*

tape¹ /teɪp/ *n* **1** [U C] **(a)** (of paper, cloth) cinta *f* **(b)** (adhesive) cinta *f* adhesiva; (Med) esparadrapo *m*; *see also* MASKING TAPE, SCOTCH TAPE® *etc* **(c)** (Sport) cinta *f* de llegada **(d)** ⇒ TAPE MEASURE **2 (a)** [U] (*magnetic ~*) (Audio, Comput, Video) cinta *f* (magnética) **(b)** [C] (Audio, Video) cinta *f*

tape² *vt* (record) grabar

tape: **~ deck** *n* platina *f*, pletina *f*; **~ measure** *n* cinta *f* métrica, metro *m*

taper *vi* afilarse, estrecharse ■ ~ *vt* afilar, estrechar

• **taper off** [*v + adv*] **(a)** «*enthusiasm*» decaer*; «*demand/sales*» disminuir* **(b)** ⇒ TAPER *vi*

tape: **~-record** /'teɪprɪ'kɔ:rd ‖ 'teɪprɪkɔ:d/ *vt* grabar; **~ recorder** *n* grabador *m*, grabadora *f*; (for cassette format) grabador *m*, grabadora *f*, casete *m* (Esp)

tapestry /'tæpəstri/ *n* (*pl* **-tries**) **(a)** [C U] (wall hanging) tapiz *m* **(b)** [U] (art form) tapicería *f*

tapeworm /'teɪpwɜ:rm ‖ 'teɪpwɜ:m/ *n* (lombriz *f*) solitaria *f*, tenia *f*

tar¹ /tɑ:r ‖ tɑ:(r)/ *n* [U] alquitrán *m*

tar² *vt* **-rr-** ‹*road/fence*› alquitranar; ‹*roof*› impermeabilizar* (*con alquitrán*)

target¹ /'tɑ:rgət ‖ 'tɑ:gɪt/ *n* **1 (a)** (thing aimed at) blanco *m*; (Mil) objetivo *m*; (board) (Sport) diana *f* **(b)** (of criticism) blanco *m* **2** (objective, goal) objetivo *m*; **to be on ~** ir* de acuerdo a lo previsto (*or* al plan de trabajo *etc*); (*before n*) ‹*date/figure*› fijado; ‹*market*› objetivo *adj inv*

target² *vt* **(a)** (select as target): **the company is ~ing the small investor** la empresa está intentando captar al pequeño inversor **(b)** (direct) ‹*advertising*› dirigir*; **to ~ benefits at those most in need** concentrar la ayuda a los más necesitados

target practice *n* [U] prácticas *fpl* del tiro

tariff /'tærəf ‖ 'tærɪf/ *n* **1** (price list) (BrE) tarifa *f* **2** (Tax) arancel *m* (aduanero)

tarmac /'tɑ:rmæk ‖ 'tɑ:mæk/ *n* [U] **(a)** **tarmac**® (AmE) (tar mixture) asfalto *m* **(b)** (surface — in airport, racetrack) pista *f*; (— on road) asfalto *m*

Tarmac® *n* (BrE) ⇒ TARMAC¹ (a)

tarnish /'tɑ:rnɪʃ ‖ 'tɑ:nɪʃ/ *vt* **(a)** ‹*silver*› deslustrar **(b)** ‹*reputation/name*› empañar

tarot card /'tærəʊ/ *n* carta *f* de tarot

tarpaulin /tɑ:r'pɔ:lən ‖ tɑ:'pɔ:lɪn/ *n* **(a)** [C] (sheet) lona *f* **(b)** [U] (material) lona *f* impermeabilizada

tarragon /'tærəgən/ *n* [U] estragón *m*

tart¹ /tɑ:rt ‖ tɑ:t/ *n* **1** (Culin) (large) tarta *f*; (individual) tartaleta *f* **2** (promiscuous woman) (colloq) fulana *f* (fam), puta *f* (vulg)

tart² *adj* **(a)** ‹*taste/apple*› ácido, agrio **(b)** ‹*remark*› cortante, áspero

tartan /'tɑ:rtn̩ ‖ 'tɑ:tn̩/ *n* **(a)** [U] (cloth) tela *f* escocesa *or* de cuadros escoceses **(b)** [C] (pattern) tartán *m*

tartar /'tɑ:rtər ‖ 'tɑ:tə(r)/ *n* [U] (Dent) sarro *m*

task /tæsk ‖ tɑ:sk/ *n* tarea *f*; ***to take sb to ~*** llamarle la atención *or* leerle* la cartilla a algn

tassel /'tæsəl/ *n* borla *f*

taste¹ /teɪst/ *n* **1** [U] **(a)** (flavor) sabor *m*, gusto *m* **(b)** (sense) gusto *m* **2** (*no pl*) (sample, small amount): **can I have a ~ of your ice cream?** ¿me dejas probar tu helado?; **we got a ~ of what was to come** fue un anticipo de lo que nos esperaba **3** [C U] (liking) gusto *m*; **to be to one's ~** ser* de su (*or* mi *etc*) gusto **4** [U] (judgment) gusto *m*; **in good/bad ~** de buen/mal gusto

taste² *vt* **(a)** (test flavor of) ‹*food/wine*› probar* **(b)** (test quality of) ‹*food*› degustar; ‹*wine*› catar **(c)** (perceive flavor): **you can ~ the sherry in it** sabe a jerez, le siento gusto a jerez (AmL) **(d)** (experience) ‹*freedom*› conocer* ■ ~ *vi* saber*; **to ~ OF sth** saber* A algo

taste bud *n* papila *f* gustativa

tasteful /'teɪstfəl/ *adj* de buen gusto

tastefully /'teɪstfəli/ *adv* con (buen) gusto

tasteless /'teɪstləs ‖ 'teɪstlɪs/ *adj* **(a)** (flavorless) insípido, soso, desabrido **(b)** (in bad taste) de mal gusto

tasty /'teɪsti/ *adj* **-tier, -tiest** sabroso, apetitoso

tattered /'tætərd ‖ 'tætəd/ *adj* ‹*clothes*› hecho jirones; ‹*pride/image*› destrozado

tatters /'tætərz ‖ 'tætəz/ *pl n*: **to be in ~** «*clothes*» estar* hecho jirones

tattoo¹ /tæ'tu:/ *n* (*pl* **-toos**) **1** (picture) tatuaje *m* **2** (display) *espectáculo militar con música*

tattoo² *vt* **-toos, -tooing, -tooed** tatuar*

tatty /'tæti/ *adj* **-tier, -tiest** (BrE colloq) ‹*clothes/shoes*› gastado, estropeado; ‹*furniture*› estropeado

taught /tɔ:t/ *past & past p of* TEACH

taunt¹ /tɔ:nt/ *vt* provocar* mediante burlas

taunt² *n* (insult) insulto *m*; (jibe) pulla *f*

Taurus /'tɔ:rəs/ *n* **(a)** (sign) (*no art*) Tauro **(b)** [C] (person) Tauro *or* tauro *mf*, taurino -na *m,f*

taut /tɔːt/ *adj* ‹*rope/sail*› tenso, tirante; ‹*skin*› tirante

tavern /'tævərn ‖ 'tævən/ *n* taberna *f*

tawdry /'tɔːdri/ *adj* **-drier, -driest** ‹*jewelry/decorations*› de oropel; ‹*decor*› de mal gusto

tawny /'tɔːni/ ▶515 *adj* **-nier, -niest** leonado, pardo rojizo *adj inv*

tawny owl *n* cárabo *m*, antillo *m*

tax[1] /tæks/ *n* [U C] (individual charge) impuesto *m*, tributo *m* (frml); (in general) impuestos *mpl*; (*before n*) **the ~ year** (in UK) el año *or* ejercicio fiscal

tax[2] *vt* **1** ‹*company/goods/earnings*› gravar; **we're being ~ed too highly** nos están cobrando demasiado en impuestos **2** (strain) ‹*resources/health*› poner* a prueba

taxable /'tæksəbəl/ *adj* ‹*goods*› sujeto a impuestos; **~ income** ingresos *mpl* gravables, ≈ base *f* imponible

taxation /tæk'seɪʃən/ *n* [U] (taxes) impuestos *mpl*, cargas *fpl* fiscales; (system) sistema *m or* régimen *m* tributario *or* fiscal

tax: **~ collector** *n* recaudador, -dora *m,f* de impuestos; **~ evasion** *n* [U] evasión *f* fiscal *or* de impuestos; (large scale) fraude *m* fiscal; **~-free** /'tæks'friː/ *adj* libre de impuestos; **~ haven** *n* paraíso *m* fiscal

taxi[1] /'tæksi/ *n* (*pl* **~s**) taxi *m*; (*before n*) **~ driver** taxista *mf*

taxi[2] *vi* **taxies**, **taxiing** *or* **taxying**, **taxied** (Aviat) rodar* por la pista de despegue/de aterrizaje, carretear (AmL)

taxidermy /'tæksə'dɜːrmi ‖ 'tæksɪˌdɜːmi/ *n* [U] taxidermia *f*

taxing /'tæksɪŋ/ *adj* ‹*problem*› difícil, complicado; ‹*job*› (mentally) que exige mucho

tax: **~man** /'tæksmæn/ (*pl* **-men** /-men/) *n* (colloq) **the ~man** Hacienda *f*, el fisco; **~payer** /'peɪər ‖ 'peɪə(r)/ *n* contribuyente *mf*; **~ return** *n* declaración *f* de la renta *or* (esp AmL) de impuestos

TB *n* [U] = **tuberculosis**

tbs, **tbsp** = **tablespoon(s)**

te /tiː/ *n* (BrE Mus) si *m*

tea /tiː/ *n* **1** [U] (drink, leaves, plant) té *m* **2** [C U] (meal) **(a)** (in the afternoon) té *m*, merienda *f* **(b)** (evening) (BrE) cena *f*, comida *f* (AmL)

tea bag *n* bolista *f* de té

teach /tiːtʃ/ (*past & past p* **taught**) *vt* ‹*subject*› dar* clases de, enseñar; ‹*course*› dar*, impartir (frml); **to ~ sb to** + INF enseñarle a algn a + INF; **who ~es you?** ¿quien te da clase?; **to ~ school** (AmE) dar* clase(s) en un colegio ■ **~** *vi* dar* clase(s)

teacher /'tiːtʃər ‖ 'tiːtʃə(r)/ *n* profesor, -sora *m,f*, docente *mf* (frml), enseñante *mf* (period); (*primary school* ~) maestro, -tra *m,f*

teacher: **~s college** *n* (AmE) (for primary education) escuela *f* normal; (for secondary education) instituto *m* de profesorado; **~ training** *n* [U] formación *f* pedagógica *or* de profesorado; (*before n*) **~ training college** (BrE) ⇒ ~S COLLEGE

tea chest *n* caja *f* de embalaje (*utilizada en mudanzas*)

teaching /'tiːtʃɪŋ/ *n* **1** [U] (profession) enseñanza *f*, docencia *f* **2** (doctrine) (*often pl*) enseñanza *f*

teaching practice *n* (BrE) práctica *f* docente

tea: **~ cloth** *n* (BrE) ⇒ TEA TOWEL; **~ cozy**, (BrE) **~ cosy** *n* cubretetera *m*; **~cup** *n* taza *f* de té

teak /tiːk/ *n* [U] (madera *f* de) teca *f*

tealeaf /'tiːliːf/ *n* (*pl* **-leaves**) hoja *f* de té

team /tiːm/ *n* **(a)** (of players, workers) equipo *m*; (*before n*) **it was a ~ effort** fue un trabajo de equipo **(b)** (of horses) tiro *m*; (of oxen) yunta *f*

team: **~mate** *n* compañero, -ra *m,f* de equipo; **~ spirit** *n* [U] espíritu *m* de equipo

teamster /'tiːmstər ‖ 'tiːmstə(r)/ *n* (AmE) camionero, -ra *m,f*

teamwork /'tiːmwɜːrk ‖ 'tiːmwɜːk/ *n* [U] trabajo *m or* labor *f* de equipo

tea: **~ party** *n* té *m*; **~pot** *n* tetera *f*

tear[1] *n* **1** /tɪr ‖ tɪə(r)/ lágrima *f*; **to be in ~s** estar* llorando **2** /ter ‖ teə(r)/ rotura *f*; (rip, slash) desgarrón *m*, rasgón *m*; *see also* WEAR[1] 1(b)

tear[2] /ter ‖ teə(r)/ (*past* **tore**; *past p* **torn**) *vt* **(a)** ‹*cloth/paper*› romper*, rasgar*; **I tore open the letter** abrí la carta (*rasgando el sobre*); **to ~ sth to pieces** *o* **bits** *o* **shreds** ‹*cloth/paper*› hacer* algo pedazos; ‹*play/essay*› hacer* algo pedazos *or* trizas *or* (fam) polvo; ‹*argument*› echar algo por tierra **(b)** (divide) (*usu pass*) dividir; **he was torn between ... and ...** se debatía entre ... y ... **(c)** (remove forcibly) **to ~ sth FROM sth** arrancar* algo DE algo ■ **~** *vi* **1** «*cloth/paper*» romperse*, rasgarse* **2** (rush) (+ *adv compl*): **to ~ along** ir* a toda velocidad

• **tear apart** [*v* + *o* + *adv*] desgarrar

• **tear down** [*v* + *o* + *adv*, *v* + *adv* + *o*] tirar abajo

• **tear off** [*v* + *o* + *adv*, *v* + *adv* + *o*] arrancar*

• **tear out** [*v* + *o* + *adv*, *v* + *adv* + *o*] arrancar*

• **tear up** [*v* + *o* + *adv*, *v* + *adv* + *o*] romper*

teardrop /'tɪrdrɑːp ‖ 'tɪədrɒp/ *n* lágrima *f*

tearful /'tɪrfəl ‖ 'tɪəfəl/ *adj* ‹*look/expression*› lloroso; ‹*farewell*› triste, emotivo

tear gas /'tɪrgæs ‖ 'tɪəgæs/ *n* [U] gas *m* lacrimógeno

tearoom /'tiːruːm, -rʊm/ *n* salón *m* de té

tease /tiːz/ *vt* tomarle el pelo a (fam); (cruelly) burlarse *or* reírse de

tea: **~ service**, **~ set** *n* juego *m* de té; **~shop** *n* (esp BrE) ⇒ TEAROOM; **~spoon** *n* **(a)** (spoon) cucharita *f*, cucharilla *f* **(b)** (quantity) cucharadita *f*; **~ strainer** *n* colador *m* (*pequeño*)

teat /tiːt/ *n* **(a)** (Zool) tetilla *f* **(b)** (of feeding bottle) (BrE) ⇒ NIPPLE (b)

tea: **~time** *n* (of afternoon snack) la hora del té, ≈ la hora de merendar; (of evening meal) (BrE) la hora de cenar *or* (AmL tb) de comer; **~ towel** *n* (BrE) paño *m or* trapo *m* de cocina

technical /'teknɪkəl/ *adj* técnico

technical college *n* (in UK) escuela *f* politécnica, ≈ instituto *m* de formación profesional (*en Esp*)

technicality /'teknɪ'kæləti/ *n* (*pl* **-ties**) (detail) detalle *m* técnico

technically /'teknɪkli/ *adv* técnicamente; (*indep*) desde el punto de vista técnico

technician /tek'nɪʃən/ *n* técnico *mf*, técnico, -ca *m,f*

technique /tek'ni:k/ *n* [C U] técnica *f*

technological /'teknə'lɑ:dʒɪkəl ‖ˌteknə'lɒdʒɪkəl/ *adj* tecnológico

technology /tek'nɑ:lədʒi ‖ tek'nɒlədʒi/ *n* [U C] (*pl* **-gies**) tecnología *f*

teddy bear /'tedi/ *n* osito *m* de peluche

tedious /'ti:diəs/ *adj* tedioso

tedium /'ti:diəm/ *n* [U] tedio *m*

teem /ti:m/ *vi* **to ~** WITH **sth**: **the forest is ~ing with birds** el bosque está repleto de pájaros; **the streets were ~ing with people** las calles hervían de gente

teenage /'ti:neɪdʒ/ *adj* ‹*girl/boy*› adolescente; ‹*fashions*› juvenil, para adolescentes

teenager /'ti:neɪdʒər ‖ 'ti:neɪdʒə(r)/ *n* adolescente *mf*

teens /ti:nz/ ▶ **451** *pl n* adolescencia *f*

tee shirt /ti:/ *n* ⇒ T-SHIRT

teeter /'ti:tər ‖ 'ti:tə(r)/ *vi* «*person*» tambalearse

teeth /ti:θ/ *pl of* TOOTH

teethe /ti:ð/ *vi*: **she's teething** le están saliendo los dientes

teething troubles /'ti:ðɪŋ/*pl n* problemas *mpl* iniciales

teetotal /'ti:'təʊtl̩/ *adj* abstemio

TEFL /'tefəl/ *n* [U] (BrE) (= **teaching English as a foreign language**) *enseñanza del inglés como lengua extranjera*

tel (= **telephone number**) Tel., fono (CS)

telecommunications /'telikə'mju:nə'keɪʃənz ‖ˌtelikəˌmju:nɪ'keɪʃənz/ *n* telecomunicaciones *fpl*

telegram /'teləgræm ‖ 'telɪgræm/ *n* telegrama *m*

telegraph /'teləgræf ‖ 'telɪgrɑ:f/ *n* **(a)** [U] (method) telégrafo *m*; (*before n*) ‹*wire/cable*› telegráfico; **~ pole** poste *m* telegráfico **(b)** [C] (message) telegrama *m*, despacho *m* telegráfico

telepathic /'telə'pæθɪk ‖ˌtelɪ'pæθɪk/ *adj* ‹*message*› telepático; ‹*person*› con telepatía, telépata

telepathy /tə'lepəθi/ *n* [U] telepatía *f*

telephone¹ /'teləfəʊn ‖ 'telɪfəʊn/ ▶ **875** *n* teléfono *m*; (*before n*) ‹*message/line*› telefónico; **~ number** (número *m* de) teléfono *m*; **~ operator** telefonista *mf*; *see also* PHONE¹

telephone² *vt* telefonear, llamar por teléfono a

telephone: **~ booth**, (BrE) **~ box** *n* cabina *f* telefónica *or* de teléfonos; **~ directory** *n* guía *f* telefónica *or* de teléfonos; **~ exchange** *n* central *f* telefónica *or* de teléfonos

telephonist /tə'lefənəst ‖ tə'lefənɪst/ *n* (BrE) telefonista *mf*

telesales /'teliseɪlz/ *pl n* televentas *fpl*

telescope /'teləskəʊp ‖ 'telɪskəʊp/ *n* telescopio *m*

telescopic /'telə'skɑ:pɪk ‖ˌtelɪs'kɒpɪk/ *adj* telescópico

teletext /'telitekst/ *n* teletex(to) *m*, videotex(to) *m*

televise /'teləvaɪz ‖ 'telɪvaɪz/ *vt* televisar

television /'teləvɪʒən ‖ 'telɪvɪʒən/ *n* **(a)** [U] (medium, industry) televisión *f*; **on ~** en *or* por (la) televisión; (*before n*) **~ licence** (in UK) *impuesto y licencia que debe obtenerse para poder usar un receptor de televisión* **(b)** [C] **~ (set)** televisor *m*

telex /'teleks/ *n* [C U] télex *m*

tell /tel/ (*past & past p* **told**) *vt* **1** (inform, reveal) decir*; **he was told that** ... le dijeron que ...; **could you ~ me the way to the station?** ¿me podría decir cómo se llega a la estación? **2** (recount, relate) ‹*joke/story*› contar*; **she's told me all about you** me ha hablado mucho de ti; **~ us about Lima** cuéntanos cómo es Lima (*or* qué tal se fue en Lima *etc*) **3** (instruct, warn) decir*; **to ~ sb to** + INF decirle* a algn QUE (+ *subj*) **4 (a)** (ascertain, know): **I could ~ from her voice that** ... noté por la voz que ...; **to ~ the time** decir la hora **(b)** (distinguish) **to ~ sth/sb** (FROM **sth/sb**) distinguir* algo/a algn (DE algo/algn); **I can't ~ the difference** yo no veo *or* no noto ninguna diferencia **5**: **all told** en total ■ **~** *vi* **1** (reveal): **promise you won't ~?** ¿prometes que no se lo vas a contar *or* decir a nadie?; **to ~ ON sb (TO sb)** (colloq) acusar a algn (A *or* CON algn) **2** (know) saber*; **you never can ~** nunca se sabe **3** (count, have an effect): **her age is beginning to ~** se le está empezando a notar la edad

● **tell apart** [*v* + *o* + *adv*] distinguir*

● **tell off** [*v* + *o* + *adv*, *v* + *adv* + *o*] (colloq) regañar, reñir* (esp Esp), retar (CS), resondrar (Per), rezongar* (AmC, Ur)

teller /'telər ‖ 'telə(r)/ *n* (in bank) cajero, -ra *m,f*

telling /'telɪŋ/ *adj* ‹*sign/remark*› revelador

telltale¹ /'telteɪl/ *adj* (*before n*) revelador

telltale² *n* (person) (colloq) soplón, -plona *m,f* (fam), acusete *mf* (fam)

temp /temp/ *n* empleado, -da *m,f* eventual *or* temporal

temper¹ /'tempər ‖ 'tempə(r)/ *n* **(a)** (*no pl*) (mood) humor *m*; (temperament, disposition) carácter *m*, genio *m*; **to have a bad ~** tener* mal genio **(b)** [C U] (rage): **to be in a ~** estar* furioso *or* hecho una furia **(c)** [C U] (composure): **to lose one's ~** perder* los estribos

temper² *vt* **(a)** (moderate) ‹*criticism*› atenuar* **(b)** (Metall) templar

temperament /'temprəmənt/ *n* [C] temperamento *m*

temperamental /'temprə'mentl̩/ *adj* ‹*person*› temperamental

temperance /'tempərəns/ *n* [U] **(a)** (moderation) (frml) templanza *f* (frml), moderación *f* **(b)** (alcohol avoidance) abstinencia *f* de bebidas; (*before n*) ‹*movement*› antialcohólico

temperate /'tempərət/ *adj* templado

temperature /'temprətʃər ‖ 'temprətʃə(r)/ ▶ **406** *n* [C U] **(a)** (Phys) temperatura *f* **(b)** (Med) (reading on thermometer) temperatura *f*; (abnormally high reading) fiebre *f*, temperatura *f* (CS); **to have** *o* **run a ~** tener* fiebre *or* (CS) temperatura

Telephone Language

Answering the phone

Hello	=	¡Sí!
	=	¡Aló! (*AmS*)
	=	¡Bueno! (*Méx*)
	=	¡Olá! (*RPl*)
	=	¡Diga! *or* ¡Dígame! (*Esp*)

The caller's opening words

hello, is that Jackie?	=	¿aló? ¿Jackie? (*AmS*) *or* (*Esp*) ¿eres Jackie?
hello, is that Mr Sánchez?	=	¿es usted el señor Sánchez?
is Jackie there, please?	=	¿está Jackie, por favor?
could I speak with *o* (*BrE*) to Jackie, please?	=	¿podría hablar con Jackie, por favor?
I wonder if I could speak with *o* (*BrE*) to Mr Bolton, please	=	¿podría hablar con el señor Bolton, por favor?
hello, this is Pete here	=	habla Pete *or* (*Esp*) soy Pete
hello, this is Donald Pearce speaking	=	buenos días/buenas tardes, habla Donald Pearce

Possible replies

(yes,) speaking	=	con él/ella (habla) *or* (*Esp*) soy yo
just a minute, please *o*	=	un momento *or* un momentito, por favor
hold on, please	=	(espere) un momento, por favor
hang on a minute	=	(espera) un momentito
hold the line, please *o* please hold	=	no cuelgue, por favor
who am I speaking to, please?	=	¿con quién hablo, por favor?
who's calling *o* speaking, please?	=	¿de parte de quién?
who shall I say is calling?	=	¿de parte de quién?
I'm afraid she isn't here at the moment	=	lo siento, (en este momento) no está
can I take a message? *o* would you like to leave a message?	=	¿quiere(s) dejar un mensaje?

The caller's response

It's OK. I'll call back *o* try again later	=	no gracias, volveré a llamar más tarde
could you tell her that *o* say that Paul called?	=	¿podría decirle que llamó Paul?
Could you ask her to call me back? She has my number	=	¿Podría decirle que me llame? Ella sabe mi teléfono

Other examples

could you put me through to the manager, please?	=	¿me comunica *or* (*Esp*) me pone con el gerente, por favor?
could I have extension 483 please?	=	¿me comunica *or* (*Esp*) me pone con extensión 483, por favor?
please leave your message after the tone	=	por favor deje su mensaje después de la señal

Telephone Numbers

The digits of telephone numbers in Spanish are often combined into larger numbers:

55–47–82	=	cincuenta y cinco – cuarenta y siete – ochenta y dos
308–12–23	=	trescientos ocho – doce – ventitrés *or* tres – cero-ocho –veintitrés
541 37 02	=	cinco – cuarenta y uno – treinta y siete – cero – dos *or* cinco – cuatro – uno – treinta y siete – cero – dos *or* quinientos cuarenta y uno – treinta y siete – cero – dos

tempest /'tempəst ‖ 'tempɪst/ *n* (liter) tempestad *f* (liter)

tempestuous /tem'pestʃuəs ‖ tem'pestjʊəs/ *adj* **(a)** ‹*relationship*› tempestuoso **(b)** ‹*sea*› (liter) tempestuoso (liter)

temple /'tempəl/ *n* **a** (Relig) templo *m* **2** (Anat) sien *f*

tempo /'tempəʊ/ *n* (*pl* **-pos** *or* **-pi** /-pi/) ritmo *m*; (Mus) tempo *m*

temporal /'tempərəl/ *adj* temporal

temporarily /'tempə'rerəli ‖ 'tempərərɪli/ *adj* temporalmente, temporariamente (AmL)

temporary /'tempəreri ‖ 'temprəri/ *adj* ‹*accommodation/arrangement*› temporal, provisional; ‹*job/work/worker*› eventual, temporal

tempt /tempt/ *vt* (*often pass*) tentar*

temptation /temp'teɪʃən/ *n* [U C] tentación *f*

tempting /'temptɪŋ/ *adj* tentador

ten[1] /ten/ **▶ 451**, **724**, **884** *n* diez *m*; *see also* FOUR[1]

ten[2] **▶ 451**, **724**, **884** *adj* diez *adj inv*

tenable /'tenəbəl/ *adj* defendible

tenacious /tə'neɪʃəs ‖ tɪ'neɪʃəs/ *adj* tenaz

tenacity /tə'næsəti ‖ tɪ'næsəti/ *n* [U] tenacidad *f*

tenancy /'tenənsi/ *n* [C U] (*pl* **-cies**) (holding, possession) tenencia *f*

tenant /'tenənt/ *n* inquilino, -na *m,f*, arrendatario, -ria *m,f*

tend /tend/ *vi* **1** (have tendency, be inclined) tender*; **to ~ to** + INF tender* A + INF **2** (attend) **to ~ TO sth/sb** ocuparse DE algo/algn ■ **~** *vt* ‹*sheep*› cuidar (de), ocuparse de; ‹*victims*› cuidar (de), atender*; ‹*garden/grave*› ocuparse de

tendency /'tendənsi/ *n* (*pl* **-cies**) tendencia *f*; (Med) propensión *f*, tendencia *f*

tender¹ /'tendər ‖ 'tendə(r)/ *adj* **(a)** (sensitive) ‹*spot*› sensible; ‹*age*› tierno **(b)** ‹*meat*› tierno **(c)** (loving) tierno

tender² *n* **(a)** [C U] (Busn) (offer) propuesta *f*, oferta *f* **(b)** [U] (*legal* ~) moneda *f* de curso legal

tender³ *vt* (frml) ‹*resignation*› presentar, ofrecer*

tenderize /'tendəraɪz/ *vt* ‹*meat*› ablandar

tenderly /'tendərli ‖ 'tendəli/ *adv* tiernamente, con ternura

tendon /'tendən/ *n* tendón *m*

tendril /'tendrəl ‖ 'tendrɪl/ *n* zarcillo *m*

tenet /'tenət ‖ 'tenɪt/ *n* principio *m*

tenfold /'tenfəʊld/ *adj/adv see* -FOLD

Tenn = **Tennessee**

tennis /'tenəs ‖ 'tenɪs/ *n* [U] tenis *m*; (*before n*) ~ **court** cancha *f or* (Esp) pista *f* de tenis; ~ **player** tenista *mf*; ~ **raquet** raqueta *f* de tenis

tenor¹ /'tenər ‖ 'tenə(r)/ *n* **1** [C U] (Mus) tenor *m* **2** (frml) (sense) tenor *m*

tenor² *adj* (*before n*) ‹*voice*› de tenor; ‹*saxophone*› tenor

ten: ~**pin bowling** *n* [U] (BrE) ⇒ ~PINS; ~**pins** *n* (+ *sing vb*) (AmE) bolos *mpl*, bowling *m*

tense¹ /tens/ *adj* **(a)** ‹*situation/person*› tenso **(b)** (taut) tenso, tirante

tense² *vt* ‹*muscles*› poner* tenso, tensar
• **tense up** [*v* + *adv*] (colloq) ponerse* tenso

tense³ *n* (Ling) tiempo *m*

tension /'tentʃən ‖ 'tenʃən/ *n* **1** [C U] **(a)** (of situation) tensión *f*, tirantez *f* **(b)** (felt by person) tensión *f* **(c)** (between two parties) conflicto *m* **2** [U] (tautness) tensión *f* **3** [U] (Elec) tensión *f*

tent /tent/ *n* tienda *f* (de campaña), carpa *f* (AmL)

tentacle /'tentɪkəl ‖ 'tentəkəl/ *n* tentáculo *m*

tentative /'tentətɪv/ *adj* **(a)** ‹*plan*› provisional, provisorio (AmS); ‹*offer*› tentativo **(b)** ‹*person*› indeciso

tenterhooks /'tentərhʊks ‖ 'tentəhʊks/ *pl n*: *to be on* ~ estar* en *or* sobre ascuas

tenth¹ /tenθ/ ▶ **540**, **725** *adj* décimo

tenth² *adv* en décimo lugar

tenth³ ▶ **540**, **543**, **725** *n* (Math) décimo *m*; (part) décima parte *f*

tenuous /'tenjuəs/ *adj* ‹*claim*› poco fundado; ‹*link*› indirecto

tenure /'tenjər ‖ 'tenjə(r)/ *n* **(a)** [U] (of property, land) tenencia *f* **(b)** [U C] (period of office) ejercicio *m*, ocupación *f*

tepid /'tepəd ‖ 'tepɪd/ *adj* tibio

term¹ /tɜːrm ‖ tɜːm/ *n* **I 1** (word) término *m* **2 (a)** (period) período *m*, periodo *m*; ~ **of** *o* (AmE also) **in office** mandato *m*; **in the short/long** ~ a corto/largo plazo **(b)** (Educ) trimestre *m*
II terms *pl* **1** (conditions) condiciones *fpl*; ***to come to*** **~*s with sth*** aceptar algo **2** (relations): **to be on good/bad ~s with sb** estar* en buenas/malas relaciones con algn **3 (a)** (sense): **in financial ~s** desde el punto de vista financiero; **in real ~s** en términos reales **(b) in terms of**: **in ~s of efficiency** en cuanto a eficiencia

term² *vt* calificar* de

terminal¹ /'tɜːrmənl ‖ 'tɜːmɪnl/ *adj* ‹*illness*› terminal; ‹*patient*› (en fase) terminal, desahuciado

terminal² *n* **(a)** (Transp) (at airport) terminal *f*; **bus** ~ terminal *f* de autobuses **(b)** (Comput) terminal *m* **(c)** (Elec) terminal *m*

terminally /'tɜːrmənəli ‖ 'tɜːmɪnəli/ *adv*: **he's ~ ill** está en fase terminal, está desahuciado

terminate /'tɜːrməneɪt ‖ 'tɜːmɪneɪt/ *vt* (frml) ‹*relationship*› poner* fin a; ‹*contract*› poner* término a; ‹*employee*› (AmE) despedir*, cesar (frml *or* period); ‹*pregnancy*› interrumpir ■ ~ *vi* «*lease/relationship*» terminarse; **this train ~s here** éste es el final del recorrido de este tren

termination /'tɜːrmə'neɪʃən ‖ ˌtɜːmɪ'neɪʃən/ *n* **(a)** [U] (of contract) (frml) terminación *f* **(b)** [U C] (Med): ~ **of pregnancy** interrupción *f* del embarazo

terminology /'tɜːrmə'nɑːlədʒi ‖ ˌtɜːmɪ'nɒlədʒi/ *n* [U C] (*pl* **-gies**) terminología *f*

terminus /'tɜːrmənəs ‖ 'tɜːmɪnəs/ *n* (*pl* **-nuses** *or* **-ni** /-niː, -naɪ ‖ -naɪ/) (of buses) terminal *f*; (of trains) estación *f* terminal

termite /'tɜːrmaɪt ‖ 'tɜːmaɪt/ *n* termita *f*

terrace /'terəs ‖ 'terəs, 'terɪs/ *n* **(a)** (patio) terraza *f* **(b)** (balcony) (AmE) terraza *f* **(c)** (on hillside) terraza *f* **(d)** (row of houses) (BrE) *hilera de casas adosadas*

terraced /'terəst ‖ 'terəst, 'terɪst/ *adj* **(a)** ‹*hillside/slope*› en terrazas *or* bancales **(b)** ‹*house*› (BrE) adosado (*en una hilera de casas uniformes*)

terrain /te'reɪn/ *n* [U C] terreno *m*

terrestrial /tə'restriəl/ *adj* terrestre

terrible /'terəbəl/ *adj* espantoso, atroz

terribly /'terəbli/ *adv* ‹*suffer*› terriblemente; ‹*sing/act*› terriblemente mal

terrier /'teriər ‖ 'teriə(r)/ *n* terrier *mf*

terrific /tə'rɪfɪk/ *adj* **(a)** (enormous) (colloq) tremendo, increíble; ‹*argument*› espantoso **(b)** (very good) (colloq) estupendo, genial (fam)

terrified /'terəfaɪd ‖ 'terɪfaɪd/ *adj* ‹*crowd*› aterrorizado, aterrado; **to be ~** OF **sth/sb** tenerle* terror *or* pánico A algo/algn

terrify /'terəfaɪ ‖ 'terɪfaɪ/ *vt* **-fies, -fying, -fied** aterrorizar*

terrifying /'terəfaɪɪŋ ‖ 'terɪfaɪɪŋ/ *adj* aterrador

territorial /'terə'tɔːriəl ‖ ˌterɪ'tɔːriəl/ *adj* territorial

territory /'terətɔːri ‖ 'terɪtəri, -tri/ *n* [U C] (*pl* **-ries**) territorio *m*

terror /'terər ‖ 'terə(r)/ *n* [U] terror *m*; **they fled in** ~ huyeron aterrorizados *or* despavoridos

terrorism /'terərɪzəm/ *n* [U] terrorismo *m*

terrorist /'terərəst ‖ 'terərɪst/ *n* terrorista *mf*

terrorize /'terəraɪz/ *vt* aterrorizar*, tener* atemorizado

terse /tɜːrs ‖ tɜːs/ *adj* seco, lacónico

test¹ /test/ *n* **(a)** (Educ) prueba *f*; (multiple-choice type) test *m* **(b)** (of machine, drug) prueba *f*; (*before n*) ‹*run/flight*› experimental, de prueba **(c)** (of blood, urine) análisis *m*; (for hearing, eyes) examen *m*

test² *vt* **(a)** ‹*student/class*› examinar, hacerle* una prueba a; ‹*knowledge/skill*› evaluar* **(b)** ‹*product*› probar*, poner* a prueba **(c)** ‹*friendship/endurance*› poner* a prueba **(d)** ‹*blood/urine*› analizar*; ‹*sight/hearing*› examinar; ‹*hypothesis*› comprobar*

testament /'testəmənt/ *n* **1** (will) testamento *m* **2** **Testament** (Bib): **the Old/New T~** el Antiguo/Nuevo Testamento

test: **~ case** *n*: *caso que sienta jurisprudencia*; **~ drive** *n* (Auto) prueba *f* de circulación en carretera

testicle /'testɪkəl/ *n* testículo *m*

testify /'testəfaɪ ‖ 'testɪfaɪ/ *vi* **-fies, -fying, -fied** (Law frml) prestar declaración, testificar*; **to ~** TO **sth** declarar *or* testificar* algo

testimonial /'testə'məʊniəl ‖ ,testɪ'məʊniəl/ *n* recomendación *f*

testimony /'testəməʊni ‖ 'testɪməni/ *n* (*pl* **-nies**) [U C] (Law) declaración *f*, testimonio *m*

testing¹ /'testɪŋ/ *n* [U] pruebas *fpl*

testing² *adj* duro, arduo

test: **~ match** *n* (Sport) partido *m* internacional; **~ paper** *n* (Educ) examen *m*, prueba *f*; **~ pilot** *n* piloto *mf* de pruebas; **~ tube** *n* probeta *f*, tubo *m* de ensayo; (*before n*) **~-tube baby** niño, -ña *m,f* probeta

tetanus /'tetn̩əs ‖ 'tetn̩əs/ *n* [U] tétano(s) *m*

tether¹ /'teðər ‖ 'teðə(r)/ *n* soga *f*

tether² *vt* atar, amarrar

Tex = **Texas**

text /tekst/ *n* [U C] texto *m*

textbook /'tekstbʊk/ *n* libro *m* de texto

textile /'tekstaɪl/ *n* [C U] textil *m*

textual /'tekstʃuəl ‖ 'tekstjʊəl/ *adj* textual

texture /'tekstʃər ‖ 'tekstʃə(r)/ *n* [U C] textura *f*

Thai¹ /taɪ/ *adj* tailandés

Thai² *n* **(a)** [C] (person) tailandés, -desa *m,f* **(b)** [U] (language) tailandés *m*

Thailand /'taɪlænd/ *n* Tailandia *f*

Thames /temz/ *n* **the ~** el Támesis

than¹ /ðæn, *weak form* ðən/ *conj* **(a)** (in comparisons) que; (with quantity) de; **I'm feeling better ~ I was** me siento mejor que antes; **more ~ $25** más de 25 dólares; **the situation is worse ~ we thought** la situación es peor de lo que pensábamos **(b)** (with alternatives): **I'd rather walk ~ go by bus** prefiero ir a pie a tomar el autobús **(c)** (when) cuando; **no sooner had I sat down ~ the bell rang** apenas me había sentado cuando sonó el timbre

than² *prep* (in comparisons) que; (with quantity) de

thank /θæŋk/ *vt* **to ~ sb** (FOR **sth**) darle* las gracias a algn (POR algo), agradecerle* (algo) a algn; **~ God/heaven(s)** menos mal, gracias a Dios; *see also* THANK YOU

thankful /'θæŋkfəl/ *adj* ‹*look/smile*› de agradecimiento, agradecido

thankfully /'θæŋkfəli/ *adv* (*indep*) menos mal, gracias a Dios

thankless /'θæŋkləs ‖ 'θæŋklɪs/ *adj* ingrato

thanks /θæŋks/ *pl n* **(a)** (expression of gratitude) agradecimiento *m* **(b)** (*as interj*) **~!** ¡gracias!; **many ~** muchas gracias **(c)** **thanks to** gracias a

Thanksgiving (Day) /'θæŋks'gɪvɪŋ/ *n* (in US) el día de Acción de Gracias

thank you *interj* ¡gracias!; **~ ~ very much** muchas gracias; **to say ~ ~** dar* las gracias; **~ ~ for coming/your help** gracias por venir/tu ayuda

that¹ /ðæt/ *pron* **1** (*pl* **those**) (demonstrative) ése, ésa; (*neuter*) eso; **those** ésos, ésas; (*to refer to sth more distant or to the remote past*) aquél, aquélla; (*neuter*) aquello; **those** aquéllos, aquéllas; **~'s wonderful!** ¡es maravilloso!; **those who have been less fortunate** los que no han tenido tanta suerte **2** (*in phrases*) **at that** (moreover) además; (thereupon): **at ~ they all burst out laughing** al oír (*or* ver *etc*) eso, todos se echaron a reír; **that is** es decir; **that's it!**: **~'s it for today** eso es todo por hoy; **now lift your left arm: ~'s it!** ahora levanta el brazo izquierdo ¡eso es! *or* ¡ahí está!; **~'s it: I've had enough!** ¡se acabó! ¡ya no aguanto más! **3** /ðət, *strong form* ðæt/ (relative) que; **it wasn't Helen (~) you saw** no fue a Helen a quien viste, no fue a Helen que viste (AmL)

that² /ðæt/ *adj* (*pl* **those**) ese, esa; **those** esos, esas; (*to refer to sth more distant, to the remote past*) aquel, aquella; **those** aquellos, aquellas

that³ /ðət, *strong form* ðæt/ *conj* que; **she said (~)** ... dijo que ...; **the news ~ our team had won** la noticia de que nuestro equipo había ganado

that⁴ /ðæt/ *adv* tan; **he can't be all ~ stupid** no es posible que sea tan tonto

thatched /θætʃt/ *adj* ‹*roof*› de paja (*or* de juncos *etc*) *or* (AmS) de quincha; ‹*cottage*› con el tejado de paja (*or* de juncos *etc*), quinchado (AmS)

thaw¹ /θɔː/ *vi* «*snow/ice*» derretirse*, fundirse; «*frozen food*» descongelarse; «*relations*» hacerse* más cordial ■ **~** *vt* ‹*frozen food*› descongelar

thaw² ▶ 920 *n* (Meteo, Pol) deshielo *m*

the¹ /*before vowel* ði, ðɪ; *before consonant* ðə, *strong form* ðiː/ ▶ 878 *def art* **1** (*sing*) el, la; (*pl*) los, las **2 (a)** (with names): **Henry ~ First** Enrique primero; **~ Smiths** los Smith **(b)** (in abstractions, generalizations) (+ *sing vb*): **~ impossible** lo imposible; **~ young** los jóvenes **3** (per): **they sell it by ~ square foot** lo venden por pie cuadrado; **I get paid by ~ hour** me pagan por hora

the² /*before vowel* ði; *before consonant* ðə/ *adv* (+ *comp*) (*as conj*) cuanto; **~ more you have, ~ more you want** cuanto más tienes, más quieres; **~ sooner, ~ better** cuanto antes, mejor

theater, (BrE) **theatre** /'θiːətər ‖ 'θɪətə(r)/ *n* **1 (a)** [C] (building) teatro *m* **(b)** [U] (theatrical world) **the ~** el teatro **2** [C] (*movie ~*) (AmE) cine *m*

theatrical /θi'ætrɪkəl/ *adj* teatral

theft /θeft/ *n* [U C] robo *m*

their /ðer ‖ ðeə(r)/ *adj*

■ **Note** The translation *su* agrees in number with the noun which it modifies; *their* is translated by *su, sus*, depending on what follows: *their father/mother* su padre/madre; *their books/magazines* sus libros/revistas. For *their* used with parts of the body, ▶ 484

(a) (*sing*) su; (*pl*) sus **(b)** (belonging to indefinite person) (*sing*) su; (*pl*) sus; **whoever called didn't**

The

The definite article the *is translated by* el *before a masculine singular noun,* la *before a feminine singular noun,* los *before a masculine plural noun,* las *before a feminine plural noun*:

the book/books = el libro/los libros
the table/tables = la mesa/las mesas

Singular feminine nouns beginning with a stressed or accented a *or* ha *take the article* el *rather than* la:

the eagle = el águila
the water = el agua

These nouns are marked in this dictionary by the symbol ‡

Exceptions to this rule are:

◆ *the letters of the alphabet* la a *and* la hache
◆ *words such as* la árabe, *where the feminine article is needed in order to differentiate gender*

The masculine singular article el *combines with the prepositions* de *and* a *to form* del *and* al:

la página del libro = the page of the book
fui al mercado = I went to the market

When/when not to use *the*

In the following cases, translations into Spanish must include the definite article, although it does not appear in English

◆ *with generic nouns, which denote a whole category*:

love is powerful = el amor es poderoso
I despise hypocrisy = detesto la hipocresía
children are a blessing = los niños son una bendición
roses are beautiful = las rosas son hermosas

◆ *with the names of certain countries and places*:

India = la India
Cairo = El Cairo
Havana = la Habana

Note that some geographical names may be used with or without the article (this is not a comprehensive list):

Argentina = (la) Argentina
Brazil = (el) Brasil
Ecuador = (el) Ecuador
Japan = (el) Japón
Paraguay = (el) Paraguay
Peru = (el) Perú
Uruguay = (el) Uruguay
Vietnam = (el) Vietnam

◆ *where a second plural noun is mentioned, with a change of gender in the Spanish*:

the horses and cows = los caballos y las vacas

The definite article is not translated in the names of monarchs or popes which contain an ordinal number in English:

Henry the Third = Enrique tercero
Elizabeth the Second = Isabel segunda

---

leave ∼ number la persona que ha llamado no dejó su teléfono

theirs /ðerz ‖ ðeəz/ *pron*

■ **Note** The translation *suyo* reflects the gender and number of the noun it is standing for; *theirs* is translated by *el suyo, la suya, los suyos, las suyas*, depending on what is being referred to.

(*sing*) suyo, -ya; (*pl*) suyos, -yas; **∼ is blue** el suyo/la suya *or* el/la de ellos es azul; **a friend of ∼** un amigo suyo *or* de ellos

them /ðem, *weak form* ðəm/ ▶ 638 *pron* **1 (a)** (as direct object) los, las; (referring to people) los *or* (Esp tb) les, las; **where did you buy ∼?** ¿dónde los/las compraste?; **he has two sons, do you know ∼?** tiene dos hijos ¿los *or* (Esp tb) les conoces? **(b)** (as indirect object) les; (with direct object pronoun present) se; **I lent ∼ some money** les presté dinero **(c)** (after preposition) ellos, ellas **2** (emphatic use) ellos, ellas; **that'll be ∼** deben de ser ellos **3** (indefinite person): **if anyone calls, tell ∼ that** … si llama alguien, dile que …

theme /θi:m/ *n* tema *m*; (*before n*) **∼ park** parque *m* temático; **∼ song** tema *m* musical; (of TV program) (AmE) música *f* de un programa

themselves /ðəm'selvz/ *pron* **(a)** (reflexive): **they bought ∼ a new car** se compraron otro coche; **they only think of ∼** sólo piensan en sí mismos; **they were by ∼** estaban solos/solas **(b)** (emphatic) ellos mismos, ellas mismas **(c)** (normal selves): **the children aren't ∼** los niños no son los de siempre **(d)** (indefinite person or persons): **if anyone's interested they can find out for ∼** si a alguien le interesa, puede averiguarlo por sí mismo

then[1] /ðen/ *adv* **1 (a)** (at that time) entonces **(b)** (in those days) en aquel entonces **2** (*after prep*): **by ∼** para entonces; **from ∼ on** a partir de ese momento, desde entonces; **(up) until** *o* **till ∼** hasta entonces **3 (a)** (next, afterward) después, luego **(b)** (in those circumstances) entonces **(c)** (besides, in addition) además **4** (in that case) entonces; ***you* do it, ∼!** ¡hazlo tú, entonces! **5 then again** (*as linker*) también

then[2] *adj* (*before n*) entonces; **the ∼ leader** el entonces líder

theologian /'θiə'ləʊdʒən/ *n* teólogo, -ga *m,f*

theological /'θiə'lɑ:dʒɪkəl ‖ ˌθiə'lɒdʒɪkəl/ *adj* teológico

theology /θi'ɑ:lədʒi ‖ θi'ɒlədʒi/ *n* [U C] (*pl* **-gies**) teología *f*

theorem /'θiərəm / *n* teorema *m*

theoretical /'θiə'retɪkəl/ *adj* teórico

theorize /'θiəraɪz/ *vi* especular, teorizar*

theory /'θiəri/ *n* [C U] (*pl* **-ries**) teoría *f*

therapeutic /'θerə'pju:tɪk/ *adj* terapéutico

therapist /'θerəpəst ‖ 'θerəpɪst/ *n* terapeuta *mf*

therapy /'θerəpi/ *n* [C U] (*pl* **-pies**) terapia *f*

there¹ /ðer ‖ ðeə(r)/ *adv* **1 (a)** (close to person being addressed) ahí; (further away) allí, ahí (esp AmL); (less precise, further) allá; **up/down ~** ahí arriba/abajo **(b) there and then** ‹*decide*› en ese mismo momento; **they mended it for me ~ and then** me lo arreglaron en el acto **2** (calling attention to sth): **~ you are** (giving sth) aquí tiene; **~ go my chances of promotion!** ¡adiós ascenso! **3** (present): **all his friends were ~** estaban todos sus amigos; **is Tony ~?** ¿está Tony?; **who's ~?** (at the door) ¿quién es?; (in the dark) ¿quién anda ahí? **4** (*as interj*) **~! that's the last of the boxes** ¡listo! ésa es la última caja; **~, ~, don't cry!** vamos, no llores

there² /ðer *weak form* ðər ‖ ðeə(r) *weak form* ðə(r)/ *pron*: **there is/are** hay; **there was** había/hubo; **there will be** habrá

there: **~about** /'ðerəbaʊt ‖ 'ðeərəbaʊt/ *adv* (AmE) ⇒ ~ABOUTS; **~abouts** /'ðerəbaʊts ‖ 'ðeərəbaʊts/ *adv* **(a)** (near that figure, time) por ahí **(b)** (in that vicinity) por allí; **~after** /ðer'æftər ‖ ðeər'ɑ:ftə(r)/ *adv* (frml) a partir de entonces; **~by** /'ðer'baɪ ‖ ðeə'baɪ, 'ðeəbaɪ/ *adv* (frml) de ese modo, así; **~fore** /'ðerfɔ:r ‖ 'ðeəfɔ:(r)/ *adv* por lo tanto, por consiguiente

there's /ðerz *weak form* ðərz ‖ ðeəz *weak form* ðəz/ **(a)** = **there is (b)** = **there has**

thermal /'θɜ:rməl ‖ 'θɜ:məl/ *adj* **(a)** ‹*stream/bath*› termal **(b)** ‹*underwear/glove*› térmico

thermometer /θər'mɑ:mətər ‖ θə'mɒmɪtə(r)/ *n* termómetro *m*

Thermos® (flask) /'θɜ:rməs ‖ 'θɜ:məs/, (AmE also) **thermos (bottle)** *n* termo *m*

thermostat /'θɜ:rməstæt ‖ 'θɜ:məstæt/ *n* termostato *m*

thesaurus /θɪ'sɔ:rəs/ *n* (*pl* **-ruses** *or* **-ri** /-raɪ/) diccionario *m* ideológico *or* de ideas afines, tesauro *m*

these /ði:z/ *pl of* THIS[1,2]

thesis /'θi:səs ‖ 'θi:sɪs/ *n* (*pl* **-ses** /-si:z/) tesis *f*; (shorter) tesina *f*

they /ðeɪ/ *pron*

■ **Note** Although *ellos* and *ellas* are given as translations of *they*, they are in practice used only for emphasis, or to avoid ambiguity: *they went to the theater* fueron al teatro; ***they*** did it ellos *or* ellas lo hicieron.

(a) (pl of he, she, it) ellos, ellas **(b)** (indefinite person or persons): **~'ve dug up the road** han levantado la calle

they'd /ðeɪd/ **(a)** = **they would (b)** = **they had**

they'll /ðeɪl/ = **they will**

they're /ðer *weak form* ðər ‖ ðeə(r) *weak form* ðeə(r)/ = **they are**

they've /ðeɪv/ = **they have**

thick /θɪk/ *adj* **-er, -est 1 (a)** ‹*layer/book/sweater*› grueso, gordo (fam); ‹*line*› grueso; **it's 5cm ~** tiene 5cm de espesor *or* de grosor **(b)** ‹*sauce/paint*› espeso **(c)** ‹*fog/smoke*› espeso, denso; ‹*fur*› tupido; ‹*beard/eyebrows*› poblado; ***through ~ and thin*** tanto en las duras como en las maduras **2** (colloq) (stupid) burro (fam), corto (fam)

thicken /'θɪkən/ *vt* ‹*sauce/paint*› espesar ■ ~ *vi* «*sauce/paint*» espesar(se); «*fog*» hacerse* más espeso *or* denso

thicket /'θɪkət ‖ 'θɪkɪt/ *n* matorral *m*

thickly /'θɪkli/ *adv* **(a)** (in a thick layer): **spread the jam ~** pon una capa gruesa de mermelada **(b)** (densely) ‹*populated*› densamente

thickness /'θɪknəs ‖ 'θɪknɪs/ *n* [U C] (of fabric, wire) grosor *m*; (of paper, wood, wall) espesor *m*, grosor *m*

thick: **~set** /'θɪk'set/ *adj* fornido; **~-skinned** /'θɪk'skɪnd/ *adj* insensible

thief /θi:f/ *n* (*pl* **thieves** /θi:vz/) ladrón, -drona *m,f*

thigh /θaɪ/ ▶ 484 *n* muslo *m*

thimble /'θɪmbəl/ *n* dedal *m*

thin¹ /θɪn/ *adj* **-nn- 1 (a)** ‹*layer/slice*› delgado, fino **(b)** ‹*person*› delgado, flaco; ‹*waist*› delgado **2 (a)** ‹*soup/sauce*› claro, poco espeso **(b)** ‹*hair*› ralo

thin² **-nn-** *vt* ‹*paint*› diluir*, rebajar; ‹*sauce*› aclarar, hacer* menos espeso ■ ~ *vi*: **his hair is ~ning** está perdiendo pelo

thing /θɪŋ/ *n* **1** (physical object) cosa *f* **2** (non-material) cosa *f*; **the same ~ happened to me** a mí me pasó lo mismo; **its a good ~ (that)** … menos mal que …; **the last ~ I expected** lo que menos me imaginaba; **he hadn't done a ~** no había hecho absolutamente nada; ***it's just one of those ~s*** son cosas que pasan **3** (affair, matter) asunto *m*; **I'm fed up with the whole ~** estoy harto del asunto **4 the thing (a)** (that which, what) lo que **(b)** (what is needed): **I've got just the ~ for you** tengo exactamente lo que necesitas *or* lo que te hace falta **(c)** (crucial point, factor): **the ~ is,** … resulta que *or* el caso es que *or* lo que pasa es que … **5 things** *pl* **(a)** (belongings, equipment) cosas *fpl* **(b)** (matters, the situation) cosas *fpl*; **if ~s don't improve** si las cosas no mejoran; **how's ~s?** (colloq) ¿qué tal? (fam) **6** (person, creature): **you poor ~!** ¡pobrecito!; **you lucky ~!** ¡qué suerte tienes! **7** (preference, fad) (colloq): **it's not my ~** no es lo mío **8** (in expressions of time): **first ~ (in the morning)** a primera hora (de la mañana)

thingamabob /'θɪŋəməbɑ:b ‖ 'θɪŋəməbɒb/, **thingamajig** /-dʒɪg/ *n* (colloq) cosa *f*, chisme *m* (Esp, Méx fam), coso *m* (AmS fam), vaina *f* (Col, Per, Ven fam)

think /θɪŋk/ (*past & past p* **thought**) *vi* **1** (use one's mind) pensar*; **to ~ ABOUT sth** pensar* EN algo; (consider) pensar* algo; **to ~ OF sth/sb** pensar* EN algo/algn; **I hadn't thought of that** no se me había ocurrido eso **2** (intend, plan) **to ~ OF -ING** pensar* + INF **3 (a)** (find, come up with): **can you ~ of anything better?** ¿se te ocurre algo mejor? **(b)** (remember) **to ~ OF sth** acordarse* DE algo; **I can't ~ of his name** no me puedo acordar de su nombre **4** (have opinion): **to ~ highly of sb** tener* muy buena opinión de algn; **he ~s a lot of you** te aprecia mucho ■ ~ *vt* **1** (reflect, ponder) pensar*; **~ what that would cost** piensa (en) lo que costaría; **that's wrong, I thought to myself** eso está mal — pensé para mí *or* para mis adentros; **I didn't ~ to look there** no se me ocurrió mirar allí **2 (a)** (suppose, imagine, expect) pensar*; **I thought you knew** pensé que lo sabías; **I can't ~ why he refused** no me explico por qué se negó **(b)** (indicating intention): **we thought we'd eat out tonight** esta noche tenemos pensado salir a cenar **3** (believe) creer*; **I ~ so/I don't ~ so** creo que sí *or* me parece que sí/creo que no *or* me parece que no; **I thought as much** ya me parecía *or* ya me lo imaginaba

• think ahead [*v* + *adv*]: **you have to ~ ahead** hay que ser previsor

• think back [*v* + *adv*] (reflect) recordar*; **~ back** haz memoria; **to ~ back** TO **sth** recordar* algo, acordarse* DE algo

• think out [*v* + *o* + *adv*, *v* + *adv* + *o*] pensar *or* plancar cuidadosamente; **a well thought-out proposal** una propuesta bien elaborada

• think over [*v* + *o* + *adv*] pensar*

• think through [*v* + *o* + *adv*, *v* + *adv* + *o*] ‹*project*› planear detenidamente; ‹*idea*› considerar detenidamente

• think up [*v* + *o* + *adv*, *v* + *adv* + *o*] ‹*excuse*› inventar; ‹*slogan*› idear

thinker /'θɪŋkər ‖ 'θɪŋkə(r)/ *n* pensador, -dora *m,f*

thinking /'θɪŋkɪŋ/ *n* [U] ideas *fpl*, pensamiento *m*; **to my (way of) ~** a mi modo de ver, en mi opinión; **good ~!** ¡buena idea!

think tank *n* gabinete *m* estratégico

thinly /'θɪnli/ *adv* **(a)** ‹*slice*› en rebanadas finas **(b)** (sparsely): **~ populated** poco poblado

thinner /'θɪnər ‖ 'θɪnə(r)/ *n* [U C] disolvente *m*, diluyente *m*

third[1] /θɜːrd ‖ θɜːd/ ▶ 540, 725 *adj* tercero

■ Note The usual translation of *third*, *tercero*, becomes *tercer* when it precedes a masculine singular noun.

third[2] *adv* **(a)** (in position, time, order) en tercer lugar **(b)** (thirdly) en tercer lugar **(c)** (*with superl*): **the ~ highest mountain** la tercera montaña en altura

third[3] ▶ 540, 543, 725 *n* **1 (a)** (Math) tercio *m* **(b)** (part) tercera parte *f*, tercio *m* **(c)** (Mus) tercera *f* **2 ~ (gear)** (Auto) (*no art*) tercera *f*

third-class /'θɜːrd'klæs ‖ ˌθɜːd'klɑːs/ *adj* (*pred* **~ class**) **(a)** (inferior) de tercera **(b)** ‹*mail*› (in US) de franqueo económico

thirdly /'θɜːrdli ‖ 'θɜːdli/ *adv* (*indep*) en tercer lugar

third: **~ party insurance** *n* seguro *m* contra terceros; **T~ World** *n* **the T~ World** el Tercer Mundo; (*before n*) ‹*nation*› tercermundista

thirst /θɜːrst ‖ θɜːst/ *n* [U] sed *f*

thirsty /'θɜːrsti ‖ 'θɜːsti/ *adj* **-tier, -tiest** ‹*person/animal*› que tiene sed; **to be ~** tener* sed

thirteen /'θɜːr'tiːn ‖ ˌθɜː'tiːn/ ▶ 451, 724, 884 *adj/n* trece *adj inv/m*; *see also* FOUR[1]

thirteenth[1] /'θɜːr'tiːnθ ‖ ˌθɜː'tiːnθ/ ▶ 540, 725 *adj* decimotercero; (before masculine singular nouns) decimotercer

thirteenth[2] *adv* en decimotercer lugar

thirteenth[3] ▶ 540, 543, 725 *n* (Math) treceavo *m*; (part) treceava parte *f*

thirtieth[1] /'θɜːrtiəθ ‖ 'θɜːtiəθ/ ▶ 540, 725 *adj* trigésimo

thirtieth[2] *adv* en trigésimo lugar

thirtieth[3] ▶ 540, 543, 884, 725 *n* (Math) treintavo *m*; (part) treintava *or* trigésima parte *f*

thirty /'θɜːrti ‖ 'θɜːti/ ▶ 540, 543, 725 *adj/n* treinta *adj inv/m*; *see also* FOUR[1]

this[1] /ðɪs/ *pron* (*pl* **these**) éste, -ta; (*neuter*) esto; **these** éstos, -tas; **what is ~?** ¿qué es esto?; **~ is John** (on photo) éste es John; (introducing) te presento a John; **is ~ where you work?** ¿aquí es donde trabajas?; **~ is Jack Smith** (on telephone) habla Jack Smith, soy Jack Smith

this[2] *adj* (*pl* **these**) este, -ta; (*pl*) estos, -tas; **look at ~ tree/house** mira este árbol/esta casa; **I like these ones** me gustan éstos/éstas

this[3] *adv*: **it's ~ big** es así de grande; **now we've come ~ far** … ya que hemos venido hasta aquí …

thistle /'θɪsəl/ *n* cardo *m*

thong /θɔːŋ ‖ θɒŋ/ *n* **(a)** (leather strip) correa *f* **(b)** (sandal) (AmE) chancla *f*, chancleta *f*

thorn /θɔːrn ‖ θɔːn/ *n* espina *f*

thorny /'θɔːrni ‖ 'θɔːni/ *adj* **-nier, -niest** ‹*plant*› espinoso; ‹*problem/issue*› espinoso, peliagudo

thorough /'θɜːrəʊ ‖ 'θʌrə/ *adj* ‹*person*› concienzudo, cuidadoso; ‹*search/investigation*› riguroso

thoroughbred /'θɜːrəbred ‖ 'θʌrəbred/ *adj* ‹*horse*› de pura sangre, de raza

thoroughfare /'θərə'fer ‖ 'θʌrəfeə(r)/ *n* **(a)** (street) (liter) calle *f*, vía *f* **(b)** (public road) vía *f* pública

thoroughly /'θɜːrəʊli ‖ 'θʌrəli/ *adv* **(a)** ‹*wash/clean*› a fondo, a conciencia; ‹*research*› rigurosamente; ‹*examine*› minuciosamente **(b)** (completely) ‹*understand*› perfectamente; **we ~ enjoyed ourselves** nos divertimos muchísimo

those /ðəʊz/ *pl of* THAT *adj, pron* 1

though[1] /ðəʊ/ *conj* aunque

though[2] *adv*: **it's easy, ~, to understand their feelings** sin embargo, es fácil comprender sus sentimientos; **the course is difficult; it's interesting, ~** el curso es difícil, pero es interesante

thought[1] /θɔːt/ *past & past p of* THINK[1]

thought[2] *n* **1 (a)** [U] (intellectual activity) pensamiento *m* **(b)** [U] (deliberation): **after much ~** tras mucho pensarlo **2** [C] **(a)** (reflection) pensamiento *m*; **what are your ~s on the matter?** ¿tú qué opinas al respecto?; **on second ~(s)** pensándolo bien **(b)** (idea) idea *f*; **I've just had a ~** se me acaba de ocurrir una idea; **the ~ never even entered my head** ni se me pasó por la cabeza

thoughtful /'θɔːtfəl/ *adj* **(a)** (kind) atento, amable; (considerate) considerado **(b)** (pensive) pensativo, meditabundo

thoughtfully /'θɔːtfəli/ *adv* pensativamente

thoughtless /'θɔːtləs ‖ 'θɔːtlɪs/ *adj* desconsiderado

thought-provoking /'θɔːtprəˌvəʊkɪŋ/ *adj* que hace pensar *or* reflexionar

thousand /'θaʊzn̩d/ ▶ 451, 724 *n* mil *m*; **a ~ tanks** mil gracias

thousandth[1] /'θaʊzəndθ/ ▶ 725 *adj* milésimo

thousandth[2] *adv* en milésimo lugar

thousandth[3] ▶543, 725 *n* (Math) milésimo *m*; (part) milésima parte *f*

thrash /θræʃ/ *vt* golpear; (as punishment) azotar; darle* una paliza a ■ ~ *vi:* ~ **(around** *o* **about)** revolverse*, retorcerse*; (in mud, water) revolcarse*
• **thrash out** [*v + o + adv, v + adv + o*] ‹*problem*› discutir, tratar de resolver

thrashing /ˈθræʃɪŋ/ *n* paliza *f*, zurra *f*

thread[1] /θred/ *n* **(a)** [C U] (filament) hilo *m*; (of plot, conversation) hilo *m* **(b)** [C] (of screw) rosca *f*, filete *m*

thread[2] *vt* ‹*needle*› enhebrar; ‹*bead*› ensartar

threadbare /ˈθredber ‖ ˈθredbeə(r)/ *adj* gastado, raído

threat /θret/ *n* amenaza *f*; **to be under ~** «*way of life*» verse* amenazado; «*factory*» estar* bajo amenaza de cierre

threaten /ˈθretn̩/ *vt* **(a)** ‹*person/stability*› amenazar* **(b)** (give warning of) ‹*action/violence*› amenazar* con ■ ~ *vi* amenazar*

threatening /ˈθretn̩ɪŋ/ *adj* amenazador

three /θriː/ ▶451, 724, 884 *adj/n* tres *adj/inv/m*; *see also* FOUR[1]

three: **~-dimensional** /ˈθriːdəˈmentʃn̩əl, -daɪ- ‖ ˌθriːdaɪˈmenʃənl, -daɪ-/ *adj* tridimensional; **~fold** *adj/adv see* -FOLD; **~-piece** /ˈθriːˈpiːs/ *adj* (*before n*): **~-piece suit** traje *m* con chaleco, terno *m*; **~-piece suite** juego *m* de living (*de sofá y dos sillones*) (AmL), tresillo *m* (Esp)

three-quarters[1] /ˈθriːˈkwɔːrtərz ‖ ˌθriːˈkwɔːtəz/ ▶543 *pron* las tres cuartas partes

three-quarters[2] *adv*: **it's ~ full** contiene el 75% *or* las tres cuartas partes de su capacidad

threshold /ˈθreʃhəʊld/ *n* **(a)** (doorway) umbral *m*; ***to be on the ~ of sth*** estar* en el umbral *or* a las puertas de algo **(b)** (of pain) umbral *m*

threw /θruː/ *past of* THROW[1]

thrift /θrɪft/ *n* [U] economía *f*, ahorro *m*; (*before n*) **~ shop** (esp AmE) *tienda que vende artículos de segunda mano con fines benéficos*

thrifty /ˈθrɪfti/ *adj* **-tier, -tiest** económico, ahorrativo

thrill[1] /θrɪl/ *n* (excitement) emoción *f*; **it was a real ~** fue verdaderamente emocionante

thrill[2] *vt* emocionar

thrilled /θrɪld/ *adj* (*pred*) **to be ~ (ABOUT/WITH sth)** estar* contentísimo *or* (fam) chocho (CON algo)

thriller /ˈθrɪlər ‖ ˈθrɪlə(r)/ *n* novela *f*/película *f* de misterio *or* de suspenso *or* (Esp) de suspense

thrilling /ˈθrɪlɪŋ/ *adj* emocionante

thrive /θraɪv/ *vi* (*past* **thrived** *or* (liter) **throve**; *past p* **thrived**) «*business/town*» prosperar; «*plant*» crecer* con fuerza

thriving /ˈθraɪvɪŋ/ *adj* (*before n*) ‹*business/town*› próspero

throat /θrəʊt/ *n* garganta *f*; (neck) cuello *m*

throb /θrɑːb ‖ θrɒb/ *vi* **-bb- (a)** «*heart/pulse*» latir con fuerza; «*engine*» vibrar **(b)** (with pain): **his leg was ~bing** tenía un dolor punzante en la pierna

throes /θrəʊz/ *pl n* (*death ~*) agonía *f*; **to be in one's death ~** agonizar*, estar agonizando

thrombosis /θrɑːmˈbəʊsəs ‖ θrɒmˈbəʊsɪs/ *n* [U C] (*pl* **-ses** /-siːz/) trombosis *f*

throne /θrəʊn/ *n* trono *m*

throng /θrɔːŋ ‖ θrɒŋ/ *n* muchedumbre *f*

throttle[1] /ˈθrɑːtl̩ ‖ ˈθrɒtl̩/ *vt* ahogar*, estrangular

throttle[2] *n* **(a)** (Auto) acelerador *m* (*que se acciona con la mano*) **(b)** (pedal) acelerador *m*

through[1] /θruː/ *prep* **1 (a)** (from one side to the other) por; **it went right ~ the wall** atravesó la pared de lado a lado; **to hear sth ~ sth** oír* algo a través de algo; **we drove ~ Munich** atravesamos Munich (*en coche*) **(b)** (past, beyond) **to be ~ sth** haber* pasado algo **2 (a)** (in time): **we worked ~ the night** trabajamos durante toda la noche; **halfway ~ his speech** en medio de su discurso; **~ the centuries** a través de los siglos **(b)** (until and including) (AmE): **Tuesday ~ Thursday** de martes a jueves; **October ~ December** desde octubre hasta diciembre inclusive **3** (by): **she spoke ~ an interpreter** habló a través de un intérprete; **I heard about it ~ a friend** me enteré a través de *or* por un amigo

through[2] *adv* **1** (from one side to the other): **it sped ~ without stopping** pasó a toda velocidad sin parar; **the red paint shows ~** se nota la pintura roja que hay debajo; *see also* GET, PULL, PUT *etc* THROUGH **2** (completely): **wet ~** mojado hasta los huesos

through[3] *adj* **1** (Transp) (*before n*) ‹*train/route*› directo; **~ traffic** tráfico *m* de paso; Ⓢ **no through road** calle sin salida **2** (finished) (colloq) (*pred*): **to be ~ WITH sb/sth** haber* terminado CON algn/algo

throughout[1] /θruːˈaʊt/ *prep* **1** (all over): **~ Europe** en toda Europa **2** (in time): **~ the weekend** (durante) todo el fin de semana; **~ his career** a lo largo de toda su carrera

throughout[2] *adv* **(a)** ‹*decorated/carpeted*› totalmente **(b)** (in time) desde el principio hasta el fin

throughway /ˈθruːweɪ/ *n* (AmE) autopista *f*

throve /θrəʊv/ *past of* THRIVE

throw[1] /θrəʊ/ (*past* **threw**; *past p* **thrown**) *vt* **1 (a)** ‹*ball/stone*› tirar, aventar* (Col, Méx, Per); ‹*grenade/javelin*› lanzar* **(b)** ‹*dice*› echar, tirar **2** (send, propel) (+ *adv compl*): **to ~ sb into jail** meter a algn preso *or* en la cárcel; **to ~ oneself into a task** meterse de lleno en una tarea **3** «*horse*» ‹*rider*› desmontar, tirar **4** (disconcert) desconcertar* **5** (have, hold) ‹*party*› hacer*, dar*
• **throw away** [*v + o + adv, v + adv + o*] **(a)** (discard) ‹*can/paper*› tirar (a la basura), botar (a la basura) (AmL exc RPl) **(b)** (waste) ‹*money*› tirar, botar (AmL exc RPl)
• **throw back** [*v + o + adv, v + adv + o*] **(a)** ‹*ball*› devolver* **(b)** (pull back) ‹*curtains*› (des)correr; ‹*bedclothes*› echar atrás
• **throw off** [*v + o + adv, v + adv + o*] **(a)** ‹*jacket/hat*› quitarse (*rápidamente*) **(b)** ‹*illness/habit*› quitarse; ‹*pursuer*› despistar
• **throw out** [*v + o + adv, v + adv + o*] **(a)** (discard) tirar (a la basura), botar (a la basura) (AmL exc RPl) **(b)** ‹*bill/proposal*› rechazar **(c)** ‹*person*› echar

• throw together [*v* + *o* + *adv*, *v* + *adv* + *o*] ‹*meal/plan*› improvisar

• throw up I [*v* + *adv* + *o*] **1** (raise) ‹*hands*› levantar *or* alzar* (*rápidamente*) **2** (bring to light) ‹*facts*› revelar (la existencia de)

II [*v* + *adv*] (vomit) (colloq) devolver*, arrojar

throw² *n* **1 (a)** (of ball) tiro *m*; (of javelin, discus) lanzamiento *m* **(b)** (of dice) tirada *f*, lance *m* **2** (AmE) **(a)** (bedspread) cubrecarna *m* **(b)** (shawl) chal *m*, echarpe *m*

thrown /θrəʊn/ *past p of* THROW¹

thrush /θrʌʃ/ *n* **1** [C] (bird) tordo *m*, zorzal *m* **2** [U] (Med) aftas *fpl*

thrust¹ /θrʌst/ *vt* (*past & past p* **thrust**) (push) empujar; (push out) sacar*; **to ~ out one's chest** sacar* pecho; **she ~ the book at me** me tendió el libro bruscamente; **he ~ his hands into his pockets** se metió las manos en los bolsillos; **to ~ sth INTO sth** ‹*knife/sword*› clavar algo EN algo

thrust² *n* **1** [C] **(a)** (with sword) estocada *f* **(b)** (push) empujón *m* **(c)** (attack, advance) ofensiva *f* **2** [U] (impetus) empuje *m*, fuerza *f*

thruway /ˈθruːweɪ/ *n* (AmE) autopista *f*

thud /θʌd/ *n* ruido *m* sordo

thug /θʌg/ *n* matón *m*

thumb¹ /θʌm/ *n* pulgar *m*

thumb² *vt* : **I ~ed a lift home** me fui a casa a dedo (fam)

thumbtack /ˈθʌmtæk/ *n* (AmE) tachuela *f*, chinche *m* (Andes), chinche *f* (AmC, Méx, RPl), chincheta *f* (Esp)

thump¹ /θʌmp/ *n* (sound, blow) golpazo *m*

thump² *vt* golpear

thunder¹ /ˈθʌndər ‖ ˈθʌndə(r)/ *n* **(a)** **▶920** [U] (Meteo) truenos *mpl* **(b)** (*no pl*) (sound — of traffic) estruendo *m*

thunder² *vi* (move loudly): **the train ~ed through the station** el tren pasó por la estación con gran estruendo ■ ~ *vt* (shout): **get out! he ~ed** —¡fuera de aquí! —bramó *or* rugió

thunder: **~ bolt** *n* rayo *m*; **~storm ▶920** *n* tormenta *f* eléctrica

thundery /ˈθʌndəri/ **▶920** *adj* tormentoso

Thursday /ˈθɜːrzdeɪ, -di ‖ ˈθɜːzdeɪ, -di/ **▶540** *n* jueves *m*; *see also* MONDAY

thus /ðʌs/ *adv* **1** (in this way) (frml) así, de este modo **2** (consequently) (*as linker*) por lo tanto, por consiguiente (frml)

thwart /θwɔːrt ‖ θwɔːt/ *vt* ‹*plan/attempt*› frustrar

thyme /taɪm/ *n* [U] tomillo *m*

thyroid (gland) /ˈθaɪrɔɪd/ *n* tiroides *f*, glándula *f* tiroidea

ti /tiː/ *n* (Mus) si *m*

tiara /tiˈɑːrə/ *n* diadema *f*

Tibet /tɪˈbet/ *n* el Tíbet

Tibetan¹ /tɪˈbetn̩/ *adj* tibetano

Tibetan² *n* **(a)** [C] (person) tibetano, -na *m,f* **(b)** [U] (language) tibetano *m*

tic /tɪk/ *n* tic *m*

tick¹ /tɪk/ *n* **1** [C] (sound) tic *m* **2** [C] (Zool) garrapata *f* **3** [C] (mark) (BrE) marca *f*, tic *m*, palomita *f* (Méx), visto *m* (Esp)

tick² *vi* «*clock/watch*» hacer* tictac ■ ~ *vt* (BrE) marcar* (*con un visto or una palomita etc*)

• tick over [*v* + *adv*] «*engine*» marchar al ralentí

ticket /ˈtɪkət ‖ ˈtɪkɪt/ *n* **1** (for bus, train) boleto *m or* (Esp) billete *m*; (for plane) pasaje *m or* (Esp) billete *m*; (for theater, museum) entrada *f*; (for baggage, coat) ticket *m*; (*before n*) **~ collector** revisor, -sora *m,f*; **~ office** (Transp) mostrador *m* (*or* ventanilla *f etc*) de venta de pasajes (*or* billetes *etc*); (Theat) taquilla *f*, boletería *f* (AmL) **2** (label) etiqueta *f*

tickle /ˈtɪkəl/ *vt* hacerle* cosquillas a ■ ~ *vi* «*wool/beard*» picar*

ticklish /ˈtɪklɪʃ/ *adj*: **to be ~** tener* cosquillas, ser* cosquilloso *or* (Méx) cosquilludo

tidal /ˈtaɪdl/ *adj* con régimen de marea

tidal wave *n* maremoto *m*

tidbit /ˈtɪdbɪt/ *n* (AmE) ⇒ TITBIT

tide /taɪd/ *n* **1** (Geog) marea *f*; **the ~ is in/out** la marea está alta/baja; **high/low ~** marea alta/baja **2** (movement) corriente *f*; (of violence) oleada *f*

• tide over [*v* + *o* + *adv*]: **this should ~ us over until next month** nos arreglaremos con esto hasta el próximo mes

tidily /ˈtaɪdli ‖ ˈtaɪdɪli/ *adv* ordenadamente, prolijamente (RPl)

tidiness /ˈtaɪdinəs ‖ ˈtaɪdinɪs/ *n* [U] orden *m*, prolijidad *f* (RPl)

tidy¹ /ˈtaɪdi/ *adj* **tidier, tidiest** ordenado, prolijo (RPl)

tidy² tidies, tidying, tidied *vt* arreglar, ordenar

• tidy up 1 [*v* + *o* + *adv*, *v* + *adv* + *o*] ‹*room/desk*› ordenar, arreglar; ‹*toys*› ordenar, recoger* **2** [*v* + *adv*] ordenar

tie¹ /taɪ/ *n* **1** (Clothing) corbata *f* **2 (a)** (bond) lazo *m*, vínculo *m* **(b)** (obligation, constraint) atadura *f*; **family ~s** obligaciones *fpl* familiares **3** (Sport) (equal score) empate *m*

tie² ties, tying, tied *vt* **1 (a)** (make) ‹*knot/bow*› hacer* **(b)** (fasten) atar, amarrar (AmL exc RPl) **2** (restrict) ‹*person*› atar **3** (Games, Sport) ‹*game*› empatar ■ ~ *vi* **1** (fasten) atarse **2** (draw) «*teams*» empatar

• tie in [*v* + *adv*] **to ~ in** (WITH **sth**) concordar* *or* cuadrar (CON algo)

• tie up [*v* + *o* + *adv*, *v* + *adv* + *o*] **(a)** ‹*parcel/animal*› atar, amarrar (AmL exc RPl) **(b) to be ~d up** (busy) estar* ocupado **(c) to be ~d up** WITH **sth** (connected) estar* ligado A *or* relacionado CON algo

tie: **~break** *n* ⇒ ~BREAKER (a); **~breaker** *n* **(a)** (in tennis) muerte *f* súbita **(b)** (in quiz game) pregunta *f* de desempate; **~pin** /ˈtaɪpɪn/ *n* alfiler *m* de corbata

tier /tɪr ‖ tɪə(r)/ *n* **(a)** (layer) hilera *f* superpuesta **(b)** (of cake) piso *m* **(c)** (in hierarchy) escalón *m*

tiger /ˈtaɪgər ‖ ˈtaɪgə(r)/ *n* (*pl* **~s** *or* ~) tigre *m*

tight¹ /taɪt/ *adj* **-er, -est 1 (a)** (fitting closely) ‹*dress/skirt*› ajustado, ceñido; (if uncomfortable) apretado **(b)** ‹*knot*› apretado **(c)** (stiff) ‹*screw/lid*› apretado, duro

(d) ‹*schedule*› apretado; ‹*budget*› limitado **2** (strict) ‹*security/control*› estricto **3** (taut) ‹*cord/thread*› tirante, tenso **4** (colloq) **(a)** (mean) ⇒ TIGHTFISTED **(b)** (drunk) (*pred*) borracho, como una cuba (fam)

tight² *adv*: **hold ~!** ¡agárrate bien *or* fuerte!; **screw the lid on ~** aprieta bien el tapón; **sleep ~!** ¡que duermas bien!

tighten /'taɪtn̩/ *vt* **(a)** ‹*nut/bolt/knot*› apretar*; ‹*rope*› tensar; **to ~ one's belt** apretarse* el cinturón **(b)** ‹*regulations*› hacer* más estricto *or* rígido **• tighten up** [*v + o + adv, v + adv + o*] ‹*laws/rules*› hacer* más estricto; **to ~ up security** reforzar* las medidas de seguridad

tight: **~fisted** /'taɪt'fɪstəd ‖ ˌtaɪt'fɪstɪd/ *adj* (colloq) agarrado (fam), amarrete (AmS fam); **~fitting** /'taɪt 'fɪtɪŋ/ *adj* ‹*jeans*› ajustado, ceñido

tightly /'taɪtli/ *adv* ‹*hold/grip*› fuerte; **~ fastened** fuertemente atado

tightrope /'taɪtrəʊp/ *n* cuerda *f* floja; (*before n*) **~ walker** funámbulo, -la *m,f*, equilibrista *mf*

tights /taɪts/ *pl n* **(a)** (for ballet etc) malla(s) *f(pl)*, leotardo(s) *m(pl)* **(b)** (BrE) ⇒ PANTYHOSE

tile¹ /taɪl/ *n* **(a)** (for floor) baldosa *f*, losa *f*; (for wall) azulejo *m* **(b)** (for roof) (BrE) teja *f*

tile² *vt* ‹*roof*› tejar; ‹*floor*› embaldosar; ‹*wall*› revestir* de azulejos, azulejar, alicatar (Esp)

till¹ /tɪl/ *conj/prep* ⇒ UNTIL[1,2]

till² *n* caja *f* (registradora)

till³ *vt* cultivar, labrar

tiller /'tɪlər ‖ 'tɪlə(r)/ *n* (Naut) caña *f or* barra *f* del timón

tilt¹ /tɪlt/ *vt* inclinar ■ **~** *vi* inclinarse

tilt² *n* [U C] inclinación *f*

timber /'tɪmbər ‖ 'tɪmbə(r)/ *n* **(a)** [U] (material) madera *f* (*para construcción*) **(b)** [U] (trees) árboles *mpl* (madereros) **(c)** [C] (beam) viga *f*, madero *m*

time¹ /taɪm/ *n* **I 1** [U] (past, present, future) tiempo *m*; **at this point** *o* **moment in ~** en este momento, en el momento presente; (*before n*) ‹*travel*› en el tiempo; **~ machine** máquina *f* del tiempo **2** [U] (time available, necessary for sth) tiempo *m*; **to make ~ for sth** hacer(se)* *or* encontrar* tiempo para algo; **just take your ~** tómate todo el tiempo que necesites *or* quieras **3** (*no pl*) (period — of days, months, years) tiempo *m*; (— of hours) rato *m*; **that was a long ~ ago** eso fue hace mucho (tiempo); **in an hour's/ten years' ~** dentro de una hora/diez años; ***for the ~ being*** por el momento, de momento **4** (*in phrases*) **all the time** (constantly) constantemente; (the whole period) todo el tiempo; **in time** (early enough) a tiempo; (eventually) con el tiempo; **in good time** con tiempo; **in no time (at all)** rapidísimo, en un abrir y cerrar de ojos **5** [U] (with respect to work): **to take** *o* (BrE also) **have ~ off** tomarse tiempo libre **6** [C] (epoch, age) (*often pl*) época *f*, tiempo *m*; **in former ~s** antiguamente; **in ~s to come** en el futuro, en tiempos venideros; ***to be behind the ~s*** ser* anticuado, estar* desfasado **II 1 (a)** ▶ 884 [U] (by clock) hora *f* **(b)** [C U] (of event) hora *f*; **we have to arrange a ~ for the next meeting** tenemos que fijar una fecha y hora para la próxima reunión; **it's ~ you left** *o* **you were leaving** es hora de que te vayas **2** [C] (point in time): **at this ~ of (the) year** en esta época del año; **at this ~ of night** a estas horas de la noche; **at all ~s** siempre; **it'll be dark by the ~ we get there** (para) cuando lleguemos ya estará oscuro **3** [C] (instance, occasion) vez *f*; **let's try one more ~** probemos otra vez *or* una vez más; **nine ~s out of ten** en el noventa por ciento de los casos **4** (*in phrases*) **about time**: **it's about ~ someone told him** ya es hora *or* ya va siendo hora de que alguien se lo diga; **about ~ (too)!** ¡ya era hora!; **at a time**: **four at a ~** de cuatro en cuatro, de a cuatro (AmL); **I can only do one thing at a ~** sólo puedo hacer una cosa a la *or* por vez; **at the same time** (simultaneously) al mismo tiempo; (however) (*as linker*) al mismo tiempo, de todas formas; **at times** a veces; **every** *o* **each time** (*as conj*) (whenever) cada vez; **from time to time** de vez en cuando; **on time** (on schedule): **the buses never run on ~** los autobuses casi nunca pasan a su hora *or* puntualmente; **she's never on ~** nunca llega temprano, siempre llega tarde **5** [C] (experience): **to have a good/bad/hard ~** pasarlo bien/mal/muy mal; **have a good ~!** ¡que te diviertas (*or* que se diviertan *etc*)!, ¡que lo pases (*or* pasen *etc*) bien! **6** [U] (Mus) compás *m*; (*before n*) **~ signature** llave *f* de tiempo **7 times** *pl* (Math): **it's four ~s bigger** es cuatro veces más grande

time² *vt* (Sport) cronometrar; **I've ~d how long it takes me** he calculado cuánto tiempo me lleva

time: **~ bomb** *n* bomba *f* de tiempo *or* de relojería; **~-consuming** /kən'suːmɪŋ ‖ kən'sjuːmɪŋ/ *adj* que lleva mucho tiempo; **~keeper** *n* **(a)** (Sport) cronometrador, -dora *m,f* **(b)** (worker) (BrE): **to be a good/bad ~keeper** ser* puntual/impuntual

timeless /'taɪmləs ‖ 'taɪmlɪs/ *adj* (liter) eterno

time limit *n* plazo *m*

timely /'taɪmli/ *adj* **-lier, -liest** oportuno

timer /'taɪmər ‖ 'taɪmə(r)/ *n* temporizador *m*; (of oven, video etc) reloj *m* (automático)

times /taɪmz/ *prep*: **3 ~ 4 is 12** 3 (multiplicado) por 4 son 12; ⇒ FOUR[1]

time: **~saving** *adj* que ahorra tiempo; **~scale** *n* escala *f* de tiempo; **~share** *n* (property) multipropiedad *f*; **~sheet** *n* hoja *f* de asistencia; **~table** *n* **(a)** (Transp) horario *m* **(b)** (esp BrE Educ) horario *m* **(c)** (schedule, programme) agenda *f*

timid /'tɪməd ‖ 'tɪmɪd/ *adj* tímido; ‹*animal*› huraño

timidly /'tɪmədli ‖ 'tɪmɪdli/ *adv* tímidamente, con timidez

timing /'taɪmɪŋ/ *n* [U] (choice of time): **the ~ of the action was disastrous** la acción fue de lo más inoportuna; **that was good ~: we've just arrived** calculaste muy bien el tiempo: acabamos de llegar

tin /tɪn/ *n* **1 (a)** [U] (metal) estaño *m* **(b)** (tinplate) (hoja)lata *f*; (*before n*) ‹*soldier*› de plomo **2** [C] (can) (esp BrE) lata *f or* (Esp tb) bote *m* (*de conservas, bebidas etc*)

tinfoil /'tɪnfɔɪl/ *n* [U] (made of tin) papel *m* de estaño; (made of aluminium) papel *m* de aluminio

tinge¹ /tɪndʒ/ *n* **(a)** (of color) tinte *m*, matiz *m* **(b)** (hint, trace) dejo *m*, matiz *m*

The Time

Basic time units

a second	=	un segundo
a minute	=	un minuto
an hour	=	una hora
a quarter of an hour	=	un cuarto de hora
half an hour	=	media hora
three quarters of an hour	=	tres cuartos de hora

Asking the time

what time is it? *o* what's the time?	=	¿qué hora es?
what time do you have? (*AmE*) *o* what time do you make it? (*BrE*)	=	¿qué hora tienes?
can you tell me the time?	=	¿me dice(s) *or* me da(s) la hora?
do you have the time?	=	¿tiene(s) hora?

Telling the time

Times on the hour are expressed as follows:

it's one o'clock	=	es la una
it's two o'clock	=	son las dos
it's three o'clock	=	son las tres
it's twelve o'clock	=	son las doce

The conjunction y *is used for times after the hour*:

it's 7:05	=	son las siete y cinco
7:10		las siete y diez
7:15		las siete y cuarto
7:20		las siete y veinte
7:25		las siete y veinticinco
7:30		las siete y media

Note that for times between these five-minute divisions of the clock, the word minutos *must be added*:

it's 8:23	=	son las ocho y veintitrés minutos
it's 4.43	=	faltan diecisiete minutos para las cinco (*most of Latin America*) *or* son las cinco menos diecisiete minutos (*Spain and the River Plate*)

For times before the hour para *is used in Latin America (with the exception of the River Plate area), and* menos *is used in Spain and the River Plate. Note the different constructions*:

		Spain and the River Plate		Most of Latin America
it's 7:35	=	son veinticinco para las ocho	=	son las ocho menos veinticinco
7:40	=	son veinte para las ocho	=	son las ocho menos veinte
7:45	=	son un cuarto para las ocho	=	son las ocho menos cuarto
7:50	=	son diez para las ocho	=	son las ocho menos diez
7:55	=	son cinco para las ocho	=	son las ocho menos cinco

Less precise expressions

it's gone 7 (o'clock) *o* it's past 7	=	son las siete pasadas
it must be about 2 (o'clock)	=	serán las dos
it's just after 5 (o'clock)	=	son las cinco y pico
it's nearly 8	=	son casi las ocho
it must be coming up to 9 (o'clock)	=	deben ser cerca de las nueve

a.m./p.m.

To specify a.m. or p.m., Spanish adds one of the following:

de la madrugada	=	(early) in the morning
de la mañana	=	in the morning
de la tarde	=	in the afternoon/evening
de la noche	=	in the evening/at night

de la madrugada *refers to the time between about 2 a.m. and 5 a.m., and* de la tarde *refers to the time from midday until about 8 p.m.*:

4 a.m.	=	las cuatro de la madrugada
6 a.m.	=	las seis de la mañana
7 p.m.	=	las siete de la tarde
9 p.m.	=	las nueve de la noche

At what time?

(at) what time did you arrive?	=	¿a qué hora llegaste?
at ten o'clock	=	a las diez
at exactly five o'clock	=	a las cinco en punto
at about 6 o'clock *o* around 6 o'clock	=	a eso de las seis *or* sobre las seis (*Esp*)

The 24-hour clock

This is used considerably more in Spanish than it is in English:

21:30	=	las veintiuna treinta
17:15	=	las diecisiete quince

The word horas *is added when talking about time on the hour*:

17:00	las diecisiete horas

tinge² *vt* (*usu pass*) (color) **to be ~d** WITH **sth** estar* matizado DE algo

tingle /'tɪŋgəl/ *vi*: **it makes your skin ~** te hace sentir un cosquilleo *or* hormigueo en la piel

tingling /'tɪŋglɪŋ/ *n* [U] cosquilleo *m*, hormigueo *m*

tinker /'tɪŋkər ‖ 'tɪŋkə(r)/ *vi* **to ~** WITH **sth** hacerle* pequeños ajustes A algo; (pej) juguetear CON algo

tinkle *vi* «*bell/glass*» tintinear

tinned /tɪnd/ *adj* (BrE) enlatado, en *or* de lata

tin: **~ opener** *n* (BrE) abrelatas *m*; **~plate** *n* [U] hojalata *f*

tint¹ /tɪnt/ *n* **(a)** [C] (of color) tinte *m*, matiz *m*; (color) tono *m* **(b)** [U] (for hair) tintura *f*, tinte *m*

tint² *vt* teñir*

tinted /'tɪntəd ‖ 'tɪntɪd/ *adj* ‹*glass*› coloreado; ‹*lenses*› con un tinte; ‹*hair*› teñido

tiny /'taɪni/ *adj* **tinier, tiniest** minúsculo, diminuto

tip¹ /tɪp/ *n* **1** (end, extremity) punta *f*; (of stick, umbrella) contera *f*, regatón *m*; (*filter ~*) filtro *m*; **to be standing on the ~s of one's toes** estar* de puntillas *or* (CS) en puntas de pie; ***on the ~ of one's tongue*** en la punta de la lengua **2** (helpful hint) consejo *m* (práctico) **3** (gratuity) propina *f* **4** (BrE) (rubbish dump) vertedero *m* (de basuras)

tip² **-pp-** *vt* **1** (give gratuity to) darle* (una) propina a **2 (a)** (tilt) inclinar **(b)** (pour, throw) tirar

- **tip off** [*v + o + adv, v + adv + o*] ‹*police/criminal*› avisar(le a), pasarle el dato a (CS), darle* un chivatazo a (Esp fam)
- **tip over 1** [*v + o + adv, v + adv + o*] volcar* **2** [*v + adv*] caerse*

tipped /tɪpt/ *adj* ‹*cigarette*› con filtro

tiptoe¹ /'tɪptəʊ/ *vi* **-toes, -toeing, -toed** caminar *or* (esp Esp) andar* de puntillas

tiptoe² *n*: **on ~** de puntillas

tiptop /'tɪp'tɑːp ‖ ˌtɪp'tɒp/ *adj* de primera, excelente; **in ~top condition** en excelente estado

tirade /taɪ'reɪd/ *n* diatriba *f*

tire¹ /taɪr ‖ 'taɪə(r)/ *vt* cansar ■ **~** *vi* **(a)** (become weary) cansarse **(b)** (become bored) **to ~** OF **sth/sb/-**ING cansarse DE algo/algn/+ INF

- **tire out** [*v + o + adv, v + adv + o*] agotar

tire², (BrE) **tyre** /taɪr ‖ 'taɪə(r)/ *n* neumático *m*, llanta *f* (AmL)

tired /taɪrd ‖ 'taɪəd/ *adj* **(a)** (weary) cansado; **to get ~** cansarse **(b)** (fed up) **to be ~** OF **sth/sb/-**ING estar* cansado DE algo/algn / + INF

tiredness /'taɪrdnəs ‖ 'taɪədnɪs/ *n* [U] cansancio *m*

tireless /'taɪrləs ‖ 'taɪəlɪs/ *adj* ‹*person*› infatigable, incansable; ‹*patience/efforts*› inagotable

tiresome /'taɪrsəm ‖ 'taɪəsəm/ *adj* ‹*person*› pesado; ‹*task*› tedioso

tiring /'taɪrɪŋ ‖ 'taɪərɪŋ/ *adj* cansador (AmS), cansado (AmC, Esp, Méx)

tissue /'tɪʃuː ‖ 'tɪʃuː, 'tɪsjuː/ *n* **1** [U C] (Anat, Bot) tejido *m* **2 (a)** [C] (paper handkerchief) pañuelo *m* de papel, Kleenex® *m* **(b)** [U] (*~ paper*) papel *m* de seda

tit /tɪt/ *n* **1** (Zool) paro *m* **2** (sl) (breast) teta *f* (fam)

titbit /'tɪtbɪt/ *n* **(a)** (of food) exquisitez *f* **(b)** (of gossip) chisme *m*

tit for tat /tæt/ *n*: **it was ~ ~ ~** fue ojo por ojo, diente por diente

title /'taɪtl̩/ *n* **1** [C] (of creative work) título *m* **2** [C] **(a)** (status) tratamiento *m* (*como Sr, Sra, Dr etc*) **(b)** (noble rank) título *m* (nobiliario *or* de nobleza) **3** (Law) [U] (right of ownership) derecho *m*

title: **~ deed** *n* (*usu pl*) título *m* de propiedad; **~holder** *n* campeón, -peona *m,f*; **~ page** *n* portada *f*, carátula *f*

titter /'tɪtər ‖ 'tɪtə(r)/ *vi* reírse* disimuladamente

tittle-tattle /'tɪtl̩ˌtætl̩/ *n* (colloq) chismes *mpl*

titular /'tɪtʃələr ‖ 'tɪtjʊlə(r)/ *adj* nominal

T-junction /'tiːˌdʒʌŋkʃən/ *n* (BrE) cruce *m* (*en forma de T*)

TN = **Tennessee**

to¹ /tuː, *weak form* tə/ *prep* **1 (a)** (indicating destination) a; **you can wear it ~ the wedding** puedes ponértelo para la boda **(b)** (indicating direction) hacia; **move a little ~ the right** córrete un poco hacia la derecha **(c)** (indicating position) a; **~ the left/right of sth** a la izquierda/derecha de algo **2 (a)** (as far as) hasta; **she can count ~ 10** sabe contar hasta 10 **(b)** (until) hasta; **I can't stay ~ the end** no puedo quedarme hasta el final; *see also* FROM 5 **3 (a)** (showing indirect object): **give it ~ me** dámelo; **I gave it ~ Rachel** se lo di a Rachel; **what did you say ~ him/them?** ¿qué le/les dijiste?; **I was talking ~ myself** estaba hablando solo **(b)** (in dedications): **~ Paul with love from Jane** para Paul, con cariño de Jane **4** (indicating proportion, relation): **how many ounces are there ~ the pound?** ¿cuántas onzas hay en una libra?; **Barcelona won by two goals ~ one** Barcelona ganó por dos (goles) a uno; **there's a 10 ~ 1 chance of ...** hay una probabilidad de uno en 10 de ... **5** (producing): **~ my horror ...** para mi horror ... **6** (indicating belonging) de; **the key ~ the front door** la llave de la puerta principal **7** **▶ 884** (telling time) (BrE): **ten ~ three** las tres menos diez, diez para las tres (AmL exc RPl)

to² /tə/ (*in infinitives*) **1 (a) ~ sing/fear/leave** cantar/temer/partir **(b)** (in order to) para; **I do it ~ save money** lo hago para ahorrar dinero **2** (*after adj or n*): **it's easy ~ do** es fácil de hacer; **you're too young ~ drink wine** eres demasiado joven para beber vino; **she was the first ~ arrive** fue la primera en llegar; **she has a lot ~ do** tiene mucho que hacer

to³ /tuː/ *adv* (shut): **I pulled the door ~** cerré la puerta

toad /təʊd/ *n* sapo *m*

toadstool /'təʊdstuːl/ *n* hongo *m* (*no comestible*)

to and fro /frəʊ/ *adv* de un lado a otro

toast¹ /təʊst/ *n* **1** [U] tostadas *fpl*, pan *m* tostado; **a piece of ~** una tostada *or* (Chi, Méx) un pan tostado; (*before n*) **~ rack** portatostadas *m* **2** [C] (tribute) brindis *m*; **we drank a ~ to him** brindamos por él

toast² *vt* **1** (Culin) tostar* **2** (drink tribute to) ‹*person/success*› brindar por

toaster /'təʊstər ‖'təʊstə(r)/ *n* tostadora *f* (eléctrica), tostador *m*

tobacco /tə'bækəʊ/ *n* [U C] (*pl* **-cos** *or* **-coes**) tabaco *m*

-to-be /tə'bi:/ *suff*: **father~/husband~** futuro padre/esposo

toboggan /tə'bɑ:gən ‖ tə'bɒgən/ *n* trineo *m*, tobogán *m*

today¹ /tə'deɪ/ ▶ 540 *adv* **(a)** (this day) hoy **(b)** (nowadays) hoy (en) día, actualmente

today² ▶ 540 *n* (*no art*) **(a)** (this day) hoy *adv*; **(as) from ~** a partir de hoy *or* del día de hoy **(b)** (present age) hoy *adv*, hoy (en) día

toddler /'tɑ:dlər ‖ 'tɒdlə(r)/ *n* niño pequeño, niña pequeña *m,f* (*entre un año y dos años y medio de edad*)

to-do /tə'du:/ *n* (colloq) (*no pl*) lío *m*, jaleo *m*

toe¹ /təʊ/ ▶ 484 *n* dedo *m* (*del pie*); **big ~** dedo *m* gordo (del pie); ***to be on one's ~s*** estar* *or* mantenerse* alerta

toe² *vt*: ***to ~ the line*** acatar la disciplina

toenail *n* uña *f* (*del pie*)

toffee /'tɑ:fi ‖ 'tɒfi/ *n* [U C] toffee *m* (*golosina hecha con azúcar y mantequilla*)

toffee-nosed /'tɑ:fi'nəʊzd ‖ 'tɒfi,nəʊzd/ *adj* (BrE colloq) estirado (fam)

tofu /'təʊfu:/ *n* [U] tofu *m*, queso *m* de soya (AmL) *or* (Esp) soja

together /tə'geðər ‖ tə'geðə(r)/ *adv* **(a)** : **they went ~** fueron juntos/juntas; **we left them alone ~** los dejamos solos a los dos; **all ~ now!** ¡todos (juntos *or* a la vez)! **(b) together with** junto con

toil¹ /tɔɪl/ *n* [U] (liter) trabajo *m* duro

toil² *vi* (liter) trabajar duro

toilet /'tɔɪlət ‖ 'tɔɪlɪt/ *n* **1** [C] (room) baño *m* (esp AmL), servicio *m* (esp Esp), váter *m* (Esp); (bowl) water *m or* (Esp) váter *m*, inodoro *m*; (*before n*) **~ paper** papel *m* higiénico; **~ roll** rollo *m* de papel higiénico **2** [U] (washing and dressing) (*before n*) **~ soap** jabón *m* de tocador; **~ water** agua *f*‡ de colonia

toiletries /'tɔɪlətriz ‖ 'tɔɪlɪtriz/ *pl n* artículos *mpl* de tocador *or* de perfumería

token¹ /'təʊkən/ *n* **1** (expression, indication): **a small ~ of gratitude** un pequeño obsequio como muestra *or* prueba de agradecimiento; **as a ~ of respect** en señal de respeto; ***by the same ~*** de igual modo **2 (a)** (coin) ficha *f* **(b)** (voucher) (BrE) vale *m*; (given as present) vale *m*, cheque-regalo *m*

token² *adj* (*before n, no comp*) ‹*fine/gesture*› simbólico

told /təʊld/ *past & past p of* TELL

tolerable /'tɑ:lərəbəl ‖ 'tɒlərəbəl/ *adj* **(a)** (endurable) tolerable **(b)** (passable) pasable

tolerance /'tɑ:lərəns ‖ 'tɒlərəns/ *n* [U] tolerancia *f*

tolerant /'tɑ:lərənt ‖ 'tɒlərənt/ *adj* tolerante

tolerate /'tɑ:ləreɪt ‖ 'tɒləreɪt/ *vt* **(a)** ‹*attitude/behavior*› tolerar **(b)** ‹*person/pain/noise*› soportar, aguantar

toleration /'tɑ:lə'reɪʃən ‖ ,tɒlə'reɪʃən/ *n* [U] tolerancia *f*

toll¹ /təʊl/ *n* **(a)** (Transp) peaje *m*, cuota *f* (Méx); (*before n*) **~ call** (AmE) llamada *f* interurbana, conferencia *f* (Esp); **~ road** carretera *f* de peaje *or* (Méx) de cuota **(b)** (cost, damage): **the climate took a ~ on his health** el clima le afectó la salud

toll² *vi* tocar*, doblar

toll: **~booth** *n* cabina *f* de peaje; **~bridge** *n* puente *m* de peaje *or* (Méx) de cuota; **~-free** /'təʊl 'fri:/ *adj* (AmE) gratuito

tomato /tə'meɪtəʊ ‖ tə'mɑ:təʊ/ *n* (*pl* **-toes**) tomate *m or* (Méx) jitomate *m*

tomb /tu:m/ *n* tumba *f*, sepulcro *m*

tomboy /'tɑ:mbɔɪ ‖ 'tɒmbɔɪ/ *n* niña *f* poco femenina, machona *f* (RPl), machetona *f* (Méx), varonera *f* (Arg)

tombstone /'tu:mstəʊn/ *n* lápida *f*

tomcat /'tɑ:mkæt ‖ 'tɒmkæt/ *n* gato *m* (macho)

tome /təʊm/ *n* (hum) libro *m*, librote *m*

tomorrow¹ /tə'mɔ:rəʊ, tə'mɑ:rəʊ ‖ tə'mɒrəʊ/ ▶ 540 *adv* mañana; **~ morning** mañana por la mañana, mañana en la mañana/tarde (AmL); **the day after ~** pasado mañana

tomorrow² ▶ 540 *n* (*no art*) **(a)** (day after today) mañana *adv* **(b)** (future) mañana *m*

tom-tom /'tɑ:mtɑ:m ‖ 'tɒmtɒm/ *n* tam-tam *m*

ton /tʌn/ *n* **1** ▶ 322 (unit of weight) tonelada *f* (*EEUU: 907kg., RU: 1.016kg.*); **this suitcase weighs a ~** (colloq) esta maleta pesa una tonelada (fam) **2** (large amount) (colloq) (*usually pl*): **~s of people/work** montones *mpl* de gente/trabajo (fam)

tone¹ /təʊn/ *n* **1 (a)** [U C] (quality of sound, voice) tono *m* **(b) tones** *pl* (sound) sonido *m*; (voice) voz *f* **(c)** [C] (Telec) señal *f* (sonora) **2** [C] (shade) tono *m*, tonalidad *f* **3** [U] **(a)** (mood, style) tono *m* **(b)** (standard, level) nivel *m* **4** [C] (Mus) (interval) tono *m*

tone² *vt* ‹*muscles/skin*› tonificar*

• **tone down** [*v + o + adv, v + adv + o*] ‹*language*› moderar; ‹*color*› atenuar*

tone-deaf /'təʊn'def/ *adj*: **to be ~** no tener* oído (musical)

tongs /tɑ:ŋz, tɔ:ŋz ‖ tɒŋz/ *pl n* tenacillas *fpl*

tongue /tʌŋ/ *n* **(a)** ▶ 484 (Anat) lengua *f*; ***to say sth ~ in cheek*** decir* algo medio burlándose *or* medio en broma **(b)** (language) lengua *f*

tongue: **~-tied** /taɪd/ *adj* tímido, cohibido; **~ twister** *n* trabalenguas *m*

tonic /'tɑ:nɪk ‖ 'tɒnɪk/ *n* **(a)** [C] (pick-me-up) tónico *m* **(b)** [U] **~ (water)** (agua *f*‡) tónica *f*

tonight¹ /tə'naɪt/ *adv* esta noche

tonight² *n* (*no art*) esta noche *f*

tonne /tʌn/ ▶ 322 *n* tonelada *f* (*métrica*)

tonsil /'tɑ:nsəl ‖ 'tɒnsəl/ *n* amígdala *f*

tonsillitis /'tɑ:nsə'laɪtəs ‖ ,tɒnsɪ'laɪtɪs/ *n* [U] amigdalitis *f*

too /tu:/ *adv* **1** (excessively) demasiado; **there were ~ many people/cars** había demasiada gente/demasiados coches; **that's ~ difficult for her to**

understand es demasiado difícil para que lo entienda **2** (as well) también **3** (very) muy; **I'm not ~ sure** no estoy muy seguro

took /tʊk/ *past of* TAKE[1]

tool /tu:l/ *n* (instrument) instrumento *m*; (workman's etc) herramienta *f*; **garden ~s** herramientas *fpl or* utensilios *mpl* de jardinería

tool: **~box** *n* caja *f* de herramientas; **~kit** *n* juego *m* de herramientas; **~shed** *n* cobertizo *m* (*para herramientas*)

toot¹ /tu:t/ *n* bocinazo *m*

toot² *vi* «*driver*» tocar* la bocina *or* el claxon, pitar ■ ~ *vt* ‹*car horn*› tocar*

tooth /tu:θ/ *n* (*pl* **teeth**) **(a)** ▶ 484 (of person, animal) diente *m*; (molar) muela *f*; **front teeth** dientes *mpl* de adelante; **back teeth** muelas *fpl*; ***to grit one's teeth*** aguantarse; (lit) apretar* los dientes; ***to have a sweet ~*** ser* goloso; ***to lie through one's teeth*** mentir* descaradamente; (*before n*) **~ decay** caries *f* dental **(b)** (of zip, saw, gear) diente *m*; (of comb) púa *f*, diente *m*

tooth: **~ache** *n* [U C] dolor *m* de muelas; **~brush** *n* cepillo *m* de dientes; **~paste** *n* [U C] dentífrico *m*, pasta *f* dentífrica *or* de dientes; **~pick** *n* palillo *m* (de dientes), escarbadientes *m*, mondadientes *m*

top¹ /tɑ:p ‖ tɒp/ *n* **1 (a)** (highest part) parte *f* superior *or* de arriba; (of mountain) cima *f*, cumbre *f*; (of tree) copa *f*; (of page) parte *f* superior; **from ~ to bottom** de arriba abajo; ***at the ~ of one's voice*** a voz en cuello *or* en grito, a grito pelado (fam) **(b)** (BrE) (of road) final *m* **2** (highest rank, position): **she came ~ of the class** sacó la mejor nota de la clase; **at the ~ of the league** (Dep) a la cabeza de la liga **3 (table) ~** tablero *m* **4** (Clothing): **a blue ~** una blusa (*or* un suéter *or* un top *etc*) azul **5 on top** (*as adv*) encima, arriba; ***to come out on ~*** salir* ganando **6 on top of** (*as prep*) encima de; **and on ~ of it all** *o* **on ~ of all that,** ... y encima *or* para colmo, ... **7** (of jar, box) tapa *f*, tapón *m* (Esp); (— of pen) capuchón *m*; ***to blow one's ~*** (colloq) explotar (fam) **8** (*spinning ~*) trompo *m*, peonza *f*

top² *adj* (*before n*) **1 (a)** ‹*layer/shelf*› de arriba, superior; ‹*note*› más alto; **on the ~ floor** en el último piso; **the ~ left-hand corner of the page** la esquina superior izquierda de la página **(b)** ‹*speed/temperature*› máximo, tope **2 (a)** (best): **to be ~ quality** ser* de primera calidad; **the service is ~ class** el servicio es de primera **(b)** (in ranked order): **our ~ priority** nuestra prioridad absoluta **(c)** (leading, senior) ‹*scientists/chefs*› más destacado; **the ~ jobs** los mejores puestos

top³ -pp- *vt* **1** (exceed, surpass) superar; ***to ~ it all*** para coronarlo, para colmo **2** (cover) **~ped with cheese** con queso por encima

• **top up** [*v + o + adv, v + adv + o*] ‹*glass*› llenar; ‹*battery*› (Auto) cargar*; ‹*income*› suplementar

topaz /'təʊpæz/ *n* [U C] topacio *m*

top: **~ hat** *n* sombrero *m* de copa; **~-heavy** /'tɑ:p'hevi ‖ ˌtɒp'hevi/ *adj* ‹*structure*› inestable (*por ser muy pesado en su parte superior*)

topic /'tɑ:pɪk ‖ 'tɒpɪk/ *n* tema *m*

topical /'tɑ:pɪkəl ‖ 'tɒpɪkəl/ *adj* de interés actual, de actualidad

topless /'tɑ:pləs ‖ 'tɒplɪs/ *adj* topless

top-level /'tɑ:p'levəl ‖ ˌtɒp'levəl/ *adj* (*before n*) ‹*talks*› de alto nivel

topography /tə'pɑ:grəfi ‖ tə'pɒgrəfi/ *n* [U C] topografía *f*

topping /'tɑ:pɪŋ ‖ 'tɒpɪŋ/ *n* [C U]: **ice-cream with chocolate ~** helado con (salsa de) chocolate por encima

topple /'tɑ:pəl ‖ 'tɒpəl/ *vi* caerse* ■ ~ *vt* **(a)** ‹*government/dictator*› derrocar*, derribar **(b)** (overturn) volcar*

top: **~-ranking** /'tɑ:p'ræŋkɪŋ ‖ ˌtɒp'ræŋkɪŋ/ *adj* (*before n*) de alto nivel; **~-secret** /'tɑ:p'si:krət ‖ ˌtɒp'si:krɪt/ *adj* (*pred* **~ secret**) secreto, reservado; **~soil** *n* [U C] *capa superior del suelo*

topsy-turvy /'tɑ:psi'tɜ:rvi ‖ ˌtɒpsi'tɜ:vi/ *adj* (colloq) ‹*room*› desordenado, patas (para) arriba (fam)

Torah /'tɔ:rə/ *n* **the ~** la *or* el Torá

torch /tɔ:rtʃ ‖ tɔ:tʃ/ *n* **(a)** (flame) antorcha *f*, tea *f* **(b)** (electric) (BrE) linterna *f*

torchlight /'tɔ:rtʃlaɪt ‖ 'tɔ:tʃlaɪt/ *n* [U]: **by ~** a la luz de la(s) antorcha(s); (*before n*) ‹*procession*› con antorchas

tore /tɔ:r ‖ tɔ:(r)/ *past of* TEAR[2]

torment¹ /'tɔ:rment ‖ 'tɔ:ment/ *n* [U C] tormento *m*

torment² /tɔ:r'ment ‖ tɔ:'ment/ *vt* atormentar, torturar; (tease) martirizar*

torn /tɔ:rn ‖ tɔ:n/ *past p of* TEAR[2]

tornado /tɔ:r'neɪdəʊ ‖ tɔ:'neɪdəʊ/ *n* (*pl* **-does** *or* **-dos**) tornado *m*

torpedo¹ /tɔ:r'pi:dəʊ ‖ tɔ:'pi:dəʊ/ *n* (*pl* **-does**) (Mil) torpedo *m*

torpedo² *vt* **-does, -doing, -doed** torpedear

torpor /'tɔ:rpər ‖ 'tɔ:pə(r)/ *n* [U] (frml) letargo *m*, sopor *m*

torrent /'tɔ:rənt ‖ 'tɒrənt/ *n* torrente *m*

torrential /tɔ:'rentʃəl ‖ tə'renʃəl/ *adj* torrencial

torrid /'tɔ:rəd ‖ 'tɒrɪd/ *adj* ‹*heat*› tórrido; ‹*affair*› apasionado

torso /'tɔ:rsəʊ ‖ 'tɔ:səʊ/ *n* (*pl* **-sos**) torso *m*

tortoise /'tɔ:rtəs ‖ 'tɔ:təs/ *n* tortuga *f*

tortoiseshell¹ /'tɔ:rtəʃel, -təsʃəl ‖ 'tɔ:təsʃel, 'tɔ:təʃəl/ *n* [U] (material) carey *m*, concha *f*

tortoiseshell² ▶ 515 *adj* (color) de color carey; ‹*cat*› pardo

tortuous /'tɔ:rtʃuəs ‖ 'tɔ:tjʊəs/ *adj* tortuoso, sinuoso

torture¹ /'tɔ:rtʃər ‖ 'tɔ:tʃə(r)/ *n* [U C] tortura *f*

torture² *vt* ‹*person/animal*› torturar; **she was ~d by doubts** las dudas la atormentaban

Tory /'tɔ:ri/ *n* (*pl* **Tories**) (in UK) tory *mf*

toss¹ /tɔ:s ‖ tɒs/ *n* **(a)** (throw) lanzamiento *m*; **with a ~ of his head** con un movimiento brusco de la cabeza **(b)** (of coin): **to win/lose the ~** ganar/perder* jugándoselo a cara o cruz (*or* sello *etc*)

toss² *vt* **(a)** (throw) ‹*ball*› tirar, lanzar*, aventar* (Col, Méx, Per); ‹*pancake*› darle* la vuelta a (*lanzándolo al aire*); **let's ~ a coin** echémoslo a cara o cruz *or* (Andes, Ven) a cara o sello *or* (Arg) a cara o ceca *or* (Méx) a águila o sol **(b)** (agitate) ‹*boat*› sacudir, zarandear **(c)** ‹*salad*› mezclar ■ ~ *vi* «*boat*» dar* bandazos; **to ~ and turn** dar* vueltas (*en la cama*)

tot /tɑːt ‖ tɒt/ *n* **(a)** (young child) pequeño, -ña *m,f*, chiquito, -ta *m,f* (esp AmL) **(b)** (of alcohol) copita *f*

• **tot up**: **-tt-** [*v* + *o* + *adv, v* + *adv* + *o*] (colloq) sumar

total¹ /'təʊtl̩/ *adj* total; ‹*failure*› rotundo

total² *n* total *m*

total³ *vt*, (BrE) **-ll- (a)** (amount to) ascender* *or* elevarse a un total de **(b)** (add up) totalizar*

totalitarian /təʊ'tælə'teriən ‖ ˌtəʊtælɪ'teəriən/ *adj* totalitario

totally /'təʊtl̩i ‖ 'təʊtəli/ *adv* totalmente, completamente

tote /təʊt/ *vt* (esp AmE colloq) ‹*weapons*› llevar

totem pole /'təʊtəm/ *n* tótem *m*

totter /'tɑːtər ‖ 'tɒtə(r)/ *vi* tambalearse

touch¹ /tʌtʃ/ *n* **1 (a)** [U] (sense) tacto *m* **(b)** [C] (physical contact): **at the ~ of a button** con sólo tocar un botón **2** [C] (small amount, degree — of humor, irony) dejo *m*, toque *m*; (— of paint) toque *m*; (of salt) pizca *f* **3** [C] (detail) detalle *m*; **to add** *o* **put the final** *o* **finishing ~es to sth** darle* los últimos toques a algo **4** [U] (communication): **to get/keep** *o* **stay in ~ with sb** ponerse*/mantenerse* en contacto con algn; **I lost ~ with her** perdí el contacto con ella

touch² *vt* **1 (a)** (be in physical contact with) tocar*; **my feet don't ~ the bottom** (of pool) no hago pie, no toco fondo **(b)** (brush, graze) rozar*, tocar* **2 (a)** (affect, concern) afectar **(b)** (move emotionally): **he was ~ed by her kindness** su amabilidad lo enterneció *or* le llegó al alma; **I was very ~ed** me emocioné ■ ~ *vi* **(a)** (with finger, hand) tocar* **(b)** «*hands*» rozarse*; «*wires*» tocarse*

• **touch down** [*v* + *adv*] (on land) aterrizar*, tomar tierra; (on moon) alunizar*

• **touch on** [*v* + *prep* + *o*] ‹*subject*› tocar*, mencionar

• **touch up** [*v* + *o* + *adv, v* + *adv* + *o*] ‹*photograph/painting*› retocar*

touch: **~-and-go** /'tʌtʃən'gəʊ/ *adj*: **I passed the exam, but it was ~-and-go** aprobé el examen, pero por poco; **how is the patient? — it's ~-and-go at the moment** ¿cómo está el paciente? — en situación crítica; **~down** *n* (on land) aterrizaje *m*; (on moon) alunizaje *m*

touching /'tʌtʃɪŋ/ *adj* enternecedor, conmovedor

touch: **~line** *n* línea *f* de banda; **~-type** *vi* mecanografiar* al tacto

touchy /'tʌtʃi/ *adj* **-chier, -chiest** ‹*person*› susceptible; ‹*subject*› delicado

tough /tʌf/ *adj* **-er, -est 1 (a)** (strong, hard-wearing) ‹*fabric/clothing*› resistente, fuerte **(b)** ‹*meat*› duro **2** ‹*person*› **(a)** (resilient) fuerte **(b)** (aggressive, violent) bravucón **3 (a)** (strict) ‹*boss/teacher*› severo; ‹*policy/discipline*› duro **(b)** ‹*exam/decision*› difícil

toughen /'tʌfən/ **~ (up)** *vt* **(a)** ‹*muscles*› endurecer*; ‹*material*› hacer* más fuerte *or* resistente **(b)** ‹*person*› hacer* más fuerte

toupee /tuː'peɪ ‖ 'tuːpeɪ/ *n* peluquín *m*, tupé *m*

tour¹ /tʊr ‖ tʊə(r), tɔː(r)/ *n* **(a)** (by bus, car) viaje *m*, gira *f*; (of castle, museum) visita *f*; (of town) visita *f* turística, recorrido *m* turístico; (*before n*) **~ guide** guía *mf* de turismo *or* (Méx) de turistas **(b)** (official visit) (to country, region) gira *f*, viaje *m*; (of factory, hospital) visita *f* **(c)** (Mus, Sport, Theat) gira *f*, tournée *f*

tour² *vt* **(a)** ‹*country/area*› recorrer, viajar por **(b)** (visit officially) visitar **(c)** (Mus, Sport, Theat) ir* de gira *or* hacer* una gira por

tourism /'tʊrɪzəm ‖ 'tʊərɪzəm, 'tɔːr-/ *n* [U] turismo *m*

tourist /'tʊrəst ‖ 'tʊərɪst, 'tɔːr-/ *n* turista *mf*; (*before n*) **~ guide** (book) guía *f* turística; (person) guía *mf* de turismo *or* (Méx) de turistas

tournament /'tʊrnəmənt ‖ 'tɔːnəmənt/ *n* torneo *m*

tourniquet /'tʊrnɪkət ‖ 'tʊənɪkeɪ/ *n* torniquete *m*

tousled /'taʊzəld/ *adj* despeinado, alborotado

tout /taʊt/ *vi*: **to ~ for customers** andar* a la caza de clientes

tow¹ /təʊ/ *n* [U] remolque *m*; **to give sb a ~** remolcar* a algn

tow² *vt* remolcar*, llevar a remolque; **they ~ed the car away** se llevaron el coche a remolque

toward /tɔːrd ‖tə'wɔːd/, (esp BrE) **towards** /tɔːrdz ‖tə'wɔːdz/ *prep* **1** (in the direction of) hacia **2** (as contribution): **she gave us $100 ~ it** nos dio 100 dólares como contribución **3** (regarding) para con, hacia; **your attitude ~ them** tu actitud para con *or* hacia ellos

towel¹ /'taʊəl/ *n* toalla *f*; (*before n*) **~ bar** *o* (BrE) **rail** toallero *m* (*de barra*)

towel² *vt*, (BrE) **-ll-** secar* con toalla

toweling, (BrE) **towelling** /'taʊəlɪŋ/ *n* [U] (tela *f* de) toalla *f*, felpa *f*

tower /'taʊər ‖ 'taʊə(r)/ *n* torre *f*

• **tower above, tower over** [*v* + *prep* + *o*] ‹*building*› descollar* sobre; ‹*person*› destacar* sobre

tower block *n* (BrE) (residential) edificio *m* *or* bloque *m* de apartamentos *or* (AmL tb) de departamentos *or* (Esp tb) de pisos, torre *f*

towering /'taʊərɪŋ/ *adj* (*before n*) **(a)** ‹*building*› altísimo **(b)** ‹*genius*› destacado

town /taʊn/ *n* [C U] (in general) ciudad *f*; (smaller) pueblo *m*, población *f*; ***to go to ~ on sth*** tirar la casa por la ventana; (*before n*) **~ center** *o* (BrE) **centre** centro *m* de la ciudad

town: **~ clerk** *n* (in US) *funcionario encargado de llevar los registros de nacimientos, defunciones etc*; **~ council** *n* (in UK) ayuntamiento *m*, municipio *m*, municipalidad *f*; **~ crier** /'kraɪər ‖ 'kraɪə(r)/ *n* pregonero *m*; **~ hall** *n* ayuntamiento *m*, municipio *m*; **~ planner** *n* urbanista *mf*; **~ planning** *n* [U] urbanismo *m*

township /'taʊnʃɪp/ *n* **(a)** (in US) (Govt) municipio *m*, municipalidad *m*, ayuntamiento *m* **(b)** (in South Africa) distrito *m* segregado

tow: **~path** *n* camino *m* de sirga; **~rope** *n* (Naut) sirga *f*; (Auto) cuerda *f* *or* cable *m* de remolque; **~ truck** *n* grúa *f*

toxic /'tɑːksɪk || 'tɒksɪk/ *adj* tóxico

toxin /'tɑːksən || 'tɒksɪn/ *n* toxina *f*

toy¹ /tɔɪ/ *n* juguete *m*

• **toy with** [*v* + *prep* + *o*] ‹*pen/food*› juguetear con; ‹*idea/possibility*› darle* vueltas a

toy² *adj* **(a)** ‹*car/gun*› de juguete **(b)** (miniature) enano

toyshop /'tɔɪʃɑːp || 'tɔɪʃɒp/ *n* juguetería *f*

trace¹ /treɪs/ *n* **(a)** [C U] (indication) señal *f*, indicio *m*, rastro *m* **(b)** [C] (small amount): **~s of poison** rastros de veneno

trace² *vt* **1 (a)** ‹*criminal/witness*› localizar*, ubicar* (AmL) **(b)** ‹*fault/malfunction*› descubrir* **2 (a)** (on tracing paper) calcar* **(b)** ‹*line/outline*› trazar*

tracing paper /'treɪsɪŋ/ *n* [U] papel *m* de calco *or* de calcar

track¹ /træk/ *n* **1** (mark) pista *f*, huellas *fpl*; **to throw sb off the ~** despistar a algn; **to keep/lose ~ of the conversation** seguir*/perder* el hilo de la conversación; **I lost all ~ of the time** no me di cuenta de la hora **2 (a)** (road, path) camino *m*, sendero *m* **(b) to be on the right/wrong ~** estar* bien/mal encaminado, ir* por buen/mal camino **3** (*race* **~**) pista *f*; (*before n*) **~ events** atletismo *m* en pista **4** [U] (track events) (AmE) atletismo *m* en pista **5** (Rail) **(a)** [C] (way) vía *f* (férrea) **(b)** [U] (rails etc) vías *fpl* **6** (song, piece of music) tema *m*, pieza *f*

track² *vt* seguirle* la pista a, rastrear

• **track down** [*v* + *o* + *adv*, *v* + *adv* + *o*] ‹*criminal/lost object*› localizar*

tracker /'trækər || 'trækə(r)/ *n* rastreador, -dora *m,f*; (*before n*) **~ dog** perro *m* rastreador

tracking /'trækɪŋ/ *n* [U] (AmE Educ) *división del alumnado en grupos de acuerdo al nivel académico*

track: **~ record** *n* historial *m*, antecedentes *mpl*; **~suit** *n* equipo *m* (de deportes), chándal *m* (Esp), pants *mpl* (Méx), buzo *m* (Chi, Per), sudadera *f* (Col))

tract /trækt/ *n* **1** (of land, sea) extensión *f* **2** (Anat) tracto *m* **3** (short treatise) tratado *m* breve

traction /'trækʃən/ *n* [U] **(a)** (Mech Eng, Med) tracción *f* **(b)** (grip) agarre *m*, adherencia *f*

tractor /'træktər || 'træktə(r)/ *n* (Agr) tractor *m*

trade¹ /treɪd/ *n* **(a)** [U] (buying, selling) comercio *m* **(b)** [U] (business, industry) industria *f* **(c)** [C] (skilled occupation) oficio *m* **(d)** (people in particular trade): **the ~** el gremio

trade² *vi* (buy, sell) comerciar ■ **~** *vt* ‹*blows/insults*› intercambiar; **to ~ sth** FOR **sth** cambiar *or* canjear algo POR algo

• **trade in** [*v* + *o* + *adv*, *v* + *adv* + *o*] entregar* como parte del pago

trade: **~mark** *n* **(a)** (symbol, name) marca *f* (de fábrica) **(b)** (distinctive characteristic) sello *m* característico; **~ name** *n* nombre *m* comercial

trader /'treɪdər || 'treɪdə(r)/ *n* comerciante *mf*

trade: **~ secret** *n* secreto *m* comercial; **~sman** /'treɪdzmən/ *n* (*pl* **-men** /-mən/) **(a)** (shopkeeper) (dated) comerciante *m*, tendero *m* **(b)** (deliveryman) proveedor *m*; **~ union** *n* sindicato *m*, gremio *m* (CS, Per); (*before n*) ‹*leader*› sindical, sindicalista, gremial (AmL)

trading /'treɪdɪŋ/ *n* [U] **(a)** (in goods) comercio *m*, actividad *f or* movimiento *m* comercial **(b)** (on stock exchange) contratación *f*, operaciones *fpl* (bursátiles)

tradition /trə'dɪʃən/ *n* [U C] tradición *f*

traditional /trə'dɪʃn̩əl || trə'dɪʃənl̩/ *adj* tradicional

traffic /'træfɪk/ *n* [U] **1** (vehicles) tráfico *m*, circulación *f*, tránsito *m* (esp AmL) **2** (goods, people transported) tránsito *m* **3** (trafficking) tráfico *m*

• **traffic in**: **-ck-** [*v* + *prep* + *o*] traficar* en

traffic: **~ circle** *n* (AmE) rotonda *f*, glorieta *f*; **~ island** *n* isla *f* peatonal; **~ jam** *n* embotellamiento *m*, atasco *m*

trafficker /'træfɪkər || 'træfɪkə(r)/ *n* traficante *mf*

traffic: **~ light** *n* (*often pl*) semáforo *m*; **~ warden** *n* (in UK) *persona que controla el estacionamiento de vehículos en las ciudades*

tragedy /'trædʒədi/ *n* [C U] (*pl* **-dies**) tragedia *f*

tragic /'trædʒɪk/ *adj* trágico

trail¹ /treɪl/ *n* **(a)** (left by animal, person) huellas *fpl*, rastro *m*; **to be on the ~ of sb/sth** seguir* la pista de algn/algo, seguirle* la pista a algn/algo **(b)** (path) sendero *m*, senda *f*

trail² *vt* **1** (drag) arrastrar **2** (follow) seguir* la pista de, seguirle* la pista a, rastrear ■ **~** *vi* **1** (drag) arrastrar **2** (lag behind) ir* a la zaga **3** «*plant*» trepar

• **trail away**, **trail off** [*v* + *adv*] irse* apagando

trailer /'treɪlər || 'treɪlə(r)/ *n* **1 (a)** (for boats, equipment) remolque *m* **(b)** (*house* **~**) (AmE) caravana *f*, tráiler *m* (AmL), casa *f* rodante (CS, Ven), cámper *f* (Chi, Méx), rulot *f* (Esp) **2** (Cin, TV) avance(s) *m(pl) or* (Esp tb) tráiler *m or* (CS) sinopsis *f*

train¹ /treɪn/ *n* **1** (Rail) tren *m*; (*before n*) **~ driver** (BrE) maquinista *mf*; **~ set** ferrocarril *m* de juguete **2 (a)** (of servants) séquito *m* **(b)** (of events) serie *f*; **to lose one's ~ of thought** perder* el hilo (de las ideas) **3** (of dress, robe) cola *f*

train² *vt* **1 (a)** (instruct) ‹*athlete*› entrenar; ‹*soldier*› adiestrar; ‹*animal*› (to perform tricks etc) amaestrar, adiestrar; ‹*employee*› capacitar; ‹*teacher*› formar **(b)** ‹*voice/ear*› educar* **(c)** ‹*plant*› guiar* **2** (aim) **to ~ sth** ON **sth/sb** ‹*gun*› apuntarle A algo/algn con algo ■ **~** *vi* **(a)** «*nurse/musician*» estudiar **(b)** (Sport) entrenar(se)

trained /treɪnd/ *adj* **(a)** ‹*worker*› calificado (esp AmL), cualificado (Esp); ‹*teacher*› un profesor titulado *or* diplomado; **a highly ~ army** un ejército muy bien adiestrado **(b)** ‹*dog*› entrenado **(c)** ‹*voice*› educado

trainee /treɪ'niː/ *n* **(a)** (in a trade) aprendiz, -diza *m,f*; (*before n*) **~ manager** *empleado que está haciendo prácticas de gerencia* **(b)** (AmE Mil) recluta *mf*

trainer /'treɪnər || 'treɪnə(r)/ *n* **1** (of athletes) entrenador, -dora *m,f*; (of performing animals) amaestrador, -dora *m,f*, adiestrador, -dora *m,f* **2** (training shoe) (BrE colloq) zapatilla *f* de deporte, tenis *m*

training /'treɪnɪŋ/ *n* [U] **(a)** (instruction) capacitación *f* **(b)** (Sport) entrenamiento *m*

traipse /treɪps/ *vi* (colloq) (+ *adv compl*): **I ~d all over town** me pateé (fam) toda la ciudad

trait /treɪt/ *n* rasgo *m*

traitor /'treɪtər ‖ 'treɪtə(r)/ *n* traidor, -dora *m,f*

tram /træm/ *n* (BrE Transp) tranvía *m*

tramp¹ /træmp/ *vi* (+ *adv compl*) **to ~ (along)** caminar *or* marchar (pesadamente)

tramp² *n* vagabundo, -da *m,f*

trample /'træmpəl/ *vt* pisotear; **they were ~d to death** murieron aplastados ■ **~** *vi* **to ~** ON **sth** pisotear algo

trampoline /'træmpəli:n/ *n* trampolín *m*, cama *f* elástica

trance /træns ‖ trɑ:ns/ *n* [C U] trance *m*

tranquil /'træŋkwəl ‖ 'træŋkwɪl/ *adj* tranquilo

tranquility, (BrE) **tranquillity** /træŋ'kwɪləti/ *n* [U] (of place, atmosphere) paz *f*, tranquilidad *f*; (of person) calma *f*, serenidad *f*

tranquilize, (BrE) **tranquillize** /'træŋkwəlaɪz ‖ 'træŋkwɪlaɪz/ *vt* sedar, dar* un sedante a

tranquilizer, (BrE) **tranquillizer** /'træŋ kwəlaɪzər ‖ 'træŋkwɪlaɪzə(r)/ *n* sedante *m*, tranquilizante *m*

transaction /trænz'ækʃən/ *n* transacción *f*, operación *f*

transatlantic /'trænzət'læntɪk/ *adj* transatlántico

transcend /træn'send/ *vt* (fml) **(a)** (go beyond) ‹*boundaries*› ir* más allá de, trascender* **(b)** (overcome) superar

transcribe /træn'skraɪb/ *vt* transcribir*

transcript /'trænskrɪpt/ *n* transcripción *f*

transcription /træn'skrɪpʃən/ *n* [U C] transcripción *f*

transfer¹ /træns'fɜ:r ‖ træns'fɜ:(r)/ *vt* **-rr- (a)** ‹*funds/account*› transferir* **(b)** ‹*property/right*› transferir*, traspasar, transmitir **(c)** ‹*call*› pasar **(d)** ‹*employee/prisoner*› trasladar; ‹*player*› (esp BrE) traspasar

transfer² /'trænsfɜ:r ‖ 'trænsfɜ:(r)/ *n* **1 (a)** [U C] (Fin, Law) transferencia *f* **(b)** [U C] (of employee) traslado *m*; (of player) (esp BrE) traspaso *m* **(c)** [U C] (of passengers) transbordo *m* **2** [C] (design) calcomanía *f*

transferable /træns'fɜ:rəbəl/ *adj* transferible; **not ~** intransferible

transferal /træns'fɜ:rəl/ *n* [U C] (AmE) ⇒ TRANSFER² 1 (a), (b)

transfix /træns'fɪks/ *vt* (*usu pass*) paralizar*

transform /træns'fɔ:rm ‖ træns'fɔ:m/ *vt* transformar

transformation /'trænsfər'meɪʃən ‖ ,trænsfə 'meɪʃən/ *n* transformación *f*

transformer /træns'fɔ:rmər ‖ træns'fɔ:mə(r)/ *n* transformador *m*

transfusion /træns'fju:ʒən/ *n* [U C] transfusión *f*

transgress /træns'gres ‖ trænz'gres/ *vt* (fml) **(a)** ‹*law*› transgredir (fml) **(b)** (go beyond) exceder, sobrepasar ■ **~** *vi* pecar*

transient /'trænziənt, 'trænʃənt ‖ 'trænziənt/ *adj* pasajero, fugaz

transistor /træn'zɪstər, -'sɪstər ‖ træn'zɪstə(r), -'sɪstə(r)/ *n* **(a)** transistor *m* **(b)** (**~** *radio*) (esp BrE) transistor *m*, radio *f or* (AmL exc CS) radio *m* a transistores

transit /'trænsət, -zət ‖ 'trænzɪt, -sɪt/ *n* [U] tránsito *m*; **passengers in ~** pasajeros *mpl* en *or* de tránsito; **it was lost in ~** se perdió en el viaje

transition /træn'zɪʃən/ *n* [U C] transición *f*

transitional /træn'zɪʃṇəl ‖ træn'zɪʃənḷ/ *adj* ‹*stage/period*› de transición

transitive /'trænsətɪv/ *adj* transitivo

translate /træns'leɪt/ *vt* traducir* ■ **~** *vi* traducir*

translation /træns'leɪʃən/ *n* [C U] traducción *f*

translator /træns'leɪtər ‖ træns'leɪtə(r)/ *n* traductor, -tora *m,f*

transmission /trænz'mɪʃən/ *n* [U C] transmisión *f*

transmit /trænz'mɪt/ *vt* **-tt-** transmitir

transmitter /'trænzmɪtər ‖ trænz'mɪtə(r)/ *n* transmisor *m*

transparency /træns'pærənsi/ *n* (*pl* **-cies**) (Phot) transparencia *f*, diapositiva *f*

transparent /træns'pærənt/ *adj* transparente

transpire /træn'spaɪr ‖ træn'spaɪə(r)/ *vi* **1 (a)** (become apparent): **it ~d that** ... resultó que ... **(b)** (happen) ocurrir, suceder **2** (Biol, Bot) transpirar

transplant¹ /træns'plænt ‖ træns'plɑ:nt/ *vt* (Hort, Med) trasplantar

transplant² /'trænsplænt ‖ 'trænsplɑ:nt/ *n* (Med) trasplante *m*

transport¹ /'trænspɔ:rt ‖ 'trænspɔ:t/ *n* transporte *m*

transport² /træns'pɔ:rt ‖træns'pɔ:t/ *vt* transportar

transportation /'trænspər'teɪʃən ‖ ,trænspɔ: 'teɪʃən/ *n* [U] transporte *m*

transpose /træns'pəʊz/ *vt* trasponer*, transponer*

transvestite /trænz'vestaɪt/ *n* travestido *m*, travesti *m*, travestí *m*

trap¹ /træp/ *n* trampa *f*

trap² *vt* **-pp (a)** ‹*animal*› cazar* (*con trampa*) **(b)** (cut off, catch) (*often pass*) atrapar; **he was ~ped in the car** quedó atrapado en el coche

trapdoor, **trap door** /træp'dɔ:r ‖ 'træpdɔ:(r)/ trampilla *f*

trapeze /træ'pi:z, trə- ‖ trə'pi:z/ *n* trapecio *m*

trapper /'træpər ‖ 'træpə(r)/ *n* trampero, -ra *m,f*

trappings /'træpɪŋz/ *pl n* **(a)** (paraphernalia): **all the ~ of success** los símbolos del éxito **(b)** (of horse) arreos *mpl*, jaeces *mpl*

trash¹ /træʃ/ *n* [U] **(a)** (refuse) (AmE) basura *f*; (*before n*) **~ bag** bolsa *f* de la basura; **~ can** cubo *m or* (CS, Per) tacho *m or* (Méx) bote *m or* (Col) caneca *f or* (Ven) tobo *m* de la basura **(b)** (worthless stuff) basura *f* **(c)** (worthless people) (AmE colloq) escoria *f*

trash² *vt* (AmE) **(a)** (dispose of) botar (a la basura) (AmL exc RPl), tirar (a la basura) (Esp, RPl) **(b)** (criticize) (colloq) ‹*movie/book*› poner* por los suelos *or* por el suelo; ‹*person*› despellejar (fam)

trashman /'træʃmæn/ *n* (*pl* **-men** /-men/) (AmE) basurero *m*

trashy /'træʃi/ *adj* **-shier, -shiest** ‹*souvenir*› barato, de porquería (fam); ‹*movie/magazine*› malo

trauma /'trɔːmə/ *n* [C U] (*pl* **-mas**) trauma *m*

traumatic /trɔː'mætɪk/ *adj* traumático, traumatizante

travel¹ /'trævəl/, (BrE) **-ll-** *vi* **1** (make journey) viajar **2** (move, go) «*vehicle*» desplazarse*, ir*; «*light/waves*» propagarse* ■ ~ *vt* ‹*country/world*› viajar por, recorrer; ‹*road/distance*› recorrer

travel² *n* (*before n*) ‹*company/brochure*› de viajes

travel: ~ **agency** *n* agencia *f* de viajes; ~ **agent** *n* agente *mf* de viajes; ~ **agent's** agencia *f* de viajes

traveler, (BrE) **-ll-** /'trævlər ‖ 'trævlə(r)/ *n* **(a)** viajero, -ra *m,f* **(b)** (itinerant person) (BrE) *persona que ha adoptado el estilo de vida errante de los gitanos*

traveler's check, (BrE) **traveller's cheque** *n* cheque *m* de viaje *or* de viajero

traveling¹, (BrE) **-ll-** /'trævlɪŋ/ *n* (*before n*) ~ **expenses** gastos *mpl* de viaje

traveling², (BrE) **-ll-** *adj* **(a)** ‹*clothes/companion*› de viaje **(b)** (itinerant) ambulante; ~ **salesman** viajante *m*

travel-sick /'trævəlsɪk/ *adj* (BrE) mareado; **to get** ~ marearse

trawler /'trɔːlər ‖ 'trɔːlə(r)/ *n* barca *f* pesquera (*utilizada para hacer pesca de arrastre*), bou *m*

tray /treɪ/ *n* bandeja *f*

treacherous /'tretʃərəs/ *adj* ‹*person*› traicionero, traidor; ‹*sea/current*› traicionero

treachery /'tretʃəri/ *n* [U C] (*pl* **-ries**) traición *f*

treacle /'triːkəl/ *n* [U] (esp BrE) melaza *f*

tread¹ /tred/ (*past* **trod**; *past p* **trodden** *or* **trod**) *vi* pisar; **to ~ in sth** pisar algo; **to ~ carefully** *o* **warily** andarse* con cuidado *or* con pie(s) de plomo ■ ~ *vt*: **she trod the earth down** apisonó la tierra; **to ~ grapes** pisar uvas; **to ~ water** flotar (*en posición vertical*)

• **tread on** [*v* + *prep* + *o*] (esp BrE) pisar

tread² *n* **1** [C U] (step, footfall) paso *m*; (steps) pasos *mpl* **2** [C U] (on tire) banda *f* de rodamiento

treadle /'tredl/ *n* pedal *m*

treason /'triːzn̩/ *n* [U] traición *f*

treasure¹ /'treʒər ‖ 'treʒə(r)/ *n* **(a)** [U] (hoard of wealth) tesoros *mpl* **(b)** [C] (sth valuable, prized) tesoro *m*; (*before n*) ~ **hunt** (Games) búsqueda *f* del tesoro

treasure² *vt* **(a)** (value greatly): **thank you for the book, I shall always ~ it** gracias por el libro, lo guardaré como algo muy especial **(b) treasured** *adj* ‹*possession*› preciado

treasurer /'treʒərər ‖ 'treʒərə(r)/ *n* tesorero, -ra *m,f*

treasury /'treʒəri/ *n* (*pl* **-ries**) **(a)** (public funds) erario *m*, tesoro *m* **(b) the Treasury** *o* **the treasury** el fisco, la hacienda pública, el tesoro (público); **Department of the T~** (in US) Departamento *m* del Tesoro (*de los Estados Unidos*), ≈ ministerio *m* de Hacienda

treat¹ /triːt/ *vt* **(a)** (+ *adv compl*) ‹*person/animal*› tratar; **you seem to ~ this whole thing as a joke** pareces tomarte a broma todo esto **(b)** (process) tratar **(c)** (deal with) (frml) ‹*subject*› tratar **(d)** (Med) ‹*patient/disease*› tratar **(e)** (entertain): **I'm ~ing you** te invito yo; **I ~ed myself to a new dress** me di el gusto de comprarme un vestido nuevo

treat² *n* gusto *m*; **I bought myself an ice cream as** *o* **for a ~** me compré un helado para darme (un) gusto

treatise /'triːtəs ‖ 'triːtɪs, -ɪz/ *n* tratado *m*

treatment /'triːtmənt/ *n* [U C] **(a)** (of person, animal, object) trato *m*; (of subject) tratamiento *m* **(b)** (of waste) tratamiento *m* **(c)** (Med) tratamiento *m*

treaty /'triːti/ *n* (*pl* **-ties**) tratado *m*

treble¹ /'trebəl/ *n* **(a)** [C] (singer) tiple *mf*; (voice) voz *f* de tiple **(b)** [U] (Audio) agudos *mpl*

treble² *vt* triplicar* ■ ~ *vi* triplicarse*

treble³ *adj* **1** (threefold) triple **2** (*before n*) (Mus) de tiple *or* soprano

treble clef *n* clave *f* de sol

tree /triː/ *n* árbol *m*; (*before n*) ~ **trunk** tronco *m*

tree: ~**-lined** *adj* (*before n*) bordeado de árboles, arbolado; ~**top** *n* copa *f* de árbol

trek¹ /trek/ *n* (hike) caminata *f*; **it's quite a ~ to the shops** hay un buen paseo hasta llegar a las tiendas

trek² *vi* **-kk-** caminar; **to go ~king** hacer* senderismo

trellis /'treləs ‖ 'trelɪs/ *n* enrejado *m*, espaldera *f*

tremble /'trembəl/ *vi* temblar*

tremendous /trɪ'mendəs/ *adj* **(a)** (great, huge) tremendo **(b)** (very good) formidable

tremendously /trɪ'mendəsli/ *adv* tremendamente

tremor /'tremər ‖ 'tremə(r)/ *n* **(a)** (quiver) temblor *m* **(b)** (*earth* ~) temblor *m* (de tierra), seísmo *m*, sismo *m* (AmL)

trench /trentʃ/ *n* zanja *f*; (Mil) trinchera *f*

trench coat *n* trinchera *f*

trend /trend/ *n* **(a)** (pattern, tendency) tendencia *f* **(b)** (fashion) moda *f*

trendy /'trendi/ *adj* **-dier, -diest** moderno

trepidation /'trepə'deɪʃən ‖ ˌtrepɪ'deɪʃən/ *n* [U] (frml) (fear) temor *m* (frml); (anxiety) inquietud *f*

trespass /'trespəs/ *vi* (Law) *entrar sin autorización en propiedad ajena*

trespasser /'trespəsər ‖ 'trespəsə(r)/ *n* intruso, -sa *m,f*; Ⓢ **trespassers will be prosecuted** ≈ prohibido el paso

tress /tres/ *n* (liter) **(a)** (lock of hair) mechón *m* **(b) tresses** *pl* (hair) cabellera *f* (liter), cabellos *mpl*

trestle /'tresəl/ *n* caballete *m*

trial¹ /'traɪəl/ *n* **1** (Law) **(a)** [C] (court hearing) proceso *m*, juicio *m* **(b)** [U] (judgment) juicio *m*; **a fair ~** un juicio imparcial; **to be on ~ for murder** estar* siendo procesado por asesinato **2** [U C] (test) prueba *f*; **clinical ~** ensayo *m* clínico; **on ~** a prueba; **by ~ and error** por ensayo y error **3** [C] (trouble): **~s and tribulations** tribulaciones *fpl* **4** (Sport) (*usu pl*) prueba *f* de selección

trial² *adj* ‹*period/flight*› de prueba; ~ **offer** oferta *f* especial (*para promover un producto nuevo*); ~ **run** prueba *f*

triangle /'traɪˌæŋgəl/ *n* (Math, Mus) triángulo *m*

triangular /traɪ'æŋgjələr ‖ traɪ'æŋgjʊlə(r)/ *adj* triangular

tribal /'traɪbəl/ *adj* tribal

tribe /traɪb/ *n* tribu *f*

tribesman /'traɪbzmən/ *n* (*pl* **-men** /-mən/) miembro *m* de una tribu

tribunal /traɪ'bju:nl̩/ *n* (court) tribunal *m*

tributary /'trɪbjəteri ‖ 'trɪbjʊtəri/ *n* (*pl* **-ries**) afluente *m*, río *m* tributario

tribute /'trɪbju:t/ *n* **1** [C U] (acknowledgment) homenaje *m*, tributo *m* (AmL); **to pay ~ to sb/sth** rendir* homenaje *or* (AmL tb) tributo a algn/algo **2** [U] (payment) tributo *m*

triceps /'traɪseps/ *n* (*pl* ~) tríceps *m*

trick¹ /trɪk/ *n* **1 (a)** (ruse) trampa *f*, ardid *m*; (*before n*) **~ photography** trucaje *m*; **a ~ question** una pregunta con trampa **(b)** (prank, joke) broma *f*, jugarreta *f* **2** (feat, skilful act) truco *m*; **to do card ~s** hacer* trucos con las cartas **3** (in card games) baza *f*

trick² *vt* engañar

trickle¹ /'trɪkəl/ *vi* (+ *adv compl*) **(a)** «*liquid*»: **sweat ~d down his forehead** le corrían gotas de sudor por la frente **(b)** (arrive, go): **letters are still trickling in** todavía se está recibiendo alguna que otra carta

trickle² *n* hilo *m*

trickster /'trɪkstər ‖ 'trɪkstə(r)/ *n* embaucador, -dora *m,f*

tricky /'trɪki/ *adj* **trickier, trickiest (a)** (difficult) ‹*task/problem*› difícil, peliagudo, que tiene sus bemoles **(b)** (sensitive) ‹*matter/problem*› delicado

tricycle /'traɪsɪkəl/ *n* triciclo *m*

trifle /'traɪfəl/ *n* **1 (a)** [C] (trivial thing) nimiedad *f* **(b)** (small amount) (*no pl*) insignificancia *f* **2** [U C] (Culin) *postre de bizcocho, jerez, crema y frutas*

• **trifle with** [*v* + *prep* + *o*] jugar* con

trifling /'traɪflɪŋ/ *adj* insignificante, sin importancia

trigger¹ /'trɪgər ‖ 'trɪgə(r)/ *n* gatillo *m*

trigger² *vt* ~ **(off)** ‹*reaction/response*› provocar*

trill /trɪl/ *n* **(a)** (in music, of birdsong) trino *m* **(b)** (Ling) vibración *f*

trilogy /'trɪlədʒi/ *n* (*pl* **-gies**) trilogía *f*

trim¹ /trɪm/ *adj* **-mm- (a)** (slim) esbelto, estilizado **(b)** (neat) ‹*uniform/suit*› elegante

trim² *n* **1** [U] (good condition): ***to be in (good) ~*** estar* en buen estado *or* en buenas condiciones **2** [C] (cut) recorte *m*

trim³ *vt* **-mm- 1** (cut) recortar **2** (decorate): **~med with velvet** con adornos de terciopelo; (round edge) ribeteado de terciopelo

trimester /traɪ'mestər ‖ traɪ'mestə(r)/ *n* (AmE) trimestre *m*

trimming /'trɪmɪŋ/ *n* **1** [U C] (on clothes) adorno *m*; (along edges) ribete *m* **2 trimmings** *pl* (offcuts) recortes *mpl*

Trinidad /'trɪnədæd ‖ 'trɪnɪdæd/ *n* Trinidad *f*; **~ and Tobago** Trinidad y Tobago

Trinity /'trɪnəti/ *n* **the (Holy) ~** la (Santísima) Trinidad

trinket /'trɪŋkət ‖ 'trɪŋkɪt/ *n* chuchería *f*, baratija *f*

trio /tri:əʊ/ *n* trío *m*

trip¹ /trɪp/ *n* **1** (journey) viaje *m*; (excursion) excursión *f*; (outing) salida *f*; **she's going on a ~ to Japan** se va de viaje al Japón; **a ~ to the zoo** una visita al zoológico **2** (stumble, fall) tropezón *m*, traspié *m*

trip² **-pp-** *vi* tropezar* ■ ~ *vt* **~ (up)** hacerle* una zancadilla a

• **trip over** [*v* + *adv*] tropezar* y caerse*

tripe /traɪp/ *n* [U] **(a)** (Culin) mondongo *m* (AmS), callos *mpl* (Esp), pancita *f* (Méx) **(b)** (nonsense) (colloq) paparruchas *fpl* (fam)

triple¹ /'trɪpəl/ *adj* triple

triple² *adv*: **~ the amount** el triple

triple³ *vt* triplicar* ■ ~ *vi* triplicarse*

triple jump *n* triple salto *m* (de longitud)

triplet /'trɪplət ‖ 'trɪplɪt/ *n* trillizo, -za *m,f*

triplicate /'trɪpləkət ‖ 'trɪplɪkət/ *n*: **in ~** por triplicado

tripod /'traɪpɑ:d ‖ 'traɪpɒd/ *n* trípode *m*

trite /traɪt/ *adj* **triter, tritest** trillado

triumph¹ /'traɪəmf ‖ 'traɪʌmf/ *n* [C U] triunfo *m*

triumph² *vi* triunfar

triumphal /traɪ'ʌmfəl/ *adj* triunfal

triumphant /traɪ'ʌmfənt/ *adj* ‹*troops/team*› triunfador; ‹*moment/entry*› triunfal; ‹*smile*› de triunfo, triunfal

trivia /'trɪviə/ *pl n* trivialidades *fpl*, nimiedades *fpl*

trivial /'trɪviəl/ *adj* ‹*events/concerns*› trivial; ‹*sum/details*› insignificante, nimio

triviality /'trɪvi'æləti/ *n* (*pl* **-ties**) [U C] trivialidad *f*

trivialize /'trɪviəlaɪz/ *vt* trivializar*

trod /trɑ:d ‖ trɒd/ *past and past p of* TREAD¹

trodden /'trɑ:dn̩ ‖ 'trɒdn̩/ *past p of* TREAD¹

trolley /'trɑ:li ‖'trɒli/ *n* **1 (a)** (~ *bus*) trolebús *m* **(b)** (~ *car*) (AmE) tranvía *m* **2** (BrE) (for food, drink) carrito *m*, mesa *f* rodante; (at airport, in supermarket, in hospital) carrito *m*

trombone /trɑ:m'bəʊn ‖ trɒm'bəʊn/ *n* trombón *m*

troop¹ /tru:p/ *n* **1** (unit) compañía *f*; (of cavalry) escuadrón *m* **2 troops** *pl*: **our ~s** nuestras tropas; **500 ~s** 500 soldados

troop² *vi* (+ *adv compl*): **to ~ in/out** entrar/salir* en tropel *or* en masa

trooper /'tru:pər ‖ 'tru:pə(r)/ *n* **(a)** (cavalryman) soldado *m* de caballería **(b)** (state police officer) (AmE) agente *mf*

trophy /'trəʊfi/ *n* (*pl* **-phies**) trofeo *m*

tropic /'trɑ:pɪk ‖ 'trɒpɪk/ *n* **(a)** (line) trópico *m*; **the T~ of Cancer/Capricorn** el trópico de Cáncer/Capricornio **(b) tropics** *pl* (area) **the ~s** el trópico

tropical /'trɑ:pɪkəl ‖ 'trɒpɪkəl/ *adj* tropical

trot¹ /trɑ:t ‖ trɒt/ *n* (*no pl*) trote *m*; ***on the ~*** (BrE colloq): **four nights on the ~** cuatro noches seguidas

trot² **-tt-** *vi* trotar

• **trot out** [*v* + *o* + *adv*, *v* + *adv* + *o*] ‹*excuses/clichés*› salir* con; ‹*facts*› recitar de memoria

trouble¹ /'trʌbəl/ *n* **1** [U C] (problems, difficulties) problemas *mpl*; (particular problem) problema *m*; **to get**

into ~ meterse en problemas *or* en líos; **to have ~ with sb/sth** tener* problemas con algn/algo; **what's the ~?** ¿qué pasa? **2** [U] (effort) molestia *f*; **I don't want to put you to any ~** no quiero ocasionarle ninguna molestia; **to go to the ~ of doing sth, to take the ~ to do sth** molestarse en hacer algo **3** [U] (strife, unrest) (*often pl*): **the ~s in Northern Ireland** los disturbios de Irlanda del Norte; **to look for ~** buscar* camorra; (*before n*) **~ spot** punto *m* conflictivo

trouble² *vt* **(a)** (worry) preocupar **(b)** (bother) molestar; **I'm sorry to ~ you** perdone *or* disculpe la molestia

troubled /'trʌbəld/ *adj* **(a)** ‹*person*› preocupado, atribulado; ‹*look*› de preocupación **(b)** (strife-torn) (journ) aquejado de problemas

trouble: **~maker** *n* alborotador, -dora *m,f*; **~shooter** /'ʃu:tər ‖ 'ʃu:tə(r)/ *n* (within company) *persona que se envía a resolver problemas, crisis etc*; (mediator) mediador, -dora *m,f*

troublesome /'trʌbəlsəm/ *adj* problemático

trough /trɔ:f ‖ trɒf/ *n* **1** (for water) abrevadero *m*, bebedero *m*; (for feed) comedero *m* **2** (Geog) hoya *f*, depresión *f*

troupe /tru:p/ *n* (Theat) compañía *f* teatral; (in circus) troupe *f*

trousers /'traʊzərz ‖ 'traʊzəz/ *pl n* pantalón *m*, pantalones *mpl*; **a pair of ~** un pantalón, unos pantalones, un par de pantalones

trouser suit *n* (BrE) traje *m* pantalón, traje *m* de chaqueta y pantalón

trousseau /'tru:səʊ/ *n* (*pl* **-x** *or* **-s** /-z/) ajuar *m*

trout /traʊt/ *n* [U C] (*pl* **trout** *or* Zool **trouts**) trucha *f*

trowel /'traʊəl/ *n* (Const) paleta *f*, llana *f*; (for gardening) desplantador *m*, palita *f*

truant /'tru:ənt/ *n*: **to play ~** faltar a clase, hacer* novillos *or* (Méx) irse* de pinta *or* (RPl) hacerse* la rata *or* la rabona *or* (Per) la vaca *or* (Chi) hacer* la cimarra *or* (Col) capar clase (fam)

truce /tru:s/ *n* tregua *f*

truck /trʌk/ *n* **1** [C] **(a)** (vehicle) camión *m*; (*before n*) **~ driver** camionero, -ra *m,f* **(b)** (BrE Rail) furgón *m*, vagón *m* **2** [U] (vegetables, fruit) (AmE) productos *mpl* de la huerta; (*before n*) **~ farm** huerta *f*

trucker /'trʌkər ‖ 'trʌkə(r)/ *n* (AmE) camionero, -ra *m,f*, transportista *mf*

trucking /'trʌkɪŋ/ *n* [U] (AmE) transporte *m* por carretera

truculent /'trʌkjələnt ‖ 'trʌkjʊlənt/ *adj* malhumorado y agresivo

trudge /trʌdʒ/ *vi* caminar con dificultad

true¹ /tru:/ *adj* **truer, truest 1 (a)** (consistent with fact, reality) ‹*story*› verídico; **to be ~** ser* cierto, ser* verdad; **to come ~** hacerse* realidad; **to hold ~** ser* válido **(b)** (accurate) (*before n*) ‹*account*› verídico **2** (real, actual, genuine) (*before n*) ‹*purpose/courage*› verdadero; ‹*friend*› auténtico, de verdad; **~ north** el norte geográfico; **it's ~ love** es amor de verdad **3** (faithful) fiel; **~ TO sth/sb** fiel A algo/algn **4** (Tech) (*pred*): **to be ~** «*wall*» estar* a plomo; «*beam*» estar* a nivel

true² *n*: **to be out of ~** no estar* a plomo

true: **~-life** /'tru:'laɪf/ *adj* (journ) (*before n*) ‹*story*› verídico; **~-to-life** /'tru:tə'laɪf/ *adj* (*pred* **~ to life**) ‹*novel/film*› realista; ‹*situation*› verosímil

truffle /'trʌfəl/ *n* trufa *f*

truly /'tru:li/ *adv* verdaderamente, realmente; ‹*grateful*› sinceramente, verdaderamente; **yours ~** (Corresp) cordiales saludos

trump /trʌmp/ *n* **(a) ~ (card)** (Games) triunfo *m*; (resource, weapon) baza *f* **(b) trumps** *pl* (suit) triunfo *m*

trumped-up /'trʌmpt'ʌp/ *adj* (*before n*) falso, fabricado

trumpet /'trʌmpət ‖ 'trʌmpɪt/ *n* trompeta *f*

trumpeter /'trʌmpətər ‖ 'trʌmpɪtə(r)/ *n* trompetista *mf*, trompeta *mf*

truncheon /'trʌntʃən/ *n* (esp BrE) porra *f*, cachiporra *f*

trunk /trʌŋk/ *n* **1 (a)** (of tree) tronco *m* **(b)** (torso) tronco *m* **2** (of elephant) trompa *f* **3 (a)** (box) baúl *m* **(b)** (of car) (AmE) maletero *m* **4 trunks** *pl* (Clothing) (for swimming) traje *m* de baño *or* (Esp tb) bañador *m* (*de hombre*)

truss /trʌs/ *vt* atar

● **truss up** [*v* + *o* + *adv*, *v* + *adv* + *o*] atar

trust¹ /trʌst/ *n* **1 (a)** [U] (confidence, faith) confianza *f* **(b)** [U C] (responsibility): **a position of ~** un puesto de confianza *or* responsabilidad **2** (Fin) **(a)** [C] (money, property) fondo *m* de inversiones **(b)** [C] (institution) fundación *f* **(c)** [U] (custody) (Law) fideicomiso *m*

trust² *vt* **1** (have confidence in) ‹*person*› confiar* en, tener* confianza en; (in negative sentences) fiarse* de; **he can't be ~ed** no es de fiar; **to ~ sb WITH sth** confiarle* algo A algn **2** (hope, assume) (frml) esperar ■ **~** *vi* **to ~ IN sb/sth** confiar* *or* tener* confianza EN algn/algo

trusted /'trʌstəd ‖ 'trʌstɪd/ *adj* (*before n*) leal, de confianza

trustee /'trʌs'ti:/ *n* **(a)** (of money, property) fideicomisario, -ria *m,f*, fiduciario, -ria *m,f* **(b)** (of institution) miembro *m* del consejo de administración

trust fund *n* fondo *m* fiduciario *or* de fideicomiso

trusting /'trʌstɪŋ/ *adj* confiado

trustworthy /'trʌst,wɜ:rði ‖ 'trʌst,wɜ:ði/ *adj* ‹*colleague/child*› digno de confianza; ‹*account/witness*› fidedigno

truth /tru:θ/ *n* (*pl* **~s** /tru:ðz/) **(a)** [U] verdad *f*; (of account, story) veracidad *f* **(b)** [C] (fact) verdad *f*

truthful /'tru:θfəl/ *adj* ‹*person*› que dice la verdad, veraz; ‹*answer*› veraz

try¹ /traɪ/ *n* (*pl* **tries**) **1** (attempt) intento *m*, tentativa *f* **2** (in rugby) ensayo *m*

try² tries, trying, tried *vt* **1 (a)** (attempt) intentar; **to ~ to** + INF tratar DE + INF, intentar + INF; **~ not to forget** procura no olvidarte **(b)** (attempt to operate): **he tried all the windows** probó a abrir todas las ventanas **2 (a)** ‹*product/technique/food*› probar*; **~ some** pruébalo, prueba un poquito **(b)** (have recourse to): **I'll ~ his work number** voy a probar a llamarlo al trabajo **3** (test, strain) ‹*courage/patience*› poner* a prueba **4 to ~ one's luck at**

sth probar* suerte con algo **5** (Law) ‹*person*› procesar, juzgar*; **to ~ sb FOR sth** juzgar* a algn POR algo ■ ~ *vi* (make attempt) intentar, probar; (make effort) esforzarse*; **you must ~ harder** tienes que esforzarte más

• **try on** [*v* + *o* + *adv*, *v* + *adv* + *o*] probarse*

• **try out** [*v* + *o* + *adv*, *v* + *adv* + *o*] ‹*product/method*› probar*; ‹*employee/player*› probar*, poner* a prueba; **to ~ sth out ON sb** probar* algo CON algn

trying /'traɪɪŋ/ *adj* ‹*day/experience*› duro

tsar /zɑ:r || zɑ:(r)/ ▶ 603 *n* zar *m*

T-shirt /'ti:ʃɜ:rt || 'ti:ʃɜ:t/ *n* camiseta *f*

tsp = **teaspoon(s)**

tub /tʌb/ *n* **(a)** (for holding liquids) cuba *f*; (for washing clothes) tina *f* **(b)** (*bath*~) bañera *f*, tina *f* (AmL) **(c)** (for ice cream) envase *m* (*gen de plástico*), tarrina *f* (Esp)

tuba /'tu:bə || 'tju:bə/ *n* tuba *f*

tubby /'tʌbi/ *adj* **-bier, -biest** (colloq) rechoncho (fam)

tube /tu:b || tju:b/ *n* **1** (pipe, container) tubo *m* **2** (television) (esp AmE colloq): **the ~** la tele (fam) **3** (BrE Transp colloq): **the ~** el metro, el subte (Arg)

tuber /'tu:bər || 'tju:bə(r)/ *n* (Bot) tubérculo *m*

tuberculosis /tʊ'bɜ:rkjə'ləʊsəs || tjʊ,bɜ:kjʊ'ləʊsɪs/ *n* [U] tuberculosis *f*

tubing /'tu:bɪŋ || 'tju:bɪŋ/ *n* [U] tubería *f*

tubular /'tu:bjələr || 'tju:bjʊlə(r)/ *adj* tubular

TUC *n* (in UK) = **Trades Union Congress**

tuck¹ /tʌk/ *n* (fold, pleat) jareta *f*, alforza *f* (CS)

tuck² *vt* meter; **he ~ed the blanket under the mattress** metió bien la manta debajo del colchón

• **tuck in 1** [*v* + *adv*] (eat) (colloq) ponerse* a comer, atacar* (fam) **2** [*v* + *o* + *adv*, *v* + *adv* + *o*] **(a)** ‹*sheet*› meter; **~ your shirt in** métete la camisa por dentro (de los pantalones) **(b)** ‹*child*› arropar

• **tuck up** [*v* + *o* + *adv*] **to ~ sb up (in bed)** arropar a algn (en la cama)

tuckered out /'tʌkərd || 'tʌkəd/ *adj* (AmE colloq) (*pred*) molido (fam), hecho polvo (fam)

Tuesday ▶ 540 /'tu:zdeɪ, -di || 'tju:zdeɪ, -di/ *n* martes *m*; *see also* MONDAY

tuft /tʌft/ *n* **(a)** (of hair) mechón *m*; (on top of head) copete *m* **(b)** (of grass) mata *f*

tug¹ /tʌg/ **-gg-** *vt* tirar de, jalar (de) (AmL exc CS) ■ ~ *vi* **to ~ AT sth** tirar DE algo, jalar (DE) algo (AmL exc CS)

tug² *n* **1** (pull) tirón *m*, jalón *m* (AmL exc CS) **2** (Naut) remolcador *m*

tug of war *n*: *juego de tira y afloja con una cuerda*

tuition /tʊ'ɪʃən || tju:'ɪʃən/ *n* [U] **(a)** (instruction) (frml) ~ (IN **sth**) clases *fpl* (DE algo); **private ~** clases *fpl* particulares **(b)** (fees) matrícula *f*

tulip /'tu:ləp || 'tju:lɪp/ *n* tulipán *m*

tumble¹ /'tʌmbəl/ *n* (fall) caída *f*

tumble² *vi* **1** (fall) caerse* **2** (roll, turn) «*acrobat*» dar* volteretas

tumble: **~down** *adj* (*before n*) en ruinas; **~ dryer** /'tʌmbəl'draɪər || 'tʌmbəl,draɪə(r)/ *n* secadora *f*

tumbler /'tʌmblər || 'tʌmblə(r)/ *n* (glass) vaso *m* (*de lados rectos*)

tummy /'tʌmi/ *n* (*pl* **-mies**) (used to or by children) barriga *f* (fam), pancita *f* (fam), tripita *f* (fam)

tumor, (BrE) **tumour** /'tu:mər || 'tju:mə(r)/ *n* tumor *m*

tumult /'tu:mʌlt || 'tju:mʌlt/ *n* [U C] tumulto *m*

tumultuous /tʊ'mʌltʃuəs || tjʊ'mʌltjʊəs/ *adj* ‹*applause*› apoteósico; ‹*protest*› tumultuoso

tuna /'tu:nə || 'tju:nə/ *n* (*pl* ~ *or* **~s**) atún *m*

tundra /'tʌndrə/ *n* [U] tundra *f*

tune¹ /tu:n || tju:n/ *n* **(a)** [C] (melody) melodía *f*; (piece) canción *f*, tonada *f*; ***to change one's ~*** cambiar de parecer **(b)** [U] (correct pitch): **to be in/out of ~** estar* afinado/desafinado

tune² *vt* **(a)** (Mus) afinar **(b)** (Auto) poner* a punto, afinar **(c)** (Rad, TV) sintonizar*

• **tune in** [*v* + *adv*] **to ~ in TO sth** sintonizar* (CON) algo

tuneful /'tu:nfəl || 'tju:nfəl/ *adj* melódico

tuner /'tu:nər || 'tju:nə(r)/ *n* **(a)** (*piano* ~) (Mus) afinador, -dora *m,f* de pianos **(b)** (Rad) sintonizador *m*

tunic /'tu:nɪk || 'tju:nɪk/ *n* **(a)** (of military uniform) guerrera *f* **(b)** (in ancient Rome) túnica *f*

tuning fork /'tu:nɪŋ || 'tju:nɪŋ/ *n* diapasón *m*

Tunisia /tu:'ni:ʒə || tju:'nɪziə/ *n* Túnez *m*

Tunisian /tu:'ni:ʒən || tju:'nɪziən/ *adj* tunecino

tunnel¹ /'tʌnl/ *n* túnel *m*; (in mine) galería *f*, socavón *m*

tunnel², (BrE) *vi* **-ll-** abrir* *or* hacer* un túnel

turban /'tɜ:rbən || 'tɜ:bən/ *n* turbante *m*

turbid /'tɜ:rbəd || 'tɜ:bɪd/ *adj* turbio

turbine /'tɜ:rbən, -baɪn || 'tɜ:baɪn/ *n* turbina *f*

turbo /'tɜ:rbəʊ || 'tɜ:bəʊ/ *n* turbocompresor *m*, turbo *m*

turbulence /'tɜ:rbjələns || 'tɜ:bjʊləns/ *n* [U] turbulencia *f*

turbulent /'tɜ:rbjələnt || 'tɜ:bjʊlənt/ *adj* turbulento

tureen /tjʊ'ri:n, tə- || tjʊə'ri:n/ *n* sopera *f*

turf¹ /tɜ:rf || tɜ:f/ *n* (*pl* **~s** *or* **turves**) **(a)** [U] (grass) césped *m* **(b)** [C] (square of grass) (esp BrE) tepe *m*

turf² *vt* ‹*garden*› encespedar, colocar* tepes en

turgid /'tɜ:rdʒəd || 'tɜ:dʒɪd/ *adj* ‹*prose*› ampuloso

Turk /tɜ:rk || tɜ:k/ *n* turco, -ca *m,f*

turkey /'tɜ:rki || 'tɜ:ki/ *n* (*pl* **~s**) [C U] pavo *m*, guajolote *m* (Méx)

Turkey /'tɜ:rki || 'tɜ:ki/ *n* Turquía *f*

Turkish¹ /'tɜ:rkɪʃ || 'tɜ:kɪʃ/ *adj* turco

Turkish² *n* [U] turco *m*

Turkish: **~ bath** *n* baño *m* turco; **~ delight** *n* [U] delicia *f* turca (*dulce gelatinoso recubierto de azúcar*)

Turkmenistan /,tɜ:rkmenɪ'stɑ:n || ,tɜ:kmenɪ'stɑ:n/ *n* Turkmenistán *m*

turmeric /'tɜ:rmərɪk || 'tɜ:mərɪk/ *n* [U] cúrcuma *f*

turmoil /'tɜ:rmɔɪl || 'tɜ:mɔɪl/ *n* [U] confusión *f*

turn¹ /tɜ:rn || tɜ:n/ *n* **1 (a)** (rotation) vuelta *f* **(b)** (change of direction) vuelta *f*, giro *m* **(c)** (bend) curva *f* **(d)** (change, alteration): **this dramatic ~ of events** este dramático giro de los acontecimientos; **to take a**

~ for the better empezar* a mejorar; **to take a ~ for the worse** empeorar, ponerse* peor; **the ~ of the century** el final del siglo (*y el principio del siguiente*) **2** (place in sequence): **whose ~ is it?** ¿a quién le toca?; **I think it's my ~** creo que me toca (el turno) a mí; ***to take ~s*** *o* ***to take it in ~(s)*** turnarse **3** (service): **to do sb a good ~** hacerle* un favor a algn **4** (bout of illness): **he had a funny ~** le dio un ataque (*or* un mareo *etc*)

turn² *vt* **1** (rotate) ‹*knob/wheel/key*› (hacer*) girar **2** (change position, direction of) ‹*head*› volver*, voltear (AmL exc RPl); **she ~ed her back on them** les volvió *or* les dio la espalda, les volteó la espalda (AmL exc RPl); **the nurse ~ed her onto her side** la enfermera la puso de lado; **3** (reverse) ‹*mattress/omelette*› darle* la vuelta a, voltear (AmL exc CS), dar* vuelta (CS); ‹*page*› pasar, volver*, dar* vuelta (CS) **4 (a)** (go around) ‹*corner*› dar* la vuelta a, dar* vuelta (CS) **(b)** (pass): **she's just ~ed 16** acaba de cumplir (los) 16 **5** (change, transform) volver*; **to ~ sth TO/INTO sth** transformar *or* convertir* algo EN algo **6** (shape — on lathe) tornear; (— on potter's wheel) hacer* ■ **~** *vi* **1** (rotate) «*handle/wheel*» girar, dar* vuelta(s) **2 (a)** (to face in different direction) «*person*» volverse*, darse* la vuelta, voltearse (AmL exc CS), darse* vuelta (CS); «*car*» dar* la vuelta, dar* vuelta (CS); **he ~ed onto his side** se volvió *or* se puso de lado **(b)** ▶ 553 (change course, direction): **to turn into a side street** meterse en una calle lateral; **to ~ left/right** girar *or* doblar *or* torcer* a la izquierda/derecha **(c)** (curve) «*road/river*» torcer* **3 (a)** (focus on): **to ~ to another subject** pasar a otro tema; **his mind ~ed to thoughts of escape** se puso a pensar en escaparse **(b)** (have recourse to): **to ~ to sb** (for protection, advice) recurrir a algn; **to ~ to drink** darse* a la bebida **4 (a)** (become): **his face ~ed red** se le puso la cara colorada; **her hair had ~ed gray** había encanecido **(b)** (be transformed) **to ~ INTO/TO sth** convertirse* EN algo **(c)** (change) «*luck/weather/tide*» cambiar **(d)** (go sour) «*milk*» agriarse* **5** (when reading): **~ to page 19** vayan a la página 19

• **turn against** [*v + o + prep + o*]: **she ~ed them against me** los puso en mi contra

• **turn around,** (BrE also) **turn round 1** [*v + adv*] darse* la vuelta, volverse*, voltearse (AmL exc CS), darse* vuelta (CS) **2** [*v + o + adv*] darle* la vuelta a, voltear (AmL exc CS), dar* vuelta (CS)

• **turn aside** [*v + adv*] darse* la vuelta, voltearse (AmL exc CS), darse* vuelta (CS)

• **turn away 1** [*v + adv*] apartarse **2** [*v + o + adv, v + adv + o*] **(a)** ‹*head/face*› volver*, voltear (AmL exc RPl), dar* vuelta (CS); **he ~ed his eyes away** apartó la mirada **(b)** (send away) ‹*business*› no aceptar; **the doorman ~ed them away** el portero no los dejó entrar

• **turn back 1** [*v + adv*] (go back) volver*, regresar **2** [*v + o + adv, v + adv + o*]: **he was ~ed back at the border** en la frontera lo hicieron regresar

• **turn down** [*v + o + adv, v + adv + o*] **(a)** (fold back) doblar **(b)** (diminish) ‹*heating/volume/temperature*› bajar **(c)** (reject) ‹*offer/candidate*› rechazar*

• **turn in 1** [*v + adv*] (go to bed) (colloq) acostarse* **2** [*v + o + adv, v + adv + o*] (hand in, over) entregar*

• **turn off 1** [*v + o + adv, v + adv + o*] ‹*light/radio/heating*› apagar*; ‹*faucet*› cerrar*; ‹*water*› cortar **2** [*v + adv*] **(a)** (from road) doblar **(b)** (switch off) apagarse*

• **turn on 1** [*v + o + adv, v + adv + o*] **(a)** ‹*light/television/oven*› encender*, prender (AmL); ‹*faucet*› abrir* **(b)** (excite) (colloq) gustar; (sexually) excitar **2** [*v + prep + o*] (attack) atacar*

• **turn out 1** [*v + o + adv, v + adv + o*] **(a)** (switch off) ‹*light*› apagar* **(b)** (empty) ‹*pockets/cupboard*› vaciar* **2** [*v + adv + o*] (produce) sacar* **3** [*v + o + adv, v + adv + o*] (force to leave) echar **4** [*v + adv*] **(a)** (attend): **several thousand ~ed out to welcome the Pope** varios miles de personas acudieron *or* fueron/vinieron a recibir al Papa **(b)** (result, prove): **everything ~ed out well** todo salió *or* bien

• **turn over 1** [*v + o + adv*] **(a)** (flip, reverse) darle* la vuelta a, voltear (AmL exc CS), dar* vuelta (CS); ‹*soil*› remover*; ‹*idea*› darle* vueltas a **(b)** (Auto) ‹*engine*› hacer* funcionar **2** [*v + o + adv, v + adv + o*] (hand over) entregar* **3** [*v + adv + o*] ‹*page*› pasar, volver*, dar* vuelta (CS) **4** [*v + adv*] (onto other side) darse* la vuelta, darse* vuelta (CS); «*car*» volcarse*

• **turn round** (esp BrE) ⇒ TURN AROUND

• **turn up 1** [*v + o + adv, v + adv + o*] **(a)** ‹*collar*› levantarse, subirse **(b)** (shorten) ‹*trousers*› acortar; ‹*hem*› subir **(c)** (increase) ‹*oven/volume*› subir; ‹*radio*› subir el volumen de **2** [*v + adv*] (colloq) **(a)** (be found) «*sth lost*» aparecer* **(b)** (arrive) (BrE) llegar*; **she didn't ~ up** no apareció

turn: **~about**, **~around** *n* giro *m*, cambio *m*; **~coat** *n* renegado, -da *m,f*

turned-up /'tɜːrnd'ʌp ‖ ˌtɜːnd'ʌp/ *adj* ‹*nose*› respingón, respingado (AmL)

turning /'tɜːrnɪŋ ‖ 'tɜːnɪŋ/ *n* (in town) bocacalle *f*; **we've missed the ~** nos hemos pasado la calle (*or* carretera *etc*)

turning point *n* momento *m* decisivo *or* crucial

turnip /'tɜːrnəp ‖ 'tɜːnɪp/ *n* [C U] nabo *m*

turn: **~out** *n* (at election) número *m* de votantes; (at public spectacle) número *m* de asistentes; **~over** *n* **1** [U] **(a)** (volume of business, sales) facturación *f* **(b)** (of stock) rotación *f* **(c)** (of staff) movimiento *m*; **2** [C] (Culin) empanada *f* (esp AmL), empanadilla *f* (esp Esp); **~pike** *n* (AmE) autopista *f* de peaje *or* (Méx) de cuota; **~ signal** *n* (AmE) intermitente *m*, direccional *f* (Col, Méx), señalizador *m* (de viraje) (Chi); **~stile** *n* torniquete *m*; **~table** *n* (Audio) (platter) plato *m*; (deck) platina *f*, tornamesa *f or m* (AmL); **~up** *n* **(a)** (hem) dobladillo *m* **(b)** (on trousers) (BrE) vuelta *f or* (RPl) botamanga *f or* (Chi) bastilla *f or* (Méx) valenciana *f*

turpentine /'tɜːrpəntaɪn ‖ 'tɜːpəntaɪn/ *n* [U] aguarrás *m*, trementina *f*

turquoise /'tɜːrkwɔɪz ‖ 'tɜːkwɔɪz/ ▶ 515 *adj* (azul) turquesa *adj inv*

turret /'tɜːrət ‖ 'tʌrɪt/ *n* torrecilla *f*

turtle /'tɜːrtl̩ ‖ 'tɜːtl/ *n* **(a)** (marine reptile) tortuga *f* marina *or* de mar **(b)** (AmE) (tortoise) tortuga *f*

turtleneck /'tɜ:rtḷnek ‖ 'tɜ:tḷnek/ *n* **(a)** ~ (**collar**) cuello *m* alto **(b)** ~ (**sweater**) suéter *m* de cuello vuelto

turves /tɜ:rvz ‖ tɜ:vz/ *pl of* TURF[1]

tusk /tʌsk/ *n* colmillo *m*

tussle /'tʌsəl/ *n* pelea *f*, lucha *f*

tut /tʌt/ *vi* **-tt-** chasquear la lengua

tutor /'tu:tər ‖ 'tju:tə(r)/ *n* profesor, -sora *m,f* particular

tutorial /tu:'tɔ:riəl ‖ tju:'tɔ:riəl/ *n*: *clase individual o con un pequeño número de estudiantes*

tutu /'tu:tu:/ *n* (*pl* **~s**) tutú *m*

tuxedo /tʌk'si:dəʊ/ *n* (*pl* **-dos** *or* **-does**) (AmE) esmoquin *m*, smoking *m*

TV *n* [C U] (= **television**) televisión *f*, tele *f* (fam), TV *f*

twang /twæŋ/ *n* (of guitar) tañido *m*; (of voice, accent): **his voice has a nasal ~** tiene la voz gangosa

tweak /twi:k/ *vt* pellizcar* (*retorciendo*)

twee /twi:/ *adj* (BrE) cursi

tweed /twi:d/ *n* [U] (Tex) tweed *m*

tweet /twi:t/ *vi* piar*, gorjear

tweezers /'twi:zərz ‖ 'twi:zəz/ *pl n* pinza(s) *f(pl)*

twelfth[1] /twelfθ/ ▶540, 725 *adj* duodécimo

twelfth[2] *adv* en duodécimo lugar

twelfth[3] ▶540, 543, 725 *n* (Math) doceavo *m*; (part) doceava parte *f*

Twelfth Night *n* Noche *f* de Reyes

twelve /twelv/ ▶451, 725, 884 *adj/n* doce *adj inv/m*; ~ **(o'clock) midnight/noon** las doce de la noche/del mediodía; *see also* FOUR[1]

twentieth[1] /'twentiəθ/ ▶540, 725 *adj* vigésimo

twentieth[2] *adv* en vigésimo lugar

twentieth[3] ▶540, 543, 725 *n* (Math) veinteavo *m*; (part) veinteava *or* vigésima parte *f*

twenty /'twenti/ ▶451, 540, 774, ▶884 *adj/n* veinte *adj inv/m*; *see also* FOUR[1]

twenty-first[1] /'twenti'fɜ:rst ‖ ˌtwenti'fɜ:st/ ▶540, 725 *adj* vigesimoprimero

twenty-first[2] *adv* en vigesimoprimer lugar

twice /twaɪs/ *adv* dos veces; **~ a year** dos veces por año; ***to think ~*** pensarlo* dos veces; **~ three is six** dos por tres es (igual a) seis; **I've got ~ as many as you** yo tengo el doble que tú

twiddle /'twɪdl/ *vt* (hacer*) girar ■ ~ *vi* **to ~** WITH **sth** juguetear CON algo

twig /twɪg/ *n* ramita *f*

twilight /'twaɪlaɪt/ *n* [U] **(a)** (dusk) crepúsculo *m* **(b)** (half-light) penumbra *f* **(c)** (period of decline) (liter) crepúsculo *m* (liter)

twin[1] /twɪn/ *n* mellizo, -za *m,f*, gemelo, -la *m,f* (esp Esp); **identical ~s** gemelos idénticos *or* (téc) univitelinos, gemelos (AmL)

twin[2] *adj* **(a)** ‹*brother/sister*› mellizo, gemelo (esp Esp) **(b)** (paired): **~ beds** camas *fpl* gemelas

twin[3] *vt* **-nn-** (BrE) (*usu pass*) **to be ~ned** WITH **sth** estar* hermanado CON algo

twine[1] /twaɪn/ *n* [U] cordel *m*, bramante *m* (Esp), cáñamo *m* (Andes), mecate *m* (AmC, Méx, Ven)

twine[2] *vi* **to ~** AROUND **sth** enroscarse* ALREDEDOR DE algo

twinge /twɪndʒ/ *n* (of pain) punzada *f*, puntada *f* (CS); (of remorse) puntada *f*

twinkle[1] /'twɪŋkəl/ *n* **(a)** (of lights, stars) centelleo *m*, titilar *m* **(b)** (in eye) brillo *m*

twinkle[2] *vi* **(a)** «*light/star*» titilar, centellear **(b)** «*eyes*» brillar

twinkling /'twɪŋklɪŋ/ *n*: ***in the ~ of an eye*** en un abrir y cerrar de ojos

twirl /twɜ:rl ‖ twɜ:l/ *vt* ‹*cane/baton*› (hacer*) girar ■ ~ *vi* «*baton*» girar; **to ~ around** girar

twist[1] /twɪst/ *vt* **1 (a)** (screw, coil) retorcer*; **to ~ sth** AROUND **sth** enrollar *or* enroscar* algo ALREDEDOR DE algo **(b)** (turn) ‹*handle/knob*› girar **2 (a)** (distort) retorcer* **(b)** (sprain) torcer* **(c)** (alter, pervert) ‹*words*› tergiversar; ‹*meaning*› torcer* ■ ~ *vi* **(a)** (wind, coil) «*rope/wire*» enrollarse, enroscarse*; «*road/river*» serpentear **(b)** (turn, rotate) girar

twist[2] *n* **1 (a)** (bend — in wire, rope) vuelta *f*, onda *f*; (— in road) recodo *m*, vuelta *f* **(b)** (turning movement) giro *m* **(c) a ~ of lemon** una rodajita de limón (*retorcida*) **2** (in story, events) giro *m* inesperado **3** (dance) twist *m*

twisted /'twɪstəd ‖ 'twɪstɪd/ *adj* retorcido

twister /'twɪstər ‖ 'twɪstə(r)/ *n* (AmE colloq) tornado *m*

twit /twɪt/ *n* (BrE colloq) imbécil *mf*

twitch[1] /twɪtʃ/ *vi* «*tail/nose*» moverse*

twitch[2] *n* tic *m*

twitter /'twɪtər ‖ 'twɪtə(r)/ *vi* **(a)** «*birds*» gorjear **(b)** «*person*» parlotear, cotorrear (fam)

two[1] /tu:/ ▶451, 724, 884 *n* dos *m*; **~ by ~** (liter) de dos en dos, de a dos (AmL); ***to put ~ and ~ together*** atar cabos; *see also* FOUR[1]

two[2] ▶451, 724, 884 *adj* dos *adj inv*

two: **~-bit** *adj* (AmE) (*before n*) (colloq) de tres al cuarto (fam); **~-dimensional** /'tu:də'mentʃnəl, -daɪ- ‖ ˌtu:dɪ'menʃənḷ, -daɪ-/ *adj* bidimensional; **~-edged** /'tu:'edʒd/ *adj* de doble filo; **~-faced** /'tu:'feɪst/ *adj* (colloq) falso, doble (Andes, Ven fam); **~fold** *adj/adv see* -FOLD; **~pence** /'tʌpəns/ *n* dos peniques *mpl*; **~-piece** *adj* ‹*swimsuit*› de dos piezas; **~-piece suit** traje *m or* (Col) vestido *m* de dos piezas, ambo *m* (CS); **~-seater** /'tu:'si:tər ‖ ˌtu:'si:tə(r)/ *n* biplaza

twosome /'tu:səm/ *n* (pair) pareja *f*

two: **~-time** *vt* (colloq) (be unfaithful to) ponerle* *or* meterle los cuernos a (fam); (double-cross) engañar; **~-tone** *adj* de dos tonos; **~-way** /'tu:'weɪ/ *adj* ‹*traffic/street*› de doble sentido *or* dirección; ‹*agreement*› bilateral; **~-way radio** aparato *m* emisor y receptor

TX = **Texas**

tycoon /taɪ'ku:n/ *n* magnate *mf*

tympani /'tɪmpəni/ *pl n* timbales *mpl*

type[1] /taɪp/ *n* **1** [C] **(a)** (sort, kind) tipo *m*; **it's a ~ of** ... (in descriptions, definitions) es una especie de ... **(b)** (typical example) tipo *m*, ejemplo *m* típico; (stereotype) estereotipo *m* **2** [U] (Print) (characters) tipo *m* (de imprenta)

type[2] *vt/i* escribir* a máquina, tipear (AmS)

type: **~cast** *vt* (*past & past p* **-cast**) ‹*actor*› encasillar (*en cierto tipo de papel*); **~face** *n* tipo *m* (de imprenta), (tipo *m* de) caracteres *mpl*, (tipo *m* de) letra *f*; **~script** *n* [C U] texto *m* mecanografiado, manuscrito *m* (*de una obra, novela etc*); **~set** *vt* (*pres p* **-setting**; *past & past p* **-set**) componer*; **~setter** /'taɪpsetər ‖ 'taɪpsetə(r)/ *n* (person) cajista *mf*, componedor, -dora *m,f*; **~write** (*past* **-wrote**; *past p* **-written**) *vt* (*usu pass*) escribir* a máquina, mecanografiar*; **~writer** *n* máquina *f* de escribir

typhoid (fever) /'taɪfɔɪd/ *n* [U] (fiebre *f*) tifoidea *f*

typhoon /taɪ'fu:n/ *n* tifón *m*

typical /'tɪpɪkəl/ *adj* típico

typically /'tɪpɪkli/ *adv* típicamente

typify /'tɪpəfaɪ ‖ 'tɪpɪfaɪ/ *vt* **-fies, -fying, -fied** tipificar*

typing /'taɪpɪŋ/ *n* [U] mecanografía *f*; (*before n*) ‹*error*› de máquina; ‹*lesson*› de mecanografía

typist /'taɪpəst ‖ 'taɪpɪst/ *n* mecanógrafo, -fa *m,f*, dactilógrafo, -fa *m,f*

typography /taɪ'pɑ:grəfi ‖ taɪ'pɒgrəfi/ *n* [U] tipografía *f*

tyrannical /tə'rænɪkəl ‖ tɪ'rænɪkəl/ *adj* tiránico

tyranny /'tɪrəni/ *n* [U] tiranía *f*

tyrant /'taɪrənt/ *n* tirano, -na *m,f*

tyre /taɪr ‖ 'taɪə(r)/ *n* (BrE) ⇒ TIRE²

Uu

U, u /ju:/ *n* U, u *f*

U (in UK) (Cin) (= **universal**) apta para todo público (AmL), todos los públicos (Esp)

ubiquitous /ju:'bɪkwətəs ‖ ju:'bɪkwɪtəs/ *adj* omnipresente (frml), ubicuo (liter)

udder /'ʌdər ‖ 'ʌdə(r)/ *n* ubre *f*

UFO *n* (= **unidentified flying object**) ovni *m*, OVNI *m*

Uganda /ju:'gændə/ *n* Uganda *f*

Ugandan /ju:'gændən/ *adj* ugandés

ugly /'ʌgli/ *adj* **uglier, ugliest** feo

UHT *adj* (BrE) (= **ultra high temperature**) UHT, UAT (AmL), uperizado (Esp)

UK *n* (= **United Kingdom**) RU *m*

Ukraine /ju:'kreɪn/ *n* Ucrania *f*

Ukrainian¹ /ju:'kreɪniən/ *adj* ucraniano, ucranio

Ukrainian² *n* **(a)** [C] (person) ucraniano, -na *m,f*, ucranio, -nia *m,f* **(b)** [U] (language) ucraniano *m*, ucranio *m*

ulcer /'ʌlsər ‖ 'ʌlsə(r)/ ▶ 484 *n* (internal) úlcera *f*; (external) llaga *f*; **a mouth ~** una llaga en la boca

ulterior /ʌl'tɪriər ‖ ʌl'tɪəriə(r)/ *adj* oculto; **~ motive** segunda intención *f*, motivo *m* oculto

ultimata /'ʌltə'meɪtə ‖ ˌʌltɪ'meɪtə/ *pl of* ULTIMATUM

ultimate¹ /'ʌltəmət ‖ 'ʌltɪmət/ *adj* **1** (eventual) ‹*aim/destination*› final **2 (a)** (utmost, supreme) ‹*sacrifice*› máximo, supremo **(b)** (most sophisticated) (journ): **the ~ sound system** lo último en sistemas de sonido, el no va más en sistemas de sonido (fam)

ultimate² *n*: **the ~ in sth** lo último en algo, el no va más en algo (fam)

ultimately /'ʌltəmətli ‖ 'ʌltɪmətli/ *adv* **(a)** (finally) en última instancia **(b)** (in the long run) a la larga

ultimatum /'ʌltə'meɪtəm ‖ˌʌltɪ'meɪtəm/ *n* (*pl* **-tums** *or* **-ta**) ultimátum *m*

ultra- /'ʌltrə/ *pref* ultra-, super- (fam)

ultrasonic /'ʌltrə'sɑ:nɪk ‖ˌʌltrə'sɒnɪk/ *adj* ultrasónico

ultrasound /'ʌltrəsaʊnd/ *n* **(a)** [U] (Phys) ultrasonido *m* **(b)** [C U] (Med) ecografía *f*

ultraviolet /'ʌltrə'vaɪələt/ *adj* ultravioleta *adj inv*

umbilical cord /əm'bɪlɪkəl ‖ ʌm'bɪlɪkəl/ *n* cordón *m* umbilical

umbrage /'ʌmbrɪdʒ/ *n*: **to take ~ (AT sth)** ofenderse *or* sentirse* agraviado (POR algo)

umbrella /ʌm'brelə/ *n* (*pl* **-las**) paraguas *m*

umpire /'ʌmpaɪr ‖ 'ʌmpaɪə(r)/ *n* árbitro, -tra *m,f*, (in baseball) umpire *mf*

umpteen /'ʌmp'ti:n/ *adj* (colloq) tropecientos (fam), miles *or* un millón de

umpteenth /'ʌmp'ti:nθ/ *adj* (colloq) enésimo; **for the ~ time** por enésima vez

un- /'ʌn/ *pref* in-, des-, no, sin, poco; *see individual words*

UN *n* (= **United Nations**) ONU *f*

unable /ʌn'eɪbəl/ *adj* (*pred*) **to be ~ to** + INF no poder* + INF

unabridged /'ʌnə'brɪdʒd/ *adj* íntegro

unacceptable /'ʌnək'septəbəl/ *adj* ‹*conduct/standard*› inaceptable, inadmisible; ‹*terms/conditions*› inadmisible

unaccompanied /'ʌnə'kʌmpənid/ *adj* **(a)** ‹*luggage*› no acompañado; ‹*person*› solo **(b)** (Mus) ‹*singing*› sin acompañamiento; ‹*instrument*› solo

unaccounted for /'ʌnə'kaʊntəd‖ˌʌnə'kaʊntɪd/ *adj* (*pred*): **the rest of the money is ~ ~** no se han dado explicaciones sobre qué sucedió con el resto del dinero; **the others are still ~ ~** los otros siguen su aparecer

unaccustomed /'ʌnə'kʌstəmd/ *adj* **(a)** (unusual) desacostumbrado, poco habitual **(b)** (unused) **to be ~ TO sth/-ING** no estar* acostumbrado A algo/+ INF

unadventurous /ˈʌnədˈventʃərəs/ *adj* poco atrevido *or* audaz
unaffected /ˈʌnəˈfektəd ‖ ˌʌnəˈfektɪd/ *adj* **(a)** (sincere, natural) ‹*person*› natural, sencillo **(b)** (not damaged, hurt) no afectado
unaided /ˈʌnˈeɪdəd ‖ ʌnˈeɪdɪd/ *adj* sin ayuda
unambitious /ˈʌnæmˈbɪʃəs/ *adj* poco ambicioso
unanimous /juːˈnænəməs ‖ juːˈnænɪməs/ *adj* unánime
unanimously /juːˈnænəməsli ‖ juːˈnænɪməsli/ *adv* ‹*vote/state*› unánimemente; ‹*elect*› por unanimidad
unanswered /ˈʌnˈænsərd ‖ ʌnˈɑːnsəd/ *adj* ‹*question/letter*› sin contestar
unappetizing /ˈʌnˈæpətaɪzɪŋ/ *adj* ‹*dish/smell*› poco apetitoso; ‹*prospect*› poco apetecible
unappreciative /ˈʌnəˈpriːʃətɪv/ *adj* ‹*person*› ingrato, desagradecido
unapproachable /ˈʌnəˈprəʊtʃəbəl/ *adj* ‹*person*› inabordable, poco accesible *or* asequible
unarmed /ˈʌnˈɑːrmd ‖ ʌnˈɑːmd/ *adj* ‹*person*› desarmado; ‹*combat*› sin armas
unassisted /ˈʌnəˈsɪstəd ‖ ˌʌnəˈsɪstɪd/ *adj* sin ayuda
unassuming /ˈʌnəˈsuːmɪŋ ‖ ˌʌnəˈsjuːmɪŋ/ *adj* sencillo, sin pretensiones
unattached /ˈʌnəˈtætʃt/ *adj* **(a)** (not affiliated) independiente **(b)** (not married) sin ataduras
unattended /ˈʌnəˈtendəd ‖ ˌʌnəˈtendɪd/ *adj* (*usu pred*) **(a)** (unwatched, unsupervised): **to leave sb ~** dejar a algn solo; **don't leave your luggage ~** vigile su equipaje en todo momento **(b)** (not dealt with) desatendido
unattractive /ˈʌnəˈtræktɪv/ *adj* poco atractivo
unauthorized /ˈʌnˈɔːθəraɪzd/ *adj* no autorizado
unavailable /ˈʌnəˈveɪləbəl/ *adj*: **that number is ~** ese número está desconectado (*or* averiado *etc*); **he is ~ for comment** no desea hacer ningún comentario
unavoidable /ˈʌnəˈvɔɪdəbəl/ *adj* inevitable
unavoidably /ˈʌnəˈvɔɪdəbli/ *adv*: **I was ~ delayed** no pude evitar llegar retrasado
unaware /ˈʌnəˈwer ‖ ˌʌnəˈweə(r)/ *adj* **(a)** (not conscious) (*pred*) **to be ~ OF sth** ignorar algo, no ser* consciente DE algo **(b)** (naive): **politically ~** sin conciencia política
unawares /ˈʌnəˈwerz ‖ ˌʌnəˈweəz/ *adv*: **to catch** *o* **take sb ~** agarrar *or* (esp Esp) coger* a algn desprevenido
unbalanced /ˈʌnˈbælənst/ *adj* **(a)** ‹*diet/composition*› desequilibrado **(b)** (mentally) desequilibrado, trastornado
unbearable /ˈʌnˈberəbəl ‖ ʌnˈbeərəbəl/ *adj* insoportable, inaguantable
unbeatable /ˈʌnˈbiːtəbəl/ *adj* ‹*team*› invencible; ‹*quality/value*› insuperable; ‹*price*› imbatible
unbeaten /ˈʌnˈbiːtn̩/ *adj* ‹*champion/army*› invicto; ‹*record*› insuperado
unbeknown /ˈʌnbɪˈnəʊn/, **unbeknownst** /-ˈnəʊnst/ *adv* (liter): **~ to me/her** sin saberlo yo/ella
unbelievable /ˈʌnbəˈliːvəbəl ‖ ˌʌnbɪˈliːvəbəl/ *adj* increíble
unbelievably /ˈʌnbəˈliːvəbli ‖ ˌʌnbɪˈliːvəbli/ *adv* increíblemente
unbelieving /ˈʌnbəˈliːvɪŋ ‖ ˌʌnbɪˈliːvɪŋ/ *adj* ‹*smile/look*› de incredulidad
unbending /ˈʌnˈbendɪŋ/ *adj* ‹*person/attitude*› inflexible; ‹*determination*› firme
unbiased /ˈʌnˈbaɪəst/ *adj* imparcial, objetivo
unblock /ˈʌnˈblɑːk ‖ ʌnˈblɒk/ *vt* desatascar*, destapar (AmL)
unbolt /ˈʌnˈbəʊlt/ *vt* ‹*gate/door*› descorrer el pestillo *or* cerrojo de
unborn /ˈʌnˈbɔːrn ‖ ʌnˈbɔːn/ *adj* ‹*child*› que todavía no ha nacido
unbreakable /ˈʌnˈbreɪkəbəl/ *adj* irrompible
unbridled /ˈʌnˈbraɪdl̩d/ *adj* desenfrenado
unbroken /ˈʌnˈbrəʊkən/ *adj* intacto, en perfecto estado; ‹*silence/run*› ininterrumpido
unbuckle /ˈʌnˈbʌkəl/ *vt* desabrochar
unbutton /ˈʌnˈbʌtn̩/ *vt* desabotonar, desabrochar
uncalled-for /ˈʌnˈkɔːldfɔːr ‖ ʌnˈkɔːlfɔː(r)/ *adj* ‹*criticism/remark*› fuera de lugar
uncanny /ˈʌnˈkæni/ *adj* raro, extraño
uncaring /ˈʌnˈkerɪŋ ‖ ʌnˈkeərɪŋ/ *adj* indiferente
unceremonious /ˈʌnˈserəˈməʊniəs ‖ ˌʌnˌserɪˈməʊniəs/ *adj* brusco, poco ceremonioso
uncertain /ˈʌnˈsɜːrtn̩ ‖ ʌnˈsɜːtn̩/ *adj* **1** **(a)** (unsure) (*pred*) **to be ~ ABOUT/OF sth** no estar* seguro DE algo **(b)** (hesitant) vacilante **2** ‹*prospects/future*› incierto **3** (vague): **in no ~ terms** muy claramente, inequívocamente
uncertainty /ˈʌnˈsɜːrtn̩ti ‖ ʌnˈsɜːtn̩ti/ *n* [U] incertidumbre *f*
unchanged /ˈʌnˈtʃeɪndʒd/ *adj* (*usu pred*): **she was quite ~** no había cambiado para nada; **the ceremony has remained ~ for centuries** la ceremonia se ha celebrado de la misma forma durante siglos
uncharacteristic /ˈʌnˈkærəktəˈrɪstɪk/ *adj* desacostumbrado, inusitado
uncharitable /ˈʌnˈtʃærətəbəl ‖ ʌnˈtʃærɪtəbəl/ *adj* ‹*act/remark*› poco caritativo
unchecked /ˈʌnˈtʃekt/ *adj* libre, sin obstáculos
uncivilized /ˈʌnˈsɪvəlaɪzd ‖ ʌnˈsɪvɪlaɪzd/ *adj* incivilizado
uncle /ˈʌŋkəl/ *n* tío *m*
unclean /ˈʌnˈkliːn/ *adj* impuro
unclear /ˈʌnˈklɪr ‖ ʌnˈklɪə(r)/ *adj* poco claro, confuso; **he was ~ about his reasons for doing it** no dio una explicación muy clara de sus motivos
uncoil /ˈʌnˈkɔɪl/ *vi* desenroscarse*
uncomfortable /ˈʌnˈkʌmfərtəbəl ‖ ʌnˈkʌmftəbəl/ *adj* incómodo
uncommon /ˈʌnˈkɑːmən ‖ ʌnˈkɒmən/ *adj* poco común *or* frecuente
uncommunicative /ˈʌnkəˈmjuːnəkeɪtɪv ‖ ˌʌnkəˈmjuːnɪkətɪv/ *adj* poco comunicativo
uncomplaining /ˈʌnkəmˈpleɪnɪŋ/ *adj* resignado

uncomplicated /ˈʌnˈkɑːmpləkeɪtəd ‖ ʌnˈkɒmplɪkeɪtɪd/ *adj* sin complicaciones; ‹*character/style*› poco complicado

uncompromising /ʌnˈkɑːmprəmaɪzɪŋ ‖ ʌnˈkɒmprəmaɪzɪŋ/ *adj* inflexible, intransigente

unconcerned /ˈʌnkənˈsɜːrnd ‖ ˌʌnkənˈsɜːnd/ *adj* indiferente

unconditional /ˈʌnkənˈdɪʃnəl ‖ ˌʌnkənˈdɪʃənl/ *adj* incondicional

unconnected /ˈʌnkəˈnektəd ‖ ˌʌnkəˈnektɪd/ *adj* (unrelated) sin conexión; **these incidents are completely ~** estos incidentes no guardan ninguna relación (entre sí)

unconscious¹ /ˈʌnˈkɑːntʃəs ‖ ʌnˈkɒnʃəs/ *adj* **1** (Med) inconsciente **2** (unaware) (*pred*) **to be ~ OF sth** no ser* consciente DE algo **3** (Psych) inconsciente

unconscious² *n* **the ~** el inconsciente

unconsciously /ʌnˈkɑːntʃəsli ‖ ʌnˈkɒnʃəsli/ *adv* inconscientemente

uncontested /ˈʌnkənˈtestəd ‖ ˌʌnkənˈtestɪd/ *adj* ‹*will*› no impugnado; ‹*leader*› indiscutible

uncontrollable /ˈʌnkənˈtrəʊləbəl/ *adj* ‹*trembling*› incontrolable; ‹*urge*› irresistible, irrefrenable; ‹*laughter*› incontenible

uncontrolled /ˈʌnkənˈtrəʊld/ *adj* incontrolado

unconventional /ˈʌnkənˈventʃnəl ‖ ˌʌnkənˈvenʃənl/ *adj* poco convencional

unconvinced /ˈʌnkənˈvɪnst/ *adj*: **I'm still ~** aún no estoy muy convencida

unconvincing /ˈʌnkənˈvɪnsɪŋ/ *adj* poco convincente

uncoordinated /ˈʌnkəʊˈɔːrdṇeɪtəd ‖ ˌʌnkəʊˈɔːdɪneɪtɪd/ *adj* ‹*person*› falto de coordinación; ‹*movements*› no coordinado

uncork /ʌnˈkɔːrk ‖ ʌnˈkɔːk/ *vt* descorchar

uncorroborated /ˈʌnkəˈrɑːbəreɪtəd ‖ ˌʌnkəˈrɒbəreɪtɪd/ *adj* no confirmado, no corroborado

uncouth /ʌnˈkuːθ/ *adj* zafio, burdo

uncover /ˈʌnˈkʌvər ‖ ʌnˈkʌvə(r)/ *vt* **(a)** (remove covering of) destapar **(b)** (expose) ‹*scandal/plot*› revelar, sacar* a la luz

unctuous /ˈʌŋktʃuəs ‖ ˈʌŋktjʊəs/ *adj* empalagoso

uncultivated /ˈʌnˈkʌltəveɪtəd ‖ ʌnˈkʌltɪveɪtɪd/ *adj* ‹*land/mind*› sin cultivar

uncurl /ˈʌnˈkɜːrl ‖ ʌnˈkɜːl/ *vt* desenrollar ■ **~** *vi* ‹‹*snake*›› desenroscarse*

uncut /ˈʌnˈkʌt/ *adj* **1 (a)** ‹*grass/hedge*› sin cortar **(b)** ‹*diamond/gem*› sin tallar, en bruto; ‹*stone/marble*› sin labrar **2** (unabridged) íntegro, completo

undamaged /ˈʌnˈdæmɪdʒd/ *adj* intacto

undaunted /ˈʌnˈdɔːntəd ‖ ʌnˈdɔːntɪd/ *adj* impertérrito

undecided /ˈʌndɪˈsaɪdəd ‖ ˌʌndɪˈsaɪdɪd/ *adj* **(a)** (wavering) (*usu pred*) indeciso **(b)** ‹*matter*› pendiente, no resuelto

undefeated /ˈʌndɪˈfiːtəd ‖ ˌʌndɪˈfiːtɪd/ *adj* invicto

undemanding /ˈʌndɪˈmændɪŋ ‖ ˌʌndɪˈmɑːndɪŋ/ *adj* ‹*job*› cómodo, que exige poco; ‹*person*› poco exigente

undeniable /ˈʌndɪˈnaɪəbəl/ *adj* innegable

undeniably /ˈʌndɪˈnaɪəbli/ *adv* sin lugar a dudas

under¹ /ˈʌndər ‖ ˈʌndə(r)/ *prep* **(a)** (beneath) debajo de, abajo de (AmL) **(b)** (less than) menos de **(c)** ‹*name/heading*› bajo **(d)** ‹*government/authority*› bajo; **he has 20 people ~ him** tiene 20 personas a su mando **(e)** (according to) según

under² *adv* **1** (less) menos; **it will cost $10 or ~** costará 10 dólares como mucho **2** (under water): **they pushed him ~** lo empujaron debajo del agua

under- /ˈʌndər/ *pref* **(a)** (below, lower): **the ~mentioned** los abajo mencionados **(b)** (less than proper): **they are ~represented on the committee** no tienen la representación que les corresponde en la comisión **(c)** (of lesser rank) sub-; **~manager** subgerente *m*

under: **~age** /ˈʌndərˈeɪdʒ/ *adj* (*before n*) ‹*person*› menor de edad; **~arm** *adj* (*before n*) (Sport) sin levantar el brazo por encima del hombro; **~carriage** *n* tren *m* de aterrizaje; **~charge** /ˈʌndərˈtʃɑːrdʒ ‖ ˌʌndəˈtʃɑːdʒ/ *vt* cobrarle de menos a; **~coat**, (AmE also) **~coating** *n* **1 (a)** [U] (paint) pintura *f* base **(b)** [C] (coating) primera mano *f* de pintura; **2** [U C] (AmE Auto) tratamiento *m* anticorrosivo del chasis; **~cover** /ˈʌndərˈkʌvər ‖ ˌʌndəˈkʌvə(r)/ *adj* secreto; **~current** *n* **(a)** (of discontent) trasfondo *m*, corriente *f* subyacente **(b)** (of water) contracorriente *f*; **~cut** /ˈʌndərˈkʌt ‖ ˌʌndəˈkʌt/ *vt* (*pres p* **-cutting**; *past & past p* **-cut**) ‹*competitor*› vender más barato que; **~done** /ˈʌndərˈdʌn ‖ ˌʌndəˈdʌn/ *adj* ‹*meat*› poco cocido, poco hecho (Esp); **~estimate** /ˈʌndərˈestəmeɪt ‖ ˌʌndərˈestɪmeɪt/ *vt* **(a)** (guess too low): **they ~estimated the cost** calcularon el costo en menos de lo que correspondía **(b)** (underrate) subestimar; **~fed** /ˈʌndərˈfed ‖ ˌʌndəˈfed/ *adj* subalimentado; **~foot** /ˈʌndərˈfʊt ‖ ˌʌndəˈfʊt/ *adv* debajo de los pies; **~go** /ˈʌndərˈgəʊ ‖ ˌʌndəˈgəʊ/ *vt* (*3rd pers sing pres* **-goes**; *pres p* **-going**; *past* **-went**; *past p* **-gone**) ‹*change/hardship*› sufrir; **he is ~going treatment** está en tratamiento; **~graduate** /ˈʌndərˈgrædʒuət ‖ ˌʌndəˈgrædʒʊət/ *n* estudiante universitario, -ria *m,f* (*de licenciatura*); (*before n*) ‹*course/student*› universitario

underground¹ /ˈʌndərgraʊnd ‖ ˈʌndəgraʊnd/ *adj* (*before n*) subterráneo; ‹*organization*› clandestino

underground² /ˈʌndərˈgraʊnd ‖ ˌʌndəˈgraʊnd/ *adv* bajo tierra

underground³ /ˈʌndərgraʊnd ‖ ˈʌndəgraʊnd/ *n* [U C] **1** *also* **Underground** (BrE Transp) metro *m*, subterráneo *m* (RPl) **2** (secret organization) movimiento *m* clandestino

under: **~growth** *n* [U] maleza *f*, monte *m* bajo; **~hand** /ˈʌndərˈhænd ‖ ˌʌndəˈhænd/, **~handed** /ˈʌndərˈhændəd ‖ ˌʌndəˈhændɪd/ *adj* ‹*person*› solapado; ‹*method/dealings*› poco limpio; **~lie** /ˈʌndərˈlaɪ ‖ ˌʌndəˈlaɪ/ *vt* (*3rd pers sing pres* **-lies**; *pres p* **-lying**; *past* **-lay**; *past p* **-lain**) subyacer* a; **~line** *vt* subrayar; **~lying** /ˈʌndərˈlaɪɪŋ ‖ ˌʌndəˈlaɪɪŋ/ *adj* (*before n*) subyacente; **~manned** /ˈʌndərˈmænd ‖ ˌʌndəˈmænd/ *adj* ‹*factory*› con personal *or* con mano de obra insuficiente; **~mine** /ˈʌndərˈmaɪn ‖ ˌʌndəˈmaɪn/ *vt* ‹*health/strength*› minar; ‹*authority*› quitar

underneath¹ /ˈʌndərˈniːθ ‖ˌʌndəˈniːθ/ *prep* debajo de, abajo de (AmL)

underneath² *adv* debajo, abajo; ‹*dig/crawl*› por debajo, por abajo

under: **~nourished** /ˈʌndərˈnɜːrɪʃt ‖ˌʌndəˈnʌrɪʃt/ *adj* desnutrido; **~paid** /ˈʌndərˈpeɪd ‖ˌʌndəˈpeɪd/ *adj* mal pagado; **~pants** *pl n* calzoncillos *mpl*, calzones *mpl* (Méx); **~pass** *n* (for traffic) paso *m* inferior; **pedestrian ~pass** pasaje *m* subterráneo; **~privileged** /ˈʌndərˈprɪvəlɪdʒd ‖ˌʌndəˈprɪvəlɪdʒd/ *adj* desfavorecido; **~rate** /ˈʌndərˈreɪt ‖ˌʌndəˈreɪt/ *vt* **(a)** ‹*ability/opponent*› subestimar **(b) ~rated** *past p* ‹*writer/play*› no debidamente apreciado *or* valorado; **~secretary** /ˈʌndərˈsekrəteri ‖ˌʌndəˈsekrətri/ *n* subsecretario, -ria *m,f*; **~sell** *vt* (*past & past p* **-sold**) ‹*competitor*› vender más barato que; **~shirt** *n* (AmE) camiseta *f* (interior); **~shorts** *pl n* (AmE) calzoncillos *mpl* (*en forma de pantalón corto*); **~side** *n* parte *f* inferior *or* de abajo; **~skirt** *n* enagua(s) *f(pl)*, viso *m*, fondo *m* (Méx); **~sold** /ˈʌndərˈsəʊld ‖ˌʌndəˈsəʊld/ *past and past p of* UNDERSELL; **~staffed** /ˈʌndərˈstæft ‖ˌʌndəˈstɑːft/ *adj*: **to be ~staffed** estar* muy escaso *or* falto de personal

understand /ˈʌndərˈstænd ‖ˌʌndəˈstænd/ (*past & past p* **-stood**) *vt* **1 (a)** (grasp meaning of) entender* **(b)** (sympathize, empathize with) comprender, entender* **2** (believe, infer): **I ~ you play tennis** tengo entendido que juega al tenis ■ ~ *vi* entender*, comprender

understandable /ˈʌndərˈstændəbəl ‖ˌʌndəˈstændəbəl/ *adj* comprensible

understanding¹ /ˈʌndərˈstændɪŋ ‖ˌʌndəˈstændɪŋ/ *n* **1** [U] **(a)** (grasp) entendimiento *m* **(b)** (interpretation) interpretación *f* **(c)** (sympathy) comprensión *f* **2** [C] (agreement, arrangement) acuerdo *m*; **we had an ~ that** … habíamos convenido que … **3** [U] **on the ~ that** bien entendido que

understanding² *adj* comprensivo

understatement /ˈʌndərˈsteɪtmənt ‖ˈʌndəsteɪtmənt/ *n* [C U]: **to say it wasn't well attended is an ~** decir que no estuvo muy concurrido es quedarse corto

understood¹ /ˈʌndərˈstʊd ‖ˌʌndəˈstʊd/ *past & past p of* UNDERSTAND

understood² *adj* (assumed): **expenses will be paid, that's ~** se sobreentiende que nos (*or* les *etc*) pagarán los gastos

under: **~study** *n* suplente *mf*, sobresaliente *mf*; **~take** /ˈʌndərˈteɪk ‖ˌʌndəˈteɪk/ *vt* (*past* **-took**; *past p* **-taken**) **(a)** ‹*responsibility*› asumir; ‹*obligation*› contraer*; ‹*task*› emprender **(b) to ~take to** + INF comprometerse A + INF; **~taker** /ˈʌndərˈteɪkər ‖ˈʌndəˌteɪkə(r)/ *n* ⇒ MORTICIAN; **~taking** /ˈʌndərˈteɪkɪŋ ‖ˌʌndəˈteɪkɪŋ/ *n* **(a)** (task) empresa *f*, tarea *f* **(b)** (promise) promesa *f*; **~tone** *n* **(a)** (low voice): **to speak in an ~tone** hablar en voz baja **(b)** (hint) trasfondo *m*; **~took** /ˈʌndərˈtʊk ‖ˌʌndəˈtʊk/ *past of* ~TAKE; **~value** /ˈʌndərˈvæljuː ‖ˌʌndəˈvæljuː/ *vt* ‹*goods*› subvalorar; ‹*person/skill*› subvalorar

underwater¹ /ˈʌndərˈwɔːtər ‖ˌʌndəˈwɔːtə(r)/ *adj* submarino

underwater² *adv* debajo del agua

under: **~wear** *n* [U] ropa *f* interior; **~weight** /ˈʌndərˈweɪt ‖ˌʌndəˈweɪt/ *adj* ‹*person/baby*› de peso más bajo que el normal; **~went** /ˈʌndərˈwent ‖ˌʌndəˈwent/ *past of* UNDERGO; **~world** *n* **(a)** (Myth) **the U~world** el infierno, el averno (liter) **(b)** (criminals): **the ~world** el hampa, los bajos fondos; **~write** /ˈʌndərˈraɪt ‖ˌʌndəˈraɪt/ *vt* (*past* **-wrote**; *past p* **-written**) **(a)** (in insurance) asegurar **(b)** (guarantee financially) ‹*project/venture*› financiar

undeserving /ˈʌndɪˈzɜːrvɪŋ ‖ˌʌndɪˈzɜːvɪŋ/ *adj* ‹*person*› de poco mérito; ‹*cause*› poco meritorio

undesirable /ˈʌndɪˈzaɪrəbəl ‖ˌʌndɪˈzaɪərəbəl/ *adj* ‹*consequence*› no deseado; ‹*person*› indeseable

undeveloped /ˈʌndɪˈveləpt/ *adj* ‹*resources/region*› sin explotar

undid /ˈʌnˈdɪd/ *past of* UNDO

undignified /ˈʌnˈdɪgnəfaɪd ‖ʌnˈdɪgnɪfaɪd/ *adj* **(a)** (lacking modesty) indecoroso **(b)** (inappropriate to status) poco digno

undisciplined /ˈʌnˈdɪsəplənd ‖ˌʌnˈdɪsɪplɪnd/ *adj* indisciplinado

undiscovered /ˈʌndɪsˈkʌvərd ‖ˌʌndɪsˈkʌvəd/ *adj* (not found) no descubierto; (unknown) desconocido

undisguised /ˈʌndɪsˈgaɪzd/ *adj* manifiesto, abierto

undisputed /ˈʌndɪˈspjuːtəd ‖ˌʌndɪˈspjuːtɪd/ *adj* ‹*champion/leader*› indiscutido; ‹*facts*› innegable

undivided /ˈʌndɪˈvaɪdəd ‖ˌʌndɪˈvaɪdɪd/ *adj*: **you have my ~ attention** tienes toda mi atención

undo /ˈʌnˈduː/ *vt* (*3rd pers sing pres* **-does**; *pres p* **-doing**; *past* **-did**; *past p* **-done**) ‹*button/jacket*› desabrochar; ‹*zipper*› abrir*; ‹*knot/parcel*› desatar, deshacer*; ‹*shoelaces*› desatar, desamarrar (AmL exc RPl)

undone /ˈʌnˈdʌn/ *adj* (*pred*) **(a)** (unfastened) desatado, desamarrado (AmL exc RPl) **(b)** (not started) sin empezar; (unfinished) sin terminar

undoubtedly /ʌnˈdaʊtədli ‖ʌnˈdaʊtɪdli/ *adv* indudablemente, sin duda

undress /ˈʌnˈdres/ *vt* desvestir*, desnudar; **to get ~ed** desvestirse*, desnudarse

undue /ˈʌnˈduː ‖ʌnˈdjuː/ *adj* (*before n*) excesivo, demasiado

unduly /ˈʌnˈduːli ‖ʌnˈdjuːli/ *adv* excesivamente, demasiado

unearth /ˈʌnˈɜːrθ ‖ʌnˈɜːθ/ *vt* **(a)** ‹*remains*› desenterrar* **(b)** ‹*fact/document*› descubrir*

unearthly /ˈʌnˈɜːrθli ‖ʌnˈɜːθli/ *adj* **-lier, -liest** sobrenatural; **at this ~ hour** a estas horas (intempestivas)

unease /ˈʌnˈiːz/ *n* [U] (nervousness) inquietud *f*; (tension, discontent) malestar *m*

uneasy /ˈʌnˈiːzi/ *adj* **-sier, -siest (a)** (anxious, troubled) inquieto, preocupado **(b)** (awkward, constrained) ‹*laugh/silence*› incómodo, molesto

uneconomical /ˈʌnˈekəˈnɑːmɪkḷ, -ˈiːkə- ‖ˌʌnˌiːkəˈnɒmɪkəl, -ˌek-/ *adj* poco económico

uneducated /ˈʌnˈedʒəkeɪtəd ‖ˌʌnˈedjʊkeɪtɪd/ *adj* sin educación, inculto

unemotional /ˈʌnɪˈməʊʃṇəl ‖ˌʌnɪˈməʊʃənḷ/ *adj* ‹*person*› indiferente; ‹*account/report*› objetivo

unemployable /'ʌnɪm'plɔɪəbəl/ *adj* inempleable

unemployed /'ʌnɪm'plɔɪd/ *adj* ‹*person*› desempleado, parado (Esp), en paro (Esp), cesante (Chi)

unemployment /'ʌnɪm'plɔɪmənt/ *n* [U] (being out of work) desempleo *m*, paro *m* (Esp), cesantía *f* (Chi); (*before n*) **~ benefit** *o* (AmE also) **compensation** subsidio *m* de desempleo, paro *m* (Esp), subsidio *m* de cesantía (Chi)

unending /ʌn'endɪŋ/ *adj* interminable, sin fin

unenthusiastic /'ʌnɪn'θu:zi'æstɪk ‖ ˌʌnɪnθju: zi'æstɪk/ *adj* poco entusiasta

unenviable /ʌn'enviəbəl/ *adj* nada envidiable

unequal /ʌn'i:kwəl/ *adj* desigual

UNESCO /ju:'neskəʊ/ *n* (*no art*) (= **United Nations Educational, Scientific and Cultural Organization**) la UNESCO

unethical /ʌn'eθɪkəl/ *adj* inmoral, poco ético

uneven /'ʌn'i:vən/ *adj* **1 (a)** (not straight) torcido **(b)** (not level) ‹*surface*› desigual, irregular, disparejo (AmL); ‹*ground*› desnivelado, desigual, disparejo (AmL) **2** ‹*color/paint*› poco uniforme, disparejo (AmL) **3** (unequal) ‹*widths/lengths/contest*› desigual

uneventful /'ʌnɪ'ventfəl/ *adj* ‹*journey*› sin incidentes; ‹*day*› tranquilo; ‹*life*› sin acontecimientos de nota

unexciting /'ʌnɪk'saɪtɪŋ/ *adj* ‹*prospect/job*› poco estimulante; ‹*food*› insulso, poco apetitoso

unexpected /'ʌnɪk'spektəd ‖ ˌʌnɪk'spektɪd/ *adj* ‹*reaction/visitor*› inesperado; ‹*result/delay*› imprevisto

unexpectedly /'ʌnɪk'spektədli ‖ ˌʌnɪk'spektɪdli/ *adv* ‹*arrive*› de improviso; ‹*happen*› de forma imprevista

unexploded /'ʌnɪk'spləʊdəd/ *adj* sin detonar

unexplored /'ʌnɪk'splɔ:rd ‖ ˌʌnɪks'plɔ:d/ *adj* inexplorado

unfailing /ʌn'feɪlɪŋ/ *adj* ‹*optimism*› indefectible, a toda prueba; ‹*interest/support*› constante

unfair /'ʌn'fer ‖ ʌn'feə(r)/ *adj* ‹*treatment/decision*› injusto; ‹*competition*› desleal; ‹*dismissal*› improcedente, injustificado; **it was ~ of him to blame you** fue injusto que te echara la culpa a ti

unfairly /ʌn'ferli ‖ ʌn'feəli/ *adj* injustamente

unfaithful /'ʌn'feɪθfəl/ *adj* ‹*spouse/lover*› infiel; ‹*follower*› desleal

unfamiliar /'ʌnfə'mɪljər ‖ ˌʌnfə'mɪliə(r)/ *adj* ‹*face/surroundings*› desconocido, nuevo

unfashionable /'ʌn'fæʃṇəbəl/ *adj* fuera de moda

unfasten /'ʌn'fæsṇ ‖ ʌn'fɑ:sṇ/ *vt* ‹*seat belt/button*› desabrochar; ‹*knot*› deshacer*, desatar

unfavorable, (BrE) **unfavourable** /'ʌn'feɪvrəbəl/ *adj* desfavorable

unfinished /'ʌn'fɪnɪʃt/ *adj* sin terminar, inacabado

unfit /'ʌn'fɪt/ *adj* **(a)** (unsuitable) ‹*mother*› inepto, incapaz; **he was ~ for the job** no estaba capacitado para el trabajo; **~ for human consumption** no apto para el consumo **(b)** (physically): **I'm ~** no estoy en forma, estoy fuera de forma

unflagging /'ʌn'flægɪŋ/ *adj* ‹*energy/enthusiasm*› inagotable; ‹*interest*› sostenido

unflattering /'ʌn'flætərɪŋ/ *adj* ‹*remark/description*› poco halagüeño; ‹*dress*› poco favorecedor

unfold /'ʌn'fəʊld/ *vt* ‹*tablecloth/map*› desdoblar, extender*; ‹*wings*› desplegar* ■ **~** *vi* **(a)** «*flower/leaf*» abrirse*; «*wings*» desplegarse* **(b)** «*story/events*» desarrollarse; «*scene*» extenderse*

unforeseen /'ʌnfɔ:r'si:n ‖ ˌʌnfɔ:'si:n/ *adj* imprevisto

unforgettable /'ʌnfər'getəbəl ‖ ˌʌnfə'getəbəl/ *adj* inolvidable

unforgivable /'ʌnfər'gɪvəbəl ‖ ˌʌnfə'gɪvəbəl/ *adj* imperdonable

unfortunate /ʌn'fɔ:rtʃṇət ‖ ʌn'fɔ:tʃənət/ *adj* desafortunado; **he has been very ~** ha tenido muy mala suerte

unfortunately /ʌn'fɔ:rtʃṇətli ‖ ʌn'fɔ:tʃənətli/ *adv* (*indep*) lamentablemente, desafortunadamente; (stronger) desgraciadamente, por desgracia

unfounded /'ʌn'faʊndəd ‖ ʌn'faʊndɪd/ *adj* infundado

unfriendly /'ʌn'frendli/ *adj* **-lier, -liest** poco amistoso; (stronger) antipático

unfulfilled /'ʌnfʊl'fɪld/ *adj* ‹*ambition/hope*› frustrado; ‹*prophecy*› no cumplido

unfurl /ʌn'fɜ:rl ‖ ʌn'fɜ:l/ *vt* desplegar*

unfurnished /'ʌn'fɜ:rnɪʃt ‖ ʌn'fɜ:nɪʃt/ *adj* sin amueblar

ungainly /ʌn'geɪnli/ *adj* desgarbado

ungracious /'ʌn'greɪʃəs/ *adj* descortés

ungrateful /ʌn'greɪtfəl/ *adj* desagradecido, ingrato, malagradecido

unguarded /'ʌn'gɑ:rdəd ‖ ʌn'gɑ:dɪd/ *adj* (incautious): **in an ~ moment** en un momento de descuido

unhappily /ʌn'hæpəli ‖ ʌn'hæpɪli/ *adv* **(a)** ‹*sigh*› tristemente, con tristeza **(b)** (unfortunately) (*indep*) lamentablemente

unhappiness /ʌn'hæpinəs ‖ ʌn'hæpinɪs/ *n* [U] infelicidad *f*; (stronger) desdicha *f*; (sadness) tristeza *f*

unhappy /ʌn'hæpi/ *adj* **-pier, -piest (a)** (sad) ‹*childhood*› infeliz; (stronger) desgraciado, desdichado **(b)** (worried) (*pred*): **I was ~ about the children being left alone** me preocupaba *or* inquietaba que los niños se quedaran solos **(c)** (discontented) (*pred*) **to be ~ ABOUT sth** no estar* contento CON algo

unharmed /ʌn'hɑ:rmd ‖ ʌn'hɑ:md/ *adj*: **he escaped ~** salió *or* resultó ileso

unhealthy /ʌn'helθi/ *adj* **-thier, -thiest (a)** ‹*person*› de mala salud; ‹*complexion*› enfermizo; ‹*climate*› poco saludable, insalubre, malsano **(b)** ‹*interest/obsession*› malsano

unheard of /ʌn'hɜ:rdɑ:v ‖ ʌn'hɜ:dɒv/ *adj* insólito

unhelpful /'ʌn'helpfəl/ *adj* ‹*assistant/secretary*› poco servicial; **he was most ~** no se mostró nada dispuesto a ayudar

unhinge /ʌn'hɪndʒ/ *vt* ‹*person/mind*› trastornar

unhurt /ʌn'hɜ:rt ‖ ʌn'hɜ:t/ *adj* ileso; **to escape ~** salir* *or* resultar ileso

unhygienic /ˈʌnharˈdʒiːnɪk/ *adj* antihigiénico

UNICEF /ˈjuːnɪsef/ *n* (*no art*) (= **United Nations International Children's Emergency Fund**) UNICEF *m or f*

unicorn /ˈjuːnəkɔːrn ‖ ˈjuːnɪkɔːn/ *n* unicornio *m*

unidentified /ˈʌnarˈdentəfaɪd ‖ ˌʌnaɪˈdentɪfaɪd/ *adj* no identificado; **~ flying object** objeto *m* volador *or* (Esp) volante no identificado

unification /ˈjuːnəfəˈkeɪʃən ‖ ˌjuːnɪfɪˈkeɪʃən/ *n* [U] unificación *f*

uniform¹ /ˈjuːnəfɔːrm ‖ ˈjuːnɪfɔːm/ *n* uniforme *m*

uniform² *adj* ‹*color/length*› uniforme; ‹*temperature/speed*› constante

uniformity /ˈjuːnəˈfɔːrməti ‖ ˌjuːnɪˈfɔːməti/ *n* [U] uniformidad *f*

unify /ˈjuːnəfaɪ ‖ ˈjuːnɪfaɪ/ *vt* **-fies, -fying, -fied** unir

unilateral /ˈjuːnɪˈlætərəl/ *adj* unilateral

unimaginable /ˈʌnəˈmædʒənəbəl ‖ ˌʌnɪˈmædʒɪnəbəl/ *adj* inimaginable

unimaginative /ˈʌnəˈmædʒənətɪv ‖ ˌʌnɪˈmædʒɪnətɪv/ *adj* ‹*person*› poco imaginativo; ‹*story/design*› falto de imaginación

unimportant /ˈʌnɪmˈpɔːrtn̩t ‖ ˌʌnɪmˈpɔːtn̩t/ *adj* ‹*matter/detail*› sin importancia

uninhabited /ˈʌnɪnˈhæbətəd ‖ ˌʌnɪnˈhæbɪtɪd/ *adj* ‹*house*› deshabitado; ‹*region/island*› despoblado

uninhibited /ˈʌnɪnˈhɪbətəd ‖ ˌʌnɪnˈhɪbɪtɪd/ *adj* desinhibido, desenfadado

unintelligent /ˈʌnɪnˈtelədʒənt ‖ ˌʌnɪnˈtelɪdʒənt/ *adj* poco inteligente

unintelligible /ˈʌnɪnˈtelədʒəbəl ‖ ˌʌnɪnˈtelɪdʒəbəl/ *adj* ininteligible

unintentional /ˈʌnɪnˈtentʃn̩əl ‖ ˌʌnɪnˈtenʃənl̩/ *adj* involuntario, no deliberado

unintentionally /ˈʌnɪnˈtentʃn̩əli ‖ ˌʌnɪnˈtenʃn̩əli/ *adv* involuntariamente, sin querer

uninterested /ˈʌnˈɪntrəstəd ‖ ʌnˈɪntrestɪd/ *adj* indiferente

uninteresting /ˈʌnˈɪntrəstɪŋ/ *adj* ‹*topic*› sin interés; ‹*person*› poco interesante

uninvited /ˈʌnɪnˈvaɪtəd ‖ ˌʌnɪnˈvaɪtɪd/ *adj*: **they came ~** vinieron sin que nadie los invitara

uninviting /ˈʌnɪnˈvaɪtɪŋ/ *adj* ‹*appearance*› poco atractivo; ‹*food*› poco apetitoso

union /ˈjuːnjən/ *n* **1** [U C] (act, state) unión *f* **2** [C] (Lab Rel) sindicato *m*, gremio *m* (CS, Per); (*before n*) ‹*official/movement*› sindical, gremial (CS, Per); **~ card** carné *m* de afiliado **3** [C] (at college, university) asociación *f or* federación *f* de estudiantes

unionize /ˈjuːnjənaɪz ‖ ˈjuːnjənaɪz/ *vt* sindicalizar* (esp AmL), sindicar* (esp Esp)

Union Jack *n* bandera *f* del Reino Unido

unique /jʊˈniːk/ *adj* (*no comp*) único

unisex /ˈjuːnəseks ‖ ˈjuːnɪseks/ *adj* unisex *adj inv*

unison /ˈjuːnəsən ‖ ˈjuːnɪsən/ *n* [U]: **in ~** al unísono

unit /ˈjuːnət ‖ ˈjuːnɪt/ *n* **1 (a)** (item) (Busn) unidad *f* **(b)** (of furniture) módulo *m* **2** (group) (Mil) unidad *f* **3** (of measurement) unidad *f* **4** (Educ) (in course) módulo *m*

unite /jʊˈnaɪt ‖ juːˈnaɪt/ *vt* unir ■ **~** *vi* unirse

united /jʊˈnaɪtəd ‖ juːˈnaɪtɪd/ *adj* unido

united: **U~ Arab Emirates** /ˈemɪrəts ‖ ˈemɪərəts/ *pl n* **the U~ Arab Emirates** los Emiratos Árabes Unidos; **U~ Kingdom** *n* **the U~ Kingdom** el Reino Unido; **U~ Nations (Organization)** *n* (+ *sing o pl vb*) **the U~ Nations (Organization)** (la Organización de) las Naciones Unidas; **U~ States** *n* (*usu* + *sing vb*) **the U~ States** los Estados Unidos; **U~ States of America** *n* (*usu* + *sing vb*) **the U~ States of America** los Estados Unidos de América

unity /ˈjuːnəti/ *n* [U C] (*pl* **-ties**) unidad *f*

universal /ˈjuːnəˈvɜːrsəl ‖ ˌjuːnɪˈvɜːsəl/ *adj* **(a)** (general) general **(b)** (worldwide) universal **(c)** (all-purpose, versatile) ‹*adaptor*› universal

universally /ˈjuːnəˈvɜːrsəli ‖ ˌjuːnɪˈvɜːsəli/ *adv* ‹*known/admired*› mundialmente, universalmente

universe /ˈjuːnəvɜːrs ‖ ˈjuːnɪvɜːs/ *n* universo *m*

university /ˈjuːnəˈvɜːrsəti ‖ ˌjuːnɪˈvɜːsəti/ *n* [C U] (*pl* **-ties**) universidad *f*; (*before n*) ‹*town/life*› universitario

unjust /ˈʌnˈdʒʌst/ *adj* injusto

unjustified /ˈʌnˈdʒʌstəfaɪd ‖ ʌnˈdʒʌstɪfaɪd/ *adj* injustificado

unkempt /ˈʌnˈkempt/ *adj* (frml) ‹*appearance*› descuidado, desarreglado; ‹*hair*› despeinado

unkind /ˈʌnˈkaɪnd/ *adj* **-er, -est** (unpleasant) poco amable; (cruel) cruel, malo; ‹*remark*› hiriente

unknown¹ /ˈʌnˈnəʊn/ *adj* desconocido

unknown² *n* **(a)** [U] (phenomenon) **the ~** lo desconocido **(b)** [C] (person) desconocida, -da *m,f*

unknown³ *adv*: **~ to her** sin ella saberlo

unlawful /ˈʌnˈlɔːfəl/ *adj* ‹*conduct*› ilegal; ‹*possession*› ilícito

unleaded /ˈʌnˈledəd ‖ ʌnˈledɪd/ *adj* sin plomo

unleash /ˈʌnˈliːʃ/ *vt* ‹*dog*› soltar*, desatar; ‹*anger/imagination*› dar(le)* rienda suelta a; ‹*war*› desencadenar

unless /ʌnˈles, ən-/ *conj* a no ser que (+ *subj*), a menos que (+ *subj*)

unlike /ˈʌnˈlaɪk/ *prep* **(a)** (not similar to) diferente *or* distinto de **(b)** (untypical of): **it's ~ you to be so optimistic** tú no sueles ser tan optimista **(c)** (in contrast to) a diferencia de

unlikely /ˈʌnˈlaɪkli/ *adj* **-lier, liest (a)** (improbable) ‹*outcome/victory*› improbable, poco probable **(b)** (far-fetched) ‹*story/explanation*› inverosímil **(c)** (odd, unexpected) insólito

unlimited /ˈʌnˈlɪmətəd ‖ ʌnˈlɪmɪtɪd/ *adj* ilimitado

unlined /ˈʌnˈlaɪnd/ *adj* **(a)** ‹*paper*› sin pautar **(b)** ‹*dress/jacket*› sin forro

unlisted /ˈʌnˈlɪstəd ‖ ʌnˈlɪstɪd/ *adj* (AmE Telec) que no figura en la guía telefónica

unlit /ˈʌnˈlɪt/ *adj* ‹*road*› sin luz, sin alumbrado

unload /ˈʌnˈləʊd/ *vt/i* descargar*

unlock /ˈʌnˈlɑːk ‖ ʌnˈlɒk/ *vt* abrir* (*algo que está cerrado con llave*)

unlucky /ˈʌnˈlʌki/ *adj* **unluckier, unluckiest** ‹*person*› sin suerte, desafortunado; ‹*day*› funesto, de mala suerte; ‹*object*› que trae mala suerte; **to be ~** tener* mala suerte

unmanageable /ˈʌnˈmænɪdʒəbəl/ *adj* ‹*child/horse*› rebelde; ‹*hair*› rebelde

unmanned /ˈʌnˈmænd/ *adj* ‹*vehicle/rocket*› sin tripulación; ‹*space flight*› no tripulado

unmarried /ˈʌnˈmærid/ *adj* soltero

unmask /ˈʌnˈmæsk ‖ ʌnˈmɑːsk/ *vt* desenmascarar

unmentionable /ˈʌnˈmentʃnəbəl ‖ ʌnˈmenʃənəbəl/ *adj* inmencionable, innombrable

unmistakable /ˈʌnməˈsteɪkəbəl ‖ ˌʌnmɪˈsteɪkəbəl/ *adj* inconfundible; ‹*proof*› inequívoco

unnamed /ˈʌnˈneɪmd/ *adj* no identificado

unnatural /ˈʌnˈnætʃərəl/ *adj* **(a)** (unusual) poco natural *or* normal **(b)** (awkward, affected) ‹*smile*› poco natural **(c)** (against nature) (frml) antinatural

unnecessarily /ˈʌnnesəˈserəli ‖ ˌʌnnesəˈserɪli, ˌʌnˈnesəserɪli/ *adv* innecesariamente

unnecessary /ʌnˈnesəseri ‖ ʌnˈnesəsəri/ *adj* innecesario

unnerve /ˈʌnˈnɜːrv ‖ ʌnˈnɜːv/ *vt* poner* nervioso, turbar (liter)

unnerving /ˈʌnˈnɜːrvɪŋ ‖ ʌnˈnɜːvɪŋ/ *adj* desconcertante, que pone nervioso

unnoticed /ˈʌnˈnəʊtəst ‖ ʌnˈnəʊtɪst/ *adj* (*pred*): **to go ∼** pasar desapercibido *or* inadvertido

unobtainable /ˈʌnəbˈteɪnəbəl/ *adj* imposible de conseguir

unobtrusive /ˈʌnəbˈtruːsɪv/ *adj* discreto

unoccupied /ˈʌnˈɑːkjəpaɪd ‖ ʌnˈɒkjʊpaɪd/ *adj* **(a)** ‹*seat/toilet*› desocupado, libre; ‹*house*› deshabitado, desocupado **(b)** (Mil) no ocupado

unofficial /ˈʌnəˈfɪʃəl/ *adj* no oficial

unofficially /ˈʌnəˈfɪʃəli/ *adv* extraoficialmente

unopened /ˈʌnˈəʊpənd/ *adj* sin abrir

unopposed /ˈʌnəˈpəʊzd/ *adj* sin oposición

unoriginal /ˈʌnəˈrɪdʒənl/ *adj* poco original, sin originalidad

unorthodox /ʌnˈɔːrθədɑːks ‖ ʌnˈɔːθədɒks/ *adj* poco ortodoxo

unpack /ˈʌnˈpæk/ *vt* ‹*bags*› sacar* las cosas de, desempacar* (AmL); ‹*suitcase*› deshacer*, desempacar* (AmL) ■ ∼ *vi* deshacer* las maletas, desempacar* (AmL)

unpaid /ˈʌnˈpeɪd/ *adj* ‹*work*› no retribuido, no remunerado; ‹*leave*› sin sueldo; ‹*debt*› pendiente, no liquidado

unpalatable /ˈʌnˈpælətəbəl/ *adj* **(a)** ‹*food/drink*› de sabor desagradable **(b)** ‹*fact/truth*› desagradable, difícil de digerir

unparalleled /ˈʌnˈpærəleld/ *adj* ‹*success/achievement*› sin paralelo, sin parangón; ‹*disaster*› sin precedentes; ‹*beauty*› incomparable

unperturbed /ˈʌnpərˈtɜːrbd ‖ ˌʌnpəˈtɜːbd/ *adj* impasible, impertérrito; **she carried on ∼** siguió sin inmutarse

unpleasant /ˈʌnˈpleznt/ *adj* desagradable

unplug /ˈʌnˈplʌg/ *vt* **-gg-** desenchufar, desconectar

unpopular /ˈʌnˈpɑːpjələr ‖ ʌnˈpɒpjʊlə(r)/ *adj* impopular; **he is ∼ with everybody** le cae muy mal a todo el mundo

unprecedented /ˈʌnˈpresədentəd ‖ ʌnˈpresɪdentɪd/ *adj* ‹*success/hostility*› sin precedentes; ‹*decision*› inaudito

unpredictable /ˈʌnprɪˈdɪktəbəl/ *adj* ‹*result/weather*› imprevisible; **she's very ∼** nunca se sabe cómo va a reaccionar

unprepared /ˈʌnprɪˈperd ‖ ˌʌnprɪˈpeəd/ *adj* **(a)** (not ready) (*pred*) **to be ∼** no estar* preparado **(b)** (not expecting) (*pred*) **to be ∼ FOR sth** no esperar algo

unprepossessing /ˈʌnpriːpəˈzesɪŋ/ *adj* poco atractivo

unprincipled /ˈʌnˈprɪnsəpəld/ *adj* sin escrúpulos *or* principios

unproductive /ˈʌnprəˈdʌktɪv/ *adj* ‹*meeting*› infructuoso

unprofessional /ˈʌnprəˈfeʃnəl ‖ ˌʌnprəˈfeʃənl/ *adj* poco profesional

unprofitable /ˈʌnˈprɑːfətəbəl ‖ ʌnˈprɒfɪtəbəl/ *adj* no rentable

unprotected /ˈʌnprəˈtektəd ‖ ˌʌnprəˈtektɪd/ *adj* sin protección; ‹*sex*› sin el uso de preservativos

unproven /ˈʌnˈpruːvən/ *adj* ‹*theory*› (que está) por demostrar *or* probar

unpublished /ˈʌnˈpʌblɪʃt/ *adj* inédito, no publicado

unpunished /ˈʌnˈpʌnɪʃt/ *adj*: **to go ∼** «*person*» quedar sin castigo; «*crime*» quedar impune

unqualified /ˈʌnˈkwɑːləfaɪd ‖ ʌnˈkwɒlɪfaɪd/ *adj* **1** (complete, total) ‹*approval*› incondicional; ‹*disaster*› absoluto; ‹*success/failure*› rotundo **2** (without qualifications) ‹*teacher/nurse*› sin titulación *or* título, no titulado; ‹*staff*› no calificado *or* (Esp) cualificado

unquestionable /ˈʌnˈkwestʃənəbəl/ *adj* ‹*sincerity/loyalty*› incuestionable, innegable

unquestioning /ˈʌnˈkwestʃənɪŋ/ *adj* ‹*obedience/faith*› ciego; ‹*loyalty*› incondicional

unravel /ˈʌnˈrævəl/ *vt*, (BrE) **-ll- (a)** ‹*threads/string*› desenredar **(b)** ‹*mystery*› desentrañar

unreadable /ˈʌnˈriːdəbəl/ *adj* **(a)** ‹*handwriting*› ilegible **(b)** ‹*novel*› muy difícil de leer

unrealistic /ˈʌnriːəˈlɪstɪk ‖ ˌʌnriəˈlɪstɪk/ *adj* ‹*expectations*› poco realista; **it's ∼ to expect that** no es realista esperar eso

unreasonable /ˈʌnˈriːznəbəl/ *adj* ‹*person*› poco razonable, irrazonable; ‹*demand/price*› excesivo, poco razonable

unrecognizable /ˈʌnˈrekəgnaɪzəbəl/ *adj* irreconocible

unrefined /ˈʌnrɪˈfaɪnd/ *adj* ‹*flour/sugar*› sin refinar, no refinado; ‹*gold*› en estado bruto; ‹*person*› poco refinado; **∼ oil** crudo *m*

unrelated /ˈʌnrɪˈleɪtəd ‖ ˌʌnrɪˈleɪtɪd/ *adj* ‹*facts/events*› no relacionados (entre sí)

unreliable /ˈʌnrɪˈlaɪəbəl/ *adj* ‹*person*› informal; ‹*information*› poco fidedigno; ‹*weather*› variable

unrepeatable /ˈʌnrɪˈpiːtəbəl/ *adj* irrepetible

unrepentant /ˈʌnrɪˈpentnt/ *adj* impenitente

unreported /ˈʌnrɪˈpɔːrtəd ‖ ˌʌnrɪˈpɔːtɪd/ *adj* ‹*crime*› no denunciado

unrepresentative /ˈʌnrepraˈzentətɪv/ *adj* poco representativo

unrequited /ˈʌnrɪˈkwaɪtəd ‖ ˌʌnrɪˈkwaɪtɪd/ *adj* ‹*love*› no correspondido

unresolved /ˈʌnrɪˈzɑːlvd ‖ ˌʌnrɪˈzɒlvd/ *adj* no resuelto

unresponsive /ˈʌnrɪˈspɑːnsɪv ‖ ˌʌnrɪˈspɒnsɪv/ *adj* ‹*audience/expression*› indiferente; ‹*pupil*› que no responde

unrest /ʌnˈrest/ *n* [U] (Pol) descontento *m*, malestar *m*; (active) disturbios *mpl*

unrestricted /ˈʌnrɪˈstrɪktəd ‖ ˌʌnrɪˈstrɪktɪd/ *adj* ilimitado

unrewarded /ˈʌnrɪˈwɔːrdəd ‖ ˌʌnrɪˈwɔːdɪd/ *adj* no recompensado

unripe /ʌnˈraɪp/ *adj* verde, que no está maduro

unrivaled, (BrE) **unrivalled** /ʌnˈraɪvəld/ *adj* incomparable, inigualable

unroll /ʌnˈrəʊl/ *vt* desenrollar

unruffled /ʌnˈrʌfəld/ *adj* **(a)** (undisturbed) ‹*manner*› sereno **(b)** (smooth) liso

unruly /ʌnˈruːli/ *adj* **-lier, -liest** ‹*class*› indisciplinado, difícil de controlar; ‹*conduct*› rebelde; ‹*child*› revoltoso

unsafe /ʌnˈseɪf/ *adj* inseguro

unsaid /ʌnˈsed/ *adj*: **to leave sth ~** callar(se) algo, no decir* algo

unsalted /ʌnˈsɔːltəd ‖ ʌnˈsɔːltɪd/ *adj* sin sal

unsatisfactory /ʌnˈsætəsˈfæktri ‖ ˌʌnsætɪsˈfæktəri/ *adj* insatisfactorio; ‹*explanation*› poco convincente

unsatisfying /ʌnˈsætəsfaɪɪŋ ‖ ʌnˈsætɪsfaɪɪŋ/ *adj* ‹*meal*› que no llena *or* satisface; ‹*job*› poco gratificante; ‹*ending*› decepcionante

unsavory, (BrE) **unsavoury** /ʌnˈseɪvəri/ *adj* desagradable

unscathed /ʌnˈskeɪðd/ *adj* (*pred*) (unhurt) ileso; (of reputation etc) indemne

unscented /ʌnˈsentəd ‖ ʌnˈsentɪd/ *adj* sin perfume

unscheduled /ʌnˈskedʒuːld ‖ ʌnˈʃedjuːld/ *adj* no programado, no previsto

unscientific /ʌnˈsaɪənˈtɪfɪk/ *adj* falto de rigor científico

unscrew /ʌnˈskruː/ *vt* ‹*screw/panel*› destornillar, desatornillar; ‹*lid*› desenroscar*

unscrupulous /ʌnˈskruːpjələs ‖ ʌnˈskruːpjʊləs/ *adj* inescrupuloso

unseat /ʌnˈsiːt/ *vt* **(a)** ‹*rider*› desmontar **(b)** ‹*government*› derribar

unseen /ʌnˈsiːn/ *adj* **(a)** (invisible) ‹*danger/obstacle*› oculto **(b)** (unnoticed) sin ser visto

unselfish /ʌnˈselfɪʃ/ *adj* ‹*person*› nada egoísta; ‹*act*› desinteresado

unsentimental /ʌnˈsentəˈmentl̩ ‖ ˌʌnsentɪˈmentl̩/ *adj* ‹*person/outlook*› poco sentimental

unsettle /ʌnˈsetl̩/ *vt* ‹*plans*› alterar; ‹*situation*› desestabilizar*; **the question clearly ~d him** la pregunta lo desconcertó visiblemente

unsettled /ʌnˈsetl̩d/ *adj* **1 (a)** (troubled) ‹*period*› agitado; ‹*childhood*› poco estable **(b)** ‹*weather*› inestable **2** (undecided) ‹*issue/dispute*› pendiente (de resolución), sin resolver; ‹*future*› incierto

unsettling /ʌnˈsetl̩ɪŋ/ *adj* inquietante; ‹*effect*› desestabilizador

unshakable, **unshakeable** /ʌnˈʃeɪkəbəl/ *adj* inquebrantable

unshaven /ʌnˈʃeɪvən/ *adj* sin afeitar, sin rasurar (esp Méx)

unsightly /ʌnˈsaɪtli/ *adj* **-lier, -liest** feo, antiestético

unsigned /ʌnˈsaɪnd/ *adj* sin firmar

unskilled /ʌnˈskɪld/ *adj* ‹*worker*› no calificado *or* (Esp) cualificado; ‹*work*› no especializado

unsociable /ʌnˈsəʊʃəbəl/ *adj* insociable, poco sociable

unsold /ʌnˈsəʊld/ *adj* no vendido

unsolicited /ˈʌnsəˈlɪsətəd ‖ ˌʌnsəˈlɪsɪtɪd/ *adj* que no se ha pedido *or* solicitado

unsolved /ʌnˈsɑːlvd ‖ ʌnˈsɒlvd/ *adj* no resuelto

unsophisticated /ˈʌnsəˈfɪstəkeɪtəd ‖ ˌʌnsəˈfɪstɪkeɪtɪd/ *adj* ‹*person*› sencillo; ‹*tastes/technology*› simple, poco sofisticado

unspeakable /ʌnˈspiːkəbəl/ *adj* ‹*evil*› incalificable, atroz; ‹*joy*› indescriptible

unspecified /ʌnˈspesəfaɪd ‖ ʌnˈspesɪfaɪd/ *adj* no especificado

unspoiled /ʌnˈspɔɪld/, (BrE also) **unspoilt** /ʌnˈspɔɪlt/ *adj* ‹*countryside*› que conserva su belleza natural

unspoken /ʌnˈspəʊkən/ *adj* ‹*agreement*› tácito; ‹*wish*› no expresado

unstable /ʌnˈsteɪbəl/ *adj* inestable; ‹*prices*› variable

unsteadily /ʌnˈstedl̩i ‖ ʌnˈstedɪli/ *adv* de modo inseguro *or* vacilante

unsteady /ʌnˈstedi/ *adj* ‹*chair/ladder*› inestable, poco firme; ‹*walk/step*› vacilante, inseguro

unstick /ʌnˈstɪk/ *vt* (*past & past p* **unstuck**) despegar*, quitar

unstuck /ʌnˈstʌk/ *adj* despegado; **to come ~** despegarse*

unsuccessful /ˈʌnsəkˈsesfəl/ *adj* ‹*attempt*› infructuoso, fallido; **they were ~ in their attempt** fracasaron en su intento

unsuccessfully /ˈʌnsəkˈsesfəli/ *adv* en vano, sin éxito

unsuitable /ʌnˈsuːtəbəl/ *adj* ‹*clothing*› poco apropiado *or* adecuado; ‹*candidate*› poco idóneo; ‹*time*› inconveniente

unsuited /ʌnˈsuːtəd ‖ ʌnˈsuːtɪd/ *adj* (*pred*) **she is ~ to this work** no sirve para este trabajo; **they are completely ~** son totalmente incompatibles

unsure /ʌnˈʃʊr ‖ ʌnˈʃʊə(r), ʌnˈʃɔː(r)/ *adj* inseguro, indeciso; **to be ~ of oneself** estar* *or* sentirse* inseguro de sí mismo

unsurpassed /ˈʌnsərˈpæst ‖ ˌʌnsəˈpɑːst/ *adj* ‹*beauty/mastery*› sin igual, sin par (liter)

unsuspecting /ˈʌnsəˈspektɪŋ/ *adj* desprevenido; **to be ~** no sospechar nada

unsweetened /ˈʌnˈswiːtn̩d/ *adj* (without sugar) sin azúcar; (without sweeteners) sin edulcorantes

unsympathetic /ˈʌnˈsɪmpəˈθetɪk/ *adj* **(a)** (showing no sympathy) ‹*person/attitude*› indiferente, poco comprensivo **(b)** (unfavorable) ‹*account*› adverso, desfavorable; **she was ~ to our cause** no veía nuestra causa con simpatía

unsystematic /ˈʌnˈsɪstəˈmætɪk/ *adj* poco sistemático

untamed /ˈʌnˈteɪmd/ *adj* ‹*animal*› sin domar; ‹*wilderness/forests*› virgen, agreste

untangle /ˈʌnˈtæŋgəl/ *vt* desenredar, desenmarañar; ‹*mystery*› desentrañar

untapped /ˈʌnˈtæpt/ *adj* sin explotar

untenable /ˈʌnˈtenəbəl/ *adj* (frml) insostenible

untended /ˈʌnˈtendəd ‖ ʌnˈtendɪd/ *adj* ‹*garden*› descuidado; ‹*patient*› desatendido

unthinkable /ˈʌnˈθɪŋkəbəl/ *adj* inconcebible, inimaginable

untidy /ˈʌnˈtaɪdi/ *adj* **-dier, -diest** ‹*room/desk/person*› desordenado; ‹*appearance*› descuidado, desprolijo (RPl); ‹*writing/schoolwork*› descuidado, desprolijo (RPl)

untie /ˈʌnˈtaɪ/ *vt* **unties, untying, untied** ‹*knot*› desatar; ‹*shoelaces*› desatar, desamarrar (AmL exc RPl); ‹*animal*› soltar*, desatar, desamarrar (AmL exc RPl)

until[1] /ʌnˈtɪl, ənˈtɪl/ *conj* hasta que

■ **Note** When used as a conjunction in positive sentences expressing the future, *until* is translated by *hasta que + subjunctive*: *we'll stay here until Carol comes back* nos quedaremos aquí hasta que llegue Carol.
In negative sentences *no* is used optionally before the verb: *he won't be satisfied until they give him his money back* no estará satisfecho hasta que (no) le devuelvan su dinero.

until[2] *prep* hasta

untimely /ˈʌnˈtaɪmli/ *adj* **(a)** ‹*death/end*› prematuro **(b)** ‹*arrival*› inoportuno, intempestivo

untold /ˈʌnˈtəʊld/ *adj* (*before n*) ‹*wealth/sums*› incalculable; ‹*misery/pleasures*› indecible, inenarrable

untouched /ˈʌnˈtʌtʃt/ *adj* **(a)** (not handled) intacto, sin tocar; **he left his food ~** no probó la comida **(b)** (safe, unharmed) intacto

untoward /ˈʌnˈtɔːrd, ˌʌntəˈwɔːrd ‖ ˈʌntəˈwɔːd/ *adj* (frml) perjudicial, adverso; **I hope nothing ~ has happened** espero que no haya pasado nada (que haya que lamentar)

untrained /ˈʌnˈtreɪnd/ *adj* falto de formación *or* capacitación; ‹*teacher*› sin título; **to the ~ eye/ear** … para (el ojo/oído de) quien no es experto …

untreated /ˈʌnˈtriːtəd ‖ ʌnˈtriːtɪd/ *adj* ‹*sewage/waste*› sin tratar *or* procesar

untried /ˈʌnˈtraɪd/ *adj* **(a)** (not tested) ‹*method*› no probado **(b)** (Law) ‹*case*› no sometido a juicio

untroubled /ˈʌnˈtrʌbəld/ *adj* tranquilo

untrue /ˈʌnˈtruː/ *adj* falso; **it is ~ (to say) that** … es falso *or* no es cierto que …

untrustworthy /ˈʌnˈtrʌstˌwɜːrði ‖ ʌnˈtrʌstˌwɜːði/ *adj* ‹*person*› de poca confianza; ‹*source*› no fidedigno

untruthful /ˈʌnˈtruːθfəl/ *adj* ‹*account/answer*› falso; ‹*person*› falso, mentiroso

unusual /ˈʌnˈjuːʒuəl/ *adj* poco corriente *or* común, fuera de lo corriente *or* común, inusual; **with ~ frankness** con inusitada *or* insólita franqueza; **did you notice anything ~ about him?** ¿le notaste algo raro *or* fuera de lo normal?

unusually /ˈʌnˈjuːʒuəli/ *adv* excepcionalmente, inusitadamente; **she was ~ talkative** estaba más conversadora que de costumbre

unveil /ˈʌnˈveɪl/ *vt* descubrir*, develar (AmL)

unwanted /ˈʌnˈwɔːntəd ‖ ʌnˈwɒntɪd/ *adj* ‹*pregnancy/child*› no deseado; ‹*object*› superfluo

unwarranted /ˈʌnˈwɔːrəntəd ‖ ʌnˈwɒrəntɪd/ *adj* injustificado

unwavering /ˈʌnˈweɪvərɪŋ/ *adj* ‹*loyalty/belief*› inquebrantable; ‹*determination*› férreo

unwelcome /ˈʌnˈwelkəm/ *adj* ‹*visit*› inoportuno; ‹*guest*› inoportuno, poco grato; ‹*news*› poco grato

unwell /ˈʌnˈwel/ *adj* mal

unwholesome /ˈʌnˈhəʊlsəm/ *adj* ‹*diet/climate*› poco sano *or* saludable; ‹*smell/person*› desagradable

unwieldy /ʌnˈwiːldi/ *adj* **-dier, -diest** pesado y difícil de manejar

unwilling /ˈʌnˈwɪlɪŋ/ *adj* mal dispuesto; **to be ~ to** + INF no querer* + INF, no estar* dispuesto a + INF

unwillingly /ˈʌnˈwɪlɪŋli/ *adv* de mala gana, a regañadientes

unwind /ˈʌnˈwaɪnd/ (*past & past p* **unwound**) *vt* desenrollar ■ ~ *vi* (colloq) relajarse

unwise /ˈʌnˈwaɪz/ *adj* poco prudente *or* sensato; **it would be ~ of you to do that** hacer eso no sería sensato

unwitting /ˈʌnˈwɪtɪŋ/ *adj* involuntario

unwittingly /ˈʌnˈwɪtɪŋli/ *adv* sin ser consciente (de ello), sin darse* cuenta

unworthy /ˈʌnˈwɜːrði ‖ ʌnˈwɜːði/ *adj* **-thier, -thiest** indigno; **to be ~ to** + INF no ser* digno DE + INF

unwound /ˈʌnˈwaʊnd/ *past & past p of* UNWIND

unwrap /ˈʌnˈræp/ *vt* **-pp-** desenvolver*

unwritten /ˈʌnˈrɪtn̩/ *adj* ‹*rule*› no escrito; ‹*agreement*› verbal, de palabra

unyielding /ˈʌnˈjiːldɪŋ/ *adj* ‹*person*› inflexible; ‹*opposition*› implacable

up[1] /ʌp/ *adv* **I 1** (in upward direction): **~ a bit … left a bit** un poco más arriba … un poco a la izquierda; **we saw them on the way ~** los vimos cuando subíamos; **from the waist ~** desde la cintura para arriba **2 (a)** (of position) arriba; **~ here/there** aquí/allí arriba; **300ft ~** a una altura de 300 pies **(b)** (upstairs, on upper floor): **I'll be ~ in a minute** subiré en un minuto **(c)** (raised): **with the blinds ~** con las persianas levantadas *or* subidas; **face ~**

boca arriba **3 (a)** (upright): **the nurse helped him ~** la enfermera lo ayudó a sentarse **(b)** (out of bed): **they're not ~ yet** todavía no se han levantado **4** (of numbers, intensity): **she had the volume ~ high** tenía el volumen muy alto; **from $25/the age of 11 ~** a partir de 25 dólares/de los 11 años **5** (at or to another place): **the path ~ to the house** el sendero hasta la casa **6** (in position, erected): **is the tent ~?** ¿ya han armado la tienda *or* (AmL) la carpa?; **the shelves are ~** los estantes están colocados *or* puestos **7** (going on) (colloq): **what's ~ with you?** ¿a ti qué te pasa?; **what's ~?** (what's the matter?) ¿qué pasa?; (as greeting) (AmE) ¿qué hay? (colloq) **8** (finished): **your time is ~** se te ha acabado el tiempo **9** (Sport) (ahead in competition): **they're two goals ~** van ganando por dos goles; ***to be one ~ on sb*** tener* una ventaja sobre algn

II (*in phrases*) **1 up against (a)** (next to) contra **(b)** (confronted by): **you don't know what you're ~ against** no sabes a lo que te enfrentas **2 up and down (a)** (vertically): **to jump ~ and down** dar* saltos; **to look sb ~ and down** mirar a algn de arriba abajo **(b)** (back and forth) de arriba abajo **3 up till** *o* **until** hasta

III up to 1 (as far as, as much as) hasta; **~ to here/now** hasta aquí/ahora **2 (a)** (equal to): **it isn't ~ to the usual standard** no es del alto nivel al que estamos acostumbrados; ⇒ COME UP TO (b) **(b)** (capable of): **she's not ~ to the job** no tiene las condiciones necesarias para el trabajo; **I'm not ~ to going out** no me siente con fuerzas (como) para salir **3** (depending on): **that's ~ to you** eso depende de ti; **it's not ~ to me to decide** no me corresponde a mí decidir **4 to be ~ to sth** (colloq): **they're ~ to something** (planning) están tramando algo, se traen algo entre manos; (doing) están haciendo algo; **what have you been ~ to lately?** ¿en qué has andado últimamente?

up² *prep* **1 (a)** (in upward direction): **to go ~ the stairs/hill** subir la escalera/colina **(b)** (at higher level): **80ft ~ the cliff** a 80 pies del pie del acantilado **2 (a)** (along): **to go ~ the river** ir* por el río; **she walked ~ and down the room** iba de un lado a otro de la habitación **(b)** (further along): **it's just ~ the road** está un poco más allá *or* adelante

up³ *n*: **~s and downs** (of life) vicisitudes *fpl*; (of marriage) altibajos *mpl*

up: **~-and-coming** /ˌʌpən'kʌmɪŋ/ *adj* (*before n*): **an ~-and-coming actor** un actor que promete; **~beat** *adj* (colloq) optimista; **~braid** /ʌp'breɪd/ *vt* (frml) reprender, reconvenir* (frml); **~bringing** /'ʌpˌbrɪŋɪŋ/ *n* (*no pl*) educación *f*; **~coming** /'ʌp'kʌmɪŋ/ *adj* (*before n*) próximo, que se acerca

update¹ /ʌp'deɪt/ *vt* poner* al día

update² /'ʌpdeɪt/ *n*: **to give sb an ~ on sth** poner* a algn al corriente *or* al tanto de algo

up: **~end** /ʌp'end/ *vt* poner* vertical, parar (AmL); **~front** /'ʌp'frʌnt/ *adv* por adelantado; **~grade** /ʌp'greɪd/ *vt* **(a)** ‹*employee*› elevar de categoría; ‹*job*› elevar la categoría de **(b)** (improve) ‹*facilities*› mejorar

upheaval /ʌp'hiːvəl/ *n* [U C] trastorno *m*; (social, political) agitación *f*

up: **~held** /ʌp'held/ *past & past p of* ~HOLD; **~hill** /'ʌp'hɪl/ *adv* cuesta arriba, en subida; **~hold** /ʌp'həʊld/ *vt* (*past & past p* **~held**) **(a)** ‹*tradition*› conservar; ‹*principle*› mantener* **(b)** (Law) ‹*decision/verdict*› confirmar

upholster /ʌp'həʊlstər ‖ ʌp'həʊlstə(r)/ *vt* tapizar*

upholstery /ʌp'həʊlstəri/ *n* [U] **(a)** (stuffing, springs) relleno *m*; (covers) tapizado *m* **(b)** (craft, trade) tapicería *f*

up: **~keep** *n* [U] (running, maintenance) mantenimiento *m*; (costs) gastos *mpl* de mantenimiento; **~lift** /ʌp'lɪft/ *vt* elevar; **~lifting** /ʌp'lɪftɪŋ/ *adj* (spiritually) que eleva el espíritu; (emotionally) que levanta el ánimo

upmarket¹ /'ʌp'mɑːrkət ‖ ˌʌp'mɑːkɪt/ *adj* de categoría, para gente pudiente

upmarket² *adv*: **to go ~** subir de categoría

upon /ə'pɑːn ‖ ə'pɒn/ *prep* (frml) **(a)** (on) sobre; **~** -ING al + INF **(b)** (indicating large numbers): **thousands ~ thousands** miles y miles

upper /'ʌpər ‖ 'ʌpə(r)/ *adj* (*before n*) **1 (a)** (spatially, numerically) superior; ‹*lip*› superior, de arriba **(b)** (in rank, importance) superior, más elevado **2** (Geog) alto; **the U~ Danube** el alto Danubio

upper: **~ class** *n* clase *f* alta; **~-class** /'ʌpər 'klæs ‖ ˌʌpə'klɑːs/ *adj* de clase alta; **~most** *adj* más alto

upright /'ʌpraɪt/ *adj* **(a)** ‹*post/position*› vertical; **to place/stand sth ~** colocar*/poner* algo de pie *or* vertical **(b)** ‹*citizen*› recto

up: **~rising** *n* levantamiento *m*, alzamiento *m*; **~river** /'ʌp'rɪvər ‖ ˌʌp'rɪvə(r)/ *adv* río arriba; **~roar** *n* [U] (noise, chaos) tumulto *m*, alboroto *m*; (outcry) protesta *f* airada; **~root** /ʌp'ruːt/ *vt* ‹*plant*› arrancar* de raíz, desarraigar* (téc); ‹*person*› desarraigar*

upset¹ /'ʌp'set/ *adj* **1** (unhappy, hurt) disgustado; (distressed) alterado; (offended) ofendido; (disappointed) desilusionado **2** (Med): **I have an ~ stomach** estoy *or* ando mal del estómago, estoy descompuesto (del estómago) (esp AmL)

upset² /'ʌp'set/ *vt* (*pres p* **upsetting**; *past & past p* **upset**) **1** (hurt) disgustar; (distress) alterar, afectar; (offend) ofender **2** (make ill): **it ~s my stomach** me cae mal, me sienta mal (al estómago) **3** ‹*plans/calculations*› desbaratar, trastornar

upset³ /'ʌpset/ *n* **1** [C U] **(a)** (upheaval) trastorno *m* **(b)** (emotional trouble) disgusto *m* **2** [C] (Med): **to have a stomach ~** estar* mal *or* (esp AmL) descompuesto del estómago

upshot /'ʌpʃɑːt ‖ 'ʌpʃɒt/ *n*: **the ~ of it all is that** ... lo que resulta de todo esto es que ...

upside down /'ʌpsaɪd/ *adj* al revés (*con la parte de arriba abajo*); **to turn sth ~ ~** poner* algo boca abajo; ‹*theory/world*› revolucionar

upstage /'ʌp'steɪdʒ/ *vt* eclipsar

upstairs /'ʌp'sterz ‖ ˌʌp'steəz/ *adv* arriba; **to go ~** subir

up: **~start** *n* advenedizo, -za *m,f*; **~state** /'ʌp 'steɪt/ *adv* (AmE): **he lives ~state** vive en el norte del estado (*fuera de la capital*); **~stream** /'ʌp 'striːm/ *adv* río *or* corriente arriba; **~surge** *n* ‹*of/in violence*› recrudecimiento *m*; ‹*in demand*› aumento *m*; **~take** *n* [U] ***to be quick on the ~take*** agarrar *or* (esp Esp) coger* las cosas al vuelo; **~tight** /'ʌp'taɪt/ *adj* (colloq) nervioso, tenso; **~-to-date** /'ʌptə'deɪt/ *adj* (*pred* **~ to date**) al día, actualizado

uptown¹ /'ʌp'taʊn/ *adj* (AmE) que va hacia el norte/hacia el distrito residencial (de la ciudad)

uptown² *adv* (AmE): **they live/went ~** viven en/fueron hacia el norte/hacia el distrito residencial de la ciudad

up: **~turn** *n* (in demand, production) repunte *m*, mejora *f*; **~turned** /'ʌp'tɜ:rnd ‖ 'ʌptɜ:nd/ *adj* ‹*nose*› respingón, respingado (AmL); ‹*table*› boca abajo, patas arriba; ‹*car/crate*› volcado

upward¹ /'ʌpwərd ‖ 'ʌpwəd/ *adj* (*before n*) ‹*direction*› hacia arriba; ‹*movement*› ascendente; ‹*tendency*› al alza

upward², (esp BrE) **upwards** /-z/ *adv* ‹*climb/look*› hacia arriba; **face ~** boca arriba

upwardly mobile /'ʌpwərdli ‖ 'ʌpwədli/ *adj* de movilidad social ascendente

uranium /jʊ'reɪniəm/ *n* [U] uranio *m*

Uranus /'jʊərənəs, jʊə'reɪnəs/ *n* Urano *m*

urban /'ɜ:rbən ‖ 'ɜ:bən/ *adj* urbano

urbane /ɜ:r'beɪn ‖ ɜ:'beɪn/ *adj* (frml) fino y cortés, urbano (frml)

urchin /'ɜ:rtʃən ‖ 'ɜ:tʃɪn/ *n* golfillo, -lla *m,f*, pilluelo, -la *m,f*

Urdu /'ʊrdu: ‖ 'ʊədu:/ *n* [U] urdu *m*

urge¹ /ɜ:rdʒ ‖ ɜ:dʒ/ *n* (wish, whim) ganas *fpl*; (creative, sexual) impulso *m*

urge² *vt* instar (frml); (entreat) pedir* con insistencia; **to ~ sb to** + INF instar a algn A QUE (+ *subj*) (frml), pedirle* A algn con insistencia QUE (+ *subj*)
• urge on [*v* + *o* + *adv*] animar, alentar*; ‹*horse*› espolear

urgency /'ɜ:rdʒənsi ‖ 'ɜ:dʒənsi/ *n* [U] urgencia *f*

urgent /'ɜ:rdʒənt ‖ 'ɜ:dʒənt/ *adj* ‹*matter/case*› urgente; ‹*tone*› apremiante

urgently /'ɜ:rdʒəntli ‖ 'ɜ:dʒəntli/ *adv* urgentemente, con urgencia

urinal /'jʊrənl̩ ‖ jʊə'raɪnl̩/ *n* (place) urinario *m*; (receptacle) orinal *m*

urinate /'jʊrəneɪt ‖ 'jʊərɪneɪt/ *vi* (frml) orinar

urine /'jʊrən ‖ 'juərɪn/ *n* [U] orina *f*

urn /ɜ:rn ‖ ɜ:n/ *n* **(a)** (vase) urna *f* **(b)** (for ashes) urna *f* funeraria **(c)** (for tea, coffee) *recipiente grande para hacer o mantener caliente té, café etc*

Uruguay /'jʊrəgwaɪ ‖ 'jʊərəgwaɪ/ *n* Uruguay *m*

Uruguayan /'jʊrə'gwaɪən ‖ ˌjʊərə'gwaɪən/ *adj* uruguayo

us /ʌs, *weak form* əs/ *pron* ▶ 638 **1 (a)** (as direct object) nos; **they helped ~** nos ayudaron **(b)** (as indirect object) nos; **he gave ~ the book** nos dio el libro; **he gave it to ~** nos lo dio **(c)** (after preposition) nosotros, -tras; **there were four of ~** éramos cuatro **2** (emphatic use) nosotros, -tras; **it was ~** fuimos nosotros

US *n* (+ *sing vb*) EEUU, EE UU, EE.UU.

USA *n* **(a)** (= **United States of America**) EEUU, EE UU, EE.UU. **(b)** (= **United States Army**) ejército *m* estadounidense *or* de los EEUU

usable, **useable** /'ju:zəbəl/ *adj* utilizable

USAF *n* (= **United States Air Force**) la Fuerza Aérea de los EEUU

usage /'ju:sɪdʒ/ *n* [U C] (Ling) uso *m*

use¹ /ju:s/ *n* **1** [U] (of machine, substance, method, word) uso *m*, empleo *m*, utilización *f*; **to be in ~** «*machine*» estar* funcionando *or* en funcionamiento; «*word*» emplearse, usarse; **to make ~ of sth** usar algo, hacer* uso de algo; **to put sth to good ~** hacer* buen uso de algo **2** [C] (application, function) uso *m* **3** [U] (usefulness): **to be of ~ to sb** serle* útil *or* de utilidad a algn, servirle* a algn; **these scissors aren't much ~** estas tijeras no sirven para nada; **it's no ~** es inútil, no hay manera, no hay caso (AmL); **what's the ~ (of -ING)?** ¿de qué sirve (+ INF)?, ¿qué sentido tiene (+ INF)? **4** (right to use): **to have the ~ of sb's car** poder* usar el coche de algn

use² /ju:z/ *vt* **1 (a)** (for task, purpose) usar; **to ~ sth AS sth** usar algo DE *or* COMO algo **(b)** (avail oneself of) ‹*service/facilities*› utilizar*, usar, hacer* uso de; **may I ~ your phone?** ¿puedo hacer una llamada *or* llamar por teléfono?; **may I ~ your toilet?** ¿puedo pasar *or* ir al baño? **2** (do with) (colloq): **I could ~ a drink** no me vendría mal un trago **3** (consume) ‹*food/fuel*› consumir, usar **4** (manipulate, exploit) (pej) utilizar*, usar (esp AmL) ■ **~** *v mod* /ju:s/ (*in neg, interrog sentences*): **I didn't ~ to visit them very often** no solía visitarlos muy a menudo; **where did you ~ to live?** ¿dónde vivías?; *see also* USED²
• use up [*v* + *o* + *adv*, *v* + *adv* + *o*] ‹*supplies/strength*› agotar, consumir; ‹*leftovers*› usar

useable *adj* ⇒ USABLE

used¹ *adj* **1** /ju:zd/ ‹*needle/stamp/car*› usado **2** /ju:st/ (accustomed) (*pred*) **to be ~ TO sth/-ING** estar* acostumbrado A algo/+ INF; **to get ~ TO sth/-ING** acostumbrarse A algo/+ INF

used² /ju:st/ *v mod* (indicating former state, habit) (*only in past*) **~ to** (+ INF): **there ~ to be** (antes) había; **I ~ to work in that shop** (antes) trabajaba en esa tienda; *see also* USE² *v mod*

useful /'ju:sfəl/ *adj* útil; **to come in ~** (BrE) ser* útil, venir* bien

useless /'ju:sləs ‖ 'ju:slɪs/ *adj* **(a)** (ineffective) inútil; **these scissors are ~** estas tijeras no sirven para nada **(b)** (not capable) (colloq) ‹*person*› inútil, negado (fam)

user /'ju:zər ‖ 'ju:zə(r)/ *n* usuario, -ria *m,f*; **drug ~** consumidor, -dora *m,f* de drogas

user-friendly /'ju:zər'frendli ‖ ˌju:zə'frendli/ *adj* fácil de usar *or* de utilizar

usher¹ /'ʌʃər ‖ 'ʌʃə(r)/ *n* **(a)** (Cin, Theat) acomodador, -dora *m,f* **(b)** (at wedding) *persona allegada a los novios que se encarga de recibir y sentar a los invitados en la iglesia*

usher² *vt*: **to ~ sb to her/his seat** conducir* a algn hasta su asiento; **he ~ed her into the room** la hizo pasar a la habitación
• usher in [*v* + *o* + *adv*, *v* + *adv* + *o*] ‹*person*› hacer* pasar; ‹*new era*› marcar* el comienzo de

usherette /ʌʃə'ret/ *n* acomodadora *f*

USN *n* = **United States Navy**

USS = **United States ship**

USSR *n* (= **Union of Soviet Socialist Republics**) URSS *f*

usual /'juːʒuəl/ *adj* ‹*method/response*› acostumbrado, habitual, usual; ‹*time/place*› de siempre, de costumbre; ‹*clothes*› de costumbre; **as ~** como de costumbre

usually /'juːʒuəli/ *adv* normalmente, usualmente; **what do you ~ do in the evenings?** ¿qué sueles hacer por las noches?

usurp /jʊ'sɜːrp || juː'zɜːp/ *vt* (frml) usurpar

UT = **Utah**

utensil /juː'tensəl || juː'tensɪl/ *n* utensilio *m*

uterus /'juːtərəs/ *n* (*pl* **-teri** /-tərаɪ/ *or* **-teruses**) útero *m*, matriz *f*

utility /juː'tɪləti/ *n* (*pl* **-ties**) (*public service* **~**) empresa *f* de servicio público

utility room *n*: *cuarto para lavar y planchar*

utilize /'juːtḷaɪz || 'juːtɪlaɪz/ *vt* (frml) utilizar*

utmost¹ /'ʌtməʊst/ *adj* (*before n*) mayor, sumo; **with the ~ care** con el mayor cuidado, con sumo cuidado; **of the ~ importance** de suma importancia

utmost² *n*: **to do one's ~** (**to** + INF) esforzarse* al máximo *or* hacer* todo lo posible (PARA + INF)

utopia, **Utopia** /juː'təʊpiə/ *n* (*pl* **-as**) utopía *f*

utter¹ /'ʌtər || 'ʌtə(r)/ *adj* (*as intensifier*) completo, total

utter² *vt* ‹*word*› decir*, pronunciar; ‹*cry*› dar*

utterly /'ʌtərli || 'ʌtəli/ *adv* (*as intensifier*) completamente, totalmente

U-turn /'juːtɜːrn || 'juːtɜːn/ *n* cambio *m* de sentido; **to make** (AmE) *o* (BrE) **do a ~** cambiar de sentido

Uzbekistan /'ʊzbekɪ'stɑːn/ *n* Uzbekistán *m*

Vv

V, **v** /viː/ *n* V, v *f*

v 1 ⇒ vs **2** (*pl* **vv**) (Bib, Lit) = **verse 3** (colloq) (= **very**) muy

V (Elec) (= **volt**(**s**)) V (*read as: voltio*(*s*))

VA *n* = **Virginia**

vacancy /'veɪkənsi/ *n* [C] (*pl* **-cies**) **(a)** (job) vacante *f* **(b)** (in hotel) habitación *f* libre

vacant /'veɪkənt/ *adj* **1 (a)** ‹*building/premises*› desocupado **(b)** ‹*post*› vacante **(c)** ‹*room*› disponible, libre; ‹*seat/space*› libre **2** (blank) ‹*look/expression*› ausente

vacate /'veɪkeɪt || veɪ'keɪt, və-/ *vt* (frml) ‹*building*› desocupar, desalojar; ‹*seat/room*› dejar libre; ‹*job/post*› abandonar, dejar

vacation¹ /veɪ'keɪʃən/ *n* [U C] (esp AmE) (from work) vacaciones *fpl*, licencia *f* (Col, Méx, RPl); (from studies) vacaciones *fpl*; **to go/be on ~** irse*/estar* de vacaciones

vacation² *vi* (AmE) pasar las vacaciones, vacacionar (Méx)

vacationer /veɪ'keɪʃṇər || və'keɪʃənə(r)/, **vacationist** /-ʃṇəst || -ʃənɪst/ *n* (AmE) turista *mf*; (in summer) veraneante *mf*

vaccinate /'væksəneɪt || 'væksɪneɪt/ *vt* vacunar

vaccination /'væksə'neɪʃən ||ˌvæksɪ'neɪʃən/ *n* [C U] vacunación *f*

vaccine /væk'siːn || 'væksiːn/ *n* [C U] vacuna *f*

vacillate /'væsəleɪt/ *vi* (hesitate) vacilar; (sway) oscilar

vacuum¹ /'vækjuəm, -juːm/ *n* vacío *m*; (*before n*) **~ pump** bomba *f* neumática

vacuum² *vi* pasar la aspiradora, aspirar (AmL)

vacuum: **~ bottle** *n* (AmE) termo *m*; **~ cleaner** *n* aspiradora *f*; **~ flask** *n* termo *m*

vagabond /'vægəbɑːnd || 'vægəbɒnd/ *n*, vagabundo, -da *m,f*

vagina /və'dʒaɪnə/ *n* vagina *f*

vagrant /'veɪgrənt/ *n* vagabundo, -da *m,f*

vague /veɪg/ *adj* **vaguer, vaguest (a)** (imprecise, unclear) ‹*term/wording/concept*› impreciso, vago **(b)** (indistinct) ‹*outline*› borroso **(c)** (absentminded) ‹*expression*› distraído; ‹*person*› distraído, despistado

vaguely /'veɪgli/ *adv* **(a)** (in imprecise, unclear way) ‹*explain/remember*› vagamente; ‹*answer/define*› con vaguedad *or* imprecisión; ‹*suspicious/ridiculous*› ligeramente; **he looks ~ like his father** tiene un ligero parecido con *or* a su padre **(b)** (absentmindedly) distraídamente

vain /veɪn/ *adj* **-er, -est 1** (self-admiring) vanidoso **2** (*before n, no comp*) **(a)** ‹*attempt*› vano; ‹*hope/belief*› vano **(b)** ‹*promise/words*› vano **(c) in vain** en vano, vanamente

vainly /'veɪnli/ *adv* (uselessly) en vano, vanamente

valentine /'væləntaɪn/ *n* **(a)** (card) *tarjeta de tono humorístico y/o amoroso que se envía anónimamente el día de San Valentín* **(b)** *also* **Valentine** (person) enamorado, -da *m,f*

Valentine's Day /'væləntaɪnz/ *n* el día de San Valentín, el día de los enamorados

valet /'vælət, 'væleɪ || 'væleɪ, 'vælɪt/ *n* **(a)** (servant) ayuda *m* de cámara **(b)** (in hotel) mozo *m* de hotel

valiant /'væljənt/ *adj* ‹*hero/deed*› valiente, valeroso; ‹*attempt*› valeroso

valid /'væləd || 'vælɪd/ *adj* válido

validate /'vælədeɪt ‖ 'vælɪdeɪt/ *vt* **(a)** (frml) ‹*theory*› dar* validez a, validar (frml) **(b)** (Law) ‹*contract/document*› validar

valley /'væli/ *n* (*pl* **-leys**) valle *m*

valor, (BrE) **valour** /'vælər ‖ 'vælə(r)/ *n* [U] (frml *o* liter) valor *m*, valentía *f*

valuable /'væljuəbəl/ *adj* valioso; ‹*time*› precioso

valuables /'væljuəbəlz/ *pl n* objetos *mpl* de valor

valuation /'vælju'eɪʃən/ *n* [C U] valoración *f*, tasación *f*, avalúo *m* (AmL)

value¹ /'vælju:/ *n* [U C] **1** (worth) valor *m* **2 values** (standards) valores *mpl*

value² *vt* **(a)** (Fin) ‹*assets/property*› tasar, valorar, avaluar* (AmL) **(b)** (regard highly) ‹*friendship/advice*› valorar, apreciar; ‹*freedom/privacy*› valorar

value-added tax /'vælju:'ædəd ‖ ˌvælju:'ædɪd/ *n* impuesto *m* al valor agregado *or* (Esp) sobre el valor añadido

valve /vælv/ *n* válvula *f*; (on musical instrument) pistón *m*

vampire /'væmpaɪr ‖ 'væmpaɪə(r)/ *n* vampiro *m*

van /væn/ *n* **(a)** (Auto) furgoneta *f*, camioneta *f* **(b)** (BrE Rail) furgón *m*

vandal /'vændl/ *n* vándalo *m*

vandalism /'vændlɪzəm/ *n* [U] vandalismo *m*

vandalize /'vændlaɪz/ *vt* destrozar*

vanguard /'vængɑ:rd ‖ 'vængɑ:d/ *n* vanguardia *f*

vanilla /və'nɪlə/ *n* [U] vainilla *f*

vanish /'vænɪʃ/ *vi* desaparecer*

vanity /'vænəti/ *n* (*pl* **-ties**) [U C] **(a)** (about appearance) vanidad *f* **(b)** (pride) orgullo *m*, vanidad *f*

vanity case *n* neceser *m*

vanquish /'væŋkwɪʃ/ *vt* (liter) vencer*

vantage point /'væntɪdʒ ‖ 'vɑ:ntɪdʒ/ *n* posición *f* ventajosa; (for view) mirador *m*

vapor, (BrE) **vapour** /'veɪpər ‖ 'veɪpə(r)/ *n* [C U] (on glass) vaho *m*; (steam) vapor *m*

vaporize /'veɪpəraɪz/ *vi* evaporarse, vaporizarse*

vapour *n* (BrE) ⇒ VAPOR

variable /'veriəbəl ‖ 'veəriəbəl/ *adj* variable

variance /'veriəns ‖ 'veəriəns/ *n* [U C]: **to be at ~ with sth** no estar* de acuerdo con algo, discrepar de algo

variant /'veriənt ‖ 'veəriənt/ *n* variante *f*

variation /'veri'eɪʃən ‖ ˌveəri'eɪʃən/ *n* [U C] variación *f*

varicose veins /'værəkəʊs ‖ 'værɪkəʊs/ *pl n* varices *fpl*, várices *fpl* (esp AmL)

varied /'verid ‖ 'veərid/ *adj* variado

variegated /'verɪgeɪtəd ‖ 'veərɪgeɪtɪd/ *adj* abigarrado, multicolor

variety /və'raɪəti/ *n* (*pl* **-ties**) **(a)** [U] (diversity) variedad *f*, diversidad *f* **(b)** [C] (assortment) **~ OF sth**: **it comes in a ~ of shades** viene en varios colores **(c)** [C] (sort) clase *f*

variety show *n* espectáculo *m* de variedades

various /'veriəs ‖ 'veəriəs/ *adj* **(a)** (several) (*before n, no comp*) varios **(b)** (different, diverse) diferentes, diversos

varnish¹ /'vɑ:rnɪʃ ‖ 'vɑ:nɪʃ/ *n* barniz *m*; (for nails) (BrE) esmalte *m*

varnish² *vt* barnizar*; **to ~ one's nails** (BrE) pintarse las uñas

vary /'veri ‖ 'veəri/, **varies, varying, varied** *vi* **(a)** (change, fluctuate) variar*; **the temperature varies between** … la temperatura oscila entre … **(b)** (differ) «*standards/prices*» variar* ■ **~** *vt* variar*; ‹*diet*› dar* variedad a

vase /veɪs, veɪz ‖vɑ:z/ *n* (for flowers) florero *m*; (ornament) jarrón *m*

vasectomy /və'sektəmi/ *n* [C U] (*pl* **-mies**) vasectomía *f*

Vaseline® /'væsəli:n/ *n* [U] vaselina *f*

vast /væst ‖ vɑ:st/ *adj* ‹*size/wealth*› inmenso, enorme; ‹*area*› vasto, extenso; ‹*knowledge*› vasto

vastly /'væstli ‖ 'vɑ:stli/ *adv* infinitamente

vat /væt/ *n* cuba *f*, tanque *m*

VAT *n* [U] (= **value-added tax**) IVA *m*

Vatican /'vætɪkən/ *n* **the ~** el Vaticano

Vatican City *n* Ciudad *f* del Vaticano

vault¹ /vɔ:lt/ *n* **1** **(a)** (strongroom) cámara *f* acorazada, bóveda *f* de seguridad (AmL) **(b)** (crypt) cripta *f* **2** (Archit) bóveda *f*

vault² *vi/vt* saltar (*apoyándose en algo*)

VCR *n* = **videocassette recorder**

VD *n* [U] = **venereal disease**

VDT *n* (esp AmE) = **visual display terminal**

VDU *n* = **visual display unit**

've /əv/ = **have**

veal /vi:l/ *n* [U] ternera *f* (*de animal muy joven y de carne pálida*)

VE-Day /'vi:'i:deɪ/ *n*: *día de la victoria aliada en Europa en la segunda guerra mundial*

veer /vɪr ‖ vɪə(r)/ *vi* «*vehicle/horse*» dar* un viraje, virar; «*wind*» cambiar de dirección; **the road ~s to the left** el camino tuerce *or* se desvía hacia la izquierda

vegan /'vi:gən/ *n* vegetariano estricto, vegetariana estricta *m,f*

vegetable /'vedʒtəbəl/ *n* **(a)** (Culin) verdura *f* **(b)** (plant) vegetal *m*; (*before n*) ‹*oil/fats*› vegetal

vegetarian¹ /'vedʒə'teriən ‖ ˌvedʒɪ'teəriən/ *n* vegetariano, -na *m,f*

vegetarian² *adj* vegetariano

vegetate /'vedʒəteɪt ‖ 'vedʒɪteɪt/ *vi* vegetar

vegetation /'vedʒə'teɪʃən ‖ ˌvedʒɪ'teɪʃən/ *n* [U] vegetación *f*

vehement /'vi:əmənt/ *adj* vehemente

vehemently /'vi:əməntli/ *adv* con vehemencia, vehementemente

vehicle /'vi:əkəl/ *n* vehículo *m*

veil¹ /veɪl/ *n* velo *m*

veil² *vt* (cover with a veil) : **to ~ one's face** taparse *or* cubrirse* con un velo, velarse (liter)

veiled /veɪld/ *adj* ‹*threat/insult*› velado

vein /veɪn/ *n* **1** (Anat, Bot, Zool) vena *f* **2** **(a)** (of ore, mineral) veta *f*, filón *m*, vena *f* **(b)** (in marble) veta *f* **3** (*no pl*) (mood, style) vena *f*

velocity /və'lɑːsəti ‖ və'lɒsəti/ *n* [U C] (*pl* **-ties**) velocidad *f*

velvet /'velvət ‖ 'velvɪt/ *n* [U] terciopelo *m*

vendetta /ven'detə/ *n* vendetta *f*

vending machine /'vendɪŋ/ *n* máquina *f* expendedora

vendor /'vendər ‖ 'vendə(r)/ *n* (Busn, Law) vendedor, -dora *m,f*

veneer /və'nɪr ‖ vɪ'nɪə(r)/ *n* [U C] (of wood, gold) enchapado *m*, chapa *f*

venerate /'venəreɪt/ *vt* venerar, reverenciar

venereal disease /və'nɪriəl ‖ və'nɪəriəl/ *n* enfermedad *f* venérea

Venetian blind /və'niːʃən/ *n* persiana *f* veneciana *or* de lamas

Venezuela /'venə'zweɪlə ‖ ˌvenɪ'zweɪlə/ *n* Venezuela *f*

Venezuelan /'venə'zweɪlən ‖ ˌvenɪ'zweɪlən/ *adj* venezolano

vengeance /'vendʒəns/ *n* [U] venganza *f*; **with a ~** (colloq) de verdad *or* con ganas

vengeful /'vendʒfəl/ *adj* vengativo

venison /'venəsən ‖ 'venɪsən/ *n* [U] (carne *f* de) venado *m*

venom /'venəm/ *n* [U] **(a)** (Zool) veneno *m* **(b)** (malice) ponzoña *f*, veneno *m*

venomous /'venəməs/ *adj* ‹*snake/spider*› venenoso; ‹*look/words*› ponzoñoso

vent¹ /vent/ *n* **(a)** (in building, tunnel) (conducto *m* de) ventilación *f*; (in chimney, furnace) tiro *m* **(b)** (*air* ~) (shaft) respiradero *m*; (grille) rejilla *f* de ventilación

vent² *vt* descargar*; **she ~ed her anger on the children** descargó su ira sobre los niños

ventilate /'ventl̩eɪt ‖ 'ventɪleɪt/ *vt* ventilar

ventilation /'ventl̩'eɪʃən ‖ ˌventɪ'leɪʃən/ *n* [U] ventilación *f*; (system) sistema *m* de ventilación

ventilator /'ventl̩eɪtər ‖ 'ventɪleɪtə(r)/ *n* (Med) respirador *m* (artificial)

ventriloquist /ven'trɪləkwəst ‖ ven'trɪləkwɪst/ *n* ventrílocuo, -cua *m,f*

venture¹ /'ventʃər ‖ 'ventʃə(r)/ *n* (Busn) empresa *f*

venture² *vi* atreverse; **to ~ out** (atreverse a) salir* ■ ~ *vt* ‹*opinion/guess*› aventurar

venue /'venjuː/ *n* (for concert) lugar *m* de actuación; (for conference, Olympics) sede *f*

Venus /'viːnəs/ *n* Venus *m*

veranda, **verandah** /və'rændə/ *n* galería *f*

verb /vɜːrb ‖ vɜːb/ *n* verbo *m*

verbal /'vɜːrbəl ‖ 'vɜːbəl/ *adj* verbal

verbatim /vər'beɪtəm ‖ vɜː'beɪtɪm/ *adv* al pie de la letra

verbose /vər'bəʊs ‖ vɜː'bəʊs/ *adj* ampuloso, verboso

verdict /'vɜːrdɪkt ‖ 'vɜːdɪkt/ *n* **(a)** (Law) veredicto *m* **(b)** (opinion) opinión *f*

verge /vɜːrdʒ ‖ vɜːdʒ/ *n* **1 (a)** (border) (BrE) borde *m* **(b) to be on the ~ of tears** estar* al borde de las lágrimas; **to be on the ~ of -ING** estar* a punto de + INF **2** (of road) (BrE) arcén *m*

• **verge on** [*v* + *prep* + *o*] rayar en

verification /'verəfə'keɪʃən ‖ ˌverɪfɪ'keɪʃən/ *n* [U] **(a)** (confirmation) confirmación *f* **(b)** (checking) verificación *f*

verify /'verəfaɪ ‖ 'verɪfaɪ/ *vt* **-fies, -fying, -fied** **(a)** (confirm) confirmar **(b)** (check) ‹*fact/statement*› verificar*

veritable /'verətəbəl ‖ 'verɪtəbəl/ *adj* (frml *or* hum) auténtico, verdadero

vermin /'vɜːrmən ‖ 'vɜːmɪn/ *n* (*pl* ~) (animals) alimañas *fpl*; (insects) bichos *mpl*

vernacular /vər'nækjələr ‖ və'nækjʊlə(r)/ *n* (native language) lengua *f* vernácula; (local speech) habla *f*‡ local

verruca /və'ruːkə/ *n* verruga *f*

versatile /'vɜːrsətl̩ ‖ 'vɜːsətaɪl/ *adj* ‹*person*› polifacético, versátil; ‹*tool*› versátil; ‹*mind*› flexible

versatility /'vɜːrsə'tɪləti ‖ ˌvɜːsə'tɪləti/ *n* [U] versatilidad *f*

verse /vɜːrs ‖ vɜːs/ *n* **1** [U] (poetry) verso *m* **2** [C] **(a)** (short poem) verso *m*, rima *f* **(b)** (stanza) estrofa *f* **(c)** [C] (in Bible) versículo *m*

versed /vɜːrst ‖ vɜːst/ *adj* (*pred*): **to be well ~ in sth** ser* muy versado en algo

version /'vɜːrʒən ‖ 'vɜːʃən/ *n* versión *f*

versus /'vɜːrsəs ‖ 'vɜːsəs/ *prep* (Law) contra; (Sport) contra, versus

vertebra /'vɜːrtəbrə ‖ 'vɜːtəbrə/ *n* (*pl* **-bras** *or* **-brae** /-breɪ/) vértebra *f*

vertebrate /'vɜːrtəbrət ‖ 'vɜːtɪbrət/ *n* vertebrado *m*

vertical /'vɜːrtɪkəl ‖ 'vɜːtɪkəl/ *adj* vertical

vertigo /'vɜːrtɪgəʊ ‖ 'vɜːtɪgəʊ/ *n* [U] vértigo *m*

verve /vɜːrv ‖ vɜːv/ *n* [U] brío *m*

very¹ /'veri/ *adv* **(a)** (extremely) muy; **she's ~ tall** es muy alta; (more emphatic) es altísima; **it was ~ hot** hacía mucho calor **(b)** (*in phrases*) **very much** ‹*like/enjoy*› mucho; **thank you ~ much** muchas gracias **(c)** (emphatic): **the ~ next day** precisamente al día siguiente; **at the ~ least** como mínimo

very² *adj* (*before n*) **(a)** (exact, precise) mismo; **for that ~ reason** por esa misma razón, por eso mismo **(b)** (actual) mismo; **its ~ existence is threatened** su misma existencia se halla amenazada **(c)** (mere, sheer) solo, mero; **the ~ mention of her name** la sola *or* mera mención de su nombre

vespers /'vespərz ‖ 'vespəz/ *pl n* vísperas *fpl*

vessel /'vesəl/ *n* **1** (Naut frml) navío *m* (frml), nave *f* (liter) **2** (receptacle) (frml) recipiente *m*; (*drinking* ~) vasija *f* **3** (Anat, Bot) vaso *m*

vest /vest/ *n* **(a)** (waistcoat) (AmE) chaleco *m* **(b)** (undergarment) (BrE) camiseta *f*

vested interest /'vestəd ‖ 'vestɪd/ *n* [U] **to have a ~ ~ in -ING/sth** tener* gran interés en + INF/algo

vestige /'vestɪdʒ/ *n* vestigio *m*

vestry /'vestri/ *n* (*pl* **-tries**) sacristía *f*

vet¹ /vet/ *n* **1** (veterinarian) veterinario, -ria *m,f* **2** (veteran) (AmE colloq) veterano, -na *m,f*

vet² *vt* **-tt-** ‹*applicant*› someter a investigación; ‹*application*› examinar

veteran /'vetərən/ *n* **(a)** (of war) veterano, -na *m,f* de guerra **(b)** (experienced person) veterano, -na *m,f*

veteran: ~ **car** *n* (BrE) coche *m* antiguo (*fabricado antes de 1919*); **V~s Day** /'vetərənz/ *n* (in US) día *m* del Armisticio

veterinarian /'vetərə'neriən ‖ ˌvetərɪ'neəriən/ *n* (AmE) médico veterinario, médica veterinaria *m,f*

veterinary /'vetərəneri ‖ 'vetrɪnəri/ *adj* veterinario; ~ **surgeon** (BrE frml) médico veterinario, médica veterinaria *m,f*

veto¹ /'vi:təʊ/ *n* (*pl* **vetoes**) [U C] veto *m*

veto² *vt* **vetoes, vetoing, vetoed** vetar

vex /veks/ *vt* **(a)** (annoy) irritar, sacar* de quicio **(b)** (worry, puzzle) desconcertar*

vexed /vekst/ *adj* **(a)** (annoyed) ‹*expression/tone*› irritado; **to be ~** estar* enojado (esp AmL), estar* enfadado (esp Esp) **(b)** (worried, puzzled) desconcertado

VHF (= **very high frequency**) VHF

via /'vaɪə, 'vi:ə ‖ 'vaɪə/ *prep* **(a)** (by way of) vía **(b)** (by means of) a través de

viable /'vaɪəbəl/ *adj* viable

viaduct /'vaɪədʌkt/ *n* viaducto *m*

vibrant /'vaɪbrənt/ *adj* **(a)** ‹*color*› vibrante; ‹*atmosphere*› efervescente **(b)** (resonant) ‹*voice*› vibrante

vibrate /'vaɪbreɪt ‖ vaɪ'breɪt/ *vi* vibrar

vibration /vaɪ'breɪʃən/ *n* [U C] vibración *f*

vicar /'vɪkər ‖ 'vɪkə(r)/ ▶ **603** *n* párroco *m*

vicarage /'vɪkərɪdʒ/ *n* vicaría *f*, casa *f* del párroco

vicarious /vɪ'keriəs ‖ vɪ'keəriəs/ *adj* indirecto

vice /vaɪs/ *n* **1** [U C] (wickedness) vicio *m* **2** [C] (BrE) ⇒ VISE

vice- /'vaɪs/ *pref* vice-

vice: ~ **president** *n* vicepresidente, -ta *m,f*; ~ **versa** /'vaɪsi'vɜ:rsə, 'vaɪs'vɜ:rsə ‖ ˌvaɪsi'vɜ:sə, ˌvaɪs'vɜ:sə/ *adv* viceversa

vicinity /vɪ'sɪnəti/ *n* [U] (frml) inmediaciones *fpl*

vicious /'vɪʃəs/ *adj* **(a)** (savage, violent) ‹*dog*› fiero; ‹*criminal*› despiadado; ‹*attack*› feroz, salvaje; ‹*crime*› atroz **(b)** (malicious) ‹*rumor*› malicioso

vicious circle *n* círculo *m* vicioso

viciously /'vɪʃəsli/ *adv* brutalmente, ferozmente

victim /'vɪktəm ‖ 'vɪktɪm/ *n* víctima *f*; **the flood ~s** los damnificados por las inundaciones

victimize /'vɪktəmaɪz ‖ 'vɪktɪmaɪz/ *vt* victimizar*

victor /'vɪktər ‖ 'vɪktə(r)/ *n* vencedor, -dora *m,f*

Victorian /vɪk'tɔ:riən/ *adj* victoriano

victorious /vɪk'tɔ:riəs/ *adj* ‹*army*› victorioso; ‹*team*› vencedor

victory /'vɪktəri/ *n* [U C] (*pl* **-ries**) victoria *f*, triunfo *m*; (Mil) victoria *f*

video¹ /'vɪdiəʊ/ *n* (*pl* **videos**) [U C] video *m* or (Esp) vídeo *m*; (*before n*) ~ **camera** videocámara *f*; ~ **recorder** aparato *m* de video or (Esp) vídeo

video² *vt* **videoes, videoing, videoed** grabar

video: **~cassette** /'vɪdiəʊkə'set/ *n* videocasete *m*; (*before n*) **~cassette recorder** magnetoscopio *m*, video *m* or (Esp) vídeo *m*; ~ **game** *n* videojuego *m*

Vienna /vi'enə/ *n* Viena *f*

Vietnam /'vi:et'nɑ:m, -næm ‖ vjet'næm/ *n* Vietnam *m*

Vietnamese¹ /vi'etnə'mi:z ‖ ˌvɪetnə'mi:z/ *adj* vietnamita

Vietnamese² *n* (*pl* ~) **(a)** [C] (person) vietnamita *mf* **(b)** [U] (language) vietnamita *m*

view¹ /vju:/ *n* **1** [U] **(a)** (sight) vista *f*; **in full ~ of sb** a la vista de algn **(b)** (range of vision): **we had a good ~ of the stage** veíamos muy bien el escenario **2** [C] (scene, vista) vista *f* **3** [C] (opinion, attitude) opinión *f*, parecer *m* **4** (plan, intention): **with a ~ to -ING** con vistas A + INF **5** (*in phrases*) **in view of** en vista de; **on view**: **to be on ~ (to the public)** exponerse* (al público)

view² *vt* **(a)** ‹*sights/scene*› ver*, mirar **(b)** (inspect) ‹*property*› ver* **(c)** (regard) ver*, considerar

viewer /'vju:ər ‖ 'vju:ə(r)/ *n* **(a)** (person) telespectador, -dora *m,f*, televidente *mf* **(b)** (for slides) visionadora *f*

view: **~finder** /'vju:'faɪndər ‖ 'vjuˌfaɪndə(r)/ *n* visor *m*; **~point** *n* punto *m* de vista

vigil /'vɪdʒəl ‖ 'vɪdʒɪl/ *n* **(a)** (watch) (liter or journ) vela *f*; **to keep a ~ over sth** velar sobre algo **(b)** (Relig) vigilia *f*

vigilance /'vɪdʒələns ‖ 'vɪdʒɪləns/ *n* [U] vigilancia *f*

vigilant /'vɪdʒələnt ‖ 'vɪdʒɪlənt/ *adj* alerta, vigilante

vigilante /ˌvɪdʒə'lænti ‖ ˌvɪdʒɪ'lænti/ *n* vigilante, -ta *m,f*

vigor, (BrE) **vigour** /'vɪgər ‖ 'vɪgə(r)/ *n* [U] vigor *m*

vigorous /'vɪgərəs/ *adj* enérgico; ‹*growth*› vigoroso

vigorously /'vɪgərəsli/ *adv* enérgicamente; ‹*deny*› rotundamente

vigour *n* [U] (BrE) ⇒ VIGOR

Viking /'vaɪkɪŋ/ *n* vikingo, -ga *m,f*

vile /vaɪl/ *adj* **viler, vilest (a)** (despicable) (liter) vil (liter) **(b)** (colloq) ‹*taste/food*› vomitivo (fam), asqueroso; ‹*color/weather*› horrible

villa /'vɪlə/ *n* **(a)** (Hist) villa *f* **(b)** (holiday house) chalet *m*

village /'vɪlɪdʒ/ *n* (large) pueblo *m*; (small) aldea *f*

villager /'vɪlədʒər ‖ 'vɪlɪdʒə(r)/ *n* (of large village) vecino, -na *m,f* or habitante *mf* del pueblo; (of small village) aldeano, -na *m,f*

villain /'vɪlən/ *n* **(a)** (in fiction) villano, -na *m,f* **(b)** (criminal) (BrE sl) maleante *mf*

vinaigrette /'vɪnɪ'gret/ *n* [U C] vinagreta *f*

vindicate /'vɪndəkeɪt ‖ 'vɪndɪkeɪt/ *vt* (frml) (justify) ‹*action*› justificar*; ‹*assertion*› confirmar; ‹*right*› reivindicar*

vindictive /vɪn'dɪktɪv/ *adj* vengativo

vine /vaɪn/ *n* (*grape~*) (on ground) vid *f*; (climbing) parra *f*

vinegar /'vɪnɪgər ‖ 'vɪnɪgə(r)/ *n* [U] vinagre *m*

vineyard /'vɪnjərd, -jɑ:rd ‖ 'vɪnjəd, -jɑ:d/ *n* viñedo *m*, viña *f*

vintage¹ /'vɪntɪdʒ/ *n* **(a)** (wine, year) cosecha *f* **(b)** (harvest, season) vendimia *f*

vintage² *adj* (*before n, no comp*) **(a)** ‹*wine*› añejo **(b)** (outstanding) ‹*year/performance*› excelente

vintage car *n* (esp BrE) coche *m* antiguo (*fabricado entre 1919 y 1930*)

vinyl /ˈvaɪnl̩/ *n* [U C] vinilo *m*

viola /viˈəʊlə/ *n* (Mus) viola *f*

violate /ˈvaɪəleɪt/ *vt* **1** ‹*agreement/rights*› violar; ‹*ban*› desobedecer* **2** ‹*shrine/grave*› profanar

violation /ˌvaɪəˈleɪʃən/ *n* [U C] violación *f*

violence /ˈvaɪələns/ *n* [U] violencia *f*

violent /ˈvaɪələnt/ *adj* **(a)** ‹*person/behavior*› violento **(b)** (strong, forceful) ‹*storm/explosion*› violento, fuerte; **he has a ~ temper** tiene muy mal genio

violently /ˈvaɪələntli/ *adv* violentamente

violet /ˈvaɪələt/ *n* **(a)** [C] (Bot) violeta *f* **(b)** **▶ 515** [U] (color) violeta *m*; (*before n*) violeta *adj inv*

violin /ˌvaɪəˈlɪn/ *n* violín *m*

violinist /ˌvaɪəˈlɪnəst ‖ ˌvaɪəˈlɪnɪst/ *n* violinista *mf*

VIP *n* (colloq) (= **very important person**) VIP *mf*

viper /ˈvaɪpər ‖ ˈvaɪpə(r)/ *n* víbora *f*

virgin¹ /ˈvɜːrdʒən ‖ ˈvɜːdʒɪn/ *n* virgen *f*

virgin² *adj* ‹*forest*› virgen; ‹*snow*› intacto

Virgo /ˈvɜːrgəʊ ‖ ˈvɜːgəʊ/ *n* (*pl* **-gos**) **(a)** (sign) (*no art*) Virgo **(b)** [C] (person) Virgo *or* virgo *mf*

virile /ˈvɪrəl ‖ ˈvɪraɪl/ *adj* viril

virtual /ˈvɜːrtʃuəl ‖ ˈvɜːtjʊəl, ˈvɜːtʃʊəl/ *adj* (*before n*) **1** (near total): **traffic is at a ~ standstill** el tráfico está prácticamente paralizado **2** (Comput, Opt) virtual

virtually /ˈvɜːrtʃuəli ‖ ˈvɜːtjʊəli, ˈvɜːtʃʊəli/ *adv* prácticamente, casi

virtue /ˈvɜːrtʃuː ‖ ˈvɜːtjuː, ˈvɜːtʃuː/ *n* **(a)** [U C] (moral excellence) virtud *f* **(b)** [C] (advantage) ventaja *f* **(c)** **by virtue of** (*as prep*) en virtud de

virtuoso /ˌvɜːrtʃuˈəʊsəʊ ‖ ˌvɜːtjʊˈəʊsəʊ, ˌvɜːtʃʊˈəʊsəʊ/ *n* (*pl* **-sos** *or* **-si** /-si/) virtuoso, -sa *m,f*

virtuous /ˈvɜːrtʃuəs ‖ ˈvɜːtjʊəs, ˈvɜːtʃʊəs/ *adj* virtuoso

virulent /ˈvɪrələnt, ˈvɪrjə- ‖ ˈvɪrʊlənt, ˈvɪrjʊ-/ *adj* virulento

virus /ˈvaɪrəs ‖ ˈvaɪərəs/ *n* (*pl* **~es**) virus *m*

visa /ˈviːzə/ *n* (*pl* **-s**) visado *m*, visa *f* (AmL)

vis-à-vis /ˌviːzəˈviː ‖ ˌviːzɑːˈviː/ *prep* con respecto a, respecto de

viscose /ˈvɪskəʊs/ *n* [U] viscosilla *f*

viscount /ˈvaɪkaʊnt/ **▶ 603** *n* vizconde *m*

viscous /ˈvɪskəs/ *adj* viscoso

vise, (BrE) **vice** /vaɪs/ *n* torno *m* *or* tornillo *m* de banco

visibility /ˌvɪzəˈbɪləti/ *n* [U] visibilidad *f*

visible /ˈvɪzəbəl/ *adj* visible; ‹*sign/improvement*› evidente

visibly /ˈvɪzəbli/ *adv* visiblemente

vision /ˈvɪʒən/ *n* **1** **(a)** [U] (faculty of sight) visión *f*, vista *f* **(b)** (visibility) visibilidad *f* **2** [U] (imagination, foresight) visión *f* (de futuro) **3** [C] (dreamlike revelation) visión *f*

visionary /ˈvɪʒəneri ‖ ˈvɪʒənri/ *n* (*pl* **-ries**) visionario, -ria *m,f*

visit¹ /ˈvɪzət ‖ ˈvɪzɪt/ *n* visita *f*; **to pay a ~ to sb** hacerle* una visita a algn

visit² *vt* visitar; ‹*friend*› visitar ■ **~** *vi* hacer* una visita; (stay) estar* de visita

visitor /ˈvɪzətər ‖ ˈvɪzɪtə(r)/ *n* (to museum, town etc) visitante *mf*; (to person's home) visita *f*

visitor center *n* (AmE) centro *m* de informaciones

visor /ˈvaɪzər ‖ ˈvaɪzə(r)/ *n* visera *f*

vista /ˈvɪstə/ *n* vista *f*

visual /ˈvɪʒuəl/ *adj* visual; **~ display unit** pantalla *f*, monitor *m*

visualize /ˈvɪʒuəlaɪz/ *vt* **(a)** (picture mentally) imaginarse, visualizar* **(b)** (expect) prever*

vital /ˈvaɪtl̩/ *adj* **(a)** (essential) esencial, fundamental **(b)** ‹*factor/issue*› decisivo, de vital importancia **(c)** ‹*organ/function*› vital

vitality /vaɪˈtæləti/ *n* [U] vitalidad *f*

vitamin /ˈvaɪtəmən ‖ ˈvɪtəmɪn, ˈvaɪt-/ *n* vitamina *f*; (*before n*) **~ pill** *o* **tablet** vitamina *f*

vivacious /vəˈveɪʃəs ‖ vɪˈveɪʃəs/ *adj* vivaz

vivid /ˈvɪvəd ‖ ˈvɪvɪd/ *adj* **(a)** ‹*color*› vivo **(b)** ‹*account/dream*› vívido **(c)** ‹*imagination*› rico

vividly /ˈvɪvədli ‖ ˈvɪvɪdli/ *adv* **(a)** ‹*colored*› vistosamente **(b)** ‹*describe*› vívidamente, gráficamente

vivisection /ˌvɪvəˈsekʃən ‖ ˌvɪvɪˈsekʃən/ *n* [U C] vivisección *f*

vixen /ˈvɪksən/ *n* (Zool) zorra *f*, raposa *f*

viz /vɪz/ *adv* a saber

VJ-Day /ˈviːˈdʒeɪdeɪ/ *n*: *día de la victoria aliada sobre el Japón*

V-neck /ˈviːnek/, (BrE also) **V-necked** /ˈviːnekt/ *adj* de escote *or* cuello en pico, de escote en V

vocabulary /vəʊˈkæbjəleri ‖ vəʊˈkæbjʊləri/ *n* (*pl* **-ries**) vocabulario *m*

vocal /ˈvəʊkəl/ *adj* vocal

vocal cords *pl n* cuerdas *fpl* vocales

vocalist /ˈvəʊkələst ‖ ˈvəʊkəlɪst/ *n* cantante *mf*

vocation /vəʊˈkeɪʃən/ *n* vocación *f*

vodka /ˈvɑːdkə ‖ ˈvɒdkə/ *n* [U C] vodka *m*

vogue /vəʊg/ *n* [C U] moda *f*

voice¹ /vɔɪs/ *n* [C U] voz *f*

voice² *vt* expresar

void¹ /vɔɪd/ *n* vacío *m*

void² *adj* **1** (liter) (*pred*) **to be ~ OF sth** estar* desprovisto de algo **2** (Law) nulo, inválido

vol (*pl* **vols**) (= **volume**) vol., t.

volatile /ˈvɑːlətl̩ ‖ ˈvɒlətaɪl/ *adj* **(a)** (Chem) volátil **(b)** ‹*person/personality*› imprevisible **(c)** ‹*situation*› volátil

volcanic /vɑːlˈkænɪk /vɒlˈkænɪk/ *adj* volcánico

volcano /vɑːlˈkeɪnəʊ /vɒlˈkeɪnəʊ/ *n* (*pl* **-noes** *or* **-nos**) volcán *m*

volition /vəʊˈlɪʃən ‖ vəˈlɪʃən/ *n* [U] (fml) volición *f* (fml); **of one's own ~** por voluntad propia, (de) motu proprio

volley¹ /ˈvɑːli ‖ ˈvɒli/ *n* **1** (of shots) descarga *f* (cerrada) **2** (Sport) volea *f*

volley² *vt/i* volear

volleyball /ˈvɑːlibɔːl ‖ ˈvɒlibɔːl/ *n* [U] vóleibol *m*, balonvolea *m*

volt /vəʊlt/ *n* voltio *m*

voltage /ˈvəʊltɪdʒ/ *n* [C U] voltaje *m*

volume /ˈvɑːljuːm ‖ ˈvɒljuːm/ *n* **1** [U C] (Phys) (of a body) volumen *m*; (of container) capacidad *f* **2** [U] (amount) cantidad *f*, volumen *m*; (of business, trade) volumen *m* **3** [U] (of sound) volumen *m* **4** [C] (book) tomo *m*, volumen *m*

voluminous /vəˈluːmənəs ‖ vəˈluːmɪnəs/ *adj* **(a)** ‹*blouse/skirt*› amplísimo **(b)** ‹*correspondence*› voluminoso

voluntarily /ˌvɑːlənˈterəli ‖ ˈvɒləntrɪli/ *adv* voluntariamente, por voluntad propia

voluntary /ˈvɑːlənteri ‖ ˈvɒləntri/ *adj* **1** (unforced) voluntario; **~ redundancy** (BrE) baja *f* incentivada **2** (unpaid) ‹*work*› voluntario; ‹*organization*› de beneficencia

volunteer¹ /ˌvɑːlənˈtɪr ‖ ˌvɒlənˈtɪər/ *n* voluntario, -ria *m,f*

volunteer² *vt* ofrecer* ■ **~** *vi* ofrecerse*; **to ~ to** + INF ofrecerse* A + INF

voluptuous /vəˈlʌptʃuəs/ *adj* voluptuoso

vomit¹ /ˈvɑːmət ‖ ˈvɒmɪt/ *vi/t* vomitar

vomit² *n* [U] vómito *m*

voodoo /ˈvuːduː/ *n* vudú *m*

voracious /vɔːˈreɪʃəs ‖ vəˈreɪʃəs/ *adj* voraz

vote¹ /vəʊt/ *n* **1 (a)** [C] (ballot cast) voto *m* **(b)** [U] (right to vote) **the ~** el sufragio, el derecho de *or* al voto **2** [C] (act) votación *f*; **to take a ~ on sth** someter algo a votación

vote² *vi* votar; **to ~ FOR sb** votar POR *or* A algn; **to ~ ON sth** someter algo a votación; **to ~ FOR/AGAINST sth** votar A FAVOR DE/EN CONTRA DE algo ■ **~** *vt* **1 (a)** (support, choose) votar por, votar **(b)** (elect) elegir* por votación **2** (decide) **to ~ to** + INF votar POR + INF

● **vote in** [*v* + *o* + *adv*, *v* + *adv* + *o*] elegir* (*por votación*)

voter /ˈvəʊtər ‖ ˈvəʊtə(r)/ *n* votante *mf*

voting /ˈvəʊtɪŋ/ *n* [U] votación *f*

vouch /vaʊtʃ/ *vi* **to ~ FOR sb** responder POR algn

voucher /ˈvaʊtʃər ‖ ˈvaʊtʃə(r)/ *n* (cash substitute) vale *m*

vow¹ /vaʊ/ *n* voto *m*, promesa *f*

vow² *vt* jurar, hacer* voto de (frml)

vowel /ˈvaʊəl/ *n* vocal *f*

voyage /ˈvɔɪɪdʒ/ *n* viaje *m*; (oversea) travesía *f*

voyager /ˈvɔɪədʒər ‖ ˈvɔɪɪdʒə(r)/ *n* (liter) viajero, -ra *m,f*; (by sea) navegante *mf*

voyeur /vwɑːˈjɜːr, ˈvɔɪ- ‖ vwɑːˈjɜː(r), ˈvɔɪ-/ *n* voyeur *mf*

vs = **versus**

VT, Vt = **Vermont**

vulgar /ˈvʌlgər ‖ ˈvʌlgə(r)/ *adj* **(a)** (coarse) ‹*person/remark*› grosero, ordinario, vulgar **(b)** (tasteless) de mal gusto, ordinario

vulgarity /vʌlˈgærəti/ *n* [U] **(a)** (coarseness) ordinariez *f*, grosería *f*, vulgaridad *f* **(b)** (tastelessness) mal gusto *m*, chabacanería *f*

vulnerable /ˈvʌlnərəbəl/ *adj* vulnerable

vulture /ˈvʌltʃər ‖ ˈvʌltʃə(r)/ *n* buitre *m*; (*turkey* ~) gallinazo *m*, zopilote *m* (AmC, Méx)

vv = **verses**

W, w /ˈdʌbəljuː/ *n* W, w *f*

W (a) (Elec) (= **watt(s)**) W **(b)** (Geog) (= **west**) O

WA = **Washington**

wad /wɑːd ‖ wɒd/ *n* (roll, bundle — of bills, notes) fajo *m*; (— of papers) montón *m*, tambache *m* (Méx); (— tied together) lío *m*

waddle /ˈwɑːdḷ ‖ ˈwɒdḷ/ *vi* «*person*» caminar *or* andar* como un pato; «*duck*» caminar balanceándose

wade /weɪd/ *vi* caminar (*por el agua, barro etc*)

● **wade through** [*v* + *prep* + *o*] (colloq) leerse* (*algo difícil, largo, aburrido etc*)

wader /ˈweɪdər ‖ ˈweɪdə(r)/ *n* **(a)** (Zool) ave *f*‡ zancuda **(b) waders** *pl* (Clothing) botas *fpl* de pescador

wading pool /ˈweɪdɪŋ/ *n* (AmE) piscina *f or* (Méx) alberca *f* inflable (*para niños*)

wafer /ˈweɪfər ‖ ˈweɪfə(r)/ *n* **(a)** (Culin) galleta *f* de barquillo, oblea *f* **(b)** (Relig) hostia *f*

wafer-thin /ˈweɪfərˈθɪn ‖ ˌweɪfəˈθɪn/ *adj* finísimo

waffle¹ /ˈwɑːfəl ‖ ˈwɒfəl/ *n* **1** [C] (Culin) wafle *m* (AmL), gofre *m* (Esp) **2** [U] (nonsense) (BrE pej) palabrería *f*; (in essay, exam) paja *f* (fam)

waffle² *vi* (esp BrE) hablar sin decir nada; (in essay, exam) meter paja (fam), payar (RPl)

waft /wɑːft ‖ ˈwɒft/ *vi* (+ *adv compl*): **the smell of coffee that ~ed from the kitchen** el olor a café que venía de la cocina

wag /wæg/ **-gg-** *vt* ‹*tail*› menear ■ **~** *vi* «*tail*» menearse, moverse*

wage¹ /weɪdʒ/ *n* (rate of pay) sueldo *m*; **wages** (actual money) sueldo *m*, paga *f*

wage² *vt*: **to ~ war** hacer* la guerra

wager¹ /ˈweɪdʒər ‖ ˈweɪdʒə(r)/ *n* apuesta *f*

wager² *vt* apostar*

waggon *n* (BrE) ⇒ WAGON

wagon /ˈwægən/ *n* **1** (drawn by animals) carro *m*; (covered) carromato *m* **2 (a)** (delivery truck) (AmE) furgoneta *f or* camioneta *f* de reparto **(b)** (BrE Rail) vagón *m* de mercancías

waif /weɪf/ *n* (liter) *persona o animal sin hogar*

wail[1] /weɪl/ *vi* «*person*» llorar; «*siren/bagpipes*» gemir*; «*wind*» aullar*

wail[2] *n* gemido *m*

waist /weɪst/ *n* (of body) (waistline) cintura *f*; (of garment) talle *m*

waist: **~band** *n* pretina *f*, cinturilla *f*; **~coat** *n* (esp BrE) chaleco *m*; **~line** *n* (of garment) talle *m*; (of body) cintura *f*

wait[1] /weɪt/ *vi* **1** esperar; **we'll have to ~ and see** habrá que esperar a ver qué pasa; **I can't ~ to see his face** me muero de ganas de ver la cara que pone; **to ~ FOR sth/sb** esperar algo/a algn; **to ~ FOR sb/sth to + INF** esperar (A) QUE algn/algo (+ *subj*) **2** (serve) **to ~ ON sb** atender* a algn ■ **~** *vt* **1** (await) esperar; **you have to ~ your turn** tienes que esperar (a) que te toque **2** (serve): **to ~ table** (AmE) servir* a la mesa

• **wait up** [*v* + *adv*] (not go to bed) **to ~ up** (FOR **sb**) esperar (A algn) levantado

wait[2] *n* (*no pl*) espera *f*; ***to lie in ~ for sb/sth*** estar* al acecho de algn/algo

waiter /'weɪtər || 'weɪtə(r)/ *n* camarero *m*, mesero *m* (AmL), mozo *m* (Col, CS), mesonero *m* (Ven)

waiting 'weɪtɪŋ/: **~ list** /*n* lista *f* de espera; **~ room** *n* sala *f* de espera

waitress /'weɪtrəs || 'weɪtrɪs/ *n* camarera *f*, mesera *f* (AmL), moza *f* (Col, CS), mesonera *f* (Ven)

waive /weɪv/ *vt* (frml) **(a)** (not apply) ‹*rule*› no aplicar*; ‹*condition*› no exigir* **(b)** (renounce) ‹*right/privilege*› renunciar a

wake[1] /weɪk/ (*past* **woke**; *past p* **woken**) *vt* despertar*; *see also* WAKE UP 1 ■ **~** *vi* despertar*, despertarse*

• **wake up 1** [*v* + *o* + *adv*, *v* + *adv* + *o*] despertar* **2** [*v* + *adv*] (become awake) despertarse*; **~ up!** ¡despiértate!; (pay attention) ¡espabílate!, ¡despabílate!; **to ~ up TO sth** ‹*to danger/fact*› darse* cuenta DE algo

wake[2] *n* **1** (of ship) estela *f*; **the hurricane left a trail of destruction in its ~** el huracán dejó una estela de destrucción a su paso **2** (for dead person) velatorio *m*

Wales /weɪlz/ *n* (el país de) Gales

walk[1] /wɔːk/ *vi* **1** (go by foot) caminar, andar* (esp Esp); (in a leisurely way) pasear; **he ~ed down/up the steps** bajó/subió los peldaños; **to ~ in/out** entrar/salir*; **to ~ up to sb** acercarse* a algn **2** (not use bus, car, etc) ir* a pie ■ **~** *vt* **1** (go along) ‹*hills/path*› recorrer **2 (a)** (take for walk) ‹*dog*› pasear, sacar* a pasear **(b)** (accompany) acompañar

• **walk away** [*v* + *adv*] alejarse

• **walk into** [*v* + *prep* + *o*] **(a)** (enter) ‹*room/building*› entrar en, entrar a (AmL) **(b)** (fall into) ‹*trap*› caer* en **(c)** (collide with) darse* contra

• **walk off 1** [*v* + *adv*] (go away) irse*, marcharse (esp Esp) **2** [*v* + *o* + *adv*, *v* + *adv* + *o*]: **we went out to ~ off our lunch** salimos a dar un paseo para bajar la comida

• **walk out** [*v* + *adv*] (Lab Rel) abandonar el trabajo (*como media reivindicatoria*)

• **walk out on** [*v* + *adv* + *prep* + *o*] ‹*lover/family*› dejar, abandonar

• **walk over** [*v* + *prep* + *o*] (colloq): **don't let him ~ all over you** no te dejes pisotear (por él)

walk[2] *n* **1** (leisurely) paseo *m*; (long) caminata *f*; **to go for a ~** ir* a pasear *or* a dar un paseo, ir* a caminar (esp AmL); **it's five minutes'** *o* **a five-minute ~ from here** está a cinco minutos de aquí a pie **2** (path) (esp AmE) camino *m* **3** (gait) manera *f* de caminar *or* andar; *see also* WALK OF LIFE

walker /'wɔːkər || 'wɔːkə(r)/ *n* **(a)** (sb that walks): **to be a fast/slow ~** caminar *or* andar* rápido/despacio **(b)** (hiker) excursionista *mf*

walkie-talkie /'wɔːki'tɔːki/ *n* walkie-talkie *m*

walk-in /'wɔːkɪn/ *adj*: **~ closet** vestidor *m*

walking[1] /'wɔːkɪŋ/ *n* [U]: **I do a lot of ~** yo camino *or* ando mucho; (*before n*) ‹*tour*› a pie; **is it within ~ distance?** ¿se puede ir a pie?

walking[2] *adj*: **she's a ~ encyclopedia** (hum) es una enciclopedia ambulante (hum); **he's a ~ miracle** vive de milagro

walking stick *n* bastón *m*

Walkman® /'wɔːkmən/ *n* (*pl* **-mans** /-mənz/) walkman® *m*

walk: **~ of life** *n*: **people from all ~s of life** gente de todas las profesiones y condiciones sociales; **~-on** *n* (*before n*) **~-on part** (Theat) papel *m* de figurante; (Cin) papel *m* de extra; **~out** *n* (from talks, meeting) *retirada en señal de protesta*; (strike) *abandono del trabajo como medida reivindicatoria*; **~over** *n* (victory by default) walkover *m* (*victoria por la no comparecencia del contrincante*); (easy victory) (colloq) paseo *m* (fam); **~way** *n* (bridge) puente *m*, pasarela *f*; (passageway) pasillo *m*; (path) sendero *m*

wall /wɔːl/ *n* **1 (a)** (freestanding) muro *m*; (of castle, city) muralla *f* **(b)** (barrier) barrera *f*; **a ~ of fire** una barrera de fuego **2** (of building, room) pared *f*, muralla *f* (Chi); (*before n*) **~ chart** gráfico *m* mural; **~ painting** mural *m* **3** (of stomach, artery) pared *f*

• **wall off** [*v* + *o* + *adv*, *v* + *adv* + *o*] separar con un muro *or* una pared *or* una tapia

• **wall up** [*v* + *o* + *adv*, *v* + *adv* + *o*] ‹*doorway/window*› tapiar; ‹*person/body*› emparedar

walled /wɔːld/ *adj* ‹*city*› amurallado; ‹*garden*› tapiado

wallet /'wɑːlət || 'wɒlɪt/ *n* **(a)** (for money) cartera *f*, billetera *f* **(b)** (folder) carpeta *f*

wallflower /'wɔːlflaʊr || 'wɔːlflaʊə(r)/ *n* **1** (Bot) alhelí *m* **2** (person) (colloq): **she was always a ~** nunca la sacaban a bailar, siempre planchaba (Bol, CS fam), siempre comía pavo (Col fam)

wallop /'wɑːləp || 'wɒləp/ *vt* (colloq) darle* una paliza a

wallow /'wɑːləʊ || 'wɒləʊ/ *vi* **(a)** (bathe) «*animal*» revolcarse* **(b)** (delight): **to ~ in self-pity** regodearse en la autocompasión

wall: **~paper** *n* [U C] papel *m* pintado, tapiz *m* de empapelar (Méx, Ven); **W~ Street** *n* Wall Street (*centro financiero de los EEUU*); **~-to-~ carpet** /'wɔːltə'wɔːl/ *n* [U C] alfombra *f* de pared a pared, moqueta *f* (Esp), moquette *f* (RPl)

walnut /ˈwɔːlnʌt/ *n* **(a)** [C] (nut) nuez *f*, nuez *f* de Castilla (Méx) **(b)** [C] ~ **(tree)** nogal *m* **(c)** [U] (wood) nogal *m*

walrus /ˈwɔːlrəs/ *n* (*pl* **~es** *or* ~) morsa *f*

waltz[1] /wɔːls, wɔːlts/ *n* vals *m*

waltz[2] *vi* valsar, valsear

wan /wɑːn ‖ wɒn/ *adj* **(a)** (pallid) ‹*face/complexion*› pálido **(b)** ‹*smile*› lánguido

wand /wɑːnd ‖ wɒnd/ *n* (of sorcerer, conjuror) varita *f* mágica

wander[1] /ˈwɑːndər ‖ ˈwɒndə(r)/ *vi* **(a)** (+ *adv compl*) (walk — in a leisurely way) pasear; (— aimlessly) deambular, vagar* **(b)** (stray): **don't let the children ~ away from the car** no dejes que los niños se alejen del coche; **don't let your mind ~!** ¡no te distraigas!

wander[2] *n* (esp BrE) (*no pl*) vuelta *f*, paseo *m*

wanderer /ˈwɑːndərər ‖ ˈwɒndərə(r)/ *n* trotamundos *mf*

wanderings /ˈwɑːndərɪŋz ‖ ˈwɒndərɪŋz/ *pl n* correrías *fpl*

wanderlust /ˈwɑːndərlʌst ‖ ˈwɒndəlʌst/ *n* [U] ansias *fpl* de conocer mundo

wane[1] /weɪn/ *vi* **(a)** «*moon*» menguar* **(b)** «*interest/popularity*» decaer*, disminuir* **(c)** **waning** *pres p* ‹*moon*› menguante; ‹*interest/popularity/influence*› decreciente

wane[2] *n*: **to be on the ~** «*moon*» estar* menguando; «*popularity*» estar* decayendo *or* disminuyendo

wangle /ˈwæŋgəl/ *vt* (colloq) agenciarse (fam)

want[1] /wɔːnt ‖ wɒnt/ *vt* **1 (a)** (require, desire) querer*; **to ~ to** + INF querer* + INF; **to ~ sb/sth to** + INF querer* QUE algn/algo (+ *subj*) **(b)** «*police*» buscar*; Ⓢ **wanted** se busca **(c)** (as price for sth) pedir* **(d)** ‹*person*› (sexually) desear **2** (need) necesitar; **you ~ to see a doctor** tienes que ver a un médico ■ ~ *vi* (lack) (frml) (*usu with neg*): **you/they will ~ for nothing** no te/les faltará nada

want[2] *n* **1** [C U] (requirement, need) necesidad *f* **2** [U] (lack, absence) falta *f*, carencia *f* (frml); **for ~ of sth** a falta de algo; **for ~ of a better word** por así decirlo **3** [U] (destitution, penury) miseria *f*

wanted /ˈwɔːntəd ‖ ˈwɒntɪd/ *adj* ‹*criminal/terrorist*› buscado (por la policía); *see also* WANT[1] 1(b)

wanton /ˈwɔːntn̩ ‖ ˈwɒntən/ *adj* **(a)** (willful) sin sentido, gratuito **(b)** (licentious) licencioso

war /wɔːr ‖ wɔː(r)/ *n* [C U] guerra *f*; **to be at ~ with sb/sth** estar* en guerra con algn/algo; **the ~ on crime** la lucha contra la delincuencia; (*before n*) **~ memorial** monumento *m* a los caídos

warble /ˈwɔːrbəl ‖ ˈwɔːbəl/ *vi* trinar, gorjear

ward /wɔːrd ‖ wɔːd/ *n* **1** (in hospital) sala *f* **2** (person) pupilo, -la *m,f*

• **ward off** [*v* + *adv* + *o*] ‹*attack*› rechazar*; ‹*blow*› desviar*; ‹*danger*› conjurar; ‹*illness*› protegerse* contra

warden /ˈwɔːrdn̩ ‖ ˈwɔːdn̩/ *n* (of castle, museum) guardián, -diana *m,f*; (of hostel, home) encargado, -da *m,f*; (of university, college) rector, -tora *m,f*; (*church~*) coadjutor *m*; (*fire ~*) (AmE) encargado, -da *m,f* de la lucha contra incendios; (*game ~*) guardabosque(s) *mf*; (of prison) (AmE) director, -tora *m,f* (*de una cárcel*)

warder /ˈwɔːrdər ‖ ˈwɔːdə(r)/ *n* (BrE) celador, -dora *m,f* (*de una cárcel*)

wardrobe /ˈwɔːrdrəʊb ‖ ˈwɔːdrəʊb/ *n* **(a)** (clothes cupboard) armario *m*, ropero *m* (esp AmL) **(b)** (set of clothes) guardarropa *m*, vestuario *m*

warehouse /ˈwerhaʊs ‖ ˈweəhaʊs/ *n* depósito *m*, almacén *m*, bodega *f* (Chi, Col, Méx)

wares /werz ‖ weəz/ *pl n* mercancía(s) *f(pl)*, mercadería(s) *f(pl)* (AmS)

war: **~fare** *n* [U] guerra *f*; **~head** /ˈwɔːrhed ‖ ˈwɔːhed/ *n* cabeza *f*, ojiva *f*

warily /ˈwerəli ‖ ˈweərɪli/ *adv* con cautela, cautelosamente

warlike /ˈwɔːrlaɪk ‖ ˈwɔːlaɪk/ *adj* guerrero

warm[1] /wɔːrm ‖ wɔːm/ *adj* **-er, -est 1** ‹*water/day*› tibio, templado; ‹*climate/wind*› cálido; **the ~est room in the house** la habitación más caliente de la casa; **I'm lovely and ~ now** estoy muy calentito ahora; **~ clothes** ropa *f* de abrigo *or* (RPl, Ven tb) abrigada *or* (Andes, Méx tb) abrigadora; **to get ~** «*person*» entrar en calor, calentarse*; «*room*» calentarse* **2 (a)** (affectionate, cordial) ‹*person*› cariñoso; ‹*welcome*› caluroso **(b)** ‹*color/atmosphere*› cálido **3** (fresh) ‹*scent/trail*› reciente, fresco

warm[2] *vt* calentar* ■ ~ *vi* **(a)** (become hotter) calentarse* **(b)** (become affectionate) **to ~ TO** *o* **TOWARD sb**: **we soon ~ed to** *o* **toward her** pronto se ganó nuestra simpatía

• **warm over** [*v* + *o* + *adv*, *v* + *adv* + *o*] (AmE Culin) calentar*

• **warm up 1** [*v* + *adv*] **(a)** (become warmer) «*place/food*» calentarse*; «*person*» entrar en calor **(b)** «*engine/apparatus*» calentarse* **(c)** (become lively) «*party/match*» animarse **(d)** (for action) «*athlete*» hacer* ejercicios de calentamiento **2** [*v* + *o* + *adv*, *v* + *adv* + *o*] **(a)** (heat) ‹*food/place*› calentar* **(b)** ‹*engine/apparatus*› calentar* **(c)** (make lively) animar

warm: **~-blooded** /ˈwɔːrmˈblʌdəd ‖ ˌwɔːmˈblʌdɪd/ *adj* (Zool) de sangre caliente; **~-hearted** /ˈwɔːrmˈhɑːrtəd ‖ ˌwɔːmˈhɑːtɪd/ *adj* afectuoso

warmly /ˈwɔːrmli ‖ ˈwɔːmli/ *adv* ‹*congratulate/welcome*› calurosamente; ‹*smile*› afectuosamente

warmth /wɔːrmθ ‖ wɔːmθ/ *n* [U] **(a)** (heat) calor *m* **(b)** (of welcome) lo caluroso **(c)** (of color, atmosphere) calidez *f*

warm-up /ˈwɔːrmʌp ‖ ˈwɔːmʌp/ *n* (exercise) ejercicio *m* de calentamiento; (practice) (pre)calentamiento *m*

warn /wɔːrn ‖ wɔːn/ *vt* **(a)** (admonish) advertir*; **we had been ~ed not to go** nos habían advertido que no fuéramos **(b)** (inform, advise) avisar, advertir*; **we were ~ed against swimming in the river** nos advirtieron que era peligroso nadar en el río

warning /ˈwɔːrnɪŋ ‖ ˈwɔːnɪŋ/ *n* **(a)** [C U] (advice, threat) advertencia *f* **(b)** [U] (prior notice) aviso *m*; **they arrived without ~** llegaron sin avisar *or* sin previo aviso

warp /wɔːrp ‖ wɔːp/ *vt* ‹*wood/metal*› alabear

warped /wɔ:rpt ‖ wɔ:pt/ *adj* ‹*timber/metal*› alabeado; ‹*record*› combado; ‹*mind/sense of humor*› retorcido

warplane /ˈwɔ:rpleɪn ‖ ˈwɔ:pleɪn/ *n* avión *m* de combate

warrant¹ /ˈwɔ:rənt ‖ ˈwɒrənt/ *n* (written authorization) (Law) orden *f* judicial; (*search* ~) orden *f* de registro *or* (AmL tb) de allanamiento; **to have a ~ for sb's arrest** tener* una orden de arresto contra algn

warrant² *vt* **1** (justify) justificar* **2** (guarantee) (*often pass*) garantizar*

warranty /ˈwɔ:rənti ‖ ˈwɒrənti/ *n* [C U] (*pl* **-ties**) garantía *f*

warren /ˈwɔ:rən ‖ ˈwɒrən/ *n* (Zool) madriguera *f* (*de conejos*), conejera *f*

warring /ˈwɔ:rɪŋ/ *adj* (*before n*) ‹*countries/tribes*› en guerra; ‹*factions*› enfrentado

warrior /ˈwɔ:rjər ‖ ˈwɒriə(r)/ *n* guerrero, -ra *m,f*

Warsaw /ˈwɔ:rsɔ: ‖ ˈwɔ:sɔ:/ *n* Varsovia *f*

warship /ˈwɔ:rʃɪp ‖ ˈwɔ:ʃɪp/ *n* buque *m* de guerra

wart /wɔ:rt ‖ wɔ:t/ *n* verruga *f*

war: **~time** *n* [U]: **in ~time** en tiempo de guerra; **~torn** *adj* devastado por la guerra

wary /ˈweri ‖ ˈweəri/ *adj* **warier, wariest** cauteloso; **to be ~ OF sb/sth** no fiarse* DE algn/algo

was /wɑ:z, *weak form* wəz ‖ wɒz, *weak form* wəz/ *past of* BE

wash¹ /wɔ:ʃ ‖ wɒʃ/ *n* **1** [C] **(a)** (act): **to have a ~** lavarse; **I'll give the car a ~** voy a lavar el coche, voy a darle una lavada al coche (AmL) **(b)** (in washing machine) lavado *m*; **your shirt is in the ~** tu camisa está lavándose **2** [U] (left by boat, plane) estela *f*

wash² *vt* **1** (clean) ‹*shirt/car/fruit*› lavar; ‹*floor*› fregar*, lavar (esp AmL); **to ~ one's face/hair** lavarse la cara/la cabeza *or* el pelo; **to ~ the dishes** fregar* *or* lavar los platos **2** (carry away) (+ *adv compl*): **the body had been ~ed ashore by the tide** la corriente había arrastrado el cuerpo hasta la orilla; *see also* WASH AWAY, WASH UP ■ ~ *vi* **(a)** (clean oneself) lavarse **(b)** (do dishes) lavar, fregar* **(c)** (do laundry) «*washing machine/person*» lavar (la ropa), hacer* la colada (Esp)

• **wash away** [*v* + *o* + *adv, v* + *adv* + *o*] **(a)** (carry away) llevarse **(b)** (cleanse) ‹*dirt*› quitar (*lavando*)

• **wash down** [*v* + *o* + *adv, v* + *adv* + *o*] **(a)** (clean) ‹*paintwork/wall*› lavar **(b)** (accompany) (colloq): **a plate of pasta ~ed down with the local wine** un plato de pasta acompañado del vino de la región

• **wash out 1** [*v* + *o* + *adv, v* + *adv* + *o*] ‹*sink/cloth*› (clean) lavar; (rinse) enjuagar* **2** [*v* + *adv*] (disappear): **the stain will ~ out** la mancha saldrá *or* se quitará al lavarlo

• **wash up 1** [*v* + *adv*] **(a)** (wash oneself) (AmE) lavarse **(b)** (wash dishes) (BrE) lavar los platos, fregar* (los platos) **2** [*v* + *o* + *adv, v* + *adv* + *o*] **(a)** (deposit) (*usu pass*) **to be ~ed up** «*body/wreckage*» ser* traído por la corriente **(b)** ‹*dishes*› (BrE) lavar, fregar*

Wash = **Washington**

washable /ˈwɔ:ʃəbəl ‖ ˈwɒʃəbəl/ *adj* lavable

wash: **~basin** *n* (BrE) ⇨ ~BOWL; **~bowl** *n* (AmE) **(a)** (in modern bathroom) lavabo *m*, lavamanos *m*, lavatorio *m* (CS), pileta *f* (RPl) **(b)** (bowl) palangana *f*, jofaina *f*, lavatorio *m* (Chi, Per); **~cloth** *n* (AmE) toallita *f* (*para lavarse*), ≈ manopla *f*

washed-out /ˈwɔ:ʃtˈaʊt ‖ ˌwɒʃtˈaʊt/ *adj* (*pred* **washed out**) **(a)** ‹*fabric*› descolorido; ‹*color*› pálido, lavado (RPl fam) **(b)** (exhausted) rendido

washer /ˈwɔ:ʃər ‖ ˈwɒʃə(r)/ *n* **1** (Tech) (ring) arandela *f*; (— on faucet) arandela *f*, junta *f*, suela *f* universal, cuerito *m* (CS fam), empaque *m* (Col, Ven) **2** ⇨ WASHING MACHINE

washing /ˈwɔ:ʃɪŋ ‖ ˈwɒʃɪŋ/ *n* **(a)** [U] (laundry — dirty) ropa *f* para lavar; (— clean) ropa *f* lavada **(b)** [U C] (act) lavado *m*

washing: **~ line** *n* (BrE) cuerda *f* para tender la ropa; **~ machine** *n* máquina *f* de lavar, lavadora *f*, lavarropas *m* (RPl); **~ powder** *n* [U C] (esp BrE) jabón *m* en polvo, detergente *m*; **~-up** /ˈwɔ:ʃɪŋˈʌp ‖ ˌwɒʃɪŋˈʌp/ *n* [U] (BrE): **to do the ~-up** lavar los platos, fregar* (los platos); (*before n*) **~-up liquid** lavavajillas *m*

wash: **~out** *n* (failure) (colloq) desastre *m* (fam); **~room** *n* baño(s) *m*(*pl*), servicios *mpl* (esp Esp)

wasn't /ˈwɑ:znt ‖ ˈwɒznt/ = **was not**

wasp /wɑ:sp ‖ wɒsp/ *n* avispa *f*

WASP /wɑ:sp ‖ wɒsp/ *n* (esp AmE) (= **white Anglo-Saxon Protestant**) *persona de la clase privilegiada de los EEUU, blanca, anglosajona y protestante*

waspish /ˈwɑ:spɪʃ ‖ ˈwɒspɪʃ/ *adj* sardónico

wastage /ˈweɪstɪdʒ/ *n* [U]: **there is too much ~ of raw material** se desperdicia demasiada materia prima; **natural ~** (of workforce) bajas *fpl* vegetativas

waste¹ /weɪst/ *n* **1** [U] (of fuel, materials) desperdicio *m*; **a ~ of time** una pérdida de tiempo; **it's a ~ of money** es tirar el dinero; **to go to ~** «*talent*» desperdiciarse; «*food*» echarse a perder **2** [U] **(a)** (refuse) residuos *mpl* **(b)** (surplus matter) material *m* sobrante **3 wastes** (*pl*): **the deserted ~s of Antarctica** las desiertas inmensidades de la Antártica

waste² *vt* **1** ‹*talents/efforts*› desperdiciar; ‹*money/electricity*› despilfarrar; ‹*food*› tirar; ‹*time*› perder*; ‹*space*› desaprovechar **2 wasted** *past p* **(a)** (misused, futile) ‹*time/money*› perdido; ‹*opportunity/space*› desperdiciado; ‹*effort*› inútil **(b)** (shrunken) ‹*body*› debilitado; ‹*limb*› atrofiado

• **waste away** [*v* + *adv*] «*person/body*» consumirse; «*muscle*» atrofiarse

waste³ *adj* **1** ‹*ground*› (barren) yermo; (not cultivated) baldío; ***to lay ~ (to) sth*** arrasar algo **2** ‹*material/matter*› de desecho

waste: **~basket** *n* (esp AmE) ⇨ WASTE-PAPER BASKET; **~ disposal unit** *n* triturador *m or* trituradora *f* de desperdicios

wasteful /ˈweɪstfəl/ *adj* ‹*person*› despilfarrador; ‹*method*› poco económico

waste: **~land** *n* [C U] (*often pl*) (barren land) páramo *m*, tierra *f* yerma *or* baldía; (uncultivated land) erial *m*; **~ paper** *n* [U] papel *m* sobrante;

~-paper basket, **~-paper bin** /ˈweɪstˈpeɪpər ‖ˌweɪstˈpeɪpə(r)/ *n* papelera *f*, papelero *m* (CS); **~ pipe** *n* tubo *m* de desagüe

watch¹ /wɑːtʃ ‖ wɒtʃ/ *n* **1** [C] (timepiece) reloj *m* (*de pulsera/de bolsillo*); (*before n*) **~ band** *o* (BrE) **strap** correa *f* de reloj **2** [U] (observation) vigilancia *f*; **to keep ~** hacer* guardia **3 (a)** [C] (period of time) guardia *f* **(b)** [C] (individual) guardia *mf*; (group) guardia *f*

watch² *vt* **1** ‹*person/expression*› observar; ‹*movie/game*› mirar; **to ~ television** ver* televisión; **we ~ed the sun go down** miramos la puesta de sol **2 (a)** (keep under observation) ‹*suspect/house*› vigilar **(b)** (look after) ‹*luggage/children*› cuidar **(c)** (pay attention to) mirar (con atención) **3** (be careful of) ‹*diet/weight*› vigilar, tener* cuidado con; **~ *it!*** (colloq) ¡cuidado! ■ **~** *vi* (look on) mirar

• watch out [*v* + *adv*] **(a)** (be careful) tener* cuidado **(b)** (look carefully) estarse* atento; **~ out for spelling mistakes** estáte atento por si hay faltas de ortografía

• watch over [*v* + *prep* + *o*] ‹*patient/child*› cuidar (de); ‹*safety/interests*› velar por

watchdog /ˈwɑːtʃdɔːg ‖ ˈwɒtʃdɒg/ *n* (dog) perro *m* guardián; (group) organismo *m* de control

watchful /ˈwɑːtʃfəl ‖ ˈwɒtʃfəl/ *adj* vigilante

watch: **~maker** *n* relojero, -ra *m,f*; **~man** /ˈwɑːtʃmən ‖ ˈwɒtʃmən/ *n* (*pl* **-men** /mən/) vigilante *m*; **~tower** *n* atalaya *f*, torre *f* de vigilancia

water¹ /ˈwɔːtər ‖ ˈwɔːtə(r)/ *n* [U] **1** agua *f*‡; **to be/lie under ~** estar*/quedar inundado; **high/low ~** marea *f* alta/baja; **to pass ~** (frml & euph) orinar, hacer* aguas menores (euph); ***to hold* ~** tenerse* en pie; (*before n*) ‹*bird/plant*› acuático; **~ sports** deportes *mpl* acuáticos **2 waters** *pl* (of sea, river) aguas *fpl*

water² *vi*: **her eyes began to ~** empezaron a llorarle los ojos; **his mouth ~ed** se le hizo agua la boca (AmL), se le hizo la boca agua (Esp) ■ **~** *vt* ‹*plant/garden/land*› regar*; ‹*livestock*› dar* de beber a

• water down [*v* + *o* + *adv*, *v* + *adv* + *o*] ‹*liquid/mixture*› diluir*; ‹*wine/beer*› aguar

water: **~ bed** *n* cama *f* de agua; **~ bottle** *n* cantimplora *f*; **~color**, (BrE) **~colour** *n* [U C] acuarela *f*; **~cress** *n* [U] berro *m*; **~fall** *n* cascada *f*, salto *m* de agua; (large) catarata *f*; **~front** *n* (beside lake, river) *zona de una ciudad que bordea un lago o río*; (docks) (esp AmE) muelles *mpl*

watering can /ˈwɔːtərɪŋ/ *n* regadera *f*

water: **~ lily** *n* nenúfar *m*; **~logged** /ˈwɔːtər lɔːgd ‖ ˈwɔːtəlɒgd/ *adj* ‹*land/soil*› anegado, inundado; ‹*shoes*› empapado; **~mark** *n* filigrana *f*; **~melon** *n* [C U] sandía *f*; **~ mill** *n* molino *m* de agua; **~ parting** *n* (AmE) ⇒ WATERSHED (a)

waterproof¹ /ˈwɔːtərpruːf ‖ ˈwɔːtəpruːf/ *adj* ‹*fabric*› impermeable; ‹*mascara*› a prueba de agua; ‹*watch*› sumergible

waterproof² *n* (esp BrE) prenda *f* impermeable

waterproof³ *vt* impermeabilizar*

water: **~-resistant** *adj* impermeabilizado, hidrófugo; **~shed** *n* (Geog) **(a)** (divide) (línea *f*) divisoria *f* de aguas **(b)** (drainage basin) (AmE) cuenca *f*; **~-ski** *vi* **-skis, -skiing, -skied** hacer* esquí acuático; **~-skiing** *n* [U] esquí *m* acuático; **~ table** *n* nivel *m* freático; **~tight** *adj* ‹*seal/container*› hermético; ‹*boat*› estanco; ‹*argument*› irrebatible, sin fisuras; ‹*alibi*› a toda prueba; **~way** *n* (river) vía *f* fluvial; (canal) vía *f or* canal *m* navegable; **~ wheel** *n* (for driving machinery) rueda *f* hidráulica; (for raising water) noria *f*; **~ wings** *pl n* flotadores *mpl* (*que se colocan en los brazos*)

watery /ˈwɔːtəri/ *adj* **(a)** (of, like water) acuoso **(b)** ‹*beer/gravy*› aguado **(c)** ‹*eyes*› lloroso

watt /wɑːt ‖ wɒt/ *n* vatio *m*

wave¹ /weɪv/ *n* **1 (a)** (of water) ola *f* **(b)** (in hair) onda *f* **(c)** (Phys) onda *f* **2** (surge, movement) oleada *f* **3** (gesture): **she gave them a ~** les hizo adiós/los saludó con la mano

wave² *vt* **1 (a)** (shake, swing) ‹*handkerchief/flag*› agitar; **to ~ sth around** agitar algo; **she ~d goodbye to him** le hizo adiós con la mano **(b)** (direct) (+ *adv compl*): **the policeman ~d us on** el policía nos hizo señas para *or* de que siguiéramos adelante **2** (curl) ‹*hair*› marcar*, ondular ■ **~** *vi* **1** (signal): **he ~d when he saw us** nos saludó con la mano al vernos; **to ~** AT *o* TO **sb** (to say goodbye) hacerle* adiós A algn con la mano; (in greeting) saludar a algn con la mano **2** (sway, flutter) «*corn/trees*» agitarse; «*flag*» ondear

• wave aside [*v* + *o* + *adv*, *v* + *adv* + *o*] **(a)** (with hand): **he ~d me aside** me hizo señas para que me hiciera a un lado **(b)** ‹*arguments/attempts*› rechazar*

wave: **~band** *n* banda *f* de frecuencia; **~length** *n* longitud *f* de onda

waver /ˈweɪvər ‖ ˈweɪvə(r)/ *vi* **1** (falter) «*person*» flaquear; «*faith*» tambalearse **2** (be indecisive) titubear

wavy /ˈweɪvi/ *adj* **wavier, waviest** ondulado

wax¹ /wæks/ *n* [U] cera *f*; (*ear~*) cera *f* (de los oídos), cerumen *m*; (*sealing ~*) lacre *m*

wax² *vt* **(a)** (treat with wax) ‹*floor/table/skis*› encerar **(b)** (to remove hair) depilar con cera ■ **~** *vi* «*moon*» crecer*; **his popularity ~ed and waned** su popularidad sufrió muchos altibajos

waxworks /ˈwækswɜːrks ‖ ˈwækswɜːks/ *n* (*pl* **~works**) (+ *sing or pl vb*) museo *m* de cera

way¹ /weɪ/ *n* **I 1** [C] **(a)** (route) camino *m*; **the ~ back** el camino de vuelta; **the ~ in/out** la entrada/salida; **it's difficult to find one's ~ around this town** es difícil orientarse en esta ciudad; **can you find your ~ there by yourself?** ¿sabes ir solo?; **I can drop the package off on my ~** de paso puedo dejar el paquete; **which ~ did you come?** ¿por dónde viniste?; **which ~ did he go?** ¿por dónde fue?; (following sb) ¿por dónde se fue?; **could you tell me the ~ to the city center?** ¿me podría decir por dónde se va al centro (de la ciudad)?; **on my ~ to work** de camino al trabajo; **the doctor is on her ~** la doctora ya va para allí/viene para aquí; **I'll tell you on the ~** te lo cuento por el camino; **I don't know the ~ up/down** no sé por dónde se sube/se baja; **to lead the ~** ir* delante; **to lose one's ~** perderse*; **there is no ~ around it** no hay otra solución; ***to go out of***

one's **~** (make a detour) desviarse* del camino; (make special effort): **they went out of their ~ to be helpful** se desvivieron por ayudar **(b)** (road, path) camino *m*, senda *f* **2** [C U] (passage, space): **to be/get in the ~** estorbar; **to stand in the ~: they stood in our ~** nos impidieron el paso; **I couldn't see it, she was standing in my ~** no podía verlo, ella me tapaba (la vista); **I won't stand in your ~** no seré yo quien te lo impida; **(get) out of the ~!** ¡hazte a un lado!; **to move sth out of the ~** quitar algo de en medio; **to keep out of sb's ~** rehuir* a algn **3** [C] (direction): **it's that ~** es en esa dirección, es por ahí; **this ~!** ¡por aquí!; **we didn't know which ~ to go** no sabíamos por dónde ir; **this ~ and that** de un lado a otro; **we're both going the same ~** vamos para el mismo lado; **look the other ~!** ¡mira para otro lado!; **whichever ~ you look at it, it's a disaster** es un desastre, lo mires por donde lo mires; **the other ~ around** al revés; **which ~ up should it be?** ¿cuál es la parte de arriba?; **to split sth three ~s** dividir algo en tres partes; **every which ~** (AmE) para todos lados; ***to go sb's ~***: **are you going my ~?** ¿vas en mi misma dirección?; **the decision went our ~** se decidió en nuestro favor; ***~ to go!*** (AmE colloq) ¡así se hace! **4** (distance) (*no pl*): **there's only a short ~ to go now** ya falta poco para llegar; **it's a long ~ from here to Rio** Río queda muy lejos de aquí; **he's come a long ~** ha venido de muy lejos; **we've come a long ~ since those days** hemos evolucionado mucho desde entonces; **a little goes a long ~** un poco cunde *or* (AmL tb) rinde mucho; **we had to walk all the ~ up** tuvimos que subir a pie hasta arriba

II 1 [C] (method, means) forma *f*, manera *f*, modo *m*; **there's no ~ of crossing the border without a passport** es imposible cruzar la frontera sin pasaporte; **it doesn't matter to me one ~ or the other** me da igual una cosa u otra; **all right, we'll do it your ~** muy bien, lo haremos a tu manera; **to do sth the hard/easy ~** hacer* algo de manera difícil/fácil; ***to have it both ~s*** quererlo* todo, querer* la chancha y los cinco reales *or* los veinte (RPl fam); ***you can't have it both ~s*** tienes que elegir entre una cosa u otra **2** [C] (manner) manera *f*, modo *m*, forma *f*; **in a subtle ~** de manera *or* modo *or* forma sutil; **he's in a bad ~** está muy mal; **that's the ~ it goes** así son las cosas, así es la vida; **it looks that ~** así *or* eso parece; **this ~ it's better for everyone** así es mejor para todos; **the ~ I see it** tal y como yo lo veo; ***to have a ~ with*** ...: **to have a ~ with children/animals** saber* cómo tratar a los niños/tener* mano con los animales; **to have a ~ with words** tener* mucha facilidad de palabra **3** [C] **(a)** (custom, characteristic): **the ~s of our people** las costumbres de nuestro pueblo; **he has a ~ of making people feel at ease** sabe hacer que la gente se sienta cómoda; ***to be set in one's ~s*** estar* muy acostumbrado a hacer las cosas de cierta manera **(b)** (wish, will): **to get/have one's (own) ~** salirse* con la suya (*or* mía *etc*) **4** [C] (feature, respect) sentido *m*, aspecto *m*; **in a ~, it's like losing an old friend** de alguna manera *or* en cierta forma es como perder a un viejo amigo; **our product is in no ~ inferior to theirs** nuestro producto no es de ninguna manera inferior al suyo

III (*in phrases*) **1 by the way** (*indep*) a propósito, por cierto **2 by way of** (*as prep*) **(a)** (via) vía, pasando por **(b)** (to serve as) a modo *or* manera de **3 in the way of** (as regards) (*as prep*): **don't expect too much in the ~ of help** en cuanto a ayuda, no esperes mucho **4 no way** (colloq): **no ~ is he going to do it** de ninguna manera lo va a hacer (fam); **no ~!** ¡ni hablar! (fam) **5 to give way (a)** (break, collapse) «*ice/rope/cable*» romperse*; «*floor*» hundirse **(b)** (succumb, give in) **to give ~ TO sth** ‹*to threats/blackmail*› ceder A *or* ANTE algo **(c)** (BrE Transp) **to give ~ (TO sb/sth)** ceder el paso (A algn/algo) **(d)** (be replaced, superseded by) **to give ~ TO sth** dejar *or* dar* paso A algo **6 under way**: **to get under ~** ponerse* en marcha; **an investigation is under ~** se está llevando a cabo una investigación

way² *adv* (colloq): **~ back in February** allá por febrero; **~ behind** muy por detrás; **they were ~ out in their calculations** se equivocaron en mucho en los cálculos; **~ past midnight** mucho después de la medianoche; **~ and away** (*as intensifier*) (AmE) con mucho, lejos (AmL fam)

way: **~lay** /ˈweɪˈleɪ/ *vt* (*past & past p* **~laid**) abordar; **~-out** /ˈweɪˈaʊt/ *adj* (*pred* **~ out**) (colloq) ultramoderno, estrambótico (fam); **~s and means** *pl n* **~s and means** (OF -ING) métodos *mpl* (DE + INF)

we /wiː, *weak form* wi/ *pron*

> **■ Note** Although *nosotros* and *nosotras* are given as translations of *we*, in practice they are used only for emphasis: *we went to the theater* fuimos al teatro; ***we*** did it nosotros *or* nosotras lo hicimos.

nosotros, -tras; **~ English** nosotros los ingleses

weak /wiːk/ *adj* **-er, -est 1 (a)** ‹*person/muscles/economy*› débil; ‹*structure*› poco sólido, endeble; ‹*handshake*› flojo; **to have a ~ heart** sufrir del corazón; **to grow ~** debilitarse **(b)** (ineffectual) ‹*character/leader*› débil **2 (a)** (not competent) ‹*student/performance*› flojo **(b)** (not convincing) ‹*argument/excuse*› poco convincente **3** (diluted) ‹*coffee/tea*› poco cargado; ‹*beer*› suave; ‹*solution*› diluido

weaken /ˈwiːkən/ *vt* debilitar ■ **~** *vi* «*person/animal*» (physically) debilitarse; «*resolve*» flaquear; «*power*» debilitarse; (relent) ceder

weakling /ˈwiːklɪŋ/ *n* alfeñique *m*

weakly /ˈwiːkli/ *adv* ‹*say*› con voz débil; **he struggled ~ and then gave in** se rindió sin apenas oponer resistencia

weakness /ˈwiːknəs ‖ ˈwiːknɪs/ *n* **1** [U] **(a)** (of body, defenses) debilidad *f*; (of structure, material) falta *f* de solidez, endeblez *f*; (of argument) pobreza *f* **(b)** (ineffectualness) falta *f* de carácter **2** [C] **(a)** (weak point — in structure, policy) punto *m* débil; (— in character) flaqueza *f*, punto *m* débil **(b)** (liking) debilidad *f*; **to have a ~ for sth** tener* debilidad por algo

weak-willed /ˈwiːkˈwɪld/ *adj* ‹*person*› de poca (fuerza de) voluntad; **to be ~** tener* poca fuerza de voluntad

weal /wi:l/ *n* verdugón *m* (*de un golpe dado con una cuerda, correa etc*)

wealth /welθ/ *n* [U] **1** riqueza *f* **2** (large quantity): **a ~ of sth** abundancia *f* de algo

wealthy /'welθi/ *adj* **-thier, -thiest** ‹*person/family*› adinerado, rico; ‹*nation/area*› rico

wean /wi:n/ *vt* ‹*baby/young*› destetar; **to ~ sb** OFF **sth**: **we ~ed him off drugs** conseguimos que dejara las drogas, conseguimos desengancharle de las drogas (Esp)

weapon /'wepən/ *n* arma *f*‡

weaponry /'wepənri/ *n* [U] armamento *m*

wear¹ /wer ‖ weə(r)/ *n* [U] **1 (a)** (use): **I've had a lot of ~ out of these shoes** les he dado mucho uso a estos zapatos; **carpets that stand hard ~** alfombras que resisten el uso constante **(b)** (damage) desgaste *m*; **~ and tear** uso *m* *or* desgaste natural **2 (a)** (wearing of clothes): **clothes for evening ~** ropa para la noche **(b)** (clothing) ropa *f*; **children's ~** ropa de niños

wear² (*past* **wore**; *past p* **worn**) *vt* **1 (a)** (at specific moment) ‹*clothes/jewelry/watch/makeup*› llevar; ‹*glasses*› llevar (puesto), usar; ‹*green/black*› vestir* de; **what perfume are you ~ing?** ¿qué perfume llevas? **(b)** (usually) ‹*clothes*› usar, ponerse*, ‹*glasses*› llevar, usar; ‹*makeup/perfume/earrings*› usar; **he ~s size 44 shoes** calza (el) 44; **she ~s her hair in a ponytail** se peina con cola de caballo **2** (through use): **the step had been worn smooth** el peldaño se había alisado con el uso; **she's worn holes in the soles** se le han agujereado las suelas ■ **~** *vi* **1** (through use) «*collar/carpet/brakes*» gastarse; ***to ~ thin*** (lit: through use) «*cloth/metal*» gastarse; «*joke*» perder* la gracia **2** (last) (+ *adv compl*) durar; **to ~ well** «*cloth/clothes*» durar mucho; «*person*» conservarse bien

• **wear away 1** [*v* + *o* + *adv*, *v* + *adv* + *o*] (erode) ‹*rock*› desgastar; ‹*pattern/inscription*› borrar **2** [*v* + *adv*] (become eroded) «*rock*» desgastarse; «*inscription*» borrarse

• **wear down 1** [*v* + *o* + *adv*, *v* + *adv* + *o*] **(a)** (by friction) ‹*heel/pencil*› gastar **(b)** (weaken) ‹*resistance*› menoscabar; ‹*person*› agotar **2** [*v* + *adv*] «*heel/tread*» gastarse

• **wear off** [*v* + *adv*] **(a)** (be removed) «*paint*» quitarse **(b)** (disappear) «*distress/numbness*» pasarse

• **wear on** [*v* + *adv*] «*winter/years*» pasar (*lentamente*); «*meeting/drought*» continuar*

• **wear out 1** [*v* + *o* + *adv*, *v* + *adv* + *o*] **(a)** (through use) ‹*shoes/carpet/batteries*› gastar **(b)** (exhaust) ‹*person*› agotar **2** [*v* + *adv*] (through use) «*shoes/towel/batteries*» gastarse

• **wear through** [*v* + *adv*] (get hole in) «*soles/cloth*» agujerearse

wearily /'wɪrəli ‖ 'wɪərɪli/ *adv* ‹*walk/move*› cansinamente; **he sighed ~** suspiró cansado

weary¹ /'wɪri ‖ 'wɪəri/ *adj* **-rier, -riest** ‹*person/legs*› cansado; ‹*sigh*› de cansancio; **to be ~** OF **sth/**-ING estar* cansado *or* harto DE algo/+ INF

weary² *vt* **-ries, -rying, -ried (a)** (tire) cansar **(b)** (annoy) hartar, cansar

weasel /'wi:zəl/ *n* (Zool) comadreja *f*

weather¹ /'weðər ‖ 'weðə(r)/ ▶ 920 *n* [U] tiempo *m*; **you can't go out in this ~** no puedes salir con este tiempo; (*before n*) ‹*map/chart*› meteorológico; **~ forecast** pronóstico *m* del tiempo

weather² *vt* **(a)** (wear) ‹*rocks*› erosionar; ‹*surface*› desgastar; ‹*skin/face*› curtir **(b)** ‹*wood*› secar* ■ **~** *vi* «*rock*» erosionarse; «*surface*» desgastarse

weather: **~beaten** *adj* ‹*face/sailor*› curtido; ‹*walls/rocks*› azotado por los elementos; **~cock** *n* veleta *f*

weathered /'weðərd ‖ 'weðəd/ *adj* ‹*rocks/brick/stone*› erosionado (*por la acción de los elementos*); ‹*wood*› curado

weather: **~man** /'weðərmæn ‖ 'weðəmæn/ *n* (*pl* **-men** /-men/) *hombre que transmite el pronóstico del tiempo por radio o televisión*; **~proof** *adj* impermeable; **~ vane** /veɪn/ *n* veleta *f*

weave /wi:v/ *vt* (*past* **wove**; *past p* **woven**) **(a)** ‹*cloth/mat*› tejer (*en telar*); ‹*basket/web*› tejer; ‹*story/plot*› tejer **(b)** (thread together) ‹*threads/branches/straw*› entretejer ■ **~** *vi* **1** (*past* **wove**; *past p* **woven**) (make cloth, baskets) tejer **2** (*past* **wove** *or* **weaved**; *past p* **woven** *or* **weaved**) «*road*» serpentear; «*person*» zigzaguear

weaver /'wi:vər ‖ 'wi:və(r)/ *n* tejedor, -dora *m,f*

weaving /'wi:vɪŋ/ *n* [U] (of cloth) tejido *m*

web /web/ *n* (*spider's ~*) telaraña *f*; **a ~ of intrigue** una red de intriga

webbed /webd/ *adj* palmeado

wed /wed/ *vt* (*past & past p* **wedded** *or* **wed**) (marry) (dated *or* journ) ‹*man/woman*› casarse con

we'd /wi:d/ **(a)** = **we had (b)** = **we would**

wedding /'wedɪŋ/ *n* **(a)** (ceremony) boda *f*, casamiento *m*, matrimonio *m* (AmS exc RPl); **to have a church/civil** (AmE) *o* (BrE) **registry-office ~** casarse por la iglesia *or* (RPl) por iglesia/por lo civil *or* (Per, RPl, Ven) por civil *or* (Chi, Méx) por el civil; (*before n*) **~ dress** vestido *m* *or* traje *m* de novia; **~ ring** alianza *f*, anillo *m* de boda, argolla *f* (de matrimonio) (Chi) **(b)** (anniversary): **silver/golden ~** bodas *fpl* de plata/oro

wedge¹ /wedʒ/ *n* **(a)** (for securing) cuña *f* **(b)** (for splitting) cuña *f* **(c)** (shape): **a ~ of cake** un trozo grande de pastel

wedge² *vt* **(a)** (secure): **to ~ a door open** ponerle* una cuña a una puerta para que no se cierre **(b)** (squeeze) meter (*a presión*)

Wednesday /'wenzdeɪ, -di/ ▶ 540 *n* miércoles *m*; *see also* MONDAY

wee¹ /wi:/ *adj* (small) (esp Scot, IrE) pequeño, chico (esp AmL); **in the ~ small hours** *o* (AmE also) **the ~ hours** a las altas horas de la madrugada

wee² *n* (BrE colloq) (*no pl*): **to have** *o* **do a ~** hacer* pis *or* pipí (fam), hacer* del uno (Méx, Per fam)

weed¹ /wi:d/ *n* **(a)** [C] (Hort) hierbajo *m*, mala hierba *f*, yuyo *m* (RPl), maleza *f* (AmL) **(b)** [U] (aquatic growth) algas *fpl*

weed² *vt* deshierbar, desherbar*, desmalezar* (AmL), sacar* los yuyos de (RPl)

• **weed out** [*v* + *o* + *adv*, *v* + *adv* + *o*] **(a)** (Hort) quitar **(b)** ‹*errors/items*› eliminar; ‹*applicants*› eliminar

The Weather

what's the weather like?	=	¿qué tiempo hace? *or* ¿cómo está el tiempo?

Where English uses the verb to be + adjective, *Spanish uses*:

◆ hacer + noun:

it's hot	=	hace calor
it's cold	=	hace frío
it's cool	=	hace fresco/fresquito
it's sunny	=	hace sol
it's windy	=	hace viento

◆ haber + noun:

it's foggy	=	hay niebla
it's misty	=	hay neblina

◆ estar + adjective:

it's cloudy	=	está nublado
it's overcast	=	está nublado *or* cubierto
it's a hot/rainy/ cloudy day	=	el día está caluroso/ lluvioso/nublado

◆ *or combinations of these*:

it's snowy	=	hay nieve *or* está nevado
it's humid	=	está muy húmedo *or* hay mucha humedad
it's muggy	=	está bochornoso *or* hace bochorno

When English uses weather *or the name of a season with* be + adjective, *Spanish does the same using* ser *or* estar:

the weather was excellent	=	el tiempo estaba excelente
summer is very hot in that region	=	el verano es muy caluroso en esa región

Note the following translation, however:

what's the weather like in Chile? (*i.e. what kind of weather do you get in Chile?*)	=	*¿cómo es el clima en Chile?*

Spanish uses impersonal verbs in a similar way to English:

it's raining	=	está lloviendo (*or*, sometimes, llueve)
it rained all day	=	llovió todo el día
it's drizzling	=	está lloviznando
it's snowing	=	está nevando
it's hailing	=	está granizando
it's spitting (*colloq*)	=	está chispeando (*colloq*)

Manifestations of the weather expressed in English with there is/are *are usually expressed in the same way in Spanish*:

there was a storm	=	hubo una tormenta
there will be scattered showers	=	habrá chubascos aislados

Note the way pronouns me/te/le *etc are used in Spanish in the following examples, where English uses the verb* have:

we had wonderful/ terrible weather	=	nos hizo un tiempo estupendo/asqueroso
we had rain all week	=	nos llovió toda la semana

weedkiller /'wi:d,kılər ‖ 'wi:d,kılə(r)/ *n* herbicida *m*

weedy /'wi:di/ *adj* **-dier, -diest (a)** (lanky) (AmE) larguirucho (fam) **(b)** (feeble, puny) (BrE colloq) enclenque

week /wi:k/ *n* **(a)** (7 days) semana *f*; **once a ∼** una vez por semana *or* a la semana; **we get paid by the ∼** nos pagan semanalmente; **(on) Tuesday ∼** *o* (BrE also) **a ∼ on Tuesday** el martes que viene no, el otro; **she arrived a ∼ (ago) yesterday** ayer hizo una semana que llegó **(b)** (working days): **I never go out in** *o* **during the ∼** nunca salgo los días de semana

week: **∼day** *n* día *m* de semana; **∼end** /'wi:kend ‖ wi:k'end/ *n* fin *m* de semana

weekly[1] /'wi:kli/ *adj* semanal

weekly[2] *adv* semanalmente; **we get paid ∼** nos pagan por semana

weekly[3] *n* (*pl* **weeklies**) semanario *m*

weep /wi:p/ *vi* (*past & past p* **wept**) **1** (cry) llorar **2** (exude liquid) «*wound/eye*» supurar

weeping willow /'wi:pıŋ/ *n* sauce *m* llorón

weepy /'wi:pi/ *adj* **-pier, -piest** (colloq) **1 (a)** ‹*person*›: **to feel ∼** tener* ganas de llorar **(b)** ‹*film/play*› que hace llorar, cebollento (Chi fam) **2** ‹*eye*› lloroso

weigh /weı/ *vt* **1** ‹*person/load/food*› pesar; **to ∼ oneself** pesarse **2** (consider) ‹*factors/arguments/evidence*› sopesar; **to ∼ one's words** medir* sus (*or* mis *etc*) palabras ■ **∼** *vi* (measure in weight) «*person/load/food*» pesar; **how much** *o* **what do you ∼?** ¿cuánto pésas?; **your inexperience will ∼ against you** tu falta de experiencia será un factor en tu contra

● **weigh down** [*v + o + adv, v + adv + o*] **(a)** (impose weight on): **the bag was ∼ing me down** la bolsa me pesaba mucho; **trees ∼ed down with fruit** árboles cargados de fruta **(b)** (depress) abrumar **(c)** ⇒ WEIGHT DOWN

● **weigh on** [*v + prep + o*]: **it still ∼ed heavily on her conscience** todavía sentía un gran cargo de conciencia; **it's been ∼ing heavily on my mind** me ha estado preocupando

● **weigh out** [*v + o + adv, v + adv + o*] pesar

● **weigh up** [*v + o + adv, v + adv + o*] ‹*situation*›

considerar; ‹*pros and cons*› sopesar; ‹*person*› evaluar*

weight[1] /weɪt/ *n* **1** [U C] (mass, heaviness) peso *m*; **the bag is 5kg in ~** la bolsa pesa 5kg; **you mustn't lift heavy ~s** no debe levantar cosas pesadas; **that has taken a ~ off my mind** eso me ha sacado un peso de encima; ***to pull one's ~***: **John isn't pulling his ~** John no trabaja como debería **2** [U] (importance, value) peso *m* **3 (a)** ▶322⌋ (unit) peso *m*; **~s and measures** pesos y medidas **(b)** (for scales, clocks) pesa *f* **(c)** (Sport) pesa *f*; (*before n*) **~ training** entrenamiento *m* con pesas

weight[2] *vt* (make heavier) darle* peso a; ‹*fishing net*› lastrar

● **weight down** [*v + o + adv, v + adv + o*] **(a)** ‹*tarpaulin/papers*› sujetar con algo pesado **(b)** ‹*body*› (to make it sink) ponerle* un lastre a

weightless /ˈweɪtləs ‖ ˈweɪtlɪs/ *adj* ingrávido

weight: **~lifter** /ˈweɪtˌlɪftər ‖ ˈweɪtˌlɪftə(r)/ *n* levantador, -dora *m,f* de pesas, pesista *mf* (Andes), halterófilo, -la *m,f*; **~lifting** /ˈweɪtˌlɪftɪŋ/ *n* [U] levantamiento *m* de pesas, halterofilia *f*

weighty /ˈweɪti/ *adj* **-tier, -tiest** ‹*argument*› de peso; ‹*matter*› importante

weir /wɪr ‖ wɪə(r)/ *n* presa *f*

weird /wɪrd ‖ wɪəd/ *adj* **-er, -est (a)** (strange) (colloq) raro, extraño **(b)** (unearthly) ‹*apparition/figure*› misterioso

welcome[1] /ˈwelkəm/ *interj* bienvenido

welcome[2] *adj* **(a)** (gladly received) ‹*guest*› bienvenido; ‹*change/news*› grato **(b)** (freely permitted): **you're ~ to use the phone** el teléfono está a tu disposición; **you're ~ to these books** puedes llevarte estos libros, si quieres **(c)** (responding to thanks): **you're ~!** ¡de nada!, ¡no hay de qué!

welcome[3] *vt* (greet) darle* la bienvenida a; (receive): **we would ~ any advice you can give us** le agradeceríamos cualquier consejo que pudiera darnos

welcome[4] *n* bienvenida *f*

welcoming /ˈwelkəmɪŋ/ *adj* **(a)** ‹*ceremony/delegation*› de bienvenida **(b)** ‹*smile/hug*› acogedor; **the little bar looked very ~** el barcito parecía muy acogedor

weld /weld/ *vt/i* soldar*

welfare /ˈwelfer ‖ ˈwelfeə(r)/ *n* [U] **1** (well-being) bienestar *m* **2** (Soc Adm) **(a)** (assistance) asistencia *f* social **(b)** (payment) (AmE) prestaciones *fpl* sociales

welfare state *n* estado *m* de bienestar

well[1] /wel/ *adv* (*comp* **better**; *superl* **best**) **1** (to high standard, satisfactorily) ‹*sing/write/work*› bien; **he's doing very ~** le van muy bien las cosas; **~ done!** ¡así se hace!, ¡muy bien!; **to go ~** «*performance/operation*» salir* bien **2** (thoroughly) ‹*wash/dry/know*› bien; **it was ~ worth the effort** realmente valió la pena; **~ and truly** (colloq): **he was ~ and truly drunk** estaba pero bien borracho **3 (a)** (considerably) (*no comp*) bastante; **until ~ into the next century** hasta bien entrado el siglo que viene **(b)** (with justification): **you may ~ ask!** ¡muy buena pregunta!; **she couldn't very ~ deny it** ¿cómo iba a negarlo? **4** (advantageously) ‹*marry*› bien; **to do ~ to + INF** hacer* bien en + INF, deber + INF; **to do ~ out of sth** salir* bien parado de algo **5** (*in phrases*) **(a) as well** (in addition) también **(b) as well as** (in addition to) además de **(c) may/might as well**: **now you've told him, you may** *o* **might as ~ give it to him!** ahora que se lo has dicho dáselo ¿total?

well[2] *adj* (*comp* **better**; *superl* **best**) **1** (healthy) bien; **how are you? — I'm very ~, thank you** ¿cómo estás? — muy bien, gracias; **get ~ soon!** ¡que te mejores! **2** (pleasing, satisfactory) bien; **it's all very ~ for him to talk, but** ... él podrá decir todo lo que quiera pero ... **3 as well**: **it would be as ~ to keep this quiet** mejor no decir nada de esto; **it's just as ~ I've got some money with me** menos mal que llevo dinero encima

well[3] *interj* **1 (a)** (introducing/continuing topic, sentence) bueno, bien **(b)** (expressing hesitation): **do you like it? — well** ... ¿te gusta? — pues *or* (esp AmL) este ... **2 (a)** (expressing surprise): **~, ~, ~! look who's here!** ¡vaya, vaya! ¡mira quién está aquí! **(b)** (expressing indignation) bueno **(c)** (dismissively) ¡bah! **(d)** (expressing resignation) bueno **3** (expressing expectation): **~? who won?** bueno ¿y quién ganó?

well[4] *n* (for water, oil, gas) pozo *m*

● **well up** [*v + adv*] «*water*» brotar, manar; **tears ~ed up in his eyes** los ojos se le llenaron de lágrimas

well- /wel/ *pref* bien

we'll /wiːl/ = **we will**

well: **~-balanced** /ˈwelˈbælənst/ *adj* (*pred* **~ balanced**) ‹*person*› equilibrado; ‹*diet*› equilibrado, balanceado; **~-behaved** /ˈwelbɪˈheɪvd/ *adj* (*pred* **~ behaved**) ‹*child*› que se porta bien, bueno; ‹*dog*› obediente; **~-being** /ˈwelˈbiːɪŋ/ *n* [U] bienestar *m*; **~-disposed** /ˈweldɪˈspəʊzd/ *adj* (*pred* **~ disposed**) dispuesto a colaborar (*or* ayudar *etc*); **~-done** /ˈwelˈdʌn/ *adj* (*pred* **~ done**) (Culin) bien cocido *or* (Esp) muy hecho; **~-dressed** /ˈwelˈdrest/ *adj* (*pred* **~ dressed**) bien vestido; **~-educated** /ˈwelˈedʒəkeɪtəd ‖ ˌwelˈedjʊkeɪtɪd/ *adj* (*pred* **~ educated**) culto; **~-founded** /ˈwelˈfaʊndəd ‖ ˌwelˈfaʊndɪd/ *adj* (*pred* **~ founded**) bien fundado; **~-groomed** /ˈwel ˈgruːmd/ *adj* (*pred* **~ groomed**) ‹*person*› bien arreglado; ‹*hair*› bien peinado; ‹*horse/garden*› bien cuidado; **~-informed** /ˈwelɪnˈfɔːrmd ‖ ˌwelɪn ˈfɔːmd/ *adj* bien informado

wellington (boot) /ˈwelɪŋtən/ *n* **(a)** (short boot) (AmE) botín *m*, bota *f* (*corta*) **(b)** (gumboot) (BrE) bota *f* de goma *or* de agua *or* de lluvia, catiusca *f* (Esp)

well: **~-kept** /ˈwelˈkept/ *adj* (*before n* **~ kept**) **(a)** ‹*house/lawns*› bien cuidado **(b)** ‹*secret*› bien guardado; **~-known** /ˈwelˈnəʊn/ *adj* (*pred* **~ known**) ‹*person*› conocido, famoso; **it is ~ known that** ... es bien sabido que ...; **~-mannered** /ˈwelˈmænərd ‖ ˌwelˈmænəd/ *adj* (*pred* **~ mannered**) de buenos modales, educado; **~-meaning** /ˈwelˈmiːnɪŋ/ *adj* (*pred* **~ meaning**) ‹*person*› bienintencionado; **he's ~ meaning, but** ... lo hace con la mejor intención, pero ...; **~-off** /ˈwelˈɔːf ‖ ˌwelˈɒf/ *adj* (*pred* **~ off**) adinerado;

~-read /'wel'red/ *adj* (*pred* **~ read**) culto; **~-to-do** /'weltə'du:/ *adj* ‹*businessman/family*› adinerado; **~-wisher** /'wel,wɪʃər ‖ 'wel,wɪʃə(r)/ *n*: **she received lots of cards from ~-wishers** recibió muchas tarjetas en que le deseaban una pronta recuperación (*or* mucha felicidad *etc*); **~-worn** /'wel'wɔ:rn ‖ ,wel'wɔ:n/ *adj* (*pred* **~ worn**) ‹*coat/carpet*› muy gastado; ‹*phrase*› muy trillado

Welsh¹ /welʃ/ *adj* galés

Welsh² *n* **(a)** [U] (language) galés *m* **(b)** (people) (+ *pl vb*) **the ~** los galeses

Welshman /'welʃmən/ *n* (*pl* **-men** /-mən/) galés *m*

welt /welt/ *n* (weal) verdugón *m*

went /went/ *past of* GO¹

wept /wept/ *past & past p of* WEEP

were /wɜ:r ‖ wɜ:(r), *weak form* wər ‖ wə(r)/ **(a)** *2nd pers sing past ind of* BE **(b)** *1st, 2nd & 3rd pers pl past ind of* BE **(c)** *subjunctive of* BE

we're /wɪr ‖ wɪə(r)/ = **we are**

weren't /wɜ:rnt ‖ wɜ:nt/ = **were not**

west¹ /west/ *n* [U] **1** (point of the compass, direction) oeste *m*; **the ~, the W~** (region) el oeste **2 the West** (the Occident) (el) Occidente *m*; (Pol, Hist) el Oeste

west² *adj* (*before n*) oeste *adj inv*, occidental; ‹*wind*› del oeste

west³ *adv* al oeste

westbound /'westbaʊnd/ *adj* que va (*or* iba *etc*) hacia el *or* en dirección oeste

westerly /'westərli ‖ 'westəli/ *adj* ‹*wind*› del oeste; **in a ~ direction** hacia el oeste, en dirección oeste

western¹ /'westərn ‖ 'westən/ *adj* **(a)** (Geog) oeste *adj inv*, del oeste, occidental; **the ~ areas of the country** las zonas oeste *or* occidentales del país **(b)** (occidental) (Geog, Pol) occidental

western² *n* western *m*, película *f* (*or* novela *f etc*) del Oeste *or* de vaqueros

Westerner, **westerner** /'westərnər ‖ 'westənə(r)/ *n* occidental *mf*

westernized /'westərnaɪzd ‖ 'westənaɪzd/ *adj* occidentalizado

west: **W~ Indian** *adj* antillano; (in UK) afroantillano; **W~ Indies** /'ɪndiz/ *pl n* **the W~ Indies** las Antillas

westward¹ /'westwərd ‖ 'westwəd/ *adj* (*before n*): **in a ~ direction** hacia el oeste, en dirección oeste

westward², (BrE) **westwards** /-z/ *adv* hacia el oeste

wet¹ /wet/ *adj* **-tt- (a)** (moist) ‹*floor/grass/clothes*› mojado; (damp) húmedo; ‹*concrete/plaster*› blando; Ⓢ **wet paint** pintura fresca *or* (Esp tb) ojo, pinta; **to get ~** mojarse **(b)** **▶ 920** (rainy) ‹*weather/day*› lluvioso

wet² *vt* (*pres p* **wetting**; *past & past p* **wet** *or* **wetted**) mojar; (dampen) humedecer*; **to ~ the bed** mojar la cama; **to ~ oneself** orinarse, hacerse* pipí (encima) (fam)

wet: **~ blanket** *n* (colloq) aguafiestas *mf* (fam); **~ suit** *n* traje *m* de neoprene *or* de neopreno

we've /wi:v/ = **we have**

whack¹ /hwæk ‖ wæk/ *n* (blow) golpe *m*; (sound) ¡zas!

whack² *vt* golpear, aporrear; ‹*person*› pegarle* a

whale /hweɪl ‖ weɪl/ *n* **1** (*pl* **~s** *or* **~**) (Zool) ballena *f* **2** (colloq) (*as intensifier*): **we had a ~ of a time** lo pasamos bomba *or* genial (fam)

wharf /hwɔ:rf ‖ wɔ:f/ *n* (*pl* **wharves** /hwɔ:rvz/) muelle *m*, embarcadero *m*

what¹ /hwɑ:t ‖ wɒt/ *pron* **1** (in questions) qué; **~'s that?** ¿qué es eso?; **~'s the problem?** ¿cuál es el problema?; **~'s 'I don't understand' in Russian?** ¿cómo se dice 'no entiendo' en ruso? **2** (*in phrases*) **or what?** (colloq) ¿o qué?; **so what?** ¿y qué?; **what about**: **but ~ about the children?** y los niños ¿qué?; **you know Julie's boyfriend? — yes, ~ about him?** ¿conoces al novio de Julie? — sí ¿por qué?; **what ... for**: **~'s this button for?** ¿para qué es este botón?; **~ are you complaining for?** ¿por qué te quejas?; **what if**: **~ if she finds out?** ¿y si se entera?; **what's-her/-his-name** (colloq): **go and ask ~'s-her-name next door** ve y pregúntale a la de al lado ¿cómo se llama? **3 (a)** (in indirect speech) qué; **she knows ~ to do** ella sabe qué hacer; **I still don't know ~'s ~ in the office** aún no sé cómo funcionan las cosas en la oficina; **(I'll) tell you ~, ...** mira, ... **(b)** (relative use) lo que; **they did ~ they could** hicieron lo que pudieron

what² *adj* **1 (a)** (in questions) qué; **~ color are the walls?** ¿de qué color son las paredes? **(b)** (in indirect speech) qué; **she didn't know ~ color to choose** no sabía qué color elegir **2** (in exclamations) qué; **~ a surprise!** ¡qué sorpresa!; **~ a lot of people!** ¡cuánta gente!

whatever¹ /hwɑ:t'evər ‖ wɒt'evə(r)/ *pron* **1** (in questions, exclamations) qué; **~ is she doing?** ¿qué (es lo que) está haciendo? **2 (a)** (no matter what): **~ you do, don't laugh!** hagas lo que hagas ¡no te vayas a reír!; **he talked about percentiles, ~ they are** habló de percentiles, que no tengo ni idea de qué son **(b)** (all that): **they let him do ~ he likes** lo dejan hacer todo lo que quiere; **~ you say** lo que tú digas, como quieras

whatever² *adj* **(a)** (no matter what): **don't give up, ~ doubts you may have** no renuncies, tengas las dudas que tengas; **all people, of ~ race or creed** todos, cualquiera sea su raza o credo **(b)** (any): **~ changes are necessary** los cambios que sean necesarios

whatever³ *adv* (*as intensifier*): **none/nothing ~** ninguno/nada en absoluto

wheat /hwi:t ‖ wi:t/ *n* [U] trigo *m*

wheatgerm /'hwi:tdʒɜ:rm ‖ 'wi:tdʒɜ:m/ *n* [U] germen *m* de trigo

wheedle /'hwi:dl̩ ‖ 'wi:dl̩/ *vt* **to ~ sth** OUT OF **sb** sonsacarle* algo a algn

wheel¹ /hwi:l ‖ wi:l/ *n* **1 (a)** (of vehicle) rueda *f* **(b)** (*potter's* **~**) torno *m* **2** (*steering* **~** *— of car*) volante *m*; (— of ship) timón *m*; **at the ~** (of car) al volante; (of ship) al timón

wheel² *vt* ‹*bicycle/wheelchair*› empujar; ‹*person*› llevar (*en silla de ruedas etc*) ■ **~** *vi* **(a)** (turn suddenly) **~ (around** *o* (BrE) **round)** «*person*» girar sobre sus (*or* mis *etc*) talones **(b)** (circle) dar* vueltas; «*birds*» revolotear

wheel: **~barrow** *n* carretilla *f*; **~chair** *n* silla *f* de ruedas; **~ clamp** *n* cepo *m*

wheeling and dealing /ˈhwiːlɪŋənˈdiːlɪŋ ‖ ˌwiːlɪŋənˈdiːlɪŋ/ *n* (colloq) tejemanejes *mpl* (fam)

wheeze /hwiːz ‖ wiːz/ *vi* «*person*» respirar con dificultad (*produciendo un sonido sibilante como los asmáticos*); «*machine*» resollar*

when¹ /hwen ‖ wen/ *adv*

■ **Note** When used as a conjunction in sentences expressing the future, *when* is translated by *cuando + subjunctive*: *we'll speak to Carol when she gets back* hablaremos con Carol cuando vuelva.

1 (in questions, indirect questions) cuándo; **that was ~ I realized that** … fue entonces cuando *or* (esp AmL tb) que me di cuenta de que …; **say ~!** di cuándo **2** (as relative): **the year ~ we got married** el año en que nos casamos; **in December, ~ we were on holiday** en diciembre, cuando estábamos de vacaciones

when² *conj* **1 (a)** (temporal sense) cuando; **I'll ask him ~ I see him** se lo preguntaré cuando lo vea **(b)** (if) si, cuando **2 (a)** (since, considering that) si, cuando **(b)** (although) cuando; **he said he was 18 ~ in fact he's only 15** dijo que tenía 18 años cuando en realidad sólo tiene 15

when³ *pron* cuándo; **~ do you have to be in London by?** ¿para cuándo tienes que estar en Londres?

whenever /hwenˈevər ‖ wenˈevə(r)/ *conj* **(a)** (every time that) siempre que; **~ I hear that song I think of Spain** siempre que *or* cada vez que escucho esa canción, me acuerdo de España **(b)** (at whatever time): **we'll go ~ you're ready** saldremos cuando estés listo

where¹ /hwer ‖weə(r)/ *adv* dónde; (indicating direction) adónde, dónde; **~'s Lewes?** ¿dónde está Lewes?; **~ are you taking me?** ¿(a)dónde me llevan?; **~ are you from?** ¿de dónde eres?

where² *conj* **(a)** donde; (indicating direction) adonde, donde **(b)** (in cases where) cuando; **~ appropriate** cuando *or* allí donde sea apropiado

whereabouts¹ /ˈhwerəbaʊts ‖ ˌweərəˈbaʊts/ *adv*: **~ in Austria do you live?** ¿en qué parte de Austria vives?

whereabouts² /ˈhwerəbaʊts ‖ ˈweərəbaʊts/ *n* (+ *sing or pl vb*) paradero *m*

whereas /hwerˈæz ‖ ˌweərˈæz/ *conj* mientras que

whereby /hwerˈbaɪ ‖ weəˈbaɪ/ *pron* (frml): **a system ~ payments are made automatically** un sistema por *or* según el cual los pagos se efectúan automáticamente

wherever¹ /hwerˈevər ‖ weərˈevə(r)/ *adv* **(a)** (in questions) dónde **(b)** (no matter where) (colloq) en cualquier parte *or* lado

wherever² *conj*: **you can use your card ~ you see this sign** puede usar su tarjeta (en cualquier establecimiento) donde vea este símbolo; **~ he goes, I'll go too** vaya donde vaya, yo iré también; **you can sit ~ you like** puedes sentarte donde quieras

wherewithal /ˈhwerwɪðɔːl ‖ ˈweəwɪðɔːl/ *n* **the ~** los medios; **we don't have the ~ to do this** no tenemos los recursos para hacer esto

whet /hwet ‖ wet/ *vt* **-tt-** ‹*interest/curiosity*› estimular; **the walk ~ted our appetites** la caminata nos abrió el apetito

whether /ˈhweðər ‖ ˈweðə(r)/ *conj*: **tell me ~ you need us or not** *o* **~ or not you need us** dime si nos necesitas o no; **I doubt ~ he knew** dudo que lo supiera; **~ you like it or not** te guste o no te guste

whey /hweɪ ‖ weɪ/ *n* [U] suero *m* (*de la leche*)

which¹ /hwɪtʃ ‖ wɪtʃ/ *pron* **1 (a)** (*in questions*) (*sing*) cuál; (*pl*) cuáles **(b)** (in indirect use) cuál; **I can never remember ~ is ~** nunca recuerdo cuál es cuál **2** (as relative): **the parcel ~ arrived this morning** el paquete que llegó esta mañana; **the newspaper in ~ the article appeared** el diario en el que *or* en el cual apareció el artículo

which² *adj* **1** (in questions) (*sing*) qué, cuál; (*pl*) qué, cuáles **2** (as relative): **we arrived at two, by ~ time they had gone** llegamos a las dos y para entonces ya se habían ido; **in ~ case** en cuyo caso

whichever¹ /hwɪtʃˈevər ‖ wɪtʃˈevə(r)/ *pron* **(a)** (no matter which): **there are several options, but ~ you choose** … hay varias opciones, pero elijas la que elijas *or* cualquiera que elijas … **(b)** (the one, ones that): **buy ~ is cheaper** compra el que sea más barato

whichever² *adj* **(a)** (no matter which): **~ party is in power** sea cual sea *or* cualquiera que sea el partido que esté en el poder **(b)** (any that): **you can write about ~ subject you know best** puedes escribir sobre el tema que mejor conozcas, sea cual sea *or* fuere

while¹ /hwaɪl ‖ waɪl/ *conj* **1** (in time) mientras; **they don't drink ~ on duty** no beben cuando están de guardia **2** (though) aunque **3** (whereas) mientras que

• **while away** [*v + adv + o, v + o + adv*]: **we had a game of chess to ~ away the time** jugamos una partida de ajedrez para pasar el rato

while² *n*: **wait a ~** (a few days, weeks) espera un tiempo; (a few minutes, hours) espera un rato; (a very short period) espera un ratito *or* un momentito; **it's been a good ~ since we had any rain** hace bastante (tiempo) que no llueve; **he was here a little ~ ago** hace un ratito estaba aquí; **(every) once in a ~** de vez en cuando

whilst /hwaɪlst ‖ waɪlst/ *conj* (BrE) ⇒ WHILE¹

whim /hwɪm ‖ wɪm/ *n* [C U] capricho *m*

whimper¹ /ˈhwɪmpər ‖ ˈwɪmpə(r)/ *vi* gimotear

whimper² *n* quejido *m*

whimsical /ˈhwɪmzɪkəl ‖ ˈwɪmzɪkəl/ *adj* ‹*person*› caprichoso; ‹*mood*› voluble

whine¹ /hwaɪn ‖ waɪn/ *vi* **(a)** «*dog*» aullar*; «*person*» gemir*; «*child*» lloriquear **(b)** (complain) (pej) quejarse

whine² *n* (of dog) aullido *m*; (of person) quejido *m*; (of engine) chirrido *m*; (of bullet) silbido *m*

whinny /ˈhwɪni ‖ ˈwɪni/ *vi* (*3rd pers sing pres* **whinnies**; *pres p* **whinnying**; *past & past p* **whinnied**) «*horse*» relinchar

whip¹ /hwɪp ‖ wɪp/ *n* (in horse riding) fusta *f*, fuete *m* (AmL exc CS); (of tamer) látigo *m*; (for punishment) azote *m*

whip² -pp- *vt* **1 (a)** (lash) ‹*horse*› pegarle* a (*con la fusta*), fustigar*; ‹*person*› azotar; ‹*child*› darle* una paliza a **(b)** (beat) ‹*egg whites*› batir; ‹*cream*› batir *or* (Esp) montar; **~ped cream** crema *f* batida *or* (Esp) nata *f* montada **2** (take quickly) (+ *adv compl*): **she ~ped out her notebook** sacó rápidamente la libreta

• whip up [*v + o + adv, v + adv + o*] **1 (a)** (arouse) ‹*trouble/unrest*› provocar*; ‹*hatred*› fomentar; ‹*support*› conseguir* **(b)** (incite) ‹*crowd*› incitar **(c)** «*wind*» ‹*sea/waves*› agitar; ‹*dust*› levantar **2 (a)** (beat, whisk) ‹*egg whites*› batir; ‹*cream*› batir, montar (Esp) **(b)** (prepare hurriedly) (colloq) ‹*meal*› improvisar

whip: **~lash injury** *n* (Med) traumatismo *m* cervical; **~-round** *n* (BrE colloq) colecta *f*, vaca *f* (AmL fam)

whir, (BrE) **whirr** /hwɜːr ‖ wɜː(r)/ *vi* **-rr-** «*machine/propellers*» runrunear, zumbar

whirl¹ /hwɜːrl ‖ wɜːl/ *vi* **(a)** (spin) «*person*» girar, dar* vueltas; «*leaves/dust*» arremolinarse **(b)** (move fast) (+ *adv compl*): **he ~ed around** se dio media vuelta rápidamente ■ ~ *vt* (+ *adv compl*) hacer* girar

whirl² *n* (turn) giro *m*, vuelta *f*; (of dust) remolino *m*; **my head was in a ~** la cabeza me daba vueltas

whirl: **~pool** *n* vorágine *f*, remolino *m*; **~wind** *n* torbellino *m*; (*before n*) **a ~wind romance** un idilio arrollador

whirr /hwɜːr ‖ wɜː(r)/ *vi* (BrE) ⇒ WHIR

whisk¹ /hwɪsk ‖ wɪsk/ *vt* **1** (Culin) batir **2** (convey quickly) (+ *adv compl*): **she was ~ed off to a meeting** se la llevaron a una reunión a toda prisa; **he ~ed away the plates** retiró los platos rápidamente

whisk² *n* (Culin) batidor *m*

whisker /ˈhwɪskər ‖ ˈwɪskə(r)/ *n* **1 (a)** [C] (single hair) pelo *m* (*de la barba*) **(b)** (narrow margin) (*no pl*) pelo *m* **2 whiskers** *pl* (of animal) bigotes *mpl*

whiskey /ˈhwɪski ‖ ˈwɪski/ *n* [U C] (*pl* **-keys**) whisky *m*, güisqui *m* (*esp americano o irlandés*)

whisky /ˈhwɪski ‖ ˈwɪski/ *n* [U C] (*pl* **-kies**) whisky *m*, güisqui *m* (*esp escocés*)

whisper¹ /ˈhwɪspər ‖ ˈwɪspə(r)/ *vi* **(a)** «*person*» cuchichear **(b)** (liter) «*wind/leaves*» susurrar (liter) ■ ~ *vt* ‹*remark/words*› susurrar

whisper² *n* **(a)** (soft voice) susurro *m*; **yes, he said in a ~** —sí —susurró **(b)** (rumor) rumor *m*

whistle¹ /ˈhwɪsəl ‖ ˈwɪsəl/ *vi* «*person/kettle/wind*» silbar; (loudly) chiflar; «*referee*» pitar; «*train*» pitar ■ ~ *vt* ‹*tune*› silbar

whistle² *n* **(a)** (instrument) silbato *m*, pito *m* **(b)** (sound — made with mouth) silbido *m*; (loud) chiflido *m*; (— made by referee's whistle) silbato *m*, pitido *m*; (— of kettle, wind, bullet) silbido *m*

white¹ /hwaɪt ‖ waɪt/ ▶**515** *adj* **-er, -est (a)** ‹*paint/cat/bread/wine/chocolate*› blanco; ‹*coffee/tea*› con leche; **she had a ~ wedding** se casó de blanco; **he went ~** se puso blanco **(b)** (Caucasian) blanco

white² ▶**515** *n* **1** [U] (color) blanco *m* **2** [C] *also* **White** (person) blanco, -ca *m,f* **3** [C] **(a)** (of egg) clara *f* **(b)** (of eye) blanco *m*

white: **~bait** *n* [U] morralla *f*, chanquetes *mpl* (Esp), cornalitos *mpl* (Arg), majuga *f* (Ur); **~-collar** /ˈwaɪtˈkɑːlər ‖ ˌwaɪtˈkɒlə(r)/ *adj* ‹*worker/job*› no manual; (clerical) de oficina; **~ elephant** *n* (building, project) elefante *m* blanco; (object) *objeto superfluo*; **~ gasoline**, **~ gas** *n* (AmE) gasolina *f or* (Andes) bencina *f or* (RPl) nafta *f* sin plomo; **~-hot** /ˈhwaɪtˈhɑːt ‖ ˌwaɪtˈhɒt/ *adj* ‹*metal*› al rojo blanco; **W~ House** *n* **the W~ House** la Casa Blanca; **~ lie** *n* mentira *f* piadosa

whiten /ˈhwaɪtn̩ ‖ ˈwaɪtn̩/ *vt* blanquear

white: **~ sauce** *n* [U] salsa *f* blanca *or* bechamel; **~ spirit** *n* [U] (BrE) espíritu *m* de petróleo (*usado como sustituto del aguarrás*)

whitewash¹ /ˈhwaɪtwɔːʃ ‖ ˈwaɪtwɒʃ/ *n* **1** [U] (Const) cal *f* **2** [C] (defeat) (colloq) paliza *f* (fam)

whitewash² *vt* ‹*wall/building*› blanquear, encalar, enjalbegar*

whiting /ˈhwaɪtɪŋ ‖ ˈwaɪtɪŋ/ *n* (*pl* **~s** *or* **~**) pescadilla *f*

Whitsun /ˈhwɪtsən ‖ ˈwɪtsən/ *n* (esp BrE) Pentecostés *f*

whittle /ˈhwɪtl̩ ‖ ˈwɪtl̩/ *vt* tallar

• whittle away [*v + o + adv, v + adv + o*] ‹*funds/resources*› ir* mermando; ‹*influence*› ir* reduciendo; ‹*rights*› ir* menoscabando

• whittle down [*v + o + adv, v + adv + o*] ‹*expenses*› recortar; ‹*applicants*› reducir* el número de

whiz, **whizz** /hwɪz ‖ wɪz/ *vi* **-zz-** (+ *adv compl*): **to ~ by** «*bullet/arrow/car*» pasar zumbando; **I ~zed through my homework** hice los deberes zumbando *or* a toda velocidad

whiz kid, **whizz kid** *n* (colloq) lince *m* (fam)

who /huː/ *pron* **1 (a)** (in questions) (*sing*) quién; (*pl*) quiénes; **~ are you writing to?** ¿a quién le estás escribiendo? **(b)** (in indirect questions) quién; **I don't know ~ you're talking about** no sé de quién estás hablando **2** (as relative): **the boy ~ won the prize** el chico que ganó el premio; **there are blankets for those ~ want them** hay mantas para quienes quieran

WHO *n* (= **World Health Organization**) OMS *f*

who'd /huːd/ **(a)** = **who had (b)** = **who would**

whodunit, **whodunnit** /huːˈdʌnət ‖ ˌhuːˈdʌnɪt/ *n* (colloq) novela *f* policíaca

whoever /huːˈevər ‖ huːˈevə(r)/ *pron* **(a)** (no matter who): **she's not coming in here, ~ she is** aquí no entra, quien quiera que sea; **~ you ask** se lo preguntes a quien se lo preguntes **(b)** (the one, ones who): **~ did this must be insane** quienquiera que haya hecho esto debe (de) estar loco; **I'll invite ~ I like** voy a invitar a quien (se) me dé la gana **(c)** (in questions) quién

whole¹ /həʊl/ *adj* **1** (entire) (*before n, no comp*): **there's a ~ bottle left** queda una botella entera; **the ~ truth** toda la verdad; **I'm fed up with the ~ affair** estoy harto del asunto **2** (*pred*) (in one piece) entero

whole² *n* **(a)** (integral unit) todo *m*; **the ~ of sth**: **a threat to the ~ of mankind** una amenaza para toda la humanidad **(b)** (*in phrases*) **as a whole**: **this will affect Europe as a ~** esto va a afectar a Europa en su totalidad; **on the whole** (*indep*) en general

wholehearted /'həʊl'hɑːrtəd ‖ ˌhəʊl'hɑːtɪd/ *adj* ‹*approval*› sin reservas; ‹*support*› incondicional

wholeheartedly /'həʊl'hɑːrtədli ‖ ˌhəʊl'hɑːtɪdli/ *adv* ‹*approve/support*› sin reservas

whole: **~meal** *adj* (BrE) integral; **~ note** *n* (AmE) semibreve *f*, redonda *f*

wholesale¹ /'həʊlseɪl/ *adj* **(a)** (Busn) (*before n*) al por mayor **(b)** ‹*destruction/slaughter*› sistemático

wholesale² *adv* **(a)** (Busn) ‹*buy/sell*› al por mayor **(b)** (on a large scale) de modo general

wholesaler /'həʊlseɪlər ‖ 'həʊlseɪlə(r)/ *n* mayorista *mf*

wholesome /'həʊlsəm/ *adj* **(a)** (healthy) ‹*food/climate*› sano **(b)** (morally good) ‹*image*› de persona sana

wholewheat /'həʊlhwiːt ‖ 'həʊlwiːt/ *adj* integral

who'll /huːl/ = **who will**

wholly /'həʊlli/ *adv* totalmente

whom /huːm/ *pron* (frml) **(a)** (in questions): **~ did you visit?** ¿a quién visitaste? **(b)** (as relative): **the cousin ~ I mentioned earlier** el primo que *or* a quien mencioné antes; **the girls, both of ~ could dance** las chicas, que ambas sabían bailar

whooping cough /'huːpɪŋ/ *n* [U] tos *f* convulsa *or* convulsiva

whoops /hwʊps ‖ wʊps/ *interj* ¡ay!, ¡epa! (AmS fam), ¡híjole! (Méx fam)

whore /hɔːr ‖ hɔː(r)/ *n* (pej) puta *f* (vulg & pey)

who's /huːz/ **(a)** = **who is (b)** = **who has**

whose¹ /huːz/ *pron* (*sing*) de quién; (*pl*) de quiénes

whose² *adj* **(a)** (in questions) (*sing*) de quién; (*pl*) de quiénes **(b)** (as relative) (*sing*) cuyo; (*pl*) cuyos

who've /huːv/ = **who have**

why¹ /hwaɪ ‖ waɪ/ *adv* por qué; **~ not?** ¿por qué no?; **~ don't you apply for the post?** ¿por qué no solicitas el puesto?; **this is ~ the attempt failed** fue por esto que el intento fracasó; **the reason ~ he couldn't attend** la razón por la cual no pudo asistir

why² *interj* ¡vaya!

why³ *n* porqué *m*

WI = **Wisconsin**

wick /wɪk/ *n* mecha *f*

wicked /'wɪkəd ‖ 'wɪkɪd/ *adj* **-er, -est (a)** (evil) ‹*person*› malvado, malo; ‹*thought*› malo; ‹*lie*› infame **(b)** (vicious) ‹*blow*› malintencionado **(c)** (mischievous) ‹*grin/laugh*› travieso

wicker /'wɪkər ‖ 'wɪkə(r)/ *n* [U] mimbre *m*

wickerwork /'wɪkərwɜːrk ‖ 'wɪkəwɜːk/ *n* [U] **(a)** (articles) artículos *mpl* de mimbre **(b)** ⇒ WICKER

wicket /'wɪkət ‖ 'wɪkɪt/ *n* **1** (in cricket) (stumps and bails) palos *mpl* **2** (window) (AmE) ventanilla *f*

wide¹ /waɪd/ *adj* **wider, widest 1** (in dimension) ‹*river/feet/trousers*› ancho; ‹*gap*› grande; ‹*desert/ocean*› vasto; **it's two meters ~** tiene *or* mide dos metros de ancho **2** (in extent, range) ‹*experience/powers/area*› amplio; **a ~ variety of things** una gran variedad de cosas **3** (off target) ‹*ball/shot*› desviado; **~ OF sth** lejos DE algo; ⇒ MARK¹ 4

wide² *adv* **wider, widest ~ apart**: **with your feet ~ apart** con los pies bien separados; **~ awake**: **to be ~ awake** estar* completamente espabilado *or* despierto; **open ~!** abra bien la boca; **~ open**: **you left the door ~ open** dejaste la puerta abierta de par en par

wide-angle lens /'waɪd'æŋgəl/ *n* granangular *m*

widely /'waɪdli/ *adv* **(a)** (extensively): **she is very ~ traveled** ha viajado mucho; **it was ~ publicized** se le dio mucha publicidad **(b)** (commonly): **a ~ held view** una opinión muy extendida **(c)** (to a large degree) ‹*vary*› mucho

widen /'waɪdn̩/ *vt* ‹*road/entrance*› ensanchar; ‹*range/debate/scope*› ampliar* ■ **~** *vi* «*road/tunnel*» ensancharse

wide: **~-ranging** /'waɪd'reɪndʒɪŋ/ *adj* ‹*powers/curriculum*› amplio; ‹*interests*› variado; ‹*effects*› de gran alcance; **~spread** *adj* ‹*custom/belief*› extendido

widow¹ /'wɪdəʊ/ *n* viuda *f*

widow² *vt*: **to be ~ed** enviudar, quedar viudo

widower /'wɪdəʊər ‖ 'wɪdəʊə(r)/ *n* viudo *m*

width /wɪdθ/ *n* **(a)** [U C] (measurement) ancho *m*, anchura *f*; **what ~ is the cloth?** ¿qué ancho tiene la tela? **(b)** [C] (in swimming pool) ancho *m*

wield /wiːld/ *vt* ‹*sword*› blandir*; ‹*power/authority*› ejercer*

wife /waɪf/ *n* (*pl* **wives**) esposa *f*, mujer *f*

wig /wɪg/ *n* peluca *f*

wiggle /'wɪgəl/ *vt* ‹*toes*› mover*; ‹*hips*› contonear

wild¹ /waɪld/ *adj* **-er, -est 1 (a)** ‹*animal*› salvaje; ‹*plant/flower*› silvestre; ‹*vegetation*› agreste **(b)** (uncivilized) ‹*tribe*› salvaje **(c)** (desolate) ‹*country*› agreste **2 (a)** (unruly) ‹*party/lifestyle*› desenfrenado **(b)** (random, uncontrolled) ‹*attempt*› desesperado; **a ~ guess** una conjetura hecha totalmente al azar **(c)** ‹*allegation/exaggeration*› absurdo **3 (a)** (violent) (liter) ‹*sea/waters*› embravecido, proceloso (liter); ‹*wind*› fuertísimo, furioso (liter) **(b)** (frantic) ‹*excitement/dancing*› desenfrenado; ‹*shouting*› desaforado; ‹*appearance/stare*› de loco; **her perfume was driving him ~** su perfume lo estaba enloqueciendo **(c)** (enthusiastic) (colloq) (*pred*) **to be ~** ABOUT **sth**: **I'm not ~ about the idea** la idea no me enloquece **(d)** (angry) (colloq) (*pred*): **it makes me ~** me saca de quicio

wild² *adv*: **these flowers grow ~** estas flores son silvestres; ***to run*** **~**: **these kids have been allowed to run ~** a estos niños los han criado como salvajes; **the garden has run ~** la maleza ha invadido el jardín

wild³ *n* [U] **the ~: an opportunity to observe these animals in the ~** una oportunidad de observar estos animales en libertad

wild: **~ boar** *n* jabalí *m*; **~ card** *n* (Comput) comodín *m*; **~cat** /ˈwaɪldkæt/ *n* (*pl* **~cats** *or* **~cat**) (European) gato *m* montés; (bobcat) (esp AmE) lince *m*

wilderness /ˈwɪldərnəs ‖ ˈwɪldənɪs/ *n* **(a)** [C U] (wasteland) páramo *m*; (jungle) jungla *f* **(b)** [U] (undeveloped land) (AmE) parque *m* natural

wild: **~fire** *n* [U] (AmE) fuego *m* arrasador; ***to spread like ~fire*** (also BrE) extenderse* como un reguero de pólvora; **~-goose chase** /ˈwaɪld ˈguːs/ *n*: **I'm not going into town again on another ~-goose chase** no pienso ir otra vez al centro a perder el tiempo para nada; **~life** *n* [U] fauna *f* y flora *f*

wildly /ˈwaɪldli/ *adv* **1 (a)** (frantically) ‹*kick/struggle/rush*› como (un) loco **(b)** (violently) ‹*rage/blow*› con furia **2 (a)** (in undisciplined fashion) ‹*live*› desordenadamente **(b)** (haphazardly, randomly) ‹*shoot/guess*› a lo loco **3** (extremely): **~ funny** comiquísimo; **~ inaccurate estimates** cálculos absolutamente errados

Wild West *n* **the ~ ~** el Lejano Oeste; (*before n*) ‹*adventure/story*› del oeste

wiles /waɪlz/ *pl n* artimañas *fpl*

wilful *adj* (BrE) ⇒ WILLFUL

will¹ /wɪl/ *v mod*

■ **Note** When translating *will* into Spanish, the future tense is not always the first option. *Ir + a + infinitive* is common in Latin American countries. For examples, see the entry below.

(*past* **would**) ['LL *es la contracción de* WILL, WON'T *de* WILL NOT *y* 'LL'VE *de* WILL HAVE] **1** (talking about the future): **he'll come on Friday** vendrá el viernes, va a venir el viernes; **he said he would come on Friday** dijo que vendría *or* iba a venir el viernes; **at the end of this month, he'll have been working here for a year** este fin de mes hará un año que trabaja aquí; **I won't let you down** no te fallaré **2 (a)** (expressing willingness): **~** *o* **would you do me a favor?** ¿quieres hacerme un favor?; **she won't tell us what happened** no nos quiere decir qué pasó **(b)** (in orders, invitations): **be quiet, ~ you!** cállate, ¿quieres?; **~ you have a drink?** ¿quieres tomar algo? **3** (expressing conjecture): **won't they be having lunch now?** ¿no estarán comiendo ahora?; **that would have been in 1947** eso debe (de) haber sido en 1947 **4 (a)** (indicating habit, characteristic): **I'll watch anything on television** yo soy capaz de mirar cualquier cosa en la televisión; **he'd get drunk every Saturday** se emborrachaba todos los sábados **(b)** (indicating capability): **this door won't shut** esta puerta no cierra *or* no quiere cerrar ■ **~** *vt* (*past & past p* **willed**) **1 (a)** (urge, try to cause): **I was ~ing her to get the answer right** estaba deseando con todas mis fuerzas que diera la respuesta correcta **(b)** (desire, ordain) (frml) «*God*» disponer*, querer* **2** (bequeath) legar*

will² *n* **1** [U] **(a)** (faculty) voluntad *f* **(b)** (willpower) voluntad *f*; **to lose the ~ to live** perder* las ansias de vivir **(c)** (desire, intention) voluntad *f*; **patients may come and go at ~** los pacientes pueden entrar y salir a voluntad; ⇒ FREE WILL **2** [C] (testament) testamento *m*

willful, (BrE) **wilful** /ˈwɪlfəl/ *adj* **1** (deliberate) ‹*misconduct/neglect*› intencionado; ‹*damage*› causado con premeditación **2** (obstinate) ‹*person*› terco

willing /ˈwɪlɪŋ/ *adj* **(a)** (eager, compliant) (*before n*) ‹*servant/worker*› servicial **(b)** (inclined) (*pred*) **to be ~ to +** INF estar* dispuesto A + INF

willingly /ˈwɪlɪŋli/ *adv* (gladly) con gusto; (readily, freely) por voluntad propia

willingness /ˈwɪlɪŋnəs ‖ ˈwɪlɪŋnɪs/ *n* [U] buena voluntad *f*, buena disposición *f*

willow /ˈwɪləʊ/ *n* sauce *m*

willpower /ˈwɪlpaʊər ‖ ˈwɪlpaʊə(r)/ *n* [U] (fuerza *f* de) voluntad

willy-nilly /ˈwɪliˈnɪli/ *adv* **(a)** (haphazardly) de cualquier manera **(b)** (like it or not) sea como sea

wilt /wɪlt/ *vi* «*plant/flower*» ponerse* mustio, marchitarse

wily /ˈwaɪli/ *adj* **wilier, wiliest** astuto

win¹ /wɪn/ (*pres p* **winning**; *past & past p* **won**) *vt* **1** (gain) ‹*prize/title*› ganar; ‹*support*› conseguir*; ‹*fame/recognition/affection*› ganarse; ‹*scholarship/promotion/contract*› conseguir* **2** (be victorious in) ‹*war/race/bet/election*› ganar ■ **~** *vi* ganar

• **win over**, (BrE also) **win round** [*v + o + adv, v + adv + o*] conquistarse a

win² *n* victoria *f*, triunfo *m*

wince /wɪns/ *vi* hacer* un gesto de dolor; (shudder) estremecerse*

winch¹ /wɪntʃ/ *n* cabrestante *m*, torno *m*

winch² *vt*: *levantar con un torno o cabrestante*

wind¹ /wɪnd/ *n* **1** ▶ 920 [C U] (Meteo) viento *m*; ***to get ~ of sth*** enterarse de algo; (*before n*) **~ power** energía *f* eólica **2** [U] (in bowels) gases *mpl* **3** [U] (breath) aliento *m* **4** [U] (Mus): **the ~** los instrumentos de viento; (*before n*) **~ instrument** instrumento *m* de viento

wind² *vt* **I** /wɪnd/ **(a)** «*exertion*» dejar sin aliento; «*blow*» cortarle la respiración a **(b)** ‹*baby*› sacarle* el aire a (fam)

II /waɪnd/ (*past & past p* **wound** /waʊnd/) **1** (coil) ‹*yarn/wool*› ovillar; **to ~ sth** AROUND *o* (esp BrE) ROUND **sth** enroscar* algo ALREDEDOR DE algo; **to ~ sth into a ball** hacer* un ovillo con algo; **to ~ the film on** (hacer*) correr la película **2 (a)** (turn) ‹*handle*› hacer* girar, darle* vueltas a; ‹*clock/watch*› darle* cuerda a **(b)** (hoist, pull) levantar ■ **~** *vi* /waɪnd/ (*past & past p* **wound** /waʊnd/) **(a)** «*river/road*» serpentear **(b) winding** *pres p* ‹*river/road*› sinuoso, serpenteante

• **wind down 1** [*v + o + adv, v + adv + o*] ‹*window*› (Auto) bajar; ‹*production/trade*› reducir* paulatinamente **2** [*v + adv*] (colloq) relajarse

• **wind up 1** [*v + o + adv, v + adv + o*] **(a)** (tighten spring) ‹*watch/toy*› darle* cuerda a **(b)** (bring to conclusion) ‹*meeting/speech*› cerrar* **(c)** (close down) ‹*company*› cerrar*, liquidar **2** [*v + o + adv*] (colloq) (make angry) torear, darle* manija a (RPl fam); (tease) tomarle el pelo a (fam) **3** [*v + adv*] **(a)** (end up, find oneself) (colloq) terminar, acabar **(b)** (conclude) «*speaker*» concluir*, terminar

wind /wɪnd/: **~fall** *n* **(a)** (fruit) *fruta caída del árbol* **(b)** (unexpected benefit): **the $100 prize was a nice little ~fall** el premio de 100 dólares le (*or* me *etc*) cayó como llovido del cielo; **~mill** *n* molino *m* de viento

window /ˈwɪndəʊ/ *n* **1 (a)** (of building) ventana *f*; (of car) ventanilla *f*; (of shop) vitrina *f* (AmL), vidriera *f* (AmL), escaparate *m* (esp Esp); ***to fly/go out (of) the ~*** «*plans*» venirse* abajo, desbaratarse; «*hopes*» desvanecerse* **(b)** (sales counter) ventanilla *f* **2** (Comput) ventana *f*, recuadro *m*

window: **~ box** *n* jardinera *f*; **~ cleaner** *n* (product) limpiacristales *m*, limpiavidrios *m* (esp Aml); (person) limpiacristales *mf*, limpiavidrios *mf* (esp AmL); **~ dressing** *n* [U] (in shop)vitrinismo *m* (AmL), vidrierismo *m* (AmL), escaparatismo *m* (esp Esp); **~ ledge** *n* alféizar *m or* repisa *f* de la ventana; **~pane** *n* vidrio *m or* (Esp) cristal *m* (*de una ventana*); **~ seat** *n* (in train, plane) asiento *m* junto a la ventanilla; **~-shop** *vi* **-pp-**: **to go ~-shopping** ir* a mirar vitrinas *or* vidrieras *or* (esp Esp) escaparates; **~sill** *n* alféizar *m or* repisa *f* de la ventana

wind /wɪnd/: **~pipe** *n* tráquea *f*; **~screen** *n* (BrE) ⇒ ~SHIELD; **~shield** *n* (AmE) parabrisas *m*; (*before n*) **~shield wiper** limpiaparabrisas *m*, limpiador *m* (Méx); **~surfer** *n* (person) tablista *mf*, surfista *mf*; (board) tabla *f* de windsurf; **~surfing** *n* [U] windsurf *m*, windsurfing *m*, surf *m* a vela; **~swept** *adj* ‹*beach/plain*› azotado por el viento; ‹*person*› despeinado; ‹*hair*› alborotado

windy /ˈwɪndi/ *adj* **-dier, -diest** ▶920 ‹*day/weather*› ventoso, de viento; **it's ~** hace viento

wine /waɪn/ *n* [U C] **(a)** (beverage) vino *m*; (*before n*) **~ cellar** bodega *f*; **~ list** carta *f* de vinos; **~ rack** botellero *m*; **~ waiter** sommelier *m*, sumiller *m* **(b)** ▶515 (color) rojo *m* granate; (*before n*) rojo granate *adj inv*

wine: **~ and dine** *vt* agasajar (*con una comida*); **~ bar** *n* bar *m* (*especializado en vinos*); **~ glass** *n* copa *f* de vino; **~growing** *n* [U] viticultura *f*; (*before n*) ‹*area/region*› vinícola; ‹*country*› productor de vino; **~tasting** /ˈwaɪn,teɪstɪŋ/ *n* **(a)** [U] (act, skill) cata *f or* catadura *f* de vinos **(b)** [C] (event) degustación *f* de vinos

wing /wɪŋ/ *n* **1** (Zool) ala *f*‡ **2** (Aviat) ala *f*‡ **3** (BrE Auto) guardabarros *m or* (Méx) salpicadera *f or* (Chi, Per) tapabarros *m* **4** (Pol) ala *f*‡ **5** (of building) ala *f*‡ **6 wings** *pl* (Theat) **the ~s** los bastidores

wingspan /ˈwɪŋspæn/ *n* envergadura *f*

wink¹ /wɪŋk/ *n* guiño *m*, guiñada *f*; **to give sb a ~** guiñarle el ojo a algn; ***not to get a ~ of sleep*** no pegar* (el *or* un) ojo

wink² *vi* **(a)** «*person*» guiñar el ojo **(b)** (flash) «*light*» parpadear

winner /ˈwɪnər ‖ ˈwɪnə(r)/ *n* ganador, -dora *m,f*

winning /ˈwɪnɪŋ/ *adj* **(a)** (victorious) (*before n*) ‹*candidate/team*› ganador; ‹*goal/shot*› de la victoria **(b)** (appealing) ‹*smile/personality*› encantador

winning post *n* (poste *m* de) llegada *f*

winnings /ˈwɪnɪŋz/ *pl n* ganancias *fpl* (*obtenidas en el juego*)

winter /ˈwɪntər ‖ ˈwɪntə(r)/ *n* [U C] invierno *m*; **in (the) ~** en invierno; (*before n*) ‹*weather*› invernal; **~ sports** deportes *mpl* de invierno

wintertime /ˈwɪntərtaɪm ‖ ˈwɪntətaɪm/ *n* [U] invierno *m*

wintry /ˈwɪntri/ *adj* **-trier, -triest** invernal

wipe¹ /waɪp/ *n* **(a)** (action): **give the table a ~ with a damp cloth** pásale un trapo húmedo a la mesa **(b)** (cloth) toallita *f*

wipe² *vt* ‹*floor/table*› limpiar, pasarle un trapo a; ‹*dishes*› secar*; **~ your nose** límpiate la nariz ■ **~** *vi* (dry dishes) secar*

• **wipe away** [*v + o + adv, v + adv + o*] ‹*tears*› secar*; ‹*memory*› borrar

• **wipe off** [*v + o + adv, v + adv + o*] **(a)** (remove) ‹*mud/oil*› limpiar **(b)** (erase) ‹*recording*› borrar

• **wipe out** [*v + o + adv, v + adv + o*] **(a)** (clean) limpiar, pasarle un trapo a **(b)** (destroy, eradicate) ‹*species/population*› exterminar; ‹*resistance*› acabar con; ‹*disease*› erradicar*; ‹*army*› aniquilar **(c)** (erase) ‹*writing/memory*› borrar

• **wipe up** [*v + o + adv, v + adv + o*] limpiar

wire¹ /waɪr ‖ ˈwaɪə(r)/ *n* **1 (a)** [C U] (metal strand) alambre *m*; (*before n*) **~ fence** alambrada *f*, alambrado *m* (AmL) **(b)** [U] (fencing, mesh) alambrada *f*, alambrado *m* (AmL) **(c)** [C] (finishing line) (AmE): **the ~** la línea de llegada, la meta **2** [C] **(a)** (Elec, Telec) cable *m* **(b)** (telegram) (colloq) telegrama *m*

wire² *vt* (Elec): **to be ~d to sth** estar* conectado a algo

wire: **~ cutters** /ˈkʌtərz ‖ ˈkʌtəz/ *pl n* cortaalambres *m*, pinzas *fpl* de corte (Méx); (large) cizalla(s) *f(pl)*; **~walker** *n* (AmE) equilibrista *mf*, funámbulo, -la *m,f*; **~ wool** *n* ⇒ STEEL WOOL

wiring /ˈwaɪrɪŋ ‖ ˈwaɪərɪŋ/ *n* [U] (Elec) cableado *m*, instalación *f* eléctrica

wiry /ˈwaɪri ‖ ˈwaɪəri/ *adj* **wirier, wiriest (a)** ‹*person*› enjuto y nervudo **(b)** ‹*hair*› áspero

Wis = **Wisconsin**

wisdom /ˈwɪzdəm/ *n* [U] sabiduría *f*

wisdom tooth *n* muela *f* del juicio

wise /waɪz/ *adj* **wiser, wisest (a)** (prudent) ‹*person*› prudente; ‹*choice/decision*› acertado **(b)** (learned, experienced) sabio; ***to be none the ~r***: **I'm none the ~r** sigo sin entender **(c)** (aware) (colloq) **to be ~ TO sth/sb**: **I'm ~ to him/his tricks** lo conozco muy bien/le conozco las mañas

• **wise up** (colloq) [*v + adv*] (d)espabilarse, avivarse (AmL fam), apiolarse (RPl fam)

-wise /waɪz/ *suff* **(a)** (with reference to): **price~/weather~** en lo que respecta al precio/tiempo **(b)** (in particular way): **length~** a lo largo

wisecrack *n* broma *f*, chiste *m*

wisely /ˈwaɪzli/ *adv* sabiamente

wish¹ /wɪʃ/ *n* **(a)** (desire) deseo *m*; **to make a ~** pedir* un deseo; **they got married against my ~es** se casaron en contra de mi voluntad **(b) wishes** *pl* (greetings): **give your mother my best ~es** dale a tu madre muchos recuerdos de mi parte, cariños a tu madre (AmL); **best ~es, Jack** saludos *or* un abrazo de Jack

wish² *vt* **(a)** (desire fervently) desear; **to ~ sth** ON **sb** desearle algo A algn; **I ~ I were rich** ¡ojalá fuera rico!; **she ~ed she hadn't told him** lamentó habérselo dicho; **I ~ you wouldn't say things like that** me disgusta mucho que digas esas cosas **(b)** (want) (frml) desear (frml) **(c)** (want for sb) desear; **~ me luck!** ¡deséame suerte!; **to ~ sb good night** darle* las buenas noches a algn ■ **~** *vi* **(a)** (make magic wish) pedir* un deseo **(b)** (want, desire): **if you ~** como quieras

wishful thinking /'wɪʃfəl/ *n* [U]: **do you know for sure that they're leaving or is it just ~ ~?** ¿sabes a ciencia cierta que se van o es simplemente lo que tú querrías?

wisp /wɪsp/ *n* (of smoke) voluta *f*; (of hair) mechón *m*

wispy /'wɪspi/ *adj* **-pier, -piest** ‹*cloud*› tenue; ‹*hair*› ralo

wistful /'wɪstfəl/ *adj* ‹*smile/thought*› nostálgico

wit /wɪt/ *n* **1** (*often pl*) (intelligence) inteligencia *f*; (ingenuity) ingenio *m*; ***to be at one's ~s' end*** estar* desesperado **2** [U] (humor) ingenio *m*

witch /wɪtʃ/ *n* bruja *f*

witch: **~craft** *n* [U] brujería *f*, hechicería *f*; **~ doctor** *n* hechicero *m*, brujo *m*

with /wɪð, wɪθ/ *prep*

■ **Note** When the translation *con* is followed by the pronouns *mí*, *ti*, and *sí*, it combines with them to form *conmigo*, *contigo*, and *consigo*: *come with me* ven conmigo; *take it with you* llévalo contigo; *he had his dog with him* tenía el perro consigo.

1 (a) (in the company of) con; **she went ~ him/them/me/you** fue con él/con ellos/conmigo/contigo **(b)** (member, employee, client etc of) en; **I've been banking ~ them for years** hace años que tengo cuenta en ese banco **2** (in descriptions): **the shirt is black ~ white stripes** la camisa es negra a *or* con rayas blancas; **the man ~ the beard** el hombre de barba; **a tall woman ~ long hair** una mujer alta con el pelo largo *or* de pelo largo; **he is married, ~ three children** está casado y tiene tres hijos **3 (a)** (indicating manner) con; **the proposal was greeted ~ derision** la propuesta fue recibida con burlas **(b)** (by means of, using) con; **she ate it ~ her fingers** lo comió con la mano **(c)** (as a result of): **trembling ~ fright** temblando de miedo

withdraw /wɪð'drɔː/ (*past* **-drew**; *past p* **-drawn**) *vt* **1 (a)** (recall, remove) ‹*troops/representative*› retirar; ‹*hand/arm*› retirar; ‹*coin/note*› retirar de la circulación; ‹*product*› retirar de la venta **(b)** ‹*money/cash*› retirar, sacar* **2 (a)** (cancel, discontinue) ‹*support/funding*› retirar; ‹*permission*› cancelar; **they threatened to ~ their labor** amenazaron con ir a la huelga **(b)** (rescind) ‹*application/charges*› retirar; ‹*demand*› renunciar a **(c)** (retract) ‹*statement/allegation*› retirar ■ **~** *vi* **(a)** «*troops/competitor/candidate*» retirarse **(b)** (socially) recluirse*; (psychologically) retraerse*

withdrawal /wɪð'drɔːəl/ *n* **1** [U C] (of troops, team, representative) retirada *f*; (of coinage) retirada *f* de la circulación; (of product) retirada *f* de la venta **2** [U] (of support, funding) retirada *f*, retiro *m* (AmL); (of application, nomination, competitor) retirada *f* **3** (Psych) retraimiento *m* **4** [C U] (of cash) retirada *f*, retiro *m* (AmL) **5** [U] (from drugs) abandono *m*; (*before n*) **~ symptoms** síndrome *m* de abstinencia

withdrawn¹ /wɪð'drɔːn/ *past p of* WITHDRAW

withdrawn² *adj* retraído

withdrew /wɪð'druː/ *past of* WITHDRAW

wither /'wɪðər ‖ 'wɪðə(r)/ *vi* «*plant/flower*» marchitarse; «*limb*» atrofiarse

withered /'wɪðərd ‖ 'wɪðəd/ *adj* ‹*plant/flower*› marchito, mustio; ‹*limb*› atrofiado

withering /'wɪðərɪŋ/ *adj* **(a)** ‹*heat*› abrasador **(b)** ‹*look*› fulminante

withhold /wɪθ'həʊld ‖ wɪð'həʊld/ *vt* (*past & past p* **-held**) ‹*payment/funds*› retener*; ‹*truth*› ocultar; ‹*consent*› negar*; ‹*information*› no revelar

within¹ /wɪð'ɪn/ *prep* **1** (inside) dentro de; **~ a radius of 20 miles** en un radio de 20 millas **2** (indicating nearness) a; **we were ~ 150m of the summit** estábamos a 150m de la cumbre **3** (in less than): **~ the time allotted** dentro del tiempo establecido; **they'll be here ~ an hour** estarán aquí en menos de una hora

within² *adv* (arch *or* liter) dentro

without /wɪð'aʊt/ *prep* sin; **do it ~ cheating** hazlo sin hacer trampas

withstand /wɪð'stænd/ *vt* (*past & past p* **-stood**) ‹*attack*› resistir; ‹*heat/pain*› soportar

witness¹ /'wɪtnəs ‖ 'wɪtnɪs/ *n* **1** [C] (person) testigo *mf*; (*before n*) **~ stand** *o* (BrE) **box** estrado *m* **2** [U] (testimony, evidence) **to be ~** TO **sth** ser* testimonio DE algo

witness² *vt* **(a)** (observe) ‹*change/event*› ser* testigo de; ‹*crime/accident*› presenciar **(b)** (authenticate) (Law) ‹*signature*› atestiguar*; ‹*will*› atestiguar* la firma de

witticism /'wɪtəsɪzəm ‖ 'wɪtɪsɪzəm/ *n* agudeza *f*; (in conversation) salida *f*

witty /'wɪti/ *adj* **-tier, -tiest** ‹*person*› ingenioso; (funny) gracioso; ‹*answer/remark*› ingenioso

wives /waɪvz/ *pl of* WIFE

wizard /'wɪzərd ‖ 'wɪzəd/ *n* mago *m*, brujo *m*

wizened /'wɪznd/ *adj* (wrinkled) arrugado; (withered) marchito

wk = **week**

wobble /'wɑːbəl ‖ 'wɒbəl/ *vi* **(a)** (tremble) «*jelly*» temblar* **(b)** (sway, waver) «*cyclist*» bambolearse; «*wheel*» bailar; «*chair*» tambalearse

wobbly /'wɑːbli ‖ 'wɒbli/ *adj* **-blier, -bliest (a)** ‹*voice*› tembloroso **(b)** ‹*wheel/tooth*› flojo; ‹*table/chair*› poco firme, que se tambalea; **my legs are ~** me tiemblan las piernas

woe /wəʊ/ *n* **(a)** [U] (sorrow) congoja *f* (liter), aflicción *f*; **~ betide you if you lose it!** ¡pobre de ti *or* ay de ti si lo pierdes! **(b) woes** *pl* (afflictions) males *mpl*

woeful /'wəʊfəl/ *adj* **(a)** (deplorable) ‹*neglect/ignorance*› lamentable **(b)** (sorrowful) (liter) ‹*person*› acongojado (liter); ‹*expression*› desconsolado

woke /wəʊk/ *past of* WAKE¹

woken /wəʊkən/ *past p of* WAKE¹

wolf¹ /wʊlf/ *n* (*pl* **wolves**) (Zool) lobo *m*

wolf² *vt* **~ (down)** devorar(se)

wolves /wʊlvz/ *pl of* WOLF[1]

woman /'wʊmən/ *n* (*pl* **women**) mujer *f*; (*before n*) **a ~ lawyer** una abogada; **a ~ friend of mine** una amiga mía

womanizer /'wʊmənaɪzər ‖ 'wʊmənaɪzə(r)/ *n* mujeriego *m*

womanly /'wʊmənli/ *adj* femenino

womb /wu:m/ *n* útero *m*, matriz *f*

women /'wɪmɪn/ *pl of* WOMAN

women's room *n* (AmE) baño *m or* (Esp) servicios *mpl* de damas *or* señoras

won /wʌn/ *past & past p of* WIN[1]

wonder[1] /'wʌndər ‖ 'wʌndə(r)/ *n* **1** [U] (awe, curiosity) asombro *m* **2** [C] (marvel, miracle) maravilla *f*; **no ~ you feel tired!** no me extraña que estés cansado!

wonder[2] *vi* **(a)** (ponder, speculate): **why do you ask? — oh, I was just ~ing** ¿por qué preguntas? — por nada **(b)** (marvel, be surprised) maravillarse; **I ~ at your patience** me maravilla la paciencia que tienes ■ ~ *vt* **(a)** (ask oneself) preguntarse; **I ~ if** *o* **whether he'll be there** me pregunto si estará **(b)** (be amazed): **I ~ (that) she didn't fire you on the spot** me sorprende que no te haya echado inmediatamente

wonder[3] *adj* (*before n*) ‹*drug/cure*› milagroso

wonderful /'wʌndərfəl ‖ 'wʌndəfəl/ *adj* maravilloso

wonderfully /'wʌndərfli ‖ 'wʌndəfəli/ *adv* maravillosamente, de maravilla

wont /wɑ:nt ‖ wəʊnt/ *n* (liter *or* hum) costumbre *f*; **as is her ~** como tiene por costumbre

won't /wəʊnt/ = **will not**

woo /wu:/ *vt* ‹*woman*› cortejar; ‹*customers/investors*› atraer*; ‹*voters*› buscar* el apoyo de

wood /wʊd/ *n* **1** [U] (material) madera *f*; (firewood) leña *f* **2** (wooded area) (*often pl*) bosque *m* **3** (in golf) [C] palo *m* de madera

wooded /'wʊdəd ‖ 'wʊdɪd/ *adj* boscoso

wooden /'wʊdn̩/ *adj* **(a)** (made of wood) de madera; **~ leg** pata *f* de palo (fam) **(b)** (stiff) ‹*expression*› rígido; ‹*performance*› acartonado

wood: **~land** /'wʊdlənd/ *n* [U] (*often pl*) bosque *m*; **~louse** *n* (*pl* **-lice**) cochinilla *f*, chanchito *m* (Andes, CS fam); **~pecker** /'wʊd,pekər ‖ 'wʊd,pekə(r)/ *n* pájaro *m* carpintero, pico *m* (barreno *or* carpintero); **~ pigeon** *n* paloma *f* torcaz; **~pile** *n* (AmE) montón *m* de leña; **~shed** *n* leñera *f*; **~wind** /'wʊdwɪnd/ *n* (*pl* **~wind** *or* **~winds**) **the ~wind(s)** los instrumentos de viento de madera; **~work** *n* [U] **(a)** (wooden fittings) carpintería *f* **(b)** (BrE) ⇒ ~WORKING; **~working** *n* [U] (AmE) (carpentry) carpintería *f*; (cabinet making) ebanistería *f*; (craftwork) artesanía *f* en madera; **~worm** *n* (*pl* **~worm**) **(a)** [C] (larva) carcoma *f* **(b)** [U] (infestation): **the table's full of ~worm** la mesa está llena de carcoma *or* está toda carcomida

woody /'wʊdi/ *adj* **-dier, -diest** leñoso

woof *n* /wʊf/ (colloq) ladrido *m*; **~ ~!** ¡guau guau!

wool /wʊl/ *n* [U] lana *f*

woolen, (BrE) **woollen** /'wʊlən/ *adj* de lana

woolens, (BrE) **woollens** /'wʊlənz/ *pl n* (Clothes) prendas *fpl* de lana

wooly, (BrE) **woolly** /'wʊli/ *adj* **-lier, -liest (a)** ‹*hat/sweater*› de lana **(b)** (unclear) ‹*thinking/argument*› vago, impreciso

word[1] /wɜ:rd ‖ wɜ:d/ *n* **1** [C] (term, expression) palabra *f*; **what's the German ~ for 'dog'?** ¿cómo se dice 'perro' en alemán?; **in other ~s** (introducing a reformulation) es decir; ***to be lost for ~s*** no encontrar* palabras **2** [C] (thing said) palabra *f*; **a ~ of advice** un consejo; **I can't hear a ~ you're saying** no te oigo nada; **I don't believe a ~ of it** no me lo creo; ***by ~ of mouth***: **the news spread by ~ of mouth** la noticia se fue transmitiendo de boca en boca; ***the last ~***: **to have the last ~** tener* la última palabra; **the last ~ in computers** la última palabra en computadoras; ***to eat one's ~s***: **I was forced to eat my ~s** me tuve que tragar lo que había dicho; ***to have a ~ with sb about sth*** hablar con algn de *or* sobre algo; ***to have ~s with sb*** tener* unas palabras con algn; ⇒ MINCE[1] **3** (assurance) (*no pl*) palabra *f*; **to keep/give one's ~** cumplir/dar* su (*or* mi *etc*) palabra; **you can take my ~ for it** te lo aseguro; ***to take sb at her/his ~*** tomarle la palabra a algn **4 (a)** [U] (news, message): **there is still no ~ of survivors** todavía no se sabe si hay supervivientes; **~ has it that** … corre la noticia *or* el rumor de que … **(b)** (instruction): **if you need a hand just say the ~** si quieres que te ayude no tienes más que pedirlo; **to give the ~ (to + INF)** dar* la orden (de + INF) **5 words** *pl* **(a)** (lyrics) letra *f* **(b)** (Theat): **he forgot his ~s** se le olvidó lo que tenía que decir

word[2] *vt* ‹*document/letter*› redactar; ‹*question*› formular

word for word *adv* ‹*repeat/copy*› palabra por palabra; ‹*translate*› literalmente

wording /'wɜ:rdɪŋ ‖ 'wɜ:dɪŋ/ *n* (of paragraph, letter) redacción *f*; (of question) formulación *f*

word: **~ processing** *n* [U] tratamiento *m or* procesamiento *m* de textos; **~ processor** /'prɑ:sesər, 'prəʊ- ‖ 'prəʊsesə(r)/ *n* procesador *m* de textos

wordy /'wɜ:rdi ‖ 'wɜ:di/ *adj* **-dier, -diest** verboso

wore /wɔ:r ‖ wɔ:(r)/ *past of* WEAR[2]

work[1] /wɜ:rk ‖ wɜ:k/ *n* **1** [U] (labor, tasks) trabajo *m*; **she put a lot of ~ into it** puso mucho esfuerzo en ello; **it's hard ~ digging** cavar es muy duro **2** [U] (employment) trabajo *m*; **to go to ~** ir* a trabajar *or* al trabajo **3** (*in phrases*) **at work**: **he's at ~** está en el trabajo, está en la oficina (*or* la fábrica *etc*); **they were hard at ~** estaban muy ocupados trabajando; **off work**: **she was off ~ for a month after the accident** después del accidente estuvo un mes sin trabajar; **he took a day off ~** se tomó un día libre; **out of work**: **to be out of ~** estar* sin trabajo *or* desocupado *or* desempleado *or* (Chi tb) cesante, estar* parado (Esp); (*before n*) **out-of-work** desocupado, desempleado, parado (Esp), cesante (Chi) **4 (a)** [C] (product, single item) obra *f*; **a ~ of art** una obra de arte **(b)** [U] (output) trabajo *m*; **a piece of ~** un trabajo; **it was the ~ of a professional** era obra de un profesional; *see also* WORKS

work[2] *vi* **1** «*person*» trabajar; **I ~ as a receptionist** trabajo de recepcionista; **to ~ hard** trabajar mucho *or* duro; **to ~ FOR sb** trabajar PARA algn; **to ~ in oils** pintar al óleo, trabajar con óleos; **he's ~ing on his car** está arreglando el coche; **scientists are ~ing on a cure** los científicos están intentando encontrar una cura; **to ~ UNDER sb** trabajar bajo la dirección de algn **2 (a)** (operate, function) «*machine/system*» funcionar; «*drug/person*» actuar*; ***it ~s both ways***: **you have to make an effort too, you know: it ~s both ways** tú también tienes que hacer el esfuerzo, ¿sabes? funciona igual *or* (esp AmL) parejo para los dos **(b)** (have required effect) «*drug/plan/method*» surtir efecto; **try it, it might ~** pruébalo, quizás resulte ■ ~ *vt* **1 (a)** (force to work) hacer* trabajar; **to ~ oneself to death** matarse trabajando **(b)** (exploit) ‹*land/soil*› trabajar; ‹*mine*› explotar **(c)** ‹*nightclubs/casinos*› trabajar en **(d)** (pay for by working): **he ~ed his passage to Australia** se costeó el pasaje a Australia trabajando en el barco **2** (cause to operate): **do you know how to ~ the machine?** ¿sabes manejar la máquina?; **this lever ~s the sprinkler system** esta palanca acciona el sistema de riego **3 (a)** (move gradually, manipulate) (+ *adv compl*): **~ the brush into the corners** mete bien el cepillo en los rincones; ***to ~ one's way***: **we ~ed our way toward the exit** nos abrimos camino hacia la salida; **she ~ed her way to the top of her profession** trabajó hasta llegar a la cima de su profesión **(b)** (shape, fashion) ‹*clay/metal*› trabajar; ‹*dough*› sobar **4 (a)** (*past & past p* **worked** *or* **wrought**) (bring about) ‹*miracle*› hacer*; *see also* WROUGHT **(b)** (arrange) (colloq) arreglar

• **work off** [*v + o + adv, v + adv + o*] **(a)** (get rid of): **you can ~ off a few kilos in the gym** puede rebajar algunos kilos en el gimnasio **(b)** ‹*debt*› amortizar*, pagar* (*trabajando*)

• **work out I** [*v + adv*] **1 (a)** (turn out) salir*, resultar; **it ~s out at $75 a head** sale (a) 75 dólares por cabeza **(b)** (be successful) «*plan*» salir* bien **2** (train, exercise) (Sport) hacer* ejercicio
II [*v + o + adv, v + adv + o*] **1 (a)** (solve) ‹*sum*› hacer*; ‹*riddle/puzzle*› resolver* **(b)** (find, calculate) ‹*percentage/probability*› calcular; **have you ~ed out the answer?** ¿lo has resuelto? **(c)** (understand) entender* **2** (devise, determine) ‹*solution/procedure*› idear; ‹*plan*› elaborar

• **work up** [*v + o + adv, v + adv + o*] **(a)** (stimulate): **they had ~ed up an appetite** se les había abierto el apetito; **I couldn't ~ up much enthusiasm** no me entusiasmaba demasiado **(b)** (excite, arouse): **she gets very ~ed up about it** se pone como loca; **they had been ~ed up into a frenzy** los habían puesto frenéticos, los habían exaltado

workable /'wɜːrkəbəl ‖ 'wɜːkəbəl/ *adj* ‹*arrangement/solution*› factible

work: **~bench** *n* banco *m* de trabajo; **~day** *n* **(a)** (part of day) jornada *f* laboral **(b)** (weekday) día *m* hábil *or* laborable *or* laboral *or* de trabajo

worker /'wɜːrkər ‖ 'wɜːkə(r)/ *n* **(a)** trabajador, -dora *m,f*; **he's a good/slow ~** trabaja bien/lentamente **(b)** (ant, bee) obrera *f*

work force *n* [U] (of nation) población *f* activa; (of company) personal *m*, plantilla *f* (Esp)

working /'wɜːrkɪŋ ‖ 'wɜːkɪŋ/ *adj* (*before n*) **1 (a)** ‹*mother/parent*› que trabaja; **~ population** población *f* activa **(b)** ‹*hours/conditions*› de trabajo; **we have a good ~ relationship** trabajamos muy bien juntos **2 (a)** (capable of operating): **it's in perfect ~ order** funciona perfectamente **(b)** (suitable for working with) ‹*hypothesis*› de trabajo; **I have a ~ knowledge of Russian** tengo conocimientos básicos de ruso

working: **~ class** *n* (*sometimes pl*) **the ~ class(es)** la clase obrera *or* trabajadora; **~-class** /'wɜːrkɪŋ'klæs ‖ ˌwɜːkɪŋ'klɑːs/ *adj* ‹*person*› de clase obrera *or* trabajadora; ‹*area*› obrero; **~ day** *n* **(a)** (weekday) día *m* hábil *or* laborable *or* laboral *or* de trabajo **(b)** ⇒ WORKDAY (a); **~ party** *n* equipo *m* de trabajo

workings /'wɜːrkɪŋz ‖ 'wɜːkɪŋz/ *pl n* (of machine) funcionamiento *m*

work: **~load** *n* (volumen *m* de) trabajo *m*; **~man** /'wɜːrkmən ‖ 'wɜːkmən/ *n* (*pl* **-men** /-mən/) obrero *m*

workmanlike /'wɜːrkmənlaɪk ‖ 'wɜːkmənlaɪk/ *adj* eficiente, profesional

workmanship /'wɜːrkmənʃɪp ‖ 'wɜːkmənʃɪp/ *n* [U] (of craftsman) trabajo *m*; (of object) factura *f*

work: **~out** *n* sesión *f* de ejercicios *or* gimnasia; **~place** *n* lugar *m* de trabajo

works /wɜːrks ‖ wɜːks/ *n* **1** (actions) (liter) (+ *pl vb*) obras *fpl* **2** (engineering operations) (+ *pl vb*) obras *fpl*; **road ~** obras viales **3** (factory) (+ *sing or pl vb*) fábrica *f* **4** (mechanism) (+ *pl vb*) mecanismo *m*

work: **~shop** *n* taller *m*; **~station** *n* (Comput) terminal *m* de trabajo; **~surface** *n* **(a)** (area) superficie *f* de trabajo **(b)** ⇒ ~TOP; **~top** *n* encimera *f*, mesada *f* (RPl)

world /wɜːrld ‖ wɜːld/ *n* **1** (earth) mundo *m*; **the longest bridge in the ~** el puente más largo del mundo; **to see the ~** ver* mundo; ***(it's a) small ~!*** el mundo es un pañuelo, ¡qué pequeño *or* (AmL) chico es el mundo!; ***to be out of this ~*** «*food/music*» ser* increíble; ***to have the best of both ~s*** tener* todas las ventajas; (*before n*) ‹*economy/peace*› mundial; ‹*politics/trade*› internacional **2 (a)** (people generally) mundo *m*; **what is the ~ coming to?** ¿adónde vamos a ir a parar? **(b)** (society): **they've gone up in the ~** han prosperado mucho (*or* hecho fortuna *etc*); **a woman/man of the ~** una mujer/un hombre de mundo **3** (specific period, group) mundo *m*; **the art ~** el mundo del arte **4** (*as intensifier*): **we are ~s apart** no tenemos nada que ver; **it did her a ~ of good** le hizo la mar de bien; **he thinks the ~ of her** tiene un altísimo concepto de ella; **to have all the time in the ~** tener* todo el tiempo del mundo; **without a care in the ~** sin ninguna preocupación **5** (Relig): **this/the other ~** este/el otro mundo

world: **W~ Bank** *n* **the W~ Bank** el Banco Mundial; **~ champion** *n* campeón, -peona *m,f* mundial; **W~ Cup** *n* **the W~ Cup** el Mundial, la Copa del Mundo; **~-famous** /'wɜːrld'feɪməs ‖ ˌwɜːld'feɪməs/ *adj* mundialmente famoso

worldly /ˈwɜːrldli ‖ ˈwɜːldli/ *adj* **(a)** ‹*goods*› material; ‹*desires*› mundano **(b)** ‹*person*› de mucho mundo; ‹*manner/charm*› sofisticado

worldly-wise /ˈwɜːrldliˈwaɪz ‖ ˌwɜːldliˈwaɪz/ *adj* de mucho mundo

world: **~ record** *n* récord *m or* marca *f* mundial; **W~ Series** *n* (in US baseball) **the W~ Series** la Serie Mundial, el campeonato mundial de béisbol; **W~ War** *n* guerra *f* mundial; **the First/Second W~ War, W~ War I/II** la primera/segunda Guerra Mundial

worldwide[1] /ˈwɜːrldˈwaɪd ‖ ˌwɜːldˈwaɪd/ *adj* mundial

worldwide[2] *adv* ‹*travel*› por todo el mundo

worm[1] /wɜːrm ‖ wɜːm/ *n* **(a)** (*earth~*) gusano *m*, lombriz *f* (de tierra) **(b)** (maggot) gusano *m* **(c)** **worms** *pl* (Med) lombrices *fpl*

worm[2] *vt* (Vet Sci) ‹*dog/cat*› desparasitar

worn[1] /wɔːrn ‖ wɔːn/ *past p of* WEAR[2]

worn[2] *adj* ‹*tire/clothes*› gastado; ‹*carpet*› raído; ‹*flagstones/steps*› desgastado

worn-out /ˈwɔːrnˈaʊt ‖ ˌwɔːnˈaʊt/ *adj* (*pred* **worn out**) **(a)** ‹*shoes/clothes*› muy gastado **(b)** (exhausted) rendido

worried /ˈwɜːrid ‖ ˈwʌrid/ *adj* ‹*look/voice*› de preocupación; ‹*person*› preocupado; **to get ~** preocuparse, inquietarse; **to be ~ ABOUT sb/sth** estar* preocupado POR algn/algo

worrier /ˈwɜːriər ‖ ˈwʌriə(r)/ *n*: **she's such a ~** se preocupa *or* se angustia tanto por todo

worry[1] /ˈwɜːri ‖ ˈwʌri/ *n* (*pl* **-ries**) [C U] preocupación *f*

worry[2] **-ries, -rying, -ried** *vt* **1** (trouble) preocupar, inquietar **2** «*dog*» ‹*sheep*› acosar ■ **~** *vi* preocuparse, inquietarse; **to ~ ABOUT sth/sb** preocuparse POR algo/algn

worrying /ˈwɜːriŋ ‖ ˈwʌriŋ/ *adj* inquietante, preocupante

worse[1] /wɜːrs ‖ wɜːs/ *adj* (*comp of* BAD[1]) peor; **to get ~** empeorar; (sicker) ponerse* peor; **things are getting ~ and ~** las cosas van de mal en peor; **to make things ~, it started snowing** por si fuera poco, empezó a nevar

worse[2] *adv* (*comp of* BADLY) peor

worse[3] *n* **the ~** el (*or* la *etc*) peor; **a change for the ~** un cambio para mal

worsen /ˈwɜːrsn̩ ‖ ˈwɜːsn̩/ *vi/t* empeorar

worse-off /ˈwɜːrsɔːf ‖ ˌwɜːsˈɒf/ *adj* (*pred* **worse off**) **(a)** (financially) en peor posición económica **(b)** (emotionally, physically) (*pred*) peor

worship[1] /ˈwɜːrʃəp ‖ ˈwɜːʃɪp/ *n* **1** [U] culto *m*, adoración *f* **2** ▶603 [C] **Worship** (as title): **Your/His W~** (of magistrate) Su Señoría; (of mayor) el señor alcalde

worship[2] *vt*, (BrE) **-pp-** ‹*God*› adorar; ‹*success/wealth*› rendir* culto a; ‹*hero*› idolatrar

worshipper /ˈwɜːrʃəpər ‖ ˈwɜːʃɪpə(r)/ *n* (Relig) fiel *m*

worst[1] /wɜːrst ‖ wɜːst/ *adj* (*superl of* BAD[1]) peor; **he's the ~ student in the class** es el peor alumno de la clase; **~ of all** lo peor de todo

worst[2] *adv* (*superl of* BADLY): **she did (the) ~ (of all) in both exams** le fue peor que a nadie en los dos exámenes

worst[3] *n* **1 the ~ (a)** (+ *sing vb*) lo peor; **his sister brings out the ~ in him** cuando está con su hermana está peor que nunca; ***if (the) ~ comes to (the) ~*** en el peor de los casos **(b)** (+ *pl vb*) los peores **2 (a) at worst** en el peor de los casos **(b) at her/his/its worst**: **I'm at my ~ in the morning** la mañana es mi peor momento del día; **this is racism at its ~** esto es racismo de la peor especie

worth[1] /wɜːrθ ‖ wɜːθ/ *adj* (*pred*) **(a)** (equal in value to) **to be ~** valer*; **it cost $300, but it was ~ the money** costó $300, pero valió la pena; **goods ~ £5,000 were stolen** robaron mercancías por valor de 5.000 libras; **this is my opinion, for what it's ~** ésta es mi opinión, si es que a alguien le interesa **(b)** (worthy of): **it's ~ a try** vale la pena intentarlo; **that's ~ knowing** es bueno saberlo; **don't argue with them, it isn't ~ it** no discutas con ellos, no vale *or* no merece la pena

worth[2] *n* [U] **(a)** (equivalent): **$2,000 dollars' ~ of furniture** muebles por valor de 2.000 dólares; **I've had my money's ~ out of this car** le he sacado mucho jugo a este coche (fam) **(b)** (of thing) valor *m*; (of person) valía *f*

worthless /ˈwɜːrθləs ‖ ˈwɜːθlɪs/ *adj* ‹*object*› sin ningún valor; ‹*person*› despreciable; **to be ~** no tener* ningún valor, no valer* nada

worthwhile /ˈwɜːrθˈhwaɪl ‖ wɜːθˈwaɪl/ *adj* ‹*enterprise/project*› que vale la pena

worthy /ˈwɜːrði ‖ ˈwɜːði/ *adj* **-thier, -thiest 1** (appropriate, equal) ‹*opponent/successor*› digno; **to be ~ OF sth/sb** ser* digno DE algo/algn **2** (good, estimable) ‹*person*› respetable; **a ~ cause** una buena causa

would /wʊd/ *v mod*

■ **Note** When *would* + a verb in English is used to form the conditional tense, it is translated by the conditional tense in Spanish.
When *would* + a verb in English is used to express habitual activity in the past, it is translated by the imperfect tense in Spanish.
For examples of both, see the entry below.

['D *es la contracción de* WOULD, WOULDN'T *de* WOULD NOT *y* 'D'VE *de* WOULD HAVE] **1** *past of* WILL[1] **2** (in conditional sentences): **I ~ if I could** lo haría si pudiera; **if I had known, I ~n't have come** si lo hubiera sabido no habría *or* no hubiera venido **3** (expressing wishes): **I wish you'd stop pestering me!** ¡deja de fastidiarme por Dios! **4** (in requests, invitations): **~ you type this for me please?** ¿me haría el favor de pasar esto a máquina?; **~ you like to come with us? — I'd love to** ¿quieres venir con nosotros? — me encantaría

would-be /ˈwʊdbiː/ *adj* (*before n*): **a ~ star/poet** un aspirante a estrella/poeta

wouldn't /ˈwʊdn̩t/ = **would not**

would've /ˈwʊdəv/ = **would have**

wound[1] /wuːnd/ *n* herida *f*

wound[2] /wuːnd/ *vt/i* herir*

wound³ /waʊnd/ *past & past p of* WIND² *vt* II, *vi*

wounded /ˈwuːndəd ‖ ˈwuːndɪd/ *adj* ‹*soldier/animal/pride*› herido; ‹*look/tone*› dolido

wove /wəʊv/ *past of* WEAVE

woven /ˈwəʊvən/ *past p of* WEAVE

WP *n* **(a)** [C] = **word processor (b)** [U] = **word processing**

wpm (= **words per minute**) palabras por minuto

wrangle¹ /ˈræŋgəl/ *vi* discutir, reñir*

wrangle² *n* altercado *m*, riña *f*

wrap¹ /ræp/ **-pp-** *vt* **(a)** (cover) ‹*parcel/gift*› envolver* **(b)** (wind, entwine): **she ~ped a shawl about her** se envolvió en un chal

• wrap up 1 [*v* + *o* + *adv*, *v* + *adv* + *o*] **(a)** ⇒ WRAP¹ *vt* (a) **(b)** (complete) (colloq) ‹*order/sale*› conseguir*; ‹*deal*› cerrar* **(c)** (conclude) (colloq) ‹*meeting*› dar* fin a **(d)** (engross) (colloq) **to be ~ped up** IN **sth**: **she's totally ~ped up in her work** no piensa más que en su trabajo, vive para su trabajo **2** [*v* + *adv*] (dress warmly) abrigarse*

wrap² *n* **(a)** (shawl) chal *m*, pañoleta *f* **(b)** (robe) (AmE) bata *f*, salto *m* de cama (CS)

wraparound /ˈræpəˌraʊnd/ *adj* ‹*skirt/dress*› cruzado

wrapper /ˈræpər ‖ ˈræpə(r)/ *n* envoltorio *m*, envoltura *f*

wrapping /ˈræpɪŋ/ *n* [C U] envoltorio *m*, envoltura *f*

wrapping paper *n* [U] (plain) papel *m* de envolver; (decorative) papel *m* de regalo

wrath /ræθ ‖ rɒθ/ *n* [U] (liter) cólera *f*, ira *f*

wreak /riːk/ *vt* (liter) ‹*destruction/chaos*› sembrar* (liter); **to ~ havoc** causar estragos

wreath /riːθ/ *n* corona *f*

wreck¹ /rek/ *n* **1** (ship) restos *mpl* del naufragio; (vehicle) restos *mpl* del avión (*or* tren *etc*) siniestrado **2** (sth, sb ruined): **the attack left him a physical ~** el ataque lo dejó hecho una ruina; **he's a nervous ~** tiene los nervios destrozados

wreck² *vt* **(a)** ‹*ship*› provocar* el naufragio de; ‹*train*› hacer* descarrilar; ‹*car*› destrozar* **(b)** (damage) destrozar* **(c)** (demolish) (AmE) ‹*house/building*› demoler* **(d)** (spoil, ruin) ‹*plans/chances*› echar por tierra; ‹*marriage/happiness*› destrozar*

wreckage /ˈrekɪdʒ/ *n* [U] (of plane, car, ship) restos *mpl*; (of house) ruinas *fpl*

wrecker /ˈrekər ‖ ˈrekə(r)/ *n* (AmE) **(a)** (demolition worker) obrero *m* de demolición *or* derribo **(b)** (car dismantler) desguazador *m or* (Méx) deshuesador *m*

wren /ren/ *n* (Zool) carrizo *m*

wrench¹ /rentʃ/ *vt* **(a)** (pull) arrancar*; **to ~ oneself away** soltarse* de un tirón *or* (AmL exc CS) de un jalón **(b)** (sprain) ‹*muscle*› desgarrarse; ‹*joint*› dislocarse*

wrench² *n* **1 (a)** (twist, pull) tirón *m*, jalón *m* (AmL exc CS) **(b)** (emotional pain) dolor *m* (*causado por una separación*) **2** (*adjustable ~*) llave *f* inglesa; *see also* MONKEY WRENCH

wrest /rest/ *vt* **to ~ sth** FROM **sb** arrancarle* algo A algn

wrestle /ˈresəl/ *vi* **(a)** (Sport) luchar **(b)** (grapple) **to ~** WITH **sb** forcejear CON algn; **to ~** WITH **sth** batallar CON algo

wrestler /ˈreslər ‖ ˈreslə(r)/ *n* luchador, -dora *m,f*

wrestling /ˈreslɪŋ/ *n* [U] lucha *f*

wretch /retʃ/ *n* (liter) **(a)** (unfortunate person) desdichado, -da *m,f*, infeliz *mf* **(b)** (despicable person) desgraciado, -da *m,f*

wretched /ˈretʃəd ‖ ˈretʃɪd/ *adj* **(a)** (abject, pitiable) ‹*existence/creature*› desdichado **(b)** (very bad) (colloq) ‹*weather*› horrible; **to feel ~** sentirse* muy mal

wriggle /ˈrɪgəl/ *vi* (move) retorcerse*; **the children ~d in their seats** los niños se movían inquietos en sus asientos

• wriggle out of [*v* + *adv* + *prep* + *o*] ‹*dress/jeans*› quitarse (*con dificultad*); **don't try to ~ out of it!** ¡no trates de escabullirte!

wring /rɪŋ/ (*past & past p* **wrung**) *vt* **1 (a)** ‹*cloth/garment*› escurrir, retorcer* **(b) to ~ sth** FROM/OUT OF **sb** ‹*confession/information*› arrancarle* algo A algn **2** ‹*neck*› retorcer*

• wring out [*v* + *o* + *adv*, *v* + *adv* + *o*] **1** ‹*cloth/swimsuit*› retorcer*, escurrir **2** ‹*water*› escurrir; ‹*truth/money*› sacar*

wrinkle¹ /ˈrɪŋkəl/ *n* arruga *f*

wrinkle² *vi* «*skin/garment*» arrugarse*

wrinkled /ˈrɪŋkəld/ *adj* arrugado

wrinkly /ˈrɪŋkli/ *adj* **-klier, -kliest** (colloq) arrugado

wrist /rɪst/ **▶ 484** *n* (Anat) muñeca *f*

wrist: **~band** *n* (bracelet) pulsera *f*; (strap) correa *f*; (sweatband) muñequera *f*; **~watch** *n* reloj *m* (de) pulsera

writ /rɪt/ *n* (Law) orden *f or* mandato *m* judicial

write /raɪt/ (*past* **wrote**; *past p* **written**) *vt* **(a)** (put in writing) escribir*; **I wrote him a letter** le escribí una carta; **to ~ sb a check** *o* (BrE) **cheque** extenderle* *or* hacerle* un cheque a algn **(b)** (write letter to) (AmE) escribirle* a ■ **~** *vi* escribir*; **to ~** TO **sb** escribirle* A algn

• write back [*v* + *adv*] **to ~ back** (TO **sb**) contestar(le A algn)

• write down [*v* + *o* + *adv*, *v* + *adv* + *o*] anotar

• write off 1 [*v* + *adv*] **to ~ off** FOR **sth**: **she wrote off for a form** escribió pidiendo que le mandaran un formulario **2** [*v* + *o* + *adv*, *v* + *adv* + *o*] **(a)** (consider beyond repair) ‹*vehicle*› declarar siniestro total **(b)** (damage beyond repair) (BrE) destrozar* **(c)** (consider a failure, disregard) ‹*marriage/project*› dar* por perdido **(d)** ‹*debt*› cancelar

• write out [*v* + *o* + *adv*, *v* + *adv* + *o*] **(a)** (write fully, copy) escribir* **(b)** (complete, fill out) ‹*prescription*› escribir*; ‹*check/receipt*› hacer*, extender* (frml)

• write up [*v* + *o* + *adv*, *v* + *adv* + *o*] ‹*report/notes*› pasar en *or* (Esp) a limpio; ‹*experiment*› redactar un informe sobre

write-off /ˈraɪtɔːf ‖ ˈraɪtɒf/ *n*: **the car was a ~** el coche fue declarado un siniestro total

writer /ˈraɪtər ‖ ˈraɪtə(r)/ *n* (author) escritor, -tora *m,f*; **the ~ of the letter** el autor de la carta; **~'s cramp** calambre *m* (*que da por escribir mucho*)

write-up /'raɪtʌp/ *n* (colloq) (review) crítica *f*, reseña *f*; (report) artículo *m*

writhe /raɪð/ *vi* «*snake*» retorcerse*; **to ~ in agony** retorcerse* de dolor

writing /'raɪtɪŋ/ *n* **(a)** [U] (script) escritura *f* **(b)** [U] (written material): **the ~'s rather blurred** la letra está algo borrosa; **in ~** por escrito; (*before n*) **~ desk** escritorio *m*; **~ pad** bloc *m*; **~ paper** papel *m* de carta **(c)** [U] (BrE) (handwriting) letra *f* **(d)** [U] (act of composing): **~ takes up a lot of my time** paso mucho tiempo escribiendo **(e)** [U] (written composition) literatura *f* **(f) writings** *pl*: **the ~s of Swift** la obra de Swift

written[1] /'rɪtn̩/ *past p of* WRITE

written[2] *adj* ‹*examination/language*› escrito; **~ permission** permiso *m* por escrito

wrong[1] /rɔːŋ ‖ rɒŋ/ *adj* **1 (a)** (incorrect, inappropriate): ‹*answer*› equivocado, incorrecto; **you've given me the ~ change** se ha equivocado al darme el cambio; **we've taken the ~ bus** nos hemos equivocado de autobús; **he went in the ~ direction** tomó *or* (esp Esp) cogió para dónde no debía; **I did it the ~ way** lo hice mal; **this is the ~ time to mention the subject** éste no es (el) momento oportuno para mencionar el tema; **she always says the ~ thing** siempre dice lo que no debe; **the picture is the ~ way up** el cuadro está al revés; **you've got your T-shirt on the ~ way round** llevas la camiseta al *or* del revés; **I'm the ~ person to ask** no soy la persona indicada para contestar esa pregunta **(b)** (mistaken) (*pred*) **to be ~** estar* equivocado; **I was ~ about her** la había juzgado mal **2** (morally): **stealing is ~** robar está mal; **you were ~ to shout at her like that** no debiste haberle gritado así, estuviste mal en gritarle así; **I haven't done anything ~** no he hecho nada malo; **what's ~ with that?** ¿qué hay de malo en eso? **3** (amiss) (*pred*): **what's ~?** ¿qué pasa?; **there's something ~ with her/with the lock** algo le pasa/algo le pasa a la cerradura; **there's nothing ~ with your heart** su corazón está perfectamente bien

wrong[2] *adv* ‹*answer*› mal, incorrectamente; **I did it all ~** lo hice todo mal; **to go ~** «*machinery*» estropearse, descomponerse* (AmL); «*plans*» salir* mal, fallar

wrong[3] *n* **(a)** [U C] (immoral action) mal *m*; (injustice) injusticia *f*; **in her eyes he can do no ~** para ella, es incapaz de hacer nada malo; **to be in the ~** estar* equivocado **(b)** [C] (Law) agravio *m*

wrong[4] *vt* (frml): **she had been ~ed by her family** su familia había sido muy injusta con ella

wrongdoing /'rɔːŋduːɪŋ ‖ 'rɒŋduːɪŋ/ *n* [U C]: **she was punished for her ~** la castigaron por sus fechorías

wrongful /'rɔːŋfəl ‖ 'rɒŋfəl/ *adj* ‹*accusation/punishment*› injusto

wrongly /'rɔːŋli ‖ 'rɒŋli/ *adv* ‹*spell/pronounce*› mal, incorrectamente; ‹*believe/assume*› equivocadamente; ‹*accuse*› injustamente

wrote /rəʊt/ *past of* WRITE

wrought /rɔːt/ (*past & past p of* WORK[2] *vt* 4(a)) (frml *or* liter): **the devastation ~ by the war** los estragos causados por la guerra

wrought iron *n* [U] hierro *m* forjado

wrung /rʌŋ/ *past & past p of* WRING

wry /raɪ/ *adj* **wrier, wriest** ‹*smile/laugh/joke*› irónico; **to make a ~ face** torcer* el gesto

WV, **W Va** = **West Virginia**

WY, **Wyo** = **Wyoming**

X, **x** /eks/ *n* **(a)** (letter) X, x *f* **(b)** (Cin) (in US) prohibida para menores de 18 años

xenophobia /'zenə'fəʊbiə/ *n* [U] xenofobia *f*

xerox /'zɪrɑːks, 'ze- ‖ 'zɪərɒks/ *vt* fotocopiar, xerografiar*

XL = **extra large**

Xmas /'krɪsməs, 'eksməs/ *n* Navidad *f*

X-rated /'eks'reɪtəd ‖ ˌeks'reɪtɪd/ *adj* (BrE) ‹*film*› sólo para adultos, clasificado X (Esp)

X-ray[1], **x-ray** /'eksreɪ/ *n* **(a)** (ray) rayo *m* X **(b)** (photograph) radiografía *f*; **I had a chest ~** me hicieron *or* me sacaron una radiografía de tórax

X-ray[2], **x-ray** *vt* hacer* *or* sacar* una radiografía de

xylophone /'zaɪləfəʊn/ *n* xilofón *m*, xilófono *m*

Yy

Y, y /waɪ/ *n* Y, y *f*

yacht /jɑːt ‖ jɒt/ *n* **(a)** (sailing boat — large) velero *m*, yate *m*; (— small) balandro *m*; (*before n*) **~ club** club *m* náutico; **~ race** regata *f* **(b)** (pleasure cruiser) yate *m*

yachting /'jɑːtɪŋ ‖ 'jɒtɪŋ/ *n* [U] navegación *f* a vela

yak /jæk/ *n* yac *m*, yak *m*

yam /jæm/ *n* **(a)** (plant, vegetable) ñame *m* **(b)** (AmE) ⇨ SWEET POTATO

yank /jæŋk/ *vt* tirar de, jalar de (AmL exc CS)

Yank /jæŋk/ *n* (BrE colloq & often pej) ⇨ YANKEE (c)

Yankee /'jæŋki/ *n* **(a)** (Hist) yanqui *mf* **(b)** (sb from Northern US) (AmE colloq) norteño, -ña *m,f* **(c)** (US citizen) (colloq: in BrE often pej) yanqui *mf* (fam & pey), gringo, -ga *m,f* (fam & pey)

yap¹ /jæp/ *vi* **-pp-** ladrar (*con ladridos agudos*)

yap² *n* ladrido *m* (*agudo*)

yard /jɑːrd ‖ jɑːd/ *n* **1 (a)** (of school, prison) patio *m* **(b)** (of house) (BrE) patio *m*; (garden) (AmE) jardín *m* **(c)** (*stock~*) corral *m* **2** (*boat~, ship~*) astillero *m* **3** ▶ 681 (measure) yarda *f* (*0,91m*)

yardstick /'jɑːrdstɪk ‖ 'jɑːdstɪk/ *n* criterio *m*

yarn /jɑːrn ‖ jɑːn/ *n* **1** [U C] (Tex) hilo *m* **2** [C] (tale) (colloq) historia *f*

yawn¹ /jɔːn/ *vi* bostezar*

yawn² *n* bostezo *m*

yawning /'jɔːnɪŋ/ *adj* (*before n*) enorme

yd ▶ 681 (*pl* **yd** *or* **yds**) = **yard**

yeah /jeə/ *interj* (colloq) sí

year /jɪr ‖ jɪə(r)/ ▶ 451, 540 *n* **1** (period of time) año *m*; **all (the) ~ round** todo el año; **by the ~ 2000** para el año 2000; **over the ~s I've grown accustomed to it** con el tiempo *or* con los años me he ido acostumbrando; **~ after ~/~ in, ~ out** año tras año; **I'm 12 ~s old** tengo doce años **2 years** *pl* (a long time): **I haven't seen him for ~s** hace años que no lo veo; **~s ago, there was a church here** años atrás, aquí había una iglesia **3** (Educ) curso *m*, año *m*

-year /jɪr ‖ jɪe(r)/ *suff*: **a third~ student** un estudiante de tercer año *or* de tercero

yearly¹ /'jɪrli ‖ 'jɪəli/ *adj* anual; **on a ~ basis** cada año

yearly² *adv* cada año; **twice ~** dos veces al *or* por año

yearn /jɜːrn ‖ jɜːn/ *vi* **to ~ to** + INF anhelar + INF; **to ~ FOR sth** añorar algo

yearning /'jɜːrnɪŋ ‖ 'jɜːnɪŋ/ *n* [U C] **~ FOR sth/to** + INF anhelo *m* *or* ansia *f*‡ DE algo/+ INF

-year-old /jər'əʊld ‖ jɪər'əʊld/ ▶ 451 *suff*: **a thirty-two~ woman** una mujer de treinta y dos años; **a six~** un niño/una niña de seis años

yeast /jiːst/ *n* [U C] levadura *f*

yell¹ /jel/ *vi/t* gritar

yell² *n* grito *m*

yellow¹ /'jeləʊ/ ▶ 515 *adj* amarillo; ‹*hair*› muy rubio *or* (Méx) güero *or* (Col) mono *or* (Ven) catire; ‹*traffic light*› (AmE) amarillo, ámbar *adj inv*

yellow² *n* **(a)** ▶ 515 [U] (color) amarillo *m* **(b)** [C] (signal) (AmE) luz *f* amarilla

yellow³ *vi* ponerse* amarillo

yellow: **~ fever** *n* [U] fiebre *f* amarilla; **~ pages**, (BrE) **Y~ Pages®** *pl n* páginas *fpl* amarillas

yelp¹ /jelp/ *vi* dar* un gañido *or* aullido

yelp² *n* gañido *m*, aullido *m*

Yemen /'jemən/ *n* Yemen *m*

yen /jen/ *n* **1** (longing) (colloq) (*no pl*) **to have a ~ to** + INF morirse* de ganas DE + INF (fam) **2** (*pl* **~**) (Fin) yen *m*

yes¹ /jes/ *interj* sí; **are you ready? — ~, I am** ¿estás listo? — sí; **you didn't tell me — ~, I did!** no me lo dijiste — ¡sí que te lo dije!

yes² *n* (*pl* **~es**) sí *m*

yes-man /'jesmæn/ *n* (*pl* **-men** /-men/) (pej): **he's a ~** es de los que dicen amén a todo

yesterday¹ /'jestərdeɪ, -di ‖ 'jestədeɪ, -di/ ▶ 540 *adv* ayer; **~ morning** ayer por la mañana, ayer en la mañana (AmL), ayer a la mañana *or* de mañana (RPl)

yesterday² ▶ 540 *n*: **~ was a busy day** ayer fue un día de mucha actividad; **the day before ~** anteayer

yet¹ /jet/ *adv* **1 (a)** (up to this or that time, till now) (*with neg*) todavía, aún; **I haven't eaten** *o* (AmE also) **I didn't eat ~** todavía *or* aún no he comido, todavía no comí (RPl); **as ~** aún, todavía **(b)** (now, so soon) (*with neg*) todavía **(c)** (thus far) (*after superl*): **it's his best book ~** es el mejor libro que ha escrito hasta ahora **2** (by now, already) (*with interrog*) ya; **has she decided** *o* (AmE also) **did she decide ~?** ¿ya se ha decidido?, ¿ya se decidió? (AmL) **3** (still) todavía, aún **4** (eventually, in spite of everything): **we may win ~** todavía podemos ganar **5** (*as intensifier*) **(a)** (even) (*with comp*) aún, todavía; **the story becomes ~ more complicated** el cuento se complica aún *or* todavía más **(b)** (in addition, besides): **~ more problems** más problemas aún; **we had to go back ~ again** tuvimos que volver otra vez más (aún) **6** (but, nevertheless) (*as linker*) sin embargo

yet² *conj* pero

yew /juː/ *n* [C U] tejo *m*

Yiddish /'jɪdɪʃ/ *n* [U] yídish *m*, yiddish *m*

yield¹ /jiːld/ *vt* **1** (surrender) ‹*position/territory*› ceder; **to ~ one's right of way** (AmE Transp) ceder

You 1

Ways of saying *you*

_Tú_ and _usted_

There are two ways of saying you *in Spanish: the formal* usted *and the informal* tú

The use of tú *has become increasingly widespread and it is now more widely used than the French equivalent* tu. *However, it is impossible to lay down hard and fast rules about when to use* tú *and when to use* usted *since the way they are used is flexible and depends on the attitude of both the speaker and the listener. The following are very general guidelines:*

(a) *The pronoun* tú *and the* tú *form of the verb (second person singular) are used between friends and family, between people on first-name terms, among young people even if they do not know each other, and when addressing children and animals*

(b) *The pronoun* usted *and the* usted *form of the verb (third person singular) are used when addressing an older person, someone in authority, or, in general, where there is a certain distance between the speakers*

(c) *However, it is important to note that in some Latin American countries, particularly Colombia, the* usted *form is often used as the familiar form, even between children*

(d) *Adults sometimes use the* usted *form when addressing children to show anger or disapproval but it can also express sympathy or affection, for example when comforting a child after a fall or when talking to a baby*

Ustedes and vosotros

In Latin America, the Canary Islands and parts of Andalusia, ustedes *is the plural of both* usted *and* tú:

no se peleen, niños
parén de discutir

In the rest of Spain, the informal plural is vosotros, *which takes the second person plural form of the verb:*

no os peleéis, niños
parad de discutir

The infinitive form is also used:

lavaros
parar, chicos

For translations of you *as direct and indirect object, and when used with prepositions, see the entry* ***you***

Vos

In some Latin American countries, the form vos *is used instead of* tú. *This usage is called* voseo, *and is common in the River Plate and parts of Central America, where* vos *is the standard form of the second person singular. (In some countries, however, this usage is considered substandard and characteristic of uneducated speech.)*

Vos *has its corresponding verb forms in the present tense and the imperative. These vary slightly from area to area. The following are the standard forms in Central America and the River Plate area:*

Present indicative

hablar vos hablás
meter vos metés
partir vos partís

Imperative

hablar	hablá	sentarse	sentate
meter	meté	moverse	movete
partir	partí	vestirse	vestite

There are also special forms for the present subjunctive and the negative imperative, although these are less widely used (many speakers use the forms corresponding to tú *in these cases, given in brackets here):*

Present subjunctive

hablar que vos hablés (que vos hables)
meter que vos metás (que vos metas)
partir que vos partás (que vos partas)

Negative imperative

hablar no hablés (no hables)
meter no metás (no metas)
partir no partás (no partas)

Note that in Uruguay the verb forms corresponding to vos *are often used with the pronoun* tú:

tú sabés que . . .
tú no te imaginás cómo . . .

The object form of vos *is* te, *but after a preposition the form* vos *remains:*

it's for you es para vos

el paso **2** ‹*crop/fruit/mineral/oil*› producir*; ‹*results*› dar* ■ ~ *vi* **1 (a)** (give way) ceder **(b)** (give priority): Ⓢ **yield** (AmE) ceda el paso **2** «*ground/ice*» ceder

yield² *n* [U C] rendimiento *m*

YMCA *n* (= **Young Men's Christian Association**) YMCA *f*, Asociación *f* Cristiana de Jóvenes

yodel /'jəʊdl̩/ *vi*, (BrE) **-ll-** cantar al estilo tirolés

yoga /'jəʊgə/ *n* [U] yoga *m*

yoghurt, **yoghourt**, **yogurt** /'jəʊgərt ‖ 'jɒgət/ *n* [U C] yogur *m*, yoghourt *m*

yoke¹ /jəʊk/ *n* **(a)** (for oxen, horses) yugo *m* **(b)** (burden, bondage) yugo *m*

yoke² *vt* ‹*oxen*› uncir*

yokel /'jəʊkəl/ *n* (pej *or* hum) pueblerino, -na *m,f or* (Méx) indio, -dia *m,f or* (Col) montañero, -ra *m,f or*

You 2

When you *is used to mean* one *in English, it can be translated in Spanish by*:

◆ the second person singular

The second person singular of the verb is used to translate you *(as subject)* + verb:

you can't do that here	=	no puedes hacer eso aquí

When you *is the direct or indirect object of the verb, the object pronoun* te *is used*:

they always try to cheat you	=	siempre intentan engañarte
they can cause you a lot of trouble	=	te pueden crear muchos problemas

This use is much more common in Spain than in Latin America

◆ the impersonal *se* with the third person singular

This is used only where you *is the subject of the verb*:

you never know	=	nunca se sabe
you can't do that here	=	aquí no se puede hacer eso

◆ *uno* with the third person singular

This can be used to translate you *as subject, direct object or indirect object; note the use of the pronoun in translations of* you *as direct or indirect object*:

you can't do that here	=	aquí uno no puede hacer eso
when a policeman stops you	=	cuando a uno lo para un policía
they can cause you a lot of trouble	=	le pueden crear a uno muchos problemas

This use is less common and more formal in tone in Spain than in Latin America, sounding to a Spaniard more like the English one.

(RPl) pajuerano, -na *m,f or* (Chi) huaso, -sa *m,f* (pey *o* hum)

yolk /jəʊk/ *n* [C U] yema *f* (de huevo)

yonder /'jɑːndər || 'jɒndə(r)/ *adv* (poet *or* dial) allá

you /juː/ ▶ 638, 935 *pron* **1** (sing) **(a)** (as subject — familiar) tú, vos (AmC, RPl); (— formal) usted; **~ liar!** ¡mentiroso! **(b)** (as direct object — familiar) te; (— formal, masculine) lo, le (Esp); (— formal, feminine) la **(c)** (as indirect object — familiar) te; (— formal) le; (— with direct object pronoun present) se; **I told ~** te dije/le dije; **I gave it to ~** te lo di/se lo di **(d)** (after prep — familiar) ti, vos (AmC, RPl); (— formal) usted **2** (pl) **(a)** (as subject, after preposition — familiar) ustedes (AmL), vosotros, -tras (Esp); (— formal) ustedes; **be quiet, ~ two** ustedes dos: ¡cállense!, vosotros dos: ¡callaos! (Esp) **(b)** (as direct object — familiar) los, las (AmL), os (Esp); (— formal, masculine) los, les (Esp); (— formal, feminine) las **(c)** (as indirect object — familiar) les (AmL), os (Esp); (— formal) les; (— with direct object pronoun present) se; **I gave ~ the book** les *or* (Esp tb) os di el libro; **I gave it to ~** se *or* (Esp tb) os lo di **3** ▶ 936 (one) **(a)** (as subject) uno, una **(b)** (as direct/indirect object) te

you'd /juːd/ **(a)** = **you had (b)** = **you would**

you'll /juːl/ = **you will**

young[1] /jʌŋ/ *adj* **younger** /'jʌŋgər || 'jʌŋgə(r)/, **youngest** /'jʌŋgəst || 'jʌŋgɪst/ **(a)** ‹*animal/person*› joven; **I have a ~er brother** tengo un hermano menor; **she is four years ~er than me** tiene cuatro años menos que yo; **a ~ man/woman** un/una joven; **a ~ lady** una señorita, una chica joven; **~ people** la gente joven, los jóvenes, la juventud; **to marry ~** casarse joven **(b)** ‹*appearance/manner/complexion*› juvenil

young[2] *pl n* (animals) crías *fpl*

youngster /'jʌŋstər || 'jʌŋstə(r)/ *n* chico, -ca *m,f*

your /jʊr, *weak form* jər || jɔː(r), *weak form* jʊə(r)/ *adj*

■ **Note** The translations *tu* and *su* agree in number with the noun which they modify; they appear as *tu*, *tus*, *su*, *sus*, depending on what follows: *your father/mother* tu padre/madre *or* su padre/madre; *your books/magazines* tus libros/revistas *or* sus libros/revistas.
The translation *vuestro* agrees in number and gender with the noun which it modifies; it appears as *vuestro*, *vuestra*, *vuestros*, *vuestras*, depending on what follows: *your father/mother* vuestro padre/vuestra madre; *your books/magazines* vuestros libros/vuestras revistas.
For *your* used with parts of the body, ▶ 484

(a) (belonging to one person) (*sing, familiar*) tu; (*pl, familiar*) tus; (*sing, formal*) su; (*pl formal*) sus; **wash ~ hands** lávate/lávese las manos **(b)** (belonging to more than one person) (*sing, familiar*) su (AmL), vuestro, -tra (Esp); (*pl, familiar*) sus (AmL), vuestros, -tras (Esp); (*sing, formal*) su; (*pl, formal*) sus; **put ~ shoes on** pónganse *or* (Esp) pone(r)os los zapatos **(c)** (one's): **if ~ name begins with A** ... si tu/su nombre empieza con A ...; **you have to take ~ shoes off in a mosque** hay que quitarse los zapatos en una mezquita

you're /jʊər || jʊə(r), jɔː(r)/ = **you are**

yours /jʊrz || jɔːz/ *pron*

■ **Note** The three translations of *yours* reflects the gender and number of the noun they are standing for; *yours* is translated by *tuyo*, *tuya*, *tuyos*, *tuyas*, *suyo*, *suya*, *suyos*, *suyas*, *vuestro*, *vuestra*, *vuestros*, *vuestras*, depending on the meaning being translated, and what is being referred to.

(a) (belonging to one person) (*sing, familiar*) tuyo, -ya; (*pl, familiar*) tuyos, -yas; (*sing, formal*) suyo, -ya; (*pl formal*) suyos, -yas; **~ is here** el tuyo/la tuya/el suyo/la suya está aquí; **a friend of ~** un amigo tuyo/suyo **(b)** (belonging to more than one person) (*sing, formal*) suyo, -ya; (*pl, formal*) suyos, -yas; (*sing, familiar*) suyo, -ya (AmL), vuestro, -tra (Esp); (*pl, familiar*) suyos, -yas (AmL), vuestros, -tras (Esp); **~ are here, children** los suyos *or* los de ustedes están aquí, niños (AmL), los vuestros están aquí, niños (Esp); **is he a friend of ~?** ¿es amigo de ustedes *or* suyo *or* (Esp) vuestro? **(c)** (Corresp): **~, Daniel** un abrazo, Daniel

yourself /jər'self ‖ jɔː'self/ *pron* **(a)** (reflexive): **describe ~** (formal) descríbase; (familiar) descríbete; **stop thinking about ~** (formal) deje de pensar en sí mismo; (familiar) deja de pensar en ti mismo; **by ~** solo/sola **(b)** (emphatic use) (formal) usted mismo, usted misma; (familiar) tú mismo, tú misma; **you're a musician ~, I hear** usted también es *or* (*familiar*) tú también eres músico, tengo entendido **(c)** (normal self): **just be ~** compórtate con naturalidad; **you're not ~ today** hoy no eres el/la de siempre **(d)** (oneself) uno mismo, una misma

yourselves /jər'selvz ‖ jɔː'selvz/ *pron* **(a)** (reflexive): **behave ~!** ¡pórtense bien! (AmL), ¡porta(r)os bien! (Esp); **by ~** solos/solas **(b)** (emphatic use) (formal) ustedes mismos/mismas; (familiar) ustedes mismos/mismas *or* (Esp) vosotros mismos/vosotras mismas **(c)** (normal selves): **just be ~** compórtense *or* (Esp) comporta(r)os con naturalidad

youth /juːθ/ *n* [U] (*pl* **youths** /juːðz/) **1** (early life) juventud *f* **2** [U] (young people) (+ *sing or pl vb*) juventud *f*; (*before n*) ‹*movement/orchestra*› juvenil; **~ club** club *m* de jóvenes **3** [C] (young man) (frml) joven *m*

youthful /'juːθfəl/ *adj* ‹*enthusiasm/manner*› juvenil; ‹*folly/ignorance*› de juventud

youth hostel *n* albergue *m* juvenil *or* de la juventud

you've /juːv/ = **you have**

yowl /jaʊl/ *vi* «*person*» dar* alaridos; «*dog*» aullar*; «*cat*» maullar*

yo-yo /'jəʊjəʊ/ *n* yo-yo *m*

yr ▶ 540 (*pl* **yrs**) = **year**

Yugoslav /'juːgəʊ'slɑːv ‖ 'juːgəslɑːv/ *adj/n* ⇒ YUGOSLAVIAN[1,2]

Yugoslavia /'juːgəʊ'slɑːviə ‖ 'jʊgə'slɑːviə/ *n* (Hist) Yugoslavia *f*

Yugoslavian¹ /'juːgəʊ'slɑːviən ‖ 'jʊgə'slɑːviən/ *adj* (Hist) yugoslavo

Yugoslavian² *n* (Hist) yugoslavo, -va *m,f*

yuppie, **yuppy** /'jʌpi/ *n* (*pl* **-pies**) (colloq) yuppy *mf* (fam)

YWCA *n* (= **Young Women's Christian Association**) YWCA *f*, Asociación *f* de Jóvenes Cristianas

Zz

Z, z /ziː ‖zed/ *n* Z, z *f*

Zaire /zɑːir ‖ zɑː'iə(r)/ *n* Zaire *m*

Zairean /zɑː'iriən ‖ zɑː'iəriən/ *adj* zaireño

Zambia /'zæmbiə/ *n* Zambia *f*

Zambian /'zæmbiən ‖ 'zæmbiən/ *adj* zambiano

zany /'zeɪni/ *adj* **zanier, zaniest** (colloq) ‹*person*› chiflado (fam); ‹*adventure*› loco

zap /zæp/ *vt* **-pp-** **(a)** (defeat, blast) (colloq) liquidar (fam) **(b)** (Comput) eliminar, borrar

zeal /ziːl/ *n* [U] (Pol, Relig) fervor *m*, celo *m*

zealot /'zelət/ *n* (fanatic) fanático, -ca *m,f*

zealous /'zeləs/ *adj* ‹*follower*› ferviente; ‹*worker*› que pone gran celo en su trabajo

zebra /'ziːbrə ‖ 'zebrə, ziː-/ *n* (*pl* **-bras** *or* **-bra**) cebra *f*

zebra crossing *n* (BrE) paso *m* de cebra

zee /ziː/, (BrE) **zed** /zed/ *n* zeta *f*

zenith /'ziːnəθ ‖ 'zenɪθ/ *n* (Astron) cenit *m*, zenit *m*; **at the ~ of her popularity** en el cenit *or* el apogeo de su popularidad

zero¹ /'zɪrəʊ, 'ziː- ‖ 'zɪərəʊ/ ▶ 724 *n* (*pl* **zeros** *or* **zeroes**) cero *m*; **the temperature fell below ~** la temperatura bajó de los cero grados; (*before n*) **~ hour** hora *f* cero

zero² ▶ 724 *adj* cero *adj inv*; **~ degrees centigrade** cero grados centígrados

zest /zest/ *n* [U] entusiasmo *m*

zigzag¹ /'zɪgzæg/ *n* zigzag *m*

zigzag² *vi* **-gg-** zigzaguear

zilch /zɪltʃ/ *n* [U] (sl) nada de nada

Zimbabwe /zɪm'bɑːbwi, -weɪ/ *n* Zimbabwe *m*, Zimbabue *m*

Zimbabwean /zɪm'bɑːbwiən/ *adj* zimbabuense, de Zimbabwe

zinc /zɪŋk/ *n* [U] cinc *m*, zinc *m*

Zionism /'zaɪənɪzəm/ *n* [U] sionismo *m*

Zionist /'zaɪənəst ‖ 'zaɪənɪst/ *adj* sionista

zip¹ /zɪp/ *n* **1** [U] (vigor) (colloq) garra *f* (fam) **2** [C] (fastener) (BrE) ⇒ ZIPPER[1]

zip² **-pp-** *vt* ‹*pocket/bag*› cerrar* la cremallera (*or* el cierre *etc*) de ■ **~** *vi* **1** (with zipper): **the suitcase ~s open/shut** la maleta se abre/cierra con cremallera (*or* cierre *etc*) **2** (move fast) (colloq): **we ~ped through the work** (nos) despachamos el trabajo en un santiamén (fam)

• **zip up** [*v* + *o* + *adv*, *v* + *adv* + *o*] ‹*bag*› cerrar*

zip: **~ code** *n* (AmE) código *m* postal; **~ fastener** *n* (BrE) ⇒ ZIPPER[1]; **~-on** *adj* (*before n*) ‹*hood/lining*› que se puede quitar, desmontable

zipper¹ /'zɪpər || 'zɪpə(r)/ *n* (AmE) cremallera *f*, cierre *m* (AmL), zíper *m* (AmC, Méx, Ven), cierre *m* relámpago (RPl) *or* (Chi) eclair

zipper² *vt* (AmE) ⇒ ZIP² *vt*

zodiac /'zəʊdiæk/ *n* **the ~** el zodíaco *or* zodiaco

zombie /'zɑːmbi || 'zɒmbi/ *n* zombie *mf*

zone /zəʊn/ *n* **(a)** (area) zona *f*; **time ~** huso *m* horario **(b)** (AmE) distrito *m*

zoo /zuː/ *n* (*pl* **zoos**) zoológico *m*, zoo *m* (esp Esp)

zoologist /zəʊ'ɑːlədʒəst || zəʊ'ɒlədʒɪst, zuː/ *n* zoólogo, -ga *m,f*

zoology /zəʊ'ɑːlədʒi || zəʊ'ɒlədʒi, zuː/ *n* [U] zoología *f*

zoom¹ /zuːm/ *n* **1** (sound) (*no pl*) zumbido *m* **2 ~ (lens)** (Cin, Phot, TV) teleobjetivo *m*, zoom *m*

zoom² *vi* (move fast) (colloq) (+ *adv compl*): **to ~ along/past** ir*/pasar zumbando (fam)

• zoom in [*v* + *adv*] **to ~ in** (ON **sth/sb**) hacer* un zoom in (SOBRE algo/algn) (*acercar rápidamente una imagen usando un teleobjetivo*)

zucchini /zʊ'kiːni/ *n* (*pl* **~** *or* **~s**) (AmE) calabacín *m*, calabacita *f* (Méx), zapallito *m* (largo *or* italiano) (CS)

Zulu¹ /'zuːluː/ *adj* zulú

Zulu² *n* **(a)** [C] (person) zulú *mf* **(b)** [U] (language) zulú *m*

Spanish verb tables

1 Guide to Verb Tables

Every Spanish verb entry in the dictionary is cross-referred to one of the conjugation models shown in the following tables. The reference is given in square brackets immediately after the headword.

All the simple tenses are shown for **hablar [A1]**, **meter [E1]**, and **partir [I1]**, the conjugation models for regular **-ar**, **-er**, and **-ir** verbs. For other verbs only the irregular tenses are given.

Compound tenses are not listed in the tables. The perfect tenses are formed with the relevant tense of the auxiliary **haber** and the past participle:

Le *he hablado* de ti
Lamento que se *haya ofendido*
El profesor nos *había visto*
Cuando *hubo terminado* de hablar, ...
Para entonces ya *habremos terminado*
Si lo *hubiera sabido, habría llamado*

The continuous tenses are formed with the relevant tense of the auxiliary **estar** and the present participle:

Estoy estudiando el problema
Cuando llegó, *estábamos cerrando*
Estuvieron esperando mucho tiempo
¿*Han estado hablando* de mí?

Other verbs such as **andar**, **ir**, and **venir** can also be used as auxiliaries to express different nuances of meaning:

Andaba diciendo que ...
A medida que lo *fui conociendo*...
¿Por qué no te *vas vistiendo*?
Hace mucho tiempo que te lo *vengo diciendo*

2 Verbs ending in -ar

▸ A1 hablar

gerundio (gerund)	participio pasado (past participle)	indicativo (indicative) presente (present)	imperfecto (imperfect)	pretérito indefinido (past simple)	futuro (future)
habl**ando**	habl**ado**	habl**o**	habl**aba**	habl**é**	habl**aré**
		habl**as**	habl**abas**	habl**aste**	habl**arás**
		habl**a**	habl**aba**	habl**ó**	habl**ará**
		habl**amos**	habl**ábamos**	habl**amos**	habl**aremos**
		habl**áis**	habl**abais**	habl**asteis**	habl**aréis**
		habl**an**	habl**aban**	habl**aron**	habl**arán**

condicional (conditional)	subjuntivo (subjunctive) presente (present)	imperfecto (imperfect)	futuro (future)	imperativo (imperative)
habl**aría**	habl**e**	habl**ara***	habl**are**	
habl**arías**	habl**es**	habl**aras**	habl**ares**	habl**a**
habl**aría**	habl**e**	habl**ara**	habl**are**	habl**e**
habl**aríamos**	habl**emos**	habl**áramos**	habl**áremos**	habl**emos**
habl**aríais**	habl**éis**	habl**arais**	habl**areis**	habl**ad**
habl**arían**	habl**en**	habl**aran**	habl**aren**	habl**en**

* all **–ar** verbs have an alternative form in which the **–ara** is replaced by **–ase**, e.g. habl**ase**, habl**ases**, habl**ase**, habl**ásemos**, habl**aseis**, habl**asen**

Spanish verb tables A2–A11

▸ A2 sacar

indicativo pretérito indefinido	subjuntivo presente	imperativo
saqué	saque	
sacaste	saques	saca
sacó	saque	saque
sacamos	saquemos	saquemos
sacasteis	saquéis	sacad
sacaron	saquen	saquen

▸ A3 pagar

indicativo pretérito indefinido	subjuntivo presente	imperativo
pagué	pague	
pagaste	pagues	paga
pagó	pague	pague
pagamos	paguemos	paguemos
pagasteis	paguéis	pagad
pagaron	paguen	paguen

▸ A4 cazar

indicativo pretérito indefinido	subjuntivo presente	imperativo
cacé	cace	
cazaste	caces	caza
cazó	cace	cace
cazamos	cacemos	cacemos
cazasteis	cacéis	cazad
cazaron	cacen	cacen

▸ A5 pensar

indicativo presente	indicativo pretérito indefinido	subjuntivo presente	imperativo
pienso	pensé, etc	piense	
piensas		pienses	piensa
piensa		piense	piense
pensamos		pensemos	pensemos
pensáis		penséis	pensad
piensan		piensen	piensen

▸ A6 empezar

indicativo presente	indicativo pretérito indefinido	subjuntivo presente	imperativo
empiezo	empecé	empiece	
empiezas	empezaste	empieces	empieza
empieza	empezó	empiece	empiece
empezamos	empezamos	empecemos	empecemos
empezáis	empezasteis	empecéis	empezad
empiezan	empezaron	empiecen	empiecen

▸ A7 regar

indicativo presente	indicativo pretérito indefinido	subjuntivo presente	imperativo
riego	regué	riegue	
riegas	regaste	riegues	riega
riega	regó	riegue	riegue
regamos	regamos	reguemos	reguemos
regáis	regasteis	reguéis	regad
riegan	regaron	rieguen	rieguen

▸ A8 rogar

indicativo presente	indicativo pretérito indefinido	subjuntivo presente	imperativo
ruego	rogué	ruegue	
ruegas	rogaste	ruegues	ruega
ruega	rogó	ruegue	ruegue
rogamos	rogamos	roguemos	roguemos
rogáis	rogasteis	roguéis	rogad
ruegan	rogaron	rueguen	rueguen

▸ A9 volcar

indicativo presente	indicativo pretérito indefinido	subjuntivo presente	imperativo
vuelco	volqué	vuelque	
vuelcas	volcaste	vuelques	vuelca
vuelca	volcó	vuelque	vuelque
volcamos	volcamos	volquemos	volquemos
volcáis	volcasteis	volquéis	volcad
vuelcan	volcaron	vuelquen	vuelquen

▸ A10 contar

indicativo presente	indicativo pretérito indefinido	subjuntivo presente	imperativo
cuento	conté, etc	cuente	
cuentas		cuentes	cuenta
cuenta		cuente	cuente
contamos		contemos	contemos
contáis		contéis	contad
cuentan		cuenten	cuenten

▸ A11 forzar

indicativo presente	indicativo pretérito indefinido	subjuntivo presente	imperativo
fuerzo	forcé	fuerce	
fuerzas	forzaste	fuerces	fuerza
fuerza	forzó	fuerce	fuerce
forzamos	forzamos	forcemos	forcemos
forzáis	forzasteis	forcéis	forzad
fuerzan	forzaron	fuercen	fuercen

Spanish verb tables A12–A21

▸ A12 degollar

indicativo presente	pretérito indefinido	subjuntivo presente	imperativo
degüello	degollé, etc	degüelle	
degüellas		degüelles	degüella
degüella		degüelle	degüelle
degollamos		degollemos	degollemos
degolláis		degolléis	degollad
degüellan		degüellen	degüellen

▸ A13 avergonzar

indicativo presente	pretérito indefinido	subjuntivo presente	imperativo
avergüenzo	avergoncé	avergüence	
avergüenzas	avergonzaste	avergüences	avergüenza
avergüenza	avergonzó	avergüence	avergüence
avergonzamos	avergonzamos	avergoncemos	avergoncemos
avergonzáis	avergonzasteis	avergoncéis	avergonzad
avergüenzan	avergonzaron	avergüencen	avergüencen

▸ A14 desosar

indicativo presente	pretérito indefinido	subjuntivo presente	imperativo
deshueso	desosé, etc	deshuese	
deshuesas		deshueses	deshuesa
deshuesa		deshuese	deshuese
desosamos		desosemos	desosemos
desosáis		desoséis	desosad
deshuesan		deshuesen	deshuesen

▸ A15 jugar

indicativo presente	pretérito indefinido	subjuntivo presente	imperativo
juego	jugué	juegue	
juegas	jugaste	juegues	juega
juega	jugó	juegue	juegue
jugamos	jugamos	juguemos	juguemos
jugáis	jugasteis	juguéis	jugad
juegan	jugaron	jueguen	jueguen

▸ A16 averiguar

indicativo pretérito indefinido	subjuntivo presente	imperativo
averigüé	averigüe	
averiguaste	averigües	averigua
averiguó	averigüe	averigüe
averiguamos	averigüemos	averigüemos
averiguasteis	averigüéis	averiguad
averiguaron	averigüen	averigüen

▸ A17 vaciar

indicativo presente	pretérito indefinido	subjuntivo presente	imperativo
vacío	vacié, etc	vacíe	
vacías		vacíes	vacía
vacía		vacíe	vacíe
vaciamos		vaciemos	vaciemos
vaciáis		vaciéis	vaciad
vacían		vacíen	vacíen

▸ A18 actuar

indicativo presente	pretérito indefinido	subjuntivo presente	imperativo
actúo	actué, etc	actúe	
actúas		actúes	actúa
actúa		actúe	actúe
actuamos		actuemos	actuemos
actuáis		actuéis	actuad
actúan		actúen	actúen

▸ A19 aislar

indicativo presente	pretérito indefinido	subjuntivo presente	imperativo
aíslo	aislé, etc	aísle	
aíslas		aísles	aísla
aísla		aísle	aísle
aislamos		aislemos	aislemos
aisláis		aisléis	aislad
aíslan		aíslen	aíslen

▸ A20 ahincar

indicativo presente	pretérito indefinido	subjuntivo presente	imperativo
ahínco	ahinqué	ahínque	
ahíncas	ahincaste	ahínques	ahínca
ahínca	ahincó	ahínque	ahínque
ahincamos	ahincamos	ahinquemos	ahinquemos
ahincáis	ahincasteis	ahinquéis	ahincad
ahíncan	ahincaron	ahínquen	ahínquen

▸ A21 arcaizar

indicativo presente	pretérito indefinido	subjuntivo presente	imperativo
arcaízo	arcaicé	arcaíce	
arcaízas	arcaizaste	arcaíces	arcaíza
arcaíza	arcaizó	arcaíce	arcaíce
arcaizamos	arcaizamos	arcaicemos	arcaicemos
arcaizáis	arcaizasteis	arcaicéis	arcaizad
arcaízan	arcaizaron	arcaícen	arcaícen

Spanish verb tables A22–A27

▸ A22 cabrahigar

indicativo		subjuntivo	imperativo
presente	pretérito indefinido	presente	
cabrahígo	cabrahigué	cabrahígue	
cabrahígas	cabrahigaste	cabrahígues	cabrahíga
cabrahíga	cabrahigó	cabrahígue	cabrahígue
cabrahigamos	cabrahigamos	cabrahiguemos	cabrahiguemos
cabrahigáis	cabrahigasteis	cabrahiguéis	cabrahigad
cabrahígan	cabrahigaron	cabrahíguen	cabrahíguen

▸ A23 aunar

indicativo		subjuntivo	imperativo
presente	pretérito indefinido	presente	
aúno	auné, etc	aúne	
aúnas		aúnes	aúna
aúna		aúne	aúne
aunamos		aunemos	aunemos
aunáis		aunéis	aunad
aúnan		aúnen	aúnen

▸ A24 andar

indicativo	subjuntivo
pretérito indefinido	imperfecto
anduve	anduviera
anduviste	anduvieras
anduvo	anduviera
anduvimos	anduviéramos
anduvisteis	anduvierais
anduvieron	anduvieran

▸ A25 dar

indicativo		subjuntivo	
presente	pretérito indefinido	presente	imperfecto
doy	di	dé	diera
das	diste	des	dieras
da	dio	dé	diera
damos	dimos	demos	diéramos
dais	disteis	deis	dierais
dan	dieron	den	dieran

▸ A26 errar

indicativo	subjuntivo	imperativo
presente	presente	
yerro	yerre	
yerras	yerres	yerra
yerra	yerre	yerre
erramos	erremos	erremos
erráis	erréis	errad
yerran	yerren	yerren

▸ A27 estar

gerundio	participio pasado	indicativo			
		presente	imperfecto	pretérito indefinido	futuro
estando	estado	estoy	estaba	estuve	estaré
		estás	estabas	estuviste	estarás
		está	estaba	estuvo	estará
		estamos	estábamos	estuvimos	estaremos
		estáis	estabais	estuvisteis	estaréis
		están	estaban	estuvieron	estarán

condicional	subjuntivo		imperativo
	presente	imperfecto	
estaría	esté	estuviera	
estarías	estés	estuvieras	está
estaría	esté	estuviera	esté
estaríamos	estemos	estuviéramos	estemos
estaríais	estéis	estuvierais	estad
estarían	estén	estuvieran	estén

Spanish verb tables E1–E3

3 Verbs ending in -er

▸ E1 meter

gerundio (gerund)	participio pasado (past participle)	indicativo (indicative) presente (present)	imperfecto (imperfect)	pretérito indefinido (past simple)	futuro (future)
met**iendo**	met**ido**	met**o**	met**ía**	met**í**	met**eré**
		met**es**	met**ías**	met**iste**	met**erás**
		met**e**	met**ía**	met**ió**	met**erá**
		met**emos**	met**íamos**	met**imos**	met**eremos**
		met**éis**	met**íais**	met**isteis**	met**eréis**
		met**en**	met**ían**	met**ieron**	met**erán**

condicional (conditional)	subjuntivo (subjunctive) presente (present)	imperfecto (imperfect)	futuro (future)	imperativo (imperative)
met**ería**	met**a**	met**iera***	met**iere**	
met**erías**	met**as**	met**ieras**	met**ieres**	met**e**
met**ería**	met**a**	met**iera**	met**iere**	met**a**
met**eríamos**	met**amos**	met**iéramos**	met**iéremos**	met**amos**
met**eríais**	met**áis**	met**ierais**	met**iereis**	met**ed**
met**erían**	met**an**	met**ieran**	met**ieren**	met**an**

* all **–er** verbs have an alternative form in which **–era** is replaced by **–ese**, e.g. met**iese**, met**ieses**, met**iese**, met**iésemos**, met**ieseis**, met**iesen**

▸ E2 vencer

indicativo presente	pretérito indefinido	subjuntivo presente	imperativo
venzo	vencí, etc	venza	
vences		venzas	vence
vence		venza	venza
vencemos		venzamos	venzamos
vencéis		venzáis	venced
vencen		venzan	venzan

▸ E3 conocer

indicativo presente	pretérito indefinido	subjuntivo presente	imperativo
conozco	conocí, etc	conozca	
conoces		conozcas	conoce
conoce		conozca	conozca
conocemos		conozcamos	conozcamos
conocéis		conozcáis	conoced
conocen		conozcan	conozcan

Spanish verb tables E4–E9

▸ E4 placer

indicativo presente	pretérito indefinido	subjuntivo presente	imperfecto	futuro	imperativo
plazco	plací	plazca	placiera	placiere	
places	placiste	plazcas	placieras	placieres	place
place	plació[1]	plazca[3]	placiera[4]	placiere[5]	plazca
placemos	placimos	plazcamos	placiéramos	placiéremos	plazcamos
placéis	placisteis	plazcáis	placierais	placiereis	placed
placen	placieron[2]	plazcan	placieran	placieren	plazcan

alternative forms, applicable only to the verb 'placer':
[1]plugo; [2]pluguieron; [3]plega or plegue; [4]pluguiera or pluguiese; [5]pluguiere.

▸ E5 yacer

indicativo presente	pretérito indefinido	subjuntivo presente	imperativo
yazco[1]	yací, etc	yazca[2]	
yaces		yazcas	yace[3]
yace		yazca	yazca
yacemos		yazcamos	yazcamos
yacéis		yazcáis	yaced
yacen		yazcan	yazcan

[1]alternative forms: yazgo or yago; [2]alternative conjugations: yazga, yazgas, etc or yaga, yagas, etc.
[3]alternative conjugations: yaz, yazga or yaga, yazgamos or yagamos, yaced, yazgan or yagan.

▸ E6 coger

indicativo presente	pretérito indefinido	subjuntivo presente	imperativo
cojo	cogí, etc	coja	
coges		cojas	coge
coge		coja	coja
cogemos		cojamos	cojamos
cogéis		cojáis	coged
cogen		cojan	cojan

▸ E7 atañer

gerundio	indicativo pretérito indefinido	subjuntivo imperfecto
atañendo	atañí	atañera
	atañiste	atañeras
	atañó	atañera
	atañimos	atañéramos
	atañisteis	atañerais
	atañeron	atañeran

▸ E8 entender

indicativo presente	pretérito indefinido	subjuntivo presente	imperativo
entiendo	entendí	entienda	
entiendes	entendiste	entiendas	entiende
entiende	entendió	entienda	entienda
entendemos	entendimos	entendamos	entendamos
entendéis	entendisteis	entendáis	entended
entienden	entendieron	entiendan	entiendan

▸ E9 mover

indicativo presente	pretérito indefinido	subjuntivo presente	imperativo
muevo	moví, etc	mueva	
mueves		muevas	mueve
mueve		mueva	mueva
movemos		movamos	movamos
movéis		mováis	moved
mueven		muevan	muevan

Spanish verb tables E10–E14

▸ E10 torcer

indicativo		subjuntivo	imperativo
presente	pretérito indefinido	presente	
tuerzo	torcí, etc	tuerza	
tuerces		tuerzas	tuerce
tuerce		tuerza	tuerza
torcemos		torzamos	torzamos
torcéis		torzáis	torced
tuercen		tuerzan	tuerzan

▸ E11 volver

participio pasado	indicativo		subjuntivo	imperativo
	presente	pretérito indefinido	presente	
vuelto	vuelvo	volví, etc	vuelva	
	vuelves		vuelvas	vuelve
	vuelve		vuelva	vuelva
	volvemos		volvamos	volvamos
	volvéis		volváis	volved
	vuelven		vuelvan	vuelvan

▸ E12 oler

indicativo		subjuntivo	imperativo
presente	pretérito indefinido	presente	
huelo	olí, etc	huela	
hueles		huelas	huele
huele		huela	huela
olemos		olamos	olamos
oléis		oláis	oled
huelen		huelan	huelan

▸ E13 leer

gerundio	indicativo	subjuntivo
	pretérito indefinido	imperfecto
leyendo	leí	leyera
	leíste	leyeras
	leyó	leyera
	leímos	leyéramos
	leísteis	leyerais
	leyeron	leyeran

▸ E14 proveer

participio pasado	indicativo	subjuntivo
	pretérito indefinido	imperfecto
provisto	proveí	proveyera
	proveíste	proveyeras
	proveyó	proveyera
	proveímos	proveyéramos
	proveísteis	proveyerais
	proveyeron	proveyeran

Spanish verb tables E15–E18

▸ E15 caber

indicativo				condicional	subjuntivo		imperativo
presente	imperfecto	pretérito indefinido	futuro		presente	imperfecto	
quepo	cabía	cupe	cabré	cabría	quepa	cupiera	
cabes	cabías	cupiste	cabrás	cabrías	quepas	cupieras	cabe
cabe	cabía	cupo	cabrá	cabría	quepa	cupiera	quepa
cabemos	cabíamos	cupimos	cabremos	cabríamos	quepamos	cupiéramos	quepamos
cabéis	cabíais	cupisteis	cabréis	cabríais	quepáis	cupierais	cabed
caben	cabían	cupieron	cabrán	cabrían	quepan	cupieran	quepan

▸ E16 caer

gerundio	participio pasado	indicativo			subjuntivo		imperativo
		presente	imperfecto	pretérito indefinido	presente	imperfecto	
cayendo	caído	caigo	caía	caí	caiga	cayera	
		caes	caías	caíste	caigas	cayeras	cae
		cae	caía	cayó	caiga	cayera	caiga
		caemos	caíamos	caímos	caigamos	cayéramos	caigamos
		caéis	caíais	caísteis	caigáis	cayerais	caed
		caen	caían	cayeron	caigan	cayeran	caigan

▸ E17 haber

indicativo				condicional	subjuntivo		imperativo
presente	imperfecto	pretérito indefinido	futuro		presente	imperfecto	
he	había	hube	habré	habría	haya	hubiera	
has	habías	hubiste	habrás	habrías	hayas	hubieras	he
ha	había	hubo	habrá	habría	haya	hubiera	haya
hemos	habíamos	hubimos	habremos	habríamos	hayamos	hubiéramos	hayamos
habéis	habíais	hubisteis	habréis	habríais	hayáis	hubierais	habed
han	habían	hubieron	habrán	habrían	hayan	hubieran	hayan

▸ E18 hacer

participio pasado	indicativo			condicional	subjuntivo		imperativo
	presente	pretérito indefinido	futuro		presente	imperfecto	
hecho	hago	hice	haré	haría	haga	hiciera	
	haces	hiciste	harás	harías	hagas	hicieras	haz
	hace	hizo	hará	haría	haga	hiciera	haga
	hacemos	hicimos	haremos	haríamos	hagamos	hiciéramos	hagamos
	hacéis	hicisteis	haréis	haríais	hagáis	hicierais	haced
	hacen	hicieron	harán	harían	hagan	hicieran	hagan

Spanish verb tables E19–E22

▸ E19 rehacer

participio pasado	indicativo			condicional	subjuntivo		imperativo
	presente	pretérito indefinido	futuro		presente	imperfecto	
rehecho	rehago	rehíce	reharé	reharía	rehaga	rehiciera	
	rehaces	rehiciste	reharás	reharías	rehagas	rehicieras	rehaz
	rehace	rehízo	rehará	reharía	rehaga	rehiciera	rehaga
	rehacemos	rehicimos	reharemos	reharíamos	rehagamos	rehiciéramos	rehagamos
	rehacéis	rehicisteis	reharéis	reharíais	rehagáis	rehicierais	rehaced
	rehacen	rehicieron	reharán	reharían	rehagan	rehicieran	rehagan

▸ E20 satisfacer

indicativo			condicional	subjuntivo		imperativo
presente	pretérito indefinido	futuro		presente	imperfecto	
satisfago	satisfice	satisfaré	satisfaría	satisfaga	satisficiera	
satisfaces	satisficiste	satisfarás	satisfarías	satisfagas	satisficieras	satisfaz[1]
satisface	satisfizo	satisfará	satisfaría	satisfaga	satisficiera	satisfaga
satisfacemos	satisficimos	satisfaremos	satisfaríamos	satisfagamos	satisficiéramos	satisfagamos
satisfacéis	satisficisteis	satisfaréis	satisfaríais	satisfagáis	satisficierais	satisfaced
satisfacen	satisficieron	satisfarán	satisfarían	satisfagan	satisficieran	satisfagan

[1]alternative form: satisface

▸ E21 poder

gerundio	participio pasado
pudiendo	podido

indicativo			condicional	subjuntivo		imperativo
presente	pretérito indefinido	futuro		presente	imperfecto	
puedo	pude	podré	podría	pueda	pudiera	
puedes	pudiste	podrás	podrías	puedas	pudieras	puede
puede	pudo	podrá	podría	pueda	pudiera	pueda
podemos	pudimos	podremos	podríamos	podamos	pudiéramos	podamos
podéis	pudisteis	podréis	podríais	podáis	pudierais	poded
pueden	pudieron	podrán	podrían	puedan	pudieran	puedan

▸ E22 poner

participio pasado	indicativo			condicional	subjuntivo		imperativo
	presente	pretérito indefinido	futuro		presente	imperfecto	
puesto	pongo	puse	pondré	pondría	ponga	pusiera	
	pones	pusiste	pondrás	pondrías	pongas	pusieras	pon
	pone	puso	pondrá	pondría	ponga	pusiera	ponga
	ponemos	pusimos	pondremos	pondríamos	pongamos	pusiéramos	pongamos
	ponéis	pusisteis	pondréis	pondríais	pongáis	pusierais	poned
	ponen	pusieron	pondrán	pondrían	pongan	pusieran	pongan

Spanish verb tables E23–E26

➤ E23 traer

gerundio	participio pasado	indicativo		subjuntivo		imperativo
		presente	pretérito indefinido	presente	imperfecto	
trayendo	traído	traigo	traje	traiga	trajera	
		traes	trajiste	traigas	trajeras	trae
		trae	trajo	traiga	trajera	traiga
		traemos	trajimos	traigamos	trajéramos	traigamos
		traéis	trajisteis	traigáis	trajerais	traed
		traen	trajeron	traigan	trajeran	traigan

➤ E24 querer

indicativo				condicional	subjuntivo		imperativo
presente	imperfecto	pretérito indefinido	futuro		presente	imperfecto	
quiero	quería	quise	querré	querría	quiera	quisiera	
quieres	querías	quisiste	querrás	querrías	quieras	quisieras	quiere
quiere	quería	quiso	querrá	querría	quiera	quisiera	quiera
queremos	queríamos	quisimos	querremos	querríamos	queramos	quisiéramos	queramos
queréis	queríais	quisisteis	querréis	querríais	queráis	quisierais	quered
quieren	querían	quisieron	querrán	querrían	quieran	quisieran	quieran

➤ E25 saber

indicativo			condicional	subjuntivo		imperativo
presente	pretérito indefinido	futuro		presente	imperfecto	
sé	supe	sabré	sabría	sepa	supiera	
sabes	supiste	sabrás	sabrías	sepas	supieras	sabe
sabe	supo	sabrá	sabría	sepa	supiera	sepa
sabemos	supimos	sabremos	sabríamos	sepamos	supiéramos	sepamos
sabéis	supisteis	sabréis	sabríais	sepáis	supierais	sabed
saben	supieron	sabrán	sabrían	sepan	supieran	sepan

➤ E26 ser

gerundio	participio pasado	indicativo			
		presente	imperfecto	pretérito indefinido	futuro
siendo	sido	soy	era	fui	seré
		eres	eras	fuiste	serás
		es	era	fue	será
		somos	éramos	fuimos	seremos
		sois	erais	fuisteis	seréis
		son	eran	fueron	serán

condicional	subjuntivo			imperativo
	presente	imperfecto	futuro	
sería	sea	fuera	fuere	
serías	seas	fueras	fueres	sé
sería	sea	fuera	fuere	sea
seríamos	seamos	fuéramos	fuéremos	seamos
seríais	seáis	fuerais	fuereis	sed
serían	sean	fueran	fueren	sean

Spanish verb tables E27–E31

➤ E27 tener

indicativo presente	pretérito indefinido	futuro	condicional	subjuntivo presente	imperfecto	imperativo
tengo	tuve	tendré	tendría	tenga	tuviera	
tienes	tuviste	tendrás	tendrías	tengas	tuvieras	ten
tiene	tuvo	tendrá	tendría	tenga	tuviera	tenga
tenemos	tuvimos	tendremos	tendríamos	tengamos	tuviéramos	tengamos
tenéis	tuvisteis	tendréis	tendríais	tengáis	tuvierais	tened
tienen	tuvieron	tendrán	tendrían	tengan	tuvieran	tengan

➤ E28 valer

indicativo presente	pretérito indefinido	futuro	condicional	subjuntivo presente	imperfecto	imperativo
valgo	valí	valdré	valdría	valga	valiera	
vales	valiste	valdrás	valdrías	valgas	valieras	vale
vale	valió	valdrá	valdría	valga	valiera	valga
valemos	valimos	valdremos	valdríamos	valgamos	valiéramos	valgamos
valéis	valisteis	valdréis	valdríais	valgáis	valierais	valed
valen	valieron	valdrán	valdrían	valgan	valieran	valgan

➤ E29 ver

participio pasado	indicativo presente	imperfecto	pretérito indefinido	subjuntivo presente	imperativo
visto	veo	veía	vi	vea	
	ves	veías	viste	veas	ve
	ve	veía	vio	vea	vea
	vemos	veíamos	vimos	veamos	veamos
	veis	veíais	visteis	veáis	ved
	ven	veían	vieron	vean	vean

➤ E30 romper

participio pasado
roto

➤ E31 verter

gerundio	indicativo presente	pretérito indefinido	subjuntivo imperfecto	imperativo
vertiendo[1]	vierto	vertí	vertiera[4]	
	viertes	vertiste	vertieras	vierte
	vierte	vertió[2]	vertiera	vierta
	vertemos	vertimos	vertiéramos	vertamos
	vertéis	vertisteis	vertierais	verted
	vierten	vertieron[3]	vertieran	viertan

alternative forms: [1]virtiendo; [2]virtió; [3]virtieron; [4]virtiera, virtieras, etc.

4 Verbs ending in -ir

▸ I1 partir

gerundio (gerund)	participio pasado (past participle)	indicativo (indicative) presente (present)	imperfecto (imperfect)	pretérito indefinido (past simple)	futuro (future)
part**iendo**	part**ido**	part**o**	part**ía**	part**í**	part**iré**
		part**es**	part**ías**	part**iste**	part**irás**
		part**e**	part**ía**	part**ió**	part**irá**
		part**imos**	part**íamos**	part**imos**	part**iremos**
		part**ís**	part**íais**	part**isteis**	part**iréis**
		part**en**	part**ían**	part**ieron**	part**irán**

condicional (conditional)	subjuntivo (subjunctive) presente (present)	imperfecto (imperfect)	futuro (future)	imperativo (imperative)
part**iría**	part**a**	part**iera***	part**iere**	
part**irías**	part**as**	part**ieras**	part**ieres**	part**e**
part**iría**	part**a**	part**iera**	part**iere**	part**a**
part**iríamos**	part**amos**	part**iéramos**	part**iéremos**	part**amos**
part**iríais**	part**áis**	part**ierais**	part**iereis**	part**id**
part**irían**	part**an**	part**ieran**	part**ieren**	part**an**

* all **-ir** verbs have an alternative form in which **-era** is replaced by **-ese**, e.g. part**iese**, part**ieses**, part**iese**, part**iésemos**, part**ieseis**, part**iesen**

▸ I2 distinguir

indicativo presente	pretérito indefinido	subjuntivo presente	imperativo
distingo	distinguí, etc	distinga	
distingues		distingas	distingue
distingue		distinga	distinga
distinguimos		distingamos	distingamos
distinguís		distingáis	distinguid
distinguen		distingan	distingan

▸ I3 delinquir

indicativo presente	pretérito indefinido	subjuntivo presente	imperativo
delinco	delinquí, etc	delinca	
delinques		delincas	delinque
delinque		delinca	delinca
delinquimos		delincamos	delincamos
delinquís		delincáis	delinquid
delinquen		delincan	delincan

▸ I4 zurcir

indicativo presente	pretérito indefinido	subjuntivo presente	imperativo
zurzo	zurcí, etc	zurza	
zurces		zurzas	zurce
zurce		zurza	zurza
zurcimos		zurzamos	zurzamos
zurcís		zurzáis	zurcid
zurcen		zurzan	zurzan

▸ I5 lucir

indicativo presente	pretérito indefinido	subjuntivo presente	imperativo
luzco	lucí, etc	luzca	
luces		luzcas	luce
luce		luzca	luzca
lucimos		luzcamos	luzcamos
lucís		luzcáis	lucid
lucen		luzcan	luzcan

Spanish verb tables I6–I13

▸ I6 reducir

indicativo presente	pretérito indefinido	subjuntivo presente	imperfecto	imperativo
reduzco	reduje	reduzca	redujera	
reduces	redujiste	reduzcas	redujeras	reduce
reduce	redujo	reduzca	redujera	reduzca
reducimos	redujimos	reduzcamos	redujéramos	reduzcamos
reducís	redujisteis	reduzcáis	redujerais	reducid
reducen	redujeron	reduzcan	redujeran	reduzcan

▸ I7 dirigir

indicativo presente	pretérito indefinido	subjuntivo presente	imperativo
dirijo	dirigí, etc	dirija	
diriges		dirijas	dirige
dirige		dirija	dirija
dirigimos		dirijamos	dirijamos
dirigís		dirijáis	dirigid
dirigen		dirijan	dirijan

▸ I8 regir

indicativo presente	pretérito indefinido	subjuntivo presente	imperativo
rijo	regí, etc	rija	
riges		rijas	rige
rige		rija	rija
regimos		rijamos	rijamos
regís		rijáis	regid
rigen		rijan	rijan

▸ I9 gruñir

gerundio	indicativo pretérito indefinido	subjuntivo imperfecto
gruñendo	gruñí	gruñera
	gruñiste	gruñeras
	gruñó	gruñera
	gruñimos	gruñéramos
	gruñisteis	gruñerais
	gruñeron	gruñeran

▸ I10 asir

indicativo presente	pretérito indefinido	subjuntivo presente	imperativo
asgo	así, etc	asga	
ases		asgas	ase
ase		asga	asga
asimos		asgamos	asgamos
asís		asgáis	asid
asen		asgan	asgan

▸ I11 sentir

gerundio	participio pasado	indicativo presente	pretérito indefinido	subjuntivo presente	imperfecto	imperativo
sintiendo	sentido	siento	sentí	sienta	sintiera	
		sientes	sentiste	sientas	sintieras	siente
		siente	sintió	sienta	sintiera	sienta
		sentimos	sentimos	sintamos	sintiéramos	sintamos
		sentís	sentisteis	sintáis	sintierais	sentid
		sienten	sintieron	sientan	sintieran	sientan

▸ I12 concernir

indicativo presente	pretérito indefinido	subjuntivo presente	imperativo
concierno	concerní, etc	concierna	
conciernes		conciernas	concierne
concierne		concierna	concierna
concernimos		concernamos	concernamos
concernís		concernáis	concernid
conciernen		conciernan	conciernan

▸ I13 adquirir

indicativo presente	pretérito indefinido	subjuntivo presente	imperativo
adquiero	adquirí, etc	adquiera	
adquieres		adquieras	adquiere
adquiere		adquiera	adquiera
adquirimos		adquiramos	adquiramos
adquirís		adquiráis	adquirid
adquieren		adquieran	adquieran

Spanish verb tables I 14–I 17

➤ I14 pedir

gerundio	participio pasado	indicativo		subjuntivo		imperativo
		presente	pretérito indefinido	presente	imperfecto	
pidiendo	pedido	pido	pedí	pida	pidiera	
		pides	pediste	pidas	pidieras	pide
		pide	pidió	pida	pidiera	pida
		pedimos	pedimos	pidamos	pidiéramos	pidamos
		pedís	pedisteis	pidáis	pidierais	pedid
		piden	pidieron	pidas	pidieran	pidan

➤ I15 ceñir

gerundio	participio pasado	indicativo			subjuntivo		imperativo
		presente	imperfecto	pretérito indefinido	presente	imperfecto	
ciñendo	ceñido	ciño	ceñía	ceñí	ciña	ciñera	
		ciñes	ceñías	ceñiste	ciñas	ciñeras	ciñe
		ciñe	ceñía	ciñó	ciña	ciñera	ciña
		ceñimos	ceñíamos	ceñimos	ciñamos	ciñéramos	ciñamos
		ceñís	ceñíais	ceñisteis	ciñáis	ciñerais	ceñid
		ciñen	ceñían	ciñeron	ciñan	ciñeran	ciñan

➤ I16 dormir

gerundio	participio pasado	indicativo		subjuntivo		imperativo
		presente	pretérito indefinido	presente	imperfecto	futuro
durmiendo	dormido	duermo	dormí	duerma	durmiera	
		duermes	dormiste	duermas	durmieras	duerme
		duerme	durmió	duerma	durmiera	duerma
		dormimos	dormimos	durmamos	durmiéramos	durmamos
		dormís	dormisteis	durmáis	durmierais	dormid
		duermen	durmieron	duerman	durmieran	duerman

➤ I17 embaír

gerundio	indicativo	subjuntivo
	pretérito indefinido	imperfecto
embayendo	embaí	embayera
	embaíste	embayeras
	embayó	embayera
	embaímos	embayéramos
	embaísteis	embayerais
	embayeron	embayeran

Spanish verb tables I 18–I 22

▸ I 18 reír

gerundio	participio pasado
riendo	reído

indicativo presente	imperfecto	pretérito indefinido	futuro	condicional	subjuntivo presente	imperfecto	imperativo
río	reía	reí	reiré	reiría	ría	riera	
ríes	reías	reíste	reirás	reirías	rías	rieras	ríe
ríe	reía	rió	reirá	reiría	ría	riera	ría
reímos	reíamos	reímos	reiremos	reiríamos	riamos	riéramos	riamos
reís	reíais	reísteis	reiréis	reiríais	riáis	rierais	reíd
ríen	reían	rieron	reirán	reirían	rían	rieran	rían

▸ I 19 argüir

gerundio	participio pasado	indicativo presente	imperfecto	pretérito indefinido	subjuntivo presente	imperfecto	imperativo
arguyendo	argüido	arguyo	argüía, etc	argüí	arguya	arguyera	
		arguyes		argüiste	arguyas	arguyeras	arguye
		arguye		arguyó	arguya	arguyera	arguya
		argüimos		argüimos	arguyamos	arguyéramos	arguyamos
		argüís		argüisteis	arguyáis	arguyerais	argüid
		arguyen		arguyeron	arguyan	arguyeran	arguyan

▸ I 20 huir

gerundio	participio pasado	indicativo presente	imperfecto	pretérito indefinido	subjuntivo presente	imperfecto	imperativo
huyendo	huido	huyo	huía, etc	huí	huya	huyera	
		huyes		huiste	huyas	huyeras	huye
		huye		huyó	huya	huyera	huya
		huimos		huimos	huyamos	huyéramos	huyamos
		huís		huisteis	huyáis	huyerais	huid
		huyen		huyeron	huyan	huyeran	huyan

▸ I 21 rehuir

indicativo presente	pretérito indefinido	subjuntivo presente	imperativo
rehúyo	rehuí, etc	rehúya	
rehúyes		rehúyas	rehúye
rehúye		rehúya	rehúya
rehuimos		rehuyamos	rehuyamos
rehuís		rehuyáis	rehuid
rehúyen		rehúyan	rehúyan

▸ I 22 prohibir

indicativo presente	pretérito indefinido	subjuntivo presente	imperativo
prohíbo	prohibí, etc	prohíba	
prohíbes		prohíbas	prohíbe
prohíbe		prohíba	prohíba
prohibimos		prohibamos	prohibamos
prohibís		prohibáis	prohibid
prohíben		prohíban	prohíban

➤ I23 reunir

indicativo		subjuntivo	imperativo
presente	pretérito indefinido	presente	
reúno	reuní, etc	reúna	
reúnes		reúnas	reúne
reúne		reúna	reúna
reunimos		reunamos	reunamos
reunís		reunáis	reunid
reúnen		reúnan	reúnan

➤ I24 decir

gerundio	participio pasado
diciendo	dicho

indicativo				condicional	subjuntivo		imperativo
presente	imperfecto	pretérito indefinido	futuro		presente	imperfecto	
digo	decía	dije	diré	diría	diga	dijera	
dices	decías	dijiste	dirás	dirías	digas	dijeras	di
dice	decía	dijo	dirá	diría	diga	dijera	diga
decimos	decíamos	dijimos	diremos	diríamos	digamos	dijéramos	digamos
decís	decíais	dijisteis	diréis	diríais	digáis	dijerais	decid
dicen	decían	dijeron	dirán	dirían	digan	dijeran	digan

➤ I25 bendecir

participio pasado	indicativo			condicional	imperativo
	presente	pretérito indefinido	futuro		
bendecido	bendigo	bendije	bendeciré	bendeciría	
	bendices	bendijiste	bendecirás	bendecirías	bendice
	bendice	bendijo	bendecirá	bendeciría	bendiga
	bendecimos	bendijimos	bendeciremos	bendeciríamos	bendigamos
	bendecís	bendijisteis	bendeciréis	bendeciríais	bendecid
	bendicen	bendijeron	bendecirán	bendecirían	bendigan

➤ I26 erguir

gerundio	indicativo		subjuntivo		imperativo
	presente	pretérito indefinido	presente	imperfecto	
irguiendo	yergo[1]	erguí	yerga[2]	irguiera	
	yergues	erguiste	yergas	irguieras	yergue[3]
	yergue	irguió	yerga	irguiera	yerga
	erguimos	erguimos	yergamos	irguiéramos	yergamos
	erguís	erguisteis	yergáis	irguierais	erguid
	yerguen	irguieron	yergan	irguieran	yergan

[1]alternative conjugation: irgo, irgues, irgue, erguimos, erguís, irguen; [2]alternative conjugation: irga, irgas, irga, irgamos, irgáis, irgan; [3]alternative conjugation: irgue, irga, irgamos, erguid, irgan.

Spanish verb tables I27–I30

▸ I27 ir

gerundio	participio pasado	indicativo presente	imperfecto	pretérito indefinido	futuro
yendo	ido	voy	iba	fui	iré
		vas	ibas	fuiste	irás
		va	iba	fue	irá
		vamos	íbamos	fuimos	iremos
		vais	ibais	fuisteis	iréis
		van	iban	fueron	irán

condicional	subjuntivo presente	imperfecto	futuro	imperativo
iría	vaya	fuera	fuere	
irías	vayas	fueras	fueres	ve
iría	vaya	fuera	fuere	vaya
iríamos	vayamos	fuéramos	fuéremos	vayamos
iríais	vayáis	fuerais	fuereis	id
irían	vayan	fueran	fueren	vayan

▸ I28 oír

gerundio	participio pasado
oyendo	oído

indicativo presente	imperfecto	pretérito	futuro	condicional	subjuntivo presente	imperfecto	imperativo indefinido
oigo	oía	oí	oiré	oiría	oiga	oyera	
oyes	oías	oíste	oirás	oirías	oigas	oyeras	oye
oye	oía	oyó	oirá	oiría	oiga	oyera	oiga
oímos	oíamos	oímos	oiremos	oiríamos	oigamos	oyéramos	oigamos
oís	oíais	oísteis	oiréis	oiríais	oigáis	oyerais	oíd
oyen	oían	oyeron	oirán	oirían	oigan	oyeran	oigan

▸ I29 salir

indicativo presente	pretérito indefinido	futuro	condicional	subjuntivo presente	imperfecto	imperativo
salgo	salí, etc	saldré	saldría	salga	saliera	
sales		saldrás	saldrías	salgas	salieras	sal
sale		saldrá	saldría	salga	saliera	salga
salimos		saldremos	saldríamos	salgamos	saliéramos	salgamos
salís		saldréis	saldríais	salgáis	salierais	salid
salen		saldrán	saldrían	salgan	salieran	salgan

▸ I30 seguir

indicativo presente	pretérito indefinido	subjuntivo presente	imperfecto	imperativo
sigo	seguí	siga	siguiera	
sigues	seguiste	sigas	siguieras	sigue
sigue	siguió	siga	siguiera	siga
seguimos	seguimos	sigamos	siguiéramos	sigamos
seguís	seguisteis	sigáis	siguierais	seguid
siguen	siguieron	sigan	siguieran	sigan

Spanish verb tables I31–I38

➤ I31 venir

gerundio	indicativo presente	pretérito indefinido	futuro	condicional	subjuntivo presente	imperfecto	imperativo
viniendo	vengo	vine	vendré	vendría	venga	viniera	
	vienes	viniste	vendrás	vendrías	vengas	vinieras	ven
	viene	vino	vendrá	vendría	venga	viniera	venga
	venimos	vinimos	vendremos	vendríamos	vengamos	viniéramos	vengamos
	venís	vinisteis	vendréis	vendríais	vengáis	vinierais	venid
	vienen	vinieron	vendrán	vendrían	vengan	vinieran	vengan

➤ I32 abolir

This is a regular verb but in the present indicative it is only used in the first and second person plural.

➤ I33 abrir

participio pasado
abierto

➤ I34 escribir

participio pasado
escrito

➤ I35 freír

gerundio	participio pasado	indicativo presente	pretérito indefinido	subjuntivo presente	imperfecto	imperativo
friendo	frito	frío	freí	fría	friera	
		fríes	freíste	frías	frieras	fríe
		fríe	frió	fría	friera	fría
		freímos	freímos	friamos	friéramos	friamos
		freís	freísteis	friáis	frierais	freíd
		fríen	frieron	frían	frieran	frían

➤ I36 imprimir

participio pasado
impreso

➤ I37 morir

gerundio	participio pasado	indicativo presente	pretérito indefinido	subjuntivo presente	imperfecto
muriendo	muerto	muero	morí	muera	muriera
		mueres	moriste	mueras	murieras
		muere	murió	muera	muriera
		morimos	morimos	muramos	muriéramos
		morís	moristeis	muráis	murierais
		mueren	murieron	mueran	murieran

➤ I38 pudrir

infinitivo	participio pasado
pudrir, podrir	podrido

All other forms are regular and are derived from the infinitive pudrir e.g. pudro, pudres, etc.

Los verbos irregulares ingleses

Las formas irregulares que sólo se usan en algunas acepciones se indican con un asterisco (e.g. **abode*).

La información completa acerca del uso, la pronunciación, etc de cada verbo se encontrará en el artículo correspondiente.

infinitive/ infinitivo	past tense/ pretérito	past participle/ participio pasado
abide	abided, *abode	abided, *abode
arise	arose	arisen
awake	awoke	awoken
be	was/were	been
bear	bore	borne
beat	beat	beaten
become	became	become
befall	befell	befallen
beget	begot, (arch) begat	begotten
begin	began	begun
behold	beheld	beheld
bend	bent	bent
beseech	beseeched, besought	beseeched, besought
beset	beset	beset
bet	bet	bet
bid	*bade, bid	*bidden, bid
bind	bound	bound
bite	bit	bitten
bleed	bled	bled
bless	blessed	blessed, (arch) blest
blow	blew	blown, *blowed
break	broke	broken
breed	bred	bred
bring	brought	brought
broadcast	broadcast	broadcast
browbeat	browbeat	browbeaten
build	built	built
burn	burned, burnt	burned, burnt
bust	busted, (BrE also) bust	busted, (BrE also) bust
buy	bought	bought
cast	cast	cast
catch	caught	caught
choose	chose	chosen
cling	clung	clung
come	came	come
cost	*cost, *costed	*cost, *costed
creep	crept	crept
crow	crowed	crowed
cut	cut	cut
deal	dealt	dealt
dig	dug	dug
dive	dived, (AmE also) dove	dived
do	did	done
draw	drew	drawn
dream	dreamed, (BrE also) dreamt	dreamed, (BrE also) dreamt
drink	drank	drunk
drive	drove	driven
dwell	dwelt, dwelled	dwelt, dwelled
eat	ate	eaten
fall	fell	fallen
feed	fed	fed
feel	felt	felt

infinitive/ infinitivo	past tense/ pretérito	past participle/ participio pasado
fight	fought	fought
find	found	found
flee	fled	fled
fling	flung	flung
floodlight	floodlit	floodlit
fly	flew	flown
forbid	forbade, forbad	forbidden
forecast	forecast, forecasted	forecast, forecasted
foresee	foresaw	foreseen
foretell	foretold	foretold
forget	forgot	forgotten
forgive	forgave	forgiven
forsake	forsook	forsaken
freeze	froze	frozen
get	got	got, (AmE also) gotten
give	gave	given
go	went	gone
grind	ground	ground
grow	grew	grown
hang	*hung, *hanged	*hung, *hanged
have	had	had
hear	heard	heard
hew	hewed	hewn, hewed
hide	hid	hidden, (arch) hid
hit	hit	hit
hold	held	held
hurt	hurt	hurt
inlay	inlaid	inlaid
input	input, inputted	input, inputted
interweave	interwove, interweaved	interwoven, interweaved
keep	kept	kept
kneel	kneeled, knelt	kneeled, knelt
knit	knitted, *knit	knitted, *knit
know	knew	known
lay	laid	laid
lead	led	led
lean	leaned, (BrE also) leant	leaned, (BrE also) leant
leap	leaped, (BrE also) leapt	leaped, (BrE also) leapt
learn	learned, (BrE also) learnt	learned, (BrE also) learnt
leave	left	left
lend	lent	lent
let	let	let
lie (*yacer etc*)	lay	lain
light	lighted, lit	lighted, lit
lose	lost	lost
make	made	made
mean	meant	meant
meet	met	met
miscast	miscast	miscast

Los verbos irregulares ingleses cont.

infinitive/ infinitivo	**past tense/ pretérito**	**past participle/ participio pasado**
misdeal	misdealt	misdealt
mishear	misheard	misheard
mishit	mishit	mishit
mislay	mislaid	mislaid
mislead	misled	misled
misread /ˈmɪsˈriːd/	misread /ˈmɪsˈred/	misread /ˈmɪsˈred/
misspell	misspelled, (BrE also) misspelt	misspelled, (BrE also) misspelt
misspend	misspent	misspent
mistake	mistook	mistaken
misunderstand	misunderstood	misunderstood
mow	mowed	mown, mowed
outbid	outbid	outbid, (AmE also) outbidden
outdo	outdid	outdone
outfight	outfought	outfought
outgrow	outgrew	outgrown
outlay	outlaid	outlaid
output	output, outputted	output, outputted
outrun	outran	outrun
outsell	outsold	outsold
outshine	outshone	outshone
overbid	overbid	overbid
overcome	overcame	overcome
overdo	overdid	overdone
overdraw	overdrew	overdrawn
overeat	overate	overeaten
overfly	overflew	overflown
overhang	overhung	overhung
overhear	overheard	overheard
overlay	overlaid	overlaid
overlie	overlay	overlain
overpay	overpaid	overpaid
override	overrode	overridden
overrun	overran	overrun
oversee	oversaw	overseen
overshoot	overshot	overshot
oversleep	overslept	overslept
overtake	overtook	overtaken
overthrow	overthrew	overthrown
partake	partook	partaken
pay	paid	paid
plead	pleaded, (AmE also) pled	pleaded, (AmE also) pled
prove	proved	proved, proven
put	put	put
quit	quit, quitted	quit, quitted
read /riːd/	read /red/	read /red/
rend	rent	rent
rid	rid	rid
ride	rode	ridden
ring	rang	rung
rise	rose	risen
run	ran	run
saw	sawed	sawed, (esp BrE) sawn
say	said	said
see	saw	seen
seek	sought	sought
sell	sold	sold
send	sent	sent
set	set	set

infinitive/ infinitivo	**past tense/ pretérito**	**past participle/ participio pasado**
sew	sewed	sewn, sewed
shake	shook	shaken
shear	sheared	*shorn, *sheared
shed	shed	shed
shine	*shone, *shined	*shone, *shined
shit	shit, shat	shit, shat
shoe	shod	shod
shoot	shot	shot
show	showed	shown, showed
shrink	shrank, shrunk	shrunk, shrunken
shut	shut	shut
sing	sang	sung
sink	sank	sunk
sit	sat	sat
slay	slew	slain
sleep	slept	slept
slide	slid	slid
sling	slung	slung
slink	slunk	slunk
slit	slit	slit
smell	smelled, (BrE also) smelt	smelled, (BrE also) smelt
sow	sowed	sowed, sown
speak	spoke	spoken
speed	*sped, *speeded	*sped, *speeded
spell	spelled, (BrE also) spelt	spelled, (BrE also) spelt
spend	spent	spent
spill	spilled, spilt	spilled, spilt
spin	spun, (arch) span	spun
spit	spat, (esp AmE) spit	spat, (esp AmE) spit
split	split	split
spoil	spoiled, (BrE also) spoilt	spoiled, (BrE also) spoilt
spread	spread	spread
spring	sprang, (AmE also) sprung	sprung
stand	stood	stood
steal	stole	stolen
stick	stuck	stuck
sting	stung	stung
stink	stank, stunk	stunk
strew	strewed	strewn, strewed
stride	strode	stridden
strike	struck	struck
string	strung	strung
strive	strove	striven
sublet	sublet	sublet
swear	swore	sworn
sweat	sweated, (AmE also) sweat	sweated, (AmE also) sweat
sweep	swept	swept
swell	swelled	swollen, (esp AmE) swelled
swim	swam	swum
swing	swung	swung
take	took	taken
teach	taught	taught
tear	tore	torn
tell	told	told
think	thought	thought
thrive	thrived, (liter) throve	thrived, (arch) thriven
throw	threw	thrown
thrust	thrust	thrust

Los verbos irregulares ingleses cont.

infinitive/ infinitivo	**past tense/ pretérito**	**past participle/ participio pasado**
tread	trod	trodden, trod
typecast	typecast	typecast
typeset	typeset	typeset
typewrite	typewrote	typewritten
undercut	undercut	undercut
undergo	underwent	undergone
underlie	underlay	underlain
undersell	undersold	undersold
understand	understood	understood
undertake	undertook	undertaken
undo	undid	undone
unstick	unstuck	unstuck
unwind	unwound	unwound
uphold	upheld	upheld
upset	upset	upset
wake	woke	woken
waylay	waylaid	waylaid
wear	wore	worn
weave	wove, *weaved	woven, *weaved
wed	wedded, wed	wedded, wed
weep	wept	wept
wet	wet, wetted	wet, wetted
win	won	won
wind *(dar cuerda etc)*	wound	wound
withdraw	withdrew	withdrawn
withhold	withheld	withheld
withstand	withstood	withstood
work	worked, *wrought	worked, *wrought
wring	wrung	wrung
write	wrote	written